THE AUTHORITY SINCE 1868

THE WORLD ALMANAC®
AND BOOK OF FACTS
1998

WORLD ALMANAC BOOKS
AN IMPRINT OF K-III REFERENCE CORPORATION
A K-III Communications Company

THE WORLD ALMANAC®
AND BOOK OF FACTS
1998

Editorial Director: Robert Famighetti
Deputy Editor: William A. McGeveran, Jr.
Senior Editor: Lori P. Wiesenfeld
Associate Editors: Beth R. Ellis, Matthew Friedlander, Mark S. O'Malley
Desktop Publishing Associate: Melissa Janssens
Chronology Editor: Donald Young
Cover: Bill Smith Studio

K-III REFERENCE CORPORATION
Director of Editorial Production: Andrea J. Pitluk
Director—Purchasing and Production: Edward A. Thomas
Managing Editor: Eileen O'Reilly

Associate Editor: Ileana Parvulescu
Production Editor: Donna J. Schindler
Publishing Systems Associate: Christy A. Gera

Desktop Publishing Assistant: Hana Shaki
Director of Indexing Services: Marjorie B. Bank
Index Editor: Walter Kronenberg

WORLD ALMANAC BOOKS
Vice President and Publisher: Richard W. Eiger

Vice President–Sales: James R. Keenley
Director of Marketing: Joyce H. Stein
Manager of Licensing: Robert Rothman

The editors acknowledge with thanks the many letters of helpful comment and criticism from readers of THE WORLD ALMANAC. Because of the volume of mail directed to the editorial offices, it is not possible to reply to each letter writer. However, every communication is read by the editors and all comments and suggestions receive careful attention. THE WORLD ALMANAC's e-mail address is Walmanac@aol.com.

THE WORLD ALMANAC does not decide wagers.

The first edition of THE WORLD ALMANAC, a 120-page volume with 12 pages of advertising, was published by the New York World in 1868. Annual publication was suspended in 1876. Joseph Pulitzer, publisher of the New York World, revived THE WORLD ALMANAC in 1886 with the goal of making it a "compendium of universal knowledge." It has been published annually since then.

THE WORLD ALMANAC and BOOK OF FACTS 1998
Copyright © 1997 by K-III Reference Corporation
A K-III Communications Company
The World Almanac and The World Almanac and Book of Facts
are registered trademarks of K-III Reference Corporation.
Library of Congress Catalog Card Number 4-3781
International Standard Serial Number (ISSN) 0084-1382
ISBN (softcover) 0-88687-820-9
ISBN (hardcover) 0-88687-821-7
Microform Edition: University Microfilms Intl.
Printed in the United States of America

The softcover and hardcover editions are distributed to the book trade by St. Martin's Press; the paperback edition is distributed to the magazine trade by ICD/The Hearst Corporation.

WORLD ALMANAC BOOKS
An Imprint of K-III Reference Corporation
One International Boulevard, Suite 444
Mahwah, New Jersey 07495-0017

CONTENTS

GENERAL INDEX

Note: Page numbers in **boldface** indicate key references. Page numbers in *italics* indicate photos.

The World Almanac

and Book of Facts 1998

SPECIAL SECTION: THE COMING MILLENNIUM

The new millennium is fast approaching. When does it actually begin? How are people going to celebrate? *The World Almanac and Book of Facts 1998* addresses these and other millennial questions, and also includes special features that highlight the millennium that is ending as well as the new one about to begin.

The calendar system used throughout most of the Western world and in parts of Asia and Africa takes the year following Christ's birth—or what was once thought to be the year—as its starting date. (The birth of Christ was originally figured as occurring in 1 BC, but modern scholars place it about 4 BC or earlier.) Thus, the Christian calendar starts with the year AD 1 (there was no year 0). A millennium is a period of 1,000 years. Counting from AD 1, then, the 2d millennium ends Dec. 31, 2000, and the 3d millennium begins Jan. 1, 2001. The year 2001 has been officially adopted by the Royal Greenwich Observatory in Cambridge, England, as the start of the new millennium. But for most people, the night to celebrate will be Dec. 31, 1999, regardless of the "official" ruling.

In the following pages, experts in various fields give their own "ten best" lists of the greatest ideas, accomplishments, and innovators of the millennium now ending. The contributors are: former Librarian of Congress and Pulitzer-Prize-winning author Daniel J. Boorstin, Pulitzer-Prize-winning author John Updike, Nobel-Prize-winning chemist Glenn T. Seaborg, gerontologist and Pultizer-Prize-winning author Robert N. Butler, M.D., and award-winning biologist Stephen Jay Gould. Other articles in this section describe how people around the world plan to celebrate New Year's Eve 1999 and deal with the "millennium bug" that threatens computers everywhere when the year 2000 arrives.

In addition, throughout the book you will find Millennium Fact Boxes, highlighting intriguing facts and dramatic changes in the past century or millennium, or the century to come. For example, you can see how much longer Americans are living today compared to 1900 and how household size has shrunk (Vital Statistics section); you can trace how the number of female college students in the U.S., extremely low in the late 1800s, grew to surpass the male total 100 years later (Education); you can compare how deaths in the U.S. from killer diseases such as tuberculosis, typhoid, and measles have been virtually eliminated since 1900, while the death rate for cancer has steadily climbed (Health); or you can find when and where total eclipses of the Sun can be viewed in the U.S. during the 21st century (Astronomy).

Ten Leading Ideas of the Second Millennium That Have Shaped Western Civilization and World History

By Daniel J. Boorstin

Daniel J. Boorstin, Librarian of Congress Emeritus, directed the Library from 1975 to 1987. He has also previously been director of the National Museum of American History, senior historian of the Smithsonian Institution, and a professor of history at the University of Chicago. His many distinguished works include The Americans: The Democratic Experience *(1973), for which he won a Pulitzer Prize.*

1. **Renaissance**—from stirrings in Italy in the 14th century. Belief that the ideas, arts, and institutions of earlier times can awaken us and enlarge our lives.

2. **Discovery**—from Spanish and Portuguese voyages of exploration in the 15th and 16th centuries. Belief that there is more still to be known, and that there are still new worlds to be found and explored.

3. **Constitutionalism and Representative Government**—from the Magna Carta (1215) and the new institutions of England and continental Europe in the 17th and 18th centuries. Commitment to the right of the governed to have a voice in their government, and so, belief in the limits of government.

4. **Invisible Worlds and Their Meanings for Us**—beginning with Galileo's (1564-1642) telescope and Leeuwenhoek's (1632-1723) microscope. The insight that much of reality (from bacteria to galaxies) is unknown and unseen without the aid of technology.

5. **Nationalism**—from the rise of national languages and literatures in Europe in the 16th century. Belief that common language, literature, arts, history, traditions, and ways of life can hold people together in community. Providing ever-new opportunities for communal fulfillment, while also bringing the risk of war between nations. In the 20th century, suggesting the broader notion of communities of nations.

6. **Individualism**—from the Protestant Reformation in the 16th century, and the rise of cities, commerce, and capitalism. Belief that the faith of the individual is essential to religious salvation, that the consent of individuals legitimates government, and that the worth of persons is to be measured by their worth as individuals and not by power or status.

7. **Rationalism and the Appeal to Science**—at least from the Renaissance and the rise of the Royal Society and other scientific institutes in England and on the European continent in the 17th century. Belief that the world of nature can be comprehended by reason and experiment and that society can be improved by knowledge gained from the social sciences and history.

8. **Progress**—at least since the Enlightenment of the 18th century. Belief that there is a tendency and a capacity in humankind toward improvement of institutions and the means of life. Reinforced by ideas of Evolution.

9. **Unlimited Communication**—beginning with printing and the rise of literacy (since the 15th century) and electronic communication (20th century). Reliance on greater communication, leading to a more universal awareness of the human condition, problems, and opportunities.

10. **Artificial Sources of Energy**—beginning with gunpowder (14th century), then steam power (18th century), electric power (19th century), the internal combustion engine (19th century), and finally electronic and atomic power (20th century). The discovery that human power and mobility are enhanced by drawing on forces beyond the human body or animal power, which can be developed and controlled.

Ten Greatest Works of Literature of the Second Millennium

By John Updike

John Updike, the acclaimed American novelist, short-story writer, poet, and literary critic, is perhaps best known for his "Rabbit" novels, beginning with Rabbit, Run *(1960) and ending with* Rabbit at Rest *(1990), one of two novels for which he won a Pulitzer Prize. His literary criticism is displayed in such works as* Hugging the Shore *(1983).*

1. **Thomas Aquinas,** *Summa Theologica,* written c. 1265-73. This medieval work of philosophy demonstrates the compatibility of faith and reason and to this day serves as a foundation of Roman Catholic apologetics. It encouraged the rise of scientific thought in Europe, and without it Dante could not have written *The Divine Comedy,* or James Joyce *Ulysses.*

2. **Dante Alighieri,** *The Divine Comedy,* written c. 1307-21. Known by the author simply as *Commedia,* this poem of 100 cantos and 14,000 lines takes the poet on a visionary voyage from Hell through Purgatory to Paradise. A triumph of schematic organization and of line-by-line vitality, it established Tuscan as the dominant dialect of Italy and remains the greatest long poem since Virgil.

3. **Miguel de Cervantes Saavedra,** *Don Quixote,* Part I, 1605; Part II, 1615. This tale, of a Spanish gentleman who read too many chivalric romances and in trying to enact them runs repeatedly afoul of a real world, is considered the first European novel. Its humor is broad, but its pathos and symbolic resonance run deep; the pairing of the idealistic, infatuated don with his earthy squire Sancho Panza encapsulates the human condition.

4. **William Shakespeare, Comedies, Histories, and Tragedies,** written c. 1590-1613, published 1623. Both the greatest poet and greatest playwright in the English language, Shakespeare wrote about 36 plays in all. Their insight into human character in action, the variety of their plots and situations, and the Protean energy of their poetic language continue to astonish readers and theater audiences.

5. **Voltaire,** *Candide,* 1759. A slim book written in three days, and published anonymously, *Candide* distills the sparkling spirit of Voltaire and the Enlightenment. Like *Don Quixote,* it dramatizes the clash between ideas and reality—the ideas are those of the philosopher Leibniz, which explained away evil, and reality is represented by the Lisbon earthquake and other sufferings endured by the titular hero and his cheerful tutor, Dr. Pangloss.

6. **Edward Gibbon,** *The History of the Decline and Fall of the Roman Empire,* 1776-88. Another monument of the Enlightenment, Gibbon's six-volume history constitutes a masterpiece of research and elegantly smooth exposition that continues to set a standard for vivid historiography and sociological analysis.

7. **Leo Tolstoy,** *War and Peace,* 1865-69. Of the many great 19th-century novels, Tolstoy's panorama of Napoleon's invasion of Russia seems the greatest—great in bulk, in empathy, in the breadth of its cast of characters, in the sweep of its speculations on human history. Vast though the canvas, the individual touch is always exact, direct, and concise.

8. **Fyodor Dostoyevsky,** *The Possessed,* 1871-72. The passionate insight that Dostoyevsky brought to the novel is at its most intense and perversely comic in this portrait of left-wing revolutionaries; even if Russia had not eventually fallen under the sway of "the devils" depicted here, the depths of the human soul sounded would make the work prophetic.

9. **Marcel Proust,** *Remembrance of Things Past,* 1913-27. The French tradition of psychological analysis is brought to its fullest flower in this prodigiously long examination of the autobiographical hero's sensibility, as his memory traces the changing perspectives that love and snobbery yield on a mordantly sketched social landscape. Proust's metaphors are marvelous.

10. **James Joyce,** *Ulysses,* 1922. A narrow, provincial subject—Dublin on one June day of 1904, as experienced by a handful of characters, foremost the young dreamer Stephen Dedalus and the middle-aged Jewish advertising salesman Leopold Bloom—becomes in Joyce's erudite, playful rendering a detailed counterpart of Homer's *Odyssey* and an epitome of realism: a book as opaque and rich as life.

Ten Greatest Scientists of the Second Millennium

By Glenn T. Seaborg

Glenn T. Seaborg, who shared the 1951 Nobel Prize in chemistry, is the co-discoverer of plutonium and a number of other elements. He was chairman of the U.S. Atomic Energy Commission from 1961 to 1971. He has taught chemistry at the University of California at Berkeley since 1939 and has been associate director of the Lawrence Berkeley National Laboratory since 1971.

1. **Leonardo da Vinci** (1452-1519). Had the earliest—and a sound—understanding of a breathtaking range of scientific topics, including the principle of inertia, the acceleration of falling bodies, the impossibility of perpetual motion, the structure of the muscles and bones of the human body, the structure and working of the heart and its valves and circulation of blood, and the motion of the earth and its moon.

2. **Isaac Newton** (1642-1727). Probably the world's greatest contributor to the fundamental laws of physics. Formulated the three laws of motion—(1) the principle of inertia, (2) the definition of force in terms of mass and acceleration, and (3) the principle that for every action there is an equal and opposite reaction. Posited the universal law of gravitational attraction. Demonstrated refraction of light into a rainbow spectrum of colors. Developed the reflecting telescope. Independent developer of calculus.

3. **Jöns Jakob Berzelius** (1779-1848). Developed the first authentic table of atomic weights. Suggested a system of symbols for the chemical elements and their compounds. Discovered the chemical elements selenium, silicon, and thorium. Introduced many chemical words, such as *catalysis, isomer, polymer, allotrope, halogen,* and *protein.*

4. **Charles Darwin** (1809-82). His book *The Origin of Species* (1859) provided the first overwhelming evidence that all organic life—including humans—evolved from ancestral forms, a concept that forever changed the fundamental tenets of biology. Posited the theory of natural selection in determining the survival of the fittest organisms and argued for the importance of secondary sexual characteristics to species' survival.

5. **Dmitri Mendeleyev** (1834-1907). Developed the first successful Periodic Table of the elements (1869-71), with which he predicted the chemical properties of three elements that were later discovered—gallium (1875), scandium (1879), and germanium (1886).

6. **Ernest Rutherford** (1871-1937). Elucidated the phenomenon of radioactive decay (1900-8). Developed the theory of the nuclear atom (1911). Demonstrated the first artificially induced nuclear reaction (1919).

7. **Albert Einstein** (1879-1955). Elucidated the photoelectric effect and Brownian motion (1905). Produced the Special Theory of Relativity (1905) and General Theory of Relativity (1915), which revolutionized our understanding of the physical world.

8. **Niels Bohr** (1885-1962). Elucidated the structure of the hydrogen atom (1913). Developed the concept of the liquid drop model of the atomic nucleus (1936-39).

9. **Werner Heisenberg** (1901-76). Developed the theory of quantum mechanics to explain atomic structure (1925). Articulated the Uncertainty Principle (1927).

10. **Enrico Fermi** (1901-54). Discoverer of nuclear reactions brought about by slow neutrons (1934). Produced the first nuclear chain reaction in uranium (Dec. 2, 1942).

Ten Most Significant Medical Advances of the Second Millennium

By Robert N. Butler, M.D.

Dr. Robert N. Butler, a noted gerontologist, has been director of the International Longevity Center since 1990 and was director of the National Institute on Aging at the National Institutes of Health (NIH) from 1976 to 1982. He is also a professor of geriatrics and adult development at New York's Mt. Sinai School of Medicine. He received a Pulitzer Prize in 1976 for his book Why Survive? Being Old in America.

1. 1520-40. Revolt against false and ancient dogmas of 16th-century medicine. German physician Phillippus Aureolus Theophrastus Bombastus von Hohenheim (1493-1541), who renamed himself Paracelsus—meaning "beyond Celsus"—in the grandiose claim that he was greater than the great ancient Roman physician Celsus, was a clinician who called for observation and sound reason in the treatment of the sick. He insisted on examining patients at their bedsides, which led to important original observations, and began to treat diseases with chemical substances instead of botanicals (plant products).

2. 1543. Introducing anatomical dissection. The insistence of Belgian physician Andreas Vesalius (1514-64) on the importance of anatomical dissection was vital to the development of our understanding of the human body and helped mark the beginning of modern medicine. His book *On the Fabric of the Human Body* was a precursor to the discovery and practice of surgery.

3. 1628. Developing an experimental model of the circulatory system. English physician William Harvey (1578-1657) successfully demonstrated the circulation of the blood and contraction of the heart. This work was basic to later contributions to the understanding and treatment of heart disease.

4. 1796. Proving the concept of immunity; developing the first vaccine. British physician Edward Jenner (1749-1823) discovered vaccination as a defense against smallpox. He experimented on a young boy, injecting him with pus from an animal infected with cowpox and, 8 weeks later, injecting him with active smallpox. The boy did not develop the disease, successfully demonstrating the theory of immunity. This laid the groundwork for Louis Pasteur's theoretical explanation of immunity and the development of modern preventive vaccines.

5. 1849-58. Establishing the principles of cellular pathology. German pathologist Rudolf Virchow (1821-1902) presented his theory of cellular pathology, leading the way for the modern concept that diseases arise primarily in individual cells, and not in organs or tissues as had been believed.

6. 1865. Promulgating the concept of self-regulation of life processes (homeostasis). French physiologist Claude Bernard (1813-78) introduced the concept of the internal environment, which is the basis of understanding homeostasis, or equilibrium, as a central principle of life. Bernard demonstrated the great importance of laboratory physiology and the necessity and principles of experimentation in the life sciences. His masterpiece, *An Introduction to the Study of Experimental Medicine*, was published in 1865.

7. Late 19th century. Corroborating scientific proof of germ theory. French microbiologist Louis Pasteur (1822-95) and German physician Robert Koch (1843-1910) definitively proved the germ theory of disease, an idea going back to at least 100 BC. Pasteur proved that fermentation was caused by living organisms he called bacteria. This led to the use of heat treatment ("pasteurization") to destroy bacteria and to the discovery that animals develop an immunity to a bacterium, e.g., the bacterium that causes rabies, when a weakened form of it is placed in their bodies. Koch demonstrated the method needed to grow bacteria cultures and isolated the specific bacteria that cause anthrax, tuberculosis, and cholera.

8. 1906. Discovering the cellular unit of the nervous system. Spanish histologist Santiago Ramón y Cajal (1852-1934) shared the 1906 Nobel Prize in physiology or medicine for his discovery that the nerve cell is the basic unit of the nervous system. It was a primary step in establishing a scientific basis for the care and treatment of nervous diseases and in understanding nerve impulses.

9. 1928/1932. Discovering antibiotics. British bacteriologist Sir Alexander Fleming (1881-1955) discovered penicillin in 1928, and German chemist Gerhard Domagk (1895-1964) discovered sulfonamides (sulfa drugs) in 1932; these antibiotics provided powerful ammunition against bacterial diseases.

10. 1944/1953. Discovering and creating a working model of DNA structure. Canadian physician Oswald Avery (1887-1955) proved in 1944 that deoxyribonucleic acid (DNA) affects hereditary traits. American biochemist James D. Watson (b. 1928) and British biophysicist Francis Crick (b. 1916) discovered in 1953 the molecular structure of DNA as the basis of heredity. These advances provided the basis of modern medicine's understanding of disease at the molecular level and of the role played by genes in the health and diseases of living organisms.

Ten Mileposts of the Second Millennium in Understanding the History of Life

By Stephen Jay Gould

Stephen Jay Gould teaches biology, geology, and the history of science at Harvard University, where he is Curator for Invertebrate Paleontology of the Museum of Comparative Zoology. He has received numerous awards for his books and articles in paleontology and other areas of science.

Greek and Roman thought, and the folk wisdom of other cultures as well, offer an anecdotal idea or two about fossils, but all the keystones of our knowledge—that fossils are the remains of organisms at all, that fossils record a very long and directional history of life on earth, and that life's sequential history unfolded by a natural process of evolution—were erected within our millennium, and at an ever-accelerating pace. I present this chronologically ordered list of 10 mileposts, 5 for general concepts followed by 5 for more specific and outstanding discoveries, as my own idiosyncratic capsule summary of this great chapter in the progress of scientific knowledge.

1. Circa 1510, in his notebook, known as the *Leicester Codex*, Leonardo da Vinci recognized fossils as remains of ancient organisms and as records of a long and sequential history. In a brilliant series of observations and deductions, Leonardo dismissed the 2 most popular theories of fossils in his time—that they are all the same age as a result of simultaneous burial in Noah's flood and that they are not organic at all, but arise from "plastic forces" within rocks. Leonardo recognized that fossils must be remains of ancient organisms, and that they must represent a long period of time because they occur in several layers of rocks and so cannot all be ascribed to one event. But Leonardo never published his notebooks, and his brilliant conclusions remained unknown.

2. 1750-1850. The emerging science of geology established a great age for the earth; the literal Biblical chronology of a mere 6,000 years—too short to permit a rich and sequential history of life recorded in numerous layers of fossils—could no longer be supported.

3. 1750-1800. The early work of geological mapping proved that fossils occur in an invariable order from the oldest to the youngest strata. Fossils could therefore be used as the primary criterion for judging the relative ages of rocks. The earth, having gained a great age (milestone number 2 above), now had a history defined by the sequential story of life's uniquely different species through time.

4. **1812.** In his great 4-volume work on the history of fossil vertebrates (*Recherches sur les ossemens fossiles,* or *Research on Fossil Bones*), Georges Cuvier indubitably established the fact that species become extinct and that older species look less and less like modern forms. (Many scientists had previously doubted the possibility of extinction, arguing that such signs of "failure" could not exist in a perfect creation.) Life's unique and sequential history was further established because extinct species never return, and therefore define the age in which they lived as a unique interval in time.

5. **1859.** Charles Darwin published *The Origin of Species* and established that "descent with modification"—or evolution along lines of genealogical transformation, and not a series of successive creations following catastrophic extinctions—produced the unique and sequential history of life.

6. **1860s and 1870s.** V. Kovalevsky in Russia, T. H. Huxley in England, and O. C. Marsh in the U.S. worked out the complex evolutionary history of horses, thus proving that evidence for evolution could be established from the fossil record.

7. **Early 1890s.** E. Du Bois, a Dutch physician and naturalist, discovered, on the island of Java, the first genuinely ancient human fossil (of the species now called *Homo erectus* and regarded as our immediate ancestor). Humans became part of the evolutionary story of all life, not a superior and separate entity. Human evolution occupies only the last 5 million years or so in a record of multicellular animal life that stretches back more than half a billion years.

8. **1909.** C. D. Walcott discovered the Burgess Shale in British Columbia. This superbly preserved fauna, including the soft parts of organisms, documented the most crucial episode in the evolution of multicellular animal life—the so-called "Cambrian explosion" (535-530 million years ago, as now known), during which virtually all the major designs of modern animal phyla appeared in the fossil record for the first time.

9. **1950s.** By learning how to find and study fossils of single-celled creatures preserved in cherts (silica, rather than the usual calcite), paleontologists began to document the earlier phases of the history of life, the biota of Precambrian times. Scientists now know that single-celled life on earth extends back 3.6 billion years.

10. **1980s.** Luis and Walter Alvarez proposed (and the work of hundreds of scientists then proved) that a large extraterrestrial object struck the earth 65 million years ago, probably triggering one of the 5 great mass extinctions that have occurred during life's multicellular history. For the first time, scientists gained a clear explanation for at least one of the great extinction events (the one that wiped out dinosaurs, along with some 50% of marine species, and gave mammals, and ultimately ourselves, a chance to evolve). Since life's history is an interplay between evolution and extinction, with both processes occurring over a great range of rates, we now have satisfactory explanations for at least some examples of all forms and stages of these crucial processes.

Marking the Millennium

By Geoffrey M. Horn

Geoffrey M. Horn is a freelance editor and writer who often writes on cultural, political, and historical topics.

Most experts agree that the 21st century will not technically start until Jan. 1, 2001. But people are already voting with their credit cards, their deposits have been made, and the verdict is in. New Year's Eve, Dec. 31, 1999, is the day people consider the end of the century and millennium, and it may be one of history's biggest merchandising events.

Whatever your notion of a romantic Millennial New Year's getaway, there is probably a tour packager or travel agent willing to sell it to you. Although bookings started early for many of the most attractive packages, some that were officially listed as sold out became available again once full details—and prices—were published.

From Machupicchu to Mickey Mouse

Crystal Cruises offers 2 millennial itineraries in Dec. 1999: the *Crystal Harmony* drops anchor at Rio for a carnival-style New Year's Eve, while the *Crystal Symphony* crosses the International Date Line in the South Pacific for a unique double New Year's Eve celebration. (After celebrating the big changeover on the western side of the date line, you cross over, and a new changeover occurs 24 hours after the first one.) If you have long dreamed of seeing in the year 2000 standing in the shadow of the Taj Mahal, watching the sun rise over Machupicchu (Peru's fabled Inca ruins), or dancing the Millennium Waltz at Vienna's Imperial Hotel, the New York-based tour packager Abercrombie & Kent can take you there.

Several island nations in the South Pacific lying close to the International Date Line on the western side have promoted themselves as the ideal place to experience the start of the new millennium. Kiribati, a nation of some 33 widely scattered islands and atolls that previously straddled the date line, actually moved the line so that the whole nation would be on the western side—and it could be the nation that ostensibly gets to see the new millennium first. However, the Royal Greenwich Observatory has concluded that the Balleny Islands, Antarctica, is probably the place to witness the dawn of the new era. This is because the midsummer sun rises early there, having been below the horizon for less than an hour. Mindful of this fact, some millennial enthusiasts have booked cruises to Antarctica, promising midnight sun, humpback whales, and no shortage of ice to keep the champagne chilled.

The *Disney Magic* cruise liner began advertising millennium cruises well before its scheduled maiden voyage in spring 1998. Among other alternatives, Cunard's published itineraries call for passengers on the *Queen Elizabeth II* to celebrate New Year's Eve 1999 at Bridgetown, Barbados. The *Royal Viking Sun* will be at Acapulco, Mexico; the *Sea Goddess I* at Virgin Gorda, British Virgin Islands; and the *Sea Goddess II* at Pulau Naira, Indonesia. Other travelers can choose to celebrate with the Fijian High Chiefs at a week-long festival of world culture, or party (figuratively) with the pharaohs near the age-old Egyptian pyramids.

High Fliers

Intrav, based in St, Louis, MO, has already reserved 2 Concorde supersonic jets for its "round the world in 17 days" millennial extravaganza. Both Dec. 1999 tours begin and end in New York City, but one group greets the new year in Hong Kong, the other in Sydney, Australia. As of fall 1997, the package price was $84,500 per passenger, with double occupancy reduced to only $75,000 a head.

Revelers seeking a lofty view at more down-to-earth prices have turned to the Eiffel Tower in Paris, Seattle's Space Needle, and other high-rise landmarks. London's planned Millennium Wheel, a 500-foot-high Ferris wheel, will offer a breathtaking view of the London skyline at only about $8 for a 20-minute ride.

In New York City, Windows on the World, the restaurant at the top of the World Trade Center, received its first millennium reservation request in 1986, while the elegant Rainbow Room had a waiting list (as of Oct. 1997) of 900 names for New Year's Eve 1999 (but no waiting list at all for Dec. 31, 2000). The posh Gleneagles golf resort in Scotland was booked up more than 3 years in advance for its traditional "Hogmanay" New Year's festivities in 1999-2000. In the Scottish Highlands, there may be a few rentable castles left at about $20,000 a week for the premillennial holiday.

Loftier Aspirations

The millennial calendar is also full of events to exalt the spirit and elevate the mind.

Christians throughout the world will celebrate the year 2000 as the 2,000th anniversary of Christ's nativity (though the exact year is now known to have been earlier). In his apostolic letter *Tertio Millennio Adveniente* (As the Third Millennium Draws Near, 1994), Pope John Paul II designated 2000 as a Holy Year and called for a "Great Jubilee" to take place in the Holy Land, in Rome, and in local churches.

A series of United Nations conferences during the millennial period will focus on topics of worldwide importance. The agenda includes the 3d Conference on the Exploration and Peaceful Uses of Outer Space, or UNISPACE III (1999 or 2000), the 2d World Conference on Natural Disaster Reduction (2000), and special General Assembly sessions on social development (2000) and children (2001). UN agencies have already proclaimed 1999 as the International Year of Older Persons and 2000 as an International Year of Thanksgiving and an International Year for the Culture of Peace.

The White House Millennium Program, led by First Lady Hillary Rodham Clinton, will publicize and coordinate various federal initiatives. Among programs announced by late 1997 were an American Cultural Showcase, hosted by the White House; a White House lecture series, cosponsored by the National Endowment for the Humanities; a series of televised Millennium Minutes, also sponsored by the NEH; and an expanded Festival of American Folklife at the Smithsonian Institution.

Other Celebrations

With the America's Cup in New Zealand and the Summer Olympics in Australia, 2000 promises to be an eventful year Down Under. Germany is also a focus of millennial interest, with a world's fair in Hannover and the planned transfer of the Bundestag, the lower house of parliament, from Bonn to Berlin. Washington, DC, celebrates its 200th year as the nation's permanent capital and the 200th anniversary of the Library of Congress.

A bevy of round-number birthdays and anniversaries in 2000 also provide cause for celebration. Hosannas will honor the memory of composer Johann Sebastian Bach on the 250th anniversary of his death. Special ceremonies will also mark the 1,200th anniversary of the coronation of Charlemagne as emperor of the Holy Roman Empire, the 500th birthday of Holy Roman Emperor Charles V, and the 600th anniversary of the death of poet Geoffrey Chaucer. The sculptor Benvenuto Cellini would have been 500 years old. Centenaries include those of sculptor Louise Nevelson, composer Aaron Copland, jazz great Louis Armstrong, and Margaret Mitchell, author of *Gone With the Wind*.

A Millennium Calendar

(Dates and details subject to change.)

1999

With the scheduled launch of the space shuttle *Atlantis*, **Jan. 14**, construction work continues on the International Space Station for the next century. Another 16 space shuttle missions are planned through **Nov. 30, 2000**.

Mayflower 2000, a full-size reconstruction of the vessel that carried the Pilgrims from England to Plymouth, MA, in 1620, sails from its berth on the Thames River in the **spring** for a 66-day voyage, with port calls at Southampton, England; New York City; and Provincetown, MA, on Cape Cod.

The Saturn-bound *Cassini* spacecraft makes its planned earth flyby in **Aug. 1999**, gaining a speed boost from earth's gravity. It is scheduled to pass Jupiter in **Dec. 2000**.

After 150 years under Portuguese sovereignty, Macau becomes a special administrative region of China toward the end of the millennium, on **Dec. 20**.

From **Dec. 24** through the end of the following year, the Vatican expects more than 13 million tourists to visit sacred sites in Italy for Holy Year 2000.

The U.S. transfers control over the Panama Canal to Panama, **Dec. 31**. Worldwide, tens of millions of people gather in thousands of cities to celebrate what, for most people, is the dawn of the new millennium.

2000

Some 4 million pilgrims are expected to visit Bethlehem, Nazareth, Jerusalem, and other sacred places in Israel and the West Bank for Holy Land 2000, **Jan. 1-Dec. 31**. Odyssey 2000, a round-the-world bicycle trek, has enlisted about 250 participants to cycle 20,000 miles across some 54 countries during the same period.

The Year of the Dragon, year 4698 on the Chinese lunar calendar, begins **Feb. 5**.

New Zealand hosts the America's Cup 2000 championship yacht races, **Feb. 26-Mar. 16**. (Challenger eliminations start in 1999.)

The first centesimal leap year since 1600 adds a day to the calendar, **Feb. 29**.

Apr. 6 marks the 1st full day of the year 1421 on the Islamic calendar.

Organizers hope to enlist more than 300 million people to participate **Apr. 22** in the largest Earth Day ever.

The Holy Shroud of Turin, Italy, is on public display, **Apr. 29-June 11**.

Up to 40 million people are expected to visit Hannover, Germany, **June 1-Oct. 31**, for the Expo 2000 world's fair.

Participation by more than 30 million people is the goal for the global March for Jesus, **June 10**, with prayer and worship processions in over 2,000 cities.

The XXVII Olympiad is held in Sydney, Australia, **Sept. 15-Oct. 1**. Sydney also hosts "Harbour of Life," an Olympic arts festival.

On **Sept. 30**, Rosh Hashanah, a Jewish holy day, marks the 1st full day of the year 5761 on the Hebrew calendar.

The U.S. elects its 1st president of the 3d millennium, **Nov. 7**.

New Millennium's Eve, **Dec. 31**. Most authorities say the 3d millennium technically begins **Jan. 1, 2001**.

Some Web Sites Relating to the Millennium

America's Cup 2000: http://www.americascup2000.org
EXPO 2000: http://www.expo2000.de/index-e.html
Greenwich 2000: http://www.greenwich2000.com/millennium/index.htm
Holy See: http://www.vatican.va/jubilee_2000/pju_en.htm
Jubilee 2000: http://www.xibalba.com/xibalba/solt/jubilee/index.html
Mayflower 2000: http://www.netstrategy.co.uk/mayflower

Millennium Alliance: http://www.cgv.org/millennium/events/index.html
Millennium 2000, Fiji Islands: http://members.aol.com/fiji2000/index.htm
Sydney 2000—Games of the XXVII Olympiad: http://www.olympic.org/games/sydney
White House Millennium Project: http://www.whitehouse.gov/Initiatives/Millennium

The Year 2000 Problem (Y2K), or The Millennium Bug

When computer systems were originally created, programmers decided to save memory in their coding by representing the year with only the last 2 digits. Because of this lack of foresight, many computers will be unable to interpret dates past the year 1999. For example, the year 2000, shown as "00," will be read as 1900. This is what technical people call the year 2000 problem, or Y2K for short. Many governments and corporations will be affected, and if certain corrections are not done in time, the general public could suffer in many possible ways, from inaccessible bank accounts to flight delays to delays in receiving Social Security checks. Home computers could be affected depending on the model or software used. Programmers are hard at work fixing the problem, and for some larger companies that means millions of lines of coding need to be reviewed. The total cost for fixing it everywhere could reach $600 billion worldwide according to some estimates, and it is possible that half of all companies that need to make adjustments will not be ready in time.

THE TOP 10 NEWS STORIES OF 1997

Billions mourned the death of Diana, Princess of Wales, killed in a Paris car crash in the early morning hours of Aug. 31. Throngs lined the path of her funeral procession, and an estimated 2 billion or more people worldwide watched the televised funeral ceremony held Sept. 6 in London's Westminster Abbey, in a massive outpouring of grief over the loss of Britain's "people's princess."

After more than 150 years as a British colony, Hong Kong was restored to Chinese rule on July 1 as a Special Administrative Region of China. Earlier in this year of transition for China, on Feb. 19, the nation's longtime "paramount leader," Deng Xiaoping, died at the age of 92.

Timothy J. McVeigh, a U.S. Army veteran with anti-government beliefs, was convicted and sentenced to death in June for the April 1995 bombing of the Alfred P. Murrah Federal Building in Oklahoma City that killed 168 people. The trial of an alleged co-conspirator, Terry L. Nichols, began in October.

After months of negotiation, Pres. Bill Clinton and the Republican-controlled Congress reached final agreement in July on two bills designed to cut taxes and balance the federal budget by the year 2002. The measures passed overwhelmingly in both houses of Congress, and Pres. Clinton signed them into law on Aug. 5.

The first mammal successfully cloned from a cell from an adult animal was reported in February by researchers at the Roslin Institute in Edinburgh, Scotland; the clone was a sheep named Dolly.

The first spacecraft to land on Mars since 1976, *Mars Pathfinder,* touched down on the planet's surface July 4 and deployed *Sojourner,* a small 22-pound roving vehicle designed to explore and analyze Martian rocks and soil. The mission provided data on the climate, atmosphere, and geology of the planet, including panoramic three-dimensional photographs of the planet's terrain in unprecedented detail.

Alleged fund-raising excesses and abuses of campaign finance laws, especially by the Clinton-Gore campaign and the Democratic National Committee, were probed by the Justice Dept. and aired in high-profile congressional hearings.

A civil jury, Feb. 4, found former football star O. J. Simpson liable in the 1994 deaths of his ex-wife, Nicole Brown Simpson, and her friend Ronald Goldman. Simpson had been acquitted of their murders in a criminal trial. The jury awarded $8.5 million in compensatory damages to the Goldman family and $12.5 million in punitive damages to each family.

Thirty-nine members of the Heaven's Gate religious cult were found dead on Mar. 26 at an estate in California after an apparent mass suicide. Among the dead was cult leader Marshall Applewhite, who had apparently maintained that a deceased co-founder of the group would pick up the cultists in a spaceship following the comet Hale-Bopp, which was then prominent in the night sky.

As rebel forces led by Laurent Kabila threatened Zaire's capital of Kinshasa, Pres. Mobutu Sese Seko, the corrupt ailing dictator who had ruled the mineral-rich Central African country for more than 30 years, fled the city May 16. Kabila's forces moved in and gained control, and Kabila was sworn in May 29 as president of the country, renamed the Democratic Republic of the Congo.

CHRONOLOGY OF THE YEAR'S EVENTS

Reported Month by Month in 3 Categories: National, International, and General

Nov. 1, 1996, to Oct. 15, 1997

NOVEMBER 1996

National

Clinton Reelected; GOP Holds Congress—Pres. Bill Clinton was reelected to a 2d term, **Nov. 5**. Vice Pres. Al Gore was reelected with him on the Democratic ticket. Republicans kept majorities in both houses of Congress.

Clinton carried 31 states and the District of Columbia, for a total of 379 electoral votes. The Republican ticket, Bob Dole for president and Jack Kemp for vice president, carried 19 states, for 159 electoral votes. A minimum of 270 electoral votes were required for election. According to official results, the Democratic ticket nationwide received 47.4 million popular votes, or 49.3% of the total, compared to 39.2 million, or 40.7%, for the Republicans. Texas billionaire Ross Perot, founder and candidate of the new Reform Party, received 8.1 million votes, or 8.4% of the total. Other candidates shared the remainder.

The president's reelection represented a stunning comeback from 1994, when his sweeping health-care reform plan died in Congress, his popularity ratings plummeted, and the Democrats lost control of Congress to the Republicans in the midterm elections. Subsequently, as the economy boomed, Clinton took moderate positions and advocated modest programs, preempting the political center. Dole, who sought to paint Clinton as a closet liberal, made a 15% across-the-board tax cut a centerpiece of his campaign. A widely respected figure, he never overcame Clinton's strong lead in the polls and was seen by some as old-fashioned. Clinton won the women's vote overwhelmingly, while dividing the votes of men, and he won majorities among blacks, Hispanics, labor union members, and young voters. The South emerged as a growing base of support for the Republicans, especially in the congressional elections. The GOP lost 8 seats in the House, retaining a 227-207 edge (3 of the contests were settled in runoffs in Dec.), with 1 independent, and gained 2 seats in the Senate for a 55-45 advantage.

Only 2 statehouses changed hands. The Republicans captured a governorship in West Virginia, and the Democrats gained one in New Hampshire. The GOP retained its 32-17 edge (there was 1 independent).

Army Studies Sexual Harassment Charges—The Army announced, **Nov. 7**, that it was investigating a large number of complaints by women soldiers that they had been sexually harassed by higher-ranking male soldiers; 2 men had been charged with rape. Since Sept., more than 2 dozen women who had just completed basic training at Aberdeen Proving Ground in Maryland had complained of abuse. Five supervisors at Aberdeen had been suspended, the Army stated, and Sec. of the Army Togo West said he had established a board of review to determine the extent of harassment in the Army. The Army announced, **Nov. 12**, that 3 male sergeants at Ft. Leonard Wood, MO, had been charged with crimes involving female soldiers. One of them pleaded guilty, **Nov. 12**, to improper relationships with trainees. Seven other noncommissioned officers at Wood had been suspended because of allegations against them.

Clinton Plans Many Changes in Cabinet—Pres. Bill Clinton began to focus on the first of what would prove to be extensive changes in his cabinet and White House staff. He said, **Nov. 8**, that Erskine Bowles, an investment banker from North Carolina, would succeed Leon Panetta, who was retiring as White House chief of staff. Bowles had been deputy chief of staff and had headed the Small Business Administration. Other resignations announced or reported **Nov. 7-13** included those of Sec. of State Warren Christopher and Defense Sec. William Perry.

Texaco Settles Suit Brought by Black Employees—Texaco reached a settlement, **Nov. 15**, in a 1994 lawsuit brought by 6 black employees, who contended that the giant oil company had passed over blacks for promotion or failed to pay them salaries comparable to those paid to white employees. The Equal Employment Opportunity Commission had concluded in June, after a court-ordered investigation, that Texaco did discriminate against blacks in promotions. The agreement followed disclosure, **Nov. 4**, of a tape in which executives reportedly discussed destroying or changing documents relevant to the lawsuit. Some civil rights leaders called for a boycott of Texaco. In the settlement, Texaco agreed to create a $115 million fund to benefit its minority employees; the latter would also get 10% pay increases, and Texaco would help create a task force, under court supervision, to oversee a diversity program. The total cost of the settlement, $176 million, was the largest of its kind. On **Nov. 19**, Richard Lundwall, a Texaco human-resources official involved in the taped conversations, was charged with obstruction of justice.

Trade Imbalance Grows With China—The Commerce Dept. reported, **Nov. 20**, that the trade deficit stood at $11.34 billion in Sept. For the 2d month in a row, the biggest deficit—$4.73 billion in Sept.—was with China; it replaced Japan, which had long had the largest trade imbalance with the United States. In other economic news, the Labor Dept. said, **Nov. 1**, that the unemployment rate had remained at 5.2% in Oct. and that 210,000 nonfarm jobs had been created during the month. The department reported, **Nov. 14**, that consumer prices had risen 0.3% in Oct. The Dow Jones industrial average posted 12 new all-time highs during the month, culminating with the close of 6547.79 on **Nov. 25**.

Democrats Return $1.47 Million in Donations—As suspicions increased that the Democrats had acted improperly in soliciting and collecting donations for the 1996 election campaign, the party continued to return gifts. Most of the funds had been acquired by John Huang, a former official at the Democratic National Committee. He had previously worked for the Commerce Dept. but had been transferred to the DNC early in 1996 after reportedly telling Pres. Bill Clinton that he could do more for him by raising money. Huang had been to the White House at least 94 times since Clinton became president. Republicans asked the Justice Dept. to appoint an independent counsel to investigate the Democrats' fund-raising, but Deputy Asst. Attorney Gen. Mark Richard said, **Nov. 29**, there was "no specific, credible evidence at this time that any individual covered by the provisions of the Independent Counsel Act has committed any federal crime." By the end of Nov., the DNC had returned $1.47 million in contributions.

International

Bulgaria, Romania Elect New Presidents—On **Nov. 3**, in a runoff, Bulgarian voters chose Petar Stoyanov of the opposition Union of Democratic Forces as president. He advocated quicker economic reform and Bulgarian membership in NATO. In another presidential runoff, **Nov. 17**, Romanians elected Emil Constantinescu, who defeated Ion Iliescu, a former Communist who had been the country's president since the overthrow of Communist rule in 1989. Constantinescu had campaigned as an anticorruption re-former and blamed Iliescu for the deterioration of Romania's economy.

Yeltsin Undergoes Heart Surgery—The long-planned heart surgery for Pres. Boris Yeltsin of Russia took place at the Moscow Cardiological Center, **Nov. 5**, when a quintuple bypass operation was performed by Dr. Renat Akchurin. Yeltsin, having previously signed a decree granting temporary powers to Prime Min. Viktor Chernomyrdin, signed a 2d decree **Nov. 6**, reassuming authority. Dr. Michael DeBakey, the U.S. heart specialist who had examined Yeltsin and recommended surgery, said, **Nov. 6**, that Yeltsin was recovering rapidly.

Pakistan Prime Minister Ousted 2d Time—Prime Min. Benazir Bhutto was removed from office for the 2d time, **Nov. 5**, in the face of widespread allegations of corruption. First installed as Pakistan's prime minister after elections in 1988, she had been dismissed by the president in 1990, only to return to power in an anticorruption campaign in 1993. Recent criticism had focused especially on Bhutto's husband, who was accused of taking bribes. In Sept., Bhutto's estranged brother and 6 of his followers were killed in a shootout with police. In Oct., street demonstrations against Bhutto resulted in arrests and more protests. After troops dispatched by military authorities surrounded Bhutto's residence, Pres. Farooq Leghari took the action to dismiss her. He picked Malik Meraj Khalid as interim prime minister, pending new elections.

500,000 Refugees Return to Rwanda—The refugee crisis in Central Africa showed signs of easing. On **Nov. 5**, leaders of 8 nations in East and Central Africa urged the UN Security Council to deploy an international force to help refugees return to Rwanda and Burundi from Zaire. More than 1 million Hutu refugees had been caught up in fighting in Zaire involving Hutu militants in the camps, Zairean Tutsi rebels, and forces of Zaire's central government. Many refugees were forced from their camps and scattered through the countryside, with little access to food and medicine. Some 500,000 refugees had then converged on one large camp. Hutu militants hid among the refugees, occasionally leaving to attack forces of Tutsi-led governments in Rwanda and Burundi.

Canada, **Nov. 12**, proposed to the Security Council that troops from Western and African nations secure critical areas and facilitate repatriation of the refugees. Pres. Bill Clinton, **Nov. 13**, backed the plan, and a number of countries offered to send troops. On **Nov. 14**, 43 U.S. soldiers, commanded by Maj. Gen. Edwin Smith, arrived in Rwanda to evaluate the problem. The Security Council, **Nov. 15**, approved a Canadian-led force to aid the refugees. However, after Zairian Tutsi rebels fired rockets into the large camp, evacuation occurred quickly, and hundreds of thousands of refugees, in a 4-day period beginning **Nov. 15**, moved toward the Rwandan border. As the refugees began pouring back into Rwanda, it became less clear whether further outside intervention was needed.

Hashimoto Heads Shaky Government in Japan—Prime Min. Ryutaro Hashimoto of Japan retained his office, **Nov. 7**, after being reelected with 262 votes by the 500-member lower house of Parliament. His Liberal Democratic Party had fallen 12 votes short of a majority in elections held in Oct. Though Hashimoto was supported by members of Parliament from 2 minor parties, these parties did not become formal coalition partners with the LDP as in the past, and Hashimoto's grip on the premiership was therefore considered weak. On **Nov. 7**, he announced a new cabinet that included only LDP members.

U.S. Troops to Stay Longer in Bosnia—Although the U.S. mission in Bosnia and Herzegovina was scheduled to end by the end of 1996, Pres. Bill Clinton announced, **Nov. 15**, that 8,500 U.S. troops would remain there, with some staying until June 1998, as part of a new NATO Stabilization Force of about 30,000. The new force would continue to seek to maintain the peace but would not help rebuild

Bosnia's infrastructure, oversee elections, or hunt for suspected war criminals. In other developments, Bosnian Serb Pres. Biljana Plavsic, **Nov. 9**, ousted Gen. Ratko Mladic as leader of the Bosnian Serb armed forces. Mladic had been indicted for war crimes. He refused to step down, and on **Nov. 12**, Pres. Slobodan Milosevic of Serbia sent an official to the Bosnian Serb capital to demand his resignation. Meanwhile, at The Hague, the Netherlands, the international tribunal on war crimes, **Nov. 29**, sentenced a Croat who had served in the Bosnian Serb army to 10 years in prison for his participation in a massacre of Muslim civilians near Srebrenica in 1995.

Russian Spacecraft Bound for Mars Crashes—The Russian spacecraft *Mars 96*, launched **Nov. 16** from Kazakhstan in the direction of the red planet, malfunctioned and crashed into the Pacific Ocean, **Nov. 17**. The cooperative space venture, involving Russia and 20 other countries, had been designed to determine if life had ever existed on Mars. Four robot landers were to land on Mars and collect data on the surface and the subsurface. U.S. officials thought that the floundering spacecraft might crash into Australia, and Pres. Bill Clinton phoned a warning to Prime Min. John Howard. However, the crash occurred in the Pacific Ocean 1,000 miles east of Easter Island. The cause of the costly failure was not immediately determined.

Serbs Protest Annulment of Elections—Opposition parties did well in municipal elections in Serbia **Nov. 17**. For the first time since World War II, a non-Communist was elected mayor of Belgrade, the capital, and the opposition also won control of the city council. Similar results were reported in a number of cities. These victories, however, were overturned in court rulings and proclamations. Large numbers of citizens began demonstrating, **Nov. 19**, against the regime of Pres. Slobodan Milosevic. A Belgrade court, **Nov. 24**, annulled the victories in city council elections there. On **Nov. 25**, more than 100,000 Serbs marched in the streets of Belgrade, and protests continued through the end of the month.

U.S. Vetoes 2d Term for UN Secretary General—The reelection of Boutros Boutros-Ghali as secretary general of the United Nations was thwarted, **Nov. 19**, when the United States cast a veto against him in the Security Council. All of the other 14 members of the Council supported him, but the United States, as one of the Council's 5 permanent members, could defeat Boutros-Ghali by voting no. The Republican-led U.S. Congress was dissatisfied with the UN's handling of its financial affairs and had insisted on a 10% personnel cut and a 2-year no-growth budget as a precondition for the payment of the dues owed by the United States, now one year in arrears. Many in Congress faulted Boutros-Ghali's leadership.

Pope Meets With Cuba's Fidel Castro—At the Vatican, Pope John Paul II met for the first time, **Nov. 19**, with Cuba's Pres. Fidel Castro, leader of the only Communist state in the Western Hemisphere. Castro had suppressed religion, confiscated church property, and jailed priests during his rule, but in 1992 the constitution was amended to allow open worship. The pope accepted an invitation to visit Cuba in 1997. He would be the first head of the Roman Catholic Church ever to visit that country.

Hijacked Passenger Jet Crashes in Ocean—On **Nov. 23**, 3 hijackers seized control of an Ethiopian passenger jet during its flight from Addis Ababa, Ethiopia, to Nairobi, Kenya. The 3 men, who were believed to be Ethiopians, ordered the pilot to fly to Australia, but the plane ran out of fuel and crashed into the Indian Ocean 500 yards from a beach resort in the Comoros, off the East African coast. People on shore aided in rescue efforts, but 127 of the 175 on board died. It was thought that all the hijackers were killed.

Asian and Pacific Leaders Focus on China—Leaders of the 18 member nations of the Asia–Pacific Economic Cooperation forum met in Manila, Philippines, **Nov. 24-25**, with concerns about China occupying much of their time. Before attending the APEC meeting, Pres. Bill Clinton and First Lady Hillary Rodham Clinton flew to Australia, **Nov. 19**, and he met with Prime Min. John Howard, **Nov. 20**. Australia was troubled by Clinton's granting of most-favored-nation trade status to China despite the latter's poor record on human rights. Addressing the Australian Parliament, **Nov. 20**, Clinton urged closer ties with China to maintain influence there. Meeting during the 2-day APEC summit, Clinton and China's Pres. Jiang Zemin agreed to exchange state visits in 1997 and 1998; the news provoked criticism from human-rights activists in the United States. On **Nov. 25**, the APEC leaders declared that they would eliminate tariffs on most computers and other high-tech products by 2000. About 80% of the world trade in these products involved the APEC nations; some nations, including China, have resisted tariff reduction over concern about protecting their industries. The First Lady arrived in Thailand for a visit **Nov. 24**; Pres. Clinton joined her there the next day, on the first such visit by a U.S. president.

General

Holyfield's TKO Takes Title From Tyson—Evander Holyfield won the World Boxing Assn. heavyweight title, **Nov. 9**, defeating the champion, Mike Tyson, with a technical knockout in the 11th round. Tyson had dominated heavyweight boxing since being released from prison in 1995. Holyfield brought a 32-3 record into the ring, compared with Tyson's 45-1 record. Holyfield, fighting aggressively, put Tyson on the canvas in the 6th round, only the 2d time he had ever been knocked down. When, in the 11th round, Tyson failed to respond to 9 Holyfield punches, the referee stopped the fight.

Simpson on Stand in Civil Trial—Former football star O. J. Simpson, who had been acquitted in a criminal trial of the murder of his ex-wife, Nicole Brown Simpson, and her friend Ronald Goldman, testified in open court for the first time, during a civil trial in Los Angeles brought by the 2 victim's families. During intense questioning, **Nov. 22, 25**, and **26**, from Daniel Petrocelli, a lawyer for the plaintiffs, Simpson denied ever striking or beating his ex-wife. However, confronted with a photograph showing Nicole Simpson with a battered appearance, after an incident in which he had pleaded guilty to spousal abuse, Simpson conceded he had been "wrongly physical." He claimed that a photograph showing him wearing expensive Bruno Magli shoes, similar to those that left bloody footprints at the scene of the murders, was a fraud. Though phone records suggested otherwise, he denied that on the day of the murders he had received a phone message from Paula Barbieri, his girlfriend, breaking off their relationship. Petrocelli argued that the call had led Simpson to blame his ex-wife for Barbieri's decision.

DECEMBER 1996

National

Conviction in Savings & Loan Scandal Thrown Out—Federal District Judge Mariana Pfaelzer, **Dec. 2**, threw out the 1993 conviction of Charles Keating on federal racketeering and securities-fraud charges. Keating, head of the failed Lincoln Savings & Loan Assn. in Irvine, CA, was a high-profile defendant in the savings and loan crisis, which involved the failure of 700 S&Ls and an expensive bailout by the federal government. In Apr. 1996, Keating's 1991 state conviction on fraud charges had been overturned because of flawed instructions given to jurors by the judge in the original trial. In reversing the federal conviction, Judge Pfaelzer said several jurors in the federal trial became predisposed against Keating after having improperly discussed his 1991 conviction. Keating had served more than 4 years in prison.

Clinton Names First Woman Secretary of State— Pres. Bill Clinton announced, **Dec. 5**, that he had chosen Madeleine Albright to serve as secretary of state during his 2d administration. Once confirmed by the Senate, she would be the first woman to hold that office and also the highest-ranking female government official in U.S. history. Albright was named to succeed Warren Christopher. An authority on European affairs, she was currently U.S. ambassador to the UN.

Clinton, **Dec. 5**, also announced that he was naming Sen. William Cohen of Maine, a Republican, to succeed William Perry as secretary of defense. He named Anthony Lake, his national security adviser, as head of the troubled Central Intelligence Agency and chose Samuel Berger, Lake's deputy at the National Security Council, to step up to the top spot there.

The next round of cabinet appointments came **Dec. 13**. Clinton chose William Daley, who had led a task force that helped win congressional approval of the North American Free Trade Agreement, to be secretary of commerce. Charlene Barshefsky was nominated as the next U.S. trade representative, and Gene Sperling was named to lead the White House's National Economic Council. Rep. Bill Richardson (D, NM), a Clinton supporter in the House who had excelled in a number of diplomatic missions, was chosen to succeed Albright at the UN. Despite speculation to the contrary, Attorney Gen. Janet Reno, who had named 4 independent counsels to conduct inquiries into administration activities, was not replaced; Clinton included her in a list of cabinet members who would stay on.

On **Dec. 20**, Clinton made appointments to fill his last 4 cabinet vacancies. Federico Peña, currently transportation secretary, was nominated to be energy secretary; Rodney Slater would succeed Peña. Alexis Herman was nominated as labor secretary, and Andrew Cuomo, son of former New York Gov. Mario Cuomo, was named secretary of housing and urban development.

Boeing Heads Big Aerospace Merger—The U.S. Federal Trade Commission announced, **Dec. 6**, that it had approved the purchase by the Boeing Co., the world's largest commercial airliner manufacturer, of Rockwell International's aerospace and weapons businesses. On **Dec. 15**, Boeing announced that it would buy McDonnell Douglas, the nation's leading producer of military aircraft, including the F-15 and F-18 fighters and the C-17 transport plane. The $13.3 billion deal required government approval.

Last U.S. House Races Settled in Runoffs—The final 3 seats in the U.S. House were determined **Dec. 10**, in Texas, in runoff elections. Because of court-ordered redistricting, the voting in 13 Texas districts had been open to any candidate, and in 3 of them no candidate had won a majority in the first round of voting in Nov. Democrats made a net gain of one seat when Nick Lampson, a former teacher and tax assessor, upset Rep. Steve Stockman (R), a freshman who had been a strongly vocal conservative in his 2 years in Washington. In another district, Rep. Ken Bentsen (D) retained his seat. In a 3d runoff, Kevin Brady won a contest between 2 Republicans.

Clintons' Defense-Fund Donations Are Returned— Trustees for the Presidential Legal Expense Trust, set up in 1994 to help Pres. Bill Clinton and First Lady Hillary Rodham Clinton pay legal costs related to several investigations, announced, **Dec. 16**, that $639,000 in questionable donations to the trust had been rejected or returned after the sources of the funds could not be verified. These donations had been raised by Charles Yah Lin Trie, an Arkansas businessman, who was appointed to a presidential commission on Asian trade. Lawyers for the defense fund had known of the questionable gifts for at least 6 months without making the matter public. Funds raised by Trie for the Democratic Party were also under review, and about $1.5 million of these funds had been returned.

Black English Defined as Separate Language—A hot debate within the ranks of American educators blossomed after **Dec. 18**, the date that the Oakland, CA, school board recognized black English as a distinct language. The language was called Ebonics, from "ebony" and "phonics." Advocates of recognizing Ebonics said that it combined English with linguistic elements found in Africa and was still used by some black Americans. The Rev. Jesse Jackson, the civil rights leader, warned, **Dec. 22**, that blacks who did not speak standard English would have difficulty finding jobs. Sec. of Education Richard Riley, **Dec. 24**, said the Clinton administration rejected the concept of Ebonics as a separate language.

Committee Says House Speaker Broke Rules—A subcommittee of the House Ethics Committee said, **Dec. 21**, that House Speaker Newt Gingrich (R, GA) had violated House ethics rules and brought discredit to the House. The committee had been investigating a course, "Renewing American Civilization," that Gingrich taught at Kennesaw State College (1993) and Reinhardt College (1994-95), both in Georgia. Both schools were tax exempt. The 4-member subcommittee concluded that GOPAC, a political action committee supportive of the Republican Party, and headed by Gingrich for many years, had helped plan, finance, and promote the course. Subcommittee members found that Gingrich, who had first said that GOPAC was involved with the course and then that it was not, had given the Ethics Committee "inaccurate, incomplete and unreliable information" about the course. In fund-raising letters for GOPAC, Gingrich had pictured the course as having a partisan role.

The subcommittee found that Gingrich had used tax-exempt donations to support the course for political purposes. It also found that the Abraham Lincoln Opportunity Foundation, a tax-exempt organization, had funded telecasts that GOPAC said would attract voters to the Republican Party. In a statement, **Dec. 21**, Gingrich said he had been "wrong" not to seek the advice of a lawyer sooner in order to ensure compliance with the law.

Stock Prices Continued to Surge in 1996—A stock market boom of awesome proportions continued through Dec. On **Dec. 27**, the Dow Jones industrial average finished at 6560.91, its 44th record close of the year. On **Dec. 31**, the Dow Jones average, having declined a bit, closed at 6448.27 for the year. This represented a 26% advance for 1996, nearly matching the 33.5% runup in 1995.

In other economic news, the Labor Dept. reported, **Dec. 6**, that the unemployment rate had risen from 5.2% to 5.4% in Nov., with 118,000 nonfarm jobs created. The department said, **Dec. 11**, that wholesale prices had jumped 0.4% in Nov. and reported on **Dec. 12** that consumer prices had risen 0.3% in the same month. The Commerce Dept. reported, **Dec. 19**, that the Oct. trade deficit was a comparatively modest $7.99 billion. The Conference Board (a business-research organization) announced, **Dec. 30**, that leading economic indicators had risen 0.1% in Nov., the same as in Oct.

International

Street Protests Continue in Belgrade—Public demonstrations against the annulment of opposition election victories continued in Belgrade, the capital of Serbia, throughout Dec. A U.S. State Dept. spokesman said, **Dec. 2**, that the Serbian government had stolen the elections. Authorities, **Dec. 3**, shut down the largest independent radio station in the capital, but then relented and allowed it to reopen, **Dec. 5**. Fact finders from the Organization for Security and Cooperation in Europe announced, **Dec. 27**, that opposition candidates in the Nov. election had won in Belgrade and 13 other cities and towns and told Serbia to reinstate the rightful winners. **Dec. 31** marked the 44th consecutive day of street protests.

Agreement Allows Iraq to Export Oil—UN Sec. Gen. Boutros Boutros-Ghali approved an agreement, **Dec. 9**, allowing Iraq to resume exports of oil so as to obtain money to alleviate critical domestic shortages of food and medicine. The new pact eased a UN trade embargo imposed on Iraq shortly after its invasion of Kuwait in 1990. An earlier UN-Iraqi agreement fell apart in Aug. 1996 when Iraq intervened in a conflict between factions of its Kurdish population. To secure a new agreement, Iraq promised to dismantle its weapons of mass destruction. Under the pact approved in Dec., Iraq could sell up to $2 billion worth of oil during a renewable 6-month period. Iraq agreed to a monitoring of how it spent the income. Production was expected to average 600,000 barrels a day, only 20% of the pre-invasion level.

New Constitution Signed in South Africa—Pres. Nelson Mandela signed into law a new democratic constitution for South Africa, **Dec. 10**, 6 days after the document, in revised form, was approved by the Constitutional Court. The historic signing took place at Sharpetown, a township that became identified with the anti-apartheid struggle after a massacre of anti-apartheid demonstrators there in 1960. Included in the new constitution was a bill of rights, to take effect immediately; other provisions were to be phased in over a 3-year period.

Second Tide of Refugees Returns to Rwanda—On **Dec. 14**, Tanzanian soldiers began forcing Rwandan refugees in northwestern Tanzania to leave their camps and return home. By year's end, some 500,000 refugees had completed the short trip to the border. In Nov., an estimated 600,000 Rwandan refugees had traveled from Zaire back to Rwanda. The refugees, mostly Hutus, had fled Rwanda to escape violence between members of Hutu and Tutsi ethnic groups.

Korean Court Cuts Ex-Presidents' Sentences—An appeals court, **Dec. 16**, reduced the sentences imposed in Aug. on 2 former presidents of South Korea. The death sentence of Chun Doo Hwan was reduced to life imprisonment, and Roh Tae Woo's term of 22½ years was reduced to 17 years. Other defendants convicted in the case received suspended sentences or were granted outright acquittals.

African Diplomat Named UN Secretary General—Kofi Annan of Ghana, who had worked for the United Nations for more than 3 decades, was elected UN secretary general, **Dec. 17**. Educated in the United States, where he received a degree in economics at Macalester College and in management at MIT, Annan had gone to work for the UN's World Health Organization. From 1993 he headed the UN's peacekeeping operations, and in 1995 he oversaw the transfer of the UN's Bosnian peacekeeping mission to NATO. After intense behind-the-scenes discussions, the Security Council, **Dec. 13**, unanimously recommended Annan's election by the Gen. Assembly. Annan, the first black African to lead the UN, was to succeed Boutros Boutros-Ghali, whose reelection had been vetoed by the United States.

Peru Rebels Seize 600 at Envoy's Residence—More than 600 hostages, including prominent government officials, were seized in Lima, Peru, **Dec. 17**, by a Marxist guerrilla group. Some 25 members of the Tupac Amaru Revolutionary Movement (MRTA) broke into the Japanese ambassador's residence about 8 P.M. during a celebration of the birthday of Emperor Akihito. Officials taken hostage included ambassadors of 12 nations, Peru's foreign and agricultural ministers, members of Congress, and the president of the Supreme Court. The captors demanded that several hundred of their imprisoned comrades be released.

The government of Pres. Alberto Fujimori had cracked down on rebel movements in Peru, including the MRTA and a larger group, the Sendero Luminoso (Shining Path). Since 1980, fighting between the government and rebels had taken 30,000 lives. While some other nations had expressed alarm at repressive measures taken by the Fujimori government, many Peruvians approved the measures, which appeared effective, and it was widely believed that the worst of the strife was over.

Two hours after the hostages were seized, the rebels freed 170 female and older captives, including Fujimori's mother and sister. Sporadic release of prisoners continued in subsequent days. On **Dec. 18**, the Red Cross brought food and water to the residence. The government, **Dec. 19**, cut off water, electricity, and telephone service. Fujimori, **Dec. 21**, offered the rebels safe passage from the residence if they freed their prisoners and gave up their weapons. On **Dec. 22**, the rebels freed 225 hostages, including all 7 from the United States. On **Dec. 31**, with the crisis 2 weeks old, 81 hostages were still being held.

Guatemalan Civil War Ends—An agreement between the Guatemalan government and leftist rebels of the Guatemalan National Revolutinary Union, signed **Dec. 29**, brought an apparent end to a 36-year civil war that had claimed more than 100,000 lives since 1960. The origins of the conflict can be traced to the overthrow of Pres. Jacobo Arbenz Guzmán in a 1954 military coup backed by the United States, after he had planned to expropriate land owned by a U.S.-based company. Over the years, the native population, suspected of supporting the rebels, suffered heavily at the hands of the armed forces. On **Dec. 4**, the 2 sides had signed a cease-fire. The final peace agreements, known as an Accord for a Firm and Lasting Peace, provided for demobilization of the 3,000 remaining rebels and a reduction in the size of the armed forces by one-third. A civilian police force was to assume domestic security responsibilities, and the government promised to deal with discrimination against indigenous Guatemalans. However, the pact did not deal with land reform, a major issue of concern to the largely landless native population.

North Koreans Apologize for Spy Incident—A tense atmosphere had existed between the 2 Koreas since Sept., when 26 North Korean commandos had landed surreptitiously in the South's territory after their spy submarine ran aground. Of these, 24 were killed, either by South Korean troops or by their own comrades, 1 was captured, and 1 was missing. On **Dec. 29**, in a statement carried on North Korea's official Radio Pyongyang, the Communist government expressed "deep regret" over the incident. On **Dec. 30**, at the border village of Panmunjon, South Korea returned the remains of the dead commandos. Also on **Dec. 30**, the United States announced that North Korea had agreed to meet with U.S. and South Korean representatives to discuss a permanent peace treaty to officially end the Korean War. The 1950-53 war had concluded only with an armistice.

General

O. J. Simpson Given Custody of His Children—On **Dec. 20**, a California Family Court judge awarded former football star O. J. Simpson custody of his 2 children by his 2d wife, Nicole Brown Simpson. Nicole Simpson and a friend, Ronald Goldman, had been murdered in 1994; O. J. Simpson was tried and found not guilty of their murders. He remained a defendant in a civil suit brought by the families of the murder victims. The children, Sydney, 11, and Justin, 8, had lived with their maternal grandparents since their mother's death.

Child Beauty Pageant Star Murdered in Colorado—In a case that drew wide national attention, JonBenet Ramsey, a 6-year-old girl who was named Little Miss Colorado 1995, was found murdered in the basement of her home in Boulder, CO, **Dec. 26**. Her parents, John and Patricia Ramsey, had reported her missing 8 hours earlier and produced what was said to be a ransom note; police reported no signs of forced entry. The parents, who were not interviewed by authorities until Apr. 30, maintained innocence of any involvement.

JANUARY 1997

National

Bombs Detonated at 2 Abortion Clinics—Two containers of flammable liquid were thrown at an abortion clinic in Tulsa, OK, **Jan. 1**, causing light damage. On **Jan. 16**, a bomb exploded in midmorning at a building in Atlanta housing an abortion clinic. An hour later, after investigators and others had come to the scene, a 2d bomb, packed with nails, exploded near the building. The first bomb had damaged the clinic but caused no injuries; 6 investigators and reporters were injured in the 2d explosion. On **Jan. 19**, 2 bombs exploded at the Tulsa site bombed earlier; the building was damaged again, but no one was injured.

House Speaker Reelected—and Reprimanded as New Congress Opens—Newt Gingrich (R, GA) was reelected Speaker of the U.S. House of Representatives, **Jan. 7**, but he subsequently received a reprimand from his colleagues. Although the Republicans held a 19-seat majority in the House, Gingrich's expected reelection had been thrown into some doubt after the House Ethics Committee concluded, in Dec., that he had violated House rules and misled the committee in its investigation of possible political use of tax-exempt donations. On **Jan. 7**, the opening day of the 105th Congress, the House considered, but defeated, 222–210, a motion to elect an interim speaker until the committee could complete its investigation. In the vote for Speaker, which followed, Gingrich received 216 votes to 205 for the Democratic leader, Richard Gephardt (MO). Nine fellow-Republicans declined to vote for Gingrich, either voting for other Republicans or, in effect, abstaining; and 1 Republican was absent. In accepting election, Gingrich apologized for any "controversy or inappropriate attention to the House" which he might have brought. On the same day, the Senate convened its opening session, with Trent Lott (MS) resuming his position as majority leader.

Jim McDermott (D, WA) resigned from the House Ethics Committee, **Jan. 14**, following allegations that he had illegally leaked to the press a tape recording of a phone conversation among Gingrich and other GOP leaders in Dec. during which they discussed how to respond to the committee's Dec. report on Gingrich. The conversation had been overheard by a Florida couple on a police scanner. They recorded it and gave a copy to McDermott. (In Apr. the couple pleaded guilty to intercepting the call, and were fined $1,000.)

The Ethics Committee, **Jan. 17**, considered a report from its counsel, James Cole, concluding that Gingrich had violated tax laws and lied to the committee. However, members of the committee were unable to agree to these conclusions. Cole stated that, with respect to a college course given by Gingrich, and supported by tax-exempt contributions, "there was an effort to have the material appear to be nonpartisan on its face yet serve as a partisan, political message for the purpose of building the Republican Party." A subcommittee drafting recommendations for punishment agreed to refrain from saying that Gingrich "knew" he had provided inaccurate information to the committee, only that he "should have known." In return, Gingrich agreed to accept a reprimand and a $300,000 fine to cover the approximate costs to the investigation incurred because of his misrepresentations. The committee, by a 7-1 vote, approved this compromise, **Jan. 17**. The full House, **Jan. 21**, approved the reprimand and fine by a 395-28 vote.

Report on "Gulf War Syndrome" Released—A report from a presidential committee failed to resolve the mystery surrounding the so-called Gulf War Syndrome, from which many veterans of the 1991 Persian Gulf War claimed to suffer. The war, though brief, may have exposed troops to chemical weapons and various pollutants, such as those produced by oil fires. Soon after the war ended, veterans in growing numbers described such symptoms as fatigue, nausea, headaches, pain in joints, and loss of memory. An initial Defense Dept. investigation concluded there was no evidence of any connection between the war and the reported maladies. However, the Presidential Advisory Committee on Gulf War Veterans' Illnesses concluded, **Jan. 7**, that the earlier investigation had been inadequate and called for further inquiry. For its part, the committee said that stress might be to blame in part, but it found little evidence that exposure to chemical weapons or pollutants was a factor. A report by scientists at the University of Texas said, **Jan. 8**, that they had identified 6 clusters of ailments suffered by veterans; the report concluded that exposure to combinations of chemicals was somehow linked to the conditions.

Economy Expanded at Faster Pace in 1996—Data released in Jan. provided a clearer picture of the state of the economy in 1996. The Labor Dept. said, **Jan. 9**, that prices charged by farmers and manufacturers for finished goods had increased by 2.8% in 1996, compared with a 2.3% increase in 1995. The department reported, **Jan. 10**, that the unemployment rate in Dec. had been 5.3%, which was slightly below the 5.6% reported for Dec. 1995. For all of 1996, 2.6 million payroll jobs were created, compared with 2.2 million in 1995. In a **Jan. 14** report, the department said consumer prices had risen 3.3% in 1996, up from 2.5% in 1995; inflation exceeded 3% for the first time in 6 years, with the higher level attributed to food and energy costs.

The Commerce Dept. reported, **Jan. 17**, that the trade deficit had stood at $8.44 billion in Nov., up from the previous month as a result of the strengthening of the U.S. dollar in international currency markets. On Wall Street, stocks continued to surge; the **Jan. 21** close of 6883.90 was the 10th all-time high posted in the new year for the Dow Jones industrial average. The Commerce Dept. said, **Jan. 31**, that gross domestic product had grown at a rate of 2.5% during 1996 (later revised to 2.4%), compared with 2.0% in 1995. The increase in the 4th quarter of 1996 had been sharp, with growth of 4.7% at an annual rate reported.

Two Women Cadets Leave Military Academy—Two of the 4 female cadets who enrolled in the Citadel, the South Carolina military academy, in fall 1996 after the school lost its legal effort to bar women, resigned from the academy, **Jan. 12**. The attitude of many male members of the cadet corps had been described as hostile toward the admission of women. The cadets, Kim Messer and Jeanie Mentavlos, said they had been assaulted and sexually harassed. Two other women continued as cadets.

Seven Black Soldiers Receive Medal of Honor—Pres. Bill Clinton awarded, **Jan 13**, the Medal of Honor, the highest U.S. award for bravery, to 7 black soldiers for their courage in action in Italy during World War II. This was the first time the medal was given to black World War II servicemen. Only one of the 7, 77-year-old Vernon J. Baker, was still living. The others, who received the award posthumously, were Edward A. Carter Jr., John R. Fox, Willy F. James Jr., Ruben Rivers, Charles L. Thomas, and George Watson.

Clinton, Gore Inaugurated for 2d Terms—Pres. Bill Clinton and Vice Pres. Al Gore took the oath of office to begin their 2d terms, **Jan. 20**. Gore was sworn in first, by Supreme Court Justice Ruth Bader Ginsburg, the first woman to administer an inaugural oath. Clinton was then sworn in by Chief Justice William Rehnquist. In his inaugural address, Clinton laid out no new policy initiatives. He took a conciliatory stance, stating that the voters, who had elected a Democratic president and a Republican Congress, expected government leaders to work together and not engage in "the politics of petty bickering and extreme partisanship they plainly deplore." He said voters wanted those in Washington "to move on with America's mission." Clinton stated that the purpose of government must be "to give all Americans an opportunity—not a guarantee, but a real opportunity—to build better lives."

Fund-Raising Scandal Continues to Plague Democrats

Fund-Raising Scandal Continues to Plague Democrats—In the face of continuing reports of legally dubious fund-raising practices, Don Fowler, outgoing chairman of the Democratic National Committee (DNC), said, **Jan. 21**, that the committee would no longer take donations from foreign nationals or from American subsidiaries of companies based outside the United States. Pres. Bill Clinton, addressing the DNC, also said that the Democrats would stop taking so-called soft money (funds donated to political parties and not subject to the same reporting requirements as money given directly to candidates), provided that the Republicans agreed to do so as well. The White House acknowledged, **Jan. 24**, that leading bankers and financial regulators had met with Clinton at the White House in May 1996. Although bankers and regulators often meet to discuss government policies on banks, this meeting was unusual because it was set up by Democratic fund-raisers. The White House also released information that day on 103 coffee meetings organized there by the DNC to help bring in donations to the 1996 Clinton reelection campaign. The documents showed that White House staffers and federal agency officials had been asked to participate in fundraising efforts targeted toward minorities, suggesting potential violations of federal laws restricting political activities by such officials.

Albright, Cohen Confirmed for Cabinet—Madeleine Albright and William Cohen, nominated by Pres. Bill Clinton to be secretary of state and secretary of defense, respectively, sailed through the Senate confirmation process in Jan. After being readily approved by Senate committees, both were confirmed by the Senate in 99-0 votes on **Jan. 22**. Albright was sworn into office **Jan. 23**, becoming the first woman to head the State Dept.

International

Israel, Palestinians Agree on Hebron Withdrawal—One of the most contentious issues between the Israelis and the Palestinians was resolved with the approval of an accord on Israeli withdrawal from Hebron, the only city from which Israel had not withdrawn under the terms of a 1995 agreement. On **Jan. 1**, an Israeli soldier had opened fire on Palestinians in a marketplace in Hebron, wounding 6. After being subdued, he said he had hoped to thwart plans for an Israeli pullout. Vowing that the incident would not interrupt their negotiations, Israeli Prime Min. Benjamin Netanyahu and Yasir Arafat, leader of the Palestinian National Authority (PNA), reached the agreement on Hebron, **Jan. 15**. Under the new accord, Israel was to pull out of 80% of Hebron, but an enclave having some 450 Israeli settlers would stay under the protection of the Israeli military, pending a final agreement. By late 1998, Israel was to pull back from all West Bank areas except settlements and certain military locations. Israeli nationalists denounced the agreement, and the Israeli cabinet approved it by only an 11-7 margin, **Jan. 16**. The science minister, Benny Begin, son of former Prime Min. Menachem Begin, resigned. The PNA cabinet approved the accord, **Jan. 16**, and the Israeli parliament approved it, 87-17, on **Jan. 17**.

Serbian Leaders Give Ground on Voting—In the face of continuing street demonstrations, Serbia's foreign minister, Milan Milutinovic, **Jan. 3**, conceded that the political opposition had won disputed elections in 3 small cities in 1996. However, he rejected the findings in a Dec. report by the Organization for Security and Cooperation in Europe indicating that the opposition had won many other contests, some in major cities. On **Jan. 8**, Pres. Slobodan Milosevic did concede that the opposition had won in Nis, Serbia's 2d-largest city. Opposition leaders said they would continue to protest until all of their claimed victories were recognized.

Austrian Chancellor Resigns—Franz Vranitzky announced, **Jan. 18**, that he was stepping down as chancellor of Austria after serving 10½ years. He had sought to improve relations with the international community which became tense in the 1980s when Pres. Kurt Waldheim, a previous UN secretary general, was accused of participating in Nazi atrocities as a German officer during World War II. Vranitzky, in 1988, publicly apologized for Austria's involvement in war crimes, and in 1993 he became the first Austrian premier to visit Israel. He had also pushed successfully for Austrian membership in the European Union. In 1996, Vranitzky's Social Democratic Party had suffered heavy losses in an election for seats in the European Parliament. In announcing his resignation, Vranitzky chose Finance Min. Viktor Klima to succeed him. Klima was a top official in the state petroleum company before joining the government as minister of public economy and transport in 1992. As finance minister, he had supported budget austerity in order to qualify Austria for membership in the economic and monetary union of the European Union.

Police Admit Killing Apartheid Foe—Five former police officers acknowledged killing a leading opponent of the old apartheid regime, the South African Truth and Reconciliation Commission announced **Jan. 28**. Steve Biko, leader of the Black Consciousness Movement, had been arrested in Aug. 1977; his death while in custody, from a massive brain hemorrhage, was reported less than a month later. Police interrogators at that time claimed he had injured his head while scuffling with the police, and an inquest found Biko's death to have been an accident. The incident provoked worldwide outrage, and the official explanation of Biko's injuries was widely rejected. In confessing to the commission, the policemen were protected by a grant of amnesty.

General

Florida Voted No. 1 in College Football—The University of Florida Gators were named in postseason polls as the top U.S. college football team. The way was cleared for Florida after previously undefeated Arizona State lost to Ohio State, 20-17, in the Rose Bowl on **Jan. 1**. In the Sugar Bowl, **Jan. 2**, Florida defeated Florida State, 52-20, handing the Seminoles their only loss of the season. Gator quarterback Danny Wuerffel, who had been awarded the Heisman Trophy as the outstanding player of the year in college football, passed for 306 yards to lead the Southeastern Conference champs to victory. On **Jan. 3**, the Associated Press media poll and the *USA Today*/CNN coaches' poll both reported the same final rankings for their top teams. The top 4, in both polls, were: 1. Florida (12-1), 2. Ohio State (11-1), 3. Florida State (11-1), 4. Arizona State (11-1).

Son of Bill Cosby Killed in Los Angeles—Ennis Cosby, 27, the son of comedian Bill Cosby, was shot to death **Jan 16** on a freeway exit ramp in Los Angeles, as he changed a flat tire on his Mercedes-Benz sports car. Police believed robbery was the most likely motive. A friend of Cosby's, who found the body, gave a description of a man she saw near the car as she drove up but was unable to identify anyone in a police lineup. Mikhail Markhasev, 18, a Russian immigrant, was arrested **Mar. 12** on suspicion of murder, after information was provided by a tipster. Ennis Cosby, a graduate student working toward a doctorate in special education at Columbia University, had been in Los Angeles during a school break visiting friends. Bill Cosby said after he heard of his son's death, "He was my hero."

Antarctic-Crossing and Ballooning Records Set—On **Jan. 18**, the Norwegian Borge Ousland completed a 1,675-mi. trek across Antarctica, the first time anyone traversed the continent alone. Beginning Nov. 15, 1996, on Berkner Island, he ended his journey at New Zealand's Scott Base 64 days later. Ousland wore skis and used a sail to take advantage of the wind.

On **Jan. 20**, American millionaire Steve Fossett landed his hot-air balloon in northern India, after a record-setting 9,672 mi. and 146 hrs., 54 min. in flight. Fossett, who launched his balloon **Jan. 13** from St. Louis, MO, flying eastward, was trying to become the first person to circumnavigate the globe in a balloon. He used up fuel faster than expected and landed once it became apparent that he could not complete the trip and might otherwise have to come down in the ocean or in hostile or rugged territory.

Green Bay Packers Are Super Bowl Champs—The Green Bay Packers, who had won the first 2 Super Bowl titles in the glory years of Coach Vince Lombardi in 1967 and 1968, finally won a 3d championship **Jan. 26**. The Packers and the New England Patriots advanced to the Super Bowl, **Jan. 12**, with victories over a pair of 2d-year expansion teams. The Packers defeated the Carolina Panthers, 30–13, for the National Football Conference title, and the Patriots downed the Jacksonville Jaguars, 20–6, for the American Football Conference championship.

The Packers, coached by Mike Holmgren, won the Super Bowl, 35–21, thwarting the Patriots with big plays. Quarterback Brett Favre threw a 54-yard touchdown pass to Andre Rison in the first quarter, and another touchdown pass, for 81 yards, to Antonio Freeman in the 2d. In the 3d quarter, Desmond Howard returned a kickoff 99 yards for a touchdown. Howard, who had 244 total yards on returns of punts and kickoffs, was voted the game's most valuable player.

FEBRUARY 1997

National

Democrats' Fund-Raising Scandal Continues to Grow—The *Washington Post* reported, **Feb. 1**, that a New Jersey man with links to organized crime had met with Pres. Bill Clinton in 1995. The Democratic National Committee (DNC) had arranged the meeting. The man, Eric Wynn, had been jailed on charges of fraud and tax evasion, and had also been convicted of stock manipulation. Wynn, who had been invited to many DNC events, was one of many prospective campaign contributors with whom Clinton had met in the runup to the 1996 election. Newspapers reported that other White House visitors had had brushes with the law. The *Post* also reported, **Feb. 12**, that the Chinese government may have channeled money to the DNC in order to influence the Clinton administration.

Documents released by the National Security Council **Feb. 14** showed that NSC officials had warned Vice Pres. Al Gore about attending a 1996 fund-raising lunch at a Buddhist temple in Los Angeles. Gore, who attended, said later that he had not known it was a fund-raiser, then said he had known it was "finance related." Donations totaling $140,000 were raised by the event, and the sources of some of the gifts were not clear.

Clinton also endorsed rewarding party contributors with such perks as golf games with him or overnight stays in the White House, according to documents released **Feb. 25** and handed over to a House committee. Included among the documents was a memorandum written to the president by Terence McAuliffe, who was finance director of the DNC at the time. The memo listed "our top ten supporters" and had Clinton's response, "Ready to start overnights right away." The White House, **Feb. 25**, named 938 persons who had stayed there overnight. The DNC said, **Feb. 28**, that it would return nearly $1.5 million in contributions that may have been illegal or improper.

Clinton Delivers State of Union Speech—In his annual State of the Union speech, delivered to a joint session of Congress **Feb. 4**, Pres. Bill Clinton offered proposals that would increase the current education budget by 20%. Saying education would be his top priority in his 2d term, he proposed tax credits for college students, tutoring to improve reading skills, more training for workers, free access to the Internet for public-school students, and establishment of national standards for teachers. The president also endorsed future campaign finance reform, including a ban on so-called soft money, restrictions on political action committees, and incentives for candidates to reduce spending. He also urged greater efforts on environmental cleanup and fighting crime, and called for changes in the 1996 welfare reform law.

In the Republican response to the president, Rep. J. C. Watts (OK), the only black Republican in Congress, said the GOP would concentrate its efforts on strengthening the family, balancing the budget, and improving race relations.

Economy Is Growing; Trade Deficit Soared in 1996—The Conference Board, a business-research organization, reported, **Feb. 4**, that leading economic indicators had risen 0.1% in Dec. The Labor Dept. said, **Feb. 7**, that the unemployment rate stood at 5.4% in Jan., compared with 5.3% in Dec., and that a total of 271,000 nonfarm jobs were created. On the inflation front, the department reported, **Feb. 14** and **18**, that prices charged by farmers and manufacturers for finished goods had declined 0.3% in Jan., while consumer prices rose 0.1%. On Wall Street, the Dow Jones industrial average posted its 13th high of the year, closing at 7067.46 on **Feb. 18**. The Commerce Dept. said, **Feb. 19**, that the U.S. trade deficit for all of 1996 was $114.23 billion, up 8.7% from the revised 1995 total of $105.06 billion. A strong U.S. dollar, which stimulated imports, was seen as responsible in part for the increase.

Biggest-Ever Wall Street Merger Announced—Morgan Stanley Group, Inc., announced, **Feb. 5**, that it would merge with Dean Witter, Discover & Co. The resulting corporation would be the biggest U.S. securities company, as measured in assets under management and market capitalization. Morgan Stanley advises major corporations, while Dean Witter's brokers advise small investors on stocks, bonds, and mutual funds. In the agreement, each Morgan Stanley share would be exchanged for 1.65 shares of Dean Witter. The new Morgan Stanley, Dean Witter, Discover & Co. would manage $270 billion in assets.

Clinton Unveils $1.69 Trillion Budget—Pres. Bill Clinton sent to Congress, **Feb. 6**, a proposal for a $1.69 trillion budget for the 1998 fiscal year. He said adoption of the budget would put the country on the course toward a balanced budget by 2002. Clinton proposed, over 5 years, to cut projected government spending by $252 billion, with 43% of the savings to come from Medicare and Medicaid. The budget proposed increased outlays for education, welfare, and health care, and about $18 billion was included to restore some benefits lost by legal immigrants in the 1996 welfare bill.

The budget would end 30 tax preferences for corporations, and expiring excise taxes would be renewed. On the other hand, Clinton proposed $98 billion in tax cuts that would mainly benefit middle-class families, students, homeowners, and older Americans. A Congressional Budget Office analysis of the budget showed that there would still be a $49 billion deficit in 2002. Republican reactions ranged from caution to outright rejection. GOP leaders said the tax cuts were too small.

Whitewater Prosecutor Stays After Flip-Flop—Pepperdine University officials announced, **Feb. 17**, that Kenneth Starr, the independent counsel investigating Whitewater and other matters related to Pres. Clinton, would resign to become dean of the law and public policy schools at Pepperdine. His decision stunned those anxious for the inquiry to continue and prompted speculation that he did not have sufficient evidence to make a case against the president or first lady. Starr, **Feb. 18**, said the investigation would still go forward. Then, on **Feb. 21**, Starr announced that he would forgo the Pepperdine position and not resign. He called his previous decision a mistake.

Clinton Takes Aim at Juvenile Crime—Pres. Bill Clinton, in legislative proposals announced **Feb. 19**, sought to head off what some analysts predicted would be a surge in juvenile crime in the United States. In general, crime rates had declined during the past few years, but enrollment of schoolchildren was higher than ever before, suggesting a possible surge in the relatively crime-prone population of adolescents and young adults. Clinton proposed to spend $495 million over 2 years to help state and local governments prosecute juvenile offenders and combat gang violence. Funds would be utilized to combat truancy and support after-school programs. Republican spending proposals in this area emphasized tougher penalties for juvenile crime and grants to states that could be used to build detention centers.

Gunman Shoots Tourists at Empire State Building—On **Feb. 23**, a gunman shot and killed a tourist from Denmark and injured 6 other people on the observation deck of the Empire State Building in New York City; afterwards he killed himself. The man, identified as 69-year-old Ali Abu Kamal, was a Palestinian teacher who had been in the U.S. since Dec. In a letter found in a pouch around his neck, he said his plan was to murder as many "Zionists" as he could in New York City.

Former FBI Agent Admits Spying—A former agent of the FBI pleaded guilty to espionage, **Feb. 28**. The agent, Earl Edwin Pitts, had been arrested in Dec. and charged with selling classified data to Russia for more than $220,000. In Pitts's plea, entered in federal court in Alexandria, VA, he admitted conspiring to commit espionage and attempted espionage. Pitts, only the 2d FBI agent ever to be convicted of spying, was sentenced **June 23** to 27 years in prison.

International

Muslim Party Wins Pakistan Election—Control of the government of Pakistan changed hands in Feb. In Nov., Pres. Farooq Leghari had dissolved the government of Prime Min. Benazir Bhutto because of allegations of corruption and called new elections. On **Feb. 3**, Bhutto's Pakistan People's Party won only 17 seats, down from the 86 it had held before. The election winner, with 134 seats, up from 72, was the Pakistan Muslim League Party, led by former Prime Min. Nawaz Sharif. Sharif was sworn in **Feb. 17**. He promised to resume peace talks with India.

Opposition Party Takes Power in Belgrade—Pres. Slobodan Milosevic of Serbia bowed to the conclusions in the Dec. report of an international mission and, on **Feb. 4**, called for a law allowing the political opposition to take power in 14 cities. A leader of the Zajendo opposition coalition said, **Feb. 4**, that daily street demonstrations would continue until all duly elected opposition city councils were seated and other demands were met. Serbia's parliament, **Feb. 11**, passed a law reinstating the opposition victories. After 89 days, Zajendo held its last protest rally in Belgrade, **Feb. 15**. Its coalition took control of the Belgrade city council, **Feb. 21**. The opposition had already taken over in the 13 other cities.

Albanians Protest Collapse of Pyramid Schemes—Investing in so-called pyramid funds had become widely popular in Albania in recent months, and those who invested early reaped large returns. But as tens of thousands of people rushed to put their money into the funds, most investors found that they had lost their stake, in many cases their life savings. The Gjallica pyramid went bankrupt on **Feb. 4**, and on that day the government began distributing available funds from the collapsed Populli pyramid fund. Although all investors were to retrieve 60% of their deposits, many did not get any of their money back. Beginning **Feb. 5**, thousands of people massed daily to demand reimbursement from the government. Authorities, **Feb. 9**, charged the director and 11 managers of the Gjallica fund

with fraud. Prem. Alexander Meksi declared a partial state of emergency in Vlore, **Feb. 10**.

President of Ecuador Ousted—Ecuadorean Pres. Abdalá Bucaram was forced from office in Feb. He had been elected easily in 1996, supported especially by the country's poor. However, his economic austerity program, including big hikes in the cost of basic utilities, prompted widespread strikes and protests. A general strike **Feb. 5-6** paralyzed the country. Bucaram brought in army troops to guard the capital. Congress, **Feb. 6**, voted, 44–34, to remove Bucaram, who also had a reputation for eccentric behavior, for "mental incapacity." He refused to step down, but in a compromise, **Feb. 9**, the vice president, Rosalia Arteaga, agreed to serve briefly. Fabian Alarcon, the president of Congress, was named interim president, **Feb. 11**, until a newly elected president could be installed.

Mexico's Drug Czar Linked to Cartel Leader—Gen. Jesús Gutiérrez Rebollo, head of Mexico's leading antidrug agency, was forced to resign, **Feb. 6**, after evidence emerged that he had taken bribes from a powerful drug cartel. Pres. Ernesto Zedillo Ponce de León had appointed Gutiérrez in Dec. to lead the National Institute to Combat Drugs, in a move to take the antidrug fight from a police force viewed as corrupt and put it under army control. Defense Min. Enrique Cervantes Aguirre announced the resignation **Feb. 18**. Cervantes said Gutiérrez, who was under arrest, had accepted money and other gifts from Amado Carrillo Fuentes, reputed leader of a drug cartel. U.S. officials said, **Feb. 19**, that Gutiérrez had been briefed on what the United States knew about the Mexican drug cartels. Mexico announced, **Feb. 25**, that 36 officers in the National Institute to Combat Drugs had been dismissed.

Pres. Bill Clinton, in a required annual report to Congress **Feb. 28**, certified that Mexico was cooperating in the fight against drugs, and hence remained eligible for military and economic aid. Colombia, however, was denied aid certification for the 2d straight year. Sec. of State Madeleine Albright said, **Feb. 28**, that drug influence extended to the highest level of the Colombian government.

North Korean Party Figure Asks Asylum—South Korea announced, **Feb. 12**, that Hwang Jang Yop, a secretary of North Korea's ruling Workers (Communist) Party, had sought asylum at the South Korean consulate in Beijing. Hwang, who was a former president of Kim Il Sung University, was the highest-level official ever to defect from North Korea. In a note released by South Korea, **Feb. 13**, Hwang said he hoped his action would help bring the 2 Koreas together. Meanwhile, on **Feb. 15**, another North Korean defector, Lee Han Yong, was shot outside his home in Bundang, South Korea; he died 10 days later. South Korean officials believed North Korean agents were responsible.

In response to a UN appeal for famine relief, the United States and South Korea announced, **Feb. 17**, that they would resume emergency food aid to North Korea. On **Feb. 21**, North Korea announced it would attend a briefing by the United States and South Korea on proposed talks to reach a final settlement of the Korean War.

China's Leader Deng Xiaoping Dies—Deng Xiaoping, who until the end remained China's "paramount leader," though he no longer held an office, died in Beijing, **Feb. 19**, at the age of 92. He would be remembered for China's free-market economic revolution, and for the brutal crackdown on anti-government demonstrators in 1989.

Born in 1904, Deng joined the Communist Party in the 1920s. He studied in the Soviet Union, before becoming secretary to the Chinese Communist Party in 1927. He was a Red army commander against the forces of Chiang Kai-shek and joined the Communist's 6,000-mi. retreat, or Long March, in 1934-35. A leader in the struggle against the Japanese during World War II and in the overthrow of the Chiang regime in 1949, Deng became secretary general of the party in 1956. Purged in 1966 during Mao Zedong's Cultural Revolution, Deng was rehabilitated in 1973. After Mao died,

Deng solidified his power in 1978 and moved toward a modernized market economy. He opposed political liberalization and allowed the army to crush demonstrations in Beijing's Tiananmen Square in 1989, with heavy loss of life. He oversaw talks establishing terms for the transfer of Hong Kong from Great Britain to China.

A nationally televised funeral, which took place on **Feb. 24**, was held at a military hospital in Beijing. Pres. Jiang Zemin, whom Deng had chosen to succeed him, eulogized Deng at a memorial service in Beijing, **Feb. 25**, ending an official 6-day mourning period.

By coincidence, Sec. of State Madeleine Albright was making her first official visit to China, **Feb. 24**. She met with Chinese leaders and expressed optimism about Sino-U.S. relations.

Israeli Housing Plan in Jerusalem Stirs Protests—The Israeli cabinet, **Feb. 26**, approved development of a large Jewish neighborhood in East Jerusalem. The area was traditionally Arab in population, but Israel wanted the city to be its undivided capital. Religious and nationalist conservatives in Israel had warned Prime Min. Benjamin Netanyahu that he must support creation of the neighborhood or his government would fall. The Palestinian National Authority strongly protested development of the area.

General

O. J. Simpson Liable in Deaths of 2 People—O. J. Simpson, who had been found not guilty in 1995 of murdering his ex-wife, Nicole, and her friend Ronald Goldman, had less success in a Santa Monica, CA, civil trial. A civil jury, **Feb. 4**, found the former football star, actor, and television pitchman liable in their deaths. Conviction in the criminal trial had required unanimity "beyond a reasonable doubt"; in the civil trial, liability required only a finding by 9 of the 12 jurors that the verdict was supported by a preponderance of the evidence. The criminal jury had been mostly black, the civil jury mostly white.

A great deal of evidence was common to both trials, with bloodstains from the victims appearing to link Simpson to their murders. In both trials, the defense contended that blood samples had been badly handled by the authorities after collection and that blood had been planted to frame Simpson. Evidence offered for the first time in the civil trial included 31 photographs of Simpson wearing expensive Bruno Magli shoes like those that had left bloody prints near the victims. Simpson, who did not testify in the criminal trial, denied ever owning such shoes in his testimony in the civil trial. At the civil trial, lawyers for the plaintiffs were allowed to read excerpts from Nicole Simpson's diary in which she wrote of threats from O. J. Simpson.

In its unanimous finding of liability, the jury awarded the Goldman family $8.5 million in compensatory damages. Nicole Simpson's family had not sought compensatory damages. Testimony in the punitive-damage phase of the trial began **Feb. 6**. On **Feb. 10** the jury ordered Simpson to pay $12.5 million in punitive damages to each of the 2 families. The verdict and damages were appealed.

Fourteen-Year-Old Becomes Youngest U.S. Figure Skating Champion—Tara Lipinski defeated defending champion Michelle Kwan at the U.S. National Figure Skating Championships held in Nashville, TN, **Feb. 15**. At the age of 14, Lipinski became the youngest to hold the title. Sixteen-year-old Kwan, who had been favored to win, fell 3 times during her long program. Todd Eldredge was the men's champion.

First Cloning of an Adult Animal Announced—News of the first mammal ever successfully cloned from a cell from an adult animal was reported **Feb. 23** in the British press. Researchers at the Roslin Institute in Edinburgh, Scotland, led by Ian Wilmut, reported directly on their work in the **Feb. 27** issue of the British journal *Nature*. In cloning, an organism is produced from only one parent,

without fertilization; the resulting organism has a genetic structure identical to that of its parent. In the past, the same scientific team had cloned sheep from the cells of embryos but had not cloned a fully developed adult sheep. In the new experiment, the researchers fused an adult sheep's udder, or mammary, cell with the unfertilized egg of another sheep. The DNA had been removed from the donor egg, eliminating the genetic characteristics of the donor. The fertilized cell was implanted in a third sheep's uterus. The clone, named Dolly, was born in July 1996.

MARCH 1997

National

Gore Defends Role in Fund-Raising—The *Washington Post* reported, **Mar. 2**, that Vice Pres. Al Gore had raised at least $40 million for the Democratic Party in 1995 and 1996, sometimes by making phone calls from the White House. Federal law prohibits soliciting campaign funds in government buildings. In 1995, Abner Mikva, then White House counsel, had notified staff members there that "no fund-raising phone calls or mail may emanate from the White House or any other federal building." Gore admitted, **Mar. 3**, that he had made a few calls from the White House but said he had been advised that "no controlling legal authority" forbade the practice. Meanwhile, administration officials acknowledged, **Mar. 5**, that in 1995 Margaret Williams, chief of staff for First Lady Hillary Rodham Clinton, had accepted a $50,000 donation to the Democratic National Committee (DNC) in the White House.

Pres. Bill Clinton said, **Mar. 10**, that 2 members of the National Security Council staff had known about a plan by China to give campaign money to Democrats, but that the FBI had asked them not to relay this information to their superiors. The FBI, **Mar. 10**, denied that any such restrictions had been made. A Senate committee, **Mar. 6**, had voted to limit the upcoming Senate investigation of 1996 campaign fund-raising practices to those that were illegal. However, some senators expressed fear that the public would complain if improper but legal practices were not investigated. The full Senate, **Mar. 11**, voted, 99–0, to look into both illegal and improper activities.

On **Mar. 17** George Tenet, acting CIA director, said his agency was investigating allegations that the DNC had asked CIA officials to intervene improperly at the White House in behalf of Roger Tamraz, a party contributor linked to overseas embezzlement and bank fraud scandals. Although an NSC staff member had recommended that Tamraz not be allowed inside the White House, he was there at least 4 times in 1996.

Former CIA Officer Admits Spying for Russia—Harold Nicholson, a former official of the CIA, pleaded guilty, **Mar. 3**, in a federal court in Alexandria, VA, to spying for Russia. He admitted having been paid more than $180,000 for providing top-secret information to Russia between 1994 and 1996. Nicholson, who had agreed to cooperate with investigators, was sentenced to 23 years and 7 months in prison.

Balanced-Budget Amendment Fails by One Vote—For the 3d time in 3 years, the Senate rejected, **Mar. 4**, a proposed constitutional amendment to require the federal government to balance its budget. The amendment would have required a balanced budget beginning in 2002; exceptions could be granted only by a vote of 60% of both houses of Congress. The 66–34 vote in favor of the amendment fell one vote short of the required two-thirds majority. All 55 Republicans and 11 of the Democrats supported the amendment.

Economic Indicators Rise; Short-term Interest Rate Is Increased—The Conference Board (a business-research organization) reported, **Mar. 4**, that leading economic indicators had risen 0.3% in Jan. The Labor Dept. said, **Mar. 7**, that the unemployment rate had edged down to 5.3% in

Feb. and that 339,000 nonfarm jobs had been added to the economy. On **Mar. 5** Alan Greenspan, chairman of the Federal Reserve Board, said that inflation still posed a potential threat and that he would support an increase in interest rates if necessary. At the same time, showing more optimism in the stock market than in a previous statement, Greenspan said that if corporate profits continued to rise, the market appeared to be properly priced.

The Labor Dept. said, **Mar. 14,** that prices charged by farmers and manufacturers for finished goods had fallen 0.4% in Feb., but also reported, **Mar. 19,** that consumer prices had risen 0.3% in the same month. The Commerce Dept. said, **Mar. 20,** that the Jan. trade deficit had stood at $12.71 billion, the largest monthly total in years.

The Fed, **Mar. 25,** raised a key short-term interest rate—the federal-funds rate, which banks charged on overnight loans to each other—up to 5.5% from 5.25%. The increase was the first since Feb. 1995. Many banks, **Mar. 25,** raised their prime rate from 8.25% to 8.5%. Amid concern about rising interest rates, the Dow Jones industrial average, on 2 consecutive trading days, **Mar. 27** and **Mar. 31,** fell a total of 297.22 points (a record for 2 days), losing 4.3% of its value.

Large Fees to Ousted Clinton Aide Revealed—The *New York Times* reported, **Mar. 6,** that former Associate Attorney Gen. Webster Hubbell had taken large sums of money from supporters of the Democratic Party. Hubbell had resigned in Mar. 1994 and pleaded guilty to 2 felony counts in Dec. 1994. Between those 2 dates, according to the *Times,* he was paid more than $400,000 from corporations, many of which contributed to the Democrats or were controlled by friends of Pres. Bill Clinton. The harshest interpretation put on the payments, which were represented as fees for legal work, was that they constituted hush money, to deter Hubbell from revealing what he knew about the Whitewater scandal that surrounded the White House.

Citadel Cadets Punished for Hazing Women—The Citadel announced, **Mar. 10,** that 10 male cadets had been disciplined for mistreating 2 female cadets. The women had later resigned from the South Carolina military academy, leaving only 2 women enrolled. One male cadet, who reportedly encouraged another to set fire to the sweatshirt worn by one of the women, was expelled. Three male cadets resigned; 2 of them had been accused of setting the fire. Other incidents of abuse had also been reported.

Clinton Injures Knee—Pres. Bill Clinton suffered a serious knee injury, **Mar. 14,** when he stumbled in Palm Beach, FL, during a visit with golfer Greg Norman. In a 2-hour operation at Bethesda Naval Hospital in Maryland that same day, surgeons reattached the torn quadriceps tendon to Clinton's kneecap. As a result of the accident, he temporarily had to rely on crutches or other support.

Clinton's Nominee to Head CIA Withdraws—Anthony Lake abandoned in Mar. what appeared to be an uphill struggle to be confirmed as director of central intelligence. In Dec., Pres. Bill Clinton had nominated Lake, then head of the National Security Council, to take over at the CIA. But support for Lake in the Senate appeared weak. Some senators were troubled because Lake was unaware, while at the NSC, that China had sought to influence the U.S. election; some also questioned Lake's management ability. In addition, Lake held stocks in oil companies even though, as NSC head, he gave the president advice that could influence oil prices. Though Lake had eventually sold the stocks, the Justice Dept. in Feb. concluded that Lake had violated conflict-of-interest laws, and he paid $5,000 in settlement. Lake withdrew his name, **Mar. 17,** Clinton, **Mar. 19,** nominated George Tenet, who had been serving as acting director since Dec. 1996.

Ten in Paramilitary Group Sentenced to Prison—Beginning **Mar. 19,** a U.S. district court judge in Phoenix, AZ, sentenced 10 members of an antigovernment paramili-tary group, the Viper Militia, to prison terms. They had been arrested in July 1996 and had pleaded guilty in Dec. to various counts, including conspiracy to make and possess unregistered destructive devices. The alleged leader, Gary Bauer, was sentenced to 9 years in prison, **Mar. 20,** for conspiracy, for providing instruction in bomb-making techniques, and for possessing machine guns.

Tobacco Company Admits Smoking Is Addictive—The Liggett Group, Inc., the 5th-largest U.S. tobacco company, agreed, **Mar. 20,** to admit that smoking is addictive and causes health problems and that the tobacco industry had sought for years to sell its products to children as young as 14. The agreement by Liggett was announced by the attorneys general of 22 states, who were seeking to recoup billions of dollars in Medicaid funds the states had expended to treat ill smokers. In a bold move that stunned the tobacco industry, Liggett also agreed to pay 25% of its pretax profits for 25 years into a fund to reimburse states and class-action plaintiffs. Liggett also agreed to release relevant documents, including those involving discussions with 4 other companies. (Those companies filed suit, **Mar. 20,** to block release of the documents.) On **Mar. 21,** Liggett issued a statement saying that nicotine is addictive and smoking "causes health problems, including lung cancer, heart and vascular disease, and emphysema."

Captain Pleads Guilty in Sex Abuse Case—Army Capt. Derrick Robertson pleaded guilty, **Mar. 20,** to having had consensual sex with a private. He was sentenced to 4 months in prison and dismissed from the Army, and his pension was revoked. He was the only officer among 10 soldiers at Aberdeen Proving Ground charged with criminal sexual misconduct.

International

State of Emergency Declared in Albania—The Albanian parliament declared a state of emergency, **Mar. 2,** amid widespread public unrest triggered by the collapse of pyramid funds in which many people had invested. On **Mar. 9,** looters took up to 40,000 firearms from a factory. On **Mar. 14,** gangs seeking to oust Pres. Sali Berisha took control of Tiranë, the capital. By **Mar. 15,** 600 people, including some foreign nationals, had been evacuated from Albania in U.S. helicopters. Government militia regained control in Tiranë, **Mar. 16.** Meanwhile, by **Mar. 19,** some 10,000 Albanian refugees had arrived in Italy, which itself declared a state of emergency because of the refugee flood. Italy decided, **Mar. 24,** to turn back Albanian ships trying to reach its coast. On **Mar. 28,** an Italian warship struck an Albanian refugee ship in the Adriatic Sea, causing an undetermined number of deaths.

Settlement Dispute Increases Middle East Tensions—Palestinians staged a general strike in East Jerusalem, the West Bank, and the Gaza Strip, **Mar. 3,** to protest a decision by Israel to construct another Jewish settlement in Arab East Jerusalem. At a meeting at the White House, **Mar. 3,** with Palestinian leader Yasir Arafat, Pres. Bill Clinton criticized the Israeli move. On **Mar. 7,** however, the United States by its veto killed an otherwise unanimous UN Security Council resolution that called the Israeli settlement illegal. In a letter delivered **Mar. 9,** King Hussein of Jordan told Prime Min. Benjamin Netanyahu of Israel that it appeared he was intentionally destroying the peace process. The latter contended, **Mar. 10,** that he was in fact reviving a failing process that he had inherited. The UN General Assembly, **Mar. 13,** approved, 130 to 2, a resolution similar to the one vetoed by the Security Council earlier; only Israel and the United States voted against it. A Jordanian soldier, **Mar. 13,** shot and killed 7 Israeli girls at a site on the Israeli-Jordanian border.

Israeli bulldozers, guarded by troops, began **Mar. 18** to clear ground for the Har Homa settlement, which would house 32,000 people. Israeli police clashed with Palestinian students in Bethlehem 2 days later. A Palestinian bomber and 3 women died in an explosion in Tel Aviv, **Mar. 21.** In a confrontation, **Mar. 29,** Israeli troops killed a Palestinian student.

South Korean President Names New Premier—A scandal involving the Hanbo Steel Industry Co. resulted in a new government in South Korea. Hanbo had been accused of exerting corrupt pressures on political leaders. In Feb., 10 businessmen and politicians had been indicted. Pres. Kim Young Sam apologized and took responsibility for the scandal, and on **Mar. 4** appointed a new premier, Koh Kun. On **Mar. 5** the president replaced 8 members of the cabinet.

Switzerland, Under Criticism, Agrees to Holocaust Victims Fund—The Swiss government announced plans **Mar. 5** to establish a $4.7 billion government-financed fund, using interest from its gold reserves, to compensate survivors of the Nazi Holocaust and their descendants, and aid victims of other human-rights abuses around the world. The government also had agreed, **Feb. 12,** to administer a separate Holocaust compensation fund set up by 3 Swiss banks, and, later, to contribute money to it. The Swiss government had been sharply criticized for bank secrecy laws which prevented a search for missing assets of Holocaust victims that had been hidden in Swiss banks by the people themselves or stolen for them and hidden there by Nazi forces, and never returned. The government had also been accused of trading in precious metals with the Nazis and helping the Nazi regime conceal stolen assets. In recent months the Swiss government had been taking steps to allow investigators to bypass banking secrecy laws.

Yeltsin Makes Internal Changes, Meets Clinton at Summit—Pres. Boris Yeltsin of Russia, on **Mar. 7,** named his chief of staff, Anatoly Chubais, to be first deputy premier in charge of the economy. On **Mar. 11,** Yeltsin asked Prem. Viktor Chernomyrdin to revamp the cabinet; the new cabinet, unveiled **Mar. 17,** was seen as stronger in support of free-market reforms. At a summit in Helsinki, **Mar. 20** and **21,** Clinton attended in a wheelchair because of a knee injury. Yeltsin expressed continuing opposition to NATO expansion that would include former Soviet allies in Eastern Europe. He anticipated a charter between Russia and NATO in which NATO would promise not to deploy nuclear weapons in new member states or to utilize bases in those countries that had been in use when the countries were in the Warsaw Pact. He promised to submit the 2d Strategic Arms Reduction Treaty to Parliament for ratification. The 2 leaders agreed to focus next on the reduction in the number of long-range nuclear warheads. Clinton said he would support Russian membership in the World Trade Organization.

Rebels in Zaire Seek Ouster of Mobutu—A rebellion in Zaire, which had gotten underway in Oct. 1996 while Pres. Mobutu Sese Seko was recovering from prostate surgery in Europe, gained momentum in Mar. After 3 decades, Mobutu's long, arbitrary, and corrupt rule had fallen into serious jeopardy. The rebels, led by Laurent Kabila, were supported by neighboring governments distressed by Mobutu's support of rebel movements in their countries. Zaire's army was reported to be undisciplined and unhappy because it often was not paid. The government had brought in mercenaries in a futile effort to stop the rebel advance. France said, **Mar. 12,** that it might send troops to Zaire if the 2 sides did not agree to a cease-fire. Kisangani, the country's 3d-largest city, fell to the rebels, **Mar. 15.** Zaire's parliament, **Mar. 18,** voted to dismiss Prem. Leon Kengo wa Dondo and to begin negotiating with Kabila. The latter, **Mar. 24,** vowed to push on to Kinshasa, the capital.

Gore, Gingrich Visit China—Vice Pres. Al Gore and House Speaker Newt Gingrich made separate trips to China in Mar., and both discussed sensitive issues between China and the United States. In Beijing, **Mar. 25,** Gore attended signings of major business agreements between China and 2 U.S. corporations. In one agreement, Boeing would sell 5 jetliners to China. In the other, General Motors, in a joint venture with a state-owned auto corporation, would build cars valued at $1.3 billion. In an awkward moment, Gore initially hesitated to join in a toast with Prem. Li Peng, celebrating the deal; aides later asserted he had not deliberately hesitated but was merely caught off guard. In a meeting with Li, **Mar. 25,** Gore discussed reports that China had funneled campaign cash to the Clinton-Gore campaign. Li said it was not true. Gore said, **Mar. 26,** that he had discussed human rights with Li and Pres. Jiang Zemin.

Gingrich headed a congressional delegation that met with Jiang and Li **Mar. 28.** The Americans brought up the subjects of religious freedom and political prisoners in China and civil liberties in Hong Kong after the midyear Chinese takeover. Gingrich said, **Mar. 30,** that he had told the Chinese leaders that the United States would intervene militarily if China attacked Taiwan.

General

Cloning of Humans Debated—The anouncement of the successful cloning of an adult sheep in Feb. prompted a debate over the ethics of human cloning. In 1994, Pres. Bill Clinton had banned the use of federal funds for human embryo research, and on **Mar. 4** he banned federal funding of human cloning research. Harold Varmus, director of the National Institutes of Health, maintained before a House committee, **Mar. 5,** that human cloning would be acceptable under certain circumstances, such as when parents wanting genetic offspring were unable to conceive children. Scientific authorities testifying before a Senate committee, **Mar. 12,** opposed an immediate ban on research into human cloning. Ian Wilmut, a leader of the research team that recently cloned the adult sheep, testified that, though human cloning might be unacceptable, cloning of mammals can be very useful, since it could lead to the production of milk with disease-fighting proteins and could help in developing treatments for such illnesses as Parkinson's disease and cystic fibrosis.

Arizona Wins NCAA Basketball Title—Arizona, which had posted a modest 19-9 record during the regular season, won the NCAA men's basketball championship in Mar. Early in the tournament, North Carolina coach Dean Smith became the winningest coach in NCAA history; Carolina's victory over Colorado, **Mar. 15,** was Smith's 877th, one more than the 876 games won by Coach Adolph Rupp of Kentucky. North Carolina won 2 more tournament games before falling to Arizona, 66-58, in the semifinals, **Mar. 29.** In the final, **Mar. 31** in Indianapolis, Arizona met the heavy favorite, Kentucky, the defending champion. Kentucky guard Anthony Epps sent the game into overtime with a successful 3-point toss with 12 seconds to play. All of Arizona's 10 overtime points came from free throws, and the final score was 84-79. Arizona guard Miles Simon was voted the tournament's most valuable player. Lute Olson was the Arizona coach.

Large Comet Sweeps Across Night Sky—An unusually large comet brought fresh beauty to the night sky in the late winter and early spring. Comet Hale–Bopp had been discovered in 1995, hurtling from the outer reaches of the solar system for its first swing past the sun in 4,200 years. Its immense size—the icy core was 25 miles wide, about 10 times the size of the average comet—made it easy to see, even in large cities. The so-called dirty snowball, warmed by the sun, shed its outer layers, producing a prominent tail millions of miles in length. Moving at close to 100,000 miles per hour, the comet made its closest approach to Earth about 122 mil mi.—**Mar. 22.**

Thirty-Nine Cultists Found Dead at Estate—Thirty-nine members of the Heaven's Gate religious cult were found dead in a large house in the community of Rancho

Santa Fe, CA, **Mar. 26,** in an apparent mass suicide. Among the dead was cult leader Marshall Applewhite, who, with a friend, Bonnie Lu Trousdale Nettles, had founded the cult in 1975. The 2 had met when he was in a Houston psychiatric hospital where she was a nurse. Applewhite apparently believed that Nettles, who died in 1985, was returning to pick up her fellow cultists in a spaceship following the comet Hale-Bopp, which was then prominent in the night sky.

The 21 women and 18 men, who had apparently been planning their deaths for some time, had moved into the estate near San Diego in Oct. They earned money for the rent and other expenses through an Internet business, Higher Source, which designed home pages on the World Wide Web for clients. Heaven's Gate promoted itself and sought recruits on its own web sites. The cult members believed that by leaving their "containers" (bodies) they could go on to attain the Level Above Human.

The deaths occurred over several days. Preparing to die, the members apparently dressed in identical black exercise outfits and black running shoes, then took a sedative (phenobarbital) mixed with vodka. Bodies were found lying on their backs on beds, with most of the faces and chests covered with purple shrouds. A packed suitcase was near each body. The 2 cult members thought to have died last had plastic bags over their heads, and other plastic bags were found in garbage cans. Rio D'Angelo, a former cult member, received a package containing a letter and 2 videotapes in which cult members described, in often joyful terms, their plans to depart the earth. D'Angelo and his supervisor went to the estate, then alerted authorities.

APRIL 1997

National

FBI Comes Under Criticism—The FBI was embarrassed by 2 reports issued in Apr. On **Apr. 1,** the Justice Dept. concluded that the agency had erred seriously in its investigation of the July 27, 1996, bombing of Olympic Park in Atlanta. Agents had reportedly sought to trick Richard Jewell, a suspect in the bombing, into being interviewed—and signing away his rights—by saying the interview was part of a "training video." Contents of the report were published **Apr. 8.**

In another report, on **Apr. 15,** the department found that FBI crime-laboratory scientists had done sloppy work and given "tilted" testimony in a number of cases. "Extremely serious" problems were found in the explosives, chemistry-toxicology, and materials analysis units. The report said conclusions were scientifically unsound and not well-documented. Fourteen agents were singled out for criticism. One, David Williams, an explosives expert, was cited for slanted testimony in the World Trade Center and Oklahoma City bombing cases.

Mayor Riordan Reelected in Los Angeles—Mayor Richard Riordan of Los Angeles, a Republican, was elected to a 2d 4-year term, **Apr. 8.** He defeated his principal opponent, State Sen. Tom Hayden, a Democrat and longtime champion of left-wing causes, by 61% to 35% in the nonpartisan election. Riordan had benefited from an improved economy and a declining crime rate.

Line-Item Veto Challenged in the Courts—Judge Thomas Jackson of the U.S. District Court in Washington, DC, held, **Apr. 10,** that the Line-Item Veto Act of 1996 was unconstitutional. That act of Congress gave the president the power to veto individual monetary expenditures within a larger spending bill. Six current or former members of Congress had challenged the law, contending that it unconstitutionally shifted the balance of power between the executive and legislative branches. However, the Clinton administration appealed Jackson's ruling to the Supreme Court, which

on **June 26** dismissed the challenge, ruling that the plaintiffs lacked the legal standing to contest the law.

Ex-Clinton Partner Gets Light Sentence—James McDougal, once a partner in Arkansas with then-Gov. Bill Clinton in the Whitewater Development Corp., was sentenced **Apr. 14** to 3 years in prison. McDougal had been convicted of seeking to enrich himself with fraudulent loans. Kenneth Starr, the independent counsel investigating the Whitewater affair, had asked U.S. District Judge George Howard Jr. to give him a light sentence because he was cooperating with the investigation. McDougal was also fined $10,000 and ordered to pay $4.2 million in restitution. In a television interview broadcast **Apr. 15,** McDougal said he was "sick and tired of lying" for Bill Clinton. Earlier, on **Apr. 10,** First Lady Hillary Rodham Clinton dismissed Whitewater as a "never-ending fictional conspiracy" and denied charges that money had been paid to former Associate Attorney Gen. Webster Hubbell to deter him from making embarrassing disclosures.

Independent Counsel on Fund-Raising Rejected—Attorney Gen. Janet Reno declined, **Apr. 14,** to appoint an independent counsel to investigate whether funds had been improperly raised for Pres. Bill Clinton's 1996 reelection campaign. Republicans had been calling for an outside inquiry. Reno said that a Justice Dept. probe had not yet found credible evidence that high-ranking executive branch officials had committed illegal acts. Thus, Reno said, the standard established for appointment of a special counsel had not been met. This marked the 4th time Reno had refused to make an appointment of this kind.

Dole Loans Gingrich Money to Pay Fine—House Speaker Newt Gingrich (R, GA) announced, **Apr. 17,** that former Sen. Robert Dole, the Republican Party's presidential nominee in 1996, would lend him $300,000 to pay the fine assessed against him in Jan. The House had approved the penalty after Gingrich admitted having used tax-exempt donations for political activities and having provided false information to a House investigating committee. Under the agreement with Dole, Gingrich would pay the loan back at a 10% interest rate, with no payments due until 2005. The plan encountered resistance in the House Ethics Committee, which announced, **May 15,** that the Speaker would borrow only half the money from Dole, using his own funds to pay the rest.

100,000 Flee Rising Floodwaters—At least 100,000 people in the United States and Canada were forced from their homes by flood-swollen rivers. Winter snows in the upper Midwest had been 3 times the normal volume. Fargo, North Dakota's biggest city, was largely undamaged because dikes had been built in preparation. But the rising Red River, **Apr. 19,** drove the 50,000 residents of Grand Forks, ND, and the 8,500 residents of East Grand Forks, MN, from their homes, many of which were damaged or destroyed. Fire in downtown Grand Forks added to the devastation. On **Apr. 23,** some 17,000 living in the Red River Valley south of Winnipeg, Manitoba, Canada, were also told to evacuate.

Stock Prices Rebound—The stock market bounced back from a late-Mar. and early-Apr. tailspin that had taken it down 10%. The Dow Jones industrial average shot up 173.38 points **Apr. 22.** In another astonishing day on Wall Street, **Apr. 29,** the Dow closed up 179.01, the 2d-highest one-day point gain yet. Strong earnings reports and diminished fears of inflation were said to be responsible.

Earlier in the month, on **Apr. 1,** the Conference Board (a business-research organization) said that the leading economic indicators had risen 0.5% in Feb. The Labor Dept. reported, **Apr. 4,** that unemployment had edged downward to 5.2% in Mar., and that 175,000 nonfarm jobs had been added to the economy. The U.S. dollar, **Apr. 10,** climbed as high as 127.14 yen, its strongest showing against the Japanese currency since 1992; the dollar also posted a 38-month high **Apr. 15** against the German mark, closing at 1.7374 marks. The Labor Dept. said, **Apr. 11,** that prices charged by manufacturers and farmers for finished goods had gone down 0.1% in Mar.

Other Labor Dept. statistics, released **Apr. 15**, indicated that consumer prices had risen only 0.1% in Mar. The Commerce Dept. reported, **Apr. 25**, that the trade deficit stood at $10.4 billion in Feb. The deptartment said, **Apr. 30,** that the U.S. economy had grown at a 5.6% annual rate in the 1st quarter, the fastest pace in 9 years, and that the federal budget deficit for the current fiscal year was now put at $75 billion, the lowest in more than 2 decades.

Senate Ratifies Chemical Weapons Treaty—With ratification by the Senate on **Apr. 24**, the United States became the 75th country to approve the Chemical Weapons Convention. Under the treaty, signatories pledged to eliminate all stocks of chemical weapons by the year 2007. Member states could ask for an inspection of any site in a member country thought to be manufacturing such weapons. Two leading Republicans, former Sen. Robert Dole and Gen. Colin Powell (ret.), appeared with Pres. Bill Clinton, **Apr. 23**, in support of the treaty. But many Republicans opposed the treaty, claiming it was unenforceable and lacked sufficient safeguards. Clinton won the support of Senate Majority Leader Trent Lott (R, MS), **Apr. 24**, by assuring him that the United States would pull out of the treaty under certain circumstances. The Senate approved the treaty, 74–26, 7 votes more than the two-thirds required for ratification. All 45 Democrats were joined by 29 of 55 Republicans in support.

Oklahoma Bombing Trial Underway—Opening arguments were presented **Apr. 24** in the first trial related to the 1995 bombing the destroyed the Murrah Federal Building in Oklahoma City and claimed 168 lives (including the life of one rescue worker). The defendant, Timothy McVeigh, was charged with conspiracy and murder. An alleged accomplice, Terry Nichols, was to be tried separately at a later date. The McVeigh trial had been moved from Oklahoma City to Denver because emotions ran so high where the crime occurred. Judge Richard Matsch presided in U.S. District Court. In his opening statement Joseph Hartzler, the government's lead prosecutor, maintained that McVeigh had carried out the bombing out of revenge for the deaths of members of the Branch Davidian cult at the hands of federal agents in Waco, TX, in 1993. Stephen Jones, McVeigh's lead lawyer, said he would establish that the defendant was innocent.

Judge Backs Government on Tobacco Regulation— On **Apr. 25**, a federal district court in Greensboro, NC, held that the Food and Drug Administration had the power to regulate the distribution, sale, and use of tobacco products. The tobacco industry had sought to overturn new FDA regulations that would restrict the ways in which tobacco was marketed. Judge William Osteen held, however, that tobacco and nicotine fit the definition of drugs and that cigarettes are drug-delivery devices. On the other hand, he ruled that free-speech protections barred the FDA from restricting the advertising of tobacco products.

Four in Army Guilty of Sexual Crimes—The Army said, **Apr. 25**, that 3 officers at Fort Bliss, TX—Maj. Eddie Brenham, Capt. Ivan Brown, and 2d Lt. Trevor Gordon— had been discharged and sentenced to prison terms ranging from 3 to 20 months for sexual misconduct. Nine other soldiers had received administrative punishment. On **Apr. 29**, an Army court-martial jury at Aberdeen Proving Ground in Maryland convicted Staff Sgt. Delmar Simpson, a former drill sergeant, of raping 6 women trainees. Simpson, who had claimed that the liaisons were consensual, was sentenced, **May 6**, to 25 years in prison. In all, 12 instructors at Aberdeen had been charged with sexual offenses.

Four Presidents Boost Volunteerism at Summit—A conference designed to encourage more Americans to offer their time as volunteers was held in Philadelphia, **Apr. 27– 29**. Pres. Bill Clinton and former presidents Gerald Ford, Jimmy Carter, and George Bush attended the Presidents' Summit for America's Future; Nancy Reagan represented her husband, former Pres. Ronald Reagan, who was incapacitated from Alzheimer's disease. Gen. Colin Powell (ret.) was general chairman. The summiteers, while acknowledging that millions of Americans already donated time in behalf of various causes, urged millions more to become involved where government could not or (in the view of some) should not venture. Special emphasis was placed on ways in which adults could help children.

Labor Secretary Approved, After Delay—The Senate, **Apr. 30**, approved, 85–13, the nomination of Alexis Herman to be secretary of labor. Approval had been delayed by Republicans expressing concern that she might have engaged in improper fund-raising activities while director of the White House Office of Public Liaison. In a conciliatory move seen as clearing the way for a favorable Senate vote, Pres. Bill Clinton, **Apr. 30**, withdrew his support for an executive order asking federal agencies to award construction projects to union labor. Herman became the only black woman in the cabinet.

International

Zaire's Regime in Turmoil as Rebels Advance— Rebels in Zaire continued to gain ground while the government was engaged in a factional struggle. On **Apr. 1**, Zaire's parliament chose Etienne Tshisekedi, an opponent of Pres. Mobutu Sese Seko, to be prime minister. Tshisekedi said, **Apr. 2**, that he would dissolve the pro-Mobutu parliament, and on **Apr. 3** he announced a cabinet from which Mobutu supporters had been excluded. Six positions were offered to—and refused by—the rebel Alliance of Democratic Forces for the Liberation of Congo (ADFL). On **Apr. 4**, the rebels, led by Laurent Kabila, captured Mbuji-Mayi, the country's major diamond-trading center. ADFL and Zairean government representatives held talks in Pretoria, South Africa, **Apr. 6–8**. The rebels captured the capital of the mineral-rich Shaba province on **Apr. 9**, giving them control of nearly half of the country. Mobutu had Tshisekedi arrested the same day, and set up a new military government. Supporters of Tshisekedi closed down Kinshasa, the capital, **Apr. 14–15**, in a general strike.

Tensions Continue Over Israeli Settlement Plan—A confrontational mood between Israelis and Palestinians continued, fueled by Israel's decision in Feb. to build a settlement in Arab East Jerusalem to house some 32,000 Jews. Two Palestinians were killed in clashes with Israeli troops **Apr. 1**. The same day King Hussein of Jordan, after meeting with Pres. Bill Clinton, in Washington, DC, said that the United States should take a more active role in mediating the Israeli-Palestinian conflict. Prime Min. Benjamin Netanyahu said, **Apr. 3**, that construction of the settlement would proceed.

Hong Kong Faces Curtailment of Rights—It appeared that the broad freedoms enjoyed by Hong Kong residents and businesspeople would be subject to some restraints after the British crown colony reverted to China's control on July 1. Tung Chee-hwa, the prospective head of the new Hong Kong government, issued a document **Apr. 9** on Civil Liberties and Social Order, indicating that all organizations would have to register with the police and that any group could be banned in the interest of national security. Organizations could not solicit or receive foreign contributions or maintain other contacts with foreigners and the police could ban protests.

Angolan Adversaries Form Unity Government—A government of national unity was launched in Angola, in accordance with a 1994 agreement. The pact had ended a civil war that spanned 19 years (1975-94) and claimed more than 500,000 lives. Seventy members of the rebel National Union for the Total Independence of Angola (UNITA) elected in 1992, finally took office in the 220-seat parliament on **Apr. 9**. UNITA was to serve as the leading opposition party in a government dominated by the Popular Movement for the Liberation of Angola (MPLA). The new government was fully underway, **Apr. 11**, when 4 UNITA ministers joined the cabinet of Pres. Jose Eduardo dos Santos. UNITA leader Jonas Savimbi declined to attend the opening ceremony. Some 6,000 UN peacekeepers remained in Angola.

India's Government Falls—The government of Indian Prime Min. H. D. Deve Gowda lost a confidence vote, **Apr. 11**, after the Congress (I) Party withdrew its support. Gowda resigned **Apr. 13**. The coalition parties chose Foreign Min. Inder K. Gujral as its new leader, **Apr. 19**, and he was sworn in as prime minister, **Apr. 21**.

Peacekeepers Land in Albania—In mid-Apr. international peacekeepers arrived in Albania, a country torn by several months of internal strife. Advance units from Italy landed in Tiranë, the capital, **Apr. 11**, and about 1,200 troops from Italy, France, and Spain arrived **Apr. 15**. The UN-sponsored force would eventually grow to 6,000.

Socialists Routed in Bulgarian Voting—After having had a caretaker government for 3 months, Bulgarians dealt a strong defeat to the Socialist Party in parliamentary voting on **Apr. 19**. The anti-Communist United Democratic Forces captured 137 seats (out of 240) to only 58 for the Socialists, who had controlled the previous parliament. Ivan Kostov, an economist, was sworn in as prime minister on **Apr. 24**.

Israeli Prime Minister Escapes Indictment—Israeli prosecutors said **Apr. 20** that a police investigation had not found enough solid evidence to indict Prime Min. Benjamin Netanyahu for "fraud and breach of trust." An investigation had been made into the appointment of Roni Bar-On as attorney general in Netanyahu's cabinet (Bar-On had later resigned). It had been charged that Netanyahu's aides brokered a deal with the Shas party to appoint Bar-On in return for Shas support for Netanyahu's coalition. Bar-on, in turn, allegedly pledged to arrange a plea bargain for Shas leader Arye Deri, who faced corruption charges. Israeli prosecutors concluded, however, that much of the evidence against Netanyahu was circumstantial and that he therefore would not be indicted.

Peruvian Troops Free Hostages; Rebels Killed in Assault—Peruvian commandos ended a 126-day standoff at the Japanese embassy in Lima, **Apr. 22,** when they stormed the building and freed 72 hostages who had been held by members of the Tupac Amaru Revolutionary Movement (MRTA). One of the hostages, hit by a bullet, later died of a heart attack. Two commandos and all 14 rebels were killed during the attack. Since the seizing of the embassy in Dec., more than 500 hostages had been released by their captors. Those freed in the final assault included the Japanese and Bolivian ambassadors and Peru's foreign minister. Hostages, alerted that an attack was imminent, opened a door and then lay on the floor. The raid began when commandos exploded a bomb in a tunnel that they had dug underneath the embassy's living room, killing 4 rebels. Commandos then stormed the building; within 40 minutes all the remaining rebels were dead. The attack was approved by Peruvian Pres. Alberto Fujimori, who had waged a long campaign to wipe out the MRTA and the Sendero Luminoso (Shining Path), another leftist guerrilla organization.

General

Tiger Woods, 21, Makes Golf History—Tiger (Eldrick) Woods, a 21-year-old golfer, captured the attention of the country by not only winning the Masters Tournament, **Apr. 13**, but also achieving several "firsts" in the process. His winning total of 270 strokes at the Augusta National Golf Club in Georgia set a tournament record, breaking the previous low of 271. His margin of victory, 12 strokes, was also a record. Woods, the son of a black man and a Thai

woman, was also the youngest Masters champion ever, and the first African-American to win any of the 4 major professional tournaments for men.

Actress "Comes Out" as Lesbian, Twice—The actress, Ellen DeGeneres, who played the title role in the ABC comedy series *Ellen*, revealed, in the **Apr. 14** issue of *Time* magazine, that she was a lesbian, and in the **Apr. 30** episode of *Ellen*, DeGeneres's character revealed her homosexuality. ABC had strongly promoted the "coming out" episode, and the show drew a large audience. *Ellen* became the first network television series to have an openly gay lead character.

Texas Separatists Give Up After Siege—A small group of armed people who proclaimed themselves the Republic of Texas precipitated a confrontation with authorities on **Apr. 27** when they kidnapped a couple near their "embassy," a tin shack outside Fort Davis, TX. The group, which authorities said had passed millions of dollars in bogus checks, claimed that the United States had illegally annexed Texas in 1845. After police surrounded the separatists the hostages were released, **Apr. 28**, in exchange for a separatist who had been arrested. Seven armed men were taken into custody **Apr. 30** en route to Fort Davis. Six individuals, including separatist leader Richard McLaren, surrendered **May 2** and 3. Two escaped on foot; one was shot to death by police, **May 5**.

MAY 1997

National

White House, Congress Agree on Balancing Budget—White House and congressional negotiators reached an agreement in May intended to result in a balanced federal budget by 2002. On **May 1**, as the 2 sides were moving toward an accord, the Congressional Budget Office announced that it had reduced its projections for budget deficits for the coming years. The strong economy accounted for the shrinking deficits. The budget agreement, announced **May 2**, provided for tax cuts totaling $135 billion, including a reduced tax on capital gains. The amount of an estate exempt from taxation would be doubled to $1.2 million. A family-friendly $500-per-child tax credit, as well as some $35 billion in college-tuition tax credits, were also part of the package.

On the revenue side, closing of loopholes and renewal of a tax on airline tickets would bring in $50 billion. Spending would be reduced by cutting Medicare payments to healthcare providers by $115 billion and trimming Medicaid costs by $15 billion. Congressional Democrats, many of whom maintained that the budget deal was weighted in favor of the rich, were nonetheless inclined to support it—especially because it allowed for increased spending on education and environment.

On **May 21** the House, 333–99, approved the agreement, and the Senate, **May 23**, voted 78–22 in favor of a slightly different version.

Court Rebuffs White House on Whitewater—The legal confrontation between the White House and Whitewater independent counsel Kenneth Starr moved nearer to resolution in May. At issue were notes taken at White House meetings in 1995 and 1996 involving First Lady Hillary Rodham Clinton, her personal attorneys, and lawyers for the White House counsel's office. Starr, who had called Mrs. Clinton the "central figure" in the Whitewater investigation, had subpoenaed notes taken by the lawyers from the counsel's office, and rejected White House claims that these notes were protected by lawyer-client privilege. A 2-1 majority of a panel of the U.S. 8th Circuit Court of Appeals in St. Louis, in a decision made public **May 2**, agreed with Starr, saying that the White House lawyers served the interests of the government and did not have a privileged lawyer-client relationship with the first lady. The White House, **May 12**, appealed the decision to the U.S. Supreme Court, but the latter, on **June 23**, refused to review the lower-court ruling.

Unemployment Falls to 24-Year Low—The Labor Dept. reported, **May 2**, that the unemployment rate had declined to 4.9% in Apr., down 0.3 point from Mar. The Apr. figure was the lowest for any month since 1973. Leading economic indicators had risen 0.1%, according to the Conference Board (a business-research organization) in Mar. The Labor Dept., **May 14**, said that prices charged by producers for finished goods declined 0.6% in Apr.—the biggest monthly drop in 4 years. The department also reported, **May 15**, that consumer prices had gone up only 0.1%. Apparently confident that inflation remained in check, a committee of the Federal Reserve Board passed up an opportunity, **May 20**, to increase short-term interest rates. The Commerce Dept. said, **May 21**, that the trade deficit had stood at $8.51 billion in Mar. On Wall Street, the Dow Jones industrial average closed, **May 27**, at an all-time high of 7383.41, the 20th record high of 1997.

Mechanical Failure Cited as a Likely Cause in TWA Crash—On **May 4**, FBI director Louis Freeh indicated that "catastrophic mechanical failure" was the most likely cause of the crash of TWA flight 800 in July 1996 (though far from being established as the cause). Freeh said evidence did not point toward a terrorist attack, although no final conclusion could yet be made. Investigators for the National Transportation Safety Board attributed the tragedy to the ignition of vapors in a fuel tank. The NTSB, **May 18**, concluded its search for debris; 95% of the aircraft had been recovered from the sea floor, and the bodies of 216 of 230 victims had been identified. On **May 30** the agency announced it would set up a privately funded airline disaster response center in New York City to coordinate release of information on air crashes to victims' relatives and the public.

Testimony Completed in Oklahoma Bombing—The trial in Denver of Timothy McVeigh, in the 1995 bombing of the Murrah Federal Building in Oklahoma City, moved along briskly in May. Jennifer McVeigh, the defendant's sister, testifying as a prosecution witness, **May 5**, said that her brother had expressed anger in 1994 over the government's 1993 assault on the Branch Davidian complex near Waco, TX. Agents of the Bureau of Alcohol, Tobacco, and Firearms had participated in the Waco raid, and other ATF agents were employed in the federal building that was bombed exactly 2 years later. Jennifer McVeigh testified that her brother had told her twice, not long before the bombing, that "something big is going to happen."

Eldon Elliott, owner of a Ryder rental outlet in Junction City, KS, identified McVeigh, **May 9**, as the man who on Apr. 17, 1995, 2 days before the bombing, rented the truck investigators believed was used in the crime. Michael Fortier, an Army friend of McVeigh, testified, **May 12**, that he and McVeigh had inspected the federal building that the latter planned to bomb. Fortier, who had agreed to cooperate with prosecutors as part of a plea bargain, said McVeigh told him he wanted to mark the anniversary of the Waco assault. Steven Burmeister, an FBI chemist, testified, **May 19**, that the clothes McVeigh wore at the time of his arrest on the day of the bombing contained traces of a chemical used in detonating cord.

No witness placed McVeigh at the scene of the bombing, and the case against him was circumstantial, but the abundance of evidence combined to make what legal experts described as a strong case. The defense sought to discredit prosecution witnesses, notably Michael Fortier and his wife, Lori, and to cast doubt on the trustworthiness of forensic evidence. Stephen Jones was the lead defense lawyer. McVeigh did not testify.

The Oklahoma state medical examiner testified, **May 22**, that a leg found in the rubble did not match any of the bodies, and the defense suggested that the leg could have been the remains of the bomber. One witness testified, **May 23**, that she had seen 2 men leaving a Ryder truck in front of the building just before the explosion; she conceded under cross-examination that one of them could have been McVeigh. Frederic Whitehurst, a former FBI crime-lab supervisor who had become an outspoken critic of the bureau, testified, **May 27**, that he had found "contamination" in the FBI work of Burmeister, but conceded he did not know specifically of any tainted evidence in the Oklahoma case. The defense, **May 28**, played recordings of wiretaps in which Fortier boasted of his skills as a story-teller and of how he could make money writing a book about the case. Closing arguments were presented **May 29**, and the jury began deliberations **May 30**.

Army's Top Sergeant Accused of Misconduct—The Army's highest-ranking enlisted soldier, Sgt. Maj. Gene McKinney, was charged, **May 7**, with 18 offenses, including adultery, assault, obstruction of justice, and mistreatment of soldiers. He was the latest to be embroiled in the military sex-harassment investigation. McKinney, **May 7**, denied the allegations. On **May 29**, Staff Sgt. Vernell Robinson, a drill instructor at Aberdeen Proving Ground in Maryland, where the scandal had first surfaced, was convicted of 19 counts of adultery, improper relations with female trainees, sodomy, obstruction of justice, and disobeying orders. Robinson, **May 30**, was sentenced to 6 months in prison and dishonorably discharged.

Clinton Apologizes for Syphilis Experiment—Pres. Bill Clinton, at a White House ceremony, apologized, **May 16**, for the "Tuskegee Study of Untreated Syphilis in the Negro Male," which was conducted between 1932 and 1972 under the auspices of the U.S. Public Health Service. Doctors, studying the long-term effects of untreated syphilis, did not tell the 399 black men who were subjects in the study that they had the disease. Treatment was withheld even after it became known in the 1940s that penicillin could cure syphilis. About 100 of the research subjects died of complications related to the disease, and many of the men's wives and children became infected. Five of 8 surviving subjects and many family members attended the White House ceremony.

Female B–52 Pilot Discharged in Adultery Case—First Lt. Kelly Flinn, who had graduated at the top of her flight-training class and become the Air Force's first woman B–52 bomber pilot, was discharged **May 29** after an investigation stemming from adultery charges against her. In Feb. she had been charged with having an affair with Marc Zigo, a married civilian, and with having sex with an enlisted man. Adultery, as well as "fraternization" between an officer and an enlisted person, were against military regulations. Flinn was also charged with falsely telling an investigator that she was not involved with Zigo. On **May 19**, Flinn asked for an honorable discharge in lieu of a court-martial. However, Air Force Sec. Sheila Widnall notified Flinn's attorney, **May 21**, that Flinn would be given a general discharge because allegations against her included dishonesty and disobedience. Flinn, who had accused the Air Force of engaging in a witch hunt, agreed to accept the general discharge, which meant forfeiting her veterans' benefits and being required to repay $18,000 in Air Force Academy tuition.

The Army, **May 29**, relieved Brig. Gen. Stephen Xenakis of his command of the Dwight David Eisenhower Army Medical Center at Fort Gordon, GA, because of an apparently "improper relationship" with a civilian nurse who was caring for his wife.

International

Blair's Labor Party Wins British Election—Eighteen years of Conservative Party rule in Great Britain came to a decisive end after **May 1** elections, which allowed Tony

Blair, the Labor Party leader, to succeed John Major as prime minister. Major, who first took office in 1990, had been trailing badly in public-opinion polls even though Britain was enjoying relative prosperity. The Conservatives were divided over whether Britain should join a unified European currency. Major, who at one time seemed cautiously optimistic toward British participation in the planned currency, the euro, declared his opposition during the campaign. Blair had called for a national referendum on the issue; he had also steered his party toward the political center, and away from its identification with socialism. Blair benefited from the sentiment, stimulated by a series of Tory scandals, that it was time for a change of political leadership.

In the parliamentary election, Labor won 418 seats in the 659-member House of Commons. Conservatives took 165 seats, barely half of their total in the outgoing Commons. The Liberal Democrats won 46 seats. Major submitted his resignation to Queen Elizabeth, **May 2;** she designated Blair as his successor the same day. The 43-year-old Blair, a lawyer, had served in Parliament since 1983. He had been elected leader of the Labor Party in 1994.

Blair announced his cabinet, **May 2** and **3.** On **May 6,** his government gave the Bank of England the power to control the country's interest rates for the first time ever.

Clinton Visits Latin Countries—Pres. Bill Clinton and First Lady Hillary Rodham Clinton visited 3 Latin American countries in May. With 8 U.S. cabinet members present in Mexico City, Presidents Clinton and Ernesto Zedillo Ponce de Leon of Mexico signed an agreement, **May 6,** providing for a broader mutual effort to fight drug trafficking. The agreement was accompanied by a U.S. acknowledgement that the U.S. was the world's leading consumer of drugs and by Mexico's admission that its drug cartels were a dominant force in the drug trade. The 2 countries signed other accords related to trade, environment, and border problems. Clinton, **May 6,** met with leaders of 2 Mexican opposition parties.

In San Jose, Costa Rica, **May 8,** Clinton met with leaders of 7 Central American and Caribbean nations and sought to reassure them that a tougher U.S. stance on immigration would not trigger a major flow of would-be immigrants back to their former homelands. In Barbados, **May 10,** Clinton attended a summit of 15 Caribbean leaders.

Bosnian Serb Convicted of War Crimes—A Bosnian Serb, Dusan Tadic, was convicted, **May 7,** by the International Criminal Tribunal of having committed atrocities as part of the Serbs' so-called ethnic-cleansing policy during the recent Balkans war. A Croat had pleaded guilty to similar charges in 1996, but Tadic's case was the first of its kind to go to trial since the prosecution of war criminals after World War II.

NATO, Russia Reach Agreement—Russia and the NATO nations agreed, **May 14,** in Moscow, on a treaty that cleared the way for NATO expansion to the east. Under the agreement, NATO would not deploy nuclear weapons or establish nuclear storage sites on the soil of the new member countries. Also, a new NATO-Russia council would give Russia a voice in NATO deliberations. Pres. Boris Yeltsin of Russia, while still opposing the inclusion of former Soviet satellite nations in NATO, said, **May 14,** that the agreement reduced the threat posed by the expansion. This agreement, the Founding Act on Mutual Relations, Cooperation, and Security, was signed in Paris, **May 27,** by Yeltsin and leaders of the NATO nations. Yeltsin said that warheads would be removed from Russian weapons aimed at the NATO countries.

Mobutu Flees Zaire, and Rebels Take Power—Pres. Mobutu Sese Seko, who had ruled Zaire for more than 30 years, looting it of billions of dollars but supported by the West as a bulwark against Communism, fled the capital (Kinshasa) **May 16,** leaving it to his rebel opponents, who had been waging a civil war. While still clinging to control,

May 4, Mobutu had met with Laurent Kabila, the rebel leader, in the neighboring Republic of the Congo, but they were unable to agree on terms under which Mobutu would yield power.

The Mobutu government collapsed, **May 16,** after top generals told the president that they would be unable to defend the capital city against an expected rebel assault. Mobutu left the city and spent the night in his ancestral village, Gbadolite, then flew on to Togo to begin a presumed exile, **May 17.** The army chief of staff and defense minister, Gen. Mahele Lieko Bokungo, who had attempted to negotiate with the rebels, was killed by soldiers loyal to Mobutu.

As rebels began entering the capital, **May 17,** Kabila declared himself head of state and suspended the constitution. After skirmishing that took 200 lives, his troops established control of Kinshasa, **May 18.** Kabila, a former Marxist who once operated a gold-mining business in Tanzania, had fitfully opposed Mobutu since the 1960s. His successful rebellion had begun late in 1996 with the support of ethnic Tutsis and neighboring governments. He now controlled a country as large as Western Europe, with a population that remained impoverished despite the nation's wealth in natural resources.

Kabila, **May 22,** named 13 ministers to a transitional government. Public demonstrations against the new government, **May 23** and **24,** resulted in a ban on such protests, **May 26,** and a ban on political party activity. Kabila was sworn in **May 29** as president of what was again called the Democratic Republic of the Congo, the country's name before Mobutu changed it. Kabila promised a new constitution, to be approved by referendum, and elections within 2 years.

"Moderate" Elected President of Iran—Mohammed Khatami, who had said he would seek to improve economic ties with the West, was elected president of Iran on **May 23.** While leftists, women, and young people rallied to Khatami, often described as a "moderate," the Islamic clerics who dominated political life in Iran generally supported a more conservative candidate. Khatami, who in his campaign speeches promised civil rights for citizens, a reduction of censorship, and improved economic ties with the West, won nearly 70% of the vote. He would succeed Ali Akbar Hashemi Rafsanjani, who was less rigidly conservative than fellow clerics and who had supported Khatami. A mid-level cleric, Khatami had been dismissed as minister of culture and Islamic guidance in 1992 after hard-line clerics called him too permissive. Khatami said, **May 27,** that U.S.-Iran relations could improve if the United States changed its attitude toward Iran.

Mutinous Soldiers Seize Power in Sierra Leone—Soldiers motivated in part by their poor living conditions overthrew Pres. Ahmed Tejan Kabbah of Sierra Leone, **May 25.** Maj. Johnny Paul Koromah, who had been jailed for his role in previous unsuccessful coup attempts, announced, **May 25,** that he had taken control of the country. Since 1991, a civil war between the government and the rebel Revolutionary United Front (RUF) had caused the death of more than 10,000 people. The mutinous soldiers allied themselves with RUF, whose own troops began pouring into Freetown, the capital. On **May 27-28,** Nigeria added 900 peacekeeping troops to the 600-strong contingent already in Sierra Leone.

Anniversary of Marshall Plan Observed—Pres. Bill Clinton, **May 28,** attended a celebration in The Hague, the Netherlands, of the 50th anniversary of the Marshall Plan. The program of U.S. economic assistance to war-ravaged Europe had been proposed by Sec. of State George Marshall in a commencement speech at Harvard University in June 1947. Some $13 billion in grants was funneled to 16 nations, speeding their economic recovery from the war and shoring up Western Europe at a time of growing Soviet expansionism. Before returning to the United States,

Clinton met with Britain's new prime minister, Tony Blair, in London, **May 29**, and spoke to the British cabinet.

General

Link Between Cockroaches and Asthma Confirmed— A federally funded study confirmed, **May 7,** a relationship that had long been suspected: Cockroaches are the leading cause of asthma in children living in inner cities in the United States. Asthma is an inflammatory disease that results in narrowed airways in the lungs. For 20 years the incidence of asthma had been increasing worldwide, and the number of U.S. cases had risen by two-thirds since 1980. Dr. Floyd Malveaux, dean of the Howard University College of Medicine, said researchers established that the roach, rather than the dust mite, was the principal villain in inner cities. Children who were allergic to a protein found in the saliva, feces, and remains of roaches had an increased chance of getting asthma.

Computer Defeats Grandmaster in Chess—Garry Kasparov, the world chess champion, was defeated by a computer, IBM's Deep Blue, in a 6-game match that concluded **May 11** in New York City. After Kasparov defeated the computer in a 1996 match, the latter underwent further programming, to the point where it could consider 200 million moves per second. In the deciding game, Kasparov resigned after only 19 moves.

JUNE 1997

National

Defendant Found Guilty in Oklahoma City Bombing—Timothy McVeigh was found guilty, **June 2**, of the 1995 bombing of a federal building in Oklahoma City that killed 168 people in all. A jury in U.S. District Court in Denver returned the unanimous verdict after 4 days of deliberation. A guilty verdict was returned in all 11 counts against McVeigh—for conspiracy to use a weapon of mass destruction, use of such a weapon, destruction of the building, and 8 counts of first-degree murder in the deaths of 8 federal law-enforcement agents. In the sentencing phase of the trial, survivors of the explosion described serious physical and emotional injuries they had suffered, and relatives of those killed spoke of their heavy loss. Defense lawyers called McVeigh a good man who had been enraged by the conduct of federal agents during sieges against citizens in Idaho and Texas. Jurors, **June 13**, unanimously recommended that McVeigh be sentenced to death.

Unemployment Rate Continues to Fall—The unemployment rate continued to edge downward. The Labor Dept. said, **June 6**, that the unemployment rate in May had been 4.8%, down 0.1% from Apr. and the lowest in 24 years. Some 138,000 nonfarm jobs had been added in May. Earlier, on **June 3**, the Conference Board (a business-research organization) reported that the leading economic indicators had declined 0.1% in Apr., the first drop in more than a year. The Labor Dept. reported, **June 13**, that prices charged by producers for finished goods had declined 0.3% in May. Other Labor Dept. statistics, relased **June 17**, showed that consumer prices rose 0.1% in May. On Wall Street, **June 20**, the Dow Jones industrial average closed at an all-time high of 7796.51, although it suffered a dip of 192 points on **June 23.**

Adultery Ends General's Shot at Top Pentagon Job—A series of sex-related scandals continued to damage military careers. The leading candidate to become chairman of the Joint Chiefs of Staff, Air Force Gen. Joseph Ralston, withdrew from consideration **June 9** after an adulterous affair in his past became known. Earlier, on **May 29**, the Army removed Brig. Gen. Stephen Xenakis as commander of Army medical operations in the Southwest after he was accused of an "improper relationship"

with a nurse who was caring for his wife. On **June 2**, the Pentagon said that Army Maj. Gen. John Longhouser, commander at the Aberdeen Proving Ground, had decided to retire after admitting an adulterous affair. On **June 6** it was reported that Rear Adm. R.M. Mitchell Jr., had been relieved of his responsibilities after an inquiry into allegations that he had made repeated advances toward a woman subordinate.

Gen. Ralston, whose appointment to become chairman of the Joint Chiefs had been anticipated, withdrew from consideration because of revelations of a past affair with a CIA civilian analyst, at a time when he was separated from his wife. Defense Sec. William Cohen had come to Ralston's defense, but Ralston's position was compromised by the recent case of First Lt. Kelly Flinn, who had been forced out of the Air Force in the wake of allegations that included adultery.

After Veto, Disaster-Aid Bill Signed—Pres. Bill Clinton, **June 12**, signed a spending bill that provided $5.6 billion in disaster aid to 35 states, including those in the Midwest that had suffered devastating floods earlier in the year. He had vetoed an earlier version of the bill because of his opposition to 2 Republican-backed provisions. One sought to avert future government shutdowns, such as the ones in 1995 and 1996 for which many Americans had blamed the GOP, by keeping agencies operating when budget agreements were delayed. The other would have barred the use of sampling techniques in conducting the national census for the year 2000. The version of the bill that Clinton signed also included $1.9 billion for U.S. peacekeeping operations overseas.

Clinton Launches Initiative on Race Relations— Pres. Bill Clinton in June opened what he foresaw as a yearlong effort to achieve reconciliation among the races in the United States. On **June 12** he appointed a presidential advisory board on race issues, chaired by historian John Hope Franklin. In a **June 14** commencement address at the University of California at San Diego, Clinton defended affirmative action programs and said that lifting "the burden of race" was "the unfinished work of our time." He said, **June 15**, that he might support a proposed formal apology to blacks for the institution of slavery. In a news conference on **Aug. 7**, however, he indicated that he hoped the idea of an apology, which was criticized by some as rhetoric of no value, "will not dominate all other things that need to be discussed about the past, the present, and the future."

Tobacco Firms, Legal Foes Reach $368 Billion Deal— Four major U.S. tobacco companies and several state attorneys general, after months of negotiations, agreed, **June 20**, to a settlement that would cost the companies $368.5 billion. Support for the agreement from the Clinton administration and the health community, as well as the required approval of Congress, remained in doubt. The attorneys general had sued the companies to recover the costs of smoking-related illnesses. They were joined by plaintiffs in class-action lawsuits and public health advocates. The unprecedented payout included $50 billion in punitive damages for the industry's deceit in concealing from the public evidence of the dangers of smoking.

The negotiations, led by Attorney Gen. Michael Moore of Mississippi, came at a time when smoking by teenagers was rising. A major component of the agreement was a commitment by the companies to cut smoking by young people. The industry would be fined heavily if youth smoking did not decline by 60% in 10 years. Marketing targeted at young people would cease, as would industry sponsorship of sporting events and concerts. The federal Food and Drug Administration would be conceded the authority to regulate tobacco products. In return, the industry would be shielded against class-action lawsuits and given immunity from punitive damage awards for past misconduct.

A committee of health experts said, **June 25**, that the agreement did not penalize the industry sufficiently and did not ensure that regulation of tobacco products would be effective.

Senate and House OK Balanced-Budget Bills—Both houses of Congress passed bills implementing the agreement reached in May that sought to achieve a balanced federal budget in 2002. The bills differed from each other in significant ways, however, and a Senate–House conference committee was left with the task of producing a final version. On **June 25** the Senate, 73–27, and the House, 270–162, passed spending bills; the House, **June 26**, 253-179, and the Senate, **June 27**, 80–18, approved tax bills. Notwithstanding the May accord, members of Congress continued to argue over provisions of both bills. Democrats, for example, complained that reductions in the tax bill favored the wealthy. Pres. Bill Clinton, **June 30**, announced his own plan for cutting taxes. It included only a small reduction in capital-gains taxes for investors in high-income brackets.

Clinton Backs Tougher Clean-Air Rules—Pres. Bill Clinton, **June 25**, approved air-quality standards that tightened limits on soot and ground-level ozone. He announced that, for the first time, the government would regulate soot particles 2.5 microns or less in diameter; these particles, when inhaled, were believed to aggravate repiratory illnesses. The new standard for ozone would limit concentrations of the gas to 80 parts per billion.

International

Voters Move France to the Left—On **June 1**, in the 2d and conclusive round of voting in the French parliamentary elections, parties of the left took power for the first time since 1986. The Socialist Party, in winning 273 seats, fell short of a majority in the 577-member National Assembly, but the Communists won 38 seats and the leftist Green environmental party took 8. The center-right coalition that had led the country captured 257 seats, down sharply from its 1993 total of 449. The results were a blow for Pres. Jacques Chirac and ensured the resignation, **June 2**, of Prem. Alain Juppé. The unpopular Juppé had already indicated he would step down after the returns were in. Unemployment stood at a 50-year high of 12.8%. During the campaign, Lionel Jospin, the Socialist leader, declared that France should not have to reduce its deficit to meet requirements of economic and monetary union with Europe. Jospin became prime minister, **June 3**, and formed a government, **June 4**, that included 2 Communists and a Green. A former minister of education, Jospin had been the unsuccessful Socialist candidate for president in 1995.

Premier of Turkey Resigns Under Pressure—Prem. Necmettin Erbakan of Turkey announced, **June 1**, that he would call new elections. The governing coalition no longer had a majority in Parliament, and Erbaken's Welfare Party had come under strong criticism from military leaders because of its Muslim fundamentalist views. Prior to Erbakan's election, Turkey had long had a secular government, buttressed by the military. Erbakan resigned **June 18**. On **June 30**, Pres. Suleyman Demirel approved a new government headed by Mesut Yilmaz, leader of the Motherland Party.

Sierra Leone Rebels Fight Nigerian Troops—Maj. Johnny Paul Koromah, new leader of Sierra Leone, announced the appointment, **June 1**, of an Armed Forces Revolutionary Council. The new rebel government faced a naval bombardment, **June 2**, from Nigerian warships off Freetown, the capital. Nigerian peacekeeping troops were already in Sierra Leone under auspices of the Community of West African States. Sierra Leone's rebel troops then fought with Nigerian troops. The Organization of African Unity, **June 3**, authorized the Nigerians to act to restore constitutional rule in Sierra Leone. U.S. troops, **June 3**,

evacuated 1,200 more foreigners from Freetown. Fighting subsided, with the rebel regime retaining power.

Liberal Party Retains Power in Canada—The **June 2** parliamentary election in Canada resulted in another victory for the Liberal Party headed by Prime Min. Jean Chretien. The Liberals lost 19 seats, however, retaining just 155 seats, a slim majority in the 301-member House of Commons. The government had introduced tough reforms aimed at erasing Canada's budget deficit. Inflation was down to 2% and job creation had been vigorous. In the election no strong rival party emerged. The Reform Party became the official opposition with 60 seats. The proseparatist Bloc Quebecois slipped to 44 seats, not much more than a majority in its only stronghold, Quebec. The New Democrats and the Progressive Conservatives won 21 and 20 seats, respectively. The latter, once the dominant force in Canadian politics, thus recouped somewhat from its devastating 2-seat showing in the 1993 election.

Ex-Ruler Pol Pot Seized in Cambodia—Pol Pot, leader of the Khmer Rouge in Cambodia and former ruler of the country, was seized by Khmer Rouge dissident guerrillas in June. The dissidents had reported arresting Pol Pot after he ordered the assassination, **June 10**, of another Khmer Rouge leader and his family. Pol Pot's capture was announced on **June 21** by First Prem. Prince Norodom Ranariddh and Second Prem. Hun Sen. They said they would ask that an international tribunal put him on trial for the more than 1 million deaths attributed to the Khmer Rouge during its calamitous years in power.

Croatia's President Tudjman Reelected—Franjo Tudjman was elected to a 3d term as president of Croatia on **June 15** with a reported 61% of the vote. International observers said, **June 16**, that the voting was flawed, partially because the state-owned news media had labeled Tudjman's opponents "enemies of the state." Tudjman, who had led Croatia to independence from Yugoslavia, had represented Croatia at the signing of the Bosnian peace agreement in Dayton, OH, in 1995.

Russia Joins Economic Summit—Leaders of the world's major industrial nations (Group of Seven) held their 23d annual meeting in Denver, CO, in June. With Russia's participation in sessions, the gathering was being dubbed the Summit of the Eight. Pres. Bill Clinton met with Prime Min. Ryutaro Hashimoto in Denver, **June 19**, to discuss the U.S. trade deficit with Japan, which had risen to $4.84 billion in April. After meeting with Pres. Boris Yeltsin of Russia, **June 20**, Clinton announced that Russia had been admitted to the Paris Club of creditor nations; the club included advanced countries that helped developing countries manage debt. European countries sought without success to persuade the United States, Canada, and Japan to adopt more specific reductions of greenhouse gases, which contributed to global warming. In a **June 22** communique, summit participants opposed human cloning, urged China to honor commitments to respect democracy in Hong Kong, and pressed the Democratic Republic of the Congo (formerly Zaire) to move toward democracy and respect human rights.

Collision Damages Russian Space Station—An unmanned cargo ship collided with the Russian space station *Mir*, **June 25**, during a docking maneuver. Three astronauts—Russians Vasily Tsibliyev and Aleksandr Lazutkin and American Michael Foale—were aboard *Mir*. They were not injured. The supply vessel missed its docking port and struck *Mir's* Spektr module, leaving a small hole and damaging a solar panel and a radiator. The mishap knocked out about half of *Mir's* power supply.

Blair Offers New Plan on Northern Ireland—British Prime Min. Tony Blair, **June 25**, modified long-standing policy on talks with Sinn Fein, political arm of the Provisional Irish Republican Army. Under the new plan of the British and Irish governments, Sinn Fein could join ongoing talks over the future of Northern Ireland without first surrendering its large stockpile of weapons. The IRA would still be required to declare a cease-fire before joining the negotiations.

Ahern Elected Prime Minister of Ireland—The Dail, lower house of Ireland's parliament, elected Bertie Ahern prime minister, **June 26.** He defeated the incumbent, John Bruton, 85-78. Ahern's Fianna Fail party had gained a plurality in parliamentary elections **June 6.** The contest marked the first time a member of Sinn Fein, political arm of the Provisional Irish Republican Army, had won election to the Dail.

General

Detroit Wins First Hockey Title in 42 Years—The Detroit Red Wings won hockey's Stanley Cup, **June 7,** with a 2-1 victory over the Philadelphia Flyers. The Red Wings, playing at home, wrapped up a 4-game sweep and captured their first championship since 1955. Niklas Lidstrom and Darren McCarty scored goals for the Red Wings; the Flyers did not score until the final 15 seconds of the game. Detroit's goaltender, Mike Vernon, was named most valuable player in the playoffs. The championship was the 7th for Detroit's coach, Scotty Bowman.

Chicago Bulls Win NBA Title Again—The Chicago Bulls won their 5th National Basketball Association title in 7 years, **June 13.** In Chicago, the home team downed the Utah Jazz, 90-86, to win the championship series, 4 games to 2. Utah led much of the way, and the game was tied when the Bulls' Steve Kerr hit a 17-ft. field goal with 5 seconds to play. The Bulls' Michael Jordan was named most valuable player in the playoffs for the 5th time.

Tyson Bites Holyfield's Ears During Title Fight—A heavyweight championship boxing match in Las Vegas, NV, was marred, **June 28,** when the challenger, Mike Tyson, bit Evander Holyfield on one ear and then the other during the 3d round. A piece of Holyfield's right ear was torn off. The referee disqualified Tyson, allowing Holyfield to retain his World Boxing Assn. crown. Tyson, who made a public apology **June 30,** said he had been angered because Holyfield had butted him with his head.

The Nevada State Athletic Commission, **July 1,** voted to hold up a $30 million purse owed to Tyson, and on **July 9** the commisson fined Tyson $3 million and revoked for one year his license to fight in Nevada. Tyson's boxing future was in question, considering that athletic commissions in other states usually followed the lead of a state that revokes a license. The license was renewable after one year, but there was no guarantee that renewal would be granted.

JULY 1997

National

Economy Appears Strong, With No Increase in Interest Rates Imminent—The Conference Board (a business-research organization) announced, **July 1,** that the leading economic indicators had risen 0.3% in May. Among encouraging numbers was a 5.0% unemployment rate for June, a 24-year low, as reported by the Labor Dept., **July 3.** The Labor Dept. also said that 217,000 nonfarm jobs had been added to the economy in June, and that producer prices in June had declined for an unprecedented 6th consecutive month, by 0.1%. The decline was attributed in part to the strong U.S. dollar, which gave Americans the option of buying foreign goods more cheaply. According to the department, **July 16,** consumer prices had risen 0.1% in June.

On Wall Street, **July 16,** the Dow Jones industrial average passed 8,000 to reach a record high, closing at 8038.88. The Commerce Dept., **July 18,** released figures indicating that the trade deficit had stood at $10.23 billion in May. Alan Greenspan, chairman of the Federal Reserve Board,

said, **July 22,** that the economy was in exceptional health and that he saw no need to raise interest rates soon. It was his view that, owing to favorable national and international conditions, productivity would continue to rise. On **July 30** the Dow Jones average finished at a record high, 8254.89, its 37th record high of the year. The Commerce Dept. reported, **July 31,** that the gross domestic product had grown 2.2% in the 2d quarter.

Clinton Skeptical on Tobacco Deal—Pres. Bill Clinton, in July, indicated a lack of enthusiasm for the sweeping agreement between tobacco companies and their legal adversaries that had been reached in June. Earlier, the state of Mississippi reached its own settlement with the companies. The state's attorney general, Michael Moore, had been a leader in the national negotiations. On **July 3,** Moore announced that 4 major tobacco companies had agreed to pay Mississippi $3.4 billion to recover Medicaid and other money spent by the state on smoking-related illnesses. On **July 9,** Clinton said that the national agreement would hamper efforts of the U.S. Food and Drug Administration to force tobacco producers to lower the nicotine content of cigarettes. Also, federal government officials were concerned that the companies would be able to deduct from their taxes the cost of their $368.5 billion settlement. This would reduce revenues to the government by $100 billion.

U.S. Spacecraft Lands on Mars—On **July 4,** for the first time in more than 2 decades, an American spacecraft landed on Mars. The Mars *Pathfinder*, launched by the National Aeronautics and Space Administration, hit the Ares Vallis area of the planet at 23 miles an hour; the impact was cushioned by airbags. On **July 6** it deployed *Sojourner*, a wheeled vehicle that moved about and measured the chemical components in rocks and soil.

Pathfinder's camera sent sharp panoramic color images of Mars back to Earth. NASA said, **July 8,** that analysis of one rock showed that it contained minerals common on Earth, including quartz and feldspar. Soil was found to contain iron, aluminum, magnesium, calcium, sulfur, and potassium. Ares Vallis is believed to have been awash in flood waters 1-3 billion years ago, and scientists hoped that data from *Sojourner* and *Pathfinder* would yield information about this and other signs of the ancient presence of water on Mars.

Senate Begins Hearings on Fund-Raising—The Senate Governmental Affairs Committee began hearings, **July 8,** into potentially illegal fund-raising practices related to the 1994 and 1996 elections. Sen. Fred Thompson (R, TN), the committee chairman, said, **July 8,** that China, through illegal contributions, had sought to influence the outcome of the 1996 election. Sen. John Glenn (D, OH), a committee member, said, **July 8,** that an important figure in the investigation, John Huang, had indicated through his lawyer that he would testify if granted immunity from prosecution. Huang was a former Democratic National Committee official who had raised large sums of money and who may have served the interests of his former employer, the Lippo Group, an Indonesian company, while also holding an important position in the Commerce Dept. The FBI, **July 14,** briefed committee members on its evidence relative to Chinese attempts to influence U.S. policy. Sens. Glenn and Joseph Lieberman (R, CT) said, **July 15,** that FBI evidence strongly indicated a Chinese plan to influence the 1996 election. The committee revealed, **July 15,** that in 1993 and 1994, while a Lippo employee, Huang had visited the White House 52 times.

The Democrats sought to determine if Haley Barbour, former chairman of the Republican National Committee (RNC), had asked for financial support from Ambrous Tung Young, a Hong Kong businessman. Michael Baroody, a former president of the National Policy Forum, a conservative think tank, testified, **July 23,** that he had resigned his NPF office because of the close relationship between the NPF and the RNC. In 1994, a U.S. subsidiary of Young Brothers Development had guaranteed a $2.1 million bank loan to the NPF. The NPF used the money to repay a $1.6 million debt to the RNC, which pumped the money into the 1994 Congressional campaign. Young Brothers later lost $700,000 when the NPF defaulted on the loan. Barbour, in testimony **July 24–25**, denied soliciting money from Young and funneling it through the NPF.

Revised TV Ratings System Adopted—NBC was the lone holdout when the major television networks agreed, **July 9**, to implement a revised and expanded television ratings system. Some viewers had complained that the original system, implemented in Jan., was not specific enough about program content that might be inappropriate for children. The new agreement supplemented the original rating catagories by assigning specific letters for different types of content—sexual content, profanity, sexually suggestive dialogue, and violence. The ratings could ultimately be used in conjunction with an electronic chip to be installed in televisions beginning in 1998. The so-called v-chip will enable consumers to block out selected programs. NBC contended the new system could lead to government censorship.

GOP Power Struggle in House Claims a Victim—Dissatisfaction among some House Republicans with Speaker Newt Gingrich (GA) reached a climax on **July 10**, when several Republicans who questioned his conservatism and leadership skills sought without success to force him to relinquish his leadership post. Gingrich then arranged for a meeting, **July 11**, between his top lieutenants—Majority Leader Dick Armey (TX), Majority Whip Tom DeLay (TX), John Boehner (OH), and Bill Paxon (NY)—and his adversaries. Reports emerged from the meeting that the leaders had not cooled the rebellion and had in fact discussed possible replacements for Gingrich. The Speaker forced Paxon, his hand-picked lieutenant, from his leadership role on **July 17**. Gingrich could not oust the others, had he so desired, because they were elected by the entire GOP caucus. Armey, **July 22**, denied plotting Gingrich's removal. DeLay and Boehner, **July 22**, declined to elaborate on their roles in the dispute.

Senate Approves Tenet to Head CIA—The Senate, **July 10**, by voice vote, approved George Tenet as director of central intelligence. Tenet, who had been acting CIA director since John Deutch resigned in Dec., had encountered no problems in confirmation hearings before the Senate Intelligence Committee in May.

Weld Fights Helms for Ambassadorship—On **July 23**, Pres. Bill Clinton nominated Mass. Gov. William Weld, widely regarded as a liberal Republican, to be U.S. ambassador to Mexico, setting the stage for a political battle between two prominent Republicans. In June, after reports circulated that Clinton would nominate Weld, Sen. Jesse Helms (R, NC), the powerful conservative chairman of the Senate Foreign Relations Committee, had already declared he would refuse to hold hearings on the nomination, which would ensure that neither the committee nor the Senate could vote on the nomination. Helms said Weld was unsuitable for the Mexico post, which would thrust him into the thick of U.S. drug policy, because he supported needle-exchange programs for drug addicts and favored the use of marijuana for medicinal purposes. Weld, **July 15**, was harshly critical of Helms and said he had no interest in meeting Helms's litmus test on social policy. After Clinton nominated Weld he resigned as governor, **July 28**; Lt. Gov. Paul Cellucci became acting governor.

Congress Passes Budget Legislation—Following agreements reached between Pres. Bill Clinton and the Republican-controlled Congress, the latter passed 2 major budget bills. The bills aimed to balance the federal budget by the year 2002. One bill, which dealt with spending, would save $115 billion in Medicare costs through lower payments to health-care providers and greater participation in managed-care programs. Some $10 billion in Medicaid

costs would be eliminated by reducing payments to hospitals that treated a high number of poor patients. At the same time, $23 billion would go to states as grants to provide health care for children, many of them uninsured. An increase in the cigarette tax would cover that cost in part. To correct what many viewed as an injustice in the 1996 welfare-reform law, the new budget contained $14 billion to restore some benefits to elderly and disabled legal immigrants.

The companion tax bill provided for a net reduction of about $95 billion in taxes. Families would get a $500 per child tax credit for children up to age 16. College tuition and book-cost credits of up to $1,500 per freshman and sophomore student also were approved. (These provisions were, however, subject to income limitations.) The top rate for long-term capital gains taxes was lowered from 28% to 20%, and the exemption for inheritance taxes was raised from $600,000 to $1 million.

After Clinton and the Republican leaders reached agreement, the House approved the spending bill on **July 30**, 346-85, and the tax bill, **July 31**, 389-43. The Senate approved both bills on **July 31**—the former, 85-15, the latter, 92-8. Large numbers of liberal House Democrats, including Minority Leader Richard Gephardt (MO), voted against both measures. They complained of tax breaks for the wealthy and said that Medicare cuts were excessive. Clinton signed the measures **Aug. 5**.

International

China Regains Control of Hong Kong—After 99 years as a British territory, Hong Kong was returned to China as of **July 1**. China had ceded Hong Kong to Britain in the 19th century, and the small colony had since become an international financial center, as well as a home and crossroads for businesspeople operating in Asia. A joint declaration on Hong Kong, signed by Britain and China in 1984, established the terms for the territory's reversion to Chinese nationality. Under the Basic Law, approved in 1990, Hong Kong was to remain semiautonomous and retain its capitalist economy for 50 years. Chinese leader Deng Xiaoping, who died in Feb. 1997, had planned for Hong Kong to function under a "one country, two systems" arrangement. Nonetheless, the future of Hong Kong remained in some doubt, especially in view of possible political restrictions.

In the handover ceremony, the British Union Jack was lowered and the Chinese flag raised. The British delegation present included Prince Charles, Prime Min. Tony Blair, and former Prime Min. Margaret Thatcher, who had participated in the 1984 negotiations. Pres. Jiang Zemin of China attended. Sec. of State Madeleine Albright represented the United States. Tung Chee-hwa, appointed by China as the territory's first chief executive under Chinese rule, was installed **July 1**, as head of what was now the Hong Kong Special Administrative Region. He had said that elections would take place within a year, and appeared eager to reassure all concerned that Hong Kong would continue to prosper.

A provisional legislature was also sworn in. It immediately imposed restrictions on political organizations and public demonstrations. Street protests against China's takeover, which had begun before midnight June 30, continued into **July 1**, but the new regime did not intervene. Martin Lee, leader of the Democratic Party, told thousands in a speech, **July 1**, that the "flame of democracy . . . will not be snuffed out."

Mexican Drug Lord Dies After Surgery—Amado Carrillo Fuentes, a billionaire drug trafficker, died in Mexico in early July after undergoing plastic surgery. Carrillo entered a hospital in Mexico City under an assumed name, **July 3**, and had 8 hours of surgery to remove fat from his midsection and change his appearance. He was found dead on the morning of **July 4**. DNA tests later established his identity. Carrillo, the reputed head of the Juarez drug cartel, was thought to have been Mexico's top drug trafficker.

New Crew to Work on Spacecraft's Problems—An unmanned Russian spacecraft took off from Kazakhstan, **July 5**, transporting supplies to the *Mir* spacecraft, whose crew had been bedeviled by problems following the collision of *Mir* and an unmanned cargo vessel in June. The supply craft, carrying food, water, oxygen, and repair and communications equipment, docked with *Mir*, **July 7**. Vasily Tsibliyev, one of the 3 astronauts aboard *Mir*, reported, **July 14**, that his heartbeat had become irregular. The Russian space agency announced, **July 21**, that a new crew would make needed repairs on the space station.

Cambodian Premier Ousted; Pol Pot Sentenced—In Cambodia, the rivalry between Prince Norodom Ranariddh and Hun Sen, who had been designated as first premier and second premier, respectively, ended abruptly **July 6**. Fighting had begun, **July 5**, between army factions supporting the 2 leaders. The next day, while Prince Ranariddh was in France, Hun Sen forced him from power. Hun Sen had criticized the prince's attempts to form an alliance with the Khmer Rouge, notorious for their brutal reign of terror when they controlled Cambodia, and he accused the prince of illegal acts. On **July 8**, forces backing Hun Sen began arresting his political opponents. A cabinet member was reported executed **July 8**. Responding to criticism, Hun Sen warned other nations, **July 10**, not to interfere in Cambodia's affairs.

Pol Pot, head of the Khmer Rouge, who had been seized by members of a dissident faction in June, was condemned to life imprisonment, **July 25**, in a trial by his former comrades. He had been accused of ordering the assassination of a rival within the Khmer Rouge and his family.

Mexico's Ruling Party Suffers Setback in Voting—On **July 6**, for the first time since it was founded in 1929, Mexico's Institutional Revolutionary Party (PRI) failed to win a majority in voting for the lower house of Congress. Recurring economic crises and widespread political corruption had hurt the PRI; it won 239 of 500 seats in the Chamber of Deputies, down from 298. The leftist Democratic Revolutionary Party (PRD), which wanted the government to take a stronger role in economic affairs and was skeptical of closer ties with the United States, won 125 seats. The conservative National Action Party (PAN) took 122 seats. The PRI held control of the Senate. However, PRD founder Cuauhtemoc Cardenas Solorzano won Mexico City's first-ever mayoral election. The PAN increased the number of governorships it held from 4 to 6.

Strife-torn Albania Gets New Government—Albania, which had deteriorated into violence and anarchy after several risky investment schemes collapsed, got a change of government in July, with new president and premier. The Socialists won a substantial majority in parliamentary elections concluded **July 6**, and the new Socialist-dominated Parlimanet elected Rexhep Mejdani, **July 24**, as Albanian president. Mejdani, in turn, named the Socialist leader, Fatos Nano, as premier. Nano promised, **July 30**, to revive the economy but said he would not reimburse those who had lost money in the investment schemes.

Three East European Nations Invited to Join NATO—The members of NATO, **July 8**, invited 3 East European nations—the Czech Republic, Hungary, and Poland—to join the organization. They were once members of the Warsaw Pact, which stood in opposition to NATO during the cold war. Russia had reluctantly agreed to NATO expansion. Russian Foreign Minister Yevgeny Primakov, **July 8**, characterized NATO's eastward expansion as a big mistake.

U.S. Helps Target Indicted War Criminals—The United States, **July 10**, gave logistical support to a British unit under NATO command as it sought to seize indicted war criminals in Bosnia. The British killed one Bosnian Serb, who had been indicted, after he resisted arrest and shot at them. Another Serb was seized. One British soldier was injured in the confrontation. The 2 Serbs had been charged with complicity in genocide.

Cease-fire Renews Hopes on Northern Ireland—The Provisional Irish Republican Army declared a cease-fire, **July 19**, in its long war to force Great Britain out of Northern Ireland. The IRA's action increased the likelihood that peace talks involving all parties would get underway soon. The cease-fire took effect **July 20**. On **July 23**, however, Northern Ireland's largest Protestant pro-union parties rejected the plan advocated by the British and Irish governments that called for "parallel decommissioning" of arms held by Catholic and Protestant fighters.

Liberia Elects President—After a 7-year civil war that had taken 150,000 lives, Liberia held a peaceful election for president, **July 19**, its first national election in 12 years. The winner was Charles Taylor, a leader of one of the warring factions, who had a reputation for brutality. International observers said that the election had been conducted fairly.

Bombs Kill 15 in Jerusalem—Suicide bombers detonated two bombs in an outdoor market in West Jerusalem, **July 30**, killing 13 people in addition to both bombers. More than 170 persons were injured. Hamas, an extremist Palestinian group, claimed responsibility. The Israeli cabinet, **July 30**, linked further participation in peace talks to the effectiveness of the Palestinian National Authority in stopping terrorist groups.

General

Martina Hingis, 16, Wins at Wimbledon—Martina Hingis of Switzerland won the women's singles championship at the Wimbledon tennis tournament in London, **July 5**. The 16-year-old was the youngest to claim that title since 1887. Hingis, who had been seeded number 1 and had won the year's Australian Open, defeated Jana Novotna of the Czech Republic, 2-6, 6-3, 6-3, in the Wimbledon final. Pete Sampras of the United States won his 4th men's singles title, **July 6**, defeating Cedric Pioline of France in the final, 6-4, 6-2, 6-4.

Fashion Designer Gianni Versace Shot to Death—Gianni Versace, the popular Italian fashion designer, was shot to death in front of his Miami Beach home, **July 15**. Versace, with the aid of "supermodels" who showcased his designs, had taken fashion to new heights of flamboyance and sensuality. Police said, **July 15**, that the prime suspect in the designer's murder was Andrew Phillip Cunanan, already wanted in 4 murders committed in the Midwest and East since Apr., including that of his former homosexual lover. A vehicle that investigators believed Cunanan had stolen from a previous victim was found near Versace's home. A massive nationwide manhunt for Cunanan began. Several miles from the Versace murder scene, on **July 23**, a caretaker became suspicious when he saw a door ajar on a houseboat. On investigating, he thought he heard a shot, and called police. After firing tear gas into the boat, assault teams entered it and found Cunanan, who apparently had committed suicide. Police said that the pistol with which Cunanan ended his life had been used to shoot Versace and another of Cunanan's victims. Cunanan's motive in the Versace killing was not immediately known.

Cloned Sheep Has Human Genes—the infant science of cloning took another step forward when researchers at the Roslin Institute near Edinburgh, Scotland—the same team that produced a cloning breakthrough in Feb.—announced, **July 24**, that they had cloned a sheep with human genes. Polly, a Poll Dorset sheep, was created by fusing human genes and skin cells of sheep embryos. The cells were implanted in the womb of an adult sheep. The new breakthrough represented yet another a step toward the day when animals' biological products could be used to treat human diseases.

Three Convicted in Cosby Extortion Plot—Autumn Jackson, 22, who claimed to be the out-of-wedlock daughter of comedian Bill Cosby, was convicted **July 25** of seeking to extort $40 million from the entertainer, having threatened otherwise to tell her story to a tabloid newspaper. Two codefendents were convicted to charges related to the attempt. Cosby had testified at the trial that he had a single sexual encounter with Jackson's mother in 1974 and had given the mother money over the years so that she would not go public with the liaison. He denied being the father of Autumn Jackson, and this issue did not figure in the trial. Lawyers for Autumn Jackson had contended that she believed she was Cosby's daughter and had been engaged in lawful negotiations for a paternity settlement.

AUGUST 1997

National

UPS, Teamsters Reach Accord After Strike—The Teamsters Union, **Aug. 4**, began a strike against United Parcel Service, which handled 12 million packages a day and represented the bulk of the shipping business in the United States. The union opposed UPS's shift toward the use of part-time employees, who were paid much less per hour than full-time workers. It also objected to UPS's desire to create a new pension plan. Some 185,000 workers went out on strike. UPS's shipping dropped by 90%, and it was estimated that the strike cost the company $600 million in revenues. Pres. Bill Clinton, **Aug. 6**, declined to utilize federal powers available to him to intervene in the dispute, but Labor Secretary Alexis Herman was influential in moving the 2 sides to a resolution. The parties reached a settlement, **Aug. 19**, that was considered generally favorable to the union. UPS agreed to create 10,000 full-time jobs by merging part-time jobs; workers in both categories would receive salary increases.

The Stock Market Rises and Falls—On Wall Street, on **Aug. 6**, the Dow Jones industrial average closed at an all-time high of 8259.31. While the economy remained strong, inflation appeared under control. The Labor Dept. had reported, **Aug. 1**, that the unemployment rate dropped back in July to 4.8%, equaling the May level and also equaling a 24-year low. Some 316,000 jobs were added to the economy in July. At the same time, the longest string ever of declines in producer prices—now 7 months in a row—had continued in July, the department said, **Aug. 13**; this time the decrease in producer prices was 0.1%. However, the stock market suffered losses later in Aug. On **Aug. 14** it was reported that the consumer price index, which had been rising only 0.1% a month, rose 0.2% in July. On **Aug. 15**, the Dow Jones industrial average plunged 247.37 points, the second-largest one-day point decline yet, closing at 7694.66, down 3.1%. At the end of the month the Dow stood at 7622.42, down 7.3% for the whole month. The Commerce Dept. said, **Aug. 20**, that the trade deficit had stood at $8.16 billion in June.

Clinton Uses Line-Item Veto for First Time—Pres. Bill Clinton, on **Aug. 11**, became the first president to use the line-item veto. Congress in 1996 had granted the president this power, which most state governors have in some form or other. In the federal version, a president could kill specific provisions in a spending bill, or eliminate a tax break, from a revenue bill if it benefited 100 or fewer persons or 10 or fewer businesses. Clinton vetoed 3 specific provisions in the new legislation. The first would have allowed New York State to receive $200 million or more in extra Medicaid payments; the second would have

permitted a few U.S. banks and financial-service companies to defer taxes on overseas income. The third provision would have deferred taxes on the sale of food-processing operations to farm cooperatives—a provision that would have principally benefited a major contributor to the Republican Party.

Earlier, on **Aug. 5**, Clinton had signed the tax and spending bills passed in July that aimed to balance the budget by 2002. The Office of Management and Budget and the Congressional Budget Office, **Aug. 6**, put out new, lowered estimates for the 1997 federal deficit—$37 billion and $34 billion, respectively.

Processor Recalls 25 Million Pounds of Beef—A new health scare involving the *E. coli* bacterium flared up in Aug. In 1993, *E. coli* contamination had been responsible for the deaths of 4 children in the Pacific Northwest. Most often, the bacteria entered food supplies when the intestines or fecal matter of slaughtered animals came in contact with meat. On **Aug. 12**, Hudson Foods Inc., a meat processor in Rogers, AR, announced it was recalling 20,000 pounds of beef after the Colorado Dept. of Public Health found that some people who had eaten Hudson Foods hamburgers had become ill. The recall was expanded to 1.2 million pounds of beef on **Aug. 15**. Inspectors for the U.S. Dept. of Agriculture found, **Aug. 18**, that the Hudson plant did not have adequate procedures for controlling quality or keeping records, and that leftover meat was mixed with the next day's supply, considered a risky practice. By **Aug. 21**, 17 people had been stricken after eating Hudson meat. On **Aug. 21**, Hudson announced a recall of 25 million pounds of beef.

Illegal Gifts Force New Teamsters Election—The struggle for power within the International Brotherhood of Teamsters was renewed when a federal official, **Aug. 22**, ordered that a new election for president of the union be held. In Dec. 1996, in a bitterly fought contest, Ron Carey had narrowly been reelected Teamsters president over James P. Hoffa, son of former Teamsters Pres. James R. Hoffa. The order for a new election came just 3 days after a settlement in the strike against United Parcel Service that was seen as favorable to the union and a boost to Carey. The federal election overseer, Barbara Quindel, found that the Carey reelection campaign had received more than $220,000 in illegal contributions. Most of this money came indirectly from a consulting company to which the union had awarded contracts or channeled funds. Carey denied knowledge of the financing scheme.

Trial Date Set for Suit Against Clinton—U.S. Circuit Court Judge Susan Webber Wright, **Aug. 22**, scheduled a trial involving Pres. Bill Clinton for May 1998. Paula Jones, a former Arkansas state employee, had accused Clinton of having made unwanted sexual advances to her in 1991. The specific legal complaint was that Clinton, then the governor, had used the power of his office to deny Jones her constitutional rights. Jones was seeking an apology and $700,000. Robert Bennett, Clinton's lawyer, said, **Aug. 22**, that Clinton would not apologize for conduct which he denied had occurred.

Florida Settles Suit With Tobacco Companies—Florida, **Aug. 25**, became the 2d state, after Mississippi, to settle a liability suit against tobacco companies. Five companies agreed to pay the state $11.3 billion to cover health costs related to the use of tobacco products. The companies would also help curb teenage smoking. Cigarette vending machines accessible to minors would disappear, as would tobacco billboard advertising near schools. The companies also agreed to release relevant documents.

Anti-Affirmative Action Measure Goes Into Effect in California—Proposition 209, a controversial anti-affirmative action measure approved by California voters in 1996, officially went into effect in the state **Aug. 28**. It barred the state from race- or gender-based preferences in school admissions, public hiring, and contracting. The U.S.

Supreme Court, **Sept. 4,** refused to extend an injunction on enforcement of the measure pending the outcome of an appeal before the Court.

International

Palestinian-Israeli Conflict Intensifies—On **Aug. 3** Israeli Prime Min. Benjamin Netanyahu said he would not honor agreements made by Israel's previous government with the Palestinians unless the Palestinian National Authority cracked down on terrorists. The next day the Israeli cabinet decided not to hand over taxes and customs fees it collected for the PNA, and Israel sent commandos, **Aug. 4,** into territory in southern Lebanon controlled by the militant Palestinian organization Hezbollah. PNA leader Yasir Arafat charged, **Aug. 5,** that Netanyahu was inventing obstacles to peace, while Netanyahu, **Aug. 6,** refused appeals from Jordan and the United States that he ease sanctions on Gaza and West Bank Palestinians. On **Aug. 8,** Hezbollah shelled Qiryat Shemona, in Upper Galilee. The PNA, **Aug. 17,** declared a phased boycott of Israeli products. On **Aug. 18,** Israel announced that it would unfreeze some of the money owed the Palestinians because they had acted against 3 men who killed an Israeli taxi driver and had cooperated somewhat in an investigation of the July bombings.

On **Aug. 18,** the Lebanese port city of Sidon was shelled by the South Lebanon Army, an ally of the Israelis. The raid claimed 10 lives, and many were wounded. Hezbollah then peppered northern Israel with 45 rockets, **Aug. 19,** causing little damage. Netanyahu called on Syria, **Aug. 19,** to restrain Hezbollah, and Israeli warplanes, **Aug. 20,** attacked targets in southern Lebanon.

Arafat, **Aug. 20,** brought together Palestinians of various factions for a conference in Gaza City, at which a Hamas leader called for confrontation with Israeli settlers. Israel, **Aug. 27,** lifted a blockade of Bethlehem, the last city to be affected by Israel's punitive reaction to the July bombings.

North Korea Attends Talks, Launches Nuclear Energy Project—North Korean representatives, **Aug. 5-7,** met with representatives of the United States, China, and South Korea in New York. The meeting was a step toward negotiating a permanent treaty to replace the armistice agreed to after the Korean War. North Korea remained in the grip of a serious famine, which the United States had sought to alleviate by promising, in July, to donate $27 million worth of grain.

North Korea moved ahead, **Aug. 19,** to officially launch an internationally funded $5 billion nuclear energy project, involving construction of two light-water nuclear power plants near Kumho. The project stemmed from a 1994 accord, under which North Korea had agreed to halt its suspected nuclear arms program.

New Cosmonauts on *Mir*; Glitches Continue—Russian cosmonauts Anatoly Solovyev and Pavel Vinogradov lifted off from Kazakhstan, **Aug. 5,** on their way to the Russian space station *Mir*. They were sent up after it appeared that the Russians already on *Mir*, Vasily Tsibliyev and Aleksander Lazutkin, could not overcome the station's technical difficulties. The 2 new cosmonauts reached *Mir* **Aug 7;** Solovyev had to dock the *Soyez* space capsule manually because *Mir*'s automated system was not working. Solovyev and Vinogradov, **Aug. 14,** repaired an oxygen-generating system that had not worked for several weeks. Meanwhile, Tsibliyev and Lazutkin landed on Earth **Aug. 14.**

Viktor Blagov of the Russian space program asserted, **Aug. 14,** that technology had not been at fault in the collision in June between *Mir* and a cargo ship. Tsibliyev and Lalzutkin charged, **Aug. 16,** that Pres. Boris Yeltsin and other officials were spreading "rumors, gossip, and lies" about them.

A cargo ship carrying supplies to *Mir* failed to dock with the space station, **Aug. 17,** after the cargo ship's computer did not respond to an electronic order from Earth. Then, on **Aug. 18,** *Mir*'s computer system failed. Solovyev docked the cargo ship manually and the crew, **Aug. 19,** replaced a defective unit in *Mir*'s computer. Solovyev and Vinogradov, **Aug. 22,** made initial repairs on the module damaged in the June collision. NASA said, **Aug. 25,** that 2 of *Mir's* 3 oxygen systems had failed, but the systems were soon restored. U.S. astronaut Michael Foale continued as a part of *Mir*'s crew throughout this time.

Four Opposition Parties Join Forces in Mexico—Four opposition parties from across the political spectrum in Mexico announced, **Aug. 12,** that they would form an alliance in the Chamber of Deputies to take power away from the long-dominant Institutional Revolutionary Party, which had lost a majority in the body in the July election. The parties that joined forces were the conservative National Action Party, the leftist Democratic Revolutionary Party, the Green Ecology Party, and the (Communist) Workers' Party. They planned to press a corruption investigation in Mexico's parliament.

NATO Forces Seize Weapons in Bosnia—A political power struggle within the Serbian portion of Bosnia-Herzegovina led to NATO intervention in Aug. Bosnian Serb Pres. Billjana Plavsic had been criticizing former Pres. Radovan Karadzic, accusing him, for example, of retaining power through the smuggling of weapons. On **Aug. 20,** British and Czech soldiers in the International Stabilization Force (SFOR), operating under NATO control, seized thousands of grenades, rifles, rocket launchers, and other weapons being kept at police stations in Banja Luka, the largest city in Serbian Bosnia. Plavsic alleged that the weapons were to be used to overthrow her. U.S. helicopters supported the SFOR action.

American soldiers in the peacekeeping force occupied the police station in Brcko, **Aug. 28,** but encountered protests from a crowd of Serbs supportive of Karadzic. Two Americans were injured, apparently by thrown stones.

General

Elvis Week Begins in Memphis—Elvis Presley's hometown in Tennessee officially dedicated the week of **Aug. 9-17** to mark the 20th anniversary of his death on Aug. 16, 1977. More than 30,000 Presley fans gathered for the annual candlelight vigil and procession at the singer's gravesite on his estate, Graceland, which is visited by more than 700,000 tourists each year. In addition to the vigil, Elvis Week in the city included riverboat cruises, dance parties, and numerous other events, as well as appearances by numerous Elvis impersonators. People in all parts of the world joined in the commemoration. From as far away as Jerusalem, fans came out in force for the ceremonial unveiling of a 17-ft. statue of the King of Rock and Roll. Presley's continuing popularity after his death has also been evidenced by an outflow of commemorative stamps and by successful marketing of a wide array of products associated with his name.

WNBA Wraps Up Its First Season—The Houston Comets vanquished the New York Liberty, 65-51, **Aug. 30,** to become the first champions of the fledgling 8-team Women's National Basketball Assn. Backed by the NBA, the professional women's league had begun its 28-game inaugural season, **June 21,** drawing crowds averaging over 9,000 fans per game. Capitalizing on its successful inauguration, the WBNA formulated plans to add 2 more teams, to expand its regular season to 30 games, and to add an All-Star game.

The rival 8-team American Basketball League (ABL), which played in the fall and winter and hence competed with men's basketball for attention, had completed its inaugural season in early 1997. The ABL finals concluded **Mar.**

11, when the Columbus Quest beat the Richmond Rage, 77-64, to win the series, 3 games to 2.

Diana, Princess of Wales, Dies in Car Crash—Diana, the Princess of Wales, was injured in an automobile accident in Paris early on **Aug. 31,** and died a few hours later. Dodi Fayed (Emad Mohammed al-Fayed), a film producer who had been Diana's frequent companion in recent weeks, was also killed in the crash, along with the driver, Henri Paul. Fayed's family owned Harrod's department store in London. Trevor Rees-Jones, a bodyguard for the Fayed family, also riding in the car, survived but was seriously injured.

After dinner at the Ritz Hotel on the night of the crash, Diana and Fayed, joined by the 2 other men, had driven away in a Mercedes shortly after midnight. They were reportedly pursued by paparazzi (freelance photographers who focus on photographing celebrities) on motorcycles. The Mercedes, believed to have been traveling at a high speed, entered an underpass below the Place de l'Alma (a bridge across the Seine River), struck a support column, and then hit a wall of the tunnel. Rescue workers needed 90 minutes to extricate the 2 passengers still alive; Diana was pronounced dead at Pitie Salpetriere hospital at 4 A.M. Six photographers and an employee of a photo agency were detained by police, who were investigating the accident.

British Prime Min. Tony Blair, **Aug. 31,** called his country "a nation in shock," and described Diana as "the people's princess." Her brother, Earl Spencer, blamed her death on the photographers who had long pursued her and on the editors who bought their photos. Prince Charles, **Aug. 31,** escorted Diana's body back to London from Paris for her funeral and burial.

Diana, 36, was divorced from Prince Charles, heir to the British throne. Their sons, William, 15, and Harry, 12, are 2d and 3d in line to inherit the throne. From the time of her marriage in 1981, the former Diana Spencer had rarely been out of the public eye, and the whole world, it seemed, had followed the travails of her life in the royal family. After her divorce, she sought a life of her own, devoting much time to charity fund-raising, while her name was linked romantically to various men. She remained widely, indeed wildly, popular inside Britain and out, and her sudden death quickly assumed the proportions of a major world event.

SEPTEMBER 1997

National

Stocks Rebound From August Slump—On **Sept. 2,** the Dow Jones industrial average abruptly reversed a downward trend, rising 257.36 points, or 3.38%, for its largest point gain ever; it closed at 7879. Inching upward from a 23-year low, the unemployment rate stood at 4.9% in Aug., the Labor Dept. reported, **Sept. 5.** The department later announced, **Sept. 16,** that consumer prices had risen 0.2% in Aug. The Commerce Dept. reported, **Sept. 18,** that the trade gap had widened to $10.34 billion in July.

Outside Counsel in Gore's Case Weighed—The *Washington Post* reported, **Sept. 3,** that $120,000 in campaign funds solicited by Vice Pres. Al Gore in 1995 and 1996 had been deposited in so-called hard money accounts of the Democratic National Committee. Gore had acknowledged making fund-raising calls from his office in the White House, but said that he had asked only for soft money. Hard money, which can be used in support of specific candidates, is closely regulated by law, while soft money is utilized for more general purposes. The newspaper article prompted the Justice Dept., **Sept. 3,** to begin a preliminary investigation into whether an independent counsel should investigate the calls made by Gore.

Three Buddhist nuns appeared before the Senate Government Affairs Committee, which was investigating fund-raising practices, **Sept. 4.** Gore had attended a luncheon at their temple in Hacienda Heights, CA, in Apr. 1996, and later said he had not known it was a fund-raiser. Tax-exempt religious institutions are forbidden by law to make political contributions. In fact, $45,000 was raised at the luncheon, and Man Ho, the administrative officer of the temple, said that Yi Chu, the treasurer, raised $55,000 more from temple members after telling them that they would be reimbursed by the temple. Man Ho said she had disposed of a document listing donors and amounts contributed, fearing it would embarrass the temple. Yi Chu testified that she had altered checks to make them appear to be loans. Documents introduced by committee Republicans **Sept. 5** appeared to establish that Gore and his staff had been aware that the temple event was a fund-raiser. In a memo, Gore stated that he planned to attend a fund-raiser in California on about that date.

Donald Fowler, national chairman of the Democratic Party in 1996, acknowledged to the committee, **Sept. 9,** that he had intervened with Clinton administration officials on behalf of some large donors. On **Sept. 18,** the committee heard from Roger Tamraz, who had given $300,000 to Democrats in 1996. Tamraz admitted he had donated in order to get the ears of those in power, observing, "It's the only reason—to get access." Tamraz, who attended a number of social events at the White House, and spoke with Pres. Bill Clinton, had been seeking U.S. support for an oil pipeline project in Central Asia. Although the administration did not support the project, Tamraz said he had gotten his money's worth and was thinking of giving $600,000 "next time."

The Justice Dept. announced, **Sept. 20,** that Attorney Gen. Janet Reno had opened a formal inquiry into whether Pres. Clinton had illegally solicited campaign donations at the White House.

Convicted of Fraud, Arizona Governor Resigns—Gov. Fife Symington of Arizona was convicted of fraud **Sept. 3,** by a federal jury in Phoenix. The 7 felony counts on which he was found guilty related to his real estate dealings before becoming governor. The jury determined that he had made false statements concerning his net worth to a Japanese bank to avoid default on a loan and that he had filed false financial statements to obtain loans from a pension fund. The governor, a Republican, resigned effective **Sept. 5,** and Sec. of State Jane Dee Hull, also a Republican, became acting governor. Symington was the 3d governor in recent years to resign because of a criminal conviction. One of the others, Guy Hunt (R) of Alabama, had a reversal of fortune earlier in 1997 when his conviction was overturned.

Sexual Harassment Found Throughout the Army—The Army, **Sept. 11,** issued a report in which it found that "sexual harassment exists throughout the Army, crossing gender, rank and racial lines." Maj. Gen. Richard Siegfried (ret.) headed the 9-month investigation which led the Army to conclude that its own leadership was to blame. Forty-seven percent of female soldiers and 30% of male soldiers said that they had experienced "unwanted sexual attention," 15% of the females reported "sexual coercion," and 7% said they had been victims of "sexual assault." Most women told investigators they had been unwilling to report misconduct for fear their complaints might damage their careers. The Army had previously issued letters of reprimand to the former commander at Aberdeen Proving Ground, where the sexual harassment scandal had first broken, and several of his deputies. Some drill sergeants had been court-martialed. In announcing that steps would be taken to improve gender relations, the Army said it would extend basic training an extra week to include instruction in ethics, and that prospective drill sergeants would undergo psychological testing and criminal background checks.

Weld Gives Up Bid to Become Envoy to Mexico—Former Gov. William Weld of Massachusetts in Sept. gave up his effort to be confirmed by the Senate as ambassador to Mexico. Sen. Jesse Helms (R, NC), chairman of the Foreign Relations Committee and an implacable opponent of Weld's nomination, presided over a committee meeting, **Sept. 12,** and, despite protests from committee members, reiterated his refusal to consider a confirmation hearing for Weld, a prominent "liberal" Republican. After declaring that he would persist in his effort to get a hearing, Weld finally announced, **Sept. 15,** that he had asked Pres. Bill Clinton to withdraw his nomination. Weld said that he was concerned that his nomination might "get embroiled" in other foreign policy issues. The 5-month confrontation battle had severely strained relations between the administration and Sen. Helms.

Plane Crashes Draw Response by Pentagon—The Pentagon, **Sept. 17,** announced a one-day stand-down, or suspension of all training flights, for safety instruction and a review of procedures, after a series of recent crashes involving U.S. military aircraft. On **Sept. 13,** an Air Force C-141 transport plane had apparently collided with a German military aircraft off the coast of Africa. On **Sept. 14,** an Air Force F-117A stealth fighter performing at an air show northeast of Baltimore crashed into a suburban area; the pilot ejected safely, but 6 people on the ground were injured. There also were 2 military air crashes on **Sept. 15**—a Navy F-18 fighter in Oman and a Marine Corps F/A-18 fighter off the coast of North Carolina—and on **Sept. 16,** 2 New Jersey Air National Guard planes collided over the Atlantic Ocean. Four crewmembers died in another accident, **Sept. 19,** when a $200 million Air Force B-1B bomber crashed in Montana.

Clinton Takes Tough Stand on Tobacco—The $368.5 billion settlement between the major tobacco companies and some 40 state attorneys general, announced in June, appeared doomed, **Sept. 17,** when Pres. Bill Clinton demanded new concessions from the companies. His requirements for a national tobacco policy included tougher penalties on the companies that could force an increase of up to $1.50 in the cost of a pack of cigarettes if smoking by teenagers did not decline. Clinton also said penalties should not be capped and should not be eligible for deduction as business expenses. In addition, he opposed any weakening of the authority of the federal Food and Drug Administration to regulate tobacco as a drug.

Teamsters Scandal Touches Democratic Party— Possible improper conduct by the Democratic Party was linked to the contest for the presidency of the Teamsters Union. The 1996 election of Ron Carey had been overturned in Aug. by a federal election overseer. On **Sept. 18,** in federal district court in New York City, Carey's campaign manager and 2 consultants pleaded guilty to having funneled illegal donations to his campaign. One of their statements to the court revealed that the Democratic National Committee had asked a foreign citizen to give $100,000 to the Carey campaign as part of a plan in which the Teamsters, in turn, would give large sums to the Democrats. The Carey campaign ultimately refused the donation, because, as an employer, the donor was not allowed to make a contribution to a union candidate. However, according to law enforcement officials, the money, instead of being returned, was funneled through a bank to a Democratic get-out-the-vote campaign in Florida. Carey, **Sept. 23,** denied he had known of the illegal contributions.

International

Bombers, Guerrillas Claim Israeli Lives—Three suicide bombings in a shopping mall in West Jerusalem, **Sept. 4,** took the lives of 4 Israelis as well as the bombers; about 190 other people were injured. On **Sept. 5,** an incursion into Lebanon, south of Sidon, by an Israeli naval unit became a disaster when Hezbollah and Amal guerrillas, later joined by Lebanese soldiers, ambushed them. Two Lebanese civilians and 12 Israeli commandos were killed.

U.S. Sec. of State Madeleine Albright visited the region and, on **Sept. 11,** urged Israel not to take actions that the Palestinians might find provocative, calling for a "time out" on expansion of Israeli settlements. A spokesperson for the Israeli government said no one could "ask us to stop expanding existing settlements, which are living organisms." Also on **Sept. 11,** Albright met in Ramallah, in the West Bank, with Yasir Arafat, chairman of the Palestinian National Authority, and urged him to make a greater effort to crack down on terrorists.

Hundreds Murdered in Algeria—Hundreds of people were slain in Algeria in a series of incidents believed linked to an upcoming election and to the long, though sporadically fought, civil war. At least 98 people had been slain in the village of Rais, south of Algiers, in late Aug., and on **Sept. 5** security forces killed 68 people described as Muslim militants, near Chrea. In the Djerba region, 4 candidates for public office were killed, **Sept. 5,** near Saida. On the night of **Sept. 5–6,** about 100 people were killed in Beni Messous, west of the capital. Security forces reportedly killed 19 militants, **Sept. 19** and **20.** In Beni-Slimane, south of Algiers, 53 civilians were killed on **Sept. 21,** and at least 85 were killed on the outskirts of Algiers, **Sept. 23.** On **Sept. 24,** the military wing of the principal Islamic opposition group called for a truce in the civil war and ordered its guerrillas "to stop combat operations."

Computer Failures Among *Mir's* Problems—On **Sept. 6,** astronauts Anatoly Solovyev and Michael Foale, during a 6-hour spacewalk, were unable to find the hole, or holes, in the *Mir* space station caused by its collision in June with a cargo ship. This failure frustrated efforts to repair the space station. On **Sept. 8,** for the 3d time in less than 2 months, the computer on *Mir* malfunctioned; a 4th computer breakdown occurred **Sept. 15.** Later on **Sept. 15,** *Mir* came within 500 to 1,000 yards of a collision with a U.S. military satellite. Mishaps on **Sept. 23** included another computer failure, a breakdown of a carbon dioxide removal system, and a leak of a mysterious brown fluid. On **Sept. 28,** David Wolf, an American, arrived to replace Foale on the *Mir* crew.

New Canadian Unity Effort Is Begun—All of Canada's premiers and territorial leaders, except the premier of Quebec, met in Calgary, Alberta, **Sept. 14,** and agreed to a proposed 7-point unity accord affirming the equality of all provinces, while identifying Quebec's government as guarantor of "the unique character of Quebec society." The proposed accord, which would not change Canada's constitution, was to be submitted for public review, like 2 earlier accords which some judged too accommodating to Quebec and which failed to gain approval. Prime Min. Jean Chrétien was to meet with the premiers in Nov. to discuss federal-provincial power-sharing issues. The controversial Calgary accord, which some regarded as an appeasement to Quebec sovereigntists, was criticized **Sept. 15** by Quebec's premier, Lucien Bouchard, as "an effort to abolish our [Quebec's] national reality."

U.S. Opposes Treaty Outlawing Land Mines—Close to 100 countries agreed, **Sept. 17,** on a treaty that would ban the production, use, or stockpiling of antipersonnel land mines. Under the treaty, which was to be submitted to the signatory countries for ratification, current stockpiles would be destroyed and any mines in place would be removed. The signatories also agreed to assist in the rehabilitation of land-mine victims. Among the countries not signing the treaty were Russia, China, India, and the United States, which had sought to amend the treaty to allow more time to develop a defensive alternative to U.S. minefields in Korea. Pres. Bill Clinton said, **Sept. 17,** that giving up land mines would jeopardize "the safety and security of our men and women in uniform." Diana, the Princess of Wales, whose support for the treaty in the months before her death included visits to land-mine victims in Angola and Bosnia, had helped bring the issue to public attention. According to one estimate, close to 10,000 civilians are killed and about 15,000 wounded each year by some 100 million land mines deployed worldwide.

General

Britain Bids Emotional Farewell to Diana—On the days leading up to the funeral of Diana, Princess of Wales, the people of Great Britain showed their grief and affection. The expression of sorrow in Britain could be measured in the huge number of flowers placed in Diana's memory at her home (Kensington Palace) and elsewhere in London. After many of her subjects criticized her for not leading the nation in mourning, Queen Elizabeth, in an unusual speech on television, **Sept. 5**, acknowledged the public expression of grief over Diana's death and expressed her own admiration for Diana and her sorrow (*see* Box). As the cause of the accident in Paris remained under investigation, the Paris prosecutor's office, on **Sept. 1**, said that Henri Paul, the driver of the car, and one of those killed, had been legally drunk when the accident occurred. On **Sept. 2**, 6 photographers and an employee of a photo agency, detained at the scene of the crash, were placed under formal investigation.

The public service for Diana, **Sept. 6**, though not a state funeral, was nonetheless an elaborate occasion. The horse-drawn coffin was escorted through London streets by members of the Welsh Guard, and was followed on foot by Prince Philip, her former father-in-law; Prince Charles, her former husband; Earl Spencer, her brother; and William and Harry, her sons. A large number of people associated with charities Diana had worked for followed. Throngs of ordinary people lined the path of the procession, and some 2,000 invited guests, among them U.S. First Lady Hillary Rodham Clinton, attended the service held in Westminster Abbey.

At the service Prime Min. Tony Blair read from the Bible, and singer Elton John, a friend of Diana's, sang and played his song "Candle in the Wind," with new lyrics in tribute to her. Earl Spencer, in an emotional and at times biting eulogy, pledged to continue Diana's efforts to guide her sons (*see* Box). Diana was buried in a private service at Althorp House, her family's home in Northamptonshire.

A Paris jeweler said, **Sept. 8**, that Dodi Fayed, with whom Diana had been romantically linked and who also died in the accident, had picked up a diamond ring on Aug. 30 that he and Diana had previously chosen. Investigators claimed, **Sept. 9**, that the driver had consumed the equivalent of about 8 glasses of wine within an hour, prior to the accident. Queen Elizabeth issued a rare public statement **Sept. 15** condemning "speculations" in the media and denying allegations that she and Prince Charles had argued over the funeral arrangements or that she had been pressured in any way.

Mother Teresa Dies, Is Buried After State Funeral—Mother Teresa, a Roman Catholic nun of Albanian parentage, who received the Nobel Peace Prize in 1979 for her decades of work in behalf of the poor and ill in India, died **Sept. 5** in Calcutta at the age of 87. Many of her admirers acclaimed her as a saint and expressed hope that the Church would accelerate the usually lengthy procedure by which an individual is canonized. As a missionary nun teaching school in India, she had decided to devote herself to the poor. In 1946 she founded the Missionaries of Charity, a religious order, whose homes, schools, and orphanages aided the needy, regardless of faith, in India and, by the 1990s, in some 100 other countries. On **Sept. 11** she received the first state funeral accorded a private citizen of India since the death of Mohandas K. Gandhi in 1948. It was attended by heads of state and other foreign dignitaries (including U.S. First Lady Hillary Rodham Clinton). Mother Teresa was buried at the headquarters of the Missionaries of Charity in a poor neighborhood of Calcutta.

Martina Hingis, Wimbledon Champ, Adds U.S. Title—Martina Hingis, the 16-year-old women's singles winner at Wimbledon, added the U.S. Open tennis title to her resume on **Sept. 7** in New York City. She had also won a 3d grand slam event in 1997, the Australian Open, in Jan. In the U.S. Open women's singles finals, she defeated Venus Williams, 17, of the U.S., 6-0, 6-4. Williams, who was unseeded, was the first black woman to play in the Open final since Althea Gibson won in 1957 and 1958. The men's Open title was won, **Sept. 7**, by Patrick Rafter of Australia, who defeated the unseeded Greg Rusedski of Great Britain, 6-3, 6-2, 4-6, 7-5.

Diet Drugs Withdrawn From the Market—Two popular diet drugs were removed from the market by their distributors, **Sept. 15**, after a request by the Food & Drug Administration because of findings that the drugs could cause heart ailments. The appetite suppressants fen fluramine and dexfenfluramine, sold under the brand names Pondimin and Redux, respectively, by Wyeth-Ayerst, a division of American Home Products Corp., were reportedly being currently used by some 600,000 people in the United States.

Ted Turner Gives $1 Billion to UN—Media mogul Ted Turner announced **Sept. 18** that he would donate a total of $1 billion to benefit United Nations agencies. He made the pledge at a UN-affiliated function in New York City. The money was to be disbursed in annual payments over 10 years, in the form of stock in the media conglomerate Time Warner Inc. It was reported that the funds would be focused on humanitarian programs.

Queen Elizabeth's Speech

Following are excerpts from Queen Elizabeth's Sept. 5 televised speech to the nation following the death of Diana, Princess of Wales:

Since last Sunday's dreadful news we have seen throughout Britain and around the world an overwhelming expression of sadness at Diana's death.

We have all been trying in our different ways to cope. It is not easy to express a sense of loss, since the initial shock is often succeeded by a mixture of other feelings—disbelief, incomprehension, anger, and concern for those who remain. . . .

So what I say to you now, as your queen and as a grandmother, I say from my heart.

First, I want to pay tribute to Diana myself. She was an exceptional and gifted human being. In good times and bad, she never lost her capacity to smile and laugh, nor to inspire others with her warmth and kindness. I admired and respected her—for her energy and commitment to others, but especially for her devotion to her two boys.

This week at Balmoral, we have all been trying to help William and Harry to come to terms with the devastating loss that they and the rest of us have suffered.

No one who knew Diana will ever forget her. Millions of others who never met her, but felt they knew her, will remember her.

I for one believe that there are lessons to be drawn from her life and from the extraordinary and moving reaction to her death. I share in your determination to cherish her memory.

This is also an opportunity for me, on behalf of my family, and especially Prince Charles and William and Harry, to thank all of you who have brought flowers, sent messages and paid your respects in so many ways to a remarkable person. These acts of kindness have been a huge source of help and comfort. . . .

I hope that tomorrow we can all, wherever we are, join in expressing our grief at Diana's loss and gratitude for her all-too-short life. It is a chance to show to the whole world the British nation united in grief and respect. . . .

OCTOBER 1-15, 1997

National

Congress, Reno Argue Over Funding Inquiry—The *New York Times* reported, **Oct. 1,** that Justice Dept. and Senate investigators were widening their investigation into how the Democrats raised and spent money during the 1996 presidential campaign. They were reportedly looking into how the Clinton-Gore campaign and the Democratic National Committee may have sought to circumvent federal law by transferring at least $32 million to the state Democratic parties. State laws were more lenient than federal law concerning the use of so-called soft money, which was tax-deductible and could be used to advance the party's agenda but not specific candidates. Ads run locally, using the money from the national party, did not directly call on viewers to vote for Pres. Bill Clinton, but they featured his name, face, and policies.

Responding, **Oct. 3,** to Rep. Henry Hyde (R, IL) and other Republicans who had asked her to appoint an independent counsel to investigate fund-raising practices by Clinton and Vice Pres. Al Gore, Attorney Gen. Janet Reno stated she had found "no evidence whatsoever" that the president solicited campaign contributions in exchange for favorable treatment. As for the now-famous White House coffees and stayovers in the Lincoln Bedroom of the White House, Reno said, "Merely entertaining his supporters . . . does not constitute a violation." Reno said, however, that the Justice Dept. was still investigating phone calls made by Clinton from the White House and that investigation into fund-raising activities by Gore would be expanded, with the option of an independent counsel still open.

Just a day later, on **Oct. 4,** the White House turned over previously unknown evidence, portions of videotapes that showed Clinton greeting wealthy supporters and fund-raisers at White House coffees. On the tapes, made public **Oct. 5,** there was no evidence that Clinton asked his visitors for money, but it was known that some donations followed the events. One event took place in the president's Oval Office, a site apparently barred under federal law from fund-raising. Some Republicans said that the newly released tapes showed that Reno had acted too quickly.

In the Senate, **Oct. 7,** a bill that would put new controls on campaign financing and advertising was thwarted by a filibuster. The McCain-Feingold bill banned soft money and sought to clearly distinguish between ads that support a candidate and those that purport to advocate positions on issues but that are often thinly veiled attacks on disfavored candidates. Majority Leader Trent Lott (R, MS), in an apparent tactic to defeat the bill, had intentionally backed an amendment that would require labor unions to get workers' permission before they could use union dues for political purposes. It was expected that, if the amendment was added to the bill, most Democrats would vote against it. An attempt to shut off debate on the amendment failed to win the necessary two-thirds vote, as did an attempt to end the filibuster on the main bill, although all 45 Democrats and 8 Republicans voted to end the filibuster.

Harold M. Ickes, who had been a White House political adviser during the 1996 campaign, answered questions from members of the Senate Government Affairs Committee, **Oct. 7-8.** He said the coffees, while helpful in generating donations, were not fund-raisers and asserted that at no time did the campaign go beyond what the law permitted.

Reno, **Oct. 9,** said she was "mad" at the White House for not having informed her of the videotapes sooner. She also rebuked those calling on her to appoint an independent counsel, saying "I want to make decisions and build cases that stand the test of time and court review." On **Oct. 14,** she ordered an extension of a Justice Dept. inquiry on Clinton's activities, with the appointment of an independent counsel still a possible result. On **Oct. 15,** Reno told the House Judiciary Committee that she had not yet found sufficient evidence to justify an independent counsel.

Global Warming Heats Up as an Issue—With the next major international conference on global warming, in Kyoto, Japan, just 2 months away, Pres. Bill Clinton sought to build public support for restrictions on the emissions of so-called greenhouse gases. These heat-trapping gases, the by-products of industrial activity and the automobile, were regarded as likely to cause an increase in temperatures around the world. Clinton invited more than 100 television weather forecasters to the White House, **Oct. 1,** where he and Vice Pres. Al Gore provided briefings on the need to set global targets for reduced emissions of greenhouse gases.

Earl Spencer's Eulogy

Following are excerpts from Earl Spencer's eulogy, given at the funeral for his sister Diana, Princess of Wales, on Sept. 6 in Westminster Abbey:

. . . . Diana was the very essence of compassion, of duty, of style, of beauty. All over the world she was a symbol of selfless humanity. . . . Someone with a natural nobility who was classless and who proved in the last year that she needed no royal title to continue to generate her particular brand of magic.

Today is our chance to say thank you for the way you brightened our lives, even though God granted you but half a life. . . .

There is a temptation to rush to canonize your memory; there is no need to do so. You stand tall enough as a human being of unique qualities not to need to be seen as a saint. . . .

There is no doubt that [Diana] was looking for a new direction in her life [recently]. She talked endlessly of getting away from England, mainly because of the treatment that she received at the hands of the newspapers. I don't think she ever understood why her genuinely good intentions were sneered at by the media, why there appeared to be a permanent quest on their behalf to bring her down. . . .

She would want us today to pledge ourselves to protecting her beloved boys William and Harry from a similar fate, and I do this here, Diana, on your behalf. . . .

And beyond that, on behalf of your mother and sisters, I pledge that we, your blood family, will do all we can to continue the imaginative and loving way in which you were steering these two exceptional young men so that their souls are not simply immersed in duty and tradition, but can sing openly as you planned.

We fully respect the heritage into which they have both been born and will always respect and encourage them in their royal role. But we, like you, recognize the need for them to experience as many different aspects of life as possible to arm them spiritually and emotionally for the years ahead. . . .

Rising tensions on the global warming issue were related to the treaty signed at the 1992 Rio de Janeiro conference, which committed signatories to trying to roll emission levels back to 1990 levels by 2000. Some countries had been pushing for more binding targets and timetables. On **Oct. 9,** as reports circulated that Clinton was being advised by aides to stretch out the timetable for compliance with tough restrictions on emissions, U.S. environmental organizations protested.

Fed Chairman Is Cautious on Inflation—Alan Greenspan, chairman of the Federal Reserve Board, who had exuded optimism on economic matters for months, said, **Oct. 8,** that he was concerned that inflation might accelerate after having been nearly invisible in recent years. His comments precipitated a sharp dip in the stock market. Earlier, on **Oct. 1,** the Conference Board reported that the leading economic indicators had risen 0.2% in Aug. The Labor Dept. reported, **Oct. 3,** that the unemployment rate had held steady at 4.9% in Sept.; workers on payrolls grew by 215,000, but that included more than 200,000 United Parcel workers returning from strike. On **Oct. 10,** the Labor Dept. said producer prices had jumped 0.5% in Sept.

"Promise Keepers" Attend Rally in Washington—Hundreds of thousands of Christian men gathered on the Mall in Washington, DC, **Oct. 4,** to reaffirm faith in God and pledge to help restore the nation and preserve the structure of the family. The rally was organized by the Promise Keepers, an evangelical group founded in 1990 by former football coach Bill McCartney. The organization estimated that 2.6 million men had attended over 60 rallies in stadiums since then. In Washington, speakers stressed the responsibilities of men as husbands and fathers, the importance of racial harmony, and the need to put a stop to abortions. These messages seemed to connect forcefully with the attendees, who sang, prayed, and applauded. Some feminist leaders claimed that the Promise Keepers advocated having wives subservient to their husbands.

Clinton Uses Line-Item Veto on Military Projects—On **Oct. 6,** Pres. Bill Clinton used his new line-item veto power to eliminate 38 military spending projects around the country. While killing plans to spend $287 million, he allowed 107 other projects costing $500 million in the Military Construction Appropriations Act to go forward. Supporters of the vetoed projects would ultimately need a two-thirds majority to override the vetoes. On **Oct. 14,** Clinton vetoed 13 items in another military spending bill having a total cost of $144 million.

Companies Settle Second-Hand Smoke Suit—Major tobacco companies, **Oct. 10,** agreed to a settlement in the class-action suit brought against them by 60,000 present and former flight attendants. The attendants and their survivors had claimed that second-hand smoke in airplanes had caused them to get cancer and other diseases. In the settlement, the companies did not acknowledge that second-hand smoke caused illnesses, and the plaintiffs agreed not to seek punitive damages if they sued as individuals in the future. In the current settlement, in Dade County Circuit Court in Miami, the companies paid nothing to the plaintiffs, though their lawyers got $49 million. The companies also agreed to spend $300 million to establish a research institute to study the detection and treatment of illnesses related to smoking.

International

Kim Jong Il Succeeds Father in North Korea—Three years after the death of Kim Il Sung, longtime ruler of North Korea, his son, Kim Jong Il, officially inherited his father's title of general secretary of the Communist Party, **Oct. 8.** Kim Il Sung had been referred to in the controlled press as the Great Leader, and his son was called the Dear Leader. Kim Jong Il's elevation came at a time when the country was reported to be in desperate straits because of famine and economic collapse. South Korea issued what was seen as a cautious welcome, hinting at a possible reconciliation between the 2 Koreas. Although Kim Jong Il had been perceived as leading the country since his father's death in July 1994, confirmation of his power was seen as a possible prelude to new initiatives on his part on the international stage.

Italian Government Falls During Austerity Debate—Prime Min. Romano Prodi of Italy resigned, **Oct. 9,** after Communist members of Parliament withdrew their support from his coalition government, over opposition to budget cutbacks. On **Oct. 13,** the Communist deputies opened talks on returning to the government.

American Foe of Land Mines Wins Peace Prize—It was announced on **Oct. 10** that the 1997 Nobel Peace Prize would be awarded to the International Campaign to Ban Landmines and to its coordinator, Jody Williams, of Putney, VT. The organization is a coalition of over 1,000 groups in more than 60 countries. It has been estimated that some 100 million mines are buried around the world and that approximately 25,000 people are killed or injured by land mines each year. The United States had not signed the new international treaty banning land mines, because of concerns over their importance to South Korea's defenses, and Williams was quick to criticize this omission, **Oct. 10.** She said it would be a sorry legacy for the Clinton administration if Pres. Clinton did not "have the courage to be the commander in chief of his military," and that it was "tragic" that he was not "on the side of humanity." On **Oct. 9,** Pres. Boris Yeltsin announced that Russia would sign the treaty; China remained a holdout.

Clinton Tours Latin America—Pres. Bill Clinton, **Oct. 12,** began a week-long visit to 3 South American countries. On his arrival in Caracas, Venezuela, **Oct. 12,** he met with Pres. Rafael Caldera and called for the lowering of trade barriers to create jobs "for all our people in the Americas, North and South." On **Oct. 13,** Clinton praised Venezuelans for opening their economy to permit private investment in nationalized industries. He flew on to Brazil the same day and met with Pres. Fernando Henrique Cardoso. On **Oct. 14** he urged Brazil to move farther in the direction of reducing greenhouse gases that appeared to be a cause of global warming.

General

Telescope Finds Massive Star Behind Dust Cloud—Scientists announced, **Oct. 7,** that they had found one of the most massive stars known, behind a dense dust cloud in the Milky Way that had previously concealed it. The star was found by a camera sensitive to infrared light, mounted on the Hubble Space Telescope, that was able to penetrate the clouds. It was 25,000 light-years distant, in the direction of the constellation Sagittarius. The rather young star, which had formed 1 to 3 million years ago, had shed much of its mass in violent eruptions of gases. The announcement of the discovery was made by the Space Telescope Science Institute in Baltimore and the University of California at Los Angeles.

Hurricane Hits Acapulco, Claims 200 Lives—A major hurricane struck Acapulco, Mexico and vicinity, **Oct. 8-10.** The death toll was put at more than 200, with many more left homeless, especially among the poor. While Acapulco's solidly build resort hotels were virtually unscathed in the face of 115-mile-per-hour winds, the hillside housing of low-income people was swept away, as 16 inches of rain fell in 3 hours. The hurricane also battered several other resort towns along Mexico's Pacific coast.

Notable Supreme Court Decisions, 1996-97

The U.S. Supreme Court term that began Oct. 7, 1996, and ended June 27, 1997, produced signed opinions in 80 cases, 5 more than in 1995-96. In 38 of these cases, including several landmark rulings, the justices reached a unanimous verdict. Another 17 decisions were reached by a 5-4 vote; in a majority of these closely decided cases, the Court's three most conservative members—Chief Justice William H. Rehnquist and Associate Justices Antonin Scalia and Clarence Thomas—were joined by two moderate conservatives, Anthony M. Kennedy and Sandra Day O'Connor.

In his 11th year as chief justice, Rehnquist wrote majority or plurality opinions in 11 cases, followed by O'Connor and John Paul Stevens with 10 apiece. As in the previous term, Stevens, a moderate liberal, was the Court's most conspicuous dissenter, casting 26 minority votes. Kennedy found himself in the minority on only 6 occasions.

Congressional Authority and States' Rights: Two major decisions rebuked Congress for overstepping its authority. On June 25, in *City of Boerne* v. *Flores*, the Court struck down the 1993 Religious Freedom Restoration Act, intended to prevent agencies at all levels of government from intruding on religious practice except when there was a "compelling need" to do so. The 6-3 majority held that Congress had improperly infringed on state prerogatives and on the power of the courts to interpret the Constitution. Two days later, in a bitterly contested 5-4 ruling (*Printz* v. *U.S.*), the Court invalidated a provision of the 1993 Brady gun-control law that had required local officials to conduct background checks on prospective handgun buyers.

Criminal Law: Strengthening the hand of law enforcement officials against sexual predators, a 5-4 majority declared that states may confine convicted sex offenders in mental institutions even after they have served their full terms in prison (*Kansas* v. *Hendricks*; June 23). Police powers in dealing with drivers and passengers during routine traffic stops were augmented in *Ohio* v. *Robinette* (8-1; Nov. 18, 1996) and *Maryland* v. *Wilson* (7-2; Feb. 19).

Election Issues: In two important voting rights cases, a 7-2 ruling limited the power of the U.S. Justice Dept. to require that states revise their redistricting plans to increase minority representation (*Reno* v. *Bossier Parish*; May 12), and a 5-4 decision upheld a Georgia congressional redistricting plan that established only one black-majority district instead of the two the Justice Department had called for (*Abrams* v. *Johnson*; June 19). By an 8-1 margin, the Court voided a Georgia law that required political candidates to submit to drug testing (*Chandler* v. *Miller*; Apr. 15). Ruling 6-3, the Court crimped the rights of minor parties by holding that states may ban "fusion tickets" that allow nominees to appear on more than one party's ballot line (*Timmons* v. *Twin Cities Area New Party*; Apr. 28).

First Amendment Rights: In a landmark 7-2 ruling that extended the right of free speech to the Internet, the justices overturned portions of the 1996 Communications Decency Act that made it a crime to transmit "indecent" material over computer networks that children might access (*Reno* v. *American Civil Liberties Union*; June 26). A 5-4 decision

upheld a 1992 federal law that required cable television systems to carry local commercial and public broadcasting stations (*Turner Broadcasting System* v. *FCC*; Mar. 31).

Overturning its own precedent in *Aguilar* v. *Felton* (1985), the Court lowered the wall between church and state by holding, 5-4, that public school systems may send teachers into parochial schools to provide remedial education for needy children (*Agostini* v. *Felton*; June 23). In *Aguilar* the Court had ruled that such instruction could not take place on the school premises.

Insider Trading: The Court held, 6-3, that insider trading laws may be used to prosecute someone who makes use of confidential information in buying or selling a stock, even when the trader has no formal connection with the company that issued the stock (*U.S.* v. *O'Hagan*; June 25).

Liability: The Court ruled, 9-0, that workers negligently exposed by their employer to asbestos dust, a known carcinogen, were not entitled to seek damages until they showed actual signs of psychological or physical impairment (*Metro-North* v. *Buckley*; June 23). In another asbestos-related case, the justices voted 6-2 to throw out a $1.3-billion class-action settlement because the class represented in the lawsuit was too diverse (*Amchem Products* v. *Windsor*; June 25).

Physician-Assisted Suicide: Upholding state laws in New York and Washington that made it a crime for doctors to help patients end their lives, the Court ruled unanimously that the Constitution does not guarantee a generalized right to physician-assisted suicide (*Washington* v. *Glucksberg* and *Vacco* v. *Quill*; June 26). In a concurring opinion, Justice O'Connor suggested that the Court might look favorably on the more narrowly defined right of "a mentally competent person who is experiencing great suffering" to control "the circumstances of his or her imminent death."

Presidential Powers: The Court unanimously rejected a request by President Bill Clinton to delay until he leaves office a lawsuit brought against him by Paula Corbin Jones, who claims he sexually harassed her in 1991 while he was Arkansas governor and she was a state employee (*Clinton* v. *Jones*, May 27). Justice Stevens found no justification for the assertion, made by Clinton's lawyers, that a sitting president has temporary immunity from civil lawsuits stemming from conduct outside the scope of his official duties.

The Court dealt the Clinton administration a second setback when it refused to review a federal appellate court ruling that notes taken by White House lawyers of discussions with First Lady Hillary Rodham Clinton were not protected by attorney-client privilege. The notes were surrendered to Whitewater independent counsel Kenneth W. Starr on June 23.

The 1996 Line-Item Veto Act survived its first major test on June 26 when the Court held, 7-2, that members of Congress who had challenged it in a suit lacked standing to sue because they had suffered no personal injury (*Raines* v. *Byrd*). The Court therefore declined to rule on the constitutionality of the measure, which allows the president to excise specific items from spending bills that are signed into law.

The 1997 Nobel Prizes

The 1997 Nobel Prize winners were announced Oct. 6-15. Each prize consisted of a large solid gold medal and a cash award worth approximately $1 million.

Chemistry: Paul D. Boyer, American, and John E. Walker, British, shared half the prize, and Jens C. Skou, Danish, won the other half, for their study of enzymes underlying the synthesis of adenosine triphosphate (ATP), an energy carrier in living cells.

Memorial Prize in Economic Science: An American, Robert C. Merton, and a Canadian-born American, Myron S. Scholes, won for devising a formula that is widely used in calculating the value of stock options. (Another American, Fischer Black, who died in 1995, was cited for his contribution to developing the formula.)

Literature: Dario Fo, an Italian playwright and performer, won for his satirical dramas, including *Comic Mystery*, *Accidental Death of an Anarchist*, and *Trumpets and Raspberries*.

Peace: The prize was awarded in two equal parts to the International Campaign to Ban Landmines and to its coordinator, Jody Williams, an American.

Physics: Two Americans, Steven Chu and William D. Phillips, and an Algerian-born Frenchman, Claude Cohen-Tannoudji, shared the prize for devising ways to cool and capture atoms with laser light so that they can be studied with great accuracy.

Physiology or Medicine: An American, Stanley B. Prusiner, won for his still-controversial discovery of prions, proteins linked to lethal brain diseases.

OBITUARIES

Deaths, Nov. 1, 1996—Oct. 15, 1997

A

Awdry, W. (Wilbert Vere), 85, Anglican minister who wrote the "Thomas the Tank Engine" children's books; Gloucestershire, England, Mar. 21, 1997.

Ayres, Lew, 88, actor who played the title role in 9 "Dr. Kildare" films; first found fame as a disillusioned German soldier in *All Quiet on the Western Front* (1930); Los Angeles, CA, Dec. 30, 1996.

B

Baker, LaVern, 67, rhythm and blues singer; inducted into Rock and Roll Hall of Fame in 1991; New York, NY, Mar. 10, 1997.

Bao Dai, 83, last emperor of Vietnam; abdicated 1945; Paris, France, July 31, 1997.

Barco, Virgilio, 75, former president of Colombia (1986-90) whose social reforms were sidetracked by drug war; Bogotá, Colombia, May 20, 1997.

Bernardin, Cardinal Joseph, 68, Roman Catholic archbishop of Chicago; general secretary and later president, National Conference of Catholic Bishops; Chicago, IL, Nov. 14, 1996.

Berry, Richard, 61, writer of the rock song "Louie, Louie"; Los Angeles, CA, Jan. 23, 1997.

Bing, Sir Rudolf, 95, autocratic former general manager of New York's Metropolitan Opera (1950-72), responsible for ushering the company into the modern era; Yonkers, NY, Sept. 2, 1997.

Blackstone, Harry Jr., 62, magician who followed in his famous father's footsteps; Loma Linda, CA, May 14, 1997.

Bokassa, Jean-Bedel, 75, ruler of the Central African Republic (1965-79) who proclaimed himself emperor; deposed after many atrocities; Bangui, Central African Republic, Nov. 3, 1996.

Brennan, William J., Jr., 91, former Supreme Court justice for 3 decades and influential champion of equal rights and due process; Arlington, VA, July 24, 1997.

Buckley, Jeff, 30, folk-rock singer and son of late musician Tim Buckley; drowned in harbor; Memphis, TN, May 29, 1997.

Burroughs, William S., 83, beat-generation writer; author of *Naked Lunch* (1959); Lawrence, KS, Aug. 2, 1997.

C

Caesar, Irving, 101, Tin Pan Alley lyricist of such tunes as "Swanee," "Tea for Two," and "Just a Gigolo"; New York, NY, Dec. 17, 1996.

Calment, Jean, 122, oldest person in the world insofar as records show; Arles, France, Aug. 4, 1997.

Calvin, Melvin, 85, biochemist who identified the Calvin Cycle, a phase crucial in photosynthesis; won a 1961 Nobel Prize; Berkeley, CA, Jan. 8, 1997.

Carné, Marcel, 90, French film director best known for *Les Enfants du Paradis* (1945); Clamart, France, Oct. 31, 1996.

Carpenter, Thelma, 77, big-band singer who sang with many jazz greats; found dead, New York, NY, May 15, 1997.

Cheatham, Doc, 91, lyrical trumpet player whose career spanned 8 decades; Washington, DC, June 2, 1997.

Claster, Nancy, 82, early hostess of TV's *Romper Room*; "Miss Nancy"; Baltimore, MD, Apr. 25, 1997.

Coleman, Peter, 77, first popularly elected governor of American Samoa (1978-85); Honolulu, HI, Apr. 28, 1997.

Cooke, Jack Kent, 84, multimillionaire who built empires in media and sports; owner of the Washington Redskins; Washington, DC, Apr. 6, 1997.

Copeland, Johnny, 60, blues singer and guitarist of the 70s and 80s; New York, NY, July 3, 1997.

Cousteau, Jacques, 87, famed oceanographer who documented undersea exploration in his best-seller *The Silent World* (1953) and Oscar-winning films; coinventor of the "Aqua-lung"; Paris, France, June 25, 1997.

D

Danilova, Alexandra, 93, ballet star and teacher who started her illustrious career at the Imperial Russian Ballet; New York, NY, July 13, 1997.

Dederich, Charles, 83, reformed alcoholic who founded Synanon, a controversial drug rehabilitation organization; Visalia, CA, Feb. 28, 1997.

De Kooning, Willem, 92, influential abstract expressionist artist known for his "Woman" paintings; altered the shape of American art; East Hampton, NY, Mar. 19, 1997.

Deng Xiaoping, 92, "paramount leader" of China from 1978; dominant figure of post-Mao China; architect of modernizations that boosted China's economy; Beijing, China, Feb. 19, 1997.

Denver, John, 53, popular singer and songwriter whose hit songs celebrated rural beauty and true love. Killed in crash of his light plane; Monterey Bay, CA, Oct. 12, 1997.

Diana, Princess of Wales, 36, society girl who became a world-famous symbol of elegance and humanitarianism after marrying Britain's Prince Charles in 1981; divorced in 1996; killed in car crash in Paris, France, Aug. 31, 1997.

Dicke, Robert, 80, physicist who predicted the Big Bang echo and challenged the theory of relativity; Princeton, NJ, Mar. 4, 1997.

Dickey, James, 73, prolific writer of poems in plain English; his novel *Deliverance* became a hit movie in the 70s; Columbia, SC, Jan. 19, 1997.

Dixon, Jeane, 79, astrologer who won fame for predicting John F. Kennedy would die in office; Washington, DC, Jan. 25, 1997.

Donoso, José, 72, Chilean author whose masterpiece was *The Obscene Bird of Night* (1973); Santiago, Chile, Dec. 7, 1996.

Dorris, Michael, 52, writer best known for *The Broken Cord*, about his son's battle with fetal alcohol syndrome; found dead from suicide; Concord, NH, Apr. 11, 1997.

Doyle, David, 67, actor who played the assistant Bosley on TV's *Charlie's Angels*; Los Angeles, CA, Feb. 26, 1997.

E

Eccles, Sir John C., 94, Australian-born neurophysiologist who shared a 1963 Nobel Prize for work with nerve cells; Contra, Switzerland, May 2, 1997.

Edel, Leon, 89, prize-winning biographer of Henry James and other American writers; Honolulu, HI, Sept. 5, 1997.

Eysenck, Hans, 81, German-born behavioral psychologist who held original and controversial theories of intelligence and personality; London, England, Sept. 4, 1997.

F

Faye, Joey, 87, legendary burlesque second banana; Englewood, NJ, Apr. 26, 1997.

Fela, Anikulapo-Kuti, 58, Africa's most famous musician and one of the leading dissidents in authoritarian Nigeria; Lagos, Nigeria, Aug. 2, 1997.

Fenneman, George, 77, sidekick to Groucho Marx on the radio and TV quiz show *You Bet Your Life*; Los Angeles, CA, May 29, 1997.

Ferreri, Marco, 68, director most famous for *La Grande Bouffe* (1973); Paris, France, May 9, 1997.

Flood, Curt, 59, All-Star center fielder for the St. Louis Cardinals who laid the groundwork for player free agency by challenging the "reserve clause"; Los Angeles, CA, Jan. 20, 1997.

Frankl, Viktor E., 92, one of the last great Viennese psychiatrists; he used his experiences as a World War II concentration camp prisoner to write the influential *Man's Search for Meaning* (1946); Vienna, Austria, Sept. 2, 1997.

Fujita, Nobuo, 85, only Japanese pilot to drop a bomb on the U.S. mainland during World War II; bombed the Oregon coast in 1942, setting off forest fires; near Tokyo, Japan, Sept. 30, 1997.

G

Ginsberg, Allen, 70, poet whose epic work *Howl!* (1956) established him as a voice of the Beat Generation; known as a master of the outrageous; New York, NY, Apr. 5, 1997.

Gordon, Irving, 81, writer of the song "Unforgettable" and the comedy sketch "Who's on First?"; Los Angeles, CA, Dec. 1, 1996.

Green, Chuck, 78, tap dance great for 6 decades, starting in the 30s; Oakland, CA, Mar. 7, 1997.

H

Haisman, Edith, 100, oldest survivor of the *Titanic*; she was 15 years old when the liner sank in 1912; Southampton, England, Jan. 20, 1997.

Hanff, Helene, 80, American writer best known for *84 Charing Cross Road* (1970), consisting of her correspondence over the years with the staff of a London bookstore; New York, NY, Apr. 9, 1997.

Harriman, Pamela, 76, U.S. ambassador to France and Democratic Party pillar; her husbands included Randolph Churchill and Averell Harriman; Paris, France, Feb. 5, 1997.

Helmsley, Harry, 87, self-made billionaire in the New York real estate industry; he and his controversial wife, Leona, faced tax evasion charges in the 80s; Scottsdale, AZ, Jan. 4, 1997.

Hershey, Alfred D., Nobel laureate who shared a 1969 prize for work with DNA; Syosset, NY, May 22, 1997.

Herzog, Chaim, 78, outspoken former Israeli president (1983-93); Tel Aviv, Israel, Apr. 17, 1997.

Hickey, William, 69, raspy-voiced character actor and acting teacher who played a Mafia don in *Prizzi's Honor* (1985); New York, NY, June 29, 1997.

Hiss, Alger, 92, former high State Department official accused of being a Communist spy; in 1950 he was convicted of perjury; New York, NY, Nov. 15, 1996.

Hogan, Ben, 84, golf legend who won 9 major championships from 1946 to 1953; one of the most creative shotmakers in the history of the game; Fort Worth, TX, July 25, 1997.

Hrabal, Bohumil, 82, the grand old man of Czech literature whose specialty was tragedy mingled with humor; Prague, Czech Republic, Feb. 3, 1997.

Huggins, Charles B., 95, surgeon who won a Nobel Prize in 1966 for cancer research; Chicago, IL, Jan. 12, 1997.

Hutson, Don, 84, star wide receiver for the Green Bay Packers (1935-45); charter member of the College and Pro Football Hall of Fame; Rancho Mirage, CA, June 26, 1997.

Huxley, Elspeth, 89, British author whose best-known work was *The Flame Trees of Thika* (1959), a fictionalized account of her childhood in Kenya; Gloucestershire, England, Jan. 10, 1997.

I

Irsay, Robert, 73, owner of the Indianapolis Colts football team; secretly moved the team from Baltimore to Indianapolis in the middle of the night in 1984; Indianapolis, IN, Jan. 14, 1997.

J

Jacobs, Helen, 88, tennis great who won 9 major championships in the 30s; East Hampton, NY, June 2, 1997.

Jaeckel, Richard, 70, actor best known for tough-guy roles in films like *The Dirty Dozen* (1967); Woodland Hills, CA, June 14, 1997.

Jagan, Cheddi, 78, Guyana's founding father, longtime opposition leader, and, since 1992, president; Washington, DC, Mar. 6, 1997.

James, Dennis, 79, veteran TV announcer, pitchman, and game show and telethon host; Palm Springs, CA, June 3, 1997.

Jayewardene, J. R. (Junius Richard), 90, former prime minister and president of Sri Lanka (1977-88); Colombo, Sri Lanka, Nov. 1, 1996.

Jepson, Helen, 92, lyric soprano who starred with the Metropolitan Opera and other companies in the 30s and 40s; Bradenton, FL, Sept. 16, 1997.

K

Kabua, Amata, 68, president of the Marshall Islands since 1979; Honolulu, HI, Dec. 20, 1996.

Kaplan, Edgar, 72, famed in the world of bridge as a player, teacher, writer, coach,

and commentator; won 28 national titles; New York, NY, Sept. 7, 1997.

Karmal, Babrak, 67, Soviet-backed president and prime minister of Afghanistan (1979-86); Moscow, Russia, Dec. 1, 1996.

Keith, Brian, 75, character actor best known as the uncle on TV's *Family Affair*; found dead, an apparent suicide; Malibu, CA, June 24, 1997.

Kemelman, Harry, 88, author of 11 mystery novels featuring a small-town rabbi as sleuth; Marblehead, MA, Dec. 15, 1996.

Kempton, Murray, 79, independent-minded columnist for *The New York Post* and *Newsday*; won a 1985 Pulitzer Prize; New York, NY, May 5, 1997.

Kendrew, John C., 80, biochemist who shared a 1962 Nobel Prize for decoding the structure of a key protein; Cambridge, England, Aug. 23, 1997.

Khan, Nusrat Fateh Ali, 48, Pakistani singer of Sufi devotional songs; a superstar in the Islamic world; London, England, Aug. 16, 1997.

Kitchell, Alma, 103, pioneering radio singer who went on to host the first radio talk shows in the 30s and 40s and first TV cooking show, beginning in 1947; Sarasota, FL, Nov. 13, 1996.

Kopelev, Lev, 85, Soviet prison camp veteran revered as a scholarly dissident writer in the 70s; Cologne, Germany, June 18, 1997.

Kuralt, Charles, 62, prize-winning CBS newsman and author who chronicled life in America with his On the Road reports; New York, NY, July 4, 1997.

Kurtz, Frank, 85, Air Force hero who flew hundreds of missions in World War II; father of actress Swoosie Kurtz, named for his warplane, the Swoose; Toluca Lake, CA, Oct. 31, 1996.

L

Lane, Burton, 84, Broadway and Hollywood composer who wrote *Finian's Rainbow*; New York, NY, Jan. 5, 1997.

Lane, Ronnie, 51, guitarist and co-founder of the English band Small Faces; Colorado, June 4, 1997.

Leakey, Mary, 83, archaeologist who, with her husband, Louis, discovered major early human remains; Nairobi, Kenya, Dec. 9, 1996.

Leonard, Sheldon, 89, actor who played underworld figures and later TV producer who helped create *The Dick Van Dyke Show*, *The Andy Griffith Show*, and *I Spy*; Beverly Hills, CA, Jan. 10, 1997.

Levine, Irwin, 58, writer of such hits as "Tie a Yellow Ribbon Round the Old Oak Tree" and "Knock Three Times"; Livingston, NJ, Jan. 22, 1997.

Lichtenstein, Roy, 73, Pop Art pioneer who gained attention beginning in the 60s with bold, posterlike pieces using comic book sources; New York, NY, Sept. 29, 1997.

Lukas, J. Anthony, 64, probing reporter and writer who won 2 Pulitzers, one for his book about school busing strife in Boston, *Common Ground* (1986); committed suicide, New York, NY, June 5, 1997.

M

Maar Dora, 89, photographer and painter who was Picasso's principal

model for his "weeping woman" portraits in the late 30s and early 40s; Paris, France, July 16, 1997.

Manley, Michael, 72, former prime minister of Jamaica and Third World spokesman; Kingston, Jamaica, Mar. 6, 1997.

Mastroianni, Marcello, 72, suave Italian actor who appeared in some 120 films, starring in *La Dolce Vita* (1960), *Divorce, Italian Style* (1962), and *8½* (1963); Paris, France, Dec. 19, 1996.

Melvin, Harold, 57, rhythm and blues singer who led the group the Blue Notes; their hits included "If You Don't Know Me By Now"; Philadelphia, PA, Mar. 24, 1997.

Meredith, Burgess, 89, versatile stage, film, and television actor; appeared in such films as *Of Mice and Men* (1939) and *Rocky* (1976); portrayed the Penguin on TV's *Batman* in the 60s; Malibu, CA, Sept. 9, 1997.

Mitchum, Robert, 79, rugged, cynically amused actor who starred in such films as *The Story of G. I. Joe* (1945), *Out of the Past* (1947), and *Cape Fear* (1962); Santa Barbara, CA, July 1, 1997.

Mobutu Sese Seko, 66, longtime dictator of Zaire (1965-97) until he was deposed by rebels in May 1997; Rabat, Morocco, Sept. 7, 1997.

Monroe, Rose Will, 77, aircraft factory employee who became known as "Rosie the Riveter," the role model for women working in the defense industry during World War II; Clarksville, IN, May 30, 1997.

Mucci, Henry A., 88, American colonel famed for a 1945 rescue of 500 prisoners from a Japanese camp in the Philippines; Melbourne, FL, Apr. 20, 1997.

Mulhare, Edward, 74, debonair Irish-born actor best known for TV's *The Ghost and Mrs. Muir* and *Knight Rider*; Van Nuys, CA, May 24, 1997.

N

Nance, Jack, 53, star of the cult movie *Eraserhead* (1978) and other David Lynch films; also appeared in TV's *Twin Peaks*; found dead of a head injury apparently sustained in a fight; South Pasadena, FL, Dec. 30, 1996.

Notorious B.I.G. (Christopher Wallace), 24, rap artist who recounted his criminal past in his music; died of gunshot wounds; Los Angeles, CA, Mar. 9, 1997.

Nyro, Laura, 49, iconoclastic singer and songwriter who wrote hits for many recording giants; songs included "And When I Die" and "Wedding Bell Blues"; Danbury, CT, Apr. 7, 1997.

P

Packard, Vance, 82, journalist who attacked the advertising industry in *The Hidden Persuaders* (1957); Martha's Vineyard, MA, Dec. 12, 1996.

Parker, (Colonel) Tom, 87, promoter and manager who orchestrated Elvis Presley's career; Las Vegas, NV, Jan. 21, 1997.

Pastrana Borrero, Misael, 74, former president of Colombia (1970-74); Bogotá, Colombia, Aug. 22, 1997.

Paulsen, Pat, 69, comedian famed for his tongue-in-cheek presidential campaigns; Tijuana, Mexico, Apr. 25, 1997.

Payton, Lawrence, 59, founding member of the Motown group the Four Tops; Southfield, MI, June 20, 1997.

Peng Zhen, 95, former Beijing mayor and Communist hard-liner who helped draft China's 1982 constitution; Beijing, China, Apr. 26, 1997.

Pinget, Robert, 78, Swiss-born novelist, playwright, member of France's Nouveau Roman literary movement; Tours, France, Aug. 25, 1997.

Pritchett, V.S. (Victor Sawdon), 96, prolific English writer esteemed for his short stories and literary criticism; London, England, Mar. 20, 1997.

Purcell, Edward, 84, physicist who shared a 1952 Nobel Prize for a method to detect the magnetism of an atom's nucleus; Cambridge, MA, Mar. 7, 1997.

R

Rey, Margret E., 90, coauthor of "Curious George" children's books with husband H. A. Rey; Cambridge, MA, Dec. 21, 1996.

Reynolds, Marjorie, 79, actress best known for *Holiday Inn* (1942) and TV's *The Life of Riley* in the 50s; Manhattan Beach, CA, Feb. 1, 1997.

Richter, Sviatoslav, 82, world-acclaimed Russian pianist; Moscow, Russia, Aug. 1, 1997.

Robbins, Harold, 81, author of *The Carpetbaggers* and a score of other escapist novels that together sold more than 50 million copies around the world; Palm Springs, CA, Oct. 14, 1997.

Rodriguez, Andres, 72, general who led a 1989 coup in Paraguay that ousted Gen. Alfredo Stroessner; later served as president; New York, NY, Apr. 21, 1997.

Rollins, Howard, 46, actor who played Virgil Tibbs on TV's *In the Heat of the Night*; film credits include *Ragtime* (1981); New York, NY, Dec. 8, 1996.

Rossi, Aldo, 66, Pulitzer Prize-winning architect known for his works of monumental simplicity and power; after being injured in car accident; Milan, Italy, Sept. 4, 1997.

Rosten, Leo, 88, writer best known for works celebrating Jewish language, humor, and culture, like *The Joys of Yiddish* (1968); New York, NY, Feb. 19, 1997.

Royko, Mike, 64, tough-minded *Chicago Tribune* columnist and voice of the working class; Chicago, IL, Apr. 29, 1997.

Rozelle, Pete, 70, National Football League commissioner (1960-89) instrumental in creating the Super Bowl and *Monday Night Football*; Rancho Santa Fe, CA, Dec. 6, 1996.

S

Sagan, Carl, 62, astronomer and author who stirred interest in the sciences with his TV series *Cosmos;* he won a 1978 Pulitzer Prize for *The Dragons of Eden;* Seattle, WA, Dec. 20, 1996.

Salam, Abdus, 70, Pakistani physicist; first Muslim scientist to win a Nobel Prize (1979); Oxford, England, Nov. 21, 1996.

Savio, Mario, 53, leading 1960s protester at Univ. of California at Berkeley; Sebastopol, CA, Nov. 6, 1996.

Sarnoff, Robert W., 78, former RCA Corporation chairman, succeeding his father; turned the company into a conglomerate by acquiring numerous unrelated businesses; New York, NY, Feb. 22, 1997.

Shabazz, Betty, 61, widow of Malcolm X and powerful voice in the civil rights movement; after suffering burns in a fire; New York, NY, June 23, 1997.

Schaefer, George, 76, Emmy Award-winning director of nearly 100 TV productions, many for the *Hallmark Hall of Fame*; Los Angeles, CA, Sept. 10, 1997.

Shanker, Albert, 68, longtime American Federation of Teachers president; New York, NY, Feb. 22, 1997.

Shelton, Reid, 72, TV and theater actor who was the original Daddy Warbucks in Broadway's *Annie*; Portland, OR, June 8, 1997.

Shoemaker, Eugene, 69, American planetary geologist who discovered many comets and asteroids including the comet named for him; killed in car accident, Alice Springs, Australia, July 18, 1997.

Singh, Ganesh Man, 84, led the struggle for democracy in Nepal and helped transform it from an absolute monarchy to a constitutional system; Nepal, Sept. 18, 1997.

Sinyavsky, Andrei, 71, Russian dissident who wrote *A Voice From the Chorus* (1973) and *Goodnight* (1984); spent 6 years in a Soviet prison camp; Paris, France, Feb. 25, 1997.

Skelton, Red, 84, radio and TV comedian known for his gentle clowning; created such memorable characters as hayseed Clem Kaddiddlehopper and tramp Freddie the Freeloader; Rancho Mirage, CA, Sept. 17, 1997.

Stewart, James, 89, actor beloved for his roles as the innocent idealistic American in such films as *It's a Wonderful Life* (1946) and *Mr. Smith Goes to Washington* (1939); he also appeared in darker classics such as *Vertigo* (1958) and *Rear Window* (1954) and won an Oscar for *The Philadelphia Story* (1940); Beverly Hills, CA, July 2, 1997.

Stone, Jon, 65, writer, producer, director, and co-creator of *Sesame Street*; New York, NY, Mar. 30, 1997.

T

Tanaka, Tomoyuki, 86, Japanese film producer who created Godzilla; Tokyo, Japan, Apr. 2, 1997.

Tartikoff, Brandon, 48, TV executive who boosted NBC with such shows as *Cheers* and *The Cosby Show*; Los Angeles, CA, Aug. 27, 1997.

Teresa, Mother, 87, Roman Catholic nun who worked for 68 years in India helping the sick and destitute; established the Order of the Missionaries of Charity (1950), which spread worldwide; she was awarded the Nobel Peace Prize in 1979; Calcutta, India, Sept. 5, 1997.

"Tiny Tim" (Herbert Khaury), 64(?), singer famed for falsetto renditions of 1920s songs, notably "Tiptoe Through the Tulips," accompanying himself on ukulele; Minneapolis, MN, Nov. 30, 1996.

Todd, Lord (Alexander Robertus), 89, Scottish biochemist whose investiga-tion of nucleic acids won him a Nobel Prize in 1957; Cambridge, England, Jan. 10, 1997.

Todorov, Stanko, 76, former Communist premier of Bulgaria (1971-90); Pernik, Bulgaria, Dec. 17, 1996.

Tombaugh, Clyde W., 90, astronomer who discovered Pluto in 1930 after a painstaking search of the night sky; Las Cruces, NM, Jan. 18, 1997.

Tsongas, Paul E., 55, former Massachusetts senator who, after a bout with cancer, was briefly the Democratic front-runner for president in 1992; Boston, MA, Jan. 18, 1997.

Tutuola, Amos, 77, Nigerian novelist whose works, including *The Palm-Wine Drinkard* (1952), drew upon African folklore; Ibadan, Nigeria, June 8, 1997.

V

Vander Meer, Johnny, 82, only major league baseball player to throw two no-hitters in consecutive starts, a feat he accomplished with the Cincinnati Reds in June 1938; Tampa, FL, Oct. 6, 1997.

Van Zandt, Townes, 52, singer and songwriter who influenced many folk and rock performers; Smyrna, TX, Jan. 2, 1997.

Vasarely, Victor, 90, patriarch of the Op Art movement in the 60s; Paris, France, Mar. 15, 1997.

Velázquez, Fidel, 97, longtime head of the Confederation of Mexican Workers and key figure in the labor movement; Mexico City, Mexico, June 21, 1997.

Versace, Gianni, 50, designer who created a worldwide fashion empire; shot to death, Miami Beach, FL, July 15, 1997.

W

Wald, George, 90, biologist who shared a Nobel Prize (1967) for research on image transfer between eye and brain; Cambridge, MA, Apr. 12, 1997.

Wannous, Saadallah, 56, one of the Arab world's leading playwrights; his caustic works were critical of the Arabs' political decline; Damascus, Syria, May 15, 1997.

Weaver, Robert C., 89, first black cabinet member and first HUD secretary; New York, NY, July 17, 1997.

Weisgall, Hugo, 84, opera composer known for his adaptation of Pirandello's *Six Characters in Search of an Author*; Manhasset, NY, Mar. 11, 1997.

White, Jesse, 79, character actor familiar to many as the Maytag Repairman on TV commercials; Los Angeles, CA, Jan. 9, 1997.

Widerberg, Bo, 66, director best known for the romantic *Elvira Madigan* (1967); Angelholm, Sweden, May 1, 1997.

Williams, Tony, 51, jazz drummer and innovator who worked with Miles Davis in the 60s; Daly City, CA, Feb. 23, 1997.

Witherspoon, Jimmy, 74, blues and jazz singer whose first hit was "Ain't Nobody's Business" (1949); Los Angeles, CA, Sept. 18, 1997.

Z

Zale, Tony, 83, middleweight boxing champion of the 40s; had 3 memorable bouts with Rocky Graziano; Portage, IN, Mar. 20, 1997.

Zinneman, Fred, 89, director of such films as *From Here to Eternity* (1953), *High Noon* (1952), and *A Man for All Seasons* (1966); London, England, Mar. 14, 1997.

Offbeat News Stories

World's Oldest Person—Jeanne Calment, said to have been the oldest person in the world according to verifiable records, died in Arles, France, Aug. 4, 1997, at the age of 122. Calment, who left no heirs, outlived a lawyer who had agreed, when she was 90, to pay her about $400 a month rent until she died, in return for then obtaining her apartment. (He died in 1996 at age 77.) Calment's title, according to the *Guinness Book of Records*, passed on to Marie-Louise Febronie Meilleur, of Corbeil, Ontario, who turned 117 on Aug. 29. Married twice, Meilleur has 75 living grandchildren and about 300 living descendants.

World's Oldest Mother—A California woman who understated her age to doctors at a clinic for in vitro fertilization gave birth late in 1996 to a healthy 6 pound 4 ounce baby at the age of 63, earning the title of "world's oldest mother." Her husband is 60, and her own mother, in her 80s, has been helping out with household chores. "Our age doesn't matter," she told an interviewer when she revealed her identity in April 1997. "We feel young at heart and we love our child."

It's a Mad, Mad World—A bus driver was recently transporting 20 patients to a mental hospital outside a city in Zimbabwe, when he reportedly stopped off for a few drinks at an illegal roadside liquor store. He returned to find his passengers gone—but not to worry: he offered rides to another 20 people and brought them to the hospital instead, warning attendants they were easily excitable. It took the facility 3 days to discover the mistake, even as the real mental patients remained at large.

Out of Control—In early 1997, Mattel, Inc., announced it was recalling its Cabbage Patch Snacktime Kids dolls, after close to 100 reports of mishaps. The battery-powered dolls, equipped with mechanical jaws that "chew" plastic French fries and carrots, did not know when to stop, and lots of children reported that the hungry critters had gone after their hair or fingers. Since the doll lacks a power switch, it can't be easily turned off while "chewing", but must be disassembled on the spot. Mattel gave $40 for each returned doll; no serious injuries were reported.

Home Delivery—A Dallas couple asleep in the front bedroom of their home were awakened with the morning paper one day in July—when a twin-engine plane carrying copies of the *New York Times* crashed into the house. "I looked up and saw I had absolutely no ceiling," said the woman, Melanie Mitro. The pilot was listed in serious condition; the couple escaped injury.

Some Don'ts for Job-Seekers—A survey of executives by Bob Levey of the *Washington Post* turned up numerous examples of unusual behavior by applicants during job interviews. Among them: bringing along a large dog, listening to a Walkman during the interview, bringing and eating lunch, blowing bubbles with bubble gum, taking off a sock to apply foot powder, taking a Polaroid picture of the interviewer, and refusing to leave unless hired.

Ready for the Worst—Just in case she should ever be abducted, a Massachusetts woman took to carrying a note in her pocketbook with the words "HELP KIDNAPPED," wrapped in a $20 bill to attract attention. Recently, however, before any abduction took place, the note fell out of her pocketbook and got picked up by a janitor, who called police. They put out an all-points bulletin in search of the victim, until they finally realized it was a false alarm.

Close Attachment—In July a 23-year-old Rhode Island woman went to an emergency room with a 24-inch lizard stuck to her chest. The reptile finally let go after being injected with a sedative; the woman was treated and released.

Crime Doesn't Pay—An apparent robbery attempt at a Lakeland, FL, bank in May went awry when the teller couldn't read the suspect's note because the handwriting was so poor; the man fled with no cash. An earlier robbery attempt, at a store in London, Ontario, went bad when the 75-year-old proprietor slugged one of the two armed gunmen on the head with a can of tomatoes. In other incidents, an accused bank robber was easily nabbed outside a Baltimore bank he had allegedly robbed; when police arrived he was standing on the sidewalk apparently counting his take. A suspect fleeing police in Johannesburg, South Africa, was cornered in the city zoo by an angry 260-pound gorilla; police finally shot the suspect, while knocking out the gorilla with a tranquilizer. And one bold fugitive, wanted in Illinois for parole violation, was so imprudent as to apply for a job as a police officer in Pine Bluff, AR; authorities quickly found him out when they ran his fingerprints through a computer database in a routine background check.

Miscellaneous Facts

—On June 19, 1997, the musical *Cats* passed by *A Chorus Line* to become the longest-running show in Broadway history, with 6,138 performances, and still going strong. Since opening on Oct. 7, 1982, the Broadway show had been seen by 8.25 million people, grossed $329 million, and reportedly used up 18,603 eyeliners, 225 gallons of makeup remover, and 2,132 pounds of hairpins.

—Aug. 16, 1997, marked the 20th anniversary of the death of rock legend Elvis Presley. He has not been forgotten. Fans by the tens of thousands attended Elvis Week (Aug. 9-17) events in Memphis, TN, ranging from an Elvis impersonator contest to a candlelight vigil at his Graceland home (which runs tours every 5 minutes 7 days a week and receives more than 700,000 visitors in a typical year). More than 1 million Elvis videos and 2 million Elvis CDs were shipped to retailers over the summer. The Elvis stamp, brought out by the U.S. Postal Service in 1993, still stands as the most profitable commemorative stamp in U.S. postal history, with a print run of 500 million.

—Betty Crocker is still alive and cooking. In fact, the Betty Crocker character, created by General Mills in 1921, now has her own Web site, at http://www.bettycrocker.com, where you can find plenty of recipes, household hints, homely sayings, and the 8 portraits of Betty that have appeared since her beginnings.

—A Times/CNN poll taken in June 1997 found that 22% of Americans believe aliens from outer space have been in contact with human beings at one time or another, and 13% believe aliens have abducted human beings in order to observe them or perform experiments on them.

—According to rankings published by *Forbes* magazine in the July 28 edition, the 3 richest people or families in the world in 1997 were (1) Bill Gates of Microsoft (worth $36.4 bil), (2) Walton family (retailers, worth $27.6 bil), and (3) financier Warren Buffett (worth $23.2 bil).

—In 1996 more than 6,100 people in China were sentenced to death and at least 4,367 were executed, according to a report by Amnesty International. The offenses ranged from murder to crimes such as stealing cows or repeatedly vandalizing strips of electric cable. Justice was often very swift; in one case cited, a man was executed May 19 for a murder allegedly committed on May 13.

—According to a company report, Salt Lake City leads U.S. cities in Jell-O consumption; it's followed by Des Moines, Milwaukee, and Pittsburgh.

—There are said to be more Barbie dolls in existence than the entire human population of the U.S., and Mattel, the manufacturer, keeps coming up with new models in tune with the latest tastes. New for 1997 (the 38th year of Barbie existence): Workin' Out Barbie, outfitted in hot pink; University Barbie, available in cheerleader outfits of 19 U.S. colleges; Talk With Me Barbie, equipped with a small computer in a pink desk and a PC-compatible CD-ROM; and Dentist Barbie, a white-coated model complete with dentist's chair, dentist's tools, and a vocabulary to match ("Let's brush!" "Great checkup!").

—What adjusted gross income do you have to make to be in the top 1% of all U.S. taxpayers? Internal Revenue statistics reported in July 1997 showed that, as of 1994, the figure was $195,726. In all, 1,149,899 returns made this cut, accounting for 14% of all income. If you reported $91,226 or more, you would be in the top 5% of those filing returns.

—According to the U.S. Postal Service, nearly 2,800 letter carriers were bitten by dogs on their route in 1996. The metropolitan postal district with the most dog bites was Miami-Ft. Lauderdale.

Historical Anniversaries

1898 — 100 Years Ago

Brooklyn, Queens, and Staten Island are consolidated with Manhattan and the Bronx, **Jan. 1**, to form the five boroughs of present-day New York City.

The U.S. battleship *Maine* arrives in Havana, Cuba, **Jan. 25**, to protect American lives and property.

The *New York Journal* publishes a private letter, **Feb. 9**, written by the Spanish minister to the U.S., Enrique de Lome, that denigrates Pres. William McKinley.

The *Maine* is blown up in Havana harbor, **Feb. 15**, killing all 260 people aboard. "Remember the *Maine*" becomes the battlecry of the ensuing Spanish-American War.

The U.S. gunboat *Nashville*, on **Apr. 22**, captures the Spanish ship *Buena Ventura*, the first prize of the Spanish-American War. A U.S. fleet under Comm. George Dewey destroys Spanish ships in Manila Bay, **May 1**.

Pres. McKinley signs a bill annexing Hawaii, **July 7**.

The Treaty of Paris is signed, **Dec. 10**, formally concluding the Spanish-American War. The U.S. is given Guam and Puerto Rico and agrees to pay Spain $20 million for the Philippines; Cuba becomes independent.

Art. Glasgow's Mackintosh School of Art is founded.

Drama. *The Seagull* by Anton Chekhov, *The Dream of a Spring Morning* by Gabriele D'Annunzio, *Drayman Henschel* by Gerhart Hauptmann, *Trelawney of the "Wells"* by Arthur Wing Pinero, *Cyrano de Bergerac* by Edmond Rostand; Konstantin Stanislavski founds the Moscow Art Theater, promulgating "method" acting.

Literature. *The Open Boat and Other Stories* by Stephen Crane, *Mr. Dooley in Peace and War* by Finley Peter Dunne, *The Turn of the Screw* by Henry James, *The War of the Worlds* by H.G. Wells, *David Harum* by Edward Noyes Westcott, "Ballad of the Reading Goal" by Oscar Wilde.

Musicals. *The Fortune Teller,* music by Victor Herbert, lyrics by Harry B. Smith.

Popular Songs. "The Rosary" by Ethelbert Nevin, lyrics by Robert Cameron Rogers; "When You Were Sweet Sixteen" by James Thornton.

Science and Technology. Marie Curie and her husband, Pierre, isolate radium, the first radioactive element. The first electromagnetic phonograph (the Telegraphone)—forerunner of the modern magnetic sound recorder—is invented by Danish engineer Valdemar Poulsen.

Miscellaneous. The American Social Science Association establishes the National Institute of Arts and Letters. Nome, AK, is founded as a result of a gold rush on the Seward Peninsula. Pepsi-Cola is introduced by New Bern, NC, pharmacist Caleb Bradham. The Goodyear Tire and Rubber Co. is founded in Akron, OH.

1948 — 50 Years Ago

Burma gains independence from Great Britain **Jan. 4**.

Mohandas K. (Mahatma) Gandhi is assassinated in New Delhi by a Hindu fanatic, **Jan. 30**.

The U.S. Supreme Court rules that religious instruction in public schools is unconstitutional, **Mar. 8**, in *McCollum v. the Board of Education.*

The World Health Organization begins operation, **Apr. 7**.

The Organization of American States is founded, **Apr. 30**.

President Harry S. Truman orders the Army to operate the railroads, **May 10**, to avert a nationwide rail strike.

Israel is proclaimed a state, **May 14**, and opens its doors to the world's Jewish population.

South Africa elects a Nationalist Afrikaner bloc, **May 26**, which ran on an apartheid platform.

Pres. Truman signs the Selective Service Act, **June 24**, which requires all men between the ages of 18 and 25 years to register for military service.

Pres. Truman signs a law, **June 25**, authorizing war-displaced persons to immigrate to America.

The first jet aircraft to cross the Atlantic arrives in Labrador from Britain, **July 12**.

The States' Rights Party, opposed to the civil rights agenda of the president, forms **July 17**; these "Dixiecrats" nominate Sen. Strom Thurmond (SC) for president.

Soviet forces, **July 24**, cut off roads and railways into Berlin from the west. In response, U.S. and British aircraft, **July 25**, begin to fly in food and supplies. The incident can be said to mark the start of the cold war.

Pres. Truman signs an executive order, **July 26**, ending racial segregation in the armed forces.

Truman is reelected, defeating New York Gov. Thomas E. Dewey (R) in a major political upset, **Nov. 2**.

T. S. Eliot is named winner of the Nobel Prize for literature, **Nov. 4**.

The UN General Assembly, meeting in Paris **Dec. 10**, adopts a Universal Declaration of Human Rights.

Alger Hiss, a State Department official accused of being a Communist spy, is indicted for perjury, **Dec. 15**.

Japanese Prime Minister Hedeki Tojo and 6 others are convicted of war crimes and hanged in occupied Japan, **Dec. 23**.

Hungarian police arrest Cardinal Jozsef Mindszenty for anti-Communist statements (announced **Dec. 27**).

Art. Willem de Kooning's *Woman,* Robert Motherwell's *Elegy to the Spanish Republic,* Jackson Pollock's *Composition No. 1,* Andrew Wyeth's *Christina's World;* Arshile Gorky takes his life on **July 3** in New York.

Drama. *Anne of the Thousand Days* by Maxwell Anderson, *The Cry of the Peacock* by Jean Anouilh, *The Antigone of Sophocles* by Bertolt Brecht, *State of Siege* by Albert Camus, *The Lady's Not for Burning* by Christopher Fry, *Mister Roberts* by Thomas Heggen and Joshua Logan, *Playbill* by Terrence Rattigan, *Summer and Smoke* by Tennessee Williams.

Literature. *Other Voices, Other Rooms* by Truman Capote, *Intruder in the Dust* by William Faulkner, *The Heart of the Matter* by Graham Greene, "The Lottery" by Shirley Jackson, *The Naked and the Dead* by Norman Mailer, *Confessions of a Mask* by Yukio Mishima, *Cry the Beloved Country* by Alan Paton, *The Pisan Cantos* by Ezra Pound, *The Young Lions* by Irwin Shaw, *The City and the Pillar* by Gore Vidal.

Movies. *Command Decision* with Clark Gable, Walter Pidgeon, Van Johnson; *A Foreign Affair* with Jean Arthur, Marlene Dietrich; *Hamlet* with Laurence Olivier; *I Remember Mama,* with Irene Dunne, Barbara Bel Geddes; *Johnny Belinda* with Jane Wyman, Lew Ayres; *Key Largo* with Humphrey Bogart, Edward G. Robinson, Lauren Bacall; *Oliver Twist* with Alec Guinness, Robert Newton, John Howard Davies; *Red River* with John Wayne, Montgomery Clift; *The Red Shoes* with Anton Walbrook, Marius Goring, Moira Shearer; *The Search* with Montgomery Clift; *The Treasure of the Sierra Madre* with Humphrey Bogart, Walter Huston, Tim Holt.

Musicals. *Kiss Me, Kate* with Alfred Drake, Patricia Morrison, Lisa Kirk, Harold Lang, music and lyrics by Cole Porter; *The Pirate* with Judy Garland, Gene Kelly, music and lyrics by Cole Porter; *Where's Charley,* with Ray Bolger, music and lyrics by Frank Loesser.

Popular Songs. "Baby, It's Cold Outside," by Frank Loesser; "Buttons and Bows" by Jay Livingston and Ray Evans; "I'll Be Home for Christmas" by Kim Gannon, Walter Kent and Buck Ram; "It's a Most Unusual Day" by Jimmy McHugh, with lyrics by Harold Adamson; "On a Slow Boat to China" by Frank Loesser; "Red Roses for a Blue Lady" by Sid Tepper and Roy Beaumont; "Sleigh Ride" by Leroy Anderson, with lyrics by Mitchell Parish; "Tennessee Waltz" by Redd Stewart and Pee Wee King.

Sports. The Winter Olympics are held in St. Moritz, Switzerland, Jan. 30-Feb. 8. The Summer Olympics are held in London, England, July 29-Aug. 14. Citation wins the Triple Crown.

Science and Technology. The controversial "Kinsey Report," compiled by Alfred Kinsey after 18,500 interviews, details the sexual behavior of American males. The Polaroid Land Camera goes on sale. The long-playing vinyl phonograph record is unveiled. Michelin introduces the first radial tires.

Television. *The Ed Sullivan Show* (initially titled *The Toast of the Town*) debuts; *Hopalong Cassidy* becomes television's first Western series.

Miscellaneous. *The Seven-Storey Mountain*, by Trappist monk Thomas Merton, becomes a best-seller. Clarence Leo Fender launches mass production of a solid-bodied electric guitar he calls the Broadcaster (renamed the Telecaster in 1950). Scrabble is copyrighted by James Brunot after he takes over the crossword game Criss-Cross and changes its name. Dial, the first deodorant soap, is introduced by Chicago's Armour and Co. The Honda motorcycle is introduced by Japanese entrepreneur Soichiro Honda. The McDonald brothers open their first restaurant.

1973 — 25 Years Ago

Great Britain, Ireland, and Denmark officially join the European Economic Community, **Jan 1.**

Richard Nixon is inaugurated for a second term as president, and Spiro Agnew as vice president, on **Jan. 20.**

The Supreme Court rules, **Jan. 22,** in *Roe* v. *Wade* that abortion in the first six months of pregnancy cannot be prohibited by law.

Henry Kissinger and Le Duc Tho of North Vietnam sign an agreement in Paris, **Jan. 27,** providing for a cease-fire in Vietnam and the end to direct involvement of U.S. ground troops in Indochina. The end of the U.S. military draft is announced. The last U.S. troops leave Vietnam, **Mar. 29.**

James W. McCord and G. Gordon Liddy are convicted, **Jan. 30,** in the Watergate scandal. E. Howard Hunt and others pleaded guilty earlier in Jan.

The Senate establishes the Select Committee on Presidential Campaign Activities, **Feb. 7,** to investigate the Watergate scandal.

Wounded Knee, SD, is occupied in protest by members of the American Indian Movement, **Feb. 27.**

The Mississippi River reaches its highest flood level in 30 years, **Apr. 11,** devastating parts of nine states.

Skylab, the first U.S. space station, is launched, **May 14,** by means of a Saturn 5 rocket.

The Senate Watergate committee opens hearings, **May 17,** under Sen. Sam J. Ervin Jr.

Juan Perón returns to Argentina, **June 20,** after nearly 18 years of exile.

Former Nixon aide John Dean, who resigned along with other top aides on **Apr. 30** in the Watergate scandal, testifies before the Watergate committee, **June 25-29,** implicating himself and others in a cover-up. Another aide, Alexander Butterfield, **July 16,** reveals the existence of a taping system in the White House.

Compromise legislation that ends bombing in Cambodia as of **Aug. 15** is signed by Pres. Nixon, **July 1.**

The Bahamas gain independence from Britain, **July 10.**

A violent coup overthrows Chile's Marxist president, Salvador Allende Gossens, **Sept. 11,** and Gen. Augusto Pinochet is named president by a military junta.

Henry Kissinger is sworn in as secretary of state, **Sept. 22,** becoming the first naturalized citizen to hold this post.

Syrian and Egyptian forces attack Israel, **Oct. 6,** beginning what becomes known as the Yom Kippur War. After fighting marked by heavy casualties on both sides, hostilities end with a cease-fire in late **Oct.**

Vice President Agnew resigns, **Oct. 10,** after pleading no contest to one income tax evasion charge.

Henry Kissinger and Le Duc Tho are named winners of the Nobel Peace Prize, **Oct. 16;** Tho declines the award.

Arab oil-producing nations impose a total embargo on shipments to the U.S., **Oct. 19-21,** to protest its Middle East policy, intensifying a world energy crisis.

In the so called Saturday Night Massacre, **Oct. 20,** Attorney Gen. Elliot Richardson and his deputy resign rather than fire Watergate special prosecutor Archibald Cox, who is fired by Solicitor General Robert Bork.

The War Power Act, requiring congressional approval for the commitment of U.S. forces abroad, becomes law **Nov. 7** after Congress overrides Pres. Nixon's veto.

Rep. Gerald Ford of Michigan is sworn in as vice president, **Dec. 6,** becoming the first to take office under the Twenty-fifth Amendment.

Art. Pablo Picasso dies, **Apr. 8,** at age 91.

Drama. *Absurd Person Singular* by Alan Ayckbourn, *Finishing Touches* by Jean Kerr, *When You Comin' Back, Red Ryder* by Mark Medoff, *Equus* by Peter Shaffer, *The Good Doctor* by Neil Simon, *Cromwell* by David Storey, *The Hot l Baltimore* by Lanford Wilson,

Journalism. *The Best and the Brightest* by David Halberstam and *Fire in the Lake: The Vietnamese and the Americans in Vietnam* by Frances Fitzgerald examine U.S. involvement in Vietnam.

Literature. *Fear of Flying* by Erica Jong, *Ninety-Two in the Shade* by Thomas McGuane, *The Black Prince* by Iris Murdoch, *Temporary Kings* by Anthony Powell, *Gravity's Rainbow* by Thomas Pynchon, *Burr* by Gore Vidal, *Breakfast of Champions* by Kurt Vonnegut.

Movies. *American Graffiti* with Richard Dreyfuss, Ron Howard; *Bang the Drum Slowly* with Michael Moriarty, Robert DeNiro; *The Day of the Jackal* with Edward Fox, Alan Badel; *The Exorcist* with Ellen Burstyn, Max von Sydow, Linda Blair; *The Last Detail* with Jack Nicholson, Otis Young, Randy Quaid; *Last Tango in Paris* with Marlon Brando, Maria Schneider; *Mean Streets* with Robert DeNiro, Harvey Keitel; *The Paper Chase* with Timothy Bottoms, Lindsay Wagner, John Houseman; *Paper Moon* with Ryan O'Neal, Tatum O'Neal, Madeline Kahn; *Serpico* with Al Pacino, John Randolph; *The Sting* with Paul Newman, Robert Redford, Robert Shaw; *Sleeper* with Woody Allen, Diane Keaton.

Musicals. *El Grande de Coca-Cola* with Ron House, Diz White, music and lyrics by the cast; *A Little Night Music* with Len Cariou, Hermione Gingold, Glynis Johns, music and lyrics by Stephen Sondheim; *Raisin* with Joe Morton, Ernestine Jackson, music by Judd Woldin, lyrics by Robert Britten; *Seesaw* with Michele Lee, Ken Howard, music by Cy Coleman, lyrics by Dorothy Fields.

Popular Songs. "Bad, Bad Leroy Brown" by Jim Croce; "Give Me Love" by George Harrison; "I Shot the Sheriff" by Bob Marley; "Killing Me Softly With His Song" by Charles Fox, lyrics by Norman Gimbel; "Superstition" and "You Are the Sunshine of My Life" by Stevie Wonder; "Tie a Yellow Ribbon Round the Ole Oak Tree" by Irwin Levine and L. Russell Brown.

Sports. Billie Jean King defeats former Wimbledon champion Bobby Riggs in a tennis match billed as the "battle of the sexes." Willie Mays retires from baseball. George Foreman becomes world heavyweight champion. Secretariat wins the Triple Crown.

Television. Detective dramas *Barnaby Jones* and *Kojak;* family drama *The Waltons.*

Miscellaneous. The Sears Tower, a $200 million, 110-story structure, opens rentable space; at the time, it is the world's tallest building, at 1,450 ft.

Notable Quotes in 1997

"We have resolved for our time a great debate over the role of government. Today we can declare: Government is not the problem, and government is not the solution. We, the American people, we are the solution."
Pres. *Bill Clinton,* in his inaugural address, Jan. 20, 1997.

"I, Robert J. Dole, do solemnly swear . . . Uh, sorry. Wrong speech."
Presidential candidate *Bob Dole,* after being awarded the Presidential Medal of Freedom by Pres. Clinton.

"To the degree I was too brash, too self-confident or too pushy, I apologize."
Speaker of the House *Newt Gingrich*, after narrowly winning reelection as Speaker.

"To those that are not here with me . . . thank you, fellas; well done, and I will always remember you."
Vernon Baker, the only living recipient among 7 black World War II veterans who received the Medal of Honor in Jan.

"He was my hero."
Comedian *Bill Cosby,* about his son, Ennis, who was killed in Los Angeles Jan. 16 when he stopped his car to change a flat tire.

"It kept nagging at me. I was pretty sure I was right that the answer couldn't be determined, and that ETS [Educational Testing Service] hadn't thought about the problem that way."
Seventeen-year-old *Colin Rizzio,* on finding a defect in an SAT math question that resulted in a recalculating of test scores.

"I can't believe we've been annoying people for this long."
The Simpsons creator *Matt Groening,* on surpassing *The Flintstones* as longest-running prime-time animated TV show.

"I didn't even know that Grammys were given to tone-deaf people."
First Lady *Hillary Rodham Clinton,* on receiving a Grammy award for a recording of her book *It Takes a Village.*

"I know I made a few little mistakes. But it was wonderful. I'm a new man. I go home exhilarated."
Former Pres. *George Bush,* after completing a parachute jump, his first since a 1944 jump as a Navy pilot.

"If you hear of me getting married, slap me."
Actress *Elizabeth Taylor,* talking to Barbara Walters on the TV show *20/20.*

"When Churchill excused himself to go to the bathroom, Truman said to the rest of us, 'This man saved the free world. Lose.' So the rest of the night, we were folding with flushes and three of a kind."
Retiring TV newsman *David Brinkley,* about a 1946 poker game he played with Harry Truman and Winston Churchill.

"It gave me an inspirational lift to know black people could do such a thing."
Archbishop *Desmond Tutu,* on how he felt as a boy in South Africa when Jackie Robinson broke the color barrier in baseball in 1947.

"Why did you offer us sneakers if you could give us scholarships?"
Fifth-grader *Andres Rodriguez,* after Donald Trump offered to buy Nike sneakers for the students at his school.

"As it turned out, we got both."
Grand Forks, ND, newspaper publisher *Mike Maidenberg,* explaining how he had promised to keep printing the paper, "come hell or high water" as floods threatened the city. Both fire and flood then devastated the city's downtown area.

"When the curtain falls, it's time to get off the stage and that's what I propose to do."
British Prime Min. *John Major,* after his May 1 election defeat, on his decision to give up leadership of his party.

"I'm definitely not a pioneer. That's for people like Jackie Robinson and Lee Elder. I'm just a product of their hard work."
Tiger Woods, after winning the Masters golf tournament.

"If you don't consider what happened in Oklahoma, Tim is a good person."
Michael Fortier, on former Army pal Timothy McVeigh, at the Oklahoma City bombing trial.

"I cried, and I cheered."
Aren Almon-Kok, whose baby daughter died in the Oklahoma City bombing, after hearing the guilty verdict.

"Well, the planes run out there and the phones work out there. The e-mail works out there. So we'll be all right."
Pres. *Bill Clinton,* on his daughter Chelsea's decision to attend Stanford University, 3,000 miles from home.

"I thought my ear had fallen off."
Heavyweight champ *Evander Holyfield,* following the boxing match in which challenger Mike Tyson bit off part of his ear.

"I have something he probably wants."
MGM Grand Hotel employee *Mitchell Libonati,* to a security guard outside Holyfield's locker-room door, after finding a piece of Holyfield's ear that Tyson bit off during their fight.

"The return of Hong Kong to the motherland after a century of vicissitudes indicates that from now on, our Hong Kong compatriots have become true masters of this Chinese land and that Hong Kong has now entered a new era of development."
Chinese president *Jiang Zemin,* after the July 1 transfer of Hong Kong from the British to the Chinese.

"We shall not forget you, and we shall watch with the closest interest as you embark on this new era of your remarkable history."
Prince Charles of Britain, on Britain's departure from Hong Kong.

"I think there will be bells ringing tonight."
Karolyn Grimes, actress who played Zuzu, Jimmy Stewart's daughter in *It's a Wonderful Life,* after Stewart's death.

"Eds: Fixes spelling of winning word."
The Associated Press, in a memo to editors written on a corrected copy of the story on the National Spelling Bee; the winning word was *euonym.*

"We are alive, thank God."
Russian cosmonaut *Vasily Tsibliev,* aboard the *Mir* space station, after a cargo ship collided with it.

"I'm just glad to be feeling better. I really thought I'd be seeing Elvis soon."
Singer *Bob Dylan,* after being released from a hospital where he was treated for a heart infection.

"I apologize and I am sorry that this apology has been so long in coming."
Pres. *Bill Clinton,* to hundreds of black men with syphilis who, as part of a federal study at Tuskegee Institute, were observed and left untreated.

"It's beginning to look a lot like Christmas."
U.S. Postal Service employee *Sandra Harding,* on the increased volume of packages due to the UPS strike.

"She was the people's princess, and that's how she will stay, how she will remain, in our hearts and in our memories forever. I feel, like everyone else in this country today, utterly devastated. We are today a nation in a state of shock."
British Prime Min. *Tony Blair,* on the death of Diana, Princess of Wales.

"Diana was the very essence of compassion, of duty, of style, of beauty. All over the world she was a symbol of selfless humanity. All over the world, a standard bearer for the rights of the truly downtrodden, a very British girl who transcended nationality."
Earl Spencer, in his eulogy to his sister.

"I give fervent thanks to God who gave this woman of unshakable faith as a gift to the church and to the world."
Pope John Paul II, on the death of Mother Teresa, in a telegram to Sister Nirmala, her successor.

"Every few seconds it changes—up an eighth, down an eighth—it's like playing a slot machine. I lose $20 million, I gain $20 million."
Media mogul *Ted Turner,* on how his desktop computer tracks the prices of his stocks.

"It's just the biggest damn mess I ever saw."
Former Pres. *Lyndon Johnson,* in a tape released by the LBJ library of a conversation in which he agonized over his decision to escalate U.S. involvement in Vietnam.

UNITED STATES GOVERNMENT

EXECUTIVE BRANCH	LEGISLATIVE BRANCH	JUDICIAL BRANCH
PRESIDENT	**CONGRESS**	**Supreme Court of the United States**
Vice President	**Senate House**	Courts of Appeals
Executive Office of the President	Architect of the Capitol	District Courts
	U.S. Botanic Garden	Territorial Courts
White House Office	General Accounting Office	Court of International Trade
Office of the Vice President	Government Printing Office	Court of Federal Claims
Council of Economic Advisers	Library of Congress	Court of Appeals for the Armed Forces
Council on Environmental Quality	Congressional Budget Office	Tax Court
National Security Council		Court of Veterans Appeals
Office of Administration		Administrative Office of the Courts
Office of Management and Budget		Federal Judicial Center
Office of National Drug Control Policy		Sentencing Commission
Office of Policy Development		
Office of Science and Technology Policy		
Office of the U.S. Trade Representative		

The Clinton Administration

As of Oct. 15, 1997; *indicates person was nominated but not confirmed by the Senate as of that date; all mailing addresses listed are for Washington, DC.

Terms of office of the president and vice president: Jan. 20, 1997, to Jan. 20, 2001. No person may be elected president of the United States for more than two 4-year terms.

President — Bill Clinton receives an annual salary of $200,000 (taxable), and an annual expense allowance of $50,000 (nontaxable) for costs resulting from official duties. In addition, up to $100,000 a year may be spent on travel expenses and $19,000 on official entertainment (both nontaxable), available for allocation within the Executive Office of the President.

Vice President — Albert Gore Jr. receives an annual salary of $171,500, plus $10,000 for expenses, all taxable.

The Cabinet Department Heads
(Salary: $148,400 per year)

Secretary of State — Madeleine K. Albright
Secretary of the Treasury — Robert E. Rubin
Secretary of Defense — William S. Cohen
Attorney General — Janet Reno
Secretary of the Interior — Bruce Babbitt
Secretary of Agriculture — Dan Glickman
Secretary of Commerce — William M. Daley
Secretary of Labor — Alexis M. Herman
Secretary of Health and Human Services — Donna E. Shalala
Secretary of Housing and Urban Development — Andrew M. Cuomo
Secretary of Transportation — Rodney E. Slater
Secretary of Energy — Federico F. Peña
Secretary of Education — Richard W. Riley
Secretary of Veterans Affairs — vacant

The White House Staff
1600 Pennsylvania Ave. NW 20500

Chief of Staff — Erskine B. Bowles
Asst. to the President & Deputy Chief of Staff — John Podesta
Asst. to the President & Deputy Chief of Staff — Sylvia Mathews
Special Envoy for the Americas and Counselor to the President — Thomas F. McLarty 3d
Senior Adviser on Policy & Strategy — Rahm Emanuel
Assistants to the President:
  Counsel to the President — Charles F. C. Ruff
  Deputy Counsel to the President — Bruce Lindsey
  Domestic Policy Council — Bruce Reed
    Office of National AIDS Policy — Sandy Thurman, dir.
  Presidential Personnel — Bob Nash
  Press Secretary — Michael McCurry
  Legislative Affairs — John Hilley
  Communications — Ann Lewis/Sidney Blumenthal
  National Economic Policy — Gene Sperling
  Intergovernmental Affairs — Mickey Ibarra
  National Security — Samuel R. Berger, act.
  Staff Secretary — Todd Stern
  Political Affairs — Craig Smith
  Public Liaison — Maria Echaveste
  Management & Administration — Virginia Apuzzo
  Counselor to the President — Doug Sosnik/Paul Begala
  Cabinet Secretary — Thurgood Marshall Jr.

Director of Presidential Scheduling — Stephanie Streett
Director of Speechwriting — Michael Waldman
Chief of Staff to the First Lady — Melanne Verveer
Chief of Staff to the Chief of Staff — Victoria Radd

Executive Agencies

Council of Economic Advisers — Janet Yellen, chair
Office of Administration — Ada Posey, act. dir.
Office of Science & Technology Policy — John H. Gibbons
Office of National Drug Control Policy — Barry R. McCaffrey
Office of Management and Budget — Franklin D. Raines, dir.
U.S. Trade Representative — Charlene Barshefsky
Council on Environmental Quality — Kathleen McGinty, chair

Department of State
2201 C St. NW 20520

Secretary of State — Madeleine K. Albright
Deputy Secretary — Strobe Talbott
Chief of Staff — Elaine K. Shocas
U.S. Ambassador to the United Nations — Bill Richardson
Under Sec. for Political Affairs — Thomas R. Pickering
Under Sec. for Management — Bonnie R. Cohen
Under Sec. for Global Affairs — Timothy E. Wirth
Under Sec. for Economic, Business, & Agricultural Affairs — Stuart Eizenstat
Under Sec. for Arms Control & International Security Affairs — Lynn E. Davis
Policy Planning Director — Gregg Craig
Chief of Protocol — Molly M. Raiser
Inspector General — Jacqueline L. Williams-Bridgers
Legal Adviser — Michael Matheson
Director Gen. of the Foreign Service & Dir. of Personnel — Anthony C. E. Quainton
Assistant Secretaries for:
  Administration — Patrick F. Kennedy
  African Affairs — Johnny Carson, act.
  Consular Affairs — Mary A. Ryan
  Democracy, Human Rights, & Labor — John Shattuck
  Diplomatic Security — Eric J. Boswell
  East Asian & Pacific Affairs — Stanley Roth
  Economic & Business Affairs — Alan Larson
  European & Canadian Affairs — Anthony Wayne
  Intelligence & Research — Jane Becket
  Inter-American Affairs — Jeffery Davidow
  International Narcotics & Law — Robert S. Gelbard
  International Organization Affairs — Princeton Lyman
  Legislative Affairs — Barbara Larkin, act.
  Near Eastern Affairs — David Welch
  Oceans, International Environmental, & Scientific Affairs — Rafe Pomerance, act.
  Politico-Military Affairs — Thomas E. McNamara
  Population, Refugees, & Migration — Phyllis E. Oakley
  Public Affairs — James P. Rubin
  South Asian Affairs — Karl Inderfurth

(continued)

Department of the Treasury
1500 Pennsylvania Ave. NW 20220

Secretary of the Treasury — Robert E. Rubin
Deputy Sec. of the Treasury — Lawrence H. Summers
Under Sec. for Domestic Finance — John Hawke
Under Sec. for International Affairs — David Lipton
Under Sec. for Enforcement — Raymond Kelly
General Counsel — Edward Knight
Inspector General — Valerie Lau
Assistant Secretaries for:
   Economic Policy — *David Wilcox
   Enforcement — James Johnson
   Fiscal Affairs — Gerald Murphy
   International Affairs — Tim Geithner
   Legislative Affairs — Linda Robertson
   Public Affairs — Howard Schloss
   Tax Policy — Donald Lubick
   Management — Nancy Killefer
   Financial Institutions — Richard Carnell
Treasurer of the U.S. — Mary Ellen Withrow
Bureaus:
   Alcohol, Tobacco, & Firearms — John W. Magaw, dir.
   Comptroller of the Currency — Eugene A. Ludwig, comm.
   Customs — Sam Banks, act. comm.
   Engraving & Printing — Larry Rolufs, dir.
   Federal Law Enforcement Training Center — Charles F. Rinkevich, dir.
   Financial Management Service — Russell Morris, comm.
   Internal Revenue Service — *Charles Rossotti, comm.
   Mint — Philip Diehl, dir.
   Public Debt — Richard L. Gregg, comm.
   U.S. Secret Service — Lewis C. Merletti, dir.
   Office of Thrift Supervision — *Ellen S. Seidman

Department of Defense
The Pentagon 20301

Secretary of Defense — William S. Cohen
Deputy Secretary — John J. Hamre
Under Sec. for Acquisition and Technol. — Paul Kaminski
Under Sec. for Policy — Walter B. Slocombe
Assistant Secretaries for:
   Command, Control, Communications, & Intelligence — Anthony M. Valletta
   Health Affairs — Dr. Edward Martin
   International Security Policy — Franklin C. Miller, act.
   Legislative Affairs — Sandra Stuart
   Personnel & Readiness — Rudy de Leon
   Program Analysis & Evaluation — William J. Lynn III
   Public Affairs — Kenneth Bacon
   Reserve Affairs — Deborah Lee
   Special Operations & Low Intensity Conflict — H. Allen Holmes
Comptroller — vacant
General Counsel — Judith Miller
Administration — Ann Reese, dir.
Operational Test & Evaluation — Phillip E. Coyle III
Chairman, Joint Chiefs of Staff — Gen. Henry Hugh Shelton
Secretary of the Army — Togo West
Secretary of the Navy — John Dalton
Secretary of the Air Force — Sheila Widnall[1]

Department of Justice
Constitution Ave. & 10th St. NW 20530

Attorney General — Janet Reno
Deputy Attorney General — Eric Holder
Associate Attorney General — *Ray Fischer
Solicitor General — Seth Waxman, act.
Office of Inspector General — Michael R. Bromwich
Assistants:
   Antitrust Division — Joel Klein
   Civil Division — Frank W. Hunger
   Civil Rights Division — *Bill Lann Lee
   Criminal Division — John C. Keeney, act.
   Environment & Natural Resources Division — Lois J. Schiffer
   Justice Programs — Laurie Robinson
   Legal Counsel — *Beth Nolan
   Policy Development — Eleanor D. Acheson
   Legislative Affairs — Andrew Fois
   Administration — Stephen R. Colgate
   Tax Division — Loretta C. Argrett
Executive Secretariat — Anna Gatons
Office of Public Affairs — Bert Brandenburg

Office of Information & Privacy — Richard L. Huff/Daniel J. Metcalf
Community Oriented Policing Services — Joseph Brann, dir.
Federal Bureau of Investigation — Louis J. Freeh, dir.
Exec. Off. for Immigration Review — Tony Moscato, dir.
Bureau of Prisons — Kathleen M. Hawk, dir.
Comm. Relations Service — Rose Ochi, dir.
Drug Enforcement Adm. — Tom Constantine
Office of Intelligence Policy & Review — James McAdams, counsel
Exec. Off. for National Security — Frederick Baron, dir.
Off. of Professional Responsibility — Michael E. Shaheen Jr.
Exec. Off. for U.S. Trustees — Joseph Patchan, dir.
Foreign Claims Comm. — Delissa Ridgeway, comm.
Exec. Off. for U.S. Attorneys — Carol DiBattiste, dir.
Immigration & Naturalization Service — Doris Meissner, comm.
Pardon Attorney — Margaret C. Love
U.S. Parole Commission — Edward F. Reilly Jr., chmn.
U.S. Marshals Service — Eduardo Gonzalez, dir.
U.S. Natl. Central Bureau of INTERPOL — John Imhoff, chief
Office of Public Liaison — Nick Gess
Office of Tribal Justice — Thomas LeClaire
Violence Against Women Act — Bonnie Campbell

Department of the Interior
1849 C St. NW 20240

Secretary of the Interior — Bruce Babbitt
Deputy Secretary — John Garamendi
Assistant Secretaries for:
   Fish, Wildlife, & Parks — vacant
   Indian Affairs — Ada E. Deer[2]
   Intergovernmental Affairs — Paddy McGuire
   Land & Minerals — Robert Armstrong
   Policy, Management, & Budget — vacant
   Water & Science — Patricia J. Beneke
Bureau of Land Management — Patrick Shea, dir.
Bureau of Reclamation — Eluid L. Martinez, comm.
Fish & Wildlife Service — Jamie Rappaport Clark, dir.
Geological Survey — Gordon P. Eaton, dir.
National Park Service — Robert G. Stanton, dir.
Surface Mining Reclamation & Enforcement — Kathy Karpan, dir.
Communications — Michael Gauldin, dir.
Office of Congressional & Legisl. Affairs — Melanie Bellar
Solicitor — John D. Leshy
External Affairs — Jana Prewitt
Exec. Secretariat & Regulatory Affairs — Julie Faulkner

Department of Agriculture
1400 Independence Ave. SW 20250

Secretary of Agriculture — Dan Glickman
Deputy Secretary — Richard Rominger
Under Secretaries for:
   Farm & Foreign Agricultural Services — Gus Schumacher Jr.
   Food, Nutrition, & Consumer Services — Shirley R. Watkins
   Food Safety — Catherine Woteki
   Natural Resources & Environment — Jim Lyons
   Research, Education, & Economics — Miley Gonzalez
   Rural Development — Jill Long Thompson
Assistant Secretaries for:
   Administration — Pearlie S. Reed, act.
   Congressional Relations — J. David Carlin
   Marketing & Regulatory Programs — Michael Dunn
General Counsel — James S. Gilliland
Inspector General — Roger C. Viadero
Chief Financial Officer — Irwin T. David, act.
Chief Information Officer — Anne F. Thomson Reed
Chief Economist — Keith Collins
Communications/Press Secretary — Tom Amontree

Department of Commerce
14th St. between Constitution & Pennsylvania Ave. NW 20230

Secretary of Commerce — William M. Daley
Deputy Secretary — Robert Mallett
Chief of Staff — Paul Donovan
General Counsel — Andrew Pincus
Assistant Secretaries:
   Chief Financial Officer & Asst. for Administration — W. Scott Gould
   Economic Development Adm. — Phillip Singerman
   Export Admin. — vacant
   Export Enforcement — vacant
   Import Administration — Robert LaRussa
   Legislative Affairs — Jane Bobbitt

Market Access & Compliance — vacant
Natl. Telecommunications Information Adm. — Clarence Irving Jr.
Oceans & Atmosphere — Terry Garcia, act.
Patent & Trademark Office & Comm. — Bruce Lehman
Trade Development — Ellis Mottur, act.
U.S. & Foreign Commercial Service — Marjory Searing, act.
Bureau of the Census — Martha Farnsworth Riche, dir.
Bureau of Economic Analysis — J. Steven Landerfeld, dir.
Under Sec. for Oceans & Atmosphere — James Baker
Under Sec. for Export Admin. — William Reinsch
Under Sec. for International Trade — Timothy J. Hauser, act.
Under Sec. for Econ. Affairs — vacant
Under Sec. for Technology — Gary Bachula, act.
Natl. Technical Info. Service — Donald Johnson
Natl. Inst. for Standards & Tech. — Robert E. Hebner, act.
Minority Business Development Agency — Courtland Cox
Public Affairs — Mary Hanley
Press Secretary — Maria Cardona

Department of Labor
200 Constitution Ave. NW 20210

Secretary of Labor — Alexis M. Herman
Deputy Secretary — Kathryn Higgins
Chief of Staff — Ted Mastroianni
Assistant Secretaries for:
　Admin. & Management — Patricia W. Lattimore, act.
　Congressional & Intergovernmental Affairs — Geri Palast
　Employment & Training — Ray Uhalde, act.
　Employment Standards — Bernard E. Anderson
　Occupational Safety & Health — Gregory Watchman, act.
　Mine Safety & Health—Davitt McAteer
　Pension & Welfare Benefits — E. Olena Berg
　Policy — vacant
　Public Affairs — Susan R. King, act.
　Veterans Employment & Training — Al Borrego, act.
Solicitor of Labor — J. Davitt McAteer, act.
Bureau of International Affairs — Andrew Samet, act.
Women's Bureau — Ida Castro
Inspector General — Charles C. Masten
Bureau of Labor Statistics — Katharine G. Abraham

Department of Health and Human Services
200 Independence Ave. SW 20201

Secretary of HHS — Donna E. Shalala
Deputy Secretary — Kevin L. Thurm
Chief of Staff — William V. Corr
Assistant Secretaries for:
　Health — *David Satcher
　Legislation — Rich Tarplin
　Management & Budget — John Callahan
　Planning & Evaluation — vacant
　Public Affairs — Melissa Skolfield
General Counsel — Harriet Rabb
Inspector General — June Gibbs Brown
Surgeon General — *David Satcher
Office of Consumer Affairs — Leslie Byrne
Administration on Aging— vacant
Health Care Financing Adm. — vacant
Administration for Children & Families — Olivia Golden, act.

Department of Housing and Urban Development
451 7th St. SW 20410

Secretary of Housing & Urban Development — Andrew M. Cuomo
Deputy Secretary — Dwight P. Robinson
Assistant Secretaries for:
　Administration — Marilynn A. Davis
　Community Planning & Development — vacant
　Fair Housing & Equal Opportunity — vacant
　Housing & Federal Housing Commissioner — Nicolas P. Retsinas
　Congressional & Intergovernmental Relations — Halbert C. DeCell III
　Policy Development & Research — vacant
　Public Affairs — vacant
　Public & Indian Housing — Kevin E. Marchman act
General Counsel — Howard Glazer, act.
Inspector General — Susan M. Gaffney
Chief Financial Officer — *Richard F. Keevey

Government National Mortgage Assn. — Kevin G. Chavers, pres.
Off. of Federal Housing Enterprise Oversight — vacant

Department of Transportation
400 7th St. SW 20590

Secretary of Transportation — Rodney E. Slater
Deputy Secretary — Mortimer L. Downey
Assistant Secretaries for:
　Administration — Melissa Spillenkothen
　Budget & Programs — Louise F. Stoll
　Governmental Affairs — Steven O. Palmer
　Aviation & International Affairs — Charles Hunnicutt
　Transportation—Frank E. Kreusi
　Public Affairs — Steve Akey
U.S. Coast Guard Commandant — Adm. Robert E. Kramek
Federal Aviation Admin. — Jane Garvey
Federal Highway Admin. — Gloria Jeff, act.
Federal Railroad Admin. — Jolene Molitoris
Maritime Admin. — John Graykowski, act.
National Highway Traffic Safety Adm. — Ricardo Martinez
Federal Transit Admin. — Gordon J. Linton
Research & Special Programs Admin. — Kelley Coyner, act.
St. Lawrence Seaway Development Corp. — David Sanders, act.

Department of Energy
1000 Independence Ave. SW 20585

Secretary of Energy — Federico F. Peña
Deputy Secretary — Betsy Moler
Under Secretary — vacant
Chief of Staff — Elgie Holstein
Deputy Chief of Staff — Liz Montoya
General Counsel — vacant
Inspector General — John C. Layton
Assistant Secretaries for:
　Congressional & Intergovernmental Affairs — J. Gary Falle, act.
　Energy Efficiency & Renewable Energy — vacant
　Defense Programs — Victor Reis
　Policy, Planning, & Program Evaluation — Marc Chupka, act.
　Environmental Restoration & Waste Management — Alvin Alm
　Administration & Human Resource Management — Archer L. Durham
　Environment, Safety, & Health — vacant
　Fossil Energy — Patricia Godley
Nuclear Energy — Terry Lash, dir.
Energy Information Adm. — Jay E. Hakes, adm.
Economic Impact & Diversity — Corlis Moody, dir.
Hearings & Appeals — George Breznay, dir.
Energy Research — Martha Krebs, dir.
Civilian Radioactive Waste Management — Lake H. Barrett, act. dir.
Nonproliferation & National Security — vacant
Chief Financial Officer — vacant
Field Management — Don Pearman
Quality Management — vacant
Energy Advisory Board — David Chaney, act. dir.
Office of Public Affairs — Brooke Anderson, dir.

Department of Education
600 Independence Ave. SW 20202

Secretary of Education — Richard W. Riley
Deputy Secretary — Marshall S. Smith, act.
Under Secretary — Judith Winston, act.
Chief of Staff — Leslie T. Thornton
Inspector General — Thomas R. Bloom
General Counsel — Jamienne Studley, act.
Assistant Secretaries for:
　Adult & Vocational Education — Patricia McNeil
　Civil Rights — Norma V. Cantu
　Educational Research & Improvement — Ricky Takai, act.
　Elementary & Secondary Educ. — Gerald N. Tirozzi
　Intergovernmental & Interagency Affairs — Mario Moreno
　Legislation & Congressional Affairs — Scott Fleming, act.
　Management — Gary Rasmussen, act.
　Postsecondary Education — David Longanecker
　Special Educ. & Rehab. Services — Judith Heumann
　Bilingual & Minority Language Affairs — Delia Pompa
　Rehab. Services Admin. — Frederic K. Schroeder, comm.

Department of Veterans Affairs
810 Vermont Ave. NW 20420
Secretary of Veterans Affairs — vacant
Deputy — Hershel W. Gober[3]
Assistant Secretaries for:
  Congressional Affairs — Philip Riggin, act.
  Management — Mark Catlett, act.
  Human Resources & Adm. — Eugene Brickhouse
  Policy & Planning — Dennis Duffy
  Public & Intergovernmental Affairs — Kathy E. Jurado

Inspector General — vacant
Under Sec. for Benefits — Stephen L. Lemons, act.
Under Sec. for Health — Kenneth W. Kizer, M.D.
National Cemetery System — Jerry W. Bowen, dir.
General Counsel — Mary Lou Keener
Board of Veterans Appeals — Roger K. Bauer, act. chair
Board of Contract Appeals — Guy H. McMichael III, chair
Small & Disadvantaged Business Utilization — Scott S. Denniston, dir.
Veterans Service Organization Liaison — Allen F. Kent

(1) Planned to resign Oct. 31, 1997. (2) Planned to resign as soon as a replacement was found. (3) Acting Secretary.

Notable U.S. Government Agencies
Source: *The U.S. Government Manual*; National Archives and Records Administration; World Almanac research

All addresses are Washington, DC, unless otherwise noted; as of Oct. 15, 1997; † indicates person was nominated but not confirmed by the Senate as of that date; * = independent agency

Bureau of Alcohol, Tobacco, and Firearms — John W. Magaw, dir. (Dept. of Treas., 650 Mass. Ave NW, 20226).

Bureau of the Census — Martha Farnsworth Riche, dir. (Dept. of Commerce, 4700 Silver Hill Rd., Suitland, MD 20746).

Bureau of Economic Analysis — J. Steven Landerfeld, dir. (Dept. of Commerce, 1441 L St. NW, 20230).

Bureau of Indian Affairs — Ada E. Deer[1], asst. sec. (Dept. of the Interior, 1849 C St. NW, 20240).

Bureau of Prisons — Kathleen M. Hawk, dir. (Dept. of Justice, 320 First St. NW, 20534).

Centers for Disease Control & Prevention — David Satcher, dir. (Dept. of HHS, 1600 Clifton Rd. NE, Atlanta, GA 30333).

***Central Intelligence Agency** — George J. Tenet, dir. (Wash., DC 20505).

***Commission on Civil Rights** — Mary Frances Berry, chair (624 9th St. NW, 20425).

***Commodity Futures Trading Commision** — Brooksley Born, chair (3 Lafayette Center, 1155 21st St. NW, 20581).

***Consumer Product Safety Commission** — Ann Brown, chair (East West Towers, 4330 East West Hwy., Bethesda, MD 20814).

***Environmental Protection Agency** — Carol M. Browner, adm. (401 M St. SW, 20460).

***Equal Employment Opportunity Commission** — Gilbert Casellas, chair (1801 L St. NW, 20507).

***Export-Import Bank of the United States** — James A. Harmon, pres. and chair (811 Vermont Ave. NW, 20571).

***Farm Credit Administration** — Marsha P. Martin, chair, Farm Credit Administration Board (1501 Farm Credit Drive, McLean, VA 22102).

Federal Aviation Administration — Jane Garvey, adm. (Dept. of Trans., 800 Independence Ave. SW, 20591).

Federal Bureau of Investigation — Louis J. Freeh, dir. (Dept. of Justice, 935 Pennsylvania Ave. NW, 20535).

***Federal Communications Commission** — William E. Kennard†, chair (1919 M St. NW, 20554).

***Federal Deposit Insurance Corporation** — Andrew Hove, act. chair (550 17th St. NW, 20429).

***Federal Election Commission** — John Warren McGarry, chair (999 E St. NW, 20463).

***Federal Emergency Management Agency** — James Lee Witt, dir. (500 C St. SW, 20472).

Federal Energy Regulatory Commission — James J. Hoecker, chair (888 1st St. NE, 20426).

Federal Highway Administration — Gloria Jeff, act. adm. (Dept. of Trans., 400 7th St. SW, 20590).

***Federal Maritime Commission** — Harold J. Creel Jr., chair (800 N. Capitol St. NW, 20573).

***Federal Mine Safety & Health Review Commission** — Mary Lu Jordan, chair (1730 K St. NW, 20006).

***Federal Reserve System** — Alan Greenspan, chair, Board of Governors (20th St. & C St. NW, 20551).

***Federal Trade Commission** — Robert Pitofsky, chair (Pennsylvania Ave. at 6th St. NW, 20580).

Fish & Wildlife Service — Jamie Rappaport Clark, dir. (Dept. of the Interior, 1849 C St. NW, 20240).

Food and Drug Administration — Michael Friedman, act. comm. (Dept. of HHS, 5600 Fishers Ln., Rockville, MD 20857).

Forest Service — Mike Dombeck, chief (Dept. of Agriculture, 201 14th St. SW, 20250).

General Accounting Office — (cong. agency) James F. Hinchman, act. comptroller gen. (441 G St. NW, 20548).

***General Services Administration** — David Barram, adm. (18th St. & F St. NW, 20405).

Government Printing Office — (cong. agency) Michael F. DiMario, public printer (732 N. Capitol St. NW, 20401).

Immigration & Naturalization Service — Doris Meissner, comm. (Dept. of Justice, 425 I St. NW, 20536).

***Inter-American Foundation** — Maria Otero, chair (901 N Stuart St., 10th floor, Arlington, VA 22203).

Internal Revenue Service — Charles Rossotti†, comm. (Dept. of Treas., 1111 Constitution Ave. NW, 20224).

Library of Congress — (cong. agency) Dr. James H. Billington, Librarian of Congress (101 Independence Ave. SE, 20540).

***National Aeronautics and Space Administration** — Daniel S. Goldin, adm. (300 E St. SW, 20546).

***National Archives & Records Administration** — John W. Carlin, archivist (8601 Adelphi Rd., College Park, MD 20740).

***National Endowment for the Arts** — Jane Alexander[2], chair (1100 Pennsylvania Ave. NW, 20506).

***National Endowment for the Humanities** — Bruce Lehman, act. chair (1100 Pennsylvania Ave. NW, 20506).

National Institutes of Health — Harold E. Varmus, dir. (Dept. of HHS, 9000 Rockville Pike, Bethesda, MD 20892).

***National Labor Relations Board** — William B. Gould IV, chair (1099 14th St. NW, 20570).

National Oceanic and Atmospheric Administration — D. James Baker, undersec. (Dept. of Commerce, 14th & Constitution Ave. NW, 20230).

National Park Service — Robert G. Stanton, dir. (Dept. of the Interior, 1849 C St. NW, 20240).

***National Railroad Passenger Corp. (Amtrak)** — Thomas M. Downs, chair, Pres. & CEO (60 Massachusetts Ave. NE, 20002).

***National Science Foundation** — Richard Zare, chair, National Science Board (4201 Wilson Blvd., Arlington, VA 22230).

***National Transportation Safety Board** — Jim Hall, chair (490 L'Enfant Plaza SW, 20594).

***Nuclear Regulatory Commission** — Shirley A. Jackson, chair (11555 Rockville Pike, Rockville, MD 20852).

Occupational Safety & Health Administration — Gregory Watchman, act. asst. sec. (Dept. of Labor, 200 Constitution Ave. NW, 20210).

***Occupational Safety & Health Review Commission** — Stuart E. Weisberg, chair (1120 20th St. NW, 20036).

***Office of Government Ethics** — Stephen D. Potts, dir. (1201 New York Ave. NW, Suite 500, 20005).

***Office of Personnel Management** — Janice Lachance, act. dir. (1900 E St. NW, 20415-0001).

***Office of Special Counsel** — Kathleen Day Koch, sp. counsel (1730 M St. NW, Suite 216, 20036).

***Peace Corps** — Mark Gearan, dir. (1990 K St. NW, 20526).

***Postal Rate Commission** — Edward J. Gleiman, chair (1333 H St. NW, 20268).

***Securities and Exchange Commission** — Arthur Levitt, chair (450 5th St. NW, 20549).

***Selective Service System** — Gil Coronado, dir. (National Headquarters, 1515 Wilson Blvd., Arlington, VA 22209-2425).

***Small Business Administration** — Aida Alvarez, adm. (409 Third St. SW, 20416).

Smithsonian Institution — (quasi-official agency) I. Michael Hayman, sec. (1000 Jefferson Dr. SW, 20560).

***Social Security Administration** — Shirley S. Chater, comm. (6401 Security Blvd., Baltimore, MD 21235).

Surgeon General — David Satcher† (Pub. Health Service, HHS, Parklawn Bldg., 5600 Fishers Ln., Rm. 18-66, Rockville, MD 20857).

***Tennessee Valley Authority** — Craven Crowell, chair, Board of Directors (400 W. Summit Hill Dr., Knoxville, TN 37902, and One Mass. Ave. NW, Suite 300, 20001).

***Trade and Development Agency** — J. Joseph Grandmaison, dir. (1621 N. Kent St., Suite 300, Arlington, VA 22209).

United States Arms Control & Disarmament Agency — John D. Holum, dir. (320 21st St. NW, 20451).

United States Coast Guard — Adm. Robert E. Kramek, commandant (Dept. of Trans., 2100 2d St. SW, 20593).

United States Customs Service — Sam Banks, act. comm. (Dept. of Treas., 1301 Constitution Ave. NW, 20229).

***United States Information Agency** — Joseph Duffey, dir. (301 4th St. SW, 20547).

***United States International Trade Commission** — Marcia E. Miller, chair (500 E St. SW, 20436).

United States Mint — Philip N. Diehl, dir. (Dept. of Treas., 633 3d St. NW, 20220).

***United States Postal Service** — Marvin Runyon, Postmaster General (475 L'Enfant Plaza SW, 20260).

United States Secret Service — Lewis C. Merletti, dir. (Dept. of Treas., 1800 G St. NW, 20223).

(1) Planned to resign as soon as a replacement was found. (2) Planned to resign Oct. 24, 1997.

CONGRESS

The One Hundred and Fifth Congress
With Official 1996 Election Results

Source: Voter News Service; World Almanac research
The 105th Congress convened on Jan. 7, 1997.

The Senate

Rep., 55; Dem., 45; Total, 100. *Incumbent. Boldface denotes the 1996 election winner. Data as of Oct. 15, 1997.

Terms are for 6 years and end Jan. 3 of the year preceding the senator's name in the following table. Annual salaries in 1997: $133,600; President Pro Tempore, Majority Leader, and Minority Leader, $148,400. To be eligible for the U.S. Senate, a person must be at least 30 years of age, a citizen of the United States for at least 9 years, and a resident of the state from which he or she is chosen. The Congress must meet annually on Jan. 3, unless it has, by law, appointed a different day.

The ZIP code of the Senate is 20510; the telephone number is 202-224-3121.

Senate officials in 1997: President Pro Tempore, Strom Thurmond; Majority Leader, Trent Lott; Majority Whip, Don Nickles; Minority Leader, Tom Daschle; Minority Whip, Wendell Ford.

D-Democrat; R-Republican; ACP-A Connecticut Party; GR-Green; I-Independent; L-Liberal; C-Conservative

Term ends	Senator (Party)/Service from[1]	1996 Election	Term ends	Senator (Party)/Service from[1]	1996 Election
	Alabama			**Iowa**	
1999	Richard C. Shelby (R)[2]/1/6/87		1999	Charles E. Grassley (R)/1981	
2003	**Jeff Sessions** (R)/1/7/97	786,436	2003	**Tom Harkin*** (D)/1985	634,166
	Roger Bedford (D)	681,651		Jim Ross Lightfoot (R)	571,807
	Alaska			**Kansas**	
1999	Frank H. Murkowski (R)/1981		1999	**Sam Brownback** (R)[4]/1/7/97	574,021
2003	**Ted Stevens*** (R)/12/24/68	177,893		Jill Docking (D)	461,344
	Jed Whittaker (GR)	29,037	2003	**Pat Roberts** (R)/1/7/97	652,677
	Theresa Nangle Obermeyer (D)	23,977		Sally Thompson (D)	362,380
	Arizona			**Kentucky**	
1999	John McCain (R)/1/6/87		1999	Wendell H. Ford (D)/12/28/74	
2001	Jon Kyl (R)/1/4/95		2003	**Mitch McConnell*** (R)/1985	724,794
	Arkansas			Steven L. Beshear (D)	560,012
1999	Dale Bumpers (D)/1975			**Louisiana**	
2003	**Tim Hutchinson** (R)/1/7/97	445,942	1999	John B. Breaux (D)/1/6/87	
	Winston Bryant (D)	400,241	2003	**Mary L. Landrieu** (D)/1/7/97	852,945
	California			Louis "Woody" Jenkins (R)	847,157
1999	Barbara Boxer (D)/1993			**Maine**	
2001	Dianne Feinstein (D)/11/10/92		2001	Olympia J. Snowe (R)/1/4/95	
	Colorado		2003	**Susan M. Collins** (R)/1/7/97	298,422
1999	Ben Nighthorse Campbell (R)[3]/1993			Joseph E. Brennan (D)	266,226
2003	**Wayne Allard** (R)/1/7/97	750,325		**Maryland**	
	Tom Strickland (D)	677,600	1999	Barbara A. Mikulski (D)/1/6/87	
	Connecticut		2001	Paul S. Sarbanes (D)/1977	
1999	Christopher J. Dodd (D)/1981			**Massachusetts**	
2001	Joe Lieberman (D,ACP)/1989		2001	Edward M. Kennedy (D)/11/7/62	
	Delaware		2003	**John F. Kerry*** (D)/1/2/85	1,334,135
2001	William V. Roth, Jr. (R)/1/1/71			William F. Weld (R)	1,143,120
2003	**Joseph R. Biden, Jr.*** (D)/1973	165,465		**Michigan**	
	Raymond J. Clatworthy (R)	105,088	2001	Spencer Abraham (R)/1/4/95	
	Florida		2003	**Carl Levin*** (D)/1979	2,195,738
1999	Bob Graham (D)/1/6/87			Ronna Romney (R)	1,500,106
2001	Connie Mack (R)/1989			**Minnesota**	
	Georgia		2001	Rod Grams (R)/1/4/95	
1999	Paul Coverdell (R)/1993		2003	**Paul David Wellstone*** (D)/1991	1,098,493
2003	**Max Cleland** (D)/1/7/97	1,103,993		Rudy Boschwitz (R)	901,282
	Guy W. Millner (R)	1,073,969		**Mississippi**	
	Hawaii		2001	Trent Lott (R)/1989	
1999	Daniel K. Inouye (D)/1963		2003	**Thad Cochran*** (R)/12/27/78	624,154
2001	Daniel K. Akaka (D)/4/28/90			James W. (Bootie) Hunt (D)	240,647
	Idaho			**Missouri**	
1999	Dirk Kempthorne (R)/1993		1999	Christopher "Kit" Bond (R)/1/6/87	
2003	**Larry E. Craig*** (R)/1991	283,532	2001	John Ashcroft (R)/1/4/95	
	Walt Minnick (D)	198,422		**Montana**	
	Illinois		2001	Conrad Burns (R)/1989	
1999	Carol Moseley-Braun (D)/1993		2003	**Max Baucus*** (D)/12/15/78	201,935
2003	**Richard J. Durbin** (D)/1/7/97	2,384,028		Dennis Rehberg (R)	182,111
	Al Salvi (R)	1,728,824		**Nebraska**	
	Indiana		2001	Bob Kerrey (D)/1989	
1999	Daniel R. Coats (R)/1989		2003	**Chuck Hagel** (R)/1/7/97	379,933
2001	Richard G. Lugar (R)/1977			Ben Nelson (D)	281,904

Term ends	Senator (Party)/Service from[1]	1996 Election
	Nevada	
1999	Harry M. Reid (D)/1/6/87	
2001	Richard H. Bryan (D)/1989	
	New Hampshire	
1999	Judd Gregg (R)/1993	
2003	**Robert Smith*** (R)/12/7/90	242,257
	"Dick" Swett (D)	227,355
	New Jersey	
2001	Frank R. Lautenberg (D)/12/27/82	
2003	**Robert G. Torricelli** (D)/1/7/97	1,519,154
	Dick Zimmer (R)	1,227,351
	New Mexico	
2001	Jeff Bingaman (D)/1983	
2003	**Pete V. Domenici*** (R)/1973	357,171
	Art Trujillo (D)	164,356
	New York	
1999	Alfonse M. D'Amato (R)/1981	
2001	Daniel Patrick Moynihan (D,L)/1977	
	North Carolina	
1999	Lauch Faircloth (R)/1993	
2003	**Jesse Helms*** (R)/1973	1,345,833
	Harvey B. Gantt (D)	1,173,875
	North Dakota	
1999	Byron L. Dorgan (D)/12/14/92	
2001	Kent Conrad (D)/1/6/87	
	Ohio	
1999	John Glenn (D)/12/24/74	
2001	Mike Dewine (R)/1/4/95	
	Oklahoma	
1999	Don Nickles (R)/1981	
2003	**James M. Inhofe*** (R)[5]/11/21/94	670,610
	Jim Boren (D)	474,162
	Oregon	
1999	Ron Wyden (D)[6]/2/6/96	
2003	**Gordon Smith** (R)/1/7/97	677,336
	Tom Bruggere (D)	624,370
	Pennsylvania	
1999	Arlen Specter (R)/1981	
2001	Rick Santorum (R)/1/4/95	
	Rhode Island	
2001	John H. Chafee (R)/12/29/76	
2003	**John F. Reed** (D)/1/7/97	230,676
	Nancy J. Mayer (R)	127,368

Term ends	Senator (Party)/Service from[1]	1996 Election
	South Carolina	
1999	Ernest F. "Fritz" Hollings (D)/11/9/66	
2003	**Strom Thurmond*** (R)/11/7/56	619,859
	Elliot Springs Close (D)	510,951
	South Dakota	
1999	Thomas A. Daschle (D)/1/6/87	
2003	**Tim Johnson** (D)/1/7/97	166,533
	Larry Pressler* (R)/1979	157,954
	Tennessee	
2001	Bill Frist (R)/1/4/95	
2003	**Fred Thompson*** (R)/12/9/94	1,091,554
	Houston Gordon (D)	654,937
	Texas	
2001	Kay Bailey Hutchison (R)/6/5/93	
2003	**Phil Gramm*** (R)/1985	3,027,680
	Victor M. Morales (D)	2,428,776
	Utah	
1999	Robert F. Bennett (R)/1993	
2001	Orrin G. Hatch (R)/1977	
	Vermont	
1999	Patrick J. Leahy (D)/1975	
2001	Jim Jeffords (R)/1989	
	Virginia	
2001	Charles S. Robb (D)/1989	
2003	**John W. Warner*** (R)/1/2/79	1,235,744
	Mark R. Warner (D)	1,115,982
	Washington	
1999	Patty Murray (D)/1993	
2001	Slade Gorton (R)/1989	
	West Virginia	
2001	Robert C. Byrd (D)/1959	
2003	**John D. Rockefeller IV*** (D)/1/15/85	456,526
	Betty A. Burks (R)	139,088
	Wisconsin	
1999	Russell D. Feingold (D)/1993	
2001	Herbert H. Kohl (D)/1989	
	Wyoming	
2001	Craig Thomas (R)/1/4/95	
2003	**Michael B. Enzi** (R)/1/7/97	114,116
	Kathy Karpan (D)	89,103

(1) Jan. 3, unless otherwise noted. (2) Democratic Sen. Richard C. Shelby announced Nov. 9, 1994, that he changed his party designation to Republican. (3) Democratic Sen. Ben Nighthorse Campbell announced Mar. 3, 1995, that he changed his party designation to Republican. (4) Senator Bob Dole resigned June 11, 1996, to run for president. Republican Sam Brownback was elected on Nov. 5, 1996, to serve out the remainder of Dole's term. (5) James M. Inhofe won a special election held Nov. 8, 1994, to fill the seat left vacant by the resignation of Sen. David Boren (D). (6) Ron Wyden won a special election (by mail) Jan. 30, 1996, to fill the seat left vacant when Republican Senator Bob Packwood resigned, Oct. 1, 1995, after the Senate Ethics Committee had concluded that Packwood had engaged in sexual and official misconduct while a senator. This was the first time a U.S. senator was elected by a mail-in vote.

The House of Representatives

Rep., 227; Dem., 206; Ind., 1; Vacant, 1; Total, 435. *Incumbent. Boldface denotes the 1996 election winner.

Data as of Oct. 15, 1997.

Members' terms to Jan. 3, 1999. Annual salaries in 1997: $133,600; Speaker of the House, $171,500; Majority Leader and Minority Leader, $148,400. To be eligible for membership, a person must be at least 25 years of age, a U.S. citizen for at least 7 years, and a resident of the state from which he or she is chosen. The ZIP code of the House is 20515; the telephone number is 202-225-3121.

House officials in 1997: Speaker, Newt Gingrich; Majority Leader, Dick Armey; Majority Whip, Tom DeLay; Minority Leader, Richard A. Gephardt; Minority Whip, David E. Bonior.

D-Democrat; R-Republican; ACP-A Connecticut Party; LB-Libertarian; C-Conservative; F-Freedom; I-Independent; IC-Independence; L-Liberal; NL-Natural Law; PS-Protect Seniors; S-Save Medicare; T-Right to Life.

Dist.	Representative (Party)	1996 Election
	Alabama	
1.	**H. L. "Sonny" Callahan*** (R)	132,206
	Don Womack (D)	69,470
2.	**Terry Everett*** (R)	132,563
	Bob Gaines (D)	74,317
3.	**Bob Riley** (R)	98,353
	T. D. (Ted) Little (D)	92,325

Dist.	Representative (Party)	1996 Election
4.	**Robert Aderholt** (R)	102,741
	Robert T. (Bob) Wilson, Jr. (D)	99,250
5.	**Bud Cramer*** (D)	126,702
	Wayne Parker (R)	94,330
6.	**Spencer Bachus*** (R)	181,336
	Mary Lynn Bates (D)	70,081
7.	**Earl F. Hilliard*** (D)	136,651

Dist.	Representative (Party)	1996 Election
2.	Ed Pastor* (D)	81,982
	Jim Buster (R)	38,786
3.	Bob Stump* (R)	175,231
	Alexander "Big Al" Schneider (D)	88,214
4.	John Shadegg* (R)	150,486
	Maria Elena Milton (D)	74,857
5.	Jim Kolbe* (R)	179,349
	Mort Nelson (D)	67,597
6.	J. D. Hayworth* (R)	121,431
	Steve Owens (D)	118,957

Arkansas

Dist.	Representative (Party)	1996 Election
1.	Marion Berry (D)	105,280
	Warren Dupwe (R)	88,436
2.	Vic Snyder (D)	114,841
	Bud Cummins (R)	104,548
3.	Asa Hutchinson (R)	137,093
	Ann Henry (D)	102,994
4.	Jay Dickey* (R)	125,956
	Vincent Tolliver (D)	72,391

California

Dist.	Representative (Party)	1996 Election
1.	Frank Riggs* (R)	110,242
	Michela Alioto (D)	96,522
2.	Wally Herger* (R)	144,913
	Roberts A. Braden (D)	80,401
3.	Vic Fazio* (D)	118,663
	Tim Lefever (R)	91,134
4.	John T. Doolittle* (R)	164,048
	Katie Hirning (D)	97,948
5.	Robert T. Matsui* (D)	142,618
	Robert S. Dinsmore (R)	52,940
6.	Lynn Woolsey* (D)	156,958
	Duane C. Hughes (R)	86,278
7.	George Miller* (D)	137,089
	Norman H. Reece (R)	42,542
8.	Nancy Pelosi* (D)	175,216
	Justin Raimondo (R)	25,739
9.	Ronald V. Dellums* (D)	154,806
	Deborah Wright (R)	37,126
10.	Ellen O. Tauscher (D)	137,726
	Bill Baker* (R)	133,633
11.	Richard Pombo* (R)	107,477
	Jason Silva (D)	65,536
12.	Tom Lantos* (D)	149,052
	Storm Jenkins (R)	49,278
13.	Fortney "Pete" Stark* (D)	114,408
	James S. Fay (R)	53,385
14.	Anna G. Eshoo* (D)	149,313
	Ben Brink (R)	71,573
15.	Tom Campbell* (R)[1]	132,737
	Dick Lane (D)	79,048
16.	Zoe Lofgren* (D)	94,020
	Chuck Wojslaw (R)	43,197
17.	Sam Farr* (D)	115,116
	Jess Brown (R)	73,856
18.	Gary A. Condit* (D)	108,827
	Bill Conrad (R)	52,695
19.	George P. Radanovich* (R)	137,402
	Paul Barile (D)	58,452
20.	Cal Dooley* (D)	65,381
	Trice Harvey (R)	45,276
21.	Bill Thomas* (R)	125,916
	Deborah A. Vollmer (D)	50,694
22.	Walter Holden Capps (D)	118,299
	Andrea Seastrand* (R)	107,987
23.	Elton Gallegly* (R)	118,880
	Robert R. Unruhe (D)	70,035
24.	Brad Sherman (D)	106,193
	Rich Sybert (R)	93,629
25.	Howard "Buck" McKeon* (R)	122,428
	Diane Trautman (D)	65,089
26.	Howard L. Berman* (D)	67,525
	Bill Glass (R)	29,332
27.	James E. Rogan (R)	95,310
	Doug Kahn (D)	82,014
28.	David Dreier* (R)	113,389
	David Levering (D)	69,037
29.	Henry A. Waxman* (D)	145,278
	Paul Stepanek (R)	52,857
30.	Xavier Becerra* (D)	58,283
	Patricia Jean Parker (R)	15,078

Dist.	Representative (Party)	1996 Election
31.	Matthew G. Martinez* (D)	69,285
	John V. Flores (R)	28,705
32.	Julian C. Dixon* (D)	124,712
	Larry Ardito (R)	18,768
33.	Lucille Roybal-Allard* (D)	47,478
	John P. Leonard (R)	8,147
34.	Esteban E. Torres* (D)	94,730
	David G. Nunez (R)	36,852
35.	Maxine Waters* (D)	92,762
	Eric Carlson (R)	13,116
36.	Jane Harman* (D)	117,752
	Susan Brooks (R)	98,538
37.	Juanita M. McDonald* (D)[2]	87,247
	Michael E. Voetee (R)	15,399
38.	Steve Horn* (R)	88,136
	Rick Zbur (D)	71,627
39.	Ed Royce* (R)	120,761
	R. O. "Bob" Davis (D)	61,392
40.	Jerry Lewis* (R)	98,821
	Robert "Bob" Conaway (D)	44,102
41.	Jay C. Kim* (R)	83,934
	Richard L. Waldron (D)	47,346
42.	George E. Brown, Jr.* (D)	52,166
	Linda M. Wilde (R)	51,170
43.	Ken Calvert* (R)	97,247
	Guy C. Kimbrough (D)	67,422
44.	Sonny Bono* (R)	110,643
	Anita Rufus (D)	73,844
45.	Dana Rohrabacher* (R)	125,326
	Sally J. Alexander (D)	68,312
46.	Loretta Sanchez (D)	47,964
	Robert K. "Bob" Dornan* (R)	46,980
47.	Christopher Cox* (R)	160,078
	Tina Louise Laine (D)	70,362
48.	Ron Packard* (R)	145,814
	Dan Farrell (D)	59,558
49.	Brian P. Bilbray* (R)	108,806
	Peter Navarro (D)	86,657
50.	Bob Filner* (D)	73,200
	Jim Baize (R)	38,351
51.	Randy "Duke" Cunningham* (R)	149,032
	Rita Tamerius (D)	66,250
52.	Duncan Hunter* (R)	116,746
	Darity Wesley (D)	53,104

Colorado

Dist.	Representative (Party)	1996 Election
1.	Diana DeGette (D)	112,631
	Joe Rogers (R)	79,540
2.	David Skaggs* (D)	145,894
	Patricia (Pat) Miller (R)	97,865
3.	Scott McInnis* (R)	183,523
	Albert L. Gurule (D)	82,953
4.	Bob Schaffer (R)	137,012
	Guy Kelley (D)	92,837
5.	Joel Hefley* (R)	188,805
	Mike Robinson (D)	73,660
6.	Dan Schaefer* (R)	146,018
	Joan Fitz-Gerald (D)	88,600

Connecticut

Dist.	Representative (Party)	1996 Election
1.	Barbara Bailey Kennelly* (D,ACP)	158,222
	Kent Sleath (R)	53,666
2.	Sam Gejdenson* (D,ACP)	115,175
	Edward W. Munster (R)	100,332
3.	Rosa L. DeLauro* (D,ACP)	150,798
	John Coppola (R)	59,335
4.	Christopher Shays* (R)	121,949
	Bill Finch (D)	75,902
5.	James H. Maloney (D,ACP)	111,974
	Gary A. Franks* (R)	98,782
6.	Nancy L. Johnson* (R)	113,020
	Charlotte Koskoff (D,ACP)	111,433

Delaware

	Representative (Party)	1996 Election
	Michael N. Castle* (R)	185,576
	Dennis E. Williams (D)	73,253

Florida

Dist.	Representative (Party)	1996 Election
1.	Joe Scarborough* (R)	175,648
	Kevin Beck (D)	66,415
2.	Allen Boyd (D)	138,100
	Bill Sutton (R)	94,030

Dist.	Representative (Party)	1996 Election
3.	**Corrine Brown*** (D)	**98,047**
	Preston James Fields (R)	62,166
4.	**Tillie K. Fowler*** (R)	**Unopposed**
5.	**Karen L. Thurman*** (D)	**161,027**
	Dave Gentry (R)	100,023
6.	**Clifford "Cliff" B. Stearns*** (R)	**161,464**
	Newell O'Brien (D)	78,886
7.	**John L. Mica*** (R)	**143,637**
	George Stuart, Jr. (D)	87,822
8.	**Bill McCollum*** (R)	**136,473**
	Al Krulick (D)	65,784
9.	**Michael Bilirakis*** (R)	**161,689**
	Jerry Provenzano (D)	73,799
10.	**C. W. Bill Young*** (R)	**114,426**
	Henry Green (D)	57,365
11.	**Jim Davis** (D)	**108,500**
	Mark Sharpe (R)	78,856
12.	**Charles T. Canady*** (R)	**122,553**
	Mike Canady (D)	76,500
13.	**Dan Miller*** (R)	**173,573**
	Sanford Gordon (D)	96,053
14.	**Porter J. Goss*** (R)	**176,961**
	Jim Nolan (D)	63,833
15.	**Dave Weldon*** (R)	**138,968**
	John L. Byron (D)	115,954
16.	**Mark Foley*** (R)	**175,674**
	Jim Stuber (D)	98,813
17.	**Carrie P. Meek*** (D)	**114,590**
	Wellington Rolle (R)	14,502
18.	**Ileana Ros-Lehtinen*** (R)	**Unopposed**
19.	**Robert Wexler** (D)	**188,745**
	Beverly Kennedy (R)	99,073
20.	**Peter Deutsch*** (D)	**159,208**
	Jim Jacobs (R)	85,717
21.	**Lincoln Diaz-Balart*** (R)	**Unopposed**
22.	**E. Clay Shaw, Jr.*** (R)	**137,070**
	Kenneth D. Cooper (D)	84,496
23.	**Alcee L. Hastings*** (D)	**102,146**
	Robert Paul Brown (R)	36,897

Georgia

Dist.	Representative (Party)	1996 Election
1.	**Jack Kingston*** (R)	**108,616**
	Rosemary D. Kaszans (D)	50,622
2.	**Sanford Bishop*** (D)	**88,256**
	Darrel Bush Ealum (R)	75,282
3.	**Michael Allen "Mac" Collins*** (R)	**120,251**
	Jim Chafin (D)	76,538
4.	**Cynthia McKinney*** (D)	**127,157**
	John M. Mitnick (R)	92,985
5.	**John Lewis*** (D)	**Unopposed**
6.	**Newt Gingrich*** (R)	**174,155**
	Michael Coles (D)	127,135
7.	**Bob Barr*** (R)	**112,009**
	Charlie Watts (D)	81,765
8.	**Saxby Chambliss*** (R)	**93,619**
	Jim Wiggins (D)	84,506
9.	**John Nathan Deal*** (R)[3]	**132,532**
	McCracken "Ken" Poston (D)	69,662
10.	**Charles Norwood, Jr.*** (R)	**96,723**
	David Bell (D)	88,054
11.	**John Linder*** (R)	**145,821**
	Tommy Stephenson (D)	80,940

Hawaii

Dist.	Representative (Party)	1996 Election
1.	**Neil Abercrombie*** (D)	**86,732**
	Orson Swindle (R)	80,053
2.	**Patsy Takemoto Mink*** (D)	**109,178**
	Tom Pico, Jr. (R)	55,729

Idaho

Dist.	Representative (Party)	1996 Election
1.	**Helen Chenoweth*** (R)	**132,344**
	Dan Williams (D)	125,899
2.	**Mike Crapo*** (R)	**157,646**
	John D. Seidl (D)	67,625

Illinois

Dist.	Representative (Party)	1996 Election
1.	**Bobby L. Rush*** (D)	**174,005**
	Noel Naughton (R)	25,659
2.	**Jesse L. Jackson, Jr.*** (D)[4]	**172,648**
	Frank H. Stratman (LB)	10,880
3.	**William O. Lipinski*** (D)	**137,153**
	Jim Nalepa (R)	67,214
4.	**Luis V. Gutierrez*** (D)	**85,278**
	William Passmore (LB)	5,857
5.	**Rod R. Blagojevich** (D)	**117,544**
	Michael Patrick Flanagan* (R)	65,768
6.	**Henry J. Hyde*** (R)	**132,401**
	Stephen de la Rosa (D)	68,807
7.	**Danny K. Davis** (D)	**149,568**
	Randy Borow (R)	27,241
8.	**Philip M. Crane*** (R)	**127,763**
	Elizabeth Anne "Betty" Hull (D)	74,068
9.	**Sidney R. Yates*** (D)	**124,319**
	Joseph Walsh (R)	71,763
10.	**John E. Porter*** (R)	**145,626**
	Philip R. Torf (D)	65,144
11.	**Gerald C. "Jerry" Weller*** (R)	**109,896**
	Clem Balanoff (D)	102,388
12.	**Jerry F. Costello*** (D)	**150,005**
	Shapley R. Hunter (R)	55,690
13.	**Harris W. Fawell*** (R)	**141,651**
	Susan W. Hynes (D)	94,693
14.	**J. Dennis Hastert*** (R)	**134,432**
	Doug Mains (D)	74,332
15.	**Thomas W. Ewing*** (R)	**121,019**
	Laurel Lunt Prussing (D)	90,065
16.	**Donald A. Manzullo*** (R)	**137,523**
	Catherine M. Lee (D)	90,575
17.	**Lane A. Evans*** (D)	**120,008**
	Mark Baker (R)	109,240
18.	**Ray LaHood*** (R)	**143,110**
	Mike Curran (D)	98,413
19.	**Glenn Poshard*** (D)	**158,668**
	Brent Winters (R)	75,751
20.	**John M. Shimkus** (R)	**120,926**
	Jay C. Hoffman (D)	119,688

Indiana

Dist.	Representative (Party)	1996 Election
1.	**Peter J. Visclosky*** (D)	**133,553**
	Michael Edward Petyo (R)	56,418
2.	**David M. McIntosh*** (R)	**123,113**
	R. Marc Carmichael (D)	85,105
3.	**Tim Roemer*** (D)	**114,288**
	Joe Zakas (R)	80,699
4.	**Mark Edward Souder*** (R)	**121,344**
	Gerald L. Houseman (D)	81,740
5.	**Steve Buyer*** (R)	**133,627**
	Douglas L. Clark (D)	67,128
6.	**Dan Burton*** (R)	**193,193**
	Carrie Jean Dillard-Trammell (D)	59,661
7.	**Edward A. Pease** (R)	**130,010**
	Robert F. Hellman (D)	72,705
8.	**John N. Hostettler*** (R)	**109,860**
	Jonathan Weinzapfel (D)	106,201
9.	**Lee H. Hamilton*** (D)	**128,123**
	Jean Leising (R)	96,442
10.	**Julia M. Carson** (D)	**85,965**
	Virginia Blankenbaker (R)	72,796

Iowa

Dist.	Representative (Party)	1996 Election
1.	**Jim Leach*** (R)	**129,242**
	Bob Rush (D)	111,595
2.	**Jim Nussle*** (R)	**127,827**
	Donna L. Smith (D)	109,731
3.	**Leonard L. Boswell*** (D)	**115,914**
	Mike Mahaffey (R)	111,895
4.	**Greg Ganske*** (R)	**133,419**
	Connie McBurney (D)	119,790
5.	**Tom Latham*** (R)	**147,576**
	MacDonald Smith (D)	75,785

Kansas

Dist.	Representative (Party)	1996 Election
1.	**Jerry Moran** (R)	**191,899**
	John Divine (D)	63,948
2.	**Jim Ryun** (R)	**131,592**
	John Frieden (D)	114,644
3.	**Vince Snowbarger** (R)	**139,169**
	Judy Hancock (D)	126,848
4.	**Todd Tiahrt*** (R)	**128,486**
	Randall Rathbun (D)	119,544

Kentucky

Dist.	Representative (Party)	1996 Election
1.	**Edward Whitfield*** (R)	**111,473**
	Dennis L. Null (D)	96,684

Dist.	Representative (Party)	1996 Election
2.	**Ron Lewis*** (R)	**125,433**
	Joe Wright (D)	90,483
3.	**Anne Meagher Northup** (R)	**126,625**
	Mike Ward* (D).	125,326
4.	**Jim Bunning*** (R).	**149,135**
	Denny Bowman (D).	68,939
5.	**Harold "Hal" Rogers*** (R).	**Unopposed**
6.	**Scotty Baesler*** (D)	**125,999**
	Ernest Fletcher (R)	100,231

Louisiana

1.	**Robert L. "Bob" Livingston*** (R)	
2.	**William J. Jefferson*** (D)	
3.	**W. J. "Billy" Tauzin*** (R)[5]	
4.	**"Jim" McCrery*** (R)	
5.	**John Cooksey** (R)	**135,990**
	Francis Thompson (D).	97,363
6.	**Richard Baker*** (R)	
7.	**Chris John** (D).	**128,449**
	Hunter Lundy (D)	113,351

In Louisiana, all candidates of all parties run against each other in an open primary, unless they are unopposed incumbents, in which case they are declared elected. All candidates who receive more than 50 percent of the primary vote are also declared elected and do not appear on the general election ballot. In 1996, candidates in Districts 1, 2, 3, 4, and 6 were declared elected.

Maine

1.	**Thomas H. Allen** (D)	**173,745**
	James B. Longley, Jr.* (R).	140,354
2.	**John E. Baldacci*** (D)	**205,439**
	Paul R. Young (R)	70,856

Maryland

1.	**Wayne T. Gilchrest*** (R).	**131,033**
	Steve R. Eastaugh (D)	81,825
2.	**Robert L. Ehrlich, Jr.*** (R)	**143,075**
	Connie Galiazzo DeJuliis (D).	88,344
3.	**Benjamin L. Cardin*** (D).	**130,204**
	Patrick L. McDonough (R)	63,229
4.	**Albert R. Wynn*** (D)	**142,094**
	John B. Kimble (R)	24,700
5.	**Steny H. Hoyer*** (D)	**121,288**
	John S. Morgan (R)	91,806
6.	**Roscoe Bartlett*** (R)	**132,853**
	Stephen Crawford (D)	100,910
7.	**Elijah E. Cummings*** (D)[6]	**115,764**
	Kenneth Kondner (R)	22,929
8.	**Constance A. Morella*** (R)	**152,538**
	Donald Mooers (D)	96,229

Massachusetts

1.	**John W. Olver*** (D)	**129,232**
	Jane Maria Swift (R)	115,801
2.	**Richard E. Neal*** (D)	**162,995**
	Mark Steele (R)	49,885
3.	**James P. McGovern** (D)	**135,044**
	Peter Blute* (R)	115,694
4.	**Barney Frank*** (D)	**183,844**
	Jonathan P. Raymond (R)	72,701
5.	**Martin T. Meehan*** (D)	**Unopposed**
6.	**John F. Tierney** (D)	**133,687**
	Peter G. Torkildsen* (R)	133,315
7.	**Edward J. Markey*** (D).	**177,053**
	Patricia H. Long (R)	76,407
8.	**Joseph P. Kennedy, II*** (D)	**147,126**
	R. Philip Hyde (R)	27,303
9.	**John Joseph Moakley*** (D)	**172,009**
	Paul V. Gryska (R)	66,079
10.	**William D. Delahunt** (D).	**160,745**
	Edward B. Teague, III (R)	123,520

Michigan

1.	**Bart Stupak*** (D)	**181,486**
	Bob Carr (R).	69,957
2.	**Peter Hoekstra*** (R)	**165,608**
	Dan Kruszynski (D).	83,603
3.	**Vernon J. Ehlers*** (R)	**169,466**
	Betsy J. Flory (D)	72,791

Dist.	Representative (Party)	1996 Election
4.	**Dave Camp*** (R)	**159,561**
	Lisa A. Donaldson (D)	79,691
5.	**James A. Barcia*** (D)	**162,675**
	Lawrence H. Sims (R)	65,542
6.	**Fred Upton*** (R)	**146,170**
	Clarence J. Annen (D)	66,243
7.	**Nick Smith*** (R)	**120,227**
	Kim H. Tunnicliff (D)	93,725
8.	**Debbie Stabenow*** (D)	**141,086**
	Dick Chrysler* (R)	115,836
9.	**Dale E. Kildee*** (D)	**136,856**
	Patrick M. Nowak (R)	89,733
10.	**David E. Bonior*** (D)	**132,829**
	Susy Heintz (R)	106,444
11.	**Joe Knollenberg*** (R)	**169,165**
	Morris Frumin (D).	99,303
12.	**Sander Levin*** (D).	**133,436**
	John Pappageorge (R)	94,235
13.	**Lynn Nancy Rivers*** (D)	**123,133**
	Joe Fitzsimmons (R)	89,907
14.	**John Conyers, Jr.*** (D) . . .	**157,722**
	William A. Ashe (R)	22,152
15.	**Carolyn Cheeks Kilpatrick** (D)	**143,683**
	Stephen Hume (R).	16,009
16.	**John D. Dingell*** (D)	**136,854**
	James R. DeSana (R)	78,723

Minnesota

1.	**Gil Gutknecht*** (R)	**137,545**
	Mary Rieder (D).	123,188
2.	**David Minge*** (D)	**144,083**
	Gary B. Revier (R)	107,807
3.	**Jim Ramstad*** (R)	**205,845**
	Stanley J. Leino (D)	87,359
4.	**Bruce F. Vento*** (D)	**145,831**
	Dennis Newinski (R)	94,110
5.	**Martin Olav Sabo*** (D)	**158,275**
	Jack Uldrich (R).	70,115
6.	**Bill Luther*** (D)	**164,921**
	Tad Jude (R)	129,989
7.	**Collin C. Peterson*** (D)	**170,936**
	Darrell McKigney (R)	80,132
8.	**James L. Oberstar*** (D)	**185,333**
	Andy Larson (R)	69,460

Mississippi

1.	**Roger F. Wicker*** (R)	**123,724**
	Henry Boyd, Jr. (D)	55,998
2.	**Bennie G. Thompson*** (D) . . .	**102,503**
	Danny Covington (R)	65,263
3.	**Charles W. "Chip" Pickering, Jr.** (R) . . .	**115,443**
	John Arthur Eaves, Jr. (D) . . .	68,658
4.	**Mike Parker*** (R)	**112,444**
	Kevin Antoine (D)	66,836
5.	**Gene Taylor*** (D)	**103,415**
	Dennis Dollar (R).	71,114

Missouri

1.	**William "Bill" Clay*** (D).	**131,659**
	Daniel F. O'Sullivan, Jr. (R) . . .	51,857
2.	**James M. Talent*** (R)	**165,999**
	Joan Kelly Horn (D)	100,372
3.	**Richard A. Gephardt*** (D) . . .	**137,300**
	Deborah Lynn "Debbie" Wheelehan (R). .	90,202
4.	**Ike Skelton*** (D)	**153,566**
	Bill Phelps (R)	81,650
5.	**Karen McCarthy*** (D)	**144,223**
	Penny Bennett (R)	61,803
6.	**Pat "Patsy Ann" Danner*** (D)	**169,006**
	Jeff Bailey (R)	72,064
7.	**Roy Blunt*** (R)	**162,558**
	Ruth Bamberger (D).	79,306
8.	**Jo Ann Emerson** (R)	**112,472**
	Emily Firebaugh (D)	83,084
9.	**Kenny Hulshof** (R)	**123,580**
	Harold L. Volkmer* (D)	117,685

Montana

Rick Hill (R)	**211,975**
Bill Yellowtail (D)	174,516

Dist.	Representative (Party)	1996 Election
	Nebraska	
1.	**Doug Bereuter*** (R)	157,108
	Patrick J. Combs (D)	67,152
2.	**Jon Christensen*** (R)	125,201
	James Martin Davis (D)	88,447
3.	**Bill Barrett*** (R)	167,758
	John Webster (D)	48,833
	Nevada	
1.	**John Ensign*** (R)	86,472
	Bob Coffin (D)	75,081
2.	**Jim Gibbons** (R)	162,310
	Thomas "Spike" Wilson (D)	97,742
	New Hampshire	
1.	**John E. Sununu** (R)	123,939
	"Joe" Keefe (D)	115,462
2.	**Charles Bass*** (R)	122,957
	Deborah Arnie Arnesen (D)	105,824
	New Jersey	
1.	**Robert E. Andrews*** (D)	160,413
	Mel Suplee (R)	44,287
2.	**Frank A. LoBiondo*** (R)	133,131
	Ruth Katz (D)	83,890
3.	**Jim Saxton*** (R)	157,503
	John Leonardi (D)	81,590
4.	**Christopher H. Smith*** (R)	146,404
	Kevin John Meara (D)	77,565
5.	**Marge Roukema*** (R)	181,323
	Bill Auer (D)	62,956
6.	**Frank Pallone, Jr.*** (D)	124,635
	Steven J. Corodemus (R)	73,402
7.	**Bob Franks*** (R)	128,821
	Larry Lerner (D)	97,285
8.	**William J. Pascrell, Jr.** (D)	98,861
	Bill Martini* (R)	92,609
9.	**Steven R. Rothman** (D)	117,646
	Kathleen A. Donovan (R)	89,005
10.	**Donald M. Payne*** (D)	127,126
	Vanessa Williams (R)	22,086
11.	**Rodney P. Frelinghuysen*** (R)	169,091
	Chris Evangel (D)	78,742
12.	**Mike Pappas** (R)	135,811
	David M. DelVecchio (D)	125,594
13.	**Robert Menendez*** (D)	115,459
	Carlos E. Munoz (R)	25,427
	New Mexico	
1.	**Steven H. Schiff*** (R)	109,290
	John Wertheim (D)	71,635
2.	**Joe Skeen*** (R)	95,091
	E. Shirley Baca (D)	74,915
3.	**Bill Redmond** (R)[7]	43,559
	Eric P. Serna (D)[7]	40,542
	New York	
1.	**Michael P. Forbes*** (R,C,IC,T)	116,620
	Nora L. Bredes (D,S)	96,496
2.	**Rick A. Lazio*** (R,C)	112,135
	Kenneth J. Herman (D,IC)	57,953
3.	**Peter T. King*** (R,C,F)	127,972
	Dal A. Lamagna (D,IC)	97,518
4.	**Carolyn McCarthy** (D,IC)	127,060
	Daniel Frisa* (R,C,F)	89,542
5.	**Gary L. Ackerman*** (D,IC,L)	125,918
	Grant M. Lally (R,C,F)	69,244
6.	**Floyd H. Flake*** (D)[8]	102,799
	Jorawar Misir (R,C,IC,F)	18,348
7.	**Thomas J. Manton*** (D)	78,848
	Rose Birtley (R,C,IC)	32,092
8.	**Jerrold L. Nadler*** (D,L)	131,943
	Michael Benjamin (R,F)	26,028
9.	**Charles E. Schumer*** (D,L)	107,107
	Robert J. Verga (R,IC,F)	30,488
10.	**Edolphus Towns*** (D,L)	99,889
	Amelia Smith-Parker (R,C,F)	8,660
11.	**Major R. Owens*** (D,L)	89,905
	Claudette Hayle (R,C,IC,F)	7,866

Dist.	Representative (Party)	1996 Election
12.	**Nydia M. Velázquez*** (D,L)	61,913
	Miguel I. Prado (R,C,T)	9,978
13.	**Susan Molinari** (R,C,F)[9]	94,660
	Tyrone G. Butler (D,L)	53,376
14.	**Carolyn B. Maloney*** (D,L)	130,175
	Jeffrey E. Livingston (R)	42,641
15.	**Charles B. Rangel*** (D,L)	113,898
	Edward R. Adams (R)	5,951
16.	**José E. Serrano*** (D,L)	95,568
	Rodney Torres (R)	2,878
17.	**Eliot L. Engel*** (D,L)	101,287
	Denis McCarthy (R,C,T)	15,892
18.	**Nita M. Lowey*** (D)	118,194
	Kerry J. Katsorhis (R,C)	59,487
19.	**Sue W. Kelly*** (R,F)	102,142
	Richard S. Klein (D,L)	86,926
20.	**Benjamin A. Gilman*** (R)	122,479
	Yash P. Aggarwal (D,L)	80,761
21.	**Michael R. McNulty*** (D,C,IC)	158,491
	Nancy Norman (R,F)	64,471
22.	**Gerald B. H. Solomon*** (R,C,T,F)	144,125
	Steve James (D)	94,192
23.	**Sherwood L. Boehlert*** (R,F)	124,626
	Bruce W. Hapanowicz (D)	50,436
24.	**John M. McHugh*** (R,C)	124,240
	Donald Ravenscroft (D)	43,692
25.	**James T. Walsh*** (R,C,IC,F)	126,691
	Marty Mack (D)	103,199
26.	**Maurice D. Hinchey*** (D,L)	122,850
	Sue Wittig (R,C,T,F)	94,125
27.	**Bill Paxon*** (R,C,T,F)	142,568
	Thomas M. Fricano (D,S)	95,503
28.	**Louise M. Slaughter*** (D)	133,084
	Geoff H. Rosenberger (R,C,F)	99,366
29.	**John J. LaFalce*** (D,L)	132,317
	David B. Callard (R,C,T,F)	81,135
30.	**Jack Quinn*** (R,C,IC,F)	121,369
	Francis J. Pordum (D,PS)	100,040
31.	**Amo Houghton*** (R,C,F)	139,734
	Bruce D. MacBain (D)	49,502
	North Carolina	
1.	**Eva M. Clayton*** (D)	108,759
	Ted Tyler (R)	54,666
2.	**Bob Etheridge** (D)	113,820
	David Funderburk* (R)	98,951
3.	**Walter B. Jones, Jr.*** (R)	118,159
	George Parrott (D)	68,887
4.	**David E. Price*** (D)	157,194
	Fred Heineman* (R)	126,466
5.	**Richard M. Burr*** (R)	130,177
	Neil Grist Cashion, Jr. (D)	74,320
6.	**Howard Coble*** (R)	167,828
	Mark Costley (D)	58,022
7.	**Mike McIntyre** (D)	87,487
	Bill Caster (R)	75,811
8.	**W. G. "Bill" Hefner*** (D)	103,129
	Curtis Blackwood (R)	81,676
9.	**Sue Myrick*** (R)	147,755
	Michel C. (Mike) Daisley (D)	83,078
10.	**T. Cass Ballenger*** (R)	158,585
	Ben Neill (D)	65,103
11.	**Charles H. Taylor*** (R)	132,860
	James Mark Ferguson (D)	91,257
12.	**Mel Watt*** (D)	124,675
	Joseph A. "Joe" Martino (R)	46,581
	North Dakota	
	Earl Pomeroy* (D)	144,833
	Kevin Cramer (R)	113,684
	Ohio	
1.	**Steve Chabot*** (R)	118,324
	Mark P. Longabaugh (D)	94,719
2.	**Rob Portman*** (R)	186,853
	Thomas R. Chandler (D)	58,715
3.	**Tony P. Hall*** (D)	144,583
	David A. Westbrock (R)	75,732
4.	**Michael G. Oxley*** (R)	147,608
	Paul McClain (D)	69,096

Dist.	Representative (Party)	1996 Election
5.	**Paul E. Gillmor*** (R)	**145,692**
	Annie Saunders (D)	81,170
6.	**Ted Strickland** (D)	**118,003**
	Frank A. Cremeans* (R)	111,907
7.	**David L. Hobson*** (R)	**158,087**
	Richard K. Blain (D)	61,419
8.	**John A. Boehner*** (R)	**165,815**
	Jeffrey D. Kitchen (D)	61,515
9.	**Marcy Kaptur*** (D)	**170,617**
	Randy Whitman (R)	46,040
10.	**Dennis J. Kucinich** (D)	**110,723**
	Martin R. Hoke* (R)	104,546
11.	**Louis Stokes*** (D)	**153,546**
	James J. Sykora (R)	28,821
12.	**John R. Kasich*** (R)	**151,667**
	Cynthia L. Ruccia (D)	78,762
13.	**Sherrod Brown*** (D)	**146,690**
	Kenneth C. Blair, Jr. (R)	87,108
14.	**Thomas C. Sawyer*** (D)	**124,136**
	Joyce George (R)	95,307
15.	**Deborah Pryce*** (R)	**156,776**
	Cliff Arnebeck (D)	64,665
16.	**Ralph Regula*** (R)	**159,314**
	Thomas E. Burkhart (D)	64,902
17.	**James A. Traficant, Jr.*** (D)	**218,283**
	James M. Cahaney (NL)	21,685
18.	**Bob Ney*** (R)	**117,365**
	Robert L. Burch (D)	108,332
19.	**Steven C. LaTourette*** (R)	**135,012**
	Thomas J. Coyne, Jr. (D)	101,152

Oklahoma

Dist.	Representative (Party)	1996 Election
1.	**Steve Largent*** (R)	**143,415**
	Randolph John Amen (D)	57,996
2.	**Tom A. Coburn*** (R)	**112,273**
	Glen D. Johnson (D)	90,120
3.	**Wes Watkins** (R)	**98,526**
	Darryl Roberts (D)	86,647
4.	**J. C. Watts, Jr.*** (R)	**106,923**
	Ed Crocker (D)	73,950
5.	**Ernest Istook*** (R)	**148,362**
	James L. Forsythe (D)	57,594
6.	**Frank D. Lucas*** (R)	**113,499**
	Paul M. Barby (D)	64,173

Oregon

Dist.	Representative (Party)	1996 Election
1.	**Elizabeth Furse*** (D)	**144,588**
	Bill Witt (R)	126,146
2.	**Robert F. (Bob) Smith** (R)	**164,062**
	Mike Dugan (D)	97,195
3.	**Earl Blumenauer*** (D)[10]	**165,922**
	Scott Bruun (R)	65,259
4.	**Peter A. DeFazio*** (D)	**177,270**
	John D. Newkirk (R)	76,649
5.	**Darlene Hooley** (D)	**139,521**
	Jim Bunn* (R)	125,409

Pennsylvania

Dist.	Representative (Party)	1996 Election
1.	**Thomas M. Foglietta*** (D)	**145,210**
	James D. Cella (R)	20,734
2.	**Chaka Fattah*** (D)	**168,887**
	Larry G. Murphy (D)	23,047
3.	**Robert A. Borski*** (D)	**121,120**
	Joseph M. McColgan (R)	54,681
4.	**Ron Klink*** (D)	**142,621**
	Paul T. Adametz (R)	79,448
5.	**John E. Peterson** (R)	**116,303**
	Ruth C. Rudy (D)	76,627
6.	**Tim Holden*** (D)	**115,193**
	Christian Y. Leinbach (R)	80,061
7.	**Curt Weldon*** (R)	**165,087**
	John F. Innelli (D)	79,875
8.	**Jim Greenwood*** (R)	**133,749**
	John P. Murray (D)	79,856
9.	**Bud Shuster*** (R)	**142,105**
	Monte Kemmlor (D)	50,650
10.	**Joseph M. McDade*** (R)	**121,670**
	Joe Cullen (D)	75,536
11.	**Paul E. Kanjorski*** (D)	**128,258**
	Stephen A. Urban (R)	60,339

Dist.	Representative (Party)	1996 Election
12.	**John P. Murtha*** (D)	**136,815**
	Bill Choby (R)	58,643
13.	**Jon D. Fox*** (R)	**120,304**
	Joseph M. Hoeffel (D)	120,220
14.	**William J. Coyne*** (D)	**122,922**
	Bill Ravotti (R)	78,921
15.	**Paul McHale*** (D)	**109,812**
	Bob Kilbanks (R)	82,803
16.	**Joseph R. Pitts** (R)	**124,511**
	James G. Blaine (D)	78,598
17.	**George W. Gekas*** (R)	**150,678**
	Paul Kettl (D)	57,911
18.	**Mike Doyle*** (D)	**120,410**
	David B. Fawcett (R)	86,829
19.	**Bill Goodling*** (R)	**130,716**
	Scott L. Chronister (D)	74,944
20.	**Frank R. Mascara*** (D)	**113,394**
	Mike McCormick (R)	97,004
21.	**Phil English*** (R)	**106,875**
	Ronald A. DiNicola (D)	104,004

Rhode Island

Dist.	Representative (Party)	1996 Election
1.	**Patrick J. Kennedy*** (D)	**121,781**
	Giovanni D. Cicione (R)	49,199
2.	**Robert A. Weygand** (D)	**118,827**
	Richard E. Wild (R)	58,458

South Carolina

Dist.	Representative (Party)	1996 Election
1.	**Mark Sanford*** (R)	**138,467**
	Joseph F. Innella (NL)	5,105
2.	**Floyd D. Spence*** (R)	**158,229**
	Maurice T. Raiford (NL)	17,713
3.	**Lindsey Graham*** (R)	**114,273**
	Debbie Dorn (D)	73,417
4.	**Bob Inglis*** (R)	**138,165**
	Darrell E. Curry (D)	54,126
5.	**John M. Spratt*** (D)	**97,335**
	Larry L. Bigham (R)	81,455
6.	**James E. Clyburn*** (D)	**120,132**
	Gary McLeod (R)	51,974

South Dakota

Dist.	Representative (Party)	1996 Election
	John R. Thune (R)	**186,393**
	Rick Weiland (D)	119,547

Tennessee

Dist.	Representative (Party)	1996 Election
1.	**William L. "Bill" Jenkins** (R)	**117,676**
	Kay C. Smith (D)	58,657
2.	**John J. Duncan, Jr.*** (R)	**150,953**
	Stephen Smith (D)	61,020
3.	**Zach Wamp*** (R)	**113,408**
	Charles N. "Chuck" Jolly (D)	85,714
4.	**Van Hilleary*** (R)	**103,091**
	Mark Stewart (D)	73,331
5.	**Bob Clement*** (D)	**140,264**
	Steven L. Edmondson (R)	46,201
6.	**Bart Gordon*** (D)	**123,846**
	Steve Gill (R)	94,599
7.	**Ed Bryant*** (R)	**136,643**
	Don Trotter (D)	73,629
8.	**John Tanner*** (D)	**123,681**
	Tom Watson (R)	55,024
9.	**Harold E. Ford, Jr.** (D)	**116,345**
	Rod DeBerry (R)	70,951

Texas

Dist.	Representative (Party)	1996 Election
1.	**Max Sandlin** (D)	**102,697**
	Ed Merritt (R)	93,105
2.	**Jim Turner** (D)	**102,908**
	Brian Babin (R)	89,838
3.	**Sam Johnson*** (R)	**142,325**
	Lee Cole (D)	47,654
4.	**Ralph M. Hall*** (D)	**132,126**
	Jerry Ray Hall (R)	71,065
5.	**Pete Sessions** (R)	**80,196**
	John Pouland (D)	70,922
6.	**Joe Barton*** (R)	**160,800**
	Janet Carroll "Skeet" Richardson (I)	26,713
7.	**Bill Archer*** (R)	**152,024**
	Al J. K. Siegmund (D)	28,187
8.	**Kevin Brady** (R)[11]	**30,368**
	Gene Fontenot (R)[11]	21,004

Dist.	Representative (Party)	1996 Election
9.	Nick Lampson (D)[11]	59,217
	Steve Stockman* (R)[11]	52,853
10.	Lloyd Doggett* (D)	132,066
	Teresa Doggett (R)	97,204
11.	Chet Edwards* (D)	99,990
	Jay Mathis (R)	74,549
12.	Kay Granger (R)	98,349
	Hugh Parmer (D)	69,859
13.	William M. "Mac" Thornberry* (R)	116,098
	Samuel Brown Silverman (D)	56,066
14.	Ron Paul (R)	99,961
	Charles "Lefty" Morris (D)	93,200
15.	Ruben Hinojosa (D)	86,347
	Tom Haughey (R)	50,914
16.	Silvestre Reyes (D)	90,260
	Rick Ledesma (R)	35,271
17.	Charles W. Stenholm* (D)	99,678
	Rudy Izzard (R)	91,429
18.	Sheila Jackson Lee* (D)	106,111
	Larry White (R)	13,956
19.	Larry Combest* (R)	156,910
	John W. Sawyer (D)	38,316
20.	Henry B. Gonzalez* (D)	88,190
	James Walker (R)	47,616
21.	Lamar Smith* (R)	205,830
	Gordon H. Wharton (D)	60,338
22.	Tom DeLay* (R)	126,056
	Scott Douglas Cunningham (D)	59,030
23.	Henry Bonilla* (R)	101,332
	Charles P. Jones (D)	59,596
24.	Martin Frost* (D)	77,847
	Ed Harrison (R)	54,551
25.	Ken Bentsen* (D)[11]	29,396
	Dolly Madison McKenna (R)[11]	21,892
26.	Dick Armey* (R)	163,708
	Jerry Frankel (D)	58,623
27.	Solomon P. Ortiz* (D)	97,350
	Joe Gardner (R)	50,964
28.	Ciro D. Rodriguez (D)[12]	14,018
	Juan F. Solis III (R) [12]	8,056
29.	Gene Green* (D)	61,751
	Jack Rodriguez (R)	28,381
30.	Eddie Bernice Johnson* (D)	61,723
	John Hendry (R)	20,664

Utah

Dist.	Representative (Party)	1996 Election
1.	James V. Hansen* (R)	150,126
	Gregory J. Sanders (D)	65,866
2.	Merrill Cook (R)	129,963
	Ross C. Anderson (D)	100,283
3.	Christopher B. Cannon (R)	106,220
	Bill Orton* (D)	98,178

Vermont

	Representative (Party)	1996 Election
	Bernie Sanders* (I)	140,678
	Susan W. Sweetser (R)	83,021
	Jack Long (D)	23,830

Virginia

Dist.	Representative (Party)	1996 Election
1.	Herbert H. "Herb" Bateman* (R)	Unopposed
2.	Owen B. Pickett* (D)	106,215
	John F. Tate (R)	57,586
3.	Robert C. "Bobby" Scott* (D)	118,603
	Elsie Goodwyn Holland (R)	25,781
4.	Norman Sisisky* (D)	160,100
	Anthony J. "Tony" Zevgolis (R)	43,516

Dist.	Representative (Party)	1996 Election
5.	Virgil H. Goode, Jr. (D)	120,323
	George C. Landrith, III (R)	70,869
6.	Robert W. "Bob" Goodlatte* (R)	133,576
	Jeffrey W. Grey (D)	61,485
7.	Thomas J. "Tom" Bliley, Jr.* (R)	189,644
	Roderic H. Slayton (D)	51,206
8.	James P. Moran, Jr.* (D)	152,334
	John E. Otey (R)	64,562
9.	Frederick C. "Rick" Boucher* (D)	122,908
	Patrick C. Muldoon (R)	58,055
10.	Frank R. Wolf* (R)	169,266
	Robert L. "Bob" Weinberg (D)	59,145
11.	Thomas M. Davis, III* (R)	138,758
	Thomas J. "Tom" Horton (D)	74,701

Washington

Dist.	Representative (Party)	1996 Election
1.	Rick White* (R)	141,948
	Jeff Coopersmith (D)	122,187
2.	Jack Metcalf* (R)	124,655
	Kevin Quigley (D)	122,728
3.	Linda Smith* (R)	123,117
	Brian Baird (D)	122,230
4.	Doc Hastings* (R)	108,647
	Rick Locke (D)	96,502
5.	George R. Nethercutt, Jr.* (R)	131,618
	Judy Olson (D)	105,166
6.	Norm Dicks* (D)	155,467
	Bill Tinsley (R)	71,337
7.	Jim McDermott* (D)	209,753
	Frank Kleschen (R)	49,341
8.	Jennifer Dunn* (R)	170,691
	Dave Little (D)	90,340
9.	Adam Smith (D)	105,236
	Randy Tate* (R)	99,199

West Virginia

Dist.	Representative (Party)	1996 Election
1.	Alan B. Mollohan* (D)	Unopposed
2.	Bob Wise* (D)	141,551
	Greg Morris (R)	63,933
3.	Nick Joe Rahall* (D)	Unopposed

Wisconsin

Dist.	Representative (Party)	1996 Election
1.	Mark W. Neumann* (R)	118,408
	Lydia C. Spottswood (D)	114,148
2.	Scott L. Klug* (R)	154,557
	Paul R. Soglin (D)	110,467
3.	Ron Kind (D)	121,967
	James E. Harsdorf (R)	112,146
4.	Gerald D. Kleczka* (D)	134,470
	Tom Reynolds (R)	98,438
5.	Tom Barrett* (D)	141,179
	Paul D. Melotik (R)	47,384
6.	Thomas E. Petri* (R)	169,213
	Al Lindskoog (D)	55,377
7.	David R. Obey* (D)	137,428
	Scott West (R)	103,365
8.	Jay Johnson (D)	129,551
	David Prosser (R)	119,398
9.	F. James Sensenbrenner, Jr.* (R)	197,910
	Floyd Brenholt (D)	67,740

Wyoming

	Representative (Party)	1996 Election
	Barbara Cubin* (R)	116,004
	Pete Maxfield (D)	85,724

The following members of Congress are nonvoting: Carlos A. Romero Barceló (D), resident commissioner, Puerto Rico; Eleanor Holmes Norton (D), District of Columbia; Robert Underwood (D), Guam; Eni F. H. Faleomavaega (D), American Samoa; Donna Christian Green (D), Virgin Islands.

(1) Tom Campbell won a Dec. 12, 1995, special election to replace Norman Y. Mineta who resigned. (2) Juanita M. McDonald won a Mar. 26, 1996, special election to replace Walter R. Tucker, who resigned after a bribery conviction. (3) John Nathan Deal changed his party designation to Republican in 1995. (4) Jesse L. Jackson, Jr. won a Dec. 12, 1995, special election to replace Mel Reynolds, who resigned after his criminal conviction relating to his having had sex with a minor. (5) W. J. "Billy" Tauzin changed his party designation to Republican in 1995. (6) Elijah E. Cummings won an Apr. 16, 1996, special election to replace Kweisi Mfume, who resigned to become president of the NAACP. (7) Bill Redmond won a May 13, 1997, special election to replace Bill Richardson, who resigned to become ambassador to the United Nations. (8) Floyd H. Flake planned to resign Nov. 15, 1997. (9) Susan Molinari resigned Aug. 2, 1997, to become a news anchor for CBS News. Her vacant seat was to be filled on Election Day, Nov. 4, 1997. (10) Earl Blumenauer won a May 21, 1996, special election to replace Ron Wyden, who was elected to fill the Senate seat of Bob Packwood. (11) Based on a 1996 Federal decision, the lines of 13 Texas districts were redrawn. A candidate had to receive a majority of the vote to win in the Nov. 5, 1996, election. In these 3 districts, no candidate received a majority; the top 2 vote-getters competed in a runoff on Dec. 10, 1996. (12) Ciro D. Rodriguez won a Mar. 15, 1997, special election to replace Frank Tejeda, who died on Jan. 30, 1997.

Congressional Committees

Senate Standing Committees

(as of Oct. 1997)

Agriculture, Nutrition, and Forestry
Chairman: Richard G. Lugar, IN
Ranking Dem.: Tom Harkin, IA
Appropriations
Chairman: Ted Stevens, AK
Ranking Dem.: Robert C. Byrd, WV
Armed Services
Chairman: Strom Thurmond, SC
Ranking Dem.: Carl Levin, MI
Banking, Housing, and Urban Affairs
Chairman: Alfonse M. D'Amato, NY
Ranking Dem.: Paul S. Sarbanes, MD
Budget
Chairman: Pete V. Domenici, NM
Ranking Dem.: Frank R. Lautenberg, NJ
Commerce, Science, and Transportation
Chairman: John McCain, AZ
Ranking Dem.: Ernest F. "Fritz" Hollings, SC

Energy and Natural Resources
Chairman: Frank H. Murkowski, AK
Ranking Dem.: Dale Bumpers, AR
Environment and Public Works
Chairman: John H. Chafee, RI
Ranking Dem.: Max Baucus, MT
Finance
Chairman: William V. Roth, Jr., DE
Ranking Dem.: Daniel Patrick Moynihan, NY
Foreign Relations
Chairman: Jesse Helms, NC
Ranking Dem.: Joseph R. Biden, DE
Governmental Affairs
Chairman: Fred Thompson, TN
Ranking Dem.: John Glenn, OH
Indian Affairs
Chairman: Ben Nighthorse Campbell, CO
Ranking Dem.: Daniel K. Inouye, HI

Judiciary
Chairman: Orrin G. Hatch, UT
Ranking Dem.: Patrick J. Leahy, VT
Labor and Human Resources
Chairman: Jim Jeffords, VT
Ranking Dem.: Edward M. Kennedy, MA
Rules and Administration
Chairman: John W. Warner, VA
Ranking Dem.: Wendell H. Ford, KY
Small Business
Chairman: Christopher "Kit" Bond, MO
Ranking Dem.: John F. Kerry, MA
Veterans' Affairs
Chairman: Arlen Specter, PA
Ranking Dem.: John D. Rockefeller IV, WV

Senate Special Committee

(as of Oct. 1997)

Aging
Chairman: Charles E. Grassley, IA
Ranking Dem.: John B. Breaux, LA

Senate Select Committees

(as of Oct. 1997)

Ethics
Chairman: Robert Smith, NH
Ranking Dem.: Harry M. Reid, NV
Intelligence
Chairman: Richard C. Shelby, AL
V. Chairman: Bob Kerrey, NE

House Select Committee

(as of Oct. 1997)

Intelligence
Chairman: Porter J. Goss, FL
Ranking Dem.: Norman Dicks, WA

Joint Committees of Congress

(as of Oct. 1997)

Economic
Chairman: Rep. Jim Saxton, NJ
V. Chairman: Sen. Connie Mack, FL

Library
Chairman: Rep. Bill Thomas, CA
V. Chairman: Sen. Ted Stevens, AK

Printing
Chairman: Sen. John W. Warner, VA
V. Chairman: Rep. Bill Thomas, CA

Taxation
Chairman: Rep. Bill Archer, TX
V. Chairman: Sen. William V. Roth, Jr., DE

House Standing Committees

(as of Oct. 1997)

Agriculture
Chairman: Robert F. (Bob) Smith, OR
Ranking Dem.: Charles W. Stenholm, TX
Appropriations
Chairman: Robert L. "Bob" Livingston, LA
Ranking Dem.: David R. Obey, WI
Banking and Financial Services
Chairman: Jim Leach, IA
Ranking Dem.: Henry B. Gonzalez, TX
Budget
Chairman: John R. Kasich, OH
Ranking Dem.: John M. Spratt, SC
Commerce
Chairman: Thomas J. "Tom" Bliley, Jr., VA
Ranking Dem.: John D. Dingell, MI
Education and the Workforce
Chairman: Bill Goodling, PA
Ranking Dem.: William L. Clay, Sr., MO

Government Reform and Oversight
Chairman: Dan Burton, IN
Ranking Dem.: Henry A. Waxman, CA
House Oversight
Chairman: Bill Thomas, CA
Ranking Dem.: Sam Gejdenson, CT
International Relations
Chairman: Benjamin A. Gilman, NY
Ranking Dem.: Lee H. Hamilton, IN
Judiciary
Chairman: Henry J. Hyde, IL
Ranking Dem.: John Conyers, Jr., MI
National Security
Chairman: Floyd D. Spence, SC
Ranking Dem.: Ronald V. Dellums, CA
Resources
Chairman: Don Young, AK
Ranking Dem.: George Miller, CA

Rules
Chairman: Gerald B. H. Solomon, NY
Ranking Dem.: John Joseph Moakley, MA
Science
Chairman: F. James Sensenbrenner, Jr., WI
Ranking Dem.: George E. Brown, Jr., CA
Small Business
Chairman: James M. Talent, MO
Ranking Dem.: John J. LaFalce, NY
Standards of Official Conduct
Chairman: James V. Hansen, UT
Ranking Dem.: Howard L. Berman, CA
Transportation and Infrastructure
Chairman: Bud Shuster, PA
Ranking Dem.: James L. Oberstar, MN
Veterans' Affairs
Chairman: Bob Stump, AZ
Ranking Dem.: Lane A. Evans, IL
Ways and Means
Chairman: Bill Archer, TX
Ranking Dem.: Charles B. Rangel, NY

Political Divisions of the U.S. Senate and House of Representatives, 1901-97

Source: *1995-1996 Congressional Directory*; Senate Library; all figures reflect immediate post-election party breakdown

Congress	Years	Senate No. of Sen.	Demo-crats	Repub-licans	Other parties	Vacant	House of Representatives No. of Rep.	Demo-crats	Repub-licans	Other parties	Vacant
57th	1901-03	90	29	56	3	2	357	153	198	5	1
58th	1903-05	90	32	58			386	178	207		1
59th	1905-07	90	32	58			386	136	250		
60th	1907-09	92	29	61		2	386	164	222		
61st	1909-11	92	32	59		1	391	172	219		
62d	1911-13	92	42	49		1	391	228	162	1	
63d	1913-15	96	51	44	1		435	290	127	18	
64th	1915-17	96	56	39	1		435	231	193	8	3
65th	1917-19	96	53	42	1		435	210[1]	216	9	
66th	1919-21	96	47	48	1		435	191	237	7	
67th	1921-23	96	37	59			435	132	300	1	2
68th	1923-25	96	43	51	2		435	207	225	3	
69th	1925-27	96	40	54	1	1	435	183	247	5	
70th	1927-29	96	47	48	1		435	195	237	3	
71st	1929-31	96	39	56	1		435	163	267	1	4
72d	1931-33	96	47	48	1		435	216[2]	218	1	
73d	1933-35	96	59	36	1		435	313	117	5	
74th	1935-37	96	69	25	2		435	322	103	10	
75th	1937-39	96	75	17	4		435	333	89	13	
76th	1939-41	96	69	23	4		435	262	169	4	
77th	1941-43	96	66	28	2		435	267	162	6	
78th	1943-45	96	57	38	1		435	222	209	4	
79th	1945-47	96	57	38	1		435	243	190	2	
80th	1947-49	96	45	51			435	188	246	1	
81st	1949-51	96	54	42			435	263	171	1	
82d	1951-53	96	48	47	1		435	234	199	2	
83d	1953-55	96	46	48	2		435	213	221	1	
84th	1955-57	96	48	47	1		435	232	203		
85th	1957-59	96	49	47			435	234	201		
86th	1959-61	98	64	34			436[3]	283	153		
87th	1961-63	100	64	36			437[4]	262	175		
88th	1963-65	100	67	33			435	258	176		1
89th	1965-67	100	68	32			435	295	140		
90th	1967-69	100	64	36			435	248	187		
91st	1969-71	100	58	42			435	243	192		
92d	1971-73	100	54	44	2		435	255	180		
93d	1973-75	100	56	42	2		435	242	192	1	
94th	1975-77	100	60	37	2		435	291	144	1	
95th	1977-79	100	61	38	1		435	292	143		
96th	1979-81	100	58	41	1		435	277	158		
97th	1981-83	100	46	53	1		435	242	192	1	
98th	1983-85	100	46	54			435	269	166		
99th	1985-87	100	47	53			435	253	182		
100th	1987-89	100	55	45			435	258	177		
101st	1989-91	100	55	45			435	260	175		
102d	1991-93	100	56	44			435	267	167	1	
103d	1993-95	100	57	43			435	258	176	1	
104th	1995-97	100	48	52			435	204	230	1	
105th	1997-99	100	45[5]	55[5]			435	207[5]	227[5]	1[5]	

(1) Democrats organized House with help of other parties. (2) Democrats organized House due to Republican deaths. (3) Proclamation declaring Alaska a state issued Jan. 3, 1959. (4) Proclamation declaring Hawaii a state issued Aug. 21, 1959. (5) As of Oct. 15, 1997, there were 55 Republicans and 45 Democrats in the Senate, and 227 Republicans, 206 Democrats, 1 Independent, and 1 vacant seat in the House of Representatives.

Congressional Bills Vetoed, 1789-1997

Source: Senate Library

	Regular vetoes	Pocket vetoes	Total vetoes	Vetoes overridden		Regular vetoes	Pocket vetoes	Total vetoes	Vetoes overridden
Washington	2	—	2	—	Benjamin Harrison	19	25	44	1
John Adams	—	—	—	—	Cleveland	42	128	170	5
Jefferson	—	—	—	—	McKinley	6	36	42	—
Madison	5	2	7	—	Theodore Roosevelt	42	40	82	1
Monroe	1	—	1	—	Taft	30	9	39	1
John Q. Adams	—	—	—	—	Wilson	33	11	44	6
Jackson	5	7	12	—	Harding	5	1	6	—
Van Buren	—	1	1	—	Coolidge	20	30	50	4
William Harrison	—	—	—	—	Hoover	21	16	37	3
Tyler	6	4	10	1	Franklin Roosevelt	372	263	635	9
Polk	2	1	3	—	Truman	180	70	250	12
Taylor	—	—	—	—	Eisenhower	73	108	181	2
Fillmore	—	—	—	—	Kennedy	12	9	21	—
Pierce	9	—	9	5	Lyndon Johnson	16	14	30	—
Buchanan	4	3	7	—	Nixon	26	17	43	7
Lincoln	2	5	7	—	Ford	48	18	66	12
Andrew Johnson	21	8	29	15	Carter	13	18	31	2
Grant	45	48	93	4	Reagan	39	39	78	9
Hayes	12	1	13	1	Bush[1]	29	15	44	1
Garfield	—	—	—	—	Clinton[2]	18	—	18	1
Arthur	4	8	12	1	Total[1]	1,466	1,065	2,531	105
Cleveland	304	110	414	2					

(1) Excluded from the figures are 2 additional bills, which Pres. Bush claimed to be vetoed but Congress considered enacted into law because the president failed to return them to Congress during a recess period. (2) As of Oct. 15, 1997. Total does not include line-item veto, exercised for the first time to veto portions of budget legislation, Aug. 11, 1997.

Judiciary of the U.S.

(data as of Oct. 1997)

Justices of the United States Supreme Court

The Supreme Court comprises the chief justice of the U.S. and 8 associate justices, all appointed by the president with advice and consent of the Senate. Salaries: chief justice, $171,500 annually; associate justice, $164,100 annually. The Supreme Court is at the U.S. Supreme Court Bldg., 1 First St. NE, Washington, DC 20543.

Members of the Supreme Court at the start of the 1997–98 term (Oct. 6, 1997): Chief justice: William H. Rehnquist; associate justices: Stephen G. Breyer, Ruth Bader Ginsburg, Anthony M. Kennedy, Sandra Day O'Connor, Antonin Scalia, David H. Souter, John Paul Stevens, Clarence Thomas.

Name,[1] apptd. from	Service Term	Yrs	Born	Died	Name,[1] apptd. from	Service Term	Yrs	Born	Died
John Jay, NY	1789-1795	5	1745	1829	William H. Moody, MA	1906-1910	3	1853	1917
John Rutledge, SC	1789-1791	1	1739	1800	Horace H. Lurton, TN	1909-1914	4	1844	1914
William Cushing, MA	1789-1810	20	1732	1810	Charles E. Hughes, NY	1910-1916	5	1862	1948
James Wilson, PA	1789-1798	8	1742	1798	Willis Van Devanter, WY	1910-1937	26	1859	1941
John Blair, VA	1789-1796	6	1732	1800	Joseph R. Lamar, GA	1910-1916	5	1857	1916
James Iredell, NC	1790-1799	9	1751	1799	*Edward D. White,* LA	1910-1921	10	1845	1921
Thomas Johnson, MD	1791-1793	1	1732	1819	Mahlon Pitney, NJ	1912-1922	10	1858	1924
William Paterson, NJ	1793-1806	13	1745	1806	James C. McReynolds, TN	1914-1941	26	1862	1946
John Rutledge,[2] SC	1795	—	1739	1800	Louis D. Brandeis, MA	1916-1939	22	1856	1941
Samuel Chase, MD	1796-1811	15	1741	1811	John H. Clarke, OH	1916-1922	5	1857	1945
Oliver Ellsworth, CT	1796-1800	4	1745	1807	*William H. Taft,* CT	1921-1930	8	1857	1930
Bushrod Washington, VA	1798-1829	31	1762	1829	George Sutherland, UT	1922-1938	15	1862	1942
Alfred Moore, NC	1799-1804	4	1755	1810	Pierce Butler, MN	1922-1939	16	1866	1939
John Marshall, VA	1801-1835	34	1755	1835	Edward T. Sanford, TN	1923-1930	7	1865	1930
William Johnson, SC	1804-1834	30	1771	1834	Harlan F. Stone, NY	1925-1941	16	1872	1946
Henry B. Livingston, NY.	1806-1823	16	1757	1823	*Charles E. Hughes,* NY	1930-1941	11	1862	1948
Thomas Todd, KY	1807-1826	18	1765	1826	Owen J. Roberts, PA	1930-1945	15	1875	1955
Joseph Story, MA	1811-1845	33	1779	1845	Benjamin N. Cardozo, NY	1932-1938	6	1870	1938
Gabriel Duval, MD	1811-1835	22	1752	1844	Hugo L. Black, AL	1937-1971	34	1886	1971
Smith Thompson, NY	1823-1843	20	1768	1843	Stanley F. Reed, KY	1938-1957	19	1884	1980
Robert Trimble, KY	1826-1828	2	1777	1828	Felix Frankfurter, MA	1939-1962	23	1882	1965
John McLean, OH	1829-1861	32	1785	1861	William O. Douglas, CT	1939-1975	36	1898	1980
Henry Baldwin, PA	1830-1844	14	1780	1844	Frank Murphy, MI	1940-1949	9	1890	1949
James M. Wayne, GA	1835-1867	32	1790	1867	*Harlan F. Stone,* NY	1941-1946	5	1872	1946
Roger B. Taney, MD	1836-1864	28	1777	1864	James F. Byrnes, SC	1941-1942	1	1879	1972
Philip P. Barbour, VA	1836-1841	4	1783	1841	Robert H. Jackson, NY	1941-1954	12	1892	1954
John Catron, TN	1837-1865	28	1786	1865	Wiley B. Rutledge, IA	1943-1949	6	1894	1949
John McKinley, AL	1837-1852	15	1780	1852	Harold H. Burton, OH	1945-1958	13	1888	1964
Peter V. Daniel, VA	1841-1860	19	1784	1860	*Fred M. Vinson,* KY	1946-1953	7	1890	1953
Samuel Nelson, NY	1845-1872	27	1792	1873	Tom C. Clark, TX	1949-1967	18	1899	1977
Levi Woodbury, NH	1845-1851	5	1789	1851	Sherman Minton, IN	1949-1956	7	1890	1965
Robert C. Grier, PA	1846-1870	23	1794	1870	*Earl Warren,* CA	1953-1969	16	1891	1974
Benjamin R. Curtis, MA	1851-1857	6	1809	1874	John Marshall Harlan, NY	1955-1971	16	1899	1971
John A. Campbell, AL	1853-1861	8	1811	1889	William J. Brennan Jr, NJ	1956-1990	33	1906	1997
Nathan Clifford, ME	1858-1881	23	1803	1881	Charles E. Whittaker, MO	1957-1962	5	1901	1973
Noah H. Swayne, OH	1862-1881	18	1804	1884	Potter Stewart, OH	1958-1981	23	1915	1985
Samuel F. Miller, IA	1862-1890	28	1816	1890	Byron R. White, CO	1962-1993	31	1917	—
David Davis, IL	1862-1877	14	1815	1886	Arthur J. Goldberg, IL	1962-1965	3	1908	1990
Stephen J. Field, CA	1863-1897	34	1816	1899	Abe Fortas, TN	1965-1969	4	1910	1982
Salmon P. Chase, OH	1864-1873	8	1808	1873	Thurgood Marshall, NY	1967-1991	24	1908	1993
William Strong, PA	1870-1880	10	1808	1895	*Warren E. Burger,* VA	1969-1986	17	1907	1995
Joseph P. Bradley, NJ	1870-1892	21	1813	1892	Harry A. Blackmun, MN	1970-1994	24	1908	—
Ward Hunt, NY	1872-1882	9	1810	1886	Lewis F. Powell Jr, VA	1972-1987	15	1907	—
John M. Harlan, KY	1877-1911	34	1833	1911	William H. Rehnquist, AZ	1972-1986	14	1924	—
William B. Woods, GA	1880-1887	6	1824	1887	John Paul Stevens, IL	1975-		1920	—
Stanley Matthews, OH	1881-1889	7	1824	1889	Sandra Day O'Connor, AZ	1981-	—	1930	—
Horace Gray, MA	1881-1902	20	1828	1902	*William H. Rehnquist,* AZ	1986-	—	1924	—
Samuel Blatchford, NY	1882-1893	11	1820	1893	Antonin Scalia, VA.	1986-	—	1936	—
Lucius Q.C. Lamar, MS	1888-1893	5	1825	1893	Anthony M. Kennedy, CA	1988-	—	1936	—
Melville W. Fuller, IL	1888-1910	21	1833	1910	David H. Souter, NH	1990-	—	1939	—
David J. Brewer, KS	1889-1910	20	1837	1910	Clarence Thomas, VA	1991-	—	1948	—
Henry B. Brown, MI	1890-1906	15	1836	1913	Ruth Bader Ginsburg, DC	1993	—	1933	—
George Shiras Jr, PA	1892-1903	10	1832	1924	Stephen Breyer, MA	1994-	—	1938	—
Howell E. Jackson, TN	1893-1895	2	1832	1895					
Edward D. White, LA	1894-1910	16	1845	1921					
Rufus W. Peckham, NY	1895-1909	13	1838	1909					
Joseph McKenna, CA	1898-1925	26	1843	1926					
Oliver W. Holmes, MA	1902-1932	29	1841	1935					
William R. Day, OH	1903-1922	19	1849	1923					

(1) Chief justices in italics. (2) Rejected Dec. 15, 1795.

U.S. Courts of Appeals

(Salaries, $141,700. CJ means Chief Judge)

Federal Circuit — Glenn L. Archer Jr, CJ; Giles S. Rich, Wilson Cowen, Bryon G. Skelton, Daniel M. Friedman, Edward S. Smith, Pauline Newman, H. Robert Mayer, Paul R. Michel, S. Jay Plager, Alan D. Lourie, Raymond C. Clevenger III, Randall R. Rader, Alvin A. Schall, William C. Bryson, Merrick B. Garland; Clerk's Office, Washington, DC 20439.

District of Columbia —Harry T. Edwards, CJ; Patricia M. Wald, Laurence H. Silberman, Stephen F. Williams, Douglas Ginsburg, David B. Sentelle, Karen LeCraft Henderson, A. Raymond Randolph, Judith W. Rogers, David S. Tatel; Clerk's Office, Washington, DC 20001.

First Circuit (ME, MA, NH, RI, Puerto Rico) — Juan R. Torruella, CJ; Bruce M. Selya, Michael Boudin, Norman H. Stahl, Sandra Lynch; Clerk's Office, Boston, MA 02109.

Second Circuit (CT, NY, VT) — Ralph K. Winter, CJ; Jon O. Newman, Amalya Lyle Kearse, Roger J. Miner, John M. Walker Jr, Joseph M. McLaughlin, Dennis Jacobs, Pierre N. Leval, Guido Calabresi, José A. Cabranes, Fred I. Parker, Frank X. Altimari, Richard J. Cardamone, Wilfred Feinberg, J. Edward Lumbard, Thomas J. Meskill, James L. Oakes, Ellsworth A. Van Graafeiland; Clerk's Office, New York, NY 10007.

Third Circuit (DE, NJ, PA, Virgin Islands) — Dolores K. Sloviter, CJ; Edward R. Becker, Walter K. Stapleton, Carol Los Mansmann, Morton I. Greenberg, Anthony J. Scirica, Robert E. Cowen, Richard L. Nygaard, Samuel A. Alito Jr, Jane R. Roth, Timothy K. Lewis, Theodore A. McKee; Clerk's Office, Philadelphia, PA 19106.

Fourth Circuit (MD, NC, SC, VA, WV) — J. Harvie Wilkinson III, CJ; Donald Stuart Russell, H. Emory Widener Jr, Kenneth K. Hall, Francis D. Murnaghan Jr, Sam J. Ervin III, William W. Wilkins Jr, Paul V. Niemeyer, Clyde H. Hamilton, J. Michael Luttig, Karen J. Williams, M. Blane Michael, Diana G. Motz; Clerk's Office, Richmond, VA 23219.

Fifth Circuit (LA., MS, TX) — Henry A. Politz, CJ; Carolyn Dineen King, E. Grady Jolly, Patrick E. Higginbotham, W. Eugene Davis, Edith H. Jones, Jerry E. Smith, John M. Duhé Jr, Jacques L. Wiener Jr, Rhesa A. Barksdale, Emilio M. Garza, Harold R. DeMoss Jr, Fortunato P. Benavides, Carl E. Stewart, Robert M. Parker, James L. Dennis; Clerk's Office, New Orleans, LA 70130.

Sixth Circuit (KY, MI, OH, TN) — Boyce F. Martin Jr, CJ; Gilbert S. Merritt; Cornelia G. Kennedy, David A. Nelson, James L. Ryan, Danny J. Boggs, Alan E. Norris, Richard F. Suhrheinrich, Eugene E. Siler Jr, Alice M. Batchelder, Martha Craig Daughtrey, Karen Nelson Moore, R. Guy Cole, Eric Clay; Clerk's Office, Cincinnati, OH 45202.

Seventh Circuit (IL, IN, WI) — Richard A. Posner, CJ; Thomas E. Fairchild; Walter J. Cummings, Wilbur F. Pell Jr, William J. Bauer, Harlington Wood Jr, Richard D. Cudahy, Jesse E. Eschbach, John L. Coffey, Joel M. Flaum, Frank H. Easterbrook, Kenneth F. Ripple, Daniel A. Manion, Michael S. Kanne, Ilana D. Rovner, Diane P. Wood, Terence T. Evans; Clerk's Office, Chicago, IL 60604.

Eighth Circuit (AR, IA, MN, MO, NE, ND, SD) — Richard S. Arnold, CJ; Theodore McMillian, George G. Fagg, Pasco M. Bowman, Roger L. Wollman, C. Arlen Beam, James B. Loken, David R. Hansen, Morris S. Arnold, Diana E. Murphy; Clerk's Office, St. Louis, MO 63101.

Ninth Circuit (AK, AZ, CA, HI, ID, MT, NV, OR, WA, Guam, N. Mariana Islands) — Procter Hug Jr, CJ; James R. Browning, Melvin Brunetti, Ferdinand F. Fernandez, Betty B. Fletcher, Michael Daly Hawkins, Andrew J. Kleinfeld, Alex Kozinski, Thomas G. Nelson, Diarmuid F. O'Scannlain, Harry Pregerson, Stephen R. Reinhardt, Pamela Ann Rymer,

Mary M. Schroeder, A. Wallace Tashima, Sidney R. Thomas, David R. Thompson, Stephen S. Trott; Clerk's Office, San Francisco, CA 94119.

Tenth Circuit (CO, KS, NM, OK, UT, WY) — Stephanie K. Seymour, CJ; John C. Porfilio, Stephen H. Anderson, Deanell R. Tacha, Bobby R. Baldock, Wade Brorby, David M. Ebel, Paul J. Kelly, Robert H. Henry, Mary Beck Briscoe, Carlos Lucero, Michael R. Murphy; Clerk's Office, Denver, CO 80257.

Eleventh Circuit (AL, FL, GA)— Joseph W. Hatchett, CJ; Gerald B. Tjoflat, Phyllis A. Kravitch, R. Lanier Anderson III, J. L. Edmondson, Emmett R. Cox, Stanley F. Birch Jr, Joel F. Dubina, Susan H. Black, Ed Carnes, Rosemary Barkett, Frank M. Hull; Clerk's Office, Atlanta GA 30303.

U.S. District Courts

(Salaries, $133,600. CJ means Chief Judge)

Alabama — Northern: Sam C. Pointer Jr, CJ; U. W. Clemon, Edwin L. Nelson, Sharon Lovelace Blackburn, C. Lynwood Smith Jr; Clerk's Office, Birmingham 35203. **Middle:** Myron H. Thompson, CJ; W. Harold Albritton, Ira DeMent; Clerk's Office, Montgomery 36101. **Southern:** Charles R. Butler Jr, CJ; A.T. Howard, R.W. Vollmer, W.B. Hand, T.V. Pittman; Clerk's Office, Mobile 36602.

Alaska — James K. Singleton, CJ; H. Russel Holland, John W. Sedwick; Clerk's Office, Anchorage 99513.

Arizona — Robert C. Broomfield, CJ; William D. Browning, Paul G. Rosenblatt, Roger G. Strand, Stephen M. McNamee, John M. Roll, Roslyn Silver, Frank R. Zappata; Clerk's Office, Phoenix 85025.

Arkansas — Eastern: Stephen M. Reasoner, CJ; George Howard Jr, Susan Webber Wright, William R. Wilson Jr, James M. Moody; Clerk's Office, Little Rock 72201-3325. **Western:** Jimm Larry Hendren, CJ; H. Franklin Waters, Harry F. Barnes; Clerk's Office, Fort Smith 72902.

California — Northern: Thelton E. Henderson, CJ; Stanley A. Weigel, Samuel Conti, Spencer Williams, William H. Orrick Jr, William A. Ingram, William W Schwarzer, Marilyn H. Patel, Charles A. Legge, D. Lowell Jensen, Fern M. Smith, Vaughn R. Walker, James Ware, Saundra Brown Armstrong, Ronald M. Whyte, Claudia Wilken, Maxine M. Chesney, Susan Illston; Clerk's Office, San Francisco 94102. **Eastern:** William B. Shubb, CJ; Lawrence K. Karlton, CJ Emeritus; David F. Levi, Oliver W. Wanger, Garland E. Burrell; Clerk's Office, Sacramento 95814. **Central:** Wm. Matthew Byrne Jr, CJ; Manuel L. Real, Mariana R. Pfaelzer, Terry J. Hatter Jr, Consuelo B. Marshall, Alicemarie H. Stotler, William J. Rea, James M. Ideman, William D. Keller, Stephen V. Wilson, J. Spencer Letts, Dickran M. Tevrizian, John G. Davies, Ronald S. W. Lew, Gary L. Taylor, Lourdes G. Baird, Linda H. McLaughlin, Audrey B. Collins, Richard A. Paez, Robert J. Timlin, George H. King, Kim M. Wardlaw, Dean D. Pregerson; Clerk's Office, Los Angeles 90012. **Southern:** Judith N. Keep, CJ; Rudi M. Brewster, Marilyn L. Huff, Irma E. Gonzalez, Napoleon A. Jones Jr, Barry T. Moskowitz, Jeffrey T. Miller, Edward J. Schwartz, Howard B. Turrentine, Gordon Thompson Jr, Leland C. Nielsen, William B. Enright, John S. Rhoades, Earl B. Gilliam; Clerk's Office, San Diego 92101.

Colorado — Richard P. Matsch, CJ; Zita L. Weinshienk, Lewis T. Babcock, Edward W. Nottingham, Daniel B. Sparr, Wiley Y. Daniel, Miller D. Walker; Clerk's Office, Denver 80294.

Connecticut — Peter C. Dorsey, CJ; Alfred V. Covello, Robert N. Chatigny, Dominic J. Squatrito, Alvin W. Thompson, Janet Bond Arterton; Clerk's Office, New Haven 06510.

Delaware — Joseph J. Farnan Jr, CJ; Sue L. Robinson, Roderick R. McKelvie; Clerk's Office, Wilmington 19801.

District of Columbia — Norma Holloway Johnson; John Garrett Penn, Thomas P. Jackson, Thomas F. Hogan, Stanley Sporkin, Royce C. Lamberth, Gladys Kessler, Paul

L. Friedman, Ricardo M. Urbina, Emmet G. Sullivan, James Robertson, Colleen Kollar-Kotelly; Clerk's Office, Washington DC 20001.

Florida — Northern: C. Roger Vinson CJ; Lacey A. Collier, Robert L. Hinkle; Clerk's Office, Tallahassee 32301. **Middle:** Elizabeth A. Kovachevich, CJ; Wm. Terrell Hodges, George Kendall Sharp, Patricia C. Fawsett, Harvey E. Schlesinger, Ralph W. Nimmons Jr, Anne C. Conway, Steven D. Merryday, Susan C. Bucklew, Henry L. Adams Jr; Clerk's Office, Jacksonville 32201. **Southern:** Edward B. Davis, CJ; Lenore C. Nesbitt, Stanley Marcus, William J. Zloch, Kenneth L. Ryskamp, Federico A. Moreno, Shelby Highsmith, Donald L. Graham, K. Michael Moore, Ursula Ungaro-Benages, Wilkie D. Ferguson Jr, Daniel T. K. Hurley, Joan A. Lenard, Donald M. Middlebrooks, Alan S. Gold; Clerk's Office, Miami 33128.

Georgia — Northern: G. Ernest Tidwell, CJ; Harold L. Murphy, Orinda D. Evans, J. Owen Forrester, Jack T. Camp, Julie E. Carnes, Clarence Cooper, Willis B. Hunt Jr, Thomas W. Thrash, Jr; Clerk's Office, Atlanta 30303. **Middle:** Duross Fitzpatrick, CJ; J. Robert Elliott, W. Louis Sands, Hugh Lawson; Clerk's Office, Macon 31202. **Southern:** Dudley H. Bowen Jr, CJ; B. Avant Edenfield, William T. Moore Jr; Clerk's Office, Savannah 31412.

Hawaii — Alan C. Kay, CJ; David A. Ezra, Helen Gillmor; Clerk's Office, Honolulu 96850.

Idaho — Edward J. Lodge, CJ; B. Lynn Winmill; Clerk's Office, Boise 83724.

Illinois — Northern: Marvin E. Aspen, CJ; Charles P. Kocoras, Paul E. Plunkett, Charles R. Norgle Sr, James F. Holderman, Ann C. Williams, Harry D. Leinenweber, James B. Zagel, James H. Alesia, Suzanne B. Conlon, George M. Marovich, George W. Lindberg, Wayne R. Andersen, Philip G. Reinhard, Ruben Castillo, Blanche M. Manning, David H. Coar, Robert W. Gettleman, Elaine E. Bucklo, Joan B. Gottschall; Clerk's Office, Chicago 60604. **Central:** Michael M. Mihm, CJ; Richard Mills, Joe Billy McDade; Clerk's Office, Springfield 62701. **Southern:** J. Phil Gilbert, CJ; William D. Stiehl, Paul E. Riley, James L. Foreman, William L. Beatty; Clerk's Office, East St. Louis 62202.

Indiana — Northern: William C. Lee, CJ; Allen Sharp, James T. Moody, Robert L. Miller Jr, Rudy Lozano; Clerk's Office, South Bend 46601. **Southern:** Sarah E. Barker, CJ; S. Hugh Dillin, Larry J. McKinney, John Daniel Tinder, David F. Hamilton; Clerk's Office, Indianapolis 46204.

Iowa — Northern: Michael J. Melloy, CJ; Mark W. Bennett; Clerk's Office, Cedar Rapids 52401. **Southern:** Charles R. Wolle, CJ; Clerk's Office, Des Moines 50309.

Kansas — G. Thomas Van Bebber, CJ; John W. Lungstrum, Monti L. Belot, Kathryn H. Vratil, John T. Marten; Clerk's Office, Wichita 67202.

Kentucky — Eastern: William Bertelsman, CJ; Henry R. Wilhoit Jr, Karl S. Forester, Joseph M. Hood, Jennifer B. Coffman; Clerk's Office, Lexington 40596-3074. **Western:** Charles R. Simpson III, CJ; John G. Heyburn II, Jennifer B. Coffman, Thomas B. Russell, Joseph P. McKinley Jr; Clerk's Office, Louisville 40202.

Louisiana — Eastern: Morley L. Sear, CJ; A. J. McNamara, Martin L. C. Feldman, Edith Brown Clement, Ginger Berrigan, Stanwood R. Duval Jr, Eldon E. Fallon, Sarah S. Vance, Mary Ann Viel Lemmo, G. Thomas Porteous Jr; Clerk's Office, New Orleans 70130. **Middle:** John V. Parker, CJ; Frank J. Polozola; Clerk's Office, Baton Rouge 70801. **Western:** F. A. Little Jr, CJ; Rebecca F. Doherty, Richard T. Haik Sr, James T. Trimble Jr, Donald E. Walter, Tucker L. Melançon; Clerk's Office, Shreveport 71101.

Maine — D. Brock Hornby, CJ; Gene Carter, Morton A. Brody; Clerk's Office, Portland 04101.

Maryland — J. Frederick Motz, CJ; Frederic N. Smalkin, William M. Nickerson, Marvin J. Garbis, Benson Everett Legg, Catherine C. Blake, Andre M. Davis, Deborah K. Chasanow, Peter J. Messitte, Alexander Williams Jr; Clerk's Office, Baltimore 21201.

Massachusetts — Joseph L. Tauro, CJ; Robert E. Keeton, William G. Young, Mark L. Wolf, Douglas P. Woodlock, Edward F. Harrington, Nathaniel M. Gorton, Richard G. Stearns, Reginald C. Lindsay, Patti B. Saris, Nancy Gertner, George A. O'Toole, Nathaniel M. Gorton, Michael A. Ponsor; Clerk's Office, Boston 02109.

Michigan — Eastern: Anna Diggs Taylor, CJ; Avern Cohn, Lawrence P. Zatkoff, Patrick J. Duggan, Bernard A. Friedman, Paul V. Gadola, Gerald E. Rosen, Robert H. Cleland, Nancy G. Edmunds, Denise Page-Hood, Paul D. Borman, John Corbett O'Meara; Clerk's Office, Detroit 48226. **Western:** Richard A. Enslen, CJ; Robert H. Bell, David W. McKeague, Gordon J. Quist; Clerk's Office, Grand Rapids 49503.

Minnesota — Paul A. Magnuson, CJ; James M. Rosenbaum, David S. Doty, Richard H. Kyle, Michael J. Davis, John R. Tunheim, Ann D. Montgomery; Clerk's Office, St. Paul 55101.

Mississippi — Northern: L. T. Senter Jr, CJ; Neal Biggers, Glen H. Davidson; Clerk's Office, Oxford 38655. **Southern:** Tom S. Lee, CJ; William H. Barbour Jr, Henry T. Wingate, Walter J. Gex III, Charles W. Pickering Sr, David Bramlette; Clerk's Office, Jackson 39201.

Missouri — Eastern: Jean C. Hamilton, CJ; Donald J. Stohr, Carol E. Jackson, Charles A. Shaw, Catherine D. Perry, E. Richard Webber; Clerk's Office, St. Louis 63101. **Western:** D. Brook Bartlett, CJ; Dean Whipple, Fernando J. Gaitan Jr, Ortrie D. Smith, Gary A. Fenner, Nanette Laughery; Clerk's Office, Kansas City 64106.

Montana — Jack D. Shanstrom, CJ; Charles C. Lovell, Donald W. Molloy; Clerk's Office, Billings 59101.

Nebraska — William G. Cambridge, CJ; Richard G. Kopf, Thomas M. Shanahan, Joseph F. Batillon; Clerk's Office, Omaha 68101.

Nevada — Lloyd D. George, CJ; Howard D. McKibben, Philip M. Pro, David W. Hagen; Clerk's Office, Las Vegas 89101, Reno 89501.

New Hampshire — Joseph A. DiClerico, CJ; Paul J. Barbadoro, Steven J. McAuliffe; Clerk's Office, Concord 03301.

New Jersey — Anne E. Thompson, CJ; John W. Bissell, Maryanne Trump Barry, Joseph H. Rodriguez, Garrett E. Brown Jr, Alfred J. Lechner Jr, Nicholas H. Politan, Alfred M. Wolin, John C. Lifland, William G. Bassler, Mary Little Parell, Joseph E. Irenas, Jerome B. Simandle, William H. Walls, Stephen M. Orlofsky, Joseph A. Greenaway Jr; Clerk's Office, Newark 07101.

New Mexico — John E. Conway, CJ; James A. Parker, C. Leroy Hansen, Martha Vazquez, Bruce D. Black; Clerk's Office, Albuquerque 87103.

New York — Northern: Thomas J. McAvoy, CJ; Frederick J. Scullin Jr, Rosemary S. Pooler, Lawrence E. Kahn; Clerk's Office, Syracuse 13261-7367. **Eastern:** Charles P. Sifton, CJ; Thomas C. Platt Jr, Raymond J. Dearie, Edward R. Korman, Reena Raggi, Arthur D. Spatt, Carol Bagley Amon, Sterling Johnson Jr, Denis R. Hurley, David G. Trager, Joanna Seybert, Allyne Ross, John Gleeson, Fredric Block; Clerk's Office, Brooklyn 11201. **Southern:** Thomas P. Griesa, CJ; Charles L. Brieant, Kevin Thomas Duffy, John E. Sprizzo, John F. Keenan, Peter K. Leisure, Miriam G. Cedarbaum, Lewis A. Kaplan, Michael B. Mukasey, Kimba Wood, Robert P. Patterson Jr, Lawrence McKenna, John S. Martin Jr, Loretta A. Preska, Sonia Sotomayer, Harold Baer Jr, Deborah A. Batts, Denny Chin, Denise L. Cote, John Koeltl, Allen G. Schwartz, Barrington D. Parker Jr, Shira A. Scheindlin, Sidney H. Stein, Jed S. Rakoff, Barbara S. Jones; Clerk's Office New York City 10007. **Western:** David G. Larimer, CJ; Richard J. Arcara, William M Skretny, John T. Curtin, John T. Elfvin, Michael A. Telesca; Clerk's Office, Buffalo 14202.

(continued)

North Carolina — Eastern: Terrence W. Boyle, CJ; James C. Fox, Malcolm J. Howard; Clerk's Office, Raleigh 27611. **Middle:** Frank W. Bullock, CJ; N. Carlton Tilley Jr, William L. Osteen Sr, James A. Beaty Jr; Clerk's Office, Greensboro 27402. **Western:** Richard L. Voorhees, CJ; Graham C. Mullen, Lacy H. Thornburg; Clerk's Office, Asheville 28801.

North Dakota — Rodney S. Webb, CJ; Patrick A. Conmy; Judge; Clerk's Office, Bismarck 58502.

Ohio — Northern: George W. White, CJ; Paul R. Matia, Lesley Brooks Wells, James G. Carr, Solomon Oliver Jr, David A. Katz, Kathleen McDonald O'Malley, Peter C. Economus, Donald C. Nugent, Patricia A. Gaughan; Clerk's Office, Cleveland 44114. **Southern:** Walter Herbert Rice, CJ; John D. Holschuh, Herman J. Weber, James L. Graham, George C. Smith, S. Arthur Spiegel, Sandra S. Beckwith, Edmund A. Sargus Jr, Susan J. Dlott, Joseph P. Kinneary; Clerk's Office, Columbus 43215.

Oklahoma — Northern: Terry C. Kern, CJ; Sven Erik Holmes, Michael Burrage; Clerk's Office, Tulsa 74103. **Eastern:** Michael Burrage CJ; Frank H. Seay; Clerk's Office, Muskogee 74401. **Western:** David L. Russell, CJ; Ralph G. Thompson, Wayne E. Alley, Robin J. Cauthron, Tim Leonard, Michael Burrage, Vicki Miles-LaGrange; Clerk's Office, Oklahoma City 73102.

Oregon — Michael R. Hogan, CJ; Malcolm M. Marsh, Robert E. Jones, Ancer L. Haggerty; Clerk's Office, Portland 97204.

Pennsylvania — Eastern: Edward N. Cahn, CJ; Norma L. Shapiro, James T. Giles, Robert F. Kelly, Franklin S. Van Antwerpen, Robert S. Gawthrop III, Lowell A. Reed Jr, Jan E. Dubois, Herbert J. Hutton, Jay C. Waldman, Ronald L. Buckwalter, Stewart Dalzell, William H. Yohn Jr, Harvey Bartle III, John R. Padova, J. Curtis Joyner, Eduardo C. Robreno, Anita B. Brody, Marjorie O. Rendell; Clerk's Office, Philadelphia 19106. **Middle:** Sylvia H. Rambo, CJ; James F. McClure Jr, Thomas I. Vanaskie; Clerk's Office, Scranton 18501. **Western:** Donald E. Ziegler; CJ; William L. Standish, D. Brooks Smith, Donald J. Lee, Donetta W. Ambrose, Gary L. Lancaster, Robert J. Cindrich, Sean J. McLaughlin; Clerk's Office, Pittsburgh 15230.

Rhode Island — Ronald R. Lagueux, CJ; Ernest C. Torres, Mary M. Lisi; Clerk's Office, Providence 02903.

South Carolina — C. Weston Houck, CJ; G. Ross Anderson Jr, Joseph F. Anderson Jr, David C. Norton, Dennis W. Shedd, Henry M. Herlong Jr, William B. Traxler Jr, Cameron McGowan Currie, Patrick Michael Duffy; Clerk's Office, Columbia 29201.

South Dakota — Richard H. Battey, CJ; Lawrence L. Piersol, Charles B. Kornmann; Clerk's Office, Sioux Falls 57104.

Tennessee — Eastern: James H. Jarvis, CJ; Thomas G. Hull, R. Allan Edgar, R. Leon Jordan, Curtis L. Collier; Clerk's Office, Knoxville 37901. **Middle:** John T. Nixon, CJ; Thomas A. Higgins, Robert L. Echols, Todd J. Campbell; Clerk's Office, Nashville 37203. **Western:** Julia S. Gibbons, CJ; James D. Todd, Jerome Turner, John Phipps McCalla, Bernice B. Donald; Clerk's Office, Memphis 38103.

Texas — Northern: Jerry Buchmeyer, CJ; Mary Lou Robinson, A. Joe Fish, Robert B. Maloney, Sidney A. Fitzwater, Samuel R. Cummings, John H. McBryde, Jorge A. Solis, Terry Means, Joe Kendall; Clerk's Office, Dallas 75242. **Southern:** George P. Kazen, CJ; Filemon B. Vela, Hayden W. Head Jr, Ricardo H. Hinojosa, Lynn N. Hughes, David Hittner, Kenneth M. Hoyt, Sim Lake, Melinda Harmon, John D. Rainey, Samuel B. Kent, Ewing Werlein Jr, Lee H. Rosenthal, Janis Graham Jack, Vanessa D. Gilmore, Nancy F. Atlas; Clerk's Office, Houston 77208. **Eastern:** Richard A. Schell, CJ; William Wayne Justice, Howell Cobb, Paul N. Brown, John Hannah Jr, David Folsom, Thad Heartfield, Joe J. Fisher; Clerk's Office, Tyler 75702. **Western:** Harry Lee Hudspeth, CJ; David Briones, Hipolito F. Garcia, Edward C. Prado, Fred

Biery, Orlando L. Garcia, James R. Nowlin, Sam Sparks, Walter S. Smith Jr, W. Royal Furgeson; Clerk's Office, San Antonio 78206.

Utah —David Sam, CJ; Dee Benson, Tena Campbell, J. Thomas Greene, Bruce Jenkins, David K. Winder; Clerk's Office, Salt Lake City 84101.

Vermont — J. Garvan Murtha, CJ, William K. Sessions III; Clerk's Office, Burlington 05402.

Virginia — Eastern: James C. Cacheris, CJ; Claude M. Hilton, James R. Spencer, Thomas S. Ellis III, Rebecca Beach Smith, Henry Coke Morgan Jr, Robert E. Payne, Raymond A. Jackson, Leonie M. Brinkema; Clerk's Office, Alexandria 22314. **Western:** Samuel G. Wilson, CJ; James P. Jones, James C. Turk; Clerk's Office, Roanoke 24006.

Washington — Eastern: Wm. Fremming Nielsen, CJ; Fred Van Sickle, Robert H. Whaley; Clerk's Office, Spokane 99210. **Western:** John C. Coughenour, CJ; Barbara Jacobs Rothstein, Carolyn R. Dimmick, Robert J. Bryan, William L. Dwyer, Thomas S. Zilly, Franklin D. Burgess; Clerk's Office, Seattle 98104.

West Virginia — Northern: Frederick P. Stamp Jr, CJ; Irene M. Keeley, W. Craig Broadwater; Clerk's Office, Wheeling 26003. **Southern:** Charles H. Haden II, CJ; John T. Copenhaver Jr, David A. Faber, Joseph R. Goodwin, Robert C. Chambers; Clerk's Office, Charleston 25329.

Wisconsin — Eastern: J. P. Stadtmueller, CJ; Rudolph T. Randa, Charles N. Clevert; Clerk's Office, Milwaukee 53202. **Western:** John C. Shabaz; CJ; Barbara B. Crabb, Clerk's Office, Madison 53701.

Wyoming — Alan B. Johnson, CJ; Clarence A. Brimmer, William F. Downes; Clerk's Office, Cheyenne 82001.

U.S. Territorial District Courts

Guam — John S. Unpingco, CJ; Clerk's Office, Agana 96910.

Northern Mariana Islands — Alex R. Munson, CJ; Clerk's Office, Saipan MP 96950.

Puerto Rico — Carmen Consuelo Cerezo, CJ; Juan M. Perez-Gimenez, Hector M. Laffitte, Jose Antonio Fuste, Salvador E. Casellas, Daniel R. Dominguez; Clerk's Office, Hato Rex 00918.

Virgin Islands — Thomas K. Moore, CJ; Raymond L. Finch; Clerk's Office, St. Croix 00820.

U.S. Court of International Trade
New York, NY 10278-0001 (Salaries, $133,600)

Chief Judge — Gregory W. Carman.

Judges — Jane A. Restani, Thomas J. Aquilino Jr, Nicholas Tsoucalas, R. Kenton Musgrave, Richard W. Goldberg, Donald C. Pogue, Evan J. Wallach.

U.S. Court of Federal Claims
Washington, DC 20005 (Salaries, $133,600)

Chief Judge — Loren A. Smith.

Judges — James F. Merow, John P. Wiese, Robert J. Yock, Lawrence S. Margolis, Christine Odell Cook Miller, Moody R. Tidwell 3d, Marian Blank Horn, Eric G. Bruggink, Bohdan A. Futey, Roger B. Andewelt, James T. Turner, Robert H. Hodges Jr, Diane Gilbert Weinstein.

U.S. Tax Court
Washington, DC 20217 (Salaries, $133,600)

Chief Judge — Mary Ann Cohen

Judges — Renato Beghe, Herbert L. Chabot, John O. Colvin, Joel Gerber, Julian I. Jacobs, Carolyn Miller Parr, Robert P. Ruwe, James S. Halpern, Carolyn P. Chiechi, David Laro, Stephen J. Swift, Thomas B. Wells, Laurence J. Whalen, Maurice B. Foley, Juan F. Vasquez, Joseph H. Gale.

U.S. Court of Veterans Appeals
Washington, D.C. 20004 (Salaries, $133,600)

Chief Judge — Frank Q. Nebeker.

Judges — Kenneth B. Kramer, John J. Farley 3d, Ronald M. Holdaway, Donald L. Ivers, Jonathan R. Steinberg.

STATE AND LOCAL GOVERNMENT

Mayors of Selected U.S. Cities

As of mid-Oct. 1997

D, Democrat; R, Republican; N-P, Non-Partisan; I, Independent; Prog. Coal., Progressive Coalition

City	Name	Next Election
Abilene, TX	Gary McCaleb, N-P	1999, May
Akron, OH	Donald L. Plusquellic, D.	1999, Nov.
Alameda, CA	Ralph J. Appezzato, N-P	1998, Nov.
Albany, GA	Thomas Coleman, D	1997, Nov.
Albany, NY	Gerald D. Jennings, D	1997, Nov.
Albuquerque, NM.	Martin Chavez, D	1997, Oct.
Alexandria, LA.	Edward Randolph Jr., D.	1998, Oct.
Alexandria, VA.	Kerry J. Donley, D	1999, May
Alhambra, CA	Paul Talbot, N-P	(¹)
Allentown, PA	William Heydt, R	1997, Nov.
Amarillo, TX	Kel Seliger, N-P	1999, May
Ames, IA.	Larry R. Curtis, N-P	1997, Nov.
Anaheim, CA.	Tom Daly, N-P	1998, Nov.
Anchorage, AK	Rick Mystrom, R	2000, Apr.
Anderson, IN	J. Mark Lawler, D	1999, Nov.
Anderson, SC	Darwin Wright, D.	1998, June
Ann Arbor, MI	Ingrid B. Sheldon, R	1998, Nov.
Annapolis, MD.	Alfred A. Hopkins, D	1997, Nov.
Appleton, WI	Timothy M. Hanna, N-P	2000, Apr.
Arcadia, CA.	Robert C. Harbicht, N-P	1998, Apr.
Arlington, MA.	Charles Lyons, D	1998, Nov.
Arlington, TX.	Elzie Odom, N-P	1999, May
Arlington Hts., IL	Arlene J. Mulder, N-P	2001, Apr.
Arvada, CO.	Robert G. Frie, N-P	1999, Nov.
Asheville, NC.	Russell Martin, N-P	1997, Nov.
Athens, GA.	Gwenn O'Looney, D	1998, Nov.
Atlanta, GA.	Bill Campbell, D	1997, Nov.
Atlantic City, NJ	James Whelan, N-P	1998, June
Augusta, GA.	Larry Sconyers, N-P	1999, Nov.
Augusta, ME.	John C. Bridge, R	1998, Nov.
Aurora, CO	Paul E. Tauer, N-P	1999, Nov.
Aurora, IL	David L. Stover, N-P	2001, Apr.
Austin, TX.	Kirk Watson, N-P.	2001, May
Bakersfield, CA	Bob Price, N-P	2000, Mar.
Baldwin Park, CA.	Bette Lowes, N-P	1999, Mar.
Baltimore, MD	Kurt Schmoke, D	1999, Nov.
Baton Rouge, LA.	Tom E. McHugh, D	1997, Nov.
Battle Creek, MI.	Ted Dearing, N-P	1997, Nov.²
Bayonne, NJ	Leonard P. Kiczek, N-P	1998, May
Baytown, TX.	Pete C. Alfaro, N-P	1998, May
Beaumont, TX.	David W. Moore, N-P	1998, May
Belleville, IL.	Mark A. Kern, N-P	2001, Apr.
Bellevue, WA.	Ron Smith, I	1998, Nov.
Bellflower, CA.	Ruth Gilson, N-P.	1998, Mar.
Bellingham, WA.	Mark Asmundson, N-P	1999, Nov.
Berkeley, CA.	Shirley Dean, N-P	1998, Dec.
Bethlehem, PA.	Kenneth R. Smith, R	1997, Nov.
Beverly Hills, CA	Meralee Goldman, N-P	1998, Apr.
Billings, MT.	Charles F. Tooley, N-P	1997, Nov.
Biloxi, MS	A. J. Holloway, Jr., R	2001, June
Binghamton, NY	Richard A. Bucci, R	1997, Nov.
Birmingham, AL.	Richard Arrington Jr., D	1999, Oct.
Bismarck, ND	Bill Sorensen, R	1998, June
Bloomfield, NJ	James P. Norton, R	1998, Nov.
Bloomington, IL.	Judy Markowitz, N-P	2001, Apr.
Bloomington, IN.	John Fernandez, D	1999, Nov.
Bloomington, MN.	Coral Houle, N-P	1997, Nov.
Boca Raton, FL.	Carol G. Hanson, N-P	1999, Mar.
Boise, ID.	Brent Coles, N-P	1997, Nov.
Bossier City, LA.	George Dement, N-P	2001, Apr.
Boston, MA	Thomas M. Menino, D	1997, Nov.
Boulder, CO	Leslie L. Durgin, N-P	1997, Nov.
Bridgeport, CT.	Joseph Ganim, D.	1997, Nov.
Bristol, CT.	Frank N. Nicastro, D	1997, Nov.
Brockton, MA.	John T. Yunits Jr., D	1997, Nov.
Broken Arrow, OK.	Jim Reynolds, N-P	1999, Apr.
Brooklyn Park, MN.	Grace Arbogast, N-P	1998, Nov.
Brownsville, TX.	Henry Gonzalez, N-P	1999, May
Bryan, TX.	Lonnie Stabler, N-P	1999, May
Buena Park, CA.	Arthur C. Brown, N-P	1997, Dec.
Buffalo, NY	Anthony M. Masiello, D	1997, Nov.
Burbank, CA.	Bob Kramer, N-P	1998, May
Burlington, VT.	Peter Clavelle, Prog. Coal.	1999, Mar.
Calumet City, IL.	Gerome P. Genova, I	2001, Apr.
Camarillo, CA.	Michael D. Morgan, N-P	1998, Dec.
Cambridge, MA.	Sheila Doyle Russell, D	1998, Jan.
Camden, NJ	Arnold Webster, D	1997, Nov.
Canton, OH.	Richard Watkins, R	1999, Nov.
Cape Coral, FL	Roger G. Butler, N-P	2000, Nov.
Carlsbad, CA	Claude Lewis, N-P	1998, Nov.
Carson, CA.	Peter D. Fajardo, N-P	1998, May.
Carson City, NV.	Ray Masayko, N-P	2000, Nov.
Casper, WY.	Kathleen Dixon, N-P	1998, Jan.
Cedar Rapids, IA	Lee R. Clancey, N-P	1997, Nov.
Champaign, IL	Dan McCollum, N-P	1999, Apr.
Chandler, AZ	Jay Tibshraeny, N-P	1998, Mar.
Charleston, SC.	Joseph P. Riley Jr., D	1999, Nov.
Charleston, WV	G. Kemp Melton, D	1999, Apr.
Charlotte, NC	Patrick McCrory, R	1997, Nov.
Charlottesville, VA	Kay Slaughter, D	1998, May
Chattanooga, TN	Jon Kinsey, N-P	2001, Mar.
Chesapeake, VA.	William E. Ward, N-P	2000, May
Chester, PA	Aaron Wilson, R	1999, Nov.
Cheyenne, WY.	Leo Pando, N-P	1997, Nov.
Chicago, IL.	Richard M. Daley, D	1999, Apr.
Chicopee, MA.	Richard J. Kos, D	1999, Nov.
Chino, CA.	Eunice M. Ulloa, R	2000, Nov.
Chula Vista, CA	Shirley Horton, I	1998, Jun.
Cicero, IL.	Betty Loren-Maltese, R	2001, Apr.
Cincinnati, OH	Roxanne Qualls, D.	1999, Nov.
Clarksville, TN	Donald W. Trotter, N-P	1998, Nov.
Clearwater, FL	Rita Garvey, N-P	2000, Apr.
Cleveland, OH	Michael R. White, D	1997, Nov.
Cleveland Hts., OH.	Carol Edwards, N-P	1998, Jan.
Clinton, IA	La Metta Wynn, N-P	1999, Nov.
Clifton, NJ	James Anzaldi, R	1998, May
Colorado Spgs., CO	Mary Lou Makepeace, R	1999, Apr.
Columbia, MO	Darwin Hindman, N-P	1998, Apr.
Columbia, SC.	Robert D. Coble, N-P	1998, Apr.
Columbus, GA.	Bobby Peters, D.	1998, Nov.
Columbus, OH.	Gregory S. Lashutka, R	1999, Nov.
Compton, CA.	Omar Bradley, N-P	2001, Apr.
Concord, CA	Bill McManigal, N-P	1997, Nov.³
Concord, NH	William Veroneau, N-P	1997, Nov.
Coon Rapids, MN.	William Thompson, N-P	1997, Nov.
Coral Gables, FL	Raul Valdes-Fauli, N-P.	1999, Apr.
Coral Springs, FL	John Sommerer, N-P	1998, Mar.
Corona, CA.	Karen Stein, N-P	1997, Dec.
Corpus Christi, TX	Loyd Neal, N-P	1999, Apr.
Costa Mesa, CA.	Peter Buffa, N-P	1999, Nov.
Council Bluffs, IA	Tom Hanafan, N-P	1997, Nov.
Covington, KY	Denny Bowman, D	1999, Nov.
Cranston, RI.	Michael A. Traficante, R	1998, Nov.
Cuyahoga Falls, OH	Donald L. Robart, R	1997, Nov.
Dallas, TX	Ronald Kirk, N-P	1998, June
Daly City, CA	Carol L. Klatt, N-P	1997, Nov.
Danbury, CT.	Gene Eriquez, D	1997, Nov.
Danville, VA.	E. Linwood Wright, N-P.	1998, July
Davenport, IA.	Patrick J. Gibbs, R	1997, Nov.
Davis, CA.	Lois Wolk, N-P	1998, Apr.
Dayton, OH	Michael R. Turner, N-P	1997, Nov.
Daytona Beach, FL.	Baron H. Asher, N-P	1997, Oct.
Dearborn , MI.	Michael Guido, N-P	1997, Nov.
Dearborn Hts., MI.	Ruth A. Canfield, N-P	1997, Nov.
Decatur, IL.	Terry M. Howley, N-P	1999, May
Delray Beach, FL	Jay Alperin, N-P	1998, Mar.
Denton, TX.	Jack Miller, N-P	1998, May
Denver, CO	Wellington Webb, N-P	1999, May
Des Moines, IA.	Robert D. Ray, N-P	1997, Nov.
Des Plaines, IL.	Paul Jung, N-P.	2001, Apr.
Detroit, MI	Dennis W. Archer, D.	1997, Nov.
Dothan, AL.	Chester L. Sowell III, N-P	2001, July
Dover, DE	James L. Hutchinson, N-P	1998, Apr.
Downey, CA.	Barbara Riley, N-P	(⁴)
Dubuque, IA.	Terrance M. Duggan, N-P	1997, Nov.
Duluth, MN.	Gary L. Doty, N-P.	1999, Nov.
Durham, NC	Sylvia S. Kerckhoff, N-P..	1997, Nov.
East Hartford, CT.	Robert DeCrescenzo, D	1997, Nov.
East Lansing, MI.	Douglas B. Jester, N-P	1997, Nov.
East Orange, NJ.	Cardell Cooper, D	1997, Nov.
Edison, NJ	George Spadoro, D	1997, Nov.
Edmond, OK	Robert Rudkin, N-P	1999, Apr.
El Cajon, CA	Joan Shoemaker, N-P	1998, Nov.
Elgin, IL	Kevin Kelly, N-P	1999, Apr.
Elizabeth, NJ	J. C. Bollwage, D	2000, Mar.
Elkhart, IN	James P. Perron, D	1999, Nov.
El Monte, CA	Patricia Wallach, D.	1999, Mar.
El Paso, TX	Carlos M. Ramirez, N-P	1999, May
Elyria, OH	Michael B. Keys, D.	1999, Nov.
Enfield, CT.	Mary Lou Strom, R	1997, Nov.
Enid, OK	Michael Cooper, N-P	1999, Mar.
Erie, PA	Joyce Savocchio, D	1997, Nov.
Escondido, CA	Sid Hollins, N-P	1998, Nov.
Euclid, OH	Paul Oyaski, D	1999, Nov.
Eugene, OR	James D. Torrey, N-P.	2000, Nov.
Evanston, IL.	Lorraine Morton, N-P	2001, Apr.

(continued)

City	Name	Next Election
Evansville, IN	Frank F. McDonald II, D.	1999, Nov.
Everett, WA.	Edward D. Hansen, N-P.	1997, Nov.
Fairbanks, AK	James C. Hayes, R	1998, Oct.
Fairfield, CA	Chuck Hamond, N-P	1997, Nov.
Fairfield, CT	Paul A. Audley, R.	1997, Nov.
Fall River, MA	Edward Lambert Jr., D.	1997, Nov.
Fargo, ND	Bruce Furness, N-P	1998, Apr.
Farmington Hills, MI	Aldo Vagnozzi, N-P	1997, Nov.
Fayetteville, NC	J. L. Dawkins, N-P	1997, Nov.
Fitchburg, MA	Ronald B. Ingemie, N-P (acting)	1997, Nov.
Flagstaff, AZ	Christopher Bavasi, N-P	2000, Apr.
Flint, MI.	Woodrow Stanley, D	1999, Nov.
Florissant, MO.	James J. Eagan, N-P.	1999, Apr.
Fontana, CA	David Eshleman, D	1998, Nov.
Ft. Collins, CO.	Ann Azari, N-P	1999, Apr.
Ft. Lauderdale, FL.	Jim Naugle, N-P	2000, Mar.
Ft. Smith, AR.	C. Raymond Baker, N-P	1998, Nov.
Ft. Wayne, IN	Paul Helmke, R.	1999, Nov.
Ft. Worth, TX.	Kenneth L. Barr, N-P	1999, May
Fountain Valley, CA	John Collins, N-P	1998, Nov.
Frankfort, KY.	William I. May Jr., N-P	1999, Nov.
Fremont, CA	Gus Morrison, N-P.	2000, Nov.
Fresno, CA	Jim Patterson, N-P.	2000, Mar.
Fullerton, CA.	Chris Norby, N-P.	1997, Dec.
Gadsden, AL.	Stephen Means, N-P.	1998, Oct.
Gainesville, FL.	Bruce Delaney, N-P	1998, May
Galveston, TX.	Henry Freudenburg III, N-P	1998, May
Gardena, CA.	Donald L. Dear, N-P	1998, Nov.
Garden Grove, CA.	Bruce Broadwater, N-P	1997, Nov.
Garland, TX.	James B. Ratliff, N-P.	1998, May
Gary, IN	Scott King, D	1999, Nov.
Gastonia, NC.	James B. Garland, N-P.	1997, Nov.
Glendale, AZ.	Elaine Scruggs, N-P	1998, Mar.
Glendale, CA.	Larry Zarian, N-P.	1998, Apr.
Grand Forks, ND	Patricia Owens, N-P	2000, June
Grand Prairie, TX.	Charles V. England, N-P	1998, May
Grand Rapids, MI.	John Logie, N-P	1999, Nov.
Greeley, CO	LaVern C. Nelson, N-P	1997, Nov.
Green Bay, WI.	Paul F. Jadin, N-P.	1999, Apr.
Greensboro, NC	Carolyn Allen, N-P.	1997, Nov.
Greenville, SC.	Knox White, R.	1999, Nov.
Greenwich, CT	Tom R. Ragland, N-P	1997, Nov.
Groton, CT	Dolores Hauber, N-P	1997, Nov.
Gulfport, MS	Bob Short, R.	2001, June
Hamden, CT	Lillian D. Clayman, D.	1997, Nov.
Hamilton, OH.	Gregory V. Jolivette, N-P	1997, Nov.
Hammond, IN	Duane W. Dedelow Jr. R	1999, Nov.
Hampton, VA.	James L. Eason, N-P.	2000, May
Harrisburg, PA.	Stephen Reed, D	1997, Nov.
Hartford, CT	Michael P. Peters, N-P	1997, Dec.
Haverhill, MA.	James A. Rurak, D	1997, Nov.
Hawthorne, CA.	Larry Guidi, N-P	1997, Nov.
Hayward, CA.	Roberta Cooper, N-P.	1998, Mar.
Helena, MT	Colleen McCarthy, N-P	1997, Nov.
Henderson, NV	James B. Gibson, N-P	2001, June
Hialeah, FL	Raul Martinez, R.	1997, Nov.
High Point, NC.	Rebecca R. Smothers, N-P	1998, Nov.
Hoboken, NJ	Anthony Russo, N-P	2001, May
Hollywood, FL.	Mara Giulianti, N-P.	1998, Mar.
Holyoke, MA.	Daniel Szostkiewicz, D	1997, Nov.
Honolulu, HI	Jeremy Harris, N-P	2000, Nov.
Houston, TX	Bob Lanier, N-P	1997, Nov.
Huntington, WV.	Jean Dean, R	2001, June
Huntington Beach, CA	Ralph Bauer, N-P	1997, Dec.
Huntington Park, CA	Jessica Maes, N-P	(4)
Huntsville, AL	Loretta Spencer, N-P.	2000, Aug.
Idaho Falls, ID.	Linda Milam, N-P	1997, Nov.
Independence, MO	Ron Stewart, N-P	1998, Apr.
Indianapolis, IN	Stephen Goldsmith, R	1999, Nov.
Inglewood, CA.	Roosevelt F. Dorn, N-P	1998, Nov.
Iowa City, IA	Naomi Novick, N-P	1998, Jan.
Irvine, CA	Christina Shea, N-P.	1998, Nov.
Irving, TX	Morris Parrish, N-P	1999, May
Irvington, NJ	Sara B. Bost, D.	1998, May
Jackson, MS	Harvey Johnson, Jr., D	2001, June
Jacksonville, FL.	John A. Delaney, R	1999, May
Janesville, WI	Bill Schneider, N-P	2000, Apr.
Jefferson City, MO.	Duane Schreimann, D	1999, Apr.
Jersey City, NJ	Bret Schundler, R	2001, May
Johnson City, TN.	Bob May, N-P	1999, Apr.
Joliet, IL	Arthur Schultz, N-P	1999, Apr.
Juneau, AK	Dennis Egan, D.	1997, Oct.
Kalamazoo, MI	Barbara Larson, N-P	1997, Nov.
Kansas City, KS.	Carol Marinovich, N-P	1999, Apr.
Kansas City, MO	Emanuel Cleaver II, D	1999, Apr.
Kenner, LA	Louis J. Congemi, R	1998, Apr.
Kenosha, WI	John Antaramian, D	2000, Apr.
Kettering, OH	Richard Hartmann, R	1997, Nov.
Killeen, TX	Raul G. Villaronga, N-P.	1998, May
Knoxville, TN	Victor Ashe, R	2000, Nov.
Kokomo, IN	James Trobaugh, R	1999, Nov.
LaCrosse, WI	John D. Medinger, N-P	2001, Apr.
Lafayette, IN.	Dave Heath, R	1999, Nov.
La Habra, CA	David Cheverton, N-P.	1997, Dec.
Lake Charles, LA	Willie L. Mount, D.	2001, May
Lakeland, FL	Ralph L. Fletcher, N-P	2000, Sept.
Lakewood, CA	Mark Titel, N-P.	1998, Mar.
Lakewood, CO	Linda Morton, D.	1999, Nov.
Lakewood, OH	Madeline Cain, D.	1999, Nov.
La Mesa, CA	Arthur Madrid, N-P.	1998, Nov.
La Mirada, CA	Pete Dames, N-P.	1998, Mar.
Lancaster, CA	Frank Roberts, N-P	1998, Apr.
Lancaster, PA.	Janice C. Stork, D	1997, Nov.
Lansing, MI	David Hollister, N-P	1997, Nov.
Laredo, TX.	Saul N. Ramirez Jr., N-P.	1998, May
Largo, FL.	Thomas Feaster, N-P	2000, Mar
Las Cruces, NM	Ruben A. Smith, D	1999, Nov.
Las Vegas, NV	Jan Laverty Jones, D	1999, June
Lawrence, KS.	Bonnie Augustine, N-P	1998, Apr.
Lawrence, MA	Mary Claire Kennedy, N-P	1997, Nov.
Lawton, OK	John T. Marley, D.	1998, Jan.
Lexington, KY.	Pam Miller, N-P	1998, Nov.
Lima, OH	David J. Berger, N-P.	1997, Nov.
Lincoln, NE	Mike Johanns, R	1999, May
Little Rock, AR.	Jim Dailey, N-P	1999, Jan.
Livermore, CA	Cathie Brown, N-P.	1997, Nov.
Livonia, MI	Jack Kirksey, N-P.	1999, Nov.
Lodi, CA.	Phillip A. Pennino, N-P.	1997, Dec.
Long Beach, CA.	Beverly O'Neill, N-P.	1998, July
Longmont, CO.	Leona Stoecker, N-P.	1997, Nov.
Longview, TX.	David L. McWhorter, N-P.	2000, May
Lorain, OH.	Joe Koziura, D	1999, Nov.
Los Angeles, CA.	Richard Riordan, N-P.	2001, Apr.
Louisville, KY	Jerry E. Abramson, D.	1998, Nov.
Lowell, MA.	Edward Caulfield, N-P	1998, Jan.
Lubbock, TX.	Windy Sitton, R	1998, Apr.
Lynchburg, VA.	James S. Whitaker, N-P.	1998, July
Lynn, MA.	Patrick J. McManus, D	1997, Nov.
Lynwood, CA	Paul Richards III, N-P.	1997, Dec.
Macon, GA.	Jim Marshall, D	1999, Nov.
Madison, WI.	Susan J.M. Bauman, N-P	1998, Apr.
Malden, MA	Richard Howard, D.	1997, Nov.
Manchester, CT	Stephen T. Cassano, N-P.	1997, Nov.
Manchester, NH	Raymond J. Wieczorek, R.	1997, Nov.
Mansfield, OH	Lydia J. Reid, D.	1999, Nov.
Marietta, GA.	Ansley L. Meaders, D.	1997, Nov.
McAllen, TX.	Leo Montalvo, R.	2001, May
Medford, MA	Michael J. McGlynn, D	1997, Nov.
Medford, OR	Jerry Lausmann, N-P	1998, Nov.
Melbourne, FL	John Buckley, N-P	2000, Nov.
Memphis, TN	Willie W. Herenton, D.	1999, Oct.
Mentor, OH	Edward Walsh, N-P	1998, Jan.
Merced, CA	Richard Bernasconi, N-P.	1997, Nov.
Meriden, CT	Joseph Marinan Jr., N-P.	1997, Dec.
Meridian, MS	John Robert Smith, R	2001, June
Mesa, AZ	Wayne Brown, N-P.	2000, May
Mesquite, TX	Mike Anderson, N-P.	1999, May
Miami, FL.	Joe Carollo, N-P.	1997, Nov.
Miami Beach, FL.	Seymour Gelber, D.	1997, Nov.
Midland, TX	Robert E. Burns, N-P	1998, May
Midwest City, OK	Eddie O. Reed, N-P	1998, Apr.
Milford, CT	Frederick Lisman, R.	1997, Nov.
Milpitas, CA	Henry Manayan, N-P	1998, Nov.
Milwaukee, WI	John O. Norquist, D	2000, Apr.
Minneapolis, MN.	Sharon Sayles Belton, D.	1997, Nov.
Minnetonka, MN	Karen J. Anderson, N-P	1997, Nov.
Mobile, AL	Michael Dow, R, I	1997, Oct.
Modesto, CA	Richard Lang, N-P	1999, Nov.
Monroe, LA	Abe E. Pierce III D	2000, Mar.
Montclair, NJ	William Farlie Jr., N-P.	2000, May
Montebello, CA.	William M. Molinari, R.	1997, Nov.
Monterey Park, CA.	Marie T. Purvis, N-P.	1998, Feb.
Montgomery, AL.	Emory Folmar, R	1999, Oct.
Montpelier, VT	Charles Kaparis, N-P	1998, Mar.
Moreno Valley, CA	Charles White, N-P.	1997, Dec.
Mt. Prospect, IL	Gerald "Skip" Farley, N-P.	2001, Apr.
Mt. Vernon, NY.	Ernest D. Davis, D	1999, Nov.
Mountain View, CA	Joseph S. Kleitman, N-P.	1998, Nov.
Muncie, IN	Dan Cannan, R	1999, Nov.
Muskogee, OK	James Bushnell, N-P	1998, Apr.
Napa, CA.	Ed Solomon, R.	2000, July
Naperville, IL	George Pradel, N-P	1999, Apr.
Nashua, NH	Donald Davidson, N-P	1999, Nov.

City	Name	Next Election
Nashville, TN	Philip N. Bredesen, D	1998, Aug.
National City, CA	George H. Waters, R	1998, Nov.
Newark, NJ	Sharpe James, D	1998, May
New Bedford, MA	Rosemary Tierney, D	1997, Nov.
New Britain, CT	Lucian Pawlak, D	1997, Nov.
New Haven, CT	John DeStefano, D	1997, Dec.
New Orleans, LA	Marc H. Morial, D	1998, Feb.
Newport Beach, CA	Janice Debay, N-P	1997, Nov.
Newport News, VA	Joe S. Frank, N-P	1998, June
New Rochelle, NY	Timothy Idoni, D	1999, Nov.
Newton, MA	Thomas Concannon Jr., N-P	1997, Nov.
New York, NY	Rudolph Giuliani, R	1997, Nov.
Niagara Falls, NY	James Galie, D	1999, Nov.
Norfolk, VA	Paul D. Fraim, N-P	1998, July
Norman, OK	Dr. William Nation, N-P	1998, Mar.
North Charleston, SC	R. Keith Summey, R	1999, July
N. Little Rock, AR	Patrick Hays, N-P	2000, Nov.
Norwalk, CA	Eleanor L. Zimmerman, N-P	1998, Apr.
Norwalk, CT	Frank J. Esposito, R	1997, Nov.
Novato, CA	Pat Eklund, N-P	1997, Nov.[5]
Oakland, CA	Elihu Mason Harris, N-P	1999, Jan.
Oak Park, IL	Barbara Furlong, N-P	2001, Apr.
Oceanside, CA	Dick Lyon, N-P	2000, Nov.
Odessa, TX	Mike Atkins, N-P	1998, May
Ogden, UT	Glenn J. Mecham, N-P	1999, Nov.
Oklahoma City, OK	Ronald J. Norick, N-P	1998, Apr.
Olympia, WA	Bob Jacobs, N-P	1999, Nov.
Omaha, NE	Hal Daub, R	2001, May
Ontario, CA	Gus James Skropos, N-P	1998, Nov.
Orange, CA	Joanne Coontz, N-P	1998, Nov.
Orlando, FL	Glenda E. Hood, N-P	2000, Apr.
Oshkosh, WI	William Castle Jr., N-P	1998, Apr.
Overland Park, KS	Ed Eilert, R	2001, Apr.
Owensboro, KY	Waymond Morris, N-P	1999, Nov.
Oxnard, CA	Manuel M. Lopez, N-P	1998, Nov.
Palm Springs, CA	William G. Kleindienst, N-P	1999, Nov.
Palo Alto, CA	Lanie Wheeler, N-P	1998, Jan.
Parma, OH	Gerald M. Boldt, D	1999, Nov.
Pasadena, CA	Chris Holden, N-P	1999, Mar.
Pasadena, TX	Johnny Isbell, N-P	2001, May
Passaic, NJ	Margie Semler, N-P	2001, May
Paterson, NJ	Martin G. Barnes, R	1997, Nov.
Pawtucket, RI	Robert E. Metivier, D	1997, Nov.
Peabody, MA	Peter Torigian, D	1997, Nov.
Pembroke Pines, FL	Alex G. Fekete, N-P	2000, Mar.
Pensacola, FL	John Fogg, N-P	1999, June
Peoria, IL	Lowell Grieves, N-P	2001, Apr.
Philadelphia, PA	Edward Rendell, D	1999, Nov.
Phoenix, AZ	Skip Rimsza, N-P	1999, Oct.
Pico Rivera, CA	Bea Proo, N-P	1998, Nov.
Pierre, SD	Gary Drewes, N-P	1999, Apr.
Pine Bluff, AR	Jerry Taylor, N-P	2000, Nov.
Pittsburgh, PA	Tom Murphy, D	1997, Nov.
Pittsfield, MA	Edward Reilly, N-P	1997, Nov.
Plainfield, NJ	Mark Fury, N-P	1997, Nov.
Plano, TX	John Longstreet, N-P	1998, May
Plantation, FL	Frank Veltri, D	1999, Mar.
Pocatello, ID	Peter J. Angstadt, N-P	1997, Nov.
Pomona, CA	Eddie Cortez, N-P	1999, Apr.
Pompano Beach, FL	William F. Griffin, N-P	1998, Mar.
Pontiac, MI	Walter Moore, N-P	1997, Nov.
Port Arthur, TX	Robert T. Morgan, D	1998, May
Portland, ME	George Campbell Jr., N-P	[4]
Portland, OR	Vera Katz, N-P	2000, Nov.
Portsmouth, VA	James W. Holley III N-P	2000, May
Providence, RI	Vincent Cianci Jr., R, I	1998, Nov.
Provo, UT	George O. Stewart, N-P	1997, Nov.
Quincy, IL	Charles W. Scholz, D	2001, Apr.
Quincy, MA	James A. Sheets, D	1997, Nov.
Racine, WI	James M. Smith, N-P	1999, Apr.
Raleigh, NC	Tom Fetzer, N-P	1997, Oct.
Rancho Cucamonga, CA	William Alexander, N-P	1998, Nov.
Rapid City, SD	Edward McLaughlin, N-P	1999, Apr.
Reading, PA	Paul Angstadt, R	1999, Nov.
Redding, CA	Patricia Andersen, N-P	1998, Apr.
Redondo Beach, CA	Gregory C. Hill, N-P	2001, Mar.
Redwood City, CA	Jim Hartnett, N-P	1997, Nov.
Reno, NV	Jeff Griffin, N-P	1999, June
Rialto, CA	John Longville, N-P	2000, Nov.
Richardson, TX	Gary Slagel, N-P	1999, May
Richmond, CA	Rosemary Corbin, D	1997, Nov.
Richmond, VA	Larry Chavis, N-P	1998, July
Riverside, CA	Ronald O. Loveridge, N-P	1997, Dec.
Roanoke, VA	David A. Bowers, D	2000, May
Rochester, MN	Charles J. Canfield, N-P	1999, Nov.
Rochester, NY	William A. Johnson Jr., D	1997, Nov.
Rochester Hills, MI	Kenneth D. Snell, N-P	1999, Nov.
Rock Hill, SC	Elizabeth D. Rhea, N-P	1998, Apr.
Rock Island, IL	Mark W. Schwiebert, N-P	2001, Apr.
Rockford, IL	Charles Box, D	2001, Apr.
Rockville, MD	Rose G. Krasnow, N-P	1997, Nov.
Rome, NY	Joseph A. Griffo, R	1999, Nov.
Rosemead, CA	Jay Imperial, N-P	1998, Mar.
Roseville, MI	Gerald K. Alsip, N-P	1997, Nov.
Roswell, NM	Thomas E. Jennings, N-P	1998, Mar.
Royal Oak, MI	Dennis G. Cowan, N-P	1997, Nov.
Sacramento, CA	Joseph Serna Jr., N-P	2000, June
Saginaw, MI	Gary L. Loster, N-P	1997, Nov.
St. Charles, MO	Robert L. Moeller, N-P	1999, Apr.
St. Clair Shores, MI	Curtis L. Dumas, N-P	1999, Nov.
St. Cloud, MN	Charles Winkleman, N-P	1997, Nov.
St. Joseph, MO	Larry Stobbs, N-P	1998, Apr.
St. Louis, MO	Clarence Harmon, D	2001, Apr.
St. Louis Park, MN	Gail Dorfman, N-P	1999, Nov.
St. Paul, MN	Norm Coleman, N-P	1997, Nov.
St. Petersburg, FL	David Fischer, N-P	2001, Mar.
Salem, OR	Michael Swaim, N-P	1998, Nov.
Salinas, CA	Alan Styles, N-P	1998, Nov.
Salt Lake City, UT	Deedee Corradini, D	1999, Nov.
San Angelo, TX	Dick Funk, N-P	1999, May
San Antonio, TX	Howard W. Peak, N-P	1999, May
San Bernardino, CA	Tom Minor, R	1997, Nov.
San Diego, CA	Susan Golding, R	2000, Nov.
Sandy City, UT	Thomas M. Dolan, N-P	1997, Nov.
San Francisco, CA	Willie Brown Jr. N-P	1999, Jan.
San Jose, CA	Susan Hammer, D	1999, Jan.
San Leandro, CA	Ellen M. Corbett, N-P	1998, May
San Mateo, CA	Gary Yates, N-P	1997, Dec.
San Rafael, CA	Albert J. Boro, N-P	1999, Nov.
Santa Ana, CA	Miguel Pulido, N-P	1998, Nov.
Santa Barbara, CA	Harriet Miller, N-P	1999, Nov.
Santa Clara, CA	Judy Nadler, N-P	1998, Nov.
Santa Clarita, CA	Clyde Smythe, N-P	1997 Dec.
Santa Cruz, CA	Cynthia S. Mathews, N-P	1997, Nov.[3]
Santa Fe, NM	Debbie Jaramillo, N-P	1998, Mar.
Santa Maria, CA	Roger Bunch, N-P	1998, Nov.
Santa Monica, CA	Pam O'Connor, N-P	1997, Sept.
Santa Rosa, CA	Sharon Wright, N-P	1998, Dec.
Sarasota, FL	Gene M. Pillot, N-P	1998, Mar.
Savannah, GA	Floyd Adams Jr., N-P	1999, Nov.
Schaumburg, IL	Al Larson, N-P	1999, Apr.
Schenectady, NY	Albert Jurczynski, R	1999, Nov.
Scottsdale, AZ	Sam Kathryn Campana, R	1998, Mar.
Scranton, PA	James P. Connors, R	1997, Nov.
Seattle, WA	Norman B. Rice, D	1997, Nov.
Sheboygan, WI	James R. Schramm, N-P	2001, Apr.
Shreveport, LA	Robert W. Williams, R	1998, Nov.
Simi Valley, CA	Gregory Stratton, N-P	1998, Nov.
Sioux City, IA	Robert Scott, N-P	1998, Jan.
Sioux Falls, SD	Gary Hanson, N-P	1999, Jan.
Skokie, IL	Jacqueline B. Gorell, N-P	2001, Apr.
Somerville, MA	Michael E. Capuano, D	1997, Nov.
South Bend, IN	Stephen J. Luecke, D	1999, Nov.
South Gate, CA	Bill Martinez, N-P	1998, Mar.
Southfield, MI	Donald F. Fracassi, R	1997, Nov.
Sparks, NV	Bruce Breslow, N-P	1999, June
Spartanburg, SC	James E. Talley, N-P	1997, Nov.
Spokane, WA	Jack Geraghty, N-P	1997, Nov.
Springfield, IL	Karen Hasara, N-P	1999, Apr.
Springfield, MA	Michael Albano, D	1997, Nov.
Springfield, MO	Leland L. Gannaway, N-P	1999, Apr.
Springfield, OH	Kevin O'Neill, N-P	1998, Jan.
Stamford, CT	Dannel P. Malloy, D	1997, Dec.
Sterling Hts., MI	Richard J. Notte, N-P	1997, Nov.
Stockton, CA	Gary Podesto, N-P	2000, Nov.
Stratford, CT	Clement F. Naples, N-P	1997, Nov.
Sunnyvale, CA	Stan Kawczynski, N-P	1997, Nov.
Suffolk, VA	Thomas Underwood, N-P	1998, July
Sunrise, FL	Steven B. Feren, N-P	2001, Mar.
Syracuse, NY	Roy A. Bernardi, R	1997, Nov.
Tacoma, WA	Brian Ebersole, N-P	1999, Nov.
Tallahassee, FL	Scott Maddox, N-P	2002, Nov.
Tampa, FL	Dick Greco, N-P	1999, Mar.
Taunton, MA	Robert Nunes, D	1997, Nov.
Taylor, MI	Cameron G. Priebe, D	1997, Nov.
Tempe, AZ	Neil Giuliano, N-P	1998, Apr.
Temple, TX	J. W. Perry, N-P	1998, May
Terre Haute, IN	James Jenkins, D	1999, Nov.
Thornton, CO	Margaret Carpenter, N-P	1999, Nov.
Thousand Oaks, CA	Judy Lazar, N-P	1997, Dec.
Titusville, FL	Larry D. Bartley, N-P	1998, Nov.
Toledo, OH	Carty Finkbeiner, N-P	1997, Nov.
Topeka, KS	Joan Wagnon, N-P	2001, Apr.
Torrance, CA	Dee Hardison, N-P	1998, Mar.
Trenton, NJ	Douglas H. Palmer, N-P	1998, May

(continued)

City	Name	Next Election	City	Name	Next Election
Troy, MI	Jeanne M. Stine, N-P	1998, Apr.	Wauwatosa, WI	Maricolette Walsh, N-P	2000, Mar.
Troy, NY	Mark Pattison, D	1998, Jan.	W. Allis, WI.	Jeannette Bell, N-P	2000, Mar.
Tucson, AZ	George Miller, D	1999, Nov.	W. Covina, CA	Ben Wong, N-P	1998, Mar.
Tulsa, OK	M. Susan Savage, D	1998, Mar.	W. Hartford, CT	Nan Glass, D	1997, Nov.
Tuscaloosa, AL	Alvin DuPont, D	1997, Oct.	W. Haven, CT.	H. Richard Borer Jr., D	1997, Dec.
Tyler, TX.	Kevin Eltise, N-P	1998, May	W. Palm Beach, FL.	Nancy M. Graham, N-P	1999, Mar.
Union City, NJ	Bruce D. Walter, D	2000, May	Westland, MI	Robert J. Thomas, D	1997, Nov.
Upland, CA	Robert R. Nolan, N-P	2000, Nov.	Westminster, CA.	Frank Fry, N-P	1998, Nov.
Utica, NY	Edward Hanna, I	1999, Nov.	Westminster, CO	Nancy Heil, N-P	1997, Nov.
Vacaville, CA.	David A. Fleming, N-P	1998, Nov.	Wheaton, IL	C. James Carr, N-P	1999, Apr.
Vallejo, CA	Gloria Exlin, N-P	1999, Nov.	White Plains, NY	S. J. Schulman, D	1997, Nov.
Vancouver, WA	Royce Pollard, N-P	1997, Nov.	Whittier, CA	Janet Henke, N-P.	1998, Apr.
Vineland, NJ	Anthony Campanella, R	2000, June	Wichita, KS	Bob Knight, N-P	1999, Apr.
Virginia Beach, VA.	Meyera E. Oberndorf, I	2000, May	Wichita Falls, TX.	Kay Yeager, N-P	1998, May
Visalia, CA	Mary Louise Vivier, N-P	1997, Nov.	Wilkes-Barre, PA	Thomas McGroarty, D	1997, Nov.
Vista, CA.	Gloria McClellan, R	1998, Dec.	Wilmington, DE.	James H. Sills Jr., D	2000, Nov.
Waco, TX	Michael Morrison, N-P	1998, May	Wilmington, NC.	Don Betz, N-P	1997, Nov.
Walnut Creek, CA.	Kathy Hicks, N-P	1997, Dec.	Winston-Salem, NC	Martha S. Wood, N-P	1997, Nov.
Waltham, MA.	William F. Stanley, D	1999, Nov.	Woodbridge, NJ	James McGreevey, D	1999, Nov.
Warren, MI	Mark Steenbergh, N-P	1999, Nov.	Woonsocket, RI	Susan D. Menard, N-P	1997, Nov.
Warren, OH.	Henry Angelo, D	1999, Nov.	Worcester, MA	Raymond Mariano, N-P	1997, Nov.
Warwick, RI.	Lincoln D. Chafee, R	1998, Nov.	Wyandotte, MI	Lawrence S. Stec, N-P	2001, Apr.
Washington, DC	Marion Barry Jr., D	1999, Jan.	Wyoming, MI	Jack Magnuson, N-P	1997, Nov.
Waterbury, CT.	Philip Giordino, R	1997, Nov.	Yakima, WA	Lynn Buchanan, N-P	1998, Jan.
Waterloo, IA	John R. Rooff III, R	1997, Nov.	Yonkers, NY.	John Spencer, R	1999, Nov.
Waukegan, IL	William F. Durkin, D	2001, Apr.	York, PA	Charles Robertson, D	1997, Nov.
Waukesha, WI	Carol Opel, N-P.	1998, Apr.	Youngstown, OH	Patrick J. Ungaro, D	1997, Nov.
			Yuma, AZ.	Marilyn R. Young, N-P	1997, Nov.

(1) Position of mayor is rotated among City Council members every 9 months. (2) City Council to elect mayor on Nov. 13, 1997. (3) City Council to elect mayor on Nov. 18, 1997. (4) Position of mayor is rotated among City Council members every 12 months. (5) City Council to elect mayor on Nov. 12, 1997.

Governors of States and Puerto Rico

As of mid-Oct. 1997

State	Capital, Zip Code	Governor	Party	Term years	Term expires	Annual salary
Alabama	Montgomery 36130	Fob James Jr.	Rep.	4	Jan. 1999	$87,643
Alaska	Juneau 99811	Tony Knowles	Dem.	4	Dec. 1998	81,648
Arizona	Phoenix 85007	Jane Dee Hull	Rep.	4	Jan. 1999	75,000
Arkansas	Little Rock 72201	Mike Huckabee	Rep.	4	Jan. 1999	60,000
California	Sacramento 95814	Pete Wilson	Rep.	4	Jan. 1999	131,000
Colorado	Denver 80203	Roy Romer	Dem.	4	Jan. 1999	70,000
Connecticut	Hartford 06106	John G. Rowland	Rep.	4	Jan. 1999	78,000
Delaware	Dover 19901	Thomas R. Carper	Dem.	4	Jan. 2001	107,000
Florida	Tallahassee 32399	Lawton Chiles	Dem.	4	Jan. 1999	110,962
Georgia	Atlanta 30334	Zell Miller	Dem.	4	Jan. 1999	103,074
Hawaii	Honolulu 96813	Benjamin Cayetano	Dem.	4	Dec. 1998	94,780
Idaho	Boise 83720	Philip E. Batt	Rep.	4	Jan. 1999	85,000
Illinois	Springfield 62706	Jim Edgar	Rep.	4	Jan. 1999	123,022
Indiana	Indianapolis 46204	Frank O'Bannon	Dem.	4	Jan. 2001	77,200
Iowa	Des Moines 50319	Terry E. Branstad	Rep.	4	Jan. 1999	98,200
Kansas	Topeka 66612	Bill Graves	Rep.	4	Jan. 1999	80,340
Kentucky	Frankfort 40601	Paul Patton	Dem.	4	Dec. 1999	86,352
Louisiana	Baton Rouge 70804	M. J. "Mike" Foster	Rep.	4	Jan. 2000	95,000
Maine	Augusta 04333	Angus King Jr.	Ind.	4	Jan. 1999	70,000
Maryland	Annapolis 21401	Parris N. Glendening	Dem.	4	Jan. 1999	120,000
Massachusetts	Boston 02113	A. Paul Cellucci	Rep.	4	Jan. 1999	100,000
Michigan	Lansing 48909	John Engler	Rep.	4	Jan. 1999	127,100
Minnesota	St. Paul 55155	Arne H. Carlson	Rep.	4	Jan. 1999	114,506
Mississippi	Jackson 39205	Kirk Fordice	Rep.	4	Jan. 2000	83,160
Missouri	Jefferson City 65102	Mel Carnahan	Dem.	4	Jan. 2001	107,269
Montana	Helena 59620	Marc Racicot	Rep.	4	Jan. 2001	78,246
Nebraska	Lincoln 68509	Ben Nelson	Dem.	4	Jan. 1999	65,000
Nevada	Carson City 89710	Bob Miller	Dem.	4	Jan. 1999	90,000
New Hampshire	Concord 03301	Jeanne Shaheen	Dem.	2	Jan. 1999	86,235
New Jersey	Trenton 08625	Christine Todd Whitman	Rep.	4	Jan. 1998	85,000
New Mexico	Santa Fe 87503	Gary Johnson	Rep.	4	Jan. 1999	90,000
New York	Albany 12224	George E. Pataki	Rep.	4	Jan. 1999	130,000
North Carolina	Raleigh 27603	James B. Hunt Jr.	Dem.	4	Jan. 2001	107,132
North Dakota	Bismarck 58505	Edward T. Schafer	Rep.	4	Jan. 2001	73,176
Ohio	Columbus 43215	George V. Voinovich	Rep.	4	Jan. 1999	115,762
Oklahoma	Oklahoma City 73105	Frank Keating	Rep.	4	Jan. 1999	70,000
Oregon	Salem 97310	John Kitzhaber	Dem.	4	Jan. 1999	88,300
Pennsylvania	Harrisburg 17120	Tom Ridge	Rep.	4	Jan. 1999	125,000
Rhode Island	Providence 02903	Lincoln C. Almond	Rep.	4	Jan. 1999	69,900
South Carolina	Columbia 29211	David M. Beasley	Rep.	4	Jan. 1999	106,078
South Dakota	Pierre 57501	William Janklow	Rep.	4	Jan. 1999	82,271
Tennessee	Nashville 37243	Don Sundquist	Rep.	4	Jan. 1999	85,000
Texas	Austin 78711	George W. Bush	Rep.	4	Jan. 1999	115,345
Utah	Salt Lake City 84114	Michael O. Leavitt	Rep.	4	Jan. 2001	85,200
Vermont	Montpelier 05609	Howard Dean	Dem.	2	Jan. 1999	96,661
Virginia	Richmond 23219	George F. Allen	Rep.	4	Jan. 1998	110,000
Washington	Olympia 98504	Mike Lowry	Dem.	4	Jan. 2001	121,000
West Virginia	Charleston 25305	Cecil H. Underwood	Rep.	4	Jan. 2001	90,000
Wisconsin	Madison 53707	Tommy G. Thompson	Rep.	4	Jan. 1999	101,861
Wyoming	Cheyenne 82002	Jim Geringer	Rep.	4	Jan. 1999	95,000
Puerto Rico	San Juan 00936	Pedro J. Rossello	NPP[1]	4	Jan. 2001	70,000

(1) New Progressive Party.

Races for Governor, 1996

Source: Voter News Service

In 1996, there were 11 state governors races, 7 of which went to the incumbent candidate. Control of the statehouses changed hands from one party to another in 2 states—New Hampshire and West Virginia. Vote totals below are official.

State	Democrat	Vote	Republican	Vote	Other	Vote
DE...	Thomas R.Carper*.....	188,300	Janet C. Rzewnicki.....	82,654		
IN ...	Frank O'Bannon	1,087,128	Stephen Goldsmith	986,982	Steve Dillon, (LB)	35,805
MO ..	Mel Carnahan*........	1,224,801	Margaret Kelly	866,268	J. Mark Oglesby, (LB)....	51,432
MT...	Judy Jacobson	76,471	Marc Racicot*	320,768		
NH...	Jeanne Shaheen	284,131	Ovide M. Lamontagne...	196,278	Fred Bramante (IR)......	10,316
NC...	James B. Hunt Jr.*.....	1,436,638	Robin Hayes........	1,097,053	Scott D. Yost, (LB)	17,559
ND...	Lee Kaldor	89,349	Edward T. Schafer*	174,937		
UT...	Jim Bradley...........	156,616	Michael O. Leavitt*	503,693	Ken Larsen, (IA)	4,741
VT...	Howard Dean*	179,544	John L. Gropper	57,161	Mary Alice Herbert, (LU) ..	4,156
WA ..	Gary Locke	1,296,492	Ellen Craswell........	940,538		
WV ..	Charlotte Pritt	287,870	Cecil H. Underwood	324,518	Wallace Johnson, (LB) ...	16,171

	New Progressive Party		Popular Democratic Party		Puerto Rican Independent Party	
Puerto Rico	Pedro Rossello*.......	1,006,331	Hector Luis Acevedo....	875,852	David Noriega Rodriquez ..	75,304

* Denotes incumbent. **Boldface** denotes winner. (LB)=Libertarian, (IR)=Reform, (IA)=Independent American, (LU)=Liberty Union

1992 Census of U.S. Governments—Popularly Elected Officials

Source: U.S. Dept. of Commerce, Economics and Statistics Administration; Bureau of the Census

A census of U.S. governments is taken at 5-year intervals (beginning in 1957). One of the major subject areas includes popularly elected officials. The term *elected officials* refers to officials who are directly elected by the voters, plus the president and the vice president of the U.S., who are elected by presidential electors rather than direct election by the people. Officials who are selected by the governing body of one or more governments are not classified as elected officials.

There were 85,006 governments in the U.S. as of Jan. 1992. In addition to the federal government and the 50 state governments, there were 84,955 units of local government. Of these, 38,978 are general-purpose local governments—3,043 county governments, and 35,935 subcounty general-purpose governments (including 19,279 municipal governments and 16,656 town or township governments). The remainder, more than half the total number, are special-purpose local governments, including 14,422 school district governments and 31,555 special district governments.

The 85,006 governments in the U.S. in 1992 had 513,200 elected officials—approximately one elected official for every 485 inhabitants. There were 542 federal and 18,828 state elected officials, which accounted for only 3.8% of the total. The majority were officials of the various local governments.

State Officials, Salaries, Party Membership

As of Oct.1997; †, ind. or other party.

Alabama

Governor — Fob James Jr., R, $87,643
Lt. Gov. — Don Siegelman, D, $12 per day, plus $50 per day expenses, plus $3,780 per mo expenses
Sec. of State — Jim Bennett, R, $61,779
Atty. Gen. — William Pryor, R, $115,695
Treasurer — Lucy Baxley, D, $61,779
Legislature: meets annually at Montgomery the 3d Tues. in Apr., 1st year of term of office; 1st Tues. in Feb., 2d and 3d yr; 2d Tues. in Jan., 4th yr. Members receive $10 per day salary, plus $50 per day expenses, plus $2,280 per mo expenses.
Senate — Dem., 22; Rep., 13. Total, 35
House — Dem., 71; Rep., 34. Total, 105

Alaska

Governor — Tony Knowles, D, $81,648
Lt. Gov. — Fran Ulmer, D, $76,188
Atty. General — Bruce Botelho, D, $84,000
Legislature: meets annually in Jan. at Juneau for 120 days with a 10-day extension possible upon 2/3 vote. First session in odd years. Members receive $24,120 annually, plus per diem as follows: beginning of session to Apr. 29, $148 per day; Apr. 30 to end of session, $160 per day.
Senate — Dem., 8; Rep., 12. Total, 20
House — Dem., 17; Rep., 22; 1 other. Total, 40

Arizona

Governor — Jane Dee Hull, R, $75,000
Sec. of State — Betsey Bayless, R, $54,600
Atty. Gen. — Grant Woods, R, $76,440
Treasurer — Tony West, R, $54,600
Legislature: meets annually in Jan. at Phoenix. Each member receives an annual salary of $15,000.
Senate — Dem., 12; Rep., 18. Total, 30
House — Dem., 22; Rep., 38. Total, 60

Arkansas

Governor — Mike Huckabee, R, $60,000
Lt. Gov. — Winthrop P. Rockefeller, R, $29,000
Sec. of State — Sharon Priest, D, $37,500
Atty. Gen. — Winston Bryant, D, $50,000
Treasurer — Jimmie Lou Fisher, D, $37,500
Auditor — Gus Wingfield, D, $37,500
General Assembly: meets odd years in Jan. at Little Rock. Members receive $12,500 annually.
Senate — Dem., 28; Rep., 7. Total, 35
House — Dem., 85; Rep., 14; 1 vacant. Total, 100

California

Governor — Pete Wilson, R, $131,000
Lt. Gov. — Gray Davis, D, $98,280
Sec. of State — Bill Jones, R, $98,280
Controller — Kathleen Connell, D, $98,280
Atty. Gen. — Dan Lungren, R, $111,384
Legislature: meets at Sacramento on the 1st Mon. in Dec. of even-numbered years; each session lasts 2 years. Members receive $78,624 annually, plus $101 per diem.
Senate — Dem., 23; Rep., 16; 1 ind. Total, 40
Assembly — Dem., 42; Rep., 37; 1 vacancy; Total, 80

Colorado

Governor — Roy Romer, D, $70,000
Lt. Gov. — Gail Schoettler, D, $48,500
Sec. of State — Victoria (Vikki) Buckley, R, $48,500
Atty. Gen. — Gale Norton, R, $60,000
Treasurer — Bill Owens, R, $48,500
General Assembly: meets annually in Jan. at Denver. Members receive $17,500 annually.
Senate — Dem., 15; Rep., 20. Total, 35
House — Dem., 24; Rep., 41. Total, 65

(continued)

Connecticut

Governor — John G. Rowland, R, $78,000
Lt. Gov. — M. Jodi Rell, R, $55,000
Sec. of State — Miles S. Rapoport, D, $50,000
Treasurer — Paul Sylvester, R, $50,000
Comptroller — Nancy S. Wyman, D, $50,000
Atty. Gen. — Richard Blumenthal, D, $60,000
General Assembly: meets annually odd years in Jan. and even years in Feb., at Hartford. Members receive $15,200 annually, plus $4,500 (senator), $3,500 (representative) per year for expenses.
Senate — Dem., 19; Rep., 17. Total, 36
House — Dem., 96; Rep., 55. Total, 151

Delaware

Governor — Thomas R. Carper, D, $107,000
Lt. Gov. — Ruth Ann Minner, D, $44,600
Sec. of State — Edward J. Freel, D, $89,900
Atty. Gen. — M. Jane Brady, R, $99,100
Treasurer — Janet C. Rzewnicki, R, $79,700
General Assembly: meets annually the 2d Tues. in Jan. and continues until June 30, at Dover. Members receive $28,300 annually, plus $5,500 expense allowance.
Senate — Dem., 13; Rep., 8. Total, 21
House — Dem., 14; Rep., 27. Total, 41

Florida[2]

Governor — Lawton Chiles, D, $110,962
Lt. Gov. — Kenneth "Buddy" McKay, D, $106,290
Sec. of State — Sandra Mortham, R, $109,841
Comptroller — Robert R. Milligan, R, $109,841
Atty. Gen. — Robert Butterworth, D, $109,841
Treasurer — Bill Nelson, D, $109,841
Legislature: meets annually at Tallahassee. Members receive $25,668 annually, plus expense allowance.
Senate — Dem., 17; Rep., 23. Total, 40
House — Dem., 55; Rep., 64; 1 vacancy. Total, 120

Georgia

Governor — Zell Miller, D, $103,074
Lt. Gov. — Pierre Howard, D, $67,319
Sec. of State — Lewis Massey, D, $82,786
Atty. Gen. — Thurbert E. Baker, D, $98,280
General Assembly: meets annually in Atlanta. Members receive $11,125 annually ($59 per diem and $4,800 expense reimbursement).
Senate — Dem., 35; Rep., 21. Total, 56
House — Dem., 112; Rep., 68. Total, 180

Hawaii

Governor — Benjamin Cayetano, D, $94,780
Lt. Gov. — Mazie K. Hirono, D, $90,041
Atty. Gen. — Margery Bronster, $85,302
Comptroller — Sam Callejo, $85,302
Dir. of Budget & Finance — Earl Anzai, $85,302
Legislature: meets annually on 3d Wed. in Jan. at Honolulu. Members receive $32,000 annually, plus expenses.
Senate — Dem., 23; Rep., 2. Total, 25
House — Dem., 44; Rep., 7. Total, 51

Idaho

Governor — Philip E. Batt, R, $85,000
Lt. Gov. — C. L. "Butch" Otter, R, $22,500
Sec. of State — Pete T. Cenarrusa, R, $67,500
Treasurer — Lydia Justice Edwards, R, $67,500
Atty. Gen. — Alan Lance, R, $75,000
Legislature: meets annually the Mon. on or nearest Jan. 9 at Boise. Members receive $12,360 annually, plus $75 per day during session if required to maintain a 2d residence, $40 if no 2d residence; plus $50 per day when engaged in legislative business when legislature is not in session.
Senate — Dem., 5; Rep., 30. Total, 35
House — Dem., 11; Rep., 59. Total, 70

Illinois

Governor — Jim Edgar, R, $123,022
Lt. Gov. — Bob Kustra, R, $86,839
Sec. of State — George H. Ryan, R, $108,549
Comptroller — Loleta A. Didrickson, R, $94,076
Atty. Gen. — Jim Ryan, R, $108,549
Treasurer — Judy Baar Topinka, R, $94,076
General Assembly: meets annually in Jan. at Springfield. Members receive $47,309 annually.
Senate — Dem., 28; Rep., 31. Total, 59
House — Dem., 60; Rep., 58. Total, 118

Indiana

Governor — Frank O'Bannon, D, $77,200
Lt. Gov. — Joseph E. Kernan, D, $64,000
Sec. of State — Sue Anne Gilroy, R, $46,000
Atty. Gen. — Jeffrey A. Modesitt, D, $59,200
Treasurer — Joyce Brinkman, R, $46,000
Auditor — Morris Wooden, R, $46,000
General Assembly: meets annually in Jan. at Indianapolis. Members receive $11,600 annually, plus $105 per day while in session, $25 per day while not in session.
Senate — Dem., 19; Rep., 31. Total, 50
House — Dem., 50; Rep., 50. Total, 100

Iowa

Governor — Terry E. Branstad, R, $98,200
Lt. Gov. — Joy Corning, R, $68,740
Sec. of State — Paul D. Pate, R, $78,050
Atty. Gen. — Tom Miller, D, $93,520
Treasurer — Michael L. Fitzgerald, D, $78,050
Auditor — Richard D. Johnson, R, $78,050
Sec. of Agriculture — Dale M. Cochran, D, $78,050
General Assembly: meets annually at Des Moines. Members receive $20,120 annually, plus expense allowance.
Senate — Dem., 22; Rep., 28. Total, 50
House — Dem., 46; Rep., 54. Total, 100

Kansas

Governor — Bill Graves, R, $80,340
Lt. Gov. — Sheila Frahm, R, $81,600
Sec. of State — Ron Thornburgh, R, $62, 412
Atty. Gen. — Carla Stovall, R, $71,772
Treasurer — Sally Thompson, D, $62,412
Legislature: meets annually in Jan. at Topeka. Members receive $63 per day salary, plus $73 per day expenses while in session, $600 per month while not in session.
Senate — Dem., 13; Rep., 27. Total, 40
House — Dem., 44; Rep., 81. Total, 125

Kentucky

Governor — Paul Patton, D, $86,352
Lt. Gov. — Steve Henry, D, $77,294
Sec. of State — John Y. Brown III, D, $77,294
Atty. Gen. —A. B. Chandler III, D, $77,294
Treasurer — John Kennedy Hamilton, D, $77,294
Auditor — Ed Hatchett, D, $77,294
General Assembly: meets even years in Jan. at Frankfort. Members receive $100 per day, plus $75 per day expenses during session and $950 per month for expenses for interim.
Senate — Dem., 20; Rep., 17; 1 vacancy. Total, 38
House — Dem., 63; Rep., 36; 1 vacancy. Total, 100

Louisiana

Governor — M. J. "Mike" Foster, R, $95,000
Lt. Gov. — Kathleen Babineaux Blanco, D, $85,000
Sec. of State — W. Fox McKeithen, R, $85,000
Atty. Gen. — Richard Ieyoub, D, $85,000
Treasurer — Ken Duncan, D, $85,000
Legislature: meets in odd-numbered years at Baton Rouge starting last Mon. in Mar., for 60 legislative days of 85 calendar days; meets in even-numbered years on last Mon. in Apr. for 30 days of 45 calendar days. Members receive $16,800 annually, plus $75 per day expenses while in session.
Senate — Dem., 25; Rep., 14. Total, 39.
House — Dem., 78; Rep., 26, 1 vacancy. Total, 105.

Maine

Governor — Angus King Jr. † $70,000
Sec. of State — Dan A. Gwadosky, D, $50,648
Atty. Gen. — Andrew Ketterer, $74,235
Treasurer — Dale McCormick, D, $50,648
State Auditor — Gail M. Chase, CIA, $54,228
Legislature: meets annually at Augusta first Wed. in Dec. and Wed. after first Tues. in Jan., in even numbered years. Members receive $10,500 for first regular session, $7,500 for 2d regular session, plus expenses; presiding officers receive 50% more.
Senate — Dem., 19; Rep., 15; 1 ind. Total, 35
House — Dem., 81; Rep., 69; 1 ind. Total, 151

Maryland

Governor — Parris N. Glendening, D, $120,000
Lt. Gov. — Kathleen Kennedy Townsend, D, $100,000
Comptroller — Louis L. Goldstein, D, $100,000
Atty. Gen. — J. Joseph Curran Jr., D, $100,000
Sec. of State — John Willis, D, $70,000
Treasurer —Richard N. Dixon, D, $100,000
General Assembly: meets 90 consecutive days annually beginning on 2d Wed. in Jan. at Annapolis. Members receive $29,700 annually, plus expenses.
Senate — Dem., 32; Rep., 15. Total, 47
House — Dem., 100; Rep., 41. Total, 141

Massachusetts

Governor — A. Paul Cellucci, R, $100,000
Lt. Gov. — (vacancy)
Sec. of State — William Francis Galvin, D, $75,000

Atty. Gen. — L. Scott Harshbarger, D, $80,000
Treasurer — Joseph Malone, R, $75,000
Auditor — A. Joseph DeNucci, D, $75,000
General Court (legislature): meets Jan. biennially in Boston. Members receive $46,410 annually.
Senate — Dem., 33; Rep., 7. Total, 40
House — Dem., 130; Rep., 30; Total, 160

Michigan

Governor — John Engler, R, $127,100
Lt. Gov. — Connie Binsfeld, R, $93,800
Sec. of State — Candice S. Miller, R, $112,000
Atty. Gen. — Frank J. Kelley, D, $112,000
Treasurer — Douglas B. Roberts (appointed), $100,000
Legislature: meets annually in Jan. at Lansing. Members receive $51,895 annually.
Senate — Dem., 16; Rep., 21; 1 vacancy. Total, 38
House — Dem., 58; Rep., 52. Total, 110

Minnesota

(DFL means Democratic-Farmer-Labor Party)
Governor — Arne H. Carlson, R, $114,506
Lt. Gov. — Joanne E. Benson, R, $62,980
Sec. of State — Joan Anderson Growe, DFL, $62,980
Atty. Gen. — Hubert H. Humphrey 3d, DFL, $89,454
Treasurer — Michael McGrath, DFL, $62,980
Auditor — Judith H. Dutcher, R, $68,709
Legislature: meets for a total of 120 days within every 2 years, at St. Paul. Members receive $29,657 annually, plus expense allowance during session.
Senate — DFL, 42; R, 24; 1 ind. Total, 67
House — DFL, 69; R, 64; 1 vacancy. Total, 134

Mississippi

Governor — Kirk Fordice, R, $83,160
Lt. Gov. — Ronnie Musgrove, D, $40,800
Sec. of State — Eric Clark, D, $75,000
Atty. Gen. — Mike Moore, D, $90,800
Treasurer — Marshall Bennett, D, $75,000
Auditor — Phil Bryant, R, $75,000
Legislature: meets annually in Jan. at Jackson. Members receive $10,000 per regular session, plus travel allowance, and $1500 per month when not in session.
Senate — Dem., 34; Rep., 18. Total, 52
House — Dem., 84; Rep., 34; 2 ind., 2 vacancies. Total, 122

Missouri

Governor — Mel Carnahan, D, $107,269
Lt. Gov. — Roger Wilson, D, $64,823
Sec. of State — Rebecca McDowell Cook, D, $86,046
Atty. Gen. — Jeremiah W. Nixon, D, $93,120
Treasurer — Bob Holden, D, $86,046
State Auditor — Margaret Kelly, R, $86,046
General Assembly: meets annually at Jefferson City on 1st Wed. after 1st Mon. in Jan. Members receive $27,580 annually.
Senate — Dem., 19; Rep., 15. Total, 34
House — Dem., 87; Rep., 75; 1 ind. Total, 163

Montana

Governor — Marc Racicot, R, $78,246
Lt. Gov. — Judy Martz, R, $53,407
Sec. of State — Mike Cooney, D, $58,658
Atty. Gen. — Joe Mazurek, D, $66,756
Legislative Assembly: meets odd years in Jan. at Helena. Members receive $58.50 per legislative day, plus $70 per day for expenses while in session.
Senate — Dem., 16; Rep., 34. Total, 50
House — Dem., 35; Rep., 65. Total, 100

Nebraska

Governor — Ben Nelson, D, $65,000
Lt. Gov. — Kim Robak, D, $47,000
Sec. of State — Scott Moore, R, $52,000
Atty. Gen. — Don Stenberg, R, $64,500
Treasurer — David Heineman, R, $49,500
Legislature: Unicameral body composed of 49 members who are elected on a nonpartisan ballot and are called senators; meets annually in Jan. at Lincoln. Members receive $12,000 annually, plus expenses.

Nevada

Governor — Robert Miller, D, $90,000
Lt. Gov. — Lonnie Hammargren, R, $20,000
Sec. of State — Dean Heller, R, $62,500
Comptroller — Darrel Daines, R, $62,500
Atty. Gen. — Frankie Sue Del Papa, D, $85,000
Treasurer — Robert Seale, R, $62,500
Legislature: meets at Carson City odd years starting on 3d Mon. in Jan. for 60 days. Members receive $130 per day salary, plus $66 per day expenses, while in session.
Senate — Dem., 9; Rep., 12. Total, 21
Assembly — Dem., 25; Rep., 17. Total, 42

New Hampshire

Governor — Jeanne Shaheen, D, $86,235
Sec. of State — William M. Gardner, D, $68,768
Atty. Gen. — Philip T. McLaughlin, D, $76,983
Treasurer — Georgie A. Thomas, R, $68,768.
General Court (Legislature): meets every year in Jan. at Concord. Members receive $200, presiding officers $250, annually.
Senate — Dem., 6; Rep., 18. Total, 24
House — Rep., 279; Dem., 112; 1 ind.; 1 lib.; 7 vac. Total, 400

New Jersey

Governor — Christine Todd Whitman, R, $85,000
Sec. of State — Lonna R. Hooks, R, $100,225
Atty. Gen. — Peter Verniero, R, $100,225
Treasurer — James A. DiEleuterio Jr, R, $100,225
Legislature: meets throughout the year at Trenton. Members receive $35,000 annually, except president of Senate and speaker of Assembly, who receive 1/3 more.
Senate — Dem., 16; Rep., 24. Total, 40
Assembly — Dem., 30; Rep., 50. Total, 80

New Mexico

Governor — Gary Johnson, R, $90,000
Lt. Gov. — Walter Bradley, R, $65,000
Sec. of State — Stephanie Gonzales, D, $65,000
Atty. Gen. — Tom Udall, D, $72,500
Treasurer — Michael A. Montoya, D, $65,000
Legislature: meets starting on the 3d Tues. in Jan. at Santa Fe; odd years for 60 days, even years for 30 days. Members receive $75 per day while in session.
Senate — Dem., 25; Rep., 17. Total, 42
House — Dem., 42; Rep., 28. Total, 70

New York

Governor — George E. Pataki, R, $130,000
Lt. Gov. — Elizabeth McCaughey, R, $110,000
Sec. of State — Alexander F. Treadwell, R, $90,832
Comptroller — H. Carl McCall, D, $110,000
Atty. Gen. — Dennis Vacco, R, $110,000
Legislature: meets annually in Jan. at Albany. Members receive $57,500 annually, plus $89 per day expenses.
Senate — Dem., 25; Rep., 36. Total, 61
Assembly — Dem., 94; Rep., 56; Total, 150

North Carolina

Governor — James B. Hunt Jr., D, $107,132
Lt. Gov. — Dennis Wicker, D, $94,552, plus expenses
Sec. of State — Elaine F. Marshall, D, $94,552
Atty. Gen. — Michael Easley, D, $94,552
Treasurer — Harlan E. Boyles, D, $94,552
General Assembly: meets odd years in Jan. at Raleigh. Members receive $13,951 annually and an expense allowance of $559 per month, plus subsistence and travel allowance while in session. Also meets in even years for a short session (about 6-8 weeks), usually in May.
Senate — Dem., 30; Rep., 20. Total, 50
House — Dem., 52; Rep., 68. Total, 120

North Dakota

Governor — Edward T. Schafer, R, $73,176
Lt. Gov. — Rosemarie Myrdal, R, $60,132
Sec. of State — Alvin A. Jaeger, R, $55,464
Atty. Gen. — Heidi Heitkamp, D, $62,592
Treasurer — Kathi Gilmore, D, $55,464
Legislative Assembly: meets odd years in Jan. at Bismarck. Members receive $250 per month salary, plus $111 per calendar day salary during session and $39 per day expenses plus any additional state or local taxes on lodging, with a limit of $650 per month.
Senate — Dem., 19; Rep., 29. Total, 48
House — Dem., 27; Rep., 71. Total, 98

Ohio

Governor — George V. Voinovich, R, $115,762
Lt. Gov. — Nancy P. Hollister, R, $59,862
Sec. of State — Bob Taft, R, $85,517
Atty. Gen. — Betty Montgomery, R, $85,517
Treasurer — J. Kenneth Blackwell, R, $85,517
Auditor — Jim Petro, R, $85,517
General Assembly: meets odd years at Columbus starting on 1st Mon. in Jan. Members receive $42,426 annually.
Senate — Dem., 12; Rep., 21. Total, 33
House — Dem., 39; Rep., 60. Total, 99

Oklahoma

Governor — Frank Keating, R, $70,000
Lt. Gov. — Mary Fallin, R, $62,500
Sec. of State — Tom Cole, R, $43,700
Atty. Gen. — Drew Edmondson, D, $75,000

(continued)

Treasurer — Robert Butkin, D, $70,000
Auditor— Clifton Scott, D, $70,000
Legislature: meets annually at noon the first Mon. in Feb. at Oklahoma City. In odd-numbered years, the session includes one day (1st Tuesday after 1st Monday) in Jan. Members receive $32,000 annually.
Senate — Dem., 33; Rep., 15. Total, 48
House — Dem., 65; Rep., 36. Total, 101

Oregon
Governor — John Kitzhaber, D, $88,300
Sec. of State — Phil Keisling, D, $67,900
Atty. Gen. — Hardy Myers, D, $72,800
Treasurer — Jim Hill, D, $67,900
Legislative Assembly: meets odd years in Jan. at Salem. Members receive $1,206 monthly, $87 expenses per day during session and when attending meetings during the interim, plus $400 expense account during interim.
Senate — Dem., 10; Rep., 20. Total, 30
House — Dem., 29; Rep., 31. Total, 60

Pennsylvania
Governor — Tom Ridge, R, $125,000
Lt. Gov. — Mark Schweiker, R, $105,000
Sec. of the Commonwealth — Yvette Kane, R, $90,000
Atty. Gen. — D. Michael Fisher, R, $104,000
Treasurer — Barbara Hafer, R, $104,000
General Assembly — convenes annually in Jan. at Harrisburg. Members receive $57,367 annually, plus expenses.
Senate — Dem., 20; Rep., 29; 1 vacancy. Total, 50.
House — Dem., 99; Rep., 104. Total, 203

Rhode Island
Governor — Lincoln C. Almond, R, $69,900
Lt. Gov. — Bernard A. Jackvony, R, $52,000
Sec. of State — James R. Langevin, D, $52,000
Atty. Gen. — Jeffrey B. Pine, R, $55,000
Treasurer — Nancy J. Mayer, R, $52,000
General Assembly: meets annually in Jan. at Providence. Members receive $10,000 annually.
Senate — Dem., 40; Rep., 10. Total, 50
House — Dem., 84; Rep., 16. Total, 100

South Carolina
Governor — David M. Beasley, R, $106,078
Lt. Gov. — Robert L. Peeler, R, $46,545
Sec. of State — Jim Miles, R, $92,007.
Comptroller Gen. — Earle E. Morris Jr., D, $92,007
Atty. Gen. — Charles M. Condon, R, $92,007
Treasurer — Richard Eckstrom, R, $92,007
General Assembly: meets annually in Jan. at Columbia. Members receive $10,400 annually, plus $88 per day for expenses.
Senate — Dem., 26; Rep., 20. Total, 46
House — Dem., 53; Rep., 69; 1 ind.; 1 vacancy. Total, 124

South Dakota
Governor — William Janklow, R, $82,271
Lt. Gov. — Carole Hillard, R, $30,766
Sec. of State — Joyce Hazeltine, R, $55,900
Treasurer — Dick Butler, D, $55,900
Atty. Gen. — Mark Barnett, R, $69,876
Auditor — Vernon Larson, R, $55,900
Legislature: meets annually in Jan. at Pierre. Members receive $4,267 for 40-day session in odd-numbered years, and $3,733 for 35-day session in even-numbered years, plus $75 per legislative day.
Senate — Dem., 13; Rep., 22. Total, 35
House — Dem., 22; Rep., 48. Total, 70

Tennessee
Governor — Don Sundquist, R, $85,000
Lt. Gov. — John S. Wilder, D, $49,500
Sec. of State — Riley C. Darnell, D, $80,700
Comptroller — William Snodgrass, D, $86,484
Atty. Gen. — John Knox Walkup, D, $107,820
General Assembly: meets annually in Jan. at Nashville. Members receive $16,500 annual salary, plus $120 per day expenses while in session.
Senate — Dem., 18; Rep., 15. Total, 33
House — Dem., 61; Rep., 38. Total, 99

Texas
Governor — George W. Bush, R, $115,345
Lt. Gov. — Bob Bullock, D, $7,200
Sec. of State — Antonio Garza Jr., R, $76,966
Comptroller — John Sharp, D, $92,217
Atty. Gen. — Dan Morales, D, $92,217
Railroad Commissioners — Carole Keeton Rylander, R, Chair; Barry Williamson, R; Charles R. Matthews, R; $92,217

(1) Salaries are effective 12/1/97.　(2) Salaries are effective 1/1/98.

Legislature: meets odd years in Jan. at Austin. Members receive $7,200 annually, plus $95 per day expenses while in session.
Senate — Dem., 17; Rep., 14. Total, 31
House — Dem., 82; Rep., 68. Total, 150

Utah
Governor — Michael O. Leavitt, R, $85,200
Lt. Gov. — Olene S. Walker, R, $66,200
Atty. Gen. — Jan Graham, D, $71,700
Treasurer — Edward T. Alter, R, $66,200
Legislature: convenes for 45 days on 2d Mon. in Jan. each year at Salt Lake City; Members receive $100 per day, plus $35 a day expenses.
Senate — Dem., 10; Rep., 19. Total, 29
House — Dem., 20; Rep., 55. Total, 75

Vermont
Governor — Howard Dean, D, $96,661
Lt. Gov. — Douglas A. Racine, D, $40,296
Sec. of State — Jim Milne, R, $60,825
Atty. Gen. — William H. Sorrell, D, $73,067
Treasurer — James Douglas, R, $60,825
Auditor — Edward Flanagan, D, $60,825
General Assembly: meets in Jan. at Montpelier (annual and biennial session). Members receive $510 per week while in session plus $100 per day for special session, plus expenses.
Senate — Dem., 12; Rep., 18. Total, 30
House — Dem., 86; Rep., 61; Prog. Coalition, 1; 2 ind. Total, 150

Virginia
Governor — George F. Allen, R, $110,000
Lt. Gov. — Donald S. Beyer Jr., D, $32,000
Atty. Gen. — Richard Cullen, R, $97,500
Sec. of the Commonwealth — Elizabeth Beamer, R, $73,023
Treasurer — Susan F. Dewey, R, $89,500
General Assembly: meets annually in Jan. at Richmond. Members receive $18,000 (senate), $17,640 (assembly) annually, plus expense and mileage allowances.
Senate — Dem., 20; Rep., 20. Total, 40
House — Dem., 52; Rep., 47; 1 ind. Total, 100

Washington
Governor — Mike Lowry, D, $121,000
Lt. Gov. — Joel Pritchard, R, $62,700
Sec. of State — Ralph Munro, R, $69,000
Atty. Gen. — Christine Gregoire, D, $93,000
Treasurer — Daniel K. Grimm, D, $84,100
Legislature: meets annually in Jan. at Olympia. Members receive $28,300 annually, plus $80 per diem while in session, and $80 per diem for attending meetings during interim.
Senate — Dem., 24; Rep., 25. Total, 49
House — Dem., 42; Rep., 56. Total, 98

West Virginia
Governor — Cecil H. Underwood, R, $90,000
Sec. of State — Ken Hechler, D, $65,000
Atty. Gen. — Darrell McGraw, D, $75,000
Treasurer — John D. Perdue, D, $65,000
Comm. of Agric. — Gus Douglass, D, $70,000
Auditor — Glen B. Gainer 3d, D, $70,000
Legislature: meets annually in Jan. at Charleston, except after gubernatorial elections, when the legislature meets in Feb. Members receive $15,000 annually.
Senate — Dem., 25; Rep., 9. Total, 34
House — Dem., 74; Rep., 26. Total, 100

Wisconsin
Governor — Tommy G. Thompson, R, $101,861
Lt. Gov. — Scott McCallum, R, $54,795
Sec. of State — Douglas La Follette, D, $49,719
Treasurer — Jack Voight, R, $49,719
Atty. Gen. — James E. Doyle, D, $97,756
Legislature: meets in Jan. at Madison. Members receive $35,070 annually, plus $75 per day expenses.
Senate — Dem., 17; Rep., 16. Total, 33
Assembly — Dem., 47; Rep., 51; 1 vacancy. Total, 99

Wyoming
Governor — Jim Geringer, R, $95,000
Sec. of State — Diana J. Ohman, R, $77,000
Atty. Gen. — William U. Hill, no statutory salary
Treasurer — Stan Smith, R, $77,000
Auditor — Dave Ferrari, R, $77,000
Legislature: meets odd years in Jan., even years in Feb., at Cheyenne. Members receive $125 per day while in session, plus $80 per day for expenses.
Senate — Dem., 9; Rep., 21. Total, 30.
House — Dem., 17; Rep., 43. Total, 60.

CABINETS OF THE U.S.

The U.S. Cabinet and Its Role

The heads of major executive departments of government constitute the Cabinet. This institution, not provided for in the U.S. Constitution, developed as an advisory body out of the desire of presidents to consult on policy matters. Aside from its advisory role, the Cabinet as such has no function and wields no executive authority. The president may or may not consult it and is not bound by its advice. Most presidents also confer with numerous advisers outside the Cabinet. A group of regular informal advisers to the president has been known in American history as a "kitchen cabinet." The formal Cabinet (which may include other officials besides department heads, as designated by the president) meets at times set by the president. Members of Pres. Bill Clinton's Cabinet listed here are as of Oct. 15, 1997.

Secretaries of State

The Department of Foreign Affairs was created by act of Congress on July 27, 1789, and the name changed to Department of State on Sept. 15.

President	Secretary	Home	Apptd.
Washington ..	Thomas Jefferson...	VA	1789
"	Edmund Randolph ..	VA	1794
"	Timothy Pickering ..	PA	1795
Adams, J.	Timothy Pickering ...	PA	1797
"	John Marshall......	VA	1800
Jefferson	James Madison	VA	1801
Madison.....	Robert Smith	MD	1809
"	James Monroe	VA	1811
Monroe	John Quincy Adams .	MA	1817
Adams, J.Q...	Henry Clay........	KY	1825
Jackson.....	Martin Van Buren ...	NY	1829
"	Edward Livingston ..	LA	1831
"	Louis McLane......	DE	1833
"	John Forsyth	GA	1834
Van Buren ...	John Forsyth	GA	1837
Harrison, W.H.	Daniel Webster....	MA	1841
Tyler	Daniel Webster	MA	1841
"	Abel P. Upshur...	VA	1843
"	John C. Calhoun..	SC	1844
Polk.......	John C. Calhoun..	SC	1845
"	James Buchanan ..	PA	1845
Taylor	James Buchanan ..	PA	1849
"	John M. Clayton ..	DE	1849
Fillmore.....	John M. Clayton ..	DE	1850
"	Daniel Webster....	MA	1850
"	Edward Everett.....	MA	1852
Pierce	William L. Marcy	NY	1853
Buchanan ...	William L. Marcy	NY	1857
"	Lewis Cass	MI.	1857
"	Jeremiah S. Black...	PA	1860
Lincoln......	Jeremiah S. Black ..	PA	1861
"	William H. Seward ..	NY	1861
Johnson, A...	William H. Seward ..	NY	1865
Grant.......	Elihu B. Washburne .	IL	1869
"	Hamilton Fish	NY	1869
Hayes	Hamilton Fish......	NY	1877
"	William M. Evarts ...	NY	1877
Garfield	William M. Evarts ...	NY	1881
"	James G. Blaine....	ME	1881
Arthur	James G. Blaine ...	ME	1881
"	F.T. Frelinghuysen ..	NJ	1881
Cleveland ...	F.T. Frelinghuysen ..	NJ	1885
"	Thomas F. Bayard ..	DE	1885
Harrison, B...	Thomas F. Bayard ..	DE	1889
"	James G. Blaine....	ME	1889
Harrison, B.	John W. Foster	IN	1892
Cleveland	Walter Q. Gresham..	IN	1893
"	Richard Olney	MA	1895
McKinley	Richard Olney	MA	1897
"	John Sherman	OH	1897
"	William R. Day	OH	1898
"	John Hay........	DC	1898
Roosevelt, T...	John Hay........	DC	1901
"	Elihu Root	NY	1905
"	Robert Bacon	NY	1909
Taft........	Robert Bacon	NY	1909
"	Philander C. Knox...	PA	1909
Wilson......	Philander C. Knox ..	PA	1913
"	William J. Bryan	NE	1913
"	Robert Lansing	NY	1915
"	Bainbridge Colby ...	NY	1920
Harding.....	Charles E. Hughes ..	NY	1921
Coolidge	Charles E. Hughes ..	NY	1923
"	Frank B. Kellogg....	MN	1925
Hoover	Frank B. Kellogg....	MN	1929
"	Henry L. Stimson ...	NY	1929
Roosevelt, F.D.	Cordell Hull	TN	1933
"	E.R. Stettinius Jr. ...	VA	1944
Truman	E.R. Stettinius Jr.	VA	1945
"	James F. Byrnes....	SC	1945
"	George C. Marshall..	PA	1947
"	Dean G. Acheson ...	CT	1949
Eisenhower ...	John Foster Dulles ..	NY	1953
"	Christian A. Herter ..	MA	1959
Kennedy	Dean Rusk	NY	1961
Johnson, L.B..	Dean Rusk	NY	1963
Nixon	William P. Rogers ...	NY	1969
"	Henry A. Kissinger ..	DC	1973
Ford	Henry A. Kissinger ..	DC	1974
Carter	Cyrus R. Vance	NY	1977
"	Edmund S. Muskie ..	ME	1980
Reagan......	Alexander M. Haig Jr.	CT	1981
"	George P. Shultz ...	CA	1982
Bush........	James A. Baker 3d ..	TX	1989
"	Lawrence S. Eagleburger	MI.	1992
Clinton.......	Warren M. Christopher......	CA	1993
"	Madeleine K. Albright	DC	1997

Secretaries of the Treasury

The Treasury Department was organized by act of Congress on Sept. 2, 1789.

President	Secretary	Home	Apptd.
Washington....	Alexander Hamilton ..	NY	1789
"	Oliver Wolcott	CT	1795
Adams, J......	Oliver Wolcott	CT	1797
"	Samuel Dexter......	MA	1801
Jefferson......	Samuel Dexter......	MA	1801
"	Albert Gallatin	PA	1801
Madison	Albert Gallatin	PA	1809
"	George W. Campbell ..	TN	1814
"	Alexander J. Dallas ..	PA	1814
"	William H. Crawford ..	GA	1816
Monroe.......	William H. Crawford ..	GA	1817
Adams, J.Q...	Richard Rush......	PA	1825
Jackson......	Samuel D. Ingham ...	PA	1829
"	Louis McLane	DE	1831
"	William J. Duane	PA	1833
"	Roger B. Taney	MD	1833
"	Levi Woodbury......	NH	1834
Van Buren....	Levi Woodbury......	NH	1837
Harrison, W.H.	Thomas Ewing	OH	1841
Tyler........	Thomas Ewing	OH	1841
"	Walter Forward	PA	1841
Tyler.........	John C. Spencer	NY	1843
"	George M. Bibb	KY	1844
Polk........	Robert J. Walker	MS	1845
Taylor........	William M. Meredith ..	PA	1849
Fillmore.......	Thomas Corwin	OH	1850
Pierce.......	James Guthrie	KY	1853
Buchanan.....	Howell Cobb	GA	1857
"	Phillip F. Thomas	MD	1860
"	John A. Dix	NY	1861
Lincoln......	Salmon P. Chase....	OH	1861
"	William P. Fessenden.	ME	1864
"	Hugh McCulloch	IN	1865
Johnson, A.....	Hugh McCulloch	IN	1865
Grant	George S. Boutwell ..	MA	1869
"	William A. Richardson.	MA	1873
"	Benjamin H. Bristow ..	KY	1874
"	Lot M. Morrill	ME	1876
Hayes........	John Sherman	OH	1877
Garfield.......	William Windom	MN	1881
Arthur........	Charles J. Folger	NY	1881

(continued)

Secretaries of the Treasury (*continued*)

President	Secretary	Home	Apptd.	President	Secretary	Home	Apptd.
Arthur	Walter Q. Gresham	IN	1884	Truman	Fred M. Vinson	KY	1945
"	Hugh McCulloch	IN	1884	"	John W. Snyder	MO	1946
Cleveland	Daniel Manning	NY	1885	Eisenhower	George M. Humphrey	OH	1953
"	Charles S. Fairchild	NY	1887	"	Robert B. Anderson	CT	1957
Harrison, B.	William Windom	MN	1889	Kennedy	C. Douglas Dillon	NJ	1961
"	Charles Foster	OH	1891	Johnson, L.B.	C. Douglas Dillon	NJ	1963
Cleveland	John G. Carlisle	KY	1893	"	Henry H. Fowler	VA	1965
McKinley	Lyman J. Gage	IL	1897	"	Joseph W. Barr	IN	1968
Roosevelt, T.	Lyman J. Gage	IL	1901	Nixon	David M. Kennedy	IL	1969
"	Leslie M. Shaw	IA	1902	"	John B. Connally	TX	1971
"	George B. Cortelyou	NY	1907	"	George P. Shultz	IL	1972
Taft	Franklin MacVeagh	IL	1909	"	William E. Simon	NJ	1974
Wilson	William G. McAdoo	NY	1913	Ford	William E. Simon	NJ	1974
"	Carter Glass	VA	1918	Carter	W. Michael Blumenthal	MI	1977
"	David F. Houston	MO	1920	"	G. William Miller	RI	1979
Harding	Andrew W. Mellon	PA	1921	Reagan	Donald T. Regan	NY	1981
Coolidge	Andrew W. Mellon	PA	1923	"	James A. Baker 3d	TX	1985
Hoover	Andrew W. Mellon	PA	1929	"	Nicholas F. Brady	NJ	1988
"	Ogden L. Mills	NY	1932	Bush	Nicholas F. Brady	NJ	1989
Roosevelt, F.D.	William H. Woodin	NY	1933	Clinton	Lloyd Bentsen	TX	1993
"	Henry Morgenthau, Jr.	NY	1934	"	Robert E. Rubin	NY	1995

Secretaries of Defense

The Department of Defense, originally designated the National Military Establishment, was created Sept. 18, 1947. It is headed by the secretary of defense, a member of the president's Cabinet. The departments of the army, of the navy, and of the air force function within the Defense Department, and since 1947 their secretaries have not been members of the president's cabinet.

President	Secretary	Home	Apptd.	President	Secretary	Home	Apptd.
Truman	James V. Forrestal	NY	1947	"	Elliot L. Richardson	MA	1973
"	Louis A. Johnson	WV	1949	"	James R. Schlesinger	VA	1973
"	George C. Marshall	PA	1950	Ford	James R. Schlesinger	VA	1974
"	Robert A. Lovett	NY	1951	"	Donald H. Rumsfeld	IL	1975
Eisenhower	Charles E. Wilson	MI	1953	Carter	Harold Brown	CA	1977
"	Neil H. McElroy	OH	1957	Reagan	Caspar W. Weinberger	CA	1981
"	Thomas S. Gates Jr.	PA	1959	"	Frank C. Carlucci	PA	1987
Kennedy	Robert S. McNamara	MI	1961	Bush	Richard B. Cheney	WY	1989
Johnson, L.B.	Robert S. McNamara	MI	1963	Clinton	Les Aspin	WI	1993
"	Clark M. Clifford	MD	1968	"	William J. Perry	CA	1994
Nixon	Melvin R. Laird	WI	1969	"	William S. Cohen	ME	1997

Secretaries of War

The War Department (which included jurisdiction over the navy until 1798) was created by act of Congress on Aug. 7, 1789, and Gen. Henry Knox was commissioned secretary of war under that act on Sept. 12, 1789.

President	Secretary	Home	Apptd.	President	Secretary	Home	Apptd.
Washington	Henry Knox	MA	1789	Grant	John A. Rawlins	IL	1869
"	Timothy Pickering	PA	1795	"	William T. Sherman	OH	1869
"	James McHenry	MD	1796	"	William W. Belknap	IA	1869
Adams, J.	James McHenry	MD	1797	"	Alphonso Taft	OH	1876
"	Samuel Dexter	MA	1800	"	James D. Cameron	PA	1876
Jefferson	Henry Dearborn	MA	1801	Hayes	George W. McCrary	IA	1877
Madison	William Eustis	MA	1809	"	Alexander Ramsey	MN	1879
"	John Armstrong	NY	1813	Garfield	Robert T. Lincoln	IL	1881
"	James Monroe	VA	1814	Arthur	Robert T. Lincoln	IL	1881
"	William H. Crawford	GA	1815	Cleveland	William C. Endicott	MA	1885
Monroe	John C. Calhoun	SC	1817	Harrison, B.	Redfield Proctor	VT	1889
Adams, J.Q.	James Barbour	VA	1825	"	Stephen B. Elkins	WV	1891
"	Peter B. Porter	NY	1828	Cleveland	Daniel S. Lamont	NY	1893
Jackson	John H. Eaton	TN	1829	McKinley	Russel A. Alger	MI	1897
"	Lewis Cass	MI	1831	"	Elihu Root	NY	1899
"	Benjamin F. Butler	NY	1837	Roosevelt, T.	Elihu Root	NY	1901
Van Buren	Joel R. Poinsett	SC	1837	"	William H. Taft	OH	1904
Harrison, W.H.	John Bell	TN	1841	"	Luke E. Wright	TN	1908
Tyler	John Bell	TN	1841	Taft	Jacob M. Dickinson	TN	1909
"	John C. Spencer	NY	1841	"	Henry L. Stimson	NY	1911
"	James M. Porter	PA	1843	Wilson	Lindley M. Garrison	NJ	1913
"	William Wilkins	PA	1844	"	Newton D. Baker	OH	1916
Polk	William L. Marcy	NY	1845	Harding	John W. Weeks	MA	1921
Taylor	George W. Crawford	GA	1849	Coolidge	John W. Weeks	MA	1923
Fillmore	Charles M. Conrad	LA	1850	"	Dwight F. Davis	MO	1925
Pierce	Jefferson Davis	MS	1853	Hoover	James W. Good	IL	1929
Buchanan	John B. Floyd	VA	1857	"	Patrick J. Hurley	OK	1929
"	Joseph Holt	KY	1861	Roosevelt, F.D.	George H. Dern	UT	1933
Lincoln	Simon Cameron	PA	1861	"	Harry H. Woodring	KS	1937
"	Edwin M. Stanton	PA	1862	"	Henry L. Stimson	NY	1940
Johnson, A.	Edwin M. Stanton	PA	1865	Truman	Robert P. Patterson	NY	1945
"	John M. Schofield	IL	1868	"	Kenneth C. Royall[1]	NC	1947

(1) Last member of the Cabinet with this title. The War Department became the Department of the Army and became a branch of the Department of Defense in 1947.

Secretaries of the Navy

The Navy Department was created by act of Congress on Apr. 30, 1798.

President	Secretary	Home	Apptd.
Adams, J.	Benjamin Stoddert	MD	1798
Jefferson	Benjamin Stoddert	MD	1801
Jefferson	Robert Smith	MD	1801
Madison	Paul Hamilton	SC	1809
Madison	William Jones	PA	1813
"	Benjamin W. Crowninshield	MA	1814
Monroe	Benjamin W. Crowninshield	MA	1817
"	Smith Thompson	NY	1818
"	Samuel L. Southard	NJ	1823
Adams, J.Q.	Samuel L. Southard	NJ	1825
Jackson	John Branch	NC	1829
"	Levi Woodbury	NH	1831
"	Mahlon Dickerson	NJ	1834
Van Buren	Mahlon Dickerson	NJ	1837
"	James K. Paulding	NY	1838
Harrison, W.H.	George E. Badger	NC	1841
Tyler	George E. Badger	NC	1841
"	Abel P. Upshur	VA	1841
"	David Henshaw	MA	1843
"	Thomas W. Gilmer	VA	1844
"	John Y. Mason	VA	1844
Polk	George Bancroft	MA	1845
"	John Y. Mason	VA	1846
Taylor	William B. Preston	VA	1849
Fillmore	William A. Graham	NC	1850
"	John P. Kennedy	MD	1852
Pierce	James C. Dobbin	NC	1853
Buchanan	Isaac Toucey	CT	1857
Lincoln	Gideon Welles	CT	1861
Johnson, A.	Gideon Welles	CT	1865
Grant	Adolph E. Borie	PA	1869
Grant	George M. Robeson	NJ	1869
Hayes	Richard W. Thompson	IN	1877
"	Nathan Goff Jr.	WV	1881
Garfield	William H. Hunt	LA	1881
Arthur	William E. Chandler	NH	1882
Cleveland	William C. Whitney	NY	1885
Harrison, B.	Benjamin F. Tracy	NY	1889
Cleveland	Hilary A. Herbert	AL	1893
McKinley	John D. Long	MA	1897
Roosevelt, T.	John D. Long	MA	1901
"	William H. Moody	MA	1902
"	Paul Morton	IL	1904
"	Charles J. Bonaparte	MD	1905
"	Victor H. Metcalf	CA	1906
"	Truman H. Newberry	MI	1908
Taft	George von L. Meyer	MA	1909
Wilson	Josephus Daniels	NC	1913
Harding	Edwin Denby	MI	1921
Coolidge	Edwin Denby	MI	1923
"	Curtis D. Wilbur	CA	1924
Hoover	Charles Francis Adams	MA	1929
Roosevelt, F.D.	Claude A. Swanson	VA	1933
"	Charles Edison	NJ	1940
"	Frank Knox	IL	1940
"	James V. Forrestal	NY	1944
Truman	James V. Forrestal[1]	NY	1945

(1) Last member of Cabinet with this title. The Navy Department became a branch of the Department of Defense when the latter was created on Sept. 18, 1947.

Attorneys General

The office of attorney general was established by act of Congress on Sept. 24, 1789. It officially reached Cabinet rank in Mar. 1792, when the first attorney general, Edmund Randolph, attended his initial Cabinet meeting. The Department of Justice, headed by the attorney general, was created June 22, 1870.

President	Attorney General	Home	Apptd.
Washington	Edmund Randolph	VA	1789
"	William Bradford	PA	1794
"	Charles Lee	VA	1795
Adams, J.	Charles Lee	VA	1797
Jefferson	Levi Lincoln	MA	1801
"	John Breckenridge	KY	1805
"	Caesar A. Rodney	DE	1807
Madison	Caesar A. Rodney	DE	1807
"	William Pinkney	MD	1811
"	Richard Rush	PA	1814
Monroe	Richard Rush	PA	1817
"	William Wirt	VA	1817
Adams, J.Q.	William Wirt	VA	1825
Jackson	John M. Berrien	GA	1829
"	Roger B. Taney	MD	1831
"	Benjamin F. Butler	NY	1833
Van Buren	Benjamin F. Butler	NY	1837
"	Felix Grundy	TN	1838
"	Henry D. Gilpin	PA	1840
Harrison, W.H.	John J. Crittenden	KY	1841
Tyler	John J. Crittenden	KY	1841
"	Hugh S. Legare	SC	1841
"	John Nelson	MD	1843
Polk	John Y. Mason	VA	1845
"	Nathan Clifford	ME	1846
"	Isaac Toucey	CT	1848
Taylor	Reverdy Johnson	MD	1849
Fillmore	John J. Crittenden	KY	1850
Pierce	Caleb Cushing	MA	1853
Buchanan	Jeremiah S. Black	PA	1857
"	Edwin M. Stanton	PA	1860
Lincoln	Edward Bates	MO	1861
"	James Speed	KY	1864
Johnson, A.	James Speed	KY	1865
"	Henry Stanbery	OH	1866
"	William M. Evarts	NY	1868
Grant	Ebenezer R. Hoar	MA	1869
"	Amos T. Akerman	GA	1870
"	George H. Williams	OR	1871
"	Edwards Pierrepont	NY	1875
"	Alphonso Taft	OH	1876
Hayes	Charles Devens	MA	1877
Garfield	Wayne MacVeagh	PA	1881
Arthur	Benjamin H. Brewster	PA	1882
Cleveland	Augustus Garland	AR	1885
Harrison, B.	William H. H. Miller	IN	1889
Cleveland	Richard Olney	MA	1893
"	Judson Harmon	OH	1895
McKinley	Joseph McKenna	CA	1897
"	John W. Griggs	NJ	1898
"	Philander C. Knox	PA	1901
Roosevelt, T.	Philander C. Knox	PA	1901
"	William H. Moody	MA	1904
"	Charles J. Bonaparte	MD	1906
Taft	George W. Wickersham	NY	1909
Wilson	J.C. McReynolds	TN	1913
"	Thomas W. Gregory	TX	1914
"	A. Mitchell Palmer	PA	1919
Harding	Harry M. Daugherty	OH	1921
Coolidge	Harry M. Daugherty	OH	1923
"	Harlan F. Stone	NY	1924
"	John G. Sargent	VT	1925
Hoover	William D. Mitchell	MN	1929
Roosevelt, F.D.	Homer S. Cummings	CT	1933
"	Frank Murphy	MI	1939
"	Robert H. Jackson	NY	1940
"	Francis Biddle	PA	1941
Truman	Thomas C. Clark	TX	1945
"	J. Howard McGrath	RI	1949
"	J.P. McGranery	PA	1952
Eisenhower	Herbert Brownell Jr.	NY	1953
"	William P. Rogers	MD	1957
Kennedy	Robert F. Kennedy	MA	1961
Johnson, L.B.	Robert F. Kennedy	MA	1963
"	N. de B. Katzenbach	IL	1964
"	Ramsey Clark	TX	1967
Nixon	John N. Mitchell	NY	1969
"	Richard G. Kleindienst	AZ	1972
"	Elliot L. Richardson	MA	1973
"	William B. Saxbe	OH	1974
Ford	William B. Saxbe	OH	1974
"	Edward H. Levi	IL	1975
Carter	Griffin B. Bell	GA	1977
"	Benjamin R. Civiletti	MD	1979
Reagan	William French Smith	CA	1981
"	Edwin Meese 3d	CA	1985
"	Richard Thornburgh	PA	1988
Bush	Richard Thornburgh	PA	1989
"	William P. Barr	NY	1991
Clinton	Janet Reno	FL	1993

Secretaries of the Interior

The Department of the Interior was created by act of Congress on Mar. 3, 1849.

President	Secretary	Home	Apptd.	President	Secretary	Home	Apptd.
Taylor	Thomas Ewing	OH	1849	Taft	Walter L. Fisher	IL	1911
Fillmore	Thomas M. T. McKennan	PA	1850	Wilson	Franklin K. Lane	CA	1913
"	Alex H. H. Stuart	VA	1850	"	John B. Payne	IL	1920
Pierce	Robert McClelland	MI	1853	Harding	Albert B. Fall	NM	1921
Buchanan	Jacob Thompson	MS	1857	"	Hubert Work	CO	1923
Lincoln	Caleb B. Smith	IN	1861	Coolidge	Hubert Work	CO	1923
"	John P. Usher	IN	1863	"	Roy O. West	IL	1929
Johnson, A.	John P. Usher	IN	1865	Hoover	Ray Lyman Wilbur	CA	1929
"	James Harlan	IA	1865	Roosevelt, F.D.	Harold L. Ickes	IL	1933
"	Orville H. Browning	IL	1866	Truman	Harold L. Ickes	IL	1945
Grant	Jacob D. Cox	OH	1869	"	Julius A. Krug	WI	1946
"	Columbus Delano	OH	1870	"	Oscar L. Chapman	CO	1949
"	Zachariah Chandler	MI	1875	Eisenhower	Douglas McKay	OR	1953
Hayes	Carl Schurz	MO	1877	"	Fred A. Seaton	NE	1956
Garfield	Samuel J. Kirkwood	IA	1881	Kennedy	Stewart L. Udall	AZ	1961
Arthur	Henry M. Teller	CO	1882	Johnson, L.B.	Stewart L. Udall	AZ	1963
Cleveland	Lucius Q.C. Lamar	MS	1885	Nixon	Walter J. Hickel	AK	1969
"	William F. Vilas	WI	1888	"	Rogers C.B. Morton	MD	1971
Harrison, B.	John W. Noble	MO	1889	Ford	Rogers C.B. Morton	MD	1971
Cleveland	Hoke Smith	GA	1893	"	Stanley K. Hathaway	WY	1975
"	David R. Francis	MO	1896	"	Thomas S. Kleppe	ND	1975
McKinley	Cornelius N. Bliss	NY	1897	Carter	Cecil D. Andrus	ID	1977
"	Ethan A. Hitchcock	MO	1898	Reagan	James G. Watt	CO	1981
Roosevelt, T.	Ethan A. Hitchcock	MO	1901	"	William P. Clark	CA	1983
"	James R. Garfield	OH	1907	"	Donald P. Hodel	OR	1985
Taft	Richard A. Ballinger	WA	1909	Bush	Manuel Lujan	NM	1989
				Clinton	Bruce Babbitt	AZ	1993

Secretaries of Agriculture

The Department of Agriculture was created by act of Congress on May 15, 1862. On Feb. 8, 1889, its commissioner was renamed secretary of agriculture and became a member of the Cabinet.

President	Secretary	Home	Apptd.	President	Secretary	Home	Apptd.
Cleveland	Norman J. Colman	MO	1889	Truman	Charles F. Brannan	CO	1948
Harrison, B.	Jeremiah M. Rusk	WI	1889	Eisenhower	Ezra Taft Benson	UT	1953
Cleveland	J. Sterling Morton	NE	1893	Kennedy	Orville L. Freeman	MN	1961
McKinley	James Wilson	IA	1897	Johnson, L.B.	Orville L. Freeman	MN	1963
Roosevelt, T.	James Wilson	IA	1901	Nixon	Clifford M. Hardin	IN	1969
Taft	James Wilson	IA	1909	"	Earl L. Butz	IN	1971
Wilson	David F. Houston	MO	1913	Ford	Earl L. Butz	IN	1974
"	Edwin T. Meredith	IA	1920	"	John A. Knebel	VA	1976
Harding	Henry C. Wallace	IA	1921	Carter	Bob Bergland	MN	1977
Coolidge	Henry C. Wallace	IA	1923	Reagan	John R. Block	IL	1981
"	Howard M. Gore	WV	1924	"	Richard E. Lyng	CA	1986
"	William M. Jardine	KS	1925	Bush	Clayton K. Yeutter	NE	1989
Hoover	Arthur M. Hyde	MO	1929	"	Edward Madigan	IL	1991
Roosevelt, F.D.	Henry A. Wallace	IA	1933	Clinton	Mike Espy	MS	1993
"	Claude R. Wickard	IN	1940	"	Dan Glickman	KS	1995
Truman	Clinton P. Anderson	NM	1945				

Secretaries of Commerce and Labor

The Department of Commerce and Labor, created by Congress on Feb. 14, 1903, was divided by Congress Mar. 4, 1913, into separate departments of Commerce and Labor. The secretary of each was made a Cabinet member.

Secretaries of Commerce and Labor

President	Secretary	Home	Apptd.
Roosevelt, T.	George B. Cortelyou	NY	1903
"	Victor H. Metcalf	CA	1904
"	Oscar S. Straus	NY	1906
Taft	Charles Nagel	MO	1909

Secretaries of Labor

President	Secretary	Home	Apptd.
Wilson	William B. Wilson	PA	1913
Harding	James J. Davis	PA	1921
Coolidge	James J. Davis	PA	1923
Hoover	James J. Davis	PA	1929
"	William N. Doak	VA	1930
Roosevelt, F.D.	Frances Perkins	NY	1933
Truman	L.B. Schwellenbach	WA	1945
"	Maurice J. Tobin	MA	1949
Eisenhower	Martin P. Durkin	IL	1953
"	James P. Mitchell	NJ	1953
Kennedy	Arthur J. Goldberg	IL	1961
"	W. Willard Wirtz	IL	1962
Johnson, L.B.	W. Willard Wirtz	IL	1963

President	Secretary	Home	Apptd.
Nixon	George P. Shultz	IL	1969
"	James D. Hodgson	CA	1970
"	Peter J. Brennan	NY	1973
Ford	Peter J. Brennan	NY	1974
"	John T. Dunlop	CA	1975
"	W.J. Usery Jr.	GA	1976
Carter	F. Ray Marshall	TX	1977
Reagan	Raymond J. Donovan	NJ	1981
"	William E. Brock	TN	1985
"	Ann D. McLaughlin	DC	1987
Bush	Elizabeth Hanford Dole	NC	1989
"	Lynn Martin	IL	1991
Clinton	Robert B. Reich	MA	1993
"	Alexis M. Herman	AL	1997

Secretaries of Commerce

President	Secretary	Home	Apptd.
Wilson	William C. Redfield	NY	1913
"	Joshua W. Alexander	MO	1919
Harding	Herbert C. Hoover	CA	1921
Coolidge	Herbert C. Hoover	CA	1923
"	William F. Whiting	MA	1928
Hoover	Robert P. Lamont	IL	1929

Hoover	Roy D. Chapin	MI	1932	Nixon	Maurice H. Stans	MN	1969
Roosevelt, F.D.	Daniel C. Roper	SC	1933	"	Peter G. Peterson	IL	1972
"	Harry L. Hopkins	NY	1939	"	Frederick B. Dent	SC	1973
"	Jesse Jones	TX	1940	Ford	Frederick B. Dent	SC	1974
"	Henry A. Wallace	IA	1945	"	Rogers C.B. Morton	MD	1975
Truman	Henry A. Wallace	IA	1945	"	Elliot L. Richardson	MA	1975
"	W. Averell Harriman	NY	1947	Carter	Juanita M. Kreps	NC	1977
"	Charles Sawyer	OH	1948	"	Philip M. Klutznick	IL	1979
Eisenhower	Sinclair Weeks	MA	1953	Reagan	Malcolm Baldrige	CT	1981
"	Lewis L. Strauss	NY	1958	"	C. William Verity Jr.	OH	1987
"	Frederick H. Mueller	MI	1959	Bush	Robert A. Mosbacher	TX	1989
Kennedy	Luther H. Hodges	NC	1961	"	Barbara H. Franklin	PA	1992
Johnson, L.B.	Luther H. Hodges	NC	1963	Clinton	Ronald H. Brown	DC	1993
"	John T. Connor	NJ	1965	"	Mickey Kantor	CA	1996
"	Alex B. Trowbridge	NJ	1967	"	William M. Daley	IL	1997
"	Cyrus R. Smith	NY	1968				

Secretaries of Housing and Urban Development

The Department of Housing and Urban Development was created by act of Congress on Sept. 9, 1965.

President	Secretary	Home	Apptd.	President	Secretary	Home	Apptd.
Johnson, L.B.	Robert C. Weaver	WA	1966	Carter	Patricia Roberts Harris	DC	1977
"	Robert C. Wood	MA	1969	"	Moon Landrieu	LA	1979
Nixon	George W. Romney	MI	1969	Reagan	Samuel R. Pierce Jr.	NY	1981
"	James T. Lynn	OH	1973	Bush	Jack F. Kemp	NY	1989
Ford	James T. Lynn	OH	1974	Clinton	Henry G. Cisneros	TX	1993
"	Carla Anderson Hills	CA	1975	"	Andrew M. Cuomo	NY	1997

Secretaries of Transportation

The Department of Transportation was created by act of Congress on Oct. 15, 1966.

President	Secretary	Home	Apptd.	President	Secretary	Home	Apptd.
Johnson, L.B.	Alan S. Boyd	FL	1966	Reagan	Andrew L. Lewis Jr.	PA	1981
Nixon	John A. Volpe	MA	1969	"	Elizabeth Hanford Dole	NC	1983
"	Claude S. Brinegar	CA	1973	"	James H. Burnley	NC	1987
Ford	Claude S. Brinegar	CA	1974	Bush	Samuel K. Skinner	IL	1989
"	William T. Coleman Jr.	PA	1975	"	Andrew H. Card Jr.	MA	1992
Carter	Brock Adams	WA	1977	Clinton	Federico F. Peña	CO	1993
"	Neil E. Goldschmidt	OR	1979	"	Rodney E. Slater	AR	1997

Secretaries of Energy

The Department of Energy was created by federal law on Aug. 4, 1977.

President	Secretary	Home	Apptd.	President	Secretary	Home	Apptd.
Carter	James R. Schlesinger	VA	1977	Reagan	John S. Herrington	CA	1985
"	Charles Duncan Jr.	WY	1979	Bush	James D. Watkins	CA	1989
Reagan	James B. Edwards	SC	1981	Clinton	Hazel R. O'Leary	MN	1993
"	Donald P. Hodel	OR	1982	"	Federico F. Peña	CO	1997

Secretaries of Health, Education, and Welfare

The Department of Health, Education, and Welfare was created by Congress on Apr. 11, 1953. On Sept. 27, 1979, it was divided by Congress into separate departments of Education and of Health and Human Services, with the secretary of each being a Cabinet member.

President	Secretary	Home	Apptd.	President	Secretary	Home	Apptd.
Eisenhower	Oveta Culp Hobby	TX	1953	Nixon	Robert H. Finch	CA	1969
"	Marion B. Folsom	NY	1955	"	Elliot L. Richardson	MA	1970
"	Arthur S. Flemming	OH	1958	"	Caspar W. Weinberger	CA	1973
Kennedy	Abraham A. Ribicoff	CT	1961	Ford	Caspar W. Weinberger	CA	1974
"	Anthony J. Celebrezze	OH	1962	"	Forrest D. Mathews	AL	1975
Johnson, L.B.	Anthony J. Celebrezze	OH	1963	Carter	Joseph A. Califano Jr.	DC	1977
"	John W. Gardner	NY	1965	"	Patricia Roberts Harris	DC	1979
"	Wilbur J. Cohen	MI	1968				

Secretaries of Health and Human Services

President	Secretary	Home	Apptd.	President	Secretary	Home	Apptd.
Carter	Patricia Roberts Harris	DC	1979	Reagan	Otis R. Bowen	IN	1985
Reagan	Richard S. Schweiker	PA	1981	Bush	Louis W. Sullivan	GA	1989
"	Margaret M. Heckler	MA	1983	Clinton	Donna E. Shalala	WI	1993

Secretaries of Education

President	Secretary	Home	Apptd.	President	Secretary	Home	Apptd.
Carter	Shirley Hufstedler	CA	1979	Bush	Lauro F. Cavazos	TX	1989
Reagan	Terrel Bell	UT	1981	"	Lamar Alexander	TN	1991
"	William J. Bennett	NY	1985	Clinton	Richard W. Riley	SC	1993
"	Lauro F. Cavazos	TX	1988				

Secretaries of Veterans Affairs

The Department of Veterans Affairs was created on Oct. 25, 1988, when Pres. Ronald Reagan signed a bill that made the Veterans Administration into a Cabinet department, effective Mar. 15, 1989.

President	Secretary	Home	Apptd.	President	Secretary	Home	Apptd.
Bush	Edward J. Derwinski	IL	1989	Clinton	Jesse Brown*	IL	1993

*Brown resigned July 1, 1997.

Directors of the Central Intelligence Agency

In 1942, Pres. Franklin D. Roosevelt established the Office of Strategic Services (OSS); it was disbanded in 1945. In 1946, Pres. Harry Truman established the Central Intelligence Group (CIG) to operate under the National Intelligence Authority (NIA). The National Security Act of 1947 replaced the NIA with the National Security Council and the CIG with the Central Intelligence Agency.

Director	Served	Appointed by President	Director	Served	Appointed by President
Adm. Sidney W. Souers	1946	Truman	William E. Colby	1973-1976	Nixon
Gen. Hoyt S. Vandenberg	1946-1947	Truman	George Bush	1976-1977	Ford
Adm. Roscoe H. Hillenkoetter	1947-1950	Truman	Adm. Stansfield Turner	1977-1981	Carter
Gen. Walter Bedell Smith	1950-1953	Truman	William J. Casey	1981-1987	Reagan
Allen W. Dulles	1953-1961	Eisenhower	William H. Webster	1987-1991	Reagan
John A. McCone	1961-1965	Kennedy	Robert M. Gates	1991-1993	Bush
Adm. William F. Raborn Jr.	1965-1966	Johnson	R. James Woolsey	1993-1995	Clinton
Richard Helms	1966-1973	Johnson	John M. Deutch	1995-1997	Clinton
James R. Schlesinger	1973	Nixon	George J. Tenet	1997-	Clinton

Speakers of the House of Representatives

(as of Oct. 15, 1997)

Party designations: A, American; D, Democratic; DR, Democratic-Republican; F, Federalist; R, Republican; W, Whig

Name	Party	State	Tenure	Name	Party	State	Tenure
Frederick Muhlenberg	F	PA	1789-1791	Theodore M. Pomeroy	R	NY	1869
Jonathan Trumbull	F	CT	1791-1793	James G. Blaine	R	ME	1869-1875
Frederick Muhlenberg	F	PA	1793-1795	Michael C. Kerr	D	IN	1875-1876
Jonathan Dayton	F	NJ	1795-1799	Samuel J. Randall	D	PA	1876-1881
Theodore Sedgwick	F	MA	1799-1801	Joseph W. Keifer	R	OH	1881-1883
Nathaniel Macon	DR	NC	1801-1807	John G. Carlisle	D	KY	1883-1889
Joseph B. Varnum	DR	MA	1807-1811	Thomas B. Reed	R	ME	1889-1891
Henry Clay	DR	KY	1811-1814	Charles F. Crisp	D	GA	1891-1895
Langdon Cheves	DR	SC	1814-1815	Thomas B. Reed	R	ME	1895-1899
Henry Clay	DR	KY	1815-1820	David B. Henderson	R	IA	1899-1903
John W. Taylor	DR	NY	1820-1821	Joseph G. Cannon	R	IL	1903-1911
Philip P. Barbour	DR	VA	1821-1823	Champ Clark	D	MO	1911-1919
Henry Clay	DR	KY	1823-1825	Frederick H. Gillett	R	MA	1919-1925
John W. Taylor	D	NY	1825-1827	Nicholas Longworth	R	OH	1925-1931
Andrew Stevenson	D	VA	1827-1834	John N. Garner	D	TX	1931-1933
John Bell	D	TN	1834-1835	Henry T. Rainey	D	IL	1933-1935
James K. Polk	D	TN	1835-1839	Joseph W. Byrns	D	TN	1935-1936
Robert M. T. Hunter	D	VA	1839-1841	William B. Bankhead	D	AL	1936-1940
John White	W	KY	1841-1843	Sam Rayburn	D	TX	1940-1947
John W. Jones	D	VA	1843-1845	Joseph W. Martin Jr.	R	MA	1947-1949
John W. Davis	D	IN	1845-1847	Sam Rayburn	D	TX	1949-1953
Robert C. Winthrop	W	MA	1847-1849	Joseph W. Martin Jr.	R	MA	1953-1955
Howell Cobb	D	GA	1849-1851	Sam Rayburn	D	TX	1955-1961
Linn Boyd	D	KY	1851-1855	John W. McCormack	D	MA	1962-1971
Nathaniel P. Banks	A	MA	1856-1857	Carl Albert	D	OK	1971-1977
James L. Orr	D	SC	1857-1859	Thomas P. O'Neill Jr.	D	MA	1977-1987
William Pennington	R	NJ	1860-1861	James Wright	D	TX	1987-1989
Galusha A. Grow	R	PA	1861-1863	Thomas S. Foley	D	WA	1989-1995
Schuyler Colfax	R	IN	1863-1869	Newt Gingrich	R	GA	1995-

Floor Leaders in the U.S. Senate Since the 1920s

Majority Leaders				Minority Leaders			
Name	Party	State	Tenure	Name	Party	State	Tenure
Charles Curtis[1]	R	KS	1925-1929	Oscar W. Underwood[2]	D	AL	1920-1923
James E. Watson	R	IN	1929-1933	Joseph T. Robinson	D	AR	1923-1933
Joseph T. Robinson	D	AR	1933-1937	Charles L. McNary	R	OR	1933-1944
Alben W. Barkley	D	KY	1937-1947	Wallace H. White	R	ME	1944-1947
Wallace H. White	R	ME	1947-1949	Alben W. Barkley	D	KY	1947-1949
Scott W. Lucas	D	IL	1949-1951	Kenneth S. Wherry	R	NE	1949-1951
Ernest W. McFarland	D	AZ	1951-1953	Henry Styles Bridges	R	NH	1951-1953
Robert A. Taft	R	OH	1953	Lyndon B. Johnson	D	TX	1953-1955
William F. Knowland	R	CA	1953-1955	William F. Knowland	R	CA	1955-1959
Lyndon B. Johnson	D	TX	1955-1961	Everett M. Dirksen	R	IL	1959-1969
Mike Mansfield	D	MT	1961-1977	Hugh D. Scott	R	PA	1969-1977
Robert C. Byrd	D	WV	1977-1981	Howard H. Baker Jr.	R	TN	1977-1981
Howard H. Baker Jr.	R	TN	1981-1985	Robert C. Byrd	D	WV	1981-1987
Robert J. Dole	R	KS	1985-1987	Robert J. Dole	R	KS	1987-1995
Robert C. Byrd	D	WV	1987-1989	Thomas A. Daschle	D	SD	1995-
George J. Mitchell	D	ME	1989-1995				
Robert J. Dole	R	KS	1995-1996				
Trent Lott	R	MS	1996-				

Note: Majority and Minority Leaders as of Oct. 1997. (1) First Republican to be designated floor leader. (2) First Democrat to be designated floor leader.

Librarians of Congress

Librarian	Served	Appointed by President	Librarian	Served	Appointed by President
John J. Beckley	1802-1807	Jefferson	Herbert Putnam	1899-1939	McKinley
Patrick Magruder	1807-1815	Jefferson	Archibald MacLeish	1939-1944	F. D. Roosevelt
George Watterston	1815-1829	Madison	Luther H. Evans	1945-1953	Truman
John Silva Meehan	1829-1861	Jackson	L. Quincy Mumford	1954-1974	Eisenhower
John G. Stephenson	1861-1864	Lincoln	Daniel J. Boorstin	1975-1987	Ford
Ainsworth Rand Spofford	1864-1897	Lincoln	James H. Billington	1987-	Reagan
John Russell Young	1897-1899	McKinley			

ECONOMICS

U.S. Budget Receipts and Outlays, 1993-97

Source: Financial Management Service, U.S. Dept. of the Treasury; fiscal 1997 figures, Office of Management & Budget

(Fiscal year ends Sept. 30)

(in millions of dollars; many figures do not add to totals because of independent rounding or omitted subcategories, including some subcategories with negative values.)

Classification	Fiscal 1993	Fiscal 1994	Fiscal 1995	Fiscal 1996
Net Receipts				
Individual income taxes	$509,680	$543,055	$590,243	$656,417
Corporation income taxes.	117,520	140,385	157,004	171,824
Social insurance taxes and contributions:				
Federal old-age and survivors insurance	281,735	302,607	284,091	311,869
Federal disability insurance	30,199	32,419	66,989	55,623
Federal hospital insurance	81,224	90,062	96,025	104,998
Railroad retirement fund.	3,781	3,723	3,942	3,872
Total employment taxes and contributions . .	396,939	428,810	451,046	476,362
Other insurance and retirement:				
Unemployment	26,556	28,004	28,878	28,584
Federal employees retirement	4,709	4,563	4,461	4,389
Non-federal employees	96	98	89	80
Total social insurance taxes and contributions	428,300	461,475	484,474	509,415
Excise taxes	48,057	55,225	57,484	54,015
Estate and gift taxes	12,577	15,225	14,763	17,189
Customs duties	18,802	20,099	19,300	18,671
Deposits of earnings by Federal Reserve Banks. . .	14,908	18,023	23,378	20,477
All other miscellaneous receipts	3,382	3,965	4,847	4,755
Net Budget Receipts.	$1,153,226	$1,257,451	$1,351,495	1,452,763
Net Outlays				
Legislative Branch	$2,406	$2,552	$2,621	$2,272
The Judiciary.	2,628	2,659	2,903	3,061
Executive Office of the President:				
The White House Office	40	40	37	39
Office of Management and Budget	55	57	56	55
Total Executive Office	194	229	213	202
Funds appropriated to the President:				
International security assistance	7,322	6,306	4,952	4,254
Multilateral assistance	1,547	1,753	2,194	2,077
Agency for International Development.	2,099	2,544	3,252	3,059
International Development Assistance.	3,855	4,445	5,557	5,229
Total funds appropriated to the President . . .	11,526	10,511	11,164	9,716
Agriculture Department:				
Food stamp program	24,602	25,549	25,554	25,359
Farm Service Agency.	NA	14,627	9,123	8,350
Forest Service.	3,292	3,353	3,765	3,411
Total Agriculture Department	63,112	60,753	56,667	54,339
Commerce Department:				
Bureau of the Census	346	250	293	260
Total Commerce Department	2,798	2,915	3,403	3,703
Defense Department—Military:				
Military personnel	75,904	73,137	70,807	66,669
Operation and maintenance	94,121	87,880	90,882	88,629
Procurement	69,936	61,769	54,984	48,912
Research, development, test, evaluation	36,968	34,786	34,710	36,561
Military construction.	4,831	4,979	6,826	6,684
Total Defense Department—Military	278,586	268,646	259,565	253,258
Defense Department—Civil	29,266	30,407	31,664	32,535
Education Department	30,290	24,699	31,321	29,900
Energy Department	16,801	17,840	17,618	16,199
Health and Human Services Department:				
Public Health Service.	18,872	19,760	20,728	21,405
Health Care Financing Adm..	266,452	285,117	310,657	354,898
Food and Drug Administration	733	801	858	865
National Institutes of Health.	9,543	10,165	10,883	10,217
Total Health and Human Services Dept.	282,781	278,901	303,075	319,802
Housing and Urban Development Department	25,181	25,845	29,045	25,512
Interior Department	6,720	6,900	7,390	6,720
Justice Department:				
Federal Bureau of Investigation	1,975	2,106	2,041	2,305
Drug Enforcement Agency	792	793	788	746
Immigration and Naturalization Service	1,551	1,543	1,805	2,246
Federal Prison System.	2,136	2,327	2,748	3,013
Total Justice Department	10,170	10,005	10,786	11,951
Labor Department:				
Unemployment Trust Fund	39,869	30,458	25,205	26,146
Total Labor Department	44,738	37,130	32,093	32,496
State Department	5,385	5,718	5,347	4,953
Transportation Department:				
Federal Aviation Administration	8,800	8,784	9,206	8,925
Total Transportation Department	34,457	37,228	38,776	38,777
Treasury Department:				
Internal Revenue Service.	18,437	21,810	25,617	28,595
Interest on the public debt	292,502	296,278	332,414	343,955
Total Treasury Department.	298,802	307,577	348,480	365,330
Veterans Affairs Department.	35,487	37,401	37,769	36,915
Environmental Protection Agency	5,930	5,855	6,349	6,046
General Services Administration	743	334	709	625
National Aeronautics and Space Administration . . .	14,305	13,695	13,377	13,882

(continued)

Classification	Fiscal 1993	Fiscal 1994	Fiscal 1995	Fiscal 1996
Office of Personnel Management	$36,794	$38,596	$41,279	$42,872
Small Business Administration	785	779	678	872
Social Security Administration[1]	328,028	345,817	362,226	375,232
Other independent agencies:				
Corporation for Natl. and Community Service[2] .	208	211	425	477
Corporation for Public Broadcasting	319	275	286	275
District of Columbia	698	698	714	712
Equal Employment Opportunity Commission . .	218	229	234	224
Export-Import Bank of the U.S.	−747	−832	−53	−560
Federal Communications Commission.	94	49	935	978
Federal Deposit Insurance Corporation	−8,412	−11,396	−17,557	−8,732
Federal Trade Commission	64	69	31	35
Legal Services Corporation	389	375	429	282
National Archives & Records Adm.	269	261	219	199
National Foundation on the Arts and Humanities	343	354	355	285
National Labor Relations Board	171	173	174	166
National Science Foundation	2,452	2,642	2,847	3,012
Nuclear Regulatory Commission.	−19	46	28	57
Railroad Retirement Board.	4,782	4,780	4,359	5,007
Securities and Exchange Commission.	99	68	122	42
Smithsonian Institution.	395	422	432	432
Tennessee Valley Authority	1,629	1,210	1,313	757
U.S. Information Agency	1,088	1,165	1,160	1,177
Total other independent agencies	−9,992	11,030	−1,470	8,577
Undistributed offsetting receipts	−119,711	−123,469	−137,635	−135,649
Net Budget Outlays	**$1,408,532**	**$1,460,553**	**$1,515,412**	**$1,560,094**
Less net receipts.	1,153,226	1,257,451	1,351,495	1,452,763
Deficit.	**$−255,306**	**$−203,102**	**$−163,917**	**$−107,331**

Fiscal 1997 Budget Totals: Receipts, $1,579.0 bil; outlays, $1,601.6 bil; deficit, $22.6 bil.

(1) The Social Security Administration (SSA), formerly a part of the Dept. of Health and Human Services, became an independent agency, Mar. 31, 1995; figures given prior to 1994 are sums of total outlays originally listed under the Health and Human Services Dept. with the heading "Social Security (Off Budget)" plus other administrative SSA outlays. (2) Formerly Action. NA=not applicable.

Summary of Receipts, Outlays, and Surpluses or Deficits, 1936-92

Source: Financial Management Service, U.S. Dept. of the Treasury

(millions of dollars)

Fiscal Year[1]	Total Receipts	Total Outlays	Surplus or Deficit (−)[2]	Fiscal Year[1]	Total Receipts	Total Outlays	Surplus or Deficit (−)[2]
1936	$3,923	$8,228	$−4,304	1965.	$116,817	$118,228	$ −1,411
1937	5,387	7,580	−2,193	1966.	130,835	134,532	−3,698
1938	6,751	6,840	−89	1967.	148,822	157,464	−8,643
1939	6,295	9,141	−2,846	1968.	152,973	178,134	−25,161
1940	6,548	9,468	−2,920	1969.	186,882	183,640	3,242
1941	8,712	13,653	−4,941	1970.	192,807	195,649	−2,842
1942	14,634	35,137	−20,503	1971.	187,139	210,172	−23,033
1943	24,001	78,555	−54,554	1972.	207,309	230,681	−23,373
1944	43,747	91,304	−47,557	1973.	230,799	245,707	−14,908
1945	45,159	92,712	−47,553	1974.	263,224	269,359	−6,135
1946	39,296	55,232	−15,936	1975.	279,090	332,332	−53,242
1947	38,514	34,496	4,018	1976.	298,060	371,779	−73,719
1948	41,560	29,764	11,796	Transition quarter[3]	81,232	95,973	−14,741
1949	39,415	38,835	580	1977.	355,559	409,203	−53,644
1950	39,443	42,562	−3,119	1978.	399,561	458,729	−59,168
1951	51,616	45,514	6,102	1979.	463,302	503,464	−40,162
1952	66,167	67,686	−1,519	1980.	517,112	590,920	−73,808
1953	69,608	76,101	−6,493	1981.	599,272	678,209	−78,936
1954	69,701	70,855	−1,154	1982.	617,766	745,706	−127,940
1955	65,451	68,444	−2,993	1983.	600,562	808,327	−207,764
1956	74,587	70,640	3,947	1984.	666,457	851,781	−185,324
1957	79,990	76,578	3,412	1985.	734,057	946,316	−212,260
1958	79,636	82,405	−2,769	1986.	769,091	990,231	−221,140
1959	79,249	92,098	−12,849	1987.	854,143	1,003,804	− 149,661
1960	92,492	92,191	301	1988.	908,166	1,063,318	−155,151
1961	94,388	97,723	−3,335	1989.	990,701	1,144,020	−153,319
1962	99,676	106,821	−7,146	1990.	1,031,308	1,251,776	−220,469
1963	106,560	111,316	−4,756	1991.	1,054,265	1,323,757	−269,492
1964	112,613	118,528	−5,915	1992.	1,090,453	1,380,794	−290,340

(1) Fiscal years 1936 to 1976 ending June 30; after 1976, fiscal years end Sept. 30. (2) May not equal difference between figures shown, because of rounding. (3) Transition quarter covers July 1, 1976-Sept. 30, 1976.

U.S. Budget Receipts and Outlays, 1789-1935

Source: U.S. Dept. of the Treasury; annual statements for years ending June 30 unless otherwise noted

(thousands of dollars)

Yearly Average	Receipts	Outlays	Yearly Average	Receipts	Outlays	Yearly Average	Receipts	Outlays
1789-1800[1]. . .	$ 5,717	$ 5,776	1866-1870. . . .	$447,301	$377,642	1901-1905 . . .	$ 559,481	$ 535,559
1801-1810[2]. . .	13,056	9,086	1871-1875. . . .	336,830	287,460	1906-1910 . . .	628,507	639,178
1811-1820[2]. . .	21,032	23,943	1876-1880. . . .	288,124	255,598	1911-1915 . . .	710,227	720,252
1821-1830[2]. . .	21,928	16,162	1881-1885. . . .	366,961	257,691	1916-1920 . . .	3,483,652	8,065,333
1831-1840[2]. . .	30,461	24,495	1886-1890. . . .	375,448	279,134	1921-1925 . . .	4,306,673	3,578,989
1841-1850[2]. . .	28,545	34,097	1891-1895. . . .	352,891	363,599	1926-1930 . . .	4,069,138	3,182,807
1851-1860 . . .	60,237	60,163	1896-1900. . . .	434,877	457,451	1931-1935 . . .	2,770,973	5,214,874
1861-1865 . . .	160,907	683,785						

(1) Average for period March 4, 1789, to Dec. 31, 1800. (2) Years ended Dec. 31, 1801 to 1842; average for 1841-1850 is for the period Jan. 1, 1841, to June 30, 1850.

Public Debt of the U.S.

Source: Bureau of Public Debt, U.S. Dept. of the Treasury

Fiscal year	Debt (billions)	Debt per cap. (dollars)	Interest paid (billions)	% of federal outlays	Fiscal year	Debt (billions)	Debt per cap. (dollars)	Interest paid (billions)	% of federal outlays
1870	$2.4	$61.06	—	—	1979	$826.5	$3,669	$59.8	11.9
1880	2.0	41.60	—	—	1980	907.7	3,985	74.9	12.7
1890	1.1	17.80	—	—	1981	997.9	4,338	95.6	14.1
1900	1.2	16.60	—	—	1982	1,142.0	4,913	117.4	15.7
1910	1.1	12.41	—	—	1983	1,377.2	5,870	128.8	15.9
1920	24.2	228	—	—	1984	1,572.3	6,640	153.8	18.1
1930	16.1	131	—	—	1985	1,823.1	7,598	178.9	18.9
1940	43.0	325	$1.0	10.5	1986	2,125.3	8,774	190.2	19.2
1945	258.7	1,849	3.8	4.1	1987	2,350.3	9,615	195.4	19.5
1950	256.1	1,688	5.7	13.4	1988	2,602.3	10,534	214.1	20.1
1955	272.8	1,651	6.4	9.4	1989	2,857.4	11,545	240.9	21.0
1960	284.1	1,572	9.2	10.0	1990	3,233.3	13,000	264.8	21.1
1965	313.8	1,613	11.3	9.6	1991	3,665.3	14,436	285.5	21.6
1970	370.1	1,814	19.3	9.9	1992	4,064.6	15,846	292.3	21.2
1975	533.2	2,475	32.7	9.8	1993	4,411.5	17,105	292.5	20.8
1976	620.4	2,852	37.1	10.0	1994	4,692.8	18,025	296.3	20.3
1977	698.8	3,170	41.9	10.2	1995	4,974.0	18,930	332.4	22.0
1978	771.5	3,463	48.7	10.6	1996	5,224.8	19,805	344.0	22.0

Note: Through 1976 the fiscal year ended June 30. From 1977 on, the fiscal year ends Sept. 30.

Consumer Price Index

The Consumer Price Index (CPI) is a measure of the average change in prices over time of basic consumer goods and services. From Jan. 1978, the Bureau of Labor Statistics began publishing CPI's for 2 population groups: (1) a CPI for all urban consumers (CPI-U), which covers about 80% of the total population; and (2) a CPI for urban wage earners and clerical workers (CPI-W), which covers about 32% of the total population. The CPI-U includes, in addition to wage earners and clerical workers, groups such as professional, managerial, and technical workers, the self-employed, short-term workers, the unemployed, retirees, and others not in the labor force.

The CPI is based on prices of food, clothing, shelter, and fuels; transportation fares; charges for doctors' and dentists' services; drug prices; and prices of the other goods and services bought for day-to-day living. The index currently measures price changes from a designated reference period, 1982-84, which equals 100.0. Use of this reference period began in Jan. 1988.

Consumer Price Indexes, First Half 1997

Source: Bureau of Labor Statistics, U.S. Dept. of Labor

(Data are semiannual averages of monthly figures)

(1982-84=100)	CPI-U (all urban consumers)		CPI-W (urban wage-earners/clerical)	
	1st half 1997	% change 2d half 1996 to 1st half 1997	1st half 1997	% change 2d half 1996 to 1st half 1997
All items	159.9	1.3	157.0	1.2
Food, beverages.	157.0	1.2	156.5	1.2
Housing	155.9	1.3	152.6	1.3
Apparel and upkeep	133.3	1.9	132.6	2.0
Transportation	144.7	0.6	144.1	0.3
Medical care.	233.4	1.6	232.8	1.6
Entertainment.	162.1	1.4	159.5	1.2
Other goods, services	221.8	1.9	218.7	2.1
Services.	178.2	1.5	175.3	1.4
Special indexes				
All items less food	160.5	1.3	157.1	1.2
Commodities less food	133.8	0.8	134.0	0.8
Nondurables.	146.1	1.2	145.9	1.2
Energy.	111.6	0.0	111.2	−0.1
All items less energy	166.3	1.3	163.4	1.2

Consumer Price Indexes (CPI-U),[1] Annual Percent Change, 1985-96

Source: Bureau of Labor Statistics, U.S. Dept. of Labor

	1985	1986	1987	1988	1989	1990	1991	1992	1993	1994	1995	1996
All items.	3.6	1.9	3.6	4.1	4.8	5.4	4.2	3.0	3.0	2.6	2.8	3.0
Food.	2.3	3.2	4.1	4.1	5.8	5.8	2.9	1.2	2.2	2.4	2.8	3.3
Shelter	5.6	5.5	4.7	4.8	4.5	5.4	4.5	3.3	3.0	3.1	3.2	3.2
Rent, residential.	6.2	5.8	4.1	3.8	3.9	5.6	6.1	2.5	2.3	2.5	2.5	2.7
Fuel and other utilities	1.6	−2.3	−1.1	−1.4	3.3	3.5	3.3	2.2	3.0	1.0	0.7	3.1
Apparel and upkeep.	2.8	0.9	4.4	4.3	2.8	4.6	3.7	2.5	1.4	−0.2	−1.0	−0.2
Private transportation.	2.5	−4.7	−3.0	3.3	4.9	5.2	2.6	2.2	2.3	3.1	3.7	2.7
New cars.	3.2	4.2	3.6	2.0	2.0	1.8	3.8	2.5	2.4	3.4	2.2	1.7
Gasoline	0.8	−21.9	−4.0	0.9	9.5	14.1	−1.8	−0.2	−1.3	0.5	1.6	6.1
Public transportation	4.5	5.9	3.5	1.8	5.0	10.1	4.4	1.7	10.3	3.0	2.3	3.4
Medical care	6.3	7.5	6.6	6.5	7.7	9.0	8.7	7.4	5.9	4.8	4.5	3.5
Entertainment	3.9	3.4	3.3	4.3	5.2	4.7	4.5	2.8	2.5	2.9	2.5	3.4
Commodities	2.1	−0.9	3.2	3.5	4.7	5.2	4.2	2.0	1.9	1.7	1.9	2.6

(1) The Consumer Price Index CPI-U measures the average change in prices of goods and services purchased by all urban consumers.

Consumer Price Indexes for Selected Items and Groups, 1970-96

Source: Bureau of Labor Statistics, U.S. Dept. of Labor

(1982-84 = 100, unless otherwise noted. Annual averages of monthly figures. For all urban consumers.)

	1970	1975	1980	1985	1990	1994	1995	1996
All Items	**38.8**	**53.8**	**82.4**	**107.6**	**130.7**	**148.2**	**152.4**	**156.9**
Food and beverages	**40.1**	**60.2**	**86.7**	**105.6**	**132.1**	**144.9**	**148.9**	**153.7**
Food	39.2	59.8	86.8	105.6	132.4	144.3	148.4	153.3
Food at home	39.9	61.8	88.4	104.3	132.3	144.1	148.8	154.3
Cereals and bakery products	37.1	62.9	83.9	107.9	140.0	163.0	167.5	174.0
Meats, poultry, fish, and eggs	44.6	67.0	92.0	100.1	130.0	137.2	138.8	144.8
Dairy products	44.7	62.6	90.9	103.2	126.5	131.7	132.8	142.1
Fruits and vegetables	37.8	56.9	82.1	106.4	149.0	165.0	177.7	183.9
Sugar and sweets	30.5	65.3	90.5	105.8	124.7	135.2	137.5	143.7
Fats and oils	39.2	73.5	89.3	106.9	126.3	133.5	137.3	140.5
Nonalcoholic beverages	27.1	41.3	91.4	104.3	113.5	123.2	131.7	128.6
Other prepared foods	39.6	58.9	83.6	106.4	131.2	147.5	151.1	156.2
Food away from home	37.5	54.5	83.4	108.3	133.4	145.7	149.0	152.7
Alcoholic beverages	52.1	65.9	86.4	106.4	129.3	151.5	153.9	158.5
Housing	**36.4**	**50.7**	**81.1**	**107.7**	**128.5**	**144.8**	**148.5**	**152.8**
Shelter	35.5	48.8	81.0	109.8	140.0	160.5	165.7	171.0
Renters' costs[1]	46.5	58.0	80.9	111.8	146.7	169.4	174.3	180.2
Maintenance and repairs	35.8	54.1	82.4	106.5	122.2	130.8	135.0	139.0
Fuel and other utilities[1]	29.1	45.4	75.4	106.5	111.6	122.8	123.7	127.5
Energy services	31.8	50.0	75.8	106.9	117.4	119.2	119.2	122.1
Household furnishings & operation	46.8	63.4	86.3	103.8	113.3	121.0	123.0	124.7
House furnishings	55.5	69.8	88.5	101.7	106.7	111.0	111.2	111.3
Apparel and upkeep	**59.2**	**72.5**	**90.9**	**105.0**	**124.1**	**133.4**	**132.0**	**131.7**
Apparel commodities	63.3	76.7	92.9	104.0	122.0	130.4	127.0	128.2
Men's and boys'	62.2	75.5	89.4	105.0	120.4	126.4	126.2	127.7
Women's and girls'	71.8	85.5	96.0	104.9	122.6	130.9	126.9	124.7
Footwear	56.8	69.6	91.8	102.3	117.4	126.0	125.4	126.6
Transportation	**37.5**	**50.1**	**83.1**	**106.4**	**120.5**	**134.3**	**139.1**	**143.0**
Private	37.5	50.6	84.2	106.2	118.8	131.4	136.3	140.0
New cars	53.0	62.9	88.4	106.1	121.4	136.0	139.0	141.4
Used cars	31.2	43.8	62.3	113.7	117.6	141.7	156.5	157.0
Gasoline	27.9	45.1	97.5	98.6	101.0	98.2	99.8	105.9
Public	35.2	43.5	69.0	110.5	142.6	172.0	175.9	181.9
Medical care	**34.0**	**47.5**	**74.9**	**113.5**	**162.8**	**211.0**	**220.5**	**228.2**
Entertainment	**47.5**	**62.0**	**83.6**	**107.9**	**132.4**	**150.1**	**153.9**	**159.1**
Other goods and services	**40.9**	**53.9**	**75.2**	**114.5**	**159.0**	**198.5**	**206.9**	**215.4**
Tobacco products	43.1	54.7	72.0	116.7	181.5	220.0	225.7	232.8
Personal care	43.5	57.9	81.9	106.3	130.4	144.6	147.1	150.1
Toilet goods and personal care appliances	42.7	58.0	79.6	107.6	128.2	141.5	143.1	144.3
Personal care services	44.2	57.7	83.7	108.9	132.8	147.9	151.5	156.6
Personal and educational expenses	35.5	48.7	70.9	119.1	170.2	223.2	235.5	247.5

(1) Dec. 1982 = 100.

Consumer Price Index by Region and Selected Cities, 1996-97

Source: Bureau of Labor Statistics, U.S. Dept. of Labor

	CPI-U Indexes[1]			% change	CPI-W Indexes[2]			% change
(1982-84 = 100)	Avg. 1996	July 1997	Aug. 1997	Aug. 1996- Aug. 1997	Avg. 1996	July 1997	Aug. 1997	Aug. 1996- Aug. 1997
U.S. city average	156.9	160.5	160.8	2.2	154.1	157.5	157.8	2.1
Northeast urban	163.6	167.6	167.8	2.3	161.1	164.7	164.9	2.2
Size A—More than 1,200,000	164.3	168.2	168.4	2.2	160.7	164.3	164.5	2.2
Size B—500,000 to 1,200,000	161.4	165.9	166.2	2.5	159.2	163.5	163.7	2.3
Size C—50,000 to 500,000	161.9	166.4	166.8	3.1	163.4	167.5	167.8	2.8
North central urban	153.0	156.6	157.2	2.5	149.6	153.1	153.6	2.5
Size A—More than 1,200,000	153.6	157.3	158.0	2.6	149.6	152.9	153.6	2.5
Size B—360,000 to 1,200,000	152.1	155.8	156.3	2.3	148.2	151.9	152.3	2.4
Size C—50,000 to 360,000	154.7	158.5	158.8	2.7	152.0	155.7	156.1	2.8
Size D—Less than 50,000	149.7	152.6	152.6	1.5	147.8	150.7	150.9	1.6
South urban	153.6	157.0	157.1	1.9	152.2	155.3	155.5	1.8
Size A—More than 1,200,000	152.7	155.8	155.9	1.8	150.9	153.9	154.0	1.7
Size B—450,000 to 1,200,000	156.3	160.5	160.8	2.5	152.5	156.2	156.5	2.2
Size C—50,000 to 450,000	153.4	156.0	156.1	1.4	153.3	155.7	155.9	1.3
Size D—Less than 50,000	152.6	156.4	156.4	2.5	153.1	156.6	157.0	2.5
West urban	157.6	161.1	161.5	2.2	154.5	157.6	158.0	2.0
Size A—More than 1,250,000	157.7	161.3	161.7	2.3	153.0	156.2	156.5	2.0
Size C—50,000 to 330,000	162.3	166.1	166.8	2.6	159.2	162.9	163.,5	2.5
Selected areas								
Chicago, IL–Gary–Lake County, IL–IN–WI	157.4	161.7	162.5	2.8	152.4	156.0	156.7	2.5
L.A.–Anaheim–Riverside, CA	157.5	159.5	159.7	1.5	152.1	153.8	154.0	1.4
New York, NY–Northern NJ–Long Island, NY–NJ–CT	166.9	170.8	170.8	2.2	163.1	166.6	166.7	2.1
Phila.–Wilm.–Trenton, PA–NJ–DE–MD	162.8	166.4	166.8	2.0	162.2	165.5	165.9	1.8
San Francisco–Oakland–San Jose, CA	155.1	160.6	161.2	3.6	152.6	157.5	158.1	3.3
Baltimore, MD	154.2	156.9	—	0.8*	153.1	155.6	—	0.6*
Boston–Lawrence–Salem, MA–NH	163.3	167.1	—	3.1*	162.2	165.8	—	3.0*
Cleveland–Akron–Lorain, OH	152.0	156.3	—	2.8*	144.3	148.2	—	2.7*
Miami–Ft. Lauderdale, FL	153.7	157.9	—	3.6*	151.8	155.5	—	3.1*
St. Louis–East St. Louis, MO–IL	149.6	153.3	—	2.3*	148.7	152.5	—	2.3*
Washington, DC–MD–VA	159.6	162.9	—	1.7*	156.9	160.2	—	1.6*
Dallas–Fort Worth, TX	148.8	—	151.2	1.1	148.9	—	151.1	1.1
Detroit–Ann Arbor, MI	152.5	—	156.9	2.8	147.7	—	151.6	2.4
Houston–Galveston–Brazoria, TX	142.7	—	145.4	1.8	142.0	—	144.9	1.9
Pittsburgh–Beaver Valley, PA	153.2	—	157.5	2.5	146.8	—	151.0	2.6

(1) For all urban consumers. (2) For urban wage-earners and clerical workers. *From July 1996 to July 1997.

Percentage Change in Consumer Prices in Selected Countries

Source: International Monetary Fund

(annual averages)

Country	1975-1980	1980-1985	1989-1990	1991-1992	1992-1993	1993-1994	1994-1995	1995-1996
Canada	8.7	7.4	4.8	1.5	1.8	0.2	2.2	1.6
France	10.5	9.6	3.4	2.4	2.1	1.7	1.8	2.0
Germany	4.1	3.9	2.7	4.0	4.1	3.0	1.8	1.5
Italy	16.3	13.7	6.4	5.1	4.5	4.0	5.2	4.0
Japan	6.5	2.7	3.1	1.7	1.3	0.7	−0.1	0.1
Spain	18.6	12.2	6.7	5.9	4.6	4.7	4.7	3.6
Sweden	10.5	9.0	10.5	2.3	4.6	2.2	2.5	0.5
Switzerland	2.3	4.3	5.4	4.1	3.3	0.8	1.8	0.8
United Kingdom	14.4	7.2	9.5	3.7	1.6	2.5	3.4	2.4
United States	8.9	5.5	5.4	3.0	3.0	2.6	2.8	3.0

Index of Leading Economic Indicators

Source: The Conference Board

The index of leading economic indicators is used to project the U.S. economy's performance. The index is made up of 10 measurements of economic activity that tend to change direction in advance of the overall economy. The index has predicted economic downturns from 8 to 20 months in advance and recoveries from 1 to 10 months in advance; however, it can be inconsistent, and has occasionally shown "false signals" of recessions.

Components

Average weekly hours of production workers in manufacturing

Average weekly initial claims for unemployment insurance, state programs

Manufacturers' new orders for consumer goods and materials, adjusted for inflation

Vendor performance (slower deliveries diffusion index)

Manufacturers' new orders, nondefense capital goods industries, adjusted for inflation

New private housing units authorized by local building permits

Stock prices, 500 common stocks

Money supply: M-2, adjusted for inflation

Interest rate spread, 10-yr Treasury bonds less federal funds

Consumer expectations (researched by Univ. of Michigan)

U.S. Gross Domestic Product, Gross National Product, Net National Product, National Income, and Personal Income

Source: Bureau of Economic Analysis, U.S. Dept. of Commerce

(billions of dollars)

	1960	1970	1980	1990	1995 R	1996
Gross domestic product	—	—	—	$5,546.1	$7,265.4	$7,636.0
Gross national product	$515.3	$1,015.5	$2,732.0	5,567.8	7,270.6	7,637.7
Less: Consumption of fixed capital	46.4	88.8	303.8	602.7	796.8	830.1
Equals: Net national product	468.9	926.6	2,428.1	4,965.1	6,473.9	6,807.6
Less: Indirect business tax and nontax liability	45.3	94.0	213.3	444.0	582.8	604.8
Business transfer payments	2.0	4.1	12.1	26.8	32.2	33.6
Statistical discrepancy	−2.8	−1.1	4.9	7.8	-28.2	−59.9
Plus: Subsidies less current surplus of government enterprises	0.4	2.9	5.7	4.5	25.2	25.4
Equals: National income	424.9	832.6	2,203.5	4,491.0	5,912.3	6,254.5
Less: Corporate profits with inventory valuation and capital consumption adjustments	49.5	74.7	177.2	380.6	650.0	735.9
Net interest	11.3	41.2	200.9	463.7	425.1	425.1
Contributions for social insurance	21.9	62.2	216.5	503.1	659.1	692.0
Wage accruals less disbursements	0.0	0.0	0.0	0.1	13.1	1.1
Plus: Government transfer payments to persons	27.5	81.8	312.6	666.3	990.0	1042.0
Personal interest income	24.9	69.3	271.9	698.2	718.9	735.7
Personal dividend income	12.9	22.2	52.9	144.4	251.9	291.2
Business transfer payments	2.0	4.1	12.1	21.3	25.0	26.0
Equals: Personal income	409.4	831.8	2,258.5	4,673.8	6,150.8	6,495.2

R = revised figures.

U.S. Gross Domestic Product

Source: Bureau of Economic Analysis, U.S. Dept. of Commerce

(billions of dollars)

	1995R	1996	First Quarter 1997[1]		1995R	1996	First Quarter 1997[1]
Gross domestic product	$7,265.4	$7,636.0	$7,933.6	Net exports of goods and services	$−86.0	$−94.8	$−98.8
Personal consumption expenditures	4,957.7	5,207.6	5,405.7	Exports	818.4	870.9	922.2
Durable goods	608.5	634.5	658.4	Goods	583.9	617.5	656.2
Nondurable goods	1,475.8	1,534.7	1,587.4	Services	234.6	253.3	266.0
Services	2,873.4	3,038.4	3,159.9	Imports	904.5	965.7	1,021.0
Gross private domestic investment	1,038.2	1,116.5	1,193.6	Goods	757.5	809.0	855.8
Fixed investment	1,008.1	1,090.7	1,127.5	Services	146.9	156.7	165.2
Nonresidential	723.0	781.4	811.3	Government consumption expenditures and gross investment	1,355.5	1,406.7	1,433.1
Structures	200.6	215.2	227.4	Federal	509.6	520.0	516.1
Producers' durable equipment	522.4	566.2	583.9	National defense	344.6	352.8	343.3
Residential	285.1	309.2	316.2	Nondefense	165.0	167.3	172.8
Change in business inventories	30.1	25.9	66.1	State and local	846.0	886.7	917.0

R = Revised figures. (1) Seasonally adjusted at annual rates.

Countries With Highest Gross Domestic Product and Per Capita GDP[1]

Source: Central Intelligence Agency, *The World Factbook 1996*; Bureau of Economic Analysis, U.S. Dept. of Commerce

Gross Domestic Product[2]
(billions of dollars; 1995 estimates unless otherwise noted)

1. United States	$7,265.4	21. Taiwan	290.5
2. China	3,500.0[4]	22. Argentina	278.5
3. Japan	2,679.2	23. Pakistan	274.2
4. Germany	1,452.2	24. Poland	226.7
5. India	1,408.7	25. South Africa	215.0
6. France	1,173.0	26. Belgium	197.0
7. United Kingdom	1,138.4	27. Venezuela	195.5
8. Italy	1,088.6	28. Malaysia	193.6
9. Brazil	976.8	29. Colombia	192.5
10. Russia	796.0[5]	30. Saudi Arabia	189.3
11. Mexico	721.4	31. Philippines	179.7
12. Indonesia	710.9	32. Sweden	177.3
13. Canada	694.0	33. Ukraine	174.6[5]
14. South Korea	590.7	34. Egypt	171.0
15. Spain	565.0	35. Switzerland	158.5
16. Thailand	416.7	36. Austria	139.3
17. Australia	405.4	37. Bangladesh	130.1
18. Turkey	345.7	38. Nigeria	122.6
19. Iran	323.5	39. Portugal	107.3
20. Netherlands	301.9	40. Chile	103.0

Per Capita Gross Domestic Product[3]
(dollars; 1995 estimates unless otherwise noted)

1. United States	$27,900	21. Bahamas	18,700
2. Monaco	25,000[6]	22. Italy	18,700
3. Luxembourg	24,800	23. New Zealand	18,300
4. Norway	24,500	24. Finland	18,200
5. Canada	24,400	25. Germany	17,900
6. U. Arab Emirates	24,000	26. Kuwait	17,000
7. Singapore	22,900	27. Andorra	16,200[8]
8. Switzerland	22,400	28. Brunei	15,800
9. Liechtenstein	22,300[7]	29. San Marino	15,800[8]
10. Australia	22,100	30. Israel	15,500
11. Denmark	21,700	31. Ireland	15,400
12. Japan	21,300	32. Spain	14,300
13. Qatar	20,820[6]	33. Taiwan	13,510
14. France	20,200	34. Cyprus	13,000[9]
15. Sweden	20,100	35. South Korea	13,000
16. Belgium	19,500	36. Trinidad & Tob.	12,100
17. Netherlands	19,500	37. Bahrain	12,000
18. United Kingdom	19,500	38. Malta	12,000
19. Austria	19,000	39. Portugal	11,000
20. Iceland	18,800	40. Slovenia	11,000

(1) International data are from CIA's *The World Factbook;* U.S. data are supplied by the Bureau of Economic Analysis. International GDP estimates are derived from purchasing power parity calculations, which involve the use of intl. dollar price weights applied to the quantities of goods and services produced in a given economy. (2) The former British colony of Hong Kong (now part of China) had a GDP of $152.4 billion in 1995. (3) The following territories have large per capita GDPs: Bermuda (UK, 1994) $28,000, Hong Kong (then UK, now China) $27,500, Cayman Islands (UK, 1994) $22,500, Aruba (Neth., 1994) $18,000, Greenland (Den.) $15,500, Faroe Islands (Den.) $15,000, Macao (Port.) $13,000. (4) 1995 estimate as extrapolated from World Bank estimate with use of official Chinese growth figures for 1993-1995. (5) 1995 estimate as extrapolated from World Bank estimate for 1994. (6) 1994 estimate. (7) 1990 estimate. (8) 1993 estimate. (9) Does not include Turkish-held area.

Chapter 11

Chapter 11 refers to the provisions in the Federal Bankruptcy Code for court-supervised reorganization of debtor companies. A company files for Chapter 11 protection when it can no longer pay its creditors or when it expects future liabilities it cannot hope to pay, such as product liability damage awards. In 1991, the U.S. Supreme Court ruled that the provision of federal bankruptcy law that permits corporations to reorganize while continuing to operate was also available for use by individuals. The Bankruptcy Reform Act of 1994 further amended Chapter 11.

Process

1. Bankruptcy filing imposes an automatic stay.
• Creditors generally cannot file or continue suits for repayment.
• Debts are frozen and creditors generally must stop collection actions. This is called the "automatic stay."
• Debtor's day-to-day operations continue.
• Spending, borrowing, and asset sales outside of the debtor's normal course of business must be approved by the court.
• Secured creditors can ask the court for exemption from the automatic stay to undertake or continue to recover the collateral that secures their claim.
2. Unsecured creditors form a committee.
• The U.S. trustee appoints the committee, which ordinarily consists of the 7 largest unsecured creditors who are willing to serve on the panel.
• The U.S. trustee can appoint additional committees to represent other creditors and shareholders.
• The committee chooses representatives to deal with the debtor company.
• The committee and U.S. trustee oversee the debtor's business operations.
• Creditors and the U.S. trustee can ask the court to appoint an examiner to investigate possible fraud or mismanagement.
• Creditors and the U.S. trustee can ask the court to order the appointment of a case trustee to run the debtor company.
• If the court orders the appointment, the U.S. trustee selects the case trustee unless a party asks that creditors be allowed to elect the case trustee.
3. The committee, other creditors, and the debtor company negotiate a reorganization plan.
• Parties negotiate a plan for the reorganization of the debtor's business and repayment of frozen debts. This step can take months or years.
• Only the debtor can file a reorganization plan with the court for the first 120 days of the bankruptcy case. The court can extend the so-called "exclusivity" period and often does so.
• If the debtor does not file a plan during the exclusivity period, if the debtor's plan is not approved by the court, or if a trustee is appointed, any party can file a plan.
• The proponent of the plan prepares a disclosure statement, which must be approved by the court at a separate hearing.

4. Creditors and shareholders vote on the plan.
• Only creditors and shareholders whose claims and interests are impaired or affected by the plan vote on it.
• A class of creditors accepts the plan if the plan is approved by creditors who hold more than half of the claims in the class by number and at least two-thirds of the claims by amount.
• A class of shareholders accepts the plan if the plan is approved by shareholders who hold at least two-thirds of the equity interest in the class by amount.
5. Judge considers the plan.
• The bankruptcy judge approves the plan if it complies with the Bankruptcy Code and all impaired classes approve.
• If at least one of the impaired classes approves the plan and it meets certain statutory tests, the judge can confirm the plan in a so-called "cramdown," even if not all impaired classes approve.
6. Reorganized company emerges.
• Generally, the debtor's debts are discharged.
• The debtor and creditors must comply with the confirmed plan.
• The automatic stay ends and a permanent injunction goes into effect against any effort to collect prepetition debts other than as provided in the plan.
• The reorganized debtor operates like a normal company.
• Only about 17% of the debtors who file Chapter 11 cases get their plans confirmed.

Expedited Procedure for Small Businesses

• The Bankruptcy Reform Act of 1994 included an expedited confirmation process to be used in Chapter 11 cases filed by small businesses.
• The debtor can elect to use the new process if it has less than $2 million in debts and its primary business is not owning or operating real estate.
• The court can order that a creditors' committee not be appointed.
• Unless the court orders otherwise, the debtor's exclusivity period for filing a plan is shortened to 100 days and all plans must be filed within 160 days.
• The court may conditionally approve the disclosure statement. This saves time by combining the court hearing on the disclosure statement with the hearing on confirmation of the plan.

State Finances
Revenue, Expenditures, Debt, and Taxes

Source: Census Bureau, U.S. Dept. of Commerce

(fiscal year 1995)

State	Revenue (millions)	Expenditures (millions)	Debt (millions)	Per capita[1] debt	Per capita[1] taxes	Per capita[1] expenditures
Alabama..........	$12,280	$11,542	$3,759	$884	$1,194	$2,714
Alaska	8,288	5,599	3,232	5,351	3,183	9,270
Arizona...........	12,593	11,162	3,037	720	1,475	2,646
Arkansas.........	7,368	6,616	1,983	798	1,365	2,663
California	118,303	109,231	48,197	1,526	1,686	3,458
Colorado..........	11,555	9,802	3,368	899	1,209	2,616
Connecticut.......	13,718	13,576	15,456	4,719	2,282	4,145
Delaware	3,441	2,980	3,524	4,916	2,224	4,156
Florida	37,359	34,750	15,370	1,085	1,311	2,453
Georgia..........	20,284	19,154	5,622	781	1,317	2,660
Hawaii	5,778	6,015	5,196	4,377	2,422	5,067
Idaho	3,845	3,360	1,303	1,120	1,490	2,889
Illinois...........	34,689	32,991	21,950	1,855	1,402	2,789
Indiana...........	16,261	15,284	5,457	940	1,386	2,634
Iowa.............	9,268	8,586	2,111	743	1,549	3,021
Kansas..........	7,374	7,116	1,145	447	1,468	2,774
Kentucky.........	12,846	11,395	7,097	1,839	1,628	2,952
Louisiana	13,956	14,461	8,520	1,962	1,077	3,331
Maine...........	4,208	4,179	3,041	2,451	1,461	3,368
Maryland.........	16,430	15,069	9,438	1,872	1,599	2,989
Massachusetts	24,101	24,282	27,734	4,566	1,910	3,998
Michigan.........	35,328	34,669	12,535	1,313	1,856	3,631
Minnesota........	18,329	16,380	4,494	975	2,023	3,553
Mississippi	8,301	7,414	1,924	713	1,335	2,749
Missouri	15,586	12,482	6,714	1,261	1,268	2,344
Montana..........	3,293	2,988	2,210	2,540	1,396	3,434
Nebraska	4,615	4,250	1,368	836	1,356	2,596
Nevada..........	5,478	4,581	1,996	1,305	1,764	2,994
New Hampshire.....	3,270	3,096	5,781	5,036	800	2,697
New Jersey........	32,675	32,605	24,358	3,066	1,713	4,104
New Mexico	6,634	6,363	1,824	1,083	1,688	3,776
New York	90,997	81,372	68,466	3,775	1,891	4,487
North Carolina.....	22,091	20,437	4,548	632	1,588	2,840
North Dakota.......	2,448	2,213	855	1,334	1,496	3,452
Ohio.............	41,306	34,990	12,295	1,103	1,362	3,138
Oklahoma.........	9,160	8,990	3,736	1,140	1,347	2,742
Oregon...........	12,986	11,030	5,482	1,745	1,365	3,512
Pennsylvania.......	40,015	39,394	14,294	1,184	1,513	3,263
Rhode Island.......	4,156	4,265	5,516	5,571	1,505	4,308
South Carolina......	12,068	11,623	5,020	1,367	1,297	3,164
South Dakota	2,090	1,880	1,663	2,282	952	2,578
Tennessee	12,900	13,432	2,822	537	1,124	2,556
Texas............	49,422	44,643	9,922	530	1,084	2,384
Utah.............	5,304	5,780	2,061	1,056	1,371	2,963
Vermont	2,074	2,014	1,668	2,851	1,370	3,442
Virginia...........	18,993	17,040	8,716	1,317	1,327	2,575
Washington........	23,576	21,200	8,820	1,624	1,877	3,904
West Virginia.......	6,629	6,262	2,586	1,415	1,494	3,425
Wisconsin.........	15,337	16,302	8,236	1,608	1,763	3,182
Wyoming..........	2,240	2,045	788	1,642	1,389	4,261
United States[2]	**903,756**	**836,894**	**427,239**	**1,629**	**1,522**	**3,192**

(1) Per capita amounts are based on population figures of the resident U.S. population (excluding the District of Columbia) as of July 1, 1995. (2) Totals in this line may not add because of rounding.

State and Local Government Receipts and Current Expenditures

Source: Bureau of Economic Analysis, U.S. Dept. of Commerce

(billions of dollars)

	1995[R]	1996	First Quarter 1997[1]		1995[R]	1996	First Quarter 1997[1]
Receipts	$999.0	$1,043.4	$1,070.9	Net interest paid	$−59.6	$−61.7	$−64.0
Personal tax and nontax receipts	189.4	200.2	208.7	Interest paid	64.1	64.6	64.6
Income taxes	140.3	149.1	155.7	Less: Interest received by			
Nontaxes	26.7	28.8	30.1	government	123.7	126.3	128.6
Other	22.4	22.3	22.9	Less: Dividends received by			
Corporate profits tax accruals ..	31.1	34.5	36.4	government	12.5	13.6	14.3
Indirect business tax and nontax				Subsidies less current surplus of			
accruals	489.3	508.9	522.0	government enterprises	−11.2	−12.3	−12.3
Sales taxes	239.4	249.8	256.2	Subsidies	0.3	0.3	0.3
Property taxes	197.4	202.3	206.2	Less: Current surplus of			
Other	52.5	56.8	59.6	government enterprises ...	11.5	12.7	12.7
Contributions for social insurance	77.3	81.4	84.2	Less: Wage accruals less			
Federal grants-in-aid	211.9	218.3	219.6	disbursements	0.0	0.0	0.0
Current expenditures	**895.9**	**900.0**	**900.1**	**Surplus or deficit (−), national**			
Consumption expenditures	698.6	730.9	751.7	**income and product**			
Transfer payments to persons ..	280.6	294.8	305.1	**accounts ....**	**103.1**	**105.3**	**104.7**

(R) Revised figures. (1) Seasonally adjusted at annual rates.

State and Local Government Current Expenditures and Gross Investment, by Function

Source: Bureau of Economic Analysis, U.S. Dept. Of Commerce

(millions of dollars)

	1995 Total[1]	1995 Current Expends.	1995 Gross Invest-ment[2]	1996 Total[1]	1996 Current Expends.	1996 Gross Invest-ment
Total	$1,043,295	$895,925	$147,370	$1,093,754	$938,012	$155,742
Central executive, legislative, and judicial activities	62,909	60,660	2,249	65,919	63,506	2,413
Administrative, legislative, and judicial activities	33,515	32,082	1,433	34,992	33,447	1,545
Tax collection and financial management..	29,394	28,578	816	30,927	30,059	868
Civilian safety	103,296	96,754	6,542	108,116	101,438	6,678
Police	45,163	43,340	1,823	47,369	45,354	2,015
Fire	18,440	17,415	1,025	19,143	18,080	1,063
Correction	39,693	35,999	3,694	41,604	38,004	3,600
Education	368,256	337,445	30,811	385,762	353,775	31,987
Elementary and secondary	279,527	260,449	19,078	293,477	273,904	19,573
Higher	65,951	55,348	10,603	68,201	56,974	11,227
Libraries	5,219	4,525	694	5,441	4,691	750
Other	17,559	17,123	436	18,643	18,206	437
Health and hospitals	32,189	26,935	5,254	34,628	29,084	5,544
Health	25,703	24,024	1,679	27,580	25,732	1,848
Hospitals	6,486	2,911	3,575	7,048	3,352	3,696
Income support, social security, and welfare	237,481	236,835	646	249,031	248,354	677
Govt. employees retirement and disability	−2,496	−2,496	...	1,156	1,156	...
Workers' compensation and temporary disability insurance	9,252	9,252	...	9,002	9,002	...
Medical care	155,017	155,017	...	163,612	163,612	...
Welfare and social services	75,708	75,062	646	75,261	74,584	677
Veterans' benefits and services	225	199	26	232	211	21
Housing and community services	25,366	3,133	22,233	26,993	2,765	24,168
Housing, comm. dev., urban renewal	6,226	2,309	3,917	6,511	2,385	4,126
Water	4,230	−3,371	7,601	4,672	−3,574	8,246
Sewerage	8,171	−834	9,005	8,900	−1,155	10,055
Sanitation	6,739	5,029	1,710	6,850	5,109	1,741
Recreational and cultural activities	14,907	11,823	3,084	15,351	12,116	3,235
Energy	−2,578	−6,958	4,380	−2,703	−7,097	4,394
Gas utilities	−349	−701	352	−342	−725	383
Electric utilities	−2,229	−6,257	4,028	−2,361	−6,372	4,011
Agriculture	4,432	4,206	226	4,544	4,309	235
Natural resources	10,277	8,267	2,010	10,657	8,535	2,122
Transportation	122,537	62,358	60,179	129,778	65,675	64,103
Highways	95,937	50,258	45,675	100,730	52,655	48,075
Water	1,430	−75	1,505	1,641	−71	1,712
Air	2,323	−1,541	3,864	2,745	−1,668	4,413
Transit and railroad	22,847	13,716	9,131	24,662	14,759	9,903
Economic development, regulation, and services	7,647	7,377	270	7,839	7,573	266
Labor training and services	5,539	5,409	130	5,067	5,445	122
Commercial activities	−12,255	−12,499	244	−13,642	−13,911	269
Publicly owned liquor store systems	−814	−824	10	−1,051	−1,063	12
Govt.-administered lotteries, parimutuels..	−11,612	−11,612	...	−12,705	−12,705	...
Other	171	−63	234	−114	−143	257
Net interest paid[2]	4,515	4,515	...	5,181	5,181	...
Other and unallocable	58,552	49,466	9,086	60,561	51,053	9,508

(1) Sum of current expenditures and gross investment. (2) Excludes interest received by social insurance funds, which is netted against expenditures for the appropriate functions.

Banks in the U.S.—Number, Deposits

Source: Federal Deposit Insurance Corp. (as of Dec. 31; 1996 data as of Sept. 23, 1997)

Comprises all FDIC-insured commercial and savings banks, including savings and loan institutions (S&Ls).

Year	Number of banks Total	Commercial banks[1] Natl.	Commercial banks[1] State	Non-members	All savings	Total deposits (millions of dollars) Total	Commercial banks[1] Natl.	Commercial banks[1] State	Non-members	All savings
1935	15,295	5,386	1,001	7,735	1,173	$ 45,102[2]	$ 24,802	$ 13,653	$ 5,669	$ 978[2]
1940	15,772	5,144	1,342	6,956	2,330	67,494	35,787	20,642	7,040	4,025
1945	15,969	5,017	1,864	6,421	2,667	151,524	77,778	41,865	16,307	15,574
1950	16,500	4,958	1,912	6,576	3,054	171,963	84,941	41,602	19,726	25,694
1955	17,001	4,692	1,847	6,698	3,764	235,211	102,796	55,739	26,198	50,478
1960	17,549	4,530	1,641	6,955	4,423	310,262	120,242	65,487	34,369	90,164
1965	18,384	4,815	1,405	7,327	4,837	467,633	185,334	78,327	51,982	151,990
1970	18,205	4,621	1,147	7,743	4,694	686,901	285,436	101,512	95,566	204,367
1975	18,792	4,744	1,046	8,595	4,407	1,157,648	450,308	143,409	187,031	376,900
1980	18,763	4,425	997	9,013	4,328	1,832,716	656,752	191,183	344,311	640,470
1985	18,033	4,959	1,070	8,378	3,626	3,140,827	1,241,875	354,585	521,628	1,022,739
1990	15,158	3,979	1,009	7,355	2,815	3,637,292	1,558,915	397,797	693,438	987,142
1993	13,220	3,304	969	6,685	2,262	3,528,487	1,576,725	476,093	701,512	774,157
1994	12,603	3,075	976	6,400	2,152	3,611,618	1,630,171	533,261	711,006	737,180
1995	11,970	2,858	1,042	6,040	2,030	3,769,477	1,695,817	614,924	716,829	741,907
1996	11,670	2,763	1,024	5,902	1,981	3,788,905	1,795,110	567,809	698,497	727,489

(1) "Nonmembers" are banks that are not members of the Federal Reserve System; "National" and "State" institutions are members. (2) Figures for 1935 do not include data for S&Ls (not available).

Largest U.S. Commercial Banks

Source: *American Banker* (as of Dec. 31, 1996)

Bank	Assets (millions)
Chase Manhattan Bank, New York, NY	$272,429
Citibank, New York, NY	241,006
Bank of America, San Francisco, CA.	180,480
Morgan Guaranty Trust Co., New York, NY	172,563
Wells Fargo Bank, San Francisco, CA.	99,165
Bankers Trust Co., New York, NY	90,430
NationsBank, Charlotte, NC	80,870
PNC Bank, Pittsburgh, PA	57,285
Bank of New York, NY	52,120
First National Bank, Chicago, IL	51,663
Republic National Bank of New York, NY.	46,953
NationsBank, South, Atlanta, GA	46,776
Fleet National Bank, Springfield, MA	46,581
First National Bank, Boston, MA	45,875
CoreStates Bank, Philadelphia, PA	42,670
First Union National Bank of Florida, Jacksonville.	39,259
Barnett Bank, Jacksonville, FL	39,209
NationsBank of Texas, Dallas	39,149
Mellon Bank, Pittsburgh, PA.	37,339
First Union National Bank of North Carolina, Charlotte	32,422
State Street Bank & Trust Co., Boston, MA	31,390
Union Bank of California, San Francisco	29,197
KeyBank, Cleveland, OH	27,813
First Union National Bank, Avondale, PA.	27,128
Comerica Bank, Detroit, MI.	27,051
Wachovia Bank of North Carolina, Winston-Salem.	$26,751
Chase Manhattan Bank (USA), Wilmington, DE	25,311
Marine Midland Bank, Buffalo, NY	23,345
Fleet Bank, Jersey City, NJ	23,116
Texas Commerce Bank, Houston	22,716
NBD Bank, Detroit, MI	22,474
Bank One, Texas, Dallas	20,886
Summit Bank (NJ), Princeton	19,615
Wachovia Bank of Georgia, Atlanta	18,919
Crestar Bank, Richmond, VA	18,264
Northern Trust Co., Chicago, IL	18,127
Norwest Bank Minnesota, Minneapolis	17,649
Bank of America Illinois, Chicago	17,075
First Bank, Minneapolis, MN.	17,055
Branch Banking & Trust Co., Winston-Salem, NC	16,596
Bank of America NW, Seattle, WA	16,568
MBNA America Bank, Wilmington, DE.	15,575
Key Bank of New York, Albany	15,486
SunTrust Bank, Atlanta, GA	15,015
Huntington National Bank, Columbus, OH	14,406
Bank One, Arizona, Phoenix	14,311
United States National Bank, Portland, OR	14,290
Harris Trust & Savings Bank, Chicago, IL	14,264
Banco Popular de Puerto Rico, San Juan	14,005
Citibank (South Dakota), Sioux Falls	13,549

U.S. Bank Failures

Source: Federal Deposit Insurance Corp.

Year	Closed or assisted	Year	Closed or assisted	Year	Closed or assisted	Year	Closed or assisted	Year	Closed or assisted
1934	61	1960	2	1971	6	1981	10	1989	207
1935	32	1961	9	1972	3	1982	42	1990	169
1936	72	1963	2	1973	6	1983	48	1991	127
1937	84	1964	8	1975	14	1984	80	1992	122
1938	81	1965	9	1976	17	1985	120	1993	41
1939	72	1966	8	1978	7	1986	145	1994	13
1940	48	1967	4	1979	10	1987	203	1995	6
1955	5	1969	9	1980	11	1988	221	1996	5
1959	3	1970	8						

World's Largest Banking Companies[1]

Source: *American Banker* (as of Dec. 31, 1996; Japan data as of Mar. 31, 1997)

Banks	Assets (millions)
Bank of Tokyo-Mitsubishi Ltd., Tokyo, Japan	$648,161
Deutsche Bank, AG, Frankfurt, Germany	575,072
Credit Agricole Mutuel, Paris, France	479,963
Dai-Ichi Kangyo Bank Ltd., Tokyo.	434,115
Fuji Bank, Ltd., Tokyo	432,992
Sanwa Bank Ltd., Osaka, Japan.	427,689
Sumitomo Bank Ltd., Osaka.	426,103
Sakura Bank, Ltd., Tokyo.	423,017
HSBC Holdings, Plc., London, United Kingdom	404,979
Norinchukin Bank, Tokyo.	375,210
Dresdner Bank, Frankfurt.	358,829
Banque Nationale de Paris	357,322
Industrial Bank of Japan Ltd., Tokyo	350,468
ABN-AMRO Bank, N.V., Amsterdam, Netherlands.	341,916
Societe Generale, Paris.	341,867
Chase Manhattan Corp., New York.	333,777
Union Bank of Switzerland, Zurich, Switzerland	326,190
NatWest Group, London	317,295
Credit Lyonnais, Paris	311,747
Barclays Plc., London	308,710
Westdeutsche Landesbank Girozentrale, Dusseldorf, Ger.	298,455
Compagnie Financiere de Paribas, Paris.	292,320
Commerzbank, Frankfurt.	290,300
Mitsubishi Trust & Banking Corp., Tokyo.	284,528
Citicorp, New York, United States.	278,941
Tokai Bank Ltd., Nagoya, Japan	$273,430
Swiss Bank Corp., Basel, Switzerland	268,519
Bayerische Vereinsbank, Munich, Germany	260,848
Mitsui Trust & Banking Co., Ltd., Tokyo	254,189
Lloyds TSB Group, Inc., London	252,292
Sumitomo Trust & Banking Co. Ltd., Osaka	248,418
BankAmerica Corp., San Francisco, United States	247,892
Long-Term Credit Bank of Japan Ltd., Tokyo	231,761
Asahi Bank, Ltd., Tokyo	230,080
Bayerische Landesbank Girozentrale, Munich	223,496
J. P. Morgan & Co., Inc., New York	221,814
Bayerische Hypotheken und Wechsel Bank, Munich	220,100
Credit Suisse First Boston, Zurich	218,870
Bankgesellschaft Berlin, AG, Berlin, Germany	218,226
Daiwa Bank Ltd., Osaka	212,967
Abbey National, Plc., London	212,307
Deutsche Genossenschaftsbank, Frankfurt	212,061
Yasuda Trust & Banking Co. Ltd., Tokyo	196,520
Toyo Trust & Banking Co. Ltd., Tokyo	192,802
NationsBank Corp., Charlotte, NC, United States	184,886
Rabobank Nederland, Utrecht, Netherlands	180,960
ING Bank, Amsterdam	178,886
Halifax Building Society, Halifax, United Kingdom.	175,111
Generale Bank, Brussels, Belgium	174,639
Istituto Bancario San Paolo di Torino, Turin, Italy	172,540

(1) Includes bank holding companies and commercial and savings banks. **Note:** Data for U.S. companies listed include assets not included in "Largest U.S. Commercial Banks" table.

Federal Deposit Insurance Corporation (FDIC)

The Federal Deposit Insurance Corporation (FDIC) is the independent deposit insurance agency created by Congress to maintain stability and public confidence in the nation's banking system. In its unique role as deposit insurer of banks and savings associations, and in cooperation with other federal and state regulatory agencies, the FDIC seeks to promote the safety and soundness of insured depository institutions in the U.S. financial system by identifying, monitoring, and addressing risks to the deposit insurance funds. The FDIC aims at promoting public understanding and sound public policies by providing financial and economic information and analyses. It seeks to minimize disruptive effects from the failure of banks and savings associations. It seeks to ensure fairness in the sale of financial products and the provision of financial services.

The FDIC's income consists of assessments on insured banks and income from investments; it receives no appropriations from Congress. The Corporation may borrow from the U.S. Treasury, not to exceed $30 billion outstanding, but the agency has made no such borrowings since it was organized in 1933. The FDIC's Bank Insurance Fund was $27.4 billion (unaudited) and the Savings Association Insurance Fund stood at $9.1 billion (unaudited), as of June 30, 1997.

Federal Reserve Board Discount Rate

The discount rate is the rate of interest set by the Federal Reserve that member banks are charged when borrowing money through the Federal Reserve System. Includes any changes through Oct. 15, 1997.

Effective date	Rate	Effective date	Rate	Effective date	Rate	Effective date	Rate	Effective date	Rate	Effective date	Rate
1980:		**1981:**		Oct. 12	9½	**1986:**		**1989:**		**1992:**	
Feb. 15	13	May 5	14	Nov. 22	9	March 7	7	Feb. 24	7	July 3	3
May 30	12	Nov. 2	13	Dec. 15	8½	April 21	6½	**1990:**		**1994:**	
June 13	11	Dec. 4	12	**1984:**		July 11	6	Dec. 18	6½	May 17	3½
July 28	10	**1982:**		April 9	9	Aug. 21	5½	**1991:**		Aug. 16	4
Sept. 26	11	July 20	11½	Nov. 21	8½	**1987:**		Apr. 30	5½	Nov. 15	4¾
Nov. 17	12	Aug. 2	11	Dec. 24	8	Sept. 4	6	Sept. 13	5	**1995:**	
Dec. 5	13	Aug. 16	10½	**1985:**		**1988:**		Nov. 6	4½	Feb. 1	5¼
		Aug. 27	10	May 20	7½	Aug. 9	6½	Dec. 20	3½	**1996:**	
										Jan. 31	5

Federal Reserve System

The Federal Reserve System is the central bank for the U.S. The system was established on Dec. 23, 1913, originally to give the country an elastic currency, to provide facilities for discounting commercial paper, and to improve the supervision of banking. Since then, the system's responsibilities have been broadened. Over the years, stability and growth of the economy, a high level of employment, stability in the purchasing power of the dollar, and reasonable balance in transactions with other countries have come to be recognized as primary objectives of governmental economic policy.

The Federal Reserve System consists of the Board of Governors, the 12 District Reserve Banks and their branch offices, and the Federal Open Market Committee. Several advisory councils help the board meet its varied responsibilities.

The hub of the system is the 7-member Board of Governors in Washington. The members of the board are appointed by the president and confirmed by the Senate, to serve 14-year terms. The president also appoints the chairman and vice chairman of the board from among the board members for 4-year terms that may be renewed. As of Sept. 1997 the board members were: Alan Greenspan, Chair; Alice M. Rivlin, Vice Chair; Edward W. Kelley Jr.; Susan M. Phillips; and Laurence H. Meyer. There were 2 vacancies as of mid-Oct. 1997.

The board is the policy-making body. In addition to its policy-making responsibilities, it supervises the budget and operations of the Reserve Banks, approves the appointments of their presidents, and appoints 3 of each District Bank's directors, including the chairman and vice chairman of each Reserve Bank's board.

The 12 Reserve Banks and their branch offices serve as the decentralized portion of the system, carrying out day-to-day operations such as circulating currency and coin and providing fiscal agency functions and payments mechanism services. The District Banks are in Boston, New York, Philadelphia, Cleveland, Richmond, Atlanta, Chicago, St. Louis, Minneapolis, Kansas City, Dallas, and San Francisco.

The system's principal function is monetary policy, which it controls using 3 tools: reserve requirements, the discount rate, and open market operations. Uniform reserve requirements, set by the board, are applied to the transaction accounts and nonpersonal time deposits of all depository institutions. Responsibility for setting the discount rate (the interest rate at which depository institutions can borrow money from the Reserve Banks) is shared by the Board of Governors and the Reserve Banks. Changes in the discount rate are recommended by the individual boards of directors of the Reserve Banks and are subject to approval by the Board of Governors.

The most important tool of monetary policy is open market operations (the purchase and sale of government securities). Responsibility for influencing the cost and availability of money and credit through the purchase and sale of government securities lies with the Federal Open Market Committee (FOMC), composed of the 7 members of the Board of Governors, the president of the Federal Reserve Bank of New York, and 4 other Federal Reserve Bank presidents, who serve one-year terms on a rotating basis. The committee bases its decisions on economic and financial developments and outlook, setting yearly growth objectives for key measures of money supply and credit. The decisions of the committee are carried out by the Domestic Trading Desk of the Federal Reserve Bank of New York.

The Federal Reserve Act prescribes a Federal Advisory Council, consisting of one member from each Federal Reserve District, who is elected annually by the Board of Directors of each of the 12 Federal Reserve Banks. The council meets with the Federal Reserve Board 4 times a year to discuss business and financial conditions and to make advisory recommendations.

The Consumer Advisory Council is a statutory body, including both consumer and creditor representatives, which advises the Board of Governors on its implementation of consumer regulations and other consumer-related matters.

Following the passage of the Monetary Control Act of 1980, the Board of Governors established the Thrift Institutions Advisory Council to provide information and views on the special needs and problems of thrift institutions. The group is composed of representatives of mutual savings banks, savings and loan associations, and credit unions.

United States Mint

Source: United States Mint, U.S. Dept. of the Treasury

The United States Mint was created on Apr. 2, 1792, by an act of Congress, which established the U.S. national coinage system. Supervision of the mint was a function of the secretary of state, but in 1799 the mint became an independent agency reporting directly to the president. The mint was made a statutory bureau of the Treasury Department in 1873, with a director appointed by the president to oversee its operations.

The mint manufactures and ships all U.S. coins for circulation to the Federal Reserve banks and branches, which issue coins to the public and the business community through depository institutions. The mint also safeguards the Treasury Department's stored gold and silver and other monetary assets.

The composition of dimes, quarters, and half dollars, traditionally produced from silver, was changed by the Coinage Act of 1965, which mandated that these coins be minted from a cupronickel-clad alloy and reduced the silver content of the half dollar to 40%. In 1970, legislative action mandated that the half dollar and a dollar coin be minted from the same alloy.

The Eisenhower dollar was minted from 1971 through 1978, when legislation called for the minting of the smaller Susan B. Anthony dollar coin. The Anthony dollar, which was minted from 1979 through 1981, marked the first time that a woman, other than a mythical figure, appeared on a U.S. coin produced for general circulation.

Mint headquarters are in Washington, DC. Mint production facilities are in Philadelphia, Denver, San Francisco, and West Point, NY. In addition, the mint is responsible for the U.S. Bullion Depository at Fort Knox, KY.

Proof coin sets, silver proof coin sets, and uncirculated coin sets are available annually from the mint. The mint also produces ongoing series of national and historic medals in honor of outstanding persons or events and sites of special meaning to the American people.

Since 1982, the mint has produced the following congressionally authorized commemorative coins: the 1982 George Washington commemorative half dollar; 1984 U.S. Olympic coins; 1986 U.S. Statue of Liberty coins; 1987 Bicentennial of the U.S. Constitution coins; 1989 U.S. Congressional coins; the 1990 Eisenhower Centennial coin; the 1991 United Services Organization 59th Anniversary coin; the 1991 Korean War Memorial coin; 1991 Mount Rushmore Anniversary coins; 1992 U.S. Olympic coins; the 1992 White House 200th Anniversary coin; 1992 Christopher Columbus Quincentenary coins; 1993 Bill of Rights coins; 1993 World War II 50th Anniversary coins; 1994 World Cup USA coins; the Thomas Jefferson 250th Anniversary coin; U.S. Veterans Commemorative coins (featuring the Prisoner of War coin, the Vietnam Veterans Memorial coin, and the Women in Military Service for America coin); the Bicentennial of the U.S. Capitol Commemorative Silver Dollar; 1995 Civil War Battlefield coins; 1995/1996 U.S. Olympic Games of the Atlanta Centennial Games; 1997 U.S. Botanic Garden Silver Dollar; 1997 Franklin Delano Roosevelt Gold coin; 1997 Gold and Silver Jackie Robinson Commemorative coins; and the 1997 National Law Enforcement Memorial Silver Dollar.

The congressionally authorized American Eagle gold, platinum, and silver bullion coins are available through dealers worldwide. The gold and platinum eagles are sold in one-ounce, half-ounce, quarter-ounce, and one-tenth-ounce sizes; the prices fluctuate with the daily market value of gold and platinum. The American eagle silver bullion coin contains one troy ounce of .999 fine silver and is priced according to the daily market value of silver. These coins also are available in proof condition, separately priced.

The mint offers free public tours and operates sales centers at the U.S. mints in Denver and Philadelphia; it also operates a sales center at Union Station in Washington, DC.

Information about mint programs and products is available from the United States Mint, Customer Service Center, 10003 Derekwood Lane, Lanham, MD 20706. Telephone: (202) 283-COIN.

Portraits on U.S. Treasury Bills, Bonds, Notes, and Savings Bonds

Denomination	Savings bonds	Treasury bills*	Treasury bonds*	Treasury notes*
$50	Washington		Jefferson	
75	Adams			
100	Jefferson		Jackson	
200	Madison			
500	Hamilton		Washington	
1,000	Franklin	H. McCulloch	Lincoln	Lincoln
5,000	Revere	J. G. Carlisle	Monroe	Monroe
10,000	J. Wilson	J. Sherman	Cleveland	Cleveland
50,000		C. Glass		
100,000		A. Gallatin	Grant	Grant
1,000,000		O. Wolcott	T. Roosevelt	T. Roosevelt
100,000,000				Madison
500,000,000				McKinley

*The U.S. Treasury discontinued issuing treasury bill, bond, and note certificates in 1986. Since then, all issues of marketable treasury securities have been available only in book-entry form, although some certificates remain in circulation.

Denominations of U.S. Currency

Since 1969 the largest denomination of U.S. currency that has been issued is the $100 bill. As larger-denomination bills reach the Federal Reserve Bank, they are removed from circulation. Because some discontinued currency is expected to be in the hands of holders for many years, the description of the various denominations below is continued.

Amt.	Portrait	Embellishment on back	Amt.	Portrait	Embellishment on back
$ 1	Washington	Great Seal of U.S.	$ 100	Franklin	Independence Hall
2	Jefferson	Signers of Declaration	500	McKinley	Ornate denominational marking
5	Lincoln	Lincoln Memorial	1,000	Cleveland	Ornate denominational marking
10	Hamilton	U.S. Treasury	5,000	Madison	Ornate denominational marking
20	Jackson	White House	10,000	Chase	Ornate denominational marking
50	Grant	U.S. Capitol	100,000*	W. Wilson	Ornate denominational marking

*For use only in transactions between Federal Reserve System and Treasury Department.

New U.S. Currency Designs

On Mar. 25, 1996, the U.S. issued a redesigned $100 note incorporating many new and modified anticounterfeiting features. The note was the first of the U.S. currency series to be redesigned. A new $50 note was to be issued Oct. 27, 1997. Additional currency was scheduled to be issued at a rate of one denomination per year. Old notes are being removed from circulation as they are returned to the Federal Reserve, but all U.S. currency will continue to be honored at full face value.

The new $100 bill has: a larger portrait, moved off-center; a watermark (seen only when held up to the light) to the right of the portrait, depicting the same person; a security thread that glows red when exposed to ultraviolet light in a dark environment; color-shifting ink that changes from green to black when viewed at different angles, to appear in the numeral on the lower, front right-hand corner of the bill; microprinting in the numeral in the note's lower, front left-hand corner and on the portrait; and other features for security, machine authentication, and processing of the currency. The redesigned $50 bill incorporates the same features as the $100 bill, with the notable addition of a low-vision feature, a large (14 mm high, as compared to 7.8 mm on the old design), dark numeral on a light background on the back of the note. The low-vision feature will appear on subsequent redesigned notes in the series. More new currency information is available on the U.S. Treasury's web site: http://www.ustreas.gov

U.S. Currency and Coin

Source: Financial Management Service, U.S. Dept. of the Treasury (Mar. 31, 1997)

Amounts Outstanding and in Circulation

Currency	Total currency and coin	Total currency	Federal Reserve notes[1]	U.S. notes	Currency no longer issued
Amounts outstanding . . .	$550,999,609,407	$526,417,139,509	$525,843,078,476	$316,997,716	$257,063,317
Less amounts held by:					
Treasury	306,077,148	12,385,128	11,832,425	361,239	191,464
Federal Reserve banks	106,159,571,664	105,486,084,845	105,486,082,485	—	2,360
Amounts in circulation . .	$444,533,960,595	$420,918,669,536	$420,345,163,566	$316,636,477	$256,869,493

Coins[2]	Total	Dollars[3]	Fractional coins
Amounts outstanding	$24,582,469,898	$2,024,703,898	$22,557,766,000
Less amounts held by:			
Treasury	293,692,020	104,238,654	189,453,366
Federal Reserve banks.	673,486,819	55,259,062	618,227,757
Amounts in circulation	$23,615,291,059	$1,865,206,182	$21,750,084,877

Currency in Circulation by Denominations

Denomination	Total currency in circulation	Federal Reserve notes[1]	U.S. notes	Currency no longer issued
$1	$6,253,758,057	$6,105,986,084	$143,481	$147,628,492
$2	1,097,154,754	964,593,312	132,548,866	12,576
$5	7,344,374,165	7,201,495,110	110,530,610	32,348,445
$10	13,383,913,360	13,361,162,340	5,950	22,745,070
$20	81,874,792,100	81,854,688,220	3,380	20,100,500
$50	46,627,618,500	46,616,125,600	—	11,492,900
$100	264,019,434,500	263,924,038,400	73,404,100	21,992,000
$500	144,595,500	144,407,500	—	188,000
$1,000	167,823,000	167,617,000	—	206,000
$5,000	1,755,000	1,700,000	—	55,000
$10,000	3,450,000	3,350,000	—	100,000
Fractional parts	485	—	—	485
Partial notes[4]	115	—	90	25
Total currency	$420,918,669,536	$420,345,163,566	$316,636,477	$256,869,493

Comparative Totals of Money in Circulation — Selected Dates

Date	Dollars (in millions)	Per capita[5]	Date	Dollars (in millions)	Per capita[5]	Date	Dollars (in millions)	Per capita[5]
Mar. 31, 1997	444,534.0	1,664.58	June 30, 1975	81,196.4	380.08	June 30, 1940	7,847.5	59.40
Mar. 31, 1996	416,280.0	1,573.15	June 30, 1970	54,351.0	265.39	June 30, 1935	5,567.1	43.75
Mar. 31, 1995	401,610.0	1,531.39	June 30, 1965	39,719.8	204.14	June 30, 1930	4,522.0	36.74
Mar. 31, 1994	371,466.0	1,428.37	June 30, 1960	32,064.6	177.47	June 30, 1925	4,815.2	41.56
Mar. 31, 1990	257,664.4	1,028.71	June 30, 1955	30,229.3	182.90	June 30, 1920	5,467.6	51.36
June 30, 1985	185,890.7	778.58	June 30, 1950	27,156.3	179.03	June 30, 1915	3,319.6	33.01
June 30, 1980	127,097.2	558.28	June 30, 1945	26,746.4	191.14	June 30, 1910	3,148.7	34.07

(1) Issued on or after July 1, 1929. (2) Excludes coin sold to collectors at premium prices. (3) Includes $481,781,898 in standard silver dollars. (4) Represents value of certain partial denominations not presented for redemption. (5) Based on Bureau of the Census estimates of population.

The requirement for a gold reserve against U.S. notes was repealed by Public Law 90-269, approved Mar. 18, 1968. Silver certificates issued on and after July 1, 1929, became redeemable from the general fund on June 24, 1968. The amount of security after those dates has been reduced accordingly.

Consumer Credit Outstanding, 1994-96

Source: Federal Reserve System

(billions of dollars)

Estimated amounts of credit outstanding as of end of year. Not seasonally adjusted.

	1994[R]	1995	1996		1994[R]	1995	1996
Total	$988.8	$1,131.9	$1,214.9	Commercial banks	$141.9	$149.1	$154.0
Ratio to disposable personal				Finance companies	61.6	70.6	86.7
income[1] (percent)	19.7	21.3	23.7	Pools of securitized assets[2]	36.4	44.4	52.4
By major holder				Revolving	357.3	435.7	522.9
Commercial banks	462.9	507.8	529.4	Commercial banks	182.0	210.3	228.6
Finance companies	134.8	152.6	152.4	Finance companies	56.8	53.5	32.5
Credit unions	119.6	131.9	144.1	Pools of securitized assets[2]	96.1	147.9	188.7
Savings institutions.	38.5	40.1	44.7	Other	313.2	342.2	298.8
Nonfinancial business. . . .	86.6	85.1	77.7	Commercial banks	139.0	148.4	146.8
Pools of securitized assets[2]	147.8	214.4	266.5	Finance companies	73.2	82.0	33.2
By major type of credit[3]				Nonfinancial business. . . .	29.8	31.5	32.8
Automobile	$319.7	$354.1	$393.2	Pools of securitized assets[2]	15.3	22.1	25.4

(1) Based on 4th quarter seasonally adjusted disposable personal income at annual rates as published by the U.S. Bureau of Economic Analysis. (2) Outstanding balances of pools upon which securities have been issued; these balances are no longer carried on the balance sheets of the loan originator. (3) Totals include estimates for certain holders for which only consumer credit totals are available. (R) Revised.

Leading U.S. Businesses in 1996

Source: *FORTUNE* Magazine

(millions of dollars in revenues)

Aerospace

Lockheed Martin	$26,875
United Technologies	23,512
Boeing	22,681
AlliedSignal	13,971
McDonnell Douglas	13,834
Textron	9,274
Northrop Grumman	8,071
General Dynamics	3,609
B.F. Goodrich	2,556

Airlines

AMR	$17,753
UAL	16,362
Delta Air Lines	12,455
Northwest Airlines	9,881
US Airways Group	8,142
Continental Airlines	6,360
Trans World Airlines	3,554
Southwest Airlines	3,406
America West Holdings	1,740
Alaska Air Group	1,592

Apparel

Nike	$6,471
VF	5,137
Reebok International	3,483
Fruit of the Loom	2,447
Liz Claiborne	2,218
Kellwood	1,466
Russell	1,244
Warnaco Group	1,064
Jones Apparel Group	1,021

Beverages

Coca-Cola	$18,546
Anheuser-Busch	10,884
Coca-Cola Enterprises	7,921
Whitman	3,111
Adolph Coors	1,732

Building Materials, Glass

Corning	$4,200
Owens-Illinois	3,976
Owens-Corning	3,832
USG	2,590
Armstrong World Inds.	2,156
Schuller	1,552

Chemicals

E. I. du Pont de Nemours	$39,689
Dow Chemical	20,053
Occidental Petroleum	10,557
Monsanto	9,262
PPG Industries	7,218
Union Carbide	6,106
W.R. Grace	5,262
FMC	5,122
Lyondell Petrochemical	5,082
Millennium Chemicals	5,057

Commercial Banks

Citicorp	$32,605
Chase Manhattan Corp.	27,421
BankAmerica Corp.	22,071
Nationsbank Corp.	17,509
J.P. Morgan & Co.	15,866
First Union Corp.	11,985
Banc One Corp.	10,272
First Chicago NBD Corp.	10,117
Bankers Trust N.Y. Corp.	9,565
Norwest Corp.	8,883

Computer and Data Services

Unisys	$6,371
First Data	4,938
Automatic Data Proc.	3,567
Comdisco	2,431
Dun & Bradstreet	2,159
Micro Warehouse	1,916
Equifax	1,811
Ceridian	1,496
A. C. Nielsen	1,359
America Online	1,094

Computer Peripherals

Seagate Technology	$8,588
Quantum	4,423
Western Digital	2,865

Lexmark International	$2,378
EMC	2,274
Storage Technology	2,040

Computers, Office Equipment

IBM	$75,947
Hewlett-Packard	38,420
Xerox	19,521
Compaq Computer	18,109
Digital Equipment	14,563
Apple Computer	9,833
Dell Computer	7,759
Sun Microsystems	7,095
Gateway 2000	5,035

Computer Software

Microsoft	$8,671
Computer Sciences	4,242
Oracle	4,223
Computer Assoc. International	3,505
Cognizant	1,731
Novell	1,375

Diversified Financials

Fed. Natl. Mortgage Assn.	$25,054
American Express	17,280
College Ret. Equities Fund	13,865
Fed. Home Loan Mortgage	12,116
Dean Witter Discover	9,029
American General	6,979
Household International	5,059
Marsh & McLennan	4,149
Student Loan Mrktg. Assn.	3,590

Electronics, Electrical Equip.

General Electric	$79,179
Motorola	27,973
Rockwell International	14,343
Raytheon	12,331
Emerson Electric	11,150
Whirlpool	8,696
Eaton	6,961

Electronics, Semiconductors

Intel	$20,847
Texas Instruments	11,713
Applied Materials	4,145
National Semiconductor	2,623
Advanced Micro Devices	1,953

Entertainment

Walt Disney	$18,739
Viacom	12,084
Time Warner	10,064
Westinghouse Electric	9,401

Food

ConAgra	$24,822
Sara Lee	18,624
RJR Nabisco Holdings	17,063
Archer Daniels Midland	13,314
IBP	12,539
CPC International	9,844
Farmland Industries	9,789
H. J. Heinz	9,112
Campbell Soup	7,678
Kellogg	6,677

Food and Drug Stores

Kroger	$25,171
American Stores	18,678
Safeway	17,269
Albertson's	13,777
Winn-Dixie Stores	12,955
Walgreen	11,778
Publix	10,526

Food Services

Pepsico	$31,645
McDonald's	10,687
Aramark	6,123
Darden Restaurants	3,192
Flagstar	2,542
Viad	2,263
Wendy's International	1,897

Forest and Paper Products

International Paper	$20,143
Kimberly-Clark	13,149
Georgia-Pacific	13,024
Weyerhaeuser	11,114
Champion International	5,880

James River Corp. of VA	$5,691
Stone Container	5,142
Boise Cascade	5,123
Mead	4,707

Furniture

Leggett & Platt	$2,466
Furniture Brands Intl.	1,697
Herman Miller	1,284

General Merchandisers

Wal-Mart Stores	$106,147
Sears Roebuck	38,236
Kmart	31,437
Dayton Hudson	25,371
J. C. Penney	23,649
Federated Dept. Stores	15,229
May Department Stores	12,601
Dillard Dept. Stores	6,412

Health Care

Columbia/HCA Healthcare	$19,909
United Healthcare	10,074
Humana	6,788
Tenet Healthcare	5,559
Medpartners	4,813
Pacificare Health Systems	4,637
Allegiance	4,387
FHP International	4,179
Wellpoint Health Networks	4,170

Hotels, Casinos, Resorts

Marriott International	$10,172
ITT	6,597
Hilton Hotels	3,940
Harrah's Entertainment	1,588
Mirage Resorts	1,368

Industrial and Farm Equip.

Caterpillar	$16,522
Deere	11,229
Ingersoll-Rand	6,703
Dresser Industries	6,562
American Standard	5,805
Case	5,409
Cummins Engine	5,257
Black & Decker	4,914
Dover	4,076

Insurance (Life and Health)

Prudential of America (Mutual)	$40,175
Metropolitan Life (Stock)	23,000
Cigna (Stock)	18,950
New York Life Ins. (Mutual)	17,347
Aetna Life & Casualty (Stock)	16,900
Teachers Ins. & Annuity (Mut.)	13,828
Nationwide Ins. Enterpr. (Stock)	12,358
Northwestern Mut. Life (Mut.)	12,110

Insurance (Property and Casualty)

State Farm Ins. (Mutual)	$42,781
American Intl. Group (Stock)	28,205
Allstate (Stock)	24,299
Travelers Group (Stock)	21,345
Loews (Stock)	19,965
ITT Hartford Group (Stock)	12,473
Liberty Mutual Group (Mut.)	10,967
Berkshire Hathaway (Stock)	10,500

Metal Products

Gillette	$9,698
Crown Cork & Seal	8,332
Tyco International	5,090
Illinois Tool Works	4,997
Masco	3,237
Newell	2,873
Stanley Works	2,671

Metals

Alcoa	$13,128
Reynolds Metals	7,016
Bethlehem Steel	4,679
Inland Steel Industries	4,584
LTV	4,135
Allegheny Teledyne	3,816
Phelps Dodge	3,787
Nucor	3,647

Motor Vehicles and Parts

General Motors	$168,369
Ford Motor	146,991
Chrysler	61,397
Tenneco	10,982
TRW	10,310

Petroleum Refining

Exxon	$119,434
Mobil	72,267
Texaco	44,561
Chevron	38,691
Amoco	32,726
USX	21,076

Pharmaceuticals

Johnson & Johnson	$21,620
Merck	19,829
Bristol-Myers Squibb	15,065
American Home Products	14,088
Pfizer	11,306
Abbott Laboratories	11,013
Eli Lilly	7,347
Pharmacia & Upjohn	7,286
Warner-Lambert	7,231

Publishing & Printing

R.R. Donnelley & Sons	$6,599
Gannett	4,665
Times Mirror	3,401
Reader's Digest Assn.	3,098
McGraw-Hill	3,075
Knight-Ridder	2,775
New York Times	2,615
Dow Jones	2,482
Tribune	2,406
American Greetings	2,012

Railroads

CSX	$10,536
Union Pacific	10,051
Burlington Northern Santa Fe	8,187
Norfolk Southern	4,770
Conrail	3,714

Rubber and Plastic Prods.

Goodyear Tire	$13,113
Rubbermaid	2,355
Premark International	2,268
Mark IV Industries	2,089

Scientific, Photographic, and Control Equipment

Eastman Kodak	$15,968
Minnesota Mining & Mfg.	14,236
Honeywell	7,312
Baxter International	5,438
Thermo Electron	2,933
Becton Dickinson	2,770
Polaroid	2,275

Securities

Merrill Lynch	$25,011
Lehman Bros. Holdings	14,260
Morgan Stanley Group	13,144
Saloman	9,002
Paine Webber Group	5,706
Bear Stearns	4,964

Soaps, Cosmetics

Procter & Gamble	$35,284
Colgate-Palmolive	8,749
Avon Products	4,814
Estée Lauder	3,195
Clorox	2,218
Revlon	2,167

Specialty Retailers

Costco	$19,566
Home Depot	19,536
Toys "R" Us	9,932
Limited	8,665
Lowe's	8,600
CVS	8,346
Woolworth[1]	8,092
Best Buy	7,217
Circuit City Group	7,029

Telecommunications

AT&T	$74,525
GTE	21,339
BellSouth	19,040
MCI Communications[2]	18,494

Ameritech	$14,917
Sprint	14,235
SBC Communications	13,898
NYNEX	13,454
Bell Atlantic	13,081
US West	12,911

Textiles

Shaw Industries	$3,201
Springs Industries	2,243
Burlington Industries	2,182
Mohawk Industries	1,795
Westpoint Stevens	1,724

Tobacco

Philip Morris	$54,553
American Brands	5,776
Universal	3,570

Toys, Sporting Goods

Mattel	$3,786
Hasbro	3,002

Transportation Equipment

Brunswick	$3,160
Trinity Industries	2,496
Harley-Davidson	1,531
Polaris Industries	1,192

Utilities, Gas and Electric

Southern	$10,358
Pacific Gas & Electric	9,610
Edison International	8,545
Entergy	7,164
Con. Edison of New York	6,960
Unicom	6,937
Texas Utilities	6,551

Wholesalers

Fleming	$16,487
Supervalu	16,486
McKesson	13,719
Sysco	13,395
Ingram Micro	12,023

(1) Woolworth announced July 17, 1997, it would close its Woolworth stores but will continue to operate Kinney and FootLocker.
(2) As of mid-Oct., MCI had received merger or acquisition offers from 3 cos.

U.S. Corporations With Largest Revenues in 1996

Source: *FORTUNE* Magazine

(millions of dollars)

Company, headquarters	Revenues	Company, headquarters	Revenues	Company, headquarters	Revenues
General Motors, Detroit, MI	$168,369	Texaco, White Plains, NY	$44,561	Procter & Gamble, Cincinnati, OH	$35,284
Ford Motor, Dearborn, MI	146,991	State Farm Insurance Cos., Bloomington, IL	42,781	Amoco, Chicago, IL	32,726
Exxon, Irving, TX	119,434	Prudential Insurance Co. of America, Newark, NJ	40,175	Citicorp, New York, NY	32,605
Wal-Mart Stores, Bentonville, AR	106,147	E. I. Du Pont de Nemours, Wilmington, DE	39,689	PepsiCo, Purchase, NY	31,645
General Electric, Fairfield, CT	79,179	Chevron, San Francisco, CA	38,691	Kmart, Troy, MI	31,437
IBM, Armonk, NY	75,947	Hewlett-Packard, Palo Alto, CA	38,420	American International Group, New York, NY	28,205
AT&T, New York, NY	74,525	Sears Roebuck, Hoffman Estates, IL	38,236	Motorola, Schaumburg, IL	27,973
Mobil, Fairfax, VA	72,267			Chase Manhattan Corp., New York, NY	27,421
Chrysler, Auburn Hills, MI	61,397				
Philip Morris, New York, NY	54,553				

Largest Corporate Mergers or Acquisitions in U.S.

Source: Securities Data Co.

(as of Oct. 1997; *italics* denote an announced merger or acquisition was not complete; year = year effective)

Company	Acquirer	Dollars	Year	Company	Acquirer	Dollars	Year
MCI Communications	*	——	*1997*	Conrail	Investor group	10.4 bil	1997
RJR Nabisco	Kohlberg Kravis Roberts	30.6 bil	1989	Getty Oil	Texaco	10.1 bil	1984
Electronic Data Sys.	shareholders	28.0 bil	1996	Boatmen's Bancshares	NationsBank	9.7 bil	1997
Lucent Technologies	shareholders	24.1 bil	1996	Paramount	Viacom	9.6 bil	1994
NYNEX	Bell Atlantic	21.3 bil	1997	American Cyanamid	American Home Products	9.6 bil	1994
McCaw Cellular Communications	AT&T	15.7 bil	1994	*Hughes Aircraft*	*Raytheon*	*9.5 bil*	*1997*
				Conoco	E. I. Du Pont de Nemours	7.6 bil	1981
Capital Cities/ABC	Walt Disney	18.8 bil	1995	US West Media Grp.	shareholders	9.3 bil	1995
Pacific Telesis Group	SBC Communications	16.5 bil	1997	US Healthcare	Aetna Life & Casualty	8.9 bil	1997
Warner Comm.	Time	14.1 bil	1990	US Bancorp	First Bank Sys.	8.9 bil	1997
Barnett Banks	*NationsBank*	*13.8 bil*	*1997*	*Salomon*	*Travelers Group*	*8.8 bil*	*1997*
Kraft	Philip Morris	13.4 bil	1988	Loral	Lockheed Martin	8.8 bil	1996
Gulf Oil	Standard Oil of CA	13.4 bil	1984	PacTel	shareholders	8.6 bil	1994
MFS Communications	WorldCom	13.6 bil	1996	Blockbuster	Viacom	8.0 bil	1994
McDonnell Douglas	Boeing	13.4 bil	1997	SmithKline Beckman	Beecham Group	7.9 bil	1989
ITT	*Starwood Lodging*	*13.3 bil*	*1997*	NCR	AT&T	7.9 bil	1991
Squibb	Bristol-Myers	12.1 bil	1989	Standard Oil	British Petroleum	7.9 bil	1987
Northrop Grumman	*Lockheed Martin*	*11.8 bil*	*1997*	PanEnergy	Duke Power	7.7 bil	1997
Allstate	shareholders	11.8 bil	1995	MCA	Matsushita Electric Ind.	7.4 bil	1991
Continental Cablevision	US WEST Media Group	11.8 bil	1996	First USA	BANC ONE	7.3 bil	1997
HFS	*CUC International*	*11.3 bil*	*1997*	Marion Merrell Dow	Hoechst AG	7.3 bil	1995
First Interstate Bancorp	Wells Fargo	10.9 bil	1996	Duracell Intl.	Gillette	7.2 bil	1996
Morgan Stanley Grp.	Dean Witter Discover	10.6 bil	1997	Turner Broadcasting	Time Warner	6.9 bil	1996
Chase Manhattan	Chemical Banking	9.9 bil	1996				

*As of mid-Oct., MCI had received merger or acquisition offers from 3 cos. Depending upon which deal, if any, is consummated, the merger or acquisition of MCI may be the largest in U.S. corporate history.

U.S. Corporate Profits by Industry[1]

Source: Bureau of Economic Analysis, U.S. Dept. of Commerce

(billions of dollars)

	1995[R]	1996	First quarter 1997[2]		1995[R]	1996	First quarter 1997[2]
Corporate profits with inventory valuation and capital consumption adjustments . . .	$650.0	$735.9	$779.6	Fabricated metal prods. . .	$12.4	$17.1	$17.4
				Industrial machinery, equip.	22.0	25.8	24.0
Domestic industries.	563.2	640.0	682.2	Electronic, other electric equip.	19.2	23.9	31.4
Financial	88.7	94.2	106.8	Motor vehicles and equip. .	-0.2	-3.2	-1.3
Nonfinancial.	474.6	545.8	575.4	Other.	25.3	29.8	25.9
Rest of the world	86.7	95.9	97.4	Nondurable goods	96.0	106.5	106.9
Receipts from rest of world . . .	120.2	132.7	139.9	Food and kindred prods. . .	27.1	28.5	28.0
Less: Payments to rest of world	33.5	36.7	42.5	Chemicals and allied prods.	30.3	31.2	28.8
Corporate profits with inventory valuation adjustment	598.4	674.1	711.9	Petroleum and coal prods.	6.0	10.0	12.4
				Other.	32.6	36.8	37.7
Domestic industries.	511.7	578.2	614.5	Transportation and public utils.	86.4	91.7	91.5
Financial	97.6	103.5	116.5	Transportation	11.4	11.7	14.9
Federal Reserve banks.	22.2	22.0	22.8	Communications	33.6	36.0	33.8
Other.	75.4	81.5	93.7	Electric, gas, sanitary srvcs.	41.4	44.0	42.8
Nonfinancial.	414.1	474.7	498.0	Wholesale trade.	26.9	38.3	49.0
Manufacturing	181.3	205.5	208.2	Retail trade	41.9	48.9	55.1
Durable goods	85.2	99.0	101.3	Other	77.6	90.3	94.2
Primary metal industries . .	6.5	5.6	3.9	Rest of the world	86.7	95.9	97.4

(1) Figures are rounded; therefore, some totals may not add. (2) Seasonally adjusted at annual rates. (R) Revised figures.

Fastest-Growing U.S. Franchises in 1996[1]

Source: Reprinted with permission from *Entrepreneur* Magazine, Jan. 1997

Company	Business	Minimum start-up cost[2]	Company	Business	Minimum start-up cost[2]
McDonald's	hamburgers, chicken, salads	$363,000	GNC Franchising Inc.	vitamin/nutrition stores	$75,000
			KFC	chicken	950,000
Yogen Fruz/Bresler's Ice Cream/ICBIY	frozen yogurt, ice cream	55,000	Re/Max Intl. Inc.	real estate services	10,000
			Pizza Hut Inc.	pizza	218,500
Subway	sandwiches, salads	54,170	Papa John's Pizza	pizza	128,500
Jani-King	commercial cleaning	1,800	Great Clips Inc.	family hair salons	64,050
7-Eleven Convenience Stores	convenience store	12,500	Holiday Inn Worldwide	hotels	varies
Snap-On Tools	professional tools & equipment	104,900	Arby's Inc.	roast beef sandwiches, subs, chicken	525,000
Novus Windshield Repair	windshield repair	11,200	Applebee's Neighborhood Grill & Bar	restaurant	1,700,000
Coverall Cleaning Concepts	commercial office cleaning	191	Servpro	cleaning & restoration services	26,400
Coldwell Banker Residential Affiliates Inc.	residential real estate brokerage	7,600	Matco Tools	automotive tools	42,500
			Dunkin' Donuts	donuts, baked goods	70,300
Blimpie Intl. Inc.	sandwiches, salads	63,920	Bruegger's Bagels	bagel bakery	249,900
Mail Boxes Etc.	postal, business, communications srvcs.	68,500	Manchu Wok	Chinese fast food	210,000
			Chem-Dry	carpet/fabric cleaning & care	8,400
Taco Bell Corp.	Mexican quick-service restaurant	191,400	Manhattan Bagel Co. Inc.	bagel bakery, deli	159,000
CleanNet USA Inc.	commercial office cleaning	1,000	Heel Quik! Inc.	shoe repair and alterations	3,500

(1) Based on the number of new franchise units added. (2) Not including franchise fee, which varies.

Largest U.S. Black-Owned Companies in 1996

Source: *Black Enterprise* Magazine

Company, Location (Business)	Sales (millions)	Company, Location (Business)	Sales (millions)
TLC Beatrice International Holdings, New York, NY (international food processor and distributor)	$2,230.0	The Bing Group, Detroit, MI (steel processing; metal stamping distributor)	$129.5
Johnson Publishing Co., Chicago, IL (publishing, broadcasting, TV production, cosmetics, hair care)	325.7	Envirotest Systems Corp., Sunnyvale, CA (vehicle emissions testing)	124.5
Philadelphia Coca-Cola Bottling Co., Philadelphia, PA (soft drink bottling)	325.0	The Anderson-Dubose Co., Solon, OH (food, paper products, and operating supplies distributor)	122.2
Pulsar Data Systems, Lanham, MD (computer systems integration and network design)	166.0	Stop Shop Save Food Markets, Baltimore, MD (supermarkets)	108.0
H. J. Russell & Co., Atlanta, GA (construction, airport concessions, real estate development)	163.8	Sylvest Management Systems Corp., Lanham, MD (computer and network integration)	107.5
Uniworld Group, New York, NY (advertising, promotion, event mktg., direct response mktg.)	157.9	Midwest Stamping Co., Bowling Green, OH (automotive metal stamping and assemblies)	106.8
Granite Broadcasting Co., New York, NY (network TV affiliates)	154.8	Mays Chemical Co., Indianapolis, IN (industrial chemicals distributor)	105.3
Convenience Corp. of America, W. Palm Beach, FL (convenience stores)	137.4	Barden Companies, Detroit, MI (radio broadcasting, real estate development, casino gaming)	93.2
Burrell Communications Group, Chicago, IL (advertising, public relations, consumer promotion, direct response mktg.)	134.7	Essence Communications, New York, NY (magazine publishing; catalog sales, entertainment)	92.8
BET Holdings, Washington, DC (cable TV network, magazine publishing)	132.7	Soft Sheen Products, Chicago, IL (hair care products manufacturer)	91.4

U.S. Capital Gains Tax

Source: U.S. Chamber of Commerce; as of Sept. 1997

The following shows how the maximum tax rate on net long-term capital gains for individuals has changed since 1960.

Year	Maximum rate (percentage)	Year	Maximum rate (percentage)	Year	Maximum rate (percentage)	Year	Maximum rate (percentage)	Year	Maximum rate (percentage)
1960	25.0	1971	32.5	1978	28.0	1987	28.0	1990	28.0[3]
1970	29.5	1972	35.0[1]	1981	20.0	1988	33.0[2]	1997	20.0[4]

(1) From 1972 to 1976, the interplay of minimum tax and maximum tax resulted in a marginal rate of 49.125%. (2) Statutory maximum of 28%, but "phase-out" notch increased marginal rate to 33%; interplay of all "phase-outs" could have increased the effective marginal rate to 49.5%. (3) The Budget Act of 1990 increased the statutory rate to 31% and capped the marginal rate at 28%; however, some taxpayers faced effective marginal rates of more than 34% because of the phase-out of personal exemptions and itemized deductions. (4) New rate is for those who, after July 28, 1997, sell capital assets held for more than 18 mos. A 10% capital gains rate applies to individuals in the 15% income tax bracket. (Those who, after July 28, 1997, sell capital assets held between 12 and 18 mos will be taxed at the old top rate of 28%. Those who sold capital assets after May 6, 1997, but before July 29, 1997, will be taxed at the 20% rate, so long as such assets were held for at least a year.) For capital assets purchased after 2000 and held for at least 5 years, a top rate of 18% applies (8% for those in the 15% income tax bracket).

1997 Federal Corporate Tax Rates

Taxable Income Amount	Tax Rate	Taxable Income Amount	Tax Rate
Not more than $50,000	15%	$335,001 to $10,000,000.	34%
$50,001 to $75,000	25%	$10,000,001 to $15,000,000	35%
$75,001 to $100,000	34%	$15,000,001 to $18,333,333	38%
$100,001 to $335,000	39%	More than $18,333,333	35%

Personal service corporations (used by professional individuals such as attorneys and doctors) pay a flat rate of 35%.

Global Stock Markets

Source: The Conference Board; not seasonally adjusted

Stock price indexes (1990=100):	1995	1996	1997 Jan.	Feb.	Mar.	Apr.	May	June
United States	164.4	202.9	236.3	237.7	227.6	240.9	255.0	266.1
Canada	129.6	154.0	178.6	180.0	171.0	174.7	186.6	188.2
France	102.1	116.0	138.5	143.5	146.2	145.2	142.2	157.3
Germany	108.4	127.6	147.0	157.8	167.8	167.1	172.2	183.8
Italy	95.8	98.0	119.8	115.4	115.3	119.5	117.9	130.0
Japan	60.0	72.9	63.6	64.4	62.5	66.4	69.6	71.5
United Kingdom	152.6	175.8	192.8	194.7	194.0	197.3	203.3	201.8

Foreign Exchange Rates, 1970-96

Source: International Monetary Fund

(National currency units per dollar except as indicated; data are annual averages)

Year	Australia[1] (dollar)	Austria (schilling)	Belgium (franc)	Canada (dollar)	Denmark (krone)	France (franc)	Germany[2] (deutsche mark)	Greece (drachma)
1970	1.1136	25.880	49.680	1.0103	7.489	5.5200	3.6480	30.00
1975	1.3077	17.443	36.799	1.0175	5.748	4.2876	2.4613	32.29
1980	1.1400	12.945	29.237	1.1693	5.634	4.2250	1.8175	42.62
1985	0.7003	20.690	59.378	1.3655	10.596	8.9852	2.9440	138.12
1989	0.7925	13.231	39.404	1.1840	7.310	6.3801	1.8800	162.42
1990	0.7813	11.370	33.418	1.1668	6.189	5.4453	1.6157	158.51
1991	0.7791	11.676	34.148	1.1457	6.396	5.6421	1.6595	182.27
1992	0.7353	10.989	32.150	1.2087	6.036	5.2938	1.5617	190.62
1993	0.6801	11.632	34.597	1.2901	6.484	5.6632	1.6533	229.25
1994	0.7317	11.422	33.456	1.3656	6.361	5.5520	1.6228	242.60
1995	0.7415	10.081	29.480	1.3724	5.602	4.9915	1.4331	231.66
1996	0.7829	10.587	30.962	1.3635	5.799	5.1155	1.5048	240.71

Year	India (rupee)	Ireland[1] (pound)	Italy (lira)	Japan (yen)	Malaysia (ringgit)	Mexico (new peso)	Netherlands (guilder)	Norway (krone)
1970	7.576	2.3959	623	357.60	3.0900	—	3.5970	7.1400
1975	8.409	2.2216	653	296.78	2.4030	—	2.5293	5.2282
1980	7.887	2.0577	856	226.63	2.1767	—	1.9875	4.9381
1985	12.369	1.0656	1,909	238.54	2.4830	—	3.3214	8.5972
1989	16.226	1.4190	1,372	137.96	2.7088	2.4615	2.1207	6.9045
1990	17.504	1.6585	1,198	144.79	2.7049	2.8126	1.8209	6.2597
1991	22.742	1.6155	1,241	134.71	2.7501	3.0184	1.8697	6.4829
1992	25.918	1.7053	1,232	126.65	2.5474	3.0949	1.7585	6.2145
1993	30.493	1.4671	1,574	111.20	2.5741	3.1156	1.8573	7.0941
1994	31.374	1.4978	1,612	102.21	2.6243	3.3751	1.8200	7.0576
1995	32.427	1.6038	1,629	94.06	2.5044	6.4194	1.6057	6.3352
1996	35.433	1.6006	1,543	108.78	2.5159	7.6009	1.6859	6.4498

Year	Portugal (escudo)	Singapore (dollar)	South Korea (won)	Spain (peseta)	Sweden (krona)	Switzerland (franc)	Thailand (baht)	United[1] Kingdom (pound)
1970	28.75	3.0800	310.57	69.72	5.1700	4.3160	21.000	2.3959
1975	25.51	2.3713	484.00	57.43	4.1530	2.5839	20.379	2.2216
1980	50.08	2.1412	607.43	71.76	4.2309	1.6772	20.476	2.3243
1985	170.39	2.2002	870.02	170.04	8.6039	2.4571	27.159	1.2963
1989	157.46	1.9503	671.46	118.38	6.4469	1.6359	25.702	1.6397
1990	142.55	1.8125	707.76	101.93	5.9188	1.3892	25.585	1.7847
1991	144.48	1.7276	733.35	103.91	6.0475	1.4340	25.517	1.7694
1992	135.00	1.6290	780.65	102.38	5.8238	1.4062	25.400	1.7655
1993	160.80	1.6158	802.67	127.26	7.7834	1.4776	25.319	1.5020
1994	165.99	1.5274	803.45	133.96	7.7160	1.3677	25.150	1.5316
1995	151.11	1.4174	771.27	124.69	7.1333	1.1825	24.915	1.5785
1996	154.24	1.4100	804.45	126.66	6.7060	1.2360	25.343	1.5617

(1) Value of one unit of foreign currency in dollars. (2) West Germany prior to 1991.

Tourism: International Visitors to the U.S., 1996

Source: Tourism Industries, International Trade Administration, Dept. of Commerce

Country of origin	Visitors (thousands)	Expenditures (millions)	Expenditures per visitor	Country of origin	Visitors (thousands)	Expenditures (millions)	Expenditures per visitor
Canada.	15,301	$6,763.0	$442	Brazil	891	NA	—
Mexico	8,530	3,001.0	352	South Korea . . .	796	NA	—
Japan	5,047	13,163.0	2,608	Italy	552	$1,440.0	$2,609
United Kingdom.	3,105	7,306.0	2,353	Australia	461	1,819.0	3,946
Germany	1,973	4,573.0	2,318	All countries . . .	46,324	69,908.0	1,509
France	990	2,255.0	2,278				

Note: Excludes international passenger fare payments and cruise travel. NA=not available.

Foreign Direct Investment[1] in the U.S. by Selected Countries and Territories

Source: Bureau of Economic Analysis; U.S. Dept. of Commerce

(millions of dollars)

	1995	1996		1995	1996
All countries[2]	$560,850	$630,045	Mexico	$1,980	$1,078
Canada	48,258	53,845	Panama	4,721	5,561
Europe[2]	357,193	410,425	Other Western Hemisphere[2] . . .	17,362	16,817
Austria	1,555	1,791	Bahamas	−1,780	−1,859
Belgium	3,676	3,979	Bermuda	1,592	921
Denmark	2,990	2,118	Netherlands Antilles	8,481	9,124
Finland	2,752	2,818	UK islands, Caribbean[2]	8,417	8,368
France	38,480	49,307	Africa	1,164	717
Germany	49,269	62,242	Middle East[2]	6,008	6,177
Ireland	7,418	9,776	Israel	1,995	1,960
Italy	2,750	2,699	Kuwait	2,527	2,572
Luxembourg	5,957	10,284	Saudi Arabia	1,310	1,484
Netherlands	65,806	73,803	Asia and Pacific[2]	122,986	134,255
Norway	2,089	2,421	Australia	7,833	9,747
Spain	2,452	1,128	Hong Kong	1,557	947
Sweden	9,581	9,470	Japan	107,933	118,116
Switzerland	35,593	35,101	Malaysia	402	445
United Kingdom	126,177	142,607	Singapore	1,548	1,468
South and Central America[2] . . .	7,878	7,810	South Korea	626	394
Brazil	751	591	Taiwan	2,139	2,298

(1) The book value of foreign direct investors' equity in, and net outstanding loans to, their U.S. affiliates. A U.S. affiliate is a U.S. business enterprise in which a single foreign direct investor owns at least 10% of the voting securities or the equivalent. (2) Totals include countries or territories not shown.

U.S. Direct Investment[1] Abroad in Selected Countries and Territories

Source: Bureau of Economic Analysis, U.S. Dept. of Commerce

(millions of dollars)

	1990	1995	1996		1990	1995	1996
All countries[2]	$424,086	$717,554	$796,494	Mexico	$9,398	$15,980	$18,747
Canada	67,033	85,441	91,587	Panama	7,409	16,216	18,256
Europe[2]	211,194	360,994	399,632	Other Western Hemisphere[2]	30,113	47,650	53,151
Austria	889	2,777	2,902	Bahamas	3,309	1,806	2,021
Belgium	9,050	17,969	18,604	Barbados	NA	755	865
Denmark	1,597	2,123	2,171	Bermuda	21,737	29,980	33,783
Finland	551	825	1,033	Dominican Republic	NA	394	465
France	18,874	32,950	34,000	Jamaica	604	1,402	1,675
Germany	27,259	44,226	44,259	Netherlands Antilles	−2,229	2,877	3,594
Greece	288	424	506	Trinidad and Tobago . . .	508	845	1,057
Ireland	6,880	8,400	11,749	UK islands, Caribbean . .	4,800	8,941	9,008
Italy	13,117	17,587	18,687	Africa[2]	4,861	6,383	7,568
Luxembourg	1,390	5,857	6,377	Egypt	1,465	1,388	1,647
Netherlands	22,658	39,344	44,667	Nigeria	161	706	978
Norway	3,815	5,133	6,103	South Africa	956	1,275	1,437
Portugal	598	1,755	1,854	Middle East[2]	3,973	7,669	8,743
Spain	7,704	10,770	11,393	Israel	756	1,662	1,886
Sweden	1,600	7,339	7,629	Saudi Arabia	1,981	3,245	3,098
Switzerland	25,199	33,532	35,751	United Arab Emirates . . .	519	660	789
Turkey	494	948	1,025	Asia and Pacific[2].	61,869	125,834	140,402
United Kingdom	68,224	122,767	142,560	Australia	14,846	25,003	28,769
Eastern Europe.	NA	4,739	6,480	China	NA	2,127	2,883
South America[2]	23,760	46,914	52,153	Hong Kong	6,187	14,206	16,022
Argentina	2,956	7,496	8,060	India	513	838	1,139
Brazil	14,918	23,706	26,166	Indonesia	3,226	6,607	7,571
Chile	1,368	5,878	6,745	Japan.	20,997	38,406	39,593
Colombia	1,728	3,352	3,468	Malaysia	1,384	4,200	5,277
Ecuador	387	833	855	New Zealand	3,131	4,845	5,519
Peru	410	1,279	2,075	Philippines	1,629	2,531	3,349
Venezuela.	1,490	3,220	3,592	Singapore	3,385	12,689	14,150
Central America[2]	17,719	33,688	38,905	South Korea.	2,178	5,169	5,510
Costa Rica	NA	870	1,205	Taiwan	0,011	4,210	4,509
Guatemala	NA	152	217	Thailand	1,585	4,315	5,254
Honduras	NA	191	145				

(1) The book value of U.S. direct investors' equity in, and net outstanding loans to, their foreign affiliates. A foreign affiliate is a foreign business enterprise in which a single U.S. investor owns at least 10% of the voting securities or the equivalent. (2) Total includes countries not shown. NA = not available.

U.S. Holdings of Foreign Stocks

Source: Bureau of Economic Analysis, U.S. Dept. Of Commerce

(billions of dollars)

	1994	1995	1996		1994	1995	1996
Western Europe.............	$288.2	$362.0	$469.5	Canada..................	$40.6	$46.9	$66.5
Of which: Switzerland......	108.8	137.6	185.4	Japan...................	108.1	128.5	126.4
Netherlands......	41.8	52.9	64.8	Latin America..............	37.9	32.0	40.7
France..........	26.7	31.3	42.8	Of which: Mexico..........	23.7	18.8	22.0
Germany........	27.3	31.7	40.4	Other countries and territories ..	111.8	129.7	172.4
Sweden.........	15.6	23.6	34.2	Of which: Hong Kong......	18.6	24.3	37.3
United Kingdom ...	20.7	30.4	33.9	Australia........	19.3	21.8	26.1
Spain...........	13.0	17.7	22.8	Total holdings..............	586.6	699.1	875.5

U.S. International Transactions

Source: Bureau of Economic Analysis, U.S. Dept. of Commerce; revised as of July 1997

(millions of dollars)

	1965	1970	1975	1980	1985	1990	1995	1996
Exports of goods, services, and income[1].............	**$42,722**	**$68,387**	**$157,936**	**$344,440**	**$382,749**	**$700,455**	**$991,490**	**$1,055,233**
Merchandise, adjusted, excluding military[2]..............	26,461	42,469	107,088	224,250	215,915	389,307	575,871	612,069
Services...............	8,824	14,171	25,497	47,584	73,155	147,824	218,739	236,764
Income receipts on U.S. assets abroad	7,437	11,748	25,351	72,606	93,679	163,324	196,880	206,400
Imports of goods, services, and income..............	**−32,708**	**−59,901**	**−132,745**	**−333,774**	**−484,037**	**−757,758**	**−1,086,539**	**−1,163,450**
Merchandise, adjusted, excluding military[2]..............	−21,510	−39,866	−98,185	−249,750	−338,088	−498,337	−749,431	−803,239
Services...............	−9,111	−14,520	−21,996	−41,491	−72,862	−120,019	−147,036	−156,634
Income payments on foreign assets in the U.S........	−2,088	−5,515	−12,564	−42,532	−73,087	−139,402	−190,072	−203,577
Unilateral transfers, net	**−4,583**	**−6,156**	**−7,075**	**−8,349**	**−22,700**	**−34,588**	**−34,046**	**−39,968**
U.S. assets abroad, net (increase/ capital outflow [−]) .	**−5,716**	**−9,337**	**−39,703**	**−86,967**	**−39,889**	**−74,011**	**−307,207**	**−352,444**
U.S. official reserve assets, net	1,225	2,481	−849	−8,155	−3,858	−2,158	−9,742	6,668
U.S. government assets, other than official reserve assets, net	−1,605	−1,589	−3,474	−5,162	−2,821	2,307	−549	−690
U.S. private assets, net	−5,336	−10,229	−35,380	−73,651	−33,211	−74,160	−296,916	−358,422
Foreign assets in the U.S., net (increase/capital inflow [+]) .	**742**	**6,359**	**17,170**	**62,612**	**146,383**	**140,992**	**451,234**	**547,555**
Statistical discrepancy (sum of above items with sign reversed)	**−457**	**−219**	**4,417**	**20,886**	**17,494**	**24,911**	**−14,931**	**−46,927**
Memorandum:								
Balance on current account ..	5,431	2,331	18,116	2,317	−123,987	−91,892	−129,095	−148,184

(1) Excludes transfers of goods and services under U.S. military grant programs. (2) Excludes exports of goods under U.S. military agency sales contracts identified in Census export documents, excludes imports of goods under direct defense expenditures identified in Census import documents, and reflects various other adjustments.

Gold Reserves of Central Banks and Governments

Source: *International Financial Statistics,* IMF; million fine troy ounces

Year end	All countries[1]	United States	Canada	Japan	Belgium	France	Germany	Italy	Nether- lands	Switzer- land	United Kingdom
1975	1,018.71	274.71	21.95	21.11	42.17	100.93	117.61	82.48	54.33	83.20	21.03
1976	1,014.23	274.68	21.62	21.11	42.17	101.02	117.61	82.48	54.33	83.28	21.03
1977	1,029.19	277.55	22.01	21.62	42.45	101.67	118.30	82.91	54.63	83.28	22.23
1978	1,036.82	276.41	22.13	23.97	42.59	101.99	118.64	83.12	54.78	83.28	22.83
1979	944.44	264.60	22.18	24.23	34.21	81.92	95.25	66.71	43.97	83.28	18.25
1980	952.99	264.32	20.98	24.23	34.18	81.85	95.18	66.67	43.94	83.28	18.84
1981	953.72	264.11	20.46	24.23	34.18	81.85	95.18	66.67	43.94	83.28	19.03
1982	949.16	264.03	20.26	24.23	34.18	81.85	95.18	66.67	43.94	83.28	19.01
1983	947.84	263.39	20.17	24.23	34.18	81.85	95.18	66.67	43.94	83.28	19.01
1984	946.79	262.79	20.14	24.23	34.18	81.85	95.18	66.67	43.94	83.28	19.03
1985	949.39	262.65	20.11	24.33	34.18	81.85	95.18	66.67	43.94	83.28	19.03
1986	949.11	262.04	19.72	24.23	34.18	81.85	95.18	66.67	43.94	83.28	19.01
1987	944.49	262.38	18.52	24.23	33.63	81.85	95.18	66.67	43.94	83.28	19.01
1988	946.65	261.87	17.14	24.23	33.67	81.85	95.18	66.67	43.94	83.28	19.00
1989	941.04	261.93	16.10	24.23	30.23	81.85	95.18	66.67	43.94	83.28	18.99
1990	939.01	261.91	14.76	24.23	30.23	81.85	95.18	66.67	43.94	83.28	18.94
1991	938.01	261.91	12.96	24.23	30.23	81.85	95.18	66.67	43.94	83.28	18.89
1992	927.55	261.84	9.94	24.23	25.04	81.85	95.18	66.67	43.94	83.28	18.61
1993	922.02	261.79	6.05	24.23	25.04	81.85	95.18	66.67	35.05	83.28	18.45
1994	917.98	261.73	3.89	24.23	25.04	81.85	95.18	66.67	34.77	83.28	18.44
1995	908.79	261.70	3.41	24.23	20.54	81.85	95.18	66.67	34.77	83.28	18.43
1996	906.10	261.66	3.09	24.23	15.32	81.85	95.18	66.67	34.77	83.28	18.43

(1) Covers IMF members with reported gold holdings. For countries not listed above, see *International Financial Statistics*.

U.S. National Income by Industry[1]

Source: Bureau of Economic Analysis, U.S. Dept. of Commerce

(billions of dollars)

	1960	1970	1975	1980	1990	1995[R]	1996
National income without capital consumption adjustment	$428.6	$835.1	$1,315.0	$2,263.9	$4,513.6	$5,888.4	$6,219.6
Domestic industries	425.1	827.8	1,297.4	2,216.3	4,492.0	5,883.2	6,217.9
Private industries.	371.6	695.4	1,088.3	1,894.5	3,830.2	5,057.8	5,362.6
Agriculture, forestry, fisheries	17.8	25.9	46.5	61.4	98.0	88.2	105.6
Mining	5.6	8.4	21.2	43.8	36.8	45.0	46.9
Construction.	22.5	47.4	69.9	126.6	222.0	266.7	285.2
Manufacturing.	125.3	215.6	317.5	532.1	859.5	1,069.2	1,110.1
Durable goods.	73.4	127.7	185.0	313.7	483.1	608.2	634.5
Nondurable goods	52.0	87.9	132.5	218.4	376.3	461.0	475.6
Transportation, public utilities	35.8	64.4	101.1	177.3	326.3	440.7	456.7
Transportation.	18.5	31.5	48.0	85.8	139.2	184.4	191.0
Communications	8.2	17.6	26.8	48.1	91.6	128.5	135.0
Electric, gas, sanitary services . . .	9.1	86.8	90.2	43.4	95.5	127.8	130.8
Wholesale trade	25.0	47.5	83.0	143.3	261.7	325.4	349.1
Retail trade	41.3	79.9	123.1	189.4	392.3	480.1	503.7
Finance, insurance, real estate . . .	51.3	96.4	143.9	279.5	684.2	1,024.4	1,095.3
Services	46.9	109.8	182.1	341.0	949.4	1,318.1	1,410.1
Government	53.5	132.4	209.1	321.8	661.1	825.3	855.3

(1) Figures may not add because of rounding. (R) Revised figures.

U.S. National Income by Type of Income[1]

Source: Bureau of Economic Analysis, U.S. Dept. of Commerce

(billions of dollars)

	1960	1970	1980	1990	1994	1995[R]	1996
National income[2]	$424.9	$832.6	$2,203.5	$4,491.0	$5,501.6	$5,912.3	$6,254.5
Compensation of employees.	296.7	618.3	1,638.2	3,297.6	4,009.8	4,215.4	4,426.9
Wages and salaries	272.8	551.5	1,372.0	2,745.0	3,257.3	3,442.6	3,633.6
Government	49.2	117.1	260.1	516.0	602.5	623.0	642.6
Other	223.7	434.3	1,111.8	2,229.0	2,654.8	2,819.6	2,991.0
Supplements to wages and salaries . . .	23.8	66.8	266.3	552.5	752.4	772.9	793.2
Employer contrib. for social ins.	12.6	34.3	127.9	278.3	350.2	366.0	385.7
Other labor income.	11.2	32.5	138.4	274.3	402.2	406.8	407.6
Proprietors' income with adjustments . . .	52.1	80.2	180.7	363.3	450.9	489.0	520.3
Farm	11.6	14.7	20.5	41.9	35.0	23.4	37.2
Nonfarm	40.5	65.4	160.1	321.4	415.9	465.5	483.1
Rental income of persons, with capital consumption adjustment	15.3	18.2	6.6	−14.2	116.6	132.8	146.3
Corp. profits with inventory adjustment	49.8	69.5	194.0	354.7	517.9	650.0	735.9
Corp. profits before tax	49.9	76.0	237.1	365.7	531.2	622.6	676.6
Corp. profits tax liability	22.7	34.4	84.8	138.7	195.3	213.2	229.0
Corp. profits after tax	27.2	41.7	152.3	227.1	335.9	409.4	447.6
Dividends.	12.9	22.5	54.7	153.5	211.0	264.4	304.8
Undistributed profits	14.3	19.2	97.6	73.6	124.8	145.0	142.8
Inventory valuation adjustment.	−0.2	−6.6	−43.1	−11.0	−13.3	−24.3	−2.5
Net interest	11.3	41.2	200.9	463.7	394.9	425.1	425.1

(1) Figures may not add because of rounding. (2) National income is the aggregate of labor and property earnings that arises in the current production of goods and services. It is the sum of employee compensation, proprietors' income, rental income, corporate profits, and net interest. It measures the total factor costs of the goods and services produced by the economy. Income is measured before deduction of taxes on income. Total national income figures include adjustments not itemized below. (3) Revised figures.

Distribution of U.S. Total Personal Income[1]

Source: Bureau of Economic Analysis, U.S. Dept. of Commerce

(billions of dollars)

Year	Personal income	Personal taxes	Disposable personal income	Personal outlays	Personal Savings Amount	Personal Savings As pct. of disposable income
1960.	$411.7	$48.7	$362.9	$339.6	$23.3	6.4%
1965.	555.8	61.9	493.9	456.2	37.8	7.6
1970.	836.1	109.0	727.1	666.1	61.0	8.4
1975.	1,315.6	156.4	1,159.2	1,054.8	104.4	9.0
1980.	2,285.7	312.4	1,973.3	1,811.5	161.8	8.2
1981.	2,560.4	360.2	2,200.2	2,001.1	199.1	9.1
1982.	2,718.7	371.4	2,347.3	2,141.8	205.5	8.8
1983.	2,891.7	369.3	2,522.4	2,355.5	167.0	6.6
1984.	3,205.5	395.5	2,810.0	2,574.4	235.7	8.4
1985.	3,439.6	437.7	3,002.0	2,795.8	206.2	6.9
1986.	3,647.5	459.9	3,187.6	2,991.1	196.5	6.2
1987.	3,877.3	514.2	3,363.1	3,194.7	168.4	5.0
1988.	4,172.8	532.0	3,640.8	3,451.7	189.1	5.2
1989.	4,489.3	594.9	3,894.5	3,706.7	187.8	4.8
1990.	4,791.6	624.8	4,166.8	3,958.1	208.7	5.0
1991.	4,968.5	624.8	4,343.7	4,097.4	246.4	5.7
1992.	5,264.2	650.5	4,613.7	4,341.0	272.6	5.9
1993.	5,480.1	689.9	4,790.2	4,575.0	214.4	4.5
1994.	5,753.1	731.4	5,021.7	4,832.3	189.4	3.8
1995[R]	6,150.8	795.1	5,355.7	5,101.1	254.6	4.8
1996.	6,495.2	886.9	5,608.3	5,368.8	239.6	4.3

(1) Figures may not add because of rounding. (R) Revised figures.

Average Yields of Long-Term Treasury, Corporate, and Municipal Bonds

Source: Office of Market Finance, U.S. Dept. of the Treasury

Period	Treasury 30-year bonds	New Aa corporate bonds[1]	New Aa municipal bonds[2]	Period	Treasury 30-year bonds	New Aa corporate bonds[1]	New Aa municipal bonds[2]
1986				**1994**			
June	7.57	9.39	7.75	June	7.40	8.16	5.96
Dec.	7.37	8.87	6.70	Dec.	7.87	8.66	6.63
1987				**1995**			
June	8.57	9.64	7.69	June	6.57	7.42	5.61
Dec.	9.12	10.22	7.83	Dec.	6.06	7.02	5.46
1988				**1996**			
June	9.00	10.08	7.67	Jan.	6.05	7.00	5.41
Dec.	9.01	10.05	7.40	Feb.	6.24	7.14	5.41
1989				Mar.	6.60	7.58	5.57
June	8.27	9.24	6.94	Apr.	6.79	7.81	5.72
Dec.	7.90	9.23	6.76	May	6.93	7.87	5.73
1990				June	7.06	8.00	5.82
June	8.46	9.69	6.98	July	7.03	7.97	5.82
Dec.	8.24	9.55	6.85	Aug.	6.84	7.68	5.69
1991				Sept.	7.03	7.84	5.62
June	8.47	9.37	6.90	Oct.	6.81	7.69	5.53
Dec.	7.70	8.55	6.43	Nov.	6.48	7.43	5.47
1992				Dec.	6.55	7.45	5.47
June	7.84	8.45	6.32	**1997**			
Dec.	7.44	8.12	6.02	Jan.	6.83	7.62	5.53
1993				Feb.	6.69	7.54	5.40
June	6.81	7.48	5.54	Mar.	6.93	7.85	5.59
Dec.	6.25	7.22	5.27				

(1) Treasury series based on 3-week moving average of reoffering yields of new corporate bonds rated Aa by Moody's Investors Service with an original maturity of at least 20 years. (2) Index of new reoffering yields on 20-year general obligations rated Aa by Moody's Investors Service.

Performance of Mutual Funds by Type

Source: CDA/Wiesenberger, Rockville, MD, 800-232-2285

(data for period ending Aug. 31, 1997)

Fund type	Fund objective	1-Yr Total return No.	1-Yr Total return Avg.	5-Yr Annual return No.	5-Yr Annual return Avg.	Fund type	Fund objective	1-Yr Total return No.	1-Yr Total return Avg.	5-Yr Annual return No.	5-Yr Annual return Avg.
Stock	Natural resources	47	24.28	23	14.93	**Bond**	Corporate-investment grade	58	10.07	23	7.08
	Equity income	175	30.98	83	15.65		Corporate high yield	173	15.46	81	10.61
	Financial services	17	48.50	14	25.99		U.S. Treasury	56	9.41	31	6.64
	Precious metals	45	−28.85	27	4.14		U.S. Government/ Agency	262	8.68	135	5.57
	Growth and current income	481	33.84	237	17.73		U.S. Government/ Short & Intermediate	205	7.40	97	4.92
	Health care	21	23.07	13	17.22		U.S. Government/ Long	39	9.55	17	6.87
	Aggressive growth	160	25.09	71	17.90		General Bond-Short & Intermediate	148	8.28	62	5.69
	Small capital gain	420	28.05	143	19.81		General Bond-Long	20	10.32	8	7.10
	Real Estate	53	32.37	9	12.41		General Bond-Investment Grade	364	9.11	140	6.19
	S&P 500 Index	69	39.11	30	18.85	**Municipal bond**	National	425	7.78	201	6.06
	Technology	58	37.57	19	24.27		California	140	8.37	73	6.37
	Utilities	94	17.41	37	10.92		New York	130	8.38	68	6.08
International stock	Emerging equity	117	10.65	7	10.22		Single state	1,239	8.16	545	6.19
	Global income	264	7.26	102	5.72						
	Global equity	257	20.18	84	14.50						
	Non-U.S. equity	629	12.24	161	11.48						
Hybrid	Asset allocation-Domestic	213	21.82	61	12.83						
	Balanced-Domestic	294	23.60	102	12.68						

Chicago Board of Trade, Contracts Traded 1987-96

	1987	1996	Percent change 1987-96		1987	1996	Percent change 1987-96
Futures group				PCS insurance	—	14,688	—
Agricultural	24,562,773	50,806,091	106.8	**Total options**	25,466,032	51,304,320	101.5
Financial	73,726,546	120,268,387	63.1	**Combined futures and options**			
Stock index	2,631,062	—	—	Agricultural	26,757,910	65,369,379	144.3
Metals	706,577	59,707	−91.5	Financial	96,987,432	156,994,150	61.9
Total futures	**101,626,958**	**171,134,185**	**68.4**	Stock index	2,631,062	—	—
Options group				Metals	716,586	60,222	−91.6
Agricultural	2,195,137	14,563,288	563.4	Insurance	—	66	—
Financial	23,260,886	36,725,763	57.9	PCS insurance	—	14,688	—
Metals	10,009	515	−94.9	**Grand total**	**127,092,990**	**222,438,505**	**75.0**
Insurance	—	66	—				

Dow Jones Industrial Average Since 1961

	High		Year		Low			High		Year		Low
Dec.	13	734.91	**1961**	Jan.	3	610.25	Nov.	20	1000.17	**1980**	Apr.	21	759.13
Jan.	3	726.01	**1962**	June	26	535.76	Apr.	27	1024.05	**1981**	Sept.	25	824.01
Dec.	18	767.21	**1963**	Jan.	2	646.79	Dec.	27	1070.55	**1982**	Aug.	12	776.92
Nov.	18	891.71	**1964**	Jan.	2	766.08	Nov.	29	1287.20	**1983**	Jan.	3	1027.04
Dec.	31	969.26	**1965**	June	28	840.59	Jan.	6	1286.64	**1984**	July	24	1086.57
Feb.	9	995.15	**1966**	Oct.	7	744.32	Dec.	16	1553.10	**1985**	Jan.	4	1184.96
Sept.	25	943.08	**1967**	Jan.	3	786.41	Dec.	2	1955.57	**1986**	Jan.	22	1502.29
Dec.	3	985.21	**1968**	Mar.	21	825.13	Aug.	25	2722.42	**1987**	Oct.	19	1738.74
May	14	968.85	**1969**	Dec.	17	769.93	Oct.	21	2183.50	**1988**	Jan.	20	1879.14
Dec.	29	842.00	**1970**	May	6	631.16	Oct.	9	2791.41	**1989**	Jan.	3	2144.64
Apr.	28	950.82	**1971**	Nov.	23	797.97	July	16	2999.75	**1990**	Oct.	11	2365.10
Dec.	11	1036.27	**1972**	Jan.	26	889.15	Dec.	31	3168.83	**1991**	Jan.	9	2470.30
Jan.	11	1051.70	**1973**	Dec.	5	788.31	June	1	3413.21	**1992**	Oct.	9	3136.58
Mar.	13	891.66	**1974**	Dec.	6	577.60	Dec.	29	3794.33	**1993**	Jan.	20	3241.95
July	15	881.81	**1975**	Jan.	2	632.04	Jan.	31	3978.36	**1994**	Apr.	4	3593.35
Sept.	21	1014.79	**1976**	Jan.	2	858.71	Dec.	13	5216.47	**1995**	Jan.	30	3832.08
Jan.	3	999.75	**1977**	Nov.	2	800.85	Dec.	27	6560.91	**1996**	Jan.	10	5032.94
Sept.	8	907.74	**1978**	Feb.	28	742.12	Aug.	6	8259.31	**1997***	Apr.	11	6391.69
Oct.	5	897.61	**1979**	Nov.	7	796.67							

*As of Oct.15

Components of the Dow Jones Averages

(as of Oct. 1997)

Dow Jones Industrial Average

AlliedSignal	Eastman Kodak	Merck
Aluminum Co. of America (Alcoa)	Exxon	Minnesota Mining & Manufacturing
American Express	General Electric	Morgan (J.P.)
AT&T	General Motors	Philip Morris
Boeing	Goodyear	Procter & Gamble
Caterpillar	Hewlett-Packard[1]	Sears
Chevron	IBM	Travelers[1]
Coca-Cola	International Paper	Union Carbide
Disney	Johnson & Johnson[1]	United Technologies
DuPont	McDonald's	Wal-Mart[1]

(1) Added to the DJIA on Mar. 17, 1997, to replace Bethlehem Steel, Texaco, Westinghouse, and Woolworth.

Dow Jones Transportation Average

Airborne Freight	CSX	UAL (United Air Lines)
Alaska Air Group	Delta Air Lines	Union Pacific
AMR (American Airlines)	Federal Express	US Airways
APL Limited	Illinois Central	USFreightways
Burlington Northern Santa Fe	Norfolk Southern	XTRA
Caliber Systems	Ryder System	Yellow Corp.
CNF Transportation	Southwest Air Lines	

Dow Jones Utility Average

American Electric Power	Edison International	Public Service Enterprise Group
Columbia Gas System	Enron	Southern Co.
Consolidated Edison of New York	Houston Industries	Texas Utilities
Consolidated Natural Gas	Pacific Gas & Electric	Unicom
Duke Power	PECO Energy	Williams Cos.

Milestones of the Dow Jones Industrial Average

First close over...		First close over...		First close over...	
100	Jan. 12, 1906	3,500	May 19, 1993	6,500	Nov. 25, 1996
500	Mar. 12, 1956	4,000	Feb. 23, 1995	7,000	Feb. 13, 1997
1,000	Nov. 14, 1972	4,500	June 16, 1995	7,500	June 10, 1997
1,500	Dec. 11, 1985	5,000	Nov. 21, 1995	8,000	July 16, 1997
2,000	Jan. 8, 1987	5,500	Feb. 8, 1996	8,100	July 24, 1997
2,500	July 17, 1987	6,000	Oct. 14, 1996	8,200	July 30, 1997
3,000	April 17, 1991				

Most Active Common Stocks in 1996

New York Exchange	Volume (millions of shares)	American Exchange	Volume (millions of shares)	NASDAQ	Volume (millions of shares)
Micron Technology Inc.	1,070.6	Viacom Inc. Class B	271.9	Intel Corp.	2,338.9
AT&T Corp.	819.0	Trans World Airlines, Inc.	199.8	Cisco Systems, Inc.	1,789.9
PepsiCo, Inc.	757.3	Echo Bay Mines Ltd.	198.5	Sun Microsystems, Inc.	1,261.4
IBM	738.6	IVAX Corp.	183.5	Microsoft Corp.	1,205.8
Wal-Mart Stores	731.5	Ampex Corp.	179.1	Oracle Corp.	1,161.6
K-Mart	621.6	XCL Ltd.	169.1	Applied Materials, Inc.	1,028.6
Compaq Computer	610.4	Hasbro, Inc.	129.3	MCI Communications	944.6
Ford Motor	608.3	Bema Gold Corporation	124.8	Tele-Communications, Inc.	934.7
Motorola Inc.	594.4	Royal Oak Mines Inc.	117.0	3Com Corp.	907.5
Bay Networks Inc.	583.6	Harken Energy Corp.	108.5	Dell Computer Corp.	903.9
Federal National Mortgage Assn.	575.7	Nabors Industries, Inc.	107.5	WorldCom, Inc.	878.8
Teléfonos de Mexico	570.2	Heary Ltd.	106.8	Informix Corp.	802.1
Philip Morris	570.0	Interdigital Communications Corp.	93.4	Novell, Inc.	791.9
Hewlett-Packard Co.	566.0	First Australia Prime Income Fund, Inc. (The)	89.8	Atmel	738.0
Hanson Plc	555.1	Gaylord Container Corporation	88.6	LM Ericsson Telephone Co.	721.9

Selected Personal Consumption Expenditures in the U.S., 1990-96

Source: Bureau of Economic Analysis, U.S. Dept. of Commerce

(billions of dollars)

	1990	1991	1992	1993[R]	1994[R]	1995[R]	1996
Food & tobacco	**648.2**	**693.8.8**	**709.5**	**733.4**	**761.7**	**783.8**	**805.7**
Food purchased for off-premise consumption	400.2	419.1	423.3	435.6	451.6	462.2	478.4
Purchased meals and beverages	193.1	223.1	228.6	243.0	254.3	264.1	268.7
Tobacco products	43.4	43.8	49.6	46.6	47.3	48.7	49.6
Clothing, accessories, jewelry	**259.3**	**265.7**	**283.5**	**298.1**	**312.7**	**323.4**	**336.3**
Shoes	31.4	31.9	33.6	34.4	36.0	36.8	38.1
Clothing and accessories less shoes	175.7	179.3	191.7	201.8	211.6	217.7	226.0
Jewelry and watches	31.3	31.4	33.2	35.6	37.7	39.3	41.6
Personal care	**59.2**	**59.1**	**63.1**	**65.1**	**68.4**	**71.9**	**75.7**
Toilet articles, preparations	36.8	39.4	41.4	43.1	45.3	47.2	49.9
Barber shops, beauty parlors, health clubs	22.4	19.7	21.8	22.0	23.0	24.7	25.7
Housing	**547.5**	**616.5**	**646.8**	**672.8**	**712.7**	**750.3**	**787.2**
Owner-occupied nonfarm dwellings—space rent	379.5	434.1	457.8	480.9	507.0	532.2	558.3
Tenant-occupied nonfarm dwellings—rent	141.1	155.8	160.5	162.1	174.0	184.6	193.6
Rental value of farm dwellings	5.2	5.2	5.3	5.5	5.8	5.9	6.1
Household operation	**437.3**	**448.4**	**470.6**	**504.1**	**535.0**	**562.8**	**591.9**
Furniture, including bedding	36.7	38.4	39.8	42.7	45.9	48.0	49.6
Kitchen and other household appliances	26.4	21.6	22.2	24.0	25.6	27.2	27.8
China, glassware, tableware, utensils	18.7	18.9	20.7	22.0	24.0	25.3	27.4
Other durable house furnishings	42.0	42.3	45.5	48.2	52.3	54.5	58.2
Semidurable house furnishings	21.2	21.6	23.2	25.0	27.2	28.9	30.1
Household utilities	136.7	145.4	148.6	160.3	163.8	168.5	177.9
Telephone, telegraph	53.8	63.5	70.3	74.5	82.6	90.2	96.9
Medical care	**597.8**	**668.7**	**733.2**	**785.5**	**826.1**	**871.6**	**912.8**
Drug preparations, sundries	60.6	70.9	75.0	78.1	81.6	85.7	90.9
Physicians	133.8	152.1	167.2	172.5	180.0	191.4	196.5
Dentists	31.6	34.7	38.5	40.8	43.9	47.6	50.9
Hospitals and nursing homes	231.3	293.4	320.0	341.1	357.0	375.9	394.2
Health insurance	36.6	37.3	42.7	53.6	55.0	53.6	56.3
Personal business	**296.0**	**318.9**	**341.7**	**357.4**	**370.4**	**389.1**	**421.1**
Brokerage charges, investment counseling	22.0	25.3	30.4	35.7	36.2	38.8	47.2
Bank service charges, trust services, safe deposit box	23.7	25.7	28.0	30.7	31.6	33.9	37.3
Legal services	49.2	42.9	46.5	47.9	48.8	49.1	52.2
Funeral, burial expenses	8.5	9.4	10.1	10.8	11.1	12.2	12.8
Transportation	**453.9**	**436.8**	**471.5**	**504.0**	**542.2**	**572.3**	**602.2**
User-operated transportation	414.0	401.4	435.7	465.5	502.6	530.1	557.7
New autos	96.6	75.3	82.1	86.4	91.2	87.1	86.1
Used autos	33.1	32.0	35.5	40.2	44.1	52.4	55.3
Repair, greasing, washing, parking, storage, rental, leasing	82.6	85.2	94.4	102.4	116.4	128.7	140.1
Gasoline and oil	108.4	103.9	106.6	107.6	109.4	114.4	122.6
Tolls	2.0	2.1	2.3	2.5	2.6	2.8	2.9
Insurance premiums less claims paid	18.1	22.6	25.5	26.8	27.5	29.4	30.9
Purchased local transportation	8.9	7.9	8.0	8.4	8.9	9.2	10.1
Mass transit systems	5.7	5.3	5.4	5.6	5.9	6.0	6.6
Taxicab	3.2	2.6	2.6	2.8	3.0	3.2	3.5
Purchased intercity transportation	30.9	27.5	27.9	30.1	30.7	33.0	34.4
Railway (excl. commutation)	0.7	0.8	0.8	0.8	0.7	0.8	0.8
Bus	1.4	1.1	1.1	1.0	1.1	1.3	1.3
Airline	26.4	23.0	23.3	25.4	25.8	27.7	28.2
Recreation	**285.7**	**292.0**	**310.8**	**340.2**	**370.2**	**402.5**	**431.1**
Books, maps	17.5	16.9	17.7	19.0	20.6	22.1	23.2
Magazines, newspapers, sheet music	23.8	21.9	21.6	22.7	24.5	25.5	26.5
Nondurable toys and sport supplies	32.1	32.8	34.2	36.6	39.7	42.2	45.4
Wheel goods, sports and photographic equipment, boats, pleasure aircraft	31.3	29.5	29.9	32.6	35.6	39.1	42.0
Video & audio prods., computers, musical instruments	50.4	57.3	61.2	68.1	78.5	85.2	89.7
Flowers, seeds, potted plants	10.3	11.3	12.3	12.7	13.4	13.9	14.9
Admissions to specified spectator amusements	14.0	15.7	16.6	18.1	19.0	20.2	22.1
Motion picture theaters	4.7	5.3	5.0	5.2	5.6	6.0	6.3
Legitimate theater, opera	4.5	6.0	6.8	7.8	8.2	8.7	9.3
Spectator sports	4.9	4.5	4.8	5.1	5.2	5.5	6.4
Clubs, fraternal organizations	8.4	9.6	10.3	11.2	11.8	12.7	13.0
Commercial participant amusements	23.1	23.8	27.2	31.5	36.2	41.5	46.2
Education and research	**86.2**	**86.1**	**93.1**	**98.5**	**104.7**	**112.2**	**119.6**
Higher education	44.0	48.0	52.0	55.5	59.0	62.2	65.2
Nursery, elementary, and secondary schools	19.8	18.0	19.3	20.1	21.4	22.8	24.0
Religious and welfare activities	**101.6**	**104.1**	**115.6**	**121.3**	**131.2**	**139.8**	**150.5**
Total personal consumption expenditures	**$3,761.2**	**$3,975.1**	**$4,219.8**	**$4,459.2**	**$4,717.0**	**$4,957.7**	**$5,207.6**

R = revised figures.

MILLENNIUM FACT BOX

Consumer Price Index, 1915-1997

Source: Bureau of Labor Statistics, U.S. Dept. of Labor

(1967 = 100. Annual averages of monthly figures, specified for all urban consumers.)

Prices as measured by the U.S. Consumer Price Index have risen dramatically during the 20th century, especially after World War II. What cost $1.00 in 1967 would have cost only about 30 cents in 1915 and about $4.79 by 1997.

1915	30.4	1935	41.1	1955	80.2	1975	161.2	1995	456.5
1920	60.0	1940	42.0	1960	88.7	1980	246.8	1997[1]	479.0
1925	52.5	1945	53.9	1965	94.5	1985	322.2		
1930	50.0	1950	72.1	1970	116.3	1990	391.4		

(1) Average for Jan. through June.

Minerals

Source: U.S. Geological Survey, U.S. Dept. of the Interior; as of mid-1997

Aluminum: the second most abundant metallic element in the earth's crust. Bauxite is the main source of aluminum; convert to aluminum equivalent by multiplying by 0.232. Guinea and Australia have 49% of the world's reserves. Aluminum is used in the U.S. principally in transportation (32%), packaging (26%), and building (16%).

Chromium: about 2/3 of the world's production of chromite, the chief source of chromium, is in India, Kazakhstan, and South Africa. The chemical and metallurgical industries use about 90% of the chromite consumed in the world.

Cobalt: used in superalloys for jet engines, chemicals (paint driers, catalysts, magnetic coatings), permanent magnets, and cemented carbides for cutting tools. Canada, Finland, Norway, Russia, Congo (formerly Zaire), and Zambia account for more than 90% of world cobalt (refinery) production. The U.S. uses about 1/3 of world consumption. Although its resources are relatively large, the U.S. has not produced cobalt since 1971; most resources are low grade, and production is not economically feasible.

Columbium: used mostly as an additive in steelmaking and in superalloys. Brazil and Canada are the world's leading columbium raw materials (feedstock) producers. There is no U.S. columbium mining industry.

Copper: uses of copper in the U.S. are in building construction (43%), electrical and electronic products (24%), industrial machinery and equipment (12%), transportation (12%), and consumer and general products (9%). The leading producer is Chile, followed by the U.S., Canada, Indonesia, Australia, Russia, China, Peru, Poland, Zambia, and Mexico. Principal mining states are Arizona, Utah, and New Mexico.

Gold: used in the U.S. in jewelry and the arts (70%), electronics and other industries (23%), and dentistry (7%). South Africa has about half the world's resources; significant quantities are also present in the U.S., Australia, Canada, the former Soviet Union, and Brazil. Gold is mined in nearly all the Western U.S. states and in Alaska.

Iron ore: the source of primary iron for the world's iron and steel industries. Major iron ore producers include Australia, Brazil, China, and the former Soviet Union.

Lead: the U.S., Australia, China, Peru, and Canada are the world's largest producers of lead. Transportation accounts for the major end use in the U.S., with 85% used in batteries, bearings, casting metals, and solders. Other uses include emergency power supply batteries, construction sheeting, sporting ammunition, and power cable coverings. The U.S. produces and consumes more than 25% of the world's lead metal, including primary and recycled material.

Manganese: essential to iron and steel production. The U.S., Japan, and Western Europe have exhausted nearly all of their economically minable manganese. South Africa and the former Soviet Union have about 75% of the world's reserves.

Nickel: vital to the stainless steel industry; used to make superalloys for the chemical and aerospace industries. Leading producers include Russia, Canada, Australia, New Caledonia, and Indonesia.

Platinum-Group Metals: the platinum group consists of 6 closely related metals: platinum, palladium, rhodium, ruthenium, iridium, and osmium. They commonly occur together in nature and are among the scarcest of the metallic elements. They are consumed in the U.S. by the following industries: automotive, electrical and electronic, chemical, and dental and medical. The automotive, chemical, and petroleum-refining industries use platinum-group metals mainly as catalysts. The former Soviet Union and South Africa have nearly all the world's reserves.

Silver: used in the following U.S. industries: photography, electrical and electronic products, sterlingware, electroplated ware, and jewelry. Silver is mined in more than 60 countries. Nevada produces more than 50% of U.S. silver, Idaho 12%.

Tantalum: a refractory metal with unique electrical, chemical, and physical properties; used in the U.S. mostly to produce electronic components, mainly tantalum capacitors. Australia, Brazil, and Canada are the leading tantalum raw-material producers. There is no U.S. tantalum mining industry.

Titanium: as a metal, titanium is used mostly in commercial and military aerospace applications. Titanium metal is produced primarily in China, Japan, Kazakhstan, Russia, and the U.S.

Vanadium: used as an alloying element in steel and aerospace titanium alloys, as a catalyst in the production of maleic and phthalic anhydride, and in the production of sulfuric acid. China, South Africa, and Russia are the world's largest producers of vanadium-bearing ores and concentrates.

Zinc: used as a protective coating on steel, as diecastings, as an alloying metal with copper to make brass, and as a component of chemical compounds in rubber and paints. It is mined in more than 50 countries. Canada is the leading producer, followed by Australia, China, Peru, the U.S., and Mexico. In the U.S., mine production comes mostly from Alaska, Tennessee, New York, and Missouri.

World Mineral Reserve Base

Source: U.S. Geological Survey, U.S. Dept. of the Interior; as of mid-1997

Mineral	Reserve Base[1]	Mineral	Reserve Base[1]
Aluminum	28,000 mil metric tons[2]	Manganese	5,000 mil metric tons
Chromium	7,500 mil metric tons	Nickel	134 mil metric tons
Cobalt	9.0 mil metric tons	Platinum-Group Metals	66 mil kilograms
Columbium	4,200 mil kilograms	Silver	420,000 metric tons
Copper	630 mil metric tons	Tantalum	26 mil kilograms
Gold	74,000 metric tons	Titanium	600 mil metric tons[4]
Iron ore	270,000 mil metric tons[3]	Vanadium	27 mil metric tons
Lead	120 mil metric tons	Zinc	330 mil metric tons

(1) Includes demonstrated resources that are currently economic (reserves) or marginally economic (marginal reserves) and some that are currently subeconomic. (2) Bauxite. (3) Crude ore. (4) Titanium dioxide (TiO_2) content.

U.S. Nonfuel Mineral Production—10 Leading States in 1996

Source: U.S. Geological Survey, U.S. Dept. of the Interior

Rank/State	Value (millions)	Percent of U.S. total	Principal minerals
1. Arizona	$3,530	9.25	Copper, sand & gravel (construction), cement, molybdenum, lime
2. Nevada	3,200	8.37	Gold, silver, sand & gravel (construction), copper, diatomite
3. California	2,840	7.43	Sand & gravel (construction), cement, boron minerals, gold, stone (crushed)
4. Minnesota	1,800	4.72	Iron ore, sand & gravel (construction), stone (crushed), sand & gravel (industrial)
5. Texas	1,780	4.67	Cement, sand & gravel (construction), stone (crushed), magnesium metal
6. Georgia	1,730	4.51	Clays, stone (crushed), cement, stone (dimension), sand & gravel (construction)
7. Utah	1,560	4.09	Copper, gold, magnesium metal, sand & gravel (construction), molybdenum
8. Florida	1,540	4.03	Phosphate rock, stone (crushed), cement, sand & gravel (construction), clays
9. Michigan	1,510	3.95	Iron ore, cement, sand & gravel (construction), magnesium compounds, stone (crushed)
10. Missouri	1,250	3.28	Lead, stone (crushed), cement, lime, zinc

U.S. Nonfuel Mineral Production

Source: U.S. Geological Survey, U.S. Dept. of the Interior

Production as measured by mine shipments, sales, or marketable production (including consumption by producers).

		1991	1992	1993	1994	1995	1996
Beryllium (metal equivalent)	metric tons	174	193	198	173	202	211
Copper (recoverable content of ores, etc.)	thousand metric tons	1,630	1,760	1,800	1,850	1,850	1,920
Gold (recoverable content of ores, etc.)	metric tons	294.1	330.2	331.0	326.2	317.0	318.0
Iron ore, usable (includes byproduct material)	million metric tons	56.8	55.6	55.7	58.4	62.5	62.1
Lead (in concentrate)	thousand metric tons	477	407	362	370	394	436
Magnesium metal (primary)	thousand metric tons	131	137	132	128	142	133
Molybdenum (content of ore and concentrate)	metric tons	53,364	49,725	36,803	46,810	58,000	56,000
Nickel (content of ore and concentrate)	metric tons	5,523	6,671	2,464	—	1,557	1,333
Silver (recoverable content of ores, etc.)	metric tons	1,860	1,800	1,640	1,480	1,560	1,570
Zinc (recoverable content of ores, etc.)	thousand metric tons	518	523	488	570	614	600
Asbestos	thousand metric tons	20	16	14	10	W	10
Barite	thousand metric tons	448	326	315	583	543	662
Boron minerals	thousand metric tons	626	554	574	550	728	581
Bromine	million kilograms	170	171	177	177	218	227
Cement (portland, masonry, etc.)	thousand metric tons	67,193	69,585	73,807	77,948	76,906	78,000E
Clays	thousand metric tons	41,017	40,237	40,700	42,200	43,100	43,100
Diatomite	thousand metric tons	610	595	599	613	687	698
Feldspar	thousand metric tons	580	725	770	765	880	890
Fluorspar	thousand metric tons	58	51	56	49	51	8
Garnet (industrial)	metric tons	50,900	54,100	44,000	51,000	53,000	68,200
Gemstones	million dollars	84.4	66.2	57.7	50.5	48.7	43.6
Gypsum	thousand metric tons	14,000	14,900	15,800	17,200	16,600	17,500
Helium (extracted from natural gas)	million cubic meters	86.4	92.0	99.3	112.0	101.0	103.2E
Helium (Grade A sold)	million cubic meters	88.1	94.4	95.6	100.0	96.1	98.1E
Iodine	thousand kilograms	1,999	1,995	1,935	1,630	1,220	1,270
Lime	thousand metric tons	15,667	16,199	16,932	17,393	18,530	19,100
Mica (scrap & flake)	thousand metric tons	103	85	88	110	108	97
Peat	thousand metric tons	632	599	616	574	660	640
Perlite (sold and used by producers)	thousand metric tons	514	541	569	644	700	684
Phosphate rock (marketable product)	thousand metric tons	48,096	46,965	35,494	41,115	43,500	45,400
Potash (K₂O equivalent)	thousand metric tons	1,749	1,705	1,506	1,400	1,480	1,390
Pumice and pumicite	thousand metric tons	401	481	469	490	529	612
Salt	thousand metric tons	35,902	34,784	38,200	39,700	40,800	10,800E
Sand and gravel (construction)	thousand metric tons	708,000	834,000	869,000	891,000	910,000	963,000
Sand and gravel (industrial)	thousand metric tons	23,224	25,195	26,220	27,900	28,900	27,800
Soda ash (sodium carbonate)	thousand metric tons	9,005	9,379	8,959	9,321	10,100	10,200
Sodium sulfate (natural)	thousand metric tons	354	337	322	298	327	306
Stone (crushed)	million metric tons	997	1,050	1,120	1,230	1,260	1,330P
Stone (dimension)	thousand metric tons	1,160	1,140	1,280	1,190	1,160	1,150
Sulfur (in all forms)	thousand metric tons	10,820	10,663	10,959	11,500	11,800	12,000
Talc	thousand metric tons	1,037	997	968	935	1,060	994
Vermiculite	thousand metric tons	180	190	190	180	170	W

(E) Estimated. (P) Preliminary figure. (W) Withheld to avoid disclosing company proprietary data. (—) No production.

U.S. Reliance on Foreign Supplies of Minerals

Source: U.S. Geological Survey, U.S. Dept. of the Interior

Mineral	Percent imported in 1996	Major sources (1992-1995)	Major uses
Arsenic	100%	China, Chile, Mexico	Wood preservatives, glass manufacturing, agricultural chemicals
Bauxite and alumina	100	Australia, Jamaica, Guinea, Brazil	Aluminum production, abrasives, chemicals, proppants, refractories
Columbium	100	Brazil, Canada, Germany	Steelmaking, superalloys
Graphite (natural)	100	Canada, Mexico, China, Madagascar, Brazil	Refractories, brake linings, lubricants, foundry dressings and molds
Manganese	100	South Africa, Gabon, Australia, Brazil	Steelmaking
Mica, sheet (natural)	100	India, Belgium, Brazil, China, Argentina	Electronic and electrical equipment
Strontium (celestite)	100	Mexico	Television picture tubes, ferrite magnets, pyrotechnics
Thallium	100	Belgium, Canada, Mexico	Superconductors materials, electronics, alloys, glass
Thorium	100	France	Ceramics, carbon arc lamps, alloys, welding electrodes
Fluorspar	99	China, South Africa, Mexico	Hydrofluoric acid, aluminum fluoride, steelmaking
Gemstones	98	Israel, Belgium, India, UK	Jewelry, carvings, gem and mineral collections
Cobalt	83	Zambia, Norway, Canada, Finland, Russia	Superalloys, cemented carbides, paint driers, magnetic alloys
Tin	83	Brazil, Bolivia, Indonesia, China	Cans and containers, electrical, transportation
Tungsten	82	China, Russia, Germany, Bolivia, UK	Machinery, lamps and lighting
Tantalum	80	Australia, Germany, Thailand, Brazil	Electronic components
Chromium	79	South Africa, Turkey, Russia, Kazakhstan, Zimbabwe	Ferroalloys, chemicals, refractories
Potash	76	Canada, Belarus, Russia, Israel, Germany	Fertilizer
Barite	66	China, India, Mexico, Morocco, Canada	Oil and gas well drilling fluids
Stone (dimension)	64	Italy, Spain, India, Canada	Construction
Nickel	63	Canada, Norway, Australia, Russia	Stainless steel, other alloys
Iodine	62	Japan, Chile	Animal feed supplements, catalysts, inks, disinfectants
Peat	58	Canada	Horticulture, agriculture

U.S. Copper, Lead, and Zinc Production, 1950-96

Source: U.S. Geological Survey, U.S. Dept. of the Interior

Year	Copper Quantity (metric tons)	Copper Value ($1,000)	Lead Quantity (metric tons)	Lead Value ($1,000)	Zinc Quantity (metric tons)	Zinc Value ($1,000)	Year	Copper Quantity (metric tons)	Copper Value ($1,000)	Lead Quantity (metric tons)	Lead Value ($1,000)	Zinc Quantity (metric tons)	Zinc Value ($1,000)
1950	827	379,122	390,839	113,078	565,516	167,000	1990	1,586	4,310,000	483,704	490,750	515,355	847,485
1960	1,037	733,706	223,774	57,722	395,013	112,365	1991	1,630	3,931,000	465,931	343,907	517,804	602,426
1965	1,226	957,028	273,196	93,959	554,429	178,284	1992	1,760	4,179,000	397,076	307,337	523,430	673,800
1970	1,560	1,984,484	518,698	178,609	484,560	163,650	1993	1,800	3,635,000	355,185	248,540	488,283	496,795
1975	1,282	1,814,763	563,783	267,230	425,792	366,097	1994	1,850	4,434,000	363,000	298,000	570,162	619,195
1980	1,181	2,666,931	550,366	515,189	317,103	261,671	1995	1,850	5,640,000	386,000	359,000	614,214	756,001
1985	1,105	1,631,000	413,955	174,008	226,545	201,607	1996	1,920	4,610,000	426,000	459,000	599,872	614,887

U.S. Pig Iron and Raw Steel Output, 1940-96

Source: American Iron and Steel Institute

(net tons)

Year	Total pig iron	Raw steel	Year	Total pig iron	Raw steel
1940	46,071,666	66,982,686	1985	50,446,000	88,259,000
1945	53,223,169	79,701,648	1989	55,873,000	97,943,000
1950	64,586,907	96,836,075	1990	54,750,000	98,906,000
1955	76,857,417	117,036,085	1991	48,637,000	87,896,000
1960	66,480,648	99,281,601	1992	52,224,000	92,949,000
1965	88,184,901	131,461,601	1993	53,082,000	97,877,000
1970	91,435,000	131,514,000	1994	54,426,000	100,579,000
1975	79,923,000	116,642,000	1995	56,097,000	104,930,000
1980	68,721,000	111,835,000	1996	54,485,000	105,309,000

Steel figures include only that portion of the capacity and production of steel for castings used by foundries operated by companies producing steel ingots.

World Gold Production, 1980-96

Source: U.S. Geological Survey, U.S. Dept. of the Interior

(troy ounces)

Year	World prod.	Africa — South Africa	Africa — Ghana	Africa — Congo (Zaire)[R]	North and South America — United States	North and South America — Canada	North and South America — Mexico	North and South America — Colombia	Other — Australia	Other — China	Other — Philippines	Other — USSR
1975	38,476,371	22,937,820	523,889	115,743	1,052,252	1,653,611	144,710	308,864	526,821	NA	502,577	NA
1980	39,197,315	21,669,468	353,000	96,452	969,782	1,627,477	195,991	510,439	547,591	NA	753,452	8,425,000
1982	43,082,814	21,355,111	331,000	135,033	1,465,686	2,081,230	214,349	472,674	866,815	1,800,000	834,439	8,550,000
1984	46,929,444	21,860,933	287,000	321,507	2,084,615	2,682,786	270,998	730,670	1,295,963	1,900,000	827,149	8,650,000
1985	49,283,691	21,565,230	299,363	257,206	2,427,232	2,815,118	265,693	1,142,385	1,881,491	1,950,000	1,062,997	8,700,000
1986	51,534,056	20,513,665	287,127	257,206	3,739,015	3,364,700	250,615	1,285,878	2,413,842	2,100,000	1,296,400	8,850,000
1987	53,033,614	19,176,500	327,598	385,809	4,947,040	3,724,000	256,822	853,600	3,558,954	2,300,000	1,048,081	8,850,000
1988	60,308,973	19,965,611	355,620	401,884	6,459,534	4,334,338	292,508	932,822	5,046,059	2,507,758	980,019	8,925,046
1989	65,335,998	19,530,290	429,470	340,798	8,543,449	5,127,850	276,914	948,640	6,544,702	2,893,567	964,265	9,773,826
1990	70,206,932	19,454,414	541,419	299,002	9,458,395	5,446,722	311,283	943,689	7,849,186	3,215,074	790,619	9,709,524
1991	70,422,599	19,326,133	845,918	282,927	9,454,311	5,676,278	326,073	1,120,260	7,530,283	3,858,089	833,219	8,359,193
1992	73,529,583	19,742,838	997,702	225,055	10,616,561	5,189,194	318,003	1,032,618	7,825,491	4,501,104	729,886	8,231,554*
1993	74,210,568	19,907,742	1,261,434	192,904	10,642,314	4,916,781	356,873	883,149	7,947,535	5,144,119	508,818	8,228,179*
1994	73,618,833	18,637,078	1,430,869	34,562	10,488,247	4,694,008	446,895	883,149	8,236,634	5,144,119	469,754	8,172,719*
1995	71,400,000	16,800,000	1,680,000	193,000	10,200,000	4,850,000	652,000	680,000	8,150,000	4,500,000	873,000	4,250,000†
1996	72,300,000	16,000,000	1,610,000	322,000	10,200,000	5,280,000	707,000	709,000	9,290,000	4,660,000	643,000	3,860,000†

NA=not available. (R) Revised to reflect improved data. (*) USSR as constituted prior to Dec. 1991. (†) Russia only.

U.S. and World Silver Production, 1930-96

Source: U.S. Geological Survey, U.S. Dept. of the Interior

(metric tons)

Year[1]	United States	World	Year[1]	United States	World	Year[1]	United States	World
1930	1,578	7,736	1970	1,400	9,670	1990	2,120	16,600
1935	1,428	6,865	1975	1,087	9,428	1991	1,860	15,600
1940	2,164	8,565	1980	1,006	10,556	1992	1,800	14,600
1945	904	5,039	1985	1,227	13,051	1993	1,640	14,300
1950	1,347	6,323	1987	1,241	14,019	1994	1,480	14,000
1955	1,134	6,967	1988	1,661	15,484	1995	1,560	15,100
1960	1,120	7,505	1989	2,008	16,041	1996	1,570	15,200[E]
1965	1,238	8,007						

(1) Largest production of silver in the United States was in 1915—2,332 metric tons. (E) Estimated.

Aluminum Summary, 1980-96

Source: U.S. Geological Survey, U.S. Dept. of the Interior

Item	Unit	1980	1985	1990	1991	1992	1993	1994	1995	1996[4]
U.S. production	1,000 metric tons	6,231	5,262	6,441	6,407	6,798	6,639	6,385	6,563	6,860
Primary aluminum	1,000 metric tons	4,654	3,500	4,048	4,121	4,042	3,695	3,299	3,375	3,577
Secondary aluminum[1]	1,000 metric tons	1,577	1,762	2,393	2,286	2,756	2,944	3,086	3,188	3,290
Primary aluminum value	Billion dollars	7.8	3.8	6.6	5.4	5.1	4.3	5.2	6.4	5.6
Price (Primary alum.)[2]	Cents/lb	76.1	48.8	74.0	59.5	57.5	53.3	71.2	85.9	71.3
Imports for consumption[1]	1,000 metric tons	647	1,420	1,514	1,490	1,725	2,544	3,382	2,975	2,810
Exports[3]	1,000 metric tons	1,346	908	1,659	1,762	1,403	1,207	1,296	1,610	1,500
World production	1,000 metric tons	15,383	15,398	19,299	19,652	19,500	19,800	19,200	19,900	20,700[E]

(1) Recoverable metal content from purchased scrap, old and new. (2) Average prices for primary aluminum, quoted by *Metals Week*. (3) Crude and semicrude (incl. metal and alloys, plates, bars, etc., and scrap). (4) All data, except primary production, have been rounded to 3 significant figures. (E) Estimated.

Economic and Financial Glossary

Source: Reviewed by Daniel Raff, associate professor of management, The Wharton School

Acquisition: The purchase of one company by another.

Arbitrage: A form of hedged investment meant to capture slight differences in the prices of 2 related securities—for example, buying gold in London and selling it at a higher price in New York. Distinct from *risk arbitrage* (defined below).

Balanced budget: A budget is balanced when receipts equal current expenditure.

Balance of payments: The difference between all payments, for some categories of transactions, made to and from foreign countries over a set period of time. A *favorable* balance exists when more payments are coming in than going out; an *unfavorable* balance, when the reverse is true. Payments may include gold, the cost of merchandise and services, interest and dividend payments, money spent by travelers, and repayment of principal on loans.

Balance of trade (trade gap): The difference between exports and imports, in both actual funds and credit. A nation's balance of trade is *favorable* when exports exceed imports and *unfavorable* when the reverse is true.

Bear market: A market in which prices are falling.

Bearer bond: A bond issued in bearer form rather than being registered in a specific owner's name. Ownership is determined by possession.

Bond: A written promise, or IOU, by the issuer to repay a fixed amount of borrowed money on a specified date and generally to make payments of interest at regular intervals in the interim.

Bull market: A market in which prices are on the rise.

Capital gain (loss): An increase (decrease) in the market value of an asset above (below) the price originally paid at the time the asset is sold.

Commercial paper: An extremely short-term corporate IOU, generally due in 270 days or less. Available in face amounts of $100,000, $250,000, $500,000, $1,000,000, and combinations thereof.

Convertible bond: A corporate bond (see below) that may be converted into a stated number of shares of common stock. Its price tends to fluctuate along with fluctuations in the price of the stock and with changes in interest rates.

Corporate bond: A bond issued by a corporation. The bond normally has a stated life and pays a fixed rate of interest. Considered safer than the common or preferred stock of the same company.

Cost of living: The cost of maintaining a standard of living measured in terms of purchased goods and services. Inflation typically measures changes in the cost of living.

Cost-of-living benefits: Benefit payments whose sum in current dollars is regularly adjusted for changes in the cost of living.

Credit crunch (liquidity crisis): A situation in which cash for lending is in short supply.

Debenture: An unsecured bond backed only by the general credit of the issuing corporation.

Deficit spending: Government spending in excess of revenues, generally financed with the sale of bonds.

Depression: A long period of economic decline when prices are low, unemployment is high, and there are many business failures.

Derivatives: Financial contracts whose values are based on, or *derived* from, the price of an underlying financial asset or price—for example, a stock or an interest rate.

Devaluation: The official lowering of a nation's currency, decreasing its value in relation to foreign currencies.

Discount rate: The rate of interest set by the Federal Reserve that member banks are charged when borrowing money through the Federal Reserve System.

Disposable income: Income after taxes that is available to persons for spending and saving.

Dividend: Discretionary payment by a corporation to its shareholders, usually in the form of cash, stock shares, or other property.

Dow Jones Industrial Average: An index of stock market prices, based on the prices of 30 leading companies on the New York Stock Exchange.

Econometrics: The use of statistical methods to study economic and financial data.

Federal Deposit Insurance Corporation (FDIC): A U.S. government-sponsored corporation that insures accounts in national banks and other qualified institutions.

Federal Reserve System: The entire banking system of the U.S., incorporating 12 Federal Reserve banks (one in each of 12 Federal Reserve districts), 24 Federal Reserve branch banks, all national banks, and state-chartered commercial banks and trust companies that have been admitted to its membership. The governors of the system greatly influence the nation's monetary and credit policies.

Full employment: The economy is said to be at full employment when everyone who wishes to work at the going wage-rate for his or her type of labor is employed, save for only the small amount of unemployment due to the fact that it takes time to switch from one job to another.

Golden parachute: Provisions in the employment contracts of executives guaranteeing substantial severance benefits if they lose their position in a corporate takeover.

Government bond: A bond issued by the U.S. Treasury, considered the safest security in the investment world. Government bonds are divided into 2 categories—those that are not marketable and those that are. *Savings bonds* cannot be bought and sold once the original purchase is made. These include the familiar Series EE bonds. You buy them at 50 percent of their face value, and when they mature, 12 years later, they can be cashed in for 100 percent of face value. Another type, Series H, are not discounted, but issued in amounts of $500, $1,000, $5,000, and $10,000 and pay their interest in semiannual checks. Marketable bonds fall into several categories. *Treasury bills* are short-term U.S. obligations, maturing in 3, 6, or 12 months. They are sold at a discount of the face value, and the minimum denomination is $10,000. *Treasury notes* mature in up to 10 years. Denominations currently range from $500 to $10,000 and up. *Treasury bonds* mature in 10 to 30 years. The minimum investment is $1,000.

Greenmail: A company buying back its own shares for more than the going market price to avoid a threatened hostile takeover.

Gross domestic product (GDP): The market value of all goods and services that have been bought for final use during a period of time. It became the official measure of the size of the U.S. economy in 1991, replacing the *Gross national product (GNP)*, which had been in use since 1941. GDP covers workers and capital employed within the nation's borders. GNP covers production by American residents, regardless of where it takes place. The switch aligned the U.S. with most other industrialized countries, making comparisons easier.

Hedge fund: A flexible investment fund for a limited number of large investors (the minimum investment is typically $1 million). Hedge funds use almost all investment techniques, including those forbidden to mutual funds, such as short-selling and heavy leveraging.

Hedging: Taking 2 positions whose gains and losses will offset each other if prices change, in order to limit financial risk.

Individual retirement account (IRA): A self-funded retirement plan that allows employed individuals to contribute up to a maximum yearly sum toward their retirement while deferring taxes until retirement.

Inflation: An increase in the level of prices.

Insider information: Important facts about the condition or plans of a corporation that have not been released to the general public.

Interest: The cost of borrowing money.

Investment bank: A financial institution that arranges the initial issuance of stocks and bonds and offers companies advice about acquisitions and divestitures.

Junk bonds: Bonds issued by companies with low credit ratings. They typically pay relatively high interest rates because of the fear of default.

Leading indicators: A series of 11 indicators from different segments of the economy used by the U.S. Commerce Department to predict when changes in the level of economic activity will occur.

Leverage: The extent to which a purchase was paid for with borrowed money. Amplifies the potential gain or loss for the purchaser.

Leveraged buyout: An acquisition of a company in which much of the purchase price is borrowed, with the debt to be repaid from future profits or by subsequently selling off company assets. Typically carried out by a small group of investors, often including incumbent management.

Liquid assets: Assets that include cash or those items that are easily converted into cash.

Margin account: A brokerage account that allows a person to trade securities on credit. A **margin call** is a demand for more collateral on the account.

Money supply: The currency held by the public, plus checking accounts in commercial banks and savings institutions.

Mortgage-backed securities: Created when a bank, builder, or government agency gathers together a group of mortgages and then sells bonds to other institutions and the public. The investors receive their proportionate share of the interest payments on the loans as well as the principal payments. Usually, the mortgages in question are guaranteed by the government.

Municipal bond: Issued by governmental units such as states, cities, local taxing authorities, and other agencies. Interest is exempt from U.S.—and sometimes state and local—income tax. *Municipal bond unit investment trusts* offer a portfolio of many different municipal bonds chosen by professionals. The income is exempt from federal income taxes.

Mutual fund: A portfolio of professionally bought and managed financial assets in which you pool your money along with thousands of other people. A share price is based on net asset value, or the value of all the investments owned by the funds, less any debt, and divided by the total number of shares. The major advantage, relative to investing individually only in a small number of stocks, is less risk—the holdings are spread out over many assets and if one or two do badly the remainder may shield you from the losses. *Bond funds* are mutual funds that deal in the bond market exclusively. *Money market mutual funds* buy in the so-called money market—institutions that need to borrow large sums of money for short terms. Usually the individual investor cannot afford the denominations required in the money market (e.g., treasury bills, commercial paper, certificates of deposit), but through a money market mutual fund the investor can take advantage of these instruments when interest rates are high as well as get the diversification advantages. These funds often offer special checking account advantages.

National debt: The debt of the national government, as distinguished from the debts of political subdivisions of the nation and of private business and individuals.

National debt ceiling: Total borrowing limit set by Congress beyond which the U.S. national debt cannot rise. This limit is periodically raised by congressional vote.

Option: A type of contractual agreement between a buyer and a seller to buy or sell shares of a security. A **call** option contract gives the right to purchase shares of a specific stock at a stated price within a given period of time. A **put** option contract gives the buyer the right to sell shares of a specific stock at a stated price within a given period of time.

Per capita income: The total income of a group divided by the number of people in the group.

Prime interest rate: The rate charged by banks on short term loans to large commercial customers with the highest credit rating.

Producer price index: A statistical measure of the change in the price of wholesale goods. It is reported for 3 different stages of the production chain: crude, intermediate, and finished goods.

Program trading: A term for trading techniques involving large numbers and large blocks of stocks, usually used in conjunction with computer programs. Techniques include *index arbitrage,* in which traders profit from price differences between stocks and futures contracts on stock indexes, and *portfolio insurance,* which is the use of stock-index futures to protect stock investors from large losses when the market drops.

Public debt: The total of a nation's debts owed by state, local, and national government. Increases in this sum, reflected in public-sector deficits, indicate how much of the nation's spending is being financed by borrowing rather than by taxation.

Recession: A mild decrease in economic activity marked by a decline in real GDP, employment, and trade, usually lasting 6 months to a year, and marked by widespread decline in many sectors of the economy.

Risk arbitrage: The purchase and/or selling of the securities of companies expected to be involved in takeover situations, in order to realize a profit.

Savings Association Insurance Fund (SAIF): Created in 1989 to insure accounts in savings and loan associations up to $100,000.

Seasonal adjustment: Statistical changes made to compensate for regular fluctuations in data that are so great they tend to distort the statistics and make comparisons meaningless. For instance, seasonal adjustments are made in midwinter for a slowdown in housing construction and for the rise in farm income in the fall after the summer crops are harvested.

Short-selling: Borrowing shares of stock from a brokerage firm and selling them, hoping to buy the shares back at a lower price, return them, and realize a profit from the decline in prices.

Stagnation: Economic slowdown in which there is little growth in GDP, capital investment, and real income.

Stock: *Common stocks* are shares of ownership in a corporation; they are the most direct way to participate in the fortunes of a company. There can be wide swings in the prices of this kind of stock. *Preferred stock* is a type of stock on which a fixed dividend must be paid before holders of common stock are issued their share of the issuing corporation's earnings. Prices are higher and yields lower than comparable bonds. However, preferred stock is attractive to corporate investors because 85% of preferred dividends are tax exempt to corporations. *Convertible preferred stock* can be converted into the common stock of the company that issued the preferred. This stock has the advantage of producing a higher yield than common stock; it also has appreciation potential. *Over-the-counter stock* is not traded on the major or regional exchanges, but rather through dealers from whom you buy directly. *Blue chip* stocks are so called because they have been leading stocks for a long time. *Growth* stocks are those whose earnings are expected to grow significantly over several years.

Stock-index futures: A futures contract is an agreement to buy or sell a specific amount of a commodity or financial instrument at a particular price at a set date in the future. Futures based on a stock index (such as the Dow Jones Industrial Average) are bets on the future price of that group of stocks.

Supply-side economics: A school of thinking about economic policy holding that lowering income tax rates will inevitably lead to enhanced economic growth and general revitalization of the economy.

Takeover: Acquisition of one company by another company or group by sale or merger. A *friendly takeover* occurs when the acquired company's management is agreeable to the merger; when management is opposed to the merger, it is an *unfriendly takeover.*

Tender offer: A public offer to buy a company's stock; usually priced at a premium above the market.

Zero coupon bond: A corporate or government bond that is issued at a deep discount from the maturity value and pays no interest during the life of the bond. It is redeemable at face value.

AGRICULTURE

U.S. Farms–Number and Acreage by State, 1996 and 1997

Source: National Agricultural Statistics Service, U.S. Dept. of Agriculture

State	Farms (1,000) 1996	1997	Acreage (mil) 1996	1997	Acreage per farm 1996	1997
U.S.	2,064	2,058	970	968	470	470
Alabama	45.0	45.0	9.8	9.7	218	216
Alaska	0.5	0.5	0.9	0.9	1,804	1,804
Arizona	7.5	7.5	35.4	35.4	4,720	4,720
Arkansas	43.0	42.5	15.0	14.8	349	348
California	82.0	84.0	30.0	30.0	366	357
Colorado	24.5	24.5	32.5	32.5	1,327	1,327
Connecticut	3.8	3.9	(Z)	(Z)	100	97
Delaware	2.5	2.4	0.6	0.6	226	235
Florida	40.0	40.0	10.3	10.3	258	258
Georgia	43.0	43.0	11.8	11.8	274	274
Hawaii	4.6	4.6	1.6	1.6	346	346
Idaho	22.0	22.0	13.5	13.5	614	614
Illinois	76.0	76.0	28.1	28.0	370	368
Indiana	61.0	62.0	15.9	15.9	261	256
Iowa	98.0	98.0	33.2	33.2	339	339
Kansas	66.0	65.0	47.8	47.8	724	735
Kentucky	88.0	88.0	14.0	13.9	159	158
Louisiana	27.0	26.5	8.7	8.5	322	321
Maine	7.4	7.3	1.3	1.3	181	184
Maryland	13.7	13.0	2.1	2.1	153	162
Massachusetts	6.1	6.2	0.6	0.6	93	92
Michigan	53.0	52.0	10.6	10.5	200	202
Minnesota	87.0	87.0	29.8	29.8	343	343
Mississippi	44.0	43.0	12.6	12.5	286	291
Missouri	104.0	102.0	30.0	29.9	288	293
Montana	22.0	23.0	59.7	59.6	2,714	2,591
Nebraska	56.0	55.0	47.0	47.0	839	855
Nevada	2.5	2.5	8.8	8.8	3,520	3,520
New Hampshire	2.4	2.4	(Z)	(Z)	179	179
New Jersey	9.2	9.4	0.8	0.8	91	88
New Mexico	13.5	13.5	43.7	43.5	3,237	3,222
New York	36.0	36.0	7.7	7.7	214	214
N. Carolina	58.0	57.0	9.2	9.0	159	158
N. Dakota	31.0	30.5	40.3	40.2	1,300	1,318
Ohio	72.0	73.0	15.1	15.1	210	207
Oklahoma	72.0	73.0	34.0	34.0	472	466
Oregon	38.5	37.5	17.5	17.5	455	467
Pennsylvania	50.0	50.0	7.7	7.7	154	154
Rhode Island	0.7	0.7	(Z)	(Z)	90	90
S. Carolina	21.5	21.5	5.0	5.0	233	233
S. Dakota	32.5	32.5	44.0	44.0	1,354	1,354
Tennessee	80.0	80.0	11.8	11.8	148	148
Texas	205.0	205.0	129.0	129.0	629	629
Utah	13.4	13.4	11.0	11.0	821	821
Vermont	6.0	6.0	1.4	1.4	225	225
Virginia	48.0	47.0	8.6	8.5	179	181
Washington	36.0	36.0	15.7	15.7	436	436
W. Virginia	20.0	20.0	3.7	3.7	185	185
Wisconsin	79.0	79.0	16.8	16.8	213	213
Wyoming	9.1	9.1	34.6	34.6	3,802	3,802

(Z) Fewer than 500,000 acres

The U.S. Farm Population

Source: Margaret Butler, U.S. Dept. of Agriculture, Economic Research Service

When first separately counted in the 1920 census, the farm population was defined as people living on farms, regardless of occupation or source of income. Many people who live on farms today have no one in the household employed primarily in agriculture, and those employed in agriculture often do not live on farms. Thirty-five percent of persons in farm operator or manager households did not live on a farm in 1992, and 38% of farm residents were members of households in which no one operated or managed a farm or received farm self-employment income. Thus, the conventional farm residence definition has lost some of its former validity and has been discontinued.

In 1994, about 5 million people lived in households associated with the operation of farms, as indicated by a household member's occupation or source of income. This farm population definition is now identified as the farm entrepreneurial population. The Midwest was home to a larger proportion of that population—44%—than any other region of the country.

Persons in Farm Occupations, 1850-1994*

Source: U.S. Dept. of Agriculture, Economic Research Service

(in thousands)

Year	Total workers[1]	Farm occupations Number	% of total	Year	Total workers[1]	Farm occupations Number	% of total
1850	7,697	4,902	63.7	1970	79,802	2,881	3.6
1870	12,925	6,850	53.0	1980	104,058	2,818	2.7
1900	29,030	10,888	37.5	1985 (Mar.)	106,214	2,949	2.8
1920	42,206	11,390	27.0	1990 (Mar.)	117,491	2,864	2.4
1930	48,686	10,321	21.2	1991 (Mar.)	116,000	2,848	2.5
1940	51,742	8,995	17.4	1992 (Mar.)	116,442	2,936	2.5
1950	59,230	6,858	11.6	1993 (Mar.)	117,238	2,988	2.5
1960	67,990	4,132	6.1	1994 (Mar.)	120,383	3,038	2.5

* These figures not compiled for years after 1994. (1) Total workers for 1985 to 1994 are employed workers ages 15 years and older; total workers for 1970 and 1980 are members of the experienced civilian labor force ages 16 years and older; total workers for 1900 to 1960 are members of the experienced civilian labor force ages 14 years and older; total workers for 1850 to 1890 are gainfully employed workers ages 10 years and older.

Livestock on Farms in the U.S., 1900-97*

Source: National Agricultural Statistics Service, U.S. Dept. of Agriculture

(in thousands)

Year (On Jan. 1)	All cattle	Milk cows	Sheep	Hogs[1]	Year (On Jan. 1)	All cattle	Milk cows	Sheep	Hogs[1]
1900	59,739	16,544	48,105	51,055	1970	112,369	12,091	20,423	57,046
1910	58,993	19,450	50,239	48,072	1980	111,242	10,758	12,699	67,318
1920	70,400	21,455	40,743	60,159	1985	109,582	10,777	10,716	54,073
1925	63,373	22,575	38,543	55,770	1990*	95,816	10,015	11,358	53,788
1930	61,003	23,032	51,565	55,705	1991*	96,393	9,966	11,174	54,416
1935	68,846	26,082	51,808	39,066	1992*	97,556	9,728	10,797	57,649
1940	68,309	24,940	52,107	61,165	1993*	99,176	9,658	10,201	58,202
1945	85,573	27,770	46,520	59,373	1994*	100,988	9,528	9,742	57,904
1950	77,963	23,853	29,826	58,937	1995*	102,755	9,487	8,886	59,990
1955	96,592	23,462	31,582	50,474	1996*	103,487	9,416	8,461	58,264
1960	96,236	19,527	33,170	59,026	1997[3]	101,209	9,281	7,937	56,171
1965[2]	109,000	16,981	25,127	56,106					

* Figures revised by USDA NASS, Jan. 1997. (1) As of Dec. 1 of preceding year. (2) From 1966, milk cows and heifers that have calved. (3) Total estimated value on farms as of Jan. 1, 1997, was (avg. value per head in parentheses): cattle $53,101,400,000 ($525.00); sheep $761,700,000 ($96.00); hogs $5,283,000,000 ($94.00).

U.S. Farms, 1940-97

Source: National Agricultural Statistics Service, U.S. Dept. of Agriculture

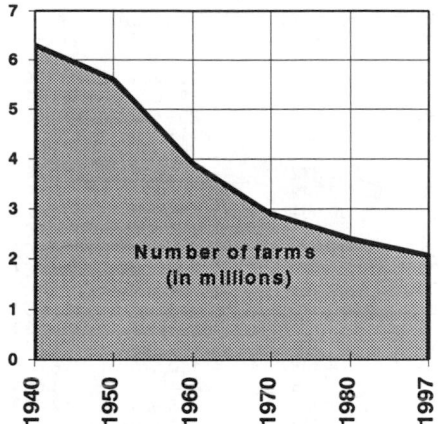

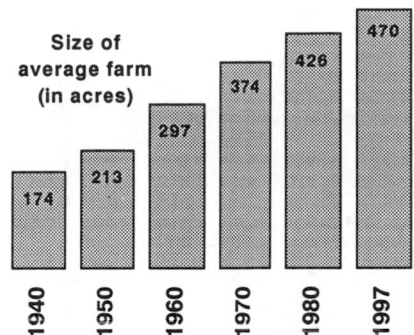

Size of average farm (in acres)

Eggs: U.S. Production, Price, and Value, 1995-96[1]

Source: National Agricultural Statistics Service, U.S. Dept. of Agriculture

State	Eggs produced[2] 1995 (mil)	1996	Price per dozen[2] 1995 (cents)	1996	Value of production 1995 (1,000 dollars)	1996	State	Eggs produced[2] 1995 (mil)	1996	Price per dozen[2] 1995 (cents)	1996	Value of production 1995 (1,000 dollars)	1996
AL ..	2,703	2,481	96.1	109.0	$216,465	$225,358	NH...	44	42	75.0	81.0	$2,750	$2,835
AR ..	3,608	3,428	97.9	105.0	294,353	299,950	NJ...	444	475	62.6	72.8	23,162	28,817
CA ..	6,444	6,569	53.7	67.1	288,369	367,317	NM...	303	306	53.0	67.5	13,383	17,213
CO..	805	827	70.6	75.6	47,361	52,101	NY...	1,071	1,042	62.6	77.1	55,871	66,949
CT ..	944	950	67.0	74.0	52,707	58,583	NC...	3,152	2,988	77.3	87.5	203,041	217,875
DE ..	138	147	113.0	119.0	12,995	14,578	ND...	47	55	38.4	58.5	1,504	2,681
FL ..	2,383	2,314	48.1	63.3	95,519	122,064	OH ..	5,964	6,502	50.9	66.2	252,973	358,694
GA ..	4,376	4,584	79.4	91.1	289,545	348,002	OK..	897	916	86.0	87.6	64,285	66,868
HI...	186	179	87.2	86.9	13,516	12,963	OR ..	709	741	61.5	73.9	36,336	45,633
ID...	238	258	60.7	70.0	12,039	15,050	PA...	5,661	5,640	56.2	62.8	265,124	295,160
IL...	762	902	68.4	68.9	43,434	51,790	RI ...	34	43	65.0	72.0	1,842	2,580
IN...	5,496	5,666	51.6	67.8	236,328	320,129	SC...	1,289	1,224	65.8	85.4	70,680	87,108
IA...	4,318	5,011	43.4	59.1	156,168	246,792	SD...	535	534	34.5	52.0	15,381	23,140
KS...	325	315	44.0	57.4	11,917	15,068	TN...	254	257	82.8	91.3	17,526	19,553
KY ..	679	664	65.4	79.2	37,006	43,824	TX...	3,922	3,986	66.3	87.5	216,961	290,646
LA ..	472	477	98.4	96.4	38,704	38,319	UT...	513	464	47.1	56.6	20,135	21,885
ME..	1,364	1,449	65.0	72.0	73,883	86,940	VT...	21	27	68.0	77.0	1,190	1,733
MD..	1,002	938	64.0	79.6	53,440	62,221	VA...	916	949	89.5	95.3	68,318	75,366
MA..	133	142	66.0	74.0	7,315	8,757	WA ..	1,455	1,413	76.9	76.4	93,241	89,961
MI..	1,388	1,318	43.5	62.3	50,315	68,426	WV ..	239	228	118.0	119.0	23,502	22,610
MN..	2,823	3,087	41.8	58.5	98,335	150,491	WI ...	849	896	43.3	60.6	30,635	45,248
MS..	1,443	1,523	99.0	121.0	119,048	153,569	WY ..	2.4	2.4	74.1	75.0	148	150
MO..	1,705	1,674	49.0	66.5	69,621	92,768	Other[3]	70	68	65.5	68.2	3,818	3,864
MT ..	105	108	57.0	66.0	4,988	5,940	**U.S.[4]**	**74,591**	**76,148**	**62.4**	**75.0**	**3,879,609**	**4,756,582**
NE ..	2,359	2,336	38.0	56.0	74,702	109,013							

(1) Estimates cover the 12-month period from Dec. 1 of the previous year through Nov. 30. (2) Average of all eggs sold by producers, including hatching eggs. (3) AK, AZ, and NV combined to avoid disclosure of individual operations; totals listed under "other." AK price estimates discontinued in 1995. (4) Total states may not equal U.S. total because of rounding.

U.S. Meat Production and Consumption, 1940-96

Source: Economic Research Service, U.S. Dept. of Agriculture

(in millions of pounds)

Year	Beef Production	Beef Consumption[2]	Veal Production	Veal Consumption[2]	Lamb and mutton Production	Lamb and mutton Consumption[2]	Pork (exclud. lard) Production	Pork (exclud. lard) Consumption[2]	All red meats[1] Production	All red meats[1] Consumption[2]	Total Poultry Production	Total Poultry Consumption[2]
1940	7,175	7,257	981	981	876	873	10,044	9,701	19,076	18,812	NA	NA
1950	9,534	9,529	1,230	1,206	597	596	10,714	10,390	22,075	21,721	3,174	3,097
1960	14,728	15,465	1,109	1,118	769	857	13,905	14,057	30,511	31,497	6,310	6,168
1970	21,684	23,451	588	613	551	669	14,699	14,957	37,522	39,689	10,193	9,981
1980	21,643	23,560	400	420	318	351	16,617	16,838	38,978	41,701	14,173	13,525
1990	22,743	24,031	327	325	363	397	15,354	16,031	38,787	40,784	23,468	22,151
1991	22,917	24,113	306	305	363	396	15,999	16,399	39,585	41,214	24,700	23,270
1992	23,086	24,261	310	312	348	388	17,233	17,474	40,977	42,435	26,201	24,394
1993	23,049	24,000	295	286	337	381	17,088	18,213	40,759	42,092	27,329	25,099
1994	24,386	25,125	293	291	308	345	17,030	17,000	42,683	43,592	29,113	25,754
1995	25,222	25,533	319	319	287	348	17,850	17.785	43,677	43,986	30,393	25,940
1996	25,526	25,875	379	379	268	334	17,118	16,846	43,291	43,434	31,974	26,614

(1) Meats may not add to total because of rounding. (2) Includes consumption and shipments of imports and beginning inventories. NA = not available.

Government Agricultural Payments by State, 1996[1]

Source: Economic Research Service, U.S. Dept. of Agriculture

(in thousands of dollars)

State	Feed Grains[2]	Wheat	Rice	Cotton[2]	Wool Act	Conservation[3]	Miscellaneous	Total
Alabama	$314	$-212	$ 0	$-4,122	$ 16	$28,821	$50,733	$75,550
Alaska	-23	0	0	0	3	1,091	187	1,258
Arizona	17	-1,169	0	-7,104	523	1,422	64,304	57,993
Arkansas	-92	-8,245	68,241	-7,380	72	14,198	295,024	361,818
California	-565	-4,526	34,272	-13,695	3,088	17,017	259,869	295,460
Colorado	-3,452	-17,016	0	0	2,522	80,438	113,609	176,101
Connecticut	-106	0	0	0	8	331	1,558	1,791
Delaware	-353	-149	0	0	1	372	5,017	4,888
Florida	134	-41	5	-351	2	7,742	15,381	22,872
Georgia	360	-1,509	0	-3,026	13	30,001	88,685	114,524
Hawaii	0	0	0	0	0	390	190	580
Idaho	-4,477	-19,910	0	0	1,591	39,664	99,141	116,009
Illinois	-66,102	-8,979	0	0	196	63,904	397,748	386,767
Indiana	-23,390	-4,150	0	0	86	33,169	207,988	213,703
Iowa	-112,154	-77	0	0	728	170,120	443,077	501,694
Kansas	-14,501	-87,960	0	-1	448	153,101	504,052	555,139
Kentucky	-1,391	-2,224	8	0	44	25,308	52,797	74,542
Louisiana	323	-410	26,773	-9,225	4	8,458	150,548	176,471
Maine	-55	0	0	0	26	2,943	1,724	4,638
Maryland	-1,123	-619	0	0	45	2,380	16,964	17,647
Massachusetts	-27	0	0	0	17	442	1,116	1,548
Michigan	-9,315	-4,477	0	0	231	22,963	100,183	109,585
Minnesota	-42,082	-24,777	0	0	589	98,834	316,240	348,804
Mississippi	135	-1,261	13,103	-15,526	4	37,322	151,148	184,925
Missouri	-2,317	-9,617	5,611	-1,666	350	113,774	183,144	289,279
Montana	-6,295	-41,498	0	0	3,504	102,895	182,268	240,874
Nebraska	-47,320	-17,669	0	0	422	76,788	376,598	388,819
Nevada	-26	-148	0	0	352	654	1,773	2,605
New Hampshire	-3	0	0	0	15	424	657	1,093
New Jersey	-125	-84	0	0	13	298	3,156	3,258
New Mexico	-534	-1,676	0	-514	2,526	19,212	39,986	59,000
New York	-2,057	-943	0	0	156	6,366	39,767	43,289
North Carolina	-197	-1,343	0	-1,367	36	8,542	70,031	75,702
North Dakota	-12,325	-77,775	0	0	961	106,282	334,377	351,520
Ohio	-10,244	-7,267	0	0	401	27,642	152,588	163,120
Oklahoma	-673	-43,057	62	-2,425	443	49,896	232,461	236,707
Oregon	-588	-9,795	0	0	1,054	28,571	55,020	74,262
Pennsylvania	-1,540	-302	0	0	216	8,265	30,472	37,111
Rhode Island	-1	0	0	0	2	61	94	156
South Carolina	770	-1,452	0	-1,859	1	12,546	32,862	42,868
South Dakota	-2,272	-15,987	0	0	2,809	68,875	176,180	229,605
Tennessee	-87	-1,889	22	-4,298	25	23,338	62,806	79,917
Texas	-6,577	-20,642	26,727	-32,338	24,620	163,559	609,429	764,778
Utah	-436	-1,196	0	0	2,565	9,822	10,251	21,006
Vermont	-76	0	0	0	33	1,333	2,745	4,035
Virginia	-502	-920	0	-39	223	6,874	24,787	30,423
Washington	-2,205	-30,507	0	0	260	54,815	133,676	156,039
West Virginia	-144	-20	0	0	136	1,946	2,620	4,538
Wisconsin	-10,573	-644	0	0	181	48,910	118,975	156,849
Wyoming	-459	-1,260	0	0	4,127	11,060	10,913	24,381
United States	**$-384,731**	**$-473,402**	**$174,824**	**$-104,936**	**$55,688**	**$1,793,179**	**$6,224,919**	**$7,285,541**

(1) Includes both cash payments and payment-in-kind (PIK) for fiscal year. (2) Negatives indicate that the current year's Advanced Deficiency Payments were less than refunds from producers to government because advances paid in the previous year were too high. (3) Includes amount paid under agriculture and conservation programs (Conservation Reserve, Agriculture Conservation, Emergency Conservation, and Great Plains Program).

U.S. Federal Food Assistance Programs, 1987-96[1]

Source: Food and Nutrition Service, U.S. Dept. of Agriculture

(in millions of dollars)

Program	1987	1988	1989	1990	1991	1992	1993	1994	1995	1996
Food stamps[2]	$11,605	$12,317	$12,932	$15,491	$18,769	$22,462	$23,653	$24,492	$24,621	$24,334
Puerto Rico nutrition asst.[3]	853	879	908	937	963	1,002	1,040	1,079	1,131	1,143
Natl. school lunch[4]	3,685	3,730	3,769	3,834	4,224	4,564	4,751	4,964	5,160	5,342
School breakfast[5]	447	482	513	596	685	787	869	959	1,048	1,119
WIC[6]	1,680	1,798	1,911	2,122	2,301	2,597	2,829	3,170	3,430	3,685
Summer food service[4]	129	133	146	164	182	204	220	230	237	250
Child/adult care[4]	548	628	697	813	945	1,104	1,223	1,354	1,464	1,534
Special milk	15	19	18	19	20	20	19	18	17	17
Nutrition for the elderly[4]	139	146	146	142	144	151	150	153	151	146
Food distrib. to Indian reserv.	63	62	65	66	65	62	62	65	65	70
Commodity supp. food prog.[4,7]	56	62	73	85	93	105	112	107	99	100
Food dist.—charitable inst.[8]	158	159	136	104	93	116	92	106	64	11
Emergency food assistance	895	645	276	257	256	236	238	218	89	44
Soup kitchens/food banks	0	0	34	77	45	36	35	48	46	35
Other costs[9]	62	58	68	71	78	92	107	120	117	143
Total[10]	**$20,335**	**$21,118**	**$21,692**	**$24,776**	**$28,863**	**$33,538**	**$35,400**	**$37,136**	**$37,739**	**$37,973**

(1) Data are for fiscal (not calendar) years. (2) Includes the federal share of state administrative expenses and other federal costs. (3) Puerto Rico participated in the Food Stamp Program from FY 1975 until July 1982, when it initiated a separate grant program. (4) Includes the value of commodities (entitlement, bonus, and cash in lieu). (5) Excludes startup costs. (6) Includes program studies and the WIC Farmers Market Nutrition Program. (7) Includes elderly feeding projects. (8) Includes summer camps. (9) Includes child nutrition state administration expenses, nutrition studies, nutrition education and training, American Samoa and Northern Marianas nutrition assistance grant, and commodity disaster relief. (10) Excludes food program administration costs.

U.S. Farm Marketings by State, 1995-96

Source: Economic Research Service, U.S. Dept. of Agriculture

(in thousands of dollars)

State/Rank[1]	1995 Farm marketings Total	1995 Crops	1995 Livestock and products	1996 Farm marketings Total	1996 Crops	1996 Livestock and products
Alabama (26).	$ 2,951,334	$ 801,784	$2,149,550	$3,173,595	$810,637	$2,362,958
Alaska (50)	27,935	21,890	6,045	29,418	23,310	6,108
Arizona (32)	1,853,669	1,049,326	804,343	2,146,417	1,307,590	838,827
Arkansas (11)	5,394,516	2,249,765	3,144,751	5,886,786	2,530,163	3,356,623
California (1)	21,281,547	15,792,837	5,488,710	23,309,526	17,096,190	6,213,336
Colorado (17)	4,051,357	1,287,188	2,764,169	4,229,447	1,470,312	2,759,135
Connecticut (42)	477,791	224,242	253,549	489,113	252,413	236,700
Delaware (39)	657,594	152,222	505,372	757,036	183,580	573,456
Florida (9)	5,984,249	4,792,116	1,192,133	6,130,658	4,942,465	1,188,193
Georgia (12)	4,688,737	2,017,742	2,670,995	5,687,046	2,407,786	3,279,260
Hawaii (44)	507,609	430,788	76,821	482,589	416,594	65,995
Idaho (25)	2,955,215	1,756,147	1,199,068	3,409,945	2,080,687	1,329,258
Illinois (5)	7,945,732	5,896,508	2,049,224	9,049,998	6,988,895	2,061,103
Indiana (14).	4,664,044	2,930,321	1,733,723	5,558,099	3,663,444	1,894,655
Iowa (3)	9,999,410	4,769,337	5,230,073	12,852,687	7,395,907	5,456,780
Kansas (7)	7,626,389	2,868,415	4,757,974	7,869,209	3,298,882	4,570,327
Kentucky (22)	3,220,241	1,571,305	1,648,936	3,550,232	1,831,347	1,718,885
Louisiana (31)	2,028,702	1,329,095	699,607	2,342,068	1,654,858	687,210
Maine (43).	457,905	187,744	270,161	485,111	223,574	261,537
Maryland (36)	1,339,209	540,508	798,701	1,533,770	633,267	900,503
Massachusetts (45)	459,517	342,080	117,437	477,698	368,631	109,067
Michigan (20)	3,381,239	1,992,076	1,389,163	3,642,927	2,194,946	1,447,981
Minnesota (6)	6,407,645	2,959,643	3,448,002	8,808,931	4,640,508	4,168,423
Mississippi (24)	2,870,975	1,180,604	1,690,371	3,462,784	1,528,505	1,934,279
Missouri (16)	4,561,575	2,098,225	2,463,350	4,950,421	2,500,276	2,450,145
Montana (33).	1,884,628	1,028,968	855,660	2,027,226	1,230,299	796,927
Nebraska (4)	8,524,549	3,119,834	5,404,715	9,454,041	4,176,780	5,277,261
Nevada (47)	299,221	109,588	189,633	286,002	132,566	153,436
New Hampshire (48) . . .	150,955	87,453	63,502	160,907	88,605	72,302
New Jersey (38)	769,991	589,332	180,659	800,958	605,395	195,563
New Mexico (34)	1,527,909	426,365	1,101,544	1,709,056	511,567	1,197,489
New York (27)	2,867,681	979,338	1,888,343	3,043,034	998,487	2,044,547
North Carolina (8)	6,439,341	3,110,371	3,328,970	7,831,309	3,403,986	4,427,323
North Dakota (23)	3,028,022	2,403,427	624,595	3,532,393	2,995,616	536,777
Ohio (15).	4,438,388	2,874,796	1,563,592	5,121,783	3,176,785	1,944,998
Oklahoma (21).	3,898,466	1,199,059	2,699,407	3,565,551	1,126,250	2,439,301
Oregon (28).	2,650,706	1,929,627	721,079	2,976,542	2,320,012	656,530
Pennsylvania (18)	3,769,178	1,164,194	2,604,984	4,142,509	1,277,932	2,864,577
Rhode Island (49)	80,422	68,335	12,087	82,867	71,573	11,294
South Carolina (35)	1,383,281	768,243	615,038	1,602,056	864,846	737,210
South Dakota (19)	3,335,563	1,633,924	1,701,639	3,683,512	2,050,747	1,632,765
Tennessee (30)	2,171,600	1,199,891	971,709	2,371,873	1,374,213	997,660
Texas (2)	12,929,651	4,817,398	8,112,253	13,053,234	5,295,205	7,758,029
Utah (37).	826,942	229,841	597,101	873,143	227,004	646,139
Vermont (41).	478,746	88,642	390,104	534,666	97,609	437,057
Virginia (29).	2,194,166	784,735	1,409,431	2,378,146	900,163	1,477,983
Washington (13)	4,768,986	3,143,459	1,625,527	5,680,980	4,016,590	1,664,390
West Virginia (46)	400,384	69,406	330,978	388,170	79,979	308,191
Wisconsin (10).	5,378,700	1,417,171	3,961,529	6,061,542	1,773,464	4,288,078
Wyoming (40)	783,407	160,315	623,092	661,979	184,338	477,641
United States	**$180,775,019**	**$92,645,620**	**$88,129,399**	**$202,338,990**	**$109,424,778**	**$92,914,212**

(1) States ranked for 1996.

Value of U.S. Agricultural Exports and Imports, 1976-96

Source: Economic Research Service, U.S. Dept. of Agriculture

(in billions of dollars, except percent)

Year	Trade balance	Exports	Percentage of all exports	Imports	Percentage of all imports	Year	Trade balance	Exports	Percentage of all exports	Imports	Percentage of all imports
1976 . .	$12.3	$22.7	20	$10.5	9	1987. . .	$7.2	$27.9	12	$20.7	5
1977 . .	10.6	24.0	20	13.4	9	1988. . .	14.3	35.3	12	21.0	5
1978 . .	13.4	27.3	21	13.9	8	1989. . .	18.1	39.7	12	21.6	5
1979 . .	15.8	32.0	19	16.2	8	1990. . .	17.7	40.4	11	22.7	5
1980 . .	23.2	40.5	19	17.3	7	1991. . .	15.1	37.8	10	22.7	5
1981 . .	26.4	43.8	19	17.3	7	1992. . .	18.2	40.6	10	24.5	5
1982 . .	23.6	39.1	18	15.5	6	1993. . .	18.3	42.9	10	24.6	4
1983 . .	18.5	34.8	18	16.3	7	1994. . .	17.4	44.0	9	26.6	4
1984 . .	19.1	38.0	18	18.9	6	1995. . .	24.9	54.7	10	29.9	4
1985 . .	11.5	31.2	15	19.7	6	1996. . .	27.3	59.9	10	32.6	4
1986 . .	5.4	26.3	13	20.9	6						

Farm Business Real Estate Debt Outstanding, by Lender Groups,[1] 1960-95

Source: Economic Research Service, U.S.Dept. of Agriculture

(in thousands of dollars)

Dec. 31	Total farm real estate debt[2]	Amounts held by principal lender groups				
		Farm Credit System[2]	Farm Services Agency[3]	Life insurance companies[4]	All operating banks	Other[5]
1960	$11,309,593	$2,222,301	$623,895	$2,651,587	$1,355,733	$4,456,068
1970	27,505,932	6,420,357	2,179,873	5,122,291	3,328,876	10,454,540
1980	89,692,429	33,224,684	7,435,059	11,997,922	7,765,058	29,269,705
1985	100,076,120	42,168,554	9,820,913	11,272,689	10,731,881	26,082,096
1986	90,407,602	35,592,540	9,713,096	10,377,063	11,942,258	22,782,645
1987	82,398,048	30,646,143	9,430,087	9,355,026	13,541,447	19,425,345
1988	77,832,498	28,445,452	8,979,749	9,039,395	14,433,688	16,934,218
1989	75,978,245	26,895,927	8,203,215	9,113,109	15,685,485	16,080,503
1990	74,731,876	25,924,490	7,639,490	9,703,958	16,288,128	15,175,805
1991	74,943,896	25,305,300	7,040,851	9,545,804	17,416,527	15,631,629
1992	75,421,266	25,407,547	6,394,446	8,765,021	18,756,852	16,095,415
1993	76,042,688	24,901,858	5,838,438	8,986,288	19,596,382	16,719,722
1994	77,679,834	24,596,715	5,465,063	9,025,132	21,079,145	17,513,779
1995	79,286,915	24,851,298	5,055,018	9,091,957	22,276,504	18,012,138

(1) Figures revised as of 1997; exclude operator households. (2) Includes data for joint stock land banks and real estate loans by Agricultural Credit Assn. (3) Includes loans made directly by Farm Services Agency for farm ownership, soil and water loans to individuals, Native American tribe land acquisition, grazing associations, and half of economic emergency loans. Also includes loans for rural housing on farm tracts and labor housing. (4) American Council of Life Insurance. (5) Estimated by ERS, USDA. Includes Commodity Credit Corporation storage and drying facility loans.

Grain, Hay, Potato, Cotton, Soybean, Tobacco Production, by State, 1996

Source: National Agricultural Statistics Service, U.S. Dept. of Agriculture

1996 State	Barley (1,000 bu)	Corn, grain (1,000 bu)	Cotton lint (1,000 b)	All hay (1,000 t)	Oats (1,000 bu)	Potatoes (1,000 cwt)	Soybeans (1,000 bu)	Tobacco (1,000 lb)	All wheat (1,000 bu)
Alabama.	—	22,960	789.0	1,752	900	1,309	10,710	—	3,520
Alaska	—	—	—	—	—	—	—	—	—
Arizona	5,670	7,000	778.0	1,347	—	2,475	—	—	16,090
Arkansas	—	28,750	1,636.0	2,310	1,800	—	112,000	—	66,960
California	13,200	35,200	2,390.0	8,008	2,250	15,651	—	—	51,750
Colorado.	9,936	133,480	—	4,054	1,820	31,890	—	—	75,500
Connecticut	—	NE	—	162	—	—	—	3,795	—
Delaware	1,564	21,450	—	64	—	1,475	7,595	—	4,134
Florida	—	9,856	130.4	624	—	9,613	1,056	20,100	380
Georgia	—	49,875	2,079.0	1,680	2,240	—	10,140	113,620	16,800
Hawaii	—	—	—	—	—	—	—	—	—
Idaho.	53,290	5,400	—	4,760	1,875	139,960	—	—	119,200
Illinois	—	1,468,800	—	3,040	4,620	1,650	398,925	—	41,800
Indiana.	—	670,350	—	2,020	1,600	1,352	203,680	14,972	27,360
Iowa	—	1,718,100	—	5,320	12,920	315	415,800	—	1,575
Kansas.	363	357,200	4.1	7,010	4,160	—	74,000	—	255,200
Kentucky	1,480	148,800	—	5,700	—	—	44,840	395,542	28,090
Louisiana	—	65,375	1,286.0	837	—	—	35,640	—	5,590
Maine	—	NE	—	336	2,100	21,175	—	—	—
Maryland	2,989	64,635	—	698	434	380	17,760	10,000	11,804
Massachusetts	—	NE	—	190	—	676	—	1,212	—
Michigan.	1,200	216,200	—	4,190	3,600	13,800	46,760	—	23,940
Minnesota.	33,280	868,750	—	5,998	15,120	24,600	224,200	—	102,382
Mississippi	—	61,710	1,876.0	2,000	—	—	54,250	—	11,270
Missouri	—	355,100	591.0	6,920	1,537	1,633	149,850	6,021	48,750
Montana	51,600	2,055	—	4,920	2,000	3,213	—	—	176,710
Nebraska	901	1,186,900	—	7,445	7,455	5,887	135,450	—	73,500
Nevada	375	—	—	1,505	—	3,160	—	—	1,650
New Hampshire	—	NE	—	117	—	—	—	—	—
New Jersey	180	11,844	—	269	—	663	4,403	—	1,748
New Mexico.	—	14,700	84.0	1,577	—	3,964	—	—	4,070
New York	—	67,410	—	3,468	4,275	7,980	—	—	6,450
North Carolina	1,300	85,500	1,002.0	1,145	1,200	3,338	34,800	585,542	25,960
North Dakota	143,000	65,520	—	4,825	19,000	28,820	24,505	—	395,130
Ohio	—	305,250	—	3,400	5,130	1,275	157,150	12,640	51,870
Oklahoma	69	24,650	134.0	5,045	600	—	7,410	—	93,100
Oregon.	9,600	5,445	—	3,244	3,395	31,684	—	—	67,605
Pennsylvania	5,025	127,330	—	4,585	7,560	4,208	11,400	15,464	9,120
Rhode Island	—	NE	—	21	—	212	—	—	—
South Carolina	200	30,020	455.0	560	1,620	—	13,500	117,810	12,150
South Dakota	6,380	370,000	—	8,200	21,600	1,596	90,780	—	139,270
Tennessee	—	78,880	675.0	3,811	—	—	40,250	109,888	17,600
Texas	374	201,600	4,345.0	7,815	3,400	3,385	7,020	—	75,400
Utah	8,200	2,730	—	2,516	648	1,176	—	—	7,760
Vermont	—	NE	—	507	—	—	—	—	—
Virginia.	5,100	39,060	159.0	2,998	—	1,800	16,320	103,543	14,575
Washington	27,280	22,200	—	3,140	1,120	94,990	—	—	182,670
West Virginia	—	4,200	—	1,066	150	—	—	2,040	495
Wisconsin	3,975	333,000	—	6,050	17,400	31,590	32,190	5,145	5,725
Wyoming	10,320	6,150	—	2,208	1,696	224	—	—	7,110
United States	**396,851**	**9,293,435**	**18,413.5**	**149,457**	**155,225**	**497,119**	**2,382,364**	**1,517,334**	**2,281,763**

NE = Not estimated. bu = bushels, b = bales (480-lbs), t = tons, cwt = hundredweight.

Production of Principal U.S. Crops, 1987-96

Source: National Agricultural Statistics Service, U.S. Dept. of Agriculture

Year	Corn for grain (1,000 bu)	Oats (1,000 bu)	Barley (1,000 bu)	Sorghum for grain (1,000 bu)	All wheat (1,000 bu)	Rye (1,000 bu)	Flax-seed (1,000 bu)	Cotton lint (1,000 b)	Cotton-seed (1,000 t)
1987	7,131,300	373,713	521,499	730,809	2,107,685	19,526	7,444	14,760.9	5,769.2
1988	4,928,681	217,600	289,994	576,686	1,812,201	14,689	1,615	15,412.5	6,061.8
1989	7,525,493	373,587	404,203	615,420	2,036,618	13,647	1,215	12,196.6	4,677.4
1990	7,934,028	357,524	422,196	573,303	2,736,428	10,176	3,812	15,505.4	5,968.5
1991	7,475,480	243,451	464,326	584,860	1,981,139	9,761	6,200	17,614.3	6,925.5
1992	9,476,698	294,229	455,090	875,022	2,466,798	11,440	3,288	16,219.5	6,230.1
1993	6,336,470	206,770	398,041	534,172	2,396,440	10,340	3,480	16,134.6	6,343.2
1994	10,102,735	229,008	374,862	649,206	2,320,981	11,341	2,922	19,662.0	7,603.9
1995	7,373,876	162,027	359,562	460,373	2,182,591	10,064	2,211	17,532.2	6,848.7
1996	9,293,435	155,225	396,851	802,974	2,281,763	9,016	1,602	18,413.5	7,143.5

Year	Tobacco (1,000 lb)	All hay (1,000 t)	Beans, dry edible (1,000 cwt)	Peas, dry edible (1,000 cwt)	Peanuts[1] (1,000 lb)	Soy-beans[2] (1,000 bu)	Potatoes (1,000 cwt)	Sweet potatoes (1,000 cwt)
1987	1,188,868	147,319	26,031	3,385	3,616,010	1,938,087	385,774	11,611
1988	1,369,500	126,010	19,253	3,868	3,980,917	1,548,841	356,438	10,945
1989	1,367,188	145,512	23,729	3,883	3,989,995	1,923,666	370,444	11,358
1990	1,626,380	146,820	32,379	2,372	3,602,770	1,925,947	402,110	12,594
1991	1,664,372	153,325	33,765	3,715	4,926,570	1,986,539	417,622	11,203
1992	1,721,671	146,903	22,615	2,535	4,284,416	2,190,354	425,367	12,005
1993	1,613,319	146,799	21,913	3,292	3,392,415	1,870,958	428,693	11,053
1994	1,582,896	150,060	29,028	2,255	4,247,455	2,516,694	467,924	13,395
1995	1,268,538	154,166	30,812	4,609	4,247,455	2,176,814	443,606	12,883
1996	1,517,334	149,457	27,354	2,282	3,661,205	2,382,364	497,119	13,456

Year	Rice (1,000 cwt)	Sugar-cane (1,000 t)	Sugar beets (1,000 t)	Pecans (1,000 t)	Almonds (1,000 t)	Wal-nuts (1,000 t)	Hazel-nuts[3] (1,000 t)	Oranges[4] (1,000 bx)	Grape-fruit[2] (1,000 bx)
1987	129,603	29,218	28,072	131.1	519.0	247.0	21.8	181,175	63,775
1988	159,897	29,904	24,810	154.1	451.9	209.0	16.5	200,250	68,700
1989	154,487	29,426	25,131	125.3	394.7	229.0	13.0	209,050	69,500
1990	156,088	28,136	27,513	102.5	519.7	227.0	21.7	184,415	49,300
1991	157,457	30,252	28,203	149.5	385.8	259.0	25.5	178,950	55,500
1992	179,658	30,363	29,143	83.0	454.4	203.0	27.7	209,610	55,265
1993	156,110	31,101	26,249	182.5	401.0	260.0	41.0	255,760	68,375
1994	197,779	30,929	31,853	99.5	584.3	232.0	21.1	240,450	65,100
1995	173,871	30,944	27,954	134.0	304.3	234.0	39.0	263,605	71,050
1996	171,321	29,462	26,680	110.8	412.0	208.0	19.0	271,790	66,200

NA=Not available. (1) Harvested for nuts. (2) Harvested for beans. (3) Formerly called filberts. (4) Crop year ending in year cited.

Principal U.S. Crops: Area Planted and Harvested, 1994-96

Source: National Agricultural Statistics Service, U.S. Dept. of Agriculture

(in thousand acres)

State	Area planted[1] 1994	1995	1996	Area harvested[1] 1994	1995	1996	State	Area planted[1] 1994	1995	1996	Area harvested[1] 1994	1995	1996
AL	2,289	2,204	2,274	2,170	2,093	2,190	NE	19,043	18,280	18,911	18,619	17,769	18,327
AZ	750	795	835	744	787	831	NV	497	516	525	491	512	522
AR	8,360	8,435	8,680	8,160	8,188	8,535	NH	98	85	84	96	83	82
CA	5,119	5,351	5,212	4,674	4,791	4,771	NJ	458	452	427	410	413	394
CO	6,103	6,104	6,456	5,632	5,748	5,511	NM	1,252	1,282	1,319	985	869	936
CT	130	112	120	123	107	115	NY	3,119	3,045	3,018	3,071	2,981	2,941
DE	510	507	501	494	499	493	NC	4,731	4,644	4,752	4,489	4,341	4,521
FL	1,090	1,079	1,108	1,048	1,036	1,083	ND	21,714	20,706	22,651	20,719	20,114	22,237
GA	4,276	4,237	4,346	3,874	3,862	3,999	OH	10,408	10,025	10,173	10,277	9,884	10,011
HI	67	50	43	67	50	43	OK	10,826	10,661	11,341	8,788	8,628	8,967
ID	4,402	4,483	4,502	4,244	4,306	4,378	OR	2,318	2,436	2,456	2,240	2,292	2,362
IL	23,801	23,221	23,926	23,393	22,526	23,183	PA	4,154	2,146	4,140	4,063	4,050	4,035
IN	12,237	11,942	12,648	12,071	11,785	12,395	RI	12	11	11	12	11	11
IA	24,207	23,502	24,247	23,967	22,872	24,057	SC	2,042	1,973	1,971	1,926	1,871	1,891
KS	22,540	22,428	24,171	21,724	21,363	20,899	SD	16,391	14,334	16,911	15,714	13,947	16,236
KY	5,558	5,716	5,849	5,353	5,461	5,645	TN	4,658	4,897	4,999	4,396	4,535	4,703
LA	3,896	3,857	4,035	3,810	3,786	3,994	TX	21,817	22,600	24,361	17,529	17,870	18,079
ME	349	364	327	339	355	316	UT	1,114	1,099	1,139	1,050	1,042	1,070
MD	1,569	1,548	1,574	1,506	1,463	1,520	VT	418	387	345	409	379	326
MA	141	134	131	135	131	125	VA	2,906	2,910	2,937	2,749	2,749	2,794
MI	7,013	6,790	7,023	6,815	6,647	6,774	WA	4,057	4,130	4,461	3,922	3,997	4,378
MN	20,077	19,577	19,971	19,534	18,972	19,587	WV	646	650	657	636	642	646
MS	4,881	4,850	4,880	4,813	4,739	4,790	WI	8,438	8,195	8,161	8,074	7,793	7,849
MO	12,674	12,055	13,275	12,466	11,687	12,794	WY	1,713	1,898	1,864	1,637	1,835	1,816
MT	9,357	9,697	10,764	8,988	9,245	10,332	U.S.[2]	324,256	318,458	334,562	308,474	301,186	313,533

(1) Crops included in area planted are corn, sorghum, oats, barley, winter wheat, rye, durum wheat, other spring wheat, rice, soybeans, peanuts, sunflower, cotton, dry edible beans, potatoes, and sugar beets. Harvested acreage is used for all hay, tobacco, and sugarcane in computing total area planted. Includes double-cropped acres and unharvested small grains planted as cover crops. (2) State figures do not add to U.S. totals because of sunflower and sugar-beet unallocated acreage.

Average Prices Received by U.S. Farmers, 1940-96

Source: Natl. Agricultural Statistics Service, U.S. Dept. of Agriculture

Figures below represent dollars per 100 lb for hogs, beef cattle, veal calves, sheep, lamb, and milk (wholesale); dollars per head for milk cows; cents per lb for chickens, broilers, turkeys, and wool; cents per dozen for eggs; weighted calendar year prices for livestock and livestock products other than wool. For 1943-63, wool prices are weighted on marketing year basis. The marketing year was changed in 1964 from a calendar year to a Dec.-Nov. basis for hogs, chickens, broilers, and eggs.

Year	Hogs	Cattle (beef)	Calves (veal)	Sheep	Lambs	Milk cows	Milk	Chickens (excl. broilers)	Broilers	Turkeys	Eggs	Wool
1940	5.39	7.56	8.83	3.95	8.10	61	1.82	13.0	17.3	15.2	18.0	28.4
1950	18.00	23.30	26.30	11.60	25.10	198	3.89	22.2	27.4	32.8	36.3	62.1
1960	15.30	20.40	22.90	5.61	17.90	223	4.21	12.2	16.9	25.4	36.1	42.0
1970	22.70	27.10	34.50	7.51	26.40	332	5.71	9.1	13.6	22.6	39.1	35.4
1975	46.10	32.20	27.20	11.30	42.10	412	8.75	9.9	26.3	34.8	54.5	44.8
1980	38.00	62.40	76.80	21.30	63.60	1,190	13.05	11.0	27.7	41.3	56.3	88.1
1984	47.10	57.30	59.90	16.40	60.10	895	13.46	15.9	33.7	48.9	72.3	79.5
1985	44.00	53.70	62.10	23.90	67.70	860	12.76	14.8	30.1	49.1	57.1	63.3
1986	49.30	52.60	61.10	25.60	69.00	820	12.51	12.5	34.5	47.1	61.6	66.8
1987	51.20	61.10	78.50	29.50	77.60	920	12.54	11.0	28.7	34.8	54.9	91.7
1988	42.30	66.60	89.20	25.60	69.10	990	12.26	9.2	33.1	38.6	52.8	138.0
1989	42.50	69.50	90.80	24.40	66.10	1,030	13.56	14.9	36.6	40.9	68.9	124.0
1990	53.70	74.60	95.60	23.20	55.50	1,160	13.74	9.3	32.6	39.4	70.9	80.0
1991	49.10	72.70	98.00	19.70	52.20	1,100	12.27	7.1	30.8	38.4	67.8	55.0
1992	41.60	71.30	89.00	25.80	59.50	1,130	13.15	8.6	31.8	37.7	57.6	74.0
1993	45.20	72.60	91.20	28.60	64.40	1,160	12.84	10.0	34.0	39.0	63.4	51.0
1994	39.90	66.70	87.20	30.90	65.60	1,170	13.01	7.6	35.0	40.4	61.4	78.0
1995	40.50	61.80	73.10	28.00	78.20	1,130	12.78	6.5	34.4	41.6	62.4	104.0
1996	51.90	58.70	58.40	29.90	82.20	1,090	14.75	6.6	38.1	43.3	75.0	70.0

Figures below represent cents per lb for cotton, apples, and peanuts; dollars per bushel for oats, wheat, corn, barley, and soybeans; dollars per 100 lb for rice, sorghum, and potatoes; dollars per ton for cottonseed and baled hay; weighted crop year prices. The marketing year is described as follows: apples, June-May; wheat, oats, barley, hay, and potatoes, July-June; cotton, rice, peanuts, and cottonseed, Aug.-July; soybeans, Sept.-Aug.; and corn and sorghum grain, Oct.-Sept.

Year	Corn	Wheat	Upland cotton*	Oats	Barley	Rice	Soy-beans	Sor-ghum	Pea-nuts	Cotton-seed	Hay	Pota-toes	Apples
1940	0.62	0.67	9.8	0.30	0.39	1.80	0.89	0.87	3.7	21.70	9.78	0.85	NA
1950	1.52	2.00	39.9	0.79	1.19	5.09	2.47	1.88	10.9	86.60	21.10	1.50	NA
1960	1.00	1.74	30.1	0.60	0.84	4.55	2.13	1.49	10.0	42.50	21.70	2.00	2.7
1970	1.33	1.33	21.9	0.62	0.97	5.17	2.85	2.04	12.8	56.40	26.10	2.21	6.5
1975	2.54	3.55	51.1	1.45	2.42	8.35	4.92	4.21	19.0	97.00	52.10	4.48	8.8
1980	3.11	3.91	74.4	1.79	2.86	12.80	7.57	5.25	25.1	129.00	71.00	6.55	12.1
1984	2.63	3.39	58.7	1.67	2.29	8.04	5.84	4.15	27.9	99.50	72.70	5.69	15.5
1985	2.23	3.08	56.8	1.23	1.98	6.53	5.05	3.45	24.4	66.00	67.60	3.92	17.3
1986	1.50	2.42	51.5	1.21	1.61	3.75	4.78	2.45	29.2	80.00	59.70	5.03	19.1
1987	1.94	2.57	63.7	1.56	1.81	7.27	5.88	3.04	28.0	82.50	65.00	4.38	12.7
1988	2.54	3.72	55.6	2.61	2.80	6.83	7.42	4.05	28.0	118.00	85.20	6.02	17.4
1989	2.36	3.72	63.6	1.49	2.42	7.35	5.69	3.75	28.0	105.00	85.40	7.36	13.9
1990	2.28	2.61	67.1	1.14	2.14	6.68	5.74	3.79	34.7	121.00	80.60	6.08	20.9
1991	2.37	3.00	56.8	1.21	2.10	7.58	5.58	4.01	28.3	71.00	71.20	4.96	25.1
1992	2.07	3.24	53.7	1.32	2.04	5.89	5.56	3.38	30.0	97.50	74.30	5.52	19.5
1993	2.50	3.26	58.1	1.36	1.99	7.98	6.40	4.13	30.4	113.00	84.70	6.18	18.4
1994	2.26	3.45	72.0	1.22	2.03	6.78	5.48	3.80	28.9	101.00	86.70	5.58	18.6
1995	3.24	4.55	75.4	1.67	2.89	9.15	6.72	5.69	29.3	106.00	82.20	6.77	24.0
1996	2.70	4.30	70.6	1.90	2.75	9.50	6.85	4.20	26.4	130.00	93.00	5.11	20.9

*Beginning in 1964, 480-lb net weight bales. NA = Not available.

Grain Storage Capacity at Principal U.S. Grain Centers, Aug. 1997

Source: Chicago Board of Trade Market Information Dept.

(in bushels)

	Capacity
Atlantic Coast	12,000,000
Great Lakes	
Toledo, OH	63,100,000
Duluth, MN	60,000,000
Chicago, IL	14,700,000
Buffalo, NY	15,200,000
Milwaukee, WI	NA
River Points	
Kansas City, MO	95,200,000
Minneapolis, MN	75,000,000
St. Joseph, MO	14,900,000
Atchison, KS	23,400,000
St. Louis, MO	9,100,000
Omaha-Council Bluffs, NE	8,400,000
Sioux City, IA	8,600,000

	Capacity
Southwest	
Texas High Plains	58,800,000
Fort Worth, TX	68,000,000
Enid, OK	NA
Gulf Points	
South Mississippi Region	45,000,000
Texas Gulf	38,800,000
Plains	
Topeka, KS	50,700,000
Salina, KS	50,600,000
Wichita, KS.	34,300,000
Lincoln, NE.	33,000,000
Hutchinson, KS.	29,600,000
Hastings-Grand Island, NE.	47,800,000
Pacific NW	
Puget Sound (incl. Portland)	32,100,000
California Ports	NA

NA= Not available.

Atlantic Coast — Albany, NY; Philadelphia, PA; Baltimore, MD; Norfolk, VA. **Gulf Points, South Mississippi Region** — New Orleans, Baton Rouge, Ama, Belle Chasse, LA; Mobile, AL. **Texas Gulf** — Houston, Galveston, Beaumont, Port Arthur, Corpus Christi, Brownsville, TX. **Pacific NW** — Seattle, Tacoma, WA; Portland, OR; Columbia River. **Texas High Plains** — Amarillo, Lubbock, Hereford, Plainview, TX.

World Wheat, Rice, and Corn Production, 1996

Source: UN Food and Agriculture Organization

(in thousands of metric tons)

Country	Wheat	Rice	Corn	Country	Wheat	Rice	Corn
Afghanistan........	1,700F	300F	360F	Laos	—	1,300	55F
Argentina	15,200	974	10,466	Madagascar........	10F	2,600	180
Australia	23,497	951	317	Malaysia	—	2,065*	45*
Austria	1,239	—	1,544	Mexico...........	3,563	455	17,300*
Bangladesh........	1,369	28,008	2F	Morocco...........	5,916	53	235
Belgium-Lux.	1,910	—	214	Myanmar........	109	20,865*	247*
Brazil	3,302	10,035	31,975	Nepal...........	1,013	3,579	1,331
Bulgaria	1,788*	8*	1,198*	Netherlands	1,269	—	87
Cambodia.........	—	3,390	60	New Zealand	261	—	160
Canada..........	30,495	—	7,300	Nigeria..........	41	3,122	5,667
Chile............	1,227	154	932	Pakistan..........	16,907	5,551*	1,300F
China	109,000F	190,100F	119,350F	Panama..........	—	230*	108F
Colombia	72	1,787	1,058	Peru	148	1,203	1,054
Croatia	741	—	1,883	Philippines	—	11,284	4,151
Cuba	—	223F	85F	Poland..........	8,792	—	363
Czech Rep........	3,732	—	143	Portugal.........	432	137	800
Denmark.........	4,834	—	—	Romania	3,168	25F	9,600
Ecuador	23	1,346	855	Russia	34,900	500F	1,100
Egypt	5,735	4,895	5,165	Slovakia	2,112	—	650
Ethiopia	1,970F	—	3,250F	South Africa	2,753*	3F	10,351*
Finland	457	—	—	Spain...........	6,002	817	3,996
France	35,946	116	14,449	Sri Lanka	—	2,684F	31F
Germany	18,922	—	2,926	Sweden	2,030	—	—
Greece	1,841	220*	1,814	Switzerland	700	—	215
Hungary	3,924	15F	5,000*	Syria	4,255*	—	200*
India...........	62,620*	120,012*	8,660*	Thailand.........	8F	21,800*	4,361*
Indonesia	—	51,165	8,925	Turkey..........	18,515	280	2,000
Iran............	11,200*	2,300*	600F	Turkmenistan	230	45*	80*
Iraq............	1,000*	270*	85F	Ukraine	13,547	82	1,870
Ireland	771	—	—	United Kingdom ...	16,031	—	—
Israel	150	—	3F	United States	62,099	7,771	236,064
Italy	8,191	1,424	8,712	Uruguay..........	628	868	119
Japan	550*	13,000F	—	Uzbekistan	1,564*	480*	200*
Kazakhstan.......	7,678	226	122	Venezuela	—	733	1,050
Kenya	350*	60F	2,223*	Vietnam	—	26,300	990F
Korea, North......	100F	2,800F	2,000F	Yugoslavia	1,850*	—	5,200*
Korea, South......	10*	6,284*	70*	**World, total**	**584,874**	**562,260**	**576,821**

Note: * Unofficial figure. F=Food and Agriculture Organization (FAO) estimate. Where production is small or nonexistent, — is indicated. Because not all countries are reported on this table, country totals do not add to world totals.

Wheat, Rice, and Corn—Exports and Imports of 10 Leading Countries

Source: UN Food and Agriculture Organization

(in thousands of metric tons)

Leading exporters	Exports[1] Wheat			Leading importers	Imports[1] Wheat		
	1993	1994	1995		1993	1994	1995
U.S.	35,666	30,571	32,420	China	7,332	8,079	11,590
Canada...........	18,210	21,378	16,960	Japan	5,814	6,352	5,965
France	18,259	12,670	16,310	Brazil...........	5,615	6,123	5,800
Australia	9,487	12,730	7,818	Italy...........	5,023	4,880	5,079
Argentina	5,777	5,172	6,913	Egypt	4,080	6,597	5,070
Germany...........	3,812	5,377	3,682	Indonesia	2,526	3,297	4,054
Hungary	94	759	2,765	Algeria..........	2,588	3,800	3,505
United Kingdom.....	3,898	3,493	2,669	Iran	2,450	3,960	3,100
Kazakhstan........	—	1,060	2,486	Spain	1,912	2,049	2,757
Denmark..........	1,332	988	1,540	Belgium-Lux.	2,169	1,937	2,719
	Rice				**Rice**		
	1993	1994	1995		1993	1994	1995
Thailand	4,989	4,859	6,198	Indonesia	24	630	3,158
India.	768	891	5,512	China	100	517	1,646
U.S.	2,680	2,822	3,084	Iran............	1,159	475	1,300
Vietnam	2,680	2,822	2,308	Brazil..........	701	987	875
Pakistan	1,032	984	1,852	Bangladesh	21	66	813
Australia	482	585	541	Korea (North).....	112	60	654
Italy	574	619	524	Saudi Arabia	577	434	605
Uruguay	505	408	462	South Africa	385	431	511
Myanmar..........	209	643	392	Malaysia	389	341	427
Argentina	263	217	390	Senegal.........	363	348	420
	Corn				**Corn**		
	1993	1994	1995		1993	1994	1995
U.S.	40,365	35,877	60,240	Japan	16,863	15,930	16,580
France	7,758	8,013	6,474	China	5,466	5,601	11,702
Argentina	4,871	4,154	6,001	Korea (South). ...	6,207	5,749	9,035
South Africa	216	4,000	1,340	Spain	2,401	2,339	2,912
Hungary	169	181	601	Mexico	211	2,747	2,687
Canada...........	357	381	444	Egypt	2,148	2,021	2,425
Belgium-Lux........	414	488	443	Malaysia	2,058	1,969	2,383
Zimbabwe	215	1,200	288	Belgium-Lux......	1,284	1,557	1,815
Germany..........	219	308	244	Netherlands	1,136	2,171	1,590
Paraguay	2	74	203	United Kingdom ...	1,508	1,602	1,501

(1) By marketing years.

World Commercial Catch of Fish, Crustaceans, and Mollusks,[1] by Major Fishing Areas, 1990-95[2]

Source: U.S. Dept. of Commerce, Natl. Oceanic and Atmospheric Admin., Natl. Marine Fisheries Service

(in thousands of metric tons; live weight)

Area	1990	1991	1992	1993	1994	1995
Marine						
Pacific Ocean	52,939	52,358	52,844	54,334	59,975	59,185
Atlantic Ocean	23,552	23,792	24,372	23,748	23,720	24,690
Indian Ocean	6,199	6,879	7,356	7,857	7,818	8,031
Total	**82,690**	**83,029**	**84,572**	**85,939**	**91,513**	**91,906**
Inland Waters						
N. America	552	551	583	578	573	549
S. America	335	331	352	376	391	415
Europe	511	493	504	497	510	528
Former USSR	988	764	682	568	490	489
Asia	10,402	10,798	11,627	13,336	15,188	17,091
Africa	1,930	1,808	1,832	1,855	1,849	1,908
Oceania	24	23	25	23	24	24
Total	**14,742**	**14,768**	**15,605**	**17,233**	**19,025**	**21,004**
Grand total	**97,432**	**97,797**	**100,177**	**103,172**	**110,538**	**112,910**

(1) Does not include marine mammals and aquatic plants. (2) Revised back to 1991.

Commercial Catch of Fish, Crustaceans, Mollusks,[1] by Selected Country, 1990-95[1]

Source: U.S. Dept. of Commerce, Natl. Oceanic and Atmospheric Admin., Natl. Marine Fisheries Service

(in thousands of metric tons; live weight)

Country	1990	1991	1992	1993	1994	1995
China	12,095	13,125	15,007	17,568	20,719	24,433
Peru	6,875	6,888	7,503	9,010	11,997	8,943
Chile	5,195	6,006	6,502	6,035	7,838	7,591
Japan	10,354	9,301	8,502	8,081	7,396	6,758
United States[3]	5,868	5,487	5,600	5,934	5,922	5,634
India	3,794	4,045	4,233	4,546	4,738	4,904
Russia	NA	7,047	5,611	4,461	3,781	4,374
Indonesia	3,044	3,352	3,439	3,685	3,917	4,118
Thailand	2,786	2,972	3,246	3,395	3,537	3,502
Norway	NA	2,173	2,561	2,562	2,551	2,808

(1) Does not include marine mammals and aquatic plants. (2) Revised back to 1991. (3) Includes weight of clam, oyster, scallop, and other mollusk shells. This weight is not included in U.S. landings statistics shown elsewhere. NA = Not available.

U.S. Commercial Landings of Fish and Shellfish, 1986-96[1]

Source: U.S. Dept. of Commerce, Natl. Oceanic and Atmospheric Admin., Natl. Marine Fisheries Service

Year	Landings for human food		Landings for industrial purposes[2]		Total	
	mil lb	mil dollars	mil lb	mil dollars	mil lb	mil dollars
1986	3,393	$2,641	2,638	$122	6,031	$2,763
1987	3,946	2,979	2,950	136	6,896	3,115
1988	4,588	3,362	2,604	158	7,192	3,520
1989	6,204	3,111	2,259	127	8,463	3,238
1990	7,041	3,366	2,363	156	9,404	3,522
1991	7,031	3,169	2,453	139	9,484	3,308
1992	7,618	3,531	2,019	147	9,637	3,678
1993	8,214	3,317	2,253	154	10,467	3,471
1994	7,936	3,751	2,525	95	10,461	3,846
1995	7,667	3,625	2,121	145	9,788	3,770
1996	7,475	3,355	2,090	132	9,565	3,487

Note: Data do not include landings outside the 50 states or products of aquaculture, except oysters and clams.

(1) Statistics on landings are shown in round weight for all items except univalve and bivalve mollusks such as clams, oysters, and scallops, which are shown in weight of meats (excluding the shell). All data are preliminary. (2) Processed into meal, oil, solubles, and shell products or used as bait or animal food.

U.S. Domestic Landings, by Regions, 1995-96[1]

Source: U.S. Dept. of Commerce, Natl. Oceanic and Atmospheric Admin., Natl. Marine Fisheries Service

Region	1995		1996	
	1,000 lb	1,000 dollars	1,000 lb	1,000 dollars
New England	592,665	$580,957	641,821	$564,169
Middle Atlantic	240,413	179,747	241,936	181,869
Chesapeake	845,632	174,229	728,830	158,736
South Atlantic	277,035	238,112	268,990	209,407
Gulf	1,464,718	724,619	1,496,875	680,304
Pacific Coast and Alaska .	6,307,767	1,756,691	6,129,410	1,610,508
Great Lakes	29,432	21,413	25,156	17,432
Hawaii	29,892	59,847	31,870	64,288
Total	**9,787,554**	**$3,735,615**	**9,564,888**	**$3,486,713**

(1) Landings are reported in round (live) weight for all items except univalve and bivalve mollusks such as clams, oysters, and scallops, which are reported in weight of meats (excluding shell). Landings for Mississippi River Drainage Area states are not available.

EMPLOYMENT

Employment and Unemployment in the U.S., 1940-96

Source: Bureau of Labor Statistics, U.S. Dept. of Labor

(civilian labor force, persons 16 years of age and older; annual averages; in thousands)

Year[1][2]	Employed	Unemployed	Unemployment rate	Year[1]	Employed	Unemployed	Unemployment rate
1940[2]	47,520	8,120	14.6%	1988	114,988	6,701	5.5%
1950	58,918	3,288	5.0	1989	117,342	6,528	5.3
1960	65,778	3,852	5.5	1990[3]	118,793	7,047	5.6
1970	78,678	4,093	4.9	1991	117,718	8,628	6.8
1980	99,303	7,637	7.1	1992	118,482	9,613	7.5
1984	105,005	8,539	7.5	1993	120,259	8,940	6.9
1985	107,150	8,312	7.2	1994[4]	123,060	7,996	6.1
1986	109,597	8,237	7.0	1995	124,900	7,404	5.6
1987	112,440	7,425	6.2	1996	126,708	7,236	5.4

(1) **Early unemployment rates:** 1915, 9.7; 1916, 4.8; 1917, 4.8; 1918, 1.4; 1919, 2.3; 1920, 4.0; 1921, 11.9; 1922, 7.6; 1923, 3.2; 1924, 5.5; 1925, 4.0; 1926, 1.9; 1927, 4.1; 1928, 4.4; 1929, 3.2; 1930, 8.7; 1931, 15.9; 1932, 23.6; 1933, 24.9; 1934, 21.7; 1935, 20.1; 1936, 16.9; 1937, 14.3; 1938, 19.0; 1939, 17.2. (2) Persons 14 years of age and older. (3) Beginning in 1990, data incorporate 1990 census-based population controls, adjusted for the estimated undercount. (4) Beginning in 1994, not strictly comparable with prior years, because of a major redesign of the survey used.

Selected Unemployment Insurance Data, by State, 1996

Source: Employment and Training Admin., U.S. Dept. of Labor; state programs only

State	Monetarily eligible claimants	First payments	Final payments	Initial claims	Benefits paid	Average weekly benefit amount	Employers subject to state law
AL	172,016	146,494	32,841	352,883	$206,157,710	$141.63	85,189
AK	48,742	45,116	19,623	103,440	113,246,187	172.04	11,710
AZ	106,978	75,866	25,274	147,471	159,386,045	150.71	93,307
AR	131,451	96,217	27,708	236,174	174,151,929	169.97	57,618
CA	1,505,450	1,178,279	495,418	3,331,628	2,806,175,023	152.44	778,860
CO	110,154	75,363	28,559	140,762	188,959,023	208.11	112,610
CT	133,036	133,086	41,834	228,759	417,787,907	222.25	93,210
DE	30,107	26,755	6,646	55,804	96,445,463	224.08	22,308
DC	22,671	22,488	11,495	35,113	86,480,302	236.21	24,179
FL	334,987	263,956	113,172	473,501	639,231,675	178.34	348,318
GA	277,991	191,862	51,221	373,358	283,557,520	165.50	164,091
HI	50,382	41,056	16,148	98,720	173,196,325	269.85	26,852
ID	56,745	48,788	14,744	120,228	95,759,835	181.65	34,233
IL	401,964	353,757	127,254	718,938	1,220,521,984	213.45	263,531
IN	190,037	128,133	39,301	278,225	233,209,351	186.81	121,255
IA	100,437	78,846	16,590	147,018	178,455,303	200.44	66,599
KS	70,832	54,528	16,137	116,508	113,911,278	202.10	63,800
KY	141,438	119,521	21,824	293,650	220,931,371	170.78	77,571
LA	104,507	76,674	21,570	175,597	142,700,403	127.62	87,982
ME	51,983	47,439	15,167	105,469	103,091,294	170.88	34,517
MD	168,001	117,818	38,667	234,999	339,193,810	194.52	121,711
MA	231,027	192,909	66,032	362,061	719,980,046	254.14	156,453
MI	561,382	403,935	106,131	852,530	946,760,026	204.87	204,600
MN	131,985	117,192	33,253	217,979	338,744,868	234.38	115,865
MS	101,589	70,353	20,496	196,049	128,287,070	140.55	49,533
MO	214,371	147,109	41,981	379,315	286,690,690	154.09	123,911
MT	36,164	29,569	9,424	61,780	59,475,828	165.40	28,378
NE	41,620	29,008	8,812	59,650	50,676,691	161.34	42,595
NV	79,860	55,521	17,943	118,286	144,205,299	194.01	36,331
NH	31,941	23,695	3,827	45,504	39,191,932	153.25	34,993
NJ	357,511	312,370	146,952	567,288	1,356,510,265	254.84	211,210
NM	44,814	30,375	10,243	62,477	73,776,648	157.13	39,551
NY	596,205	541,784	263,380	1,122,048	1,824,318,748	205.78	441,337
NC	350,825	235,074	37,745	858,922	381,766,863	192.74	152,641
ND	18,090	14,663	5,185	27,793	32,339,839	174.83	18,652
OH	356,685	268,939	64,198	615,142	699,761,322	202.44	224,499
OK	63,492	48,568	16,003	125,479	97,729,029	175.31	71,145
OR	165,828	145,835	46,460	363,773	367,260,839	190.53	93,670
PA	567,418	467,434	135,550	1,159,206	1,502,210,748	219.08	235,229
PR	136,998	126,610	62,415	263,067	215,059,292	93.69	46,965
RI	59,048	54,102	22,554	120,536	183,120,078	228.15	30,488
SC	169,228	113,719	25,534	343,408	192,220,173	165.32	79,391
SD	12,305	9,339	1,016	21,440	15,550,388	150.36	21,148
TN	231,349	176,346	54,456	474,162	312,045,433	154.58	105,900
TX	540,637	350,443	177,954	713,770	920,386,899	188.95	365,970
UT	46,201	34,364	8,253	56,514	67,733,683	197.68	44,014
VT	26,608	22,899	4,172	43,065	47,962,310	168.11	19,631
VA	2,148	2,167	1,807	3,078	7,461,539	155.39	n/a
VI	176,929	113,520	27,005	336,012	195,183,693	172.62	149,237
WA	272,730	223,630	76,871	542,320	795,249,361	210.08	165,135
WV	67,614	59,990	11,100	00,080	140,087,009	175.86	38,035
WI	258,779	234,291	43,483	504,788	469,636,256	202.49	116,203
WY	16,321	13,130	4,172	27,610	30,162,239	181.23	17,401
U.S.	**10,177,611**	**7,989,615**	**2,738,963**	**18,509,147**	**20,634,905,504**	**189.45**	**6,169,555**

Unemployment Rates, by Selected Country, 1975-97

Source: Bureau of Labor Statistics, U.S. Dept. of Labor; civilian labor force, seasonally adjusted; Oct. 1997

Time period	U.S.	Canada	Australia	Japan	France	Germany[1]	Italy[2]	Sweden	United Kingdom
1975	8.5	6.9	4.9	1.9	4.2	3.4	3.4	1.6	4.6
1980	7.1	7.5	6.1	2.0	6.5	2.8	4.4	2.0	7.0
1981	7.6	7.6	5.8	2.2	7.6	4.0	4.9	2.5	10.5
1982	9.7	11.0	7.2	2.4	8.3	5.6	5.4	3.1	11.3
1983	9.6	11.9	10.0	2.7	8.6	6.9[3]	5.9	3.5	11.8
1984	7.5	11.3	9.0	2.8	10.0	7.1	5.9	3.1	11.7R
1985	7.2	10.5	8.3	2.6	10.5	7.2	6.0	2.8	11.2
1986	7.0	9.6	8.1	2.8	10.6	6.6	7.5[3]	2.6	11.2
1987	6.2	8.9	8.1	2.9	10.8	6.3	7.9	2.2[3]	10.3
1988	5.5	7.8	7.2	2.5	10.3	6.3	7.9	1.9	8.6
1989	5.3	7.5	6.2	2.3	9.6	5.7	7.8	1.6	7.2R
1990	5.6[3]	8.1	6.9	2.1	9.1	5.0	7.0	1.8	6.9R
1991	6.8	10.4	9.6	2.1	9.6	4.3P	6.9[3]	3.1	8.8R
1992	7.5	11.3	10.8	2.2	10.4[3]	4.6P	7.3P	5.6	10.1
1993	6.9	11.2	10.9	2.5	11.8	5.7P	10.2P[3]	9.3	10.5
1994	6.1[3]	10.4	9.7	2.9	12.3	6.5P	11.3P	9.6	9.7R
1995	5.6	9.5	8.5	3.2	11.8	6.5P	12.0P	9.1	8.7R
1996	5.4	9.7	8.6	3.4	12.6	7.2P	12.1P	9.9	8.2R,P
1st quarter	5.6	9.5	8.5	3.3	12.2	6.9	12.0	9.5	8.3R
2d quarter....	5.4	9.6	8.5	3.5	12.5	7.1	12.5	9.7	8.3R
3d quarter....	5.3	9.8	8.7	3.4	12.7	7.2	11.9	9.9	8.2R
4th quarter ...	5.3	9.9	8.6	3.3	12.8	7.5	12.0	10.3	7.9R
1997									
1st quarter ...	5.3	9.6	8.7	3.3	12.7	7.7	12.3	10.6	7.5R
2d quarter....	4.9	9.4	8.7	3.5	12.7	7.8	12.7	10.6	7.2R

NA=Not available. P=Preliminary. R=Revised. **Note:** For the sake of making comparisions, U.S. unemployment rate concepts were applied to unemployment data collected from Canada, Australia, Japan, France, Germany, Italy, Sweden, and the United Kingdom. Quarterly and monthly figures for France and Germany were calculated by applying annual adjustment factors to current published data and therefore should be viewed as less precise indicators of unemployment under U.S. concepts than the annual figures. (1) All figures for region of former West Germany. (2) Quarterly rates are for the first month of the quarter. (3) As a result of revisions in survey methodology, there are breaks in the data series for the U.S. (1990, 1994), France (1992), Germany (1983), Italy (1986, 1991, 1993), and Sweden (1987); data prior to a survey change are not fully comparable to data released after a survey change.

Employed Persons, by Occupation and Sex, 1995-96

Source: Bureau of Labor Statistics, U.S. Dept. of Labor

(in thousands)

Occupation	Total 16 years and older 1995	Total 16 years and older 1996	Men 16 years and older 1995	Men 16 years and older 1996	Women 16 years and older 1995	Women 16 years and older 1996
Total	124,900	126,708	67,377	68,207	57,523	58,501
Managerial and professional specialty	35,318	36,497	18,378	18,744	16,940	17,754
Executive, administrative, and managerial	17,186	17,746	9,840	9,979	7,346	7,767
Officials and administrators, public administration.	710	716	371	384	339	332
Other executive, administrative, and managerial..	12,151	12,656	7,471	7,703	4,680	4,953
Management-related occupations	4,325	4,374	1,998	1,892	2,327	2,481
Professional specialty	18,132	18,752	8,539	8,764	9,593	9,987
Engineers	1,934	1,960	1,771	1,793	163	167
Mathematical and computer scientists	1,195	1,345	813	933	382	412
Natural scientists	519	536	377	379	142	157
Health diagnosing occupations	1,002	960	773	715	229	245
Health assessment and treating occupations	2,762	2,812	393	403	2,369	2,409
Teachers, college and university	846	889	464	502	382	387
Teachers, except college and university........	4,507	4,724	1,142	1,207	3,365	3,517
Lawyers and judges......................	926	911	684	647	242	264
Other professional specialty occupations	4,440	4,616	2,122	2,186	2,318	2,430
Technical, sales, and administrative support	37,417	37,683	13,310	13,489	24,107	24,194
Technicians and related support	3,909	3,926	1,900	1,865	2,009	2,061
Sales occupations.........................	15,119	15,404	7,634	7,782	7,485	7,622
Administrative support, including clerical	18,389	18,353	3,776	3,842	14,613	14,511
Service occupations	16,930	17,177	6,774	6,967	10,155	10,210
Precision production, craft, and repair	13,524	13,587	12,323	12,368	1,201	1,219
Mechanics and repairers....................	4,423	4,521	4,248	4,335	175	185
Construction trades........................	5,098	5,108	4,978	4,981	120	127
Other precision production, craft, and repair.......	4,004	3,959	3,097	3,052	907	906
Operators, fabricators, and laborers..............	18,068	18,197	13,675	13,750	4,393	4,447
Machine operators, assemblers, and inspectors....	7,907	7,874	4,958	4,902	2,949	2,972
Transportation and material moving occupations ...	5,171	5,302	4,682	4,799	490	504
Motor vehicle operators	3,904	4,025	3,474	3,575	429	450
Other transportation and material moving occupations	1,268	1,277	1,207	1,223	60	54
Handlers, equipment cleaners, helpers, and laborers	4,990	5,021	4,035	4,049	955	971
Construction laborers......................	780	809	754	778	26	31
Other handlers, equipment cleaners, etc........	4,210	4,212	3,281	3,272	929	940
Farming, forestry, and fishing	3,642	3,566	2,916	2,889	726	677

Note: Totals may not add because of independent rounding.

Unemployment Insurance

Source: Unemployment Insurance Service, U.S. Dept. of Labor; September 1997

Unlike old-age and survivors insurance, which is entirely a federal program, the unemployment insurance program is a federal-state system that provides insured wage earners partial replacement for lost wages during a period of involuntary unemployment. The program protects most wage and salary workers. During fiscal year 1996, an estimated 118 million workers in commerce, industry, agriculture, and government were covered under the federal-state system.

Each state, as well as the District of Columbia, Puerto Rico, and the Virgin Islands, has its own law and operates its own program. The amount and duration of the weekly benefits are determined by state laws, based on prior wages and length of employment. States are required to extend the duration of benefits when unemployment rises to and remains above specified state levels; costs of extended benefits are shared by the state and federal governments.

Under the Federal Unemployment Tax Act, the federal tax rate is 6.2% on the first $7,000 paid to each employee of employers with one or more employees in 20 weeks of the year or with a quarterly payroll of $1,500 or more. A credit of up to 5.4% is allowed for taxes paid under state unemployment insurance laws that meet certain criteria, leaving the net federal rate at 0.8% of taxable wages; subject employers also pay a state unemployment tax. Governmental agencies and certain nonprofit organizations are not subject to the federal tax; such entities reimburse states for benefits paid to former employees.

The secretary of labor certifies states for administrative grants to operate the program (under the Social Security Act) and for employer tax credit (under the Federal Unemployment Tax Act).

Benefits are financed solely by employer contributions, except in Alaska and Pennsylvania, where employees also contribute. Benefits are paid through the states' public employment offices, at which unemployed workers must register for work and to which they must report regularly for referral to a possible job during the time when they are drawing weekly benefit payments. During fiscal year 1996, $22.8 billion in benefits was paid under all unemployment insurance programs to 8.3 million beneficiaries. Beneficiaries received an average weekly payment of $188.87 for total unemployment, which lasted an average of 14.9 weeks.

U.S. Unemployment Rates by Selected Characteristics, 1994-97

Source: Bureau of Labor Statistics, U.S. Dept. of Labor; seasonally adjusted, quarterly averages

Characteristic	1994			1995				1996				1997	
	II	III	IV	I	II	III	IV	I	II	III	IV	I	II
Total (all civilian workers)	6.2	6.0	5.6	5.5	5.6	5.7	5.6	5.6	5.4	5.3	5.3	5.3	4.9
Men, 20 years and older	5.4	5.3	4.9	4.7	4.9	4.9	4.8	4.9	4.7	4.5	4.4	4.5	4.1
Women, 20 years and older	5.5	5.3	4.9	4.9	5.0	5.0	4.8	4.9	4.8	4.7	4.8	4.7	4.4
Both sexes, 16 to 19 years	18.2	17.5	16.6	16.7	17.3	17.8	17.6	17.3	16.5	16.6	16.6	17.0	15.9
White	5.3	5.2	4.9	4.8	4.9	4.9	4.9	4.9	4.7	4.6	4.6	4.5	4.1
Black and other	10.6	10.2	9.8	9.4	9.6	10.0	9.2	9.5	9.3	9.2	9.2	9.5	9.1
Black	11.6	10.8	10.6	10.2	10.4	11.0	9.9	10.6	10.3	10.5	10.6	10.9	10.2
Hispanic origin	10.2	10.0	9.2	9.4	9.2	9.2	9.5	9.6	9.2	8.7	8.0	8.3	7.7
Married men, spouse present	3.7	3.5	3.3	3.2	3.4	3.4	3.2	3.1	3.0	3.0	3.0	2.8	2.7
Married women, spouse present	4.1	4.1	3.8	3.8	3.9	4.1	3.8	3.7	3.7	3.4	3.6	3.3	3.2
Women who maintain families	9.0	8.5	8.7	8.4	8.5	7.7	7.5	7.8	7.8	8.6	8.5	9.1	7.7
Occupation													
Managerial and professional specialty	2.6	2.5	2.4	2.4	2.4	2.5	2.5	2.4	2.4	2.3	2.3	2.1	2.0
Technical, sales, and administrative support	5.1	4.8	4.5	4.4	4.6	4.4	4.3	4.5	4.4	4.5	4.6	4.3	4.1
Precision production, craft, and repair	6.5	5.9	5.6	5.7	6.1	6.4	5.9	5.7	5.4	5.4	5.5	5.0	4.7
Operators, fabricators, and laborers	9.0	8.9	8.4	7.9	8.3	8.5	8.2	8.3	8.0	7.6	7.7	8.1	7.3
Farming, forestry, and fishing	7.3	9.1	8.0	7.7	8.2	7.6	8.0	7.9	8.0	6.7	7.5	7.4	7.0
Industry													
Nonagricultural private wage and salary workers	6.4	6.2	5.8	5.6	5.8	5.9	5.8	5.7	5.6	5.4	5.4	5.3	5.0
Goods-producing industries	6.9	6.7	6.3	6.1	6.5	6.6	6.5	6.3	6.1	5.7	5.9	5.7	5.3
Mining	6.3	5.9	4.3	5.0	4.5	4.0	7.4	6.0	3.9	4.2	6.1	4.7	2.4
Construction	11.9	10.9	10.8	11.1	11.7	12.0	11.5	10.7	10.0	9.4	9.7	9.6	8.5
Manufacturing	5.5	5.5	5.0	4.6	5.0	5.1	5.0	5.0	4.9	4.6	4.7	4.4	4.3
Durable goods	5.2	5.5	4.5	4.1	4.4	4.5	4.5	4.8	4.6	4.1	4.5	4.0	3.5
Nondurable goods	5.9	5.5	5.6	5.3	5.9	5.9	5.7	5.3	5.3	5.3	5.1	5.1	5.4
Service-producing industries	6.1	6.0	5.6	5.4	5.5	5.6	5.5	5.5	5.4	5.3	5.2	5.2	4.9
Transportation and public utilities	5.0	4.7	4.5	4.7	4.4	4.4	4.3	4.0	4.3	4.1	4.0	4.1	3.1
Wholesale and retail trade	7.4	7.3	7.0	6.4	6.5	6.7	6.4	6.6	6.5	6.3	6.2	6.4	6.2
Finance, insurance, and real estate	3.6	3.8	3.3	3.3	3.5	3.2	3.0	2.6	2.6	2.8	3.0	3.2	3.0
Services	6.0	5.7	5.4	5.3	5.5	5.5	5.5	5.6	5.5	5.3	5.1	4.9	4.7
Government workers	3.5	3.4	3.0	3.0	3.0	2.9	2.8	2.8	3.0	2.9	2.9	2.9	2.5
Agricultural wage/salary workers	9.3	12.0	10.0	10.3	11.7	10.4	11.9	10.6	10.3	9.2	10.4	8.9	9.1

Note: Beginning in Jan. 1997, data reflect revised population controls used in the household survey.

Annual Earnings, by Educational Attainment, Sex, Race, and Hispanic Origin, 1995

Source: Bureau of the Census, U.S. Dept. of Commerce; averages per person, ages 18 and over

Characteristic	Total	Not a high school graduate	High school graduate	Some college or an associate degree	Bachelor's degree	Advanced degree
Total	$26,792	$14,013	$21,431	$23,862	$36,980	$56,667
Male	33,251	16,748	26,333	29,851	46,111	69,588
Female	19,414	9,790	15,970	17,962	26,841	37,813
White	27,556	14,224	22,161	24,040	37,711	57,054
Black	20,537	12,956	17,072	21,824	29,666	46,654
Hispanic origin[1]	18,262	13,068	18,333	19,923	30,602	45,612

(1) May be of any race.

Occupational Illnesses, by Industry and Type of Illness, 1995

Source: Bureau of Labor Statistics, U.S. Dept. of Labor

(percent distribution)

Occupational illness	Private sector[1]	Goods producing				Service producing				
		Agri-culture[2]	Min-ing[3]	Con-struc-tion	Manu-facturing	Trans. and pub. utilities	Whole-sale	Retail	Fi-nance[4]	Service
Total [2,040,900 cases] ...	100.0	100.0	100.0	100.0	100.0	100.0	100.0	100.0	100.0	100.0
Nature of injury, illness:										
Sprains, strains..........	43.0	37.3	42.3	38.0	37.7	50.6	45.1	40.3	36.5	49.7
Bruises, contusions.......	9.4	8.3	11.0	7.5	9.0	10.5	9.3	10.9	8.0	9.2
Cuts, lacerations.........	7.5	11.5	6.4	8.7	8.8	4.9	6.3	10.9	5.2	4.6
Fractures	6.1	5.3	11.1	10.2	6.1	5.9	6.8	5.6	5.3	4.6
Carpal tunnel syndrome....	1.5	0.6	—	0.7	2.8	0.8	1.1	1.2	4.7	1.1
Heat burns	1.8	0.3	1.7	1.5	1.7	0.4	0.9	4.1	0.8	1.4
Tendinitis	1.1	0.7	—	0.5	1.9	0.9	0.8	0.8	1.4	0.9
Chemical burns..........	0.7	0.6	0.6	0.6	0.9	0.4	0.3	0.7	0.2	0.8
Amputations	0.6	0.7	0.7	0.6	1.1	0.3	0.6	0.3	0.1	0.2
Multiple injuries..........	3.0	3.4	5.6	3.2	2.9	2.8	3.9	3.1	4.4	2.6
Source of injury, illness:										
Chemicals/chem. products..	1.9	1.5	8.3	1.2	2.3	1.4	0.9	1.7	2.2	2.1
Containers	14.1	10.1	5.4	5.0	13.9	20.4	22.9	20.2	9.9	8.6
Furniture, fixtures	3.7	0.8	0.3	1.6	2.6	1.6	2.7	6.3	6.0	5.3
Machinery	7.0	7.4	10.8	6.9	11.5	2.9	6.8	6.9	7.2	4.0
Parts and materials	11.1	8.2	17.7	23.8	17.5	8.7	13.6	6.2	4.6	3.7
Worker motion or position...	14.7	15.2	5.5	12.8	18.7	14.6	13.3	12.0	19.9	13.6
Floor, ground surface	15.5	13.3	16.3	18.2	10.0	16.3	12.9	19.7	22.8	17.5
Tools, instruments, equip. ...	6.0	8.5	8.9	10.4	6.6	3.1	4.1	6.6	4.6	5.0
Vehicles	7.8	9.4	7.1	4.9	4.6	19.1	12.4	6.1	7.5	6.7
Health care patient	4.8	—	—	—	—	1.1	0.1	—	0.8	19.9
Event or exposure:										
Contact with object/equip.	27.5	32.2	38.5	33.0	33.9	22.4	29.1	29.7	18.0	18.7
Struck by object	13.2	15.9	20.8	17.1	14.4	10.2	14.8	15.8	9.6	9.2
Struck against object	7.0	8.1	7.7	8.0	7.6	6.3	6.7	8.1	5.5	5.7
Caught in object	4.6	5.1	8.4	4.0	8.3	3.3	5.2	3.6	1.4	2.1
Fall to lower level	5.1	6.4	8.3	11.9	3.1	6.9	5.2	4.1	6.9	4.2
Fall to same level	11.0	8.4	9.7	7.4	7.4	9.6	8.7	16.1	16.1	13.8
Slips, trips (without fall)	2.9	3.5	1.1	2.6	2.4	3.9	2.7	3.0	3.2	3.1
Overexertion............	27.4	20.0	26.4	22.5	25.9	28.5	31.1	24.1	21.7	33.2
Overexertion in lifting.....	16.4	11.2	10.1	13.0	14.4	17.1	20.1	16.7	12.8	19.3
Repetitive motion	4.0	2.1	0.8	1.9	8.4	2.0	2.6	2.5	8.6	2.6
Exposed to harmful substance............	5.1	5.0	5.8	4.4	5.4	3.5	2.9	6.3	5.2	5.5
Transportation accidents ...	3.6	5.5	2.4	3.2	1.7	8.7	5.7	2.3	5.7	3.5
Fires, explosions.........	0.2	0.2	—	0.4	0.2	0.1	0.2	0.2	—	0.2
Assault, by person........	1.1	0.1	—	0.1	0.1	0.4	0.2	1.2	1.3	3.4

Note: Dashes (—) indicate data that are not available or data that do not meet publication guidelines. Because of rounding and classifications not shown, percentages may not add to 100. All injuries and illnesses reported involved days away from work. (1) Private sector includes all industries except government, but excludes farms with fewer than 11 employees. (2) Agriculture includes forestry and fishing, but excludes farms with fewer than 11 employees. (3) Data conforming to OSHA definition for mining operators in coal, metal, and nonmetal mining and for employers in railroad transportation are provided to the Bureau of Labor Statistics by the Mine Safety and Health Administration, U.S. Dept. of Labor; and by the Federal Railroad Administration, U.S. Dept. of Transportation. Independent mining contractors are excluded from the coal, metal, and nonmetal industries. (4) Finance includes insurance and real estate.

Fatal Occupational Injuries, 1996

Source: Bureau of Labor Statistics, U.S. Dept. of Labor

Event or exposure	Fatalities		Event or exposure	Fatalities	
	Number	Percentage		Number	Percentage
Transportation incidents........	**2,556**	**42**	**Contact with objects and equipment..................**	**1,005**	**16**
Highway....................	1,324	22	Struck by object..................	579	9
Collision between vehicles	656	11	Struck by falling object	402	7
Vehicle struck stationary object. ..	240	4	Struck by flying object...........	58	1
Noncollision	348	6	Caught in or compressed by equipment or objects...................	283	5
Nonhighway (farm, industrial premises)	369	6	Caught in or crushed in collapsing materials	130	2
Aircraft.....................	320	5	**Exposure to harmful substances or environments ....**	**523**	**9**
Worker struck by a vehicle........	349	6	Contact with electric current	279	5
Water vehicle	107	2	Contact with temperature extremes....	32	1
Railway	75	1	Exposure to caustic, noxious, or allergenic substances	119	2
Assaults and violent acts	**1,144**	**19**	Oxygen deficiency	92	2
Homicide	912	15	**Fires and explosions ....**	**184**	**3**
Shooting..................	751	12	**Other events or exposures.......**	**16**	**—**
Stabbing..................	79	1	**Total........................**	**6,112**	**100**
Self-inflicted injury..............	199	3			
Falls	**684**	**11**			
Fall to lower level	607	10			
Fall on same level..............	49	1			

Note: Totals for major categories may include subcategories not shown separately. Percentages, based on incidence rate per total fatalities, may not add to totals because of rounding.

Civilian Employment of the Federal Government, May 1997

Source: Statistical Analysis and Services Division, U.S. Office of Personnel Management

(payroll in thousands of dollars, for May 1997)

Agency	All Areas Employment	All Areas Payroll	United States Employment	United States Payroll	Wash., DC, MSA Employment	Wash., DC, MSA Payroll	Overseas Employment	Overseas Payroll
Total, all agencies[1]	2,813,121	$9,488,999	2,706,871	$9,150,660	328,853	$1,398,772	106,250	$338,339
Legislative Branch	32,250	119,927	32,240	119,860	30,887	113,87111	10	67
Congress	18,249	62,909	8,249	62,909	18,249	62,909	—	—
U.S. Senate	7,013	24,876	7,013	24,876	7,013	24,876	—	—
House of Representatives . . .	11,220	37,974	11,220	37,974	11,220	37,974	—	—
Architect of the Capitol	1,844	5,535	1,844	5,535	1,844	5,535	—	—
Congressional Budget Ofc	234	1,208	234	1,208	234	1,208	—	—
General Accounting Ofc	3,359	17,874	3,355	17,848	2,388	13,011	4	26
Government Printing Ofc	3,602	13,011	3,602	13,011	3,254	12,007	—	—
Library of Congress	4,432	16,831	4,426	16,790	4,405	16,728	6	41
U.S. Tax Court	292	1,454	292	1,454	287	1,430	—	—
Judicial Branch	29,888	117,584	29,542	116,324	1,768	8,854	346	1,260
Supreme Court	373	1,860	373	1,860	373	1,860	—	—
U.S. Courts	29,515	115,724	29,169	114,464	1,395	6,994	346	1,260
Executive Branch	2,750,983	9,251,488	2,645,089	8,914,476	296,198	1,276,047	105,894	337,012
Exec Ofc of the President	1,552	7,764	1,545	7,721	1,545	7,721	7	43
White House Office	382	1,640	382	1,640	382	1,640	—	—
Ofc of Vice President	19	127	19	127	19	127	—	—
Ofc of Mgmt & Budget	501	2,744	501	2,744	501	2,744	—	—
Office of Administration	174	700	174	700	174	700	—	—
Council Economic Advisors . .	29	141	29	141	29	141	—	—
Ofc of Policy Development . .	28	151	28	151	28	151	—	—
National Security Council . . .	40	199	40	199	40	199	—	—
Ofc of Natl Drug Control	88	482	88	482	88	482	—	—
Ofc of U.S. Trade Rep	155	897	148	854	148	854	7	43
Executive Departments	1,683,040	5,936,514	1,597,221	5,657,178	219,501	955,397	85,819	279,336
State	24,033	83,132	8,379	29,242	7,251	24,489	15,654	53,890
Treasury	156,394	534,396	155,237	529,190	21,371	99,515	1,157	5,206
Defense, Total	766,086	2,653,580	705,367	2,462,237	71,932	289,733	60,719	191,343
Defense, Mil Funct Total	738,543	2,577,049	677,892	2,385,980	70,915	286,171	60,651	191,062
Defense, Civ Funct Total	27,543	76,531	27,475	76,250	1,017	3,562	68	281
Dept of the Army	255,836	728,997	230,122	654,830	21,187	49,234	25,714	74,167
Army, Mil Funct Total	228,294	652,467	202,648	578,581	20,170	5,672	25,646	73,886
Army, Civil Funct Total . . .	27,542	76,530	27,474	76,249	1,017	3,562	68	281
Corps of Engineers	27,454	76,170	27,386	75,889	929	3,202	68	281
Dept of the Navy	209,645	896,034	199,271	862,254	30,198	136,287	10,374	33,780
Dept of the Air Force	173,931	598,319	166,241	566,115	5,503	33,348	7,690	32,204
Defense Log Agcy	48,109	160,178	47,138	158,010	3,123	12,193	971	2,168
Other Def Act (excl DLA) .	78,565	270,052	62,595	221,028	11,921	58,671	15,970	49,024
Justice	113,881	456,586	111,763	447,308	20,471	100,767	2,118	9,278
Interior	70,843	222,076	70,521	221,019	7,805	30,769	322	1,057
Agriculture	102,542	314,909	101,183	311,456	11,547	47,480	1,359	3,453
Commerce	34,497	130,100	33,719	127,323	18,795	80,410	778	2,777
Labor	15,497	59,853	15,463	59,716	5,230	22,322	34	137
Health and Human Services .	59,378	234,509	59,177	233,642	26,697	114,365	201	867
Housing & Urban Dev	11,094	46,352	11,006	45,999	3,057	14,849	88	353
Transportation	63,050	327,641	62,554	325,089	9,755	51,099	496	2,552
Energy	17,257	88,810	17,250	88,747	6,000	37,394	7	63
Education	4,540	19,389	4,534	19,363	3,122	13,855	6	26
Veterans Affairs	243,948	765,181	241,068	756,847	6,468	28,350	2,880	8,334
Independent Agencies	1,066,391	3,307,210	1,046,323	3,249,577	75,152	312,929	20,068	57,633
Bd of Gov, Fed Rsrv Sys	1,721	8,444	1,721	8,444	1,721	8,444	—	—
Environmtl Protect Agcy	17,566	76,799	17,537	76,671	5,803	28,003	29	128
Equal Employ Opp Comm . . .	2,625	10,565	2,625	10,565	668	2,987	—	—
Federal Communicatns Comm	2,086	9,681	2,084	9,669	1,717	8,241	2	12
Fed Emergency Mgmt Agcy .	6,158	20,277	5,866	19,710	1,930	7,192	292	567
General Svcs Admin	14,195	53,294	14,113	53,070	4,701	20,074	82	224
Natl Aero & Space Admin . . .	19,993	95,636	19,972	95,516	4,357	21,919	21	120
Natl Fnd Arts & Humanities . .	334	1,533	334	1,533	334	1,533	—	—
Peace Corps	1,136	2,143	665	1,970	535	1,736	471	173
Securities & Exchnge Comm .	2,825	12,973	2,825	12,973	1,796	8,284	—	—
Smithsonian Inst. (total)	5,112	16,532	4,940	16,054	4,529	14,541	172	478
Social Security Admin	67,250	222,575	66,721	221,032	1,504	6,094	529	1,543
U.S. Postal Service	852,738	2,471,726	848,724	2,458,249	23,006	72,896	4,014	13,477

(1) Totals include agencies not listed.

MILLENNIUM FACT BOX

Civilian Employment of the Federal Government, 1821-1990

The total number of civilians working for the federal government rose from several thousand in the early 19th century to over 3.5 million in 1990. (Since then, however, there has been a decline, to about 2.8 million as of 1997.)

Year	Employment	Year	Employment	Year	Employment
1821	6,914	1881	100,020	1940	1,042,420
1831	11,491	1891	157,442	1950	1,960,708
1841	18,038	1901	239,476	1960	2,398,704
1851	26,274	1910	388,708	1970	2,981,574
1861	00,072	1920	655,265	1980	3,121,783
1871	51,020	1930	601,319	1990	3,508,463

Distribution of Wage and Salary Workers Paid Hourly Rates, Second Quarter 1997

Source: Bureau of Labor Statistics, U.S. Dept. of Labor; unpublished tabulations from Current Population Survey

(in thousands)

	Total hourly workers	$4.75[1] or less	Less than $10.00	$10.00 or more
Sex and age				
Total, 16 years and older	70,536	3,795	40,849	29,687
16 to 24 years	15,998	2,019	14,216	1,782
20 to 24 years	9,866	841	8,276	1,590
25 years and older	54,538	1,777	26,633	27,905
25 to 54 years	47,407	1,405	22,532	24,875
25 to 34 years	17,726	682	9,904	7,822
35 to 44 years	17,622	460	7,558	10,064
45 to 54 years	12,059	263	5,069	6,990
55 years and older	7,131	372	4,102	3,029
55 to 64 years	5,531	198	2,874	2,657
65 years and older	1,600	174	1,227	373
Men, 16 years and older.	35,782	1,530	17,714	18,068
16 to 24 years	8,385	945	7,180	1,205
20 to 24 years	5,294	394	4,235	1,059
25 years and older	27,398	585	10,536	16,862
Women, 16 years and older	34,754	2,266	23,135	11,619
16 to 24 years	7,614	1,074	7,037	577
20 to 24 years	4,573	446	4,041	532
25 years and older	27,140	1,192	16,098	11,042
Race and Hispanic origin				
White				
Total, 16 years and older	58,212	3,211	2,958	25,254
Men.	29,851	1,272	14,312	15,539
Women	28,361	1,939	18,645	9,716
Black				
Total, 16 years and older	9,313	478	6,110	3,203
Men.	4,420	222	2,619	1,801
Women	4,892	257	3,490	1,402
Hispanic origin				
Total, 16 years and older	8,570	598	6,068	2,502
Men.	5,240	303	3,472	1,768
Women	3,330	295	2,596	734
Full- and part-time status				
Full-time workers				
Total, 16 years and older	53,327	1,500	7,031	26,296
Men.	30,278	660	13,044	17,234
Women	23,048	838	13,986	9,062
Part-time workers				
Total, 16 years and older	17,099	2,290	13,756	3,343
Men.	5,439	866	4,641	798
Women	11,660	1,424	9,115	2,545

Note: Data exclude the incorporated self-employed and are not seasonally adjusted. Totals may not add because of independent rounding. The data are from unpublished work tables and should not be considered as though part of a BLS news release. All the standard caveats that are normally issued with annual unpublished minimum wage data apply to these quarterly tabulations as well. (1) $4.75 = minimum wage, Oct. 1, 1996-Sept. 1, 1997.

Federal Minimum Hourly Wage Rates Since 1950

Source: Bureau of Labor Statistics, U.S. Dept. of Labor

The Fair Labor Standards Act of 1938 and subsequent amendments provide for minimum wage-coverage applicable to workers in specified nonsupervisory employment categories. Exempt from coverage are executives and administrators or professionals.

Effective date	Nonfarm Workers Under laws prior to 1966[1]	Percent, of avg earnings[2]	Under 1966 and later provis.[3]	Farm Workers[4]	Effective date	Nonfarm Workers Under laws prior to 1966[1]	Percent, of avg earnings[2]	Under 1966 and later provis.[3]	Farm Workers[4]
Jan. 25, 1950 . . .	$0.75	54	NA	NA	Jan. 1, 1975	$2.10	45	$2.00	$1.80
Mar. 1, 1956. . . .	1.00	52	NA	NA	Jan. 1, 1976	2.30	46	2.20	2.00
Sept. 3, 1961 . . .	1.15	50	NA	NA	Jan. 1, 1977	(5)	(5)	2.30	2.20
Sept. 3, 1963 . . .	1.25	51	NA	NA	Jan. 1, 1978	2.65	44	2.65	2.65
Feb. 1, 1967. . . .	1.40	50	$1.00	$1.00	Jan. 1, 1979	2.90	45	2.90	2.90
Feb. 1, 1968. . . .	1.60	54	1.15	1.15	Jan. 1, 1980	3.10	43	3.10	3.10
Feb. 1, 1969. . . .	(5)	(5)	1.30	1.30	Jan. 1, 1981	3.35	42	3.35	3.35
Feb. 1, 1970. . . .	(5)	(5)	1.45	(5)	Apr. 1, 1990.	3.80[6]	35	3.80[6]	3.80[6]
Feb. 1, 1971. . . .	(5)	(5)	1.60	(5)	Apr. 1, 1991.	4.25[6]	38	4.25[6]	4.25[6]
May 1, 1974	2.00	46	1.90	1.60	Oct. 1, 1996.	4.75[7]	37	4.75[7]	4.75[7]
					Sept. 1, 1997. . . .	5.15	NA	5.15	5.15

NA = not applicable. (1) Applies to workers covered prior to 1961 Amendments and, after Sept. 1965, to workers covered by 1961 Amendments. Rates set by 1961 Amendments were: Sept. 1961, $1.00; Sept. 1964, $1.15; and Sept. 1965, $1.25. (2) Percent of gross average hourly earnings of production workers in manufacturing. (3) Applies to workers newly covered by Amendments of 1966, 1974, and 1977, and Title IX of Education Amendments of 1972. (4) Included in coverage as of 1966, 1974, and 1977 Amendments. (5) No change in rate. (6) Training wage for workers age 16-19 in first six months of first job: Apr. 1, 1990, $3.35; Apr. 1, 1991, $3.62. The training wage expired Mar. 31, 1993. (7) Under 1996 legislation, a subminimum training wage of $4.25 an hour was established for employees under 20 years of age during their first 90 consecutive calendar days of employment with an employer. For workers receiving gratuities, the minimum wage remained $2.13 per hour.

Hourly Compensation Costs, by Selected Country, 1975-95

Source: Bureau of Labor Statistics, U.S. Dept. of Labor

(in U.S. dollars, compensation for production workers in manufacturing)

Country/Territory	1975	1985	1990	1995	Country/Territory	1975	1985	1990	1995
United States	$6.36	$13.01	$14.91	$17.20	Finland	$4.61	$8.16	$21.03	$24.78
Canada	5.96	10.94	15.83	16.03	France	4.52	7.52	15.23	19.34
Mexico	1.47	1.59	1.64	1.51	Germany[1]	6.35	9.60	21.96	31.88
Australia	5.62	8.20	13.07	14.40	Greece	1.69	3.66	6.71	8.95
Hong Kong[2]	0.76	1.73	3.20	4.82	Ireland	3.03	5.92	11.76	13.83
Israel	2.25	4.06	8.55	10.59	Italy	4.67	7.63	17.74	16.48
Japan	3.00	6.34	12.80	23.66	Luxembourg	6.35	7.72	16.37	NA
Korea, South	0.32	1.23	3.71	7.40	Netherlands	6.58	8.75	18.29	24.18
New Zealand	3.21	4.47	8.33	10.11	Norway	6.77	10.37	21.47	24.38
Singapore	0.84	2.47	3.78	7.28	Portugal	1.58	1.53	3.77	5.35
Sri Lanka	0.28	0.28	0.35	NA	Spain	2.53	4.66	11.33	12.70
Taiwan	0.40	1.50	3.95	5.82	Sweden	7.18	9.66	20.93	21.36
Austria	4.51	7.58	17.75	25.38	Switzerland	6.09	9.66	20.86	29.28
Belgium	6.41	8.97	19.22	26.88	United Kingdom	3.37	6.27	12.71	13.77
Denmark	6.28	8.13	17.96	24.19					

NA=Not available. (1) Former West Germany. (2) Now part of China.

Top 15 Metropolitan Areas, by Average Annual Salary, 1995

Source: Bureau of Labor Statistics, U.S. Dept. of Labor

Rank	Metropolitan area	Average annual salary[1]	Rank	Metropolitan area	Average annual salary[1]
1.	San Jose, CA	$42,409	8.	Bergen–Passaic, NJ	$35,746
2.	New York, NY	42,272	9.	Washington, DC–MD–VA–WV	34,891
3.	San Francisco, CA	37,975	10.	Detroit, MI	34,706
4.	Middlesex–Somerset–Hunterdon, NJ	37,925	11.	Jersey City, NJ	34,621
5.	New Haven–Bridgeport–Stamford–		12.	Kokomo, IN	33,967
	Danbury–Waterbury, CT	37,546	13.	Hartford, CT	33,948
6.	Newark NJ	37,224	14.	Anchorage, AK	33,650
7.	Trenton, NJ	36,614	15.	Flint, MI	33,389

Note: Jacksonville, NC, recorded the **lowest annual pay level** among metropolitan statistical areas in 1995—$16,951—followed by Myrtle Beach, SC ($17,910), McAllen–Edinburg–Mission, TX ($18,031), Yuma, AZ (18,286), and Brownsville–Harlingen–San Benito, TX ($18,566). The average annual salary in the 5 bottom-ranked metropolitan areas averaged 36-42% below the nationwide metropolitan average of $29,105. A total of 14 metropolitan areas reported average pay levels below $20,000 annually. (1) Data are preliminary and include workers covered by Unemployment Insurance and Unemployment Compensation for Federal Employees programs.

Average Hours and Earnings of Production Workers, 1967-96[1]

Source: Bureau of Labor Statistics, U.S. Dept. of Labor

(annual averages)

	Weekly hours	Hourly earnings	Weekly earnings		Weekly hours	Hourly earnings	Weekly earnings
1967	38.0	$2.68	$101.84	1982	34.8	$7.68	$267.26
1968	37.8	2.85	107.73	1983	35.0	8.02	280.70
1969	37.7	3.04	114.61	1984	35.2	8.32	292.86
1970	37.1	3.23	119.83	1985	34.9	8.57	299.09
1971	36.9	3.45	127.31	1986	34.8	8.76	304.85
1972	37.0	3.70	136.90	1987	34.8	8.98	312.50
1973	36.9	3.94	145.39	1988	34.7	9.28	322.02
1974	36.5	4.24	154.76	1989	34.6	9.66	334.24
1975	36.1	4.53	163.53	1990	34.5	10.01	345.35
1976	36.1	4.86	175.45	1991	34.3	10.32	353.98
1977	36.0	5.25	189.00	1992	34.4	10.57	363.61
1978	35.8	5.69	203.70	1993	34.5	10.83	373.64
1979	35.7	6.16	219.91	1994	34.7	11.12	385.86
1980	35.3	6.66	235.10	1995	34.5	11.43	394.34
1981	35.2	7.25	255.20	1996	34.4	11.81	406.26

(1) Data relate to private-industry production workers in mining and manufacturing; to construction workers in construction; and to nonsupervisory workers in transportation and public utilities; wholesale and retail trade; finance, insurance, and real estate; and services.

Educational Attainment by Labor-Force Status and Occupation, Mar. 1996

Source: Bureau of the Census, Dept. of Commerce

Characteristics	Number of persons (1,000)	Percentage with High school degree or more	Percentage with Some college or more	Percentage with Bachelor's degree or more
Civilian labor force, 25 years and older	111,919	88.7	55.9	28.4
Employed	106,662	89.4	56.8	29.1
Not employed	5,257	74.8	37.2	13.2
Not in the labor force	55,742	67.6	32.4	13.9
Total, employed persons, 25-64 years old	102,890	89.8	57.1	29.3
Executive, admin., and managerial	15,938	97.3	77.2	48.6
Professional specialty occupations	16,924	99.4	93.8	75.9
Technicians and related support occupations	3,324	98.3	80.6	32.1
Sales occupations	11,413	94.0	60.5	29.6
Administrative support occupations, includ. clerical	15,152	96.6	55.3	15.5
Private household occupations	548	59.5	21.4	6.4
Other service occupations	11,556	79.7	36.1	8.2
Farming, forestry, and fishing	2,455	70.4	30.4	9.9
Precision products, craft, and repair	11,483	82.7	35.3	7.1
Machine operators, assemblers, and inspectors	6,569	73.4	23.3	4.4
Transportation and material moving	4,443	80.6	29.4	5.4
Handlers, equip. cleaners, helpers, and laborers	3,087	72.7	23.8	5.4

Median Weekly Earnings of Full-Time Wage and Salary Workers by Age, Sex, and Union Affiliation, 1995-96

Source: Bureau of Labor Statistics, U.S. Dept. of Labor

Sex and age	1995				1996			
	Total	Members of unions[1]	Repre-sented by unions[2]	Non-union	Total	Members of unions[1]	Repre-sented by unions[2]	Non-union
Total, 16 years and older	$479	$602	$598	$447	$490	$615	$610	$462
16 to 24 years	292	375	373	287	298	371	362	294
25 years and older	510	613	610	486	520	625	621	498
25 to 34 years	451	542	534	433	463	554	548	447
35 to 44 years	550	621	619	520	559	636	632	530
45 to 54 years	582	665	663	536	594	687	686	552
55 to 64 years	514	614	614	482	535	620	616	505
65 years and older	389	509	506	362	384	510	510	367
Men, 16 years and older	538	640	638	507	557	653	651	520
16 to 24 years	303	388	388	298	307	375	369	303
25 years and older	588	654	652	563	599	669	668	580
25 to 34 years	490	583	579	475	499	591	587	485
35 to 44 years	624	665	663	612	632	683	683	617
45 to 54 years	685	705	706	670	698	718	721	682
55 to 64 years	623	655	659	607	643	667	664	633
65 years and older	441	615	619	400	477	589	593	424
Women, 16 years and older . . .	406	527	523	386	418	549	543	398
16 to 24 years	275	349	345	272	284	358	339	280
25 years and older	428	539	536	408	444	560	555	420
25 to 34 years	403	492	488	393	415	497	495	405
35 to 44 years	453	553	552	427	463	561	556	439
45 to 54 years	464	595	593	423	481	620	616	445
55 to 64 years	403	501	501	383	420	524	523	395
65 years and older	353	435	425	333	334	417	413	321

Note: Data refer to the sole or principal job of full-time workers. Excluded are self-employed workers whose businesses are incorporated, although they technically qualify as wage and salary workers. (1) Data refer to members of a labor union or an employee association similar to a union. (2) Data refer to members of a labor union or an employee association similar to a union, as well as to workers who report no union affiliation but whose jobs are covered by a union or an employee association contract.

Work Stoppages (Strikes and Lockouts) in the U.S., 1960-96

Source: Bureau of Labor Statistics, U.S. Dept. of Labor; involving 1,000 workers or more

Year	Number of stoppages[1]	Workers involved[1] (thousands)	Work days idle[1] (thousands)	Year	Number of stoppages[1]	Workers involved[1] (thousands)	Work days idle[1] (thousands)
1960.	222	896	13,260	1983.	81	909	17,461
1965.	268	999	15,140	1984.	62	376	8,499
1970.	381	2,468	52,761	1985.	54	324	7,079
1971.	298	2,516	35,538	1986.	69	533	11,861
1972.	250	975	16,764	1987.	46	174	4,481
1973.	317	1,400	16,260	1988.	40	118	4,381
1974.	424	1,796	31,809	1989.	51	452	16,996
1975.	235	965	17,563	1990.	44	185	5,926
1976.	231	1,519	23,962	1991.	40	392	4,584
1977.	298	1,212	21,258	1992.	35	364	3,989
1978.	219	1,006	23,774	1993.	35	182	3,981
1979.	235	1,021	20,409	1994.	45	322	5,020
1980.	187	795	20,844	1995.	31	192	5,771
1981.	145	729	16,908	1996.	37	273	4,887
1982.	96	656	9,061				

(1) The number of stoppages and workers relate to stoppages that began in the year. Days of idleness include all stoppages in effect. Workers are counted more than once if they were involved in more than one stoppage during the year.

Work Stoppages Involving 5,000 Workers or More, Beginning in 1996

Source: Bureau of Labor Statistics, U.S. Dept. of Labor

Employer, location, and union	Began	Ended	Workers involved[1]	Estimated days idle in 1996[1]
Commercial Building Realty Advisory Board, New York, NY; Service Employees (SEIU)	1/4	2/4	30,000	630,000
San Diego public schools, San Diego, CA; San Diego Education Assn.	2/1	2/8	5,000	30,000
Ingalls Shipbuilding, Inc., Pascagoula, MS; Metal Trades Council (MTC)	2/14	2/15	7,600	14,200
General Motors Corp., Dayton, OH; Automobile Workers (UAW)	3/5	3/22	136,000[2]	1,260,000
Retail grocery chains—Safeway and King Sooper, Denver, CO, area; Food and Commercial Workers (UFCW)	5/14	6/26	12,000	372,000
Northern Illinois Mason Empolyers Assn., Chicago, IL; Bricklayers (BAC)	6/1	6/12	6,500	52,000
McDonnell Douglas Aerospace, St. Louis, MO; Machinists (IAM)	6/5	9/16	6,700	482,400
League of Voluntary Hospitals, New York, NY; Service Employees (SEIU)	6/24	8/28	5,600	272,600
General Motors Corp., Janesville, WI; Automobile Workers (UAW)	10/30	11/6	5,100	30,600

(1) Workers and days idle are rounded to the nearest 100. (2) Includes workers idled because of material shortages.

Labor Union Directory

Source: Bureau of Labor Statistics, U.S. Dept. of Labor; AFL-CIO; World Almanac research, as of Sept. 1997.

(*) Independent union; all others affiliated with AFL-CIO.

American Federation of Labor & Congress of Industrial Organizations (AFL-CIO), 815 16th St. NW, Washington, DC 20006; founded 1955; John J. Sweeney, Pres. (since 1995); 13.1 mil. members.

Actors and Artistes of America, Associated (AAAA), 165 W 46th St., New York, NY 10036; founded 1919; Theodore Bikel, Pres.; no individual members, 7 National Performing Arts Unions are affiliates; approx. 100,000 combined membership.

Actors' Equity Association, 165 W 46th St., New York, NY 10036; founded 1913; Ron Silver, Pres. (since 1991); 39,000 active members.

Air Line Pilots Association, 535 Herndon Parkway, PO Box 1169, Herndon, VA 20172; founded 1931; J. Randolph Babbitt, Pres. (since 1990); 45,000 members.

Aluminum, Brick & Glass Workers International Union (ABGWIU), 3362 Hollenberg Drive, Bridgeton, MO 63044; founded 1953 (merged with steelworkers, Jan. 20, 1997).

Automobile, Aerospace & Agricultural Implement Workers of America, International Union, United (UAW), 8000 E Jefferson Ave., Detroit, MI 48214; founded 1935; Stephen P. Yokich, Pres. (since 1995); 1.3 mil. members, 1,130 locals.

Bakery, Confectionery & Tobacco Workers International Union (BC&T), 10401 Connecticut Ave., Kensington, MD 20895; founded 1886; Frank Hurt, Pres. (since 1992); 125,000 members.

Boilermakers, Iron Shipbuilders, Blacksmiths, Forgers and Helpers, International Brotherhood of (IBBISB/BF&H), 753 State Ave., Suite 570, Kansas City, KS 66101; founded 1880; Charles W. Jones, Int'l Pres. (since 1983); 82,419 members, 337 locals.

Bricklayers and Allied Craftworkers, International Union of, 815 15th St. NW, Washington, DC 20005; founded 1865; John T. Joyce, Intl Pres. (since 1979); 100,000 members, 400 locals.

Carpenters and Joiners of America, United Brotherhood of, 101 Constitution Ave. NW, Washington, DC 20001; founded 1881; Douglas J. McCarron, Gen. Pres. (since 1995); 500,000 members, 1,000 locals.

Chemical Workers Union, International (ICWU), 1655 W Market St., Akron, OH 44313; founded 1944 (merged with Food and Commercial Workers, July 1, 1996).

Clothing and Textile Workers Union, Amalgamated (ACTWU), 15 Union Square, New York, NY 10003; founded 1976 (merged with International Ladies' Garment Workers' to form Needletrades, Industrial, and Textile Employees, June 1995.

Communications Workers of America (CWA), 501 3d St. NW, Washington, DC 20001; founded 1938; Morton Bahr, Pres. (since 1985); 630,000 members, 1,400 locals.

Distillery, Wine & Allied Workers International Union (DWU), 66 Grand Ave., Englewood, NJ 07631; founded 1940 (merged with Food and Commercial Workers, Oct. 1, 1995).

***Education Association, National,** 1201 16th St. NW, Washington, DC 20036; founded 1857; Bob Chase, Pres. (since 1996); 2.3 mil. members, 13,500 affiliates.

Electrical Workers, International Brotherhood of (IBEW), 1125 15th St. NW, Washington, DC 20005; founded 1891; John J. Barry, Intl Pres. (since 1986); 800,000 members, 1,134 locals.

Electronic, Electrical, Salaried, Machine and Furniture Workers, International Union of (IUE), 1126 16th St. NW, Washington, DC 20036; founded 1949; Edward Fire, Pres. (since 1997); 130,000 members, 450 locals.

Engineers, International Union of Operating (IUOE), 1125 17th St. NW, Washington, DC 20036; founded 1896; Frank Hanley, Gen. Pres.; 400,000 members, 183 locals.

Farm Workers of America, United (UFW), 29700 Woodford Tehachapi Rd., PO Box 62, Keene, CA 93531; founded 1962; Arturo S. Rodríguez, Pres. (since 1993); 50,000 members.

***Federal Employees, National Federation of (NFFE),** 1016 16th St. NW, Suite 300, Washington, DC 20036; founded 1917; James D. Cunningham Sr., Pres. (since); 150,000 members, 350 locals.

Fire Fighters, International Association of, 1750 New York Ave. NW, Washington, DC 20006; founded 1918; Alfred K. Whitehead, Gen. Pres. (since 1988); 225,000 members, 2,280 locals.

Firemen and Oilers, National Conference of, 1100 Circle 75 Parkway, Suite 1585, Atlanta, GA 30339; founded 1898; Jimmy L. Walker, Pres.; 26,000 members, 210 locals.

Flight Attendants, Association of, 1275 K St. NW, Washington, DC 20036-4090; founded 1945; Patricia A. Friend, Pres.; 42,000 members.

Food and Commercial Workers International Union, United (UFCW), 1775 K St. NW, Washington, DC 20006-1598; founded 1979 following merger; Douglas H. Dority, Intl Pres. (since 1994); 1.4 mil. members, 997 locals.

Garment Workers of America, United (UGWA), 4207 Lebanon Rd., Hermitage, TN 37076; founded 1891 (merged with Food and Commercial Workers, Dec. 1, 1994).

Garment Workers' Union, International Ladies' (ILGWU), 1710 Broadway, New York, NY 10019; founded 1900 (merged with Amalgamated Clothing and Textile Workers to form Needletrades, Industrial, and Textile Employees, June 1995.

Glass, Molders, Pottery, Plastics & Allied Workers Intl. Union (GMP), 608 E Baltimore Pike, PO Box 607, Media, PA 19063; founded 1842; James H. Rankin, Intl Pres. (since 1997); 68,000 members, 390 locals.

Government Employees, American Federation of (AFGE), 80 F St. NW, Washington, DC 20001; founded 1932; John N. Sturdivant, Natl. Pres. (since 1988); 210,000 members, 1,200 locals.

Grain Millers, American Federation of (AFGM), 4949 Olson Memorial Hwy., Minneapolis, MN 55422; founded 1936; Larry R. Jackson, Gen. Pres. (since 1991); 27,000 members, 200 locals.

Graphic Communications International Union (GCIU), 1900 L St. NW, Washington, DC 20036; founded 1983; James J. Norton, Pres. (since 1985); 160,000 members, 450 locals.

Hotel Employees and Restaurant Employees International Union, 1219 28th St. NW, Washington, DC 20007; Edward T. Hanley, Gen. Pres. (since 1973); 400,000 members, 190 locals.

Iron Workers, International Association of Bridge, Structural, Ornamental and Reinforcing, 1750 New York Ave. NW, Suite 400, Washington, DC 20006; founded 1896; Jake West, Gen. Pres. (since 1989); 120,000 members, 242 locals.

Laborers' International Union of North America (LIUNA), 905 16th St. NW, Washington, DC 20006-1765; founded 1903; Arthur A. Coia, Gen. Pres. (since 1993); 750,000 members, 624 locals.

Leather Goods, Plastics Novelty and Service Workers' Union, International, 265 W 14th St., New York, NY 10011; Andrew McKenzie, Gen. Pres. (since 1992); 6,000 members, 85 locals.

Letter Carriers, National Association of (NALC), 100 Indiana Ave. NW, Washington, DC 20001-2144; founded 1889; Vincent R. Sombrotto, Pres. (since 1978); 315,000 members, 3,000 locals.

Locomotive Engineers, Brotherhood of (BLE), The Standard Bldg. Mezzanine, 1370 Ontario St., Cleveland, OH 44113-1702; founded 1863; Clarence V. Monin, Intl Pres. (since 1996); 55,000 members, 623 divisions.

Longshoremen's Association, International (ILA), 17 Battery Pl., New York, NY 10004; John Bowers, Pres., (since 1987); 65,000 members, 340 locals.

***Longshore & Warehouse Union, International (ILWU),** 1188 Franklin St., San Francisco, CA 94109-6800; founded 1937; Brian McWilliams, Pres. (since 1994); 60,000 members, 74 locals.

Machinists and Aerospace Workers, International Association of (IAM), 9000 Machinists Pl., Upper Marlboro, MD 20772-2687; founded 1888; R. Thomas Buffenbarger, Intl Pres. (since 1997); 731,780 members, 1,370 locals.

Maintenance of Way Employees, Brotherhood of (BMWE), 26555 Evergreen Rd., Suite 200, Southfield, MI 48076; founded 1887; Mac A. Fleming, Pres. (since 1990); 50,000 members, 790 locals.

Marine Engineer Beneficial Assn. (MEBA), 444 N Capitol St. NW, Suite 800, Washington, DC 20001; founded 1875; Alex Shandrowsky, Pres. (since 1996); 1,212 members, 25 locals.

Maritime Union, National (NMU), 30 Montgomery St., 8th floor, Jersey City, NJ 07302; Rene Lioeanjie, Pres. (since 1997); 50,000 members.

(continued)

Mine Workers of America, United (UMWA), 900 15th St. NW, Washington, DC 20005; founded 1890; Cecil Roberts, Intl Pres. (since 1995); 130,000 members, 600 locals.

Musicians of the United States and Canada, American Federation of (AF of M), 1501 Broadway, Suite 600, New York, NY 10036; founded 1896; Steve Young, Pres. (since 1995); 125,000 members, 324 locals.

Needletrades, Industrial, and Textile Employees, Union of (UNITE), 1710 Broadway, New York, NY 10019; founded 1995; Jay Mazur, Pres (since 1995); 285,000 members, 1,138 locals.

Newspaper Guild-Communications Workers of America (CWA) The, 501 3d St. NW, Washington, DC. 20001-2797; founded 1933; Linda Foley, Pres. (since 1995); 34,000 members, 72 locals.

*Nurses Association, American (ANA), 600 Maryland Ave. SW, Suite 100W, Washington, DC 20024-2571; founded 1897; Beverly L. Malone, PhD, RN, FAAN, Pres. (since 1996); 177,408 members, 53 constituent state & territorial assns.

Office and Professional Employees International Union (OPEIU), 265 W 14th St., Suite 610, New York, NY 10011; founded 1945 (AFL Charter); Michael Goodwin, Intl Pres. (since 1994); 130,000 members, 200 locals.

Oil, Chemical and Atomic Workers International Union (OCAW), 255 Union Blvd., PO Box 281200, Lakewood, CO 80228-8200; Robert E. Wages, Pres. (since 1991); 87,000 members, 350 locals.

Painters and Allied Trades, International Brotherhood of (IBPAT), 1750 New York Ave. NW, Washington, DC 20006; founded 1887; A. L. "Mike" Monroe, Gen. Pres.; 128,243 members, 550 locals.

Paperworkers International Union, United (UPIU), 3340 Perimeter Hill Dr., Nashville, TN 37211; founded 1884; Boyd Young, Pres. (since 1996); 255,000 members, 1,300 locals.

*Plant Guard Workers of America, International Union, United (UPGWA), 25510 Kelly Rd., Roseville, MI 48066; founded 1948; Gene McConville, Pres. (since 1990); 20,000 members, 180 locals.

Plasterers' and Cement Masons' International Association of the United States & Canada, Operative, 14405 Laurel Pl., Suite 300, Laurel, MD; 20707; founded 1864; John Dougherty, Gen. Pres.; 50,000 members, 135 locals.

Plumbing and Pipe Fitting Industry of the United States and Canada, United Association of Journeymen and Apprentices of, the, 901 Massachusetts Ave. NW, Washington, DC 20001; founded 1889; Martin J. Maddaloni, Gen. Pres. (since 1997); 292,000 members, 417 locals.

*Police, National Fraternal Order of, 1410 Donelson Pike, A-17, Nashville, TN 37217; Gilbert G. Gallegos, Natl. Pres. (since 1995); 270,000 members, 1,992 affiliates.

Police Associations, International Union of, 1421 Prince St., Suite 330, Alexandria, VA 22314; Sam A. Cabral, Pres. (since 1995); 50,000 members, 400 locals.

*Postal Supervisors, National Association of, 1727 King St., Suite 400, Alexandria, VA 22314-2753; Vincent Palladino, Pres. (since 1992); 36,000 members, 400 locals.

Postal Workers Union, American (APWU), 1300 L St. NW, Washington, DC 20005; founded 1971; Moe Biller, Pres. (since 1980); 350,000 members, 1,850 locals.

Retail, Wholesale and Department Store Union, 30 E 29th St., New York, NY 10016; Lenore Miller, Pres.; 100,000 members, 157 locals.

Roofers, Waterproofers & Allied Workers, United Union of, 1660 L St. NW, Suite 800, Washington, DC 20036; founded 1906; Earl J. Kruse, Pres. (since 1985); 25,000 members, 110 locals.

Rubber, Cork, Linoleum and Plastic Workers of America, United (URW), 570 White Pond Dr., Akron, OH 44320-1156; founded 1935 (merged with Steelworkers, July 1, 1995).

*Rural Letter Carriers' Association, National, 1630 Duke St., 4th floor, Alexandria, VA 22314; founded 1903; Steven Smith, Pres. (since 1997); 96,000 members; 50 state org.

Seafarers International Union of North America (SIUNA), 5201 Auth Way, Camp Springs, MD 20746; founded 1938; Michael Sacco, Pres. (since 1988); 85,000 members, 18 affiliates.

Service Employees International Union (SEIU), 1313 L St. NW, Washington, DC 20005; founded 1921; Andrew L. Stern, Pres. (since 1996); 1,110,000 members, 493 locals.

Sheet Metal Workers' International Association (SMWIA), 1750 New York Ave. NW, Washington, DC 20006; founded 1888; Arthur Moore, Gen. Pres. (since 1993); 150,000 members, 203 locals.

State, County and Municipal Employees, American Federation of (AFSCME), 1625 L St. NW, Washington, DC 20036; Gerald McEntee, Pres. (since 1981); 1.3 mil. members, 3,617 locals.

Steelworkers of America, United (USWA), 5 Gateway Center, Pittsburgh, PA 15222; founded 1936; George Becker, Intl Pres. (since 1994); 550,000 members, 2,300 locals.

Teachers, American Federation of (AFT), 555 New Jersey Ave. NW, Washington, DC 20001; founded 1916; Sandra Feldman, Pres. (since 1997); 940,000 members, 2,378 locals.

Teamsters, Chauffeurs, Warehousemen and Helpers of America, International Brotherhood of (IBT), 25 Louisiana Ave. NW, Washington, DC 20001; founded 1903; Ronald R. Carey, Pres. (since 1992); 1.4 mil. members, 569 locals.

Television and Radio Artists, American Federation of, 260 Madison Ave., 7th floor, New York, NY 10016; founded 1937; Shelby Scott, Pres. (since 1993); 75,000 members, 30 locals.

Theatrical Stage Employees, Moving Picture Technicians, Artists and Allied Crafts of the United States and Canada, International Alliance of (IATSE), 1515 Broadway, Suite 601, New York, NY 10036; founded 1893; Thomas C. Short, Intl Pres. (since 1994); 90,000 members, 555 locals.

Transit Union, Amalgamated (ATU), 5025 Wisconsin Ave. NW, Washington, DC 20016; founded 1892; James LaSala, Intl Pres. (since 1986); 155,000 members, 275 locals.

Transportation-Communications International Union (TCU), 3 Research Place, Rockville, MD 20850; founded 1899; Robert A. Scardelletti, Intl Pres. (since 1991); 95,000 members, 450 locals.

Transportation Union, United (UTU), 14600 Detroit Ave., Cleveland, OH 44107; founded 1969; Charles L. Little, Pres. (since 1995); 80,000 members, 688 locals.

Transport Workers Union of America, 80 West End Ave., New York, NY 10023; founded 1934; Sonny Hall, Intl Pres. (since 1993); 125,000 members, 92 locals.

*Treasury Employees Union, National (NTEU), 901 E St. NW, Suite 600, Washington, DC 20004; founded 1938; Robert M. Tobias, Natl. Pres. (since 1983); 150,000 represented, 226 chapters.

United Textile Workers of America, Council of (CUTWA), 763 Walnut Knoll Lane, Cordova, TN 38018; founded 1901 (merged with Food and Commercial Workers, Nov. 1, 1995).

*University Professors, American Association of (AAUP), 1012 14th St. NW, Washington, DC 20005; founded 1915; James Perley, Pres.; 44,000 members, 850 chapters.

Utility Workers Union of America (UWUA), 815 16th St. NW, Washington, DC 20006; founded 1945; Donald E. Wightman, Natl. Pres. (since 1996); 50,000 members, 225 locals.

U.S. Union Membership, 1930-96

Source: Bureau of Labor Statistics, U.S. Dept. of Labor

Year	Labor force[1] (thousands)	Union members[2] (thousands)	Percentage of labor force	Year	Labor force[1] (thousands)	Union members[2] (thousands)	Percentage of labor force
1930	29,424	3,401	11.6	1986	96,903	16,975	17.5
1935	27,053	3,584	13.2	1987	99,303	16,913	17.0
1940	32,376	8,717	26.9	1988	101,407	17,002	16.8
1945	40,394	14,322	35.5	1989	103,480	16,960	16.4
1950	45,222	14,267	31.5	1990	103,905	16,740	16.1
1955	50,675	16,802	33.2	1991	102,786	16,568	16.1
1960	54,234	17,049	31.4	1992	103,688	16,390	15.8
1965	60,815	17,299	28.4	1993	105,067	16,598	15.8
1970	70,920	19,381	27.3	1994	107,989	16,748	15.5
1975	76,945	19,611	25.5	1995	110,038	16,360	14.9
1980	90,564	19,843	21.9	1996	111,960	16,269	14.5
1985	94,521	16,996	18.0				

(1) Does not include agricultural employment; from 1985, does not include self-employed or unemployed persons. (2) From 1930 to 1980 data are the number of dues-paying members of traditional trade unions, with members counted regardless of employment status; from 1985, figures also include members of employee associations that engage in collective bargaining with employers.

NATIONAL DEFENSE

Data as of Oct. 1, 1997.

Chief Commanding Officers of the U.S. Military

Chairman, Joint Chiefs of Staff
Gen. Henry Hugh Shelton

Vice Chairman
Gen. Joseph W. Ralston

The Joint Chiefs of Staff consists of the Chairman and Vice Chairman of the Joint Chiefs of Staff; the Chief of Staff, U.S. Army; the Chief of Naval Operations; the Chief of Staff, U.S. Air Force; and the Commandant of the Marine Corps.

Army

	Date of Rank
Chief of Staff	
Reimer, Dennis J.	June 21, 1991
Other Generals	
Bramlett, David A.	Sept. 1, 1996
Clark , Wesley K.	June 21, 1996
Crouch, William W.	Jan. 1, 1995
Griffith, Ronald H.	June 6, 1995
Hartzog, William W.	Dec. 1, 1994
Shelton, Henry H.	Mar. 1, 1996
Shoomaker, Peter J.	Pending Senate confirmation.
Tilelli, John H., Jr.	July 19, 1994
Wilson, Johnnie E.	May 1, 1996

Air Force

	Date of Rank
Chief of Staff	
Ryan, Michael E.	Apr. 4, 1996
Other Generals	
Babbitt, George T., Jr.	June 1, 1997
Eberhart, Ralph E.	Aug. 1, 1997
Estes, Howell M., III	Oct. 1, 1996
Habiger, Eugene E.	Mar. 1, 1996
Hawley, Richard E.	Aug. 1, 1995
Jamerson, James L.	Sept. 1, 1994
Kross, Walter	Aug. 1, 1996
Myers, Richard B.	Sept. 1, 1997
Newton, Lloyd W.	Apr. 1, 1997
Ralston, Joseph W.	July 1, 1995

Navy

	Date of Rank
Chief of Naval Operations	
Adm. Jay L. Johnson (aviator)	Apr. 1, 1996
Other Admirals	
Bowman, Frank L. (submariner)	Oct. 1, 1996
Clemins, Archie R. (submariner)	Jan. 1, 1997
Gehman, Harold W., Jr. (surface warfare)	Oct. 1, 1996
Larson, Charles R. (submariner)	Mar. 1, 1990
Lopez, Thomas J. (surface warfare)	July 31, 1996
Prueher, Joseph W. (aviator)	June 1, 1995
Reason, J. Paul (surface warfare)	Feb. 1, 1997

Marine Corps

Commandant of the Marine Corps (CMC)
Gen. Charles C. Krulak .... July 1, 1995

Assistant Commandant of the Marine Corps (ACMC)
Gen. Richard I. Neal .... Sept. 27, 1996

Coast Guard

Commandant, with rank of Admiral
Robert E. Kramek .... June 1, 1994

Vice Commandant, with rank of Vice Admiral
Richard D. Herr .... June 30, 1994

Unified Defense Commands Commanders in Chief

U.S. European Command, Stuttgart-Vaihingen, Germany — Gen. Wesley K. Clark (USA) (concurrently NATO Supreme Allied Commander, Europe)

U.S. Pacific Command, Honolulu, HI — Adm. Joseph W. Prueher (USN)

U.S. Atlantic Command, Norfolk, VA — Adm. Harold W. Gehman, Jr. (USN) (concurrently NATO Supreme Allied Commander, Atlantic)

U.S. Special Operations Command, MacDill AFB, Florida — Gen. Peter J. Shoomaker* (USA)
*Pending Senate confirmation.

U.S. Transportation Command, Scott AFB, Illinois — Gen. Walter Kross (USAF)

U.S. Central Command, MacDill AFB, Florida — Gen. Anthony C. Zinni (USMC)

U.S. Southern Command, Quarry Heights, Panama — Lt. Gen. Charles E. Wilhelm (USMC)

U.S. Space Command, Peterson AFB, Colorado — Gen. Howell M. Estes III (USAF)

U.S. Strategic Command, Offutt AFB, Nebraska — Gen. Eugene E. Habiger (USAF)

North Atlantic Treaty Organization International Commands

Supreme Allied Commander, Europe (SACEUR) — Gen. Wesley K. Clark (USA)

Deputy Supreme Allied Commander, Europe (DSACEUR) — Gen. Sir Jeremy MacKenzie (UKA)

Supreme Allied Commander, Atlantic — Adm. Harold W. Gehman, Jr. (USN)

Commander in Chief, Allied Forces Southern Europe — Adm. Thomas J. Lopez (USN)

Commander in Chief, Allied Forces Central Europe — Gen. D. Stoeckmann (GEA)

Commander in Chief, Allied Forces Northwestern Europe — Air Chief Marshal Sir John Cheshire (RAF)

Chairman, NATO Military Committee — Gen. Klaus Naumann (GEA)

Principal U.S. Military Training Centers

Army

Name, PO address	Zip	Nearest city	Name, PO address	Zip	Nearest city
Aberdeen Proving Ground, MD	21005	Aberdeen	Fort Lee, VA.	23801	Petersburg
Carlisle Barracks, PA	17013	Carlisle	Fort McClellan, AL	36205	Anniston
Fort Benning, GA	31905	Columbus	Fort Rucker, AL	36362	Dothan
Fort Bliss, TX	79916	El Paso	Fort Sill, OK	73503	Lawton
Fort Bragg, NC	28307	Fayetteville	Fort Leonard Wood, MO	65473	Rolla
Fort Devens, MA.	01433	Ayer	Joint Readiness, Ft. Polk, LA	71459	Leesville
Fort Gordon, GA	30905	Augusta	National Training Center	92311	Barstow, CA
Fort Huachuca, AZ	85613	Sierra Vista	The Judge Advocate General		
Fort Jackson, SC	29207	Columbia	School, VA	22901	Charlottesville
Fort Knox, KY	40121	Louisville			
Fort Leavenworth, KS	66027	Leavenworth			

Navy

Name	Zip	Nearest city	Name	Zip	Nearest city
Naval Education & Training Ctr.	32508	Pensacola, FL	Naval Education & Training Ctr.	02841	Newport, RI
Naval Air Training Center	78419	Corpus Christi,TX	Naval Post Graduate School. .	93943	Monterey, CA
Training Command, Atlantic Fleet	23511	Norfolk, VA	Naval Submarine School	06349	Groton, CT
Training Command, Pacific Fleet	92143	San Diego, CA	Naval Training Ctr., Great Lakes	60088	N. Chicago, IL
Naval Aviation Schools Command	32508	Pensacola, FL	Naval War College	02841	Newport, RI

Marine Corps

Name, PO address	Zip	Nearest city	Name, PO address	Zip	Nearest city
MCB Camp Lejeune, NC.	28542	Jacksonville	MCAS Cherry Point, NC	28533	Havelock
MCB Camp Pendleton, CA . . .	92055	Oceanside	MCAS Miramar, CA	92145	San Diego
MCB Kaneohe Bay, HI	96863	Kailua	MCAS New River, NC.	28545	Jacksonville
MCAGCC Twentynine Palms, CA	92278	Palm Springs	MCAS Beaufort, SC	29904	Beaufort
MCCDC Quantico, VA.	22134	Quantico	MCAS Yuma, AZ	85369	Yuma
MCRD Parris Island, SC	29905	Beaufort	MCMWTC Bridgeport, CA. . . .	93517	Bridgeport
MCRD San Diego, CA.	92140	San Diego			

MCB = Marine Corps Base. MCCDC = Marine Corps Combat Development Command. MCAS = Marine Corps Air Station. MCRD = Marine Corps Recruit Depot. MCAGCC = Marine Corps Air-Ground Combat Center. MCMWTC = Marine Corps Mountain Warfare Training Center.

Air Force

Name, PO address	Zip	Nearest city	Name, PO address	Zip	Nearest city
Goodfellow AFB, TX	76908	San Angelo	Maxwell AFB, AL.	36112	Montgomery
Keesler AFB, MS.	39534	Biloxi			
Lackland AFB, TX	78236	San Antonio	Sheppard AFB, TX.	76311	Wichita Falls

All are Air Education and Training Command Bases.

Personal Salutes and Honors

The United States national salute, 21 guns, is also the salute to a national flag. The independence of the U.S. is commemorated by the salute to the Union — one gun for each state — fired at noon on July 4, at all military posts provided with suitable artillery.

A 21-gun salute on arrival and departure, with 4 ruffles and flourishes, is rendered to the president of the United States, to an ex-president, and to a president-elect. The national anthem or "Hail to the Chief," as appropriate, is played for the president, and the national anthem for the others. A 21-gun salute on arrival and departure, with 4 ruffles and flourishes, also is rendered to the sovereign or chief of state of a foreign country or a member of a reigning royal family; the national anthem of his or her country is played. The music is considered an inseparable part of the salute and immediately follows the ruffles and flourishes without pause. For the Honors March, generals receive the "General's March," admirals receive the "Admiral's March," and all others receive the 32-bar medley of "The Stars and Stripes Forever."

Grade, title, or office	Salute (in guns) Arriving	Leaving	Ruffles and flourishes	Music
Vice president of United States.	19		4	Hail, Columbia
Speaker of the House.	19		4	Honors March
U.S. or foreign ambassador	19		4	Nat. anthem of official
Premier or prime minister.	19		4	Nat. anthem of official
Secretary of Defense, Army, Navy, or Air Force	19	19	4	Honors March
Other cabinet members, Senate president pro tempore, governor, or chief justice of U.S..	19		4	Honors March
Chairman, Joint Chiefs of Staff.	19	19	4	
Army chief of staff, chief of naval operations, Air Force chief of staff, Marine commandant	19	19	4	Honors March
General of the Army, general of the Air Force, fleet admiral. . . .	19	19	4	
generals, admirals	17	17	4	
Assistant secretaries of Defense, Army, Navy, or Air Force	17	17	4	Honors March
Chair of a committee of Congress.	17		4	Honors March

Other salutes (on arrival only) include: 15 guns, along with 3 ruffles and flourishes, for U.S. envoys or ministers and foreign envoys or ministers accredited to the U.S.; 15 guns, for a lieutenant general or vice admiral; 13 guns, along with 2 ruffles and flourishes, for a major general or rear admiral (upper half) and for U.S. ministers resident and ministers resident accredited to the U.S.; 11 guns, along with 1 ruffle and flourish, for a brigadier general or rear admiral (lower half) and for U.S. charges d'affaires and like officials accredited to the U.S.; with 11 guns, and no ruffles and flourishes, for consuls general accredited to the U.S.

Military Units, U.S. Army and Air Force

Army Units. Squad: In infantry usually 10 enlisted personnel under a staff sergeant. **Platoon:** In infantry 4 squads under a lieutenant. **Company:** Headquarters section and 4 platoons under a captain. (Company-size unit in the artillery is a battery; in the cavalry, a troop.) **Battalion:** Hdqts. and 4 or more companies under a lieutenant colonel. (Battalion-size unit in the cavalry is a squadron.) **Brigade:** Hdqts. and 3 or more battalions under a colonel. **Division:** Hdqts. and 3 brigades with artillery, combat support, and combat service support units under a major general. **Army Corps:** Two or more divisions with corps troops under a lieutenant general. **Field Army:** Hdqts. and 2 or more corps with field Army troops under a general.

Air Force Units. Flight: Numerically designated flights are the lowest level unit in the Air Force. They are used primarily where there is a need for small mission elements to be incorporated into an organized unit. **Squadron:** A squadron is the basic unit in the Air Force. It is used to designate the mission units in operational commands. **Group:** The group is a flexible unit composed of 2 or more squadrons whose functions may be operational, support, or administrative in nature. **Wing:** An operational wing normally has 2 or more assigned mission squadrons in an area such as combat, flying training, or airlift. **Numbered Air Forces:** Normally an operationally oriented agency, the numbered air force is designed for the control of 2 or more wings with the same mission and/or geographical location. **Major Command:** A major subdivision of the Air Force that is assigned a major segment of the USAF mission.

The Federal Service Academies

U.S. Military Academy, West Point, NY. Founded 1802. Awards BS degree and Army commission for a 5-year service obligation. For admissions information, write Admissions Office, USMA, West Point, NY 10996.

U.S. Naval Academy, Annapolis, MD. Founded 1845. Awards BS degree and Navy or Marine Corps commission for a 5-year service obligation. For admissions information, write Dean of Admissions, Naval Academy, Annapolis, MD 21402.

U.S. Air Force Academy, Colorado Springs, CO. Founded 1954. Awards BS degree and Air Force commission for a 6-year service obligation. For admissions information, write Registrar, U.S. Air Force Academy, CO 80840-5025.

U.S. Coast Guard Academy, New London, CT. Founded 1876. Awards BS degree and Coast Guard commission for a 5-year service obligation. For admissions information, write Director of Admissions, Coast Guard Academy, New London, CT 06320.

U.S. Merchant Marine Academy, Kings Point, NY. Founded 1943. Awards BS degree, a license as a deck, engineer, or dual officer, and a U.S. Naval Reserve commission. Service obligations vary according to options taken by the graduate. For admissions information, write Admission Office, U.S. Merchant Marine Academy, Kings Point, NY 11024.

U.S. Army, Navy, Air Force, Marine Corps, and Coast Guard Insignia

Source: Dept. of the Army, Dept. of the Navy, Dept. of the Air Force, U.S. Dept. of Defense

Army

General of the Armies — Gen. John J. Pershing, the only person to have held this rank, in life, was authorized to prescribe his own insignia, but never wore in excess of four stars. The rank originally was established posthumously by Congress for George Washington in 1799, and he was promoted to the rank by joint resolution of Congress, approved by Pres. Gerald Ford, Oct. 19, 1976.

General of the Army — Five silver stars fastened together in a circle and the coat of arms of the United States in gold color metal with shield and crest enameled.

General	Four silver stars
Lieutenant General	Three silver stars
Major General	Two silver stars
Brigadier General	One silver star
Colonel	Silver eagle
Lieutenant Colonel	Silver oak leaf
Major	Gold oak leaf
Captain	Two silver bars
First Lieutenant	One silver bar
Second Lieutenant	One gold bar

Warrant Officers

Grade Five — Silver bar with 4 enamel silver squares
Grade Four — Silver bar with 4 enamel black squares
Grade Three — Silver bar with 3 enamel black squares
Grade Two — Silver bar with 2 enamel black squares
Grade One — Silver bar with 1 enamel black squares

Noncommissioned Officers

Sergeant Major of the Army (E-9) — Same as Command Sergeant Major (below) but with 2 stars. Also wears distinctive red and white shield on lapel.

Command Sergeant Major (E-9) — Three chevrons above 3 arcs with a 5-pointed star with a wreath around the star between the chevrons and arcs.

Sergeant Major (E-9) — Three chevrons above 3 arcs with a 5-pointed star between the chevrons and arcs.

First Sergeant (E-8) — Three chevrons above 3 arcs with a lozenge between the chevrons and arcs.

Master Sergeant (E-8) — Three chevrons above 3 arcs.
Sergeant First Class (E-7) — Three chevrons above 2 arcs.
Staff Sergeant (E-6) — Three chevrons above 1 arc.
Sergeant (E-5) — Three chevrons.
Corporal (E-4) — Two chevrons.

Specialists

Specialist (E-4) — Eagle device only.

Other enlisted

Private First Class (E-3) — One chevron above one arc.
Private (E-2) — One chevron.
Private (E-1) — None.

Air Force

Insignia for Air Force officers are identical to those of the Army. Insignia for enlisted personnel are worn on both sleeves and consist of a star and an appropriate number of rockers. Chevrons appear above 5 rockers for the top 3 noncommissioned officer ranks, as follows (in ascending order): Master Sergeant, 1 chevron; Senior Master Sergeant, 2 chevrons; and Chief Master Sergeant, 3 chevrons. The insignia of the Chief Master Sergeant of the Air Force has 3 chevrons and a wreath around the star design.

Navy

The following are worn on the lower sleeves of the Service Dress Blue uniform. They are of gold embroidery.

Rank	Insignia
Fleet Admiral*	1 two inch with 4 one-half inch
Admiral	1 two inch with 3 one-half inch
Vice Admiral	1 two inch with 2 one-half inch
Rear Admiral (upper half)	1 two inch with 1 one-half inch
Rear Admiral (lower half) .	1 two inch
Captain	4 one-half inch
Commander	3 one-half inch
Lieutenant Commander	2 one-half inch with 1 one-quarter inch between
Lieutenant	2 one-half inch
Lieutenant (j.g.)	1 one-half inch with one-quarter inch above
Ensign	1 one-half inch

Warrant Officer-W-4 — ½" stripe with 1 break
Warrant Officer W-3 — ½" stripe with 2 breaks, 2" apart
Warrant Officer W-2 — ½" stripe with 3 breaks, 2" apart
Warrant Officer W-1 — ¼" stripe with 3 breaks, 2" apart

Enlisted personnel (noncommissioned petty officers)—A rating badge worn on the upper left sleeve, consisting of a spread eagle, appropriate number of chevrons, and centered specialty mark.

*The rank of Fleet Admiral is reserved for wartime use only.

Marine Corps

Marine Corps' distinctive cap and collar ornament is the Marine Corps Emblem—a combination of the American eagle, a globe, and an anchor. Marine Corps and Army officer insignia are similar. Marine Corps enlisted insignia, although basically similar to Army's, feature crossed rifles beneath the chevrons. Marine Corps enlisted rank insignia are as follows:

Sergeant Major of the Marine Corps (E-9) — Same as Sergeant Major (below) but with Marine Corps emblem in the center instead of the star.

Sergeant Major (E-9) — Three chevrons above 4 rockers with a 5-pointed star in the center.

Master Gunnery Sergeant (E-9) — Three chevrons above 4 rockers with a bursting bomb insignia in the center.

First Sergeant (E-8) — Three chevrons above 3 rockers with a diamond in the middle.

Master Sergeant (E-8) — Three chevrons above 3 rockers with crossed rifles in the middle.

Gunnery Sergeant (E-7) — Three chevrons above 2 rockers with crossed rifles in the middle.

Staff Sergeant (E-6) —Three chevrons above 1 rocker with crossed rifles in the middle.

Sergeant (E-5) — Three chevrons above crossed rifles.
Corporal (E-4) — Two chevrons above crossed rifles.
Lance Corporal (E-3) — One chevron above crossed rifles.
Private First Class (E-2) — One chevron.
Private (E-1) — None.

Coast Guard

Coast Guard insignia follow Navy custom, with certain minor changes such as the officer cap insignia. The Coast Guard shield is worn on both sleeves of officers and on the right sleeve of all enlisted personnel.

U.S. Army Personnel on Active Duty[1]

Source: Department of the Army, U.S. Dept. of Defense

Date[2]	Total strength	Commissioned officers			Warrant officers		Enlisted personnel		
		Total	Male	Female[3]	Male[4]	Female	Total	Male	Female
1940	267,767	17,563	16,624	939	763	—	249,441	249,441	—
1942	3,074,184	203,137	190,662	12,475	3,285	—	2,867,762	2,867,762	—
1943	6,993,102	557,657	521,435	36,222	21,919	0	6,413,526	6,358,200	55,325
1944	7,992,868	740,077	692,351	47,726	36,893	10	7,215,888	7,144,601	71,287
1945	8,266,373	835,403	772,511	62,892	56,216	44	7,374,710	7,283,930	90,780
1946	1,889,690	257,300	240,643	16,657	9,826	18	1,622,546	1,605,847	16,699
1950	591,487	67,784	63,375	4,409	4,760	22	518,921	512,370	6,551
1955	1,107,606	111,347	106,173	5,174	10,552	48	985,659	977,943	7,716
1960	871,348	91,056	86,832	4,224	10,141	39	770,112	761,833	8,279
1965	967,049	101,812	98,029	3,783	10,285	23	854,929	846,409	8,520
1970	1,319,735	143,704	138,469	5,235	23,005	13	1,153,013	1,141,537	11,476
1975	781,316	89,756	85,184	4,572	13,214	22	678,324	640,621	37,703
1980 (Sept. 30)	772,661	85,339	77,843	7,496	13,265	113	673,944	612,593	61,351
1985 (Sept. 30)	776,244	94,103	83,563	10,540	15,296	288	666,557	598,639	67,918
1990 (Mar. 31)	746,220	91,330	79,520	11,810	15,177	470	639,713	567,015	72,698
1993 (Mar. 31)	590,324	76,714	66,336	10,378	12,359	441	500,810	443,942	56,868
1994	553,627	74,956	64,281	10,675	12,448	535	465,688	405,664	60,024
1995	521,036	72,646	62,250	10,396	12,053	599	435,807	377,832	57,975
1996 (May 31). . .	493,330	68,850	58,875	9,975	11,456	660	408,511	351,669	56,842
1997 (May 31). . .	487,297	67,986	58,270	9,716	11,021	719	403,072	342,817	60,255

(1) Represents strength of the active Army, including Philippine Scouts, retired Regular Army personnel on extended active duty, and National Guard and Reserve personnel on extended active duty; excludes U.S. Military Academy cadets, contract surgeons, and National Guard and Reserve personnel not on extended active duty.
(2) June 30, unless otherwise noted; data for 1940 to 1946 include personnel in the Army Air Forces and its predecessors (Air Service and Air Corps).
(3) Includes women doctors, dentists, and Medical Service Corps officers for 1946 and subsequent years, women in the Army Nurse Corps for all years, and the Women's Army Corps and Women's Medical Specialists Corps (dietitians, physical therapists, and occupational specialists) for 1943 and subsequent years.
(4) Act of Congress approved Apr. 27, 1926, directed the appointment as warrant officers of field clerks still in active service. Includes flight officers as follows: 1943, 5,700; 1944, 13,615; 1945, 31,117; 1946, 2,580.

U.S. Navy Personnel on Active Duty

Date	Officers	Nurses	Enlisted	Officer Candidates	Total
1940 (June)	13,162	442	144,824	2,569	160,997
1945 (June)	320,293	11,086	2,988,207	61,231	3,380,817
1950 (June)	42,687	1,964	331,860	5,037	381,538
1960 (June)	67,456	2,103	544,040	4,385	617,984
1970 (June)	78,488	2,273	605,899	6,000	692,660
1980 (June)[1]	63,100	—	464,100	—	527,200
1990 (Sept.)	74,429	—	530,133	—	604,562
1991 (Oct.)	70,824	—	494,923	—	565,747
1992 (Mar.)	71,826	—	500,459	—	572,285
1993 (Mar.)	66,787	—	445,409	—	512,196
1994 (Apr.)	64,430	—	418,378	—	482,808
1995 (May)	61,075	—	402,626	—	463,701
1996 (June)	60,013	—	376,595	—	436,608
1997 (June)	57,341	—	340,616	—	397,957

(1) Starting in 1980, "Nurses" are included with "Officers," and "Officer Candidates" are included with "Enlisted."

U.S. Marine Corps Personnel on Active Duty

(midyear personnel figures)

Year	Officers	Enlisted	Total	Year	Officers	Enlisted	Total	Year	Officers	Enlisted	Total
1940	1,800	26,545	28,345	1980	18,198	170,271	188,469	1994	18,430	159,949	178,379
1945	37,067	437,613	474,680	1990	19,958	176,694	196,652	1995	18,017	153,929	171,946
1950	7,254	67,025	74,279	1991	19,753	174,287	194,040				
1960	16,203	154,418	170,621	1992	19,132	165,397	184,529	1996	18,146	154,141	172,287
1970	24,941	234,796	259,737	1993	18,878	161,205	180,083	1997	18,089	154,240	172,329

U.S. Air Force Personnel on Active Duty

(as of May 1)

Year[1]	Strength	Year[1]	Strength	Year[1]	Strength	Year[1]	Strength
1907	3	1942	764,415	1970	791,078	1993	444,351
1918	195,023	1943	2,197,114	1980	557,969	1994	426,327
1920	9,050	1944	2,372,292	1986	608,200	1995	400,051
1930	13,531	1945	2,282,259	1990	535,233	1996	389,400
1940	51,165	1950	411,277	1991	510,432	1997	378,681
1941	152,125	1960	814,213	1992	470,315		

(1) Prior to 1947, data are for U.S. Army Air Corps and Air Service of the Signal Corps.

U.S. Coast Guard Personnel on Active Duty

(midyear personnel figures)

Year	Total	Officers	Cadets	Enlisted	Year	Total	Officers	Cadets	Enlisted
1970	37,689	5,512	653	31,524	1988 . . .	37,723	6,530	887	30,306
1975	36,788	5,630	1,177	29,981	1989 . . .	37,453	6,614	867	29,972
1980	39,381	6,463	877	32,041	1990 . . .	37,308	6,475	820	29,860
1981	39,760	6,519	981	32,260	1991 . . .	38,280	7,095	900	30,285
1982	38,248	6,431	902	30,915	1992 . . .	39,185	7,348	919	30,918
1983	39,708	6,535	811	32,362	1993 . . .	38,832	7,724	691	30,417
1984	38,705	6,790	759	31,156	1994 . . .	37,284	7,401	881	29,002
1985	38,595	6,775	733	31,087	1995 . . .	36,731	7,489	841	28,401
1986	37,284	6,577	754	29,953	1996 . . .	35,229	7,270	830	27,129
1987	38,576	6,644	859	31,073	1997 . . .	34,717	7,079	868	26,770

Defense Contracts

Source: U.S. Dept. of Defense

(in thousands of dollars)

The 50 companies (including their subsidiaries) receiving the largest dollar volume of prime contract awards from the Department of Defense during fiscal year 1996.

Lockheed Martin	$11,998,430	ITT Industries	$670,969	Standard Missile	$372,116
McDonnell Douglas	9,938,973	GTE	599,073	Logicon	332,440
General Motors	3,240,326	Tracor	580,599	Avondale Industries	328,065
Raytheon	3,011,905	Halliburton Energy Srvcs.	573,635	The Renco Group	326,446
General Dynamics	2,670,030	AT&T	529,037	Tenneco	324,550
Northrop Grumman	2,604,705	Texas Instruments	528,569	MIT	319,444
United Technologies	2,257,695	AlliedSignal	511,804	Nassco Holdings	301,456
Boeing	1,724,044	Rolls-Royce PLC	462,445	Chrysler	300,080
Litton Industries	1,709,112	Alliant Techsystems	456,551	Motorola	290,091
General Electric	1,530,029	Black & Decker	452,589	U.S. Dept. of Energy	284,350
Westinghouse Electric	1,440,714	Aetna Services	451,499	IBM	280,096
Boeing North American	1,287,683	Exxon	446,735	Atlantic Richfield	279,439
Textron	1,193,762	BDM International	407,467	Longbow LLC	273,786
Science Applications Intl.	1,066,291	Olin	398,459	Worldcorp	270,884
United Defense LP	876,614	Unisys	381,588	Harris	268,894
TRW	786,749	DynCorp	379,994	Honeywell	263,609
Computer Sciences	711,956	Mitre	374,724		

Women in the Armed Forces

Source: U.S. Dept. of Defense

Women in the Army, Navy, Air Force, Marines, and Coast Guard are fully integrated with male personnel. Expansion of military women's programs began in the Department of Defense in fiscal year 1973.

Admission of women to the service academies began in the fall of 1976.

Under rules instituted in 1993, women were allowed to fly combat aircraft and serve aboard warships. Women remained restricted from service in ground combat units.

Between Apr. 1993 and July 1994, almost 260,000 positions in the armed forces were opened to women. In July 1994, 80.2% of all jobs and 92% of all career fields in the military had been opened to women. As of June 30, 1997, women made up 13.6% of the armed forces.

Women Active Duty Troops in 1997

Service	% Women
Army	14.6
Navy	12.7
Marines	5.3
Air Force	17.0
Coast Guard	9.5

Women on Active Duty, All Services*: 1973-97

Year	% Women	Year	% Women
1973	2.5	1987	10.2
1975	4.6	1993	11.6
1981	8.9	1997	13.6

*Not including the Coast Guard, which is a part of the Dept. of Transportation.

African American Service in U.S. Wars

American Revolution. About 5,000 blacks served in the Continental Army, mostly in integrated units, some in all-black combat units.

Civil War. Some 200,000 blacks served in the Union Army; 38,000 were killed, and 22 won the Medal of Honor (the nation's highest award).

World War I. About 367,000 blacks served in the armed forces, 100,000 in France.

World War II. More than 1 million blacks served in the armed forces; all-black fighter and bomber AAF units and infantry divisions gave distinguished service. (By 1954, the armed forces were completely desegregated.)

Vietnam War. 274,937 blacks served in the armed forces (1965-74); 5,681 were killed in combat.

Persian Gulf War. About 104,000 blacks served in the Kuwaiti theater—20% of U.S. soldiers, compared with 8.7% for World War II and 9.8% for Vietnam.

Veteran Population

Source: U.S. Dept. of Veterans Affairs; as of July 1997

(in thousands)

Total veterans in civilian life[a,b]	**25,551**
Total wartime veterans	**19,614**
Total Persian Gulf War	1,864
Persian Gulf War with service in Vietnam era	288
Persian Gulf War with no prior wartime service	1,575
Total Vietnam era	8,212
Vietnam era with service in Korean conflict	491
Vietnam era with no prior wartime service	7,721
Total Korean conflict	4,290
Korean conflict with service in WWII	673
Korean conflict with no prior wartime service	3,617
World War II	6,694
World War I	7
Total peacetime veterans	**5,937**
Total post-Vietnam era	3,027
Service between Korean conflict and Vietnam era only	2,767
Other peacetime	143

Note: Detail may not add to total shown due to rounding. (a) The category "wartime veterans" equals the sum of Persian Gulf War (no service in Vietnam era), Vietnam era (no service in Korean conflict), Korean conflict (no service in World War II), World War II, and World War I. The data refer only to veterans living in the U.S. and Puerto Rico since data on veterans living elsewhere are not available. (b) There are an indeterminate number of Mexican Border period veterans, 18 of whom were receiving benefits in July 1997.

Veterans Compensation and Pension Case Payments

Source: 1900-1980: Dept. of Veterans Affairs; 1990-1996: Natl. Center for Veteran Analysis and Statistics

Fiscal year	Living veteran cases	Deceased veteran cases	Total cases	Total expenditures (dollars)	Fiscal year	Living veteran cases	Deceased veteran cases	Total cases	Total expenditures (dollars)
1900	752,510	241,019	993,529	$138,462,130	1970	3,127,338	1,487,176	4,614,514	$5,253,839,611
1910	602,622	318,461	921,083	159,974,056	1980	3,195,395	1,450,785	4,646,180	11,046,637,368
1920	419,627	349,916	769,543	316,418,030	1990	2,746,329	837,596	3,583,925	14,674,411,000
1930	542,610	298,223	840,833	418,432,809	1993	2,660,030	713,758	3,373,788	16,881,938,000
1940	610,122	239,176	849,298	429,138,465	1994	2,658,704	683,200	3,341,904	17,188,447,000
1950	2,368,238	658,123	3,026,361	2,009,462,298	1995	2,668,576	661,679	3,330,255	17,765,045,000
1960	3,008,935	950,802	3,959,737	3,314,761,383	1996	2,671,026	637,232	3,308,258	17,055,809,000

Active Duty U.S. Military Personnel Strengths, Worldwide

Source: U.S. Dept. of Defense

(as of Mar. 31, 1997)

U.S. Territories & Special Locations

U.S., 48 contiguous states	995,803
Alaska	16,623
Hawaii	36,712
Guam	4,803
Johnston Atoll	257
Puerto Rico	2,445
Transients	28,715
Afloat	130,951
Total[1]	**1,216,318**

Europe

Albania	143
Belgium	1,677
Bosnia and Herzegovina	7,906
Croatia	756
Germany	63,377
Greece	460
Greenland	127
Hungary	2,622
Iceland	1,771
Italy	12,192
Macedonia	464
Netherlands	681
Norway	108
Portugal	1,074
Spain	2,438
Turkey	3,056
United Kingdom	11,562
Afloat	2,753
Total[1]	**113,547**

East Asia & Pacific

Australia	636
Japan	37,137
Korea, South	37,213
Singapore	171
Thailand	127
Afloat	15,492
Total[1]	**91,035**

North Africa, Middle East & South Asia

Bahrain	810
Diego Garcia	744
Egypt	1,164
Kuwait	1,129
Saudi Arabia	2,541
Afloat	2,136
Total[1]	**8,839**

Other Western Hemisphere

Canada	199
Cuba (Guantánamo)	1,793
Haiti	346
Honduras	386
Panama	6,101
Afloat	166
Total[1]	**9,534**
Total Worldwide[2]	**1,443,138**

(1) Countries and areas with fewer than 100 assigned U.S. military members not listed; regional totals include personnel stationed in those countries and areas. (2) Total worldwide includes U.S. military personnel stationed in Sub-Saharan Africa (255), former Soviet republics (102), and Antarctica (23), as well as undistributed personnel (3,485 total—2,317 ashore, 1,168 afloat).

The Medal of Honor

The Medal of Honor is the highest military award for bravery that can be given to any individual in the United States. The first Army Medals were awarded on Mar. 25, 1863, and the first Navy Medals went to sailors and Marines on Apr. 3, 1863.

The Medal of Honor, established by Joint Resolution of Congress, July 12, 1862 (amended by Acts of Congress, July 9, 1918, and July 25, 1963), is awarded in the name of Congress to a person who, while a member of the armed forces, distinguishes himself or herself conspicuously by gallantry and intrepidity at the risk of life above and beyond the call of duty while engaged in an action against any enemy of the United States; while engaged in military operations involving conflict with an opposing foreign force; or while serving with friendly foreign forces engaged in an armed conflict against an opposing armed force in which the United States is not a belligerent party. The deed performed must have been one of personal bravery or self-sacrifice so conspicuous as to clearly distinguish the individual above his or her comrades and must have involved risk of life. Incontestable proof of the performance of service is required, and each recommendation for award of this decoration is considered on the standard of extraordinary merit.

Prior to World War I, the 2,625 Army Medal of Honor awards up to that time were reviewed to determine which past awards met new stringent criteria. The Army removed 911 names from the list, most of them former members of a volunteer infantry group during the Civil War who had been induced to extend their enlistments when they were promised the medal.

Since that review, Medals of Honor have been awarded in the following numbers:

World War I	124	Korean War	131
Peacetime (1920-40)	18	Vietnam War	239
World War II	440	Somalia	2

The figure for World War II includes 7 African-American soldiers who were awarded Medals of Honor (6 of them posthumously) in Jan. 1997. Previously, no black soldier had received the medal for World War II service; an Army inquiry begun in 1993 concluded that the prevailing political climate and Army practices of the time had prevented proper recognition of heroism on the part of black soldiers in that war.

MILLENNIUM FACT BOX

U.S. Armed Forces, 1789 to 1996[1]

1789................. 718	1850 20,824	1910............... 139,344	1960 2,503,631
1801................. 7,108	1860 27,958	1920............... 343,302	1970 3,064,760
1810.............. 11,554	1870 50,632	1930............... 255,648	1980 2,050,627
1820.............. 15,113	1880 37,894	1940............... 458,365	1990 2,043,705
1830.............. 11,942	1890 38,666	1945.......... 12,055,884	1996 1,471,722
1840.............. 21,616	1900 125,923	1950............ 1,459,462	

Note: Figures may not equal those reported elsewhere in *The World Almanac*, because of different reporting dates and differences in units included. [1]Personnel on active duty.

For Further Information on the U.S. Armed Forces

Army — Office of the Chief of Public Affairs, Attention: Public Communications Division—CR, Army 1500 Wash., DC 20310-1500. **Web** site: http://www.army.mil

Navy — Chief of Information, 1200 Navy Pentagon, Wash., DC 20350-1200. **Web** site: http://www.navy.mil

Air Force — Office of Public Affairs, 1690 Air Force, Pentagon, Wash., DC 20330-1690. **Web** site: http://www.af.mil

Marine Corps — Commandant of the Marine Corps (Code PA), Headquarters, U.S. Marine Corps, Wash. DC 20380-1775. **Web** site: http://www.usmc.mil

Coast Guard — Commandant (G-CP), U.S. Coast Guard, 2100 Second St. SW, Wash., DC 20593-0001. **Web** site: http://www.dot.gov/dotinfo/uscg

Additional information on all the U.S. Armed Forces branches, as well as many other related organizations, can be accessed through DefenseLINK, the official Internet site of the Dept. of Defense: http://www.defenselink.mil

Armed Forces per 1,000 Persons, 1995[1]

Source: U.S. Arms Control and Disarmament Agency

Afghanistan 0.9	Czech Republic . . . 6.6	Kuwait 11.0	Singapore 18.0
Albania. 16.2	Denmark 5.2	Lebanon 14.9	Slovakia 9.7
Argentina 1.9	Egypt. 6.9	Libya 14.5	South Africa. 2.4
Australia. 3.2	El Salvador 3.8	Mexico. 1.9	Spain 5.4
Austria 5.6	Finland. 6.3	Mongolia 8.6	Sweden. 5.8
Belarus. 11.1	France 8.7	Morocco. 6.7	Switzerland 4.0
Belgium 4.6	Germany 4.2	Netherlands 4.3	Syria 21.2
Bolivia 4.0	Greece. 20.3	Nicaragua 3.4	Taiwan 20.0
Bosnia and	Hungary. 7.0	Norway 8.7	Thailand 4.9
Herzegovina. . . . 18.0	India. 1.4	Oman 17.1	Turkey. 13.1
Brazil 1.8	Indonesia. 1.4	Pakistan 4.6	Ukraine 9.3
Bulgaria 10.0	Iran 6.8	Philippines. 1.5	United Arab
Cambodia. 8.5	Iraq 18.9	Poland. 7.2	Emirates. 20.5
Canada 2.5	Israel 34.9	Portugal 7.9	United Kingdom . . . 4.0
Chile 7.2	Italy 7.6	Qatar. 18.7	Venezuela. 3.5
China 2.4	Japan. 1.9	Romania 9.5	Vietnam. 7.6
Colombia 4.0	Jordan 27.3	Russia. 9.4	Yugoslavia 7.1
Croatia. 12.1	Korea, North. 44.3	Rwanda 5.5	Zaire (now Congo) . 1.1
Cuba 6.4	Korea, South 14.5	Saudi Arabia 9.3	

(1) Includes active-duty personnel performing national security functions. Does not include reserves or paramilitary forces.

Nations With Largest Armed Forces, by Active-Duty Troop Strength, 1996

Source: *The Military Balance, 1996-97* (International Institute for Strategic Studies, published by Oxford University Press, UK)

	Active troops (thousands)	Reserve troops	Defense expend. ($ bil)[1]	Tanks (MBT) (army only)	Cruisers/ Frigates/ Destroyers	Sub- marines	Combat aircraft FGA (air force only)	fighters
1. **China**	2,935.0	1,200+	31.7	8,000-8,500	36F/18D	63	400+	4000 est.
2. **U.S.**	1,483.8	1,880.6	266.4[2]	10,497	31C/49F/52D*	95	52 tactic. ftr. sqn	
3. **Russia**	1,270.0	20,000	82.0	16,800	24C/120F/21D*	133	775	425
4. India	1,145.0	535.0	8.3	3,500	19F/5D*	19	17 sqn	20 sqn
5. N. Korea	1,054.0	4,700.0	5.2	3,400	3F	25	529 total FGA/ftr.	
6. S. Korea	660.0	4,500.0	14.4	2,050	33F/7D	4	255	130
7. Turkey	639.0	378.7	6.0	4,280	16F/5D	15	11 sqn	7 sqn
8. Pakistan	587.0	513.0	3.6	2,050+	8F/3D	9	123	243
9. Vietnam	572.0	3-4,000	1.0	1,300	8F	—	65	125
10. Iran	513.0	350.0	2.5	1,440	3F/2D	2	150	115
11. Egypt	440.0	254.0	2.4	3,650	6F/1D	8	135	338
12. Syria	421.0	500.0	2.0	4,600	2F	3	154	300
13. Ukraine	400.8	1,000.0	1.1	4,026	4 total	3	200	425
14. **France**	398.9	337.0	48.0	880	1C/36F/4D*	17	9 sqn	6 sqn
15. Iraq	382.5	650.0	2.7	2,700	1F	—	130	180
16. Taiwan	376.0	1,657.5	13.1	630+	18F/18D	4	327 total FGA/ftr.	
17. Germany	358.4	304.9	41.8	2,988	11F/3D	17	8 sqn	.8 sqn
18. Italy	325.2	584.0	20.0	1,164	1C/26F/4D*	8	7 sqn	8 sqn
19. Myanmar	321.0	NA	1.9	106	—	—	24	36
20. Indonesia	299.2	400.0	2.8	355†	17F	2	52	12
21. Brazil	295.0	1,115.0	6.9	61	15F/3D*	5	86	16
22. Thailand	254.0	200.0	3.9	253+	12F	—	47	42
23. Poland	248.5	466.0	2.6	1,721	1F/1D	3	115	299
24. Japan	235.5	47.9	50.2	1,130	51F/9D	17	50	249
25. Romania	228.4	427.0	0.9	1,255	5F/1D	1	88	256
26. **UK**	226.0	327.4	34.2	2,541	23F/12D*	14	11 sqn	6 sqn
27. Spain	206.8	438.0	8.5	682	17F*	8	3 sqn	7 sqn
28. Morocco	194.0	150.0	1.3	524	1F	—	19	12
29. Israel	175.0	430.0	7.2	4,300	—	2	413 total FGA/ftr.[3]	
30. Mexico	175.0	300.0	2.7	—	4F/3D	—	10	

Boldface denotes nations with known strategic nuclear capability. MBT =main battle tank. FGA=fighter, ground attack; Sqn= squadron (12-24 aircraft). †=light tanks only. *Denotes navies with aircraft carriers, as follows: U.S. 12, Russia 1, India 2, France 2, Italy 1, Brazil 1, UK 3, Spain 1. (1) 1995 figures unless otherwise noted. (2) 1996. (3) Plus 250 in storage. NA = not available.

Nuclear Arms Treaties and Negotiations: A Historical Overview

(as of Sept. 1997)

Aug. 5, 1963—Limited Test Ban Treaty signed in Moscow by U.S., USSR, and Britain; prohibited testing of nuclear weapons in space, above ground, and under water.

Jan. 27, 1967—Outer Space Treaty banned the introduction of nuclear weapons and other weapons of mass destruction into orbit around the earth, their installation on the moon or other celestial body, or their station in space.

July 1, 1968—Nuclear Nonproliferation Treaty, with U.S., USSR, and Great Britain as major signers, limited spread of nuclear material for military purposes by agreement not to assist nonnuclear nations in getting or making nuclear weapons. Extended indefinitely, May 11, 1995.

May 26, 1972—Strategic Arms Limitation Treaty (SALT I) signed in Moscow by U.S. and USSR. This short-term agreement imposed a 5-year freeze on both testing and deployment of intercontinental ballistic missiles (ICBMs) as well as submarine-launched ballistic missiles (SLBMs). In the area of defensive nuclear weapons, the separate **ABM Treaty** limited antiballistic missiles to 2 sites of 100 antiballistic missile launchers in each country (amended in 1974 to one site in each country). ABM Treaty amended Sept. 1997 to allow flexibility in development of shorter-range nuclear weapons.

July 3, 1974—ABM Treaty Revision (protocol on antiballistic missile systems) and **Threshold Test Ban Treaty** on limiting underground testing of nuclear weapons to 150 kilotons were signed by U.S. and USSR in Moscow.

Sept. 1977—U.S. and USSR agreed to continue to abide by SALT I, despite its expiration date.

June 18, 1979—SALT II, signed in Vienna by the U.S. and USSR, constrained offensive nuclear weapons, limiting each side to 2,400 missile launchers and heavy bombers; ceiling to apply until Jan. 1, 1985. Treaty also set a subceiling of 1,320 ICBMs and SLBMs with multiple warheads on each side. SALT II never reached the Senate floor for ratification because Pres. Jimmy Carter withdrew support following Dec. 1979 Soviet invasion of Afghanistan.

Dec. 8, 1987—Intermediate-Range Nuclear Forces (INF) Treaty signed in Washington, D.C., by USSR leader Mikhail Gorbachev and U.S. Pres. Ronald Reagan, eliminating all U.S. and Soviet intermediate- and shorter-range nuclear missiles from Europe and Asia. Ratified, with conditions, by U.S. Senate on May 27, 1988; by USSR on June 1, 1988. Entered into force June 1, 1988.

July 31, 1991—Strategic Arms Reduction Treaty (START I) signed in Moscow by USSR and U.S. to reduce strategic offensive arms by about 30% in 3 phases over 7 years. START I was the first treaty to mandate reductions by the superpowers. Treaty was approved by U.S. Senate Oct. 1, 1992. With the Soviet Union breakup in Dec. 1991, 4 former Soviet republics became independent nations with strategic nuclear weapons—Russia, Ukraine, Kazakhstan, and Belarus. The last 3 agreed in principle in 1992 to transfer their nuclear weapons to Russia and ratify START I. The Russian Supreme Soviet voted to ratify, Nov. 4, 1992, but Russia decided not to provide instruments of ratification until the other 3 republics ratified START I and acceded to the Nuclear Nonproliferation Treaty (NPT) as nonnuclear nations. By late 1994, all 3 nations had done so, and NPT entered into force on Dec. 5, 1994. In Dec. 1996, Belarus was the last of the 3 to give up its nuclear weapons.

Jan. 3, 1993—START II signed in Moscow by U.S. and Russia. Potentially the broadest disarmament pact in history, it called for both sides to reduce their long-range nuclear arsenals to about one-third of their then-current levels within a decade and disable and dismantle launching systems. The U.S. ratified START II on Jan. 26, 1996. On Sept. 26, 1997, the U.S. and Russia signed an agreement that would delay the dismantling of launching systems under START II to the end of 2007 (they would still be disabled by 2003). The accord was expected to facilitate Russian ratification of START II. Russia and the U.S. also agreed in writing to work toward further strategic arms cuts in a 3d round of START negotiations.

Sept. 24, 1996—Comprehensive Test Ban Treaty (CTBT) signed by U.S. and Russia. The CTBT bans all nuclear weapon tests and other nuclear explosions. It is intended to help prevent the nuclear powers from developing more advanced weapons, while limiting the ability of other states to acquire such devices. As of Sept. 1997, the CTBT had been signed by 146 nations and ratified by 8. The U.S. and Russia had not yet ratified it.

Monthly Military Pay Scale

Source: U.S. Dept. of Defense; effective Jan. 1, 1997

Rank/Grade	Years of Service						
	2	4	8	12	16	20	26
General—O-10	$7,619.10	$7,619.10	$7,911.60	$8,349.90	$8,947.20	$9,546.30	$10,140.90
Lt. General—O-9	6,693.90	6,836.70	7,010.40	7,302.00	7,911.60	8,349.90	8,947.20
Major General—O-8	6,085.50	6,229.80	6,693.90	7,010.40	7,302.00	7,911.60	8,106.60
Brig. General—O-7	5,243.10	5,243.10	5,478.30	5,795.70	6,693.90	7,154.40	7,154.40
Colonel—O-6	3,997.50	4,259.70	4,259.70	4,259.70	5,100.90	5,478.30	6,285.60
Lt. Colonel—O-5	3,417.00	3,653.40	3,653.40	3,966.60	4,549.20	4,955.70	5,128.80
Major—O-4	2,987.10	3,186.30	3,388.50	3,823.20	4,173.30	4,287.90	4,287.90
Captain—O-3	2,548.50	3,014.70	3,272.10	3,619.80	3,708.60	3,708.60	3,708.60
1st Lt.—O-2	2,170.80	2,695.80	2,751.60	2,751.60	2,751.60	2,751.60	2,751.60
2d Lt.—O-1	1,796.10	2,170.80	2,170.80	2,170.80	2,170.80	2,170.80	2,170.80
Chief Warrant—W-4	2,491.80	2,548.50	2,781.90	3,101.40	3,359.40	3,560.70	3,966.60
Warrant Officer—W-1	1,765.80	1,913.40	2,085.90	2,260.20	2,433.60	2,608.20	2,608.20
Sgt. Major—E-9	0.00	0.00	0.00	2,762.40	2,889.90	3,011.70	3,478.50
Master Sgt.—E-8	0.00	0.00	2,265.60	2,391.90	2,519.10	2,639.70	3,106.50
Sgt. 1st class—E-7	1,707.90	1,833.00	1,955.70	2,081.40	2,237.10	2,329.20	2,794.80
Staff Sgt.—E-6	1,483.50	1,610.70	1,731.30	1,887.30	2,009.40	2,040.00	2,040.00
Sergeant—E-5	1,299.90	1,422.30	1,577.70	1,700.40	1,731.30	1,731.30	1,731.30
Corporal—E-4	1,176.30	1,341.60	1,394.70	1,394.70	1,394.70	1,394.70	1,394.70
Pvt. 1st class—E-3	1,107.00	1,196.70	1,196.70	1,196.70	1,196.70	1,196.70	1,196.70
Private—E-2	1,010.10	1,010.10	1,010.10	1,010.10	1,010.10	1,010.10	1,010.10
Recruit—E-1	900.90	900.90	900.90	900.90	900.90	900.90	900.90

Chairmen of the Joint Chiefs of Staff

Gen. of the Army Omar N. Bradley, USA	8/16/49–8/14/53	Gen. George S. Brown, USAF	7/1/74 – 6/20/78
Adm. Arthur W. Radford, USN	8/15/53– 8/14/57	Gen. David C. Jones, USAF	6/21/78 – 6/18/82
Gen. Nathan F. Twining, USAF	8/15/57 – 9/30/60	Gen. John W. Vessey Jr., USA	6/18/82 – 9/30/85
Gen. Lyman L. Lemnitzer, USA	10/1/60 – 10/30/62	Adm. William J. Crowe, Jr., USN	10/1/85 – 9/30/89
Gen. Maxwell D. Taylor, USA	10/1/62 – 7/3/64	Gen. Colin L. Powell, USA	10/1/89 – 9/30/93
Gen. Earle G. Wheeler, USA	7/3/64 – 7/2/70	Gen. John M. Shalikashvili, USA	10/1/93 – 9/30/97
Adm. Thomas H. Moorer, USN	7/3/70 – 6/30/74	Gen. Henry H. Shelton, USA	10/1/97–

Casualties in Principal Wars of the U.S.
Source: U.S. Dept. of Defense, U.S. Coast Guard

Data prior to World War I are based on incomplete records in many cases. Casualty data are confined to dead and wounded personnel and, therefore, exclude personnel captured or missing in action who were subsequently returned to military control. Dash (—) indicates information is not available. Off. = officers.

War	Branch of service	Number serving	Casualties Battle deaths	Casualties Other deaths	Casualties Wounds not mortal[7]	Casualties Total
Revolutionary War	Total	—	**4,435**	—	**6,188**	—
1775-83	Army	184,000	4,044	—	6,004	—
	Navy	to	342	—	114	—
	Marines	250,000	49	—	70	—
War of 1812	Total	286,730[8]	**2,260**	—	**4,505**	**6,765**
1812-15	Army	—	1,950	—	4,000	5,950
	Navy	—	265	—	439	704
	Marines	—	45	—	66	111
Mexican War	Total	78,789[8]	**1,733**	**11,550**	**4,152**	**17,435**
1846-48	Army	—	1,721	11,550	4,102	17,373
	Navy	—	1	—	3	4
	Marines	—	11	—	47	58
	Coast Guard[12]	71 off.	—	—	—	—
Civil War	Total	2,213,582[8]	**140,415**	**224,097**	**281,881**	**646,392**
Union forces	Army	2,128,948	138,154	221,374	280,040	639,568
1861-65	Navy	—	2,112	2,411	1,710	6,233
	Marines	84,415	148	312	131	591
Confederate forces	Total		**74,524**	**59,297**	—	**133,821**
(estimate)[1]	Army	600,000	—	—	—	—
1863-66	Navy	to	—	—	—	—
	Marines	1,500,000	—	—	—	—
	Coast Guard[12]	219 off.	1	—	—	—
Spanish-American	Total	307,420	**385**	**2,061**	**1,662**	**4,108**
War	Army[3]	280,564	369	2,061	1,594	4,024
1898	Navy	22,875	10	0	47	57
	Marines	3,321	6	0	21	27
	USCG[12]	660	0	—	—	—
World War I	Total	4,743,826	**53,513**	**63,195**	**204,002**	**320,710**
April 6, 1917-	Army[4]	4,057,101	50,510	55,868	193,663	300,041
Nov. 11, 1918	Navy	599,051	431	6,856	819	8,106
	Marines	78,839	2,461	390	9,520	12,371
	Coast Guard	8,835	111	81	—	192
World War II	Total	16,353,659	**292,131**	**115,185**	**671,846**	**1,079,162**
Dec. 7, 1941-	Army[5]	11,260,000	234,874	83,400	565,861	884,135
Dec. 31, 1946[2]	Navy[6]	4,183,466	36,950	25,664	37,778	100,392
	Marines	669,100	19,733	4,778	68,207	91,718
	Coast Guard	241,093	574	1,343	—	1,917
Korean War[9]	Total	5,764,143	**33,667**	**3,249**	**103,284**	**140,200**
June 25, 1950-	Army	2,834,000	27,709	2,452	77,596	107,757
July 27, 1953	Navy	1,177,000	493	160	1,576	2,226
	Marines	424,000	4,267	339	23,744	28,353
	Air Force	1,285,000	1,198	298	368	1,864
	Coast Guard	44,143	—	—	—	—
Vietnam War[10]	Total	8,752,000	**47,393**	**10,800**	**153,363**	**211,556**
Aug. 4, 1964-	Army	4,368,000	30,929	7,272	96,802	135,003
Jan. 27, 1973	Navy	1,842,000	1,631	931	4,178	6,740
	Marines	794,000	13,085	1,753	51,392	66,230
	Air Force	1,740,000	1,741	842	931	3,514
	Coast Guard	8,000	7	2	60	69
Persian Gulf War	Total	467,939[11, 12]	**148**	**151**	**467**	**766**
1991	Army	246,682	98	105	—	—
	Navy	98,852	6	14	—	—
	Marines	71,254	24	26	—	—
	Air Force	50,751	20	6	—	—
	Coast Guard	400	—	—	—	—

(1) Authoritative statistics for the Confederate forces are not available. An estimated 26,000-31,000 Confederate personnel died in Union prisons.
(2) Data are for the period Dec. 1, 1941, through Dec. 31, 1946, when hostilities were officially terminated by Presidential Proclamation, but few battle deaths or wounds not mortal were incurred after the Japanese acceptance of Allied peace terms on Aug. 14, 1945. Numbers serving Dec. 1, 1941-Aug. 31, 1945, were: Total—14,903,213; Army—10,420,000; Navy—3,883,520; and Marine Corps—599,693.
(3) Number serving covers the period April 21-Aug. 13, 1898, while dead and wounded data are for the period May 1-Aug. 31, 1898. Active hostilities ceased on Aug. 13, 1898, but ratifications of the treaty of peace were not exchanged between the United States and Spain until April 11, 1899.
(4) Includes Army Air Forces battle deaths and wounds not mortal, as well as casualties suffered by American forces in northern Russia to Aug. 25, 1919, and in Siberia to April 1, 1920. Other deaths covered the period April 1, 1917-Dec. 31, 1918.
(5) Includes Army Air Forces.
(6) Battle deaths and wounds not mortal include casualties incurred in Oct. 1941 due to hostile action.
(7) Marine Corps data for World War II, the Spanish-American War, and prior wars represent the number of individuals wounded, whereas all other data in this column represent the total number (incidence) of wounds.
(8) As reported by the Commissioner of Pensions in his Annual Report for Fiscal Year 1903.
(9) As a result of an ongoing Dept. of Defense review of available Korean War casualty record information, updates to previously reported figures for battle deaths and other deaths are reflected in this table.
(10) Number serving covers the period Aug. 4, 1964-Jan. 27, 1973 (date of ceasefire). Includes casualties incurred in Mayaguez Incident. Wounds not mortal exclude 150,332 persons not requiring hospital care.
(11) Estimated, because deployment figures changed continually.
(12) Actually the U.S. Revenue Cutter Services, predecessor to the U.S. Coast Guard.

TAXES

Federal Income Tax

Source: George W. Smith III, CPA, Nationally Syndicated Tax Author and Columnist

On Aug. 5, 1997, Pres. Bill Clinton signed into law the Taxpayer Relief Act of 1997, the most significant tax legislation in over a decade. It includes more than 800 amendments to the Internal Revenue Tax Code, including 285 new tax sections. The law contains over $150 billion in tax cuts and will have a major impact on taxpayers well into the 21st century.

Highlights of Taxpayer Relief Act of 1997

Starting Dates. The complexity of the law is compounded by the various starting dates. Of the major provisions, 36 are retroactive, over 100 began when the bill was signed into law, and 69 start Jan. 1, 1998. Five major provisions of the law become effective after 1998.

On Aug. 11, Pres. Clinton vetoed two items in the so-called Taxpayer Relief Act. This represents the first time a president has vetoed provisions of enacted legislation using the authority of the recently enacted line-item veto.

Capital Gains. After July 28, 1997, the maximum long-term capital gains tax rate for individual taxpayers is lowered to 20% from the previous 28% maximum, for qualified investments held more than 18 months, or more than 12 months if the investment was sold after May 6 but before July 29. For taxpayers in the 15% bracket, the maximum net capital gains rate is even lower, 10%.

Qualified investments sold after July 28, 1997, and held more than 12 months but less than 18 months will be taxed as a "midterm gain" at the old maximum rate of 28%.

Five-Year Period. Starting Jan. 1, 2001, a lower capital gains rate of 18% may apply if the taxpayer held the investment more than five years, 8% if in the 15% tax bracket. If the taxpayer is in a bracket higher than 15%, the five-year holding period applies only to investments acquired after Dec. 31, 2000. If in the 15% bracket, the investment does not have to be acquired after the year 2000 in order to have the five-year period begin.

More on Capital Gains. Capital gains on collectible items such as art, antiques, jewelry, stamps, and coins continue to be taxed at a maximum 28%. However, certain newly minted gold and silver coins issued by the federal government and coins issued under state law become subject to the lower capital gains rates. Gain attributable to depreciation deducted from depreciable real estate will now be recaptured at a maximum 25% tax rate. The balance will be taxed at a maximum rate of 20%. The rules for deducting capital losses remain the same.

Individual Retirement Accounts (IRAs). Starting in 1998 there are a number of new IRA regulations:

(a) An individual will not be considered an active participant in an employer-sponsored plan and will not be disqualified from making a deductible IRA contribution because the individual's spouse is an active participant in a plan. The spouse who does not participate in a qualified retirement plan may make a maximum deductible IRA contribution (up to $2,000) provided adjusted gross income on the couple's joint tax return is $150,000 or less. The amount deductible starts to phase out when adjusted gross income is over $150,000, with full phase-out at $160,000.

(b) The new law raises the adjusted gross income (AGI) limits for which an IRA deduction is allowed. The new maximum amounts are phased in annually through the year 2007.

(c) The new law allows IRA distributions for qualifying first-time home buying expenses of up to $10,000 without penalty, effective for 1998 and later years.

(d) Starting in 1998, a new type of IRA is available to taxpayers called a Roth IRA. Contributions made to it are not deductible. However, distributions of funds held in the account for five years or longer and paid on or after the date on which an individual attains age 59½ are tax-free. Also tax-free are any funds paid to the estate or beneficiary on or after an individual's death, funds paid that are attributable to the individual being disabled, or payments up to $10,000 used for a first-time home purchase. There are some restrictions, depending on adjusted gross income.

(e) Beginning in 1998, a trust or custodial account can be created or organized exclusively for paying qualified higher education expenses of the account holder. Annual nondeductible contributions of up to $500 a year per child may be made until the beneficiary reaches age 18. Earnings on contributions will be distributed tax-free when used to pay qualified higher education expenses for the IRA beneficiary. However, there are limitations depending on gross income.

Retirement Distributions. The Taxpayer Relief Act repeals the 15% excise tax on excess distributions from qualified retirement plans, tax-sheltered annuities, and IRAs. The 15% excise tax on excess retirement accumulations is also repealed. Prior legislation *suspended* the excise tax penalty only on excess distributions for 1997, 1998, and 1999, but did not repeal it.

Sale of Home. Retroactive to May 7, 1997, homeowners filing a joint income tax return may, under the new law, exclude up to $500,000 in gain from the sale of their principal residence. This election is reusable every two years. Various provisions related to "unforeseen events," five-year ownership, marital status, and certain other situations may apply.

For single taxpayers the excludable amount is $250,000. Married couples who do not share a principal residence but file a joint tax return also may claim the $250,000 exclusion for a qualifying sale or exchange of each spouse's principal residence.

Vacation and rental homes also may qualify for the exclusion if they are converted into the taxpayer's principal residence and the two-year residency requirement is met. A yacht or houseboat can qualify if either is considered the owner's primary residence. Land next to a home also can qualify for the $250,000 exclusion, if the land is used as part of the owner's principal residence.

The Taxpayer Relief Act repeals the previous two-year reporting requirement for home gains and the one-time $125,000 exclusion for persons age 55 or older.

Dependent Standard Deduction. For 1998, the new law increases the basic standard deduction for dependents who can be claimed on another taxpayer's return to the greater of $700 or the dependent's earned income (salary, wages, etc.) plus $250, not to exceed the basic standard deduction for nondependent individuals.

Child Tax Credit. Beginning in 1998, a $400 credit against federal taxes is allowed for each child under the age of 17 who can be claimed as a dependent and is the taxpayer's son or daughter, a descendant of the son or daughter, a stepchild, or an eligible foster child. The credit increases to $500 per child starting in 1999.

Higher-income taxpayers must reduce the allowable child credit by $50 for each $1,000 (or fraction thereof) by which modified adjusted gross income exceeds $110,000 for a joint return, $75,000 for an unmarried individual, and $55,000 for married individuals filing separate returns.

Low-income families with children may use the credit to offset their income taxes as well as Social Security taxes paid for the year.

Education Tax Incentives. Starting in 1998, individuals can claim a nonrefundable HOPE scholarship credit up to a maximum of $1,500 per student against their federal income taxes for qualified tuition and related expenses. The credit can be used for each of the first two years of postsecondary education in a degree or certificate program at an eligible institution. The credit does not apply to room and board or cost of books.

Taxpayers can claim a nonrefundable lifetime learning credit against their federal income taxes equal to 20% of qualified tuition and fees paid after June 30, 1998, for the taxpayer, spouse or dependents. The maximum amount of the credit per taxpayer is $1,000 ($5,000 × 20%) for expenses paid in taxable years before 2003, and $2,000 ($10,000 × 20%) thereafter. This credit is allowed only for tax years in which the HOPE credit is not claimed for the same student's tuition.

Both education credits are reduced or eliminated based on income. The credit phase-out begins with modified AGI exceeding $40,000 for singles ($80,000 on a joint return), with full phase-out at $50,000 for singles ($100,000 joint). These amounts are to be inflation-adjusted after 2001.

Student Loan Interest. Starting in 1998, the new law allows taxpayers who pay interest on qualified higher education loans taken for themselves, spouses, or any dependents to deduct interest paid during the first 60 months in which interest payments are required on the loan. However, dependents of another taxpayer may not deduct interest they themselves pay. Married individuals must file a joint return in order to claim the deduction.

The maximum interest deduction for 1998 is $1,000; it increases to $1,500 for 1999, $2,000 in the year 2000, and $2,500 thereafter. This is an "above-the-line" page one deduction that is allowed whether or not the taxpayer itemizes on Schedule A. There is also a phase-out for any taxpayer whose income exceeds a certain level.

Employer-Paid Tuition. Beginning after June 30, 1997, tuition, fees, and related education expenses paid by an employer under an employer's educational assistance program, up to $5,250 annually, are tax-free to an employee through May 31, 2000. Most graduate-level courses do not qualify.

Office in Home. Beginning in 1999, taxpayers will be able to claim deductions for an office in their home when they conduct administrative or management activities for their business, providing they do not perform substantial administrative activities at another fixed location.

Self-Employed Health Insurance. The Taxpayer Relief Act eventually will allow a 100% page-one, Form 1040 deduction for health insurance for the self-employed business person. The deduction for 1997 is 40% of the cost of the health insurance. This percentage increases to 45% for 1998 and 1999, and 50% for 2000, with annual increases over the next seven years to a full 100% deduction in 2007.

Charitable Mileage Rate. Starting in 1998, the new law increases the deduction for individuals who use their passenger automobile in volunteer work for qualified charities to 14 cents per mile. The standard mileage rate for 1997 remains at 12 cents per mile.

Corporate AMT Tax. For 1998, the corporate alternative minimum tax (AMT) is repealed for small businesses, providing the preceding three-year average of $5 million or less annual gross receipts test is met. A corporation will continue to be exempt from AMT as long as its average gross receipts for the prior three years do not exceed $7.5 million.

Estimated Tax Penalties. For tax years beginning after 1997, taxpayers do not have to pay a penalty for underpayment of estimated tax unless the amount of the underpayment is $1,000 or more, up from the previous $500.

Foreign Income. The foreign earned-income exclusion has been increased to $72,000 starting in 1998 and increases annually thereafter by $2,000 until it reaches $80,000 in the year 2002. After that, the amount will be indexed for inflation.

Estate and Gift Tax. Beginning in 1998 and through 2006, the estate and gift tax unified credit increases annually in a series of steps. The current $600,000 exemption will increase annually to a maximum $1 million in 2006.

Beginning in 1999, the $10,000-per-person annual exclusion for gifts will be indexed for inflation and rounded to the next lowest multiple of $1,000.

Other Recent Changes

Nonworking IRA Deduction. Starting Jan. 1, 1997, the maximum tax-deferred IRA retirement contribution for a married couple filing a joint tax return was increased from $2,250 to $4,000 per year (not to exceed total combined income). Each spouse can contribute up to $2,000 annually, even if the spouse had little or no income. There are exceptions.

Retirement Planning. The Small Business Act of 1996 (a) eliminated 5-year averaging for lump sum distributions from qualified retirement plans beginning after 1999. However, prior rules that applied to individuals who attained age 50 before Jan. 1, 1986, remained in effect. (b) As of Jan. 1, 1997, the definition of a highly compensated employee is a 5% owner or an employee who earns more than $80,000 and is in the top 20% of employees ranked by compensation.

Age 70½ Plus. As of 1997, any employee who continues to work beyond age 70½ and is not a 5% owner of the business can continue to defer retirement plan distributions (and any resulting income tax liability) until a later date.

Seniors' Earnings Limits. Starting in 1997, individuals age 65-69 may, without jeopardizing their Social Security benefits, earn up to $13,500, with annual increases reaching $30,000 by 2002. Individuals age 65 to 69 will lose $1 of benefits in 1997 for every $3 of earned income in excess of the $13,500 threshold.

Age 62 to 64. The maximum amount individuals age 62 to 64 may earn without losing any Social Security benefits was adjusted for inflation to $8,640 for 1997. Individuals age 62 to 64 lose $1 of their Social Security benefits in 1997 for every $2 of earned income exceeding $8,640.

Age 70 or Over. Individuals who are age 70 or over will not lose any benefits regardless of earnings.

Death Benefits. Qualified accelerated death benefits paid under a life insurance contract to terminally ill persons (certified as expected to die within 24 months) are excluded from gross income starting Jan. 1, 1997. A similar exclusion applies to the sale or assignment of death benefits under a life insurance contract to a person engaged in the business of purchasing insurance contracts on the lives of terminally or chronically ill persons. Accelerated death benefits paid to a chronically ill person under a long-term care rider are tax-free, up to $175 per day.

Adoption Credit. An adoption expense credit is available for up to $5,000 of qualified expenses for each eligible adopted person. The credit limit is per person, not per year, and increases to $6,000 for an eligible person with special needs. Adoption expenses paid through a nondiscriminatory employee adoption-assistance program may be excluded from gross income.

Long-Term Care. The Health Insurance Act of 1996 allows long-term care insurance contracts issued in 1997 or later to be treated in the same way as health insurance contracts for income tax purposes. Premiums are a deductible medical expense up to annual limits based on age. Long-term care benefits received under a qualifying policy will be tax-free, subject to certain per diem restrictions.

Medical Savings Accounts (MSAs). MSAs are intended to meet medical costs not covered by a high-deductible health plan. Starting in 1997, MSAs may be offered only by employers who, on the average, had no more than 50 employees in either of the two preceding years and provided high-deductible health plans. Self-employed individuals may use MSAs to pay health care expenses.

The annual insurance deductible amount for an MSA to qualify must be between $1,500 and $2,250 for individuals and between $3,000 and $4,500 for families. The distributions from MSAs are tax-free if used for qualified medical expenses. *Penalty:* Distributions not used for medical expenses are subject to regular income tax plus a 15% penalty. Penalty does not apply after age 65 or upon death or disability.

Self-Employed Exclusion. Self-employed individuals can exclude from income any payments received for injury or sickness under a self-insured plan similar to traditional accident or health insurance plans.

Damage Awards. Tax-free treatment for payment of damages received after Aug. 20, 1996, is limited to physical injury or sickness. Damages received for emotional distress that are not attributable to a physical injury or sickness, or to actual medical expenses, are now taxable.

Social Security Taxes. The maximum wage base for withholding Social Security tax increased to $65,400 for 1997; the tax rate remains at 6.2%. The Medicare tax rate remains at 1.45% and applies to total wages. There is no maximum wage base for Medicare. These tax rates are paid by both employer and employee. Self-employed individuals pay both parts, 12.4% and 2.9%, on net earnings.

Elective Withholding. Starting Jan. 1, 1997, taxpayers who receive Social Security benefits (and certain other payments) from the federal government may elect to have federal income tax withheld at a rate of 7%, 15%, 28%, or 31%. States are now required to permit elective federal withholding from unemployment compensation at a rate of 15%.

Business Equipment. The election to expense instead of depreciating the cost of certain business assets is called a "Section 179 Expense Election." The maximum amount deductible for 1997 is $18,000, with annual increases reaching $25,000 by 2003.

Auto Mileage. For 1997, the standard mileage tax rate deduction for business use of an automobile was increased to 31.5 cents a mile for all business miles driven. The standard mileage rate cannot be used for leased cars. The mileage rate for charitable use remains at 12 cents a mile for 1997 (raised to 14 cents for 1998). The medical and moving rates remain at 10 cents per mile.

Corporate Eligibility. Beginning in 1997, the maximum number of eligible shareholders of an S corporation was increased from 35 to 75. Previously, it was limited to 35. S corporations can now own 80% or more of a C corporation.

SIMPLE Retirement Plan. Congress enacted a new retirement plan titled Savings Incentive Match Plan for Employees (SIMPLE), for businesses with 100 or fewer employees, including self-employed individuals. This plan became effective Jan. 1, 1997. It is generally easy to implement and cost effective to administrate. The SIMPLE plan is similar to a 401(k) retirement plan in that employees can elect to defer compensation, therefore deferring taxes.

Payroll Tax Reporting. Starting Jan. 1, 1998, the IRS requires businesses that had federal employment taxes of more than $50,000 for the calendar year 1995 to begin making all federal tax deposit payments electronically, using the government's new Electronic Federal Tax Payment System (EFTPS). Failure to do so will result in a 10% penalty for each deposit not made through EFTPS. The electronic tax deposit rules apply to all federal taxes. For more information call the IRS Customer Service at 1-800-945-8400 or 1-800-555-4477.

Electronic Services. Federal tax forms, tax legislation, court decisions, and other information are now available electronically from the IRS as follows:

via modem: 1-705-321-8020
via the IRS's Internet Home Page addresses:
   Telnet: iris.irs.ustreas.gov
   FTP: htp.irs.ustreas.gov
   World Wide Web: http://www.irs.ustreas.gov

Other Tax Law Provisions

Retirement. The maximum dollar amount on individuals' elective deferrals to their 401(k) retirement plans is adjusted annually for inflation. The maximum amount for 1997 is $9,500. Participants in a 40l(k) plan may generally withdraw funds from their retirement plan without penalty when the funds are "necessary" to satisfy "immediate and heavy financial needs."

A recent federal law provides that a state may not impose an income tax on any individual's retirement income if the person is no longer a resident of that state.

"Nanny Tax." Employers are not required to withhold taxes for household workers such as nannies, gardeners, and cooks who receive less than $1,000 per year. In addition, all household workers under the age of 18 (students, etc.) are exempt from employment taxes unless working in a household is their principal occupation. Employers have to apply for an employer identification number and issue employee wage statements (Form W-2).

Children's Income. Parents may elect to include on their income tax return the unearned income of a dependent child under age 14 whose income is more than $650 but less than $6,500. The income must consist solely of interest and dividends. Form 8814, *Parent's Election to Report Child's Interest and Dividends*, must be attached to the parents' tax return. This election is not available if estimated tax payments were made in the child's name.

If a dependent child with taxable income cannot file an income tax return, the parent, guardian, or other legally responsible person must file a return for the child. The parent or guardian may be held liable for any unpaid tax.

Education Expenses. For 1997, an individual may not claim a dependency exemption for a child who qualifies as a full-time student and is over age 23 at the end of the year, unless the child's gross income is less than $2,650.

Interest earned on U.S. Series EE bonds issued after 1989 may be exempt from federal income tax under certain circumstances if the bonds are used to pay tuition and fees for a taxpayer, spouse, or dependent. Your banker can assist you with details.

Interest. Borrowers can generally deduct the points paid on their mortgage loan. The IRS has also affirmed that the buyer can deduct "seller-paid points" on the purchase of a principal residence.

Interest paid on investments is deductible, but only up to the amount of net investment income. Capital gains income also can be included as investment income when figuring the limitation. However, the taxpayer will have to reduce the amount of net long-term capital gain eligible for capital gains treatment in order to offset the additional investment interest deduction.

Intangibles. Congress now allows for patents, trademarks, and certain other intangible assets to be amortized over a 15-year period. The cost of goodwill and customer/patient lists are included in this 15-year write-off period.

Business Expenses. The deduction for qualified business meals and entertainment expenses is limited to 50% of the cost. A receipt is required for business meals, entertainment, and transportation costs above $75. Adequate records must be kept substantiating the time, place, date, and business purpose of the expense.

Expenses paid for business assignments away from home in a single location that last for more than one year are not considered temporary nor are they deductible. Travel expenses paid for other individuals (including a spouse) traveling with the taxpayer on a business trip are not deductible unless the individual (1) is an employee, (2) has a bona fide business purpose for the travel, and (3) would otherwise be allowed to deduct the travel expense.

Dues paid to business, social, athletic, luncheon, sporting, and country clubs, including airport and hotel clubs, are not deductible. However, dues paid to the Chamber of Commerce and business Economic Clubs remain deductible.

Gift Giving. Taxpayers deducting individual charitable contributions of $250 or more must obtain written substantiation from the charity. If the statement or receipt is for more than $75, the charity must include a breakdown of the payment indicating how much is a (deductible) contribution and what (if any) was the (nondeductible) value of goods or services (including meals) received.

Federal Empowerment Zones. A 20% employment tax credit is available to most employers for qualified wages paid to each full or part-time employee who is a resident of one of 9 federal empowerment zones. These are distressed areas designated for economic revitalization by the U.S. government. The 20% credit is applied toward the employer's income tax liability for the first $15,000 of wages paid per employee. The maximum credit per employee is $3,000. The full 20% credit has been extended through the year 2001 but is reduced to 15% for 2002, 10% for 2003, and 5% for 2004. To qualify, an employee must perform substantially all employment services within the zone and in the employer's trade or business.

Social Security Numbers. For 1997, taxpayers can lose their head of household filing status, dependency exemption, dependent care credit, and earned income credit, if the Social Security number of a dependent is not included on their tax return. For information on getting a number, call the Social Security Administration at 1-800-772-1213.

1998 Tax Payments. Individual federal estimated tax payment due dates for 1998 are: 1st Quarter, Apr. 15, 1998; 2nd Quarter, June 15, 1998; 3rd Quarter, Sept. 15, 1998; 4th Quarter, Jan. 15, 1999.

If taxpayers do not have the necessary funds to pay their federal income taxes when due, they may apply for monthly installment payments by attaching Form 9465 to the tax return. Penalty and interest will continue to accrue on any balance owed. There is a $43 fee if the request is approved.

Tax Refunds. Taxpayers can request to have their refund electronically deposited directly into their checking or savings account. According to the IRS, refunds to taxpayers who file their returns electronically are issued within 21 days.

Services. The IRS provides videotaped instructions to assist taxpayers, not only in English but also in Spanish. These tapes are available at participating libraries. Many federal tax instructions, publications, and forms are printed in Spanish. For more information, call 1-800-TAX-FORM, and ask for free IRS Publication 1SP, Derechos del Contribuyente.

The IRS telephone service for hearing-impaired persons is available for taxpayers who have access to TDD equipment. The toll-free number is 1-800-829-4059.

Who Must File

Generally, a U.S. citizen or a resident alien will have to file a 1997 income tax return if the person's gross income for the year is at least as much as the amount shown in the following table:

Filing Status	1997 Gross Income
Single	
• Under 65	$ 6,800
• 65 or older	7,800
Married filing jointly	
• Both spouses under 65	12,200
• One spouse 65 or older	13,000
• Both spouses 65 or older	13,800
Married filing separately	2,650
Head of Household	
• Under 65	8,700
• 65 or older	9,700
Qualifying widow(er)	
• Under 65	9,550
• 65 or older	10,350

Some Additional Filing Requirements. A tax return must be filed if:

• Taxpayer had net earnings of $400 or more from self-employment for the year.
• Taxpayer received advance earned income credit payments during the year from an employer or is entitled to receive a refundable earned income credit.
• Taxpayer paid estimated income tax payments during 1997 or expects an income tax refund.
• Gross income is less than the filing requirement amount but additional taxes are owed for:
—Social Security tax on unreported tips.
—Alternative minimum tax
—Recapture of investment credit
— Tax attributable to qualified retirement distributions (including IRAs), annuities, and modified endowment contracts.

When to File

U.S. individual income tax returns for 1997 are required to be filed with the IRS no later than Wed., Apr. 15, 1998. An individual who cannot file on time should file Form 4868, *Application for Automatic Extension of Time to File U.S. Individual Income Tax Return.* Form 4868 gives the taxpayer an automatic 4-month extension of time to file, until Mon., Aug. 17, 1998. This is not, however, an extension of time to pay the tax. The taxpayer will owe interest and may be charged a penalty on any federal income tax owed and not paid to the IRS by Apr. 15, 1998.

Which Tax Return to File

Most U.S. citizens can use one of the following basic income tax forms: 1040EZ, 1040A or 1040. Forms 1040EZ and 1040A are shorter and simpler than Form 1040.

You may be able to use the shortest of the 3 forms, Form 1040EZ, if:

• You are single or married filing jointly and do not claim any dependents.
• You are not 65 or older or blind.
• You have income only from wages, salaries, tips, taxable scholarships or fellowships, unemployment compensation, or Alaska Permanent Fund dividends, and do not have over $400 of taxable interest income.
• Your taxable income is less than $50,000.
• You do not itemize deductions, claim any adjustments to income, or have tax credits other than the earned income credit.
• You did not receive any advance earned income credit payments.
• You did not make any estimated tax payments.
• You file on or before Wed., Apr. 15, 1998. You cannot use Form 1040EZ after Apr. 15 even if you have filed for an extension.

You may be able to use Form 1040A if:

• You have income from wages, salaries, tips, taxable scholarships or fellowships, interest, and dividends.
• You have income from Individual Retirement Account (IRA) distributions, pensions, annuities, unemployment compensation, and taxable Social Security or railroad retirement benefits.
• Your taxable income is less than $50,000.
• You do not itemize deductions.
• You claim a deduction for qualified contributions to an IRA.

• You claim a credit for child and dependent care expenses, credit for the elderly or the disabled, or the earned income credit.
• You report employment taxes on wages paid to household employees on Schedule H.
• You take the education exclusion for interest income earned from Series EE U.S. Savings Bonds.
• You received advance earned income credit payments.
• You owe alternative minimum tax.
• You have made estimated tax payments.
• You filed for an extension of time to file.

You will have to file Form 1040 if any of the following situations apply:

• Your taxable income is $50,000 or more.
• You itemize deductions.
• You receive any nontaxable dividends or capital gain distributions.
• You have foreign bank accounts and/or foreign trusts.
• You have taxable refunds of state or local income taxes.
• You have business, farm, or rental income.
• You sold or exchanged capital assets or business property.
• You have miscellaneous income not allowed on Form 1040EZ or 1040A, such as alimony.
• You have additional adjustments to income such as alimony or moving expenses.
• You can claim a foreign tax credit or certain other credits to which you are entitled.
• You have other taxes such as self-employment tax or Social Security tax on tips.
• You are required to file additional forms, such as **Form 2106**, Employee Business Expenses; **Form 2555**, Foreign Earned Income; **Form 3903**, Moving Expenses; **Form 4972**, Tax on Lump-Sum Distributions.

1997 Individual Income Tax Rates

Single

Tax Rate	Taxable Income
15%	$0 to $24, 650
28%	$24,651 to $59,750
31%	$59,751 to $ 124,650
36%	$124,651 to $271,050
39.6%	More than $271,050

Married Filing Jointly or Qualifying Widow(er)

Tax Rate	Taxable Income
15%	$0 to $41,200
28%	$41,201 to $99,600
31%	$99,601 to $151,750
36%	$151,751 to $271,050
39.6%	More than $271,050

Married Filing Separately

Tax Rate	Taxable Income
15%	$0 to $20,600
28%	$20,601 to $49,800
31%	$49,801 to $75,875
36%	$75,876 to $135,525
39.6%	More than $135,525

(continued)

Head of Household	
Tax Rate	**Taxable Income**
15%	$0 to $33,050
28%	$33,051 to $85,350
31%	$85,351 to $138,200
36%	$138,201 to $271,050
39.6%	More than $271,050

Estates and Trusts	
Tax Rate	**Taxable Income**
15%	$0 to $1,650
28%	$1,651 to $3,900

Estates and Trusts	
Tax Rate	**Taxable Income**
31%	$3,901 to $5,950
36%	$5,951 to $8,100
39.6%	More than $8,100

The alternative minimum tax rate for noncorporate taxpayers is 26% for alternative minimum taxable income less the exemption amount up to $175,000 ($87,500 for married individuals filing separately). Above that dollar level, a 28% rate applies.

Dependent and Personal Exemptions

The deductible exemption amount for 1997 has been increased to $2,650 for each individual taxpayer or dependent. The exemption amount has been adjusted by the IRS for inflation each year since 1990.

Exemption Phaseout. The deduction for each exemption is reduced by 2% for each $2,500 ($1,250 for married filing separately) or fraction thereof by which adjusted gross income for 1997 exceeds the following amounts:

Married filing jointly	$181,800
Qualifying widow(er)	$181,800
Head of household	$151,500
Single	$ 88,475
Married filing separately	$ 90,900

The exemption amount is fully phased out when adjusted gross income is more than $122,500 ($61,250 for married filing separately) over the above threshold amount.

Standard Deduction

The standard deduction is a flat dollar amount that is subtracted from the adjusted gross income of taxpayers who do not itemize their deductions. The amount of the basic standard deduction depends on the taxpayer's filing status and is adjusted annually for inflation.

1997 Basic Standard Deduction

Single:	$4,150
Married filing jointly or qualifying widow(er):	$6,900
Married filing separately:	$3,450
Head of household:	$6,050

These figures are not applicable if an individual can be claimed as a dependent on another person's tax return.

Caution: Taxpayers with itemized deductions totaling more than the above amounts usually should itemize instead of using the standard deduction.

An individual claimed as a dependent on another person's income tax return generally may claim on his or her own tax return only the larger of $650 or the amount of earned income up to the amount of the basic standard deduction that the taxpayer would normally be allowed.

Earned income includes wages, salaries, commissions, and tips. It also includes net profit from self-employment received as compensation for personal services rendered. Any part of a scholarship or fellowship grant that must be included in gross income is also considered earned income.

Elderly or blind taxpayers may claim an **additional standard deduction** in addition to the **basic standard deduction**. Taxpayers who are age 65 or over or blind at the end of 1997 qualify. Individuals who claim the additional standard deduction because of blindness must attach a doctor's statement to their income tax return.

Tax Tip: For tax purposes, an individual is considered 65 years of age beginning on the day preceding his or her 65th birthday. Consequently, a taxpayer whose 65th birthday falls on Jan. 1, 1998, is entitled to take the additional standard deduction for 1997.

1997 Additional Standard Deduction

Single or head of household, age 65 or older OR blind	$1,000
Single or head of household, age 65 or older AND blind	$2,000
Married filing jointly or qualifying widow(er), age 65 or older OR blind (per person)	$ 800
Married filing jointly or qualifying widow(er), age 65 or older AND blind (per person)	$1,600
Married filing separately, age 65 or older OR blind	$ 800
Married filing separately, age 65 or older AND blind	$1,600

Adjustments to Income

Individual Retirement Accounts (IRAs)

Taxpayers may contribute to their IRAs even if they are covered by an employer-sponsored qualified retirement plan. However, the amount that can be deducted on their income tax return depends on total income: Married taxpayers filing jointly in 1997 with adjusted gross income (AGI) of $40,000 or less may take the maximum IRA deduction allowed, regardless of whether either spouse is an active participant in a qualified retirement plan. Single taxpayers in a qualified retirement plan may deduct up to the maximum IRA contribution provided their AGI is $25,000 or less. Above these amounts, the IRA deduction begins to phase out over the next $10,000 of AGI if a taxpayer is an active participant in a qualified retirement plan.

Single taxpayers not covered by a qualified employer retirement plan may deduct an IRA contribution up to the lesser of $2,000 or the amount of their earned income, regardless of their total income. Married taxpayers filing jointly may take an IRA deduction provided neither spouse is an active participant in a qualified retirement plan. The

Small Business Act of 1996 allows a maximum contribution up to $2,000 to an IRA account for each spouse on a jointly filed return as of 1997.

New for 1997, IRA payouts used to pay medical expenses in excess of 7.5% of adjusted gross income are exempt from the 10% penalty for early withdrawal. In addition, the penalty will not apply to IRA distributions taken early by certain unemployed, formerly unemployed, or self-employed individuals to pay for their health insurance premiums.

There are significant changes to the IRA laws starting in 1998.

Moving Expenses

Taxpayers who change jobs or are transferred to another job location during the year usually can deduct part of their moving expenses. These expenses include travel and the cost of moving household goods to their new home. The cost of meals while moving is no longer deductible.

To qualify, the move must be a result of changing job locations or starting a new job and must meet distance and time tests. The new job must be at least 50 miles farther from the former home than was the old job. Employees also must work full time for at least 39 weeks during the first 12 months after they arrive in the general area of their new job.

Taxpayers no longer have to itemize on Schedule A to deduct moving expenses. These expenses are now an adjustment to income and should instead be reported on page 1, Form 1040. Moves within the United States are reported on Form 3903, *Moving Expenses.*

Itemized Deductions

If the total amount of itemized deductions is more than the standard deduction, you generally should itemize your deductions on your income tax return. Itemized deductions are reported on Schedule A, Form 1040.
• Cosmetic surgery for congenital abnormality, personal injury resulting from an accident or trauma, or a disfiguring disease is allowed as a medical deduction. Only the total amount of medical expenses that exceeds 7.5% of the taxpayer's adjusted gross income is deductible.
• Most mortgage interest paid on a taxpayer's primary residence and 2d home is fully deductible.
• Interest paid on home equity loans is deductible, but only on the first $100,000 of equity debt.
• Investment interest expense is deductible only to the extent of net investment income. Any investment interest expense not deducted is carried over to future years.
• State and local income taxes, real estate taxes and personal property taxes are fully deductible. Sales taxes are not.
• Casualty and theft losses are deductible subject to the $100 limitation rule for each occurrence and the 10% of adjusted gross income provision.
• Miscellaneous items, such as union and professional dues, tax preparation fees, safe-deposit box rental expense, and employee business expenses are deductible, but only the amount that exceeds 2% of adjusted gross income.

• Amounts spent for business tools and supplies used at work are deductible expenses if they wear out within 1 year from the date of purchase. Tools expected to last more than a year will have to be depreciated. These expenses also are subject to the 2% rule.
• Armed forces reservists can deduct the unreimbursed cost of their uniforms if regulations restrict them from wearing them except while on duty as a reservist.
Individuals can deduct gambling losses, including the cost of lottery tickets, on Schedule A, but only up to the amount of their gambling winnings reported on Page 1, Form 1040. Unreimbursed employee business expenses, including travel, automobile, telephone, and gifts, are also deductible on Schedule A as miscellaneous itemized deductions. Only 50% of the cost of customer meals and entertainment is deductible. All deductible employee business expenses are also subject to the 2% adjusted gross income rule.
Many itemized deductions otherwise allowed are further reduced by the smaller of these two figures: 3% of a taxpayer's adjusted gross income in excess of the 1997 threshold amount, $121,200 ($60,600 for married taxpayers filing separately) or 80% of the amount of these itemized deductions otherwise allowable for the year. This provision does not apply to medical expenses, investment interest expense, casualty losses, or gambling losses to the extent of gambling winnings.

1997 Earned Income Credit

Low-income workers who have dependent children and maintain a household may be eligible for a refundable earned income credit, based on income such as wages and tips.
The maximum earned income credit for an individual with one qualifying child is $2,210. However, the credit is gradually phased out as earned income increases; it disappears once adjusted gross income reaches $25,760. For an individual with 2 or more qualifying children, the maximum credit is $3,656 and is phased out, disappearing once adjusted gross income reaches $29,290.
The IRS has a chart showing the earned income credit at various income levels. The IRS will also help individuals filing for the credit if they need assistance. An individual may qualify for the credit even if not otherwise required to file a return. However, a tax return *must be filed* to receive the refund.

The credit has been extended to include persons who do not have a qualifying child; the maximum credit is $332. To qualify: (1) earned income and adjusted gross income must be less than $9,500, (2) an individual or spouse must be at least 25 years old and less than 65, and (3) an individual cannot be claimed as a dependent on another person's return.
The Welfare Reform Act of 1996 added several restrictions to the earned income credit: (1) The credit cannot be taken by individuals who are not authorized to be employed in the U.S. (2) Individuals must include their own Social Security number and, if married, their spouse's Social Security number on the return claiming the credit. (3) The individual's "disqualified" income cannot exceed $2,250. Disqualified income includes interest, dividends and, if greater than zero, net rent, royalty income, and capital-gains net income.

Taxable Social Security Benefits

Up to 50% of Social Security benefits may be taxable income if the person's total income is:
• over $25,000 but less than $34,000 for single, head of household, qualifying widow(er), or married and filing separately, *and the spouses lived apart for all of the year.*
• over $32,000 but less than $44,000 for married individuals filing jointly.

For people with incomes exceeding the maximum $34,000 or $44,000 amounts, 85% of Social Security benefits are taxable. Below these amounts, 50% is still included in taxable income. If the taxpayer is married, filing separately, and lived with a spouse at any time during the year, the amounts are reduced to zero.
Generally, Social Security benefits will not be taxable if they are the only income received during the year.

IRS Tax Audit

Although only about one out of every 100 individual tax returns will be audited in 1997, the IRS is very good at selecting returns for audit that will yield additional taxes. Nevertheless, if your return is selected, it does not necessarily mean you will incur any additional tax liability.

If you do not agree with the examiner's report, you can meet with the examiner's supervisor to discuss your case further. If you still do not agree, you have the right to appeal the findings through a separate Appeals Office. You can also appeal to the U.S. Tax Court.

Your Rights as a Taxpayer

Congress passed the *Taxpayer Bill of Rights 1* in 1989, requiring that the IRS explain, in easy-to-understand language, any actions it proposes to take against a taxpayer and that it relax some of its audit and collection procedures.
In 1996 Congress enacted the Taxpayer Bill of Rights 2. This law created an Office of the Taxpayer Advocate within the IRS, with authority to order IRS personnel to issue refund checks and meet deadlines for resolving disputes. This legisla-

tion also requires the agency to pay a taxpayer's legal fees if the latter wins the case and the IRS cannot show it was "substantially justified" in pursuing it. The IRS is also required to accept the postmark of a qualified courier as proof of timely mailing.
Individuals can learn more about this legislation by obtaining a free copy of IRS Publication 1, *Your Rights as a Taxpayer;* call 1-800-TAX-FORM.

State Government Individual Income Taxes

Source: Reproduced with permission from *CCH State Tax Guide*, published and copyrighted by CCH Inc., 2700 Lake Cook Road, Riverwoods, IL 60115

Below are basic state tax rates on taxable income, for 1997 unless otherwise indicated. Alaska, Florida, Nevada, South Dakota, Texas, Washington, and Wyoming did not have state income taxes and are thus not listed. For further details, see notes which follow.

Alabama
1st	$1,000	2%
Next	$5,000	4%
Over	$6,000	5%

Arizona
First	$20,000	2.9%
Next	$30,000	3.30%
Next	$50,000	3.90%
Next	$200,000	4.80%
$300,001 and over		5.17%

Arkansas
1st	$2,999	1%
Next	$3,000	2.50%
Next	$3,000	3.50%
Next	$6,000	4.50%
Next	$10,000	6%
$25,000 or over.		7%

California
$0 to $9,816.		1%
$9,817 to $23,264.		2%
$23,265 to $36,714.		4%
$36,715 to $50,968.		6%
$50,969 to $64,414.		8%
$64,415 and over.		9.30%

Colorado
5% of fed. taxable income.

Connecticut
First	$12,500	3%
Over	$12,500	4.50%

Delaware
$2,001 to $5,000.		3.10%
Next	$5,000	4.85%
Next	$10,000	5.80%
Next	$5,000	6.15%
Next	$5,000	6.45%
Over	$30,000	6.90%

District of Columbia
1st	$10,000	6%
2d	$10,000	8%
Over	$20,000	9.50%

Georgia
1st	$1,000	1%
Next	$2,000	2%
Next	$2,000	3%
Next	$2,000	4%
Next	$3,000	5%
Over	$10,000	6%

Hawaii
First	$3,000	2%
Next	$2,000	4%
Next	$2,000	6%
Next	$4,000	7.25%
Next	$10,000	8%
Next	$10,000	8.75%
Next	$10,000	9.50%
Over	$41,000	10%

Idaho
1st	$1,000	2%
2d	$1,000	4%
3rd	$1,000	4.50%
4th	$1,000	5.50%
5th	$1,000	6.50%
Next	$2,500	7.50%

Illinois
3% of taxable net income

Indiana
3.4% of adj. gross income

Iowa
$0 to $1,112		0.40%
$1,113 to $2,224.		0.80%
$2,225 to $4,448.		2.70%
$4,449 to $10,008.		5%
$10,009 to $16,680.		6.80%
$16,681 to $22,240.		7.20%
$22,241 to $33,360.		7.55%
$32,361 to $50,040.		8.80%
Over	$50,040	9.98%

Kansas
1st	$30,000	3.50%
Next	$30,000	6.25%
Over	$60,000	6.45%

Kentucky
1st	$3,000	2%
Next	$1,000	3%
Next	$1,000	4%
Next	$3,000	5%
$8,000 and over		6%

Louisiana
1st	$10,000	2%
Next	$40,000	4%
Over	$50,000	6%

Maine
Less than $4,150.		2%
$4,150 to $8,249.		4.50%
$8,250 to $16,499.		7%
$16,500 or more		8.50%

Maryland
1st	$1,000	2%
2d	$1,000	3%
2d	$1,000	4%
Over	$3,000	5%

Massachusetts
Interest, dividends, certain cap. gains.		12%
Certain cap. gains income		0-5%
All other income.		5.95%

Michigan
4.4% of taxable income

Minnesota
$0 to 24,140		6%
$24,141 to 95,920		8%
Over $95,920		8.50%

Mississippi
1st	$5,000	3%
Next	$5,000	4%
Over	$10,000	5%

Missouri
1st	$1,000	1.50%
2d	$1,000	2%
3rd	$1,000	2.50%
4th	$1,000	3%
5th	$1,000	3.50%

6th	$1,000	4%
7th	$1,000	4.50%
8th	$1,000	5%
9th	$1,000	5.50%
Over	$9,000	6%

Montana
$0 to $1,899	2%
$1,900 to $3,799	3%
	less $19
$3,800 to $7,599	4%
	less $57
$7,600 to $11,399	5%
	less $133
$11,400 to $15,199	6%
	less $247
$15,200 to $18,999	7%
	less $399
$19,000 to $26,499	8%
	less $589
$26,500 to $37,899	9%
	less $854
$37,900 to $66,399	10%
	less $1,233
$66,399 and over	11%
	less $1,897

Nebraska
1st	$4,000	2.62%
Next	$26,000	3.65%
Next	$16,750	5.24%
Over	$46,750	6.99%

New Hampshire
5% of interest and dividends

New Jersey
1st	$20,000	1.40%
Next	$30,000	1.75%
Next	$20,000	2.45%
Next	$10,000	3.50%
Next	$70,000	5.53%
Over	$150,000	6.37%

New Mexico
Not over $8,000.		1.70%
$8,001 to $16,000.		3.20%
$16,001 to $24,000.		4.70%
$24,001 to $40,000.		6%
$40,001 to $64,000.		7.10%
$64,001 to $100,000.		7.90%
Over $100,000.		8.50%

New York
First	$11,000.	4%
Next	$5,000.	5%
Next	$6,000.	6%
Over	$26,000.	7.125%

North Carolina
Up to	$21,250.	6%
Next	$78,750.	7%
Over	$100,000.	7.75%

North Dakota
1st	$3,000.	2.67%
Next	$2,000.	4%
Next	$3,000.	5.33%
Next	$7,000.	6.67%
Next	$10,000.	8%
Next	$10,000.	9.33%

Next	$15,000.	10.67%
Over	$50,000.	12%

Ohio
First	$5,000.	0.693%
Next	$5,000.	1.387%
Next	$5,000.	2.775%
Next	$5,000.	3.469%
Next	$20,000.	4.162%
Next	$40,000.	4.857%
Next	$20,000.	5.550%
Next	$100,000.	6.444%
Over	$200,000.	7.004%

Oklahoma
1st	$2,000.	0.50%
Next	$3,000.	1%
Next	$2,500.	2%
Next	$2,300.	3%
Next	$2,400.	4%
Next	$2,800.	5%
Next	$6,000.	6%
Remainder.		7%

Oregon
1st	$2,250.	5%
Next	$3,450.	7%
Over	$5,700.	9%

Pennsylvania 2.80%

Rhode Island
27.5% of federal liability

South Carolina
First	$2,280.	2.50%
Next	$2,280.	3%
Next	$2,280.	4%
Next	$2,280.	5%
Next	$2,280.	6%
Over	$11,400.	7%

Tennessee
6% of interest and dividends

Utah
1st	$1,500.	2.30%
Next	$1,500.	3.30%
Next	$1,500.	4.20%
Next	$1,500.	5.20%
Next	$1,500.	6%
Over	$7,500.	7%

Vermont
25% of federal income tax

Virginia
1st	$3,000.	2%
Next	$2,000.	3%
Next	$12,000.	5%
Over	$17,000.	5.75%

West Virginia
First	$10,000.	3%
Next	$15,000.	4%
Next	$15,000.	4.50%
Next	$20,000.	6%
Over	$60,000.	6.50%

Wisconsin
$0 to $10,000.		4.9%
$10,001 to $20,000.		6.55%
$20,001 and over.		6.93%

Alabama: Rates shown are for married persons filing jointly. Single persons, heads of families, married persons filing separately, and estates or trusts are taxed at 2% on the first $500 taxable income, 4% on the next $2,500, 5% on any excess over $3,000.

Arizona: Effective Jan. 1, 1997, for married persons filing jointly and heads of households, rates are as shown. Effective Aug. 1, 1997, for single taxpayers, the rates range from 2.9% of the first $10,000 of taxable income to 5.17% of income over $150,000.

California: The rates shown are the 1996 inflation-adjusted rates for residents who are joint taxpayers or surviving spouses with dependents. For single taxpayers, married persons filing separately, and fiduciaries, the rates range from 1% on the first $4,908 of taxable income to 9.3% on taxable income over $32,207. For unmarried heads of households, the rates range from 1% on the first $9,817 of taxable income to 9.3% on taxable income over $43,839. A 7% alternative minimum tax is imposed.

Colorado: Alternative minimum tax imposed. Qualified taxpayers may pay alternative tax of 0.5% of gross receipts from sales.

Connecticut: The tax rates shown are for married individuals filing jointly. For unmarried individuals and married individuals filing separately, rates are 3% on the first $6,250 of Conn. taxable income and $187.50 plus 4.5% of the excess over $6,250. For heads of households, rates are 3% of the first $10,000 of Conn. taxable income and $300 plus 4.5% of the excess over $10,000. For trusts or estates, rates are 4.5% of Conn. taxable income. For tax year beginning in 1998, rates are: (1) for unmarried individuals and married individuals filing separately, 3% on the first $7,500 of Conn. taxable income and $225 plus 4.5% of the excess over $7,500; (2) for heads of households, 3% of the first $12,000 of Conn. taxable income and $360 plus 4.5% of the excess over $12,000; (3) for married individuals, 3% of the first $15,000 of Conn. taxable income and $450 plus 4.5% of the excess over $15,000; and (4) for trusts or estates, 4.5% of Conn. taxable income. Payroll withholding rates will not be adjusted until July 1, 1998. Resident estates and trusts continue to be subject to the 4.5% income tax rate on all of their income. Additional state minimum tax imposed on resident individuals, trusts, and estates.

District of Columbia: The tax on unincorporated business is 9.975%. Minimum tax, $100.

Georgia: Rates shown are for married persons filing jointly and heads of households. Single persons pay at rates ranging from 1% on taxable net income not over $750 to 6% on taxable net income over $7,000. Married persons filing separately pay at rates ranging from 1% on taxable net income not over $500 to 6% on taxable net income over $5,000.

Hawaii: Rates shown are for taxpayers filing jointly and surviving spouses. Special rate tables are provided for heads of households, unmarried individuals and married individuals filing separately, and estates and trusts.

Idaho: Each person (joint returns deemed one person) filing return pays additional $10.

Illinois: Each person (joint returns deemed one person) filing return pays additional $10.

Iowa: Rates shown are 1997 rates. For 1998, rates range between 0.36% of first $1,000 of taxable income and 8.98% of taxable income over $45,000 (dollar amounts not adjusted for inflation). An alternative minimum tax is imposed equal to 75% of the maximum state individual income tax rate for the tax year of the state alternative minimum taxable income.

Kansas: Rates shown are for married individuals filing joint returns. For single individuals and married individuals filing separate returns, the rates are 4.4% of the first $20,000 of Kansas taxable income, 7.5% of the next $10,000, and 7.75% of the excess over $30,000. For tax year 1997, for single individuals and married individuals filing separate returns, the rate is 4.1% of the first $20,000 of taxable income. The rate for taxable income that is more than $20,000 but less than $30,001 is $820 plus 7.5% of the excess over $20,000. The rate for taxable income over $30,000 is $1,570 plus 7.75% of the excess over $30,000. For tax year 1998, for single individuals and married individuals filing separate returns, the rate is 3.5% of the first $15,000 of taxable income. (This rate will remain unchanged for tax years 1999 and 2000.) The rate for taxable income that is more than $15,000 but less than $30,001 is $525 plus 6.75% of the excess over $15,000. The rate for taxable income over $30,000 is $1,537.50 plus 7.75% of the excess over $30,000. For tax year 1999, for single individuals and married individuals filing separate returns with taxable income over $15,000 but less than $30,001, the rate is $525 plus 6.25% of the excess over $15,000. This rate will not change for tax year 2000. The rate for taxable income over $30,000 is $1,462.50 plus 7.45% of the excess over $30,000. For tax year 2000, for single individuals and married individuals filing separate returns with more than $30,000 in taxable income, the rate is $1,462.50 plus 6.45% of the excess over $30,000.

Louisiana: These are the maximum tax rates for individuals. For joint returns, the tax is determined as if net income and the personal exemption credits were reduced by one-half. Actual tax is determined from tax tables.

Maine: Rates shown are 1996 rates for single individuals and married persons filing separately. For unmarried or legally separated individuals who qualify as heads of household, tax rates range from 2% if taxable income is less than $6,200 to 8.5% if taxable income is $24,750 or more. For married individuals filing jointly and widows or widowers permitted to file a joint federal return, tax rates range from 2% if taxable income is less than $8,250 to 8.5% if taxable income is $33,000 or more. 1997 rates to be set administratively, based on inflation. Additional state minimum tax is imposed.

Maryland: For tax years beginning after 1997 but before 1999, income over $3,000 is taxed at a rate of 4.95%. For a tax year beginning after 1998 but before 2000, income over $3,000 will be taxed at a rate of 4.9%. For a tax year beginning after 1999 but before 2001, income over $3,000 will be taxed at a rate of 4.85%. For a tax year beginning after 2000 but before 2002, income over $3,000 will be taxed at a rate of 4.8%. For a tax year beginning after 2001, income over $3,000 will be taxed at a rate of 4.75%.

Michigan: Persons with business activity in Michigan are also subject to a single business tax on an adjusted tax base.

Minnesota: Rates shown are 1997 amounts for married individuals filing jointly and surviving spouses. For single individuals, the tax is 6% on the first $16,510 of taxable income, 8% on taxable income over $16,510 but not over $54,250, and 8.5% on taxable income over $54,250; for married individuals filing separately, the tax is 6% on the first $12,070 of taxable income, 8% on taxable income over $12,070 but not over $47,960, and 8.5% on taxable income over $47,960; for unmarried heads of households, the tax is 6% on the first $20,330 of taxable income, 8% on income over $20,330 but not over $81,700, and 8.5% on income over $81,700. A 7% alternative minimum tax is imposed.

Montana: Rates shown are 1996 amounts, as indexed for inflation. Minimum tax, $1.

Nebraska: Rates shown are for married couples filing jointly and qualified surviving spouses. Rates for married couples filing separately range from 2.62% of the first $2,000 to 6.99% of taxable income over $23,375. Rates for heads of household range from 2.62% of the first $3,800 to 6.99% of taxable income over $35,000. Rates for single individuals range from 2.62% of the first $2,400 to 6.99% of taxable income over $26,500. Rates for estates range from 2.62% of the first $500 to 6.99% for taxable income over $15,150.

New Jersey: Rates shown are for married persons filing jointly, heads of households, and surviving spouses. The rates for married persons filing separately, unmarried individuals, and estates and trusts range from 1.4% of the first $20,000 of taxable income to 6.37% of taxable income over $75,000.

New Mexico: Rates shown are for married persons filing jointly and surviving spouses. For married persons filing separately, the rates range from 1.7% on the first $4,000 of taxable income to 8.5% on taxable income over $50,000. For heads of household, rates range from 1.7% on the first $7,000 of taxable income to 8.5% on taxable income over $83,000. For single individuals, estates and trusts, rates range from 1.7% of the first $5,500 of taxable income to 8.5% of taxable income over $65,000. Qualified taxpayers may pay alternative tax of 0.75% of gross receipts from New Mexico sales.

New York: The rates shown are the figures for married individuals filing jointly and surviving spouses. Separate schedules are set out for heads of households (ranging between 4% on the first $7,500 of taxable income and 7.125% on taxable income over $17,000) and for unmarried individuals, married individuals filing separately, and estates and trusts (ranging between 4% of the first $5,500 of taxable income and 7.125% of taxable income over $13,000). The rates are reduced for tax years beginning after 1996. In addition, individuals, estates, and trusts are subject to a 6% tax on minimum taxable income.

North Carolina: Rates shown are for married persons filing jointly. For heads of households the rates are 6% on the first $17,000, 7% of next $63,000, 7.75% of excess over $80,000. For unmarried individuals other than surviving spouses and heads of households the rate is 6% of first $12,750, 7% of next $47,250, 7.75% of excess over $60,000. For married filing separately the rate is 6% of first $10,625, 7% of next $39,375, 7.75% of excess over $50,000.

North Dakota: Individuals, estates and trusts are allowed an optional method of computing the tax. The optional tax is 14% of the taxpayer's adjusted federal income tax liability for the tax year.

Ohio: For the 1997 tax year, these tax rates may be reduced by the tax commissioner, by a percentage determined by the Office of Budget and Management according to a complicated formula based on budget surpluses.

Oklahoma: Rates shown are for heads of households, married persons filing jointly, and a surviving spouse not deducting federal income taxes. Single persons, married persons filing separately, and estates and trusts not deducting federal income taxes pay at rates ranging from 0.5% on the first $1,000 of taxable income to 7% on taxable income over $10,000. Optional rates (ranging from 0.5% to 10%) are enacted for taxpayers who deduct federal income taxes.

Oregon: Rates shown are 1997 amounts for single or married filing separately. Rates for joint filers, heads of households, and qualifying widow(er)s are 5% of the first $4,500; 7% for $4,501 to $11,400; and 9% over $11,400.

Utah: Rates shown are for married persons filing jointly and heads of households. Married taxpayers filing separately, single taxpayers and estates and trusts pay at rates ranging from 2.35% on taxable income not over $750 to 7% on taxable income over $3,750. Rates for single taxpayers, estates and trusts, and married couples filing separately range from 2.3% of the first $750 of taxable income to 7% of taxable income over $3,750.

West Virginia: A minimum tax is also imposed, equal to the excess by which an amount equal to 25% of any federal minimum tax or alternative minimum tax for the tax year exceeds the total tax due for the tax year.

Wisconsin: Rates shown are for married persons filing jointly. Rates for married persons filing separately range from 4.9% of the first $5,000 of taxable income to 6.93% of income over $10,000. The rates for fiduciaries and single individuals range from 4.9% of the first $7,500 of taxable income to 6.93% of taxable income over $15,001. Alternative minimum tax is imposed. For tax years ending after Apr. 1, 1991, Apr. 1, 1992, and Apr. 1, 1993, and for tax years beginning in 1994, 1995, and 1996, a surcharge is imposed on individuals, estates, trusts, and partnerships, except an entity with gross receipts of less than $1,000, at the rate of the greater of $25 or 0.4345% of net business income. The maximum surcharge is $9,800. An individual, estate, trust, or partnership engaged in farming with a net farm profit of $1,000 or more is subject to a surcharge of $25, regardless of whether the entity is otherwise subject to a surcharge. (The Department of Revenue must establish annual surcharge rates necessary to generate a sufficient level of revenue to fund appropriations from the recycling fund.)

AEROSPACE
Memorable Moments in Human Spaceflight

Sources: National Aeronautics and Space Administration; Congressional Research Service; World Almanac research

Note: U.S. space missions are in boldface. Other missions were sponsored by the Soviet Union or, later, the Commonwealth of Independent States. All dates are Eastern standard time. EVA = extravehicular activity. ASTP = Apollo-Soyuz Test Project. Number of total flights by each crew member is given in parentheses when flight listed is not the first.

Dates	Mission[1]	Crew (no. of flights)	Duration (hr:min)	Remarks
4/12/61	Vostok 1	Yuri A. Gagarin	1:48	1st human orbital flight
5/5/61	**Mercury-Redstone 3**	**Alan B. Shepard Jr.**	0:15	**1st American in space**
7/21/61	**Mercury-Redstone 4**	**Virgil I. Grissom**	0:15	**Spacecraft sank, Grissom rescued**
8/6/61-8/7/61	Vostok 2	Gherman S. Titov	25:18	1st spaceflight of more than 24 hrs
2/20/62	**Mercury-Atlas 6**	**John H. Glenn Jr.**	4:55	**1st American in orbit; 3 orbits**
5/24/62	**Mercury-Atlas 7**	**M. Scott Carpenter**	4:56	**Manual retrofire error caused 250-mi landing overshoot**
8/11/62-8/15/62	Vostok 3	Andrian G. Nikolayev	94:22	Vostok 3 and 4 made 1st group flight
8/12/62-8/15/62	Vostok 4	Pavel R. Popovich	70:57	On 1st orbit it came within 3 mi of Vostok 3
5/15/63-5/16/63	**Mercury-Atlas 9**	**L. Gordon Cooper**	34:19	**1st U.S. evaluation of effects of one day in space on a person; 22 orbits**
6/14/63-6/19/63	Vostok 5	Valery F. Bykovsky	119:06	Vostok 5 and 6 made 2d group flight
6/16/63-6/19/63	Vostok 6	Valentina V. Tereshkova	70:50	1st woman in space; passes within 3 mi of Vostok 5
10/12/64-10/13/64	Voskhod 1	Vladimir M. Komarov, Konstantin P. Feoktistov, Boris B. Yegorov	24:17	1st 3-person orbital flight; 1st without space suits
3/18/65-3/19/65	Voskhod 2	Pavel I. Belyayev, Aleksei A. Leonov	26:02	Leonov made 1st "space walk" (10 min)
3/23/65	**Gemini-Titan 3**	**Grissom (2), John W. Young**	4:53	**1st piloted spacecraft to change its orbital path**
6/3/65-6/7/65	**Gemini-Titan 4**	**James A. McDivitt, Edward H. White 2d**	97:56	**White was 1st American to "walk in space" (36 min)**
12/15/65-12/16/65	**Gemini-Titan 6**	**Schirra (2), Thomas P. Stafford**	25:51	**Completed 1st U.S. space rendezvous, with Gemini 7**
12/4/65-12/18/65	**Gemini-Titan 7**	**Frank Borman, James A. Lovell**	330:35	**Longest-duration Gemini flight**
3/16/66	**Gemini-Titan 8**	**Neil A. Armstrong, David R. Scott**	10:41	**1st docking of one space vehicle with another; mission aborted, control malfunction; 1st Pacific landing**
7/18/66-7/21/66	**Gemini-Titan 10**	**Young (2), Michael Collins**	70:47	**1st use of Agena target vehicle's propulsion systems; 1st orbital docking**
11/11/66-11/15/66	**Gemini-Titan 12**	**Lovell (2), Edwin W. "Buzz" Aldrin Jr.**	94:34	**Final Gemini mission; 5½ hr EVA**
4/23/67-4/24/67	Soyuz 1	Komarov (2)	26:40	Crashed on reentry, killing Komarov
10/11/68-10/22/68	**Apollo-Saturn 7**	**Schirra (3), Donn F. Eisele, R. Walter Cunningham**	260:09	**1st piloted flight of Apollo spacecraft command-service module only; live TV footage of crew**
12/21/68-12/27/68	**Apollo-Saturn 8**	**Borman (2), Lovell (3), William A. Anders**	147:00	**1st lunar orbit and piloted lunar return reentry (command-service module only); views of lunar surface televised to Earth**
1/14/69-1/17/69	Soyuz 4	Vladimir A. Shatalov	71:21	Docked with Soyuz 5
1/15/69-1/18/69	Soyuz 5	Boris V. Volyanov, Aleksei S. Yeliseyev, Yevgeny V. Khrunov	72:54	Docked with 4; Yeliseyev and Khrunov transferred to Soyuz 4 via a spacewalk
3/3/69-3/13/69	**Apollo-Saturn 9**	**McDivitt (2), D. Scott (2), Russell L. Schweickart**	241:00	**1st piloted flight of lunar module**
5/18/69-5/26/69	**Apollo-Saturn 10**	**Stafford (3), Young (3), Cernan(2)**	192:03	**1st lunar module orbit of Moon, 50,000 ft from Moon surface**
7/16/69-7/24/69	**Apollo-Saturn 11**	**Armstrong (2), Collins (2), Aldrin (2)**	195:18	**1st lunar landing made by Armstrong and Aldrin (7/20); collected 48.5 lb of soil, rock samples; lunar stay time 21:36:21**
10/11/69-10/16/69	Soyuz 6	Georgi S. Shonin, Valery N. Kubasov	118:43	1st welding of metals in space
10/12/69-10/17/69	Soyuz 7	Anatoly V. Flipchenko, Vladislav N. Volkov, Viktor V. Gorbatko	118:40	Space lab construction test made; Soyuz 6, 7, and 8: 1st time 3 spacecraft, 7 crew members orbited the Earth at once
10/13/69[2]	Soyuz 8	Shatalov (2), Yeliseyev (2)	118:51	Part of space lab construction team
11/14/69-11/24/69	**Apollo-Saturn 12**	**Conrad (3), Richard F. Gordon Jr. (2), Alan L. Bean**	244:36	**Conrad and Bean made 2d Moon landing (11/18); collected 74.7 lb of samples, lunar stay time 31:31**
4/11/70-4/17/70	**Apollo-Saturn 13**	**Lovell (4), Fred W. Haise Jr., John L. Swigart Jr.**	142:54	**Aborted after service module oxygen tank ruptured; crew returned safely using lunar module**

Dates	Mission[1]	Crew (no. of flights)	Duration (hr:min)	Remarks
1/31/71- 2/9/71	Apollo-Saturn 14	A. Shepard (2), Stuart A. Roosa, Edgar D. Mitchell	216:01	Shepard and Mitchell made 3d Moon landing (2/3); collected 96 lb of lunar samples; lunar stay 33:31
4/19/71[2]	Salyut 1[3]	(Occupied by Soyuz 11 crew)		1st space station
4/22/71[2]	Soyuz 10	Shatalov (3), Yeliseyev (3), Nikolay N. Rukavishnikov	47:46	1st successful docking with a space station; failed to enter space station
6/6/71- 6/30/71	Soyuz 11	Georgi T. Dobrovolskiy, V. Volkov (2), Viktor I. Patsayev	570:22	Docked and entered Salyut 1 space station; orbited in Salyut 1 for 23 days, crew died during reentry from loss of pressurization
7/26/71- 8/7/71	Apollo-Saturn 15	D. Scott (3), James B. Irwin, Alfred M. Worden	295:12	Scott and Irwin made 4th Moon landing (7/30); 1st lunar rover use; 1st deep space walk; 170 lb of samples; 66:55 stay
4/16/72- 4/27/72	Apollo-Saturn 16	Young (4), Charles M. Duke Jr., Thomas K. Mattingly 2d	265:51	Young and Duke made 5th Moon landing (4/20); colleced 213 lb of lunar samples; lunar stay 71:2
12/7/72- 12/19/72	Apollo-Saturn 17	Cernan (3), Ronald E. Evans, Harrison H. Schmitt	301:51	Cernan and Schmitt made 6th lunar landing (12/11); collected 243 lb of samples; record lunar stay of more than 75 hr
5/14/73[2]	Skylab 1[4]	(Occupied by Skylab 2, 3, and 4 crews)		1st U.S. space station
5/25/73- 6/22/73	Skylab 2	Conrad (4), Joseph P. Kerwin, Paul J. Weitz	672:49	1st Amer. piloted orbiting space station; crew repaired damage caused during boost
7/28/73- 9/25/73	Skylab 3	Bean (2), Owen K. Garriott, Jack R. Lousma	1,427:09	Crew systems and operational tests; exceeded pre-mission plans for scientific activities; 13 hrs EVA 13:44
11/16/73- 2/8/74	Skylab 4	Gerald P. Carr, Edward G. Gibson, William Pogue	2,017:15	Final Skylab mission
7/15/75- 7/21/75	Soyuz 19 (ASTP)	Leonov (2), Kubasov (2)	143:31	U.S.-USSR joint flight; crews linked up in space (7/17), conducted experiments, shared meals, and held a joint news conference
7/15/75- 7/24/75	Apollo (ASTP)	Vance Brand, Stafford (4), Donald K. Slayton	217:28	Joint flight with Soyuz 19
12/10/77[2]	Soyuz 26	Yuri V. Romanenko, Georgiy M. Grechko (2)	2,314:00	1st multiple docking to a space station (Soyuz 26 and 27 docked at Salyut 6)
1/10/78[2]	Soyuz 27	Vladimir A. Dzhanibekov	142:59	See Soyuz 26
3/2/78[2]	Soyuz 28	Aleksei A. Gubarev (2), Vladimir Remek	190:16	1st international crew launch; Remek was 1st Czech in space
4/12/81- 4/14/81	Columbia (STS-1)	Young (5), Robert L. Crippen	54:21	1st space shuttle flight
11/11/82- 11/16/82	Columbia (STS-5)	Brand (2), Robert Overmyer, William Lenoir, Joseph Allen	122:14	1st reuse of space shuttle; 1st 4-person crew
6/18/83- 6/24/83	Challenger (STS-7)	Crippen (2), Frederick Hauck, Sally K. Ride, John M. Fabian, Norman Thagard	146:24	Ride was 1st U.S. woman in space; 1st 5-person crew
6/27/83[2]	Soyuz T-9	Vladimir A. Lyakhov (2), A. P. Aleksandrov	3,585:46	Docked at Salyut 7; 1st construction in space
8/30/83- 9/5/83	Challenger (STS-8)	Truly (2), Daniel Brandenstein, William Thornton, Guion Bluford, Dale Gardner	145:09	Bluford was 1st U.S. black in space
11/28/83- 12/8/83	Columbia (STS-9)	Young (6), Brewster Shaw Jr., Robert Parker, Garriott (2), Byron Lichtenberg, Ulf Merbold	247:47	1st 6-person crew; 1st Spacelab mission
2/3/84- 2/11/84	Challenger (41-B)	Brand (3), Robert Gibson, Ronald McNair, Bruce McCandless, Robert Stewart	191:16	1st untethered EVA
4/6/84- 4/13/84	Challenger (41-C)	Crippen (3), Francis R. Scobee, George D. Nelson, Terry J. Hart, James D. van Hoften	167:40	1st in-orbit satellite repair
7/17/84[2]	Soyuz T-12	Dzhanibekov (4), Svetlana Y. Savitskaya (2), Igor P. Volk,	283:14	Docked at Salyut 7; Savitskaya was 1st woman to perform EVA
10/5/84- 10/13/84	Challenger (41-G)	Crippen (4), Jon A. McBride, Kathryn D. Sullivan, Ride (2), Marc Garneau, David C. Leestma, Paul D. Scully-Power	197:24	1st 7-person crew
11/8/84- 11/16/84	Discovery (51-A)	Hauck (2); David M. Walker, Dr. Anna L. Fisher, J. Allen (2), D. Gardner (2)	191:45	1st satellite retrieval/repair
4/12/85- 4/19/85	Discovery (51-D)	Karol J. Bobko, Donald E. Williams, Jake Garn, Charles D. Walker, Jeffrey A. Hoffman, S. David Griggs, M. Rhea Seddon	167:55	Garn was 1st senator in space
6/17/85- 6/24/85	Discovery (51-G)	Brandenstein (2), John O. Creighton, Shannon W. Lucid, Steven R. Nagel, Fabian (2), Prince Sultan Salman al Saud, Patrick Baudry	169:39	Launched 3 satellites; Salman al-Saud was 1st Arab in space; Baudry was 1st French person on U.S. mission
10/3/85- 10/7/85	Atlantis (51-J)	Bobko (3), Ronald J. Grabe, David C. Hilmers, Stewart (2), William A. Pailes	97:47	1st Atlantis flight

(continued)

Dates	Mission[1]	Crew (no. of flights)	Duration (hr:min)	Remarks
10/30/85-11/6/85	Challenger (61-A)	Hartsfield (3), Steven R. Nagel, Buchli (2), Bluford (2), Bonnie J. Dunbar, Wubbo J. Ockels, Richard Furrer, Ernst Messerschmid	168:45	1st 8-person crew; 1st German Spacelab mission
11/26/85-12/3/85	Atlantis (61-B)	Shaw (2), Bryan D. O'Connor, Sherwood C. Spring, Mary L. Cleave, Jerry L. Ross, C. Walker (3), Rodolfo Neri	165:05	Space structures assembly test; Neri was 1st Mexican in space
1/12/86-1/18/86	Columbia (61-C)	R. Gibson (2), Charles F. Bolden Jr., Hawley (2), G. Nelson (2), Franklin R. Chang-Diaz, Robert J. Cenker, Bill Nelson	146:04	B. Nelson was 1st U.S. Representative in space; material and astronomy experiments conducted
1/28/86	Challenger (51-L)	Scobee (2), Michael J. Smith, Judith A. Resnik (2), Ellison S. Onizuka (2), Ronald E. McNair, Gregory B. Jarvis, Christa McAuliffe		Exploded 73 sec after liftoff; all were killed
2/20/86[2]	Mir[3]	Space station with 6 docking ports		
3/13/86[2]	Soyuz T-15	Leonid Kizim (3), Vladimr Solovyov (2)	3,000:01	Ferry between stations; docked at Mir
2/5/87-12/29/87	Soyuz TM-2	Romanenko (3), Aleksandr I. Laveikin	7,835:38	Romanenko set endurance record, since broken
12/21/87-12/21/88	Soyuz TM-4	V. Titov (2), Muso Manarov, Anatoly Levchenko	8,782:39	Docked at Mir
9/29/88-10/3/88	Discovery (STS-26)	Hauck (3), Richard O. Covey (2), Hilmers (2), G. Nelson (2), John M. Lounge (2)	97:00	Redesigned shuttle makes 1st flight
4/24/90-4/29/90	Discovery (STS-31)	McCandless (2), Sullivan (2), Loren J. Shriver (2), Bolden (2), Steven A. Hawley (3)	121:16	Launched Hubble Space Telescope
5/7/92-5/16/92	Endeavour (STS-49)	Brandenstein (4), Kevin C. Chilton, Bruce E. Melnick (2), Pierre J. Thuot (2), Richard J. Hieb (2), Kathryn Thornton (2), Tom Akers (2)	213:30	1st 3-person EVA; satellite recovery and redeployment
9/12/92-9/21/92	Endeavour (STS-47)	R. Gibson (4), Curtis L. Brown Jr., Mark Lee (2), Jay Apt (2), N. Jan Davis, Mae Carol Jemison, Mamoru Mohri	190:30	Jemison was 1st black woman in space; Lee and Davis were 1st married couple to travel together in space; 1st Japanese Spacelab
4/8/93-4/17/93	Discovery (STS-56)	Kenneth D. Cameron, Stephen S. Oswald (2), C. Michael Foale (2), Ellen Ochoa, Kenneth D. Cockrell	222:08	2d atmospheric mission; Ochoa was 1st Hispanic woman in space
12/2/93-12/13/93	Endeavour (STS-61)	Covey (3), Kenneth D. Bowersox (2), Claude Nicollier (2), Story Musgrave (5), Akers (3), K. Thornton (3), Hoffman (4)	259:58	Hubble Space Telescope repaired; Akers set new U.S. EVA duration record (29 hr, 40 min)
2/3/94-2/11/94	Discovery (STS-60)	Bolden (3), Kenneth S. Reightier Jr. (2), Davis, (2), Chang-Diaz (3), Ronald M. Sega, Sergei K. Krikalev	199:10	Krikalev was 1st Russian on U.S. shuttle
2/3/95-2/11/95	Discovery (STS-63)	James D. Wetherbee (3), Eileen M. Collins, Bernard A. Harris (2), Foale (3), Janice Voss (2), V. Titov (4)	198:29	Discovery and Russian space station rendezvous
3/14/95-3/22/95	Soyuz TM-21	Thagard (2), Vladimir Dezhurov, Gennadi Strekalov	2,688[5]	Docked with Mir 3/16/95; Thagard was the 1st Amer. aboard the Russ. spacecraft; Valery Polyakov returned to Earth, 3/22/95, after a record stay in space (439 days)
3/2/95-3/18/95	Endeavour (STS-67)	Oswald (3), William G. Gregory, Samuel T. Durrance (2), Ronald Parise (2), Wendy B. Lawrence, Tamara Jernigan (3), John M. Grunsfeld	399:09	Shuttle data made available on the Internet; astronomy research conducted
6/27/95-7/7/95	Atlantis (STS-71)	R. Gibson (5), Charles J. Precourt (2), Ellen S. Baker (3), Gregory J. Harbaugh (3), Dunbar (4), Anatoly Y. Solovyev (4) (to Mir), Nikolai M. Budarin (to Mir), Thagard (5) (from Mir), Strekalov (from Mir), Dezhurov (from Mir)	269:47	1st Mir docking; exchanged crew members with Mir; Thagard, with his stay on Mir, had spent 115 days in space
10/20/95-11/5/95	Columbia (STS-73)	Bowersox (3), Kent Rominger, K. Thornton (4), Catherine Coleman, Michael Lopez-Alegria, Fred Leslie, Albert Sacco	381:52	Most ever first-time space flyers; near-weightlessness experiments conducted in microgravity laboratory
11/8/95-11/20/95	Atlantis (STS-74)	Cameron (3), James D. Halsell Jr. (2), Chris Hadfield, Ross (5), William McArthur (2)	196:30	2d Mir docking (11/15-11/18); erected a 15-ft permanent docking tunnel to Mir for future use by U.S. orbiters
1/11/96-1/20/96	Endeavour (STS-72)	Brian Duffy (3), Brent W. Jett Jr., Winston E. Scott, Leroy Chiao (2), Daniel T. Barry, Koichi Wakata	214:01	Released NASA space probe; retrieved Japanese satellite; 13 hrs EVA
2/22/96-3/9/96	Columbia (STS-75)	Andrew M. Allen (3), Scott J. Horowitz, Chang-Diaz (5), Umberto Guidoni, Hoffman (5), Maurizio Cheli, Nicollier (3)	377:40	Lost an Italian satellite when its tether was severed; microgravity experiments performed; singe marks found on 2 O-rings
3/22/96-3/31/96	Atlantis (STS-76)	Chilton (3), Richard A. Searfoss (2), Sega (2), Richard Clifford (3) Linda Godwin (3), Lucid (5) (to Mir)	221:15	3d Mir docking (5 days); Lucid to Mir; 2-person EVA

Dates	Mission[1]	Crew (no. of flights)	Duration (hr:min)	Remarks
6/20/96-7/7/96	Columbia (STS-78)	Terence T. Henricks (4), Kevin R. Kregel (2), Susan J. Helms (3), Richard M. Linnehan, Charles E. Brady, Jean-Jacques Favier, Robert Brent Thirsk	405:48	Studied weightlessness with the Life/Microgravity Spacelab on board
9/16/96-9/26/96	Atlantis (STS-79)	Apt (4), Terry Wilcutt (2), William Readdy (3), Akers (4), Carl E. Walz (3), Lucid (5) (from *Mir*), John Blaha (5) (to *Mir*)	243:19	Docked with *Mir* 9/18/96; exchanged crew members, including Lucid, who set U.S. and women's individual duration in space record (188 days)
11/19/96-12/7/96	Columbia (STS-80)	Cockrell (3), Rominger (2), Jernigan (4), Thomas D. Jones (3), Musgrave (6)	423:53	Longest-duration shuttle flight; Musgrave was oldest person ever in space; 2 science satellites deployed and retrieved; 2 space walks canceled
1/12/97-1/22/97	Atlantis (STS-81)	Mike Baker (4), Jett (2), Jeff Wisoff (3), Grunsfeld (2), Marsha Ivins (4), Jerry Linenger (2) (to *Mir*), Blaha (5) (from *Mir*)	243:30	Docked with *Mir* 1/14-1/19/97; Linenger to *Mir*; Blaha from *Mir*, spent 128 days in space
2/11/97-2/21/97	Discovery (STS-82)	Bowersox (4), Horowitz (2), Joe Tanner (4), Hawley (4), Harbaugh (4), Lee (4), Steve Smith (2)	238:47	Increased capabilities of Hubble Space Telescope; 5 EVAs used to service it
5/15/97-5/24/97	Atlantis (STS-84)	Precourt (3), E. Collins (2), Jean-François Clervoy (2), Carlos Noriega, Ed Lu, Elena Kondakova, Foale (4) (to *Mir*), Linenger (2) (from *Mir*)	221:20	Docked with *Mir* 5/16-5/21/97; Foale to *Mir*; Linenger from *Mir*, 132 days in space, 2d longest time for an American; stay on *Mir* marked by troubles incl. fire 2/23
7/1/97-7/17/97	Columbia (STS-94)	Halsell (4), Susan L. Still (2), Janice Voss (4), Donald A. Thomas (4), Michael Gernhardt (3), Roger Crouch (2), Greg Linteris (2)	376:46	Reflight of Microgravity Science Laboratory-1 mission (STS-83) that was aborted 4/8/97 because of problem with fuel cell
9/25/97-10/6/97	Atlantis (STS-86)	Wetherbee (4), Michael J. Bloomfield, V. Titov (4), Scott Parazynski (2), Jean-Loup Chrétien (3), Lawrence (2), David Wolf (2) (to *Mir*), Foale (4) (from *Mir*)	236:24	Docked with *Mir* 9/27-10/3/97; delivered new computer to *Mir*; Wolf to *Mir*; Foale from *Mir*; stay on *Mir* marked by collision with cargo ship 6/25, worst such collision ever

Note: As of Oct. 1997, there have been 87 space shuttle flights, 62 since the 1986 *Challenger* explosion. Active shuttles include the *Columbia* (23 flights), the *Discovery* (23), the *Atlantis* (20), and the *Endeavour* (11). (The *Challenger* completed 9 missions.)

Four Soviets died in spaceflights: Komarov was killed on Soyuz 1 (1967) when the parachute lines tangled during descent; the 3-person Soyuz 11 crew (1971) was asphyxiated. Seven Americans died in the *Challenger* explosion, and 3 astronauts—Virgil I. Grissom, Edward H. White, and Roger B. Chaffee—died in the Jan. 27, 1967, Apollo 1 fire on the ground at Cape Kennedy, FL.

(1) For space shuttle flights, mission name is in parentheses following the name of the orbiter. (2) Launch date. (3) Space stations, such as the *Salyuts* and *Mir*, have been used to house crews since 1971. (4) Skylab 1 deteriorated and fell from orbit without burning up upon entering the atmosphere. Pieces fell on Australia and the Indian Ocean; no one was injured. (5) Approximate crew duration for Thagard's stay. Crew did not return together.

Individuals Who Have Flown in Space, 1961-96
Source: Congressional Research Service; as of Dec. 31, 1996

Country	No. of individs.	Country	No. of individs.	Country	No. of individs.	Country	No. of individs.
United States	235	Canada[2]	6	India[1]	1	Romania[1]	1
Russia/CIS	87	Cuba[1]	1	Italy[2]	3	Saudi Arabia[2]	1
Afghanistan[1]	1	Czechoslovakia[1]	1	Japan[1,2]	4	Switzerland[2]	1
Austria[1]	1	France[1,2]	7	Mexico[2]	1	Syria[1]	1
Belgium[2]	1	Germany[1,2]	9	Mongolia[1]	1	United Kingdom[1]	1
Bulgaria[1]	2	Hungary[1]	1	Netherlands[2]	1	Vietnam[1]	1
				Poland[1]	1	**Total**	**370**

Note: All cosmonauts who were citizens of the USSR at the time of launch are included under "Russia/CIS." "Germany" includes former E and W Germany. (1) On Russian/CIS-sponsored mission. (2) On U.S.-sponsored mission.

Summary of Worldwide Successful Announced Payloads, 1957-96
Source: National Aeronautics and Space Administration
(A payload is something carried into space by a rocket.)

Year	Total[1]	USSR/CIS[2]	United States	Japan	China	European Space Agency	France	United Kingdom	India	Germany	Canada
1957-59	24	6	18	—	—	—	—	—	—	—	—
1960-69	1,035	399	614	—	—	2	4	1	—	—	—
1970-79	1,366	1,028	247	18	8	5	14	6	1	3	4
1980-89	1,431	1,132	191	26	16	14	5	4	9	7	5
1990	159	96	31	7	5	1	2	5	1	1	0
1991	157	101	30	2	1	4	6	2	1	1	2
1992	128	77	27	3	2	1	3	0	2	1	1
1993	104	59	29	1	1	2	2	0	1	0	0
1994	109	64	27	4	5	1	0	0	2	2	0
1995	87	45	24	2	1	2	3	0	1	1	1
1996	69	23	32	1	2	10	0	00	1	0	0
Total	**4,669**	**3,030**	**1,270**	**64**	**41**	**42**	**39**	**18**	**19**	**16**	**13**

(1) Includes launches sponsored by countries not shown. (2) Figures for 1986-91 are for the Soviet Union; 1992-96 figures are for the Commonwealth of Independent States.

Notable U.S. Planetary Science Missions

Source: National Aeronautics and Space Administration

Spacecraft	Launch date (GMT)	Mission	Remarks
Mariner 2	Aug. 27, 1962	Venus	Passed within 22,000 mi of Venus 12/14/62; contact lost 1/3/63 at 54 million mi
Ranger 7	July 28, 1964	Moon	Yielded over 4,000 photos of lunar surface
Mariner 4	Nov. 28, 1964	Mars	Passed behind Mars 7/14/65; took 22 photos from 6,000 mi
Ranger 8	Feb. 17, 1965	Moon	Yielded over 7,000 photos of lunar surface
Surveyor 3	Apr. 17, 1967	Moon	Scooped and tested lunar soil
Mariner 5	June 14, 1967	Venus	In solar orbit; closest Venus fly-by 10/19/67
Mariner 6	Feb. 24, 1969	Mars	Came within 2,000 mi of Mars 7/31/69; collected data, photos
Mariner 7	Mar. 27, 1969	Mars	Came within 2,000 mi of Mars 8/5/69
Mariner 9	May 30, 1971	Mars	First craft to orbit Mars 11/13/71; sent back more than 7,000 photos
Pioneer 10	Mar. 2, 1972	Jupiter	Passed Jupiter 12/4/73; exited the planetary system 6/13/83; transmission ended 3/31/97 at 6.39 billion mi
Pioneer 11	Apr. 5, 1973	Jupiter, Saturn	Passed Jupiter 12/3/74; Saturn 9/1/79; discovered an additional ring and 2 moons around Saturn; operating in outer solar system; transmission ended 9/95
Mariner 10	Nov. 3, 1973	Venus, Mercury	Passed Venus 2/5/74; arrived Mercury 3/29/74. First time gravity of one planet (Venus) used to whip spacecraft toward another (Mercury)
Viking 1	Aug. 20, 1975	Mars	Landed on Mars 7/20/76; did scientific research, sent photos; functioned 6½ years
Viking 2	Sept. 9, 1975	Mars	Landed on Mars 9/3/76; functioned 3½ years
Voyager 1	Sept. 5, 1977	Jupiter, Saturn	Encountered Jupiter 3/5/79, provided evidence of Jupiter ring; passed near Saturn 11/12/80
Voyager 2	Aug. 20, 1977	Jupiter, Saturn, Uranus, Neptune	Encountered Jupiter 7/9/79; Saturn 8/25/81; Uranus 1/24/86; Neptune 8/25/89
Pioneer Venus 1	May 20, 1978	Venus	Entered Venus orbit 12/4/78; spent 14 years studying planet; ceased operating 10/19/92
Pioneer Venus 2	Aug. 8, 1978	Venus	Encountered Venus 12/9/78; probes impacted on surface
Magellan	May 4, 1989	Venus	Orbit and map Venus; monitored geological activity on surface; ceased operating 10/12/94
Galileo	Oct. 18, 1989	Jupiter	Used Earth's gravity to propel it toward Jupiter; encountered Venus Feb. 1990; encountered Jupiter 12/7/95; released probe to Jovian surface; encountered moons Ganymede, Europa, Io, and Callisto
Mars Observer	Sept. 25, 1992	Mars	Communication was lost 8/21/93
Near Earth Asteroid Rendezvous (NEAR)	Feb. 17, 1996	The asteroid Eros	Expected rendezvous with Eros, early 1999; to orbit and study the asteroid for about 1 year
Mars Global Surveyor	Nov. 7, 1996	Mars	Began orbiting Mars 9/11/97; began 2-year mapping survey of entire Martian surface; discovered magnetism on planet
Mars Pathfinder	Dec. 4, 1996	Mars	Landed on Mars 7/4/97; rover Sojourner began on-site measurements of the Martian climate and soil composition, sending thousands of surface images
Cassini	Oct. 15, 1997	Saturn	Scheduled to reach Saturn in 2004; to study planet's atmosphere, rings, and moons; probe will land on moon Titan

Notable Proposed U.S. Space Missions

Source: National Aeronautics and Space Administration; as of Oct. 1997

Planned Launch date	Mission	Purpose
Nov. 1997	Lunar Prospector	Search for resources on the Moon, particularly water
Nov. 1997	Spartan 201	Study of the Sun
1998	Earth Observing System	Provide long-term data sets of interactions between Earth's land, atmosphere, water, and life
1998	Landsat-7	Continue the record of remote-sensing measurements of Earth's land surface
1998	Advanced X-ray Astrophysics Facility	Study of dark matter, stellar evolution, galactic clusters
Feb. 1999	Stardust	Gather dust samples from comet Wild-2 and return samples to Earth
Not set	Pluto Fast Fly-by	First fly-by of Pluto for photographic survey and other studies
2001	Space InfraRed Telescope Facility	High-sensitivity observations of celestial sources

Note: All spacecraft to be launched by expendable rockets.

Traffic at World Airports, 1996

Source: Airports Council International-North America

Airport	Passenger Arrivals and Departures	Airport	Passenger Arrivals and Departures
London, UK (Heathrow)	56,037,813	Toronto, Ontario (Lester B. Pearson Intl.)	24,204,641
Tokyo/Haneda, Japan (Tokyo Intl.)	46,631,475	Rome, Italy (Fiumicino)	23,035,764
Frankfurt, Germany (Rhein/Main)	38,761,174	Madrid, Spain (Barajas)	21,856,673
Seoul, South Korea (Kimpo Intl.)	34,707,549	Sydney, Australia (Kingsford Smith)	19,705,876
Paris, France (Charles De Gaulle)	31,823,741	Mexico City, Mexico (Mexico City)	16,265,384
Hong Kong, China (Hong Kong Intl.)	30,212,327	Zurich, Switzerland (Zurich)	16,251,166
Amsterdam, Netherlands (Schiphol)	27,753,088	Copenhagen, Denmark (Copenhagen)	15,857,390
Paris, France (Orly)	27,364,985	Munich, Germany (Munich)	15,686,095
Tokyo, Japan (Narita)	25,408,196	Taipei, Taiwan (Chiang Kai-shek)	15,613,624
Bangkok, Thailand (Bangkok Intl.)	24,993,486	Palma de Mallorca, Spain (Palma de Mallorca)	15,377,437
Singapore (Changi)	24,514,248	Manchester, UK (Manchester)	14,842,950
London, UK (Gatwick)	24,327,480	Dusseldorf, Germany (Dusseldorf)	14,417,261

Note: Excludes U.S. airports. Includes only those airports participating in the Airports Council International Annual Airport Traffic Statistics collection.

Traffic at U.S. Airports, 1996

Source: Airports Council International-North America

Airport	Passenger Arrivals and Departures	Airport	Passenger Arrivals and Departures
Chicago (O'Hare–ORD)	69,133,189	Phoenix (Sky Harbor Intl.–PHX)	30,376,584
Atlanta (Hartsfield Intl.–ATL)	63,344,730	Minneapolis/St. Paul (MSP)	29,612,167
Dallas/Ft. Worth (DFW)	58,034,503	Newark (EWR)	29,072,591
Los Angeles (LAX)	57,974,559	St. Louis (Lambert St. Louis Intl.–STL)	27,274,846
San Francisco (SFO)	39,247,308	Houston (IAH)	26,475,801
Miami (MIA)	33,504,579	Orlando (MCO)	25,548,773
Denver (DEN)	32,264,312	Boston (Logan Intl.–BOS)	25,042,667
New York (J. F. Kennedy Intl.–JFK)	31,015,239	Seattle-Tacoma (SEA)	24,324,600
Detroit (DTW)	30,614,038	Honolulu (HNL)	24,247,332
Las Vegas (McCarran Intl.–LAS)	30,470,957	Charlotte (CLT)	21,847,510

U.S. Scheduled Airline Traffic, 1994-96

Source: Air Transport Association of America

	1994	1995	1996
Passenger traffic			
Revenue passengers enplaned (000)	528,848	547,773	581,201
Revenue passenger miles (000)	519,381,688	540,656,211	578,408,509
Available seat miles (000)	784,330,936	807,077,839	834,688,294
Revenue passenger load factor (%)	66.2	67.0	69.3
Cargo traffic (ton miles)	**16,061,707**	**16,920,976**	**17,698,336**
Revenue freight and express (ton miles)	13,729,157	14,577,522	15,244,952
Revenue U.S. Mail (ton miles)	2,269,550	2,343,454	2,453,384
Financial			
Passenger revenue ($000)	$65,421,539	$69,594,423	$75,315,600
Net profit ($000)	−$344,115	$2,313,591	$2,824,328
Employees	**539,759**	**546,987**	**564,425**

Leading U.S. Passenger Airlines, 1996

Source: Air Transport Association of America

(in thousands)

Airline	Passengers	Airline	Passengers	Airline	Passengers
Delta	97,201	Alaska	11,758	Atlantic Southeast	3,632
United	81,863	Simmons	6,010	American Trans Air	3,431
American	79,324	Hawaiian	5,338	ValuJet	3,003
USAir[1]	56,639	Aloha	5,059	Continental Micronesia	2,601
Southwest	55,372	Reno	4,930	Trans States	2,121
Northwest	52,682	Mesa	4,307	Carnival	1,770
Continental	35,743	Continental Express	4,100	Air Wisconsin	1,757
Trans World	23,281	Horizon Air	3,753	Western Pacific	1,754
America West	18,130				

(1) Name changed in 1997 to US Airways.

Airline On-Time Arrivals, 1995-96

Source: Office of General Counsel, U.S. Dept. of Transportation

(percent of arrivals within 15 min. of scheduled time, for leading airlines)

	Airline	1996	1995	1995 rank
1.	Southwest	81.8	82.3	1
2.	Continental	76.6[1]	79.5	4
3.	Northwest	76.6[1]	80.7	2
4.	USAir[2]	75.7	79.8	3
5.	United	73.8	77.7	5
6.	American	72.2	77.5	7
7.	Delta	71.2	76.2	9
8.	America West	70.8	77.6	6
9.	Alaska	68.6	76.7	8
10.	TWA	68.5	74.3	10
	Average for all 10 airlines	**74.5**	**78.7**	

Note: All domestic scheduled-service passenger flights, including those with mechanical delays, are included. A canceled flight is counted as a delay. The on-time performance database tracks only these 10 leading airlines, which account for more than 90% of domestic operating revenues. (1) When figures are carried out to several decimal places, Continental had the better on-time performance of these two carriers. (2) Name changed in 1997 to US Airways.

U.S. Airline Safety, Scheduled Commercial Carriers, 1981-96

Source: Air Transport Association of America

	Departures (millions)	Fatal accidents	Fatalities	Fatal accidents per 100,000 departures		Departures (millions)	Fatal accidents	Fatalities	Fatal accidents per 100,000 departures
1981	5.2	4	4	0.077	1989	6.6	8	131	0.121
1982[1]	5.0	4	234	0.060	1990	6.9	6	39	0.087
1983	5.0	4	15	0.079	1991	6.8	4	62	0.059
1984	5.4	1	4	0.018	1992	7.1	4	33	0.057
1985	5.8	4	197	0.069	1993	7.2	1	1	0.014
1986[1]	6.4	2	5	0.016	1994	7.5	4	200	0.053
1987[1]	6.6	4	231	0.046	1995	8.1	2	166	0.025
1988[1]	6.7	3	285	0.030	1996	8.2	3	342	0.036

(1) Sabotage-caused accidents are included in the number of fatal accidents and fatalities, but not in the calculation of accident rates.

Aircraft Operating Statistics, 1996

Source: Air Transport Association of America; figures are averages for most commonly used models

	No. of seats	Speed airborne (mph)	Flight length (mi)	Fuel (gal per hr)	Operating cost per hr		No. of seats	Speed airborne (mph)	Flight length (mi)	Fuel (gal per hr)	Operating cost per hr
B747-100	410	518	2,882	3,633	$6,567	MD-90	154	441	782	817	$1,711
B747-400	400	539	5,063	3,445	7,075	B727-200	148	440	742	1,288	2,396
B747-200/300 .	369	529	3,321	3,759	7,790	B727-F.......	0	444	586	1,367	4,810
B747-F	0	508	2,313	3,695	8,853	A320-100/200..	148	458	1,101	816	2,126
L-1011-100/200	305	498	1,363	2,399	5,081	B737-400	144	414	702	792	2,106
B-777	291	513	2,451	2,037	4,194	MD-80	141	432	798	924	2,033
DC-10-10	286	498	1,493	2,233	5,092	B737-300	131	416	602	836	1,943
DC-10-40	284	504	1,963	2,647	4,684	DC-9-50	121	374	345	898	1,925
DC-10-30	272	516	2,379	2,625	5,859	B737-100/200..	112	388	442	831	1,899
A300-600	266	467	1,126	1,671	5,123	B737-500	110	412	570	743	1,730
MD-11	260	524	3,253	2,400	6,335	DC-9-40	109	387	487	837	1,789
L-1011-500 ...	222	523	2,995	2,454	4,764	DC-9-30	100	389	468	818	1,749
B767-300ER ..	216	495	2,331	1,590	3,616	F-100........	97	384	500	705	1,858
B757-200	187	464	1,167	1,048	2,637	DC-9-10	71	380	413	737	1,614
B767-200ER ..	181	486	2,135	1,432	3,195						

National Aviation Hall of Fame

The National Aviation Hall of Fame at Dayton, OH, is dedicated to honoring the outstanding pioneers of air and space.

Allen, William M.
Andrews, Frank M.
Armstrong, Neil A.
Arnold, Henry H. "Hap"
Atwood, John Leland
Balchen, Bernt
Baldwin, Thomas S.
Beachey, Lincoln
Beech, Olive A.
Beech, Walter H.
Bell, Alexander Graham
Bell, Lawrence D.
Bellanca, Giuseppe Mario
Bendix, Vincent T.
Boeing, William E.
Bong, Richard I.
Borman, Frank
Boyd, Albert
Bradley, Mark E.
Brown, George "Scratchley"
Brukner, Clayton John
Byrd, Richard E.
Cessna, Clyde V.
Chamberlin, Clarence D.
Chanute, Octave
Chennault, Claire L.
Cochran (Odlum), Jacqueline
Collins, Michael
Combs, Harry B.
Conrad Jr., Charles
Crawford, Frederick C.
Crossfield, A. Scott
Cunningham, Alfred A.
Curtiss, Glenn H.
Dargue, Herbert Arthur
Davis Jr., Benjamin O.
DeSeversky, Alexander P.
Doolittle, James H.
Douglas, Donald W.
Draper, Charles S.

Eaker, Ira C.
Earhart (Putnam), Amelia
Eielson, C. Benjamin
Ellyson, Theodore G.
Ely, Eugene B.
Everest, Frank K.
Fairchild, Sherman M.
Fleet, Reuben H.
Fokker, Anthony H.G.
Ford, Henry
Foss, Joseph
Foulois, Benjamin D.
Frye, Jack
Gabreski, Francis S.
Gentile, Dominic "Don"
Gilruth, Robert R.
Glenn Jr., John H.
Goddard, George W.
Goddard, Robert H.
Godfrey, Arthur
Goldwater, Barry M.
Grissom, Virgil I.
Gross, Robert E.
Grumman, Leroy R.
Guggenheim, Harry F.
Haughton, Daniel J.
Hegenberger, Albert F.
Heinemann, Edward H.
Hoover, Robert A.
Hughes, Howard R.
Ingalls, David S.
James Jr., Daniel "Chappie"
Jeppesen, Elrey B.
Johnson, Clarence L.
Johnston, Alvin M. "Tex"
Jones, Thomas V.
Kenney, George C.
Kettering, Charles F.
Kindelberger, James H.
Kittinger Jr., Joseph William

Knabenshue, A. Roy
Knight, William J.
Lahm, Frank P.
Langley, Samuel P.
Lear Sr., William P.
LeMay, Curtis E.
LeVier, Anthony W.
Lindbergh, Anne M.
Lindbergh, Charles A.
Link, Edwin A.
Lockheed, Allan H.
Loening, Grover
Luke Jr., Frank
Macready, Carl B.
Macready, John A.
Martin, Glenn L.
McCampbell, David
McDonnell, James S.
Meyer, John C.
Mitchell, William "Billy"
Mitscher, Marc A.
Montgomery, John J.
Moorer, Thomas H.
Moss, Sanford A.
Neumann, Gerhard
Nichols, Ruth R.
Norden, Carl L.
Northrop, John K.
Pangborn, Clyde Edward
Patterson, William A.
Piper Sr., William T.
Pitcairn, Harold Frederick
Post, Wiley H.
Read, Albert C.
Reeve, Robert C.
Rentschler, Frederick B.
Richardson, Holden C.
Rickenbacker, Edward V.
Rodgers, Calbraith P.
Rogers, Will

Rushworth, Robert A.
Rutan, Elbert "Burt" L.
Ryan, T. Claude
Schirra, Walter M.
Schriever, Bernard A.
Selfridge, Thomas E.
Shepard Jr., Alan B.
Sikorsky, Igor I.
Six, Robert F.
Slayton, Donald K. "Deke"
Smith, C.R.
Spaatz, Carl A.
Sperry Sr., Elmer A.
Sperry Sr., Lawrence B.
Stafford, Thomas Patten
Stanley, Robert M.
Stapp, John P.
Stearman, Lloyd C.
Taylor, Charles E.
Thomas, Lowell
Tibbets Jr., Paul W.
Towers, John H.
Trippe, Juan T.
Turner, Roscoe
Twining, Nathan F.
Vandenberg, Hoyt
von Braun, Wernher
von Karman, Theodore
von Ohain, Hans P.
Vought, Chance M.
Wade, Leigh
Walden, Henry W.
Wells, Edward
Wilson, Thornton A.
Woolman, Collett Everman "C.E."
Wright, Orville
Wright, Wilbur
Yeager, Charles E.
Young, John W.

Some Notable Aviation Firsts[1]

1903 — On Dec. 17, near Kitty Hawk, NC, brothers Wilbur and Orville Wright made the first human-carrying, powered flight. Each made 2 flights; the longest, about 852 ft, lasted 59 sec.

1907 — U.S. airplane manufacturing company formed by Glenn H. Curtiss.

1908 — First airplane passenger, Lt. Frank P. Lahm, rode with Wilbur Wright in a brief (6 min, 24 sec) flight.

1911 — The first transportation of mail by airplane officially approved by the U.S. Postal Service began on Sept. 23. It lasted one week. In 1918, limited scheduled air mail service began. By 1921, scheduled transcontinental airmail service began between New York City and San Francisco.

1914 — The first scheduled passenger airline service began. It operated between St. Petersburg and Tampa, FL.

1919 — The first airline food, a basket lunch, was served as part of a commercial airline service.

1930 — Ellen Church became the first flight attendant.

1939 — On Aug. 27, the German Heinkel He 178 made the first successful flight powered by a jet engine.

1947 — Mach 1, the sound barrier, was broken by Amer. Charles E. ("Chuck") Yeager in a Bell X-1 rocket-powered aircraft.

1947 — Largest airplane ever flown, Howard Hughes's "Spruce Goose," flew 1 mi at an altitude of 80 ft.

1953 — Jacqueline Cochran became the first woman to fly faster than sound.

1960 — Convair B-58, the first supersonic bomber, was introduced.

1968 — The supersonic speed of Mach 2 was accomplished for the first time, in a Tupolev Tu-144. The plane had an approximate maximum speed of 1,200 mph.

1970 — The Tupolev Tu-144, during commercial transport, exceeded Mach 2. It reached about 1,335 mph at 53,475 ft.

1976 — The Concorde began the first scheduled supersonic commercial service.

(1) Excludes notable around-the-world and international trips.

Some Notable Around-the-World and Intercontinental Trips

	From/To	Miles	Time	Date
Nellie Bly.	New York/New York		72d 06h 11m	1889
George Francis Train	New York/New York		67d 12h 03m	1890
Charles Fitzmorris	Chicago/Chicago		60d 13h 29m	1901
J. W. Willis Sayre.	Seattle/Seattle		54d 09h 42m	1903
J. Alcock-A.W. Brown [1]	Newfoundland/Ireland	1,960	16h 12m	June 14-15, 1919
Two U.S. Army airplanes	Seattle/Seattle	26,103	35d 01h 11m	1924
Richard E. Byrd, Floyd Bennett [2]	Spitsbergen (Nor.)/N. Pole.	1,545	15h 30m	May 9, 1926
Amundsen-Ellsworth-Nobile Polar Expedition (in a dirigible)	Spitsbergen (Nor.)/over N. Pole to Teller, Alaska		80h	May 11-14,1926
E.S. Evans and L. Wells (*New York World*)	New York/New York	18,410[3]	28d 14h 36m 05s	June 16-July 14, 1926
Charles Lindbergh [4]	New York/Paris.	3,610	33h 29m 30s	May 20-21, 1927
Amelia Earhart, W. Stultz, L. Gordon	Newfoundland/Wales		20h 40m	June 17-18, 1928
Graf Zeppelin	Friedrichshafen, Ger./Lakehurst, NJ .	6,630	4d 15h 46m	Oct. 11-15, 1928
Graf Zeppelin	Friedrichshafen, Ger./Lakehurst, NJ .	21,700	20d 04h	Aug. 14-Sept. 4, 1929
Wiley Post and Harold Gatty (Monoplane Winnie Mae)	New York/New York	15,474	8d 15h 51m	July 1, 1931
C. Pangborn-H. Herndon Jr. [5] . .	Misawa, Japan/Wenatchee, Wash. .	4,458	41h 34m	Oct. 3-5, 1931
Amelia Earhart [6]	Newfoundland/Ireland	2,026	14h 56m	May 20-21, 1932
Wiley Post (Monoplane Winnie Mae)[7]	New York/New York	15,596	115h 36m 30s	July 15-22, 1933
Hindenburg Zeppelin	Lakehurst, NJ/Frankfort, Ger.		42h 53m	Aug. 9-11, 1936
H. R. Ekins (Scripps-Howard Newspapers in race) (Zeppelin Hindenburg to Germany, air-planes from Frankfurt)	Lakehurst, NJ/Lakehurst, NJ	25,654	18d 11h 14m 33s	Sept. 30-Oct. 19, 1936
Howard Hughes and 4 assistants	New York/New York	14,824	3d 19h 08m 10s	July 10-13, 1938
Douglas Corrigan.	New York/Dublin.		28h 13m	July 17-18, 1938
Mrs. Clara Adams (Pan American Clipper)	Port Washington, NY/ Newark, NJ.		16d 19h 04m	June 28-July 15, 1939
Globester, U.S. Air Transport Command	Washington, DC/Washington, DC . .	23,279	149h 44m	Oct. 4, 1945
Capt. William P. Odom (A-26 Reynolds Bombshell)	New York/New York	20,000	78h 55m 12s	Apr. 12-16, 1947
America, Pan American 4-engine Lockheed Constellation [8]	New York/New York	22,219	101h 32m	June 17-30, 1947
Col. Edward Eagan	New York/New York	20,559	147h 15m	Dec. 13, 1948
USAF B-50 Lucky Lady II (Capt. James Gallagher) [9]	Ft. Worth, TX/Ft. Worth, TX	23,452	94h 01m	Feb. 26-Mar. 2, 1949
Col. D. Schilling, USAF [10]	England/Limestone, ME.	3,300	10h 01m	Sept. 22, 1950
C.F. Blair Jr.	Norway/Alaska	3,300	10h 29m	May 29, 1951
Two U.S. S-55.	Massachusetts/Scotland	3,410	42h 30m	July 15-31, 1952
Canberra Bomber [11]	N. Ireland/Newfoundland	2073	04h 34m	Aug. 26, 1952
	Newfoundland/N. Ireland	2073	03h 25m	Aug. 26, 1952
Three USAF B-52 Strato-fortresses [12]	Merced, CA/CA.	24,325	45h 19m	Jan. 15-18, 1957
Max Conrad	Chicago/Rome	5,000	34h 03m	Mar. 5-6, 1959
USSR TU-114 [13]	Moscow/New York	5,092	11h 06m	June 28, 1959
Boeing 707-320.	New York/Moscow	c.5,090	08h 54m	July 23, 1959
Peter Gluckmann (solo)	San Francisco/San Francisco.	22,800	29d	Aug. 22-Sept. 20, 1959
Sue Snyder	Chicago/Chicago	21,219	62h 59m	June 22-24, 1960
Max Conrad (solo)	Miami/Miami.	25,946	8d 18h 35m 57s	Feb. 28-Mar. 8, 1961
Sam Miller & Louis Fodor	New York/New York		46h 28m	Aug. 3-4, 1963
Robert & Joan Wallick	Manila/Manila.	23,129	5d 06h 17m 10s	June 2-7, 1966
Arthur Godfrey, Richard Merrill Fred Austin, Karl Keller	New York/New York	23,333	86h 9m 01s	June 4-7, 1966
Trevor K. Brougham.	Darwin, Australia/Darwin	24,800	5d 05h 57m	Aug. 5-10, 1972
Walter H. Mullikin, Albert Frink, Lyman Watt, Frank Cassaniti, Edward Shields	New York/New York	23,137	1d 22h 50s	May 1-3, 1976
Arnold Palmer	Denver/Denver	22,985	57h 7m 12s	May 17-19, 1976
Boeing 747[14]	San Francisco/San Francisco.	26,382	57h 25m 42s	Oct. 28-31, 1977
Richard Rutan & Jeana Yeager[15]	Edwards AFB, CA.	24,986	09d 03m 44s	Dec. 14-23, 1986
Concorde.	New York/New York	1,114 mph	31h 27m 49s	Aug. 15-16, 1995
Col. Douglas L. Raaberg and crew, B1 bomber[16]	Dyess AFB, Abilene, TX/Dyess AFB.	6,250	36h 13m 36s	June 3, 1995
Linda Finch[17]	Oakland, CA/Oakland, CA	26,000	73d	Mar. 17-May 28, 1997

(1) Nonstop transatlantic flight. (2) Claim of reaching N. Pole in dispute; if claim is untrue, then Amundsen-Ellsworth-Nobile were the first to fly over N. Pole. (3) Includes mileage by train and auto, 4,110; by plane, 6,300; by steamship, 8,000. (4) Solo transatlantic flight in the Ryan monoplane "Spirit of St. Louis." (5) Nonstop transpacific flight. (6) First woman's transoceanic solo flight. (7) First to fly solo around N circumference of the world and first to fly twice around the world. (8) Inception of regular commercial global air service. (9) First nonstop round-the-world flight, refueled 4 times in flight. (10) Nonstop jet transatlantic flight. (11) Transatlantic round trip on same day. (12) First nonstop global flight by jet planes, refueled in flight by KC-97 aerial tankers; average speed approx. 525 mph. (13) Nonstop between Moscow and New York. (14) Speed record around the world over both Earth's poles. (15) Circled Earth nonstop without refueling. (16) Refueled in flight 6 times. Tested B-1B bomber by bombing 3 pre-arranged target sites on 3 continents. (17) Followed the intended around-the-world flight route (1937) of Amelia Earhart.

METEOROLOGY

National Weather Service Watches and Warnings

Source: National Weather Service, NOAA, U.S. Dept. of Commerce; *Glossary of Meteorology,* American Meteorological Society

National Weather Service forecasters issue a *Severe Thunderstorm* or *Tornado Watch* for a specific area when a severe convective storm that usually covers a relatively small geographic area or moves in a narrow path is sufficiently intense to threaten life and/or property. Examples include thunderstorms with large hail, damaging winds, and/or tornadoes. Additionally, excessive localized convective rains are classified as severe storms but are often the product of severe local storms. Such rainfall may result in related phenomena that threaten life and property, such as flash floods. Although cloud-to-ground lightning is not a criterion for severe local storms, it is acknowledged to be highly dangerous and a leading cause of deaths and injuries from thunderstorms.

A *Watch* alerts people that threatening weather is likely. Under a Watch, persons should remain alert for approaching storms, activate a plan for action, and monitor ongoing events closely. A *Warning* means that severe weather is occurring or has been indicated by radar; **immediate** action should be taken by people in the storm's path.

Severe Thunderstorm—A thunderstorm that produces a tornado, winds of at least 50 knots (58 mph), and/or hail at least 3/4 inch in diameter. A thunderstorm with winds of at least 35 knots (40 mph) and/or hail at least 1/2 inch in diameter is defined as approaching severe. A *Severe Thunderstorm Watch* is issued for a specific area where such storms are most likely to develop. A *Severe Thunderstorm Warning* indicates that a severe thunderstorm has been sighted or indicated by radar.

Tornado—A violent rotating column of air (winds over 200 mph), usually pendant to a cumulonimbus cloud, with circulation reaching the ground. A tornado nearly always starts as a funnel cloud and may be accompanied by a loud roaring noise. On a local scale, it is the most destructive of all atmospheric phenomena. Tornado paths have varied in length from a few feet to more than 100 miles (avg. 5 mi); in diameter from a few feet to more than a mile (avg. 220 yd); average forward speed, 30 mph.

Cyclone—An atmospheric circulation of winds rotating counterclockwise in the northern hemisphere and clockwise in the southern hemisphere. Tornadoes, hurricanes, and the lows shown on weather maps are all examples of cyclones of various size and intensity. Cyclones are usually accompanied by precipitation or stormy weather.

Subtropical Storm—An atmospheric circulation of one-minute sustained surface winds, 34 knots (39 mph) or more. Depending on its characteristics and intensity, it can develop into a tropical storm or a hurricane.

Tropical Storm—An atmospheric circulation of one-minute sustained surface winds within a range of 34 to 63 knots (39 to 73 mph). A *Tropical Storm Watch* is an announcement that a tropical storm or tropical storm conditions may pose a threat to coastal areas generally within 36 hours. A *Tropical Storm Warning* is an announcement that tropical storm conditions pose a threat along a specified segment of coastline within 24 hours.

Hurricane—A severe cyclone originating over tropical ocean waters and having one-minute sustained surface winds 64 knots (73 mph) or higher. (West of the international date line, in the western Pacific, such storms are known as *typhoons.*) The area of hurricane-force winds forms a circle or an oval, sometimes as wide as 300 mi in diameter. In the lower latitudes, hurricanes usually move west or northwest at 10 to 15 mph. When the center approaches 25° to 30° North Latitude, the direction of motion often changes to northeast, with increased forward speed.

Blizzard—A severe weather condition characterized by strong winds bearing a great amount of snow. The National Weather Service specifies winds of 35 mph or higher and sufficient falling and/or blowing snow to frequently reduce visibility to less than 1/4 mi. for a duration of at least 3 hours.

Flood—Flooding takes many forms. *River Flood:* A natural process that occurs when rains, sometimes coupled with melting snow, fill river basins with too much water, too quickly; in some locations, torrential rains from decaying hurricanes or tropical systems can also be a major cause of river flooding. *Coastal Flooding:* Winds generated from tropical storms and hurricanes or intense offshore low pressure systems can drive ocean water inland and cause significant flooding. Coastal floods can also be produced by sea waves called *tsunamis,* sometimes referred to as tidal waves; these waves are produced by earthquakes or volcanic activity. *Flash Flooding:* Usually due to copious amounts of rain falling in a short period of time, flash flooding typically occurs within 6 hours of the rain event. Flash floods account for the majority of flood deaths in the U.S. *Urban Flooding:* Urbanization significantly increases runoff over what would occur on natural terrain, making flash flooding in these areas extremely dangerous. During periods of urban flooding, streets can become swift-moving rivers, and basements can become death traps as they fill with water. *Ice Jam Flooding:* Ice can accumulate at natural or artificial obstructions and stop the flow of water. As the water flow is stopped, water builds up and flooding can occur upstream. If the jam suddenly gives way, the gush of ice and water can cause serious downstream flash flooding.

Flash Flood or Flood Watch: Persons should be alert that flash flooding or flooding is possible within a designated area.

Flash Flood or Flood Warning: Flash flooding or flooding has been reported or is imminent, and all necessary precautions should be taken immediately.

Urban and Small Stream Advisory: Small streams, streets, and low-lying areas such as railroad underpasses and urban storm drains are flooding.

National Weather Service Marine Warnings and Advisories

Small Craft Advisory: A Small Craft Advisory alerts mariners to sustained (exceeding 2 hours) weather and/or sea conditions, either present or forecast, potentially hazardous to small boats. Although there is no definition of a small craft, hazardous conditions generally include winds of 18 to 33 knots and/or dangerous wave conditions. It is the responsibility of the mariner, based on experience and on the location and size or type of boat, to determine if the conditions are hazardous. When a mariner becomes aware of a Small Craft Advisory, he or she should immediately obtain the latest marine forecast to determine the reason for the advisory.

Gale Warning indicates that winds within the range 34 to 47 knots, not directly associated with a tropical storm, are forecast for the area.

Tropical Storm Warning indicates that winds of 34 to 63 knots are forecast in a specified coastal area within 24 hours or less. Issued only for winds of tropical weather systems.

Storm Warning indicates that winds 48 knots or above, not directly associated with a tropical storm, are forecast for the area.

Hurricane Warning indicates that winds 64 knots or greater are forecast for the area within 24 hours. Issued only for winds produced by tropical weather systems.

Special Marine Warning: A warning for potentially hazardous weather conditions, usually of short duration (2 hours or less) and producing wind speeds of 34 knots or more, not adequately covered by existing marine warnings.

Primary sources of dissemination are commercial radio, TV, U.S. Coast Guard radio stations, and NOAA VHF-FM broadcasts. These NOAA broadcasts on 162.40 to 162.55 MHz can usually be received 20-40 mi from the transmitting antenna site, depending on terrain and quality of the receiver used. Where transmitting antennas are on high ground, the range may be somewhat greater, reaching 60 mi or more.

Monthly Normal Temperatures, Precipitation

Source: National Climatic Data Center, NESDIS, NOAA, U.S. Dept. of Commerce

The temperatures below are based on records for the 30-year period 1961-90. For stations that did not have continuous records from the same site for the entire 30 years, the means have been adjusted to the record at the present site.
Airport stations, unless otherwise indicated. * = city station; T = temperature in Fahrenheit; P = precipitation in inches; L = less than 0.05 inch.

	Jan.		Feb.		Mar.		Apr.		May		June		July		Aug.		Sept.		Oct.		Nov.		Dec.	
Station	T	P	T	P	T	P	T	P	T	P	T	P	T	P	T	P	T	P	T	P	T	P	T	P
Albany, NY	21	2.4	24	2.3	34	2.9	46	3.0	58	3.4	67	3.6	72	3.2	70	3.5	61	3.0	50	2.8	40	3.2	27	2.9
Albuquerque, NM	34	0.4	40	0.5	47	0.5	55	0.5	64	0.5	74	0.6	79	1.4	76	1.6	69	1.0	57	0.9	44	0.4	35	0.5
Anchorage, AK	15	0.8	19	0.8	26	0.7	36	0.7	47	0.7	54	1.1	58	1.7	56	2.4	48	2.7	35	2.0	21	1.1	16	1.1
Asheville, NC	36	3.3	39	3.9	47	4.6	55	3.4	63	4.4	69	4.2	73	4.5	72	4.7	66	3.9	56	3.6	48	3.6	40	3.5
Atlanta, GA	41	4.8	45	4.8	54	5.8	62	4.3	69	4.3	76	3.6	79	5.0	78	3.7	73	3.4	62	3.1	53	3.9	45	4.3
Atlantic City, NJ	31	3.5	33	3.1	42	3.6	50	3.6	60	3.3	69	2.6	75	3.8	73	4.1	66	2.9	55	2.8	46	3.6	36	3.3
Baltimore, MD	32	3.1	35	3.1	44	3.4	53	3.1	63	3.7	73	3.7	77	3.7	76	3.9	69	3.4	57	3.0	47	3.3	37	3.4
Barrow, AK	-13	0.2	-18	0.2	-15	0.2	-2	0.2	19	0.2	34	0.3	39	0.9	38	1.0	31	0.6	14	0.5	-2	0.3	-11	0.2
Birmingham, AL	42	5.1	46	4.7	54	6.2	62	5.0	69	4.9	76	3.7	80	5.3	79	3.6	73	3.9	63	2.8	53	4.3	45	5.1
Bismarck, ND	9	0.5	16	0.4	28	0.8	43	1.7	55	2.2	64	2.7	71	2.1	68	1.7	57	1.5	46	0.9	29	0.5	14	0.5
Boise, ID	29	1.5	36	1.2	43	1.3	49	1.2	58	1.1	67	1.8	74	0.4	73	0.4	63	0.8	52	0.8	40	1.5	30	1.4
Boston, MA	29	3.6	30	3.6	39	3.7	48	3.6	58	3.3	68	3.1	74	2.8	72	3.2	65	3.1	55	3.3	45	4.2	34	4.0
Buffalo, NY	24	2.7	25	2.3	34	2.7	45	2.9	57	3.1	66	3.6	71	3.1	69	4.2	62	3.5	51	3.1	41	3.8	29	3.7
Burlington, VT	16	1.8	18	1.6	31	2.2	44	2.8	56	3.1	65	3.5	71	3.7	68	4.1	59	3.3	48	2.9	37	3.1	23	2.4
Caribou, ME	9	2.4	12	1.9	25	2.4	38	2.5	51	3.1	61	2.9	66	4.0	63	4.1	54	3.5	43	3.1	31	3.6	15	3.2
Charleston, SC	48	3.5	51	3.3	58	4.3	65	2.7	73	4.0	78	6.4	82	6.8	81	7.2	76	4.7	67	2.9	58	2.5	51	3.2
Chicago, IL	21	1.5	25	1.4	37	2.7	49	3.6	59	3.3	69	3.8	73	3.7	72	4.2	64	3.8	53	2.4	40	2.9	27	2.5
Cleveland, OH	25	2.0	27	2.2	37	2.9	48	3.1	58	3.5	68	3.7	72	3.5	70	3.4	64	3.4	53	2.5	43	3.2	31	3.1
Columbus, OH	26	2.2	30	2.2	41	3.3	51	3.2	61	3.9	69	4.0	73	4.3	72	3.7	66	3.0	54	2.2	43	3.2	32	2.9
Dallas-Ft. Worth, TX	43	1.8	48	2.2	57	2.8	66	3.5	73	4.9	81	3.0	85	2.3	85	2.2	77	3.4	67	3.5	56	2.3	47	1.8
Denver, CO	30	0.5	33	0.6	39	1.3	48	1.7	57	2.4	67	1.8	74	1.9	71	1.5	62	1.2	51	1.0	39	0.9	31	0.6
Des Moines, IA	19	1.0	25	1.1	37	2.3	51	3.4	62	3.7	72	4.5	77	3.8	74	4.2	65	3.5	54	2.6	39	1.8	24	1.3
Detroit, MI	23	1.8	25	1.7	36	2.6	47	3.0	58	2.9	68	3.6	72	3.2	71	3.4	63	2.9	51	2.1	40	2.7	28	2.8
Dodge City, KS	30	0.5	35	0.6	43	1.6	55	2.0	64	3.0	74	3.1	80	3.2	78	2.7	69	1.9	57	1.3	43	0.8	32	0.6
Duluth, MN	7	1.2	12	0.8	24	1.9	39	2.3	51	3.0	60	3.8	66	3.6	64	4.0	54	3.8	44	2.5	28	1.8	13	1.2
Fairbanks, AK	-10	0.5	-4	0.4	11	0.4	31	0.3	49	0.6	60	1.4	63	1.9	57	2.0	46	1.0	25	0.9	3	0.8	-7	0.9
Fresno, CA	46	2.0	51	1.8	55	1.9	61	1.0	69	0.3	77	0.1	82	L	80	L	75	0.2	65	0.5	54	1.4	45	1.4
Galveston, TX*	53	3.3	55	2.3	62	2.2	69	2.4	76	3.6	81	4.4	83	4.0	84	4.5	80	5.9	73	2.8	64	3.4	56	3.5
Grand Junction, CO	25	0.6	34	0.5	43	0.9	52	0.7	62	0.9	72	0.5	79	0.6	76	0.8	67	0.8	55	1.0	40	0.7	29	0.6
Grand Rapids, MI	22	1.8	24	1.4	34	2.6	46	3.4	58	3.1	67	3.7	72	3.2	70	3.6	61	4.2	50	2.8	38	3.3	27	2.9
Hartford, CT	25	3.4	28	3.2	38	3.6	49	3.9	60	4.1	69	3.8	74	3.2	72	3.7	63	3.8	52	3.6	42	4.0	30	3.9
Helena, MT	20	0.6	26	0.4	34	0.7	43	1.0	53	1.8	62	1.9	69	1.1	67	1.3	55	1.2	45	0.6	32	0.5	21	0.6
Honolulu, HI	73	3.6	73	2.2	74	2.2	76	1.5	78	1.1	79	0.5	81	0.6	81	0.4	81	0.8	80	2.3	77	3.0	74	3.8
Houston, TX	50	3.2	54	3.3	61	2.7	68	4.2	75	4.7	80	4.0	83	3.3	82	3.7	78	4.9	70	3.7	61	3.4	54	3.7
Huron, SD	13	0.4	19	0.8	32	1.2	46	2.0	58	2.7	68	3.3	74	2.3	72	2.0	61	1.4	49	1.4	32	0.7	18	0.5
Indianapolis, IN	26	2.3	30	2.5	41	3.8	52	3.7	63	4.0	72	3.5	75	4.5	73	3.6	67	2.9	55	2.6	43	3.2	31	3.3
Jackson, MS	44	5.2	48	4.7	57	5.8	65	5.6	72	5.1	79	3.2	82	4.5	81	3.8	76	3.6	65	3.3	56	4.8	48	5.9
Jacksonville, FL	52	3.3	55	3.9	61	3.7	67	2.8	73	3.6	79	5.7	82	5.6	81	7.9	78	7.0	70	2.9	62	2.1	55	2.7
Juneau, AK	24	4.5	28	3.7	33	3.3	40	2.8	47	3.4	53	3.1	56	4.2	55	5.3	49	6.7	42	7.8	32	4.9	27	4.4
Kansas City, MO	26	1.1	31	1.1	43	2.5	55	3.1	64	5.0	73	4.7	79	4.4	76	4.0	68	4.9	57	3.3	43	1.9	30	1.6
Knoxville, TN	36	4.2	40	4.1	49	5.1	58	3.7	65	4.1	73	4.0	77	4.7	76	3.1	70	3.1	58	2.8	49	3.8	40	4.5
Lander, WY	20	0.5	25	0.6	34	1.2	43	2.1	53	2.3	63	1.5	71	0.8	69	0.5	58	1.1	47	1.1	31	0.8	21	0.6
Lexington, KY	31	2.9	35	3.2	45	4.4	55	3.9	64	4.5	72	3.7	76	5.0	75	3.9	68	3.2	57	2.6	46	3.4	36	4.0
Little Rock, AR	39	3.9	44	4.4	53	5.3	62	6.2	70	7.0	78	7.8	82	8.2	81	8.1	74	7.4	63	6.3	52	5.2	43	4.3
Los Angeles, CA*	58	2.9	60	3.1	61	2.6	63	1.0	66	0.2	70	L	74	L	75	0.1	74	0.5	70	0.3	63	2.0	58	2.0
Louisville, KY	32	2.9	36	3.3	46	4.7	56	4.2	65	4.6	73	3.5	77	4.5	76	3.5	70	3.2	58	2.7	47	3.7	37	3.6
Marquette, MI*	12	2.2	14	1.7	24	2.8	37	2.6	50	3.0	59	3.5	65	2.9	63	3.4	54	4.1	44	3.6	30	2.9	17	2.6
Memphis, TN	40	3.7	44	4.4	53	5.4	63	5.5	71	5.0	79	3.6	83	3.8	81	3.4	74	3.5	63	3.0	53	5.1	44	5.7
Miami, FL	67	2.0	69	2.1	72	2.4	75	2.9	79	6.2	81	9.3	83	5.7	83	7.6	82	7.6	78	5.6	74	2.7	69	1.8
Milwaukee, WI	19	1.6	23	1.5	33	2.7	44	3.5	55	2.8	65	3.2	71	3.5	69	3.5	62	3.4	50	2.4	38	2.5	24	2.3
Minneapolis, MN	12	1.0	18	0.9	31	1.9	46	2.4	59	3.4	68	4.1	74	3.5	71	3.6	61	2.7	49	2.2	33	1.6	18	1.1
Mobile, AL	50	4.8	53	5.5	61	6.4	68	4.5	75	5.7	80	5.0	82	6.9	82	7.0	78	5.9	68	2.9	60	4.1	53	5.3
Moline, IL	20	1.5	25	1.2	37	3.0	50	3.9	61	4.3	71	4.3	75	5.0	73	4.2	65	4.0	53	2.9	40	2.5	25	2.2
Nashville, TN	36	3.6	40	3.8	50	4.9	59	4.4	68	4.9	76	3.6	79	4.0	78	3.5	72	3.5	60	2.6	50	4.1	41	4.6
Newark, NJ	31	3.4	33	3.0	42	3.9	52	3.8	63	4.1	73	3.2	78	4.5	76	3.9	69	3.7	58	3.1	47	3.9	36	3.5
New Orleans, LA	51	5.1	54	6.0	62	4.9	69	4.5	75	4.6	80	5.8	82	6.1	82	6.2	78	5.5	69	3.1	61	4.4	55	5.8
New York, NY*	32	3.4	34	3.3	42	4.1	53	4.2	63	4.4	72	3.7	77	4.4	76	4.0	68	3.9	58	3.6	48	4.5	37	3.9
Norfolk, VA	39	3.8	41	3.5	49	3.7	57	3.1	66	3.8	74	3.8	78	5.1	77	4.8	72	3.9	61	3.2	53	2.9	44	3.2
Oklahoma City, OK	36	1.1	41	1.6	50	2.7	60	2.8	68	5.2	77	4.3	82	2.6	81	2.6	73	3.8	62	3.2	50	2.0	39	1.4
Omaha, NE	21	0.7	27	0.8	39	2.0	52	2.7	62	4.5	72	3.9	77	3.5	74	3.2	65	3.7	53	2.3	39	1.5	25	1.0
Philadelphia, PA	30	3.2	33	2.8	42	3.5	52	3.6	63	3.8	72	3.7	77	4.3	76	3.8	68	3.4	56	2.6	46	3.3	36	3.4
Phoenix, AZ	54	0.7	58	0.7	62	0.9	70	0.2	79	0.1	88	0.1	94	0.8	92	1.0	86	0.9	75	0.7	62	0.7	54	1.0
Pittsburgh, PA	26	2.5	29	2.4	39	3.4	50	3.2	60	3.6	68	3.7	72	3.8	71	3.2	64	3.0	52	2.4	42	2.9	32	2.9
Portland, ME	21	3.5	23	3.3	33	3.7	43	4.1	53	3.6	62	3.4	69	3.1	67	2.9	59	3.1	49	3.9	39	5.2	27	4.6
Portland, OR	40	5.4	44	3.9	47	3.6	51	2.4	57	2.1	64	1.5	68	0.6	69	1.1	63	1.8	55	2.7	46	5.3	40	6.1
Providence, RI	28	4.1	30	3.7	37	4.3	47	4.0	57	3.5	67	2.8	73	3.0	71	4.0	64	3.5	54	3.8	44	4.2	33	4.5
Raleigh, NC	39	3.6	42	3.4	50	3.7	59	2.9	67	3.7	74	3.7	78	4.4	77	4.4	71	3.3	60	2.7	51	2.9	43	3.1
Rapid City, SD	22	0.4	27	0.5	34	1.0	45	1.9	55	2.7	65	3.1	72	2.0	71	1.7	60	1.2	49	1.1	35	0.6	24	0.5
Reno, NV	33	1.1	38	1.0	43	0.7	49	0.4	57	0.7	65	0.5	72	0.3	70	0.3	60	0.4	51	0.4	40	0.9	33	1.0
Richmond, VA	37	3.2	39	3.2	48	3.6	57	3.0	66	3.8	74	3.6	78	5.0	77	4.4	70	3.3	59	3.5	50	3.2	40	3.3
St. Louis, MO	29	1.8	34	2.1	45	3.6	57	3.5	66	4.0	75	3.7	80	3.9	78	2.9	70	3.1	58	2.7	46	3.3	34	3.0
Salt Lake City, UT	28	1.1	34	1.2	42	1.9	50	2.1	59	1.8	69	0.9	78	0.8	76	0.9	65	1.3	53	1.4	41	1.3	30	1.4
San Antonio, TX	49	1.7	54	1.8	62	1.5	69	2.5	76	4.2	82	3.8	85	2.2	85	2.5	79	3.4	70	3.2	60	2.6	52	1.5
San Diego, CA	57	1.8	59	1.5	60	1.8	62	0.8	64	0.2	67	0.1	71	L	73	0.1	71	0.2	68	0.4	62	1.5	57	1.6
San Francisco, CA	49	4.4	52	3.2	53	3.1	56	1.4	58	0.2	62	0.1	63	L	64	0.1	65	0.2	61	1.2	55	2.9	49	3.1
San Juan, PR	77	2.8	77	2.1	78	2.3	79	3.8	81	5.9	82	4.0	83	4.4	83	5.3	82	5.3	82	5.7	80	5.9	78	4.7
Sault Ste. Marie, MI*	13	2.4	14	1.7	24	2.3	38	2.4	51	2.7	58	3.1	64	2.7	63	3.6	55	3.7	45	3.2	33	3.5	19	2.9
Savannah, GA	49	3.6	52	3.2	59	3.8	66	3.0	74	4.1	79	5.7	82	6.4	81	7.4	77	4.5	67	2.4	59	2.2	52	3.0
Scottsbluff, NE	25	0.5	30	0.5	36	1.1	47	1.6	56	2.8	67	2.6	74	2.1	72	1.1	61	1.1	50	0.8	36	0.6	26	0.6
Seattle, WA	41	5.4	44	4.0	47	3.8	50	2.5	56	1.8	61	1.6	65	0.9	66	1.2	61	1.9	54	3.3	46	5.7	42	6.0
Spokane, WA	27	2.0	33	1.5	39	1.5	46	1.2	54	1.4	62	1.3	69	0.7	68	0.7	59	0.7	47	1.0	35	2.2	28	2.4
Springfield, MO	31	1.8	36	2.2	46	3.9	56	4.2	65	4.4	73	5.1	78	2.9	77	3.5	69	4.6	58	[illegible]	[illegible]	[illegible]	[illegible]	[illegible]
Syracuse, NY	22	2.3	24	2.2	34	2.8	46	3.3	57	3.3	65	3.8	70	3.8	68	3.5	62	3.8	51	3.2	41	3.7	28	3.2
Tampa, FL	60	2.0	62	3.1	67	3.0	71	1.2	77	3.1	81	5.5	82	6.6	82	7.6	81	6.0	75	2.0	68	1.8	62	2.2
Washington, DC	31	2.7	34	2.8	43	3.2	53	3.1	62	4.0	71	3.9	76	3.5	74	3.9	67	3.4	55	3.2	45	3.3	35	3.2
Wilmington, DE	31	3.0	33	2.9	43	3.4	52	3.4	63	3.8	72	3.6	76	4.2	75	3.4	68	3.4	56	2.9	46	3.3	36	3.5

Normal High and Low Temperatures, Precipitation

Source: National Climatic Data Center, NESDIS, NOAA, U.S. Dept. of Commerce

The normal temperatures below are based on records for the 30-year period 1961-90. The extreme temperatures (through 1990) are listed for the stations shown and may not agree with the state records shown on page 182.

Airport stations, unless otherwise indicated. * = city station. The minus (−) sign indicates temperatures below zero. Temperatures are Fahrenheit.

State	Station	Normal temperature January Max.	Normal temperature January Min.	Normal temperature July Max.	Normal temperature July Min.	Extreme temperature Highest	Extreme temperature Lowest	Normal annual precipitation (inches)
Alabama	Mobile	60	40	91	73	104	3	63.96
Alaska	Anchorage	21	8	65	52	85	−34	15.91
Alaska	Barrow	−7	−19	45	34	79	−56	4.49
Arizona	Phoenix	66	41	106	81	122	17	7.66
Arkansas	Little Rock	49	29	92	72	112	−5	72.10
California	Los Angeles*	68	49	84	65	112	28	14.77
California	San Diego	66	49	76	66	111	29	9.9
California	San Francisco	56	42	72	54	106	20	19.70
Colorado	Denver	43	16	88	59	104	−30	15.40
Connecticut	Hartford	33	16	85	62	102	−26	44.14
Delaware	Wilmington	39	22	86	67	102	−14	40.84
District of Columbia	Washington–National	42	27	89	71	104	−5	38.63
Florida	Jacksonville	64	41	91	72	105	7	51.32
Florida	Miami	75	59	89	76	98	30	55.91
Georgia	Atlanta	50	32	88	70	105	−8	50.77
Georgia	Savannah	60	38	91	72	105	3	49.22
Hawaii	Honolulu	80	66	88	74	94	53	22.02
Idaho	Boise	36	22	90	58	111	−25	12.11
Illinois	Chicago	29	13	84	63	104	−27	35.82
Illinois	Moline	28	11	86	65	106	−27	39.08
Indiana	Indianapolis	34	17	86	65	104	−23	39.94
Iowa	Des Moines	28	11	87	67	108	−24	33.12
Kentucky	Lexington	39	22	86	66	103	−21	44.55
Kentucky	Louisville	40	23	87	67	105	−20	44.39
Louisiana	New Orleans	61	42	91	73	102	11	61.88
Maine	Caribou	19	−2	77	55	96	−41	36.60
Maine	Portland	30	11	79	58	103	−39	44.34
Maryland	Baltimore	40	23	87	67	105	−7	40.76
Massachusetts	Boston	36	22	82	65	102	−12	41.51
Michigan	Detroit	30	16	83	61	104	−21	32.62
Michigan	Sault Ste. Marie*	21	5	76	51	98	−36	34.23
Minnesota	Duluth	16	−2	77	55	97	−39	30.00
Minnesota	Minneapolis-St. Paul	21	3	84	63	105	−34	28.32
Mississippi	Jackson	56	33	92	71	106	2	55.37
Missouri	Kansas City	35	17	89	68	109	−23	37.62
Missouri	St. Louis	38	21	89	70	107	−18	37.51
Montana	Helena	30	10	85	53	105	−42	11.60
Nebraska	Omaha	31	11	88	66	114	−23	29.86
Nebraska	Scottsbluff	38	12	90	59	109	−42	15.27
Nevada	Reno	45	21	92	51	105	−16	7.53
New Jersey	Atlantic City	40	21	85	65	106	−11	40.29
New Mexico	Albuquerque	47	22	93	64	105	−17	8.88
New York	Albany	30	11	84	60	100	−28	36.17
New York	Buffalo	30	17	80	62	99	−20	38.58
New York	New York–La Guardia	37	26	84	69	107	−3	42.12
North Carolina	Asheville	47	25	83	62	100	−16	47.59
North Carolina	Raleigh	49	29	88	68	105	−9	41.43
North Dakota	Bismarck	20	−2	84	56	109	−44	15.47
Ohio	Cleveland	32	18	82	61	104	−19	36.63
Ohio	Columbus	34	19	84	63	102	−19	38.09
Oregon	Portland	45	34	80	57	107	−3	36.30
Pennsylvania	Philadelphia	38	23	86	67	104	−7	41.41
Pennsylvania	Pittsburgh	34	19	83	62	103	−18	36.85
Rhode Island	Providence	37	19	82	63	104	−13	45.53
South Carolina	Charleston	58	38	90	73	104	6	51.53
South Dakota	Huron	24	2	87	62	112	−39	20.08
South Dakota	Rapid City	34	11	86	58	110	−30	16.64
Tennessee	Memphis	49	31	92	73	108	−13	52.10
Tennessee	Nashville	46	27	90	69	107	−17	47.30
Texas	Galveston*	58	47	87	79	101	8	42.28
Texas	Houston	61	40	93	72	107	7	46.07
Utah	Salt Lake City	36	19	92	64	107	−30	16.18
Vermont	Burlington	25	8	81	60	101	−30	34.47
Virginia	Norfolk	47	31	86	70	104	−3	44.64
Virginia	Richmond	46	26	88	68	105	−12	43.16
Washington	Seattle-Tacoma	45	35	75	55	99	0	37.19
Washington	Spokane	33	21	83	54	108	−25	16.49
Wisconsin	Milwaukee	26	12	80	62	103	−26	32.93
Wyoming	Lander	31	8	86	56	101	−37	13.01

Mean Annual Snowfall (inches) based on record through 1990: Boston, MA, 42; Sault Ste. Marie, MI, 113; Albany, NY, 65.2; Burlington, VT, 78.6; Lander, WY, 66; Juneau, AK, 105.8.

Wettest Spot: Mount Waialeale, HI, on the island of Kauai, is the rainiest place in the world, according to the National Geographic Society, with an average annual rainfall of 460 inches.

Highest Temperature: A temperature of 136° F observed at Azizia (Al Aziziyah), near Tripoli, Libya, on Sept. 13, 1922, is generally accepted as the world's highest temperature recorded under standard conditions.

The record high in the United States was 134° F in Death Valley, CA, July 10, 1913.

Lowest Temperature: A record low temperature of −128.6° F was recorded at the Soviet Antarctica station Vostok on July 21, 1983.

The record low in the United States was −80° F at Prospect Creek, AK, Jan. 23, 1971.

The lowest official temperature on the North American continent was recorded at −81° F in Feb. 1947, at an airport in the Yukon called Snag.

These are the meteorological champions—the official temperature extremes—but there are many other claimants to thermometer fame. However, sun readings are unofficial records, since meteorological data to qualify officially must be taken on instruments in a sheltered and ventilated location.

Annual Climatological Data

Source: National Climatic Data Center, NESDIS, NOAA, U.S. Dept. of Commerce

1995

Station	Elev. ft	Temperature °F Highest	Date	Lowest	Date	Precipitation Total (in.)	Greatest in 24 hours	Date	Sleet or snow Total (in.)	Greatest in 24 hours	Date	Fastest wind MPH	Date	No. of days Clear*	Cloudy*	Prec. .01 in. or more	Snow, sleet 1 in. or more
Albany, NY	275	99	7/14	−18	2/7	34.08	2.67	10/20	54.8	13.3	2/4	47	8/31	—	—	118	14
Albuquerque, NM	5,311	103	7/28	16	12/26	5.68	0.99	9/7	9.8	4.5	1/4	41	3/28	151	91	50	3
Anchorage, AK	114	78	6/11	−15	1/13	13.76	1.02	8/12	52.0	12.0	3/16	43	2/14	61	244	93	14
Asheville, NC	2,140	93	8/18	6	2/9	55.39	4.22	10/4	3.5	3.1	2/7	33	10/5	72	179	123	2
Atlanta, GA	1,010	102	8/15	13	12/10	52.77	7.27	10/3	0.4	0.4	2/6	41	5/15	—	—	115	0
Atlantic City, NJ[3]	64	100	7/15	6	2/6	35.70	3.06	8/5	0.8	0.4	2/15	47	11/11	—	—	100	23
Baltimore, MD	148	102	7/15	5	2/6	36.93	2.76	8/5	11.3	7.2	2/3	36	2/5	96	175	118	2
Barrow, AK	31	64	7/8	−51	2/1	2.75	0.42	7/5	24.0	2.0	3/17	38	12/19	40	213	51	6
Birmingham, AL	620	103	8/18	13	12/10	55.12	6.94	10/3	1.0	0.8	2/6	—	—	—	—	121	0
Bismarck, ND	1,647	98	8/17	−28	3/8	18.90	1.80	5/8	64.2	7.7	1/16	48	7/12	78	186	104	19
Boise, ID	2,838	102	7/28	9	1/2	14.02	0.75	5/1	14.5	4.8	2/12	38	4/7	—	—	109	3
Boston, MA	15	100	7/14	1	2/7	35.10	3.31	10/5	41.5	11.0	12/19	43	4/4	106	178	127	11
Buffalo, NY	705	97	7/15	−1	2/12	33.99	2.22	10/5	142.8	37.9	12/9	39	12/9	—	—	169	29
Burlington, VT	332	100	7/14	−13	2/6	32.19	1.88	8/3	102.5	17.7	2/4	35	11/11	69	197	154	30
Caribou, ME[4]	624	93	8/10	−33	1/11	34.41	2.58	10/27	—	21.2	2/4	32	4/5	—	—	159	35
Charleston, SC	40	102	8/14	19	2/9	49.59	2.55	8/23	T	T	11/5	36	1/7	—	—	131	0
Chicago, IL	658	104	7/13	−4	12/9	32.88	2.57	11/10	30.9	3.7	1/21	36	4/18	96	163	121	13
Cleveland, OH	777	98	7/14	−1	2/12	39.05	2.53	1/15	82.1	12.0	12/19	45	3/20	—	—	149	23
Columbus, OH	813	97	7/15	−3	2/12	45.30	3.22	8/4	34.9	4.3	12/19	32	4/11	70	204	142	15
Dallas-Ft. Worth, TX	551	105	7/28	16	12/10	35.40	3.68	3/12	T	T	11/28	39	7/5	—	—	73	0
Denver, CO	5,282	99	8/8	−7	1/1	18.27	1.13	7/13	—	—	—	45	3/22	—	—	94	—
Des Moines, IA[3]	938	101	7/13	−6	12/10	31.03	2.54	5/8	24.7	8.1	1/5	38	12/8	—	—	109	8
Detroit, MI	637	100	7/14	−2	2/5	28.82	1.45	7/26	29.7	5.1	1/6	39	7/13	—	—	136	11
Duluth, MN	1,428	94	7/30	−22	12/11	34.30	2.71	8/24	123.6	12.1	12/13	41	7/31	66	207	149	38
Fairbanks, AK	436	88	5/11	−48	1/26	8.85	1.07	6/25	28.9	3.7	2/10	25	8/29	71	189	79	12
Fresno, CA	328	108	7/28	32	1/2	17.29	2.43	3/9	T	T	6/15	29	1/4	—	—	71	0
Grand Rapids, MI	793	98	6/20	−7	2/12	35.25	2.73	6/2	83.6	5.8	11/11	36	10/27	—	—	148	26
Hartford, CT	169	100	7/15	−9	2/7	40.92	2.71	10/5	43.2	9.7	2/4	44	11/12	87	186	120	11
Helena, MT	3,828	98	8/6	−21	12/8	12.37	1.18	5/11	27.2	5.1	4/9	51	6/15	—	—	102	7
Honolulu, HI	7	94	7/15	56	2/12	13.60	3.96	2/27	0.0	0.0	—	28	4/17	86	92	81	0
Houston, TX	96	103	7/28	27	12/10	44.63	4.14	12/17	T	T	1/2	35	3/7	100	161	104	0
Huron, SD	1,281	98	7/11	−18	3/8	29.97	2.02	5/26	67.9	8.6	10/23	38	12/8	82	180	103	16
Indianapolis, IN	795	99	7/14	−1	12/9	35.46	2.39	5/13	29.7	8.0	12/19	43	6/21	82	185	119	10
Jackson, MS[3]	291	100	7/28	18	12/29	59.03	4.32	4/22	0.0	0.0	—	37	11/11	—	—	102	0
Jacksonville, FL	26	100	7/16	20	2/9	50.25	4.52	8/24	T	T	12/22	32	5/19	87	144	127	0
Kansas City, MO	979	99	7/11	−4	1/7	34.69	3.39	5/16	10.4	3.4	12/8	38	10/23	—	—	101	2
Knoxville, TN[5]	979	100	8/16	8	2/9	42.83	2.30	5/18	3.7	2.0	1/30	45	11/11	—	—	121	2
Lander, WY	5,557	97	7/29	−10	1/1	19.68	1.29	5/26	105.5	13.7	10/21	39	3/21	118	134	95	31
Lexington, KY	966	97	7/14	1	2/12	50.08	4.25	6/26	12.4	3.0	3/8	31	11/11	80	189	123	3
Little Rock, AR	257	105	8/20	13	12/10	37.01	2.18	10/2	8.1	7.0	1/22	—	—	—	—	98	1
Los Angeles, CA	97	93	10/2	44	3/24	23.28	3.50	1/3	0.0	0.0	—	29	1/5	132	120	42	0
Louisville, KY	477	96	8/31	4	12/10	40.89	2.68	5/17	6.0	2.6	2/7	39	8/8	—	—	116	3
Marquette, MI	1,415	96	6/18	−17	12/13	38.96	2.09	9/6	223.6	16.2	2/3	—	—	—	—	173	53
Memphis, TN	258	100	8/19	13	12/10	56.90	4.12	6/30	3.7	2.5	2/6	—	—	—	—	101	1
Miami, FL	7	97	8/15	39	2/9	79.30	5.02	6/20	0.0	0.0	—	33	5/17	71	123	138	0
Milwaukee, WI	679	103	7/13	−5	12/9	31.34	2.65	8/16	46.2	9.7	11/27	47	8/28	—	—	130	13
Minn.-St. Paul, MN	834	101	7/13	−11	2/11	25.66	1.85	8/5	40.3	7.1	12/8	40	7/14	74	210	132	12
Mobile, AL	211	99	8/16	22	12/10	80.49	8.86	5/9	T	T	12/22	38	10/4	96	149	107	0
Moline, IL	592	100	7/13	−5	1/5	34.27	2.92	5/23	37.3	15.1	1/19	38	10/23	—	—	113	7
Nashville, TN	590	99	8/30	9	12/10	48.84	3.05	9/12	3.3	1.0	2/7	29	11/11	93	149	119	2
Newark, NJ	7	104	7/15	6	2/6	37.67	3.63	7/17	26.1	9.5	12/19	41	4/4	88	161	115	6
New Orleans, LA	4	100	8/20	26	12/11	65.33	12.40	5/8	T	T	12/22	35	11/11	112	142	101	0
New York, NY	132	102	7/15	6	2/6	40.42	3.36	7/17	26.2	10.8	2/4	29	11/14	—	—	118	6
Norfolk, VA	24	101	7/15	15	2/7	35.82	2.29	6/12	0.3	0.3	2/8	29	4/10	110	157	108	0
Oklahoma City, OK	1,285	102	9/3	11	12/10	36.77	3.31	5/26	14.0	4.0	1/22	74	7/23	—	—	87	3
Philadelphia, PA	5	103	7/15	5	2/6	31.53	1.81	10/27	14.0	8.8	2/3	36	10/14	—	—	108	4
Phoenix, AZ	1,109	121	7/28	37	12/23	9.51	1.59	8/20	0.0	0.0	—	41	7/30	—	—	31	0
Pittsburgh, PA	1,137	100	7/15	−4	2/12	28.89	2.12	7/17	49.7	7.1	11/14	35	11/11	68	209	145	12
Portland, ME	43	96	7/14	−10	2/7	41.29	2.73	11/14	73.5	13.1	2/4	45	2/4	—	—	135	17
Portland, OR[3]	21	99	7/17	16	2/14	43.33	2.82	11/10	4.0	3.6	2/12	51	12/12	—	—	158	1
Providence, RI[3]	51	99	7/15	1	2/7	38.24	2.87	10/5	15.5	7.5	2/4	38	11/12	—	—	125	3
Raleigh, NC	416	100	8/14	12	2/9	48.59	4.24	10/4	2.2	1.0	2/7	37	5/19	112	144	109	1
Rapid City, SD	3,162	102	8/17	−15	12/9	19.65	1.63	6/21	41.2	8.5	3/3	52	12/8	—	—	116	10
Reno, NV[3]	4,404	100	8/4	10	12/25	12.56	1.85	12/11	13.1	4.2	1/4	48	3/9	—	—	64	5
Richmond, VA[6]	164	100	7/15	9	2/7	34.44	1.88	3/8	3.9	1.9	1/29	40	3/8	—	—	99	2
St. Louis, MO	535	101	8/18	4	12/9	41.68	6.55	5/16	14.4	5.3	12/19	40	10/26	100	168	122	4
Salt Lake City, UT	4,221	106	7/29	11	2/15	16.92	1.01	9/29	40.3	7.0	2/11	43	6/5	115	160	96	13
San Antonio, TX	788	103	7/28	25	12/10	22.66	3.87	9/19	T	T	1/2	34	7/3	—	—	74	0
San Diego, CA	13	90	2/19	43	1/18	17.04	2.30	1/4	0.0	0.0	—	32	1/4	138	118	47	0
San Francisco, CA	8	95	6/25	38	2/15	27.42	3.18	12/11	T	T	3/23	54	12/12	137	144	87	0
San Juan, PR	13	96	9/18	66	3/16	55.95	3.95	5/15	0.0	0.0	—	32	9/6	128	77	197	0
Sault Ste. Marie, MI	718	94	6/18	−20	2/9	45.84	4.11	8/30	208.8	27.8	12/10	38	4/3	60	227	190	49
Savannah, GA	46	100	8/18	20	2/9	51.11	8.71	8/25	T	T	2/7	40	5/15	103	157	113	0
Scottsbluff, NE	3,943	103	8/7	−22	1/4	16.70	1.31	5/6	44.4	9.1	1/16	45	12/4	—	—	100	18
Seattle, WA	400	96	6/30	22	2/14	42.60	2.30	11/28	0.2	0.2	2/12	41	12/12	66	215	144	0
Spokane, WA[7]	2,356	93	7/20	2	2/14	19.85	1.08	3/14	9.0	3.3	2/14	46	12/12	—	—	111	14
Springfield, MO	1,278	101	8/31	−5	12/10	41.86	2.54	4/10	24.8	13.5	1/18	38	11/6	—	—	118	5
Syracuse, NY	410	96	8/3	−11	2/7	31.34	2.98	10/21	136.8	10.1	11/14	41	7/6	—	—	159	37
Tampa, FL	19	97	8/15	28	2/9	54.13	5.29	6/24	0.0	0.0	—	40	11/8	—	—	118	0
Washington, DC	10	99	7/15	7	2/6	39.80	3.36	10/14	11.9	4.5	2/3	37	11/11	93	168	105	4
Wilmington, DE	74	99	7/15	4	2/6	39.27	2.57	10/14	18.6	7.5	2/3	46	4/9	—	—	116	4

*To get partly cloudy days, deduct the total of clear and cloudy days from 365 (1 yr). (T) Trace. (—) Data not available or incomplete. (1) Date shown is the starting date of the storm (in some cases it lasted more than one day). (2) Sustained for at least 1 minute, not peak gust. (3) Snow/sleet data compiled through Nov. (4) Snow/sleet data not available for Jan. (5) Snow/sleet data not available for Nov. (6) Snow/sleet and wind data compiled through Nov. (7) Snow/sleet data compiled through Sept.

Record Temperatures by State Through 1996

Source: National Climatic Data Center, NESDIS, NOAA, U.S. Dept. of Commerce

State	Lowest °F	Highest °F	Latest date	Station	Approximate elevation in feet
Alabama	−27		Jan. 30, 1966	New Market	760
		112	Sept. 5, 1925	Centerville	345
Alaska	−80		Jan. 23, 1971	Prospect Creek	1,100
		100	June 27, 1915	Fort Yukon	420*
Arizona	−40		Jan. 7, 1971	Hawley Lake	8,180
		128	June 29, 1994 [1]	Lake Havasu City	505
Arkansas	−29		Feb. 13, 1905	Pond	1,250
		120	Aug. 10, 1936	Ozark	396
California	−45		Jan. 20, 1937	Boca	5,532
		134	July 10, 1913	Greenland Ranch	−178
Colorado	−61		Feb. 1, 1985	Maybell	5,920
		118	July 11, 1888	Bennett	5,484
Connecticut	−32		Feb. 16, 1943	Falls Village	585
		106	July 15, 1995	Danbury	450
Delaware	−17		Jan. 17, 1893	Millsboro	20
		110	July 21, 1930	Millsboro	20
Florida	−2		Feb. 13, 1899	Tallahassee	193
		109	June 29, 1931	Monticello	207
Georgia	−17		Jan. 27, 1940	CCC Camp F-16	1,000*
		112	July 24, 1952	Louisville	132
Hawaii	12		May 17, 1979	Mauna Kea Obs. 111.2.	13,770
		100	Apr. 27, 1931	Pahala	850
Idaho	−60		Jan. 18, 1943	Island Park Dam	6,285
		118	July 28, 1934	Orofino	1,027
Illinois	−35		Feb. 3, 1996 [1]	Mount Carroll	817
		117	July 14, 1954	East St. Louis	410
Indiana	−36		Jan. 19, 1994	New Whiteland	785
		116	July 14, 1936	Collegeville	672
Iowa	−47		Feb. 3, 1996 [1]	Elkader	770
		118	July 20, 1934	Keokuk	614
Kansas	−40		Feb. 13, 1905	Lebanon	1,812
		121	July 24, 1936 [1]	Alton (near)	1,651
Kentucky	−37		Jan. 19, 1994	Shelbyville	730
		114	July 28, 1930	Greensburg	581
Louisiana	−16		Feb. 13, 1899	Minden	194
		114	Aug. 10, 1936	Plain Dealing	268
Maine	−48		Jan. 19, 1925	Van Buren	510
		105	July 10, 1911 [1]	North Bridgton	450
Maryland	−40		Jan. 13, 1912	Oakland	2,461
		109	July 10, 1936 [1]	Cumberland; Frederick	623; 325
Massachusetts	−35		Jan. 12, 1981	Chester	640
		107	Aug. 2, 1975	Chester; New Bedford	640; 120
Michigan	−51		Feb. 9, 1934	Vanderbilt	785
		112	July 13, 1936	Mio	963
Minnesota	−60		Feb. 2, 1996	Tower	1,430
		114	July 6, 1936 [1]	Moorhead	904
Mississippi	−19		Jan. 30, 1966	Corinth	420
		115	July 29, 1930	Holly Springs	600
Missouri	−40		Feb. 13, 1905	Warsaw	700
		118	July 14, 1954 [1]	Warsaw; Union	705; 560
Montana	−70		Jan. 20, 1954	Rogers Pass	5,470
		117	July 5, 1937	Medicine Lake	1,950
Nebraska	−47		Feb. 12, 1899	Camp Clarke	3,700
		118	July 24, 1936 [1]	Minden	2,169
Nevada	−50		Jan. 8, 1937	San Jacinto	5,200
		125	June 29, 1994 [1]	Laughlin	605
New Hampshire	−46		Jan. 28, 1925	Pittsburg	1,575
		106	July 4, 1911	Nashua	125
New Jersey	−34		Jan. 5, 1904	River Vale	70
		110	July 10, 1936	Runyon	18
New Mexico	−50		Feb. 1, 1951	Gavilan	7,350
		122	June 27, 1994	Waste Isolat. Pilot Plt.	3,418
New York	−52		Feb. 18, 1979 [1]	Old Forge	1,720
		108	July 22, 1926	Troy	35
North Carolina	−34		Jan. 21, 1985	Mt. Mitchell	6,525
		110	Aug. 21, 1983	Fayetteville	213
North Dakota	−60		Feb. 15, 1936	Parshall	1,929
		121	July 6, 1936	Steele	1,857
Ohio	−39		Feb. 10, 1899	Milligan	800
		113	July 21, 1934 [1]	Gallipolis (near)	673
Oklahoma	−27		Jan. 18, 1930	Watts	958
		120	June 27, 1994 [1]	Tipton	1,350
Oregon	−54		Feb. 10, 1933 [1]	Seneca	4,700
		119	Aug. 10, 1898	Pendleton	1,074
Pennsylvania	−42		Jan. 5, 1904	Smethport	1,500
		111	July 10, 1936 [1]	Phoenixville	100
Rhode Island	−25		Feb. 5, 1996	Greene	425
		104	Aug. 2, 1975	Providence	51
South Carolina	−19		Jan. 21, 1985	Caesars Head	3,115
		111	June 28, 1954 [1]	Camden	170
South Dakota	−58		Feb. 17, 1936	McIntosh	2,277
		120	July 5, 1936	Gannvalley	1,750
Tennessee	−32		Dec. 30, 1917	Mountain City	2,471
		113	Aug. 9, 1930 [1]	Perryville	377

State	Lowest °F	Highest °F	Latest date	Station	Approximate elevation in feet
Texas	−23		Feb. 8, 1933 [1]	Seminole	3,275
		120	Aug. 12, 1936	Seymour	1,291
Utah	−69		Feb. 1, 1985	Peter's Sink	8,092
		117	Jul. 5, 1985	Saint George	2,880
Vermont	−50		Dec. 30, 1933	Bloomfield	915
		105	July 4, 1911	Vernon	310
Virginia	−30		Jan. 22, 1985	Mountain Lake Bio. Station	3,870
		110	July 15, 1954	Balcony Falls	725
Washington	−48		Dec. 30, 1968	Mazama; Winthrop 2,120; 1,755	
		118	Aug. 5, 1961 [1]	Ice Harbor Dam	475
West Virginia	−37		Dec. 30, 1917	Lewisburg	2,200
		112	July 10, 1936 [1]	Martinsburg	435
Wisconsin	−54		Jan. 24, 1922	Danbury	908
		114	July 13, 1936	Wisconsin Dells	900
Wyoming	−66		Feb. 9, 1933	Riverside R.S.	6,650
		114	July 12, 1900	Basin	3,500

* Estimated (1) Also on earlier dates at the same or other places.

World Temperature and Precipitation

Source: World Meteorological Organization

Average daily maximum and minimum temperatures and annual precipitation are based on records for the 30-year period 1961-90. The length of record of extreme temperatures includes all available years of data for a given location and is usually for a longer period; record temperatures may have been measured at a different location within the city. Surface elevations are supplied by the WMO and may differ from city elevation figures in other sections of *The World Almanac*. NA = not available.

Station	Surface elevation (feet)	Temperature °F — Average Daily January Max.	January Min.	July Max.	July Min.	Extreme Max.	Extreme Min.	Average annual precipitation (inches)
Algiers, Algeria	82	61.7	42.6	87.1	65.3	NA	NA	27.0
Athens, Greece	49	56.1	44.6	88.9	73.0	NA	NA	14.6
Auckland, New Zealand	20	74.8	61.2	58.5	46.4	NA	NA	49.4
Bangkok, Thailand	66	89.6	69.8	90.9	77.0	104	51	59.0
Berlin, Germany	190	35.2	26.8	73.6	55.2	107	−4	23.3
Bogotá, Colombia	8,357	67.3	41.7	64.6	45.5	75	21	32.4
Bombay (Mumbai), India	36	85.3	66.7	86.2	77.5	110	46	85.4
Bucharest, Romania	298	34.7	22.1	83.8	60.1	105	−18	23.4
Budapest, Hungary	456	34.2	24.8	79.7	59.7	103	−10	20.3
Buenos Aires, Argentina	82	85.8	67.3	59.7	45.7	104	22	45.2
Cairo, Egypt	243	65.8	48.2	93.9	71.1	118	34	1.0
Cape Town, South Africa	138	79.0	60.3	63.3	44.6	105	28	20.5
Caracas, Venezuela	2,739	79.9	60.8	81.3	66.0	96	45	36.1
Casablanca, Morocco	203	62.8	47.1	77.7	66.7	NA	NA	16.8
Copenhagen, Denmark	16	35.6	28.4	68.9	55.0	NA	NA	NA
Damascus, Syria	2,004	54.3	32.9	97.2	61.9	NA	NA	5.6
Dublin, Ireland	279	45.7	36.5	66.0	52.5	86	8	28.8
Geneva, Switzerland	1,364	38.3	27.9	76.3	53.2	101	−3	35.6
Havana, Cuba	164	78.4	65.5	88.3	74.8	NA	NA	46.9
Hong Kong, China	203	65.5	56.5	88.7	79.9	97	32	87.2
Istanbul, Turkey	108	47.8	37.2	82.8	65.3	105	7	27.4
Jerusalem, Israel	2,483	53.4	39.4	83.8	63.0	107	26	23.2
Lagos, Nigeria	125	90.0	72.3	82.8	72.1	NA	NA	59.3
Lima, Peru	43	79.0	66.9	66.4	59.4	NA	NA	0.2
London, England	203	44.1	32.7	71.1	52.3	99	2	29.7
Manila, Philippines	79	85.8	74.8	89.1	76.8	NA	NA	49.6
Mexico City, Mexico	7,570	70.3	43.7	73.8	53.2	NA	NA	33.4
Montreal, Canada	118	21.6	5.2	79.2	59.7	100	−36	37.0
Nairobi, Kenya	5,897	77.9	50.9	71.6	48.6	NA	NA	41.9
Paris, France	213	42.8	33.6	75.2	55.2	105	−1	25.6
Prague, Czech Republic	1,197	32.7	22.5	73.9	53.2	98	−16	20.7
Reykjavik, Iceland	200	35.4	26.6	55.9	46.9	76	−3	31.5
Rome, Italy	79	53.8	35.4	88.2	62.1	NA	NA	33.0
San Salvador, El Salvador	2,037	86.5	61.3	86.2	66.4	105	45	68.3
Sao Paolo, Brazil	2,598	81.1	65.7	71.2	53.1	NA	NA	57.4
Shanghai, China	23	45.9	32.9	88.9	76.6	104	10	43.8
Singapore	52	85.8	73.6	87.4	75.6	NA	NA	84.6
Stockholm, Sweden	171	30.7	23.0	71.4	56.1	97	−26	21.2
Sydney, Australia	10	79.5	65.5	62.4	43.9	114	32	46.4
Tehran, Iran	3,906	45.0	30.0	98.2	75.2	109	−5	9.1
Tokyo, Japan	118	49.1	34.2	83.8	72.1	NA	NA	55.4
Toronto, Canada	567	27.5	12.0	80.2	57.6	105	−26	30.8

Hurricane and Tornado/Wind Storm Classifications

Source: National Weather Service, NOAA, U.S. Dept. of Commerce

The Saffir-Simpson Hurricane Scale is a 1-5 rating based on a hurricane's present intensity. The scale is used to give an estimate of the potential property damage and flooding expected along the coast from a hurricane landfall. Wind speed is the determining factor in the scale. The Fujita (or F) Scale, created by T. Theodore Fujita, is used to classify tornadoes or other severe wind storms. The F Scale uses rating numbers from 0-5, based on the amount and type of wind damage.

Saffir-Simpson Scale (Hurricanes)

Category	Wind Speed	Severity	Storm Surge [1]
1	74-95 MPH	Weak	4-5 feet
2	96-110 MPH	Moderate	6-8 feet
3	111-130 MPH	Strong	9-12 feet
4	131-155 MPH	Very Strong	13-18 feet
5	> 155 MPH	Devastating	> 18 feet

(1) Above normal tides.

Fujita Scale (Tornadoes/Wind Storms)

Rank	Wind Speed	Damage	Strength
F-0	Up to 72 MPH	Light	Weak
F-1	73-112 MPH	Moderate	Weak
F-2	113-157 MPH	Considerable	Strong
F-3	158-206 MPH	Severe	Strong
F-4	207-260 MPH	Devastating	Violent
F-5	> 261 MPH	Incredible	Violent

Hurricane Names in 1998

Source: National Weather Service, NOAA, U.S. Dept. of Commerce

Names assigned to Atlantic hurricanes, 1998 — Alex, Bonnie, Charley, Danielle, Earl, Frances, Georges, Hermine, Ivan, Jeanne, Karl, Lisa, Mitch, Nicole, Otto, Paula, Richard, Shary, Tomas, Virginie, Walter.

Names assigned to Eastern Pacific hurricanes, 1998 — Agatha, Blas, Celia, Darby, Estelle, Frank, Georgette, Howard, Isis, Javier, Kay, Lester, Madeline, Newton, Orlene, Paine, Roslyn, Seymour, Tina, Virgil, Winifred, Xavier, Yolanda, Zeke.

Tides and Their Causes

Source: U.S. Dept. of Commerce, Natl. Oceanic & Atmospheric Admin. (NOAA), Natl. Ocean Service (NOS)

The tides are a natural phenomenon involving the alternating rise and fall in the large fluid bodies of the earth caused by the combined gravitational attraction of the sun and moon. The combination of these two variable force influences produces the complex recurrent cycle of the tides. Tides may occur in both oceans and seas, to a limited extent in large lakes, the atmosphere and, to a very minute degree, in the earth itself. The period between succeeding tides varies as the result of many factors and force influences.

The tide-generating force represents the difference between (1) the centrifugal force produced by the revolution of the earth around the common center-of-gravity of the earth-moon system and (2) the gravitational attraction of the moon acting upon the earth's overlying waters. Since, on the average, the moon is only 238,852 miles from the earth compared with the sun's much greater distance of 92,956,000 miles, this closer distance outranks the much smaller mass of the moon compared with that of the sun, and the moon's tide-raising force is, accordingly, 2.5 times that of the sun.

The effect of the tide-generating forces of the moon and sun acting tangentially to the earth's surface (the so-called "tractive force") tends to cause a maximum accumulation of the waters of the oceans at two diametrically opposite positions on the surface of the earth and to withdraw compensating amounts of water from all points 90° removed from the positions of these tidal bulges. As the earth rotates beneath the maxima and minima of these tide-generating forces, a sequence of two high tides, separated by two low tides, ideally is produced each day (semidiurnal tide).

Twice in each lunar month, when the sun, moon, and earth are directly aligned, with the moon between the earth and the sun (at new moon) or on the opposite side of the earth from the sun (at full moon), the sun and the moon exert their gravitational force in a mutual or additive fashion. The highest high tides and lowest low tides are produced at these times. These are called *spring* tides. At two positions 90° in between, the gravitational forces of the moon and sun—imposed at right angles—tend to counteract each other to the greatest extent,

and the range between high and low tides is reduced. These are called *neap* tides. This semi-monthly variation between the spring and neap tides is called the *phase inequality*.

The inclination of the moon's monthly orbit to the equator and the inclination of the sun during the earth's yearly orbit to the equator produce a difference in the height of succeeding high tides and in the extent of depression of succeeding low tides that is known as the *diurnal inequality*. In most cases, this produces a type of tide called a *mixed tide*. In extreme cases, these phenomena can result in only one high tide and one low tide each (*diurnal tide*). There are also other monthly and yearly variations in the tide due to the elliptical shape of the orbits themselves.

The datum for Charting and Predictions is Mean Lower Low Water (MLLW). This became effective Jan. 1989 according to the convention of 1980, which prescribed that data on all United States coastlines would be the same; namely, Mean Higher High Water (MHHW), Mean High Water (MHW), Mean Tide Level (MTL), Mean Sea Level (MSL), Mean Low Water (MLW), Mean Lower Low Water (MLLW). Diurnal range of tide is the difference in height between MHHW and MLLW. Mean range of tide is the difference in height between MHW and MLW.

The actual range of tide in the waters of the open oceans may amount to only 1 to 3 feet. However, as the ocean tide approaches shoal waters and its effects are augmented the tidal range may be greatly increased. In Nova Scotia along the narrow channel of the Bay of Fundy, the range of tides, or difference between high and low waters, may reach 43-1/2 feet or more (under spring tide conditions) due to resonant amplification.

At New Orleans, the periodic rise and fall of the diurnal tide is affected by the seasonal stages of the Mississippi River, being about 10 inches at low stage and zero at high. The Canadian Tide Tables for 1972 gave a maximum range of nearly 50 feet at Leaf Basin, Ungava Bay, Quebec.

In every case, actual high or low tide can vary considerably from the average, as a result of weather conditions such as strong winds, abrupt barometric pressure changes, or prolonged periods of extreme high or low pressure.

The Average Rise and Fall of Tides[1]

Places	Ft.	In.	Places	Ft.	In.	Places	Ft.	In.
Baltimore, MD	1	8	Hampton Roads, VA	2	10	St. John's, Nfld.	2	7[2]
Boston, MA	10	4	Key West, FL	1	10	St. Petersburg, FL	2	3
Charleston, SC	5	10	Mobile, AL	1	6	San Diego, CA.	5	9
Cristobal, Panama	1	1	New London, CT	3	1	Sandy Hook, NJ.	5	2
Eastport, ME	19	4	Newport, RI	3	11	San Francisco, CA.	5	10
Ft. Pulaski, GA	7	6	New York, NY	5	1	Seattle, WA.	11	4
Galveston, TX	1	5	Philadelphia, PA	6	9	Vancouver, B.C.	10	6
Halifax, N.S.	4	5[2]	Portland, ME	9	11	Washington, DC	3	2

(1) Diurnal range. (2) Mean range.

Speed of Winds in the U.S.

Source: National Climatic Data Center, NESDIS, NOAA, U.S. Dept. of Commerce

Miles per hour — average through 1995. High through 1995. Wind velocities in true values.

Station	Avg.	High	Station	Avg.	High	Station	Avg.	High
Albuquerque, NM	8.9	52	Helena, MT	7.7	73	Mt. Washington, NH.	35.3	231
Anchorage, AK.	7.1	75	Honolulu, HI	11.3	46	New Orleans, LA	8.1	69
Atlanta, GA	9.1	60	Houston, TX	7.9	51	New York, NY(b)	9.4	39
Baltimore, MD	9.1	80	Indianapolis, IN	9.6	46	Omaha, NE.	10.5	58
Bismarck, ND	10.2	54	Jacksonville, FL.	7.9	46	Philadelphia, PA	9.5	73
Boston, MA	12.5	54	Kansas City, MO	10.7	48	Phoenix, AZ	6.2	43
Buffalo, NY	11.9	91	Las Vegas, NV	9.3	53	Pittsburgh, PA.	9.1	58
Cape Hatteras, NC.	11.1	60	Lexington, KY	9.2	46	Portland, OR.	7.9	88
Casper, WY.	12.8	81	Little Rock, AR.	7.8	65	Rochester, NY.	9.7	52
Chicago, IL	10.4	58	Los Angeles, CA	6.2	49	St. Louis, MO	9.7	52
Cleveland, OH.	10.5	53	Louisville, KY.	8.3	46	Salt Lake City, UT	8.8	71
Dallas-Ft. Worth, TX.	10.7	73	Memphis, TN	8.8	51	San Diego, CA.	7.0	56
Denver, CO.	8.6	46	Miami, FL	9.2	(a)86	San Francisco, CA.	8.7	47
Des Moines, IA	10.7	76	Milwaukee, WI	11.5	54	Seattle, WA.	9.0	63
Detroit, MI.	10.4	48	Minn.-St. Paul, MN.	10.5	51	Spokane, WA.	8.9	59
Hartford, CT	8.4	44	Mobile, AL	8.9	63	Washington, DC	9.4	46

(a) Highest velocity ever recorded in Miami area was 132 mph, at former station in Miami Beach in Sept. 1926. (b) Data for Central Park; Battery Place data through 1960, avg. 14.5, high 113.

Wind Chill Table

Source: National Weather Service, NOAA, U.S. Dept. of Commerce

Both temperature and wind cause heat loss from body surfaces. A combination of cold and wind makes a body feel colder than the actual temperature. The table shows, for example, that a temperature of 20 degrees Fahrenheit, plus a wind of 20 miles per hour, causes a body heat loss equal to that in minus 10 degrees with no wind. In other words, a 20-mph wind makes 20 degrees feel like minus 10.

Top line of figures shows actual temperatures in degrees Fahrenheit. Column at left shows wind speeds. (Wind speeds greater than 45 mph have little additional chilling effect.)

MPH	35	30	25	20	15	10	5	0	−5	−10	−15	−20	−25	−30	−35	−40	−45
5	33	27	21	16	12	7	0	−5	−10	−15	−21	−26	−31	−36	−42	−47	−52
10	22	16	10	3	−3	−9	−15	−22	−27	−34	−40	−46	−52	−58	−64	−71	−77
15	16	9	2	−5	−11	−18	−25	−31	−38	−45	−51	−58	−65	−72	−78	−85	−92
20	12	4	−3	−10	−17	−24	−31	−39	−46	−53	−60	−67	−74	−81	−88	−95	−103
25	8	1	−7	−15	−22	−29	−36	−44	−51	−59	−66	−74	−81	−88	−96	−103	−110
30	6	−2	−10	−18	−25	−33	−41	−49	−56	−64	−71	−79	−86	−93	−101	−109	−116
35	4	−4	−12	−20	−27	−35	−43	−52	−58	−67	−74	−82	−89	−97	−105	−113	−120
40	3	−5	−13	−21	−29	−37	−45	−53	−60	−69	−76	−84	−92	−100	−107	−115	−123
45	2	−6	−14	−22	−30	−38	−46	−54	−62	−70	−78	−85	−93	−102	−109	−117	−125

Heat Index

The heat index is a measure of the contribution that high humidity makes with abnormally high temperatures in reducing the body's ability to cool itself. For example, the index shows that for an actual air temperature of 100 degrees Fahrenheit and a relative humidity of 50%, the effect on the human body would be same as 120 degrees. Sunstroke and heat exhaustion are likely when the heat index reaches 105. This index is a measure of what hot weather "feels like" to the average person for various temperatures and relative humidities.

Relative Humidity	Air Temperature*										
	70	75	80	85	90	95	100	105	110	115	120
	Apparent Temperature*										
0%	64	69	73	78	83	87	91	95	99	103	107
10%	65	70	75	80	85	90	95	100	105	111	116
20%	66	72	77	82	87	93	99	105	112	120	130
30%	67	73	78	84	90	96	104	113	123	135	148
40%	68	74	79	86	93	101	110	123	137	151	
50%	69	75	81	88	96	107	120	135	150		
60%	70	76	82	90	100	114	132	149			
70%	70	77	85	93	106	124	144				
80%	71	78	86	97	113	136					
90%	71	79	88	102	122						
100%	72	80	91	108							

*Degrees Fahrenheit.

Ultraviolet (UV) Index Forecast

Source: National Weather Service, NOAA, U.S. Dept. of Commerce

The National Weather Service (NWS), the Environmental Protection Agency (EPA), and the Centers for Disease Control and Prevention (CDC) developed the UV Index in an effort to raise the visibility of the risks associated with prolonged exposure to ultraviolet radiation. The NWS, EPA, and CDC began offering an experimental UV index on a limited basis on June 28, 1994, in response to increasing incidence of skin cancer, cataracts, and other effects from exposure to the sun's harmful rays. The NWS UV Index is now a regular element of atmospheric forecasts.

UV Index number and forecast. The UV Index number, ranging between 0 and 10+, is an indication of the amount of UV radiation reaching the earth's surface over the one-hour period around noon. The lower the number, the less the amount of UV radiation. The UV Index forecast is produced by the NWS Climate Prediction Center, Camp Springs, MD, about a day in advance of the time for which the forecast is effective. The forecast is based on several factors: latitude, day of year, time of day, total ozone in the atmosphere, elevation, and predicted cloud conditions at solar noon time. A forecast is given for 58 listed cities. The index is valid for a radius of about 30 miles around a listed city; however, adjustments should be made for a number of factors.

Ozone. Total ozone is measured by a NOAA polar orbiting satellite. This measurement is combined with the aforementioned factors to help determine how much atmosphere the UV rays must pass through to reach the surface; the greater the distance and more ozone, the lower the UV radiation at the surface.

Cloudiness. Rapid changes in cloud amount can alter the predicted UV Index. Increased cloudiness will lower the index number.

Reflectivity. Reflective surfaces will intensify UV exposure to varying degrees. For example, grass reflects 2.5% to

3% of the UV radiation reaching the surface; sand, 20% to 30%; snow and ice, 80% to 90%; water, up to 100% (depending on the angle of reflection).

Elevation. Trips to the mountains and to the beach will increase exposure to UV radiation. At higher elevations, the distance by which UV radiation has to travel to reach the surface is shortened, so there is less atmosphere to absorb the rays. For every 4,000 ft. one travels above sea level, the UV Index increases by 1 unit. The presence of snow and the lack of pollutants in the atmosphere also intensify UV exposure at higher altitudes. At the beach, several factors increase UV exposure: light-colored sand and water reflect UV rays, and people usually wear less clothing and often lie in a horizontal position.

Latitude. The closer someone is to the equator, the higher the UV radiation level. It makes good sense to cover exposed areas and wear sunglasses when traveling in tropical regions. (A person can suffer a bad sunburn in the Tropics even during winter.).

Accuracy. By gathering data from 20 UV sensors (June-Oct. 1994), the NWS determined 32% of UV Index forecasts were correct, 76% were within plus or minus 1 UV Index unit, and about 90% were within plus or minus 2 units. Unpredictable cloudiness, haze, and pollution contribute to forecast error.

SPF number. The UV Index is not linked in any way to the SPF number found on suntan lotions and sunscreens. For an explanation of the SPF factor for a particular product, contact the manufacturer or the Food and Drug Administration.

Further information. For questions about health aspects or what precautions to take after learning the UV Index number, call the U.S. EPA hot line (800-296-1996) or a doctor/optometrist. For questions about scientific aspects, call the NWS at 301-713-0622.

ENVIRONMENT

Hazardous Waste Sites in the U.S., 1997

Source: Environmental Protection Agency, *National Priorities List,* Apr. 1997

State	Final Gen	Final Fed	Proposed Gen	Proposed Fed	Total	State	Final Gen	Final Fed	Proposed Gen	Proposed Fed	Total
Alabama	9	3	1	0	13	New Hampshire	17	1	0	0	18
Alaska	1	6	0	0	7	New Jersey	99	6	1	0	106
Arizona	7	3	0	0	10	New Mexico	8	1	1	0	10
Arkansas	12	0	0	0	12	New York	74	4	1	0	79
California	67	23	4	0	94	North Carolina	21	2	0	0	23
Colorado	12	3	2	0	17	North Dakota	0	0	0	0	0
Connecticut	14	1	0	0	15	Ohio	31	3	2	2	38
Delaware	17	1	0	0	18	Oklahoma	9	1	1	0	11
District of Columbia	0	0	0	0	0	Oregon	8	2	1	0	11
Florida	46	6	2	0	54	Pennsylvania	94	6	2	0	102
Georgia	13	2	1	0	16	Rhode Island	10	2	0	0	12
Hawaii	1	3	0	0	4	South Carolina	24	2	0	0	26
Idaho	6	2	2	0	10	South Dakota	1	1	0	0	2
Illinois	34	4	3	0	41	Tennessee	11	3	0	1	15
Indiana	30	0	1	0	31	Texas	22	4	2	0	28
Iowa	15	1	1	0	17	Utah	8	4	4	0	16
Kansas	9	1	0	1	11	Vermont	8	0	0	0	8
Kentucky	15	1	0	0	16	Virginia	18	7	0	0	25
Louisiana	14	1	3	0	18	Washington	35	14	1	0	50
Maine	9	3	0	0	12	West Virginia	4	2	1	0	7
Maryland	8	5	2	1	16	Wisconsin	40	0	0	0	40
Massachusetts	22	8	0	0	30	Wyoming	2	1	0	0	3
Michigan	72	0	1	1	74	Puerto Rico	9	1	0	0	10
Minnesota	28	2	0	0	30	Guam	1	1	0	0	2
Mississippi	1	0	2	0	3	American Samoa	0	0	0	0	0
Missouri	19	3	0	0	22	Trust Territories	0	0	0	0	0
Montana	8	0	1	0	9	Virgin Islands	2	0	0	0	2
Nebraska	9	1	0	0	10	**Totals**	**1,055**	**151**	**43**	**6**	**1,255**
Nevada	1	0	0	0	1						

Note: Gen = general superfund sites; Fed = federal facility sites.

Toxics Release Inventory, 1994-95

Source: Environmental Protection Agency

Reported industrial releases of toxic chemicals into the environment by major manufacturing facilities (excluding power plants and mining facilities) decreased 4.9% from the 1994 figure and 45.6% from the figure for 1988, the baseline year. Totals below may not add because of rounding.

Pollutant releases	1995 mil lb	1994 mil lb	Top industries, total releases	1995 mil lb	1994 mil lb
Air releases	1,562	1,556	Chemicals	788	851
Underground injection	235	349	Primary metals	331	313
On-site land releases	275	289	Paper	233	246
Surface water releases	136	66	Plastics	112	119
Total	**2,209**	**2,260**	Transportation equipment	110	122
Pollutant transfers			**Top carcinogens, air/water/land releases**		
To recycling	2,214	2,456	Dichloromethane	57	63
To energy recovery	512	464	Styrene	42	40
To treatment	288	319	Trichloroethylene	25	30
To disposal/other	281	298	Formaldehyde	19	12
To publicly owned treatment works	240	255	Acetaldehyde	14	13
Total	**3,535**	**3,792**	Chloroform	11	11

Top 10 States, Total Releases, 1994-95

Source: Environmental Protection Agency

(air, water, land, and underground injection; ranked for 1995)

State	1995 mil lb	1994 mil lb	State	1995 mil lb	1994 mil lb
Texas	284	250	Illinois	100	98
Louisiana	172	153	North Carolina	86	89
Ohio	122	117	Florida	84	94
Tennessee	111	156	Indiana	80	65
Alabama	103	95	Utah	76	66

Emissions of Principal Pollutants, 1986-1995

Source: U.S. Environmental Protection Agency, Office of Air Quality Planning and Standards

(in thousand short tons)

Source	1986	1987	1988	1989	1990	1991	1992	1993	1994	1995
Carbon monoxide[1]	109,199	108,012	115,849	103,144	100,650	97,376	94,043	94,133	98,779	92,099
Lead	7.3	6.9	6.5	6.0	5.7	5.3	4.9	4.9	5.0	5.0
Nitrogen oxides[2]	22,348	22,403	23,618	23,222	23,038	22,672	22,847	23,276	23,661	21,779
Volatile organic compounds[2]	24,991	24,778	25,719	23,935	23,599	22,877	22,420	22,575	23,281	22,865
Particulate matter[3]	3,096	2,968	3,071	3,039	2,708	2,677	2,729	2,669	2,696	2,547
Sulfur oxides	22,442	22,204	22,647	22,785	22,433	22,068	21,836	21,517	21,047	18,319
Total	**182,083**	**180,372**	**190,911**	**176,104**	**172,434**	**167,675**	**163,880**	**164,175**	**169,469**	**157,614**

(1) The observed increase in carbon monoxide emissions between 1993 and 1994 is attributed to 2 sources: transportation emissions (up 2%) and wildfire emissions (up 160%). (2) Ozone, a major air pollutant and the primary constituent of smog, is not emitted directly to the air but is formed by sunlight acting on emissions of nitrogen oxides and volatile organic compounds. (3) Does not include natural sources.

U.S. Carbon Monoxide Emission Estimates, 1986-95

Source: U.S. Environmental Protection Agency, Office of Air Quality Planning and Standards; in thousand short tons

Source	1986	1987	1988	1989	1990	1991	1992	1993	1994	1995
Fuel combustion	7,548	6,960	7,372	7,441	5,064	5,356	5,601	4,953	4,884	3,960
Industrial processes	7,067	6,851	7,034	7,013	6,914	6,815	6,909	7,009	7,160	7,439
Transportation	87,330	85,381	85,581	80,568	77,500	76,675	74,759	75,471	77,490	74,246
Miscellaneous	7,254	8,820	15,863	8,121	11,173	8,530	6,774	6,700	9,245	6,455
Total[1]	109,199	108,012	115,849	103,144	100,650	97,376	94,043	94,133	98,779	92,099

(1) Totals may not add because of rounding.

U.S. Lead Emission Estimates, 1986-95

Source: U.S. Environmental Protection Agency, Office of Air Quality Planning and Standards; in short tons

Source	1986	1987	1988	1989	1990	1991	1992	1993	1994	1995
Fuel combustion	516	510	511	505	500	495	491	495	493	493
Industrial processes	2,972	3,004	3,090	3,161	3,278	3,081	2,734	2,869	2,957	2,914
Transportation	3,808	3,343	2,911	2,368	1,888	1,704	1,637	1,580	1,577	1,578
Miscellaneous	0	0	0	0	0	0	0	0	0	0
Total[1]	7,296	6,857	6,513	6,034	5,666	5,280	4,862	4,945	5,028	4,986

(1) Totals may not add because of rounding.

U.S. Nitrogen Oxides Emission Estimates, 1986-95

Source: U.S. Environmental Protection Agency, Office of Air Quality Planning and Standards; in thousand short tons

Source	1986	1987	1988	1989	1990	1991	1992	1993	1994	1995
Fuel Combustion	10,668	10,897	11,457	11,552	11,483	11,382	11,421	11,696	11,631	10,077
Industrial Processes	872	841	860	852	851	837	853	866	888	872
Transportation	10,550	10,315	10,575	10,526	10,331	10,170	10,325	10,495	10,767	10,601
Miscellaneous	257	351	726	292	373	283	249	219	374	228
Total[1]	22,348	22,403	23,618	23,222	23,038	22,672	22,847	23,276	23,661	21,779

(1) Totals may not add because of rounding.

Air Quality of Selected U.S. Metropolitan Areas[1], 1987-95

Source: U.S. Environmental Protection Agency, Office of Air Quality Planning and Standards

Metropolitan statistical area	1987	1988	1989	1990	1991	1992	1993	1994	1995
Atlanta, GA	27	21	3	17	6	5	17	4	19
Bakersfield, CA	70	91	56	48	49	16	49	45	45
Baltimore, MD	28	43	9	12	20	5	14	17	14
Boston, MA/NH	5	15	4	1	3	1	3	1	1
Chicago, IL	17	23	4	3	8	7	1	8	4
Dallas, TX	13	14	7	8	1	3	5	1	13
Denver, CO	37	19	11	9	7	7	3	2	2
Detroit, MI	9	17	10	3	8	1	2	8	11
El Paso, TX	32	16	33	27	13	17	10	10	4
Fresno, CA	49	29	47	29	33	27	28	11	19
Hartford, CT	20	27	11	7	14	9	9	10	9
Houston, TX	67	61	41	59	42	30	26	29	54
Las Vegas, NV/AZ	7	31	46	22	15	5	8	12	7
Los Angeles/Long Beach, CA	201	239	226	180	184	185	146	136	103
Miami, FL	4	5	4	1	2	0	0	0	0
Minneapolis/St. Paul, MN/WI	14	3	7	3	2	1	0	5	3
New Haven/Meriden, CT	20	16	7	10	22	3	11	8	8
New York, NY	44	46	18	18	22	4	6	8	8
Orange County, CA	58	65	66	48	42	43	25	14	6
Phoenix/Mesa, AZ	42	27	30	9	4	10	7	9	13
Pittsburgh, PA	10	20	9	11	4	2	5	2	7
Riverside/San Bernardino, CA	171	181	178	144	144	155	142	122	110
Sacramento, CA	52	73	60	43	44	21	10	11	16
St. Louis, MO/IL	17	20	13	8	6	3	6	12	14
Salt Lake City/Ogden, UT	7	11	15	2	19	10	3	10	1
San Diego, CA	61	84	90	60	39	37	17	16	14
San Francisco, CA	1	2	1	1	0	0	0	0	1
Seattle/Bellevue/Everett, WA	14	20	8	5	2	1	0	0	0
Ventura, CA	54	83	59	36	49	25	16	24	30
Washington, DC/MD/VA/WV	26	37	8	5	17	2	13	7	8

(1) Data indicate the number of days metropolitan statistical areas failed to meet acceptable air-quality standards at trend sites (Pollutant Standards Index rating over 100).

U.S. Watersheds

Source: U.S. Environmental Protection Agency

On Oct. 2, 1997, the U.S. Environmental Protection Agency (EPA) released its first comprehensive assessment of the 2,111 U.S. watersheds in the continental U.S. (A watershed is a water drainage area, or land areas bounded by ridges that catch rain and snow and drain to rivers, lakes, and groundwater within the drainage area.) The EPA concluded that 16% of these watersheds have good water quality, 36% have moderate water quality, and 21% have more serious problems; there is insufficient information to fully characterize the remaining 27%. The data indicate that polluted runoff from urban and rural areas is a major contributor to water quality problems, threatening water quality even in currently healthy watersheds.

The EPA categorized the watersheds by combining nationally available data from 15 individual databases, from both public and private sources, into a single Index of Watershed Indicators. The indicators include seven used to assess watershed conditions (quality) and eight used to assess vulnerability to degradation from pollution. You can find information about your own watershed on the Internet by going to the following Web site: http://www.epa.gov/surf/index2.html

U.S. List of Endangered and Threatened Species

Source: Fish and Wildlife Service, U.S. Dept. of Interior; as of Aug. 31, 1997

Group	Endangered — U.S. only	Endangered — Foreign only	Threatened — U.S. only	Threatened — Foreign only	Total listed species	Species with recovery plans
Mammals	57	251	7	16	331	39
Birds	75	178	15	6	274	72
Reptiles	14	65	18	14	111	30
Amphibians	9	8	7	1	25	11
Fishes	67	11	41	0	119	75
Snails	15	1	7	0	23	19
Clams	56	2	6	0	64	44
Crustaceans	15	0	3	0	18	6
Insects	24	4	9	0	37	21
Arachnids	5	0	0	0	5	4
Animals, subtotal	**337**	**520**	**113**	**37**	**1,007**	**321**
Flowering plants	514	1	113	0	628	380
Conifers	2	0	0	2	4	1
Ferns and others	26	0	2	0	28	21
Plant, subtotal	**542**	**1**	**115**	**2**	**660**	**402**
Grand total	**879**	**521**	**228**	**39**	**1,667**[1]	**723**[2]

(1) When separate populations of a species are listed as endangered and as threatened, those species are tallied twice. Those species are the argali, chimpanzee, leopard, gray wolf, piping plover, roseate tern, green sea turtle, saltwater crocodile, Steller sea lion, and olive ridley sea turtle. (2) There are 461 approved recovery plans. Some recovery plans cover more than one species, and a few species have separate plans covering different parts of their ranges. Recovery plans are drawn up only for listed species that occur in the U.S.

Some Endangered Species

Source: Fish and Wildlife Service, U.S. Dept. of the Interior

Common name	Scientific name	Range
Armadillo, giant	Pridontes maximus (giganteus)	Venezuela, Guyana to Argentina
Bat, gray	Myotis grisescens	Central, southeastern U.S.
Bison, wood	Bison bison athabascae	Canada, northwestern U.S.
Bobcat	Felis rufus escuinapae	Central Mexico
Camel, Bactrian	Camelus bactrianus	Mongolia, China
Caribou, woodland	Rangifer tarandus caribou	U.S., Canada
Cheetah	Acinonyx jubatus	Africa to India
Chimpanzee, pygmy	Pan paniscus	Congo (formerly Zaire)
Condor, California	Gymnogyps californianus	U.S. (OR, CA, AZ), Mexico (Baja)
Cougar, eastern	Felis concolor couguar	Eastern N America
Crane, hooded	Grus monacha	Japan, Russia
Crane, whooping	Grus americana	Canada, Mexico, U.S. (Rocky Mts. to Carolinas)
Crocodile, American	Crocodylus acutus	U.S. (FL), Mexico, central and S America
Curlew, Eskimo	Numenius borealis	Alaska, N Canada to Argentina
Dolphin, Chinese river	Lipotes vexillifer	China
Elephant, Asian	Elephas maximus	S central & southeastern Asia
Falcon, American peregrine	Falco peregrinus anatum	Canada to Mexico
Fox, northern swift	Vulpes velox hebes	U.S., Canada
Frog, Israel painted	Discoglossus nigriventer	Israel
Gorilla	Gorilla gorilla	Central & W Africa
Hawk, Hawaiian	Buteo solitarius	U.S. (HI)
Hyena, brown	Hyaena brunnea	S Africa
Kangaroo, Tasmanian forester	Macropus giganteus tasmaniensis	Australia (Tasmania)
Leopard	Panthera pardus	Africa & Asia
Lion, Asiatic	Panthera leo persica	Turkey to India
Macaw, indigo	Anodorhynchus leari	Brazil
Manatee, West Indian (Florida)	Trichechus manatus	Southeastern U.S., Caribbean Sea, S America
Ocelot	Felis pardalis	U.S. (TX, AZ) to Central & S America
Ostrich, West African	Struthio camelus spatzi	W Sahara
Otter, marine	Lutra felina	Peru south to Straits of Magellan
Panda, giant	Ailuropoda melanoleuca	China
Panther, Florida	Felis concolor coryi	U.S. (LA, AR east to SC, FL)
Parakeet, golden	Aratinga guarouba	Brazil
Parrot, imperial	Amazona imperialis	West Indies (Dominica)
Python, Indian	Python molurus molurus	Sri Lanka, India
Rhinoceros, black	Diceros bicornis	Sub-Saharan Africa
Rhinoceros, northern white	Ceratotherium simum cottoni	Congo (formerly Zaire), Sudan, Uganda, Central African Rep.
Salamander, Chinese giant	Andrias davidanus davidanus	Western China
Sea turtle, leatherback	Dermochelys coriacea	Tropical, temperate, & subpolar seas
Squirrel, Carolina northern flying	Glaucomys sabrinus coloratus	U.S. (NC, TN)
Stork, Oriental white	Ciconia ciconia boyciana	China, Japan, Korea, Russia
Tiger	Panthera tigris	Asia
Tortoise, Galapagos	Geochelone elephantopus	Ecuador (Galapagos Islands)
Turtle, Plymouth red-bellied	Pseudemys rubiventris bangsi	U.S. (MA)
Whale, gray	Eschrichtius robustus	N Pacific Ocean
Whale, humpback	Megaptera novaeangliae	Oceania
Wolf, red	Canis rufus	Southeastern U.S. to central TX
Woodpecker, ivory-billed	Campephilus principalis	S central and southeastern U.S., Cuba
Yak, wild	Bos grunniens mutus	China (Tibet), India
Zebra, mountain	Equus zebra zebra	S Africa

Classification

Source: *Funk & Wagnalls New Encyclopedia*

In biology, classification is the identification, naming, and grouping of organisms into a formal system. The 2 fields that are most directly concerned with classification are taxonomy and systematics. Although the 2 disciplines overlap considerably, taxonomy is more concerned with nomenclature (naming) and with constructing hierarchical systems, and systematics with uncovering evolutionary relationships. Two kingdoms of living forms, Plantae and Animalia, have been recognized since Aristotle established the first taxonomy in the 4th century BC. In addition, there are the following 3 kingdoms: Protista (one-celled organisms), Monera (bacteria and blue-green algae; also known as the kingdom Procaryotae), and Fungi. The 7 basic categories of classification (from most general to most specific) are: kingdom, phylum (or division), class, order, family, genus, and species. Below are 2 examples:

Zoological hierarchy

Kingdom	Phylum	Class	Order	Family	Genus	Species Name	Common name
Animalia	Chordata	Mammalia	Primates	Hominidae	Homo	Homo sapiens	Human

Botanical hierarchy

Kingdom	Division*	Class	Order	Family	Genus	Species Name	Common name
Plantae	Magnoliophyta	Magnoliopsida	Magnoliales	Magnoliaceae	Magnolia	M. virginiana	Sweet Bay

* In botany, the division is generally used in place of the phylum.

Gestation, Longevity, and Incubation of Animals

Information reviewed and updated by Ronald M. Nowak, ed. *Walker's Mammals of the World* (5th ed., Johns Hopkins University Press, 1991). Average longevity figures supplied by Ronald T. Reuther. These apply to animals in captivity; the potential life span of animals is rarely attained in nature. Figures on gestation and incubation are averages based on estimates by leading authorities.

Animal	Gestation (days)	Average longevity (years)	Maximum longevity (yr-mo)	Animal	Gestation (days)	Average longevity (years)	Maximum longevity (yr-mo)
Ass.	365	12	47	Leopard	98	12	23
Baboon	187	20	45	Lion	100	15	30
Bear: Black	219	18	36-10	Monkey (rhesus)	166	15	37
Grizzly	225	25	50	Moose	240	12	27
Polar	240	20	38	Mouse (meadow)	21	3	4
Beaver	105	5	50	Mouse (dom. white)	19	3	6
Bison	285	15	40	Opossum (American)	13	1	5
Camel (Bactrian)	406	12	50	Pig (domestic)	112	10	27
Cat (domestic)	63	12	28	Puma	90	12	20
Chimpanzee	230	20	53	Rabbit (domestic)	31	5	13
Chipmunk	31	6	8	Rhinoceros (black)	450	15	45
Cow	284	15	30	Rhinoceros (white)	480	20	50
Deer (white-tailed)	201	8	20	Sea lion (California)	350	12	30
Dog (domestic)	61	12	20	Sheep (domestic)	154	12	20
Elephant (African)	660	35	70	Squirrel (gray)	44	10	23-6
Elephant (Asian)	645	40	77	Tiger	105	16	26-3
Elk	250	15	26-8	Wolf (maned)	63	5	13
Fox (red)	52	7	14	Zebra (Grant's)	365	15	50
Giraffe	425	10	33-7				
Goat (domestic)	151	8	18	**Incubation time** (days)			
Gorilla	258	20	54	Chicken			21
Guinea pig	68	4	8	Duck			30
Hippopotamus	238	41	54-4	Goose			30
Horse	330	20	50	Pigeon			18
Kangaroo (gray)	36	7	24	Turkey			26

Speeds of Animals

Source: *Natural History* magazine, Mar. 1974. Copyright © The American Museum of Natural History, 1974

Animal	mph	Animal	mph	Animal	mph
Cheetah	70	Mongolian wild ass	40	Human	27.89
Pronghorn antelope	61	Greyhound	39.35	Elephant	25
Wildebeest	50	Whippet	35.50	Black mamba snake	20
Lion	50	Rabbit (domestic)	35	Six-lined race runner	18
Thomson's gazelle	50	Mule deer	35	Wild turkey	15
Quarterhorse	47.5	Jackal	35	Squirrel	12
Elk	45	Reindeer	32	Pig (domestic)	11
Cape hunting dog	45	Giraffe	32	Chicken	9
Coyote	43	White-tailed deer	30	Spider (Tegenaria atrica)	1.17
Gray fox	42	Wart hog	30	Giant tortoise	0.17
Hyena	40	Grizzly bear	30	Three-toed sloth	0.15
Zebra	40	Cat (domestic)	30	Garden snail	0.03

Most of these measurements are for maximum speeds over approximate quarter mile distances. Exceptions are the lion and elephant, whose speeds were clocked in the act of charging; the whippet, which was timed over a 200-yd course; the cheetah, timed over a 100-yd distance; the human, timed for a 15-yd segment of a 100-yd run (of 13.6 sec); and the black mamba, six-lined race runner, spider, giant tortoise, three-toed sloth, and garden snail, which were measured over various small distances.

Major Venomous Animals

Snakes

Asian pit viper — from 2 ft to 5 ft long; throughout Asia; reactions and mortality vary, but most bites cause tissue damage, and mortality is generally low.

Australian brown snake — 4 ft to 7 ft long; very slow onset of cardiac or respiratory distress; moderate mortality, but because death can be sudden and unexpected, it is the most dangerous of the Australian snakes; antivenom.

Barba Amarilla or fer-de-lance — up to 7 ft long; from tropical Mexico to Brazil; severe tissue damage common; moderate mortality; antivenom.

Black mamba — up to 14 ft long, fast-moving; S and C Africa; rapid onset of dizziness, difficulty breathing, erratic heartbeat; mortality high, nears 100% without antivenom.

Boomslang — less than 6 ft long; in African savannahs; rapid onset of nausea and dizziness, often followed by slight recovery and then sudden death from internal hemorrhaging; bites rare, mortality high; antivenom.

Bushmaster — up to 12 ft long; wet tropical forests of C and S America; few bites occur, but mortality rate is high.

Common or Asian cobra — 4 ft to 8 ft long; throughout southern Asia; considerable tissue damage, sometimes paralysis; mortality probably not more than 10%; antivenom.

Copperhead — less than 4 ft long; from New England to Texas; pain and swelling; very seldom fatal; antivenom seldom needed.

Coral snake — 2 ft to 5 ft long; in Americas south of Canada; bite may be painless; slow onset of paralysis, impaired breathing; mortalities rare, but high without antivenom and mechanical respiration.

Cottonmouth water moccasin — up to 5 ft long; wetlands of southern U.S. from Virginia to Texas. Rapid onset of severe pain, swelling; mortality low, but tissue destruction can be extensive; antivenom.

Death adder — less than 3 ft long; Australia; rapid onset of faintness, cardiac and respiratory distress; at least 50% mortality without antivenom.

Desert horned viper — in dry areas of Africa and western Asia; swelling and tissue damage; low mortality; antivenom.

European viper — 1 ft to 3 ft long; bleeding and tissue damage; mortality low; antivenom.

Gaboon viper — more than 6 ft long; fat; 2-in. fangs; south of the Sahara; massive tissue damage, internal bleeding; few recorded bites.

King cobra — up to 16 ft long; throughout southern Asia; rapid swelling, dizziness, loss of consciousness, difficulty breathing, erratic heartbeat; mortality varies sharply with amount of venom involved, but most bites involve nonfatal amounts; antivenom.

Krait — up to 5 ft long; in SE Asia; rapid onset of sleepiness; numbness; as much as 50% mortality even with use of antivenom.

Puff adder — up to 5 ft long; fat; south of the Sahara and throughout the Middle East; rapid large swelling, great pain, dizziness; moderate mortality, often from internal bleeding; antivenom.

Rattlesnake — 2 ft to 6 ft long; throughout W Hemisphere; rapid onset of severe pain, swelling; mortality low, but amputation of affected digits is sometimes necessary; antivenom. Mojave rattler may produce temporary paralysis.

Ringhals, or spitting, cobra — 5 ft to 7 ft long; southern Africa; squirts venom through holes in front of fangs as a defense; venom is severely irritating, can cause blindness.

Russell's viper or tic-polonga — more than 5 ft long; throughout Asia; internal bleeding; bite reports common; moderate mortality rate; antivenom.

Saw-scaled or carpet viper — as much as 2 ft long; in dry areas from India to Africa; severe bleeding, fever; high mortality, causes more human fatalities than any other snake; antivenom.

Sea snakes — throughout Pacific, Indian oceans except NE Pacific; almost painless bite, variety of muscle pain, paralysis; mortality rate low, many bites not envenomed; some antivenoms.

Sharp-nosed pit viper or one hundred pace snake — up to 5 ft long; in S Vietnam, Taiwan, and China; the most toxic of Asian pit vipers; very rapid onset of swelling and tissue damage, internal bleeding; moderate mortality; antivenom.

Taipan — up to 11 ft long; in Australia and New Guinea; rapid paralysis with severe breathing difficulty; mortality nears 100% without antivenom.

Tiger snake — 2 ft to 6 ft long; S Australia; pain, numbness, mental disturbances with rapid onset of paralysis; may be the most deadly of all land snakes, although antivenom is quite effective.

Yellow or Cape cobra — 7 ft long; in S Africa; most toxic venom of any cobra; rapid onset of swelling, breathing and cardiac difficulties; mortality is high without treatment; antivenom.

Note: Not all bites by venomous snakes are actually envenomed. Any animal bite, however, carries the danger of tetanus, and anyone suffering a venomous snake bite should seek medical attention. Antivenoms do not cure; they are only an aid in the treatment of bites. Mortality rates above are for envenomed bites; low mortality, c. 2% or less; moderate, 2%-5%; high, 5%-15%.

Lizards

Gila monster — as much as 24 in. long, with heavy body and tail; in high desert in SW U.S. and N Mexico; immediate severe pain and transient low blood pressure; no recent mortality.

Mexican beaded lizard — similar to Gila monster, Mexican west coast; reaction and mortality rate similar to Gila monster.

Insects

Ants, bees, wasps, hornets, etc. Global distribution. Usual reaction is piercing pain in area of sting. Not directly fatal, except in cases of massive multiple stings. However, many people suffer allergic reactions — swelling and rashes — and a few may die within minutes from severe sensitivity to the venom (anaphylactic shock).

Spiders, Scorpions

Atrax spider — also known as funnel whip spider; several varieties, often large; in Australia; slow onset of breathing, circulation difficulties; low mortality; antivenom.

Black widow — small, round-bodied with red hourglass marking; the widow and its relatives are found in tropical and temperate zones; severe musculoskeletal pain, weakness, breathing difficulty, convulsions; may be more serious in small children; low mortality; antivenom. The **redback** spider of Australia has the hourglass marking on its back, rather than on its front, but is otherwise identical to the black widow.

Brown recluse, or fiddleback, spider — small, oblong body; throughout U.S.; pain with later ulceration at place of bite; in severe cases fever, nausea, and stomach cramps; ulceration may last months; very low mortality.

Scorpion — crablike body with stinger in tail, various sizes, many varieties throughout tropical and subtropical areas; various symptoms may include severe pain spreading from the wound, numbness, severe agitation, cramps; severe reaction may include respiratory failure; low mortality, usually in children; antivenoms.

Tarantula — large, hairy spider found around the world; the American tarantula, and probably all other tarantulas, are harmless to humans, though their bite may cause some pain and swelling.

Sea Life

Cone-shell — mollusk in small, beautiful shell; in the S Pacific and Indian oceans; shoots barbs into victims; paralysis; low mortality.

Octopus — global distribution, usually in warm waters; all varieties produce venom, but only a few can cause death; rapid onset of paralysis with breathing difficulty.

Portuguese man-of-war — jellyfishlike, with tentacles up to 70 ft long; in most warm water areas; immediate severe pain; not directly fatal, though shock may cause death in rare cases.

Sea wasp — jellyfish, with tentacles up to 30 ft long, in the S Pacific; very rapid onset of circulatory problems; high mortality because of speed of toxic reaction; antivenom.

Stingray — several varieties of differing sizes; found in tropical and temperate seas and some fresh water; severe pain, rapid onset of nausea, vomiting, breathing difficulties; wound area may ulcerate, gangrene may appear; seldom fatal.

Stonefish — brownish fish that lies motionless as a rock on bottom in shallow water; throughout S Pacific and Indian oceans; extraordinary pain, rapid paralysis; low mortality; antivenom available, amount determined by number of puncture wounds; warm water relieves pain.

Major U.S. Public Zoological Parks

Source: *World Almanac* questionnaire, 1997; budget and attendance in millions

Zoo	Budget	Atten-dance	Acres	Species	Some major attractions
Albuquerque Biological Park	$14.5	1.0	170	1,894[1]	Polar Bear Exhibit, Shark Tank *for further information: (505) 764-6200.*
Arizona-Sonora Desert Museum (Tucson)	5.5	0.6	100	1,500	Desert grasslands, Hummingbird aviary, Mountain Woodlands *for further information: (520) 883-1380.*
Audubon (New Orleans)	9.5	0.8	58	360	White alligators, Louisiana Swamp, Reptile Encounter *for further information: (504) 581-IMAX.*
Baltimore	8.1	0.6	180	284	Children's zoo, Chimpanzee Forest, African Watering Hole *for further information: (410) 366-LION.*
Bronx Zoo (NYC)	38.0	2.0	265	560	Jungle World, Baboon Reserve, Asian Rain Forest *for further information: (718) 367-1010.*
Buffalo Zoological Gardens	4.3	0.4	23.5	177	Gorilla Troop, Children's Zoo, Maned Wolves Exhibit *for further information: (716) 837-3900.*
Chicago (Brookfield)	41.0	2.1	216	400+	7 Seas Panorama, Tropic World, Habitat Africa!, The Swamp *for further information: (708) 485-0263 x-352.*
Cincinnati	NA	1.3	67	750	Blakely's Barn, Wings of the World, Jungle Trails *for further information: (800) 94-HIPPO.*
Cleveland Metroparks Zoo	10.0	1.3	165	599	Rain forest, Wildlife of the Great Lakes, Wolf Wilderness *for further information: (216) 661-6500 x-233.*
Columbus (Powell, OH)	18.5	1.3	404	700	Discovery Reef, Gorilla habitat, All of N. America *for further information: (614) 645-3400.*
Dallas Zoo	7.4	0.5	85	387	Wilds of Africa, Chimpanzee Forest, Gorilla Exhibit *for further information: (214) 670-5656.*
Denver	9.0	1.7	80	600	Tropical Discovery, Primate Panorama, Northern Shores *for further information: (303) 331-4100.*
Detroit Zoological Park	10.5	1.1	125	270	Penguinarium, Great Apes of Harambee, Interpretive Gallery *for further information: (248) 398-0900.*
Houston Zoological Gardens	12.0	1.4	55	730	Pigmy Hippo Habitat, World of Primates, Asian Elephants *for further information: (713) 525-3300.*
Lincoln Park Zoological Gardens (Chicago)	11.7	4.0	35	246	Great Ape house, polar bear pool, Farm-in-the-Zoo *for further information: (312) 742-2000.*
Los Angeles Zoo	17.2	1.3	80	400	Tiger Falls, Great ape families, Walk through aviary *for further information: (213) 666-4090.*
Louisville Zoological Garden	6.3	0.6	74	370	New Islands Exhibit, Seal and Sea Lion training *for further information: (502) 459-2181.*
Memphis Zoo	7.6	0.7	70	400	Cat Country, Primate Canyon, Animals of the Night *for further information: (901) 276-WILD.*
Metro Washington Park (Portland, OR)	15	1.1	64	188	Asian elephants, Alaska Tundra, African rain forest *for further information: (503) 226-1561.*
Miami Metrozoo	7.0	0.5	740	250	African Plains, Children's Zoo, Koalas, Komodo Dragons *for further information: (305) 251-0401.*
Milwaukee County Zoo	14.0	1.4	200	300	Aquatic and Reptile Center, wolf woods, bear dens *for further information: (414) 771-3040.*
Minnesota Zoo	15.0	1.1	500	385	Discovery Bay, Tropical Trail, Clubhouse Cove *for further information: (800) 366-7811.*
National (Washington, DC)	24.0	3.0	163	500	Amazonia, Panda Exhibit, Komodo Dragons *for further information: (202) 673-4666.*
Oklahoma City Zoological Park	8.3	0.8	110	657	Aquaticus, Great EscApe Cat Forest, African Lakes. *for further information: (405) 424-3344.*
Omaha/Henry Doorly Zoo	11.0	1.6	130	629	Indoor rain forest, Cat complex, aquarium, Imax theater *for further information: (402) 733-8401.*
Point Defiance (Tacoma, WA)	6.9	0.5	29	295	Arctic Tundra, Southeast Asia, Discovery Reef, The Farm *for further information: (253) 591-5337.*
Philadelphia, Zoological Society of	15.5	1.1	42	395	Carnivore Kingdom, white lions, red pandas *for further information: (215) 243-5277.*
Phoenix	2.8	1.0	125	NA	Africa Trail, Arizona Trail, Tropics Trail, Children's Trail *for further information: (602) 273-1341 x-7422.*
Riverbanks (Columbia, SC)	5.4	0.9	170	546	Aquarium Reptile Complex, Botanical Garden, Coral Reef *for further information: (803) 779-8717.*
St. Louis Zoo	21.0	2.6	90	740	Big Cat Country, The Living World, Jungle of the Apes *for further information: (314) 781-0900.*
San Diego Zoo	NA	3.0	100	800	Tiger River, Gorilla Tropics, Polar Bear Plunge, Giant Pandas *for further information: (619) 231-1515.*
San Diego (Wild Animal Park)	NA	1.6	2,200	300+	Heart of Africa, Mombassa Lagoon, Hidden Jungle *for further information: (760) 747-8702.*
San Francisco	12.0	0.9	125	270	Primate Discovery Center, Aye-Aye exhibit, Gorilla World *for further information: (415) 753-7080.*
Toledo	9.0	0.9	31	525	Hippoquarium, aquarium, African Savanna, Children's Zoo *for further information: (419) 385-5721.*
Tulsa Zoo and Living Museum	3.5	0.5	70	250	Elephant Encounter, Chimpanzee Connection, Sea Lions *for further information: (918) 669-6601.*
Woodland Park Zoo (Seattle)	10.0	1.1	90	285	Tropical rain forest, Elephant Forest, Tropical Asia *for further information: (206) 684-4800.*
Zoo Atlanta	9.5	0.0	00.5	200	Masai Mara, Ford African Rain Forest, Asian Forest *for further information: (404) 624-5600.*

Note: NA = Not Available. (1) Includes plant species.

Major Canadian Public Zoological Parks

Source: *World Almanac* questionnaire, 1997; budget in millions of dollars (Canadian), attendance in millions

Zoo	Budget	Atten-dance	Acres	Species	Major attractions
Calgary	$14.0	0.8	170	291	Canadian Wilds, Prehistoric Park, Dorothy Harvie Garden *for further information: (800) 588-9993.*
Granby (Quebec)	4.5	0.3	70	225	Reptile House, Africa Pavilion, Big Cats Pavilion *for further information: (514) 372-9113 x-102.*
Toronto Zoo, Metropolitan	21.9	0.9	710	459	Komodo Dragons, Naked Mole Rats, Conservation Centre *for further information: (416) 392-5900.*
Vancouver Aquarium	10.0	0.9	2.2	697	Killer Whales, Amazon Gallery, Arctic Canada *for further information: (604) 685-3364.*
Winnipeg (Assiniboine Park)	2.4	0.5	54	271	Kinsmen Discovery Center, Tropical House *for further information: (204) 986-6922.*

Top 50 American Kennel Club Registrations

Source: American Kennel Club, New York, NY; dogs registered during calendar year shown

Breed	Rank 1996	Number registered 1996	Rank 1995	Number registered 1995	Breed	Rank 1996	Number registered 1996	Rank 1995	Number registered 1995
Labrador Retriever	1	149,505	1	132,051	Chow Chow	26	13,587	20	17,722
Rottweiler	2	89,867	2	93,656	Bulldog	27	13,468	30	12,092
German Shepherd Dog	3	79,076	3	78,088	Pekingese	28	13,157	28	13,081
Golden Retriever	4	68,993	4	64,107	Collie	29	12,542	29	12,850
Beagle	5	56,946	5	57,063	Bichon Frise	30	12,199	34	10,817
Poodle	6	56,803	6	54,784	Chinese Shar-Pei	31	12,178	27	13,174
Dachshund	7	48,426	8	44,680	Great Dane	32	12,052	33	11,015
Cocker Spaniel	8	45,305	7	48,065	Lhasa Apso	33	11,903	31	12,060
Yorkshire Terrier	9	40,216	10	36,881	Brittany	34	11,539	32	11,618
Pomeranian	10	39,712	9	37,894	Akita	35	11,161	35	10,661
Shih Tzu	11	38,055	12	34,947	West Highland White Terrier	36	8,171	36	7,773
Chihuahua	12	36,562	14	33,542	Saint Bernard	37	7,519	37	6,537
Boxer	13	36,398	15	31,894	Pembroke Welsh Corgi	38	7,452	38	6,520
Shetland Sheepdog	14	33,577	13	33,721	Weimaraner	39	7,314	39	6,312
Dalmatian	15	32,972	11	36,714	Australian Shepherd	40	6,026	40	5,940
Miniature Schnauzer	16	31,834	16	30,256	Scottish Terrier	41	5,578	41	5,311
Siberian Husky	17	25,557	17	24,291	Chesapeake Bay Retriever	42	5,540	42	5,069
Miniature Pinscher	18	20,355	19	17,810	Mastiff	43	4,807	45	4,245
Pug	19	18,398	24	15,927	Alaskan Malamute	44	4,616	43	4,510
Doberman Pinscher	20	17,919	18	18,141	Great Pyrenees	45	4,521	44	4,465
Boston Terrier	21	17,816	23	16,031	Cairn Terrier	46	4,256	46	4,102
Basset Hound	22	17,032	22	16,055	Samoyed	47	3,678	47	4,088
Maltese	23	16,902	21	16,179	Airedale Terrier	48	3,316	48	3,307
German Shorthaired Pointer	24	15,024	26	14,113	Schipperke	49	3,138	49	3,162
English Springer Spaniel	25	14,715	25	15,039	Newfoundland	50	2,984	51	2,862

Cat Breeds

Source: Cat Fanciers' Assn., Manasquan, NJ

Only a small percentage of house cats in the U.S. are pedigreed or registered with one of the official registering bodies, the largest of which is the Cat Fanciers' Assn., Inc., sponsor of more than 600 clubs. The Cat Fanciers' Assn. recognized 36 breeds as of Dec. 31, 1996 (in order of registration totals): Persian, Maine Coon, Siamese, Abyssinian, Exotic, Oriental, Scottish Fold, American Shorthair, Birman, Ocicat, Burmese, Cornish Rex, Tonkinese, Devon Rex, Russian Blue, Manx, Somali, Colorpoint Shorthair, Ragdoll, British Shorthair, Norwegian Forest Cat, Egyptian Mau, Japanese Bobtail, American Curl, Balinese, Chartreux, Turkish Angora, Javanese, Singapura, Bombay, Korat, Selkirk Rex, American Wirehair, Havana Brown, Turkish Van, and European Burmese.

Trees of the U.S.

Source: American Forests, Washington, DC, 1997

Approximately 850 native and naturalized species of trees are grown in the U.S. The oldest living tree is believed to be a bristlecone pine tree in California named Methusalah, estimated to be 4,700 years old. The world's largest known living tree, the General Sherman giant sequoia in California, weighs more than 6,167 tons—as much as 41 blue whales or 740 elephants.

American Forests recognizes and lists the "National Champion" (largest known, by total mass) of each U.S. tree species. Anyone can nominate candidates for this National Register of Big Trees; for information, write to American Forests, PO Box 2000, Washington, DC 20013. Listed below, in alphabetical order, are ten National Champion trees selected by American Forests as worthy of note.

Selected National Champion Trees

Tree Type	Girth at 4.5 ft. (in.)	Height (ft.)	Crown Spread (ft.)	Total Points	Location
American Beech[1]	279	115	138	429	Harwood, MD
Black Willow	400	76	92	499	Grand Traverse County, MI
Coast Douglas-Fir	438	329	60	782	Coos County, OR
Coast Redwood[2]	867	313	101	1,205	Prairie Creek, CA
Giant Sequoia	998	275	107	1,300	Sequoia National Park, CA
Loblolly Pine	188	148	83	357	Warren, AZ
Pinyon Pine	213	69	52	295	Cuba, NM
Sugar Maple	233	87	100	345	Kingston, NH
Sugar Pine	442	232	29	681	Dorrington, CA
White Oak	374	79	102	479	Wye Mills State Park, MD

(1) Replaces American Elm, which was damaged by fire. (2) Remeasurement in 1997.

1997 IN
PICTURES

NASA

In July, NASA's Pathfinder became the first spacecraft to visit Mars since 1976; above, the roving Sojourner vehicle encounters the rock dubbed "Yogi" as it explores the Martian surface near the landing site.

NATIONAL SCENE

Pres. Bill Clinton and First Lady Hillary Rodham Clinton, with their daughter, Chelsea, wave to crowds in Washington, DC, after his inauguration Jan. 20 for a new term.

Shortly after becoming the nation's first female secretary of state in January, Madeleine Albright, on a world tour, meets with Chinese Pres. Jiang Zemin in Beijing.

With Speaker of the House Newt Gingrich, Budget Committee chairman John Kasich, and others looking on, Pres. Clinton, Aug. 5, signs a bipartisan package of tax and spending cuts aimed at balancing the federal budget by 2002.

Retired Gen. Colin Powell, chair of a national volunteerism summit, pitches in by picking up trash on a Philadelphia street; four present or former U.S. presidents joined in the three-day summit in late April.

On Apr. 19, 1997, two years after a bomb destroyed a government office building in Oklahoma City, relatives and friends of the victims gather to mourn the tragedy. Timothy McVeigh (inset) was convicted in the bombing in June and sentenced to death.

Thirty-nine members of the Heaven's Gate religious cult were found dead Mar. 26 in their California compound after a ritual suicide; the cultists and their leader, Marshall Applewhite (inset), apparently believed they would be carried to another world on a spaceship arriving behind the Hale-Bopp comet.

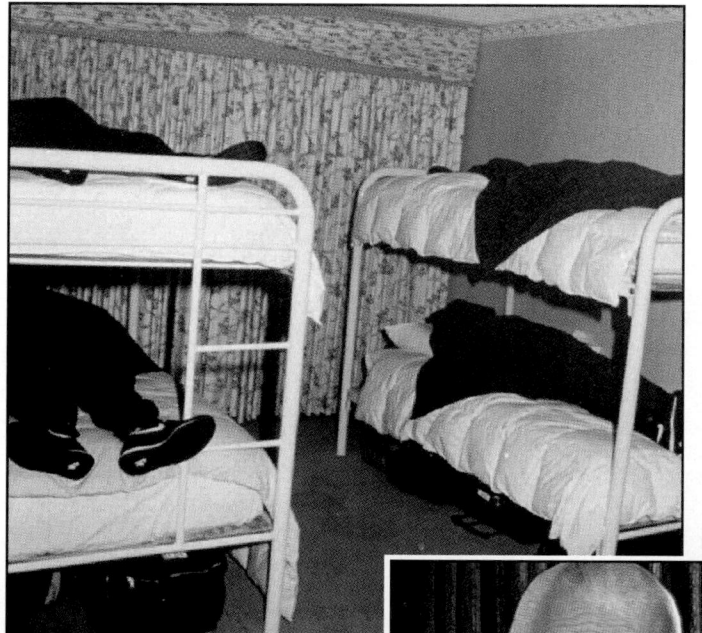

NATURAL DISASTERS

AP/WIDE WORLD PHOTOS

All 50,000 residents of Grand Forks, ND, had to evacuate the town Apr. 19, as floodwaters poured in from the swollen Red River; at left, Pres. Clinton flies over Grand Forks in a helicopter to survey the massive damage.

TED S. WARREN/AUSTIN AMERICAN STATESMAN/SIPA PRESS

AP/WIDE WORLD PHOTOS

At least six tornadoes ripped through central Texas on May 27; one of them killed 27 people in a housing subdivision in Jarrell. At right, a funnel cloud touches down along Interstate 35, north of the town; above, a view of the destruction left behind.

CRIME AND COURT CASES

In a shocking crime that led to a prolonged investigation, six-year-old beauty pageant winner JonBenet Ramsey (inset) was found murdered in her Boulder, CO, home below (guarded by a sheriff's deputy).

Former football star O. J. Simpson, with bodyguard, leaves a Santa Monica, CA, courtroom Feb. 4, after a civil jury found him liable for damages in the 1994 murders of his ex-wife and her friend.

People gather at the doorsteps of Gianni Versace's Miami Beach mansion, where the designer (inset) was gunned down July 15. A manhunt for his suspected killer ended July 23, when Andrew Cunanan, a fugitive suspected in four other murders, killed himself on a houseboat nearby.

PEOPLE

Mother Teresa, the Catholic nun who devoted her life to the dying and destitute of all faiths, died in Calcutta, India, on Sept. 5 at the age of 87.

Pres. Bill Clinton and First Lady Hillary Rodham Clinton, with their daughter, Chelsea, after her high school graduation in June from Sidwell Friends School in Washington, DC.

Seven soldiers became the first African-Americans ever granted Medals of Honor for heroism during World War II. Among those attending the awards ceremony in January were (left to right): the widow of 1st Lt. John Fox, the niece of Maj. Charles Thomas, and Lt. Joseph Baker, the only one of the seven still living.

Former Pres. George Bush gives a thumbs-up signal after completing a 12,500-foot parachute jump at a U.S. Army facility near Yuma, AZ, Mar. 25. Bush, 72, had made his last jump in 1944 as a U.S. Navy pilot, when his plane was shot down over the Pacific in World War II.

Entertainer Bill Cosby and his wife, Camille, leave their New York City home, Jan. 16, after learning that their only son, Ennis, 27, was shot to death while changing a flat tire on a California highway.

First Lt. Kelly Flinn, the Air Force's first female B-52 pilot, with her attorney. Charged in connection with an affair she had with a married civilian, Flinn agreed in May to accept a general discharge from the military rather than face a court-martial.

SCIENCE AND TECHNOLOGY

Ian Wilmut, an embryologist at a Scottish research institute, poses in March with Dolly, a seven-month-old ewe that his research team cloned from an adult animal– the first such cloning ever reported.

PIERRE VILLARD/SIPA PRESS

ILKKA UIMONEN/SYGMA

Russian grandmaster Garry Kasparov ponders a move against IBM's wily Deep Blue chess computer, in New York City in May. Kasparov was beaten in a six game-match, marking the first time a chess champion lost to a computer in a traditional match.

Jacques Cousteau, the world-famous French undersea explorer and filmmaker, died June 25 in Paris, at the age of 87.

AP/WIDE WORLD PHOTOS

AP/WIDE WORLD PHOTOS

Aboard Russia's trouble-plagued Mir space station, cosmonaut Aleksander Lazutkin (left), with U.S. astronaut Michael Foale (center) and cosmonaut Vasily Tsibliyev, talks with ground controllers. A few days earlier, on June 25, the three survived a crash with an unmanned cargo craft during a practice docking, which knocked out about half the station's power supply.

200

Photos continue on page 777

ENERGY

U.S. Energy Summary, 1996

Source: Energy Information Administration, U.S. Dept. of Energy, *Annual Energy Review 1996*

In 1996, strong economic growth contributed to the 5th consecutive year of growth in U.S. energy consumption, which rose 3.2% to an all-time high of nearly 94 quadrillion British thermal units (Btu), according to preliminary data. The increase resulted from a rise in the consumption of petroleum, coal, renewable energy, and natural gas; the use of nuclear electric power declined by 0.1%. Petroleum consumption increased by 0.51 million barrels per day to 18.23 million barrels per day. The consumption of coal was at an all-time high of 1.01 billion short tons in 1996, up 4.6% from the 1995 level. Renewable energy consumption rose by 7.9% to a record level of 7.4 quadrillion Btu; conventional hydroelectric power, which was at an all-time high, accounted for 81% of the increase and for 53% of renewable energy consumption.

The energy intensity of the economy, which is measured in terms of energy consumption per dollar of gross domestic product, increased for the 1st time in 5 years. About 14,000 Btu of energy were consumed for each 1992 dollar in 1996, compared with about 19,000 Btu in the early 1970s.

U.S. total energy production rose 2.1% to a record 72.6 quadrillion Btu in 1996. Most of the increase was attributed to growth in production of coal, renewable energy, and natural gas. Coal production increased 2.9% to a record 1.06 billion short tons, while renewable energy production grew 7.6% to reach an all-time high of 7.1 quadrillion Btu. Crude oil (including lease condensate) production dropped 0.15 quadrillion Btu to 13.7 quadrillion Btu, its lowest level in 42 years.

U.S. net imports of energy increased to an all-time high of 19.0 quadrillion Btu in 1996, an increase of 6.1% from the 1995 level. Almost all of the increase was accounted for by petroleum net imports, which increased by 6.9% to 18.04 quadrillion Btu, just 0.2 quadrillion Btu below the record level set in 1977. U.S. net imports of petroleum totaled 8.4 million barrels per day in 1996. Members of OPEC supplied 4.2 million barrels per day, just under half the total. Coal remained the primary U.S. energy export; coal exports rose 2.3% to 91 million short tons in 1996.

U.S. Energy Overview, 1960-96

Source: Energy Information Administration, U.S. Dept. of Energy, *Annual Energy Review 1996*

(in quadrillion Btu)

Activity and energy source	1960	1965	1970	1975	1980	1985	1990[1]	1994	1995	1996[P]
Production	**41.49**	**49.34**	**62.07**	**59.86**	**64.76**	**64.87**	**70.76**[R]	**70.68**[R]	**71.12**[R]	**72.61**
Fossil fuels	39.87	47.23	59.19	54.73	59.01	57.54	58.56	57.91[R]	57.41[R]	58.41
Coal	10.82	13.06	14.61	14.99	18.60	19.33	22.46	22.07	21.98[R]	22.61
Natural gas (dry)	12.66	15.78	21.67	19.64	19.91	16.98	18.36	19.35[R]	19.10[R]	19.53
Crude oil[2]	14.93	16.52	20.40	17.73	18.25	18.99	15.57	14.10	13.89[R]	13.74
Natural gas plant liquids	1.46	1.88	2.51	2.37	2.25	2.24	2.17	2.39	2.44	2.53
Nuclear electric power	0.01	0.04	0.24	1.90	2.74	4.15	6.16	6.84	7.18[R]	7.17
Hydroelectric pumped storage[3]	(4)	(4)	(4)	(4)	(4)	(4)	−0.04	−0.03	−0.03	−0.03
Renewable energy	1.61	2.07	2.65	3.23	3.01	3.18	6.07[R]	5.97[R]	6.56[R]	7.06
Conventional hydroelectric power[5]	1.61	2.06	2.63	3.15	2.90	2.97	3.01	2.67	3.21[R]	3.59
Geothermal energy	(*)	(*)	0.01	0.07	0.11	0.20	0.33[R]	0.36	0.31	0.34
Biofuels[6]	(*)	(*)	(*)	(*)	(*)	0.01	2.63	2.84[R]	2.95[R]	3.02
Solar energy	0	0	0	0	0	0	0.07	0.07	0.07	0.07
Wind energy	0	0	0	0	0	(*)	0.02	0.04	0.03[R]	0.04
Imports	**4.23**	**5.92**	**8.39**	**14.11**	**15.97**	**12.10**	**18.99**	**22.71**	**22.48**[R]	**23.68**
Natural gas	0.16	0.47	0.85	0.98	1.01	0.95	1.55	2.68	2.90[R]	2.90
Crude oil[7]	2.20	2.65	2.81	8.72	11.19	6.81	12.77	15.34	15.63[R]	16.24
Petroleum products[8]	1.80	2.75	4.66	4.23	3.46	3.80	4.35	3.91	3.23[R]	3.86
Other[9]	0.07	0.04	0.07	0.19	0.31	0.54	0.32	0.78	0.72[R]	0.68
Exports	**1.48**	**1.85**	**2.66**	**2.36**	**3.72**	**4.23**	**4.91**	**4.12**	**4.58**	**4.69**
Coal	1.02	1.38	1.94	1.76	2.42	2.44	2.77	1.88	2.32	2.37
Crude oil	0.43	0.39	0.55	0.44	1.16	1.66	1.82	1.99	1.99	2.06
Other[10]	0.03	0.09	0.18	0.16	0.14	0.14	0.31	0.26	0.27	0.26
Adjustments[11]	**−0.43**	**−0.72**	**−1.37**	**−1.07**	**−1.05**	**1.24**	**−0.75**[R]	**−0.05**[R]	**1.92**[R]	**2.21**
Consumption[12]	**43.80**	**52.68**	**66.43**	**70.55**	**75.96**	**73.98**	**84.09**[R]	**89.21**[R]	**90.94**[R]	**93.81**
Fossil fuels	42.14	50.58	63.52	65.35	69.98	66.22	71.95[R]	76.06[R]	76.94[R]	79.29
Coal	9.84	11.58	12.26	12.66	15.42	17.48	19.10	20.02[R]	20.08[R]	20.99
Coal coke net imports	−0.01	−0.02	−0.06	0.01	−0.04	−0.01	(*)	0.02	0.03	(*)
Natural gas[13]	12.39	15.77	21.79	19.95	20.39	17.83	19.30	21.29[R]	22.16[R]	22.59
Petroleum[14]	19.92	23.25	29.52	32.73	34.20	30.92	33.55	34.73	34.66[R]	35.72
Nuclear electric power	0.01	0.04	0.24	1.90	2.74	4.15	6.16	6.84	7.18[R]	7.17
Hydroelectric pumped storage[3]	(4)	(4)	(4)	(4)	(4)	(4)	−0.04	−0.03	−0.03	−0.03
Renewable energy	1.66	2.06	2.67	3.29	3.23	3.61	6.17[R]	6.28[R]	6.85[R]	7.39
Conventional hydroelectric power[5,15]	1.66	2.06	2.65	3.22	3.12	3.40	3.10	2.96	3.47[R]	3.91
Geothermal energy[16]	(*)	(*)	0.01	0.07	0.11	0.20	0.35[R]	0.38	0.33[R]	0.35
Biofuels[6]	(*)	(*)	(*)	(*)	(*)	0.01	2.63	2.84[R]	2.95[R]	3.02
Solar energy	0	0	0	0	0	0	0.07	0.07	0.07	0.07
Wind energy	0	0	0	0	0	(*)	0.02	0.04	0.03[R]	0.04

(1) Starting in 1990, expanded coverage of nonelectric utility use of renewable energy resulted an increase in total energy production and consumption figures. (2) Includes lease condensate. (3) Total pumped storage facility production minus energy used for pumping. (4) Before 1990, pumped storage is included in conventional hydroelectric power. (5) Starting in 1990, pumped storage is removed and expanded coverage of industrial use of hydroelectric power is included. (6) These include wood, wood waste, peat, wood liquors, railroad ties, pitch, wood sludge, municipal solid waste, agricultural waste, straw, tires, landfill gases, fish oils, and/or other waste. (7) Includes imports of crude oil for the Strategic Petroleum Reserve, which began in 1977. (8) Include imports of unfinished oils and natural gas plant liquids. (9) Coal, electricity, and coal coke. (10) Natural gas, petroleum products, electricity, and coal coke. (11) A balancing item. Includes stock changes, losses, gains, miscellaneous blending components, and unaccounted-for supply. (12) Starting in 1990, "Consumption" includes the part of net imports of electricity derived from nonrenewable energy sources. (13) Includes supplemental gaseous fuels. (14) Petroleum products supplied, including natural gas plant liquids and crude oil burned as fuel. (15) Starting in 1990, includes only the part of net imports of electricity derived from hydroelectric power. (16) Includes electricity imports from Mexico derived from geothermal energy. R=revised data. P=preliminary data. (*)=Less than 0.005 quadrillion Btu. **Note:** Totals may not equal sum of components as a result of independent rounding.

World Energy Consumption and Production Trends

Source: Energy Information Administration, U.S. Dept. of Energy, International Database, Aug. 1997

The world's consumption of primary energy—petroleum, natural gas, coal, net hydroelectric, nuclear, geothermal, solar, wind electric power, and biofuels (primarily for the United States)—increased from 357 quadrillion Btu (British thermal units) in 1994 to 365 quadrillion Btu in 1995. The 29 countries of the Organization for Economic Cooperation and Development (OECD), which includes some of the world's largest economies (the United States, Japan, and Germany), continued to dominate global energy use. OECD nations accounted for more than 58% of the world's primary energy consumption in 1995. World production of primary energy increased from 355 quadrillion Btu in 1994 to 363 quadrillion Btu in 1995. World production of petroleum in 1995 was almost 68 million barrels per day, or 142 quadrillion Btu; petroleum remained the most heavily used source of energy.

In 1995, 3 countries—the United States, Russia, and China—were the world's leading producers (40%) and consumers (42%) of energy. Russia and the United States alone supplied 31% of the world total. The United States alone accounted for 25% of the world's total energy consumption. The United States consumed 28% more energy than it produced—an imbalance of 19.8 quadrillion Btu.

World's Major Producers of Primary Energy, 1995

Source: Energy Information Administration, International Energy Database, Aug. 1997, quadrillion Btu

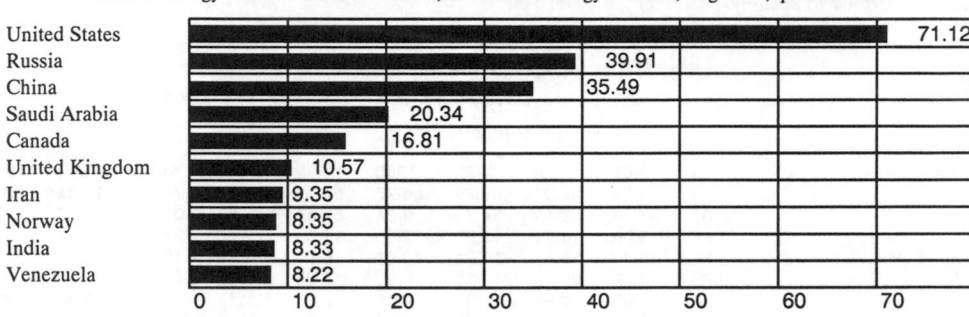

World's Major Consumers of Primary Energy, 1995

Source: Energy Information Administration, International Energy Database, Aug. 1997, quadrillion Btu

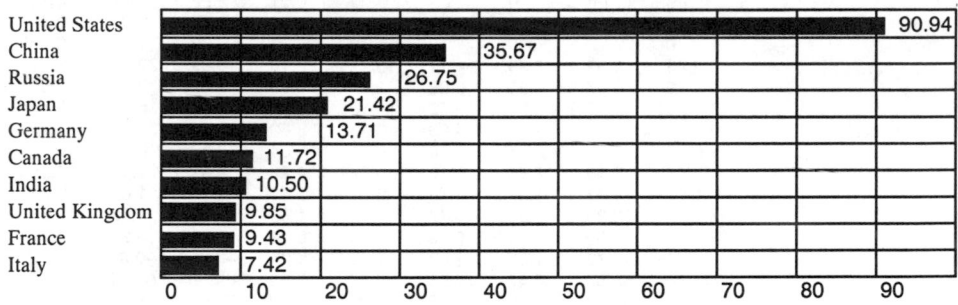

U.S. Petroleum Trade, 1973-96

Source: Energy Information Administration, U.S. Dept. of Energy, *Monthly Energy Review,* June 1997

(in thousands of barrels per day; average for the year)

Year	Imports from Persian Gulf[1]	Total imports	Total exports	Net imports[2]	Petroleum products supplied	Year	Imports from Persian Gulf[1]	Total imports	Total exports	Net imports[2]	Petroleum products supplied
1973	848	6,256	231	6,025	17,308	1985	311	5,067	781	4,286	15,726
1974	1,039	6,112	221	5,892	16,653	1986	912	6,224	785	5,439	16,281
1975	1,165	6,056	209	5,846	16,322	1987	1,077	6,678	764	5,914	16,665
1976	1,840	7,313	223	7,090	17,461	1988	1,541	7,402	815	6,587	17,283
1977	2,448	8,807	243	8,565	18,431	1989	1,861	8,061	859	7,202	17,325
1978	2,219	8,363	362	8,002	18,847	1990	1,966	8,018	857	7,161	16,988
1979	2,069	8,456	471	7,985	18,513	1991	1,845	7,627	1,001	6,626	16,714
1980	1,519	6,909	544	6,365	17,056	1992	1,778	7,888	950	6,938	17,033
1981	1,219	5,996	595	5,401	16,058	1993	1,782	8,620	1,003	7,618	17,237
1982	696	5,113	815	4,298	15,296	1994	1,728	8,996	942	8,054	17,718
1983	442	5,051	739	4,312	15,231	1995	1,573	8,835	949	7,886	17,725
1984	506	5,437	722	4,715	15,726	1996	1,604	9,399	981	8,419	18,234

(1) Bahrain, Iran, Iraq, Kuwait, Qatar, Saudi Arabia, and the United Arab Emirates. (2) Net imports are total imports minus total exports. **Notes:** Beginning in Oct. 1977, imports for the Strategic Petroleum Reserves are included. U.S. geographic coverage includes the 50 states and the District of Columbia. U.S. exports include shipments to U.S. territories, and imports include receipts from U.S. territories. Figures in this table may not add, because of independent rounding.

Appliance Use in U.S. Households, 1978-93

Source: Energy Information Administration, U.S. Dept. of Energy, *Annual Energy Review 1996*

(percentage of households)

Appliance	1978	1980	1982	1984	1987	1990	1993	Change 1980-93
Total households	100	100	100	100	100	100	100	—
Type of appliances								
Electric appliances								
Television set (color)	NA	82	85	88	93	96	98	16
Television set (B/W)	NA	51	47	43	36	31	20	-31
Clothes washer	75	75	72	74	76	76	77	2
Range (stove-top burner)	53	54	53	54	57	58	61	7
Oven, regular or microwave	54	59	59	63	79	88	91	32
Oven, microwave	8	14	21	34	61	79	84	70
Clothes dryer	45	47	45	46	51	53	57	10
Separate freezer	35	38	37	37	34	35	35	-3
Dishwasher	35	37	36	38	43	45	45	8
Dehumidifier	NA	9	9	9	10	12	9	(1)
Waterbed heaters	NA	NA	NA	10	14	15	12	NA
Window or ceiling fan	NA	NA	28	35	46	51	60	NA
Whole house fan	NA	NA	8	8	9	10	4	NA
Evaporative cooler	NA	4	4	4	3	4	3	-1
Pump for well water	NA	NA	NA	NA	NA	15	13	NA
Swimming-pool pump[2]	NA	4	3	NA	NA	5	5	1
Gas appliances[3]								
Range (stove-top burner)	48	46	47	45	43	42	38	-8
Oven	47	42	42	42	41	41	36	-6
Clothes dryer	14	14	15	16	15	16	15	1
Outdoor gas grill	NA	9	11	13	20	26	29	20
Outdoor gas light	2	2	2	1	1	1	1	-1
Swimming pool heater[4]	NA	NA	NA	1	1	2	1	NA
Refrigerators[5]								
One	86	86	86	88	86	84	85	-1
Two or more	14	14	13	12	14	15	15	1
Air conditioning								
Central[6]	23	27	28	30	36	39	44	17
Individual room units[6]	33	30	30	30	30	29	25	-5
None	44	43	42	40	36	32	32	-11
Portable kerosene heaters	(1)	(1)	3	6	6	5	2	2

(1) Less than 0.5%. (2) All reported swimming pools were assumed to have an electric pump for filtering and circulating the water, except for 1993, when a filtering system was made explicit. (3) Includes natural gas or liquefied petroleum gases. (4) In 1984 and 1987, figure also includes heaters for jacuzzis and hot tubs. (5) Fewer than 0.5% of the households did not have a refrigerator. (6) Households with both central and individual room units are counted only under "Central." NA= not available. **Note:** Percentages may not add because of independent rounding.

Energy Consumption and Consumption per Capita by State, 1994

Source: Energy Information Administration, U.S. Dept. of Energy, State Energy Data System; preliminary data

	Consumption				Consumption per Capita			
Rank State	Trillion Btu	Rank State	Trillion Btu	Rank State	Million Btu	Rank State	Million Btu
1. Texas	10,388.5	28. Colorado	1,050.5	1. Alaska	1,050.8	28. Georgia	336.9
2. California. . .	7,556.9	29. Oregon	1,038.2	2. Louisiana	884.5	29. Oregon	336.3
3. Ohio	3,968.4	30. Iowa	1,034.7	3. Wyoming	862.8	30. Michigan.	325.6
4. New York . .	3,868.0	31. Arizona	1,033.8	4. Texas	564.2	31. New Jersey. . . .	322.3
5. Pennsylvania	3,832.2	32. Arkansas . . .	956.5	5. North Dakota . . .	538.9	32. South Dakota . .	321.5
6. Louisiana . .	3,817.8	33. West Virginia .	817.2	6. West Virginia . . .	448.1	33. Pennsylvania . .	317.7
7. Illinois	3,708.1	34. Connecticut . .	797.2	7. Alabama	446.3	34. Illinois.	315.3
8. Florida	3,382.4	35. Alaska.	633.3	8. Kentucky	445.5	35. North Carolina. .	313.3
9. Michigan . . .	3,090.3	36. Utah	594.8	9. Maine	441.3	36. Utah	311.6
10. New Jersey .	2,546.8	37. New Mexico .	590.8	10. Indiana.	439.3	37. District of	
11. Indiana	2,528.2	38. Nebraska . . .	560.1	11. Montana.	430.8	Columbia	310.3
12. Georgia. . . .	2,377.7	39. Maine	546.9	12. Oklahoma	424.2	38. Missouri	305.6
13. North Carolina	2,215.0	40. Nevada	514.4	13. Kansas	420.2	39. Virginia	304.8
14. Washington .	2,088.5	41. Idaho	441.3	14. Mississippi. . . .	398.0	40. Colorado.	286.9
15. Virginia	1,996.7	42. Wyoming . . .	410.8	15. Washington . . .	391.2	41. Vermont	263.0
16. Tennessee .	1,955.4	43. Montana	368.8	16. Arkansas	389.9	42. Maryland	256.6
17. Alabama . . .	1,883.5	44. North Dakota .	344.5	17. Idaho.	389.0	43. Arizona	253.5
18. Wisconsin . .	1,714.4	45. New		18. Tennessee. . . .	377.8	44. New	
19. Kentucky. . .	1,705.3	Hampshire. . .	285.5	19. Delaware	374.9	Hampshire	251.4
20. Missouri . . .	1,613.3	46. Delaware	265.4	20. South Carolina .	373.2	45. Rhode Island. . .	249.5
21. Minnesota . .	1,562.7	47. Hawaii	259.6	21. Iowa	365.5	46. Massachusetts .	246.2
22. Massachusetts	1,487.5	48. Rhode Island .	248.1	22. Ohio	357.4	47. Connecticut. . . .	243.4
23. Oklahoma . .	1,381.6	49. South Dakota .	232.5	23. New Mexico. . . .	356.9	48. Florida	242.3
24. South Carolina	1,359.6	50. District of		24. Nevada	351.8	49. California	240.6
25. Maryland. . .	1,283.0	Columbia. . . .	176.0	25. Nebraska	344.8	50. Hawaii	220.3
26. Kansas	1,071.9	51. Vermont	152.6	26. Minnesota	342.1	51. New York	213.1
27. Mississippi . .	1,062.9	**Total U.S.**	**88,886.3**	27. Wisconsin	337.3	**Total U.S.**	**341.4**

World Crude Oil and Natural Gas Reserves, Jan. 1, 1996

Sources: Energy Information Administration, U.S. Dept. of Energy, *Annual Energy Review 1996; Oil and Gas Journal,* PennWell Publishing Co., Dec. 1995; *World Oil,* Gulf Publishing Co., Aug. 1996

Region and country	Crude oil (billion barrels) Oil and Gas Journal	World Oil	Natural gas (trillion cubic feet) Oil and Gas Journal	World Oil	Region and country	Crude oil (billion barrels) Oil and Gas Journal	World Oil	Natural gas (trillion cubic feet) Oil and Gas Journal	World Oil
North America	**77.0**	**76.7**	**300.6**	**298.6**	Iraq............	100.0	99.2	109.5	108.0
Canada.........	4.9	5.6	67.0	65.8	Kuwait..........	96.5	95.0	52.9	56.7
Mexico.........	49.8	48.8	68.4	67.7	Oman...........	5.1	3.3	25.2	20.1
United States	22.4	22.4	165.1	165.1	Qatar	3.7	3.9	250.0	244.8
Central and South America	**78.9**	**85.0**	**203.5**	**210.7**	Saudi Arabia......	261.2	261.3	185.9	194.1
Argentina........	2.2	2.4	18.6	21.9	Syria...........	2.5	2.6	7.0	7.9
Bolivia..........	0.1	0.1	4.5	0.0	United Arab Emirates	98.1	63.5	204.6	201.1
Brazil..........	4.2	6.2	5.2	7.3	Yemen	4.0	3.0	15.0	17.0
Colombia........	3.5	5.5	10.0	12.0	Other	0.0	0.0	0.2	1.1
Ecuador........	2.1	3.4	3.8	4.0	**Africa.**	**73.2**	**78.7**	**334.6**	**357.7**
Peru...........	0.8	0.7	7.0	7.0	Algeria	9.2	10.0	128.0	131.3
Trinidad and Tobago	0.5	0.6	10.6	12.2	Angola	5.4	3.1	1.8	1.8
Venezuela	64.5	65.6	139.9	142.8	Cameroon........	0.4	0.0	3.9	3.9
Other...........	1.0	0.6	4.0	3.5	Congo Republic....	1.5	1.3	4.3	4.3
Western Europe	**15.8**	**31.6**	**170.9**	**241.4**	Egypt..........	3.9	3.8	22.1	19.1
Denmark	1.0	1.0	4.0	3.9	Libya..........	29.5	34.7	45.8	46.2
Germany	0.3	0.4	11.3	11.6	Nigeria	20.8	21.3	109.7	124.4
Italy...........	0.6	0.7	13.2	10.5	Tunisia	0.4	0.4	2.6	2.7
Netherlands	0.1	0.1	65.2	64.1	Other	2.0	4.0	16.4	24.0
Norway	8.4	24.2	47.5	121.9	**Far East and Oceania.**	**44.0**	**54.8**	**328.5**	**403.4**
United Kingdom ...	4.3	4.5	23.3	24.7	Australia	1.6	3.4	20.1	94.8
Other...........	1.0	0.8	6.4	4.7	Brunei..........	1.4	1.1	14.0	13.9
Eastern Europe and Former USSR	**59.0**	**191.0**	**1,999.5**	**1,951.2**	China..........	24.0	31.0	59.0	46.3
Hungary.........	0.1	0.1	3.4	3.4	India...........	5.8	5.3	25.0	25.5
Romania	1.6	1.0	13.0	4.7	Indonesia	5.2	5.9	68.9	72.3
Former USSR.....	57.0	189.7	1,977.0	1,936.6	Malaysia	4.3	5.2	68.0	80.2
Other[1]	0.2	0.2	6.2	6.6	New Zealand......	0.1	0.1	2.8	2.3
Middle East.	**659.6**	**589.4**	**1,597.2**	**1,491.0**	Pakistan	0.2	0.2	27.0	17.5
Bahrain	0.2	0.0	5.3	5.4	Papua New Guinea .	0.4	0.6	3.0	14.6
Iran............	88.2	57.7	741.6	634.8	Thailand	0.2	0.3	5.9	5.7
					Other	0.8	1.7	34.8	30.4
					World.	**1,007.4**	**1,107.3**	**4,934.9**	**4,954.0**

(1) Albania, Bulgaria, Czech Republic, Poland, and Slovakia. **Notes:** Data for Kuwait and Saudi Arabia include one-half of the reserves in the Neutral Zone between Kuwait and Saudi Arabia. All reserve figures except those for the former USSR and natural gas reserves in Canada are proved reserves recoverable with present technology and prices. Former USSR figures are "explored reserves," which include proved, probable, and some partially possible. The Canadian natural gas figures include proved and some probable. The latest Energy Information Administration data for the U.S. are for Dec. 31, 1995. Totals may not equal sum of components as a result of independent rounding.

Gasoline Retail Prices, U.S. City Average, 1973-96

Source: Energy Information Administration, U.S. Dept. of Energy, *Monthly Energy Review,* June 1997

(cents per gallon, including taxes)

Average	Leaded regular	Unleaded regular	Unleaded premium	All types[1]	Average	Leaded regular	Unleaded regular	Unleaded premium	All types[1]
1973	38.8	NA	NA	NA	1985	111.5	120.2	134.0	119.6
1974	53.2	NA	NA	NA	1986	85.7	92.7	108.5	93.1
1975	56.7	NA	NA	NA	1987	89.7	94.8	109.3	95.7
1976	59.0	61.4	NA	NA	1988	89.9	94.6	110.7	96.3
1977	62.2	65.6	NA	NA	1989	99.8	102.1	119.7	106.0
1978	62.6	67.0	NA	65.2	1990	114.9	116.4	134.9	121.7
1979	85.7	90.3	NA	88.2	1991	NA	114.0	132.1	119.6
1980	119.1	124.5	NA	122.1	1992	NA	112.7	131.6	119.0
1981[2]	131.1	137.8	147.0[3]	135.3	1993	NA	110.8	130.2	117.3
1982	122.2	129.6	141.5	128.1	1994	NA	111.2	130.5	117.4
1983	115.7	124.1	138.3	122.5	1995	NA	114.7	133.6	120.5
1984	112.9	121.2	136.6	119.8	1996	NA	123.1	141.3	128.8

(1) Also includes types of motor gasoline not shown separately. (2) In Sept. 1981, the Bureau of Labor Statistics changed the weights used in the calculation of average motor gasoline prices. Starting in Sept. 1981, gasohol is included in the average for all types, and unleaded premium is weighted more heavily. (3) Based on Sept. through Dec. data only. **Notes:** Geographic coverage for 1973-77 is 56 urban areas; for 1978 and later, 85 urban areas. NA = not available.

Nuclear Electricity Gross Generation by Selected Country, Mar. 1997

Source: Energy Information Administration, U.S. Dept. of Energy, *Monthly Energy Review,* June 1997

(billion kilowatt-hours; E = estimate)

Argentina	0.7	France	33.8	Lithuania	1.3	Sweden	7.3[E]
Belgium	4.4	Germany.......	15.3	Mexico........	1.0	Switzerland	2.4
Brazil..........	0.4	Hungary	1.4	Netherlands	0.4	Taiwan........	3.1
Bulgaria	1.8	India..........	0.9	Russia	10.7	Ukraine........	8.4[E]
Canada	8.4	Japan	26.2	South Africa	0.7	United Kingdom ..	9.6[E]
Finland........	1.9	Korea, South....	6.1[E]	Spain.........	3.8	United States ...	52.9

World Nuclear Power

Source: International Atomic Energy Agency, Dec. 31, 1996

Country	Reactors in operation No. of units	Reactors in operation Total MW(e)	Reactors under construction No. of units	Reactors under construction Total MW(e)	Nuclear electricity supplied in 1996 TW(e).h[1]	Nuclear electricity supplied in 1996 % of total	Total operating experience to Dec. 31, 1996 Years	Total operating experience to Dec. 31, 1996 Months
Argentina	2	935	1	692	6.92	11.43	36	7
Armenia	1	376	—	—	2.10	36.72	29	4
Belgium	7	5,712	—	—	41.40	57.18	142	7
Brazil	1	626	1	1,245	2.29	0.74	14	9
Bulgaria	6	3,538	—	—	18.08	42.24	89	1
Canada	21	14,902	—	—	87.52	15.97	369	9
China	3	2,167	2	1,200	13.62	1.27	11	5
Czech Republic. .	4	1,648	2	1,824	12.85	20.00	42	8
Finland	4	2,355	—	—	18.68	28.13	71	4
France	57	59,948	3	4,355	378.20	77.36	935	3
Germany	20	22,282	—	—	152.80	30.29	530	7
Hungary	4	1,729	—	—	14.18	40.76	46	2
India	10	1,695	4	808	7.42	2.21	139	1
Iran	—	—	2	2,146	—	—	—	—
Japan.	53	42,369	2	2,111	298.20	33.99	756	1
Kazakhstan	1	70	—	—	0.09	0.15	23	6
Korea, South . . .	11	9,120	5	3,870	70.33	35.77	111	10
Lithuania	2	2,370	—	—	12.67	83.44	22	6
Mexico	2	1,308	—	—	7.88	5.19	9	11
Netherlands	2	504	—	—	3.90	4.79	51	9
Pakistan	1	125	1	300	0.31	0.56	25	3
Romania	1	650	1	650	0.91	1.75	0	6
Russia	29	19,843	4	3,375	108.82	13.10	555	6
Slovakia	4	1,632	4	1,552	11.26	44.53	65	5
Slovenia	1	632	—	—	4.36	37.87	15	3
South Africa	2	1,842	—	—	11.76	6.33	24	3
Spain	9	7,207	—	—	53.80	31.97	156	2
Sweden	12	10,040	—	—	71.40	52.38	231	2
Switzerland.	5	3,077	—	—	23.72	44.45	108	10
Taiwan	6	4,884	—	—	36.33	29.07	92	1
Ukraine	16	13,765	4	3,800	79.58	43.76	190	2
United Kingdom .	35	12,928	—	—	85.90	26.04	1,098	4
United States . . .	110	100,685	—	—	674.78	21.92	2,138	7
Total	**442**	**350,964**	**36**	**27,928**	**2,312.06**	**—**	**8,135**	**7**

(1) 1 terawatt-hour [TW(e).h] = 10^6 megawatt-hour [MW(e).h]. For an average power plant, 1 TW(e).h = 0.39 megatonnes of coal equivalent (input) and 0.23 megatonnes of oil equivalent (input). **Note:** In 1996, no reactors were shut down.

U.S. Nuclear Reactor Units and Power Plant Operations

Source: Energy Information Administration, U.S. Dept. of Energy, *Monthly Energy Review,* June 1997

	Number of reactor units Licensed for operation Operable	Licensed for operation In startup	Construction permits Granted	Construction permits Pending	On order	Announced	Total	Total design capacity (million KWs)	Nuclear-based electricity generation (million net KW-hours)	Nuclear portion of domestic electricity generation (percent)
1976. . .	61	1	71	63	16	2	214	212	191,104	9.4
1977. . .	65	2	78	49	13	2	209	203	250,883	11.8
1978. . .	70	0	88	32	5	0	195	191	276,403	12.5
1979. . .	68	0	90	24	3	0	185	180	255,155	11.4
1980. . .	70	1	82	12	3	0	168	162	251,116	11.0
1981. . .	74	0	76	11	2	0	163	157	272,674	11.9
1982. . .	77	2	60	3	2	0	144	134	282,773	12.6
1983. . .	80	3	53	0	2	0	138	129	293,677	12.7
1984. . .	86	6	38	0	2	0	132	123	327,634	13.6
1985. . .	95	3	30	0	2	0	130	121	383,691	15.5
1986. . .	100	7	19	0	2	0	128	119	414,038	16.6
1987. . .	107	4	14	0	2	0	127	119	455,270	17.7
1988. . .	108	3	12	0	0	0	123	115	526,973	19.5
1989. . .	110	1	10	0	0	0	121	113	529,355	19.0
1990. . .	111	0	8	0	0	0	119	111	576,862	20.5
1991. . .	111	0	8	0	0	0	119	111	612,565	21.7
1992. . .	109	0	8	0	0	0	117	111	618,776	22.1
1993. . .	109	0	7	0	0	0	116	110	610,291	21.2
1994. . .	109	0	7	0	0	0	116	110	640,140	22.0
1995. . .	109	1	6	0	0	0	116	110	673,402	22.5
1996. . .	110	0	6	0	0	0	116	110	674,729	21.9

TRADE AND TRANSPORTATION

U.S. Trade With Selected Countries and Major Areas, 1996

Source: Office of Trade and Economic Analysis, U.S. Dept. of Commerce

(millions of dollars)

Country/Area	U.S. trade balance with	Rank	Exports to	Rank	Imports from	Rank
Japan	$-47,580.2	1	$67,606.8	2	$115,187.0	2
China	-39,520.0	2	11,992.6	15	51,512.6	4
Canada	-21,682.3	3	134,210.3	1	155,892.6	1
Mexico	-17,505.8	4	56,791.5	3	74,297.3	3
Germany	-15,450.1	5	23,495.0	6	38,945.1	5
Taiwan	-11,447.1	6	18,460.2	7	29,907.3	6
Italy	-9,527.8	7	8,797.1	16	18,324.8	11
Malaysia	-9,282.6	8	8,546.2	17	17,828.8	12
Venezuela	-8,423.7	9	4,749.4	24	13,173.1	13
Nigeria	-5,159.9	10	818..4	57	5,978.3	26
Indonesia	-4,273.1	11	3,976.8	28	8,249.9	18
France	-4,190.3	12	14,455.5	10	18,645.8	10
Thailand	-4,138.6	13	7,197.5	20	11,336.1	14
Sweden	-3,722.2	14	3,430.5	30	7,152.7	21
Singapore	-3,623.1	15	16,720.0	8	20,343.1	9
Saudi Arabia	-3,155.9	16	7,311.3	19	10,467.2	15
India	-2,841.2	17	3,328.3	32	6,169.5	25
Angola	-2,633.2	18	268.3	77	2,901.5	34
Norway	-2,433.5	19	1,559.0	47	3,992.5	30
Philippines	-2,019.0	20	6,142.4	21	8,161.4	19
Gabon	-1,927.6	21	56.1	125	1,983.7	42
Algeria	-1,490.5	22	635.2	60	2,125.7	34
Sri Lanka	-1,181.9	23	211.1	90	1,393.0	50
Ireland	-1,135.2	24	3,668.7	29	4,803.9	27
Bangladesh	-1,132.9	25	210.1	91	1,343.0	51
North America	-39,188.1	NA	191,001.8	NA	230,189.9	NA
Western Europe	-16,058.3	NA	141,542.8	NA	157,601.1	NA
European Union (EU)	-15,236.2	NA	127,710.4	NA	142,946.6	NA
European Free Trade Association	-1,913.8	NA	10,198.4	NA	12,112.1	NA
Eastern Europe	280.3	NA	7,266.8	NA	6,986.5	NA
Former Soviet Republics	387.6	NA	5,077.7	NA	4,690.1	NA
Organization for Economic Cooperation & Development (OECD) in Europe	-16,087.5	NA	140,766.4	NA	156,853.9	NA
Pacific Rim Countries	-101,790.2	NA	188,243.1	NA	290,033.3	NA
Asia—Near East	114.5	NA	19,966.2	NA	19,851.6	NA
Asia—Newly Industrialized Countries (NICS)	-7,002.3	NA	75,767.6	NA	82,769.9	NA
South Asia	-5,257.8	NA	5,046.4	NA	10,304.2	NA
Assn. of Southeast Asian Nations (ASEAN)	-23,010.0	NA	42,957.6	NA	65,967.6	NA
South/Central America	3,052.3	NA	52,599.3	NA	49,547.0	NA
Twenty Latin American Republics	-16,120.2	NA	103,724.4	NA	119,844.6	NA
Central American Common Market	-412.2	NA	6,361.8	NA	6,774.0	NA
Latin American Free Trade Association (LAFTA)	-16,694.8	NA	92,311.3	NA	109,066.1	NA
North Atlantic Treaty Organization (NATO) Allies	-33,263.4	NA	255,037.2	NA	288,300.6	NA
Organization of Petroleum Exporting Countries (OPEC)	-22,010.3	NA	22,274.8	NA	44,285.0	NA
Unidentified[1]	628.8	NA	628.8	NA	(-)	NA
Total	$-170,214.3	NA	$625,075.0	NA	$795,289.3	NA

(1) The export totals reflect shipments of certain grains, oilseeds, and satellites that are not included in the country/area totals.
NA – Not applicable. Note: Details may not equal totals because of rounding.

Definitions of areas as used in the above table:

North America—Canada, Mexico.
Western Europe—Andorra, Austria, Belgium, Bosnia and Herzegovina, Croatia, Cyprus, Denmark, Faroe Islands, Finland, France, Germany, Gibraltar, Greece, Iceland, Ireland, Italy, Liechtenstein, Luxembourg, Macedonia, Malta and Gozo, Monaco, Netherlands, Norway, Portugal, San Marino, Slovenia, Spain, Svalbard/Jan Mayen Island, Sweden, Switzerland, Turkey, United Kingdom, Vatican City, Yugoslavia.
European Union—Statistics cover Belgium, Denmark, France, Germany, Greece, Ireland, Italy, Luxembourg, Netherlands, Portugal, Spain, United Kingdom.
European Free Trade Association—Austria, Finland, Iceland, Liechtenstein, Norway, Sweden, Switzerland.
Eastern Europe—Albania, Armenia, Azerbaijan, Belarus, Bulgaria, Czech Republic, Estonia, Georgia, Hungary, Kazakhstan, Kyrgyzstan, Latvia, Lithuania, Moldova, Poland, Romania, Russia, Slovakia, Tajikistan, Turkmenistan, Ukraine, Uzbekistan.
Former Soviet Republics—Armenia, Azerbaijan, Belarus, Estonia, Georgia, Kazakhstan, Kyrgyzstan, Latvia, Lithuania, Moldova, Russia, Tajikistan, Turkmenistan, Ukraine, Uzbekistan.
OECD—Austria, Belgium, Denmark, Finland, France, Germany, Greece, Iceland, Ireland, Italy, Liechtenstein, Luxembourg, Monaco, Netherlands, Norway, Portugal, San Marino, Spain, Svalbard/Jan Mayen Island, Sweden, Switzerland, Turkey, United Kingdom.
Pacific Rim Countries/Territories—Australia, Brunei, China, Hong Kong (now part of China), Indonesia, Japan, South Korea, Macao, Malaysia, New Zealand, Papua New Guinea, Philippines, Singapore, Taiwan.
Asia—Near East—Bahrain, Iran, Iraq, Israel, Jordan, Kuwait, Lebanon, Oman, Qatar, Saudi Arabia, Syria, United Arab Emirates, Yemen.
Asia—Newly Industrialized Countries (NICS)—Hong Kong (now part of China), Korea, Singapore, Taiwan.
South Asia—Afghanistan, Bangladesh, India, Nepal, Pakistan, Sri Lanka.
ASEAN—Statistics cover Brunei, Indonesia, Malaysia, Philippines, Singapore, Thailand.
South/Central America—Anguilla, Antigua and Barbuda, Argentina, Aruba, Bahamas, Barbados, Belize, Bermuda, Bolivia, Brazil, British Virgin Islands, Cayman Islands, Chile, Colombia, Costa Rica, Cuba, Dominica, Dominican Republic, Ecuador, El Salvador, Falkland Islands, French Guiana, Grenada, Guadeloupe, Guatemala, Guyana, Haiti, Honduras, Jamaica, Martinique, Montserrat, Netherland Antilles, Nicaragua, Panama, Paraguay, Peru, St. Kitts and Nevis, St. Lucia, St. Vincent and the Grenadines, Suriname, Trinidad and Tobago, Turks and Caicos Islands, Uruguay, Venezuela.
Twenty Latin American Republics—Argentina, Bolivia, Brazil, Chile, Colombia, Costa Rica, Cuba, Dominican Republic, Ecuador, El Salvador, Guatemala, Haiti, Honduras, Mexico, Nicaragua, Panama, Paraguay, Peru, Uruguay, Venezuela.
Central American Common Market—Costa Rica, El Salvador, Guatemala, Honduras, Nicaragua.
LAFTA—Argentina, Bolivia, Brazil, Chile, Colombia, Ecuador, Mexico, Paraguay, Peru, Uruguay, Venezuela.
NATO Allies—Belgium, Canada, Denmark, France, Germany, Greece, Iceland, Ireland, Italy, Liechtenstein, Luxembourg, Monaco, Netherlands, Norway, Portugal, San Marino, Spain, Svalbard/Jan Mayan Island, Sweden, Switzerland, Turkey, United Kingdom.
OPEC—Algeria, Gabon, Indonesia, Iran, Iraq, Kuwait, Libya, Nigeria, Qatar, Saudi Arabia, United Arab Emirates, Venezuela.

U.S. Exports and Imports by Principal Commodity Groupings, 1996

Source: Office of Trade and Economic Analysis, U.S. Dept. of Commerce

(millions of dollars)

Item	Exports	Imports	Item	Exports	Imports
Total	$625,075	$795,289	Jewelry	$618	$4,361
Agricultural commodities	59,385	32,575	Lighting, plumbing	1,362	2,580
Animal feeds	4,188	634	Metal manufactures	9,216	10,842
Cereal flour	1,172	1,212	Metalworking machinery	5,247	6,789
Coffee	4	2,491	Nickel	307	1,140
Corn	8,625	116	Optical goods	1,383	2,327
Cotton, raw and linters	2,741	305	Paper and paperboard	9,853	11,629
Hides and skins	1,516	133	Photographic equipment	3,745	5,266
Live animals	531	1,592	Plastic articles	4,444	5,306
Meat and preparations	6,967	2,316	Platinum	248	1,720
Oils/fats, vegetable	1,024	1,426	Pottery	96	1,569
Rice	1,031	157	Power generating mach.	22,415	22,509
Soybeans	7,447	31	Printed materials	4,353	2,699
Sugar	5	1,003	Records/magnetic media	6,556	4,078
Tobacco, unmanufactured	1,396	1,053	Rubber articles	983	1,465
Vegetables and fruit	7,324	7,512	Rubber tires and tubes	1,962	3,074
Wheat	6,296	247	Scientific instruments	20,645	12,407
Other agricultural	5,504	8,887	Ships, boats	1,013	1,069
Manufactured goods	486,171	658,782	Silver and bullion	638	568
ADP equipment; office machinery	39,702	66,474	Spacecraft	636	232
Airplanes	18,976	3,942	Specialized ind. mach.	25,701	18,512
Airplane parts	11,707	3,471	Televisions, VCRs, etc.	19,853	34,186
Aluminum	3,493	4,834	Textile yarn, fabric	7,837	10,255
Artwork/antiques	887	2,792	Toys/games/sporting goods	3,698	14,721
Basketware, etc.	2,240	3,012	Travel goods	308	3,583
Chemicals - cosmetics	4,350	2,444	Vehicles	50,181	102,551
Chemicals - dyeing	2,732	2,164	Watches/clocks/parts	277	2,804
Chemicals - fertilizers	3,072	1,406	Wood manufactures	1,690	4,042
Chemicals - inorganic	4,706	4,953	**Mineral fuel**	12,181	78,086
Chemicals - medicinal	7,144	7,082	Coal	3,856	607
Chemicals - organic	14,809	14,807	Crude oil	560	54,931
Chemicals - plastics	15,464	7,438	Liquefied propane/butane	302	1,264
Chemicals - other	9,684	4,578	Mineral fuels, other	3,170	1,823
Clothing	7,298	41,557	Natural gas	261	4,564
Copper	1,587	2,960	Petroleum preparations	3,952	14,004
Electrical machinery	57,189	75,488	**Selected commodities:**		
Footwear	764	12,753	Alcoholic bev., distilled	387	2,045
Furniture and bedding	3,333	9,432	Cigarettes	4,738	68
Gem diamonds	151	6,600	Cork, wood, lumber	5,513	7,537
General industrial mach.	26,700	25,289	Crude fertilizers	1,530	1,179
Glass and glassware	2,512	3,092	Fish and preparations	2,938	6,657
Gold, nonmonetary	6,641	2,735	Metal ores; scrap	4,276	4,034
Iron and steel mill products	4,805	13,383	Pulp and waste paper	4,037	2,648

Note: Details may not equal totals as a result of rounding.

U.S. Exports and Imports, 1950-96

Source: Office of Trade and Economic Analysis, U.S. Dept. of Commerce

(millions of dollars)

Year	Exports	Imports	Year	Exports	Imports	Year	Exports	Imports
1950	$9,997	$8,954	1975	$107,652	$98,503	1992	$448,164	$532,665
1955	14,298	11,566	1980	220,626	244,871	1993	465,091	580,659
1960	19,659	15,073	1985	213,133	345,276	1994	512,626	663,256
1965	26,742	21,520	1990	394,030	495,042	1995	584,742	743,445
1970	42,681	40,356	1991	421,730	485,453	1996	625,075	795,289

World Trade Organization (WTO)

Following World War II, the major economic powers of the world negotiated a set of rules for reducing and limiting trade barriers and for settling trade disputes. These rules were called the General Agreement on Tariffs and Trade (GATT). Headquarters to oversee the administration of the GATT were established in Geneva, Switzerland. Periodically, rounds of multilateral trade negotiations under the GATT were carried out. The 8th round, begun in 1986 in Punta del Este, Uruguay, and dubbed the Uruguay Round, concluded on Dec. 15, 1993, when 117 countries completed a new trade-liberalization agreement. The name for the GATT was changed to the World Trade Organization (WTO), which officially came into being Jan. 1, 1995.

The North American Free Trade Agreement (NAFTA)

NAFTA, a comprehensive plan for free trade between the U.S., Canada, and Mexico, took effect on Jan. 1, 1994. Major provisions are as follows:

Agriculture—Tariffs on all farm products are to be eliminated over 15 years. Domestic price-support systems may continue provided they do not distort trade.

Automobiles—After 8 years, at least 62.5% of an automobile's value must have been produced in North America for it to qualify for duty-free status. Tariffs are to be phased out over 10 years.

Banking—U.S. and Canadian banks may acquire Mexican commercial banks accounting for as much as 8% of the industry's capital. All limits on ownership end in 2004.

Disputes—Special judges have jurisdiction to resolve disagreements within strict timetables.

Energy—Mexico continues to bar foreign ownership of its oil fields but, starting in 2004, U.S. and Canadian companies can bid on contracts offered by Mexican oil and electricity monopolies.

Environment—The agreement cannot be used to overrule national and state environmental, health, or safety laws.

Immigration—All 3 countries must ease restrictions on the movement of business executives and professionals.

Jobs—Barriers designed to limit Mexican migration to the U.S. remain in force.

Patent and copyright protection—Mexico strengthened its laws providing protection to intellectual property.

Textiles—A "rule of origin" provision requires most garments to be made from yarn and fabric produced in North America. Most tariffs are being phased out over 5 years.

Tariffs—Tariffs on 10,000 customs goods will be eliminated over 15 years. One-half of U.S. exports to Mexico will be considered duty-free within 5 years.

Trucking—Trucks will have free access on crossborder routes and throughout the 3 countries by 1999.

Shortest Navigable Distances[1] Between Ports

Source: Defense Mapping Agency, Hydrographic/Topographic Center

Distances shown are in nautical mi (1,852 m, or about 6,076.115 ft). For statute mi, multiply by 1.15.

From	To	Distance	From	To	Distance
New York, New York	Barcelona, Spain	3,714	Colón,[2] Panama	Buenos Aires, Argentina	5,385
"	Cape Town, South Africa	6,786	"	Galveston, Texas	1,508
"	Cherbourg, France	3,134	"	Gibraltar[3]	4,332
"	Copenhagen, Denmark	3,720	"	Hamburg, Germany	5,061
"	Galveston, Texas	1,935	"	Helsinki, Finland	5,970
"	Glasgow, Scotland	3,210	"	Lagos, Nigeria	5,050
"	Hamburg, Germany	3,654	"	Lisbon, Portugal	4,152
"	Havana, Cuba	1,186	"	Oslo, Norway	5,053
"	Helsinki, Finland	4,257	"	Piraeus, Greece	5,759
"	Oslo, Norway	3,644	"	Port Said, Egypt	6,251
"	Piraeus, Greece	4,688	"	St. John's, Nfld.	2,695
"	Southampton, England	3,169	"	Southampton, England	4,576
Montreal, Canada	Algiers, Algeria	3,842	San Francisco, Calif.	Bombay, India	9,794
"	Barcelona, Spain	3,939	"	Calcutta, India	9,384
"	Cape Town, South Africa	7,118	"	Colón, Panama	3,285
"	Gibraltar[2]	3,429	Vancouver, Canada	Calcutta, India	8,727
"	Halifax, Nova Scotia	895	"	Melbourne, Australia	7,365
"	Havana, Cuba	3,326	Panama, Panama	Jakarta, Indonesia	10,603
"	Istanbul, Turkey	5,226	Port Said, Egypt	Ho Chi Minh City, Vietnam	5,684
"	Kingston, Jamaica	3,269	"	Hong Kong	6,489
"	Lagos, Nigeria	6,505	"	Manila, Philippines	6,365
"	Marseille, France	4,116	"	Melbourne, Australia	7,886
"	Naples, Italy	4,406	"	Singapore	5,035
"	Oslo, Norway	3,957	"	Yokohama, Japan	7,924
"	Piraeus, Greece	4,856	Cape Town,[4] S. Africa	Jakarta, Indonesia	5,276
"	Port Said, Egypt	5,348	"	Melbourne, Australia	6,600
"	Southampton, England	3,397	"	Singapore	5,614
			Singapore	Jakarta, Indonesia	525

(1) Traveling through station points. (2) Colón, on the Atlantic, is 44 nautical mi from Panama (port) on the Pacific. (3) Gibraltar (port) is 24 nautical mi E of the Strait of Gibraltar. (4) Cape Town is 35 nautical mi NW of the Cape of Good Hope.

50 Busiest U.S. Ports, 1995

Source: Corps of Engineers, Dept. of the Army, U.S. Dept. of Defense

(ports ranked by tonnage handled; all figures in tons)

Rank	Port	Total	Domestic	Foreign	Imports	Exports
1.	South Louisiana, LA, Port of	204,482,591	106,972,579	97,510,012	28,867,399	68,642,613
2.	Houston, TX	135,231,322	63,694,434	71,536,888	42,859,905	28,676,983
3.	New York, NY and NJ	119,341,574	71,281,214	48,060,360	38,728,644	9,331,716
4.	Baton Rouge, LA	83,612,788	45,384,087	38,228,701	26,564,120	11,664,581
5.	Valdez, AK	80,955,084	80,881,706	73,378	0	73,378
6.	New Orleans, LA	76,984,036	37,962,557	39,021,479	18,770,926	20,250,553
7.	Plaquemine, LA, Port of	72,897,301	48,466,434	24,430,867	7,854,328	16,576,539
8.	Corpus Christi, TX	70,456,033	25,885,340	44,570,693	38,624,945	5,945,748
9.	Long Beach, CA	53,227,490	19,738,999	33,488,491	15,994,553	17,493,938
10.	Tampa, FL	51,911,335	31,812,115	20,099,220	6,069,656	14,029,564
11.	Mobile, AL	50,972,223	25,083,220	25,889,003	11,711,441	14,177,562
12.	Texas City, TX	50,402,938	19,213,208	31,189,730	29,980,279	1,209,451
13.	Port Arthur, TX	49,799,977	6,763,743	43,036,234	36,864,423	6,171,811
14.	Pittsburgh, PA	48,849,508	48,849,508	0	0	0
15.	Norfolk Harbor, VA	47,658,182	10,283,351	37,374,831	5,543,382	31,831,449
16.	Lake Charles, LA	46,569,641	19,740,706	26,828,935	21,615,421	5,213,514
17.	Los Angeles, CA	46,478,586	19,063,467	27,415,119	13,550,393	13,864,726
18.	Duluth-Superior, MN & WI	45,049,184	34,932,890	10,116,294	1,425,472	8,690,822
19.	Baltimore, MD	44,695,812	13,098,369	31,597,443	14,359,323	17,238,120
20.	Philadelphia, PA	40,634,284	12,763,551	27,870,733	27,151,633	719,100
21.	Portland, OR	31,255,509	13,616,851	17,638,658	2,714,802	14,923,856
22.	Marcus Hook, PA	30,818,134	14,549,103	16,269,031	16,222,985	46,046
23.	St. Louis, MO & IL	30,137,632	30,137,632	0	0	0
24.	Huntington, WV	28,265,731	28,265,731	0	0	0
25.	Pascagoula, MS	26,926,582	9,481,727	17,444,855	14,735,302	2,709,553
26.	Seattle, WA	26,179,838	6,041,194	20,138,644	7,567,122	12,571,522
27.	Chicago, IL	25,329,030	22,082,501	3,246,529	2,206,262	1,040,267
28.	Paulsboro, NJ	24,780,664	11,645,610	13,135,054	12,984,722	150,332
29.	Newport News, VA	23,365,005	5,170,196	18,194,809	1,794,695	16,400,114
30.	Beaumont, TX	20,937,132	14,922,961	6,014,171	4,026,335	1,987,836
31.	Tacoma, WA	20,878,751	7,026,469	13,852,282	4,009,359	9,842,923
32.	Richmond, CA	20,839,258	15,034,485	5,804,773	3,649,403	2,155,370
33.	Freeport, TX	19,661,621	5,475,882	14,185,739	12,271,130	1,914,609
34.	Detroit, MI	18,660,925	15,002,672	3,658,253	3,051,172	607,081
35.	Port Everglades, FL	18,367,389	10,238,202	8,129,187	6,254,011	1,875,176
36.	Savannah, GA	17,379,724	3,566,640	13,813,084	6,437,974	7,375,110
37.	Boston, MA	16,744,386	9,637,706	7,106,680	6,363,958	742,722
38.	Memphis, TN	15,944,945	15,944,945	0	0	0

Rank	Port	Total	Domestic	Foreign	Imports	Exports
39.	Indiana Harbor, IN	15,700,153	15,019,457	680,696	640,254	40,442
40.	Jacksonville, FL.	15,692,999	8,740,054	6,952,945	5,062,499	1,890,446
41.	San Juan, PR	15,477,965	10,900,245	4,577,720	3,775,480	802,240
42.	Cleveland, OH	15,393,496	12,323,290	3,070,206	2,655,471	414,735
43.	Lorain, OH.	14,964,284	14,839,878	124,406	124,406	0
44.	Toledo, OH	14,074,499	7,240,352	6,834,147	1,376,781	5,457,366
45.	Oakland, CA	13,224,118	2,523,900	10,700,218	4,330,630	6,369,588
46.	Anacortes, WA.	13,109,828	11,120,181	1,989,647	538,040	1,451,607
47.	Cincinnati, OH	13,068,362	13,068,362	0	0	0
48.	New Castle, DE	12,455,809	4,874,803	7,581,006	7,540,893	40,113
49.	Honolulu, HI	11,545,102	9,374,582	2,170,520	1,923,739	246,781
50.	Portland, ME	11,456,007	2,015,780	9,440,227	9,295,191	145,036

Major Merchant Fleets of the World

Source: Maritime Administration, U.S. Dept of Commerce

Fleets of oceangoing steam and motor ships totaling 1,000 gross tons or more as of Jan. 1997. Excludes ships operating exclusively on the Great Lakes and inland waterways and special types such as channel ships, icebreakers, cable ships, and merchant ships owned by any military force. Gross tonnage is a volume measurement; each cargo gross ton represents 100 cubic ft of enclosed space. Deadweight (Dwt) tonnage is carrying capacity of a ship in long tons (2,240 lb). Tonnage figures may not add, because of rounding.

(tonnage in thousands)

	Total			General cargo			Bulk carriers			Tankers		
	No. of ships	Gross tons	Dwt tons	No. of ships	Gross tons	Dwt tons	No. of ships	Gross tons	Dwt tons	No. of ships	Gross tons	Dwt tons
All countries[1]	26,858	463,540	720,040	11,471	72,676	89,472	5,694	155,053	271,037	6,384	171,447	300,350
United States.	495	12,785	17,511	147	1,849	2,484	15	345	575	173	5,955	10,378
Privately owned . . .	302	10,043	13,944	30	527	704	15	345	575	145	5,464	9,492
Government owned	193	2,742	3,567	117	1,322	1,780	—	—	—	28	491	886
Algeria	73	891	1,082	28	184	261	9	172	289	24	494	495
Antigua & Barbuda. . .	379	1,969	2,550	264	884	1,146	9	175	289	11	26	37
Bahamas	954	23,800	37,549	443	4,828	6,078	142	4,518	7,901	241	11,871	21,946
Belize	177	680	1,008	147	496	744	13	122	177	13	49	72
Bermuda.	72	3,363	5,064	13	173	157	8	237	423	30	2,380	3,973
Brazil	188	4,356	7,191	31	157	217	53	1,891	3,319	83	1,946	3,266
Bulgaria	105	1,120	1,613	44	262	329	34	532	834	14	200	322
China	1,513	15,402	23,454	791	4,824	6,798	345	6,648	11,137	233	2,213	3,594
Cyprus	1,476	23,935	38,662	610	4,477	6,182	555	12,787	22,115	166	4,469	8,108
Denmark (DIS)[2]	315	4,945	7,193	163	505	628	11	514	955	71	1,869	3,293
Egypt	110	1,058	1,658	69	344	475	18	492	824	14	189	330
Finland	84	972	876	29	119	140	6	80	121	13	238	377
Germany.	404	5,419	6,556	172	773	938	1	45	75	31	254	381
Greece	874	26,855	48,211	132	1,042	1,560	406	11,056	19,534	266	13,607	26,081
Honduras	256	698	1,036	206	496	727	10	97	157	28	81	127
Hong Kong	223	8,045	13,857	45	713	870	124	6,074	11,327	15	393	693
India.	305	6,717	11,290	64	514	724	140	3,149	5,276	93	2,959	5,174
Indonesia	444	2,013	3,122	287	877	1,355	18	224	348	118	814	1,302
Iran.	123	3,432	6,091	45	507	691	47	1,024	1,700	28	1,896	3,693
Isle of Man	110	2,739	4,435	21	198	225	19	755	1,401	37	1,241	2,320
Italy	352	5,245	7,564	50	188	250	36	1,549	2,880	194	2,163	3,438
Japan	744	14,944	21,997	148	815	665	182	4,778	8,771	299	7,286	10,998
Kerguelen islands . . .	72	2,503	4,263	17	52	65	5	444	805	33	1,503	2,865
Korea (North)	98	577	786	84	438	593	9	107	173	1	2	4
Korea (South)	449	6,636	10,173	151	653	712	124	3,660	6,666	105	550	928
Liberia	1,587	59,085	96,515	269	3,907	4,025	461	16,883	29,676	642	32,742	58,170
Malaysia	303	3,944	5,892	121	570	832	50	1,272	2,264	96	1,668	2,295
Malta	1,113	18,948	31,717	441	3,046	4,157	337	7,213	12,368	265	7,784	14,374
Marshall Islands.	106	4,642	7,831	22	137	142	34	949	1,648	31	2,679	5,097
Netherlands.	445	4,187	4,952	302	1,455	1,889	8	204	320	71	932	1,437
Norway.	111	628	859	68	146	139	11	106	171	24	267	514
Norway (NIS)[3]	626	18,540	29,295	177	2,168	2,346	102	3,736	6,661	285	10,871	19,350
Panama	3,998	79,188	120,397	1,528	11,648	12,213	1,086	32,746	57,137	893	23,948	41,304
Philippines	534	8,315	13,328	199	1,432	1,642	232	6,326	11,069	65	166	256
Poland	125	2,014	2,987	47	475	523	69	1,452	2,400	4	28	40
Portugal	73	678	1,185	45	141	195	7	121	229	17	391	739
Romania.	223	2,336	3,567	161	949	1,337	39	869	1,412	12	423	757
Russia	1,655	8,822	11,126	1,203	4,584	4,945	129	1,793	2,726	271	1,969	3,011
Saint Vincent.	683	6,442	10,112	420	2,384	3,265	121	2,573	4,441	99	1,215	2,150
Singapore	753	16,053	25,240	166	1,871	1,983	126	4,267	7,757	331	7,206	12,618
Spain	81	536	840	20	59	81	1	3	6	16	318	542
Sweden	198	2,324	2,219	68	518	393	9	40	60	69	646	1,080
Syria.	119	376	541	114	331	467	4	44	72	-	-	-
Taiwan	202	5,961	9,161	40	151	223	55	2,441	4,548	19	957	1,657
Thailand	286	1,902	3,072	160	958	1,449	35	482	817	82	378	698
Turkey	516	6,056	10,110	238	836	1,309	177	4,175	7,241	74	786	1,386
Ukraine.	415	3,143	3,709	326	2,133	2,539	21	457	746	29	92	127
United Kingdom.	140	2,665	2,815	27	75	95	6	62	97	60	1,070	1,600
Vanuatu	98	1,490	1,870	48	425	389	32	708	1,185	12	140	207
Vietnam	108	423	665	94	345	534	5	48	81	9	30	50

(1) Includes combination passenger and cargo ships and other type of vessels not listed separately. (2) Danish international ship registry. (3) Norwegian international ship registry.

New Passenger Cars Imported Into the U.S., by Country of Origin,[1] 1968-96

Source: Bureau of the Census, Foreign Trade Division

	Japan	Germany[2]	Italy	United Kingdom	Sweden	France	South Korea	Mexico	Canada	Total[3]
1968 . . .	169,849	707,972	33,843	96,787	52,515	39,551	NA	NA	500,881	1,620,452
1969 . . .	260,005	642,157	41,569	104,050	41,008	24,457	NA	NA	691,146	1,846,717
1970 . . .	381,338	674,945	42,523	76,257	57,844	37,114	NA	NA	692,783	2,013,420
1971 . . .	703,672	770,807	51,469	106,710	61,925	23,316	NA	0	802,281	2,587,484
1972 . . .	697,788	676,967	64,614	72,038	64,541	14,713	NA	9	842,300	2,485,901
1973 . . .	624,805	677,465	56,102	64,140	58,626	8,219	NA	4,469	871,557	2,437,345
1974 . . .	791,791	619,757	107,071	72,512	60,817	21,331	NA	3,914	817,559	2,572,557
1975 . . .	695,573	370,012	102,344	67,106	51,993	15,647	NA	0	733,766	2,074,653
1976 . . .	1,128,936	349,804	82,500	77,190	37,466	21,916	NA	0	825,590	2,536,749
1977 . . .	1,341,530	423,492	55,437	56,889	39,370	19,215	NA	NA	849,814	2,790,144
1978 . . .	1,563,047	416,231	69,689	54,478	56,140	28,502	NA	6	833,061	3,024,982
1979 . . .	1,617,328	495,565	72,456	46,911	65,907	27,887	NA	4	677,008	3,005,523
1980 . . .	1,991,502	338,711	46,899	32,517	61,496	47,386	NA	1	594,770	3,116,448
1981 . . .	1,911,525	234,052	21,635	12,728	68,042	42,477	NA	1	563,943	2,856,286
1982 . . .	1,801,185	259,385	9,402	13,023	89,231	50,032	NA	27	702,495	2,926,407
1983 . . .	1,871,192	239,807	5,442	17,261	114,726	40,823	NA	2	835,665	3,133,836
1984 . . .	1,948,714	335,032	8,582	19,833	114,854	37,788	NA	NA	1,073,425	3,559,427
1985 . . .	2,527,467	473,110	8,689	24,474	142,640	42,882	NA	13,647	1,144,805	4,397,679
1986 . . .	2,618,711	451,699	11,829	27,506	148,700	10,869	169,309	41,983	1,162,226	4,691,297
1987 . . .	2,417,509	377,542	8,648	50,059	138,565	26,707	399,856	126,266	926,927	4,589,010
1988 . . .	2,123,051	264,249	6,053	31,636	108,006	15,990	455,741	148,065	1,191,357	4,450,213
1989 . . .	2,051,525	216,881	9,319	29,378	101,571	4,885	270,609	133,049	1,151,122	4,042,728
1990 . . .	1,867,794	245,286	11,045	27,271	93,084	1,976	201,475	215,986	1,220,221	3,944,602
1991 . . .	1,762,347	171,097	2,886	14,862	62,905	1,727	186,740	249,498	1,109,248	3,612,665
1992 . . .	1,598,919	205,248	1,791	10,997	76,832	65	130,110	266,111	1,119,223	3,447,200
1993 . . .	1,501,953	180,383	1,178	20,029	58,742	23	122,943	299,634	1,371,856	3,604,361
1994 . . .	1,488,159	178,774	1,010	28,217	63,867	58	213,962	360,367	1,525,746	3,909,079
1995 . . .	1,114,360	204,932	1,031	42,450	82,593	14	131,718	462,800	1,552,691	3,624,428
1996 . . .	1,012,785	234,381	1,125	43,890	86,593	5	140,572	550,620	1,589,980	3,698,604

(1) Excludes passenger cars assembled in U.S. foreign trade zones. (2) Figures prior to 1991 are for West Germany. (3) Includes countries not shown separately.

Passenger Car Production, U.S. Plants[1]

Source: American Automobile Manufacturers Assn.

	1995	1996
Chrysler Corp.		
Neon	116,584	100,358
Breeze	7,987	85,347
Total Plymouth	**124,571**	**185,705**
Cirrus	83,401	37,870
Neon	0	12,992
LeBaron J Coupe	23,227	0
Concorde	14,344	1,209
Total Chrysler-Plymouth	**245,593**	**237,776**
Neon	130,863	133,906
Stratus	114,514	109,550
Intrepid	84,792	35,291
Viper	1,084	1,669
Total Dodge	**331,253**	**280,416**
Total Chrysler Corp.	**576,846**	**518,192**
Ford Motor Co.		
Contour	146,536	154,962
Thunderbird	94,027	77,094
Taurus	410,409	436,786
Escort	216,086	236,718
Mustang	143,947	130,488
Total Ford	**1,011,005**	**1,036,048**
Cougar	48,830	34,495
Mystique	51,595	52,624
Sable	124,883	119,727
Lincoln Town Car	99,291	94,695
Mark	15,961	15,415
Continental	42,332	34,925
Tracer	1,813	37,890
Total Lincoln-Mercury	**384,705**	**389,711**
Total Ford Motor Co.	**1,395,710**	**1,425,769**
General Motors Corp.		
Caprice	89,056	66,263
Corvette	19,478	12,282
Beretta-Corsica	221,484	109,656
Cavalier	241,496	272,403
Geo Prizm	94,441	65,557
Malibu	0	11,550
Total Chevrolet	**665,955**	**537,711**
Grand Prix	144,330	108,939
Grand Am	266,046	244,066
Bonneville H.	80,565	82,820
Sunfire	83,514	106,019
Total Pontiac	**574,455**	**641,844**
DeVille (K)	110,273	95,464
Fleetwood	13,445	9,411
Eldorado	23,670	20,113
Seville	38,725	37,261
Total Cadillac	**186,113**	**162,249**
Aurora	28,496	28,967
Delta 88	71,594	59,762
Oldsmobile 98	18,785	8,520
Achieva	49,119	40,187
Cutlass	0	2,935
Cutlass Supreme	93,126	87,475
Ciera	130,096	72,186
Total Oldsmobile	**391,216**	**300,032**
LeSabre	149,866	146,761
Roadmaster	24,840	14,007
Park Avenue	47,932	48,671
Riviera	25,660	21,593
Century	93,012	59,893
Skylark	52,569	51,613
Total Buick	**393,879**	**342,538**
Saturn	301,540	313,937
Toyota Cavalier	1,978	11,701
Total General Motors Corp. . .	**2,515,136**	**2,210,012**
Diamond Star		
Mitsubishi Eclipse	60,695	65,049
Mitsubishi Galant	55,523	57,013
Dodge Avenger	42,326	33,638
Chrysler Sebring	39,402	26,727
Eagle Talon	20,215	10,534
Total Mitsubishi Motor	**218,161**	**192,961**
BMW		
3 Series	11,872	9,666
Z3 Roadster	0	40,880
Total BMW	**11,872**	**50,546**
Honda		
Accord	373,227	424,462
Civic	179,768	186,838
Acura CL	0	23,048
Total Honda	**552,995**	**634,348**
Auto Alliance		
Probe	50,653	33,716
Mazda MX-6/626	98,909	95,726
Total Auto Alliance	**149,562**	**129,442**
Nissan		
Altima	164,522	141,714
Sentra	121,037	105,612
200 SX	47,675	30,543
Total Nissan	**333,234**	**277,869**
Subaru Legacy	80,660	98,747
Toyota		
Avalon	105,611	78,759
Corolla	135,112	158,974
Camry	275,834	307,618
Total Toyota	**516,557**	**545,351**
Total Passenger Cars	**6,350,733**	**6,083,227**

(1) Not all models are listed.

Selected Motor Vehicle Statistics

Source: Federal Highway Administration; U.S. Dept. of Transportation; Insurance Institute for Highway Safety; 1995 figures where not otherwise specified.

State	Driver's age Jan 1, 1996 (1) Regular	(2) Juvenile	State gas tax cents/gal. (July 1, 1997)	Safety belt use law(3) (Aug. 1, 1997)	Licensed drivers per 1,000 resident pop.	Registered motor vehicles per 1,000 resident pop.	Licensed drivers per registered motor vehicle	Gallons of fuel used per vehicle	Miles per gallon	Annual miles driven per vehicle	Vehicle miles per licensed driver
Alabama	16	-	18	S	813	835	0.97	839	16.99	14,250	14,649
Alaska	16	-	8	S	720	898	0.80	691	11.01	7,604	9,491
Arizona	16	-	18	S	623	681	0.91	850	16.24	13,800	15,099
Arkansas	16	-	18.6	S	712	649	1.10	1,121	14.73	16,522	15,067
California	16-18	14	18	P	638	710	0.90	674	18.28	12,321	13,723
Colorado	16	16	22	S	728	750	0.97	711	17.54	12,468	12,853
Connecticut	16-18	-	36	P	717	801	0.90	556	19.24	10,695	11,939
Delaware	16-18	-	23	S	732	825	0.89	693	18.32	12,696	14,315
Dist. of Col.	18	-	20	S	611	438	1.39	779	18.33	14,277	10,235
Florida	16	-	12.8	S	778	732	1.06	721	17.10	12,325	11,593
Georgia	16	-	7.5	P	672	850	0.79	845	16.50	13,951	17,640
Hawaii	15	-	16	P	617	676	0.91	512	19.34	9,905	10,846
Idaho	17	15	25	S	693	897	0.77	684	17.22	11,788	15,257
Illinois	16-18	-	19	S	610	758	0.80	637	16.47	10,497	13,062
Indiana	16-18	-	15	S	639	874	0.73	755	16.85	12,727	17,417
Iowa	16-18	-	20	P	671	990	0.68	643	14.35	9,235	13,638
Kansas	16	14-15	18	S	690	813	0.85	737	16.38	12,067	14,204
Kentucky	16	-	16.4	S	657	682	0.96	966	16.16	15,617	16,208
Louisiana	15-17	15	20	P	597	757	0.79	733	16.04	11,763	14,901
Maine	16-17	16	19	S	696	779	0.89	746	17.44	13,021	14,563
Maryland	16-18	16	23.5	P	663	725	0.92	674	18.23	12,282	13,421
Massachusetts	18	16 1/2	21	S	693	741	0.94	612	17.43	10,674	11,411
Michigan	16-18	14	15	S	697	804	0.87	689	16.21	11,168	12,871
Minnesota	16-18	15	20	S	599	842	0.71	685	16.58	11,353	15,962
Mississippi	16	-	18.4	S	628	795	0.79	827	16.67	13,790	17,458
Missouri	16	-	17	S	674	799	0.84	834	16.73	13,948	16,545
Montana	15-16	13	27	S	659	1,113	0.59	627	15.49	9,705	16,382
Nebraska	16	14	25.5	S	704	896	0.79	744	14.49	10,778	13,724
Nevada	16	14	24	S	683	684	1.00	880	15.16	13,344	13,377
New Hampshire	16-18	16	18.7	No	785	977	0.80	552	17.19	9,486	11,811
New Jersey	17	16	10.5	S	680	743	0.91	659	15.67	10,330	11,291
New Mexico	15-16	-	18.875	P	696	880	0.79	784	18.19	14,253	18,021
New York	17-18	16	22.80	P	578	566	1.02	623	17.99	11,202	10,989
North Carolina	16-18	-	22.6	P	699	790	0.88	765	17.49	13,384	15,125
North Dakota	16	14	20	S	700	1,083	0.65	673	14.00	9,422	14,584
Ohio	16-18	14	22	S	697	880	0.79	612	16.80	10,274	12,967
Oklahoma	16	-	17	P	658	871	0.75	776	17.36	13,476	17,856
Oregon	16	14	24	P	809	887	0.91	630	17.13	10,784	11,816
Pennsylvania	17-18	16	25.815	S	675	703	0.96	692	16.10	11,146	11,592
Rhode Island	16-18	-	29	S	677	706	0.96	593	16.63	9,863	10,287
South Carolina	16	15	16	S	692	771	0.90	849	16.10	13,667	15,233
South Dakota	16	14	21	S	708	972	0.73	752	14.38	10,823	14,866
Tennessee	16	14	20	S	711	1,027	0.69	630	16.53	10,409	15,034
Texas	16-18	15	20	P	661	731	0.90	785	16.87	13,236	14,641
Utah	16	-	24.5	S	643	741	0.87	770	16.86	12,980	14,959
Vermont	18	16	16	S	779	842	0.93	781	16.14	12,607	13,621
Virginia	16-19	-	17.5	S	699	848	0.82	705	17.65	12,437	15,082
Washington	16-18	-	23	S	693	829	0.84	643	17.00	10,938	13,080
West Virginia	16-18	16	25.35	S	714	780	0.92	764	15.99	12,223	13,354
Wisconsin	16-18	14	23.8	S	703	780	0.90	712	18.08	12,870	14,270
Wyoming	16	14	9	S	721	1,252	0.58	878	13.33	11,714	20,341
Average					672	767	0.88	711	16.91	12,022	13,717

(1) Unrestricted operation of private passenger car. When 2 ages are shown, license issued at lower age on completion of approved driver education course. (2) Juvenile license issued with consent of parent or guardian. (3) P = officer may stop vehicle for a violation (primary); S = an officer may issue seat belt citation only when vehicle is stopped for another moving violation (secondary).

U.S. Car Sales by Vehicle Size and Type, 1985-96

Source: American Automobile Manufacturers Assn.

Year	Small (%)	Midsize (%)	Large (%)	Luxury (%)	Total (%)
1996	27.3	49.4	11.6	13.5	100.0
1995	27.1	48.5	10.8	13.6	100.0
1994	29.2	45.6	11.7	13.5	100.0
1993	32.8	43.3	11.1	12.8	100.0
1992	32.9	44.5	9.2	13.4	100.0
1991	33.0	44.9	8.3	13.9	100.0
1990	32.8	44.8	9.4	13.0	100.0
1989	36.6	41.9	11.9	11.6	100.0
1988	37.6	42.5	10.0	9.9	100.0
1987	38.4	42.3	9.1	10.2	100.0
1986	37.6	42.5	9.8	10.1	100.0
1985	37.9	42.1	9.8	10.2	100.0

U.S. Car Sales by Type of Buyer, 1980-96

Source: American Automobile Manufacturers Assn.

| Year | Sales in thousands | | | | % of total sales | |
	Consumer	Business	Government	Total	Consumer	Business
1996	4,031	4,306	161	8,499	47.4	50.7
1995	4,308	4,204	160	8,672	49.9	48.7
1994	4,624	4,496	115	9,235	51.3	47.3
1993	4,669	3,941	108	8,718	53.6	45.2
1992	4,558	3,683	113	8,354	54.6	44.1
1991	4,538	3,752	97	8,387	54.1	44.8
1990	5,768	3,567	149	9,484	60.8	37.6
1989	6,375	3,402	136	9,913	64.3	34.3
1988	6,802	3,699	138	10,639	63.9	34.8
1987	6,748	3,395	135	10,278	65.7	33.0
1986	7,658	3,666	127	11,450	66.9	32.0
1985	7,083	3,822	134	11,039	64.2	34.6
1984	6,590	3,669	135	10,394	63.4	35.3
1983	6,054	3,006	119	9,179	66.0	32.7
1982	5,285	2,593	102	7,980	66.2	32.5
1981	5,623	2,787	116	8,535	66.0	32.7
1980	6,062	2,791	126	8,979	67.5	31.1

Domestic and Imported Retail Car Sales in the U.S., 1980-96

Source: American Automobile Manufacturers Assn.

Calendar year	Domestic	Imports From Japan	From Germany	From other countries	Total imports	Total U.S. sales	Import % Total	Import % Japan	U.S.-sponsored imports
1980	6,581,307	1,905,968	305,219	186,700	2,397,887	8,979,194	26.7	21.2	223,310
1981	6,208,760	1,858,896	282,881	185,502	2,327,279	8,536,039	27.3	21.8	174,665
1982	5,758,586	1,801,969	247,080	174,508	2,223,557	7,982,143	27.9	22.6	139,767
1983	6,795,295	1,915,621	279,748	191,403	2,386,772	9,182,067	26.0	20.9	136,798
1984	7,951,523	1,906,206	344,416	188,220	2,438,842	10,390,365	23.5	18.3	116,965
1985	8,204,542	2,217,837	423,983	195,925	2,837,745	11,042,287	25.7	20.1	206,252
1986	8,214,897	2,382,614	443,721	418,286	3,244,621	11,459,518	28.3	20.8	314,358
1987	7,080,858	2,190,405	347,881	657,465	3,195,751	10,276,609	31.1	21.3	348,154
1988	7,526,038	2,022,602	280,099	700,991	3,003,692	10,529,730	28.5	19.2	393,412
1989	7,072,902	1,897,143	248,561	553,660	2,699,364	9,772,266	27.6	19.4	340,425
1990	6,896,888	1,719,384	265,116	418,823	2,403,323	9,300,211	25.8	18.5	296,778
1991	6,136,757	1,500,309	192,776	344,814	2,037,899	8,174,656	24.9	18.4	280,673
1992	6,276,557	1,451,766	200,851	283,938	1,936,555	8,213,112	23.6	17.7	228,927
1993	6,741,667	1,328,445	186,177	261,570	1,776,192	8,517,859	20.9	15.6	185,284
1994	7,255,303	1,239,450	192,241	303,489	1,735,214	8,990,517	19.3	13.8	95,399
1995	7,128,712	981,462	207,555	317,269	1,506,257	8,634,964	17.4	11.4	99,657
1996	7,253,582	726,940	237,984	308,247	1,273,171	8,526,753	14.9	8.5	72,166

World Motor Vehicle Production, 1950-96

Source: American Automobile Manufacturers Assn.

(in thousands)

Year	United States	Canada	Europe	Japan	Other	World total	U.S. % of world total
1996	11,799	2,397	17,728	10,346	9,244	51,513	22.9
1995	11,985	2,417	17,001	10,196	8,405	50,008	24.0
1994	12,263	2,321	16,195	10,554	8,167	49,500	24.7
1993	10,898	2,246	15,208	11,228	7,205	46,785	23.5
1992	9,729	1,961	17,628	12,499	6,269	48,088	24.5
1991	8,811	1,888	17,804	13,245	5,180	46,928	18.9
1990	9,783	1,928	18,866	13,487	4,496	48,554	20.2
1985	11,653	1,933	16,113	12,271	2,939	44,909	26.0
1980	8,010	1,324	15,496	11,043	2,692	38,565	20.8
1970	8,284	1,160	13,049	5,289	1,637	29,419	28.2
1960	7,905	398	6,837	482	866	16,488	47.9
1950	8,006	388	1,991	32	160	10,577	75.7

Note: As far as can be determined, production refers to vehicles locally manufactured.

Motor Vehicle Production by Selected Countries, 1996

Source: American Automobile Manufacturers Assn.

Country	Passenger cars	Commercial vehicles	Total	Country	Passenger cars	Commercial vehicles	Total
Argentina	269,439	43,711	313,150	Japan	7,863,763	2,482,023	10,345,786
Australia.	302,615	19,423	322,038	Korea, South	2,264,709	548,005	2,812,714
Austria.	97,386	8,703	106,089	Malaysia	180,000	0	180,000
Belgium	367,536	69,062	436,598	Mexico	797,682	421,742	1,219,424
Brazil	1,466,900	345,700	1,812,600	Netherlands.	145,206	33,000	178,206
Canada	1,279,312	1,117,731	2,397,043	Poland	352,750	47,921	400,671
China.	381,510	1,074,670	1,456,180	Spain	2,213,102	199,207	2,412,309
Commonwealth of				Sweden	367,799	95,362	463,161
Indep. States . .	857,550	178,973	1,036,523	Taiwan	264,943	101,083	366,026
Czech Republic . .	263,327	8,684	272,011	Turkey	207,757	68,990	276,747
France	3,147,622	442,965	3,590,587	United Kingdom . . .	1,686,134	238,263	1,924,397
Germany	4,539,583	303,320	4,842,909	United States	6,083,227	5,715,678	11,798,905
India	395,844	365,648	761,492				
Italy	1,317,995	227,370	1,545,365	Total	37,318,281	14,194,882	51,513,163

Top-Selling Passenger Cars in the U.S. by Calendar Year, 1992-96
(Domestic and Import)

Source: American Automobile Manufacturers Assn.

1996

1. Ford Taurus	401,049	8. Chevrolet Lumina	237,973	15. Dodge Neon	139,831		
2. Honda Accord	382,298	9. Pontiac Grand Am	222,477	16. Buick LeSabre	131,316		
3. Toyota Camry	359,433	10. Toyota Corolla	209,048	17. Nissan Sentra	129,596		
4. Honda Civic	286,350	11. Ford Contour	174,187	18. Nissan Maxima	128,395		
5. Ford Escort	284,644	12. Chevrolet Corsica/Beretta	149,117	19. Ford Mustang	122,674		
6. Saturn	278,574	13. Nissan Altima	147,910	20. Mercury Sable	114,164		
7. Chevrolet Cavalier	277,222	14. Dodge Intrepid	145,402				

1995

1. Ford Taurus	366,266	8. Pontiac Grand Am	234,226	15. Dodge Intrepid	147,576
2. Honda Accord	341,384	9. Chevrolet Lumina	214,595	16. Buick LeSabre	141,410
3. Toyota Camry	328,595	10. Toyota Corolla	213,636	17. Ford Mustang	136,962
4. Honda Civic	289,435	11. Chevrolet Cavalier	212,767	18. Nissan Sentra	134,854
5. Saturn	285,674	12. Chevrolet Corsica/Beretta	192,361	19. Pontiac Grand Prix	131,747
6. Ford Escort	285,570	13. Ford Contour	174,214	20. Oldsmobile Ciera	128,860
7. Dodge/Plymouth Neon	240,189	14. Nissan Altima	148,172		

1994		1993		1992	
1. Ford Taurus	397,031	1. Ford Taurus	360,448	1. Ford Taurus	409,751
2. Honda Accord	367,615	2. Honda Accord	330,030	2. Honda Accord	393,477
3. Ford Escort	336,967	3. Toyota Camry	299,737	3. Toyota Camry	286,602
4. Toyota Camry	321,979	4. Chevrolet Cavalier	273,617	4. Ford Escort	236,622
5. Saturn	286,003	5. Ford Escort	269,034	5. Honda Civic/CRX	219,228
6. Honda Civic	267,023	6. Honda Civic	255,579	6. Chevrolet Lumina	218,114
7. Pontiac Grand Am	262,310	7. Saturn	229,356	7. Chevrolet Cavalier	212,374
8. Chevrolet Corsica/Beretta	222,129	8. Chevrolet Lumina	219,683	8. Pontiac Grand Am	210,332
9. Toyota Corolla	210,926	9. Ford Tempo	217,644	9. Ford Tempo	207,173
10. Chevrolet Cavalier	187,263	10. Pontiac Grand Am	214,761	10. Saturn	196,126

The Most Popular Colors, by Type of Vehicle, 1996 Model Year

Source: American Automobile Manufacturers Assn.

Luxury cars		Full size/ intermediate cars		Compact/sports cars		Light trucks and vans	
Color	Percentage	Color	Percentage	Color	Percentage	Color	Percentage
Light brown	17.8	Dark green	18.8	Med./dark green	21.2	White	23.6
White	14.6	White	17.5	White	14.4	Med./dark green	20.7
White metallic	13.0	Light brown	10.3	Black	12.9	Black	10.3
Dark green	11.8	Medium red	9.5	Light brown	10.4	Bright red	7.6
Black	9.0	Black	7.3	Medium red	9.0	Medium red	6.1
Dark blue	7.5	Silver	5.7	Bright red	8.7	Dark red	5.8
Medium red	7.3	Medium blue	5.2	Dark blue	5.0	Light brown	5.1
Light green	5.4	Dark red	4.7	Teal	4.8	Teal/aqua	5.0
Dark red	5.4	Bright red	4.0	Silver	4.3	Med./dark blue	4.6
Silver	3.3	Purple	3.9	Purple	3.5	Silver	3.6
Medium gray	2.7	Teal/aqua	3.3	Bright blue	3.3	Purple	2.1
Light blue	1.0	Medium gray	3.0	Light green	1.0	Light blue	1.8
Other	1.2	Other	6.8	Other	1.5	Other	3.7

MILLENNIUM FACT BOX

Growth of the Automobile in the U.S.[1]

Pioneer automakers were active in the U.S. in the 1890s, and Henry Ford produced his first experimental car in 1893. Automobiles became increasingly popular as a means of transportation rather than strictly for sport, and the automobile industry expanded rapidly for much of the century, with a falloff during WW I when plants converted to the production of war materials. But it wasn't until 1913, when Ford introduced the conveyor belt to carry automobile parts on an assembly line, that the automobile industry really began to meet the growing demand of Americans for auto-mobiles of all types. The number of cars registered in the U.S. for both private and public use, as shown here, leveled off in the 1990s, and in some years actually decreased.

Year	Cars Reg.	Year	Cars Reg.	Year	Cars Reg.	Year	Cars Reg.
1900	8,000	1935	22,567,827	1970	89,243,557	1989	143,081,443
1905	77,400	1940	27,465,826	1975	106,705,934	1990	143,549,627
1910	458,377	1945	25,796,985	1980	121,600,843	1991	142,955,623
1915	2,332,426	1950	40,339,077	1985	131,664,029	1992	144,213,429
1920	8,131,522	1955	52,144,739	1986	135,431,112	1993	146,314,296
1925	17,481,001	1960	61,671,390	1987	137,323,632	1994	133,929,662
1930	23,034,753	1965	75,257,588	1988	141,251,695	1995	136,066,045

(1) There were no publicly owned vehicles before 1925; statistics also exclude military vehicles for all years. Alaska and Hawaii data included since 1960.

Licensed Drivers, by Age

Source: Federal Highway Administration, U.S. Dept. of Transportation

Age	1994 Male	1994 Female	1994 Total	1995 Male	1995 Female	1995 Total	1985 Total	Percent change total drivers 1985-95
under 16	29,493	26,828	56,321	30,833	27,827	58,660	99,000[1]	-40.75[1]
16	765,937	704,584	1,470,521	811,717	751,854	1,563,571	1,635,000	-4.37
17	1,147,918	1,052,924	2,200,842	1,169,351	1,081,243	2,250,594	2,380,000	-5.44
18	1,311,200	1,181,937	2,493,137	1,341,761	1,221,265	2,563,026	2,778,000	-7.74
19	1,436,846	1,291,126	2,727,972	1,407,905	1,280,369	2,688,274	3,118,000	-13.78
(19 and under)	4,691,394	4,257,399	8,948,793	4,761,567	4,362,558	9,124,125	10,010,000	-8.85
20	1,483,343	1,352,749	2,836,091	1,501,614	1,378,437	2,880,051	3,346,000	-13.93
21	1,517,155	1,404,366	2,921,521	1,510,552	1,402,840	2,913,392	3,636,000	-19.87
22	1,618,962	1,511,063	3,130,025	1,549,402	1,453,907	3,003,309	3,794,000	-20.84
23	1,796,150	1,686,492	3,482,642	1,645,621	1,555,962	3,201,583	3,953,000	-19.01
24	1,859,410	1,749,570	3,608,980	1,809,413	1,717,698	3,527,110	4,005,000	-11.93
(20-24)	8,275,019	7,704,240	15,979,259	8,016,601	7,508,844	15,525,445	18,734,000	-17.13
25-29	9,294,140	8,806,159	18,100,299	9,234,547	8,822,290	18,056,837	20,453,000	-11.72
30-34	10,743,221	10,147,503	20,890,724	10,255,668	10,028,055	20,283,723	19,048,000	6.49
35-39	10,340,903	10,131,633	20,472,537	10,381,712	10,277,348	20,659,060	17,038,000	21.25
40-44	9,321,870	9,164,014	18,485,884	9,512,860	9,465,126	18,977,987	13,269,000	43.02
45-49	8,159,613	8,009,774	16,169,387	8,469,713	8,401,960	16,871,673	10,743,000	57.05
50-54	6,349,025	6,195,086	12,544,111	6,493,069	6,397,959	12,891,029	9,825,000	31.21
55-59	5,092,733	4,939,940	10,032,673	5,167,725	5,057,785	10,225,511	9,910,000	3.18
60-64	4,567,868	4,419,678	8,987,547	4,530,005	4,428,256	8,958,261	9,200,000	-2.63
65-69	4,280,619	4,247,325	8,527,944	4,248,092	4,234,797	8,482,889	7,473,000	13.51
70-74	3,577,798	3,649,303	7,227,101	3,582,678	3,702,020	7,284,698	11,165,000	48.43
75-79	2,421,968	2,486,334	4,908,302	2,465,550	2,577,527	5,043,077	NA	NA
80-84	1,340,945	1,379,120	2,720,065	1,358,182	1,439,180	2,797,361	NA	NA
85 and over	736,823	672,017	1,408,840	736,399	710,409	1,446,808	NA	NA
Total	89,193,940	86,209,525	175,403,465	89,214,367	87,414,115	176,628,482	156,868,000	12.60

(1) Comparisons between "licensed" drivers under age 16 in 1985 and in 1995 are not entirely valid because of a change in definition in 1990, which interpreted "licensed" drivers more strictly than before.

Highway Speed Limits, by State

Source: National Motorists Association

Under the National Highway System Designation Act, signed Nov. 28, 1995, by Pres. Bill Clinton, states were allowed to set their own highway speed limits, as of Dec. 8, 1995. Under federal legislation enacted in 1974 during the energy crisis, states had been, in effect, restricted to a National Maximum Speed Limit (NMSL) of 55 miles per hour (raised in 1987 to 65 mph on rural interstates). New maximum speed limits by state are given in the table below; all speeds are given in miles per hour. Most data current as of Oct. 1, 1997.

State	Cars Interstate	Cars Other Primary	Trucks Interstate	Trucks Other Primary	State	Cars Interstate	Cars Other Primary	Trucks Interstate	Trucks Other Primary
AL	70	65	70	65	MT	*/65	*/55	65[1]	60[1]/55
AK	65	55	65	55	NE	75	55	75	55
AZ	75	55	75	55	NV	75	70	75	70
AR	70	55	65	55	NH	65	55	65	55
CA	70	65	55	55	NJ	55	50	55	50
CO	75	65	75	65	NM	75	65	75	65
CT	55	55	55	55	NY	65	55	65[2]	55
DE	65	50	65	50	NC	70	55	70	55
FL	70	65	70	65	ND	70	65/55	70	65/55
GA	70	65	70	65	OH	65	65	55	55
HI	55	55	55	55	OK	75	70	75	70
ID	75	65	75	65	OR	65	55	55	55
IL	65	65	55	65	PA	65	55	65	55
IN	65	55	60	55	RI	65	55	65	55
IA	65	65	65	65	SC	65	55	65	55
KS	70	65	70	65	SD	75	65	65	55
KY	65	55	65	55	TN	65	65	65	65
LA	70	65	70	65	TX	70/65	70/65	60/55	60/55
ME	65	55	65	55	UT	75	65	75	65
MA	65	55	65	55	VT	65	50	65	50
MA	65	65	65	65	VA	65	55	65	55
MI	70	70	55	55	WA	70	55	60	55
MN	70	65	70	65	WV	70	55	70	55
MS	70	70	70	70	WI	65	65	65	65
MO	70	70	70	70	WY	75	65	75	65

(1) 55 mph for triple-trailer trucks. (2) 55 mph for double-trailer trucks on the Thruway.

Note: Where two speeds are given, the first is for daytime and the second for nighttime. "Daytime" means from one-half hour before sunrise to one-half hour after sunset; "nighttime" means at any other hour.

* Denotes that drivers are required to restrict themselves to "reasonable and prudent" speeds, i.e., they must operate on a public street or highway in a careful and prudent manner, and at a rate of speed no greater than is reasonable and proper under the conditions existing at the point of operation, taking into account the amount and character of traffic, condition of brakes, weight of vehicle, grade and width of highway, condition of surface, and freedom of obstruction to view ahead, and they must not drive so as to unduly or unreasonably endanger the life, limb, property, or other rights of a person entitled to the use of the street or highway.

Road Mileage Between Selected U.S. Cities

	Atlanta	Boston	Chicago	Cincin-nati	Cleve-land	Dallas	Denver	Des Moines	Detroit	Houston
Atlanta, Ga.	...	1,037	674	440	672	795	1,398	870	699	789
Boston, Mass..	1,037	...	963	840	628	1,748	1,949	1,280	695	1,804
Chicago, Ill.	674	963	...	287	335	917	996	327	266	1,067
Cincinnati, Oh.	440	840	287	...	244	920	1,164	571	259	1,029
Cleveland, Oh.	672	628	335	244	...	1,159	1,321	652	170	1,273
Dallas Tex.	795	1,748	917	920	1,159	...	781	684	1,143	243
Denver, Col.	1,398	1,949	996	1,164	1,321	781	...	669	1,253	1,019
Detroit, Mich.	699	695	266	259	170	1,143	1,253	584	...	1,265
Houston, Tex.	789	1,804	1,067	1,029	1,273	243	1,019	905	1,265	...
Indianapolis, Ind. . .	493	906	181	106	294	865	1,058	465	278	987
Kansas City, Mo.. . .	798	1,391	499	591	779	489	600	195	743	710
Los Angeles, Cal. . .	2,182	2,979	2,054	2,179	2,367	1,387	1,059	1,727	2,311	1,538
Memphis, Tenn. . . .	371	1,296	530	468	712	452	1,040	599	713	561
Milwaukee, Wis. . . .	761	1,050	87	374	422	991	1,029	361	353	1,142
Minneapolis, Minn. .	1,068	1,368	405	692	740	936	841	252	671	1,157
New Orleans, La. . .	479	1,507	912	786	1,030	496	1,273	978	1,045	356
New York, N.Y.. . . .	841	206	802	647	473	1,552	1,771	1,119	637	1,608
Omaha, Neb.	986	1,412	459	693	784	644	537	132	716	865
Philadelphia, Pa.. . .	741	296	738	567	413	1,452	1,691	1,051	573	1,508
Pittsburgh, Pa.	687	561	452	287	129	1,204	1,411	763	287	1,313
Portland Ore.	2,601	3,046	2,083	2,333	2,418	2,009	1,238	1,786	2,349	2,205
St. Louis, Mo..	541	1,141	289	340	529	630	857	333	513	779
San Francisco	2,496	3,095	2,142	2,362	2,467	1,753	1,235	1,815	2,399	1,912
Seattle, Wash.	2,618	2,976	2,013	2,300	2,348	2,078	1,307	1,749	2,279	2,274
Tulsa, Okla.	772	1,537	683	736	925	257	681	443	909	478
Washington, DC . . .	608	429	671	481	346	1,319	1,616	984	506	1,375

	India-napolis	Kansas City	Los Angeles	Louis-ville	Memphis	Mil-waukee	Minne-apolis	New Orleans	New York	Omaha
Atlanta, Ga.	493	798	2,182	382	371	761	1,068	479	841	986
Boston, Mass..	906	1,391	2,979	941	1,296	1,050	1,368	1,507	206	1,412
Chicago, Ill.	181	499	2,054	292	530	87	405	912	802	459
Cincinnati, Oh.	106	591	2,179	101	468	374	692	786	647	693
Cleveland Oh.	294	779	2,367	345	712	422	740	1,030	473	784
Dallas, Tex.	865	489	1,387	819	452	991	936	496	1,552	644
Denver, Col.	1,058	600	1,059	1,120	1,040	1,029	841	1,273	1,771	537
Detroit, Mich.	278	743	2,311	360	713	353	671	1,045	637	716
Houston, Tex.	987	710	1,538	928	561	1,142	1,157	356	1,608	865
Indianapolis, Ind. . .	...	485	2,073	111	435	268	586	796	713	587
Kansas City, Mo.. . .	485	...	1,589	520	451	537	447	806	1,198	201
Los Angeles, Cal. . .	2,073	1,589	...	2,108	1,817	2,087	1,889	1,883	2,786	1,595
Memphis, Tenn. . . .	435	451	1,817	367	...	612	826	390	1,100	652
Milwaukee, Wis. . . .	268	537	2,087	379	612	...	332	994	889	493
Minneapolis, Minn. .	586	447	1,889	697	826	332	...	1,214	1,207	357
New Orleans, La. . .	796	806	1,883	685	390	994	1,214	...	1,311	1,007
New York, N.Y.. . . .	713	1,198	2,786	748	1,100	889	1,207	1,311	...	1,251
Omaha, Neb.	587	201	1,595	687	652	493	357	1,007	1,251	...
Philadelphia, Pa.. . .	633	1,118	2,706	668	1,000	825	1,143	1,211	100	1,183
Pittsburgh, Pa.	353	838	2,426	388	752	539	857	1,070	368	895
Portland, Ore.	2,272	1,809	959	2,320	2,259	2,010	1,678	2,505	2,885	1,654
St. Louis, Mo..	235	257	1,845	263	285	363	552	673	948	449
San Francisco	2,293	1,835	379	2,349	2,125	2,175	1,940	2,249	2,934	1,683
Seattle, Wash.	2,194	1,839	1,131	2,305	2,290	1,940	1,608	2,574	2,815	1,638
Tulsa, Okla.	631	248	1,452	659	401	757	695	647	1,344	387
Washington, DC . . .	558	1,043	2,631	582	867	758	1,076	1,078	233	1,116

	Phila-delphia	Pitts-burgh	Port-land	St. Louis	Salt Lake City	San Fran-cisco	Seattle	Toledo	Tulsa	Wash., DC
Atlanta, Ga.	741	687	2,601	541	1,878	2,496	2,618	640	772	608
Boston, Mass..	296	561	3,046	1,141	2,343	3,095	2,976	739	1,537	429
Chicago, Ill.	738	452	2,083	289	1,390	2,142	2,013	232	683	671
Cincinnati, Oh.	567	287	2,333	340	1,610	2,362	2,300	200	736	481
Cleveland Oh..	413	129	2,418	529	1,715	2,467	2,348	111	925	346
Dallas, Tex.	1,452	1,204	2,009	630	1,242	1,753	2,078	1,084	257	1,319
Denver, Col.	1,691	1,411	1,238	857	504	1,235	1,307	1,218	681	1,616
Detroit, Mich.	576	287	2,349	513	1,647	2,399	2,279	59	909	506
Houston, Tex..	1,508	1,313	2,205	779	1,438	1,912	2,274	1,206	478	1,375
Indianapolis, Ind. . .	633	353	2,272	235	1,504	2,293	2,194	219	631	558
Kansas City, Mo.. . .	1,118	838	1,809	257	1,086	1,835	1,839	687	248	1,043
Los Angeles, Cal. . .	2,706	2,426	959	1,845	715	379	1,131	2,276	1,452	2,631
Memphis, Tenn. . . .	1,000	752	2,259	285	1,535	2,125	2,290	654	401	867
Milwaukee, Wis. . . .	825	539	2,010	363	1,423	2,175	1,940	319	757	758
Minneapolis, Minn. .	1,143	857	1,678	552	1,186	1,940	1,608	637	695	1,076
New Orleans, La. . .	1,211	1,070	2,505	673	1,738	2,249	2,574	986	647	1,078
New York, N.Y.. . . .	100	368	2,885	948	2,182	2,934	2,815	578	1,344	233
Omaha, Neb.	1,183	895	1,654	449	931	1,683	1,638	681	387	1,116
Philadelphia, Pa.. . .	...	288	2,821	868	2,114	2,866	2,751	514	1,264	133
Pittsburgh, Pa.	288	...	2,535	588	1,826	2,578	2,465	228	984	221
Portland, Ore..	2,821	2,535	...	2,060	767	636	172	2,315	1,913	2,754
St. Louis, Mo..	868	588	2,060	...	1,337	2,089	2,081	454	396	793
San Francisco	2,866	2,578	636	2,089	752	...	808	2,364	1,760	2,799
Seattle, Wash.	2,751	2,465	172	2,081	836	808	...	2,245	1,982	2,684
Tulsa, Okla.	1,264	984	1,913	396	1,172	1,760	1,982	850	...	1,189
Washington, DC . . .	133	221	2,754	793	2,047	2,799	2,684	447	1,189	...

Air Distances Between Selected World Cities in Statute Miles
Point-to-point measurements are usually from City Hall.

	Bangkok	Beijing	Berlin	Cairo	Cape Town	Caracas	Chicago	Hong Kong	Hono-lulu	Lima
Bangkok.........	...	2,046	5,352	4,523	6,300	10,555	8,570	1,077	6,609	12,244
Beijing	2,046	...	4,584	4,698	8,044	8,950	6,604	1,217	5,077	10,349
Berlin...........	5,352	4,584	...	1,797	5,961	5,238	4,414	5,443	7,320	6,896
Cairo	4,523	4,698	1,797	...	4,480	6,342	6,141	5,066	8,848	7,726
Cape Town.......	6,300	8,044	5,961	4,480	...	6,366	8,491	7,376	11,535	6,072
Caracas.........	10,555	8,950	5,238	6,342	6,366	...	2,495	10,165	6,021	1,707
Chicago.........	8,570	6,604	4,414	6,141	8,491	2,495	...	7,797	4,256	3,775
Hong Kong.......	1,077	1,217	5,443	5,066	7,376	10,165	7,797	...	5,556	11,418
Honolulu	6,609	5,077	7,320	8,848	11,535	6,021	4,256	5,556	...	5,947
London	5,944	5,074	583	2,185	5,989	4,655	3,958	5,990	7,240	6,316
Los Angeles	7,637	6,250	5,782	7,520	9,969	3,632	1,745	7,240	2,557	4,171
Madrid	6,337	5,745	1,165	2,087	5,308	4,346	4,189	6,558	7,872	5,907
Melbourne	4,568	5,643	9,918	8,675	6,425	9,717	9,673	4,595	5,505	8,059
Mexico City	9,793	7,753	6,056	7,700	8,519	2,234	1,690	8,788	3,789	2,639
Montreal.........	8,338	6,519	3,740	5,427	7,922	2,438	745	7,736	4,918	3,970
Moscow	4,389	3,607	1,006	1,803	6,279	6,177	4,987	4,437	7,047	7,862
New York........	8,669	6,844	3,979	5,619	7,803	2,120	714	8,060	4,969	3,639
Paris	5,877	5,120	548	1,998	5,786	4,732	4,143	5,990	7,449	6,370
Rio de Janeiro	9,994	10,768	6,209	6,143	3,781	2,804	5,282	11,009	8,288	2,342
Rome...........	5,494	5,063	737	1,326	5,231	5,195	4,824	5,774	8,040	6,750
San Francisco	7,931	5,918	5,672	7,466	10,248	3,902	1,859	6,905	2,398	4,518
Singapore	883	2,771	6,164	5,137	6,008	11,402	9,372	1,605	6,726	11,689
Stockholm	5,089	4,133	528	2,096	6,423	5,471	4,331	5,063	6,875	7,166
Tokyo	2,865	1,307	5,557	5,958	9,154	8,808	6,314	1,791	3,859	9,631
Warsaw	5,033	4,325	322	1,619	5,935	5,559	4,679	5,147	7,366	7,215
Washington, DC ...	8,807	6,942	4,181	5,822	7,895	2,047	596	8,155	4,838	3,509

	London	Los Angeles	Madrid	Mel-bourne	Mexico City	Mon-treal	Mos-cow	New Delhi	New York	Paris
Bangkok.........	5,944	7,637	6,337	4,568	9,793	8,338	4,389	1,813	8,669	5,877
Beijing	5,074	6,250	5,745	5,643	7,753	6,519	3,607	2,353	6,844	5,120
Berlin...........	583	5,782	1,165	9,918	6,056	3,740	1,006	3,598	3,979	548
Cairo	2,185	7,520	2,087	8,675	7,700	5,427	1,803	2,758	5,619	1,998
Cape Town.......	5,989	9,969	5,308	6,425	8,519	7,922	6,279	5,769	7,803	5,786
Caracas.........	4,655	3,632	4,346	9,717	2,234	2,438	6,177	8,833	2,120	4,732
Chicago.........	3,958	1,745	4,189	9,673	1,690	745	4,987	7,486	714	4,143
Hong Kong.......	5,990	7,240	6,558	4,595	8,788	7,736	4,437	2,339	8,060	5,990
Honolulu	7,240	2,557	7,872	5,505	3,789	4,918	7,047	7,412	4,969	7,449
London	...	5,439	785	10,500	5,558	3,254	1,564	4,181	3,469	214
Los Angeles	5,439	...	5,848	7,931	1,542	2,427	6,068	7,011	2,451	5,601
Madrid	785	5,848	...	10,758	5,643	3,448	2,147	4,530	3,593	655
Melbourne	10,500	7,931	10,758	...	8,426	10,395	8,950	6,329	10,359	10,430
Mexico City	5,558	1,542	5,643	8,426	...	2,317	6,676	9,120	2,090	5,725
Montreal.........	3,254	2,427	3,448	10,395	2,317	...	4,401	7,012	331	3,432
Moscow	1,564	6,068	2,147	8,950	6,676	4,401	...	2,698	4,683	1,554
New York........	3,469	2,451	3,593	10,359	2,090	331	4,683	7,318	...	3,636
Paris	214	5,601	655	10,430	5,725	3,432	1,554	4,102	3,636	...
Rio de Janeiro	5,750	6,330	5,045	8,226	4,764	5,078	7,170	8,753	4,801	5,684
Rome...........	895	6,326	851	9,929	6,377	4,104	1,483	3,684	4,293	690
San Francisco	5,367	347	5,803	7,856	1,887	2,543	5,885	7,691	2,572	5,577
Singapore	6,747	8,767	7,080	3,759	10,327	9,203	5,228	2,571	9,534	6,673
Stockholm	942	5,454	1,653	9,630	6,012	3,714	716	3,414	3,986	1,003
Tokyo	5,959	5,470	6,706	5,062	7,035	6,471	4,660	3,638	6,757	6,053
Warsaw	905	5,922	1,427	9,598	6,337	4,022	721	3,277	4,270	852
Washington, DC ...	3,674	2,300	3,792	10,180	1,885	489	4,876	7,500	205	3,840

	Rio de Janeiro	Rome	San Fran-cisco	Singa-pore	Stock-holm	Tehran	Tokyo	Vienna	Warsaw	Wash., DC
Bangkok.........	9,994	5,494	7,931	883	5,089	3,391	2,865	5,252	5,033	8,807
Beijing	10,768	5,063	5,918	2,771	4,133	3,490	1,307	4,648	4,325	6,942
Berlin...........	6,209	737	5,672	6,164	528	2,185	5,557	326	322	4,181
Cairo	6,143	1,326	7,466	5,137	2,096	1,234	5,958	1,481	1,619	5,822
Cape Town.......	3,781	5,231	10,248	6,008	6,423	5,241	9,154	5,656	5,935	7,895
Caracas.........	2,804	5,195	3,902	11,402	5,471	7,320	8,808	5,372	5,559	2,047
Chicago.........	5,282	4,824	1,859	9,372	4,331	6,502	6,314	4,698	4,679	596
Hong Kong.......	11,009	5,774	6,905	1,605	5,063	3,843	1,791	5,431	5,147	8,155
Honolulu	8,288	8,040	2,398	6,726	6,875	8,070	3,859	7,632	7,366	4,838
London	5,750	895	5,367	6,747	942	2,743	5,959	771	905	3,674
Los Angeles	6,330	6,326	347	8,767	5,454	7,682	5,470	6,108	5,922	2,300
Madrid	5,045	851	5,803	7,080	1,653	2,978	6,706	1,128	1,427	3,792
Melbourne	8,226	9,929	7,856	3,759	9,630	7,826	5,062	9,790	9,598	10,180
Mexico City	4,764	6,377	1,887	10,327	6,012	8,184	7,035	6,320	6,337	1,885
Montreal.........	5,078	4,104	2,543	9,203	3,714	5,880	6,471	4,009	4,022	489
Moscow	7,170	1,483	5,885	5,228	716	1,532	4,660	1,043	721	4,876
New York........	4,801	4,293	2,572	9,534	3,986	6,141	6,757	4,234	4,270	205
Paris	5,684	690	5,577	6,673	1,003	2,625	6,053	645	852	3,840
Rio de Janeiro	...	5,707	6,613	9,785	6,683	7,374	11,532	6,127	6,455	4,779
Rome...........	5,707	...	6,259	6,229	1,245	2,127	6,142	477	820	4,497
San Francisco	6,613	6,259	...	8,448	5,399	7,362	5,150	5,994	5,854	2,441
Singapore	9,785	6,229	8,448	...	5,936	4,103	3,300	6,035	5,843	9,662
Stockholm	6,683	1,245	5,399	5,936	...	2,173	5,053	780	494	4,183
Tokyo	11,532	6,142	5,150	3,300	5,053	4,775	...	5,689	5,347	6,791
Warsaw	6,455	820	5,854	5,843	494	1,879	5,689	347	...	4,472
Washington, DC ...	4,779	4,497	2,441	9,662	4,183	6,341	6,791	4,438	4,472	...

EDUCATION

Historical Overview of Public Elementary and Secondary Schools

Source: National Center for Education Statistics, U.S. Dept. of Education

Pupils and teachers (thousands)	1959-60[1]	1969-70[1]	1979-80[1]	1989-90[1]	1990-91[1]	1991-92[1]	1992-93[1]	1993-94[1]	1994-95[1]
Total U.S. population	179,323	201,385	224,567	246,819	249,402	252,137	255,028	257,783	260,372
Population 5-17 years of age	43,881	52,386	48,041	44,947	45,306	45,918	46,662	47,419	48,155
Percentage 5-17 years of age	24.5	26	21.4	18.2	18.2	18.2	18.3	18.4	18.5
Enrollment (thousands)									
Elementary and secondary	36,087	45,550	41,651	40,543	41,217	42,047	42,816	43,465	44,111
Kindergarten & grades 1-8	27,602	32,513	28,034	29,152	29,878	30,506	31,081	31,504	31,898
Grades 9-12	8,485	13,037	13,616	11,390	11,338	11,541	11,735	11,961	12,213
Percentage pop. 5-17 enrolled	82.2	87	86.7	90.2	91.0	91.6	91.8	91.7	91.6
Percentage in high schools	23.5	28.6	32.7	28.1	27.5	27.4	27.4	27.5	27.7
High school graduates (thousands)	1,627	2,589	2,748	2,320	2,235	2,212	2,233	2,221	2,274
Average school term (in days)	178.0	178.9	178.5	*	179.8	*	*	*	*
Total instructional staff (thousands)	1,457	2,286	2,406	2,986	3,051	3,104	3,140	3,209	3,281
Teachers, librarians, and other non-supervisory instructional staff (thousands)	1,393	2,195	2,300	2,860	2,924	2,975	3,017	3,088	3,161
Revenue & expenditures (millions)									
Total revenue	$14,747	$40,267	$96,881	$208,548	$223,341	$234,486	$247,626	$260,142	$273,138
Total expenditures	15,613	40,683	95,962	212,473	229,430	241,567	252,935	265,285	278,966
Current elem. and secondary	12,239	34,218	86,984	188,229	202,038	211,216	220,948	231,543	243,845
Capital outlay	2,662	4,659	6,506	17,781	19,771	20,797	22,172	23,747	24,454
Other	133	636	598	2,983	3,296	4,392	4,379	4,682	5,149
Interest on school debt	490	1,171	1,874	3,776	4,325	5,162	5,437	5,335	5,519
Salaries and pupil cost				(data in unadjusted dollars)					
Avg. annual salary of instruct. staff[2]	$5,174	$9,047	$16,715	$32,638	$34,412	$35,550	$36,454	$37,383	$38,501
Expenditure per capita total pop.	87	202	427	861	920	958	992	1,029	1,071
Current expenditure per pupil ADA[3]	375	816	2,272	4,972	5,258	5,421	5,584	5,767	5,988

* = Data not collected. (1) Because of a modification in scope, data on expenditures for elementary and secondary schools for 1959-60 and later years are not entirely comparable with data for prior years. (2) Includes supervisors, principals, teachers, and nonsupervisory instructional staff. (3) ADA means average daily attendance in elementary and secondary day schools. **Note:** Because of rounding, details may not add to totals.

Programs for the Disabled, 1987-96[1]

Source: Office of Special Education and Rehabilitative Services, U.S. Dept. of Education

(Number of children up to 21 years old served annually in educational programs for the disabled; in thousands.)

Type of Disability	1987-88	1988-89	1989-90	1990-91	1991-92	1992-93	1993-94	1994-95	1995-96
All disabilities	4,446	4,544	4,641	4,771	4,949	5,125	5,309	5,378	5,573
Learning disabilities	1,928	1,987	2,050	2,130	2,234	2,354	2,408	2,489	2,579
Speech impairments	953	967	973	987	997	996	1,014	1,015	1,022
Mental retardation	582	564	548	536	538	519	536	555	570
Serious emotional disturbance	373	376	381	391	399	401	414	427	438
Hearing impairments	56	56	57	58	60	60	64	64	67
Orthopedic impairments	47	47	48	49	51	52	56	60	63
Other health impairments	45	43	52	55	58	65	82	106	133
Visual impairments	22	23	22	23	24	23	24	24	25
Multiple disabilities	77	85	86	96	97	102	108	88	93
Deafness/blindness	12	2	2	1	1	1	1	1	1
Autism and other	*	*	*	*	5	19	24	29	39
Preschool disabilities[2]	361	394	422	441	484	531	578	519	544

Note: Counts are based on reports from the 50 states, the District of Columbia, and Puerto Rico. Increases since 1987-88 are due in part to new legislation enacted in fall 1986, which mandated public school special education services for all disabled children ages 3-5. Details may not add to totals because of rounding.

* = Data not collected. (1) Includes students served under Chapter I and Individuals With Disabilities Education Act (IDEA). (2) Includes preschool children 3-5 years and 0-5 years served under Chapter I and IDEA respectively.

Technology in Public Schools, 1994-97

Source: Quality Education Data, Inc., Denver, CO

Technology	Number of schools				Percentage of schools			
	1994	1995	1996	1997	1994	1995	1996	1997
Schools with laser disc players[1]	17,489	24,534	28,497	30,417	21.0	29.1	29.3	35.5
Elementary[2]	9,247	13,292	15,447	16,614	18.0	26.0	25.2	31.8
Junior high[3]	3,580	4,924	5,766	6,124	26.0	36.0	38.9	43.5
Senior high[4]	4,548	5,990	6,933	7,322	27.0	35.4	36.6	42.5
Schools with modems[1]	22,611	30,768	37,889	40,876	27.0	37.0	39.0	47.7
Elementary[2]	10,878	16,010	20,250	22,234	21.0	31.0	33.0	42.6
Junior high[3]	4,246	5,652	6,929	7,417	31.0	41.1	46.7	52.7
Senior high[4]	7,402	8,790	10,277	10,781	44.0	52.0	54.2	62.6
Schools with networks[1]	17,522	24,604	29,875	32,299	21.0	29.2	30.7	37.7
Elementary[2]	7,545	11,693	14,868	16,441	15.0	23.0	24.2	31.5
Junior high[3]	3,220	4,599	5,590	6,035	24.0	33.4	37.7	42.8
Senior high[4]	6,576	8,159	9,166	9,565	39.0	48.3	48.4	55.5
Schools with CD-ROMs[1]	20,943	34,480	43,499	46,388	25.0	41.0	44.7	54.1
Elementary[2]	9,791	18,343	24,353	26,377	19.0	36.0	39.7	50.5
Junior high[3]	4,261	6,510	7,952	8,410	31.0	47.4	53.6	59.7
Senior high[4]	6,713	9,327	10,756	11,140	40.0	55.2	56.7	64.6

(1) Includes schools for special and adult education, not shown separately. (2) Includes grades K-12, preschool, preschool through 3, K-6, and K-8. (3) Includes schools with grade spans of 4-8 and 7-9. (4) Includes grades 7-12, 9-12, 10-12, vocational technical, and alternative high schools.

Enrollment and Teachers in Public Schools, Fall 1995*

Source: National Center for Education Statistics, U.S. Dept. of Education; National Education Association

	Local school districts	Classroom teachers	Total enrollment	Pupils per teacher	Teacher's avg. pay[1]	Instr. aides	Expend. per pupil
U.S.	14,772	2,598,220	44,840,481	17.3	$38,509	494,289	$5,998
Alabama	127	44,056	746,149	16.9	32,549	6,657	4,405
Alaska	56	7,379	127,618	17.3	50,647	1,751	8,963
Arizona	227	38,017	743,566	19.6	33,350	9,613	4,778
Arkansas	314	26,449	453,257	17.1	29,975	3,523	4,459
California	1,001	230,849	5,536,406	24.0	43,474	56,822	4,992
Colorado	176	35,388	656,279	18.5	36,175	5,919	5,443
Connecticut	166	36,070	517,935	14.4	50,426	7,520	8,817
Delaware	19	6,463	108,461	16.8	41,436	861	7,030
District of Columbia	1	5,305	79,802	15.0	45,012	327	9,335
Florida	67	114,938	2,176,222	18.9	33,881	24,111	5,718
Georgia	181	79,480	1,311,126	16.5	36,042	21,709	5,193
Hawaii	1	10,500	187,180	17.8	35,842	937	6,078
Idaho	112	12,784	243,097	19.0	31,818	1,914	4,210
Illinois	914	113,538	1,943,623	17.1	42,679	21,137	6,136
Indiana	294	55,821	977,263	17.5	38,575	14,421	5,826
Iowa	390	32,318	502,343	15.5	33,225	6,083	5,483
Kansas	304	30,729	463,008	15.1	35,837	4,760	5,817
Kentucky	176	39,120	659,821	16.9	33,950	10,916	5,217
Louisiana	66	46,980	797,366	17.0	28,347	10,026	4,761
Maine	285	15,392	213,569	13.9	33,800	3,776	6,428
Maryland	24	47,819	805,544	16.8	41,148	7,318	7,245
Massachusetts	352	62,710	915,007	14.6	43,806	12,867	7,287
Michigan	557	83,179	1,641,456	19.7	44,251	14,318	6,994
Minnesota	397	46,971	835,166	17.8	37,975	6,088	6,000
Mississippi	153	28,997	506,272	17.5	27,720	8,758	4,080
Missouri	536	57,951	889,881	15.4	34,342	7,228	5,383
Montana	481	10,076	165,547	16.4	29,950	1,938	5,692
Nebraska	680	20,028	289,744	14.5	31,768	3,578	5,935
Nevada	17	13,878	265,041	19.1	37,340	1,489	5,160
New Hampshire	178	12,346	194,171	15.7	36,867	3,519	5,859
New Jersey	607	86,706	1,197,381	13.8	49,349	13,936	9,774
New Mexico	89	19,398	329,640	17.0	29,715	4,574	4,586
New York	717	181,559	2,813,230	15.5	49,560	28,001	9,623
North Carolina	119	73,201	1,183,090	16.2	31,225	22,287	5,077
North Dakota	243	7,501	119,100	15.9	27,711	1,471	4,775
Ohio	661	107,347	1,836,015	17.1	38,831	10,092	6,162
Oklahoma	551	39,364	616,393	15.7	29,270	7,186	4,845
Oregon	248	26,680	527,914	19.8	40,900	6,381	6,436
Pennsylvania	501	104,921	1,787,533	17.0	47,429	14,831	7,109
Rhode Island	36	10,482	149,799	14.3	43,019	1,458	7,469
South Carolina	95	39,922	645,586	16.2	32,659	7,558	4,797
South Dakota	177	9,641	144,685	15.0	26,764	2,302	4,775
Tennessee	140	53,403	893,770	16.7	33,789	9,992	4,388
Texas	1,044	240,371	3,748,167	15.6	32,644	43,046	5,222
Utah	40	20,039	477,121	23.8	31,750	5,037	3,656
Vermont	284	7,676	105,565	13.8	37,200	2,931	6,750
Virginia	141	74,731	1,079,854	14.4	35,837	12,072	5,327
Washington	296	46,907	956,572	20.4	37,860	8,582	5,906
West Virginia	55	21,073	307,112	14.6	33,159	2,957	6,107
Wisconsin	427	55,033	870,175	15.8	38,950	8,361	6,930
Wyoming	49	6,734	99,859	14.8	31,721	1,350	6,160

*Full-time elementary and secondary day schools only. (1) 1996-97; National Education Association estimate.

Mathematics and Reading Achievement of U.S. Students

Source: National Assessment of Educational Progress, National Center for Education Statistics, U.S. Dept. of Education

Percent of students who scored at or above proficient level in national tests. NA = not administered.

State	Grade 4 Mathematics 1992	1996	Grade 4 Reading 1992	1994	Grade 8 Mathematics 1992	1996	State	Grade 4 Mathematics 1992	1996	Grade 4 Reading 1992	1994	Grade 8 Mathematics 1992	1996
AL	43	48	20	23	39	45	MT	NA	71	NA	35	NA	75
AK	NA	65	NA	NA	NA	68	NE	67	70	31	34	70	76
AZ	53	57	21	24	55	57	NV	NA	57	38	36	NA	NA
AR	47	54	23	24	44	52	NJ	68	68	35	33	NA	NA
CA	46	46	19	18	50	51	NM	50	51	23	21	48	51
CO	61	67	25	28	64	67	NY	57	64	27	27	57	61
CT	67	75	34	38	64	70	NC	50	64	25	30	47	56
DE	55	54	24	23	52	55	ND	72	75	35	38	78	77
DC	23	20	NA	NA	22	20	OR	NA	65	NA	NA	NA	67
FL	52	55	21	23	49	54	PA	65	68	32	30	NA	NA
GA	53	53	25	26	48	51	RI	54	61	28	32	56	60
HI	52	53	17	19	46	51	SC	48	48	22	20	48	48
IN	60	72	30	33	60	68	TN	47	58	23	27	47	53
IA	72	74	36	35	76	78	TX	56	69	24	26	53	59
KY	51	60	23	26	51	56	UT	66	69	30	30	67	70
LA	39	44	15	15	37	38	VT	NA	67	NA	NA	NA	72
ME	75	75	36	41	72	77	VA	59	62	31	26	57	58
MD	55	59	24	26	54	57	WA	NA	67	NA	27	NA	67
MA	68	71	36	36	63	68	WV	52	63	25	26	47	54
MI	61	68	NA	NA	58	67	WI	71	74	33	35	71	75
MN	71	76	31	33	74	75	WY	69	64	33	32	67	68
MS	36	42	14	18	33	36	U.S. Avg.	57	62	27	28	56	61
MO	62	66	30	31	62	64							

Revenues[1] for Public Elementary and Secondary Schools, by Source, 1996-97

Source: National Education Association

(estimated; in thousands)

State	Total	Federal Amount	%	State Amount	%	Local and intermediate Amount	%
U.S.	$299,995,450	$20,612,840	6.9	$146,679,858	48.9	$132,702,752	44.2
Alabama	3,694,147*	347,664*	9.4*	2,550,628*	69.0*	795,855*	21.5*
Alaska	1,142,869*	143,562*	12.6*	726,473*	63.6*	272,834*	23.9*
Arizona.	4,083,066*	350,081*	8.6*	1,706,128	41.8*	2,026,857*	49.6*
Arkansas.	2,267,043	1,88,709*	8.3*	1,495,045	65.9*	583,289*	25.7*
California.	34,367,662	2,909,463	8.5	20,832,065	60.6	10,626,134	30.9
Colorado	4,021,795*	225,628*	5.6*	1,773,781*	44.1*	2,022,386*	50.3*
Connecticut	4,837,454*	215,230*	4.4*	1,865,517*	38.6*	2,756,707*	57.0*
Delaware	889,807	63,210	7.1	598,642	67.3	277,955	25.6
District of Columbia	495,824*	70,380*	14.2*	—	—	425,444*	85.8*
Florida	13,896,990	972,473	7.0	6,759,952	48.6	6,164,565	44.4
Georgia.	8,114,570*	559,623	6.9*	4,230,891*	52.1*	3,324,056	41.0*
Hawaii	1,317,337	106,412	8.1	1,185,388	90.0	25,537	1.9
Idaho	1,240,328*	84,899	6.8*	791,946*	63.8*	363,483*	29.3*
Illinois.	12,997,255*	972,772*	7.5*	3,512,766*	27.0*	8,511,717*	65.5*
Indiana	6,850,695	341,153	5.0	3,603,266	52.6	2,906,276	42.4
Iowa.	3,115,526	154,247	5.0	1,668,900	53.6	1,292,379	41.5
Kansas	3,000,805	163,782	5.5	1,730,473	57.7	1,106,550	36.9
Kentucky	3,725,827*	331,937*	8.9*	2,480,230*	66.6*	913,660*	24.5*
Louisiana.	4,037,664*	512,689*	12.7*	2,037,510*	50.5*	1,487,465	36.8*
Maine.	1,422,500	97,200	6.8	665,954	46.8	659,346	46.4
Maryland	5,782,642	323,866	5.6	2,314,652	40.0	3,144,124	54.4
Massachusetts	7,145,072*	382,652*	5.4*	2,570,881*	36.0*	4,191,539*	58.7*
Michigan	12,805,391*	848,225*	6.6*	8,684,901*	67.8*	3,727,805*	25.6*
Minnesota	5,913,284*	279,774*	4.7*	3,321,593*	56.2*	2,311,917*	39.1*
Mississippi	2,400,183*	324,740*	13.5*	1,384,323	57.7	691,120*	28.8*
Missouri	5,439,929*	339,406*	6.2*	2,128,046*	39.1*	2,972,477*	54.6*
Montana	1,004,021	96,872	9.6	470,835	46.9	436,314	43.5
Nebraska.	1,607,933	68,294	4.2	618,105	38.4	921,534	57.3
Nevada.	1,631,609	70,537	4.3	547,023	33.5	1,014,049	62.2
New Hampshire.	1,303,780*	39,306*	3.0*	86,525*	6.6*	1,177,949*	90.3*
New Jersey	12,500,110*	456,546*	3.7*	4,915,719*	39.3*	7,127,845*	57.0*
New Mexico	2,086,351*	204,381*	9.8*	1,424,216*	68.3*	457,754*	21.9*
New York	26,559,743	1,587,000	6.0*	10,405,000	39.2	14,567,743	54.8
North Carolina.	6,389,731*	573,075*	9.0	4,266,007*	66.8*	1,550,649*	24.3*
North Dakota	639,315	75,142	11.8	271,063	42.4	293,110	45.8
Ohio.	11,948,477	710,728	5.9	4,929,344	41.3	6,308,405	52.8
Oklahoma	3,007,275	269,000	8.9	1,880,000	62.5	858,275	28.5
Oregon	3,375,900	240,700	7.1	1,871,300	55.4	1,263,900	37.4
Pennsylvania	14,775,401*	824,199*	5.6*	6,113,888*	41.4*	7,837,314*	53.0*
Rhode Island	1,183,561*	42,929*	3.6*	493,615*	41.7*	647,017*	54.7*
South Carolina.	3,908,700	321,200	8.2	1,796,500	46.0	1,791,000	45.8
South Dakota	747,471	73,597	9.8	238,874	32.0	435,000	58.2
Tennessee.	4,239,950	356,694	8.4	2,152,517	50.8	1,730,739	40.8
Texas.	22,869,794	1,842,651	8.1	9,970,988	43.6	11,056,155	48.3
Utah.	2,145,000	134,000	6.2	1,348,000	62.8	663,000	30.9
Vermont	788,065*	39,517*	5.0*	227,629*	28.9*	520,919*	66.1*
Virginia	6,384,388*	363,391*	5.7*	2,315,018*	36.3*	3,705,979	58.0*
Washington	6,476,816	405,954	6.3	4,446,743	68.7	1,624,119	25.1
West Virginia	2,080,634	174,414	8.4	1,305,844	62.8	600,376	28.9
Wisconsin	6,682,088	292,936*	4.4*	3,642,522	54.5	2,746,630	41.1
Wyoming.	653,132	40,000	6.1	322,632	49.4	290,500	44.5

* Indicates NEA estimate. (1) Included as revenue receipts are all appropriations from general funds of federal, state, county, and local governments; receipts from taxes levied for school purposes; income from permanent school funds and endowments; and income from leases of school lands and miscellaneous sources (interest on bank deposits, tuition, gifts, school lunch charges, etc.).

Public High School Graduation Rates, 1994-95

Source: National Center for Education Statistics, U.S. Dept. of Education

	Grad. rate (%)[1]	Rank		Grad. rate (%)[1]	Rank		Grad. rate (%)[1]	Rank
U.S.	68.6		Kentucky.	70.3	31	North Dakota.	86.8	2T
Alabama	60.2	44	Louisiana	58.7	49	Ohio	74.6	22
Alaska	68.2	35	Maine	72.3	29	Oklahoma	75.3	18
Arizona	63.2	42	Maryland	73.9	23	Oregon	68.9	33T
Arkansas	73.1	25T	Massachusetts . . .	76.0	15	Pennsylvania.	77.3	14
California	64.0	39T	Michigan	68.9	33T	Rhode Island.	72.6	28
Colorado	73.1	25T	Minnesota	86.8	2T	South Carolina. . . .	55.1	51
Connecticut	75.0	19T	Mississippi	60.1	45T	South Dakota	86.6	4
Delaware	64.7	38	Missouri	72.7	27	Tennessee	63.8	41
District of Columbia	60.1	45T	Montana	85.6	5	Texas	59.7	47
Florida	59.1	48	Nebraska	84.3	7	Utah	79.1	11
Georgia	56.6	50	Nevada.	65.1	37	Vermont	89.4	1
Hawaii	75.0	19T	New Hampshire. . .	74.9	21	Virginia	71.9	30
Idaho	79.5	10	New Jersey	83.5	8	Washington.	73.4	24
Illinois	75.5	16	New Mexico	64.0	39T	West Virginia	75.4	17
Indiana	70.1	32	New York	61.8	43	Wisconsin	81.7	9
Iowa	85.1	6	North Carolina	65.5	36	Wyoming.	78.2	12
Kansas	77.4	13						

Note: T=Tied in rank with one or more states. (1) Graduates as percentage of fall 1991 9th-grade enrollment.

Institutions of Higher Education–Charges, 1969-70 to 1997-98

Source: National Center for Education Statistics, U.S. Dept. of Education; The College Board

Figures for 1969-70 are average charges for full-time resident degree-credit students; figures for later years are average charges per full-time equivalent student. Room and board are based on full-time students. These figures are enrollment-weighted, according to the number of full-time-equivalent undergraduates, and thus vary from averages given elsewhere.

	Tuition and required fees			Board rates (7-day basis)[1]			Dormitory charges		
	All institutions	2-yr	4-yr	All institutions	2-yr	4-yr	All institutions	2-yr	4-yr
Public (in-state)									
1969-70	$323	$178	$427	$511	$465	$540	$369	$ 308	$395
1979-80	583	355	840	867	894	898	715	572	749
1989-90	1,356	756	2,035	1,635	1,581	1,728	1,513	962	1,561
1990-91	1,454	824	2,159	1,691	1,594	1,767	1,612	1,050	1,658
1991-92	1,624	937	2,410	1,780	1,612	1,852	1,731	1,074	1,789
1992-93	1,782	1,025	2,349	1,841	1,668	1,854	1,756	1,106	1,816
1993-94	1,942	1,125	2,537	1,880	1,681	1,895	1,873	1,190	1,934
1994-95	2,057	1,192	2,681	1,949	1,712	1,967	1,959	1,232	2,023
1995-96[2]	NA	1,330	2,811	NA	—[3]	3,932[4]	NA	—[4]	—[4]
1996-97[2]	NA	1,465	2,975	NA	—[3]	4,167[4]	NA	—[4]	—[4]
1997-98[2]	NA	1,501	3,111	NA	—[3]	4,361[4]	NA	—[4]	—[4]
Private									
1969-70	1,533	1,034	1,809	561	546	608	436	413	503
1979-80	3,130	2,062	3,811	955	924	1,078	827	769	999
1989-90	8,147	5,196	10,348	1,948	1,811	2,339	1,923	1,663	2,411
1990-91	8,772	5,570	11,379	2,074	1,989	2,470	2,063	1,744	2,654
1991-92	9,434	5,752	12,192	2,252	2,090	2,727	2,221	1,789	2,860
1992-93	9,942	6,059	10,294	2,344	1,875	2,354	2,348	1,970	2,362
1993-94	10,572	6,370	10,952	2,434	1,970	2,445	2,490	2,067	2,506
1994-95	11,111	6,914	11,481	2,509	2,023	2,520	2,587	2,233	2,601
1995-96[2]	NA	6,339	12,216	NA	4,063[4]	5,166[4]	NA	—[4]	—[4]
1996-97[2]	NA	6,613	12,994	NA	4,346[4]	5,363[4]	NA	—[4]	—[4]
1997-98[2]	NA	6,855	13,664	NA	4,543[4]	5,549[4]	NA	—[4]	—[4]

(1) Data for 1989-90 through 1993-94 reflect 20 meals per week rather than 7 days per week. (2) 1995-96 through 1997-98 figures supplied by the College Board; earlier figures from National Center for Educational Statistics. (3) Sample too small to provide meaningful information. (4) Board and dormitory figures for 1995-96 through 1997-98 are combined. NA = not available.

MILLENNIUM FACT BOX

U.S. Higher Education Trends

During the 20th century, enrollments in institutions of higher education rose rapidly, as did the proportion of women attending college. By the year 2000 the proportion of female college graduates was expected to be 56%, compared with 19% in 1900.

Year	1889-90	1899-1900	1909-10	1919-20	1929-30	1939-40
Total Institutions	998	977	951	1,041	1,409	1,708
Total Fall Enrollment	156,756	237,592	355,213	597,880	1,100,737	1,494,203
Total Bachelor's Degrees	15,539	27,410	37,199	48,622	122,484	186,500
Men	12,857	22,173	28,762	31,980	73,615	109,546
Women	2,682	5,237	8,437	16,642	48,869	76,954

Year	1949-50	1959-60	1969-70	1979-80	1989-90	1999-2000[1]
Total Institutions	1,851	2,008	2,525	3,152	3,535	3,800[2]
Total Fall Enrollment	2,659,021	3,639,847	8,004,660	11,569,899	13,538,560	14,800,000
Total Bachelor's Degrees	432,058	392,440	792,656	929,417	1,051,344	1,138,000
Men	328,841	254,063	451,380	473,611	491,696	500,000
Women	103,217	138,377	341,276	455,806	559,648	637,000

(1) Enrollment and bachelor's degree figures are U.S. Dept. of Education projections; totals do not add because of rounding. (2) Estimated.

American College Testing (ACT) Program Mean Scores and Characteristics of College-Bound Students, 1988-97

Source: The American College Testing Program

(for school year ending in year shown)

	Unit[1]	1988[2]	1989[2]	1990[2]	1991[2]	1992[2]	1993[2]	1994[2]	1995[2]	1996[2]	1997[2]
Composite Scores . . . Points. . . .		20.8	20.6	20.6	20.6	20.6	20.7	20.8	20.8	20.9	21.0
Male . . . . Points		19.6	19.3	21.0	20.9	20.9	21.0	20.9	21.0	21.0	21.1
Female . . . . Points		18.1	18.0	20.3	20.4	20.5	20.5	20.7	20.7	20.8	20.8
English Score . . . . . . Points. . . .		18.5	18.4	20.5	20.3	20.2	20.3	20.3	20.2	20.3	20.3
Male . . . . Points		18.0	17.8	20.1	19.8	19.8	19.8	19.8	19.8	19.8	19.9
Female . . . . Points		19.0	18.9	20.9	20.7	20.6	20.6	20.7	20.6	20.7	20.7
Math Score. . . . . Points. . . .		17.2	17.1	19.9	20.0	20.0	20.1	20.2	20.2	20.2	20.6
Male . . . . Points		18.4	18.3	20.7	20.6	20.7	20.8	20.8	20.9	20.9	21.3
Female . . . . Points		16.1	16.1	19.3	19.4	19.5	19.6	19.6	19.7	19.7	20.1
Participants											
Total Number . . . . 1,000.		842	855	817	796	832	875	892	945	925	959
Male . . . . Percent . . .		46	46	46	45	45	45	45	44	44	44
White . . . . Percent . . .		81	80	79	79	79	79	79	80	79	79
Black. . . . . Percent . . .		9	9	9	9	9	9	9	9	9	9
Composite Scores											
27 or above . . . . Percent . . .		14	14	12	11	12	12	13	13	13	10
18 or below . . . . . . Percent . . .		31	32	35	35	35	35	34	34	34	26

(1) Minimum point score, 1; maximum score, 36. Test scores and characteristics of college-bound students are based on the performance of all ACT-tested students who graduated in the spring of a given school year and who took the ACT Assessment during junior or senior year of high school. (2) Beginning with the Oct. 1989 test (1990 scores), an entirely new ACT Assessment was introduced. The Enhanced ACT Assessment increases the emphasis on rhetorical skills in the measurement of writing proficiency, increases the number of advanced math items, and includes a new reading test that features inferential and reasoning skills and a test designed to measure science reasoning. The Enhanced ACT also provides subscores in English, mathematics, and reading. The composite scores for 1988-89 have been converted to provide a basis of comparison; all 1990-97 scores are for the Enhanced ACT. It is not possible to compare directly these data and data from earlier years.

Recentering of SAT I Scores

Source: The College Board

The SAT I is a 3-hour test of both verbal and mathematical abilities which, like the ACT test, is used for evaluating applicants for admission to colleges and universities. In 1995, the College Board, which creates and administers the SAT I, as well as other tests such as the SAT II achievement tests in individual subjects, recentered the scoring scale for the SAT I. It did so by reestablishing the original mean score of 500 on the 200-800 scale. This scale had not been adjusted since 1941, when it reflected only the norm of some 10,000 students, frequently from private secondary schools and applying mostly to the nation's most selective private colleges and universities. Over the years, the mean score had shifted below 500 as a larger number of students began taking the test, and verbal and math scores had ceased to be comparable. Now the scores represent a more diverse college-bound population that encompasses approximately 2 million students nationwide.

The rank order of scores, expressed as percentiles, has not been affected by the recentering. Students' relative standing in respect to one another and the difficulty level of the test remain unchanged, and now a direct comparison can be drawn between the verbal test and the math test. However, numerical scores are not directly comparable to scores originally reported in years before the recentering. The scores listed in the following tables concerning the SATs have been recentered and, therefore, are not the actual scores that were reported for the years shown.

To obtain a free score converter, while supplies last, individuals can write to SAT Score Converter, 45 Columbus Ave., New York, NY 10023. Further information on the SAT can be obtained at the College Board web site—http://www.collegeboard.org

SAT Mean Verbal and Math Scores of College-Bound Seniors, 1987-97[1]

Source: The College Board

(Recentered scale)

	Unit	1987	1988	1989	1990	1991	1992	1993	1994	1995	1996	1997
Verbal Scores	Points	507	505	504	500	499	500	500	499	504	505	505
Male	Points	512	512	510	505	503	504	504	501	505	507	507
Female	Points	502	499	498	496	495	496	497	497	502	503	503
Math Scores.	Points	501	501	502	501	500	501	503	504	506	508	511
Male	Points	523	521	523	521	520	521	524	523	525	527	530
Female	Points	481	483	482	483	482	484	484	487	490	492	494

(1) For 1987-95, individual student scores were converted to the recentered score, and then the mean was recomputed. For 1996 and 1997, most students received scores on the recentered scale. (Any score on the original scale was converted to the recentered score prior to computing the mean.)

SAT Mean Scores by State, 1987 and 1994-97

Source: The College Board

(Recentered scale)

	1987		1994		1995		1996		1997		% Grads. Taking
	Verbal	Math	Verbal	Math	Verbal	Math	Verbal	Math	Verbal	Math	SAT[1]
Alabama	553	535	556	547	565	555	565	558	561	555	8
Alaska	521	504	510	502	521	513	521	513	520	517	48
Arizona	539	526	519	519	524	520	525	521	523	522	29
Arkansas	556	540	552	537	556	542	566	550	567	558	6
California	500	507	489	506	492	509	495	511	496	514	45
Colorado	542	535	532	534	538	538	536	538	536	539	30
Connecticut	515	499	502	497	507	502	507	504	509	507	79
Delaware	517	496	505	491	505	494	508	495	505	498	65
Dist. of Columbia	482	462	479	468	485	471	489	473	490	475	60
Florida	501	497	490	492	497	496	498	496	499	499	50
Georgia	478	470	474	474	483	477	484	477	486	481	63
Hawaii	481	502	477	504	483	507	485	510	483	512	54
Idaho	548	524	537	529	544	532	543	536	544	539	15
Illinois	539	540	553	562	563	574	564	575	562	578	14
Indiana	492	487	488	493	492	494	494	494	494	497	57
Iowa	588	586	580	586	589	595	590	600	589	601	5
Kansas	572	562	568	565	576	571	579	571	578	575	9
Kentucky	554	538	549	543	552	542	549	544	548	546	12
Louisiana	548	530	556	549	560	552	559	550	560	553	10
Maine	510	493	497	490	504	497	504	498	507	504	67
Maryland	513	502	505	503	506	503	507	504	507	507	64
Massachusetts	511	500	502	500	505	502	507	504	508	508	80
Michigan	534	533	547	554	559	565	557	565	557	566	11
Minnesota	548	549	569	576	580	591	582	593	582	592	9
Mississippi	561	540	559	546	572	557	569	557	567	551	4
Missouri	549	538	560	554	569	566	570	569	567	568	9
Montana	555	548	540	542	549	553	546	547	545	548	22
Nebraska	563	562	557	559	568	570	567	568	562	564	9
Nevada	516	508	506	508	511	508	508	507	508	509	32
New Hampshire	527	512	515	510	520	515	520	514	521	518	70
New Jersey	502	493	494	500	496	503	498	505	497	508	69
New Mexico	559	544	550	546	559	549	554	548	554	545	12
New York	501	495	492	497	495	498	497	499	495	502	74
North Carolina	477	468	482	482	488	482	490	486	490	488	59
North Dakota	583	573	570	573	587	602	596	599	588	595	5
Ohio	532	521	533	531	536	535	536	535	535	536	25
Oklahoma	560	539	557	554	565	553	566	557	568	560	8
Oregon	521	509	513	515	525	522	523	521	525	524	50
Pennsylvania	505	491	494	489	496	489	498	492	498	495	72
Rhode Island	509	492	496	488	502	490	501	491	499	493	70
South Carolina	474	466	473	473	478	473	480	474	479	474	56
South Dakota	587	577	558	563	579	576	574	566	574	570	4
Tennessee	563	543	562	553	571	560	563	552	564	556	13
Texas	493	486	489	500	495	501	495	500	494	501	49
Utah	577	557	582	573	585	576	583	575	576	570	4
Vermont	518	500	504	498	506	499	506	500	508	502	69
Virginia	511	499	501	495	504	494	507	496	506	497	69
Washington	532	519	511	512	519	517	519	519	523	523	46
West Virginia	534	519	516	507	525	509	526	506	524	508	18
Wisconsin	550	551	562	572	574	585	577	586	576	590	7
Wyoming	557	551	535	541	551	544	544	544	543	543	12
National Average	**507**	**501**	**499**	**504**	**504**	**506**	**505**	**508**	**505**	**511**	**42**

(1) Based on number of high school graduates in 1997, as projected by the Western Interstate Commission for Higher Education, and number of students in the class of 1997 who took the SAT. **Note:** The College Board states that comparing states or ranking them on the basis of SAT scores alone is invalid, and the College Board strongly discourages doing so.

Salaries of College Professors, 1996-97

Source: American Association of University Professors

	Men	Type of institution		Women	Type of institution	
Academic rank	Public	Private/ Independent	Church-related	Public	Private/ Independent	Church-related
Doctoral level						
Professor	$73,140	$93,293	$78,667	$66,117	$84,574	$73,836
Associate	53,100	61,345	56,956	49,661	58,039	53,184
Assistant	44,961	52,756	46,892	41,921	48,891	44,004
Master's level						
Professor	60,947	65,330	63,913	58,394	61,609	57,284
Associate	49,383	50,692	50,005	46,943	48,435	46,577
Assistant	41,058	41,342	40,656	39,185	39,743	38,756
General 4-year						
Professor	55,120	63,060	49,674	52,721	58,537	46,637
Associate	45,451	47,548	41,428	43,977	45,706	39,542
Assistant	38,251	38,696	34,622	36,723	38,098	33,843
2-year						
Professor	54,103	44,836	36,502	50,378	39,880	32,235
Associate	45,149	39,455	31,606	42,407	34,458	28,304
Assistant	39,088	34,717	26,710	37,162	31,693	25,507

Top 50 Public Libraries in the U.S. and Canada

Source: Public Library Data Service, Statistical Report 1997, Public Library Association

Ranked at end of the 1996 fiscal year by population served.

Population served	Library name and location	No. of branches[1]	No. of holdings	Circulation	Annual acquisition expenditures
3,593,729	Los Angeles Public Library (CA)	66	5,254,608	9,663,530	$7,615,185
3,324,500	Los Angeles Public Library, County of (CA)	85	6,943,249	14,152,507	3,592,585
3,070,302	New York Public Library, The Branch Libraries (NY)	84	11,473,683	11,138,629	6,702,000
2,783,726	Chicago Public Library (IL)	79	9,561,679	7,839,041	11,000,000
2,300,664	Brooklyn Public Library (NY)	59	6,386,447	10,178,332	7,182,920
1,950,000	Queens Borough Public Library (NY)	62	8,640,540	15,280,937	7,791,000
1,794,783	Houston Public Library (TX)	34	5,829,327	5,906,886	5,839,133
1,790,900	Phoenix Public Library (AZ)	11	1,764,965	5,686,766	2,900,507
1,684,608	Miami-Dade Public Library System (FL)	30	3,454,995	10,667,327	5,495,836
1,585,577	Free Library of Philadelphia (PA)	52	7,983,088	6,530,277	5,148,923
1,377,922	Broward County Library System (FL)	32	1,985,088	6,970,894	4,377,058
1,336,449	Carnegie Library of Pittsburgh (PA)	18	6,664,198	3,029,038	1,338,066
1,296,731	San Antonio Public Library (TX)	18	1,660,470	3,450,299	2,165,277
1,261,999	Orange County Public Library (CA)	27	2,507,128	5,658,762	4,787,410
1,213,000	San Diego Public Library (CA)	32	2,473,994	6,370,488	2,007,214
1,171,600	Hawaii State Public Library System (HI)	49	3,517,989	8,196,376	2,750,074
1,108,361	Sacramento Public Library (CA)	22	1,343,224	3,587,046	1,745,766
1,090,600	Riverside City and County Public Library (CA)	27	1,631,997	3,553,463	346,534
1,047,265	Harris County Public Library (TX)	25	2,061,653	4,753,399	1,567,060
1,030,678	Montréal, Bibliothèque de (Quebec)	24	2,509,733	5,133,370	2,719,051
1,030,150	Dallas Public Library (TX)	22	2,722,736	4,077,655	2,131,084
1,027,974	Detroit Public Library (MI)	25	2,768,782	1,594,963	2,822,573
1,012,620	King County Library System (WA)	39	NA	12,610,610	5,388,462
1,003,464	Providence Public Library (RI)	9	1,189,815	686,093	558,818
973,000	San Bernardino County Library (CA)	27	1,091,335	2,375,144	488,000
968,532	Buffalo & Erie County Public Library (NY)	53	NA	8,827,234	2,982,516
914,623	San Diego County Library (CA)	32	1,099,557	2,817,907	911,000
906,300	Fairfax County Public Library (VA)	23	2,115,076	9,224,102	2,964,725
892,874	Tampa-Hillsborough County Public Library (FL)	17	2,163,613	3,436,618	3,003,634
877,970	Las Vegas Clark County Library District (NV)	23	1,931,904	5,013,000	4,089,520
866,228	Cincinnati & Hamilton County, Public Library of (OH)	41	8,485,820	12,564,004	6,140,060
856,989	San Jose Public Library System (CA)	17	1,317,535	5,000,199	2,456,117
844,847	Memphis & Shelby County Public Libraries (TN)	21	1,714,196	3,803,242	1,870,404
843,000	St. Louis County Library (MO)	17	2,907,108	9,037,668	3,400,872
819,000	Montgomey County Dept. of Public Libraries (MD)	22	2,534,723	9,105,295	4,481,580
779,900	Contra Costa County Library (Pleasant Hill, CA)	22	1,063,042	3,795,557	1,318,794
770,684	Indianapolis-Marion County Public Library (IN)	21	1,951,119	8,275,441	4,374,349
767,482	Jacksonville Public Libraries (FL)	17	2,687,930	3,693,283	1,985,567
767,059	Calgary Public Library (Alberta)	14	2,126,171	10,693,283	2,814,907
766,394	Atlanta-Fulton Public Library (GA)	32	2,045,696	2,444,531	2,188,149
764,854	Tucson-Pima Library (AZ)	18	1,144,000	5,158,354	1,992,600
764,053	Prince George's County Memorial Library System (MD)	21	1,813,310	4,626,353	2,766,181
744,506	Orange County Library System (FL)	11	1,739,300	4,622,091	2,505,177
743,640	Columbus Metropolitan Library (OH)	19	2,384,752	11,862,449	6,199,775
724,200	San Francisco Public Library (CA)	26	2,308,901	4,3450,72	5,071,856
717,500	Enoch Pratt Free Library (Baltimore, MD)	28	2,705,320	1,270,239	2,254,885
717,400	Macomb County Library (MI)	0	139,929	250,495	315,575
713,968	Rochester Public Library (NY)	10	1,270,991	1,553,131	957,000
705,138	Baltimore County Public Library (MD)	15	1,777,905	10,339,570	3,730,481
697,742	Hennepin County Library (MN)	26	2,083,637	10,309,551	4,444,317

(1) Main branch not included. NA= not available.

Number of Public Libraries and Operating Income, by State

Source: U.S. Dept. of Education; National Center for Education Statistics

(data for fiscal year 1994 unless otherwise indicated; operating income in thousands)

State	No. of libraries	Operating income[1]	State	No. of libraries	Operating income[1]	State	No. of libraries	Operating income[1]
Alabama	207	$46,080	Kentucky	116	$44,137	Ohio	250	$410,086
Alaska	87	18,473	Louisiana	65	64,639	Oklahoma	112	35,203
Arizona	39	69,868	Maine	232	18,924[2]	Oregon	124	62,828
Arkansas	35	22,369	Maryland	24	123,219	Pennsylvania	445	162,847[2]
California	170	565,539	Massachusetts	373	138,451	Rhode Island	51	19,486
Colorado	120	88,067	Michigan	380	179,172[2]	S. Carolina	40	46,184
Connecticut	194	91,112	Minnesota	132	107,275	S. Dakota	113	10,553
Delaware	29	9,086	Mississippi	47	23,914	Tennessee	140	53,983
District of Columbia	1	22,339	Missouri	147	101,283	Texas	496	186,600[2]
Florida	97	232,344	Montana	82	11,352	Utah	69	34,790
Georgia	54	100,850	Nebraska	269	24,049[2]	Vermont	200	8,460[2]
Hawaii	1	24,855	Nevada	23	57,480	Virginia	90	129,189
Idaho	107	15,149	New Hampshire	229	22,032	Washington	69	150,275
Illinois	606	357,589	New Jersey	309	241,644	W. Virginia	97	17,658
Indiana	238	155,861	New Mexico	73	20,231	Wisconsin	381	114,160
Iowa	518	49,091	New York	741	607,897	Wyoming	23	10,776
Kansas	324	49,744	N. Carolina	74	96,542	U.S. Total	8,921	$5,260,087
			N. Dakota	78	6,352			

(1) Income represents total operating income and/or total income from all sources, as reported by libraries. Some totals may be underestimated because of nonresponse. (2) These libraries reported data for fiscal year 1993.

American Colleges and Universities
General Information for the 1996–97 Academic Year
Source: Peterson's, Copyright 1997

These listings include only accredited undergraduate degree-granting institutions in the United States and U.S. territories that have a total institutional enrollment of 1,000 or more. Four-year colleges (those that award a bachelor's as their highest undergraduate degree) are listed first, followed by two-year colleges (those that award an associate as their highest or primary undergraduate degree). Data reported only for institutions that provided updated information on Peterson's Annual Survey of Undergraduate Institutions for the 1996–97 academic year.

All institutions are coeducational except those where the zip code is directly followed by: (1)–men only, (2)–primarily men, (3)–women only, (4)–primarily women.

Year is that of founding.

Governing official is the chief executive officer.

Institutional control: 1–independent (nonprofit), 2–independent-religious, 3–proprietary (profit making), 4–federal, 5–state, 6–commonwealth (Puerto Rico), 7–territory (U.S. territories), 8–county, 9–district, 10–city, 11–state and local, 12–state related.

Highest degree offered: B–bachelor's, M–master's, F–first professional, D–doctorate.

Enrollment is the total number of matriculated undergraduate and (if applicable) graduate students.

Faculty is the total number of faculty members teaching undergraduate courses and (if available) graduate courses.

Any data not reported are indicated as NR.

Four-Year Colleges

Name, address	Year	Governing official, control, and highest degree offered		Enroll-ment	Faculty
Abilene Christian U, Abilene, TX 79699-9100	1906	Dr. Royce Money	2-D	4,397	278
Acad of Art Coll, San Francisco, CA 94105-3410	1929	Ms. Elisa Stephens	3-M	4,568	493
Adams State Coll, Alamosa, CO 81102	1921	Dr. J. Thomas Gilmore	5-M	2,444	159
Adelphi U, Garden City, NY 11530	1896	Dr. James A. Norton	1-D	5,969	549
Adrian Coll, Adrian, MI 49221-2575	1859	Dr. Stanley P. Caine	2-B	1,049	92
Alabama A&M U, Normal, AL 35762-1357	1875	Dr. John T. Gibson	5-D	5,263	366
Alabama State U, Montgomery, AL 36101-0271	1867	Dr. William H. Harris	5-M	5,554	328
Albany State U, Albany, GA 31705-2717	1903	Dr. Portia Shields	5-M	3,150	173
Albertus Magnus Coll, New Haven, CT 06511-1189	1925	Dr. Julia M. McNamara	2-M	1,177	61
Albion Coll, Albion, MI 49224-1831	1835	Dr. Melvin L. Vulgamore	2-B	1,527	118
Albright Coll, Reading, PA 19612-5234	1856	Dr. Ellen S. Hurwitz	2-B	1,193	109
Alcorn State U, Lorman, MS 39096-9402	1871	Dr. Clinton Bristow, Jr.	5-M	3,073	211
Alfred U, Alfred, NY 14802-1205	1836	Dr. Edward G. Coll, Jr.	1-D	2,397	200
Allegheny Coll, Meadville, PA 16335	1815	Dr. Richard J. Cook	2-B	1,846	195
Allegheny U of the Health Sciences, Philadelphia, PA 19102-1192	1848	Mr. Sherif S. Abdelhak	1-D	3,154	1,360
Allentown Coll of St Francis de Sales, Center Valley, PA 18034-9568	1962	Rev. Daniel Gambet, OSFS	2-M	2,158	93
Alma Coll, Alma, MI 48801-1599	1886	Dr. Alan J. Stone	2-B	1,363	147
Alvernia Coll, Reading, PA 19607-1799	1958	Dr. Laurence W. Mazzeno, III	2-B	1,347	112
Alverno Coll, Milwaukee, WI 53234-3922 (3)	1887	Sr. Joel Read	2-M	2,191	197
Amber U, Garland, TX 75041-5595	1971	Dr. Douglas W. Warner	2-M	1,610	65
American International Coll, Springfield, MA 01109-3189	1885	Dr. Harry J. Courniotes	1-D	1,986	93
American Military U, Manassas Park, VA 20111	1991	Mr. James P. Etter	3-M	1,000	130
American U, Washington, DC 20016-8001	1893	Dr. Benjamin Ladner	2-D	11,285	976
American U of Puerto Rico, Bayamón, PR 00960-2037	1963	Mr. Juan B. Nazario-Negron	1-B	3,110	235
Amherst Coll, Amherst, MA 01002	1821	Dr. Tom Gerety	1-B	1,607	187
Anderson U, Anderson, IN 46012-3495	1917	Dr. James L. Edwards	2-D	2,136	197
Andrews U, Berrien Springs, MI 49104	1874	Dr. Niels-Erik Andreasen	2-D	3,133	328
Angelo State U, San Angelo, TX 76909	1928	Dr. E. James Hindman	5-M	6,200	250
Anna Maria Coll, Paxton, MA 01612	1946	Dr. Bernard S. Parker	2-M	1,927	85
Appalachian State U, Boone, NC 28608	1899	Dr. Francis T. Borkowski	5-D	11,909	763
Aquinas Coll, Grand Rapids, MI 49506-1799	1886	Mr. R. Paul Nelson	2-M	2,385	173
Arizona State U, Tempe, AZ 85287-2203	1885	Dr. Lattie F. Coor	5-D	38,664	1,913
Arizona State U West, Phoenix, AZ 85069-7100	1984	Dr. Elaine P. Maimon	5-M	3,898	301
Arkansas State U, State University, AR 72467	1909	Dr. Leslie Wyatt	5-D	9,828	481
Arkansas Tech U, Russellville, AR 72801-2222	1909	Dr. Robert C. Brown	5-M	4,490	275
Armstrong Atlantic State U, Savannah, GA 31419-1997	1935	Dr. Robert A. Burnett	5-M	5,617	349
Art Ctr Coll of Design, Pasadena, CA 91103-1999	1930	Mr. David R. Brown	1-M	1,477	427
Asbury Coll, Wilmore, KY 40390-1198	1890	Dr. David J. Gyertson	2-B	1,167	115
Ashland U, Ashland, OH 44805-3702	1878	Dr. G. William Benz	2-M	5,733	213
Assumption Coll, Worcester, MA 01615-0005	1904	Dr. Joseph H. Hagan	2-M	2,596	211
Athens State Coll, Athens, AL 35611-1902	1822	Dr. Jerry F. Bartlett	5-B	2,800	135
Auburn U, Auburn University, AL 36849-0001	1856	Dr. William V. Muse	5-D	21,778	1,260
Auburn U at Montgomery, Montgomery, AL 36124-4023	1967	Dr. Roy H. Saigo	5-M	5,645	364
Audrey Cohen Coll, New York, NY 10013-1919	1964	Ms. Alída Mesrop	1-M	1,180	92
Augsburg Coll, Minneapolis, MN 55454-1351	1869	Dr. Charles S. Anderson	2-M	2,862	325
Augustana Coll, Rock Island, IL 61201-2296	1860	Dr. Thomas Tredway	2-B	2,214	181
Augustana Coll, Sioux Falls, SD 57197	1860	Dr. Ralph H. Wagoner	2-M	1,750	159
Augusta Coll, Augusta, GA 30904-2200	1925	Dr. William A. Bloodworth, Jr.	5-M	5,561	275
Aurora U, Aurora, IL 60506-4892	1893	Dr. Thomas H. Zarle	1-M	2,016	240
Austin Coll, Sherman, TX 75090-4440	1849	Dr. Oscar C. Page	2-M	1,149	98
Austin Peay State U, Clarksville, TN 37044-0001	1927	Dr. Sal D. Rinella	5-M	8,187	486
Averett Coll, Danville, VA 24541-3692	1859	Dr. Frank R. Campbell	2-M	2,540	249
Avila Coll, Kansas City, MO 64145-1698	1916	Dr. Larry Kramer	2-M	1,275	142
Azusa Pacific U, Azusa, CA 91702-7000	1899	Dr. Richard E. Felix	2-D	4,547	431
Babson Coll, Babson Park, MA 02157-0310	1919	Mr. Leo I. Higdon, Jr.	1-M	3,270	189
Baker Coll of Flint, Flint, MI 48507-5508	1911	Dr. Julianne T. Princinsky	1-B	4,039	156
Baker Coll of Mount Clemens, Clinton Township, MI 48035-4701	1990	Mr. F. James Cummins	1-B	1,081	64
Baker Coll of Muskegon, Muskegon, MI 49442-3497	1888	Dr. Rick Amidon	1-B	1,711	120
Baker Coll of Owosso, Owosso, MI 48867-4400	1984	Mrs. Denise Bannan	1-B	1,812	109
Baker U, Baldwin City, KS 66006-0065	1858	Dr. Daniel M. Lambert	2-M	2,508	83
Baldwin-Wallace Coll, Berea, OH 44017-2088	1845	Dr. Neal Malicky	2-M	4,621	276
Ball State U, Muncie, IN 47306-1099	1918	Dr. John E. Worthen	5-D	18,594	1,086
Bard Coll, Annandale-on-Hudson, NY 12504	1860	Dr. Leon Botstein	1-M	1,244	151
Barnard Coll, New York, NY 10027-6598 (3)	1889	Dr. Judith R. Shapiro	1-B	2,294	279
Barry U, Miami Shores, FL 33161-6695	1940	Sr. Jeanne O'Laughlin, OP, PhD	2-D	7,016	550

Name, address	Year	Governing official, control, and highest degree offered		Enrollment	Faculty
Barton Coll, Wilson, NC 27893	1902	Dr. James B. Hemby, Jr.	2-B	1,295	80
Baruch Coll of the City U of NY, New York, NY 10010-5585	1919	Dr. Matthew Goldstein	11-D	15,223	770
Bates Coll, Lewiston, ME 04240-6028	1855	Dr. Donald W. Harward	1-B	1,672	174
Bayamón Central U, Bayamón, PR 00960-1725	1970	Rev. Vincent A. M. Van Rooij, OP	2-M	3,144	147
Baylor U, Waco, TX 76798	1845	Dr. Robert B. Sloan, Jr.	2-D	12,391	664
Beaver Coll, Glenside, PA 19038-3295	1853	Dr. Bette E. Landman	2-M	2,567	331
Belhaven Coll, Jackson, MS 39202-1789	1883	Dr. Roger Parrott	2-M	1,256	87
Bellarmine Coll, Louisville, KY 40205-0671	1950	Dr. Joseph J. McGowan, Jr.	2-M	2,180	171
Bellevue U, Bellevue, NE 68005-3098	1965	Dr. John B. Muller	1-M	2,600	93
Belmont U, Nashville, TN 37212-3757	1951	Dr. William E. Troutt	2-M	2,926	350
Beloit Coll, Beloit, WI 53511-5596	1846	Mr. Victor E. Ferrall, Jr.	1-B	1,273	128
Bemidji State U, Bemidji, MN 56601-2699	1919	Dr. M. James Bensen	5-M	4,019	201
Benedict Coll, Columbia, SC 29204	1870	Dr. David H. Swinton	2-B	2,138	142
Benedictine U, Lisle, IL 60532-0900	1887	Dr. William J. Carroll	2-D	2,579	245
Bentley Coll, Waltham, MA 02154-4705	1917	Dr. Joseph M. Cronin	1-M	6,169	360
Berea Coll, Berea, KY 40404	1855	Dr. Larry D. Shinn	1-B	1,524	134
Berklee Coll of Music, Boston, MA 02215-3693	1945	Dr. Lee Eliot Berk	1-B	2,809	293
Berry Coll, Mount Berry, GA 30149-0159	1902	Dr. Gloria M. Shatto	1-M	2,085	126
Bethel Coll, Mishawaka, IN 46545-5591	1947	Dr. Norman Bridges	2-M	1,467	115
Bethel Coll, St Paul, MN 55112-6999	1871	Dr. George K. Brushaber	2-M	2,584	213
Bethune-Cookman Coll, Daytona Beach, FL 32114-3099	1904	Dr. Oswald P. Bronson, Sr.	2-B	2,335	200
Biola U, La Mirada, CA 90639-0001	1908	Dr. Clyde Cook	2-D	3,039	240
Birmingham-Southern Coll, Birmingham, AL 35254	1856	Dr. Neal R. Berte	2-M	1,492	134
Black Hills State U, Spearfish, SD 57799-9500	1883	Dr. Thomas O. Flickema	5-M	2,866	105
Bloomfield Coll, Bloomfield, NJ 07003-9981	1868	Dr. John F. Noonan	2-B	2,054	217
Bloomsburg U of Pennsylvania, Bloomsburg, PA 17815-1905	1839	Dr. Jessica Kozloff	5-M	7,438	395
Bluefield State Coll, Bluefield, WV 24701-2198	1895	Dr. Robert E. Moore	5-B	2,609	162
Bluffton Coll, Bluffton, OH 45817-1196	1899	Dr. Lee Snyder	2-M	1,090	91
Boise State U, Boise, ID 83725-0399	1932	Dr. Charles Ruch	5-D	15,137	849
Boricua Coll, New York, NY 10032-1560	1974	Dr. Victor G. Alicea	1-M	1,052	116
Boston Coll, Chestnut Hill, MA 02167-9991	1863	Rev. William P. Leahy, SJ	2-D	14,830	982
Boston U, Boston, MA 02215	1839	Mr. Jon Westling	1-D	29,664	2,834
Bowdoin Coll, Brunswick, ME 04011-2546	1794	Mr. Robert H. Edwards	1-B	1,581	158
Bowie State U, Bowie, MD 20715	1865	Dr. Nathanael Pollard, Jr.	5-M	5,067	251
Bowling Green State U, Bowling Green, OH 43403	1910	Dr. Sidney A. Ribeau	5-D	17,564	866
Bradley U, Peoria, IL 61625-0002	1897	Dr. John R. Brazil	1-M	5,900	454
Brandeis U, Waltham, MA 02254-9110	1948	Dr. Jehuda Reinharz	1-D	4,219	485
Brenau U, Gainesville, GA 30501-3697 (4)	1878	Dr. John S. Burd	1-M	2,225	230
Brewton-Parker Coll, Mt Vernon, GA 30445-0197	1904	Dr. Y. Lynn Holmes	2-B	1,582	183
Briar Cliff Coll, Sioux City, IA 51104-2100	1930	Sr. Margaret Wick	2-B	1,116	71
Bridgewater Coll, Bridgewater, VA 22812-1599	1880	Dr. Phillip C. Stone	2-B	1,033	95
Bridgewater State Coll, Bridgewater, MA 02325-0001	1840	Dr. Adrian Tinsley	5-M	8,711	449
Brigham Young U, Provo, UT 84602-1001	1875	Dr. Merrill J. Bateman	2-D	30,563	1,691
Brigham Young U–Hawaii Cmps, Laie, Oahu, HI 96762-1294	1955	Dr. Eric B. Shumway	2-B	2,287	149
Brooklyn Coll of the City U of NY, Brooklyn, NY 11210-2889	1930	Dr. Vernon E. Lattin	11-M	13,267	907
Brown U, Providence, RI 02912	1764	Mr. E. Gordon Gee	1-D	7,626	682
Bryant Coll, Smithfield, RI 02917-1287	1863	Mr. Ronald K. Machtley	1-M	3,332	206
Bryn Mawr Coll, Bryn Mawr, PA 19010-2899 (3)	1885	Dr. Nancy J. Vickers	1-D	1,886	232
Bucknell U, Lewisburg, PA 17837	1846	Dr. Wiliam D. Adams	1-M	3,573	280
Buena Vista U, Storm Lake, IA 50588	1891	Dr. Frederick V. Moore	2-M	1,173	102
Butler U, Indianapolis, IN 46208-3485	1855	Dr. Geoffrey Bannister	1-M	3,932	389
Cabrini Coll, Radnor, PA 19087-3698	1957	Dr. Antoinette Iadarola	2-M	2,042	162
Caldwell Coll, Caldwell, NJ 07006-6195	1939	Sr. Patrice Werner	2-M	1,750	108
California Baptist Coll, Riverside, CA 92504-3206	1950	Dr. Ron Ellis	2-M	2,687	117
California Coll for Health Sciences, National City, CA 91950-6605	1978	Mr. Kenneth B. Scheiderman	3-M	9,100	17
California Coll of Arts and Crafts, San Francisco, CA 94107	1907	Mr. Lorne Buchman	1-M	1,056	260
California Inst of Tech, Pasadena, CA 91125-0001	1891	Dr. Thomas E. Everhart	1-D	1,902	353
California Inst of the Arts, Valencia, CA 91355-2340	1961	Dr. Steven D. Lavine	1-M	1,125	279
California Lutheran U, Thousand Oaks, CA 91360-2787	1959	Dr. Luther S. Luedtke	2-M	2,457	209
California Polytechnic State U, San Luis Obispo, San Luis Obispo, CA 93407	1901	Dr. Warren J. Baker	5-M	17,000	888
California State Polytechnic U, Pomona, Pomona, CA 91768-2557	1938	Dr. Bob Suzuki	5-M	16,803	994
California State U, Bakersfield, Bakersfield, CA 93311-1099	1970	Dr. Tomas A. Arciniega	5-M	5,435	315
California State U, Chico, Chico, CA 95929-0722	1887	Dr. Manuel A. Esteban	5-M	13,919	816
California State U, Dominguez Hills, Carson, CA 90747-0001	1960	Dr. Robert Detweiler	5-M	10,400	724
California State U, Fresno, Fresno, CA 93740	1911	Dr. John D. Welty	5-D	17,213	950
California State U, Fullerton, Fullerton, CA 92834-9480	1957	Dr. Milton A. Gordon	5-M	24,040	1,228
California State U, Hayward, Hayward, CA 94542-3000	1957	Dr. Norma Rees	5-M	12,734	703
California State U, Long Beach, Long Beach, CA 90840-0119	1949	Dr. Robert C. Maxson	5-M	27,431	1,423
California State U, Los Angeles, Los Angeles, CA 90032-8530	1947	Dr. James M. Rosser	5-M	18,849	1,091
California State U, Northridge, Northridge, CA 91330	1958	Dr. Blenda J. Wilson	5-M	25,020	1,453
California State U, Sacramento, Sacramento, CA 95819-6048	1947	Dr. Donald R. Gerth	5-M	23,420	1,214
California State U, San Bernardino, San Bernardino, CA 92407-2397	1965	Dr. Anthony H. Evans	5-M	12,153	571
California State U, San Marcos, San Marcos, CA 92096	1990	Dr. Alexander Gonzalez	5-M	3,841	264
California State U, Stanislaus, Turlock, CA 95382	1957	Dr. Marvalene Hughes	5-M	6,100	345
California U of Pennsylvania, California, PA 15419-1394	1852	Dr. Angelo Armenti, Jr.	5-M	5,636	355
Calumet Coll of Saint Joseph, Whiting, IN 46394-2195	1951	Dr. Dennis C. Rittenmeyer	2-B	1,018	110
Calvin Coll, Grand Rapids, MI 49546-4388	1876	Dr. Gaylen J. Byker	2-M	4,051	324
Cameron U, Lawton, OK 73505-6377	1908	Dr. Don Davis	5-M	5,231	321
Campbellsville U, Campbellsville, KY 42718-2799	1906	Dr. Kenneth W. Winters	2-D	1,530	117
Campbell U, Buies Creek, NC 27506	1887	Dr. Norman A. Wiggins	2-F	6,920	349
Canisius Coll, Buffalo, NY 14208-1098	1870	Rev. Vincent M. Cooke, S.J.	2-M	4,746	383
Capital U, Columbus, OH 43209-2394	1830	Dr. Josiah H. Blackmore	2-F	4,035	381
Cardinal Stritch U, Milwaukee, WI 53217-3985	1937	Sr. Mary Lea Schneider	2-M	5,526	572
Carleton Coll, Northfield, MN 55057-4001	1866	Dr. Stephen R. Lewis, Jr.	1-B	1,698	198
Carlow Coll, Pittsburgh, PA 15213-3165 (4)	1929	Dr. Grace Ann Geibel, RSM	2-M	2,339	229
Carnegie Mellon U, Pittsburgh, PA 15213-3891	1900	Dr. Jared L. Cohon	1-D	7,758	777
Carroll Coll, Helena, MT 59625-0002	1909	Dr. Matthew J. Quinn	2-B	1,352	122
Carroll Coll, Waukesha, WI 53186-5593	1846	Dr. Frank Falcone	2-M	2,464	174
Carson-Newman Coll, Jefferson City, TN 37760	1851	Dr. J. Cordell Maddox	2-M	2,265	172
Carthage Coll, Kenosha, WI 53140-1994	1847	Dr. F. Gregory Campbell	2-M	2,164	124
Case Western Reserve U, Cleveland, OH 44106	1826	Dr. Agnar Pytte	1-D	9,970	1,963
Castleton State Coll, Castleton, VT 05735	1787	Dr. Martha K. Farmer	5-M	1,854	179
Catawba Coll, Salisbury, NC 28144-2488	1851	Mr. J. Fred Corriher, Jr.	2-M	1,178	100
The Catholic U of America, Washington, DC 20064	1887	Br. Patrick Ellis, FSC, PhD	2-D	5,974	654
Cedar Crest Coll, Allentown, PA 18104-6196 (4)	1867	Dr. Dorothy Gulbenkian Blaney	2-M	1,699	154

Name, address	Year	Governing official, control, and highest degree offered		Enroll-ment	Faculty
Cedarville Coll, Cedarville, OH 45314-0601	1887	Dr. Paul H. Dixon	2-B	2,509	188
Central Coll, Pella, IA 50219-1999	1853	Dr. Thomas Iverson	2-B	1,299	127
Central Connecticut State U, New Britain, CT 06050-4010	1849	Dr. Richard L. Judd	5-M	9,520	729
Central Methodist Coll, Fayette, MO 65248-1198	1854	Dr. Marianne Inman	2-M	1,152	76
Central Michigan U, Mount Pleasant, MI 48859	1892	Dr. Leonard E. Plachta	5-D	16,597	866
Central Missouri State U, Warrensburg, MO 64093	1871	Dr. Ed Elliott	5-M	10,770	500
Central State U, Wilberforce, OH 45384	1887	Dr. George Ayres	5-M	1,976	121
Central Washington U, Ellensburg, WA 98926	1891	Dr. Ivory V. Nelson	5-M	8,569	341
Chadron State Coll, Chadron, NE 69337	1911	Dr. Samuel H. Rankin	5-M	2,983	164
Chaminade U of Honolulu, Honolulu, HI 96816-1578	1955	Dr. Mary Wesselkamper	2-M	2,674	175
Chapman U, Orange, CA 92866	1861	Dr. James Doti	2-F	3,673	352
Charleston Southern U, Charleston, SC 29423-8087	1964	Dr. Jairy C. Hunter, Jr.	2-M	2,329	122
Charter Oak State Coll, Newington, CT 06111-2646	1973	Dr. Merle W. Harris	5-B	1,252	NR
Chestnut Hill Coll, Philadelphia, PA 19118-2695 (3)	1924	Sr. Carol J. Vale, SSJ, PhD	2-M	1,340	151
Cheyney U of Pennsylvania, Cheyney, PA 19319	1837	Dr. Donald Mullett	5-M	1,360	113
Chicago State U, Chicago, IL 60628	1867	Dr. Dolores Cross	5-M	9,412	482
Christian Brothers U, Memphis, TN 38104-5581	1871	Br. Michael J. McGinniss, FSC	2-M	1,785	162
Christopher Newport U, Newport News, VA 23606-2998	1961	Mr. Paul S. Trible, Jr.	5-M	4,558	340
The Citadel, The Military Coll of South Carolina, Charleston, SC 29409	1842	Maj. Gen. John S. Grinalds	5-M	4,319	190
City Coll of the City U of NY, New York, NY 10031-6977	1847	Dr. Yolanda T. Moses	11-D	12,494	1,054
City U, Bellevue, WA 98004-6442	1973	Dr. Michael A. Pastore	1-M	12,875	1,259
Clarion U of Pennsylvania, Clarion, PA 16214	1867	Dr. Diane L. Reinhard	5-M	5,886	366
Clark Atlanta U, Atlanta, GA 30314	1869	Dr. Thomas W. Cole, Jr.	2-D	5,798	NR
Clarke Coll, Dubuque, IA 52001-3198	1843	Dr. Catherine Dunn, BVM	2-M	1,082	118
Clarkson U, Potsdam, NY 13699	1896	Dr. Denny G. Brown	1-D	2,670	172
Clark U, Worcester, MA 01610-1477	1887	Dr. Richard P. Traina	1-D	2,732	172
Clayton Coll & State U, Morrow, GA 30260-0285	1969	Dr. Richard Skinner	5-B	4,687	250
Clemson U, Clemson, SC 29634	1889	Dr. Constantine W. Curris	5-D	16,537	1,301
Cleveland State U, Cleveland, OH 44115	1964	Dr. Claire A. Van Ummersen	5-D	15,522	810
Clinch Valley Coll of the U of Virginia, Wise, VA 24293	1954	Dr. L. Jay Lemons	5-B	1,387	90
Coastal Carolina U, Conway, SC 29528-6054	1954	Dr. Ronald R. Ingle	5-M	4,477	255
Coe Coll, Cedar Rapids, IA 52402-5070	1851	Dr. James R. Phifer	2-M	1,247	143
Colby Coll, Waterville, ME 04901	1813	Mr. William R. Cotter	1-B	1,764	155
Colegio Universitario del Este, Carolina, PR 00984-2010	1949	Mr. Alberto Maldonado Ruiz, Esq.	1-B	4,405	105
Colgate U, Hamilton, NY 13346-1386	1819	Dr. Neil R. Grabois	1-M	2,859	257
Coll Misericordia, Dallas, PA 18612-1098	1924	Dr. Albert B. Anderson	2-M	1,736	158
Coll of Charleston, Charleston, SC 29424-0002	1770	Dr. Alexander M. Sanders, Jr.	5-B	11,053	700
Coll of Insurance, New York, NY 10007-2165	1962	Dr. Ellen Thrower	1-M	2,379	93
Coll of Mount St Joseph, Cincinnati, OH 45233-1670	1920	Sr. Francis Marie Thrailkill, OSU	2-M	2,205	210
Coll of Mount Saint Vincent, Riverdale, NY 10471-1093	1911	Dr. Mary C. Stuart	1-M	1,500	123
The Coll of New Jersey, Ewing, NJ 08628	1855	Dr. Harold Eickhoff	5-M	6,704	612
Coll of New Rochelle, New Rochelle, NY 10805-2308 (4)	1904	Dr. Stephen J. Sweeny	1-M	2,698	219
Coll of Notre Dame, Belmont, CA 94002-1997	1851	Dr. Margaret Huber	2-M	1,743	194
Coll of Notre Dame of Maryland, Baltimore, MD 21210-2476 (3)	1873	Dr. Dorothy M. Brown	2-M	3,237	84
Coll of Our Lady of the Elms, Chicopee, MA 01013-2839 (3)	1928	Dr. Kathleen Keating, SSJ	2-M	1,133	105
Coll of Saint Benedict, Saint Joseph, MN 56374 (3)	1913	Ms. Mary Lyons	2-B	1,958	152
Coll of St Catherine, St Paul, MN 55105-1789 (3)	1905	Dr. Anita Pampusch	2-M	2,695	161
Coll of Saint Elizabeth, Morristown, NJ 07960-6989 (4)	1899	Sr. Francis Raftery	2-M	1,694	167
Coll of St Francis, Joliet, IL 60435-6188	1920	Dr. James A. Doppke	2-M	1,500	138
Coll of Saint Mary, Omaha, NE 68124-2377 (3)	1923	Dr. Maryanne Stevens	2-B	1,069	138
The Coll of Saint Rose, Albany, NY 12203-1419	1920	Dr. R. Mark Sullivan	1-M	3,857	216
Coll of St Scholastica, Duluth, MN 55811-4199	1912	Dr. Daniel H. Pilon	2-M	2,101	160
Coll of Santa Fe, Santa Fe, NM 87505-7634	1947	Dr. James A. Fries	1-M	1,469	178
Coll of Staten Island of the City U of NY, Staten Island, NY 10314-6600	1955	Dr. Marlene Springer	11-M	12,208	765
Coll of the Holy Cross, Worcester, MA 01610-2395	1843	Rev. Gerard C. Reedy, SJ	2-B	2,636	265
Coll of the Ozarks, Pt Lookout, MO 65726	1906	Dr. Jerry C. Davis	2-B	1,525	115
The Coll of West Virginia, Beckley, WV 25802-2830	1933	Dr. Charles H. Polk	1-B	1,983	121
Coll of William and Mary, Williamsburg, VA 23187-8795	1693	Mr. Timothy J. Sullivan	5-D	7,722	696
The Coll of Wooster, Wooster, OH 44691	1866	Dr. R. Stanton Hales, Jr.	2-B	1,650	163
Colorado Christian U, Lakewood, CO 80226-7499	1914	Dr. Ronald R. Schmidt	2-M	3,006	202
The Colorado Coll, Colorado Springs, CO 80903-3294	1874	Dr. Kathryn Mohrman	1-M	2,099	178
Colorado Sch of Mines, Golden, CO 80401-1887	1874	Dr. George S. Ansell	5-D	3,203	290
Colorado State U, Fort Collins, CO 80523-0015	1870	Dr. Albert C. Yates	5-D	21,970	1,004
Colorado Tech U, Colorado Springs, CO 80907-3896	1965	Mr. David D. O'Donnell	3-D	1,521	92
Columbia Coll, Chicago, IL 60605-1997	1890	Dr. John B. Duff	1-M	8,066	1,148
Columbia Coll, New York, NY 10027	1754	Dr. Austin E. Quigley	1-B	3,726	NR
Columbia Coll, Columbia, SC 29203-5998 (3)	1854	Dr. Peter T. Mitchell	2-M	1,321	90
Columbia International U, Columbia, SC 29230-3122	1923	Dr. Johnny V. Miller	2-M	1,032	33
Columbia Union Coll, Takoma Park, MD 20912-7794	1904	Dr. Charles Scriven	2-B	1,163	43
Columbia U, Sch of Engineering & Applied Sci, New York, NY 10027	1864	Dr. Zvi Galil	1-D	1,093	94
Columbia U, Sch of General Studies, New York, NY 10027	1754	Dr. Gillian Lindt	1-B	900	450
Columbia U, Sch of Nursing, New York, NY 10032-3702 (4)	1892	Dr. Mary O. Mundinger	1-D	600	40
Columbus Coll of Art and Design, Columbus, OH 43215-1758	1879	Dr. Edward Lathy	1-B	1,494	152
Columbus State U, Columbus, GA 31907-5645	1958	Dr. Frank D. Brown	5-M	5,536	221
Concord Coll, Athens, WV 24712-1000	1872	Dr. Jerry L. Beasley	5-B	2,357	151
Concordia Coll, Moorhead, MN 56562	1891	Dr. Paul J. Dovre	2-B	2,928	292
Concordia U, Irvine, CA 92612-3299	1972	Dr. D. Ray Halm	2-M	1,027	114
Concordia U, River Forest, IL 60305-1499	1864	Dr. George C. Heider	2-M	2,107	193
Concordia U, St Paul, MN 55104-5494	1893	Dr. Robert Holst	2-M	1,259	117
Concordia U, Portland, OR 97211-6099	1905	Dr. Charles E. Schlimpert	2-M	1,020	127
Concordia U Wisconsin, Mequon, WI 53097-2402	1881	Dr. M. J. Stelmachowicz	2-M	3,659	150
Connecticut Coll, New London, CT 06320-4196	1911	Dr. Claire L. Gaudiani	1-M	1,918	181
Converse Coll, Spartanburg, SC 29302-0006 (3)	1889	Dr. Sandra C. Thomas	1-M	1,250	83
Coppin State Coll, Baltimore, MD 21216-3698	1900	Dr. Calvin W. Burnett	5-M	3,643	132
Cornell Coll, Mount Vernon, IA 52314-1098	1853	Dr. Leslie H. Garner, Jr.	2-B	1,105	129
Cornell U, Ithaca, NY 14853-0001	1865	Dr. Hunter R. Rawlings	1-D	18,849	1,541
Cornerstone Coll, Grand Rapids, MI 49505-5897	1941	Dr. Rex Rogers	2-B	1,082	106
Creighton U, Omaha, NE 68178-0001	1878	Rev. Michael G. Morrison, SJ	2-D	6,158	1,361
Culver-Stockton Coll, Canton, MO 63435-1299	1853	Dr. Edwin B. Strong, Jr.	2-B	1,031	75
Cumberland Coll, Williamsburg, KY 40769-1372	1889	Dr. James Taylor	2-M	1,614	95
Cumberland U, Lebanon, TN 37087-3554	1842	Dr. Clair Eugene Martin	1-M	1,062	100
Curry Coll, Milton, MA 02186-9984	1879	Mr. Kenneth Quigley	1-M	1,909	170
Daemen Coll, Amherst, NY 14226-3592	1947	Dr. Martin J. Anisman	1-M	1,815	164
Dakota State U, Madison, SD 57042-1799	1881	Dr. Jerald Tunheim	5-B	1,231	81
Dallas Baptist U, Dallas, TX 75211-9299	1965	Dr. Gary R. Cook	2-M	3,283	179

Name, address	Year	Governing official, control, and highest degree offered		Enrollment	Faculty
Dartmouth Coll, Hanover, NH 03755	1769	Mr. James O. Freedman	1-D	5,300	487
Davenport Coll of Business, Grand Rapids, MI 49503	1866	Mr. Donald W. Maine	1-B	2,719	162
Davenport Coll of Business, Kalamazoo Cmps, Kalamazoo, MI 49006-2791 (4)	1866	Dr. Patricia Dolly	1-B	1,200	78
Davenport Coll of Business, Lansing Cmps, Lansing, MI 48933-2197	1979	Mr. Don Colizzi	1-B	1,218	105
David Lipscomb U, Nashville, TN 37204-3951	1891	Dr. Stephen Flatt	2-M	2,543	183
David N Myers Coll, Cleveland, OH 44115-1096	1848	Dr. Arnold G. Tew	1-B	1,178	100
Davidson Coll, Davidson, NC 28036-1719	1837	Mr. Robert F. Vagt	2-B	1,613	151
Delaware State U, Dover, DE 19901-2277	1891	Dr. William B. DeLauder	5-M	3,328	176
Delaware Valley Coll, Doylestown, PA 18901-2697	1896	Dr. Joshua Feldstein	1-B	1,380	129
Delta State U, Cleveland, MS 38733-0001	1925	Dr. F. Kent Wyatt	5-D	3,860	291
Denison U, Granville, OH 43023	1831	Dr. Michele Tolela Myers	1-B	2,017	163
Denver Tech Coll, Denver, CO 80224-1658	1945	Mr. Raul Valdez Pages	3-M	1,500	85
DePaul U, Chicago, IL 60604-2287	1898	Rev. John P. Minogue, CM	2-D	17,294	1,344
DePauw U, Greencastle, IN 46135-1772	1837	Dr. Robert G. Bottoms	2-B	2,147	220
Detroit Coll of Business, Dearborn, MI 48126-3799	1962	Dr. James Mendola	1-B	3,374	195
Detroit Coll of Business, Warren Cmps, Warren, MI 48092-5209	1975	Ms. Janet Guggenheim	1-B	2,041	85
DeVry Inst of Tech, Phoenix, AZ 85021-2995	1967	Mr. James A. Dugan	3-B	2,862	85
DeVry Inst of Tech, Long Beach, CA 90806	1984	Dr. Rose Marie Dishman	3-B	1,366	77
DeVry Inst of Tech, Pomona, CA 91768-2642	1983	Dr. Rose Marie Dishman	3-B	3,037	117
DeVry Inst of Tech, Decatur, GA 30030-2198	1969	Dr. Ronald Bush	3-B	3,109	134
DeVry Inst of Tech, Addison, IL 60101-6106	1982	Mr. Jerry R. Dill	3-B	3,468	102
DeVry Inst of Tech, Chicago, IL 60618-5994	1931	Dr. E. Arthur Stunnard	3-B	3,192	101
DeVry Inst of Tech, Kansas City, MO 64131-3698	1931	Mr. Charles R. Levalley	3-B	2,130	76
DeVry Inst of Tech, Columbus, OH 43209-2764	1952	Dr. Galen H. Graham	3-B	2,647	79
DeVry Inst of Tech, Irving, TX 75063-2440	1969	Dr. Francis V. Cannon	3-B	2,419	138
Dickinson Coll, Carlisle, PA 17013-2896	1773	Dr. A. Lee Fritschler	1-B	1,709	171
Dickinson State U, Dickinson, ND 58601-4896	1918	Dr. Philip W. Conn	5-B	1,701	103
Dillard U, New Orleans, LA 70122-3097	1869	Dr. Samuel DuBois Cook	2-B	1,563	124
Doane Coll, Crete, NE 68333-2430	1872	Dr. Frederic D. Brown	2-M	1,795	112
Dominican Coll of Blauvelt, Orangeburg, NY 10962-1210	1952	Sr. Kathleen Sullivan	1-M	1,811	178
Dominican Coll of San Rafael, San Rafael, CA 94901-2298	1890	Dr. Joseph R. Fink	2-M	1,417	167
Dominican U, River Forest, IL 60305-1099	1901	Dr. Donna M. Carroll	2-M	1,818	172
Dordt Coll, Sioux Center, IA 51250-1697	1955	Dr. Carl E. Zylstra	2-M	1,269	93
Dowling Coll, Oakdale, NY 11769-1999	1955	Dr. Victor P. Meskill	1-M	6,046	424
Drake U, Des Moines, IA 50311-4516	1881	Dr. Michael R. Ferrari	1-D	5,376	267
Drew U, Madison, NJ 07940-1493	1867	Mr. Thomas H. Kean	2-D	2,174	134
Drexel U, Philadelphia, PA 19104-2875	1891	Dr. Constantine N. Papadakis	1-D	9,590	732
Drury Coll, Springfield, MO 65802-3791	1873	Dr. John E. Moore, Jr.	1-M	1,620	122
Duke U, Durham, NC 27708-0586	1838	Dr. Nannerl O. Keohane	2-D	11,589	2,105
Duquesne U, Pittsburgh, PA 15282-0001	1878	Dr. John E. Murray, Jr.	2-D	9,400	808
D'Youville Coll, Buffalo, NY 14201-1084	1908	Dr. Denise A. Roche, GNSH	1-M	1,915	164
Earlham Coll, Richmond, IN 47374-4095	1847	Mr. Douglas Bennett	2-B	1,005	108
East Carolina U, Greenville, NC 27858-4353	1907	Dr. Richard Eakin	5-D	16,805	1,181
East Central U, Ada, OK 74820-6899	1909	Dr. Bill S. Cole	5-M	4,369	225
Eastern Coll, St Davids, PA 19087-3696	1932	Dr. Roberta Hestenes	2-M	2,348	207
Eastern Connecticut State U, Willimantic, CT 06226-2295	1889	Dr. David G. Carter	5-M	4,590	199
Eastern Illinois U, Charleston, IL 61920-3099	1895	Dr. David L. Jorns	5-M	11,711	659
Eastern Kentucky U, Richmond, KY 40475-3101	1906	Dr. Hanly Funderburk	5-M	16,060	855
Eastern Mennonite U, Harrisonburg, VA 22801-2462	1917	Dr. Joseph L. Lapp	2-F	1,150	122
Eastern Michigan U, Ypsilanti, MI 48197	1849	Dr. William E. Shelton	5-D	22,541	1,195
Eastern New Mexico U, Portales, NM 88130	1934	Dr. Everett L. Frost	5-M	3,617	226
Eastern Oregon U, La Grande, OR 97850-2899	1929	Dr. David E. Gilbert	5-M	1,876	103
Eastern Washington U, Cheney, WA 99004-2431	1882	Dr. Marshall Drummond	5-M	7,589	538
East Stroudsburg U of Pennsylvania, East Stroudsburg, PA 18301-2999	1893	Dr. Robert Dillman	5-M	5,552	277
East Tennessee State U, Johnson City, TN 37614-0734	1911	Dr. Roy S. Nicks	5-D	11,859	935
East Texas Baptist U, Marshall, TX 75670-1498	1912	Dr. Bob E. Riley	2-M	1,222	103
Eckerd Coll, St Petersburg, FL 33711	1958	Dr. Peter H. Armacost	2-B	1,466	116
Edgewood Coll, Madison, WI 53711-1998	1927	Dr. James A. Ebben	2-M	2,032	152
Edinboro U of Pennsylvania, Edinboro, PA 16444	1857	Dr. Frank G. Pogue, Jr.	5-M	7,178	313
Elizabeth City State U, Elizabeth City, NC 27909-7806	1891	Dr. Mickey L. Burnim	5-B	2,000	149
Elizabethtown Coll, Elizabethtown, PA 17022-2298	1899	Dr. Theodore E. Long	2-B	1,728	152
Elmhurst Coll, Elmhurst, IL 60126-3296	1871	Dr. Bryant L. Cureton	2-B	2,701	218
Elmira Coll, Elmira, NY 14901	1855	Dr. Thomas K. Meier	1-M	1,117	74
Elon Coll, Elon College, NC 27244	1889	Dr. J. Fred Young	2-M	3,588	235
Embry-Riddle Aeronautical U, Prescott, AZ 86301-3720	1978	Dr. Jeff Ashworth	1-B	1,435	85
Embry-Riddle Aeronautical U, Daytona Beach, FL 32114-3900	1926	Dr. Steven M. Sliwa	1-M	4,135	211
Embry-Riddle Aeronautical U, Extended Cmps, Daytona Beach, FL 32114-3900	1970	Dr. Leon E. Flancher	1-M	11,716	2,649
Emerson Coll, Boston, MA 02116-1511	1880	Dr. Jacqueline W. Liebergott	1-D	3,441	295
Emmanuel Coll, Boston, MA 02115 (3)	1919	Sr. Janet Eisner, SND	2-M	1,564	111
Emory U, Atlanta, GA 30322-1100	1836	Dr. William M. Chace	2-D	11,270	2,486
Emporia State U, Emporia, KS 66801-5087	1863	Dr. Robert E. Glennen	5-D	5,772	327
Eugene Lang Coll, New Sch for Social Research, New York, NY 10011-8601	1978	Dr. Beatrice Banu	1-B	383	63
Evangel Coll, Springfield, MO 65802-2191	1955	Dr. Robert H. Spence	2-B	1,574	122
The Evergreen State Coll, Olympia, WA 98505	1967	Dr. Jane L. Jervis	5-M	3,714	183
Fairfield U, Fairfield, CT 06430-5195	1942	Rev. Aloysius P. Kelley, SJ	2-M	5,111	342
Fairleigh Dickinson U, Teaneck-Hackensack, Teaneck, NJ 07666-1914	1942	Dr. Francis J. Mertz	1-D	6,934	767
Fairmont State Coll, Fairmont, WV 26554	1865	Dr. Janet Dudley-Eshbach	5-B	6,555	437
Fashion Inst of Tech, New York, NY 10001-5992	1944	Dr. Allan F. Hershfield	11-M	8,489	844
Faulkner U, Montgomery, AL 36109-3398	1942	Dr. Billy D. Hilyer	2-F	2,376	125
Fayetteville State U, Fayetteville, NC 28301-4298	1867	Dr. Willis B. McLeod	5-D	3,951	234
Felician Coll, Lodi, NJ 07644-2198	1942	Sr. Theresa Martin	2-M	1,250	97
Ferris State U, Big Rapids, MI 49307-2742	1884	Dr. William Sederburg	5-F	9,495	601
Ferrum Coll, Ferrum, VA 24088-9001	1913	Dr. Jerry M. Boone	2-B	1,075	97
Finch U of Health Sciences/Chicago Medical Sch, North Chicago, IL 60064-3095	1912	Mr. Herman M. Finch	1-D	1,440	23
Fitchburg State Coll, Fitchburg, MA 01420-2697	1894	Dr. Michael P. Riccards	5-M	3,701	415
Flagler Coll, St Augustine, FL 32085-1027	1968	Dr. William L. Proctor	1-B	1,526	123
Florida A&M U, Tallahassee, FL 32307	1887	Dr. Frederick Humphries	5-D	10,448	727
Florida Atlantic U, Boca Raton, FL 33431-0991	1961	Dr. Anthony James Catanese	5-D	18,362	688
Florida Inst of Tech, Melbourne, FL 32901-6975	1958	Dr. Lynn Edward Weaver	1-D	4,185	445

Name, address	Year	Governing official, control, and highest degree offered		Enroll-ment	Faculty
Florida International U, Miami, FL 33199	1965	Dr. Modesto A. Maidique	5-D	24,413	NR
Florida Memorial Coll, Miami, FL 33054	1879	Dr. Albert E. Smith	2-B	1,457	NR
Florida Metropolitan U-Orlando Coll, North, Orlando, FL 32810-5674	1953	Mrs. Ouida B. Kirby	3-M	1,375	86
Florida Metropolitan U-Tampa Coll, Tampa, FL 33614-5899	1890	Mr. Joel Boyd	3-M	1,250	45
Florida Southern Coll, Lakeland, FL 33801-5698	1885	Dr. Thomas L. Reuschling	2-M	1,964	143
Florida State U, Tallahassee, FL 32306	1857	Dr. Talbot D'Alemberte	5-D	30,264	1,470
Fontbonne Coll, St Louis, MO 63105-3098	1917	Dr. Dennis C. Golden	2-M	1,882	198
Fordham U, New York, NY 10458	1841	Rev. Joseph A. O'Hare, SJ	2-D	13,723	1,139
Fort Hays State U, Hays, KS 67601-4099	1902	Dr. Edward H. Hammond	5-M	5,540	302
Fort Lewis Coll, Durango, CO 81301-3999	1911	Mr. Joel M. Jones	5-B	4,600	241
Fort Valley State U, Fort Valley, GA 31030-3298	1895	Dr. Oscar L. Prater	5-F	3,024	152
Framingham State Coll, Framingham, MA 01701-9101	1839	Dr. Raymond Kieft	5-M	5,155	295
Franciscan U of Steubenville, Steubenville, OH 43952-6701	1946	Rev. Michael Scanlan, TOR	2-M	1,927	137
Francis Marion U, Florence, SC 29501-0547	1970	Dr. Lee A. Vickers	5-M	3,722	219
Franklin and Marshall Coll, Lancaster, PA 17604-3003	1787	Dr. Richard Kneedler	1-B	1,822	174
Franklin Pierce Coll, Rindge, NH 03461-0060	1962	Dr. George J. Hagerty	1-B	1,327	112
Franklin U, Columbus, OH 43215-5399	1902	Dr. Paul J. Otte	1-M	4,049	230
Freed-Hardeman U, Henderson, TN 38340-2399	1869	Dr. Milton R. Sewell	2-M	1,564	101
Fresno Pacific U, Fresno, CA 93702-4709	1944	Dr. Allen Carden	2-M	1,000	188
Friends U, Wichita, KS 67213	1898	Dr. Biff Green	1-M	2,169	119
Frostburg State U, Frostburg, MD 21532-1099	1898	Dr. Catherine R. Gira	5-M	5,418	314
Furman U, Greenville, SC 29613-0688	1826	Dr. David E. Shi	1-M	2,734	194
Gallaudet U, Washington, DC 20002-3625	1864	Dr. I. King Jordan	1-D	2,034	330
Gannon U, Erie, PA 16541	1925	Msgr. David A. Rubino, PhD	2-M	3,327	290
Gardner-Webb U, Boiling Springs, NC 28017	1905	Dr. M. Christopher White	2-M	2,739	174
Geneva Coll, Beaver Falls, PA 15010-3599	1848	Dr. John H. White	2-M	1,782	115
George Fox U, Newberg, OR 97132-2697	1891	Dr. Edward F. Stevens	2-D	2,188	116
George Mason U, Fairfax, VA 22030-4444	1957	Dr. Alan G. Merten	5-D	24,368	1,350
Georgetown Coll, Georgetown, KY 40324-1696	1829	Dr. William H. Crouch, Jr.	2-M	1,514	125
Georgetown U, Washington, DC 20057	1789	Rev. Leo J. O'Donovan, SJ	2-D	12,629	2,085
The George Washington U, Washington, DC 20052	1821	Mr. Stephen J. Trachtenberg	1-D	18,986	2,214
Georgia Coll and State U, Milledgeville, GA 31061	1889	Dr. Ralph W. Hemphill	5-M	5,534	343
Georgia Inst of Tech, Atlanta, GA 30332-0001	1885	Dr. Gerald W. Clough	5-D	12,985	686
Georgian Court Coll, Lakewood, NJ 08701-2697 (4)	1908	Sr. Barbara Williams	2-M	1,919	194
Georgia Southern U, Statesboro, GA 30460	1906	Dr. Nicholas Henry	5-D	14,312	650
Georgia Southwestern State U, Americus, GA 31709-4693	1906	Dr. Michael L. Hanes	5-M	2,522	133
Georgia State U, Atlanta, GA 30303-3083	1913	Dr. Carl V. Patton	5-D	23,410	1,437
Gettysburg Coll, Gettysburg, PA 17325-1411	1832	Dr. Gordon A. Haaland	1-B	2,000	220
Glenville State Coll, Glenville, WV 26351-1200	1872	Dr. William K. Simmons	5-B	2,179	167
GMI Engineering & Management Inst, Flint, MI 48504-4898	1919	Dr. James E. A. John	1-M	3,225	154
Golden Gate U, San Francisco, CA 94105-2968	1853	Dr. Thomas M. Stauffer	1-D	6,119	523
Goldey-Beacom Coll, Wilmington, DE 19808-1999	1886	Dr. Mohammad Ilyas	1-M	1,600	73
Gonzaga U, Spokane, WA 99258	1887	Rev. Edward Glynn, SJ	2-D	4,479	283
Gordon Coll, Wenham, MA 01984-1899	1889	Dr. R. Judson Carlberg	2-M	1,259	115
Goshen Coll, Goshen, IN 46526-4794	1894	Dr. Shirley H. Showalter	2-B	1,014	126
Goucher Coll, Baltimore, MD 21204-2794	1885	Dr. Judy Jolley Mohraz	1-M	1,303	139
Governors State U, University Park, IL 60466	1969	Dr. Paula Wolff	5-M	6,082	280
Graceland Coll, Lamoni, IA 50140	1895	Dr. William T. Higdon	2-M	1,260	95
Grambling State U, Grambling, LA 71245	1901	Dr. Raymond A. Hicks	5-D	8,000	224
Grand Canyon U, Phoenix, AZ 85017-3030	1949	Dr. Bill Williams	2-M	2,119	196
Grand Valley State U, Allendale, MI 49401-9403	1960	Mr. Arend D. Lubbers	5-M	14,662	769
Grand View Coll, Des Moines, IA 50316-1599	1896	Rev. Thomas W. Thomsen	2-B	1,468	135
Grantham Coll of Engineering, Slidell, LA 70460-6815 (2)	1951	Mr. John D. Ward	3-B	1,430	8
Greensboro Coll, Greensboro, NC 27401-1875	1838	Dr. Craven E. Williams	2-B	1,023	99
Grinnell Coll, Grinnell, IA 50112-0805	1846	Dr. Pamela A. Ferguson	1-B	1,314	155
Grove City Coll, Grove City, PA 16127-2104	1876	Dr. John H. Moore	2-M	2,329	144
Guilford Coll, Greensboro, NC 27410-4173	1837	Dr. Donald W. McNemar	2-B	1,071	132
Gustavus Adolphus Coll, St Peter, MN 56082-1498	1862	Dr. Axel D. Steuer	2-B	2,376	225
Gwynedd-Mercy Coll, Gwynedd Valley, PA 19437-0901	1948	Dr. Linda M. Bevilacqua, OP	2-M	1,721	181
Hamilton Coll, Clinton, NY 13323-1296	1812	Dr. Eugene M. Tobin	1-B	1,715	201
Hamline U, St Paul, MN 55104-1284	1854	Dr. Larry G. Osnes	2-D	3,335	296
Hampshire Coll, Amherst, MA 01002	1965	Dr. Gregory S. Prince, Jr.	1-B	1,068	94
Hampton U, Hampton, VA 23668	1868	Dr. William R. Harvey	1-D	6,035	389
Hannibal-LaGrange Coll, Hannibal, MO 63401-1940	1858	Dr. Woodrow Burt	2-B	1,050	82
Hanover Coll, Hanover, IN 47243-0108	1827	Dr. Russell L. Nichols	2-B	1,051	106
Harding U, Searcy, AR 72149-0001	1924	Dr. David B. Burks, Jr.	2-M	4,081	246
Hardin-Simmons U, Abilene, TX 79698-0001	1891	Dr. Lanny Hall	2-F	2,279	179
Harris-Stowe State Coll, St Louis, MO 63103-2136	1857	Dr. Henry Givens, Jr.	5-B	1,723	122
Hartwick Coll, Oneonta, NY 13820-4020	1797	Dr. Richard A. Detweiler	1-B	1,494	126
Harvard U, Cambridge, MA 02138	1636	Dr. Neil Rudenstine	1-D	18,310	2,134
Hastings Coll, Hastings, NE 68902-0269	1882	Dr. Richard Hoover	2-M	1,107	98
Haverford Coll, Haverford, PA 19041-1392	1833	Dr. Thomas Tritton	1-B	1,137	109
Hawaii Pacific U, Honolulu, HI 96813-2785	1965	Mr. Chatt Wright	1-M	8,270	539
Heidelberg Coll, Tiffin, OH 44883-2462	1850	Dr. Richard H. Owens	2-M	1,386	101
Henderson State U, Arkadelphia, AR 71999-0001	1890	Dr. Charles D. Dunn	5-M	3,527	223
Heritage Coll, Toppenish, WA 98948-9599	1907	Dr. Kathleen Ross, SNJM	1-M	1,187	154
High Point U, High Point, NC 27262-3598	1924	Dr. Jacob C. Martinson	2-M	2,596	184
Hillsdale Coll, Hillsdale, MI 49242-1298	1844	Dr. George C. Roche, III	1-B	1,163	113
Hobart and William Smith Colleges, Geneva, NY 14456-3397	1822	Dr. Richard H. Hersh	1-B	1,794	159
Hofstra U, Hempstead, NY 11550-1090	1935	Dr. James M. Shuart	1-D	12,279	978
Hollins Coll, Roanoke, VA 24020-1688 (3)	1842	Dr. Janet E. Rasmussen	1-M	1,030	90
Holy Family Coll, Philadelphia, PA 19114-2094	1954	Sr. Francesca Onley	2-M	2,590	253
Hood Coll, Frederick, MD 21701-8575 (4)	1893	Mrs. Shirley D. Peterson	2-M	1,870	98
Hope Coll, Holland, MI 49422-9000	1866	Dr. John H. Jacobson, Jr.	2-B	2,849	270
Houghton Coll, Houghton, NY 14744	1883	Dr. Daniel R. Chamberlain	2-B	1,249	133
Houston Baptist U, Houston, TX 77074-3298	1960	Dr. E. Douglas Hodo	2-M	2,243	138
Howard Payne U, Brownwood, TX 76801-2715	1889	Dr. Don Newbury	2-B	1,468	124
Howard U, Washington, DC 20059-0002	1867	Mr. H. Patrick Swygert, Esq.	1-D	10,332	1,808
Humboldt State U, Arcata, CA 95521-8299	1913	Dr. Alistair W. McCrone	5-M	7,686	637
Humphreys Coll, Stockton, CA 95207-3896	1896	Dr. Robert G. Humphreys	1-F	1,083	70
Hunter Coll of the City U of NY, New York, NY 10021-5085	1870	Mr. David A. Caputo	11-M	18,250	1,095
Husson Coll, Bangor, ME 04401-2999	1898	Dr. William H. Beardsley	1-M	1,946	93
ICI U, Irving, TX 75063-2631	1967	Dr. George M. Flattery	2-M	8,628	285
Idaho State U, Pocatello, ID 83209	1901	Dr. Richard Bowen	5-D	12,154	693
Illinois Inst of Tech, Chicago, IL 60616-3793	1890	Mr. Lewis Collens	1-D	6,287	535
Illinois State U, Normal, IL 61790-2200	1857	Dr. David A. Strand	5-D	19,409	944

Name, address	Year	Governing official, control, and highest degree offered		Enrollment	Faculty
Illinois Wesleyan U, Bloomington, IL 61702-2900	1850	Dr. Minor Myers, Jr.	1-B	1,928	169
Immaculata Coll, Immaculata, PA 19345-0900 (4)	1920	Sr. Marie Roseanne Bonfini	2-D	2,391	164
Indiana Inst of Tech, Fort Wayne, IN 46803-1297	1930	Mr. Donald J. Andorfer	1-B	1,321	29
Indiana State U, Terre Haute, IN 47809-1401	1865	Dr. John W. Moore	5-D	10,934	706
Indiana U Bloomington, Bloomington, IN 47405	1820	Dr. Kenneth R. R. Gros Louis	5-D	34,700	1,635
Indiana U East, Richmond, IN 47374-1289	1971	Dr. David J. Fulton	5-B	2,302	195
Indiana U Kokomo, Kokomo, IN 46904-9003	1945	Dr. Emita B. Hill	5-M	2,965	195
Indiana U Northwest, Gary, IN 46408-1197	1959	Dr. Hilda Richards	5-M	5,149	350
Indiana U of Pennsylvania, Indiana, PA 15705	1875	Dr. Lawrence K. Pettit	5-D	13,680	823
Indiana U–Purdue U Fort Wayne, Fort Wayne, IN 46805-1499	1917	Dr. Michael A. Wartell	5-M	10,749	674
Indiana U–Purdue U Indianapolis, Indianapolis, IN 46202-2896	1969	Mr. Gerald L. Bepko	5-D	27,011	2,084
Indiana U South Bend, South Bend, IN 46634-7111	1922	Dr. Kenneth L. Perrin	5-M	7,544	599
Indiana U Southeast, New Albany, IN 47150-6405	1941	Dr. F. C. Richardson	5-M	5,396	376
Indiana Wesleyan U, Marion, IN 46953-4999	1920	Dr. James Barnes	2-M	5,069	133
Inter American U of PR, Aguadilla Cmps, Aguadilla, PR 00605	1957	Ms. Hilda Baco	1-B	3,629	163
Inter American U of PR, Arecibo Cmps, Arecibo, PR 00614-4050	1957	Dr. Zaida Vega	1-B	4,220	253
Inter Amer U of PR, Barranquitas Cmps, Barranquitas, PR 00794	1957	Dr. Irene Fernandez Aponte	1-B	1,687	90
Inter American U of PR, Bayamón Cmps, Bayamón, PR 00957	NR	Mr. Felix Torres	1-B	4,673	242
Inter American U of PR, Fajardo Cmps, Fajardo, PR 00738-7003	1965	Mrs. Yolanda Robles Garcia	1-B	1,964	111
Inter American U of PR, Guayama Cmps, Guayama, PR	1958	Dr. Samuel F. Febres-Santiago	1-B	2,027	89
Inter American U of PR, Metropolitan Cmps, Hato Rey, PR 00919	1960	Dr. Manuel J. Fernos	1-M	13,910	NR
Inter American U of PR, Ponce Cmps, Mercedita, PR 00715-2201	1962	Ms. Marilina Wayland	1-B	3,503	182
Inter American U of PR, San Germán Cmps, San Germán, PR 00683-5008	1912	Prof. Agnes Mojica	1-M	6,286	354
Iona Coll, New Rochelle, NY 10801-1890	1940	Br. James A. Liguori, CFC	1-M	5,588	400
Iowa State U of Science and Tech, Ames, IA 50011	1858	Dr. Martin C. Jischke	5-D	24,899	1,568
Ithaca Coll, Ithaca, NY 14850-7020	1892	Dr. James J. Whalen	1-M	5,683	528
Jackson State U, Jackson, MS 39217	1877	Dr. James E. Lyons, Sr.	5-D	6,218	399
Jacksonville State U, Jacksonville, AL 36265-9982	1883	Dr. Harold J. McGee	5-M	7,688	352
Jacksonville U, Jacksonville, FL 32211-3394	1934	Mr. Paul S. Tipton	1-M	2,321	244
James Madison U, Harrisonburg, VA 22807	1908	Dr. Ronald E. Carrier	5-D	12,963	758
Jamestown Coll, Jamestown, ND 58405	1883	Dr. James Walker	2-B	1,094	73
Jersey City State Coll, Jersey City, NJ 07305-1957	1927	Dr. Carlos Hernandez	5-M	7,450	262
John Brown U, Siloam Springs, AR 72761-2121	1919	Dr. A. LeVon Balzer	2-M	1,379	93
John Carroll U, University Heights, OH 44118-4581	1886	Rev. John J. Shea, SJ	2-M	4,197	381
John F Kennedy U, Orinda, CA 94563-2689	1964	Mr. Charles E. Glasser	1-D	1,859	732
John Jay Coll of Criminal Justice, the City U of NY, New York, NY 10019-1093	1964	Dr. Gerald Lynch	11-M	10,724	689
Johns Hopkins U, Baltimore, MD 21218-2699	1876	Dr. William K. Brody	1-D	4,979	419
Johnson & Wales U, Providence, RI 02903-3703	1914	Dr. John A. Yena	1-D	7,851	319
Johnson & Wales U, Charleston, SC 29403	1984	Dr. Barry L. Gleim	1-B	1,246	46
Johnson C Smith U, Charlotte, NC 28216	1867	Dr. Dorothy Cowser Yancy	1-B	1,427	88
Johnson State Coll, Johnson, VT 05656-9405	1828	Dr. Robert Hahn	5-M	1,591	114
Juniata Coll, Huntingdon, PA 16652-2119	1876	Dr. Robert W. Neff	1-B	1,161	100
Kalamazoo Coll, Kalamazoo, MI 49006-3295	1833	Dr. James F. Jones, Jr.	1-B	1,302	101
Kansas Newman Coll, Wichita, KS 67213-2084	1933	Sr. Tarcisia Roths	2-M	1,989	305
Kansas State U, Manhattan, KS 66506	1863	Dr. Jon Wefald	5-D	20,325	1,405
Kean Coll of New Jersey, Union, NJ 07083	1855	Dr. Ronald Applbaum	5-M	10,404	916
Keene State Coll, Keene, NH 03435-2604	1909	Dr. Stanley J. Yarosewick	5-M	4,021	347
Kennesaw State Coll, Kennesaw, GA 30144-5591	1963	Dr. Betty L. Siegel	5-M	12,537	543
Kent State U, Kent, OH 44242-0001	1910	Dr. Carol A. Cartwright	5-D	20,600	1,351
Kentucky State U, Frankfort, KY 40601	1886	Dr. Mary L. Smith	12-M	2,356	147
Kenyon Coll, Gambier, OH 43022-9623	1824	Dr. Robert A. Oden, Jr.	1-B	1,547	146
King's Coll, Wilkes-Barre, PA 18711-0801	1946	Rev. James Lackenmier, CSC	2-M	2,279	176
Knox Coll, Galesburg, IL 61401	1837	Mr. Frederick C. Nahm	1-B	1,134	112
Kutztown U of Pennsylvania, Kutztown, PA 19530	1866	Dr. David E. McFarland	5-M	7,843	430
Lafayette Coll, Easton, PA 18042-1798	1826	Mr. Arthur J. Rothkopf	2-B	2,185	232
Lake Forest Coll, Lake Forest, IL 60045-2399	1857	Dr. David Spadafora	1-M	1,106	115
Lake Superior State U, Sault Sainte Marie, MI 49783-1699	1946	Dr. Robert D. Arbuckle	5-M	3,392	172
Lamar U, Beaumont, TX 77710	1923	Dr. Rex Cottle	5-D	8,418	554
Lambuth U, Jackson, TN 38301	1843	Mr. W. Ellis Arnold, III	2-B	1,036	92
Lander U, Greenwood, SC 29649-2099	1872	Dr. William C. Moran	5-M	2,722	166
Langston U, Langston, OK 73050-0838	1897	Dr. Ernest L. Holloway	5-M	4,008	199
La Roche Coll, Pittsburgh, PA 15237-5898	1963	Msgr. William Kerr	2-M	1,641	151
La Salle U, Philadelphia, PA 19141-1199	1863	Br. Joseph Burke	2-M	5,130	300
La Sierra U, Riverside, CA 92515	1922	Dr. Lawrence T. Geraty	2-D	1,607	115
Lawrence Tech U, Southfield, MI 48075-1058	1932	Dr. Charles M. Chambers	1-M	3,916	333
Lawrence U, Appleton, WI 54912-0599	1847	Dr. Richard Warch	1-B	1,218	158
Lebanon Valley Coll, Annville, PA 17003-0501	1866	Dr. G. David Pollick	2-M	1,879	173
Lee U, Cleveland, TN 37311-4475	1918	Dr. Paul Conn	2-B	2,477	187
Lehigh U, Bethlehem, PA 18015-3094	1865	Dr. Peter Likins	1-D	6,275	489
Lehman Coll of the City U of NY, Bronx, NY 10468-1589	1931	Dr. Ricardo R. Fernandez	11-M	9,413	601
Le Moyne Coll, Syracuse, NY 13214-1399	1946	Rev. Robert A. Mitchell, SJ	2-M	2,713	224
LeMoyne-Owen Coll, Memphis, TN 38126-6595	1862	Mr. George Robert Johnson, Jr.	2-M	1,104	86
Lenoir-Rhyne Coll, Hickory, NC 28603	1891	Dr. Ryan A. LaHurd	2-M	1,579	120
Lesley Coll, Cambridge, MA 02138-2790 (3)	1909	Ms. Margaret A. McKenna	1-D	6,166	920
LeTourneau U, Longview, TX 75607-7001	1946	Dr. Alvin O. Austin	2-M	2,059	154
Lewis & Clark Coll, Portland, OR 97219-7899	1867	Dr. Michael Mooney	1-F	3,074	300
Lewis-Clark State Coll, Lewiston, ID 83501-2698	1893	Dr. James Hottois	5-B	2,978	303
Lewis U, Romeoville, IL 60446	1932	Br. James Gaffney, FSC	2-M	4,310	274
Liberty U, Lynchburg, VA 24502	1971	Dr. John M. Borek, Jr.	2-D	5,581	244
Lincoln Memorial U, Harrogate, TN 37752-1901	1897	Dr. Scott D. Miller	1-M	2,003	116
Lincoln U, Jefferson City, MO 65102	1866	Dr. Wendell G. Rayburn, Sr.	5-M	2,979	202
Lincoln U, Lincoln University, PA 19352	1854	Dr. Niara Sudarkasa	12-M	1,810	138
Lindenwood Coll, St Charles, MO 63301-1695	1827	Dr. Dennis Spellmann	2-M	4,293	162
Lindsey Wilson Coll, Columbia, KY 42728-1298	1903	Dr. Walter S. Reuling	2-M	1,317	60
Linfield Coll, McMinnville, OR 97128-6894	1849	Dr. Vivian A. Bull	2-B	1,594	121
Lock Haven U of Pennsylvania, Lock Haven, PA 17745-2390	1870	Dr. Craig Dean Willis	5-M	3,549	211
Logan Coll of Chiropractic, Chesterfield, MO 63006-1065	1935	Dr. George A. Goodman	1-F	1,054	85
Loma Linda U, Loma Linda, CA 92350	1905	Dr. B. Lyn Behrens	2-D	3,308	1,162
Long Island U, Brooklyn Cmps, Brooklyn, NY 11201-8423	1926	Dr. David J. Steinberg	1-D	8,264	559
Long Island U, C W Post Cmps, Brookville, NY 11548-1300	1954	Dr. David J. Steinberg	1-D	9,172	956
Long Island U, Southampton Coll, Southampton, NY 11968-9822	1963	Dr. David J. Steinberg	1-M	1,491	111
Longwood Coll, Farmville, VA 23909-1800	1839	Dr. William F. Dorrill	5-M	3,023	222
Loras Coll, Dubuque, IA 52004-0178	1839	Dr. Joachim W. Froehlich	2-M	1,815	136
Louisiana State U and A&M Coll, Baton Rouge, LA 70803-3103	1860	Dr. William L. Jenkins	5-D	26,842	1,301

Name, address	Year	Governing official, control, and highest degree offered		Enroll-ment	Faculty
Louisiana State U in Shreveport, Shreveport, LA 71115-2399	1965	Dr. Vincent J. Marsala	5-M	3,945	206
Louisiana State U Medical Ctr, New Orleans, LA 70112-2223	1931	Dr. Mervin L. Trail	5-D	2,965	NR
Louisiana Tech U, Ruston, LA 71272	1894	Dr. Daniel D. Reneau	5-D	9,313	459
Lourdes Coll, Sylvania, OH 43560-2898	1958	Sr. Ann Francis Klimkowski, OSF	2-B	1,540	120
Loyola Coll, Baltimore, MD 21210-2699	1852	Rev. Harold Ridley, SJ	2-D	6,245	442
Loyola Marymount U, Los Angeles, CA 90045-8350	1911	Rev. Thomas P. O'Malley, SJ	2-F	6,729	518
Loyola U Chicago, Chicago, IL 60611-2196	1870	Rev. John J. Piderit, SJ	2-D	13,759	961
Loyola U New Orleans, New Orleans, LA 70118-6195	1912	Rev. Bernard Patrick Knoth, SJ	2-F	5,203	414
Lubbock Christian U, Lubbock, TX 79407-2099	1957	Dr. L. Ken Jones	2-M	1,232	97
Luther Coll, Decorah, IA 52101-1045	1861	Dr. Jeffrey Baker	2-B	2,409	215
Luther Rice Bible Coll and Sem, Lithonia, GA 30038-2418 (2)	1962	Dr. James Flanagan	2-D	1,285	33
Lycoming Coll, Williamsport, PA 17701-5192	1812	Dr. James E. Douthat	2-B	1,489	109
Lynchburg Coll, Lynchburg, VA 24501-3199	1903	Dr. Charles O. Warren, Jr.	2-M	1,842	167
Lyndon State Coll, Lyndonville, VT 05851	1911	Dr. Margaret R. Williams	5-M	1,137	108
Lynn U, Boca Raton, FL 33431-5598	1962	Dr. Donald E. Ross	1-M	1,652	168
Macalester Coll, St Paul, MN 55105-1899	1874	Dr. Michael McPherson	2-B	1,797	210
Madonna U, Livonia, MI 48150-1173	1947	Sr. Mary Francilene	2-M	3,972	283
Maharishi U of Management, Fairfield, IA 52557	1971	Dr. Bevan Morris	1-D	1,025	90
Malone Coll, Canton, OH 44709-3897	1892	Dr. Ronald G. Johnson	2-M	2,069	163
Manchester Coll, North Manchester, IN 46962-1225	1889	Dr. Parker G. Marden	2-M	1,054	104
Manhattan Coll, Riverdale, NY 10471	1853	Br. Thomas J. Scanlan	2-M	3,076	244
Manhattanville Coll, Purchase, NY 10577-2132	1841	Mr. Richard A. Berman	1-M	1,500	207
Mankato State U, Mankato, MN 56002-8400	1868	Dr. Richard R. Rush	5-M	12,695	715
Mannes Coll of Music, New Sch for Social Research, New York, NY 10024-4402	1916	Dr. Joel Lester	1-M	288	216
Mansfield U of Pennsylvania, Mansfield, PA 16933	1857	Mr. Rod C. Kelchner	5-M	2,897	201
Marian Coll, Indianapolis, IN 46222-1997	1851	Dr. Daniel A. Felicetti	2-B	1,304	135
Marian Coll of Fond du Lac, Fond du Lac, WI 54935-4699	1936	Dr. Alan D. Osterndorf	2-M	2,432	131
Marietta Coll, Marietta, OH 45750-4000	1835	Dr. Lauren R. Wilson	1-M	1,256	104
Marist Coll, Poughkeepsie, NY 12601-1387	1929	Dr. Dennis J. Murray	1-M	4,372	415
Marquette U, Milwaukee, WI 53201-1881	1881	Rev. Robert A. Wild, SJ	2-D	10,539	996
Marshall U, Huntington, WV 25755-2020	1837	Dr. J. Wade Gilley	5-D	11,066	719
Mars Hill Coll, Mars Hill, NC 28754	1856	Dr. Max Lennon	2-B	1,050	123
Mary Baldwin Coll, Staunton, VA 24401 (4)	1842	Dr. Cynthia H. Tyson	2-M	2,132	122
Marygrove Coll, Detroit, MI 48221-2599 (4)	1905	Dr. John E. Shay, Jr.	2-M	2,510	58
Maryland Inst, Coll of Art, Baltimore, MD 21217-4192	1826	Mr. Fred Lazarus	1-M	1,064	161
Marylhurst Coll, Marylhurst, OR 97036-0261	1893	Dr. Nancy A. Wilgenbusch	2-M	1,228	278
Marymount Manhattan Coll, New York, NY 10021-4597	1936	Dr. Regina S. Peruggi	1-B	2,015	156
Marymount U, Arlington, VA 22207-4299	1950	Sr. Eymard Gallagher, RSHM	2-M	3,845	355
Maryville U of Saint Louis, St Louis, MO 63141-7299	1872	Dr. Keith Lovin	1-M	3,196	272
Mary Washington Coll, Fredericksburg, VA 22401-5358	1908	Dr. William M. Anderson, Jr.	5-M	3,745	243
Marywood U, Scranton, PA 18509-1598	1915	Sr. Mary Reap, IHM	2-D	2,926	250
Massachusetts Coll of Art, Boston, MA 02115-5882	1873	Dr. Katherine Sloan	5-M	1,487	189
Mass Coll of Pharmacy and Allied Health Sciences, Boston, MA 02115-5896	1823	Mr. Charles F. Monahan, Jr.	1-D	1,451	195
Massachusetts Inst of Tech, Cambridge, MA 02139-4307	1861	Dr. Charles M. Vest	1-D	9,947	896
The McGregor Sch of Antioch U, Yellow Springs, OH 45387-1609	1988	Dr. Steven Brzezinski	1-M	1,057	89
McKendree Coll, Lebanon, IL 62254-1299	1828	Dr. James M. Dennis	2-B	1,787	154
McMurry U, Abilene, TX 79697	1923	Dr. Robert E. Shimp	2-B	1,400	115
McNeese State U, Lake Charles, LA 70609-2495	1939	Dr. Robert D. Hebert	5-M	8,059	300
Medgar Evers Coll of the City U of NY, Brooklyn, NY 11225-2298	1969	Dr. Edison O. Jackson	11-B	5,402	359
Medical Coll of Georgia, Augusta, GA 30912-1003	1828	Dr. Francis J. Tedesco	5-D	2,048	775
Medical U of South Carolina, Charleston, SC 29425-0002	1824	Dr. James B. Edwards	5-D	2,334	2,062
Mercer U, Macon, GA 31207-0003	1833	Dr. R. Kirby Godsey	2-F	6,960	325
Mercer U, Cecil B Day Cmps, Atlanta, GA 30341-4155	1968	Dr. R. Kirby Godsey	2-D	1,900	48
Mercy Coll, Dobbs Ferry, NY 10522-1189	1951	Dr. Jay Sexter	1-M	7,364	665
Mercyhurst Coll, Erie, PA 16546	1926	Dr. William P. Garvey	2-M	2,712	164
Meredith Coll, Raleigh, NC 27607-5298 (3)	1891	Dr. John E. Weems	2-M	2,574	227
Merrimack Coll, North Andover, MA 01845-5800	1947	Mr. Richard J. Santagati	2-B	2,804	178
Mesa State Coll, Grand Junction, CO 81502-2647	1925	Dr. Ray N. Kieft	5-B	4,724	272
Messiah Coll, Grantham, PA 17027	1909	Dr. Rodney J. Sawatsky	2-B	2,517	211
Methodist Coll, Fayetteville, NC 28311-1420	1956	Dr. M. Elton Hendricks	2-B	1,736	104
Metropolitan State Coll of Denver, Denver, CO 80217-3362	1963	Dr. Sheila Kaplan	5-B	17,177	880
Metropolitan State U, St Paul, MN 55106-5000	1971	Dr. Susan A. Cole	5-M	5,245	497
Miami U, Oxford, OH 45056	1809	Dr. James C. Garland	12-D	16,103	1,063
Michigan State U, East Lansing, MI 48824-1020	1855	Mr. M. Peter McPherson	5-D	41,545	3,239
Michigan Tech U, Houghton, MI 49931-1295	1885	Dr. Curtis J. Tompkins	5-D	6,195	407
MidAmerica Nazarene U, Olathe, KS 66062-1899	1966	Dr. Richard Spindle	2-M	1,394	117
Middlebury Coll, Middlebury, VT 05753-6002	1800	Dr. John M. McCardell, Jr.	1-D	2,097	215
Middle Tennessee State U, Murfreesboro, TN 37132	1911	Dr. James E. Walker	5-D	17,924	972
Midland Lutheran Coll, Fremont, NE 68025-4200	1883	Dr. Carl L. Hansen	2-B	1,062	70
Midwestern State U, Wichita Falls, TX 76308-2096	1922	Dr. Louis J. Rodriguez	5-M	5,643	281
Miles Coll, Birmingham, AL 35208	1905	Mr. Albert J. H. Sloan, II	2-B	1,234	56
Millersville U of Pennsylvania, Millersville, PA 17551-0302	1855	Dr. Joseph A. Caputo	5-M	7,474	422
Millikin U, Decatur, IL 62522-2084	1901	Dr. Curtis L. McCray	2-B	1,930	203
Millsaps Coll, Jackson, MS 39210-0001	1890	Dr. George M. Harmon	2-M	1,377	107
Mills Coll, Oakland, CA 94613-1000 (3)	1852	Dr. Janet L. Holmgren	1-M	1,182	154
Milwaukee Sch of Engineering, Milwaukee, WI 53202-3109	1903	Dr. Hermann Viets	1-M	2,957	220
Minot State U, Minot, ND 58707-0002	1913	Dr. H. Erik Shaar	5-M	3,602	233
Mississippi Coll, Clinton, MS 39058	1826	Dr. Howell Todd	2-F	3,321	229
Mississippi State U, Mississippi State, MS 39762	1878	Dr. Donald W. Zacharias	5-D	14,064	832
Mississippi U for Women, Columbus, MS 39701-9998 (4)	1884	Dr. Clyda S. Rent	5-M	3,278	189
Mississippi Valley State U, Itta Bena, MS 38941-1400	1946	Dr. William W. Sutton	5-M	2,200	168
Missouri Baptist Coll, St Louis, MO 63141-8698	1968	Dr. R. Alton Lacey	2-B	2,423	82
Missouri Southern State Coll, Joplin, MO 64801-1595	1937	Dr. Julio Leon	5-B	5,258	283
Missouri Valley Coll, Marshall, MO 65340-3197	1889	Dr. J. Kenneth Bryant	2-B	1,214	68
Missouri Western State Coll, St Joseph, MO 64507-2294	1915	Dr. Janet Gorman Murphy	5-B	5,109	303
Molloy Coll, Rockville Centre, NY 11571-5002	1955	Dr. Martin Snyder	1-M	2,346	278
Monmouth U, West Long Branch, NJ 07764-1898	1933	Dr. Rebecca Stafford	1-M	5,110	374
Montana State U–Billings, Billings, MT 59101-9984	1927	Dr. Ronald P. Sexton	5-M	4,006	224
Montana State U–Bozeman, Bozeman, MT 59717	1893	Dr. Michael P. Malone	5-D	11,611	625
Montana State U–Northern, Havre, MT 59501-7751	1929	Dr. William Daehling	5-M	1,702	118
Montana Tech of The U of Montana, Butte, MT 59701-8997	1895	Dr. Lindsay D. Norman, Jr.	5-M	1,860	123
Montclair State U, Upper Montclair, NJ 07043-1624	1908	Dr. Irvin D. Reid	5-M	12,993	774
Montreat Coll, Montreat, NC 28757-1267	1916	Mr. William W. Hurt	2-M	1,000	49
Moody Bible Inst, Chicago, IL 60610-3284	1886	Dr. Joseph M. Stowell, III	2-M	1,553	144
Moorhead State U, Moorhead, MN 56563-0002	1885	Dr. Roland Barden	5-M	6,194	340

Name, address	Year	Governing official, control, and highest degree offered		Enroll- ment	Faculty
Moravian Coll, Bethlehem, PA 18018-6650	1742	Dr. Ervin J. Rooke	2-M	1,952	157
Morehead State U, Morehead, KY 40351	1922	Dr. Ronald Eaglin	5-M	8,344	429
Morehouse Coll, Atlanta, GA 30314 (1)	1867	Dr. Walter E. Massey	1-B	2,926	231
Morgan State U, Baltimore, MD 21251	1867	Dr. Earl Richardson	5-D	5,889	340
Morningside Coll, Sioux City, IA 51106-1751	1894	Dr. Jerry Israel	2-M	1,137	118
Morris Brown Coll, Atlanta, GA 30314-4140	1881	Dr. Samuel D. Jolley, Jr.	2-B	2,153	158
Mount Aloysius Coll, Cresson, PA 16630-1900	1939	Sr. Mary Ann Dillon	2-B	1,012	120
Mount Holyoke Coll, South Hadley, MA 01075-1414 (3)	1837	Ms. Joanne V. Creighton	1-M	1,898	213
Mount Mary Coll, Milwaukee, WI 53222-4597 (3)	1913	Dr. Patricia O'Donoghue	2-M	1,287	152
Mount Mercy Coll, Cedar Rapids, IA 52402-4797	1928	Dr. Thomas R. Feld	2-B	1,131	107
Mount Olive Coll, Mount Olive, NC 28365	1951	Dr. J. William Byrd	2-B	1,341	81
Mount Saint Mary Coll, Newburgh, NY 12550-3494	1960	Sr. Ann Sakac	1-M	1,978	167
Mount St Mary's Coll, Los Angeles, CA 90049-1597 (4)	1925	Sr. Karen M. Kennelly	2-M	1,411	238
Mount Saint Mary's Coll and Sem, Emmitsburg, MD 21727-7799	1808	Mr. George R. Houston, Jr.	2-F	1,884	142
Mount Union Coll, Alliance, OH 44601-3993	1846	Dr. Harold M. Kolenbrander	2-B	1,731	112
Mount Vernon Nazarene Coll, Mount Vernon, OH 43050-9500	1964	Dr. E. LeBron Fairbanks	2-M	1,685	82
Muhlenberg Coll, Allentown, PA 18104-5586	1848	Mr. Arthur R. Taylor	2-B	1,953	198
Murray State U, Murray, KY 42071-0009	1922	Dr. Kern Alexander	5-M	8,636	384
Muskingum Coll, New Concord, OH 43762	1837	Dr. Samuel W. Speck, Jr.	2-M	1,411	105
National-Louis U, Evanston, IL 60201-1730	1886	Dr. Orley R. Herron	1-D	7,430	287
Nazareth Coll of Rochester, Rochester, NY 14618-3790	1924	Dr. Rose Marie Beston	1-M	2,761	178
Nebraska Wesleyan U, Lincoln, NE 68504-2796	1887	Dr. John W. White, Jr.	2-B	1,562	152
Neumann Coll, Aston, PA 19014-1298	1965	Dr. Rosalie M. Mirenda	2-M	1,142	144
New Coll of California, San Francisco, CA 94102-5206	1971	Dr. Peter Gabel	1-F	1,600	90
New Hampshire Coll, Manchester, NH 03106-1045	1932	Dr. Richard A. Gustafson	1-M	5,614	223
New Jersey Inst of Tech, Newark, NJ 07102-1982	1881	Dr. Saul K. Fenster	5-D	7,837	534
New Mexico Highlands U, Las Vegas, NM 87701	1893	Mr. Selimo Rael	5-M	2,751	169
New Mexico Inst of Mining and Tech, Socorro, NM 87801	1889	Dr. Daniel H. Lopez	5-D	1,461	108
New Mexico State U, Las Cruces, NM 88003-8001	1888	Dr. William Conroy	5-D	14,748	664
New Orleans Baptist Theological Sem, New Orleans, LA 70126-4858	1917	Dr. Charles S. Kelley, Jr.	2-D	1,822	28
New Sch Bach of Arts, New Sch for Social Research, New York, NY 10011-8603	1919	Ms. Elizabeth D. Dickey	1-D	330	820
New York Inst of Tech, Old Westbury, NY 11568-8000	1955	Dr. Matthew Schure	1-F	9,396	921
New York U, New York, NY 10012-1019	1831	Dr. L. Jay Oliva	1-D	36,056	4,722
Niagara U, Niagara University, NY 14109	1856	Rev. Paul L. Golden, CM.	1-M	2,935	206
Nicholls State U, Thibodaux, LA 70310	1948	Dr. Donald J. Ayo	5-M	7,210	278
Nichols Coll, Dudley, MA 01571	1815	Dr. James J. Darazsdi	1-M	1,501	54
Norfolk State U, Norfolk, VA 23504-3907	1935	Dr. Harrison B. Wilson	5-D	8,352	616
North Adams State Coll, North Adams, MA 01247-4100	1894	Dr. Thomas D. Aceto	5-M	1,745	136
North Carolina Ag and Tech State U, Greensboro, NC 27411	1891	Dr. Edward B. Fort	5-D	7,533	516
North Carolina Central U, Durham, NC 27707-3129	1910	Mr. Julius L. Chambers	5-F	5,400	427
North Carolina State U, Raleigh, NC 27695	1887	Dr. Larry K. Monteith	5-D	27,169	2,623
North Central Bible Coll, Minneapolis, MN 55404-1322	1930	Dr. Gordon L. Anderson	2-B	1,008	64
North Central Coll, Naperville, IL 60566-7063	1861	Dr. Harold R. Wilde	2-M	2,623	205
North Dakota State U, Fargo, ND 58105	1890	Dr. Thomas R. Plough	5-D	9,688	497
Northeastern Illinois U, Chicago, IL 60625-4699	1961	Dr. Salme H. Steinberg	5-M	10,035	472
Northeastern State U, Tahlequah, OK 74464-2399	1846	Dr. Larry Williams	5-D	8,735	449
Northeastern U, Boston, MA 02115-5096	1898	Dr. Richard M. Freeland	1-D	24,579	2,130
Northeast Louisiana U, Monroe, LA 71209-0001	1931	Mr. Lawson L. Swearingen, Jr.	5-D	11,116	574
Northern Arizona U, Flagstaff, AZ 86011	1899	Dr. Clara M. Lovett	5-D	19,605	935
Northern Illinois U, De Kalb, IL 60115-2854	1895	Dr. John E. LaFourette	5-D	21,609	1,208
Northern Kentucky U, Highland Heights, KY 41099	1968	Dr. James C. Votruba	5-F	11,505	701
Northern Michigan U, Marquette, MI 49855-5301	1899	Dr. Judith I. Bailey	5-M	8,034	354
Northern State U, Aberdeen, SD 57401-7198	1901	Dr. John Hutchinson	5-M	2,634	135
North Georgia Coll & State U, Dahlonega, GA 30597-1001	1873	Dr. Delmas J. Allen	5-M	3,198	202
North Park U, Chicago, IL 60625-4895	1891	Dr. David G. Horner	2-D	1,815	86
Northwestern Coll, Orange City, IA 51041-1996	1882	Dr. James E. Bultman	2-B	1,160	103
Northwestern Coll, St Paul, MN 55113-1598	1902	Dr. Donald Ericksen	2-B	1,362	132
Northwestern Oklahoma State U, Alva, OK 73717-2799	1897	Dr. Joe J. Struckle	5-M	1,790	106
Northwestern State U of Louisiana, Natchitoches, LA 71497	1884	Dr. Randall Webb	5-D	9,037	318
Northwestern U, Evanston, IL 60208	1851	Dr. Henry S. Bienen	1-D	12,213	2,373
Northwest Missouri State U, Maryville, MO 64468-6001	1905	Dr. Dean L. Hubbard	5-M	6,154	259
Northwest Nazarene Coll, Nampa, ID 83686-5897	1913	Dr. Richard Hagood	2-M	1,201	105
Northwood U, Midland, MI 48640-2398	1959	Dr. David E. Fry	1-M	1,549	57
Norwich U, Northfield, VT 05663	1819	Dr. Richard Schneider	1-M	2,556	179
Notre Dame Coll, Manchester, NH 03104-2299	1950	Dr. Carol J. Descoteaux, CSC	2-M	1,017	127
Nova Southeastern U, Fort Lauderdale, FL 33314-7721	1964	Dr. Ovid C. Lewis	1-D	14,951	1,124
Nyack Coll, Nyack, NY 10960-3698	1882	Dr. David E. Schroeder	2-M	1,312	123
Oakland City U, Oakland City, IN 47660-1099	1885	Dr. James W. Murray	2-M	1,087	67
Oakland U, Rochester, MI 48309-4401	1957	Dr. Gary D. Russi	5-D	13,965	697
Oakwood Coll, Huntsville, AL 35896	1896	Dr. Benjamin F. Reaves	2-B	1,666	124
Oberlin Coll, Oberlin, OH 44074-1090	1833	Dr. Nancy Schrom Dye	1-B	2,861	251
Occidental Coll, Los Angeles, CA 90041-3392	1887	Dr. John B. Slaughter	1-M	1,534	199
Oglethorpe U, Atlanta, GA 30319-2797	1835	Dr. Donald S. Stanton	1-M	1,227	121
Ohio Dominican Coll, Columbus, OH 43219-2099	1911	Sr. Mary Andrew Matesich	2-B	1,883	110
Ohio Northern U, Ada, OH 45810-1599	1871	Dr. DeBow Freed	2-F	2,931	271
The Ohio State U, Columbus, OH 43210	1870	Dr. E. Gordon Gee	5-D	48,352	3,518
The Ohio State U at Lima, Lima, OH 45804-3576	1960	Dr. Violet I. Meek	5-B	1,281	72
The Ohio State U at Marion, Marion, OH 43302-5695	1958	Dr. F. Dominic Dottavio	5-B	1,312	82
Ohio State U–Mansfield Cmps, Mansfield, OH 44906-1599	1958	Dr. John O. Riedl	5-B	1,343	64
Ohio State U–Newark Cmps, Newark, OH 43055-1797	1957	Dr. Rafael L. Cortado	5-B	1,611	89
Ohio U, Athens, OH 45701-2979	1804	Dr. Robert Glidden	5-D	18,997	1,204
Ohio U–Chillicothe, Chillicothe, OH 45601-0629	1946	Dr. Delbert E. Meyer	5-B	1,565	118
Ohio U–Eastern, St Clairsville, OH 43950-9724	1957	Dr. James W. Newton	5-B	1,050	110
Ohio U–Lancaster, Lancaster, OH 43130-1097	1968	Dr. Charles P. Bird	5-M	1,500	129
Ohio U–Zanesville, Zanesville, OH 43701-2695	1946	Dr. Craig D. Laubenthal	5-M	1,195	49
Ohio Wesleyan U, Delaware, OH 43015	1842	Dr. Thomas B. Courtice	2-B	1,815	156
Oklahoma Baptist U, Shawnee, OK 74801-2558	1910	Dr. Bob R. Agee	2-M	2,361	150
Oklahoma Christian U of Science and Arts, Oklahoma City, OK 73136-1100	1950	Dr. Kevin Jacobs	2-M	1,562	127
Oklahoma City U, Oklahoma City, OK 73106-1402	1904	Dr. Jerald C. Walker	2-F	4,696	383
Oklahoma Panhandle State U, Goodwell, OK 73939-0430	1909	Dr. John Goodwin	5-B	1,366	73
Oklahoma State U, Stillwater, OK 74078	1890	Dr. James E. Halligan	5-D	19,201	1,158
Old Dominion U, Norfolk, VA 23529	1930	Dr. James V. Koch	5-D	11,400	1,143
Olivet Nazarene U, Kankakee, IL 60901-0592	1907	Dr. John C. Bowling	2-M	2,256	145
Oral Roberts U, Tulsa, OK 74171-0001	1963	Mr. Richard L. Roberts	2-D	3,761	223

Name, address	Year	Governing official, control, and highest degree offered		Enrollment	Faculty
Oregon Health Sciences U, Portland, OR 97201-3098	1974	Dr. Peter O. Kohler	12-D	1,812	76
Oregon Inst of Tech, Klamath Falls, OR 97601-8801	1947	Dr. Lawrence J. Wolf	5-M	2,339	162
Oregon State U, Corvallis, OR 97331	1868	Dr. Paul G. Risser	5-D	13,784	2,204
Otterbein Coll, Westerville, OH 43081	1847	Dr. C. Brent DeVore	2-M	2,526	159
Ouachita Baptist U, Arkadelphia, AR 71998-0001	1886	Dr. Ben M. Elrod	2-B	1,604	150
Our Lady of Holy Cross Coll, New Orleans, LA 70131-7399	1916	Rev. Thomas E. Chambers, CSC	2-M	1,316	99
Our Lady of the Lake U of San Antonio, San Antonio, TX 78207-4689	1895	Sr. Elizabeth Anne Sueltenfuss	2-D	3,468	217
Pace U, New York, NY 10038	1906	Dr. Patricia Ewers	1-D	11,915	1,007
Pacific Lutheran U, Tacoma, WA 98447	1890	Dr. Loren J. Anderson	2-M	3,463	338
Pacific Union Coll, Angwin, CA 94508	1882	Dr. D. Malcolm Maxwell	2-M	1,544	125
Pacific U, Forest Grove, OR 97116-1797	1849	Dr. Faith Gabelnick	1-F	1,750	176
Palm Beach Atlantic Coll, West Palm Beach, FL 33416-4708	1968	Dr. Paul R. Corts	2-M	1,830	152
Palmer Coll of Chiropractic, Davenport, IA 52803-5287	1897	Dr. Virgil V. Strang	1-F	1,922	135
Park Coll, Parkville, MO 64152-4358	1875	Dr. Donald J. Breckon	2-M	1,207	100
Parsons Sch of Design, New Sch for Social Research, New York, NY 10011-8878	1896	Ms. Lesley Cadman	1-M	1,881	407
Penn State U Abington Coll, Abington, PA 19001-3918	1950	Dr. Karen Wiley Sandler	12-B	3,262	162
Penn State U Altoona Coll, Altoona, PA 16601-3760	1929	Dr. Allen C. Meadors	12-B	3,475	192
Penn State U at Erie, The Behrend Coll, Erie, PA 16563	1948	Dr. John M. Lilley	12-M	3,207	208
Penn State U Berks-Lehigh Valley Coll, Reading, PA 19610-6009	1924	Dr. Frederick H. Gaige	12-B	2,423	155
Penn State U Harrisburg Cmps of the Capital Coll, Middletown, PA 17057-4898	1966	Dr. John G. Bruhn	12-D	3,417	227
Penn State U Univ Park Cmps, University Park, PA 16802-1503	1855	Dr. Graham B. Spanier	12-D	39,782	2,231
Pepperdine U, Malibu, CA 90263-0001	1937	Dr. David Davenport	2-D	7,896	296
Peru State Coll, Peru, NE 68421	1867	Dr. Robert L. Burns	5-M	1,800	121
Pfeiffer U, Misenheimer, NC 28109-0960	1885	Dr. Zane E. Eargle	2-M	1,534	52
Philadelphia Coll of Bible, Langhorne, PA 19047-2990	1913	Dr. W. Sherrill Babb	2-M	1,187	116
Philadelphia Coll of Pharmacy and Science, Philadelphia, PA 19104-4495	1821	Dr. Philip P. Gerbino	1-D	2,021	205
Philadelphia Coll of Textiles and Science, Philadelphia, PA 19144-5497	1884	Dr. James P. Gallagher	1-M	3,402	227
Piedmont Coll, Demorest, GA 30535-0010	1897	Dr. W. Ray Cleere	2-M	1,128	110
Pittsburg State U, Pittsburg, KS 66762-5880	1903	Dr. John R. Darling	5-M	6,426	313
Plymouth State Coll of the U System of NH, Plymouth, NH 03264-1595	1871	Dr. Donald P. Wharton	5-M	4,000	200
Point Loma Nazarene Coll, San Diego, CA 92106-2899	1902	Dr. Jim L. Bond	2-M	2,491	251
Point Park Coll, Pittsburgh, PA 15222-1984	1960	Dr. Katherine Henderson	1-M	2,297	195
Polytechnic U, Brooklyn Cmps, Brooklyn, NY 11201-2990	1854	Dr. David C. Chang	1-D	2,219	293
Polytechnic U of Puerto Rico, Hato Rey, PR 00919	1966	Mr. Ernesto Vazquez-Barquet	1-M	4,461	249
Pomona Coll, Claremont, CA 91711	1887	Dr. Peter W. Stanley	1-B	1,420	154
Pontifical Catholic U of Puerto Rico, Ponce, PR 00731-6382	1948	Mrs. Marcelina Velez de Santiago	2-M	11,470	636
Portland State U, Portland, OR 97207-0751	1946	Dr. Judith Ramaley	5-D	14,768	746
Prairie View A&M U, Prairie View, TX 77446-0188	1878	Dr. Charles A. Hines	5-M	5,999	329
Pratt Inst, Brooklyn, NY 11205-3899	1887	Dr. Thomas F. Schutte	1-M	3,363	502
Presbyterian Coll, Clinton, SC 29325	1880	Dr. Kenneth B. Orr	2-B	1,153	114
Princeton U, Princeton, NJ 08544-1019	1746	Mr. Harold T. Shapiro	1-D	6,340	890
Providence Coll, Providence, RI 02918	1917	Rev. Philip A. Smith, OP	2-D	5,621	391
Purchase Coll, State U of NY, Purchase, NY 10577-1400	1967	Mr. Bill Lacy	5-M	2,396	250
Purdue U, West Lafayette, IN 47907-1968	1869	Dr. Steven C. Beering	5-D	35,156	2,204
Purdue U Calumet, Hammond, IN 46323-2094	1951	Dr. James Yackel	5-M	9,402	457
Purdue U North Central, Westville, IN 46391-9528	1967	Dr. Dale W. Alspaugh	5-M	3,399	221
Queens Coll, Charlotte, NC 28274-0002	1857	Dr. Billy O. Wireman	2-M	1,564	106
Queens Coll of the City U of NY, Flushing, NY 11367-1597	1937	Dr. Allen Lee Sessoms	11-M	17,073	1,035
Quincy U, Quincy, IL 62301-2699	1860	Rev. Dr. Eugene Kole, OFM	2-M	1,141	104
Quinnipiac Coll, Hamden, CT 06518-1904	1929	Dr. John L. Lahey	1-F	5,117	381
Radford U, Radford, VA 24142	1910	Dr. Douglas Covington	5-M	8,270	505
Ramapo Coll of New Jersey, Mahwah, NJ 07430-1680	1969	Dr. Robert A. Scott	5-M	4,001	298
Randolph-Macon Coll, Ashland, VA 23005-5505	1830	Dr. Ladell Payne	2-B	1,101	151
Reed Coll, Portland, OR 97202-8199	1909	Dr. Steven Koblik	1-M	1,325	128
Regis Coll, Weston, MA 02193-1571 (3)	1927	Dr. Sheila Megley, RSM	2-M	1,401	141
Regis U, Denver, CO 80221-1099	1877	Rev. Michael J. Sheeran, SJ	2-M	7,039	109
Rensselaer Polytechnic Inst, Troy, NY 12180-3590	1824	Dr. R. Byron Pipes	1-D	6,250	342
Rhode Island Coll, Providence, RI 02908-1924	1854	Dr. John Nazarian	5-M	7,150	640
Rhode Island Sch of Design, Providence, RI 02903-2784	1877	Mr. Roger Mandle	1-M	2,003	315
Rhodes Coll, Memphis, TN 38112-1690	1848	Dr. James H. Daughdrill, Jr.	2-M	1,425	145
Rice U, Houston, TX 77005	1912	Dr. Malcolm Gillis	1-D	4,225	575
The Richard Stockton Coll of New Jersey, Pomona, NJ 08240-9988	1971	Dr. Vera King Farris	5-M	5,512	297
Rider U, Lawrenceville, NJ 08648-3001	1865	Dr. J. Barton Luedeke	1-M	4,640	369
Rivier Coll, Nashua, NH 03060-5086	1933	Sr. Jeanne Perreault	2-M	2,798	190
Roanoke Coll, Salem, VA 24153-3794	1842	Dr. David M. Gring	2-B	1,694	164
Robert Morris Coll, Chicago, IL 60601-2592	1913	Mr. Michael Viollt	1-B	3,734	246
Robert Morris Coll, Moon Township, PA 15108-1189	1921	Dr. Edward A. Nicholson	1-M	4,907	296
Roberts Wesleyan Coll, Rochester, NY 14624-1997	1866	Dr. William C. Crothers	2-M	1,337	121
Rochester Inst of Tech, Rochester, NY 14623-5604	1829	Dr. Albert J. Simone	1-D	12,933	1,076
Rockford Coll, Rockford, IL 61108-2393	1847	Dr. William A. Shields	1-M	1,309	132
Rockhurst Coll, Kansas City, MO 64110-2561	1910	Rev. Peter B Ely, SJ	2-M	2,866	199
Roger Williams U, Bristol, RI 02809	1956	Mr. Anthony J. Santoro	1-F	3,875	300
Rollins Coll, Winter Park, FL 32789-4499	1885	Dr. Rita Bornstein	1-M	3,297	256
Roosevelt U, Chicago, IL 60605-1394	1945	Dr. Theodore L. Gross	1-D	6,663	530
Rose-Hulman Inst of Tech, Terre Haute, IN 47803-3920	1874	Dr. Samuel F. Hulbert	1-M	1,574	133
Rowan U, Glassboro, NJ 08028-1701	1923	Dr. Herman D. James	5-M	9,213	350
Rush U, Chicago, IL 60612-3832	1969	Dr. Leo M. Henikoff	1-D	1,474	170
Russell Sage Coll, Troy, NY 12180-4115 (3)	1916	Dr. Jeanne K. Neff	1-B	1,038	193
Rutgers, State U of NJ, Camden Coll of Arts & Scis, Camden, NJ 08102	1927	Dr. Robert A. Catlin	5-B	2,223	NR
Rutgers, State U of NJ, Coll of Engineering, Piscataway, NJ 08855-0909	1864	Dr. Ellis H. Dill	5-B	2,156	NR
Rutgers, State U of NJ, Coll of Nursing, Newark, NJ 07102-1896	1956	Dr. Hurdis M. Griffith	5-D	370	NR
Rutgers, State U of NJ, Coll of Pharmacy, Piscataway, NJ 08855-0789	1927	Dr. John Louis Colaizzi	5-D	986	NR
Rutgers, State U of NJ, Cook Coll, New Brunswick, NJ 08903-0231	1921	Dr. Bruce C. Carlton	5-B	3,160	NR
Rutgers, State U of NJ, Douglass Coll, New Brunswick, NJ 08903-0270 (3)	1918	Dr. Martha A. Cotter	5-B	2,965	NR

Name, address	Year	Governing official, control, and highest degree offered		Enroll-ment	Faculty
Rutgers, State U of NJ, Livingston Coll, New Brunswick, NJ 08903	1969	Dr. Arnold G. Hyndman	5-B	3,032	NR
Rutgers, State U of NJ, Mason Gross Sch of Arts, New Brunswick, NJ 08903-0270	1976	Dr. Marilyn F. Somville	5-D	725	NR
Rutgers, State U of NJ, Newark Coll of Arts & Scis, Newark, NJ 07102-1896	1946	Dr. David Hosford	5-B	3,684	NR
Rutgers, State U of NJ, Rutgers Coll, New Brunswick, NJ 08903-2101	1766	Dr. Carl Kirschner	5-B	10,317	NR
Rutgers, State U of NJ, U Coll–Camden, Camden, NJ 08102-1401	1950	Dr. Robert A. Catlin	5-B	714	NR
Rutgers, State U of NJ, U Coll–Newark, Newark, NJ 07102-1896	1934	Dr. David Hosford	5-B	1,776	NR
Rutgers, State U of NJ, U Coll–New Brunswick, New Brunswick, NJ 08903	1934	Dr. Emmitt Dennis	5-B	2,911	NR
Sacred Heart U, Fairfield, CT 06432-1000	1963	Dr. Anthony J. Cernera	2-M	5,545	349
Saginaw Valley State U, University Center, MI 48710	1963	Dr. Eric R. Gilbertson	5-M	7,338	461
St Ambrose U, Davenport, IA 52803-2898	1882	Dr. Edward J. Rogalski	2-M	2,680	200
Saint Anselm Coll, Manchester, NH 03102-1310	1889	Rev. Jonathan DeFelice, OSB	2-B	1,928	159
Saint Augustine's Coll, Raleigh, NC 27610-2298	1867	Dr. Bernard W. Franklin	2-B	1,584	114
St Bonaventure U, St Bonaventure, NY 14778-2284	1858	Dr. Robert J. Wickenheiser	2-M	2,723	117
St Cloud State U, St Cloud, MN 56301-4498	1869	Dr. Bruce Grube	5-D	14,048	662
St Edward's U, Austin, TX 78704-6489	1885	Dr. Patricia Hayes	2-M	3,082	235
St Francis Coll, Brooklyn Heights, NY 11201-4398	1884	Dr. Frank J. Macchianola	1-B	2,077	160
Saint Francis Coll, Loretto, PA 15940-0600	1847	Rev. Christian R. Oravec	2-M	1,886	182
St John Fisher Coll, Rochester, NY 14618-3597	1948	Dr. Katherine E. Keough	2-M	2,333	164
Saint John's U, Collegeville, MN 56321 (1)	1857	Br. Dietrich Reinhart, OSB	2-M	1,796	172
St John's U, Jamaica, NY 11439	1870	Rev. Donald J. Harrington, CM	2-D	16,804	1,050
Saint Joseph Coll, West Hartford, CT 06117-2700 (4)	1932	Dr. Winifred E. Coleman	2-M	1,922	82
Saint Joseph's Coll, Standish, ME 04084-5263	1912	Dr. David House	2-M	1,105	94
St Joseph's Coll, New York, Brooklyn, NY 11205-3688	1916	Sr. George Aquin O'Connor	1-B	1,263	133
St Joseph's Coll, Suffolk Cmps, Patchogue, NY 11772-2399	1916	Sr. George Aquin O'Connor	1-M	2,593	253
Saint Joseph's U, Philadelphia, PA 19131-1395	1851	Rev. Nicholas S. Rashford, SJ	2-M	6,963	405
St Lawrence U, Canton, NY 13617-1455	1856	Dr. Daniel F. Sullivan	1-M	2,096	181
Saint Leo Coll, Saint Leo, FL 33574-2008	1889	Dr. Arthur F. Kirk, Jr.	2-M	1,651	125
Saint Louis U, St Louis, MO 63103-2097	1818	Rev. Lawrence Biondi, SJ	2-D	10,572	2,609
Saint Mary-of-the-Woods Coll, Saint Mary-of-the-Woods, IN 47876 (3)	1840	Dr. Barbara Doherty, SP	2-M	1,266	55
Saint Mary's Coll, Notre Dame, IN 46556 (3)	1844	Dr. Marilou Eldred	2-B	1,474	179
Saint Mary's Coll of California, Moraga, CA 94575	1863	Br. Craig J. Franz, FSC,Ph.D.	2-M	4,204	194
St Mary's Coll of Maryland, St Mary's City, MD 20686	1840	Dr. Jane Margaret O'Brien	5-B	1,478	164
Saint Mary's U of Minnesota, Winona, MN 55987-1399	1912	Br. Louis DeThomasis, FSC	2-M	9,321	665
St Mary's U of San Antonio, San Antonio, TX 78228-8507	1852	Rev. John Moder, SM	2-D	4,096	322
Saint Michael's Coll, Colchester, VT 05439	1904	Dr. Marc VanderHeyden	2-M	2,641	249
St Norbert Coll, De Pere, WI 54115-2099	1898	Dr. Thomas A. Manion	2-M	2,122	175
St Olaf Coll, Northfield, MN 55057-1098	1874	Dr. Mark U. Edwards, Jr.	2-B	2,959	347
Saint Peter's Coll, Jersey City, NJ 07306-5997	1872	Rev. James N. Loughran, SJ	2-M	3,863	408
St Thomas Aquinas Coll, Sparkill, NY 10976	1952	Dr. Margaret M. Fitzpatrick, SC	1-M	2,100	115
St Thomas U, Miami, FL 33054-6459	1961	Rev. Msgr. Franklyn M. Casale	2-F	2,262	133
Saint Vincent Coll, Latrobe, PA 15650	1846	Rev. Martin R. Bartel, OSB	2-B	1,215	105
Saint Xavier U, Chicago, IL 60655-3105	1847	Dr. Richard Yanikoski	2-M	4,200	261
Salem State Coll, Salem, MA 01970-5353	1854	Dr. Nancy D. Harrington	5-M	10,132	409
Salisbury State U, Salisbury, MD 21801-6837	1925	Dr. William C. Merwin	5-M	5,308	NR
Salve Regina U, Newport, RI 02840-4192	1934	Dr. Therese Antone, RSM	2-D	1,844	197
Samford U, Birmingham, AL 35229-0002	1841	Dr. Thomas E. Corts	2-F	4,473	429
Sam Houston State U, Huntsville, TX 77341	1879	Dr. Bobby K. Marks	5-D	12,564	516
San Diego State U, San Diego, CA 92182	1897	Dr. Stephen L. Weber	5-D	29,331	2,264
San Francisco State U, San Francisco, CA 94132-1722	1899	Dr. Robert A. Corrigan	5-M	27,420	1,546
San Jose State U, San Jose, CA 95192-0001	1857	Dr. Robert L. Caret	5-M	25,874	1,784
Santa Clara U, Santa Clara, CA 95053-0001	1851	Rev. Paul L. Locatelli, SJ	2-D	7,863	592
Sarah Lawrence Coll, Bronxville, NY 10708	1926	Dr. Alice Stone Ilchman	1-M	1,329	232
Savannah Coll of Art and Design, Savannah, GA 31402-3146	1978	Mr. Richard G. Rowan	1-M	3,093	155
Savannah State U, Savannah, GA 31404	1890	Dr. John T. Wolfe, Jr.	5-B	3,211	155
Sch of the Art Inst of Chicago, Chicago, IL 60603-3103	1866	Mr. Anthony Jones	1-M	2,012	392
Sch of Visual Arts, New York, NY 10010-3994	1947	Mr. David Rhodes	3-M	3,047	736
Seattle Pacific U, Seattle, WA 98119-1997	1891	Dr. Philip W. Eaton	2-D	3,293	208
Seattle U, Seattle, WA 98122	1891	Rev. Stephen V. Sundborg, SJ	2-D	5,990	397
Seton Hall U, South Orange, NJ 07079-2697	1856	Msgr. Robert Sheeran	2-D	8,518	715
Shawnee State U, Portsmouth, OH 45662-4344	1986	Dr. Clive Veri	5-B	3,505	239
Shaw U, Raleigh, NC 27601-2399	1865	Dr. Talbert O. Shaw	2-B	2,262	249
Shenandoah U, Winchester, VA 22601-5195	1875	Dr. James A. Davis	2-D	1,871	242
Shepherd Coll, Shepherdstown, WV 25443-3210	1871	Dr. David L. Dunlop	5-B	3,845	257
Shippensburg U of Pennsylvania, Shippensburg, PA 17257-2299	1871	Dr. Anthony F. Ceddia	5-M	6,683	355
Shorter Coll, Rome, GA 30165-4298	1873	Dr. Larry Lee McSwain	2-B	1,577	73
Siena Coll, Loudonville, NY 12211-1462	1937	Fr. Kevin Macklin, OFM	2-M	3,212	252
Siena Heights Coll, Adrian, MI 49221-1796	1919	Dr. Richard Artman	2-M	2,002	110
Silver Lake Coll, Manitowoc, WI 54220-9319	1869	Sr. Barbara Belinske	2-M	1,144	132
Simmons Coll, Boston, MA 02115 (3)	1899	Dr. Daniel Cheever	1-D	3,740	381
Simpson Coll, Redding, CA 96003-8606	1921	Dr. James M. Grant	2-M	1,169	58
Simpson Coll, Indianola, IA 50125-1297	1860	Dr. Stephen G. Jennings	2-B	1,805	161
Skidmore Coll, Saratoga Springs, NY 12866-1632	1903	Dr. David H. Porter	1-M	2,244	200
Slippery Rock U of Pennsylvania, Slippery Rock, PA 16057	1889	Dr. G. Warren Smith, II	5-D	7,291	395
Smith Coll, Northampton, MA 01063 (3)	1871	Ms. Ruth Simmons	1-D	2,788	276
Sonoma State U, Rohnert Park, CA 94928-3609	1960	Dr. Ruben Arminana	5-M	6,999	435
South Carolina State U, Orangeburg, SC 29117-0001	1896	Dr. Leroy Davis	5-D	4,993	229
South Dakota Sch of Mines and Tech, Rapid City, SD 57701-3995	1885	Dr. Richard J. Gowen	5-D	2,218	145
South Dakota State U, Brookings, SD 57007	1881	Dr. Robert T. Wagner	5-D	8,350	539
Southeastern Coll of the Assemblies of God, Lakeland, FL 33801-6099	1935	Dr. James Hennesy	2-B	1,090	85
Southeastern Louisiana U, Hammond, LA 70402	1925	Dr. Sally Clausen	5-M	14,592	615
Southeastern Oklahoma State U, Durant, OK 74701-0609	1909	Mr. Glen Johnson	5-M	3,831	202
Southeast Missouri State U, Cape Girardeau, MO 63701-4799	1873	Dr. Dale F. Nitzschke	5-M	8,200	436
Southern Adventist U, Collegedale, TN 37315-0370	1892	Dr. Gordon Bietz	2-M	1,650	133
Southern Arkansas U–Magnolia, Magnolia, AR 71753	1909	Dr. Steven G. Gamble	5-M	2,592	154
Southern California Coll, Costa Mesa, CA 92626-6597	1920	Mr. Wayne E. Kraiss	2-M	1,226	57
Southern Connecticut State U, New Haven, CT 06515-1355	1893	Mr. Michael J. Adanti	5-M	11,412	719
Southern Illinois U at Carbondale, Carbondale, IL 62901-6806	1869	Dr. Donald L. Beggs	5-D	21,863	1,612
Southern Illinois U at Edwardsville, Edwardsville, IL 62026-0001	1957	Dr. Nancy Belck	5-F	11,151	750
Southern Methodist U, Dallas, TX 75275	1911	Dr. R. Gerald Turner	2-D	9,464	752
Southern Nazarene U, Bethany, OK 73008-2694	1899	Dr. Loren P. Gresham	2-M	1,828	137
Southern Oregon U, Ashland, OR 97520	1926	Dr. Stephen Reno	5-M	4,247	270

Name, address	Year	Governing official, control, and highest degree offered		Enroll-ment	Faculty
Southern Polytechnic State U, Marietta, GA 30060-2896	1948	Dr. Daniel S. Papp	5-M	3,871	203
Southern U and A&M Coll, Baton Rouge, LA 70813	1880	Dr. Marvin L. Yates	5-D	9,800	603
Southern Utah U, Cedar City, UT 84720-2498	1897	Dr. Gerald R. Sherratt	5-M	5,640	217
Southern Wesleyan U, Central, SC 29630-1020	1906	Dr. David J. Spittal	2-M	1,298	37
Southwest Baptist U, Bolivar, MO 65613-2597	1878	Dr. C. Pat Taylor	2-M	3,096	204
Southwestern Adventist U, Keene, TX 76059	1894	Dr. Marvin E. Anderson	2-M	1,030	80
Southwestern Oklahoma State U, Weatherford, OK 73096-3098	1901	Dr. Joe Anna Hibler	5-M	4,506	240
Southwestern U, Georgetown, TX 78626	1840	Dr. Roy B. Shilling, Jr.	2-B	1,226	152
Southwest Missouri State U, Springfield, MO 65804-0094	1905	Dr. John H. Keiser	5-M	15,535	821
Southwest State U, Marshall, MN 56258-1598	1963	Dr. Doug Sweetland	5-M	2,900	124
Southwest Texas State U, San Marcos, TX 78666	1899	Dr. Jerome Supple	5-D	20,776	931
Spalding U, Louisville, KY 40203-2188	1814	Dr. Thomas R. Oates	2-D	1,423	144
Spelman Coll, Atlanta, GA 30314-4399 (3)	1881	Dr. Johnnetta B. Cole	1-B	1,961	209
Spring Arbor Coll, Spring Arbor, MI 49283-9799	1873	Dr. James Chapman	2-M	1,069	103
Springfield Coll, Springfield, MA 01109-3797	1885	Dr. Randolph W. Bromery	1-D	2,923	232
Spring Hill Coll, Mobile, AL 36608-1791	1830	Rev. William J. Rewak, SJ	2-M	1,445	90
Stanford U, Stanford, CA 94305-9991	1891	Mr. Gerhard Casper	1-D	13,811	1,488
State U of NY at Albany, Albany, NY 12222-0001	1844	Dr. Karen R. Hitchcock	5-D	14,215	835
State U of NY at Binghamton, Binghamton, NY 13902-6000	1946	Dr. Lois B. DeFleur	5-D	11,976	683
State U of NY at Buffalo, Buffalo, NY 14260	1846	Mr. William R. Greiner	5-D	23,577	1,734
State U of NY at New Paltz, New Paltz, NY 12561-2499	1828	Dr. Roger W. Bowen	5-M	7,539	555
State U of NY at Oswego, Oswego, NY 13126	1861	Dr. Deborah F. Stanley	5-M	8,264	391
State U of NY at Stony Brook, Stony Brook, NY 11794	1957	Dr. Shirley Strum Kenny	5-D	17,309	1,610
State U of NY Coll at Brockport, Brockport, NY 14420-2997	1867	Dr. Paul Yu	5-M	8,723	509
State U of NY Coll at Buffalo, Buffalo, NY 14222-1095	1867	Dr. Muriel A. Moore	5-M	11,184	654
State U of NY Coll at Cortland, Cortland, NY 13045	1868	Dr. Judson H. Taylor	5-M	6,278	441
State U of NY Coll at Fredonia, Fredonia, NY 14063	1826	Dr. Dennis L. Hefner	5-M	4,556	292
State U of NY Coll at Geneseo, Geneseo, NY 14454-1401	1871	Dr. Christopher Dahl	5-M	5,564	322
State U of NY Coll at Old Westbury, Old Westbury, NY 11568-0210	1965	Dr. L. Eudora Pettigrew	5-B	3,790	233
State U of NY Coll at Oneonta, Oneonta, NY 13820	1889	Dr. Alan B. Donovan	5-M	5,616	325
State U of NY Coll at Plattsburgh, Plattsburgh, NY 12901	1889	Dr. Horace A. Judson	5-M	5,624	346
State U of NY Coll at Potsdam, Potsdam, NY 13676	1816	Dr. William Merwin	5-M	4,073	272
State U of NY Coll of Environ Sci and Forestry, Syracuse, NY 13210-2779	1911	Dr. Ross S. Whaley	5-D	1,740	127
State U of NY Empire State Coll, Saratoga Springs, NY 12866-4391	1971	Dr. James W. Hall	5-M	7,123	329
State U of NY Health Science Ctr at Brooklyn, Brooklyn, NY 11203-2098	1858	Dr. Eugene Feigelson	5-D	1,604	156
State U of NY Health Science Ctr at Syracuse, Syracuse, NY 13210-2334	1950	Dr. Gregory L. Eastwood	5-D	1,020	45
State U of NY Inst of Tech at Utica/Rome, Utica, NY 13504-3050	1966	Dr. Peter J. Cayan	5-M	2,317	155
State U of West Georgia, Carrollton, GA 30118	1933	Dr. Beheruz N. Sethna	5-M	8,560	375
Stephen F Austin State U, Nacogdoches, TX 75962	1923	Dr. Daniel D. Angel	5-D	11,671	680
Stetson U, DeLand, FL 32720-3781	1883	Dr. H. Douglas Lee	1-F	2,784	215
Stevens Inst of Tech, Hoboken, NJ 07030	1870	Dr. Harold J. Raveche	1-D	3,382	195
Stonehill Coll, Easton, MA 02357	1948	Rev. Bartley MacPhaidin, CSC	2-B	2,041	195
Strayer Coll, Washington, DC 20005-2603	1892	Mr. Ron K. Bailey	3-M	8,172	284
Suffolk U, Boston, MA 02108-2770	1906	Mr. David J. Sargent	1-D	6,401	619
Sullivan Coll, Louisville, KY 40205	1864	Mr. A.R. Sullivan	3-M	2,321	88
Sul Ross State U, Alpine, TX 79832	1920	Dr. R. Vic Morgan	5-M	2,458	70
Susquehanna U, Selinsgrove, PA 17870-1001	1858	Dr. Joel L. Cunningham	2-B	1,568	156
Swarthmore Coll, Swarthmore, PA 19081-1397	1864	Dr. Alfred H. Bloom	1-B	1,437	187
Syracuse U, Syracuse, NY 13244-0003	1870	Dr. Kenneth A. Shaw	1-D	14,719	1,378
Tarleton State U, Stephenville, TX 76402	1899	Dr. Dennis P. McCabe	5-M	6,369	332
Taylor U, Upland, IN 46989-1001	1846	Dr. Jay L. Kesler	2-B	1,866	144
Teikyo Post U, Waterbury, CT 06723-2540	1890	Dr. Phyllis C. DeLeo	1-B	1,550	24
Temple U, Philadelphia, PA 19122-6096	1884	Mr. Peter J. Liacouras	12-D	25,469	2,457
Tennessee State U, Nashville, TN 37209-1561	1912	Dr. James A. Hefner	5-D	8,643	473
Tennessee Tech U, Cookeville, TN 38505	1915	Dr. Angelo A. Volpe	5-D	8,173	472
Texas A&M International U, Laredo, TX 78041-1900	1969	Dr. J. Charles Jennett	5-M	2,510	121
Texas A&M U, College Station, TX 77843-1244	1876	Dr. Ray M. Bowen	5-D	41,892	2,307
Texas A&M U at Galveston, Galveston, TX 77553-1675	1962	Dr. Viola E. Florez	5-B	1,203	86
Texas A&M U–Commerce, Commerce, TX 75429-3011	1889	Dr. Jerry D. Morris	5-D	7,546	383
Texas A&M U–Corpus Christi, Corpus Christi, TX 78412-5503	1947	Dr. Robert R. Furgason	5-D	5,671	343
Texas A&M U–Kingsville, Kingsville, TX 78363	1925	Dr. Manuel L. Ibanez	5-D	6,113	337
Texas A&M U–Texarkana, Texarkana, TX 75505-5518	1971	Dr. Stephen R. Hensley	5-M	1,187	40
Texas Christian U, Fort Worth, TX 76129-0002	1873	Dr. William E. Tucker	2-D	6,961	493
Texas Lutheran U, Seguin, TX 78155-5999	1891	Dr. Jon Moline	2-B	1,234	97
Texas Southern U, Houston, TX 77004-4584	1947	Mr. James M. Douglas, Esq.	5-D	9,518	524
Texas Tech U, Lubbock, TX 79409	1923	Mr. John T. Montford	5-D	24,717	990
Texas Wesleyan U, Fort Worth, TX 76105-1536	1890	Dr. Jake B. Schrum	2-F	2,966	245
Texas Woman's U, Denton, TX 76204 (4)	1901	Dr. Carol Surles	5-D	9,788	623
Thomas Edison State Coll, Trenton, NJ 08608-1176	1972	Dr. George A. Pruitt	5-M	8,585	443
Thomas Jefferson U, Philadelphia, PA 19107	1824	Dr. Paul C. Brucker	1-M	1,175	223
Thomas More Coll, Crestview Hills, KY 41017-3495	1921	Rev. William F. Cleves	2-M	1,345	174
Tiffin U, Tiffin, OH 44883-2161	1888	Dr. George Kidd, Jr.	1-M	1,151	84
Touro Coll, New York, NY 10010	1971	Dr. Bernard Lander	1-F	8,876	810
Towson U, Towson, MD 21252-0001	1866	Dr. Hoke L. Smith	5-M	15,105	973
Trevecca Nazarene U, Nashville, TN 37210-2834	1901	Dr. Millard Reed	2-M	1,547	127
Trinity Coll, Hartford, CT 06106-3100	1823	Dr. Evan S. Dobelle	1-M	2,134	255
Trinity Coll, Washington, DC 20017-1094 (3)	1897	Ms. Patricia A. McGuire	2-M	1,453	136
Trinity Coll of Vermont, Burlington, VT 05401-1470 (4)	1925	Dr. Lorna Edmunson	2-M	1,042	132
Trinity International U, Deerfield, IL 60015-1284	1897	Dr. Gregory Waybright	2-D	2,160	157
Trinity U, San Antonio, TX 78212-7200	1869	Dr. Ronald K. Calgaard	2-M	2,495	265
Tri-State U, Angola, IN 46703-1764	1884	Dr. R. John Reynolds	1-B	1,146	91
Troy State U, Troy, AL 36082	1887	Dr. Jack Hawkins, Jr.	5-M	6,211	359
Troy State U Dothan, Dothan, AL 36304-0368	1961	Dr. Michael Malone	5-M	2,150	144
Troy State U Montgomery, Montgomery, AL 36103-4419	1957	Dr. Glenda M. Curry	5-M	3,360	187
Truman State U, Kirksville, MO 63501-4221	1867	Dr. Jack Magruder	5-M	6,261	390
Tufts U, Medford, MA 02155	1852	Dr. John DiBiaggio	1-D	8,183	1,084
Tulane U, New Orleans, LA 70118-5669	1834	Dr. Eamon M. Kelly	1-D	11,246	746
Tusculum Coll, Greeneville, TN 37743-9997	1794	Dr. Robert E. Knott	2-M	1,516	131
Tuskegee U, Tuskegee, AL 36088	1881	Dr. Benjamin F. Payton	1-F	3,124	306
Union Coll, Schenectady, NY 12308-2311	1795	Dr. Roger H. Hull	1-M	2,335	190
The Union Inst, Cincinnati, OH 45206-1925	1964	Dr. Robert T. Conley	1-D	2,016	122
Union U, Jackson, TN 38305-3697	1823	Dr. David S. Dockery	2-M	1,975	157
United States Air Force Acad, USAF Academy, CO 80840-5025	1954	Maj. Gen. Tad Oelstrom	4-B	4,308	558
United States International U, San Diego, CA 92131-1799	1952	Dr. Garry D. Hays	1-D	1,873	111

Name, address	Year	Governing official, control, and highest degree offered		Enrollment	Faculty
United States Military Acad, West Point, NY 10996	1802	Lt. Gen. Daniel W. Christman	4-B	4,016	547
United States Naval Acad, Annapolis, MD 21402-5000	1845	Adm. Charles Larson	4-B	4,000	600
Universidad del Turabo, Gurabo, PR 00778-3030	1972	Dr. Dennis Alicea	1-M	7,320	NR
Universidad Metropolitana, Río Piedras, PR 00928-1150	1980	Dr. Rene L. Labarca Bonnet	1-M	4,700	NR
The U of Akron, Akron, OH 44325-0001	1870	Dr. Marion Ruebel	5-D	24,252	1,739
The U of Alabama, Tuscaloosa, AL 35487	1831	Dr. Andrew A. Sorensen	5-D	17,565	1,011
The U of Alabama at Birmingham, Birmingham, AL 35294	1969	Mr. Paul Hardin	5-D	15,274	1,796
The U of Alabama in Huntsville, Huntsville, AL 35899	1950	Dr. Frank Franz	5-D	4,982	421
U of Alaska Anchorage, Anchorage, AK 99508-8060	1954	Mr. Edward Lee Gorsuch	5-M	13,049	982
U of Alaska Fairbanks, Fairbanks, AK 99775-7480	1917	Dr. Joan K. Wadlow	5-D	5,197	717
U of Alaska Southeast, Juneau, AK 99801-8625	1972	Dr. Marshall Lind	5-M	2,944	134
U of Arizona, Tucson, AZ 85721	1885	Dr. Manuel T. Pacheco	5-D	33,504	1,592
U of Arkansas, Fayetteville, AR 72701-1201	1871	Dr. Daniel E. Ferritor	5-D	14,577	884
U of Arkansas at Little Rock, Little Rock, AR 72204-1099	1927	Dr. Charles E. Hathaway	5-D	10,720	653
U of Arkansas at Monticello, Monticello, AR 71656	1909	Dr. Fred J. Taylor	5-M	2,124	126
U of Arkansas at Pine Bluff, Pine Bluff, AR 71601-2799	1873	Dr. Lawrence A. Davis, Jr.	5-M	3,242	213
U of Arkansas for Medical Sciences, Little Rock, AR 72205-7199	1879	Dr. Harry P. Ward	5-D	1,851	NR
U of Baltimore, Baltimore, MD 21201-5779	1925	Dr. H. Mebane Turner	5-F	4,361	273
U of Biblical Studies and Sem, Bethany, OK 73008	1976	NR	2-M	1,400	12
U of Bridgeport, Bridgeport, CT 06601	1927	Dr. Richard L. Rubenstein	1-D	2,142	260
U of California, Berkeley, Berkeley, CA 94720	1868	Dr. Chang-Lin Tien	5-D	29,630	1,787
U of California, Davis, Davis, CA 95616	1905	Dr. Larry N. Vanderhoef	5-D	23,931	1,597
U of California, Irvine, Irvine, CA 92697	1965	Dr. Laurel L. Wilkening	5-D	17,281	997
U of California, Los Angeles, Los Angeles, CA 90095	1919	Dr. Albert Carnesale	5-D	34,935	3,228
U of California, Riverside, Riverside, CA 92521-0102	1954	Dr. Raymond L. Orbach	5-D	9,063	430
U of California, San Diego, La Jolla, CA 92093-5003	1959	Dr. Robert C. Dynes	5-D	18,119	1,436
U of California, Santa Barbara, Santa Barbara, CA 93106	1909	Dr. Henry T. Yang	5-D	18,531	849
U of California, Santa Cruz, Santa Cruz, CA 95064	1965	Dr. M. R. C. Greenwood	5-D	10,215	556
U of Central Arkansas, Conway, AR 72035-0001	1907	Dr. Winfred L. Thompson	5-M	8,994	522
U of Central Florida, Orlando, FL 32816	1963	Dr. John C. Hitt	5-D	27,278	NR
U of Central Oklahoma, Edmond, OK 73034-5209	1890	Mr. George Nigh	5-M	14,481	676
U of Central Texas, Killeen, TX 76540-1416	1973	Dr. Pauline Moseley	1-M	1,039	57
The U of Charleston, Charleston, WV 25304-1099	1888	Dr. Edwin H. Welch	1-M	1,424	NR
U of Chicago, Chicago, IL 60637-1513	1891	Mr. Hugo F. Sonneschein	1-D	12,117	1,639
U of Cincinnati, Cincinnati, OH 45221	1819	Dr. Joseph A. Steger	5-D	19,139	953
U of Colorado at Boulder, Boulder, CO 80309	1876	Dr. Judith E. N. Albino	5-D	24,622	1,500
U of Colorado at Colorado Springs, Colorado Springs, CO 80933-7150	1965	Dr. Linda Bunnell Shade	5-D	5,840	390
U of Colorado at Denver, Denver, CO 80217-3364	1912	Ms. Georgia Lesh-Laurie	5-D	10,844	614
U of Colorado Health Sciences Ctr, Denver, CO 80262	1883	Dr. Vincent A. Fulginiti	5-D	2,156	1,109
U of Connecticut, Storrs, CT 06269	1881	Dr. Philip E. Austin	5-D	15,541	1,148
U of Dallas, Irving, TX 75062-4799	1955	Rev. Msgr. Milam Joseph	2-D	2,771	188
U of Dayton, Dayton, OH 45469-1611	1850	Br. Raymond L. Fitz, SM	2-D	10,320	809
U of Delaware, Newark, DE 19716	1743	Dr. David P. Roselle	12-D	18,115	1,038
U of Denver, Denver, CO 80208	1864	Mr. Daniel Ritchie	1-D	8,714	420
U of Detroit Mercy, Detroit, MI 48219-0900	1877	Dr. Maureen A. Fay, OP	2-D	7,284	582
U of Evansville, Evansville, IN 47722-0002	1854	Dr. James S. Vinson	2-M	3,185	183
The U of Findlay, Findlay, OH 45840-3653	1882	Dr. Kenneth E. Zirkle	2-M	3,743	267
U of Florida, Gainesville, FL 32611-8140	1853	Dr. John V. Lombardi	5-D	39,932	2,225
U of Georgia, Athens, GA 30602	1785	Dr. Michael F. Adams	5-D	29,404	3,173
U of Great Falls, Great Falls, MT 59405	1932	Dr. Frederick W. Gilliard	2-M	1,291	107
U of Guam, Mangilao, GU 96923	1952	Dr. Jose T. Nededog	7-M	3,654	230
U of Hartford, West Hartford, CT 06117-1599	1877	Dr. Humphrey Tonkin	1-D	7,068	904
U of Hawaii at Hilo, Hilo, HI 96720-4091	1970	Dr. Kenneth Perrin	5-B	2,870	281
U of Hawaii at Manoa, Honolulu, HI 96822	1907	Dr. Kenneth P. Mortimer	5-D	17,023	1,425
U of Houston, Houston, TX 77204-2163	1927	Dr. Arthur K. Smith	5-D	30,774	1,927
U of Houston–Clear Lake, Houston, TX 77058-1098	1974	Dr. William A. Staples	5-M	6,968	411
U of Houston–Downtown, Houston, TX 77002-1001	1974	Dr. Max Castillo	5-B	7,947	394
U of Houston–Victoria, Victoria, TX 77901-4450	1973	Dr. Karen S. Haynes	5-M	1,809	85
U of Idaho, Moscow, ID 83844-4140	1889	Dr. Robert A. Hoover	5-D	11,727	625
U of Illinois at Chicago, Chicago, IL 60607-7128	1946	Dr. David C. Broski	5-D	24,583	2,723
U of Illinois at Springfield, Springfield, IL 62794-9243	1969	Dr. Naomi B. Lynn	5-M	4,611	237
U of Illinois at Urbana–Champaign, Champaign, IL 61820-5711	1867	Dr. Michael Aiken	5-D	36,164	1,843
U of Indianapolis, Indianapolis, IN 46227-3697	1902	Dr. G. Benjamin Lantz, Jr.	2-D	3,861	337
The U of Iowa, Iowa City, IA 52242	1847	Dr. Mary Sue Coleman	5-D	27,921	1,803
U of Kansas, Lawrence, KS 66045	1866	Dr. Robert E. Hemenway	5-D	27,407	2,084
U of Kentucky, Lexington, KY 40506-0032	1865	Dr. Charles T. Wethington, Jr.	5-D	23,431	2,222
U of La Verne, La Verne, CA 91750-4443	1891	Dr. Stephen Morgan	1-D	2,965	NR
U of Louisville, Louisville, KY 40292-0001	1798	Dr. John W. Shumaker	5-D	21,020	1,757
U of Maine, Orono, ME 04469	1865	Dr. Frederick E. Hutchinson	5-D	9,928	634
U of Maine at Farmington, Farmington, ME 04938-1990	1863	Dr. Theodora J. Kalikow	5-B	2,391	156
U of Maine at Presque Isle, Presque Isle, ME 04769-2888	1903	Dr. W. Michael Easton	5-B	1,347	97
U of Mary, Bismarck, ND 58504-9652	1959	Sr. Thomas Welder	2-M	2,016	129
U of Mary Hardin-Baylor, Belton, TX 76513	1845	Dr. Jerry G. Bawcom	2-M	2,265	157
U of Maryland, Baltimore County, Baltimore, MD 21228-5398	1963	Dr. Freeman A. Hrabowski	5-D	9,932	664
U of Maryland, Coll Park, College Park, MD 20742	1856	Dr. William E. Kirwan	5-D	31,471	1,849
U of Maryland Eastern Shore, Princess Anne, MD 21853-1299	1886	Dr. Dolores Spikes	5-D	3,166	280
U of Maryland U Coll, College Park, MD 20742-1600	1947	Dr. T. Benjamin Massey	5-M	33,435	1,393
U of Massachusetts Amherst, Amherst, MA 01003-0001	1863	Dr. David K. Scott	5-D	23,108	1,310
U of Massachusetts Boston, Boston, MA 02125-3393	1964	Dr. Sherry H. Penney	5-D	10,216	817
U of Massachusetts Dartmouth, North Dartmouth, MA 02747-2300	1895	Dr. Peter H. Cressy	5-D	5,103	417
U of Massachusetts Lowell, Lowell, MA 01854-2881	1894	Dr. William T. Hogan	5-D	12,731	615
The U of Memphis, Memphis, TN 38152	1912	Dr. V. Lane Rawlins	5-D	19,271	1,217
U of Miami, Coral Gables, FL 33124	1925	Mr. Edward T. Foote, II	1-D	13,677	2,370
U of Michigan, Ann Arbor, MI 48109	1817	Dr. Homer A. Neal	5-D	36,525	3,520
U of Michigan–Dearborn, Dearborn, MI 48128-1491	1959	Dr. James C. Renick	5-M	8,324	383
U of Michigan–Flint, Flint, MI 48502-2186	1956	Dr. Charlie Nelms	5-M	6,236	242
U of Minnesota, Duluth, Duluth, MN 55812-2496	1947	Dr. Kathryn A. Martin	5-M	7,501	400
U of Minnesota, Morris, Morris, MN 56267	1959	Dr. David C. Johnson	5-B	1,970	123
U of Minnesota, Twin Cities Cmps, Minneapolis, MN 55455-0213	1851	Dr. Nils Hasselmo	5-D	37,018	2,828
U of Mississippi, University, MS 38677-9702	1844	Dr. Robert C. Khayat	5-D	10,280	595
U of Mississippi Medical Ctr, Jackson, MS 39216-4505	1955	Dr. A. Wallace Conerly	5-D	1,806	644
U of Missouri–Columbia, Columbia, MO 65211	1839	Dr. Charles A. Kiesler	5-D	22,483	1,603
U of Missouri–Kansas City, Kansas City, MO 64110-2499	1929	Dr. Eleanor B. Schwartz	5-D	10,298	729
U of Missouri–Rolla, Rolla, MO 65409	1870	Dr. John T. Park	5-D	5,264	378
U of Missouri–St Louis, St Louis, MO 63121-4499	1963	Dr. Blanche M. Touhill	5-D	23,344	970
U of Mobile, Mobile, AL 36663-0220	1961	Dr. Michael A. Magnoli	2-M	2,241	151
The U of Montana–Missoula, Missoula, MT 59812-0002	1893	Dr. George M. Dennison	5-D	11,886	635

Name, address	Year	Governing official, control, and highest degree offered		Enrollment	Faculty
U of Montevallo, Montevallo, AL 35115	1896	Dr. Robert M. McChesney	5-M	3,206	202
U of Nebraska at Kearney, Kearney, NE 68849-0001	1903	Dr. Gladys Styles Johnston	5-M	7,620	422
U of Nebraska at Omaha, Omaha, NE 68182	1908	Dr. Del D. Weber	5-D	15,000	996
U of Nebraska–Lincoln, Lincoln, NE 68588	1869	Dr. James Moeser	5-D	23,887	1,512
U of Nebraska Medical Ctr, Omaha, NE 68198-0001	1869	Dr. William O. Berndt	5-D	2,718	709
U of Nevada, Las Vegas, Las Vegas, NV 89154-9900	1957	Dr. Carol Harter	5-D	19,682	1,138
U of Nevada, Reno, Reno, NV 89557	1874	Dr. Joseph N. Crowley	5-D	11,652	649
U of New England, Biddeford, ME 04005-9526	1953	Dr. Sandra Featherman	1-F	1,892	181
U of New Hampshire, Durham, NH 03824	1866	Dr. Joan R. Leitzel	5-D	12,454	890
U of New Haven, West Haven, CT 06516-1916	1920	Dr. Lawrence J. DeNardis	1-D	5,438	546
U of New Mexico, Albuquerque, NM 87131-2039	1889	Dr. Richard E. Peck	5-D	23,617	2,006
U of New Orleans, New Orleans, LA 70148	1958	Dr. Gregory M. St.L. O'Brien	5-D	15,665	727
U of North Alabama, Florence, AL 35632-0001	1830	Mr. Robert L. Potts	5-M	5,529	280
U of North Carolina at Asheville, Asheville, NC 28804-3299	1927	Dr. Patsy Reed	5-M	3,092	261
The U of North Carolina at Chapel Hill, Chapel Hill, NC 27599	1789	Dr. Michael K. Hooker	5-D	24,141	2,640
U of North Carolina at Charlotte, Charlotte, NC 28223-0001	1946	Dr. James H. Woodward, Jr.	5-D	15,795	911
U of North Carolina at Greensboro, Greensboro, NC 27412-0001	1891	Dr. Patricia A. Sullivan	5-D	12,323	718
U of North Carolina at Pembroke, Pembroke, NC 28372-1510	1887	Dr. Joseph B. Oxendine	5-M	3,006	211
U of North Carolina at Wilmington, Wilmington, NC 28403-3201	1947	Dr. James R. Leutze	5-M	9,077	512
U of North Dakota, Grand Forks, ND 58202	1883	Dr. Kendall Baker	5-D	11,300	720
U of Northern Colorado, Greeley, CO 80639	1890	Dr. Howard M. Skinner	5-D	10,306	537
U of Northern Iowa, Cedar Falls, IA 50614	1876	Dr. Robert D. Koob	5-D	12,957	808
U of North Florida, Jacksonville, FL 32224-2645	1965	Dr. Adam W. Herbert	5-D	10,909	596
U of North Texas, Denton, TX 76203-6737	1890	Dr. Alfred F. Hurley	5-D	24,957	994
U of Notre Dame, Notre Dame, IN 46556	1842	Rev. Dr. Edward A. Malloy, CSC	2-D	9,927	927
U of Oklahoma, Norman, OK 73019-0390	1890	Mr. David L. Boren	5-D	20,026	1,037
U of Oklahoma Health Sciences Ctr, Oklahoma City, OK 73190	1890	Dr. Joseph J. Ferretti	5-D	2,757	961
U of Oregon, Eugene, OR 97403	1872	Mr. David Frohnmayer	5-D	17,269	1,192
U of Osteopathic Medicine and Health Sciences, Des Moines, IA 50312-4104	1898	Dr. Richard Ryan	1-F	1,350	108
U of Pennsylvania, Philadelphia, PA 19104	1740	Dr. Judith Rodin	1-D	21,171	3,853
U of Phoenix, Phoenix, AZ 85072-2069	1976	Mr. William Gibbs	3-M	31,000	3,407
U of Pittsburgh, Pittsburgh, PA 15260	1787	Mr. Mark A. Nordenberg	12-D	25,479	3,465
U of Pittsburgh at Bradford, Bradford, PA 16701-2812	1963	Dr. Richard E. McDowell	12-B	1,274	109
U of Pittsburgh at Greensburg, Greensburg, PA 15601-5860	1963	Dr. Norman W. Scanlon	12-B	1,381	90
U of Pittsburgh at Johnstown, Johnstown, PA 15904-2990	1927	Dr. Albert L. Etheridge	12-B	3,143	183
U of Portland, Portland, OR 97203-5798	1901	Rev. David T. Tyson, CSC	2-M	2,639	240
U of Puerto Rico, Aguadilla Regional Coll, Aguadilla, PR 00604-0160	1972	Prof. Juana Segarra Jaramillo	6-B	3,312	133
U of Puerto Rico at Arecibo, Arecibo, PR 00613	1967	Dra. Josefa Garcia Firpi	6-B	4,715	263
U of Puerto Rico at Ponce, Ponce, PR 00732-7186	1970	Prof. Rafael Capo	6-B	4,126	190
U of Puerto Rico, Cayey U Coll, Cayey, PR 00737	1967	Mr. Jose Luis Monserrate	6-B	3,758	197
U of Puerto Rico, Humacao U Coll, Humacao, PR 00791	1962	Dr. Roberto Marrero	6-B	4,294	265
U of Puerto Rico, Mayagüez Cmps, Mayagüez, PR 00681-5000	1911	Dr. Stuart J. Ramos	6-D	12,594	640
U of Puerto Rico Medical Sciences Cmps, San Juan, PR 00936-5067	1950	Dr. Jorge L. Sanchez	6-D	2,712	759
U of Puerto Rico, Río Piedras, San Juan, PR 00931	1903	Dr. Manuel G. Tejera	6-D	19,234	1,476
U of Puget Sound, Tacoma, WA 98416-0005	1888	Dr. Susan Resneck Pierce	1-M	3,039	234
U of Redlands, Redlands, CA 92373-0999	1907	Dr. James R. Appleton	1-M	3,584	661
U of Rhode Island, Kingston, RI 02881	1892	Dr. Robert L. Carothers	5-F	13,261	642
U of Richmond, University of Richmond, VA 23173	1830	Dr. Richard L. Morrill	2-F	4,366	452
U of Rio Grande, Rio Grande, OH 45674	1876	Dr. Barry M. Dorsey	1-M	2,057	135
U of Rochester, Rochester, NY 14627-0001	1850	Mr. Thomas H. Jackson	1-D	8,172	1,295
U of St Thomas, St Paul, MN 55105-1096	1885	Rev. Dennis Dease	2-D	10,324	694
U of St Thomas, Houston, TX 77006-4694	1947	Dr. Joseph M. McFadden	2-D	2,504	204
U of San Diego, San Diego, CA 92110-2492	1949	Dr. Alice B. Hayes	2-D	6,603	514
U of San Francisco, San Francisco, CA 94117-1080	1855	Rev. John P. Schlegel, SJ	2-D	7,888	760
U of Science and Arts of Oklahoma, Chickasha, OK 73018-0001	1908	Dr. Roy Troutt	5-B	1,523	74
U of Scranton, Scranton, PA 18510-4622	1888	Rev. J. A. Panuska, SJ	2-M	4,906	412
U of South Alabama, Mobile, AL 36688-0002	1963	Dr. Frederick P. Whiddon	5-D	12,041	844
U of South Carolina, Columbia, SC 29208	1801	Dr. John M. Palms	5-D	25,488	1,379
U of South Carolina–Aiken, Aiken, SC 29801-6309	1961	Dr. Robert E. Alexander	5-M	3,027	205
U of South Carolina–Spartanburg, Spartanburg, SC 29303-4932	1967	Dr. John C. Stockwell	5-M	3,549	214
U of South Dakota, Vermillion, SD 57069-2390	1862	Dr. Betty Turner Asher	5-D	7,028	456
U of Southern California, Los Angeles, CA 90089	1880	Dr. Steven B. Sample	1-D	27,558	2,601
U of Southern Colorado, Pueblo, CO 81001-4901	1933	Dr. Tito Guerrero, III	5-M	4,109	162
U of Southern Indiana, Evansville, IN 47712-3590	1965	Dr. H. Ray Hoops	5-M	7,763	416
U of Southern Maine, Portland, ME 04104-9300	1878	Dr. Richard L. Pattenaude	5-F	9,966	546
U of Southern Mississippi, Hattiesburg, MS 39406-5167	1910	Dr. Horace W. Fleming	5-D	12,497	700
U of South Florida, Tampa, FL 33620-9951	1956	Mrs. Betty Castor	5-D	30,938	1,654
U of Southwestern Louisiana, Lafayette, LA 70504	1898	Dr. Ray P. Authement	5-D	16,742	670
The U of Tampa, Tampa, FL 33606-1490	1931	Dr. Ronald L. Vaughn	1-M	2,712	195
U of Tennessee at Chattanooga, Chattanooga, TN 37403-2598	1886	Dr. Frederick W. Obear	5-M	8,296	547
The U of Tennessee at Martin, Martin, TN 38238-1000	1927	Dr. Margaret N. Perry	5-M	5,491	376
U of Tennessee, Knoxville, Knoxville, TN 37996	1794	Dr. William T. Snyder	5-D	25,517	1,517
U of Tennessee, Memphis, Memphis, TN 38163-0002	1911	Mr. William R. Rice	5-D	2,092	914
The U of Texas at Arlington, Arlington, TX 76019-0407	1895	Dr. Robert E. Witt	5-D	20,544	1,215
The U of Texas at Austin, Austin, TX 78712	1883	Dr. Peter Flawn	5-D	48,008	2,431
The U of Texas at Brownsville, Brownsville, TX 78520-4991	1973	Dr. Juliet Garcia	5-M	2,752	399
The U of Texas at Dallas, Richardson, TX 75083-0688	1969	Dr. Franklyn G. Jenifer	5-D	9,378	426
The U of Texas at El Paso, El Paso, TX 79968-0001	1913	Dr. Diana Natalicio	5-D	15,386	799
The U of Texas at San Antonio, San Antonio, TX 78249	1969	Dr. Samuel A. Kirkpatrick	5-D	17,547	783
The U of Texas at Tyler, Tyler, TX 75799-0001	1971	Dr. George F. Hamm	5-M	3,789	219
U of Texas Health Science Ctr at San Antonio, San Antonio, TX 78284-6200	1976	Dr. John P. Howe, III	5-D	2,721	1,213
U of Texas-Houston Health Science Ctr, Houston, TX 77225-0036	1972	Dr. M. David Low	5-D	3,111	1,046
U of Texas Medical Branch at Galveston, Galveston, TX 77555	1891	Dr. Thomas N. James	5-D	2,204	1,295
The U of Texas of the Permian Basin, Odessa, TX 79762-0001	1969	Dr. Charles A. Sorber	5-M	2,193	128
The U of Texas–Pan American, Edinburg, TX 78539-2999	1927	Dr. Miguel A. Nevarez	5-D	12,692	622
U of Texas Southwestern Medical Ctr at Dallas, Dallas, TX 75235-9002	1943	Dr. C. Kern Wildenthal	5-D	1,714	108
U of the Arts, Philadelphia, PA 19102-4944	1870	Mr. Peter Solmssen	1-M	1,399	256
U of the District of Columbia, Washington, DC 20008-1175	1976	Dr. Tilden J. LeMelle	9-M	7,464	615
U of the Incarnate Word, San Antonio, TX 78209-6397	1881	Dr. Louis J. Agnese, Jr.	2-M	3,287	287
U of the Pacific, Stockton, CA 95211-0197	1851	Mr. Donald V. DeRosa	1-D	4,785	614
U of the Sacred Heart, San Juan, PR 00914-0383	1935	Dr. Jose Jaime Rivera	2-M	5,199	366
U of the South, Sewanee, TN 37383-1000	1857	Dr. Samuel R. Williamson	2-D	1,346	151
U of the State of NY, Regents Coll, Albany, NY 12203-5159	1970	Mr. C. Wayne Williams	1-B	18,432	NR

Name, address	Year	Governing official, control, and highest degree offered		Enroll- ment	Faculty
U of the Virgin Islands, Charlotte Amalie, St Thomas, VI 00802-9990	1962	Dr. Orville Kean	7-M	2,898	269
U of Toledo, Toledo, OH 43606-3398	1872	Dr. Frank E. Horton	5-D	21,692	1,355
U of Tulsa, Tulsa, OK 74104-3189	1894	Dr. Robert W. Lawless	2-D	4,236	408
U of Utah, Salt Lake City, UT 84112	1850	Dr. Jerilyn S. McIntyre	5-D	24,930	1,454
U of Vermont, Burlington, VT 05405-0160	1791	Mr. Thomas P. Salmon	5-D	8,929	1,030
U of Virginia, Charlottesville, VA 22903	1819	Mr. John T. Casteen, III	5-D	17,959	2,095
U of Washington, Seattle, WA 98195	1861	Dr. Richard McCormick	5-D	34,368	3,892
The U of West Alabama, Livingston, AL 35470	1835	Dr. Donald C. Hines	5-M	2,153	121
U of West Florida, Pensacola, FL 32514-5750	1963	Dr. Morris L. Marx	5-D	8,054	429
U of Wisconsin–Eau Claire, Eau Claire, WI 54702-4004	1916	Dr. Larry Schnack	5-M	10,503	515
U of Wisconsin–Green Bay, Green Bay, WI 54311-7001	1968	Dr. Mark L. Perkins	5-M	5,220	274
U of Wisconsin–La Crosse, La Crosse, WI 54601-3742	1909	Dr. Judith L. Kuipers	5-M	9,046	449
U of Wisconsin–Madison, Madison, WI 53706-1380	1848	Dr. David Ward	5-D	39,826	2,545
U of Wisconsin–Milwaukee, Milwaukee, WI 53201-0413	1956	Dr. John H. Schroeder	5-D	21,877	1,354
U of Wisconsin–Oshkosh, Oshkosh, WI 54901-8621	1871	Dr. John E. Kerrigan	5-M	10,382	529
U of Wisconsin–Parkside, Kenosha, WI 53141-2000	1968	Dr. Eleanor J. Smith	5-M	4,254	275
U of Wisconsin–Platteville, Platteville, WI 53818-3099	1866	Dr. David Markee	5-M	4,998	280
U of Wisconsin–River Falls, River Falls, WI 54022-5001	1874	Dr. Gary A. Thibodeau	5-M	5,359	278
U of Wisconsin–Stevens Point, Stevens Point, WI 54481-3897	1894	Dr. Howard Thoyre	5-M	8,360	426
U of Wisconsin–Stout, Menomonie, WI 54751	1891	Dr. Charles Sorensen	5-M	7,322	364
U of Wisconsin–Superior, Superior, WI 54880-2873	1893	Dr. Julius E. Erlenbach	5-M	2,647	160
U of Wisconsin–Whitewater, Whitewater, WI 53190-1790	1868	Dr. H. Gaylon Greenhill	5-M	10,398	471
U of Wyoming, Laramie, WY 82071	1886	Dr. Philip L. Dubois	5-D	11,251	720
U System Coll for Lifelong Learning, Concord, NH 03301	1972	Dr. Victor Montana	11-B	2,187	350
Urbana U, Urbana, OH 43078-2091	1850	Dr. Francis E. Hazard	2-B	1,179	75
Ursinus Coll, Collegeville, PA 19426-1000	1869	Dr. John Strassburger	2-B	1,196	135
Ursuline Coll, Pepper Pike, OH 44124-4398 (4)	1871	Dr. Anne Marie Diederich	2-M	1,312	133
Utah State U, Logan, UT 84322	1888	Dr. George H. Emert	5-D	20,808	780
Utica Coll of Syracuse U, Utica, NY 13502-4892	1946	Dr. Michael K. Simpson	1-B	1,748	168
Valdosta State U, Valdosta, GA 31698	1906	Dr. Hugh C. Bailey	5-D	9,810	472
Valley City State U, Valley City, ND 58072	1890	Dr. Ellen Earle Chaffee	5-B	1,121	89
Valparaiso U, Valparaiso, IN 46383-6493	1859	Dr. Alan F. Harre	2-F	3,472	359
Vanderbilt U, Nashville, TN 37240-1001	1873	Mr. Joe B. Wyatt	1-D	10,253	2,084
Vassar Coll, Poughkeepsie, NY 12604	1861	Dr. Frances D. Fergusson	1-M	2,330	231
Villa Julie Coll, Stevenson, MD 21153	1952	Dr. Carolyn Manuszak	1-M	1,866	141
Villanova U, Villanova, PA 19085-1699	1842	Rev. Edmund J. Dobbin, OSA	2-D	10,182	770
Virginia Commonwealth U, Richmond, VA 23284-9005	1838	Dr. Eugene P. Trani	5-D	21,681	2,502
Virginia Military Inst, Lexington, VA 24450 (2)	1839	Maj. Gen. Josiah Bunting, III	5-B	1,218	127
Virginia Polytechnic Inst and State U, Blacksburg, VA 24061-0202	1872	Dr. Paul E. Torgersen	5-D	24,812	1,574
Virginia State U, Petersburg, VA 23806-2096	1882	Mr. Eddie N. Moore, Jr.	5-M	4,014	254
Virginia Union U, Richmond, VA 23220-1170	1865	Dr. S. Dallas Simmons	2-D	1,551	104
Virginia Wesleyan Coll, Norfolk, VA 23502-5599	1961	Dr. William T. Greer, Jr.	2-B	1,460	100
Viterbo Coll, La Crosse, WI 54601-4797	1890	Dr. William J. Medland	2-M	1,914	173
Wagner Coll, Staten Island, NY 10301	1883	Dr. Norman R. Smith	1-M	2,002	196
Wake Forest U, Winston-Salem, NC 27109	1834	Dr. Thomas K. Hearn, Jr.	1-D	5,910	1,658
Walla Walla Coll, College Place, WA 99324-1198	1892	Dr. W. G. Nelson	2-M	1,763	193
Walsh Coll of Accountancy and Business Admin, Troy, MI 48007-7006	1922	Dr. David A. Spencer	1-M	3,428	127
Walsh U, North Canton, OH 44720-3396	1958	Dr. Kenneth N. Hamilton, Jr.	2-M	1,381	122
Wartburg Coll, Waverly, IA 50677-1003	1852	Dr. Robert Vogel	2-B	1,467	116
Washburn U of Topeka, Topeka, KS 66621	1865	Dr. Jerry Farley	10-F	6,248	430
Washington and Jefferson Coll, Washington, PA 15301-4801	1781	Dr. Howard J. Burnett	1-B	1,128	101
Washington and Lee U, Lexington, VA 24450	1749	Dr. John W. Elrod	1-F	2,006	194
Washington Coll, Chestertown, MD 21620-1197	1782	Dr. John S. Toll	1-M	1,009	93
Washington State U, Pullman, WA 99164-1610	1890	Dr. Samuel H. Smith	5-D	20,121	1,234
Washington U, St Louis, MO 63130-4899	1853	Dr. Mark S. Wrighton	1-D	10,767	2,354
Wayland Baptist U, Plainview, TX 79072-6998	1908	Dr. Wallace E. Davis, Jr.	2-M	4,009	92
Waynesburg Coll, Waynesburg, PA 15370-1222	1849	Mr. Timothy R. Thyreen	2-M	1,288	99
Wayne State Coll, Wayne, NE 68787	1910	Dr. Donald J. Mash	5-M	3,828	228
Wayne State U, Detroit, MI 48202	1868	Mr. David Adamany	5-D	31,185	2,701
Weber State U, Ogden, UT 84408-1001	1889	Dr. Paul H. Thompson	5-M	13,906	487
Webster U, St Louis, MO 63119-3194	1915	Dr. Richard S. Meyers	1-D	12,319	508
Wellesley Coll, Wellesley, MA 02181 (3)	1870	Ms. Diana Chapman Walsh	1-B	2,319	320
Wentworth Inst of Tech, Boston, MA 02115-5998	1904	Dr. John F. Van Domelen	1-B	2,264	120
Wesleyan U, Middletown, CT 06459-0260	1831	Dr. Douglas J. Bennet, Jr.	1-D	3,279	344
Wesley Coll, Dover, DE 19901	1873	Dr. Reed M. Stewart	2-B	1,325	95
West Chester U of Pennsylvania, West Chester, PA 19383	1871	Dr. Madeleine Wing Adler	5-M	11,261	706
Western Carolina U, Cullowhee, NC 28723	1889	Dr. John W. Bardo	5-D	6,511	508
Western Connecticut State U, Danbury, CT 06810-6885	1903	Dr. James R. Roach	5-M	5,607	331
Western Illinois U, Macomb, IL 61455-1390	1899	Dr. Donald S. Spencer	5-M	12,184	659
Western International U, Phoenix, AZ 85021-2718	1978	Mr. Michael J. Siedien	3-M	1,200	65
Western Kentucky U, Bowling Green, KY 42101-3576	1906	Dr. Barbara Birch	5-M	14,613	867
Western Maryland Coll, Westminster, MD 21157-4390	1867	Dr. Robert H. Chambers	1-M	2,592	204
Western Michigan U, Kalamazoo, MI 49008	1903	Dr. Diether H. Haenicke	5-D	25,699	1,232
Western Montana Coll of The U of Montana, Dillon, MT 59725-3598	1893	Dr. Sheila M. Stearns	5-B	1,115	75
Western New England Coll, Springfield, MA 01119-2654	1919	Dr. Anthony S. Caprio	1-F	4,574	294
Western New Mexico U, Silver City, NM 88062-0680	1893	Dr. John E. Counts	5-M	2,533	145
Western Oregon U, Monmouth, OR 97361	1856	Dr. Betty J. Youngblood	5-M	4,030	261
Western State Coll of Colorado, Gunnison, CO 81231	1901	Dr. Harry L. Peterson, Jr.	5-B	2,534	143
Western Washington U, Bellingham, WA 98225-5996	1893	Dr. Karen Morse	5-M	11,039	523
Westfield State Coll, Westfield, MA 01086	1838	Dr. Frederick Woodward	5-M	4,878	328
West Liberty State Coll, West Liberty, WV 26074	1837	Dr. Ronald M. Zaccari	5-B	2,412	142
Westminster Coll, New Wilmington, PA 16172-0001	1852	R. Thomas Williamson	2-M	1,584	122
Westminster Coll of Salt Lake City, Salt Lake City, UT 84105-3697	1875	Dr. Peggy A. Stock	1-M	1,922	193
Westmont Coll, Santa Barbara, CA 93108-1099	1940	Dr. David K. Winter	2-B	1,320	119
West Texas A&M U, Canyon, TX 79016-0001	1909	Dr. Russell C. Long	5-M	6,482	346
West Virginia State Coll, Institute, WV 25112-1000	1891	Dr. Hazo W. Carter, Jr.	5-B	4,545	253
West Virginia U, Morgantown, WV 26506-6201	1867	Mr. David C. Hardesty, Jr.	5-D	21,743	1,592
West Virginia U Inst of Tech, Montgomery, WV 25136	1895	Dr. John P. Carrier	5-M	2,486	199
West Virginia Wesleyan Coll, Buckhannon, WV 26201	1890	Mr. William R. Haden	2-M	1,592	144
Wheaton Coll, Wheaton, IL 60187-5593	1860	Dr. Duane Litfin	2-D	2,697	284
Wheaton Coll, Norton, MA 02766	1834	Dr. Dale Rogers Marshall	1-B	1,350	133
Wheeling Jesuit U, Wheeling, WV 26003-6295	1954	Fr. Thomas S. Acker, SJ	2-M	1,527	102
Wheelock Coll, Boston, MA 02215 (4)	1888	Dr. Marjorie Bakken	1-M	1,360	183
Whitman Coll, Walla Walla, WA 99362-2083	1859	Dr. Thomas Cronin	1-D	1,309	174
Whittier Coll, Whittier, CA 90608-0634	1887	Dr. James L. Ash, Jr.	1-F	2,165	172
Whitworth Coll, Spokane, WA 99251-0001	1890	Dr. William P. Robinson	2-M	2,026	102

Name, address	Year	Governing official, control, and highest degree offered		Enroll- ment	Faculty
Wichita State U, Wichita, KS 67260	1895	Dr. Eugene Morgan Hughes	5-D	14,264	758
Widener U, Chester, PA 19013-5792	1821	Dr. Robert J. Bruce	1-D	8,150	435
Wilkes U, Wilkes-Barre, PA 18766-0002	1933	Dr. Christopher N. Breiseth	1-M	2,800	225
Willamette U, Salem, OR 97301-3931	1842	Dr. Jerry E. Hudson	2-F	2,501	211
William Carey Coll, Hattiesburg, MS 39401-5499	1906	Dr. James Edwards	2-M	2,254	172
William Jewell Coll, Liberty, MO 64068-1843	1849	Dr. W. Christian Sizemore	2-B	1,172	160
William Paterson U of New Jersey, Wayne, NJ 07470-8420	1855	Dr. Arnold Speert	5-M	8,941	326
Williams Coll, Williamstown, MA 01267	1793	Dr. Harry C. Payne	1-M	2,138	265
William Woods U, Fulton, MO 65251-1098	1870	Dr. Jahnae Barnett	2-M	1,151	93
Wilmington Coll, New Castle, DE 19720-6491	1967	Dr. Audrey K. Doberstein	1-D	5,500	480
Wilmington Coll, Wilmington, OH 45177	1870	Dr. Daniel DiBiasio	2-B	1,092	102
Wingate U, Wingate, NC 28174	1896	Dr. Jerry E. McGee	2-M	1,275	105
Winona State U, Winona, MN 55987-5838	1858	Dr. Darrell Krueger	5-M	7,500	350
Winston-Salem State U, Winston-Salem, NC 27110-0003	1892	Dr. Alvin J. Schexnider	5-B	2,781	182
Winthrop U, Rock Hill, SC 29733	1886	Dr. Anthony DiGiorgio	5-M	5,402	428
Wittenberg U, Springfield, OH 45501-0720	1845	Dr. L. Baird Tipson	2-B	2,000	166
Wofford Coll, Spartanburg, SC 29303-3663	1854	Dr. Joab M. Lesesne	2-B	1,115	84
Woodbury U, Burbank, CA 91510	1884	Dr. Kenneth R. Nielsen	1-M	1,132	150
Worcester Polytechnic Inst, Worcester, MA 01609-2280	1865	Dr. Edward A. Parrish, Jr.	1-D	3,648	267
Worcester State Coll, Worcester, MA 01602-2597	1874	Dr. Kalyan K. Ghosh	5-M	5,369	268
Wright State U, Dayton, OH 45435	1964	Dr. Harley E. Flack	5-D	15,697	950
Xavier U, Cincinnati, OH 45207-2111	1831	Rev. James E. Hoff, SJ	2-D	6,423	490
Xavier U of Louisiana, New Orleans, LA 70125-1098	1925	Dr. Norman C. Francis	2-F	3,526	258
Yale U, New Haven, CT 06520	1701	Mr. Richard C. Levin	1-D	11,047	2,920
Yeshiva U, New York, NY 10033-3201	1886	Dr. Norman Lamm	1-D	5,246	676
York Coll of Pennsylvania, York, PA 17405-7199	1787	Dr. George W. Waldner	1-M	5,046	350
York Coll of the City U of New York, Jamaica, NY 11451-0001	1967	Dr. Charles C. Kidd, Sr.	11-B	6,335	440
Youngstown State U, Youngstown, OH 44555-0002	1908	Dr. Leslie H. Cochran	5-D	12,801	784

Two-Year Colleges

The highest undergraduate degree offered for all two-year colleges is the associate degree.

Name, address	Year	Governing official, control, and highest degree offered		Enroll- ment	Faculty
Abraham Baldwin Ag Coll, Tifton, GA 31794-2601	1933	Dr. Harold J. Loyd	5	2,553	118
Adirondack Comm Coll, Queensbury, NY 12804	1960	Dr. Roger Andersen	11	3,487	240
Aiken Tech Coll, Aiken, SC 29802-0696	1972	Dr. Kathleen A. Noble	11	2,143	119
Aims Comm Coll, Greeley, CO 80632-0069	1967	Dr. George R. Conger	9	6,869	370
Alabama Southern Comm Coll, Monroeville, AL 36460	1965	Dr. John A. Johnson	5	1,800	107
Alamance Comm Coll, Graham, NC 27253-8000	1959	Dr. W. Ronald McCarter	5	3,340	145
Albuquerque Tech Vocational Inst, Albuquerque, NM 87106-4096	1965	Dr. Alex A. Sanchez	5	15,555	601
Alexandria Tech Coll, Alexandria, MN 56308-3707	1961	Mr. Larry Shellito	5	1,705	89
Allan Hancock Coll, Santa Maria, CA 93454-6399	1920	Dr. Ann Foxworthy	11	7,403	404
Allegany Coll of Maryland, Cumberland, MD 21502	1961	Dr. Donald L. Alexander	11	2,735	206
Allen County Comm Coll, Iola, KS 66749-1607	1923	Mr. John Masterson	11	1,747	140
Allentown Business Sch, Allentown, PA 18103-3880	1869	Ms. Virginia Carpenter	3	1,000	50
Alpena Comm Coll, Alpena, MI 49707-1495	1952	Dr. Donald L. Newport	11	2,028	89
Alvin Comm Coll, Alvin, TX 77511-4898	1949	Dr. A. Rodney Allbright	11	3,873	141
Amarillo Coll, Amarillo, TX 79178-0001	1929	Dr. Luther Bud Joyner	11	7,314	424
American River Coll, Sacramento, CA 95841-4286	1955	Dr. Marie Smith	9	19,854	790
Angelina Coll, Lufkin, TX 75902-1768	1968	Dr. Larry M. Phillips	11	3,984	201
Anne Arundel Comm Coll, Arnold, MD 21012-1895	1961	Dr. Martha A. Smith	11	11,278	570
Anoka-Ramsey Comm Coll, Coon Rapids, MN 55433-3499	1965	Dr. Patrick M. Johns	5	4,510	170
Anson Comm Coll, Polkton, NC 28135-0126	1962	Dr. Donald P. Altieri	5	1,326	102
Antelope Valley Coll, Lancaster, CA 93536-5426	1929	Dr. Linda Spink	11	9,027	400
Arapahoe Comm Coll, Littleton, CO 80160-9002	1965	Dr. James F. Weber	5	7,346	298
Arizona Western Coll, Yuma, AZ 85366-0929	1962	Dr. Don Schoening	11	5,763	230
Arkansas State U–Beebe Branch, Beebe, AR 72012-1000	1927	Dr. Eugene McKay	5	1,827	89
The Art Inst of Atlanta, Atlanta, GA 30326-1018	1949	Mr. Hal R. Griffith	3	1,455	96
The Art Inst of Dallas, Dallas, TX 75231-9959	1978	Mr. Thomas M. Hauser	3	1,200	84
The Art Inst of Fort Lauderdale, Fort Lauderdale, FL 33316-3000	1968	Mr. David Pauldine	3	2,100	150
The Art Inst of Houston, Houston, TX 77056-4115	1978	Mr. Steve R. Gregg	3	1,111	78
The Art Inst of Philadelphia, Philadelphia, PA 19103-5198	1966	Dr. Stacey R. Sauchuk	3	1,850	120
The Art Inst of Pittsburgh, Pittsburgh, PA 15222-3269	1921	Dr. Dennis J. Fantaski	3	2,400	107
The Art Inst of Seattle, Seattle, WA 98121-1642	1982	Leslie E. Pritchard	3	2,304	200
Asheville-Buncombe Tech Comm Coll, Asheville, NC 28801-4897	1959	Mr. K. Ray Bailey	5	4,058	434
Asnuntuck Comm-Tech Coll, Enfield, CT 06082-3800	1972	Dr. Harvey S. Irlen	5	2,051	112
Athens Area Tech Inst, Athens, GA 30601-1500	1958	Dr. Kenneth C. Easom	5	1,653	100
Atlanta Metropolitan Coll, Atlanta, GA 30310-4498	1974	Dr. Harold E. Wade	5	1,992	73
Atlantic Comm Coll, Mays Landing, NJ 08330-2699	1966	Dr. John May	8	5,682	310
Augusta Tech Inst, Augusta, GA 30906	1961	Mr. Jack B. Patrick	5	2,437	189
Austin Comm Coll, Austin, TX 78752-4390	1972	Dr. Bill Segura	9	26,000	1,406
Bainbridge Coll, Bainbridge, GA 31717	1972	Dr. Edward D. Mobley	5	1,031	47
Bakersfield Coll, Bakersfield, CA 93305-1299	1913	Dr. Robert Allison	11	12,000	496
Baltimore City Comm Coll, Baltimore, MD 21215-7893	1947	Dr. James D. Tschechtelin	5	5,970	493
Barstow Coll, Barstow, CA 92311-6699	1959	Mr. Maynard Sommer	11	2,632	128
Barton County Comm Coll, Great Bend, KS 67530-9283	1969	Dr. Veldon L. Law	11	10,000	292
Bay de Noc Comm Coll, Escanaba, MI 49829-2511	1963	Dr. Dwight E. Link	8	2,155	143
Beaufort County Comm Coll, Washington, NC 27889-1069	1967	Dr. Ron Champion	5	1,154	110
Bee County Coll, Beeville, TX 78102-2197	1965	Dr. Norman Wallace	8	2,734	140
Belleville Area Coll, Belleville, IL 62221-5899	1946	Mr. Larry Schmalenberger	9	14,646	NR
Bellevue Comm Coll, Bellevue, WA 98007-6484	1966	Mrs. B. Jean Floten	5	10,266	572
Belmont Tech Coll, St Clairsville, OH 43950-9735	1971	Dr. Wesley R. Channell	5	1,700	101
Bergen Comm Coll, Paramus, NJ 07652-1595	1965	Dr. Judith K. Winn	8	12,296	657
Berkeley Coll, West Paterson, NJ 07424-3353	1931	Mr. Kevin L. Luing	3	1,652	113
Berkeley Coll, New York, NY 10017-4604	1945	Mr. Robert J. Hurd	3	1,227	76
Berkshire Comm Coll, Pittsfield, MA 01201-5786	1960	Dr. Barbara A. Viniar	5	2,351	180
Bessemer State Tech Coll, Bessemer, AL 35021-0308	1966	Dr. W. Michael Bailey	5	1,612	100
Bevill State Comm Coll, Sumiton, AL 35148	1969	Dr. Harold Wade	5	4,597	63
Big Bend Comm Coll, Moses Lake, WA 98837-3299	1962	Dr. William C. Bonaudi	5	1,777	154
Bishop State Comm Coll, Mobile, AL 36603-5898	1965	Dr. Yvonne Kennedy	5	3,661	249
Bismarck State Coll, Bismarck, ND 58501-1299	1939	Dr. Donna Thigpen	5	2,406	117
Black Hawk Coll, Moline, IL 61265-5899	1946	Dr. Judith A. Redwine	11	6,335	488
Blackhawk Tech Coll, Janesville, WI 53547-5009	1968	Dr. James C. Catania	9	3,000	293
Black River Tech Coll, Pocahontas, AR 72455	1972	Mr. Richard Gaines	5	1,189	70

Name, address	Year	Governing official, control, and highest degree offered		Enroll-ment	Faculty
Blinn Coll, Brenham, TX 77833-4049.	1883	Dr. Donald E. Voelter.	11	9,209	376
Blue Mountain Comm Coll, Pendleton, OR 97801-1000	1962	Dr. Virginia Harrington	11	2,754	256
Blue Ridge Comm Coll, Flat Rock, NC 28731-9624.	1969	Dr. David W. Sink	11	2,496	176
Blue Ridge Comm Coll, Weyers Cave, VA 24486-0080.	1965	Dr. James R. Perkins.	5	1,788	137
Borough of Manhattan Comm Coll of City U of NY, New York, NY 10007-1079.	1963	Dr. Antonio Perez.	11	16,186	1,128
Bossier Parish Comm Coll, Bossier City, LA 71111-5801	1967	Mr. Thomas N. Carleton	11	4,706	158
Bowling Green State U-Firelands Coll, Huron, OH 44839-9791	1968	Dr. R. Darby Williams.	5	1,370	79
Bramson ORT Tech Inst, Forest Hills, NY 11375-4239	1977	Dr. Ephraim Buhks.	1	1,200	57
Brazosport Coll, Lake Jackson, TX 77566-3199.	1948	Dr. Millicent M. Valek.	11	3,426	178
Brevard Comm Coll, Cocoa, FL 32922-6597	1960	Dr. Maxwell C. King.	5	14,557	1,468
Briarcliffe Coll, Bethpage, NY 11714	1966	Mr. Richard Turan.	3	1,243	101
Bristol Comm Coll, Fall River, MA 02720-7395.	1965	Ms. Eileen Farley.	5	5,075	256
Bronx Comm Coll of City U of NY, Bronx, NY 10453	1959	Dr. Carolyn Grubbs Williams	11	8,450	390
Brookdale Comm Coll, Lincroft, NJ 07738-1597	1967	Dr. Peter F. Burnham.	8	11,868	443
Brookhaven Coll, Farmers Branch, TX 75244-4997	1978	Dr. Walter G. Bumphus.	8	9,060	525
Broome Comm Coll, Binghamton, NY 13902-1017	1946	Dr. Donald A. Dellow.	11	5,402	344
Broward Comm Coll, Fort Lauderdale, FL 33301-2298.	1960	Dr. Willis N. Holcombe.	5	25,273	775
Brown Inst, Minneapolis, MN 55407-1932.	1946	Mr. Ronald G. Andersen.	3	1,300	96
Bucks County Comm Coll, Newtown, PA 18940-1525.	1964	Dr. James J. Linksz.	8	9,204	452
Bunker Hill Comm Coll, Boston, MA 02129.	1973	Mr. Maurice F. O'Shea.	5	5,695	145
Burlington County Comm Coll, Pemberton, NJ 08068-1599	1966	Dr. Robert Messina.	8	6,140	310
Butler County Comm Coll, El Dorado, KS 67042-3280	1927	Dr. Jacqueline Uietti.	11	7,506	573
Butler County Comm Coll, Butler, PA 16003-1203	1965	Dr. Frederick F. Bartok.	8	3,098	220
Butte Coll, Oroville, CA 95965-8399.	1966	Dr. Betty M. Dean.	9	12,300	561
Cabrillo Coll, Aptos, CA 95003-3194	1959	Mr. John D. Hurd.	9	11,805	552
Caldwell Comm Coll and Tech Inst, Hudson, NC 28638-2397	1964	Dr. Kenneth A. Boham	5	3,127	225
Camden County Coll, Blackwood, NJ 08012-0200	1967	Dr. Phyllis Della Vecchia	11	12,669	627
Cañada Coll, Redwood City, CA 94061-1099	1968	Dr. Marie E. Rosenwasser	9	5,640	231
Cape Cod Comm Coll, West Barnstable, MA 02668-1599	1961	Dr. Richard A. Kraus	5	3,630	256
Cape Fear Comm Coll, Wilmington, NC 28401-3993	1959	Mr. Eric B. McKeithan	5	3,500	211
Capital Comm Tech Coll, Hartford, CT 06105-2354.	1946	Dr. Ira Rubenzahl	5	2,900	174
Carl Albert State Coll, Poteau, OK 74953-5208	1934	Dr. Joe E. White	5	1,933	160
Carl Sandburg Coll, Galesburg, IL 61401-9576	1967	Dr. Donald G. Crist	11	3,000	208
Carroll Comm Coll, Westminster, MD 21157.	1996	Dr. Joseph F. Shields	11	2,532	210
Casper Coll, Casper, WY 82601-4699.	1945	Dr. LeRoy Strausner	9	3,960	185
Catawba Valley Comm Coll, Hickory, NC 28602-9699	1960	Dr. Cuyler A. Dunbar	11	3,401	250
Catonsville Comm Coll, Catonsville, MD 21228-5381	1957	Dr. Frederick J. Walsh	8	9,458	534
Cayuga County Comm Coll, Auburn, NY 13021-3099	1953	Dr. Dennis Golladay	11	2,872	182
Cecil Comm Coll, North East, MD 21901-1999.	1968	Dr. Robert L. Gell	8	1,078	175
Cedar Valley Coll, Lancaster, TX 75134-3799	1977	Dr. Carol J. Spencer.	5	3,136	130
Central Alabama Comm Coll, Alexander City, AL 35011-0699	1965	Dr. James H. Cornell	5	2,386	140
Central Arizona Coll, Coolidge, AZ 85228-9779	1961	Dr. John J. Klein	8	14,950	440
Central Carolina Comm Coll, Sanford, NC 27330-9000	1962	Dr. Marvin R. Joyner	11	3,056	192
Central Carolina Tech Coll, Sumter, SC 29150-2499	1963	Dr. Keith W. Bird, Jr.	5	2,300	144
Central Comm Coll–Grand Island Cmps, Grand Island, NE 68802-4903	1976	Dr. William Giddings.	11	2,124	165
Central Comm Coll–Hastings Cmps, Hastings, NE 68902-1024	1966	Dr. LaVern Franzen	11	2,812	111
Central Comm Coll–Platte Cmps, Columbus, NE 68602-1027.	1968	Dr. M. Richard Shaink	11	2,154	100
Central Florida Comm Coll, Ocala, FL 34478-1388	1957	Dr. Charles Dassance	11	6,010	213
Centralia Coll, Centralia, WA 98531-4099	1925	Dr. Henry P. Kirk	5	1,800	121
Central Lakes Coll, Brainerd, MN 56401-3904	1938	Ms. Sally Jane Ihne	5	3,300	140
Central Ohio Tech Coll, Newark, OH 43055-1767	1971	Dr. Rafael L. Cortada	5	1,636	149
Central Oregon Comm Coll, Bend, OR 97701-5998	1949	Dr. Robert L. Barber	9	3,363	176
Central Piedmont Comm Coll, Charlotte, NC 28235-5009	1963	Dr. Paul A. Zeiss.	11	15,420	1,877
Central Texas Coll, Killeen, TX 76540-1800	1967	Dr. James R. Anderson	11	8,600	328
Central Virginia Comm Coll, Lynchburg, VA 24502-4907	1966	Dr. Belle S. Wheelan	5	3,749	200
Central Wyoming Coll, Riverton, WY 82501-2273	1966	Dr. JoAnne McFarland.	11	1,825	110
Century Comm and Tech Coll, White Bear Lake, MN 55110.	1970	Dr. James Meznek.	5	7,000	280
Cerritos Coll, Norwalk, CA 90650-6298.	1956	Dr. Fred Gaskin.	11	20,717	690
Cerro Coso Comm Coll, Ridgecrest, CA 93555-9571	1973	Dr. Daniel Roe Darnell.	5	3,855	262
Chabot Coll, Hayward, CA 94545-5001.	1961	Dr. Sam Schauerman	5	13,416	933
Chaffey Coll, Rancho Cucamonga, CA 91737-3002	1883	Dr. Jerry W. Young	9	12,651	540
Champlain Coll, Burlington, VT 05402-0670.	1878	Dr. Roger H. Perry	1	2,127	161
Chandler-Gilbert Comm Coll, Chandler, AZ 85225-2479.	1985	Ms. Arnette S. Ward.	9	3,500	195
Charles County Comm Coll, La Plata, MD 20646-0910	1958	Dr. John Sine.	11	5,879	355
Charles Stewart Mott Comm Coll, Flint, MI 48503-2089	1923	Dr. Allen Arnold.	9	9,009	420
Chattahoochee Tech Inst, Marietta, GA 30060	1961	Dr. Harlon Crimm	5	2,066	76
Chattahoochee Valley State Comm Coll, Phenix City, AL 36869-7928	1974	Dr. Richard J. Federinko	5	2,010	108
Chattanooga State Tech Comm Coll, Chattanooga, TN 37406-1018	1965	Dr. James L. Catanzaro	5	9,335	615
Chemeketa Comm Coll, Salem, OR 97309-7070.	1955	Dr. Gerard Berger.	11	9,033	685
Chesapeake Coll, Wye Mills, MD 21679-0008	1965	Dr. Stuart M. Bounds	11	2,082	141
Chesterfield-Marlboro Tech Coll, Cheraw, SC 29520-1007.	1967	Dr. Ronald W. Hampton	11	1,028	66
Chipola Jr Coll, Marianna, FL 32446-3065	1947	Dr. H. Dale O'Daniel.	5	2,357	142
Chippewa Valley Tech Coll, Eau Claire, WI 54701-6120	1912	Dr. William A. Ihlenfeldt.	9	3,800	400
Cincinnati State Tech and Comm Coll, Cincinnati, OH 45223-2690.	1966	Dr. Ronald Wright	5	5,377	351
Cisco Jr Coll, Cisco, TX 76437-9321	1940	Dr. Roger C. Schustereit	11	2,553	98
Citrus Coll, Glendora, CA 91741-1899.	1915	Dr. Louis E. Zellers.	11	10,448	392
City Colls of Chicago, Harold Washington Coll, Chicago, IL 60601-2449.	1962	Ms. Nancy DeSombre.	11	7,577	243
City Colls of Chicago, Harry S Truman Coll, Chicago, IL 60640-5616	1956	Dr. Phoebe K. Helm.	11	4,620	160
City Colls of Chicago, Kennedy-King Coll, Chicago, IL 60621-3733	1935	Dr. Wayne Watson	11	2,539	106
City Colls of Chicago, Malcolm X Coll, Chicago, IL 60612-3145.	1911	Ms. Zerrie D. Campbell.	11	3,480	93
City Colls of Chicago, Olive-Harvey Coll, Chicago, IL 60628-1645	1970	Dr. Lawrence M. Cox.	11	3,959	133
City Colls of Chicago, Richard J Daley Coll, Chicago, IL 60652-1242	1960	Dr. Ted Martinez, Jr.	11	4,679	155
City Colls of Chicago, Wilbur Wright Coll, Chicago, IL 60634-1591	1934	Mr. Raymond F. LeFevour	11	7,510	218
Clackamas Comm Coll, Oregon City, OR 97045-7998	1966	Dr. John S. Keyser.	9	8,694	524
Clark Coll, Vancouver, WA 98663-3598.	1933	Dr. Earl P. Johnson.	5	10,700	320
Clark State Comm Coll, Springfield, OH 45501-0570	1962	Dr. Karen E. Nagle.	5	2,496	161
Cleveland Comm Coll, Shelby, NC 28152.	1965	Dr. L. Steve Thornburg.	5	1,873	91
Cleveland Inst of Electronics, Cleveland, OH 44114-3636 (2)	1934	Mr. John R. Drinko.	3	2,173	7
Cleveland State Comm Coll, Cleveland, TN 37320-3570	1967	Dr. Carl Hite.	5	3,670	182
Clinton Comm Coll, Clinton, IA 52732-6299	1946	Ms. Karen Vickers.	5	1,161	75
Clinton Comm Coll, Plattsburgh, NY 12901-9573	1969	Dr. Jay L. Fennell.	11	1,644	179
Cloud County Comm Coll, Concordia, KS 66901-1002.	1965	Dr. James D. Ihly	11	3,112	218
Clovis Comm Coll, Clovis, NM 88101-8381	1971	Dr. Jay Gurley.	5	3,964	209

Name, address	Year	Governing official, control, and highest degree offered		Enroll- ment	Faculty
Coastal Carolina Comm Coll, Jacksonville, NC 28546-6877	1964	Dr. Ronald K. Lingle, Jr.	11	3,190	195
Coastal Georgia Comm Coll, Brunswick, GA 31520-3644	1961	Dr. Dorothy L. Lord	5	1,900	79
Coastline Comm Coll, Fountain Valley, CA 92708-2597	1976	Dr. Leslie N. Purdy	11	11,665	350
Cochise Coll, Sierra Vista, AZ 85635-2317	1977	Dr. Walter S. Patton	11	1,961	253
Coconino County Comm Coll, Flagstaff, AZ 86003	1991	Dr. V. Phillip Tullar	5	3,895	200
Coffeyville Comm Coll, Coffeyville, KS 67337-5063	1923	Dr. Ronald E. Thomas	11	1,901	65
Colby Comm Coll, Colby, KS 67701-4099	1964	Dr. Mikel Ary	11	1,138	63
Coll of Alameda, Alameda, CA 94501-2109	1970	Dr. George Herring	11	5,030	166
Coll of DuPage, Glen Ellyn, IL 60137-6599	1967	Dr. Michael T. Murphy	11	33,920	1,819
Coll of Eastern Utah, Price, UT 84501-2699	1937	Mr. Brent Haddock	5	3,170	128
Coll of Lake County, Grayslake, IL 60030-1198	1967	Dr. Gretchen J. Naff	9	14,867	776
Coll of Marin, Kentfield, CA 94904	1926	Dr. James E. Middleton	11	8,845	464
Coll of St Catherine–Minneapolis, Minneapolis, MN 55454-1494	1964	Dr. Anita M. Pampusch	2	1,237	116
Coll of San Mateo, San Mateo, CA 94402-3784	1922	Mr. Peter Landsberger	11	11,506	476
Coll of Southern Idaho, Twin Falls, ID 83303-1238	1964	Mr. Gerald R. Meyerhoeffer	11	5,502	260
Coll of the Canyons, Santa Clarita, CA 91355-1899	1969	Dr. Dianne G. Van Hook	11	6,446	260
Coll of the Desert, Palm Desert, CA 92260-9305	1959	Dr. William R. Kroonen	11	9,710	320
Coll of the Mainland, Texas City, TX 77591-2499	1967	Mr. Larry L. Stanley	11	3,564	180
Coll of the Redwoods, Eureka, CA 95501-9300	1964	Dr. Cedric A. Sampson	11	6,968	376
Coll of the Sequoias, Visalia, CA 93277-2234	1925	Dr. Kamiran S. Badrkhan	11	9,078	445
Coll of the Siskiyous, Weed, CA 96094-2899	1957	Dr. Martha Romero	11	2,900	178
Collin County Comm Coll, McKinney, TX 75070-2906	1985	Dr. John H. Anthony	11	10,580	613
The Colorado Inst of Art, Denver, CO 80203-2903	1952	Mr. David C. Zorn	3	1,520	123
Colorado Mountn Coll, Alpine Cmps, Steamboat Springs, CO 80487	1965	Mr. John Vickery	9	1,262	132
Columbia Basin Coll, Pasco, WA 99301-3397	1955	Dr. Lee R. Thornton	5	6,761	350
Columbia Coll, Sonora, CA 95370	1968	Dr. Jim R. Riggs	11	2,644	121
Columbia-Greene Comm Coll, Hudson, NY 12534-0327	1969	Dr. Terry A. Cline	11	1,578	115
Columbia State Comm Coll, Columbia, TN 38402-1315	1966	Dr. O. Rebecca Hawkins	5	3,968	239
Columbus State Comm Coll, Columbus, OH 43216-1609	1963	Dr. Valeriana M. Moeller	5	16,330	910
Columbus Tech Inst, Columbus, GA 31904-6572	1961	Mr. Eugene Demonet	5	1,540	NR
Comm Coll of Allegheny County, Pittsburgh, PA 15233	1966	Dr. J. David Griffin	8	16,984	3,436
Comm Coll of Aurora, Aurora, CO 80011-9036	1983	Dr. Larry Carter	5	4,440	197
Comm Coll of Beaver County, Monaca, PA 15061-2588	1966	Dr. Margaret Williams-Betlyn	5	2,352	149
Comm Coll of Denver, Denver, CO 80217-3363	1970	Dr. Byron McClenney	5	11,897	596
Comm Coll of Philadelphia, Philadelphia, PA 19130-3991	1964	Dr. Frederick W. Capshaw	11	18,713	1,182
Comm Coll of Rhode Island, Warwick, RI 02886-1807	1964	Mr. Edward Liston	5	11,717	697
Comm Coll of Southern Nevada, North Las Vegas, NV 89030-4296	1971	Dr. Richard Moore	5	24,678	862
Comm Coll of the Air Force, Maxwell Air Force Base, AL 36112-6613	1972	Col. Tamzy J. House	4	404,289	6,328
Comm Coll of Vermont, Waterbury, VT 05676-0120	1970	Ms. Barbara Murphy	5	3,907	524
Compton Comm Coll, Compton, CA 90221-5393	1927	Mr. Ulis C. Williams	11	5,700	347
Connors State Coll, Warner, OK 74469-9700	1908	Dr. Ronald D. Garner	5	2,149	137
Contra Costa Coll, San Pablo, CA 94806-3195	1948	Dr. D. Candy Rose	11	3,000	222
Copiah-Lincoln Comm Coll, Wesson, MS 39191-0457	1928	Dr. Howell C. Garner	11	1,785	115
Copiah-Lincoln Comm Coll–Natchez Cmps, Natchez, MS 39120-8446	1972	Dr. Howell C. Garner	11	1,685	42
Corning Comm Coll, Corning, NY 14830-3297	1956	Dr. Eduardo J. Marti	11	3,220	188
Cosumnes River Coll, Sacramento, CA 95823-5799	1970	Dr. Merilee R. Lewis	9	12,656	425
County Coll of Morris, Randolph, NJ 07869-2086	1966	Dr. Edward J. Yaw	8	8,910	517
Cowley County Comm Coll and Voc-Tech Sch, Arkansas City, KS 67005-2662	1922	Dr. Patrick J. McAtee	11	3,287	184
Crafton Hills Coll, Yucaipa, CA 92399-1799	1972	Dr. Luis S. Gomez	11	5,103	184
Craven Comm Coll, New Bern, NC 28562-4984	1965	Dr. Lewis S. Redd	5	2,207	202
Crowder Coll, Neosho, MO 64850-9160	1963	Dr. Kent A. Farnsworth	11	1,778	168
Cuesta Coll, San Luis Obispo, CA 93403-8106	1964	Dr. Grace N. Mitchell	9	8,126	309
Culinary Inst of America, Hyde Park, NY 12538-1499	1946	Mr. Ferdinand E. Metz	1	2,067	120
Cumberland County Coll, Vineland, NJ 08360-0517	1963	Dr. Roland J. Chapdelaine	11	2,460	118
Cuyahoga Comm Coll, Eastern Cmps, Highland Hills, OH 44122-6104	1971	Dr. Lawrence Simpson	11	4,959	201
Cuyahoga Comm Coll, Metropolitan Cmps, Cleveland, OH 44115-3123	1963	Dr. Alex Johnson	11	5,616	320
Cuyahoga Comm Coll, Western Cmps, Parma, OH 44130-5199	1966	Mr. Ronald M. Sobel	11	11,207	580
Cuyamaca Coll, El Cajon, CA 92019-4304	1978	Dr. Sherrill L. Amador	5	4,469	NR
Cypress Coll, Cypress, CA 90630-5897	1966	Dr. Christine Johnson	11	14,580	434
Dabney S Lancaster Comm Coll, Clifton Forge, VA 24422	1964	Dr. Richard R. Teaff	5	1,722	160
Dalton Coll, Dalton, GA 30720-3797	1963	Dr. James A. Burran	5	3,006	106
Danville Area Comm Coll, Danville, IL 61832-5199	1946	Dr. Harry J. Braun	11	2,662	134
Danville Comm Coll, Danville, VA 24541-4088	1967	Dr. B. Carlyle Ramsey	5	3,835	149
Darton Coll, Albany, GA 31707-3098	1965	Dr. Peter J. Sireno	5	2,265	150
Davidson County Comm Coll, Lexington, NC 27293-1287	1958	Dr. J. Bryan Brooks	11	2,193	346
Daytona Beach Comm Coll, Daytona Beach, FL 32120-2811	1958	Dr. Philip R. Day, Jr.	5	12,063	773
Dean Coll, Franklin, MA 02038-1994	1865	Dr. Paula M. Rooney	1	1,950	111
De Anza Coll, Cupertino, CA 95014-5793	1967	Dr. Martha J. Kanter	11	24,721	945
DeKalb Coll, Decatur, GA 30034-3897	1964	Dr. Jacquelyn Belcher	5	15,690	1,050
DeKalb Tech Inst, Clarkston, GA 30021	1961	Dr. Paul M. Starnes	5	4,347	492
Delaware County Comm Coll, Media, PA 19063-1094	1967	Dr. Richard D. De Cosmo	11	9,807	438
Delaware Tech & Comm Coll, Jack F Owens Cmps, Georgetown, DE 19947	1967	Dr. G. Timothy Kavel	5	3,221	155
Delaware Tech & Comm Coll, Stanton/Wilmington Cmps, Newark, DE 19713	1968	Mr. Lawrence H. Miller	5	6,706	454
Delaware Tech & Comm Coll, Terry Cmps, Dover, DE 19904	1972	Dr. Marguerite M. Johnson	5	1,944	131
Delgado Comm Coll, New Orleans, LA 70119-4399	1921	Dr. Ione Elioff	5	14,112	679
Del Mar Coll, Corpus Christi, TX 78404-3897	1935	Dr. Terry L. Dicianna	11	10,386	535
Delta Coll, University Center, MI 48710	1961	Dr. Peter D. Boyse	9	9,418	515
Des Moines Area Comm Coll, Ankeny, IA 50021-8995	1966	Dr. Joseph Borgen	11	10,287	NR
DeVry Inst, North Brunswick, NJ 08902-3362	1969	Mr. Robert Bocchino	3	2,918	95
Dixie Coll, St George, UT 84770-3876	1911	Dr. Robert Huddleston	5	3,132	198
Dodge City Comm Coll, Dodge City, KS 67801-2399	1935	Dr. Richard Drum	11	2,676	163
Doña Ana Branch Comm Coll, Las Cruces, NM 88003-8001	1973	Dr. James L. McLaughlin	11	3,949	NR
Dundalk Comm Coll, Baltimore, MD 21222-4694	1970	Dr. Felix T. Haynes	8	2,946	157
Dunwoody Inst, Minneapolis, MN 55403	1914	Mr. Frank Starke	1	1,191	75
Durham Tech Comm Coll, Durham, NC 27703-5023	1961	Dr. Phail Wynn, Jr.	5	2,746	442
Dutchess Comm Coll, Poughkeepsie, NY 12601-1595	1957	Dr. D. David Conklin	11	6,233	415
Dyersburg State Comm Coll, Dyersburg, TN 38024	1969	Dr. Karen A. Bowyer	5	2,321	153
East Arkansas Comm Coll, Forrest City, AR 72335-9598	1974	Dr. George McCormick	5	1,199	101
East Central Coll, Union, MO 63084-0529	1968	Dr. Dale Gibson	9	3,049	181

Name, address	Year	Governing official, control, and highest degree offered		Enrollment	Faculty
East Central Comm Coll, Decatur, MS 39327-0129	1928	Dr. Eddie M. Smith	11	1,828	115
Eastern Arizona Coll, Thatcher, AZ 85552-0769	1888	Mr. Gherald L. Hoopes, Jr.	11	2,686	232
Eastern New Mexico U–Roswell, Roswell, NM 88202-6000	1958	Dr. Joseph Roberts	5	2,797	150
Eastern Oklahoma State Coll, Wilburton, OK 74578-4999	1908	Dr. Bill Hill	5	2,263	54
Eastern Wyoming Coll, Torrington, WY 82240-1699	1948	Dr. Jack L. Bottenfield	11	1,651	136
Eastfield Coll, Mesquite, TX 75150-2099	1970	Dr. Robert Aguero	11	8,056	105
East Georgia Coll, Swainsboro, GA 30401-2699	1973	Dr. Jeremiah J. Ashcroft	5	1,015	41
East Los Angeles Coll, Monterey Park, CA 91754-6001	1945	Mr. Ernest H. Moreno	11	15,100	450
East Mississippi Comm Coll, Scooba, MS 39358-0158	1927	Dr. Thomas L. Davis	11	1,482	70
Edgecombe Comm Coll, Tarboro, NC 27886-9399	1968	Dr. Hartwell H. Fuller, Jr.	11	2,011	135
Edison Comm Coll, Fort Myers, FL 33906-6210	1962	Dr. Kenneth Walker	11	9,836	724
Edison State Comm Coll, Piqua, OH 45356-9253	1973	Dr. Kenneth A. Yowell	5	2,721	183
Edmonds Comm Coll, Lynnwood, WA 98036-5999	1967	Dr. Jack Oharah	11	10,089	440
Education America–Tampa Tech Inst Cmps, Tampa, FL 33612-8410	1948	Mr. William D. Polmear	3	1,150	48
Elaine P Nunez Comm Coll, Chalmette, LA 70043-1249	1992	Dr. Carol S. Hopson	5	1,670	104
El Camino Coll, Torrance, CA 90506-0001	1947	Mr. Thomas Fallo	9	22,675	533
El Centro Coll, Dallas, TX 75202-3604	1966	Dr. Wright L. Lassiter, Jr.	8	4,170	363
Elgin Comm Coll, Elgin, IL 60123-7193	1949	Dr. Roy Flores	11	9,104	459
El Paso Comm Coll, El Paso, TX 79998-0500	1969	Dr. Adriana Barrera	8	22,264	1,304
Enterprise State Jr Coll, Enterprise, AL 36331-1300	1965	Dr. Stafford L. Thompson	5	1,897	125
Erie Comm Coll, City Cmps, Buffalo, NY 14203-2601	1971	Dr. Louis M. Ricci	11	3,112	258
Erie Comm Coll, North Cmps, Williamsville, NY 14221-7095	1946	Dr. Louis M. Ricci	11	6,434	443
Erie Comm Coll, South Cmps, Orchard Park, NY 14127-2199	1974	Dr. Louis M. Ricci	11	3,391	288
Essex Comm Coll, Baltimore, MD 21237-3899	1957	Dr. Leila Gonzalez Sullivan	11	8,516	507
Essex County Coll, Newark, NJ 07102-1798	1966	Dr. Zachary Yamba	8	8,952	270
Eugenio Maria de Hostos Comm Coll of City U of NY, Bronx, NY 10451	1968	Dr. Isaura Santiago	11	4,836	423
Everett Comm Coll, Everett, WA 98201-1327	1941	Dr. Susan C. Carroll	5	7,303	288
Evergreen Valley Coll, San Jose, CA 95135-1598	1975	Dr. Noella Vela	11	9,002	300
Fashion Inst of Design & Merchandising, LA Cmps, Los Angeles, CA 90015-1421	1969	Ms. Tonian Hohberg	3	4,083	110
Fashion Inst of Design & Merchandising, SF Cmps, San Francisco, CA 94108-5829	1973	Mrs. Barbara Cupper	3	1,744	26
Fayetteville Tech Comm Coll, Fayetteville, NC 28303-0236	1961	Dr. Craig Allen	5	7,316	756
Feather River Comm Coll District, Quincy, CA 95971-6023	1968	Dr. Donald Donato	11	1,200	95
Fergus Falls Comm Coll, Fergus Falls, MN 56537-1009	1960	Mr. Dan F. True	5	1,488	78
Finger Lakes Comm Coll, Canandaigua, NY 14424-8395	1965	Dr. Daniel T. Hayes	11	3,768	230
Fiorello H LaGuardia Comm Coll of City U of NY, Long Island City, NY 11101-3071	1970	Dr. Raymond C. Bowen	11	10,341	604
Flathead Valley Comm Coll, Kalispell, MT 59901-2622	1967	Dr. David Beyer	11	1,142	111
Florence-Darlington Tech Coll, Florence, SC 29501-0548	1963	Dr. Charles W. Gould	5	2,939	209
Florida Comm Coll at Jacksonville, Jacksonville, FL 32202-4030	1963	Dr. Edgar C. Napier	5	18,660	1,494
Florida Keys Comm Coll, Key West, FL 33040-4397	1965	Dr. William A. Seeker	5	2,200	94
Florida National Coll, Hialeah, FL 33012	1982	Mr. Jose Regueiro	3	1,100	70
Floyd Coll, Rome, GA 30162-1864	1970	Dr. H. Lynn Cundiff	5	3,048	66
Foothill Coll, Los Altos Hills, CA 94022-4599	1958	Dr. Bernadine Chuck Fong	11	15,500	578
Forsyth Tech Comm Coll, Winston-Salem, NC 27103-5197	1964	Dr. Desna L. Wallin	5	4,895	535
Fort Scott Comm Coll, Fort Scott, KS 66701	1919	Dr. Laura Meeks	11	1,651	59
Fox Valley Tech Coll, Appleton, WI 54913-2277	1967	Dr. H. Victor Baldi	11	6,100	1,241
Frank Phillips Coll, Borger, TX 79008-5118	1948	Dr. William A. Griffin, Jr.	11	1,026	96
Frederick Comm Coll, Frederick, MD 21702-2097	1957	Dr. Lee J. Betts	11	4,233	272
Fresno City Coll, Fresno, CA 93741-0002	1910	Dr. Daniel L. Larios	9	18,103	832
Front Range Comm Coll, Westminster, CO 80030-2105	1968	Dr. Thomas Gonzales	5	11,027	765
Fullerton Coll, Fullerton, CA 92832-2095	1913	Dr. Vera M. Martinez	11	18,339	678
Full Sail Ctr for the Recording Arts, Winter Park, FL 32792-7437	1979	E. Haddock/J. Phelps	3	1,020	95
Fulton-Montgomery Comm Coll, Johnstown, NY 12095-3790	1964	Dr. Priscilla J. Bell	11	1,799	94
Gadsden State Comm Coll, Gadsden, AL 35902-0227	1985	Dr. Victor Ficker	5	6,243	288
Gainesville Coll, Gainesville, GA 30503-1358	1964	Dr. Katherine Fuller	5	2,652	111
Galveston Coll, Galveston, TX 77550-7496	1967	Dr. Carlisle B. Rathburn, III	11	2,328	133
Garden City Comm Coll, Garden City, KS 67846-6399	1919	Dr. James H. Tangeman	9	2,334	148
Garland County Comm Coll, Hot Springs, AR 71913	1973	Dr. Tom Spencer	11	1,866	106
Gaston Coll, Dallas, NC 28034-1499	1963	Dr. Patricia Skinner	11	6,532	370
Gateway Comm Coll, Phoenix, AZ 85034-1795	1968	Dr. Phil Randolph	11	6,804	300
Gateway Comm-Tech Coll, New Haven, CT 06511-5918	1968	Dr. Diana Van Der Ploeg	5	4,537	310
Gateway Tech Coll, Kenosha, WI 53144-1690	1911	Dr. Carole M. Johnson	11	6,800	489
Gavilan Coll, Gilroy, CA 95020-9599	1919	Dr. Glenn E. Mayle	11	4,029	164
Genesee Comm Coll, Batavia, NY 14020-9704	1966	Dr. Stuart Steiner	11	4,059	219
George Corley Wallace State Comm Coll, Selma, AL 36702-1049	1966	Dr. Julius Ray Brown	5	1,750	78
George C Wallace State Comm Coll, Dothan, AL 36303-9234	1949	Dr. Larry Beaty	5	4,000	180
Georgia Military Coll, Milledgeville, GA 31061-3398	1879	Maj. Gen. Peter J. Boylam, Jr.	11	3,495	179
Germanna Comm Coll, Locust Grove, VA 22508-0339	1970	Dr. Francis S. Turnage	5	2,596	135
Glendale Comm Coll, Glendale, AZ 85302-3090	1965	Dr. Tessa Martinez Pollack	11	16,235	687
Glendale Comm Coll, Glendale, CA 91208-2894	1927	Dr. John A. Davitt	11	15,337	345
Glen Oaks Comm Coll, Centreville, MI 49032-9719	1965	Dr. Philip G. Ward	11	1,447	96
Gloucester County Coll, Sewell, NJ 08080	1967	Dr. Richard H. Jones	8	4,811	215
Gogebic Comm Coll, Ironwood, MI 49938	1932	Dr. Donald J. Foster	11	1,399	91
Golden West Coll, Huntington Beach, CA 92647-2748	1966	Dr. Kenneth D. Yglesias	11	12,177	410
Gordon Coll, Barnesville, GA 30204-1762	1852	Dr. Jerry M. Williamson	5	2,227	99
Grand Rapids Comm Coll, Grand Rapids, MI 49503-3201	1914	Mr. Richard Calkins	9	13,028	511
Grays Harbor Coll, Aberdeen, WA 98520-7599	1930	Dr. Jewell Manspeaker	5	2,708	200
Grayson County Coll, Denison, TX 75020-8299	1964	Dr. Alan Scheibmeir	11	3,004	176
Great Basin Coll, Elko, NV 89801-3348	1967	Dr. Ronald K. Remington	5	2,817	289
Great Lakes Coll, Midland, MI 48642	1907	Mr. William Guerriero	1	1,400	124
Greenfield Comm Coll, Greenfield, MA 01301-9739	1962	Dr. Charles C. Wall	5	1,694	146
Green River Comm Coll, Auburn, WA 98092-3699	1965	Mr. Richard A. Rutkowski	5	8,544	497
Greenville Tech Coll, Greenville, SC 29606-5616	1962	Dr. Thomas E. Barton, Jr.	5	8,480	539
Grossmont Coll, El Cajon, CA 92020-1799	1961	Dr. Richard M. Sanchez	11	15,000	653
Guilford Tech Comm Coll, Jamestown, NC 27282-0309	1958	Dr. Don Cameron	11	6,894	385
Gulf Coast Comm Coll, Panama City, FL 32401-1058	1957	Dr. Robert L. McSpadden	5	4,208	315
Gwinnett Tech Inst, Lawrenceville, GA 30246-1505	1984	Ms. Sharon J. Rigsby	5	4,000	84
Hagerstown Jr Coll, Hagerstown, MD 21742-6590	1946	Dr. Norman P. Shea	8	2,917	203
Harford Comm Coll, Bel Air, MD 21015-1698	1957	Dr. Claudia E. Chiesi	11	4,625	468
Harrisburg Area Comm Coll, Harrisburg, PA 17110-2999	1964	Dr. Paul R. Hurley, Jr.	11	10,715	612
Hartnell Coll, Salinas, CA 93901-1697	1920	Dr. Edward J. Valeau	9	7,500	363
Hawkeye Comm Coll, Waterloo, IA 50704-8015	1967	Dr. Dan Brobst	11	3,538	207
Haywood Comm Coll, Clyde, NC 28721-9453	1964	Mr. Wayne Hawkins	11	1,262	118

Name, address	Year	Governing official, control, and highest degree offered		Enroll-ment	Faculty
Heartland Comm Coll, Bloomington, IL 61701	1990	Dr. Jonathan Astroth	9	3,343	191
Henry Ford Comm Coll, Dearborn, MI 48128-1495	1938	Dr. Andrew A. Mazzara	9	13,300	994
Herkimer County Comm Coll, Herkimer, NY 13350	1966	Dr. Ronald F. Williams	11	2,466	111
Hesser Coll, Manchester, NH 03103-7245	1900	Mr. Linwood W. Galeucia	3	3,000	99
Hibbing Comm Coll, Hibbing, MN 55746-3300	1916	Dr. Anthony Kuznik	5	1,042	65
Highland Comm Coll, Freeport, IL 61032-9341	1962	Dr. Ruth Mercedes Smith	11	2,650	169
Highland Comm Coll, Highland, KS 66035-0068	1858	Dr. Betty Stevens	11	2,654	195
Highline Comm Coll, Des Moines, WA 98198-9800	1961	Dr. Edward M. Command	5	7,185	223
Hill Coll of the Hill Jr Coll District, Hillsboro, TX 76645-0619	1923	Dr. W. R. Auvenshine	9	2,500	80
Hillsborough Comm Coll, Tampa, FL 33631-3127	1968	Mr. Jeff Hockaday	5	18,307	746
Hinds Comm Coll, Raymond, MS 39154	1917	Dr. Clyde Muse	11	10,726	890
Hocking Coll, Nelsonville, OH 45764-9588	1968	Dr. John J. Light	5	5,071	253
Holmes Comm Coll, Goodman, MS 39079-0369	1928	Dr. Starkey A. Morgan, Sr.	11	2,639	125
Holyoke Comm Coll, Holyoke, MA 01040-1099	1946	Dr. David M. Bartley	5	3,558	235
Horry-Georgetown Tech Coll, Conway, SC 29528-6066	1965	Dr. D. Kent Sharples	11	3,279	240
Housatonic Comm-Tech Coll, Bridgeport, CT 06604-4704	1965	Dr. Janis M. Wertz	5	2,654	137
Houston Comm Coll System, Houston, TX 77270-7849	1971	Ms. Ruth Burgos-Sasscer	11	35,585	2,387
Howard Coll, Big Spring, TX 79720-3702	1945	Dr. Cheryl T. Sparks	11	2,400	165
Howard Comm Coll, Columbia, MD 21044-3197	1966	Dr. Dwight A. Burrill	11	4,954	318
Hudson County Comm Coll, Jersey City, NJ 07306	1974	Dr. Glen Gabert	11	4,249	237
Hudson Valley Comm Coll, Troy, NY 12180-6096	1953	Dr. Stephen M. Curtis	11	9,644	511
Hutchinson Comm Coll and Area Vocational Sch, Hutchinson, KS 67501-5894	1928	Dr. Edward E. Berger	11	3,621	264
Illinois Central Coll, East Peoria, IL 61635-0001	1967	Dr. Thomas K. Thomas	11	12,115	658
Illinois Eastern Comm Colls, Frontier Comm Coll, Fairfield, IL 62837-2601	1976	Mr. Jerry Hefley	11	2,302	128
Illinois Eastern Comm Colls, Lincoln Trail Coll, Robinson, IL 62454	1969	Dr. John Arabatgis	11	1,216	70
Illinois Eastern Comm Colls, Olney Central Coll, Olney, IL 62450	1962	Dr. Hans Andrews	11	1,128	94
Illinois Eastern Comm Colls, Wabash Valley Coll, Mount Carmel, IL 62863-2657	1960	Dr. Harry K. Benson	11	1,461	84
Illinois Valley Comm Coll, Oglesby, IL 61348-9692	1924	Dr. Jean Goodnow	9	4,281	189
Imperial Valley Coll, Imperial, CA 92251-0158	1922	Dr. Gilbert M. Dominguez	11	5,841	310
Independence Comm Coll, Independence, KS 67301-0708	1925	Mr. Neil Edds	5	1,848	153
Indiana Business Coll, Indianapolis, IN 46204-1108	1902	Mr. Kenneth J. Konesco	3	1,700	70
Indian Hills Comm Coll, Ottumwa, IA 52501-1398	1966	Dr. Lyle A. Hellyer	11	3,424	143
Indian River Comm Coll, Fort Pierce, FL 34981-5599	1960	Dr. Edwin R. Massey	5	6,890	860
Instituto Comercial de Puerto Rico Jr Coll, Hato Rey, PR 00919-0304	1946	Mrs. Genoveva Christian	3	1,754	88
Interboro Inst, New York, NY 10019-3602	1888	Mr. Bruce R. Kalish	3	1,049	44
Inver Hills Comm Coll, Inver Grove Heights, MN 55076-3224	1969	Dr. Steve Wallace	5	4,793	220
Iowa Central Comm Coll, Fort Dodge, IA 50501-5798	1966	Dr. Robert A. Paxton	11	2,828	206
Iowa Lakes Comm Coll, Estherville, IA 51334-2295	1967	Mr. James E. Billings	11	2,428	40
Iowa Western Comm Coll, Council Bluffs, IA 51502	1966	Dr. Dan Kinney	9	3,887	218
Irvine Valley Coll, Irvine, CA 92720-4399	1979	Mr. Raghu Mathur	11	10,300	344
Isothermal Comm Coll, Spindale, NC 28160-0804	1965	Dr. Willard L. Lewis	5	1,706	92
Itasca Comm Coll, Grand Rapids, MN 55744	1922	Dr. Joe Sertich	5	1,308	68
Itawamba Comm Coll, Fulton, MS 38843-1099	1947	Dr. David Cole	11	3,500	102
Ivy Tech State Coll–Central Indiana, Indianapolis, IN 46206-1763	1963	Dr. Meredith L. Carter	5	5,355	326
Ivy Tech State Coll–Columbus, Columbus, IN 47203-1868	1963	Mr. Homer B. Smith	5	2,881	200
Ivy Tech State Coll–Eastcentral, Muncie, IN 47302-9448	1968	Dr. J. Robert Jeffs	5	2,540	249
Ivy Tech State Coll–Kokomo, Kokomo, IN 46903-1373	1968	Dr. Stephen J. Daily	5	1,659	141
Ivy Tech State Coll–Lafayette, Lafayette, IN 47905-5266	1968	Dr. Elizabeth J. Doversberger	5	2,311	146
Ivy Tech State Coll–Northcentral, South Bend, IN 46619-3837	1968	Dr. Carl F. Lutz	5	2,552	226
Ivy Tech State Coll–Northeast, Fort Wayne, IN 46805-1430	1969	Mr. Jon L. Rupright	5	3,305	280
Ivy Tech State Coll–Northwest, Gary, IN 46409-1499	1963	Dr. Darnell Cole	5	2,933	221
Ivy Tech State Coll–Southcentral, Sellersburg, IN 47172-1829	1968	Mr. Jeff L. Pittman	5	1,744	128
Ivy Tech State Coll–Southwest, Evansville, IN 47710-3398	1963	Mr. Daniel L. Schenk	5	2,765	235
Ivy Tech State Coll–Wabash Valley, Terre Haute, IN 47802	1966	Dr. Sam E. Borden	5	2,345	167
Ivy Tech State Coll–Whitewater, Richmond, IN 47374-1220	1963	Mr. James Steck	5	1,062	112
Jackson Comm Coll, Jackson, MI 49201-8399	1928	Dr. Lee Howser	8	7,100	435
Jackson State Comm Coll, Jackson, TN 38301-3797	1967	Dr. Walter L. Nelms	5	3,513	193
James H Faulkner State Comm Coll, Bay Minette, AL 36507-2619	1965	Dr. Gary L. Branch	5	3,042	157
Jamestown Comm Coll, Jamestown, NY 14701-1999	1950	Dr. Gregory T. DeCinque	11	3,343	263
Jefferson Coll, Hillsboro, MO 63050-2441	1963	Dr. Gregory D. Adkins	11	3,934	190
Jefferson Comm Coll, Watertown, NY 13601	1961	Dr. John W. Deans	11	3,500	193
Jefferson Comm Coll, Steubenville, OH 43952-3598	1966	Dr. Edward L. Florak	11	1,437	114
Jefferson Davis Comm Coll, Brewton, AL 36426	1965	Dr. Richard E. Brogdon	5	1,600	66
Jefferson State Comm Coll, Birmingham, AL 35215-3098	1965	Dr. Judy M. Merritt	11	6,065	286
John A Logan Coll, Carterville, IL 62918-9900	1967	Dr. Ray Hancock	11	5,022	246
John C Calhoun State Comm Coll, Decatur, AL 35609-2216	1965	Dr. Richard Carpenter	5	7,278	316
John M Patterson State Tech Coll, Montgomery, AL 36116-2699	1962	Mr. J. L. Taunton	5	1,144	63
Johnson County Comm Coll, Overland Park, KS 66210-1299	1967	Dr. Charles J. Carlsen	11	15,073	686
John Tyler Comm Coll, Chester, VA 23831	1967	Dr. Marshall W. Smith	5	5,058	224
John Wood Comm Coll, Quincy, IL 62301-9147	1974	Dr. William Simpson	9	2,300	156
Joliet Jr Coll, Joliet, IL 60431-8938	1901	Dr. Thomas E. Gamble	11	10,417	496
Jones County Jr Coll, Ellisville, MS 39437-3901	1928	Dr. Ronald Whitehead	11	4,480	175
J Sargeant Reynolds Comm Coll, Richmond, VA 23285-5622	1972	Dr. S. A. Burnette	5	6,284	482
Kalamazoo Valley Comm Coll, Kalamazoo, MI 49003-4070	1966	Dr. Marilyn J. Schlack	11	11,090	425
Kankakee Comm Coll, Kankakee, IL 60901-0888	1966	Dr. Larry D. Huffman	11	3,651	143
Kansas City Kansas Comm Coll, Kansas City, KS 66112-3003	1923	Dr. Thomas R. Burke	11	6,000	357
Kaskaskia Coll, Centralia, IL 62801-7878	1966	Dr. Alice Mumaw-Jacobs	11	2,996	211
Kellogg Comm Coll, Battle Creek, MI 49017-3397	1956	Dr. Paul R. Ohm	11	7,920	325
Kent State U, Ashtabula Cmps, Ashtabula, OH 44004-2299	1958	Dr. Gary C. Ensign	5	1,100	74
Kent State U, Stark Cmps, Canton, OH 44720-7599	1967	Dr. William G. Bittle	5	2,607	170
Kent State U, Trumbull Cmps, Warren, OH 44483-1998	1954	Dr. David A. Allen, Jr.	5	1,918	100
Kent State U, Tuscarawas Cmps, New Philadelphia, OH 44663-9403	1962	Dr. Gregg L. Andrews	5	1,323	102
Kilgore Coll, Kilgore, TX 75662-3299	1935	Dr. William M. Holda	11	4,388	260
Kingsborough Comm Coll of City U of NY, Brooklyn, NY 11235	1963	Mr. Leon M. Goldstein	11	14,536	784
Kings River Comm Coll, Reedley, CA 93654-2099	1926	Dr. Richard J. Giese	11	6,704	221
Kingwood Coll, Kingwood, TX 77339-3801	1984	Dr. Stephen C. Head	11	3,354	244
Kirkwood Comm Coll, Cedar Rapids, IA 52406-2068	1966	Dr. Norm Nielsen	11	10,594	NR
Kirtland Comm Coll, Roscommon, MI 48653-9699	1966	Dr. Dorothy N. Franke	9	1,352	95
Kishwaukee Coll, Malta, IL 60150	1967	Dr. Norman L. Jenkins	11	4,500	198
Labette Comm Coll, Parsons, KS 67357-4299	1923	Dr. Joseph C. Birmingham	11	2,598	234
Lake Area Tech Inst, Watertown, SD 57201	1964	Mr. Gary Williams	5	1,044	65

Name, address	Year	Governing official, control, and highest degree offered		Enrollment	Faculty
Lake City Comm Coll, Lake City, FL 32025	1962	Dr. Muriel Kay Heimer	5	2,377	204
Lake Land Coll, Mattoon, IL 61938-9366	1966	Dr. Robert K. Luther	11	4,710	290
Lakeland Comm Coll, Kirtland, OH 44094-5198	1967	Dr. Ralph R. Doty	11	8,378	575
Lake Michigan Coll, Benton Harbor, MI 49022-1899	1946	Dr. Richard Pappas	9	3,260	240
Lakeshore Tech Coll, Cleveland, WI 53015-1414	1967	Dr. Dennis Ladwig	11	2,409	300
Lake-Sumter Comm Coll, Leesburg, FL 34788-8751	1962	Dr. Robert Westrick	11	2,700	117
Lake Tahoe Comm Coll, South Lake Tahoe, CA 96150-4524	1975	Dr. Guy F. Lease	11	3,000	177
Lake Washington Tech Coll, Kirkland, WA 98034	1949	Dr. Donald W. Fowler	9	2,787	307
Lamar U–Orange, Orange, TX 77630-5899	1969	Dr. J. Michael Shahan	5	1,513	74
Lamar U–Port Arthur, Port Arthur, TX 77641-0310	1909	Dr. Sam Monroe	5	2,476	141
Lane Comm Coll, Eugene, OR 97405-0640	1964	Dr. Jerry Moskus	11	9,441	537
Laney Coll, Oakland, CA 94607-4893	1953	Mr. Earnest C. Crutchfield	11	10,454	315
Lansing Comm Coll, Lansing, MI 48901-7210	1957	Dr. Abel B. Sykes, Jr.	11	16,136	920
Laramie County Comm Coll, Cheyenne, WY 82007-3299	1968	Dr. Charles Bohlen	8	4,282	255
Laredo Comm Coll, Laredo, TX 78040-4395	1946	Dr. Ramon H. Dovalina	11	7,408	308
Lassen Coll, Susanville, CA 96130	1925	Mr. Robert J. Shepherd	11	2,951	204
Lawson State Comm Coll, Birmingham, AL 35221-1798	1965	Dr. Perry W. Ward	5	1,701	107
Lee Coll, Baytown, TX 77522-0818	1934	Dr. Jackson N. Sasser	9	5,938	333
Lehigh Carbon Comm Coll, Schnecksville, PA 18078-2598	1967	Dr. James R. Davis	11	4,185	257
Lenoir Comm Coll, Kinston, NC 28502-0188	1960	Dr. Lonnie H. Blizzard	5	2,069	163
Lewis and Clark Comm Coll, Godfrey, IL 62035-2466	1970	Dr. Dale T. Chapman	9	5,408	305
Lima Tech Coll, Lima, OH 45804-3597	1971	Dr. James J. Countryman	5	2,583	167
Lincoln Land Comm Coll, Springfield, IL 62794-9256	1967	Dr. Norman Stephens, Jr.	9	11,016	245
Linn-Benton Comm Coll, Albany, OR 97321	1966	Mr. Jon Carnahan	11	5,455	475
Long Beach City Coll, Long Beach, CA 90808-1780	1927	Dr. E. Jan Kehoe	5	25,100	900
Longview Comm Coll, Lee's Summit, MO 64081-2105	1969	Mr. Aldo W. Leker	11	6,079	268
Lorain County Comm Coll, Elyria, OH 44035	1963	Dr. Roy Church	11	7,047	347
Lord Fairfax Comm Coll, Middletown, VA 22645-0047	1969	Dr. Marilyn C. Beck	5	3,410	152
Los Angeles City Coll, Los Angeles, CA 90029-3590	1929	Mr. Jose Robledo	9	15,217	625
Los Angeles Harbor Coll, Wilmington, CA 90744-2397	1949	Mr. James L. Heinselman	11	7,603	259
Los Angeles Mission Coll, Sylmar, CA 91342-3244	1974	Dr. William Norlund	11	6,569	115
Los Angeles Pierce Coll, Woodland Hills, CA 91371-0001	1947	Dr. E. Bing Inocencio	11	18,212	519
Los Angeles Southwest Coll, Los Angeles, CA 90047-4810	1967	Dr. Mary E. Lee	11	5,802	223
Los Angeles Trade-Tech Coll, Los Angeles, CA 90015-4108	1925	Dr. Hosni A. Nabi	11	14,853	600
Los Angeles Valley Coll, Van Nuys, CA 91401-4096	1949	Dr. Tyree Wieder	11	17,084	482
Los Medanos Coll, Pittsburg, CA 94565-5197	1970	Dr. Raul Rodriguez	9	7,311	236
Louisiana State U at Alexandria, Alexandria, LA 71302-9121	1960	Dr. Robert Cavanaugh	5	2,431	87
Louisiana State U at Eunice, Eunice, LA 70535-1129	1967	Dr. William J. Nunez, III	5	2,649	120
Lower Columbia Coll, Longview, WA 98632-0310	1934	Dr. Vernon R. Pickett	5	4,081	160
Lurleen B Wallace State Jr Coll, Andalusia, AL 36420-1418	1969	Dr. Seth Hammett	5	1,147	71
Luzerne County Comm Coll, Nanticoke, PA 18634-9804	1966	NR	8	6,137	399
Macomb Comm Coll, Warren, MI 48093-3896	1954	Dr. Albert L. Lorenzo	9	24,500	841
Macon Coll, Macon, GA 31206	1968	Dr. S. Aaron Hyatt	5	3,600	164
Macon Tech Inst, Macon, GA 31206-3628	1966	Dr. Melton Palmer, Jr.	5	2,300	NR
Madison Area Tech Coll, Madison, WI 53704-2599	1911	Dr. Beverly S. Simone	9	19,050	1,881
Manatee Comm Coll, Bradenton, FL 34206-7046	1957	Dr. Stephen J. Korcheck	5	7,308	260
Manchester Comm-Tech Coll, Manchester, CT 06045-1046	1963	Dr. Jonathan M. Daube	5	5,400	205
Maple Woods Comm Coll, Kansas City, MO 64156-1299	1969	Dr. Stephen R. Brainard	11	4,558	189
Marion Tech Coll, Marion, OH 43302-5694	1971	Dr. John Richard Bryson	12	1,800	105
Marshalltown Comm Coll, Marshalltown, IA 50158-4760	1927	Mr. David Felland	9	1,248	107
Massachusetts Bay Comm Coll, Wellesley Hills, MA 02181-5359	1961	Mr. Roger A. Van Winkle	5	4,518	279
Massasoit Comm Coll, Brockton, MA 02402-3996	1966	Dr. Robert R. Rose	5	5,602	357
McDowell Tech Comm Coll, Marion, NC 28752-9724	1964	Dr. Robert M. Boggs	5	1,115	58
McHenry County Coll, Crystal Lake, IL 60012-2761	1967	Dr. Daniel J. La Vista	11	4,809	235
McLennan Comm Coll, Waco, TX 76708-1499	1965	Dr. Dennis F. Michaelis	8	5,561	284
Mendocino Coll, Ukiah, CA 95482-0300	1973	Dr. Carl J. Ehmann	11	3,823	193
Merced Coll, Merced, CA 95348-2898	1962	NR	11	7,063	421
Mercer County Comm Coll, Trenton, NJ 08690-1004	1966	Dr. Thomas D. Sepe	11	6,565	361
Meridian Comm Coll, Meridian, MS 39307	1937	Dr. William F. Scaggs	11	3,205	255
Merritt Coll, Oakland, CA 94619-3196	1953	Dr. Wise Allen	11	5,123	201
Mesa Comm Coll, Mesa, AZ 85202-4866	1965	Dr. Larry K. Christiansen	11	23,108	852
Metropolitan Comm Coll, East St Louis, IL 62201-1100	1996	Dr. Janet Finch	8	1,268	83
Metropolitan Comm Coll, Omaha, NE 68103-0777	1974	Dr. J. Richard Gilliland	11	10,759	557
Miami-Dade Comm Coll, Miami, FL 33132-2296	1960	Dr. Eduardo J. Padron	11	51,019	2,070
Miami U–Hamilton Cmps, Hamilton, OH 45011-3399	1968	Dr. Jack Rhodes	5	2,612	170
Miami U–Middletown Cmps, Middletown, OH 45042-3497	1966	Dr. Michael P. Governanti	5	2,629	165
Middle Georgia Coll, Cochran, GA 31014-1599	1884	Dr. Joe Ben Welch	5	2,061	120
Middlesex Comm Coll, Bedford, MA 01730-1655	1970	Dr. Carole A. Cowan	5	5,945	377
Middlesex Comm–Tech Coll, Middletown, CT 06457-4889	1966	Ms. Dianne E. Williams	5	2,611	130
Middlesex County Coll, Edison, NJ 08818-3050	1964	Dr. John Bakum	8	11,000	552
Midland Coll, Midland, TX 79705-6099	1969	Dr. David E. Daniel	11	4,000	194
Midlands Tech Coll, Columbia, SC 29202-2408	1974	Dr. James L. Hudgins	11	9,728	668
Mid Michigan Comm Coll, Harrison, MI 48625-9447	1965	Dr. Ronald G. Yerch	11	3,304	227
Mid-Plains Comm Coll, North Platte, NE 69101-9491	1965	Dr. Gregg Fitch	9	2,025	97
Mid-State Tech Coll, Wisconsin Rapids, WI 54494-5599	1917	Mr. Brian Oehler	11	4,297	90
Milwaukee Area Tech Coll, Milwaukee, WI 53233-1443	1912	Dr. John R. Birkholz	9	23,099	1,759
Mineral Area Coll, Park Hills, MO 63601	1922	Dr. Dixie A. Kohn	9	2,458	133
Minneapolis Comm and Tech Coll, Minneapolis, MN 55403-1779		Mr. Phillip Davis	5	5,777	435
MiraCosta Coll, Oceanside, CA 92056-3899	1934	Dr. Tim T. L. Dong	5	8,038	388
Mission Coll, Santa Clara, CA 95054-1897	1977	Dr. Michael Rao	11	8,530	376
Mississippi County Comm Coll, Blytheville, AR 72316-1109	1975	Dr. John P. Sullins	5	2,205	72
Mississippi Delta Comm Coll, Moorhead, MS 38761-0668	1926	Dr. Bobby Garvin	9	2,497	130
Mississippi Gulf Coast Comm Coll, Perkinston, MS 39573-0047	1911	Dr. Willis H. Lott	9	9,687	753
Mitchell Comm Coll, Statesville, NC 28677-5293	1852	Dr. Douglas O. Eason	5	1,550	90
Moberly Area Comm Coll, Moberly, MO 65270-1304	1927	Dr. Evelyn E. Jorgenson	11	2,014	95
Modesto Jr Coll, Modesto, CA 95350-5800	1921	Dr. Maria Sheehan	11	14,148	470
Mohave Comm Coll, Kingman, AZ 86401-1299	1971	Mr. Michael Tacha	5	5,486	349
Mohawk Valley Comm Coll, Utica, NY 13501-5394	1946	Dr. Michael I. Schafer	11	4,423	274
Monroe Coll, Bronx, NY 10468-5407	1933	Mr. Stephen J. Jerome	3	2,752	108
Monroe Comm Coll, Rochester, NY 14623-5780	1961	Dr. Peter A. Spina	11	12,951	1,143
Monroe County Comm Coll, Monroe, MI 48161-9047	1964	Mr. Gerald D. Welch	8	3,737	201
Montana State U Coll of Tech-Great Falls, Great Falls, MT 59405	1969	Mr. Willard R. Weaver	5	1,020	NR
Montcalm Comm Coll, Sidney, MI 48885-0300	1965	Dr. Donald C. Burns	11	1,945	153
Monterey Peninsula Coll, Monterey, CA 93940-4799	1947	Dr. Kirk Avery	5	8,300	388
Montgomery Coll, Conroe, TX 77384		Dr. William D. Law, Jr.	11	3,000	179
Montgomery Coll–Germantown Cmps, Germantown, MD 20876	1975	Dr. Robert E. Parilla	11	3,488	187
Montgomery Coll–Rockville Cmps, Rockville, MD 20850-1196	1965	Dr. Robert E. Parilla	11	13,144	698
Montgomery Coll–Takoma Park Cmps, Takoma Park, MD 20912	1946	Dr. Robert E. Parilla	11	4,500	223

Name, address	Year	Governing official, control, and highest degree offered		Enrollment	Faculty
Montgomery County Comm Coll, Blue Bell, PA 19422-0796	1964	Dr. Edward M. Sweitzer	8	8,704	558
Moorpark Coll, Moorpark, CA 93021-1695	1967	Dr. James W. Walker	8	11,780	450
Moraine Park Tech Coll, Fond du Lac, WI 54936-1940	1967	Dr. John J. Shanahan	11	5,811	351
Moraine Valley Comm Coll, Palos Hills, IL 60465-0937	1967	Dr. Vernon O. Crawley	11	13,234	570
Morgan Comm Coll, Fort Morgan, CO 80701-4399	1967	Dr. John McKay	5	1,200	142
Morton Coll, Cicero, IL 60650-4398	1924	Dr. John A. Neuhaus	11	4,830	214
Motlow State Comm Coll, Tullahoma, TN 37388-8100	1969	Dr. A. Frank Glass	5	3,160	210
Mountain Empire Comm Coll, Big Stone Gap, VA 24219-0700	1972	Dr. Robert H. Sandel	5	2,700	150
Mountain View Coll, Dallas, TX 75211-6599	1970	Dr. Monique Amerman	8	5,569	264
Mt Hood Comm Coll, Gresham, OR 97030-3300	1966	Dr. Joel Vela	11	7,171	547
Mount Ida Coll, Newton Centre, MA 02159-3310	1899	Dr. Bryan E. Carlson	1	2,009	222
Mt San Antonio Coll, Walnut, CA 91789-1399	1946	Dr. William H. Feddersen	9	32,000	799
Mt San Jacinto Coll, San Jacinto, CA 92583-2399	1963	Dr. Roy B. Mason, II	11	5,627	215
Mount Wachusett Comm Coll, Gardner, MA 01440-1000	1963	Dr. Daniel M. Asquino	5	2,814	112
Murray State Coll, Tishomingo, OK 73460-3130	1908	Dr. Glen Pedersen	5	1,706	73
Muscatine Comm Coll, Muscatine, IA 52761-5396	1929	Dr. Victor G. McAvoy	5	1,262	95
Muskegon Comm Coll, Muskegon, MI 49442-1493	1926	Dr. Frank P Marczak	11	5,169	150
Muskingum Area Tech Coll, Zanesville, OH 43701-2694	1969	Dr. Lynn H. Willett	11	2,135	104
Napa Valley Coll, Napa, CA 94558-6236	1942	Dr. Diane E. Carey	11	7,000	304
Nash Comm Coll, Rocky Mount, NC 27804-0488	1967	Dr. J. Reid Parrott, Jr.	5	1,880	106
Nashville State Tech Inst, Nashville, TN 37209-4515	1970	Dr. George H. Van Allen	5	7,013	294
Nassau Comm Coll, Garden City, NY 11530-6793	1959	Dr. Sean A. Fanelli	11	20,620	1,523
Naugatuck Valley Comm–Tech Coll, Waterbury, CT 06708-3000	1992	Dr. Richard L. Sanders	5	5,239	299
Navajo Comm Coll, Tsaile, AZ 86556	1968	Dr. Tommy Lewis, Jr.	4	1,718	152
Navarro Coll, Corsicana, TX 75110-4899	1946	Dr. Gerald Burson	11	3,211	175
Neosho County Comm Coll, Chanute, KS 66720-2699	1936	Dr. James O. Hill	11	1,185	96
Newbury Coll, Brookline, MA 02146-5750	1962	Mr. Edward J. Tassinari	1	1,032	114
The New England Banking Inst, Boston, MA 02111-2671	1909	Mr. Robert A. Regan	1	1,744	360
New England Inst of Tech, Warwick, RI 02886-2244	1940	Dr. Richard I. Gouse	1	2,200	168
New Hampshire Comm Tech Coll, Nashua/Claremont, Nashua, NH 03063	1967	Dr. Keith W. Bird	5	1,037	63
New Hampshire Tech Inst, Concord, NH 03301-7412	1964	Dr. William Simonton, Jr.	5	1,453	145
New Mexico Jr Coll, Hobbs, NM 88240-9123	1965	Dr. Charles D. Hays	11	2,882	129
New Mexico State U–Alamogordo, Alamogordo, NM 88310	1958	Dr. Janine Twomey	5	2,100	134
New Mexico State U–Carlsbad, Carlsbad, NM 88220-3509	1950	Dr. Douglas E. Burghan	5	1,077	72
New River Comm Coll, Dublin, VA 24084-1127	1969	Dr. Edwin L. Barnes	5	1,577	170
Niagara County Comm Coll, Sanborn, NY 14132-9460	1962	Mr. Gerald L. Miller	11	5,118	449
Nicolet Area Tech Coll, Rhinelander, WI 54501-0518	1968	Dr. Adrian Lorbetske	11	1,433	84
Normandale Comm Coll, Bloomington, MN 55431-4399	1968	Dr. Thomas J. Horak	5	7,365	230
Northampton County Area Comm Coll, Bethlehem, PA 18017-7599	1967	Dr. Robert J. Kopecek	11	5,542	464
North Arkansas Coll, Harrison, AR 72601	1974	Dr. Bill Baker	11	1,551	123
North Central Michigan Coll, Petoskey, MI 49770-8717	1958	Mr. Robert B. Graham	8	2,032	146
North Central Tech Coll, Mansfield, OH 44901-0698	1961	Dr. Ronald E. Abrams	5	2,523	182
Northcentral Tech Coll, Wausau, WI 54401-1880	1912	Dr. Robert Ernst	9	3,500	218
North Central Texas Coll, Gainesville, TX 76240-4699	1924	Dr. Ronnie Glasscock	8	4,133	175
North Country Comm Coll, Saranac Lake, NY 12983-2046	1967	Dr. Gail Rogers Rice	11	1,167	158
North Dakota State Coll of Science, Wahpeton, ND 58076	1903	Dr. Jerry Olson	5	2,581	159
Northeast Alabama Comm Coll, Rainsville, AL 35986-0159	1963	Dr. Charles M. Pendley	5	1,838	51
Northeast Comm Coll, Norfolk, NE 68702-0469	1973	Dr. James C. Underwood	11	4,285	194
Northeastern Jr Coll, Sterling, CO 80751-2344	1941	Dr. Bruce C. Perryman	5	3,408	79
Northeastern Oklahoma A&M Coll, Miami, OK 74354-6434	1919	Dr. Jerry D. Carroll	5	2,244	100
Northeast Iowa Comm Coll, Peosta Cmps, Peosta, IA 52068-9776	1970	Mr. Don Roby	11	1,700	66
Northeast Mississippi Comm Coll, Booneville, MS 38829	1948	Mr. Joe M. Childers	5	3,000	126
Northeast State Tech Comm Coll, Blountville, TN 37617-0246	1966	Dr. William W. Locke	5	3,636	246
Northeast Texas Comm Coll, Mount Pleasant, TX 75456-1307	1985	Dr. Charles B. Florio	11	2,070	114
Northeast Wisconsin Tech Coll, Green Bay, WI 54307-9042	1913	Dr. Gerald D. Prindiville	11	7,187	215
Northern Essex Comm Coll, Haverhill, MA 01830	1960	Dr. David F. Hartleb	5	5,597	457
Northern New Mexico Comm Coll, Española, NM 87532	1909	Dr. Sigfredo Maestas	5	1,652	160
Northern Oklahoma Coll, Tonkawa, OK 74653-0310	1901	Dr. Joe Kinzer	5	2,350	80
Northern Virginia Comm Coll, Annandale, VA 22003-3796	1965	Dr. Richard J. Ernst	5	37,307	1,347
North Florida Comm Coll, Madison, FL 32340-1602	1958	Dr. Beverly Grissom	5	1,023	37
North Harris Coll, Houston, TX 77073	1972	Dr. John E. Pickelman	11	9,398	196
North Hennepin Comm Coll, Minneapolis, MN 55445-2231	1966	Dr. Yvette Jackson	5	5,177	220
North Idaho Coll, Coeur d'Alene, ID 83814-2199	1933	Dr. Ron Bell	11	3,644	270
North Iowa Area Comm Coll, Mason City, IA 50401-7299	1918	Dr. David Buettner	11	2,728	107
North Lake Coll, Irving, TX 75038-3899	1977	Dr. David C. England	8	6,233	342
Northland Comm and Tech Coll, Thief River Falls, MN 56701	1965	Dr. Orley Gunderson	5	1,214	82
Northland Pioneer Coll, Holbrook, AZ 86025-0610	1974	Dr. Gary Passer	11	4,779	400
North Seattle Comm Coll, Seattle, WA 98103-3599	1970	Dr. Constance Rice	5	15,387	374
North Shore Comm Coll, Danvers, MA 01923-4093	1965	Dr. George Traicoff	5	4,238	339
NorthWest Arkansas Comm Coll, Bentonville, AR 72712	1989	Dr. Bob C. Burns	11	2,950	201
Northwest Coll, Powell, WY 82435-1898	1946	Dr. John P. Hanna	11	1,906	181
Northwestern Coll, Lima, OH 45805-1498	1920	Dr. Loren R. Jarvis	1	1,800	67
Northwestern Connecticut Comm-Tech Coll, Winsted, CT 06098-1798	1965	Dr. R. Eileen Baccus	5	1,839	94
Northwestern Michigan Coll, Traverse City, MI 49686-3061	1951	Dr. Ilse Burke	11	3,918	93
Northwest Indian Coll, Bellingham, WA 98226	1978	Dr. Robert J. Lorence	4	1,500	63
Northwest Mississippi Comm Coll, Senatobia, MS 38668-1701	1927	Dr. David M. Haraway	11	4,200	200
Northwest-Shoals Comm Coll, Muscle Shoals, AL 35662	1961	Dr. Larry McCoy	5	4,522	174
Northwest State Comm Coll, Archbold, OH 43502-9542	1968	Dr. Larry G. McDougle	5	2,119	136
Northwest Tech Coll, Bemidji, MN 56601	1993	Mr. Ray Cross	5	5,000	400
Norwalk Comm-Tech Coll, Norwalk, CT 06854-1655	1961	Dr. William H. Schwab	5	5,357	302
Oakland Comm Coll, Bloomfield Hills, MI 48304-2266	1964	Mr. Richard T. Thompson	11	24,941	788
Oakton Comm Coll, Des Plaines, IL 60016-1268	1969	Dr. Margaret B. Lee	9	10,404	625
Ocean County Coll, Toms River, NJ 08754-2001	1964	Dr. Milton Shaw	8	7,704	349
Odessa Coll, Odessa, TX 79764-7127	1946	Dr. Vance W. Gipson	11	4,894	208
Ohio U–Southern Cmps, Ironton, OH 45638-2214	1956	Dr. Bill Dingus	5	2,564	125
Ohlone Coll, Fremont, CA 94539-5884	1967	Dr. Floyd M. Hogue	11	8,400	434
Okaloosa-Walton Comm Coll, Niceville, FL 32578-1295	1963	Dr. James R. Richburg	11	5,820	274
Oklahoma City Comm Coll, Oklahoma City, OK 73159-4419	1969	Dr. Robert P. Todd	5	10,215	363
Oklahoma State U, Oklahoma City, Oklahoma City, OK 73107-6120	1961	Dr. James Hooper	5	4,000	205
Oklahoma State U, Okmulgee, Okmulgee, OK 74447-3901	1946	Dr. Robert Klabenes	5	2,205	138
Olympic Coll, Bremerton, WA 98337-1699	1946	Ms. Donna M. Allen	5	12,038	339
Onondaga Comm Coll, Syracuse, NY 13215	1962	Mr. Barrett Jones	11	7,200	477
Orangeburg-Calhoun Tech Coll, Orangeburg, SC 29118-8299	1968	Dr. Jeffery R. Olson	11	1,765	141
Orange Coast Coll, Costa Mesa, CA 92628-5005	1947	Ms. Margaret A. Gratton	11	22,392	813
Orange County Comm Coll, Middletown, NY 10940-6437	1950	Dr. Preston Pulliams	11	5,794	317

Name, address	Year	Governing official, control, and highest degree offered		Enroll-ment	Faculty
Otero Jr Coll, La Junta, CO 81050-3415	1941	Dr. Joe M. Treece	5	1,000	53
Owensboro Comm Coll, Owensboro, KY 42303-1899	1986	Dr. David Brauer	5	2,614	124
Owens Comm Coll, Findlay, OH 45840	1983	Mr. Daniel H. Brown	5	1,659	145
Owens Comm Coll, Toledo, OH 43699-1947	1966	Mr. Daniel H. Brown	5	10,432	622
Oxnard Coll, Oxnard, CA 93033-6699	1975	Dr. Steven S. Arvizu	8	5,073	288
Ozarks Tech Comm Coll, Springfield, MO 65802		Dr. Norman K. Myers	9	3,507	150
Palm Beach Comm Coll, Lake Worth, FL 33461-4796	1933	Dr. Edward M. Eissey	5	16,016	772
Palo Alto Coll, San Antonio, TX 78224-2499	1987	Dr. Ernest A. Martinez	11	7,499	317
Palomar Coll, San Marcos, CA 92069-1487	1946	Dr. George R. Boggs	11	24,013	1,097
Palo Verde Coll, Blythe, CA 92225-1118	1947	Dr. Donald F. Averill	11	1,200	69
Panola Coll, Carthage, TX 75633-2397	1947	Dr. W. F. Edmonson	11	1,772	104
Paradise Valley Comm Coll, Phoenix, AZ 85032-1200	1985	Dr. Raul Cardenas	11	5,786	263
Paris Jr Coll, Paris, TX 75460-6298	1924	Mr. Bobby R. Walters	11	2,450	117
Parkland Coll, Champaign, IL 61821-1899	1967	Dr. Zelema M. Harris	9	8,074	466
Pasadena City Coll, Pasadena, CA 91106-2041	1924	Dr. James P. Kossler	11	21,673	824
Pasco-Hernando Comm Coll, Dade City, FL 33523-7599	1972	Dr. Robert W. Judson, Jr.	5	5,808	246
Passaic County Comm Coll, Paterson, NJ 07505-1179	1968	Dr. Steven M. Rose	8	3,717	276
Patrick Henry Comm Coll, Martinsville, VA 24115-5311	1962	Dr. Max Wingett	5	2,700	113
Paul D Camp Comm Coll, Franklin, VA 23851-0737	1971	Dr. Jerome J. Friga	5	1,523	59
Pearl River Comm Coll, Poplarville, MS 39470	1909	Dr. Ted J. Alexander	11	2,727	167
Peirce Coll, Philadelphia, PA 19102-4603	1865	Dr. Arthur J. Lendo	1	1,200	123
Pellissippi State Tech Comm Coll, Knoxville, TN 37933-0990	1974	Dr. Allen G. Edwards	5	7,794	412
Peninsula Coll, Port Angeles, WA 98362-2779	1961	Dr. Wallace Sigmar	5	3,550	149
Pennsylvania Coll of Tech, Williamsport, PA 17701-5778	1965	Dr. Robert Breuder	12	4,744	350
Penn State U Delaware County Cmps of the Commonwealth Coll, Media, PA 19063-5596	1966	Dr. Edward S. J. Tomezsko	12	1,567	96
Penn State U DuBois Cmps of the Commonwealth Coll, DuBois, PA 15801-3199	1935	Dr. Joseph Strasser	12	1,035	64
Penn State U Hazleton Cmps of the Commonwealth Coll, Hazleton, PA 18201-1291	1934	Dr. Karen Doyle Walton	12	1,391	78
Penn State U Mont Alto Cmps of the Commonwealth Coll, Mont Alto, PA 17237-9703	1929	Dr. David H. Goldenberg	12	1,205	71
Penn State U Shenango Cmps of the Commonwealth Coll, Sharon, PA 16146-1537	1965	Dr. Albert N. Skomra	12	1,033	87
Penn State U Worthington Scranton Cmps Commonwealth Coll, Dunmore, PA 18512-1699	1923	Dr. James D. Gallagher	12	1,419	88
Penn State U York Cmps of the Commonwealth Coll, York, PA 17403-3298	1926	Dr. Donald A. Gogniat	12	2,079	128
Penn Valley Comm Coll, Kansas City, MO 64111	1969	Dr. E. Paul Williams	11	4,133	233
Pensacola Jr Coll, Pensacola, FL 32504-8998	1948	Dr. Horace E. Hartsell	5	12,000	819
Phillips Comm Coll of the U of Arkansas, Helena, AR 72342-0785	1965	Dr. Steven Jones	11	2,287	70
Phoenix Coll, Phoenix, AZ 85013-4234	1920	Dr. Marie Pepicello	11	11,266	540
Piedmont Tech Coll, Greenwood, SC 29648-1467	1966	Dr. Lex D. Walters	5	3,276	130
Piedmont Virginia Comm Coll, Charlottesville, VA 22902-7589	1972	Dr. Deborah M. DiCroce	5	4,436	262
Pierce Coll, Lakewood, WA 98498-1999	1967	Dr. George Delaney	5	10,294	579
Pikes Peak Comm Coll, Colorado Springs, CO 80906-5498	1968	Dr. Marijane Axtell Paulsen	5	6,626	498
Pima Comm Coll, Tucson, AZ 85709-1010	1966	Dr. Robert Jensen	5	27,960	1,567
Pitt Comm Coll, Greenville, NC 27835-7007	1961	Dr. Charles E. Russell	11	4,668	240
Polk Comm Coll, Winter Haven, FL 33881-4299	1964	Dr. Maryly VanLeer Peck	5	6,000	260
Porterville Coll, Porterville, CA 93257-6058	1927	Dr. Bonnie L. Rogers	5	2,778	140
Portland Comm Coll, Portland, OR 97280-0990	1961	Dr. Daniel F. Moriarty	11	27,594	1,215
Potomac State Coll of West Virginia U, Keyser, WV 26726-2698	1901	Dr. Kathryn A. Brailer	5	1,108	83
Prairie State Coll, Chicago Heights, IL 60411-8226	1958	Dr. T. Lightfield	11	5,000	289
Pratt Comm Coll and Area Vocational Sch, Pratt, KS 67124-8317	1938	Dr. William Wojciechowski	9	1,341	54
Prince George's Comm Coll, Largo, MD 20774-2199	1958	Dr. Robert I. Bickford	8	11,696	574
Pueblo Comm Coll, Pueblo, CO 81004-1499	1933	Dr. Joe May	5	4,127	310
Pulaski Tech Coll, North Little Rock, AR 72118	1945	Mr. Benjamin Wyatt	5	1,643	88
Queensborough Comm Coll of City U of NY, Bayside, NY 11364	1958	Dr. Kurt R. Schmeller	11	10,907	701
Quincy Coll, Quincy, MA 02169-4522	1958	Dr. G. Jeremiah Ryan	10	5,200	69
Quinebaug Valley Comm-Tech Coll, Danielson, CT 06239-1440	1971	Ms. Dianne E. Williams	5	1,170	81
Quinsigamond Comm Coll, Worcester, MA 01606-2092	1963	Dr. Sandra Kurtinitis	5	4,770	371
Rancho Santiago Coll, Santa Ana, CA 92706-3398	1915	Dr. Vivian B. Blevins	5	20,714	1,799
Randolph Comm Coll, Asheboro, NC 27204-1009	1962	Dr. Larry K. Linker	5	1,427	73
Rappahannock Comm Coll, Glenns, VA 23149-0287	1970	Dr. Norman H. Scott	12	2,129	130
Raritan Valley Comm Coll, Somerville, NJ 08876-1265	1965	Dr. Cary A. Israel	8	5,470	289
Reading Area Comm Coll, Reading, PA 19603-1706	1971	Dr. Gust Zogas	8	2,756	249
Redlands Comm Coll, El Reno, OK 73036	1938	Dr. Larry F. Devane	5	1,938	133
Red Rocks Comm Coll, Lakewood, CO 80228-1255	1969	Dr. Dorothy A. Horrell	5	3,280	276
Red Wing/Winona Tech Coll, Winona, MN 55987	1992	Mr. Jim Johnson	5	1,560	84
Rend Lake Coll, Ina, IL 62846-9801	1967	Mr. Mark S. Kern	5	4,378	180
Richard Bland Coll of the Coll of William and Mary, Petersburg, VA 23805-7100	1961	Dr. James B. McNeer	5	1,237	48
Richland Coll, Dallas, TX 75243-2199	1972	Dr. Stephen Mittelstet	11	13,391	665
Richland Comm Coll, Decatur, IL 62521-8513	1971	Dr. Charles R. Novak	9	3,388	215
Richmond Comm Coll, Hamlet, NC 28345-1189	1964	Mr. Joseph W. Grimsley	5	1,146	100
Ricks Coll, Rexburg, ID 83460-4107	1888	Dr. Steven D. Bennion	2	7,755	387
Ridgewater Coll, Willmar, MN 56201-1097	1961	Dr. Mary Retterer	5	3,840	236
Rio Hondo Coll, Whittier, CA 90601-1699	1960	Dr. Jesus Carreon	11	14,500	710
Rio Salado Coll, Tempe, AZ 85281-6950	1978	Dr. Linda Thor	11	9,006	469
Riverland Comm Coll, Austin, MN 55912	1940	Mr. John Gedker	5	2,571	161
Riverside Comm Coll, Riverside, CA 92506-1293	1916	Dr. Salvatore Rotella	11	20,845	550
Roane State Comm Coll, Harriman, TN 37748-5011	1971	Dr. Sherry L. Hoppe	5	5,803	337
Robeson Comm Coll, Lumberton, NC 28359-1420	1965	Mr. Fred W. Williams, Jr.	5	1,594	114
Rochester Comm and Tech Coll, Rochester, MN 55904-4999	1915	Dr. Donald D. Supalla	5	4,350	225
Rockingham Comm Coll, Wentworth, NC 27375-0038	1964	Dr. Robert C. Keys	5	1,907	114
Rockland Comm Coll, Suffern, NY 10901-3699	1959	Dr. Antonette Cleveland	11	6,446	586
Rock Valley Coll, Rockford, IL 61114-5699	1964	Dr. Karl J. Jacobs	9	8,676	222
Rogers U, Claremore, OK 74017-3252	1909	Mr. Rodger Randle	5	3,118	270
Rogue Comm Coll, Grants Pass, OR 97527-9298	1970	Dr. Harvey Bennett	11	2,425	459
Rose State Coll, Midwest City, OK 73110-2799	1968	Dr. Larry Nutter	11	7,831	383
Rowan-Cabarrus Comm Coll, Salisbury, NC 28145-1595	1963	Dr. Richard L. Brownell	5	3,500	130
Roxbury Comm Coll, Roxbury Crossing, MA 02120-3400	1973	Dr. Grace C. Brown	5	2,600	172
Sacramento City Coll, Sacramento, CA 95822-1386	1916	Dr. Robert M. Harris	11	16,345	375
Saddleback Coll, Mission Viejo, CA 92692-3697	1967	Dr. Ned Doffoney	11	16,917	606
Saint Augustine Coll, Chicago, IL 00640-3501	1980	Fr. Carlos A. Plazas	1	1,298	121

Name, address	Year	Governing official, control, and highest degree offered		Enrollment	Faculty
Saint Charles County Comm Coll, St Peters, MO 63376-0975	1986	Dr. John M. McGuire	5	4,564	231
St Clair County Comm Coll, Port Huron, MI 48061-5015	1923	Dr. Christa Adams	8	4,132	270
St Cloud Tech Coll, St Cloud, MN 56303-1240	1948	Dr. Harold Erickson	5	2,558	121
St Johns River Comm Coll, Palatka, FL 32177-3807	1958	Dr. R. L. McLendon, Jr.	5	3,500	157
St Louis Comm Coll at Florissant Valley, St Louis, MO 63135-1499	1963	Dr. Irving P. McPhail	9	7,664	380
St Louis Comm Coll at Forest Park, St Louis, MO 63110-1316	1962	Dr. Henry D. Shannon	9	8,197	366
St Louis Comm Coll at Meramec, Kirkwood, MO 63122-5720	1963	Mr. Richard A. Black	9	13,570	570
St Paul Tech Coll, St Paul, MN 55102-1800	1922	Dr. Donovan Schwichtenberg	12	3,400	565
St Petersburg Jr Coll, St Petersburg, FL 33731-3489	1927	Dr. Carl M. Kuttler, Jr.	11	17,535	899
St Philip's Coll, San Antonio, TX 78203-2098	1898	Dr. Charles A. Taylor	9	7,867	462
Salem Comm Coll, Carneys Point, NJ 08069-2799	1972	Dr. Peter B. Contini	8	1,228	74
Salt Lake Comm Coll, Salt Lake City, UT 84130-0808	1948	Dr. Frank W. Budd	5	21,348	1,148
San Bernardino Valley Coll, San Bernardino, CA 92410-2748	1926	Dr. Sharon Coballero	11	10,156	375
Sandhills Comm Coll, Pinehurst, NC 28374-8299	1963	Dr. John Dempsey	11	2,489	148
San Diego City Coll, San Diego, CA 92101-4787	1914	Dr. Jerome Hunter	11	12,652	250
San Diego Mesa Coll, San Diego, CA 92111-4998	1964	Dr. Constance Carroll	9	22,677	676
San Jacinto Coll–North Cmps, Houston, TX 77049-4599	1974	Dr. Edwin E. Lehr	11	4,080	213
San Jacinto Coll–South Cmps, Houston, TX 77089-6099	1979	Dr. Raymond M. Hawkins	11	5,411	220
San Joaquin Delta Coll, Stockton, CA 95207-6370	1935	Dr. L. H. Horton, Jr.	9	17,504	NR
San Jose City Coll, San Jose, CA 95128-2799	1921	Dr. Chui L. Tsang	9	9,918	390
San Juan Coll, Farmington, NM 87402-4699	1958	Dr. James C. Henderson	8	4,231	252
Santa Barbara City Coll, Santa Barbara, CA 93109-2394	1908	Dr. Peter R. MacDougall	9	11,288	562
Santa Fe Comm Coll, Gainesville, FL 32606-6200	1966	Dr. Larry W. Tyree	11	12,058	611
Santa Monica Coll, Santa Monica, CA 90405-1628	1929	Dr. Piedad F. Robertson	11	22,127	664
Santa Rosa Jr Coll, Santa Rosa, CA 95401-4395	1918	Dr. Robert F. Agrella	11	27,885	1,062
Sauk Valley Comm Coll, Dixon, IL 61021	1965	Dr. Richard L. Behrendt	9	2,635	152
Savannah Tech Inst, Savannah, GA 31405		Mr. John D. Stewart	5	1,832	112
Schenectady County Comm Coll, Schenectady, NY 12305-2294	1968	Dr. Gabriel J. Basil	11	3,510	211
Schoolcraft Coll, Livonia, MI 48152-2696	1961	Dr. Richard W. McDowell	9	9,307	421
Scott Comm Coll, Bettendorf, IA 52722-6804	1966	Dr. Lenny E. Stone	11	3,800	235
Scottsdale Comm Coll, Scottsdale, AZ 85250-2699	1969	Dr. Arthur W. De Cabooter	11	9,765	447
Seattle Central Comm Coll, Seattle, WA 98122-2400	1966	Dr. Charles H. Mitchell	5	10,333	388
Seminole Comm Coll, Sanford, FL 32773-6199	1966	Dr. E. Ann McGee	11	6,924	502
Seminole State Coll, Seminole, OK 74818-0351	1931	Dr. Jim Utterback	5	1,600	85
Seward County Comm Coll, Liberal, KS 67905-1137	1969	Dr. James Grote	11	1,899	147
Shasta Coll, Redding, CA 96049-6006	1948	Dr. Douglas M. Treadway	11	10,650	397
Shawnee Comm Coll, Ullin, IL 62992-9725	1967	Dr. Terry G. Ludwig	11	2,109	166
Shelby State Comm Coll, Memphis, TN 38174-0568	1970	Mr. Mark L. Stansbury	5	5,862	342
Shelton State Comm Coll, Tuscaloosa, AL 35405	1979	Dr. Thomas E. Umphrey	5	5,167	268
Sheridan Coll, Sheridan, WY 82801-1500	1948	Dr. Stephen Maier	11	2,683	215
Shoreline Comm Coll, Seattle, WA 98133-5696	1964	Mr. Gary L. Oertli	5	8,575	333
Sierra Coll, Rocklin, CA 95677-3397	1936	Dr. Kevin M. Ramirez	5	13,567	518
Sinclair Comm Coll, Dayton, OH 45402-1460	1887	Dr. David H. Ponitz	11	19,360	880
Skagit Valley Coll, Mount Vernon, WA 98273-5899	1926	Dr. Lydia Ledesma	5	6,538	344
Skyline Coll, San Bruno, CA 94066-1698	1969	Ms. Linda Graef Salter	8	8,104	268
Snead State Comm Coll, Boaz, AL 35957	1935	Dr. William H. Osborn	5	1,589	70
Snow Coll, Ephraim, UT 84627-1203	1888	Dr. Gerald Day	5	2,546	155
Solano Comm Coll, Suisun City, CA 94585-3197	1945	Mr. Stan R. Arterberry	11	9,909	374
South Arkansas Comm Coll, El Dorado, AR 71731-7010	1975	Dr. Ben Whitfield	5	1,000	81
South Central Tech Coll, North Mankato, MN 56003	1946	Dr. Ken Mills	5	3,590	NR
Southeast Arkansas Tech Coll, Pine Bluff, AR 71603	1991	Dr. Terry J. Puckett	5	1,277	100
Southeast Comm Coll, Lincoln Cmps, Lincoln, NE 68520-1299	1973	Mrs. Jeanette Volker	9	5,305	565
Southeastern Baptist Theological Sem, Wake Forest, NC 27588-1889	1950	Dr. Paige Patterson	2	1,358	45
Southeastern Comm Coll, Whiteville, NC 28472-0151	1964	Dr. Stephen C. Scott	5	1,575	145
Southeastern Comm Coll, North Cmps, West Burlington, IA 52655-0605	1968	Dr. R. Gene Gardner	11	1,881	94
Southeastern Illinois Coll, Harrisburg, IL 62946-9804	1960	Dr. Ben Cullers	5	2,964	184
Southeast Tech Inst, Sioux Falls, SD 57107-9910	1968	Mr. Terry Sullivan	5	2,830	110
Southern Maine Tech Coll, South Portland, ME 04106	1946	Dr. Wayne H. Ross	5	2,412	148
Southern State Comm Coll, Hillsboro, OH 45133-9487	1975	Dr. Lawrence N. Dukes	5	1,576	97
Southern Union State Comm Coll, Wadley, AL 36276	1922	Dr. Roy W. Johnson	5	6,499	217
Southern U at Shreveport–Bossier City Cmps, Shreveport, LA 71107	1964	Dr. Jerome G. Greene, Jr.	5	1,202	75
Southern West Virginia Comm and Tech Coll, Mount Gay, WV 25637	1971	Dr. Travis P. Kirkland	5	3,014	184
South Florida Comm Coll, Avon Park, FL 33825-9356	1965	Dr. Catherine P. Cornelius	5	1,600	213
South Georgia Coll, Douglas, GA 31533-5098	1906	Dr. Edward D. Jackson, Jr.	5	1,130	54
South Mountain Comm Coll, Phoenix, AZ 85040	1979	Dr. John A. Cordova	11	2,423	184
South Plains Coll, Levelland, TX 79336-6595	1958	Dr. Gary D. McDaniel	11	5,844	356
South Puget Sound Comm Coll, Olympia, WA 98512-6292	1970	Dr. Kenneth J. Minnaert	5	5,310	231
South Seattle Comm Coll, Seattle, WA 98106-1499	1970	Dr. Peter Ku	5	2,837	194
Southside Virginia Comm Coll, Alberta, VA 23821-9719	1970	Dr. John J. Cavan	5	1,605	182
South Suburban Coll, South Holland, IL 60473-1270	1927	Dr. Bruce Aldrich	11	6,185	369
South Texas Comm Coll, McAllen, TX 78501	1993	NR	9	6,050	108
Southwestern Coll, Chula Vista, CA 91910-7299	1961	Mr. Joseph M. Conte	11	15,771	626
Southwestern Comm Coll, Creston, IA 50801	1966	Dr. Richard L. Byerly	5	1,228	69
Southwestern Comm Coll, Sylva, NC 28779	1964	Dr. Cecil Groves	5	1,735	NR
Southwestern Michigan Coll, Dowagiac, MI 49047-9793	1964	Mr. David C. Briegel	11	2,339	197
Southwestern Oregon Comm Coll, Coos Bay, OR 97420-2912	1961	Dr. Stephen J. Kridelbaugh	11	1,814	243
Southwest Mississippi Comm Coll, Summit, MS 39666	1918	Dr. Horace C. Holmes	9	1,660	89
Southwest Missouri State U–West Plains, West Plains, MO 65775	1963	Dr. Marvin O. Looney	5	1,138	20
Southwest Texas Jr Coll, Uvalde, TX 78801-6297	1946	Mr. Billy Word	11	3,256	166
Southwest Virginia Comm Coll, Richlands, VA 24641	1968	Dr. Charles R. King	5	4,235	235
Southwest Wisconsin Tech Coll, Fennimore, WI 53809-9778	1967	Dr. Richard A. Rogers	11	3,870	101
Spartanburg Tech Coll, Spartanburg, SC 29305-4386	1961	Dr. Dan Terhune	5	2,562	NR
Spokane Comm Coll, Spokane, WA 99207-5399	1963	Dr. James Williams	5	5,400	358
Spokane Falls Comm Coll, Spokane, WA 99224-5288	1967	Dr. Vern Loland	5	5,700	565
Spoon River Coll, Canton, IL 61520-9801	1959	Dr. Keith Miller	5	1,922	189
Springfield Tech Comm Coll, Springfield, MA 01105-1296	1967	Dr. Andrew M. Scibelli	5	6,211	308
Stanly Comm Coll, Albemarle, NC 28001-7458	1971	Dr. Mike Taylor	5	1,660	76
Stark State Coll of Tech, Canton, OH 44720-7299	1970	Dr. John J. McGrath	11	4,096	210
State Fair Comm Coll, Sedalia, MO 65301-2199	1966	Dr. Marvin Fielding	9	2,277	98
State Tech Inst at Memphis, Memphis, TN 38134-7693	1967	Dr. M. Douglas Call	5	10,195	620
State U of NY at Farmingdale, Farmingdale, NY 11735	1912	Dr. Frank A. Cipriani	5	5,697	285
State U of NY Coll of A&T at Cobleskill, Cobleskill, NY 12043	1916	Dr. Kenneth E. Wing	5	2,213	145
State U of NY Coll of A&T at Morrisville, Morrisville, NY 13408	1908	Dr. Frederick W. Woodward	5	2,758	171
State U of NY Coll of Tech at Alfred, Alfred, NY 14802	1908	Dr. William Rezak	5	3,100	176

Name, address	Year	Governing official, control, and highest degree offered		Enroll-ment	Faculty
State U of NY Coll of Tech at Canton, Canton, NY 13617	1906	Dr. Joseph L. Kennedy	5	2,004	107
State U of NY Coll of Tech at Delhi, Delhi, NY 13753	1913	Dr. Mary Ellen Duncan	5	1,903	135
Suffolk County Comm Coll–Ammerman Cmps, Selden, NY 11784-2851	1962	Dr. John F. Cooper	11	13,154	782
Suffolk County Comm Coll–Western Cmps, Brentwood, NY 11717.	1974	Mr. Salvatore J. LaLima	11	6,097	349
Sullivan County Comm Coll, Loch Sheldrake, NY 12759-5151	1962	Dr. Jeffrey B. Willens	11	1,781	106
Surry Comm Coll, Dobson, NC 27017-0304	1965	Dr. James Reeves	5	3,036	98
Sussex County Comm Coll, Newton, NJ 07860	1981	Dr. William A. Connor	11	2,376	188
Tacoma Comm Coll, Tacoma, WA 98466	1965	Dr. Pamela Trausue	5	5,356	299
Tallahassee Comm Coll, Tallahassee, FL 32304-2895	1966	Dr. T. K. Wetherell	11	9,737	372
Tarrant County Jr Coll, Fort Worth, TX 76102-6599	1967	Dr. Leonardo de la Garza	8	25,174	1,159
Tech Career Institutes, New York, NY 10001-2705	1909	Mr. Tom Coleman	3	3,700	192
Tech Coll of the Lowcountry, Beaufort, SC 29901-1288	1972	Dr. Anne S. McNutt	5	1,600	69
Temple Coll, Temple, TX 76504-7435	1926	Dr. Marc A. Nigliazzo	9	2,450	125
Terra State Comm Coll, Fremont, OH 43420-9670	1968	Dr. Charlotte J. Lee	5	2,512	159
Texarkana Coll, Texarkana, TX 75599-0001	1927	Dr. Carl M. Nelson	11	4,038	196
Texas State Tech Coll, Sweetwater, TX 79556-4108	1970	Dr. Clay G. Johnson	5	1,019	93
Texas State Tech Coll–Harlingen, Harlingen, TX 78550-3697	1967	Dr. J. Gilbert Leal	5	3,082	151
Texas State Tech Coll–Waco/Marshall Cmps, Waco, TX 76705-1695	1965	Dr. Fred L. Williams	5	3,448	331
Thomas Nelson Comm Coll, Hampton, VA 23670-0407	1968	Dr. Shirley R. Pippins	5	7,192	320
Three Rivers Comm Coll, Poplar Bluff, MO 63901-2393	1966	Dr. James S. Spencer	11	3,000	67
Three Rivers Comm-Tech Coll, Norwich, CT 06360	1963	Dr. Booker T. DeVaughn	5	3,707	192
Tidewater Comm Coll, Portsmouth, VA 23703	1968	Dr. Larry Whitworth	5	16,199	760
Tomball Coll, Tomball, TX 77375-4036	1988	Dr. Diane Troyer	11	3,805	230
Tompkins Cortland Comm Coll, Dryden, NY 13053-9533	1968	Dr. Carl Haynes	11	2,262	196
Treasure Valley Comm Coll, Ontario, OR 97914-3423	1962	Dr. Berton L. Glandon	11	3,625	110
Tri-County Tech Coll, Pendleton, SC 29670-0587	1962	Dr. Don C. Garrison	5	3,293	251
Trident Tech Coll, Charleston, SC 29423-8067	1964	Dr. Mary Thornley	11	9,079	523
Trinidad State Jr Coll, Trinidad, CO 81082-2396	1925	Dr. Harold Deselms	5	2,281	140
Trinity Valley Comm Coll, Athens, TX 75751-2765	1946	Mr. Ron Baugh	11	4,995	224
Triton Coll, River Grove, IL 60171-9983	1964	Dr. George Jorndt	5	12,690	712
Truckee Meadows Comm Coll, Reno, NV 89512-3901	1971	Dr. John Richardson	5	9,338	464
Truett-McConnell Coll, Cleveland, GA 30528-9799	1946	Dr. T. Clark Bryan	2	2,090	162
Tulsa Comm Coll, Tulsa, OK 74135-6198	1968	Dr. Dean P. VanTrease	5	20,000	1,200
Tunxis Comm Tech Coll, Farmington, CT 06032-3026	1969	Dr. Cathryn Addy	5	3,675	175
Tyler Jr Coll, Tyler, TX 75711-9020	1926	Dr. William R. Crowe	11	7,984	364
UAB Walker Coll, Jasper, AL 35501-4967	1938	Dr. J. Foster Watkins	5	1,005	41
Ulster County Comm Coll, Stone Ridge, NY 12484	1961	Mr. Robert T. Brown	11	2,638	175
Umpqua Comm Coll, Roseburg, OR 97470-0226	1964	Dr. James M. Kraby	11	2,100	148
Union County Coll, Cranford, NJ 07016-1528	1933	Dr. Thomas H. Brown	11	9,598	436
The U of Akron–Wayne Coll, Orrville, OH 44667-9192	1972	Dr. Marion Ruebel	5	1,458	109
U of Alaska Anchorage, Kenai Peninsula Coll, Soldotna, AK 99669-9798	1964	Ms. Ginger Steffy	5	1,813	109
U of Alaska, Prince William Sound Comm Coll, Valdez, AK 99686-0097	1978	Dr. JoAnne C. McDowell	5	1,508	75
U of Arkansas Comm Coll at Hope, Hope, AR 71801	1966	Mr. Johnny Rapert	5	1,053	62
U of Cincinnati Clermont Coll, Batavia, OH 45103-1785	1972	Dr. James McDonough	5	2,266	163
U of Cincinnati Raymond Walters Coll, Cincinnati, OH 45236-1007	1967	Dr. Barbara A. Bardes	5	2,771	265
U of Hawaii–Hawaii Comm Coll, Hilo, HI 96720-4091	1954	Ms. Sandra Sakaguchi	5	2,500	149
U of Hawaii–Honolulu Comm Coll, Honolulu, HI 96817-4598	1920	Dr. Peter R. Kessinger	5	4,127	185
U of Hawaii–Kapiolani Comm Coll, Honolulu, HI 96816-4421	1957	Mr. John F. Morton	5	7,283	317
U of Hawaii–Kauai Comm Coll, Lihue, HI 96766-9591	1965	Mr. David Iha	5	1,178	71
U of Hawaii–Leeward Comm Coll, Pearl City, HI 96782-3366	1968	Dr. Barbara B. Polk	5	5,987	243
U of Hawaii–Maui Comm Coll, Kahului, HI 96732	1967	Dr. Clyde Sakamoto	5	2,815	148
U of Hawaii–Windward Comm Coll, Kaneohe, HI 96744-3528	1972	Dr. Peter T. Dyer	5	1,666	80
U of Kentucky, Ashland Comm Coll, Ashland, KY 41101-3683	1937	Mr. Roger C. Noe	5	2,477	136
U of Kentucky, Elizabethtown Comm Coll, Elizabethtown, KY 42701-3081	1964	Dr. Charles E. Stebbins	5	3,381	181
U of Kentucky, Hazard Comm Coll, Hazard, KY 41701-2403	1968	Dr. G. Edward Hughes	5	2,358	156
U of Kentucky, Henderson Comm Coll, Henderson, KY 42420-4623	1963	Dr. Patrick R. Lake	5	1,396	96
U of Kentucky, Hopkinsville Comm Coll, Hopkinsville, KY 42241-2100	1965	Dr. Jim Kerley	5	2,898	158
U of Kentucky, Jefferson Comm Coll, Louisville, KY 40202-2005	1968	Dr. Richard Green	5	9,273	490
U of Kentucky, Lexington Comm Coll, Lexington, KY 40506-0235	1965	Dr. Janice N. Friedel	5	5,505	302
U of Kentucky, Madisonville Comm Coll, Madisonville, KY 42431-9185	1968	Dr. Arthur D. Stumpf	5	2,533	167
U of Kentucky, Maysville Comm Coll, Maysville, KY 41056	1967	Dr. James C. Shires	5	1,409	111
U of Kentucky, Paducah Comm Coll, Paducah, KY 42002-7380	1932	Dr. Leonard O'Hara	5	2,842	143
U of Kentucky, Prestonsburg Comm Coll, Prestonsburg, KY 41653-1815	1964	Dr. Deborah Lee Floyd	5	2,698	132
U of Kentucky, Somerset Comm Coll, Somerset, KY 42501-2973	1965	Dr. Rollin J. Watson	5	2,498	153
U of Kentucky, Southeast Comm Coll, Cumberland, KY 40823-1099	1960	Dr. W. Bruce Ayers	5	2,466	107
U of Maine at Augusta, Augusta, ME 04330-9410	1965	Dr. Owen F. Cargol	5	3,589	207
U of New Mexico–Los Alamos Branch, Los Alamos, NM 87544-2233	1980	Dr. Carlos B. Ramirez	5	1,023	96
U of New Mexico–Valencia Cmps, Los Lunas, NM 87031-7633	1981	Dr. Alice V. Letteney	5	1,550	93
U of Puerto Rico, Colegio Regional de la Montaña, Utuado, PR 00641-2500	1979	Prof. Ramon Colon Murphy	6	1,217	63
U of South Carolina at Beaufort, Beaufort, SC 29902-4601	1959	Dr. Chris P. Plyler	5	1,055	81
U of South Carolina at Lancaster, Lancaster, SC 29721-0889	1959	Dr. Joseph Pappin, III	5	1,153	52
U of South Carolina at Sumter, Sumter, SC 29150-2498	1966	Dr. C. Leslie Carpenter	5	1,396	73
U of Wisconsin Ctr–Fox Valley, Menasha, WI 54952-8002	1933	Dr. James W. Perry	5	1,250	58
U of Wisconsin Ctr–Waukesha County, Waukesha, WI 53188-2720	1966	Dr. Mary S. Knudten	5	1,681	77
Utah Valley State Coll, Orem, UT 84058-0001	1941	Dr. Kerry D. Romesburg	5	14,756	607
Valencia Comm Coll, Orlando, FL 32802-3028	1967	Dr. Paul C. Gianini, Jr.	5	23,748	978
Vance-Granville Comm Coll, Henderson, NC 27536-0917	1969	Dr. Ben F. Currin	5	4,234	262
Ventura Coll, Ventura, CA 93003-3899	1925	Dr. Larry Calderon	11	11,381	451
Vernon Regional Jr Coll, Vernon, TX 76384-4092	1972	Dr. Wade Kirk	11	1,854	98
Victoria Coll, Victoria, TX 77901-4494	1925	Dr. Jimmy Goodson	8	3,598	120
Victor Valley Coll, Victorville, CA 92392-5849	1961	Mr. Nicholas L. Halisky	5	8,000	325
Vincennes U, Vincennes, IN 47591-5202	1801	Dr. Phillip M. Summers	5	6,500	400
Vincennes U Jasper Cmps, Jasper, IN 47546-9393	1970	Dr. Chris Croll	5	1,260	62
Virginia Highlands Comm Coll, Abingdon, VA 24212-0828	1967	Dr. F. David Wilkin, Jr.	5	1,834	131
Virginia Western Comm Coll, Roanoke, VA 24038	1966	Dr. Charles L. Downs	5	7,201	290
Vista Comm Coll, Berkeley, CA 94704-5102	1974	Dr. Barbara Beno	11	3,318	125

Name, address	Year	Governing official, control, and highest degree offered		Enroll-ment	Faculty
Volunteer State Comm Coll, Gallatin, TN 37066-3188	1970	Dr. Hal R. Ramer	5	6,887	417
Wake Tech Comm Coll, Raleigh, NC 27603-5696	1958	Dr. Bruce I. Howell	11	7,330	423
Walker Tech Inst, Rock Springs, GA 30739	1966	NR	5	1,052	NR
Wallace State Comm Coll, Hanceville, AL 35077-2000	1966	Dr. James C. Bailey	5	5,409	301
Walla Walla Comm Coll, Walla Walla, WA 99362-9267	1967	Dr. Steven L. VanAusdle	5	4,633	444
Walters State Comm Coll, Morristown, TN 37813-6899	1970	Dr. Jack E. Campbell	5	6,039	253
Warren County Comm Coll, Washington, NJ 07882-9605	1981	Dr. Vincent De Sanctis	11	1,619	61
Washington State Comm Coll, Marietta, OH 45750-9225	1971	Dr. Carson K. Miller	5	2,019	132
Washtenaw Comm Coll, Ann Arbor, MI 48106	1965	Dr. Gunder A. Myran	11	10,560	759
Waubonsee Comm Coll, Sugar Grove, IL 60554-9799	1966	Dr. John J. Swalec	9	7,666	501
Waukesha County Tech Coll, Pewaukee, WI 53072-4601	1923	Dr. Richard T. Anderson	11	4,700	520
Wayne Comm Coll, Goldsboro, NC 27533-8002	1957	Dr. Edward H. Wilson, Jr.	11	2,647	133
Wayne County Comm Coll, Detroit, MI 48226-3010	1967	Dr. Curtis L. Ivery	11	11,266	400
Weatherford Coll, Weatherford, TX 76086-5699	1869	Dr. Jim Boyd	11	2,277	94
Wenatchee Valley Coll, Wenatchee, WA 98801-1799	1939	Dr. Woody Ahn	11	3,368	203
Westark Comm Coll, Fort Smith, AR 72913-3649	1928	Mr. Joel R. Stubblefield	11	5,432	240
Westchester Comm Coll, Valhalla, NY 10595-1698	1946	Dr. Joseph N. Hankin	11	11,127	788
Western Iowa Tech Comm Coll, Sioux City, IA 51102-5199	1966	Dr. Robert E. Dunker	5	3,200	157
Western Nebraska Comm Coll, Scottsbluff, NE 69361	1921	Dr. James R. Garcia	11	3,911	136
Western Nevada Comm Coll, Carson City, NV 89703-7316	1971	Dr. James Randolph	5	5,143	358
Western Oklahoma State Coll, Altus, OK 73521-1397	1926	Dr. Ray Brown	5	1,459	78
Western Piedmont Comm Coll, Morganton, NC 28655-9978	1964	Dr. Jim A. Richardson	5	2,562	132
Western Texas Coll, Snyder, TX 79549-9502	1969	Dr. Harry L. Krenek	11	1,033	55
Western Wisconsin Tech Coll, La Crosse, WI 54602-0908	1911	Dr. James Lee Rasch	9	4,438	184
Western Wyoming Comm Coll, Rock Springs, WY 82902-0428	1959	Dr. T. L. Boggs	11	3,094	232
West Hills Comm Coll, Coalinga, CA 93210-1399	1932	Dr. Frank P. Gornick	5	3,167	107
West Los Angeles Coll, Culver City, CA 90230-3500	1969	Dr. Evelyn C. Wong	11	7,400	320
Westmoreland County Comm Coll, Youngwood, PA 15697	1970	Dr. Daniel C. Krezenski	8	6,245	390
West Shore Comm Coll, Scottville, MI 49454-9716	1967	Dr. William M. Anderson	9	1,452	71
West Valley Coll, Saratoga, CA 95070-5698	1963	Dr. Marchelle Fox	11	14,224	560
West Virginia Northern Comm Coll, Wheeling, WV 26003	1972	Dr. Linda S. Dunn	5	2,554	158
West Virginia U at Parkersburg, Parkersburg, WV 26101-9577	1971	Dr. Eldon L. Miller	5	3,439	176
Wharton County Jr Coll, Wharton, TX 77488-3298	1946	Dr. Frank R. Vivelo	11	3,958	224
Whatcom Comm Coll, Bellingham, WA 98226-8003	1970	Dr. Harold G. Heiner	5	2,727	167
Wilkes Comm Coll, Wilkesboro, NC 28697	1965	Dr. Gordon Burns	5	2,240	171
William Rainey Harper Coll, Palatine, IL 60067-7398	1965	Dr. Paul N. Thompson	11	14,000	1,018
Wilson Tech Comm Coll, Wilson, NC 27893-3310	1958	Dr. Frank L. Eagles	5	1,379	92
Wisconsin Indianhead Tech Coll, New Richmond Cmps, New Richmond, WI 54017-1738	1972	Mr. Tim Schreiner	9	1,300	65
Wisconsin Indianhead Tech Coll, Rice Lake Cmps, Rice Lake, WI 54868-2435	1941	Dr. Vasant Kumar	9	1,136	79
Wood Coll, Mathiston, MS 39752-0289	1886	Dr. Robert Sandin	2	1,500	35
Wor-Wic Comm Coll, Salisbury, MD 21804	1976	Dr. Arnold H. Maner	11	1,989	103
Wytheville Comm Coll, Wytheville, VA 24382-3308	1967	Dr. William F. Snyder	5	2,559	137
Yakima Valley Comm Coll, Yakima, WA 98907-1647	1928	Dr. Linda Kaminski	5	3,446	292
Yavapai Coll, Prescott, AZ 86301-3297	1966	Dr. Doreen Dailey	11	6,121	487
York Tech Coll, Rock Hill, SC 29730-3395	1961	Dr. Dennis F. Merrell	5	3,528	236
Yuba Coll, Marysville, CA 95901-7699	1927	Dr. Stephen Epler	11	9,860	500

Tuition and College Costs, 1997-98

According to Peterson's Guides Annual Survey of Undergraduate Institutions, the average cost of tuition, mandatory fees, and room and board at four-year private colleges reached $17,501 in 1997-98. The average comparable cost at four-year public colleges was $7,331 for state residents and $12,420 for others. Tuition and fees at two-year private colleges averaged $7,094. The same costs at two-year public colleges averaged $1,864 for state residents and $4,612 for nonresidents. The 10 most expensive four-year institutions, counting tuition, fees, and room and board, were: Sarah Lawrence College ($30,295); Harvard University ($30,080); University of Chicago ($30,080); Hampshire College ($30,045); Yale University ($29,950); Brown University ($29,900); New York University ($29,900); Columbia College ($29,872); Columbia University, School of Engineering and Applied Science ($29,872); Boston University ($29,848).

College Freshman Attitudes, 1996
Source: *The American Freshman: National Norms for Fall 1996*

According to the 31st annual survey of college freshmen conducted by the American Council on Education and UCLA, an increasing proportion of students beginning college in 1996 expected to get a job to help pay for their college expenses—41.1%, compared to 39.5% the previous year and 34.7% in 1989. A record 38.4% reported that they spent one or more hours per week doing volunteer work (up from a low of 26.6% when the question was first asked in 1987). The percent who felt frequently "overwhelmed by all I have to do" rose to an all-time high of 29.4%.

The percentage of freshmen citing "financial assistance" as a "very important" reason for selecting their college increased to an all-time high of 33.1% in 1996, compared to 31.6% the previous year and a low of 13.6% in 1976. The percent indicating that they chose a college because its "graduates gain admission to top graduate/professional schools" rose to a record 29.6%. The percent who chose a college because "graduates get good jobs" reached an eight-year high of 46.8%. A record 66.3% of freshmen planned to earn graduate or professional degrees. Interest in teaching reached a 23-year high, with 10.2% of freshmen (31.7% of women and 5.7% of men) planning to become elementary or secondary school teachers. Interest in medical careers remained steady, matching 1995's record high of 6.4%. The percent of freshmen planning on business careers hit a 20-year low of 14.0%, down from a high of 24.6% in 1987. A record low of 3.3% had plans to become lawyers, compared to a high of 5.4% in 1989.

Record numbers of freshmen reported having taken three years of math (95.1%), two years of biological science (41.3%), two years of physical science (52.6%), and one-half year of computer science (58.3%) to prepare for college. Also, a record 84.4% reported having taken at least two years of a foreign language. For whatever reason, the percentage of freshmen who reported being frequently "bored in class" rose to an all-time high of 35.6%.

More freshmen described themselves as "liberal" or "far left" (24.6%, up from 23.8%) and "conservative" or "far right" (22.7%, up from 21.9%) than in 1995. The percent of students that considered themselves "middle-of-the-road" fell from 54.3% to 52.7%. The opinion that "If two people like each other, it's all right for them to have sex even if they've known each other for a very short time" was supported by an all-time low of 41.6%, down from a high of 51.9% in 1987.

ARTS AND MEDIA

Some Notable Movies, Sept. 1996-Aug. 1997

Movie	Stars	Director
Absolute Power	Clint Eastwood, Gene Hackman, Laura Linney, Ed Harris	Clint Eastwood
Air Force One	Harrison Ford, Gary Oldman, Glenn Close	Wolfgang Petersen
Batman and Robin	George Clooney, Chris O'Donnell, Arnold Schwarzenegger, Alicia Silverstone	Joel Schumacher
Beavis and Butt-Head Do America	Mike Judge, David Spade, Eric Bogosian, Cloris Leachman (voices)	Mike Judge
Big Night	Stanley Tucci, Tony Shalhoub	Stanley Tucci
Breaking the Waves	Emily Watson, Stellan Skarsgard, Katrin Cartlidge	Lars Von Trier
Con Air	Nicolas Cage, John Malkovich, John Cusack	Simon West
Contact	Jodie Foster, Matthew McConaughey, James Woods	Robert Zemeckis
Cop Land	Sylvester Stallone, Robert DeNiro, Ray Liotta, Harvey Keitel	James Mangold
Dante's Peak	Pierce Brosnan, Linda Hamilton	Roger Donaldson
Devil's Own, The	Harrison Ford, Brad Pitt, Margaret Colin, Ruben Blades	Alan J. Pakula
Donnie Brasco	Johnny Depp, Al Pacino, Michael Madsen, Bruno Kirby, James Russo, Anne Heche	Mike Newell
English Patient, The	Ralph Fiennes, Kristin Scott Thomas, Juliette Binoche, Willem Dafoe	Anthony Minghella
Everyone Says I Love You	Woody Allen, Alan Alda, Goldie Hawn, Julia Roberts	Woody Allen
Evita	Madonna, Antonio Banderas, Jonathan Pryce	Alan Parker
Face/Off	John Travolta, Nicolas Cage, Joan Allen, Gina Gershon	John Woo
Fifth Element, The	Bruce Willis, Gary Oldman, Ian Holm, Milla Jovovich	Luc Besson
First Wives Club, The	Bette Midler, Goldie Hawn, Diane Keaton	Hugh Wilson
Fly Away Home	Jeff Daniels, Anna Paquin, Dana Delany, Terry Kinney	Carroll Ballard
G. I. Jane	Demi Moore, Viggo Mortensen, Anne Bancroft	Ridley Scott
Hamlet	Kenneth Branagh, Kate Winslet, Derek Jacobi, Julie Christie	Kenneth Branagh
Jerry Maguire	Tom Cruise, Cuba Gooding Jr., Renee Zellweger, Kelly Preston	Cameron Crowe
Kolya	Zdenak Sverak, Andrej Chalimon, Irena Livanova, Ondrez Vetchy	Jan Sverak
Liar, Liar	Jim Carrey, Jennifer Tilly, Justin Cooper	Tom Shadyak
Looking for Richard	Alec Baldwin, Al Pacino, Aidan Quinn, Winona Ryder, Kevin Spacey	Al Pacino
Lost Highway	Bill Pullman, Patricia Arquette, Balthazar Getty, Robert Blake	David Lynch
Lost World, The: Jurassic Park	Jeff Goldblum, Julianne Moore, Pete Postlethwaite, Arliss Howard	Steven Spielberg
Mars Attacks!	Jack Nicholson, Glenn Close, Pierce Brosnan, Sarah Jessica Parker	Tim Burton
Marvin's Room	Meryl Streep, Leonardo DiCaprio, Diane Keaton, Robert DeNiro	Jerry Zaks
Men in Black	Will Smith, Tommy Lee Jones, Vincent D'Onofrio, Linda Fiorentino	Barry Sonnenfeld
Michael Collins	Liam Neeson, Aidan Quinn, Stephen Rea, Alan Rickman, Julia Roberts	Neil Jordan
Mirror Has Two Faces, The	Barbra Streisand, Jeff Bridges, Lauren Bacall	Barbra Streisand
Mother	Albert Brooks, Debbie Reynolds, Rob Morrow	Albert Brooks
My Best Friend's Wedding	Julia Roberts, Dermot Mulroney, Cameron Diaz, Rupert Everett	P. J. Hogan
101 Dalmatians	Glenn Close, Jeff Daniels, Joely Richardson, Joan Plowright	Stephen Herek
People vs. Larry Flynt, The	Woody Harrelson, Courtney Love, Edward Norton	Milos Forman
Private Parts	Howard Stern, Mary McCormack, Robin Quivers	Betty Thomas
Ransom	Mel Gibson, Rene Russo, Gary Sinise, Delroy Lindo	Ron Howard
Rosewood	Ving Rhames, Jon Voight, Don Cheadle, Esther Rolle, Elise Neal	John Singleton
Scream	Neve Campbell, Drew Barrymore, Skeet Ulrich, Courteney Cox	Wes Craven
Secrets and Lies	Timothy Spall, Brenda Blethyn, Phyllis Logan, Marianne Jean-Baptiste	Mike Leigh
Selena	Jennifer Lopez, Edward James Olmos	Gregory Nava
She's So Lovely	Sean Penn, Robin Wright Penn, John Travolta	Nick Cassavettes
Shine	Armin Mueller-Stahl, Noah Taylor, Geoffrey Rush, Lynn Redgrave	Scott Hicks
Sleepers	Kevin Bacon, Robert DeNiro, Dustin Hoffman, Brad Pitt, Jason Patric	Barry Levinson
Sling Blade	Billy Bob Thornton, John Ritter, Dwight Yoakum, J.T. Walsh	Billy Bob Thornton
Spawn	Michael Jai White, Theresa Randle, Martin Sheen, John Leguizamo	Mark Dippe
Speed 2: Cruise Control	Sandra Bullock, Jason Patric, Willem Dafoe	Jan De Bont
Star Trek: First Contact	Patrick Stewart, Brent Spiner, James Cromwell	Jonathan Frakes
William Shakespeare's Romeo and Juliet	Leonardo DiCaprio, Claire Danes, Brian Dennehy, John Leguizamo	Baz Luhrmann

Top 50 Movies, 1996

Source: *Variety,* Jan. 13-Jan. 19, 1997; box-office grosses in the U.S. and Canada during calendar year 1996

Rank/Title	Gross (millions)	Rank/Title	Gross (millions)	Rank/Title	Gross (millions)
1. Independence Day	$306.2	19. The Cable Guy	$60.2	35. The Mirror Has Two Faces.	$40.5
2. Twister	241.7	20. Courage Under Fire	59.0	36. Dead Man Walking*	39.3
3. Mission Impossible	181.0	21. Jack	58.5	37. Sense and Sensibility*	39.0
4. The Rock	134.1	22. 12 Monkeys	57.0	38. Happy Gilmore	38.6
5. The Nutty Professor	128.8	23. Executive Decision	56.7	39. The Ghost and the Darkness	37.7
6. Ransom	125.8	24. Primal Fear	56.1	40. Michael	35.1
7. The Birdcage	124.1	25. Jingle All the Way	54.5	41. The Truth About Cats and Dogs	34.8
8. 101 Dalmatians	109.7	26. Tin Cup	53.9	42. A Thin Line Between Love and Hate	34.8
9. A Time to Kill	108.8	27. Sleepers	52.5	43. Muppet Treasure Island	34.3
10. Phenomenon	104.5	28. Dragonheart	51.4	44. Set It Off	34.3
11. The First Wives Club	103.7	29. Up Close and Personal	51.1	45. Waiting to Exhale*	33.7
12. Eraser	101.3	30. Jumanji*	46.7	46. Matilda	33.5
13. The Hunchback of Notre Dame	99.9	31. Toy Story*	45.7	47. Striptease	33.2
14. Star Trek: First Contact	86.2	32. Beavis and Butt-Head Do America	44.5	48. Heat*	32.9
15. Space Jam	83.0	33. William Shakespeare's Romeo and Juliet	44.0	49. The Long Kiss Goodnight	32.8
16. Mr. Holland's Opus	82.6	34. Grumpier Old Men*	43.5	50. Homeward Bound II	32.8
17. Broken Arrow	70.8				
18. Jerry Maguire	63.7				

*1995 release; 1996 gross only.

All-Time Top 50 American Movies Through 1996

Source: *Variety* magazine

Rank/Title/Date	Gross[1] (millions)	Rank/Title/Date	Gross[1] (millions)	Rank/Title/Date	Gross[1] (millions)
1. E.T.: The Extra-Terrestrial (1982)	$399.8	19. Aladdin (1992)	$217.4	36. Apollo 13 (1995)	$172.1
2. Jurassic Park (1993)	357.1	20. Back to the Future (1985)	208.2	37. Three Men and a Baby (1987)	167.8
3. Forrest Gump (1994)	329.7	21. Terminator 2 (1991)	204.8	38. Robin Hood: Prince of Thieves (1991)	165.5
4. Star Wars (1977)	322.7	22. Indiana Jones and the Last Crusade (1989)	197.2	39. The Exorcist (1973)	165.0
5. The Lion King (1993)	312.9	23. Gone With the Wind (1939)	191.7	40. Batman Returns (1992)	162.8
6. Independence Day (1996)	306.2	24. Dances With Wolves (1990)	184.2	41. The Sound of Music (1965)	160.5
7. Home Alone (1990)	285.8	25. Batman Forever (1995)	184.0	42. The Firm (1993)	158.3
8. Return of the Jedi (1983)	263.7	26. The Fugitive (1993)	183.9	43. Fatal Attraction (1987)	156.6
9. Jaws (1975)	260.0	27. Mission Impossible (1996)	181.0	44. The Sting (1973)	156.0
10. Batman (1989)	251.2	28. Indiana Jones and the Temple of Doom (1984)	179.9	45. Who Framed Roger Rabbit? (1988)	154.1
11. Raiders of the Lost Ark (1981)	242.4	29. Pretty Woman (1990)	178.4	46. Beverly Hills Cop II (1987)	153.7
12. Twister (1996)	241.7	30. Tootsie (1982)	177.2	47. Grease (1978)	153.1
13. Ghostbusters (1984)	238.6	31. Top Gun (1986)	176.8	48. Rambo: First Blood Part II (1985)	150.4
14. Beverly Hills Cop (1984)	234.8	32. Snow White and the Seven Dwarfs (1937)	175.3	49. Gremlins (1984)	148.2
15. Toy Story (1995)	228.1	33. Crocodile Dundee (1986)	174.6	50. Lethal Weapon 2 (1989)	147.3
16. The Empire Strikes Back (1980)	222.7	34. Home Alone 2 (1992)	173.6		
17. Mrs. Doubtfire (1993)	219.2	35. Rain Man (1989)	172.8		
18. Ghost (1990)	217.6				

(1) Gross is in absolute dollars based on box office sales in the U.S. and Canada. Ticket prices favor recent films, but older films have the advantage of reissues.

Most Popular Movie Videos

Source: Alexander & Associates/Video Flash, New York, NY

Top 10 Rentals, 1996	All Time Top 10 Rentals[1]	Top 10 Sales, 1996	All Time Top 10 Sales[2]
1. Braveheart	1. Top Gun	1. Toy Story	1. The Lion King
2. Babe	2. Pretty Woman	2. Pocahontas	2. Aladdin
3. Twister	3. Home Alone	3. Babe	3. Beauty and the Beast
4. Seven	4. Ghost	4. The Aristocats	4. Snow White and the Seven Dwarfs
5. Independence Day	5. The Little Mermaid	5. Independence Day	5. Forrest Gump
6. The Net	6. Terminator 2: Judgment Day	6. Twister	6. 101 Dalmatians
7. Jumanji	7. Beauty and the Beast	7. Aladdin	7. Jurassic Park
8. Casino	8. Cinderella	8. Oliver & Company	8. The Little Mermaid
9. Waterworld	9. Dances With Wolves	9. Jumanji	9. Toy Story
10. Toy Story	10. Forrest Gump	10. Indian in the Cupboard	10. E.T.: The Extra-Terrestrial

(1) Rented Mar. 1, 1987-Dec. 31, 1996. (2) Sold Feb. 16, 1988-Dec. 31, 1996.

National Film Registry, 1989-96

Source: National Film Registry, Library of Congress

"Culturally, historically, or esthetically significant" films placed on the National Film Registry, Library of Congress. Films selected in 1996 are in **boldface**.

Adam's Rib (1949)
The Adventures of Robin Hood (1938)
The African Queen (1951)
All About Eve (1950)
All That Heaven Allows (1955)
All Quiet on the Western Front (1930)
An American in Paris (1951)
American Graffiti (1973)
Annie Hall (1977)
The Apartment (1960)
The Awful Truth (1937)
Badlands (1973)
The Band Wagon (1953)
The Bank Dick (1940)
The Battle of San Pietro (1945)
The Best Years of Our Lives (1946)
Big Business (1929)
The Big Parade (1925)
The Birth of a Nation (1915)
The Black Pirate (1926)
Blacksmith Scene (1893)
Blade Runner (1982)
The Blood of Jesus (1941)
Bonnie and Clyde (1967)
Bringing Up Baby (1938)
Broken Blossoms (1919)
Cabaret (1972)
Carmen Jones (1954)
Casablanca (1942)
Castro Street (1966)

Cat People (1942)
Chan Is Missing (1982)
The Cheat (1915)
Chinatown (1974)
Chulas Fronteras (1976)
Citizen Kane (1941)
City Lights (1931)
The Conversation (1974)
The Cool World (1963)
A Corner in Wheat (1909)
The Crowd (1928)
David Holzman's Diary (1968)
The Day the Earth Stood Still (1951)
The Deer Hunter (1978)
Destry Rides Again (1939)
Detour (1946)
Dodsworth (1936)
Dog Star Man (1964)
Double Indemnity (1944)
Dr. Strangelove (or, How I Learned to Stop Worrying and Love the Bomb) (1964)
Duck Soup (1933)
Eaux D'Artifice (1953)
El Norte (1983)
E.T.: The Extra-Terrestrial (1982)
The Exploits of Elaine (1914)
Fantasia (1940)
Fatty's Tintype Tangle (1915)
Flash Gordon serial (1936)
Footlight Parade (1933)
Force of Evil (1948)

The Forgotten Frontier (1931)
The Four Horsemen of the Apocalypse (1921)
Frankenstein (1931)
Frank Film (1973)
Freaks (1932)
The Freshman (1925)
Fury (1936)
The General (1927)
Gerald McBoing Boing (1951)
Gertie the Dinosaur (1914)
Gigi (1958)
The Godfather (1972)
The Godfather, Part II (1974)
The Gold Rush (1925)
Gone With the Wind (1939)
The Graduate (1967)
The Grapes of Wrath (1940)
The Great Train Robbery (1903)
Greed (1924)
Harlan County, U.S.A. (1976)
The Heiress (1949)
Hell's Hinges (1916)
High Noon (1952)
High School (1968)
His Girl Friday (1940)
Hospital (1970)
The Hospital (1971)
How Green Was My Valley (1941)
I Am a Fugitive From a Chain Gang (1932)

Intolerance (1916)
Invasion of the Body Snatchers (1956)
It Happened One Night (1934)
It's a Wonderful Life (1946)
The Italian (1915)
Jammin' the Blues (1944)
The Jazz Singer (1927)
Killer of Sheep (1977)
King Kong (1933)
The Lady Eve (1941)
Lassie Come Home (1943)
The Last of the Mohicans (1920)
Lawrence of Arabia (1962)
The Learning Tree (1969)
Letter From an Unknown Woman (1948)
Life and Times of Rosie the Riveter (1980)
Louisiana Story (1948)
Love Me Tonight (1932)
The Manchurian Candidate (1962)
Manhatta (1921)
Magical Maestro (1952)
The Magnificent Ambersons (1942)
The Maltese Falcon (1941)
March of Time: Inside Nazi Germany—1938 (1938)
Marty (1955)
M*A*S*H (1970)
Meet Me in St. Louis (1944)

Meshes of the Afternoon (1943)
Midnight Cowboy (1969)
Mildred Pierce (1945)
Modern Times (1936)
Morocco (1930)
A Movie (1958)
Mr. Smith Goes to Washington (1939)
My Darling Clementine (1946)
Nanook of the North (1922)
Nashville (1975)
A Night at the Opera (1935)
The Night of the Hunter (1955)
Ninotchka (1939)
North by Northwest (1959)
Nothing but a Man (1964)
On the Waterfront (1954)
One Flew Over the Cuckoo's Nest (1975)
The Outlaw Josey Wales (1976)
Out of the Past (1947)
Paths of Glory (1957)

The Philadelphia Story (1940)
Pinocchio (1940)
A Place in the Sun (1951)
Point of Order (1964)
The Poor Little Rich Girl (1917)
Primary (1960)
The Prisoner of Zenda (1937)
The Producers (1968)
Psycho (1960)
Pull My Daisy (1959)
Raging Bull (1980)
Rebel Without a Cause (1955)
Red River (1948)
Ride the High Country (1962)
Rip Van Winkle (1896)
The River (1937)
Road to Morocco (1942)
Safety Last (1923)
Salesman (1969)
Salt of the Earth (1954)
Scarface (1932)
The Searchers (1956)

Seventh Heaven (1927)
Shadow of a Doubt (1943)
Shadows (1959)
Shane (1953)
She Done Him Wrong (1933)
Sherlock, Jr. (1924)
Shock Corridor (1963)
Show Boat (1936)
Singin' in the Rain (1952)
Snow White (1933)
Snow White and the Seven Dwarfs (1937)
Some Like It Hot (1959)
Stagecoach (1939)
Star Wars (1977)
Sullivan's Travels (1941)
Sunrise (1927)
Sunset Boulevard (1950)
Sweet Smell of Success (1957)
Tabu (1933)
Taxi Driver (1976)
Tevye (1939)
The Thief of Bagdad (1924)
To Be or Not To Be (1942)

To Fly (1976)
To Kill a Mockingbird (1962)
Topaz (1943-45)
Top Hat (1935)
Touch of Evil (1958)
The Treasure of the Sierra Madre (1948)
Trouble in Paradise (1932)
2001: A Space Odyssey (1968)
Verbena Tragica (1939)
Vertigo (1958)
What's Opera, Doc? (1957)
Where Are My Children? (1916)
The Wind (1928)
Within Our Gates (1920)
The Wizard of Oz (1939)
A Woman Under the Influence (1974)
Woodstock (1970)
Yankee Doodle Dandy (1942)
Zapruder Film (1963)

Record Long-Run Broadway Plays[1]

Source: The League of American Theatres and Producers, Inc., New York, NY

On June 19, 1997, *Cats* staged its 6,138th performance, putting it ahead of *A Chorus Line* as the longest running Broadway show in history.

Title	Performances	Title	Performances	Title	Performances
A Chorus Line	6,137	South Pacific	1,925	Dreamgirls	1,521
*Cats	6,117	Magic Show	1,920	Mame	1,508
Oh! Calcutta! (revival)	5,962	Gemini	1,819	Same Time, Next Year	1,453
*Les Miserables	4,183	Deathtrap	1,793	Arsenic and Old Lace	1,444
*Phantom of the Opera	3,902	Harvey	1,775	The Sound of Music	1,443
42nd Street	3,485	Dancin'	1,774	How to Succeed in Business	
Grease	3,388	La Cage aux Folles	1,761	Without Really Trying	
Fiddler on the Roof	3,242	Hair	1,750	(original)	1,417
Life With Father	3,224	The Wiz	1,672	Me and My Girl	1,409
Tobacco Road	3,182	Born Yesterday	1,642	Hellzapoppin	1,404
Hello Dolly	2,844	Crazy for You	1,638	The Music Man	1,365
My Fair Lady	2,717	Ain't Misbehavin'	1,604	Funny Girl	1,348
*Miss Saigon	2,560	Best Little Whorehouse in		Mumenschanz	1,328
Annie	2,377	Texas	1,584	Oh! Calcutta! (original)	1,314
Man of La Mancha	2,329	Mary, Mary	1,572	*Beauty and the Beast	1,312
Abie's Irish Rose	2,327	Evita	1,567	Brighton Beach Memoirs	1,299
Oklahoma!	2,212	Voice of the Turtle	1,557	Angel Street	1,295
Pippin	1,944	Barefoot in the Park	1,530	Lightnin'	1,291

(1) Number of performances through June 1, 1997. * Still running June 1, 1997.

Some Notable Broadway Theater Openings, 1996-97 Season

A Doll's House. A revival of the Henrik Ibsen drama. Directed by Anthony Page. With Janet McTeer and Anthony Page.

An American Daughter. A drama about a member of a prominent family awaiting senate confirmation as surgeon general. By Wendy Wasserstein. Directed by Daniel Sullivan. With Kate Nelligan, Hal Holbrook, Lynne Thigpen, and Peter Riegert.

Annie. A revival of the 1977 musical. Book by Thomas Meehan. Music by Charles Strouse. Lyrics by Martin Charnin. Directed by Charnin. With Nell Carter, Conrad John Schuck, and Brittny Kissinger.

Barrymore. A play about actor John Barrymore's attempt to recreate his legendary performance as Richard III. By William Luce. Directed by Gene Saks. With Christopher Plummer.

Chicago. A revival of the 1975 musical of love and murder. Book by Fred Ebb and Bob Fosse. Music and lyrics by John Kander and Ebb. Directed by Walter Bobbie. With Bebe Neuwirth, Ann Reinking, Joel Grey, and James Naughton.

The Gin Game. A revival of the 1977 drama about two older people. Book by D. L. Coburn. Directed by Charles Nelson Reilly. With Julie Harris and Charles Durning.

Jekyll and Hyde. A musical based on the Robert Louis Stevenson story. Book by Leslie Bricusse. Music by Frank Wildhorn. Lyrics by Bricusse. Directed by Robin Phillips. With Robert Cuccioli, Linda Eder, and Christiane Noll.

The Last Night of Ballyhoo. A romantic comedy about two women preparing for a major social event, the premiere of *Gone*

With the Wind, in 1939 Atlanta. Book by Alfred Uhry. Directed by Ron Lagomarsino. With Dana Ivey, Arija Bareikis, Terry Beaver, Jessica Hecht, Stephen Largay, Paul Rudd, and Celia Weston.

The Life. A musical about life on the street in the 1980s in Manhattan's Times Square. Book by David Newman, Ira Gasman, and Cy Coleman. Music by Coleman. Lyrics by Gasman. Directed by Michael Blakemore. With Pamela Isaacs, Kevin Ramsey, Lillias White, and Sam Harris.

Once Upon a Mattress. A revival of the 1959 musical comedy, based on the Hans Christian Andersen tale "Princess and the Pea." Book by Jay Thompson, Marshall Barer, and Dean Fuller. Music by Mary Rodgers. Lyrics by Barer. Directed by Gerald Gutierrez. With Sarah Jessica Parker.

Present Laughter. A revival of the Noel Coward comedy. Directed by Scott Elliott. With Frank Langella and Allison Janney.

Skylight. A drama about the meeting of two people after a three-year separation. By David Hare. Directed by Richard Eyre. With Michael Gambon and Lia Williams.

Titanic. A musical about the ill-fated ocean liner. Book by Peter Stone. Music and lyrics by Maury Yeston. Directed by Richard Jones. With Michael Cerveris, John Cunningham, Allan Corduner, Alma Cuervo, David Garrison, and Larry Keith.

The Young Man From Atlanta. A drama set in the 1950s in Houston about a couple attempting to cope with their only child's death. By Horton Foote. Directed by Robert Falls. With Rip Torn and Shirley Knight.

Some Notable Nonprofit Professional Theater Companies in the U.S.

Source: Theatre Communications Group, Inc., July 1997

Theater Company	City	State	Theater Company	City	State
Actors Theatre of Louisville	Louisville	KY	Intiman Theatre	Seattle	WA
Alabama Shakespeare Festival	Montgomery	AL	Long Wharf Theatre	New Haven	CT
Alley Theater	Houston	TX	Manhattan Theatre Club	New York	NY
Alliance Theatre Company	Atlanta	GA	Mark Taper Forum	Los Angeles	CA
American Conservatory Theatre	San Francisco	CA	McCarter Theatre	Princeton	NJ
American Repertory Theatre	Cambridge	MA	Milwaukee Repertory Theater	Milwaukee	WI
Arena Stage	Washington	DC	Missouri Repertory Theatre	Kansas City	MO
Arizona Theatre Company	Tucson	AZ	Oregon Shakespeare Festival	Ashland	OR
Asolo Center for Performing Arts	Sarasota	FL	People's Light and Theatre Company	Malvern	PA
Berkeley Repertory Theatre	Berkeley	CA	Pittsburgh Public Theater	Pittsburgh	PA
Center Stage	Baltimore	MD	Roundabout Theatre Company	New York	NY
Children's Theatre Company, The	Minneapolis	MN	San Jose Repertory Theatre	San Jose	CA
Cincinnati Playhouse in the Park	Cincinnati	OH	Seattle Children's Theatre	Seattle	WA
Cleveland Play House, The	Cleveland	OH	Seattle Repertory Theatre	Seattle	WA
Dallas Theater Center	Dallas	TX	South Coast Repertory	Costa Mesa	CA
Denver Center Theater Company	Denver	CO	Steppenwolf Theatre Company	Chicago	IL
GeVa Theatre	Rochester	NY	Studio Arena Theatre	Buffalo	NY
Goodman Theatre	Chicago	IL	TheatreWorks/USA	New York	NY
Great Lakes Theater Festival	Cleveland	OH	Trinity Repertory Theatre	Providence	RI
Guthrie Theater Foundation	Minneapolis	MN	Yale Repertory Theatre	New Haven	CT
Hartford Stage Company	Hartford	CT			
Huntington Theatre Company	Boston	MA			

Some Notable U.S. Symphony Orchestras

Source: American Symphony Orchestra League, 1156 Fifteenth St. NW, Suite 800, Washington, DC 20005; data as of Sept. 1997

Symphony Orchestra[1]	Music Director[2]	Symphony Orchestra[1]	Music Director[2]
Alabama Symphony (AL)	—	Music of the Baroque (IL)	Thomas S. Wikman
American Composers (NY)	Dennis Russell Davies	Naples Philharmonic (FL)	Christopher Seaman
American (NY)	Leon Botstein	Nashville Symphony (TN)	Kenneth S. Schermerhorn
Atlanta (GA)	Yoel Levi	National (Washington, DC)	Leonard Slatkin
Austin (TX)	—	New Haven (CT)	Michael Palmer
Baltimore (MD)	David Zinman	New Jersey (Newark)	Zdenek Macal
Baton Rouge (LA)	James Paul	New Mexico (Albuquerque)	David Lockington
Boston (MA)	Seiji Ozawa	New West (CA)	Boris Brott
Brooklyn Philharmonic (NY)	Robert Spano	New World Symphony (Miami Beach, FL)	Michael Tilson Thomas
Buffalo Philharmonic (NY)	Maximiano Valdez	New York Chamber Sym. of the 92nd St. Y (NYC)	Gerard Schwarz
Cedar Rapids (IA)	Christian Tiemeyer	New York Philharmonic (NYC)	Kurt Masur
Charleston (SC)	David Stahl	New York Pops (NY)	Skitch Henderson
Charlotte (NC)	Peter McCoppin	North Carolina (Raleigh)	Gerhardt Zimmermann
Chattanooga, & Opera Assn. (TN)	Robert Bernhardt	Northeastern Pennsylvania (Philadelphia)	Hugh Keelan
Chicago (IL)	Daniel Barenboim	Ohio Chamber Orchestra (OH)	—
Chicago Sinfonietta (IL)	Paul Freeman	Oklahoma City Philharmonic (OK)	Joel A. Levine
Cincinnati (OH)	Jesus Lopez-Cobos	Omaha (NE)	Victor Yampolsky
Cleveland (OH)	Christoph von Dohnányi	Oregon (Portland)	James DePreist
Colorado (Denver)	Marin Alsop	Pacific Symphony (Irvine, CA)	Carl St. Clair
Colorado Springs (CO)	Yaacov Bergman	Pasadena (CA)	Jorge Mester
Columbus (OH)	Alessandro Siciliani	Philadelphia (PA)	Wolfgang Sawallisch
Dallas (TX)	Andrew Litton	Phoenix (AZ)	Hermann Michael
Dayton Philharmonic (OH)	Neal Gittleman	Philharmonia Baroque (CA)	Nicholas McGegan
Delaware (Wilmington)	Stephen Gunzenhauser	Pittsburgh (PA)	Mariss Jansons
Des Moines (IA)	Joseph S. Giunta	Portland (ME)	Toshiyuki Shimada
Detroit (MI)	Neeme Jarvi	Rhode Island Philharmonic Orch. (Providence)	Larry Rachleff
El Paso (TX)	Gurer Aykal	Richmond Symphony (VA)	George Manahan
Erie Philharmonic (PA)	Peter Bay	Rochester Philharmonic Orch. (NY)	Robert Bernhardt
The Florida Orchestra (Tampa)	Jahja Ling	St. Louis (MO)	Hans Vonk
Florida Philharmonic (Ft. Lauderdale)	James Judd	St. Paul Chamber Orch. (MN)	Hugh Wolff
Florida Symphonic Pops (Boca Raton)	Crafton Beck	San Antonio (TX)	Christopher P. Wilkins
Florida West Coast (FL)	Leif Bjaland	San Francisco (CA)	Michael Tilson Thomas
Fort Wayne Philharmonic (IN)	Edward Chivzel	San Jose (CA)	Leonid Grin
Fort Worth (TX)	John Giordano	Santa Barbara (CA)	Gisele Ben-Dor
Grand Rapids (MI)	Catherine Comet	Savannah (GA)	Philip B. Greenberg
Grant Park (Chicago, IL)	Hugh Wolff	Seattle (WA)	Gerard Schwarz
Harrisburg (PA)	Richard Westerfield	Shreveport (LA)	Dennis Simons
Hartford (CT)	Michael Lankester	Spokane (WA)	Fabio Mechetti
Houston (TX)	Christoph Eschenbach	Springfield (MA)	Mark Russell Smith
Hudson Valley Philharmonic (Poughkeepsie, NY)	Randall Craig Fleischer	Syracuse (NY)	Fabio Mechetti
Indianapolis (IN)	Raymond Leppard	Toledo (OH)	Andrew Massey
Jacksonville (FL)	Roger Nierenberg	Tucson (AZ)	George Hanson
Kalamazoo (MI)	Yoshimi Takeda	Tulsa Philharmonic (OK)	Kenneth Jean
Kansas City (MO)	Joseph Silverstein	Utah (Salt Lake City)	Joseph Silverstein
Knoxville (TN)	Kirk Trevor	Virginia Symphony (Norfolk)	JoAnn Falletta
Long Beach (CA)	JoAnn Falletta	West Virginia (Charleston)	Thomas B. Conlin
Long Island Philharmonic (NY)	David Lockington	Wichita (KS)	Zuohuang Chen
Los Angeles Chamber Orch. (CA)	Iona Brown	Winston-Salem Piedmont Triad Symphony (NC)	Peter J. Perret
Los Angeles Philharmonic (CA)	Esa-Pekka Salonen		
Louisville Orchestra (KY)	Max Bragado-Darman		
Memphis (TN)	—		
Milwaukee (WI)	Andreas Delfs		
Minnesota (Minneapolis)	Eiji Oue		
Mississippi (Jackson)	Colman Pearce		

(1) Orchestra name = place name + Symphony Orchestra, unless otherwise noted. (2) General title; listed is highest-ranking member of conducting personnel. — indicates that a new music director was being sought.

U.S. Opera Companies With Budgets of $500,000 or More

Source: OPERA America, 1156 15th Street NW, Washington, DC 20005-1704; July 1997

Academy of Vocal Arts Opera Theatre (Philadelphia, PA); K. James McDowell, dir.
Albuquerque Civic Light Opera (NM); Reuben Murray, exec. dir.
American Music Theater Festival (Phila.); Marjorie Samoff, prod. dir.
American Musical Theater of San Jose (CA); Dianna Shuster, dir.
Anchorage Opera (AK); Peter Brown, gen. dir.
Arizona Opera Co. (Tucson); Glynn Ross, gen. dir.
Aspen Opera Theatre Center (CO); Edward Dwooney, gen. mgr.
Atlanta Opera (GA); Alfred Kennedy, exec. dir.
Augusta Opera (GA); Edward Bradberry, gen. dir.
Austin Lyric Opera (TX); Joseph McClain, gen. dir.
Baltimore Opera Co. (MD); Michael Harrison, gen. dir.
Boston Festival Opera Ltd.; David Spiro, art. dir.
Boston Lyric Opera Co.; Janice Mancini Del Sesto, gen. dir.
Brooklyn Academy of Music; Harvey Lichtenstein, exec. prod.
Central City Opera (Denver, CO); Pelham Pearce, gen. mgr.
Chautauqua Opera (NY); Jay Lesenger, gen. dir.
Chicago Opera Theater; Mark Tiarks, gen. dir.
Cincinnati Opera; Paul A. Stuhlreyer III, mng. dir.
Cleveland Opera; David Bamberger, gen. dir.
Connecticut Opera (Hartford); George Osborne, gen. dir.
Dallas Opera; Plato Karayanis, gen. dir.
Dayton Opera Assn. (OH); Paul A. Stuhlreyer III, gen. dir.
Des Moines Metro Opera (Indianola, IA); Jerilee Mace, exec. dir.
Florentine Opera (Milwaukee), Dennis Hanthorn, gen. mgr.
Florida Grand Opera; Robert Heuer, gen. mgr.
Fort Worth Opera; William Walker, gen. dir.
Fullerton Civic Light Opera (CA); Griff Duncan, gen. mgr.
Glimmerglass Opera (Cooperstown, NY); Esther Nelson, gen. dir.
Goodspeed Opera House (E. Haddam, CT); Michael Price, exec. dir.
Greater Buffalo Opera (NY); Gary Burgess, gen. dir.
Hawaii Opera Theatre; Henry Akina, gen. dir.
Houston Grand Opera Assn.; David Gockley, gen. dir
Indianapolis Opera Company; James Caraher, art. dir.
Kentucky Opera Assn. (Louisville); William P. Winkler, exec. dir.
Knoxville Opera (TN); Robert Lyall, gen. dir.
L.A. Opera; Peter Hemmings, gen. dir.
Light Opera Works (Evanston, IL); Bridget McDonough, mgr. dir.
Long Beach Civic Light Opera (CA); Luke Yankee, prod. art. dir.
Long Beach Opera (CA); Michael Milenski, gen. dir.
Lyric Opera of Chicago; William Mason, gen. dir.
Lyric Opera of Kansas City (MO); Russell Patterson, gen. dir./art. dir.
Metro Lyric Opera (NJ); Era M. Tognoli, gen. & art. dir.
Metropolitan Opera Assn. (NYC); Joseph Volpe, gen. mgr.
Michigan Opera Theatre (Detroit); David DiChiera, gen. dir.
Minnesota Opera Co. (St. Paul); Kevin Smith, gen. dir.
Music-Theatre Group (NY & Stockbridge, MA); Lyn Austin, prod. dir.
Nashville Opera Association; Carol Peterman, exec. dir
Nevada Opera (Reno); Frank D. Kistler, gen. dir.
New England Marionette Opera (Peterborough, NH); Edward Leach, gen. dir.
New Jersey State Opera (Newark); Alfredo Silipigni, art. dir.

New Orleans Opera Assn.; Ray Anthony Delia, exec. dir.
New York City Opera Natl. Co.; Clifford Kellas, tour coordinator
New York City Opera; Paul Kellogg, gen. dir.
New York Gilbert & Sullivan Players, Inc. (NYC); Albert Bergeret, art. dir.
Ohio Light Opera; James Stuart, art. dir
Opera Carolina (Charlotte, NC); James Wright, gen. dir.
Opera Colorado (Denver); Nathaniel Merrill, art. dir.
Opera Company of Boston; Sarah Caldwell, art. dir.
Opera Company of Philadelphia; Robert B. Driver, gen. dir.
Opera Festival of NJ (Princeton Junction); Deborah S. Sandler, gen. dir.
Opera Grand Rapids (MI); Robert Lyall, gen. dir.
Opera Memphis (TN); Michael Ching, gen./art. dir
Opera Northeast (NY); Donald Westwood, art. dir.
Opera Omaha (NE); Jane Hill, exec. dir.
Opera Orchestra of NY (NYC); Eve Queler, art dir
Opera Pacific (Irvine, CA); Patrick L. Veitch, gen. dir.
Opera San Jose (CA); Irene Dalis, gen. dir.
Opera Theatre of St. Louis (MO); Charles MacKay, gen. dir.
Opera/Columbus (OH); William F. Russell, gen. dir.
Opera Delaware (Wilmington); Leland Kimball, gen. dir.
Orlando Opera Co. (FL); Robert Swedberg, gen. dir.
Palm Beach Opera (FL); Herbert P. Benn, gen. dir.
Pittsburgh Civic Light Opera; Van Kaplan, exec. dir.
Pittsburgh Opera; Mark Weinstein, exec. dir.
Playwrights Horizons (NYC); Tim Sanford, art. dir.
Portland Opera Assn. (OR); Robert Bailey, exec. dir.
Sacramento Opera Assn. (CA); Marianne H. Oaks, gen. dir.
St. Ann Center for Restoration and the Arts (Brooklyn, NY); Susan Feldman, art. dir.
San Bernardino Civic Light Opera Association (CA); Keith Stava, gen. mgr.
San Diego Civic Light Opera Assn.; Leon Drew, gen. mgr.
San Diego Opera Assn.; Ian Campbell, gen. dir.
San Francisco Opera; Lotfi Mansouri, gen. dir.
San Francisco Opera Center; Christopher Hahn, dir.
Santa Barbara Civic Light Opera (CA); Paul Iannacone, exec. prod.
Santa Fe Opera (NM); John Crosby, dir.
Sarasota Opera Assn. (FL); Deane Allyn, exec. dir.
Seattle Opera Assn.; Speight Jenkins, gen. dir.
Skylight Opera Theatre (Milwaukee); Joan Lounsbery, mng. dir.
Southeastern Regional Opera (SC); Einar Anderson, art. dir.
Summer Opera Theatre Company (DC); Elaine Walter, gen. mgr.
Syracuse Opera (NY); Catherine Wolff, gen. dir.
Teatro de la Opera (PR); José A. Rey, art. dir.
Tri-Cities Opera (Binghamton, NY); Susan MacLennan, exec. dir.
Tulsa Opera (OK); Carol Crawford, gen. dir.
Utah Festival Opera Company; Michael Ballam, gen. dir.
Utah Opera (Salt Lake City); Anne Ewers, gen. dir.
Virginia Opera (Norfolk); Peter Mark, gen. dir.
Washington Opera (DC); Patricia Mossel, exec. dir.
Wolf Trap Opera (Vienna, VA); Peter Russell, gen. dir.

Some Notable U.S. Dance Companies

Source: Reviewed by Gary Parks, Reviews Editor, *Dance* magazine

African-American Dance Ensemble, Durham, NC
Alvin Ailey American Dance Theater, New York, NY
Aman Folk Ensemble, Los Angeles, CA
American Ballet Theatre, New York, NY
American Indian Dance Theater, New York, NY
American Repertory Ballet, Princeton, NJ
Atlanta Ballet, GA
Ballet Austin, Austin, TX
Ballet Concierto de Puerto Rico, Santurce, PR
Ballet Florida, West Palm Beach, FL
Ballet Hispanico of New York, New York, NY
BalletMet Columbus, Columbus, OH
Ballet Tech, New York, NY
Ballet West, Salt Lake City, UT
Les Ballets Trockadero de Monte Carlo, New York, NY
Tandy Beal and Company, Santa Cruz, CA
Maria Benitez Teatro Flamenco, Santa Fe, NM
Boston Ballet, Boston, MA
Trisha Brown Company, New York, NY
Donald Byrd/The Group, New York, NY
Chen & Dancers, New York, NY
Yoshiko Chuma and the School of Hard Knocks, New York, NY
Cincinnati Ballet, Cincinnati, OH
Cleveland San Jose Ballet, Cleveland, OH
Colorado Ballet, Denver, CO
Merce Cunningham Dance Company, New York, NY
Dallas Black Dance Theatre, Dallas, TX
Dance Alloy, Pittsburgh, PA
Dance Theatre of Harlem, New York, NY
Della Davidson Dance Company, San Francisco, CA

Dayton Ballet, Dayton, OH
Dayton Contemporary Dance Company, Dayton, OH
Eiko & Koma, New York, NY
Eisenhower Dance Ensemble, Rochester, MI
Eugene Ballet Company, Eugene, OR
Garth Fagan Dance, Rochester, NY
Fort Worth Dallas Ballet, Fort Worth, TX
Gus Giordano Jazz Dance Chicago, Evanston, IL
Joe Goode Performance Group, San Francisco, CA
David Gordon/Pick Up Co., New York, NY
Martha Graham Dance Co., New York, NY
Hartford Ballet, Hartford, CT
Erick Hawkins Dance Co., New York, NY
Joseph Holmes Dance Theater, Chicago, IL
Houston Ballet, Houston, TX
Hubbard Street Dance Chicago, Chicago, IL
Indianapolis Ballet Theatre, Indianapolis, IN
Isaacs, McCaleb & Dancers, San Diego, CA
Jazzdance by Danny Buraczeski, Minneapolis, MN
Jazz Tap Ensemble, Los Angeles, CA
Margaret Jenkins Dance Company, San Francisco, CA
The Joffrey Ballet, Chicago, IL
Bill T. Jones/Arnie Zane Dance Company, New York, NY
Demetrius Klein Dance Company, Lake Worth, FL
Ko-Thi Dance Company, Milwaukee, WI
Liz Lerman Dance Exchange, Washington, DC
Limón Dance Company, New York, NY
LINES Contemporary Ballet, San Francisco, CA
Loretta Livingston and Dancers, Los Angeles, CA
Murray Louis and Nikolais Dance, New York, NY

(continued)

Some Notable U.S. Dance Companies *(continued)*

Lar Lubovitch Dance Company, New York, NY
Malashock Dance Company, San Diego, CA
Susan Marshall and Company, New York, NY
Miami City Ballet, Miami Beach, FL
Elisa Monte Dance Company, New York, NY
Mark Morris Dance Group, New York, NY
Jennifer Muller/The Works, New York, NY
Muntu Dance Theatre, Chicago, IL
Nevada Dance Theatre, Las Vegas, NV
New York City Ballet, New York, NY
North Carolina Dance Theatre, Charlotte, NC
Oakland Ballet, Oakland, CA
ODC/San Francisco, San Francisco, CA
Ohio Ballet, Akron, OH
Oregon Ballet Theatre, Portland, OR
Pacific Northwest Ballet, Seattle, WA
Parsons Dance Company, New York, NY
Pennsylvania Ballet, Philadelphia, PA
Pepatián, Bronx, NY
Stephen Petronio Company, New York, NY
Philadanco, Philadelphia, PA

Pilobolus Dance Theater, Washington, CT
Pittsburgh Ballet Theatre, Pittsburgh, PA
Richmond Ballet, Richmond, VA
Ririe-Woodbury Dance Company, Salt Lake City, UT
Cleo Parker Robinson Dance Ensemble, Denver, CO
San Francisco Ballet, San Francisco, CA
Carlota Santana Spanish Dance Arts Co., New York, NY
James Sewell Ballet, Minneapolis, MN
Sharir Dance Company, Austin, TX
Solomons Company/Dance, New York, NY
State Ballet of Missouri, Kansas City, MO
Elizabeth Streb Ringside, New York, NY
Paul Taylor Dance Company, New York, NY
Tharp!, New York, NY
Trinity Irish Dance Company, Evanston, IL
Tulsa Ballet, Tulsa, OK
Urban Bush Women, New York, NY
Washington Ballet, Washington, DC
June Watanabe in Company, San Rafael, CA
Zivili, Granville, OH

100 Best-Selling U.S. Magazines, 1996

Source: Audit Bureau of Circulations, Schaumburg, IL

General magazines, exclusive of groups and comics; also excluding magazines that failed to file reports to ABC by press time. Based on total average paid circulation during the 6 months ending Dec. 31, 1996.

Magazine	Circulation	Magazine	Circulation	Magazine	Circulation
1. NRTA/AARP Bulletin	20,567,352	34. Martha Stewart Living	2,025,182	69. Vanity Fair	1,115,760
2. Modern Maturity	20,528,786	35. Money	1,993,119	70. The American Hunter	1,114,553
3. Reader's Digest	15,072,260	36. V.F.W. Magazine	1,980,947	71. Scholastic Parent &	
4. TV Guide	13,013,938	37. Ebony	1,803,566	Child	1,095,681
5. NationalGeographic		38. Popular Science	1,793,192	72. PC World	1,091,987
Magazine	9,025,003	39. Field & Stream	1,750,180	73. The Family Handyman	1,089,755
6. Better Homes and		40. Parents	1,737,249	74. Us	1,083,639
Gardens	7,605,325	41. Country Living	1,674,925	75. Endless Vacation	1,083,582
7. Family Circle	5,239,074	42. Life	1,601,069	76. Scouting	1,062,843
8. Good Housekeeping	4,951,240	43. American Rifleman	1,545,242	77. Parenting Magazine	1,060,360
9. Ladies' Home Journal	4,544,416	44. Golf Digest	1,515,829	78. Country Home	1,043,599
10. Woman's Day	4,317,604	45. Woman's World	1,504,067	79. Sesame Street	
11. McCall's	4,290,216	46. Soap Opera Digest	1,468,333	Magazine	1,032,627
12. Time	4,102,168	47. Sunset	1,431,549	80. AAA Going Places	1,029,054
13. Car & Travel Magazine	3,975,761	48. Popular Mechanics	1,428,356	81. Home	1,017,227
14. People Weekly	3,449,852	49. Cooking Light	1,379,055	82. Motor Trend	1,013,326
15. Prevention	3,311,244	50. Men's Health	1,373,817	83. PC/Computing	1,005,213
16. Playboy	3,236,517	51. Outdoor Life	1,353,061	84. Penthouse	1,005,006
17. Newsweek	3,194,769	52. First for Women	1,331,399	85. Essence	1,000,208
18. Sports Illustrated	3,173,639	53. 'Teen	1,327,893	86. Travel & Leisure	990,115
19. Redbook	2,926,702	54. Rolling Stone	1,298,631	87. Disney Adventures	977,349
20. The American Legion		55. Golf Magazine	1,292,980	88. Weight Watchers	
Magazine	2,777,351	56. Entertainment		Magazine	976,063
21. Home & Away	2,719,931	Weekly	1,280,230	89. In Style	950,680
22. Avenues	2,549,695	57. Boys' Life	1,267,283	90. Health	943,543
23. Southern Living	2,490,542	58. Consumers Digest	1,259,422	91. Victoria	943,125
24. Cosmopolitan	2,486,393	59. The Elks Magazine	1,250,475	92. Shape	931,893
25. National Enquirer	2,480,349	60. Discover	1,228,111	93. American Homestyle &	
26. Seventeen	2,442,090	61. New Woman	1,222,143	Gardening	930,155
27. Motorland	2,376,974	62. Mademoiselle	1,206,054	94. Jet	925,308
28. U.S. News & World		63. Bon Appetit	1,197,505	95. Elle	924,242
Report	2,260,857	64. Vogue	1,190,018	96. Globe	905,338
29. Star	2,220,711	65. Self	1,159,305	97. True Story Plus	904,813
30. NEA Today	2,168,447	66. PC Magazine	1,151,473	98. Country America	902,122
31. YM	2,153,815	67. Kiplinger's Personal		99. Today's Homeowner	901,266
32. Glamour	2,115,488	Finance Magazine	1,148,760	100. Business Week	893,771
33. Smithsonian	2,095,819	68. Car and Driver	1,122,047		

Some Notable Books, 1997

Source: List published by American Library Association, Chicago, IL, 1997, for books published in 1996 calendar year

Fiction

Behind the Scenes at the Museum, Kate Atkinson
Ship Fever and Other Stories, Andrea Barrett
Drown, Junot Diaz
The Woman Who Walked Into Doors, Roddy Doyle
Middle Son, Deborah Iida
A Fine Balance, Rohinton Mistry
Asking for Love, Roxana Robinson
Funny Boy, Shyam Selvadurai
Last Orders, Graham Swift
After Rain, William Trevor
The Night in Question, Tobias Wolff

Poetry

The Spirit Level, Seamus Heaney
The Legend of Light, Bob Hicok
Otherwise, Jane Kenyon

Nonfiction

Undaunted Courage: Meriwether Lewis, Thomas Jefferson, and the Opening of the American West, Stephen E. Ambrose
Great Books: My Adventure with Homer, Rousseau, Woolf, and Other Indestructible Writers of the Western World, David Denby
Like Judgment Day: The Ruin and Redemption of a Town Called Rosewood, Michael D'Orso

Dubious Conceptions: The Politics of Teenage Pregnanacy, Kristin Luker
A History of Reading, Alberto Manguel
The Color of Water: A Black Man's Tribute to His White Mother, James McBride
Angela's Ashes, Frank McCourt
God Has Ninety-Nine Names: Reporting From a Militant Middle East, Judith Miller
Showing My Color: Impolite Essays on Race and Identity, Clarence Page
Sojourner Truth: A Life, a Symbol, Nell Irvin Painter
The Song of the Dodo, David Quammen
Longitude: The True Story of a Lone Genius Who Solved the Greatest Scientific Problem of His Time, Dava Sobel

Notable Books for Children and Young Adults, 1997

Source: From list published by American Library Association, Chicago, IL, 1997, for books published in the 1996 calendar year

All Ages

Come Sunday, Nikki Grimes
When Birds Could Talk and Bats Could Sing: The Adventures of Bruh Sparrow, Sis Wren, and Their Friends Virgina Hamilton
Maples in the Mist: Children's Poems From the Tang Dynasty, Minfong Ho
Grandmother Bryant's Pocket, Jacqueline Briggs Martin
The Graphic Alphabet, David Pelletier
Earth Always Endures: Native American Poems, Neil Philip
Nursery Tales Around the World, Judy Sierra
O Jerusalem, Jane Yolen
Beni's Family Cookbook for the Jewish Holidays, Jane Breskin Zalben

Younger Readers

The Story of Little Babaji, Helen Bannerman
Fanny's Dream, Caralyn Buehner
My Brother, Ant, Betsy Byars
Animal Crackers: A Delectable Collection of Pictures, Poems, and Lullabies for the Very Young, Jane Dyer
Where Once There Was a Wood, Denise Fleming
Lilly's Purple Plastic Purse, Kevin Henkes
Hush! A Thai Lullaby, Minfong Ho
Sam and the Tigers: A New Telling of Little Black Sambo, Julius Lester
Jelly Beans for Sale, Bruce McMillan
My Very First Mother Goose, Iona Opie, ed.
The Paperboy, Dav Pilkey
The Squiggle, Carole Lexa Schaefer
The Day Gogo Went to Vote: South Africa, April 1994, Elinor Batezat Sisulu

Middle Grade Readers

Growing Up in Coal Country, Susan Campbell Bartoletti
Anastasia's Album, Hugh Brewster
Train to Somewhere, Eve Bunting
The Rooster's Gift, Pam Conrad
Eleanor, Barbara Cooney
The Apprenticeship of Lucas Whitaker, Cynthia DeFelice
The Bone Detectives: How Forensic Anthropologists Solve Crimes and Uncover Mysteries of the Dead, Donna M. Jackson

Small Steps: The Year I Got Polio, Peg Kehret
Wilma Unlimited: How Wilma Rudolph Became the World's Fastest Woman, Kathleen Krull
Mysterious Tales of Japan, Rafe Martin
Toussaint L'Ouverture: The Fight for Haiti's Freedom, Walter Dean Myers
Ogbo: Sharing Life in an African Village, Ifeoma Onyefulu
Jip, His Story, Katherine Paterson
Four Perfect Pebbles: A Holocaust Story, Lila Perl and Marion Blumenthal Lazen
Bill Pickett: Rodeo-Ridin' Cowboy, Andrea D. Pickney
What Zeesie Saw on Delancey Street, Elsa Okon Rael
Minty: A Story of Young Harriet Tubman, Alan Schroeder
Starry Messenger, Peter Sis
Leonardo Da Vinci, Diane Stanley
Orphan Train Rider: One Boy's True Story, Andrea Warren
Golem, David Wisniewski
The Friends, Kazumi Yumoto

Junior High School Age-Readers

Cold Shoulder Road, Joan Aiken
Granny the Pag, Nina Bawden
A Girl Named Disaster, Nancy Farmer
The Abracadabra Kid: A Writer's Life, Sid Fleischman
The Life and Death of Crazy Horse, Russell Freedman
The View from Saturday, E.L. Konigsburg
Winning Ways: A Photohistory of American Women in Sports, Sue Macy
The Moorchild, Eloise McGraw
Sabriel, Garth Nix
The Golden Compass, Philip Pullman
John Steinbeck, Catherine Reef
Remembering Mog, Colby Rodowsky
The Smithsonian Book of First Ladies: Their Lives, Times, and Issues, Edith P. Mayo, ed.
Big Annie of Calumet: A True Story of the Industrial Revolution, Jerry Stanley
The Thief, Megan Whalen Turner
Belle Prater's Boy, Ruth White

Young Adult (Teenage)—Fiction

Beyond the Western Sea:, The Escape From Home, Avi
The Lost Years of Merlin, T.A. Barron

The China Garden, Liz Berry
Pastwatch: The Redemption of Christopher Columbus, Orson Scott Card
My Father's Scar, Michael Cart
Another Kind of Monday, William E. Coles
Trout Summer, Jane Leslie Conly
The Voice on the Radio, Caroline B. Cooney
That Summer, Sarah Dessen
Bruises, Anke De Vries
A Girl Named Disaster, Nancy Farmer
The Cuckoo's Child, Suzanne Freeman
Nathan's Run, John Gilstrap
Wildside, Steven Gould
Don't You Dare Read This, Mrs. Dunphrey, Margaret Peterson Haddix
Running Out of Time, Margaret Peterson Haddix
My Sister's Bones, Cathi Hanauer
Mr. Was, Pete Hautman
The Music of Dolphins, Karen Hesse
Far North, Will Hobbs
Land Girls, Angela Huth
The Window, Jeanette Ingold
The Sandy Bottom Orchestra, Garrison Keillor and Jenny Lind Nilson
Danger Zone, David Klass
Johnny Voodoo, Dakota Lane
Run for Your Life, Marilyn Levy
After the War, Carol Matas
Adem's Cross, Alice Mead
Gideon's People, Carolyn Meyer
Slam!, Walter Dean Meyers
Song of the Magdalene, Donna Jo Napoli
Sabriel, Garth Nix
Jip, His Story, Katherine Paterson
The Final Journey, Gudrun Pausewang
Don't Think Twice, Ruth Pennebaker
The Golden Compass, Philip Pullman
Hang a Thousand Trees With Ribbons, Ann Rinaldi
The Sin Eater, Gary D. Schmidt
Another Way to Dance, Martha Southgate
Crash, Jerry Spinelli
Dangerous Skies, Suzanne Fisher Staples
The Ornament Tree, Jean Thesman
Rats Saw God, Rob Thomas
The Thief, Megan Whalen Turner
Wrestling Sturbridge, Rich Wallace
I Want to Buy a Vowel, John Welter
Gulf, Robert Westall
Belle Prater's Boy, Ruth White

Best-Selling Books, 1996

Source: *Publishers Weekly,* Apr.7, 1997

Rankings are determined by sales figures provided by publishers, based on copies "shipped and billed" in 1996, minus returns through Feb. 24, 1997.

Hardcover Fiction

1. *The Runaway Jury,* John Grisham
2. *Executive Orders,* Tom Clancy
3. *Desperation,* Stephen King
4. *Airframe,* Michael Crichton
5. *The Regulators,* Richard Bachman
6. *Malice,* Danielle Steele
7. *Silent Honor,* Danielle Steele
8. *Primary Colors,* Anonymous
9. *Cause of Death,* Patricia Cornwell
10. *The Tenth Insight,* James Redfield
11. *The Deep End of the Ocean,* Jacquelyn Mitchard
12. *How Stella Got Her Groove Back,* Terry McMillan
13. *Moonlight Becomes You,* Mary Higgins Clark
14. *My Gal Sunday,* Mary Higgins Clark
15. *The Celestine Prophecy,* James Redfield

Hardcover Nonfiction

1. *Make the Connection,* Oprah Winfrey and Bob Greene
2. *Men Are From Mars, Women Are From Venus,* John Gray
3. *The Dilbert Principle,* Scott Adams
4. *Simple Abundance,* Sarah Ban Breathnach
5. *The Zone,* Barry Sears with Bill Lawren
6. *Bad As I Wanna Be,* Dennis Rodman
7. *In Contempt,* Christopher Darden
8. *A Reporter's Life,* Walter Conkrite
9. *Dogbert's Top Secret Management Handbook,* Scott Adams
10. *My Sergei: A Love Story,* Ekaterina Gordeeva with E.M. Swift

11. *Gift and Mystery,* Pope John Paul II
12. *I'm Not Really Here,* Tim Allen
13. *Rush Limbaugh Is a Big Fat Idiot and Other Observations,* Al Franken
14. *James Herriot's Favorite Dog Stories,* James Herriot
15. *My Story,* Sarah, Duchess of York

Trade Paperback

1. *A 3rd Serving of Chicken Soup for the Soul,* eds., Jack Canfield and Mark Hansen
2. *Snow Falling on Cedars,* David Guterson
3. *It's a Magical World: A Calvin and Hobbes Collection,* Bill Watterson
4. *There's Treasure Everywhere: A Calvin and Hobbes Collection,* Bill Watterson
5. *Chicken Soup for the Woman's Soul,* eds., Jack Canfield, Mark Victor Hansen, Jennifer Read Hawthorne and Marci Shimoff
6. *A Journal of Daily Renewal: The Companion to Make the Connection,* Bob Greene and Oprah Winfrey
7. *Windows 95 for Dummies,* Andy Rathbone
8. *Fugitive From the Cubicle Police: A Dilbert Book,* Scott Adams
9. *The Last Chapter and Worse: A Far Side Collection,* Gary Larson
10. *The English Patient (movie tie-in),* Michael Ondaatje
11. *Reviving Ophelia,* Mary Pipher
12. *Microsoft Windows 95 Resource Kit,* Microsoft Publishers
13. *Still Pumped From Using the Mouse: A Dilbert Book,* Scott Adams
14. *SSN: A Strategy Guide to Submarine Warfare,* Tom Clancy
15. *Dr. Atkins' New Diet Revolution,* Robert Atkins

Mass-Market Paperback

1. *The Rainmaker*, John Grisham
2. *The Green Mile, Part 1: The Two Dead Girls*, Stephen King
3. *The Green Mile, Part 2: The Mouse on the Mile*, Stephen King
4. *The Green Mile, Part 3: Coffey's Hands*, Stephen King
5. *The Green Mile, Part 5: Night Journey*, Stephen King
6. *The Green Mile, Part 4: The Bad Death of Eduard Delacroix*, Stephen King
7. *The Green Mile, Part 6: Coffey on the Mile*, Stephen King
8. *The Gift*, Danielle Steele
9. *Lightninig*, Danielle Steele
10. *The Lost World*, Michael Crichton
11. *Let Me Call You Sweetheart*, Mary Higgins Clark
12. *The Horse Whisperer*, Nicholas Evans
13. *Rose Madder*, Stephen King
14. *Tom Clancy's Op-Center (III): Games of the State*, Tom Clancy and Steve Pieczenik
15. *From Potter's Field*, Patricia Cornwell

Almanacs, Atlases, and Annuals

1. *The World Almanac and Book of Facts 1997*, ed. Robert Famighetti
2. *The Universal Almanac 1997*, ed. John Wright
3. *The World Almanac for Kids 1997*, ed. Judith Levey
4. *What Color Is Your Parachute? 1996*, Richard Nelson Bolles
5. *The World Almanac and Book of Facts 1996*, ed. Robert Famighetti

Leading U.S. Daily Newspapers, 1996

Source: *1997 Editor & Publisher International Yearbook*

(Circulation as of Sept. 30, 1996; m = morning, e = evening)

As of Feb. 1, 1997, the number of U.S. daily newspapers had declined to 1,520, a net loss of 13, since Feb. 1, 1996. Average daily circulation for the 6-month period ending Sept. 30, 1996 was 56,983,290, down 1,210,101 from that for the same period in 1995. The large decrease can be partially attributed to newspaper circulation cutbacks in areas that do not generate profit or advertising revenue. Sunday editions increased by 2, to a total of 890, during 1996. Average Sunday circulation for the 6-month period ending Sept. 30, 1996, fell 731,482, to 60,797,814, despite the addition of Sunday editions of the *New York Post* and *Journal Newspapers of Fairfax*, VA. The decline in both daily and Sunday circulation can be partially traced to large drops in the circulation of the *Detroit News* and *Free Press*.

Newspaper		Circulation		Newspaper		Circulation
1. *Wall Street Journal* (New York, NY)	(m)	1,783,532	51.	*Express-News* (San Antonio, TX)	(m)	215,593
2. *USA Today* (Arlington, VA)	(m)	1,591,629	52.	*Courant* (Hartford, CT)	(m)	208,844
3. *Times* (New York, NY)	(m)	1,071,120	53.	*Times-Dispatch* (Richmond, VA)	(m)	208,632
4. *Times* (Los Angeles, CA)	(m)	1,029,073	54.	*Enquirer* (Cincinnati, OH)	(m)	205,233
5. *Post* (Washington, DC)	(m)	789,198	55.	*Daily Oklahoman* (Oklahoma City, OK)	(m)	203,705
6. *Daily News* (New York, NY)	(m)	734,277	56.	*Pioneer Press* (St. Paul, MN)	(m)	203,601
7. *Tribune* (Chicago, IL)	(m)	680,535	57.	*Virginian-Pilot* (Norfolk, VA)	(m)	201,683
8. *Newsday* (Long Island, NY)	(m)	564,754	58.	*Daily News* (Los Angeles, CA)	(m)	200,655
9. *Chronicle* (Houston, TX)	(m)	545,348	59.	*Post-Intelligencer* (Seattle, WA)	(m)	198,385
10. *Sun-Times* (Chicago, IL)	(m)	496,030	60.	*Times-Union* (Jacksonville, FL)	(m)	187,207
11. *Chronicle* (San Francisco, CA)	(m)	486,977	61.	*American-Statesman* (Austin, TX)	(m)	181,272
12. *Morning News* (Dallas, TX)	(m)	478,181	62.	*Palm Beach Post* (West Palm Beach, FL)	(m)	175,003
13. *Globe* (Boston, MA)	(m)	471,024	63.	*Daily News* (Philadelphia, PA)	(m)	174,595
14. *Post* (New York, NY)	(m)	429,642	64.	*Democrat-Gazette* (Little Rock, AR)	(m)	172,223
15. *Inquirer* (Philadelphia, PA)	(m)	427,175	65.	*Journal* (Providence, RI)	(m)	171,824
16. *Star-Ledger* (Newark, NJ)	(m)	405,869	66.	*Commercial Appeal* (Memphis, TN)	(m)	170,952
17. *Star Tribune* (Minneapolis, MN)	(m)	393,740	67.	*Register* (Des Moines, IA)	(m)	169,898
18. *Plain Dealer* (Cleveland, OH)	(m)	386,256	68.	*News* (Birmingham, AL)	(m)	167,865
19. *Arizona Republic* (Phoenix, AZ)	(m)	382,122	69.	*Press-Enterprise* (Riverside, CA)	(m)	160,004
20. *Union-Tribune* (San Diego, CA)	(all day)	372,081	70.	*World* (Tulsa, OK)	(m)	158,610
21. *Free Press* (Detroit, MI)	(m)	363,385	71.	*Daily News* (Dayton, OH)	(m)	158,295
22. *Herald* (Miami, FL)	(m)	361,279	72.	*Asbury Park Press* (Neptune, NJ)	(all day)	156,473
23. *Register* (Orange County, CA)	(m)	353,812	73.	*Bee* (Fresno, CA)	(m)	152,591
24. *Times* (St. Petersburg, FL)	(m)	340,878	74.	*News & Observer* (Raleigh, NC)	(m)	150,951
25. *Oregonian* (Portland, OR)	(all day)	338,586	75.	*Record* (Hackensack, NJ)	(m)	150,122
26. *Post* (Denver, CO)	(m)	334,436	76.	*Beacon Journal* (Akron, OH)	(m)	148,914
27. *Post-Dispatch* (St. Louis, MO)	(all day)	321,461	77.	*Review-Journal* (Las Vegas, NV)	(m)	147,927
28. *Rocky Mountain News* (Denver, CO)	(m)	316,910	78.	*Blade* (Toledo, OH)	(m)	147,365
29. *Constitution* (Atlanta, GA)	(m)	308,301	79.	*Tennessean* (Nashville, TN)	(m)	146,788
30. *Sun* (Baltimore, MD)	(m)	304,412	80.	*Democrat and Chronicle* (Rochester, NY)	(m)	142,572
31. *Journal Sentinel* (Milwaukee, WI)	(m)	287,673	81.	*Press* (Grand Rapids, MI)	(e)	139,978
32. *Mercury News* (San Jose, CA)	(m)	285,735	82.	*Morning Call* (Allentown, PA)	(m)	130,317
33. *Herald* (Boston, MA)	(m)	284,794	83.	*Daily Herald* (Arlington Heights, IL)	(m)	129,202
34. *Star* (Kansas City, MO)	(m)	279,305	84.	*News Tribune* (Tacoma, WA)	(m)	128,432
35. *Bee* (Sacramento, CA)	(m)	276,758	85.	*Tribune* (Salt Lake City, UT)	(m)	127,978
36. *Sentinel* (Orlando, FL)	(all day)	262,802	86.	*News Journal* (Wilmington, DE)	(all day)	125,637
37. *News* (Buffalo, NY)	(all day)	262,045	87.	*State* (Columbia SC)	(m)	122,053
38. *Times-Picayune* (New Orleans, LA)	(m)	259,577	88.	*Spokesman-Review* (Spokane, WA)	(m)	118,555
39. *Tribune* (Tampa, FL)	(m)	255,142	89.	*Journal* (Atlanta, GA)	(e)	118,260
40. *Sun-Sentinel* (Fort Lauderdale, FL)	(m)	255,050	90.	*News-Sentinel* (Knoxville, TN)	(m)	115,636
41. *Dispatch* (Columbus, OH)	(m)	253,549	91.	*Journal* (Albuquerque, NM)	(m)	113,253
42. *Post-Gazette* (Pittsburgh, PA)	(m)	240,992	92.	*Telegram & Gazette* (Worcester, MA)	(m)	112,976
43. *News* (Detroit, MI)	(e)	237,917	93.	*Examiner* (San Francisco, CA)	(e)	112,382
44. *Observer* (Charlotte, NC)	(m)	236,050	94.	*Herald-Leader* (Lexington, KY)	(m)	111,623
45. *Courier-Journal* (Louisville, KY)	(m)	232,539	95.	*Herald-Tribune* (Sarasota, FL)	(m)	110,179
46. *Star* (Indianapolis, IN)	(m)	230,095	96.	*Post & Courier* (Charleston, SC)	(m)	108,162
47. *World-Herald* (Omaha, NE)	(all day)	227,721	97.	*Times* (Roanoke, VA)	(m)	106,902
48. *Times* (Seattle, WA)	(e)	226,287	98.	*Clarion-Ledger* (Jackson, MS)	(m)	105,571
49. *Investor's Business Daily* (Los Angeles, CA)	(m)	222,972	99.	*Gazette* (Colorado Springs, CO)	(m)	103,553
50. *Star-Telegram* (Fort Worth, TX)	(m)	221,860	100.	*Advertiser* (Honolulu, HI)	(m)	103,522

Leading Canadian Daily Newspapers, 1996

Source: *1997 Editor & Publisher International Yearbook*

(Circulation as of Sept. 30, 1996; m = morning)

For the year ending Feb. 1, 1997, the number of Canadian dailies declined by 1, to 106. Canadian daily circulation fell by 178,429, to 4,702,656, in the 6-month period ending Sept. 30, 1996. During the same period, Sunday circulation decreased by 78,113, to 3,031,815.

Newspaper		Circulation	Newspaper		Circulation
Star (Toronto, ON)	(m)	468,279	*La Presse* (Montreal, QC)	(m)	164,998
Globe and Mail (Toronto, ON)	(m)	303,870	*Province* (Vancouver, BC)	(m)	149,624
Le Journal (Montreal, QC)	(m)	262,178	*Gazette* (Montreal, QC)	(m)	142,635
Sun (Toronto, ON)	(m)	228,731	*Journal* (Edmonton, AB)	(m)	136,526
Sun (Vancouver, BC)	(m)	177,181	*Citizen* (Ottawa, ON)	(m)	130,102

U.S. Commercial Radio Stations, by Format, 1991-97

Source: M Street Corporation, Nashville, TN © 1997; counts are for Aug. of each year

Stations, by primary format	1991	1992	1993	1994	1995	1996	1997
Country	2,457	2,552	2,612	2,642	2,608	2,558	2,502
Adult Contemporary (AC)	2,088	1,963	1,895	1,784	1,661	1,592	1,521
News, Talk, Business, Sports	527	648	841	1,028	1,165	1,262	1,313
Religion (Teaching and Music)	799	837	915	926	970	996	1,054
Rock (Album, Modern, Classic)	529	592	643	721	808	868	942
Oldies	704	731	701	714	718	725	753
Spanish and Ethnic	370	385	421	470	492	515	549
Adult Standards	408	412	421	435	469	474	536
Urban, Black, Urban AC	311	313	321	328	342	348	358
Top-40	675	578	441	358	324	314	351
Easy Listening	210	171	116	106	85	91	87
Variety	81	72	68	63	63	65	51
Jazz	53	52	45	43	58	54	50
Classical, Fine Arts	51	48	45	44	39	41	46
Pre-Teen	4	3	13	19	26	30	35
Comedy	0	0	0	1	0	0	0
Off Air	308	352	345	369	323	298	162
Changing formats/not available	19	15	14	6	9	6	3
Total stations	9,594	9,724	9,890	10,057	10,160	10,237	10,313

Top-Grossing North American Concert Tours, 1985-96

Source: Pollstar; Fresno, CA

Artist (Year)	Total gross[1]	Cities/ Shows	Artist (Year)	Total gross[1]	Cities/ Shows
1. The Rolling Stones (1994)	$121.2	43/60	11. The Grateful Dead (1993)	$45.6	29/81
2. Pink Floyd (1994)	103.5	39/59	12. Kiss (1996)	43.6	75/92
3. The Rolling Stones (1989)	98.0	33/60	13. Boyz II Men (1995)	43.2	133/134
4. The Eagles (1994)	79.4	32/54	14. Billy Joel (1990)	43.0	53/95
5. The New Kids on the Block (1990)	74.1	122/152	15. The Who (1989)	41.7	27/39
6. U2 (1992)	67.0	61/73	16. Bruce Springsteen & the E St. Band (1985)	39.1	21/40
7. The Eagles (1995)	63.3	46/58	17. R.E.M. (1995)	38.7	63/81
8. Barbra Streisand (1994)	58.9	6/22	18. Paul McCartney (1990)	37.9	21/32
9. The Grateful Dead (1994)	52.4	29/84	19. Bon Jovi (1989)	36.7	129/143
10. Elton John/Billy Joel (1994)	47.7	14/21	20. U2 (1987)	35.1	50/79

(1) In mils. Not adjusted for inflation.

Sales of Recorded Music and Music Videos, by Genre and Format, 1992-96

Source: Recording Industry Assn. of America, Washington, D.C.

Breakdown by percentage of all recorded music sold.

Genre	1992	1993	1994	1995	1996
Rock	31.6	30.2	35.1	33.5	32.6
Country	17.4	18.7	16.3	16.7	14.7
Urban Contemp.	9.8	10.6	9.6	11.3	12.1
Pop	11.5	11.9	10.3	10.1	9.3
Rap	8.6	9.2	7.9	6.7	8.9
Gospel	2.8	3.2	3.3	3.1	4.3
Classical	3.7	3.3	3.7	2.9	3.4
Jazz	3.8	3.1	3.0	3.0	3.3
Oldies	0.8	1.0	0.8	1.0	0.8
Soundtracks	0.7	0.7	1.0	0.9	0.8
New Age	1.2	1.0	1.0	0.7	0.7
Children's	0.5	0.4	0.4	0.5	0.7
Other	5.4	4.6	5.3	7.0	5.2

Format	1992	1993	1994	1995	1996
Compact disc (CD)	46.5	51.1	58.4	65.0	68.4
Cassette	43.6	38.0	32.1	25.1	19.3
LP	1.3	0.3	0.8	0.5	0.6
Singles (all types)	7.5	9.2	7.4	7.5	9.3
Music video	1.0	1.3	0.8	0.9	1.0

Note: Totals may not equal 100% because of "Don't know/no answer" responses to survey.

MILLENNIUM FACT BOX

Half a Century of Number-One Hits

Source: Billboard Magazine

Popular music in America goes back to the early days, and songs like "Believe Me If All Those Endearing Young Charms" (1808) or "Turkey in the Straw" (c. 1834) are still remembered today. From 1946 onward, it is possible to measure the popularity of songs each year by sales on the pop music charts; below is a list of the top pop singles for selected years, followed by the recording artist.

1946 "Prisoner of Love," Perry Como
1950 "Good Night Irene," Gordon Jenkins and the Weavers
1955 "Cherry Pink and Apple Blossom White," Perez Prado
1960 "Theme From *A Summer Place*," Percy Faith
1965 "Wooly Bully," Sam the Sham and the Pharaohs
1970 "Bridge Over Troubled Water," Simon and Garfunkel

1975 "Love Will Keep Us Together," Captain and Tennille
1980 "Call Me," Blondie
1985 "Careless Whisper," Wham!
1990 "Hold On," Wilson Philips
1995 "Gangsta's Paradise," Coolio Featuring L.V.
1996 "Macarena (Bayside Boys Mix)," Los Del Rio

Sales of Recorded Music and Music Videos, by Units Shipped and Value, 1988-96

Source: Recording Industry Assn. of America, Washington, D.C.

(in millions, net after returns)

Format	1988	1989	1990	1991	1992	1993	1994	1995	1996	% change 1995-96
Compact disc (CD)										
Units shipped	149.7	207.2	286.5	333.3	407.5	495.4	662.1	722.9	778.9	7.7
Dollar value	2,089.9	2,587.5	3,451.6	4,337.7	5,326.5	6,511.4	8,464.5	9,377.4	9,934.7	5.9
CD single										
Units shipped	1.6	−0.1	1.1	5.7	7.3	7.8	9.3	21.5	43.2	100.9
Dollar value	9.8	−0.7	6.0	35.1	45.1	45.8	56.1	110.9	184.1	66.0
Cassette										
Units shipped	450.1	446.2	442.2	360.1	366.4	339.5	345.4	272.6	225.3	−17.4
Dollar value	3,385.1	3,345.8	3,472.4	3,019.6	3,116.3	2,915.8	2,976.4	2,303.6	1,905.3	−17.3
Cassette single										
Units shipped	22.5	76.2	87.4	69.0	84.6	85.6	81.1	70.7	59.9	−15.3
Dollar value	57.3	194.6	257.9	230.4	298.8	298.5	274.9	236.3	189.3	−19.9
LP/EP										
Units shipped	72.4	34.6	11.7	4.8	2.3	1.2	1.9	2.2	2.9	31.8
Dollar value	532.2	220.3	86.5	29.4	13.5	10.6	17.8	25.1	36.8	46.6
Vinyl single										
Units shipped	65.6	36.6	27.6	22.0	19.8	15.1	11.7	10.2	10.1	−1.0
Dollar value	180.4	116.4	94.4	63.9	66.4	51.2	47.2	46.7	47.5	1.7
Music video										
Units shipped	NA	6.1	9.2	6.1	7.6	11.0	11.2	12.6	16.9	34.1
Dollar value	NA	115.4	172.3	118.1	157.4	213.3	231.1	220.3	236.1	7.2
Total units	761.9	806.7	865.7	801.0	895.5	955.6	1,122.7	1,112.7	1,137.2	2.2
Total value	6,254.8	6,579.4	7,541.1	7,834.2	9,024.0	10,046.6	12,068.0	12,320.3	12,533.8	1.7

NA = Not applicable. (1) Cassette singles were introduced in the second half of the year. The figure here represents 6-month sales. (2) Total includes discontinued configurations not itemized in the table.

Multi-Platinum and Platinum Awards for Recorded Music and Music Videos, 1996

Source: Recording Industry Assn. of America, Washington, D.C.

To achieve platinum status, an album must reach a minimum sale of 1 mil units in LPs, tapes, and CDs, with a manufacturer's dollar volume of at least $2 mil based on one-third of the suggested retail list price for each record, tape, or CD sold. To achieve multi-platinum status, an album must reach a minimum sale of at least 2 mil units in LPs, tapes, and CDs, with a manufacturer's dollar volume of at least $4 mil based on one-third of the list price. Singles must sell 1 mil units to achieve a platinum award and at least 2 mil to achieve a multi-platinum award. EP singles count as 2 units. Double-CD sets count as 2 units. Music videos (long form) must sell 100,000 units to qualify for a platinum award and must sell more than 200,000 units for a multi-platinum award. Video singles, which must have a maximum running time of 15 minutes and no more than 2 songs per title, must sell 50,000 units to qualify for a platinum award and at least 100,000 units to qualify for a multi-platinum award.

Awards listed were for albums and singles released in 1996 and for music videos released at any time. No multi-platinum or platinum video singles were awarded in 1996.

Albums, Multi-Platinum

(numbers in parentheses = millions sold)

The Beatles, *The Beatles Anthology, Vol. 2* (3)
Toni Braxton, *Secrets* (3)
Celine Dion, *Falling Into You* (7)
Fugees, *The Score* (5)
Hootie and the Blowfish, *Fairweather Johnson* (2)
Kenny G, *The Moment* (2)
Dave Matthews Band, *Crash* (2)
Metallica, *Load* (3)
NAS, *It Was Written* (2)
Tupac Shakur, *All Eyez on Me* (7)
Keith Sweat, *Keith Sweat* (2)

Albums, Platinum

Ace of Base, *The Bridge*
Alice in Chains, *Unplugged*
Tori Amos, *Boys for Pele*
Clint Black, *Greatest Hits*
Blackstreet, *Another Level*
Michael Bolton, *This Is the Time-Christmas Album*
Brooks & Dunn, *Borderline*
Deana Carter, *Did I Shave My Legs for This?*
Counting Crows, *Recovering the Satellites*
The Cranberries, *To the Faithful Departed*
Sheryl Crow, *Sheryl Crow*
Gloria Estefan, *Destiny*
Journey, *Trial by Fire*
Wynnona Judd, *Revelations*
La Bouche, *Sweet Dreams*
Tracy Lawrence, *Time Marches On*
Donna Lewis, *Now in a Minute*
Marilyn Manson, *Antichrist Superstar*
Mindy McCready, *Ten Thousand Angels*
George Michael, *Older*
New Edition, *Home Again*
Nirvana, *From the Muddy Banks of the Wishkah*

Outkast, *Aliens*
R.E.M., *New Adventures in Hi-Fi*
Rage Against the Machine, *Evil Empire*
S.W.V., *New Beginning*
Adam Sandler, *What the Hell Happened to Me?*
Soundgarden, *Down on the Upside*
Soundtrack, *The Crow: City of Angels*
Soundtrack, *Hunchback of Notre Dame*
Soundtrack, *The Nutty Professor*
Soundtrack, *Set It Off*
Soundtrack, *Sunset Park*
Soundtrack, William Shakespeare's *Romeo and Juliet*
Sting, *Mercury Falling*
Stone Temple Pilots, *Tiny Music Songs From the Vatican Gift Shop*
George Strait, *Clear Blue Sky*
Tony Rich Project, *Words*
Too Short, *Gettin' It (Album Number Ten)*
Luther Vandross, *Your Secret Love*
Various, *Jock Jams, Vol. 2*
Bryan White, *Between Now and Forever*
"Weird Al" Yankovic, *Bad Hair Day*

Singles, Multi-Platinum

(number in parenthesis = millions sold)

Bone Thugs 'n Harmony, "Tha Crossroads" (2)
Mariah Carey, "One Sweet Day" (2)
Tupac Shakur, "How Do U Want It" (2)

Singles, Platinum

Blackstreet, "No Diggity"
Mary J. Blige, "Not Gon' Cry"
Toni Braxton, "You're Makin' Me High"
Toni Braxton, "Un-Break My Heart"
Busta Rhymes, "Woo-Hah"
Mariah Carey, "Always Be My Baby"
Tracy Chapman, "Give Me One Reason"
Celine Dion, "Because You Loved Me"
Celine Dion, "It's All Coming Back to Me Now"

Ginuwine, "Pony"
Junior M.A.F.I.A., "Gettin' Money"
LL Cool J, "Loungin' "
Quad City DJ's, "C'mon n' Ride It (The Train)
R. Kelly, "I Can't Sleep"
R. Kelly w/ R. Isley, "Down Low (Nobody Has to Know)"
Keith Sweat, "Twisted"
Keith Sweat, "Nobody"

Music Videos, Multi-Platinum

Carreras, Domingo, Pavarotti, *Three Tenors in Concert, 1994*
Michael Jackson, *Dangerous—The Short Films*
Metallica, *A Year and a Half in the Life of...Pt. 1*
Metallica, *A Year and a Half in the Life of...Pt. 2*
Pink Floyd, *Pulse*
Various, *Kids Sing Praise, Vol. 1*

Music Videos, Platinum

Big Idea Productions, *Where's God When I'm Scared?*
Big Idea Productions, *The Toy That Saved My Life*
Michael Bolton, *Soul & Passion*
Mariah Carey, *MTV Unplugged*
Mariah Carey, *Mariah Carey at Madison Square Garden*
Carman, *The Standard*
Eric Clapton, *Cream of Clapton*
Bob Marley and the Wailers, *The Bob Marley Story*
Shania Twain, *The Woman in Me*
Various, *Kids Sing Praise, Vol. 2*
Various, *Mother Goose Gospel Video, Vol. 1*
Andrew Lloyd Webber, *The Premiere Collection Encore*

Top-Selling Video Games, 1996

Source: The NPD TRSTS Video Games Tracking Service, The NPD Group, Inc., Port Washington, NY; ranked by units sold

Title
1. Nintendo 64 Super Mario 64
2. Super Nintendo Donkey Kong Country 2
3. Super Nintendo Donkey Kong Country 3
4. Sony Playstation Madden '97
5. Nintendo 64 Wave Race 64
6. Super Nintendo Super Mario RPG
7. Sony Playstation Tekken 2
8. Nintendo 64 Star Wars: Shadow of the Empire

Title
9. Sony Playstation Resident Evil
10. Nintendo 64 Mortal Kombat Trilogy
11. Nintendo 64 Killer Instinct Gold
12. Super Nintendo Super Mario World 2: Yoshi's Island
13. Sony Playstation Crash Bandicoot
14. Nintendo 64 Pilot Wings 64
15. Genesis Madden NFL '97

U.S. Television Set Owners

Source: Nielsen Media Research; Dec. 31, 1996

Of the 97 million homes (98% of U.S. households) that owned at least one TV set in 1996:

99% had color televisions
36% had 2 TV sets

38% had 3 or more TV sets
82% had a VCR

66% received basic cable
33% received premium cable

Some Television Addresses, Phone Numbers, Internet Sites

BROADCAST

ABC–American Broadcasting Company
77 W 66th St.
New York, NY 10023   (212) 456-7777
Web site: http://www.abc.com

CBS–Columbia Broadcasting System, Inc.
51 W 52nd St.
New York, NY 10019   (212) 975-4321
Web site: http://www.cbs.com

NBC–National Broadcasting Company
30 Rockefeller Plaza
New York, NY 10112   (212) 664-4444
Web site: http://nbc.com

Fox Television
205 E 67th St.
New York, NY 10021   (212) 452-5555
Web site: http://www.fox.com

PBS–Public Broadcasting Service
1320 Braddock Place
Alexandria, VA 22314   (703) 739-5000
Web site: http://www.pbs.org

CABLE

A&E–Arts & Entertainment Network
235 E 45th St.
New York, NY 10017   (212) 210-1400
Web site: http://www.aetv.com

AMC–American Movie Classics
Rainbow Media Holdings, Inc.
150 Crossways Park W
Woodbury, NY 11797   (516) 364-2222
Web site: http://www.amctv.com

BET–Black Entertainment Television
1 BET Plaza, 1900 W Place, NE
Washington, DC 20018   (202) 608-2000
Web site: http://www.msbet.com

CNBC–Consumer News and Business Channel
2200 Fletcher Ave.
Fort Lee, NJ 07024   (201) 585-2622
Web site: http://www.cnbc.com

CNN–Cable News Network
One CNN Center, Box 105366
Atlanta, GA 30348-5366 (404) 827-1500
Web site: http://www.cnn.com

C-SPAN–Cable-Satellite Public Affairs Network
400 N Capitol St. NW, Suite 650
Washington, DC 20001   (202) 737-3220
Web site: http://www.c-span.org

DIS–The Disney Channel
3800 W Alameda Ave.
Burbank, CA 91505   (818) 569-7500
Web site: http://www.disneychannel.com

ESPN–ESPN, Inc.
ESPN Plaza, 935 Middle St.
Bristol, CT 06010   (860) 585-2000
Web site: http://espn.com

LIF–Lifetime
309 W 49th St.
New York, NY 10019   (212) 424-7000
Web site: http://www.lifetimetv.com

MSNBC
1 MSNBC Plaza
Secaucus, NJ 07094   (201) 583-5000
Web site: http://www.msnbc.com

MTV–Music Television
MTV Networks, Inc.
1515 Broadway
New York, NY 10036   (212) 258-8000
Web site: http://www.mtv.com

NICK–Nickelodeon/Nick at Nite
MTV Networks, Inc.
1515 Broadway
New York, NY 10036   (212) 258-8000
Web sites: http://www.nick.com
              http://www.nick-at-nite.com

TBS–Turner Broadcasting System
Turner Entertainment Group
One CNN Center, Box 105366
Atlanta, GA 30348-5366
(404) 827-1700
Web site: http://www.turner.com

TDC–The Discovery Channel
Discovery Communications
7700 Wisconsin Ave., Suite 700
Bethesda, MD 20814   (301) 986-0444
Web site: http://www.discovery.com

USA–USA Network
USA Networks
1230 Ave. of the Americas
New York, NY 10020   (212) 408-9100
Web site: http://www.usanetwork.com

Number of Cable TV Systems, 1974-97

Source: *Television and Cable Factbook*, Warren Publishing, Inc., Washington, DC; estimates as of Jan. 1

Year	Systems	Year	Systems	Year	Systems	Year	Systems
1974	3,158	1980	4,225	1986	7,500	1992	11,073
1975	3,506	1981	4,375	1987	7,900	1993	11,108
1976	3,681	1982	4,825	1988	9,500	1994	11,214
1977	3,832	1983	5,600	1989	9,050	1995	11,215
1978	3,875	1984	6,200	1990	9,575	1996	11,220
1979	4,160	1985	6,000	1991	10,704	1997	10,943

Top 20 Cable Video Networks, 1997

Source: *Cable Television Developments,* Natl. Cable Television Assn., Jan.-Mar. 1997; ranked by number of subscribers

Rank	Network[1]	Affiliates	Subscribers (mils)	Rank	Network[1]	Affiliates	Subscribers (mils)
1.	ESPN (1979)	27,600	71.1	11.	Arts & Entertainment Network (1984)	12,000	66.9
2.	CNN (1980)	11,528	71.0	12.	MTV: Music Television (1981)	9,176	66.7
3.	TNT (Turner Network Television) (1988)	10,538	70.5	13.	Nickelodeon (1979)	11,788	66.0
					Nick at Nite (1985)	11,711	66.0
4.	TBS (1976)	11,668	69.9	14.	The Weather Channel (1982)	6,500	64.2
5.	C-SPAN (1979)	6,003	69.7	15.	Headline News (1982)	6,470	64.0
6.	USA Network (1980)	12,500	69.7	16.	AMC (American Movie Classics) (1984)	NA	61.5
7.	The Discovery Channel (1985)	NA	69.5	17.	CNBC (1989)	11,711	60.0
8.	TNN (The Nashville Network) (1983	17,636	68.9	18.	QVC Network (1986)	5,895[2]	58.2
9.	LIFETIME Television (1984)	8,300	67.0	19.	VH-1 (Video Hits One) (1985)	6,088[3]	56.3
10.	The Family Channel (1977)	13,352	66.9	20.	The Learning Channel (1980)	NA	55.0

NA = Not available. **Note:** Data include noncable affiliates. (1) Date in parentheses is year service began. (2) As of 10/96. (3) As of 1/97.

U.S. Households With Cable Television, 1977-96

Source: Nielsen Media Research, New York, NY

Year	Basic cable subscribers	Percentage of households with TVs	Year	Basic cable subscribers	Percentage of households with TVs
1977	12,168,450	16.6	1987	44,970,880	50.5
1978	13,391,910	17.9	1988	48,636,520	53.8
1979	14,814,380	19.4	1989	52,564,470	57.1
1980	17,671,490	22.6	1990	54,871,330	59.0
1981	23,219,200	28.3	1991	55,786,390	60.6
1982	29,340,570	35.0	1992	57,211,600	61.5
1983	34,113,790	40.5	1993	58,834,440	62.5
1984	37,290,870	43.7	1994	60,483,600	63.4
1985	39,872,520	46.2	1995	62,956,470	65.7
1986	42,237,140	48.1	1996	64,654,160	66.7

Average Television Viewing Time, 1997

Source: Nielsen Media Research, May 1997 (hours:minutes per week)

Group	Age	Mon.-Fri. 10 AM- 4:30 PM	Mon.-Fri. 4:30 PM- 7:30 PM	Mon.-Sun. 8-11 PM	Sat. 7 AM-1 PM	Mon.-Fri. 11:30 PM- 1 AM
Women	18+	5:10	3:42	9:03	0:40	1:22
	18-24	4:33	2:54	6:31	0:36	1:22
	25-54	4:19	3:00	8:28	0:39	1:28
	55+	7:09	5:24	11:12	0:45	1:31
Men	18+	3:05	2:50	8:21	0:36	1:26
	18-24	3:09	2:16	5:59	0:27	1:19
	25-54	2:34	2:21	8:06	0:37	1:29
	55+	4:21	4:17	10:21	0:38	1:21
Teens	12-17	1:53	2:49	6:00	0:40	0:44
Children	2-5	5:37	2:58	4:26	1:06	0:25
	6-11	1:41	2:39	4:54	1:02	0:22
Total		**3:48**	**3:17**	**7:37**	**1:11**	**0:41**

TV Viewing Shares, Broadcast Years 1987-1996[1]

Source: *Cable TV Facts,* Cable Advertising Bureau, New York, NY

	All Television Households[2]										All Cable Households[2]										Pay Cable Households[2]									
	'87	'88	'89	'90	'91	'92	'93	'94	'95	'96	'87	'88	'89	'90	'91	'92	'93	'94	'95	'96	'87	'88	'89	'90	'91	'92	'93	'94	'95	'96
Network Affiliates	64	61	58	55	53	54	53	52	48	46	53	52	49	46	46	47	46	44	41	40	48	48	45	43	41	43	42	42	38	36
Indep. TV Stations[3]	20	20	20	20	21	20	21	21	22	21	17	17	16	16	17	16	17	17	17	17	16	17	16	16	16	16	16	17	17	18
Public TV Stations	4	4	3	3	3	3	4	4	3	3	3	3	3	3	2	3	3	3	3	3	3	3	2	2	2	2	2	3	2	3
Basic Cable	13	15	17	21	24	24	25	26	30	33	23	25	28	32	35	35	36	37	42	43	23	24	27	30	34	33	35	36	41	43
Pay Cable	4	7	7	6	6	6	5	5	6	6	10	11	11	10	9	8	8	8	8	8	17	18	18	18	17	17	16	15	15	14

(1) Broadcast year (season) ends in May of the year shown, began the previous Sept. (2) Share figures refer to percentage of the viewing audience for all television viewing, 24 hours/day. As a result of multiset use and rounding of numbers, share figures add to more than 100. (3) Independent shares include those for Fox.

Favorite Syndicated Programs, 1996-97

Source: Nielsen Media Research, Sept. 16, 1996-May 21, 1997

Average audience percentages, or ratings, are estimates of the percentage of TV-owning households watching a program.

Rank	Program	Avg. audience (%)	Rank	Program	Avg. audience (%)
1.	Wheel of Fortune (Mon.-Fri.)	11.8	11.	Entertainment Tonight	6.2
2.	Home Improvement (Mon.-Fri.)	9.7	12.	MMN Home Team Baseball	6.1
2.	Jeopardy	9.7	12.	Portfolio XV	6.1
4.	National Geographic on Assignment (Oct.)	8.2	12.	WCW Wrestling	6.1
4.	Oprah Winfrey Show	8.2	15.	Century 16	6.0
6.	Seinfeld (Mon.-Sat.)	7.8	16.	Xena	5.8
7.	Buena Vista I	7.4	17.	Journeys of Hercules	5.7
8.	National Geographic on Assignment (Feb.)	7.1	18.	Star Trek-Deep Space Nine	5.6
9.	ESPN NFL Regular Season	6.6	19.	Wheel of Fortune (Weekend)	5.6
10.	Simpsons (Mon.-Fri.)	6.5	20.	NFL on TNT '96 Regular Season	5.5

TV Parental Guidelines

On Dec. 19, 1996, representatives of the television industry announced the creation of TV Parental Guidelines, a rating system intended to give parents advance information about the content of programs. The guidelines, modeled after the Motion Picture Ratings System and developed by a broad spectrum of industry representatives, began to appear on broadcast and cable television programs in Jan. 1997. On July 10, 1997, most of the television industry, after negotiations with advocacy groups, agreed to add the labels D, L, S, and V to the existing ratings. The added labels, which went into effect by Oct. 1, provide more specific information about the degree of violence, coarse language, and sexually suggestive content. Some of the networks that did not add the labels Oct. 1 began to add their own parental advisories to shows.

There are two categories of ratings, one for children's programs and one for programs not specifically designed for children. The ratings are as follows:

The following categories apply to programs designed solely for children:

All Children. *This program is designed to be appropriate for all children.* Whether animated or live action, the themes and elements in this program are specifically designed for a very young audience, including children ages 2-6. This program is not expected to frighten younger children.

Directed to Older Children. *This program is designed for children age 7 and above.* It may be more appropriate for children who have acquired the developmental skills needed to distinguish between make-believe and reality. Themes and elements in this program may include mild physical or comedic violence, or may frighten children under the age of 7. Therefore, parents may wish to consider the suitability of this program for their very young children. Programs containing fantasy violence that may be more intense or more combative than other programs in this category are designated as **TV-Y7-FV.**

The following categories apply to programs designed for the entire audience:

General Audience. *Most parents would find this program suitable for all ages.* Although this rating does not signify a program designed specifically for children, most parents may let younger children

watch this program unattended. It contains little or no violence, no strong language, and little or no sexual dialog or situations.

Parental Guidance Suggested. *This program may contain some material that some parents would find unsuitable for younger children.* Many parents may want to watch it with their younger children. The theme itself may call for parental guidance and/or the program contains one or more of the following: moderate violence (V), some suggestive sexual situations (S), infrequent coarse language (L), some suggestive dialog (D).

Parents Strongly Cautioned. *This program may contain some material that many parents would find unsuitable for children under 14 years of age.* Parents are strongly urged to exercise greater care in monitoring this program and are cautioned against letting children under the age of 14 watch unattended. This program contains one or more of the following: intense violence (V), intense sexual situations (S), strong coarse language (L), intensely suggestive dialog (D).

Mature Audience Only. *This program is specifically designed to be viewed by adults and therefore may be unsuitable for children under 17.* This program contains one or more of the following: graphic violence (V), explicit sexual activity (S), crude indecent language (L).

When a program is broadcast, the appropriate icon should appear in the upper left corner of the picture frame for the first 15 seconds. If the program is longer than 1 hour, the icon should be repeated at the beginning of the 2d hour. Guidelines are also displayed in TV listings in newspapers and magazines.

Favorite Prime-Time Television Programs, 1996-97

Source: Nielsen Media Research

Data are for regularly scheduled network programs (Sept. 16, 1996-May 21, 1997); ranked by average audience percentage. Average audience percentages, or ratings, are estimates of the percentage of all TV-owning households that are watching a particular program. Audience share percentages are estimates of the percentage of the those watching TV that are tuned into a particular program.

Rank	Program	Average audience (%)	Audience share (%)	Rank	Program	Average audience (%)	Audience share (%)
1.	E.R.	21.2	35	24.	NBC Monday Night Movies	11.0	17
2.	Seinfeld	20.5	32	24.	Caroline in the City	11.0	17
3.	Suddenly Susan	17.0	27	28.	3rd Rock From the Sun	10.8	17
4.	Friends	16.8	28	28.	Law and Order	10.8	19
4.	Naked Truth	16.8	27	30.	Ellen	10.6	17
6.	Fired Up	16.5	26	31.	Dateline NBC-Friday	10.5	18
7.	NFL Monday Night Football	16.2	27	31.	Cybill	10.5	16
8.	Single Guy	14.1	23	31.	Chicago Hope	10.5	18
9.	Home Improvement	14.0	22	34.	Murphy Brown	10.4	16
10.	Touched by An Angel	13.6	21	35.	Roseanne	10.1	17
11.	60 Minutes	13.3	23	36.	CBS Tuesday Movie	10.0	16
11.	20/20	12.8	23	37.	Ink	9.6	15
13.	NYPD Blue	12.5	21	38.	Life's Work	9.5	15
14.	CBS Sunday Night Movie	12.1	19	38.	Something So Right	9.5	15
15.	Primetime Live	11.9	20	40.	ABC Sunday Night Movie	9.4	15
16.	Frasier	11.8	18	41.	Sabrina, the Teenage Witch	9.3	17
17.	Spin City	11.7	18	41.	CBS Wednesday Movie	9.3	15
18.	NBC Sunday Night Movie	11.5	18	43.	King of the Hill	9.2	14
18.	Drew Carey Show	11.5	18	43.	The Practice	9.2	16
20.	X-Files	11.4	17	45.	Grace Under Fire	9.1	15
20.	Dateline NBC-Tuesday	11.4	19	45.	The Nanny	9.1	16
22.	Soul Man	11.2	19	45.	Pearl	9.1	15
22.	Cosby	11.2	18	45.	Diagnosis Murder	9.1	15
24.	Walker, Texas Ranger	11.0	20	49.	Early Edition	9.0	16
24.	Mad About You	11.0	18	50.	Family Matters	8.8	17

All-Time Top Television Programs

Source: Nielsen Media Research, Jan. 1961-Jan. 26, 1997

Estimates exclude unsponsored or joint network telecasts or programs under 30 minutes long. Ranked by rating (percentage of TV-owning households tuned in to the program).

Rank	Program	Telecast date	Network	Rating (%)	Avg. audience (000)
1.	M*A*S*H (last episode)	2/28/83	CBS	60.2	50,150
2.	Dallas (Who Shot J.R.?)	11/21/80	CBS	53.3	41,470
3.	Roots-Pt. 8	1/30/77	ABC	51.1	36,380
4.	Super Bowl XVI	1/24/82	CBS	49.1	40,020
5.	Super Bowl XVII	1/30/83	NBC	48.6	40,480
6.	XVII Winter Olympics - 2d Wed.	2/23/94	CBS	48.5	45,690
7.	Super Bowl XX	1/26/86	NBC	48.3	41,490
8.	Gone With the Wind-Pt. 1	11/7/76	NBC	47.7	33,960
9.	Gone With the Wind-Pt. 2	11/8/76	NBC	47.4	33,750
10.	Super Bowl XII	1/15/78	CBS	47.2	34,410
11.	Super Bowl XIII	1/21/79	NBC	47.1	35,090
12.	Bob Hope Christmas Show	1/15/70	NBC	46.6	27,260
13.	Super Bowl XVIII	1/22/84	CBS	46.4	38,800
13.	Super Bowl XIX	1/20/85	ABC	46.4	39,390
15.	Super Bowl XIV	1/20/80	CBS	46.3	35,330
16	Super Bowl XXX	1/28/96	NBC	46.0	44,150
16.	ABC Theater (The Day After)	11/20/83	ABC	46.0	38,550
18.	Roots-Pt. 6	1/28/77	ABC	45.9	32,680
18.	The Fugitive	8/29/67	ABC	45.9	25,700
20.	Super Bowl XXI	1/25/87	CBS	45.8	40,030
21.	Roots-Pt. 5	1/27/77	ABC	45.7	32,540
22.	Super Bowl XXVIII	1/29/94	NBC	45.5	42,860
22.	Cheers (last episode)	5/20/93	NBC	45.5	42,360
24.	Ed Sullivan	2/9/64	CBS	45.3	23,240
25.	Super Bowl XXVII	1/31/93	NBC	45.1	41,990
26.	Bob Hope Christmas Show	1/14/71	NBC	45.0	27,050
27.	Roots-Pt. 3	1/25/77	ABC	44.8	31,900
28.	Super Bowl XI	1/9/77	NBC	44.4	31,610
28.	Super Bowl XV	1/25/81	NBC	44.4	34,540
30.	Super Bowl VI	1/16/72	CBS	44.2	27,450
31.	XVII Winter Olympics - 2d Fri.	2/25/94	CBS	44.1	41,540
31.	Roots-Pt. 2	1/24/77	ABC	44.1	31,400
33.	Beverly Hillbillies	1/8/64	CBS	44.0	22,570
34.	Roots-Pt. 4	1/26/77	ABC	43.8	31,190
34.	Ed Sullivan	2/16/64	CBS	43.8	22,445
36.	Super Bowl XXIII	1/22/89	NBC	43.5	39,320
37.	Academy Awards	4/7/70	ABC	43.4	25,390
38.	Super Bowl XXXI	1/26/97	FOX	43.3	42,000
39.	Thorn Birds-Pt. 3	3/29/83	ABC	43.2	35,990
40.	Thorn Birds-Pt. 4	3/30/83	ABC	43.1	35,900
41.	CBS NFC Championship	1/10/82	CBS	42.9	34,960
42.	Beverly Hillbillies	1/15/64	CBS	42.8	21,960
43.	Super Bowl VII	1/14/73	NBC	42.7	27,670
44.	Thorn Birds-Pt. 2	3/28/83	ABC	42.5	35,400

Top-Rated TV Shows of Each Season, 1950-51 to 1996-97

Source: Nielsen Media Research; regular series programs, Sept.-May season

Season	Program	Rating[1]	TV-owning households (in thousands)	Season	Program	Rating[1]	TV-owning households (in thousands)
1950-51	Texaco Star Theatre	61.6	10,320	1974-75	All in the Family	30.2	68,500
1951-52	Godfrey's Talent Scouts	53.8	15,300	1975-76	All in the Family	30.1	69,600
1952-53	I Love Lucy	67.3	20,400	1976-77	Happy Days	31.5	71,200
1953-54	I Love Lucy	58.8	26,000	1977-78	Laverne & Shirley	31.6	72,900
1954-55	I Love Lucy	49.3	30,700	1978-79	Laverne & Shirley	30.5	74,500
1955-56	$64,000 Question	47.5	34,900	1979-80	60 Minutes	28.2	76,300
1956-57	I Love Lucy	43.7	38,900	1980-81	Dallas	31.2	79,900
1957-58	Gunsmoke	43.1	41,920	1981-82	Dallas	28.4	81,500
1958-59	Gunsmoke	39.6	43,950	1982-83	60 Minutes	25.5	83,300
1959-60	Gunsmoke	40.3	45,750	1983-84	Dallas	25.7	83,800
1960-61	Gunsmoke	37.3	47,200	1984-85	Dynasty	25.0	84,900
1961-62	Wagon Train	32.1	48,555	1985-86	Cosby Show	33.8	85,900
1962-63	Beverly Hillbillies	36.0	50,300	1986-87	Cosby Show	34.9	87,400
1963-64	Beverly Hillbillies	39.1	51,600	1987-88	Cosby Show	27.8	88,600
1964-65	Bonanza	36.3	52,700	1988-89	Roseanne	25.5	90,400
1965-66	Bonanza	31.8	53,850	1989-90	Roseanne	23.4	92,100
1966-67	Bonanza	29.1	55,130	1990-91	Cheers	21.6	93,100
1967-68	Andy Griffith	27.6	56,670	1991-92	60 Minutes	21.7	92,100
1968-69	Rowan & Martin Laugh-In	31.8	58,250	1992-93	60 Minutes	21.6	93,100
1969-70	Rowan & Martin Laugh-In	26.3	58,500	1993-94	Home Improvement	21.9	94,200
1970-71	Marcus Welby, MD	29.6	60,100	1994-95	Seinfeld	20.5	95,400
1971-72	All in the Family	34.0	62,100	1995-96	E.R.	22.0	95,900
1972-73	All in the Family	33.3	64,800	1996-97	E.R.	21.2	97,000
1973-74	All in the Family	31.2	66,200				

(1) Rating is percent of TV-owning households tuned in to the program. Data prior to 1988-89 exclude Alaska and Hawaii.

100 Leading U.S. Advertisers, 1996

Source: Competitive Media Reporting and Publishers Information Bureau, New York, © Copyright 1997

(in thousands of dollars)

Rank	Advertiser	Ad spending	Rank	Advertiser	Ad spending	Rank	Advertiser	Ad spending
1.	General Motors	$1,712,102.0	35.	Ford Motor Co. dealers assn.	$333,385.2	68.	SBC Communications	$165,301.6
2.	Procter & Gamble	1,493,456.0	36.	Toyota Motor Co.		69.	Wendy's Intl.	155,630.6
3.	Philip Morris	1,236,978.4		(local dealers)	326,463.6	70.	Microsoft	155,551.9
4.	Chrysler	1,119,851.1	37.	Anheuser-Busch	317,065.1	71.	Toyota auto dealers assn.	47,646.1
5.	Ford	897,666.1	38.	Bristol-Myers Squibb Co.	315,354.9	72.	Wal-Mart Stores	145,135.5
6.	Johnson & Johnson	840,483.7	00.	JC Penney	305,718.8	73.	Schering-Plough	145,017.7
7.	Walt Disney	775,620.6	40.	Political Advertising	284,133.2	74.	Pfizer	144,789.9
8.	Pepsico	767,978.2	41.	Mars	281,608.8	75.	Hershey Foods	143,975.8
9.	Time Warner	747,319.7	42.	Mattel	278,314.1	76.	Dean Witter Discover	142,211.9
10.	AT&T	659,750.2	43.	American Express	274,870.7	77.	Philips Electronics	139,225.4
11.	Ford Motor Co. (local dealers)	616,798.1	44.	Sprint	274,024.5	78.	Darden Restaurants	138,723.4
12.	McDonalds	599,132.9	45.	Dayton Hudson	272,134.8	79.	Honda Motor Co.	
13.	Unilever PLC	593,808.2	46.	IBM	263,913.2		(local dealers)	138,221.6
14.	Sears Roebuck & Co.	592,543.9	47.	Seagram	261,349.6	80.	Glaxo Wellcome	137,316.3
15.	Grand Metropolitan PLC	579,529.2	48.	SmithKline Beecham	252,246.4	81.	Cadbury Schweppes	137,240.3
16.	News Corp.	573,463.6	49.	K-Mart	242,875.7	82.	Mitsubishi	135,562.0
17.	Toyota Motor	545,745.8	50.	Chrysler Corp. (local dealers)	242,715.1	83.	Montgomery Ward	135,475.3
18.	General Motors dealers assn	477,723.3	51.	Mazda	238,759.4	84.	Best Buy	135,234.7
19.	Nestlé	477,460.1	52.	Valassis Communications	234,376.9	85.	Kimberly-Clark	134,872.4
20.	General Motors		53.	RJR Nabisco Holdings	222,529.3	86.	Bell Atlantic	134,627.0
	(local dealers)	447,601.3	54.	Bayer Group	221,050.3	87.	SC Johnson & Sons	133,330.9
21.	American Home Products	446,425.3	55.	Visa Intl.	219,883.7	88.	Dillard Dept. Stores	133,043.1
22.	Nissan Motor Co.	439,390.3	56.	Chrysler Corp. dealer assn.	217,464.2	89.	Wm. Wrigley Jr. Co.	131,783.7
23.	National Amusements	426,920.7	57.	Hasbro	212,538.2	90.	General Electric	131,754.8
24.	Sony	418,612.9	58.	Gillette	200,717.1	91.	MacAndrews and	
25.	Kellogg Co.	410,352.4	59.	Nike	196,028.7		Forbes Holdings	131,348.1
26.	Federated Dept. Stores	407,389.9	60.	Nissan Motor Co.		92.	BAT Industries	130,801.8
27.	General Mills	401,142.7		(local dealers)	194,449.9	93.	Credit Lyonnais	130,385.7
28.	Honda Motor Co.	392,410.5	61.	Campbell Soup	194,349.1	94.	Prudential Insurance	130,026.1
29.	Circuit City Stores	390,157.1	62.	Novartis Agricultural	193,511.9	95.	Eastman Kodak	129,874.0
30.	May Depart. Stores	384,453.5	63.	Quaker Oats	184,733.8	96.	BellSouth	128,614.6
31.	Warner-Lambert	371,497.9	64.	Sara Lee	176,799.9	97.	Home Depot	128,022.7
32.	U.S. Government	365,885.2	65.	Clorox	173,140.6	98.	John A. Benckiser	122,061.2
33.	Coca-Cola	336,756.6	66.	Tandy	172,788.9	99.	Levi Strauss	121,426.6
34.	MCI Communications	333,495.7	67.	Ralston Purina	171,920.2	100.	Adolph Coors	120,809.3

U.S. Ad Spending by Selected Categories, 1996

Source: Competitive Media Reporting and Publishers Information Bureau, New York, © Copyright 1997

(in thousands of dollars, Jan.-Dec. 1996)

Category	Total ad spending	Magazine	Sunday magazines	Local newspaper	Network TV	Spot TV	Syndicated TV	Cable TV	Network radio
Automotive	$11,616,573.4	$1,445,580.5	$39,714.5	$3,990,466.1	$1,974,660.0	$3,192,801.6	$97,547.4	$442,385.0	$53,627.4
Retail	9,375,505.4	320,933.0	87,021.6	4,695,739.0	776,159.0	2,523,196.4	75,005.0	270,780.5	125,558.6
Business, consumer services	8,435,456.4	899,946.3	52,631.6	2,057,887.0	1,433,357.5	2,098,155.6	177,650.2	650,437.3	139,265.9
Entertainment . .	5,422,421.2	80,976.6	2,067.7	584,902.2	1,967,168.8	1,930,035.7	204,013.1	365,748.6	11,460.2
Food	4,018,560.5	664,488.5	48,164.8	23,077.3	1,413,256.0	847,946.9	406,638.9	423,339.9	65,789.9
Toiletries & cosmetics . . .	3,602,301.4	641,053.5	135,084.6	149,305.1	1,350,650.0	514,300.0	298,649.8	334,259.4	95,835.1
Drugs & remedies	3,326,315.8	992,512.9	21,605.3	6,877.9	1,380,061.5	268,980.0	290,493.8	319,067.9	27,525.4
Travel & hotels .	2,593,892.3	519,922.8	36,154.6	1,024,089.6	181,198.7	306,299.8	5,543.0	161,769.3	40,094.8
Direct response cos.	2,039,111.5	1,074,336.3	7,375.8	113,846.1	350,450.2	92,130.7	14,065.5	138,649.5	17,423.3
Computers, office equip. . .	1,668,775.9	109,917.6	3,326.7	5,836.0	789,213.9	276.301.6	203,833.5	192,386.3	42,498.7
Candy, snacks, & soft drinks . .	1,650,215.2	907,468.0	340,848.1	129,243.4	27,757.9	73,170.3	10,264.3	52,457.9	31,398.7
Insurance & real estate	1,635,914.7	198,189.5	10,528.2	572,860.7	278,728.7	298,891.8	7,798.6	99,102.6	20,807.8
Publishing & media	1,438,744.7	356,104.1	12,914.0	272,850.1	72,665.1	289,645.8	23,681.2	151,927.0	73,267.0
Sporting goods, toys	1,357,229.8	664,060.1	35,141.9	8,716.3	386,685.0	70,197.2	27,029.5	135,175.9	1,721.0
Apparel, footwear	1,264,511.8	258,545.0	3,457.1	6,447.9	349,441.3	219,215.0	171,524.7	241,112.9	1,404.9
Household equip.	922,568.6	190,551.5	20,701.2	22,266.9	260,122.7	162,086.9	65,170.1	158,446.0	9,397.2
Beer & wine. . . .	905,179.4	168,571.5	16,081.0	9,431.1	362,985.8	124,140.5	76,325.6	123,809.0	16,374.7
Electronic equip. .	802,839.8	38,348.0	572.7	7,284.1	412,961.4	159,698.6	6,422.0	88,520.1	5,517.7
Soaps & cleansers	657,406.4	332,982.0	6,956.9	25,472.3	97,027.7	2,924.5	16,659.2	15,273.2	61.0
Cigarettes	595,392.9	97,342.8	3,895.7	777.6	251,042.6	82,747.2	67,608.1	85,192.8	3,753.7
Jewelry, optical .	564,370.5	269,705.7	11,751.0	7,593.0	166,770.2	38,699.6	38,699.6	13,049.3	36,039.9
Building materials	441,935.2	141,841.2	9,842.9	24,198.8	69,955.2	81,676.6	11,738.9	84,629.0	4,985.6
Household furnishings . . .	377,530.3	201,167.0	1,235.2	56,028.0	0.0	175.0	0.0	113.0	0.0
Gasoline, lubricants	353,286.3	69,588.3	4,535.1	11,604.9	110,021.1	70,159.2	29,034.7	48,140.0	1,741.5
Horticulture, farming	332,498.7	167,504.2	8,156.1	21,914.4	61,026.0	38,286.0	5,374.8	17,919.1	3,531.1
Miscellaneous . .	326,417.3	16,706.2	995.1	8,118.7	76,334.6	125,712.6	4,114.5	29,136.2	4,202.7
Pets & pet foods	264,905.1	25,368.3	16,942.0	50,836.9	30,885.0	60,209.2	11,918.0	34,349.8	18,875.7
Liquor	225,992.8	186,123.0	4,499.3	3,406.4	0.0	599.9	.0	25.2	0.0
Freight, industrial	199,571.4	47,484.0	107.1	6,035.4	77,206.3	31,363.7	1,102.0	13,005.1	2,322.2
Industrial materials	164,369.3	65,193.5	34.3	5,779.9	31,721.7	25,260.3	3,759.1	13,103.5	4,389.7
Bus. propositions	68,844.8	41,034.2	43.2	6,568.8	0.0	2,331.2	0.0	700.3	0.0
Airplanes (not travel)	32,557.4	10,198.2	0.0	7,474.6	0.0	996.5	0.0	1,035.3	0.0
Total.	**66,710,858.6**	**11,213,758.1**	**942,393.6**	**13,928,813.1**	**14,739,557.4**	**14,017,723.7**	**2,326,105.4**	**4,728,350.0**	**805,924.3**

DISASTERS

Disasters are reported as of Sept. 1997. Listings are selective and generally do not include disasters having relatively low fatalities in a particular category.

Some Notable Shipwrecks Since 1854

(Figures indicate estimated lives lost.)

1854, Mar.—City of Glasgow; Brit. steamer missing in N Atlantic; 480.

1854, Sept. 27—Arctic; U.S. (Collins Line) steamer sunk in collision with French steamer *Vesta* near Cape Race; 285-351.

1856, Jan. 23—Pacific; U.S. (Collins Line) steamer missing in N Atlantic; 186-286.

1858, Sept. 23—Austria; German steamer destroyed by fire in N Atlantic; 471.

1863, Apr. 27—Anglo-Saxon; Brit. steamer wrecked at Cape Race; 238.

1865, Apr. 27—Sultana; Mississippi River steamer blew up near Memphis, TN; 1,450.

1869, Oct. 27—Stonewall; steamer burned on Mississippi River below Cairo, IL; 200.

1870, Jan. 25—City of Boston; Brit. (Inman Line) steamer vanished between New York and Liverpool; 177.

1870, Oct. 19—Cambria; Brit. steamer wrecked off N Ireland; 196.

1872, Nov. 7—Mary Celeste; U.S. half-brig sailed from New York for Genoa; found abandoned in Atlantic 4 weeks later in mystery of sea; crew never heard from; loss of life unknown.

1873, Jan. 22—Northfleet; Brit. steamer foundered off Dungeness, England; 300.

1873, Apr. 1—Atlantic; Brit. (White Star) steamer wrecked off Nova Scotia; 585.

1873, Nov. 23—Ville du Havre; French steamer sank after collision with Brit. sailing ship *Loch Earn*; 226.

1875, May 7—Schiller; German steamer wrecked off Scilly Isles; 312.

1875, Nov. 4—Pacific; U.S. steamer sank after collision off Cape Flattery; 236.

1878, Sept. 3—Princess Alice; Brit. steamer sank after collision in Thames River; 700.

1878, Dec. 18—Byzantin; French steamer sank after collision in Dardanelles; 210.

1881, May 24—Victoria; steamer capsized in Thames River, Canada; 200.

1883, Jan. 19—Cimbria; German steamer sank in collision with Brit. steamer *Sultan* in North Sea; 389.

1887, Nov. 15—Wah Yeung; Brit. steamer burned at sea; 400.

1890, Feb. 17—Duburg; Brit. steamer wrecked, China Sea; 400.

1890, Sept. 19—Ertogrul; Turkish frigate foundered off Japan; 540.

1891, Mar. 17—Utopia; Brit. steamer sank in collision with Brit. ironclad *Anson* off Gibraltar; 562.

1895, Jan. 30—Elbe; German steamer sank in collision with Brit. steamer *Craithie* in North Sea; 332.

1895, Mar. 11—Reina Regenta; Spanish cruiser foundered near Gibraltar; 400.

1898, Feb. 15—Maine; U.S. battleship blown up in Havana Harbor; 260.

1898, July 4—La Bourgogne; French steamer sank in collision with Brit. sailing ship *Cromartyshire* off Nova Scotia; 549.

1898, Nov. 26—Portland; U.S. steamer wrecked off Cape Cod; 157.

1904, June 15—General Slocum; excursion steamer burned in East River, New York City; 1,030.

1904, June 28—Norge; Danish steamer wrecked on Rockall Island, Scotland; 620.

1906, Aug. 4—Sirio; Italian steamer wrecked off Cape Palos, Spain; 350.

1908, Mar. 23—Matsu Maru; Japanese steamer sank in collision near Hakodate, Japan; 300.

1909, Aug. 1—Waratah; Brit. steamer, Sydney to London, vanished; 300.

1910, Feb. 9—General Chanzy; French steamer wrecked off Minorca, Spain; 200.

1911, Sept. 25—Liberté; French battleship exploded at Toulon; 285.

1912, Mar. 5—Principe de Asturias; Spanish steamer wrecked off Spain; 500.

1912, Apr. 14-15—Titanic; Brit. (White Star) steamer hit iceberg in N Atlantic; 1,503.

1912, Sept. 28—Kichemaru; Japanese steamer sank off Japanese coast; 1,000.

1914, May 29—Empress of Ireland; Brit. (Canadian Pacific) steamer sunk in collision with Norwegian collier in St. Lawrence River; 1,014.

1915, May 7—Lusitania; Brit. (Cunard Line) steamer torpedoed and sunk by German submarine off Ireland; 1,198.

1915, July 24—Eastland; excursion steamer capsized in Chicago River; 812.

1916, Feb. 26—Provence; French cruiser sank in Mediterranean; 3,100.

1916, Mar. 3—Principe de Asturias; Spanish steamer wrecked near Santos, Brazil; 558.

1916, Aug. 29—Hsin Yu; Chinese steamer sank off Chinese coast; 1,000.

1917, Dec. 6—Mont Blanc, Imo; French ammunition ship and Belgian steamer collided in Halifax Harbor; 1,600.

1918, Apr. 25—Kiang-Kwan; Chinese steamer sank in collision off Hankow; 500.

1918, July 12—Kawachi; Japanese battleship blew up in Tokayama Bay; 500.

1918, Oct. 25—Princess Sophia; Canadian steamer sank off Alaskan coast; 398.

1919, Jan. 17—Chaonia; French steamer lost in Straits of Messina, Italy; 460.

1919, Sept. 9—Valbanera; Spanish steamer lost off Florida coast; 500.

1921, Mar. 18—Hong Kong; steamer wrecked in South China Sea; 1,000.

1922, Aug. 26—Niitaka; Japanese cruiser sank in storm off Kamchatka, USSR; 300.

1924, June 12—USS Mississippi; U.S. battleship; explosions in gun turret, off San Pedro, CA; 48.

1927, Oct. 25—Principessa Mafalda; Italian steamer blew up, sank off Porto Seguro, Brazil; 314.

1928, Nov. 12—Vestris; Brit. steamer sank in gale off Virginia; 113.

1934, Sept. 8—Morro Castle; U.S. steamer, Havana to New York, burned off Asbury Park, NJ; 134.

1939, May 23—Squalus; U.S. submarine sank off Portsmouth, NH; 26.

1939, June 1—Thetis; Brit. submarine sank in Liverpool Bay; 99.

1942, Feb. 18—Truxtun and Pollux; U.S. destroyer and cargo ship ran aground, sank off Newfoundland; 204.

1942, Oct. 2—Curacao; Brit. cruiser sank after collision with liner Queen Mary; 338.

1944, Dec. 17-18—3 U.S. Third Fleet destroyers sank during typhoon in Philippine Sea; 790.

1947, Jan. 19—Himera; Greek steamer hit a mine off Athens; 392.

1947, Apr. 16—Grandcamp; French freighter exploded in Texas City, TX, harbor, starting fires; 510.

1948, Nov.—Chinese army evacuation ship exploded and sank off S Manchuria; 6,000.

1948, Dec. 3—Kiangya; Chinese refugee ship wrecked in explosion S of Shanghai; 1,100+.

1949, Sept. 17—Noronic; Canadian Great Lakes Cruiser burned at Toronto dock; 130.

1952, Apr. 26—Hobson and Wasp; U.S. destroyer and aircraft carrier collided in Atlantic; 176.

1954, May 26—Pennington; sank off RI coast; 103.

1954, Sept. 26—Toya Maru; Japanese ferry sank in Tsugaru Strait, Japan; 1,172.

1956, July 26—Andrea Doria and Stockholm; Italian liner and Swedish liner collided off Nantucket; 51.

1957, July 14—Eshghabad; Soviet ship ran aground in Caspian Sea; 270.

1960, Dec. 19—Constellation; U.S. aircraft carrier, caught fire in Brooklyn Navy Yard, NY; 49.

1961, July 8—Save; Portuguese ship ran aground off Mozambique; 259.

1962, Apr. 8—Dara; Brit. liner exploded and sank in Persian Gulf; 236.

1963, Apr. 10—Thresher; U.S. Navy atomic submarine sank in N Atlantic; 129.

1964, Feb. 10—Voyager and Melbourne; Australian destroyer *Voyager* sank after collision with Australian aircraft carrier *Melbourne* off New South Wales; 82.

1965, Nov. 13—Yarmouth Castle; Panamanian registered cruise ship burned and sank off Nassau; 89.

1967, July 29—Forrestal; U.S. aircraft carrier caught fire off N Vietnam; 134.

1968, Jan. 25—Dakar; Israeli submarine vanished in Mediterranean Sea; 69.

1968, late May—Scorpion; U.S. nuclear submarine sank in Atlantic near Azores; 99 (located Oct. 31).

1969, June 2—Evans; U.S. destroyer cut in half by Australian carrier *Melbourne*, S China Sea; 74.

1970, Mar. 4—Eurydice; French submarine sank in Mediterranean near Toulon; 57.

1970, Dec. 15—Namyong-Ho; South Korean ferry sank in Korea Strait; 308.

1974, May 1—Motor launch capsized off Bangladesh; 250.

1974, Sept. 26—Soviet destroyer burned and sank in Black Sea; 200+.

1975, Nov. 10—Edmund Fitzgerald; U.S. cargo ship sank during storm on Lake Superior; 29.

1976, Oct. 20—George Prince and **Frosta;** ferryboat and Norwegian tanker collided on Mississippi R. at Luling, LA; 77.

1976, Dec. 25—Patria; Egyptian liner caught fire and sank in the Red Sea; 100.

1979, Aug. 14—23 yachts competing in Fastnet yacht race sank or abandoned during storm in S Irish Sea; 18.

1981, Jan. 27—Tamponas II; Indonesian passenger ship caught fire and sank in Java Sea; 580.

1981, May 26—Nimitz; U.S. Marine combat jet crashed on deck of U.S. aircraft carrier; 14.

1983, Feb. 12—Marine Electric; coal freighter sank during storm off Chincoteague, VA; 33.

1983, May 25—10th of Ramadan; Nile steamer caught fire and sank in Lake Nasser; 357.

1986, Apr. 20—ferry sinks near Barisal, Bangladesh; 262.

1986, Aug. 31—Soviet passenger ship **Admiral Nakhimov** and Soviet freighter *Pyotr Vasev* collided in Black Sea; 398.

1987, Mar. 6—Brit. ferry capsized off Zeebrugge, Belg.; 189.

1987, Dec. 20—Philippine ferry *Dona Paz* and oil tanker *Victor* collided in Tablas Strait; 3,000+.

1988, Aug. 6—Indian ferry capsized on Ganges R.; 400+.

1989, Apr. 19—USS Iowa; U.S. battleship; explosion in gun turret; 47.

1989, Aug. 20—Brit. barge *Bowbelle* struck Brit. pleasure cruiser *Marchioness* on Thames R. in central London; 56.

1989, Sept. 10—Romanian pleasure boat and Bulgarian barge collided on Danube R.; 161.

1991, Apr. 10—Auto ferry and oil tanker collided outside Livorno Harbor, Italy; 140.

1991, Dec. 14—Salem Express; ferry rammed coral reef near Safaga, Egypt; 462.

1993, Feb. 17—Neptune; ferry capsized off Port-au-Prince, Haiti; 500+.

1993, Oct. 10—West Sea Ferry; capsized in Yellow Sea near W South Korea during storm; 285.

1994, Sept. 28—Estonia; ferry sank in Baltic Sea when water entered through bow door; 1,049.

1996, May 21—Bukoba; ferry sank in Lake Victoria; 500.

1997, Feb. 20—Tamil refugee boat sank off Sri Lanka; 165.

1997, Mar. 28—Albanian refugee boat sank in Adriatic Sea after being rammed by Italian navy warship *Sibilla;* 83.

1997, Sept. 8—Pride of la Gonâve; Haitian ferry sank off Montrouis, Haiti; 200+.

Some Notable Aircraft Disasters Since 1937

Date	Aircraft	Site of accident	Deaths
1937, May 6	German zeppelin Hindenburg	Burned at mooring, Lakehurst, NJ	36[1]
1944, Aug. 23	U.S. Air Force B-24 Liberator bomber	Hit school, Freckleton, England	61[1]
1945, July 28	U.S. Army B-25	Hit Empire State Building, New York, NY	14[1]
1952, Dec. 20	U.S. Air Force C-124	Fell, burned, Moses Lake, WA	87
1953, Mar. 3	Canadian Pacific Comet Jet	Karachi, Pakistan	11[2]
1953, June 18	U.S. Air Force C-124	Crashed, burned near Tokyo	129
1955, Oct. 6	United Airlines DC-4	Crashed in Medicine Bow Peak, WY	66
1955, Nov. 1	United Airlines DC-6B	Exploded, crashed near Longmont, CO	44[3]
1956, June 20	Venezuelan Super-Constellation	Crashed in Atlantic off Asbury Park, NJ	74
1956, June 30	TWA Super-Const., United DC-7	Collided over Grand Canyon, AZ	128
1960, Dec. 16	United DC-8 jet, TWA Super-Const.	Collided over New York City	134[4]
1962, Mar. 16	Flying Tiger Super-Constellation	Vanished in W Pacific	107
1962, June 3	Air France Boeing 707 jet	Crashed on takeoff from Paris	130
1962, June 22	Air France Boeing 707 jet	Crashed in storm, Guadeloupe, W.I.	113
1963, June 3	Chartered Northwest Airlines DC-7	Crashed in Pacific off British Columbia	101
1963, Nov. 29	Trans-Canada Airlines DC-8F	Crashed after takeoff from Montreal	118
1965, May 20	Pakistani Boeing 720-B	Crashed at Cairo, Egypt, airport	121
1966, Jan. 24	Air India Boeing 707 jetliner	Crashed on Mont Blanc, France-Italy	117
1966, Feb. 4	All-Nippon Boeing 727	Plunged into Tokyo Bay	133
1966, Mar. 5	BOAC Boeing 707 jetliner	Crashed on Mount Fuji, Japan	124
1966, Dec. 24	U.S. military-chartered CL-44	Crashed into village in South Vietnam	129[1]
1967, Apr. 20	Swiss Britannia turboprop	Crashed at Nicosia, Cyprus	126
1967, July 19	Piedmont Boeing 727, Cessna 310	Collided in air, Hendersonville, NC	82
1968, Apr. 20	S. African Airways Boeing 707	Crashed on takeoff, Windhoek, South-West Africa	122
1968, May 3	Braniff International Electra	Crashed in storm near Dawson, TX	85
1969, Mar. 16	Venezuelan DC-9	Crashed after takeoff from Maracaibo, Venezuela	155[5]
1969, Dec. 8	Olympic Airways DC-6B	Crashed near Athens in storm	93
1970, Feb. 15	Dominican DC-9	Crashed into sea on takeoff from Santo Domingo	102
1970, July 3	British chartered jetliner	Crashed near Barcelona, Spain	112
1970, July 5	Air Canada DC-8	Crashed near Toronto International Airport	108
1970, Aug. 9	Peruvian turbojet	Crashed after takeoff from Cuzco, Peru	101[1]
1970, Nov. 14	Southern Airways DC-9	Crashed in mountains near Huntington, WV	75[6]
1971, July 30	All-Nippon Boeing 727 and Japanese Air Force F-86	Collided over Morioka, Japan	162[7]
1971, Sept. 4	Alaska Airlines Boeing 727	Crashed into mountain near Juneau, AK	111
1972, Aug. 14	East German Ilyushin-62	Crashed on takeoff, East Berlin	156
1972, Oct. 13	Aeroflot Ilyushin-62	Soviet airline crashed near Moscow	176
1972, Dec. 3	Chartered Spanish airliner	Crashed on takeoff, Canary Islands	155
1972, Dec. 29	Eastern Airlines Lockheed Tristar	Crashed on approach to Miami Intl. Airport	101
1973, Jan. 22	Chartered Boeing 707	Burst into flames during landing, Kano Airport, Nigeria	176
1973, Feb. 21	Libyan jetliner	Shot down by Israeli fighter planes over Sinai	108
1973, Apr. 10	British Vanguard turboprop	Crashed during snowstorm at Basel, Switzerland	104
1973, June 3	Soviet Supersonic TU-144	Crashed near Goussainville, France	14[8]
1973, July 11	Brazilian Boeing 707	Crashed on approach to Orly Airport, Paris	122
1973, July 31	Delta Airlines jetliner	Crashed, landing in fog at Logan Airport, Boston	89
1973, Dec. 23	French Caravelle jet	Crashed in Morocco	106
1974, Mar. 3	Turkish DC-10 jet	Crashed at Ermenonville near Paris	346
1974, Apr. 23	Pan American 707 jet	Crashed in Bali, Indonesia	107
1974, Dec. 1	TWA-727	Crashed in storm, Upperville, VA	92
1974, Dec. 4	Dutch-chartered DC-8	Crashed in storm near Colombo, Sri Lanka	191
1975, Apr. 4	Air Force Galaxy C-5A	Crashed near Saigon, S Vietnam, after takeoff carrying orphans	172
1975, June 24	Eastern Airlines 727 jet	Crashed in storm, JFK Airport, NY	113
1975, Aug. 3	Chartered 707	Hit mountainside, Agadir, Morocco	188
1976, Sept. 10	British Airways Trident, Yugoslav DC-9	Collided near Zagreb, Yugoslavia	176
1976, Sept. 19	Turkish 727	Hit mountain, S Turkey	155
1976, Oct. 13	Bolivian 707 cargo jet	Crashed in Santa Cruz, Bolivia	100[9]
1977, Mar. 27	KLM 747, Pan American 747	Collided on runway, Tenerife, Canary Islands	582
1977, Nov. 19	TAP Boeing 727	Crashed on Madeira	130
1977, Dec. 4	Malaysian Boeing 737	Hijacked, then exploded in mid-air over Straits of Johore	100
1977, Dec. 13	U.S. DC-3	Crashed after takeoff at Evansville, IN	29[10]

(continued)

Some Notable Aircraft Disasters Since 1937 (*continued*)

Date	Aircraft	Site of accident	Deaths
1978, Jan. 1	Air India 747	Exploded, crashed into sea off Bombay	213
1978, Sept. 25	Boeing 727, Cessna 172	Collided in air, San Diego, CA	150
1978, Nov. 15	Chartered DC-8	Crashed near Colombo, Sri Lanka	183
1979, May 25	American Airlines DC-10	Crashed after takeoff at O'Hare Intl. Airport, Chicago	275[11]
1979, Aug. 17	Two Soviet Aeroflot jetliners	Collided over Ukraine	173
1979, Nov. 26	Pakistani Boeing 707	Crashed near Jidda, Saudi Arabia	156
1979, Nov. 28	New Zealand DC-10	Crashed into mountain in Antarctica	257
1980, Mar. 14	Polish Ilyushin 62	Crashed making emergency landing, Warsaw	87[12]
1980, Aug. 19	Saudi Arabian Tristar	Burned after emergency landing, Riyadh	301
1981, Dec. 1	Yugoslavian DC-9	Crashed into mountain in Corsica	178
1982, Jan. 13	Air Florida Boeing 737	Crashed into Potomac R. after takeoff	78
1982, July 9	Pan Am Boeing 727	Crashed after takeoff in Kenner, LA	153[13]
1983, Sept. 1	S. Korean Boeing 747	Shot down after violating Soviet airspace	269
1983, Nov. 27	Colombian Boeing 747	Crashed near Barajas Airport, Madrid	183
1985, Feb. 19	Spanish Boeing 727	Crashed into Mt. Oiz, Spain	148
1985, June 23	Air-India Boeing 747	Crashed into Atlantic Ocean S of Ireland	329
1985, Aug. 2	Delta Air Lines L-1011	Crashed at Dallas-Ft. Worth Intl. Airport	137
1985, Aug. 12	Japan Air Lines Boeing 747	Crashed into Mt. Ogura, Japan	520[14]
1985, Dec. 12	Arrow Air DC-8	Crashed after takeoff in Gander, Newfoundland	256[15]
1986, Mar. 31	Mexican Boeing 727	Crashed NW of Mexico City	166
1986, Aug. 31	Aeromexico DC-9	Collided with Piper PA-28 over Cerritos, CA	82[16]
1987, May 9	Polish Ilyushin 62M	Crashed after takeoff in Warsaw, Poland	183
1987, Aug. 16	Northwest Airlines MD-82	Crashed after takeoff in Romulus, MI	156
1987, Nov. 28	S. African Boeing 747	Crashed into Indian Ocean near Mauritius	159
1987, Nov. 29	S. Korean Boeing 707	Exploded over Thai-Burmese border	155
1988, Mar. 17	Colombian Boeing 707	Crashed into mountainside near Venezuela border	137
1988, July 3	Iranian A300 Airbus	Shot down by U.S. Navy warship *Vincennes* over Persian Gulf	290
1988, Dec. 21	Pan Am Boeing 747	Exploded and crashed in Lockerbie, Scotland	270[17]
1989, Feb. 8	U.S. Boeing 707	Crashed into mountain in Azores Islands off Portugal	144
1989, June 7	Suriname DC-8	Crashed near Paramaribo Airport, Suriname	168
1989, July 19	United Airlines DC-10	Crashed while landing in Sioux City, IA	111
1989, Sept. 19	French DC-10	Exploded in air over Niger	171
1991, May 26	Lauda-Air Boeing 767-300	Exploded over rural Thailand	223
1991, July 11	Nigerian DC-8	Crashed while landing at Jidda, Saudi Arabia	261
1991, Oct. 5	Indonesian military transport	Crashed after takeoff from Jakarta	137[1]
1992, July 31	Thai Airbus A-300-310	Crashed into mountain S. of Kathmandu, Nepal	113
1992, Oct. 4	El Al Boeing 747-200F	Crashed into 2 apartment bldgs., Amsterdam, Netherlands	120[1]
1994, Jan. 3	Aeroflot TU-154	Crashed and exploded after takeoff in Irkhutsk, Russia	125[18]
1994, Apr. 26	China Airlines Airbus A-300-600R	Crashed at Japan's Nagoya Airport	264
1994, June 16	China Northwest Airlines TU-154	Crashed 10 min. after takeoff	160
1994, Sept. 8	USAir Boeing 737-300	Crashed in Aliquippa, PA, near Pittsburgh Intl. Airport	132
1994, Oct. 31	American Eagle ATR-72-210	Crashed in field near Roselawn, IN	68
1995, Aug. 11	Aviateca Boeing 737	Crashed into Chichontepec volcano, El Salvador	65
1995, Dec. 20	American Airlines Boeing 757	Crashed into mountain 50 mi N of Cali, Colombia	160
1996, Jan. 8	Antonova 32 cargo jet	Crashed into central market, Kinshasa, Zaire	350+[1]
1996, Feb. 6	Turkish Boeing 757	Crashed into Atlantic Ocean, off Dominican Republic	189
1996, Apr. 25	T-43, a military version of a Boeing 737	Crashed into mountain near Dubrovnik, Croatia	35[19]
1996, May 11	ValuJet DC-9	Crashed into the Florida Everglades after takeoff	110
1996, July 17	Trans World Airlines Boeing 747	Exploded and crashed in Atlantic Ocean, off Long Isl., NY	230
1996, Aug. 29	Vnukovo TU-154	Crashed into mountain on Arctic island of Spitsbergen	141
1996, Oct. 2	Aeroperu Boeing 757	Crashed in Pacific after takeoff from Lima, Peru	70
1996, Oct. 31	Brazilian TAM Fokker-100	Crashed into houses in São Paulo, Brazil	98[20]
1996, Nov. 7	Nigerian Boeing 727	Crashed into a lagoon 40 mi SE of Lagos, Nigeria	143
1996, Nov. 12	Saudi Arabian Boeing 747, Kazakh Ilyushin-76 cargo plane	Collided in midair near New Delhi, India	349[21]
1996, Nov. 23	Ethiopian Boeing 767	Hijacked, then crashed in Indian Ocean off the Comoros	127
1997, Jan. 9	Comair Embraer 120	Crashed on approach into Detroit Metro. Airport	29
1997, Feb. 4	2 Sikorsky CH-53 transport helicopters	Collided in midair over northern Galilee, Israel	73
1997, May 8	China Southern Airlines Boeing 737	Crashed on approach into Shenzhen's Huangtian Airport	35
1997, July 11	Cubana de Aviación Antonov-24	Crashed into the Caribbean off SE Cuba	44
1997, Aug. 6	Korean Air Boeing 747-300	Crashed into jungle on Guam on approach into airport	228
1997, Sept. 3	Vietnamese Airlines Tupolev Tu-134	Crashed on approach into Phnom Penh airport	64
1997, Sept. 14	American C-141 cargo plane, German Tupolev TU-154	Collided in midair off SW Africa	33
1997, Sept. 26	Indonesian Airbus A-300	Crashed near Medan, Indonesia, airport	234

(1) Incl. those on ground and in buildings. (2) First fatal crash of commercial jet plane. (3) Caused by bomb planted by John G. Graham in insurance plot to kill his mother, a passenger. (4) Incl. all 128 aboard planes and 6 on ground. (5) Killed 84 on the plane and 71 on the ground. (6) Incl. 43 Marshall University football players and coaches. (7) Airliner-fighter crash; pilot of fighter parachuted to safety, was arrested for negligence. (8) First supersonic plane crash; killed 6 crewmen and 8 on ground; there were no passengers. (9) Crew of 3 killed; 97, mostly children, killed on the ground. (10) Incl. Univ. of Evansville basketball team. (11) Highest death toll in U.S. aviation history. (12) Incl. 22 members of U.S. boxing team. (13) Incl. 8 on the ground. (14) Worst single-plane disaster. (15) Incl. 248 members of U.S. 101st Airborne Division. (16) Incl. 15 on the ground. (17) Incl. 11 on the ground. (18) Incl. 1 on the ground. (19) Incl. U.S. Sec. of Commerce Ronald Brown. (20) Incl. 2 on the ground. (21) World's worst midair collision.

Some Notable Railroad Disasters

Date	Location	Deaths	Date	Location	Deaths
1876, Dec. 29	Ashtabula, OH	92	1907, Jan. 2	Volland, KS	33
1880, Aug. 11	Mays Landing, NJ	40	1907, Jan. 19	Fowler, IN	29
1887, Aug. 10	Chatsworth, IL	81	1907, Feb. 16	New York, NY	22
1888, Oct. 10	Mud Run, PA	55	1907, Feb. 23	Colton, CA	26
1891, June 14	Nr. Basel, Switzerland	100	1907, May 11	Lompoc, CA	36
1896, July 30	Atlantic City, NJ	60	1907, July 20	Salem, MI	33
1903, Dec. 23	Laurel Run, PA	53	1908, Sept. 25	Young's Point, MT	21
1904, Aug. 7	Eden, CO	96	1909, Jan. 15	Dotsero, CO	21
1904, Sept. 24	New Market, TN	56	1910, Mar. 1	Wellington, WA	96
1906, Mar. 16	Florence, CO	35	1910, Mar. 21	Green Mountain, IA	55
1906, Oct. 28	Atlantic City, NJ	40	1911, Aug. 25	Manchester, NY	29
1906, Dec. 30	Washington, DC	53	1912, July 4	East Corning, NY	39

Date	Location	Deaths	Date	Location	Deaths
1912, July 5	Ligonier, PA	23	1952, July 9	Rzepin, Poland	
1914, Aug. 5	Tipton Ford, MO	43	1952, Oct. 8	Harrow, England	1
1914, Sept. 15	Lebanon, MO	28	1953, Mar. 27	Conneaut, OH	2
1915, May 22	Nr. Gretna, Scotland	227	1955, Apr. 3	Guadalajara, Mexico	300
1916, Mar. 29	Amherst, OH	27	1956, Jan. 22	Los Angeles, CA	30
1917, Sept. 28	Kellyville, OK	23	1956, Feb. 28	Swampscott, MA	13
1917, Dec. 12	Modane, France	543[1]	1956, Sept. 5	Springer, NM	20
1917, Dec. 20	Shepherdsville, KY	46	1957, June 11	Vroman, CO	12
1918, June 22	Ivanhoe, IN	68	1957, Sept. 1	Kendal, Jamaica	178
1918, July 9	Nashville, TN	101	1957, Sept. 29	Montgomery, W Pakistan	250
1918, Nov. 1	Brooklyn, NY	97	1957, Dec. 4	London, England	90
1919, Jan. 12	South Byron, NY	22	1958, May 8	Rio de Janeiro, Brazil	128
1919, Dec. 20	Onawa, ME	23	1958, Sept. 15	Elizabethport, NJ	48
1921, Feb. 27	Porter, IN	37	1960, Mar. 1	Bakersfield, CA	14
1921, Dec. 5	Woodmont, PA	27	1960, Nov. 14	Pardubice, Czech.	110
1922, Aug. 5	Sulphur Spring, MO	34	1962, Jan. 8	Woerden, Netherlands	91
1922, Dec. 13	Humble, TX	22	1962, May 3	Tokyo, Japan	163
1923, Sept. 27	Lockett, WY	31	1962, July 28	Steelton, PA	19
1925, June 16	Hackettstown, NJ	50	1964, July 26	Porto, Portugal	94
1925, Oct. 27	Victoria, MS	21	1966, Dec. 28	Everett, MA	13
1926, Sept. 5	Waco, CO	30	1970, Feb. 1	Buenos Aires, Argentina	236
1928, Aug. 24	IRT subway, Times Sq., NY	18	1971, June 10	Salem, IL	11
1937, July 16	Nr. Patna, India	107	1972, June 16	Vierzy, France	107
1938, June 19	Saugus, MT	47	1972, July 21	Seville, Spain	76
1939, Aug. 12	Harney, NV	24	1972, Oct. 6	Saltillo, Mexico	208
1939, Dec. 22	Near Magdeburg, Germany	132	1972, Oct. 30	Chicago, IL	45
1939, Dec. 22	Near Friedrichshafen, Germany	99	1974, Aug. 30	Zagreb, Yugoslavia	153
1940, Apr. 19	Little Falls, NY	31	1975, Feb. 28	London subway train	41
1940, July 31	Cuyahoga Falls, OH	43	1977, Jan. 18	Granville, Australia	83
1943, Aug. 29	Wayland, NY	27	1977, Feb. 4	Chicago, IL, elevated train	11
1943, Sept. 6	Frankford Junction, Philadelphia, PA	79	1981, June 6	Bihar, India	500+
1943, Dec. 16	Between Rennert and Buie, NC	72	1982, Jan. 27	El Asnam, Algeria	130
1944, Jan. 16	Leon Prov., Spain	500	1982, July 11	Tepic, Mexico	120
1944, Mar. 2	Salerno, Italy	521	1983, Feb. 19	Empalme, Mexico	100
1944, July 6	High Bluff, TN	35	1987, Jan. 4	Essex, MD	16
1944, Aug. 4	Near Stockton, GA	47	1988, Dec. 12	London, England	115
1944, Sept. 14	Dewey, IN	29	1989, Jan. 15	Maizdi Khan, Bangladesh	110+
1944, Dec. 31	Bagley, UT	50	1990, Jan. 4	Sindh Prov., Pakistan	210+
1945, Aug. 9	Michigan, ND	34	1991, May 14	Shigaraki, Japan	42
1946, Mar. 20	Aracaju, Mexico	185	1993, Sept. 22	Big Bayou Conot, AL	47
1946, Apr. 25	Naperville, IL	45	1994, Mar. 8	Nr. Durban, South Africa	63
1947, Feb. 18	Gallitzin, PA	24	1994, Sept. 22	Tolunda, Angola	300
1949, Oct. 22	Nr. Dwor, Poland	200+	1995, Mar. 20	Tokyo subway	12[2]
1950, Feb. 17	Rockville Centre, NY	31	1995, Aug. 20	Firozabad, India	300+
1950, Sept. 11	Coshocton, OH	33	1996, Feb. 16	Silver Spring, MD	12
1950, Nov. 22	Richmond Hill, NY	79	1997, Mar. 3	Punjab State, Pakistan	125
1951, Feb. 6	Woodbridge, NJ	84	1997, Mar. 31	Huarte Arakil, Spain	21
1951, Nov. 12	Wyuta, WY	17	1997, Apr. 29	Rongjiawan Station, Hunan, China	58
1951, Nov. 25	Woodstock, AL	17	1997, May 4	Rwanda	100+
1952, Mar. 4	Nr. Rio de Janeiro, Brazil	119	1997, Sept. 14	Central India	77

(1) World's worst train wreck; passenger train derailed. (2) Sarin nerve gas released in subway.

Principal U.S. Mine Disasters Since 1900

Source: Bureau of Mines, U.S. Dept. of the Interior; Mine Safety and Health Admin., U.S. Dept. of Labor

(Prior to 1970, only disasters with losses of 75 or more lives are listed; since 1970, all disasters in which 5 or more people were killed are listed. All are bituminous-coal mines unless otherwise noted.)

Date	Location	Deaths	Date	Location	Deaths
1900, May 1	Scofield, UT	200	1924, Apr. 28	Benwood, WV	119
1902, May 19	Coal Creek, TN	184	1926, Jan. 13	Wilburton, OK	91
1902, July 10	Johnstown, PA	112	1927, Apr. 30	Everettville, WV	97
1903, June 30	Hanna, WY	169	1928, May 19	Mather, PA	195
1904, Jan. 25	Cheswick, PA	179	1930, Nov. 5	Millfield, OH	82
1905, Feb. 26	Virginia City, AL	112	1940, Jan. 10	Bartley, WV	91
1907, Jan. 29	Stuart, WV	84	1947, Mar. 25	Centralia, IL	111
1907, Dec. 6	Monongah, WV	361	1951, Dec. 21	West Frankfort, IL	119
1907, Dec. 19	Jacobs Creek, PA	239	1968, Nov. 20	Farmington, WV	78
1908, Nov. 28	Marianna, PA	154	1970, Dec. 30	Hyden, KY	38
1909, Nov. 13	Cherry, IL	259	1971, Apr. 12	Rosiclare, IL[3]	7
1910, Jan. 31	Primero, CO	75	1972, May 2	Kellogg, ID[2]	91
1910, May 5	Palos, AL	90	1972, July 22	Blacksville, WV	9
1910, Nov. 8	Delagua, CO	79	1972, Dec. 16	Itmann, WV	5
1911, Apr. 8	Littleton, AL	128	1976, Mar. 9	Oven Fork, KY	15
1911, Dec. 9	Briceville, TN	84	1976, Mar. 11	Oven Fork, KY	8
1912, Mar. 26	Jed, WV	83	1977, Mar. 1	Tower City, PA	9
1913, Apr. 23	Finleyville, PA	96	1978, Apr. 4	Duty, VA	5
1913, Oct. 22	Dawson, NM	263	1979, June 8	Franklin, LA[3]	5
1914, Apr. 28	Eccles, WV	181	1980, Nov. 7	Clothier, WV	5
1915, Mar. 2	Layland, WV	112	1981, Apr. 15	Redstone, CO	15
1917, Apr. 27	Hastings, CO	121	1981, Dec. 7	Topmost, KY	8
1917, June 8	Butte, MT[2]	163	1981, Dec. 8	Whitwell, TN	13
1919, June 5	Wilkes-Barre, PA[1]	92	1982, Jan. 20	Craynor, KY	7
1922, Nov. 6	Spangler, PA	77	1983, June 21	Dante, VA	7
1922, Nov. 22	Dolomite, AL	90	1984, Dec. 19	Huntington, UT	27
1923, Feb. 8	Dawson, NM	120	1986, Feb. 6	Fairview, WV	5
1923, Aug. 14	Kemmerer, WY	99	1989, Sept. 13	Sturgis, KY	10
1924, Mar. 8	Castle Gate, UT	171	1992, Dec. 7	Norton, VA	8

Note: World's worst mine disaster killed 1,549 workers in Honkeiko Colliery in Manchuria, Apr. 25, 1942. (1) Anthracite mine. (2) Metal mine. (3) Nonmetal mine.

Some Notable U.S. Tornadoes Since 1925

Date	Location	Deaths	Date	Location	Deaths
25, Mar. 18	MO, IL, IN	689	1968, May 15	Midwest	71
927, Apr. 12	Rock Springs, TX	74	1969, Jan. 23	MS	32
927, May 9	AR, Poplar Bluff, MO.	92	1971, Feb. 21	Mississippi delta	110
1927, Sept. 29	St. Louis, MO.	90	1973, May 26-27	South, Midwest (series)	47
1930, May 6	Hill, Navarro, Ellis Co., TX.	41	1974, Apr. 3-4	AL, GA, TN, KY, OH	315
1932, Mar. 21	AL (series of tornadoes)	268	1977, Apr. 4	AL, MS, GA.	22
1936, Apr. 5	MS, GA	455	1979, Apr. 10	TX, OK.	60
1936, Apr. 6	Gainesville, GA	203	1980, June 3	Grand Island, NE (series)	4
1938, Sept. 29	Charleston, SC.	32	1982, Mar. 2-4	South, Midwest (series)	17
1942, Mar. 16	Central to NE Mississippi.	75	1982, May 29	Southern IL	10
1942, Apr. 27	Rogers and Mayes Co., OK.	52	1983, May 18-22	TX	12
1944, June 23	OH, PA, WV, MD	150	1984, Mar. 28	NC, SC.	57
1945, Apr. 12	OK-AR.	102	1984, Apr. 21-22	MS	15
1947, Apr. 9	TX, OK, KS	169	1984, Apr. 26	OK-MN (series)	17
1948, Mar. 19	Bunker Hill and Gillespie, IL.	33	1985, May 31	NY, PA, OH, Ont. (series)	75
1949, Jan. 3	LA and AR.	58	1987, May 22	Saragosa, TX	29
1952, Mar. 21	AR, MO, TN (series)	208	1989, Nov. 15	Huntsville, AL.	18
1953, May 11	Waco, TX	114	1989, Nov. 16	Newburgh, NY.	9
1953, June 8	MI, OH	142	1990, June 2-3	Midwest, Great Lakes	13
1953, June 9	Worcester and vicinity, MA	90	1990, Aug. 28	Northern IL	25
1953, Dec. 5	Vicksburg, MS	38	1991, Apr. 26	KS, OK.	23
1955, May 25	KS, MO, OK, TX.	115	1992, Nov. 21-23	South, Midwest	26
1957, May 20	KS, MO.	48	1994, Mar. 27-28	AL, TN, GA, NC, SC (series)	52
1958, June, 4	NW Wisconsin	30	1994, Apr. 26	Central TX	4
1959, Feb. 10	St. Louis, MO.	21	1995, May 6-7	southern OK, northern TX	23
1960, May 5, 6	Southeastern OK, AR	30	1995, May 19-20	TX to MD (series)	4
1965, Apr. 11	IN, IL, OH, MI, WI	271	1996, Apr. 14	Northern AR	7
1966, Mar. 3	Jackson, MS	57	1996, Apr. 21	Western AR (series)	4
1966, Mar. 3	MS, AL	61	1997, Mar. 1	Central AR	26
1967, Apr. 21	IL, MI.	33	1997, May 27	Jarrell, TX.	27

Some Notable Hurricanes, Typhoons, Blizzards, Other Storms

Names of hurricanes and typhoons in italics: H.—hurricane; T.—typhoon

Date	Location	Deaths	Date	Location	Deaths
1888, Mar. 11-14	Blizzard, eastern U.S.	400	1970, Oct. 15	T. *Titang*, Philippines	526
1900, Aug.-Sept.	H., Galveston, TX.	6,000	1970, Nov. 13	Cyclone, Bangladesh.	300,000
1906, Sept. 19-24	H., LA, MS.	350	1971, Aug. 1	T. *Rose*, Hong Kong	130
1906, Sept. 18	Typhoon, Hong Kong	10,000	1972, June 19-29	H. *Agnes*, FL to NY	118
1915, Sept. 29	H., LA	500	1972, Dec. 3	T. *Theresa*, Philippines	169
1926, Sept. 11-22	H., FL, AL	243	1973, June-Aug.	Monsoon rains, India	1,217
1926, Oct. 20	H., Cuba	600	1974, June 11	Storm Dinah, Luzon Isl., Phil.	71
1928, Sept. 6-20	H., southern FL	1,836	1974, July 11	T. *Gilda*, Japan, S. Korea	108
1930, Sept. 3	H., Dominican Republic	2,000	1974, Sept. 19-20	H. *Fifi*, Honduras	2,000
1935, Aug. 29-Sept. 10	H., Caribbean, southeastern U.S.	400+	1974, Dec. 25	Cyclone leveled Darwin, Austral..	50
1938, Sept. 21	H., Long Island, NY; New England	600	1975, Sept. 13-27	H. *Eloise*, Caribbean, NE U.S.	71
1940, Nov. 11-12	Blizzard, NE, Midwest U.S.	144	1976, May 20	T. *Olga*, floods, Philippines.	215
1942, Oct. 15-16	H., Bengal, India	40,000	1977, July 25, 31	T. *Thelma*, T. *Vera*, Taiwan	39
1944, Sept. 9-16	H., NC to New England.	46	1978, Oct. 27	T. *Rita*, Philippines	c. 400
1947, Dec. 26	Blizzard, New York, NY, N Atlantic states	55	1979, Aug. 30-Sept. 7	H. *David*, Caribbean, E U.S.	1,100
1952, Oct. 22	Typhoon, Philippines	440	1980, Aug. 4-11	H. *Allen*, Caribbean, TX	272
1954, Aug. 30	H. *Carol*, northeastern U.S.	68	1981, Nov. 25	T. *Irma*, Luzon Isl., Phil.	176
1954, Oct. 5-18	H. *Hazel*, E Canada, U.S.; Haiti	347	1983, June	Monsoon, India	900
1955, Aug. 12-13	H. *Connie*, NC, SC, VA, MD	43	1983, Aug. 18	H. *Alicia*, southern TX	17
1955, Aug. 7-21	H. *Diane*, eastern U.S.	400	1984, Sept. 2	T. *Ike*, S Philippines.	1,363
1955, Sept. 19	H. *Hilda*, Mexico	200	1985, May 25	Cyclone, Bangladesh.	10,000
1955, Sept. 22-28	H. *Janet*, Caribbean	500	1985, Oct. 26-Nov. 6	H. *Juan*, SE U.S.	97
1956, Feb. 1-29	Blizzard, W Europe.	1,000	1987, Nov. 25	T. *Nina*, Philippines	650
1957, June 25-30	H. *Audrey*, TX to AL	390	1988, Sept. 10-17	H. *Gilbert*, Caribbean, Gulf of Mexico	260
1958, Feb. 15-16	Blizzard, northeastern U.S.	171	1989, Sept. 16-22	H. *Hugo*, Caribbean, SE U.S.	504
1959, Sept. 17-19	T. *Sarah*, Japan, S. Korea	2,000	1990, May 6-11	Cyclones, SE India	450
1959, Sept. 26-27	T. *Vera*, Honshu, Japan	4,466	1991, Apr. 30	Cyclone, Bangladesh.	139,000
1960, Sept. 4-12	H. *Donna*, Caribbean, E U.S..	148	1991, Nov. 5	Tropical storm, Samar and Leyte, Philippines	7,000+
1961, Sept. 11-14	H. *Carla*, TX.	46	1992, Aug. 24-26	H. *Andrew*, southern FL, LA.	14
1961, Oct. 31	H. *Hattie*, Br. Honduras	400	1993, Mar. 13-14	Blizzard, eastern U.S.	200
1963, May 28-29	Windstorm, Bangladesh	22,000	1993, June	Monsoon, Bangladesh.	2,000
1963, Oct. 4-8	H. *Flora*, Caribbean	6,000	1994, Nov. 8-18	Storm Gordon, Caribbean, FL	830
1964, Oct. 4-7	H. *Hilda*, LA, MS, GA	38	1995, Sept. 4-6	H. *Luis*, Caribbean	14
1964, June 30	T. *Winnie*, N Philippines	107	1995, Sept. 13-22	H. *Marilyn*, Virgin Isls., Carib.	13
1964, Sept. 5	T. *Ruby*, Hong Kong and China.	735	1995, Oct. 2-4	H. *Opal*, S Mexico, FL, AL	59
1965, May 11-12	Windstorm, Bangladesh	17,000	1995, Nov. 2-3	T. *Angela*, Philippines	600+
1965, June 1-2	Windstorm, Bangladesh	30,000	1996, Jan. 7-8	Blizzard, northeastern U.S..	100
1965, Sept. 7-12	H. *Betsy*, FL, MS, LA	74	1996, July 8-13	H. *Bertha*, Carib., eastern U.S.	15
1965, Dec. 15	Windstorm, Bangladesh	10,000	1996, Aug. 22	Blizzard, Himalayas, N India.	239
1966, June 4-10	H. *Alma*, Honduras, SE U.S.	51	1996, Aug. 29-Sept. 6	H. *Fran*, Carib., NC, VA, WV.	28
1966, Sept. 24-30	H. *Inez*, Carib., FL, Mexico	293	1996, Sept. 9-10	H. *Hortense*, Caribbean.	24
1967, July 9	T. *Billie*, SW Japan	347	1996, Sept. 9	T. *Sally*, S China.	114
1967, Sept. 5-23	H. *Beulah*, Carib., Mex., TX.	54	1996, Nov. 6	Cyclone, Andhra Pradesh, India.	1,000+
1967, Dec. 12-20	Blizzard, Southwest U.S.	51	1996, Nov. 24-25	Ice storms, TX to MO.	26
1968, Nov. 18-28	T. *Nina*, Philippines	63	1996, Dec. 25	Tropical storm, E Malaysia	100+
1969, Aug. 17-18	H. *Camille*, MS, LA.	256	1997, May 19	Cyclone, Bangladesh.	108
1970, July 30-Aug. 5	H. *Celia*, Cuba, FL, TX	31	1997, May 26	Rain storm, Philippines	29
1970, Aug. 20-21	H. *Dorothy*, Martinique	42	1997, July 2	Storms, southeastern MI	16
1970, Sept. 15	T. *Georgia*, Philippines	300	1997, Aug. 18	Typhoon, Taiwan.	24
1970, Oct. 14	T. *Sening*, Philippines	583	1997, Sept. 27	Cyclone, S Bangladesh	c. 35

Some Notable Floods, Tidal Waves

Date	Location	Deaths	Date	Location	De
1228	Holland	100,000	1972, June 9	Rapid City, SD	2
1642	China	300,000	1972, Aug. 7	Luzon Isl., Philippines	4
1883, Aug. 27	Indonesia	36,000	1972, Aug. 19-31	Pakistan	1,5
1887	Huang He River, China	900,000	1974, Mar. 29	Tubaro, Brazil	1,00
1889, May 31	Johnstown, PA	2,209	1974, Aug. 12	Monty-Long, Bangladesh	2,50(
1900, Sept. 8	Galveston, TX	5,000	1976, June 5	Teton Dam collapse, ID	11
1903, June 15	Heppner, OR	325	1976, July 31	Big Thompson Canyon, CO	139
1911	Chang Jiang River, China	100,000	1976, Nov. 17	East Java, Indonesia	136
1913, Mar. 25-27	OH, IN	732	1977, July 19-20	Johnstown, PA	68
1915, Aug. 17	Galveston, TX	275	1977, Nov. 6	Toccoa, GA	39
1928, Mar. 13	Dam collapse, Saugus, CA	450	1978, June-Sept.	N India	1,200
1928, Sept. 13	Lake Okeechobee, FL	2,000	1979, Jan.-Feb.	Brazil	204
1931, Aug.	Huang He River, China	3,700,000	1979, July 17	Lomblem Isl., Indonesia	539
1937, Jan. 22	OH, MS Valleys	250	1979, Aug. 11	Morvi, India	15,000
1939	N China	200,000	1980, Feb. 13-22	Southern CA, AZ	26
1946, Apr. 1	HI, AK	159	1981, Apr.	N China	550
1947, Sept. 20	Honshu Island, Japan	1,900	1981, July	Sichuan, Hubei Prov., China	1,300
1951, Aug.	Manchuria	1,800	1982, Jan. 23	Nr. Lima, Peru	600
1953, Jan. 31	W Europe	2,000	1982, May 12	Guangdong, China	430
1954, Aug. 17	Farahzad, Iran	2,000	1982, Sept. 17-21	El Salvador, Guatemala	1,300+
1955, Oct. 7-12	India, Pakistan	1,700	1984, Aug-Sept.	South Korea	200+
1959, Nov. 1	W Mexico	2,000	1985, July 19	Dam collapse, N Italy	361
1959, Dec. 2	Frejus, France	412	1987, Aug.-Sept.	N Bangladesh	1,000+
1960, Oct. 10	Bangladesh	6,000	1988, Sept.	N India	1,000+
1960, Oct. 31	Bangladesh	4,000	1990, June 14	Shadyside, OH	23
1962, Feb. 17	North Sea coast, Germany	343	1991, Dec. 18-26	TX	18
1962, Sept. 27	Barcelona, Spain	445	1992, Feb. 9-15	Southern CA	13
1963, Oct. 9	Dam collapse, Vaiont, Italy	1,800	1993, July-Aug.	Midwest	48
1966, Nov. 3-4	Florence, Venice, Italy	113	1994, July	GA, AL	32
1967, Jan. 18-24	E Brazil	894	1995, Jan. 30-Feb. 9	NW Europe	40
1967, Mar. 19	Rio de Janeiro, Brazil	436	1995, Mar. 8-15	CA	15
1967, Nov. 26	Lisbon, Portugal	464	1995, July	Hunan Province, China	1,200
1968, Aug. 7-14	Gujarat State, India	1,000	1995, Aug. 19	SW Morocco	136
1968, Oct. 7	NE India	780	1995, Dec. 25	KwaZulu Natal, South Africa	166
1969, Jan. 18-26	Southern CA	100	1996, Jan.	Northeastern U.S.	15+
1969, Mar. 17	Mundau Valley, Alagoas, Brazil	218	1996, Feb. 17	Biak Isl., Indonesia	105
1969, Aug. 20-22	Western VA	189	1996, April	Afghanistan	100+
1969, Sept. 15	South Korea	250	1996, June-July	S China	315
1969, Oct. 1-8	Tunisia	500	1996, Aug. 7	Pyrenees Mts., Spain	71
1970, May 20	Central Romania	160	1996, Dec.-1997, Jan.	Northwestern U.S.	29
1970, July 22	Himalayas, India	500	1997, Feb.-Mar.	Bolivia	16
1971, Feb. 26	Rio de Janeiro, Brazil	130	1997, Mar.	Ohio R. Valley	35
1972, Feb. 26	Buffalo Creek, WV	118	1997, July	Poland, Czech Republic	98

Some Major Earthquakes

Source: Global Volcanism Network, Smithsonian Institution; U.S. Geological Survey, Dept. of the Interior; World Almanac research

Magnitude of earthquakes (Mag.) is measured on the Richter scale; each higher number represents a tenfold increase in energy measured in ground motion. Adopted in 1935, the scale is applied to earthquakes here as far back as reliable seismograms are available.

Date	Location	Deaths	Mag.	Date	Location	Deaths	Mag.
526, May 20	Antioch, Syria	250,000	NA	1927, May 22	Nan-Shan, China	200,000	8.3
856	Corinth, Greece	45,000	"	1932, Dec. 25	Gansu, China	70,000	7.6
1057	Chihli, China	25,000	"	1933, Mar. 2	Japan	2,990	8.9
1169, Feb. 11	Near Mt. Etna, Sicily	15,000[1]	"	1933, Mar. 10	Long Beach, CA	115	6.2
1268	Cilicia, Asia Minor	60,000	"	1934, Jan. 15	India, Bihar-Nepal	10,700	8.4
1290, Sept. 27	Chihli, China	100,000	"	1935, May 30	Quetta, India	50,000	7.5
1293, May 20	Kamakura, Japan	30,000	"	1939, Jan. 25	Chillan, Chile	28,000	8.3
1531, Jan. 26	Lisbon, Portugal	30,000	"	1939, Dec. 26	Erzincan, Turkey	30,000	8.0
1556, Jan. 24	Shaanxi, China	830,000	"	1946, Dec. 20	Honshu, Japan	1,330	8.4
1667, Nov.	Shemaka, Caucasia	80,000	"	1948, June 28	Fukui, Japan	5,390	7.3
1693, Jan. 11	Catania, Italy	60,000	"	1949, Aug. 5	Pelileo, Ecuador	6,000	6.8
1730, Dec. 30	Hokkaido, Japan	137,000	"	1950, Aug. 15	Assam, India	1,530	8.7
1737, Oct. 11	India, Calcutta	300,000	"	1953, Mar. 18	NW Turkey	1,200	7.2
1755, June 7	N Persia	40,000	"	1956, June 10-17	N Afghanistan	2,000	7.7
1755, Nov. 1	Lisbon, Portugal	60,000	8.75*	1957, July 2	N Iran	1,200	7.4
1783, Feb. 4	Calabria, Italy	30,000	NA	1957, Dec. 13	W Iran	1,130	7.3
1797, Feb. 4	Quito, Ecuador	41,000	"	1960, Feb. 29	Agadir, Morocco	12,000	5.9
1811-12	New Madrid, MO (series)	NA	8.7*	1960, May 21-30	S Chile	5,000	9.5
1822, Sept. 5	Asia Minor, Aleppo	22,000	NA	1962, Sept. 1	NW Iran	12,230	7.3
1828, Dec. 28	Echigo, Japan	30,000	"	1963, July 26	Skopje, Yugoslavia	1,100	6.0
1868, Aug. 13-15	Peru, Ecuador	40,000	"	1964, Mar. 27	Alaska	131	9.2
1875, May 16	Venezuela, Colombia	16,000	"	1966, Aug. 19	E Turkey	2,520	7.1
1886, Aug. 31	Charleston, SC	60	6.6	1968, Aug. 31	NE Iran	12,000	7.3
1896, June 15	Japan, sea wave	27,120	NA	1970, Jan. 4	Yunnan Prov., China	10,000	7.5
1905, Apr. 4	Kangra, India	19,000	8.6	1970, Mar. 28	W Turkey	1,100	7.3
1906, Apr. 18-19	San Francisco, CA	503[2]	8.3	1970, May 31	N Peru	66,000	7.8
1906, Aug. 17	Valparaiso, Chile	20,000	8.6	1971, Feb. 9	San Fernando Val., CA	65	6.6
1907, Oct. 21	Central Asia	12,000	8.1	1972, Apr. 10	S Iran	5,054	7.1
1908, Dec. 28	Messina, Italy	83,000	7.5	1972, Dec. 23	Managua, Nicaragua	5,000	6.2
1915, Jan. 13	Avezzano, Italy	29,980	7.5	1974, Dec. 28	Pakistan (9 towns)	5,200	6.3
1918, Oct. 11	Mona Passage, P.R.	116	7.5	1975, Sept. 6	Turkey (Lice, etc.)	2,300	6.7
1920, Dec. 16	Gansu, China	200,000	8.6	1976, Feb. 4	Guatemala	23,000	7.5
1923, Sept. 1	Yokohama, Japan	143,000	8.3	1976, May 6	NE Italy	1,000	6.5
1925, Mar. 16	Yunnan, China	5,000	7.1	1976, June 25	Irian Jaya, New Guinea	422	7.1

Date	Location	Deaths	Mag.	Date	Location	Deaths	Mag.
., July 27	Tangshan, China.....	255,000	8.0	1990, June 20	W Iran	40,000+	7.7
6, Aug. 16	Mindanao, Philippines..	8,000	7.8	1990, July 16	Luzon, Philippines.....	1,621	7.8
6, Nov. 24	NW Iran-USSR border .	5,000	7.3	1991, Feb. 1	Pakistan, Afgh. border..	1,200	6.8
77, Mar. 4	Romania............	1,500	7.2	1991, Oct. 19	N India.............	2,000	7.0
977, Aug. 19	Indonesia	200	8.0	1992, Mar. 13, 15	E Turkey	4,000	6.2/6.0
1977, Nov. 23	NW Argentina........	100	8.2	1992, June 28	S California	1	7.5/6.6
1978, Sept. 16	NE Iran............	15,000	7.8	1992, Dec. 12	Flores Isl., Indonesia ..	2,500	7.5
1979, Sept. 12	Indonesia	100	8.1	1993, July 12	off Hokkaido, Japan ...	200+	7.7
1979, Dec. 12	Colombia, Ecuador ...	800	7.9	1993, Sept. 29	Maharashtra, S India...	9,748[3]	6.3
1980, Oct. 10	NW Algeria	3,500	7.7	1994, Jan. 17	Northridge, CA	61	6.8
1980, Nov. 23	S Italy.............	3,000	7.2	1994, Feb. 15	S Sumatra, Indon.	215	7.0
1981, June 11	S Iran.............	3,000	6.9	1994, June 6	Cauca, SW Colombia ..	1,000	6.8
1981, July 28	S Iran.............	1,500	7.3	1994, Aug. 19	N Algeria	164	6.0
1982, Dec. 13	W Arabian Peninsula ..	2,800	6.0	1995, Jan. 16	Kobe, Japan.........	5,502	6.9
1983, May 26	N Honshu, Japan.....	81	7.7	1995, May 27	Sakhalin Isl., Russia ..	1,989	7.5
1983, Oct. 30	E Turkey...........	1,342	6.9	1995, Oct. 1	SW Turkey	73	6.0
1985, Mar. 3	Chile..............	146	7.8	1995, Oct. 9	W coast, Mexico......	c. 40+	7.6
1985, Sept. 19	Michoacan, Mexico ...	9,500	8.1	1996, Feb. 3	SW China...........	200+	7.0
1986, Oct. 10	El Salvador.........	1,000+	5.5	1996, Feb. 17	Irian Jaya, Indonesia ..	53	7.5
1987, Mar. 6	Colombia-Ecuador ...	4,000+	7.0	1997, Feb. 4	Turkmen.-Iran border ..	79	6.9
1988, Aug. 20	India-Nepal border....	1,450	6.6	1997, Feb. 27	W Pakistan..........	100+	7.3
1988, Nov. 6	China-Burma border...	1,000	7.3	1997, Feb. 28	NW Iran............	1000+	6.1
1988, Dec. 7	Turkey-USSR border ..	25,000	7.0	1997, May 10	N Iran	1,560	7.5
1989, Oct. 17	San Francisco Bay area.	62	7.1	1997, May 21	Madhya Pradesh, India	40+	6.1
1990, May 30	N Peru	115	6.3	1997, July 9	NE Venezuela........	82	6.9
				1997, Sept. 26	Central Italy	11	5.5/5.7

(*) estimated from earthquake intensity. NA=not available. (1) Once thought to have been a volcanic eruption; evidence indicates a destructive earthquake and tsunami occurred on this date. (2) With subsequent fires, death toll rose to 700. (3) Official death toll released by Indian government. Other sources reported estimates of 30,000 deaths.

Other Recent Earthquakes

Source: Global Volcanism Network, Smithsonian Institution; dates are Greenwich Mean Time

Date	Location	Magnitude	Date	Location	Magnitude
1996, July 15	Guerrero, Mexico	6.5	Nov. 6	Bonin Isls.	6.6
July 21	Sulawesi Isl., Indonesia	6.9	Nov. 19	E Kashmir	6.8
Aug. 2	Solomon Isls.	7.1	Dec. 2	E of Kyushu, Japan	6.7
Aug. 5	SE of Fiji Isls.	6.5	1997, Jan. 11	SW Mexico	7.1
Aug. 5	Tonga	6.7	Mar. 11	Mindanao, Philippines	6.8
Sept. 5	NE of Easter Isl.	7.1	Apr. 21	SW Pacific, between Santa	
Sept. 5	SE of Taiwan	6.6		Cruz Isls. and Vanuatu	7.5
Oct. 9	Cyprus	6.8	Apr. 22	Trinidad and Tobago	6.7
Oct. 13	Solomon Isls.	7.0	May 3	Kermadec Isls.	6.9
Oct. 18	S Japan	6.6	July 16	Central Chile	6.5

Some Notable Fires Since 1835

(See also Notable Explosions Since 1910.)

Date	Location	Deaths	Date	Location	Deaths
1835, Dec. 16	New York, NY, 500 bldgs. destroyed	—	1946, Dec. 12	N, NY, ice plant, tenement....	37
1845, May	Canton, China, theater	1,670	1949, Apr. 5	Effingham, IL, hospital.......	77
1871, Oct. 8	Chicago, $196 million loss;		1950, Jan. 7	Davenport, IA, Mercy Hospital..	41
	17,000 bldgs. destroyed ...	250	1953, Mar. 29	Largo, FL, nursing home	35
1871, Oct. 8	Peshtigo, WI, forest fire......	1,182	1953, Apr. 16	Chicago, metalworking plant...	35
1872, Nov. 9	Boston, 800 bldgs. destroyed .	—	1957, Feb. 17	Warrenton, MO, home for aged.	72
1876, Dec. 5	Brooklyn, NY, theater	295	1958, Mar. 19	New York, NY, loft building....	24
1877, June 20	St. John, New Brunswick.....	100	1958, Dec. 1	Chicago, parochial school.....	95
1881, Dec. 8	Ring Theater, Vienna	850	1958, Dec. 16	Bogotá, Colombia, store......	83
1887, May 25	Opera Comique, Paris.......	200	1959, June 23	Stalheim, Norway, resort hotel .	34
1887, Sept. 4	Exeter, England, theater	200	1960, Mar. 12	Pusan, Korea, chemical plant ..	68
1894, Sept. 1	MN, forest fire.............	413	1960, July 14	Guatemala City, mental hospital	225
1897, May 4	Paris, charity bazaar	150	1960, Nov. 13	Amude, Syria, movie theater...	152
1900, June 30	Hoboken, NJ, docks	326	1961, Jan. 6	Thomas Hotel, San Francisco..	20
1902, Sept. 20	Birmingham, AL, church	115	1961, Dec. 8	Hartford, CT, hospital........	16
1903, Dec. 30	Iroquois Theater, Chicago....	602	1961, Dec. 17	Niteroi, Brazil, circus	323
1908, Jan. 13	Rhoads Theater, Boyertown, PA	170	1963, May 4	Diourbel, Senegal, theater	64
1908, Mar. 4	Collinwood, OH, school......	176	1963, Nov. 18	Surfside Hotel, Atlantic City, NJ	25
1911, Mar. 25	Triangle Shirtwaist factory, NY, NY	146	1963, Nov. 23	Fitchville, OH, rest home	63
1913, Oct. 14	Mid Glamorgan, Wales, colliery	439	1963, Dec. 29	Roosevelt Hotel, Jacksonville, FL	22
1918, Apr. 13	Norman, OK, state hospital ...	38	1964, May 8	Manila, apartment bldg.	30
1918, Oct. 12	Cloquet, MN, forest fire......	400	1964, Dec. 18	Fountaintown, IN, nursing home	20
1919, June 20	Mayagüez Theater, San Juan,		1965, Mar. 1	LaSalle, Quebec, apartment...	28
	Puerto Rico	150	1965, Aug. 11-16	Watts riot fires, CA..........	30+
1923, May 17	Camden, SC, school........	76	1966, Mar. 11	Numata, Japan, 2 ski resorts ..	31
1924, Dec. 24	Babb's Switch, OK, school....	35	1966, Aug. 13	Melbourne, Australia, hotel....	29
1929, May 15	Cleveland, OH, clinic........	125	1966, Sept. 12	Anchorage, AK, hotel........	14
1930, Apr. 21	Columbus, OH, penitentiary...	320	1966, Oct. 17	New York, NY, bldg. (firefighters)	12
1931, July 24	Pittsburgh, PA, home for aged.	48	1966, Dec. 7	Erzurum, Turkey, barracks....	68
1934, Dec. 11	Hotel Kerns, Lansing, MI	34	1967, Feb. 7	Montgomery, AL, restaurant ...	25
1938, May 16	Atlanta, GA, Terminal Hotel...	35	1967, May 22	Brussels, Belgium, store......	322
1940, Apr. 23	Natchez, MS, dance hall	198	1967, July 16	Jay, FL, state prison.........	37
1942, Nov. 28	Cocoanut Grove, Boston.....	491	1968, Feb. 26	Shrewsbury, England, hospital .	22
1942, Dec. 12	St. John's, Nfld., hostel	100	1968, May 11	Vijayawada, India, wedding hall	58
1943, Sept. 7	Gulf Hotel, Houston, TX	55	1968, Nov. 18	Glasgow, Scotland, factory....	24
1944, July 6	Ringling Circus, Hartford, CT..	168	1969, Dec. 2	Notre Dame, Can., nursing home	54
1946, June 5	LaSalle Hotel, Chicago	61	1970, Jan. 9	Marietta, OH, nursing home ...	27
1946, Dec. 7	Winecoff Hotel, Atlanta	119	1970, Mar. 20	Seattle, WA, hotel	19

Date	Location	Deaths	Date	Location	Deaths
?70, Nov. 1	Grenoble, France, dance hall	145	1983, Feb. 13	Turin, Italy, movie theater	.....
1970, Dec. 20	Tucson, AZ, hotel	28	1983, Dec. 17	Madrid, Spain, discotheque	...
1971, Mar. 6	Burghoezli, Switzerland, psychiatric clinic	28	1984, May 11	Great Adventure Amusement Pk., NJ	.....
1971, Apr., 20	Bangkok, Thailand, hotel	24	1985, Apr. 21	Tabaco, Phil., movie theater	...
1971, Dec., 25	Seoul, South Korea, hotel	162	1985, Apr. 26	Buenos Aires, Arg., hospital	
1972, May 13	Osaka, Japan, nightclub	116	1985, May 11	Bradford, England, soccer stadium	5
1972, July 5	Sherborne, England, hospital	30	1986, Dec. 31	Puerto Rico, Dupont Plaza Hotel	96
1973, Feb. 6	Paris, France, school	21	1987, May 6-June 2	N China, forest fire	193
1973, June 24	New Orleans, LA, bar	32	1987, Nov. 17	London, England, subway	30
1973, Nov. 6	Fukui, Japan, train	28	1988, Mar. 20	Lashio, Burma, 2,000 buildings	134
1973, Nov. 29	Kumamoto, Japan, dept. store	107	1990, Mar. 25	Bronx, NY, social club	87
1973, Dec. 2	Seoul, South Korea, theater	50	1991, Mar. 3	Addis Ababa, Ethiopia, munitions dump	260+
1974, Feb. 1	São Paulo, Brazil, bank building	189	1991, Sept. 3	Hamlet, NC, processing plant	25
1974, June 30	Port Chester, NY, discotheque	24	1991, Oct. 20-21	Oakland, Berkeley, CA, wildfire	24
1974, Nov. 3	Seoul, S. Korea, hotel, disco	88	1993, Apr. 19	Waco, TX, cult compound	72
1975, Dec. 12	Mina, Saudi Arabia, tent city	138	1994, May 10	Bangkok, Thailand, toy factory	213
1976, Oct. 24	Bronx, NY, social club	25	1994, July 4-10	Glenwood Springs, CO (firefighters)	14
1977, Feb. 25	Moscow, Russia, Rossiya hotel	45	1994, Dec. 10	Karamay, China, theater	300
1977, May 28	Southgate, KY, nightclub	164	1994, Nov. 2	Durunka, Egypt, burning fuel flood	500
1977, June 9	Abidjan, Ivory Coast, nightclub	41	1995, Oct. 28	Baku, Azerbaijan, subway train	300
1977, June 26	Columbia, TN, jail	42	1995, Dec. 23	Mandi Dabwali, India, school	500+
1977, Nov. 14	Manila, Philippines, hotel	47	1996, Mar. 19	Quezon City, Philippines, nightclub	150+
1978, Jan. 28	Kansas City, Coates House Hotel	16	1996, Mar. 28	Bogor, Indonesia, shopping mall	78
1978, Aug. 19	Abadan, Iran, movie theater	425+	1996, Apr. 11	Düsseldorf, Germany, airport	16
1979, July 14	Saragossa, Spain, hotel	80	1996, Oct. 22	Caracas, Venezuela, jail	25
1979, Dec. 31	Chapais, Quebec, social club	42	1996, Nov. 20	Hong Kong building	39
1980, May 20	Kingston, Jamaica, nursing home	157	1997, Feb. 23	Baripada, India, worship site	164
1980, Nov. 21	MGM Grand Hotel, Las Vegas	84	1997, Apr. 15	Mina, Saudi Arabia, encampment	343
1980, Dec. 4	Stouffer Inn, Harrison, NY	26	1997, June 7	Thanjavur, India, temple	60+
1981, Jan. 9	Keansburg, NJ, boarding home	30	1997, June 13	New Delhi, India, movie theater	60
1981, Feb. 10	Las Vegas Hilton	8	1997, July 11	Pattaya, Thailand, hotel	90
1981, Feb. 14	Dublin, Ireland, discotheque	44	1997, Sept. 29	Home for retarded children, nr. Colina, Chile	30
1982, Sept. 4	Los Angeles, apartment house	24			
1982, Nov. 8	Biloxi, MS, county jail	29			

Some Notable Explosions Since 1910

Date	Location	Deaths	Date	Location	Deaths
1910, Oct. 1	Los Angeles Times Bldg.	21	1967, Dec. 25	Apartment bldg., Moscow, USSR	20
1913, Mar. 7	Dynamite, Baltimore harbor	55	1968, Apr. 6	Sports store, Richmond, IN	43
1915, Sept. 27	Gasoline tank car, Ardmore, OK	47	1970, Apr. 8	Subway construction, Osaka, Japan	73
1917, Apr. 10	Munitions plant, Eddystone, PA	133	1971, June 24	Tunnel, Sylmar, CA	17
1917, Dec. 6	Halifax Harbor, Canada	1,654	1971, June 28	School, fireworks, Puebla, Mexico	13
1918, May 18	Chemical plant, Oakdale, PA	193	1971, Oct. 21	Shopping center, Glasgow, Scotland	20
1918, July 2	Explosives, Split Rock, NY	50	1973, Feb., 10	Liquefied gas tank, Staten Island, NY	40
1918, Oct. 4	Shell plant, Morgan Station, NJ	64	1975, Dec. 27	Chasnala, India, mine	431
1919, May 22	Food plant, Cedar Rapids, IA	44	1976, Apr. 13	Lapua, Finland, munitions works	40
1920, Sept. 16	Wall Street, NY, NY, bomb	30	1977, Nov. 11	Freight train, Iri, South Korea	57
1921, Sept. 21	Chem. storage facility, Oppau, Ger.	561	1977, Dec. 22	Grain elevator, Westwego, LA	35
1924, Jan. 3	Food plant, Pekin, IL	42	1978, Feb. 24	Derailed tank car, Waverly, TN	12
1927, May 18	Bath school, Lansing, MI	38	1978, July 11	Propylene tank truck, Spanish coastal campsite	150
1928, April 13	Dance hall, West Plains, MO	40			
1937, Mar. 18	New London, TX, school	311	1980, Oct. 23	School, Ortuella, Spain	64
1940, Sept. 12	Hercules Powder, Kenvil, NJ	55	1982, Apr. 25	Antiques exhibition, Todi, Italy	33
1942, June 5	Ordnance plant, Elwood, IL	49	1982, Nov. 2	Salang Tunnel, Afghanistan	1,000-3,000
1944, Apr. 14	Bombay, India, harbor	700			
1944, July 17	Port Chicago, CA, pier	322	1984, Feb. 25	Oil pipeline, Cubatao, Brazil	508
1944, Oct. 21	Liquid gas tank, Cleveland	135	1984, June 21	Naval supply depot, Severomorsk, USSR	200+
1947, Apr. 16	Texas City, TX, pier	576	1984, Nov. 19	Gas storage area, NE Mexico City	334
1948, July 28	Farben works, Ludwigshafen, Ger.	184	1984, Dec. 3	Chemical plant, Bhopal, India	3,849
1950, May 19	Munitions barges, S. Amboy, NJ	30	1984, Dec. 5	Coal mine, Taipei, Taiwan	94
1956, Aug. 7	Dynamite trucks, Cali, Colombia	1,100	1985, June 25	Fireworks factory, Hallett, OK	21
1958, Apr. 18	Sunken munitions ship, Okinawa, Japan	40	1988, Apr. 10	Pakistani army ammunitions dump nr. Rawalpindi and Islamabad	100
1958, May 22	Nike missiles, Leonardo, NJ	10	1988, May 5	Shell Oil Company, Norco, LA	7
1959, Apr. 10	World War II bomb, Philippines	38	1988, July 6	Oil rig, North Sea	167
1959, June 28	Rail tank cars, Meldrin, GA	25	1989, June 3	Gas pipeline, between Ufa, Asha, USSR	650+
1959, Aug. 7	Dynamite truck, Roseburg, OR	13			
1959, Nov. 2	Jamuri Bazar, India, explosives	46	1992, Mar. 3	Coal mine, Kozlu, Turkey	270+
1959, Dec. 13	Dortmund, Ger., 2 apt. bldgs	26	1992, Apr. 22	Sewer, Guadalajara, Mexico	190
1960, Mar. 4	Belgian munitions ship, Havana, Cuba	100	1992, May 9	Coal mine, Plymouth, Nova Scotia	26
1960, Oct. 25	Gas, Windsor, Ont., store	11	1993, Feb. 26	World Trade Center, NY, NY	6
1962, Jan. 16	Gas pipeline, Edson, Alberta	8	1994, July 18	Jewish community center, Buenos Aires, Argentina	100
1962, Oct. 3	Telephone Co. office, NY, NY	23			
1963, Jan. 2	Packing plant, Terre Haute, IN	16	1995, Apr. 19	Federal office building, Oklahoma City	168[1]
1963, Mar. 9	Dynamite plant, S. Africa	45			
1963, Aug. 13	Explosives dump, Gauhaiti, India	32	1995, Apr. 29	Subway construction, South Korea	110
1963, Oct. 31	State Fair Coliseum, Indianapolis, IN	73	1995, Nov. 13	Military facility, Riyadh, Saudi Arabia	7
1964, July 23	Bone, Algeria, harbor munitions	100	1996, Jan. 31	Bank, Colombo, Sri Lanka	53
1965, Mar. 4	Gas pipeline, Natchitoches, LA	17	1996, Feb. 25	Jerusalem and Ashkelon, Israel	27
1965, Aug. 9	Missile silo, Searcy, AR	53	1996, Mar. 3-4	Jerusalem and Tel Aviv, Israel	33
1965, Oct. 21	Bridge, Tila Bund, Pakistan	80	1996, June 25	U.S. military housing complex, nr. Dhahran, Saudi Arabia	19
1965, Oct. 30	Cartagena, Colombia	48			
1965, Nov. 24	Armory, Keokuk, IA	20	1996, July 24	Train, Colombo, Sri Lanka	54
1966, Oct. 13	Chemical plant, La Salle, Quebec	11	1996, Nov. 10	Cemetery, Moscow, Russia	13
1967, Feb. 17	Chemical plant, Hawthorne, NJ	11			

	Location	Deaths	Date	Location	
Nov. 16	Russian military apartment, Dagestan region, Russia	68	1997, Jan. 18	Near courthouse, Lahore, Pakistan	25
3, Nov. 21	Building, San Juan, Puerto Rico	29	1997, Mar. 19	Ammunition depot, Jalalabad, Afghanistan	16
96, Nov. 27	Coal mine, Shanxi province, China	91+	1997, July 8	Train, Punjab, India	36
96, Dec. 2	Train, Haryana, India	12	1997, July 9	Military airfield, S Romania	16
996, Dec. 30	Train, Assam, India	59+	1997, July 30	Market, Jerusalem	15
997, Jan. 7	Shopping district, Algiers, Algeria	13			

(1) Includes a rescue worker who died during the rescue effort.

Notable Nuclear Accidents

Oct. 7, 1957 — A fire in the Windscale plutonium production reactor N of Liverpool, England, released radioactive material. In 1983, the British government said that 39 people had probably died of cancer as a result.

1957 — A chemical explosion in Kasli, USSR (now in Russia), in tanks containing nuclear waste, spread radioactive material and forced a major evacuation.

Jan. 3, 1961 — An experimental reactor at a federal installation near Idaho Falls, ID, killed 3 workers—the only deaths in U.S. reactor operations. The plant had high radiation levels, but damage was contained.

Oct. 5, 1966 — A sodium cooling system malfunction caused a partial core meltdown at the Enrico Fermi demonstration breeder reactor, near Detroit, MI. Radiation contained.

Jan. 21, 1969 — A coolant malfunction from an experimental underground reactor at Lucens Vad, Switzerland, resulted in the release of a large amount of radiation into a cavern, which was then sealed.

Mar. 22, 1975 — A technician checking for air leaks with a lighted candle caused a $100 million fire at the Brown's Ferry reactor in Decatur, AL. The fire burned out electrical controls, lowering the cooling water to dangerous levels.

Mar. 28, 1979 — The worst commercial nuclear accident in the U.S. occurred as equipment failures and human mistakes led to a loss of coolant and a partial core meltdown at the Three Mile Island reactor in Middletown, PA.

Feb. 11, 1981 — Eight workers were contaminated when over 100,000 gallons of radioactive coolant leaked into the containment building of TVA's Sequoyah 1 plant in Tennessee.

Apr. 25, 1981 — Some 100 workers were exposed to radioactive material during repairs of a nuclear plant at Tsuruga, Japan.

Jan. 6, 1986 — A cylinder of nuclear material burst after being improperly heated at a Kerr-McGee plant at Gore, OK. One worker died and 100 were hospitalized.

Apr. 26, 1986 — In the worst accident in the history of the nuclear power industry, fires and explosions resulting from an unauthorized experiment conducted at the Chernobyl nuclear power plant near Kiev, USSR (now in Ukraine), left at least 31 dead in the immediate aftermath and spread significant quantities of radioactive material over much of Europe. An estimated 135,000 people were evacuated from areas around Chernobyl, some of which were rendered uninhabitable for years. As a result of the radiation released into the atmosphere, tens of thousands of excess cancer deaths (as well as increased rates of birth defects) were expected in succeeding decades.

Record Oil Spills

The number of tons can be multiplied by 7 to estimate roughly the number of barrels spilled; the exact number of barrels in a ton varies with the type of oil. Each barrel contains 42 gallons.

Name, place	Date	Cause	Tons
Ixtoc I oil well, S Gulf of Mexico	June 3, 1979	Blowout	600,000
Nowruz oil field, Persian Gulf	Feb. 1983	Blowout	600,000 (est.)
Atlantic Empress & *Aegean Captain*, off Trinidad and Tobago	July 19, 1979	Collision	300,000
Castillo de Bellver, off Cape Town, South Africa	Aug. 6, 1983	Fire	250,000
Amoco Cadiz, near Portsall, France	Mar. 16, 1978	Grounding	223,000
Torrey Canyon, off Land's End, England	Mar. 18, 1967	Grounding	119,000
Sea Star, Gulf of Oman	Dec. 19, 1972	Collision	115,000
Urquiola, La Coruna, Spain	May 12, 1976	Grounding	100,000
Hawaiian Patriot, N Pacific	Feb. 25, 1977	Fire	99,000
Othello, Tralhavet Bay, Sweden	Mar. 20, 1970	Collision	60,000-100,000

Other Notable Oil Spills

Name, place	Date	Cause	Gallons
Persian Gulf	began Jan. 23, 1991	Spillage by Iraq	130,000,000[1]
Braer, off Shetland Islands	Jan. 5, 1993	Grounding	26,000,000
Aegean Sea, off N Spain	Dec. 3, 1992	Unknown	21,500,000
Sea Empress, off SW Wales	Feb. 15, 1996	Grounding	18,000,000
World Glory, off South Africa	June 13, 1968	Hull failure	13,524,000
Exxon Valdez, Prince William Sound, AK	Mar. 24, 1989	Grounding	10,080,000
Keo, off MA	Nov. 5, 1969	Hull failure	8,820,000
Storage tank, Sewaren, NJ	Nov. 4, 1969	Tank rupture	8,400,000
Ekofisk oil field, North Sea	Apr. 22, 1977	Well blowout	8,200,000
Argo Merchant, Nantucket, MA	Dec. 15, 1976	Grounding	7,700,000
Pipeline, West Delta, LA	Oct. 15, 1967	Dragging anchor	6,720,000
Tanker off Japan	Nov. 30, 1971	Ship broke in half	6,258,000
Usinsk, Russian Arctic	Aug. 12, 1994	Pipeline rupture	4,300,000
Storage tank, Monongahela River	Jan. 2, 1988	Tank rupture	3,800,000 (est.)[2]

(1) Est. by Saudi Arabia. Some estimates as low as 25 mil gal. (2) Other estimates are as high as 84.6 mil gal.

Historic Assassinations Since 1865

1865—Apr. 14. U.S. Pres. Abraham Lincoln shot by John Wilkes Booth in Washington, DC; died Apr. 15.

1881—Mar. 13. Alexander II, of Russia.—July 2. U.S. Pres. James A. Garfield shot by Charles J. Guiteau, Washington, DC; died Sept. 19.

1894—June 24. Pres. Sadi Carnot of France, by Italian anarchist, Sante Caserio, in Lyon.

1898—Sept. 10. Empress Elizabeth of Austria, stabbed by Italian anarchist Luigi Luccheni.

1900—July 29. Umberto I, king of Italy.

1901—Sept. 6. U.S. Pres. William McKinley in Buffalo, NY; died Sept. 14. Leon Czolgosz executed for the crime.

1908—Feb. 1. King Carlos I of Portugal and his son Luis Felipe, in Lisbon.

1913—Feb. 23. Mex. Pres. Francisco I. Madero and Vice Pres. Jose Pino Suarez.—Mar. 18. George, king of Greece.

1914—June 28. Archduke Francis Ferdinand of Austria-Hungary and his wife in Sarajevo, Bosnia (later part of Bosnia and Herzegovina), by Gavrilo Princip.

1916—Dec. 30. Grigori Rasputin, politically powerful Russian monk.

1918—July 12. Grand Duke Michael of Russia, at Perm.—July 16. Nicholas II, abdicated as czar of Russia; his wife, the Czarina Alexandra; their son, Czarevitch Alexis; their daughters, Grand Duchesses Olga, Tatiana, Marie, Anastasia; and 4 members of their household, executed by Bolsheviks at Ekaterinburg.

1920—May 20. Mexican Pres. Gen. Venustiano Carranza in Tlaxcalantongo.

1922—Aug. 22. Michael Collins, Irish revolutionary.—Dec. 16. Polish Pres.Gabriel Narutowicz in Warsaw.

1923—July 20. Gen. Francisco "Pancho" Villa, ex-rebel leader, in Parral, Mexico.

1928—July 17. Gen. Alvaro Obregon, president-elect of Mexico, in San Angel, Mexico.

1932—May 6. Pres. Paul Doumer of France shot by Russian émigré, Pavel Gorgulov, in Paris.

1934—July 25. In Vienna, Austrian Chancellor Engelbert Dollfuss by Nazis.

1935—Sept. 8. U.S. Sen. Huey P. Long shot in Baton Rouge, LA, by Dr. Carl Austin Weiss, who was slain by Long's bodyguards; Long died Sept. 10.

1940—Aug. 20. Leon Trotsky (Lev Bronstein), 63, exiled Russian war minister, near Mexico City, by Ramon Mercador del Rio, a Spaniard.

1948—Jan. 30. Mohandas K. Gandhi, 78, shot in New Delhi, India, by Nathuram Vinayak Godse.—Sept. 17. Count Folke Bernadotte, UN mediator for Palestine, by Jewish extremists in Jerusalem.

1951—July 20. King Abdullah ibn Hussein of Jordan.—Oct. 16. Prime Min. Liaquat Ali Khan of Pakistan shot in Rawalpindi.

1956—Sept. 21. Pres. Anastasio Somoza of Nicaragua, shot in Leon; died Sept. 29.

1957—July 26. Pres. Carlos Castillo Armas of Guatemala, in Guatemala City by one of his own guards.

1958—July 14. King Faisal of Iraq; his uncle, Crown Prince Abdullah; and July 15, Prem. Nuri as-Said, by rebels in Baghdad.

1959—Sept. 25. Prime Min. Solomon Bandaranaike of Ceylon, by Buddhist monk in Colombo.

1961—Jan. 17. Ex-Prem. Patrice Lumumba of the Congo, in Katanga Province—May 30. Dominican dictator Rafael Leonidas Trujillo Molina, near Ciudad Trujillo.

1963—June 12. Medgar W. Evers, NAACP's Mississippi field secretary, by Byron De Law Beckwith in Jackson, MS.—Nov. 2. Pres. Ngo Dinh Diem of South Vietnam and his brother, Ngo Dinh Nhu, in a military coup.—Nov. 22. U.S. Pres. John F. Kennedy shot in Dallas, TX; accused Lee Harvey Oswald murdered by Jack Ruby while awaiting trial.

1965—Jan. 21. Iranian Prem. Hassan Ali Mansour in Tehran; 4 executed.—Feb. 21. Malcolm X, black nationalist, shot in New York City.

1966—Sept. 6. Prime Min. Hendrik F. Verwoerd of South Africa stabbed to death in parliament at Cape Town.

1968—Apr. 4. Rev. Dr. Martin Luther King Jr. fatally shot in Memphis, TN; James Earl Ray convicted of crime.—June 5. Sen. Robert F. Kennedy (D, NY) shot in Los Angeles; Sirhan Sirhan, convicted of crime.

1971—Nov. 28. Prime Min. Wasfi Tal of Jordan, in Cairo, by Palestinian guerrillas.

1973—Mar. 2. U.S. Amb. Cleo A. Noel Jr., U.S. Ch⸻ d'Affaires George C. Moore, and Belgian Cha⸻ d'Affaires Guy Eid killed by Palestinian guerrillas Khartoum, Sudan.

1974—Aug. 19. U.S. Amb. to Cyprus, Rodger P. Davies killed by sniper's bullet in Nicosia.

1975—Feb. 11. Pres. Richard Ratsimandrava, of Madagascar, shot in Tananarive.—Mar. 25. King Faisal of Saudi Arabia shot by nephew Prince Musad Abdel Aziz, in royal palace, Riyadh.—Aug. 15. Bangladesh Pres. Sheik Mujibur Rahman killed in coup.

1976—Feb. 13. Nigerian head of state, Gen. Murtala Ramat Mohammed, by self-styled "young revolutionaries."

1977—Mar. 16. Kamal Jumblat, Lebanese Druse chieftain, shot near Beirut.—Mar. 18. Congo Pres. Marien Ngouabi shot in Brazzaville.

1978—July 9. Former Iraqi Prem. Abdul Razak Al-Naif shot in London.

1979—Feb. 14. U.S. Amb. Adolph Dubs shot by Afghan Muslim extremists in Kabul.—Aug. 27. Lord Mountbatten, World War II hero, and 2 others killed when a bomb exploded on his fishing boat off the coast of Co. Sligo, Ire. IRA claimed responsibility.—Oct. 26. South Korean Pres. Park Chung Hee and 6 bodyguards fatally shot by Kim Jae Kyu, head of South Korean CIA, and 5 aides in Seoul.

1980—Apr. 12. Liberian Pres. William R. Tolbert slain in military coup.—Sept. 17. Former Nicaraguan Pres. Anastasio Somoza Debayle shot in Paraguay.

1981—Oct. 6. Egyptian Pres. Anwar al-Sadat shot by commandos while reviewing military parade in Cairo.

1982—Sept. 14. Lebanese Pres.-elect Bashir Gemayel killed by bomb in east Beirut.

1983—Aug. 21. Philippine opposition leader Benigno Aquino Jr. shot by gunman at Manila International Airport.

1984—Oct. 31. Indian Prime Min. Indira Gandhi shot and killed by 2 Sikh bodyguards, in New Delhi.

1986—Feb. 28. Swedish Prem. Olof Palme shot by gunman on Stockholm street.

1987—June 1. Lebanese Prem. Rashid Karami killed when bomb exploded aboard a helicopter.

1988—Apr. 16. PLO military chief Khalil Wazir (Abu Jihad) gunned down by Israeli commandos in Tunisia.

1989—Aug. 18. Colombian presidential candidate Luis Carlos Galan killed by Medellín cartel drug traffickers at campaign rally in Bogotá.—Nov. 22. Lebanese Pres. Rene Moawad killed when bomb exploded next to his motorcade.

1990—Mar. 22. Presidential candidate Bernando Jamamillo Ossa shot by gunman at an airport in Bogotà.

1991—May 21. Rajiv Gandhi, former prime min. of India, killed by bomb during election rally in Madras.

1992—June 29. Mohammed Boudiaf, Pres. of Algeria, shot by gunman in Annaba.

1993—May 1. Ranasinghe Premadasa, Pres. of Sri Lanka, killed by bomb in Colombo.

1994—Mar. 23. Luis Donaldo Colosio, Mexican presidential candidate, shot by gunman Mario Aburto Martinez. —Apr. 6. Burundian Pres. Cyprien Ntaryamira and Rwandan Pres. Juvenal Habyarimana killed, with 8 others, when their plane was apparently shot down.

1995—Nov. 4. Yitzhak Rabin, prime min. of Israel, shot by gunman Yigal Amir at peace rally in Tel Aviv.

1996—Oct. 2. Andrei Lukanov, former Bulgarian prime minister, shot outside his home by an unidentified gunman.

Assassination Attempts

1912—Oct. 14. Former U.S. Pres.Theodore Roosevelt shot and wounded by demented man in Milwaukee, WI.

1933—Feb. 15. In Miami, FL, Joseph Zangara, anarchist, shot at Pres.-elect Franklin D. Roosevelt, but a woman seized his arm, and the bullet fatally wounded Mayor Anton J. Cermak, of Chicago, who died Mar. 6. Zangara was electrocuted on Mar. 20, 1933.

1944—July 20. Adolf Hitler was injured when a bomb, planted by a German officer, exploded in Hitler's headquarters. One aide was killed and 12 were injured in the explosion.

1950—Nov. 1. In an attempt to assassinate Pres. Truman, 2 members of a Puerto Rican nationalist movement—Griselio Torresola and Oscar Collazo—tried to shoot their way into Blair House. Torresola was killed, and a guard, Pvt. Leslie Coffelt, was fatally shot.

1970—Nov. 27. Pope Paul VI unharmed by knife-wielding assailant who attempted to attack him in Manila airport.

1972—May 15. Alabama Gov. George Wallace shot in Laurel, MD, by Arthur Bremer; seriously crippled.

1975—Sept. 5. Pres. Gerald R. Ford unharmed when a Secret Service agent grabbed a pistol aimed at him by Lynette (Squeaky) Fromme, a Charles Manson follower, in Sacramento.—Sept. 22. Pres. Ford unharmed when Sara Jane Moore fired a revolver at him.

1980—May 29. Civil rights leader Vernon E. Jordan Jr. shot and wounded in Ft. Wayne, IN.

1981—Jan. 16. Irish political activist Bernadette Devlin McAliskey and her husband shot and seriously wounded by 3 members of a Protestant paramilitary group in Co. Tyrone, Ire.—Mar. 30. Pres. Ronald Reagan, along with Press Sec. James Brady, Secret Service agent Timothy J. McCarthy, and Washington, DC, policeman Thomas Delahanty shot and seriously wounded by John W. Hinckley Jr. in Washington, DC.—May 13. Pope John Paul II and 2 bystanders shot and wounded by Mehmet Ali Agca, an escaped Turkish murderer, in St. Peter's Square, Rome.

1982—May 12. Pope John Paul II unharmed when a man with a knife was overpowered by guards, in Fatima, Portugal.

1984—Oct. 12. British Prime Min. Margaret Thatcher narrowly escaped injury when a bomb, said to have been planted by the IRA, exploded at the Grand Hotel in Brighton, England, during a Conservative Party conference. (Four died, including a member of Parliament.)

1986—Sept. 7. Chilean Pres. Gen. Augusto Pinochet Ugarte escaped unharmed when his motorcade was attacked by rebels using rockets, bazookas, grenades, and rifles.

1994—Oct. 29. Pres. Bill Clinton unharmed when Francisco Duran, later convicted of attempted assassination, shot at a tourist resembling Clinton outside the White House.

1995—June 26. Egyptian Pres. Hosni Mubarak unharmed when gunmen fired on his motorcade in Addis Ababa, Ethiopia. Four died, including 2 Ethiopian police officers.

1997—Feb. 12. Colombian Pres. Ernesto Samper Pizano unharmed when a bomb exploded on a runway in Barranquilla as his plane was preparing to land.—Apr. 30. Tajik Pres. Imamali Rakhmanov injured when a grenade was thrown at him (2 others were killed).

Notable U.S. Kidnappings Since 1924

Robert Franks, 13, in Chicago, **May 22, 1924,** by 2 youths, Richard Loeb and Nathan Leopold, who killed boy. Demand for $10,000 ignored. Loeb died in prison; Leopold paroled 1958.

Charles A. Lindbergh Jr., 20 mos. old, in Hopewell, NJ, **Mar. 1, 1932;** found dead **May 12.** Ransom of $50,000 paid to man identified as Bruno Richard Hauptmann, 35, paroled German convict who entered U.S. illegally. Hauptmann was convicted after spectacular trial at Flemington, and electrocuted in Trenton, NJ, prison, **Apr. 3, 1936.**

William A. Hamm Jr., 39, in St. Paul, **June 15, 1933.** $100,000 paid. Alvin Karpis given life, paroled in 1969.

Charles F. Urschel, in Oklahoma City, **July 22, 1933.** Released **July 31** after $200,000 paid. George (Machine Gun) Kelly and 5 others given life.

Brooke L. Hart, 22, in San Jose, CA. Thomas Thurmond and John Holmes arrested after demanding $40,000 ransom. When Hart's body was found in San Francisco Bay, **Nov. 26, 1933,** a mob attacked the jail at San Jose and lynched the 2 kidnappers.

George Weyerhaeuser, 9, in Tacoma, WA, **May 24, 1935.** Returned home **June 1** after $200,000 paid. Kidnappers given 20 to 60 years.

Charles Mattson, 10, in Tacoma, WA, **Dec. 27, 1936.** Found dead **Jan. 11, 1937.** Kidnapper asked $28,000, failed to contact.

Arthur Fried, in White Plains, NY, **Dec. 4, 1937.** Body not found. Two kidnappers executed.

Robert C. Greenlease, 6, taken from Kansas City, MO, school **Sept. 28, 1953,** and held for $600,000. Body found Oct. 7. Bonnie Brown Heady and Carl A. Hall pleaded guilty and were executed.

Peter Weinberger, 32 days old, Westbury, NY, **July 4, 1956,** for $2,000 ransom, not paid. Child found dead. Angelo John LaMarca, 31, convicted, executed.

Lee Crary, 8, in Everett, WA, **Sept. 22, 1957;** $10,000 ransom, not paid. He escaped after 3 days, led police to George E. Collins, who was convicted.

Frank Sinatra Jr., 19, from hotel room in Lake Tahoe, CA, **Dec. 8, 1963.** Released **Dec. 11** after his father paid $240,000 ransom. Three men sentenced to prison.

Barbara Jane Mackle, 20, abducted **Dec. 17, 1968,** from Atlanta, GA, motel; was found unharmed 3 days later, buried in a coffin-like wooden box 18 inches underground, after her father had paid $500,000 ransom; Gary Steven Krist sentenced to life, Ruth Eisenmann-Schier to 7 years.

Mrs. Roy Fuchs, 35, and 3 children held hostage 2 hours, **May 14, 1969,** in Long Island, NY, released after her husband, a bank manager, paid kidnappers $129,000 in bank funds; 4 men arrested, ransom recovered.

Virginia Piper, 49, abducted **July 27, 1972,** from her home in suburban Minneapolis; found unharmed near Duluth 2 days later after her husband paid $1 million ransom.

Patricia "Patty" Hearst, 19, taken from her Berkeley, CA, apartment **Feb. 4, 1974.** "Symbionese Liberation Army" captors demanded her father, publisher Randolph Hearst, give millions to poor. Implicated in San Francisco bank holdup, **Apr. 15.** FBI, **Sept. 18, 1975,** captured her and others; they were indicted on various charges. Patricia Hearst convicted of bank robbery, **Mar. 20, 1976;** released from prison under executive clemency, **Feb. 1, 1979.** In 1978, William and Emily Harris were sentenced to 10 years to life for the kidnapping; both paroled in 1983.

J. Reginald Murphy, 40, an editor of *Atlanta* (GA) *Constitution,* kidnapped **Feb. 20, 1974;** freed **Feb. 22** after newspaper paid $700,000 ransom. William A. H. Williams arrested; most of the money recovered.

E. B. Reville, Hepzibah, GA, banker, and wife, Jean, kidnapped **Sept. 30, 1974.** Ransom of $30,000 paid. He was found alive; Jean Reville was found dead **Oct. 2.**

Jack Teich, Kings Point, NY, steel executive, seized **Nov. 12, 1974;** released **Nov. 19** after payment of $750,000.

Adam Walsh, 6, abducted from a Hollywood, FL, department store, **July 27, 1981.** Although his severed head was found 2 weeks later at Vero Beach, FL, his body was never recovered. John Walsh, Adam's father, became active in raising awareness about missing children.

Sidney J. Reso, oil company executive, seized **Apr. 29, 1992;** died **May 3;** Arthur D. Seale and wife, Irene, arrested **June 19.** Arthur Seale pleaded guilty, sentenced to life in prison; Irene Seale sentenced to 20-year prison term.

Polly Klaas, 12, Petaluma, CA, abducted at knife point, **Oct. 1, 1993,** during a slumber party at her home. Police arrested Richard Allen Davis on **Nov. 30;** he led them to her body, found **Dec. 4** in wooded area of Cloverdale, CA. Davis was found guilty **June 18, 1996,** and was sentenced to death **Sept. 26.**

Marshall I. Wais, 79, owner of 2 San Francisco steel companies, kidnapped **Nov. 19, 1996,** from his San Francisco home. Released unharmed the same day after $500,000 ransom paid; Thomas William Taylor and Michael K. Robinson arrested the same day.

ASTRONOMY AND CALENDAR

Edited by Dr. Lee T. Shapiro, Planetarium Director
Morehead Planetarium, University of North Carolina at Chapel Hill

Celestial Events Summary, 1998

(Greenwich Mean Time, or GMT)

1998 will be a good year for meteor showers. Watch for the Quadrantids around Jan. 3, the Orionids near Oct. 21, and the Geminids about Dec. 13. Watch particularly for the Leonids around Nov. 17, as 1998 may be a forerunner to the expected Leonid meteor storm in 1999. The year will also be a good one for lunar occultations, with a strong start of 3 events each in Jan. and Feb. and 7 in Mar. During the year, the Moon will occult Aldebaran 12 times, Jupiter 11 times, Regulus 7 times, Mars and Saturn 3 times, Venus twice, and Mercury once.

At the start of the year, Venus, Mars, Jupiter, and Saturn are all visible in the early evening, but one by one they disappear, until by late Mar. they have left the evening sky. Although Venus will be at its best in the morning sky from mid-Feb. through mid-Aug., these 4 planets will all be seen best in the morning sky during the first week or 2 of Aug. During Sept. and Oct., Jupiter and Saturn are up most of the night. Mars, so prominent in 1997, is noticeable mainly in the morning sky during the second half of the year. At year's end, Jupiter and Saturn dominate the early evening sky, while Mars is the prominent object in the early morning sky.

About an hour and a half before sunrise on the morning of Apr. 23, look for the 3 brightest celestial objects—the Moon, Venus, and Jupiter—grouped together in the east. Venus passes Jupiter on Apr. 23, and 5 weeks later on May 29 passes Saturn, both events visible in the morning sky. Again in the early morning before sunrise, look for Venus and Mars paired together low in the NE around August 5, while Jupiter and Saturn are prominent high in the south.

Astronomical Positions Defined

Two celestial bodies are in **conjunction** when they are due N and S of each other, either in **Right Ascension** (with respect to the N celestial pole) or in **Celestial Longitude** (with respect to the N ecliptic pole). If the bodies are seen near each other, they will rise and set at nearly the same time. They are in **opposition** when their Right Ascensions differ by exactly 12 hours, or when their Celestial Longitudes differ by 180°. One of the 2 objects in opposition will rise while the other is setting. **Quadrature** refers to the arrangement where the coordinates of 2 bodies differ by exactly 90°. These terms may refer to the relative positions of any 2 bodies as seen from Earth, but one of the bodies is so frequently the Sun that mention of the Sun is omitted; otherwise, both bodies are named. The geocentric angular separation between the Sun and an object is termed **elongation**. Elongation is limited only for Mercury and Venus; the greatest elongation for each of these bodies is noted in the appropriate table and is approximately the time for longest observation. The term **perihelion** means nearest to the Sun, and **aphelion**, farthest from the Sun. An **occultation** of a planet or a star is an **eclipse** of it by some other body, usually the Moon.

Celestial Events Highlights, 1998

(GMT, or as indicated)

January

Mercury, low in the E before sunrise, pairs with Venus on the 26th.

Venus is low in the southwest after sunset at beginning of the month but is lost in the Sun's glare at mid-month as it passes by inferior conjunction on the 16th, to re-emerge low in the southeast before sunrise.

Mars starts the year bright and ends the year bright, closest to the Sun on the 7th and passing Jupiter on the 21st, low in the evening sky at astronomical twilight.

Jupiter, still visible in the early evening sky in the southeast, is the 3d-brightest object normally visible in the night sky after the Moon and Venus.

Saturn, at its dimmest this month, is seen in Pisces during the first half of the night.

Moon passes Mars and Jupiter on the 1st, occults Saturn on the 5th (one of 3 occultations of Saturn this year), occults Aldebaran on the 9th (there are 12 occultations of Aldebaran this year), passes Venus and Mercury on the 27th, Jupiter again on the 29th, and Mars again on the 30th.

Jan. 1—Mars 4° S of Moon; Jupiter 3° S of Moon.

Jan. 4—Earth at perihelion, 91.4 mil mi from the Sun.

Jan. 5—Saturn 0.2° N of Moon, Saturn occulted by Moon.

Jan. 6—Mercury at greatest western elongation of 23° (W of Sun and rising before the Sun).

Jan. 7—Mars at perihelion, 128 mil mi from Sun.

Jan. 9—Star Aldebaran in constellation Taurus 0.4° S of Moon, Aldebaran occulted by Moon; Neptune 4° S of Venus.

Jan. 16—Venus at inferior conjunction, between Earth and Sun.

Jan. 19—Neptune in conjunction with Sun.

Jan. 20—Sun enters Capricornus.

Jan. 21—Mars 0.2° S of Jupiter.

Jan. 22—Neptune enters Capricornus; Mars enters Aquarius.

Jan. 24—Jupiter enters Aquarius.

Jan. 26—Mercury 8° S of Venus.

Jan. 27—Venus 3° N of Moon; Mercury 5° S of Moon.

Jan. 28—Uranus in conjunction with Sun.

Jan. 29—Jupiter 2° S of Moon.

Jan. 30—Mars 1.7° S of Moon.

February

Mercury closes with the Sun, hidden in the glare, with superior conjunction on the 22d.

Venus, brilliant but low in the southeast, rises a couple of hours before sunrise.

Mars enters Pisces during the last week of the month very low in the WSW at sunset.

Jupiter is now too close to the Sun to be seen, in conjunction on 23d.

Saturn, getting lower in the sky in the early evening, is still relatively dim in Pisces.

Moon occults Saturn on the 1st, occults Aldebaran on the 5th, passes Venus on the 23d, Neptune and Uranus on the 24th, and occults Mars on the 27th (one of 3 this year).

Feb. 1—Saturn 0.6° N of Moon, occulted by Moon.

Feb. 2—Neptune 2° N of Mercury.

Feb. 5—Aldebaran 0.2° S of Moon, Aldebaran occulted by Moon; Venus stationary, resumes direct motion.

Feb. 8—Uranus 1.4° N of Mercury.

Feb. 17—Sun enters Aquarius.

Feb. 22—Mercury in superior conjunction with the Sun, on the far side of its orbit from Earth.

Feb. 23—Jupiter in conjunction with the Sun; Venus 1.6° N of Moon.

Feb. 24—Neptune and Uranus 3° S of Moon.

Feb. 25—Mars enters Pisces.

Feb. 26—Total solar eclipse; see details under eclipses.

Feb. 27—Mars 0.7° N of Moon, Mars occulted by Moon.

March

Mercury emerges low into the early evening sky in the last 1 week into Mar., pairing with Mars on the 11th and beginning retrograde motion on the 27th.

Venus still bright and low in SE before sunrise, occulted by the Moon on the 24th.

Mars disappears into the glow of sunset and is not visible for most of the month, but spends a few days briefly passing through the constellation of Cetus.

Jupiter reemerges from the glare of the Sun in the early morning during 2d half of the month.

Saturn is very low in the sky after sunset and is lost in the glare of sunset by the end of the month.

Moon occults Saturn on the 1st (one of 7 lunar occultations this month); Vesta on the 2d, Aldebaran on the 5th, Juno on the 13th, passes Neptune on the 23d, Uranus on the 24th, occults Venus on the 24th, Jupiter on the 26th (there are 11 occultations of Jupiter this year), and on the 30th passes Mercury and occults Vesta.

Mar. 1—Saturn 1° N of Moon, occulted by Moon.

Mar. 2—Moon occults minor planet Vesta, which is 0.1° S of Moon.

Mar. 5—Aldebaran 0.2° S of Moon, occulted by Moon.

Mar. 7—Neptune 4° S of Venus.

Mar. 11—Mars 1.2° S of Mercury.

Mar. 12—Pluto stationary, begins retrograde motion.

Mar. 13—Penumbral lunar eclipse, hardly noticeable, but see details under eclipses; Moon occults minor planet Juno which is 0.9° S of Moon; Sun enters Pisces.

Mar. 14—Mars enters Cetus.

Mar. 16—Mars enters Pisces.

Mar. 19—Uranus 3° S of Venus.

Mar. 20—Mercury at greatest eastern elongation of 19° (E of Sun and setting after the Sun); Vernal Equinox at 19:55 GMT (2:55 PM EST), spring begins in the northern hemisphere, autumn in the southern hemisphere.

Mar. 23—Neptune 3° S of Moon.

Mar. 24—Uranus 3° S of Moon; Venus 0.09° S of Moon, Venus occulted by Moon.

Mar. 26—Jupiter 0.8° S of Moon, occulted by Moon.

Mar. 27—Mercury stationary, begins retrograde motion; Venus greatest western elongation of 47°.

Mar. 30—Mars 4° S of Mercury; Moon occults minor planet Vesta, which is 1.2° N of Moon.

April

Mercury passes inferior conjunction on the 6th, stays hidden from view into mid-month when it reappears in the morning sky and resumes direct motion on the 19th.

Venus bright and low in the ESE before sunrise, occulted by the Moon on the 23rd.

Mars enters Aries but cannot be seen this month because of its proximity to the Sun.

Jupiter makes a wonderful triple with the Moon and Venus just before dawn in the east.

Saturn in conjunction with the Sun; cannot be observed.

Moon occults Aldebaran on the 1st, passes Neptune and Uranus on the 20th, occults Jupiter and Venus on the 23d, Mercury on the 24th, and Aldebaran on the 28th.

Apr. 1—Aldebaran 0.2° S of Moon, Aldebaran occulted by Moon.

Apr. 6—Mercury in inferior conjunction.

Apr. 12—Mars enters Aries.

Apr. 13—Saturn in conjunction with Sun.

Apr. 19—Mercury stationary, resumes direct motion.

Apr. 20—Neptune and Uranus 3° S of Moon; Sun enters Aries.

Apr. 23—Jupiter 0.3° S of Venus; Jupiter 0.2° S of Moon, Jupiter occulted by Moon; Venus 0.08° N of Moon, Venus occulted by Moon.

Apr. 24—Mercury 0.9° N of Moon, occulted by Moon.

Apr. 28—Aldebaran 0.4° S of Moon, occulted by Moon.

May

Mercury visible low in the E in the early morning sky, pairing with Saturn on the 12th.

Venus lower in the E is bright and rising as astronomical twilight begins.

Mars is in conjunction this month and still not visible.

Jupiter is prominent in the ESE a couple of hours before sunrise and enters Pisces at the end of the month.

Saturn appears in the early morning sky, still in the constellation of Pisces, pairing with Venus on the 29th.

Moon passes Neptune on the 17th, Uranus on the 18th, occults Jupiter on the 20th, passes Venus on the 22d, Saturn on the 23d, and Mercury on the 24th.

May 4—Neptune stationary, begins retrograde motion; Mercury at greatest western elongation of 27°.

May 12—Saturn 0.8° N of Mercury; Mars in conjunction with Sun.

May 15—Sun and Mars enter Taurus.

May 17—Neptune 3° S of Moon; Uranus stationary, begins retrograde motion.

May 18—Uranus 3° S of Moon.

May 20—Jupiter 0.4° N of Moon, occulted by Moon.

May 22—Venus 1.7° N of Moon.

May 23—Saturn 1.7 N of Moon.

May 24—Mercury 3° N of Moon.

May 28—Pluto at opposition.

May 29—Saturn 0.3° S of Venus; Jupiter enters Pisces.

June

Mercury disappears into the Sun's glare early in the month passing superior conjunction on the 10th, but reemerges after mid-month in the evening sky.

Venus very low in ENE as astronomical twilight begins.

Mars still too close to the Sun for observation.

Jupiter now rising about the middle of the night, prominent in the southeast at dawn.

Saturn now higher in the sky in the early morning before sunrise.

Moon occults Regulus on the 1st, passes Neptune on the 13th, Uranus on the 14th, occults Jupiter on the 17th, passes Saturn on the 19th, Venus on the 21st, occults Aldebaran on the 22d, passes Mercury on the 25th, and occults Regulus again on the 28th.

June 1—Star Regulus in the constellation Leo 1° N of Moon, Regulus occulted by Moon.

June 10—Mercury in superior conjunction with the Sun.

June 13—Neptune 2° S of Moon.

June 14—Uranus 3° S of Moon.

June 17—Jupiter 0.8° N of Moon, occulted by Moon.

June 19—Saturn 2° N of Moon.

June 21—Northern Solstice at 14:03 GMT (10:30 AM EDT), summer begins in the northern hemisphere, winter in the southern hemisphere; Venus 3° N of Moon.

June 22—Aldebaran 0.4° S of Moon, occulted by Moon; Sun enters Gemini.

June 25—Mercury 5° N of Moon.

June 27—Star Pollux of constellation Gemini 0.8° N of Mercury.

June 28—Regulus 0.8° N of Moon, occulted by Moon.

July

Mercury visible in the early evening in the W, begins retrograde motion on the 30th.

Venus very low in NE as astronomical twilight begins.

Mars enters Gemini after 1 week and finally reappears very low in ENE before dawn.

Jupiter shines brightly in Pisces rising about 3 hours after sunset, begins retrograde motion on the 18th.

Saturn, high in the sky at sunrise, enters the constellation of Cetus past the middle of the month.

Moon passes Neptune on the 10th, Uranus on the 11th, occults Jupiter on the 14th, passes Saturn on the 17th, occults Ceres on the 18th, Aldebaran on the 19th, passes Venus on the 21st, Mars on the 22d, Mercury on the 25th, and occults Regulus on the 25th.

July 3—Aldebaran 4° S of Venus.

July 4—Earth at aphelion, 94.5 mil mi from the Sun.

July 7—Mars enters Gemini.

July 10—Neptune 2° S of Moon.

July 11—Uranus 3° S of Moon.

July 14—Jupiter 1° N of Moon, occulted by Moon.

July 17—Mercury at greatest eastern elongation of 27°; Saturn 2° N of Moon.

July 18—Jupiter stationary, begins retrograde motion; Moon occults minor planet Ceres, 1.1° S of Moon.

July 19—Aldebaran 0.3° S of Moon, Aldebaran occulted by Moon; Saturn enters Cetus.

July 20—Pluto enters Scorpius.

July 21—Venus 4° N of Moon.

July 22—Mars 5° N of Moon; Sun enters Cancer.

July 23—Neptune at opposition.

July 25—Mercury 2° S of Moon; Regulus 0.7° N of Moon, Regulus occulted by Moon.

July 30—Mercury stationary, begins retrograde motion.

August

Mercury, visible in early evening in the W during 1st week, disappears into the Sun's glare, passing inferior conjunction on the 14th, reappears in the E in the morning at the end of the month as it resumes direct motion on the 23d.

Venus, low in the NE before sunrise, passes Pollux in Gemini on the 8th.

Mars makes a pretty pair with Venus low in the NE on the morning of the 5th and enters Cancer on the 18th.

Jupiter, slowly brightening, rises a couple of hours after sunset and enters Aquarius at the end of the month.

Saturn is now rising a few hours after sunset and getting brighter, begins retrograde on the 16th.

Moon passes Neptune and Uranus on the 7th, occults Jupiter on the 11th, passes Saturn on the 13th, occults Ceres on the 15th, Aldebaran on the 16th, passes Mars on the 19th, and Venus on the 20th.

Aug. 3—Uranus at opposition.

Aug. 5—Mars 0.8° N of Venus.

Aug. 7—Neptune 2° S of Moon; Uranus 3° S of Moon.

Aug. 8—Penumbral lunar eclipse, hardly noticeable, but see details under eclipses; Pollux 7° N of Venus.

Aug. 11—Jupiter 0.9° N of Moon, Jupiter occulted by Moon; Pollux 6° N of Mars; Sun enters Leo.

Aug. 13—Saturn 2° N of Moon.

Aug. 14—Mercury in inferior conjunction.

Aug. 15—Moon occults minor planet Ceres, which is 0.9° S of Moon.

Aug. 16—Aldebaran 0.2° S of Moon, Aldebaran occulted by Moon; Saturn stationary, begins retrograde motion.

Aug. 18—Pluto stationary, resumes direct motion; Mars enters Cancer.

Aug. 19—Mars 4° N of Moon.

Aug. 20—Venus 3° N of Moon.

Aug. 21-22—Annular solar eclipse; see details under eclipses.

Aug. 23—Mercury stationary, resumes direct motion.

Aug. 25—Mercury 3° S of Venus.

Aug. 31—Mercury at greatest western elongation of 18°; Jupiter enters Aquarius.

September

Mercury appears in the E in the early morning during 1st half of the month, pairs with Venus on the 11th, then disappears into the Sun's glare to pass superior conjunction on the 25th.

Venus, getting lower in the E, is lost in the glare of the Sun after mid-month.

Mars enters Leo after mid-month at its faintest and still low in E early in the morning.

Jupiter, rising just after sunset, is at its brightest for the year, reaching opposition at mid-month.

Saturn enters Pisces at mid-month, now more than 50% brighter than it was in January.

Moon passes Neptune on the 3d, Uranus on the 4th, occults Jupiter on the 7th, passes Saturn on the 9th, occults Aldebaran on the 12th, passes Mars on the 17th, occults Regulus on the 18th, passes Neptune again on the 30th.

Sep. 3—Neptune 2° S of Moon.

Sep. 4—Uranus 3° S of Moon.

Sep. 6—Regulus 0.8° S of Venus; Penumbral lunar eclipse, hardly noticeable, but see details under eclipses.

Sep. 7—Jupiter 0.5° N of Moon, Jupiter occulted by Moon; Regulus 0.8° S of Mercury.

Sep. 8—Neptune enters Sagittarius.

Sep. 9—Saturn 2° N of Moon.

Sep. 11—Mercury 0.4° N of Venus.

Sep. 12—Aldebaran 0.3° S of Moon, Aldebaran occulted by Moon; Moon occults minor planet Ceres, which is 0.9° S of Moon.

Sep. 16—Jupiter at opposition; Saturn enters Pisces.

Sep. 17—Mars 2° N of Moon; Sun enters Virgo.

Sep. 18—Regulus 0.6° N of Moon, Regulus occulted by Moon; Mars enters Leo; Pluto enters Ophiuchus.

Sep. 23—Autumnal Equinox at 5:37 GMT (1:37 AM EDT), autumn begins in the northern hemisphere, spring begins in the southern hemisphere.

Sep. 25—Mercury in superior conjunction with the Sun.

Sep. 30—Neptune 2° S of Moon.

October

Mercury emerges into the evening sky after 1st third of the month.

Venus, in superior conjunction with the Sun on the 30th, is not visible during the month.

Mars passes close to Regulus in Leo at the end of the 1st week, slowly getting higher in the morning sky.

Jupiter, prominent in the southeast at sunset, is still up for most of the night.

Saturn, now rising at sunset, reaches 0 magnitude by mid-month, is up all night long with opposition on the 23d.

Moon passes Uranus on the 1st, occults Pallas and Jupiter on the 4th, passes Saturn on the 7th, occults Aldebaran on the 9th, Regulus on the 15th, Mars on the 16th, passes Mercury on the 21st, passes Uranus and Neptune on the 28th, and occults Jupiter on the 31st.

Oct. 1—Uranus 3° S of Moon.

Oct. 4—Moon occults minor planet Pallas which is 1° S of Moon; Jupiter 0.2° N of Moon, Jupiter occulted by Moon.

Oct. 6—Regulus 0.9° S of Mars.

Oct. 7—Saturn 1.8° N of Moon.

Oct. 9—Aldebaran 0.4° S of Moon, occulted by Moon; Moon occults Ceres, which is 0.9° S of Moon.

Oct. 11—Neptune stationary, resumes direct motion.

Oct. 15—Regulus 0.5° N of Moon, occulted by Moon.

Oct. 16—Mars 1° N of Moon, occulted by Moon.

Oct. 19—Uranus stationary, resumes direct motion.

Oct. 21—Mercury 7° S of Moon.

Oct. 23—Saturn at opposition.

Oct. 28—Neptune and Uranus 2° S of Moon.

Oct. 30—Venus in superior conjunction with the Sun.

Oct. 31—Jupiter 0.2° N of Moon, occulted by Moon.

November

Mercury remains visible in the early evening sky until the last week, begins retrograde on the 21st.

Venus still too close to the Sun and not visible.

Mars enters Virgo at mid-month and begins to brighten.

Jupiter, dimming a little, is in SSE at astronomical twilight, resumes direct motion on the 14th.

Saturn begins to decline in brightness after mid-month, but is in the sky until nearly dawn.

Moon passes Saturn on the 3d, occults Aldebaran and Ceres on the 6th, Regulus on the 11th, Mars on the 13th, passes Mercury on the 20th, Neptune on the 24th, Uranus on the 25th, occults Jupiter on the 28th, and passes Saturn on the 30th.

Nov. 1—Sun enters Libra.

Nov. 3—Saturn 1.7° N of Moon.

ov. 6—Aldebaran 0.6° S of Moon, Aldebaran occulted Moon, Moon occults minor planet Ceres, which is 0.3° of Moon.

Nov. 9—Star Antares of constellation Scorpius 1.9° S of Mercury.

Nov. 11—Mercury at greatest eastern elongation of 23°; Regulus 0.3° N of Moon, Regulus occulted by Moon.

Nov. 13—Mars 0.5° S of Moon, occulted by Moon.

Nov. 14—Jupiter stationary, resumes direct motion; Neptune enters Capricornus.

Nov. 16—Mars enters Virgo.

Nov. 20—Mercury 7° S of Moon.

Nov. 21—Mercury stationary, begins retrograde motion.

Nov. 24—Neptune 1.9° S of Moon; Sun enters Scorpius.

Nov. 25—Uranus 2° S of Moon.

Nov. 28—Jupiter 0.6° N of Moon, occulted by Moon.

Nov. 30—Pluto in conjunction with the Sun; Saturn 1.8° N of Moon.

December

Mercury passes inferior conjunction on the 1st, then re-emerges after 1st week into the early morning sky

Venus reemerges in the early evening sky in the SW after mid-month.

Mars furthest from the Sun at mid-month and at its brightest at year's end.

Jupiter, although still prominent in the S at sunset with Saturn, is setting before the middle of the night.

Saturn falls in brightness, but is still visible in [..] until after midnight, resuming direct motion on the 30th.

Moon occults Ceres and Aldebaran on the 3d, Regulus on the 9th, passes Mars on the 12th, Mercury on the 17th, Neptune on the 21st, Uranus on the 22d, occults Jupiter on the 25th, passes Saturn on the 27th, and occults Aldebaran on the 30th.

Dec. 1—Mercury in inferior conjunction; Sun enters Ophiuchus.

Dec. 3—Moon occults minor planet Ceres, which is 1.2° N of Moon; Aldebaran 0.6° S of Moon, Aldebaran occulted by Moon.

Dec. 9—Regulus 0.01° N of Moon, occulted by Moon.

Dec. 11—Mercury stationary, resumes direct motion.

Dec. 12—Mars 1.8° S of Moon.

Dec. 16—Mars at aphelion, 155 mil mi from Sun.

Dec. 17—Mercury 3° S of Moon.

Dec. 19—Sun enters Sagittarius.

Dec. 20—Mercury at greatest western elongation of 22°.

Dec. 21—Neptune 1.7° S of Moon.

Dec. 22—Southern Solstice at 1:56 GMT (8:56 PM EST Dec. 21), winter begins in the northern hemisphere, summer begins in the southern hemisphere; Antares 7° S of Mercury; Uranus 1.8° S of Moon.

Dec. 25—Jupiter 1.2° N of Moon, occulted by Moon.

Dec. 27—Saturn 2° N of Moon.

Dec. 30—Saturn stationary, resumes direct motion; Aldebaran 0.6° S of Moon, Aldebaran occulted by Moon.

Leonid Meteor Storm

When a chunk of material, ice or rock, plunges into Earth's atmosphere and burns up in a fiery display, the event is a **meteor.** While the chunk of material is still in space, it is a **meteoroid.** If a portion of the material survives passage through the atmosphere and reaches the ground, the remnant on the ground is a **meteorite.**

Meteors come from 2 basic sources. Sporadic meteors, which occur throughout the year, seem to originate from the asteroid belt. Other meteors, which come in groups and seem to occur at the same time each year, are called meteor showers and seem to originate as leftover material from comets. As a comet orbits the Sun and the Sun slowly boils away some of the comet's material, the comet leaves a trail of tiny particles dispersed along the comet's path. If Earth's orbit and this path intersect, then once a year, as Earth reaches that point in its orbit, there will be a **meteor shower.**

Meteor showers vary in strength, but usually the 3 best meteor showers of the year are the Perseids around Aug. 12, the Orionids around Oct. 21, and the Geminids around Dec. 13. The showers feature meteors at the rate of about 60 per hour. Best observing conditions occur with the absence of moonlight, usually when the Moon's phase is between waning crescent and waxing 1st quarter. Meteor showers are also usually better after the middle of the night, since in analogy with more raindrops on a car's front window, one is facing in Earth's forward direction.

After 2 spectacular comets in 2 years, Comet Hyakutake in 1996 and Comet Hale-Bopp in 1997, there is the likelihood of a spectacular meteor storm either in 1998 or 1999. For most meteor showers the cometary debris is relatively uniformly scattered along the comet's orbit. However, in the case of the Leonid meteor shower, which occurs every year around Nov. 17, the cometary debris, from Comet Temple-Tuttle, seems to be bunched up in one stretch. That means most years when Earth crosses the orbit of this comet, the meteor shower produced is relatively weak. However, approximately every 33 years Earth encounters the bunched-up debris. This last occurred in 1966 when observers on the W coast of the U.S. were treated to an awesome display of meteors in the early morning hours, as the rate peaked at 150,000 meteors per hour. Sometimes the storm is a disappointment, as it was in 1899 and 1933; at other times it is a roaring success, as in 1833 and 1866. In 1998 the Moon will be a couple of days before New Moon at the time of the Leonid meteor shower, and in 1999 the Moon will be 1 day past Waxing Quarter, so both years will be good opportunities to look for the Leonid meteor storm.

Planets and the Sun

The planets of the solar system, in order of their mean distance from the Sun, are Mercury, Venus, Earth, Mars, Jupiter, Saturn, Uranus, Neptune, and Pluto. Both Uranus and Neptune are visible through good binoculars, but Pluto is so distant and so small that only large telescopes or long-exposure photographs can make it visible.

Because Mercury and Venus are nearer to the Sun than is Earth, their motions about the Sun are seen from Earth as wide swings first to one side of the Sun and then to the other, although both planets are passing continuously around the Sun in orbits that are almost circular. When their passage takes them either between Earth and the Sun or beyond the Sun as seen from Earth, they are invisible to us. Because of the laws that govern the motions of planets about the Sun, both Mercury and Venus require much less time to pass between Earth and the Sun than around the far side of the Sun; so their periods of visibility and invisibility are unequal.

The planets that lie farther from the Sun than does Earth may be seen for longer periods and are invisible only when so located in our sky that they rise and set at about the same time as the Sun—and thus become overwhelmed by the Sun's great brilliance. Although several of the giant planets seem to emit their own energy, they are observed from Earth as a result of sunlight reflecting from their surfaces or cloud layers. Mercury and Venus, because they are between Earth and the Sun, show phases very much as the Moon does. The planets farther from the Sun are always seen as full, although Mars does occasionally present a slightly gibbous phase—like the Moon when not quite full.

The planets appear to move rapidly among the stars because of being closer. The stars are also in motion, some of them at tremendous speeds, but they are so far away that their motion does not change their apparent positions in the heavens sufficiently to be perceived. The nearest star is about 7,000 times farther away than the most distant planet in our solar system.

Planets of the Solar System

AU= astronomical unit (92.9 mil mi, the mean distance of the Earth from the Sun); d = 1 Earth synodic (solar) day (24 hrs); sidereal day = the rotation period of a planet measured with respect to the stars; synodic day = the rotation period of a planet measured with respect to the Sun (the "true" day, i.e. the time from midday to midday, or from sunrise to sunrise).

Mercury

Distance from Sun	
Perihelion	28.6 mil mi
Semi-major axis	0.38710 AU
Aphelion	43.4 mil mi
Period of revolution around Sun	87.97 d
Orbital eccentricity	0.20563
Orbital inclination	7° 0′ 18″
Synodic day (midday to midday)	175.97 d
Sidereal day	58.65 d
Rotational inclination	~0.1°
Mass (Earth = 1)	0.0553
Mean radius	1,516 mi
Mean density (Earth = 1)	0.98
Natural satellites	0
Average surface temperature	333° F

Mercury, the nearest planet to the Sun, is the 2d-smallest of the 9 planets known to be orbiting the Sun. Its diameter is 3,032 mi; its mean distance from the Sun is 36,000,000 mi.

Mercury moves with great speed in its journey about the Sun, averaging about 30 mi a second to complete its circuit in about 88 Earth days. Mercury rotates upon its axis over a period of nearly 59 days, thus exposing all its surface periodically to the Sun. Because its orbital period is only about 50% longer than its sidereal rotation, the solar (synodic) day on Mercury, or the time from one sunrise to the next, is about 176 days, twice as long as a Mercurian year. It is believed that the surface passing before the Sun may reach a temperature of about 840° F, while the temperature on the nighttime side may fall as low as –300° F. Although Mercury is the closest planet to the Sun, it has by far the largest range of temperature change from day to night.

Uncertainty about conditions on Mercury and its motion arises from its shorter angular distance from the Sun as seen from Earth. Mercury is always too much in line with the Sun to be observed against a dark sky, but is always seen during either morning or evening twilight.

Mariner 10 passed Mercury 3 times in 1974 and 1975. Less tha half of the surface was photographed, revealing a degree of cratering similar to that of the Moon. A very thin atmosphere of hydrogen and helium may be made up of gases of the solar wind temporarily concentrated by the presence of Mercury. The discovery of a weak but permanent magnetic field was a surprise to scientists. It has been held that both a fluid core and rapid rotation are necessary for the generation of a planetary magnetic field. Mercury may demonstrate the contrary; the field may reveal something about the history of Mercury.

Venus

Distance from Sun	
Perihelion	66.8 mil mi
Semi-major axis	0.72333 AU
Aphelion	67.7 mil mi
Period of revolution around Sun	224.70 d
Orbital eccentricity	0.00679
Orbital inclination	3° 23′ 41″
Synodic day (midday to midday)	116.75 d (retrograde)
Sidereal day	243.02 d (retrograde)
Rotational inclination	177.3°
Mass (Earth = 1)	0.8151
Mean radius	3,761 mi
Mean density (Earth = 1)	0.943
Natural satellites	0
Average surface temperature	870° F

Venus, slightly smaller than Earth, moves about the Sun at a mean distance of 67,000,000 mi in 225 Earth days. Its synodical revolution—its return to the same relationship with Earth and the Sun, which is a result of the combination of its own motion with that of Earth—is 584 days. As a result, every 19 months Venus is nearer to Earth than any other planet in the solar system. The planet is covered with a dense, white, cloudy atmosphere that conceals whatever is below it. This same cloud reflects sunlight efficiently so that when Venus is favorably situated, it is the 3d-brightest object in the sky, exceeded only by the Sun and the Moon.

Spectral analysis of sunlight reflected from Venus's cloud tops has shown features that can best be explained by identifying material of the clouds as sulfuric acid. Infrared spectroscopy from a balloon-borne telescope nearly 20 mi above Earth's surface gave indications of a small amount of water vapor present in the same region of the atmosphere of Venus. In 1956, radio astronomers at the Naval Research Laboratories in Washington, DC, found a temperature for Venus of about 600° F. Subsequent work and data from the *Mariner 2* space probe in 1962 confirmed a high temperature. *Mariner 2* was unable to detect the existence of a magnetic field even as weak as 1/100,000 of Earth's magnetic field.

In 1967, a Soviet space probe, *Venera 4*, and the American *Mariner 5* arrived at Venus within a few hours of each other. *Venera 4* was designed to allow an instrument package to land gently on the surface via parachute. It ceased to transmit information in about 75 minutes when its temperature reading went above 500° F. After considerable controversy, it was agreed that the instrument package still had 20 mi to go to reach the surface. *Mariner 5* went around the night side of Venus at a distance of about 6,000 mi. Its radio signals passed to Earth through Venus's atmosphere twice (once on the night side and once on the day side). The results were startling. Venus's atmosphere is nearly all carbon dioxide and must exert a pressure at the planet's surface of as much as 90 times Earth's normal sea-level pressure of one atmosphere. Because Earth and Venus are about the same size and were presumably formed at the same time by the same general process and from the same mixture of chemical elements, one is faced with the question: Which is the planet with the unusual history—Earth or Venus? Recent measurements indicate that Venus has a surface temperature of almost 900° F as a result of an extreme greenhouse effect. Because of the thick atmosphere, the temperature is essentially the same both day and night.

Radar astronomers using powerful transmitters as well as sensitive receivers and computers succeeded in determining the rotation period of Venus. It turns out to be 243 days clockwise—in other words, contrary to the spin of the other planets and to its own motion around the Sun. If it were exactly 243.16 days, Venus would present the same face toward Earth at every inferior conjunction. This rate and sense of rotation allows a solar day (sunrise to sunrise) on Venus of 116.8 Earth days. Any part of Venus will receive sunlight on its clouds for more than 58 days and then return to darkness for 58 days. Earth-based radar observations have shown surface features below the clouds. Large craters, continent-size highlands, and extensive, dry "ocean" basins were identified.

Mariner 10 passed Venus before traveling on to Mercury in 1974. The carbon dioxide molecule found in such abundance in the atmosphere is rather opaque to certain ultraviolet wavelengths, enabling sensitive television cameras to photograph the Venusian cloud cover. Photos radioed to Earth showed a spiral pattern in the clouds from the equator to the poles.

In 1978, two U.S. *Pioneer* probes arrived at Venus. One went into orbit around Venus; the other split into 5 separate probes targeted for widely spaced entry points to sample different conditions. The probes confirmed expected high surface temperatures and high winds aloft. Winds of about 200 mi per hour there may account for the transfer of heat into the night side despite the low rotation speed of the planet. However, surface winds were light at the time. Atmosphere and cloud chemistries were examined in detail, providing much data for continued analysis. The probes detected 4 layers of clouds and more light on the surface than expected solely from sunlight. This light allowed Soviet scientists to obtain, in 1975 and later in 1982, 4 photos of rocks on the surface. Sulfur seems to play a large role in the chemistry of Venus, and reactions involving sulfur may be responsible for the glow. To learn more about the weather and atmospheric circulation on Venus, the orbiter took daily photos of the daylight-side cloud cover. It confirmed the cloud pattern and its circulation shown by *Mariner 10*. The orbiter's radar produced maps of the entire planet showing the large features mentioned above.

The Venus orbiter *Magellan* was launched in 1989. It was equipped to observe Venus by a side-scanning radar system, together with one to gather data on the variations in elevations directly beneath the craft. *Magellan* mapped all but a small fraction of the planet. The side-looking radar illuminated the surface and its features with radio waves and recorded the strength and distance of the returning echoes. Computer processing produced a view of the landscape as if it had been seen through a clear atmosphere from above, near sunset, with a visibility better than about 500 feet on Venus. Information on vertical relief had a resolution of about 30 feet.

Craters more than 20 mi wide are believed to have been caused by impacting bodies. Theia Mons, a huge shield volcano, has a diameter of over 500 mi and a height of over 3 mi. (Compare this to the largest Hawaiian volcano, which is only about 125 mi in diameter, but with a height of nearly 5.5 mi from the ocean floor.) Many lava flows have been seen, and some old craters and plains seem to be filled with lava.

Most of the surface is believed to be younger than 1 bil to 500 mil years old. Modifications of previously existing surface features have been caused by weathering and by tectonic actions such as faulting. Tectonic actions on Venus are distinctly different from such actions on Earth. The intense heat at the surface can prevent surface materials from cooling to the same brittle condition as on Earth. No activity on Venus seems to be similar to Earth's moving tectonic plates, but local stretching and compressing may produce rift valleys and higher plains and mountains. Although there is no weathering due to water, the action of winds is in evidence. Extensive sand dunes have been seen, and windblown deposits indicate stable wind patterns for very long periods of time. Although there are deep regions, somewhat similar to Earth's ocean basins, there is no water to fill them. The orbit of *Magellan* was adjusted to a nearly circular shape about 300 mi from the planet's surface in 1993. In this mode, variation in *Magellan*'s orbital speed revealed information on irregularities in the gravitational field, presumably due to details in the internal structure of the planet. Although *Magellan* ceased operating in Oct. 1994, its data about the topography of Venus's surface will keep teams of analysts and theoreticians busy for years.

Mars

Mars is the first planet beyond Earth, away from the Sun. Mars's diameter is about 4,213 mi. Although Mars's orbit is nearly circular, it is somewhat more eccentric than the orbits of many of the other planets, and Mars is more than 25 mil mi farther from the Sun in some parts of its year than it is in others. Mars takes 687 Earth days to make one circuit of the Sun, traveling at about 15 mi a second. The

Distance from Sun	
Perihelion	128.4 mil mi
Semi-major axis	1.52364 AU
Aphelion	154.8 mil mi
Period of revolution around Sun	686.98 d (1.88 y)
Orbital eccentricity	0.09342
Orbital inclination	1° 51′ 0″
Synodic day (midday to midday)	24h 41m 58s
Sidereal day	24h 37m 22s
Rotational inclination	25.19°
Mass (Earth = 1)	0.1075
Mean radius	2,106 mi
Mean density (Earth = 1)	0.713
Natural satellites	2
Average surface temperature	−76° F

planet rotates upon its axis in almost the same period of time as Earth—24 hours and 37 minutes. Mars's mean distance from the Sun is 141 mil mi, so its temperature would be lower than that on Earth even if its atmosphere were not so thin. *Mariner 4*, in 1965, reported that atmospheric pressure on Mars is between 1% and 2% of Earth's atmospheric pressure. As is the case with Venus, the thin atmosphere appears to be composed largely of carbon dioxide. No evidence of free water was found by *Mariner 4*.

The planet is exposed to an influx of cosmic radiation about 100 times as intense as that on Earth.

Deductions from years of telescopic observation indicate that about 5/8 of the surface of Mars is a desert of reddish rock, sand, and soil. The rest is covered by irregular patches that appear generally green, in hues that change through the year. These were formerly held to be some sort of primitive vegetation, but with the findings of *Mariner 4* of a complete lack of water and oxygen, it appeared that such growth would not be possible. The nature of the green areas became a mystery. They may be regions covered with volcanic salts whose color changes with changing temperatures and atmospheric conditions, or they may be gray rather than green. (When large gray areas are placed beside large red areas, the gray areas appear green to the eye.)

Mars's axis of rotation is inclined from a vertical to the plane of its orbit about the Sun by about 25°, and therefore Mars has seasons as does Earth. White caps form about the winter pole of Mars, growing in the winter and shrinking in the summer. These polar caps are now believed to be both water ice and carbon dioxide ice. It is the carbon dioxide that is seen to come and go with the seasons. The water ice is apparently in many layers with dust between them, indicating climatic cycles.

Markings forming a network of fine lines, crossing much of the surface of Mars, have been seen by diligent observers. A few of the 21 photographs sent back to Earth by *Mariner 4* covered areas crossed by canals; the pictures show faint, ill-defined, broad, dark markings, the nature of which could not be positively determined. *Mariners 6* and *7* in 1969 sent back many photographs of higher quality. These showed cratering similar to the earlier views, but in addition showed other types of terrain. Some regions seemed featureless over large areas; others were chaotic, showing high relief without apparent organization into mountain chains or craters. *Mariner 9*, the first spacecraft to orbit Mars (1971), transmitted more than 10,000 photographs covering 100% of the surface. Although these photos and other data show that Mars resembles no other planet we know, scientists using terrestrial terms describe features that seem to be clearly of volcanic origin. One of these features is Olympus Mons, apparently a shield volcano whose caldera is more than 50 mi wide and whose outer slopes are more than 300 mi in diameter; it stands more than 15 mi above the surrounding plain—the tallest known mountain in the solar system. Some features may have been produced by cracking (faulting) of the surface and the sliding of one region over or past another. Many craters seem to have been produced by impacting bodies that may have come from the nearby asteroid belt. Features near the S pole may have been produced by glaciers no longer present. Valles Marineris, a huge series of inter-related canyons, stretches more than 3,000 mi.

Although the Russians landed a probe on the Martian surface in 1971, it transmitted for only 90 seconds. In 1976, the U.S. landed 2 *Viking* spacecraft on the Martian surface. The landers had devices aboard to perform chemical analyses of the soil in search of evidence of life; results were inconclusive. The 2 *Viking* orbiters returned the best pictures up to then of Martian topographic features. Scientists believe many of these features can be explained only if Mars once had large quantities of flowing water.

In 1997, 2 more U.S. spacecraft—the Mars *Pathfinder* and the Mars *Global Surveyor*—went to the red planet to continue exploration aided by monitoring with the Hubble Space Telescope. Preliminary geological results from the *Pathfinder*, which landed July 4, indicate that in its beginning stages Mars melted to a sufficient extent to separate into dense and lighter layers. The *Surveyor*, which went into orbit around Mars on Sept. 11, has already reported the presence of a very weak magnetic field that may have been stronger in the distant past.

Mars's position in its orbit and its speed around that orbit in relation to Earth's position and speed bring the planet fairly close to Earth on occasions about 2 years apart and then move Mars and Earth too far apart for favorable observation. Every 15-17 years, the close approaches are especially favorable for observation.

Mars has 2 satellites, discovered in 1877 by Asaph Hall. The outer satellite, Deimos, revolves around the planet in about 31 hours. The inner satellite, Phobos, whips around Mars in a little more than 7 hours, making 3 trips around the planet each Martian day. Since it orbits Mars faster than the planet rotates, Phobos rises in the W and sets in the E, opposite to what other bodies appear to do in the Martian sky. *Mariner* and *Viking* photos show these satellites to be irregularly shaped and pitted with numerous craters. Phobos also exhibits a system of linear grooves, each about 1/3 mi across and roughly parallel. Phobos measures about 8 by 12 mi and Deimos about 5 by 7.5 mi.

Of the tens of thousands of meteorites found on Earth, approximately a dozen of them may have originated on Mars. In 1996, a NASA research team concluded that a meteorite found in 1984 on an Antarctic ice field not only might be a rock blasted from the surface of Mars but also might contain evidence that life existed on Mars more than 3.5 bil years ago. The meteorite has been age-dated to about 4.5 bil years. The scientists theorize that 3.5 bil years ago, Mars may have been warmer and wetter, and microscopic life may have formed and left evidence in the rock, including possible fossilized microscopic organisms. Then, 16 mil years ago, it is believed that a huge asteroid or comet struck Mars, blasting material, including this rock, into space. The rock may have entered Earth's atmosphere about 13,000 years ago, landing in Antarctica. The evidence is intriguing, but not conclusive, and even if the above conclusions are correct they indicate the presence only of microscopic life, at a time far in the past.

Jupiter

Jupiter is the largest of the planets. Its equatorial diameter is nearly 89,000 mi, 11 times the diameter of Earth. Its polar diameter is about 6,000 mi shorter. This noticeable oblateness is a result of the liquidity of the planet and its extremely rapid rate of rotation; a day is less than 10 Earth hours long. For a planet this size, this rotational speed is amazing. A point on Jupiter's equator moves at a speed of 22,000 mi per hour, as compared with 1,000 mi for a point on Earth's equator. Jupiter is at an average distance of 480 mil mi from the Sun and takes almost 12 Earth years to make one complete circuit of the Sun.

Distance from Sun	
Perihelion	460.2 mil mi
Semi-major axis	5.20260 AU
Aphelion	507.0 mil mi
Period of revolution around Sun	11.86 y
Orbital eccentricity	0.04846
Orbital inclination	1° 18′ 17″
Synodic day (midday to midday)	9h 55m 33s
Sidereal day	9h 55m 30s
Rotational inclination	3.12°
Mass (Earth = 1)	317.83
Mean radius	43,441 mi
Mean density (Earth = 1)	0.24
Natural satellites	16
Average temperature*	−160° F

*i.e., temperature where atmosphere pressure equals 1 Earth atmosphere.

The major chemical constituents of Jupiter's atmosphere are molecular hydrogen (H_2) and helium (He). Minor constituents include methane (CH_4), ammonia (NH_3), ethane (C_2H_6), and water (H_2O). The temperature at the tops of the clouds may be about −280° F. The clouds are probably ammonia ice crystals, becoming ammonia droplets lower down. There may be a space before water ice crystals show up as clouds: in turn, these become water droplets near the bottom of the entire cloud layer. The total atmosphere may be only a few hundred mi in depth, pulled down by the surface gravity (the equivalent of 2.36 times Earth's gravity) to a relatively thin layer. Of course, the gases become denser with depth, until they may turn into a slush or slurry. Perhaps there is no real interface between the gaseous atmosphere and the hydrogen ocean that accounts for most of Jupiter's volume. *Pioneer 10* and *11*, passing Jupiter in 1973 and 1974, provided evidence for considering Jupiter almost entirely liquid hydrogen. Long before a rocky core about the size of Earth is reached, scientists believe hydrogen mixed with helium becomes a liquid metal at very high temperature and pressure. Jupiter's cloudy atmosphere is a fairly good reflector of sunlight and makes it appear far brighter than any of the stars.

Fourteen of Jupiter's 16 known satellites were found through Earth-based observations. Four of the moons are large and bright, rivaling Earth's Moon and the planet Mercury in diameter, and may be seen through binoculars. They move rapidly around Jupiter, and their change of position from night to night is extremely interesting to watch. The other satellites are much smaller, and in all but one instance much farther from Jupiter, and cannot be seen except through powerful telescopes. The 4 outermost satellites revolve around Jupiter clockwise as seen from the north, contrary to the motions of the great majority of the satellites in the solar system and to the direction of revolution of the planets around the Sun. These moons may be captured asteroids. Jupiter's mass is more than twice the mass of all the other planets put together.

Photographs from *Pioneer 10* and *11* were far surpassed by those of *Voyager 1* and *2*, both of which rendezvoused with Jupiter in 1979. Thousands of high-resolution multicolor pictures show rapid variations of features both large and small. The Great Red Spot exhibited internal counterclockwise rotation. Much turbulence was seen in adjacent material passing N or S of it. The satellites Amalthea, Io, Europa, Ganymede, and Callisto were photographed, some in great detail. Each is individual and unique, with no similarities to other known planets or satellites. Io has active volcanoes that probably have ejected material into a doughnut-shaped ring enveloping its orbit about Jupiter. This is not to be confused with the thin, flat disklike ring closer to Jupiter's surface.

Beginning July 16, 1994, the 21 large fragments of Comet Shoemaker Levy 9 collided with Jupiter in a dramatic 6-day barrage. Moving at 134,000 mph, stretched out like a 21-car freight train, the fragments impacted one after another against the side of Jupiter facing away from Earth. Massive plumes of gas erupted from the impact sites, forming brilliant fireballs and leaving dark blotches and smears behind. One of the largest chunks, labeled the G fragment, impacted with the force of 6 mil megatons of TNT, 100,000 times the power of the largest nuclear bomb ever detonated. It produced a plume 1,200-1,600 mi high and 5,000 mi wide and left a dark discoloration larger than Earth. These impacts were closely observed and produced a massive amount of data for scientists to analyze.

Scientists produced their own impact, when the *Galileo* spacecraft went into orbit around Jupiter and released an atmospheric probe into the Jovian atmosphere in Dec. 1995. The cone-shaped probe, traveling at a speed of more than 106,000 mph, survived deceleration forces of 228 times Earth's gravity as it plunged 400 mi, relaying information about Jupiter's atmosphere for 57 minutes before expiring. Initial findings revealed a relatively dry atmosphere for the planet, with about 1/5 the atmosphere for the amount of water expected from studies of the Comet Shoemaker-Levy 9 impacts. There were also higher-than-expected concentrations of helium. The probe gave evidence of wind speeds of more than 4,000 mph and a relative absence of lightning. These findings, together with data transmitted from the *Galileo* spacecraft still orbiting the planet with flybys of various Jovian moons, raise many unresolved questions about Jupiter and its satellites.

Saturn

Distance from Sun	
Perihelion	837.4 mil mi
Semi-major axis	9.53877 AU
Aphelion	936.0 mil mi
Period of revolution around Sun	29.46 y
Orbital eccentricity	0.05317
Orbital inclination	2° 29′ 7″
Synodic day (midday to midday)	10h 30m 2s
Sidereal day	10h 30m 0s
Rotational Inclination	26.73°
Mass (Earth = 1)	95.16
Mean radius	36,184 mi
Mean density (Earth = 1)	0.124
Natural satellites	18
Average temperature*	−220° F

*i.e., temperature where atmosphere pressure equals 1 Earth atmosphere.

Saturn, last of the planets visible to the unaided eye, is almost twice as far from the Sun as Jupiter, almost 900 mil mi. It is 2d in size to Jupiter, but its mass is much smaller. Saturn's specific gravity is less than that of water. Its diameter is almost 75,000 mi at the equator; its rotational speed spins it completely around in a little more than 10 hours, and its atmosphere is much like that of Jupiter, except that its temperature at the top of its cloud layer is at least 100° F lower. At about 300° F below zero, the ammonia would be frozen out of Saturn's clouds. The theoretical construction of Saturn resembles that of Jupiter; it likely has a small dense center surrounded by a layer of liquid and a deep atmosphere.

Until *Pioneer 11* passed Saturn in 1979, only 10 satellites of the planet were known from ground-based observations. *Pioneer 11* discovered 2 more, and the other 6 were found in the *Voyager 1* and *2* flybys, which also yielded more information about Saturn's icy satellites. In 1995, astronomers using the Hubble Space Telescope detected evidence for previously unknown moons of Saturn, but these results have not been confirmed.

Saturn's ring system begins about 7,000 mi above the visible disk of Saturn, lying above its equator and extending about 35,000 mi into space. The diameter of the ring system visible from Earth is about 170,000 mi; the rings are

estimated to be no thicker than 10 mi. In 1973, radar observation showed the ring particles to be large chunks of material averaging a meter on a side.

Voyager 1 and *2* observations showed the rings to be considerably more complex than had been believed. To the untrained eye, the *Voyager* photographs could be mistaken for pictures of a colorful phonograph record. In October, 1997 the Cassini spacecraft was to be launched; it was scheduled to reach Saturn in 2004, to study this planet, its rings, and its satellites.

Uranus

Distance from Sun	
Perihelion	1,698.8 mil mi
Semi-major axis	19.17914 AU
Aphelion	1,867.2 mil mi
Period of revolution around Sun	84.01 y
Orbital eccentricity	0.04724
Orbital inclination	0° 46′ 24″
Synodic day (midday to midday)	17h 14m 23s (retrograde)
Sidereal day	17h 14m 24s (retrograde)
Rotational inclination	97.86°
Mass (Earth = 1)	14.54
Mean radius	15,759 mi
Mean density (Earth = 1)	0.239
Natural satellites	15
Average temperature*	−320° F

*i.e., temperature where atmosphere pressure equals 1 Earth atmosphere.

Voyager 2, after passing Saturn in 1981, headed for a rendezvous with Uranus, culminating in a flyby in 1986. This encounter answered many questions and raised others.

Uranus, discovered by Sir William Herschel on Mar. 13, 1781, lies at a distance of 1.8 bil mi from the Sun, taking 84 years to make its circuit around our star. Uranus has a diameter of about 32,000 mi and spins once in some 17.4 hours, according to flyby magnetic data. One of the most fascinating features of Uranus is how far over it is tipped. Its N pole lies 98° from being directly up and down to its orbit plane. Thus, its seasons are extreme. When the Sun rises at the N pole, it stays up for 42 Earth years; then it sets, and the N pole is in darkness (and winter) for 42 Earth years.

Uranus has 15 moons (the 5 largest having been known before the flyby), which have orbits lying in the plane of the planet's equator. In that plane there is also a complex of rings, 9 of which were discovered in 1978. Invisible from Earth, the 9 original rings were found by observers watching Uranus pass before a star. As they waited, they saw their photoelectric equipment register several short eclipses of the star; then the planet occulted the star as expected. After the star came out from behind Uranus, the star winked out several more times. Subsequent observations and analyses indicated the 9 narrow, nearly opaque rings circling Uranus. Evidence from the *Voyager 2* flyby has shown the ring particles to be predominantly a yard or so in diameter.

In addition to photos of the 10 new, very small satellites, *Voyager 2* returned detailed photos of the 5 large satellites. As in the case of other satellites newly observed in the *Voyager* program, these bodies proved to be entirely different from one another and from any others. Miranda has grooved markings, reminiscent of Jupiter's Ganymede, but often arranged in a chevron pattern. Ariel shows rifts and channels. Umbriel is extremely dark, prompting some observers to regard its surface as among the oldest in the system. Titania has rifts and fractures, but not the evidence of flow found on Ariel. Oberon's main feature is its surface saturated with craters, unrelieved by other formations.

Uranus is likely to have a rocky core, surrounded by a thick, icy mantle or perhaps a liquid mantle of water, methane, and ammonia, on top of which is a slushy layer of hydrogen and helium that gradually becomes an atmosphere.

In addition to its rotational tilt, Uranus's magnetic field axis is tipped an incredible 58.6° from its rotational axis and is displaced about 1/3 of its radius away from the planet's center.

Neptune

Distance from Sun	
Perihelion	2,770.1 mil mi
Semi-major axis	30.05749 AU
Aphelion	2,818.0 mil mi
Period of revolution around Sun	164.79 y
Orbital eccentricity	0.00858
Orbital inclination	1° 46′ 5″
Synodic day (midday to midday)	16h 6m 37s
Sidereal day	16h 6m 36s
Rotational inclination	29.56°
Mass (Earth = 1)	17.15
Mean radius	15,301 mi
Mean density (Earth = 1)	0.297
Natural satellites	8
Average temperature*	−330° F

*i.e., temperature where atmosphere pressure equals 1 Earth atmosphere.

Neptune, currently the most distant planet from the Sun (until 1999), lies at an average distance of 2.8 bil mi. It was the last planet visited in *Voyager 2*'s epic 12-year trek (1977-89) from Earth.

As with the other giant planets, Neptune may have no solid surface, or exact diameter. However, a mean value of 30,600 mi may be assigned to a diameter between atmosphere levels where the pressure is about the same as sea level on Earth. Without a solid surface it is challenging to determine a "true" rotation rate for a giant planet. Astronomers use a determination of the rotation rate of the planet's magnet field to indicate the internal rotation rate, which in the case of Neptune is 16.1 hours. Neptune orbits the Sun in 164.8 years in a nearly circular orbit. Neptune was not discovered until 1846; not until 2010 will Neptune have completed one full trip around the Sun since its discovery.

Voyager 2, which passed 3,000 mi from Neptune's N pole, found a magnetic field that is considerably asymmetric to the planet's structure, similar to, but not so extreme as, that found at Uranus.

Neptune's atmosphere was seen to be quite blue, with quickly changing white clouds often suspended high above an apparent surface. There is a feature called the Great Dark Spot, reminiscent of the Great Red Spot of Jupiter, even to the counterclockwise rotation expected in a high-pressure system in the southern hemisphere. Observations with the Hubble Space Telescope have shown that the Great Dark Spot originally seen by *Voyager* has apparently dissipated, but a new dark spot has since appeared. Atmospheric constituents are mostly hydrocarbon compounds. Although lightning and auroras have been found on other giant planets, only the aurora phenomenon has been seen on Neptune.

Six new satellites were definitively discerned around Neptune by *Voyager 2*. Five of these satellites orbit Neptune in a half day or less. Of the 8 satellites of Neptune in all, the largest, Triton, is in a retrograde orbit, suggesting that it was captured rather than being coeval with Neptune. Triton's large size, sufficient to raise significant tides on the planet, may one day, billions of years from now, cause Triton to come close enough to Neptune for it to be torn apart. Nereid was found in 1949 and has the highest orbital eccentricity (0.75) of any moon. Its long looping orbit suggests that it, too, was captured. Each of the satellites that has been photographed by the 2 *Voyagers* in the planetary encounters has been different from any of the other satellites, and certainly different from any of the planets. Only about half of Triton has been observed, but its terrain shows cratering and a strange regional feature described as

resembling the skin of a cantaloupe. Triton has a tenuous atmosphere of nitrogen with a trace of hydrocarbons and evidence of active geysers injecting material into it. At −390° F, the winter time parts of Triton are the coldest regions yet found in the solar system.

Voyager 2 also confirmed the existence of at least 3 rings composed of very fine particles. There may be some clumpiness in the rings structure. It is not known whether Neptune's satellites influence the formation or maintenance of the rings.

As with the other giant planets, Neptune is emitting more energy than it receives from the Sun. *Voyager* found the excess to be 2.7 times the solar contribution. Cooling from internal heat sources and from the heat of formation of the planets is thought to be responsible.

Pluto

Distance from Sun	
Perihelion	2,762.5 mil mi
Semi-major axis	39.52874 AU
Aphelion	4,586.5 mil mi
Period of revolution around Sun	247.69 y
Orbital eccentricity	0.2482
Orbital inclination	17° 7′ 17″
Synodic day (midday to midday)	6d 9h 18m (retrograde)
Sidereal day	6d 9h 18m (retrograde)
Rotational inclination	122.46°
Mass (Earth = 1)	0.0021
Mean radius	707 mi
Mean density (Earth = 1)	0.3714
Natural satellites	1
Average surface temperature	−370° F

Although Pluto on the average stays about 3.6 bil mi from the Sun, its orbit is so eccentric that its minimum distance of 2.76 bil mi is less than the current distance of Neptune. Thus, Pluto, until 1999, is temporarily the 8th planet from the Sun. At its mean distance, Pluto takes 247.7 years to circumnavigate the Sun, a 3/2 resonance with Neptune. Until recently, this was about all that was known of Pluto.

About a century ago, a hypothetical planet was believed to lie beyond Neptune and Uranus because neither planet followed the paths predicted by astronomers even when all known gravitational influences were considered. In what was little more than a guess, a mass of 1 Earth was assigned to the mysterious body, and mathematical searches were begun. Amid some controversy about the validity of the predictive process, Pluto was discovered nearly where it had been predicted to lie. It was found by Clyde Tombaugh at the Lowell Observatory in Flagstaff, AZ, in 1930.

At the U.S. Naval Observatory, also in Flagstaff, in 1978, James Christy obtained a photograph of Pluto that was distinctly elongated. Repeated observations of this shape and its variation were convincing evidence of the discovery of a satellite of Pluto, now named Charon. Subsequent observations show it to be 730 mi across, more than 12,000 mi from Pluto, and taking 6.4 days to move around Pluto. In this same length of time, Pluto and Charon both rotate once around their individual axes. The Pluto-Charon system thus appears to rotate as virtually a rigid body. Gravitational laws allow these interactions to give the mass of Pluto as 0.0021 of Earth. This mass, together with a new diameter for Pluto of 1,413 mi, make the density about twice that of water. Theorists predict that Pluto has a rocky core, surrounded by a thick mantle of ice.

It is now clear that Pluto, the body found by Tombaugh, could not have influenced Neptune and Uranus to go astray. Although a 10th planet might be out there somewhere, theorists no longer believe that there are unexplained pertubations in the orbit of Uranus or Neptune that might be caused by it. Astronomers have discovered more than 2 dozen asteroid-size objects, somewhat beyond Pluto, in a region called the Kuiper belt, where some comets are believed to originate.

Because the rotational axis of the system is tipped from the reference plane of the solar system by about 98.3°, there is only a short interval every half solar period when Pluto and Charon alternately eclipse each other. Both worlds are approximately spherical, but they are otherwise different. Pluto is red; Charon gray. Charon's surface is identified as water ice; Pluto's surface is frozen methane.

Large regions on Pluto are dark, others light; Pluto has spots and, perhaps, polar caps. Although extremely cold, Pluto's methane surface produces a tenuous atmosphere that may be slowly escaping into space, perhaps going to Charon. When Pluto occulted a star, the star's light faded in such a way as to have passed through a haze layer lying above the planet's surface, indicating an inversion of temperatures—110 K above and 50 K below—suggesting Pluto has primitive weather.

Morning and Evening Stars, 1998

(Greenwich Mean Time)

	Morning	Evening		Morning	Evening
Jan.	Mercury Venus from Jan. 16 Uranus from Jan. 28 Neptune from Jan. 19 Pluto	Venus to Jan. 16 Mars Jupiter Saturn Uranus to Jan. 28 Neptune to Jan. 19	July	Venus Mars Jupiter Saturn Uranus Neptune to July 23	Mercury Neptune from July 23 Pluto
Feb.	Mercury to Feb. 22 Venus Jupiter from Feb. 23 Uranus Neptune Pluto	Mercury from Feb. 22 Mars Jupiter to Feb. 23 Saturn	Aug.	Mercury from Aug. 14 Venus Mars Jupiter Saturn Uranus to Aug. 3	Mercury to Aug. 13 Uranus from Aug. 3 Neptune Pluto
Mar.	Venus Jupiter Uranus Neptune Pluto	Mercury Mars Saturn	Sept.	Mercury to Sep. 25 Venus Mars Jupiter to Sep. 16 Saturn	Mercury from Sep. 25 Jupiter from Sep. 16 Uranus Neptune Pluto
Apr.	Mercury from Apr. 6 Venus Jupiter Saturn from Apr. 13 Uranus Neptune Pluto	Mercury to Apr. 6 Mars Saturn to Apr. 13	Oct.	Venus to Oct. 30 Mars Saturn to Oct. 23	Mercury Venus from Oct. 30 Jupiter Saturn from Oct. 23 Uranus Neptune Pluto
May	Mercury Venus Mars from May 12 Jupiter Saturn Uranus Neptune Pluto to May 28	Mars to May 12 Pluto from May 28	Nov.	Mars Pluto from Nov. 30	Mercury Venus Jupiter Saturn Uranus Neptune Pluto to Nov. 30
June	Mercury to June 10 Venus Mars Jupiter Saturn Uranus Neptune	Mercury from June 10 Pluto	Dec.	Mercury from Dec. 1 Mars Pluto	Mercury to Dec. 1 Venus Jupiter Saturn Uranus Neptune

Greenwich Sidereal Time for 0ʰ GMT, 1998

(Add 12 hours to obtain Right Ascension of Mean Sun)

Date	d	h	m	Date	d	h	m	Date	d	h	m
Jan.	1	6	41.8	May	1	14	34.9	Sept.	8	23	07.4
	11	7	21.2		11	15	14.3		18	23	46.9
	21	8	00.6		21	15	53.7		28	0	26.3
	31	8	40.1		31	16	33.2	Oct.	8	1	05.7
Feb.	10	9	19.5	June	10	17	12.6		18	1	45.1
	20	9	58.9		20	17	52.0		28	2	24.6
Mar.	2	10	38.3		30	18	31.4	Nov.	7	3	04.0
	12	11	17.8	July	10	19	10.9		17	3	43.4
	22	11	57.2		20	19	50.3		27	4	22.8
Apr.	1	12	36.6		30	20	29.7	Dec.	7	5	02.3
	11	13	16.0	Aug.	9	21	09.2		17	5	41.7
	21	13	55.5		19	21	48.6		27	6	21.1
					29	22	28.0				

Star Tables

These tables include stars of visual magnitude 2.4 and brighter (the lower the number, the brighter the star). Stars of variable magnitude are designated by v. Coordinates are for mid-1998. If no parallax figures are given, the trigonometric parallax figure is smaller than the margin for error and the distance given is obtained by indirect methods. Greek letters in the star names were adopted to indicate perceived degree of relative brightness within the constellation, alpha being the brightest.

To find the time when the star is on the meridian, subtract Right Ascension of Mean Sun (from sidereal timetable above) from the star's Right Ascension, first adding 24h to the latter, if necessary. Mark this result PM, if less than 12h, but if greater than 12, subtract 12h and mark the remainder AM.

Star	Magni-tude	Paral-lax "	Light yrs.	Right ascen. h	Right ascen. m	Decli-nation ° '
α Andromedae (Alpheratz)	2.06	0.02	90	0	08.3	+29 05
β Cassiopeiae (Caph)	2.27v	0.07	45	0	09.1	+59 08
α Phoenicia (Ankaa)	2.39	0.04	93	0	26.2	−42 19
α Cassiopeiae (Schedar)	2.23	0.01	150	0	40.4	+56 31
β Ceti (Deneb Kaitos)	2.04	0.06	57	0	43.5	−18 00
β Andromedae (Mirach)	2.06	0.04	76	1	09.6	+35 36
α Eridani (Achnerar)	0.46	0.02	118	1	37.6	−57 14
γ Andromedae (Almaak)	2.26		260	2	03.8	+42 19
α Arietis (Hamal)	2.00	0.04	76	2	07.1	+23 27
ο Ceti (Mira)	2.00	0.01	103	2	19.2	− 3 00
α Ursae Minoris (Polaris)	2.02v		680	2	29.7	+89 15
β Persei (Algol)	2.12v	0.03	105	3	08.0	+40 57
α Persei (Mirphak)	1.80	0.03	150	3	24.2	+49 51
α Tauri (Aldebaran)	0.85v	0.05	68	4	35.8	+16 30
β Orionis (Rigel)	0.12v		900	5	14.4	− 8 12
α Aurigae (Capella)	0.08v	0.07	45	5	16.5	+46 00
γ Orionis (Bellatrix)	1.64	0.03	470	5	25.0	+ 6 21
β Tauri (Elnath)	1.65	0.02	300	5	26.2	+28 36
δ Orionis (Mintaka)	2.23v		1500	5	31.9	− 0 18
ε Orionis (Alnilam)	1.70		1600	5	36.1	− 1 12
ζ Orionis (Alnitak)	2.05	0.02	1600	5	40.5	− 1 57
κ Orionis (Saiph)	2.06	0.01	2100	5	47.7	− 9 40
α Orionis (Betelgeuse)	0.50v		520	5	55.1	+ 7 24
β Aurigae (Menkalinan)	1.90v	0.04	88	5	59.4	+44 57
β Canis Majoris (Mirzam)	1.98	0.01	750	6	22.6	−17 57
α Carinae (Canopus)	−0.72	0.02	98	6	23.9	−52 42
γ Geminorum (Alhena)	1.93	0.03	105	6	37.6	+16 24
α Canis Majoris (Sirius)	−1.46	0.38	8.7	6	45.1	−16 43
ε Canis Majoris (Adhara)	1.50		680	6	58.5	−28 58
δ Canis Majoris (Wezen)	1.86		2100	7	08.3	−26 24
α Geminorum (Castor)	1.99	0.07	45	7	34.4	+31 53
α Canis Minoris (Procyon)	0.38	0.29	11.3	7	39.2	+ 5 14
β Geminorum (Pollux)	1.14	0.09	35	7	45.2	+28 02
ζ Puppis (Naos)	2.25		2400	8	03.5	−40 00
γ Velorum (Al Suhail)	1.82		520	8	09.5	−47 20
ε Carinae (Avior)	1.86		340	8	22.5	−59 30
δ Velorum	1.96	0.04	76	8	44.7	−54 42
λ Velorum (Suhail)	2.21	0.02	750	9	07.9	−43 26
β Carinae (Miaplacidus)	1.68	0.04	86	9	13.2	−69 43
ι Carinae (Tureis)	2.25		750	9	17.0	−59 16
α Hydrae (Alphard)	1.98	0.02	94	9	27.5	− 8 39
α Leonis (Regulus)	1.35	0.04	84	10	08.3	+11 59

Star	Magni-tude	Paral-lax "	Light yrs.	Right ascen. h	Right ascen. m	Decli-nation ° '
β Ursae Majoris (Merak)	2.37	0.04	78	11	01.7	+56 24
α Ursae Majoris (Dubhe)	1.79	0.03	105	11	03.6	+61 46
β Leonis (Denebola)	2.14	0.08	43	11	49.0	+14 35
α Crucis (Acrux)	1.58		370	12	26.5	−63 06
γ Crucis (Gacrux)	1.63		220	12	31.1	−57 06
γ Centauri	2.17		160	12	41.3	−48 56
β Crucis (Becrux)	1.25v		490	12	47.6	−59 41
ε Ursae Majoris (Alioth)	1.77v	0.01	68	12	53.9	+55 58
ζ Ursae Majoris (Mizar)	2.27	0.04	88	13	23.9	+54 56
α Virginis (Pica)	0.97v	0.02	220	13	25.1	−11 09
ε Centauri	2.30v		570	13	39.8	−53 28
ε Ursae Majoris (Alkaid)	1.86		210	13	47.5	+49 20
β Centauri (Hadar)	0.61v	0.02	490	14	03.7	−60 22
η Centauri (Menkent)	2.06	0.06	55	14	06.6	−36 22
α Bootis (Arcturus)	−0.04	0.09	36	14	15.6	+19 12
ε Centauri	2.31v		390	14	35.4	−42 09
α Centauri (Rigel Kentaurus)	−0.01	0.75	4.3	14	39.5	−60 50
α Lupi	2.30v		430	14	41.8	−47 23
ε Bootis (Izar)	2.40	0.01	103	14	44.9	+27 06
β Ursae Minoris (Kochab)	2.08	0.03	105	14	50.7	+74 10
α Coronae Borealis (Gemma)	2.23v	0.04	76	15	34.6	+26 43
δ Scorpii (Dschubba)	2.32		590	16	00.3	−22 37
α Scorpii (Antares)	0.96v	0.02	520	16	29.3	−26 26
α Trianguli Australis (Atria)	1.92	0.02	82	16	48.6	−69 01
ε Scorpii	2.29	0.05	66	16	50.1	−34 17
λ Scorpii (Shaula)	1.63v		310	17	33.5	−37 06
α Ophiuchi (Rasalhague)	2.08	0.06	58	17	34.9	+12 34
θ Scorpii	1.87	0.02	650	17	37.2	−43 00
γ Draconis (Eltanin)	2.23	0.02	108	17	56.6	+51 30
ε Sagittarii (Kaus Australis)	1.85	0.02	124	18	24.1	−34 23
α Lyrae (Vega)	0.03	0.12	26.5	18	36.9	+38 47
ο Sagittarii (Nunki)	2.02		300	18	55.2	−26 18
α Aquilae (Altair)	0.77	0.20	16.5	19	50.7	+ 8 52
γ Cygni (Sadr)	2.20		750	20	22.2	+40 15
α Pavonis (Peacock)	1.94		310	20	25.5	−56 44
α Cygni (Deneb)	1.25		1600	20	41.4	+45 16
ε Pegasi (Enif)	2.39		780	21	44.1	+ 9 52
α Gruis (Al Nair)	1.74	0.05	64	22	08.1	−46 58
β Gruis	2.11v		280	22	42.6	−46 53
α Piscis Austrinis (Fomalhaut)	1.16	0.14	22.6	22	57.6	−29 38

Astronomical Constants; Speed of Light

The following were adopted as part of the International Astronomical Union System of Astronomical Constants (1976): **Speed of light,** 299,792.458 km per sec., or about 186,282 statute mi per sec.; **solar parallax,** 8″.794148; **Astronomical Unit,** 149,597,870 km, or about 92,976,000 mi; **constant of nutation,** 9″.2025; and **constant of aberration,** 20″.49552.

Beginnings of the Universe

One of the dominating astronomical discoveries of the 20th century was the realization that the galaxies of the universe all seem to be moving away from us. It turned out that they are not just moving away from us, but are all moving away from one another—that is, the universe seems to be expanding. Hence, scientists conclude that the universe must once, very long ago, have been extremely compact and dense. Although there are alternatives to this theory and still many questions unresolved, much of the observational evidence currently available supports the idea that the universe we know began its existence between 8 and 20 billion years ago as an explosion of a super-dense, super-small concentration of matter.

This explosion of matter giving birth to the universe is called the **Big Bang.** On the subatomic level, according to this theory, there were vast changes of energy and matter and the way physical laws operated during the first 5 minutes. After those minutes the percentages of the basic matter of the universe—hydrogen, helium, and lithium—were set. Everything was so compact and so hot that radiation dominated the early universe and there were no stable, un-ionized atoms. At first, the universe was opaque, in the sense that any energy emitted was quickly absorbed and then re-emitted by free electrons. As the universe expanded, the density and the temperature continued to drop. A few hundred thousand years after the initial Big Bang, the temperature had dropped far enough that electrons and nuclei could combine to form stable atoms as the universe became transparent. Once that had occurred the radiation, which had been trapped, was free to escape.

In the 1940s, George Gamov and others predicted that astronomers should be able to see remnants of this escaped radiation. Astronomers continued to refine the theories and were preparing to build equipment to search for this background radiation when physicists Arno Penzias and Robert Wilson of the Bell Telephone Laboratories in NJ inadvertently beat them to the punch (the 2 were later awarded a Nobel Prize). Despite the Big Bang's success at predicting the existence of **cosmic background radiation,** there are still many unresolved questions, and astronomers are still working on modifications of the theory.

Constellations

Culturally, constellations are imagined patterns among the stars that, in some cases, have been recognized through millennia of tradition. In the early days of astronomy, knowledge of the constellations was necessary in order to function as an astronomer. For today's astronomers, constellations are simply areas on the entire sky in which interesting objects await observation and interpretation.

Because Western culture has prevailed in establishing modern science, equally viable and interesting constellations and celestial traditions of other cultures (of Asia or Africa, for example) are not well-known outside their regions of origin. Even the patterns with which we are most familiar today have undergone considerable change over the centuries, because the Western heritage embraces teachings of cultures disparate in time as well as place.

Today 88 constellations are recognized. Although many of these have their origins in ancient days, some are "modern," contrived out of unformed stars by astronomers a few centuries ago. Unformed stars were those usually too faint or inconveniently placed to be included in depicting the more prominent constellations.

When astronomers began to travel to S Africa in the 16th and 17th centuries, they found a sky that itself was unformed and showed numerous brilliant stars. Thus, we find constellations in the southern hemisphere that depict technological marvels of the time, as well as some arguably traditional forms, such as the "fly."

Many of the commonly recognized constellations had their origins in ancient Asia Minor—Syria, Babylonia, etc. These were adopted by the Greeks and Romans, who translated their names and stories into their own languages, modifying some details in the process. After the declines of these cultures, most such knowledge entered oral tradition or remained hidden in monastic libraries. Beginning in the 8th cent., the Muslim explosion spread through the Mediterranean world. Wherever possible, everything was translated into Arabic to be taught in the universities the Muslims established all over their new-found world.

In the 13th cent., Alphonsus XX of Spain, an avid student of astronomy, succeeded in having Ptolemy's *Almagest,* as its Arabian title was known, translated into Latin. It thus became widely available to European scholars. In the process, the constellation names were translated, but the star names were retained in their Arabic forms. Transliterating Arabic into the Roman alphabet has never been an exact art, so many of the star names we use today only seem Arabic to those who are not scholars.

Names of stars often indicated what parts of the traditional figures they represented: Deneb, the tail of the swan; Betelgeuse, the armpit of the giant. Thus, the names were an indication of the position in the sky of a particular star, provided one recognized the traditional form of the mythic figure.

Usage of Latin names for the constellations couples often inconceivable creatures, represented in unimaginable configurations, with names that often seem unintelligible. Avoiding traditional names, astronomers may designate the brighter stars in a constellation with Greek letters, usually in order of brightness. Thus, the "alpha star" is often the brightest star of that constellation. The "of" implies possession, so the genitive (possessive) form of the constellation name is used, as in Alpha Orionis, the first star of Orion (Betelgeuse). Astronomers usually use a 3-letter form for the constellation name, as indicated here.

Until the 1920s, astronomers used curved boundaries for the constellation areas. As these were rather arbitrary at best, the International Astronomical Union adopted new constellation boundaries that ran due north-S and east-W , filling the sky much as the contiguous states fill up the area of the "lower 48" United States.

Within these boundaries, and occasionally crossing them, popular "asterisms" are recognized: the so-called Big Dipper is a small part of the constellation Ursa Major, the big bear; the Sickle is the traditional head and mane of Leo, the lion; one of the horntips of Taurus, the bull, properly belongs to Auriga, the charioteer; the northE star of the Great Square of Pegasus is Alpha Andromedae.

It is unlikely that further change will occur in the realm of the celestial constellations.

Name	Genitive	Abbrev.	Meaning
Andromeda	Andromedae	And	Chained Maiden
Antlia	Antliae	Ant	Air Pump
Apus	Apodis	Aps	Bird of Paradise
Aquarius	Aquarii	Aqr	Water Bearer
Aquila	Aquilae	Aql	Eagle
Ara	Arae	Ara	Altar
Aries	Arietis	Ari	Ram
Auriga	Aurigae	Aur	Charioteer
Bootes	Bootis	Boo	Herdsmen
Caelum	Caeli	Cae	Chisel
Camelopardalis	Camelopardalis	Cam	Giraffe
Cancer	Cancri	Cnc	Crab
Canes Venatici	Canum Venaticorum	CVn	Hunting Dogs
Canis Major	Canis Majoris	CMa	Great Dog
Canis Minor	Canis Minoris	CMi	Little Dog
Capricornus	Capricorni	Cap	Sea-goat
Carina	Carinae	Car	Keel
Cassiopeia	Cassiopeiae	Cas	Queen
Centaurus	Centauri	Cen	Centaur
Cepheus	Cephei	Cep	King
Cetus	Ceti	Cet	Whale
Chamaeleon	Chamaeleontis	Cha	Chameleon
Circinus	Circini	Cir	Compasses (art)
Columba	Columbae	Col	Dove
Coma Berenices	Comae Berenices	Com	Berenice's Hair
Corona Australis	Coronae Australis	CrA	Southern Crown
Corona Borealis	Coronae Borealis	CrB	Northern Crown
Corvus	Corvi	Crv	Crow
Crater	Crateris	Crt	Cup
Crux	Crucis	Cru	Cross (southern)
Cygnus	Cygni	Cyg	Swan
Delphinus	Delphini	Del	Dolphin
Dorado	Doradus	Dor	Goldfish
Draco	Draconis	Dra	Dragon
Equuleus	Equulei	Equ	Little Horse
Eridanus	Eridani	Eri	River
Fornax	Fornacis	For	Furnace
Gemini	Geminorum	Gem	Twins
Grus	Gruis	Gru	Crane (bird)
Hercules	Herculis	Her	Hercules
Horologium	Horologii	Hor	Clock
Hydra	Hydrae	Hya	Water Snake (female)
Hydrus	Hydri	Hyi	Water Snake (male)
Indus	Indi	Ind	Indian
Lacerta	Lacertae	Lac	Lizard
Leo	Leonis	Leo	Lion
Leo Minor	Leonis Minoris	LMi	Little Lion
Lepus	Leporis	Lep	Hare
Libra	Librae	Lib	Balance
Lupus	Lupi	Lup	Wolf
Lynx	Lyncis	Lyn	Lynx
Lyra	Lyrae	Lyr	Lyre
Mensa	Mensae	Men	Table Mountain
Microscopium	Microscopii	Mic	Microscope
Monoceros	Monocerotis	Mon	Unicorn
Musca	Muscae	Mus	Fly
Norma	Normae	Nor	Square (rule)
Octans	Octantis	Oct	Octant
Ophiuchus	Ophiuchi	Oph	Serpent Bearer
Orion	Orionis	Ori	Hunter
Pavo	Pavonis	Pav	Peacock
Pegasus	Pegasi	Peg	Flying Horse
Perseus	Persei	Per	Hero
Phoenix	Phoenicis	Phe	Phoenix
Pictor	Pictoris	Pic	Painter
Pisces	Piscium	Psc	Fishes
Piscis Austrinius	Piscis Austrini	PsA	Southern Fish
Puppis	Puppis	Pup	Stern (deck)
Pyxis	Pyxidis	Pyx	Compass (sea)
Reticulum	Reticuli	Ret	Reticle
Sagitta	Sagittae	Sge	Arrow
Sagittarius	Sagittarii	Sgr	Archer
Scorpius	Scorpii	Sco	Scorpion
Sculptor	Sculptoris	Scl	Sculptor
Scutum	Scuti	Sct	Shield
Serpens	Serpentis	Ser	Serpent
Sextans	Sextantis	Sex	Sextant
Taurus	Tauri	Tau	Bull
Telescopium	Telescopii	Tel	Telescope
Triangulum	Trianguli	Tri	Triangle
Triangulum Australe	Trianguli Australis	TrA	Southern Triangle
Tucana	Tucanae	Tuc	Toucan
Ursa Major	Ursae Majoris	UMa	Great Bear
Ursa Minor	Ursae Minoris	UMi	Little Bear
Vela	Velorum	Vel	Sail
Virgo	Virginis	Vir	Maiden
Volans	Volantis	Vol	Flying Fish
Vulpecula	Vulpeculae	Vul	Fox

Rising and Setting of Planets, 1998

Greenwich Mean Time (0 designates midnight)

Venus, 1998

Date	20° N Latitude Rise h m	20° N Latitude Set h m	30° N Latitude Rise h m	30° N Latitude Set h m	40° N Latitude Rise h m	40° N Latitude Set h m	50° N Latitude Rise h m	50° N Latitude Set h m	60° N Latitude Rise h m	60° N Latitude Set h m
Jan. 1	8 01	19 12	8 16	18 56	8 35	18 38	9 00	18 12	9 42	17 31
11	7 00	18 15	7 14	18 02	7 31	17 45	7 53	17 22	8 30	16 45
21	5 54	17 12	6 07	16 59	6 23	16 43	6 44	16 21	7 18	15 47
31	4 57	16 16	5 10	16 03	5 26	15 47	5 48	15 26	6 22	14 51
Feb. 10	4 18	15 36	4 31	15 22	4 47	15 06	5 10	14 44	5 45	14 08
20	3 53	15 10	4 07	14 57	4 24	14 40	4 47	14 16	5 24	13 39
Mar. 2	3 40	14 56	3 53	14 43	4 10	14 26	4 34	14 02	5 11	13 25
12	3 32	14 51	3 45	14 37	4 02	14 21	4 24	13 59	5 00	13 23
22	3 28	14 51	3 40	14 39	3 55	14 24	4 15	14 03	4 48	13 31
Apr. 1	3 25	14 54	3 35	14 44	3 48	14 31	4 05	14 14	4 32	13 48
11	3 22	15 00	3 30	14 52	3 40	14 43	3 53	14 30	4 13	14 10
21	3 20	15 07	3 25	15 02	3 31	14 56	3 39	14 48	3 51	14 36
May 1	3 16	15 15	3 18	15 13	3 20	15 12	3 23	15 09	3 27	15 06
11	3 13	15 24	3 12	15 26	3 09	15 28	3 06	15 31	3 02	15 37
21	3 11	15 33	3 05	15 39	2 59	15 46	2 50	15 55	2 36	16 10
31	3 09	15 44	3 00	15 53	2 49	16 04	2 34	16 20	2 10	16 44
Jun. 10	3 09	15 55	2 56	16 08	2 41	16 24	2 20	16 45	1 46	17 20
20	3 11	16 08	2 55	16 24	2 36	16 44	2 09	17 11	1 24	17 57
30	3 15	16 22	2 57	16 40	2 34	17 04	2 02	17 36	1 07	18 32
Jul. 10	3 23	16 36	3 03	16 57	2 38	17 22	2 01	17 59	0 57	19 04
20	3 34	16 50	3 13	17 11	2 46	17 38	2 08	18 17	0 58	19 26
30	3 47	17 03	3 26	17 24	3 00	17 50	2 21	18 29	1 13	19 37
Aug. 9	4 02	17 13	3 42	17 33	3 17	17 58	2 42	18 33	1 40	19 34
19	4 18	17 21	4 00	17 38	3 38	18 00	3 08	18 30	2 16	19 22
29	4 33	17 26	4 19	17 40	4 01	17 58	3 36	18 22	2 56	19 02
Sep. 8	4 48	17 29	4 38	17 39	4 24	17 52	4 06	18 10	3 37	18 38
18	5 03	17 29	4 56	17 36	4 47	17 44	4 36	17 55	4 18	18 12
28	5 16	17 29	5 14	17 31	5 11	17 34	5 06	17 38	4 59	17 44
Oct. 8	5 30	17 28	5 32	17 26	5 34	17 24	5 36	17 20	5 40	17 16
18	5 44	17 27	5 50	17 21	5 57	17 14	6 07	17 03	6 22	16 48
28	5 59	17 28	6 09	17 18	6 21	17 05	6 38	16 48	7 05	16 21
Nov. 7	6 14	17 31	6 28	17 17	6 46	16 59	7 10	16 35	7 48	15 56
17	6 31	17 37	6 49	17 19	7 11	16 57	7 41	16 27	8 32	15 36
27	6 49	17 46	7 09	17 26	7 34	17 00	8 10	16 24	9 12	15 22
Dec. 7	7 06	17 58	7 28	17 36	7 56	17 09	8 35	16 30	9 44	15 20
17	7 22	18 13	7 45	17 51	8 12	17 23	8 52	16 44	10 04	15 32
27	7 36	18 30	7 57	18 09	8 24	17 43	9 01	17 05	10 07	16 00

Mars, 1998

Date	20° N Latitude Rise h m	20° N Latitude Set h m	30° N Latitude Rise h m	30° N Latitude Set h m	40° N Latitude Rise h m	40° N Latitude Set h m	50° N Latitude Rise h m	50° N Latitude Set h m	60° N Latitude Rise h m	60° N Latitude Set h m
Jan 1	8 38	19 46	8 54	19 30	9 14	19 10	9 42	18 42	10 29	17 56
11	8 26	19 42	8 40	19 28	8 58	19 11	9 21	18 47	10 00	18 09
21	8 13	19 38	8 25	19 26	8 39	19 12	8 59	18 53	9 29	18 22
31	8 00	19 33	8 09	19 24	8 20	19 13	8 35	18 58	8 58	18 35
Feb. 10	7 45	19 27	7 51	19 21	7 59	19 13	8 10	19 03	8 26	18 47
20	7 30	19 21	7 34	19 18	7 38	19 13	7 44	19 08	7 53	18 59
Mar. 2	7 14	19 15	7 15	19 14	7 17	19 13	7 18	19 12	7 20	19 10
12	6 59	19 08	6 57	19 10	6 55	19 13	6 52	19 16	6 47	19 21
22	6 43	19 02	6 38	19 06	6 33	19 12	6 26	19 19	6 14	19 32
Apr. 1	6 27	18 55	6 20	19 02	6 11	19 11	6 00	19 23	5 41	19 42
11	6 12	18 48	6 02	18 57	5 50	19 09	5 34	19 26	5 09	19 52
21	5 57	18 41	5 45	18 53	5 30	19 08	5 09	19 29	4 37	20 02
May 1	5 42	18 34	5 28	18 48	5 10	19 06	4 46	19 31	4 06	20 12
11	5 28	18 27	5 12	18 44	4 52	19 04	4 23	19 33	3 36	20 21
21	5 15	18 20	4 57	18 38	4 34	19 01	4 02	19 34	3 07	20 29
31	5 03	18 13	4 43	18 33	4 18	18 58	3 43	19 33	2 41	20 36
Jun. 10	4 51	18 05	4 30	18 27	4 03	18 53	3 25	19 31	2 17	20 40
20	4 40	17 57	4 18	18 19	3 50	18 47	3 10	19 27	1 57	20 41
30	4 30	17 49	4 07	18 11	3 39	18 40	2 57	19 21	1 41	20 38
Jul. 10	4 20	17 39	3 57	18 02	3 28	18 30	2 47	19 12	1 29	20 29
20	4 10	17 29	3 48	17 51	3 19	18 19	2 38	19 00	1 22	20 16
30	4 00	17 17	3 39	17 39	3 11	18 06	2 31	18 46	1 19	19 58
Aug. 9	3 51	17 04	3 30	17 25	3 03	17 51	2 25	18 29	1 18	19 36
19	3 41	16 50	3 21	17 10	2 56	17 35	2 21	18 10	1 19	19 11
29	3 30	16 35	3 12	16 54	2 49	17 16	2 17	17 49	1 21	18 44
Sep. 8	3 20	16 19	3 03	16 36	2 42	16 57	2 13	17 26	1 24	18 14
18	3 09	16 02	2 54	16 17	2 35	16 36	2 09	17 02	1 26	17 44
28	2 57	15 44	2 44	15 57	2 27	16 14	2 05	16 36	1 28	17 12
Oct. 8	2 44	15 26	2 33	15 37	2 19	15 51	2 00	16 10	1 29	16 40
18	2 31	15 06	2 22	15 15	2 11	15 27	1 55	15 42	1 30	16 07
28	2 18	14 46	2 11	14 53	2 02	15 02	1 49	15 14	1 30	15 34
Nov. 7	2 04	14 25	1 59	14 31	1 52	14 37	1 43	14 46	1 28	15 00
17	1 49	14 04	1 46	14 08	1 41	14 12	1 36	14 18	1 26	14 27
27	1 34	13 42	1 32	13 44	1 30	13 46	1 28	13 49	1 23	13 53
Dec. 7	1 18	13 20	1 18	13 20	1 19	13 20	1 19	13 19	1 19	13 19
17	1 02	12 58	1 04	12 56	1 06	12 53	1 09	12 50	1 14	12 45
27	0 44	12 35	0 48	12 31	0 52	12 27	0 58	12 21	1 07	12 12

Jupiter, 1998

Date		20° N Latitude Rise h m	Set h m	30° N Latitude Rise h m	Set h m	40° N Latitude Rise h m	Set h m	50° N Latitude Rise h m	Set h m	60° N Latitude Rise h m	Set h m
Jan	1	9 16	20 36	9 29	20 23	9 45	20 07	10 07	19 45	10 41	19 11
	11	8 44	20 06	8 56	19 53	9 11	19 39	9 32	19 18	10 04	18 46
	21	8 12	19 36	8 24	19 25	8 38	19 11	8 57	18 51	9 27	18 21
	31	7 41	19 07	7 52	18 56	8 05	18 43	8 23	18 25	8 51	17 57
Feb	10	7 09	18 38	7 19	18 28	7 31	18 16	7 48	17 59	8 14	17 33
	20	6 38	18 09	6 47	18 00	6 58	17 49	7 14	17 33	7 37	17 10
Mar	2	6 06	17 40	6 15	17 32	6 25	17 21	6 39	17 07	7 00	16 46
	12	5 35	17 11	5 42	17 03	5 52	16 54	6 04	16 41	6 24	16 22
	22	5 03	16 42	5 10	16 35	5 18	16 27	5 29	16 15	5 47	15 58
Apr	1	4 31	16 12	4 37	16 06	4 44	15 59	4 54	15 49	5 10	15 33
	11	3 58	15 43	4 04	15 37	4 11	15 30	4 19	15 22	4 33	15 08
	21	3 26	15 12	3 31	15 07	3 36	15 02	3 44	14 54	3 56	14 43
May	1	2 53	14 41	2 57	14 37	3 02	14 32	3 08	14 26	3 18	14 16
	11	2 19	14 10	2 23	14 06	2 27	14 02	2 33	13 57	2 41	13 48
	21	1 45	13 38	1 48	13 35	1 52	13 31	1 57	13 26	2 04	13 19
	31	1 11	13 05	1 13	13 02	1 16	12 59	1 20	12 55	1 26	12 49
Jun	10	0 35	12 31	0 37	12 28	0 40	12 26	0 43	12 23	0 48	12 18
	20	23 56	11 55	0 01	11 54	0 03	11 51	0 06	11 49	0 10	11 45
				23 57		23 59	(Jupiter rises twice on this date & latitudes)				
	30	23 19	11 19	23 20	11 17	23 22	11 16	23 24	11 13	23 28	11 10
Jul	10	22 41	10 41	22 42	10 40	22 44	10 38	22 46	10 36	22 49	10 33
	20	22 02	10 03	22 03	10 01	22 05	9 59	22 07	9 57	22 11	9 54
	30	21 22	9 22	21 23	9 21	21 25	9 19	21 28	9 16	21 31	9 13
Aug	9	20 41	8 41	20 43	8 39	20 45	8 37	20 48	8 34	20 52	8 29
	19	19 59	7 58	20 01	7 56	20 04	7 53	20 07	7 50	20 12	7 45
	29	19 16	7 14	19 19	7 11	19 22	7 08	19 26	7 04	19 32	6 58
Sep	8	18 33	6 29	18 36	6 26	18 40	6 23	18 45	6 18	18 52	6 11
	18	17 50	5 44	17 53	5 41	17 57	5 37	18 03	5 31	18 11	5 23
	28	17 06	4 59	17 10	4 56	17 15	4 51	17 21	4 45	17 31	4 35
Oct	8	16 23	4 15	16 28	4 11	16 33	4 06	16 40	3 59	16 50	3 48
	18	15 41	3 32	15 46	3 27	15 51	3 22	15 59	3 14	16 10	3 03
	28	15 00	2 49	15 04	2 45	15 10	2 39	15 18	2 31	15 30	2 19
Nov	7	14 19	2 08	14 24	2 03	14 30	1 58	14 38	1 50	14 50	1 38
	17	13 39	1 29	13 44	1 24	13 50	1 18	13 58	1 10	14 10	0 58
	27	13 01	0 51	13 06	0 46	13 11	0 40	13 19	0 33	13 31	0 21
Dec	7	12 23	0 14	12 28	0 10	12 33	0 04	12 41	23 53	12 52	23 42
	17	11 47	23 35	11 51	23 31	11 56	23 26	12 03	23 19	12 13	23 09
	27	11 11	23 01	11 15	22 57	11 20	22 53	11 25	22 47	11 34	22 38

Saturn, 1998

Date		20° N Latitude Rise h m	Set h m	30° N Latitude Rise h m	Set h m	40° N Latitude Rise h m	Set h m	50° N Latitude Rise h m	Set h m	60° N Latitude Rise h m	Set h m
Jan	1	12 04	0 20	12 01	0 23	11 57	0 26	11 52	0 31	11 45	0 39
	11	11 26	23 38	11 23	23 41	11 19	23 45	11 14	23 50	11 05	0 02
	11					(Saturn sets twice on this date & latitude)					23 59
	21	10 48	23 01	10 45	23 04	10 41	23 09	10 35	23 14	10 26	23 23
	31	10 11	22 25	10 07	22 28	10 03	22 33	9 57	22 39	9 47	22 48
Feb	10	9 34	21 49	9 30	21 53	9 25	21 58	9 19	22 04	9 09	22 15
	20	8 57	21 14	8 53	21 18	8 48	21 23	8 41	21 30	8 30	21 42
Mar	2	8 21	20 39	8 17	20 44	8 11	20 49	8 03	20 57	7 51	21 09
	12	7 46	20 05	7 41	20 10	7 35	20 16	7 26	20 24	7 13	20 37
	22	7 10	19 30	7 05	19 36	6 58	19 42	6 49	19 51	6 35	20 06
Apr	1	6 35	18 56	6 29	19 02	6 22	19 09	6 12	19 19	5 57	19 34
	11	5 59	18 22	5 53	18 29	5 45	18 36	5 35	18 47	5 19	19 03
	21	5 24	17 49	5 17	17 55	5 09	18 03	4 58	18 14	4 41	18 32
May	1	4 49	17 15	4 42	17 21	4 33	17 30	4 21	17 42	4 03	18 00
	11	4 13	16 40	4 06	16 48	3 57	16 57	3 45	17 09	3 25	17 29
	21	3 38	16 06	3 30	16 14	3 21	16 23	3 08	16 36	2 47	16 57
	31	3 02	15 32	2 54	15 40	2 44	15 49	2 31	16 03	2 09	16 24
Jun	10	2 26	14 57	2 18	15 05	2 08	15 15	1 54	15 29	1 32	15 51
	20	1 50	14 21	1 41	14 30	1 31	14 40	1 16	14 55	0 54	15 18
	30	1 13	13 45	1 05	13 54	0 54	14 05	0 39	14 20	0 16	14 43
Jul	10	0 36	13 09	0 27	13 18	0 16	13 29	0 01	13 44	23 34	14 08
	10			(Saturn rises twice on this date & latitude)				23 57			
	20	23 55	12 32	23 46	12 41	23 35	12 52	23 19	13 07	22 55	13 32
	30	23 17	11 54	23 08	12 03	22 57	12 15	22 41	12 30	22 17	12 54
Aug	9	22 38	11 16	22 29	11 25	22 18	11 36	22 02	11 52	21 38	12 16
	19	21 59	10 36	21 50	10 45	21 39	10 57	21 23	11 12	20 59	11 37
	29	21 20	9 56	21 11	10 05	20 59	10 17	20 44	10 32	20 20	10 56
Sep	8	20 39	9 16	20 30	9 25	20 19	9 36	20 04	9 51	19 40	10 15
	18	19 59	8 34	19 50	8 43	19 39	8 54	19 24	9 09	19 01	9 32
	28	19 17	7 52	19 09	8 01	18 58	8 12	18 44	8 26	18 21	8 49
Oct	8	18 36	7 10	18 27	7 18	18 17	7 29	18 03	7 43	17 41	8 05
	18	17 54	6 27	17 46	6 36	17 36	6 46	17 22	6 59	17 01	7 21
	28	17 12	5 45	17 04	5 53	16 54	6 02	16 41	6 15	16 20	6 36
Nov	7	16 30	5 02	16 23	5 10	16 13	5 19	16 00	5 32	15 40	5 52
	17	15 48	4 20	15 41	4 27	15 32	4 36	15 19	4 49	15 00	5 08
	27	15 07	3 38	15 00	3 45	14 51	3 54	14 39	4 06	14 19	4 25
Dec	7	14 26	2 56	14 19	3 03	14 10	3 12	13 58	3 24	13 39	3 43
	17	13 46	2 16	13 39	2 23	13 30	2 31	13 18	2 43	12 59	3 02
	27	13 06	1 36	12 59	1 43	12 50	1 52	12 38	2 03	12 19	2 22

Aurora Borealis and Aurora Australis

The Aurora Borealis, also called the Northern Lights, is a broad display of rather faint light in the northern skies at night. The Aurora Australis, a similar phenomenon, appears at the same time in southern skies. The aurora appears in a wide variety of forms. Sometimes it is seen as a quiet glow, almost foglike in character; sometimes as vertical streamers in which there may be considerable motion; sometimes as a series of luminous expanding arcs. There are many colors, with white, yellow, and red predominating.

The auroras are most vivid and most frequently seen at about 20 degrees from the magnetic poles, along the northern coast of the N American continent and the eastern part of the northern coast of Europe. The Aurora Borealis has been seen as far S as Key West, and the Aurora Australis has been seen as far N as Australia and New Zealand. Such occurrences are rare, however.

The Sun produces a stream of charged particles, called the solar wind. These particles, mainly electrons and protons, approach Earth at speeds on the order of 300 mi per second. Some of these particles are trapped by Earth's magnetic field, forming the Van Allen belts—two donut shaped radiation bands around Earth. Excess amounts of these charged particles, often produced by solar flares, follow Earth's magnetic lines of force toward Earth's magnetic poles. High in the atmosphere, collisions between solar and terrestrial atoms result in the glow in the upper atmosphere called the aurora. The glow may be vivid where the lines of magnetic force converge near the magnetic poles.

The auroral displays appear at heights ranging from 50 to about 600 mi and have given us a means of estimating the extent of Earth's atmosphere.

The auroras are often accompanied by magnetic storms whose forces, also guided by the lines of force of Earth's magnetic field, disrupt electrical communication.

Eclipses, 1998
(Greenwich Mean Time)

There are 5 eclipses in 1998, 1 total eclipse of the Sun, 1 annular eclipse of the Sun, and 3 penumbral eclipses of the Moon. Penumbral eclipses of the Moon are not very noticeable.

I. Total Eclipse of the Sun, Feb. 26

The path of totality begins at sunrise in the middle of the Pacific Ocean about 3,000 km southeast of Hawaii. Moving eastward, it passes over part of the Galapagos Islands and enters S America crossing southern Panama, northern Colombia, northwestern Venezuela, and a few islands in the Caribbean Sea. The path crosses the Atlantic and ends at sunset about 1,000 km W of Morocco and Africa.

Circumstances of the Eclipse

Event	Date	h	m
Partial eclipse begins	Feb. 26	14	50
Total eclipse begins	26	15	48
Central eclipse at midday	26	17	36
Total eclipse ends	26	19	9
Partial eclipse ends	26	20	6

II. Penumbral Eclipse of the Moon, Mar. 13

Penumbral eclipses of the Moon are not very noticeable, since direct sunlight still reaches all portions of the daytime side of the Moon. Unlike partial or total Lunar eclipses, there is no distinct shadow (the umbra) observable on the Moon. The beginning of the eclipse will be visible in most of N America, Central America, S America, Europe, Africa, Greenland, and western Asia. The end of the eclipse will be visible in N America, Central America, S America, Greenland, western France, the British Isles, extreme western Africa, Spain, Portugal, and extreme eastern Asia.

Circumstances of the Eclipse

Event	Date	h	m
Penumbral eclipse begins	Mar. 13	2	14
Middle of eclipse	13	4	20
Penumbral eclipse ends	13	6	26

III. Penumbral eclipse of the Moon, Aug. 8

See comment about penumbral eclipses of the Moon at II above. The beginning of the eclipse will be visible in eastern N America, Central America, S America, Africa, Europe, southern Greenland, and extreme western Asia. The end of the eclipse will be visible in most of N America (except the northwest), Central America, S America, Africa (except the extreme east), most of Europe, and southern Greenland.

Circumstances of the Eclipse

Event	Date	h	m
Penumbral eclipse begins	Aug. 8	1	32
Middle of eclipse	8	2	25
Penumbral eclipse ends	8	3	18

IV. Annular eclipse of the Sun, Aug. 21-22

The path of the annular eclipse is in the southern hemisphere, starting in the Indian Ocean, crossing Sumatra, then Malaysia, between Celebes and Mindanao, N of New Guinea, and ending in the southern Pacific Ocean.

Circumstances of the Eclipse

Event	Date	h	m
Partial eclipse begins	Aug. 21	23	10
Total eclipse begins	22	0	15
Central eclipse at midday	22	2	14
Total eclipse ends	22	3	56
Partial eclipse ends	22	5	2

V. Penumbral eclipse of the Moon, Sept. 6

See comment about penumbral eclipses of the Moon at II above. The beginning of the eclipse will be visible in N America and S America (except in the extreme east), Central America, extreme eastern Asia, Australia (except the extreme west), and New Zealand. The end of the eclipse will be visible in western N America, Australia, New Zealand, and the eastern half of Asia.

Circumstances of the Eclipse

Event	Date	h	m
Penumbral eclipse begins	Sept. 6	9	14
Middle of eclipse	6	11	10
Penumbral eclipse ends	6	13	6

The Planets: Motion, Distance, and Brightness

Planet	Mean daily motion ʺ	Orbital velocity mi per sec.	Sidereal revolution days	Synodic revolution days	Distance from Sun in millions of mi Max.	Min.	Distance from Earth in millions of mi Max.	Min.	Light at[1] peri-helion	ap-helion
Mercury	14,732	29.75	88.0	115.9	43.4	28.6	138	48	10.57	4.59
Venus	5,768	21.76	224.7	583.9	67.7	66.8	162	24	1.94	1.89
Earth	3,548	18.51	365.3	—	94.5	91.4	—	—	1.03	0.97
Mars	1,886	14.99	687.0	779.9	154.8	128.4	249	34	0.524	0.361
Jupiter	299	8.12	4,332.6	398.9	507.0	460.2	602	366	0.0408	0.0336
Saturn	120	5.99	10,759.2	378.1	936.0	837.4	1,030	743	0.0123	0.0099
Uranus.	42	4.23	30,685.4	369.7	1,867.2	1,698.8	1,962	1,604	0.0030	0.0025
Neptune	21	3.38	60,189.0	367.5	2,818.0	2,770.1	2,912	2,676	0.00113	0.00109
Pluto	14	2.95	90,465.0	366.7	4,586.5	2,762.5	4,681	2,668	0.00113	0.00041

(1) Light at perihelion and aphelion is solar illumination in units of mean illumination at Earth.

Planets and the Sun, by Selected Characteristics

Sun and planets	Semi-diameter at unit dis-tance ′ ʺ	at mean least dis-tance ′ ʺ	in mi mean s.d.	Volume[1]	Mass[1]	Den-sity[1]	Sidereal period of rotation d	h	m	s	Gravity at surface[1]	Re-flect-ing power Pct°	Daytime sur-face temp. °F
Sun	959.62	—	432,449	1,299,370	332,946	0.26	24	16	48		27.90	—	+10,000
Mercury	3.37	5.5	1,516	0.056	0.0553	0.98	58	15	36		0.38	0.11	725
Venus	8.34	30.1	3,761	0.8570	0.8151	0.94	243	R			0.91	0.65	870
Earth	—	—	3,959	1.000	1.000	1.00		23	56	4.2	1.00	0.37	68
Moon	2.40	932.4	1,080	0.0203	0.0123	0.61	27	7	44		0.17	0.12	212
Mars	4.69	8.95	2,106	0.1506	0.1075	0.71		24	37	22	0.38	0.15	−76
Jupiter	98.35	23.4	43,441	1,321	317.83	0.24		9	55	30	2.36	0.52	−160
Saturn	82.83	9.7	36,184	764	95.16	0.12		10	30	0	0.92	0.47	−218
Uranus.	35.4	1.9	15,759	63	14.54	0.24		17	14	R	0.89	0.51	−323
Neptune	33.4	1.2	15,301	58	17.15	0.30		16	7		1.12	0.41	−330
Pluto	1.9	0.05	707	0.006	0.0021	0.37	6	9	18	R	0.07	0.3	−369

(1) Earth = 1.   R = Retrograde rotation of Venus and Uranus.

The Sun

The Sun, the controlling body of Earth's solar system, is a star often described as average. Yet, the Sun's mass and luminosity are greater than that of 80% of the stars in Earth's galaxy. On the other hand, most of the stars that can be easily seen on any clear night are bigger and brighter than the Sun. It is the Sun's proximity to Earth that makes it appear tremendously large and bright. The Sun is 400,000 times as bright as the full moon and gives Earth 6 million times as much light as do all the other stars put together. A series of thermonuclear reactions involving the atoms of the elements of which it is composed produces the heat and light that make life possible on Earth.

The Sun has a diameter of 864,000 mi and, on average, is 92,980,000 mi from Earth. It is 1.41 times as dense as water. The light of the Sun reaches Earth in 499 seconds, or in slightly more than 8 minutes. The average solar surface temperature has been measured at a value of 5,800 K, or about 10,000° F. The interior temperature of the Sun is theorized to be about 27,000,000° F.

When Sunlight is analyzed with a spectroscope, it is found to consist of a continuous spectrum composed of all the colors of the rainbow in order, crossed by many dark lines. The "absorption lines" are produced by gaseous materials in the atmosphere of the Sun. More than 60 of the natural terrestrial elements have been identified in the Sun, all in gaseous form because of the Sun's intense heat.

Spheres and Corona

The radiating surface of the Sun is called the **photosphere**, and just above it is the **chromosphere**. The chromosphere is visible to the naked eye only at times of total solar eclipses, appearing then to be a pinkish-violet layer with occasional great prominences projecting above its general level. With proper instruments, the chromosphere can be seen or photographed whenever the Sun is visible without waiting for a total eclipse. Above the chromosphere is the **corona,** also visible to the naked eye only at times of total eclipse. Instruments also permit the brighter portions of the corona to be studied whenever conditions are favorable. The pearly light of the corona surges millions of mi from the Sun. Iron, nickel, and calcium are believed to be principal contributors to the composition of the corona, all in a state of extreme attenuation and high ionization that indicates temperatures on the order of a million degrees Fahrenheit.

Sunspots

There is an intimate connection between Sunspots and the corona. At times of low Sunspot activity, the fine streamers of the corona are longer above the Sun's equator than over the polar regions of the Sun; during periods of high Sunspot activity, the corona extends fairly evenly outward from all regions of the Sun, but to a much greater distance in space. Sunspots are dark, irregularly shaped regions whose diameters may reach lengths of tens of thousands of mi. The average life of a Sunspot group is from 2 to 3 weeks, but some Sunspot groups have lasted for more than a year by being carried repeatedly around as the Sun rotated upon its axis.

The record for the duration of a Sunspot is 18 months. Sunspots reach a low point, on average, every 11.3 years, with a peak of activity occurring irregularly between 2 successive minima. We are a little past the beginning of Sunspot cycle #23, and the number of sunspots should increase over the next few years.

The Zodiac

The Sun's apparent yearly path among the stars is known as the ecliptic. The zone, 18° wide, 9° on each side of the **ecliptic**, is known as the **zodiac**. Inside this zone are the apparent paths of the Sun, Moon, Earth, and the other planets. Only Pluto regularly strays outside this band on the celestial sphere. The zodiac is used both astrologically and astronomically. Though the two had a common beginning, they are no longer the same.

Beginning at the point on the ecliptic that marks the position of the Sun at the vernal equinox and proceeding eastward, the astrological zodiac is divided into 12 signs of 30° each, shown below. These signs are named from the 12 constellations of the zodiac with which the signs coincided in the time of the astronomer Hipparchus, about 2,000 years ago. Owing to the precession of the equinoxes, that is to say, to the retrograde motion of the equinoxes along the ecliptic, each sign in the zodiac has, in the course of 2,000 years, moved backward about 30° into the constellation W of it; the sign Aries is now in the constellation Pisces, for example, and so on. The vernal equinox will move from Pisces into Aquarius about the middle of the 26th century.

The astronomical constellations of the zodiac, unlike the astrological signs, are no longer equal in size. The ecliptic actually moves through parts of 13, not 12, astronomical constellations, the 13th being Ophiuchus. Also, the constellation of the scorpion is called Scorpius, while the sign is called Scorpio. Because of the width of the zodiac, it actually cuts through parts of 26 different constellations, not just 12.

The signs of the zodiac, with their Latin and English names, are as follows:

Spring	1.	♈	Aries	The Ram
	2.	♉	Taurus	The Bull
	3.	♊	Gemini	The Twins
Summer	4.	♋	Cancer	The Crab
	5.	♌	Leo	The Lion
	6.	♍	Virgo	The Virgin
Autumn	7.	♎	Libra	The Balance
	8.	♏	Scorpio	The Scorpion
	9.	♐	Sagittarius	The Archer
Winter	10.	♑	Capricorn	The Goat
	11.	♒	Aquarius	The Water Bearer
	12.	♓	Pisces	The Fishes

Although the ecliptic does not pass through the constellation of Cetus, it comes so close that on Mar. 28, 1998, the disk of the Sun will clip a corner of Cetus. The constellations of the zodiac with the approximate dates that the Sun is in each constellation in 1998, are as follows:

Jan. 1 - Jan. 19	....	Sagittarius
Jan. 20 - Feb. 16	....	Capricornus
Feb. 17 - Mar. 12	....	Aquarius
Mar. 13 - Apr. 19	....	Pisces
Apr. 20 - May 14	....	Aries
May 15 - June 21	....	Taurus
June 22 - July 21	....	Gemini
July 22 - Aug. 10	....	Cancer
Aug. 11 - Sept. 16	....	Leo
Sept. 17 - Oct. 31	....	Virgo
Nov. 1 - Nov. 23	....	Libra
Nov. 24 - Nov. 30	....	Scorpius
Dec. 1 - Dec. 18	....	Ophiuchus
Dec. 19 - Dec. 31	....	Sagittarius

The Moon

Distance from Earth	
Perigee	225,745 mi
Semi-major axis	238,856 mi
Aphelion	251,967 mi
Period of revolution	27.322 d
Synodic orbital period	29.53 d
(period of phases)	
Orbital eccentricity	0.0549
Orbital enclination	5° 8′ 42″
Sidereal day (rotation period)	27.322 d
Rotational inclination	6.68°
Mass (Earth = 1)	0.0123
Mean radius	1,080 mi
Mean density (Earth = 1)	0.6051
Average surface temperature	−10° F

The Moon completes a circuit around Earth in a period whose mean or average duration is 27 days, 7 hours, 43.2 minutes. This is the Moon's **sidereal period**. Because of the motion of the Moon in common with Earth around the Sun, the mean duration of the lunar month—the period from one New Moon to the next New Moon—is 29 days, 12 hours, 44.05 minutes. This is the Moon's **synodic period**.

The mean distance of the Moon from Earth is 238,856 mi. Because the orbit of the Moon about Earth is not circular but elliptical, however, the maximum distance from Earth that the Moon may reach is 251,967 mi and the least distance is 225,745 mi. (All distances are from the center of one body to the center of the other.)

The Moon's diameter is 2,160 mi. If we deduct the radius of the Moon, 1,080 mi, and the radius of Earth, 3,959 mi, from the minimum distance, or **perigee**, the figure for the nearest approach of the bodies' surfaces comes to 220,706 mi.

The Moon rotates on its axis in a period of time that is exactly equal to its sidereal revolution about Earth: 27.322 days. Thus the backside or farside of the Moon always faces away from Earth. This does not mean that the backside is always dark, since the Sun is the main source of light in the Solar System. The farside of the Moon gets just as much direct sunlight as the nearside. At New Moon phase, the farside of the Moon is fully lit. With its long day and night, the daytime temperature can reach 260° F, while the coldest nighttime temperature may reach −280° F. This day to night temperature change is exceeded only by that on Mercury.

The Moon's revolution about Earth is irregular because of its elliptical orbit. The Moon's rotation, however, is regular, and this, together with the irregular revolution, produces what is called "libration in longitude," which permits the observer on Earth to see first farther around the E side and then farther around the W side of the Moon. The Moon's variation N or S of the ecliptic permits one to see farther over first one pole and then the other of the Moon; this is called "libration in latitude." These two libration effects permit observers on Earth to see a total of about 60% of the Moon's surface over a period of time. The hidden side of the Moon was first photographed in 1959 by the Soviet space vehicle *Lunik III*. The farside does appear noticeably different from the nearside, in that the farside has practically none of the large lava plains, called maria, which are so prominent on the nearside of the Moon. Although the Apollo missions indicated that the Moon lacked any water, in late 1996, the U.S. Dept. of Defense announced that the Clementine spacecraft, which was launched in 1994, may have detected ice in a deep crater near the Moon's south pole.

Tides on Earth are caused mainly by the Moon, because of its proximity to Earth. The ratio of the tide-raising power of the Moon to that of the Sun is 11 to 5.

Harvest Moon and Hunter's Moon

The Harvest Moon, the full Moon nearest the autumnal equinox, ushers in a period of several successive days when the Moon rises soon after sunset. This phenomenon gives farmers in temperate latitudes extra hours of light in which to harvest their crops before frost and winter come. The 1998 Harvest Moon falls on Oct. 5 GMT. Harvest Moon in the southern hemisphere temperate latitudes falls on Mar. 13.

The next full Moon after Harvest Moon is called the Hunter's Moon, It is accompanied by a similar but less marked phenomenon. In 1998, the Hunter's Moon occurs on Nov. 4, northern hemisphere; Apr. 11, southern hemisphere.

Moon's Perigee and Apogee, 1998

(Greenwich Mean Time)

Perigee						Apogee					
Date	Hour		Date	Hour		Date	Hour		Date	Hour	
Jan. 3	9		July 16	14		Jan. 18	21		July 30	12	
Jan. 30	14		Aug. 11	12		Feb. 15	15		Aug. 27	6	
Feb. 27	20		Sept. 8	6		Mar. 15	1		Sept. 23	22	
Mar. 28	7		Oct. 6	13		Apr. 11	2		Oct. 21	5	
Apr. 25	18		Nov. 4	1		May 8	9		Nov. 17	6	
May 24	0		Dec. 2	12		June 5	0		Dec. 14	17	
June 20	17		Dec. 30	18		July 2	17				

Moon Phases, 1998

(Greenwich Mean Time)

New Moon				Waxing Quarter				Full Moon				Waning Quarter			
Month	d	h	m	Month	d	h	m	Month	d	h	m	Month	d	h	m
Jan.	28	6	1	Jan.	5	14	18	Jan.	12	17	24	Jan.	20	19	40
Feb.	26	17	26	Feb.	3	22	53	Feb.	11	10	23	Feb.	19	15	27
Mar.	28	3	14	Mar.	5	8	41	Mar.	13	4	34	Mar.	21	7	38
Apr.	26	11	41	Apr.	3	20	18	Apr.	11	22	23	Apr.	19	19	53
May	25	19	32	May	3	10	4	May	11	14	29	May	19	4	35
June	24	3	50	June	2	1	45	June	10	4	18	June	17	10	38
July	23	13	44	July	1	18	43	July	9	16	1	July	16	15	13
Aug.	22	2	3	July	31	12	5	Aug.	8	2	10	Aug.	14	19	48
Sept.	20	17	1	Aug.	30	5	6	Sept.	6	11	21	Sept.	13	1	58
Oct.	20	10	9	Sept.	28	21	11	Oct.	5	20	12	Oct.	12	11	11
Nov.	19	4	27	Oct.	28	11	46	Nov.	4	5	18	Nov.	11	0	28
Dec.	18	22	42	Nov.	27	0	23	Dec.	3	15	19	Dec.	10	17	53
				Dec.	26	10	46								

Earth: Size, Computation of Time, Seasons

Distance from the Sun	
Perihelion	91.4 mil mi
Semi-major axis	1.00002 AU
Aphelion	94.5 mil mi
Period of revolution	365.3d
Orbital eccentricity	0.01670
Orbital inclination	0° 0′ 0″
Sidereal day (Rotation period)	23h 56m 4.2s
Synodic day (midday to midday)	24h 0m 0s
Rotational inclination	23.45°
Mass (Earth = 1)	1.000
Mean radius	3,959 mi
Mean density (Earth = 1)	1.00
Natural satellites	1
Average surface temperature	45° F

Size and Dimensions

Earth is the 5th-largest planet and the 3d from the Sun. Its mass is 6 sextillion, 588 quintillion short tons. Using the parameters of an ellipsoid adopted by the International Astronomical Union in 1964 and recognized by the International Union of Geodesy and Geophysics in 1967, the length of the equator is 24,901.55 mi, the length of a meridian is 24,859.82 mi, the equatorial diameter is 7,926.41 mi, and the area of this reference ellipsoid is approximately 196,938,800 sq. mi.

Earth is considered a solid, rigid mass with a dense core of magnetic, probably metallic material with a radius of about 2,200 mi. The outer 2/3 part of the core is probably liquid. Around the core is a thick shell or mantle of dense rock. A section of the mantle, the aesthenosphere, is somewhat plasticlike and under slow steady pressure can flow like a liquid. The mantle, in turn, is covered by a thin crust forming the solid granite and basalt base of the continents and ocean basins. Over broad areas of Earth's surface, the crust has a thin cover of sedimentary rock such as sandstone, shale, and limestone formed by weathering of Earth's surface and deposition of sands, clays, and plant and animal remains.

The temperature in Earth increases about 1° F with every 100 to 200 feet in depth, in the upper 100 km of Earth, and the temperature near the core is believed to be near the melting point of the core materials under the conditions at that depth. The heat of Earth is believed to be derived from radioactivity in the rocks, pressures developed within Earth, and the original heat of formation.

Atmosphere of Earth

Earth's atmosphere is a blanket composed of nitrogen, oxygen, and argon, in amounts of about 77%, 21%, and 1% by volume. Also present in minute quantities are carbon dioxide, hydrogen, neon, helium, krypton, and xenon. Water vapor displaces other gases and varies from nearly zero to about 4% by volume. The atmosphere rests on Earth's surface with the weight equivalent to a layer of water 34 ft deep. For about 300,000 ft upward, the gases remain in the proportions stated. Gravity holds the gases to Earth. The weight of the air compresses it at the bottom so that the greatest density is at Earth's surface. Pressure, as well as density, decreases as height increases because the weight pressing upon any layer is always less than that pressing upon the layers below.

The temperature of the air drops with increased height until the **tropopause** is reached. Altitude of the tropopause may vary from 25,000 to 60,000 ft. The atmosphere below the tropopause is the **troposphere,** which contains 90% of the air and the tallest mountains. This is also where most weather phenomena occur. The atmosphere for about 20 mi above the tropopause is the **stratosphere,** where the temperature generally increases with height except at high latitudes in winter. The stratophere also contains ozone, which prevents ultraviolet rays from reaching Earth's surface. The height of the **ozone** layer varies from approximately 12 to 21 mi above Earth. Traces exist as low as 6 mi and as high as 35 mi. A temperature maximum near the 30-mi level is called the **stratopause.**

Above this boundary is the **mesosphere,** where the temperature decreases with height to a minimum, the **meso-**

pause, at a height of 50 mi. Extending above the mesosphere to the outer fringes of the atmosphere is the **thermosphere,** a region where temperature increases with height to a value measured in thousands of degrees Fahrenheit. The lower portion of this region, extending from 50 to about 400 mi in altitude, is characterized by a high ion density and is thus called the **ionosphere.** The outer region is called the **exosphere;** this is the region where gas molecules traveling at high speed may escape into outer space, above 600 mi.

Latitude, Longitude

Position on the globe is measured by means of meridians and parallels. Meridians, which are imaginary lines drawn around Earth through the poles, determine **longitude.** The meridian running through Greenwich, England, is the **prime meridian of longitude,** and all others are either E or west. Parallels, which are imaginary circles parallel with the equator, determine **latitude.** The length of a degree of longitude varies as the cosine of the latitude. At the equator a degree is 69.171 statute mi; this is gradually reduced toward the poles. Value of a longitude degree at the poles is zero.

Latitude is reckoned by the number of degrees N or S of the equator, an imaginary circle on Earth's surface everywhere equidistant between the two poles. According to the International Astronomical Union ellipsoid of 1964, the length of a degree of latitude is 68.708 statute mi at the equator and varies slightly N and S because of the oblate form of the globe; at the poles it is 69.403 statute mi.

Definitions of Time

Earth rotates on its axis and follows an elliptical orbit around the Sun. The rotation makes the Sun appear to move across the sky from E to west. This rotation determines day and night, and the complete rotation, in relation to the Sun, is called the **apparent** or **true solar day.** A sundial thus measures **apparent solar time.** This length of time varies, but an average determines the **mean solar day** of 24 hours.

The mean solar day and **mean solar time** are in universal use for civil purposes. Mean solar time may be obtained from apparent solar time by correcting observations of the Sun for the **equation of time.** Mean solar time may be as much as 16 minutes behind or 14 minutes ahead of apparent solar time.

Sidereal time is the measure of time defined by the diurnal motion of the vernal equinox and is determined from observation of the meridian transits of stars. One complete rotation of Earth relative to the equinox is called the **sidereal day.** The **mean sidereal day** is 23 hours, 56 minutes, 4.091 seconds of mean solar time.

The interval required for Earth to make one absolute revolution around the Sun is a **sidereal year;** it consisted of 365 days, 6 hours, 9 minutes, and 9.5 seconds of mean solar time (approximately 24 hours per day) in 1900 and has been increasing at the rate of 0.0001 second annually.

The **tropical year,** upon which our calendar is based, is the interval between 2 consecutive returns of the Sun to the vernal equinox. The tropical year consisted of 365 days, 5 hours, 48 minutes, and 46 seconds in 1900. It has been decreasing at the rate of 0.530 second per century. The **calendar year** begins at 12 o'clock midnight precisely, local clock time, on the night of Dec. 31-Jan. 1. The day and the calendar month also begin at midnight by the clock.

On Jan. 1, 1972, the Bureau International des Poids et Mesures in Paris introduced International Atomic Time (TAI) as the most precisely determined time scale for astronomical usage. The fundamental unit of TAI in the international system of units is the second, defined as the duration of 9,192,631,770 periods of the radiation corresponding to the transition between 2 hyperfine levels of the ground state of the cesium 133 atom. Universal time (UT), which serves as the basis for civil timekeeping, is officially defined by a formula which relates UT to mean sidereal time in Greenwich, England.

The Zones and Seasons

The 5 zones of Earth's surface are the Torrid, lying between the Tropics of Cancer and Capricorn; the N Temperate, between Cancer and the Arctic Circle; the S Temperate, between Capricorn and the Antarctic Circle; and the 2 Frigid Zones, between the Polar Circles and the Poles.

The inclination or tilt of Earth's axis with respect to the Sun determines the seasons. These are commonly marked in the N Temperate Zone, where spring begins at the vernal equinox, summer at the summer solstice, autumn at the autumnal equinox, and winter at the winter solstice.

In the S Temperate Zone, the seasons are reversed. Spring begins at the autumnal equinox, summer at the winter solstice, etc.

If Earth's axis were perpendicular to the plane of Earth's orbit around the Sun, there would be no change of seasons. Day and night would be of nearly constant length, and there would be equable conditions of temperature. But the axis is tilted 23° 27′ away from a perpendicular to the orbit, and only in Mar. and Sept. is the axis at right angles to the Sun.

The points at which the Sun crosses the equator are the equinoxes, when day and night are most nearly equal. The points at which the Sun is at a maximum distance from the equator are the solstices. Days and nights are then most unequal. However, at the equator, day and night are equal throughout the year.

In June, the North Pole is tilted 23° 27′ toward the Sun, and the days in the northern hemisphere are longer than the nights, while the days in the southern hemisphere are shorter than the nights. In December, the North Pole is tilted 23° 27′ away from the Sun, and the situation is reversed.

The Seasons in 1998

In 1998 the 4 seasons will begin as shown below. (Add one hour to Eastern Standard Time for Atlantic Time; subtract one hour for Central, 2 hours for Mountain, 3 hours for Pacific, 4 hours for Alaska, 5 hours for Hawaii-Aleutian. Also shown is Greenwich Mean Time.)

Seasons	Date	GMT	EST
Vernal Equinox	Mar. 20	19:55	14:55
Summer Solstice	June 21	14:03	9:03
Autumnal Equinox	Sept. 23	5:37	0:37
Winter Solstice	Dec. 22	1:56	20:56*

*previous day

Poles of Earth

The geographic (rotation) poles, or points where Earth's axis of rotation cuts the surface, are not absolutely fixed in the body of Earth. The pole of rotation describes an irregular curve about its mean position.

Two periods have been detected in this motion: (1) an annual period due to seasonal changes in barometric pressure, to load of ice and snow on the surface, and to other phenomena of seasonal character; (2) a period of about 14 months due to the shape and constitution of Earth.

In addition, there are small but as yet unpredictable irregularities. The whole motion is so small that the actual pole at any time remains within a circle of 30 or 40 feet in radius centered at the mean position of the pole.

The pole of rotation for the time being is of course the pole having a latitude of 90° and an indeterminate longitude.

Magnetic Poles

The **north magnetic pole** of Earth is that region where the magnetic force is vertically downward, and the **south**

magnetic pole is that region where the magnetic force is vertically upward. A compass placed at the magnetic poles experiences no directive force in azimuth.

There are slow changes in the distribution of Earth's magnetic field. These changes were at one time attributed in part to a periodic movement of the magnetic poles around the geographical poles, but later evidence refutes this theory and points, rather, to a slow migration of "disturbance" foci over Earth.

There appear shifts in position of the magnetic poles due to the changes in Earth's magnetic field. The center of the area designated as the north magnetic pole was estimated to be in about latitude 70.5° N and longitude 96° W in 1905; from recent nearby measurements and studies of the secular changes, the position in 1970 was estimated as latitude 76.2° N and longitude 101° W. Improved data rather than actual motion account for at least part of the change.

The position of the south magnetic pole in 1912 was near 71° S and longitude 150° E. In 1970 it was estimated at latitude 66° S and longitude 139.1° E.

The direction of the horizontal components of the magnetic field at any point is known as magnetic N at that point, and the angle by which it deviates E or W of true N is known as the magnetic declination or, in the mariner's terminology, the **variation of the compass.**

A compass without error points in the direction of magnetic north. (In general, this is not the direction of the magnetic north pole.) If one follows the direction indicated by the N end of the compass, he or she will travel along a rather irregular curve that eventually reaches the north magnetic pole (though not usually by a great-circle route). However, the action of the compass should not be thought of as due to any influence of the distant pole, but simply as an indication of the distribution of Earth's magnetism at the place of observation.

Rotation of Earth

The **speed of rotation** of Earth about its axis has been found to be slightly variable. The variations may be classified as:

(A) **Secular.** Tidal friction acts as a brake on the rotation and causes a slow secular increase in the length of the day, about 1 millisecond per century.

(B) **Irregular.** The speed of rotation may increase for a number of years, about 5 to 10, and then start decreasing. The maximum difference from the mean in the length of the day during a century is about 5 milliseconds. The accumulated difference in time has amounted to approximately 44 seconds since 1900. The cause is probably motion in the interior of Earth.

(C) **Periodic.** Seasonal variations exist with periods of 1 year and 6 months. The cumulative effect is such that each year, Earth is late about 30 milliseconds near June 1 and is ahead about 30 milliseconds near Oct. 1. The maximum seasonal variation in the length of the day is about 0.5 millisecond. It is believed that the principal cause of the annual variation is the seasonal change in the wind patterns of the northern and southern hemispheres. The semiannual variation is due chiefly to tidal action of the Sun, which distorts the shape of Earth slightly.

The secular and irregular variations were discovered by comparing time based on the rotation of Earth with time based on the orbital motion of the Moon about Earth and of the planets about the Sun. The periodic variation was determined largely with the aid of quartz-crystal clocks. The introduction of the cesium-beam atomic clock in 1955 made it possible to determine in greater detail than before the nature of the irregular and periodic variations.

Chronological Eras, 1998

The year 1998 of the Christian Era comprises the latter part of the 222d and the beginning of the 223d year of the independence of the U.S.

Era	Year	Begins in 1998	Era	Year	Begins in 1997
Byzantine	7507	Sept. 14	Grecian (Seleucidae)	2310	Sept. 14 or Oct. 14
Jewish	5759	Sept. 20[1]			
Roman (Ab Urbe Condita)	2751	Jan. 14	Diocletian	1715	Sept. 11
Nabonassar (Babylonian)	2747	Apr. 24	Indian (Saka)	1920	Mar. 22
Japanese	2658	Jan. 1	Islamic/Muslim (Hijra)	1419	Apr. 27[1]

(1) Year begins at sunset.

Chronological Cycles, 1998

Dominical Letter	D	Golden Number (Lunar Cycle)	IV	Roman Indiction	6
Epact	2	Solar Cycle	19	Julian Period (year of)	6711

Twilight

Twilight is that evening period of waning light from the time of sunset to dark, often termed dusk. Morning twilight, a time of increasing light, is called **dawn.** The source of this light is the Sun shining on the atmosphere above the observer. Twilight is a time of very slowly changing sky illumination with no abrupt variations. Nevertheless, there are 3 commonly accepted divisions in this smooth continuum defined by the distance the Sun lies below the astronomical horizon: civil twilight, nautical twilight, and astronomical twilight. The **astronomical horizon** is that great circle lying 90° from the zenith, the point directly over the observer's head. Twilight ends in the evening or begins in the morning at a particular time. Nominally, evening events are repeated in reverse order in the morning. **Civil twilight** is the time from the moment of sunset, when the Sun's apparent upper edge is just at the horizon, until the center of the Sun is 6° directly below the horizon. In many states, this is the time in the evening when automobile headlights must be turned on, not to see better, but to be seen by other drivers. After this time, a newspaper becomes increasingly difficult to read in the absence of artificial light. **Nautical twilight** ends when the Sun's center is 12° below the horizon. By this time in the evening, the bright stars used by navigators have appeared, and the horizon may still be seen. After this time, the horizon is more difficult to perceive, preventing navigators from sighting stars. **Astronomical twilight** ends in the evening when the Sun is 18° below the horizon and the sky is dark enough, at least away from the Sun's location, to allow astronomical work to proceed. Sunlight, however, is still shining on the higher levels of the atmosphere from the observer's zenith to the horizon toward the Sun. Although not named as a period of twilight, when the Sun is 24° below the horizon, no part of the observer's atmosphere, even toward the Sun, receives any sunlight. In the tropics, the Sun moves nearly vertically, accomplishing its 6°, 12°, or 18° depression very quickly. In the polar regions, the Sun's diurnal motion may actually be nearly along the horizon, prolonging the twilight period

or even not permitting darkness to fall at all. In mid-latitudes, civil twilight may last about a half hour; nautical, an hour; and astronomers can go to work in about 90 minutes. The twilight tables given in *The World Almanac* are for the beginning of morning twilight and the end of evening astronomical twilight, and are presented for reference only. Although the instant of the Sun's horizontal depression may be calculated precisely, the phenomena associated with the event are sufficiently imprecise that the table is not recalculated each year.

Astronomical Twilight—Meridian of Greenwich

Date		20° Morn. h m	20° Even. h m	30° Morn. h m	30° Even. h m	40° Morn. h m	40° Even. h m	50° Morn. h m	50° Even. h m	60° Morn. h m	60° Even. h m
Jan.	1	5 17	6 51	5 31	6 37	5 45	6 23	6 00	6 08	6 18	5 49
	11	5 20	6 56	5 33	6 44	5 45	6 31	5 58	6 18	6 14	6 03
	21	5 21	7 02	5 32	6 51	5 42	6 41	5 53	6 30	6 04	6 19
Feb.	1	5 20	7 08	5 28	6 59	5 36	6 52	5 42	6 46	5 47	6 41
	11	5 17	7 12	5 23	7 06	5 27	7 03	5 29	7 01	5 27	7 03
	21	5 12	7 16	5 14	7 13	5 15	7 13	5 12	7 17	5 02	7 26
Mar.	1	5 07	7 18	5 07	7 19	5 04	7 22	4 56	7 30	4 40	7 47
	11	4 59	7 22	4 55	7 25	4 48	7 33	4 35	7 47	4 08	8 14
	21	4 50	7 25	4 43	7 32	4 31	7 44	4 11	8 05	3 33	8 44
Apr.	1	4 40	7 28	4 29	7 40	4 11	7 57	3 43	8 26	2 47	9 24
	11	4 30	7 32	4 15	7 47	3 53	8 10	3 16	8 48	1 56	10 11
	21	4 21	7 36	4 02	7 56	3 35	8 24	2 48	9 12		
May	1	4 13	7 42	3 50	8 04	3 17	8 38	2 17	9 39		
	11	4 06	7 47	3 40	8 14	3 00	8 53	1 45	10 10		
	21	4 01	7 53	3 31	8 22	2 46	9 08	1 10	10 47		
June	1	3 57	7 59	3 25	8 31	2 35	9 22				
	11	3 56	8 03	3 22	8 37	2 29	9 31				
	21	3 57	8 06	3 23	8 41	2 28	9 36				
July	1	4 00	8 07	3 26	8 41	2 32	9 35				
	11	4 05	8 06	3 32	8 38	2 42	9 28				
	21	4 10	8 03	3 40	8 32	2 54	9 18	1 12	10 57		
Aug.	1	4 16	7 56	3 49	8 23	3 09	9 02	1 53	10 17		
	11	4 21	7 49	3 58	8 12	3 24	8 45	2 23	9 45		
	21	4 25	7 41	4 06	7 59	3 38	8 27	2 50	9 15		
Sept.	1	4 29	7 30	4 14	7 45	3 52	8 07	3 15	8 43	1 55	10 01
	11	4 33	7 20	4 21	7 31	4 04	7 48	3 36	8 16	2 39	9 11
	21	4 35	7 10	4 28	7 18	4 15	7 30	3 54	7 50	3 14	8 30
Oct.	1	4 38	7 01	4 34	7 05	4 26	7 12	4 12	7 26	3 44	7 54
	11	4 40	6 53	4 40	6 53	4 36	6 56	4 28	7 04	4 10	7 22
	21	4 43	6 46	4 46	6 43	4 46	6 42	4 43	6 45	4 34	6 53
Nov.	1	4 47	6 40	4 53	6 34	4 57	6 29	5 00	6 26	4 59	6 27
	11	4 51	6 37	5 00	6 28	5 07	6 20	5 14	6 13	5 20	6 07
	21	4 55	6 36	5 07	6 25	5 17	6 14	5 28	6 04	5 39	5 52
Dec.	1	5 01	6 37	5 14	6 24	5 26	6 12	5 40	5 58	5 55	5 42
	11	5 06	6 40	5 20	6 26	5 34	6 12	5 49	5 57	6 08	5 38
	21	5 12	6 45	5 26	6 30	5 41	6 16	5 56	6 00	6 16	5 41
	31	5 16	6 50	5 30	6 36	5 44	6 22	6 00	6 07	6 18	5 48

MILLENNIUM FACT BOX

Eclipses in the 21st Century

During the 21st century Halley's Comet will return (2061-62), and there will be 8 total solar eclipses visible in the continental U.S. The first comes after a long gap; the last one to be seen was on Feb. 26, 1979, in the northwestern U.S.

Date	Path of Totality
Aug. 21, 2017	Oregon to South Carolina
Apr. 8, 2024	Mexico to Texas and up through Maine
Aug. 23, 2044	Montana to North Dakota
Aug. 12, 2045	N California to Florida
Mar. 30, 2052	Florida to Georgia
May 11, 2078	Louisiana to North Carolina
May 1, 2079	New Jersey to the lower edge of New England
Sept. 14, 2099	North Dakota to Virginia

Total Solar Eclipses, 1950-2010

Total solar eclipses actually take place nearly as often as total lunar eclipses; they occur at a rate of about 3 every 4 years, while total lunar eclipses come at a rate of about 5 every 6 years. However, total lunar eclipses are visible over at least half Earth, while total solar eclipses can be seen only along a very narrow path up to a few hundred mi wide and a few thousand mi long. Total solar eclipses are thus a rarity for most people. Unlike lunar eclipses, solar eclipses can be dangerous to observe. This is not because the Sun emits more potent rays during an eclipse, but because the Sun is always dangerous to observe directly and people are particularly likely to stare at it during a solar eclipse.

Date	Duration[1]		Width	Path of Totality
	m	s	(mi)	
1950, Sept. 12	1	13	83	Arctic Ocean, Siberia, Pacific Ocean
1952, Feb. 25	3	09	85	Africa, Middle East, Soviet Union
1954, June 30	2	35	95	U.S., Canada, Iceland, Europe, Middle East
1955, June 20	7	07	157	SE Asia, Philippines, Pacific Ocean
1956, June 8	4	44	266	S Pacific Ocean
1958, Oct. 12	5	10	129	Pacific Ocean, Chile, Argentina
1959, Oct. 2	3	01	75	New England, Atlantic Ocean, Africa
1961, Feb. 15	2	45	160	Europe, Soviet Union
1962, Feb. 5	4	08	91	Borneo, New Guinea, Pacific Ocean
1963, July 20	1	39	63	Pacific Ocean, Alaska, Canada, Maine
1965, May 30	5	15	123	New Zealand, Pacific Ocean
1966, Nov. 12	1	57	52	Pacific Ocean, S America, Atlantic Ocean
1968, Sept. 22	0	39	64	Soviet Union, China
1970, Mar. 7	3	27	95	Pacific Ocean, Mexico, Eastern U.S., Canada
1972, July 10	2	35	109	Siberia, Alaska, Canada
1973, June 30	7	03	159	Atlantic Ocean, Central Africa, Indian Ocean
1974, June 20	5	08	214	Indian Ocean, Australia
1976, Oct. 23	4	46	123	Africa, Indian Ocean, Australia
1977, Oct. 12	2	37	61	Pacific Ocean, Colombia, Venezuela
1979, Feb. 26	2	49	185	NW U.S., Canada, Greenland
1980, Feb. 16	4	08	92	Africa, Indian Ocean, India, Burma, China
1981, July 31	2	02	67	Soviet Union, Pacific Ocean
1983, June 11	5	10	123	Indian Ocean, Indonesia, New Guinea
1984, Nov. 22	1	59	53	New Guinea, Pacific Ocean
1985, Nov. 12	1	58	430	Antarctica
1986, Oct. 3h	0	01	1	N Atlantic Ocean
1987, Mar. 29h	0	07	3	S Atlantic Ocean, Africa
1988, Mar. 18	3	46	104	Sumatra, Borneo, Philippines, Pacific Ocean
1990, July 22	2	32	125	Finland, Soviet Union, Aleutian Islands
1991, July 11	6	53	160	Hawaii, Mexico, Central America, Colombia, Brazil
1992, June 30	5	20	182	S Atlantic Ocean
1994, Nov. 3	4	23	117	Peru, Bolivia, Paraguay, Brazil
1995, Oct. 24	2	09	48	Iran, India, SE Asia
1997, Mar. 9	2	50	221	Mongolia, Siberia
1998, Feb. 26	4	08	94	Galapagos Islands, Panama, Colombia, Venezuela
1999, Aug. 11	2	22	69	Europe, Middle East, India
2001, June 21	4	56	125	Atlantic Ocean, Africa, Madagascar
2002, Dec. 4	2	04	54	S Africa, Indian Ocean, Australia
2003, Nov. 23	1	57	338	Antarctica
2005, Apr. 8h	0	42	17	Pacific Ocean, NW S America
2006, Mar. 29	4	07	114	Atlantic Ocean, Africa, Asia
2008, Aug. 1	2	27	144	Arctic Ocean, Asia
2009, July 22	6	39	160	Asia, Pacific Ocean
2010, July 11	5	20	160	Atlantic Ocean

h = indicates annular-total hybrid eclipse. (1) Duration refers to length of time at optimal viewing area.

Calculation of Rise Times

The Daily Calendar pages contain rise and set times for the Sun and Moon for the Greenwich Meridian at N latitudes 20°, 30°, 40°, 50°, and 60°. You probably live somewhere W of the Greenwich meridian, 0° longitude, and within the range of latitudes in the table. Notice that from day to day, the values for the Sun at any particular latitude do not change very much. This slow variation for the Sun means that no important correction needs to be made from one day to the next, once a proper correction for your latitude has been made. Thus, whenever the Sun rises or sets at the 0° meridian, that will also be the time of that phenomenon at your Standard Time meridian. Any correction necessary for you to be able to observe that phenomenon from your location will be to account for your distance from the Standard Time meridian and for your latitude.

The Moon, however, moves its own diameter, about one-half degree, in an hour, or about 13.2° in one complete turn of Earth—one day. Most of this is eastward against the background stars of the sky, but some is also N or S of the equator. If there is little change on the same day of the times over the range of latitudes, the Moon is near the celestial equator. All this motion considerably affects the times of rise or set, as you can see from the adjacent entries in the table. Thus, it is necessary to take your longitude into account in addition to your latitude. If you have no need for total accuracy, simply note that the time will be between the 4 values you find surrounding your location and the dates of interest.

The process of finding more accurate corrections is called interpolation. In the example, linear interpolation involving simple differences is used. In extreme cases, higher order interpolation should be used. If such cases are important to you, it is suggested that you plot the times, draw smooth curves through the plots, and interpolate by eye between the relevant curves. Some people find this exercise fun.

Let's find the times of the moonrise for the August Waxing Quarter Moon and sunset the same day at Iowa City, IA.

First, where is Iowa City, IA? Find Iowa City's latitude and longitude in the "Latitude, Longitude, and Altitude of U.S. and Canadian Cities" table found in the World Exploration and Geography section of *The World Almanac*. You must also know the time zone in which the city is located, which you can estimate from the "International Time Zones" map in the map section of *The World Almanac*.

I. Iowa City, IA: 41° 39′ 37″ N
91° 31′ 53″ W

IA. Convert these values to decimals:
37/60 = 0.62
39 + 0.62 = 39.62
39.62/60 = 0.66
41 + 0.66 = 41.66 N
53/60 = 0.88
31 + 0.88 = 31.88
31.88/60 = 0.53
91 + 0.53 = 91.53 W

IB. Fraction Iowa City lies between 40° and 50°:
41.66 − 40 = 1.66; 1.66/10 = 0.166

IC. Fraction world must turn between Greenwich and Iowa City:
91.53/360 = 0.254

ID. Iowa City is in the Central Standard Time zone and the CST meridian is 90°, thus 91.53 is 91.53 − 90 = 1.53° W of the Central Standard Meridian. In 24 hours, there are 24 × 60 = 1,440 minutes; 1,440/360 = 4 minutes for every degree around Earth. So events happen 4 × 1.53 = 6.1 minutes later in Iowa City than at the 90° meridian. (If the location is E of the Standard Meridian, events happen earlier.)

IE. The values IB and IC are interpolates for Iowa City; ID is the time correction from local to Standard time for Iowa City. These values need never be calculated again for Iowa City.

IIA. To find the time of moonrise we start from the table of Moon Phases, 1998, we see that August's Waxing Quarter Moon occurs on Aug. 30. We need the Greenwich times for moonrise at latitudes 40° and 50°, and for Aug. 30 and 31, the day of the Waxing Quarter Moon and the next day. These values are found in the Astronomy Daily Calendar 1998: we then compute the difference between the two latitudes.

	40°	Diff.	50°
Aug. 30	13:05	0:27	13:32
Aug. 31	14:00	0:30	14:30

IIB. We want IB and the Aug. 30 time difference:
0.166 × 27 = 4.5

Add this to the Aug. 30, 40° rise time:
13:05 + 4.5 = 13:09.5

And for Aug. 31:
0.166 × 30 = 5.0

Add this to the Aug. 31, 40° rise time:
14:00 + 5.0 = 14:05.0

These 2 times are for the latitude of Iowa City, but for the Greenwich meridian.

IIC. To get the time for Iowa City meridian, take the difference between these 2 times just determined,
14:05.0 − 13:09.5 = 55.5 minutes,

and find what fraction of this 24-hour change took place while Earth turned between Greenwich and Iowa City, 0.254 (See IC)
55.5 × 0.254 = 14.1 minutes after 13:09.5

Thus 13:09.5 + 14.1 = 13:23.6 is the time the Waxing Quarter Moon will rise in the local time of Iowa City.

IID. But this happens 6.1 minutes (See ID) later by CST clock time at Iowa City, thus
13:23.6 + 6.1 = 13:29.7 CST

But this is summer, and daylight time is in effect;
13:30 + 1:00 = 14:30 CDT is the rise time for the Waxing Quarter Moon at Iowa City the afternoon of August 30, 1998.

IIIA. To find the time of sunset we need the Greenwich times for sunset at latitudes 40° and 50°. These values are found in the Astronomy Daily Calendar 1998: we then compute the difference between the two latitudes.

	40°	Diff.	50°
Aug. 30	18:35	0:14	18:49

IIIB. We want IB and the Aug. 30 time difference:
0.166 × 14 = 2.3

Add this to the Aug. 30, 40° set time:
18:35 + 2.3 = 18:37.3

This is the local time for the latitude of Iowa City.

IIIC. But this happens 6.1 minutes (See ID) later by CST clock time at Iowa City, thus
18:37.3 + 6.1 = 18:43.4 CST

But this is summer, and daylight time is in effect;
18:43 + 1:00 = 19:43 CDT is sunset at Iowa City on August 30, 1998.

January 1998

1st Month   **31 days**

Greenwich Mean Time

NOTE: For each day, numbers on first line indicate Sun. *Italic* numbers on second line indicate *Moon*. Degrees are North Latitude.

Moon Phases: FM = full moon; LQ = last quarter; NM = new moon; FQ = first quarter.
Sun's distance is in Astronomical Units.

CAUTION: Must be converted to local time. For instructions see "Calculation of Rise Times."

Day of month, of week, of year / *Moon Phase*	Sun on Meridian h m s / *Moon Distance*	Sun's Declination ° ' / *Distance*	20° Rise Sun / *Moon*	20° Set Sun / *Moon*	30° Rise Sun / *Moon*	30° Set Sun / *Moon*	40° Rise Sun / *Moon*	40° Set Sun / *Moon*	50° Rise Sun / *Moon*	50° Set Sun / *Moon*	60° Rise Sun / *Moon*	60° Set Sun / *Moon*
1 TH	12 03 31	-23 02	6 35	17 32	6 56	17 11	7 22	16 45	7 59	16 09	9 02	15 05
1	*.9833*	*.9833*	*8 46*	*20 31*	*8 59*	*20 20*	*9 15*	*20 05*	*9 36*	*19 46*	*10 10*	*19 14*
2 FR	12 04 00	-22 57	6 35	17 33	6 56	17 12	7 22	16 46	7 58	16 10	9 02	15 06
2	*.9833*		*9 35*	*21 31*	*9 44*	*21 23*	*9 56*	*21 14*	*10 12*	*21 00*	*10 36*	*20 40*
3 SA	12 04 27	-22 52	6 36	17 33	6 56	17 13	7 22	16 47	7 58	16 11	9 01	15 08
3	*.9833*		*10 21*	*22 30*	*10 27*	*22 27*	*10 34*	*22 22*	*10 43*	*22 16*	*10 58*	*22 06*
4 SU	12 04 55	-22 46	6 36	17 34	6 57	17 13	7 22	16 48	7 58	16 12	9 01	15 10
4	*.9833*		*11 07*	*23 29*	*11 08*	*23 30*	*11 10*	*23 30*	*11 13*	*23 31*	*11 17*	*23 32*
5 MO	12 05 22	-22 39	6 36	17 35	6 57	17 14	7 22	16 49	7 58	16 13	9 00	15 11
5	*14 19 FQ*	*.9832*	*11 51*	*none*	*11 49*	*none*	*11 46*	*none*	*11 42*	*none*	*11 36*	*none*
6 TU	12 05 48	-22 33	6 37	17 35	6 57	17 15	7 22	16 50	7 58	16 14	8 59	15 13
6	*.9833*		*12 36*	*0 28*	*12 29*	*0 32*	*12 22*	*0 38*	*12 11*	*0 46*	*11 55*	*0 57*
7 WE	12 06 14	-22 25	6 37	17 36	6 57	17 16	7 22	16 51	7 57	16 15	8 58	15 15
7	*.9833*		*13 22*	*1 26*	*13 12*	*1 35*	*12 59*	*1 45*	*12 43*	*2 00*	*12 17*	*2 22*
8 TH	12 06 40	-22 18	6 37	17 36	6 57	17 17	7 22	16 52	7 57	16 17	8 57	15 17
8	*.9833*		*14 10*	*2 25*	*13 57*	*2 37*	*13 40*	*2 52*	*13 18*	*3 12*	*12 43*	*3 44*
9 FR	12 07 05	-22 09	6 37	17 37	6 57	17 17	7 22	16 53	7 56	16 18	8 56	15 19
9	*.9833*		*15 00*	*3 23*	*14 44*	*3 38*	*14 25*	*3 56*	*13 58*	*4 21*	*13 16*	*5 03*
10 SA	12 07 29	-22 01	6 37	17 38	6 57	17 18	7 22	16 54	7 56	16 19	8 55	15 21
10	*.9834*		*15 52*	*4 21*	*15 35*	*4 37*	*15 14*	*4 58*	*14 45*	*5 26*	*13 57*	*6 14*
11 SU	12 07 53	-21 52	6 37	17 38	6 57	17 19	7 21	16 55	7 55	16 21	8 54	15 23
11	*.9834*		*16 46*	*5 16*	*16 29*	*5 33*	*16 07*	*5 55*	*15 37*	*6 25*	*14 48*	*7 15*
12 MO	12 08 16	-21 43	6 38	17 39	6 57	17 20	7 21	16 56	7 55	16 22	8 52	15 25
12	*17 25 FM*	*.9834*	*17 40*	*6 09*	*17 24*	*6 26*	*17 03*	*6 47*	*16 35*	*7 16*	*15 48*	*8 04*
13 TU	12 08 39	-21 33	6 38	17 40	6 57	17 21	7 21	16 57	7 54	16 23	8 51	15 27
13	*.9835*		*18 34*	*6 59*	*18 19*	*7 14*	*18 01*	*7 33*	*17 36*	*7 59*	*16 55*	*8 42*
14 WE	12 09 01	-21 22	6 38	17 40	6 57	17 21	7 20	16 58	7 54	16 25	8 49	15 29
14	*.9835*		*19 26*	*7 45*	*19 14*	*7 58*	*18 59*	*8 14*	*18 39*	*8 36*	*18 06*	*9 11*
15 TH	12 09 23	-21 12	6 38	17 41	6 57	17 22	7 20	16 59	7 53	16 26	8 48	15 31
15	*.9836*		*20 18*	*8 27*	*20 09*	*8 38*	*19 57*	*8 50*	*19 42*	*9 08*	*19 18*	*9 35*
16 FR	12 09 43	-21 01	6 38	17 42	6 57	17 23	7 20	17 00	7 52	16 28	8 46	15 34
16	*.9837*		*21 07*	*9 07*	*21 01*	*9 14*	*20 54*	*9 23*	*20 45*	*9 35*	*20 30*	*9 54*
17 SA	12 10 03	-20 49	6 38	17 42	6 56	17 24	7 19	17 01	7 51	16 29	8 45	15 36
17	*.9837*		*21 56*	*9 45*	*21 54*	*9 49*	*21 51*	*9 54*	*21 47*	*10 00*	*21 41*	*10 10*
18 SU	12 10 23	-20 37	6 38	17 43	6 56	17 25	7 19	17 02	7 50	16 31	8 43	15 38
18	*.9838*		*22 44*	*10 22*	*22 45*	*10 22*	*22 46*	*10 23*	*22 48*	*10 24*	*22 51*	*10 26*
19 MO	12 10 41	-20 25	6 38	17 44	6 56	17 26	7 18	17 03	7 49	16 32	8 41	15 41
19	*.9839*		*23 32*	*10 58*	*23 36*	*10 55*	*23 42*	*10 52*	*23 49*	*10 47*	*none*	*10 41*
20 TU	12 10 59	-20 13	6 38	17 44	6 56	17 27	7 18	17 05	7 48	16 34	8 40	15 43
20	*19 41 LQ*	*.9840*	*none*	*11 35*	*none*	*11 29*	*none*	*11 21*	*none*	*11 12*	*0 01*	*10 56*
21 WE	12 11 16	-20 00	6 38	17 45	6 55	17 27	7 17	17 06	7 47	16 36	8 38	15 46
21	*.9841*		*0 21*	*12 13*	*0 28*	*12 04*	*0 38*	*11 53*	*0 51*	*11 38*	*1 12*	*11 14*
22 TH	12 11 33	-19 46	6 38	17 46	6 55	17 28	7 17	17 07	7 46	16 37	8 36	15 48
22	*.9842*		*1 11*	*12 54*	*1 22*	*12 42*	*1 35*	*12 27*	*1 54*	*12 07*	*2 23*	*11 35*
23 FR	12 11 49	-19 32	6 38	17 46	6 55	17 29	7 16	17 08	7 45	16 39	8 34	15 50
23	*.9843*		*2 02*	*13 38*	*2 16*	*13 24*	*2 33*	*13 06*	*2 56*	*12 41*	*3 34*	*12 01*
24 SA	12 12 04	-19 18	6 37	17 47	6 54	17 30	7 15	17 09	7 44	16 40	8 32	15 53
24	*.9844*		*2 56*	*14 26*	*3 11*	*14 10*	*3 31*	*13 49*	*3 59*	*13 21*	*4 44*	*12 35*
25 SU	12 12 18	-19 04	6 37	17 48	6 54	17 31	7 15	17 10	7 43	16 42	8 30	15 56
25	*.9845*		*3 51*	*15 19*	*4 08*	*15 01*	*4 29*	*14 40*	*4 59*	*14 10*	*5 48*	*13 20*
26 MO	12 12 31	-18 49	6 37	17 48	6 54	17 32	7 14	17 12	7 42	16 44	8 28	15 58
26	*.9846*		*4 46*	*16 15*	*5 03*	*15 58*	*5 25*	*15 37*	*5 55*	*15 07*	*6 45*	*14 17*
27 TU	12 12 44	-18 34	6 37	17 49	6 53	17 33	7 13	17 13	7 41	16 45	8 26	16 01
27	*.9847*		*5 41*	*17 15*	*5 58*	*16 59*	*6 18*	*16 40*	*6 46*	*16 12*	*7 32*	*15 28*
28 WE	12 12 56	-18 18	6 37	17 49	6 53	17 34	7 12	17 14	7 39	16 47	8 23	16 03
28	*6 02 NM*	*.9848*	*6 35*	*18 16*	*6 49*	*18 03*	*7 07*	*17 47*	*7 31*	*17 25*	*8 09*	*16 49*
29 TH	12 13 07	-18 02	6 36	17 50	6 52	17 34	7 11	17 15	7 38	16 49	8 21	16 06
29	*.9849*		*7 27*	*19 18*	*7 38*	*19 09*	*7 51*	*18 57*	*8 10*	*18 41*	*8 39*	*18 15*
30 FR	12 13 17	-17 46	6 36	17 51	6 52	17 35	7 11	17 16	7 37	16 50	8 19	16 08
30	*.9851*		*8 16*	*20 20*	*8 23*	*20 15*	*8 32*	*20 08*	*8 44*	*19 59*	*9 03*	*19 44*
31 SA	12 13 26	-17 30	6 36	17 51	6 51	17 36	7 10	17 18	7 35	16 52	8 17	16 11
31	*.9852*		*9 03*	*21 21*	*9 06*	*21 20*	*9 10*	*21 19*	*9 16*	*21 17*	*9 24*	*21 14*

February 1998

2d Month   **28 days**

Greenwich Mean Time

NOTE: For each day, numbers on first line indicate Sun. *Italic* numbers on second line indicate *Moon*. Degrees are North Latitude.

Moon Phases: FM = full moon; LQ = last quarter; NM = new moon; FQ = first quarter.
Sun's distance is in Astronomical Units.

CAUTION: Must be converted to local time. For instructions see "Calculation of Rise Times."

Day of month, of week, of year / Moon Phase	Sun on Meridian / Moon Phase (h m s)	Sun's Declination ° ' / Distance	20° Rise Sun/Moon	20° Set Sun/Moon	30° Rise Sun/Moon	30° Set Sun/Moon	40° Rise Sun/Moon	40° Set Sun/Moon	50° Rise Sun/Moon	50° Set Sun/Moon	60° Rise Sun/Moon	60° Set Sun/Moon
1 SU	12 13 35	-17 13	6 36	17 52	6 50	17 37	7 09	17 19	7 34	16 54	8 14	16 14
32		*.9853*	*9 49*	*22 22*	*9 48*	*22 25*	*9 47*	*22 29*	*9 46*	*22 34*	*9 43*	*22 42*
2 MO	12 13 42	-16 56	6 35	17 52	6 50	17 38	7 08	17 20	7 32	16 56	8 12	16 16
33		*.9855*	*10 35*	*23 21*	*10 30*	*23 28*	*10 24*	*23 37*	*10 16*	*23 49*	*10 03*	*none*
3 TU	12 13 49	-16 38	6 35	17 53	6 49	17 39	7 07	17 21	7 31	16 57	8 10	16 19
34 22 54 FQ		*.9856*	*11 21*	*none*	*11 12*	*none*	*11 01*	*none*	*10 47*	*none*	*10 24*	*0 08*
4 WE	12 13 55	-16 21	6 35	17 53	6 49	17 40	7 06	17 22	7 29	16 59	8 07	16 22
35		*.9857*	*12 08*	*0 20*	*11 56*	*0 31*	*11 41*	*0 44*	*11 21*	*1 03*	*10 49*	*1 32*
5 TH	12 14 00	-16 03	6 34	17 54	6 48	17 40	7 05	17 24	7 28	17 01	8 05	16 24
36		*.9859*	*12 57*	*1 18*	*12 42*	*1 32*	*12 24*	*1 49*	*11 59*	*2 13*	*11 19*	*2 51*
6 FR	12 14 04	-15 45	6 34	17 55	6 47	17 41	7 04	17 25	7 26	17 02	8 02	16 27
37		*.9860*	*13 48*	*2 15*	*13 31*	*2 31*	*13 11*	*2 51*	*12 42*	*3 18*	*11 56*	*4 04*
7 SA	12 14 08	-15 26	6 33	17 55	6 47	17 42	7 03	17 26	7 25	17 04	8 00	16 29
38		*.9862*	*14 40*	*3 10*	*14 23*	*3 27*	*14 01*	*3 49*	*13 32*	*4 18*	*12 43*	*5 07*
8 SU	12 14 11	-15 07	6 33	17 56	6 46	17 43	7 02	17 27	7 23	17 06	7 57	16 32
39		*.9864*	*15 33*	*4 03*	*15 16*	*4 20*	*14 55*	*4 41*	*14 26*	*5 11*	*13 38*	*5 59*
9 MO	12 14 13	-14 48	6 32	17 56	6 45	17 44	7 01	17 28	7 21	17 08	7 55	16 35
40		*.9865*	*16 26*	*4 53*	*16 11*	*5 09*	*15 52*	*5 29*	*15 25*	*5 56*	*14 42*	*6 41*
10 TU	12 14 14	-14 29	6 32	17 57	6 44	17 45	6 59	17 30	7 20	17 09	7 52	16 37
41		*.9867*	*17 19*	*5 40*	*17 05*	*5 54*	*16 49*	*6 11*	*16 27*	*6 35*	*15 51*	*7 13*
11 WE	12 14 14	-14 10	6 31	17 57	6 43	17 45	6 58	17 31	7 18	17 11	7 49	16 40
42 10 24 FM		*.9869*	*18 10*	*6 23*	*18 00*	*6 35*	*17 47*	*6 49*	*17 29*	*7 08*	*17 02*	*7 39*
12 TH	12 14 14	-13 50	6 31	17 58	6 43	17 46	6 57	17 32	7 16	17 13	7 47	16 43
43		*.9871*	*19 00*	*7 04*	*18 53*	*7 13*	*18 44*	*7 23*	*18 32*	*7 37*	*18 13*	*7 59*
13 FR	12 14 12	-13 30	6 30	17 58	6 42	17 47	6 56	17 33	7 15	17 15	7 44	16 45
44		*.9873*	*19 49*	*7 43*	*19 45*	*7 48*	*19 41*	*7 55*	*19 34*	*8 04*	*19 25*	*8 17*
14 SA	12 14 10	-13 10	6 30	17 59	6 41	17 48	6 55	17 34	7 13	17 16	7 41	16 48
45		*.9874*	*20 38*	*8 20*	*20 37*	*8 22*	*20 37*	*8 24*	*20 36*	*8 28*	*20 35*	*8 33*
15 SU	12 14 08	-12 49	6 29	17 59	6 40	17 49	6 53	17 36	7 11	17 18	7 39	16 51
46		*.9876*	*21 26*	*8 56*	*21 29*	*8 55*	*21 32*	*8 53*	*21 38*	*8 51*	*21 46*	*8 48*
16 MO	12 14 04	-12 29	6 29	18 00	6 39	17 49	6 52	17 37	7 09	17 20	7 36	16 53
47		*.9878*	*22 14*	*9 33*	*22 20*	*9 28*	*22 28*	*9 23*	*22 39*	*9 15*	*22 56*	*9 03*
17 TU	12 14 00	-12 08	6 28	18 00	6 38	17 50	6 51	17 38	7 07	17 21	7 33	16 56
48		*.9881*	*23 03*	*10 10*	*23 12*	*10 03*	*23 24*	*9 53*	*23 40*	*9 40*	*none*	*9 20*
18 WE	12 13 56	-11 47	6 28	18 01	6 37	17 51	6 49	17 39	7 06	17 23	7 31	16 58
49		*.9883*	*23 53*	*10 50*	*none*	*10 39*	*none*	*10 25*	*none*	*10 07*	*0 06*	*9 39*
19 TH	12 13 50	-11 26	6 27	18 01	6 36	17 52	6 48	17 40	7 04	17 25	7 28	17 01
50 15 28 LQ		*.9885*	*none*	*11 31*	*0 05*	*11 18*	*0 20*	*11 01*	*0 42*	*10 38*	*1 16*	*10 02*
20 FR	12 13 44	-11 04	6 26	18 01	6 36	17 52	6 47	17 41	7 02	17 27	7 25	17 04
51		*.9887*	*0 44*	*12 16*	*0 59*	*12 01*	*1 17*	*11 42*	*1 43*	*11 15*	*2 25*	*10 32*
21 SA	12 13 38	-10 43	6 26	18 02	6 35	17 53	6 45	17 42	7 00	17 28	7 22	17 06
52		*.9889*	*1 37*	*13 05*	*1 53*	*12 48*	*2 14*	*12 27*	*2 43*	*11 58*	*3 30*	*11 10*
22 SU	12 13 30	-10 21	6 25	18 02	6 34	17 54	6 44	17 44	6 58	17 30	7 19	17 09
53		*.9891*	*2 31*	*13 58*	*2 48*	*13 41*	*3 09*	*13 20*	*3 40*	*12 50*	*4 29*	*12 00*
23 MO	12 13 22	-9 59	6 24	18 03	6 33	17 55	6 43	17 45	6 56	17 32	7 17	17 11
54		*.9894*	*3 25*	*14 55*	*3 42*	*14 39*	*4 03*	*14 18*	*4 32*	*13 50*	*5 21*	*13 02*
24 TU	12 13 14	-9 37	6 24	18 03	6 32	17 55	6 41	17 46	6 54	17 33	7 14	17 14
55		*.9896*	*4 19*	*15 56*	*4 34*	*15 41*	*4 53*	*15 23*	*5 20*	*14 58*	*6 02*	*14 17*
25 WE	12 13 05	-9 15	6 23	18 03	6 31	17 56	6 40	17 47	6 52	17 35	7 11	17 17
56		*.9898*	*5 12*	*16 58*	*5 24*	*16 46*	*5 40*	*16 32*	*6 02*	*16 13*	*6 36*	*15 41*
26 TH	12 12 55	-8 52	6 22	18 04	6 29	17 57	6 38	17 48	6 50	17 37	7 08	17 19
57 17 27 NM		*.9901*	*6 03*	*18 01*	*6 12*	*17 53*	*6 23*	*17 44*	*6 39*	*17 31*	*7 03*	*17 11*
27 FR	12 12 45	-8 30	6 22	18 04	6 28	17 57	6 37	17 49	6 48	17 38	7 05	17 22
58		*.9903*	*6 52*	*19 04*	*6 57*	*19 01*	*7 04*	*18 57*	*7 13*	*18 51*	*7 26*	*18 43*
28 SA	12 12 34	-8 07	6 21	18 05	6 27	17 58	6 35	17 50	6 46	17 40	7 02	17 24
59		*.9905*	*7 40*	*20 07*	*7 41*	*20 08*	*7 43*	*20 10*	*7 44*	*20 12*	*7 47*	*20 15*

March 1998

3d Month

31 days

Greenwich Mean Time

NOTE: For each day, numbers on first line indicate Sun. *Italic* numbers on second line indicate *Moon*.
Degrees are North Latitude.

Moon Phases: FM = full moon; LQ = last quarter; NM = new moon; FQ = first quarter.
Sun's distance is in Astronomical Units.

CAUTION: Must be converted to local time. For instructions see "Calculation of Rise Times."

Day of month, of week, of year / Moon Phase	Sun on Meridian / Moon Phase h m s	Sun's Declination ° ′ / Distance	20° Rise Sun/Moon	20° Set Sun/Moon	30° Rise Sun/Moon	30° Set Sun/Moon	40° Rise Sun/Moon	40° Set Sun/Moon	50° Rise Sun/Moon	50° Set Sun/Moon	60° Rise Sun/Moon	60° Set Sun/Moon
1 SU	12 12 23	-7 45	6 20	18 05	6 26	17 59	6 34	17 52	6 44	17 42	6 59	17 27
60		.9908	8 28	21 09	8 25	21 15	8 21	21 22	8 15	21 31	8 07	21 45
2 MO	12 12 11	-7 22	6 19	18 05	6 25	18 00	6 32	17 53	6 42	17 43	6 56	17 29
61		.9910	9 16	22 11	9 08	22 20	8 59	22 32	8 47	22 48	8 29	23 13
3 TU	12 11 59	-6 59	6 19	18 06	6 24	18 00	6 31	17 54	6 40	17 45	6 53	17 32
62		.9913	10 04	23 11	9 53	23 24	9 40	23 40	9 21	none	8 53	none
4 WE	12 11 46	-6 36	6 18	18 06	6 23	18 01	6 29	17 55	6 38	17 47	6 50	17 34
63		.9915	10 54	none	10 40	none	10 23	none	9 59	0 02	9 22	0 37
5 TH	12 11 32	-6 13	6 17	18 06	6 22	18 02	6 28	17 56	6 36	17 48	6 47	17 37
64	8 42 FQ	.9917	11 45	0 10	11 29	0 25	11 09	0 44	10 41	1 11	9 57	1 54
6 FR	12 11 19	-5 50	6 16	18 07	6 21	18 02	6 26	17 57	6 34	17 50	6 45	17 39
65		.9920	12 37	1 06	12 20	1 23	11 59	1 44	11 29	2 13	10 41	3 01
7 SA	12 11 05	-5 26	6 15	18 07	6 20	18 03	6 25	17 58	6 31	17 52	6 42	17 42
66		.9922	13 29	2 00	13 12	2 17	12 51	2 38	12 22	3 08	11 33	3 57
8 SU	12 10 50	-5 03	6 15	18 07	6 18	18 04	6 23	17 59	6 29	17 53	6 39	17 44
67		.9925	14 22	2 51	14 06	3 07	13 46	3 27	13 19	3 55	12 34	4 41
9 MO	12 10 35	-4 40	6 14	18 08	6 17	18 04	6 22	18 00	6 27	17 55	6 36	17 47
68		.9927	15 14	3 38	15 00	3 52	14 43	4 11	14 19	4 36	13 41	5 16
10 TU	12 10 20	-4 16	6 13	18 08	6 16	18 05	6 20	18 01	6 25	17 56	6 33	17 49
69		.9930	16 05	4 22	15 54	4 34	15 40	4 49	15 21	5 10	14 50	5 43
11 WE	12 10 04	-3 53	6 12	18 08	6 15	18 06	6 18	18 02	6 23	17 58	6 30	17 52
70		.9933	16 55	5 03	16 47	5 13	16 37	5 24	16 23	5 40	16 01	6 05
12 TH	12 09 48	-3 29	6 11	18 09	6 14	18 06	6 17	18 03	6 21	18 00	6 27	17 54
71		.9935	17 45	5 42	17 40	5 48	17 33	5 56	17 25	6 07	17 12	6 23
13 FR	12 09 32	-3 06	6 10	18 09	6 13	18 07	6 15	18 04	6 19	18 01	6 24	17 57
72	4 35 FM	.9938	18 33	6 19	18 31	6 23	18 30	6 27	18 27	6 32	18 23	6 40
14 SA	12 09 15	-2 42	6 10	18 09	6 11	18 07	6 14	18 05	6 17	18 03	6 21	17 59
73		.9941	19 21	6 56	19 23	6 56	19 25	6 56	19 28	6 55	19 33	6 55
15 SU	12 08 58	-2 18	6 09	18 10	6 10	18 08	6 12	18 07	6 14	18 05	6 18	18 02
74		.9943	20 09	7 33	20 14	7 29	20 21	7 25	20 30	7 19	20 44	7 10
16 MO	12 08 41	-1 55	6 08	18 10	6 09	18 09	6 10	18 08	6 12	18 06	6 15	18 04
75		.9946	20 58	8 10	21 06	8 03	21 17	7 55	21 31	7 43	21 54	7 26
17 TU	12 08 24	-1 31	6 07	18 10	6 08	18 09	6 09	18 09	6 10	18 08	6 12	18 07
76		.9949	21 47	8 48	21 59	8 38	22 13	8 26	22 32	8 10	23 03	7 44
18 WE	12 08 07	-1 07	6 06	18 11	6 07	18 10	6 07	18 10	6 08	18 09	6 09	18 09
77		.9952	22 37	9 28	22 51	9 16	23 09	9 00	23 33	8 39	none	8 06
19 TH	12 07 49	-0 43	6 05	18 11	6 05	18 11	6 06	18 11	6 06	18 11	6 06	18 11
78		.9955	23 29	10 11	23 45	9 57	none	9 38	none	9 13	0 12	8 32
20 FR	12 07 32	-0 20	6 04	18 11	6 04	18 11	6 04	18 12	6 04	18 12	6 03	18 14
79		.9957	none	10 58	none	10 41	0 04	10 21	0 32	9 52	1 18	9 06
21 SA	12 07 14	+0 04	6 04	18 11	6 03	18 12	6 02	18 13	6 01	18 14	6 00	18 16
80	7 39 LQ	.9960	0 21	11 48	0 38	11 30	0 59	11 09	1 29	10 39	2 18	9 49
22 SU	12 06 56	+0 28	6 03	18 12	6 02	18 12	6 01	18 14	5 59	18 16	5 56	18 19
81		.9963	1 13	12 41	1 30	12 24	1 52	12 03	2 22	11 33	3 11	10 44
23 MO	12 06 38	+0 51	6 02	18 12	6 01	18 13	5 59	18 15	5 57	18 17	5 53	18 21
82		.9966	2 05	13 38	2 22	13 22	2 42	13 03	3 10	12 36	3 56	11 51
24 TU	12 06 20	+1 15	6 01	18 12	5 59	18 14	5 58	18 16	5 55	18 19	5 50	18 24
83		.9969	2 57	14 37	3 11	14 24	3 29	14 08	3 53	13 46	4 32	13 09
25 WE	12 06 02	+1 39	6 00	18 12	5 58	18 14	5 56	18 17	5 53	18 20	5 47	18 26
84		.9973	3 48	15 39	3 59	15 29	4 13	15 17	4 32	15 01	5 01	14 34
26 TH	12 05 44	+2 02	5 59	18 13	5 57	18 15	5 54	18 18	5 50	18 22	5 44	18 29
85		.9975	4 37	16 42	4 45	16 36	4 54	16 29	5 07	16 19	5 26	16 04
27 FR	12 05 26	+2 26	5 58	18 13	5 56	18 16	5 53	18 19	5 48	18 24	5 41	18 31
86		.9978	5 26	17 45	5 29	17 44	5 34	17 42	5 39	17 40	5 48	17 37
28 SA	12 05 08	+2 49	5 57	18 13	5 55	18 16	5 51	18 20	5 46	18 25	5 38	18 33
87	3 15 NM	.9980	6 15	18 49	6 14	18 52	6 12	18 56	6 11	19 02	6 08	19 10
29 SU	12 04 50	+3 13	5 57	18 13	5 53	18 17	5 49	18 21	5 44	18 27	5 35	18 36
88		.9983	7 03	19 53	6 58	20 00	6 51	20 10	6 43	20 23	6 29	20 43
30 MO	12 04 32	+3 36	5 56	18 14	5 52	18 17	5 48	18 22	5 42	18 28	5 32	18 38
89		.9986	7 53	20 56	7 44	21 07	7 32	21 22	7 17	21 41	6 53	22 12
31 TU	12 04 14	+3 59	5 55	18 14	5 51	18 18	5 46	18 23	5 40	18 30	5 29	18 41
90		.9989	8 44	21 58	8 31	22 12	8 15	22 30	7 54	22 55	7 20	23 36

April 1998

4th Month   **30 days**

Greenwich Mean Time

NOTE: For each day, numbers on first line indicate Sun. *Italic* numbers on second line indicate *Moon*.
Degrees are North Latitude.

Moon Phases: FM = full moon; LQ = last quarter; NM = new moon; FQ = first quarter.
Sun's distance is in Astronomical Units.

CAUTION: Must be converted to local time. For instructions see "Calculation of Rise Times."

Day of month, of week, of year / Moon Phase	Sun on Meridian (h m s)	Sun's Declination °´ / Distance	20° Rise Sun/Moon	20° Set Sun/Moon	30° Rise Sun/Moon	30° Set Sun/Moon	40° Rise Sun/Moon	40° Set Sun/Moon	50° Rise Sun/Moon	50° Set Sun/Moon	60° Rise Sun/Moon	60° Set Sun/Moon
1 WE	12 03 56	+4 23	5 54	18 14	5 50	18 19	5 45	18 24	5 37	18 31	5 26	18 43
91		*.9992*	*9 37*	*22 58*	*9 21*	*23 14*	*9 02*	*23 35*	*8 36*	*none*	*7 53*	*none*
2 TH	12 03 38	+4 46	5 53	18 14	5 49	18 19	5 43	18 25	5 35	18 33	5 23	18 46
92		*.9995*	*10 30*	*23 54*	*10 13*	*none*	*9 52*	*none*	*9 23*	*0 03*	*8 35*	*0 50*
3 FR	12 03 20	+5 09	5 52	18 15	5 47	18 20	5 41	18 26	5 33	18 35	5 20	18 48
93	*20 19 FQ*	*.9997*	*11 24*	*none*	*11 07*	*0 11*	*10 45*	*0 33*	*10 15*	*1 03*	*9 26*	*1 52*
4 SA	12 03 03	+5 32	5 51	18 15	5 46	18 20	5 40	18 27	5 31	18 36	5 17	18 51
94		*1.0000*	*12 18*	*0 47*	*12 01*	*1 04*	*11 41*	*1 25*	*11 12*	*1 54*	*10 26*	*2 41*
5 SU	12 02 46	+5 55	5 50	18 15	5 45	18 21	5 38	18 28	5 29	18 38	5 14	18 53
95		*1.0003*	*13 10*	*1 36*	*12 56*	*1 51*	*12 37*	*2 10*	*12 12*	*2 37*	*11 31*	*3 19*
6 MO	12 02 28	+6 18	5 50	18 16	5 44	18 22	5 37	18 29	5 27	18 39	5 11	18 55
96		*1.0006*	*14 02*	*2 21*	*13 50*	*2 34*	*13 35*	*2 51*	*13 14*	*3 13*	*12 40*	*3 49*
7 TU	12 02 11	+6 40	5 49	18 16	5 43	18 22	5 35	18 30	5 25	18 41	5 08	18 58
97		*1.0009*	*14 52*	*3 03*	*14 43*	*3 14*	*14 31*	*3 27*	*14 16*	*3 44*	*13 51*	*4 12*
8 WE	12 01 55	+7 03	5 48	18 16	5 42	18 23	5 33	18 31	5 22	18 42	5 05	19 00
98		*1.0011*	*15 41*	*3 42*	*15 35*	*3 50*	*15 28*	*3 59*	*15 18*	*4 12*	*15 02*	*4 31*
9 TH	12 01 38	+7 25	5 47	18 16	5 40	18 23	5 32	18 32	5 20	18 44	5 02	19 03
99		*1.0014*	*16 30*	*4 20*	*16 27*	*4 24*	*16 24*	*4 30*	*16 19*	*4 37*	*16 12*	*4 47*
10 FR	12 01 22	+7 47	5 46	18 17	5 39	18 24	5 30	18 33	5 18	18 46	4 59	19 05
100		*1.0017*	*17 18*	*4 57*	*17 19*	*4 58*	*17 19*	*4 59*	*17 21*	*5 00*	*17 23*	*5 03*
11 SA	12 01 06	+8 10	5 45	18 17	5 38	18 25	5 29	18 34	5 16	18 47	4 56	19 08
101	*22 25 FM*	*1.0020*	*18 06*	*5 33*	*18 10*	*5 31*	*18 15*	*5 28*	*18 22*	*5 24*	*18 33*	*5 17*
12 SU	12 00 50	+8 32	5 45	18 17	5 37	18 25	5 27	18 35	5 14	18 49	4 53	19 10
102		*1.0023*	*18 54*	*6 10*	*19 02*	*6 04*	*19 11*	*5 57*	*19 24*	*5 47*	*19 44*	*5 33*
13 MO	12 00 34	+8 54	5 44	18 18	5 36	18 26	5 26	18 36	5 12	18 50	4 50	19 13
103		*1.0026*	*19 44*	*6 48*	*19 54*	*6 39*	*20 07*	*6 28*	*20 25*	*6 13*	*20 54*	*5 50*
14 TU	12 00 19	+9 15	5 43	18 18	5 35	18 26	5 24	18 37	5 10	18 52	4 47	19 15
104		*1.0028*	*20 34*	*7 27*	*20 47*	*7 16*	*21 04*	*7 01*	*21 26*	*6 41*	*22 04*	*6 10*
15 WE	12 00 04	+9 37	5 42	18 18	5 34	18 27	5 23	18 38	5 08	18 53	4 44	19 17
105		*1.0031*	*21 25*	*8 10*	*21 40*	*7 55*	*21 59*	*7 38*	*22 26*	*7 13*	*23 10*	*6 34*
16 TH	11 59 50	+9 58	5 41	18 18	5 32	18 28	5 21	18 39	5 06	18 55	4 41	19 20
106		*1.0034*	*22 16*	*8 55*	*22 33*	*8 38*	*22 54*	*8 18*	*23 24*	*7 50*	*none*	*7 05*
17 FR	11 59 36	+10 20	5 41	18 19	5 31	18 28	5 20	18 40	5 04	18 57	4 38	19 22
107		*1.0037*	*23 08*	*9 43*	*23 25*	*9 25*	*23 47*	*9 04*	*none*	*8 34*	*0 13*	*7 44*
18 SA	11 59 22	+10 41	5 40	18 19	5 30	18 29	5 18	18 41	5 02	18 58	4 36	19 25
108		*1.0040*	*23 59*	*10 34*	*none*	*10 17*	*none*	*9 55*	*0 17*	*9 25*	*1 08*	*8 34*
19 SU	11 59 09	+11 02	5 39	18 19	5 29	18 30	5 17	18 42	5 00	19 00	4 33	19 27
109	*19 54 LQ*	*1.0043*	*none*	*11 28*	*0 16*	*11 12*	*0 37*	*10 51*	*1 06*	*10 23*	*1 54*	*9 35*
20 MO	11 58 56	+11 22	5 38	18 20	5 28	18 30	5 15	18 43	4 58	19 01	4 30	19 30
110		*1.0046*	*0 49*	*12 25*	*1 05*	*12 10*	*1 24*	*11 52*	*1 50*	*11 28*	*2 32*	*10 47*
21 TU	11 58 44	+11 43	5 38	18 20	5 27	18 31	5 14	18 44	4 56	19 03	4 27	19 32
111		*1.0048*	*1 38*	*13 23*	*1 51*	*13 12*	*2 07*	*12 58*	*2 29*	*12 38*	*3 03*	*12 07*
22 WE	11 58 32	+12 04	5 37	18 20	5 26	18 31	5 13	18 45	4 54	19 04	4 24	19 35
112		*1.0051*	*2 27*	*14 23*	*2 36*	*14 15*	*2 48*	*14 06*	*3 03*	*13 53*	*3 28*	*13 32*
23 TH	11 58 21	+12 23	5 36	18 21	5 25	18 32	5 11	18 46	4 52	19 06	4 21	19 37
113		*1.0054*	*3 14*	*15 24*	*3 20*	*15 21*	*3 26*	*15 17*	*3 36*	*15 10*	*3 50*	*15 01*
24 FR	11 58 10	+12 43	5 36	18 21	5 24	18 33	5 10	18 47	4 50	19 07	4 18	19 40
114		*1.0057*	*4 01*	*16 27*	*4 03*	*16 28*	*4 04*	*16 29*	*4 06*	*16 30*	*4 10*	*16 33*
25 SA	11 57 59	+13 03	5 35	18 21	5 23	18 33	5 08	18 48	4 48	19 09	4 15	19 42
115		*1.0059*	*4 49*	*17 30*	*4 46*	*17 36*	*4 42*	*17 42*	*4 37*	*17 51*	*4 30*	*18 05*
26 SU	11 57 49	+13 23	5 34	18 22	5 22	18 34	5 07	18 49	4 46	19 11	4 13	19 45
116	*11 42 NM*	*1.0062*	*5 38*	*18 34*	*5 31*	*18 44*	*5 22*	*18 56*	*5 10*	*19 12*	*4 51*	*19 38*
27 MO	11 57 40	+13 42	5 34	18 22	5 21	18 35	5 06	18 50	4 44	19 12	4 10	19 47
117		*1.0065*	*6 29*	*19 38*	*6 18*	*19 52*	*6 04*	*20 08*	*5 45*	*20 31*	*5 16*	*21 07*
28 TU	11 57 31	+14 01	5 33	18 22	5 20	18 35	5 04	18 51	4 42	19 14	4 07	19 50
118		*1.0067*	*7 22*	*20 41*	*7 08*	*20 57*	*6 50*	*21 17*	*6 25*	*21 44*	*5 47*	*22 29*
29 WE	11 57 22	+14 20	5 32	18 23	5 19	18 36	5 03	18 52	4 41	19 15	4 04	19 52
119		*1.0070*	*8 17*	*21 41*	*8 00*	*21 59*	*7 40*	*22 20*	*7 11*	*22 50*	*6 25*	*23 40*
30 TH	11 57 14	+14 39	5 32	18 23	5 18	18 37	5 02	18 53	4 39	19 17	4 01	19 55
120		*1.0072*	*9 12*	*22 38*	*8 55*	*22 55*	*8 33*	*23 17*	*8 03*	*23 47*	*7 13*	*none*

May 1998

5th Month   **31 days**

Greenwich Mean Time

NOTE: For each day, numbers on first line indicate Sun. *Italic* numbers on second line indicate *Moon*. Degrees are North Latitude.

Moon Phases: FM = full moon; LQ = last quarter; NM = new moon; FQ = first quarter.
Sun's distance is in Astronomical Units.

CAUTION: Must be converted to local time. For instructions see "Calculation of Rise Times."

Day of month, of week, of year / *Moon Phase*	Sun on Meridian h m s / *Distance*	Sun's Decli-nation ° ´	20° Rise Sun/*Moon*	20° Set Sun/*Moon*	30° Rise Sun/*Moon*	30° Set Sun/*Moon*	40° Rise Sun/*Moon*	40° Set Sun/*Moon*	50° Rise Sun/*Moon*	50° Set Sun/*Moon*	60° Rise Sun/*Moon*	60° Set Sun/*Moon*
1 FR	11 57 07	+14 57	5 31	18 23	5 17	18 37	5 01	18 54	4 37	19 18	3 59	19 57
121	*1.0075*		*10 08*	*23 30*	*9 51*	*23 46*	*9 30*	*none*	*9 00*	*none*	*8 11*	*0 37*
2 SA	11 57 00	+15 15	5 30	18 24	5 17	18 38	4 59	18 55	4 35	19 20	3 56	20 00
122	*1.0077*		*11 03*	*none*	*10 47*	*none*	*10 28*	*0 07*	*10 01*	*0 35*	*9 17*	*1 20*
3 SU *10 05 FQ*	11 56 54	+15 33	5 30	18 24	5 16	18 38	4 58	18 56	4 33	19 21	3 53	20 02
123	*1.0080*		*11 56*	*0 18*	*11 43*	*0 32*	*11 26*	*0 50*	*11 03*	*1 14*	*10 27*	*1 53*
4 MO	11 56 48	+15 51	5 29	18 25	5 15	18 39	4 57	18 57	4 32	19 23	3 51	20 05
124	*1.0082*		*12 48*	*1 02*	*12 37*	*1 13*	*12 24*	*1 28*	*12 06*	*1 48*	*11 38*	*2 18*
5 TU	11 56 42	+16 08	5 29	18 25	5 14	18 40	4 56	18 58	4 30	19 24	3 48	20 07
125	*1.0085*		*13 38*	*1 42*	*13 30*	*1 51*	*13 21*	*2 02*	*13 09*	*2 16*	*12 50*	*2 39*
6 WE	11 56 38	+16 25	5 28	18 25	5 13	18 40	4 55	18 59	4 28	19 26	3 45	20 10
126	*1.0087*		*14 26*	*2 21*	*14 22*	*2 26*	*14 17*	*2 33*	*14 11*	*2 42*	*14 01*	*2 56*
7 TH	11 56 33	+16 42	5 28	18 26	5 12	18 41	4 53	19 00	4 27	19 27	3 43	20 12
127	*1.0089*		*15 14*	*2 57*	*15 14*	*2 59*	*15 13*	*3 02*	*15 12*	*3 06*	*15 11*	*3 11*
8 FR	11 56 30	+16 58	5 27	18 26	5 12	18 42	4 52	19 01	4 25	19 29	3 40	20 14
128	*1.0092*		*16 02*	*3 33*	*16 05*	*3 32*	*16 09*	*3 31*	*16 14*	*3 29*	*16 22*	*3 26*
9 SA	11 56 26	+17 15	5 27	18 26	5 11	18 42	4 51	19 02	4 23	19 30	3 38	20 17
129	*1.0094*		*16 51*	*4 10*	*16 57*	*4 05*	*17 05*	*4 00*	*17 16*	*3 52*	*17 32*	*3 41*
10 SU	11 56 24	+17 31	5 26	18 27	5 10	18 43	4 50	19 03	4 22	19 32	3 35	20 19
130	*1.0096*		*17 40*	*4 47*	*17 49*	*4 39*	*18 01*	*4 30*	*18 18*	*4 17*	*18 43*	*3 57*
11 MO *14 30 FM*	11 56 22	+17 46	5 26	18 27	5 09	18 44	4 49	19 04	4 20	19 33	3 33	20 22
131	*1.0099*		*18 30*	*5 26*	*18 42*	*5 16*	*18 58*	*5 02*	*19 20*	*4 44*	*19 54*	*4 15*
12 TU	11 56 20	+18 02	5 25	18 28	5 09	18 44	4 48	19 05	4 19	19 35	3 30	20 24
132	*1.0101*		*19 21*	*6 08*	*19 36*	*5 54*	*19 55*	*5 38*	*20 21*	*5 14*	*21 03*	*4 38*
13 WE	11 56 19	+18 17	5 25	18 28	5 08	18 45	4 47	19 06	4 17	19 36	3 28	20 27
133	*1.0103*		*20 13*	*6 52*	*20 30*	*6 37*	*20 50*	*6 17*	*21 20*	*5 50*	*22 08*	*5 06*
14 TH	11 56 19	+18 31	5 24	18 28	5 07	18 46	4 46	19 07	4 16	19 38	3 25	20 29
134	*1.0106*		*21 05*	*7 40*	*21 22*	*7 23*	*21 44*	*7 01*	*22 15*	*6 31*	*23 06*	*5 42*
15 FR	11 56 19	+18 46	5 24	18 29	5 07	18 46	4 45	19 08	4 15	19 39	3 23	20 31
135	*1.0108*		*21 56*	*8 30*	*22 14*	*8 13*	*22 35*	*7 51*	*23 06*	*7 20*	*23 56*	*6 28*
16 SA	11 56 20	+19 00	5 24	18 29	5 06	18 47	4 44	19 09	4 13	19 40	3 21	20 34
136	*1.0110*		*22 47*	*9 23*	*23 03*	*9 06*	*23 23*	*8 45*	*23 51*	*8 15*	*none*	*7 26*
17 SU	11 56 22	+19 14	5 23	18 30	5 06	18 47	4 43	19 10	4 12	19 42	3 18	20 36
137	*1.0112*		*23 35*	*10 19*	*23 49*	*10 03*	*none*	*9 44*	*none*	*9 18*	*0 36*	*8 34*
18 MO	11 56 24	+19 27	5 23	18 30	5 05	18 48	4 42	19 11	4 11	19 43	3 16	20 38
138	*1.0114*		*none*	*11 15*	*none*	*11 03*	*0 07*	*10 47*	*0 30*	*10 25*	*1 08*	*9 50*
19 TU *4 36 LQ*	11 56 26	+19 40	5 23	18 30	5 04	18 49	4 42	19 12	4 09	19 44	3 14	20 41
139	*1.0116*		*0 23*	*12 13*	*0 34*	*12 04*	*0 47*	*11 52*	*1 05*	*11 36*	*1 34*	*11 11*
20 WE	11 56 30	+19 53	5 22	18 31	5 04	18 49	4 41	19 13	4 08	19 46	3 12	20 43
140	*1.0119*		*1 09*	*13 12*	*1 16*	*13 07*	*1 25*	*13 00*	*1 37*	*12 51*	*1 55*	*12 36*
21 TH	11 56 33	+20 06	5 22	18 31	5 03	18 50	4 40	19 14	4 07	19 47	3 10	20 45
141	*1.0121*		*1 54*	*14 12*	*1 57*	*14 11*	*2 01*	*14 09*	*2 07*	*14 07*	*2 15*	*14 04*
22 FR	11 56 38	+20 18	5 22	18 32	5 03	18 51	4 39	19 14	4 06	19 48	3 08	20 47
142	*1.0123*		*2 40*	*15 13*	*2 39*	*15 16*	*2 38*	*15 20*	*2 36*	*15 25*	*2 34*	*15 33*
23 SA	11 56 42	+20 30	5 22	18 32	5 03	18 51	4 39	19 15	4 04	19 50	3 06	20 49
143	*1.0125*		*3 26*	*16 15*	*3 21*	*16 22*	*3 15*	*16 31*	*3 06*	*16 44*	*2 53*	*17 04*
24 SU	11 56 48	+20 41	5 21	18 32	5 02	18 52	4 38	19 16	4 03	19 51	3 04	20 52
144	*1.0126*		*4 15*	*17 18*	*4 06*	*17 29*	*3 54*	*17 43*	*3 39*	*18 03*	*3 15*	*18 34*
25 MO *19 33 NM*	11 56 54	+20 52	5 21	18 33	5 02	18 52	4 37	19 17	4 02	19 52	3 02	20 54
145	*1.0128*		*5 06*	*18 21*	*4 53*	*18 36*	*4 38*	*18 54*	*4 16*	*19 19*	*3 42*	*20 00*
26 TU	11 57 00	+21 03	5 21	18 33	5 01	18 53	4 37	19 18	4 01	19 53	3 00	20 56
146	*1.0130*		*6 00*	*19 23*	*5 45*	*19 40*	*5 25*	*20 01*	*4 58*	*20 30*	*4 15*	*21 19*
27 WE	11 57 07	+21 13	5 21	18 34	5 01	18 54	4 36	19 19	4 00	19 55	2 58	20 58
147	*1.0132*		*6 56*	*20 23*	*6 39*	*20 41*	*6 17*	*21 03*	*5 48*	*21 33*	*4 58*	*22 24*
28 TH	11 57 14	+21 23	5 21	18 34	5 01	18 54	4 35	19 19	3 59	19 56	2 56	21 00
148	*1.0134*		*7 53*	*21 19*	*7 36*	*21 36*	*7 14*	*21 57*	*6 43*	*22 27*	*5 52*	*23 16*
29 FR	11 57 22	+21 33	5 20	18 34	5 00	18 55	4 35	19 20	3 59	19 57	2 54	21 02
149	*1.0135*		*8 50*	*22 10*	*8 34*	*22 26*	*8 13*	*22 45*	*7 44*	*23 11*	*6 56*	*23 54*
30 SA	11 57 30	+21 42	5 20	18 35	5 00	18 55	4 34	19 21	3 58	19 58	2 53	21 03
150	*1.0137*		*9 46*	*22 57*	*9 31*	*23 10*	*9 13*	*23 26*	*8 48*	*23 48*	*8 07*	*none*
31 SU	11 57 38	+21 51	5 20	18 35	5 00	18 56	4 34	19 22	3 57	19 59	2 51	21 05
151	*1.0138*		*10 39*	*23 40*	*10 27*	*23 50*	*10 13*	*none*	*9 52*	*none*	*9 20*	*0 23*

June 1998

6th Month   **30 days**

Greenwich Mean Time

NOTE: For each day, numbers on first line indicate Sun. *Italic* numbers on second line indicate *Moon*.
Degrees are North Latitude.

Moon Phases: FM = full moon; LQ = last quarter; NM = new moon; FQ = first quarter.
Sun's distance is in Astronomical Units.

CAUTION: Must be converted to local time. For instructions see "Calculation of Rise Times."

Day of month, of week, of year / Moon Phase	Sun on Meridian h m s / Distance	Sun's Declination ° ′	20° Rise Sun/Moon	20° Set Sun/Moon	30° Rise Sun/Moon	30° Set Sun/Moon	40° Rise Sun/Moon	40° Set Sun/Moon	50° Rise Sun/Moon	50° Set Sun/Moon	60° Rise Sun/Moon	60° Set Sun/Moon
1 MO	11 57 47	+22 00	5 20	18 36	4 59	18 56	4 33	19 23	3 56	20 00	2 50	21 07
152		*1.0140*	*11 31*	*none*	*11 22*	*none*	*11 11*	*0 02*	*10 56*	*0 19*	*10 33*	*0 46*
2 TU	11 57 57	+22 08	5 20	18 36	4 59	18 57	4 33	19 23	3 55	20 01	2 48	21 09
153	*1 46 FQ*	*1.0141*	*12 21*	*0 19*	*12 15*	*0 26*	*12 09*	*0 35*	*11 59*	*0 46*	*11 45*	*1 04*
3 WE	11 58 06	+22 15	5 20	18 36	4 59	18 57	4 33	19 24	3 55	20 02	2 47	21 09
154		*1.0143*	*13 09*	*0 57*	*13 07*	*1 01*	*13 05*	*1 05*	*13 02*	*1 11*	*12 57*	*1 20*
4 TH	11 58 16	+22 23	5 20	18 37	4 59	18 58	4 32	19 25	3 54	20 03	2 46	21 12
155		*1.0144*	*13 57*	*1 33*	*13 59*	*1 34*	*14 01*	*1 34*	*14 03*	*1 34*	*14 08*	*1 34*
5 FR	11 58 27	+22 30	5 20	18 37	4 59	18 58	4 32	19 25	3 54	20 04	2 44	21 14
156		*1.0146*	*14 45*	*2 10*	*14 50*	*2 06*	*14 57*	*2 02*	*15 05*	*1 57*	*15 18*	*1 49*
6 SA	11 58 38	+22 36	5 20	18 38	4 59	18 59	4 32	19 26	3 53	20 05	2 43	21 15
157		*1.0147*	*15 34*	*2 46*	*15 43*	*2 40*	*15 53*	*2 32*	*16 07*	*2 21*	*16 29*	*2 04*
7 SU	11 58 48	+22 43	5 20	18 38	4 58	18 59	4 31	19 26	3 52	20 06	2 42	21 16
158		*1.0148*	*16 24*	*3 25*	*16 35*	*3 15*	*16 50*	*3 03*	*17 09*	*2 47*	*17 41*	*2 21*
8 MO	11 59 00	+22 48	5 20	18 38	4 58	19 00	4 31	19 27	3 52	20 06	2 41	21 18
159		*1.0149*	*17 15*	*4 05*	*17 29*	*3 53*	*17 47*	*3 37*	*18 11*	*3 16*	*18 51*	*2 42*
9 TU	11 59 11	+22 54	5 20	18 39	4 58	19 00	4 31	19 28	3 52	20 07	2 40	21 19
160		*1.0151*	*18 07*	*4 49*	*18 24*	*4 34*	*18 44*	*4 15*	*19 12*	*3 49*	*19 59*	*3 07*
10 WE	11 59 23	+22 59	5 20	18 39	4 58	19 01	4 31	19 28	3 51	20 08	2 39	21 20
161	*4 19 FM*	*1.0152*	*19 00*	*5 36*	*19 18*	*5 19*	*19 39*	*4 58*	*20 10*	*4 28*	*21 01*	*3 40*
11 TH	11 59 35	+23 03	5 20	18 39	4 58	19 01	4 31	19 29	3 51	20 08	2 39	21 21
162		*1.0153*	*19 53*	*6 26*	*20 10*	*6 08*	*20 33*	*5 46*	*21 03*	*5 15*	*21 55*	*4 23*
12 FR	11 59 47	+23 07	5 20	18 40	4 58	19 01	4 31	19 29	3 51	20 09	2 38	21 22
163		*1.0154*	*20 44*	*7 19*	*21 01*	*7 01*	*21 22*	*6 39*	*21 51*	*6 09*	*22 39*	*5 18*
13 SA	12 00 00	+23 11	5 20	18 40	4 58	19 02	4 31	19 30	3 51	20 10	2 37	21 23
164		*1.0155*	*21 34*	*8 14*	*21 49*	*7 58*	*22 07*	*7 38*	*22 33*	*7 10*	*23 14*	*6 23*
14 SU	12 00 12	+23 14	5 20	18 40	4 58	19 02	4 31	19 30	3 50	20 10	2 37	21 24
165		*1.0156*	*22 22*	*9 11*	*22 34*	*8 57*	*22 49*	*8 40*	*23 09*	*8 16*	*23 41*	*7 37*
15 MO	12 00 25	+23 17	5 20	18 40	4 58	19 02	4 31	19 30	3 50	20 11	2 36	21 25
166		*1.0157*	*23 08*	*10 08*	*23 17*	*9 58*	*23 27*	*9 45*	*23 42*	*9 26*	*none*	*8 57*
16 TU	12 00 38	+23 20	5 21	18 41	4 59	19 03	4 31	19 31	3 50	20 11	2 36	21 26
167		*1.0158*	*23 53*	*11 06*	*23 58*	*10 59*	*none*	*10 51*	*none*	*10 39*	*0 04*	*10 21*
17 WE	12 00 51	+23 22	5 21	18 41	4 59	19 03	4 31	19 31	3 50	20 12	2 36	21 26
168	*10 39 LQ*	*1.0159*	*none*	*12 04*	*none*	*12 02*	*0 03*	*11 58*	*0 11*	*11 53*	*0 23*	*11 46*
18 TH	12 01 04	+23 24	5 21	18 41	4 59	19 03	4 31	19 31	3 50	20 12	2 36	21 27
169		*1.0160*	*0 37*	*13 03*	*0 38*	*13 05*	*0 39*	*13 06*	*0 40*	*13 09*	*0 42*	*13 12*
19 FR	12 01 17	+23 25	5 21	18 42	4 59	19 04	4 31	19 32	3 50	20 12	2 36	21 27
170		*1.0161*	*1 22*	*14 03*	*1 18*	*14 08*	*1 14*	*14 16*	*1 08*	*14 25*	*1 00*	*14 40*
20 SA	12 01 30	+23 26	5 21	18 42	4 59	19 04	4 31	19 32	3 50	20 13	2 36	21 27
171		*1.0162*	*2 08*	*15 03*	*2 00*	*15 13*	*1 51*	*15 25*	*1 39*	*15 42*	*1 20*	*16 08*
21 SU	12 01 43	+23 26	5 21	18 42	4 59	19 04	4 31	19 32	3 51	20 13	2 36	21 28
172		*1.0163*	*2 56*	*16 05*	*2 45*	*16 18*	*2 31*	*16 35*	*2 12*	*16 57*	*1 43*	*17 34*
22 MO	12 01 56	+23 26	5 22	18 42	5 00	19 04	4 31	19 32	3 51	20 13	2 36	21 28
173		*1.0163*	*3 48*	*17 07*	*3 33*	*17 23*	*3 15*	*17 42*	*2 51*	*18 10*	*2 12*	*18 55*
23 TU	12 02 09	+23 26	5 22	18 42	5 00	19 04	4 32	19 33	3 51	20 13	2 36	21 28
174		*1.0164*	*4 42*	*18 07*	*4 25*	*18 25*	*4 04*	*18 46*	*3 35*	*19 17*	*2 49*	*20 07*
24 WE	12 02 22	+23 25	5 22	18 43	5 00	19 05	4 32	19 33	3 51	20 13	2 37	21 28
175	*3 51 NM*	*1.0164*	*5 38*	*19 05*	*5 20*	*19 23*	*4 58*	*19 45*	*4 27*	*20 15*	*3 37*	*21 06*
25 TH	12 02 35	+23 24	5 22	18 43	5 00	19 05	4 32	19 33	3 52	20 13	2 37	21 28
176		*1.0165*	*6 35*	*19 59*	*6 18*	*20 15*	*5 56*	*20 36*	*5 26*	*21 04*	*4 36*	*21 51*
26 FR	12 02 48	+23 22	5 23	18 43	5 01	19 05	4 33	19 33	3 52	20 13	2 38	21 27
177		*1.0165*	*7 32*	*20 49*	*7 16*	*21 03*	*6 57*	*21 21*	*6 29*	*21 45*	*5 44*	*22 25*
27 SA	12 03 00	+23 20	5 23	18 43	5 01	19 05	4 33	19 33	3 53	20 13	2 38	21 27
178		*1.0166*	*8 28*	*21 34*	*8 14*	*21 46*	*7 57*	*22 00*	*7 34*	*22 20*	*6 57*	*22 50*
28 SU	12 03 13	+23 18	5 23	18 43	5 01	19 05	4 33	19 33	3 53	20 13	2 39	21 27
179		*1.0166*	*9 21*	*22 16*	*9 11*	*22 24*	*8 58*	*22 35*	*8 40*	*22 49*	*8 12*	*23 11*
29 MO	12 03 25	+23 15	5 24	18 43	5 02	19 05	4 34	19 33	3 54	20 13	2 40	21 26
180		*1.0166*	*10 12*	*22 55*	*10 05*	*23 00*	*9 57*	*23 06*	*9 45*	*23 15*	*0 06*	*23 28*
30 TU	12 03 37	+23 12	5 24	18 43	5 02	19 06	4 34	19 33	3 54	20 13	2 41	21 26
181		*1.0167*	*11 02*	*23 32*	*10 58*	*23 34*	*10 51*	*23 38*	*10 48*	*23 39*	*10 39*	*23 43*

July 1998

7th Month

31 days

Greenwich Mean Time

NOTE: For each day, numbers on first line indicate Sun. *Italic* numbers on second line indicate *Moon*. Degrees are North Latitude.

Moon Phases: FM = full moon; LQ = last quarter; NM = new moon; FQ = first quarter.
Sun's distance is in Astronomical Units.

CAUTION: Must be converted to local time. For instructions see "Calculation of Rise Times."

Day of month, of week, of year	Sun on Meridian *Moon* Phase h m s	Sun's Decli-nation ° ′ *Distance*	20° Rise Sun *Moon* h m	20° Set Sun *Moon* h m	30° Rise Sun *Moon* h m	30° Set Sun *Moon* h m	40° Rise Sun *Moon* h m	40° Set Sun *Moon* h m	50° Rise Sun *Moon* h m	50° Set Sun *Moon* h m	60° Rise Sun *Moon* h m	60° Set Sun *Moon* h m
1 WE	12 03 49	+23 08	5 24	18 43	5 02	19 05	4 35	19 33	3 55	20 12	2 42	21 25
182	*18 44 FQ*	*1.0167*	*11 51*	*none*	*11 51*	*none*	*11 51*	*none*	*11 51*	*none*	*11 51*	*23 57*
2 TH	12 04 00	+23 04	5 24	18 43	5 03	19 05	4 35	19 33	3 55	20 12	2 43	21 24
183		*1.0167*	*12 39*	*0 08*	*12 42*	*0 07*	*12 47*	*0 04*	*12 52*	*0 02*	*13 02*	*none*
3 FR	12 04 11	+22 59	5 25	18 44	5 03	19 05	4 36	19 32	3 56	20 12	2 44	21 23
184		*1.0167*	*13 27*	*0 45*	*13 34*	*0 40*	*13 43*	*0 33*	*13 54*	*0 25*	*14 13*	*0 12*
4 SA	12 04 22	+22 55	5 25	18 44	5 04	19 05	4 36	19 32	3 57	20 11	2 45	21 22
185		*1.0167*	*14 16*	*1 22*	*14 26*	*1 14*	*14 39*	*1 03*	*14 56*	*0 50*	*15 24*	*0 28*
5 SU	12 04 33	+22 49	5 25	18 44	5 04	19 05	4 37	19 32	3 58	20 11	2 47	21 21
186		*1.0167*	*15 07*	*2 01*	*15 20*	*1 50*	*15 36*	*1 36*	*15 58*	*1 17*	*16 35*	*0 47*
6 MO	12 04 43	+22 44	5 26	18 44	5 04	19 05	4 37	19 32	3 58	20 10	2 48	21 20
187		*1.0167*	*15 58*	*2 44*	*16 14*	*2 29*	*16 33*	*2 12*	*17 00*	*1 48*	*17 44*	*1 10*
7 TU	12 04 53	+22 38	5 26	18 44	5 05	19 05	4 38	19 31	3 59	20 10	2 50	21 19
188		*1.0167*	*16 51*	*3 29*	*17 08*	*3 13*	*17 30*	*2 53*	*18 00*	*2 25*	*18 49*	*1 39*
8 WE	12 05 02	+22 31	5 26	18 43	5 05	19 04	4 39	19 31	4 00	20 09	2 51	21 18
189		*1.0167*	*17 45*	*4 18*	*18 02*	*4 00*	*18 25*	*3 39*	*18 56*	*3 08*	*19 48*	*2 18*
9 TH	12 05 11	+22 24	5 27	18 43	5 06	19 04	4 39	19 31	4 01	20 09	2 53	21 17
190	*16 02 FM*	*1.0166*	*18 38*	*5 10*	*18 55*	*4 53*	*19 17*	*4 31*	*19 47*	*3 59*	*20 37*	*3 08*
10 FR	12 05 20	+22 17	5 27	18 43	5 06	19 04	4 40	19 30	4 02	20 08	2 54	21 15
191		*1.0166*	*19 29*	*6 06*	*19 45*	*5 49*	*20 05*	*5 28*	*20 32*	*4 59*	*21 16*	*4 10*
11 SA	12 05 28	+22 09	5 28	18 43	5 07	19 04	4 41	19 30	4 03	20 07	2 56	21 14
192		*1.0166*	*20 19*	*7 04*	*20 32*	*6 49*	*20 49*	*6 30*	*21 11*	*6 04*	*21 46*	*5 22*
12 SU	12 05 35	+22 01	5 28	18 43	5 07	19 04	4 41	19 29	4 04	20 07	2 58	21 12
193		*1.0166*	*21 07*	*8 02*	*21 17*	*7 50*	*21 29*	*7 35*	*21 45*	*7 15*	*22 11*	*6 42*
13 MO	12 05 43	+21 53	5 28	18 43	5 08	19 03	4 42	19 29	4 05	20 06	2 59	21 11
194		*1.0165*	*21 53*	*9 01*	*21 59*	*8 53*	*22 06*	*8 42*	*22 16*	*8 28*	*22 32*	*8 06*
14 TU	12 05 49	+21 44	5 29	18 43	5 08	19 03	4 43	19 28	4 06	20 05	3 01	21 09
195		*1.0165*	*22 37*	*10 00*	*22 39*	*9 55*	*22 42*	*9 50*	*22 45*	*9 43*	*22 50*	*9 32*
15 WE	12 05 56	+21 35	5 29	18 43	5 09	19 03	4 44	19 28	4 07	20 04	3 03	21 07
196		*1.0165*	*23 21*	*10 58*	*23 19*	*10 58*	*23 17*	*10 58*	*23 13*	*10 58*	*23 08*	*10 58*
16 TH	12 06 02	+21 26	5 29	18 43	5 09	19 02	4 44	19 27	4 08	20 03	3 05	21 06
197	*15 14 LQ*	*1.0164*	*none*	*11 57*	*none*	*12 01*	*23 53*	*12 07*	*23 43*	*12 14*	*23 27*	*12 25*
17 FR	12 06 07	+21 16	5 30	18 42	5 10	19 02	4 45	19 27	4 09	20 02	3 07	21 04
198		*1.0164*	*0 06*	*12 56*	*0 00*	*13 05*	*none*	*13 15*	*none*	*13 29*	*23 49*	*13 51*
18 SA	12 06 12	+21 06	5 30	18 42	5 11	19 02	4 46	19 26	4 11	20 01	3 09	21 02
199		*1.0163*	*0 53*	*13 56*	*0 43*	*14 08*	*0 31*	*14 23*	*0 14*	*14 43*	*none*	*15 16*
19 SU	12 06 16	+20 55	5 31	18 42	5 11	19 01	4 47	19 25	4 12	20 00	3 11	21 00
200		*1.0163*	*1 42*	*14 56*	*1 28*	*15 11*	*1 12*	*15 30*	*0 49*	*15 55*	*0 14*	*16 37*
20 MO	12 06 20	+20 44	5 31	18 42	5 12	19 01	4 47	19 25	4 13	19 59	3 13	20 58
201		*1.0162*	*2 33*	*15 56*	*2 17*	*16 12*	*1 58*	*16 34*	*1 30*	*17 03*	*0 47*	*17 52*
21 TU	12 06 23	+20 33	5 31	18 41	5 12	19 00	4 48	19 24	4 14	19 58	3 15	20 56
202		*1.0161*	*3 27*	*16 53*	*3 10*	*17 11*	*2 48*	*17 33*	*2 18*	*18 04*	*1 29*	*18 55*
22 WE	12 06 26	+20 21	5 32	18 41	5 13	19 00	4 49	19 23	4 16	19 57	3 17	20 54
203		*1.0161*	*4 23*	*17 48*	*4 05*	*18 05*	*3 43*	*18 27*	*3 13*	*18 56*	*2 22*	*19 45*
23 TH	12 06 28	+20 09	5 32	18 41	5 13	18 59	4 50	19 22	4 17	19 55	3 20	20 52
204	*13 45 NM*	*1.0160*	*5 19*	*18 39*	*5 03*	*18 55*	*4 42*	*19 14*	*4 13*	*19 41*	*3 25*	*20 24*
24 FR	12 06 29	+19 57	5 32	18 40	5 14	18 59	4 51	19 22	4 18	19 54	3 22	20 50
205		*1.0159*	*6 15*	*19 27*	*6 01*	*19 40*	*5 43*	*19 56*	*5 17*	*20 18*	*4 36*	*20 53*
25 SA	12 06 30	+19 44	5 33	18 40	5 15	18 58	4 52	19 21	4 19	19 53	3 24	20 47
206		*1.0158*	*7 10*	*20 10*	*6 58*	*20 20*	*6 43*	*20 33*	*6 23*	*20 50*	*5 51*	*21 15*
26 SU	12 06 31	+19 32	5 33	18 40	5 15	18 57	4 53	19 20	4 21	19 51	3 26	20 45
207		*1.0157*	*8 03*	*20 51*	*7 54*	*20 58*	*7 43*	*21 06*	*7 29*	*21 17*	*7 06*	*21 34*
27 MO	12 06 30	+19 18	5 34	18 39	5 16	18 57	4 54	19 19	4 22	19 50	3 28	20 43
208		*1.0156*	*8 53*	*21 29*	*8 48*	*21 32*	*8 42*	*21 37*	*8 33*	*21 42*	*8 20*	*21 50*
28 TU	12 06 30	+19 05	5 34	18 39	5 16	18 56	4 54	19 18	4 23	19 49	3 31	20 41
209		*1.0155*	*9 43*	*22 06*	*9 41*	*22 06*	*9 39*	*22 06*	*9 37*	*22 05*	*9 33*	*22 05*
29 WE	12 06 28	+18 51	5 34	18 38	5 17	18 56	4 55	19 17	4 25	19 47	3 33	20 38
210		*1.0154*	*10 31*	*22 42*	*10 33*	*22 39*	*10 36*	*22 34*	*10 39*	*22 29*	*10 44*	*22 19*
30 TH	12 06 26	+18 37	5 35	18 38	5 18	18 55	4 56	19 16	4 26	19 46	3 35	20 36
211		*1.0153*	*11 20*	*23 19*	*11 25*	*23 12*	*11 32*	*23 04*	*11 41*	*22 52*	*11 55*	*22 35*
31 FR	12 06 23	+18 22	5 35	18 38	5 18	18 54	4 57	19 15	4 27	19 44	3 38	20 33
212	*12 06 FQ*	*1.0151*	*12 08*	*23 58*	*12 17*	*23 47*	*12 28*	*23 35*	*12 42*	*23 18*	*13 06*	*22 52*

August 1998

8th Month   **31 days**

Greenwich Mean Time

NOTE: For each day, numbers on first line indicate Sun. *Italic* numbers on second line indicate *Moon*. Degrees are North Latitude.

Moon Phases: FM = full moon; LQ = last quarter; NM = new moon; FQ = first quarter.
Sun's distance is in Astronomical Units.

CAUTION: Must be converted to local time. For instructions see "Calculation of Rise Times."

Day of month, of week, of year / Moon Phase	Sun on Meridian / Distance	Sun's Declination ° ´	20° Rise Sun/Moon	20° Set Sun/Moon	30° Rise Sun/Moon	30° Set Sun/Moon	40° Rise Sun/Moon	40° Set Sun/Moon	50° Rise Sun/Moon	50° Set Sun/Moon	60° Rise Sun/Moon	60° Set Sun/Moon
1 SA	12 06 20	+18 07	5 35	18 37	5 19	18 53	4 58	19 14	4 29	19 43	3 40	20 31
213	*1.0150*		*12 58*	*none*	*13 09*	*none*	*13 24*	*none*	*13 44*	*23 47*	*14 16*	*23 13*
2 SU	12 06 16	+17 52	5 36	18 37	5 19	18 53	4 59	19 13	4 30	19 41	3 42	20 28
214	*1.0149*		*13 48*	*0 38*	*14 03*	*0 25*	*14 20*	*0 09*	*14 45*	*none*	*15 26*	*23 39*
3 MO	12 06 11	+17 37	5 36	18 36	5 20	18 52	5 00	19 12	4 32	19 40	3 45	20 26
215	*1.0147*		*14 40*	*1 21*	*14 56*	*1 06*	*15 17*	*0 47*	*15 45*	*0 21*	*16 33*	*none*
4 TU	12 06 06	+17 21	5 36	18 36	5 21	18 51	5 01	19 11	4 33	19 38	3 47	20 23
216	*1.0146*		*15 33*	*2 08*	*15 51*	*1 51*	*16 12*	*1 30*	*16 43*	*1 01*	*17 34*	*0 13*
5 WE	12 06 00	+17 05	5 37	18 35	5 21	18 50	5 02	19 10	4 35	19 36	3 50	20 21
217	*1.0145*		*16 26*	*2 59*	*16 44*	*2 41*	*17 06*	*2 19*	*17 37*	*1 48*	*18 28*	*0 57*
6 TH	12 05 54	+16 49	5 37	18 34	5 22	18 50	5 03	19 08	4 36	19 35	3 52	20 18
218	*1.0143*		*17 19*	*3 53*	*17 36*	*3 36*	*17 56*	*3 14*	*18 25*	*2 44*	*19 12*	*1 53*
7 FR	12 05 46	+16 32	5 37	18 34	5 22	18 49	5 04	19 07	4 37	19 33	3 54	20 16
219	*1.0142*		*18 10*	*4 51*	*18 25*	*4 35*	*18 43*	*4 15*	*19 07*	*3 47*	*19 47*	*3 02*
8 SA / *2 11 FM*	12 05 39	+16 15	5 38	18 33	5 23	18 48	5 05	19 06	4 39	19 31	3 57	20 13
220	*1.0140*		*19 00*	*5 50*	*19 12*	*5 37*	*19 26*	*5 20*	*19 45*	*4 57*	*20 15*	*4 20*
9 SU	12 05 30	+15 58	5 38	18 33	5 24	18 47	5 06	19 05	4 40	19 30	3 59	20 10
221	*1.0139*		*19 48*	*6 50*	*19 56*	*6 40*	*20 05*	*6 28*	*20 18*	*6 11*	*20 37*	*5 45*
10 MO	12 05 22	+15 41	5 38	18 32	5 24	18 46	5 06	19 04	4 42	19 28	4 01	20 08
222	*1.0137*		*20 34*	*7 51*	*20 38*	*7 45*	*20 42*	*7 38*	*20 48*	*7 28*	*20 57*	*7 12*
11 TU	12 05 12	+15 23	5 39	18 31	5 25	18 45	5 07	19 02	4 43	19 26	4 04	20 05
223	*1.0135*		*21 20*	*8 51*	*21 19*	*8 49*	*21 18*	*8 47*	*21 17*	*8 45*	*21 16*	*8 41*
12 WE	12 05 02	+15 06	5 39	18 31	5 25	18 44	5 08	19 01	4 45	19 24	4 06	20 02
224	*1.0134*		*22 05*	*9 51*	*22 00*	*9 54*	*21 55*	*9 57*	*21 47*	*10 02*	*21 35*	*10 09*
13 TH	12 04 52	+14 48	5 39	18 30	5 26	18 43	5 09	19 00	4 46	19 22	4 09	19 59
225	*1.0132*		*22 52*	*10 51*	*22 43*	*10 58*	*22 32*	*11 07*	*22 18*	*11 18*	*21 55*	*11 37*
14 FR / *19 50 LQ*	12 04 41	+14 29	5 40	18 30	5 27	18 42	5 10	18 58	4 48	19 21	4 11	19 57
226	*1.0130*		*23 40*	*11 51*	*23 27*	*12 02*	*23 12*	*12 15*	*22 52*	*12 34*	*22 19*	*13 03*
15 SA	12 04 29	+14 11	5 40	18 29	5 27	18 41	5 11	18 57	4 49	19 19	4 14	19 54
227	*1.0129*		*none*	*12 50*	*none*	*13 05*	*23 56*	*13 22*	*23 30*	*13 46*	*22 49*	*14 25*
16 SU	12 04 17	+13 52	5 40	18 28	5 28	18 40	5 12	18 56	4 51	19 17	4 16	19 51
228	*1.0127*		*0 30*	*13 49*	*0 15*	*14 06*	*none*	*14 26*	*none*	*14 54*	*23 27*	*15 41*
17 MO	12 04 05	+13 33	5 40	18 27	5 28	18 39	5 13	18 54	4 52	19 15	4 18	19 48
229	*1.0125*		*1 22*	*14 47*	*1 05*	*15 04*	*0 44*	*15 26*	*0 15*	*15 56*	*none*	*16 47*
18 TU	12 03 52	+13 14	5 41	18 27	5 29	18 38	5 14	18 53	4 54	19 13	4 21	19 45
230	*1.0123*		*2 16*	*15 42*	*1 59*	*15 59*	*1 37*	*16 21*	*1 06*	*16 51*	*0 15*	*17 41*
19 WE	12 03 38	+12 55	5 41	18 26	5 30	18 37	5 15	18 52	4 55	19 11	4 23	19 42
231	*1.0121*		*3 11*	*16 33*	*2 54*	*16 49*	*2 33*	*17 10*	*2 03*	*17 37*	*1 14*	*18 23*
20 TH	12 03 24	+12 35	5 41	18 25	5 30	18 36	5 16	18 50	4 57	19 09	4 26	19 40
232	*1.0119*		*4 07*	*17 21*	*3 51*	*17 35*	*3 32*	*17 53*	*3 05*	*18 17*	*2 21*	*18 55*
21 FR	12 03 10	+12 15	5 42	18 24	5 31	18 35	5 17	18 49	4 58	19 07	4 28	19 37
233	*1.0118*		*5 01*	*18 06*	*4 48*	*18 17*	*4 32*	*18 31*	*4 09*	*18 50*	*3 34*	*19 19*
22 SA / *2 04 NM*	12 02 55	+11 55	5 42	18 24	5 31	18 34	5 18	18 47	5 00	19 05	4 30	19 34
234	*1.0115*		*5 54*	*18 47*	*5 44*	*18 55*	*5 32*	*19 05*	*5 15*	*19 19*	*4 48*	*19 39*
23 SU	12 02 40	+11 35	5 42	18 23	5 32	18 33	5 19	18 46	5 01	19 03	4 33	19 31
235	*1.0113*		*6 45*	*19 26*	*6 39*	*19 31*	*6 31*	*19 37*	*6 20*	*19 45*	*6 02*	*19 56*
24 MO	12 02 24	+11 15	5 42	18 22	5 32	18 32	5 20	18 44	5 03	19 01	4 35	19 28
236	*1.0111*		*7 35*	*20 04*	*7 32*	*20 05*	*7 29*	*20 07*	*7 24*	*20 09*	*7 16*	*20 12*
25 TU	12 02 08	+10 54	5 43	18 21	5 33	18 31	5 21	18 43	5 04	18 59	4 38	19 25
237	*1.0109*		*8 24*	*20 40*	*8 25*	*20 38*	*8 26*	*20 36*	*8 26*	*20 32*	*8 28*	*20 26*
26 WE	12 01 51	+10 33	5 43	18 21	5 33	18 30	5 22	18 41	5 06	18 57	4 40	19 22
238	*1.0107*		*9 13*	*21 17*	*9 17*	*21 12*	*9 22*	*21 05*	*9 29*	*20 55*	*9 39*	*20 41*
27 TH	12 01 34	+10 13	5 43	18 20	5 34	18 29	5 23	18 40	5 07	18 55	4 42	19 19
239	*1.0105*		*10 01*	*21 55*	*10 09*	*21 46*	*10 18*	*21 35*	*10 30*	*21 20*	*10 50*	*20 58*
28 FR	12 01 16	+9 52	5 43	18 19	5 35	18 27	5 24	18 38	5 09	18 53	4 45	19 16
240	*1.0102*		*10 50*	*22 34*	*11 00*	*22 22*	*11 13*	*22 07*	*11 31*	*21 48*	*12 00*	*21 17*
29 SA	12 00 58	+9 30	5 44	18 18	5 35	18 26	5 25	18 37	5 10	18 51	4 47	19 13
241	*1.0100*		*11 39*	*23 15*	*11 53*	*23 01*	*12 09*	*22 43*	*12 32*	*22 19*	*13 09*	*21 40*
30 SU / *5 08 FQ*	12 00 40	+9 09	5 44	18 17	5 36	18 25	5 26	18 35	5 12	18 49	4 49	19 10
242	*1.0098*		*12 30*	*0 00*	*12 46*	*23 43*	*13 06*	*23 23*	*13 32*	*22 55*	*14 16*	*22 09*
31 MO	12 00 22	+8 10	5 44	18 16	5 36	18 24	5 26	18 34	5 13	18 47	4 52	19 07
243	*1.0095*		*13 21*	*none*	*13 39*	*none*	*14 00*	*none*	*14 30*	*23 38*	*15 19*	*22 48*

September 1998

9th Month

30 days

Greenwich Mean Time

NOTE: For each day, numbers on first line indicate Sun. *Italic* numbers on second line indicate *Moon*.
Degrees are North Latitude.

Moon Phases: FM = full moon; LQ = last quarter; NM = new moon; FQ = first quarter.
Sun's distance is in Astronomical Units.

CAUTION: Must be converted to local time. For instructions see "Calculation of Rise Times."

Day of month, of week, of year	Sun on Meridian / *Moon Phase* h m s	Sun's Declination ° ´ / *Distance*	20° Rise Sun *Moon* h m	20° Set Sun *Moon* h m	30° Rise Sun *Moon* h m	30° Set Sun *Moon* h m	40° Rise Sun *Moon* h m	40° Set Sun *Moon* h m	50° Rise Sun *Moon* h m	50° Set Sun *Moon* h m	60° Rise Sun *Moon* h m	60° Set Sun *Moon* h m
1 TU	12 00 03	+8 26	5 44	18 15	5 37	18 23	5 27	18 32	5 15	18 45	4 54	19 04
244		*1.0093*	*14 14*	*0 48*	*14 31*	*0 30*	*14 53*	*0 08*	*15 24*	*none*	*16 16*	*23 37*
2 WE	11 59 44	+8 04	5 45	18 15	5 37	18 22	5 28	18 30	5 16	18 42	4 57	19 01
245		*1.0090*	*15 06*	*1 39*	*15 23*	*1 22*	*15 45*	*1 00*	*16 14*	*0 29*	*17 04*	*none*
3 TH	11 59 24	+7 42	5 45	18 14	5 38	18 20	5 29	18 29	5 18	18 40	4 59	18 58
246		*1.0088*	*15 58*	*2 35*	*16 13*	*2 18*	*16 33*	*1 57*	*16 59*	*1 28*	*17 43*	*0 39*
4 FR	11 59 04	+7 20	5 45	18 13	5 38	18 19	5 30	18 27	5 19	18 38	5 01	18 55
247		*1.0085*	*16 48*	*3 33*	*17 01*	*3 18*	*17 17*	*3 00*	*17 39*	*2 34*	*18 14*	*1 53*
5 SA	11 58 44	+6 58	5 45	18 12	5 39	18 18	5 31	18 26	5 20	18 36	5 04	18 52
248		*1.0083*	*17 37*	*4 33*	*17 47*	*4 21*	*17 59*	*4 07*	*18 14*	*3 47*	*18 39*	*3 15*
6 SU	11 58 24	+6 36	5 45	18 11	5 40	18 17	5 32	18 24	5 22	18 34	5 06	18 49
249	*11 22 FM*	*1.0081*	*18 25*	*5 34*	*18 31*	*5 26*	*18 38*	*5 17*	*18 47*	*5 04*	*19 01*	*4 43*
7 MO	11 58 04	+6 13	5 46	18 10	5 40	18 16	5 33	18 22	5 23	18 32	5 08	18 46
250		*1.0078*	*19 12*	*6 36*	*19 14*	*6 33*	*19 15*	*6 28*	*19 17*	*6 22*	*19 20*	*6 13*
8 TU	11 57 43	+5 51	5 46	18 09	5 41	18 14	5 34	18 21	5 25	18 30	5 11	18 43
251		*1.0076*	*19 59*	*7 38*	*19 56*	*7 39*	*19 52*	*7 40*	*19 47*	*7 42*	*19 39*	*7 45*
9 WE	11 57 22	+5 28	5 46	18 08	5 41	18 13	5 35	18 19	5 26	18 27	5 13	18 40
252		*1.0073*	*20 47*	*8 40*	*20 40*	*8 46*	*20 30*	*8 53*	*20 18*	*9 02*	*20 00*	*9 16*
10 TH	11 57 01	+5 06	5 46	18 07	5 42	18 12	5 36	18 17	5 28	18 25	5 15	18 37
253		*1.0070*	*21 36*	*9 42*	*21 25*	*9 52*	*21 11*	*10 04*	*20 52*	*10 20*	*20 23*	*10 46*
11 FR	11 56 40	+4 43	5 46	18 07	5 42	18 11	5 37	18 16	5 29	18 23	5 18	18 34
254		*1.0068*	*22 26*	*10 44*	*22 12*	*10 57*	*21 54*	*11 13*	*21 30*	*11 36*	*20 51*	*12 12*
12 SA	11 56 19	+4 20	5 47	18 06	5 43	18 09	5 38	18 14	5 31	18 21	5 20	18 31
255		*1.0065*	*23 19*	*11 44*	*23 02*	*12 00*	*22 42*	*12 19*	*22 13*	*12 47*	*21 27*	*13 31*
13 SU	11 55 58	+3 57	5 47	18 05	5 43	18 08	5 39	18 13	5 32	18 19	5 22	18 28
256	*1 59 LQ*	*1.0063*	*none*	*12 42*	*23 55*	*13 00*	*23 33*	*13 21*	*23 03*	*13 51*	*22 12*	*14 41*
14 MO	11 55 37	+3 34	5 47	18 04	5 44	18 07	5 40	18 11	5 34	18 16	5 25	18 25
257		*1.0060*	*0 12*	*13 38*	*none*	*13 56*	*none*	*14 18*	*23 58*	*14 48*	*23 08*	*15 39*
15 TU	11 55 15	+3 11	5 47	18 03	5 44	18 06	5 41	18 09	5 35	18 14	5 27	18 22
258		*1.0058*	*1 07*	*14 30*	*0 50*	*14 47*	*0 28*	*15 08*	*none*	*15 37*	*none*	*16 24*
16 WE	11 54 54	+2 48	5 48	18 02	5 45	18 04	5 42	18 08	5 37	18 12	5 29	18 19
259		*1.0055*	*2 02*	*15 19*	*1 46*	*15 34*	*1 26*	*15 52*	*0 58*	*16 17*	*0 12*	*16 58*
17 TH	11 54 33	+2 25	5 48	18 01	5 45	18 03	5 42	18 06	5 38	18 10	5 32	18 16
260		*1.0052*	*2 56*	*16 04*	*2 42*	*16 16*	*2 24*	*16 31*	*2 01*	*16 52*	*1 22*	*17 24*
18 FR	11 54 11	+2 02	5 48	18 00	5 46	18 02	5 43	18 04	5 40	18 08	5 34	18 13
261		*1.0050*	*3 48*	*16 46*	*3 37*	*16 55*	*3 24*	*17 06*	*3 05*	*17 22*	*2 35*	*17 45*
19 SA	11 53 50	+1 39	5 48	17 59	5 47	18 01	5 44	18 03	5 41	18 05	5 36	18 10
262		*1.0047*	*4 40*	*17 25*	*4 32*	*17 31*	*4 22*	*17 38*	*4 09*	*17 48*	*3 49*	*18 03*
20 SU	11 53 29	+1 15	5 48	17 58	5 47	17 59	5 45	18 01	5 43	18 03	5 39	18 07
263	*17 03 NM*	*1.0044*	*5 30*	*18 03*	*5 26*	*18 05*	*5 20*	*18 08*	*5 13*	*18 12*	*5 02*	*18 18*
21 MO	11 53 08	+0 52	5 49	17 57	5 48	17 58	5 46	17 59	5 44	18 01	5 41	18 04
264		*1.0041*	*6 19*	*18 39*	*6 18*	*18 38*	*6 17*	*18 37*	*6 16*	*18 36*	*6 14*	*18 33*
22 TU	11 52 46	+0 29	5 49	17 56	5 48	17 57	5 47	17 58	5 46	17 59	5 44	18 01
265		*1.0039*	*7 08*	*19 16*	*7 10*	*19 12*	*7 14*	*19 06*	*7 19*	*18 59*	*7 26*	*18 48*
23 WE	11 52 26	+0 05	5 49	17 56	5 49	17 56	5 48	17 56	5 47	17 57	5 46	17 58
266		*1.0036*	*7 56*	*19 53*	*8 02*	*19 45*	*8 10*	*19 36*	*8 20*	*19 23*	*8 37*	*19 03*
24 TH	11 52 05	-0 18	5 49	17 55	5 49	17 54	5 49	17 54	5 49	17 54	5 48	17 55
267		*1.0033*	*8 44*	*20 31*	*8 54*	*20 21*	*9 06*	*20 07*	*9 22*	*19 49*	*9 47*	*19 21*
25 FR	11 51 44	-0 41	5 49	17 54	5 50	17 53	5 50	17 53	5 50	17 52	5 51	17 52
268		*1.0030*	*9 33*	*21 12*	*9 46*	*20 58*	*10 01*	*20 41*	*10 23*	*20 19*	*10 57*	*19 42*
26 SA	11 51 23	-1 05	5 50	17 53	5 50	17 52	5 51	17 51	5 52	17 50	5 53	17 48
269		*1.0027*	*10 23*	*21 54*	*10 38*	*21 39*	*10 57*	*21 19*	*11 22*	*20 52*	*12 04*	*20 09*
27 SU	11 51 03	-1 28	5 50	17 52	5 51	17 51	5 52	17 49	5 53	17 48	5 55	17 45
270		*1.0024*	*11 13*	*22 40*	*11 30*	*22 23*	*11 51*	*22 01*	*12 20*	*21 32*	*13 08*	*20 42*
28 MO	11 50 43	-1 51	5 50	17 51	5 51	17 50	5 53	17 48	5 55	17 46	5 58	17 42
271	*21 12 FQ*	*1.0021*	*12 04*	*23 29*	*12 22*	*23 11*	*12 44*	*22 49*	*13 15*	*22 18*	*14 06*	*21 26*
29 TU	11 50 23	-2 15	5 50	17 50	5 52	17 48	5 54	17 46	5 56	17 43	6 00	17 39
272		*1.0019*	*12 55*	*none*	*13 13*	*none*	*13 35*	*23 42*	*14 06*	*23 12*	*14 57*	*22 21*
30 WE	11 50 03	-2 38	5 51	17 49	5 53	17 47	5 55	17 44	5 58	17 41	6 02	17 36
273		*1.0016*	*13 46*	*0 21*	*14 02*	*0 04*	*14 23*	*none*	*14 51*	*none*	*15 38*	*23 28*

October 1998

10th Month   **31 days**

Greenwich Mean Time

NOTE: For each day, numbers on first line indicate Sun. *Italic* numbers on second line indicate *Moon*. Degrees are North Latitude.

Moon Phases: FM = full moon; LQ = last quarter; NM = new moon; FQ = first quarter.
Sun's distance is in Astronomical Units.

CAUTION: Must be converted to local time. For instructions see "Calculation of Rise Times."

Day of month, of week, of year	Sun on Meridian / Moon Phase h m s	Sun's Decli-nation ° ' / Distance	20° Rise Sun / Moon h m	20° Set Sun / Moon h m	30° Rise Sun / Moon h m	30° Set Sun / Moon h m	40° Rise Sun / Moon h m	40° Set Sun / Moon h m	50° Rise Sun / Moon h m	50° Set Sun / Moon h m	60° Rise Sun / Moon h m	60° Set Sun / Moon h m
1 TH	11 49 43	-3 01	5 51	17 48	5 53	17 46	5 56	17 43	6 00	17 39	6 05	17 33
274		1.0013	*14 35*	*1 16*	*14 50*	*1 01*	*15 08*	*0 41*	*15 32*	*0 13*	*16 12*	*none*
2 FR	11 49 24	-3 25	5 51	17 47	5 54	17 45	5 57	17 41	6 01	17 37	6 07	17 30
275		1.0010	*15 24*	*2 14*	*15 36*	*2 01*	*15 50*	*1 45*	*16 09*	*1 22*	*16 39*	*0 45*
3 SA	11 49 05	-3 48	5 51	17 47	5 54	17 43	5 58	17 40	6 03	17 35	6 10	17 27
276		1.0007	*16 12*	*3 14*	*16 20*	*3 04*	*16 29*	*2 52*	*16 42*	*2 35*	*17 02*	*2 09*
4 SU	11 48 46	-4 11	5 52	17 46	5 55	17 42	5 59	17 38	6 04	17 33	6 12	17 24
277		1.0004	*17 00*	*4 15*	*17 03*	*4 10*	*17 07*	*4 03*	*17 13*	*3 53*	*17 22*	*3 37*
5 MO	11 48 28	-4 34	5 52	17 45	5 55	17 41	6 00	17 36	6 06	17 30	6 14	17 21
278	20 13 FM	1.0001	*17 47*	*5 18*	*17 46*	*5 17*	*17 45*	*5 15*	*17 44*	*5 13*	*17 41*	*5 09*
6 TU	11 48 10	-4 57	5 52	17 44	5 56	17 40	6 01	17 35	6 07	17 28	6 17	17 18
279		.9998	*18 36*	*6 21*	*18 30*	*6 25*	*18 23*	*6 29*	*18 15*	*6 34*	*18 01*	*6 43*
7 WE	11 47 53	-5 20	5 52	17 43	5 57	17 39	6 02	17 33	6 09	17 26	6 19	17 15
280		.9995	*19 25*	*7 25*	*19 16*	*7 33*	*19 04*	*7 43*	*18 48*	*7 56*	*18 24*	*8 16*
8 TH	11 47 35	-5 43	5 53	17 42	5 57	17 37	6 03	17 32	6 10	17 24	6 22	17 12
281		.9993	*20 17*	*8 29*	*20 04*	*8 41*	*19 47*	*8 56*	*19 25*	*9 16*	*18 50*	*9 48*
9 FR	11 47 19	-6 06	5 53	17 41	5 58	17 36	6 04	17 30	6 12	17 22	6 24	17 09
282		.9990	*21 11*	*9 33*	*20 55*	*9 48*	*20 35*	*10 06*	*20 08*	*10 32*	*19 24*	*11 14*
10 SA	11 47 02	-6 29	5 53	17 41	5 58	17 35	6 05	17 29	6 13	17 20	6 26	17 06
283		.9987	*22 06*	*10 34*	*21 48*	*10 51*	*21 26*	*11 12*	*20 56*	*11 42*	*20 06*	*12 31*
11 SU	11 46 47	-6 52	5 53	17 40	5 59	17 34	6 06	17 27	6 15	17 18	6 29	17 04
284		.9984	*23 02*	*11 33*	*22 44*	*11 50*	*22 22*	*12 13*	*21 51*	*12 43*	*21 00*	*13 35*
12 MO	11 46 32	-7 14	5 54	17 39	6 00	17 33	6 07	17 25	6 17	17 16	6 31	17 01
285	11 12 LQ	.9981	*23 57*	*12 27*	*23 41*	*12 44*	*23 20*	*13 06*	*22 51*	*13 36*	*22 02*	*14 25*
13 TU	11 46 17	-7 37	5 54	17 38	6 00	17 32	6 08	17 24	6 18	17 14	6 34	16 58
286		.9979	*none*	*13 17*	*none*	*13 33*	*none*	*13 52*	*23 53*	*14 19*	*23 12*	*15 02*
14 WE	11 46 03	-7 59	5 54	17 37	6 01	17 31	6 09	17 22	6 20	17 11	6 36	16 55
287		.9976	*0 52*	*14 03*	*0 37*	*14 17*	*0 19*	*14 33*	*none*	*14 55*	*none*	*15 31*
15 TH	11 45 49	-8 21	5 55	17 37	6 02	17 30	6 10	17 21	6 21	17 09	6 39	16 52
288		.9973	*1 45*	*14 46*	*1 33*	*14 56*	*1 18*	*15 09*	*0 57*	*15 26*	*0 24*	*15 53*
16 FR	11 45 36	-8 44	5 55	17 36	6 02	17 28	6 11	17 19	6 23	17 07	6 41	16 49
289		.9970	*2 37*	*15 26*	*2 28*	*15 33*	*2 17*	*15 41*	*2 01*	*15 53*	*1 38*	*16 11*
17 SA	11 45 24	-9 06	5 55	17 35	6 03	17 27	6 12	17 18	6 25	17 05	6 44	16 46
290		.9967	*3 27*	*16 03*	*3 21*	*16 07*	*3 14*	*16 11*	*3 05*	*16 17*	*2 51*	*16 26*
18 SU	11 45 12	-9 28	5 56	17 34	6 04	17 26	6 13	17 17	6 26	17 03	6 46	16 43
291		.9965	*4 16*	*16 40*	*4 14*	*16 40*	*4 11*	*16 40*	*4 08*	*16 41*	*4 03*	*16 41*
19 MO	11 45 00	-9 49	5 56	17 34	6 04	17 25	6 14	17 15	6 28	17 01	6 49	16 40
292		.9962	*5 04*	*17 16*	*5 06*	*17 13*	*5 08*	*17 09*	*5 10*	*17 03*	*5 15*	*16 55*
20 TU	11 44 50	-10 11	5 56	17 33	6 05	17 24	6 15	17 14	6 29	16 59	6 51	16 38
293	10 10 NM	.9959	*5 52*	*17 53*	*5 57*	*17 46*	*6 04*	*17 38*	*6 12*	*17 27*	*6 26*	*17 10*
21 WE	11 44 40	-10 33	5 57	17 32	6 06	17 23	6 16	17 12	6 31	16 57	6 54	16 35
294		.9956	*6 41*	*18 31*	*6 49*	*18 21*	*7 00*	*18 09*	*7 14*	*17 52*	*7 37*	*17 27*
22 TH	11 44 31	-10 54	5 57	17 32	6 06	17 22	6 18	17 11	6 33	16 56	6 56	16 32
295		.9953	*7 30*	*19 10*	*7 41*	*18 57*	*7 56*	*18 42*	*8 15*	*18 20*	*8 47*	*17 46*
23 FR	11 44 22	-11 15	5 58	17 31	6 07	17 21	6 19	17 10	6 34	16 54	6 59	16 29
296		.9951	*8 19*	*19 52*	*8 33*	*19 37*	*8 51*	*19 18*	*9 16*	*18 52*	*9 56*	*18 10*
24 SA	11 44 14	-11 36	5 58	17 30	6 08	17 20	6 20	17 08	6 36	16 52	7 01	16 26
297		.9948	*9 09*	*20 36*	*9 26*	*20 19*	*9 46*	*19 58*	*10 14*	*19 29*	*11 01*	*18 41*
25 SU	11 44 07	-11 57	5 58	17 30	6 08	17 19	6 21	17 07	6 38	16 50	7 04	16 24
298		.9945	*10 00*	*21 23*	*10 17*	*21 06*	*10 39*	*20 43*	*11 10*	*20 12*	*12 01*	*19 20*
26 MO	11 44 00	-12 18	5 59	17 29	6 09	17 18	6 22	17 05	6 39	16 48	7 06	16 21
299		.9942	*10 50*	*22 14*	*11 08*	*21 56*	*11 30*	*21 33*	*12 01*	*21 02*	*12 54*	*20 10*
27 TU	11 43 54	-12 38	5 59	17 28	6 10	17 18	6 23	17 04	6 41	16 46	7 09	16 18
300		.9940	*11 39*	*23 06*	*11 56*	*22 50*	*12 18*	*22 29*	*12 48*	*21 59*	*13 38*	*21 11*
28 WE	11 43 49	-12 58	6 00	17 28	6 11	17 17	6 24	17 03	6 43	16 44	7 11	16 15
301	11 47 FQ	.9937	*12 28*	*none*	*12 43*	*23 47*	*13 03*	*23 28*	*13 29*	*23 03*	*14 13*	*22 21*
29 TH	11 43 45	-13 18	6 00	17 27	6 11	17 16	6 25	17 02	6 44	16 43	7 14	16 13
302		.9934	*13 15*	*0 01*	*13 28*	*none*	*13 44*	*none*	*14 06*	*none*	*14 41*	*23 40*
30 FR	11 43 41	-13 38	6 00	17 27	6 12	17 15	6 26	17 00	6 46	16 41	7 16	16 10
303		.9931	*14 02*	*0 58*	*14 11*	*0 47*	*14 23*	*0 32*	*14 39*	*0 12*	*15 04*	*none*
31 SA	11 43 38	-13 58	6 01	17 26	6 13	17 14	6 28	16 59	6 48	16 39	7 19	16 07
304		.9929	*14 48*	*1 57*	*14 53*	*1 49*	*15 01*	*1 39*	*15 10*	*1 25*	*15 25*	*1 04*

November 1998

11th Month
Greenwich Mean Time
30 days

NOTE: For each day, numbers on first line indicate Sun. *Italic* numbers on second line indicate *Moon*. Degrees are North Latitude.

Moon Phases: FM = full moon; LQ = last quarter; NM = new moon; FQ = first quarter. Sun's distance is in Astronomical Units.

CAUTION: Must be converted to local time. For instructions see "Calculation of Rise Times."

Day of month, of week, of year	Sun on Meridian / *Moon Phase* (h m s)	Sun's Declination ° ′ / *Distance*	20° Rise Sun/*Moon*	20° Set Sun/*Moon*	30° Rise Sun/*Moon*	30° Set Sun/*Moon*	40° Rise Sun/*Moon*	40° Set Sun/*Moon*	50° Rise Sun/*Moon*	50° Set Sun/*Moon*	60° Rise Sun/*Moon*	60° Set Sun/*Moon*
1 SU	11 43 36	-14 17	6 01	17 26	6 14	17 13	6 29	16 58	6 49	16 37	7 22	16 05
305		*.9926*	*15 34*	*2 57*	*15 35*	*2 53*	*15 37*	*2 49*	*15 40*	*2 42*	*15 43*	*2 32*
2 MO	11 43 35	-14 37	6 02	17 25	6 14	17 12	6 30	16 57	6 51	16 36	7 24	16 02
306		*.9923*	*16 21*	*3 59*	*16 18*	*3 59*	*16 14*	*4 00*	*16 09*	*4 02*	*16 02*	*4 03*
3 TU	11 43 34	-14 56	6 02	17 25	6 15	17 12	6 31	16 56	6 53	16 34	7 27	16 00
307		*.9921*	*17 10*	*5 02*	*17 02*	*5 07*	*16 53*	*5 14*	*16 41*	*5 23*	*16 23*	*5 37*
4 WE	11 43 35	-15 14	6 03	17 24	6 16	17 11	6 32	16 55	6 54	16 32	7 29	15 57
308	*5 19 FM*	*.9918*	*18 01*	*6 07*	*17 50*	*6 16*	*17 35*	*6 29*	*17 16*	*6 45*	*16 47*	*7 11*
5 TH	11 43 36	-15 33	6 03	17 24	6 17	17 10	6 33	16 53	6 56	16 31	7 32	15 55
309		*.9916*	*18 55*	*7 12*	*18 40*	*7 26*	*18 22*	*7 43*	*17 57*	*8 06*	*17 16*	*8 44*
6 FR	11 43 38	-15 51	6 04	17 23	6 18	17 09	6 34	16 52	6 57	16 29	7 34	15 52
310		*.9913*	*19 52*	*8 17*	*19 34*	*8 33*	*19 13*	*8 54*	*18 44*	*9 22*	*17 55*	*10 09*
7 SA	11 43 40	-16 09	6 04	17 23	6 18	17 09	6 36	16 51	6 59	16 28	7 37	15 50
311		*.9911*	*20 50*	*9 19*	*20 32*	*9 37*	*20 09*	*9 59*	*19 38*	*10 31*	*18 45*	*11 23*
8 SU	11 43 44	-16 27	6 05	17 22	6 19	17 08	6 37	16 50	7 01	16 26	7 39	15 47
312		*.9909*	*21 48*	*10 18*	*21 30*	*10 36*	*21 08*	*10 58*	*20 38*	*11 29*	*19 47*	*12 21*
9 MO	11 43 49	-16 44	6 05	17 22	6 20	17 07	6 38	16 49	7 02	16 25	7 42	15 45
313		*.9906*	*22 45*	*11 12*	*22 29*	*11 28*	*22 09*	*11 49*	*21 41*	*12 18*	*20 56*	*13 04*
10 TU	11 43 54	-17 01	6 06	17 22	6 21	17 07	6 39	16 48	7 04	16 23	7 45	15 42
314		*.9904*	*23 40*	*12 01*	*23 26*	*12 15*	*23 10*	*12 33*	*22 47*	*12 57*	*22 10*	*13 36*
11 WE	11 44 00	-17 18	6 06	17 21	6 22	17 06	6 40	16 47	7 06	16 22	7 47	15 40
315	*0 29 LQ*	*.9902*	*none*	*12 45*	*none*	*12 57*	*none*	*13 11*	*23 52*	*13 30*	*23 25*	*14 01*
12 TH	11 44 07	-17 34	6 07	17 21	6 22	17 06	6 41	16 47	7 07	16 20	7 50	15 38
316		*.9899*	*0 32*	*13 26*	*0 22*	*13 34*	*0 10*	*13 45*	*none*	*13 58*	*none*	*14 20*
13 FR	11 44 15	-17 51	6 07	17 21	6 23	17 05	6 42	16 46	7 09	16 19	7 52	15 36
317		*.9897*	*1 23*	*14 04*	*1 16*	*14 09*	*1 08*	*14 15*	*0 57*	*14 23*	*0 39*	*14 36*
14 SA	11 44 24	-18 07	6 08	17 21	6 24	17 05	6 44	16 45	7 11	16 18	7 55	15 33
318		*.9895*	*2 13*	*14 41*	*2 09*	*14 43*	*2 05*	*14 44*	*2 00*	*14 47*	*1 52*	*14 50*
15 SU	11 44 34	-18 22	6 09	17 20	6 25	17 04	6 45	16 44	7 12	16 16	7 57	15 31
319		*.9893*	*3 01*	*15 17*	*3 01*	*15 15*	*3 02*	*15 13*	*3 02*	*15 09*	*3 03*	*15 04*
16 MO	11 44 44	-18 38	6 09	17 20	6 26	17 04	6 46	16 43	7 14	16 15	8 00	15 29
320		*.9890*	*3 49*	*15 54*	*3 53*	*15 48*	*3 58*	*15 41*	*4 04*	*15 32*	*4 15*	*15 18*
17 TU	11 44 56	-18 52	6 10	17 20	6 26	17 03	6 47	16 42	7 16	16 14	8 02	15 27
321		*.9888*	*4 37*	*16 31*	*4 45*	*16 22*	*4 54*	*16 11*	*5 06*	*15 56*	*5 26*	*15 34*
18 WE	11 45 08	-19 07	6 10	17 20	6 27	17 03	6 48	16 42	7 17	16 13	8 05	15 25
322		*.9886*	*5 26*	*17 09*	*5 37*	*16 58*	*5 50*	*16 43*	*6 08*	*16 23*	*6 37*	*15 52*
19 TH	11 45 21	-19 21	6 11	17 20	6 28	17 02	6 49	16 41	7 19	16 12	8 07	15 23
323	*4 28 NM*	*.9884*	*6 16*	*17 51*	*6 29*	*17 36*	*6 46*	*17 18*	*7 09*	*16 53*	*7 47*	*16 14*
20 FR	11 45 35	-19 35	6 12	17 19	6 29	17 02	6 50	16 40	7 20	16 10	8 10	15 21
324		*.9882*	*7 06*	*18 34*	*7 22*	*18 18*	*7 42*	*17 57*	*8 09*	*17 28*	*8 55*	*16 42*
21 SA	11 45 50	-19 49	6 12	17 19	6 30	17 02	6 52	16 40	7 22	16 09	8 12	15 19
325		*.9880*	*7 57*	*19 21*	*8 14*	*19 03*	*8 36*	*18 41*	*9 07*	*18 09*	*9 58*	*17 18*
22 SU	11 46 05	-20 02	6 13	17 19	6 31	17 01	6 53	16 39	7 23	16 08	8 14	15 17
326		*.9878*	*8 47*	*20 10*	*9 05*	*19 52*	*9 28*	*19 29*	*10 00*	*18 57*	*10 53*	*18 04*
23 MO	11 46 22	-20 15	6 13	17 19	6 31	17 01	6 54	16 39	7 25	16 07	8 17	15 15
327		*.9876*	*9 37*	*21 02*	*9 55*	*20 44*	*10 17*	*20 22*	*10 48*	*19 52*	*11 40*	*19 01*
24 TU	11 46 39	-20 27	6 14	17 19	6 32	17 01	6 55	16 38	7 26	16 06	8 19	15 14
328		*.9874*	*10 25*	*21 55*	*10 42*	*21 40*	*11 02*	*21 20*	*11 31*	*20 53*	*12 17*	*20 08*
25 WE	11 46 56	-20 40	6 15	17 19	6 33	17 01	6 56	16 38	7 28	16 06	8 21	15 12
329		*.9872*	*11 12*	*22 50*	*11 26*	*22 37*	*11 44*	*22 21*	*12 08*	*21 58*	*12 47*	*21 22*
26 TH	11 47 15	-20 51	6 15	17 19	6 34	17 00	6 57	16 37	7 29	16 05	8 24	15 10
330		*.9870*	*11 58*	*23 46*	*12 09*	*23 37*	*12 23*	*23 25*	*12 41*	*23 08*	*13 11*	*22 42*
27 FR	11 47 34	-21 03	6 16	17 19	6 35	17 00	6 58	16 37	7 31	16 04	8 26	15 09
331	*0 24 FQ*	*.9868*	*12 42*	*none*	*12 50*	*none*	*12 59*	*none*	*13 12*	*none*	*13 31*	*none*
28 SA	11 47 54	-21 14	6 17	17 19	6 36	17 00	6 59	16 36	7 32	16 03	8 28	15 07
332		*.9866*	*13 26*	*0 44*	*13 30*	*0 38*	*13 34*	*0 31*	*13 40*	*0 21*	*13 49*	*0 05*
29 SU	11 48 15	-21 24	6 17	17 19	6 36	17 00	7 00	16 36	7 34	16 03	8 30	15 06
333		*.9865*	*14 11*	*1 42*	*14 10*	*1 41*	*14 09*	*1 39*	*14 08*	*1 36*	*14 06*	*1 32*
30 MO	11 48 36	-21 34	6 18	17 19	6 37	17 00	7 01	16 36	7 35	16 02	8 32	15 04
334		*.9863*	*14 57*	*2 42*	*14 52*	*2 45*	*14 45*	*2 49*	*14 37*	*2 54*	*14 25*	*3 01*

December 1998

12th Month

Greenwich Mean Time

31 days

NOTE: For each day, numbers on first line indicate Sun. *Italic* numbers on second line indicate *Moon*. Degrees are North Latitude.

Moon Phases: FM = full moon; LQ = last quarter; NM = new moon; FQ = first quarter.
Sun's distance is in Astronomical Units.

CAUTION: Must be converted to local time. For instructions see "Calculation of Rise Times."

Day of month, of week, of year	Sun on Meridian Moon Phase h m s	Sun's Declination ° ' Distance	20° Rise Sun Moon h m	20° Set Sun Moon h m	30° Rise Sun Moon h m	30° Set Sun Moon h m	40° Rise Sun Moon h m	40° Set Sun Moon h m	50° Rise Sun Moon h m	50° Set Sun Moon h m	60° Rise Sun Moon h m	60° Set Sun Moon h m
1 TU	11 48 58	-21 44	6 18	17 19	6 38	17 00	7 02	16 35	7 36	16 01	8 34	15 03
335		.9861	15 45	3 44	15 36	3 52	15 24	4 01	15 09	4 13	14 45	4 33
2 WE	11 49 21	-21 53	6 19	17 19	6 39	17 00	7 03	16 35	7 38	16 01	8 36	15 02
336		.9860	16 37	4 48	16 24	5 00	16 08	5 14	15 46	5 34	15 11	6 06
3 TH	11 49 44	-22 02	6 20	17 20	6 40	17 00	7 04	16 35	7 39	16 00	8 38	15 01
337	15 20 FM	.9858	17 32	5 53	17 16	6 08	16 56	6 27	16 29	6 53	15 44	7 36
4 FR	11 50 08	-22 11	6 20	17 20	6 40	17 00	7 05	16 35	7 40	16 00	8 40	15 00
338		.9857	18 30	6 58	18 13	7 15	17 50	7 37	17 19	8 07	16 28	8 58
5 SA	11 50 32	-22 19	6 21	17 20	6 41	17 00	7 06	16 35	7 41	15 59	8 42	14 59
339		.9855	19 30	8 00	19 12	8 19	18 49	8 41	18 18	9 13	17 25	10 06
6 SU	11 50 57	-22 26	6 22	17 20	6 42	17 00	7 07	16 35	7 43	15 59	8 44	14 58
340		.9854	20 30	8 59	20 13	9 16	19 52	9 38	19 22	10 09	18 33	10 59
7 MO	11 51 22	-22 33	6 22	17 20	6 43	17 00	7 08	16 35	7 44	15 59	8 46	14 57
341		.9852	21 28	9 52	21 13	10 08	20 55	10 27	20 29	10 54	19 48	11 38
8 TU	11 51 48	-22 40	6 23	17 21	6 43	17 00	7 09	16 35	7 45	15 58	8 47	14 56
342		.9851	22 23	10 40	22 12	10 53	21 57	11 09	21 37	11 31	21 05	12 06
9 WE	11 52 15	-22 46	6 23	17 21	6 44	17 00	7 10	16 35	7 46	15 58	8 49	14 55
343		.9850	23 17	11 23	23 08	11 33	22 58	11 46	22 44	12 02	22 22	12 27
10 TH	11 52 42	-22 52	6 24	17 21	6 45	17 01	7 11	16 35	7 47	15 58	8 50	14 55
344	17 55 LQ	.9849	none	12 04	none	12 10	23 57	12 18	23 49	12 29	23 36	12 45
11 FR	11 53 09	-22 58	6 25	17 22	6 45	17 01	7 11	16 35	7 48	15 58	8 52	14 54
345		.9847	0 07	12 41	0 03	12 44	none	12 48	none	12 52	none	13 00
12 SA	11 53 37	-23 02	6 25	17 22	6 46	17 01	7 12	16 35	7 49	15 58	8 53	14 54
346		.9846	0 57	13 18	0 55	13 17	0 54	13 16	0 52	13 15	0 49	13 13
13 SU	11 54 05	-23 07	6 26	17 22	6 47	17 01	7 13	16 35	7 50	15 58	8 54	14 53
347		.9845	1 45	13 54	1 47	13 50	1 50	13 44	1 55	13 38	2 01	13 27
14 MO	11 54 34	-23 11	6 26	17 23	6 47	17 02	7 14	16 35	7 51	15 58	8 56	14 53
348		.9844	2 33	14 30	2 39	14 23	2 46	14 14	2 57	14 01	3 13	13 42
15 TU	11 55 03	-23 14	6 27	17 23	6 48	17 02	7 14	16 36	7 52	15 58	8 57	14 53
349		.9843	3 21	15 08	3 31	14 58	3 43	14 44	3 58	14 26	4 24	13 58
16 WE	11 55 32	-23 18	6 28	17 23	6 49	17 02	7 15	16 36	7 52	15 58	8 58	14 53
350		.9842	4 11	15 49	4 23	15 35	4 39	15 18	5 00	14 55	5 34	14 18
17 TH	11 56 01	-23 20	6 28	17 24	6 49	17 03	7 16	16 36	7 53	15 59	8 59	14 53
351		.9841	5 01	16 31	5 16	16 15	5 35	15 56	6 01	15 28	6 44	14 44
18 FR	11 56 30	-23 22	6 29	17 24	6 50	17 03	7 16	16 37	7 54	15 59	9 00	14 53
352	22 43 NM	.9841	5 52	17 17	6 09	17 00	6 30	16 38	7 00	16 07	7 50	15 16
19 SA	11 57 00	-23 24	6 29	17 25	6 50	17 04	7 17	16 37	7 55	15 59	9 01	14 53
353		.9840	6 43	18 06	7 01	17 48	7 24	17 25	7 56	16 53	8 49	15 59
20 SU	11 57 30	-23 25	6 30	17 25	6 51	17 04	7 18	16 37	7 55	16 00	9 01	14 54
354		.9839	7 34	18 58	7 52	18 40	8 15	18 17	8 47	17 46	9 40	16 53
21 MO	11 58 00	-23 26	6 30	17 26	6 52	17 04	7 18	16 38	7 56	16 00	9 02	14 54
355		.9838	8 24	19 51	8 41	19 35	9 02	19 14	9 32	18 45	10 21	17 57
22 TU	11 58 30	-23 26	6 31	17 26	6 52	17 05	7 19	16 38	7 56	16 01	9 02	14 55
356		.9838	9 11	20 46	9 27	20 32	9 46	20 14	10 12	19 50	10 53	19 10
23 WE	11 59 00	-23 26	6 31	17 27	6 53	17 05	7 19	16 39	7 57	16 01	9 03	14 55
357		.9837	9 57	21 42	10 10	21 31	10 25	21 17	10 46	20 58	11 19	20 28
24 TH	11 59 30	-23 25	6 32	17 27	6 53	17 06	7 20	16 39	7 57	16 02	9 03	14 56
358		.9836	10 42	22 38	10 51	22 31	11 02	22 22	11 17	22 09	11 40	21 50
25 FR	11 59 59	-23 24	6 32	17 28	6 53	17 07	7 20	16 40	7 58	16 03	9 03	14 57
359		.9836	11 25	23 35	11 30	23 31	11 36	23 27	11 45	23 22	11 58	23 13
26 SA	12 00 29	-23 23	6 33	17 28	6 54	17 07	7 20	16 41	7 58	16 03	9 03	14 58
360	10 47 FQ	.9835	12 08	none	12 09	none	12 10	none	12 12	none	12 14	none
27 SU	12 00 59	-23 21	6 33	17 29	6 54	17 08	7 21	16 41	7 58	16 04	9 04	14 59
361		.9835	12 51	0 32	12 48	0 33	12 44	0 35	12 39	0 36	12 31	0 39
28 MO	12 01 28	-23 18	6 33	17 29	6 55	17 08	7 21	16 42	7 58	16 05	9 04	15 00
362		.9834	13 37	1 31	13 29	1 36	13 20	1 43	13 08	1 52	12 50	2 06
29 TU	12 01 57	-23 15	6 34	17 30	6 55	17 09	7 21	16 43	7 58	16 06	9 03	15 01
363		.9834	14 25	2 32	14 13	2 41	14 00	2 53	13 41	3 09	13 12	3 35
30 WE	12 02 26	-23 12	6 34	17 31	6 55	17 10	7 21	16 44	7 59	16 06	9 03	15 02
364		.9833	15 17	3 34	15 02	3 47	14 44	4 01	14 19	4 27	13 39	5 04
31 TH	12 02 55	-23 09	6 35	17 31	6 56	17 10	7 22	16 44	7 59	16 07	9 03	15 03
365		.9833	16 12	4 37	15 55	4 54	15 33	5 14	15 04	5 42	14 16	6 29

Perpetual Calendar

The number shown for each year indicates which Gregorian calendar to use. For 1583-1802, see "Gregorian Calendar" on page 312. For 1803-20, use numbers for 1983-2000, respectively. For Julian Calendar, see "Julian Calendar" on page 312.

Year		Year		Year		Year		Year	
1821	2	1847	6	1873	4	1899	1	1925	5
1822	3	1848	14	1874	5	1900	2	1926	6
1823	4	1849	2	1875	6	1901	3	1927	7
1824	12	1850	3	1876	14	1902	4	1928	8
1825	7	1851	4	1877	2	1903	5	1929	3
1826	1	1852	12	1878	3	1904	13	1930	4
1827	2	1853	7	1879	4	1905	1	1931	5
1828	10	1854	1	1880	12	1906	2	1932	13
1829	5	1855	2	1881	7	1907	3	1933	1
1830	6	1856	10	1882	1	1908	11	1934	2
1831	7	1857	5	1883	2	1909	6	1935	3
1832	8	1858	6	1884	10	1910	7	1936	11
1833	4	1859	7	1885	5	1911	1	1937	6
1834	5	1860	8	1886	6	1912	9	1938	7
1835	6	1861	3	1887	7	1913	4	1939	1
1836	13	1862	4	1888	8	1914	5	1940	9
1837	1	1863	5	1889	3	1915	6	1941	4
1838	2	1864	13	1890	4	1916	14	1942	5
1839	3	1865	1	1891	5	1917	2	1943	6
1840	11	1866	2	1892	13	1918	3	1944	14
1841	6	1867	3	1893	1	1919	4	1945	2
1842	7	1868	11	1894	2	1920	12	1946	3
1843	1	1869	6	1895	3	1921	7	1947	4
1844	9	1870	7	1896	11	1922	1	1948	12
1845	4	1871	1	1897	6	1923	2	1949	7
1846	5	1872	9	1898	7	1924	10	1950	1

Year		Year		Year		Year		Year	
1951	2	1977	7	2003	4	2029	2	2055	6
1952	10	1978	1	2004	12	2030	3	2056	14
1953	5	1979	2	2005	7	2031	4	2057	2
1954	6	1980	10	2006	1	2032	12	2058	3
1955	7	1981	5	2007	2	2033	7	2059	4
1956	8	1982	6	2008	10	2034	1	2060	12
1957	3	1983	7	2009	5	2035	2	2061	7
1958	4	1984	8	2010	6	2036	10	2062	1
1959	5	1985	3	2011	7	2037	5	2063	2
1960	13	1986	4	2012	8	2038	6	2064	10
1961	1	1987	5	2013	3	2039	7	2065	5
1962	2	1988	13	2014	4	2040	8	2066	6
1963	3	1989	1	2015	5	2041	3	2067	7
1964	11	1990	2	2016	13	2042	4	2068	8
1965	6	1991	3	2017	1	2043	5	2069	3
1966	7	1992	11	2018	2	2044	13	2070	4
1967	1	1993	6	2019	3	2045	1	2071	5
1968	9	1994	7	2020	11	2046	2	2072	13
1969	4	1995	1	2021	6	2047	3	2073	1
1970	5	1996	9	2022	7	2048	11	2074	2
1971	6	1997	4	2023	1	2049	6	2075	3
1972	14	1998	5	2024	9	2050	7	2076	11
1973	2	1999	6	2025	4	2051	1	2077	6
1974	3	2000	14	2026	5	2052	9	2078	7
1975	4	2001	2	2027	6	2053	4	2079	1
1976	12	2002	3	2028	14	2054	5	2080	9

The remainder of the page consists of fourteen reference calendars, numbered 1 through 6 and including the sample years 1997, 1998, and 1999, each showing all twelve months (JANUARY, FEBRUARY, MARCH, APRIL, MAY, JUNE, JULY, AUGUST, SEPTEMBER, OCTOBER, NOVEMBER, DECEMBER) with day headings S M T W T F S.

The page is a perpetual calendar reference chart containing eight numbered year-type calendars (7, 8, 9, 10, 11, 12, 13, 14), each showing all twelve months (JANUARY through DECEMBER) with day columns S M T W T F S.

Julian and Gregorian Calendars; Leap Year; Century

Calendars based on the movements of the sun and moon have been used since ancient times, but none has been perfect. The **Julian calendar**, under which Western nations measured time until AD 1582, was authorized by Julius Caesar in 46 BC, the year 709 of Rome. His expert was a Greek, Sosigenes. The Julian calendar, on the assumption that the length of the true year was 365 1/4 days, gave every 4th year 366 days. St. Bede the Venerable, an Anglo-Saxon monk, announced in AD 730 that the 365 1/4-day Julian year was 11 min, 14 sec too long, a cumulative error of about a day every 128 years, but nothing was done about it for more than 800 years.

By 1582 the accumulated error was estimated to amount to 10 days. In that year Pope Gregory XIII decreed that the day following Oct. 4, 1582, should be called Oct. 15, thus dropping 10 days and initiating what became known as the **Gregorian calendar**.

However, with common years 365 days and a 366-day leap year every 4th year, the error in the length of the year would have recurred at the rate of a little more than 3 days every 400 years. Therefore, 3 of every 4 centesimal years (years ending in 00) were made common years, not leap years. Thus, 1600 was a leap year; 1700, 1800, and 1900 were not, but 2000 will be. **Leap years** are those years divisible by 4, except centesimal years, which are common unless divisible by 400.

The Gregorian calendar was adopted at once by France, Italy, Spain, Portugal, and Luxembourg. Within 2 years most German Catholic states, Belgium, and parts of Switzerland and the Netherlands were brought under the new calendar, and Hungary followed in 1587. The rest of the Netherlands, along with Denmark and the German Protestant states, made the change in 1699-1700. (German Protestants retained the Julian calendar's reckoning of the movable feast of Easter until 1776.)

The British government imposed the Gregorian calendar on all its possessions, including the American colonies, in 1752. The British decreed that the day following Sept. 2, 1752, should be called Sept. 14, a loss of 11 days. All dates preceding were marked OS, for Old Style. In addition, New Year's Day was moved to Jan. 1 from Mar. 25 (e.g., under the old reckoning, Mar. 24, 1700, had been followed by Mar. 25, 1701). George Washington's birthdate, which was Feb. 11, 1731, OS, became Feb. 22, 1732, NS (New Style). In 1753 Sweden too went Gregorian, but retaining the Julian calendar's rules for Easter until 1844.

In 1793 the French revolutionary government adopted a calendar of 12 months of 30 days with 5 extra days in September of each common year and a 6th every 4th year. Napoleon reinstated the Gregorian calendar in 1806.

The Gregorian system later spread to non-European regions, first in the European colonies and then in the independent countries, replacing traditional calendars at least for official purposes. Japan in 1873, Egypt in 1875, China in 1912, and Turkey in 1925 made the change, usually in conjunction with political upheavals. In China, the republican government began reckoning years from its 1911 founding — e.g., 1948 was designated the year 37. After 1949, the Communists adopted the Common, or Christian Era, year count, even for the traditional lunar calendar.

In 1918 the revolutionary government in the Soviet Union decreed that the day after Jan. 31, 1918, OS, would become Feb. 14, 1918, NS. Greece followed in 1923. (The Russian Orthodox Church has retained the Julian calendar, as have various Middle Eastern Christian sects.) For the first time in history, all major cultures have one calendar.

To convert from the Julian to the Gregorian calendar, add 10 days to dates Oct. 5, 1582, through Feb. 28, 1700; after that date add 11 days through Feb. 28, 1800; 12 days through Feb. 28, 1900; and 13 days through Feb. 28, 2100.

A **century** consists of 100 consecutive years. The 1st century AD may be said to have consisted of the years 1 through 100. The 20th century by this reckoning consists of the years 1901 through 2000 and would end Dec. 31, 2000, as would the millennium. The 21st century will begin Jan. 1, 2001.

Julian Calendar

To find which of the 14 calendars printed on pages 310-11 applies to any year, starting Jan. 1, under the Julian system, find the century for the desired year in the 3 leftmost columns below. Read across and find the year in the 4 top rows. Then read down. The number in the intersection is the calendar designation for that year.

Year (last 2 figures of desired year)

Century			01 02 03 04	05 06 07 08	09 10 11 12	13 14 15 16	17 18 19 20	21 22 23 24	25 26 27 28
			29 30 31 32	33 34 35 36	37 38 39 40	41 42 43 44	45 46 47 48	49 50 51 52	53 54 55 56
			57 58 59 60	61 62 63 64	65 66 67 68	69 70 71 72	73 74 75 76	77 78 79 80	81 82 83 84
		00	85 86 87 88	89 90 91 92	93 94 95 96	97 98 99			
0	700 1400	12	7 1 2 10	5 6 7 8	3 4 5 13	1 2 3 11	6 7 1 9	4 5 6 14	2 3 4 12
100	800 1500	11	6 7 1 9	4 5 6 14	2 3 4 12	7 1 2 10	5 6 7 8	3 4 5 13	1 2 3 11
200	900 1600	10	5 6 7 8	3 4 5 13	1 2 3 11	6 7 1 9	4 5 6 14	2 3 4 12	7 1 2 10
300	1000 1700	9	4 5 6 14	2 3 4 12	7 1 2 10	5 6 7 8	3 4 5 13	1 2 3 11	6 7 1 9
400	1100 1800	8	3 4 5 13	1 2 3 11	6 7 1 9	4 5 6 14	2 3 4 12	7 1 2 10	5 6 7 8
500	1200 1900	14	2 3 4 12	7 1 2 10	5 6 7 8	3 4 5 13	1 2 3 11	6 7 1 9	4 5 6 14
600	1300 2000	13	1 2 3 11	6 7 1 9	4 5 6 14	2 3 4 12	7 1 2 10	5 6 7 8	3 4 5 13

Gregorian Calendar

Choose the desired year from the table below or from page 310 (for years 1803 to 2080). The number after each year designates which calendar to use for that year, as shown on pages 310-11. (The Gregorian calendar was inaugurated Oct. 15, 1582. From that date to Dec. 31, 1582, use calendar 6.)

1583-1802

Year		Year		Year		Year		Year		Year		Year		Year		Year		Year		Year	
1583	7	1603	4	1623	1	1643	5	1663	2	1683	6	1703	2	1723	6	1743	3	1763	7	1783	4
1584	8	1604	12	1624	9	1644	13	1664	10	1684	14	1704	10	1724	14	1744	11	1764	8	1784	12
1585	3	1605	7	1625	4	1645	1	1665	5	1685	2	1705	5	1725	2	1745	6	1765	3	1785	7
1586	4	1606	1	1626	5	1646	2	1666	6	1686	3	1706	6	1726	3	1746	7	1766	4	1786	1
1587	5	1607	2	1627	6	1647	3	1667	7	1687	4	1707	7	1727	4	1747	1	1767	5	1787	2
1588	13	1608	10	1628	14	1648	11	1668	8	1688	12	1708	8	1728	12	1748	9	1768	13	1788	10
1589	1	1609	5	1629	2	1649	6	1669	3	1689	7	1709	3	1729	7	1749	4	1769	1	1789	5
1590	2	1610	6	1630	3	1650	7	1670	4	1690	1	1710	4	1730	1	1750	5	1770	2	1790	6
1591	3	1611	7	1631	4	1651	1	1671	5	1691	2	1711	5	1731	2	1751	6	1771	3	1791	7
1592	11	1612	8	1632	12	1652	9	1672	13	1692	10	1712	13	1732	10	1752	14	1772	11	1792	8
1593	6	1613	3	1633	7	1653	4	1673	1	1693	5	1713	1	1733	5	1753	2	1773	6	1793	3
1594	7	1614	4	1634	1	1654	5	1674	2	1694	6	1714	2	1734	6	1754	3	1774	7	1794	4
1595	1	1615	5	1635	2	1655	6	1675	3	1695	7	1715	3	1735	7	1755	4	1775	1	1795	5
1596	9	1616	13	1636	10	1656	14	1676	11	1696	8	1716	11	1736	8	1756	12	1776	9	1796	13
1597	4	1617	1	1637	5	1657	2	1677	6	1697	3	1717	6	1737	3	1757	7	1777	4	1797	1
1598	5	1618	2	1638	6	1658	3	1678	7	1698	4	1718	7	1738	4	1758	1	1778	5	1798	2
1599	6	1619	3	1639	7	1659	4	1679	1	1699	5	1719	1	1739	5	1759	2	1779	6	1799	3
1600	14	1620	11	1640	8	1660	12	1680	9	1700	6	1720	9	1740	6	1760	10	1780	14	1800	4
1601	2	1621	6	1641	3	1661	7	1681	4	1701	7	1721	4	1741	1	1761	5	1781	2	1801	5
1602	3	1622	7	1642	4	1662	1	1682	5	1702	1	1722	5	1742	2	1762	6	1782	3	1802	6

The Julian Period

How many days have you lived? To determine this, multiply your age by 365, add the number of days since your last birthday, and account for all leap years. Chances are your calculations will go wrong somewhere. Astronomers, however, find it convenient to express dates and time intervals in days rather than in years, months, and days. This is done by placing events within the Julian period.

The Julian period was devised in 1582 by the French classical scholar Joseph Scaliger (1540-1609) and named after his father, Julius Caesar Scaliger, not after the Julian calendar. Scaliger began Julian Day (JD) #1 at noon, Jan. 1, 4713 BC, the most recent time that 3 major chronological cycles began on the same day: 1) the 28-year solar cycle,

after which dates in the Julian calendar (e.g., Feb. 11) return to the same days of the week (e.g., Monday); (2) the 19-year lunar cycle, after which the phases of the moon return to the same dates of the year; and (3) the 15-year indiction cycle, used in ancient Rome to regulate taxes. It will take 7,980 years to complete the period, the product of 28, 19, and 15.

Noon of Dec. 31, 1997, marks the beginning of JD 2,450,814; that many days will have passed since the start of the Julian period. The JD at noon of any date in 1998 may be found by adding to this figure the day of the year for that date, which can be obtained from the left half of the "Days Between Two Dates" chart.

Days Between Two Dates

This table covers a period of 2 ordinary years. To use the table, find the **boldface number** for each date and subtract the smaller from the larger. Example—For days between Feb. 10, 1997, and Dec. 15, 1998, subtract 41 from 714; answer is 673 days. For leap year, such as 2000, one day must be added: answer for days between Feb. 10, 1999, and Dec. 15, 2000, would be 674.

First Year

Date	Jan.	Feb.	Mar.	April	May	June	July	Aug.	Sept.	Oct.	Nov.	Dec.
1	1	32	60	91	121	152	182	213	244	274	305	335
2	2	33	61	92	122	153	183	214	245	275	306	336
3	3	34	62	93	123	154	184	215	246	276	307	337
4	4	35	63	94	124	155	185	216	247	277	308	338
5	5	36	64	95	125	156	186	217	248	278	309	339
6	6	37	65	96	126	157	187	218	249	279	310	340
7	7	38	66	97	127	158	188	219	250	280	311	341
8	8	39	67	98	128	159	189	220	251	281	312	342
9	9	40	68	99	129	160	190	221	252	282	313	343
10	10	41	69	100	130	161	191	222	253	283	314	344
11	11	42	70	101	131	162	192	223	254	284	315	345
12	12	43	71	102	132	163	193	224	255	285	316	346
13	13	44	72	103	133	164	194	225	256	286	317	347
14	14	45	73	104	134	165	195	226	257	287	318	348
15	15	46	74	105	135	166	196	227	258	288	319	349
16	16	47	75	106	136	167	197	228	259	289	320	350
17	17	48	76	107	137	168	198	229	260	290	321	351
18	18	49	77	108	138	169	199	230	261	291	322	352
19	19	50	78	109	139	170	200	231	262	292	323	353
20	20	51	79	110	140	171	201	232	263	293	324	354
21	21	52	80	111	141	172	202	233	264	294	325	355
22	22	53	81	112	142	173	203	234	265	295	326	356
23	23	54	82	113	143	174	204	235	266	296	327	357
24	24	55	83	114	144	175	205	236	267	297	328	358
25	25	56	84	115	145	176	206	237	268	298	329	359
26	26	57	85	116	146	177	207	238	269	299	330	360
27	27	58	86	117	147	178	208	239	270	300	331	361
28	28	59	87	118	148	179	209	240	271	301	332	362
29	29	—	88	119	149	180	210	241	272	302	333	363
30	30	—	89	120	150	181	211	242	273	303	334	364
31	31	—	90	—	151	—	212	243	—	304	—	365

Second Year

Date	Jan.	Feb.	Mar.	April	May	June	July	Aug.	Sept.	Oct.	Nov.	Dec.
1	366	397	425	456	486	517	547	578	609	639	670	700
2	367	398	426	457	487	518	548	579	610	640	671	701
3	368	399	427	458	488	519	549	580	611	641	672	702
4	369	400	428	459	489	520	550	581	612	642	673	703
5	370	401	429	460	490	521	551	582	613	643	674	704
6	371	402	430	461	491	522	552	583	614	644	675	705
7	372	403	431	462	492	523	553	584	615	645	676	706
8	373	404	432	463	493	524	554	585	616	646	677	707
9	374	405	433	464	494	525	555	586	617	647	678	708
10	375	406	434	465	495	526	556	587	618	648	679	709
11	376	407	435	466	496	527	557	588	619	649	680	710
12	377	408	436	467	497	528	558	589	620	650	681	711
13	378	409	437	468	498	529	559	590	621	651	682	712
14	379	410	438	469	499	530	560	591	622	652	683	713
15	380	411	439	470	500	531	561	592	623	653	684	714
16	381	412	440	471	501	532	562	593	624	654	685	715
17	382	413	441	472	502	533	563	594	625	655	686	716
18	383	414	442	473	503	534	564	595	626	656	687	717
19	384	415	443	474	504	535	565	596	627	657	688	718
20	385	416	444	475	505	536	566	597	628	658	689	719
21	386	417	445	476	506	537	567	598	629	659	690	720
22	387	418	446	477	507	538	568	599	630	660	691	721
23	388	419	447	478	508	539	569	600	631	661	692	722
24	389	420	448	479	509	540	570	601	632	662	693	723
25	390	421	449	480	510	541	571	602	633	663	694	724
26	391	422	450	481	511	542	572	603	634	664	695	725
27	392	423	451	482	512	543	573	604	635	665	696	726
28	393	424	452	483	513	544	574	605	636	666	697	727
29	394	—	453	484	514	545	575	606	637	667	698	728
30	395	—	454	485	515	546	576	607	638	668	699	729
31	396	—	455	—	516	—	577	608	—	669	—	730

Chinese Calendar, Asian Festivals

Source: Chinese Information and Culture Center, New York, NY

The Chinese calendar (like the Islamic calendar; see Religion section) is a lunar calendar. It is divided into 12 months of 29 or 30 days (compensating for the lunar month's mean duration of 29 days, 12 hr, 44.05 min). This calendar is synchronized with the solar year by the addition of extra months at fixed intervals.

The Chinese calendar runs on a 60-year cycle. The cycles 1876-1935 and 1936-95, with the years grouped under their 12 animal designations, are printed below, along with the first 24 years of the current cycle. It began in 1996 and will last until 2055. The year 1998 (Lunar Year 4696) is found in the 3d column, under Tiger, and is known as a Year of the Tiger. Readers can find the animal name for the year of their birth, marriage, etc., in the same chart. (Note: The first 3-7 weeks of each Western year belong to the previous Chinese year and animal designation.)

Both the Western (Gregorian) and traditional lunar calendars are used publicly in China and in North and South Korea, and 2 New Year's celebrations are held. In Taiwan, in overseas Chinese communities, and in Vietnam, the lunar calendar is used only to set the dates for traditional festivals, with the Gregorian system in general use.

The 4-day Chinese New Year, Hsin Nien, the 3-day Vietnamese New Year festival, Tet, and the 3-to-4-day Korean festival, Suhl, begin at the 2d new moon after the winter solstice. Because the date is fixed according to the date of the new moon in the Far East, which is west of the International Date Line, the date may be one day later than that of the new moon in the U.S. The day may fall, therefore, between Jan. 21 and Feb. 19 of the Gregorian calendar. Jan. 28 marks the start of the new Chinese year in 1998.

Rat	Ox	Tiger	Hare (Rabbit)	Dragon	Snake	Horse	Sheep (Goat)	Monkey	Rooster	Dog	Pig
1876	1877	1878	1879	1880	1881	1882	1883	1884	1885	1886	1887
1888	1889	1890	1891	1892	1893	1894	1895	1896	1897	1898	1899
1900	1901	1902	1903	1904	1905	1906	1907	1908	1909	1910	1911
1912	1913	1914	1915	1916	1917	1918	1919	1920	1921	1922	1923
1924	1925	1926	1927	1928	1929	1930	1931	1932	1933	1934	1935
1936	1937	1938	1939	1940	1941	1942	1943	1944	1945	1946	1947
1948	1949	1950	1951	1952	1953	1954	1955	1956	1957	1958	1959
1960	1961	1962	1963	1964	1965	1966	1967	1968	1969	1970	1971
1972	1973	1974	1975	1976	1977	1978	1979	1980	1981	1982	1983
1984	1985	1986	1987	1988	1989	1990	1991	1992	1993	1994	1995
1996	1997	1998	1999	2000	2001	2002	2003	2004	2005	2006	2007
2008	2009	2010	2011	2012	2013	2014	2015	2016	2017	2018	2019

Standard Time, Daylight Saving Time, and Others

Source: National Imagery and Mapping Agency; U.S. Dept. of Transportation

Standard Time

Standard Time is reckoned from the Prime Meridian of Longitude in Greenwich, England. The world is divided into 24 zones, each 15° of arc, or one hour in time apart. The Greenwich meridian (0°) extends through the center of the initial zone, and the zones to the east are numbered from 1 to 12, with the prefix "minus" indicating the number of hours to be subtracted to obtain Greenwich Time. Each zone extends 7.5° on either side of its central meridian.

Westward zones are similarly numbered, but prefixed "plus" showing the number of hours that must be added to get Greenwich Time. Although these zones apply generally to sea areas, the Standard Time maintained in many countries does not coincide with zone time. A graphical representation of the zones is shown on the Standard Time Zone Chart of the World published by the National Imagery and Mapping Agency, Distribution Division, N/ACC3, National Ocean Service, Riverdale, MD 20737-1199; telephone: (800) 638-8972.

The U.S. and possessions are divided into 10 Standard Time zones. Each zone is approximately 15° of longitude in width. All places in each zone use, instead of their own local time, the time counted from the transit of the "mean sun" across the Standard Time meridian that passes near the middle of that zone. These time zones are designated as Atlantic, Eastern, Central, Mountain, Pacific, Alaska, Hawaii-Aleutian, Samoa, Wake Island, and Guam, and the time in these zones is reckoned from the 60th, 75th, 90th, 105th, 120th, 135th, 150th, and 165th meridians west of Greenwich and the 165th and 150th meridians east of Greenwich. The time zone line wanders to conform to local geographical regions. The time in the various zones in the U.S. and U.S. territories is earlier than Greenwich Time by 4, 5, 6, 7, 8, 9, 10, and 11 hours, respectively. However, Wake Island and Guam cross the International Date Line and are 12 and 10 hours later than Greenwich Time, respectively.

24-Hour Time

Twenty-four-hour time is widely used in scientific work throughout the world. In the U.S. it is used also in operations of the armed forces. In Europe it is frequently used by the transportation networks in preference to the 12-hour AM and PM system. With the 24-hour system, the day begins at midnight and is designated 0000 through 2359.

International Date Line

The Date Line, approximately coinciding with the 180th meridian, separates the calendar dates. The date must be advanced one day when crossing in a westerly direction and set back one day when crossing in an easterly direction. The Date Line frequently deviates from the 180th meridian because of decisions made by individual nations affected. The line is deflected eastward through the Bering Strait and westward of the Aleutians to prevent separating these areas by date. The line is again deflected eastward of the Tonga and New Zealand Islands in the South Pacific for the same reason. More recently it was deflected much farther eastward to include all of Kiribati. The line is established by international custom; there is no international authority prescribing its exact course.

Daylight Saving Time

Daylight Saving Time is achieved by advancing the clock one hour. Daylight Saving Time in the U.S. begins each year at 2 AM on the first Sunday in Apr. and ends at 2 AM on the last Sunday in Oct.

Daylight Saving Time was first observed in the U.S. during World War I, and then again during World War II. In the intervening years, some states and communities observed Daylight Saving Time using whatever beginning and ending dates they chose. In 1966, Congress passed the Uniform Time Act, which provided that any state or territory that chooses to observe Daylight Saving Time must begin and end on the federal dates. Any state could, by law, exempt itself; a 1972 amendment to the act authorized states split by time zones to observe Daylight Saving Time in one time zone and standard time in the other time zone. Currently, Arizona, Hawaii, the eastern time zone portion of Indiana, Puerto Rico, the U.S. Virgin Islands, and American Samoa do not observe Daylight Saving Time.

Congress and the secretary of transportation both have authority to change time zone boundaries. Since 1966 there have been a number of changes to U.S. time zone boundaries. Efforts to conserve energy have also prompted various changes to the times that Daylight Saving Time was observed in the past.

International Usage

Adjusting clock time to be able to use the added daylight on summer evenings is common throughout the world.

Canada, which extends over 6 time zones, observes Daylight Saving Time from the first Sunday of Apr. until the last Sunday of Oct. Saskatchewan remains on standard time throughout the year. Communities elsewhere in Canada also may choose to exempt themselves from Daylight Saving Time. Mexico, which occupies 3 time zones, observes Daylight Saving Time during the same period as Canada.

Member nations of the European Union (EU) observe a "summer-time period," the EU's version of Daylight Saving Time, from the last Sunday of March until the last Sunday in Oct.

Russia, which extends over 11 time zones, maintains its Standard Time 1 hour fast for its zone designation. Additionally, it proclaims Daylight Saving Time from the 4th Sunday in March until the 4th Sunday in Sept.

China, which extends across 5 time zones, has decreed that the entire country be placed on Greenwich Time plus 8 hours. Daylight Saving Time is not observed. Japan, which lies within one time zone, also does not modify its legal time during the summer months.

Many countries in the Southern Hemisphere maintain Daylight Saving Time, generally from Oct. to Mar.; however, most countries near the equator do not deviate from Standard Time.

See also the "International Time Zones" map on page 484.

Standard Time Differences—World Cities

The time indicated in the table is fixed by law and is called the legal time or, more generally, Standard Time. Use of Daylight Saving Time varies widely. * Indicates morning of the following day. At 12:00 noon, Eastern Standard Time, the Standard Time (in 24-hour time) in selected cities is as follows:

City	Time		City	Time		City	Time		City	Time
Addis Ababa	20 00		Casablanca	17 00		Madrid	18 00		Sarajevo	18 00
Amsterdam	18 00		Copenhagen	18 00		Manila	1 00*		Seoul	2 00*
Athens	19 00		Dhaka	23 00		Mecca	20 00		Shanghai	1 00*
Auckland	5 00*		Dublin	17 00		Melbourne	3 00*		Singapore	1 00*
Baghdad	20 00		Geneva	18 00		Montevideo	14 00		Stockholm	18 00
Bangkok	0 00*		Helsinki	19 00		Moscow	20 00		Sydney	3 00*
Beijing	1 00*		Ho Chi Minh City	0 00*		Munich	18 00		Taipei	1 00*
Belfast	17 00		Hong Kong	1 00*		Nagasaki	2 00*		Tashkent	22 00
Berlin	18 00		Istanbul	19 00		Nairobi	20 00		Tehran	20 30
Bogotá	12 00		Jakarta	0 00*		New Delhi	22 30		Tel Aviv	19 00
Bombay (Mumbai)	22 30		Jerusalem	19 00		Oslo	18 00		Tokyo	2 00*
Brussels	18 00		Johannesburg	19 00		Paris	18 00		Vladivostok	3 00*
Bucharest	19 00		Karachi	22 00		Prague	18 00		Vienna	18 00
Budapest	18 00		Kathmandu	22 45		Quito	12 00		Warsaw	18 00
Buenos Aires	14 00		Kiev	19 00		Rio de Janeiro	14 00		Wellington	5 00*
Cairo	19 00		Lagos	18 00		Rome	18 00		Yangon (Rangoon)	23 30
Calcutta	22 30		Lima	12 00		St. Petersburg	20 00		Yokohama	2 00*
Cape Town	19 00		Lisbon	17 00		Santiago	13 00		Zurich	18 00
Caracas	13 00		London	17 00						

Standard Time Differences—North American Cities

At 12:00 noon, Eastern Standard Time, the Standard Time in North American cities is as follows:

City	Time		City	Time		City	Time	
Akron, OH	12 00	Noon	Galveston, TX	11 00	AM	Philadelphia, PA	12 00	Noon
Albuquerque, NM	10 00	AM	Grand Rapids, MI	12 00	Noon	*Phoenix, AZ	10 00	AM
Atlanta, GA	12 00	Noon	Halifax, NS	1 00	PM	Pierre, SD	11 00	AM
Austin, TX	11 00	AM	Hartford, CT	12 00	Noon	Pittsburgh, PA	12 00	Noon
Baltimore, MD	12 00	Noon	Havana, Cuba	12 00	Noon	Portland, ME	12 00	Noon
Birmingham, AL	11 00	AM	Helena, MT	10 00	AM	Portland, OR	9 00	AM
Bismarck, ND	11 00	AM	*Honolulu, HI	7 00	AM	Providence, RI	12 00	Noon
Boise, ID	10 00	AM	Houston, TX	11 00	AM	Quebec, Que.	12 00	Noon
Boston, MA	12 00	Noon	*Indianapolis, IN	12 00	Noon	*Regina, Sask.	11 00	AM
Buffalo, NY	12 00	Noon	Jacksonville, FL	12 00	Noon	Reno, NV	9 00	AM
Butte, MT	10 00	AM	Juneau, AK	8 00	AM	Richmond, VA	12 00	Noon
Calgary, Alta.	10 00	AM	Kansas City, MO	11 00	AM	Rochester, NY	12 00	Noon
Charleston, SC	12 00	Noon	*Kingston, Jamaica	12 00	Noon	Sacramento, CA	9 00	AM
Charleston, WV	12 00	Noon	Knoxville, TN	12 00	Noon	St. John's, Nfld.	1 30	PM
Charlotte, NC	12 00	Noon	Lexington, KY	12 00	Noon	St. Louis, MO	11 00	AM
Charlottetown, PEI.	1 00	PM	Lincoln, NE	11 00	AM	St. Paul, MN	11 00	AM
Chattanooga, TN	12 00	Noon	Little Rock, AR	11 00	AM	Salt Lake City, UT	10 00	AM
Cheyenne, WY	10 00	AM	Los Angeles, CA	9 00	AM	San Antonio, TX	11 00	AM
Chicago, IL	11 00	AM	Louisville, KY	12 00	Noon	San Diego, CA	9 00	AM
Cleveland, OH	12 00	Noon	*Mexico City, Mexico	11 00	AM	San Francisco, CA	9 00	AM
Colorado Spr., CO	10 00	AM	Memphis, TN	11 00	AM	*San Juan, PR	1 00	PM
Columbus, OH	12 00	Noon	Miami, FL	12 00	Noon	Santa Fe, NM	10 00	AM
Dallas, TX	11 00	AM	Milwaukee, WI	11 00	AM	Savannah, GA	12 00	Noon
*Dawson, Yuk.	9 00	AM	Minneapolis, MN	11 00	AM	Seattle, WA	9 00	AM
Dayton, OH	12 00	Noon	Mobile, AL	11 00	AM	Shreveport, LA	11 00	AM
Denver, CO	10 00	AM	Montreal, Que	12 00	Noon	Sioux Falls, SD	11 00	AM
Des Moines, IA	11 00	AM	Nashville, TN	11 00	AM	Spokane, WA	9 00	AM
Detroit, MI	12 00	Noon	Nassau, Bahamas	12 00	Noon	Tampa, FL	12 00	Noon
Duluth, MN	11 00	AM	New Haven, CT	12 00	Noon	Toledo, OH	12 00	Noon
Edmonton, Alta.	10 00	AM	New Orleans, LA	11 00	AM	Topeka, KS	11 00	AM
El Paso, TX	10 00	AM	New York, NY	12 00	Noon	Toronto, Ont.	12 00	Noon
Erie, PA	12 00	Noon	Nome, AK	8 00	AM	*Tucson, AZ	10 00	AM
Evansville, IN	11 00	AM	Norfolk, VA	12 00	Noon	Tulsa, OK	11 00	AM
Fairbanks, AK	8 00	AM	Oklahoma City, OK	11 00	AM	Vancouver, BC	9 00	AM
Flint, MI.	12 00	Noon	Omaha, NE	11 00	AM	Washington, DC	12 00	Noon
*Fort Wayne, IN	12 00	Noon	Ottawa, Ont.	12 00	Noon	Wichita, KS	11 00	AM
Fort Worth, TX.	11 00	AM	*Panama City, Panama	12 00	Noon	Wilmington, DE	12 00	Noon
Frankfort, KY	12 00	Noon	Peoria, IL	11 00	AM	Winnipeg, Man.	11 00	AM

Note: This same table can be used for Daylight Saving Time when it is in effect, but allowance must be made for cities that do not observe it; they are marked with an asterisk. Daylight Saving Time is one hour later than Standard Time.

U.S. Legal or Public Holidays, 1998

Technically, the U.S. observes no national holidays; each state has jurisdiction over its holidays, which are designated by legislative enactment or executive proclamation. The president and the U.S. Congress can legally designate holidays only for the District of Columbia and for federal employees. In practice, however, most states observe the federal legal public holidays. Federal legal public holidays are New Year's Day, Martin Luther King Jr. Day, Presidents' Day, Memorial Day, Independence Day, Labor Day, Columbus Day, Veterans Day, Thanksgiving, and Christmas.

Chief Legal or Public Holidays

When a holiday falls on a Sunday or a Saturday, it is usually observed on the following Monday or the preceding Friday. For some holidays, government and business closing practices vary. In most states, the office of the secretary of state can provide details for holiday closings. The following will be legal or public holidays in most states in 1998:

Jan. 1 (Thurs.) — New Year's Day
Jan. 19 (3d Mon. in Jan.) — Martin Luther King Jr. Day
Feb. 12 (Thurs.) — Lincoln's Birthday
Feb. 16 (3d Mon. in Feb.) — Washington's Birthday, or Presidents' Day, or Washington-Lincoln Day
May 25 (last Mon. in May) — Memorial Day, or Decoration Day

July 4 (Sat.) — Independence Day
Sept. 7 (1st Mon. in Sept.) — Labor Day
Nov. 11 (Wed.) — Veterans Day
Nov. 26 (4th Thurs. in Nov.) — Thanksgiving
Dec. 25 (Fri.) — Christmas Day
In some states, the following will be legal or public holidays in 1998:
Apr. 10 (Fri.) — Good Friday. (In some states, observed for half or part of day.)
Oct. 12 (2d Mon. in Oct.) — Columbus Day, or Discoverers' Day, or Pioneers' Day
Nov. 3 (1st Tues. after 1st Mon. in Nov.) — Election Day

Selected International Holidays, 1998

Jan. 26 — Australia Day obsvd., Australia
Feb. 5 — Constitution Day, Mexico
Feb. 21-24 — Carnival, Brazil
Mar. 9 — Commonwealth Day, Canada, Great Britain
Mar. 17 — St. Patrick's Day, Ireland
Mar. 21 — Benito Juarez's Birthday, Mexico
Apr. 8 — Buddha's Birthday, Korea, Japan
Apr. 23 — National Sovereignty Day, Turkey
May 5 — Cinco de Mayo (Battle of Puebla Day), Mexico
May 17 — Constitution Day, Norway
May 18 — Victoria Day, Canada
May 30 — Dragon Boat Festival, China
June 19 — Midsummer Eve, Baltics, Scandinavia
July 1 — Canada Day, Canada

July 14 — Bastille Day, France
Aug. 30 — St. Rose of Lima, Peru
Sept. 7 — Labor Day, Canada
Sept. 16 — Independence Day, Mexico
Sept. 19 — St. Gennaro, Italy
Oct. 3 — German Unification Day, Germany
Oct. 12 — Día de la Raza, Mexico
Oct. 12 — Thanksgiving Day, Canada
Nov. 1-2 — Day of the Dead, Mexico
Nov. 5 — Guy Fawkes Day, Great Britain
Nov. 11 — Remembrance Day, Canada
Dec. 12 — Jamhuri Day, Kenya; Guadalupe Day, Mexico
Dec. 26 — Boxing Day, Australia, Canada, Great Britain, New Zealand

AWARDS — MEDALS — PRIZES
The Alfred B. Nobel Prize Winners

Alfred B. Nobel (1833-96), inventor of dynamite, bequeathed $9,000,000, the interest to be distributed yearly to those who had most benefited humankind in physics, chemistry, medicine-physiology, literature, and promotion of peace. These prizes were first awarded in 1901. The first Nobel Memorial Prize in Economic Science was awarded in 1969, funded by the central bank of Sweden. If the year is omitted, no award was given. In 1996, each prize was worth more than $1 mil. For 1997 Nobel Winners, see page 67.

Physics

1996	David M. Lee, Douglas D. Osheroff, Robert C. Richardson, all U.S.	1973	Ivar Giaever, U.S.; Leo Esaki, Jpn.; Brian D. Josephson, Br.
1995	Martin Perl, Frederick Reines, both U.S.	1972	John Bardeen, Leon N. Cooper, John R. Schrieffer, all U.S.
1994	Bertram N. Brockhouse, Can.; Clifford G. Shull, U.S.	1971	Dennis Gabor, Br.
1993	Joseph H. Taylor, Russell A. Hulse, both U.S.	1970	Louis Neel, Fr.; Hannes Alfven, Swed.
1992	Georges Charpak, Pol.-Fr.	1969	Murray Gell-Mann, U.S.
1991	Pierre-Giles de Gennes, Fr.	1968	Luis W. Alvarez, U.S.
1990	Richard E. Taylor, Can.; Jerome I. Friedman, Henry W. Kendall, both U.S.	1967	Hans A. Bethe, U.S.
		1966	Alfred Kastler, Fr.
1989	Norman F. Ramsey, U.S.; Hans G. Dehmelt, Ger.-U.S.; Wolfgang Paul, Ger.	1965	Richard P. Feynman, Julian S. Schwinger, both U.S.; Shinichiro Tomonaga, Jpn.
1988	Leon M. Lederman, Melvin Schwartz, Jack Steinberger, all U.S.	1964	Nikolai G. Basov, Aleksander M. Prochorov, both USSR; Charles H. Townes, U.S.
1987	K. Alex Müller, Swiss; J. Georg Bednorz, Ger.	1963	Maria Goeppert-Mayer, Eugene P. Wigner, both U.S.; J. Hans D. Jensen, Ger.
1986	Ernest Ruska, Ger.; Gerd Binnig, Ger.; Heinrich Rohrer, Swiss	1962	Lev. D. Landau, USSR
1985	Klaus von Klitzing, Ger.	1961	Robert Hofstadter, U.S.; Rudolf L. Mossbauer, Ger.
1984	Carlo Rubbia, It.; Simon van der Meer, Dutch	1960	Donald A. Glaser, U.S.
1983	Subrahmanyan Chandrasekhar, William A. Fowler, both U.S.	1959	Owen Chamberlain, Emilio G. Segre, both U.S.
1982	Kenneth G. Wilson, U.S.	1958	Pavel Cherenkov, Ilya Frank, Igor Y. Tamm, all USSR
1981	Nicolaas Bloembergen, Arthur Schaalow, both U.S.; Kai M. Siegbahn, Swed.	1957	Tsung-dao Lee, Chen Ning Yang, both U.S.
1980	James W. Cronin, Val L. Fitch, both U.S.	1956	John Bardeen, Walter H. Brattain, William Shockley, all U.S.
1979	Steven Weinberg, Sheldon L. Glashow, both U.S.; Abdus Salam, Pakistani	1955	Polykarp Kusch, Willis E. Lamb, both U.S.
		1954	Max Born, Br.; Walter Bothe, Ger.
1978	Pyotr Kapitsa, USSR; Arno Penzias, Robert Wilson, both U.S.	1953	Frits Zernike, Dutch
		1952	Felix Bloch, Edward M. Purcell, both U.S.
1977	John H. Van Vleck, Philip W. Anderson, both U.S.; Nevill F. Mott, Br.	1951	Sir John D. Cockroft, Br.; Ernest T. S. Walton, Ir.
1976	Burton Richter, Samuel C.C. Ting, both U.S.	1950	Cecil F. Powell, Br.
		1949	Hideki Yukawa, Jpn.
1975	James Rainwater, U.S.; Ben Mottelson, U.S.-Dan.; Aage Bohr, Dan.	1948	Patrick M. S. Blackett, Br.
		1947	Sir Edward V. Appleton, Br.
		1946	Percy Williams Bridgman, U.S.
		1945	Wolfgang Pauli, U.S.
1974	Martin Ryle, Antony Hewish, both Br.	1944	Isidor Isaac Rabi, U.S.
1943	Otto Stern, U.S.		
1939	Ernest O. Lawrence, U.S.		
1938	Enrico Fermi, It.-U.S.		
1937	Clinton J. Davisson, U.S.; Sir George P. Thomson, Br.		
1936	Carl D. Anderson, U.S.;Victor F. Hess, Aus.		
1935	Sir James Chadwick, Br.		
1933	Paul A. M. Dirac, Br.; Erwin Schrodinger, Austria		
1932	Werner Heisenberg, Ger.		
1930	Sir Chandrasekhara V. Raman, Indian		
1929	Prince Louis-Victor de Broglie, Fr.		
1928	Owen W. Richardson, Br.		
1927	Arthur H. Compton, U.S.; Charles T. R. Wilson, Br.		
1926	Jean B. Perrin, Fr.		
1925	James Franck, Gustav Hertz, both Ger.		
1924	Karl M. G. Siegbahn, Swed.		
1923	Robert A. Millikan, U.S.		
1922	Niels Bohr, Dan.		
1921	Albert Einstein, Ger.-U.S.		
1920	Charles E. Guillaume, Fr.		
1919	Johannes Stark, Ger.		
1918	Max K. E. L. Planck, Ger.		
1917	Charles G. Barkla, Br.		
1915	Sir William H. Bragg, Sir William L. Bragg, both Br.		
1914	Max von Laue, Ger.		
1913	Heike Kamerlingh-Onnes, Dutch		
1912	Nils G. Dalen, Swed.		
1911	Wilhelm Wien, Ger.		
1910	Johannes D. van der Waals, Dutch		
1909	Carl F. Braun, Ger.; Guglielmo Marconi, It.		
1908	Gabriel Lippmann, Fr.		
1907	Albert A. Michelson, U.S.		
1906	Sir Joseph J. Thomson, Br.		
1905	Philipp E. A. von Lenard, Ger.		
1904	John W. Strutt, Lord Rayleigh, Br.		
1903	Antoine Henri Becquerel, Pierre Curie, both Fr.; Marie Curie, Pol.-Fr.		
1902	Hendrik A. Lorentz, Pieter Zeeman, both Dutch		
1901	Wilhelm C. Roentgen, Ger.		

Chemistry

1996	Harold W. Kroto, Br.; Robert F. Curl Jr.; Richard E. Smalley, both U.S.	1975	John Cornforth, Austral.-Br.; Vladimir Prelog, Yugo.-Swiss
1995	Paul Crutzen, Dutch; Mario Molina, Mex.-U.S.; Sherwood Rowland, U.S.	1974	Paul J. Flory, U.S.
		1973	Ernst Otto Fischer, Ger.; Geoffrey Wilkinson, Br.
1994	George A. Olah, U.S.		
1993	Kary B. Mullis, U.S.; Michael Smith, Br.-Can.	1972	Christian B. Anfinsen, Stanford Moore, William H. Stein, all U.S.
1992	Rudolph A. Marcus, Can.-U.S.	1971	Gerhard Herzberg, Canadian
1991	Richard R. Ernst, Swiss	1970	Luis F. Leloir, Arg.
1990	Elias James Corey, U.S.	1969	Derek H. R. Barton, Br.; Odd Hassel, Nor.
1989	Thomas R. Cech, Sidney Altman, both U.S.	1968	Lars Onsager, U.S.
1988	Johann Deisenhofer, Robert Huber, Hartmut Michel, all Ger.	1967	Manfred Eigen, Ger.; Ronald G. W. Norrish, George Porter, both Br.
1987	Donald J. Cram, Charles J. Pedersen, both U.S.; Jean-Marie Lehn, Fr.	1966	Robert S. Mulliken, U.S.
		1965	Robert B. Woodward, U.S.
1986	Dudley Herschbach, Yuan T. Lee, both U.S.; John C. Polanyi, Can.	1964	Dorothy C. Hodgkin, Br.
		1963	Giulio Natta, It.; Karl Ziegler, Ger.
1985	Herbert A. Hauptman, Jerome Karle, both U.S.	1962	John C. Kendrew, Max F. Perutz, both Br.
1984	Bruce Merrifield, U.S.	1961	Melvin Calvin, U.S.
1983	Henry Taube, Can.	1960	Willard F. Libby, U.S.
1982	Aaron Klug, S. Afr.	1959	Jaroslav Heyrovsky, Czech.
1981	Kenichi Fukui, Jpn.; Roald Hoffmann, U.S.	1958	Frederick Sanger, Br.
		1957	Sir Alexander R. Todd, Br.
1980	Paul Berg, Walter Gilbert, both U.S.; Frederick Sanger, Br.	1956	Sir Cyril N. Hinshelwood, Br.; Nikolai N. Semenov, USSR
1979	Herbert C. Brown, U.S.; George Wittig, Ger.	1955	Vincent du Vigneaud, U.S.
		1954	Linus C. Pauling, U.S.
1978	Peter Mitchell, Br.	1953	Hermann Staudinger, Ger.
1977	Ilya Prigogine, Belg.	1952	Archer J. P. Martin, Richard L. M. Synge, both Br.
1976	William N. Lipscomb, U.S.		
1951	Edwin M. McMillan, Glenn T. Seaborg, both U.S.		
1950	Kurt Alder, Otto P. H. Diels, both Ger.		
1949	William F. Giauque, U.S.		
1948	Arne W. K. Tiselius, Swed.		
1947	Sir Robert Robinson, Br.		
1946	James B. Sumner, John H. Northrop, Wendell M. Stanley, all U.S.		
1945	Artturi I. Virtanen, Fin.		
1944	Otto Hahn, Ger.		
1943	Georg de Hevesy, Hung.		
1939	Adolf F. J. Butenandt, Ger.; Leopold Ruzicka, Swiss		
1938	Richard Kuhn, Ger.		
1937	Walter N. Haworth, Br.; Paul Karrer, Swiss		
1936	Peter J. W. Debye, Dutch		
1935	Frederic & Irene Joliot-Curie, both Fr.		
1934	Harold C. Urey, U.S.		
1932	Irving Langmuir, U.S.		
1931	Friedrich Bergius, Karl Bosch, both Ger.		
1930	Hans Fischer, Ger.		
1929	Sir Arthur Harden, Br.; Hans von Euler-Chelpin, Swed.		
1928	Adolf O. R. Windaus, Ger.		
1927	Heinrich O. Wieland, Ger.		
1926	Theodor Svedberg, Swed.		
1925	Richard A. Zsigmondy, Ger.		
1923	Fritz Pregl, Aus.		
1922	Francis W. Aston, Br.		
1921	Frederick Soddy, Br.		
1920	Walther H. Nernst, Ger.		
1918	Fritz Haber, Ger.		

1915	Richard M. Willstatter, Ger.
1914	Theodore W. Richards, U.S.
1912	Victor Grignard, Paul Sabatier, both Fr.
1911	Marie Curie, Pol.-Fr.

1910	Otto Wallach, Ger.
1909	Wilhelm Ostwald, Ger.
1908	Ernest Rutherford, Br.
1907	Eduard Buchner, Ger.
1906	Henri Moissan, Fr.

1905	Adolf von Baeyer, Ger.
1904	Sir William Ramsay, Br.
1903	Svante A. Arrhenius, Swed.
1902	Emil Fischer, Ger.
1901	Jacobus H. van't Hoff, Dutch

Physiology or Medicine

1996	Peter C. Doherty, Austral.; Rolf M. Zinkernagel, Swiss
1995	Edward B. Lewis, Eric F. Wieschaus, both U.S.; Christiane Nuesslein-Volhard, Ger.
1994	Alfred G. Gilman, Martin Rodbell, both U.S.
1993	Phillip A. Sharp, U.S.; Richard J. Roberts, Br.
1992	Edmond H. Fisher, Edwin G. Krebs, both U.S.
1991	Edwin Neher, Bert Sakmann, both Ger.
1990	Joseph E. Murray, E. Donnall Thomas, both U.S.
1989	J. Michael Bishop, Harold E. Varmus, both U.S.
1988	Gertrude B. Elion, George H. Hitchings, both U.S; Sir James Black, Br.
1987	Susumu Tonegawa, Jpn.
1986	Rita Levi-Montalcini, It.-U.S., Stanley Cohen, U.S.
1985	Michael S. Brown, Joseph L. Goldstein, both U.S.
1984	Cesar Milstein, Br.-Arg.; Georges J. F. Koehler, Ger.; Niels K. Jerne, Br.-Dan.
1983	Barbara McClintock, U.S.
1982	Sune Bergstrom, Bengt Samuelsson, both Swed.; John R. Vane, Br.
1981	Roger W. Sperry, David H. Hubel, Tosten N. Wiesel, all U.S.
1980	Baruj Benacerraf, George Snell, both U.S.; Jean Dausset, Fr.
1979	Allan M. Cormack, U.S.; Godfrey N. Hounsfield, Br.
1978	Daniel Nathans, Hamilton O. Smith, both U.S.; Werner Arber, Swiss
1977	Rosalyn S. Yalow, Roger C.L. Guillemin, Andrew V. Schally, all U.S.
1976	Baruch S. Blumberg, Daniel Carleton Gajdusek, both U.S.
1975	David Baltimore, Howard Temin, both U.S.; Renato Dulbecco, It.-U.S.
1974	Albert Claude, Lux.-U.S.; George Emil Palade, Rom.-U.S.; Christian Rene de Duve, Belg.

1973	Karl von Frisch, Ger.; Konrad Lorenz, Ger.-Aus.; Nikolaas Tinbergen, Br.
1972	Gerald M. Edelman, U.S.; Rodney R. Porter, Br.
1971	Earl W. Sutherland Jr., U.S.
1970	Julius Axelrod, U.S.; Sir Bernard Katz, Br.; Ulf von Euler, Swed.
1969	Max Delbrück, Alfred D. Hershey, Salvador Luria, all U.S.
1968	Robert W. Holley, H. Gobind Khorana, Marshall W. Nirenberg, all U.S.
1967	Ragnar Granit, Swed.; Haldan Keffer Hartline, George Wald, both U.S.
1966	Charles B. Huggins, Francis Peyton Rous, both U.S.
1965	François Jacob, Andre Lwoff, Jacques Monod, all Fr.
1964	Konrad E. Bloch, U.S.; Feodor Lynen, Ger.
1963	Sir John C. Eccles, Austral.; Alan L. Hodgkin, Andrew F. Huxley, both Br.
1962	Francis H. C. Crick, Maurice H. F. Wilkins, both Br.; James D. Watson, U.S.
1961	Georg von Bekesy, U.S.
1960	Sir F. MacFarlane Burnet, Austral.; Peter B. Medawar, Br.
1959	Arthur Kornberg, Severo Ochoa, both U.S.
1958	George W. Beadle, Edward L. Tatum, Joshua Lederberg, all U.S.
1957	Daniel Bovet, It.
1956	Andre F. Cournand, Dickinson W. Richards Jr., both U.S.; Werner Forssmann, Ger.
1955	Alex H. T. Theorell, Swed.
1954	John F. Enders, Frederick C. Robbins, Thomas H. Weller, all U.S.
1953	Hans A. Krebs, Br.; Fritz A. Lipmann, U.S.
1952	Selman A. Waksman, U.S.
1951	Max Theiler, U.S.
1950	Philip S. Hench, Edward C. Kendall, both U.S.; Tadeus Reichstein, Swiss
1949	Walter R. Hess, Swiss; Antonio Moniz, Port.
1948	Paul H. Müller, Swiss

1947	Carl F. Cori, Gerty T. Cori, both U.S.; Bernardo A. Houssay, Arg.
1946	Hermann J. Muller, U.S.
1945	Ernst B. Chain, Sir Alexander Fleming, Sir Howard W. Florey, all Br.
1944	Joseph Erlanger, Herbert S. Gasser, both U.S.
1943	Henrik C. P. Dam, Dan.; Edward A. Doisy, U.S.
1939	Gerhard Domagk, Ger.
1938	Corneille J. F. Heymans, Belg.
1937	Albert Szent-Gyorgyi, Hung.-U.S.
1936	Sir Henry H. Dale, Br.; Otto Loewi, U.S.
1935	Hans Spemann, Ger.
1934	George R. Minot, William P. Murphy, G. H. Whipple, all U.S.
1933	Thomas H. Morgan, U.S.
1932	Edgar D. Adrian, Sir Charles S. Sherrington, both Br.
1931	Otto H. Warburg, Ger.
1930	Karl Landsteiner, U.S.
1929	Christiaan Eijkman, Dutch; Sir Frederick G. Hopkins, Br.
1928	Charles J. H. Nicolle, Fr.
1927	Julius Wagner-Jauregg, Austrian
1926	Johannes A. G. Fibiger, Dan.
1924	Willem Einthoven, Dutch
1923	Frederick G. Banting, Can.; John J. R. Macleod, Scot.
1922	Archibald V. Hill, Br.; Otto F. Meyerhof, Ger.
1920	Schack A. S. Krogh, Dan.
1919	Jules Bordet, Belg.
1914	Robert Barany, Aus.
1913	Charles R. Richet, Fr.
1912	Alexis Carrel, Fr.
1911	Allvar Gullstrand, Swed.
1910	Albrecht Kossel, Ger.
1909	Emil T. Kocher, Swiss
1908	Paul Ehrlich, Ger.; Elie Metchnikoff, Fr.
1907	Charles L. A. Laveran, Fr.
1906	Camillo Golgi, It.; Santiago Ramon y Cajal, Span.
1905	Robert Koch, Ger.
1904	Ivan P. Pavlov, Russ.
1903	Niels R. Finsen, Dan.
1902	Sir Ronald Ross, Br.
1901	Emil A. von Behring, Ger.

Literature

1996	Wislawa Szymborska, Pol.
1995	Seamus Heaney, Ir.
1994	Kenzaburo Oe, Jpn.
1993	Toni Morrison, U.S.
1992	Derek Walcott, W. Ind.
1991	Nadine Gordimer, S. Afr.
1990	Octavio Paz, Mex.
1989	Camilo José Cela, Span.
1988	Naguib Mahfouz, Egy.
1987	Joseph Brodsky, USSR-U.S.
1986	Wole Soyinka, Nig.
1985	Claude Simon, Fr.
1984	Jaroslav Siefert, Czech.
1983	William Golding, Br.
1982	Gabriel Garcia Marquez, Colombian-Mex.
1981	Elias Canetti, Bulg.-Br.
1980	Czeslaw Milosz, Pol.-U.S.
1979	Odysseus Elytis, Gk.
1978	Isaac Bashevis Singer, U.S.
1977	Vicente Aleixandre, Span.
1976	Saul Bellow, U.S.
1975	Eugenio Montale, It.
1974	Eyvind Johnson, Harry Edmund Martinson, both Swed.
1973	Patrick White, Austral.
1972	Heinrich Böll, Ger.
1971	Pablo Neruda, Chil.
1970	Aleksandr I. Solzhenitsyn, USSR
1969	Samuel Beckett, Ir.
1968	Yasunari Kawabata, Jpn.
1967	Miguel Angel Asturias, Guate.

1966	Samuel Joseph Agnon, Isr.; Nelly Sachs, Swed.
1965	Mikhail Sholokhov, USSR
1964	Jean Paul Sartre, Fr. (Prize declined)
1963	Giorgos Seferis, Gk.
1962	John Steinbeck, U.S.
1961	Ivo Andric, Yugo.
1960	Saint-John Perse, Fr.
1959	Salvatore Quasimodo, It.
1958	Boris L. Pasternak, USSR (Prize declined)
1957	Albert Camus, Fr.
1956	Juan Ramon Jimenez, Span.
1955	Halldor K. Laxness, Ice.
1954	Ernest Hemingway, U.S.
1953	Sir Winston Churchill, Br.
1952	Francois Mauriac, Fr.
1951	Par F. Lagerkvist, Swed.
1950	Bertrand Russell, Br.
1949	William Faulkner, U.S.
1948	T.S. Eliot, Br.
1947	Andre Gide, Fr.
1946	Hermann Hesse, Ger.-Swiss
1945	Gabriela Mistral, Chil.
1944	Johannes V. Jensen, Dan.
1939	Frans E. Sillanpaa, Fin.
1938	Pearl O. Buck, U.S.
1937	Roger Martin du Gard, Fr
1936	Eugene O'Neill, U.S.
1934	Luigi Pirandello, It.
1933	Ivan A. Bunin, USSR

1932	John Galsworthy, Br.
1931	Erik A. Karlfeldt, Swed.
1930	Sinclair Lewis, U.S.
1929	Thomas Mann, Ger.
1928	Sigrid Undset, Nor.
1927	Henri Bergson, Fr.
1926	Grazia Deledda, It.
1925	George Bernard Shaw, Ir.-Br.
1924	Wladyslaw S. Reymont, Pol.
1923	William Butler Yeats, Ir.
1922	Jacinto Benavente, Span.
1921	Anatole France, Fr.
1920	Knut Hamsun, Nor.
1919	Carl F. G. Spitteler, Swiss
1917	Karl A. Gjellerup, Henrik Pontoppidan, both Dan.
1916	Verner von Heidenstam, Swed.
1915	Romain Rolland, Fr.
1913	Rabindranath Tagore, Ind.
1912	Gerhart Hauptmann, Ger.
1911	Maurice Maeterlinck, Belg.
1910	Paul J. L. Heyse, Ger.
1909	Selma Lagerlof, Swed.
1908	Rudolf C. Eucken, Ger.
1907	Rudyard Kipling, Br.
1906	Giosue Carducci, It.
1905	Henryk Sienkiewicz, Pol.
1904	Frederic Mistral, Fr.; Jose Echegaray, Span
1903	Bjornsterne Bjornson, Nor.
1902	Theodor Mommsen, Ger.
1901	Rene F. A. Sully Prudhomme, Fr.

Peace

1996	Bishop Carlos Ximenes Belo, José Ramos-Horta, both Timorese	1971	Willy Brandt, Ger.	1931	Jane Addams, Nicholas Murray Butler, both U.S.
1995	Joseph Rotblat, Pol.-Br.; Pugwash Conference	1970	Norman E. Borlaug, U.S.	1930	Nathan Soderblom, Swed.
		1969	Intl. Labor Organization	1929	Frank B. Kellogg, U.S.
1994	Yasir Arafat, Pal.; Shimon Peres, Yitzhak Rabin, both Isr.	1968	Rene Cassin, Fr.	1927	Ferdinand E. Buisson, Fr.; Ludwig Quidde, Ger.
1993	Frederik W. de Klerk, Nelson Mandela, both S. Afr.	1965	UN Children's Fund (UNICEF)	1926	Aristide Briand, Fr.; Gustav Stresemann, Ger.
		1964	Martin Luther King Jr., U.S.		
		1963	International Red Cross, League of Red Cross Societies		
1992	Rigoberta Menchú, Guat.	1962	Linus C. Pauling, U.S.	1925	Sir J. Austen Chamberlain, Br.; Charles G. Dawes, U.S.
1991	Aung San Suu Kyi, Myanmarese	1961	Dag Hammarskjold, Swed.		
1990	Mikhail S. Gorbachev, USSR	1960	Albert J. Luthuli, S. Afr.	1922	Fridtjof Nansen, Nor.
1989	Dalai Lama, Tib.	1959	Philip J. Noel-Baker, Br.	1921	Karl H. Branting, Swed.; Christian L. Lange, Nor.
1988	United Nations Peacekeeping Forces	1958	Georges Pire, Belg.		
		1957	Lester B. Pearson, Can.	1920	Leon V.A. Bourgeois, Fr.
1987	Oscar Arias Sanchez, Costa Rican	1954	Office of the UN High Commissioner for Refugees	1919	Woodrow Wilson, U.S.
1986	Elie Wiesel, Rom.-U.S.			1917	International Red Cross
1985	Intl. Physicians for the Prevention of Nuclear War, U.S.	1953	George C. Marshall, U.S.	1913	Henri La Fontaine, Belg.
		1952	Albert Schweitzer, Fr.	1912	Elihu Root, U.S.
1984	Bishop Desmond Tutu, S. Afr.	1951	Leon Jouhaux, Fr.	1911	Tobias M.C. Asser, Dutch; Alfred H. Fried, Aus.
1983	Lech Walesa, Pol.	1950	Ralph J. Bunche, U.S.		
1982	Alva Myrdal, Swed.; Alfonso Garcia Robles, Mex.	1949	Lord John Boyd Orr of Brechin Mearns, Br.	1910	Permanent Intl. Peace Bureau
				1909	Auguste M. F. Beernaert, Belg.; Paul H. B. B. d'Estournelles de Constant, Fr.
1981	Office of UN High Commissioner for Refugees	1947	Friends Service Council, Br.; American Friends Service Committee, U.S.		
1980	Adolfo Perez Esquivel, Arg.	1946	Emily G. Balch, John R. Mott, both U.S.	1908	Klas P. Arnoldson, Swed.; Fredrik Bajer, Dan.
1979	Mother Teresa of Calcutta, Alb.-Ind.				
1978	Anwar Sadat, Egy.; Menachem Begin, Isr.	1945	Cordell Hull, U.S.	1907	Ernesto T. Moneta, It.; Louis Renault, Fr.
		1944	International Red Cross	1906	Theodore Roosevelt, U.S.
1977	Amnesty International	1938	Nansen International Office for Refugees	1905	Baroness Bertha von Suttner, Austrian
1976	Mairead Corrigan, Betty Williams, both N. Ir.			1904	Institute of International Law
		1937	Viscount Cecil of Chelwood, Br.	1903	Sir William R. Cremer, Br.
1975	Andrei Sakharov, USSR	1936	Carlos de Saavedra Lamas, Arg.	1902	Elie Ducommun, Charles A. Gobat, both Swiss
1974	Eisaku Sato, Jpn.; Sean MacBride, Ir.	1935	Carl von Ossietzky, Ger.		
1973	Henry Kissinger, U.S.; Le Duc Tho, N. Viet. (Tho declined)	1934	Arthur Henderson, Br.	1901	Jean H. Dunant, Swiss; Frederic Passy, Fr.
		1933	Sir Norman Angell, Br.		

Nobel Memorial Prize in Economic Science

1996	James A. Mirrlees, Br.; William Vickrey, Can.-U.S.	1987	Robert M. Solow, U.S.	1976	Milton Friedman, U.S.
		1986	James M. Buchanan, U.S.	1975	Tjalling Koopmans, Dutch-U.S.; Leonid Kantorovich, USSR
1995	Robert E. Lucas Jr., U.S.	1985	Franco Modigliani, It.-U.S.		
1994	John C. Harsanyi, John F. Nash, both U.S.	1984	Richard Stone, Br.	1974	Gunnar Myrdal, Swed.; Friedrich A. von Hayek, Austrian
		1983	Gerard Debreu, Fr.-U.S.		
1993	Robert W. Fogel, Douglass C. North, both U.S.	1982	George J. Stigler, U.S.	1973	Wassily Leontief, U.S.
		1981	James Tobin, U.S.	1972	Kenneth J. Arrow, U.S.; John R. Hicks, Br.
1992	Gary S. Becker, U.S.	1980	Lawrence R. Klein, U.S.		
1991	Ronald H. Coase, Br.-U.S.	1979	Theodore W. Schultz, U.S.; Sir Arthur Lewis, Br.	1971	Simon Kuznets, U.S.
1990	Harry M. Markowitz, William F. Sharpe, Merton H. Miller, all U.S.			1970	Paul A. Samuelson, U.S.
		1978	Herbert A. Simon, U.S.	1969	Ragnar Frisch, Norwegian; Jan Tinbergen, Dutch
1989	Trygve Haavelmo, Nor.	1977	Bertil Ohlin, Swedish; James E. Meade, Br.		
1988	Maurice Allais, Fr.				

Pulitzer Prizes in Journalism, Letters, and Music

The Pulitzer Prizes were endowed by Joseph Pulitzer (1847-1911), publisher of the *New York World*, in a bequest to Columbia University and are awarded annually by the president of the university on recommendation of the Pulitzer Prize Board for work done during the preceding year. All prizes are now $3,000 (originally $500) in each category, except Meritorious Public Service, for which a gold medal is given. If a year is omitted, no award was given that year.

Journalism

Meritorious Public Service

1918—New York Times. Also special award to Minna Lewinson and Henry Beetle Hough
1919—Milwaukee Journal
1921—Boston Post
1922—New York World
1923—Memphis (TN) Commercial Appeal
1924—New York World
1926—Enquirer-Sun, Columbus, GA
1927—Canton (OH) Daily News
1928—Indianapolis (IN) Times
1929—New York Evening World
1931—Atlanta (GA) Constitution
1932—Indianapolis (IN) News
1933—New York World-Telegram
1934—Medford (OR) Mail-Tribune
1935—Sacramento (CA) Bee
1936—Cedar Rapids (IA) Gazette
1937—St.Louis Post-Dispatch
1938—Bismarck (ND) Tribune
1939—Miami (FL) Daily News
1940—Waterbury (CT) Republican and American
1941—St.Louis Post-Dispatch
1942—Los Angeles Times
1943—Omaha World Herald
1944—New York Times
1945—Detroit Free Press
1946—Scranton (PA) Times.

1947—Baltimore Sun
1948—St. Louis Post-Dispatch
1949—Nebraska State Journal
1950—Chicago Daily News; St. Louis Post-Dispatch
1951—Miami (FL) Herald and Brooklyn Eagle
1952—St. Louis Post-Dispatch
1953—Whiteville (NC) News Reporter; Tabor City (NC) Tribune
1954—Newsday (Long Island, NY)
1955—Columbus (GA) Ledger and Sunday Ledger-Enquirer
1956—Watsonville (CA) Register-Pajaronian
1957—Chicago Daily News
1958—Arkansas Gazette, Little Rock
1959—Utica (NY) Observer-Dispatch and Utica Daily Press
1960—Los Angeles Times
1961—Amarillo (TX) Globe-Times
1962—Panama City (FL) News-Herald
1963—Chicago Daily News
1964—St.Petersburg (FL) Times
1965—Hutchinson (KS) News
1966—Boston Globe
1967—Louisville (KY) Courier-Journal; Milwaukee Journal
1968—Riverside (CA) Press-Enterprise
1969—Los Angeles Times
1970—Newsday (Long Island, NY)
1971—Winston Salem (NC) Journal & Sentinel
1972—New York Times
1973—Washington Post
1974—Newsday (Long Island, NY)

1975—Boston Globe
1976—Anchorage (AK) Daily News
1977—Lufkin (TX) News
1978—Philadelphia Inquirer
1979—Point Reyes (CA) Light
1980—Gannett News Service
1981—Charlotte (NC) Observer
1982—Detroit News
1983—Jackson (MS) Clarion-Ledger
1984—Los Angeles Times
1985—Ft. Worth (TX) Star-Telegram
1986—Denver Post
1987—Pittsburgh Press
1988—Charlotte (NC) Observer
1989—Anchorage (AK) Daily News
1990—Philadelphia Inquirer, Gilbert M. Gaul; Washington (NC) Daily News
1991—Des Moines (IA) Register, Jane Schorer
1992—Sacramento (CA) Bee, Tom Knudson
1993—Miami (FL) Herald
1994—Akron (OH) Beacon Journal
1995—Virgin Islands Daily News, St. Thomas
1996—News & Observer, Raleigh (NC)
1997—Times-Picayune, New Orleans (LA)

Reporting

This category originally embraced all fields. Later, separate categories were made for national and international reporting.

1917—Herbert Bayard Swope, New York World
1918—Harold A. Littledale, New York Evening Post
1920—John J. Leary Jr., New York World
1921—Louis Seibold, New York World
1922—Kirke L. Simpson, Associated Press (AP)
1923—Alva Johnston, New York Times
1924—Magner White, San Diego Sun
1925—James W. Mulroy, Alvin H. Goldstein, Chicago Daily News
1926—William Burke Miller, Louisville (KY) Courier-Journal
1927—John T. Rogers, St. Louis Post-Dispatch
1929—Paul Y. Anderson, St. Louis Post-Dispatch
1930—Russell D. Owens, New York Times. Also $500 to W.O. Dapping, Auburn (NY) Citizen
1931—A.B. MacDonald, Kansas City (MO) Star
1932—W.C. Richards, D.D. Martin, J.S. Pooler, F.D. Webb, J.N.W. Sloan, Detroit Free Press
1933—Francis A. Jamieson, AP
1934—Royce Brier, San Francisco Chronicle
1935—William H. Taylor, New York Herald Tribune
1936—Lauren D. Lyman, New York Times
1937—John J. O'Neill, NY Herald Tribune; William L. Laurence, NY Times; Howard W. Blakeslee, AP; Gobind Behari Lal, Universal Service; and David Dietz, Scripps-Howard Newspapers
1938—Raymond Sprigle, Pittsburgh Post-Gazette
1939—Thomas L. Stokes, Scripps-Howard Newspaper Alliance
1940—S. Burton Heath, New York World-Telegram
1941—Westbrook Pegler, New York World-Telegram
1942—Stanton Delaplane, San Francisco Chronicle
1943—George Weller, Chicago Daily News
1944—Paul Schoenstein, New York Journal-American
1945—Jack S. McDowell, San Francisco Call-Bulletin
1946—William L. Laurence, New York Times
1947—Frederick Woltman, New York World-Telegram
1948—George E. Goodwin, Atlanta Journal
1949—Malcolm Johnson, New York Sun
1950—Meyer Berger, New York Times
1951—Edward S. Montgomery, San Francisco Examiner
1952—George de Carvalho, San Francisco Chronicle
    (1) General or Spot; (2) Special or Investigative
1953—(1) Providence (RI) Journal and Evening Bulletin; (2) Edward J. Mowery, New York World-Telegram & Sun
1954—(1) Vicksburg (MS) Sunday Post-Herald; (2) Alvin Scott McCoy, Kansas City (MO) Star
1955—(1) Mrs. Caro Brown, Alice (TX) Daily Echo; (2) Roland K. Towery, Cuero (TX) Record
1956—(1) Lee Hills, Detroit Free Press; (2) Arthur Daley, New York Times
1957—(1) Salt Lake Tribune; (2) Wallace Turner and William Lambert, Portland Oregonian
1958—(1) Fargo, (ND) Forum; (2) George Beveridge, Washington (DC) Evening Star
1959—(1) Mary Lou Werner, Washington Evening Star; (2) John Harold Brislin, Scranton (PA) Tribune, and The Scrantonian
1960—(1) Jack Nelson, Atlanta Constitution; (2) Miriam Ottenberg, Washington (DC) Evening Star
1961—(1) Sanche de Gramont, New York Herald Tribune; (2) Edgar May, Buffalo (NY) Evening News
1962—(1) Robert D. Mullins, Deseret News, Salt Lake City; (2) George Bliss, Chicago Tribune
1963—(1) Shared by Sylvan Fox, William Longgood, and Anthony Shannon, New York World-Telegram & Sun; (2) Oscar Griffin Jr., Pecos (TX) Independent and Enterprise

1964—(1) Norman C. Miller, Wall Street Journal; (2) Shared by James V. Magee, Albert V. Gaudiosi, and Frederick A. Meyer, Philadelphia Bulletin
1965—(1) Melvin H. Ruder, Hungry Horse News, Columbia Falls, MT; (2) Gene Goltz, Houston Post
1966—(1) Los Angeles Times Staff; (2) John A. Frasca, Tampa (FL) Tribune
1967—(1) Robert V. Cox, Chambersburg (PA) Public Opinion; (2) Gene Miller, Miami (FL) Herald
1968—(1) Detroit Free Press Staff; (2) J. Anthony Lukas, New York Times
1969—(1) John Fetterman, Louisville Courier-Journal and Times; (2) Albert L. Delugach, St. Louis Globe Democrat, and Denny Walsh, Life
1970—(1) Thomas Fitzpatrick, Chicago Sun-Times; (2) Harold Eugene Martin, Montgomery Advertiser & Alabama Journal
1971—(1) Akron (OH) Beacon Journal Staff; (2) William Hugh Jones, Chicago Tribune
1972—(1) Richard Cooper and John Machacek, Rochester (NY) Times-Union; (2) Timothy Leland, Gerard M. O'Neill, Stephen A. Kurkjian and Anne De Santis, Boston Globe
1973—(1) Chicago Tribune; (2) Sun Newspapers of Omaha
1974—(1) Hugh F. Hough, Arthur M. Petacque, Chicago Sun-Times; (2) William Sherman, New York Daily News
1975—(1) Xenia (OH) Daily Gazette; (2) Indianapolis Star
1976—(1) Gene Miller, Miami (FL) Herald; (2) Chicago Tribune
1977—(1) Margo Huston, Milwaukee Journal; (2) Acel Moore, Wendell Rawls Jr., Philadelphia Inquirer
1978—(1) Richard Whitt, Louisville (KY) Courier-Journal; (2) Anthony R. Dolan, Stamford (CT) Advocate
1979—(1) San Diego (CA) Evening Tribune; (2) Gilbert M. Gaul, Elliot G. Jaspin, Pottsville (PA) Republican
1980—(1) Philadelphia Inquirer; (2) Stephen A. Kurkjian, Alexander B. Hawes Jr., Nils Bruzelius, Joan Vennochi, Robert M. Porterfield, Boston Globe
1981—(1) Longview (WA) Daily News staff; (2) Clark Hallas and Robert B. Lowe, Arizona Daily Star
1982—(1) Kansas City (MO) Star, Kansas City Times; (2) Paul Henderson, Seattle Times
1983—(1) Fort Wayne (IN) News-Sentinel; (2) Loretta Tofani, Washington Post
1984—(1) New York Newsday; (2) Boston Globe
1985—(1) Thomas Turcol, Virginian-Pilot and Ledger-Star, Norfolk, VA; (2) William K. Marimow, Philadelphia Inquirer; Lucy Morgan & Jack Reed, St. Petersburg (FL) Times
1986—(1) Edna Buchanan, Miami (FL) Herald; (2) Jeffrey A. Marx & Michael M. York, Lexington (KY) Herald-Leader
1987—(1) Akron (OH) Beacon Journal; (2) Daniel R. Biddle, H.G. Bissinger, Fredric N. Tulsky, Philadelphia Inquirer; John Woestendiek, Philadelphia Inquirer
1988—(1) Alabama Journal; Lawrence (MA) Eagle-Tribune; (2) Walt Bogdanich, Wall Street Journal
1989—(1) Louisville (KY) Courier-Journal; (2) Bill Dedman, Atlanta Journal and Constitution
1990—(1) San Jose (CA) Mercury News; (2) Lon Kilzer, Chris Ison, Star Tribune, Minneapolis-St. Paul
1991—(1) Miami (FL) Herald; (2) Joseph T. Hallinan, Susan M. Headden, Indianapolis Star
1992—(1) New York Newsday; (2) Lorraine Adams, Dan Malone, Dallas Morning News
1993—(1) Los Angeles Times; Jeff Brazil, Steve Berry, Orlando (FL) Sentinel
1994—(1) New York Times staff; (2) Providence (RI) Journal-Bulletin staff
1995—(1) Los Angeles Times staff; (2) Brian Donovan, Stephanie Saul, New York Newsday
1996—(1) New York Times, Robert D. McFadden; (2) The Orange County (CA) Register staff
1997—(1) Long Island (NY) Newsday, staff; (2) Eric Nalder, Deborah Nelson, Alex Tizon, Seattle Times

Criticism or Commentary

(1) Criticism; (2) Commentary
1970—(1) Ada Louise Huxtable, New York Times; (2) Marquis W. Childs, St. Louis Post-Dispatch
1971—(1) Harold C. Schonberg, New York Times; (2) William A. Caldwell, The Record, Hackensack, NJ
1972—(1) Frank Peters Jr., St. Louis Post-Dispatch; (2) Mike Royko, Chicago Daily News
1973—(1) Ronald Powers, Chicago Sun-Times; (2) David S. Broder, Washington Post
1974—(1) Emily Genauer, New York Newsday; (2) Edwin A. Roberts Jr., National Observer
1975—(1) Roger Ebert, Chicago Sun Times; (2) Mary McGrory, Washington Star
1976—(1) Alan M. Kriegsman, Washington Post; (2) Walter W. (Red) Smith, New York Times
1977—(1) William McPherson, Washington Post; (2) George F. Will, Washington Post Writers Group
1978—(1) Walter Kerr, New York Times; (2) William Safire, New York Times

(continued)

Criticism or Commentary (continued)

1979—(1) Paul Gapp, Chicago Tribune; (2) Russell Baker, New York Times
1980—(1) William A. Henry III, Boston Globe; (2) Ellen Goodman, Boston Globe
1981—(1) Jonathan Yardley, Washington Star; (2) Dave Anderson, New York Times
1982—(1) Martin Bernheimer, Los Angeles Times; (2) Art Buchwald, Los Angeles Times Syndicate
1983—(1) Manuela Hoelterhoff, Wall Street Journal; (2) Claude Sitton, Raleigh (NC) News & Observer
1984—(1) Paul Goldberger, New York Times; (2) Vermont Royster, Wall Street Journal
1985—(1) Howard Rosenberg, Los Angeles Times; (2) Murray Kempton, New York Newsday
1986—(1) Donal J. Henahan, New York Times; (2) Jimmy Breslin, New York Daily News
1987—(1) Richard Eder, Los Angeles Times; (2) Charles Krauthammer, Washington Post
1988—(1) Tom Shales, Washington Post; (2) Dave Barry, Miami (FL) Herald
1989—(1) Michael Skube, News and Observer, Raleigh, NC; (2) Clarence Page, Chicago Tribune
1990—(1) Allan Temko, San Francisco Chronicle; (2) Jim Murray, Los Angeles Times
1991—(1) David Shaw, Los Angeles Times; (2) Jim Hoagland, Washington Post
1992—(1) No award; (2) Anna Quindlen, New York Times
1993—(1) Michael Dirda, Washington Post; (2) Liz Balmaseda, Miami (FL) Herald
1994—(1) Lloyd Schwartz, Boston Phoenix; (2) William Raspberry, Washington Post
1995—(1) Margo Jefferson, New York Times; (2) Jim Dwyer, New York Newsday
1996—(1) Robert Campbell, Boston Globe; (2) E.R. Shipp, New York Daily News
1997—(1) Tim Page, Washington Post; (2) Eileen McNamara, Boston Globe

National Reporting

1942—Louis Stark, New York Times
1944—Dewey L. Fleming, Baltimore Sun
1945—James B. Reston, New York Times
1946—Edward A. Harris, St. Louis Post-Dispatch
1947—Edward T. Folliard, Washington Post
1948—Bert Andrews, New York Herald Tribune; Nat S. Finney, Minneapolis Tribune
1949—Charles P. Trussell, New York Times
1950—Edwin O. Guthman, Seattle Times
1952—Anthony Leviero, New York Times
1953—Don Whitehead, AP
1954—Richard Wilson, Des Moines (IA) Register
1955—Anthony Lewis, Washington Daily News
1956—Charles L. Bartlett, Chattanooga (TN) Times
1957—James Reston, New York Times
1958—Relman Morin, AP; Clark Mollenhoff, Des Moines (IA) Register & Tribune
1959—Howard Van Smith, Miami (FL) News
1960—Vance Trimble, Scripps-Howard, Washington, DC
1961—Edward R. Cony, Wall Street Journal
1962—Nathan G. Caldwell and Gene S. Graham, Nashville Tennessean
1963—Anthony Lewis, New York Times
1964—Merriman Smith, UPI
1965—Louis M. Kohlmeier, Wall Street Journal
1966—Haynes Johnson, Washington (DC) Evening Star
1967—Monroe Karmin and Stanley Penn, Wall Street Journal
1968—Howard James, Christian Science Monitor; Nathan K. Kotz, Des Moines (IA) Register
1969—Robert Cahn, Christian Science Monitor
1970—William J. Eaton, Chicago Daily News
1971—Lucinda Franks & Thomas Powers, UPI
1972—Jack Anderson, United Feature Syndicate
1973—Robert Boyd and Clark Hoyt, Knight Newspapers
1974—James R. Polk, Washington (DC) Star-News; Jack White, Providence (RI) Journal-Bulletin
1975—Donald L. Barlett and James B. Steele, Philadelphia Inquirer
1976—James Risser, Des Moines (IA) Register
1977—Walter Mears, AP
1978—Gaylord D. Shaw, Los Angeles Times
1979—James Risser, Des Moines (IA) Register
1980—Charles Stafford, Bette Swenson Orsini, St. Petersburg (FL) Times
1981—John M. Crewdson, New York Times
1982—Rick Atkinson, Kansas City Times
1983—Boston Globe
1984—John Noble Wilford, New York Times
1985—Thomas J. Knudson, Des Moines (IA) Register
1986—Craig Flournoy & George Rodrigue, Dallas Morning News; Arthur Howe, Philadelphia Inquirer
1987—Miami (FL) Herald; New York Times

1988—Tim Weiner, Philadelphia Inquirer
1989—Donald L. Barlett & James B. Steele, Philadelphia Inquirer
1990—Ross Anderson, Bill Dietrich, Mary Ann Gwinn, Eric Nalder, Seattle Times
1991—Marjie Lundstrom, Rochelle Sharpe, Gannett News Service
1992—Jeff Taylor, Mike McGraw, Kansas City (MO) Star
1993—David Maraniss, Washington Post
1994—Eileen Welsome, Albuquerque Tribune
1995—Tony Horwitz, Wall Street Journal
1996—Alix M. Freedman, Wall Street Journal
1997—Staff, Wall Street Journal

International Reporting

1942—Laurence Edmund Allen, AP
1943—Ira Wolfert, North American Newspaper Alliance
1944—Daniel DeLuce, AP
1945—Mark S. Watson, Baltimore Sun
1946—Homer W. Bigart, New York Herald Tribune
1947—Eddy Gilmore, AP
1948—Paul W. Ward, Baltimore Sun
1949—Price Day, Baltimore Sun
1950—Edmund Stevens, Christian Science Monitor
1951—Keyes Beech and Fred Sparks, Chicago Daily News; Homer Bigart and Marguerite Higgins, New York Herald Tribune; Relman Morin and Don Whitehead, AP
1952—John M. Hightower, AP
1953—Austin C. Wehrwein, Milwaukee Journal
1954—Jim G. Lucas, Scripps-Howard Newspapers
1955—Harrison Salisbury, New York Times
1956—William Randolph Hearst Jr., Frank Conniff, Hearst Newspapers; Kingsbury Smith, INS
1957—Russell Jones, UPI
1958—New York Times
1959—Joseph Martin and Philip Santora, New York Daily News
1960—A.M. Rosenthal, New York Times
1961—Lynn Heinzerling, AP
1962—Walter Lippmann, New York Herald Tribune Syndicate
1963—Hal Hendrix, Miami (FL) News
1964—Malcolm W. Browne, AP; David Halberstam, New York Times
1965—J.A. Livingston, Philadelphia Bulletin
1966—Peter Arnett, AP
1967—R. John Hughes, Christian Science Monitor
1968—Alfred Friendly, Washington Post
1969—William Tuohy, Los Angeles Times
1970—Seymour M. Hersh, Dispatch News Service
1971—Jimmie Lee Hoagland, Washington Post
1972—Peter R. Kann, Wall Street Journal
1973—Max Frankel, New York Times
1974—Hedrick Smith, New York Times
1975—William Mullen and Ovie Carter, Chicago Tribune
1976—Sydney H. Schanberg, New York Times
1978—Henry Kamm, New York Times
1979—Richard Ben Cramer, Philadelphia Inquirer
1980—Joel Brinkley, Jay Mather, Louisville (KY) Courier-Journal
1981—Shirley Christian, Miami (FL) Herald
1982—John Darnton, New York Times
1983—Thomas L. Friedman, New York Times; Loren Jenkins, Washington Post
1984—Karen Elliot House, Wall Street Journal
1985—Josh Friedman, Dennis Bell, Ozler Muhammad, New York Newsday
1986—Lewis M. Simons, Pete Carey, Katherine Ellison, San Jose (CA) Mercury News
1987—Michael Parks, Los Angeles Times
1988—Thomas L. Friedman, New York Times
1989—Glenn Frankel, Washington Post; Bill Keller, New York Times
1990—Nicholas D. Kirstof, Sheryl WuDunn, New York Times
1991—Caryle Murphy, Washington Post; Serge Schmemann, New York Times
1992—Patrick J. Sloyan, New York Newsday
1993—John F. Burns, New York Times; Roy Gutman, New York Newsday
1994—Dallas Morning News team
1995—Mark Fritz, AP
1996—David Rohde, Christian Science Monitor
1997—John F. Burns, New York Times

Washington or Foreign Correspondence

Category was merged with others in 1948.
1929—Paul Scott Mowrer, Chicago Daily News
1930—Leland Stowe, New York Herald Tribune
1931—H.R. Knickerbocker, Philadelphia Public Ledger and New York Evening Post
1932—Walter Duranty, New York Times, and Charles G. Ross, St. Louis Post-Dispatch
1933—Edgar Ansel Mowrer, Chicago Daily News
1934—Frederick T. Birchall, New York Times
1935—Arthur Krock, New York Times
1936—Wilfred C. Barber, Chicago Tribune

1937—Anne O'Hare McCormick, New York Times
1938—Arthur Krock, New York Times
1939—Louis P. Lochner, AP
1940—Otto D. Tolischus, New York Times
1941—Bronze plaque to commemorate work of American correspondents on war fronts
1942—Carlos P. Romulo, Philippines Herald
1943—Hanson W. Baldwin, New York Times
1944—Ernest Taylor Pyle, Scripps-Howard Newspaper Alliance
1945—Harold V. (Hal) Boyle, AP
1946—Arnaldo Cortesi, New York Times
1947—Brooks Atkinson, New York Times

Editorial Writing

1917—New York Tribune
1918—Louisville (KY) Courier-Journal
1920—Harvey E. Newbranch, Omaha Evening World-Herald
1922—Frank M. O'Brien, New York Herald
1923—William Allen White, Emporia (KS) Gazette
1924—Frank Buxton, Boston Herald, Special Prize; Frank I. Cobb, New York World
1925—Robert Lathan, Charleston (SC) News and Courier
1926—Edward M. Kingsbury, New York Times
1927—F. Lauriston Bullard, Boston Herald
1928—Grover C. Hall, Montgomery (AL) Advertiser
1929—Louis Isaac Jaffe, Norfolk Virginian-Pilot
1931—Chas. Ryckman, Fremont (NE) Tribune
1933—Kansas City (MO) Star
1934—E. P. Chase, Atlantic (IA) News Telegraph
1936—Felix Morley, Washington Post; George B. Parker, Scripps-Howard Newspapers
1937—John W. Owens, Baltimore Sun
1938—W.W. Waymack, Des Moines (IA) Register and Tribune
1939—Ronald G. Callvert, Portland Oregonian
1940—Bart Howard, St. Louis Post-Dispatch
1941—Reuben Maury, New York Daily News
1942—Geoffrey Parsons, New York Herald Tribune
1943—Forrest W. Seymour, Des Moines (IA) Register & Tribune
1944—Henry J. Haskell, Kansas City (MO) Star
1945—George W. Potter, Providence (RI) Journal-Bulletin
1946—Hodding Carter, Greenville (MS) Delta Democrat-Times
1947—William H. Grimes, Wall Street Journal
1948—Virginius Dabney, Richmond (VA) Times-Dispatch
1949—John H. Crider, Boston Herald; Herbert Elliston, Washington Post
1950—Carl M. Saunders, Jackson (MI) Citizen-Patriot
1951—William H. Fitzpatrick, New Orleans States
1952—Louis LaCoss, St. Louis Globe Democrat
1953—Vermont C. Royster, Wall Street Journal
1954—Don Murray, Boston Herald
1955—Royce Howes, Detroit Free Press
1956—Lauren K. Soth, Des Moines (IA) Register and Tribune
1957—Buford Boone, Tuscaloosa (AL) News
1958—Harry S. Ashmore, Arkansas Gazette
1959—Ralph McGill, Atlanta Constitution
1960—Lenoir Chambers, Norfolk Virginian-Pilot
1961—William J. Dorvillier, San Juan (Puerto Rico) Star
1962—Thomas M. Storke, Santa Barbara (CA) News-Press
1963—Ira B. Harkey Jr., Pascagoula (MS) Chronicle
1964—Hazel Brannon Smith, Lexington (MS) Advertiser
1965—John R. Harrison, Gainesville (FL) Sun
1966—Robert Lasch, St. Louis Post-Dispatch
1967—Eugene C. Patterson, Atlanta Constitution
1968—John S. Knight, Knight Newspapers
1969—Paul Greenberg, Pine Bluff (AR) Commercial
1970—Philip L. Geyelin, Washington Post
1971—Horance G. Davis Jr., Gainesville (FL) Sun
1972—John Strohmeyer, Bethlehem (PA) Globe-Times
1973—Roger B. Linscott, Berkshire Eagle, Pittsfield, MA
1974—F. Gilman Spencer, Trenton (NJ) Trentonian
1975—John D. Maurice, Charleston (WV) Daily Mail
1976—Philip Kerby, Los Angeles Times
1977—Warren L. Lerude, Foster Church, and Norman F. Cardoza, Reno Evening Gazette and Nevada State Journal
1978—Meg Greenfield, Washington Post
1979—Edwin M. Yoder, Washington Star
1980—Robert L. Bartley, Wall Street Journal
1982—Jack Rosenthal, New York Times
1983—Editorial board, Miami Herald
1984—Albert Scardino, Georgia Gazette
1985—Richard Aregood, Philadelphia Daily News
1986—Jack Fuller, Chicago Tribune
1987—Jonathan Freedman, Tribune (San Diego)
1988—Jane Healy, Orlando (FL) Sentinel
1989—Lois Wille, Chicago Tribune
1990—Thomas J. Hylton, Pottstown (PA) Mercury
1991—Ron Casey, Harold Jackson, Joey Kennedy, Birmingham (AL) News
1992—Maria Henson, Lexington (KY) Herald-Leader
1994—R. Bruce Dold, Chicago Tribune
1995—Jeffrey Good, St. Petersburg (FL) Times

1996—Robert B. Semple Jr., New York Times
1997—Michael Gartner, Ames (IA) Daily Tribune

Editorial Cartooning

1922—Rollin Kirby, New York World
1924—Jay N. Darling, Des Moines (IA) Register
1925—Rollin Kirby, New York World
1926—D. R. Fitzpatrick, St. Louis Post-Dispatch
1927—Nelson Harding, Brooklyn Eagle
1928—Nelson Harding, Brooklyn Eagle
1929—Rollin Kirby, New York World
1930—Charles Macauley, Brooklyn Eagle
1931—Edmund Duffy, Baltimore Sun
1932—John T. McCutcheon, Chicago Tribune
1933—H. M. Talburt, Washington Daily News
1934—Edmund Duffy, Baltimore Sun
1935—Ross A. Lewis, Milwaukee Journal
1937—C. D. Batchelor, New York Daily News
1938—Vaughn Shoemaker, Chicago Daily News
1939—Charles G. Werner, Daily Oklahoman
1940—Edmund Duffy, Baltimore Sun
1941—Jacob Burck, Chicago Times
1942—Herbert L. Block, Newspaper Enterprise Assn.
1943—Jay N. Darling, Des Moines (IA) Register
1944—Clifford K. Berryman, Washington Star
1945—Bill Mauldin, United Feature Syndicate
1946—Bruce Alexander Russell, Los Angeles Times
1947—Vaughn Shoemaker, Chicago Daily News
1948—Reuben L. (Rube) Goldberg, New York Sun
1949—Lute Pease, Newark (NJ) Evening News
1950—James T. Berryman, Washington Star
1951—Reginald W. Manning, Arizona Republic
1952—Fred L. Packer, New York Mirror
1953—Edward D. Kuekes, Cleveland Plain Dealer
1954—Herbert L. Block, Washington Post & Times-Herald
1955—Daniel R. Fitzpatrick, St. Louis Post-Dispatch
1956—Robert York, Louisville (KY) Times
1957—Tom Little, Nashville Tennessean
1958—Bruce M. Shanks, Buffalo Evening News
1959—Bill Mauldin, St. Louis Post-Dispatch
1961—Carey Orr, Chicago Tribune
1962—Edmund S. Valtman, Hartford Times
1963—Frank Miller, Des Moines (IA) Register
1964—Paul Conrad, Denver Post
1966—Don Wright, Miami (FL) News
1967—Patrick B. Oliphant, Denver Post
1968—Eugene Gray Payne, Charlotte (NC) Observer
1969—John Fischetti, Chicago Daily News
1970—Thomas F. Darcy, New York Newsday
1971—Paul Conrad, Los Angeles Times
1972—Jeffrey K. MacNelly, Richmond News-Leader
1974—Paul Szep, Boston Globe
1975—Garry Trudeau, Universal Press Syndicate
1976—Tony Auth, Philadelphia Inquirer
1977—Paul Szep, Boston Globe
1978—Jeffrey K. MacNelly, Richmond News Leader
1979—Herbert L. Block, Washington Post
1980—Don Wright, Miami (FL) News
1981—Mike Peters, Dayton (OH) Daily News
1982—Ben Sargent, Austin American-Statesman
1983—Richard Lochner, Chicago Tribune
1984—Paul Conrad, Los Angeles Times
1985—Jeffrey K. MacNelly, Chicago Tribune
1986—Jules Feiffer, Village Voice (NY)
1987—Berke Breathed, Washington Post
1988—Doug Marlette, Atlanta Constitution, Charlotte (NC) Observer
1989—Jack Higgins, Chicago Sun-Times
1990—Tom Toles, Buffalo News
1991—Jim Borgman, Cincinnati Enquirer
1992—Signe Wilkinson, Philadelphia Daily News
1993—Stephen R. Benson, Arizona Republic
1994—Michael P. Ramirez, Commercial Appeal, Memphis, TN
1995—Mike Luckovich, Atlanta Constitution
1996—Jim Morin, Miami (FL) Herald
1997—Walt Handelsman, New Orleans (LA) Times-Picayune

Spot News Photography

1942—Milton Brooks, Detroit News
1943—Frank Noel, AP
1944—Frank Filan, AP; Earl L. Bunker, Omaha World-Herald
1945—Joe Rosenthal, AP
1947—Arnold Hardy, amateur, Atlanta, GA
1948—Frank Cushing, Boston Traveler
1949—Nathaniel Fein, New York Herald Tribune
1950—Bill Crouch, Oakland (CA) Tribune
1951—Max Desfor, AP
1952—John Robinson and Don Ultang, Des Moines (IA) Register & Tribune
1953—William M. Gallagher, Flint (MI) Journal
1954—Mrs. Walter M. Schau, amateur
1955—John L. Gaunt Jr., Los Angeles Times
1956—New York Daily News

(continued)

Spot News Photography *(continued)*

1957—Harry A. Trask, Boston Traveler
1958—William C. Beall, Washington Daily News
1959—William Seaman, Minneapolis Star
1960—Andrew Lopez, UPI
1961—Yasushi Nagao, Mainichi Newspapers, Tokyo
1962—Paul Vathis, AP
1963—Hector Rondon, La Republica, Caracas, Venezuela
1964—Robert H. Jackson, Dallas Times-Herald
1965—Horst Faas, AP
1966—Kyoichi Sawada, UPI
1967—Jack R. Thornell, AP
1968—Rocco Morabito, Jacksonville (FL) Journal
1969—Edward Adams, AP
1970—Steve Starr, AP
1971—John Paul Filo, Valley Daily News & Daily Dispatch of Tarentum & New Kensington, PA
1972—Horst Faas and Michel Laurent, AP
1973—Huynh Cong Ut, AP
1974—Anthony K. Roberts, AP
1975—Gerald H. Gay, Seattle Times
1976—Stanley Forman, Boston Herald American
1977—Neal Ulevich, AP; Stanley Forman, Boston Herald American
1978—John H. Blair, UPI
1979—Thomas J. Kelly III, Pottstown (PA) Mercury
1980—UPI
1981—Larry C. Price, Ft. Worth (TX) Star-Telegram
1982—Ron Edmonds, AP
1983—Bill Foley, AP
1984—Stan Grossfeld, Boston Globe
1985—The Register, Santa Ana, CA
1986—Carol Guzy & Michel duCille, Miami (FL) Herald
1987—Kim Komenich, San Francisco Examiner
1988—Scott Shaw, Odessa (TX) American
1989—Ron Olshwanger, St. Louis Post-Dispatch
1990—Oakland (CA) Tribune photo staff
1991—Greg Marinovich, AP
1992—Associated Press staff
1993—Ken Geiger, William Snyder, Dallas Morning News
1994—Paul Watson, Toronto Star
1995—Carol Guzy, Washington Post
1996—Charles Porter IV, AP
1997—Annie Wells, Santa Rosa (CA) Press Democrat

Feature Photography

1968—Toshio Sakai, UPI
1969—Moneta Sleet Jr., Ebony
1970—Dallas Kinney, Palm Beach (FL) Post
1971—Jack Dykinga, Chicago Sun-Times
1972—Dave Kennerly, UPI
1973—Brian Lanker, Topeka (KS) Capitol-Journal
1974—Slava Veder, AP
1975—Matthew Lewis, Washington Post
1976—Louisville (KY) Courier-Journal and Louisville Times
1977—Robin Hood, Chattanooga (TN) News-Free Press
1978—J. Ross Baughman, AP
1979—Staff photographers, Boston Herald American
1980—Erwin H. Hagler, Dallas Times-Herald
1981—Taro M. Yamasaki, Detroit Free Press
1982—John H. White, Chicago Sun-Times
1983—James B. Dickman, Dallas Times-Herald
1984—Anthony Suad, Denver Post
1985—Stan Grossfeld, Boston Globe; Larry C. Price, Phila. Inquirer
1986—Tom Gralish, Philadelphia Inquirer
1987—David Peterson, Des Moines (IA) Register
1988—Michel duCille, Miami (FL) Herald
1989—Manny Crisostomo, Detroit Free Press
1990—David C. Turnley, Detroit Free Press
1991—William Snyder, Dallas Morning News
1992—John Kaplan, Block Newspapers (Toledo, OH)
1993—AP staff
1994—Kevin Carter, New York Times
1995—AP staff
1996—Stephanie Welsh, Newhouse News Service
1997—Alexander Zemlianichenko, AP

Special Citation

1938—Edmonton (Alberta) Journal, bronze plaque
1941—New York Times

Fiction

1918—Ernest Poole, *His Family*
1919—Booth Tarkington, *The Magnificent Ambersons*
1921—Edith Wharton, *The Age of Innocence*
1922—Booth Tarkington, *Alice Adams*
1923—Willa Cather, *One of Ours*
1924—Margaret Wilson, *The Able McLaughlins*
1925—Edna Ferber, *So Big*
1926—Sinclair Lewis, *Arrowsmith* (refused prize)

1944—Byron Price and Mrs. William Allen White. Also to Richard Rodgers and Oscar Hammerstein 2d, for musical *Oklahoma!*
1945—Press cartographers for war maps
1947—(Pulitzer centennial year) Columbia Univ. and the Graduate School of Journalism; St. Louis Post-Dispatch
1948—Dr. Frank Diehl Fackenthal
1951—Cyrus L. Sulzberger, New York Times
1952—Max Kase, New York Journal-American, Kansas City (MO) Star
1953—New York Times; Lester Markel
1957—Kenneth Roberts, for his historical novels
1958—Walter Lippmann, New York Herald Tribune
1960—Garrett Mattingly, for *The Armada*
1961—American Heritage *Picture History of the Civil War*
1964—Gannett Newspapers
1973—James T. Flexner, for biography of George Washington
1976—John Hohenberg, for services to American journalism
1977—Alex Haley, for *Roots*
1978—Richard Lee Strout, Christian Science Monitor and New Republic; E.B. White
1984—Theodore Geisel ("Dr. Seuss")
1985—William Schuman, composer, educational leader
1987—Joseph Pulitzer Jr.
1992—Art Spiegelman, for *Maus*
1996—Herb Caen, San Francisco Chronicle

Feature Writing

1979—Jon D. Franklin, Baltimore Evening Sun
1980—Madeleine Blais, Miami (FL) Herald Tropic Magazine;
1981—Teresa Carpenter, Village Voice, New York City
1982—Saul Pett, AP
1984—Peter M. Rinearson, Seattle Times
1985—Alice Steinbach, Baltimore Sun
1986—John Camp, St. Paul Pioneer Press & Dispatch
1987—Steve Twomey, Philadephia Inquirer
1988—Jacqui Banaszynski, St. Paul Pioneer Press Dispatch
1989—David Zucchino, Philadelphia Inquirer
1990—Dave Curtin, Colorado Springs Gazette Telegraph
1991—Sheryl James, St. Petersburg (FL) Times
1992—Howell Raines, New York Times
1993—George Lardner Jr., Washington Post
1994—Isabel Wilkerson, New York Times
1995—Ron Suskind, Wall Street Journal
1996—Rick Bragg, New York Times
1997—Lisa Pollak, Baltimore Sun

Explanatory Journalism

1985—Jon Franklin, Baltimore Evening Sun
1986—New York Times staff
1987—Jeff Lyon & Peter Gorner, Chicago Tribune
1988—Daniel Hertzberg, James B. Stewart, Wall Street Journal
1989—David Hanners, William Snyder, Karen Blessen, Dallas Morning News
1990—David A. Vise, Steve Coll, Washington Post
1991—Susan C. Faludi, Wall Street Journal
1992—Robert S. Capers, Eric Lipton, Hartford (CT) Courant
1993—Mike Toner, Atlanta Journal-Constitution
1994—Ronald Kotulak, Chicago Tribune
1995—Leon Dash, Lucian Perkins, Washington Post
1996—Laurie Garrett, New York Newsday
1997—Michael Vitez, Ron Cortes, April Saul, Philadelphia Inquirer

Specialized Reporting (1985-90)

1985—Randall Savage, Jackie Crosby, Macon (GA) Telegraph & News
1986—Andrew Schneider & Mary Pat Flaherty, Pittsburgh Press
1987—Alex S. Jones, New York Times
1988—Dean Baquet, William Gaines, Ann Marie Lipinski, Chicago Tribune
1989—Edward Humes, Orange County (CA) Register
1990—Tamar Stieber, Albuquerque Journal

Beat Reporting

1991—Natalie Angier, New York Times
1992—Deborah Blum, Sacramento (CA) Bee
1993—Paul Ingrassia, Joseph B. White, Wall Street Journal
1994—Eric Freedman, Jim Mitzelfeld, Detroit News
1995—David Shribman, Boston Globe
1996—Bob Keeler, New York Newsday
1997—Byron Acohido, Seattle Times

Letters

1927—Louis Bromfield, *Early Autumn*
1928—Thornton Wilder, *Bridge of San Luis Rey*
1929—Julia M. Peterkin, *Scarlet Sister Mary*
1930—Oliver LaFarge, *Laughing Boy*
1931—Margaret Ayer Barnes, *Years of Grace*
1932—Pearl S. Buck, *The Good Earth*
1933—T. S. Stribling, *The Store*
1934—Caroline Miller, *Lamb In His Bosom*
1935—Josephine W. Johnson, *Now in November*
1936—Harold L. Davis, *Honey in the Horn*

1937—Margaret Mitchell, *Gone With the Wind*
1938—John P. Marquand, *The Late George Apley*
1939—Marjorie Kinnan Rawlings, *The Yearling*
1940—John Steinbeck, *The Grapes of Wrath*
1942—Ellen Glasgow, *In This Our Life*
1943—Upton Sinclair, *Dragon's Teeth*
1944—Martin Flavin, *Journey in the Dark*
1945—John Hersey, *A Bell for Adano*
1947—Robert Penn Warren, *All the King's Men*
1948—James A. Michener, *Tales of the South Pacific*
1949—James Gould Cozzens, *Guard of Honor*
1950—A. B. Guthrie Jr., *The Way West*
1951—Conrad Richter, *The Town*
1952—Herman Wouk, *The Caine Mutiny*
1953—Ernest Hemingway, *The Old Man and the* Sea
1955—William Faulkner, *A Fable*
1956—MacKinlay Kantor, *Andersonville*
1958—James Agee, *A Death in the Family*
1959—Robert Lewis Taylor, *The Travels of Jaimie McPheeters*
1960—Allen Drury, *Advise and Consent*
1961—Harper Lee, *To Kill a Mockingbird*
1962—Edwin O'Connor, *The Edge of Sadness*
1963—William Faulkner, *The Reivers*
1965—Shirley Ann Grau, *The Keepers of the House*
1966—Katherine Anne Porter, *Collected Stories*
1967—Bernard Malamud, *The Fixer*
1968—William Styron, *The Confessions of Nat Turner*
1969—N. Scott Momaday, *House Made of Dawn*
1970—Jean Stafford, *Collected Stories*
1972—Wallace Stegner, *Angle of Repose*
1973—Eudora Welty, *The Optimist's Daughter*
1975—Michael Shaara, *The Killer Angels*
1976—Saul Bellow, *Humboldt's Gift*
1978—James Alan McPherson, *Elbow Room*
1979—John Cheever, *The Stories of John Cheever*
1980—Norman Mailer, *The Executioner's Song*
1981—John Kennedy Toole, *A Confederacy of Dunces*
1982—John Updike, *Rabbit Is Rich*
1983—Alice Walker, *The Color Purple*
1984—William Kennedy, *Ironweed*
1985—Alison Lurie, *Foreign Affairs*
1986—Larry McMurtry, *Lonesome Dove*
1987—Peter Taylor, *A Summons to Memphis*
1988—Toni Morrison, *Beloved*
1989—Anne Tyler, *Breathing Lessons*
1990—Oscar Hijuelos, *The Mambo Kings Play Songs of Love*
1991—John Updike, *Rabbit at Rest*
1992—Jane Smiley, *A Thousand Acres*
1993—Robert Olen Butler, *A Good Scent From a Strange Mountain*
1994—E. Annie Proulx, *The Shipping News*
1995—Carol Shields, *The Stone Diaries*
1996—Richard Ford, *Independence Day*
1997—Steven Millhauser, *Martin Dressler: The Tale of an American Dreamer*

Drama

1918—Jesse Lynch Williams, *Why Marry?*
1920—Eugene O'Neill, *Beyond the Horizon*
1921—Zona Gale, *Miss Lulu Bett*
1922—Eugene O'Neill, *Anna Christie*
1923—Owen Davis, *Icebound*
1924—Hatcher Hughes, *Hell-Bent for Heaven*
1925—Sidney Howard, *They Knew What They Wanted*
1926—George Kelly, *Craig's Wife*
1927—Paul Green, *In Abraham's Bosom*
1928—Eugene O'Neill, *Strange Interlude*
1929—Elmer Rice, *Street Scene*
1930—Marc Connelly, *The Green Pastures*
1931—Susan Glaspell, *Alison's House*
1932—George S. Kaufman, Morrie Ryskind, and Ira Gershwin, *Of Thee I Sing*
1933—Maxwell Anderson, *Both Your Houses*
1934—Sidney Kingsley, *Men in White*
1935—Zoe Akins, *The Old Maid*
1936—Robert E. Sherwood, *Idiot's Delight*
1937—George S. Kaufman and Moss Hart, *You Can't Take It With You*
1938—Thornton Wilder, *Our Town*
1939—Robert E. Sherwood, *Abe Lincoln in Illinois*
1940—William Saroyan, *The Time of Your Life*
1941—Robert E. Sherwood, *There Shall Be No Night*
1943—Thornton Wilder, *The Skin of Our Teeth*
1945—Mary Chase, *Harvey*
1946—Russel Crouse and Howard Lindsay, *State of the Union*
1948—Tennessee Williams, *A Streetcar Named Desire*
1949—Arthur Miller, *Death of a Salesman*
1950—Richard Rodgers, Oscar Hammerstein 2d, and Joshua Logan, *South Pacific*
1952—Joseph Kramm, *The Shrike*
1953—William Inge, *Picnic*
1954—John Patrick, *Teahouse of the August Moon*

1955—Tennessee Williams, *Cat on a Hot Tin Roof*
1956—Frances Goodrich and Albert Hackett, *The Diary of Anne Frank*
1957—Eugene O'Neill, *Long Day's Journey Into Night*
1958—Ketti Frings, *Look Homeward, Angel*
1959—Archibald MacLeish, *J. B.*
1960—George Abbott, Jerome Weidman, Sheldon Harnick, and Jerry Bock, *Fiorello*
1961—Tad Mosel, *All the Way Home*
1962—Frank Loesser and Abe Burrows, *How to Succeed in Business Without Really Trying*
1965—Frank D. Gilroy, *The Subject Was Roses*
1967—Edward Albee, *A Delicate Balance*
1969—Howard Sackler, *The Great White Hope*
1970—Charles Gordone, *No Place to Be Somebody*
1971—Paul Zindel, *The Effect of Gamma Rays on Man-in-the-Moon Marigolds*
1973—Jason Miller, *That Championship Season*
1975—Edward Albee, *Seascape*
1976—Michael Bennett, James Kirkwood, Nicholas Dante, Marvin Hamlisch, and Edward Kleban, *A Chorus Line*
1977—Michael Cristofer, *The Shadow Box*
1978—Donald L. Coburn, *The Gin Game*
1979—Sam Shepard, *Buried Child*
1980—Lanford Wilson, *Talley's Folly*
1981—Beth Henley, *Crimes of the Heart*
1982—Charles Fuller, *A Soldier's Play*
1983—Marsha Norman, *'night, Mother*
1984—David Mamet, *Glengarry Glen Ross*
1985—Stephen Sondheim and James Lapine, *Sunday in the Park With George*
1987—August Wilson, *Fences*
1988—Alfred Uhry, *Driving Miss Daisy*
1989—Wendy Wasserstein, *The Heidi Chronicles*
1990—August Wilson, *The Piano Lesson*
1991—Neil Simon, *Lost in Yonkers*
1992—Robert Schenkkan, *The Kentucky Cycle*
1993—Tony Kushner, *Angels in America: Millennium Approaches*
1994—Edward Albee, *Three Tall Women*
1995—Horton Foote, *The Young Man From Atlanta*
1996—Jonathan Larson, *Rent*

History (U.S.)

1917—J. J. Jusserand, *With Americans of Past and Present Days*
1918—James Ford Rhodes, *History of the Civil War*
1920—Justin H. Smith, *The War With Mexico*
1921—William Sowden Sims, *The Victory at Sea*
1922—James Truslow Adams, *The Founding of New England*
1923—Charles Warren, *The Supreme Court in United States History*
1924—Charles Howard McIlwain, *The American Revolution: A Constitutional Interpretation*
1925—Frederick L. Paxton, *A History of the American Frontier*
1926—Edward Channing, *A History of the U.S.*
1927—Samuel Flagg Bemis, *Pinckney's Treaty*
1928—V. L Parrington, *Main Currents in American Thought*
1929—Fred A. Shannon, *The Organization and Administration of the Union Army, 1861-65*
1930—Claude H. Van Tyne, *The War of Independence*
1931—Bernadotte E. Schmitt, *The Coming of the War, 1914*
1932—Gen. John J. Pershing, *My Experiences in the World War*
1933—Frederick J. Turner, *The Significance of Sections in American History*
1934—Herbert Agar, *The People's Choice*
1935—Charles McLean Andrews, *The Colonial Period of American History*
1936—Andrew C. McLaughlin, *The Constitutional History of the United States*
1937—Van Wyck Brooks, *The Flowering of New England*
1938—Paul Herman Buck, *The Road to Reunion, 1865-1900*
1939—Frank Luther Mott, *A History of American Magazines*
1940—Carl Sandburg, *Abraham Lincoln: The War Years*
1941—Marcus Lee Hansen, *The Atlantic Migration, 1607-1860*
1942—Margaret Leech, *Reveille in Washington*
1943—Esther Forbes, *Paul Revere and the World He Lived In*
1944—Merle Curti, *The Growth of American Thought*
1945—Stephen Bonsal, *Unfinished Business*
1946—Arthur M. Schlesinger Jr., *The Age of Jackson*
1947—James Phinney Baxter 3d, *Scientists Against Time*
1948—Bernard De Voto, *Across the Wide Missouri*
1949—Roy F. Nichols, *The Disruption of American Democracy*
1950—O. W. Larkin, *Art and Life in America*
1951—R. Carlyle Buley, *The Old Northwest: Pioneer Period 1815-1840*
1952—Oscar Handlin, *The Uprooted*
1953—George Dangerfield, *The Era of Good Feelings*
1954—Bruce Catton, *A Stillness at Appomattox*
1955—Paul Horgan, *Great River: The Rio Grande in North American History*
1956—Richard Hofstadter, *The Age of Reform*
1957—George F. Kennan, *Russia Leaves the War*

(continued)

1958—Bray Hammond, *Banks and Politics in America—From the Revolution to the Civil War*
1959—Leonard D. White and Jean Schneider, *The Republican Era; 1869-1901*
1960—Margaret Leech, *In the Days of McKinley*
1961—Herbert Feis, *Between War and Peace: The Potsdam Conference*
1962—Lawrence H. Gibson, *The Triumphant Empire: Thunderclouds Gather in the West*
1963—Constance McLaughlin Green, *Washington: Village and Capital, 1800-1878*
1964—Sumner Chilton Powell, *Puritan Village: The Formation of a New England Town*
1965—Irwin Unger, *The Greenback Era*
1966—Perry Miller, *Life of the Mind in America*
1967—William H. Goetzmann, *Exploration and Empire: The Explorer and Scientist in the Winning of the American West*
1968—Bernard Bailyn, *The Ideological Origins of the American Revolution*
1969—Leonard W. Levy, *Origin of the Fifth Amendment*
1970—Dean Acheson, *Present at the Creation: My Years in the State Department*
1971—James McGregor Burns, *Roosevelt: The Soldier of Freedom*
1972—Carl N. Degler, *Neither Black nor White*
1973—Michael Kammen, *People of Paradox: An Inquiry Concerning the Origins of American Civilization*
1974—Daniel J. Boorstin, *The Americans: The Democratic Experience*
1975—Dumas Malone, *Jefferson and His Time*
1976—Paul Horgan, *Lamy of Santa Fe*
1977—David M. Potter, *The Impending Crisis*
1978—Alfred D. Chandler Jr., *The Visible Hand: The Managerial Revolution in American Business*
1979—Don E. Fehrenbacher, *The Dred Scott Case: Its Significance in American Law and Politics*
1980—Leon F. Litwack, *Been in the Storm So Long*
1981—Lawrence A. Cremin, *American Education: The National Experience, 1783-1876*
1982—C. Vann Woodward, ed., *Mary Chesnut's Civil War*
1983—Rhys L. Issac, *The Transformation of Virginia, 1740-1790*
1985—Thomas K. McCraw, *Prophets of Regulation*
1986—Walter A. McDougall, ... *The Heavens and the Earth*
1987—Bernard Bailyn, *Voyagers to the West*
1988—Robert V. Bruce, *The Launching of Modern American Science, 1846-1876*
1989—Taylor Branch, *Parting the Waters: America in the King Years, 1954-63*; and James M. McPherson, *Battle Cry of Freedom: The Civil War Era*
1990—Stanley Karnow, *In Our Image: America's Empire in the Philippines*
1991—Laurel Thatcher Ulrich, *A Midwife's Tale: The Life of Martha Ballard,* based on her diary, 1785-1812
1992—Mark E. Neely Jr., *The Fate of Liberty: Abraham Lincoln and Civil Liberties*
1993—Gordon S. Wood, *The Radicalism of the American Revolution*
1995—Doris Kearns Goodwin, *No Ordinary Time: Franklin and Eleanor Roosevelt: The Home Front in World War II*
1996—Alan Taylor, *William Cooper's Town: Power and Persuasion on the Frontier of the Early American Republic*
1997—Jack N. Rakove, *Original Meanings: Politics and Ideas in the Making of the Constitution*

Biography or Autobiography

1917—Laura E. Richards and Maude Howe Elliott, assisted by Florence Howe Hall, *Julia Ward Howe*
1918—William Cabell Bruce, *Benjamin Franklin, Self-Revealed*
1919—Henry Adams, *The Education of Henry Adams*
1920—Albert J. Beveridge, *The Life of John Marshall*
1921—Edward Bok, *The Americanization of Edward Bok*
1922—Hamlin Garland, *A Daughter of the Middle Border*
1923—Burton J. Hendrick, *The Life and Letters of Walter H. Page*
1924—Michael Pupin, *From Immigrant to Inventor*
1925—M. A. DeWolfe Howe, *Barrett Wendell and His Letters*
1926—Harvey Cushing, *Life of Sir William Osler*
1927—Emory Holloway, *Whitman: An Interpretation in Narrative*
1928—Charles Edward Russell, *The American Orchestra and Theodore Thomas*
1929—Burton J. Hendrick, *The Training of an American: The Earlier Life and Letters of Walter H. Page*
1930—Marquis James, *The Raven* (Sam Houston)
1931—Henry James, *Charles W. Eliot*
1932—Henry F. Pringle, *Theodore Roosevelt*
1933—Allan Nevins, *Grover Cleveland*
1934—Tyler Dennett, *John Hay*
1935—Douglas Southall Freeman, *R. E. Lee*
1936—Ralph Barton Perry, *The Thought and Character of William James*
1937—Allan Nevins, *Hamilton Fish: The Inner History of the Grant Administration*
1938—Divided between Odell Shepard, *Pedlar's Progress* (Bronson Alcott), and Marquis James, *Andrew Jackson*

1939—Carl Van Doren, *Benjamin Franklin*
1940—Ray Stannard Baker, *Woodrow Wilson, Life and Letters*
1941—Ola Elizabeth Winslow, *Jonathan Edwards*
1942—Forrest Wilson, *Crusader in Crinoline* (Harriet Beecher Stowe)
1943—Samuel Eliot Morison, *Admiral of the Ocean Sea* (Christopher Columbus)
1944—Carleton Mabee, *The American Leonardo: The Life of Samuel F. B. Morse*
1945—Russell Blaine Nye, *George Bancroft: Brahmin Rebel.*
1946—Linny Marsh Wolfe, *Son of the Wilderness* (John Muir)
1947—William Allen White, *The Autobiography of William Allen White*
1948—Margaret Clapp, *Forgotten First Citizen: John Bigelow*
1949—Robert E. Sherwood, *Roosevelt and Hopkins*
1950—Samuel Flag Bemis, *John Quincy Adams and the Foundations of American Foreign Policy*
1951—Margaret Louise Colt, *John C. Calhoun: American Portrait*
1952—Merlo J. Pusey, *Charles Evans Hughes*
1953—David J. Mays, *Edmund Pendleton, 1721-1803*
1954—Charles A. Lindbergh, *The Spirit of St. Louis*
1955—William S. White, *The Taft Story*
1956—Talbot F. Hamlin, *Benjamin Henry Latrobe*
1957—John F. Kennedy, *Profiles in Courage*
1958—Douglas Southall Freeman (Vols. I-VI) and John Alexander Carroll and Mary Wells Ashworth (Vol. VII), *George Washington*
1959—Arthur Walworth, *Woodrow Wilson: American Prophet*
1960—Samuel Eliot Morison, *John Paul Jones*
1961—David Donald, *Charles Sumner and the Coming of the Civil War*
1963—Leon Edel, *Henry James: Vol. II, The Conquest of London, 1870-1881; Vol. III, The Middle Years, 1881-1895*
1964—Walter Jackson Bate, *John Keats*
1965—Ernest Samuels, *Henry Adams*
1966—Arthur M. Schlesinger Jr., *A Thousand Days*
1967—Justin Kaplan, *Mr. Clemens and Mark Twain*
1968—George F. Kennan, *Memoirs (1925-1950)*
1969—B. L. Reid, *The Man From New York: John Quinn and His Friends*
1970—T. Harry Williams, *Huey Long*
1971—Lawrence Thompson, *Robert Frost: The Years of Triumph, 1915-1938*
1972—Joseph P. Lash, *Eleanor and Franklin*
1973—W. A. Swanberg, *Luce and His Empire*
1974—Louis Sheaffer, *O'Neill, Son and Artist*
1975—Robert A. Caro, *The Power Broker: Robert Moses and the Fall of New York*
1976—R.W.B. Lewis, *Edith Wharton: A Biography*
1977—John E. Mack, *A Prince of Our Disorder: The Life of T. E. Lawrence*
1978—Walter Jackson Bate, *Samuel Johnson*
1979—Leonard Baker, *Days of Sorrow and Pain: Leo Baeck and the Berlin Jews*
1980—Edmund Morris, *The Rise of Theodore Roosevelt*
1981—Robert K. Massie, *Peter the Great: His Life and World*
1982—William S. McFeely, *Grant: A Biography*
1983—Russell Baker, *Growing Up*
1984—Louis R. Harlan, *Booker T. Washington*
1985—Kenneth Silverman, *The Life and Times of Cotton Mather*
1986—Elizabeth Frank, *Louise Bogan: A Portrait*
1987—David J. Garrow, *Bearing the Cross: Martin Luther King Jr. and the Southern Christian Leadership Conference*
1988—David Herbert Donald, *Look Homeward: A Life of Thomas Wolfe*
1989—Richard Ellmann, *Oscar Wilde*
1990—Sebastian de Grazia, *Machiavelli in Hell*
1991—Steven Naifeh and Gregory White Smith, *Jackson Pollock: An American Saga*
1992—Lewis B. Puller Jr., *Fortunate Son: The Healing of a Vietnam Vet*
1993—David McCullough, *Truman*
1994—David Levering Lewis, *W.E.B. DuBois: Biography of a Race, 1868-1919*
1995—Joan D. Hedrick, *Harriet Beecher Stowe: A Life*
1996—Jack Miles, *God: A Biography*
1997—Frank McCourt, *Angela's Ashes: A Memoir*

American Poetry

Before this prize was established in 1922, awards were made from gifts provided by the Poetry Society: **1918**—*Love Songs*, by Sara Teasdale; **1919**—*Old Road to Paradise*, by Margaret Widdemer; *Corn Huskers*, by Carl Sandburg.
1922—Edwin Arlington Robinson, *Collected Poems*
1923—Edna St. Vincent Millay, *The Ballad of the Harp-Weaver; A Few Figs From Thistles; Eight Sonnets in American Poetry, 1922; A Miscellany*
1924—Robert Frost, *New Hampshire: A Poem With Notes and Grace Notes*
1925—Edwin Arlington Robinson, *The Man Who Died Twice*
1926—Amy Lowell, *What's O'Clock*
1927—Leonora Speyer, *Fiddler's Farewell*
1928—Edwin Arlington Robinson, *Tristram*

American Poetry *(continued)*

1929—Stephen Vincent Benet, *John Brown's Body*
1930—Conrad Aiken, *Selected Poems*
1931—Robert Frost, *Collected Poems*
1932—George Dillon, *The Flowering Stone*
1933—Archibald MacLeish, *Conquistador*
1934—Robert Hillyer, *Collected Verse*
1935—Audrey Wurdemann, *Bright Ambush*
1936—Robert P. Tristram Coffin, *Strange Holiness*
1937—Robert Frost, *A Further Range*
1938—Marya Zaturenska, *Cold Morning Sky*
1939—John Gould Fletcher, *Selected Poems*
1940—Mark Van Doren, *Collected Poems*
1941—Leonard Bacon, *Sunderland Capture*
1942—William Rose Benet, *The Dust Which Is God*
1943—Robert Frost, *A Witness Tree*
1944—Stephen Vincent Benet, *Western Star*
1945—Karl Shapiro, *V-Letter and Other Poems*
1947—Robert Lowell, *Lord Weary's Castle*
1948—W. H. Auden, *The Age of Anxiety*
1949—Peter Viereck, *Terror and Decorum*
1950—Gwendolyn Brooks, *Annie Allen*
1951—Carl Sandburg, *Complete Poems*
1952—Marianne Moore, *Collected Poems*
1953—Archibald MacLeish, *Collected Poems*
1954—Theodore Roethke, *The Waking*
1955—Wallace Stevens, *Collected Poems*
1956—Elizabeth Bishop, *Poems, North and South*
1957—Richard Wilbur, *Things of This World*
1958—Robert Penn Warren, *Promises: Poems 1954-1956*
1959—Stanley Kunitz, *Selected Poems 1928-1958*
1960—W. D. Snodgrass, *Heart's Needle*
1961—Phyllis McGinley, *Times Three: Selected Verse From Three Decades*
1962—Alan Dugan, *Poems*
1963—William Carlos Williams, *Pictures From Breughel*
1964—Louis Simpson, *At the End of the Open Road*
1965—John Berryman, *77 Dream Songs*
1966—Richard Eberhart, *Selected Poems*
1967—Anne Sexton, *Live or Die*
1968—Anthony Hecht, *The Hard Hours*
1969—George Oppen, *Of Being Numerous*
1970—Richard Howard, *Untitled Subjects*
1971—William S. Merwin, *The Carrier of Ladders*
1972—James Wright, *Collected Poems*
1973—Maxine Winokur Kumin, *Up Country*
1974—Robert Lowell, *The Dolphin*
1975—Gary Snyder, *Turtle Island*
1976—John Ashbery, *Self-Portrait in a Convex Mirror*
1977—James Merrill, *Divine Comedies*
1978—Howard Nemerov, *Collected Poems*
1979—Robert Penn Warren, *Now and Then: Poems 1976-1978*
1980—Donald Justice, *Selected Poems*
1981—James Schuyler, *The Morning of the Poem*
1982—Sylvia Plath, *The Collected Poems*
1983—Galway Kinnell, *Selected Poems*
1984—Mary Oliver, *American Primitive*
1985—Carolyn Kizer, *Yin*
1986—Henry Taylor, *The Flying Change*
1987—Rita Dove, *Thomas and Beulah*
1988—William Meredith, *Partial Accounts: New and Selected Poems*

1989—Richard Wilbur, *New and Collected Poems*
1990—Charles Simic, *The World Doesn't End*
1991—Mona Van Duyn, *Near Changes*
1992—James Tate, *Selected Poems*
1993—Louise Glück, *The Wild Iris*
1994—Yusef Komunyakaa, *Neon Vernacular*
1995—Philip Levine, *The Simple Truth*
1996—Jorie Graham, *The Dream of the Unified Field*
1997—Lisel Mueller, *Alive Together: New and Selected Poems*

General Nonfiction

1962—Theodore H. White, *The Making of the President 1960*
1963—Barbara W. Tuchman, *The Guns of August*
1964—Richard Hofstadter, *Anti-Intellectualism in American Life*
1965—Howard Mumford Jones, *O Strange New World*
1966—Edwin Way Teale, *Wandering Through Winter*
1967—David Brion Davis, *The Problem of Slavery in Western Culture*
1968—Will and Ariel Durant, *Rousseau and Revolution*
1969—Norman Mailer, *The Armies of the Night*; Rene Jules Dubos, *So Human an Animal: How We Are Shaped by Surroundings and Events*
1970—Eric H. Erikson, *Gandhi's Truth*
1971—John Toland, *The Rising Sun*
1972—Barbara W. Tuchman, *Stilwell and the American Experience in China, 1911-1945*
1973—Frances FitzGerald, *Fire in the Lake: The Vietnamese and the Americans in Vietnam*; Robert Coles, *Children of Crisis*, Volumes II & III
1974—Ernest Becker, *The Denial of Death*
1975—Annie Dillard, *Pilgrim at Tinker Creek*
1976—Robert N. Butler, *Why Survive? Being Old in America*
1977—William W. Warner, *Beautiful Swimmers*
1978—Carl Sagan, *The Dragons of Eden*
1979—Edward O. Wilson, *On Human Nature*
1980—Douglas R. Hofstadter, *Gödel, Escher, Bach: An Eternal Golden Braid*
1981—Carl E. Schorske, *Fin-de-Siecle Vienna: Politics and Culture*
1982—Tracy Kidder, *The Soul of a New Machine*
1983—Susan Sheehan, *Is There No Place on Earth for Me?*
1984—Paul Starr, *Social Transformation of American Medicine*
1985—Studs Terkel, *The Good War*
1986—Joseph Lelyveld, *Move Your Shadow*; J. Anthony Lukas, *Common Ground*
1987—David K. Shipler, *Arab and Jew*
1988—Richard Rhodes, *The Making of the Atomic Bomb*
1989—Neil Sheehan, *A Bright Shining Lie: John Paul Vann and America in Vietnam*
1990—Dale Maharidge and Michael Williamson, *And Their Children After Them*
1991—Bert Holldobler and Edward O. Wilson, *The Ants*
1992—Daniel Yergin, *The Prize: The Epic Quest for Oil*
1993—Garry Wills, *Lincoln at Gettysburg*
1994—David Remnick, *Lenin's Tomb: The Last Days of the Soviet Empire*
1995—Jonathan Weiner, *The Beak of the Finch: A Story of Evolution in Our Time*
1996—Tina Rosenberg, *The Haunted Land: Facing Europe's Ghosts After Communism*
1997—Richard Kluger, *Ashes to Ashes: America's Hundred-Year Cigarette War, the Public Health, and the Unabashed Triumph of Philip Morris*

Music

1943—William Schuman, *Secular Cantata No. 2, A Free Song*
1944—Howard Hanson, *Symphony No. 4, Op. 34*
1945—Aaron Copland, *Appalachian Spring*
1946—Leo Sowerby, *The Canticle of the Sun*
1947—Charles E. Ives, *Symphony No. 3*
1948—Walter Piston, *Symphony No. 3*
1949—Virgil Thomson, *Louisiana Story*
1950—Gian-Carlo Menotti, *The Consul*
1951—Douglas Moore, *Giants in the Earth*
1952—Gail Kubik, *Symphony Concertante*
1954—Quincy Porter, *Concerto for Two Pianos and Orchestra*
1955—Gian-Carlo Menotti, *The Saint of Bleecker Street*
1956—Ernest Toch, *Symphony No. 3*
1957—Norman Dello Joio, *Meditations on Ecclesiastes*
1958—Samuel Barber, *Vanessa*
1959—John La Montaine, *Concerto for Piano and Orchestra*
1960—Elliott Carter, *Second String Quartet*
1961—Walter Piston, *Symphony No. 7*
1962—Robert Ward, *The Crucible*
1963—Samuel Barber, *Piano Concerto No. 1*
1966—Leslie Bassett, *Variations for Orchestra*
1967—Leon Kirchner, *Quartet No. 3*
1968—George Crumb, *Echoes of Time and The River*
1969—Karel Husa, *String Quartet No. 3*
1970—Charles W. Wuorinen, *Time's Encomium*
1971—Mario Davidovsky, *Synchronisms No. 6*
1972—Jacob Druckman, *Windows*

1973—Elliott Carter, *String Quartet No. 3*
1974—Donald Martino, *Notturno.* (Special Citation) Roger Sessions
1975—Dominick Argento, *From the Diary of Virginia Woolf*
1976—Ned Rorem, *Air Music.* Special Award (posth.) to Scott Joplin
1977—Richard Wernick, *Visions of Terror and Wonder*
1978—Michael Colgrass, *Deja Vu for Percussion and Orchestra*
1979—Joseph Schwantner, *Aftertones of Infinity*
1980—David Del Tredici, *In Memory of a Summer Day*
1982—Roger Sessions, *Concerto for Orchestra.* (Special Citation) Milton Babbitt
1983—Ellen T. Zwilich, *Three Movements for Orchestra*
1984—Bernard Rands, *Canti del Sole*
1985—Stephen Albert, *Symphony, RiverRun*
1986—George Perle, *Wind Quintet IV*
1987—John Harbison, *The Flight Into Egypt*
1988—William Bolcom, *12 New Etudes for Piano*
1989—Roger Reynolds, *Whispers Out of Time*
1990—Mel Powell, *Duplicates: A Concerto for Two Pianos and Orchestra*
1991—Shulamit Ran, *Symphony*
1992—Wayne Peterson, *The Face of the Night, The Heart of the Dark*
1993—Christopher Rouse, *Trombone Concerto*
1994—Gunther Schuller, *Of Reminiscences and Reflections*
1995—Morton Gould, *Stringmusic*
1996—George Walker, *Lilacs*
1997—Wynton Marsalis, *Blood on the Fields*

Miscellaneous Book Awards

Awarded in 1996 or 1997

Academy of American Poets Awards. Tanning Prize, $100,000: Adrienne Rich; Lenore Marshall Prize, $10,000: Charles Wright; James Laughlin Award, $5,000: Tony Hoagland, *Donkey Gospel*; Walt Whitman Award, $1,000: Barbara Ras, *Bite Every Sorrow*; Landon Translation Award, $1,000: David Hinton, *The Selected Poems of Li Po, The Late Poems of Meng Chiao, Landscape Over Zero*

American Academy of Arts and Letters. Gold medal for poetry: John Ashbery; Award of Merit for the Novel, $5,000: Richard Ford; academy awards in literature, $7,500 each: fiction: Charles Baxter, Maureen Howard, Jayne Anne Phillips, Jane Smiley; translation: Lane Dunlop; poetry: Allen Grossman; nonfiction: Luc Sante; drama: Wallace Shawn; Rosenthal Foundation Award in Literature, $5,000: Mary Kay Zuravleff, *The Frequency of Souls*; Sue Kaufman Prize for first fiction, $2,500: Brad Watson, *Last Days of the Dog-Men;* Witter Bynner Poetry Prize, $2,500: Mark Doty; Michael Braude Award for light verse, $5,000: Robert Conquest; Harold D. Vursell Memorial Award, $5,000: Elizabeth McCracken, *The Giant's House*; Morton Dauwen Zabel Award, $5,000: Wendy Lesser; E. M. Forster Award, $12,500: Glyn Maxwell

Booker Prize, British award for fiction, $35,000: Graham Swift, *Last Orders*

Curtis Benjamin Award, for creative publishing: Thomas J. McCormack, St. Martin's Press

Caldecott Medal, by American Library Assn., for most distinguished American picture book: David Wisniewski, *Golem*

Christopher Awards, by The Christophers, for expression of highest values of human spirit, bronze medallion each: Gov. Robert P. Casey, *Fighting for Life*; Jimmy Carter, *Living Faith*; Patricia Raybon, *My First White Friend: Confessions on Race, Love, and Forgiveness*; Jim and Brian Doyle, *Two Voices: A Father and Son Discuss Family and Faith;* Stephen E. Ambrose, *Undaunted Courage: Meriwether Lewis, Thomas Jefferson, and the Opening of the American West*

Francis Parkman Prize, by Society of American Historians: Drew Gilpin Faust, *Mothers of Invention*

Coretta Scott King Award, by the American Library Assn. for African American authors and illustrators of outstanding books for children and young adults: Author: Walter Dean Myers *Slam!;* Illustrator: Jerry Pinkney, *Minty: A Story of Young Harriet Tubman*

Lincoln Prize, by Lincoln and Soldiers Institute at Gettysburg College, for lifetime contribution to Civil War studies, $50,000 and a bronze bust of Lincoln: Don E. Fehrenbacher, lifetime achievement

National Book Awards, by National Book Foundation, $10,000 each: fiction: Andrea Barrett, *Ship Fever and Other Stories;* nonfiction: James Caroll, *An American Requiem: God, My Father, and the War that Came Between Us*; poetry: Hayden Carruth, *Scrambled Eggs and Whiskey: Poems 1991-1995*; young people's literature: Victor Martinez, *Parrot in the Oven: Mi Vida;* Medal for Distinguished Contribution to American Letters: Toni Morrison

National Book Critics Circle Awards. Fiction: Gina Berriault, *Women in Their Beds;* nonfiction: Jonathan Raban, *Bad Land;* criticism: William Gass, *Finding a Form;* biography and autobiography: Frank McCourt, *Angela's Ashes;* poetry: Robert Hass, *Sun Under Wood;* reviewing: Dennis Drabelle; contribution to American arts & letters: Albert Murray

Golden Kite Awards, by Society of Children's Book Writiers and Illustrators: fiction: Eloise McGraw, *The Moorchild;* nonfiction: Peg Kehret, *Small Steps;* picture-illustration: Holly Berry, *Market Day*; picture book text: Diane Stanley, *Saving Sweetness*

PEN/Faulkner Award, for fiction, $15,000: Gina Berriault, *Women in Their Beds*

Edgar Allan Poe Awards, by the Mystery Writers of America: Grand Master award: Ruth Rendell; best novel: *The Chatham School Affair*, Thomas H. Cook

Whiting Writers' Award, by the Whiting Foundation for outstanding talent and promise: Anderson Ferrell, Cristina Garcia, Molly Gloss, Brigit Pegeen Kelly, Brian Kiteley, Chris Offutt, Elizabeth Spires, Patricia Storace, Judy Troy, A.J. Verdelle

Newbery Medal Books

The Newbery Medal is awarded annually by the Association for Library Service to Children, a division of the American Library Association, to the author of the most distinguished contribution to American literature for children.

Year Awarded	Book, Author	Year Awarded	Book, Author
1922	*The Story of Mankind*, Hendrik Willem van Loon	1961	*Island of the Blue Dolphins*, Scott O'Dell
1923	*The Voyages of Dr. Dolittle*, Hugh Lofting	1962	*The Bronze Bow*, Elizabeth George Speare
1924	*The Dark Frigate*, Charles Boardman Hawes	1963	*A Wrinkle in Time*, Madeleine L'Engle
1925	*Tales From Silver Lands*, Charles Joseph Finger	1964	*It's Like This, Cat*, Emily Cheney Neville
1926	*Shen of the Sea*, Arthur Bowie Chrisman	1965	*Shadow of a Bull*, Maja Wojciechowska
1927	*Smoky, the Cowhorse*, Will James	1966	*I, Juan de Pareja*, Elizabeth Borton de Trevino
1928	*Gay-Neck*, Dhan Gopal Mukerji	1967	*Up a Road Slowly*, Irene Hunt
1929	*The Trumpeter of Krakow*, Eric P. Kelly	1968	*From the Mixed-Up Files of Mrs. Basil E. Frankweiler*, E. L. Konigsburg
1930	*Hitty, Her First Hundred Years*, Rachel Field		
1931	*The Cat Who Went to Heaven*, Elizabeth Coatsworth	1969	*The High King*, Lloyd Alexander
1932	*Waterless Mountain*, Laura Adams Armer	1970	*Sounder*, William H. Armstrong
1933	*Young Fu of the Upper Yangtze*, Elizabeth Foreman Lewis	1971	*The Summer of the Swans*, Betsy Byars
1934	*Invincible Louisa*, Cornelia Lynde Meigs	1972	*Mrs. Frisby and the Rats of NIMH*, Robert C. O'Brien
1935	*Dobry*, Monica Shannon	1973	*Julie of the Wolves*, Jean George
1936	*Caddie Woodlawn*, Carol Ryrie Brink	1974	*The Slave Dancer*, Paula Fox
1937	*Roller Skates*, Ruth Sawyer	1975	*M. C. Higgins the Great*, Virginia Hamilton
1938	*The White Stag*, Kate Seredy	1976	*Grey King*, Susan Cooper
1939	*Thimble Summer*, Elizabeth Enright	1977	*Roll of Thunder, Hear My Cry*, Mildred D. Taylor
1940	*Daniel Boone*, James Daugherty	1978	*Bridge to Terabithia*, Katherine Paterson
1941	*Call It Courage*, Armstrong Sperry	1979	*The Westing Game*, Ellen Raskin
1942	*The Matchlock Gun* Walter D. Edmonds	1980	*A Gathering of Days*, Joan Blos
1943	*Adam of the Road*, Elizabeth Janet Gray	1981	*Jacob Have I Loved*, Katherine Paterson
1944	*Johnny Tremain*, Esther Forbes	1982	*A Visit to William Blake's Inn: Poems for Innocent and Experienced Travelers*, Nancy Willard
1945	*Rabbit Hill*, Robert Lawson		
1946	*Strawberry Girl*, Lois Lenski	1983	*Dicey's Song*, Cynthia Voigt
1947	*Miss Hickory*, Carolyn S. Bailey	1984	*Dear Mr. Henshaw*, Beverly Cleary
1948	*Twenty-One Balloons*, William Pène Du Bois	1985	*The Hero and the Crown*, Robin McKinley
1949	*King of the Wind*, Marguerite Henry	1986	*Sarah, Plain and Tall*, Patricia MacLachlan
1950	*The Door in the Wall*, Marguerite de Angeli	1987	*The Whipping Boy*, Sid Fleischman
1951	*Amos Fortune, Free Man*, Elizabeth Yates	1988	*Lincoln: A Photobiography*, Russell Freedman
1952	*Ginger Pye*, Eleanor Estes	1989	*Joyful Noise: Poems for Two Voices*, Paul Fleischman
1953	*Secret of the Andes*, Ann Nolan Clark	1990	*Number the Stars*, Lois Lowry
1954	*. . . And Now Miguel*, Joseph Krumgold	1991	*Maniac Magee*, Jerry Spinelli
1955	*The Wheel on the School*, Meindert DeJong	1992	*Shiloh*, Phyllis Reynolds Naylor
1956	*Carry On, Mr. Bowditch*, Jean Lee Latham	1993	*Missing May*, Cynthia Rylant
1957	*Miracles on Maple Hill*, Virginia Sorensen	1994	*The Giver*, Lois Lowry
1958	*Rifles for Watie*, Harold Keith	1995	*Walk Two Moons*, Sharon Creech
1959	*The Witch of Blackbird Pond*, Elizabeth George Speare	1996	*The Midwife's Apprentice*, Karen Cushman
1960	*Onion John*, Joseph Krumgold	1997	*The View From Saturday*, E. L. Konigsburg

Journalism

National Journalism Awards, by Scripps Howard Foundation, for print journalism. Service to literacy, $2,500 each: *Gaston Gazette,* Gastonia, NC and *WTHR-TV,* Indianapolis; human interest writing, $2,500: John Lang, *Scripps Howard News Service;* editorial writing, $2,000: Michael G. Gartner, *Daily Tribune,* Ames, IA; environmental reporting, $2,000 each: Ken Ward Jr., *Charleston (WV) Gazette,* and *Mobile (AL) Register;* public service reporting, $2,500 each: Maureen Magee, *Ventura County (CA) Star,* and Alison Young, *Detroit Free Press;* service to First Amendment, $2,500: *Honolulu Star-Bulletin;* excellence in broadcast journalism, $2,000 each: *WWSB-TV,* Sarasota, FL; *WCPO-TV,* Cincinnati, OH ; *KNAU-FM Radio,* Flagstaff, AZ; *WCBS Radio,* New York, NY; college cartooning, $2,000: Jody D. Lindke, University of Nevada

National Magazine Awards, by American Society of Magazine Editors and Columbia Univ. Graduate School of Journalism. General excellence, circulation over 1 million: *Vanity Fair,* 400,000 to 1 million: *Outside;* 100,000 to 400,000: *Wired;* under 100,000: *I.D.;* single topic issue: *Scientific American;* special interests: *Smithsonian;* feature writing: *Sports Illustrated;* fiction: *The New Yorker;* design: *I.D.;* photography: *National Geographic;* reporting: *Outside;* personal service: *Glamour;* public interest: *Fortune;* essays & criticism:*The New Yorker;* special award for general excellence in new media: *Money*

Overseas Press Club Awards, by Dateline for work abroad. Hal Boyle Award (newspaper or wire service reporting): John-Thor Dahlburg, *Los Angeles Times,* "Afghanistan: Legacy of Fear"; Bob Considine Award (newspaper or wire-service interpretation): *Wall Street Journal,* Tokyo Bureau, "Unmasking the Mandarins: The Failure of Japan's Bureaucracy"; Robert Capa Gold Medal (published photographic reporting requiring exceptional courage and enterprise): Corrine Dufka, Reuters, "Liberia: From a Dead Man's Wallet"; Olivier Rebbot Award (photography in mags. and books): Yunghi Kim, *Contact Press Images/Time/*U.S. News & World Report, "The Forgotten Comfort Women of Korea"; John Faber Award (photography in newspapers and wire services): Carol Guzy, *Washington Post,* "Exodus: Return to Rwanda"; Lowell Thomas Award (radio news or interpretation): Lisa Rolland, *ABC News Radio,* Land Mines: The Survivor's Perspective"; David Kaplan Award (TV spot news reporting): Ron Allen, correspondent, Carol Grisanti, producer, *NBC News,* "Rwanda: Another Tale of Tragedy"; Edward R. Murrow Award (TV interpretation or documentary): Peter Arnett, Bernard Shaw, John Holliman, *CNN,* "CNN Presents: Back to Baghdad"; Ed Cunningham Memorial Award (magazine reporting) *Newsweek* team, "China: Friend or Foe?"; Thomas Nast Award (cartooning): Signe Wilkinson, *Philadelphia Daily News;* Morton Frank Award (business reporting): David McClintick, *Fortune,* "The Predator"; Malcolm Forbes Award (business reporting in newspapers or wire service): R.C. Longworth, *Chicago Tribune,* "Global Squeeze"; Carl Spielvogel Award (business reporting in broadcast media): Adam Smith (Jerry Goodman), Alvin H. Permutter, Peter Forges, *Alvin H. Permutter Inc.,* and Thirteen/WNET, "Adam Smith: European Crackup?"; Cornelius Ryan Award (nonfiction book): Peter Maas, *Love Thy Neighbor: A Story of War;* Madeline Dane Ross Award (foreign reporting in any medium concerned with human condition): *Chicago Tribune,* "Gambling With Life"; Eric and Amy Burger Award (reporting in any medium on human rights): Gilbert A. Lewthwaite, Gregory Kane, *Baltimore Sun,* "Witness to Slavery," Whitman Basson Award (reporting in any medium on international environmental issues): Jeff Wheelwright, *Discover* Magazine, "The Air of Ostrava"

George Foster Peabody Awards, by the Univ. of Georgia. *People's Century,* BBC, London, WGBH-TV, Boston; *The American Experience: The Battle Over Citizen Kane,* The American Experience and Lennon Documentary Group/ WGBH-TV, Boston; *The Great War and the Shaping of the 20th Century,* KCET-TV, Los Angeles and BBC; *Survivors of the Holocaust,* Turner Original Productions, Atlanta, and Steven Spielberg in assoc. with Survivors of the Shoah Visual History Foundation; *The X-Files,* Fox, Ten Thirteen Productions in assoc. with Twentieth Television; *Journey of the African-American Athlete,* HBO, Sports, NY, *Law & Order,* NBC, Wolf Films in assoc. with Universal Television; *Pride and Prejudice,* A&E Television Networks and BBC; *The Simpsons,* Fox, Gracie Films, Los Angeles, in assoc. with Twentieth Television; *NYPD Blue,* ABC, Steven Bochco Productions; Mobil Masterpiece Theatre's *House of Cards, To Play the King,* and *The Final Cut,* BBC, WGBH-TV, Boston; *How Do You Spell God?,* HBO, New York; *Wise Up!,* Carlton Television for Channel 4, London; *Edith Ann's Christmas,* ABC, Tomlin and Wagner Theatricalz, Kurtz & Friends, Los Angeles; *One to One: Mentoring,* WCCO-TV, Minneapolis; *Black Radio: Telling It Like It Was,* Radio Smithsonian, Washington, DC, for Public Radio Intl.; *Remorse: The 14 Stories of Eric Morse,* Sound Portrait Productions, New York, for Natl. Public Radio; *This American Life,* WBEZ-FM, Chicago; *Kinetic City Super Crew,* Amer. Assoc. for the Advancement of Science, Washington, DC; *Who's Guarding the Guardians?,* WCVB-TV, Boston; *Newsnight—Afghanistan,* BBC News, London; *Passport to Kill,* WNBC-TV, New York; *Vote for Me: Politics in America,* Center for New American Media, Midnight Films and WETA-TV, Washington, DC; *The Celluloid Closet,* Telling Pictures, HBO, Channel 4, London, and ZDF-Arté (Germany/France); Frontline: *The Gate of Heavenly Peace,* Long Bow Group, Inc., and Independent Television service for Frontline/WGBH-TV, Boston; *Paradise Lost: The Child Murders at Robin Hood Hills,* HBO, Creative Thinking International Ltd., New York; *Frontline: The Choice '96,* Frontline/WGBH-TV, Boston, and Helen Whitney Productions; NOVA: *Odyssey of Life,* NOVA/WGBH-TV, Boston, Agaton Film and Television, Swedish Television, SVTI, ZDF-Arté (Germany/France) and Channel 4, London; KOMO-TV, Seattle, for excellence in television programming; Peter Gzowski of CBS Radio, Toronto, and Bud Greenspan each received a personal Peabody Award

George Polk Awards, by Long Island Univ., for excellence in journalism. National: Elizabeth Marchak, *The Plain Dealer,* Cleveland, OH; transportation: Byron Acohido, *The Seattle Times;* local: Kevin Collison, *The Buffalo News;* magazine: Anne-Marie Cusac, *The Progressive;* foreign: John F. Burns, *The New York Times;* foreign television: Christiane Amanpour, Anita Pratap, CNN; economics: *New York Times;* political: *Los Angeles Times;* cultural: Chuck Philips, *Los Angeles Times;* national television: Matt Meagher, Tim Peek, *Inside Edition;* criticism: Blair Kamin, *Chicago Tribune*

Reuben Awards, by National Cartoonists Society. Best cartoonist of 1997: Sergio Aragones

The Spingarn Medal

The Spingarn Medal has been awarded annually since 1915 (except in 1938) by the National Association for the Advancement of Colored People for the highest achievement by a black American in the previous year.

1915 Ernest E. Just	1936 John Hope	1958 Daisy Bates and the	1977 Alex Haley
1916 Charles Young	1937 Walter White	Little Rock Nine	1978 Andrew Young
1917 Harry T. Burleigh	1939 Marian Anderson	1959 Edward Kennedy (Duke)	1979 Mrs. Rosa L. Parks
1918 William S. Braithwaite	1940 Louis T. Wright	Ellington	1980 Dr. Rayford W. Logan
1919 Archibald H. Grimké	1941 Richard Wright	1960 Langston Hughes	1981 Coleman Young
1920 W. E. B. Du Bois	1942 A. Philip Randolph	1961 Kenneth B. Clark	1982 Dr. Benjamin E. Mays
1921 Charles S. Gilpin	1943 William H. Hastie	1962 Robert C. Weaver	1983 Lena Horne
1922 Mary B. Talbert	1944 Charles Drew	1963 Medgar W. Evers	1984 Thomas Bradley
1923 George W.Carver	1945 Paul Robeson	1964 Roy Wilkins	1985 Bill Cosby
1924 Roland Hayes	1946 Thurgood Marshall	1965 Leontyne Price	1986 Dr. Benjamin L. Hooks
1925 James W. Johnson	1947 Dr. Percy L. Julian	1966 John H. Johnson	1987 Percy E. Sutton
1926 Carter G. Woodson	1948 Channing H. Tobias	1967 Edward W. Brooke	1988 Frederick D. Patterson
1927 Anthony Overton	1949 Ralph J. Bunche	1968 Sammy Davis Jr.	1989 Jesse Jackson
1928 Charles W. Chesnutt	1950 Charles H. Houston	1969 Clarence M. Mitchell Jr.	1990 L. Douglas Wilder
1929 Mordecai W. Johnson	1951 Mabel K. Staupers	1970 Jacob Lawrence	1991 Gen. Colin L. Powell
1930 Henry A. Hunt	1952 Harry T. Moore	1971 Leon H. Sullivan	1992 Barbara Jordan
1931 Richard B. Harrison	1953 Paul R. Williams	1972 Gordon Parks	1993 Dorothy I. Height
1932 Robert R. Moton	1954 Theodore K. Lawless	1973 Wilson C. Riles	1994 Maya Angelou
1933 Max Yergan	1955 Carl Murphy	1974 Damon Keith	1995 John Hope Franklin
1934 William T. B. Williams	1956 Jack R. Robinson	1975 Henry (Hank) Aaron	1996 A. Leon Higginbotham
1935 Mary McLeod Bethune	1957 Martin Luther King Jr.	1976 Alvin Ailey	1997 Carl T. Rowan

Miscellaneous Awards

American Academy of Arts and Letters, (1997) gold medal in music: Gunther Schuller; award for distinguished service to the Arts: Kitty Carlisle Hart; Arnold W. Brunner Memorial Prize in Architecture: Henry Ciriani; academy awards, $7,500 each, in Architecture: Daniel Libeskind; in Art: Enrique Chagoya, Tim Hawkinson, Bill Jensen, Harvey Quaytman, James Seawright; in Music: Curt Cacioppo, Brian Fennelly, Morris Rosenzweig, Marilyn Shrude; Rosenthal Award, for Art, $5,000: Eve Aschheim

Charles Frankel Prizes, by National Endowment for the Humanities, for those who have increased public awareness of the humanities, $5,000 each (1996): Rita Dove, Doris Kearns Goodwin, Daniel Kemmis, Arturo Madrid, and Bill Moyers

National Inventor of the Year Awards, by Intellectual Property Owners (1997): (shared) Dale J. Kempf; Daniel W. Norbeck; Hing L. Sham; Chen Zhao, of Abbott Laboratories; Joseph P. Vacca; Bruce D. Dorsey; James P. Guare; M. Katharine Holloway; Randall W. Hungate, of Merck & Co., Inc.

John F. Kennedy Center for the Performing Arts Awards, for contribution to U.S. cultural life (1996): Edward Albee, Benny Carter, Johnny Cash, Jack Lemmon and Maria Tallchief (1997): Lauren Bacall, Bob Dylan, Charlton Heston, Jessye Norman, Edward Villella

National Medal of the Arts, by White House, for outstanding contributions to cultural life in the U.S. (1996): Edward Albee, Sarah Caldwell, Harry Callahan, Zelda Fichlander, Eduardo "Lalo" Guerrero, Lionel Hampton, Bella Lewitzky, Vera List, Robert Redford, Maurice Sendak, Stephen J. Sondheim, Boys Choir of Harlem

Pritzker Architecture Prize, by the Hyatt Foundation, $100,000: (1997) Sverre Fehn

1997 Teacher of the Year, by the Council of Chief State School Officers and Scholastic Inc.: Sharon Draper, Cincinnati, OH

1997 Library of the Year Award, by Gale Research, Inc., and Library Journal, $10,000 grant: Ann Arbor Public Library, Ann Arbor, MI

Templeton Prize for Progress in Religion, by Templeton Foundation, about $1.2 million: Pandurang Shastri Athavale.

Westinghouse Talent Search, 1st place, $40,000 scholarship: Adam Cohen, New York, NY; 2d place, $30,000 scholarship: Carrie Shilyansky, San Marino, CA; 3d place, $20,000 scholarship: Nicholas Eriksson, Missoula, MT; 4th place, $15,000 scholarship: Davesh Maulik, Roslyn, NY; 5th place, $15,000 scholarship: Emily Levy, North Miami Beach, FL; 6th place, $15,000 scholarship: Dev Kumar, Dallas, TX; 7th place, $10,000 scholarship: Ann Seiferle-Valencia, Farmington, NM; 8th place, $10,000 scholarship: Dylan Schwindt, Cortez, CO; 9th place, $10,000 scholarship: Rose Payyapilli, Brooklyn, NY; 10th place, $10,000 scholarship: Whitney Bowe, Cedarhurst, NY

Miss America Winners

1921	Margaret Gorman, Washington, DC	1965	Vonda Kay Van Dyke, Phoenix, Arizona
1922-23	Mary Campbell, Columbus, Ohio	1966	Deborah Irene Bryant, Overland Park, Kansas
1924	Ruth Malcolmson, Philadelphia, Pennsylvania	1967	Jane Anne Jayroe, Laverne, Oklahoma
1925	Fay Lamphier, Oakland, California	1968	Debra Dene Barnes, Moran, Kansas
1926	Norma Smallwood, Tulsa, Oklahoma	1969	Judith Anne Ford, Belvidere, Illinois
1927	Lois Delander, Joliet, Illinois	1970	Pamela Anne Eldred, Birmingham, Michigan
1933	Marion Bergeron, West Haven, Connecticut	1971	Phyllis Ann George, Denton, Texas
1935	Henrietta Leaver, Pittsburgh, Pennsylvania	1972	Laurie Lea Schaefer, Columbus, Ohio
1936	Rose Coyle, Philadelphia, Pennsylvania	1973	Terry Anne Meeuwsen, DePere, Wisconsin
1937	Bette Cooper, Bertrand Island, New Jersey	1974	Rebecca Ann King, Denver, Colorado
1938	Marilyn Meseke, Marion, Ohio	1975	Shirley Cothran, Fort Worth, Texas
1939	Patricia Donnelly, Detroit, Michigan	1976	Tawney Elaine Godin, Yonkers, New York
1940	Frances Marie Burke, Philadelphia, Pennsylvania	1977	Dorothy Kathleen Benham, Edina, Minnesota
1941	Rosemary LaPlanche, Los Angeles, California	1978	Susan Perkins, Columbus, Ohio
1942	Jo-Caroll Dennison, Tyler, Texas	1979	Kylene Barker, Galax, Virginia
1943	Jean Bartel, Los Angeles, California	1980	Cheryl Prewitt, Ackerman, Mississippi
1944	Venus Ramey, Washington, D.C.	1981	Susan Powell, Elk City, Oklahoma
1945	Bess Myerson, New York City, New York	1982	Elizabeth Ward, Russellville, Arkansas
1946	Marilyn Buferd, Los Angeles, California	1983	Debra Maffett, Anaheim, California
1947	Barbara Walker, Memphis, Tennessee	1984	Vanessa Williams, Milwood, New York*
1948	BeBe Shopp, Hopkins, Minnesota		Suzette Charles, Mays Landing, New Jersey
1949	Jacque Mercer, Litchfield, Arizona	1985	Sharlene Wells, Salt Lake City, Utah
1951	Yolande Betbeze, Mobile, Alabama	1986	Susan Akin, Meridian, Mississippi
1952	Coleen Kay Hutchins, Salt Lake City, Utah	1987	Kellye Cash, Memphis, Tennessee
1953	Neva Jane Langley, Macon, Georgia	1988	Kaye Lani Rae Rafko, Monroe, Michigan
1954	Evelyn Margaret Ay, Ephrata, Pennsylvania	1989	Gretchen Carlson, Anoka, Minnesota
1955	Lee Meriwether, San Francisco, California	1990	Debbye Turner, Columbia, Missouri
1956	Sharon Ritchie, Denver, Colorado	1991	Marjorie Vincent, Oak Park, Illinois
1957	Marian McKnight, Manning, South Carolina	1992	Carolyn Suzanne Sapp, Honolulu, Hawaii
1958	Marilyn Van Derbur, Denver, Colorado	1993	Leanza Cornett, Jacksonville, Florida
1959	Mary Ann Mobley, Brandon, Mississippi	1994	Kimberly Aiken, Columbia, South Carolina
1960	Lynda Lee Mead, Natchez, Mississippi	1995	Heather Whitestone, Birmingham, Alabama
1961	Nancy Fleming, Montague, Michigan	1996	Shawntel Smith, Muldrow, Oklahoma
1962	Maria Fletcher, Asheville, North Carolina	1997	Tara Dawn Holland, Overland Park, Kansas
1963	Jacquelyn Mayer, Sandusky, Ohio	1998	Kate Shindle, Evanston, Illinois
1964	Donna Axum, El Dorado, Arkansas		

* Resigned July 23, 1984.

Entertainment Awards

1996-97 Emmy Awards

Prime-Time Emmy Awards

Drama series: *Law & Order,* NBC
Comedy series: *Frasier,* NBC
Miniseries: *Prime Suspect 5: Errors of Judgement,* PBS
Television movie: *Miss Evers' Boys,* HBO
Variety, music, comedy special: *Chris Rock: Bring the Pain,* HBO
Variety, music, comedy series: *Tracey Takes On. . .,* HBO
Lead actor, drama series: Dennis Franz, *NYPD Blue,* ABC
Lead actress, drama series: Gillian Anderson, *The X-Files,* Fox
Lead actor, comedy series: John Lithgow, *3rd Rock From the Sun,* NBC
Lead actress, comedy series: Helen Hunt, *Mad About You,* NBC
Lead actor, miniseries/special: Armand Assante, *Gotti,* HBO
Lead actress, miniseries/special: Alfre Woodard, *Miss Evers' Boys,* HBO

Supporting actor, drama series: Hector Elizondo, *Chicago Hope,* CBS
Supporting actress, drama series: Kim Delaney, *NYPD Blue,* ABC
Supporting actor, comedy series: Michael Richards, *Seinfeld,* NBC
Supporting actress, comedy series: Kristen Johnston, *3rd Rock From the Sun,* NBC
Supporting actor, miniseries/special: Beau Bridges, *The Second Civil War,* HBO
Supporting actress, miniseries/special: Diana Rigg, *Rebecca,* PBS
Individual performance, variety/music program: Bette Midler, *Bette Midler: Diva Las Vegas,* HBO
Directing, drama series: Mark Tinker, *NYPD Blue: Where's Swaldo?,* ABC

Daytime Emmy Awards

Drama series: *General Hospital*, ABC
Actress: Jess Walton, *The Young & the Restless*, CBS
Actor: Justin Deas, *Guiding Light*, CBS
Supporting actress: Michelle Stafford, *The Young & the Restless*, CBS
Supporting actor: Ian Buchanan, *The Bold & the Beautiful*, CBS
Directing team: *The Young and the Restless*, CBS

Writing team: (dual) *All My Children*, ABC, *The Young & the Restless*, CBS
Game/audience participation show: *The Price Is Right*, CBS
Game show host: Pat Sajak
Children's series: *Reading Rainbow*, PBS
Animated children's program: *Animaniacs*, WB
Outstanding talk show: *The Oprah Winfrey Show*, SYN
Talk show host: Rosie O'Donnell

1997 Tony (Antoinette Perry) Awards

Play: *The Last Night of Ballyhoo*, by Alfred Uhry
Musical: *Titanic*, music and lyrics by Maury Yeston
Book of a musical: *Titanic*, by Peter Stone
Actor, play: Christopher Plummer, *Barrymore*
Actress, play: Janet McTeer, *A Doll's House*
Actor, musical: James Naughton, *Chicago*
Actress, musical: Bebe Neuwirth, *Chicago*
Musical score: *Titanic*
Director, play: Anthony Page, *A Doll's House*
Director, musical: Walter Bobbie, *Chicago*
Play revival: *A Doll's House*

Musical revival: *Chicago*
Featured actor, play: Owen Teale, *A Doll's House*
Featured actress, play: Lynne Thigpen, *An American Daughter*
Featured actor, musical: Chuck Cooper, *The Life*
Featured actress, musical: Lillias White, *The Life*
Choreography: Ann Reinking, *Chicago*
Costume design: Judith Dolan, *Candide*
Scenic design: Stewart Laing, *Titanic*
Lighting design: Ken Billington, *Chicago*
Orchestration: Jonathan Tunick, *Titanic*
Lifetime achievement: Bernard B. Jacobs
Regional theater: Berkeley Repertory Theatre, Berkeley, CA

1997 Golden Globe Awards

Movies
Drama: *The English Patient*
Musical/comedy: *Evita*
Actress, drama: Brenda Blethyn, *Secrets and Lies*
Actor, drama: Geoffrey Rush, *Shine*
Actress, musical/comedy: Madonna, *Evita*
Actor, musical/comedy: Tom Cruise, *Jerry Maguire*
Supp. actress, drama: Lauren Bacall, *The Mirror Has Two Faces*
Supp. actor, drama: Edward Norton, *Primal Fear*
Director: Milos Forman, *The People vs. Larry Flynt*
Screenplay: Scott Alexander and Larry Karaszewski, *The People vs. Larry Flynt*
Foreign-language film: *Kolya* (Czech Republic)
Original score: Gabriel Yared, *The English Patient*
Original song: *You Must Love Me*, from *Evita*
Cecil B. De Mille award for lifetime achievement: Dustin Hoffman

Television
Series, drama: *The X-Files*, Fox
Actress, drama: Gillian Anderson, *The X-Files*
Actor, drama: David Duchovny, *The X-Files*
Series, musical/comedy: *3rd Rock From the Sun*, NBC
Actress, musical/comedy: Helen Hunt, *Mad About You*
Actor, musical/comedy: John Lithgow, *3rd Rock From the Sun*
Miniseries, movie made for TV: *Rasputin*, HBO
Actress, miniseries, movie made for TV: Helen Mirren, *Losing Chase*
Actor, miniseries, movie made for TV: Alan Rickman, *Rasputin*
Supporting actress, miniseries, movie made for TV: Kathy Bates, *The Late Shift*
Supporting actor, miniseries, movie made for TV: Ian McKellen, *Rasputin*

Academy Awards (Oscars) for 1927-1996

1927-28
Picture: *Wings*
Actor: Emil Jannings, *The Way of All Flesh*
Actress: Janet Gaynor, *Seventh Heaven*
Director: Frank Borzage, *Seventh Heaven*; Lewis Milestone, *Two Arabian Knights*

1928-29
Picture: *Broadway Melody*
Actor: Warner Baxter, *In Old Arizona*
Actress: Mary Pickford, *Coquette*
Director: Frank Lloyd, *The Divine Lady*

1929-30
Picture: *All Quiet on the Western Front*
Actor: George Arliss, *Disraeli*
Actress: Norma Shearer, *The Divorcee*
Director: Lewis Milestone, *All Quiet on the Western Front*

1930-31
Picture: *Cimarron*
Actor: Lionel Barrymore, *Free Soul*
Actress: Marie Dressler, *Min and Bill*
Director: Norman Taurog, *Skippy*

1931-32
Picture: *Grand Hotel*
Actor: Fredric March, *Dr. Jekyll and Mr. Hyde*; Wallace Beery, *The Champ* (tie)
Actress: Helen Hayes, *The Sin of Madelon Claudet*
Director: Frank Borzage, *Bad Girl*
Special: Walt Disney, *Mickey Mouse*

1932-33
Picture: *Cavalcade*
Actor: Charles Laughton, *The Private Life of Henry VIII*
Actress: Katharine Hepburn, *Morning Glory*
Director: Frank Lloyd, *Cavalcade*

1934
Picture: *It Happened One Night*
Actor: Clark Gable, *It Happened One Night*

Actress: Claudette Colbert, *It Happened One Night*
Director: Frank Capra, *It Happened One Night*

1935
Picture: *Mutiny on the Bounty*
Actor: Victor McLaglen, *The Informer*
Actress: Bette Davis, *Dangerous*
Director: John Ford, *The Informer*

1936
Picture: *The Great Ziegfeld*
Actor: Paul Muni, *Story of Louis Pasteur*
Actress: Luise Rainer, *The Great Ziegfeld*
Sup. Actor: Walter Brennan, *Come and Get It*
Sup. Actress: Gale Sondergaard, *Anthony Adverse*
Director: Frank Capra, *Mr. Deeds Goes to Town*

1937
Picture: *Life of Emile Zola*
Actor: Spencer Tracy, *Captains Courageous*
Actress: Luise Rainer, *The Good Earth*
Sup. Actor: Joseph Schildkraut, *Life of Emile Zola*
Sup. Actress: Alice Brady, *In Old Chicago*
Director: Leo McCarey, *The Awful Truth*

1938
Picture: *You Can't Take It With You*
Actor: Spencer Tracy, *Boys Town*
Actress: Bette Davis, *Jezebel*
Sup. Actor: Walter Brennan, *Kentucky*
Sup. Actress: Fay Bainter, *Jezebel*
Director: Frank Capra, *You Can't Take It With You*

1939
Picture: *Gone With the Wind*
Actor: Robert Donat, *Goodbye Mr. Chips*
Actress: Vivien Leigh, *Gone With the Wind*
Sup. Actor: Thomas Mitchell, *Stage Coach*

Sup. Actress: Hattie McDaniel, *Gone With the Wind*
Director: Victor Fleming, *Gone With the Wind*

1940
Picture: *Rebecca*
Actor: James Stewart, *The Philadelphia Story*
Actress: Ginger Rogers, *Kitty Foyle*
Sup. Actor: Walter Brennan, *The Westerner*
Sup. Actress: Jane Darwell, *The Grapes of Wrath*
Director: John Ford, *The Grapes of Wrath*

1941
Picture: *How Green Was My Valley*
Actor: Gary Cooper, *Sergeant York*
Actress: Joan Fontaine, *Suspicion*
Sup. Actor: Donald Crisp, *How Green Was My Valley*
Sup. Actress: Mary Astor, *The Great Lie*
Director: John Ford, *How Green Was My Valley*

1942
Picture: *Mrs. Miniver*
Actor: James Cagney, *Yankee Doodle Dandy*
Actress: Greer Garson, *Mrs. Miniver*
Sup. Actor: Van Heflin, *Johnny Eager*
Sup. Actress: Teresa Wright, *Mrs. Miniver*
Director: William Wyler, *Mrs. Miniver*

1943
Picture: *Casablanca*
Actor: Paul Lukas, *Watch on the Rhine*
Actress: Jennifer Jones, *The Song of Bernadette*
Sup. Actor: Charles Coburn, *The More the Merrier*
Sup. Actress: Katina Paxinou, *For Whom the Bell Tolls*
Director: Michael Curtiz, *Casablanca*

(continued)

Academy Awards (continued)

1944

Picture: *Going My Way*
Actor: Bing Crosby, *Going My Way*
Actress: Ingrid Bergman, *Gaslight*
Sup. Actor: Barry Fitzgerald, *Going My Way*
Sup. Actress: Ethel Barrymore, *None But the Lonely Heart*
Director: Leo McCarey, *Going My Way*

1945

Picture: *The Lost Weekend*
Actor: Ray Milland, *The Lost Weekend*
Actress: Joan Crawford, *Mildred Pierce*
Sup. Actor: James Dunn, *A Tree Grows in Brooklyn*
Sup. Actress: Anne Revere, *National Velvet*
Director: Billy Wilder, *The Lost Weekend*

1946

Picture: *The Best Years of Our Lives*
Actor: Fredric March, *The Best Years of Our Lives*
Actress: Olivia de Havilland, *To Each His Own*
Sup. Actor: Harold Russell, *The Best Years of Our Lives*
Sup. Actress: Anne Baxter, *The Razor's Edge*
Director: William Wyler, *The Best Years of Our Lives*

1947

Picture: *Gentleman's Agreement*
Actor: Ronald Colman, *A Double Life*
Actress: Loretta Young, *The Farmer's Daughter*
Sup. Actor: Edmund Gwenn, *Miracle on 34th Street*
Sup. Actress: Celeste Holm, *Gentleman's Agreement*
Director: Elia Kazan, *Gentleman's Agreement*

1948

Picture: *Hamlet*
Actor: Laurence Olivier, *Hamlet*
Actress: Jane Wyman, *Johnny Belinda*
Sup. Actor: Walter Huston, *Treasure of Sierra Madre*
Sup. Actress: Claire Trevor, *Key Largo*
Director: John Huston, *Treasure of Sierra Madre*

1949

Picture: *All the King's Men*
Actor: Broderick Crawford, *All the King's Men*
Actress: Olivia de Havilland, *The Heiress*
Sup. Actor: Dean Jagger, *Twelve O'Clock High*
Sup. Actress: Mercedes McCambridge, *All the King's Men*
Director: Joseph L. Mankiewicz, *Letter to Three Wives*

1950

Picture: *All About Eve*
Actor: Jose Ferrer, *Cyrano de Bergerac*
Actress: Judy Holliday, *Born Yesterday*
Sup. Actor: George Sanders, *All About Eve*
Sup. Actress: Josephine Hull, *Harvey*
Director: Joseph L. Mankiewicz, *All About Eve*

1951

Picture: *An American in Paris*
Actor: Humphrey Bogart, *The African Queen*
Actress: Vivien Leigh, *A Streetcar Named Desire*
Sup. Actor: Karl Malden, *A Streetcar Named Desire*
Sup. Actress: Kim Hunter, *A Streetcar Named Desire*
Director: George Stevens, *A Place in the Sun*

1952

Picture: *The Greatest Show on Earth*
Actor: Gary Cooper, *High Noon*
Actress: Shirley Booth, *Come Back, Little Sheba*
Sup. Actor: Anthony Quinn, *Viva Zapata!*
Sup. Actress: Gloria Grahame, *The Bad and the Beautiful*
Director: John Ford, *The Quiet Man*

1953

Picture: *From Here to Eternity*
Actor: William Holden, *Stalag 17*
Actress: Audrey Hepburn, *Roman Holiday*
Sup. Actor: Frank Sinatra, *From Here to Eternity*
Sup. Actress: Donna Reed, *From Here to Eternity*
Director: Fred Zinnemann, *From Here to Eternity*

1954

Picture: *On the Waterfront*
Actor: Marlon Brando, *On the Waterfront*
Actress: Grace Kelly, *The Country Girl*
Sup. Actor: Edmond O'Brien, *The Barefoot Contessa*
Sup. Actress: Eva Marie Saint, *On the Waterfront*
Director: Elia Kazan, *On the Waterfront*

1955

Picture: *Marty*
Actor: Ernest Borgnine, *Marty*
Actress: Anna Magnani, *The Rose Tattoo*
Sup. Actor: Jack Lemmon, *Mister Roberts*
Sup. Actress: Jo Van Fleet, *East of Eden*
Director: Delbert Mann, *Marty*

1956

Picture: *Around the World in 80 Days*
Actor: Yul Brynner, *The King and I*
Actress: Ingrid Bergman, *Anastasia*
Sup. Actor: Anthony Quinn, *Lust for Life*
Sup. Actress: Dorothy Malone, *Written on the Wind*
Director: George Stevens, *Giant*

1957

Picture: *The Bridge on the River Kwai*
Actor: Alec Guinness, *The Bridge on the River Kwai*
Actress: Joanne Woodward, *The Three Faces of Eve*
Sup. Actor: Red Buttons, *Sayonara*
Sup. Actress: Miyoshi Umeki, *Sayonara*
Director: David Lean, *The Bridge on the River Kwai*

1958

Picture: *Gigi*
Actor: David Niven, *Separate Tables*
Actress: Susan Hayward, *I Want to Live*
Sup. Actor: Burl Ives, *The Big Country*
Sup. Actress: Wendy Hiller, *Separate Tables*
Director: Vincente Minnelli, *Gigi*

1959

Picture: *Ben-Hur*
Actor: Charlton Heston, *Ben-Hur*
Actress: Simone Signoret, *Room at the Top*
Sup. Actor: Hugh Griffith, *Ben-Hur*
Sup. Actress: Shelley Winters, *Diary of Anne Frank*
Director: William Wyler, *Ben-Hur*

1960

Picture: *The Apartment*
Actor: Burt Lancaster, *Elmer Gantry*
Actress: Elizabeth Taylor, *Butterfield 8*
Sup. Actor: Peter Ustinov, *Spartacus*
Sup. Actress: Shirley Jones, *Elmer Gantry*
Director: Billy Wilder, *The Apartment*

1961

Picture: *West Side Story*
Actor: Maximilian Schell, *Judgment at Nuremberg*
Actress: Sophia Loren, *Two Women*
Sup. Actor: George Chakiris, *West Side Story*
Sup. Actress: Rita Moreno, *West Side Story*
Director: Jerome Robbins, Robert Wise, *West Side Story*

1962

Picture: *Lawrence of Arabia*
Actor: Gregory Peck, *To Kill a Mockingbird*
Actress: Anne Bancroft, *The Miracle Worker*
Sup. Actor: Ed Begley, *Sweet Bird of Youth*
Sup. Actress: Patty Duke, *The Miracle Worker*
Director: David Lean, *Lawrence of Arabia*

1963

Picture: *Tom Jones*
Actor: Sidney Poitier, *Lilies of the Field*
Actress: Patricia Neal, *Hud*
Sup. Actor: Melvyn Douglas, *Hud*
Sup. Actress: Margaret Rutherford, *The V.I.P.s*
Director: Tony Richardson, *Tom Jones*

1964

Picture: *My Fair Lady*
Actor: Rex Harrison, *My Fair Lady*
Actress: Julie Andrews, *Mary Poppins*
Sup. Actor: Peter Ustinov, *Topkapi*
Sup. Actress: Lila Kedrova, *Zorba the Greek*
Director: George Cukor, *My Fair Lady*

1965

Picture: *The Sound of Music*
Actor: Lee Marvin, *Cat Ballou*
Actress: Julie Christie, *Darling*
Sup. Actor: Martin Balsam, *A Thousand Clowns*
Sup. Actress: Shelley Winters, *A Patch of Blue*
Director: Robert Wise, *The Sound of Music*

1966

Picture: *A Man for All Seasons*
Actor: Paul Scofield, *A Man for All Seasons*
Actress: Elizabeth Taylor, *Who's Afraid of Virginia Woolf?*
Sup. Actor: Walter Matthau, *The Fortune Cookie*
Sup. Actress: Sandy Dennis, *Who's Afraid of Virginia Woolf?*
Director: Fred Zinnemann, *A Man for All Seasons*

1967

Picture: *In the Heat of the Night*
Actor: Rod Steiger, *In the Heat of the Night*
Actress: Katharine Hepburn, *Guess Who's Coming to Dinner*
Sup. Actor: George Kennedy, *Cool Hand Luke*
Sup. Actress: Estelle Parsons, *Bonnie and Clyde*
Director: Mike Nichols, *The Graduate*

1968

Picture: *Oliver!*
Actor: Cliff Robertson, *Charly*
Actress: Katharine Hepburn, *The Lion in Winter;* Barbra Streisand, *Funny Girl* (tie)
Sup. Actor: Jack Albertson, *The Subject Was Roses*
Sup. Actress: Ruth Gordon, *Rosemary's Baby*
Director: Sir Carol Reed, *Oliver!*

1969

Picture: *Midnight Cowboy*
Actor: John Wayne, *True Grit*
Actress: Maggie Smith, *The Prime of Miss Jean Brodie*
Sup. Actor: Gig Young, *They Shoot Horses, Don't They?*
Sup. Actress: Goldie Hawn, *Cactus Flower*
Director: John Schlesinger, *Midnight Cowboy*

1970

Picture: *Patton*
Actor: George C. Scott, *Patton* (refused)
Actress: Glenda Jackson, *Women in Love*
Sup. Actor: John Mills, *Ryan's Daughter*
Sup. Actress: Helen Hayes, *Airport*
Director: Franklin Schaffner, *Patton*

1971

Picture: *The French Connection*
Actor: Gene Hackman, *The French Connection*
Actress: Jane Fonda, *Klute*
Sup. Actor: Ben Johnson, *The Last Picture Show*
Sup. Actress: Cloris Leachman, *The Last Picture Show*
Director: William Friedkin, *The French Connection*

1972
Picture: *The Godfather*
Actor: Marlon Brando, *The Godfather* (refused)
Actress: Liza Minnelli, *Cabaret*
Sup. Actor: Joel Grey, *Cabaret*
Sup. Actress: Eileen Heckart, *Butterflies Are Free*
Director: Bob Fosse, *Cabaret*

1973
Picture: *The Sting*
Actor: Jack Lemmon, *Save the Tiger*
Actress: Glenda Jackson, *A Touch of Class*
Sup. Actor: John Houseman, *The Paper Chase*
Sup. Actress: Tatum O'Neal, *Paper Moon*
Director: George Roy Hill, *The Sting*

1974
Picture: *The Godfather, Part II*
Actor: Art Carney, *Harry and Tonto*
Actress: Ellen Burstyn, *Alice Doesn't Live Here Anymore*
Sup. Actor: Robert DeNiro, *The Godfather, Part II*
Sup. Actress: Ingrid Bergman, *Murder on the Orient Express*
Director: Francis Ford Coppola, *The Godfather, Part II*

1975
Picture: *One Flew Over the Cuckoo's Nest*
Actor: Jack Nicholson, *One Flew Over the Cuckoo's Nest*
Actress: Louise Fletcher, *One Flew Over the Cuckoo's Nest*
Sup. Actor: George Burns, *The Sunshine Boys*
Sup. Actress: Lee Grant, *Shampoo*
Director: Milos Forman, *One Flew Over the Cuckoo's Nest*

1976
Picture: *Rocky*
Actor: Peter Finch, *Network*
Actress: Faye Dunaway, *Network*
Sup. Actor: Jason Robards, *All the President's Men*
Sup. Actress: Beatrice Straight, *Network*
Director: John G. Avildsen, *Rocky*

1977
Picture: *Annie Hall*
Actor: Richard Dreyfuss, *The Goodbye Girl*
Actress: Diane Keaton, *Annie Hall*
Sup. Actor: Jason Robards, *Julia*
Sup. Actress: Vanessa Redgrave, *Julia*
Director: Woody Allen, *Annie Hall*

1978
Picture: *The Deer Hunter*
Actor: Jon Voight, *Coming Home*
Actress: Jane Fonda, *Coming Home*
Sup. Actor: Christopher Walken, *The Deer Hunter*
Sup. Actress: Maggie Smith, *California Suite*
Director: Michael Cimino, *The Deer Hunter*

1979
Picture: *Kramer vs. Kramer*
Actor: Dustin Hoffman, *Kramer vs. Kramer*
Actress: Sally Field, *Norma Rae*
Sup. Actor: Melvyn Douglas, *Being There*
Sup. Actress: Meryl Streep, *Kramer vs. Kramer*
Director: Robert Benton, *Kramer vs. Kramer*

1980
Picture: *Ordinary People*
Actor: Robert DeNiro, *Raging Bull*
Actress: Sissy Spacek, *Coal Miner's Daughter*
Sup. Actor: Timothy Hutton, *Ordinary People*
Sup. Actress: Mary Steenburgen, *Melvin & Howard*
Director: Robert Redford, *Ordinary People*

1981
Picture: *Chariots of Fire*
Actor: Henry Fonda, *On Golden Pond*
Actress: Katharine Hepburn, *On Golden Pond*
Sup. Actor: John Gielgud, *Arthur*
Sup. Actress: Maureen Stapleton, *Reds*
Director: Warren Beatty, *Reds*

1982
Picture: *Gandhi*
Actor: Ben Kingsley, *Gandhi*
Actress: Meryl Streep, *Sophie's Choice*
Sup. Actor: Louis Gossett Jr., *An Officer and a Gentleman*
Sup. Actress: Jessica Lange, *Tootsie*
Director: Richard Attenborough, *Gandhi*

1983
Picture: *Terms of Endearment*
Actor: Robert Duvall, *Tender Mercies*
Actress: Shirley MacLaine, *Terms of Endearment*
Sup. Actor: Jack Nicholson, *Terms of Endearment*
Sup. Actress: Linda Hunt, *The Year of Living Dangerously*
Director: James L. Brooks, *Terms of Endearment*

1984
Picture: *Amadeus*
Actor: F. Murray Abraham, *Amadeus*
Actress: Sally Field, *Places in the Heart*
Sup. Actor: Haing S. Ngor, *The Killing Fields*
Sup. Actress: Peggy Ashcroft, *A Passage to India*
Director: Milos Forman, *Amadeus*

1985
Picture: *Out of Africa*
Actor: William Hurt, *Kiss of the Spider Woman*
Actress: Geraldine Page, *The Trip to Bountiful*
Sup. Actor: Don Ameche, *Cocoon*
Sup. Actress: Anjelica Huston, *Prizzi's Honor*
Director: Sydney Pollack, *Out of Africa*

1986
Picture: *Platoon*
Actor: Paul Newman, *The Color of Money*
Actress: Marlee Matlin, *Children of a Lesser God*
Sup. Actor: Michael Caine, *Hannah and Her Sisters*
Sup. Actress: Dianne Wiest, *Hannah and Her Sisters*
Director: Oliver Stone, *Platoon*

1987
Picture: *The Last Emperor*
Actor: Michael Douglas, *Wall Street*
Actress: Cher, *Moonstruck*
Sup. Actor: Sean Connery, *The Untouchables*
Sup. Actress: Olympia Dukakis, *Moonstruck*
Director: Bernardo Bertolucci, *The Last Emperor*

1988
Picture: *Rain Man*
Actor: Dustin Hoffman, *Rain Man*
Actress: Jodie Foster, *The Accused*
Sup. Actor: Kevin Kline, *A Fish Called Wanda*
Sup. Actress: Geena Davis, *The Accidental Tourist*
Director: Barry Levinson, *Rain Man*

1989
Picture: *Driving Miss Daisy*
Actor: Daniel Day-Lewis, *My Left Foot*
Actress: Jessica Tandy, *Driving Miss Daisy*
Sup. Actor: Denzel Washington, *Glory*
Sup. Actress: Brenda Fricker, *My Left Foot*
Director: Oliver Stone, *Born on the Fourth of July*

1990
Picture: *Dances With Wolves*
Actor: Jeremy Irons, *Reversal of Fortune*
Actress: Kathy Bates, *Misery*
Sup. Actor: Joe Pesci, *Goodfellas*
Sup. Actress: Whoopi Goldberg, *Ghost*
Director: Kevin Costner, *Dances With Wolves*

1991
Picture: *The Silence of the Lambs*
Actor: Anthony Hopkins, *The Silence of the Lambs*

Actress: Jodie Foster, *The Silence of the Lambs*
Sup. Actor: Jack Palance, *City Slickers*
Sup. Actress: Mercedes Ruehl, *The Fisher King*
Director: Jonathan Demme, *The Silence of the Lambs*

1992
Picture: *Unforgiven*
Actor: Al Pacino, *Scent of a Woman*
Actress: Emma Thompson, *Howards End*
Sup. Actor: Gene Hackman, *Unforgiven*
Sup. Actress: Marisa Tomei, *My Cousin Vinny*
Director: Clint Eastwood, *Unforgiven*

1993
Picture: *Schindler's List*
Actor: Tom Hanks, *Philadelphia*
Actress: Holly Hunter, *The Piano*
Sup. Actor: Tommy Lee Jones, *The Fugitive*
Sup. Actress: Anna Paquin, *The Piano*
Director: Steven Spielberg, *Schindler's List*

1994
Picture: *Forrest Gump*
Actor: Tom Hanks, *Forrest Gump*
Actress: Jessica Lange, *Blue Sky*
Sup. Actor: Martin Landau, *Ed Wood*
Sup. Actress: Dianne Wiest, *Bullets Over Broadway*
Director: Robert Zemeckis, *Forrest Gump*

1995
Picture: *Braveheart*
Actor: Nicolas Cage, *Leaving Las Vegas*
Actress: Susan Sarandon, *Dead Man Walking*
Sup. Actor: Kevin Spacey, *The Usual Suspects*
Sup. Actress: Mira Sorvino, *Mighty Aphrodite*
Director: Mel Gibson, *Braveheart*

1996
Picture: *The English Patient*
Actor: Geoffrey Rush, *Shine*
Actress: Frances McDormand, *Fargo*
Sup. Actor: Cuba Gooding Jr., *Jerry Maguire*
Sup. Actress: Juliette Binoche, *The English Patient*
Director: Anthony Minghella, *The English Patient*
Foreign Film: *Kolya*, Czech Republic
Original Screenplay: Ethan and Joel Coen, *Fargo*
Adapted Screenplay: Billy Bob Thornton, *Sling Blade*
Cinematography: John Seale, *The English Patient*
Art Direction: Stuart Craig, *The English Patient*
Film Editing: Walter Murch, *The English Patient*
Original Song: "You Must Love Me," *Evita*, Andrew Lloyd Webber and Tim Rice
Original musical or comedy score: Rachel Portman, *Emma*
Original dramatic score: Gabriel Yared, *The English Patient*
Costume: Ann Roth, *The English Patient*
Makeup: Rick Baker and David Leroy Anderson, *The Nutty Professor*
Sound: Walter Murch, Mark Berger, David Parker, and Chris Newman, *The English Patient*
Documentary Feature: *When We Were Kings*
Documentary Short Subject: *Breathing Lessons: The Life and Work of Mark O'Brien*
Short Film, Live: *Dear Diary*
Short Film, Animated: *Quest*
Visual Effects: Volker Engel, Douglas Smith, Clay Pinney, and Joseph Viskocil, *Independence Day*
Scientific and Technical Oscar: Imax Corp.
Honorary Award: Michael Kidd, choreographer
Irving G. Thalberg Memorial Award: Saul Zaentz, producer

Selected Grammy Awards for 1996

Record: "Change the World," Eric Clapton
Album: *Falling Into You*, Celine Dion
Song: "Change the World," Gordon Kennedy, Wayne Kirk-patrick, and Tommy Sims
New artist: LeAnn Rimes
Female pop vocalist: Toni Braxton, "Unbreak My Heart"
Male pop vocalist: Eric Clapton, "Change the World"
Pop album: *Falling Into You*, Celine Dion
Group or duo pop performance w/ vocal: The Beatles, "Free as a Bird"
Traditional pop album: *Here's to the Ladies*, Tony Bennett
Rock vocalist, female: Sheryl Crow, "If It Makes You Happy"
Rock vocalist, male: Beck, "Where It's At"
Rock song: "Give Me One Reason," Tracy Chapman
Rock album: *Sheryl Crow*, Sheryl Crow
R & B vocalist, female: Toni Braxton, "You're Makin' Me High"
R & B vocalist, male: Luther Vandross, "Your Secret Love"
R & B song: "Exhale (Shoop Shoop)," Babyface
R & B album: *Words,* Tony Rich Project
Rap solo: LL Cool J, "Hey Lover"

Rap album: *The Score*, Fugees
Jazz vocalist: Cassandra Wilson, "New Moon Daughter"
Contemporary jazz album: *High Life*, Wayne Shorter
Contemporary blues album: *Just Like You*, Keb' Mo'
Traditional blues album: *Deep in the Blues*, James Cotton
Country vocalist, female: LeAnn Rimes, "Blue"
Country vocalist, male: Vince Gill, "Worlds Apart"
Country song: "Blue," Bill Mack
Country album: *The Road to Ensenada*, Lyle Lovett
Contemporary folk album: *The Ghost of Tom Joad*, Bruce Springsteen
Traditional folk album: *Pete*, Pete Seeger
Reggae album: *Hall of Fame: A Tribute to Bob Marley's 50th Anniversary*, Bunny Wailer
Spoken word or non-musical album: *It Takes a Village*, Hillary Rodham Clinton
Producer of the Year: Babyface
Opera recording: *Britten: Peter Grimes*, Richard Hickox, conductor
Classical album: *Corigliano: Of Rage and Rememberance (Symphony No. 1, etc.)*, Leonard Slatkin, conductor

Grammy Awards for 1958-95

Source: National Academy of Recording Arts & Sciences

Record	Year	Album
Domenico Modugno, "Nel Blu Dipinto Di Blu (Volare)"	1958	Henry Mancini, *The Music From Peter Gunn*
Bobby Darin, "Mack the Knife"	1959	Frank Sinatra, *Come Dance With Me*
Percy Faith, "Theme From a Summer Place"	1960	Bob Newhart, *Button Down Mind*
Henry Mancini, "Moon River"	1961	Judy Garland, *Judy at Carnegie Hall*
Tony Bennett, "I Left My Heart in San Francisco"	1962	Vaughn Meader, *The First Family*
Henry Mancini, "The Days of Wine and Roses"	1963	Barbra Streisand, *The Barbra Streisand Album*
Stan Getz, Astrud Gilberto, "The Girl From Ipanema"	1964	Stan Getz, Astrud Gilberto, *Getz/Gilberto*
Herb Alpert, "A Taste of Honey"	1965	Frank Sinatra, *September of My Years*
Frank Sinatra, "Strangers in the Night"	1966	Frank Sinatra, *A Man and His Music*
5th Dimension, "Up, Up and Away"	1967	The Beatles, *Sgt. Pepper's Lonely Hearts Club Band*
Simon & Garfunkel, "Mrs. Robinson"	1968	Glen Campbell, *By the Time I Get to Phoenix*
5th Dimension, "Aquarius/Let the Sunshine In"	1969	Blood Sweat and Tears, *Blood, Sweat and Tears*
Simon & Garfunkel, "Bridge Over Troubled Water"	1970	Simon & Garfunkel, *Bridge Over Troubled Water*
Carole King, "It's Too Late"	1971	Carole King, *Tapestry*
Roberta Flack, "The First Time Ever I Saw Your Face"	1972	George Harrison and friends, *The Concert for Bangla Desh*
Roberta Flack, "Killing Me Softly With His Song"	1973	Stevie Wonder, *Innervisions*
Olivia Newton-John, "I Honestly Love You"	1974	Stevie Wonder, *Fulfillingness' First Finale*
Captain & Tennille, "Love Will Keep Us Together"	1975	Paul Simon, *Still Crazy After All These Years*
George Benson, "This Masquerade"	1976	Stevie Wonder, *Songs in the Key of Life*
Eagles, "Hotel California"	1977	Fleetwood Mac, *Rumours*
Billy Joel, "Just the Way You Are"	1978	Bee Gees, *Saturday Night Fever*
The Doobie Brothers, "What a Fool Believes"	1979	Billy Joel, *52nd Street*
Christopher Cross, "Sailing"	1980	Christopher Cross, *Christopher Cross*
Kim Carnes, "Bette Davis Eyes"	1981	John Lennon, Yoko Ono, *Double Fantasy*
Toto, "Rosanna"	1982	Toto, *Toto IV*
Michael Jackson, "Beat It"	1983	Michael Jackson, *Thriller*
Tina Turner, "What's Love Got to Do With It"	1984	Lionel Richie, *Can't Slow Down*
USA for Africa, "We Are the World"	1985	Phil Collins, *No Jacket Required*
Steve Winwood, "Higher Love"	1986	Paul Simon, *Graceland*
Paul Simon, "Graceland"	1987	U2, *The Joshua Tree*
Bobby McFerrin, "Don't Worry, Be Happy"	1988	George Michael, *Faith*
Bette Midler, "Wind Beneath My Wings"	1989	Bonnie Raitt, *Nick of Time*
Phil Collins, "Another Day in Paradise"	1990	Quincy Jones, *Back on the Block*
Natalie Cole, with Nat "King" Cole, "Unforgettable"	1991	Natalie Cole, with Nat "King" Cole, *Unforgettable*
Eric Clapton, "Tears in Heaven"	1992	Eric Clapton, *Unplugged*
Whitney Houston, "I Will Always Love You"	1993	Whitney Houston, *The Bodyguard*
Sheryl Crow, "All I Wanna Do"	1994	Tony Bennett, *MTV Unplugged*
Seal, "Kiss From a Rose"	1995	Alanis Morissette, *Jagged Little Pill*

Other Entertainment Awards

Cannes Film Festival Awards, (1997) Palme d'Or: (dual) *Unagi (The Eel)*, Shohei Imamura, *Ta'm E Guilass (The Taste of Cherry)*, Abbas Kiarostami; Grand Prix: *The Sweet Hereafter*, Atom Egoyan; best actress: Kathy Burke, *Nil by Mouth*; best actor: Sean Penn, *She's So Lovely*; best director: Wong Kar-Wai, *Happy Together*; best screenplay: James Schamus, *The Ice Storm*; Special Jury prize: *Western*, Manuel Poirier; best first feature: *Sazaku*, Naomi Kawase; 50th anniversary prize: Youssef Chahine; best technical achievement: Thierry Arbogast, cinematographer, *The Fifth Element* and *She's So Lovely*; Palme d'Or (short): *Is It the Design or Is It the Wrapper?*, Tessa Sheridan

Christopher Awards, by the Christophers: movies: *Fly Away Home*, *Marvin's Room*, *Mr. Holland's Opus*, *The Spitfire Grill*; television: ABC News Turning Point: *Race for a Miracle: The Brad and Vicki Margus Story*; *The American Experience: TR, The Story of Theodore Roosevelt*; *The Boys Next Door*, *A Brother's Promise: The Dan Jansen Story*; *Color Me Perfect*; Nightline: *The Gift*

Directors Guild of America Awards, feature film: Anthony Minghella, *The English Patient*; documentary: Al Pacino, *Looking for Richard*

National Society of Film Critics Awards (for 1996) film: *Breaking the Waves*; actor: Eddie Murphy, *The Nutty Profes-*

sor; actress: Emily Watson, *Breaking the Waves;* director: Lars von Trier, *Breaking the Waves;* supporting actor: (tie) Martin Donovan, *The Portrait of a Lady* and Tony Shalhoub, *Big Night;* supporting actress: Barbara Hershey, *The Portrait of a Lady;* cinematography: Robby Muller, *Breaking the Waves* and *Dead Man;* screenplay: Albert Brooks and Monica Johnson, *Mother;* foreign language film: *La Ceremonie;* documentary: *When We Were Kings;* Special citation: James Katz and Robert Harris for their restoration of *Vertigo*.

Sundance Film Festival Awards, (1997) Grand Jury Prize: (drama) *Sunday*, Jonathan Nossiter; (documentary) *Girls Like Us*, Jane C. Wagner and Tina DiFeliciantonio. Directing Award: (drama) *Hurricane*, Morgan J. Freeman; (docu.) *Licensed to Kill*, Arthur Dong; Audience Award: (drama) *Hurricane*, and *Love Jones* (shared); (docu.) *Paul Monette: The Brink of Summer's End*. Filmmakers Trophy: (drama) *In the Company of Men*; (docu.) *Licensed to Kill*. Cinematography Award: (drama) *Hurricane*; (docu.) *My America...or Honk if You Love Buddha*; Waldo Salt Screenwriting Award: *Sunday*. Freedom of Expression Award: *Family Name* and *Fear and Learning at Hoover Elementary* (shared). Latin American Cinema Award: *Landscapes of Memory*; Short Filmmaking Award: *Man About Town*.

NOTED PERSONALITIES
Widely Known Americans of the Present

Political leaders, journalists, and other widely known living persons. This list excludes many in categories listed elsewhere in Noted Personalities, such as Entertainers of the Present, or in the Sports section. As of Sept. 1997.

Name (Birthplace)	Birthdate
Mortimer Adler (New York, NY)	12/2/02
Roger Ailes (Knoxville, TN)	7/3/40
Madeleine K. Albright (Prague, Czech.)	5/15/37
Lamar Alexander (Knoxville, TN)	7/3/40
Stephen E. Ambrose (Decatur, IL)	1/10/36
Jack Anderson (Long Beach, CA)	10/19/22
Walter H. Annenberg (Milwaukee, WI)	3/13/08
Roone Arledge (Forest Hills, NY)	7/8/31
Richard K. Armey (Cando, ND)	7/7/40
Neil Armstrong (Wapakoneta, OH)	8/5/30
Bruce Babbitt (Los Angeles, CA)	6/27/38
F. Lee Bailey (Waltham, MA)	6/10/33
James Baker (Houston, TX)	4/28/30
Russell Baker (Loudoun Co., VA)	8/14/25
Dave Barry (Armonk, NY)	7/3/47
Marion Barry (Itta Bena, MS)	3/6/36
Sidney K. Barthelmy (New Orleans, LA)	3/17/42
William J. Bennett (Brooklyn, NY)	7/31/43
Lloyd Bentsen (Mission, TX)	2/11/21
Samuel "Sandy" Berger (Sharon, CT)	10/28/45
Joseph R. Biden Jr. (Scranton, PA)	11/20/42
Harry Blackmun (Nashville, IL)	11/12/08
David Bonior (Detroit, MI)	6/6/45
Daniel Boorstin (Atlanta, GA)	10/1/14
Erskine Bowles (Monterey, CA)	6/28/38
Barbara Boxer (Brooklyn, NY)	11/11/40
Ben Bradlee (Boston, MA)	8/26/21
Bill Bradley (Crystal City, MO)	7/28/43
Ed Bradley (Philadelphia, PA)	6/22/41
James Brady (Grand Rapids, MI)	9/17/44
Jimmy Breslin (Jamaica, NY)	10/17/30
Stephen Breyer (San Francisco, CA)	8/15/38
David Brinkley (Wilmington, NC)	7/10/20
David Broder (Chicago Heights, IL)	9/11/29
Jane Brody (Brooklyn, NY)	5/19/41
Tom Brokaw (Webster, SD)	2/6/40
Joyce Brothers (New York, NY)	9/20/28
Helen Gurley Brown (Green Forest, AR)	2/18/22
Jerry Brown (San Francisco, CA)	4/7/38
Jesse Brown (Chicago, IL)	3/27/44
Pat Buchanan (Wash., DC)	11/2/38
Art Buchwald (Mt. Vernon, NY)	10/20/25
William F. Buckley Jr. (New York, NY)	11/24/25
Warren Buffett (Omaha, NE)	8/30/30
Leo Buscaglia (Los Angeles, CA)	3/31/24
Barbara Bush (Rye, NY)	6/8/25
George Bush (Milton, MA)	6/12/24
George W. Bush (New Haven, CT)	7/6/46
Robert N. Butler (New York, NY)	1/21/27
Robert Byrd (N. Wilkesboro, NC)	11/20/17
Ron Carey (New York, NY)	3/22/36
Jimmy Carter (Plains, GA)	10/1/24
Rosalynn Carter (Plains, GA)	8/18/27
James Carville Jr. (Fort Benning, GA)	10/25/44
Julia Child (Pasadena, CA)	8/15/12
Noam Chomsky (Philadelphia, PA)	12/7/28
Warren Christopher (Scranton, ND)	10/27/25
Connie Chung (Wash., DC)	8/20/46
Liz Claiborne (Brussels, Belg.)	3/31/29
Marcia Clark (Berkeley, CA)	8/31/53
Bill Clinton (Hope, AR)	8/19/46
Chelsea Clinton (Little Rock, AR)	2/27/80
Hillary Rodham Clinton (Chicago, IL)	10/26/47
Johnnie L. Cochran Jr.(Shreveport, LA)	10/2/37
William Cohen (Bangor, ME)	8/28/40
Henry Steele Commager (Pittsburgh, PA)	10/25/02
Joan Ganz Cooney (Phoenix, AZ)	10/30/29
Bob Costas (New York, NY)	3/22/52
Katie Couric (Wash., DC)	1/7/57
Walter Cronkite (St. Joseph, MO)	11/4/16
Andrew Cuomo (New York, NY)	12/6/57
Mario Cuomo (Queens, NY)	6/15/32
Richard M. Daley (Chicago, IL)	4/24/42
William Daley (Chicago, IL)	8/9/48
Alfonse M. D'Amato (Brooklyn, NY)	8/1/37
Thomas Daschle (Aberdeen, SD)	12/9/47
Tom D. DeLay (Laredo, TX)	4/8/47
Ronald Dellums (Oakland, CA)	11/24/35
Alan Dershowitz (Brooklyn, NY)	9/1/38
Barry Diller (San Francisco, CA)	2/2/42
Christopher Dodd (Willimantic, CT)	5/27/44
Elizabeth Dole (Salisbury, NC)	7/29/36
Robert Dole (Russell, KS)	7/22/23
Pete Domenici (Albuquerque, NM)	5/7/32
Sam Donaldson (El Paso, TX)	3/11/34
Elizabeth Drew (Cincinnati, OH)	11/16/35
Michael S. Dukakis (Boston, MA)	11/3/33
Marian Wright Edelman (Bennettsville, SC)	6/6/39
Michael Eisner (New York, NY)	3/7/42
Rahm Emmanuel (Chicago, IL)	11/29/59
Nora Ephron (New York, NY)	5/19/41
Myrlie Evers-Williams (Vicksburg, MS)	3/17/33
James Fallows (Philadelphia, PA)	8/2/49
Jerry Falwell (Lynchburg, VA)	8/11/33
Louis Farrakhan (New York, NY)	5/11/33
Dianne Feinstein (San Francisco, CA)	6/22/33
Geraldine Ferraro (Newburgh, NY)	8/26/35
Shelby Foote (Greenville, MS)	11/17/16
Malcolm "Steve" Forbes Jr. (Morristown, NJ)	7/18/47
Betty Ford (Chicago, IL)	4/8/18
Gerald R. Ford (Omaha, NE)	7/14/13
Wendell Ford (Owensboro, KY)	9/8/24
Louis Freeh (Jersey City, NJ)	1/6/50
Betty Friedan (Peoria, IL)	2/4/21
Milton Friedman (Brooklyn, NY)	7/31/12
John Kenneth Galbraith (Iona Station, Ont.)	10/15/08
Bill Gates (Seattle, WA)	10/28/55
Henry Louis Gates Jr. (Keyser, WV)	9/16/50
David Geffen (Brooklyn, NY)	2/21/43
Richard Gephardt (St. Louis, MO)	1/31/41
Louis Gerstner (Mineola, NY)	3/1/42
Charles Gibson (Evanston, IL)	3/9/43
Newt Gingrich (Harrisburg, PA)	6/17/43
Ruth Bader Ginsburg (Brooklyn, NY)	3/15/33
Rudolph Giuliani (New York, NY)	5/28/44
John Glenn (Cambridge, OH)	7/18/21
Dan Glickman (Wichita, KS)	11/24/44
Barry M. Goldwater (Phoenix, AZ)	1/1/09
Ellen Goodman (Newton, MA)	4/11/41
Doris Kearns Goodwin (Rockville Centre, NY)	1/4/43
Al Gore Jr. (Wash., DC)	3/31/48
Tipper Gore (Wash., DC)	8/19/48
Robert A. Gottlieb (New York, NY)	4/29/31
Stephen Jay Gould (New York, NY)	9/10/41
Billy Graham (Charlotte, NC)	11/7/18
Katharine Graham (New York, NY)	6/16/17
Phil Gramm (Ft. Benning, GA)	7/8/42
Jeff Greenfield (New York, NY)	6/10/43
Meg Greenfield (Seattle, WA)	12/27/30
Alan Greenspan (New York, NY)	3/6/26
Bryant Gumbel (New Orleans, LA)	9/29/48
David Halberstam (New York, NY)	4/10/34
Paul Harvey (Tulsa, OK)	9/4/18
Orrin Hatch (Homestead Park, PA)	3/22/34
Howell Heflin (Poulan, GA)	6/19/21
Jesse Helms (Monroe, NC)	10/18/21
Leona Helmsley (New York, NY)	c1920
Heloise (Waco, TX)	4/15/51
Alexis Herman (Mobile, AL)	7/16/47
H. Wayne Huizenga (Evergreen Park, IL)	12/29/39
Al Hunt (Charlottesville, VA)	12/4/42
Kay Bailey Hutchison (Galveston, TX)	7/22/43
Lee A. Iacocca (Allentown, PA)	10/15/24
Carl Icahn (Queens, NY)	1936
Patricia Ireland (Oak Park, IL)	10/19/45
Jesse Jackson (Greenville, SC)	10/8/41
Stephen Jobs (California)	2/24/55
Lady Bird Johnson (Karnack, TX)	12/22/12
Vernon E. Jordan Jr. (Atlanta, GA)	8/15/35
John R. Kasich (McKees Rocks, PA)	5/13/52
Donna Karan (Forest Hills, NY)	10/2/48
Nancy Kassebaum Baker (Topeka, KS)	7/29/32
Jeffrey Katzenberg (New York, NY)	1950
Jack Kemp (Los Angeles, CA)	7/13/35
Anthony Kennedy (Sacramento, CA)	7/23/36
Caroline Kennedy (Boston, MA)	11/27/57
Edward M. Kennedy (Brookline, MA)	2/22/32
John F. Kennedy Jr. (Wash., DC)	11/25/60
Jack Kevorkian (Pontiac, MI)	5/26/28
Coretta Scott King (Marion, AL)	4/27/27
Larry King (Brooklyn, NY)	11/19/34
Michael Kinsley (Detroit, MI)	3/9/51
Larry Kirkland (Camden, SC)	3/12/22
Jeane Kirkpatrick (Duncan, OK)	11/19/26
Henry Kissinger (Fuerth, Germany)	5/27/23
Calvin Klein (New York, NY)	11/19/42
Edward I. Koch (New York, NY)	12/12/24
C. Everett Koop (Brooklyn, NY)	10/14/16

Name (Birthplace)	Birthdate	Name (Birthplace)	Birthdate
Ted Koppel (Lancashire, England)	2/8/40	Laurance S. Rockefeller (New York, NY)	5/26/10
William Kristol (New York, NY)	12/23/52	Andy Rooney (Albany, NY)	1/14/19
Ann Landers (Sioux City, IA)	7/4/18	Robert Rubin (New York, NY)	8/29/38
Estee Lauder (New York, NY)	9/1/08	Louis Rukeyser (New York, NY)	1/30/33
Matt Lauer (New York, NY)	1957	Tim Russert (Buffalo, NY)	5/7/50
Ralph Lauren (Bronx, NY)	10/14/39	William Safire (New York, NY)	12/17/29
Norman Lear (New Haven, CT)	7/27/22	Paul Samuelson (Gary, IN)	5/15/15
Jim Lehrer (Wichita, KS)	5/19/34	Diane Sawyer (Glasgow, KY)	12/22/45
Anthony Lewis (New York, NY)	3/27/27	Antonin Scalia (Trenton, NJ)	3/11/36
Rush Limbaugh (Cape Girardeau, MO)	1/12/51	Arthur Schlesinger Jr. (Columbus, OH)	10/15/17
Anne Morrow Lindbergh (Englewood, NJ)	1906	Patricia Schroeder (Portland, OR)	7/30/40
Frank Lorenzo (New York, NY)	5/19/40	Robert Schuller (Alton, IA)	9/16/26
Trent Lott (Grenada, MS)	10/9/41	H. Norman Schwarzkopf (Trenton, NJ)	8/22/34
Shannon Lucid (Shanghai, China)	1/14/43	Willard Scott (Alexandria, VA)	3/7/34
Richard G. Lugar (Indianapolis, IN)	4/4/32	Brent Scowcroft (Ogden, UT)	3/19/25
Joan Lunden (Sacramento, CA)	9/19/50	Glenn T. Seaborg (Ishpeming, MI)	4/19/12
William Manchester (Attleboro, MA)	4/1/22	Donna E. Shalala (Cleveland, OH)	2/14/41
Janet Maslin (New York, NY)	8/12/49	Bernard Shaw (Chicago, IL)	1940
Mary Matalin (Chicago, IL)	8/19/53	Henry Hugh Shelton (Speed, NC)	1/2/42
John McCain III (Panama Canal Zone)	8/29/36	Maria Shriver (Chicago, IL)	11/6/55
George McGovern (Avon, SD)	7/19/22	George P. Shultz (New York, NY)	12/13/20
Michael McCurry (Charleston, SC)	10/27/54	Alan K. Simpson (Cody, WY)	9/2/31
John McLaughlin (Providence, RI)	3/29/27	O. J. Simpson (San Francisco, CA)	7/9/47
Robert McNamara (San Francisco, CA)	6/9/16	Rodney Slater (Tutwyler, MS)	2/23/55
Howard Metzenbaum (Cleveland, OH)	6/4/17	Liz Smith (Ft. Worth, TX)	2/2/23
Kweisi Mfume (Baltimore, MD)	10/24/48	David H. Souter (Melrose, MA)	9/17/39
Barbara Mikulski (Baltimore, MD)	7/20/36	Susan Sontag (New York, NY)	1/28/33
Kate Millett (St. Paul, MN)	9/14/34	George Soros (Budapest, Hungary)	8/12/30
Susan Molinari (Staten Island, NY)	3/27/58	Arlen Specter (Wichita, KS)	2/12/30
Walter Mondale (Ceylon, MN)	1/5/28	Benjamin Spock (New Haven, CT)	5/2/03
Carol Moseley-Braun (Chicago, IL)	8/16/47	Lesley Stahl (Lynn, MA)	12/16/41
Bill Moyers (Hugo, OK)	6/5/34	Kenneth Starr (Vernon, TX)	1946
Daniel P. Moynihan (Tulsa, OK)	3/16/27	Shelby Steele (Chicago, IL)	1/1/46
Rupert Murdoch (Melbourne, Australia)	3/11/31	George Steinbrenner (Rocky River, OH)	7/4/30
Ralph Nader (Winsted, CT)	2/27/34	Gloria Steinem (Toledo, OH)	3/25/34
Don Nickles (Ponca City, OK)	12/6/48	George Stephanopoulos (Fall River, MA)	2/10/61
Oliver North (San Antonio, TX)	10/7/43	David J. Stern (New York, NY)	9/22/42
Eleanor Holmes Norton (Wash., DC)	6/13/37	John Paul Stevens (Chicago, IL)	4/20/20
Robert Novak (Joliet, IL)	2/26/31	Martha Stewart (Nutley, NJ)	8/3/41
Sam Nunn (Perry, GA)	9/8/38	John J. Sweeney (New York, NY)	5/5/34
Sandra Day O'Connor (El Paso, TX)	3/26/30	Arthur Ochs Sulzberger Jr. (Mt. Kisco, NY)	9/22/51
Hazel O'Leary (Newport News, VA)	5/17/37	John H. Sununu (Havana, Cuba)	7/2/39
Charles Osgood (New York, NY)	1/8/33	Paul Tagliabue (Jersey City, NJ)	11/24/40
Michael Ovitz (Encino, CA)	12/4/46	Susan Taylor (New York, NY)	1/23/46
Camille Paglia (Endicott, NY)	1947	George Tenet (Queens, NY)	1/5/53
Leon F. Panetta (Monterey, CA)	6/28/38	Studs Terkel (New York, NY)	5/16/12
Rosa Parks (Tuskegee, AL)	2/4/13	Clarence Thomas (Savannah, GA)	6/23/48
Jane Pauley (Indianapolis, IN)	10/31/50	R. David Thomas (Atlantic City, NJ)	7/2/32
Bill Paxon (Buffalo, NY)	4/29/54	Fred Thompson (Sheffield, AL)	8/19/42
Federico Pena (Laredo, TX)	3/15/55	Hunter S. Thompson (Louisville, KY)	7/18/37
H. Ross Perot (Texarkana, TX)	6/27/30	J. Strom Thurmond (Edgefield, SC)	12/5/02
George Plimpton (New York, NY)	3/18/27	Laurence Tisch (New York, NY)	3/15/23
Norman Podhoretz (New York, NY)	1/16/30	Alvin Toffler (New York, NY)	10/4/28
Alvin F. Poussaint (New York, NY)	5/15/34	John Toland (LaCrosse, WI)	6/29/12
Colin Powell (New York, NY)	4/5/37	Calvin Trillin (Kansas City, MO)	12/5/35
Lewis Powell Jr. (Suffolk, VA)	9/19/07	Margaret Truman (Independence, MO)	2/17/24
Dan Quayle (Indianapolis, IN)	2/4/47	Donald Trump (New York, NY)	1946
Anna Quindlen (Philadelphia, PA)	7/8/53	Ted Turner (Cincinnati, OH)	11/19/38
Jane Bryant Quinn (Niagara Falls, NY)	2/5/39	Peter Ueberroth (Chicago, IL)	9/2/37
Franklin Raines (Seattle, WA)	1/14/49	Jack Valenti (Houston, TX)	9/5/21
Dan Rather (Wharton, TX)	10/31/31	Abigail Van Buren (Sioux City, IA)	7/4/18
Nancy Reagan (New York, NY)	7/6/23	George Wallace (Clio, AL)	8/25/19
Ronald Reagan (Tampico, IL)	2/6/11	Mike Wallace (Brookline, MA)	5/9/18
Sumner M. Redstone (Boston, MA)	5/27/23	Barbara Walters (Boston, MA)	9/25/31
Ralph Reed (Portsmouth, VA)	6/24/61	J. C. Watts (Eufaula, OK)	11/18/57
William Rehnquist (Milwaukee, WI)	10/1/24	Caspar Weinberger (San Francisco, CA)	8/18/17
Robert B. Reich (Scranton, PA)	6/24/46	Jann Wenner (New York, NY)	1/7/46
Janet Reno (Miami, FL)	7/21/38	Cornel West (Tulsa, OK)	6/2/53
Ann Richards (Waco, TX)	9/3/33	Bill White (Lakewood, FL)	1/28/34
Bill Richardson (Pasadena, CA)	11/15/47	Byron White (Ft. Collins, CO)	6/8/17
Sally K. Ride (Encino, CA)	5/26/51	Christine Todd Whitman (New York)	9/26/46
Richard Riley (Greenville, SC)	1/2/33	Tom Wicker (Hamlet, NC)	6/18/26
Richard Riordan (Flushing, NY)	1930	Elie Wiesel (Sighet, Romania)	9/30/28
Cokie Roberts (New Orleans, LA)	12/27/43	L. Douglas Wilder (Richmond, VA)	1/17/31
Oral Roberts (nr. Ada, OK)	1/24/18	George Will (Champaign, IL)	5/4/41
Pat Robertson (Lexington, VA)	3/22/30	Pete Wilson (Lake Forest, IL)	8/23/33
David Rockefeller (New York, NY)	6/12/15	William Junius Wilson (Derry Twp., PA)	12/20/35
John D. "Jay" Rockefeller 4th (New York, NY)	6/18/37	Coleman Young (Tuscaloosa, AL)	5/24/18

Selected Architects and Some of Their Achievements

Max Abramovitz, b 1908, Avery Fisher Hall, NYC; U.S. Steel Bldg. (now USX Towers), Pittsburgh, PA.

Henry Bacon, 1866-1924, Lincoln Memorial, Wash., DC.

Pietro Belluschi, 1899-1994, Juilliard School of Music, Lincoln Center, Pan Am Bldg. (now MetLife Bldg.) (with Walter Gropius), all NYC.

Marcel Breuer, 1902-81, Whitney Museum of American Art (with Hamilton Smith), NYC.

Charles Bulfinch, 1763-1844, State House, Boston; Capitol (part), Wash., DC.

Gordon Bunshaft, 1909-90, Lever House, Park Ave, NYC; Hirshhorn Museum, Wash., DC.

Daniel H. Burnham, 1846-1912, Union Station, Wash. DC; Flatiron Bldg., NYC.

Irwin Chanin, 1892-1988, theaters, skyscrapers, NYC.

Ralph Adams Cram, 1863-1942, Cath. of St. John the Divine, NYC; U.S. Military Acad. (part), West Point, NY.

R. Buckminster Fuller, 1895-1983, U.S. Pavilion (geodesic domes), Expo 67, Montreal.

Cass Gilbert, 1859-1934, Custom House, Woolworth Bldg., NYC; Supreme Court Bldg., Wash., DC.

Bertram G. Goodhue, 1869-1924, Capitol, Lincoln, NE; St. Thomas's Church, St. Bartholomew's Church, NYC.

Walter Gropius, 1883-1969, Pan Am Bldg. (now MetLife Bldg.) (with Pietro Belluschi), NYC.

Lawrence Halprin, b 1916, Ghirardelli Sq., San Francisco; Nicollet Mall, Minneapolis; FDR Memorial, Wash., DC.

Peter Harrison, 1716-75, Touro Synagogue, Redwood Library, Newport, RI.

Wallace K. Harrison, 1895-1981, Metropolitan Opera House, Lincoln Center, NYC.

Thomas Hastings, 1860-1929, NY Public Library (with John Carrère), Frick Mansion, NYC.

James Hoban, 1762-1831, White House, Wash., DC.

Raymond Hood, 1881-1934, Rockefeller Center (part), Daily News, NYC; Tribune, Chicago, IL.

Richard M. Hunt, 1827-95, Metropolitan Museum (part), NYC; National Observatory, Wash., DC.

William Le Baron Jenney, 1832-1907, Home Insurance (demolished 1931), Chicago, IL.

Philip C. Johnson, b 1906, AT&T headquarters (now 550 Madison Ave.), NYC; Transco Tower, Houston, TX.

Albert Kahn, 1869-1942, General Motors Bldg., Detroit, MI.

Louis Kahn, 1901-74, Salk Laboratory, La Jolla, CA; Yale Art Gallery, New Haven, CT.

Christopher Grant LaFarge, 1862-1938, Roman Catholic Chapel, West Point, NY.

Benjamin H. Latrobe, 1764-1820, Capitol (part), Wash., DC; State Capitol Bldg., Richmond, VA.

William Lescaze, 1896-1969, Philadelphia Savings Fund Society; Borg-Warner Bldg., Chicago.

Maya Lin, b 1959, Vietnam Veterans Memorial, Wash., DC.

Bernard R. Maybeck, 1862-1957, Hearst Hall, Univ. of CA, Berkeley; First Church of Christ Scientist, Berkeley, CA.

Charles F. McKim, 1847-1909, Public Library, Boston; Columbia Univ. (part), NYC.

Charles M. McKim, b 1920, KUHT-TV Transmitter Bldg., Lutheran Church of the Redeemer, Houston, TX.

Richard Meier, b. 1934, Getty Center Museum Los Angeles, CA; High Museum of Art, Atlanta, GA.

Ludwig Mies van der Rohe, 1886-1969, Seagram Bldg., (with Philip C. Johnson), NYC; National Gallery, Berlin.

Robert Mills, 1781-1855, Washington Monument, Wash., DC.

Charles Moore, 1925-93, Sea Ranch, near San Francisco; Piazza d'Italia, New Orleans, LA.

Richard J. Neutra, 1892-1970, Mathematics Park, Princeton, NJ; Orange Co. Courthouse, Santa Ana, CA.

Gyo Obata, b 1923, Natl. Air & Space Museum, Smithsonian Inst., Wash., DC; Dallas-Ft. Worth Airport.

Frederick L. Olmsted, 1822-1903, Central Park, NYC; Fairmount Park, Philadelphia, PA.

I(eoh) M(ing) Pei, b 1917, East Wing, Natl. Gallery of Art, Wash., DC; Pyramid, The Louvre, Paris; Rock & Roll Hall of Fame and Museum, Cleveland, OH.

Cesar Pelli, b 1926, World Financial Center, Carnegie Hall Tower, NYC; Petronas Twin Towers, Malaysia.

William Pereira, 1909-85, Cape Canaveral; Transamerica Bldg., San Francisco, CA.

John Russell Pope, 1874-1937, National Gallery, Wash., DC.

John Portman, b 1924, Peachtree Center, Atlanta, GA.

George Browne Post, 1837-1913, NY Stock Exchange; Capitol, Madison, WI.

James Renwick Jr., 1818-95, Grace Church, St. Patrick's Cath., NYC; Corcoran (now Renwick) Gallery, Wash., DC.

Henry H. Richardson, 1838-86, Trinity Church, Boston, MA.

Kevin Roche, b 1922, Oakland Museum, Oakland, CA; Fine Arts Center, University of Massachusetts, Amherst.

James Gamble Rogers, 1867-1947, Columbia-Presbyterian Medical Center, NYC; Northwestern Univ., Evanston, IL.

John Wellborn Root, 1887-1963, Palmolive Bldg., Chicago; Hotel Statler, Wash., DC.

Paul Rudolph, b 1918, Jewitt Art Center, Wellesley Colllege, MA; Art & Architecture Bldg., Yale Univ., New Haven, CT.

Eero Saarinen, 1910-61, Gateway to the West Arch, St. Louis, MO; Trans World Flight Center, NYC.

Louis Skidmore, 1897-1962, Atomic Energy Commission town site, Oak Ridge, TN; Terrace Plaza Hotel, Cincinnati, OH.

Clarence S. Stein, 1882-1975, Temple Emanu-El, NYC.

Edward Durell Stone, 1902-78, U.S. Embassy, New Delhi, India; (H. Hartford) Gallery of Modern Art, NYC.

Louis H. Sullivan, 1856-1924, Auditorium Bldg., Chicago, IL.

Richard Upjohn, 1802-78, Trinity Church, NYC.

Max O. Urbahn, 1912-95, Vehicle Assembly Bldg., Cape Canaveral, FL.

Ralph T. Walker, 1889-1973, NY Telephone Bldg. (now NYNEX); IBM Research Lab, Poughkeepsie, NY.

Roland A. Wank, 1898-1970, Cincinnati Union Terminal, OH; head architect (1933-44), Tennessee Valley Authority.

Stanford White, 1853-1906, Washington Arch in Washington Square Park, first Madison Square Garden, NYC.

Frank Lloyd Wright, 1867 (or 1869)-1959, Imperial Hotel, Tokyo; Guggenheim Museum, NYC; Unity Church, Oak Park, IL; Robie House, Chicago, IL; Taliesin, Spring Green, WI.

William Wurster, 1895-1973, Ghirardelli Sq., San Francisco; Cowell College, UC, Berkeley, CA.

Minoru Yamasaki, 1912-86, World Trade Center, NYC.

Noted Artists, Photographers, and Sculptors of the Past

Artists are painters unless otherwise indicated.

Berenice Abbott, 1898-1991, (U.S.) photographer. Documentary of New York City, *Changing New York* (1939).

Ansel Easton Adams, 1902-84, (U.S.) photographer. Landscapes of the American Southwest.

Washington Allston, 1779-1843, (U.S.) landscapist. *Belshazzar's Feast.*

Albrecht Altdorfer, 1480-1538, (Ger.) landscapist.

Andrea del Sarto, 1486-1530, (It.) frescoes. *Madonna of the Harpies.*

Fra Angelico, c1400-55, (It.) Renaissance muralist. *Madonna of the Linen Drapers' Guild.*

Diane Arbus, 1923-71, (U.S.) photographer. Disturbing images.

Alexsandr Archipenko, 1887-1964, (U.S.) sculptor. *Boxing Match, Medranos.*

Eugène Atget, 1856-1927, (Fr.) photographer. Parisian life.

John James Audubon, 1785-1851, (U.S.) *Birds of America.*

Hans Baldung-Grien, 1484-1545, (Ger.) *Todentanz.*

Ernst Barlach, 1870-1938, (Ger.) Expressionist sculptor. *Man Drawing a Sword.*

Frederic-Auguste Bartholdi, 1834-1904, (Fr.) *Liberty Enlightening the World, Lion of Belfort.*

Fra Bartolommeo, 1472-1517, (It.) *Vision of St. Bernard.*

Aubrey Beardsley, 1872-98, (Br.) illustrator. *Salome, Lysistrata, Morte d'Arthur, Volpone.*

Max Beckmann, 1884-1950, (Ger.) Expressionist. *The Descent From the Cross.*

Gentile Bellini, 1426-1507, (It.) Renaissance. *Procession in St. Mark's Square.*

Giovanni Bellini, 1428-1516, (It.) *St. Francis in Ecstasy.*

Jacopo Bellini, 1400-70, (It.) *Crucifixion.*

George Wesley Bellows, 1882-1925, (U.S.) sports artist, portraitist, landscapist. *Stag at Sharkey's, Edith Olavell.*

Thomas Hart Benton, 1889-1975, (U.S.) American regionalist. *Threshing Wheat, Arts of the West.*

Gianlorenzo Bernini, 1598-1680, (It.) Baroque sculpture. *The Assumption.*

Albert Bierstadt, 1830-1902, (U.S.) landscapist. *The Rocky Mountains, Mount Corcoran.*

George Caleb Bingham, 1811-79, (U.S.) *Fur Traders Descending the Missouri.*

William Blake, 1752-1827, (Br.) engraver. *Book of Job, Songs of Innocence, Songs of Experience.*

Rosa Bonheur, 1822-99, (Fr.) *The Horse Fair.*

Pierre Bonnard, 1867-1947, (Fr.) Intimist. *The Breakfast Room, Girl in a Straw Hat.*

Gutzon Borglum, 1871-1941, (U.S.) sculptor. Mt. Rushmore Memorial.

Hieronymus Bosch, 1450-1516, (Flem.) religious allegories. *The Crowning With Thorns.*

Sandro Botticelli, 1444-1510, (It.) Renaissance. *Birth of Venus, Adoration of the Magi, Guiliano de'Medici.*

Margaret Bourke-White, 1906-71, (U.S.) photographer, photojournalist. WW2, USSR, rural South during the Depression.

Mathew Brady, c1823-96, (U.S.) photographer. Official photographer of the Civil War.

Constantin Brancusi, 1876-1957, (Rom.) Nonobjective sculptor. *Flying Turtle, The Kiss.*

Georges Braque, 1882-1963, (Fr.) Cubist. *Violin and Palette.*

Pieter Bruegel the Elder, c1525-69, (Flem.) *The Peasant Dance, Hunters in the Snow, Magpie on the Gallows.*

Pieter Bruegel the Younger, 1564-1638, (Flem.) *Village Fair, The Crucifixion.*

Edward Burne-Jones, 1833-98, (Br.) Pre-Raphaelite artist-craftsman. *The Mirror of Venus.*

Alexander Calder, 1898-1976, (U.S.) sculptor. *Lobster Trap and Fish Tail.*

Julia Cameron, 1815-79, (Br.) photographer. Considered one of the most important portraitists of the 19th cent.

Robert Capa (Andrei Friedmann), 1913-54, (Hung.-U.S.) photographer. War photojournalist; invasion of Normandy.

Michelangelo Merisi da Caravaggio, 1573-1610, (It.) Baroque. *The Supper at Emmaus.*

Emily Carr, 1871-1945, (Can.) landscapist. *Blunden Harbour, Big Raven, Rushing Sea of Undergrowth.*

Carlo Carrà, 1881-1966, (It.) Metaphysical school. *Lot's Daughters, The Enchanted Room.*

Mary Cassatt, 1844-1926, (U.S.) Impressionist. *The Cup of Tea, Woman Bathing, The Boating Party.*

George Catlin, 1796-1872, (U.S.) American Indian life. *Gallery of Indians, Buffalo Dance.*

Benvenuto Cellini, 1500-71, (It.) Mannerist sculptor, goldsmith. *Perseus and Medusa, Salt Cellar of Francis I.*

Paul Cézanne, 1839-1906, (Fr.) *Card Players, Mont-Sainte-Victoire With Large Pine Trees.*

Marc Chagall, 1887-1985, (Russ.) Jewish life and folklore. *I and the Village, The Praying Jew.*

Jean Simeon Chardin, 1699-1779, (Fr.) still lifes. *The Kiss, The Grace.*

Frederick Church, 1826-1900, (U.S.) Hudson River school. *Niagara, Andes of Ecuador.*

Giovanni Cimabue, 1240-1302, (It.) Byzantine mosaicist. *Madonna Enthroned With St. Francis.*

Claude Lorrain (Claude Gellée), 1600-82, (Fr.) ideal-landscapist. *The Enchanted Castle.*

Thomas Cole, 1801-48, (U.S.) Hudson River school. *The Ox-Bow, In the Catskills.*

John Constable, 1776-1837, (Br.) landscapist. *Salisbury Cathedral From the Bishop's Grounds.*

John Singleton Copley, 1738-1815, (U.S.) portraitist. *Samuel Adams, Watson and the Shark.*

Lovis Corinth, 1858-1925, (Ger.) Expressionist. *Apocalypse.*

Jean-Baptiste-Camille Corot, 1796-1875, (Fr.) landscapist. *Souvenir de Mortefontaine, Pastorale.*

Correggio, 1494-1534, (It.) Renaissance muralist. *Mystic Marriages of St. Catherine.*

Gustave Courbet, 1819-77, (Fr.) Realist. *The Artist's Studio.*

Lucas Cranach the Elder, 1472-1553, (Ger.) Protestant Reformation portraitist. *Luther.*

Imogen Cunningham, 1883-1976, (U.S.) photographer, portraitist. Plant photography.

Nathaniel Currier, 1813-88, and **James M. Ives**, 1824-95, (both U.S.) lithographers. *A Midnight Race on the Mississippi, American Forest Scene—Maple Sugaring.*

John Steuart Curry, 1897-1946, (U.S.) Americana, murals. *Baptism in Kansas.*

Salvador Dalí, 1904-89, (Sp.) Surrealist. *Persistence of Memory, The Crucifixion.*

Honoré Daumier, 1808-79, (Fr.) caricaturist. *The Third-Class Carriage.*

Jacques-Louis David, 1748-1825, (Fr.) Neoclassicist. *The Oath of the Horatii.*

Arthur Davies, 1862-1928, (U.S.) Romantic landscapist. *Unicorns, Leda and the Dioscuri.*

Willem de Kooning, 1904-1997, (Dutch-U.S.) abstract expressionist. *Excavation, Woman I, Door to the River.*

Edgar Degas, 1834-1917, (Fr.) *The Ballet Class.*

Eugène Delacroix, 1798-1863, (Fr.) Romantic. *Massacre at Chios, Liberty Leading the People.*

Paul Delaroche, 1797-1856, (Fr.) historical themes. *Children of Edward IV.*

Luca Della Robbia, 1400-82, (It.) Renaissance terracotta artist. *Cantoria* (singing gallery), Florence cathedral.

Donatello, 1386-1466, (It.) Renaissance sculptor. *David, Gattamelata.*

Jean Dubuffet, 1902-85, (Fr.) painter, sculptor, printmaker. *Group of Four Trees.*

Marcel Duchamp, 1887-1968, (Fr.) Dada artist. *Nude Descending a Staircase, No. 2.*

Raoul Dufy, 1877-1953, (Fr.) Fauvist. *Chateau and Horses.*

Asher Brown Durand, 1796-1886, (U.S.) Hudson River school. *Kindred Spirits.*

Albrecht Dürer, 1471-1528, (Ger.) Renaissance painter, engraver, woodcuts. *St. Jerome in His Study, Melencolia I.*

Anthony van Dyck, 1599-1641, (Flem.) Baroque portraitist. *Portrait of Charles I Hunting.*

Thomas Eakins, 1844-1916, (U.S.) Realist. *The Gross Clinic.*

Alfred Eisenstaedt, 1898-1995, (Ger.-U.S.) photographer, photojournalist. Famous for V-J Day, Aug. 14, 1945, photograph of sailor and nurse in Times Square, NYC.

Peter Henry Emerson, 1856-1936, (Br.) photographer. Promoted photography as an independent art form.

Jacob Epstein, 1880-1959, (Br.) religious and allegorical sculptor. *Genesis, Ecce Homo.*

Jan van Eyck, c1390-1441, (Flem.) naturalistic panels. *Adoration of the Lamb.*

Roger Fenton, 1819-68, (Br.) photographer. Crimean War.

Anselm Feuerbach, 1829-80, (Ger.) Romantic Classicist. *Judgment of Paris, Iphigenia.*

John Bernard Flannagan, 1895-1942, (U.S.) animal sculptor. *Triumph of the Egg.*

Jean-Honoré Fragonard, 1732-1806, (Fr.) Rococo. *The Swing.*

Daniel Chester French, 1850-1931, (U.S.) *The Minute Man of Concord;* seated *Lincoln,* Lincoln Memorial, Wash., DC.

Caspar David Friedrich, 1774-1840, (Ger.) Romantic landscapes. *Man and Woman Gazing at the Moon.*

Thomas Gainsborough, 1727-88, (Br.) portraitist. *The Blue Boy, The Watering Place, Orpin the Parish Clerk.*

Alexander Gardner, 1821-82, (U.S.) photographer. Civil War; railroad construction; Great Plains Indians.

Paul Gauguin, 1848-1903, (Fr.) Post-impressionist. *The Tahitians, Spirit of the Dead Watching.*

Lorenzo Ghiberti, 1378-1455, (It.) Renaissance sculptor. Gates of Paradise baptistery doors, Florence.

Alberto Giacometti, 1901-66, (Swiss) attenuated sculptures of solitary figures. *Man Pointing.*

Giorgione, c1477-1510, (It.) Renaissance. *The Tempest.*

Giotto di Bondone, 1267-1337, (It.) Renaissance. *Presentation of Christ in the Temple.*

François Girardon, 1628-1715, (Fr.) Baroque sculptor of classical themes. *Apollo Tended by the Nymphs.*

Vincent van Gogh, 1853-90, (Dutch) *The Starry Night, L'Arlesienne, Bedroom at Arles, Self-Portrait.*

Arshile Gorky, 1905-48, (U.S.) Surrealist. *The Liver Is the Cock's Comb.*

Francisco de Goya y Lucientes, 1746-1828, (Sp.) *The Naked Maja, The Disasters of War* (etchings).

El Greco, 1541-1614, (Sp.) *View of Toledo, Assumption of the Virgin.*

Horatio Greenough, 1805-52, (U.S.) Neo-classical sculptor.

Matthias Grünewald, 1480-1528, (Ger.) mystical religious themes. *The Resurrection.*

Frans Hals, c1580-1666, (Dutch) portraitist. *Laughing Cavalier, Gypsy Girl.*

Austin Hansen, 1910-96, (U.S.) photographer. Harlem, NY, life.

Childe Hassam, 1859-1935, (U.S.) Impressionist. *Southwest Wind, July 14 Rue Daunon.*

Edward Hicks, 1780-1849, (U.S.) folk painter. *The Peaceable Kingdom.*

Lewis Wickes Hine, 1874-1940, (U.S.) photographer. Studies of immigrants, children in industry.

Hans Hofmann, 1880-1966, (U.S.) early abstract Expressionist. *Spring, The Gate.*

William Hogarth, 1697-1764, (Br.) caricaturist. *The Rake's Progress.*

Katsushika Hokusai, 1760-1849, (Jpn.) printmaker. *Crabs.*

Hans Holbein the Elder, 1460-1524, (Ger.) late Gothic. *Presentation of Christ in the Temple.*

Hans Holbein the Younger, 1497-1543, (Ger.) portraitist. *Henry VIII, The French Ambassadors.*

Winslow Homer, 1836-1910, (U.S.) naturalist painter, marine themes. *Marine Coast, High Cliff.*

Edward Hopper, 1882-1967, (U.S.) realistic urban scenes. *Sunlight in a Cafeteria.*

Jean-Auguste-Dominique Ingres, 1780-1867, (Fr.) Classicist. *Valpincon Bather.*

George Inness, 1825-94, (U.S.) luminous landscapist. *Delaware Water Gap.*

William Henry Jackson, 1843-1942, (U.S.) photographer. American West, building of Union Pacific Railroad.

Donald Judd, 1928-94, (U.S.) sculptor, major Minimalist.

Frida Kahlo, 1907-54, (Mex.) painter; *Self-Portrait With Monkey.*

Vasily Kandinsky, 1866-1944, (Russ.) Abstractionist. *Capricious Forms, Improvisation 38 (second version).*

Paul Klee, 1879-1940, (Swiss) Abstractionist. *Twittering Machine, Pastoral, Death and Fire.*

Gustav Klimt, 1862-1918, (Austrian) cofounder of Vienna Secession Movement, *The Kiss*

Oscar Kokoschka, 1886-1980, (Austrian) Expressionist. *View of Prague, Harbor of Marseilles.*

Kathe Kollwitz, 1867-1945, (Ger.) printmaker, social justice themes. *The Peasant War.*

Gaston Lachaise, 1882-1935, (U.S.) figurative sculptor. *Standing Woman.*

John La Farge, 1835-1910, (U.S.) muralist. *Red and White Peonies, The Ascension.*

Dorothea Lange, 1895-1965, (U.S.), photographer. Depression photographs, migrant farm workers.

Fernand Léger, 1881-1955, (Fr.) machine art. *The Cyclists.*

Leonardo da Vinci, 1452-1519, (It.) *Mona Lisa, Last Supper, The Annunciation.*

Emanuel Leutze, 1816-68, (U.S.) historical themes. *Washington Crossing the Delaware.*

Roy Lichtenstein, 1923-97, (U.S.) pop artist.

Jacques Lipchitz, 1891-1973, (Fr.) Cubist sculptor. *Harpist.*

Filippino Lippi, 1457-1504, (It.) Renaissance.

Fra Filippo Lippi, 1406-69, (It.) Renaissance. *Coronation of the Virgin, Madonna and Child With Angels.*

Morris Louis, 1912-62, (U.S.) abstract Expressionist. *Signa, Stripes, Alpha-Phi.*

Aristide Maillol, 1861-1944, (Fr.) sculptor. *L'Harmonie.*

Édouard Manet, 1832-83, (Fr.) forerunner of Impressionism. *Luncheon on the Grass, Olympia.*

Andrea Mantegna, 1431-1506, (It.) Renaissance frescoes. *Triumph of Caesar.*

Franz Marc, 1880-1916, (Ger.) Expressionist. *Blue Horses.*

John Marin, 1870-1953, (U.S.) Expressionist seascapes. *Maine Island.*

Reginald Marsh, 1898-1954, (U.S.) satirical artist. *Tattoo and Haircut.*

Masaccio, 1401-28, (It.) Renaissance. *The Tribute Money.*

Henri Matisse, 1869-1954, (Fr.) Fauvist. *Woman With the Hat.*

Michelangelo Buonarroti, 1475-1564, (It.) *Pietà, David, Moses, The Last Judgment,* Sistine Chapel ceiling.

Jean-Francois Millet, 1814-75, (Fr.) painter of peasant subjects. *The Gleaners, The Man With a Hoe.*

Joan Miró, 1893-1983, (Sp.) Exuberant colors, playful images. Catalan landscape, *Dutch Interior.*

Amedeo Modigliani, 1884-1920, (It.) *Reclining Nude.*

Piet Mondrian, 1872-1944, (Dutch) Abstractionist. *Composition With Red, Yellow and Blue.*

Claude Monet, 1840-1926, (Fr.) Impressionist. *The Bridge at Argenteuil, Haystacks.*

Henry Moore, 1898-1986, (Br.) sculptor of large-scale, abstract works. *Reclining Figure* (several).

Gustave Moreau, 1826-98, (Fr.) Symbolist. *The Apparition, Dance of Salome.*

James Wilson Morrice, 1865-1924, (Can.) landscapist. *The Ferry, Quebec, Venice, Looking Over the Lagoon.*

William Morris, 1834-1896 (Br.) decorative artist, leader of the Arts and Crafts movement.

Grandma Moses, 1860-1961, (U.S.) folk painter. *Out for the Christmas Trees, Thanksgiving Turkey.*

Edvard Munch, 1863-1944, (Nor.) Expressionist. *The Cry.*

Bartolome Murillo, 1618-82, (Sp.) Baroque religious artist. *Vision of St. Anthony, The Two Trinities.*

Eadweard Muybridge, 1830-1904, (Br.-U.S.) photographer. Studies of motion, *Animal Locomotion.*

Nadar (Gaspar-Félix Tournachon) 1820-1910, (Fr.) photographer, caricaturist, portraitist. Invented photo-essay.

Barnett Newman, 1905-70, (U.S.) abstract Expressionist. *Stations of the Cross.*

Isamu Noguchi, 1904-88, (U.S.) abstract sculptor, designer. *Kouros, BirdC(MU),* sculptural gardens.

Georgia O'Keeffe, 1887-1986, (U.S.) Southwest motifs. *Cow's Skull: Red, White, and Blue, The Shelton With Sunspots.*

José Clemente Orozco, 1883-1949, (Mex.) frescoes. *House of Tears, Pre-Columbian Golden Age.*

Timothy H. O'Sullivan, 1840-82, (U.S.) Civil War photographer.

Charles Willson Peale, 1741-1827, (U.S.) Amer. Revolutionary portraitist. *The Staircase Group,* U.S. presidents.

Rembrandt Peale, 1778-1860, (U.S.) portraitist. Thomas Jefferson.

Pietro Perugino, 1446-1523, (It.) Renaissance. *Delivery of the Keys to St. Peter.*

Pablo Picasso, 1881-1973, (Sp.) painter, sculptor. *Guernica; Dove; Head of a Woman; Head of a Bull, Metamorphosis.*

Piero della Francesca, c1415-92, (It.) Renaissance. *Duke of Urbino, Flagellation of Christ.*

Camille Pissarro, 1830-1903, (Fr.) Impressionist. *Boulevard des Italiens, Morning, Sunlight; Bather in the Woods.*

Jackson Pollock, 1912-56, (U.S.) abstract Expressionist. *Autumn Rhythm.*

Nicolas Poussin, 1594-1665, (Fr.) Baroque pictorial classicism. *St. John on Patmos.*

Maurice B. Prendergast, c 1860-1924, (U.S.) Post-impressionist water colorist. *Umbrellas in the Rain.*

Pierre-Paul Prud'hon, 1758-1823, (Fr.) Romanticist. *Crime Pursued by Vengeance and Justice.*

Pierre Cecile Puvis de Chavannes, 1824-98, (Fr.) muralist. *The Poor Fisherman.*

Raphael Sanzio, 1483-1520, (It.) Renaissance. *Disputa, School of Athens, Sistine Madonna.*

Man Ray, 1890-1976, (U.S.) Dada artist. *Observing Time, The Lovers, Marquis de Sade.*

Odilon Redon, 1840-1916, (Fr.) Symbolist painter, lithographer. *In the Dream, Vase of Flowers.*

Rembrandt van Rijn, 1606-69, (Dutch) *The Bridal Couple, The Night Watch.*

Frederic Remington, 1861-1909, (U.S.) painter, sculptor. Portrayer of the American West, *Bronco Buster.*

Pierre-Auguste Renoir, 1841-1919, (Fr.) Impressionist. *The Luncheon of the Boating Party, Dance in the Country.*

Joshua Reynolds, 1723-92, (Br.) portraitist. *Mrs. Siddons As the Tragic Muse.*

Diego Rivera, 1886-1957, (Mex.) frescoes. *The Fecund Earth.*

Henry Peach Robinson, 1830-1901 (Br.) photographer. A leader of "high art" photography.

Norman Rockwell, 1894-1978, (U.S.) painter, illustrator. *Saturday Evening Post* covers.

Auguste Rodin, 1840-1917, (Fr.) sculptor. *The Thinker.*

Mark Rothko, 1903-70, (U.S.) abstract Expressionist. *Light, Earth and Blue.*

Georges Rouault, 1871-1958, (Fr.) Expressionist. *Three Judges.*

Henri Rousseau, 1844-1910, (Fr.) primitive exotic themes. *The Snake Charmer.*

Theodore Rousseau, 1812-67, (Swiss-Fr.) landscapist. *Under the Birches, Evening.*

Peter Paul Rubens, 1577-1640, (Flem.) Baroque. *Mystic Marriage of St. Catherine.*

Jacob van Ruisdael, c1628-82, (Dutch) landscapist. *Jewish Cemetery.*

Charles M. Russell, 1866-1926, (U.S.) Western life.

Salomon van Ruysdael, c1600-70, (Dutch) landscapist. *River with Ferry-Boat.*

Albert Pinkham Ryder, 1847-1917, (U.S.) seascapes and allegories. *Toilers of the Sea.*

Augustus Saint-Gaudens, 1848-1907, (U.S.) memorial statues. *Farragut, Mrs. Henry Adams (Grief).*

Andrea Sansovino, 1460-1529, (It.) Renaissance sculptor. *Baptism of Christ.*

Jacopo Sansovino, 1486-1570, (It.) Renaissance sculptor. *St. John the Baptist.*

John Singer Sargent, 1856-1925, (U.S.) Edwardian society portraitist. *The Wyndham Sisters, Madam X.*

Georges Seurat, 1859-91, (Fr.) Pointillist. *Sunday Afternoon on the Island of Grande Jatte.*

Gino Severini, 1883-1966, (It.) Futurist and Cubist. *Dynamic Hieroglyph of the Bal Tabarin.*

Ben Shahn, 1898-1969, (U.S.) social and political themes. Sacco and Vanzetti series, *Seurat's Lunch, Handball.*

Charles Sheeler, 1883-1965, (U.S.) abstractionist.

David Alfaro Siqueiros, 1896-1974, (Mex.) political muralist. *March of Humanity.*

John F. Sloan, 1871-1951, (U.S.) depictions of New York City.

David Smith, 1906-65, (U.S.) welded metal sculpture. *Hudson River Landscape, Zig, Cubi* series.

Edward Steichen, 1879-1973, (U.S.) photographer. Credited with transforming photography into an art form.

Alfred Stieglitz, 1864-1946, (U.S.) photographer, editor; helped create acceptance of photography as art.

Paul Strand, 1890-1976, (U.S.) photographer. People, nature, landscapes.

Gilbert Stuart, 1755-1828, (U.S.) portraitist. George Washington, Thomas Jefferson, James Madison.

Thomas Sully, 1783-1872, (U.S.) portraitist. *Col. Thomas Handasyd Perkins, The Passage of the Delaware.*

William Henry Fox Talbot, 1800-77, (Br.) photographer. *Pencil of Nature,* early photographically illustrated book.

George Tames, 1919-94, (U.S.) photographer. Chronicled presidents, political leaders.

Yves Tanguy, 1900-55, (Fr.) Surrealist. *Rose of the Four Winds, Mama, Papa Is Wounded!*

Giovanni Battista Tiepolo, 1696-1770, (It.) Rococo frescoes. *The Crucifixion.*

Jacopo Tintoretto, 1518-94, (It.) Mannerist. *The Last Supper.*

Titian, c1485-1576, (It.) Renaissance. *Venus and the Lute Player, The Bacchanal.*

Jose Rey Toledo, 1916-94, (U.S.) Native American artist. Captured the essence of tribal dances on canvas.

Henri de Toulouse-Lautrec, 1864-1901, (Fr.) *At the Moulin Rouge.*

John Trumbull, 1756-1843, (U.S.) historical themes. *The Declaration of Independence.*

J(oseph) M(allord) W(illiam) Turner, 1775-1851, (Br.) Romantic landscapist. *Snow Storm.*

Paolo Uccello, 1397-1475, (It.) Gothic-Renaissance. *The Rout of San Romano.*

Maurice Utrillo, 1883-1955, (Fr.) Impressionist. *Sacre-Coeur de Montmartre.*

John Vanderlyn, 1775-1852, (U.S.) Neo-classicist. *Ariadne Asleep on the Island of Naxos.*

Diego Velázquez, 1599-1660, (Sp.) Baroque. *Las Meninas, Portrait of Juan de Pareja.*

Jan Vermeer, 1632-75, (Dutch) interior genre subjects. *Young Woman With a Water Jug.*

Paolo Veronese, 1528-88, (It.) devotional themes, vastly peopled canvases. *The Temptation of St. Anthony.*

Andrea del Verrocchio, 1435-88, (It.) Florentine sculptor. *Colleoni.*

Maurice de Vlaminck, 1876-1958, (Fr.) Fauvist landscapist.

Andy Warhol, 1928-87, (U.S.) Pop Art. *Campbell's Soup Cans, Marilyn Diptych.*

Antoine Watteau, 1684-1721, (Fr.) Rococo painter of "scenes of gallantry." *The Embarkation for Cythera.*

George Frederic Watts, 1817-1904, (Br.) painter and sculptor of grandiose allegorical themes. *Hope.*

Benjamin West, 1738-1820, (U.S.) realistic historical themes. *Death of General Wolfe.*

Edward Weston, 1886-1958, (U.S.) photographer. Landscapes of American West.

James Abbott McNeill Whistler, 1834-1903, (U.S.) *Arrangement in Grey and Black, No. 1: The Artist's Mother.*

Archibald M. Willard, 1836-1918, (U.S.) *The Spirit of '76.*

Grant Wood, 1891-1942, (U.S.) Midwestern regionalist. *American Gothic, Daughters of Revolution.*

Ossip Zadkine, 1890-1967, (Russ.) School of Paris sculptor. *The Destroyed City, Musicians, Christ.*

Noted Black Americans of the Past

Ralph David Abernathy, 1926-90, organizer, 1957, pres., 1968, Southern Christian Leadership Conference.

Crispus Attucks, c1723-70, leader of group of colonists that clashed with British soldiers in 1770 Boston Massacre.

James Baldwin, 1924-87, author, playwright; *Go Tell It on the Mountain, Tell Me How Long the Train's Been Gone.*

Benjamin Banneker, 1731-1806, inventor, astronomer, mathematician, gazetteer.

James P. Beckwourth, 1798-c 1867, western fur trader, scout; Beckwourth Pass in N California named for him.

Mary McCleod Bethune, 1875-1955, adviser to FDR and Truman; founder, pres., Bethune-Cookman College.

Henry Blair, 19th cent., pioneer inventor; obtained patents for a corn-planter, 1834, and cotton-planter, 1836.

Edward Bouchet, 1852-1918, first black to earn a PhD at a U.S. university (Yale, 1876); first elected to Phi Beta Kappa.

Sterling A. Brown, 1901-89, poet, literature professor; helped establish African-American literary criticism.

William Wells Brown, 1815-84, novelist, dramatist; first American black to publish a novel.

Ralph Bunche, 1904-71, first black to win the Nobel Peace Prize, 1950; undersecretary of the UN, 1950.

George Washington Carver, 1864-1943, botanist, chemist, and educator; revolutionized the economy of the South.

Charles Waddell Chesnutt, 1858-1932, author known primarily for his short stories, including *The Conjure Woman.*

James Cleveland, 1931-91, composer, musician, singer; first black gospel artist to appear in Carnegie Hall.

Countee Cullen, 1903-46, poet, played a prominent role in the Harlem Renaissance of the 1920s; *The Black Christ.*

Benjamin O. Davis Sr., 1877-1970, first black general, 1940, in U.S. Army.

William L. Dawson, 1886-1970, Illinois congressman, first black chairman of a major U.S. House committee.

Aaron Douglas, 1900-79, painter; called father of black American art.

Frederick Douglass, 1817-95, author, editor, orator, diplomat; edited the abolitionist weekly, *The North Star.*

St. Clair Drake, 1911-90, black studies pioneer, *Black Metropolis* (1945, with Horace R. Cayton); author.

Charles Richard Drew, 1904-50, physician, pioneered in development of blood banks; director of American Red Cross blood donor project in WW2.

William Edward Burghardt (W.E.B.) Du Bois, 1868-1963, historian, sociologist; a founder of the NAACP, 1909, and of its magazine *The Crisis.*

Paul Laurence Dunbar, 1872-1906, poet, novelist; won fame with *Lyrics of Lowly Life,* 1896.

Jean Baptiste Point du Sable, c1750-1818, pioneer trader and first settler of Chicago, 1779.

Henry O. Flipper, 1856-1940, first black to graduate, 1877, from West Point.

Marcus Garvey, 1887-1940, founded Universal Negro Improvement Assn., 1911.

Ewart Guinier, 1911-90, trade unionist; first chairman of Harvard Univ.'s Dept. of African American Studies.

Jupiter Hammon, c1720-1800, poet; first black American to have his works published, 1761.

Lorraine Hansberry, 1930-65, playwright; won New York Drama Critics Circle Award, 1959; *A Raisin in the Sun.*

William H. Hastie, 1904-76, first black federal judge, appointed 1937; governor of Virgin Islands, 1946-49.

Matthew A. Henson, 1866-1955, member of Peary's 1909 expedition to the North Pole; placed U.S. flag at the pole.

Chester Himes, 1909-84, novelist. *Cotton Comes to Harlem.*

William A. Hinton, 1883-1959, physician, developed tests for syphilis; first black prof., 1949, at Harvard Med. School.

Charles Hamilton Houston, 1895-1950, lawyer, Howard University instructor, and champion of minority rights.

Langston Hughes, 1902-67, poet, lyric writer, author; a major influence in the Harlem Renaissance of the 1920s.

Daniel James Jr., 1920-78, first black 4-star general, 1975; commander, North American Air Defense Command.

Henry Johnson, 1897-1929, first American decorated by France in WW1 with the Croix de Guerre.

James Weldon Johnson, 1871-1938, poet, novelist, diplomat; lyricist for *Lift Every Voice and Sing.*

Barbara Jordan, 1936-96, congresswoman, orator, educator; first black woman to win a seat in the Texas senate (1966.

Ernest Everett Just, 1883-1941, marine biologist; studied egg development; author, *Biology of Cell Surfaces,* 1941.

Martin Luther King Jr., 1929-68, minister, civil rights leader; led Montgomery, AL, boycott that brought 1956 Supreme Court decision barring segregation on buses; founder, pres.,

Southern Christian Leadership Conference, 1957; Nobel laureate (1964); assassinated.

Lewis H. Latimer, 1848-1928, associate of Edison; supervised installation of first electric street lighting in NYC.

Mickey Leland, 1944-89, U.S. representative from Texas, 1978 until death; chairman of Congressional Black Caucus.

Henry Lewis, 1932-1996, (U.S.) conductor; first black conductor and musical director of major American orchestra.

Malcolm X (Little), 1925-65, Black Muslim, black nationalist leader; promoted black pride; assassinated.

Thurgood Marshall, 1908-93, first black U.S. solicitor general, 1965; first black justice of U.S. Supreme Court, 1967-91; led to desegregation victory in Supreme Court decision *Brown* v. *Board of Education of Topeka,* 1954.

Jan Matzeliger, 1852-89, invented lasting machine, patented 1883, which revolutionized the shoe industry.

Benjamin Mays, 1895-1984, educator, civil rights leader; headed Morehouse College, 1940-67.

Ronald McNair, 1950-86, physicist, astronaut; killed in *Challenger* explosion.

Dorie Miller, 1919-43, Navy hero of Pearl Harbor attack.

Willard Motley, 1912-65, novelist; *Knock on Any Door.*

Elijah Muhammad, 1897-1975, founded Black Muslims, 1931.

Pedro Alonzo Niño, navigator of Columbus's Niña, 1492.

Frederick D. Patterson, 1901-88, founder of United Negro College Fund, 1944.

Harold R. Perry, 1916-91, first black American Roman Catholic bishop in the 20th cent., 1966; first black clergyman to deliver opening prayer in U.S. Congress, 1964.

Adam Clayton Powell Jr., 1908-72, early civil rights leader, congressman, 1945-69.

Joseph H. Rainey, 1832-87, first black elected to U.S. House of Representatives, 1869, from South Carolina.

A. Philip Randolph, 1889-1979, organized Brotherhood of Sleeping Car Porters, 1925; an organizer of 1941 and 1963 March on Washington movements.

Hiram R. Revels, 1822-1901, first black U.S. senator, elected in Mississippi, served 1870-71.

Norbert Rillieux, 1806-94; invented a vacuum pan evaporator, 1846, revolutionizing sugar-refining industry.

Paul Robeson, 1898-1976, actor, singer, civil rights activist; graduated first in class at Rutgers, 1918, Phi Beta Kappa.

Jackie Robinson, 1919-72, first black baseball player to play in the major leagues, 1947, and be inducted into the Baseball Hall of Fame, 1962.

Max Robinson, 1939-88, TV journalist, first black to anchor network news, 1978.

John B. Russwurm, 1799-1851, with **Samuel E. Cornish,** 1793-1858, founded, 1827, nation's first black newspaper, *Freedom's Journal,* in NYC.

Bayard Rustin, 1910-87, an organizer of the 1963 March on Washington; exec. director, A. Philip Randolph Institute.

Peter Salem, at the Battle of Bunker Hill, June 17, 1775, shot and killed British commander Maj. John Pitcairn.

Stephen Spottswood, 1897-1974, NAACP chairman, 1961-74.

Carl Stokes, 1927-1996, first black mayor of a major American city (Cleveland); (1967-72).

Willard Townsend, 1895-1957, organized the United Transport Service Employees (redcaps), 1935.

Sojourner Truth, 1797-1883, born Isabella Baumfree; preacher, abolitionist; worked for black educational opportunities.

Harriet Tubman, 1823-1913, Underground Railroad conductor, nurse and spy for Union Army in the Civil War.

Nat Turner, 1800-31, led most significant of more than 200 slave revolts in U.S., in Southampton, VA; hanged.

Booker T. Washington, 1856-1915, founder, 1881, and first pres. of Tuskegee Institute; author, *Up From Slavery.*

Harold Washington, 1922-87, first black mayor of Chicago.

Robert C. Weaver, 1907-97, first black person appointed to cabinet; secretary of HUD.

Ida B. Wells (Barnett), 1862-1931, journalist who waged anti-lynching crusade.

Phillis Wheatley, c1753-84, poet; 2d American woman and first black woman to be published, 1770.

Walter White, 1893-1955, exec. secretary, NAACP, 1931-55.

Roy Wilkins, 1901-81, exec. director, NAACP, 1955-77.

Daniel Hale Williams, 1858-1931, performed one of first two open-heart operations, 1893; first black elected a fellow of the American College of Surgeons.

Granville T. Woods, 1856-1910, invented third-rail system now used in subways, and automatic air brake.

Carter G. Woodson, 1875-1950, historian; founded Assn. for the Study of Negro Life and History.

Frank Yerby, 1916-91, First best-selling American black novelist; *The Foxes of Harrow.*

Noted Business Leaders, Industrialists, and Philanthropists of the Past

Elizabeth Arden (F. N. Graham), 1884-1966, (U.S.) Canadian-born founder of cosmetics empire.

Philip D. Armour, 1832-1901, (U.S.) industrialist; streamlined meatpacking.

John Jacob Astor, 1763-1848, (U.S.) German-born fur trader, banker, real estate magnate; at death, richest in U.S.

Francis W. Ayer, 1848-1923, (U.S.) ad industry pioneer.

August Belmont, 1816-90, (U.S.) German-born financier.

James B. (Diamond Jim) Brady, 1856-1917, (U.S.) financier, philanthropist, legendary bon vivant.

Adolphus Busch, 1839-1913, (U.S.) German-born businessman; established brewery empire.

Asa Candler, 1851-1929, (U.S.) founded Coca-Cola Co.

Andrew Carnegie, 1835-1919, (U.S.) Scottish-born industrialist; philanthropist; founded Carnegie Steel Co., a keystone of U.S. Steel Corp. (1901).

Tom Carvel, 1908-89, (Gr.-U.S.) founded ice cream chain.

William Colgate, 1783-1857, (Br.-U.S.) Br.-born businessman, philanthropist; founded soap-making empire.

Jay Cooke, 1821-1905, (U.S.) financier; sold $1 billion in Union bonds during Civil War.

Peter Cooper, 1791-1883, (U.S.) industrialist, inventor, philanthropist; founder Cooper Union (1859).

Ezra Cornell, 1807-74, (U.S.) businessman, philanthropist; headed Western Union, established university.

Erastus Corning, 1794-1872, (U.S.) financier; headed N.Y. Central.

Charles Crocker, 1822-88, (U.S.) railroad builder, financier.

Samuel Cunard, 1787-1865, (Can.) pioneered trans-Atlantic steam navigation.

Marcus Daly, 1841-1900, (U.S.) Irish-born copper magnate.

George T. Delacorte, 1893-1991, (U.S.) publisher; Central Park donations included Alice in Wonderland statue.

W. Edwards Deming, 1900-93, (U.S.) quality-control expert who revolutionized Japanese manufacturing.

Walt Disney, 1901-66, (U.S.) pioneer in cinema animation; built entertainment empire.

Herbert H. Dow, 1866-1930, (U.S.) founder of chemical co.

James Duke, 1856-1925, (U.S.) founded American Tobacco, Duke Univ.

Eleuthere I. du Pont, 1771-1834, (Fr.-U.S.) gunpowder manufacturer; founded one of the largest business empires.

Thomas C. Durant, 1820-85, (U.S.) railroad official, financier.

William C. Durant, 1861-1947, (U.S.) industrialist; formed General Motors.

George Eastman, 1854-1932, (U.S.) inventor; manufacturer of photographic equipment.

Marshall Field, 1834-1906, (U.S.) merchant; founded Chicago's largest department store.

Harvey Firestone, 1868-1938, (U.S.) founded tire company.

Avery Fisher, 1906-94, (U.S.) industrialist, philanthropist, founded Fisher electronics.

Henry M. Flagler, 1830-1913, (U.S.) financier; helped form Standard Oil; developed Florida as resort state.

Malcolm Forbes, 1919-90, (U.S.) magazine publisher.

Henry Ford, 1863-1947, (U.S.) auto maker; developed first popular low-priced car.

Henry Ford 2d, 1917-87, (U.S.) headed auto company founded by grandfather.

Henry C. Frick, 1849-1919, (U.S.) steel and coke magnate who had a prominent role in the development of U.S. Steel.

Jakob Fugger (Jakob the Rich), 1459-1525, (Ger.) headed leading banking, trading house, in 16th-cent. Europe.

Alfred C. Fuller, 1885-1973, (U.S.) Canadian-born businessman; founded brush company.

Elbert H. Gary, 1846-1927, (U.S.) one of the organizers of U.S. Steel; chairman of the board of directors, 1903-27.

Jean Paul Getty, 1892-1976, (U.S.) founded oil empire.

Amadeo P. Giannini, 1870-1949, (U.S.) founded Bank of America.

Stephen Girard, 1750-1831, (U.S.) French-born financier, philanthropist; richest man in U.S. at his death.

Jay Gould, 1836-92, (U.S.) railroad magnate, financier, speculator.

Hetty Green, 1834-1916, (U.S.) financier, the "witch of Wall St."; richest woman in U.S. in her day.

William Gregg, 1800-67, (U.S.) launched textile industry in the South.

Meyer Guggenheim, 1828-1905, (U.S.) Swiss-born merchant, philanthropist; built merchandising, mining empires.

Armand Hammer, 1898-1990, (U.S.) headed Occidental Petroleum; promoted U.S.-Soviet ties.

Edward H. Harriman, 1848-1909, (U.S.) railroad financier, administrator; headed Union Pacific.

William Randolph Hearst, 1863-1951, (U.S.) a dominant figure in American journalism; built vast publishing empire.

Henry J. Heinz, 1844-1919, (U.S.) founded food empire.

James J. Hill, 1838-1916, (U.S.) Canadian-born railroad magnate, financier; founded Great Northern Railway.

Conrad N. Hilton, 1888-1979, (U.S.) hotel chain founder.

Howard Hughes, 1905-76, (U.S.) industrialist, aviator, movie maker.

H. L. Hunt, 1889-1974, (U.S.) oil magnate.

Collis P. Huntington, 1821-1900, (U.S.) railroad magnate.

Henry E. Huntington, 1850-1927, (U.S.) railroad builder, philanthropist.

Walter L. Jacobs, 1898-1985, (U.S.) founder of the first rental car agency, which later became Hertz.

Howard Johnson, 1896-1972, (U.S.) founded restaurants.

Henry J. Kaiser, 1882-1967, (U.S.) industrialist; built empire in steel, aluminum.

Minor C. Keith, 1848-1929, (U.S.) railroad magnate; founded United Fruit Co.

Will K. Kellogg, 1860-1951, (U.S.) businessman, philanthropist; founded breakfast food co.

Richard King, 1825-85, (U.S.) cattleman; founded half-million-acre King Ranch in Texas.

William S. Knudsen, 1879-1948, (U.S.) Danish-born auto industry executive.

Samuel H. Kress, 1863-1955, (U.S.) businessman, art collector, philanthropist; founded "dime store" chain.

Ray A. Kroc, 1902-84, (U.S.) founded McDonald's fast food.

Alfred Krupp, 1812-87, (Ger.) armaments magnate.

William Levitt, 1907-94, (U.S.) industrialist, "suburb maker".

Thomas Lipton, 1850-1931, (Scot.) merchant, tea empire.

James McGill, 1744-1813, (Scot.-Can.) founded university.

Andrew W. Mellon, 1855-1937, (U.S.) financier, industrialist; benefactor of National Gallery of Art.

Charles E. Merrill, 1885-1956, (U.S.) financier; developed firm of Merrill Lynch.

John Pierpont Morgan, 1837-1913, (U.S.) most powerful figure in finance and industry at the turn of the cent..

Malcolm Muir, 1885-1979, (U.S.) created *Business Week* magazine; headed *Newsweek,* 1937-61.

Samuel Newhouse, 1895-1979, (U.S.) publishing and broadcasting magnate; built communications empire.

Aristotle Onassis, 1906-75, (Gr.) shipping magnate.

William S. Paley, 1901-90, (U.S.) built CBS communications empire.

George Peabody, 1795-1869, (U.S.) merchant, financier, philanthropist.

James C. Penney, 1875-1971, (U.S.) businessman; developed department store chain.

William C. Procter, 1862-1934, (U.S.) headed soap company.

John D. Rockefeller, 1839-1937, (U.S.) industrialist; established Standard Oil.

John D. Rockefeller Jr., 1874-1960, (U.S.) philanthropist; established foundation; provided land for United Nations.

Meyer A. Rothschild, 1743-1812, (Ger.) founded international banking house.

Thomas Fortune Ryan, 1851-1928, (U.S.) financier; a founder of American Tobacco.

Russell Sage, 1816-1906, (U.S.) financier.

David Sarnoff, 1891-1971, (U.S.) broadcasting pioneer; established first radio network, NBC.

Richard Sears, 1863-1914, (U.S.) founded mail-order co.

Werner von Siemens, 1816-92, (Ger.) industrialist; inventor.

Alfred P. Sloan, 1875-1966, (U.S.) industrialist, philanthropist; headed General Motors.

A. Leland Stanford, 1824-93, (U.S.) railroad official, philanthropist; founded university.

Nathan Straus, 1848-1931, (U.S.) German-born merchant, philanthropist; headed Macy's.

Levi Strauss, c1829-1902, (U.S.) pants manufacturer.

Clement Studebaker, 1831-1901, (U.S.) wagon, carriage manufacturer.

Gustavus Swift, 1839-1903, (U.S.) pioneer meatpacker.

Gerard Swope, 1872-1957, (U.S.) industrialist, economist; headed General Electric.

James Walter Thompson, 1847-1928, (U.S.) ad executive.

Alice Tully, 1902-93, (U.S.) philanthropist, arts patron.

Theodore N. Vail, 1845-1920, (U.S.) organized Bell Telephone system; headed AT&T.

Cornelius Vanderbilt, 1794-1877, (U.S.) financier; established steamship, railroad empires.

Henry Villard, 1835-1900, (U.S.) German-born railroad executive, financier.

George Westinghouse, 1846-1914, (U.S) inventor, manufacturer; organized Westinghouse Electric Co., 1886.

Charles R. Walgreen, 1873-1939, (U.S.) founded drugstore chain.

DeWitt Wallace, 1889-1981, (U.S.) and **Lila Wallace,** 1889-1984, (U.S.) cofounders of *Reader's Digest* magazine.

Sam Walton, 1918-92, (U.S.) founder of Wal-Mart stores.

John Wanamaker, 1838-1922, (U.S.) pioneered department-store merchandising.

Aaron Montgomery Ward, 1843-1913, (U.S.) established first mail-order firm.

Thomas J. Watson, 1874-1956, (U.S.) IBM head, 1914-56.

John Hay Whitney, 1905-82, (U.S.) publisher, sportsman, philanthropist.

Charles E. Wilson, 1890-1961, (U.S.) auto industry executive; public official.

Frank W. Woolworth, 1852-1919, (U.S.) created 5 & 10 chain.

William Wrigley Jr., 1861-1932, (U.S.) founded chewing gum co.

Noted American Cartoonists

Scott Adams, b 1957, Dilbert.
Charles Addams, 1912-88, macabre cartoons.
Brad Anderson, b 1924, Marmaduke.
Peter Arno, 1904-68, *New Yorker* urban characterizations.
Tex Avery, 1908-80, animator of Bugs Bunny, Porky Pig.
Arthur Babbitt, 1907-92, Disney cartoonist.
George Baker, 1915-75, The Sad Sack.
C. C. Beck, 1910-89, Captain Marvel.
Jim Berry, b 1932, Berry's World.
Herb Block (Herblock), b 1909, political cartoonist.
George Booth, b 1926, *New Yorker* cartoonist.
Berkeley Breathed, b 1957, Bloom County.
Clare Briggs, 1875-1930, Mr. & Mrs.
Dik Browne, 1917-89, Hi & Lois, Hagar the Horrible.
Marjorie Buell, 1904-93, Little Lulu.
Ernie Bushmiller, 1905-82, Nancy.
Milton Caniff, 1907-88, Terry & the Pirates, Steve Canyon.
Al Capp, 1909-79, Li'l Abner.
Roz Chast, b 1954, *New Yorker* "bonfire of the banalities."
Paul Conrad, 1924, political cartoonist.
Roy Crane, 1901-77, Captain Easy, Buz Sawyer.
Robert Crumb, b 1943, "Underground" cartoonist.
Shamus Culhane, 1908-96, animator.
Jay N. Darling (Ding), 1876-1962, political cartoonist.
Jack Davis, b 1926, *Mad* magazine.
Jim Davis, b 1945, Garfield.
Billy DeBeck, 1890-1942, Barney Google.
Rudolph Dirks, 1877-1968, The Katzenjammer Kids.
Walt Disney, 1901-66, producer of animated cartoons, created Mickey Mouse and Donald Duck.
Steve Ditko, b 1927, Spider-Man.
Mort Drucker, b 1929, *Mad* magazine.
Will Eisner, b 1917, The Spirit.
Jules Feiffer, b 1929, satirical *Village Voice* cartoonist.
Bud Fisher, 1884-1954, Mutt & Jeff.
Ham Fisher, 1900-55, Joe Palooka.
James Montgomery Flagg, 1877-1960, illustrator, created the famous Uncle Sam recruiting poster during WWI.
Max Fleischer, 1883-1972, Betty Boop.
Hal Foster, 1892-1982, Tarzan, Prince Valiant.
Fontaine Fox, 1884-1964, Toonerville Folks.
Isadore "Friz" Freleng, 1905-95, animator, Yosemite Sam, Porky Pig, Sylvestor and Tweety.
Al Frueh, 1880-1968, *New Yorker* cartoonist.
Rube Goldberg, 1883-1970, Boob McNutt.
Chester Gould, 1900-85, Dick Tracy.
Harold Gray, 1894-1968, Little Orphan Annie.
Matt Groening, b 1954, Life In Hell, The Simpsons.
Cathy Guisewite, b 1950, Cathy.
Bill Hanna, b 1910, & **Joe Barbera,** b 1911, animators of Tom & Jerry, Huckleberry Hound, Yogi Bear, Flintstones.
Johnny Hart, b 1931, BC, Wizard of Id.
Alfred Harvey, 1913-94, created Casper the Friendly Ghost
Jimmy Hatlo, 1898-1963, Little Iodine.
John Held Jr., 1889-1958, "Jazz Age" cartoonist.
George Herriman, 1881-1944, Krazy Kat.
Harry Hershfield, 1885-1974, Abie the Agent.
Al Hirschfeld, b 1903, *N.Y. Times* theater caricaturist.
Burne Hogarth, 1911-96, Tarzan.
Helen Hokinson, 1900-49, satirized clubwomen.
Nicole Hollander, b 1939, Sylvia.
Lynn Johnston, b 1947, For Better or For Worse.
Chuck Jones, b 1912, animator, Bugs Bunny, Porky Pig.

Mike Judge, b. 1962, Beavis and Butt-head, King of the Hill.
Bob Kane, b 1916, Batman.
Bil Keane, b 1922, The Family Circus.
Walt Kelly, 1913-73, Pogo.
Hank Ketcham, b 1920, Dennis the Menace.
Ted Key, b 1912, Hazel.
Frank King, 1883-1969, Gasoline Alley.
Jack Kirby, 1917-94, Fantastic Four, The Incredible Hulk.
Rollin Kirby, 1875-1952, political cartoonist.
B(ernard) Kliban, 1935-91, cat books.
Edward Koren, b 1935, *New Yorker* woolly characters.
Harvey Kurtzman, 1921-93, *Mad* magazine.
Walter Lantz, 1900-94, Woody Woodpecker.
Gary Larson, b 1950, The Far Side.
Mell Lazarus, b 1929, Momma, Miss Peach.
Stan Lee, b 1922, Marvel Comics.
David Levine, b 1926, *N.Y. Review of Books* caricatures.
Doug Marlette, b 1949, editorial cartoonist, Kudzu.
Don Martin, b 1931, *Mad* magazine.
Bill Mauldin, b 1921, depicted squalid life of the G.I. in WW2.
Jeff MacNelly, b 1947, political cartoonist, Shoe.
Winsor McCay, 1872-1934, Little Nemo.
John T. McCutcheon, 1870-1949, midwestern rural life.
George McManus, 1884-1954, Bringing Up Father.
Dale Messick, b 1906, Brenda Starr.
Norman Mingo, 1896-1980, Alfred E. Neuman.
Bob Montana, 1920-75, Archie.
Dick Moores, 1909-86, Gasoline Alley.
Willard Mullin, 1902-78, sports cartoonist, created Dodgers "Bum" and Mets "Kid."
Russell Myers, b 1938, Broom Hilda.
Thomas Nast, 1840-1902, political cartoonist, created Democratic donkey and Republican elephant.
Pat Oliphant, b 1935, political cartoonist.
Frederick Burr Opper, 1857-1937, Happy Hooligan.
Richard Outcault, 1863-1928, Yellow Kid, Buster Brown.
Mike Peters, b 1943, editorial cartoons. Mother Goose & Grimm.
George Price, 1901-95, *New Yorker* lower-class life.
Alex Raymond, 1909-56, Flash Gordon, Jungle Jim.
Forrest (Bud) Sagendorf, 1915-94, Popeye
Art Sansom, 1920-91, The Born Loser.
Charles Schulz, b 1922, Peanuts.
Elzie C. Segar, 1894-1938, creator of Popeye
Joe Shuster, 1914-92, & **Jerry Siegel,** 1914-96, Superman.
Sydney Smith, 1887-1935, The Gumps.
Otto Soglow, 1900-75, Little King, Canyon Kiddies.
Art Spiegelman, b 1948, Raw, Maus.
William Steig, b 1907, *New Yorker* cartoonist.
James Swinnerton, 1875-1974, Little Jimmy.
Paul Terry, 1887-1971, animator of Mighty Mouse.
Bob Thaves, b 1924, Frank and Ernest.
James Thurber, 1894-61, *New Yorker* cartoonist.
Garry Trudeau, b 1948, Doonesbury.
Mort Walker, b 1923, Beetle Bailey.
Bill Watterson, b 1958, Calvin and Hobbes.
Russ Westover, 1887-1966, Tillie the Toiler.
Frank Willard, 1893-1958, Moon Mullins.
J. R. Williams, 1888-1957, The Willets Family, Out Our Way.
Gahan Wilson, b 1930, cartoonist of the macabre.
Tom Wilson, b 1931, Ziggy.
Art Young, 1866-1943, political radical and satirist.
Chic Young, 1901-73, Blondie.

Noted Historians, Economists, and Social Scientists of the Past

Brooks Adams, 1848-1927, (U.S.) historian, political theoretician; *The Law of Civilization and Decay.*
Henry Adams, 1838-1918, (U.S.) historian; *History of the United States of America, The Education of Henry Adams.*
Francis Bacon, 1561-1626, (Eng.) philosopher, essayist, and statesman; championed observation and induction.
George Bancroft, 1800-91, (U.S.) historian; wrote 10-volume *History of the United States.*
Jack Barbash, 1911-94, (U.S.) labor economist who helped create the AFL-CIO.
Charles A. Beard, 1874-1948, (U.S.) historian; *The Economic Basis of Politics.*
Bede (the Venerable), c673-735, (Eng.) scholar, historian.
Ruth Benedict, 1887-1948, (U.S.) anthropologist; studied Indian tribes of the Southwest.
Bruno Bettelheim, 1903-90, (Aust.-U.S.) psychoanalyst specializing in autistic children; *The Uses of Enchantment.*
Louis Blanc, 1811-82, (Fr.) Socialist leader and historian whose ideas were a link between utopian and Marxist socialism.
Leonard Bloomfield, 1887-1949, (U.S.) linguist; *Language.*
Franz Boas, 1858-1942, (U.S.) German-born anthropologist; studied American Indians.
Van Wyck Brooks, 1886-1963, (U.S.) historian; critic of New England culture, especially literature.

Edmund Burke, 1729-97, (Ir.) British parliamentarian and political philosopher; influenced many Federalists.
Joseph Campbell, 1904-87, (U.S.) author, editor, teacher; wrote books on mythology, folklore.
Thomas Carlyle, 1795-1881, (Sc.) historian, critic; *Sartor Resartus, Past and Present, The French Revolution.*
Edward Channing, 1856-1931, (U.S.) historian; wrote 6-volume *History of the United States.*
John R. Commons, 1862-1945, (U.S.) economist, labor historian; *Legal Foundations of Capitalism.*
Benedetto Croce, 1866-1952, (It.) philosopher, statesman, and historian; *Philosophy of the Spirit.*
Bernard A. De Voto, 1897-1955, (U.S.) historian; wrote trilogy on American West; edited Mark Twain manuscripts.
Ariel Durant, 1898-1981, & **Will Durant,** 1885-1981, (U.S.) historians; *The Story of Civilization.*
Emile Durkheim, 1858-1917, (Fr.) a founder of modern sociology; *The Rules of Sociological Method.*
Friedrich Engels, 1820-95, (Ger.) political writer; with Marx wrote the *Communist Manifesto.*
Erik Erikson, 1902-94, (U.S.) psychoanalyst, author; theory of developmental stages of life, *Childhood and Society.*
Irving Fisher, 1867-1947, (U.S.) economist; contributed to the development of modern monetary theory.

John Fiske, 1842-1901, (U.S.) historian and lecturer; popularized Darwinian theory of evolution.

Charles Fourier, 1772-1837, (Fr.) utopian socialist.

Sir James George Frazer, 1854-1941, (Br.) anthropologist; studied myth in religion; *The Golden Bough.*

Henry George, 1839-97, (U.S.) economist, reformer; led single-tax movement.

Edward Gibbon, 1737-94, (Br.) historian; wrote *The History of the Decline and Fall of the Roman Empire.*

Francesco Guicciardini, 1483-1540, (It.) historian; wrote *Storia d'Italia,* principal historical work of the 16th cent.

Thomas Hobbes, 1588-1679, (Eng.) philosopher, political theorist; *Leviathan.*

Richard Hofstadter, 1916-70, (U.S.) historian; *The Age of Reform.*

John Maynard Keynes, 1883-1946, (Br.) economist; principal advocate of deficit spending.

Russell Kirk, 1918-94, (U.S.), social philosopher; *The Conservative Mind.*

Alfred L. Kroeber, 1876-1960, (U.S.) cultural anthropologist; studied Indians of North and South America.

Christopher Lasch, 1932-94, (U.S.) social critic, historian; *The Culture of Narcissism.*

James L. Laughlin, 1850-1933, (U.S.) economist; helped establish Federal Reserve System.

Lucien Lévy-Bruhl, 1857-1939, (Fr.) philosopher; studied the psychology of primitive societies; *Primitive Mentality.*

Kurt Lewin, 1890-1947, (U.S.) German-born psychologist, studied human motivation and group dynamics.

John Locke, 1632-1704, (Eng.) philosopher and political theorist; *Two Treatises of Government.*

Konrad Lorenz, 1904-89, (Austrian) ethologist; pioneer in study of animal behavior.

Thomas B. Macaulay, 1800-59, (Br.) historian, statesman.

Niccolò Machiavelli, 1469-1527, (It.) writer, statesman. *The Prince, Discourses on Livy.*

Bronislaw Malinowski, 1884-1942, (Pol.) considered the father of social anthropology.

Thomas R. Malthus, 1766-1834, (Br.) economist; famed for *Essay on the Principle of Population.*

Karl Mannheim, 1893-1947, (Hung.) sociologist, historian; *Ideology and Utopia.*

Karl Marx, 1818-83, (Ger.) political philosopher, proponent of Communism; *Communist Manifesto, Das Kapital.*

Giuseppe Mazzini, 1805-72, (It.) political philosopher.

George H. Mead, 1863-1931, (U.S.) philosopher, social psychologist.

Margaret Mead, 1901-78, (U.S.) cultural anthropologist; popularized field, *Coming of Age in Samoa.*

James Mill, 1773-1836, (Sc.) philosopher, historian, economist; a proponent of utilitarianism.

Perry G. Miller, 1905-63, (U.S.) historian; interpreted 17th-cent. New England.

Theodor Mommsen, 1817-1903, (Ger.) historian; *The History of Rome.*

Charles-Louis Montesquieu, 1689-1755, (Fr.) social philosopher; *The Spirit of Laws.*

Samuel Eliot Morison, 1887-1976, (U.S.) historian; chronicled voyages of early explorers.

Lewis Mumford, 1895-1990, (U.S.) sociologist, critic; *The Culture of Cities.*

Gunnar Myrdal, 1898-1987, (Swed.) economist, social scientist; *Asian Drama: An Inquiry Into the Poverty of Nations.*

Joseph Needham, 1900-95, (Br.) scientific historian; *Science and Civilization in China.*

Allan Nevins, 1890-1971, (U.S.) historian, biographer; *The Ordeal of the Union.*

José Ortega y Gasset, 1883-1955, (Sp.) philosopher; advocated control by elite, *The Revolt of the Masses.*

Robert Owen, 1771-1858, (Br.) political philosopher, reformer; pioneer in cooperative movement.

Thomas (Tom) Paine, 1737-1809, (U.S.) political theorist, writer. *Common Sense.*

Vilfredo Pareto, 1848-1923, (It.) economist, sociologist.

Francis Parkman, 1823-93, (U.S.) historian; *France and England in North America.*

William Prescott, 1796-1859, (U.S.) early American historian; *The Conquest of Peru.*

Pierre Joseph Proudhon, 1809-65, (Fr.) social theorist; the father of anarchism, *The Philosophy of Property.*

François Quesnay, 1694-1774, (Fr.) economic theorist.

David Ricardo, 1772-1823, (Br.) economic theorist; advocated free international trade.

James H. Robinson, 1863-1936, (U.S.) historian, educator.

Carl Rogers, 1902-87, (U.S.) psychotherapist, author.

Jean-Jacques Rousseau, 1712-78, (Fr.) social philosopher; the father of romantic sensibility; *Confessions.*

Lee Salk, 1926-92, (U.S.) child psychologist, author.

Edward Sapir, 1884-1939, (Ger.-U.S.) anthropologist; studied ethnology and linguistics of some U.S. Indian groups.

Ferdinand de Saussure, 1857-1913, (Swiss) a founder of modern linguistics.

Hjalmar Schacht, 1877-1970, (Ger.) economist.

Joseph Schumpeter, 1883-1950, (Czech.-U.S.) economist, sociologist; theorized on capitalism and business development.

George Simmel, 1858-1918, (Ger.) sociologist, philosopher; helped establish German sociology.

B(urrhus) F(rederick) Skinner, 1904-89, (U.S.) psychologist; behaviorism.

Adam Smith, 1723-90, (Br.) economist; advocated laissez-faire economy and free trade, *The Wealth of Nations.*

Jared Sparks, 1789-1866, (U.S.) historian, educator, editor; *The Library of American Biography.*

Oswald Spengler, 1880-1936, (Ger.) philosopher and historian; *The Decline of the West.*

William G. Sumner, 1840-1910, (U.S.) social scientist, economist; laissez-faire economy, Social Darwinism.

Hippolyte Taine, 1828-93, (Fr.) historian; basis of naturalistic school; *The Origins of Contemporary France.*

Frank W. Taussig, 1859-1940, (U.S.) economist, educator.

A(lan) J(ohn) P(ercivale) Taylor, 1906-89, (Br.) historian; *The Origins of the Second World War.*

Nikolaas Tinbergen, 1907-88, (Dutch-Br.) ethologist; pioneer in study of animal behavior.

Alexis de Tocqueville, 1805-59, (Fr.) political scientist, historian; *Democracy in America.*

Francis E. Townsend, 1867-1960, (U.S.) led old-age pension movement, 1933.

Arnold Toynbee, 1889-1975, (Br.) historian; *A Study of History,* sweeping analysis of hist. of civilizations.

Heinrich von Treitschke, 1834-96, (Ger.) historian, political writer; *A History of Germany in the 19th Cent.*

George Trevelyan, 1838-1928, (Br.) historian, statesman; favored "literary" over "scientific" history; *History of England.*

Barbara Tuchman, 1912-89, (U.S.) author of popular history books, *The Guns of August, The March of Folly.*

Frederick J. Turner, 1861-1932, (U.S.) historian, educator; *The Frontier in American History.*

Thorstein B. Veblen, 1857-1929, (U.S.) economist, social philosopher; *The Theory of the Leisure Class.*

Giovanni Vico, 1668-1744, (It.) historian, philosopher; regarded by many as first modern historian; *New Science.*

Izaak Walton, 1593-1683, (Eng.) wrote biographies; political-philosophical study of fishing, *The Compleat Angler.*

Sidney J., 1859-1947, and **Beatrice,** 1858-1943, **Webb,** (Br.) leading figures in Fabian Society and Labor Party.

Walter P. Webb, 1888-1963, (U.S.) historian of the West.

Max Weber, 1864-1920, (Ger.) sociologist; *The Protestant Ethic and the Spirit of Capitalism.*

Notable Military and Naval Leaders of the Past

Creighton Abrams, 1914-74, (U.S.) commanded forces in Vietnam, 1968-72.

Harold Alexander, 1891-1969, (Br.) led Allied invasion of Italy, 1943, WW2.

Ethan Allen, 1738-89, (U.S.) headed Green Mountain Boys; captured Ft. Ticonderoga, 1775, Amer. Rev.

Edmund Allenby, 1861-1936, (Br.) in Boer War, WW1; led Egyptian expeditionary force, 1917-18.

Benedict Arnold, 1741-1801, (U.S.) victorious at Saratoga; tried to betray West Point to British, Amer. Rev.

Henry "Hap" Arnold, 1886-1950, (U.S.) commanded Army Air Force in WW2.

John Barry, 1745-1803, (U.S.) won numerous sea battles during Amer. Rev.

Pierre Beauregard, 1818-93, (U.S.) Confed. general, ordered bombardment of Ft. Sumter that began the Civil War.

Gebhard von Blücher, 1742-1819, (Ger.) helped defeat Napoleon at Waterloo.

Napoleon Bonaparte, 1769-1821, (Fr.) defeated Russia and Austria at Austerlitz, 1805; invaded Russia, 1812; defeated at Waterloo, 1815.

Edward Braddock, 1695-1755, (Br.) commanded forces in French and Indian War.

Omar N. Bradley, 1893-1981, (U.S.) headed U.S. ground troops in Normandy invasion, 1944, WW2.

John Burgoyne, 1722-92, (Br.) defeated at Saratoga, Amer. Rev.

Claire Lee Chennault, 1893-1958, (U.S.) general, headed Flying Tigers in WW2.

Mark W. Clark, 1896-1984, (U.S.) helped plan N. African invasion in WW2; commander of UN forces, Korean War.

Karl von Clausewitz, 1780-1831, (Prussian) military theorist.

Lucius D. Clay, 1897-1978, (U.S.) led Berlin airlift, 1948-49.

Henry Clinton, 1700-95, (Br.) commander of forces in Amer. Rev., 1778-81.

Cochise, c 1815-74, (Nat. Am.) chief of Chiricahua band of Apache Indians in Southwest.

Charles Cornwallis, 1738-1805, (Br.) victorious at Brandywine, 1777; surrendered at Yorktown, Amer. Rev.

Crazy Horse, 1849-77, (Nat. Am.) Sioux war chief victorious at the battle of Little Big Horn

George Armstrong Custer, 1839-76, (U.S.) U.S. army officer defeated and killed at the battle of Little Big Horn.

Moshe Dayan, 1915-81, (Isr.) directed campaigns in the 1967, 1973 Arab-Israeli wars.

Stephen Decatur, 1779-1820, (U.S.) naval hero of Barbary wars, War of 1812.

Anton Denikin, 1872-1947, (Russ.) led White forces in Russian civil war.

George Dewey, 1837-1917, (U.S.) destroyed Spanish fleet at Manila, 1898, Spanish-American War.

Karl Doenitz, 1891-1980, (Ger.) submarine commander in chief and naval commander during WW2; briefly claimed to be head of state after Hitler's death; convicted of war crimes.

Hugh C. Dowding, 1883-1970, (Br.) headed RAF, 1936-40, WW2.

Jubal Early, 1816-94, (U.S.) Confed. general led raid on Washington, 1864, Civil War.

Dwight D. Eisenhower, 1890-1969, (U.S.) commanded Allied forces in Europe, WW2.

David Farragut, 1801-70, (U.S.) Union admiral, captured New Orleans, Mobile Bay, Civil War.

Ferdinand Foch, 1851-1929, (Fr.) headed victorious Allied armies, 1918, WW1.

Nathan Bedford Forrest, 1821-77, (U.S.) Confed. general, led raids against Union supply lines, Civil War.

Frederick the Great, 1712-86, (Prussian) led Prussia in Seven Years War.

Horatio Gates, 1728-1806, (U.S.) commanded army at Saratoga, Amer. Rev.

Geronimo, 1829-1909 (Nat. Am.) leader of Chiricahua band of Apache Indians.

Charles G. Gordon, 1833-85, (Br.) led forces in China, Crimean War; killed at Khartoum.

Ulysses S. Grant, 1822-85, (U.S.) headed Union army, Civil War, 1864-65; forced Lee's surrender, 1865.

Nathanael Greene, 1742-86, (U.S.) defeated British in Southern campaign, 1780-81.

Heinz Guderian, 1888-1953, (Ger.) tank theorist, led panzer forces in Poland, France, Russia, WW2.

Douglas Haig, 1861-1928, (Br.) led British armies in France, 1915-18, WW1.

William F. Halsey, 1882-1959, (U.S.) defeated Japanese fleet at Leyte Gulf, 1944, WW2.

Sir Arthur Travers Harris, 1895-1984, (Br.) led Britain's WW2 bomber command.

Richard Howe, 1726-99, (Br.) commanded navy in Amer. Rev., 1776-78; June 1 victory against French, 1794.

William Howe, 1729-1814, (Br.) commanded forces in Amer. Rev., 1776-78.

Isaac Hull, 1773-1843, (U.S.) sunk British frigate *Guerriere,* War of 1812.

Thomas (Stonewall) Jackson, 1824-63, (U.S.) Confed. general led Shenandoah Valley campaign, Civil War.

Joseph Joffre, 1852-1931, (Fr.) headed Allied armies, won Battle of the Marne, 1914, WW1.

Chief Joseph, c 1840-1904, (Nat. Am.) chief of the Nez Percé, led his tribe across 3 states seeking refuge in Canada; surrendered about 30 mi from Canadian border.

John Paul Jones, 1747-92, (U.S.) commanded *Bonhomme Richard* in victory over Serapis, Amer. Rev., 1779.

Stephen Kearny, 1794-1848, (U.S.) headed Army of the West in Mexican War.

Ernest J. King, 1878-1956, (U.S.) chief WW2 naval strategist.

Horatio H. Kitchener, 1850-1916, (Br.) led forces in Boer War; victorious at Khartoum; organized army in WW1.

Henry Knox, 1750-1806, (U.S.) general in Amer. Rev.; first secretary of war under U.S. Constitution.

Lavrenti Kornilov, 1870-1918, (Russ.) commander-in-chief, 1917; led counter-revolutionary march on Petrograd.

Thaddeus Kosciusko, 1746-1817, (Pol.) aided Amer. Rev.

Mikhail Kutuzov, 1745-1813, (Russ.) fought French at Borodino, Napoleonic Wars, 1812; abandoned Moscow; forced French retreat.

Marquis de Lafayette, 1757-1834, (Fr.) aided Amer. Rev.

T(homas) E. Lawrence (of Arabia), 1888-1935, (Br.) organized revolt of Arabs against Turks in WW1.

Henry (Light-Horse Harry) Lee, 1756-1818, (U.S.) cavalry officer in Amer. Rev.

Robert E. Lee, 1807-70, (U.S.) Confed. general defeated at Gettysburg, Civil War; surrendered to Grant, 1865.

Lyman Lemnitzer, 1899-1988, (U.S.) WW2 hero, later general, chairman of Joint Chiefs of Staff.

James Longstreet, 1821-1904, (U.S.) aided Lee at Gettysburg, Civil War.

Douglas MacArthur, 1880-1964, (U.S.) commanded forces in SW Pacific in WW2; headed occupation forces in Japan, 1945-51; UN commander in Korean War.

Erich von Manstein, 1887-1973, (Ger.) served in WW1 and WW2, planned invasion of France (1940), convicted of war crimes.

Carl Gustaf Mannerheim, 1867-1951, (Finn.) army officer and pres. of Finland 1944-46.

Francis Marion, 1733-95, (U.S.) led guerrilla actions in South Carolina during Amer. Rev.

Duke of Marlborough, 1650-1722, (Br.) led forces against Louis XIV in War of the Spanish Succession.

George C. Marshall, 1880-1959, (U.S.) chief of staff in WW2; authored Marshall Plan.

George B. McClellan, 1826-85, (U.S.) Union general, commanded Army of the Potomac, 1861-62, Civil War.

George Meade, 1815-72, (U.S.) commanded Union forces at Gettysburg, Civil War.

Billy Mitchell, 1879-1936, (U.S.) WW1 air-power advocate; court-martialed for insubordination, later vindicated.

Helmuth von Moltke, 1800-91, (Ger.) victorious in Austro-Prussian, Franco-Prussian wars.

Louis de Montcalm, 1712-59, (Fr.) headed troops in Canada, French and Indian War; defeated at Quebec, 1759.

Bernard Law Montgomery, 1887-1976, (Br.) stopped German offensive at Alamein, 1942, WW2; helped plan Normandy invasion.

Daniel Morgan, 1736-1802, (U.S.) victorious at Cowpens, 1781, Amer. Rev.

Louis Mountbatten, 1900-79, (Br.) Supreme Allied Commander of SE Asia, 1943-46, WW2.

Joachim Murat, 1767-1815, (Fr.) led cavalry at Marengo, Austerlitz, and Jena, Napoleonic Wars.

Horatio Nelson, 1758-1805, (Br.) naval commander destroyed French fleet at Trafalgar.

Michel Ney, 1769-1815, (Fr.) commanded forces in Switz., Aust., Russ., Napoleonic Wars; defeated at Waterloo.

Chester Nimitz, 1885-1966, (U.S.) commander of naval forces in Pacific in WW2.

George S. Patton, 1885-1945, (U.S.) led assault on Sicily, 1943, Third Army invasion of Europe, WW2.

Oliver Perry, 1785-1819, (U.S.) won Battle of Lake Erie in War of 1812.

John Pershing, 1860-1948, (U.S.) commanded Mexican border campaign, 1916, American Expeditionary Force, WW1.

Henri Philippe Pétain, 1856-1951, (Fr.) defended Verdun, 1916; headed Vichy government in WW2.

George E. Pickett, 1825-75, (U.S.) Confed. general famed for "charge" at Gettysburg, Civil War.

Hyman Rickover, 1900-86, (U.S.) father of nuclear navy.

Erwin Rommel, 1891-1944, (Ger.) headed Afrika Korps, WW2.

Gerd von Rundstedt, 1875-1953, (Ger.) supreme commander in West, 1942-45, WW2.

Aleksandr Samsonov, 1859-1914, (Russ.) led invasion of E. Prussia, WW1, defeated at Tannenberg, 1914.

Winfield Scott, 1786-1866, (U.S.) hero of War of 1812; headed forces in Mexican war, took Mexico City.

Philip Sheridan, 1831-88, (U.S.) Union cavalry officer, headed Army of the Shenandoah, 1864-65, Civil War.

William T. Sherman, 1820-91, (U.S.) Union general, sacked Atlanta during "march to the sea," 1864, Civil War.

Carl Spaatz, 1891-1974, (U.S.) directed strategic bombing against Germany, later Japan, in WW2.

Raymond Spruance, 1886-1969, (U.S.) victorious at Midway Island, 1942, WW2.

Joseph W. Stilwell, 1883-1946, (U.S.) headed forces in the China, Burma, India theater in WW2.

J.E.B. Stuart, 1833-64, (U.S.) Confed. cavalry commander, Civil War.

George H. Thomas, 1816-70, (U.S.) saved Union army at Chattanooga, 1863; won at Nashville, 1864, Civil War.

Aleksandr Suvorov, 1729-1800, (Rus.) victorious commander of Allied Russian and Austrian armies against Ottoman Turks in Russo-Turkish War.

Semyon Timoshenko, 1895-1970, (USSR) defended Moscow, Stalingrad, WW2; led winter offensive, 1942-43.

Alfred von Tirpitz, 1849-1930, (Ger.) responsible for submarine blockade in WW1.

Jonathan M. Wainwright, 1883-1953, (U.S.) forced to surrender on Corregidor, 1942, WW2.

George Washington, 1732-99, (U.S.) led Continental army, 1775-83, Amer. Rev.

Archibald Wavell, 1883-1950, (Br.) commanded forces in N. and E. Africa, and SE Asia in WW2.

Anthony Wayne, 1745-96, (U.S.) captured Stony Point, 1779, Amer. Rev.

Duke of Wellington, 1769-1852, (Br.) defeated Napoleon at Waterloo, 1815.

James Wolfe, 1727-59, (Br.) captured Quebec from French, 1759, French and Indian War.

Isoroku Yamamoto, 1884-1943, (Jpn.) com. in chief of Japanese fleet and naval planner before and during WW2.

Georgi Zhukov, 1895-1974, (Russ.) defended Moscow, 1941, led assault on Berlin, 1945, WW2.

Noted Philosophers and Religious Figures of the Past

For other Greeks and Romans, see Historical Figures chapter. See also Religion chapter.

Lyman Abbott, 1835-1922, (U.S.) clergyman, reformer; advocate of Christian Socialism.

Pierre Abelard, 1079-1142, (Fr.) philosopher, theologian, teacher; used dialectic method to support Christian dogma.

Felix Adler, 1851-1933, (U.S.) German-born founder of the Ethical Culture Society.

Thomas Aquinas, 1225-74, (It.) preeminent medieval philosopher-theologian; saint; *Summa Theologica.*

Aristotle, 384-322 BC, (Gr.) pioneering wide-ranging realistic philosopher, logician, ethician, naturalist.

Augustine, 354-430, (N Africa) philosopher, theologian, bishop; *Confessions, City of God On the Trinity.*

J. L. Austin, 1911-60, (Br.) ordinary-language philosopher.

Averroes (Ibn Rushd), 1126-98, (Sp.) Islamic philosopher, physician.

Avicenna (Ibn Sina), 980-1037, (Iran.) Islamic philosopher, scientist.

A(lfred) J(ules) Ayer, 1910-89, (Br.) philosopher; logical positivist; *Language, Truth, and Logic.*

Roger Bacon, c1214-94, (Eng.) philosopher and scientist.

Bahaullah (Mirza Husayn Ali), 1817-92, (Pers.) founder of Bahá'í faith.

Karl Barth, 1886-1968, (Swiss) theologian; a leading force in 20th-cent. Protestantism.

Thomas à Becket, 1118-70, (Eng.) archbishop of Canterbury; opposed Henry II; murdered by King's men.

St. Benedict, c480-547, (It.) founded the Benedictines.

Jeremy Bentham, 1748-1832, (Br.) philosopher, reformer; enunciated utilitarianism.

Henri Bergson, 1859-1941, (Fr.) philosopher of evolution.

George Berkeley, 1685-1753, (Ir.) idealist philosopher, churchman.

John Biddle, 1615-62, (Eng.) founder of English Unitarianism.

Jakob Boehme, 1575-1624, (Ger.) theosophist and mystic.

Dietrich Bonhoeffer, 1906-1945 (Ger.) Lutheran theologian, pastor; executed as opponent of Nazis.

William Brewster, 1567-1644, (Eng.) headed Pilgrims.

Emil Brunner, 1889-1966, (Swiss) Protestant theologian.

Giordano Bruno, 1548-1600, (It.) philosopher, pantheist.

Martin Buber, 1878-1965, (Ger.) Jewish philosopher, theologian; *I and Thou.*

Buddha (Siddhartha Gautama), c563-c 483 BC, (Ind.) philosopher; founded Buddhism.

John Calvin, 1509-64, (Fr.) theologian; a key figure in the Protestant Reformation.

Rudolph Carnap, 1891-1970, (U.S.) German-born philosopher; a founder of logical positivism.

William Ellery Channing, 1780-1842, (U.S.) clergyman; early spokesman for Unitarianism.

Auguste Comte, 1798-1857, (Fr.) philosopher; originated positivism.

Confucius, 551-479 BC, (Chin.) founder of Confucianism.

John Cotton, 1584-1652, (Eng.) Puritan theologian.

Thomas Cranmer, 1489-1556, (Eng.) churchman; wrote much of *Book of Common Prayer.*

René Descartes, 1596-1650, (Fr.) philosopher, mathematician; "father of modern philosophy." *Discourse on Method.*

John Dewey, 1859-1952, (U.S.) philosopher, educator; instrumentalist theory of knowledge; helped inaugurate progressive education movement.

Denis Diderot, 1713-84, (Fr.) philosopher, encyclopedist.

John Duns Scotus, c1266-1308, (Sc.) Franciscan philosopher and theologian.

Mary Baker Eddy, 1821-1910, (U.S.) founder of Christian Science; *Science and Health.*

Jonathan Edwards, 1703-58, (U.S.) preacher, theologian.

(Desiderius) Erasmus, c1466-1536, (Du.) Renaissance humanist; *On the Freedom of the Will.*

Johann Fichte, 1762-1814, (Ger.) idealist philosopher.

George Fox, 1624-91, (Br.) founder of Society of Friends.

St. Francis of Assisi, 1182-1226, (It.) founded Franciscans.

al-Ghazali, 1058-1111, Islamic philosopher.

Georg W. F. Hegel, 1770-1831, (Ger.) idealist philosopher; *Phenomenology of Mind.*

Martin Heidegger, 1889-1976, (Ger.) existentialist philosopher; affected many fields; *Being and Time.*

Johann G. Herder, 1744-1803, (Ger.) philosopher, cultural historian; a founder of German Romanticism.

Thomas Hobbes, 1588-1679, (Eng.) philosopher, political theorist; *Leviathan.*

David Hume, 1711-76, (Sc.) leading empiricist philosopher; *Enquiry Concerning Human Understanding.*

Jan Hus, 1369-1415, (Czech.) religious reformer.

Edmund Husserl, 1859-1938, (Ger.) philosopher; founded the phenomenological movement.

Thomas Huxley, 1825-95, (Br.) philosopher, educator.

William Inge, 1860-1954, (Br.) theologian; explored mystic aspects of Christianity.

William James, 1842-1910, (U.S.) philosopher, psychologist; pragmatist; studied religious experience.

Karl Jaspers, 1883-1969, (Ger.) existentialist philosopher.

Joan of Arc, 1412-1431, (Fr.) national heroine and patron saint of France; key figure in the Hundred Years' War.

Immanuel Kant, 1724-1804, (Ger.) philosopher; preeminent founder of modern critical philosophy; *Critique of Pure Reason.*

Thomas à Kempis, c1380-1471, (Ger.) monk, devotional writer; probably wrote *Imitation of Christ.*

Soren Kierkegaard, 1813-55, (Dan.) religious philosopher; precursor of existentialism; *Either/Or, The Sickness Unto Death.*

John Knox, 1505-72, (Sc.) leader of the Protestant Reformation in Scotland.

Lao-Tzu, 604-531 BC, (Chin.) philosopher; considered the founder of the Taoist religion.

Gottfried von Leibniz, 1646-1716, (Ger.) rationalistic philosopher, logician, mathematician.

John Locke, 1632-1704, (Eng.) political theorist, empiricist philosopher; *Essay Concerning Human Understanding.*

Ignatius Loyola, 1491-1556, (Sp.) founder of the Jesuits.

Martin Luther, 1483-1546, (Ger.) leader of the Protestant Reformation, founded Lutheran church.

Maimonides, 1135-1204, (Sp.) major Jewish philosopher.

Gabriel Marcel, 1889-1973, (Fr.) Roman Catholic existentialist philosopher, dramatist, and critic.

Jacques Maritain, 1882-1973, (Fr.) Neo-Thomist philosopher.

Cotton Mather, 1663-1728, (U.S.) defender of orthodox Puritanism; founded Yale, 1701.

Philipp Melanchthon, 1497-1560, (Ger.) theologian, humanist; an important voice in the Reformation.

Maurice Merleau-Ponty, 1908-61, (Fr.) existentialist philosopher.

Thomas Merton, 1915-68, (U.S.) Trappist monk, spiritual writer; *The Seven Storey Mountain.*

John Stuart Mill, 1806-73, (Br.) philosopher, economist; libertarian political theorist; *Utilitarianism.*

Muhammad, c570-632, (Arab) the prophet of Islam.

Dwight Moody, 1837-99, (U.S.) evangelist.

G(eorge) E(dward) Moore, 1873-1958, (Br.) philosopher, ethical theorist; *Principia Ethica,* "A Defense of Common Sense."

Elijah Muhammad, 1897-1975, (U.S.) leader of the Black Muslim sect.

Heinrich Muhlenberg, 1711-87, (Ger.) organized the Lutheran Church in America.

John H. Newman, 1801-90, (Br.) Roman Catholic convert, cardinal; led Oxford Movement; *Apologia pro Vita Sua.*

Reinhold Niebuhr, 1892-1971, (U.S.) Protestant theologian.

Friedrich Nietzsche, 1844-1900, (Ger.) philosopher; *The Birth of Tragedy, Beyond Good and Evil, Thus Spake Zarathustra.*

Blaise Pascal, 1623-62, (Fr.) philosopher, mathematician; *Pensées.*

St. Patrick, c389-c 461, (BR.) brought Christianity to Ireland.

St. Paul, ?-c 67, a key proponent of Christianity; his epistles are first Christian theological writing.

Norman Vincent Peale, 1898-1993, (U.S.) religious leader, author; *The Power of Positive Thinking.*

C(harles) S. Peirce, 1839-1914, (U.S.) philosopher, logician; originated concept of pragmatism, 1878.

Plato, c 428-347 BC, (Gr.) philosopher; wrote classic Socratic dialogues; argued for independent reality of ideas; *Republic.*

Plotinus, (Rom.) 205-70, a founder of neo-Platonism; *Enneads.*

Josiah Royce, 1855-1916, (U.S.) idealist philosopher.

Bertrand Russell, 1872-1970, (Br.) philosopher, logician; one of the founders of modern logic; a prolific popular writer.

Charles T. Russell, 1852-1916, (U.S.) founder of Jehovah's Witnesses.

Gilbert Ryle, 1900-76, (Br.) analytic philosopher; *The Concept of Mind.*

George Santayana, 1863-1952, (U.S.) philosopher, writer, critic. *The Sense of Beauty, The Realms of Being.*

Jean-Paul Sartre, 1905-80, (Fr.) philosopher, novelist, playwright. *Nausea, No Exit, Being and Nothingness.*

Friedrich von Schelling, 1775-1854, (Ger.) philosopher of romantic movement.

Friedrich Schleiermacher, 1768-1834, (Ger.) theologian; a founder of modern Protestant theology.

Arthur Schopenhauer, 1788-1860, (Ger.) philosopher; *The World as Will and Idea.*

Albert Schweitzer, 1875-1965, (Ger.) theologian, social philosopher, medical missionary.

Joseph Smith, 1805-44, (U.S.) founded Latter-day Saints (Mormon) movement, 1830.

Socrates, 469-399 BC, (Gr.) influential philosopher immortalized by Plato.

Herbert Spencer, 1820-1903, (Br.) philosopher of evolution.

Baruch de Spinoza, 1632-77, (Dutch) rationalist philosopher; *Ethics.*

Billy Sunday, 1862-1935, (U.S.) evangelist.

Pierre Teilhard de Chardin, 1881-1955, (Fr.) Jesuit priest, paleontologist, philosopher-theologian; *The Divine Milieu.*

Daisetz Teitaro Suzuki, 1870-1966, (Jpn.) Buddhist scholar.

Emanuel Swedenborg, 1688-1772, (Swed.) philosopher, mystic.

Paul Tillich, 1886-1965, (U.S.) German-born philosopher and theologian; brought depth psychology to Protestantism.

John Wesley, 1703-91, (Br.) theologian, evangelist; founded Methodism.

Alfred North Whitehead, 1861-1947, (Br.) philosopher, mathematician; *Process and Reality.*

William of Occam, c1285-c1349 (Eng.) medieval scholastic philosopher; nominalist.

Roger Williams, c 1603-83, (U.S.) clergyman; championed religious freedom and separation of church and state.

Ludwig Wittgenstein, 1889-1951, (Austrian) philosopher; major influence on contemporary language philosophy; *Tractatus Logico-Philosophicus, Philosophical Investigations.*

John Wycliffe, 1320-84, (Eng.) theologian, reformer.

Brigham Young, 1801-77, (U.S.) Mormon leader after Smith's assassination; colonized Utah.

Huldrych Zwingli, 1484-1531, (Swiss) theologian; led Swiss Protestant Reformation.

Noted Political Leaders of the Past

(Modern royalty; U.S. presidents, vice presidents, Supreme Court justices, signers of Decl. of Indep. listed elsewhere.)

Abu Bakr, 573-634, Muslim leader, first caliph, chosen successor to Muhammad.

Dean Acheson, 1893-1971, (U.S.) secretary of state; architect of cold war foreign policy.

Samuel Adams, 1722-1803, (U.S.) patriot, Boston Tea Party firebrand.

Konrad Adenauer, 1876-1967, (Ger.) W. German chancellor.

Emilio Aguinaldo, 1869-1964, (Philip.) revolutionary; fought against Spain and the U.S.

Akbar, 1542-1605, greatest Mogul emperor of India.

Salvador Allende Gossens, 1908-1973, (Chilean) Marxist pres. 1970-73; ousted and dried in coup.

Herbert H. Asquith, 1852-1928, (Br.) liberal prime min.; instituted major social reform.

Atahualpa, ?-1533, Inca (ruling chief) of Peru.

Kemal Ataturk, 1881-1938, (Turk.) founded modern Turkey.

Clement Attlee, 1883-1967, (Br.) Labor party leader, prime min.; enacted natl. health, nationalized many industries.

Stephen F. Austin, 1793-1836, (U.S.) led Texas colonization.

Mikhail Bakunin, 1814-76, (Russ.) revolutionary; leading exponent of anarchism.

Arthur J. Balfour, 1848-1930, (Br.) foreign secretary under Lloyd George; issued Balfour Declaration backing Zionism.

Bernard M. Baruch, 1870-1965, (U.S.) financier, govt. adviser.

Fulgencio Batista y Zaldívar, 1901-73, (Cuban) Cuban pres. (1940-44, 1952-59) and dictator, overthrown by Castro.

Lord Beaverbrook, 1879-1964, (Br.) financier, statesman, newspaper owner.

Menachem Begin, 1913-92, (Isr.) Israeli prime min., shared 1978 Nobel Peace Prize.

Eduard Benes, 1884-1948, (Czech.) pres. during interwar and post-WW2 eras.

David Ben-Gurion, 1886-1973, (Isr.) first prime min. of Israel, 1948-53, 1955-63.

Thomas Hart Benton, 1782-1858, (U.S.) Missouri senator; championed agrarian interests and westward expansion.

Aneurin Bevan, 1897-1960, (Br.) Labor party leader.

Ernest Bevin, 1881-1951, (Br.) Labor party leader, foreign minister; helped lay foundation for NATO.

Otto von Bismarck, 1815-98, (Ger.) statesman known as the Iron Chancellor; uniter of Germany, 1870.

James G. Blaine, 1830-93, (U.S.) Republican politician, diplomat; influential in launching Pan-American movement.

Léon Blum, 1872-1950, (Fr.) socialist leader, writer; headed first Popular Front government.

Simón Bolívar, 1783-1830, (Venez.) S. Amer. Rev.ary who liberated much of the continent from Spanish rule.

William E. Borah, 1865-1940, (U.S.) isolationist senator; helped block U.S. membership in League of Nations.

Cesare Borgia, 1476-1507, (It.) soldier, politician; an outstanding figure of the Italian Renaissance.

Willy Brandt, 1913-92, (Ger.) statesman, chancellor of West Germany, 1969-74; promoted East/West peace, *Ostpolitik.*

Leonid Brezhnev, 1906-82, (USSR) Soviet leader, 1964-82.

William J. Brennan Jr., 1906-97, (U.S.) associate justice of the U.S. Supreme Court (1956-90); a leading liberal force.

Aristide Briand, 1862-1932, (Fr.) foreign minister; chief architect of Locarno Pact and anti-war Kellogg-Briand Pact.

William Jennings Bryan, 1860-1925, (U.S.) Democratic, populist leader, orator; 3 times lost race for presidency.

William C. Bullitt, 1891-1967, (U.S.) diplomat; first ambassador to USSR, ambassador to France.

Ralph Bunche, 1904-71, (U.S.) a founder and key diplomat of United Nations for more than 20 years.

John C. Calhoun, 1782-1850, (U.S.) political leader; champion of states' rights and a symbol of the Old South.

Robert Castlereagh, 1769-1822, (Br.) foreign secretary; guided Grand Alliance against Napoleon.

Camillo Benso Cavour, 1810-61, (It.) statesman; largely responsible for uniting Italy under the House of Savoy.

Nicolae Ceausescu, 1918-89, (Romanian) Communist leader, head of state 1967-89.

Austen Chamberlain, 1863-1937, (Br.) statesman who shared the Nobel Peace Prize and was instrumental in the finalization of the Locarno Treatise, both in 1925 .

Neville Chamberlain, 1869-1940, (Br.) Conservative prime min. whose appeasement of Hitler led to Munich Pact.

Chiang Kai-shek, 1887-1975, (Chin.) Nationalist Chinese pres. whose government was driven from mainland to Taiwan.

Winston Churchill, 1874-1965, (Br.) prime min., soldier, author; guided Britain through WW2.

Galeazzo Ciano, 1903-44, (It.) fascist foreign minister; helped create Rome-Berlin Axis, executed by Mussolini.

Henry Clay, 1777-1852, (U.S.) "The Great Compromiser," one of the most influential pre-Civil War political leaders.

Georges Clemenceau, 1841-1929, (Fr.) twice prem., Wilson's antagonist at Paris Peace Conference after WW1.

DeWitt Clinton, 1769-1828, (U.S.) political leader; responsible for promoting idea of the Erie Canal.

Robert Clive, 1725-74, (Br.) first administrator of Bengal; laid foundation for British Empire in India.

Jean Baptiste Colbert, 1619-83, (Fr.) statesman; influential under Louis XIV, created the French navy.

Oliver Cromwell, 1599-1658, (Br.) Lord Protector of England, led parliamentary forces during Civil War.

Curzon of Kedleston, 1859-1925, (Br.) viceroy of India, foreign secretary; major force in post-WW1 world.

Édouard Daladier, 1884-1970, (Fr.) radical socialist politician, arrested by Vichy, interned by Germans until 1945.

Georges Danton, 1759-94, (Fr.) a leading figure in the French Revolution.

Jefferson Davis, 1808-89, (U.S.) pres. of the Confed. States of America.

Charles G. Dawes, 1865-1951, (U.S.) statesman, banker; advanced plan to stabilize post-WW1 German finances.

Alcide De Gasperi, 1881-1954, (It.) prime min.; founder of Christian Democratic party.

Charles De Gaulle, 1890-1970, (Fr.) general, statesman; first pres. of the Fifth Republic.

Deng Xiaoping, 1904-97, (Chin.) "paramount leader" of China; backed economic modernization.

Eamon de Valera, 1882-1975, (Ir.-U.S.) statesman; led fight for Irish independence.

Thomas E. Dewey, 1902-71, (U.S.) New York governor; twice loser in try for presidency.

Ngo Dinh Diem, 1901-63, (Viet.) South Vietnamese pres.; assassinated in government takeover.

Everett M. Dirksen, 1896-1969, (U.S.) Senate Republican minority leader, orator.

Benjamin Disraeli, 1804-81, (Br.) prime min.; considered founder of modern Conservative party.

Engelbert Dollfuss, 1892-1934, (Austrian) chancellor; assassinated by Austrian Nazis.

Andrea Doria, 1466-1560, (It.) Genoese admiral, statesman; called "Father of Peace" and "Liberator of Genoa."

Stephen A. Douglas, 1813-61, (U.S.) Democratic leader, orator; opposed Lincoln for the presidency.

Alexander Dubcek, 1921-92, (Czech.) statesman whose attempted liberalization was crushed, 1968.

John Foster Dulles, 1888-1959, (U.S.) secretary of state under Eisenhower, cold war policy-maker.

Friedrich Ebert, 1871-1925, (Ger.) Social Democratic movement leader; 1st pres. of Weimar Republic, 1919-25.

Sir Anthony Eden, 1897-1977, (Br.) foreign secretary, prime min. during Suez invasion of 1956.

Ludwig Erhard, 1897-1977, (Ger.) economist, West German chancellor; led nation's economic rise after WW2.

Hamilton Fish, 1808-93, (U.S.) secretary of state, successfully mediated disputes with Great Britain, Latin America.

James V. Forrestal, 1892-1949, (U.S.) secretary of navy, first secretary of defense.

Francisco Franco, 1892-1975, (Sp.) leader of rebel forces during Spanish Civil War and dictator of Spain.

Benjamin Franklin, 1706-90, (U.S.) printer, publisher, author, inventor, scientist, diplomat.

Louis de Frontenac, 1620-98, (Fr.) governor of New France (Canada); encouraged explorations, fought Iroquois.

J. William Fulbright, 1905-95, (U.S.) U.S. senator; leading figure in U.S. foreign policy during cold war years.

Hugh Gaitskell, 1906-63, (Br.) Labor party leader; major force in reversing its stand for unilateral disarmament.

Albert Gallatin, 1761-1849, (U.S.) secretary of treasury who was instrumental in negotiating end of War of 1812.

Léon Gambetta, 1838-82, (Fr.) statesman, politician; one of the founders of the Third Republic.

Indira Gandhi, 1917-84, (In.) daughter of Jawaharlal Nehru, prime min. of India, 1966-77, 1980-84; assassinated.

Mohandas K. Gandhi, 1869-1948, (In.) political leader, ascetic; led movement against British rule; assassinated.

Giuseppe Garibaldi, 1807-82, (It.) patriot, soldier; a leader in the Risorgimento, Italian unification movement.

Genghis Khan, c1167-1227, Mongol conqueror, ruler of vast Asian empire.

William E. Gladstone, 1809-98, (Br.) prime min. 4 times; dominant force of Liberal party from 1868 to 1894.

Paul Joseph Goebbels, 1897-1945, (Ger.) Nazi propagandist, master of mass psychology.

Klement Gottwald, 1896-1953, (Czech.) Communist leader; ushered Communism into his country.

Che (Ernesto) Guevara, 1928-67, (Arg.) guerrilla leader; prominent in Cuban revolution; killed in Bolivia.

Alexander Hamilton, 1755-1804, (U.S.) first treasury secretary; champion of strong central government.

Dag Hammarskjold, 1905-61, (Swed.) statesman; UN secretary-general.

John Hay, 1838-1905, (U.S.) secretary of state; primarily associated with Open Door Policy toward China.

Patrick Henry, 1736-99, (U.S.) major revolutionary figure, remarkable orator.

Édouard Herriot, 1872-1957, (Fr.) Radical Socialist leader; twice prem., pres. of National Assembly.

Theodor Herzl, 1860-1904, (Hung.) founded modern Zionism.

Heinrich Himmler, 1900-45, (Ger.) notorious head of Nazi SS and Gestapo.

Paul von Hindenburg, 1847-1934, (Ger.) field marshal, WW1; 2d pres. of Weimar Republic, 1925-34.

Adolf Hitler, 1889-1945, (Ger.) dictator; wrote *Mein Kampf*, built Nazism, launched WW2, presided over the Holocaust.

Ho Chi Minh, 1890-1969, (Viet.) N Vietnamese pres., Vietnamese Communist leader.

Harry L. Hopkins, 1890-1946, (U.S.) New Deal administrator; closest adviser to FDR during WW2.

Edward M. House, 1858-1938, (U.S.) diplomat; confidential adviser to Woodrow Wilson.

Samuel Houston, 1793-1863, (U.S.) leader of struggle to win control of Texas from Mexico.

Cordell Hull, 1871-1955, (U.S.) secretary of state, 1933-44; initiated reciprocal trade to lower tariffs, helped organize UN.

Hubert H. Humphrey, 1911-78, (U.S.) Minnesota Democrat, senator, vice pres.; spent 32 years in public service.

Jinnah, Muhammad Ali, 1876-1948, (Pak.) founder, first governor-general of Pakistan.

Benito Juarez, 1806-72, (Mex.) rallied his country against foreign threats, sought to create democratic, federal republic.

Frank B. Kellogg, 1856-1937, (U.S.) secretary of state; negotiated Kellogg-Briand Pact to outlaw war.

Robert F. Kennedy, 1925-68, (U.S.) attorney general, senator; assassinated while seeking pres.ial nomination.

Aleksandr Kerensky, 1881-1970, (Russ.) headed provisional government after Feb. 1917 revolution.

Ruhollah Khomeini, 1900-89, (Iranian), religious leader with Islamic title "ayatollah," directed overthrow of shah, 1979.

Nikita Khrushchev, 1894-1971, (USSR) prem., first secretary of Communist party; initiated de-Stalinization.

Kim Il Sung, 1912-94, (Korean) N Korean dictator, 1948-94.

Lajos Kossuth, 1802-94, (Hung.) principal figure in 1848 Hungarian revolution.

Pyotr Kropotkin, 1842-1921, (Russ.) anarchist; championed the peasants but opposed Bolshevism.

Kublai Khan, c1215-94, Mongol emperor; founder of Yüan dynasty in China.

Béla Kun, 1886-c1939, (Hung.) member of 3d Communist Intl., tried to foment worldwide revolution.

Robert M. LaFollette, 1855-1925, (U.S.) Wisconsin public official; leader of progressive movement.

Pierre Laval, 1883-1945, (Fr.) politician, Vichy foreign minister; executed for treason.

Andrew Bonar Law, 1858-1923, (Br.) Conservative party politician; led opposition to Irish home rule.

Vladimir Ilyich Lenin (Ulyanov), 1870-1924, (Russ.) revolutionary; founder of Bolshevism, Soviet leader 1917-24.

Ferdinand de Lesseps, 1805-94, (Fr.) diplomat, engineer; conceived idea of Suez Canal

Rene Levesque, 1922-87, (Can.) prem. of Quebec, 1976-85; led unsuccessful fight to separate from Canada.

Maxim Litvinov, 1876-1951, (Pol.-Russ.) revolutionary, commissar of foreign affairs; favored cooperation with West.

Liu Shaoqi, c1898-1974, (Chin.) Communist leader; fell from grace during Cultural Revolution.

David Lloyd George, 1863-1945, (Br.) Liberal party prime min.; laid foundations for modern welfare state.

Henry Cabot Lodge, 1850-1924, (U.S.) Republican senator; led opposition to participation in League of Nations.

Huey P. Long, 1893-1935, (U.S.) Louisiana political demagogue, governor; assassinated.

Rosa Luxemburg, 1871-1919, (Ger.) revolutionary; leader of the German Social Democratic party and Spartacus party.

J. Ramsay MacDonald, 1866-1937, (Br.) first Labor party prime min. of Great Britain.

Harold Macmillan, 1895-1986, (Br.) prime min. of Great Britain, 1957-63.

Joseph R. McCarthy, 1908-57, (U.S.) senator, extremist in searching out alleged Communists and pro-Communists.

Makarios III, 1913-77, (Cypriot) Greek Orthodox archbishop; first pres. of Cyprus.

Mao Zedong, 1893-1976, (Chin.) chief Chinese Marxist theorist, revolutionary, political leader; led Chinese revolution establishing his nation as Communist state.

Jean Paul Marat, 1743-93, (Fr.) revolutionary, politician; identified with radical Jacobins; assassinated.

José Martí, 1853-95, (Cub.) patriot, poet; leader of Cuban struggle for independence.

Jan Masaryk, 1886-1948, (Czech.) foreign minister; died by mysterious alleged suicide following Communist coup.

Thomas G. Masaryk, 1850-1937, (Czech.) statesman, philosopher; first pres. of Czechoslovak Republic.

Jules Mazarin, 1602-61, (Fr.) cardinal, statesman; prime min. under Louis XIII and queen regent Anne of Austria.

Giuseppe Mazzini, 1805-72, (It.), reformer dedicated to Risorgimento movement for renewal of Italy.

Tom Mboya, 1930-69, (Kenyan) political leader; instrumental in securing independence for Kenya.

Cosimo I de' Medici, 1519-74, (It.) Duke of Florence, grand duke of Tuscany.

Lorenzo de' Medici, the Magnificent, 1449-92, (It.) merchant prince; a towering figure in Italian Renaissance.

Catherine de Médicis, 1519-89, (Fr.) queen consort of Henry II, regent of France; influential in Catholic-Huguenot wars.

Golda Meir, 1898-1978, (Isr.) a founder of the state of Israel and prime min., 1969-74.

Klemens W. N. L. Metternich, 1773-1859, (Austria) statesman; arbiter of post-Napoleonic Europe.

François Mitterrand, 1916-96, (Fr.) pres. of France, 1981-95; proponent of European unity.

Mobutu Sese Seko, 1930-97, (Zaire) president of Zaire (now Congo) (1965-97); exiled after 1997 rebellion.

Guy Mollet, 1905-75, (Fr.) social politician, resistance leader.

Henry Morgenthau Jr., 1891-1967, (U.S.) secy. of treasury; fund-raiser for New Deal and U.S. WW2 activities.

Gouverneur Morris, 1752-1816, (U.S.) statesman, diplomat; financial expert who helped plan decimal coinage system.

Benito Mussolini, 1883-1945, (It.) dictator and leader of the Italian fascist state; assassinated.

Imre Nagy, c1896-1958, (Hung.) Communist prem.; assassinated after Soviets crushed 1956 uprising.

Gamal Abdel Nasser, 1918-70, (Egypt.) leader of Arab unification, 2d Egyptian pres..

Jawaharlal Nehru, 1889-1964, (Indian) prime min.; guided India through its early years of independence.

Kwame Nkrumah, 1909-72, (Ghan.) 1st prime min., 1957-60, and pres., 1960-66, of Ghana.

Frederick North, 1732-92, (Br.) prime min.; his inept policies led to loss of American colonies.

Daniel O'Connell, 1775-1847, (Ir.) political leader; known as The Liberator.

Omar, c581-644, Muslim leader; 2d caliph, led Islam to become an imperial power.

Thomas P. (Tip) O'Neill Jr., 1912-94, (U.S.) U.S. congressman, Speaker of the House, 1977-86.

Ignace Paderewski, 1860-1941, (Pol.) statesman, pianist; composer, briefly prime min., an ardent patriot.

Viscount Palmerston, 1784-1865, (Br.) Whig-Liberal prime min., foreign minister; embodied British nationalism.

Andreas George Papandreou, 1919-1996, (Gk.) leftist politician, served 2 times as prem., (1981-89, 1993-96).

Georgios Papandreou, 1888-1968, (Gk.) Republican politician; served 3 times as prime min..

Franz von Papen, 1879-1969, (Ger.) politician; played major role in overthrow of Weimar Republic and rise of Hitler.

Charles Stewart Parnell, 1846-1891, (Ir.) nationalist leader, "uncrowned king of Ireland."

Lester Pearson, 1897-1972, (Can.) diplomat, Liberal party leader, prime min..

Robert Peel, 1788-1850, (Br.) reformist prime min., founder of Conservative party.

Juan Perón, 1895-1974, (Arg.) pres. of Argentina (1946-55 and 1973-74).

Joseph Pilsudski, 1867-1935, (Pol.) statesman; instrumental in reestablishing Polish state in the 20th cent..

Charles Pinckney, 1757-1824, (U.S.) founding father; his Pinckney plan was largely incorporated into constitution.

Christian Pineau, 1905-95, (Fr.) leader of French Resistance during WW2; French foreign minister, 1956-58.

William Pitt, the Elder, 1708-78, (Br.) statesman; called the "Great Commoner," transformed Britain into imperial power.

William Pitt, the Younger, 1759-1806, (Br.) prime min. during French Revolutionary wars.

Georgi Plekhanov, 1857-1918, (Russ.) revolutionary, social philosopher; called "father of Russian Marxism."

Raymond Poincaré, 1860-1934, (Fr.) 9th pres. of the Republic; advocated harsh punishment of Germany after WW1.

Georges Pompidou, 1911-74, (Fr.) Gaullist political leader; pres. 1969-74.

Grigori Potemkin, 1739-91, (Russ.) field marshal; favorite of Catherine II.

Yitzhak Rabin, 1922-95, (Isr.) military, political leader; prime min. of Israel, 1974-77, 1992-95; assassinated.

Edmund Randolph, 1753-1813, (U.S.) attorney; prominent in drafting, ratification of constitution.

John Randolph, 1773-1833, (U.S.) Southern planter; strong advocate of states' rights.

Jeannette Rankin, 1880-1973, (U.S.) pacifist; first woman member of U.S. Congress.

Walter Rathenau, 1867-1922, (Ger.) industrialist, statesman.

Sam Rayburn, 1882-1961, (U.S.) Democratic leader; representative for 47 years, House Speaker for 17.

Paul Reynaud, 1878-1966, (Fr.) statesman; prem. in 1940 at the time of France's defeat by Germany.

Syngman Rhee, 1875-1965, (Korean) first pres. of S. Korea.

Cecil Rhodes, 1853-1902, (Br.) imperialist, industrial magnate; established Rhodes scholarships in his will

Cardinal de Richelieu, 1585-1642, (Fr.) statesman; known as "red eminence," chief minister to Louis XIII.

Maximilien Robespierre, 1758-94, (Fr.) leading figure in French Revolution, and Reign of Terror.

Nelson Rockefeller, 1908-79, (U.S.) Republican governor of NY, 1959-73; U.S. vice pres., 1974-77.

George W. Romney, 1907-95, (U.S.) pres. of American Motors; 3-term Republican governor of Michigan.

Eleanor Roosevelt, 1884-1962, (U.S.) First Lady, humanitarian, United Nations diplomat.

Elihu Root, 1845-1937, (U.S.) lawyer, statesman, diplomat; leading Republican supporter of the League of Nations.

Dean Rusk, 1909-95, (U.S.) statesman; secretary of state, 1961-69, during Vietnam War.

John Russell, 1792-1878, (Br.) Liberal prime min. during the Irish potato famine.

Anwar al-Sadat, 1918-81, (Egypt.) pres., 1970-1981, promoted peace with Israel; nobel laureate; assassinated.

António de Salazar, 1889-1970, (Port.) longtime dictator.

José de San Martin, 1778-1850, South Amer. Rev.ary; protector of Peru.

Eisaku Sato, 1901-75, (Jpn.) prime min.; presided over Japan's post-WW2 emergence as major world power.

Abdul Aziz Ibn Saud, c1880-1953, king of Saudi Arabi, 1932-53.

Philipp Scheidemann, 1865-1939, (Ger.) Social Democratic leader; first chancellor of the German republic.

Robert Schuman, 1886-1963, (Fr.) statesman; founded European Coal and Steel Community.

Carl Schurz, 1829-1906, (U.S.) German-American political leader, journalist, orator, dedicated reformer.

Kurt Schuschnigg, 1897-1977, (Aust.) chancellor; unsuccessful in stopping his country's annexation by Germany.

William H. Seward, 1801-72, (U.S.) anti-slavery activist; as U.S. secretary of state purchased Alaska.

Carlo Sforza, 1872-1952, (It.) foreign minister, anti-fascist.

Sitting Bull, c1831-90, (Nat. Am.) Sioux leader in Battle of Little Bighorn over George A. Custer, 1876.

Alfred E. Smith, 1873-1944, (U.S.) New York Democratic governor; first Roman Catholic to run for presidency.

Margaret Chase Smith, 1897-1995, (U.S.) congresswoman, senator; 1st woman elected to both houses of Congress.

Jan C. Smuts, 1870-1950, (S. African) statesman, philosopher, soldier, prime min..

Paul Henri Spaak, 1899-1972, (Belg.) statesman, socialist leader.

Joseph Stalin, 1879-1953, (USSR) Soviet dictator, 1924-53; instituted forced collectivization, massive purges, and labor camps, causing millions of deaths.

Edwin M. Stanton, 1814-69, (U.S.) secretary of war, 1862-68, during the Civil War.

Edward R. Stettinius Jr., 1900-49, (U.S.) industrialist, secretary of state who coordinated aid to WW2 allies.

Adlai E. Stevenson, 1900-65, (U.S.) Democratic leader, diplomat, Illinois governor, pres.ial candidate.

Henry L. Stimson, 1867-1950, (U.S.) statesman; served in 5 administrations, foreign policy adviser in 30s and 40s.

Gustav Stresemann, 1878-1929, (Ger.) chancellor, foreign minister; strove to regain friendship for post-WW1 Germany.

Sukarno, 1901-70, (Indon.) dictatorial first pres. of the Indonesian republic.

Sun Yat-sen, 1866-1925, (Chin.) revolutionary; leader of Kuomintang, regarded as the father of modern China.

Robert A. Taft, 1889-1953, (U.S.) conservative Senate leader, called "Mr. Republican."

Charles de Talleyrand, 1754-1838, (Fr.) statesman, diplomat; the major force of the Congress of Vienna of 1814-15.

U Thant, 1909-74 (Bur.) statesman, UN secretary-general.

Norman M. Thomas, 1884-1968, (U.S.) social reformer; 6 times unsuccessful Socialist party pres.ial candidate.

Josip Broz Tito, 1892-1980, (Yug.) pres. of Yugoslavia from 1953, WW2 guerrilla chief, postwar rival of Stalin.

Imiro Togliatti, 1893-1964, (It.) major leader of Italian Communist party.

Hideki Tojo, 1885-1948, (Jpn.) statesman, soldier; prime min. during most of WW2.

François Toussaint L'Ouverture, c1744-1803, (Haitian) patriot, martyr; thwarted French colonial aims.

Leon Trotsky, 1879-1940, (Russ.) revolutionary, founded Red Army, expelled from party in conflict with Stalin; assassinated.

Rafael L. Trujillo Molina, 1891-1961, (Dom.) dictator of Dominican Republic, 1930-61; assassinated.

Moise K. Tshombe, 1919-69, (Cong.) pres. of secessionist Katanga, prem. of Congo (later Zaire).

William M. Tweed, 1823-78, (U.S.) politician; absolute leader of Tammany Hall, NYC's Democratic political machine.

Walter Ulbricht, 1893-1973, (Ger.) Communist leader of German Democratic Republic.

Arthur H. Vandenberg, 1884-1951, (U.S.) senator; proponent of anti-Communist bipartisan foreign policy after WW2.

Eleutherios Venizelos, 1864-1936, (Gk.) most prominent Greek statesman in early 20th cent.; expanded territory.

Hendrik F. Verwoerd, 1901-66, (S. African) prime min.; rigorously applied apartheid policy despite protest.

Robert Walpole, 1676-1745, (Br.) statesman; generally considered Britain's first prime min..

Daniel Webster, 1782-1852, (U.S.) orator, politician; advocate of business interests during Jacksonian agrarianism.

Chaim Weizmann, 1874-1952, (Russ.-Isr.) Zionist leader, scientist; first Israeli pres..

Wendell L. Willkie, 1892-1944, (U.S.) Republican who tried to unseat FDR when he ran for his 3d term.

Harold Wilson, 1916-95, (Br.) Labor party leader; prime min., 1964-70, 1974-76.

Emiliano Zapata, c1879-1919, (Mex.) revolutionary; major influence on modern Mexico.

Zhou Enlai, 1898-1976, (Chin.) diplomat, prime min.; a leading figure of the Chinese Communist party.

Noted Scientists of the Past

For pre-modern scientists see also Noted Philosophers, pp. 343-44, and Historical Figures chapter.

Howard H. Aiken, 1900-73, (U.S.) mathematician; credited with designing forerunner of digital computer.

Albertus Magnus, 1193-1280, (Ger.) theologian, philosopher; established medieval Christian study of natural science.

Alhazen (Ibn al-Haytham), 965-1040, mathematician, astronomer, theorist in optics.

Andre-Marie Ampère, 1775-1836, (Fr.) scientist known for contributions to electrodynamics.

Amedeo Avogadro, 1776-1856, (It.) chemist, physicist; advanced important theories on properties of gases.

John V. Atanasoff, 1903-95, (U.S.) physicist and co-inventor with Clifford Berry of first electronically digital computer, the Atanasoff-Berry Computer (ABC).

John Bardeen, 1908-91, (U.S.) co-inventor of the transistor.

A. C. Becquerel, 1788-1878, (Fr.) physicist; pioneer in electro-chemical science.

A. H. Becquerel, 1852-1908, (Fr.) physicist; discovered radioactivity in uranium.

Alexander Graham Bell, 1847-1922, (U.S.) inventor; first to patent and commercially exploit the telephone, 1876.

Daniel Bernoulli, 1700-82, (Swiss) mathematician; advanced kinetic theory of gases and fluids.

Clifford Berry, 1918-1963, (U.S.) co-inventor with John V. Atanasoff of the first electronically digital computer, the ABC.

Jöns Jakob Berzelius, 1779-1848, (Swed.) chemist; developed modern chemical symbols and formulas.

Henry Bessemer, 1813-98, (Br.) engineer; invented Bessemer steel-making process.

Louis Blériot, 1872-1936, (Fr.) engineer; pioneer aviator, invented and constructed monoplanes.

Niels Bohr, 1885-1962, (Dan.) physicist; leading figure in the development of quantum theory.

Max Born, 1882-1970, (Ger.) physicist known for research in quantum mechanics.

Satyendranath Bose, 1894-1974, (In.) physicist, chemist, mathematician; forerunner of modern quantum theory.

Walter Brattain, 1902-87, (U.S.) inventor; worked on invention of transistor.

Louis de Broglie, 1893-1987, (Fr.) physicist; best known for wave theory.

Robert Bunsen, 1811-99, (Ger.) chemist; invented Bunsen burner.

Luther Burbank, 1849-1926, (U.S.) plant breeder whose work developed plant breeding into a modern science.

Vannevar Bush, 1890-1974, (U.S.) electrical engineer; developed differential analyzer, 1st electronic analogue computer.

Marvin Camras, 1916-95, (U.S.) inventor, electrical engineer; invented magnetic tape recording.

Alexis Carrel, 1873-1944, (Fr.) surgeon, biologist; developed methods of suturing blood vessels and transplanting organs.

Rachel Carson, 1907-64, (U.S.) marine biologist; spurred concern for environment with *The Sea Around Us* (1951).

George Washington Carver, 1864-1943, (U.S.) botanist, chemist, and educator.

Henry Cavendish, 1731-1810, (Br.) chemist, physicist; discovered hydrogen.

James Chadwick, 1891-1974, (Br.) physicist; discovered the neutron.

Darly Chapin, 1906-95, (U.S.) physicist; co-developer of the solar energy cell.

Jean M. Charcot, 1825-93, (Fr.) neurologist known for work on hysteria, hypnotism, sclerosis.

Albert Claude, 1899-1983, (Belg.) a founder of modern cell biology.

John D. Cockcroft, 1897-1967, (Br.) nuclear physicist; with E. T. S. Walton constructed first atomic particle accelerator.

Nicolaus Copernicus, 1473-1543, (Pol.) astronomer who first postulated heliocentric solar system.

Jacques Yves Cousteau, 1910-1997, (Fr.) naval officer and marine explorer; co-inventor of the "Aqualung".

Seymour Cray, 1925-96, (U.S.) computer industry pioneer; developed supercomputers.

William Crookes, 1832-1919, (Br.) physicist, chemist; discovered thallium, invented a cathode-ray tube, radiometer.

Marie Curie, 1867-1934, (Pol.-Fr.) physical chemist known for work on radium and its compounds.

Pierre Curie, 1859-1906, (Fr.) physical chemist known for work, with his wife Marie, on radioactivity.

Gottlieb Daimler, 1834-1900, (Ger.) engineer, inventor; pioneer automobile manufacturer.

John Dalton, 1766-1844, (Br.) chemist, physicist; formulated atomic theory, made first table of atomic weights.

Charles Darwin, 1809-82, (Br.) naturalist; established theory of organic evolution; *Origin of Species.*

Humphry Davy, 1778-1829, (Br.) chemist; research in electrochemistry led to isolation of potassium, sodium, calcium, barium, boron, magnesium, and strontium.

Lee De Forest, 1873-1961, (U.S.) inventor; pioneer in development of wireless telegraphy, sound pictures, television.

Max Delbruck, 1907-81, (U.S.) pioneer in modern molecular genetics.

Rudolf Diesel, 1858-1913, (Ger.) mechanical engineer; patented Diesel engine.

Christian Doppler, 1803-53, (Aust.) physicist; showed change in energy wavelengths caused by motion, Doppler effect.

J. Presper Eckert Jr., 1919-95, (U.S.) co-inventor with John W. Mauchly of the first large-scale digital computer, the Eniac.

Thomas A. Edison, 1847-1931, (U.S.) inventor; held more than 1,000 patents, including incandescent electric lamp.

Paul Ehrlich, 1854-1915, (Ger.) bacteriologist; pioneer in modern immunology and bacteriology.

Albert Einstein, 1879-1955, (Ger.-U.S.) theoretical physicist; known for formulation of relativity theory.

John F. Enders, 1897-1985, (U.S.) virologist who helped discover vaccines against polio, measles, and mumps.

Leonhard Euler, 1707-83, (Swiss) mathematician, physicist; authored first calculus book.

Gabriel Fahrenheit, 1686-1736, (Ger.) physicist; introduced Fahrenheit scale for thermometers.

Michael Faraday, 1791-1867, (Br.) chemist, physicist; known for work in field of electricity.

Philo T. Farnsworth, 1906-71, (U.S.) made key contributions to electronic television including the image dissector tube.

Pierre de Fermat, 1601-65, (Fr.) mathematician; founded modern theory of numbers and calculus of probabilities.

Enrico Fermi, 1901-54, (It.-U.S.) physicist; one of primary architects of the nuclear age.

Galileo Ferraris, 1847-97, (It.) physicist; electrical engineer, discovered principle of rotary magnetic field.

Richard Feynman, 1918-88, (U.S.) a leading theoretical physicist; also a popular writer.

Camille Flammarion, 1842-1925, (Fr.) astronomer; popularized study of astronomy.

Alexander Fleming, 1881-1955, (Br.) bacteriologist; discovered penicillin.

Jean B. J. Fourier, 1768-1830, (Fr.) mathematician; discovered theorem governing periodic oscillation.

James Franck, 1882-1964, (Ger.) physicist; proved value of quantum theory.

Sigmund Freud, 1856-1939, (Austrian) psychiatrist; founder of psychoanalysis.

Galileo Galilei, 1564-1642, (It.) astronomer, physicist; a founder of the experimental method.

Luigi Galvani, 1737-98, (It.) physician, physicist; known as founder of galvanism.

Carl Friedrich Gauss, 1777-1855, (Ger.) mathematician, astronomer, physicist.

Joseph Gay-Lussac, 1778-1850, (Fr.) chemist, physicist; investigated behavior of gases; law of combining volumes.

Josiah W. Gibbs, 1839-1903, (U.S.) theoretical physicist, chemist; founded chemical thermodynamics.

Robert H. Goddard, 1882-1945, (U.S.) physicist; father of modern rocketry.

George W. Goethals, 1858-1928, (U.S.) army engineer; built Panama Canal.

William C. Gorgas, 1854-1920, (U.S.) sanitarian, U.S. army surgeon-general; his work to prevent yellow fever, malaria helped ensure construction of Panama Canal.

Ernest Haeckel, 1834-1919, (Ger.) zoologist, evolutionist; a strong proponent of Darwin.

Otto Hahn, 1879-1968, (Ger.) chemist; worked on atomic fission.

J. B. S. Haldane, 1892-1964, (Br.) scientist; known for work as geneticist and application of mathematics to science.

James Hall, 1761-1832, (Br.) geologist, chemist; founded experimental geology, geochemistry.

Edmund Halley, 1656-1742, (Br.) astronomer; calculated the orbits of many planets.

William Harvey, 1578-1657, (Eng.) physician, anatomist; discovered circulation of the blood.

Werner Heisenberg, 1901-76, (Ger.) physicist; developed matrix mechanics and uncertainty principle.

Hermann von Helmholtz, 1821-94, (Ger.) physicist, anatomist, physiologist.

William Herschel, 1738-1822, (Br.) astronomer; discovered Uranus.

Heinrich Hertz, 1857-94, (Ger.) physicist; his discoveries led to wireless telegraphy.

David Hilbert, 1862-1943, (Ger.) mathematician; formulated 1st satisfactory set of axioms for modern Euclidean geometry.

Edwin P. Hubble, 1889-1953, (U.S.) astronomer; produced first observational evidence of expanding universe.

Alexander von Humboldt, 1769-1859, (Ger.) explorer, naturalist, earth scientist; originated ecology, geophysics.

Julian Huxley, 1887-1975, (Br.) biologist; a gifted exponent and philosopher of science.

Edward Jenner, 1749-1823, (Br.) physician; discovered vaccination.

William Jenner, 1815-98, (Br.) physician, pathological anatomist.

Frederic Joliot-Curie, 1900-58, (Fr.) physicist; with his wife continued work of Curies on radioactivity.

Irene Joliot-Curie, 1897-1956, (Fr.) physicist; continued work of Curies in radioactivity.

James P. Joule, 1818-89, (Br.) physicist; determined relation. between heat and mech. energy (conservation of energy).

Carl Jung, 1875-1961, (Swiss) psychiatrist; founder of analytical psychology.

William Thomson Kelvin, 1824-1907, (Br.) mathematician, physicist; known for work on heat and electricity.

Sister Elizabeth Kenny, 1886-1952, (Austral.) nurse; developed method of treatment for polio.

Johannes Kepler, 1571-1630, (Ger.) astronomer; discovered important laws of planetary motion.

Al-Khowarizmi, early 9th cent., (Arab.), mathematician.

Georges Köhler, 1946-95, (Ger.) immunologist; co-inventor of monoclonal antibody technique.

Joseph Lagrange, 1736-1813, (Fr.) geometer, astronomer; number theorist, analytical and celestial mechanics.

Jean B. Lamarck, 1744-1829, (Fr.) naturalist; forerunner of Darwin in evolutionary theory.

Edwin Land, 1910-91, (U.S.) invented Polaroid camera.

Irving Langmuir, 1881-1957, (U.S.) physical chemist; colloid research and biochemistry.

Pierre S. Laplace, 1749-1827, (Fr.) astronomer, physicist; put forth nebular hypothesis of origin of solar system.

Antoine Lavoisier, 1743-94, (Fr.) chemist; founder of modern chemistry.

Ernest O. Lawrence, 1901-58, (U.S.) physicist; invented the cyclotron.

Jerome Lejeune, 1927-94, (Fr.) geneticist; discovered the cause of Down's syndrome.

Louis 1903-72, and **Mary Leakey,** 1913-96, (Br.) early hominid paleoanthropologists; discovered remains in Africa.

Anton van Leeuwenhoek, 1632-1723, (Dutch) microscopist; father of microbiology.

Justus von Liebig, 1803-73, (Ger.) chemist; established quantitative organic chemical analysis.

Joseph Lister, 1827-1912, (Br.) pioneered antiseptic surgery.

Percival Lowell, 1855-1916, (U.S.) astronomer; predicted the existence of Pluto.

Louis, 1864-1984, and **Auguste Lumière,** 1862-1954, (Fr.) invented cinematograph.

Guglielmo Marconi, 1874-1937, (It.) physicist; known for his development of wireless telegraphy.

John W. Mauchly, 1908-80, (U.S.) co-inventor with J. Presper Eckert of the first large-scale digital computer, the Eniac.

James Clerk Maxwell, 1831-79, (Br.) physicist; known especially for his work in electricity and magnetism.

Maria Goeppert Mayer, 1906-72, (Ger.-U.S.) physicist; independently developed theory of structure of atomic nuclei.

Barbara McClintock, 1902-92, (U.S.) geneticist; significant studies in the nature of mobile genetic elements.

Lise Meitner, 1878-1968, (Austrian) physicist whose work contributed to the development of the atomic bomb.

Gregor J. Mendel, 1822-84, (Austrian) botanist, monk; his experimental work was the cornerstone of modern genetics.

Dmitri Mendeleyev, 1834-1907, (Russ.) chemist; developed first successful Periodic Table of the Elements.

Franz Mesmer, 1734-1815, (Ger.) physician; developed theory of animal magnetism.

Albert A. Michelson, 1852-1931, (U.S.) physicist; established speed of light as a fundamental constant.

Robert A. Millikan, 1868-1953, (U.S.) physicist; studied elementary electronic charge and photoelectric effect.

Thomas Hunt Morgan, 1866-1945, (U.S.) geneticist, embryologist; established chromosome theory of heredity.

Isaac Newton, 1642-1727, (Eng.) natural philosopher, mathematician; discovered law of gravitation, laws of motion.

Robert N. Noyce, 1927-89, (U.S.) inventor of the microchip, which revolutionized the electronics industry.

J. Robert Oppenheimer, 1904-67, (U.S.) physicist; director of Los Alamos during development of the atomic bomb.

Wilhelm Ostwald, 1853-1932, (Ger.) physical chemist, philosopher; primary founder of physical chemistry.

Robert Morris Page, 1903-92, (U.S.) physicist; a leading figure in development of radar technology.

Louis Pasteur, 1822-95, (Fr.) chemist; originated process of pasteurization.

Clair C. Patterson, 1922-95, (U.S.) geochemist; made first accurate determination of Earth's age, 4.6 bil years.

Linus C. Pauling, 1901-94, (U.S.) chemist; specializing in chemical bonds; political activist.

Max Planck, 1858-1947, (Ger.) physicist; originated and developed quantum theory.

Roy J. Plunkett, 1922-94, (U.S.) chemist; created Teflon ™.

Henri Poincaré, 1854-1912, (Fr.) mathematician, physicist; influenced cosmology, relativity, and topology.

Joseph Priestley, 1733-1804, (Br.) chemist; one of the discoverers of oxygen.

Isidor Isaac Rabi, 1899-1988, (U.S.) physicist; pioneered atom exploration.

Walter S. Reed, 1851-1902, (U.S.) army pathologist, bacteriologist; proved mosquitoes transmit yellow fever.

Bernhard Riemann, 1826-66, (Ger.) mathematician; aidedto development of calculus and mathematical physics.

Wilhelm Roentgen, 1845-1923, (Ger.) physicist; discovered the X ray.

Ernest Rutherford, 1871-1937, (Br.) physicist; discovered the atomic nucleus.

Albert B. Sabin, 1906-93, (Russ.-U.S.), developed oral polio live-virus vaccine (1954), which was licensed in 1961.

Carl Sagan, 1934-96, (U.S.) astronomer, science writer and popularizer.

Jonas Salk, 1914-95, (U.S.) developed the first successful polio vaccine, which came into widespread use in 1950s.

Giovanni Schiaparelli, 1835-1910, (It.) astronomer; hypothesized canals on the surface of Mars.

Angelo Secchi, 1818-78, (It.) astronomer; pioneer in classifying stars by their spectra.

Harlow Shapley, 1885-1972, (U.S.) astronomer; noted for his studies of the galaxy.

Eugen Shoemaker, 1928-97, (U.S.) planetary geologist; noted for his discovery of comets, maily Shoemaker-Levy (1993).

Roger Sperry, 1913-94, (U.S.) brain expert; studied relationship between the right and left sides of the brain.

Charles P. Steinmetz, 1865-1923, (Ger.-U.S.) electrical engineer; developed basic ideas on alternating current.

Frederick Stewart, 1904-93, (Br.) botanist, cell biologist; studies considered foundations of molecular biology.

George Stibitz, 1904-95. (U.S.), invented first digital computer.

Leo Szilard, 1898-1964, (Hung.-U.S.) physicist; helped create first sustained nuclear reaction.

Nikola Tesla, 1856-1943, (Serb.-U.S.) electrical engineer; contributed to most developments in electronics.

Rudolf Virchow, 1821-1902, (Ger.) pathologist; a founder of cellular pathology.

Alessandro Volta, 1745-1827, (It.) physicist; pioneer in electricity.

Werner von Braun, 1912-77, (Ger.-U.S.) pioneered development of rockets for warfare and space exploration.

Alfred Russell Wallace, 1823-1913, (Br.) naturalist; proposed concept of evolution similar to Darwin's.

August von Wasserman, 1866-1925, (Ger.) bacteriologist; discovered reaction used as test for syphilis.

James E. Watt, 1736-1819, (Br.) mechanical engineer, inventor; invented modern steam-condensing engine.

Alfred L. Wegener, 1880-1930, (Ger.) meteorologist, geophysicist; postulated theory of continental drift.

Norbert Wiener, 1894-1964, (U.S.) mathematician; founder of the science of cybernetics.

Eugene Wigner, 1902-95, (U.S.) quantum theorist, nuclear physicist; helped perfect world's first nuclear reactor.

Sewall Wright, 1889-1988, (U.S.) evolutionary theorist.

Ferdinand von Zeppelin, 1838-1917, (Ger.) soldier, aeronaut, airship designer.

Noted Social Reformers, Humanitarians, and Educators of the Past

Jane Addams, 1860-1935, (U.S.) cofounder of Hull House; won Nobel Peace Prize, 1931.

Susan B. Anthony, 1820-1906, (U.S.) a leader in temperance, anti-slavery, and woman suffrage movements.

Henry Barnard, 1811-1900, (U.S.) public school reformer.

Thomas Barnardo, 1845-1905, (Br.) social reformer; pioneered in care of destitute children.

Clara Barton, 1821-1912, (U.S.) organizer of the American Red Cross.

Henry Ward Beecher, 1813-87, (U.S.) clergyman, abolitionist.

Sarah G. Blanding, 1899-1985, (U.S.) head of Vassar College, 1946-64.

Amelia Bloomer, 1818-94, (U.S.) suffragette, social reformer.

William Booth, 1829-1912, (Br.) founded Salvation Army.

John Brown, 1800-59, (U.S.) abolitionist who led murder of 5 pro-slavery men, was hanged.

Nicholas Murray Butler, 1862-1947, (U.S.) educator; headed Columbia Univ., 1902-45; Nobel Peace Prize, 1931.

Frances X. (Mother) Cabrini, 1850-1917, (It.-U.S.) Italian-born nun; founded charitable institutions; first American canonized as a saint, 1946.

Carrie Chapman Catt, 1859-1947, (U.S.) suffragette; helped win passage of the 19th amendment.

Cesar Chavez, 1927-93, (U.S.) labor leader; helped establish United Farm Workers of America.

Clarence Darrow, 1857-1938, (U.S.) lawyer; defender of "underdog," opponent of capital punishment.

Dorothy Day, 1897-1980, (U.S.) founder of Catholic Worker movement.

Eugene V. Debs, 1855-1926, (U.S.) labor leader; led Pullman strike, 1894; 4-time Socialist presidential candidate.

Melvil Dewey, 1851-1931, (U.S.) devised decimal system of library-book classification.

Dorothea Dix, 1802-87, (U.S.) crusader for the mentally ill.

Thomas Dooley, 1927-61, (U.S.) "jungle doctor," noted for efforts to supply medical aid to developing countries.

William Lloyd Garrison, 1805-79, (U.S.) abolitionist.

Giovanni Gentile, 1875-1944, (It.) philosopher, educator; reformed Italian educational system.

Emma Goldman, 1869-1940, (Russ.-U.S.) published anarchist *Mother Earth,* birth-control advocate.

Samuel Gompers, 1850-1924, (U.S.) labor leader.

Michael Harrington, 1928-89, (U.S.) exposed poverty in affluent U.S. in *The Other America,* 1963.

Sidney Hillman, 1887-1946, (U.S.) labor leader; helped organize CIO.

John Holt, 1924-85, (U.S.) educator and author.

Samuel G. Howe, 1801-76, (U.S.) social reformer; changed public attitudes toward the handicapped.

Helen Keller, 1880-1968, (U.S.) crusader for better treatment for the handicapped; deaf and blind herself.

Maggie Kuhn, 1905-95, (U.S.) founded Gray Panthers, 1970.

William Kunstler, 1919-95, (U.S.) civil liberties attorney.

John L. Lewis, 1880-1969, (U.S.) labor leader; headed United Mine Workers, 1920-60.

Horace Mann, 1796-1859, (U.S.) pioneered modern public school system.

William H. McGuffey, 1800-73, (U.S.) whose *Reader* was a mainstay of 19th-cent. U.S. public education.

Alexander Meiklejohn, 1872-1964, (U.S.) Br.-born educator; championed academic freedom and experimental curricula.

Karl Menninger, 1893-1990, (U.S.) with brother William found Menninger Clinic, and Menninger Foundation in Topeka, KS.

Maria Montessori, 1870-1952, (It.) educator, physician; originated Montessori method of student self-motivation.

Lucretia Mott, 1793-1880, (U.S.) reformer, pioneer feminist.

Philip Murray, 1886-1952, (U.S.) Scottish-born labor leader.

Florence Nightingale, 1820-1910, (Br.) founder of modern nursing.

Emmeline Pankhurst, 1858-1928, (Br.) woman suffragist.

Elizabeth P. Peabody, 1804-94, (U.S.) education pioneer; founded 1st kindergarten in U.S., 1860.

Walter Reuther, 1907-70, (U.S.) labor leader; headed UAW.

Jacob Riis, 1849-1914, (U.S.) crusader for urban reforms.

Margaret Sanger, 1883-1966, (U.S.) social reformer; pioneered the birth-control movement.

Elizabeth Seton, 1774-1821, (U.S.) nun; est. parochial school education in U.S.; first native-born American saint.

Earl of Shaftesbury (A. A. Cooper), 1801-85, (Br.) social reformer.

Elizabeth Cady Stanton, 1815-1902, (U.S.) woman suffrage pioneer.

Lucy Stone, 1818-93, (U.S.) feminist, abolitionist.

Mother Teresa of Calcutta, 1910-97, (Albanian) Rom. Catholic nun who founded Missionaries of Charity to care for the sick and dying poor; won 1979 Nobel Peace Prize.

Philip Vera Cruz, 1905-94, (Filipino-U.S.) helped to found the United Farm Workers Union.

William Wilberforce, 1759-1833, (Br.) social reformer; prominent in struggle to abolish the slave trade.

Emma Hart Willard, 1787-1870, (U.S.) pioneered higher education for women.

Frances E. Willard, 1839-98, (U.S.) temperance, women's rights leader.

Mary Wollstonecraft, 1759-97, (Br.) wrote *Vindication of the Rights of Women*.

Notable Writers of the Present

Name (Birthplace)	Birthdate	Name (Birthplace)	Birthdate
Chinua Achebe (Ogidi, Nigeria)	11/16/30	Garrison Keillor (Anoka, MN)	8/7/42
Alice Adams (Fredericksburg, VA)	8/14/26	William Kennedy (Albany, NY)	1/16/28
Edward Albee (Wash., DC)	3/12/28	Stephen King (Portland, ME)	9/21/47
Jorge Amado (Bahia, Brazil)	8/1/12	Barbara Kingsolver (Annapolis, MD)	4/8/55
Martin Amis (Oxford, Eng.)	8/25/49	Maxine Hong Kingston (Stockton, CA)	10/27/40
Maya Angelou (St. Louis, MO)	4/4/28	Galway Kinnell (Providence, RI)	2/1/27
Oscar Arias Sanchez (Heredia, Costa Rica)	9/13/41	John Knowles (Fairmont, WV)	9/16/26
John Ashbery (Rochester, NY)	1927	Kenneth Koch (Cincinnati, OH)	2/27/25
Margaret Atwood (Ottawa, Ont.)	11/18/39	Dean Koontz (Everett, PA)	7/9/45
Louis Auchincloss (Lawrence, NY)	9/27/17	Judith Krantz (NYC)	1/9/28
John Barth (Cambridge, MD)	5/27/30	Maxine Kumin (Philadelphia, PA)	6/6/25
Ann Beattie (Wash., DC)	9/7/47	John Le Carré (Poole, Eng.)	10/19/31
Saul Bellow (Lachine, Que.)	7/10/15	Ursula LeGuin (Berkeley, CA)	10/21/29
Peter Benchley (NYC)	5/8/40	Madeleine L'Engle (NYC)	11/29/18
Thomas Berger (Cincinnati, OH)	7/20/24	Elmore Leonard (New Orleans, LA)	10/11/25
Judy Blume (Elizabeth, NJ)	2/12/38	Doris Lessing (Kermanshah, Persia)	10/22/19
Ray Bradbury (Waukegan, IL)	8/22/20	Ira Levin (NYC)	8/27/29
Barbara Taylor Bradford (Leeds, Eng.)	5/10/33	Robert Ludlum (NYC)	5/25/27
Gwendolyn Brooks (Topeka, KS)	6/7/17	Alison Lurie (Chicago, IL)	9/3/26
Hortense Calisher (NYC)	12/20/11	Nagib Mahfuz (Cairo, Egypt)	12/11/11
Tom Clancy (Baltimore, MD)	1947	Norman Mailer (Long Branch, NJ)	1/31/23
Mary Higgins Clark (NYC)	12/24/31	David Mamet (Chicago, IL)	11/30/47
Beverly Cleary (McMinnville, OR)	4/12/16	Bobbie Ann Mason (nr. Mayfield, KY)	5/1/40
Evan S. Connell (Kansas City, MO)	8/17/24	Cormac McCarthy (Providence, RI)	7/20/33
Pat Conroy (Atlanta, GA)	10/26/45	Frrank McCourt (Brooklyn, NY)	1930
Robin Cook (NYC)	5/4/40	Colleen McCullough (Wellington, N.S.W.)	6/1/37
Harry Crews (Alma, GA)	6/6/35	Thomas McGuane (Wyandotte, MI)	12/11/39
Michael Crichton (Chicago, IL)	10/23/42	Larry McMurtry (Wichita Falls, TX)	6/3/36
Janet Dailey (Storm Lake, IA)	5/21/44	James A. Michener (NYC)	2/3/07
Joan Didion (Sacramento, CA)	12/5/34	Arthur Miller (NYC)	10/17/15
E. L. Doctorow (NYC)	1/6/31	Wright Morris (Central City, NE)	1/6/10
Takako Doi (Hyogo, Jap.)	11/30/28	Toni Morrison (Lorain, OH)	2/18/31
Rita Dove (Akron, OH)	8/28/52	Alice Munro (Wingham, Ont.)	7/10/31
John Gregory Dunne (Hartford, CT)	5/25/32	Iris Murdoch (Dublin, Ire.)	7/15/19
Louise Erdrich (Little Falls, MN)	7/6/54	V. S. Naipaul (Port-of-Spain, Trin.)	8/17/32
Laura Esquivel (Mexico City, Mexico)	1950	Joyce Carol Oates (Lockport, NY)	6/16/38
Howard Fast (NYC)	11/11/14	Tim O'Brien (Austin, MN)	10/1/46
Horton Foote (Wharton, TX)	3/14/16	Cynthia Ozick (NYC)	4/17/28
Frederick Forsyth (Ashford, Eng.)	1938	Grace Paley (NYC)	12/11/22
Paula Fox (NYC)	4/22/23	Octavio Paz (Mexico City, Mex.)	3/31/14
Marilyn French (NYC)	11/21/29	Marge Piercy (Detroit, MI)	3/31/36
Carlos Fuentes (Mexico City, Mex.)	11/11/28	Robert Pinsky (Long Branch, NJ)	10/20/40
Charles Fuller (Philadelphia, PA)	3/5/39	Chaim Potok (NYC)	2/17/29
William Gaddis (NYC)	1922	Reynolds Price (Macon, NC)	2/1/33
Gabriel Garcia Marquez (Aracata, Colombia)	3/6/28	E. Annie Proulx (Norwich, CT)	8/22/35
Frank Gilroy (NYC)	10/13/25	Mario Puzo (NYC)	10/15/20
Gail Godwin (Birmingham, AL)	6/18/37	Thomas Pynchon (Glen Cove, NY)	5/8/37
William Goldman (Chicago, IL)	8/12/31	David Rabe (Dubuque, IA)	3/10/40
Nadine Gordimer (Springs, S. Africa)	11/20/23	Ishmael Reed (Chattanooga, TN)	2/22/38
Mary Gordon (Long Island, NY)	12/8/49	Anne Rice (New Orleans, LA)	10/14/41
Sue Grafton (Louisville, KY)	4/24/40	Adrienne Rich (Baltimore, MD)	5/16/29
Günter Grass (Danzig, Ger.)	10/16/27	Philip Roth (Newark, NJ)	3/19/33
Shirley Ann Grau (New Orleans, LA)	7/8/29	Salman Rushdie (Bombay, India)	6/19/47
John Grisham (Jonesboro, AR)	2/8/55	J. D. Salinger (NYC)	1/1/19
John Guare (NYC)	2/5/38	Lawrence Sanders (NYC)	1920
Arthur Hailey (Luton, Eng.)	4/5/20	Maurice Sendak (NYC)	6/10/28
Robert Hass (San Francisco, CA)	1941	Sidney Sheldon (Chicago, IL)	2/11/17
Vaclav Havel (Prague, Czech.)	10/5/36	Sam Shepard (Ft. Sheridan, IL)	11/5/43
John Hawkes (Stamford, CT)	8/17/25	Carol Shields (Oak Park, IL)	6/2/35
Joseph Heller (Brooklyn, NY)	5/1/23	Shel Silverstein (Chicago, IL)	1932
Mark Helprin (NYC)	6/28/47	Neil Simon (NYC)	7/4/27
S. E. Hinton (Tulsa, OK)	1948	Jane Smiley (Los Angeles, CA)	9/26/49
Ted Hughes (Mytholmroyd, Eng.)	8/17/30	Aleksandr Solzhenitsyn (Kislovodsk, Russia)	12/11/10
John Irving (Exeter, NH)	3/2/42	Wole Soyinka (Abeokuta, Nigeria)	7/13/34
John Jakes (Chicago, IL)	3/31/32	Mickey Spillane (Brooklyn, NY)	3/9/18
P. D. James (Oxford, Eng.)	8/3/20	Danielle Steel (NYC)	8/14/47
Erica Jong (NYC)	3/26/42		

Name (Birthplace)	Birthdate	Name (Birthplace)	Birthdate
Richard Stern, (NYC)	2/25/28	Kurt Vonnegut Jr. (Indianapolis, IN)	11/11/22
Mary Stewart (Sunderland, Eng.)	9/17/16	Alice Walker (Eatonton, GA)	2/9/44
Robert Stone (Brooklyn, NY)	8/21/37	Robert James Waller (Rockford, IA)	8/1/39
Tom Stoppard (Zlin, Czech.)	7/13/37	Joseph Wambaugh (East Pittsburgh, PA)	1/22/37
William Styron (Newport News, VA)	6/11/25	Wendy Wasserstein (NYC)	10/10/50
Amy Tan (Oakland, CA)	2/19/52	Eudora Welty (Jackson, MS)	4/13/09
Paul Theroux (Medford, MA)	4/10/41	John Edgar Wideman (Pittsburgh, PA)	6/14/41
Scott F. Turow (Chicago, IL)	4/12/49	August Wilson (Pittsburgh, PA)	4/27/45
Anne Tyler (Minneapolis, MN)	10/25/41	Lanford Wilson (Lebanon, MO)	4/13/37
John Updike (Shillington, PA)	3/18/32	Tom Wolfe (Richmond, VA)	3/2/31
Leon Uris (Baltimore, MD)	8/3/24	Tobias Wolff (Birmingham, AL)	6/19/45
Gore Vidal (West Point, NY)	10/3/25	Herman Wouk (NYC)	5/27/15

Poets Laureate

There is no record of the origin of the office of Poet Laureate of England. Henry III (1216-72) reportedly had a Versificator Regis, or King's Poet, who was paid 100 shillings a year. Other poets said to have filled the role and received payment include Geoffrey Chaucer (d 1400), Edmund Spenser (d 1599), Ben Jonson (d 1637), and Sir William d'Avenant (d. 1668).

The first official English poet laureate was John Dryden, appointed in 1668, for life (as is customary). Thomas Shadwell was appointed in 1689; followed by Nahum Tate, 1692; Nicholas Rowe, 1715; Rev. Laurence Eusden, 1718; Colley Cibber, 1730; William Whitehead, 1757; Rev. Thomas Warton, 1785; Henry James Pye,

1790; Robert Southey in 1813; William Wordsworth, 1843; Alfred, Lord Tennyson, 1850; Alfred Austin, 1896; Robert Bridges, 1913; John Masefield, 1930; C. Day Lewis, 1968; Sir John Betjeman, 1972; Ted Hughes, 1984.

In the U.S., the appointment is made by the Librarian of Congress and is not for life. Robert Penn Warren was named the first U.S. Poet Laureate, effective Sept. 1986. Later appointments were: 1987, Richard Wilbur; 1988, Howard Nemerov; 1990, Mark Strand; 1991, Joseph Brodsky; 1992, Mona Van Duyn, first female poet laureate; 1993, Rita Dove, first black poet laureate; 1995, Robert Hass; 1997, Robert Pinsky.

Noted Writers of the Past

Not including Greeks and Romans listed in Historical Figures chapter.

James Agee, 1909-55, (U.S.) novelist. *A Death in the Family.*

Conrad Aiken, 1889-1973, (U.S.) poet, critic. *Ushant.*

Louisa May Alcott, 1832-88, (U.S.) novelist. *Little Women.*

Sholom Aleichem, 1859-1916, (Russ.) Yiddish writer. *Tevye's Daughter, Adventures of Mottel, The Old Country.*

Vicente Aleixandre, 1898-1984, (Sp.) poet. *La destrucción o el amor, Dialogolos del conocimiento.*

Horatio Alger, 1832-1899, (U.S.) "rags-to-riches" books.

Kingsley Amis, 1922-95, (Br.) novelist, critic. *Lucky Jim.*

Hans Christian Andersen, 1805-75, (Dan.) author of fairy tales. *The Princess and the Pea, The Ugly Duckling.*

Maxwell Anderson, 1888-1959, (U.S.) playwright. *What Price Glory?, High Tor, Winterset, Key Largo.*

Sherwood Anderson, 1876-1941, (U.S.) short-story writer. "Death in the Woods"; *Winesburg, Ohio* (collection).

Matthew Arnold, 1822-88, (Br.) poet, critic. "Thrysis," "Dover Beach," "The Gypsy Scholar"; "Culture and Anarchy."

Isaac Asimov, 1920-92, (U.S.) science-fiction writer. *I Robot.*

W(yston) H(ugh) Auden, 1907-73, (Br.) poet, playwright, literary critic. "The Age of Anxiety."

Jane Austen, 1775-1817, (Br.) novelist. *Pride and Prejudice, Sense and Sensibility, Emma, Mansfield Park.*

Isaac Babel, 1894-1941, (Russ.) short-story writer, playwright. *Odessa Tales, Red Cavalry.*

James Baldwin, 1924-87, author, playwright; *The Fire Next Time, Blues for Mister Charlie, Just Above My Head.*

Honoré de Balzac, 1799-1850, (Fr.) novelist. *Le Père Goriot, Cousine Bette, Eugénie Grandet.*

James M. Barrie, 1860-1937, (Br.) playwright, novelist. *Peter Pan, Dear Brutus, What Every Woman Knows.*

Charles Baudelaire, 1821-67, (Fr.) symbolist poet. *Les Fleurs du Mal.*

L(yman) Frank Baum, 1856-1919, (U.S.) writer. *Wizard of Oz* series.

Simone de Beauvoir, 1908-86, (Fr.) novelist, essayist. *The Second Sex, Memoirs of a Dutiful Daughter.*

Samuel Beckett, 1906-89, (Ir.) novelist, playwright. *Waiting for Godot, Endgame* (plays); *Murphy, Watt, Molloy* (novels).

Brendan Behan, 1923-64, (Ir.) playwright. *The Quare Fellow, The Hostage, Borstal Boy.*

Robert Benchley, 1889-1945, (U.S.) humorist.

Stephen Vincent Benét, 1898-1943, (U.S.) poet, novelist. *John Brown's Body.*

John Berryman, 1914-72, (U.S.) poet. *Homage to Mistress Bradstreet.*

Ambrose Bierce, 1842-1914, (U.S.) short-story writer, journalist. *In the Midst of Life, The Devil's Dictionary.*

Elizabeth Bishop, 1911-79, (U.S.) poet. *North and South—A Cold Spring.*

William Blake, 1757-1827, (Br.) poet, artist. *Songs of Innocence, Songs of Experience, The Marriage of Heaven and Hell.*

Giovanni Boccaccio, 1313-75, (It.) poet. *Decameron.*

Heinrich Böll, 1917-85, (Ger.) novelist, short-story writer. *Group Portrait With Lady.*

Jorge Luis Borges, 1900-86, (Arg.) short-story writer, poet, essayist. *Labyrinths.*

James Boswell, 1740-95, (Sc.) biographer. *The Life of Samuel Johnson.*

Pierre Boulle, (1913-94), (Fr.) novelist. *The Bridge Over the River Kwai, Planet of the Apes.*

Anne Bradstreet, c1612-72, (U.S.) poet. *The Tenth Muse Lately Sprung Up in America.*

Bertolt Brecht, 1898-1956, (Ger.) dramatist, poet. *The Threepenny Opera, Mother Courage and Her Children.*

Charlotte Brontë, 1816-55, (Br.) novelist. *Jane Eyre.*

Emily Brontë, 1818-48, (Br.) novelist. *Wuthering Heights.*

Elizabeth Barrett Browning, 1806-61, (Br.) poet. *Sonnets From the Portuguese, Aurora Leigh.*

Joseph Brodsky, 1940-96, (Russ.-U.S.) poet. *A Part of Speech, Less Than One, To Urania.*

Robert Browning, 1812-89, (Br.) poet. "My Last Duchess," "Fra Lippo Lippi," *The Ring and The Book.*

Pearl S. Buck, 1892-1973, (U.S.) novelist. *The Good Earth.*

Mikhail Bulgakov, 1891-1940, (Russ.) novelist, playwright. *The Heart of a Dog, The Master and Margarita.*

John Bunyan, 1628-88, (Br.) writer. *Pilgrim's Progress.*

Anthony Burgess, 1917-93, (Br.) author. *A Clockwork Orange.*

Frances Hodgson Burnett, 1849-1924, (U.S.) novelist. *The Secret Garden.*

Robert Burns, 1759-96, (Sc.) poet. "Flow Gently, Sweet Afton," "My Heart's in the Highlands," "Auld Lang Syne."

Virginia Lee Burton, 1909-68, (U.S.), children's author. *Mike Mulligan and His Steam Shovel, The Little House.*

Edgar Rice Burroughs, 1875-1950, (U.S.) novelist. *Tarzan of the Apes.*

William S. Burroughs, 1914-97, (U.S.) novelist. *Naked Lunch.*

George Gordon, Lord Byron, 1788-1824, (Br.) poet. *Don Juan, Childe Harold, Manfred, Cain.*

Italo Calvino, 1923-85, (It.) novelist, short-story writer. *If on a Winter's Night a Traveler.*

Albert Camus, 1913-60, (Fr.) writer. *The Stranger, The Fall.*

Karel Capek, 1890-1938, (Czech.) playwright, novelist, essayist. *R.U.R. (Rossum's Universal Robots).*

Truman Capote, 1924-84, (U.S.) author. *Other Voices, Other Rooms, Breakfast at Tiffany's, In Cold Blood.*

Lewis Carroll (Charles Dodgson), 1832-98, (Br.) writer, mathematician. *Alice's Adventures in Wonderland.*

Giacomo Casanova, 1725-98, (It.) adventurer, memoirist.

Willa Cather, 1873-1947, (U.S.) novelist. *O Pioneers!, My Ántonia, Death Comes for the Archbishop.*

Miguel de Cervantes Saavedra, 1547-1616, (Sp.) novelist, dramatist, poet. *Don Quixote.*

Raymond Chandler, 1888-1959, (U.S.) writer of detective fiction. Philip Marlowe series.

Geoffrey Chaucer, c 1340-1400, (Br.) poet. *The Canterbury Tales, Troilus and Criseyde.*

John Cheever, 1912-82, (U.S.) short-story writer, novelist. *The Wapshot Scandal*, "The Country Husband."

Anton Chekhov, 1860-1904, (Russ.) short-story writer, dramatist. *Uncle Vanya, The Cherry Orchard, The Three Sisters.*

G(ilbert) K(eith) Chesterton, 1874-1936, (Br.) critic, novelist, relig. apologist. Father Brown series of mysteries.

Kate Chopin, 1851-1904, (U.S.) writer. *The Awakening.*

Agatha Christie, 1890-1976, (Br.) mystery writer; created Miss Marple, Hercule Poirot; *And Then There Were None, Murder on the Orient Express, Murder of Roger Ackroyd.*

James Clavell, 1925-94, (Br.-U.S.) novelist. *Noble House, Shogun, King Rat.*

Jean Cocteau, 1889-1963, (Fr.) writer, visual artist, filmmaker. *The Beauty and the Beast, Les Enfants Terribles.*

Samuel Taylor Coleridge, 1772-1834, (Br.) poet, critic. "Kubla Khan," "The Rime of the Ancient Mariner."

(Sidonie) Colette, 1873-1954, (Fr.) novelist. *Claudine, Gigi.*

Joseph Conrad, 1857-1924, (Br.) novelist. *Lord Jim, Heart of Darkness, The Nigger of the Narcissus, Nostromo.*

James Fenimore Cooper, 1789-1851, (U.S.) novelist. Leatherstocking Tales, *The Last of the Mohicans.*

Pierre Corneille, 1606-84, (Fr.) dramatist. *Medeé, Le Cid.*

Hart Crane, 1899-1932, (U.S.) poet. "The Bridge."

Stephen Crane, 1871-1900, (U.S.) novelist, short-story writer. *The Red Badge of Courage,* "The Open Boat."

E. E. Cummings, 1894-1962, (U.S.) fiction writer. *Tulips and Chimneys.*

Roald Dahl, 1916-90, (Br.-U.S.) writer. *Charlie and the Chocolate Factory, James and the Giant Peach.*

Gabriele D'Annunzio, 1863-1938, (It.) poet, novelist, dramatist. *The Child of Pleasure, The Intruder, The Victim.*

Dante Alighieri, 1265-1321, (It.) poet. *The Divine Comedy.*

Robertson Davies, 1913-95, (Can.) novelist, playwright, essayist. Salterton Trilogy, Deptford Trilogy, Cornish Trilogy.

Daniel Defoe, 1660-1731, (Br.) writer. *Robinson Crusoe, Moll Flanders, Journal of the Plague Year.*

Peter De Vries, 1910-93, (U.S.) journalist, writer. *The Tunnel of Love, Let Me Count the Ways.*

Charles Dickens, 1812-70, (Br.) novelist. *David Copperfield, Oliver Twist, Great Expectations, A Tale of Two Cities.*

James Dickey, 1923-1997, (U.S.) poet, novelist. *Deliverance.*

Emily Dickinson, 1830-86, (U.S.) lyric poet. "Because I could not stop for Death. . .", "Success is counted sweetest. . ."

Isak Dinesen (Karen Blixen), 1885-1962, (Dan.) author. *Out of Africa, Seven Gothic Tales, Winter's Tales.*

John Donne, 1573-1631, (Br.) poet, divine. *Songs and Sonnets.*

José Donoso, 1924-1996, (Chil.) surreal novelist and short story writer. *The Obscene Bird of Night.*

John Dos Passos, 1896-1970, (U.S.) novelist. *U.S.A.*

Fyodor Dostoyevsky, 1821-81, (Russ.) novelist. *Crime and Punishment, The Brothers Karamazov, The Possessed.*

Arthur Conan Doyle, 1859-1930, (Br.) novelist. Sherlock Holmes mystery stories.

Theodore Dreiser, 1871-1945, (U.S.) novelist. *An American Tragedy, Sister Carrie.*

John Dryden, 1631-1700, (Br.) poet, dramatist, critic. *All for Love, Mac Flecknoe, Absalom and Achitophel.*

Alexandre Dumas, 1802-70, (Fr.) novelist, dramatist. *The Three Musketeers, The Count of Monte Cristo.*

Alexandre Dumas (fils), 1824-95, (Fr.) dramatist, novelist. *La Dame aux Camélias, Le Demi-Monde.*

Ilya G. Ehrenburg, 1891-1967, (Russ.) writer. *The Thaw.*

George Eliot (Mary Ann Evans or Marian Evans), 1819-80, (Br.) novelist. *Silas Marner, Middlemarch.*

T(homas) S(tearns) Eliot, 1888-1965, (Br.) poet, critic. *The Waste Land,* "The Love Song of J. Alfred Prufrock."

Stanley Elkin, 1930-95, (U.S.) novelist, short story writer. *A Modern Comedy, George Mills, Searches and Seizures.*

Ralph Ellison, 1914-94, (U.S.), writer. *Invisible Man.*

Ralph Waldo Emerson, 1803-82, (U.S.) poet, essayist. "Brahma," "Nature," "The Over-Soul," "Self-Reliance."

James T. Farrell, 1904-79, (U.S.) novelist. *Studs Lonigan.*

William Faulkner, 1897-1962, (U.S.) novelist. *Sanctuary, Light in August, The Sound and the Fury, Absalom, Absalom!*

Edna Ferber, 1887-1968, (U.S.) novelist, short-story writer, playwright. *So Big, Cimarron, Show Boat.*

Henry Fielding, 1707-54, (Br.) novelist. *Tom Jones.*

F(rancis) Scott Fitzgerald, 1896-1940, (U.S.) short-story writer, novelist. *The Great Gatsby, Tender Is the Night.*

Gustave Flaubert, 1821-80, (Fr.) novelist. *Madame Bovary.*

Ian Fleming, 1908-64, (Br.) novelist; created James Bond spy thrillers.

Ford Madox Ford, 1873-1939, (Br.) novelist, critic, poet. *The Good Soldier.*

C(ecil) S(cott) Forester, 1899-1966, (Br.) writer. Horatio Hornblower books.

E(dward) M(organ) Forster, 1879-1970, (Br.) novelist. *A Passage to India, Howards End.*

Anatole France, 1844-1924, (Fr.) writer. *Penguin Island, My Friend's Book, The Crime of Sylvestre Bonnard.*

Robert Frost, 1874-1963, (U.S.) poet. "Birches," "Fire and Ice," "Stopping by Woods on a Snowy Evening."

John Galsworthy, 1867-1933, (Br.) novelist, dramatist. The Forsyte Saga.

Erle Stanley Gardner, 1889-1970, (U.S.) mystery writer; created Perry Mason.

Jean Genet, 1911-86, (Fr.) playwright, novelist. *The Maids.*

Kahlil Gibran, 1883-1931, (Lebanese-U.S.) mystical novelist, essayist, poet. *The Prophet.*

André Gide, 1869-1951, (Fr.) writer. *The Immoralist, The Pastoral Symphony, Strait Is the Gate.*

Allen Ginsberg, 1926-1997, (U.S.) Beat poet. "Howl", "Kaddish," "The Fall of America: Poems of These States".

Jean Giraudoux, 1882-1944, (Fr.) novelist, dramatist. *Electra, The Madwoman of Chaillot, Ondine, Tiger at the Gate.*

Johann Wolfgang von Goethe, 1749-1832, (Ger.) poet, dramatist, novelist. *Faust, Sorrows of Young Werther.*

Nikolai Gogol, 1809-52, (Russ.) short-story writer, dramatist, novelist. *Dead Souls, The Inspector General.*

William Golding, 1911-93, (Br.) novelist. *Lord of the Flies.*

Oliver Goldsmith, 1730?-74, (Br.-Ir.) dramatist, novelist. *The Vicar of Wakefield, She Stoops to Conquer.*

Maxim Gorky, 1868-1936, (Russ.) dramatist, novelist. *The Lower Depths.*

Robert Graves, 1895-1985, (Br.) poet, classical scholar, novelist. *I, Claudius; The White Goddess.*

Thomas Gray, 1716-71, (Br.) poet. "Elegy Written in a Country Churchyard," "The Progress of Poesy."

Graham Greene, 1904-91, (Br.) novelist. *The Power and the Glory, The Heart of the Matter, The Ministry of Fear.*

Zane Grey, 1872-1939, (U.S.) writer of western stories.

Jakob Grimm, 1785-1863, (Ger.) philologist, folklorist; with brother **Wilhelm Grimm,** 1786-1859, collected *Grimm's Fairy Tales.*

Alex Haley, 1921-92, (U.S.) author. *Roots.*

Dashiell Hammett, 1894-1961, (U.S.) detective-story writer; created Sam Spade. *The Maltese Falcon, The Thin Man.*

Knute Hamsun, 1859-1952 (Nor.) novelist. *Hunger.*

Thomas Hardy, 1840-1928, (Br.) novelist, poet. *The Return of the Native, Tess of the D'Urbervilles, Jude the Obscure.*

Joel Chandler Harris, 1848-1908, (U.S.) short-story writer. Uncle Remus series.

Moss Hart, 1904-61, (U.S.) playwright. *Once in a Lifetime, You Can't Take It With You, The Man Who Came to Dinner.*

Bret Harte, 1836-1902, (U.S.) short-story writer, poet. *The Luck of Roaring Camp.*

Jaroslav Hasek, 1883-1923, (Czech.) writer, playwright. *The Good Soldier Schweik.*

Nathaniel Hawthorne, 1804-64, (U.S.) novelist, short-story writer. *The Scarlet Letter,* "Young Goodman Brown."

Heinrich Heine, 1797-1856, (Ger.) poet. *Book of Songs.*

Lillian Hellman, 1905-84, (U.S.) playwright, author of memoirs. *The Little Foxes, An Unfinished Woman, Pentimento.*

Ernest Hemingway, 1899-1961, (U.S.) novelist, short-story writer. *A Farewell to Arms, For Whom the Bell Tolls.*

O. Henry (W. S. Porter), 1862-1910, (U.S.) short-story writer. "The Gift of the Magi."

James Herriot (James Alfred Wight), 1916-95, (Br.) novelist, veterinarian. *All Creatures Great and Small.*

John Hersey, 1914-93, (U.S.) novelist, journalist. *Hiroshima, A Bell for Adano.*

Hermann Hesse, 1877-1962, (Ger.) novelist, poet. *Death and the Lover, Steppenwolf, Siddhartha.*

James Hilton, 1900-54, (Br.) novelist. *Lost Horizon.*

Oliver Wendell Holmes, 1809-94, (U.S.) poet, novelist. *The Autocrat of the Breakfast-Table.*

A(lfred) E. Housman, 1859-1936, (Br.) poet. *A Shropshire Lad.*

William Dean Howells, 1837-1920, (U.S.) novelist, critic. *The Rise of Silas Lapham.*

Langston Hughes, 1902-67, (U.S.) poet, playwright. *The Weary Blues, One-Way Ticket, Shakespeare in Harlem.*

Victor Hugo, 1802-85, (Fr.) poet, dramatist, novelist. *Notre Dame de Paris, Les Misérables.*

Zora Neale Hurston, 1903-60, (U.S.) novelist, folklorist. *Their Eyes Were Watching God, Mules and Men.*

Aldous Huxley, 1894-1963, (Br.) writer. *Brave New World.*

Henrik Ibsen, 1828-1906, (Nor.) dramatist, poet. *A Doll's House, Ghosts, The Wild Duck, Hedda Gabler.*

William Inge, 1913-73, (U.S.) playwright. *Picnic; Come Back, Little Sheba; Bus Stop.*

Eugene Ionesco, 1910-94, (Fr.) surrealist dramatist. *The Bald Soprano, The Chairs.*

Washington Irving, 1783-1859, (U.S.) writer. "Rip Van Winkle," "The Legend of Sleepy Hollow."

Christopher Isherwood, 1904-1986, (Br.) novelist, playwright. *The Berlin Stories.*

Shirley Jackson, 1919-65, (U.S.) writer. "The Lottery."

Henry James, 1843-1916, (U.S.) novelist, short-story writer, critic. *The Portrait of a Lady, The Ambassadors, Daisy Miller.*

Robinson Jeffers, 1887-1962, (U.S.) poet, dramatist. *Tamar and Other Poems, Medea.*

Samuel Johnson, 1709-84, (Br.) author, scholar, critic. *Dictionary of the English Language, Vanity of Human Wishes.*

Ben Jonson, 1572-1637, (Br.) dramatist, poet. *Volpone.*

James Joyce, 1882-1941, (Ir.) writer. *Ulysses, Dubliners, A Portrait of the Artist as a Young Man, Finnegans Wake.*

Franz Kafka, 1883-1924, (Ger.) novelist, short-story writer. *The Trial, Amerika, The Castle, The Metamorphosis.*

George S. Kaufman, 1889-1961, (U.S.) playwright. *The Man Who Came to Dinner, You Can't Take It With You, Stage Door.*

Nikos Kazantzakis, 1883?-1957, (Gk.) novelist. *Zorba the Greek, A Greek Passion.*

John Keats, 1795-1821, (Br.) poet. "Ode on a Grecian Urn," "Ode to a Nightingale," "La Belle Dame Sans Merci."

Jack Kerouac, 1922-1969, (U.S.), author, Beat poet. *On the Road, The Dharma Bums,* "Mexico City Blues."

Joyce Kilmer, 1886-1918, (U.S.) poet. "Trees."

Rudyard Kipling, 1865-1936, (Br.) author, poet. "The White Man's Burden," "Gunga Din," *The Jungle Book.*

Jean de la Fontaine, 1621-95, (Fr.) poet. *Fables choisies.*

Pär Lagerkvist, 1891-1974, (Swed.) poet, dramatist, novelist. *Barabbas, The Sybil.*

Selma Lagerlöf, 1858-1940, (Swed.) novelist. *Jerusalem, The Ring of the Lowenskolds.*

Alphonse de Lamartine, 1790-1869, (Fr.) poet, novelist, statesman. *Méditations poétiques.*

Charles Lamb, 1775-1834, (Br.) essayist. *Specimens of English Dramatic Poets, Essays of Elia.*

Giuseppe di Lampedusa, 1896-1957, (It.) novelist. *The Leopard.*

William Langland, c1332-1400, (Eng.) poet. *Piers Plowman.*

Ring Lardner, 1885-1933, (U.S.) short-story writer, humorist.

Louis L'Amour, 1908-88, (U.S.) western author, screenwriter. *Hondo, The Cherokee Trail.*

D(avid) H(erbert) Lawrence, 1885-1930, (Br.) novelist. *Sons and Lovers, Women in Love, Lady Chatterley's Lover.*

Mikhail Lermontov, 1814-41, (Russ.) novelist, poet. "Demon," *Hero of Our Time.*

Alain-René Lesage, 1668-1747, (Fr.) novelist. *Gil Blas de Santillane.*

Gotthold Lessing, 1729-81, (Ger.) dramatist, philosopher, critic. *Miss Sara Sampson, Minna von Barnhelm.*

C(live) S(taples) Lewis, 1898-1963, (Br.) critic, novelist, religious writer. *Allegory of Love; The Lion, the Witch and the Wardrobe, Out of the Silent Planet.*

Sinclair Lewis, 1885-1951, (U.S.) novelist. *Babbitt, Main Street, Arrowsmith, Dodsworth.*

Vachel Lindsay, 1879-1931, (U.S.) poet. *General William Booth Enters Into Heaven, The Congo.*

Hugh Lofting, 1886-1947, (Br.) writer. *Dr. Doolittle series.*

Jack London, 1876-1916, (U.S.) novelist, journalist. *Call of the Wild, The Sea-Wolf, White Fang.*

Henry Wadsworth Longfellow, 1807-82, (U.S.) poet. *Evangeline, The Song of Hiawatha.*

Amy Lowell, 1874-1925, (U.S.) poet, critic. "Lilacs."

James Russell Lowell, 1819-91, (U.S.) poet, editor. *Poems, The Biglow Papers.*

Robert Lowell, 1917-77, (U.S.) poet. "Lord Weary's Castle".

Archibald MacLeish, 1892-1982, (U.S.) poet. *Conquistador.*

Bernard Malamud, 1914-86, (U.S.) short-story writer, novelist. "The Magic Barrel," *The Assistant, The Fixer.*

Stéphane Mallarmé, 1842-98, (Fr.) poet. *Poésies.*

Thomas Malory, ?-1471, (Br.) writer. *Morte d'Arthur.*

Andre Malraux, 1901-76, (Fr.) novelist. *Man's Fate.*

Osip Mandelstam, 1891-1938, (Russ.) poet. *Stone, Tristia.*

Thomas Mann, 1875-1955, (Ger.) novelist, essayist. *Buddenbrooks, The Magic Mountain,* "Death in Venice."

Katherine Mansfield, 1888-1923, (Br.) short-story writer. "Bliss."

Christopher Marlowe, 1564-93, (Br.) dramatist, poet. *Tamburlaine the Great, Dr. Faustus, The Jew of Malta.*

John Masefield, 1878-1967, (Br.) poet. "Sea Fever," "Cargoes," *Salt Water Ballads.*

Edgar Lee Masters, 1869-1950, (U.S.) poet, biographer. *Spoon River Anthology.*

W(illiam) Somerset Maugham, 1874-1965, (Br.) author. *Of Human Bondage, The Moon and Sixpence.*

Guy de Maupassant, 1850-93, (Fr.) novelist, short-story writer. "A Life," "Bel-Ami," "The Necklace."

François Mauriac, 1885-1970, (Fr.) novelist, dramatist. *Viper's Tangle, The Kiss to the Leper.*

Vladimir Mayakovsky, 1893-1930, (Russ.) poet, dramatist. *The Cloud in Trousers.*

Mary McCarthy, 1912-89, (U.S.) critic, novelist, memoirist. *Memories of a Catholic Girlhood.*

Carson McCullers, 1917-67, (U.S.) novelist. *The Heart Is a Lonely Hunter, Member of the Wedding.*

Herman Melville, 1819-91, (U.S.) novelist, poet. *Moby-Dick, Typee, Billy Budd, Omoo.*

H(enry) L(ewis) Mencken, 1880-1956, (U.S.) author, critic, editor. *Prejudices, The American Language.*

George Meredith, 1828-1909, (Br.) novelist, poet. *The Ordeal of Richard Feverel, The Egoist.*

Prosper Mérimée, 1803-70, (Fr.) author. *Carmen.*

James Merrill, 1926-95, (U.S.) poet. *Divine Comedies.*

Edna St. Vincent Millay, 1892-1950, (U.S.) poet. *The Harp Weaver and Other Poems, A Few Figs From Thistles.*

Henry Miller, 1891-1980, (U.S.) erotic novelist. *Tropic of Cancer.*

A(lan) A(lexander) Milne, 1882-1956, (Br.) author. *Winnie-the-Pooh.*

John Milton, 1608-74, (Br.) poet, writer. *Paradise Lost, Comus, Lycidas, Areopagitica.*

Mishima Yukio (Hiraoka Kimitake), 1925-70, (Jpn.) writer. *Confessions of a Mask.*

Gabriela Mistral, 1889-1957, (Chil.) poet. *Sonnets of Death.*

Margaret Mitchell, 1900-49, (U.S.) novelist. *Gone With the Wind.*

Jean Baptiste Molière, 1622-73, (Fr.) dramatist. *Le Tartuffe, Le Misanthrope, Le Bourgeois Gentilhomme.*

Ferenc Molnár, 1878-1952, (Hung.) dramatist, novelist. *Liliom, The Guardsman, The Swan.*

Michel de Montaigne, 1533-92, (Fr.) essayist. *Essais.*

Eugenio Montale, 1896-1981, (It.) poet.

Clement C. Moore, 1779-1863, (U.S.) poet, educator. "A Visit From Saint Nicholas."

Marianne Moore, 1887-1972, (U.S.) poet.

Sir Thomas More, 1478-1535, (Br.) writer, statesman, saint. *Utopia.*

Murasaki Shikibu, c978-1031?, (Jpn.) novelist. *The Tale of Genji.*

Alfred de Musset, 1810-57, (Fr.) poet, dramatist. *La Confession d'un Enfant du Siècle.*

Vladimir Nabokov, 1899-1977, (Russ.-U.S.) novelist. *Lolita.*

Ogden Nash, 1902-71, (U.S.) poet of light verse.

Pablo Neruda, 1904-73, (Chil.) poet. *Twenty Love Poems and One Song of Despair, Toward the Splendid City.*

Sean O'Casey, 1884-1964, (Ir.) dramatist. *Juno and the Paycock, The Plough and the Stars.*

Frank O'Connor (Michael Donovan), 1903-66, (Ir.) short-story writer. "Guests of a Nation."

Flannery O'Connor, 1925-64, (U.S.) novelist, short-story writer. *Wise Blood,* "A Good Man Is Hard to Find."

Clifford Odets, 1906-63, (U.S.) playwright. *Waiting for Lefty, Awake and Sing, Golden Boy, The Country Girl.*

John O'Hara, 1905-70, (U.S.) novelist, short-story writer. *From the Terrace, Appointment in Samarra, Pal Joey.*

Omar Khayyam, c1028-1122, (Per.) poet. *Rubaiyat.*

Eugene O'Neill, 1888-1953, (U.S.) playwright. *Emperor Jones, Anna Christie, Long Day's Journey Into Night.*

George Orwell, 1903-50, (Br.) novelist, essayist. *Animal Farm, Nineteen Eighty-Four.*

John Osborne, 1929-95, (Br.) dramatist, novelist. *Look Back in Anger, The Entertainer.*

Dorothy Parker, 1893-1967, (U.S.) poet, short-story writer. *Enough Rope, Laments for the Living.*

Boris Pasternak, 1890-1960, (Russ.) poet, novelist. *Doctor Zhivago.*

Samuel Pepys, 1633-1703, (Br.) public official, diarist.

S(idney) J(oseph) Perelman, 1904-79, (U.S.) humorist. *The Road to Miltown, Under the Spreading Atrophy.*

Charles Perrault, 1628-1703, (Fr.) writer. *Tales From Mother Goose (Sleeping Beauty, Cinderella).*

Petrarch (Francesco Petrarca), 1304-74, (It.) poet. *Africa, Trionfi, Canzoniere.*

Luigi Pirandello, 1867-1936, (It.) novelist, dramatist. *Six Characters in Search of an Author.*

Sylvia Plath, 1932-63, (U.S.) author, poet. *The Bell Jar.*

Edgar Allan Poe, 1809-49, (U.S.) poet, short-story writer, critic. "Annabel Lee," "The Raven," "The Purloined Letter."

Alexander Pope, 1688-1744, (Br.) poet. *The Rape of the Lock, The Dunciad, An Essay on Man.*

Katherine Anne Porter, 1890-1980, (U.S.) novelist, short-story writer. *Ship of Fools.*

Ezra Pound, 1885-1972, (U.S.) poet. *Cantos.*

Marcel Proust, 1871-1922, (Fr.) novelist. *Remembrance of Things Past.*

Aleksandr Pushkin, 1799-1837, (Russ.) poet, novelist. *Boris Godunov, Eugene Onegin, The Bronze Horseman.*

François Rabelais, 1495-1553, (Fr.) writer. *Gargantua.*

Jean Racine, 1639-99, (Fr.) dramatist. *Andromaque, Phèdre, Bérénice, Britannicus.*

Ayn Rand, 1905-82, (Russ.-U.S.) novelist, moral theorist. *The Fountainhead, Atlas Shrugged.*

Erich Maria Remarque, 1898-1970, (Ger.-U.S.) novelist. *All Quiet on the Western Front.*

Samuel Richardson, 1689-1761, (Br.) novelist. *Pamela; or Virtue Rewarded.*

Rainer Maria Rilke, 1875-1926, (Ger.) poet. *Life and Songs, Duino Elegies, Poems From the Book of Hours.*

Arthur Rimbaud, 1854-91, (Fr.) poet. *A Season in Hell.*

Edwin Arlington Robinson, 1869-1935, (U.S.) poet. "Richard Cory," "Miniver Cheevy," *Merlin.*

Theodore Roethke, 1908-63, (U.S.) poet. *Open House, The Waking, The Far Field.*

Romain Rolland, 1866-1944, (Fr.) novelist, biographer. *Jean-Christophe.*

Pierre de Ronsard, 1524-85, (Fr.) poet. *Sonnets pour Hélène, La Franciade.*

Edmond Rostand, 1868-1918, (Fr.) poet, dramatist. *Cyrano de Bergerac.*

Damon Runyon, 1880-1946, (U.S.) short-story writer, journalist. *Guys and Dolls, Blue Plate Special.*

John Ruskin, 1819-1900, (Br.) critic, social theorist. *Modern Painters, The Seven Lamps of Architecture.*

Antoine de Saint-Exupéry, 1900-44, (Fr.) writer. *Wind, Sand and Stars, The Little Prince.*

Saki, or H(ector) H(ugh) Munro, 1870-1916, (Br.) writer. *The Chronicles of Clovis.*

George Sand (Amandine Lucie Aurore Dupin), 1804-76, (Fr.) novelist. *Indiana, Consuelo.*

Carl Sandburg, 1878-1967, (U.S.) poet. *The People, Yes; Chicago Poems, Smoke and Steel, Harvest Poems.*

William Saroyan, 1908-81, (U.S.) playwright, novelist. *The Time of Your Life, The Human Comedy.*

May Sarton, 1914-95, (Belg.-U.S.) poet, novelist. *Encounter in April, Anger.*

Dorothy L. Sayers, 1893-1957, (br.) mystery writer; created Lord Peter Wimsey.

Richard Scarry, 1920-94, (U.S.) author of children's books. *Richard Scarry's Best Story Book Ever.*

Friedrich von Schiller, 1759-1805, (Ger.) dramatist, poet, historian. *Don Carlos, Maria Stuart, Wilhelm Tell.*

Sir Walter Scott, 1771-1832, (Sc.) novelist, poet. *Ivanhoe.*

Jaroslav Seifert, 1902-86, (Czech.) poet.

Dr. Seuss (Theodor Seuss Geisel), 1904-91, (U.S.) children's book author and illustrator. *The Cat in the Hat.*

William Shakespeare, 1564-1616, (Br.) dramatist, poet. *Romeo and Juliet, Hamlet, King Lear, Julius Caesar,* sonnets.

George Bernard Shaw, 1856-1950, (Ir.-Br.) playwright, critic. *St. Joan, Pygmalion, Major Barbara, Man and Superman.*

Mary Wollstonecraft Shelley, 1797-1851, (Br.) novelist, feminist. *Frankenstein, The Last Man.*

Percy Bysshe Shelley, 1792-1822, (Br.) poet. *Prometheus Unbound, Adonais,* "Ode to the West Wind," "To a Skylark."

Richard B. Sheridan, 1751-1816, (Br.) dramatist. *The Rivals, School for Scandal.*

Robert Sherwood, 1896-1955, (U.S.) playwright, biographer. *The Petrified Forest, Idiot's Delight, Abe Lincoln in Illinois.*

Mikhail Sholokhov, 1906-84, (Russ.) writer. *The Silent Don.*

Upton Sinclair, 1878-1968, (U.S.) novelist. *The Jungle.*

Isaac Bashevis Singer, 1904-91, (Pol.-U.S.) novelist, short story writer, in Yiddish. *The Magician of Lublin.*

C(harles) P(ercy) Snow, 1905-80, (Br.) novelist, scientist. *Strangers and Brothers, Corridors of Power.*

Stephen Spender, 1909-95, (Br.) poet, critic, novelist. *Twenty Poems,* "Elegy for Margaret."

Edmund Spenser, 1552-99, (Br.) poet. *The Faerie Queen.*

Christina Stead, 1903-83, (Austral.) novelist, short-story writer. *The Man Who Loved Children.*

Richard Steele, 1672-1729, (Br.) essayist, playwright, began the *Tatler* and *Spectator. The Conscious Lovers.*

Lincoln Steffens, 1866-1936, (U.S.) editor, writer. *The Shame of the Cities.*

Gertrude Stein, 1874-1946, (U.S.) writer. *Three Lives.*

John Steinbeck, 1902-68, (U.S.) novelist. *The Grapes of Wrath, Of Mice and Men, The Winter of Our Discontent.*

Stendhal (Marie Henri Beyle), 1783-1842, (Fr.) novelist. *The Red and the Black, The Charterhouse of Parma.*

Laurence Sterne, 1713-68, (Br.) novelist. *Tristram Shandy.*

Wallace Stevens, 1879-1955, (U.S.) poet. *Harmonium, The Man With the Blue Guitar, Notes Toward a Supreme Fiction.*

Robert Louis Stevenson, 1850-94, (Br.) novelist, poet, essayist. *Treasure Island, A Child's Garden of Verses.*

Bram Stoker, 1845-1910, (Br.) writer. *Dracula.*

Rex Stout, 1886-1975, (U.S.) mystery writer; created Nero Wolfe.

Harriet Beecher Stowe, 1811-96, (U.S.) novelist. *Uncle Tom's Cabin.*

Lytton Strachey, 1880-1932, (Br.) biographer, critic. *Eminent Victorians, Queen Victoria, Elizabeth and Essex.*

August Strindberg, 1849-1912, (Swed.) dramatist, novelist. *The Father, Miss Julie, The Creditors.*

Jonathan Swift, 1667-1745, (Br.) satirist, poet. *Gulliver's Travels,* "A Modest Proposal."

Algernon C. Swinburne, 1837-1909, (Br.) writer. *Atalanta in Calydon.*

John M. Synge, 1871-1909, (Ir.) poet, dramatist. *Riders to the Sea, The Playboy of the Western World.*

Rabindranath Tagore, 1861-1941, (Ind.) author, poet. *Sadhana, The Realization of Life, Gitanjali.*

Booth Tarkington, 1869-1946, (U.S.) novelist. *Seventeen.*

Peter Taylor, 1917-94, (U.S.) novelist. *A Summons to Memphis.*

Sara Teasdale, 1884-1933, (U.S.) poet. *Helen of Troy and Other Poems, Rivers to the Sea, Flame and Shadow.*

Alfred, Lord Tennyson, 1809-92, (Br.) poet. *Idylls of the King, In Memoriam,* "The Charge of the Light Brigade."

William Makepeace Thackeray, 1811-63, (Br.) novelist. *Vanity Fair, Henry Esmond, Pendennis.*

Dylan Thomas, 1914-53, (Welsh) poet. *Under Milk Wood, A Child's Christmas in Wales.*

Henry David Thoreau, 1817-62, (U.S.) writer, philosopher, naturalist. *Walden,* "Civil Disobedience."

James Thurber, 1894-1961, (U.S.) humorist, cartoonist. "The Secret Life of Walter Mitty," *My Life and Hard Times.*

J(ohn) R(onald) R(euel) Tolkien, 1892-1973, (Br.) writer. *The Hobbit, Lord of the Rings* trilogy.

Leo Tolstoy, 1828-1910, (Russ.) novelist, short-story writer. *War and Peace, Anna Karenina,* "The Death of Ivan Ilyich."

Anthony Trollope, 1815-82, (Br.) novelist. *The Warden, Barchester Towers,* the Palliser novels.

Ivan Turgenev, 1818-83, (Russ.) novelist, short-story writer. *Fathers and Sons, First Love, A Month in the Country.*

Amos Tutuola 1920-97 (Nigerian) novelist. *The Palm-Wine Drinkard, My Life in the Bush of Ghosts.*

Mark Twain (Samuel Clemens), 1835-1910, (U.S.) novelist, humorist. *The Adventures of Huckleberry Finn, Tom Sawyer; Life on the Mississippi.*

Sigrid Undset, 1881-1949, (Nor.) novelist, poet. *Kristin Lavransdatter.*

Paul Valéry, 1871-1945, (Fr.) poet, critic. *La Jeune Parque, The Graveyard by the Sea.*

Jules Verne, 1828-1905, (Fr.) novelist. *Twenty Thousand Leagues Under the Sea.*

François Villon, 1431-63?, (Fr.) poet. *The Lays, The Grand Testament.*

Voltaire (F.M. Arouet), 1694-1778, (Fr.) writer of "philosophical romances"; philosopher, historian; *Candide.*

Robert Penn Warren, 1905-89, (U.S.) novelist, poet, critic. *All the King's Men.*

Evelyn Waugh, 1903-66, (Br) novelist. *The Loved One; Brideshead Revisited; A Handful of Dust.*

H(erbert) G(eorge) Wells, 1866-1946, (Br.) novelist. *The Time Machine, The Invisible Man, The War of the Worlds.*

Rebecca West, 1893-1983, (Br.) novelist, critic, journalist. *Black Lamb and Grey Falcon.*

Edith Wharton, 1862-1937, (U.S.) novelist. *The Age of Innocence, The House of Mirth, Ethan Frome.*

E(lwyn) B(rooks) White, 1899-1985, (U.S.), essayist, novelist. *Here Is New York, Charlotte's Web, Stuart Little.*

Patrick White, 1912-90, (Austral.) novelist. *The Tree of Man.*

T(erence) H(anbury) White, 1906-64, (Br.) author. *The Once and Future King, A Book of Beasts.*

Walt Whitman, 1819-92, (U.S.) poet. *Leaves of Grass.*

John Greenleaf Whittier, 1807-92, (U.S.) poet, journalist. *Snow-Bound.*

Oscar Wilde, 1854-1900, (Ir.) novelist, playwright. *The Picture of Dorian Gray, The Importance of Being Earnest.*

Laura Ingalls Wilder, 1867-1957, (U.S.) novelist. Little House on the Prairie series of children's books.

Thornton Wilder, 1897-1975, (U.S.) playwright. *Our Town, The Skin of Our Teeth, The Matchmaker.*

Tennessee Williams, 1911-83, (U.S.) playwright. *A Streetcar Named Desire, Cat on a Hot Tin Roof, The Glass Menagerie.*

William Carlos Williams, 1883-1963, (U.S.) poet, physician. *Tempers, Al Que Quiere! Paterson;* "This Is Just to Say."

Edmund Wilson, 1895-1972, (U.S.) critic, novelist. *Axel's Castle, To the Finland Station.*

P(elham) G(renville) Wodehouse, 1881-1975, (Br.-U.S.) humorist. The "Jeeves" novels, *Anything Goes.*

Thomas Wolfe, 1900-38, (U.S.) novelist. *Look Homeward, Angel; You Can't Go Home Again; Of Time and the River.*

Virginia Woolf, 1882-1941, (Br.) novelist, essayist. *Mrs. Dalloway, To the Lighthouse, The Waves, A Room of One's Own.*

William Wordsworth, 1770-1850, (Br.) poet. "Tintern Abbey," "Ode: Intimations of Immortality," *The Prelude.*

Richard Wright, 1908-60, novelist, short story writer. *Native Son, Black Boy, Uncle Tom's Children.*

William Butler Yeats, 1865-1939, (Ir.) poet, playwright. "The Second Coming," *The Wild Swans at Coole.*

Émile Zola, 1840-1902, (Fr.) novelist. *Nana, Thérèsè Raquin.*

Composers of Classical and Avant Garde Music

Carl Philipp Emanuel Bach, 1714-88, (Ger.) Cantatas, passions, numerous keyboard and instrumental works.

Johann Christian Bach, 1735-82, (Ger.) Concertos, operas, sonatas.

Johann Sebastian Bach, 1685-1750, (Ger.) St. Matthew Passion, The Well-Tempered Clavier.

Samuel Barber, 1910-81, (U.S.) Adagio for Strings, Vanessa.

Béla Bartók, 1881-1945, (Hung.) Concerto for Orchestra, The Miraculous Mandarin.

Beach, Amy (Mrs. H. H. A. Beach), 1867-1944, (U.S.) The Year's at the Spring, Fireflies, The Chambered Nautilus

Ludwig van Beethoven, 1770-1827, (Ger.) Concertos (Emperor), sonatas (Moonlight, Pathetique), 9 symphonies.

Vincenzo Bellini, 1801-35, (It.) I Puritani, La Sonnambula, Norma.

Alban Berg, 1885-1935, (Austrian) Wozzeck, Lulu.

Hector Berlioz, 1803-69, (Fr.) Damnation of Faust, Symphonie Fantastique, Requiem.

Leonard Bernstein, 1918-90, (U.S.) Chichester Psalms, Jeremiah Symphony, Mass.

Georges Bizet, 1838-75, (Fr.) Carmen, Pearl Fishers.

Ernest Bloch, 1880-1959, (Swiss-U.S.) Macbeth (opera), Schelomo, Voice in the Wilderness.

Luigi Boccherini, 1743-1805, (It.) Chamber music and guitar pieces.

Alexander Borodin, 1833-87, (Russ.) Prince Igor, In the Steppes of Central Asia, Polovtzian Dances.

Pierre Boulez, b 1925, (Fr.) LeVisage nuptial, Edats/Multiple, Domaines.

Johannes Brahms, 1833-97, (Ger.) Liebeslieder Waltzes, Acad. Festival Overture, chamber music, 4 symphonies.

Benjamin Britten, 1913-76, (Br.) Peter Grimes, Turn of the Screw, A Ceremony of Carols, War Requiem.

Anton Bruckner, 1824-96, (Austrian) 9 symphonies.

Dietrich Buxtehude, 1637-1707, (Dan.) Organ works, vocal music.

William Byrd, 1543-1623, (Br.) Masses, motets.

John Cage, (1912-92), (U.S.) Winter Music, Fontana Mix.

Emmanuel Chabrier, 1841-94, (Fr.) Le Roi Malgré Lui, Espana.

Gustave Charpentier, 1860-1956, (Fr.) Louise.

Frédéric Chopin, 1810-49, (Pol.) Mazurkas, waltzes, etudes, nocturnes, polonaises (Polonaise No. 6 in A flat major [Heroic]), sonatas.

Aaron Copland, 1900-90, (U.S.) Appalachian Spring, Fanfare for the Common Man, Lincoln Portrait.

Claude Debussy, 1862-1918, (Fr.) Pelleas et Melisande, La Mer, Prelude to the Afternoon of a Faun.

Gaetano Donizetti, 1797-1848, (It.) Elixir of Love, Lucia di Lammermoor, Daughter of the Regiment.

Paul Dukas, 1865-1935, (Fr.) Sorcerer's Apprentice.

Antonin Dvorak, 1841-1904, (Czech.) Songs My Mother Taught Me, Symphony in E Minor (From the New World).

Edward Elgar, 1857-1934, (Br.) Enigma Variations, Pomp and Circumstance.

Manuel de Falla, 1876-1946, (Sp.) El Amor Brujo, La Vida Breve, The Three-Cornered Hat.

Gabriel Fauré, 1845-1924, (Fr.) Requiem, Elègie for Cello and Piano.

Cesar Franck, 1822-90, (Belg.) Symphony in D minor, Violin Sonata.

George Gershwin, 1898-1937, (U.S.) Rhapsody in Blue, An American in Paris, Porgy and Bess.

Philip Glass, b 1937, (U.S.) Einstein on the Beach, The Voyage.

Mikhail Glinka, 1804-57, (Russ.) A Life for the Tsar, Ruslan and Ludmilla.

Christoph W. Gluck, 1714-87, (Ger.) Alceste, Iphigènie en Tauride.

Charles Gounod, 1818-93, (Fr.) Faust, Romeo and Juliet.

Edvard Grieg, 1843-1907, (Nor.) Peer Gynt Suite, Concerto in A minor for piano.

George Frideric Handel, 1685-1759, (Ger.-Br.) Messiah, Water Music.

Howard Hanson, 1896-1981, (U.S.) Symphonies No. 1 (Nordic) and No. 2 (Romantic).

Roy Harris, 1898-1979, (U.S.) Symphonies.

(Franz) Joseph Haydn, 1732-1809, (Austrian) Symphonies (Clock, London, Toy), chamber music, oratorios.

Paul Hindemith, 1895-1963, (U.S.) Mathis der Maler.

Gustav Holst, 1874-1934, (Br.) The Planets.

Arthur Honegger, 1892-1955, (Fr.) Judith, Le Roi David, Pacific 231.

Alan Hovhaness, b 1911, (U.S.) Symphonies, Magnificat.

Engelbert Humperdinck, 1854-1921, (Ger.) Hansel and Gretel.

Charles Ives, 1874-1954, (U.S.) Concord Sonata, symphonies.

Aram Khachaturian, 1903-78, (Russ.) Ballets, piano pieces, Sabre Dance.

Zoltán Kodaly, 1882-1967, (Hung.) Háry János, Psalmus Hungaricus.

Fritz Kreisler, 1875-1962, (Austrian) Caprice Viennois, Tambourin Chinois.

Edouard Lalo, 1823-92, (Fr.) Symphonie Espagnole.

Ruggero Leoncavallo, 1857-1919, (It.) Pagliacci.

Franz Liszt, 1811-86, (Hung.) 20 Hungarian rhapsodies, symphonic poems.

Edward MacDowell, 1861-1908, (U.S.) To a Wild Rose.

Gustav Mahler, 1860-1911, (Austrian) Das Lied von der Erde.

Pietro Mascagni, 1863-1945, (It.) Cavalleria Rusticana.

Jules Massenet, 1842-1912, (Fr.) Manon, Le Cid, Thaïs.

Felix Mendelssohn, 1809-47, (Ger.) A Midsummer Night's Dream, Songs Without Words, violin concerto.

Gian-Carlo Menotti, b 1911, (It.-U.S.) The Medium, The Consul, Amahl and the Night Visitors.

Claudio Monteverdi, 1567-1643, (It.) Opera, masses, madrigals.

Modest Moussorgsky, 1839-81, (Russ.) Boris Godunov, Pictures at an Exhibition.

Wolfgang Amadeus Mozart, 1756-91, (Austrian) Chamber music, concertos, operas (Magic Flute, Marriage of Figaro), 41 symphonies.

Jacques Offenbach, 1819-80, (Fr.) Tales of Hoffmann.

Carl Orff, 1895-1982, (Ger.) Carmina Burana.

Johann Pachelbel, 1653-1706, (Ger.) Canon and Gigue in D major.

Ignacy Paderewski, 1860-1941, (Pol.) Minuet in G.

Niccolò Paganini, 1782-1840, (It.) Caprices for violin solo.

Giovanni Palestrina, c1525-94, (It.) Masses, madrigals.

Krzystof Pendercki, b 1933, (Pol.) Psalmus, Polymorphia, De natura sonoris.

Francis Poulenc, 1899-1963, (Fr.) Dialogues des Carmèlites.

Sergei Prokofiev, 1891-1953, (Russ.) Classical Symphony, Love for Three Oranges, Peter and the Wolf.

Giacomo Puccini, 1858-1924, (It.) La Boheme, Manon Lescaut, Tosca, Madama Butterfly.

Henry Purcell, 1659-95, (Eng.) Dido and Aeneas.

Sergei Rachmaninoff, 1873-1943, (Russ.) Concertos, preludes (Prelude in C sharp minor), symphonies.

Maurice Ravel, 1875-1937, (Fr.) Boléro, Daphnis et Chloè, Piano Concerto in D for Left Hand Alone.

Nikolai Rimsky-Korsakov, 1844-1908, (Russ.) Golden Cockerel, Capriccio Espagnol, Scheherazade, Russian Easter Overture, Flight of the Bumblebee.

Gioacchino Rossini, 1792-1868, (It.) Barber of Seville, Othello, William Tell.

Camille Saint-Saëns, 1835-1921, (Fr.) Carnival of Animals (The Swan), Samson and Delilah, Danse Macabre.

Alessandro Scarlatti, 1660-1725, (It.) Cantatas, oratorios, operas.

Domenico Scarlatti, 1685-1757, (It.) Harpsichord works.

Arnold Schoenberg, 1874-1951, (Austrian) Pelleas and Melisande, Pierrot Lunaire, Verklärte Nacht.

Franz Schubert, 1797-1828, (Austrian) Chamber music (Trout Quintet), lieder, symphonies (Unfinished).

Robert Schumann, 1810-56, (Ger.) Die Frauenliebe und Leben, Träumerei.

Dimitri Shostakovich, 1906-75, (Russ.) Symphonies, Lady Macbeth of the District Mzensk.

Jean Sibelius, 1865-1957, (Finn.) Finlandia.

Bedrich Smetana, 1824-84, (Czech.) The Bartered Bride.

Karlheinz Stockhausen, b 1928, (Ger.) KontraPunkte, Kontakte for Electronic Instruments.

Richard Strauss, 1864-1949, (Ger.) Salome, Elektra, Der Rosenkavalier, Thus Spake Zarathustra.

Igor Stravinsky, 1882-1971, (Russ.) Noah and the Flood, The Rake's Progress, The Rite of Spring.

Toru Takemitsu, 1930-96, (Jpn.) Requiem for Strings, Dorian Horizon.

Peter I. Tchaikovsky, 1840-93, (Russ.) Nutcracker, Swan Lake, The Sleeping Beauty.

Virgil Thomson, 1896-1989, (U.S.) Opera, film music, Four Saints in Three Acts.

Ralph Vaughan Williams, 1872-1958, (Eng.) Fantasiz on a Theme by Thomas Tallis, symphonies, vocal music.

Giuseppe Verdi, 1813-1901, (It.) Aida, Rigoletto, Don Carlo, Il Trovatore, La Traviata, Falstaff, Macbeth.

Heitor Villa-Lobos, 1887-1959, (Brazil) Bachianas Brasileiras.

Antonio Vivaldi, 1678-1741, (It.) Concerto grossos (The Four Seasons).

Richard Wagner, 1813-83, (Ger.) Rienzi, Tannhäuser, Lohengrin, Tristan und Isolde.

Carl Maria von Weber, 1786-1826, (Ger.) Der Freischutz.

Composers of Operettas, Musicals, and Popular Music

Richard Adler, b 1921, (U.S.) *Pajama Game; Damn Yankees.*

Milton Ager, 1893-1979, (U.S.) I Wonder What's Become of Sally; Hard Hearted Hannah; Ain't She Sweet?

Arthur Altman, 1910-94, (U.S.) *All or Nothing at All.*

Leroy Anderson, 1908-75, (U.S.) Syncopated Clock.

Paul Anka, b 1941, (Can.) My Way; *Tonight Show* theme.

Harold Arlen, 1905-86, (U.S.) Stormy Weather; Over the Rainbow; Blues in the Night; That Old Black Magic.

Burt Bacharach, b 1928, (U.S.) Raindrops Keep Fallin' on My Head; Walk on By; What the World Needs Now Is Love.

Ernest Ball, 1878-1927, (U.S.) Mother Machree; When Irish Eyes Are Smiling.

Irving Berlin, 1888-1989, (U.S.) *Annie Get Your Gun; Call Me Madam;* God Bless America; White Christmas.

Leonard Bernstein, 1918-90, (U.S.) *On the Town; Wonderful Town; Candide; West Side Story.*

Eubie Blake, 1883-1983, (U.S.) *Shuffle Along;* I'm Just Wild About Harry.

Jerry Bock, b 1928, (U.S.) *Mr. Wonderful; Fiorello; Fiddler on the Roof; The Rothschilds.*

Carrie Jacobs Bond, 1862-1946, (U.S.) I Love You Truly.

Nacio Herb Brown, 1896-1964, (U.S.) Singing in the Rain; You Were Meant for Me; All I Do Is Dream of You.

Hoagy Carmichael, 1899-1981, (U.S.) Stardust; Georgia on My Mind; Old Buttermilk Sky.

George M. Cohan, 1878-1942, (U.S.) Give My Regards to Broadway; You're a Grand Old Flag; Over There.

Cy Coleman, b 1929, (U.S.) *Sweet Charity;* Witchcraft.

John Frederick Coots, 1897-?, (U.S.) Santa Claus Is Coming to Town, You Go to My Head, For All We Know.

Noel Coward, 1899-1973, (Br.) *Bitter Sweet;* Mad Dogs and Englishmen; Mad About the Boy.

Neil Diamond, b 1941, (U.S.) I'm a Believer; Sweet Caroline.

Walter Donaldson, 1893-1947, (U.S.) My Buddy; Carolina in the Morning; Makin' Whoopee.

Vernon Duke, 1903-69, (U.S.) April in Paris.

Bob Dylan, b 1941, (U.S.) Blowin' in the Wind.
Gus Edwards, 1879-1945, (U.S.) School Days; By the Light of the Silvery Moon; In My Merry Oldsmobile.
Sherman Edwards, 1919-81, (U.S.) See You in September; Wonderful! Wonderful!
Duke Ellington, 1899-1974, (U.S.) Sophisticated Lady; Satin Doll; It Don't Mean a Thing; Solitude.
Sammy Fain, 1902-89, (U.S.) I'll Be Seeing You; Love Is a Many-Splendored Thing.
Fred Fisher, 1875-1942, (U.S.) Peg O' My Heart; Chicago.
Stephen Collins Foster, 1826-64, (U.S.) My Old Kentucky Home; Old Folks at Home.
Rudolf Friml, 1879-1972, (Czech-U.S.) *The Firefly; Rose Marie; Vagabond King; Bird of Paradise.*
John Gay, 1685-1732, (Br.) *The Beggar's Opera.*
George Gershwin, 1898-1937, (U.S.) Someone to Watch Over Me; I've Got a Crush on You; Embraceable You.
Morton Gould, 1913-96, (U.S.) Fall River Suite, Holocaust Suite, Spirituals for Orchestra, Stringmusic.
Ferde Grofe, 1892-1972, (U.S.) Grand Canyon Suite.
Marvin Hamlisch, b 1944, (U.S.) The Way We Were, Nobody Does It Better, *A Chorus Line.*
Ray Henderson, 1896-1970, (U.S.) *George White's Scandals;* That Old Gang of Mine; Five Foot Two, Eyes of Blue.
Victor Herbert, 1859-1924, (Ir.-U.S.) *Mlle. Modiste; Babes in Toyland; The Red Mill; Naughty Marietta; Sweethearts.*
Jerry Herman, b 1933, (U.S.) *Hello Dolly; Mame.*
Brian Holland, b 1941, **Lamont Dozier,** b 1941, **Eddie Holland,** b 1939, (all U.S.) Heat Wave; Stop! In the Name of Love; Baby, I Need Your Loving.
Antonio Carlos Jobim, 1927-94, (Brazil) *The Girl From Ipanema, Desafinado, One Note Samba.*
Billy (William Martin) Joel, b 1949, (U.S.) *Just the Way You Are, Honesty,* Piano Man.
Scott Joplin, 1868-1917, (U.S.) *Treemonisha.*
John Kander, b 1927, (U.S.) *Cabaret; Chicago; Funny Lady.*
Jerome Kern, 1885-1945, (U.S.) *Sally; Sunny; Show Boat.*
Carole King, b 1942, (U.S.) Will You Love Me Tomorrow?; Natural Woman; One Fine Day; Up on the Roof.
Burton Lane, 1912-1997, (U.S.) *Finian's Rainbow.*
Franz Lehar, 1870-1948, (Hung.) *Merry Widow.*
Jerry Leiber, & **Mike Stoller,** both b 1933, (both U.S.) Hound Dog; Searchin'; Yakety Yak; Love Me Tender.
Mitch Leigh, b 1928, (U.S.) *Man of La Mancha.*
John Lennon, 1940-80, & **Paul McCartney,** b 1942, (both Br.) I Want to Hold Your Hand; She Loves You.
Frank Loesser, 1910-69, (U.S.) *Guys and Dolls; Where's Charley?; The Most Happy Fella; How to Succeed ....*
Frederick Loewe, 1901-88, (Austrian-U.S.) *Brigadoon; Paint Your Wagon; My Fair Lady; Camelot.*
Andrew Lloyd Webber, b 1948, (Br.) *Jesus Christ Superstar, Evita, Cats, The Phantom of the Opera.*
Henry Mancini, 1924-94, (U.S.) Moon River; Days of Wine and Roses; Pink Panther Theme.
Barry Mann, b 1939, & **Cynthia Weil,** b 1937, (both U.S.) You've Lost That Loving Feeling.
Jimmy McHugh, 1894-1969, (U.S.) Don't Blame Me; I'm in the Mood for Love; I Feel a Song Coming On.
Alan Menken, b 1950, (U.S.) *Little Shop of Horrors.*
Joseph Meyer, 1894-1987, (U.S.) If You Knew Susie; California, Here I Come; Crazy Rhythm.
Chauncey Olcott, 1858-1932, (U.S.) Mother Machree.

Jerome "Doc" Pomus, 1925-91, (U.S.) Save the Last Dance for Me, A Teenager in Love.
Cole Porter, 1893-1964, (U.S.) *Anything Goes; Kiss Me Kate; Can Can; Silk Stockings.*
Smokey Robinson, b 1940, (U.S.) Shop Around; My Guy; My Girl; Get Ready.
Richard Rodgers, 1902-79, (U.S.) *Oklahoma!; Carousel; South Pacific; The King and I; The Sound of Music.*
Sigmund Romberg, 1887-1951, (Hung.) *Maytime; The Student Prince; Desert Song; Blossom Time.*
Harold Rome, 1908-93, (U.S.) *Pins and Needles; Call Me Mister; Wish You Were Here; Fanny; Destry Rides Again.*
Vincent Rose, b 1880-1944, (U.S.) Avalon; Whispering; Blueberry Hill.
Harry Ruby, 1895-1974, (U.S.) Three Little Words; Who's Sorry Now?
Arthur Schwartz, 1900-84, (U.S.) *The Band Wagon;* Dancing in the Dark; By Myself; That's Entertainment.
Neil Sedaka, b 1939, (U.S.) Breaking Up Is Hard to Do.
Paul Simon, b 1942, (U.S.) Sounds of Silence; I Am a Rock; Mrs. Robinson; Bridge Over Troubled Waters.
Stephen Sondheim, b 1930, (U.S.) *A Little Night Music; Company; Sweeney Todd; Sunday in the Park With George.*
John Philip Sousa, 1854-1932, (U.S.) *El Capitan;* Stars and Stripes Forever.
Oskar Straus, 1870-1954, (Austrian) *Chocolate Soldier.*
Johann Strauss, 1825-99, (Austrian) *Gypsy Baron; Die Fledermaus;* waltzes: Blue Danube, Artist's Life.
Charles Strouse, b 1928, (U.S.) *Bye Bye, Birdie; Annie.*
Jule Styne, 1905-94, (Br.-U.S.) *Gentlemen Prefer Blondes; Bells Are Ringing; Gypsy; Funny Girl.*
Arthur S. Sullivan, 1842-1900, (Br.) *H.M.S. Pinafore, Pirates of Penzance; The Mikado.*
Deems Taylor, 1885-1966, (U.S.) *Peter Ibbetson.*
Harry Tobias, 1895-94, (U.S.) *I'll Keep the Lovelight Burning.*
Egbert van Alstyne, 1882-1951, (U.S.) In the Shade of the Old Apple Tree; Memories; Pretty Baby.
Jimmy Van Heusen, 1913-90, (U.S.) Moonlight Becomes You; Swinging on a Star; All the Way; Love and Marriage.
Albert von Tilzer, 1878-1956, (U.S.) I'll Be With You in Apple Blossom Time; Take Me Out to the Ball Game.
Harry von Tilzer, 1872-1946, (U.S.) Only a Bird in a Gilded Cage; On a Sunday Afternoon.
Fats Waller, 1904-43, (U.S.) Honeysuckle Rose; Ain't Misbehavin'.
Harry Warren, 1893-1981, (U.S.) You're My Everything; We're in the Money; I Only Have Eyes for You.
Jimmy Webb, b 1946, (U.S.) Up, Up and Away; By the Time I Get to Phoenix; Didn't We?; Wichita Lineman.
Kurt Weill, 1900-50, (Ger.-U.S.) *Threepenny Opera; Lady in the Dark; Knickerbocker Holiday; One Touch of Venus.*
Percy Wenrich, 1887-1952, (U.S.) When You Wore a Tulip; Moonlight Bay; Put On Your Old Gray Bonnet.
Richard A. Whiting, 1891-1938, (U.S.) Till We Meet Again; Sleepytime Gal; Beyond the Blue Horizon; My Ideal.
John Williams, b 1932, (U.S.) *Jaws, E.T., Star Wars* series, *Raiders of the Lost Ark* series.
Meredith Willson, 1902-84, (U.S.) *The Music Man.*
Stevie Wonder, b 1950, (U.S.) You Are the Sunshine of My Life; Signed, Sealed, Delivered, I'm Yours.
Vincent Youmans, 1898-1946, (U.S.) *Two Little Girls in Blue; Wildflower; No, No, Nanette; Hit the Deck; Rainbow; Smiles.*

Lyricists

Howard Ashman, 1950-91, (U.S.) Little Shop of Horrors, The Little Mermaid.
Johnny Burke, 1908-84, (U.S.) Misty; Imagination.
Irving Caesar, 1895-1996, (U.S.) Swanee, Tea for Two, Just a Gigolo.
Sammy Cahn, 1913-93, (U.S.) High Hopes; Love and Marriage; The Second Time Around; It's Magic.
Leonard Cohen, b 1934, (Can.) Suzanne, Stranger Song.
Betty Comden, b 1919, (U.S.) and **Adolph Green,** b 1915, (U.S.) The Party's Over; Just in Time; New York, New York.
Hal David, b 1921, (U.S.) What the World Needs Now Is Love.
Buddy De Sylva, 1895-1950, (U.S.) When Day Is Done; Look for the Silver Lining; April Showers.
Howard Dietz, 1896-1983, (U.S.) Dancing in the Dark; You and the Night and the Music; That's Entertainment.
Al Dubin, 1891-1945, (U.S.) Tiptoe Through the Tulips; Anniversary Waltz; Lullaby of Broadway.
Fred Ebb, b 1936, (U.S.) Cabaret, Zorba, Woman of the Year.
Dorothy Fields, 1905-74, (U.S.) On the Sunny Side of the Street; Don't Blame Me; The Way You Look Tonight.
Ira Gershwin, 1896-1983, (U.S.) The Man I Love; Fascinating Rhythm; S'Wonderful; Embraceable You.
William S. Gilbert, 1836-1911, (Br.) The Mikado; H.M.S. Pinafore, Pirates of Penzance.
Gerry Goffin, b 1939, (U.S.) Will You Love Me Tomorrow, Take Good Care of My Baby, Up on the Roof.

Mack Gordon, 1905-59, (Pol.-U.S.) You'll Never Know; The More I See You; Chattanooga Choo-Choo.
Oscar Hammerstein II, 1895-1960, (U.S.) Ol' Man River; Oklahoma; Carousel.
E. Y. (Yip) Harburg, 1898-1981, (U.S.) Brother, Can You Spare a Dime; April in Paris; Over the Rainbow.
Lorenz Hart, 1895-1943, (U.S.) Isn't It Romantic; Blue Moon; Lover; Manhattan; My Funny Valentine.
DuBose Heyward, 1885-1940, (U.S.) Summertime.
Gus Kahn, 1886-1941, (U.S.) Memories; Ain't We Got Fun.
Alan J. Lerner, 1918-86, (U.S.) Brigadoon; My Fair Lady; Camelot; Gigi; On a Clear Day You Can See Forever.
Johnny Mercer, 1909-76, (U.S.) Blues in the Night; Come Rain or Come Shine; Laura; That Old Black Magic.
Bob Merrill, b 1921, (U.S.) People; Don't Rain on My Parade.
Jack Norworth, 1879-1959, (U.S.) Take Me Out to the Ball Game; Shine On Harvest Moon.
Mitchell Parish, 1901-93, (U.S.) Stairway to the Stars; Stardust.
Andy Razaf, 1895-1973, (U.S.) Honeysuckle Rose, Ain't Misbehavin', S'posin'.
Leo Robin, 1900-84, (U.S.) Thanks for the Memory; Hooray for Love; Diamonds Are a Girl's Best Friend.
Paul Francis Webster, 1907-84, (U.S.) Secret Love, The Shadow of Your Smile, Love Is a Many-Splendored Thing.
Jack Yellen, 1892-1991, (U.S.) Down by the O-Hi-O; Ain't She Sweet; Happy Days Are Here Again.

Some Notable Figures of the Past in Dance

Source: Reviewed by Gary Parks, Reviews editor, *Dance* magazine

Alvin Ailey, 1931-89, (U.S.) modern dancer, choreographer; melded modern dance and Afro-Caribbean techniques.

Frederick Ashton, 1904-88, (Br.) ballet choreographer; director of Great Britain's Royal Ballet, 1963-70.

Fred Astaire, 1899-1987, (U.S.) dancer, actor; teamed with dancer/actress **Ginger Rogers** (1911-95) in movie musicals.

George Balanchine, 1904-83, (Russ.-U.S.) ballet choreographer, teacher; most influential exponent of the neoclassical style, founded, with Lincoln Kirstein, School of American Ballet and New York City Ballet.

Carlo Blasis, 1803-78, (It.) ballet dancer, choreographer, writer; his teaching methods are standards of classical dance.

August Bournonville, 1805-79, (Dan.) ballet dancer, choreographer, teacher; developed a distinctly Danish style known for its exuberance and lightness.

Enrico Cecchetti, 1850-1928, (It.) ballet dancer, leading dancers of Russia's Imperial Ballet; his technique is basis for Britain's Imperial Society of Teachers of Dancing.

Gower Champion, 1921-80, (U.S.) dancer, choreographer, director; with his wife **Marge,** b 1923, (U.S.), choreographed and danced in Broadway musicals and films.

John Cranko, 1927-73, (S. African) choreographer; created narrative ballets based on literary works.

Agnes de Mille, 1909-93, (U.S.) ballet dancer, choreographer; known for using American themes, she choreographed the ballet *Rodeo* and the musical *Oklahoma.*

Sergei Diaghilev, 1872-1929, (Russ.) impresario; founded Les Ballet Russes; saw ballet as an art unifying dance, drama, music, and decor.

Alexandra Danilova, 1903-97, (Russ.) ballet dancer; noted teacher at the School of American Ballet.

Isadora Duncan, 1877-1927, (U.S.) expressive dancer who united free movement with serious music; one of the founders of modern dance.

Fanny Elssler, 1810-84, (Austrian) ballerina of the Romantic period; known for dramatic skill and sensual style.

Michel Fokine, 1880-1942, (Russ.) ballet dancer, choreographer, teacher; rejected strict classicism in favor of dramatically expressive style.

Margot Fonteyn, 1919-91, (Br.) prima ballerina, Royal Ballet of Great Britain; famed performance partner of Rudolf Nureyev.

Bob Fosse, 1927-87, (U.S.) jazz dancer, choreographer, director; Broadway musicals and film.

Martha Graham, 1893-1991, (U.S.) modern dancer, choreographer, created and codified her own dramatic technique.

Martha Hill, 1901-95, (U.S.) educator; leading figure in modern dance; founder American Dance Festival.

Doris Humphrey, 1895-1958, (U.S.) modern dancer, choreographer, writer, teacher; known for her intellect and choreographic range.

Robert Joffrey, 1930-88, (U.S.) ballet dancer, choreographer; co-founded with **Gerald Arpino,** b 1928, (U.S.), the Joffrey Ballet.

Kurt Jooss, 1901-79, (Ger.) choreographer, teacher; created expressionist works using modern and classical techniques.

Tamara Karsavina, 1885-1978, (Russ.) prima ballerina of Russia's Imperial Ballet and Diaghilev's Ballets Russes; partner of Nijinsky.

Nora Kaye, 1920-87, (U.S.) ballerina with Metropolitan Opera Ballet and Ballet Theater (now American Ballet Theatre).

Lincoln Kirstein, 1907-96 (U.S.) brought ballet as an art form to U.S.; founded, with George Balanchine, School of American Ballet and New York City Ballet.

Serge Lifar, 1905-86, (Russ.-F.) prem. danseur, choreographer; director of dance at Paris Opera, 1930-45, 1947-58.

José Limón, 1908-72, (Mex.-U.S.) modern dancer, choreographer, teacher; developed technique based on Humphrey.

Catherine Littlefield, 1908-51, (U.S.) ballet dancer, choreographer, teacher; pioneer of American ballet.

Léonide Massine, 1896-1979, (Russ.-U.S.) ballet dancer, choreographer; created "symphonic ballet" using concert music previously thought unsuitable for dance.

Kenneth MacMillan, 1929-92, (Br.) ballet dancer, choreographer; director of Royal Ballet of Great Britain 1970-77.

Vaslav Nijinsky, 1890-50, (Russ.) prem. danseur, choreographer; leading member of Diaghilev's Ballets Russes; his ballets were revolutionary for their time.

Alwin Nikolais, 1910-93, (U.S.) modern choreographer; created dance theater utilizing mixed media effects.

Jean-George Noverre, 1727-1810, (Fr.) ballet choreographer, teacher, writer; his theories on dramatic ballet remain influential; called the "Shakespeare of the dance."

Rudolf Nureyev, 1938-93, (Russ.) prem. danseur, choreographer; leading male dancer of his generation; director of dance at Paris Opera, 1983-89.

Ruth Page, 1903-91, (U.S.) ballet dancer, choreographer; danced and directed ballet at Chicago Lyric Opera.

Anna Pavlova, 1881-1931, (Russ.) prima ballerina; toured all over the world with her own company to great acclaim.

Marius Petipa, 1818-1910, (Fr.) ballet dancer, choreographer; as ballet master of the Imperial Ballet, he established Russian classicism as leading style of late 19th cent..

Pearl Primus, 1919-95, (Trinidad-U.S.) modern dancer, choreographer, scholar; combined African, Caribbean, and African-American styles.

Bill (Bojangles) Robinson, 1878-1949, (U.S.) tap dancer; called the King of Tapology, he attained fame on stage and screen rare for an African-American of his era.

Ruth St. Denis, 1877-1968, (U.S.) interpretive dancer, choreographer, teacher; touring widely, she influenced many early modern dancers.

Ted Shawn, 1891-1972, (U.S.) modern dancer, choreographer; teamed with Ruth St. Denis to form Denishawn dance company and school.

Marie Taglioni, 1804-84, (It.) ballerina, teacher; in title role of *La Sylphide* established image of the ethereal ballerina.

Antony Tudor, 1908-87, (Br.) choreographer, teacher; exponent of the "psychological ballet."

Mary Wigman, 1886-1973, (Ger.) modern dancer, choreographer, teacher; influential in European expressionist dance.

Agrippina Vaganova, 1879-1951, (Russ.) ballet teacher, director; codified Soviet ballet technique that developed virtuosity.

Selected Notable Opera Singers of the Past

Frances Alda, 1883-1952, (NZ.) soprano
Paul Althouse, 1889-1954, (U.S.) tenor
Pasquale Amato, 1878-1942, (It.) baritone
Marian Anderson, 1902-93, (U.S.) contralto
Jussi Björling, 1911-60, (Swed.) tenor
Lucrezia Bori, 1887-1960, (It.) soprano
Maria Callas, 1923-77, (U.S.) soprano
Emma Calvé, 1858-1942, (Fr.) soprano
Enrico Caruso, 1873-1921, (It.) tenor
Feodor Chaliapin, 1873-1938, (Russ.) bass
Boris Christoff, 1914-93, (Bulg.) bass
Richard Crooks, 1900-72, (U.S.) tenor
Giuseppe De Luca, 1876-1950, (It.) baritone
Edouard De Reszke, 1853-1917, (Pol.) bass
Jean De Reszke, 1850-1925, (Pol.) tenor
Emmy Destinn, 1878-1930, (Czech.) soprano
Emma Eames, 1865-1952, (U.S.) soprano
Geraldine Farrar, 1882-1967, (U.S.) soprano

Kirsten Flagstad, 1895-1962, (Nor.) soprano.
Olive Fremstad, 1871-1951, (Swed.-U.S.) soprano
Amelita Galli-Curci, 1882-1963, (It.) soprano
Mary Garden, 1874-1967, (Br.) soprano
Beniamino Gigli, 1890-1957, (It.) tenor
Tito Gobbi, 1913-84, (It.) baritone
Frieda Hempel, 1885-1955, (Ger.) soprano
Maria Jeritza, 1887-1982, (Czech.) soprano
Alexander Kipnis, 1891-1978, (Russ.-U.S.) bass
Lilli Lehmann, 1848-1929, (Ger.) soprano
Lotte Lehmann, 1888-1976, (Ger.-U.S.) soprano
Jenny Lind, 1820-87, (Swed.) soprano
John McCormack, 1884-1945, (Ir.) tenor
Blanche Marchesi, 1863-1940, (Fr.) soprano
Nellie Melba, 1861-1931, (Austral.) soprano.

Lauritz Melchior, 1890-1973, (Dan.) tenor
Zinka Milanov, 1906-89, (Yugo.) soprano
Lillian Nordica, 1857-1914, (U.S.) soprano
Adelina Patti, 1843-1919, (It.) soprano
Peter Pears, 1910-86, (Eng.) tenor
Jan Peerce, 1904-84, (U.S.) tenor
Ezio Pinza, 1892-1957, (It.) bass
Lily Pons, 1898-1976, (Fr.) soprano
Rosa Ponselle, 1897-1981, (U.S.) soprano
Marcella Sembrich, 1858-1935, (Pol.) soprano
Eleanor Steber, 1916-90, (U.S.) soprano
Luisa Tetrazzini, 1871-1940, (It.) soprano
Lawrence Tibbett, 1896-1960, (U.S.) baritone
Richard Tucker, 1913-75, (U.S.) tenor
Pauline Viardot, 1821-1910, (Fr.) mezzo-soprano
Leonard Warren, 1911-60, (U.S.) baritone

Some Notable Blues and Jazz Artists of the Past

Julian "Cannonball" Adderley, 1928-75, alto sax
Louis "Satchmo" Armstrong, 1900-71, trumpet, singer; originated the "scat" vocal
Mildred Bailey, 1907-51, blues singer
Chet Baker, 1929-88, trumpet
Count Basie, 1904-84, orchestra leader, piano
Sidney Bechet, 1897-1959, early innovator, soprano sax
Bix Beiderbecke, 1903-31, cornet, piano, composer

Tommy Benford, 1906-94, drummer
Bunny Berigan, 1909-42, trumpet, singer
Barney Bigard, 1906-80, clarinet
Ed Blackwell, 1929-92, drummer
Jimmy Blanton, 1921-42, bass
Charles "Buddy" Bolden, 1868-1931, cornet; formed first jazz band, in the 1890s
Big Bill Broonzy, 1893-1958, blues singer, guitar

Clifford Brown, 1930-56, trumpet
Don Byas, 1912-72, tenor sax
Cab Calloway, 1907-94, band leader
Harry Carney, 1910-74, baritone sax
Sidney Catlett, 1910-51, drums
Doc Cheatham, 1905-97, jazz and big band trumpeter
Don Cherry, 1937-95, lyrical jazz trumpeter
Charlie Christian, 1919-42, guitar
Kenny Clarke, 1914-85, pioneer of modern drums
Buck Clayton, 1911-91, trumpet, arranger
James Cleveland, 1931-91, gospel singer
Al Cohn, 1925-88, tenor sax, composer
Cozy Cole, 1909-81, drums
John Coltrane, 1926-67, tenor sax innovator
Eddie Condon, 1904-73, guitar, band leader; Dixieland
Tadd Dameron, 1917-65, piano, composer
Eddie "Lockjaw" Davis, 1921-86, tenor sax
Miles Davis, 1926-91, trumpet; pioneer of cool jazz
Wild Bill Davison, 1906-89, cornet, early Chicago jazz
Paul Desmond, 1924-77, alto sax
Vic Dickenson, 1906-84, trombone, composer
Willy Dixon, 1915-92, songwriter, blues, "You Shook Me"
Warren "Baby" Dodds, 1898-1959, Dixieland drummer
Johnny Dodds, 1892-1940, clarinet
Jimmy Dorsey, 1904-57, clarinet, alto sax; band leader
Tommy Dorsey, 1905-56, trombone; band leader
Roy Eldridge, 1911-89, trumpet, drums, singer
Duke Ellington, 1899-1974, piano, band leader, composer
Bill Evans, 1929-80, piano
Gil Evans, 1912-88, composer, arranger, piano
Ella Fitzgerald, 1918-1996, jazz vocalist, "first lady of song"
"Red" Garland, 1923-84; piano
Erroll Garner, 1921-77, piano, composer, "Misty"
Stan Getz, 1927-91, tenor sax
Dizzy Gillespie, 1917-93, trumpet, composer; bop developer
Benny Goodman, 1909-86, clarinet, band and combo leader
Dexter Gordon, 1923-90, tenor sax; bop-derived style
Bobby Hackett, 1915-76, trumpet, cornet
W. C. Handy, 1873-1958, composer, "St Louis Blues"
Coleman Hawkins, 1904-69, tenor sax; "Body and Soul"
Fletcher Henderson, 1898-1952, orchestra leader, arranger
Woody Herman, 1913-87, clarinet, alto sax, band leader
Jay C. Higginbotham, 1906-73, trombone
Earl "Fatha" Hines, 1905-83, piano, songwriter
Johnny Hodges, 1906-70, alto sax
Billie Holiday, 1915-59, blues singer, "Strange Fruit"
John Lee Hooker, b. 1917, blues singer and guitarist,
Sam "Lightnin'" Hopkins, 1912-82, blues singer, guitarist
Howlin' Wolf, 1910-1976, blues singer; harmonica, guitar
Mahalia Jackson, 1911-72, gospel singer
Blind Lemon Jefferson, 1897-1930, blues singer, guitar
Little Willie John, 1937-68, singer, songwriter
Bunk Johnson, 1879-1949, cornet, trumpet
James P. Johnson, 1891-1955, piano, composer
Robert Johnson, 1912-38, blues songwriter, singer,guitarist
Jo Jones, 1911-85, drums
Philly Joe Jones, 1923-85, drums
Thad Jones, 1923-86, trumpet, cornet
Scott Joplin, 1868-1917, ragtime composer
Louis Jordan, 1908-75, singer, alto sax
Stan Kenton, 1912-79, orchestra leader, composer, piano
Albert King, 1923-92, blues guitarist
Gene Krupa, 1909-73, drums, band and combo leader
Scott LaFaro, 1936-61, bass
Huddie Ledbetter (Leadbelly), 1888-1949, blues singer, guitar
Mel Lewis, 1929-90, drummer, orchestra leader
Jimmie Lunceford, 1902-47, band leader, sax

Jimmy McPartland, 1907-91, trumpet
Carmen McRae, 1920-94, jazz singer
Glenn Miller, 1904-44, trombone, dance band leader
Charles Mingus, 1922-79, bass, composer, combo leader
Thelonious Monk, 1920-82, piano, composer, combo leader;
  a developer of bop
Wes Montgomery, 1925-68, guitar
"Jelly Roll" Morton, 1885-1941, composer, piano, singer
Bennie Moten, 1894-1935, piano
Gerry Mulligan, 1927-96, baritone sax, songwriter, "cool school"
Turk Murphy, 1915-87, trombone, band leader
Theodore "Fats" Navarro, 1923-50, trumpet
Red Nichols, 1905-65, cornet, combo leader
King Oliver, 1885-1938, cornet, band leader; Louis Armstrong
Sy Oliver, 1910-88, Swing Era arranger, composer, conductor
Kid Ory, 1886-1973, trombone, "Muskrat Ramble"
Charlie "Bird" Parker, 1920-55, alto sax, composer; rated by
  many as greatest jazz improviser
Joe Pass, 1929-94, guitarist
Art Pepper, 1925-82, alto sax
Oscar Pettiford, 1922-60, a leading bassist in the bop era
Bud Powell, 1924-66, piano; modern jazz pioneer
Don Pullen, 1942-95, piano; percussive pianist
Sun Ra, 1915?-93, jazz bandleader, pianist, composer
Gertrude "Ma" Rainey, 1886-1939, blues singer
Don Redman, 1900-64, composer, arranger
Django Reinhardt, 1910-53, guitar; Belgian gypsy, first Euro-
  pean to influence American jazz
Buddy Rich, 1917-87, drums, band leader
Red Rodney, 1928-94, trumpeter
Frank Rosolino, 1926-78, trombone
Jimmy Rowles, 1918-96, jazz composer, accompanist
Jimmy Rushing, 1903-72, blues singer
Pee Wee Russell, 1906-69, clarinet
Zoot Sims, 1925-85, tenor, alto sax; clarinet
Zutty Singleton, 1898-1975, Dixieland drummer
Bessie Smith, 1894-1937, blues singer
Clarence "Pinetop" Smith, 1904-29, piano, singer; pioneer of
  boogie woogie
Willie "The Lion" Smith, 1897-1973, stride style pianist
Muggsy Spanier, 1906-67, cornet, band leader
Billy Strayhorn, 1915-67, composer, piano
Sonny Stitt, 1924-82, alto, tenor sax
Art Tatum, 1910-56, piano; technical virtuoso
Art Taylor, 1929-95, jazz drummer, bandleader
Jack Teagarden, 1905-64, trombone, singer
Dave Tough, 1908-48, drums
Lennie Tristano, 1919-78, piano, composer
Joe Turner, 1911-85, blues singer
Sarah Vaughan, 1924-90, singer
Joe Venuti, 1904-78, first great jazz violinist
T-Bone Walker, 1910-75, guitarist; pioneered electric blues
  guitar sound
Thomas "Fats" Waller, 1904-43, piano, singer, composer
Dinah Washington, 1924-63, singer
Ethel Waters, 1896-1977, jazz and blues singer
Muddy Waters, 1915-83, blues singer, songwriter
Johnny Watson, 1935-96, rhythm and blues guitarist
Chick Webb, 1902-39, band leader, drums
Ben Webster, 1909-73, tenor sax
Paul Whiteman, 1890-1967, jazz orchestra leader.
Charles "Cootie" Williams, 1908-85, trumpet, band leader
Mary Lou Williams, 1914-81, piano, composer
Teddy Wilson, 1912-86, piano, composer
Kai Winding, 1922-83, trombone, composer
Jimmy Yancey, 1894-1951, piano
Lester "Pres" Young, 1909-59, tenor sax, composer.

Noted Country Music Artists of the Past

Roy Acuff, 1903-92, guitarist, singer, songwriter, "Wabash
  Cannon Ball"
Boudleaux Bryant, 1920-87, songwriter, singer; "Hey Joe"
Carter Family (original members, "Mother" Maybelle 1909-78;
  Alvin, 1891-1960, Sara, 1898-1979) "Wildwood Flower"
Patsy Cline, 1932-63, singer; "Crazy"
Vernon Dalhart, 1883-1948, singer; "The Death of Floyd Collins"
Lester Flatt, 1914-79, singer, guitarist; "Foggy Mountain Breakdown"
Red Foley, 1910-68, singer; "Blues in My Heart"
Tennessee Ernie Ford, 1919-91, singer, songwriter; "Shotgun Boogie"
Lefty Frizzell, 1928-75, singer, guitarist; "Long Black Veil"
Kendall L. Hayes, 1936-95, song writer; "Walk On By"
Uncle Dave Macon, 1870-1952, singer, banjo player and comedian.
J. D. Miller, 1923-96, songwriter; "Honky-Tonk Angels"
Roger Miller, 1936-92, singer, songwriter; "King of the Road"
Bill Monroe, 1911-96, singer, songwriter, and mandolin player
  considered "father of Bluegrass music"; "Mule Skinner Blues"
Minnie Pearl, 1912-96, comedienne, Grand Ole Opry star.
Jim Reeves, 1924-64, singer, songwriter; "Four Walls"
Charlie Rich (Silver Fox), 1932-95, singer, songwriter; "The
  Most Beautiful Girl"

Tex Ritter, 1907-74, singer, songwriter; "Jingle, Jangle, Jingle"
Marty Robbins, 1925-82, singer, songwriter; "A White Sport
  Coat and a Pink Carnation"
Jimmie Rodgers, 1897-1933, singer, songwriter; "T for Texas"
Fred Rose, 1898-1954, songwriter, singer, musician, "Blue
  Eyes Cryin' in the Rain"
Original Sons of the Pioneers, Len Slye (Roy Rogers), b
  1912, Bob Nolan, 1908-80, singers, songwriters, "Tumbling
  Tumbleweed"; Tim Spencer, 1905-74, singer, songwriter,
  "Careless Kisses"; Hugh Farr, 1903-80, Karl Farr, 1909-61,
  Lloyd Perryman, 1917-77, singers
Merle Travis, 1917-83, singer, guitarist, songwriter; "16 Tons"
Ernest Tubb, 1914-84, singer, songwriter and guitarist; "The
  Yellow Rose of Texas"
Conway Twitty, 1933-93, singer, songwriter; "Hello Darlin' "
Dottie West, 1932-91, singer, songwriter; "Here Comes My
  Baby"
Hank Williams Sr., 1923-53, singer, songwriter; "Your Cheatin'
  Heart"
Bob Wills, 1905-75, singer, bandleader, songwriter; "San An-
  tonio Rose"

Some Rock and Roll, Rhythm and Blues, and Rap Artists

AC/DC: "Back in Black"
Bryan Adams: "Cuts Like a Knife"
Aerosmith: "Sweet Emotion"
*The Allman Brothers Band (1995): "Ramblin' Man"
*The Animals (1994): "House of the Rising Sun"
Paul Anka: "Lonely Boy"
The Association: "Cherish"
Frankie Avalon: "Venus"
*La Vern Baker (1991): "I Cried a Tear"
*†Hank Ballard and the Midnighters (1990): "Work With Me, Annie"
*The Band (1994): "The Weight"
*The Beach Boys (1988): "Good Vibrations"
Beastie Boys: "(You Gotta) Fight for Your Right (to Party)"
*The Beatles (1988): Sgt. Pepper's Lonely Hearts Club Band
Beck: "Loser"
*The Bee Gees (1997): "Stayin' Alive"
Pat Benatar: "Hit Me With Your Best Shot"
*Chuck Berry (1986): "Johnny B. Goode"
The Big Bopper: "Chantilly Lace"
Black Sabbath: "Paranoid"
*Bobby "Blue" Bland (1992): "Turn On Your Love Light"
Mary J. Blige: My Life
Blind Faith: "Can't Find My Way Home"
Blondie: "Heart of Glass"
Blood, Sweat, and Tears: "Spinning Wheel"
Gary "U.S." Bonds: "Quarter to Three"
Bon Jovi: "Livin' on a Prayer"
*Booker T. and the Mgs (1992): "Green Onions"
Earl Bostic: "Flamingo"
*David Bowie (1996): "Space Oddity"
Boyz II Men: "I'll Make Love to You"
Toni Braxton: "Un-Break My Heart"
*James Brown (1986): "Papa's Got a Brand New Bag"
*Ruth Brown (1993): "Lucky Lips"
Jackson Browne: "Doctor My Eyes"
*Buffalo Springfield (1997): "For What It's Worth"
Bush: "Glycerine"
*The Byrds (1991): "Turn! Turn! Turn!"
Mariah Carey: "Vision of Love"
The Cars: "Shake It Up"
*Johnny Cash (1992): "I Walk the Line"
*Ray Charles (1986): "Georgia on My Mind"
Cheap Trick: "Surrender"
Chubby Checker: "The Twist"
Chicago: "Saturday in the Park"
Eric Clapton: "Layla"
The Clash: "Rock the Casbah"
*The Coasters (1987): "Yakety Yak"
*Eddie Cochran (1987): "Summertime Blues"
Joe Cocker: "With a Little Help From My Friends"
Phil Collins: "Against All Odds"
Sean "Puff Daddy" Combs: "I'll Be Missing You"
*Sam Cooke (1986): "You Send Me"
Coolio: "Gangsta's Paradise"
Alice Cooper: "School's Out"
Elvis Costello: "Alison"
*Cream (1993): "Sunshine of Your Love"
*Creedence Clearwater Revival (1993): "Proud Mary"
*Crosby, Stills, and Nash (1997): "Suite: Judy Blue Eyes"
Sheryl Crow: "All I Want to Do"
The Cure: "Boys Don't Cry"
The Crystals: "Da Doo Ron Ron"
Cypress Hill: "Insane in the Brain"
Danny and the Juniors: "At the Hop"
*Bobby Darin (1990): "Splish Splash"
Spencer Davis Group: "Gimme Some Lovin' "
Deep Purple: "Smoke on the Water"
Def Leppard: "Photograph"
Depeche Mode: "Strange Love"
*Bo Diddley (1987): "Who Do You Love?"
*†Dion and the Belmonts (1989): "A Teenager in Love"
Celine Dion: "Because You Loved Me"
Dire Straits: "Money for Nothing"
*Fats Domino (1986): "Blueberry Hill"

Donovan: "Mellow Yellow"
The Doobie Brothers: "What a Fool Believes"
*The Doors (1993): "Light My Fire"
*The Drifters (1988): "Save the Last Dance for Me"
Duran Duran: "Hungry Like the Wolf"
*Bob Dylan (1988): "Like a Rolling Stone"
The Eagles: "Hotel California"
Earth, Wind, and Fire: "Shining Star"
*Duane Eddy (1994): "Rebel-Rouser"
Emerson, Lake, and Palmer: "Lucky Man"
En Vogue: "Hold On"
The Eurythmics: "Sweet Dreams (Are Made of This)"
*The Everly Brothers (1986): "Wake Up, Little Susie"
The Five Satins: "In the Still of the Night"
Fleetwood Mac: Rumours
*The Four Seasons (1990): "Sherry"
*The Four Tops (1990): "I Can't Help Myself (Sugar Pie, Honey Bunch)"
*Aretha Franklin (1987): "Respect"
Peter Gabriel: "Shock the Monkey"
Marvin Gaye (1987): "I Heard It Through the Grapevine"
Genesis: "No Reply at All"
Grand Funk Railroad: "We're an American Band"
Grand Master Flash and the Furious Five: "The Message"
*The Grateful Dead (1994): "Uncle John's Band"
*Al Green (1995): "Let's Stay Together"
Guns N' Roses: "Sweet Child o' Mine"
*†Bill Haley and His Comets (1987): "Rock Around the Clock"
Hall and Oates: "Kiss on My List"
Hanson: "MMMBop"
Heart: "Barracuda"
*Jimi Hendrix (1992): "Purple Haze"
Herman's Hermits: "Mrs. Brown, You've Got a Lovely Daughter"
*†Buddy Holly and the Crickets (1986): "That'll Be the Day"
*John Lee Hooker (1991): "Boogie Chillun"
Hootie and the Blowfish: Cracked Rear View
Whitney Houston: "I Will Always Love You"
*The Impressions (1991): "For Your Precious Love"
INXS: "Need You Tonight"
*The Isley Brothers (1992): "It's Your Thing"
*The Jackson Five (1997): "ABC"
Janet Jackson: Rhythm Nation
Michael Jackson: Thriller
*Etta James (1993): "Tell Mama"
Tommy James & The Shondells: "Crimson and Clover"
Jay and the Americans: "This Magic Moment"
*Jefferson Airplane (1996): "White Rabbit"
Jethro Tull: Aqualung
Jewel: "You Were Meant for Me"
Joan Jett: "I Love Rock 'n' Roll"
Billy Joel: "Piano Man"
*Elton John (1994): "Candle in the Wind"
*Little Willie John (1996): "Sleep"
*Janis Joplin (1995): "Me and Bobby McGee"
K.C. and the Sunshine Band: "Get Down Tonight"
*B.B. King (1987): "The Thrill Is Gone"
Carole King: Tapestry
*The Kinks (1990): "You Really Got Me"
Kiss: "Rock 'n' Roll All Night"
*Gladys Knight and the Pips (1996): "Midnight Train to Georgia"
*Led Zeppelin (1995): Stairway to Heaven"
Brenda Lee: "I'm Sorry"
*John Lennon (1994): "Imagine"
*Jerry Lee Lewis (1986): "Whole Lotta Shakin' Going On"
Little Anthony and the Imperials: "Tears on My Pillow"
*Little Richard (1986): "Tutti Frutti"
Live: "Lightning Crashes"
L. L. Cool J: "Mama Said Knock You Out"
The Lovin' Spoonful: "Summer in the City"

*Frankie Lymon and the Teenagers (1993): "Why Do Fools Fall in Love?"
Lynyrd Skynyrd: "Free Bird"
Madonna: "Material Girl"
The Mamas and the Papas: "Monday, Monday"
*Bob Marley (1994): Exodus
*Martha and the Vandellas (1995): "Dancin' in the Streets"
The Marvelettes: "Please, Mr. Postman"
Paul McCartney: "Band on the Run"
Don McLean: "American Pie"
*Clyde McPhatter (1987): "A Lover's Question"
Meat Loaf: "Paradise by the Dashboard Light"
John (Cougar) Mellencamp: "Jack and Diane"
Men at Work: "Who Can It Be Now?"
Metallica: "Enter Sandman"
George Michael: "Faith"
*Joni Mitchell (1997): "Big Yellow Taxi"
The Monkees: "I'm a Believer"
Moody Blues: "Nights in White Satin"
Alanis Morissette: "Ironic"
*Van Morrison (1993): "Brown-Eyed Girl"
*Ricky Nelson (1987): "Hello, Mary Lou"
Nine Inch Nails: "Closer"
Nirvana: Nevermind
The Notorious B.I.G.: "Mo Money Mo Problems"
Oasis: "Wonderwall"
*Roy Orbison (1987): "Oh, Pretty Woman"
Ozzy Osbourne: "Crazy Train"
*Parliament/Funkadelic (1997): "One Nation Under a Groove"
Pearl Jam: "Jeremy"
*Carl Perkins (1987): "Blue Suede Shoes"
Peter, Paul, and Mary: "Leavin' on a Jet Plane"
Tom Petty and the Heartbreakers: "Refugee"
*Wilson Pickett (1991): "Land of 1,000 Dances"
*Pink Floyd (1996): The Wall
*The Platters (1990): "The Great Pretender"
The Police: "Every Breath You Take"
Poco: "Crazy Love"
Iggy Pop: "Lust for Life"
*Elvis Presley (1986): "Love Me Tender"
The Pretenders: "Brass in Pocket"
Lloyd Price: "Stagger Lee"
Prince/⚥ (TAFKAP): "Purple Rain"
Procol Harum: "A Whiter Shade of Pale"
Public Enemy: "Fight the Power"
Queen: "Bohemian Rhapsody"
The Ramones: "I Wanna Be Sedated"
*Otis Redding (1989): "(Sittin' on) The Dock of the Bay"
Red Hot Chili Peppers: "Under the Bridge"
*Jimmy Reed (1991): "Ain't That Loving You, Baby?"
Lou Reed: "Walk on the Wild Side"
R.E.M.: "Losing My Religion"
The Righteous Brothers: "You've Lost That Lovin' Feelin' "
Johnny Rivers: "Poor Side of Town"
*†Smokey Robinson and the Miracles (1987): "Shop Around"
*The Rolling Stones (1989): "Satisfaction"
The Ronettes: "Be My Baby"
Linda Ronstadt: "You're No Good"
Run-D.M.C.: "Raisin' Hell"
Salt-N-Pepa: "Shoop"
*Sam and Dave (1992): "Soul Man"
Santana: "Black Magic Woman"
Seal: "Kiss From a Rose"
Neil Sedaka: "Breaking Up Is Hard to Do"
The Sex Pistols: "Anarchy in the U.K."
Tupac Shakur: "How Do U Want It"
Del Shannon: "Runaway"
*The Shirelles (1996): "Soldier Boy"
Carly Simon: "You're So Vain"
Paul Simon: "50 Ways to Leave Your Lover"
*Simon and Garfunkel (1990): "Bridge Over Troubled Water"
*Sly and the Family Stone (1993): "Everyday People"
Smashing Pumpkins: "Today"
Patti Smith: "Because the Night"

Soundgarden: "Black Hole Sun"
Spice Girls: "Wannabe"
Bruce Springsteen: "Born to Run"
Squeeze: "Tempted"
Steely Dan: "Rikki Don't Lose That Number"
Steppenwolf: "Born to Be Wild"
***Rod Stewart (1994):** "Maggie Mae"
Sting: "If You Love Somebody, Set Them Free"
The Sugar Hill Gang: "Rapper's Delight"
Donna Summer: "Bad Girls"
***The Supremes (1988):** "Stop! In the Name of Love"
Talking Heads: "Once in a Lifetime"
James Taylor: "You've Got a Friend"

***The Temptations (1989):** "My Girl"
Three Dog Night: "Joy to the World"
TLC: "Waterfalls"
T. Rex: "Bang a Gong (Get It On)"
***Big Joe Turner (1987):** "Shake, Rattle & Roll"
***Ike and Tina Turner (1991):** "Proud Mary"
***Tina Turner (1991):** "What's Love Got to Do With It?"
The Turtles: "Happy Together"
U2: "With or Without You"
Ritchie Valens: "La Bamba"
Van Halen: "Running With the Devil"
Stevie Ray Vaughan: "Crossfire"
***The Velvet Underground (1996):** "Sweet Jane"

Dionne Warwick: "I Say a Little Prayer"
***Muddy Waters (1987):** "I Can't Be Satisfied"
Mary Wells: "My Guy"
***The Who (1990):** *Tommy*
***Jackie Wilson (1987):** "That's Why"
***Stevie Wonder (1989):** "You Are the Sunshine of My Life"
***The Yardbirds (1992):** "For Your Love"
Yes: "Roundabout"
***Neil Young (1995):** "Down by the River"
***The Young Rascals/The Rascals (1997):** "Good Lovin' "
***†Frank Zappa/Mothers of Invention (1995):** *Sheik Yerbouti*
ZZ Top: "Legs"

*Inducted into Rock and Roll Hall of Fame as a performer between 1986 and 1997; year of induction in parentheses. † Only individual performer is a member of the Rock and Roll Hall of Fame. *Italics* = Album; quotation marks = single.

Entertainment Personalities — Where and When Born

actors, musicians, dancers, singers, producers, directors, radio-TV performers

(as of Sept. 1997)

Name	Birthplace	Birthdate	Name	Birthplace	Birthdate
Abbado, Claudio	Milan, Italy	6/26/33	Arquette, Patricia	New York, NY.	4/8/68
Abdul, Paula	San Fernando, CA	6/19/62	Arquette, Rosanna	New York, NY.	8/10/59
Abraham, F. Murray	Pittsburgh, PA.	10/24/39	Arroyo, Martina	New York, NY.	2/2/37
Adams, Bryan	Kingston, Ontario.	11/5/59	Arthur, Beatrice	New York, NY.	5/13/26
Adams, Don	New York, NY.	4/19/26	Ashley, Elizabeth	Ocala, FL.	8/30/41
Adams, Edie	Kingston, PA	4/16/29	Asner, Ed	Kansas City, MO.	11/15/29
Adams, Joey	New York, NY.	1/6/11	Assante, Armand	New York, NY.	10/4/49
Adams, Mason	New York, NY.	2/26/19	Astin, John	Baltimore, MD.	3/30/30
Adjani, Isabelle	Paris, France	6/27/55	Atkins, Chet	Luttrell, TN.	6/20/24
Agar, John	Chicago, IL.	1/31/21	Attenborough, Richard	Cambridge, England	8/29/23
Agutter, Jenny	London, England	12/20/52	Auberjonois, Rene	New York, NY.	6/1/40
Aiello, Danny	New York, NY.	6/20/33	Aumont, Jean-Pierre	Paris, France	1/5/09
Aimee, Anouk	Paris, France	4/27/34	Austin, Patti	New York, NY.	8/10/48
Albanese, Licia	Bari, Italy	7/22/13	Autry, Alan	Shreveport, LA	7/31/52
Alberghetti, Anna Maria.	Pesaro, Italy.	5/15/36	Autry, Gene	Tioga, TX.	9/29/07
Albert, Eddie	Rock Island, IL	4/22/08	Avalon, Frankie	Philadelphia, PA	9/18/39
Albert, Marv	New York, NY.	6/12/43	Ax, Emmanuel.	Lvov, Ukraine	6/8/49
Alda, Alan	New York, NY.	1/28/36	Axton, Hoyt.	Duncan, OK.	3/25/38
Alexander, Jane	Boston, MA	10/28/39	Aykroyd, Dan	Ottawa, Ontario.	7/1/52
Alexander, Jason	Newark, NJ	9/23/59	Aznavour, Charles	Paris, France	5/22/24
Allen, Debbie	Houston, TX.	1/16/50	Babyface	Indianapolis, IN.	4/10/59
Allen, Joan	Rochelle, IL	8/20/56	Bacall, Lauren	New York, NY.	9/16/24
Allen, Karen	Carrollton, IL.	10/5/51	Bacon, Kevin	Philadelphia, PA	7/8/58
Allen, Steve	New York, NY.	12/26/21	Baez, Joan	Staten Island, NY	1/9/41
Allen, Tim	Denver, CO	6/13/53	Bain, Conrad	Lethbridge, Alberta.	2/4/23
Allen, Woody	Brooklyn, NY	12/1/35	Baio, Scott	Brooklyn, NY	9/22/61
Alley, Kirstie	Wichita, KS	1/12/55	Baker, Anita	Toledo, OH	1/26/58
Allman, Gregg	Nashville, TN	12/7/47	Baker, Carroll	Johnstown, PA	5/28/31
Allyson, June	New York, NY.	10/7/17	Baker, Joe Don	Groesbeck, TX	2/12/36
Alonso, Maria Conchita.	Cienfuegos, Cuba	6/29/57	Baker, Kathy	Midland, TX	6/8/50
Alpert, Herb	Los Angeles, CA	3/31/35	Bakula, Scott	St. Louis, MO	10/9/55
Altman, Robert	Kansas City, MO.	2/20/25	Baldwin, Alec	Massapequa, NY.	4/3/58
Ames, Ed	Boston, MA	7/9/27	Baldwin, Daniel	Massapequa, NY.	—
Amos, John	Newark, NJ	12/27/42	Baldwin, Stephen.	Massapequa, NY.	5/12/66
Amos, Tori	North Carolina	8/22/64	Baldwin, William	Massapequa, NY.	2/21/63
Anderson, Gillian	Chicago, IL.	8/9/68	Ballard, Kaye	Cleveland, OH	11/20/26
Anderson, Harry	Newport, RI	10/14/49	Bancroft, Anne	New York, NY.	9/17/31
Anderson, Ian	Dunfermline, Scotland	8/10/47	Banderas, Antonio	Málaga, Spain	8/10/60
Anderson, Kevin	Illinois	1/13/60	Banks, Tyra	Los Angeles, CA.	12/3/73
Anderson, Loni	St. Paul, MN.	8/5/46	Bannon, Jack	Los Angeles, CA.	6/14/40
Anderson, Lynn	Grand Forks, ND.	9/26/47	Baranski, Christine	Buffalo, NY.	5/2/52
Anderson, Melissa Sue.	Berkeley, CA	9/26/62	Barbeau, Adrienne	Sacramento, CA	6/11/45
Anderson, Richard	Long Branch, NJ	8/8/26	Bardot, Brigitte	Paris, France	9/28/34
Anderson, Richard Dean.	Minneapolis, MN.	1/23/50	Barker, Bob	Darrington, WA.	12/12/23
Andersson, Bibi.	Stockholm, Sweden	11/11/35	Barkin, Ellen	New York, NY.	4/16/55
Andress, Ursula.	Bern, Switzerland	3/19/36	Barrie, Barbara	Chicago, IL.	5/23/31
Andrews, Anthony	London, England	1/12/48	Barry, Gene	New York, NY.	6/14/19
Andrews, Julie.	Walton, England	10/1/35	Barty, Billy	Millsboro, PA	10/25/24
Andrews, Patty	Minneapolis, MN.	2/16/20	Barrymore, Drew	Los Angeles, CA.	2/22/75
Aniston, Jennifer	Sherman Oaks, CA.	2/11/69	Bartoli, Cecilia.	Rome, Italy	6/4/66
Anka, Paul	Ottawa, Ontario.	7/30/41	Bartolucci, Bernardo.	Parma, Italy	3/16/40
Ann-Margret	Stockholm, Sweden	4/28/41	Baryshnikov, Mikhail	Riga, Latvia	1/28/48
Applegate, Christina.	Los Angeles, CA.	11/25/72	Basinger, Kim	Athens, GA	12/8/53
Archer, Anne.	Los Angeles, CA.	8/25/47	Bassett, Angela	New York, NY.	8/16/58
Arkin, Adam	Brooklyn, NY	8/19/56	Bassey, Shirley	Cardiff, Wales.	1/8/37
Arkin, Alan	New York, NY.	3/26/34	Bateman, Jason	Rye, NY.	1/14/69
Arnaz, Desi Jr.	Los Angeles, CA.	1/19/53	Bateman, Justine.	Rye, NY.	2/19/66
Arnaz, Lucie	Los Angeles, CA.	7/17/51	Bates, Alan.	Allestree, England	2/17/34
Arness, James	Minneapolis, MN.	5/26/23	Bates, Kathy	Memphis, TN	6/28/48
Arnold, Eddy	Henderson, TN	5/15/18	Battle, Kathleen	Portsmouth, OH	8/13/48
Arnold, Tom	Ottumwa, IA	3/6/59	Baxter, Meredith	Los Angeles, CA.	6/21/47

Name	Birthplace	Birthdate	Name	Birthplace	Birthdate
Bean, Orson	Burlington, VT	7/22/28	Brewer, Teresa	Toledo, OH	5/7/31
Beatty, Ned	Louisville, KY	7/6/37	Bridges, Beau	Hollywood, CA	12/9/41
Beatty, Warren	Richmond, VA	3/30/37	Bridges, Jeff	Los Angeles, CA	12/4/49
Beck (Hansen)	Los Angeles, CA	7/8/70	Bridges, Lloyd	San Leandro, CA	1/15/13
Beck, Jeff	Surrey, England	6/24/44	Brimley, Wilford	Salt Lake City, UT	9/27/34
Beck, John	Chicago, IL	1/28/43	Brinkley, Christie	Malibu, CA	2/2/54
Bedelia, Bonnie	New York, NY	3/25/48	Broderick, Matthew	New York, NY	3/21/62
Begley, Ed, Jr.	Los Angeles, CA	9/16/49	Brolin, James	Los Angeles, CA	7/18/40
Belafonte, Harry	New York, NY	3/1/27	Bronson, Charles	Ehrenfeld, PA	11/3/22
Bel Geddes, Barbara	New York, NY	10/31/22	Brooks, Albert	Beverly Hills, CA	7/22/47
Belmondo, Jean-Paul	Neuilly-sur-Seine, France	4/9/33	Brooks, Garth	Tulsa, OK	2/7/62
Belushi, Jim	Chicago, IL	6/15/54	Brooks, James L	North Bergen, NJ	5/9/40
Belzer, Richard	Bridgeport, CT	8/4/44	Brooks, Mel	New York, NY	6/28/26
Benatar, Pat	Brooklyn, NY	1/10/53	Brosnan, Pierce	Co. Meath, Ireland	5/16/53
Benedict, Dirk	Helena, MT	3/1/45	Brown, Blair	Washington, DC	1948
Bening, Annette	Topeka, KS	5/29/58	Brown, Bobby	Boston, MA	2/5/69
Benjamin, Richard	New York, NY	5/22/38	Brown, Bryan	Sydney, Australia	6/23/47
Bennett, Tony	New York, NY	8/3/26	Brown, James	Pulaski, TN	6/17/28
Benson, George	Pittsburgh, PA	3/22/43	Brown, Les	Reinerton, PA	3/14/12
Benson, Robby	Dallas, TX	1/21/56	Browne, Jackson	Heidelberg, Germany	10/9/48
Berenger, Tom	Chicago, IL	5/31/50	Browne, Roscoe Lee	Woodbury, NJ	5/2/25
Bergen, Candice	Beverly Hills, CA	5/9/46	Brubeck, Dave	Concord, CA	12/6/20
Bergen, Polly	Knoxville, TN	7/14/30	Bryson, Peabo	Greenville, SC	4/13/51
Bergman, Ingmar	Uppsala, Sweden	7/14/18	Buckley, Betty	Ft. Worth, TX	7/3/47
Berle, Milton	New York, NY	7/12/08	Buffett, Jimmy	Pascagoula, MS	12/25/46
Berlinger, Warren	Brooklyn, NY	8/31/37	Bujold, Genevieve	Montreal, Quebec	7/1/42
Berman, Lazar	Leningrad, Russia	2/26/30	Bullock, Sandra	Arlington, VA	7/26/67
Berman, Shelley	Chicago, IL	2/3/26	Bumbry, Grace	St. Louis, MO	1/4/37
Bernard, Crystal	Dallas, TX	9/30/64	Burghoff, Gary	Bristol, CT	5/24/40
Bernhard, Sandra	Flint, MI	6/6/55	Burke, Delta	Orlando, FL	7/30/56
Bernsen, Corbin	N. Hollywood, CA	9/7/54	Burnett, Carol	San Antonio, TX	4/26/33
Berry, Chuck	St. Louis, MO	10/18/26	Burrows, Darren E.	Winfield, KS	9/12/66
Berry, Halle	Cleveland, OH	8/14/68	Burstyn, Ellen	Detroit, MI	12/7/32
Berry, Ken	Moline, IL	11/3/33	Burton, LeVar	Landstuhl, W Germany	2/16/57
Bertinelli, Valerie	Wilmington, DE	4/23/60	Burton, Tim	Burbank, CA	8/25/58
Bialik, Mayim	San Diego, CA	12/12/75	Buscemi, Steve	Brooklyn, NY	12/13/57
Bikel, Theodore	Vienna, Austria	5/2/24	Busey, Gary	Goose Creek, TX	6/29/44
Billingsley, Barbara	Los Angeles, CA	12/22/22	Busfield, Timothy	Lansing, MI	6/12/57
Binoche, Juliette	Paris, France	4/9/64	Butler, Brett	Montgomery, AL	1/30/58
Birney, David	Washington, DC	4/23/39	Buttons, Red	New York, NY	2/5/19
Bishop, Joey	Bronx, NY	2/3/18	Buzzi, Ruth	Westerly, RI	7/24/36
Bisset, Jacqueline	Weybridge, England	9/13/44	Byrne, David	Dumbarton, Scotland	5/14/52
Bissett, Josie	Seattle, WA	10/5/69	Caan, James	New York, NY	3/26/39
Björk (Gudmundsdottir)	Rheinberg, Iceland	10/21/66	Caballe, Montserrat	Barcelona, Spain	4/12/33
Black, Clint	Katy, TX	2/4/62	Caesar, Sid	Yonkers, NY	9/8/22
Black, Karen	Park Ridge, IL	7/1/42	Cage, Nicolas	Long Beach, CA	1/7/64
Blades, Ruben	Panama City, Panama	7/16/48	Cain, Dean	Mt. Clemens, MI	7/31/66
Blair, Linda	St. Louis, MO	1/22/59	Caine, Michael	London, England	3/14/33
Blake, Robert	Nutley, NJ	9/18/33	Caldwell, Sarah	Maryville, MO	3/6/24
Bledsoe, Tempestt	Chicago, IL	8/1/73	Caldwell, Zoe	Melbourne, Australia	9/14/33
Bloom, Claire	London, England	2/15/31	Calhoun, Rory	Los Angeles, CA	8/8/23
Blyth, Ann	Mt. Kisco, NY	8/16/28	Cameron, Kirk	Panorama City, CA	10/12/70
Bochco, Steven	New York, NY	12/16/43	Camp, Hamilton	London, England	10/30/34
Bogarde, Dirk	London, England	3/28/20	Campanella, Joseph	New York, NY	11/21/27
Bogosian, Eric	Boston, MA	4/24/53	Campbell, Glen	Billstown, AR	4/22/36
Bogdanovich, Peter	Kingston, NY	7/30/39	Campbell, Naomi	London, England	5/22/70
Bologna, Joseph	Brooklyn, NY	12/30/38	Campbell, Neve	Toronto, Ontario	10/3/73
Bolton, Michael	New Haven, CT.	2/26/53	Campion, Jane	Wellington, New Zealand	1955
Bonet, Lisa	San Francisco, CA	11/16/67	Cannell, Stephen J.	Los Angeles, CA	2/5/42
Bonham-Carter, Helena	London, England	5/26/66	Cannon, Dyan	Tacoma, WA	1/4/37
Bon Jovi, Jon	Sayreville, NJ	3/2/62	Capshaw, Kate	Ft. Worth, TX	1953
Bono (Vox)	Dublin, Ireland	5/10/60	Carey, Drew	Cleveland, OH	5/23/61
Bono, Sonny	Detroit, MI	2/16/35	Carey, Mariah	Huntington, NY	3/27/70
Boone, Debby	Hackensack, NJ	9/22/56	Cariou, Len	Winnipeg, Canada	9/30/39
Boone, Pat	Jacksonville, FL	6/1/34	Carlin, George	New York, NY	5/12/37
Borge, Victor	Copenhagen, Denmark	1/3/09	Carlisle, Kitty	New Orleans, LA	9/3/15
Borgnine, Ernest	Hamden, CT.	1/24/17	Carmen, Eric	Cleveland, OH.	8/11/49
Bosson, Barbara	Charleroi, PA	11/1/39	Carney, Art	Mt. Vernon, NY	11/4/18
Bosco, Philip	Jersey City, NJ	9/26/30	Carpenter, Mary Chapin	Princeton, NJ	2/21/58
Bosley, Tom	Chicago, IL	10/1/27	Caron, Leslie	Boulogne, France	7/1/31
Bostwick, Barry	San Mateo, CA	2/24/45	Carr, Vikki	El Paso, TX	7/19/41
Bottoms, Timothy	Santa Barbara, CA	8/30/51	Carradine, David	Hollywood, CA	10/8/36
Bowie, David	London, England	1/8/47	Carradine, Keith	San Mateo, CA	8/8/49
Boxleitner, Bruce	Elgin, IL	5/12/50	Carreras, Jose	Barcelona, Spain	12/5/46
Boy George	London, England	6/14/61	Carrere, Tia	Honolulu, HI	1/2/66
Boyle, Peter	Philadelphia, PA	10/18/33	Carrey, Jim	Jackson Point, Canada	1/17/62
Bracco, Lorraine	Brooklyn, NY	10/2/55	Carroll, Diahann	Bronx, NY	7/17/35
Bracken, Eddie	New York, NY	2/7/20	Carroll, Pat	Shreveport, LA	5/5/27
Branagh, Kenneth	Belfast, N. Ireland	12/10/60	Carson, Johnny	Corning, IA	10/23/25
Brando, Marlon	Omaha, NE	4/3/24	Carter, Benny	New York, NY	8/8/07
Brandy (Norwood)	McComb, MS	2/11/79	Carter, Dixie	McLemoresville, TN	5/25/39
Braugher, Andre	Chicago, Il	7/1/—	Carter, Jack	New York, NY	6/24/23
Braxton, Toni	Severn, MD	1968	Carter, June	Maces Spring, VA	6/23/29
Brennan, Eileen	Los Angeles, CA	9/3/35	Carter, Lynda	Phoenix, AZ	7/24/51
Brenner, David	Philadelphia, PA	2/4/45	Carter, Nell	Birmingham, AL	9/13/48

Name	Birthplace	Birthdate	Name	Birthplace	Birthdate
Carter, Ron	Royal Oak Twp, MI	5/4/37	Coyote, Peter	New York, NY	1942
Caruso, David	Forest Hills, NY	1/17/56	Cox, Ronny	Cloudcroft, NM	8/23/38
Carvey, Dana	Missoula, MT	4/2/55	Crain, Jeanne	Barstow, CA	5/25/25
Casadesus, Gaby	Marseilles, France	8/9/01	Crawford, Cindy	DeKalb, IL	2/20/66
Cash, Johnny	Kingsland, AR	2/26/32	Crawford, Michael	Salisbury, England	1/19/42
Cash, Rosanne	Memphis, TN	5/24/55	Crenna, Richard	Los Angeles, CA	11/30/26
Cass, Peggy	Boston, MA	5/21/24	Crespin, Regine	Marseilles, France	2/23/26
Cassidy, David	New York, NY	4/12/50	Cronyn, Hume	London, Ontario	7/18/11
Cates, Phoebe	New York, NY	7/16/63	Crosby, David	Los Angeles, CA	8/14/41
Cathbert, Lacey	Purvis, MS	9/30/82	Cross, Ben	London, England	12/16/47
Cavett, Dick	Gibbon, NE	11/19/36	Crouse, Lindsay	New York, NY	5/12/48
Chamberlain, Richard	Beverly Hills, CA	3/31/35	Crow, Sheryl	Kennett, MO	2/11/62
Chan, Jackie	Hong Kong	4/7/54	Crowe, Cameron	Palm Springs, CA	7/13/57
Channing, Carol	Seattle, WA	1/31/23	Crowell, Rodney	Houston, TX	8/17/50
Channing, Stockard	New York, NY	2/13/44	Cruise, Tom	Syracuse, NY	7/3/62
Chaplin, Geraldine	Santa Monica, CA	7/31/44	Crystal, Billy	Long Beach, NY	3/14/47
Chapman, Tracy	Cleveland, OH	3/30/64	Culkin, Macaulay	New York, NY	8/26/80
Charisse, Cyd	Amarillo, TX	3/8/21	Cullum, John	Knoxville, TN	3/2/30
Charles, Ray	Albany, GA	9/23/30	Culp, Robert	Oakland, CA	8/16/30
Charo	Murcia, Spain	1/15/51	Cummings, Constance	Seattle, WA	5/15/10
Chase, Chevy	New York, NY	10/8/43	Curry, Tim	Cheshire, England	4/19/46
Cheadle, Don	Kansas City, MO	11/29/64	Curtin, Jane	Cambridge, MA	9/6/47
Checker, Chubby	Philadelphia, PA	10/3/41	Curtis, Jamie Lee	Los Angeles, CA	11/22/58
Cher	El Centro, CA	5/20/46	Curtis, Keene	Salt Lake City, UT	2/15/23
Chiklis, Michael	Lowell, MA	8/30/63	Curtis, Tony	New York, NY	6/3/25
Chong, Rae Dawn	Vancouver, Canada	2/28/62	Cusack, Joan	Evanston, IL	10/11/62
Chong, Thomas	Edmonton, Alberta	5/24/38	Cusack, John	Evanston, IL	6/28/66
Christie, Julie	Assam, India	4/14/40	Cyrus, Billy Ray	Flatwoods, KY	8/25/61
Christopher, William	Evanston, IL	10/20/32	Dafoe, Willem	Appleton, WI	7/22/55
Church, Thomas Hayden	El Paso, TX	6/17/—	Dahl, Arlene	Minneapolis, MN	8/11/28
Clapton, Eric	Surrey, England	3/30/45	Dale, Jim	Rothwell, England	8/15/35
Clark, Dick	Mt. Vernon, NY	11/30/29	Dalton, Abby	Las Vegas, NV	8/15/32
Clark, Petula	Ewell, Surrey, England	11/15/32	Dalton, Timothy	Colwyn Bay, Wales	3/21/44
Clark, Roy	Meherrin, VA	4/15/33	Daltrey, Roger	London, England	3/1/44
Clay, Andrew Dice	Brooklyn, NY	9/29/58	Daly, Timothy	Suffern, NY	3/1/58
Clayburgh, Jill	New York, NY	4/30/44	Daly, Tyne	Madison, WI	2/21/47
Cleese, John	Weston-Super-Mare, England	10/27/39	Damone, Vic	Brooklyn, NY	6/12/28
Cliburn, Van	Shreveport, LA	7/12/34	Danes, Claire	New York, NY	4/12/79
Clooney, George	Lexington, KY	5/6/61	D'Angelo, Beverly	Columbus, OH	11/15/54
Clooney, Rosemary	Maysville, KY	5/23/28	Dangerfield, Rodney	Babylon, NY	11/22/22
Close, Glenn	Greenwich, CT	3/19/47	Daniels, Charlie	Wilmington, NC	10/28/36
Coburn, James	Laurel, NE	8/31/28	Daniels, Jeff	Georgia	2/19/55
Coca, Imogene	Philadelphia, PA	11/18/08	Daniels, William	Brooklyn, NY	3/31/27
Coen, Ethan	St. Louis Park, MN	9/21/57	Danner, Blythe	Philadelphia, PA	2/3/44
Coen, Joel	St. Louis Park, MN	11/29/54	Danson, Ted	San Diego, CA	12/29/47
Cole, Gary	Park Ridge, IL	9/20/57	Danza, Tony	New York, NY	4/21/50
Cole, Natalie	Los Angeles, CA	2/6/50	Darby, Kim	Hollywood, CA	7/8/48
Cole, Olivia	Memphis, TN	11/26/42	Davidson, John	Pittsburgh, PA	12/13/41
Coleman, Dabney	Austin, TX	1/3/32	Davis, Ann B.	Schenectady, NY	5/5/26
Coleman, Gary	Zion, IL	2/8/68	Davis, Clifton	Chicago, IL	10/4/45
Coleman, Ornette	Fort Worth, TX	3/9/30	Davis, Geena	Wareham, MA	1/21/57
Collins, Joan	London, England	5/23/33	Davis, Judy	Perth, Australia	1955
Collins, Judy	Seattle, WA	5/1/39	Davis, Mac	Lubbock, TX	1/21/42
Collins, Pauline	Exmouth, England	9/3/40	Davis, Ossie	Cogdell, GA	12/18/17
Collins, Phil	London, England	1/30/51	Dawber, Pam	Farmington Hills, MI	10/18/51
Comden, Betty	Brooklyn, NY	5/3/19	Dawson, Richard	Hampshire, England	11/20/32
Como, Perry	Canonsburg, PA	5/18/12	Day, Doris	Cincinnati, OH	4/3/24
Connery, Sean	Edinburgh, Scotland	8/25/30	Day-Lewis, Daniel	London, England	4/29/57
Connick, Harry Jr.	New Orleans, LA	9/11/67	Dean, Jimmy	Plainview, TX	8/10/28
Conniff, Ray	Attleboro, MA	11/6/16	De Camp, Rosemary	Prescott, AZ	11/14/10
Connors, Mike	Fresno, CA	8/15/25	DeCarlo, Yvonne	Vancouver, BC	9/1/22
Conrad, Robert	Chicago, IL	3/1/35	Dee, Frances	Los Angeles, CA	11/26/07
Constantine, Michael	Reading, PA	5/22/27	Dee, Ruby	Cleveland, OH	10/27/23
Conti, Tom	Paisley, Scotland	11/22/41	Dee, Sandra	Bayonne, NJ	4/23/42
Conway, Tim	Willoughby, OH	12/15/33	DeFranco, Buddy	Camden, NJ	2/17/23
Cook, Barbara	Atlanta, GA	10/25/27	DeGeneres, Ellen	Metairie, LA	1/26/58
Cooke, Alistair	Manchester, England	11/20/08	DeHaven, Gloria	Los Angeles, CA	7/23/25
Coolidge, Rita	Nashville, TN	5/1/45	De Havilland, Olivia	Tokyo, Japan	7/1/16
Cooper, Alice	Detroit, MI	2/4/48	Delaney, Kim	Philadelphia, PA	11/29/64
Cooper, Jackie	Los Angeles, CA	9/15/21	Delany, Dana	New York, NY	3/11/56
Copperfield, David	Metuchen, NJ	9/16/56	DeLaurentis, Dino	Torre Annunziata, Italy	8/8/19
Coppola, Francis Ford	Detroit, MI	4/7/39	Delon, Alain	Sceaux, France	11/8/35
Corbin, Barry	Lamesa, TX	10/16/40	DeLuise, Dom	Brooklyn, NY	8/1/33
Corby, Ellen	Racine, WI	6/3/13	Demme, Jonathan	Rockville Centre, NY	2/22/44
Cord, Alex	New York, NY	8/3/31	DeMornay, Rebecca	Santa Rosa, CA	11/29/61
Corea, Chick	Chelsea, MA	6/12/41	Deneuve, Catherine	Paris, France	10/22/43
Corelli, Franco	Ancona, Italy	4/8/23	De Niro, Robert	New York, NY	8/17/43
Corey, Jeff	New York, NY	8/10/14	Dennehy, Brian	Bridgeport, CT	7/9/38
Corley, Pat	Dallas, TX	6/1/30	Denver, Bob	New Rochelle, NY	1/9/35
Cosby, Bill	Philadelphia, PA	7/12/37	Denver, John	Roswell, NM	12/31/43
Costas, Bob	New York, NY	3/22/52	DePalma, Brian	Newark, NJ	9/11/40
Costello, Elvis	London, England	8/25/54	Depardieu, Gerard	Chateauroux, France	12/27/48
Costner, Kevin	Compton, CA	1/18/55	Depp, Johnny	Owensboro, KY	6/9/63
Courtenay, Tom	Hull, England	2/25/37	Derek, Bo	Long Beach, CA	11/20/56
Cox, Courteney	Birmingham, AL	6/15/64	Derek, John	Hollywood, CA	8/12/26

Name	Birthplace	Birthdate	Name	Birthplace	Birthdate
Dern, Bruce	Chicago, IL.	6/4/36	Evigan, Greg.	S. Amboy, NJ	10/14/53
Dern, Laura	Santa Monica, CA	2/1/67	Fabares, Shelley	Santa Monica, CA	1/19/42
Devane, William	Albany, NY.	9/5/37	Fabian (Forte)	Philadelphia, PA	2/6/43
DeVito, Danny.	Neptune, NJ.	11/17/44	Fabio	Milan, Italy	3/15/61
DeWitt, Joyce	Wheeling, WV.	4/23/49	Fabray, Nanette.	San Diego, CA	10/27/20
Dey, Susan.	Pekin, IL.	12/10/52	Fairbanks, Douglas Jr.	New York, NY.	12/9/09
Diamond, Neil	Brooklyn, NY	1/24/41	Fairchild, Morgan.	Dallas, TX.	2/3/50
Diaz, Cameron	San Diego, CA	8/30/72	Falana, Lola	Philadelphia, PA.	9/11/46
DiCaprio, Leonardo	Los Angeles, CA.	11/11/74	Falk, Peter.	New York, NY.	9/16/27
Dickinson, Angie	Kulm, ND.	9/30/31	Farentino, James.	Brooklyn, NY	2/24/38
Diddley, Bo.	McComb, MS	12/20/28	Fargo, Donna	Mt. Airy, NC.	11/10/45
Diller, Phyllis	Lima, OH.	7/17/17	Farina, Dennis.	Chicago, IL.	2/29/44
Dillman, Bradford.	San Francisco, CA.	4/14/30	Farley, Chris.	Madison, WI.	2/15/64
Dion, Celine	Charlemagne, Quebec	3/30/68	Farr, Jamie.	Toledo, OH.	7/1/34
Dillon, Matt.	New Rochelle, NY.	2/18/64	Farrell, Eileen	Willimantic, CT.	2/13/20
Dobson, Kevin.	New York, NY.	3/18/44	Farrell, Mike	St. Paul, MN.	2/6/39
Doherty, Shannen	Memphis, TN.	4/21/71	Farrow, Mia	Los Angeles, CA.	2/9/45
Dolenz, Mickey.	Los Angeles, CA.	3/8/45	Faustino, David	California.	3/3/74
Domingo, Placido.	Madrid, Spain	1/21/41	Fawcett, Farrah	Corpus Christi, TX.	2/2/47
Domino, Fats	New Orleans, LA.	2/26/28	Faye, Alice	New York, NY.	5/5/12
Donahue, Phil.	Cleveland, OH.	12/21/35	Feinstein, Michael	Columbus, OH.	9/7/56
Donahue, Troy	New York, NY.	1/27/36	Feldon, Barbara.	Pittsburgh, PA	3/12/41
D'Onofrio, Vincent	Brooklyn, NY	6/30/59	Feliciano, Jose	Lares, Puerto Rico.	9/10/45
Dotrice, Roy	Guernsey, England	5/26/23	Fell, Norman.	Philadelphia, PA.	3/24/24
Douglas, Kirk	Amsterdam, NY	12/9/16	Feldshuh, Tovah	New York, NY.	12/27/53
Douglas, Michael	New Brunswick, NJ	9/25/44	Fenn, Sherilyn.	Detroit, MI	2/1/65
Down, Leslie-Ann	London, England.	3/17/54	Ferrell, Conchata	Charleston, WV.	3/28/43
Downey, Robert Jr.	New York, NY.	4/4/65	Ferrer, Mel	Elberon, NJ	8/25/17
Downs, Hugh	Akron, OH.	2/14/21	Fiedler, John.	Platville, WI	2/3/25
Drescher, Fran	Queens, NY	9/30/57	Field, Sally	Pasadena, CA	11/6/46
Drew, Ellen.	Kansas City, MO.	11/23/15	Fiennes, Ralph	Suffolk, England	12/22/62
Dreyfuss, Richard	Brooklyn, NY	10/29/47	Finney, Albert	Salford, England.	5/9/36
Dryer, Fred.	Hawthorne, CA.	7/6/46	Fiorentino, Linda	Philadelphia, PA.	3/9/60
Duchovny, David	New York, NY.	8/7/60	Firth, Colin	Grayshott, England.	9/10/60
Duffy, Julia	Minneapolis, MN.	6/27/51	Firth, Peter.	Yorkshire, England.	10/27/53
Duffy, Patrick	Townsend, MT	3/17/49	Fischer-Dieskau, Dietrich	Berlin, Germany.	5/28/25
Dukakis, Olympia.	Lowell, MA.	6/20/31	Fishburne, Laurence	Augusta, GA.	7/30/61
Duke, Patty.	New York, NY.	12/14/46	Fisher, Carrie	Beverly Hills, CA.	10/21/56
Dukes, David	San Francisco, CA.	6/6/45	Fisher, Eddie	Philadelphia, PA.	8/10/28
Dullea, Keir.	Cleveland, OH.	5/30/36	Fitzgerald, Geraldine	Dublin, Ireland	11/24/13
Dunaway, Faye	Bascom, FL	1/14/41	Flack, Roberta.	Black Mountain, NC.	2/10/39
Duncan, Sandy	Henderson, TX	2/20/46	Flanagan, Fionnula	Dublin, Ireland	12/10/41
Dunham, Katherine	Joliet, IL.	6/22/10	Fleming, Rhonda.	Hollywood, CA.	8/10/23
Dunne, Griffin	New York, NY.	6/8/55	Fletcher, Louise.	Birmingham, AL	7/22/34
Dunst, Kirsten	New Jersey	4/30/82	Foch, Nina	Leyden, Netherlands	4/20/24
Durbin, Deanna	Winnipeg, Manitoba	12/4/21	Fogelberg, Dan	Peoria, IL.	8/13/51
Durning, Charles	Highland Falls, NY.	2/28/23	Foley, Dave	Toronto, Ontario	1/4/63
Dussault, Nancy	Pensacola, FL.	6/30/36	Fonda, Bridget	Los Angeles, CA.	1/27/64
Dutton, Charles S.	Baltimore, MD.	1/30/51	Fonda, Jane	New York, NY.	12/21/37
Duvall, Robert.	San Diego, CA	1/5/31	Fonda, Peter.	New York, NY.	2/23/40
Duvall, Shelley	Houston, TX	7/7/49	Fontaine, Joan	Tokyo, Japan	10/22/17
Dylan, Bob.	Duluth, MN.	5/24/41	Ford, Faith	Alexandria, LA	9/14/64
Dysart, Richard	Augusta, ME.	3/30/29	Ford, Glenn	Quebec, Canada.	5/1/16
Easton, Sheena.	Bellshill, Scotland	4/27/59	Ford, Harrison	Chicago, IL.	7/13/42
Eastwood, Clint	San Francisco, CA.	5/31/30	Forman, Milos	Caslav, Czechoslovakia.	2/18/32
Ebert, Roger	Urbana, IL.	6/18/42	Forsythe, John	Penns Grove, NJ.	1/29/18
Ebsen, Buddy	Belleville, IL.	4/2/08	Foster, Jodie.	New York, NY.	11/19/62
Eden, Barbara.	Tucson, AZ	8/23/34	Fox, James.	London, England.	5/19/39
Edwards, Anthony	Santa Barbara, CA	7/19/63	Fox, Matthew	Crowheart, WY.	1967
Edwards, Blake	Tulsa, OK	7/26/22	Fox, Michael J.	Edmonton, Alberta.	6/9/61
Edwards, Ralph	Merino, CO	6/13/13	Foxworth, Robert.	Houston, TX.	11/1/41
Eichhorn, Lisa	Reading, PA.	2/4/52	Foxworthy, Jeff	Atlanta, GA.	9/6/57
Eikenberry, Jill.	New Haven, CT.	1/21/47	Frampton, Peter	Kent, England.	4/22/50
Ekberg, Anita	Malmo, Sweden	9/29/31	Franciosa, Anthony	New York, NY.	10/25/28
Ekland, Britt	Stockholm, Sweden.	10/6/42	Francis, Anne	Ossining, NY	9/16/30
Elam, Jack	Miami, AZ	11/13/16	Francis, Arlene	Boston, MA	10/20/08
Elizondo, Hector	New York, NY.	12/22/36	Francis, Connie	Newark, NJ	12/12/38
Elliott, Bob	Boston, MA	3/26/23	Franken, Al.	New York, NY.	5/21/51
Elliot, Chris	New York, NY.	1960	Frankenheimer, John	Malba, NY	2/19/30
Elliott, Sam	Sacramento, CA	8/9/44	Franklin, Aretha	Memphis, TN.	3/25/42
Enberg, Dick.	Auburn Hills, MI	1/5/35	Franklin, Bonnie	Santa Monica, CA.	1/6/44
Englund, Robert.	Hollywood, CA.	6/6/48	Frann, Mary	St. Louis, MO	2/27/43
Elvira	Manhattan, KS	9/17/51	Franz, Dennis	Maywood, IL	10/28/44
Enya	Gweedore, Ireland.	5/17/61	Fraser, Brendan	Indianapolis, IN.	12/3/67
Ephron, Nora	New York, NY.	5/19/41	Freeman, Al Jr.	San Antonio, TX.	3/21/34
Estefan, Gloria	Havana, Cuba.	9/1/57	Freeman, Morgan	Memphis, TN.	6/1/37
Estevez, Emilio	New York, NY.	5/12/62	Fricker, Brenda	Dublin, Ireland	2/17/45
Estrada, Erik	New York, NY.	3/16/49	Friedkin, William	Chicago, IL.	8/29/39
Etheridge, Melissa	Leavenworth, KS.	5/29/61	Frost, David	Tenterden, England.	4/7/39
Evans, Dale	Uvalde, TX.	10/31/12	Fuentes, Daisy	Havana, Cuba	11/17/66
Evans, Linda	Hartford, CT	11/18/42	Funicello, Annette	Utica, NY.	10/22/42
Evans, Robert.	New York, NY.	6/29/30	Funt, Allen	New York, NY.	9/16/14
Everett, Chad	South Bend, IN	6/11/36	Gabor, Zsa Zsa	Budapest, Hungary	2/6/17
Everly, Don.	Brownie, KY.	2/1/37	Gabriel, John	Niagara Falls, NY	5/25/31
Everly, Phil.	Chicago, IL.	1/19/39	Gabriel, Peter	London, England.	2/13/50

Name	Birthplace	Birthdate	Name	Birthplace	Birthdate
Galway, James	Belfast, Ireland	12/8/39	Griffith, Melanie	New York, NY	8/9/57
Garagiola, Joe	St. Louis, MO	2/12/26	Grimes, Tammy	Lynn, MA	1/30/34
Garcia, Andy	Havana, Cuba	4/12/56	Grizzard, George	Roanoke Rapids, NC	4/1/28
Garofalo, Janeane	New Jersey	9/28/64	Grodin, Charles	Pittsburgh, PA	4/21/35
Garfunkel, Art	New York, NY	11/5/41	Grosbard, Ulu	Antwerp, Belgium	1/19/29
Garland, Beverly	Santa Cruz, CA	10/17/26	Gross, Michael	Chicago, IL	6/21/47
Garner, James	Norman, OK	4/7/28	Guest, Christopher	New York, NY	2/5/48
Garr, Teri	Lakewood, OH	12/11/45	Guillaume, Robert	St. Louis, MO	11/30/37
Garrett, Betty	St. Joseph, MO	5/23/19	Guinness, Alec	London, England	4/2/14
Garth, Jennie	Champaign, IL	4/3/72	Gumbel, Greg	New Orleans, LA	5/3/46
Gatlin, Larry	Seminole, TX	5/2/48	Guthrie, Arlo	New York, NY	7/10/47
Gayle, Crystal	Paintsville, KY	1/9/51	Guttenberg, Steve	New York, NY	8/24/58
Gaynor, Mitzi	Chicago, IL	9/4/30	Guy, Buddy	Lettsworth, LA	7/30/36
Gazzara, Ben	New York, NY	8/28/30	Guy, Jasmine	Boston, MA	3/10/64
Geary, Anthony	Coalville, UT	5/29/47	Hackett, Buddy	Brooklyn, NY	8/31/24
Geary, Cynthia	Jackson, MS	3/21/66	Hackman, Gene	San Bernardino, CA	1/30/30
Gedda, Nicolai	Stockholm, Sweden	7/11/25	Hagen, Uta	Gottingen, Germany	6/12/19
Gere, Richard	Philadelphia, PA	8/31/49	Haggard, Merle	Bakersfield, CA	4/6/37
Getty, Estelle	New York, NY	7/25/24	Hagman, Larry	Weatherford, TX	9/21/31
Ghostley, Alice	Eve, MO	8/14/26	Haid, Charles	San Francisco, CA	6/2/44
Giannini, Giancarlo	Spezia, Italy	8/1/42	Hale, Barbara	DeKalb, IL	4/18/22
Gibb, Barry	Isle of Man, England	9/1/46	Hall, Arsenio	Cleveland, OH	2/12/55
Gibb, Maurice	Manchester, England	12/22/49	Hall, Daryl	Pottstown, PA	10/11/48
Gibb, Robin	Manchester, England	12/22/49	Hall, Deidre	Milwaukee, WI	10/31/48
Gibbons, Leeza	South Carolina	3/26/57	Hall, Huntz	New York, NY	8/15/19
Gibbs, Marla	Chicago, IL	6/14/31	Hall, Monty	Winnipeg, Manitoba	8/25/25
Gibson, Debbie	New York, NY	8/31/70	Hall, Tom T.	Olive Hill, KY	5/25/36
Gibson, Henry	Germantown, PA	9/21/35	Hamill, Mark	Oakland, CA	9/25/51
Gibson, Mel	Peekskill, NY	1/3/56	Hamilton, George	Memphis, TN	8/12/39
Gielgud, John	London, England	4/14/04	Hamilton, Linda	Salisbury, MD	9/26/56
Gifford, Frank	Santa Monica, CA	8/16/30	Hamlin, Harry	Pasadena, CA	10/30/51
Gifford, Kathie Lee	Paris, France	8/16/53	Hammer	Oakland, CA	3/29/63
Gilbert, Sara	Santa Monica, CA	1/29/75	Hampton, Lionel	Birmingham, AL	4/12/13
Gilbert, Melissa	Los Angeles, CA	5/8/64	Hancock, Herbie	Chicago, IL	4/12/40
Gilberto, Astrud	Salvador, Brazil	3/30/40	Hanks, Tom	Oakland, CA	7/9/56
Gill, Vince	Norman, OK	4/12/57	Hannah, Daryl	Chicago, IL	12/3/60
Gillette, Anita	Baltimore, MD	8/16/38	Hardison, Kadeem	New York, NY	7/24/66
Gilley, Mickey	Natchez, MS	3/9/36	Harewood, Dorian	Dayton, OH	8/6/51
Gilpin, Peri	Waco, TX	5/27/—	Harmon, Mark	Burbank, CA	9/2/51
Ginty, Robert	New York, NY	11/14/48	Harper, Jessica	Chicago, IL	10/10/49
Givens, Robin	New York, NY	11/27/64	Harper, Tess	Mammoth Springs, AR	8/15/50
Glaser, Paul Michael	Cambridge, MA	3/25/42	Harper, Valerie	Suffern, NY	8/22/40
Glenn, Scott	Pittsburgh, PA	1/26/42	Harrelson, Woody	Midland, TX	7/23/61
Gless, Sharon	Los Angeles, CA	5/31/43	Harrington, Pat	New York, NY	8/13/29
Glover, Crispin	New York, NY	9/20/64	Harris, Barbara	Evanston, IL	7/25/35
Glover, Danny	San Francisco, CA	7/22/47	Harris, Ed	Englewood, NJ	11/28/50
Glover, Savion	Newark, NJ	1973	Harris, Emmylou	Birmingham, AL	4/2/47
Godard, Jean Luc	Paris, France	12/3/30	Harris, Julie	Grosse Pte. Park, MI	12/2/25
Goldberg, Whoopi	New York, NY	11/13/49	Harris, Neil Patrick	Albuquerque, NM	6/15/73
Goldblum, Jeff	Pittsburgh, PA	10/22/52	Harris, Richard	Co. Limerick, Ireland	10/1/33
Goldthwait, Bobcat	Syracuse, NY	5/1/62	Harris, Rosemary	Ashby, England	9/19/30
Goldwyn, Tony	Los Angeles, CA	5/20/60	Harrison, George	Liverpool, England	2/25/43
Gooding Jr., Cuba	Bronx, NY	1/2/68	Harrison, Gregory	Avalon, CA	5/31/50
Goodman, John	St. Louis, MO	6/20/52	Harry, Deborah	Miami, FL	7/1/45
Gorme, Eydie	Bronx, NY	8/16/32	Hart, Mary	Madison, SD	11/8/51
Gorshin, Frank	Pittsburgh, PA	4/5/34	Hart, Melissa Joan	Sayville, NY	4/18/76
Gossett, Louis Jr.	Brooklyn, NY	5/27/36	Hartley, Mariette	New York, NY	6/21/40
Gould, Elliott	Brooklyn, NY	8/29/38	Hartman, David	Pawtucket, RI	5/19/35
Gould, Harold	Schenectady, NY	12/10/23	Hartman, Lisa	Houston, TX	6/1/56
Goulet, Robert	Lawrence, MA	11/26/33	Hartman, Phil	Ontario, Canada	9/24/48
Gowdy, Curt	Green River, WY	7/31/19	Hasselhoff, David	Baltimore, MD	7/17/52
Graham, Virginia	Chicago, IL	7/4/12	Hatcher, Teri	Sunnyvale, CA	12/8/64
Grammer, Kelsey	St. Thomas, Virgin Islands	2/20/55	Hauer, Rutger	Breukelen, Netherlands	1/23/44
Granger, Farley	San Jose, CA	7/1/25	Haver, June	Rock Island, IL	6/10/26
Grant, Amy	Augusta, GA	12/25/60	Havoc, June	Seattle, WA	11/8/16
Grant, Hugh	London, England	9/9/60	Hawke, Ethan	Austin, TX	11/6/70
Grant, Lee	New York, NY	10/31/29	Hawn, Goldie	Washington, DC	11/21/45
Graves, Peter	Minneapolis, MN	3/18/26	Hayden, Melissa	Toronto, Ontario	4/25/23
Gray, Linda	Santa Monica, CA	9/12/40	Hayek, Salma	Coatzacoalcos, Mexico	9/2/68
Gray, Spaulding	Barrington, RI	6/5/41	Hayes, Isaac	Covington, TN	8/20/42
Grayson, Kathryn	Winston-Salem, NC	2/9/22	Hays, Robert	Bethesda, MD	7/24/47
Greco, Jose	Abruzzi, Italy	12/23/18	Heard, John	Washington, DC	3/7/45
Green, Adolph	New York, NY	12/2/15	Hearn, George	Memphis, TN	1935
Green, Al	Forrest City, AR	4/13/46	Heche, Anne	Aurora, OH	5/25/69
Greene, Shecky	Chicago, IL	4/8/26	Heckart, Eileen	Columbus, OH	3/29/19
Greenwood, Bruce	Quebec, Canada	8/12/56	Hellgott, David	Melbroune, Australia	5/19/47
Greer, Jane	Washington, DC	9/9/24	Helmond, Katherine	Galveston, TX	7/5/34
Gregory, Cynthia	Los Angeles, CA	7/8/46	Hemingway, Mariel	Mill Valley, CA	11/21/61
Gregory, Dick	St. Louis, MO	10/12/32	Hemmings, David	Guildford, England	11/18/41
Gregory, James	Bronx, NY	12/23/11	Hemsley, Sherman	Philadelphia, PA	2/1/38
Grey, Jennifer	New York, NY	3/22/60	Henderson, Florence	Dale, IN	2/14/34
Grey, Joel	Cleveland, OH	4/11/32	Henderson, Skitch	Halstad, MN	1/27/18
Grier, David Alan	Detroit, MI	6/30/55	Henley, Don	Gilmer, TX	7/22/47
Griffin, Merv	San Mateo, CA	7/6/25	Henner, Marilu	Chicago, IL	4/6/52
Griffith, Andy	Mount Airy, NC	6/1/26	Henning, Doug	Ft. Garry, Manitoba	5/3/47

Name	Birthplace	Birthdate	Name	Birthplace	Birthdate
Henry, Buck	New York, NY	12/9/30	Jackson, Kate	Birmingham, AL	10/29/48
Hepburn, Katharine	Hartford, CT	5/12/07	Jackson, Michael	Gary, IN.	8/29/58
Herman, Pee-Wee	Peekskill, NY	8/27/52	Jackson, Milt	Detroit, MI	1/1/22
Herrmann, Edward	Washington, DC	7/21/43	Jackson, Samuel L.	Chattanooga, TN.	12/21/48
Hershey, Barbara	Los Angeles, CA	2/5/48	Jacobi, Derek	London, England.	10/22/38
Hesseman, Howard	Lebanon, OR	2/27/40	Jagger, Mick	Dartford, England	7/26/43
Heston, Charlton	Evanston, IL	10/4/24	James, Etta	Los Angeles, CA	1938
Hewett, Christopher	Sussex, England	4/5/—	Janis, Conrad	New York, NY.	2/11/28
Hewitt, Jennifer Love	Waco, TX.	2/21/79	Jarmusch, Jim	Akron, OH	1/22/53
Hildegarde	Adell, WI	2/1/06	Jarreau, Al	Milwaukee, WI	3/12/40
Hill, Arthur	Melfort, Sask.	8/1/22	Jarrette, Keith	Allentown, PA.	5/8/45
Hill, Steven	Seattle, WA	2/24/22	Jeffreys, Anne	Goldsboro, NC	1/26/23
Hill, George Roy	Minneapolis, MN	12/20/22	Jennings, Waylon	Littlefield, TX.	6/15/37
Hiller, Wendy	Stockport, England	8/15/12	Jeter, Michael	Lawrenceburg, TN.	8/20/52
Hillerman, John	Denison, TX.	12/30/32	Jett, Joan	Philadelphia, PA	9/22/60
Hines, Gregory	New York, NY.	2/14/46	Jewel (Kilcher)	Homer, AK.	5/3/74
Hines, Roy	Boston, MA	3/13/26	Jewison, Norman	Toronto, Ontario	7/21/26
Hines, Jerome	Hollywood, CA	11/8/21	Jillian, Ann	Cambridge, MA.	1/29/50
Hingle, Pat	Miami, FL.	7/19/24	Joel, Billy	Bronx, NY	5/9/49
Hirsch, Judd	New York, NY.	3/15/35	John, Elton	Middlesex, England	3/25/47
Hirt, Al	New Orleans, LA.	11/7/22	Johns, Glynis	Durban, S Africa	10/5/23
Ho, Don	Kakaako, Oahu, HI.	8/13/30	Johnson, Arte	Benton Harbor, MI.	1/20/29
Hoffman, Dustin	Los Angeles, CA.	8/8/37	Johnson, Beverly	Buffalo, NY.	10/13/52
Hogan, Paul	New South Wales, Australia	10/8/39	Johnson, Don	Flatt Creek, MO	12/15/49
Holbrook, Hal	Cleveland, OH	2/17/25	Johnson, J. J.	Indianapolis, IN.	1/22/24
Holder, Geoffrey	Trinidad	8/1/30	Johnson, Kristen	Washington, DC	9/20/67
Holliman, Earl	Delhi, LA	9/11/28	Johnson, Van	Newport, RI	8/25/16
Holliday, Polly	Jasper, AL	8/2/37	Jones, Charlie	Ft. Smith, AR	11/9/30
Holly, Lauren	Bristol, PA	10/28/63	Jones, Davy	Manchester, England	12/30/45
Holm, Celeste	New York, NY.	4/29/19	Jones, Dean	Morgan City, AL	1/25/35
Hooker, John Lee	Clarksdale, MS	8/22/17	Jones, Elvin	Pontiac, MI.	9/9/27
Hooks, Jan	Decatur, GA	4/23/57	Jones, George	Saratoga, TX	9/12/31
Hope, Bob	London, England.	5/29/03	Jones, Grace	Spanishtown, Jamaica	5/19/52
Hopkins, Anthony	Port Talbot, South Wales	12/31/37	Jones, Henry	Philadelphia, PA	8/1/12
Hopkins, Bo	Greenville, SC	2/2/42	Jones, Jack	Hollywood, CA	1/14/38
Hopkins, Telma	Louisville, KY	10/28/48	Jones, James Earl	Tate Co., MS	1/17/31
Hopper, Dennis	Dodge City, KS.	5/17/36	Jones, Jennifer	Tulsa, OK	3/2/19
Horne, Lena	Brooklyn, NY	6/30/17	Jones, Quincy	Chicago, IL.	3/14/33
Horne, Marilyn	Bradford, PA.	1/16/34	Jones, Shirley	Smithton, PA	3/31/34
Hornsby, Bruce	Williamsburg, VA.	11/23/54	Jones, Tom	Pontypridd, Wales	6/7/40
Horsley, Lee	Muleshoe, TX.	5/15/55	Jones, Tommy Lee	San Saba, TX.	9/15/46
Hoskins, Bob.	Suffolk, England	10/26/42	Jourdan, Louis	Marseilles, France	6/19/19
Houston, Whitney	E Orange, NJ	8/9/63	Judd, Naomi	Ashland, KY.	1/11/46
Howard, Ken	El Centro, CA	3/28/44	Judd, Wynonna	Ashland, KY.	5/3/64
Howard, Ron	Duncan, OK	3/1/54	Jump, Gordon	Dayton, OH	4/1/32
Howell, C. Thomas	Los Angeles, CA	12/7/66	Kahn, Madeline	Boston, MA	9/29/42
Howes, Sally Ann	London, England.	7/20/30	Kanaly, Steve	Burbank, CA.	3/14/46
Hughes, Barnard	Bedford Hills, NY.	7/16/15	Kane, Carol	Cleveland, OH	6/18/52
Hulce, Tom	Whitewater, WI	12/6/53	Karlen, John	New York, NY.	5/28/33
Humperdinck, Engelbert	Madras, India	5/3/36	Karn, Richard	Seattle, WA	2/17/56
Hunt, Helen	Los Angeles, CA.	6/15/63	Karras, Alex	Gary, IN.	7/15/35
Hunt, Linda	Morristown, NJ	4/2/45	Kasem, Casey.	Detroit, MI	4/27/33
Hunter, Holly	Conyers, GA.	3/20/58	Kavner, Julie.	Los Angeles, CA.	9/7/51
Hunter, Kim	Detroit, MI	11/12/22	Kazan, Elia	Istanbul, Turkey	9/7/09
Hunter, Tab	New York, NY.	7/11/31	Kazan, Lainie	New York, NY.	5/15/42
Hurley, Elizabeth	Hampshire, England	6/10/65	Keach, Stacy	Savannah, GA	6/2/41
Hurt, John	Chesterfield, England.	1/22/40	Keaton, Diane	Santa Ana, CA	1/5/46
Hurt, Mary Beth	Marshalltown, IA	9/26/46	Keaton, Michael	Pittsburgh, PA	9/9/51
Hurt, William	Washington, DC	3/20/50	Keel, Howard	Gillespie, IL	4/13/17
Hussey, Ruth	Providence, RI	10/30/14	Keeshan, Bob	Lynbrook, NY.	6/27/27
Huston, Anjelica	Santa Monica, CA.	7/8/51	Keitel, Harvey	Brooklyn, NY	5/13/39
Hutton, Betty.	Battle Creek, MI	2/26/21	Keith, David	Knoxville, TN	5/8/54
Hutton, Lauren	Charleston, SC	11/17/44	Kellerman, Sally	Long Beach, CA	6/2/37
Hutton, Timothy	Malibu, CA.	8/16/60	Kelley, DeForest	Atlanta, GA	1/20/20
Hyman, Earle	Rocky Mount, NC	10/11/26	Kennedy, George.	New York, NY.	2/18/25
Ian, Janis	New York, NY.	4/7/51	Kennedy, Jayne.	Washington, DC	11/27/51
Ice-T	Newark, NJ	2/16/58	Kenny G.	Seattle, WA	6/5/56
Idle, Eric	Durham, England	3/29/43	Kent, Allegrara	Los Angeles, CA.	8/11/37
Idol, Billy	London, England.	11/30/55	Kercheval, Ken	Wolcottville, IN	7/15/35
Iman	Mogadishu, Somalia	7/25/55	Kerns, Joanna	San Francisco, CA	2/12/53
Iglesias, Julio	Madrid, Spain	9/23/43	Kerr, Deborah	Helensburgh, Scotland	9/30/21
Imus, Don	Riverside, CA	7/23/40	Kessel, Barney	Muskogee, OK	10/17/23
Ireland, Kathy	Santa Barbara, CA	3/8/63	Khan, Chaka	Great Lakes, IL	3/23/53
Ingram, James	Akron, OH	2/16/56	Kidder, Margot	Yellowknife, N.W.T.	10/17/48
Irons, Jeremy	Cowes, England	9/19/48	Kidman, Nicole	Honolulu, HI.	6/21/67
Irving, Amy	Palo Alto, CA	9/10/53	Kiley, Richard	Chicago, IL.	3/31/22
Irving, George S.	Springfield, MA	11/1/22	Kilmer, Val	Los Angeles, CA.	12/31/59
Ivey, Judith	El Paso, TX	9/4/51	Kimbrough, Charles	St. Paul, MN.	5/23/36
Ivory, James	Berkeley, CA	6/7/28	King, Alan.	Brooklyn, NY	12/26/27
Jackee	Winston-Salem, NC	8/14/56	King, B. B.	Itta Bena, MS	9/16/25
Jackson, Anne	Allegheny, PA.	9/3/25	King, Carole	Brooklyn, NY	2/9/42
Jackson, Glenda	Liverpool, England.	5/9/36	King, Larry	Brooklyn, NY	11/19/33
Jackson, Janet	Gary, IN.	5/16/66	King, Perry	Alliance, OH.	4/30/48
Jackson, Jermaine	Gary, IN.	12/11/54	Kingsley, Ben	Yorkshire, England	12/31/43
Jackson, La Toya	Gary, IN.	5/29/56	Kinnear, Greg	Logansport, IN	6/17/63

Name	Birthplace	Birthdate	Name	Birthplace	Birthdate
Kinski, Nastassja	Berlin, W. Germany	1/24/60	Lewis, Jerry Lee	Ferriday, LA	9/29/35
Kirby, Bruno	New York, NY	4/28/49	Lewis, John	La Grange, IL	5/30/20
Kirby, Durward	Covington, KY	8/24/12	Lewis, Juliette	San Fernando Valley, CA	6/21/73
Kirkland, Gelsey	Bethlehem, PA	12/29/53	Lewis, Richard	New York, NY	6/29/47
Kitt, Eartha	North, SC	1/26/28	Lewis, Shari	New York, NY	1/17/34
Klein, Robert	New York, NY	2/8/42	Light, Judith	Trenton, NJ	2/9/50
Klemperer, Werner	Cologne, Germany	3/22/19	Lightfoot, Gordon	Orillia, Ontario	11/17/38
Kline, Kevin	St. Louis, MO	10/24/47	Linden, Hal	New York, NY	3/20/31
Klugman, Jack	Philadelphia, PA	4/27/22	Linkletter, Art	Saskatchewan, Canada	7/17/12
Knight, Gladys	Atlanta, GA	5/28/44	Linn-Baker, Mark	St. Louis, MO	6/17/53
Knotts, Don	Morgantown, WV	7/21/24	Liotta, Ray	Newark, NJ	12/18/55
Konitz, Lee	Chicago, IL	10/13/27	Lithgow, John	Rochester, NY	10/19/45
Kopell, Bernie	New York, NY	6/21/33	Little, Rich	Ottawa, Ontario	11/26/38
Korman, Harvey	Chicago, IL	2/15/27	Little Richard	Macon, GA	12/5/32
Kotto, Yaphet	New York, NY	11/15/37	L. L. Cool J	New York, NY	1/14/68
Kramer, Stanley	New York, NY	9/29/13	Lloyd, Christopher	Stamford, CT	10/22/38
Kristofferson, Kris	Brownsville, TX	6/22/36	Lloyd, Emily	England	9/29/70
Kubrick, Stanley	Bronx, NY	7/26/28	Lloyd Webber, Andrew	London, England	3/22/48
Kudrow, Lisa	Encino, CA	5/30/63	Locke, Sondra	Shelbyville, TN	5/28/47
Kurtz, Swoosie	Omaha, NE	9/6/44	Lockhart, June	New York, NY	6/25/25
LaBelle, Patti	Philadelphia, PA	5/24/44	Locklear, Heather	Los Angeles, CA	9/25/61
Ladd, Cheryl	Huron, SD	7/12/51	Loggia, Robert	New York, NY	1/3/30
Ladd, Diane	Meridian, MS	11/29/32	Loggins, Kenny	Everett, WA	1/17/47
Lahti, Christine	Detroit, MI	4/5/50	Lollobrigida, Gina	Subiaco, Italy	7/4/27
Laine, Cleo	Middlesex, England	10/28/27	Lom, Herbert	Prague, Czechoslovakia	1/9/17
Laine, Frankie	Chicago, IL	3/30/13	Long, Shelley	Ft. Wayne, IN	8/23/49
Lake, Ricki	New York, NY	9/21/68	Lopez, Jennifer	Bronx, NY	1970
Lamarr, Hedy	Vienna, Austria	11/9/13	Lord, Jack	New York, NY	12/30/30
Lamas, Lorenzo	Santa Monica, CA	1/20/58	Loren, Sophia	Rome, Italy	9/20/34
Lambert, Christopher	New York, NY	3/29/57	Loring, Gloria	New York, NY	12/10/46
Landau, Martin	New York, NY	6/20/34	Loudon, Dorothy	Boston, MA	9/17/33
Landis, John	Chicago, IL	8/3/50	Louis-Dreyfus, Julia	New York, NY	1/13/61
Lane, Diane	New York, NY	1/22/63	Love, Courtney	San Francisco, CA	7/9/64
Lane, Nathan	Jersey City, NJ	2/3/56	Lovett, Lyle	Klein, TX	11/1/57
lang, k.d.	Consort, Alberta	11/2/61	Lovitz, Jon	Tarzana, CA	7/21/57
Lang, Stephen	New York, NY	7/11/52	Loveless, Patty	Pikeville, KY	1/4/57
Lange, Hope	Redding Ridge, CT	11/28/31	Lowe, Rob	Charlottesville, VA	3/17/64
Lange, Jessica	Cloquet, MN	4/20/49	Lucas, George	Modesto, CA	5/14/44
Langella, Frank	Bayonne, NJ	1/1/40	Lucci, Susan	Scarsdale, NY	12/23/48
Langford, Frances	Lakeland, FL	4/4/13	Luckinbill, Laurence	Ft. Smith, AR	11/21/34
Lansbury, Angela	London, England	10/16/25	Ludwig, Christa	Berlin, Germany	3/16/28
Laredo, Ruth	Detroit, MI	11/20/37	Lumet, Sidney	Philadelphia, PA	6/25/24
Larroquette, John	New Orleans, LA	11/25/47	LuPone, Patti	Northport, NY	4/21/49
LaSalle, Eriq	Hartford, CT	6/23/63	Lynch, David	Missoula, MT	1/20/46
Lauper, Cyndi	New York, NY	6/20/53	Lynley, Carol	New York, NY	2/13/42
Laurie, Piper	Detroit, MI	1/22/32	Lynn, Loretta	Butcher Hollow, KY	4/14/35
Lavin, Linda	Portland, ME	10/15/37	Ma, Yo Yo	Paris, France	10/7/55
Lawless, Lucy	Mount Albert, New Zealand	3/28/68	Maazel, Lorin	Paris, France	3/6/30
Lawrence, Carol	Melrose Park, IL	9/5/34	MacArthur, James	Los Angeles, CA	12/8/37
Lawrence, Martin	Frankfurt, Germany	4/16/65	MacCorkindale, Simon	Cambridge, England	2/12/52
Lawrence, Joey	Montgomery, PA	4/20/76	MacDowell, Andie	Gaffney, SC	4/21/58
Lawrence, Steve	Brooklyn, NY	7/8/35	MacGraw, Ali	Pound Ridge, NY	4/1/38
Lawrence, Vicki	Inglewood, CA	3/26/49	MacLachlan, Kyle	Yakima, WA	2/22/59
Leach, Robin	London, England	8/29/41	MacLaine, Shirley	Richmond, VA	4/24/34
Leachman, Cloris	Des Moines, IA	4/4/26	MacLeod, Gavin	Mt. Kisco, NY	2/28/30
Lear, Norman	New Haven, CT	7/27/22	MacNee, Patrick	London, England	2/6/22
Learned, Michael	Washington, DC	4/9/39	MacNeil, Cornell	Minneapolis, MN	9/24/22
LeBlanc, Matt	Newton, MA	5/25/68	MacPherson, Elle	Sydney, Australia	3/29/64
LeBon, Simon	Bushey, England	10/27/58	Macchio, Ralph	Long Island, NY	11/4/62
Lee, Ang	Taiwan	10/23/54	Macy, Bill	Revere, MA	5/18/22
Lee, Brenda	Atlanta, GA	12/11/44	Macy, William H.	Miami, FL	3/13/50
Lee, Christopher	London, England	5/27/22	Madden, John	Austin, MN	4/10/36
Lee, Michele	Los Angeles, CA	6/24/42	Madigan, Amy	Chicago, IL	9/11/51
Lee, Pamela Anderson	Comox, Canada	7/1/67	Madonna (Ciccone)	Bay City, MI	8/16/58
Lee, Peggy	Jamestown, ND	5/26/20	Maher, Bill	Rivervale, NJ	1/20/–
Lee, Spike	Atlanta, GA	3/20/57	Mahoney, John	Manchester, England	6/20/40
Leeves, Jane	East Grinstead, England	4/13/63	Majors, Lee	Wyandotte, MI	4/23/40
Legrand, Michel	Paris, France	2/24/32	Malden, Karl	Chicago, IL	3/22/13
Leguizamo, John	Bogota, Colombia	7/22/65	Malkovich, John	Christopher, IL	12/9/53
Leibman, Ron	New York, NY	10/11/37	Malone, Dorothy	Chicago, IL	1/30/25
Leigh, Janet	Merced, CA	7/6/27	Manchester, Melissa	Bronx, NY	2/15/51
Leigh, Jennifer Jason	Los Angeles, CA	2/5/62	Mandel, Howie	Toronto, Ontario	11/29/55
Leighton, Laura	Iowa City, IA	3/14/69	Mandrell, Barbara	Houston, TX	12/25/48
Lemmon, Jack	Boston, MA	2/8/25	Mangione, Chuck	Rochester, NY	11/29/40
Lennox, Annie	Aberdeen, Scotland	12/25/54	Manilow, Barry	New York, NY	6/17/46
Leno, Jay	New Rochelle, NY	4/28/50	Mann, Herbie	New York, NY	4/16/30
Leonard, Robert Sean	Westwood, NJ	2/28/69	Manoff, Dinah	New York, NY	1/25/58
Leoni, Tea	New York, NY	2/25/66	Mantegna, Joe	Chicago, IL	11/13/47
Leslie, Joan	Detroit, MI	1/26/25	Marceau, Marcel	Strasbourg, France	3/22/23
Leto, Jared	Bossier City, LA	12/26/71	Marchand, Nancy	Buffalo, NY	6/19/28
Letterman, David	Indianapolis, IN	4/12/47	Marin, Cheech	Los Angeles, CA	7/13/46
Levine, James	Cincinnati, OH	6/23/43	Marinaro, Ed	New York, NY	3/31/00
Levinson, Barry	Baltimore, MD	6/2/32	Markova, Alicia	London, England	12/1/10
Lewis, Huey	New York, NY	7/5/51	Marriner, Neville	Lincoln, England	4/15/24
Lewis, Jerry	Newark, NJ	3/16/26	Marsalis, Branford	New Orleans, LA	8/26/60

Name	Birthplace	Birthdate	Name	Birthplace	Birthdate
Marsalis, Wynton	New Orleans, LA	10/18/61	Miller, Penelope Ann	Los Angeles, CA	1/13/64
Marsh, Jean	London, England	7/1/34	Mills, Donna	Chicago, IL	12/11/42
Marshall, E. G.	Owatonna, MN	6/18/10	Mills, John	Suffolk, England	2/22/08
Marshall, Garry	New York, NY	11/13/34	Milner, Martin	Detroit, MI	12/28/27
Marshall, Penny	New York, NY	10/15/43	Milnes, Sherrill	Downers Grove, IL	1/10/35
Marshall, Peter	Huntington, WV	3/30/27	Milsap, Ronnie	Robinsville, NC	1/16/44
Martin, Dick	Detroit, MI	1/30/23	Minghella, Anthony	Isle of Wight, England	1/6/54
Martin, Steve	Waco, TX	4/14/45	Minnelli, Liza	Los Angeles, CA	3/12/46
Martin, Tony	San Francisco, CA	12/25/13	Mirren, Helen	London, England	7/2/46
Martins, Peter	Copenhagen, Denmark	10/27/46	Mitchell, Joni	McLeod, Alberta	11/7/43
Mason, Jackie	Sheboygan, WI	6/9/31	Mr. T	Chicago, IL	5/21/52
Mason, Marsha	St. Louis, MO	4/3/42	Modine, Matthew	Loma Linda, CA	3/22/59
Masterson, Mary Stuart	Los Angeles, CA	6/28/66	Moffat, Donald	Plymouth, England	12/26/30
Mastrantonio, Mary Eliz.	Lombard, IL	11/17/58	Moffo, Anna	Wayne, PA	6/27/27
Masur, Kurt	Brieg, Germany	7/18/27	Molinaro, Al	Kenosha, WI	6/24/19
Masur, Richard	New York, NY	11/20/48	Moll, Richard	Pasadena, CA	1/13/43
Mathers, Jerry	Sioux City, IA	6/2/48	Montalban, Ricardo	Mexico City, Mexico	11/25/20
Matheson, Tim	Glendale, CA	12/31/47	Moody, Ron	London, England	1/8/24
Mathis, Johnny	San Francisco, CA	9/30/35	Moore, Clayton	Chicago, IL	9/14/14
Matlin, Marlee	Morton Grove, IL	8/24/65	Moore, Demi	Roswell, NM	11/11/62
Matthau, Walter	New York, NY	10/1/20	Moore, Dudley	London, England	4/19/35
Mature, Victor	Louisville, KY	1/29/16	Moore, Mary Tyler	Brooklyn, NY	12/29/36
May, Elaine	Philadelphia, PA	4/21/32	Moore, Melba	New York, NY	10/29/45
Mayfield, Curtis	Chicago, IL	6/3/42	Moore, Roger	London, England	10/14/27
Mayo, Virginia	St. Louis, MO	11/30/20	Moore, Terry	Los Angeles, CA	1/1/29
Mazursky, Paul	Brooklyn, NY	4/25/30	Moranis, Rick	Toronto, Ontario	4/18/53
McArdle, Andrea	Philadelphia, PA	11/5/63	Moreno, Rita	Humacao, PR	12/11/31
McBride, Patricia	Teaneck, NJ	8/23/42	Morgan, Harry	Detroit, MI	4/10/15
McCallum, David	Glasgow, Scotland	9/19/33	Moriarty, Michael	Detroit, MI	4/5/41
McCambridge, Mercedes	Joliet, IL	3/17/18	Morissette, Alanis	Ottawa, Ontario	6/1/74
McCarthy, Andrew	Westfield, NJ	11/29/62	Morita, Pat	Isleton, CA	6/28/32
McCarthy, Jenny	Chicago, IL	11/1/72	Morris, Howard	New York, NY	9/4/25
McCarthy, Kevin	Seattle, WA	2/15/14	Morrison, Van	Belfast, N. Ireland	8/31/45
McCartney, Paul	Liverpool, England	6/18/42	Morrissey	Manchester, England	5/22/59
McCarver, Tim	Memphis, TN	10/16/41	Morrow, Rob	New Rochelle, NY	9/21/62
McClanahan, Rue	Healdton, OK	2/21/36	Morse, Robert	Newton, MA	5/18/31
McConaughey, Matthew	Uvalde, Texas	11/4/69	Morton, Joe	New York, NY	10/18/47
McCoo, Marilyn	Jersey City, NJ	9/30/43	Moses, William	Los Angeles, CA	11/17/59
McCormack, Mary	Plainsfield, NJ	4/8/69	Moss, Kate	London, England	1/16/74
McDermott, Dylan	Waterbury, CT	10/26/62	Muldaur, Diana	New York, NY	8/19/38
McDonnell, Mary	Wilkes-Barre, PA	1952	Mulgrew, Kate	Dubuque, IA	4/29/55
McDormand, Frances	Illinois	6/23/57	Mull, Martin	Chicago, IL	8/18/43
McDowall, Roddy	London, England	9/28/28	Mueller-Stahl, Armin	Tilsit, E. Prussia	12/17/20
McDowell, Malcolm	Leeds, England	6/13/43	Mulligan, Richard	New York, NY	11/13/32
McEntire, Reba	McAlester, OK	3/28/55	Mulroney, Dermot	Alexandria, VA	10/31/63
McFerrin, Bobby	New York, NY	3/11/50	Munsel, Patrice	Spokane, WA	5/14/25
McGavin, Darren	Spokane, WA	5/7/22	Murphy, Ben	Jonesboro, AR	3/6/42
McGillis, Kelly	Newport Beach, CA	7/9/57	Murphy, Eddie	Brooklyn, NY	4/3/61
McGoohan, Patrick	New York, NY	3/19/28	Murphy, Michael	Los Angeles, CA	5/5/38
McGovern, Elizabeth	Evanston, IL	7/18/61	Murray, Anne	Springhill, Nova Scotia	6/20/45
McGovern, Maureen	Youngstown, OH	7/27/49	Murray, Bill	Evanston, IL	9/21/50
McGregor, Ewan	Crieff, Scotland	3/31/71	Murray, Don	Hollywood, CA	7/31/29
McGuire, Al	New York, NY	9/7/31	Musburger, Brent	Portland, OR	5/26/39
McGuire, Dorothy	Omaha, NE	6/14/19	Muti, Riccardo	Naples, Italy	7/28/41
McKean, Michael	New York, NY	10/17/47	Myers, Mike	Toronto, Ontario	5/23/63
McKechnie, Donna	Pontiac, MI	11/16/42	Nabors, Jim	Sylacauga, AL	6/12/33
McKellen, Ian	Burnley, England	5/25/39	Nash, Graham	Blackpool, England	2/2/42
McMahon, Ed	Detroit, MI	3/6/23	Naughton, James	Middletown, CT	7/6/46
McNichol, Kristy	Los Angeles, CA	9/11/62	Neal, Patricia	Packard, KY	1/20/26
McParland, Marion	Stough, England	3/20/20	Nealon, Kevin	Bridgeport, CT	11/18/53
McRaney, Gerald	Collins, MS	8/19/48	Neeson, Liam	Ballymena, N. Ireland	6/7/52
Meadows, Jayne	Wu Chang, China	9/27/20	Neill, Sam	Ulster, N. Ireland	9/14/47
Meara, Anne	New York, NY	9/20/29	Nelligan, Kate	London, Ontario	3/16/51
Meat Loaf	Dallas, TX	9/27/47	Nelson, Craig T.	Spokane, WA	4/4/46
Mehta, Zubin	Bombay, India	4/29/36	Nelson, Ed	New Orleans, LA	12/21/28
Mellencamp, John	Seymour, IN	10/7/51	Nelson, Judd	Portland, ME	11/28/59
Mendes, Sergio	Niteroi, Brazil	2/11/41	Nelson, Tracy	Santa Monica, CA	10/25/63
Menuhin, Yehudi	New York, NY	4/22/16	Nelson, Willie	Abbott, TX	4/30/33
Mercer, Marian	Akron, OH	11/26/35	Nero, Peter	New York, NY	5/22/34
Merchant, Natalie	Jamestown, NY	10/26/63	Nesmith, Mike	Dallas, TX	12/30/42
Merrick, David	St. Louis, MO	11/27/12	Neuwirth, Bebe	Princeton, NJ	12/31/58
Merrill, Dina	New York, NY	12/9/25	Neville, Aaron	New Orleans, LA	1/24/41
Merrill, Robert	Brooklyn, NY	6/4/19	Newhart, Bob	Oak Park, IL	9/5/29
Metcalf, Laurie	Carbondale, IL	6/16/55	Newley, Anthony	Hackney, England	9/24/31
Michael, George	Watford, England	6/26/63	Newman, Paul	Cleveland, OH	1/26/25
Michaels, Al	New York, NY	11/12/44	Newman, Randy	Los Angeles, CA	11/28/43
Michaels, Lorne	Toronto, Canada	11/17/44	Newton, Wayne	Norfolk, VA	4/3/42
Midler, Bette	Paterson, NJ	12/1/45	Newton-John, Olivia	Cambridge, England	9/26/47
Midori	Osaka, Japan	10/25/71	Nicholas, Denise	Detroit, MI	7/12/44
Milano, Alyssa	New York, NY	12/19/72	Nicholas, Fayard	Philadelphia, PA	10/20/14
Miles, Sarah	Ingatestone, England	12/31/41	Nicholas, Harold	Philadelphia, PA	3/27/24
Miles, Vera	near Boise City, OK	8/23/29	Nichols, Mike	Berlin, Germany	11/6/31
Miller, Ann	Houston, TX	4/12/19	Nicholson, Jack	Neptune, NJ	4/28/37
Miller, Dennis	Pittsburgh, PA	11/3/53	Nicks, Stevie	Phoenix, AZ	5/26/48
Miller, Mitch	Rochester, NY	7/4/11	Nielsen, Leslie	Regina, Sask	2/11/26

Name	Birthplace	Birthdate
Nilsson, Birgit	Karup, Sweden	5/17/18
Nimoy, Leonard	Boston, MA	3/26/31
Nolte, Nick	Omaha, NE	2/8/40
Norman, Jessye	Augusta, GA.	9/15/45
Norris, Chuck	Ryan, OK.	3/10/40
North, Sheree	Los Angeles, CA	1/17/33
Norton, Edward	Columbia, MD.	1969
Noth, Christopher	Madison, WI	11/13/57
Novak, Kim	Chicago, IL.	2/13/33
Nuyen, France	Marseille, France	7/31/39
Oates, John	New York, NY.	4/7/48
O'Brian, Hugh	Rochester, NY	4/19/25
O'Brien, Conan	Brookline, MA.	4/18/63
O'Brien, Margaret	San Diego, CA	1/15/37
Ocean, Billy	Fyzabad, Trinidad	1/21/50
O'Connor, Carroll	New York, NY.	8/2/24
O'Connor, Donald	Chicago, IL.	8/28/25
O'Connor, Sinead	Dublin, Ireland	12/8/66
Odetta	Birmingham, AL	12/31/30
O'Donnell, Chris	Winnetka, IL.	6/26/70
O'Donnell, Rosie	Commack, NY	3/21/62
O'Hara, Maureen	Dublin, Ireland	8/17/20
O'Herlihy, Dan.	Wexford, Ireland	5/1/19
Oldman, Gary	London, England.	3/21/58
Olin, Ken	Chicago, IL.	7/30/54
Olin, Lena.	Stockholm, Sweden	3/22/55
Olmos, Edward James	E. Los Angeles, CA	2/24/47
Olsen, Ashley	California	6/13/86
Olsen, Mary-Kate.	California	6/13/86
Olsen, Merlin.	Logan, UT	9/15/40
O'Neal, Ryan	Los Angeles, CA	4/20/41
O'Neal, Tatum	Los Angeles, CA.	11/5/63
O'Neill, Ed	Youngstown, OH.	4/12/46
Ontkean, Michael.	Vancouver, B.C.	1/24/46
Orbach, Jerry	New York, NY.	10/20/35
Orlando, Tony	New York, NY.	4/3/44
Ormond, Julia	Epsom, England	1/4/65
Osbourne, Ozzy	Birmingham, England.	12/3/46
O'Shea, Milo	Dublin, Ireland	6/2/26
Oslin, K.T.	Crosset, AR	1942
Osmond, Donny	Ogden, UT	12/9/57
Osmond, Marie	Ogden, UT	10/13/59
O'Sullivan, Maureen	Boyle, Ireland	5/17/11
O'Toole, Annette	Houston, TX.	4/1/53
O'Toole, Peter.	Connemara, Ireland	8/2/32
Owens, Buck.	Sherman, TX	8/12/29
Oz, Frank.	Herford, England	5/25/44
Ozawa, Seiji	Shenyang, China.	9/1/35
Paar, Jack	Canton, OH	5/1/18
Pacino, Al.	New York, NY.	4/25/40
Packer, Billy	Wellsville, NY	2/25/40
Page, Jimmy	Heston, England	1/9/44
Page, Patti	Claremore, OK	11/8/27
Paige, Janis	Tacoma, WA	9/16/22
Palance, Jack	Lattimer, PA	2/18/20
Palin, Michael	Sheffield, England	5/5/43
Palmer, Betsy	East Chicago, IN	11/1/29
Palmer, Robert	Bately, England.	1/19/49
Palminteri, Chazz.	Bronx, NY	5/15/51
Paltrow, Gwyneth.	Los Angeles, CA.	9/28/73
Papas, Irene	Chiliomedion, Greece.	3/9/26
Paquin, Anna	Wellington, New Zealand	6/24/82
Parker, Alan	London, England.	2/14/40
Parker, Eleanor	Cedarville, OH	6/26/22
Parker, Fess	Ft. Worth, TX	8/16/25
Parker, Jameson	Baltimore, MD.	11/18/47
Parker, Jean	Deer Lodge, MT	8/11/12
Parker, Mary-Louise	Fort Jackson, SC.	8/2/64
Parker, Sarah Jessica	Nelsonville, OH.	3/25/65
Parsons, Estelle	Lynn, MA	11/20/27
Parton, Dolly	Sevierville, TN	1/19/46
Patinkin, Mandy.	Chicago, IL.	11/30/52
Patric, Jason.	Queens, NY.	6/17/66
Pavarotti, Luciano	Modena, Italy	10/12/35
Paxton, Bill	Fort Worth, TX.	5/17/55
Paycheck, Johnny	Greenfield, OH.	5/31/41
Peck, Gregory	La Jolla, CA	4/5/16
Pendergrass, Teddy	Philadelphia, PA	3/26/50
Penn, Arthur	Philadelphia, PA	9/27/22
Penn, Robin Wright	Dallas, TX	4/8/66
Penn, Sean.	Burbank, CA.	8/17/60
Penny, Joe	London, England.	9/14/56
Perez, Rosie	Brooklyn, NY	9/6/64
Perkins, Elizabeth	New York, NY	11/18/60
Perlman, Itzhak	Tel Aviv, Israel	8/31/45
Perlman, Rhea	Brooklyn, NY	3/31/48
Perlman, Ron	New York, NY.	4/13/50
Perrine, Valerie	Galveston, TX.	9/3/43
Perry, Luke	Fredericktown, OH	10/11/66
Perry, Mathew.	Williamstown, MA	8/19/69
Persoff, Nehemiah	Jerusalem	8/14/20
Pesci, Joe	Newark, NJ	2/9/43
Peters, Bernadette	New York, NY.	2/28/48
Peters, Brock	New York, NY.	7/2/27
Peters, Roberta	New York, NY.	5/4/30
Peterson, Oscar	Montreal, Quebec	8/15/25
Petty, Tom	Gainesville, FL	10/20/53
Pfeiffer, Michelle	Santa Ana, CA	4/29/57
Philbin, Regis	New York, NY.	8/25/34
Phillips, Lou Diamond	Philippines	2/17/62
Phillips, Mackenzie	Alexandria, VA	11/10/59
Phillips, Michelle	Long Beach, CA	6/4/44
Pickett, Wilson	Prattville, AL.	3/18/41
Pierce, David Hyde.	Albany, NY	4/3/59
Pinchot, Bronson	New York, NY.	5/20/59
Pinkett, Jada	Baltimore, MD.	8/18/71
Pirner, David	Green Bay, WI	4/16/64
Piscopo, Joe	Passaic, NJ	6/17/51
Pitt, Brad	Shawnee, OK.	12/18/64
Plant, Robert.	W. Bromwich, England	8/20/48
Pleshette, Suzanne	New York, NY.	1/31/37
Plowright, Joan	Brigg, England	10/28/29
Plummer, Amanda	New York, NY.	3/23/57
Plummer, Christopher.	Toronto, Ontario	12/13/27
Poitier, Sidney.	Miami, FL.	2/20/27
Polanski, Roman	Paris, France	8/18/33
Pollack, Sydney.	Lafayette, IN.	7/1/34
Ponti, Carlo	Milan, Italy	12/11/13
Pop, Iggy	Ann Arbor, MI	4/21/47
Posey, Parker	Baltimore, MD.	11/8/64
Post, Markie	Palo Alto, CA	11/4/50
Poston, Tom	Columbus, OH	10/17/27
Potts, Annie	Nashville, TN	10/28/52
Povich, Maury	Washington, DC	1/17/39
Powell, Jane	Portland, OR	4/1/28
Powers, Stefanie	Hollywood, CA	11/2/42
Prentiss, Paula	San Antonio, TX	3/4/39
Presley, Priscilla	New York, NY.	5/24/46
Preston, Billy.	Houston, TX.	9/9/46
Previn, Andre	Berlin, Germany	4/6/29
Price, Leontyne	Laurel, MS.	2/10/27
Price, Ray	Perryville, TX	1/12/26
Pride, Charlie	Sledge, MS	3/18/39
Priestley, Jason.	Vancouver, British Columbia.	8/28/69
Prince/♀ (TAFKAP)	Minneapolis, MN	6/7/58
Principal, Victoria.	Fukuoka, Japan	1/3/45
Prosky, Robert	Philadelphia, PA.	12/13/30
Pryce, Jonathan	Wales	6/1/47
Pryor, Richard.	Peoria, IL.	12/1/40
Puente, Tito	New York, NY.	4/20/23
Pulliam, Keshia Knight	Newark, NJ	4/9/79
Pullman, Bill	Hornell, NY	12/17/54
Purcell, Sarah	Richmond, IN	10/8/48
Pyle, Denver	Bethune, CO	5/11/20
Quaid, Dennis	Houston, TX.	4/9/54
Quaid, Randy	Houston, TX.	10/1/50
Queen Latifah	East Orange, NJ	3/18/70
Quinn, Aidan.	Chicago, IL.	3/8/59
Quinn, Anthony	Chihuahua, Mexico	4/21/15
Quinn, Martha	Albany, NY.	5/11/59
Rabb, Ellis	Memphis, TN	6/20/30
Rabbitt, Eddie	Brooklyn, NY	11/27/41
Rachins, Alan	Cambridge, MA.	10/10/47
Rae, Charlotte.	Milwaukee, WI	4/22/26
Raffi	Cairo, Italy	7/8/48
Raitt, Bonnie	Burbank, CA.	11/8/49
Ramey, Samuel.	Colby, KS	3/28/42
Rampal, Jean-Pierre	Marseilles, France.	1/7/22
Randall, Tony	Tulsa, OK	2/26/20
Randolph, John	New York, NY.	6/1/15
Randolph, Joyce	Detroit, MI	10/21/25
Raphael, Sally Jessy	Easton, PA.	2/25/43
Rashad, Phylicia	Houston, TX.	6/17/48
Ratzenberger, John	Bridgeport, CT	4/6/47
Rawls, Lou	Chicago, IL.	12/1/36
Raymond, Gene	New York, NY.	8/13/08
Reagan, Ronald	Tampico, IL	2/6/11
Reddy, Helen	Melbourne, Australia	10/25/41
Redford, Robert.	Santa Monica, CA.	8/18/37
Redgrave, Lynn	London, England.	3/8/43

Name	Birthplace	Birthdate	Name	Birthplace	Birthdate
Redgrave, Vanessa	London, England	1/30/37	Russo, Rene	Burbank, CA	2/17/54
Reed, Jerry	Atlanta, GA	3/20/37	Rutherford, Ann	Toronto, Ontario	11/2/20
Reed, Lou	Long Island, NY	3/2/43	Ruttan, Susan	Oregon City, OR	9/16/50
Reed, Oliver	London, England	2/13/38	Ryan, Meg	Fairfield, CT	11/19/61
Reed, Rex	Ft. Worth, TX	10/2/38	Ryan, Roz	Detroit, MI	7/7/51
Reese, Della	Detroit, MI	7/6/31	Rydell, Bobby	Philadelphia, PA	4/26/42
Reeve, Christopher	New York, NY	9/25/52	Ryder, Winona	Winona, MN	10/29/71
Reeves, Keanu	Beirut, Lebanon	9/2/64	Sabato, Antonio Jr.	Italy	2/29/72
Regalbuto, Joe	New York, NY	8/24/—	Sade	Ibadan, Nigeria	1/16/59
Reid, Tim	Norfolk, VA	12/19/44	Sagal, Katie	Los Angeles, CA	1956
Reilly, Charles Nelson	New York, NY	1/13/31	Saget, Bob	Philadelphia, PA	5/17/56
Reiner, Carl	Bronx, NY	3/20/22	Sahl, Mort	Montreal, Quebec	5/11/27
Reiner, Rob	Bronx, NY	3/6/45	Saint, Eva Marie	Newark, NJ	7/4/24
Reinhold, Judge	Wilmington, DE	5/21/56	Sandler, Adam	Brooklyn, NY	9/9/66
Reinking, Ann	Seattle, WA	11/10/50	St. James, Susan	Los Angeles, CA	8/14/46
Reiser, Paul	New York, NY	3/30/57	St. John, Jill	Los Angeles, CA	8/19/40
Reitman, Ivan	Czechoslovakia	10/27/46	Sajak, Pat	Chicago, IL	10/26/47
Resnik, Regina	New York, NY	8/30/24	Saks, Gene	New York, NY	11/8/21
Reynolds, Burt	Waycross, GA	2/11/36	Sales, Soupy	Franklinton, NC	1/8/26
Reynolds, Debbie	El Paso, TX	4/1/32	Samms, Emma	London, England	8/28/60
Reznor, Trent	Mercer, PA	5/17/65	Sands, Julian	Yorkshire, England	1/15/58
Ricci, Christina	Santa Monica, CA	2/12/80	Sanford, Isabel	New York, NY	8/29/17
Richards, Keith	Kent, England	12/18/43	Sarandon, Susan	New York, NY	10/4/46
Richards, Michael	Culver City, CA	7/21/49	Sarnoff, Dorothy	New York, NY	5/25/17
Richardson, Miranda	Lancashire, England	3/3/58	Sartain, Gailard	Tulsa, OK	9/18/46
Richardson, Natasha	London, England	5/11/63	Savage, Fred	Highland Park, IL.	7/9/76
Richardson, Patricia	Bethesda, MD	2/23/51	Saxon, John	Brooklyn, NY	8/5/35
Richie, Lionel	Tuskegee, AL	6/20/50	Sayles, John	Schenectady, NY	9/28/50
Rickles, Don	New York, NY	5/8/26	Scaggs, Boz	Dallas, TX	6/8/44
Rickman, Alan	Hammersmith, England	2/21/46	Scalia, Jack	Brooklyn, NY	11/10/51
Riegert, Peter	New York, NY	4/11/47	Schallert, William	Los Angeles, CA	7/6/22
Rigg, Diana	Doncaster, England	7/20/38	Scheider, Roy	Orange, NJ	11/10/32
Rimes, LeAnn	Jackson, MS	8/28/82	Schell, Maria	Vienna, Austria	1/15/26
Ringwald, Molly	Roseville, CA	2/18/68	Schell, Maximilian	Vienna, Austria	12/8/30
Ritter, John	Burbank, CA	9/17/48	Schenkel, Chris	Bippus, IN	8/21/23
Rivera, Chita	Washington, DC	1/23/33	Schiffer, Claudia	Germany	8/24/71
Rivera, Geraldo	New York, NY	7/4/43	Schneider, John	Mt. Kisco, NY	4/8/54
Rivers, Joan	Brooklyn, NY	6/8/37	Schneider, Rob	San Francisco, CA	10/31/—
Roach, Max	Elizabeth City, NC	1/10/24	Schroder, Rick	Staten Island, NY	4/3/70
Robards, Jason Jr.	Chicago, IL	7/26/22	Schwarzenegger,		
Robbins, Jerome	New York, NY	10/11/18	Arnold	Graz, Austria	7/30/47
Robbins, Tim	W. Covina, CA	10/16/58	Schwarzkopf, Elisabeth	Jarotschin, Poland	12/9/15
Roberts, Doris	St. Louis, MO	11/4/29	Schwimmer, David	Queens, NY	11/12/67
Roberts, Eric	Biloxi, MS	4/18/56	Sciorra, Annabella	New York, NY	3/24/64
Roberts, Julia	Smyrna, GA	10/28/67	Scofield, Paul	Hurst, Pierpont, England	1/21/22
Roberts, Pernell	Waycross, GA	5/18/30	Scolari, Peter	New Rochelle, IL.	9/12/54
Roberts, Tony	New York, NY	10/22/39	Scorsese, Martin	New York, NY	11/17/42
Robertson, Cliff	La Jolla, CA	9/9/25	Scott, George C.	Wise, VA	10/18/27
Robertson, Dale	Harrah, OK	7/14/23	Scott, Lizabeth	Scranton, PA	9/29/22
Robinson, Smokey	Detroit, MI	2/19/40	Scott, Martha	Jamesport, MO	9/22/14
Roche, Eugene	Boston, MA	9/22/28	Scotto, Renata	Savona, Italy	2/24/35
Rodgers, Jimmy	Camas, WA	9/18/33	Scully, Vin	New York, NY	11/29/27
Rodriquez, Johnny	Sabinal, TX	12/10/51	Seagal, Steven	Lansing, MI	4/10/51
Rogers, Fred	Latrobe, PA	3/20/28	Secor, Kyle	Tacoma, WA	5/31/—
Rogers, Kenny	Houston, TX	8/21/38	Sedaka, Neil	New York, NY	3/13/39
Rogers, Mimi	Coral Gables, FL	1/27/56	Seeger, Pete	New York, NY	5/3/19
Rogers, Roy	Cincinnati, OH	11/5/12	Segal, George	Great Neck, NY	2/13/34
Rogers, Wayne	Birmingham, AL	4/7/33	Seidelman, Susan	Philadelphia, PA	12/11/52
Rolle, Esther	Pompano Beach, FL	11/8/33	Seinfeld, Jerry	New York, NY	4/29/55
Rollins, Sonny	New York, NY	9/7/29	Sellecca, Connie	New York, NY	5/25/55
Ronstadt, Linda	Tucson, AZ	7/15/46	Selleck, Tom	Detroit, MI	1/29/45
Rooney, Mickey	Brooklyn, NY	9/23/20	Severinsen, Doc	Arlington, OR	7/7/27
Rose, Axl	Lafayette, IN	2/6/62	Seymour, Jane	Middlesex, England	2/15/51
Rose Marie	New York, NY	8/15/25	Shackelford, Ted	Oklahoma City, OK	6/23/46
Roseanne	Salt Lake City, UT	11/3/52	Shaffer, Paul	Thunder Bay, Ontario	11/28/49
Ross, Diana	Detroit, MI	3/26/44	Shandling, Garry	Chicago, IL	11/29/49
Ross, Katharine	Hollywood, CA	1/29/42	Shankar, Ravi	Benares, India	4/7/20
Ross, Marion	Albert Lea, MN	10/25/28	Sharif, Omar	Alexandria, Egypt	4/10/32
Rossellini, Isabella	Rome, Italy	6/18/52	Shatner, William	Montreal, Quebec	3/22/31
Rostropovich, Mstislav	Baku, Azerbaijan	3/12/27	Shaughnessy, Charles	London, England	2/9/—
Roth, David Lee	Bloomington, IN	10/10/55	Shaver, Helen	St. Thomas, Ontario	2/24/51
Roth, Tim	London, England	5/14/61	Shaw, Artie	New York, NY	5/23/10
Rotten, Johnny	England	1/31/56	Shea, John	N. Conway, NH	4/14/49
Rourke, Mickey	Schnectady, NY	7/16/53	Shearer, Harry	Los Angeles, CA	12/23/43
Rowlands, Gena	Cambria, WI	6/19/34	Shearer, Moira	Scotland	1/17/26
Ruehl, Mercedes	Queens, NY	2/28/48	Shearing, George	London, England	8/13/19
Rush, Barbara	Denver, CO	1/4/30	Sheedy, Ally	New York, NY	6/12/62
Rush, Geoffrey	Toowoomba, Australia	1951	Sheen, Charlie	Los Angeles, CA	9/3/65
Russell, Jane	Bemidji, MN	6/21/21	Sheen, Martin	Dayton, OH	8/3/40
Russell, Ken	Southampton, England	7/3/27	Shelley, Carole	London, England	8/16/39
Russell, Kurt	Springfield, MA	3/17/51	Shepard, Sam	Ft. Sheridan, IL.	11/5/43
Russell, Mark	Buffalo, NY	8/23/32	Shepherd, Cybill	Memphis, TN	2/18/49
Russell, Leon	Lawton, OK	4/2/41	Sheridan, Nicollette	Northington, England	11/21/63
Russell, Nipsey	Atlanta, GA	10/13/24	Shields, Brooke	New York, NY	5/31/65
Russell, Theresa	San Diego, CA	3/20/57	Shire, Talia	New York, NY	4/25/46

Name	Birthplace	Birthdate	Name	Birthplace	Birthdate
Short, Bobby	Danville, IL	9/15/24	Stewart, Patrick	Mirfield, England	7/13/40
Short, Martin	Hamilton, Ontario	3/26/50	Stewart, Rod	London, England	1/10/45
Show, Grant	Detroit, MI	4/27/62	Stickney, Dorothy	Dickinson, ND	6/21/1896
Shue, Andrew	South Orange, NJ	2/20/67	Stiers, David Ogden	Peoria, IL	10/31/42
Shue, Elisabeth	Wilmington, DE	10/6/63	Stiller, Ben	New York, NY	1966
Shull, Richard B.	Evanston, IL	2/24/29	Stiller, Jerry	New York, NY	6/8/29
Sidney, Sylvia	New York, NY	8/8/10	Stills, Stephen	Dallas, TX	1/3/45
Siepi, Cesare	Milan, Italy	2/10/23	Sting	Newcastle, England	10/2/51
Sikking, James B.	Los Angeles, CA	3/5/34	Stipe, Michael	Decatur, GA	1/4/60
Sills, Beverly	Brooklyn, NY	5/25/29	Stockwell, Dean	Hollywood, CA	3/5/36
Silver, Ron	New York, NY	7/2/46	Stoltz, Eric	American Samoa	9/30/61
Silverman, Jonathan	Los Angeles, CA	8/5/66	Stone, Dee Wallace	Kansas City, KS	12/14/48
Silverstone, Alicia	San Francisco, CA	10/4/76	Stone, Oliver	New York, NY	9/15/46
Simmons, Gene	Haifa, Israel	8/25/49	Stone, Sharon	Meadville, PA	3/10/58
Simmons, Jean	London, England	1/31/29	Stookey, Paul	Baltimore, MD	12/30/37
Simmons, Richard	New Orleans, LA	7/12/48	Storch, Larry	New York, NY	1/8/23
Simon, Carly	New York, NY	6/25/45	Storm, Gale	Bloomington, TX	4/5/22
Simon, Paul	Newark, NJ	10/13/41	Stowe, Madeleine	Los Angeles, CA	8/18/58
Simone, Nina	Tyron, NC	2/21/33	Straight, Beatrice	Old Westbury, NY	8/2/18
Sinatra, Frank	Hoboken, NJ	12/12/15	Strait, George	Pearsall, TX	5/18/52
Sinbad	Benton Harbor, MI	11/10/56	Strasser, Robin	New York, NY	5/7/45
Sinise, Gary	Blue Island, IL	3/7/55	Stratas, Teresa	Toronto, Ontario	5/26/38
Singleton, John	Los Angeles, CA	1/6/68	Strauss, Peter	New York, NY	2/20/47
Siskel, Gene	Chicago, IL	1/26/46	Streep, Meryl	Summit, NJ	6/22/49
Skerritt, Tom	Detroit, MI	8/25/33	Streisand, Barbra	Brooklyn, NY	4/24/42
Slater, Christian	New York, NY	8/19/69	Stringfield, Sherry	Colorado Springs, CO	6/24/67
Slater, Helen	Massapequa, NY	12/14/63	Stritch, Elaine	Detroit, MI	2/2/26
Slezak, Erika	Hollywood, CA	8/5/46	Struthers, Sally	Portland, OR	7/28/48
Slick, Grace	Chicago, IL	10/30/39	Stuarti, Enzo	Rome, Italy	3/3/25
Smirnoff, Yakov	Odessa, Russia	1/24/51	Sullivan, Susan	New York, NY	11/18/44
Smith, Allison	New York, NY	12/9/69	Sumac, Yma	Ichocan, Peru	9/10/27
Smith, Buffalo Bob	Buffalo, NY	11/27/17	Summer, Donna	Boston, MA	12/31/48
Smith, Jaclyn	Houston, TX	10/26/47	Sutherland, Donald	St. John, New Brunswick	7/17/34
Smith, Keely	Norfolk, VA	3/9/35	Sutherland, Joan	Sydney, Australia	11/7/26
Smith, Maggie	Ilford, England	12/28/34	Sutherland, Kiefer	London, England	12/20/66
Smith, Will	Philadelphia, PA	9/25/68	Swayze, Patrick	Houston, TX	8/18/54
Smits, Jimmy	New York, NY	7/9/55	Swit, Loretta	Passaic, NJ	11/4/37
Smothers, Dick	New York, NY	11/20/39	Takei, George	Los Angeles, CA	4/20/39
Smothers, Tom	New York, NY	2/2/37	Tallchief, Maria	Fairfax, OK	1/24/25
Snipes, Wesley	Orlando, FL	7/31/63	Tarantino, Quentin	Knoxville, TN	3/27/63
Snow, Hank	Nova Scotia, Canada	5/9/14	Taylor, Billy	Greenville, SC	7/24/21
Solti, Georg	Budapest, Hungary	10/21/12	Taylor, Elizabeth	London, England	2/27/32
Somers, Suzanne	San Bruno, CA	10/16/46	Taylor, James	Boston, MA	3/12/48
Sommer, Elke	Berlin, Germany	11/5/41	Taylor, Rip	Washington, DC	1/13/30
Sorbo, Kevin	Mound, MN	9/24/58	Taylor, Rod	Sydney, Australia	1/11/29
Sorvino, Mira	Tenafly, NJ	9/28/70	Te Kanawa, Kiri	Gisborne, New Zealand	3/6/44
Sorvino, Paul	Brooklyn, NY	2/17/54	Tebaldi, Renata	Pesaro, Italy	2/1/22
Sothern, Ann	Valley City, ND	1/22/09	Temple, Shirley	Santa Monica, CA	4/23/28
Soul, David	Chicago, IL	8/28/43	Tennant, Victoria	London, England	9/30/50
Spacek, Sissy	Quitman, TX	12/25/49	Tennille, Toni	Montgomery, AL	5/8/43
Spacey, Kevin	S. Orange, NJ	7/26/59	Tesh, John	Garden City, NY	7/9/52
Spade, David	Birmingham, MI	7/22/65	Tharp, Twyla	Portland, IN	7/1/41
Spader, James	Boston, MA	2/7/60	Thicke, Alan	Kirkland Lake, Ontario	3/1/47
Spano, Joe	San Francisco, CA	7/7/46	Thomas, Jay	New Orleans, LA	7/12/48
Spector, Phil	Bronx, NY	12/25/40	Thomas, Jonathan Taylor	Bethlehem, PA	9/8/81
Spelling, Aaron	Dallas, TX	4/22/28	Thomas, Kristin Scott	Cornwall, England	1960
Spelling, Tori	Los Angeles, CA	5/16/73	Thomas, Marlo	Detroit, MI	11/21/43
Spielberg, Steven	Cincinnati, OH	12/18/47	Thomas, Philip Michael	Columbus, OH	5/26/49
Springfield, Dusty	London, England	4/16/39	Thomas, Richard	New York, NY	6/13/51
Springfield, Rick	Sydney, Australia	8/23/49	Thompson, Emma	London, England	4/15/59
Springsteen, Bruce	Freehold, NJ	9/23/49	Thompson, Jack	Sydney, Australia	8/31/40
Stack, Robert	Los Angeles, CA	1/13/19	Thompson, Lea	Rochester, MN	5/31/61
Stafford, Jo	Coalinga, CA	11/12/18	Thompson, Sada	Des Moines, IA	9/27/29
Stahl, Richard	Detroit, MI	1/4/32	Thorne-Smith, Courtney	San Francisco, CA	11/8/68
Stallone, Sylvester	New York, NY	7/6/46	Thornton, Billy Bob	Hot Springs, AR	8/4/55
Stamos, John	Cypress, CA	8/19/63	Thurman, Uma	Boston, MA	4/29/70
Stamp, Terence	Stepney, England	7/22/39	Tiegs, Cheryl	Minnesota	9/25/47
Stang, Arnold	New York, NY	9/28/25	Tillis, Mel	Tampa, FL	8/8/32
Stanley, Kim	Tularosa, NM	2/11/25	Tilly, Meg	Texada, B.C.	2/14/60
Stanton, Harry Dean	West Irvine, KY	7/14/26	Tilson Thomas, Michael	Hollywood, CA	12/21/44
Stapleton, Jean	New York, NY	1/19/23	Todd, Richard	Dublin, Ireland	6/11/19
Stapleton, Maureen	Troy, NY	6/21/25	Tomei, Marisa	New York, NY	12/4/64
Starr, Ringo	Liverpool, England	7/7/40	Tomlin, Lily	Detroit, MI	9/1/39
Steenburgen, Mary	Newport, AR	2/8/53	Tomlinson, David	Scotland	5/7/17
Steiger, Rod	W. Hampton, NY	4/14/25	Torme, Mel	Chicago, IL	9/13/25
Stephens, James	Mt. Kisco, NY	5/18/51	Tork, Peter	Washington, DC	2/13/44
Stern, Daniel	Stamford, CT	5/28/57	Torn, Rip	Temple, TX	2/6/31
Stern, Howard	New York, NY	1/12/54	Townsend, Robert	Chicago, IL	2/6/57
Stern, Isaac	Kreminiecz, Russia	7/21/20	Townshend, Peter	Chiswick, England	5/19/45
Sternhagen, Frances	Washington, DC	1/13/30	Travanti, Daniel J.	Kenosha, WI	3/7/40
Stevens, Andrew	Memphis, TN	6/10/55	Travers, Mary	Louisville, KY	11/9/36
Stevens, Cat	London, England	7/21/48	Travis, Nancy	New York, NY	9/21/61
Stevens, Connie	Brooklyn, NY	8/8/38	Travis, Randy	Marshville, NC	5/4/59
Stevens, Rise	New York, NY	6/11/13	Travolta, John	Englewood, NJ	2/10/54
Stevens, Stella	Yazoo City, MS	10/1/36	Trebek, Alex	Sudbury, Ontario	7/22/40
Stevenson, Parker	Philadelphia, PA	6/4/52	Trevor, Claire	New York, NY	3/8/09
Stewart, Jon	Lawrence, NJ	1963	Tritt, Travis	Marietta, GA	2/9/63

Name	Birthplace	Birthdate	Name	Birthplace	Birthdate
Tucker, Michael	Baltimore, MD	2/6/44	Wheaton, Wil	Burbank, CA	7/29/72
Tucker, Tanya	Seminole, TX	10/10/58	Whitaker, Forest	Longview, TX	7/15/61
Tune, Tommy	Wichita Falls, TX	2/28/39	White, Barry	Galveston, TX	9/12/44
Turner, Janine	Lincoln, NE	12/6/62	White, Betty	Oak Park, IL	1/17/22
Turner, Kathleen	Springfield, MO	6/19/54	White, Jaleel	Los Angeles, CA	11/27/76
Turner, Tina	Brownsville, TN	11/26/39	White, Vanna	N Myrtle Beach, SC	2/18/57
Turturro, John	Brooklyn, NY	2/28/57	Whiting, Margaret	Detroit, MI	7/22/24
Twiggy	London, England	9/19/46	Whitmore, James	White Plains, NY	10/1/21
Tyler, Liv	Portland, ME	7/1/77	Widmark, Richard	Sunrise, MN	12/26/14
Tyler, Steven	Boston, MA	3/26/48	Wiest, Dianne	Kansas City, MO	3/28/48
Tyson, Cicely	New York, NY	12/19/33	Wilder, Billy	Vienna, Austria	6/22/06
Uecker, Bob	Milwaukee, WI	1/26/35	Wilder, Gene	Milwaukee, WI	6/11/35
Uggams, Leslie	New York, NY	5/25/43	Williams, Andy	Wall Lake, IA	12/3/30
Ullman, Tracey	Slough, England	12/30/59	Williams, Barry	Santa Monica, CA	9/30/54
Ullmann, Liv	Tokyo, Japan	12/16/38	Williams, Billy Dee	New York, NY	4/6/37
Underwood, Blair	Tacoma, WA	8/25/64	Williams, Cindy	Van Nuys, CA	8/22/47
Urich, Robert	Toronto, Ohio	12/19/47	Williams, Esther	Los Angeles, CA	8/8/23
Ustinov, Peter	London, England	4/16/21	Williams, Hal	Columbus, OH	12/14/38
Vaccaro, Brenda	Brooklyn, NY	11/18/39	Williams, Hank Jr.	Shreveport, LA	5/26/49
Vale, Jerry	New York, NY	7/8/31	Williams, JoBeth	Houston, TX	1949
Valente, Caterina	Paris, France	1/14/31	Williams, Montel	Baltimore, MD	7/3/56
Valli, Frankie	Newark, NJ	5/3/37	Williams, Paul	Omaha, NE	9/19/40
Van Ark, Joan	New York, NY	6/16/43	Williams, Robin	Chicago, IL	7/21/52
Vance, Courtney B.	Detroit, MI	3/12/60	Williams, Treat	Rowayton, CT	12/1/51
Vandross, Luther	New York, NY	4/20/51	Williams, Vanessa	New York, NY	3/18/63
Van Damme, Jean-Claude	Brussels, Belgium	10/18/60	Williamson, Nicol	Hamilton, Scotland	9/14/38
Van Dyke, Dick	West Plains, MO	12/13/25	Willis, Bruce	W. Germany	3/19/55
Van Dyke, Jerry	Danville, IL	7/27/31	Wilson, Demond	Valdosta, GA	10/13/46
Van Halen, Eddie	Nijmegen, Netherlands	1/26/57	Wilson, Elizabeth	Grand Rapids, MI	4/4/25
Van Patten, Dick	New York, NY	12/9/28	Wilson, Flip	Jersey City, NJ	12/8/33
Van Peebles, Mario	Mexico	1/15/57	Wilson, Nancy	Chillicothe, OH	2/20/37
Vaughn, Robert	New York, NY	11/22/32	Windom, William	New York, NY	9/28/23
Vaughn, Vince	Minneapolis, MN	1970	Winfield, Paul	Los Angeles, CA	5/22/41
Vedder, Eddie	Evanston, IL	12/23/65	Winfrey, Oprah	Kosciusko, MS	1/29/54
Verdon, Gwen	Los Angeles, CA	1/13/25	Winger, Debra	Cleveland, OH	5/16/55
Vereen, Ben	Miami, FL	10/10/46	Winkler, Henry	New York, NY	10/30/45
Verrett, Shirley	New Orleans, LA	5/31/31	Winningham, Mare	Phoenix, AZ	5/6/59
Vickers, Jon	Prince Albert, Sask.	10/26/26	Winslet, Kate	Reading, England	10/5/75
Vincent, Jan-Michael	Denver, CO	7/15/44	Winter, Johnny	Beaumont, TX	2/23/44
Vinson, Helen	Beaumont, TX	9/17/07	Winters, Jonathan	Dayton, OH	11/11/25
Vinton, Bobby	Canonsburg, PA	4/16/35	Winters, Shelley	St. Louis, MO	8/18/22
Vitale, Dick	E Rutherford, NJ	6/9/40	Winwood, Steve	Birmingham, England	5/12/48
Voight, Jon	Yonkers, NY	12/29/38	Wiseman, Joseph	Montreal, Quebec	5/15/18
Von Stade, Frederica	Somerville, NJ	6/1/45	Withers, Jane	Atlanta, GA	4/12/26
Von Sydow, Max	Lund, Sweden	4/10/29	Witt, Alicia	Worcester, MA	8/21/75
Wagner, Jack	Washington, MO	10/3/59	Wolf, Scott	Boston, MA	6/4/68
Wagner, Lindsay	Los Angeles, CA	6/22/49	Wonder, Stevie	Saginaw, MI	5/13/50
Wagner, Robert	Detroit, MI	2/10/30	Woo, John	Guangzhau, China.	5/1/46
Wahl, Ken	Chicago, IL	2/14/56	Wood, Elijah	Cedar Rapids, IA	1/28/81
Wain, Bea	Bronx, NY	4/30/17	Woodard, Alfre	Tulsa, OK	11/2/53
Waite, Ralph	White Plains, NY	6/22/29	Woods, James	Vernal, NJ	4/18/47
Waits, Tom	Pomona, CA	12/7/49	Woodward, Edward	Croyden, England	6/1/30
Walden, Robert	New York, NY	9/25/43	Woodward, Joanne	Thomasville, GA	2/27/30
Walken, Christopher	New York, NY	3/31/43	Wopat, Tom	Lodi, WI	9/9/50
Wallach, Eli	Brooklyn, NY	12/7/15	Worth, Irene	Nebraska	6/23/16
Walston, Ray	Laurel, MS	11/2/24	Wray, Fay	Alberta, Canada	9/10/07
Walter, Jessica	New York, NY	1/31/44	Wright, Martha	Seattle, WA	3/23/26
Ward, Fred	San Diego, CA	1943	Wright, Max	Detroit, MI	8/2/43
Ward, Sela	Meridian, MS	8/11/56	Wright, Steven	New York, NY	12/6/55
Ward, Simon	London, England	10/19/41	Wright, Teresa	New York, NY	10/27/18
Warden, Jack	Newark, NJ	9/18/20	Wyatt, Jane	Campgaw, NJ	8/10/11
Warner, Malcolm-Jamal	Jersey City, NJ	8/18/70	Wyle, Noah	Hollywood, CA	6/4/71
Warren, Lesley Ann	New York, NY	8/16/46	Wyman, Jane	St. Joseph, MO	1/4/14
Warrick, Ruth	St. Joseph, MO	6/29/16	Wynette, Tammy	Red Bay, AL	5/5/42
Warwick, Dionne	E Orange, NJ	12/12/41	Yankovic, Weird Al	Los Angeles, CA	10/23/59
Washington, Denzel	Mt. Vernon, NY	12/28/54	Yanni	Kalamata, Greece	11/4/54
Waters, John	Baltimore, MD	4/22/46	Yarborough, Glenn	Milwaukee, WI	1/12/30
Waters, Roger	Great Bookham, England	9/9/44	Yarrow, Peter	New York, NY	5/31/38
Waterston, Sam	Cambridge, MA	11/15/40	Yearwood, Trisha	Monticello, GA	9/19/64
Watts, Andre	Nuremberg, Germany	6/20/46	Yoakam, Dwight	Pikesville, KY	10/23/56
Wayans, Damon	New York, NY	9/4/60	York, Michael	Fulmer, England	3/27/42
Wayans, Keenan Ivory	New York, NY	6/8/58	York, Susannah	London, England	1/9/42
Waxman, Al	Toronto, Ontario	3/2/35	Young, Alan	Northumberland, England	11/19/19
Weathers, Carl	New Orleans, LA	1/14/48	Young, Burt	New York, NY	4/30/40
Weaver, Dennis	Joplin, MO	6/4/24	Young, Loretta	Salt Lake City, UT	1/6/13
Weaver, Fritz	Pittsburgh, PA	1/19/26	Young, Neil	Toronto, Ontario	11/12/45
Weaver, Sigourney	New York, NY	10/8/49	Young, Robert	Chicago, IL	2/22/07
Weir, Peter	Sydney, Australia	8/8/44	Young, Sean	Louisville, KY	11/20/59
Weitz, Bruce	Norwalk, CT	5/27/43	Youngman, Henny	Liverpool, England	1/12/06
Welch, Raquel	Chicago, IL	9/5/40	Zeffirelli, Franco	Florence, Italy	2/12/23
Weld, Tuesday	New York, NY	8/27/43	Zellweger, Renee	Katy, TX	1969
Wells, Kitty	Nashville, TN	8/30/19	Zemeckis, Robert	Chicago, IL	5/14/51
Wendt, George	Chicago, IL	10/17/48	Zerbe, Anthony	Long Beach, CA	5/20/36
West, Adam	Walla Walla, WA	9/19/29	Zimbalist, Efrem Jr.	New York, NY	11/30/23
Wettig, Patricia	Cincinnati, OH	12/4/51	Zimbalist, Stephanie	Encino, CA	10/8/56
Whalley-Kilme, Joanne	Manchester, England	8/25/64	Zukerman, Pinchas	Tel Aviv, Israel	7/16/48
			Zuniga, Daphne	San Francisco, CA	10/28/62

Entertainment Personalities of the Past

See also other lists. Data as of Sept. 1997.

Born	Died	Name	Born	Died	Name	Born	Died	Name
1895	1974	Abbott, Bud	1934	1993	Bixby, Bill	1967	1994	Cobain, Kurt
1887	1995	Abbott, George	1911	1960	Bjoerling, Jussi	1911	1976	Cobb, Lee J.
1903	1992	Acuff, Roy	1895	1973	Blackmer, Sidney	1877	1961	Coburn, Charles
1872	1953	Adams, Maude	1931	1989	Blake, Amanda	1878	1942	Cohan, George M.
1855	1926	Adler, Jacob P.	1921	1995	Blaine, Vivian	1902	1986	Cohen, Myron
1903	1984	Adler, Luther	1908	1989	Blanc, Mel	1903	1996	Colbert, Claudette
1898	1933	Adoree, Renee	1928	1972	Blocker, Dan	1919	1965	Cole, Nat "King"
1902	1986	Aherne, Brian	1909	1979	Blondell, Joan	1890	1965	Collins, Ray
1931	1989	Ailey, Alvin	1888	1959	Blore, Eric	1891	1958	Colman, Ronald
1918	1994	Akins, Claude	1901	1975	Blue, Ben	1908	1934	Columbo, Russ
1909	1964	Albertson, Frank	1899	1957	Bogart, Humphrey	1921	1992	Connors, Chuck
1907	1981	Albertson, Jack	1880	1965	Boland, Mary	1920	1994	Conrad, William
1894	1956	Allen, Fred	1895	1969	Boles, John	1917	1982	Conried, Hans
1906	1964	Allen, Gracie	1904	1987	Bolger, Ray	1911	1975	Conte, Richard
1913	1996	Allen, Mel	1903	1960	Bond, Ward	1914	1984	Coogan, Jackie
1883	1950	Allgood, Sara	1892	1981	Bondi, Beulah	1904	1995	Cook, Elisha
1908	1993	Ameche, Don	1917	1981	Boone, Richard	1935	1964	Cooke, Sam
1903	1993	Ames, Leon	1833	1893	Booth, Edwin	1901	1961	Cooper, Gary
1902	1993	Anderson, Marian	1796	1852	Booth, Junius Brutus	1888	1971	Cooper, Gladys
1909	1992	Andrews, Dana	1898	1992	Booth, Shirley	1896	1973	Cooper, Melville
1913	1967	Andrews, Laverne	1905	1965	Bow, Clara	1914	1968	Corey, Wendell
1918	1995	Andrews, Maxine	1874	1946	Bowes, Maj. Edward	1893	1974	Cornell, Katherine
1887	1933	Arbuckle, Fatty (Roscoe)	1928	1977	Boyd, Stephen	1890	1972	Correll, Charles (Andy)
1908	1990	Arden, Eve	1898	1972	Boyd, William	1905	1979	Costello, Dolores
1900	1976	Arlen, Richard	1899	1978	Boyer, Charles	1906	1959	Costello, Lou
1868	1946	Arliss, George	1893	1939	Brady, Alice	1905	1994	Cotten, Joseph
1888	1945	Armetta, Henry	1894	1974	Brennan, Walter	1899	1973	Coward, Noel
1909?	1996	Amsterdam, Morey	1904	1979	Brent, George	1924	1973	Cox, Wally
1900	1971	Armstrong, Louis	1891	1951	Brice, Fanny	1908	1983	Crabbe, Buster
1917	1986	Arnaz, Desi	1916	1994	Brazzi, Rossano	1928	1978	Crane, Bob
1890	1956	Arnold, Edward	1891	1959	Broderick, Helen	1911	1986	Crawford, Broderick
1905	1974	Arquette, Cliff	1892	1973	Brown, Joe E.	1904	1977	Crawford, Joan
1900	1991	Arthur, Jean	1926	1966	Bruce, Lenny	1880	1942	Crews, Laura Hope
1907	1991	Ashcroft, Peggy	1895	1953	Bruce, Nigel	1880	1974	Crisp, Donald
1899	1987	Astaire, Fred	1910	1982	Bruce, Virginia	1942	1973	Croce, Jim
1906	1987	Astor, Mary	1915	1985	Brynner, Yul	1904	1977	Crosby, Bing
1885	1946	Atwill, Lionel	1903	1979	Buchanan, Edgar	1910	1986	Crothers, Scatman
1905	1967	Auer, Mischa	1938	1982	Buono, Victor	1908	1990	Cummings, Robert
1900	1972	Austin, Gene	1885	1970	Burke, Billie	1878	1968	Currie, Finlay
1908	1996	Ayres, Lew	1911	1967	Burnette, Smiley	1913	1994	Cushing, Peter
1913	1989	Backus, Jim	1896	1996	Burns, George	1914	1978	Dailey, Dan
1918	1990	Bailey, Pearl	1917	1993	Burr, Raymond	1923	1965	Dandridge, Dorothy
1892	1968	Bainter, Fay	1925	1984	Burton, Richard	1894	1963	Daniell, Henry
1906	1975	Baker, Josephine	1897	1946	Busch, Mae	1901	1971	Daniels, Bebe
1904	1983	Balanchine, George	1883	1966	Bushman, Francis X.	1936	1973	Darin, Bobby
1911	1989	Ball, Lucille	1896	1946	Butterworth, Charles	1921	1965	Darnell, Linda
1919	1996	Balsam, Martin	1893	1971	Byington, Spring	1879	1967	Darwell, Jane
1882	1956	Bancroft, George	1904	1972	Cabot, Bruce	1909	1986	Da Silva, Howard
1903	1968	Bankhead, Tallulah	1918	1977	Cabot, Sebastian	1866	1949	Davenport, Harry
1890	1952	Banks, Leslie	1899	1986	Cagney, James	1908	1989	Davis, Bette
1890	1955	Bara, Theda	1895	1956	Calhern, Louis	1907	1961	Davis, Joan
1810	1891	Barnum, Phineas T.	1923	1977	Callas, Maria	1925	1990	Davis, Sammy Jr.
1879	1959	Barrymore, Ethel	1907	1994	Calloway, Cab	1931	1955	Dean, James
1882	1942	Barrymore, John	1933	1976	Cambridge, Godfrey	1917	1993	Defore, Don
1878	1954	Barrymore, Lionel	1865	1940	Campbell, Mrs. Patrick	1905	1968	Dekker, Albert
1848	1905	Barrymore, Maurice	1950	1994	Candy, John	1908	1983	Del Rio, Dolores
1897	1963	Barthelmess, Richard	1892	1964	Cantor, Eddie	1892	1983	Demarest, William
1914	1984	Basehart, Richard	1897	1991	Capra, Frank	1905	1993	DeMille, Agnes
1904	1984	Basie, Count	1878	1947	Carey, Harry	1881	1959	DeMille, Cecil B.
1923	1985	Baxter, Anne	1913	1994	Carey, Macdonald	1937	1992	Dennis, Sandy
1889	1951	Baxter, Warner	1906	1996	Carné, Marcel	1891	1967	Denny, Reginald
1909	1997	Beal, John	1950	1983	Carpenter, Karen	1901	1974	DeSica, Vittorio
1904	1965	Beatty, Clyde	1906	1988	Carradine, John	1905	1977	Devine, Andy
1902	1962	Beavers, Louise	1880	1961	Carrillo, Leo	1924	1991	Dewhurst, Colleen
1884	1946	Beery, Noah, Sr.	1892	1972	Carroll, Leo G.	1942	1972	De Wilde, Brandon
1913	1994	Beery, Noah Jr.	1905	1965	Carroll, Nancy	1907	1974	De Wolfe, Billy
1889	1949	Beery, Wallace	1910	1963	Carson, Jack	1920	1985	Diamond, Selma
1901	1970	Begley, Ed	1873	1921	Caruso, Enrico	1901	1992	Dietrich, Marlene
1904	1991	Bellamy, Ralph	1876	1973	Casals, Pablo	1879	1947	Digges, Dudley
1949	1982	Belushi, John	1929	1989	Cassavetes, John	1901	1966	Disney, Walt
1906	1968	Benaderet, Bea	1893	1969	Castle, Irene	1894	1949	Dix, Richard
1906	1964	Bendix, William	1887	1918	Castle, Vernon	1905	1958	Donat, Robert
1904	1965	Bennett, Constance	1922	1991	Caulfield, Joan	1889	1972	Donlevy, Brian
1910	1990	Bennett, Joan	1873	1938	Chaliapin, Feodor	1901	1981	Douglas, Melvyn
1943	1987	Bennett, Michael	1919	1980	Champion, Gower	1907	1959	Douglas, Paul
1894	1974	Benny, Jack	1918	1961	Chandler, Jeff	1889	1956	Draper, Ruth
1924	1970	Benzell, Mimi	1883	1930	Chaney, Lon	1881	1965	Dresser, Louise
1917	1996	Beradino, John	1905	1973	Chaney, Lon Jr.	1869	1934	Dressler, Marie
1899	1966	Berg, Gertrude	1942	1981	Chapin, Harry	1820	1897	Drew, Mrs. John
1903	1978	Bergen, Edgar	1889	1977	Chaplin, Charles	1923	1996	Dru, Joanne
1915	1982	Bergman, Ingrid	1893	1961	Chatterton, Ruth	1909	1951	Duchin, Eddy
1895	1976	Berkeley, Busby	1908	1996	Cherrill, Virginia	1917	1990	Duff, Howard
1923	1986	Bernardi, Herschel	1888	1972	Chevalier, Maurice	1890	1974	Dumbrille, Douglass
1844	1923	Bernhardt, Sarah	1888	1960	Clark, Bobby	1889	1965	Dumont, Margaret
1893	1943	Bernie, Ben	1914	1968	Clark, Fred	1878	1927	Duncan, Isadora
1939	1996	Bessell, Ted	1920	1966	Clift, Montgomery	1905	1967	Dunn, James
1889	1967	Bickford, Charles	1932	1963	Cline, Patsy	1898	1990	Dunne, Irene
			1892	1967	Clyde, Andy	1893	1980	Durante, Jimmy

Born	Died	Name	Born	Died	Name	Born	Died	Name
1907	1968	Duryea, Dan	1882	1974	Goldwyn, Samuel	1915	1992	Ireland, John
1858	1924	Duse, Eleanora	1909	1986	Goodman, Benny	1838	1905	Irving, Henry
1894	1929	Eagels, Jeanne	1915	1969	Gorcey, Leo	1909	1995	Ives, Burl
1914	1993	Eckstine, Billy	1906	1995	Gordon, Gale	1875	1942	Jackson, Joe
1901	1967	Eddy, Nelson	1896	1985	Gordon, Ruth	1911	1972	Jackson, Mahalia
1933	1996	Edelman, Herb	1899	1982	Gosden, Freeman (Amos)	1926	1997	Jaeckel, Richard
1897	1971	Edwards, Cliff	1869	1944	Gottschalk, Ferdinand	1891	1984	Jaffe, Sam
1879	1945	Edwards, Gus	1829	1869	Gottschalk, Louis	1903	1991	Jagger, Dean
1928	1996	Edwards, Vince	1916	1973	Grable, Betty	1917	1997	James, Dennis
1899	1974	Ellington, Duke	1894	1991	Graham, Martha	1916	1983	James, Harry
1941	1974	Elliot, Cass	1925	1981	Grahame, Gloria	1889	1956	Janis, Elsie
1891	1967	Elman, Mischa	1913	1993	Granger, Stewart	1886	1950	Jannings, Emil
1881	1951	Errol, Leon	1904	1986	Grant, Cary	1930	1980	Janssen, David
1888	1976	Evans, Edith	1915	1987	Greene, Lorne	1900	1974	Jenkins, Allen
1901	1989	Evans, Maurice	1879	1954	Greenstreet, Sydney	1898	1981	Jessel, George
1909	1994	Ewell, Tom	1874	1948	Griffith, David Wark	1918	1996	Johnson, Ben
1883	1939	Fairbanks, Douglas	1912	1980	Griffith, Hugh	1892	1962	Johnson, Chic
1914	1970	Farmer, Frances	1925	1995	Guardino, Harry	1886	1950	Jolson, Al
1870	1929	Farnum, Dustin	1912	1967	Guthrie, Woody	1889	1942	Jones, Buck
1876	1953	Farnum, William	1875	1959	Gwenn, Edmund	1933	1983	Jones, Carolyn
1882	1967	Farrar, Geraldine	1926	1993	Gwynne, Fred	1911	1965	Jones, Spike
1904	1971	Farrell, Glenda	1892	1950	Hale, Alan	1943	1970	Joplin, Janis
1897	1961	Fay, Frank	1918	1990	Hale, Alan Jr.	1902	1982	Jory, Victor
1895	1962	Fazenda, Louise	1925	1981	Haley, Bill	1905	1981	Joslyn, Allyn
1900	1993	Feld, Fritz	1899	1979	Haley, Jack	1940	1994	Julia, Raul
1933	1982	Feldman, Marty	1902	1985	Hamilton, Margaret	1910	1966	Kane, Helen
1920	1993	Fellini, Federico	1847	1919	Hammerstein, Oscar	1887	1969	Karloff, Boris
1919	1997	Fenneman, George	1893	1964	Hardwicke, Cedric	1893	1970	Karns, Roscoe
1912	1992	Ferrer, Jose	1892	1957	Hardy, Oliver	1949	1984	Kaufman, Andy
1898	1985	Fetchit, Stepin	1911	1937	Harlow, Jean	1913	1987	Kaye, Danny
1894	1979	Fiedler, Arthur	1904	1995	Harris, Phil	1811	1868	Kean, Charles
1918	1973	Field, Betty	1908	1990	Harrison, Rex	1806	1880	Kean, Mrs. Charles
1898	1979	Fields, Gracie	1870	1946	Hart, William S.	1787	1833	Kean, Edmund
1879	1946	Fields, W.C.	1928	1973	Harvey, Laurence	1895	1966	Keaton, Buster
1931	1978	Fields, Totie	1910	1973	Hawkins, Jack	1910	1993	Keeler, Ruby
1916	1977	Finch, Peter	1890	1973	Hayakawa, Sessue	1921	1997	Keith, Brian
1902	1975	Fine, Larry	1885	1969	Hayes, Gabby	1894	1973	Kellaway, Cecil
1865	1932	Fiske, Minnie Maddern	1900	1993	Hayes, Helen	1898	1979	Kelly, Emmett
1888	1961	Fitzgerald, Barry	1902	1971	Hayward, Leland	1912	1996	Kelly, Gene
1895	1962	Flagstad, Kirsten	1917	1975	Hayward, Susan	1929	1982	Kelly, Grace
1900	1971	Flippen, Jay C.	1918	1987	Hayworth, Rita	1910	1981	Kelly, Patsy
1909	1959	Flynn, Errol	1896	1937	Healy, Ted	1907	1968	Kelton, Pert
1925	1974	Flynn, Joe	1910	1971	Heflin, Van	1926	1959	Kendall, Kay
1910	1968	Foley, Red	1901	1987	Heifetz, Jascha	1914	1990	Kennedy, Arthur
1905	1982	Fonda, Henry	1873	1918	Held, Anna	1890	1948	Kennedy, Edgar
1920	1978	Fontaine, Frank	1955	1996	Hemingway, Margaux	1886	1956	Kibbee, Guy
1887	1983	Fontanne, Lynn	1942	1970	Hendrix, Jimi	1888	1964	Kilbride, Percy
1919	1991	Fonteyn, Margot	1912	1969	Henie, Sonja	1923	1986	Knight, Ted
1895	1973	Ford, John	1908	1992	Henreid, Paul	1901	1980	Kostelanetz, Andre
1901	1976	Ford, Paul	1936	1990	Henson, Jim	1919	1962	Kovacs, Ernie
1919	1991	Ford, Tennessee Ernie	1929	1993	Hepburn, Audrey	1885	1974	Kruger, Otto
1899	1966	Ford, Wallace	1886	1956	Hersholt, Jean	1921	1991	Kulp, Nancy
1927	1987	Fosse, Bob	1928	1997	Hickey, William	1913	1964	Ladd, Alan
1901	1970	Foster, Preston	1925	1992	Hill, Benny	1895	1967	Lahr, Bert
1922	1991	Foxx, Redd	1899	1980	Hitchcock, Alfred	1919	1973	Lake, Veronica
1857	1928	Foy, Eddie	1914	1955	Hodiak, John	1915	1982	Lamas, Fernando
1933?	1990	Franchi, Sergio	1894	1973	Holden, Fay	1914	1996	Lamour, Dorothy
1903	1968	Francis, Kay	1918	1981	Holden, William	1913	1994	Lancaster, Burt
1934	1991	Franciscus, James	1922	1965	Holliday, Judy	1902	1986	Lanchester, Elsa
1893	1966	Frawley, William	1905	1992	Holloway, Sterling	1917	1995	Lane, Pricilla
1870	1955	Friganza, Trixie	1936	1959	Holly, Buddy	1919	1948	Landis, Carole
1890	1958	Frisco, Joe	1888	1951	Holt, Jack	1904	1972	Landis, Jessie Royce
1907	1980	Froman, Jane	1918	1973	Holt, Tim	1936	1991	Landon, Michael
1916	1994	Furness, Betty	1898	1978	Homolka, Oscar	1884	1944	Langdon, Harry
1901	1960	Gable, Clark	1967	1995	Hoon, Shannon	1853	1929	Langtry, Lillie
1920	1995	Gabor, Eva	1902	1972	Hopkins, Miriam	1921	1959	Lanza, Mario
1905	1990	Garbo, Greta	1858	1935	Hopper, DeWolf	1917	1996	LaRue, Lash (Alfred)
1942	1995	Garcia, Jerry	1915	1970	Hopper, William	1870	1950	Lauder, Harry
1922	1992	Gardenia, Vincent	1904	1989	Horowitz, Vladimir	1899	1962	Laughton, Charles
1922	1990	Gardner, Ava	1886	1970	Horton, Edward Everett	1890	1965	Laurel, Stan
1913	1952	Garfield, John	1874	1926	Houdini, Harry	1923	1984	Lawford, Peter
1922	1969	Garland, Judy	1902	1988	Houseman, John	1898	1952	Lawrence, Gertrude
1908	1996	Garson, Greer	1903	1952	Howard, Curly	1908	1991	Lean, David
1939	1984	Gaye, Marvin	1881	1965	Howard, Eugene	1940	1973	Lee, Bruce
1906	1984	Gaynor, Janet	1867	1961	Howard, Joe	1907	1952	Lee, Canada
1902	1978	Geer, Will	1890	1943	Howard, Leslie	1914	1970	Lee, Gypsy Rose
1900	1954	George, Gladys	1897	1975	Howard, Moe	1899	1991	LeGallienne, Eva
1958	1988	Gibb, Andy	1895	1955	Howard, Shemp	1888	1976	Lehmann, Lotte
1892	1962	Gibson, Hoot	1885	1955	Howard, Tom	1913	1967	Leigh, Vivien
1894	1971	Gilbert, Billy	1916	1988	Howard, Trevor	1922	1976	Leighton, Margaret
1895	1936	Gilbert, John	1885	1949	Howard, Willie	1940	1980	Lennon, John
1907	1990	Gilford, Jack	1925	1985	Hudson, Rock	1898	1981	Lenya, Lotte
1855	1937	Gillette, William	1890	1977	Hull, Henry	1870	1941	Leonard, Eddie
1897	1987	Gingold, Hermione	1886	1957	Hull, Josephine	1907	1997	Leonard, Sheldon
1898	1968	Gish, Dorothy	1895	1958	Humphrey, Doris	1900	1987	LeRoy, Mervyn
1893	1993	Gish, Lillian	1925	1969	Hunter, Jeffrey	1906	1972	Levant, Oscar
1916	1987	Gleason, Jackie	1921	1996	Hunter, Ross	1905	1980	Levene, Sam
1886	1959	Gleason, James	1901	1962	Husing, Ted	1902	1971	Lewis, Joe E.
1884	1938	Gluck, Alma	1906	1987	Huston, John	1892	1971	Lewis, Ted
1919	1991	Gobel, George	1884	1950	Huston, Walter	1919	1987	Liberace
1905	1990	Goddard, Paulette	1895	1969	Ingram, Rex	1820	1887	Lind, Jenny
1903	1983	Godfrey, Arthur	1895	1980	Iturbi, Jose	1920	1995	Lindfors, Viveca
1949	1995	Godunov, Alexander	1936	1990	Ireland, Jill	1894	1989	Lillie, Beatrice

Born	Died	Name	Born	Died	Name	Born	Died	Name
1893	1971	Lloyd, Harold	1910	1994	Morgan, Dennis	1918	1987	Preston, Robert
1870	1922	Lloyd, Marie	1890	1949	Morgan, Frank	1911	1993	Price, Vincent
1891	1957	Lockhart, Gene	1900	1941	Morgan, Helen	1911	1978	Prima, Louis
1913	1969	Logan, Ella	1915	1994	Morgan, Henry	1954	1977	Prinze, Freddie
1909	1942	Lombard, Carole	1908	1992	Morley, Robert	1936	1996	Prowse, Juliet
1902	1977	Lombardo, Guy	1901	1970	Morris, Chester	1946	1989	Radner, Gilda
1927	1974	Long, Richard	1934	1996	Morris, Greg	1895	1980	Raft, George
1895	1975	Lopez, Vincent	1914	1959	Morris, Wayne	1890	1967	Rains, Claude
1888	1968	Lorne, Marion	1943	1971	Morrison, Jim	1902	1994	Ralston, Esther
1904	1964	Lorre, Peter	1932	1982	Morrow, Vic	1892	1967	Rathbone, Basil
1912	1962	Lovejoy, Frank	1915	1977	Mostel, Zero	1897	1960	Ratoff, Gregory
1890	1971	Lowe, Edmund	1897	1969	Mowbray, Alan	1926	1991	Ray, Aldo
1905	1993	Loy, Myrna	1923	1997	Mulhare, Edward	1927	1990	Ray, Johnnie
1892	1947	Lubitsch, Ernst	1927	1996	Mulligan, Gerry	1916	1994	Raye, Martha
1882	1956	Lugosi, Bela	1895	1967	Muni, Paul	1941	1967	Redding, Otis
1894	1971	Lukas, Paul	1915	1970	Munshin, Jules	1908	1985	Redgrave, Michael
1892	1977	Lunt, Alfred	1924	1971	Murphy, Audie	1921	1986	Reed, Donna
1918	1995	Lupino, Ida	1902	1992	Murphy, George	1932	1992	Reed, Robert
1926	1982	Lynde, Paul	1885	1965	Murray, Mae	1914	1959	Reeves, George
1926	1971	Lynn, Diana	1896	1970	Nagel, Conrad	1873	1943	Reinhardt, Max
1903	1965	MacDonald, Jeanette	1900	1973	Naish, J. Carroll	1935	1991	Remick, Lee
1902	1969	MacLane, Barton	1898	1961	Naldi, Nita	1909	1971	Rennie, Michael
1908	1991	MacMurray, Fred	1943	1997	Nance, Jack	1941	1996	Rettig, Tommy
1921	1986	MacRae, Gordon	1908	1994	Natwick, Mildred	1932	1995	Rich, Charlie
1909	1973	Macready, George	1914	1994	Nelson, Harriet (Hillard)	1902	1983	Richardson, Ralph
1922	1996	Madison, Guy	1906	1975	Nelson, Ozzie	1921	1985	Riddle, Nelson
1908	1973	Magnani, Anna	1940	1985	Nelson, Rick	1898	1977	Ritchard, Cyril
1924	1994	Mancini, Henry	1885	1967	Nesbit, Evelyn	1907	1974	Ritter, Tex
1890	1975	Main, Marjorie	1890	1950	Nijinsky, Vaslav	1905	1969	Ritter, Thelma
1932	1995	Malle, Louis	1893	1974	Nilsson, Anna Q.	1901	1965	Ritz, Al
1932	1967	Mansfield, Jayne	1909	1983	Niven, David	1906	1986	Ritz, Harry
1905	1980	Mantovani, Annunzio	1902	1985	Nolan, Lloyd	1903	1985	Ritz, Jimmy
1897	1975	March, Fredric	1894	1930	Normand, Mabel	1925	1982	Robbins, Marty
1945	1981	Marley, Bob	1972	1997	Notorious B.I.G.	1898	1976	Robeson, Paul
1890	1966	Marshall, Herbert	1899	1968	Novarro, Ramon	1878	1949	Robinson, Bill
1917	1995	Martin, Dean	1938	1993	Nureyev, Rudolf	1893	1973	Robinson, Edward G.
1913	1990	Martin, Mary	1903	1978	Oakie, Jack	1905	1977	Rochester (E. Anderson)
1920	1981	Martin, Ross	1860	1926	Oakley, Annie	1921	1991	Roddenberry, Gene
1924	1987	Marvin, Lee	1928	1982	Oates, Warren	1897	1933	Rodgers, Jimmie
1888	1964	Marx, Arthur (Harpo)	1911	1979	Oberon, Merle	1911	1995	Rogers, Ginger
1901	1979	Marx, Herbert (Zeppo)	1915	1985	O'Brien, Edmond	1879	1935	Rogers, Will
1890	1977	Marx, Julius (Groucho)	1899	1983	O'Brien, Pat	1905	1994	Roland, Gilbert
1886	1961	Marx, Leonard (Chico)	1908	1981	O'Connell, Arthur	1950	1996	Rollins, Howard
1893	1977	Marx, Milton (Gummo)	1921	1993	O'Connell, Helen	1907	1994	Romero, Cesar
1909	1984	Mason, James	1880	1959	O'Connor, Una	1880	1962	Rooney, Pat
1896	1983	Massey, Raymond	1908	1968	O'Keefe, Dennis	1899	1966	Rose, Billy
1924	1996	Mastroianni, Marcello	1880	1938	Oland, Warner	1922	1987	Rowan, Dan
1885	1957	Mayer, Louis B.	1860	1932	Olcott, Chauncey	1887	1982	Rubinstein, Artur
1895	1973	Maynard, Ken	1883	1942	Oliver, Edna May	1886	1970	Ruggles, Charles
1935	1995	McClure, Doug	1907	1989	Olivier, Laurence	1924	1961	Russell, Gail
1884	1945	McCormack, John	1892	1963	Olsen, Ole	1861	1922	Russell, Lillian
1905	1990	McCrea, Joel	1927	1994	O'Neal, Patrick	1911	1976	Russell, Rosalind
1895	1952	McDaniel, Hattie	1849	1920	O'Neill, James	1892	1972	Rutherford, Margaret
1928	1993	McFarland, George "Spanky"	1936	1988	Orbison, Roy	1903	1973	Ryan, Irene
1899	1981	McHugh, Frank	1899	1985	Ormandy, Eugene	1909	1973	Ryan, Robert
1907	1991	McIntire, John	1876	1949	Ouspenskaya, Maria	1933	1994	Sargent, Dick
1883	1959	McLaglen, Victor	1887	1972	Owen, Reginald	1877	1968	St. Denis, Ruth
1907	1971	McMahon, Horace	1860	1941	Paderewski, Ignace	1884	1955	Sakall, S.Z.
1907	1979	McNeill, Don	1924	1987	Page, Geraldine	1885	1936	Sale (Chic), Charles
1911	1995	McQueen, Butterfly	1889	1954	Pallette, Eugene	1906	1972	Sanders, George
1930	1980	McQueen, Steve	1914	1986	Palmer, Lilli	1924	1994	Savalas, Telly
1924	1996	Meadows, Audrey	1894	1958	Pangborn, Franklin	1895	1964	Schildkraut, Joseph
1920	1980	Medford, Kay	1914	1992	Parks, Bert	1889	1965	Schipa, Tito
1880	1946	Meek, Donald	1914	1975	Parks, Larry	1882	1951	Schnabel, Artur
1861	1931	Melba, Nellie	1881	1940	Pasternack, Josef A.	1920	1981	Scott, Hazel
1890	1973	Melchior, Lauritz	1837	1908	Pastor, Tony (Vaudevillian)	1898	1987	Scott, Randolph
1890	1963	Menjou, Adolphe	1907	1969	Pastor, Tony (Bandleader)	1914	1965	Scott, Zachary
1902	1966	Menken, Helen	1843	1919	Patti, Adelina	1843	1896	Scott-Siddons, Mrs.
1925	1994	Mercouri, Melina	1840	1889	Patti, Carlotta	1938	1979	Seberg, Jean
1909	1997	Meredith, Burgess	1885	1931	Pavlova, Anna	1892	1974	Seeley, Blossom
1908	1984	Merman, Ethel	1912	1989	Payne, John	1893	1987	Segovia, Andres
1905	1986	Milland, Ray	1912	1996	Pearl, Minnie	1971	1995	Selena
1904	1944	Miller, Glenn	1904	1984	Peerce, Jan	1925	1980	Sellers, Peter
1898	1936	Miller, Marilyn	1899	1967	Pendleton, Nat	1902	1965	Selznick, David O.
1913	1982	Mills, Harry	1905	1941	Penner, Joe	1884	1960	Sennett, Mack
1903	1955	Minnevitch, Borrah	1928	1994	Peppard, George	1924	1975	Serling, Rod
1939	1976	Mineo, Sal	1932	1992	Perkins, Anthony	1970	1996	Shakur, Tupac
1913	1955	Miranda, Carmen	1970	1993	Phoenix, River	1927	1978	Shaw, Robert
1918	1994	Mitchell, Cameron	1915	1963	Piaf, Edith	1891	1972	Shawn, Ted
1892	1962	Mitchell, Thomas	1893	1979	Pickford, Mary	1868	1949	Shean, Al
1917	1997	Mitchum, Robert	1897	1984	Pidgeon, Walter	1902	1983	Shearer, Norma
1880	1940	Mix, Tom	1892	1957	Pinza, Ezio	1915	1967	Sheridan, Ann
1926	1962	Monroe, Marilyn	1898	1963	Pitts, Zasu	1917	1994	Shore, Dinah
1911	1973	Monroe, Vaughn	1919	1995	Pleasance, Donald	1875	1953	Shubert, Lee
1921	1991	Montand, Yves	1904	1976	Pons, Lily	1755	1831	Siddons, Mrs. Sarah
1917	1951	Montez, Maria	1897	1981	Ponselle, Rosa	1921	1985	Signoret, Simone
1933	1995	Montgomery, Elizabeth	1904	1963	Powell, Dick	1912	1985	Silvers, Phil
1904	1981	Montgomery, Robert	1912	1993	Powell, Eleanor	1900	1976	Sim, Alastair
1901	1947	Moore, Grace	1892	1984	Powell, William	1938	1995	Sinclair, Madge
1914	1999	Moore, Garry	1913	1958	Power, Tyrone	1913	1997	Skelton, Red
1876	1962	Moore, Victor	1905	1986	Preminger, Otto	1858	1942	Skinner, Otis
1906	1974	Moorehead, Agnes	1935	1977	Presley, Elvis			

Born	Died	Name	Born	Died	Name	Born	Died	Name
1863	1948	Smith, C. Aubrey	1903	1968	Tone, Franchot	1904	1984	Weissmuller, Johnny
1907	1986	Smith, Kate	1867	1957	Toscanini, Arturo	1903	1992	Welk, Lawrence
1854	1932	Sousa, John Philip	1898	1968	Tracy, Lee	1915	1985	Welles, Orson
1884	1957	Sparks, Ned	1900	1967	Tracy, Spencer	1896	1975	Wellman, William
1908	1994	Stander, Lionel	1903	1972	Traubel, Helen	1892	1980	West, Mae
1907	1990	Stanwyck, Barbara	1894	1975	Treacher, Arthur	1924	1996	Weston, Jack
1934	1970	Stevens, Inger	1853	1917	Tree, Herbert Beerbohm	1895	1968	Wheeler, Bert
1929	1996	Stevenson, McLean	1890	1973	Truex, Ernest	1919	1997	White, Jesse
1908	1997	Stewart, James	1932	1984	Truffaut, Francois	1889	1938	White, Pearl
1882	1977	Stokowski, Leopold	1919	1986	Tucker, Forrest	1891	1967	Whiteman, Paul
1879	1953	Stone, Lewis	1913	1975	Tucker, Richard	1865	1948	Whitty, May
1904	1980	Stone, Milburn	1884	1966	Tucker, Sophie	1910	1995	Wickes, Mary
1898	1959	Sturges, Preston	1920	1995	Turner, Lana	1918	1989	Wilde, Cornel
1911	1960	Sullavan, Margaret	1874	1940	Turpin, Ben	1912	1979	Wilding, Michael
1912	1994	Sullivan, Barry	1908	1959	Twelvetrees, Helen	1877	1922	Williams, Bert
1902	1974	Sullivan, Ed	1933	1993	Twitty, Conway	1923	1953	Williams, Hank Sr.
1903	1956	Sullivan, Francis L.	1895	1926	Valentino, Rudolph	1905	1975	Wills, Bob
1892	1946	Summerville, Slim	1901	1986	Vallee, Rudy	1903	1978	Wills, Chill
1899	1983	Swanson, Gloria	1912	1979	Vance, Vivian	1917	1972	Wilson, Marie
1904	1969	Swarthout, Gladys	1922	1996	Van Fleet, Jo	1884	1969	Winninger, Charles
1904	1996	Talbot, Lyle	1924	1990	Vaughan, Sarah	1904	1959	Withers, Grant
1893	1957	Talmadge, Norma	1893	1943	Veidt, Conrad	1907	1961	Wong, Anna May
1899	1972	Tamiroff, Akim	1926	1981	Vera-Ellen	1938	1981	Wood, Natalie
1909	1994	Tandy, Jessica	1958	1979	Vicious, Sid	1892	1978	Wood, Peggy
1878	1947	Tanguay, Eva	1885	1957	Von Stroheim, Erich	1888	1963	Woolley, Monty
1885	1966	Taylor, Deems	1906	1981	Von Zell, Harry	1902	1981	Wyler, William
1899	1958	Taylor, Estelle	1942	1995	Walker, Junior	1886	1966	Wynn, Ed
1887	1946	Taylor, Laurette	1922	1992	Walker, Nancy	1916	1986	Wynn, Keenan
1911	1969	Taylor, Robert	1914	1951	Walker, Robert	1929	1992	York, Dick
1847	1928	Terry, Ellen	1887	1980	Walsh, Raoul	1890	1960	Young, Clara Kimball
1899	1936	Thalberg, Irving	1876	1962	Walter, Bruno	1913	1978	Young, Gig
1912	1991	Thomas, Danny	1876	1958	Warner, H. B.	1887	1953	Young, Roland
1892	1960	Thomas, John Charles	1924	1963	Washington, Dinah	1902	1979	Zanuck, Darryl F.
1882	1976	Thorndike, Sybil	1900	1977	Waters, Ethel	1940	1993	Zappa, Frank
1896	1960	Tibbett, Lawrence	1914	1995	Wayne, David	1907	1997	Zinneman, Fred
1920	1991	Tierney, Gene	1907	1979	Wayne, John	1869	1932	Ziegfeld, Florenz
1932?	1996	Tiny Tim	1891	1966	Webb, Clifton	1873	1976	Zukor, Adolph
1909	1958	Todd, Michael	1920	1982	Webb, Jack			

Original Names of Selected Entertainers

Edie Adams: Elizabeth Edith Enke
Eddie Albert: Edward Albert Heimberger
Alan Alda: Alphonso D'Abruzzo
Fred Allen: John Sullivan
Woody Allen: Allen Konigsberg
June Allyson: Ella Geisman
Julie Andrews: Julia Wells
Eve Arden: Eunice Quedens
Beatrice Arthur: Bernice Frankel
Jean Arthur: Gladys Greene
Fred Astaire: Frederick Austerlitz
Alan Autry: Carlos Brown
Babyface: Kenneth Edmonds
Lauren Bacall: Betty Joan Perske
Anne Bancroft: Anna Maria Italiano
Gene Barry: Eugene Klass
Orson Bean: Dallas Burrows
Pat Benatar: Patricia Andrejewski
Robbie Benson: Robert Segal
Tony Bennett: Anthony Benedetto
Busby Berkeley: William Berkeley Enos
Irving Berlin: Israel Baline
Jack Benny: Benjamin Kubelsky
Joey Bishop: Joseph Gottlieb
Robert Blake: Michael Gubitosi
Bono (Vox): Paul Hewson
Victor Borge: Borge Rosenbaum
David Bowie: David Robert Jones
Boy George: George Alan O'Dowd
Fanny Brice: Fanny Borach
Charles Bronson: Charles Buchinski
Albert Brooks: Albert Einstein
Mel Brooks: Melvin Kaminsky
George Burns: Nathan Birnbaum
Ellen Burstyn: Edna Gilhooley
Richard Burton: Richard Jenkins
Red Buttons: Aaron Chwatt
Nicolas Cage: Nicholas Coppola
Michael Caine: Maurice Micklewhite
Maria Callas: Maria Kalogeropoulos
Vikki Carr: Florencia Casillas
Diahann Carroll: Carol Diahann Johnson
Cyd Charisse: Tula Finklea
Ray Charles: Ray Charles Robinson
Chubby Checker: Ernest Evans
Cher: Cherilyn Sarkisian
Patsy Cline: Virginia Patterson Hensley
Lee J. Cobb: Leo Jacoby

Claudette Colbert: Lily Chauchoin
Michael Connors: Kreker Ohanian
Robert Conrad: Conrad Robert Falk
Alice Cooper: Vincent Furnier
David Copperfield: David Kotkin
Howard Cosell: Howard Cohen
Elvis Costello: Declan McManus
Lou Costello: Louis Cristillo
Peter Coyote: Peter Cohon
Joan Crawford: Lucille Le Sueur
Michael Crawford: Michael Dumble-Smith
Tom Cruise: Thomas Mapother IV
Tony Curtis: Bernard Schwartz
Vic Damone: Vito Farinola
Rodney Dangerfield: Jacob Cohen
Bobby Darin: Walden Robert Cassotto
Doris Day: Doris von Kappelhoff
James Dean: James Byron
Yvonne De Carlo: Peggy Middleton
Sandra Dee: Alexandra Zuck
John Denver: Henry John
    Deutschendorf Jr.
Bo Derek: Mary Cathleen Collins
John Derek: Derek Harris
Danny DeVito: Daniel Michaeli
Angie Dickinson: Angeline Brown
Bo Diddley: Elias Bates
Phyllis Diller: Phyllis Driver
Diana Dors: Diana Fluck
Kirk Douglas: Issur Danielovitch
Melvyn Douglas: Melvyn Hesselberg
Bob Dylan: Robert Zimmerman
Sheena Easton: Sheena Shirley Orr
Barbara Eden: Barbara Huffman
Elvira: Cassandra Paterson
Ron Ely: Ronald Pierce
Enya: Eithne Ni Bhraonian
Dale Evans: Frances Smith
Chad Everett: Raymond Cramton
Tom Ewell: S. Yewell Tompkins
Douglas Fairbanks: Douglas Ullman
Morgan Fairchild: Patsy McClenny
Jamie Farr: Jameel Farah
Alice Faye: Ann Leppert
Stepin Fetchit: Lincoln Perry
Sally Field: Sally Mahoney
W.C. Fields: William Claude Dukenfield
Peter Finch: William Mitchell

Barry Fitzgerald: William Shields
Joan Fontaine: Joan de Havilland
John Ford: Sean O'Fearna
John Forsythe: John Freund
Jodie Foster: Alicia Christian Foster
Redd Foxx: John Sanford
Anthony Franciosa: Anthony Papaleo
Arlene Francis: Arlene Kazanjian
Connie Francis: Concetta Franconero
Greta Garbo: Greta Gustafsson
Vincent Gardenia: Vincent Scognamiglio
John Garfield: Julius Garfinkle
Judy Garland: Frances Gumm
James Garner: James Bumgarner
Crystal Gayle: Brenda Gayle Webb
Kathie Lee Gifford: Kathie Epstein
Paulette Goddard: Marion Levy
Whoopi Goldberg: Caryn Johnson
Eydie Gorme: Edith Gormezano
Stewart Granger: James Stewart
Cary Grant: Archibald Leach
Lee Grant: Lyova Rosenthal
Joel Grey: Joe Katz
Robert Guillaume: Robert Williams
Buddy Hackett: Leonard Hacker
Hammer: Stanley Kirk Burrell
Jean Harlow: Harlean Carpentier
Rex Harrison: Reginald Carey
Laurence Harvey: Larushka Skikne
Helen Hayes: Helen Brown
Susan Hayward: Edythe Marriner
Rita Hayworth: Margarita Cansino
Pee-Wee Herman: Paul Reubenfeld
Barbara Hershey: Barbara Herzstine
William Holden: William Beedle
Billie Holliday: Eleanora Fagan
Judy Holliday: Judith Tuvim
Harry Houdini: Ehrich Weiss
Curly, Moe, Shemp Howard: Horwitz
Leslie Howard: Leslie Stainer
Rock Hudson: Roy Scherer Jr. (later
    Fitzgerald)
Engelbert Humperdinck: Arnold Dorsey
Kim Hunter: Janet Cole
Mary Beth Hurt: Mary Supinger
Betty Hutton: Betty Thornberg
Ice-T: Tracy Morrow
Billy Idol: William Broad

David Janssen: David Meyer
Anne Jillian: Anne Nauseda
Elton John: Reginald Dwight
Don Johnson: Donald Wayne
Al Jolson: Asa Yoelson
Jennifer Jones: Phyllis Isley
Tom Jones: Thomas Woodward
Louis Jourdan: Louis Gendre
Wynonna Judd: Christina Ciminella
Boris Karloff: William Henry Pratt
Danny Kaye: David Kaminsky
Diane Keaton: Diane Hall
Michael Keaton: Michael Douglas
Howard Keel: Harold Leek
Chaka Khan: Yvette Stevens
Carole King: Carole Klein
Larry King: Larry Zeigler
Ben Kingsley: Krishna Banji
Nastassja Kinski: Nastassja Naksyznyski
Ted Knight: Tadeus Wladyslaw Konopka
Cheryl Ladd: Cheryl Stoppelmoor
Veronica Lake: Constance Ockleman
Hedy Lamarr: Hedwig Kiesler
Dorothy Lamour: Mary Kaumeyer
Michael Landon: Eugene Orowitz
Mario Lanza: Alfredo Cocozza
Queen Latifah: Dana Owens
Stan Laurel: Arthur Jefferson
Steve Lawrence: Sidney Leibowitz
Brenda Lee: Brenda Mae Tarpley
Bruce Lee: Lee Yuen Kam
Gypsy Rose Lee: Rose Louise Hovick
Michelle Lee: Michelle Dusiak
Peggy Lee: Norma Egstrom
Janet Leigh: Jeanette Morrison
Vivien Leigh: Vivian Hartley
Huey Lewis: Hugh Cregg
Jerry Lewis: Joseph Levitch
Hal Linden: Harold Lipshitz
Carole Lombard: Jane Peters
Jack Lord: John Joseph Ryan
Sophia Loren: Sophia Scicoloni
Peter Lorre: Laszio Lowenstein
Myrna Loy: Myrna Williams
Bela Lugosi: Bela Ferenc Blasko
Moms Mabley: Loretta Mary Aitken
Shirley MacLaine: Shirley Beaty
Elle MacPherson: Eleanor Gow
Madonna: Madonna Louise Ciccone

Lee Majors: Harvey Lee Yeary 2d
Karl Malden: Malden Sekulovich
Barry Manilow: Barry Alan Pincus
Jayne Mansfield: Vera Jane Palmer
Fredric March: Frederick Bickel
Peter Marshall: Pierre LaCock
Walter Matthau: Walter Matuschanskayasky
Dean Martin: Dino Crocetti
Meat Loaf: Marvin Lee Aday
Ethel Merman: Ethel Zimmerman
George Michael: Georgios Panayiotou
Ray Milland: Reginald Truscott-Jones
Ann Miller: Lucille Collier
Joni Mitchell: Roberta Joan Anderson
Marilyn Monroe: Norma Jean
  Mortenson (later Baker)
Yves Montand: Ivo Livi
Ron Moody: Ronald Moodnick
Demi Moore: Demetria Guynes
Garry Moore: Thomas Garrison Morfit
Rita Moreno: Rosita Alverio
Harry Morgan: Harry Bratsburg
Mr. T: Lawrence Tero
Paul Muni: Muni Weisenfreund
Mike Nichols: Michael Igor Peschowsky
Chuck Norris: Carlos Ray
Notrorious B.I.G.: Christopher Wallace
Hugh O'Brian: Hugh Krampke
Maureen O'Hara: Maureen Fitzsimons
Patti Page: Clara Ann Fowler
Jack Palance: Walter Palanuik
Bert Parks: Bert Jacobson
Minnie Pearl: Sarah Ophelia Cannon
Bernadette Peters: Bernadette Lazzaro
Edith Piaf: Edith Gassion
Slim Pickens: Louis Lindley
Mary Pickford: Gladys Smith
Stephanie Powers: Stefania Federkiewicz
Paula Prentiss: Paula Ragusa
Robert Preston: Robert Preston Meservey
Prince ♀ (TAFKAP): Prince Rogers
  Nelson
Tony Randall: Leonard Rosenberg
Johnnie Ray: John Alvin
Martha Raye: Margaret O'Reed
Donna Reed: Donna Belle Mullenger
Della Reese: Delloreese Patricia Early
Joan Rivers: Joan Sandra Molinsky
Edward G. Robinson: Emmanuel
  Goldenberg
Ginger Rogers: Virginia McMath

Roy Rogers: Leonard Slye
Mickey Rooney: Joe Yule Jr.
Johnny Rotten: John Lydon
Lillian Russell: Helen Leonard
Theresa Russell: Theresa Paup
Winona Ryder: Winona Horowitz
Soupy Sales: Milton Hines
Susan Sarandon: Susan Tomaling
Randolph Scott: George Randolph Crane
Jane Seymour: Joyce Frankenberg
Omar Sharif: Michael Shalhoub
Charlie Sheen: Carlos Irwin Estevez
Martin Sheen: Ramon Estevez
Beverly Sills: Belle Silverman
Talia Shire: Talia Coppola
Phil Silvers: Philip Silversmith
Sinbad: David Atkins
Suzanne Somers: Suzanne Mahoney
Ann Sothern: Harriette Lake
Robert Stack: Robert Modini
Barbara Stanwyck: Ruby Stevens
Jean Stapleton: Jeanne Murray
Ringo Starr: Richard Starkey
Connie Stevens: Concetta Ingolia
Sting: Gordon Sumner
Donna Summer: La Donna Gaines
Rip Taylor: Charles Elmer Jr.
Robert Taylor: Spangler Brugh
Danny Thomas: Muzyad Yakhoob, later
  Amos Jacobs
Tiny Tim: Herbert Khaury
Rip Torn: Elmore Rual Torn Jr.
Randy Travis: Randy Traywick
Sophie Tucker: Sophia Kalish
Tina Turner: Annie Mae Bullock
Twiggy: Leslie Hornby
Conway Twitty: Harold Lloyd Jenkins
Rudolph Valentino: Rudolpho
  D'Antonguolla
Frankie Valli: Frank Castelluccio
Sid Vicious: John Simon Ritchie
David Wayne: Wayne McMeekan
John Wayne: Marion Morrison
Clifton Webb: Webb Hollenbeck
Raquel Welch: Raquel Tejada
Gene Wilder: Jerome Silberman
Shelley Winters: Shirley Schrift
Stevie Wonder: Stevland Morris
Natalie Wood: Natasha Gurdin
Jane Wyman: Sarah Jane Fulks
Gig Young: Byron Barr

Selected Royal Families of Europe

Name (Birthplace)	Birthdate
Belgium	
King Albert II (Brussels)	6/6/34
Queen Paola (Calabria, Italy)	9/11/37
Prince Philippe (Brussels)	4/15/60
Princess Astrid (Brussels)	6/5/62
Prince Laurent (Brussels)	10/19/63
United Kingdom	
Queen Elizabeth, Queen Mother (London)	8/4/00
Queen Elizabeth II (London)	4/21/26
Prince Philip (Corfu, Greece)	6/10/21
Prince Charles (London)	11/14/48
Prince William (London)	6/21/82
Prince Henry, or Harry (London)	9/15/84
Princess Anne (London)	8/15/50
Prince Andrew (London)	2/19/60
Princess Beatrice (London)	8/8/88
Princess Eugenie (London)	3/23/90
Prince Edward (London)	3/10/64
Princess Margaret (Glamis, Scotland)	8/21/30
Denmark	
Queen Margrethe II (Copenhagen)	4/16/40
Prince Henrik (France)	6/11/34
Prince Frederik (Copenhagen)	5/26/68
Prince Joachim (Copenhagen)	6/7/69
Princess Alexandra (Hong Kong)	6/30/64
Liechtenstein	
Prince Hans-Adam II (Liechtenstein)	2/14/45
Princess Marie	—
Crown Prince Alois (Liechtenstein)	6/11/68
Prince Maximilian (Liechtenstein)	5/16/69
Prince Constantin (Liechtenstein)	3/15/70
Princess Tatjana (Liechtenstein)	4/10/73
Luxembourg	
Grand Duke Jean (Berg Castle, Luxembourg)	1/5/21
Grand Duchess Joséphine-Charlotte (Belgium)	10/11/27

Name (Birthplace)	Birthdate
Princess Marie-Astrid (Luxembourg)	2/17/54
Prince Henri (Luxembourg)	4/16/55
Prince Jean (Luxembourg)	5/15/57
Princess Margaretha (Luxembourg)	5/15/57
Prince Guillaume (Luxembourg)	5/1/63
Monaco	
Prince Rainier III (Monaco)	5/31/23
Prince Albert (Monte Carlo)	3/14/58
Princess Caroline (Monte Carlo)	1/23/57
Princess Stephanie (Monaco-Ville, Monaco)	2/1/65
Netherlands	
Queen Beatrix (Baarn, Netherlands)	1/31/38
Prince Claus (Dotzingen, Germany)	6/9/26
Prince Willem-Alexander (Utrecht, Netherlands)	4/27/67
Prince Johan Friso (Utrecht, Netherlands)	9/25/68
Prince Constantijn (Utrecht, Netherlands)	10/11/69
Norway	
King Harald V (Skaugum, Norway)	2/21/37
Queen Sonja (Oslo)	7/4/37
Princess Märtha Louise (Oslo)	9/22/71
Crown Prince Haakon (Oslo)	7/20/73
Spain	
King Juan Carlos I (Rome, Italy)	1/5/38
Queen Sofía (Athens, Greece)	11/2/38
Princess Elena (Madrid)	12/20/63
Princess Cristina (Madrid)	6/13/65
Crown Prince Felipe (Madrid)	1/30/68
Sweden	
King Carl XVI Gustav (Stockholm)	4/30/46
Queen Silvia	12/00/10
Crown Princess Victoria (Stockholm)	7/14/77
Prince Carl Philip (Stockholm)	5/13/79
Princess Madeleine (Stockholm)	6/10/82

UNITED STATES POPULATION

A Profile of America's Diversity—The View From the Census Bureau, 1997

by
Dr. Martha Farnsworth Riche
Director, Bureau of the Census
U.S. Department of Commerce

I am often asked to describe the typical American. There is no such person! America's population is extraordinarily diverse, as Census Bureau data show. Here are some examples:

Racial and Ethnic Composition

On Apr. 1, 1997, there were an estimated 267.0 million people living in the U.S., compared to Census Day, Apr. 1, 1990, 7 years earlier, when the nation's population stood at 248.7 mil. Of the 1997 population, 33.8 mil (13%) were black; the American Indian/Eskimo/Aleut populations made up 2.3 mil (1%); Asians and Pacific Islanders numbered 10.0 mil (4%). An estimated 29.0 mil (11%) were of Hispanic origin (persons of Hispanic origin may be of any race). About 194.4 mil (73%) of the total population classified themselves as non-Hispanic white.

Business Owners

This diversity reaches the ranks of the nation's business owners. There were 620,912 African-Americans owning firms in the U.S. as of 1992, a total of 4% of all U.S. firms. Hispanic-owned firms numbered 862,605, a total of 5% of all firms in the U.S. About 6.4 mil, or one-third of all businesses in the nation—were owned by women.

Age Structure

On Apr. 1, 1997, 69.3 mil Americans (26%) were under 18 years old. At the other end of the continuum, 34.0 mil (13%) were age 65 or older. At the farthest tip were the centenarians—people 100 years old or more. About 59,000 fell into this exclusive group. The median age—with half of all Americans above and half below—was 34.9 years, the oldest it has ever been.

Income Spectrum

The nation's families had a median income of $40,611 in 1995, and 9% of all families had incomes of $100,000 and over. About 11% of families were below the official government poverty level in 1995.

Marriage and Families

In 1996, 55% of men and 52% of women aged 15 and older were married.

Of 100 mil households in 1996, 70% contained families. Married couples maintained 77% of all families, while women with no husband present maintained 18%.

About half of the nation's 70 mil families contained children. Most families with children (25 mil) included both a mother and a father; 8 mil had a mother only, and 2 mil contained only a father.

Of the 30 mil households without families, 83% consisted of one person living alone.

Education

While 18% of Americans aged 25 and older lacked a high school diploma in 1996, 24% had a bachelor's degree or higher. These proportions differed greatly by age group. For example, 88% of 35- to 44-year-olds had a high school diploma and 26% had a bachelor's degree or more. But among those aged 75 or older, only 59% had a high school diploma and only 13% had a bachelor's degree or more.

State and Local Taxes

Reflecting diverse economies and histories, state and local governments rely on different kinds of tax revenues. For example, in 1994 property taxes provided 66% of all New Hampshire's state and local tax revenues, at least 40% of all tax revenues in 6 other states (ME, MI, MT, NJ, RI, and VT), but less than 15% of the revenues in 4 states (AL, AR, DE, and NM). Other significant tax revenue sources in 1994 included general sales taxes (over 40% of the revenues for 3 states, WA, TN, and NM), individual income taxes (over 33% in 3 states, MD, MA, and OR), and severance taxes on the extraction of natural resources (42% in AK). While some states relied heavily on general sales and individual income taxes, others did not use them at all; 4 states levied no general sales tax and 7 states had no individual income tax.

The Foreign-Born Population

In 1996, an estimated 24.6 mil Americans, or 9.3% of the population, were foreign-born, the highest level since prior to World War II. More than one-fourth of these immigrants—6.7 mil—were born in Mexico. Other common immigrant homelands included the Philippines (1.2 mil), China (801,000), Cuba (772,000), India (757,000), Vietnam (740,000), El Salvador (701,000), Canada (660,000), Korea (550,000), Germnay (523,000), and the Dominican Republic (515,000).

The Lay of the Land

The nation's settlement landscape is just as disparate as the U.S. population. Urban areas were home to the majority of Americans in 1990 (75%). The most populous cities in 1994 were New York (7.3 mil), Los Angeles (3.4 mil), Chicago (2.7 mil), Houston (1.7 mil), and Philadelphia (1.5 mil). Among all cities with 1994 populations more than 100,000, the fastest-growing from 1990 to 1994 were Henderson, NV (whose population rose 57%), Palmdale, CA (47%), Chandler, AZ (33%), Las Vegas, NV (27%), and Plano, TX (23%).

On the other hand, about 25% of Americans lived in rural areas as of 1990. In 1992, the U.S. had 1.9 mil farms. These farms included an average of 491 acres; 166,000 were smaller than 10 acres and 71,000 were 2,000 acres or larger. As of 1990, 7% of rural residents lived on a farm, down from 53% in 1940.

Businesses and Workers

In 1992, more than 87.6 mil persons worked for the nearly 4.7 mil employer businesses in the U.S. The majority of these businesses (more than 3.2 mil, or nearly 70%) had annual receipts of less than $500,000; these smaller firms employed a relatively small number of workers, around 10.5 mil persons—12% of the total. The remaining more than 1.4 mil employer businesses employed nearly 77.1 mil persons.

International Trade

America's diversity extends to the list of its leading trading partners. These include Canada ($70.5 bil in combined imports and exports during the first quarter of 1996), Japan ($45.8 bil), Mexico ($29.7 bil), Germany ($15.0 bil), the United Kingdom ($14.1 bil), China ($13.1 bil), South Korea ($12.5 bil), Taiwan ($11.2 bil), Singapore ($9.4 bil), and France ($8.1 bil).

What the New Millennium May Hold

The Census Bureau does not have a crystal ball, but the data we collect do give us an idea of what may happen—if current trends continue. According to our projections, the U.S. will have 393.9 mil people in the year 2050—49% more than the population today.

We expect the population then will be even more diverse than it is now. The non-Hispanic white share of the population is projected to fall from the current 73% to 53% by 2050. Meanwhile, persons of Hispanic origin should increase from 11% to 24% of the population. Asians and Pacific Islanders should see their population climb from 4% to 9%. Increases are expected to be smaller for African Americans (13% to 15%) and the American Indian, Eskimo, and Aleut populations (from slightly under 1% to slightly more than 1%).

Agewise, we anticipate that there will be relatively more persons aged 65 or older (a projected 20% of the popula-tion in 2050, compared to 13% now) and fewer children (24% in 2050, down from 26% currently).

We also expect the mix of families and households to change in the coming years. As the population continues to age, relatively fewer families would have children (a pro-jected 41% in 2010, down from 50% in 1994). And it is projected that, among families with children, a lower pro-portion will include two married parents (72% in 2010, down from 74% in 1994). Meanwhile, households main-tained by a person living alone should rise from 24% to 27% of all households.

The American Community Survey—Toward More Up-to-date Demographic Data

Source: Bureau of the Census, U.S. Dept. of Commerce

Communities make decisions every year—not every 10 years. That's why the Census Bureau is developing the American Community Survey (ACS), a large monthly household survey that will more frequently update eco-nomic, social, and housing data for communities, now collected only once every decade. Topics to be covered include income, poverty, immigration, educational attain-ment, commuting patterns, housing conditions, household composition, and race and Hispanic origin.

In 1997, the survey was being conducted in 8 test sites around the nation to evaluate costs, procedures, and new ways to use the information; the development phase will continue through 2002, with a gradual expansion in number of sites. The Census Bureau plans for the survey to be in full operation in every county by 2003.

According to Census Bureau plans, the ACS, beginning in 2001, will provide a new social and economic profile every year for all states, cities, counties, and metropolitan areas with populations of 250,000 or more. Starting in 2004, ACS data will be available for areas with population groups of 65,000 or more. In 2010 the ACS form will be used in place of the present census long form.

Information for smaller areas and smaller population groups will be available as multiyear estimates are up-dated every year. For example, data for neighborhoods (census tracts) that are comparable in quality to statistics from the decennial census will be available starting in 2008 as 5-year averages (2003-7) and will be updated every year thereafter (2004-8, 2005-9, 2006-10, etc.).

Billions of government and business dollars are allo-cated among states, communities, and population groups based on their social, economic, and housing conditions. The ACS is intended to provide states and communities with accurate and timely information so this money may be spent wisely. Specific uses of the data include tracking the well-being of children, fami-lies, and the elderly; determining the need for high-ways, schools, and hospitals; and designing community programs for welfare, health care, work-force diversifi-cation, and job-training. Businesses can use survey in-formation to help decide when to expand current sites and when to build new ones, as well as how best to tar-get their markets.

The Plan for Census 2000

Source: Bureau of the Census, U.S. Dept. of Commerce; World Almanac Research

When Thomas Jefferson delivered the first U.S. census to Pres. George Washington in 1790, he wrote the returns in black and his estimate of the true totals in red. Since then there has always been some gap between the census count and the true total, whatever it may be. Despite the Census Bureau's efforts, the 1990 census is believed by some to have missed more than 4 million people. With the year 2000 approaching, the Bureau has been aiming toward a new approach in its effort to truly account for everyone. Traditional enumeration methods are expensive and may be only marginally effective in accounting for every individ-ual. So the Bureau designed a plan for a less costly and, it believes, more accurate Census 2000, built around 4 fun-damental strategies: partnership, simplicity, new technol-ogy, and use of sampling methods.

The first strategy consists of forming close partnerships with state, local, and tribal governments; community groups; the Postal Service; and private companies. The Census Bureau is working with these groups to find ways to make local residents more aware of the census and its importance, to compile more accurate address lists, and to hire and train temporary census workers.

The 2d strategy is to make the census simpler and easier for respondents, so as to increase the response rate. This in-volves such tactics as designing more user-friendly forms, placing forms in public places, using both English- and Spanish-language questionnaires in areas with high concen-trations of Hispanics, making multiple contacts with households rather than sending only the form, and offering more ways to respond—such as via toll-free telephone numbers and the Internet.

A 3d change involves drawing upon the dramatic ad-vances in computing that have occurred since the last census. When processing forms, the Census Bureau will be able to scan them directly into computers with so-phisticated software that is designed to read handwriting and to spot duplications, such as when one spouse re-turns a form by mail while the other fills one out over the phone. New technologies also will enable data seekers to find information they may want from Census 2000 by simply sitting at their computers and pointing and click-ing with a mouse.

A final proposed change is the use of statistical methods. The Census Bureau concluded that using temporary employ-ees in 1990 to try to find every nonresponding household greatly boosted the cost of conducting the census without re-sulting in maximum accuracy. For Census 2000, pending approval by Congress, the Bureau planned to supplement interviews of nonresponding households with sampling methods aimed at accounting for 100% of the population. More specifically, the goal was to contact directly at least 90% of households in each neighborhood and use sampling to make scientific estimates of the rest.

To check the quality of its work and to reach its goal of accounting for 100% of the population, the Census Bureau planned to take a 2d independent sample of 750,000 hous-ing units. It would check the results from the mail-in, tele-phone interviews, and personal visits. It was hoped that this quality check would eliminate the undercount and lead to a "one number census" that is right the first time.

Some critics, however, have questioned whether the under-count is as large as contended by the Census Bureau and/or have opposed the use of sampling methods in the census Many Republicans in Congress share this view, and, as of Sept. 1997, prospects for implementation of the sampling plan remained uncertain.

Race and Hispanic Origin for the U.S., 1990 and 1980

Source: Bureau of the Census, U.S. Dept. of Commerce

Race	1990 Census Number	1990 Census Percent	1980 Census Number	1980 Census Percent	% change 1980-90
All persons........................	248,709,873[1]	100.0	226,545,805	100.0	9.8
White	199,686,070	80.3	188,371,622	83.1	6.0
Black.................	29,986,060	12.1	26,495,025	11.7	13.2
American Indian, Eskimo, or Aleut	1,959,234	0.8	1,420,400	0.6	37.9
American Indian.................	1,878,285	0.8	1,364,033	0.6	37.7
Eskimo	57,152	0.0	42,162	0.0	35.6
Aleut	23,797	0.0	14,205	0.0	67.5
Asian-Pacific Islander	7,273,662	2.9	3,500,439[2]	1.5	107.8
Chinese.................	1,645,472	0.7	806,040	0.4	104.1
Filipino.................	1,406,770	0.6	774,652	0.3	81.6
Japanese.................	847,562	0.3	700,974	0.3	20.9
Asian Indian.................	815,447	0.3	361,531	0.2	125.6
Korean.................	798,849	0.3	354,593	0.2	125.3
Vietnamese.................	614,547	0.2	261,729	0.1	134.8
Hawaiian.................	211,014	0.1	166,814	0.1	26.5
Samoan.................	62,964	0.0	41,948	0.0	50.1
Guamanian	49,345	0.0	32,158	0.0	53.4
Other Asian-Pacific Islander	821,692	0.3	NA	NA	NA
Other race.................	9,804,847	3.9	6,758,319	3.0	45.1
Hispanic and non-Hispanic origin					
Hispanic origin[3]	22,354,059	9.0	14,608,673	6.4	53.0
Mexican.................	13,495,938	5.4	8,740,439	3.9	54.4
Puerto Rican	2,727,754	1.1	2,013,945	0.9	35.4
Cuban.................	1,043,932	0.4	803,226	0.4	30.0
Other Hispanic.................	5,086,435	2.0	3,051,063	1.3	66.7
Not of Hispanic origin.................	226,355,814	91.0	211,937,132	93.6	6.8

Percent totals may not add because of rounding. NA=Not available. (1) The race data shown here are based on the U.S. population as tabulated in the 1990 census. Figures do not reflect corrections to the 1990 population census; the corrected 1990 U.S. population is 248,718,301. (2) The 1980 count of 3,500,439 Asian-Pacific Islanders based on 100% tabulations includes only the 9 specific Asian-Pacific Islander groups listed separately in the 1980 race item. A figure of 3,726,440, from sample tabulations, is more comparable to the 1990 count since it includes those groups. (3) Persons of Hispanic origin may be of any race.

Definitions of Race and Hispanic Origin Groups

Source: Bureau of the Census, U.S. Dept. of Commerce

The concept of race as used by the Census Bureau does not reflect any clear-cut scientific definition of biological stock. The data for race represent self-classification by respondents. Persons could identify their race by classifying themselves in one of the categories listed on the census form, that is, white, black, American Indian, Eskimo, Aleut, Chinese, Filipino, Japanese, Asian Indian, Korean, Vietnamese, Hawaiian, Samoan, Guamanian, Other API (Asian-Pacific Islander), or Other race. Data for API groups not listed on the census questionnaire but contained in Census Bureau tables—Cambodian, Hmong, Laotian, Thai, Bangladeshi, Burmese, Indonesian, Malayan, Okinawan, Pakistani, Sri Lankan, Tongan, Tahitian, Northern Mariana Islander, Palauan, and Fijian—were tabulated from write-in responses from those who identified themselves as "Other API" or "Other race." The "Other race" cate-

gory includes persons not included in the race categories described above. Persons reporting in the "Other race" category and writing in the name of a Hispanic origin group, are included. In reality, no specific race can be determined from the classification "Hispanic." Persons of Spanish/Hispanic origin may be of any race.

Persons of Spanish/Hispanic origin or descent are those who classify themselves in one of the Hispanic origin categories listed on the census questionnaire—for example, Mexican, Puerto Rican, or Cuban—as well as those who indicated that they were of "other" Spanish/Hispanic origin. Included are those whose origins are from Spanish-speaking countries of the Caribbean, from Central or South America, or from Spain, or are identifying themselves generally as Spanish, Spanish-American, Hispano, Hispanic, Latino, etc.

Estimated Population of American Colonies, 1630-1780

Source: Bureau of the Census, U.S. Dept. of Commerce

(in thousands)

Colony	1780	1770	1750	1740	1720	1700	1690	1670	1650	1630
Total........................	2,780.4	2,148.1	1,170.8	905.6	466.2	250.9	210.4	111.9	50.4	4.6
Maine (counties)[1].............	49.1	31.3	...	...	...	...	...	...	1.0	0.4
New Hampshire[2]	87.8	62.4	27.5	23.3	9.4	5.0	4.2	1.8	1.3	0.5
Vermont[3]	47.6	10.0	...	...	...	...	...	...	...	...
Plymouth and Massachusetts[1,2,4] .	268.6	235.3	188.0	151.6	91.0	55.9	56.9	35.3	15.6	0.9
Rhode Island[2]	52.9	58.2	33.2	25.3	11.7	5.9	4.2	2.2	0.8	...
Connecticut[2]	206.7	183.9	111.3	89.6	58.8	26.0	21.6	12.6	4.1	...
New York[2]	210.5	162.9	76.7	63.7	36.9	19.1	13.9	5.8	4.1	0.4
New Jersey[2]	139.6	117.4	71.4	51.4	29.8	14.0	8.0	1.0	...	...
Pennsylvania[2]	327.3	240.1	119.7	85.6	31.0	18.0	11.4	...	...	...
Delaware[2]	45.4	35.5	28.7	19.9	5.4	2.5	1.5	0.7	0.2	...
Maryland[2]	245.5	202.6	141.1	116.1	66.1	29.6	24.0	13.2	4.5	...
Virginia[2].	538.0	447.0	231.0	180.4	87.8	58.6	53.0	35.3	18.7	2.5
North Carolina[2]	270.1	197.2	73.0	51.8	21.3	10.7	7.6	3.8	...	...
South Carolina[2]	180.0	124.2	64.0	45.0	17.0	5.7	3.9	0.2	...	...
Georgia[2]	56.1	23.4	5.2	2.0	...	...	...	...	...	...
Kentucky[5]	45.0	15.7	...	...	...	...	...	...	...	...
Tennessee[6]	10.0	1.0	...	...	...	...	...	...	...	...

(1) For 1660-1750, Maine counties are included with Massachusetts. Maine was part of Massachusetts until it became a separate state in 1820. (2) One of the original 13 states. (3) Admitted to statehood in 1791. (4) Plymouth became a part of the Province of Massachusetts in 1691. (5) Admitted to statehood in 1792. (6) Admitted to statehood in 1796.

U.S. Area and Population: 1790-1990

Source: Bureau of the Census, U.S. Dept. of Commerce

Census date	Area (sq mi) Gross	Land	Water	Population Number	per sq mi of land	Increase over preceding census Number	%
1990 (Apr. 1).............	3,787,319[1]	3,536,278	251,041[1]	248,718,301	70.3	22,176,098	9.8
1980 (Apr. 1).............	3,618,770	3,539,289	79,481	226,542,203	64.0	23,240,172	11.4
1970 (Apr. 1).............	3,618,770	3,536,855	81,915	203,302,031	57.5	23,978,856	13.4
1960 (Apr. 1)[2]...........	3,618,770	3,540,911	77,859	179,323,175	50.6	27,997,377	18.5
1950 (Apr. 1).............	3,618,770	3,552,206	66,564	151,325,798	42.6	19,161,229	14.5
1940 (Apr. 1).............	3,618,770	3,554,608	64,162	132,164,569	37.2	8,961,945	7.3
1930 (Apr. 1).............	3,618,770	3,551,608	67,162	123,202,624	34.7	17,181,087	16.2
1920 (Jan. 1).............	3,618,770	3,546,931	71,839	106,021,537	29.9	13,793,041	15.0
1910 (Apr. 15)...........	3,618,770	3,547,045	71,725	92,228,496	26.0	16,016,328	21.0
1900 (June 1)...........	3,618,770	3,547,314	71,456	76,212,168	21.5	13,232,402	21.0
1890 (June 1)...........	3,612,299	3,540,705	71,594	62,979,766	17.8	12,790,557	25.5
1880 (June 1)...........	3,612,299	3,540,705	71,594	50,189,209	14.2	11,630,838	30.2
1870 (June 1)...........	3,612,299	3,540,705	71,594	38,558,371	10.9	7,115,050	22.6
1860 (June 1)...........	3,021,295	2,969,640	51,655	31,443,321	10.6	8,251,445	35.6
1850 (June 1)...........	2,991,655	2,940,042	51,613	23,191,876	7.9	6,122,423	35.9
1840 (June 1)...........	1,792,552	1,749,462	43,090	17,068,953[2]	9.8	4,203,433	32.7
1830 (June 1)...........	1,792,552	1,749,462	43,090	12,866,020[2]	7.4	3,227,567	33.5
1820 (June 1)...........	1,792,552	1,749,462	43,090	9,638,453	5.5	2,398,572	33.1
1810 (Aug. 6)...........	1,722,685	1,681,828	40,857	7,239,881	4.3	1,931,398	36.4
1800 (Aug. 4)...........	891,364	864,746	26,618	5,308,483	6.1	1,379,269	35.1
1790 (Aug. 2)...........	891,364	864,746	26,618	3,929,214	4.5	—	—

(1) Includes inland, coastal, Great Lakes, and territorial water. Data for prior years cover inland water only. (2) U.S. total includes persons (5,318 in 1830 and 6,100 in 1840) on public ships in the service of the U.S. not credited to any region, division, or state.
Note: Percent changes are computed on the basis of change in population since the preceding census date, so the period covered therefore is not always exactly 10 years.
Population density figures given for various years represent the area within the boundaries of the U.S. that was under the jurisdiction on the date in question, including in some cases considerable areas not organized or settled and not actually covered by the census. In 1870, for example, Alaska was not covered by the census.
Population figures shown here may reflect corrections made to the initial tabulated census counts.

Population, by Sex, Race, Residence, and Median Age, 1790-1997

Source: Bureau of the Census, U.S. Dept. of Commerce

(in thousands, except as indicated)

Date	Sex Male	Female	Race White	Black Number	Percent	Other	Residence Urban	Rural	Median Age (years) All races	White	Black
Conterminous U.S.[1]											
1790 (Aug. 2)	NA	NA	3,172	757	19.3	NA	202	3,728	NA	NA	NA
1810 (Aug. 6)	NA	NA	5,862	1,378	19.0	NA	525	6,714	NA	16.0	NA
1820 (Aug. 7)	4,897	4,742	7,867	1,772	18.4	NA	693	8,945	16.7	16.6	17.2
1840 (June 1)	8,689	8,381	14,196	2,874	16.8	NA	1,845	15,224	17.8	17.9	17.6
1860 (June 1)	16,085	15,358	26,923	4,442	14.1	79	6,217	25,227	19.4	19.7	17.5
1870 (June 1)	19,494	19,065	33,589	4,880	12.7	89	9,902	28,656	20.2	20.4	18.5
1880 (June 1)	25,519	24,637	43,403	6,581	13.1	172	14,130	36,026	20.9	21.4	18.0
1890 (June 1)	32,237	30,711	55,101	7,489	11.9	358	22,106	40,841	22.0	22.5	17.8
1900 (June 1)	38,816	37,178	66,809	8,834	11.6	351	30,160	45,835	22.9	23.4	19.4
1920 (Jan. 1)	53,900	51,810	94,821	10,463	9.9	427	54,158	51,553	25.3	25.5	22.3
1930 (Apr. 1)	62,137	60,638	110,287	11,891	9.7	597	68,955	53,820	26.5	26.9	23.5
1940 (Apr. 1)	66,062	65,608	118,215	12,866	9.8	589	74,424	57,246	29.0	29.5	25.3
United States											
1950 (Apr. 1)	74,833	75,864	135,150	15,045	9.9	1,131	96,467	54,230	30.2	30.7	26.2
1960 (Apr. 1)	88,331	90,992	158,832	18,872	10.5	1,620	125,269	54,054	29.5	30.3	23.5
1970 (Apr. 1)[2]	98,912	104,300	177,749	22,580	11.1	2,883	149,647	53,565	28.1	28.9	22.4
1980 (Apr. 1)[3]	110,053	116,493	194,713	26,683	11.8	5,150	167,051	59,495	30.0	30.9	24.9
1983 (July 1, est)	113,647	120,145	199,420	27,867	11.9	6,505	NA	NA	30.8	31.7	25.9
1985 (July 1, est)	115,730	122,194	202,031	28,569	12.0	7,324	NA	NA	31.4	32.3	26.6
1990 (Apr. 1)[4]	121,239	127,470	199,686	29,986	12.1	9,233	187,053	61,656	32.9	34.4	28.1
1992 (July 1, est)	124,511	130,500	212,910	31,654	12.4	10,447	NA	NA	33.4	34.4	28.5
1994 (July 1, est)	127,261	133,111	216,480	32,647	12.5	11,245	NA	NA	34.0	35.0	29.0
1995 (July 1, est)	128,569	134,321	218,149	33,095	12.6	11,646	NA	NA	34.3	35.3	29.2
1996 (July 1, est)	129,810	135,474	219,749	33,503	12.6	12,031	NA	NA	34.6	35.7	29.5
1997 (May 1, est.)	130,798	136,379	220,975	33,856	12.7	12,346	NA	NA	34.9	35.9	29.6

NA=Not available. **Note:** Urban and rural definitions may change from census to census. The figures in this table have been adjusted to be consistent with the 1990 urban and rural definitions. (1) Excludes Alaska and Hawaii. (2) The revised 1970 resident population count is 203,302,031, which incorporates changes due to errors found after tabulations were completed. The race and sex data shown here reflect the official 1970 census count; the residence data come from the tabulated count. (3) The race data shown for Apr. 1, 1980, have been modified. (4) The data shown are based on the U.S. population as tabulated in the 1990 census. Figures do not reflect corrections to the 1990 population. The corrected 1990 U.S. population is 248,718,301.

U.S. Population by Official

State	1790[1]	1800[1]	1810[1]	1820	1830	1840	1850	1860	1870	1880	1890
AL	....	1	9	127,901	309,527	590,756	771,623	964,201	996,992	1,262,505	1,513,401
AK	....	....	....	....	....	....	....	....	....	33,426	32,052
AZ	....	....	....	....	....	....	....	....	9,658	40,440	88,243
AR	....	....	1	14,273	30,388	97,574	209,897	435,450	484,471	802,525	1,128,211
CA	....	....	....	....	....	....	92,597	379,994	560,247	864,694	1,213,398
CO	....	....	....	....	....	....	....	34,277	39,864	194,327	413,249
CT	238	251	262	275,248	297,675	309,978	370,792	460,147	537,454	622,700	746,258
DE	59	64	73	72,749	76,748	78,085	91,532	112,216	125,015	146,608	168,493
DC	....	8	16	23,336	30,261	33,745	51,687	75,080	131,700	177,624	230,392
FL	....	....	....	....	34,730	54,477	87,445	140,424	187,748	269,493	391,422
GA	83	163	252	340,989	516,823	691,392	906,185	1,057,286	1,184,109	1,542,180	1,837,353
HI	....	....	....	....	....	....	....	....	....	....	....
ID.	....	....	....	....	....	....	....	....	14,999	32,610	88,548
IL.	....	....	12	55,211	157,445	476,183	851,470	1,711,951	2,539,891	3,077,871	3,826,352
IN.	....	6	25	147,178	343,031	685,866	988,416	1,350,428	1,680,637	1,978,301	2,192,404
IA.	....	....	....	....	....	43,112	192,214	674,913	1,194,020	1,624,615	1,912,297
KS	....	....	....	....	....	....	....	107,206	364,399	996,096	1,428,108
KY	74	221	407	564,317	687,917	779,828	982,405	1,155,684	1,321,011	1,648,690	1,858,635
LA	....	....	77	153,407	215,739	352,411	517,762	708,002	726,915	939,946	1,118,588
ME	97	152	229	298,335	399,455	501,793	583,169	628,279	626,915	648,936	661,086
MD	320	342	381	407,350	447,040	470,019	583,034	687,049	780,894	934,943	1,042,390
MA	379	423	472	523,287	610,408	737,699	994,514	1,231,066	1,457,351	1,783,085	2,238,947
MI	....	....	5	8,896	31,639	212,267	397,654	749,113	1,184,059	1,636,937	2,093,890
MN	....	....	....	....	....	....	6,077	172,023	439,706	780,773	1,310,283
MS	....	8	31	75,448	136,621	375,651	606,526	791,305	827,922	1,131,597	1,289,600
MO	....	....	20	66,586	140,455	383,702	682,044	1,182,012	1,721,295	2,168,380	2,679,185
MT	....	....	....	....	....	....	....	....	20,595	39,159	142,924
NE	....	....	....	....	....	....	....	28,841	122,993	452,402	1,062,656
NV	....	....	....	....	....	....	....	6,857	42,491	62,266	47,355
NH	142	184	214	244,161	269,328	284,574	317,976	326,073	318,300	346,991	376,530
NJ	184	211	246	277,575	320,823	373,306	489,555	672,035	906,096	1,131,116	1,444,933
NM	....	....	....	....	....	....	61,547	93,516	91,874	119,565	160,282
NY	340	589	959	1,372,812	1,918,608	2,428,921	3,097,394	3,880,735	4,382,759	5,082,871	6,003,174
NC	394	478	556	638,829	737,987	753,419	869,039	992,622	1,071,361	1,399,750	1,617,949
ND	....	....	....	....	....	....	....	....	2,405[2]	36,909	190,983
OH	....	45	231	581,434	937,903	1,519,467	1,980,329	2,339,511	2,665,260	3,198,062	3,672,329
OK	....	....	....	....	....	....	....	....	....	....	258,657
OR	....	....	....	....	....	....	12,093	52,465	90,923	174,768	317,704
PA	434	602	810	1,049,458	1,348,233	1,724,033	2,311,786	2,906,215	3,521,951	4,282,891	5,258,113
RI	69	69	77	83,059	97,199	108,830	147,545	174,620	217,353	276,531	345,506
SC	249	346	415	502,741	581,185	594,398	668,507	703,708	705,606	995,577	1,151,149
SD	....	....	....	....	....	....	....	....	4,8372	11,7762	348,600
TN	36	106	262	422,823	681,904	829,210	1,002,717	1,109,801	1,258,520	1,542,359	1,767,518
TX	....	....	....	....	....	....	212,592	604,215	818,579	1,591,749	2,235,527
UT	....	....	....	....	....	....	11,380	40,273	86,786	143,963	210,779
VT	85	154	218	235,981	280,652	291,948	314,120	315,098	330,551	332,286	332,422
VA	692	808	878	938,261	1,044,054	1,025,227	1,119,348	1,219,630	1,225,163	1,512,565	1,655,980
WA	....	....	....	....	....	....	....	1,201	11,594	23,955	357,232
WV	56	79	105	136,808	176,924	224,537	302,313	376,688	442,014	618,457	762,794
WI	....	....	....	....	....	30,945	305,391	775,881	1,054,670	1,315,497	1,693,330
WY	....	....	....	....	....	....	....	....	9,118	20,789	62,555
U.S.	3,929	5,308	7,240	9,638,453	12,866,020[3]	17,068,953[3]	23,191,876	31,443,321	38,558,371	50,189,209	62,979,766

Note: Where possible, population shown is that of the 1990 area of the state. Members of the Armed Forces overseas or other U.S. nationals abroad are not included. Totals have been revised to include corrections of initial tabulated counts.
(1) Totals for 1790, 1800, and 1810 are in thousands. (2) 1860 figure is for Dakota Territory; 1870 figures are for parts of Dakota Territory. (3) U.S. total includes persons (5,318 in 1830 and 6,100 in 1840) on public ships in the service of the U.S. not credited to any region, division, or state.

Congressional Apportionment

Source: Bureau of the Census, U.S. Dept. of Commerce

	1990	1980		1990	1980		1990	1980		1990	1980		1990	1980
AL ...	7	7	ID	2	2	MN ...	8	8	ND ...	1	1	VT	1	1
AK ...	1	1	IL	20	22	MS ...	5	5	OH ...	19	21	VA ...	11	10
AZ ...	6	5	IN	10	10	MO ...	9	9	OK ...	6	6	WA ...	9	8
AR ...	4	4	IA	5	6	MT ...	1	2	OR ...	5	5	WV ...	3	4
CA ...	52	45	KS	4	5	NE ...	3	3	PA	21	23	WI	9	9
CO ...	6	6	KY	6	7	NV ...	2	2	RI	2	2	WY ...	1	1
CT ...	6	6	LA ...	7	8	NH ...	2	2	SC	6	6			
DE ...	1	1	ME ...	2	2	NJ	13	14	SD	1	1	Totals...	435	435
FL ...	23	19	MD ...	8	8	NM ...	3	3	TN	9	9			
GA ...	11	10	MA ...	10	11	NY ...	31	34	TX	30	27			
HI	2	2	MI	16	18	NC ...	12	11	UT	3	3			

The Constitution, in Article 1, Section 2, provided for a census of the population every 10 years to establish a basis for apportionment of representatives among the states. This apportionment largely determines the number of electoral votes allotted to each state.

The number of representatives of each state in Congress is determined by the state's population, but each state is entitled to one representative regardless of population. A congressional apportionment has been made after each decennial census except that of 1920.

Under provisions of a law that became effective Nov. 15, 1941, representatives are apportioned by the method of equal proportions. In the application of this method, the apportionment is made so that the average population per representative has the least possible variation between one state and any other. The first House of Representatives, in 1789, had 65 members, as provided by the Constitution. As the population grew, the number of representatives was increased, but the total membership has been fixed at 435 since the apportionment based on the 1910 census.

Census, 1790-1990

1900	1910	1920	1930	1940	1950	1960	1970	1980	1990
1,828,697	2,138,093	2,348,174	2,646,248	2,832,961	3,061,743	3,266,740	3,444,354	3,894,025	4,040,389
63,592	64,356	55,036	59,278	72,524	128,643	226,167	302,583	401,851	550,043
122,931	204,354	334,162	435,573	499,261	749,587	1,302,161	1,775,399	2,716,546	3,665,339
1,311,564	1,574,449	1,752,204	1,854,482	1,949,387	1,909,511	1,786,272	1,923,322	2,286,357	2,350,624
1,485,053	2,377,549	3,426,861	5,677,251	6,907,387	10,586,223	15,717,204	19,971,069	23,667,764	29,758,213
539,700	799,024	939,629	1,035,791	1,123,296	1,325,089	1,753,947	2,209,596	2,889,735	3,294,473
908,420	1,114,756	1,380,631	1,606,903	1,709,242	2,007,280	2,535,234	3,032,217	3,107,564	3,287,116
184,735	202,322	223,003	238,380	266,505	318,085	446,292	548,104	594,338	666,168
278,718	331,069	437,571	486,869	663,091	802,178	763,956	756,668	638,432	606,900
528,542	752,619	968,470	1,468,211	1,897,414	2,771,305	4,951,560	6,791,418	9,746,961	12,938,071
2,216,331	2,609,121	2,895,832	2,908,506	3,123,723	3,444,578	3,943,116	4,587,930	5,462,982	6,478,149
154,001	191,874	255,881	368,300	422,770	499,794	632,772	769,913	964,691	1,108,229
161,772	325,594	431,866	445,032	524,873	588,637	667,191	713,015	944,127	1,006,734
4,821,550	5,638,591	6,485,280	7,630,654	7,897,241	8,712,176	10,081,158	11,110,285	11,427,409	11,430,602
2,516,462	2,700,876	2,930,390	3,238,503	3,427,796	3,934,224	4,662,498	5,195,392	5,490,214	5,544,156
2,231,853	2,224,771	2,404,021	2,470,939	2,538,268	2,621,073	2,757,537	2,825,368	2,913,808	2,776,831
1,470,495	1,690,949	1,769,257	1,880,999	1,801,028	1,905,299	2,178,611	2,249,071	2,364,236	2,477,588
2,147,174	2,289,905	2,416,630	2,614,589	2,845,627	2,944,806	3,038,156	3,220,711	3,660,324	3,686,891
1,381,625	1,656,388	1,798,509	2,101,593	2,363,880	2,683,516	3,257,022	3,644,637	4,206,116	4,220,164
694,466	742,371	768,014	797,423	847,226	913,774	969,265	993,722	1,125,043	1,227,928
1,188,044	1,295,346	1,449,661	1,631,526	1,821,244	2,343,001	3,100,689	3,923,897	4,216,933	4,780,753
2,805,346	3,366,416	3,852,356	4,249,614	4,316,721	4,690,514	5,148,578	5,689,170	5,737,093	6,016,425
2,420,982	2,810,173	3,668,412	4,842,325	5,256,106	6,371,766	7,823,194	8,881,826	9,262,044	9,295,287
1,751,394	2,075,708	2,387,125	2,563,953	2,792,300	2,982,483	3,413,864	3,806,103	4,075,970	4,375,665
1,551,270	1,797,114	1,790,618	2,009,821	2,183,796	2,178,914	2,178,141	2,216,994	2,520,770	2,575,475
3,106,665	3,293,335	3,404,055	3,629,367	3,784,664	3,954,653	4,319,813	4,677,623	4,916,766	5,116,901
243,329	376,053	548,889	537,606	559,456	591,024	674,767	694,409	786,690	799,065
1,066,300	1,192,214	1,296,372	1,377,963	1,315,834	1,325,510	1,411,330	1,485,333	1,569,825	1,578,417
42,335	81,875	77,407	91,058	110,247	160,083	285,278	488,738	800,508	1,201,675
411,588	430,572	443,083	465,293	491,524	533,242	606,921	737,681	920,610	1,109,252
1,883,669	2,537,167	3,155,900	4,041,334	4,160,165	4,835,329	6,066,782	7,171,112	7,365,011	7,730,188
195,310	327,301	360,350	423,317	531,818	681,187	951,023	1,017,055	1,303,302	1,515,069
7,268,894	9,113,614	10,385,227	12,588,066	13,479,142	14,830,192	16,782,304	18,241,391	17,558,165	17,990,778
1,893,810	2,206,287	2,559,123	3,170,276	3,571,623	4,061,929	4,556,155	5,084,411	5,880,095	6,632,448
319,146	577,056	646,872	680,845	641,935	619,636	632,446	617,792	652,717	638,800
4,157,545	4,767,121	5,759,394	6,646,697	6,907,612	7,946,627	9,706,397	10,657,423	10,797,603	10,847,115
790,391	1,657,155	2,028,283	2,396,040	2,336,434	2,233,351	2,328,284	2,559,463	3,025,487	3,145,576
413,536	672,765	783,389	953,786	1,089,684	1,521,341	1,768,687	2,091,533	2,633,156	2,842,337
6,302,115	7,665,111	8,720,017	9,631,350	9,900,180	10,498,012	11,319,366	11,800,766	11,864,720	11,882,842
428,556	542,610	604,397	687,497	713,346	791,896	859,488	949,723	947,154	1,003,464
1,340,316	1,515,400	1,683,724	1,738,765	1,899,804	2,117,027	2,382,594	2,590,713	3,120,729	3,486,310
401,570	583,888	636,547	692,849	642,961	652,740	680,514	666,257	690,768	696,004
2,020,616	2,184,789	2,337,885	2,616,556	2,915,841	3,291,718	3,567,089	3,926,018	4,591,023	4,877,203
3,048,710	3,896,542	4,663,228	5,824,715	6,414,824	7,711,194	9,579,677	11,198,655	14,225,513	16,986,335
276,749	373,351	449,396	507,847	550,310	688,862	890,627	1,059,273	1,461,037	1,722,850
343,641	355,956	352,428	359,611	359,231	377,747	389,881	444,732	511,456	562,758
1,854,184	2,061,612	2,309,187	2,421,851	2,677,773	3,318,680	3,966,949	4,651,448	5,346,797	6,189,197
518,103	1,141,990	1,356,621	1,563,396	1,736,191	2,378,963	2,853,214	3,413,244	4,132,353	4,866,669
958,820	1,221,119	1,463,701	1,729,205	1,901,974	2,005,552	1,860,421	1,744,237	1,950,186	1,793,477
2,069,042	2,333,860	2,632,067	2,939,006	3,137,587	3,434,575	3,951,777	4,417,821	4,705,642	4,891,769
92,531	145,965	194,402	225,565	250,742	290,529	330,066	332,416	469,557	453,589
76,212,168	92,228,496	106,021,537	123,202,624	132,164,569	151,325,798	179,323,175	203,302,031	226,542,203	248,718,301

U.S. Center of Population, 1790-1990

Source: Bureau of the Census, U.S. Dept. of Commerce

The U.S. Center of Population is considered here as the center of population gravity, or that point upon which the U.S. would balance if it were a rigid plane without weight and the population distributed thereon, with each individual assumed to have equal weight and to exert an influence on a central point proportional to his or her distance from that point. The 1990 center is 818.6 miles from the 1790 center of population and is 39.5 miles SW of the 1980 center.

Year	N Lat °	′	″	W Long °	′	″	Approximate location
1790	39	16	30	76	11	12	23 miles east of Baltimore, MD
1800	39	16	6	76	56	30	18 miles west of Baltimore, MD
1810	39	11	30	77	37	12	40 miles northwest by west of Washington, DC (in VA)
1820	39	5	42	78	33	0	16 miles east of Moorefield, WV[1]
1830	38	57	54	79	16	54	19 miles west-southwest of Moorefield, WV[1]
1840	39	2	0	80	18	0	16 miles south of Clarksburg, WV[1]
1850	38	59	0	81	19	0	23 miles southeast of Parkersburg, WV[1]
1860	39	0	24	82	48	48	20 miles south by east of Chillicothe, OH
1870	39	12	0	83	35	42	48 miles east by north of Cincinnati, OH
1880	39	4	8	84	39	40	8 miles west by south of Cincinnati, OH (in KY)
1890	39	11	56	85	32	53	20 miles east of Columbus, IN
1900	39	9	36	85	48	54	6 miles southeast of Columbus, IN
1910	39	10	12	86	32	20	In the city of Bloomington, IN
1920	39	10	21	86	43	15	8 miles south-southeast of Spencer, Owen Co., IN
1930	39	3	45	87	8	6	3 miles northeast of Linton, Greene Co., IN
1940	38	56	54	87	22	35	2 miles southeast by east of Carlisle, Haddon township, Sullivan Co., IN
1950 (inc. Alaska & Hawaii)	38	48	15	88	22	8	3 miles northeast of Louisville, Clay Co., IL
1960	38	35	58	89	12	35	6½ miles northwest of Centralia, Clinton Co., IL
1970	38	27	47	89	42	22	5 miles east southeast of Mascoutah, St. Clair Co., IL
1000	38	8	13	90	34	26	¼ mile west of De Soto, Jefferson Co., MO
1990	37	52	20	91	12	55	9.7 miles northwest of Steelville, MO

(1) West Virginia was set off from Virginia on Dec. 31, 1862, and was admitted as a state on June 20, 1863.

Immigrants Admitted, by Top 30 Metropolitan Areas of Intended Residence, 1996

Source: Immigration and Naturalization Service, U.S. Dept. of Justice

(fiscal year 1996)

Metropolitan Statistical Area	Number	Percentage	Metropolitan Statistical Area	Number	Percentage
New York, NY	133,168	14.5	Philadelphia, PA–NJ	13,034	1.4
Los Angeles–Long Beach, CA	64,285	7.0	Detroit, MI	11,929	1.3
Miami, FL	41,527	4.5	Jersey City, NJ	11,399	1.2
Chicago, IL	39,989	4.4	Nassau–Suffolk, NY	10,594	1.2
Washington, DC–MD–VA	34,327	3.7	Seattle–Bellevue–Everett, WA	10,429	1.1
Houston, TX	21,387	2.3	Riverside–San Bernardino, CA	10,314	1.1
Boston–Lawrence–Lowell–Brockton, MA	18,726	2.0	Fort Lauderdale, FL	10,290	1.1
San Diego, CA	18,226	2.0	Atlanta, GA	9,870	1.1
San Francisco, CA	18,171	2.0	Middlesex–Somerset–Hunterdon, NJ	9,286	1.0
Newark, NJ	17,939	2.0	El Paso, TX	8,701	0.9
Orange County, CA	17,580	1.9	Minneapolis–St. Paul, MN–WI	7,615	0.8
Dallas, TX	15,915	1.7	Sacramento, CA	6,953	0.8
Oakland, CA	15,759	1.7	West Palm Beach–Boca Raton, FL	6,553	0.7
Bergen–Passaic, NJ	15,682	1.7	Honolulu, HI	6,553	0.7
San Jose, CA	13,854	1.5	Fort Worth–Arlington, TX	6,274	0.7
			Total immigrants admitted to U.S.	**915,900**	**100.0**

Immigrants Admitted, by State of Intended Residence, 1996

Source: Immigration and Naturalization Service, U.S. Dept. of Justice

(fiscal year 1996)

State	Number of immigrants	State	Number of immigrants	State	Number of immigrants	State	Number of immigrants
AL	1,782	KS	4,303	NY	154,095	WV	583
AK	1,280	KY	2,019	NC	7,011	WI	3,607
AZ	8,900	LA	4,092	ND	606	WY	280
AR	1,494	ME	1,028	OH	10,237		
CA	201,529	MD	20,732	OK	3,511		
CO	8,895	MA	23,085	OR	7,554	Other:	
CT	10,874	MI	17,253	PA	16,938	Guam	2,820
DE	1,377	MN	8,977	RI	3,098	N Mariana Isls.	176
DC	3,784	MS	1,073	SC	2,151	Puerto Rico	8,560
FL	79,461	MO	5,690	SD	519	Virgin Isls.	1,384
GA	12,608	MT	449	TN	4,343	Armed Service Posts	109
HI	8,436	NE	2,150	TX	83,385	Other or	
ID	1,825	NV	5,874	UT	4,250	unknown	10
IL	42,517	NH	1,512	VT	654	**Total**	**915,900**
IN	4,692	NJ	63,303	VA	21,375		
IA	3,037	NM	5,780	WA	18,833		

U.S. Foreign-Born Population, 1996

Source: Bureau of the Census, U.S. Dept. of Commerce

Percentage of U.S. Population That Is Foreign-Born, 1900-96

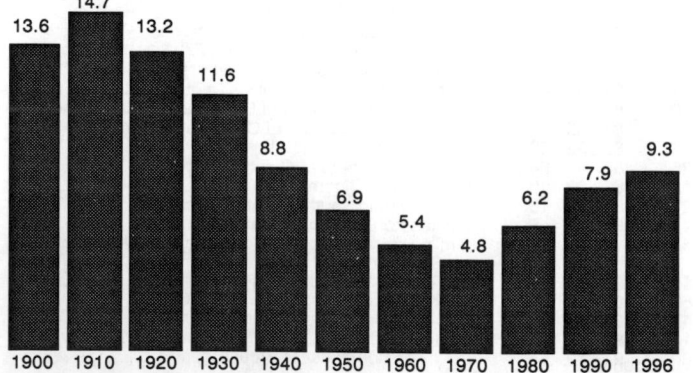

Year	1900	1910	1920	1930	1940	1950	1960	1970	1980	1990	1996
%	13.6	14.7	13.2	11.6	8.8	6.9	5.4	4.8	6.2	7.9	9.3

Highest-Ranking Countries of Birth of U.S. Foreign-Born Population, 1996

Country	Number (in thousands)
Mexico	6,679
Philippines	1,164
China	801
Cuba	772
India	757
Vietnam	740
El Salvador	701
Canada	660
Korea	550
Germany	523
Dominican Republic	515

Population by State, 1990-96

Source: Bureau of the Census, U.S. Dept. of Commerce

Rank	State	1996 population	1990 population	Percentage change 1990-96	Rank	State	1996 population	1990 population	Percentage change 1990-96
	U.S.	265,283,783	248,718,301	6.7	26.	SC	3,698,746	3,486,310	6.1
1.	CA	31,878,234	29,758,213	7.1	27.	OK	3,300,902	3,145,576	4.9
2.	TX	19,128,261	16,986,335	12.6	28.	CT.....	3,274,238	3,287,116	-0.4
3.	NY	18,184,774	17,990,778	1.1	29.	OR	3,203,735	2,842,337	12.7
4.	FL.	14,399,985	12,938,071	11.3	30.	IA	2,851,792	2,776,831	2.7
5.	PA	12,056,112	11,882,842	1.5	31.	MS	2,716,115	2,575,475	5.5
6.	IL	11,846,544	11,430,602	3.6	32.	KS.	2,572,150	2,477,588	3.8
7.	OH	11,172,782	10,847,115	3.0	33.	AR	2,509,793	2,350,624	6.8
8.	MI	9,594,350	9,295,287	3.2	34.	UT.	2,000,494	1,722,850	16.1
9.	NJ	7,987,933	7,730,188	3.3	35.	WV	1,825,754	1,793,477	1.8
10.	GA	7,353,225	6,478,149	13.5	36.	NM	1,713,407	1,515,069	13.1
11.	NC	7,322,870	6,632,448	10.4	37.	NE	1,652,093	1,578,417	4.7
12.	VA	6,675,451	6,189,197	7.9	38.	NV	1,603,163	1,201,675	33.4
13.	MA	6,092,352	6,016,425	1.3	39.	ME	1,243,316	1,227,928	1.3
14.	IN	5,840,528	5,544,156	5.3	40.	ID	1,189,251	1,006,734	18.1
15.	WA	5,532,939	4,866,669	13.7	41.	HI	1,183,723	1,108,229	6.8
16.	MO	5,358,692	5,116,901	4.7	42.	NH	1,162,481	1,109,252	4.8
17.	TN	5,319,654	4,877,203	9.1	43.	RI	990,225	1,003,464	−1.3
18.	WI	5,159,795	4,891,769	5.5	44.	MT	879,372	799,065	10.1
19.	MD	5,071,604	4,780,753	6.1	45.	SD	732,405	696,004	5.2
20.	MN	4,657,758	4,375,665	6.4	46.	DE	724,842	666,168	8.8
21.	AZ	4,428,068	3,665,339	20.8	47.	ND	643,539	638,800	0.7
22.	LA	4,350,579	4,220,164	3.1	48.	AK.	607,007	550,043	10.4
23.	AL	4,273,084	4,040,389	5.8	49.	VT.....	588,654	562,758	4.6
24.	KY	3,883,723	3,686,891	5.3	50.	DC	543,213	606,900	−10.5
25.	CO	3,822,676	3,294,473	16.0	51.	WY	481,400	453,589	6.1

Note: Population figures for 1990 include corrections to the original tabulated population.

Density of Population by State, 1920-90

Source: Bureau of the Census, U.S. Dept. of Commerce

(per square mile, land area only)

State	1920	1960	1980	1990	State	1920	1960	1980	1990	State	1920	1960	1980	1990
AL....	45.8	64.2	76.6	79.6	LA....	39.6	72.2	94.5	96.9	OH ...	141.4	236.6	263.3	264.9
AK*...	0.1	0.4	0.7	1.0	ME ...	25.7	31.3	36.3	39.8	OK....	29.2	33.8	44.1	45.8
AZ....	2.9	11.5	23.9	32.3	MD ...	145.8	313.5	428.7	489.2	OR	8.2	18.4	27.4	29.6
AR....	33.4	34.2	43.9	45.1	MA ...	479.2	657.3	733.3	767.6	PA....	194.5	251.4	264.3	265.1
CA....	22.0	100.4	151.4	190.8	MI	63.8	137.7	162.6	163.6	RI	566.4	819.3	897.8	960.3
CO	9.1	16.9	27.9	31.8	MN ...	29.5	43.1	51.2	55.0	SC....	55.2	78.7	103.4	115.8
CT....	286.4	520.6	637.8	678.4	MS ...	38.6	46.0	53.4	54.9	SD....	8.3	9.0	9.1	9.2
DE....	113.5	225.2	307.6	340.8	MO ...	49.5	62.6	71.3	74.3	TN....	56.1	86.2	111.6	118.3
DC....7,292.9	12,523.9	10,132.3	9,882.8	MT....	3.8	4.6	5.4	5.5	TX....	17.8	36.4	54.3	64.9
FL....	17.7	91.5	180.0	239.6	NE....	16.9	18.4	20.5	20.5	UT....	5.5	10.8	17.8	21.0
GA....	49.3	67.8	94.1	111.9	NV....	0.7	2.6	7.3	10.9	VT....	38.6	42.0	55.2	60.8
HI*...	39.9	98.5	150.1	172.5	NH....	49.1	67.2	102.4	123.7	VA....	57.4	99.6	134.7	156.3
ID	5.2	8.1	11.5	12.2	NJ....	420.0	805.5	986.2	1,042.0	WA ...	20.3	42.8	62.1	73.1
IL	115.7	180.4	205.3	205.6	NM ...	2.9	7.8	10.7	12.5	WV ...	60.9	77.2	80.8	74.5
IN	81.3	128.8	152.8	154.6	NY....	217.9	350.6	370.6	381.0	WI ...	47.6	72.6	86.5	90.1
IA	43.2	49.2	52.1	49.7	NC....	52.5	93.2	120.4	136.1	WY ...	2.0	3.4	4.9	4.7
KS....	21.6	26.6	28.9	30.3	ND	9.2	9.1	9.4	9.3	U.S....	29.9*	50.6	64.0	70.3
KY....	60.1	76.2	92.3	92.8										

(*) For purposes of comparison, Alaska and Hawaii are included in above tabulation for 1920, even though not states then.

25 Largest Counties, by Population, 1990-96

Source: Bureau of the Census, U.S. Dept of Commerce

County	1996 population	1990 population	Percentage change, 1990-96	County	1996 population	1990 population	Percentage change, 1990-96
Los Angeles, CA	9,127,751	8,863,052	3.0	San Bernardino, CA. .	1,598,358	1,418,380	12.7
Cook, IL	5,096,540	5,105,044	−0.2	New York, NY	1,533,774	1,487,536	3.1
Harris, TX	3,126,966	2,818,101	11.0	Philadelphia, PA ...	1,478,002	1,585,577	−6.8
San Diego, CA	2,655,463	2,498,016	6.3	Broward, FL.	1,438,228	1,255,531	14.6
Orange, CA	2,636,888	2,410,668	9.4	Riverside, CA.	1,417,425	1,170,413	21.1
Maricopa, AZ	2,611,327	2,122,101	23.1	Middlesex, MA.....	1,412,561	1,398,468	1.0
Kings, NY.........	2,273,966	2,300,664	−1.2	Cuyahoga, OH.....	1,401,552	1,412,140	−0.7
Dade, FL	2,076,175	1,937,194	7.2	Suffolk, NY	1,356,896	1,321,768	2.7
Wayne, MI	2,039,819	2,111,687	−3.4	Alameda, CA......	1,328,139	1,276,702	4.0
Dallas, TX	2,000,192	1,852,810	8.0	Bexar, TX	1,318,322	1,185,394	11.2
Queens, NY	1,980,643	1,951,598	1.5	Tarrant, TX	1,305,185	1,170,103	11.5
King, WA	1,619,411	1,507,305	7.4	Nassau, NY	1,303,389	1,287,444	1.2
Santa Clara, CA	1,599,604	1,497,577	6.8				

Note: The following are the smallest counties, by 1996 population: Yellowstone National Park, MT (40); Kalawao County, HI (87); Loving County, TX (141); King County, TX (336); Arthur County, NE (428); Kenedy County, TX (438); Petroleum County, MT (533); San Juan County, CO (564); McPherson County, NE (565); and Blaine County, NE (651).

Metropolitan Areas, 1990-94

Source: Bureau of the Census, U.S. Dept. of Commerce

(CMSAs and MSAs of more than 600,000 persons listed by 1994 population estimates)

Metropolitan statistical areas (MSAs) are defined for federal statistical use by the Office of Management and Budget (OMB), with technical asistance from the Bureau of the Census. Most individual metropolitan areas with populations over 1 mil may, under specified circumstances, be subdivided into component Primary Metropolitan Statistical Areas (PMSAs), in which case the area as a whole is designated a Consolidated Metropolitan Statistical Area (CMSA).

Effective June 30, 1995, the Office of Management and Budget designated 253 MSAs, 72 PMSAs, and 18 CMSAs for the U.S. and Puerto Rico based on standards published in the Federal Register on Mar. 30, 1990, as applied to 1990 census data.

CMSAs and MSAs	Population 1990	Population 1994	Percentage change 1990-94
New York–Northern New Jersey–Long Island, NY–NJ–CT–PA CMSA....	19,549,649	19,796,430	1.3
Los Angeles–Riverside–Orange County, CA CMSA	14,531,529	15,302,275	5.3
Chicago–Gary–Kenosha, IL–IN–WI CMSA	8,239,820	8,526,804	3.5
Washington–Baltimore, DC–MD–VA–WV CMSA	6,726,395	7,051,495	4.8
San Francisco–Oakland–San Jose, CA CMSA ..	6,249,881	6,513,322	4.2
Philadelphia–Wilmington–Atlantic City, PA–NJ–DE–MD CMSA	5,893,019	5,959,301	1.1
Boston–Worcester–Lawrence, MA–NH–ME–CT CMSA..........	5,455,403	5,497,284	0.8
Detroit–Ann Arbor–Flint, MI CMSA	5,187,171	5,255,700	1.3
Dallas–Fort Worth, TX CMSA	4,037,282	4,362,483	8.1
Houston–Galveston–Brazoria, TX CMSA ...	3,731,029	4,098,776	9.9
Miami–Fort Lauderdale, FL CMSA	3,192,725	3,408,038	6.7
Atlanta, GA...........	2,959,500	3,330,997	12.6
Seattle–Tacoma–Bremerton, WA CMSA .	2,970,300	3,225,517	8.6
Cleveland, Akron, OH CMSA	2,859,644	2,898,855	1.4
Minneapolis–St. Paul, MN–WI	2,538,776	2,688,455	5.9
San Diego, CA	2,498,016	2,632,078	5.4
St. Louis, MO–IL.......	2,492,348	2,536,080	1.8
Phoenix–Mesa, AZ	2,238,498	2,473,384	10.5
Pittsburgh, PA.........	2,394,811	2,402,012	0.3
Denver–Boulder–Greeley, CO CMSA..........	1,980,140	2,189,994	10.6
Tampa–St. Petersburg–Clearwater, FL	2,067,959	2,156,546	4.3
Portland–Salem, OR–WA CMSA	1,793,476	1,982,238	10.5
Cincinnati–Hamilton, OH–KY–IN, CMSA.......	1,817,569	1,894,071	4.2
Kansas City, MO.......	1,582,874	1,647,241	4.1
Milwaukee–Racine, WI CMSA	1,607,183	1,637,278	1.9
Sacramento–Yolo, CA . CMSA	1,481,220	1,587,898	7.2
Norfolk–Virginia Beach–Newport News, VA–NC	1,444,710	1,529,207	5.8
Indianapolis, IN........	1,380,491	1,461,693	5.9
San Antonio, TX	1,324,749	1,437,306	8.5

CMSAs and MSAs	Population 1990	Population 1994	Percentage change 1990-94
Columbus, OH........	1,345,450	1,422,875	5.8
Orlando, FL..........	1,224,844	1,361,489	11.2
New Orleans, LA	1,285,262	1,308,904	1.8
Charlotte–Gastonia–Rock Hill, NC–SC	1,162,140	1,260,390	8.5
Buffalo–Niagara Falls, NY	1,189,340	1,189,237	0.0
Salt Lake City–Odgen, UT..........	1,072,227	1,178,338	9.9
Hartford, CT..........	1,157,585	1,151,413	−0.5
Providence–Fall River–Warwick, RI–MA.....	1,134,350	1,129,172	−0.5
Greensboro–Winston–Salem–High Point, NC	1,050,304	1,107,051	5.4
Rochester, NY........	1,062,470	1,090,596	2.6
Las Vegas, NV–AZ	852,646	1,076,267	26.2
Nashville, TN........	985,026	1,069,648	8.6
Memphis, TN–AR–MS ..	1,007,306	1,056,096	4.8
Oklahoma City, OK	958,839	1,007,302	5.1
Grand Rapids–Muskegon–Holland, MI	937,891	984,990	5.0
Louisville, KY–IN	949,012	980,855	3.4
Jacksonville, FL.......	906,727	971,829	7.2
Raleigh–Durham–Chapel Hill, NC	858,485	965,127	12.4
Austin–San Marcos, TX .	846,227	963,981	13.9
Dayton–Springfield, OH .	951,270	956,382	0.5
West Palm Beach–Boca Raton, FL	863,503	954,539	10.5
Richmond–Petersburg, VA...............	865,640	916,674	5.9
Albany–Schenectady–Troy, NY	861,623	875,240	1.6
Honolulu, HI..........	836,231	874,330	4.6
Greenville–Spartanburg–Anderson, SC	830,539	873,356	5.2
Birmingham, AL.......	839,942	872,222	3.8
Fresno, CA	755,580	834,663	10.5
Syracuse, NY.........	742,237	753,980	1.6
Tulsa, OK	708,954	743,107	4.8
Tucson, AZ	666,957	731,523	9.7
El Paso, TX..........	591,610	664,813	12.4
Omaha, NE–IA	639,580	662,811	3.6
Albuquerque, NM......	589,131	645,533	9.6
Scranton–Wilkes-Barre–Hazleton, PA	638,524	636,993	−0.2
Knoxville, TN	585,960	631,107	7.7
Toledo, OH	614,128	613,945	0.0
Allentown–Bethlehem–Easton, PA	595,208	611,765	2.8
Harrisburg–Lebanon–Carlisle, PA	587,986	609,715	3.7
Bakersfield, CA	544,981	609,332	11.8
Youngstown–Warren, OH	600,895	604,123	0.5

Final 1990 census figures showed that the nation in that year had 40 metropolitan areas of at least 1 mil population, including 5 that had reached that size since 1980. The 40 areas had 132.9 mil people, or 53.4% of the U.S. population, in 1990. It is estimated that since the 1990 census, the populations of 3 additional metropolitan areas (Las Vegas, NV–AZ; Nashville, TN; and Oklahoma City, OK) have increased to more than 1 mil. By 1994, 54.5% of the population lived in metropolitan areas that had a total of at least 1 mil inhabitants.

Some 207.7 mil people resided in metropolitan areas in 1994, an increase of more than 9.6 mil (4.9%) since 1990. The population outside metropolitan areas totaled 52.7 mil in 1994, up 2.0 mil (3.9%) from 1990. The metropolitan population in 1994 was 79.8% of the U.S. total, compared with 79.4% in 1990 and 76.2% in 1980.

Population of 100 Largest U.S. Cities, 1850-1994

Source: Bureau of the Census, U.S. Dept. of Commerce (100 most populous cities ranked by July 1, 1994, population estimates)

Rank	City	1994	1990	1980	1970	1950	1900	1850
1.	New York, NY	7,333,253	7,322,564	7,071,639	7,895,563	7,891,957	3,437,202	696,115
2.	Los Angeles, CA	3,448,613	3,485,557	2,968,528	2,811,801	1,970,358	102,479	1,610
3.	Chicago, IL	2,731,743	2,783,726	3,005,072	3,369,357	3,620,962	1,698,575	29,963
4.	Houston, TX	1,702,086	1,629,902	1,595,138	1,233,535	596,163	44,633	2,396
5.	Philadelphia, PA	1,524,249	1,585,577	1,688,210	1,949,996	2,071,605	1,293,697	121,376
6.	San Diego, CA	1,151,977	1,110,623	875,538	697,471	334,387	17,700	...
7.	Phoenix, AZ	1,048,949	983,403	789,704	584,303	106,818	5,544	...
8.	Dallas, TX	1,022,830	1,007,618	904,599	844,401	434,462	42,638	...
9.	San Antonio, TX	998,905	935,393	785,940	654,153	408,442	53,321	3,488
10.	Detroit, MI	992,038	1,027,974	1,203,368	1,514,063	1,849,568	285,704	21,019
11.	San Jose, CA	816,884	782,224	629,400	459,913	95,280	21,500	...
12.	Indianapolis, IN[1]	752,279	731,327	700,807	736,856	427,173	169,164	8,091
13.	San Francisco, CA	734,676	723,959	678,974	715,674	775,357	342,782	34,776
14.	Baltimore, MD	702,979	736,014	786,741	905,787	949,708	508,957	169,054
15.	Jacksonville, FL[1]	665,070	635,230	540,920	504,265	204,517	28,429	1,045
16.	Columbus, OH	635,913	632,945	565,021	540,025	375,901	125,560	17,882
17.	Milwaukee, WI	617,044	628,088	636,297	717,372	637,392	285,315	20,061
18.	Memphis, TN	614,289	610,337	646,174	623,988	396,000	102,320	8,841
19.	El Paso, TX	579,307	515,342	425,259	322,261	130,485	15,906	...
20.	Washington, DC	567,094	606,900	638,432	756,668	802,178	278,718	40,001
21.	Boston, MA	547,725	574,283	562,994	641,071	801,444	560,892	136,881
22.	Seattle, WA	520,947	516,259	493,846	530,831	467,591	80,671	...
23.	Austin, TX	514,013	465,648	345,890	253,539	132,459	22,258	629
24.	Nashville, TN[1]	504,505	488,374	455,651	426,029	174,307	80,865	10,165
25.	Denver, CO	493,559	467,610	492,686	514,678	415,786	133,859	...
26.	Cleveland, OH	492,901	505,616	573,822	750,879	914,808	381,768	17,034
27.	New Orleans, LA	484,149	496,938	557,927	593,471	570,445	287,104	116,375
28.	Oklahoma City, OK	463,201	444,724	404,014	368,164	243,504	10,037	...
29.	Fort Worth, TX	451,814	447,619	385,164	393,455	278,778	26,688	...
30.	Portland, OR	450,777	438,802	368,148	379,967	373,628	90,426	...
31.	Kansas City, MO	443,878	434,829	448,028	507,330	456,622	163,752	...
32.	Charlotte, NC	437,797	395,925	315,474	241,420	134,042	18,091	1,065
33.	Tucson, AZ	434,726	405,323	330,537	262,933	45,454	7,531	...
34.	Long Beach, CA	433,852	429,321	361,498	358,879	250,767	2,252	...
35.	Virginia Beach, VA	430,295	393,089	262,199	172,106	5,390	...	...
36.	Albuquerque, NM	411,994	384,619	332,920	244,501	96,815	6,238	...
37.	Atlanta, GA	396,052	393,929	425,022	495,039	331,314	89,872	2,572
38.	Fresno, CA	386,551	354,091	217,491	165,655	91,669	12,470	...
39.	Honolulu, HI[2]	385,881	365,272	365,048	324,871	248,034	39,306	...
40.	Tulsa, OK	374,851	367,302	360,919	330,350	182,740	1,390	...
41.	Sacramento, CA	373,964	369,365	275,741	257,105	137,572	29,282	6,820
42.	Miami, FL	373,024	358,648	346,681	334,859	249,276	1,681	...
43.	St. Louis, MO	368,215	396,685	452,801	622,236	856,796	575,238	77,860
44.	Oakland, CA	366,926	372,242	339,337	361,561	384,575	66,960	...
45.	Pittsburgh, PA	358,883	369,879	423,959	520,089	676,806	321,616	46,601
46.	Cincinnati, OH	358,170	364,114	385,409	453,514	503,998	325,902	115,435
47.	Minneapolis, MN	354,590	368,383	370,951	434,400	521,718	202,718	...
48.	Omaha, NE	345,033	335,719	313,939	346,929	251,117	102,555	...
49.	Las Vegas, NV	327,878	258,204	164,674	125,787	24,624	...	...
50.	Toledo, OH	322,550	332,943	354,635	383,062	303,616	131,822	3,829
51.	Colorado Springs, CO	316,480	280,430	215,105	135,517	45,472	21,085	...
52.	Mesa, AZ	313,649	288,104	152,404	63,049	16,790	722	...
53.	Buffalo, NY	312,965	328,175	357,870	462,768	580,132	352,387	42,261
54.	Wichita, KS	310,236	304,017	279,838	276,554	168,279	24,671	...
55.	Santa Ana, CA	290,827	293,827	204,023	155,710	45,533	4,933	...
56.	Arlington, TX	286,922	261,717	160,113	90,229	7,692	1,079	...
57.	Tampa, FL	285,523	280,015	271,577	277,714	124,681	15,839	...
58.	Anaheim, CA	282,133	266,406	219,494	166,408	14,556	1,456	...
59.	Corpus Christi, TX	275,419	257,428	232,134	204,525	108,287	4,703	...
60.	Louisville, KY	270,308	269,555	298,694	361,706	369,129	204,731	43,194
61.	Birmingham, AL	264,527	265,347	284,413	300,910	326,037	38,415	...
62.	St. Paul, MN	262,071	272,235	270,230	309,866	311,349	163,065	1,112
63.	Newark, NJ	258,751	275,221	329,248	381,930	438,776	246,070	38,894
64.	Anchorage, AK	253,649	226,338	174,431	48,081	11,254	...	...
65.	Aurora, CO	250,717	222,103	158,588	74,974	11,421	202	...
66.	Riverside, CA	241,644	226,546	170,591	140,089	46,764	7,973	...
67.	Norfolk, VA	241,426	261,250	266,979	307,951	213,513	46,624	14,326
68.	St. Petersburg, FL	238,585	240,318	238,647	216,159	96,738	1,575	...
69.	Lexington, KY	237,612	225,366	204,165	108,137	55,534	26,369	8,159
70.	Raleigh, NC	236,707	212,092	150,255	122,830	65,679	13,643	4,518
71.	Rochester, NY	231,170	230,356	241,741	295,011	332,488	162,608	36,403
72.	Baton Rouge, LA	227,482	219,531	220,394	165,921	125,629	11,269	3,905
73.	Jersey City, NJ	226,022	228,517	223,532	260,350	299,017	206,433	6,856
74.	Stockton, CA	222,633	210,943	148,283	109,963	70,853	17,506	...
75.	Akron, OH	221,886	223,019	237,177	275,425	274,605	42,728	3,266
76.	Mobile, AL	204,490	196,263	200,452	190,026	129,009	38,469	20,515
77.	Lincoln, NE	203,076	191,972	171,932	149,518	98,884	40,169	...
78.	Richmond, VA	201,108	202,798	219,214	249,332	230,310	85,050	27,570
79.	Shreveport, LA	196,982	198,518	206,989	182,064	127,206	16,013	1,728
80.	Greensboro, NC	196,167	183,894	155,642	144,076	74,389	10,035	...
81.	Montgomery, AL	195,471	187,543	177,857	133,386	106,525	30,346	8,728
82.	Madison, WI	194,586	190,766	170,616	171,809	96,056	19,164	1,525
83.	Lubbock, TX	194,467	186,206	174,361	149,101	71,747	...	...
84.	Garland, TX	184,216	180,635	138,857	81,437	10,571	819	...

(continued)

Rank	City	1994	1990	1980	1970	1950	1900	1850
85.	Hialeah, FL...............	194,120	188,008	145,254	102,452	19,676	...	...
86.	Des Moines, IA	193,965	193,189	191,003	201,404	177,965	62,139	...
87.	Jackson, MS	193,097	196,637	202,895	153,968	98,271	7,816	1,881
88.	Spokane, WA	192,781	177,165	171,300	170,516	161,721	36,848	...
89.	Bakersfield, CA	191,060	174,978	105,611	69,515	34,784	4,836	...
90.	Grand Rapids, MI	190,395	189,126	181,843	197,649	176,515	87,565	2,686
91.	Huntington Beach, CA	189,220	181,519	170,505	115,960	5,237	...	...
92.	Columbus, GA[1]	186,470	178,681	169,441	155,028	79,611	17,614	9,621
93.	Fremont, CA	183,575	173,339	131,945	100,869	...	...	...
94.	Yonkers, NY	183,490	188,082	195,351	204,297	152,798	47,931	...
95.	Fort Wayne, IN	183,359	172,971	172,391	178,269	133,607	45,115	4,282
96.	Tacoma, WA	183,060	176,664	158,501	154,407	143,673	37,714	...
97.	San Bernardino, CA........	181,718	164,164	118,794	104,251	63,058	6,150	...
98.	Chesapeake, VA..........	180,577	151,982	114,486	89,580	...	...	...
99.	Newport News, VA.........	179,127	171,439	144,903	138,177	42,358	19,635	...
100.	Dayton, OH...............	178,540	182,005	193,536	243,023	243,872	85,333	10,977

Note: The Apr. 1, 1990, census counts include count resolution corrections and geographic changes. (1) Indianapolis, IN; Jacksonville, FL; Nashville-Davidson, TN; and Columbus, GA, are parts of consolidated city-county governments. Populations of other incorporated places in the county have been excluded from the population totals shown here. For years that predate the establishment of a consolidated city-county government, city population is shown. (2) Locations in Hawaii are called "census designated places (CDPs)." Although these areas are not incorporated, they are recognized for census purposes as large urban places. Honolulu CDP is coextensive with Honolulu Judicial District within the city and county of Honolulu.

U.S. Population, by Age, Sex, and Household, 1990

Source: Bureau of the Census, U.S. Dept. of Commerce; 1990 Census

Total population......................	248,709,873[1]	**Sex**		
Age		Male		121,239,418
Under 5 years	18,354,443	Female		127,470,455
5 to 17 years......................	45,249,989	**Households by type**		
18 to 20 years.....................	11,726,868	Total households.............		**91,947,410**
21 to 24 years.....................	15,010,898	Family households (families)..............		64,517,947
25 to 44 years.....................	80,754,835	Married-couple families...............		50,708,322
45 to 54 years.....................	25,223,086	Percentage of total households		55.1
55 to 59 years.....................	10,531,756	Other family, male householder.........		3,143,582
60 to 64 years.....................	10,616,167	Other family, female householder.		10,666,043
65 to 74 years.....................	18,106,558	Nonfamily households		27,429,463
75 to 84 years.....................	10,055,108	Percentage of total households		29.8
85 years and over	3,080,165	Householder living alone...............		22,580,420
		Householder 65 years and over		8,824,845
Median age........................	32.9	Persons living in households.............		242,012,129
Under 18 years	63,604,432	Persons per household...................		2.63
Percentage of total population...........	25.6	Persons living in group quarters		6,697,744
65 years and over	31,241,831	Institutionalized persons		3,334,018
Percentage of total population...........	12.6	Other persons in group quarters		3,363,726

(1) Data shown are based on the U.S. population as tabulated in the 1990 census, and do not reflect corrections to the 1990 population. The corrected 1990 U.S. population is 248,718,301.

Projections of Total Population, by Age, 1995-2050

Source: Bureau of the Census, U.S. Dept. of Commerce

	1995		2000		2010		2050	
Age	Population[1]	Percentage distribution	Population[1]	Percentage distribution	Population[1]	Percentage distribution	Population[1]	Percentage distribution
Total	262,820	100.0	274,634	100.0	297,716	100.0	393,931	100.0
Under 5 years	19,591	7.5	18,987	6.9	20,012	6.7	27,106	6.9
5-13 years	34,378	13.1	36,043	13.1	35,605	12.0	47,804	12.1
14-17 years	14,773	5.6	15,752	5.7	16,894	5.7	21,207	5.4
18-24 years	24,926	9.5	26,258	9.6	30,138	10.1	36,333	9.2
25-34 years	40,863	15.5	37,233	13.6	38,292	12.9	49,365	12.5
35-44 years	42,514	16.2	44,659	16.3	38,521	12.9	47,393	12.0
45-54 years	31,092	11.8	37,030	13.5	43,564	14.6	43,494	11.0
55-64 years	21,139	8.0	23,961	8.7	35,283	11.9	42,368	10.8
65 years and over	33,543	12.8	34,709	12.6	39,408	13.2	78,859	20.0
85 years and over	3,634	1.4	4,259	1.6	5,671	1.9	18,223	4.6
100 years and over	54	0.0	72	0.0	131	0.0	834	0.2

Note: All figures shown are for July 1 of the given year, exclude Armed Forces overseas, and are middle series population projections. For the series shown, different assumptions were made regarding fertility rates (lifetime births per woman), life expectancy, and immigration in the coming decades. Assumptions were based on July 1 estimates of U.S. population consistent with the 1990 decennial census, as enumerated. Yearly net immigration was assumed to be 820,000. Percentage distribution may not equal 100, because of overlapping categories shown and rounding. (1) In thousands.

Poverty Level by Family Size, 1994-96

Source: Bureau of the Census, U.S. Dept. of Commerce

	1994	1995	1996		1994	1995	1996
1 person..................	$7,547	$7,763	$7,995	3 persons................	$11,821	$12,158	$12,516
Under 65 years	7,710	7,929	8,163	4 persons................	15,141	15,569	16,036
65 years and over	7,108	7,309	7,525	5 persons................	17,900	18,408	18,952
2 persons	9,661	9,933	10,233	6 persons................	20,235	20,804	21,389
Householder under 65 years.	9,979	10,259	10,564	7 persons................	22,923	23,552	24,268
Householder 65 years and				8 persons................	25,427	26,237	27,091
over..................	8,967	9,219	9,491	9 persons or more.........	30,300	31,280	31,971

Poverty Rate

Source: Bureau of the Census, U.S. Dept. of Commerce

The poverty rate is the proportion of the population whose income falls below the government's official poverty level, which is adjusted each year for inflation. The national poverty rate was 13.7% in 1996, statistically unchanged from the 1995 rate of 13.8%. Children remained overrepresented among the poor, with a poverty rate of 20.5%. As a group the elderly were slightly underrepresented.

Poverty by Family Status, Sex, and Race, 1986-96

Source: Bureau of the Census, U.S. Dept. of Commerce

(numbers in thousands)

	1996 No.	%[1]	1995 No.	%[1]	1994 No.	%[1]	1990 No.	%[1]	1986 No.	%[1]
Total poor	36,529	13.7	36,425	13.8	38,059	14.5	33,585	13.5	32,370	13.6
In families	27,376	12.2	27,501	12.3	28,965	13.1	25,232	12.0	24,754	12.0
Head of household	7,708	11.0	7,532	10.8	8,053	11.6	7,098	10.7	7,023	10.9
Related children	13,764	19.8	13,999	20.2	14,610	21.2	12,715	19.9	12,257	19.8
Unrelated individuals	8,452	20.8	8,247	20.9	8,287	21.5	7,446	20.7	6,846	21.6
In families, female householder, no husband present	13,796	35.8	14,205	36.5	14,380	38.6	12,578	37.2	11,944	38.3
Head of household	4,167	32.6	4,057	32.4	4,232	34.6	3,768	33.4	3,613	34.6
Related children	7,990	49.3	8,364	50.3	8,427	52.9	7,363	53.4	6,943	54.4
Unrelated female individuals	5,145	24.2	4,865	23.5	5,012	24.9	4,589	24.0	4,311	25.1
All other families	13,580	7.3	13,296	7.2	14,605	7.9	12,654	7.1	12,811	7.3
Head of household	3,541	6.2	3,475	6.1	3,821	6.7	3,330	6.0	3,410	6.3
Related children	5,774	10.9	5,635	10.7	6,183	11.7	5,352	10.7	5,313	10.8
Unrelated male individuals	3,308	17.0	3,382	18.0	3,276	17.8	2,857	16.9	2,536	17.5
Total white poor	24,650	11.2	24,423	11.2	25,379	11.7	22,326	10.7	22,183	11.0
In families	17,621	9.6	17,593	9.6	18,474	10.1	15,916	9.0	16,393	9.4
Head of household	5,059	8.6	4,994	8.5	5,312	9.1	4,622	8.1	4,811	8.6
Related children	8,488	15.5	8,474	15.5	8,826	16.3	7,696	15.1	7,714	15.3
Female householder, no spouse present	2,276	27.3	2,200	26.6	2,329	29.0	2,010	26.8	2,041	28.2
Unrelated individuals	6,463	18.9	6,336	19.0	6,292	19.3	5,739	18.6	5,198	19.2
Total black poor	9,694	28.4	9,872	29.3	10,196	30.6	9,837	31.9	8,983	31.1
In families	7,993	27.6	8,189	28.5	8,447	29.6	8,160	31.0	7,410	29.7
Head of household	2,206	26.1	2,127	26.4	2,212	27.3	2,193	29.3	1,987	28.0
Related children	4,411	39.5	4,644	41.5	4,787	43.3	4,412	44.2	4,039	42.7
Female householder, no spouse present	1,724	43.7	1,701	45.1	1,715	46.1	1,648	48.1	1,488	50.1
Unrelated individuals	1,606	32.2	1,551	32.6	1,617	34.8	1,491	35.1	1,431	38.5

(1) Percentage of total U.S. population in that general category who fell below poverty level and are enumerated here. For example, of all black female heads of households in 1996, 43.7%, or 1,724,000, were poor.

Persons Below Poverty Level, 1960-96

Source: Bureau of the Census, U.S. Dept. of Commerce

Year	Number below poverty level (in millions) All races[1]	White	Black	Hispanic origin[2]	Percentage below poverty level All races[1]	White	Black	Hispanic origin[2]	Avg. income cutoffs for family of 4 at poverty level[3]
1960	39.9	28.3	NA	NA	22.2	17.8	NA	NA	$3,022
1970	25.4	17.5	7.5	NA	12.6	9.9	33.5	NA	3,968
1980	29.3	19.7	8.6	3.5	13.0	10.2	32.5	25.7	8,414
1990	33.6	22.3	9.8	6.0	13.5	10.7	31.9	28.1	13,359
1991	35.7	23.7	10.2	6.3	14.2	11.3	32.7	28.7	13,924
1992	38.0	25.3	10.8	7.6	14.8	11.9	33.4	29.6	14,335
1993	39.3	26.2	10.9	8.1	15.1	12.2	33.1	30.6	14,763
1994	38.1	25.4	10.2	8.4	14.5	11.7	30.6	30.7	15,141
1995	36.4	24.4	9.9	8.6	13.8	11.2	29.3	30.3	15,569
1996	36.5	24.7	9.7	8.7	13.7	11.2	28.4	29.4	16,036

NA = Not available. **Note:** Because of a change in the definition of poverty, data prior to 1980 are not directly comparable to data since 1980. (1) Includes other races not shown separately. (2) Persons of Hispanic origin may be of any race. (3) Figures for 1960-80 represent only nonfarm families.

Persons in Poverty, by State, 1995-96

Source: Bureau of the Census, U.S. Dept. of Commerce

State	1996 Percentage	1995 Percentage	State	1996 Percentage	1995 Percentage	State	1996 Percentage	1995 Percentage	State	1996 Percentage	1995 Percentage
AL	17.1	18.3	IL	12.3	12.4	MT	16.2	13.4	RI	10.8	10.5
AK	7.7	8.7	IN	8.6	11.7	NE	9.9	9.2	SC	16.5	16.9
AZ	18.3	16.0	IA	10.9	11.5	NV	9.6	11.1	SD	13.2	14.5
AR	16.1	15.1	KS	11.0	12.9	NH	5.9	6.5	TN	15.7	15.1
CA	16.8	17.3	KY	15.9	16.6	NJ	8.5	8.5	TX	17.0	18.3
CO	9.7	8.9	LA	20.1	22.7	NM	25.4	23.2	UT	8.1	8.2
CT	10.7	10.3	ME	11.2	10.3	NY	16.6	16.8	VT	11.5	9.0
DE	9.5	9.3	MD	10.2	10.4	NC	12.4	13.4	VA	11.3	10.6
DC	23.2	21.7	MA	10.6	10.4	ND	11.5	11.2	WA	12.2	12.1
FL	15.2	15.6	MI	11.7	13.2	OH	12.1	12.8	WV	17.6	17.7
GA	13.5	13.1	MN	9.5	10.5	OK	10.9	16.9	WI	8.7	8.8
HI	11.2	9.5	MS	22.1	21.7	OR	11.6	11.5	WY	12.1	10.8
ID	13.2	13.3	MO	9.5	13.6	PA	11.9	12.4			

Aid to Families With Dependent Children, Fiscal Year 1996

Source: Admin. for Children and Families, Off. of Planning, Research, and Evaluation, Div. of Data Collection and Analysis, U.S Dept. of HHS

State	Total assistance payments[1]	Average monthly caseload	Average monthly recipients	Average monthly children	Average monthly payment per Family	Person
Alabama	$75,110	42,393	105,204	79,272	$147.65	$59.50
Alaska	107,436	12,253	36,192	23,218	730.67	247.37
Arizona	228,321	63,404	171,533	118,166	300.09	110.92
Arkansas	51,188	22,747	58,166	42,009	187.53	73.34
California	5,907,518	895,960	2,625,833	1,804,831	549.46	187.48
Colorado	129,207	35,447	98,525	67,672	303.76	109.28
Connecticut	322,918	58,117	161,733	108,146	463.02	166.38
Delaware	34,733	10,388	23,367	15,766	278.62	123.87
District of Columbia	120,830	25,721	70,201	48,244	391.48	143.43
Florida	679,704	211,975	560,561	394,797	267.21	101.05
Georgia	384,454	130,387	352,607	250,608	245.71	90.86
Guam	14,100	2,137	7,853	5,512	549.96	149.63
Hawaii	173,247	21,960	66,539	44,219	657.43	216.97
Idaho	30,068	9,008	22,926	15,910	278.18	109.29
Illinois	832,931	224,148	655,396	455,591	309.67	105.91
Indiana	153,464	52,873	147,995	103,991	241.87	86.41
Iowa	131,080	32,785	89,208	59,193	333.18	122.45
Kansas	97,921	25,148	68,497	48,026	324.49	119.13
Kentucky	191,443	71,827	174,882	120,253	222.11	91.23
Louisiana	130,054	70,581	235,551	161,763	153.55	46.01
Maine	98,560	20,461	55,878	35,283	401.42	146.99
Maryland	285,168	74,106	204,105	140,400	320.67	116.43
Massachusetts	559,912	88,365	236,842	152,821	528.03	197.01
Michigan	775,931	178,002	527,110	353,883	363.26	122.67
Minnesota	332,573	58,250	171,109	116,071	475.78	161.97
Mississippi	67,825	47,954	129,052	95,992	117.86	43.80
Missouri	253,823	82,717	231,891	162,369	255.71	91.21
Montana	45,465	10,836	31,192	20,521	349.66	121.47
Nebraska	53,480	14,166	38,724	26,887	314.60	115.09
Nevada	48,359	14,827	37,561	27,179	271.80	107.29
New Hampshire	49,762	9,538	24,200	15,833	434.76	171.36
New Jersey	352,257	111,983	288,486	195,397	262.14	101.75
New Mexico	152,727	33,852	101,123	65,352	375.97	125.86
New York	2,929,347	431,717	1,183,749	770,530	565.44	206.22
North Carolina	299,518	113,127	277,841	191,105	220.64	89.84
North Dakota	21,037	4,892	13,399	9,051	358.35	130.84
Ohio	762,816	206,722	545,918	381,807	307.50	116.44
Oklahoma	121,852	38,809	104,845	74,122	261.65	96.85
Oregon	154,539	33,444	86,940	59,912	385.07	148.13
Pennsylvania	821,949	190,329	543,502	367,871	359.88	126.03
Puerto Rico	63,448	50,888	154,891	105,322	103.90	34.14
Rhode Island	125,311	21,226	58,397	39,021	491.96	178.82
South Carolina	100,870	45,770	119,184	89,068	183.65	70.53
South Dakota	21,555	5,995	16,282	11,889	299.60	110.32
Tennessee	189,760	99,096	260,257	180,845	159.58	60.76
Texas	494,970	254,953	684,020	483,883	161.78	60.30
Utah	64,234	14,767	40,330	27,070	362.47	132.73
Vermont	55,604	9,058	25,294	15,684	511.58	183.19
Virgin Islands	4,174	1,399	4,953	3,664	248.73	70.23
Virginia	199,229	64,937	161,928	114,030	255.67	102.53
Washington	584,799	98,933	274,160	177,225	492.59	177.75
West Virginia	101,484	36,562	95,085	61,591	231.31	88.94
Wisconsin	291,044	60,058	170,224	122,864	403.84	142.48
Wyoming	16,824	4,732	12,839	9,113	296.29	109.20
U.S. Total	$20,295,932	4,551,730	12,644,076	8,670,839	$371.58	$133.76

Note: Under 1996 legislation, the AFDC program was converted to a state block-grant program (Temporary Assistance to Needy Families [TANF]). Conversion dates vary from state to state, starting from Sept. 30, 1996. As of July 1, 1997, 11 states were operating under the new program. (1) Total assistance payments given in thousands. These include federal, state, and local payments for AFDC-Basic and AFDC-Unemployed Parent, Title IV-A Payments under JOBS, Home Repair, and payments to Indian tribes.

Income Distribution by Population Fifths, 1996

Source: Bureau of the Census, U.S. Dept. of Commerce

	Upper limit of each fifth[1]					Percentage distribution of total income					
Families	Lowest	Second	Third	Fourth	Top 5%[2]	Lowest fifth	Second fifth	Third fifth	Fourth fifth	Top fifth	Top 5%
All races	$19,680	$34,315	$51,086	$75,316	$128,000	4.2	10.0	15.8	23.1	46.8	20.3
White	21,729	36,250	53,304	77,420	132,200	4.7	10.3	15.9	22.9	46.2	20.0
Black	10,356	20,000	33,500	54,500	89,839	3.2	8.7	15.2	24.4	48.5	19.4

(1) The highest fifth does not have an upper limit. (2) Lower limit for top 5%.

Mean Income Received by Population Fifths, 1970-96

Source: Bureau of the Census, U.S. Dept. of Commerce

Year	Lowest fifth	Second fifth	Third fifth	Fourth fifth	Highest fifth	Top 5%	Year	Lowest fifth	Second fifth	Third fifth	Fourth fifth	Highest fifth	Top 5%
1996	$8,596	$21,097	$35,486	$54,922	$115,514	$201,220	1991	$8,127	$20,308	$33,733	$51,423	$ 98,612	$153,890
1995	8,350	20,397	34,106	52,429	109,411	188,828	1990	8,390	21,024	34,726	52,356	101,604	161,794
1994	7,982	19,769	33,303	51,823	108,947	188,231	1985	8,211	20,296	33,617	50,555	93,254	140,143
1993	7,817	19,676	32,982	51,256	106,789	183,285	1980	8,301	20,034	32,974	48,551	85,279	123,359
1992	7,917	19,749	33,273	51,076	98,968	157,080	1970	7,487	19,908	32,059	45,192	80,016	122,817

Note: Average incomes were adjusted for inflation. Because of a change in survey methodology, data prior to 1992 are not directly comparable to later data. Restrictions are placed on the level of income reported. Actual income reported may exceed the amount recorded in the Census Bureau's survey. In 1993, the restrictions were changed; as a result, earlier data are not directly comparable to data since 1993.

U.S. Places of 5,000 or More Population—With ZIP and Area Codes

Source: U.S. Bureau of the Census, Dept. of Commerce; Bellcore

The following is a list of places of 5,000 or more inhabitants recognized by the Bureau of the Census, U.S. Dept. of Commerce, based on data collected in the 1990 Decennial Census. More recent estimates were not available for all cities as of late 1997. This list includes places that are incorporated under the laws of their respective states as cities, boroughs, towns, and villages, with the following exceptions: boroughs in Alaska and towns in the 6 New England states (Connecticut, Maine, Massachusetts, New Hampshire, Rhode Island, and Vermont), New York, and Wisconsin. Unincorporated places that the Census Bureau designates as "census designated places (CDPs)" are also included. These unincorporated communities, marked (u), are statistically compatible with incorporated communities because of their population density. CDP boundaries can change from one census to another. Hawaii is the only state that has no incorporated places recognized by the Census Bureau; all places shown for Hawaii are CDPs.

This list also includes, in *italics*, minor civil divisions (MCDs) for the following states: Connecticut, Maine, Massachusetts, New Hampshire, New Jersey, Rhode Island, Vermont, and Wisconsin. MCDs are areas that are not incorporated under the laws of the state and that are not recognized by the Census Bureau as CDPs, but are often the primary political or administrative divisions of a county. These areas may also serve as general-purpose local governments.

The geographical boundaries for places marked with a dagger (†) changed from the 1980 census to the 1990 census.

An asterisk (*) denotes that the ZIP code given is for general delivery; named streets and/or post office boxes within the community may differ. Consult the local postmaster for the correct ZIP code for specific addresses within the community.

Area codes, given in parentheses, refer only to home and business telephone numbers. Overlay area codes are excluded. When 2 area codes are listed for one locale, consult local operators for further assistance.

For some places, no area code and/or ZIP code is available.

Alabama

ZIP	Place		1990	1980
35007	Alabaster	(205)	14,619	7,079
35950	Albertville	(205)	14,507	12,039
35010	Alexander City	(205)	14,917	13,807
36420	Andalusia	(334)	9,269	10,415
*36201	Anniston	(205)	26,638	29,135
35016	Arab	(205)	6,321	6,053
35611	Athens	(205)	16,901	14,558
*36502	Atmore	(334)	8,046	8,789
35954	Attalla	(205)	6,859	7,737
*36830	Auburn	(334)	33,830	28,471
36507	Bay Minette	(334)	7,168	7,455
*35020	Bessemer	(205)	33,581	31,729
*35203	Birmingham	(205)	265,347	284,413
35957	Boaz	(205)	6,928	7,151
*36426	Brewton	(334)	5,885	6,680
35215	Center Point(u)	(205)	22,658	23,317
36611	Chickasaw	(205)	6,649	7,402
35045	Clanton	(205)	7,669	5,832
*35055	Cullman	(205)	13,367	13,084
36322	Daleville	(334)	5,117	4,250
36526	Daphne	(205)	11,291	3,406
*35601	Decatur	(205)	48,778	42,002
36732	Demopolis	(334)	7,512	7,678
*36302	Dothan	(334)	53,721	48,750
*36330	Enterprise	(334)	20,119	18,033
*36027	Eufaula	(334)	13,220	12,097
35064	Fairfield	(205)	12,200	13,242
36532	Fairhope	(334)	8,490	7,286
*35630	Florence	(205)	36,426	37,029
35214	Forestdale(u)	(205)	10,395	10,814
35967	Fort Payne	(205)	11,838	11,485
36362	Fort Rucker(u)	(205)	7,593	8,932
35068	Fultondale	(205)	6,400	6,217
*35901	Gadsden	(205)	42,523	47,565
35071	Gardendale	(205)	9,251	8,005
36037	Greenville	(334)	7,494	7,807
35976	Guntersville	(205)	7,038	7,041
35570	Hamilton	(205)	5,787	5,093
35640	Hartselle	(205)	10,867	8,858
35209	Homewood	(205)	23,644	21,412
*35244	Hoover	(205)	40,000	18,996
35023	Hueytown	(205)	15,280	13,452
*35801	Huntsville	(205)	159,880	142,513
35210	Irondale	(205)	9,458	6,510
36545	Jackson	(334)	5,819	6,073
36265	Jacksonville	(205)	10,283	9,735
*35501	Jasper	(205)	13,553	11,894
36863	Lanett	(205)	8,985	8,922
35094	Leeds	(205)	10,009	8,638
35758	Madison	(205)	14,792	4,057
35228	Midfield	(205)	5,559	6,182
36054	Millbrook	(205)	6,046	3,101
*36601	Mobile	(334)	196,263	200,452
*36460	Monroeville	(334)	6,993	5,674
*36104	Montgomery	(334)	187,543	177,857
*35223	Mountain Brook	(205)	19,810	19,718
35667	Muscle Shoals	(205)	9,611	8,911
35476	Northport	(205)	17,297	14,291
*36801	Opelika	(334)	22,122	21,896
36467	Opp	(334)	7,011	7,204
36203	Oxford	(205)	9,537	8,939
*36360	Ozark	(334)	13,030	13,188
35124	Pelham	(205)	9,356	6,759
*35125	Pell City	(205)	7,945	6,616
36867	Phenix City	(334)	25,311	26,928
36272	Piedmont	(205)	5,347	5,544
35126	Pinson-Clay-Chalkville(u)	(205)	10,987	....
35127	Pleasant Grove	(205)	8,458	7,102
*36067	Prattville	(334)	19,910	18,647

ZIP	Place		1990	1980
36610	Prichard	(205)	34,320	39,541
35906	Rainbow City	(205)	7,667	6,299
36274	Roanoke	(334)	6,362	5,809
35653	Russellville	(205)	7,812	8,195
36201	Saks(u)	(205)	11,138	11,118
36571	Saraland	(205)	11,760	9,833
36572	Satsuma	(205)	5,194	3,822
35768	Scottsboro	(205)	13,786	14,758
*36701	Selma	(334)	23,755	26,684
35660	Sheffield	(205)	10,380	11,903
35901	Southside	(205)	5,580	5,141
35150	Sylacauga	(205)	12,520	12,708
35160	Talladega	(205)	18,175	19,128
36078	Tallassee	(334)	5,112	4,763
35217	Tarrant City	(205)	8,046	8,148
*36582	Theodore(u)	(205)	6,509	6,392
36619	Tillman's Corner(u)	(205)	17,988	15,941
36081	Troy	(334)	13,051	13,124
35173	Trussville	(205)	8,283	3,507
*35401	Tuscaloosa	(205)	77,866	75,211
35674	Tuscumbia	(205)	8,413	9,137
36083	Tuskegee	(334)	12,257	13,327
*36854	Valley†	(205)	8,215	8,946
35216	Vestavia Hills	(205)	19,550	15,722

Alaska (907)

ZIP	Place	1990	1980
*99501	Anchorage	226,338	174,431
*99708	College(u)	11,249	4,043
99702	Eielson AFB(u)	5,251	5,232
*99701	Fairbanks	30,843	22,645
*99801	Juneau	26,751	19,528
99611	Kenai	6,327	4,324
*99901	Ketchikan	8,263	7,198
*99615	Kodiak	6,365	4,756
99639	Ninilchik(u)	10,523	341
99835	Sitka	8,588	7,803

Arizona

ZIP	Place		1990	1980
*85220	Apache Junction	(602)	18,092	9,935
85323	Avondale	(602)	16,182	8,168
85603	Bisbee	(520)	6,288	7,154
85326	Buckeye	(602)	4,436	3,434
*86430	Bullhead City†	(520)	21,951	10,719
86322	Camp Verde†	(520)	6,243	3,824
*85222	Casa Grande	(520)	19,076	14,971
*85225	Chandler	(602)	89,862	29,673
86503	Chinle(u)	(520)	5,059	2,815
85228	Coolidge	(520)	6,934	6,851
86326	Cottonwood	(520)	5,918	4,550
86326	Cottonwood-Verde Village(u)	(520)	7,037	....
*85607	Douglas	(520)	13,137	13,058
85335	El Mirage	(602)	5,001	4,307
85231	Eloy	(520)	7,211	6,240
*86004	Flagstaff	(520)	45,857	34,743
85232	Florence	(520)	7,321	3,391
85726	Flowing Wells(u)	(520)	14,013	....
	Fortuna Foothills(u)	(520)	7,737	....
*85269	Fountain Hills†	(602)	10,030	2,771
*85234	Gilbert	(602)	29,122	5,717
*85301	Glendale	(602)	147,864	97,172
*85501	Globe	(520)	6,062	6,886
85338	Goodyear	(602)	6,258	2,747
*85622	Green Valley(u)	(520)	13,231	7,999
85283	Guadalupe	(602)	5,458	4,506
86401	Kingman	(520)	12,722	9,257
*86100	Lake Havasu City	(520)	24,363	15,909
*85201	Mesa	(602)	288,104	152,404

ZIP	Place		1990	1980
86440	Mohave Valley(u)	(520)	6,962	....
.....	New Kingman-Butler(u) ...	(520)	11,627	....
*85621	Nogales	(520)	19,489	15,683
85737	Oro Valley	(520)	6,670	1,489
86040	Page	(520)	6,598	4,907
85253	Paradise Valley	(602)	11,773	11,085
*85541	Payson	(520)	8,377	5,068
*85345	Peoria	(602)	50,675	12,171
*85026	Phoenix	(602)	983,403	789,704
*86301	Prescott	(520)	26,592	19,865
*86301	Prescott Valley	(520)	8,904	2,284
*85546	Safford	(520)	7,359	7,010
*85251	Scottsdale	(602)	130,075	88,622
*86336	Sedona†	(520)	7,720	5,319
85901	Show Low	(520)	5,020	4,298
*85635	Sierra Vista	(520)	32,983	24,937
85635	Sierra Vista Southeast(u)..	(520)	9,237	....
85350	Somerton	(520)	5,282	3,969
85713	South Tucson	(520)	5,171	6,554
*85351	Sun City(u)	(602)	38,126	40,505
85375	Sun City West(u)	(602)	15,997	3,772
85248	Sun Lakes(u)	(602)	6,578	1,925
85374	Surprise	(602)	7,122	3,723
*85282	Tempe	(602)	141,993	106,919
86045	Tuba City(u)	(520)	7,323	5,045
*85726	Tucson	(520)	405,323	330,537
86047	Winslow	(520)	9,279	7,921
*85364	Yuma	(520)	56,966	42,481

Arkansas

ZIP	Place		1990	1980
71923	Arkadelphia	(870)	10,014	10,005
71822	Ashdown	(870)	5,150	4,218
*72501	Batesville	(870)	9,187	8,447
72714	Bella Vista(u)	(501)	9,083	2,589
*72015	Benton	(501)	18,177	17,717
72712	Bentonville	(501)	11,257	8,756
72315	Blytheville	(870)	22,523	23,844
72022	Bryant	(501)	5,269	2,682
72023	Cabot	(501)	8,319	4,806
71701	Camden	(870)	14,701	15,356
72830	Clarksville	(501)	5,833	5,237
*72032	Conway	(501)	26,481	20,375
71635	Crossett	(870)	6,282	6,706
71639	Dumas	(870)	5,520	6,091
*71730	El Dorado	(870)	23,146	25,270
*72701	Fayetteville	(501)	42,247	36,608
72335	Forrest City	(870)	13,364	13,803
*72901	Fort Smith	(501)	72,798	71,626
*72601	Harrison	(870)	9,936	9,567
72543	Heber Springs	(501)	5,628	4,589
72342	Helena	(870)	7,491	9,598
71801	Hope	(870)	9,768	10,290
*71901	Hot Springs	(501)	32,462	35,781
71909	Hot Springs Village(u) ...	(501)	6,361	2,083
*72076	Jacksonville†	(501)	29,101	27,589
72401	Jonesboro	(870)	46,535	31,530
*72201	Little Rock	(501)	175,727	159,151
71753	Magnolia	(870)	11,151	11,909
72104	Malvern	(501)	9,236	10,163
72360	Marianna	(870)	6,033	6,220
72113	Maumelle†	(501)	6,714	1,368
71953	Mena	(501)	5,475	5,154
71655	Monticello	(870)	8,119	8,259
72110	Morrilton	(501)	6,551	7,355
72653	Mountain Home	(870)	9,027	8,066
72112	Newport	(870)	7,459	8,339
*72114	North Little Rock	(501)	61,829	64,388
72370	Osceola	(870)	8,930	8,881
*72450	Paragould	(870)	18,540	15,248
*71601	Pine Bluff	(870)	57,140	56,636
72455	Pocahontas	(870)	6,151	5,995
*72756	Rogers	(501)	24,692	17,429
*72801	Russellville	(501)	21,260	14,518
*72143	Searcy	(501)	15,180	13,612
72120	Sherwood	(501)	18,878	10,423
72761	Siloam Springs	(501)	8,151	7,940
*72764	Springdale	(501)	29,945	23,458
72160	Stuttgart	(870)	10,420	10,941
75502	Texarkana	(870)	22,631	21,459
72472	Trumann	(501)	6,346	6,395
72956	Van Buren	(501)	14,899	12,020
71671	Warren	(870)	6,455	7,646
72390	West Helena	(870)	10,137	11,367
*72301	West Memphis	(870)	28,259	28,138
72396	Wynne	(870)	8,817	7,927

California

Area code (925) goes into effect on Mar. 14, 1998. Before then, use (510).
Area code (949) goes into effect on Apr. 18, 1998. Before then, use (714).
Area code (323) goes into effect on June 13, 1998. Before then, use (213).
Area code (831) goes into effect on July 11, 1998. Before then, use (408).

ZIP	Place		1990	1980
94301	Adelanto	(805)	6,791	2,164
*91376	Agoura Hills†	(818)	20,391	11,399
*94501	Alameda	(510)	73,979	63,852
94507	Alamo(u)	(925)	12,277	8,505
94706	Albany	(510)	16,327	15,130

ZIP	Place		1990	1980
*91802	Alhambra .... (323)/	(626)	82,087	64,767
92656	Aliso Viejo(u)	(949)	7,612	....
90249	Alondra Park(u)	(310)	12,215	12,189
*91901	Alpine(u) (San Diego)..	(619)	9,695	5,368
*91001	Altadena(u)	(626)	42,658	40,983
95945	Alta Sierra(u)	(530)	5,709	2,168
94589	American Canyon(u)	(707)	7,706	5,712
*92803	Anaheim	(714)	266,406	219,494
96007	Anderson	(530)	8,299	7,381
*94509	Antioch	(925)	62,195	42,683
*92307	Apple Valley†	(760)	46,079	16,748
*95003	Aptos(u)	(831)	9,061	7,039
*91006	Arcadia	(626)	48,284	45,993
95521	Arcata	(707)	15,211	12,849
95825	Arden-Arcade(u)	(916)	92,040	87,570
*93420	Arroyo Grande	(805)	14,432	11,290
*90701	Artesia	(562)	15,464	14,301
93203	Arvin	(805)	9,286	6,863
94577	Ashland(u)	(510)	16,590	13,893
93422	Atascadero	(805)	23,138	16,232
94025	Atherton	(650)	7,163	7,797
95301	Atwater	(209)	22,282	17,530
*95603	Auburn	(530)	10,653	7,540
95201	August(u)	(209)	6,376	5,445
93204	Avenal	(209)	9,770	4,137
91746	Avocado Heights(u)	(626)	14,232	11,733
91702	Azusa	(626)	41,203	29,380
*93302	Bakersfield	(805)	174,978	105,611
91706	Baldwin Park	(626)	69,330	50,554
92220	Banning	(909)	20,572	14,020
*92312	Barstow	(760)	21,472	17,690
94565	Bay Point(u)	(925)	17,453	10,244
93402	Baywood-Los Osos(u) ...	(805)	14,377	10,933
95903	Beale AFB(u)	(530)	6,912	6,329
92223	Beaumont	(909)	9,685	6,818
90201	Bell	(323)	34,365	25,450
*90706	Bellflower	(323)	61,815	53,441
90201	Bell Gardens .. (213)/(323)/	(562)	42,315	34,117
94002	Belmont	(650)	24,165	24,505
94510	Benicia	(707)	24,437	15,376
95005	Ben Lomond(u)	(831)	7,884	7,238
*94704	Berkeley	(510)	102,724	103,328
*90210	Beverly Hills.... (213)/(310)/	(323)	31,971	32,646
92315	Big Bear Lake†	(909)	5,351	4,896
94506	Black Hawk(u)	(925)	6,199	....
92316	Bloomington(u)	(909)	15,116	12,781
*92225	Blythe	(760)	8,448	6,805
93637	Bonadella Ranchos-Madera Ranchos(u).	(209)	5,705	3,272
91902	Bonita(u)	(619)	12,542	6,257
92021	Bostonia(u)	(619)	13,670	....
95006	Boulder Creek(u)	(831)	6,725	5,662
95416	Boyes Hot Springs(u)	(707)	5,973	4,177
92227	Brawley	(760)	18,923	14,946
*92622	Brea .... (562)/	(714)	32,873	27,913
94513	Brentwood	(925)	7,563	4,434
*90622	Buena Park	(714)	68,784	64,165
*91510	Burbank	(818)	93,649	84,625
*94010	Burlingame	(650)	26,666	26,173
*92231	Calexico	(760)	18,633	14,412
*93504	California City	(805)	5,955	2,743
*93010	Camarillo	(805)	52,297	37,797
93428	Cambria(u)	(805)	5,382	3,061
95682	Cameron Park(u)	(530)	11,897	5,607
95008	Campbell	(408)	36,048	26,843
92055	Camp Pendleton North(u)..	(949)	10,373	2,065
92055	Camp Pendleton South(u)..	(949)	11,299	7,952
92587	Canyon Lake(u)	(909)	7,938	2,039
95010	Capitola	(831)	10,171	9,095
*92008	Carlsbad	(760)	63,292	35,490
*95608	Carmichael(u)	(916)	48,702	43,108
*93013	Carpinteria	(805)	13,747	10,835
*90745	Carson	(310)	83,995	81,221
92077	Casa de Oro-Mt. Helix(u)..	(619)	30,727	19,651
*94544	Castro Valley(u)	(510)	48,619	43,810
95012	Castroville	(831)	5,272	4,396
*92235	Cathedral City†	(760)	30,085	11,096
95307	Ceres	(209)	26,413	13,281
90703	Cerritos	(562)	53,244	53,020
91724	Charter Oak(u)	(626)	8,858	6,840
94541	Cherryland(u)	(510)	11,088	9,425
92223	Cherry Valley(u)	(909)	5,945	5,012
*95926	Chico	(530)	39,970	26,716
*91708	Chino	(909)	59,682	40,165
91709	Chino Hills(u)	(909)	27,608	....
93610	Chowchilla	(209)	5,930	5,122
*91910	Chula Vista	(619)	135,160	83,927
91702	Citrus(u)	(626)	9,481	12,450
*95621	Citrus Heights(u)	(916)	107,439	85,911
91711	Claremont	(909)	32,610	31,028
94517	Clayton	(925)	7,317	4,325
95422	Clearlake†	(707)	11,804	8,343
*93612	Clovis	(209)	50,323	33,021
92236	Coachella	(760)	16,896	9,129
93210	Coalinga	(209)	8,212	6,593
92324	Colton	(909)	40,213	21,310
90022	Commerce ...... (323)/	(562)	12,135	10,509
*90221	Compton	(310)	90,454	81,350
*94520	Concord	(925)	111,308	103,763
93212	Corcoran	(209)	13,360	6,454

ZIP	Place	1990	1980	ZIP	Place	1990	1980
96021	Corning . . . . (530)	5,870	4,745	92546	Hemet. . . . . (909)	36,094	22,531
*91718	Corona . . . . (909)	75,943	37,791	94547	Hercules . . . . (510)	16,829	5,963
*92118	Coronado. . . . . (619)	26,540	18,790	90254	Hermosa Beach . . . . (310)	18,219	18,070
*94925	Corte Madera . . . . (415)	8,272	8,074	*92340	Hesperia† . . . . (760)	50,418	20,612
*92628	Costa Mesa . . . . . . (714)//(949)	96,357	82,562	92346	Highland† . . . . (909)	34,439	21,720
94931	Cotati . . . . (707)	5,714	3,346	94010	Hillsborough . . . . (650)	10,667	10,372
94556	Country Club(u) . . . . (209)	9,325	9,585	*95023	Hollister . . . . (831)	19,318	11,488
*91722	Covina . . . . (626)	43,332	32,746	91720	Home Gardens(u) . . . . . . (909)	7,780	5,783
92325	Crestline(u) . . . . (909)	8,594	6,715	*92647	Huntington Beach . . . . . . (714)	181,519	170,505
90201	Cudahy . . . . (323)	22,817	18,275	90255	Huntington Park . . . . (323)	56,129	45,932
*90230	Culver City . . . . (230)/(310)/(323)	38,793	38,139	*91932	Imperial Beach . . . . (619)	26,512	22,689
*95014	Cupertino. . . . . (408)	39,967	34,297	*92201	Indio . . . . (760)	36,850	21,611
90630	Cypress. . . . . (714)	42,655	40,738	*90301	Inglewood . . . . (213)/(310)/(323)	109,602	94,162
*94015	Daly City . . . . (415)//(650)	92,088	78,519	.....	Interlaken(u).	6,404	....
92629	Dana Point† . . . . (949)	31,896	21,271	95640	Ione . . . . (916)	6,516	2,207
*94526	Danville† . . . . (925)	31,306	26,143	*92719	Irvine . . . . (714)//(949)	110,330	62,134
95616	Davis . . . . (530)	46,322	36,640	93117	Isla Vista(u) . . . . (805)	20,395	....
90250	Del Aire(u) . . . . (310)	8,040	8,487	94914	Kentfield(u) . . . . (415)	6,030	....
*93215	Delano . . . . (805)	22,762	16,491	93630	Kerman . . . . (209)	5,448	4,002
93953	Del Monte Forest(u) . . . . . (831)	5,069	....	93930	King City . . . . (831)	7,634	5,495
*92240	Desert Hot Springs . . . . . (760)	11,668	5,941	93631	Kingsburg . . . . (209)	7,245	5,115
*91765	Diamond Bar . . . . (909)	53,672	....	*91011	La Cañada Flintridge . . . . (818)	19,378	20,153
93618	Dinuba . . . . (209)	12,743	9,907	*91224	La Crescenta-Montrose(u) . (818)	16,968	16,531
94514	Discovery Bay(u). . . . . . . (925)	5,351	1,326	90045	Ladera Heights(u) . . . . . . (310)	6,316	6,647
95620	Dixon . . . . (707)	10,417	7,541	94549	Lafayette . . . . (925)	23,366	20,837
*90241	Downey . . . . (562)	91,444	82,602	.....	Laguna(u)	9,828	....
*91009	Duarte. . . . . (626)	20,716	16,766	*92607	Laguna Beach . . . . (949)	23,170	17,858
94568	Dublin† . . . . (925)	23,229	13,496	*92654	Laguna Hills(u) . . . . (949)	46,731	33,600
93219	Earlimart(u) . . . . (805)	5,881	4,578	92607	Laguna Niguel† . . . . (949)	44,723	12,237
90220	East Compton(u) . . . . (310)	7,967	6,435	*90631	La Habra . . . . (562)//(949)	51,263	45,232
.....	East Foothills(u)	14,898	16,890	90631	La Habra Heights . . . . . . (562)	6,226	4,786
92343	East Hemet(u) . . . . (909)	17,611	14,712	92352	Lake Arrowhead(u) . . . . . . (909)	6,539	6,272
90638	East La Mirada(u) . . . . . . (562)	9,367	9,688	*92531	Lake Elsinore† . . . . (909)	18,316	5,982
90022	East Los Angeles(u). . (323)/(562)	126,379	110,017	92530	Lakeland Village(u) . . . . . (909)	5,159	2,796
94303	East Palo Alto† . . . . (650)	23,451	18,106	93535	Lake Los Angeles(u) . . . . (805)	7,977	....
91117	East Pasadena(u)	5,910	....	92040	Lakeside(u) . . . . (619)	39,412	23,921
93257	East Porterville(u) . . . . . . (209)	5,790	5,218	*90714	Lakewood . . . . (562)	73,553	74,511
.....	East San Gabriel(u) . . . . . (626)	12,736	....	*91941	La Mesa . . . . (619)	52,911	50,308
*93523	Edwards AFB(u) . . . . (805)	7,423	8,554	*90638	La Mirada . . . . (562)//(714)	40,452	40,986
*92020	El Cajon. . . . . (619)	88,693	73,892	93241	Lamont(u) . . . . (805)	11,517	9,616
*92244	El Centro . . . . (760)	31,405	23,996	*93539	Lancaster . . . . (805)	97,300	48,027
94530	El Cerrito . . . . (510)	22,869	22,731	90623	La Palma . . . . (562)//(714)	15,392	15,399
95762	El Dorado Hills(u) . . . . . . (916)	6,395	3,453	*91747	La Puente . . . . (626)	36,955	30,882
*95624	Elk Grove(u) . . . . (916)	17,483	10,959	92253	La Quinta† . . . . (909)	11,215	4,027
*91734	El Monte . . . . (626)	106,162	79,494	95401	La Riviera(u) . . . . (916)	10,986	10,906
*93446	El Paso de Robles . . . . . . (805)	18,583	9,163	95403	Larkfield-Wikiup(u) . . . . . . (707)	6,779	....
93030	El Rio(u) . . . . (805)	6,419	5,674	*94939	Larkspur . . . . (415)	11,068	11,064
90245	El Segundo . . . . (310)	15,223	13,752	95330	Lathrop† . . . . (209)	6,841	4,112
*94802	El Sobrante(u) . . . . (510)	9,852	10,535	91750	La Verne . . . . (909)	30,843	23,508
92630	El Toro(u) . . . . (949)	62,685	38,153	*90260	Lawndale. . . . . (310)	27,331	23,460
92709	El Toro Station(u) . . . . . . (949)	6,869	7,632	*91945	Lemon Grove . . . . (619)	23,984	20,780
*94612	Emeryville. . . . . (510)	5,740	3,714	93245	Lemoore . . . . (209)	13,622	8,832
*92024	Encinitas† . . . . (760)	55,406	36,550	90304	Lennox(u) . . . . (310)	22,757	18,445
*92025	Escondido . . . . (760)	108,648	64,355	95648	Lincoln . . . . (916)	7,248	4,132
*95501	Eureka . . . . (707)	27,025	24,153	95901	Linda(u). . . . . (530)	13,033	10,225
93221	Exeter . . . . (209)	7,276	5,606	93247	Lindsay . . . . (209)	8,338	6,936
*94930	Fairfax. . . . . (415)	6,931	7,391	95062	Live Oak(u) (Santa Cruz) . . (831)	15,212	11,482
94533	Fairfield . . . . (707)	78,650	58,099	*94550	Livermore . . . . (925)	56,741	48,349
95628	Fair Oaks(u) (Sacramento) . (916)	26,867	22,602	95334	Livingston . . . . (209)	7,317	5,326
96052	Fairview(u) (Trinity)	9,045	....	*95240	Lodi . . . . (209)	51,874	35,221
*92028	Fallbrook(u) . . . . (760)	22,095	14,041	92354	Loma Linda . . . . (909)	18,470	10,694
93223	Farmersville . . . . (209)	6,235	5,544	90717	Lomita . . . . (213)	19,442	18,807
95018	Felton(u) . . . . (831)	5,350	4,564	*93436	Lompoc. . . . . (805)	37,649	26,267
*93015	Fillmore . . . . (805)	11,992	9,602	*90801	Long Beach . . . . (310)//(562)	429,321	361,498
90001	Florence-Graham(u) . . . . . (323)	57,147	48,662	95650	Loomis† . . . . (916)	5,705	3,663
95828	Florin(u). . . . . (916)	24,330	16,523	*90720	Los Alamitos . . (562)//(562)//(949)	11,788	11,529
*95630	Folsom . . . . (916)	29,802	11,003	*94022	Los Altos . . . . (650)	26,599	25,769
*92334	Fontana. . . . . (909)	87,535	36,804	94022	Los Altos Hills. . . . . (650)	7,514	7,421
95841	Foothill Farms(u) . . . . (916)	17,135	13,700	*90086	Los Angeles (213)/(310)/(323)/(818)	3,485,557	2,968,528
95437	Fort Bragg . . . . (707)	6,078	5,019	93635	Los Banos . . . . (209)	14,519	10,341
95540	Fortuna. . . . . (707)	8,788	7,591	*95030	Los Gatos . . . . (408)	27,357	26,906
94404	Foster City . . . . (650)	28,176	23,287	91709	Los Serranos(u) . . . . (909)	7,099	....
92728	Fountain Valley . . . . (714)	53,691	55,080	94903	Lucas Valley-Marinwood(u). . (415)	5,982	6,409
95019	Freedom(u) . . . . (831)	8,361	6,416	90262	Lynwood . . . . . (213)/(310)/(323)	61,945	48,289
*94537	Fremont . . . . (510)	173,339	131,945	93250	Mc Farland . . . . (805)	7,005	5,151
*93706	Fresno. . . . . (209)	354,091	217,491	95521	McKinleyville(u) . . . . (707)	10,749	7,772
*92634	Fullerton . . . . (714)	114,144	102,246	*93638	Madera . . . . (209)	29,282	21,732
95632	Galt . . . . (209)	8,889	5,514	93637	Madera Acres(u) . . . . (209)	5,245	2,173
*90247	Gardena . . . . (310)	49,841	45,165	95954	Magalia(u) . . . . (530)	8,987	....
95205	Garden Acres(u) . . . . (209)	8,547	7,361	*90266	Manhattan Beach . . . . . . (310)	32,063	31,542
*92642	Garden Grove. . . . . (714)	143,965	123,307	*95336	Manteca . . . . (209)	40,773	24,925
92394	George AFB(u) . . . . (760)	5,085	7,061	92518	March AFB(u). . . . . (909)	5,523	3,607
*95020	Gilroy . . . . (408)	31,487	21,641	93933	Marina . . . . (831)	26,512	20,647
92509	Glen Avon(u) . . . . (909)	12,663	8,444	*90291	Marina Del Rey(u) . . . . . . (310)	7,431	6,336
*91209	Glendale . . . . . (323)/(626)//(818)	180,038	139,060	94553	Martinez . . . . (925)	31,808	22,582
91741	Glendora . . . . (626)	47,832	38,500	95901	Marysville . . . . (530)	12,324	9,898
93561	Golden Hills(u)	5,423	....	90270	Maywood . . . . (323)	27,893	21,810
92313	Grand Terrace . . . . (909)	10,946	8,498	93640	Mendota . . . . (209)	6,821	5,038
*95945	Grass Valley. . . . . (530)	9,048	6,697	*94025	Menlo Park . . . . (650)	28,403	26,438
93308	Greenacres(u) . . . . (805)	7,379	5,381	92359	Mentone(u) . . . . (909)	5,675	....
93927	Greenfield (Monterey) . . . . (831)	7,464	4,181	*95340	Merced . . . . (209)	56,155	36,423
93433	Grover City. . . . . (805)	11,602	8,827	94030	Millbrae . . . . (650)	20,414	20,058
93434	Guadalupe . . . . (805)	5,479	3,629	*94941	Mill Valley . . . . (415)	13,038	12,967
91745	Hacienda Heights(u) . . . . . (626)	52,354	49,422	*95035	Milpitas . . . . (408)	50,690	37,820
94019	Half Moon Bay . . . . (650)	8,886	7,282	91752	Mira Loma(u) . . . . (909)	15,786	7,394
*93230	Hanford . . . . (209)	30,463	20,958	93641	Mira Monte(u). . . . . (805)	7,744	....
90716	Hawaiian Gardens(u) . . . . (323)	13,639	10,548	*92691	Mission Viejo† . . . . (949)	72,820	48,503
*90250	Hawthorne . . . . . (213)/(310)/(323)	71,349	56,437	*95350	Modesto . . . . (209)	164,746	106,963
*94544	Hayward . . . . (510)	111,343	93,585	*91017	Monrovia . . . . (626)	35,733	30,531
95448	Healdsburg . . . . (707)	9,460	7,217	91763	Montclair . . . . (909)	28,434	22,628

ZIP	Place	1990	1980
90640	Montebello (323)	59,564	52,929
93940	Monterey (831)	31,954	27,558
*91754	Monterey Park (323)/(626)/(818)	60,738	54,338
*93021	Moorpark† (805)	25,494	7,798
*94556	Moraga (925)	15,987	15,014
*92552	Moreno Valley† (909)	118,779	28,139
*95037	Morgan Hill (408)	23,928	17,060
*93442	Morro Bay (805)	9,664	9,064
*94041	Mountain View (650)	67,365	58,655
92405	Muscoy(u) (714)	7,541	6,188
*94558	Napa (707)	61,865	50,879
*91950	National City (619)	54,249	48,772
92363	Needles (760)	5,191	4,120
94560	Newark (510)	37,861	32,126
*92658	Newport Beach (949)	66,643	62,556
93444	Nipomo(u) (805)	7,109	5,247
91760	Norco (909)	23,302	19,732
95603	North Auburn(u) (530)	10,301	7,619
94025	North Fair Oaks(u) (650)	13,912	10,308
95660	North Highlands(u) (916)	42,105	37,825
90650	Norwalk (562)	94,279	84,901
*94947	Novato (415)	47,585	43,916
95361	Oakdale (209)	11,978	8,474
*94617	Oakland (510)	372,242	339,337
94561	Oakley(u) (925)	18,374	2,816
93445	Oceano(u) (805)	6,169	4,478
*92054	Oceanside (760)	128,090	76,698
93308	Oildale(u) (805)	26,553	23,382
*93023	Ojai (805)	7,613	6,816
95961	Olivehurst(u) (530)	9,738	8,929
*91761	Ontario (909)	133,179	88,820
95060	Opal Cliffs(u) (831)	5,940	5,041
*92613	Orange (714)	110,658	91,450
93646	Orange Cove (209)	5,604	4,026
95662	Orangevale(u) (916)	26,266	20,585
94563	Orinda† (925)	16,642	17,030
95963	Orland (530)	5,052	4,031
93647	Orosi(u) (209)	5,486	4,076
*95965	Oroville (530)	11,885	8,683
95965	Oroville East(u) (530)	8,462	....
*93030	Oxnard (805)	142,560	108,195
94044	Pacifica (650)	37,670	36,866
93950	Pacific Grove (831)	16,117	15,755
95968	Palermo(u) (530)	5,260	2,572
93590	Palmdale (805)	68,946	12,277
92260	Palm Desert (760)	23,252	11,801
.....	Palm Desert Country(u)	5,626	....
*92262	Palm Springs (760)	40,144	32,359
*94303	Palo Alto (650)	55,900	55,225
90274	Palos Verdes Estates (310)	13,512	14,376
*95969	Paradise (530)	25,401	22,571
90723	Paramount (562)	47,669	36,407
95823	Parkway-So. Sacramento(u) (916)	31,903	26,815
93648	Parlier (209)	7,938	2,902
*91109	Pasadena (323)/(626)/(818)	131,586	118,072
	Paso Robles. See El Paso de Robles		
95363	Patterson (209)	8,626	3,908
92509	Pedley(u)	8,869	....
*92572	Perris (909)	21,500	6,827
*94952	Petaluma (707)	43,166	33,834
*90660	Pico Rivera (562)	59,177	53,387
*94612	Piedmont (510)	10,602	10,498
94564	Pinole (510)	17,460	14,253
*93449	Pismo Beach (805)	7,669	5,364
94565	Pittsburg (925)	47,607	33,465
92670	Placentia (714)	41,259	35,041
95667	Placerville (530)	8,286	6,739
94523	Pleasant Hill (925)	31,583	25,547
*94566	Pleasanton (925)	50,570	35,160
*91769	Pomona (909)	131,700	92,742
*93257	Porterville (209)	29,521	19,707
*93041	Port Hueneme (805)	20,322	17,803
92064	Poway† (619)	43,396	33,439
93907	Prunedale(u) (831)	7,393	....
*93551	Quartz Hill(u) (805)	9,626	7,421
92065	Ramona(u) (760)	13,040	8,173
*95670	Rancho Cordova(u) (916)	48,731	42,881
*91729	Rancho Cucamonga (909)	101,409	55,250
92270	Rancho Mirage (760)	9,778	6,281
*90275	Rancho Palos Verdes (310)	41,667	36,577
91941	Rancho San Diego(u) (619)	6,977	....
92688	Rancho Santa Margarita(u) (949)	11,390	....
96080	Red Bluff (530)	12,363	9,490
*96049	Redding (530)	66,462	42,103
*92373	Redlands (909)	60,395	43,619
*90277	Redondo Beach (310)	60,167	57,102
*94063	Redwood City (650)	66,072	54,951
93654	Reedley (209)	15,791	11,071
*92377	Rialto (909)	72,395	37,862
*94802	Richmond (510)	86,019	74,676
*93555	Ridgecrest (760)	28,295	15,929
95003	Rio Del Mar(u) (831)	8,919	7,067
95673	Rio Linda(u) (916)	9,481	7,359
95366	Ripon (209)	7,455	3,509
95367	Riverbank (209)	8,591	5,695
*92502	Riverside (909)	226,546	170,591
*95677	Rocklin (916)	18,806	7,344
94572	Rodeo(u) (510)	7,589	8,286
*94928	Rohnert Park (707)	36,326	22,965
90274	Rolling Hills Estates (310)	7,789	7,701
93560	Rosamond(u) (805)	7,430	2,869
95401	Roseland(u) (707)	8,779	7,915
91770	Rosemead (626)	51,638	42,604
95826	Rosemont(u) (916)	22,851	18,888
*95678	Roseville (916)	44,685	24,347
90720	Rossmoor(u) (714)	9,893	10,457
91748	Rowland Heights(u) (818)	42,647	28,258
92509	Rubidoux(u) (909)	24,367	17,048
*95814	Sacramento (916)	369,365	275,741
*93907	Salinas (831)	108,777	80,479
*94960	San Anselmo (415)	11,735	12,067
*92401	San Bernardino (909)	164,164	118,794
*94066	San Bruno (650)	38,961	35,417
*93001	San Buenaventura (Ventura) (805)	92,557	73,774
94070	San Carlos (650)	26,382	24,710
*92674	San Clemente (949)	41,100	27,325
*92138	San Diego (619)	1,110,623	875,538
92065	San Diego Country Estates(u) (760)	6,874	....
91773	San Dimas (909)	32,398	24,014
*91341	San Fernando (818)	22,580	17,731
*94142	San Francisco (415)	723,959	678,974
*91778	San Gabriel (626)	37,120	30,072
93657	Sanger (209)	16,839	12,542
*92581	San Jacinto (909)	16,210	7,098
*95113	San Jose (408)	782,224	629,400
*92675	San Juan Capistrano (949)	26,183	18,959
*94577	San Leandro (510)	68,223	63,952
94580	San Lorenzo(u) (510)	19,987	20,545
*93401	San Luis Obispo (805)	41,958	34,252
*92069	San Marcos (760)	38,974	17,479
*91118	San Marino (626)	12,959	13,307
*94402	San Mateo (650)	85,619	77,640
94806	San Pablo (510)	25,158	19,750
*94915	San Rafael (415)	48,410	44,700
94583	San Ramon† (925)	35,303	20,511
*92711	Santa Ana (714)/(949)	293,827	204,023
*93102	Santa Barbara (805)	85,571	74,414
*95050	Santa Clara (408)	93,613	87,700
*91380	Santa Clarita (805)	110,690	....
*95060	Santa Cruz (831)	49,711	41,483
90670	Santa Fe Springs (562)	15,520	14,520
93454	Santa Maria (805)	61,552	39,685
*90401	Santa Monica (310)	86,905	88,314
*93060	Santa Paula (805)	25,062	20,658
*95402	Santa Rosa (707)	113,261	82,658
92071	Santee† (619)	52,902	40,298
*95070	Saratoga (408)	28,061	29,261
*94965	Sausalito (415)	7,152	7,338
*95066	Scotts Valley (831)	8,667	6,891
90740	Seal Beach (714)	25,098	25,975
93955	Seaside (831)	38,826	36,567
*95472	Sebastopol (707)	7,008	5,595
93662	Selma (209)	14,757	10,942
93263	Shafter (805)	8,409	7,010
*91025	Sierra Madre (626)	10,762	10,837
90806	Signal Hill (562)	8,371	5,734
*93065	Simi Valley (805)	100,218	77,500
92075	Solana Beach† (619)	12,956	12,250
93960	Soledad (831)	7,161	5,928
95476	Sonoma (707)	8,168	6,054
95073	Soquel(u) (831)	9,188	6,212
91733	South El Monte (626)	20,850	16,623
90280	South Gate (323)/(562)	86,284	66,784
*96151	South Lake Tahoe (530)	21,586	20,681
95965	South Oroville(u) (530)	7,463	7,246
*91030	South Pasadena (213)/(323)/(626)/(818)	23,936	22,681
*94080	South San Francisco (650)	54,312	49,393
91770	South San Gabriel(u) (626)	7,700	5,421
91744	South San Jose Hills(u) (626)	17,814	16,076
90605	South Whittier(u) (562)	49,514	43,815
95991	South Yuba(u) (530)	8,816	7,530
*91977	Spring Valley(u) (619)	55,331	40,191
94305	Stanford(u) (650)	18,097	11,045
90680	Stanton (714)	30,491	23,723
*95208	Stockton (209)	210,943	148,283
94585	Suisun City (707)	22,704	11,087
*92586	Sun City(u) (714)	14,930	8,460
*94086	Sunnyvale (408)	117,324	106,618
96130	Susanville (530)	7,279	6,520
93268	Taft (805)	5,902	5,316
94941	Tamalpais-Homestead Valley(u) (415)	9,601	8,511
*93581	Tehachapi (805)	6,182	4,126
*92589	Temecula† (909)	27,177	4,289
91780	Temple City (626)	31,153	28,972
95965	Thermalito(u) (530)	5,646	4,961
*91359	Thousand Oaks (805)	104,381	77,072
94920	Tiburon (415)	7,554	6,685
*90503	Torrance (310)	133,107	129,881
*95376	Tracy (209)	33,558	18,428
*93274	Tulare (209)	33,249	22,530
*95380	Turlock (209)	42,224	26,287
*92681	Tustin (714)/(949)	50,689	32,248
92705	Tustin Foothills(u) (714)	24,358	26,174
*92277	Twentynine Palms† (760)	11,821	8,802
92278	Twentynine Palms Base(u) (760)	10,606	7,079
95060	Twin Lakes(u) (831)	5,379	4,502
95482	Ukiah (707)	14,632	12,035
94587	Union City (510)	53,762	39,406

ZIP	Place		1990	1980
*91785	Upland	(909)	63,374	47,647
*95687	Vacaville	(707)	71,476	43,367
91744	Valinda(u)	(626)	18,735	18,712
*94590	Vallejo	(707)	109,199	80,303
92343	Valle Vista(u)	(909)	8,751	5,474
93437	Vandenberg AFB(u)	(805)	9,846	8,136
93436	Vandenberg Village(u)	(805)	5,971	5,839
	Ventura. *See San Buenaventura*			
*92393	Victorville	(760)	40,674	14,220
90043	View Park-Windsor Hills(u)	(310)	11,769	12,101
92667	Villa Park	(714)	6,299	7,137
.....	Vincent(u)		13,713	....
*93277	Visalia	(209)	75,659	49,729
*92083	Vista	(760)	71,865	35,834
*91788	Walnut	(909)	29,105	12,478
*94596	Walnut Creek	(925)	60,569	54,033
90255	Walnut Park(u)	(213)	14,722	11,811
93280	Wasco	(805)	12,412	9,613
*95076	Watsonville	(831)	31,099	23,662
90044	West Athens(u)	(310)	8,859	8,531
90502	West Carson(u)	(323)	20,143	17,997
90247	West Compton(u)	(310)	5,451	5,907
*91793	West Covina	(626)	96,226	80,292
90069	West Hollywood†	(310)/(323)	36,118	35,754
91359	Westlake Village†	(805)	7,455	6,130
92684	Westminster	(714)	78,293	71,133
90047	Westmont(u)	(323)	31,044	27,916
91746	West Puente Valley(u)	(626)	20,254	20,445
95691	West Sacramento†	(916)	28,898	24,482
*90606	West Whittier-Los Nietos(u)	(562)	24,164	21,001
*90605	Whittier	(562)	77,671	68,558
92595	Wildomar(u)	(909)	10,411	....
95490	Willits	(707)	5,027	4,008
90222	Willowbrook(u)	(323)	32,772	30,962
95988	Willows	(530)	5,988	4,777
95492	Windsor(u)	(707)	13,371	....
95388	Winton(u)	(209)	7,559	4,995
92502	Woodcrest(u)	(909)	7,796	....
93286	Woodlake	(209)	5,678	4,343
*95695	Woodland	(530)	40,230	30,235
94062	Woodside	(650)	5,034	5,291
*92686	Yorba Linda	(714)	52,422	28,254
96097	Yreka	(530)	6,948	5,916
*95991	Yuba City	(530)	27,385	18,736
92399	Yucaipa†	(909)	32,824	27,654
*92286	Yucca Valley(u)	(760)	13,701	8,294

Colorado

ZIP	Place		1990	1980
*80840	Air Force Academy	(719)	9,062	8,655
81101	Alamosa	(719)	7,579	6,830
80401	Applewood(u)	(303)	11,069	12,040
*80004	Arvada	(303)	89,218	84,576
*81611	Aspen	(970)	5,049	3,678
*80017	Aurora	(303)	222,103	158,588
80908	Black Forest(u)	(719)	8,143	3,372
*80302	Boulder	(303)	83,295	76,685
80601	Brighton	(303)	14,203	12,773
*80020	Broomfield	(303)	24,638	20,730
*81212	Canon City	(719)	12,687	13,037
80104	Castle Rock	(303)	8,710	3,921
80120	Castlewood(u)	(303)	24,392	16,413
80110	Cherry Hills Village	(303)	5,245	5,127
81220	Cimarron Hills(u)	(719)	11,160	6,597
81520	Clifton(u)	(970)	12,671	5,223
*80903	Colorado Springs	(719)	280,430	215,105
80120	Columbine(u)	(303)	23,969	23,523
*80022	Commerce City	(303)	16,466	16,234
81321	Cortez	(970)	7,284	7,095
*81625	Craig	(970)	8,091	8,133
*80202	Denver	(303)	467,610	492,686
80022	Derby(u)	(303)	6,043	8,578
*81301	Durango	(970)	12,439	11,649
*80110	Englewood	(303)	29,396	30,021
80620	Evans	(970)	5,876	5,063
80439	Evergreen(u)	(303)	7,582	6,376
80221	Federal Heights	(303)	9,342	7,838
80913	Fort Carson(u)	(719)	11,309	13,219
*80525	Fort Collins	(970)	87,491	65,092
80621	Fort Lupton	(970)	5,159	4,251
80701	Fort Morgan	(970)	9,068	8,768
80817	Fountain	(719)	10,175	8,324
81504	Fruitvale(u)	(303)	5,222	....
81522	Gateway(u)	(970)	7,510	....
*81601	Glenwood Springs	(970)	6,561	4,637
*80401	Golden	(303)	13,127	12,237
*81501	Grand Junction	(970)	29,255	27,956
*80631	Greeley	(970)	60,454	53,006
*80111	Greenwood Village	(303)	7,589	5,729
80501	Gunbarrel(u)	(303)	9,388	5,172
80126	Highlands Ranch(u)	(303)	10,181	....
80127	Ken Caryl(u)	(303)	24,391	10,661
80026	Lafayette	(303)	14,708	8,985
81050	La Junta	(719)	7,678	8,338
*80226	Lakewood	(303)	126,475	113,808
81052	Lamar	(719)	8,343	7,713
*80126	Littleton	(303)	33,711	28,631
*80501	Longmont	(303)	51,529	42,942
80027	Louisville	(303)	12,003	5,593

ZIP	Place		1990	1980
*80538	Loveland	(970)	37,357	30,215
*81401	Montrose	(970)	8,854	8,722
80233	Northglenn	(303)	27,195	29,847
80649	Orchard Mesa(u)	(303)	5,977	4,876
80134	Parker†	(303)	5,450	290
*81003	Pueblo	(719)	98,640	101,686
81503	Redlands(u)	(970)	9,355	....
80911	Security-Widefield(u)	(719)	23,822	18,768
80221	Sherrelwood(u)	(303)	16,636	17,629
80122	Southglenn(u)	(303)	43,087	37,787
*80477	Steamboat Springs	(970)	6,695	5,098
80751	Sterling	(970)	10,362	11,385
80906	Stratmoor(u)	(719)	5,854	5,519
80229	Thornton	(303)	55,031	42,054
81082	Trinidad	(719)	8,580	9,663
80229	Welby(u)	(303)	10,218	9,668
80030	Westminster	(303)	74,619	50,211
80221	Westminster East(u)	(303)	5,197	6,002
*80033	Wheat Ridge	(303)	29,419	30,293
80550	Windsor	(970)	5,062	4,277

Connecticut

See note on page 389

ZIP	Place		1990	1980
06401	Ansonia	(203)	18,403	19,039
06001	Avon	(860)	13,937	11,201
06403	Beacon Falls	(203)	5,083	3,995
06037	Berlin	(860)	16,787	15,121
06801	Bethel	(203)	17,541	16,004
06002	Bloomfield	(860)	19,483	18,608
06405	Branford	(203)	27,603	23,363
*06602	Bridgeport	(203)	141,686	142,546
*06010	Bristol	(860)	60,640	57,370
06804	Brookfield	(203)	14,113	12,872
06234	Brooklyn	(860)	6,681	5,691
06013	Burlington	(860)	7,026	5,660
06019	Canton	(860)	8,268	7,635
06040	Central Manchester(u)	(860)	30,934	31,058
06410	Cheshire	(203)	25,684	21,788
06413	Clinton	(860)	12,767	11,195
06415	Colchester	(860)	10,980	7,761
06340	Conning Towers-Nautilus Park(u)	(860)	10,013	9,665
06238	Coventry	(860)	10,063	8,895
06416	Cromwell	(860)	12,286	10,265
*06810	Danbury	(203)	65,585	60,470
06820	Darien	(203)	18,130	18,892
06418	Derby	(203)	12,199	12,346
06422	Durham	(860)	5,732	5,143
06423	East Haddam	(860)	6,676	5,621
06424	East Hampton	(860)	10,428	8,572
*06101	East Hartford(u)	(860)	50,452	52,563
06512	East Haven(u)	(203)	26,144	25,036
06333	East Lyme	(860)	15,340	13,870
06016	East Windsor	(860)	10,081	8,925
06425	Easton	(203)	6,303	5,962
06029	Ellington	(860)	11,197	9,711
*06082	Enfield	(860)	45,532	42,695
06426	Essex	(860)	5,904	5,078
06430	Fairfield	(203)	53,418	54,849
*06032	Farmington	(860)	20,608	16,407
06033	Glastonbury Center(u)	(860)	7,082	7,049
06035	Granby	(860)	9,369	7,956
*06830	Greenwich	(203)	58,441	59,565
06351	Griswold	(860)	10,384	8,967
06340	Groton	(860)	45,144	41,062
06340	Groton Borough	(860)	9,837	10,086
06437	Guilford	(203)	19,848	17,375
06438	Haddam	(860)	6,769	6,383
*06514	Hamden	(203)	52,434	51,071
*06101	Hartford	(860)	139,739	136,392
06791	Harwinton	(860)	5,228	4,889
06082	Hazardville(u)	(860)	5,179	5,436
06248	Hebron	(860)	7,079	5,453
06037	Kensington(u)	(860)	8,306	7,502
06239	Killingly	(860)	15,889	14,519
06249	Lebanon	(860)	6,041	4,762
06339	Ledyard	(860)	14,913	13,735
06759	Litchfield	(860)	8,365	7,605
06443	Madison	(203)	15,485	14,031
06040	Manchester	(860)	51,618	49,761
06250	Mansfield	(860)	21,103	20,634
06447	Marlborough	(860)	5,535	4,746
*06450	Meriden	(203)	59,479	57,118
06762	Middlebury	(203)	6,145	5,995
06457	Middletown	(860)	42,762	39,040
06460	Milford	(203)	49,938	48,168
06468	Monroe	(203)	16,896	14,010
06353	Montville	(860)	16,673	16,455
06770	Naugatuck	(203)	30,625	26,456
*06050	New Britain	(860)	75,491	73,840
06840	New Canaan	(203)	17,864	17,931
06810	New Fairfield	(203)	12,911	11,260
06057	New Hartford	(860)	5,769	4,884
*06511	New Haven	(203)	100,414	126,089
*06111	Newington(u)	(860)	29,208	28,841
06320	New London	(860)	28,540	28,842
06776	New Milford	(860)	23,629	19,420

ZIP	Place		1990	1980
06470	Newtown	(203)	20,779	19,107
06471	North Branford	(203)	12,996	11,554
06473	North Haven(u)	(203)	22,249	22,080
*06856	Norwalk	(203)	78,331	77,767
06360	Norwich	(860)	37,391	38,074
06779	Oakville(u)	(860)	8,741	8,737
06371	Old Lyme	(860)	6,535	6,159
06475	Old Saybrook	(860)	9,552	9,287
06477	Orange	(203)	12,830	13,237
06478	Oxford	(203)	8,685	6,634
02891	Pawcatuck(u)	(860)	5,289	5,216
06374	Plainfield	(860)	14,363	12,774
06062	Plainville	(860)	17,392	16,401
06782	Plymouth	(860)	11,822	10,732
06480	Portland	(860)	8,418	8,383
06365	Preston	(860)	5,006	4,644
06712	Prospect	(203)	7,775	6,807
06260	Putnam	(860)	6,835	6,855
06260	Putnam†	(860)	9,031	8,580
06898	Redding	(203)	7,927	7,272
06877	Ridgefield Center(u)	(203)	6,363	6,066
06877	Ridgefield	(203)	20,919	20,120
06067	Rocky Hill	(860)	16,554	14,559
06483	Seymour	(203)	14,288	13,434
06484	Shelton	(203)	35,418	31,314
06082	Sherwood Manor(u)	(860)	6,357	6,303
06070	Simsbury	(860)	22,023	21,161
06071	Somers	(860)	9,108	8,473
06488	Southbury	(203)	15,818	14,156
06489	Southington	(860)	38,518	36,879
06074	South Windsor	(860)	22,090	17,198
06082	Southwood Acres(u)	(860)	8,963	9,779
06075	Stafford	(860)	11,091	9,268
*06904	Stamford	(203)	108,056	102,466
06378	Stonington	(860)	16,919	16,220
06268	Storrs(u)	(860)	12,198	11,394
06497	Stratford(u)	(203)	49,389	50,541
06078	Suffield	(860)	11,427	9,294
06786	Terryville(u)	(860)	5,426	5,234
06787	Thomaston	(860)	6,947	6,272
06277	Thompson	(860)	8,668	8,141
06082	Thompsonville(u)	(860)	8,458	8,151
06084	Tolland	(860)	11,001	9,694
06790	Torrington	(860)	33,687	30,987
06611	Trumbull(u)	(203)	32,000	32,989
06066	Vernon	(860)	29,841	27,974
06492	Wallingford	(203)	40,822	37,274
*06701	Waterbury	(203)	108,961	103,266
06385	Waterford	(860)	17,930	17,843
06795	Watertown	(860)	20,456	19,489
06107	West Hartford(u)	(860)	60,110	61,301
06516	West Haven	(203)	54,021	53,184
06498	Westbrook	(860)	5,414	5,216
06883	Weston	(203)	8,648	8,284
*06880	Westport(u)	(203)	24,407	25,290
06109	Wethersfield(u)	(860)	25,651	26,013
06226	Willimantic(u)†	(860)	14,746	14,652
06279	Willington	(860)	5,979	4,694
06897	Wilton	(203)	15,989	15,351
06094	Winchester	(860)	11,524	10,841
06280	Windham	(860)	22,039	21,062
06095	Windsor	(860)	27,817	25,204
06096	Windsor Locks(u)	(860)	12,358	12,190
06098	Winsted	(860)	8,254	8,092
06716	Wolcott	(203)	13,700	13,008
06525	Woodbridge	(203)	7,924	7,761
06798	Woodbury	(203)	8,131	6,942
06281	Woodstock	(860)	6,008	5,117

Delaware (302)

ZIP	Place	1990	1980
19713	Brookside(u)	15,307	15,255
19703	Claymont(u)	9,800	10,022
*19901	Dover	27,630	23,507
19809	Edgemoor(u)	5,853	7,397
19805	Elsmere	5,935	6,493
19963	Milford	6,032	5,366
*19711	Newark	26,463	25,247
19800	Pike Creek(u)	10,163	....
19973	Seaford	5,689	5,256
19977	Smyrna	5,231	4,750
19804	Stanton(u)	5,028	5,495
19803	Talleyville(u)	6,346	6,880
*19899	Wilmington	71,529	70,195
19720	Wilmington Manor	8,568	9,233

District of Columbia (202)

ZIP	Place	1990	1980
*20090	Washington	606,900	638,432

Florida

ZIP	Place		1990	1980
*32714	Altamonte Springs	(407)	35,167	21,105
.....	Andover(u)		6,251	....
33572	Apollo Beach(u)	(813)	6,025	4,014
*32712	Apopka	(407)	13,611	6,019

ZIP	Place		1990	1980
33821	Arcadia	(941)	6,488	6,002
32233	Atlantic Beach	(904)	11,636	7,847
33823	Auburndale	(941)	8,846	6,501
33280	Aventura(u)	(305)	14,914	9,698
33825	Avon Park	(941)	8,078	8,026
32857	Azalea Park(u)	(407)	8,926	8,301
*33830	Bartow	(941)	14,716	14,780
.....	Bay Hill(u)		5,346	....
34667	Bayonet Point(u)	(813)	21,860	16,455
33505	Bayshore Gardens(u)	(813)	17,062	14,945
33589	Beacon Square(u)	(813)	6,265	6,513
34233	Bee Ridge	(941)	6,406	3,313
32073	Bellair-Meadowbrook Terrace(u)	(813)	15,606	12,144
33430	Belle Glade	(561)	16,177	16,535
*32802	Belle Isle	(407)	5,272	2,848
34420	Belleview	(352)	19,386	15,439
*34464	Beverly Hills(u)	(352)	6,163	5,024
*33509	Bloomingdale(u)	(813)	13,912	....
.....	Boca Del Mar(u)		17,754	....
*33431	Boca Raton	(561)	61,486	49,447
*33923	Bonita Springs(u)	(941)	13,600	5,435
*33436	Boynton Beach	(561)	46,284	35,624
*34206	Bradenton	(941)	43,769	30,228
*33509	Brandon(u)	(813)	57,985	41,826
32503	Brent(u)	(850)	21,624	21,872
33317	Broadview Park(u)	(954)	6,109	6,022
33313	Broadview-Pompano Park(u)	(954)	5,230	5,223
*34601	Brooksville	(352)	7,589	5,582
33311	Browardale(u)	(954)	6,257	7,409
33142	Brownsville(u)	(813)	15,607	18,058
34743	Buena Ventura Lakes(u)		14,148	....
32404	Callaway	(850)	12,253	7,154
32920	Cape Canaveral	(407)	8,014	5,733
*33990	Cape Coral	(941)	74,991	32,103
33055	Carol City(u)	(305)	53,331	47,349
*33688	Carrollwood(u)	(813)	7,195	....
*33601	Carrollwood Village(u)	(813)	15,051	....
*32707	Casselberry	(407)	18,849	15,037
33401	Century Village(u)	(305)	8,363	10,619
*34618	Clearwater	(813)	98,699	85,170
*34711	Clermont	(352)	6,910	5,461
33440	Clewiston	(941)	6,085	5,219
*32922	Cocoa	(407)	17,710	16,096
*32931	Cocoa Beach	(407)	12,123	10,926
32922	Cocoa West(u)	(407)	6,160	6,432
*33063	Coconut Creek	(954)	27,269	6,288
33064	Collier Manor-Cresthaven(u)	(954)	7,322	7,045
33801	Combee Settlement(u)	(813)	5,463	5,400
32809	Conway(u)	(407)	13,159	24,027
33328	Cooper City	(954)	21,335	10,140
33114	Coral Gables	(305)	40,091	43,241
*33060	Coral Springs	(954)	78,864	37,349
33157	Coral Terrace(u)	(305)	23,255	22,702
*32536	Crestview	(850)	9,886	7,617
33803	Crystal Lake(u)	(813)	5,300	6,827
33157	Cutler(u)	(305)	16,201	15,608
33157	Cutler Ridge(u)	(305)	21,268	20,886
33884	Cypress Gardens(u)	(941)	9,188	8,043
33919	Cypress Lake(u)	(941)	10,491	8,721
*33525	Dade City	(352)	5,633	4,923
33004	Dania	(954)	13,183	11,796
33314	Davie	(954)	47,143	20,500
*32114	Daytona Beach	(904)	61,991	54,176
32713	De Bary	(407)	7,176	4,980
*33441	Deerfield Beach	(954)	46,997	39,193
32433	DeFuniak Springs	(850)	5,200	5,563
*32720	De Land	(904)	16,622	15,354
*33444	Delray Beach	(561)	47,184	34,329
33617	Del Rio(u)	(813)	8,248	7,409
*32763	Deltona(u)	(407)	50,828	15,710
*32541	Destin†	(850)	8,090	3,913
.....	Doctor Phillips(u)		7,963	....
*34698	Dunedin	(813)	34,427	30,203
33610	East Lake-Orient Park(u)	(813)	6,171	5,612
33940	East Naples(u)	(941)	22,951	12,127
*32132	Edgewater	(904)	15,351	6,726
32542	Eglin AFB(u)	(850)	8,347	7,574
33614	Egypt Lake(u)	(813)	14,580	11,932
34680	Elfers(u)	(813)	12,356	11,396
*34223	Englewood(u)	(941)	15,025	10,229
32534	Ensley(u)	(850)	16,362	14,422
*32726	Eustis	(352)	12,856	9,453
32804	Fairview Shores(u)	(305)	13,192	10,174
*32034	Fernandina Beach	(904)	8,765	7,224
32730	Fern Park(u)	(407)	8,294	8,904
32514	Ferry Pass(u)	(850)	26,301	16,910
33034	Florida City	(305)	5,978	6,174
32960	Florida Ridge(u)	(561)	12,218	4,988
32714	Forest City(u)	(407)	10,638	6,819
.....	Forest Island Park(u)		5,988	....
*33310	Fort Lauderdale	(954)	149,238	153,279
*33902	Fort Myers	(941)	44,947	36,638
*33931	Fort Myers Beach(u)	(941)	9,284	5,753
*33922	Fort Myers Shores(u)	(941)	5,460	4,426
*34981	Fort Pierce	(561)	36,830	33,802
33452	Fort Pierce North(u)	(561)	5,833	5,929
34982	Fort Pierce South(u)	(561)	5,320	3,324
*32548	Fort Walton Beach	(850)	21,407	20,829
*32043	Fruit Cove(u)	(904)	5,904	3,906

ZIP	Place		1990	1980
34230	Fruitville(u)	(941)	9,808	2,551
*32602	Gainesville	(352)	85,075	81,371
33801	Gibsonia(u)	(813)	5,168	5,011
33534	Gibsonton(u)	(813)	7,706	....
32960	Gifford(u)	(561)	6,278	6,240
33138	Gladeview(u)	(954)	15,637	18,919
33143	Glenvar Heights(u)	(305)	14,823	13,216
33999	Golden Gate(u)	(941)	14,148	4,327
33055	Golden Glades(u)	(305)	25,474	23,154
32733	Goldenrod(u)	(407)	12,362	13,677
32560	Gonzalez(u)	(850)	7,669	6,084
33170	Goulds(u)	(305)	7,284	7,078
.....	Greater Northdale(u)		16,318	....
33463	Greenacres City	(561)	18,683	8,870
*32561	Gulf Breeze	(850)	5,530	5,478
33581	Gulf Gate Estates(u)	(813)	11,622	9,248
33707	Gulfport	(941)	11,709	11,180
*33844	Haines City	(941)	11,683	10,799
*33009	Hallandale	(305)/(954)	30,997	36,517
.....	Hammocks(u)		10,897	....
.....	Hamptons at Boca Raton(u)		11,686	....
*33010	Hialeah	(305)	188,004	145,254
33016	Hialeah Gardens	(305)	7,727	2,700
.....	Highpoint		13,818	....
*33455	Hobe Sound(u)	(561)	11,507	6,822
*34689	Holiday(u)	(813)	19,360	18,392
32117	Holly Hill	(904)	11,141	9,953
*33022	Hollywood	(954)	121,720	121,323
*33030	Homestead	(305)	26,694	20,668
33039	Homestead AFB(u)	(305)	5,153	7,594
34447	Homosassa Springs(u)†	(352)	6,271	1,426
*34667	Hudson(u)	(813)	7,344	5,799
33934	Immokalee(u)	(941)	14,120	11,038
32937	Indian Harbour Beach	(407)	6,933	5,967
*34450	Inverness	(352)	5,797	4,095
33880	Inwood(u)	(941)	6,824	6,668
.....	Iona(u)	(941)	9,565	....
33162	Ives Estates(u)	(305)	13,531	10,613
*32203	Jacksonville	(904)	635,230	540,920
32250	Jacksonville Beach	(904)	17,839	15,462
33880	Jan Phyl Village(u)	(941)	5,308	2,785
33568	Jasmine Estates(u)	(813)	17,136	11,995
*34957	Jensen Beach(u)	(561)	9,884	6,642
*33458	Jupiter	(561)	24,907	9,868
33183	Kendale Lakes(u)	(305)	48,524	32,769
33256	Kendall(u)	(305)	87,271	73,758
.....	Kendall Lakes West(u)	(305)	6,038	....
33149	Key Biscayne(u)	(305)	8,854	6,313
33037	Key Largo(u)	(305)	11,336	7,447
*33040	Key West	(305)	24,832	24,382
*33573	Kings Point(u)	(305)	12,422	8,724
*34744	Kissimmee	(407)	30,337	15,487
*32159	Lady Lake	(352)	8,071	1,193
*32055	Lake City	(904)	9,626	9,257
*33804	Lakeland	(941)	70,576	47,406
33801	Lakeland Highlands(u)	(941)	9,972	10,426
32569	Lake Lorraine(u)	(850)	6,779	5,427
33054	Lake Lucerne(u)	(305)	9,478	9,762
33612	Lake Magdalene(u)	(813)	15,973	13,256
*32746	Lake Mary	(407)	5,929	2,853
33403	Lake Park	(561)	6,704	6,909
.....	Lakes by the Bay(u)		5,615	....
32073	Lakeside(u)	(904)	29,137	10,534
*33853	Lake Wales	(941)	9,670	8,466
34951	Lakewood Park(u)	(561)	7,211	3,411
*33461	Lake Worth	(561)	28,564	27,048
34639	Land O'Lakes(u)	(813)	7,892	4,515
33462	Lantana	(561)	8,392	8,048
*34640	Largo	(813)	65,910	57,958
33313	Lauderdale Lakes	(954)	27,341	25,426
33313	Lauderhill	(954)	49,015	37,271
34272	Laurel(u)	(941)	8,245	6,368
33714	Lealman(u)	(813)	21,748	19,873
*34748	Leesburg	(352)	14,783	13,191
*33936	Lehigh Acres(u)	(813)	13,611	9,604
33033	Leisure City(u)	(305)	19,379	17,905
33074	Lighthouse Point	(954)	10,378	11,488
33177	Lindgren Acres(u)	(305)	22,290	11,986
32060	Live Oak	(904)	6,332	6,732
32860	Lockhart(u)	(407)	11,636	10,569
34228	Longboat Key	(941)	5,937	4,843
*32750	Longwood	(407)	13,316	10,029
33549	Lutz(u)	(813)	10,552	5,555
32444	Lynn Haven	(850)	9,270	6,239
.....	McGregor(u)		6,504	....
*32751	Maitland	(407)	8,932	8,763
33550	Mango(u) †	(813)	8,700	6,493
33050	Marathon(u)	(305)	8,857	7,568
*33937	Marco(u)	(941)	9,493	4,694
33063	Margate	(954)	42,985	35,900
*32446	Marianna	(850)	6,292	7,006
*32901	Melbourne	(407)	60,034	46,536
32666	Melrose Park(u)	(954)	6,477	5,672
33561	Memphis(u)	(941)	6,760	5,501
*32953	Merritt Island(u)	(407)	32,886	30,708
*33101	Miami	(305)	358,648	346,681
*33152	Miami Beach	(305)	92,639	96,298
33023	Miami Gardens-Utopia-Carver(u)	(954)	7,448	9,100
00014	Miami Lakes(u)	(003)	12,750	9,809
33153	Miami Shores	(305)	10,084	9,244
33166	Miami Springs	(305)	13,268	12,350
32976	Micco(u)	(561)	8,757	3,585
*32068	Middleburg(u)	(904)	6,223	....
*32570	Milton	(850)	7,216	7,206
32754	Mims(u)	(407)	9,412	7,583
33023	Miramar	(954)	40,663	32,813
32757	Mount Dora	(352)	7,316	5,883
32526	Myrtle Grove(u)	(850)	17,402	14,238
*33940	Naples	(941)	19,505	17,581
33940	Naples Park(u)	(941)	8,002	5,438
33092	Naranja(u)†	(305)	5,790	10,381
32266	Neptune Beach	(904)	6,816	5,248
*34653	New Port Richey	(813)	14,044	11,196
33552	New Port Richey East(u)	(813)	9,683	6,147
*32168	New Smyrna Beach	(904)	16,549	13,557
32578	Niceville	(850)	10,509	8,543
33269	Norland(u)	(305)	22,109	19,471
33308	North Andrews Gardens(u)	(954)	9,002	8,994
33141	North Bay Village	(305)	5,383	4,920
33918	North Fort Myers(u)	(941)	30,027	22,808
33068	North Lauderdale	(954)	26,473	18,653
33961	North Miami	(305)	50,001	42,566
33160	North Miami Beach	(305)	35,361	36,553
33940	North Naples(u)	(941)	13,422	7,950
33408	North Palm Beach	(561)	11,284	11,344
34287	North Port	(941)	11,973	6,205
34234	North Sarasota(u)	(941)	6,702	4,997
33334	Oakland Park	(305)	26,326	22,944
33860	Oak Ridge(u)	(813)	15,388	15,477
*34478	Ocala	(352)	42,045	37,170
32548	Ocean City(u)	(850)	5,422	5,582
32761	Ocoee	(407)	12,778	7,803
33163	Ojus(u)	(305)	15,519	17,344
34677	Oldsmar	(813)	8,361	2,608
33265	Olympia Heights(u)	(305)	37,792	33,112
*33054	Opa-Locka	(305)	15,283	14,460
33054	Opa-Locka North(u)	(305)	6,568	5,721
*32763	Orange City	(904)	5,347	2,795
*32073	Orange Park	(904)	9,488	8,766
*32802	Orlando	(407)	164,674	128,291
32861	Orlo Vista(u)	(407)	5,990	6,474
*32174	Ormond Beach	(904)	29,721	21,436
32074	Ormond By-The-Sea(u)	(904)	8,157	7,665
*32765	Oviedo	(407)	11,114	3,074
32571	Pace(u)	(850)	6,277	5,006
.....	Page Park-Pine Manor(u)		5,116	....
33476	Pahokee	(561)	6,822	6,346
*32177	Palatka	(904)	10,447	10,175
*32906	Palm Bay	(407)	62,543	18,560
33480	Palm Beach	(561)	9,814	9,729
33403	Palm Beach Gardens	(561)	22,990	14,407
32136	Palm Coast(u)	(904)	14,287	2,837
*34221	Palmetto	(941)	9,268	8,637
33157	Palmetto Estates(u)	(305)	12,293	11,116
*34683	Palm Harbor(u)	(813)	50,256	5,215
*33601	Palm River-Clair Mel(u)	(813)	13,691	14,447
33460	Palm Springs	(561)	9,763	8,166
33012	Palm Springs North(u)	(305)	5,300	5,838
32082	Palm Valley(u)	(904)	9,960	....
*32401	Panama City	(850)	34,396	33,346
33029	Pembroke Pines	(954)	65,566	35,776
*32502	Pensacola	(850)	59,198	57,619
33257	Perrine(u)	(305)	15,576	16,129
32347	Perry	(850)	7,151	8,254
32859	Pine Castle(u)	(407)	8,276	9,992
32858	Pine Hills(u)	(407)	35,322	31,029
.....	Pine Island Ridge	(954)	5,244	....
*34665	Pinellas Park	(813)	43,571	32,811
33168	Pinewood(u)	(305)	15,518	14,346
33318	Plantation	(954)	66,814	48,653
*33566	Plant City	(813)	22,754	17,064
*33060	Pompano Beach	(954)	72,411	52,618
33064	Pompano Beach Highlands(u)	(954)	17,915	16,154
*33952	Port Charlotte(u)	(941)	41,535	25,770
32124	Port Orange	(904)	35,399	18,756
32927	Port St. John(u)	(407)	8,933	1,837
*34981	Port St. Lucie	(561)	55,761	14,690
34992	Port Salerno(u)	(561)	7,786	4,511
33032	Princeton(u)	(305)	7,073	....
*33950	Punta Gorda	(941)	10,637	6,797
*32351	Quincy	(850)	7,452	8,591
33156	Richmond Heights(u)	(305)	8,583	8,577
33312	Riverland(u)	(954)	5,376	5,919
33569	Riverview(u)	(813)	6,478	....
33419	Riviera Beach	(561)	27,646	26,489
*32955	Rockledge	(407)	16,023	11,877
33411	Royal Palm Beach	(561)	15,532	3,423
*33570	Ruskin(u)	(813)	6,046	5,117
34695	Safety Harbor	(813)	15,120	6,461
*32084	Saint Augustine	(904)	11,695	11,985
*34769	Saint Cloud	(407)	12,684	7,840
*33733	Saint Petersburg	(813)	240,318	238,647
33736	Saint Petersburg Beach	(813)	9,200	9,354
33912	San Carlos Park(u)	(941)	11,785	3,590
33432	Sandalfoot Cove(u)	(305)	14,214	5,299
*32771	Sanford	(407)	32,387	23,176
33957	Sanibel	(941)	5,468	3,363
*34230	Sarasota	(941)	50,897	48,868

ZIP	Place		1990	1980
33577	Sarasota Springs(u)	(941)	16,088	13,860
32937	Satellite Beach	(407)	9,889	9,163
33055	Scott Lake(u)	(305)	14,588	14,154
*32958	Sebastian	(561)	10,248	2,831
*33870	Sebring	(941)	8,841	8,736
33584	Seffner(u)	(813)	5,371	....
*34640	Seminole	(813)	9,251	4,856
*34242	Siesta Key(u)	(941)	7,772	7,010
34472	Silver Springs Shores(u)	(352)	6,421	3,983
32809	Sky Lake(u)	(407)	6,202	6,692
32703	South Apopka(u)	(407)	6,360	5,687
33505	South Bradenton(u)	(941)	20,398	14,297
32121	South Daytona	(904)	12,488	11,252
34277	Southgate(u)	(813)	7,324	7,322
34233	South Gate Ridge(u)	(941)	5,924	4,259
33243	South Miami	(305)	10,404	10,895
33157	South Miami Heights(u)	(305)	30,030	23,559
33707	South Pasadena	(813)	5,644	4,188
32937	South Patrick Shores(u)	(407)	10,249	9,816
34230	South Sarasota(u)	(941)	5,298	4,267
33595	South Venice(u)	(813)	11,951	8,075
32401	Springfield	(904)	8,719	7,220
*34601	Spring Hill(u)	(352)	31,117	6,468
32091	Starke	(904)	5,226	5,306
*34994	Stuart	(561)	11,936	9,467
33573	Sun City Center(u)	(813)	8,326	5,605
33160	Sunny Isles(u)	(305)	11,772	12,564
*33322	Sunrise	(954)	65,683	39,681
33283	Sunset(u)	(305)	15,810	13,531
33144	Sweetwater	(305)	13,909	8,067
*32301	Tallahassee	(850)	124,773	81,548
33320	Tamarac	(954)	44,822	29,376
33144	Tamiami(u)	(305)	33,845	17,607
*33602	Tampa	(813)	280,015	271,577
*34689	Tarpon Springs	(813)	17,874	13,251
32778	Tavares	(352)	7,383	4,398
*33601	Temple Terrace	(813)	16,444	11,097
*32780	Titusville	(407)	39,394	31,910
32601	Town 'n' Country(u)	(813)	60,946	37,834
33706	Treasure Island	(813)	7,266	6,316
32867	Union Park(u)	(407)	6,890	19,175
33620	University West(u)†	(813)	23,760	24,514
32401	Upper Grand Lagoon(u)	(850)	7,855	3,314
32580	Valparaiso	(850)	6,316	6,142
*34285	Venice	(941)	17,052	12,153
33595	Venice Gardens(u)	(813)	7,701	6,568
*32960	Vero Beach	(561)	17,350	16,176
32960	Vero Beach South(u)	(561)	16,973	12,636
.....	Villages of Oriole(u)	(561)	5,698	....
33901	Villas(u)	(813)	9,898	8,724
32507	Warrington(u)	(850)	16,040	15,792
33314	Washington Park(u)	(954)	6,930	7,240
32703	Wekiva Springs(u)	(407)	23,026	13,386
33414	Wellington(u)	(561)	20,670	4,622
33155	Westchester(u)	(305)	29,883	29,272
.....	Westgate-Belvedere Homes(u)		6,880	....
33138	West Little River(u)	(305)	33,575	32,492
32904	West Melbourne	(407)	8,398	5,078
33144	West Miami	(305)	5,727	6,076
*33406	West Palm Beach	(561)	67,764	63,305
.....	West Park(u)		10,347	9,003
32505	West Pensacola(u)	(850)	22,107	24,371
33168	Westview(u)	(305)	9,668	9,102
33165	Westwood Lakes(u)	(305)	11,522	11,478
.....	Whiskey Creek(u)		5,061	....
33305	Wilton Manors	(954)	11,804	12,742
33803	Winston(u)	(813)	9,118	9,315
*34787	Winter Garden	(407)	9,863	6,789
*33880	Winter Haven	(941)	24,725	21,119
*32789	Winter Park	(407)	22,623	22,339
*32707	Winter Springs	(407)	22,151	10,475
32547	Wright(u)	(904)	18,945	13,011
32097	Yulee(u)	(904)	6,915	3,168
*33540	Zephyrhills	(813)	8,220	5,742

Georgia

ZIP	Place		1990	1980
31620	Adel	(912)	5,093	5,592
*31706	Albany	(912)	78,804	74,425
*30201	Alpharetta	(770)	13,002	3,128
31709	Americus	(912)	16,516	16,120
*30603	Athens	(706)	45,734	42,549
*30301	Atlanta	(404)	393,929	425,022
*30903	Augusta	(706)	44,707	47,532
31717	Bainbridge	(912)	10,803	10,553
30032	Belvedere Park(u)	(404)	18,089	17,766
31723	Blakely	(912)	5,595	5,880
*31520	Brunswick	(912)	16,433	17,605
*30518	Buford	(404)	8,771	6,578
31728	Cairo	(912)	9,035	8,777
*30701	Calhoun	(706)	7,135	5,563
31730	Camilla	(912)	5,124	5,414
30032	Candler-McAfee(u)	(404)	29,491	27,306
*30117	Carrollton	(770)	16,029	14,078
30120	Cartersville	(770)	12,037	9,247
30125	Cedartown	(770)	7,976	8,619
30366	Chamblee	(404)	7,668	7,137
30021	Clarkston	(404)	5,385	4,539

ZIP	Place		1990	1980
30337	College Park	(404)	20,645	24,632
*31908	Columbus	(706)	178,681	169,441
30027	Conley(u)	(404)	5,528	6,033
*30208	Conyers	(404)	7,380	6,567
31015	Cordele	(912)	10,833	11,184
.....	Country Club Estates(u)	.....	7,500	....
30209	Covington	(770)	9,860	10,586
*30720	Dalton	(706)	22,218	20,581
31742	Dawson	(912)	5,295	5,699
*30030	Decatur (DeKalb)	(404)	17,304	18,404
31520	Dock Junction(u)	(912)	7,094	6,189
30362	Doraville	(404)	7,626	7,414
31533	Douglas	(912)	10,464	10,980
*30134	Douglasville	(404)	11,635	7,641
30333	Druid Hills(u)	(404)	12,174	12,700
*31021	Dublin	(912)	16,312	16,083
30136	Duluth	(404)	9,821	2,956
30356	Dunwoody(u)	(404)	26,302	17,768
31023	Eastman	(912)	5,241	5,330
30364	East Point	(404)	34,595	37,486
30635	Elberton	(706)	5,682	5,686
30809	Evans(u)	(706)	13,713	....
30060	Fair Oaks(u)	(404)	6,996	8,486
30535	Fairview(u)	(706)	6,444	6,558
30214	Fayetteville	(404)	5,827	2,715
31750	Fitzgerald	(912)	8,901	10,187
*30050	Forest Park	(404)	16,958	18,782
31905	Fort Benning South(u)	(706)	14,617	15,074
30905	Fort Gordon(u)	(706)	9,140	14,069
30742	Fort Oglethorpe	(706)	5,880	5,443
31314	Fort Stewart(u)	(912)	13,774	15,031
31030	Fort Valley	(912)	8,198	9,000
30605	Gaines School(u)	(706)	11,354	....
*30501	Gainesville	(770)	17,885	15,280
31408	Garden City	(912)	7,410	6,895
31754	Georgetown(u)	(912)	5,554	2,785
30316	Gresham Park(u)	(404)	9,000	6,232
*30223	Griffin	(770)	21,325	20,728
30354	Hapeville	(404)	5,483	6,166
31313	Hinesville	(912)	21,596	11,309
31545	Jesup	(912)	8,958	9,418
30144	Kennesaw	(404)	8,936	5,095
31548	Kingsland	(912)	5,474	2,008
30728	La Fayette	(706)	6,313	6,517
*30240	La Grange	(706)	25,574	24,204
30741	Lakeview(u)	(706)	5,237	5,403
*30245	Lawrenceville	(404)	17,250	8,928
*30247	Lilburn	(404)	9,295	3,765
30057	Lithia Springs(u)	(404)	11,403	9,145
30059	Mableton(u)	(404)	25,725	25,111
*31201	Macon	(912)	107,365	116,896
*30060	Marietta	(404)	44,129	30,821
30917	Martinez(u)	(706)	33,731	16,472
31061	Milledgeville	(912)	17,727	12,176
*30655	Monroe	(770)	9,759	8,854
*30260	Morrow	(404)	5,168	3,791
*31768	Moultrie	(912)	14,865	15,105
30087	Mountain Park(u)	(404)	11,025	9,425
*30263	Newnan	(770)	12,497	11,449
*30071	Norcross	(404)	5,947	3,363
30319	North Atlanta(u)	(404)	27,812	30,521
30033	North Decatur(u)	(404)	13,936	11,830
30033	North Druid Hills(u)	(404)	14,170	12,438
30032	Panthersville(u)	(404)	9,874	11,366
30269	Peachtree City	(404)	19,027	6,429
31069	Perry	(912)	9,452	9,453
30073	Powder Springs	(404)	6,862	3,381
31643	Quitman	(912)	5,292	5,188
30074	Redan(u)	(404)	24,376	....
*30274	Riverdale	(404)	9,455	7,121
*30161	Rome	(706)	30,325	28,915
*30077	Roswell	(404)	47,986	23,337
31558	Saint Marys	(912)	8,204	3,596
31522	Saint Simons Island(u)	(912)	12,026	6,566
31082	Sandersville	(912)	6,290	6,137
30358	Sandy Springs(u)	(404)	67,842	46,877
*31402	Savannah	(912)	137,812	141,654
30079	Scottdale(u)	(404)	8,636	8,770
*30080	Smyrna	(404)	30,981	20,312
30278	Snellville	(404)	12,084	8,514
30901	South Augusta(u)	(706)	55,998	51,072
*30458	Statesboro	(912)	15,854	14,866
*30086	Stone Mountain	(404)	6,544	4,867
30747	Summerville	(706)	5,025	4,878
30401	Swainsboro	(912)	7,361	7,602
31791	Sylvester	(912)	6,023	5,860
30286	Thomaston	(706)	9,127	9,682
*31792	Thomasville	(912)	17,554	18,463
30824	Thomson	(706)	6,862	7,001
*31794	Tifton	(912)	14,215	13,749
30577	Toccoa	(706)	8,720	8,869
*30084	Tucker(u)	(404)	25,781	25,399
30291	Union City	(404)	8,887	4,780
*31603	Valdosta	(912)	40,038	37,596
30474	Vidalia	(912)	11,118	10,393
30180	Villa Rica	(770)	6,542	3,420
30339	Vinings(u)	(404)	7,417	....
*31088	Warner Robins	(912)	43,861	39,893
*31501	Waycross	(912)	16,410	19,371
30830	Waynesboro	(706)	5,669	5,760

ZIP	Place		1990	1980
30901	West Augusta(u)	(706)	27,637	24,242
31410	Wilmington Island(u)	(912)	11,230	7,546
30680	Winder	(770)	7,373	6,705

Hawaii (808)

See note on page 389

ZIP	Place	1990	1980
96701	Aiea(u)	8,906	32,879
96818	Aliamanu(u)	8,835	....
96706	Ewa Beach(u)	14,315	14,369
.....	Halawa(u)	13,408	....
96744	Heeia(u)	5,010	5,432
96853	Hickam Housing(u)	6,553	4,425
*96720	Hilo(u)	37,808	35,269
*96820	Honolulu(u)	365,272	365,048
96732	Kahului(u)	16,889	12,978
96734	Kailua(u)	9,126	4,751
96863	Kailua(u)	36,818	35,812
96744	Kaneohe(u)	35,448	29,919
.....	Kaneohe Station(u)	11,662	11,615
96746	Kapaa(u)	8,149	4,467
96753	Kihei(u)	11,107	5,644
*96761	Lahaina(u)	9,073	6,095
96762	Laie(u)	5,577	4,643
96766	Lihue(u)	5,536	4,000
96792	Maili(u)	6,059	5,026
96792	Makaha(u)	7,990	6,582
96706	Makakilo(u)	9,828	7,691
96768	Makawao(u)	5,405	2,900
96789	Mililani Town(u)	29,359	21,365
96792	Nanakuli(u)	9,575	8,185
96782	Pearl City(u)	30,993	42,575
96788	Pukalani(u)	5,879	3,950
96786	Schofield Barracks(u)	19,597	18,851
.....	Village Park(u)	7,407	....
96786	Wahiawa(u)	17,386	16,911
96792	Waianae(u)	8,758	7,941
96793	Wailuku(u)	10,688	10,260
.....	Waimalu(u)	29,967	....
96796	Waimea(u)	5,972	1,179
96797	Waipahu(u)	31,435	29,139
96797	Waipio(u)	11,812	....
96786	Waipio Acres(u)	5,304	4,091

Idaho (208)

ZIP	Place	1990	1980
83401	Ammon	5,002	4,669
83221	Blackfoot	9,646	10,065
*83707	Boise City	125,551	102,249
83318	Burley	8,702	8,761
*83605	Caldwell	18,400	17,699
83202	Chubbuck	7,794	7,052
*83814	Coeur D'Alene	24,561	19,913
83714	Garden City	6,369	4,571
*83402	Idaho Falls	43,973	39,739
83338	Jerome	6,529	6,891
83501	Lewiston	28,082	27,986
*83642	Meridian	9,596	6,658
83843	Moscow	18,398	16,513
83647	Mountain Home	7,913	7,540
83648	Mountain Home AFB(u)	5,936	6,403
*83651	Nampa	28,365	25,112
83661	Payette	5,672	5,448
*83201	Pocatello	46,117	46,340
83854	Post Falls	7,349	5,736
83440	Rexburg	14,298	11,559
83350	Rupert	5,455	5,476
83864	Sandpoint	5,203	4,460
*83301	Twin Falls	27,634	26,209

Illinois

ZIP	Place		1990	1980
60101	Addison	(630)	32,053	29,826
60102	Algonquin	(847)	11,693	5,834
60658	Alsip	(708)	18,227	17,134
62002	Alton	(618)	33,064	34,171
60002	Antioch	(847)	6,105	4,419
*60005	Arlington Heights	(847)	75,463	66,116
*60505	Aurora	(630)	99,556	81,293
*60010	Barrington	(847)	9,538	9,029
60103	Bartlett	(630)	19,395	13,254
61607	Bartonville	(309)	5,671	6,137
60510	Batavia	(630)	17,076	12,574
60085	Beach Park†	(847)	9,492	8,468
62618	Beardstown	(217)	5,270	6,338
*62220	Belleville	(618)	42,806	41,580
60104	Bellwood	(708)	20,241	19,811
61008	Belvidere	(815)	15,962	15,176
60106	Bensenville	(630)	17,767	16,106
62812	Benton	(618)	7,216	7,778
60163	Berkeley	(708)	5,137	5,467
60402	Berwyn	(708)	45,426	46,849
62010	Bethalto	(618)	9,507	8,630
60108	Bloomingdale	(630)	16,614	12,656

ZIP	Place		1990	1980
*61701	Bloomington	(309)	51,889	44,189
60406	Blue Island	(708)	21,203	21,855
60440	Bolingbrook	(630)	40,843	37,261
60538	Boulder Hill(u)	(630)	8,894	9,333
60914	Bourbonnais	(815)	13,929	13,280
60915	Bradley	(815)	10,918	11,015
60455	Bridgeview	(708)	14,402	14,155
60153	Broadview	(708)	8,538	8,618
60513	Brookfield	(708)	18,876	19,395
60089	Buffalo Grove	(847)	36,417	22,230
60459	Burbank	(708)	27,600	28,462
60521	Burr Ridge	(630)	7,684	3,838
62206	Cahokia	(618)	17,550	18,904
60409	Calumet City	(708)	37,840	39,697
60643	Calumet Park	(708)	8,418	8,788
61520	Canton	(309)	13,959	14,626
*62901	Carbondale	(618)	27,033	26,414
62626	Carlinville	(217)	5,416	5,439
62821	Carmi	(618)	5,626	6,107
*60188	Carol Stream	(630)	31,759	15,472
60110	Carpentersville	(847)	23,049	23,272
60013	Cary	(847)	10,043	6,640
62801	Centralia	(618)	14,274	15,126
62206	Centreville	(618)	7,489	9,747
*61821	Champaign	(217)	63,502	58,267
61920	Charleston	(217)	20,398	19,355
62629	Chatham	(217)	6,074	5,597
62233	Chester	(618)	8,204	8,401
*60607	Chicago	(312)/(773)	2,783,726	3,005,072
60411	Chicago Heights	(708)	32,966	37,026
60415	Chicago Ridge	(708)	13,643	13,473
61523	Chillicothe	(309)	5,959	6,176
60650	Cicero	(708)	67,436	61,232
60514	Clarendon Hills	(630)	6,994	6,870
61727	Clinton	(217)	7,437	8,014
62234	Collinsville	(618)	22,424	19,475
62236	Columbia	(618)	5,524	4,269
60478	Country Club Hills	(708)	15,431	14,676
60525	Countryside	(708)	5,961	6,242
60435	Crest Hill	(815)	10,999	9,252
60445	Crestwood	(708)	10,823	10,852
60417	Crete	(708)	6,773	5,417
61610	Creve Coeur	(309)	5,938	6,851
*60014	Crystal Lake	(815)	24,696	18,590
*61832	Danville	(217)	33,828	38,985
60561	Darien	(630)	18,148	14,956
*62525	Decatur	(217)	83,900	93,939
60015	Deerfield	(847)	17,327	17,432
60115	De Kalb	(815)	35,076	33,157
*60018	Des Plaines	(847)	53,414	53,568
61021	Dixon	(815)	15,134	15,710
60419	Dolton	(708)	23,956	24,766
*60515	Downers Grove	(630)	46,845	42,259
62832	Du Quoin	(618)	6,697	6,594
62024	East Alton	(618)	7,063	7,096
61244	East Moline	(309)	20,147	20,907
61611	East Peoria	(309)	21,378	22,385
*62201	East St. Louis	(618)	40,944	55,200
62025	Edwardsville	(618)	14,582	12,480
62401	Effingham	(217)	11,927	11,270
*60120	Elgin	(847)	77,010	63,668
*60009	Elk Grove Village	(847)	33,429	28,679
60126	Elmhurst	(630)	42,029	44,276
60635	Elmwood Park	(708)	23,206	24,016
*60201	Evanston	(847)	73,233	73,706
60642	Evergreen Park	(708)	20,874	22,260
62837	Fairfield	(618)	5,442	5,944
62208	Fairview Heights	(618)	14,351	12,111
62839	Flora	(618)	5,093	5,379
60422	Flossmoor	(708)	8,651	8,423
60130	Forest Park	(708)	14,918	15,177
60020	Fox Lake	(847)	7,539	6,831
60423	Frankfort	(815)	7,180	4,357
.....	Frankfort Square(u)	(815)	6,227	....
60131	Franklin Park	(847)	18,485	17,507
61032	Freeport	(815)	25,840	26,266
60030	Gages Lake(u)	(847)	8,349	3,814
*61401	Galesburg	(309)	33,530	35,305
61254	Geneseo	(309)	5,990	6,373
60134	Geneva	(630)	12,625	9,881
62034	Glen Carbon	(618)	7,774	5,197
60022	Glencoe	(847)	8,499	9,200
60139	Glendale Heights	(630)	27,915	23,251
*60137	Glen Ellyn	(630)	24,919	23,691
60025	Glenview	(847)	37,052	32,060
60425	Glenwood	(708)	9,289	10,538
62035	Godfrey(u)	(618)	5,436	....
.....	Goodings Grove(u)	(815)	14,054	....
62040	Granite City	(618)	32,766	36,815
60030	Grayslake	(847)	7,388	5,260
62246	Greenville	(618)	5,108	5,271
60031	Gurnee	(847)	13,715	7,179
*60103	Hanover Park	(630)	32,918	28,719
62946	Harrisburg	(618)	9,318	10,410
60033	Harvard	(815)	5,975	5,100
60426	Harvey	(708)	29,771	35,810
60056	Harwood Heights	(708)	7,680	8,228
60429	Hazel Crest	(708)	13,334	13,973
62948	Herrin	(618)	10,857	10,708
60457	Hickory Hills	(708)	13,021	13,778

ZIP	Place		1990	1980
62249	Highland	(618)	7,546	7,122
*60035	Highland Park	(847)	30,575	30,599
60040	Highwood	(847)	5,331	5,455
60162	Hillside	(708)	7,672	8,279
*60521	Hinsdale	(630)	16,029	16,726
*60195	Hoffman Estates	(847)	46,363	37,272
60430	Homewood	(708)	19,278	19,724
60942	Hoopeston	(217)	5,871	6,411
60067	Inverness	(847)	6,516	4,046
60143	Itasca	(630)	6,947	7,129
*62650	Jacksonville	(217)	19,327	20,284
62052	Jerseyville	(618)	7,382	7,506
*60436	Joliet	(815)	77,217	77,956
60458	Justice	(708)	11,137	10,552
60901	Kankakee	(815)	27,541	29,633
61443	Kewanee	(309)	12,969	14,508
60525	La Grange	(708)	15,362	15,693
60525	La Grange Park	(708)	12,861	13,359
60044	Lake Bluff	(847)	5,486	4,434
60045	Lake Forest	(847)	17,836	15,245
60102	Lake in the Hills	(847)	5,900	5,651
60047	Lake Zurich	(847)	14,927	8,225
60438	Lansing	(708)	28,131	29,039
61301	La Salle	(815)	9,717	10,347
60439	Lemont	(630)	7,359	5,640
*60048	Libertyville	(847)	19,174	16,520
62656	Lincoln	(217)	15,418	16,327
60645	Lincolnwood	(847)	11,365	11,921
60046	Lindenhurst	(847)	8,044	6,220
60532	Lisle	(630)	19,584	13,638
62056	Litchfield	(217)	6,883	7,204
60441	Lockport	(815)	9,401	9,192
60148	Lombard	(630)	39,408	36,879
*61130	Loves Park	(815)	15,457	13,192
60411	Lynwood	(708)	6,535	4,195
60534	Lyons (Cook)	(708)	9,828	9,925
*60050	McHenry	(815)	16,343	10,737
61115	Machesney Park†	(815)	19,042	19,514
61455	Macomb	(309)	19,952	19,863
62959	Marion	(618)	14,545	14,031
60426	Markham (Cook)	(708)	13,136	15,172
62258	Mascoutah	(618)	5,511	4,962
60443	Matteson	(708)	11,378	10,223
61938	Mattoon	(217)	18,441	19,293
*60153	Maywood	(708)	27,139	27,998
*60160	Melrose Park	(708)	20,859	20,735
61342	Mendota	(815)	7,017	7,134
62960	Metropolis	(618)	6,734	7,171
60445	Midlothian	(708)	14,372	14,274
61264	Milan	(309)	5,753	6,371
60448	Mokena	(708)	6,128	4,578
*61265	Moline	(309)	43,080	46,407
61462	Monmouth	(309)	9,489	10,706
60450	Morris	(815)	10,274	8,833
61550	Morton	(309)	13,799	14,178
60053	Morton Grove	(847)	22,373	23,747
62863	Mount Carmel	(618)	8,287	8,908
60056	Mount Prospect	(847)	53,168	52,634
62864	Mount Vernon	(618)	17,082	17,193
60060	Mundelein	(847)	21,224	17,053
62966	Murphysboro	(618)	9,176	9,866
*60540	Naperville	(630)	85,806	42,601
60451	New Lenox	(815)	9,698	5,792
60714	Niles	(847)	28,375	30,363
61761	Normal	(309)	40,023	35,672
60634	Norridge	(708)	14,459	16,483
60542	North Aurora	(630)	6,010	5,205
*60062	Northbrook	(708)	32,572	30,778
60064	North Chicago	(847)	34,978	38,774
60164	Northlake	(708)	12,505	12,166
60546	North Riverside	(708)	6,180	6,764
60521	Oak Brook	(630)	9,087	6,676
60452	Oak Forest	(708)	26,202	25,040
*60455	Oak Lawn	(708)	56,182	60,590
*60303	Oak Park	(708)	53,648	54,887
62269	O'Fallon	(618)	16,064	12,173
62450	Olney	(618)	8,661	9,026
60477	Orland Hills	(708)	5,510	2,784
60462	Orland Park	(708)	35,720	23,045
61350	Ottawa	(815)	17,528	18,166
*60067	Palatine	(847)	38,894	32,171
60463	Palos Heights	(708)	11,478	11,096
60465	Palos Hills	(708)	17,803	16,654
62557	Pana	(217)	5,796	6,040
61944	Paris	(217)	9,016	9,885
60466	Park Forest	(708)	24,656	26,222
60068	Park Ridge	(847)	36,175	38,704
*61554	Pekin	(309)	32,254	33,967
*61601	Peoria	(309)	113,504	124,160
61603	Peoria Heights	(309)	6,930	7,453
61354	Peru	(815)	9,302	10,886
60545	Plano	(630)	5,104	4,875
61764	Pontiac	(815)	11,428	11,227
61356	Princeton	(815)	7,197	7,342
60070	Prospect Heights	(847)	15,236	11,823
*62301	Quincy	(217)	39,682	42,554
61866	Rantoul	(217)	17,212	20,161
60471	Richton Park	(708)	10,523	9,403
60627	Riverdale	(708)	13,671	13,233

ZIP	Place		1990	1980
60305	River Forest	(708)	11,669	12,392
60171	River Grove	(708)	9,961	10,368
60546	Riverside	(708)	8,774	9,236
60472	Robbins	(708)	7,498	8,853
62454	Robinson	(618)	6,740	7,285
61068	Rochelle	(815)	8,769	8,982
61071	Rock Falls	(815)	9,669	10,633
*61125	Rockford	(815)	139,704	139,712
*61201	Rock Island	(309)	40,630	46,821
60008	Rolling Meadows	(847)	22,598	20,167
60446	Romeoville	(815)	14,101	15,519
*60172	Roselle	(630)	20,803	17,034
60073	Round Lake Beach	(847)	16,406	12,921
*60174	Saint Charles	(630)	22,620	17,492
62881	Salem	(618)	7,470	7,813
60548	Sandwich	(815)	5,607	5,356
60411	Sauk Village	(708)	9,926	10,906
*60194	Schaumburg	(847)	68,586	53,355
60176	Schiller Park	(847)	11,189	11,458
62225	Scott AFB(u)	(618)	7,245	8,648
60436	Shorewood	(815)	6,264	4,714
61282	Silvis	(309)	6,926	7,130
*60077	Skokie	(847)	59,432	60,278
60177	South Elgin	(847)	7,474	5,970
60473	South Holland	(708)	22,105	24,977
*62703	Springfield	(217)	105,417	100,054
61362	Spring Valley	(815)	5,246	5,822
60475	Steger	(708)	8,592	9,269
61081	Sterling	(815)	15,142	16,281
60402	Stickney	(708)	5,678	5,893
60107	Streamwood	(630)	31,197	23,456
61364	Streator	(815)	14,121	14,795
60501	Summit	(708)	9,971	10,110
62221	Swansea	(618)	8,201	5,529
60178	Sycamore	(815)	9,896	9,219
62568	Taylorville	(217)	11,133	11,386
60477	Tinley Park	(708)	37,115	26,178
62294	Troy	(618)	6,019	3,772
60466	University Park	(708)	6,204	6,245
61801	Urbana	(217)	36,383	35,978
62471	Vandalia	(618)	6,114	5,338
60061	Vernon Hills	(847)	15,319	9,827
60181	Villa Park	(630)	22,279	23,155
60555	Warrenville	(630)	11,389	7,519
61571	Washington	(309)	10,136	10,364
62204	Washington Park	(618)	7,431	8,223
62298	Waterloo	(618)	5,030	4,646
60970	Watseka	(815)	5,424	5,543
60084	Wauconda	(847)	6,294	5,688
*60085	Waukegan	(847)	69,481	67,653
60154	Westchester	(708)	17,301	17,730
*60185	West Chicago	(630)	14,808	12,550
60558	Western Springs	(708)	11,956	12,876
62896	West Frankfort	(618)	8,526	9,437
60559	Westmont	(630)	21,402	17,353
61604	West Peoria(u)	(309)	5,314	5,219
*60187	Wheaton	(630)	51,441	43,043
*60090	Wheeling	(847)	29,911	23,266
60514	Willowbrook	(630)	8,701	4,953
60091	Wilmette	(847)	26,694	28,221
60190	Winfield	(630)	7,096	4,422
60093	Winnetka	(847)	12,210	12,772
60096	Winthrop Harbor	(847)	6,240	5,427
60097	Wonder Lake(u)	(815)	6,664	5,917
60191	Wood Dale	(630)	12,394	11,251
*60517	Woodridge	(630)	26,359	21,763
62095	Wood River	(618)	11,490	12,446
60098	Woodstock	(815)	14,368	11,725
60482	Worth	(708)	11,208	11,592
60099	Zion	(847)	19,783	17,865

Indiana

ZIP	Place		1990	1980
46001	Alexandria	(765)	5,709	6,028
*46011	Anderson	(765)	59,459	64,695
46703	Angola	(219)	5,851	5,486
46706	Auburn	(219)	9,386	8,122
47421	Bedford	(812)	13,817	14,410
46107	Beech Grove	(317)	13,383	13,196
*47408	Bloomington	(812)	60,633	52,663
46714	Bluffton	(219)	9,104	8,705
47601	Boonville	(812)	6,686	6,300
47834	Brazil	(812)	7,640	7,852
46112	Brownsburg	(317)	7,628	6,242
*46032	Carmel	(317)	25,380	18,272
46303	Cedar Lake	(219)	8,885	8,754
47111	Charlestown	(812)	5,889	5,596
46304	Chesterton	(219)	9,118	8,531
47129	Clarksville (Clark Co.)	(812)	19,838	15,164
47842	Clinton	(765)	5,040	5,267
46725	Columbia City	(219)	5,700	5,091
*47201	Columbus	(812)	31,802	30,614
47331	Connersville	(765)	15,550	17,023
47933	Crawfordsville	(765)	13,584	13,325
46307	Crown Point	(219)	17,728	16,455
46733	Decatur	(219)	8,642	8,649
46514	Dunlap(u)	(219)	5,705	5,397

ZIP	Place		1990	1980
46311	Dyer	(219)	10,923	9,555
46312	East Chicago	(219)	33,892	39,786
*46515	Elkhart	(219)	43,627	41,305
46036	Elwood	(765)	9,494	10,867
*47708	Evansville	(812)	126,272	130,496
46038	Fishers	(317)	7,189	2,008
*46802	Fort Wayne	(219)	172,971	172,391
46041	Frankfort	(765)	14,754	15,168
46131	Franklin	(317)	12,932	11,563
46738	Garrett	(219)	5,349	4,751
*46401	Gary	(219)	116,646	151,968
46933	Gas City	(765)	6,296	6,370
*46526	Goshen	(219)	23,794	19,665
46530	Granger(u)	(219)	20,241	....
46135	Greencastle	(765)	8,984	8,403
46140	Greenfield	(317)	11,657	11,288
47240	Greensburg	(812)	9,286	9,254
*46142	Greenwood	(317)	26,507	19,327
46319	Griffith	(219)	17,914	17,026
*46320	Hammond	(219)	84,236	93,714
47348	Hartford City	(765)	6,960	7,622
46322	Highland	(219)	23,696	25,935
46342	Hobart	(219)	21,822	22,987
47542	Huntingburg	(812)	5,236	5,376
46750	Huntington	(219)	16,389	16,202
*46206	Indianapolis	(317)	731,327	700,807
*47546	Jasper	(812)	10,030	9,097
*47130	Jeffersonville	(812)	21,968	21,220
46755	Kendallville	(219)	7,773	7,299
*46902	Kokomo	(765)	44,996	47,808
*47901	Lafayette	(765)	43,758	43,011
.....	Lakes of the Four Seasons(u)	(219)	6,556	....
46405	Lake Station	(219)	13,899	15,087
*46350	La Porte	(219)	21,507	21,796
46226	Lawrence	(317)	26,779	25,591
46052	Lebanon	(765)	12,059	11,456
47441	Linton	(812)	5,814	6,315
46947	Logansport	(219)	16,865	17,731
46356	Lowell	(219)	6,430	5,827
47250	Madison	(812)	12,006	12,472
*46952	Marion	(765)	32,607	35,874
46151	Martinsville	(765)	11,677	11,311
46410	Merrillville	(219)	27,257	27,677
*46360	Michigan City	(219)	33,822	36,850
*46544	Mishawaka	(219)	42,635	40,201
47960	Monticello	(219)	5,237	5,162
46158	Mooresville	(317)	5,541	5,349
47620	Mount Vernon	(812)	7,217	7,656
*47302	Muncie	(765)	71,170	77,216
46321	Munster	(219)	19,949	20,671
46550	Nappanee	(219)	5,474	4,694
*47150	New Albany	(812)	36,322	37,103
47362	New Castle	(765)	17,753	20,056
46774	New Haven	(219)	9,338	6,714
46060	Noblesville	(317)	17,655	12,253
46962	North Manchester	(219)	6,383	5,998
47265	North Vernon	(812)	5,129	5,768
47130	Oak Park(u)	(812)	5,630	5,871
46970	Peru	(765)	12,843	13,764
46168	Plainfield	(317)	10,438	9,191
46563	Plymouth	(219)	8,291	7,693
46368	Portage	(219)	29,062	27,409
47371	Portland	(219)	6,483	7,074
47670	Princeton	(812)	8,127	8,976
47978	Rensselaer	(219)	5,045	4,944
*47374	Richmond	(765)	38,705	41,349
46975	Rochester	(219)	5,969	5,050
46173	Rushville	(765)	5,533	6,113
47167	Salem	(812)	5,619	5,290
46375	Schererville	(219)	20,155	13,209
47170	Scottsburg	(812)	5,334	5,068
47172	Sellersburg	(812)	5,914	3,211
47274	Seymour	(812)	15,579	15,050
46176	Shelbyville	(765)	15,347	14,989
*46624	South Bend	(219)	105,511	109,727
46383	South Haven(u)	(219)	6,112	6,679
46224	Speedway	(317)	13,092	12,641
47586	Tell City	(812)	8,088	8,704
*47808	Terre Haute	(812)	55,430	61,125
*46383	Valparaiso	(219)	24,414	22,247
47591	Vincennes	(812)	19,867	20,857
46992	Wabash	(219)	12,127	12,985
*46580	Warsaw	(219)	10,968	10,647
47501	Washington	(812)	10,864	11,325
*47901	West Lafayette	(765)	26,144	21,247
46391	Westville	(219)	5,255	2,887
46394	Whiting	(219)	5,155	5,630
47394	Winchester	(765)	5,095	5,659
46077	Zionsville	(317)	5,281	3,948

Iowa

ZIP	Place		1990	1980
50511	Algona	(515)	6,015	6,289
50009	Altoona	(515)	7,242	5,764
*50010	Ames	(515)	47,198	45,775
52205	Anamosa	(319)	5,100	4,958
50021	Ankeny	(515)	18,482	15,429

ZIP	Place		1990	1980
50022	Atlantic	(712)	7,432	7,789
52722	Bettendorf	(319)	28,139	27,381
50036	Boone	(515)	12,392	12,602
52601	Burlington	(319)	27,208	29,529
51401	Carroll	(712)	9,579	9,705
50613	Cedar Falls	(319)	34,298	36,322
*52401	Cedar Rapids	(319)	108,772	110,243
52544	Centerville	(515)	5,936	6,558
50616	Charles City	(515)	7,878	8,778
51012	Cherokee	(712)	6,026	7,004
51632	Clarinda	(712)	5,104	5,458
50428	Clear Lake	(515)	8,183	7,458
*52732	Clinton	(319)	29,201	32,828
50325	Clive	(515)	7,462	6,064
52241	Coralville	(319)	10,347	7,687
*51501	Council Bluffs	(712)	54,315	56,449
50801	Creston	(515)	7,911	8,429
*52802	Davenport	(319)	95,333	103,264
52101	Decorah	(319)	8,063	7,991
51442	Denison	(712)	6,604	6,675
*50318	Des Moines	(515)	193,189	191,003
*52001	Dubuque	(319)	57,538	62,374
51334	Estherville	(712)	6,720	7,518
52556	Fairfield	(515)	9,768	9,428
50501	Fort Dodge	(515)	25,894	29,423
52627	Fort Madison	(319)	11,614	13,520
50112	Grinnell	(515)	8,902	8,868
*51537	Harlan	(712)	5,148	5,357
50644	Independence	(319)	5,972	6,392
50125	Indianola	(515)	11,340	10,843
*52240	Iowa City	(319)	59,735	50,508
50126	Iowa Falls	(515)	5,435	6,174
52632	Keokuk	(319)	12,451	13,536
50138	Knoxville	(515)	8,232	8,143
51031	Le Mars	(712)	8,454	8,276
52057	Manchester	(319)	5,137	4,942
52060	Maquoketa	(319)	6,130	6,313
52302	Marion	(319)	20,442	19,474
50158	Marshalltown	(515)	25,178	26,938
*50401	Mason City	(515)	29,040	30,144
52641	Mount Pleasant	(319)	7,959	7,322
52761	Muscatine	(319)	22,881	23,467
50201	Nevada	(515)	6,009	5,912
50208	Newton	(515)	14,799	15,292
50211	Norwalk	(515)	5,726	2,676
50662	Oelwein	(319)	6,493	7,564
52577	Oskaloosa	(515)	10,600	10,989
52501	Ottumwa	(515)	24,488	27,381
50219	Pella	(515)	9,270	8,349
50220	Perry	(515)	6,652	7,053
*51566	Red Oak	(712)	6,264	6,810
51601	Shenandoah	(712)	5,572	6,274
51250	Sioux Center	(712)	5,074	4,588
*51101	Sioux City	(712)	80,505	82,003
51301	Spencer	(712)	11,066	11,726
50588	Storm Lake	(712)	8,769	8,814
50322	Urbandale	(515)	23,500	17,869
52349	Vinton	(319)	5,103	5,040
52353	Washington	(319)	7,074	6,584
*50701	Waterloo	(319)	66,467	75,985
50677	Waverly	(319)	8,539	8,444
50595	Webster City	(515)	7,894	8,572
*50265	West Des Moines	(515)	31,702	21,894
50311	Windsor Heights	(515)	5,190	5,474

Kansas

ZIP	Place		1990	1980
67410	Abilene	(785)	6,242	6,572
67005	Arkansas City	(316)	12,762	13,201
66002	Atchison	(913)	10,656	11,407
67010	Augusta	(316)	7,848	6,968
66012	Bonner Springs	(913)	6,413	6,266
66720	Chanute	(316)	9,488	10,506
67337	Coffeyville	(316)	12,917	15,185
67701	Colby	(785)	5,510	5,544
66901	Concordia	(785)	6,152	6,847
67037	Derby	(316)	14,691	9,786
67801	Dodge City	(316)	21,129	18,001
67042	El Dorado	(316)	11,495	11,551
66801	Emporia	(316)	25,512	25,287
66442	Fort Riley North(u)	(785)	12,848	16,086
66701	Fort Scott	(316)	8,362	8,893
67846	Garden City	(316)	24,097	18,256
67530	Great Bend	(316)	15,427	16,608
67601	Hays	(785)	17,814	16,301
67060	Haysville	(316)	8,364	8,006
*67501	Hutchinson	(316)	39,308	40,284
67301	Independence	(316)	10,030	10,598
66749	Iola	(316)	6,351	6,938
66441	Junction City	(785)	20,642	19,305
*66102	Kansas City	(913)	149,800	161,148
66043	Lansing	(913)	7,120	5,307
*66044	Lawrence	(785)	65,608	52,738
66048	Leavenworth	(913)	38,495	33,656
66209	Leawood	(913)	10,000	13,360
66210	Lenexa	(913)	34,110	18,639
*67901	Liberal	(316)	16,573	14,911
67460	McPherson	(316)	12,422	11,753

ZIP	Place		1990	1980
*66502	Manhattan	(785)	37,737	32,644
66202	Merriam	(913)	11,819	10,794
66202	Mission	(913)	9,504	8,643
67114	Newton	(316)	16,700	16,332
*66061	Olathe	(913)	63,402	37,258
66067	Ottawa	(785)	10,667	11,016
66202	Overland Park	(913)	111,790	81,784
67219	Park City†	(316)	5,054	4,056
67357	Parsons	(316)	11,919	12,898
66762	Pittsburg	(316)	17,789	18,770
66202	Prairie Village	(913)	23,186	24,657
67124	Pratt	(316)	6,687	6,885
66205	Roeland Park	(913)	7,706	7,962
*67401	Salina	(785)	42,299	41,843
66203	Shawnee	(913)	37,962	29,653
*66601	Topeka	(785)	119,883	118,690
67880	Ulysses	(316)	5,474	4,653
67152	Wellington	(316)	8,517	8,212
*67209	Wichita	(316)	304,017	279,838
67156	Winfield	(316)	11,931	10,736

Kentucky

ZIP	Place		1990	1980
41001	Alexandria	(606)	5,592	4,735
*41101	Ashland	(606)	23,622	27,064
40004	Bardstown	(502)	6,712	6,155
41073	Bellevue	(606)	6,997	7,678
40403	Berea	(606)	9,129	8,226
*42101	Bowling Green	(502)	41,688	40,450
40261	Buechel(u)	(502)	7,081	6,855
41005	Burlington(u)	(606)	6,070	....
*42718	Campbellsville	(502)	9,592	8,715
42330	Central City	(502)	5,015	5,214
*40701	Corbin	(606)	7,644	8,075
*41011	Covington	(606)	43,646	49,585
41031	Cynthiana	(606)	6,497	5,881
*40422	Danville	(606)	12,559	12,942
41074	Dayton	(606)	6,576	6,979
40243	Douglass Hills	(502)	5,431	4,384
41017	Edgewood	(606)	8,143	7,243
*42701	Elizabethtown	(502)	18,167	15,380
41018	Elsmere	(606)	6,847	7,203
41018	Erlanger	(606)	15,979	14,466
40118	Fairdale(u)	(502)	6,563	7,315
40291	Fern Creek(u)	(502)	16,406	16,866
41139	Flatwoods	(606)	7,799	8,354
*41042	Florence	(606)	18,586	15,586
42223	Fort Campbell North(u)	(502)	18,861	17,211
40121	Fort Knox(u)	(502)	21,495	31,055
41017	Fort Mitchell	(606)	7,438	7,294
41075	Fort Thomas	(606)	16,032	16,012
41011	Fort Wright	(606)	6,404	4,481
*40601	Frankfort	(502)	26,535	25,973
*42134	Franklin	(502)	7,607	7,738
40324	Georgetown	(502)	11,414	10,972
*42141	Glasgow	(502)	12,351	12,958
40330	Harrodsburg	(606)	7,335	7,265
*41701	Hazard	(606)	5,416	5,371
42420	Henderson	(502)	25,945	24,834
40228	Highview(u)	(502)	14,814	13,286
40229	Hillview	(502)	6,119	5,196
*42240	Hopkinsville	(502)	29,809	27,318
41051	Independence	(606)	10,444	7,998
*40299	Jeffersontown	(502)	23,223	15,795
40342	Lawrenceburg	(502)	5,911	5,167
40033	Lebanon	(502)	5,695	6,590
*40507	Lexington	(606)	225,366	204,165
*40741	London	(606)	5,757	4,002
*40232	Louisville	(502)	269,555	298,694
40252	Lyndon	(502)	8,037	1,553
42431	Madisonville	(502)	16,203	16,979
42066	Mayfield	(502)	9,935	10,705
41056	Maysville	(606)	7,169	7,983
40965	Middlesboro	(606)	11,328	12,251
40253	Middletown	(502)	5,016	414
42633	Monticello	(606)	5,357	5,677
40351	Morehead	(606)	8,357	7,789
40353	Mount Sterling	(606)	5,362	5,820
40047	Mount Washington	(502)	5,256	3,997
42071	Murray	(502)	14,442	14,248
40218	Newburg(u)	(502)	21,647	24,612
*41071	Newport	(606)	18,871	21,587
*40356	Nicholasville	(606)	13,603	10,400
40259	Okolona(u)	(502)	18,902	20,039
*42301	Owensboro	(502)	53,577	54,450
*42003	Paducah	(502)	27,256	29,315
*40361	Paris	(606)	8,730	7,935
*41501	Pikeville	(606)	6,324	4,756
40268	Pleasure Ridge Park(u)	(502)	25,131	27,332
42445	Princeton	(502)	6,940	7,073
*40160	Radcliff	(502)	19,778	14,656
*40475	Richmond	(606)	21,183	21,705
42276	Russellville	(502)	7,454	7,520
40216	Saint Dennis(u)	(502)	10,326	....
40206	Saint Matthews	(502)	15,691	13,519
*40066	Shelbyville	(502)	6,155	5,329
40256	Shively	(502)	15,535	16,645

ZIP	Place		1990	1980
*42501	Somerset	(606)	10,735	10,649
41015	Taylor Mill	(606)	5,530	4,509
40272	Valley Station(u)	(502)	22,840	24,474
40383	Versailles	(606)	7,269	6,427
41016	Villa Hills	(606)	7,370	4,384
41101	Westwoods(u)	(606)	5,300	5,973
40769	Williamsburg	(606)	5,493	5,560
*40391	Winchester	(606)	15,799	15,216

Louisiana

ZIP	Place		1990	1980
*70510	Abbeville	(318)	11,184	12,391
*71301	Alexandria	(318)	49,049	51,648
70032	Arabi(u)	(504)	8,787	10,248
70094	Avondale(u)	(504)	5,813	6,699
*70714	Baker	(504)	13,087	12,865
*71220	Bastrop	(318)	13,916	15,527
*70821	Baton Rouge	(504)	219,531	220,394
70360	Bayou Cane(u)	(504)	15,876	15,723
70037	Belle Chasse(u)	(504)	8,512	5,412
*70427	Bogalusa	(504)	14,280	16,976
*71111	Bossier City	(318)	52,721	50,817
70517	Breaux Bridge	(318)	6,694	5,922
70094	Bridge City(u)	(504)	8,327	....
70811	Brownfields(u)	(504)	5,229	....
71291	Brownsville-Bawcomville(u)	(318)	7,397	7,252
71322	Bunkie	(318)	5,044	5,364
70520	Carencro	(318)	5,518	3,712
*70043	Chalmette(u)†	(504)	31,860	33,847
71291	Claiborne(u)	(318)	8,300	6,278
*70433	Covington	(504)	7,691	7,892
*70526	Crowley	(318)	13,983	16,036
70345	Cut Off(u)	(504)	5,325	5,049
*70726	Denham Springs	(504)	8,381	8,563
70634	De Ridder	(318)	9,868	10,337
70047	Destrehan	(504)	8,031	2,382
70346	Donaldsonville	(504)	7,949	7,901
70072	Estelle(u)	(504)	14,091	12,724
70535	Eunice	(318)	11,162	12,479
71459	Fort Polk South	(318)	10,911	12,498
70538	Franklin	(318)	9,004	9,584
70820	Gardere	(504)	7,209	....
*70737	Gonzales	(504)	7,208	7,287
71245	Grambling	(318)	5,512	4,226
*70053	Gretna	(504)	17,208	20,615
*70401	Hammond	(504)	15,871	15,226
70123	Harahan	(504)	9,927	11,384
*70058	Harvey(u)	(504)	21,222	22,709
*70360	Houma	(504)	30,495	32,602
70544	Jeanerette	(318)	6,205	6,511
70502	Jefferson(u)	(504)	14,521	15,550
70546	Jennings	(318)	11,305	12,401
*70062	Kenner	(504)	72,033	66,382
70445	Lacombe(u)	(504)	6,523	5,146
*70501	Lafayette	(318)	94,438	80,584
*70601	Lake Charles	(318)	70,580	75,226
71254	Lake Providence	(318)	5,380	6,361
*70068	La Place(u)	(504)	24,194	16,112
70373	Larose(u)	(504)	5,772	5,234
*71446	Leesville	(318)	7,638	9,054
*70448	Mandeville	(504)	7,474	6,076
71052	Mansfield	(318)	5,389	6,485
71351	Marksville	(318)	5,526	5,113
*70072	Marrero(u)	(504)	36,671	36,548
70075	Meraux(u)	(504)	8,849	....
70812	Merrydale(u)	(318)	10,395	....
*70009	Metairie(u)	(504)	149,428	164,160
*71055	Minden	(318)	13,661	15,084
*71203	Monroe	(318)	54,909	57,597
*70380	Morgan City	(504)	14,531	16,114
70612	Moss Bluff(u)	(318)	8,039	7,004
*71457	Natchitoches	(318)	16,609	16,664
*70560	New Iberia	(318)	31,828	32,766
*70140	New Orleans	(504)	496,938	557,927
70760	New Roads	(504)	5,303	3,924
71463	Oakdale	(318)	6,837	7,155
70808	Oak Hills Place	(504)	5,479	....
*70570	Opelousas	(318)	19,091	18,903
70392	Patterson	(504)	5,166	4,693
*71360	Pineville	(318)	12,255	12,034
*70764	Plaquemine	(504)	7,101	7,521
70454	Ponchatoula	(504)	5,425	5,469
70767	Port Allen	(504)	6,277	6,114
70601	Prien(u)	(318)	6,448	6,224
70394	Raceland(u)	(504)	5,564	6,302
70578	Rayne	(318)	8,502	9,066
71037	Red Chute(u)	(318)	5,431	....
70084	Reserve(u)	(504)	8,847	7,288
70123	River Ridge(u)	(504)	14,800	17,146
*71270	Ruston	(318)	20,071	20,585
70582	Saint Martinville	(318)	7,226	7,965
70087	Saint Rose(u)	(504)	6,259	....
70817	Shenandoah(u)		13,429	....
*71102	Shreveport	(318)	198,518	206,989
*70458	Slidell	(504)	24,124	26,718
71075	Springhill	(318)/(504)	5,668	6,516
*70663	Sulphur	(318)	20,125	19,709

ZIP	Place		1990	1980
*71282	Tallulah	(318)	8,526	11,341
70056	Terrytown(u)	(504)	23,787	23,548
*70301	Thibodaux	(504)	14,125	15,810
70053	Timberlane(u)	(504)	12,614	11,579
70809	Village Saint George(u)	(504)	6,242	....
70586	Ville Platte	(318)	9,037	9,201
70092	Violet(u)	(504)	8,574	11,678
70094	Waggaman(u)	(504)	9,405	9,004
70669	Westlake	(318)	5,007	5,246
*71291	West Monroe	(318)	14,096	14,993
*70094	Westwego	(504)	11,218	12,663
71483	Winnfield	(318)	6,138	7,311
71295	Winnsboro	(318)	5,755	5,921
70791	Zachary	(504)	9,036	7,297

Maine (207)

See note on page 389

ZIP	Place	1990	1980
*04210	Auburn	24,309	23,128
*04330	Augusta	21,325	21,819
*04401	Bangor	33,181	31,643
04530	Bath	9,799	10,246
04915	Belfast	6,355	6,243
03901	*Berwick*	5,995	4,149
*04005	Biddeford	20,710	19,638
04412	Brewer	9,021	9,017
04011	Brunswick Center(u)	14,683	10,990
04011	*Brunswick*	20,906	17,366
04093	*Buxton*	6,494	5,775
04843	*Camden*	5,060	4,584
04107	*Cape Elizabeth*	8,854	7,838
04736	Caribou	9,415	9,916
04021	*Cumberland*	5,836	5,284
03903	*Eliot*	5,329	4,948
04605	Ellsworth	5,975	5,179
04937	*Fairfield*	6,718	6,113
04105	*Falmouth*	7,610	6,853
04938	Farmington	7,436	6,730
04032	*Freeport*	6,905	5,863
04345	Gardiner	6,746	6,485
04038	*Gorham*	11,856	10,101
04039	*Gray*	5,904	4,344
04444	*Hampden*	5,974	5,250
*04079	*Harpswell*	5,012	3,796
04730	Houlton Center(u)	5,627	5,730
04730	*Houlton*	6,613	6,766
04239	*Jay*	5,080	5,080
04043	*Kennebunk*	8,004	6,621
03904	Kittery Center(u)	5,151	5,465
03904	*Kittery*	9,372	9,314
*04240	Lewiston	39,757	40,481
04750	*Limestone*	9,922	8,719
04457	*Lincoln*	5,587	5,066
04250	*Lisbon*	9,457	8,769
04751	Loring AFB(u)	7,829	6,572
04462	Millinocket Center(u)	6,922	7,567
04462	*Millinocket*	6,956	7,567
04963	*Oakland*	5,595	5,162
04064	Old Orchard Beach Ctr.(u)	7,789	6,023
04064	*Old Orchard Beach*	7,789	6,291
04468	Old Town	8,317	8,422
04473	Orono Center(u)	9,789	9,891
04473	*Orono*	10,573	10,578
*04101	Portland	64,358	61,572
04769	Presque Isle	10,550	11,172
04841	Rockland	7,972	7,919
04276	Rumford Compact(u)	5,419	6,256
04276	*Rumford*	7,078	8,240
04072	Saco	15,181	12,921
04073	Sanford Center(u)	10,296	10,268
04073	*Sanford*	20,463	18,020
*04074	*Scarborough*	12,518	11,347
04976	Skowhegan Center(u)	6,990	6,517
04976	*Skowhegan*	8,725	8,098
03908	*South Berwick*	5,877	4,046
*04101	South Portland	23,163	22,712
04084	*Standish*	7,678	5,946
04086	*Topsham*	8,746	6,431
*04901	Waterville	17,173	17,779
04090	*Wells*	7,778	8,211
*04092	Westbrook	16,121	14,976
04062	*Windham*	13,020	11,282
04901	Winslow Center(u)	5,436	5,903
04901	*Winslow*	7,997	8,057
04364	*Winthrop*	5,986	5,889
04096	*Yarmouth*	7,862	6,585
03909	*York*	9,818	8,465

Maryland

ZIP	Place		1990	1980
21001	Aberdeen	(410)	13,087	11,533
21005	Aberdeen Proving Ground(u)	(410)	5,267	5,722
20783	Adelphi(u)	(301)	13,524	12,530
20335	Andrews AFB(u)	(410)	10,000	10,064
*21401	Annapolis	(410)	33,195	31,740

ZIP	Place		1990	1980
21227	Arbutus(u)	(410)	19,750	20,163
21012	Arnold(u)	(410)	20,261	12,285
20916	Aspen Hill(u)	(301)	45,494	47,455
21220	Ballenger Creek†	(410)	5,546	2,659
*21203	Baltimore	(410)	736,014	786,741
*21014	Bel Air	(410)	8,942	7,814
21050	Bel Air North(u)	(410)	14,880	5,043
21014	Bel Air South(u)	(410)	26,421	9,140
*20705	Beltsville(u)	(301)	14,476	12,760
*20814	Bethesda(u)	(301)	62,936	63,022
20710	Bladensburg	(301)	8,064	7,691
*20715	Bowie	(301)	37,642	33,695
21220	Bowleys Quarters(u)	(410)	5,595	....
21225	Brooklyn Park(u)	(410)	10,987	11,508
21716	Brunswick	(301)	5,117	4,572
20866	Burtonsville(u)	(410)	5,853	2,046
20818	Cabin John(u)	(301)	5,341	5,135
20619	California(u)	(410)	7,626	5,770
20705	Calverton(u)	(301)	12,046	7,649
21613	Cambridge	(410)	11,514	11,703
20748	Camp Springs(u)	(301)	16,392	16,118
21401	Cape St. Clair(u)	(410)	7,878	6,022
21234	Carney(u)	(410)	25,578	21,488
21228	Catonsville(u)	(410)	35,233	33,208
20657	Chesapeake Ranch Estates(u)	(301)	5,423	....
20784	Cheverly	(301)	6,023	5,751
*20815	Chevy Chase(u)	(301)	8,559	12,232
20783	Chillum(u)	(301)	31,309	32,775
20735	Clinton(u)	(301)	19,987	16,438
20904	Cloverly(u)	(301)	7,904	5,153
*21030	Cockeysville(u)	(410)	18,668	17,013
20914	Colesville(u)	(301)	18,819	14,359
*20740	College Park	(301)	23,714	23,614
*21045	Columbia(u)	(410)/(301)	75,883	52,518
20743	Coral Hills(u)	(410)	11,032	11,602
21114	Crofton(u)	(410)	12,781	12,009
*21502	Cumberland	(301)	23,712	25,933
20872	Damascus(u)	(301)	9,817	4,129
*20747	District Heights	(301)	6,711	6,799
21222	Dundalk(u)	(410)	65,800	71,293
21601	Easton	(410)	9,372	7,536
20737	East Riverdale(u)	(301)	14,187	14,104
21219	Edgemere(u)	(410)	9,226	9,078
21040	Edgewood(u)	(410)	23,903	19,455
21784	Eldersburg(u)	(410)	9,720	4,959
21227	Elkridge(u)	(410)	12,953	....
*21921	Elkton	(410)	9,073	6,468
*21043	Ellicott City(u)	(410)	41,396	21,784
21221	Essex(u)	(410)	40,872	39,614
20904	Fairland(u)	(301)	19,828	5,154
21047	Fallston(u)	(410)	5,730	5,572
21061	Ferndale(u)	(410)	16,355	14,314
20747	Forestville(u)	(301)	16,731	16,401
20755	Fort Meade(u)	(301)	12,509	14,083
20744	Fort Washington(u)	(301)	24,032	....
*21701	Frederick	(301)	40,186	28,086
20744	Friendly(u)	(301)	9,028	8,848
21532	Frostburg	(301)	8,069	7,715
*20877	Gaithersburg	(301)	39,676	26,424
21055	Garrison(u)	(410)	5,045	....
*20874	Germantown(u)	(301)	41,145	9,721
20706	Glenarden	(301)	5,025	4,993
*21061	Glen Burnie(u)	(410)	37,305	37,263
20769	Glenn Dale(u)	(301)	9,689	4,829
20772	Greater Upper Marlboro		11,528	....
*20770	Greenbelt	(301)	20,561	17,332
21122	Green Haven(u)	(410)	14,416	6,577
21771	Green Valley(u)	(301)	9,424	4,504
*21740	Hagerstown	(301)	35,306	34,132
21740	Halfway(u)	(301)	8,873	8,659
21078	Havre de Grace	(410)	8,952	8,763
20903	Hillandale(u)	(301)	10,318	9,686
20748	Hillcrest Heights(u)	(301)	17,136	17,021
*20780	Hyattsville	(301)	13,864	12,709
20794	Jessup(u)	(410)	6,537	4,288
21085	Joppatowne(u)	(410)	11,084	11,348
20785	Kentland(u)	(301)	7,967	8,596
20772	Kettering(u)	(301)	9,901	6,972
21122	Lake Shore(u)	(410)	13,269	10,181
20785	Landover(u)	(301)	5,052	5,374
20787	Langley Park(u)	(301)	17,474	14,038
20706	Lanham-Seabrook(u)	(301)	16,792	15,814
21227	Lansdowne-Baltimore Highlands(u)	(410)	15,509	16,759
20646	La Plata	(301)	5,841	2,484
20772	Largo(u)	(301)	9,475	5,557
*20707	Laurel	(301)	19,086	12,103
20653	Lexington Park(u)	(410)	9,943	10,361
21090	Linthicum(u)	(410)	7,547	7,457
21207	Lochearn(u)	(410)	25,240	26,908
21037	Londontowne(u)	(410)	6,992	6,052
21784	Long Meadow(u)†	(410)	5,594	1,203
*21093	Lutherville-Timonium(u)	(410)	16,442	16,871
20748	Marlow Heights(u)	(301)	5,885	5,824
20772	Marlton(u)	(301)	5,523	....
20707	Maryland City(u)	(301)	6,813	6,949
21093	Mays Chapel(u)	(410)	10,102	5,213
21220	Middle River(u)	(410)	24,616	26,756
21207	Milford Mill(u)	(410)	22,547	20,354
20717	Mitchellville(u)	(301)	12,593	....

ZIP	Place		1990	1980
20879	Montgomery Village(u)	(301)	32,315	18,725
20712	Mount Rainier	(301)	7,954	7,361
21402	Naval Academy(u)	(410)	5,420	5,367
20784	New Carrollton	(301)	12,002	12,632
20815	North Bethesda(u)	(301)	29,656	22,671
20895	North Kensington(u)	(301)	8,607	9,039
20707	North Laurel(u)	(301)	15,008	6,093
20878	North Potomac(u)	(301)	18,456	....
21842	Ocean City	(410)	5,146	4,946
21113	Odenton(u)	(410)	12,833	13,270
*20832	Olney(u)	(301)	23,019	13,026
21206	Overlea(u)	(410)	12,137	12,965
21117	Owings Mills(u)	(410)	9,474	9,526
*20745	Oxon Hill-Glassmanor(u)†	(301)	35,794	36,267
20785	Palmer Park(u)	(301)	7,019	7,986
21234	Parkville(u)	(410)	31,617	35,159
21401	Parole(u)	(410)	10,054	3,377
21122	Pasadena(u)	(410)	10,012	7,439
21128	Perry Hall(u)	(410)	22,723	13,455
21208	Pikesville(u)	(410)	24,815	22,555
*20850	Potomac(u)	(301)	45,634	40,313
21227	Pumphrey(u)	(410)	5,483	5,666
21133	Randallstown(u)	(301)	26,277	25,927
.....	Redland(u)	(301)	16,145	10,528
21136	Reisterstown(u)	(410)	19,314	19,385
21122	Riviera Beach(u)	(410)	11,376	8,812
*20850	Rockville	(301)	44,830	43,811
20772	Rosaryville(u)	(301)	8,976	....
21237	Rosedale(u)	(410)	18,703	19,956
.....	Rossmoor(u)	.....	6,182	....
21221	Rossville(u)	(410)	9,492	8,646
20602	Saint Charles(u)	(301)	28,717	13,921
*21801	Salisbury	(410)	20,592	16,429
20763	Savage-Guilford(u)	(410)	9,669	2,928
20743	Seat Pleasant	(301)	5,359	5,217
21144	Severn(u)	(410)	24,499	20,147
21146	Severna Park(u)	(410)	25,879	21,253
*20907	Silver Spring(u)	(301)	76,046	72,893
21061	South Gate(u)	(410)	27,564	24,185
20895	South Kensington(u)	(301)	8,777	9,344
20707	South Laurel(u)	(301)	18,591	18,034
*20746	Suitland-Silver Hills(u)	(301)	35,111	32,164
*20907	Takoma Park	(301)	16,724	16,231
*20748	Temple Hills(u)	(301)	6,865	6,630
21285	Towson(u)	(410)	49,445	51,083
*20602	Waldorf(u)	(301)	15,058	9,782
20743	Walker Mill(u)	(301)	10,920	10,651
*21157	Westminster	(410)	13,060	8,808
20902	Wheaton-Glenmont(u)	(301)	53,720	48,598
21162	White Marsh(u)	(410)	8,183	....
20903	White Oak(u)	(301)	18,671	13,700
21207	Woodlawn(u) (Baltimore)	(410)	32,907	29,453
21284	Woodlawn(u) (Prince George's)	(410)	5,329	5,306

Massachusetts

See note on page 389

ZIP	Place		1990	1980
02351	Abington(u)	(617)	13,817	13,887
01720	Acton	(508)	17,872	17,544
02743	Acushnet	(508)	9,554	8,704
01220	Adams Center(u)	(413)	6,356	6,857
01220	Adams	(413)	9,445	10,381
01001	Agawam	(413)	27,323	26,271
01913	Amesbury Center(u)	(508)	12,109	12,236
01913	Amesbury	(508)	14,997	13,971
*01002	Amherst Center(u)	(413)	17,824	17,773
*01002	Amherst	(413)	35,228	33,229
*01810	Andover(u)	(508)	8,242	8,445
*01810	Andover	(508)	29,151	26,370
02174	Arlington(u)	(617)	44,630	48,219
01430	Ashburnham	(508)	5,433	4,075
01721	Ashland	(508)	12,066	9,165
01331	Athol Center(u)	(508)	8,732	8,708
01331	Athol	(508)	11,451	10,634
02703	Attleboro	(508)	38,383	34,196
01501	Auburn	(508)	15,005	14,845
01432	Ayer	(508)	6,871	6,993
02630	Barnstable	(508)	40,949	30,898
01730	Bedford	(617)	12,996	13,067
01007	Belchertown	(413)	10,579	8,339
02019	Bellingham	(508)	14,877	14,300
02178	Belmont(u)	(617)	24,720	26,100
01915	Beverly	(508)	38,195	37,655
*01821	Billerica	(508)	37,609	36,727
01504	Blackstone	(508)	8,023	6,570
*02205	Boston	(617)	574,283	562,994
02532	Bourne	(508)	16,064	13,874
01921	Boxford	(508)	6,266	5,374
*02205	Braintree(u)	(617)	33,836	36,337
02631	Brewster	(508)	8,440	5,226
02324	Bridgewater	(508)	21,249	17,202
*02403	Brockton	(508)	92,788	95,172
02146	Brookline(u)	(617)	54,718	55,062
01803	Burlington	(617)	23,302	23,486
*02139	Cambridge	(617)	95,802	95,322
02021	Canton	(617)	18,530	18,182

ZIP	Place		1990	1980
02330	Carver	(508)	10,590	6,988
*02632	Centerville	(508)	9,190	3,640
01507	Charlton	(508)	9,576	6,719
02633	Chatham	(508)	6,579	6,071
01824	Chelmsford(u)	(508)	32,383	31,174
02150	Chelsea	(617)	28,710	25,431
*01020	Chicopee	(413)	56,632	55,112
01510	Clinton	(508)	13,222	12,771
01778	Cochituate(u)	(508)	6,046	6,126
02025	Cohasset	(617)	7,075	7,174
01742	Concord	(508)	17,076	16,293
*01226	Dalton	(413)	7,155	6,797
01923	Danvers(u)	(508)	24,174	24,100
02714	Dartmouth	(508)	27,244	23,966
*02026	Dedham(u)	(617)	23,782	25,298
01342	Deerfield	(413)	5,018	4,517
02638	Dennis	(508)	13,864	12,360
02715	Dighton	(508)	5,631	5,352
01516	Douglas	(508)	5,438	3,730
01826	Dracut	(508)	25,594	21,249
01571	Dudley	(508)	9,540	8,717
*02332	Duxbury	(617)	13,895	11,807
02333	East Bridgewater	(508)	11,104	9,945
02536	East Falmouth(u)	(508)	5,577	5,181
01027	Easthampton	(413)	15,537	15,580
01028	East Longmeadow	(413)	13,367	12,905
02334	Easton	(508)	19,807	16,623
02149	Everett	(617)	35,701	37,195
02719	Fairhaven	(508)	16,132	15,759
*02722	Fall River	(508)	92,703	92,574
*02540	Falmouth	(508)	27,960	23,640
01420	Fitchburg	(508)	41,194	39,580
01433	Fort Devens(u)	(508)	8,973	9,546
02035	Foxborough(u)	(508)	5,706	5,697
01701	Framingham	(508)	64,989	65,113
02038	Franklin Center(u)	(508)	9,965	9,296
02038	Franklin	(508)	22,095	18,217
02702	Freetown	(508)	8,522	7,058
01440	Gardner	(508)	20,125	17,900
01833	Georgetown	(508)	6,384	5,687
*01930	Gloucester	(508)	28,716	27,768
01519	Grafton	(508)	13,035	11,238
01033	Granby	(413)	5,565	5,380
01230	Great Barrington	(413)	7,725	7,405
*01301	Greenfield Center(u)	(413)	14,016	14,198
01302	Greenfield	(413)	18,666	18,436
01450	Groton	(508)	7,511	6,154
01834	Groveland	(508)	5,214	5,040
02338	Halifax	(617)	6,526	5,513
01936	Hamilton	(508)	7,280	6,960
02339	Hanover	(617)	11,912	11,358
02341	Hanson	(617)	9,028	8,617
01451	Harvard	(508)	12,329	12,170
02645	Harwich	(508)	10,275	8,971
*01830	Haverhill	(508)	51,418	46,865
02043	Hingham	(617)	19,821	20,339
02343	Holbrook(u)	(617)	11,041	11,140
01520	Holden	(508)	14,628	13,336
01746	Holliston	(508)	12,926	12,622
*01040	Holyoke	(413)	43,704	44,678
01747	Hopedale	(508)	5,666	3,905
01748	Hopkinton	(508)	9,191	7,114
01749	Hudson Center(u)	(508)	14,267	14,156
01749	Hudson	(508)	17,233	16,408
02045	Hull(u)	(617)	10,466	9,714
02601	Hyannis(u)	(508)	14,120	9,118
01938	Ipswich	(508)	11,873	11,158
02364	Kingston	(617)	9,045	7,362
02347	Lakeville	(508)	7,785	5,931
01523	Lancaster	(508)	6,661	6,334
*01842	Lawrence	(508)	70,207	63,175
01238	Lee	(413)	5,849	6,247
01524	Leicester	(508)	10,191	9,446
01240	Lenox	(413)	5,069	6,523
01453	Leominster	(508)	38,145	34,508
02173	Lexington(u)	(617)	28,974	29,479
01773	Lincoln	(617)	7,666	7,098
01460	Littleton	(508)	7,051	6,970
*01028	Longmeadow(u)	(413)	15,467	16,301
*01853	Lowell	(508)	103,439	92,418
01056	Ludlow	(413)	18,820	18,150
01462	Lunenburg	(508)	9,117	8,405
*01901	Lynn	(617)	81,245	78,471
01940	Lynnfield(u)	(617)	11,274	11,267
02148	Malden	(617)	53,884	53,386
01944	Manchester-by-the-Sea (formerly Manchester)	(508)	5,286	5,424
02048	Mansfield	(508)	16,568	13,453
01945	Marblehead(u)	(617)	19,971	20,126
01752	Marlborough	(508)	31,813	30,617
02050	Marshfield	(617)	21,531	20,916
02648	Marstons Mills(u)	(508)	8,017	....
02649	Mashpee	(508)	7,884	3,700
02739	Mattapoisett	(508)	5,850	5,597
01754	Maynard(u)	(508)	10,325	9,590
02052	Medfield	(508)	10,531	10,220
02155	Medford	(617)	57,407	58,076
02053	Medway	(508)	9,931	8,447
*02176	Melrose	(617)	28,150	30,055
01860	Merrimac	(508)	5,166	4,451

ZIP	Place		1990	1980
01844	Methuen	(508)	39,990	36,701
02346	Middleborough Center(u)	(508)	6,837	7,012
02346	Middleborough	(508)	17,867	16,404
01757	Milford Center(u)	(508)	23,339	21,720
01757	Milford	(508)	25,355	23,390
01527	Millbury	(508)	12,228	11,808
02054	Millis	(508)	7,613	6,908
02186	Milton(u)	(617)	25,725	25,860
01057	Monson	(413)	7,776	7,315
01351	Montague	(413)	8,316	8,011
*02554	Nantucket	(508)	6,012	5,087
01760	Natick	(508)	30,510	29,461
*02205	Needham(u)	(617)	27,557	27,901
*02740	New Bedford	(508)	99,922	98,478
01951	Newbury	(508)	5,623	4,529
01950	Newburyport	(508)	16,317	15,900
*02205	Newton	(617)	82,585	83,622
02056	Norfolk	(508)	9,270	6,363
01247	North Adams	(413)	16,797	18,063
01002	North Amherst(u)	(413)	6,239	5,616
*01060	Northampton	(413)	29,289	29,286
01845	North Andover	(508)	22,792	20,129
*02760	North Attleborough	(508)	25,038	21,095
01532	Northborough	(508)	11,929	10,568
01534	Northbridge	(508)	13,371	12,246
01864	North Reading	(508)	12,002	11,455
02766	Norton	(508)	14,265	12,690
02061	Norwell	(617)	9,279	9,182
02062	Norwood(u)	(617)	28,700	29,711
01364	Orange	(508)	7,312	6,844
02653	Orleans	(508)	5,838	5,306
01540	Oxford Center(u)	(508)	5,969	6,369
01540	Oxford	(508)	12,588	11,680
01069	Palmer	(413)	12,054	11,389
*01960	Peabody	(508)	47,264	45,976
02359	Pembroke	(617)	14,544	13,487
01463	Pepperell	(508)	10,098	8,061
01866	Pinehurst(u)	(508)	6,614	6,588
*01201	Pittsfield	(413)	48,622	51,974
02762	Plainville	(508)	6,871	5,857
*02360	Plymouth Center(u)	(508)	7,258	7,232
*02360	Plymouth	(508)	45,608	35,913
*02205	Quincy	(617)	84,985	84,743
02368	Randolph(u)	(617)	30,093	28,218
02767	Raynham	(508)	9,867	9,085
01867	Reading(u)	(617)	22,539	22,678
02769	Rehoboth	(508)	8,656	7,570
02151	Revere	(617)	42,786	42,423
02370	Rockland	(617)	16,123	15,695
01966	Rockport	(508)	7,482	6,345
*01970	Salem	(508)	38,091	38,276
01952	Salisbury	(508)	6,882	5,973
02563	Sandwich	(508)	15,489	8,727
01906	Saugus(u)	(617)	25,549	24,746
02066	Scituate	(617)	16,786	17,317
02771	Seekonk	(508)	13,046	12,269
02067	Sharon	(617)	15,517	13,601
01464	Shirley	(508)	6,118	5,124
01545	Shrewsbury	(508)	24,146	22,674
*02722	Somerset(u)	(508)	17,655	18,813
*02205	Somerville(u)	(617)	76,210	77,372
01002	South Amherst	(413)	5,053	4,861
01772	Southborough	(508)	6,628	6,193
01550	Southbridge Center(u)	(508)	13,631	12,882
01550	Southbridge	(508)	17,816	16,665
01075	South Hadley	(413)	16,685	16,399
01077	Southwick	(413)	7,667	7,382
02664	South Yarmouth(u)	(508)	10,358	7,525
01562	Spencer Center(u)	(508)	6,306	6,350
01562	Spencer	(508)	11,645	10,774
*01101	Springfield	(413)	156,983	152,319
01564	Sterling	(508)	6,481	5,440
02180	Stoneham	(617)	22,203	21,424
02072	Stoughton	(617)	26,777	26,710
01775	Stow	(508)	5,328	5,144
01566	Sturbridge	(508)	7,775	5,976
01776	Sudbury	(508)	14,358	14,027
01590	Sutton	(508)	6,824	5,855
01907	Swampscott(u)	(617)	13,650	13,837
02777	Swansea	(508)	15,411	15,461
02780	Taunton	(508)	49,832	45,001
01468	Templeton	(508)	6,438	6,070
01876	Tewksbury	(508)	27,266	24,635
01983	Topsfield	(508)	5,754	5,709
01469	Townsend	(508)	8,496	7,201
01879	Tyngsborough	(508)	8,642	5,683
01569	Uxbridge	(508)	10,415	8,374
01880	Wakefield(u)	(617)	24,825	24,895
02081	Walpole	(508)	20,223	18,859
*02205	Waltham	(617)	57,878	58,200
01082	Ware Center(u)	(413)	6,533	6,806
01082	Ware	(413)	9,808	8,953
02571	Wareham	(508)	19,232	18,457
*02205	Watertown(u)	(617)	33,284	34,384
01778	Wayland	(508)	11,874	12,170
01570	Webster Center(u)	(508)	11,849	11,175
01570	Webster	(508)	10,100	11,400
02181	Wellesley	(617)	26,615	27,209
01581	Westborough	(508)	14,133	13,619
01583	West Boylston	(508)	6,611	6,204

ZIP	Place		1990	1980
02379	West Bridgewater	(508)	6,389	6,359
01742	West Concord(u)	(508)	5,761	5,331
*01085	Westfield	(413)	38,372	36,465
01886	Westford	(508)	16,392	13,434
01473	Westminster	(508)	6,191	5,139
02193	Weston	(617)	10,200	11,169
02790	Westport	(508)	13,852	13,763
*01089	West Springfield(u)	(413)	27,537	27,042
02090	Westwood	(617)	12,557	13,212
02673	West Yarmouth	(508)	5,409	3,852
*02205	Weymouth(u)	(617)	54,063	55,601
01588	Whitinsville(u)	(508)	5,639	5,379
02382	Whitman	(617)	13,240	13,534
01095	Wilbraham	(413)	12,635	12,053
01267	Williamstown	(413)	8,220	8,741
01887	Wilmington(u)	(508)	17,651	17,471
01475	Winchendon	(508)	8,805	7,019
01890	Winchester(u)	(617)	20,267	20,701
02152	Winthrop(u)	(617)	18,127	19,294
*01801	Woburn	(617)	35,943	36,626
*01613	Worcester	(508)	169,759	161,799
02093	Wrentham	(508)	9,006	7,580
02675	Yarmouth	(508)	21,174	18,449

Michigan

ZIP	Place		1990	1980
49221	Adrian	(517)	22,097	21,276
49224	Albion	(517)	10,066	11,059
49401	Allendale(u)	(616)	6,950	....
48101	Allen Park	(313)	31,092	34,196
48801	Alma	(517)	9,034	9,652
49707	Alpena	(517)	11,354	12,214
*48106	Ann Arbor	(734)	109,608	107,969
*48321	Auburn Hills†	(248)	17,076	15,388
*49016	Battle Creek	(616)	53,516	35,724
*48707	Bay City	(517)	38,936	41,593
48505	Beecher(u)	(517)	14,465	17,178
48809	Belding	(616)	5,969	5,634
*49022	Benton Harbor	(616)	12,818	14,707
49022	Benton Heights(u)	(616)	5,465	6,787
48072	Berkley	(248)	16,960	18,637
48025	Beverly Hills	(248)	10,610	11,598
49307	Big Rapids	(616)	12,603	14,361
*48012	Birmingham	(248)	19,997	21,689
48301	Bloomfield(u)	(810)	42,137	42,876
48722	Bridgeport(u)	(517)	8,569	....
48116	Brighton	(810)	5,686	4,268
48601	Buena Vista(u)		8,196	....
*48501	Burton	(810)	27,437	29,976
49601	Cadillac	(616)	10,104	10,199
*48187	Canton(u)	(734)	57,047	....
48724	Carrollton(u)	(517)	6,521	7,482
48015	Center Line	(810)	9,026	9,293
48813	Charlotte	(517)	8,083	8,251
48017	Clawson	(248)	13,874	15,103
*48046	Clinton(u)	(517)	85,866	72,400
49036	Coldwater	(517)	9,607	9,461
49321	Comstock Park(u)	(616)	6,530	5,506
49508	Cutlerville(u)	(616)	11,228	8,256
48423	Davison	(810)	5,693	6,087
*48120	Dearborn	(313)	89,286	90,660
*48127	Dearborn Heights	(313)	60,838	67,706
*48231	Detroit	(313)	1,027,974	1,203,368
49047	Dowagiac	(616)	6,418	6,307
49506	East Grand Rapids	(616)	10,807	10,914
*48826	East Lansing	(517)	50,677	51,392
48021	Eastpointe	(810)	35,283	38,280
49001	Eastwood(u)	(616)	6,340	7,186
48229	Ecorse	(313)	12,180	14,447
49829	Escanaba	(906)	13,659	14,355
49022	Fair Plain(u)	(616)	8,051	8,289
*48333	Farmington	(248)	10,170	11,022
48333	Farmington Hills	(248)	74,614	58,056
48430	Fenton	(810)	8,434	8,098
48220	Ferndale	(248)	25,084	26,227
48134	Flat Rock	(734)	7,290	6,853
*48501	Flint	(810)	140,925	140,925
48433	Flushing	(810)	8,542	8,624
49506	Forest Hills(u)	(616)	16,690	....
48026	Fraser	(810)	13,899	14,560
*48135	Garden City	(734)	31,846	35,640
48439	Grand Blanc	(810)	7,760	6,848
49417	Grand Haven	(616)	11,951	11,763
48837	Grand Ledge	(517)	7,562	6,920
*49501	Grand Rapids	(616)	189,126	181,843
*49418	Grandville	(616)	15,624	12,412
48838	Greenville	(616)	8,101	8,019
48138	Grosse Ile(u)	(734)	9,781	9,320
*48231	Grosse Pointe	(313)	5,681	5,901
48230	Grosse Pointe Farms	(313)	10,092	10,551
48230	Grosse Pointe Park	(313)	12,857	13,562
48230	Grosse Pointe Woods	(313)	17,715	18,886
48212	Hamtramck	(313)	18,372	21,300
48225	Harper Woods	(313)	14,903	16,361
48045	Harrison(u)	(517)	24,685	23,649
48840	Haslett(u)	(517)	10,230	7,025
49058	Hastings	(616)	6,549	6,418
48030	Hazel Park	(248)	20,051	20,914

ZIP	Place		1990	1980
48203	Highland Park	(313)	20,121	27,909
49242	Hillsdale	(517)	8,175	7,432
*49423	Holland	(616)	30,745	26,281
48442	Holly	(248)	5,595	4,874
48842	Holt(u)	(517)	11,744	10,097
49931	Houghton	(906)	7,498	7,512
*48843	Howell	(517)	8,147	6,976
49426	Hudsonville	(616)	6,170	4,844
48070	Huntington Woods	(248)	6,419	6,937
48141	Inkster	(313)/(734)	30,772	35,190
48846	Ionia	(616)	5,990	5,920
*49801	Iron Mountain	(906)	8,525	8,341
49938	Ironwood	(906)	6,849	7,741
49849	Ishpeming	(906)	7,200	7,538
*49204	Jackson	(517)	37,425	39,739
*49428	Jenison(u)	(616)	17,882	16,330
*49001	Kalamazoo	(616)	80,277	79,722
49518	Kentwood	(616)	37,826	30,438
49801	Kingsford	(906)	5,480	5,290
49843	K.I. Sawyer AFB(u)	(906)	6,577	7,345
48144	Lambertville(u)	(734)	7,860	6,341
*48901	Lansing	(517)	127,321	130,414
48446	Lapeer	(810)	7,759	6,198
48146	Lincoln Park	(313)	41,832	45,105
*48150	Livonia	(734)	100,850	104,814
49431	Ludington	(616)	8,507	8,937
48071	Madison Heights	(248)	32,196	35,375
49660	Manistee	(616)	6,734	7,665
49855	Marquette	(906)	21,977	23,288
49068	Marshall	(616)	6,941	7,201
48040	Marysville	(810)	8,515	7,345
48854	Mason	(517)	6,768	6,019
48122	Melvindale	(313)	11,216	12,322
49858	Menominee	(906)	9,398	10,099
*48640	Midland	(517)	38,053	37,269
*48381	Milford	(248)	5,500	5,041
48161	Monroe	(734)	22,902	23,531
*48046	Mount Clemens	(810)	18,405	18,991
*48804	Mount Pleasant	(517)	23,299	23,746
*49440	Muskegon	(616)	39,809	40,823
49444	Muskegon Heights	(616)	13,176	14,611
*48047	New Baltimore	(810)	5,798	5,439
49120	Niles	(616)	12,458	13,115
49505	Northview(u)	(616)	13,712	11,662
48167	Northville	(248)	6,226	5,698
49441	Norton Shores	(616)	21,755	22,025
*48376	Novi	(248)	32,998	22,525
48237	Oak Park	(248)	30,468	31,537
*48805	Okemos(u)	(517)	20,216	8,882
48867	Owosso	(517)	16,322	16,455
49770	Petoskey	(616)	6,056	6,097
48170	Plymouth	(734)	9,560	9,986
48170	Plymouth Township(u)	(734)	23,646	....
*48343	Pontiac	(248)	71,136	76,715
49081	Portage	(616)	41,042	38,157
*48061	Port Huron	(810)	33,694	33,981
*48231	Redford(u)	(313)	54,387	58,441
48218	River Rouge	(313)	11,314	12,912
48192	Riverview	(734)	13,894	14,569
*48308	Rochester	(248)	7,130	7,203
48306	Rochester Hills†	(248)	61,766	40,704
48174	Romulus	(313)/(734)	22,897	24,857
48066	Roseville	(810)	51,412	54,311
*48068	Royal Oak	(248)	65,410	70,893
*48605	Saginaw	(517)	69,512	77,508
48604	Saginaw Township North(u)	(517)	23,018	....
48603	Saginaw Township South(u)	(517)	13,987	....
48079	Saint Clair	(810)	5,116	4,780
*48080	Saint Clair Shores	(313)	68,107	76,210
48879	Saint Johns	(517)	7,392	7,376
49085	Saint Joseph	(616)	9,214	9,622
48176	Saline	(734)	6,663	6,483
49783	Sault Sainte Marie	(906)	14,689	14,448
49455	Shelby(u)	(616)	48,655	....
48609	Shields(u)	(517)	6,634	....
*48037	Southfield	(248)	75,727	75,568
48195	Southgate	(734)	30,771	32,058
49090	South Haven	(616)	5,563	5,943
48178	South Lyon	(248)	6,479	5,214
48161	South Monroe(u)	(734)	5,266	4,232
49015	Springfield	(248)	5,582	5,917
*48311	Sterling Heights	(810)	117,810	108,999
49091	Sturgis	(616)	10,130	9,468
48180	Taylor	(313)/(734)	70,811	77,568
49286	Tecumseh	(517)	7,462	7,320
48182	Temperance(u)	(734)	6,542	....
49093	Three Rivers	(616)	7,464	7,015
*49685	Traverse City	(616)	15,155	15,516
48183	Trenton	(734)	20,586	22,762
*48099	Troy	(248)	72,884	67,102
*48318	Utica	(810)	5,081	5,282
49504	Walker	(616)	17,279	15,088
*48390	Walled Lake	(248)	6,278	4,748
*48090	Warren	(810)	144,864	161,134
48329	Waterford(u)	(248)	66,692	64,250
48917	Waverly(u)	(517)	15,614	....
48184	Wayne	(734)	19,899	21,159
*48325	West Bloomfield(u)	(248)	54,843	41,962
48185	Westland	(313)/(734)	84,724	84,603
49019	Westwood(u)	(616)	8,957	8,519

ZIP	Place		1990	1980
48393	Wixom	(248)	8,550	6,705
48183	Woodhaven	(734)	11,631	10,902
48753	Wurtsmith AFB(u)	(517)	5,080	5,166
*48192	Wyandotte	(734)	30,938	34,006
49509	Wyoming	(616)	63,891	59,616
*48197	Ypsilanti	(734)	24,846	24,031
49464	Zeeland	(616)	5,417	4,764

Minnesota

ZIP	Place		1990	1980
56007	Albert Lea	(507)	18,310	19,200
56308	Alexandria	(320)	8,029	7,608
55304	Andover	(612)	15,216	9,387
*55303	Anoka	(612)	17,192	15,634
55124	Apple Valley	(612)	34,598	21,818
55112	Arden Hills	(612)	9,199	8,012
55912	Austin	(507)	21,926	23,020
56601	Bemidji	(218)	11,165	10,949
55449	Blaine	(612)	38,975	28,558
*55420	Bloomington	(612)	86,335	81,831
56401	Brainerd	(218)	12,353	11,489
55429	Brooklyn Center	(612)	28,887	31,230
55443	Brooklyn Park	(612)	56,381	43,332
55313	Buffalo	(612)	6,856	4,560
*55337	Burnsville	(612)	51,288	35,674
55008	Cambridge	(612)	5,094	3,287
55316	Champlin	(612)	16,849	9,006
55317	Chanhassen	(612)	11,732	6,359
55318	Chaska	(612)	11,339	8,346
55719	Chisholm	(218)	5,290	5,930
55720	Cloquet	(218)	10,885	11,142
55421	Columbia Heights	(612)	18,910	20,029
55433	Coon Rapids	(612)	52,978	35,826
55340	Corcoran	(612)	5,199	4,252
55016	Cottage Grove	(612)	22,935	18,994
56716	Crookston	(218)	8,119	8,628
55428	Crystal	(612)	23,788	25,543
*56501	Detroit Lakes	(218)	6,635	7,106
*55806	Duluth	(218)	85,493	92,811
55121	Eagan	(612)	47,409	20,700
55005	East Bethel	(612)	8,050	6,626
56721	East Grand Forks	(218)	8,658	8,537
*55344	Eden Prairie	(612)	39,311	16,263
55424	Edina	(612)	46,075	46,073
55330	Elk River	(612)	11,143	6,785
56031	Fairmont	(507)	11,265	11,506
55113	Falcon Heights	(612)	5,380	5,291
55021	Faribault	(507)	17,085	16,241
55024	Farmington	(612)	5,940	4,370
*56537	Fergus Falls	(218)	12,362	12,519
55025	Forest Lake	(612)	5,833	4,596
55432	Fridley	(612)	28,335	30,228
55427	Golden Valley	(612)	20,971	22,775
*55744	Grand Rapids	(218)	7,976	7,934
*55304	Ham Lake	(612)	8,924	7,832
55033	Hastings	(612)	15,478	12,827
55810	Hermantown	(218)	6,761	6,759
*55746	Hibbing	(218)	18,046	21,193
*55343	Hopkins	(612)	16,529	15,336
55350	Hutchinson	(320)	11,459	9,244
56649	International Falls	(218)	8,301	5,611
*55075	Inver Grove Heights	(612)	22,477	17,171
55042	Lake Elmo	(612)	5,900	5,296
55044	Lakeville	(612)	24,854	14,790
55014	Lino Lakes	(612)	8,807	4,966
55355	Litchfield	(320)	6,041	5,904
55117	Little Canada	(612)	8,971	7,102
56345	Little Falls	(320)	7,371	7,250
55115	Mahtomedi	(612)	5,633	3,851
*56001	Mankato	(507)	31,405	28,646
55311	Maple Grove	(612)	38,736	20,525
55109	Maplewood	(612)	30,954	26,990
56258	Marshall	(507)	12,023	11,161
55118	Mendota Heights	(612)	9,388	7,288
*55440	Minneapolis	(612)	368,383	370,951
55345	Minnetonka	(612)	48,370	38,683
56265	Montevideo	(320)	5,499	5,845
*55362	Monticello	(612)	5,045	4,693
*56560	Moorhead	(218)	32,295	29,998
56267	Morris	(320)	5,613	5,367
55364	Mound	(612)	9,634	9,280
55112	Mounds View	(612)	12,541	12,593
55112	New Brighton	(612)	22,207	23,269
54427	New Hope	(612)	21,853	23,087
56073	New Ulm	(507)	13,132	13,755
55057	Northfield	(507)	14,684	12,562
56001	North Mankato	(507)	10,662	9,145
55109	North Saint Paul	(612)	12,376	11,921
55128	Oakdale	(612)	18,377	12,123
55323	Orono	(612)	7,285	6,845
55060	Owatonna	(507)	19,386	18,632
55421	Plymouth	(612)	50,889	31,615
55372	Prior Lake	(612)	11,482	7,284
55303	Ramsey	(612)	12,408	10,093
55066	Red Wing	(612)	15,134	13,736
55423	Richfield	(612)	35,710	37,851
55422	Robbinsdale	(612)	14,396	14,422
*55901	Rochester	(507)	70,729	57,906
55068	Rosemount	(612)	8,622	5,083

ZIP	Place		1990	1980
55113	Roseville	(612)	33,485	35,820
55418	Saint Anthony	(612)	7,727	7,981
*56301	Saint Cloud	(320)	48,812	42,566
55426	Saint Louis Park	(612)	43,787	42,931
*55101	Saint Paul	(612)	272,235	270,230
56082	Saint Peter	(507)	9,481	9,056
56377	Sartell	(320)	5,409	3,427
56379	Sauk Rapids	(320)	7,823	5,793
56378	Savage	(612)	9,906	3,954
55379	Shakopee	(612)	11,739	9,941
55126	Shoreview	(612)	24,587	17,300
55331	Shorewood	(612)	5,917	4,646
55075	South Saint Paul	(612)	20,197	21,235
55432	Spring Lake Park	(612)	6,532	6,477
*55082	Stillwater	(612)	13,882	12,290
56701	Thief River Falls	(218)	8,010	9,105
55127	Vadnais Heights	(612)	11,041	5,111
*55792	Virginia	(218)	9,410	11,056
56387	Waite Park	(320)	5,020	3,496
56093	Waseca	(507)	8,385	8,219
55118	West Saint Paul	(612)	19,248	18,527
55110	White Bear Lake	(612)	24,622	22,538
56201	Willmar	(320)	17,531	15,895
55987	Winona	(507)	25,435	25,075
55125	Woodbury	(612)	20,075	10,297
56187	Worthington	(507)	9,977	10,243

Mississippi (601)

ZIP	Place	1990	1980
39730	Aberdeen	6,837	7,184
38821	Amory	7,093	7,307
38606	Batesville	6,403	5,162
*39520	Bay Saint Louis	8,063	7,850
*39530	Biloxi	46,319	49,311
38829	Booneville	7,955	6,199
*39042	Brandon	11,077	9,626
39601	Brookhaven	10,243	10,800
39046	Canton	10,062	11,116
38614	Clarksdale	19,717	21,137
38732	Cleveland	15,384	14,524
*39056	Clinton	21,847	14,660
39429	Columbia	6,815	7,733
*39701	Columbus	23,799	27,503
38834	Corinth	11,820	13,180
39059	Crystal Springs	5,643	4,902
39532	D'Iberville†	6,566	6,236
39074	Forest	5,062	5,229
39553	Gautier†	10,088	10,392
*38701	Greenville	45,226	40,613
*38930	Greenwood	18,906	20,115
*38901	Grenada	10,864	11,508
39564	Gulf Hills(u)	5,004	4,512
*39501	Gulfport	40,775	39,676
*39401	Hattiesburg	41,906	40,829
*38635	Holly Springs	7,261	7,285
38637	Horn Lake	9,069	4,326
38751	Indianola	11,809	8,050
*39205	Jackson	196,637	202,895
39090	Kosciusko	6,986	7,415
*39440	Laurel	18,827	21,897
38756	Leland	6,366	6,667
39560	Long Beach	15,804	14,199
39339	Louisville	7,165	7,323
39648	McComb	11,797	12,331
*39110	Madison	7,471	2,241
*39302	Meridian	41,036	46,577
*39567	Moss Point	17,837	18,998
*39120	Natchez	19,460	22,209
38652	New Albany	6,775	7,072
*39564	Ocean Springs	14,673	14,504
39567	Orange Grove(u)	15,676	13,476
38655	Oxford	10,026	9,882
*39567	Pascagoula	25,899	29,318
39571	Pass Christian	5,557	5,014
39288	Pearl	19,588	18,602
39465	Petal	7,883	8,476
39350	Philadelphia	6,758	6,434
39466	Picayune	10,633	10,361
*39157	Ridgeland	11,714	5,461
38663	Ripley	5,371	4,271
39533	Saint Martin(u)	6,349	....
38671	Southaven†	17,949	16,441
39759	Starkville	18,458	16,139
*38801	Tupelo	30,685	23,905
*39180	Vicksburg	20,909	25,434
39576	Waveland	5,369	4,186
39367	Waynesboro	5,143	5,349
.....	West Hattiesburg(u)	5,450	....
39773	West Point	8,489	8,811
38967	Winona	5,724	6,177
39194	Yazoo City	12,427	12,092

Missouri

ZIP	Place		1990	1980
63123	Affton(u)	(314)	21,106	23,181
63010	Arnold	(314)	18,828	19,141
65605	Aurora	(417)	6,459	6,437
*63011	Ballwin	(314)	21,406	12,656
63137	Bellefontaine Neighbors	(314)	10,918	10,082

ZIP	Place		1990	1980
64012	Belton	(816)	18,145	12,708
63134	Berkeley	(314)	12,250	15,922
63031	Black Jack	(314)	6,131	5,293
*64015	Blue Springs	(816)	40,103	25,936
65613	Bolivar	(417)	6,845	5,919
65233	Boonville	(816)	7,095	6,959
63114	Breckenridge Hills	(314)	5,181	5,666
63144	Brentwood	(314)	8,150	8,209
63044	Bridgeton	(314)	17,732	18,445
*63701	Cape Girardeau	(573)	34,475	34,361
64836	Carthage	(417)	10,747	11,104
63830	Caruthersville	(573)	7,389	7,958
63834	Charleston	(573)	5,085	5,230
63017	Chesterfield†	(314)	38,630	28,384
64601	Chillicothe	(816)	8,799	9,089
63105	Clayton	(314)	13,926	14,306
64735	Clinton	(816)	8,703	8,366
*65201	Columbia	(573)	69,133	62,061
63128	Concord(u)	(314)	19,859	20,896
63126	Crestwood	(314)	11,229	12,815
63141	Creve Coeur	(314)	12,289	11,743
63136	Dellwood	(314)	5,245	6,200
63020	De Soto	(314)	5,993	5,993
63131	Des Peres	(314)	8,388	7,953
63841	Dexter	(573)	7,506	7,043
63011	Ellisville	(314)	7,183	6,233
64024	Excelsior Springs	(816)	10,373	10,424
63640	Farmington	(573)	11,596	8,270
63135	Ferguson	(314)	22,290	24,549
63028	Festus	(314)	8,105	7,574
*63033	Florissant	(314)	51,038	55,721
65473	Fort Leonard Wood(u)	(573)	15,863	21,262
65251	Fulton	(573)	10,033	11,046
64118	Gladstone	(816)	26,243	24,990
65254	Glasgow Village(u)	(573)	5,199	....
63122	Glendale	(314)	5,945	6,035
64030	Grandview	(816)	24,973	24,561
63401	Hannibal	(573)	18,004	18,811
64701	Harrisonville	(816)	7,696	6,372
63042	Hazelwood	(314)	15,512	13,098
*64050	Independence	(816)	112,301	111,797
63755	Jackson	(573)	9,256	7,827
*65101	Jefferson City	(573)	35,517	33,619
63136	Jennings	(314)	15,841	16,934
*64801	Joplin	(417)	40,866	39,126
*64108	Kansas City	(816)	434,829	448,028
63857	Kennett	(573)	10,941	10,145
63501	Kirksville	(816)	17,152	17,167
63122	Kirkwood	(314)	27,291	27,739
63124	Ladue (St. Louis Co.)	(314)	8,795	9,369
63367	Lake Saint Louis	(314)	7,536	3,843
65536	Lebanon	(417)	9,983	9,507
*64063	Lee's Summit	(816)	46,418	28,741
63125	Lemay(u)	(314)	18,005	35,424
64068	Liberty	(816)	20,459	16,251
63552	Macon	(816)	5,571	5,680
63863	Malden	(573)	5,123	6,096
63011	Manchester	(314)	6,447	6,351
63143	Maplewood	(314)	9,962	10,960
65340	Marshall	(816)	12,711	12,781
63043	Maryland Heights†	(314)	25,440	26,413
64468	Maryville	(816)	10,663	9,558
63129	Mehlville(u)	(314)	27,557	....
65265	Mexico	(573)	11,290	12,276
65270	Moberly	(816)	12,839	13,418
65708	Monett	(417)	6,529	6,148
63026	Murphy(u)	(314)	9,342	8,121
64850	Neosho	(417)	9,254	9,493
64772	Nevada	(417)	8,597	9,044
63121	Normandy	(314)	5,063	5,174
63121	Northwoods	(314)	5,106	5,831
63129	Oakville(u)	(314)	31,750	....
63366	O'Fallon	(314)	17,427	8,677
63132	Olivette	(314)	7,573	7,952
63114	Overland	(314)	17,987	19,620
63775	Perryville	(573)	6,933	7,343
63120	Pine Lawn	(314)	5,083	6,570
*63901	Poplar Bluff	(573)	16,841	17,139
64083	Raymore	(816)	5,592	3,154
64133	Raytown	(816)	30,601	31,831
65738	Republic	(417)	6,290	4,485
64085	Richmond	(816)	5,738	5,499
63117	Richmond Heights	(314)	10,448	11,516
63124	Rock Hill	(314)	5,217	5,702
65401	Rolla	(573)	14,090	13,303
63074	Saint Ann	(314)	14,449	15,523
*63301	Saint Charles	(314)	50,634	37,379
63114	Saint John	(314)	7,502	7,854
*64501	Saint Joseph	(816)	71,852	76,691
*63166	Saint Louis	(314)	396,685	452,801
63376	Saint Peters	(314)	40,660	15,700
63126	Sappington(u)	(314)	10,917	11,388
*65301	Sedalia	(816)	19,800	20,927
63119	Shrewsbury	(314)	6,416	5,077
63801	Sikeston	(573)	17,641	17,431
63138	Spanish Lake(u)	(314)	20,322	20,032
*65801	Springfield	(417)	140,494	133,116
63080	Sullivan	(573)	5,661	5,461
63006	Town and Country	(314)	9,503	3,187
64683	Trenton	(816)	6,129	6,811
63084	Union	(314)	6,048	5,506

ZIP	Place		1990	1980
63130	University City	(314)	40,087	42,690
64093	Warrensburg	(816)	15,244	13,807
63090	Washington	(314)	10,704	9,251
64870	Webb City	(417)	7,449	7,309
63119	Webster Groves	(314)	22,992	23,097
65775	West Plains	(417)	8,913	7,741

Montana (406)

ZIP	Place	1990	1980
59711	Anaconda	10,356	12,518
*59101	Billings	81,125	66,818
*59715	Bozeman	22,660	21,645
*59701	Butte	33,336	37,205
*59401	Great Falls	55,125	56,884
59501	Havre	10,201	10,891
*59601	Helena	24,609	23,938
.....	Helena Valley West Central(u)	6,327	....
*59901	Kalispell	11,917	10,689
59044	Laurel	5,686	5,481
59457	Lewistown	6,097	7,104
59047	Livingston	6,701	6,994
59402	Malmstrom AFB(u)	5,938	6,675
59301	Miles City	8,461	9,602
*59801	Missoula	42,918	33,351
59801	Orchard Homes(u)	10,317	10,837
59270	Sidney	5,217	5,726

Nebraska

ZIP	Place		1990	1980
69301	Alliance	(308)	9,765	9,920
68310	Beatrice	(402)	12,352	12,891
*68005	Bellevue	(402)	30,948	21,813
*68008	Blair	(402)	6,860	6,418
69337	Chadron	(308)	5,588	5,933
68108	Chalco(u)	(402)	7,337	....
*68601	Columbus	(402)	19,480	17,328
68025	Fremont	(402)	23,680	23,979
69341	Gering	(308)	7,946	7,760
*68802	Grand Island	(308)	39,487	33,180
*68901	Hastings	(402)	22,837	23,045
68949	Holdrege	(308)	5,671	5,624
*68847	Kearney	(308)	24,396	21,158
68128	La Vista	(402)	9,840	9,588
68850	Lexington	(308)	6,600	7,040
*68501	Lincoln	(402)	191,972	171,932
69001	McCook	(308)	8,112	8,404
68410	Nebraska City	(402)	6,547	7,127
*68701	Norfolk	(402)	21,476	19,449
*69101	North Platte	(308)	22,605	24,509
68113	Offutt AFB West(u)	(402)	10,883	8,787
69153	Ogallala	(308)	5,095	5,638
*68108	Omaha	(402)	335,719	313,939
*68046	Papillion	(402)	10,378	6,399
68048	Plattsmouth	(402)	6,415	6,295
68127	Ralston	(402)	6,236	5,143
*69361	Scottsbluff	(308)	13,711	14,156
68434	Seward	(402)	5,641	5,713
69162	Sidney	(308)	5,959	6,010
68776	South Sioux City	(402)	9,677	9,339
68787	Wayne	(402)	5,142	5,240
68467	York	(402)	7,940	7,723

Nevada (702)

ZIP	Place	1990	1980
*89005	Boulder City	12,567	9,590
*89701	Carson City	40,443	32,022
89112	East Las Vegas(u)	11,087	6,449
*89801	Elko	14,836	8,758
.....	Enterprise(u)	6,412	....
*89406	Fallon	6,430	4,262
89408	Fernley(u)	5,164	....
89410	Gardnerville Ranchos(u)	7,455	3,542
*89015	Henderson	64,948	24,363
*89450	Incline Village-Crystal Bay(u)	7,119	6,225
*89125	Las Vegas	258,204	164,674
89191	Nellis AFB(u)	8,377	7,476
*89030	North Las Vegas	47,849	42,739
89041	Pahrump(u)	7,424	....
89109	Paradise(u)	124,682	84,818
*89501	Reno	133,850	100,756
*89431	Sparks	53,367	40,780
*89801	Spring Creek(u)†	5,866	4,155
.....	Spring Valley(u)	51,726	....
89110	Sunrise Manor(u)	95,362	44,155
89433	Sun Valley(u)	11,391	8,822
89101	Winchester(u)	23,365	19,728
*89445	Winnemucca	6,102	4,140

New Hampshire (603)

See note on page 389

ZIP	Place	1990	1980
03031	Amherst	9,068	8,243
03811	Atkinson	5,188	4,397
03825	Barrington	6,164	4,404
03102	Bedford	12,563	9,481

ZIP	Place	1990	1980
03220	Belmont	5,796	4,026
03570	Berlin	11,824	13,084
03304	Bow	5,500	4,015
03743	Claremont	13,902	14,557
*03301	Concord	36,006	30,400
03818	Conway	7,940	7,158
03038	Derry Compact(u)	20,446	12,248
03038	Derry	29,603	18,875
*03820	Dover	25,042	22,377
03824	Durham Compact(u)	9,236	8,448
03824	Durham	11,818	10,652
03042	Epping	5,162	3,460
03833	Exeter Compact(u)	9,556	8,947
03833	Exeter	12,481	11,024
03835	Farmington	5,739	4,630
03235	Franklin	8,304	7,901
03246	Gilford	5,867	4,841
03045	Goffstown	14,621	11,315
03841	Hampstead	6,732	3,785
*03842	Hampton Compact(u)	7,989	6,779
*03842	Hampton	12,278	10,493
03755	Hanover Compact(u)	6,538	6,861
03755	Hanover	9,212	9,119
03049	Hollis	5,705	4,679
03106	Hooksett	9,002	7,303
03051	Hudson	19,530	14,022
03452	Jaffrey	5,361	4,349
03431	Keene	22,430	21,449
03848	Kingston	5,591	4,111
*03246	Laconia	15,743	15,575
*03766	Lebanon	12,183	11,134
03501	Litchfield	5,516	4,150
03561	Littleton	5,827	5,558
03053	Londonderry Compact(u)	10,114	....
03053	Londonderry	19,781	13,598
*03103	Manchester	99,332	90,936
03054	Merrimack	22,156	15,406
03055	Milford Compact(u)	8,015	6,269
03055	Milford	11,795	8,685
*03060	Nashua	79,662	67,865
03857	Newmarket	7,157	4,290
03773	Newport	6,110	6,229
03076	Pelham	9,408	8,090
03275	Pembroke	6,561	6,561
03458	Peterborough	5,239	4,895
03865	Plaistow	7,316	5,609
03264	Plymouth	5,811	5,094
*03801	Portsmouth	25,925	26,254
03077	Raymond	8,713	5,453
*03867	Rochester	26,630	21,560
03079	Salem	25,746	24,124
03874	Seabrook	6,503	5,917
03878	Somersworth	11,249	10,350
03275	Suncook(u)	5,214	4,698
*03431	Swanzey	6,236	5,183
03281	Weare	6,193	3,232
03087	Windham	9,000	5,664

New Jersey

See note on page 389

ZIP	Place		1990	1980
08201	Absecon	(609)	7,298	6,859
07401	Allendale	(201)	5,900	5,901
07712	Asbury Park	(732)	16,799	17,015
*08401	Atlantic City	(609)	37,986	40,199
08106	Audubon	(609)	9,205	9,533
07001	Avenel(u)	(732)	15,504	....
08007	Barrington	(609)	6,792	7,418
08002	Bayonne	(201)	61,464	65,047
08722	Beachwood	(732)	9,324	7,687
07109	Belleville(u)†	(973)	34,213	35,367
*08031	Bellmawr	(609)	12,603	13,721
07719	Belmar	(732)	5,877	6,771
07621	Bergenfield	(201)	24,458	25,568
07922	Berkeley Heights Twp.(u)	(908)	11,980	12,549
08009	Berlin	(609)	5,672	5,786
07924	Bernardsville	(908)	6,597	6,715
08012	Blackwood(u)	(609)	5,120	5,219
07003	Bloomfield(u)†	(973)	45,061	47,792
07403	Bloomingdale	(973)	7,530	7,867
07603	Bogota	(201)	7,824	8,344
07005	Boonton	(973)	8,343	8,620
08805	Bound Brook	(732)	9,487	9,710
*08723	Brick Twp.(u)	(732)	66,473	53,629
08302	Bridgeton	(609)	18,942	18,795
08807	Bridgewater Twp.(u)	(732)/(908)	32,509	29,175
08203	Brigantine	(609)	11,354	8,318
08015	Browns Mills(u)	(609)	11,429	10,568
07828	Budd Lake(u)	(973)	7,272	6,523
08016	Burlington	(609)	9,835	10,246
07405	Butler	(973)	7,392	7,616
*07006	Caldwell(u)†	(973)	7,549	7,624
*08101	Camden	(609)	87,492	84,910
07072	Carlstadt	(201)	5,510	6,166
08069	Carney's Point Twp. (u)	(609)	8,443	8,396
07008	Carteret	(732)	19,025	20,598
07009	Cedar Grove Twp.(u)(Essex)	(973)	12,053	12,600
07928	Chatham	(973)	8,007	8,537

ZIP	Place		1990	1980	ZIP	Place		1990	1980
*08034	Cherry Hill Twp.(u)	(609)	69,319	68,785	07644	Lodi	(201)/(973)	22,355	23,956
08077	Cinnaminson Twp.(u)	(609)	14,583	16,072	07740	Long Branch	(732)	28,658	29,819
07066	Clark Twp.(u)	(732)/(908)	14,629	16,699	*07946	Long Hill Twp.(u)	(973)	7,826	7,275
08312	Clayton	(609)	6,155	6,013	07071	Lyndhurst Twp.(u)	(201)	18,262	20,326
08021	Clementon	(609)	5,601	5,764	08641	McGuire AFB(u)	(609)	7,580	7,853
07010	Cliffside Park	(201)	20,393	21,464	07940	Madison	(973)	15,850	15,357
*07015	Clifton	(973)	71,984	74,388	08859	Madison Park(u)	(732)	7,490	7,447
07624	Closter	(201)	8,094	8,164	*07430	Mahwah Twp.(u)	(201)	17,905	12,127
08108	Collingswood	(609)	15,289	15,838	08736	Manasquan	(732)	5,369	5,354
07067	Colonia(u)	(732)	18,238	....	08835	Manville	(908)	10,567	11,278
07016	Cranford Twp.(u)	(908)	22,633	24,573	08052	Maple Shade Twp.(u)	(609)	19,211	20,525
07626	Cresskill	(201)	7,558	7,609	07040	Maplewood Twp.(u)	(973)	21,756	22,950
08759	Crestwood Village(u)	(732)	8,030	7,965	08402	Margate City	(609)	8,431	9,179
*07801	Dover	(973)	15,115	14,681	07746	Marlboro Twp.(u)	(732)	27,974	17,560
07628	Dumont	(201)	17,187	18,334	08053	Marlton(u)	(609)	10,228	9,411
08812	Dunellen	(732)	6,528	6,593	07747	Matawan	(732)	9,239	8,837
08816	East Brunswick Twp.(u)	(732)	43,548	37,711	07607	Maywood	(201)	9,536	9,895
07936	East Hanover Twp.(u)	(973)	9,926	9,319	08619	Mercerville-Hamilton Sq.(u).	(609)	26,873	25,446
*07019	East Orange	(973)	73,552	77,878	08840	Metuchen	(732)	12,804	13,762
07073	East Rutherford	(201)/(973)	7,902	7,849	08846	Middlesex	(732)	13,055	13,480
07724	Eatontown	(732)	13,800	12,703	07748	Middletown Twp.(u)	(732)	68,183	62,574
07020	Edgewater	(201)	5,001	4,628	07432	Midland Park	(201)	7,047	7,381
08010	Edgewater Park Twp.(u)	(609)	8,388	9,273	07041	Millburn Twp.(u)	(973)	18,630	19,543
*08818	Edison Twp.(u)	(732)/(908)	88,680	70,193	08850	Milltown (Middlesex)	(732)	6,968	7,136
*07207	Elizabeth	(908)	110,002	106,201	08332	Millville	(609)	25,992	24,815
07407	Elmwood Park	(201)	17,623	18,377	08094	Monroe Twp. (Gloucester)(u)	(609)	26,703	21,639
07630	Emerson	(201)	6,930	7,793	*07042	Montclair(u)	(973)	37,729	38,321
07631	Englewood	(201)	24,850	23,701	07645	Montvale	(201)	6,946	7,318
07632	Englewood Cliffs	(201)	5,634	5,698	07045	Montville Twp.(u)	(973)	15,600	14,290
08618	Ewing Twp.(u)	(609)	34,185	34,842	08057	Moorestown-Lenola(u)	(609)	13,242	13,695
07004	Fairfield(u)	(973)	7,615	7,987	07950	Morris Plains	(973)	5,219	5,305
07704	Fair Haven	(732)	5,270	5,679	*07960	Morristown	(973)	16,189	16,614
07410	Fair Lawn	(201)/(973)	30,548	32,229	07092	Mountainside	(908)	6,657	7,118
07022	Fairview (Bergen)	(201)	10,733	10,519	08060	Mount Holly Twp.(u)	(609)	10,639	10,818
07023	Fanwood	(908)	7,115	7,767	08087	Mystic Island(u)	(609)	7,400	4,929
08518	Florence-Roebling(u)	(609)	8,564	7,677	*07753	Neptune Twp.(u)	(732)	28,148	28,366
07932	Florham Park	(973)	8,521	9,359	*07102	Newark	(973)	275,221	329,248
08863	Fords(u)	(732)	14,392	....	*08901	New Brunswick	(732)	41,711	41,442
08640	Fort Dix(u)	(609)	10,205	14,297	07646	New Milford	(201)	15,990	16,876
07024	Fort Lee	(201)	31,997	32,449	07974	New Providence	(908)	11,439	12,426
07417	Franklin Lakes	(201)	9,873	8,769	07860	Newton	(973)	7,521	7,748
*08873	Franklin Twp.				07031	North Arlington	(201)	13,790	16,587
	(Somerset)(u)	(732)/(908)	42,780	31,358	07047	North Bergen Twp.(u)	(201)	48,414	47,019
07728	Freehold	(732)	10,742	10,020	08902	North Brunswick Twp.(u)†	(732)	31,287	22,220
07026	Garfield	(201)	26,727	26,803	07006	North Caldwell(u)†	(973)	6,706	5,832
08753	Gilford Park(u)	(732)	8,668	6,528	08225	Northfield	(609)	7,305	7,795
08028	Glassboro	(609)	15,614	14,574	07508	North Haledon	(973)	7,987	8,177
08029	Glendora(u)	(609)	5,201	5,632	07060	North Plainfield	(908)	18,820	19,108
07028	Glen Ridge(u)†	(973)	7,076	7,855	08260	North Wildwood	(609)	5,017	4,714
07452	Glen Rock	(201)	10,883	11,497	07110	Nutley(u)†	(973)	27,099	28,998
08030	Gloucester City	(609)	12,649	13,121	07436	Oakland	(201)	11,997	13,443
07093	Guttenberg	(201)	8,268	7,340	*08758	Ocean Twp. (Ocean)(u)	(609)/(732)	5,416	3,731
*07602	Hackensack	(201)	37,049	36,039	*08050	Ocean Acres(u)	(609)	5,587	4,850
07840	Hackettstown	(908)	8,120	8,850	08226	Ocean City	(609)	15,512	13,949
08033	Haddonfield	(609)	11,633	12,337	07757	Oceanport	(732)	6,146	5,888
08035	Haddon Heights	(609)	7,860	8,361	08857	Old Bridge(u)	(732)	22,151	21,815
*07510	Haledon	(973)	6,951	6,607	08857	Old Bridge Twp.(u)	(732)	56,493	51,515
*08609	Hamilton Twp. (Mercer)(u)	(609)	86,553	82,801	07649	Oradell	(201)	8,024	8,658
08037	Hammonton	(609)	12,208	12,298	*07051	Orange(u)†	(973)	29,925	31,136
07981	Hanover Twp.(u)	(973)	11,538	11,846	07650	Palisades Park	(201)	14,536	13,732
07029	Harrison	(973)	13,425	12,242	08065	Palmyra	(609)	7,056	7,085
07604	Hasbrouck Heights	(201)	11,488	12,166	07652	Paramus	(201)	25,004	26,474
*07510	Hawthorne	(973)	17,084	18,200	07656	Park Ridge	(201)	8,102	8,515
07730	Hazlet Twp.(u)	(732)	21,976	23,013	07054	Parsippany-Troy Hills Twp.(u)	(973)	48,478	49,868
08904	Highland Park (Middlesex)	(732)	13,279	13,396	07055	Passaic	(973)	58,041	52,463
08520	Hightstown	(609)	5,126	4,581	*07510	Paterson	(973)	140,891	137,970
07642	Hillsdale	(201)	9,750	10,495	08066	Paulsboro	(609)	6,577	6,944
07205	Hillside Twp.(u)	(908)/(973)	21,044	21,440	08110	Pennsauken Twp.(u)	(609)	34,738	33,775
07030	Hoboken	(201)	33,397	42,460	08069	Penns Grove	(609)	5,228	5,760
08753	Holiday City-Berkeley(u)	(732)	14,293	9,019	08070	Pennsville Center(u)	(609)	12,218	12,467
.....	Holiday City South(u)	(732)	5,452	....	07440	Pequannock Twp.(u)	(973)	12,844	13,776
07843	Hopatcong	(973)	15,586	15,531	*08861	Perth Amboy	(732)	41,967	38,951
08525	Hopewell Twp. (Mercer)(u)	(609)	11,590	10,893	08865	Phillipsburg	(908)	15,757	16,647
07111	Irvington(u)†	(973)	59,774	61,473	08021	Pine Hill	(609)	9,854	8,684
08830	Iselin(u)	(732)	16,141	....	*08854	Piscataway Twp.(u)	(732)/(908)	47,089	42,223
*08527	Jackson Twp.(u)	(732)	33,283	25,644	08071	Pitman	(609)	9,365	9,744
08831	Jamesburg	(732)	5,294	4,114	*07061	Plainfield	(908)	46,577	45,555
*07303	Jersey City	(201)	228,517	223,532	08232	Pleasantville	(609)	16,027	13,435
07734	Keansburg	(732)	11,069	10,613	08742	Point Pleasant	(732)	18,177	17,747
07032	Kearny	(201)/(973)	34,874	35,735	08742	Point Pleasant Beach	(732)	5,112	5,415
08824	Kendall Park(u)	(908)	7,127	7,419	07442	Pompton Lakes	(973)	10,539	10,660
07033	Kenilworth	(908)	7,574	8,221	*08540	Princeton	(609)	12,016	12,035
07735	Keyport	(732)	7,586	7,413	07508	Prospect Park	(973)	5,053	5,142
07405	Kinnelon	(973)	8,470	7,770	07065	Rahway	(732)	25,325	26,723
07871	Lake Mohawk(u)	(973)	8,930	8,498	08057	Ramblewood(u)	(609)	6,181	6,475
08701	Lakewood(u)	(732)	26,095	22,863	07446	Ramsey	(201)	13,228	12,899
08879	Laurence Harbor(u)	(732)	6,361	6,737	07869	Randolph Twp.(u)	(973)	19,974	17,828
08648	Lawrenceville(u)	(609)	6,446	....	08869	Raritan	(908)	5,798	6,128
*08733	Leisure Village West-Pine Lake Park(u)	(732)	10,139	....	07701	Red Bank	(732)	10,636	12,031
07605	Leonia	(201)	8,365	8,027	07657	Ridgefield	(201)	9,996	10,294
07035	Lincoln Park	(973)	10,978	8,806	07660	Ridgefield Park	(201)	12,454	12,738
07738	Lincroft(u)	(732)	6,193	....	*07451	Ridgewood	(201)/(973)	24,152	25,208
07036	Linden	(732)/(908)	36,701	37,836	07456	Ringwood	(973)	12,623	12,625
08021	Lindenwold	(609)	18,734	18,196	07661	River Edge	(201)	10,603	11,111
08221	Linwood	(609)	6,866	6,144	08075	Riverside Twp.(u)	(609)	7,974	7,941
07424	Little Falls Twp.(u)	(973)	11,294	11,496	07675	River Vale(u)	(201)	9,410	9,489
07643	Little Ferry	(201)	9,989	9,399	07726	Robertsville(u)	(732)	9,841	8,461
07739	Little Silver	(732)	5,721	5,548	07662	Rochelle Park Twp.	(201)	5,587	5,603
07039	Livingston Twp.(u)	(973)	26,609	28,040	07866	Rockaway	(973)	6,243	6,852
					07203	Roselle	(908)	20,314	20,641

ZIP	Place		1990	1980
07204	Roselle Park.	(908)	12,805	13,377
07760	Rumson.	(732)	6,701	7,623
08078	Runnemede	(609)	9,042	9,461
*07070	Rutherford	(201)	17,790	19,068
07663	Saddle Brook Twp.(u).	(201)/(973)	13,296	14,084
08079	Salem	(609)	6,883	6,959
08872	Sayreville.	(732)	34,998	29,969
07076	Scotch Plains Twp.(u)	(732)/(908)	21,150	20,774
*07094	Secaucus.	(201)	14,061	13,719
08753	Silverton	(732)	9,175	7,236
08083	Somerdale	(609)	5,440	5,900
*08873	Somerset(u)	(732)	22,070	21,731
08244	Somers Point	(609)	11,216	10,330
08876	Somerville	(908)	11,632	11,973
08879	South Amboy	(732)	7,851	8,322
07079	South Orange Twp. (u)	(973)	16,390	15,864
07080	South Plainfield. . . .	(732)/(908)	20,489	20,521
08882	South River	(732)	13,692	14,361
07871	Sparta Twp.(u)	(973)	15,157	13,333
08884	Spotswood.	(732)	7,983	7,840
07081	Springfield Twp. (u) . . .	(908)/(973)	13,420	13,955
07762	Spring Lake Heights.	(732)	5,341	5,424
08084	Stratford	(609)	7,614	8,005
07747	Strathmore(u)	(732)	7,060	....
07876	Succasunna-Kenvil(u)	(201)	11,781	10,931
*07901	Summit	(908)	19,757	21,071
07666	Teaneck Twp.(u)	(201)	37,825	39,007
07670	Tenafly	(201)	13,326	13,552
07724	Tinton Falls	(732)	12,361	7,740
*08753	Toms River(u).	(973)	7,524	7,465
*07512	Totowa	(973)	10,177	11,448
*08650	Trenton	(609)	88,675	92,124
08520	Twin Rivers(u)	(609)	7,715	7,742
07083	Union Twp. (Union)(u)	(908)	50,024	50,184
07735	Union Beach.	(732)	6,156	6,354
07087	Union City	(201)	58,012	55,593
07458	Upper Saddle River	(201)	7,198	7,958
08406	Ventnor City	(609)	11,005	11,704
07044	Verona(u)†.	(973)	13,597	14,166
08251	Villas(u)	(609)	8,136	5,909
08360	Vineland	(609)	54,780	53,753
07463	Waldwick	(201)	9,757	10,802
07057	Wallington	(201)/(973)	10,828	10,741
07465	Wanaque.	(201)/(973)	9,711	10,025
07882	Washington	(908)	6,474	6,429
07675	Washington Twp.(Bergen)(u)	(201)	9,245	9,550
07060	Watchung	(908)	5,110	5,290
*07470	Wayne Twp.(u)	(973)	47,025	46,474
07087	Weehawken Twp.(u)	(201)	12,385	13,168
07006	West Caldwell(u)†	(973)	10,422	11,407
*07091	Westfield	(732)/(908)	28,870	30,447
07728	West Freehold(u)	(732)	11,166	9,929
07764	West Long Branch	(732)	7,690	7,380
07480	West Milford Twp.(u)†	(973)	25,430	22,750
07093	West New York.	(201)	38,125	39,194
07052	West Orange(u)†.	(973)	39,103	39,510
07424	West Paterson	(973)	10,982	11,293
07675	Westwood	(201)	10,446	10,714
07885	Wharton	(973)	5,405	5,485
08610	White Horse(u)	(609)	9,397	10,098
07886	White Meadow Lake(u). . . .	(973)	8,002	8,429
08094	Williamstown	(609)	10,891	5,768
08046	Willingboro Twp.(u)	(609)	36,291	39,912
08095	Winslow Twp.(u)	(609)	30,087	20,034
07095	Woodbridge(u)	(732)	17,434	....
*07095	Woodbridge Twp.(u)	(732)	93,092	90,074
08096	Woodbury	(609)	10,904	10,353
07675	Woodcliff Lake	(201)	5,303	5,644
07075	Wood-Ridge	(201)/(973)	7,506	7,929
07481	Wyckoff Twp.(u)	(201)	15,372	15,500
08620	Yardville-Groveville(u)	(609)	9,248	9,414
07726	Yorketown(u)	(609)	6,313	5,330

New Mexico (505)

ZIP	Place	1990	1980
*88310	Alamogordo	27,596	24,024
*87101	Albuquerque.	384,619	332,920
88021	Anthony(u)	5,160	3,285
*88210	Artesia.	10,610	10,385
87410	Aztec	5,480	5,512
87002	Belen	6,547	5,617
87004	Bernalillo	5,960	2,988
87413	Bloomfield	5,214	4,881
*88220	Carlsbad	24,952	25,496
*88101	Clovis	30,954	31,194
87048	Corrales.	5,453	2,791
*88030	Deming	10,970	9,964
*87532	Espanola	8,389	6,803
*87401	Farmington.	33,997	31,222
*87301	Gallup.	19,157	18,167
87020	Grants	8,626	11,439
*88240	Hobbs	29,121	29,153
88330	Holloman AFB(u).	5,891	7,245
*88001	Las Cruces	62,360	45,086
87701	Las Vegas	14,753	14,322
87544	Los Alamos(u)	11,455	11,039
87031	Los Lunas	6,013	3,525
88260	Lovington.	9,322	9,727

ZIP	Place		1990	1980
87107	North Valley(u)		12,507	12,984
87114	Paradise Hills(u).		5,513	5,096
88130	Portales.		10,690	9,940
87740	Raton		7,372	8,225
*87124	Rio Rancho†		32,512	9,985
*88201	Roswell		44,260	39,676
87115	Sandia(u).		6,742	5,288
*87501	Santa Fe		56,537	49,160
87420	Shiprock(u)		7,687	7,237
*88061	Silver City		10,683	9,887
87801	Socorro.		8,159	7,173
87105	South Valley(u)		35,701	38,898
88063	Sunland Park†		8,179	4,313
87901	Truth or Consequences . . .		6,221	5,219
88401	Tucumcari		6,827	6,765
87544	White Rock(u)		6,192	6,560
87327	Zuni Pueblo(u)		5,857	5,551

New York

See note on page 389

ZIP	Place		1990	1980
10901	Airmont(u)	(914)	7,835	....
*12201	Albany.	(518)	100,031	101,727
11507	Albertson(u)	(516)	5,166	5,561
14411	Albion	(716)	5,863	4,897
14226	Amherst.	(716)	111,711	108,706
11701	Amityville	(516)	9,286	9,076
12010	Amsterdam	(518)	20,714	21,872
12603	Arlington(u)	(914)	11,948	11,305
*13021	Auburn	(315)	31,258	32,548
*11702	Babylon.	(516)	12,249	12,388
11510	Baldwin(u)	(516)	22,719	31,630
11510	Baldwin Harbor(u).	(516)	7,899	....
13027	Baldwinsville	(315)	6,591	6,446
12020	Ballston Spa.	(518)	5,194	4,711
14020	Batavia	(716)	16,310	16,703
14810	Bath	(607)	5,801	6,042
11705	Bayport(u)	(516)	7,702	9,282
11706	Bay Shore(u)	(516)	21,279	10,784
11709	Bayville	(516)	7,193	7,034
11751	Baywood(u)	(516)	7,351	....
12508	Beacon	(914)	13,243	12,937
11710	Bellmore(u)	(516)	16,438	18,106
11714	Bethpage(u)	(516)	15,761	16,840
*13902	Binghamton	(607)	53,008	55,860
11716	Bohemia(u)	(516)	9,556	9,308
11717	Brentwood(u)	(516)	45,218	44,321
10510	Briarcliff Manor	(914)	7,070	7,115
14610	Brighton (u)	(716)	34,455	35,776
14420	Brockport.	(716)	8,749	9,776
10708	Bronxville.	(914)	6,028	6,267
*14205	Buffalo	(716)	328,175	357,870
*14424	Canandaigua	(716)	10,725	10,419
13617	Canton	(315)	6,379	7,055
11514	Carle Place(u)	(516)	5,107	5,470
11516	Cedarhurst.	(516)	5,716	6,162
11720	Centereach(u)	(516)	26,720	30,136
11934	Center Moriches(u)	(516)	5,987	5,703
11721	Centerport(Suffolk)(u)	(516)	5,333	6,576
11722	Central Islip(u)	(516)	26,028	19,734
*14225	Cheektowaga(u)	(716)	84,387	92,145
10977	Chestnut Ridge†	(914)	7,517	8,217
12065	CliftonPark.	(518)	30,117	
12043	Cobleskill.	(518)	5,268	5,272
12047	Cohoes	(518)	16,825	18,144
12205	Colonie	(518)	8,019	8,869
11725	Commack(u)	(516)	36,124	34,719
10920	Congers(u).	(914)	8,003	7,123
11726	Copiague(u)	(516)	20,769	20,132
11727	Coram(u)	(516)	30,111	24,752
14830	Corning	(607)	11,938	12,953
13045	Cortland	(607)	19,801	20,138
*10520	Croton-on-Hudson.	(914)	7,018	6,889
14437	Dansville	(716)	5,002	4,979
11729	Deer Park(u)	(516)	28,840	30,394
12054	Delmar(u)	(518)	8,360	8,423
14043	Depew	(716)	17,673	19,819
13214	DeWitt(u).	(315)	8,244	9,024
11746	Dix Hills(u)	(516)	25,849	26,693
10522	Dobbs Ferry	(914)	9,940	10,053
14048	Dunkirk	(716)	13,989	15,310
14052	East Aurora	(716)	6,647	6,803
10709	Eastchester(u)	(914)	18,537	20,305
12302	East Glenville(u)	(518)	6,518	6,537
11576	East Hills.	(516)	6,746	7,160
11730	East Islip(u)	(516)	14,325	13,852
11758	East Massapequa(u)	(516)	19,550	13,987
11554	East Meadow(u)	(516)	36,909	39,317
11731	East Northport(u)	(516)	20,411	20,187
11772	East Patchogue(u).	(516)	20,195	18,139
14445	East Rochester	(716)	6,932	7,596
11518	East Rockaway	(516)	10,152	10,917
11786	East Shoreham(u)	(516)	5,461	....
*14901	Elmira	(607)	33,724	35,327
11003	Elmont(u).	(516)	28,612	27,592
11731	Elwood(u)	(516)	10,916	11,847
*13760	Endicott.	(607)	13,531	14,457
13762	Endwell(u)	(607)	12,602	13,745
13219	Fairmount(u)	(315)	12,266	13,415

ZIP	Place		1990	1980	ZIP	Place		1990	1980
14450	Fairport	(716)	5,943	5,970	11501	Mineola	(516)	19,005	20,757
11735	Farmingdale	(516)	8,022	7,946	10950	Monroe	(914)	6,672	5,996
11738	Farmingville(u)	(516)	14,842	13,398	10952	Monsey(u)	(914)	13,986	12,380
*11001	Floral Park	(516)	15,947	16,805	12701	Monticello	(914)	6,597	6,306
13603	Fort Drum(u)	(315)	11,578	....	10970	Mount Ivy(u)	(914)	6,013	....
11768	Fort Salonga(u)	(516)	9,176	9,550	10549	Mount Kisco	(914)	9,108	8,025
11010	Franklin Square(Nassau)(u)	(516)	28,205	29,051	11766	Mount Sinai(u)	(516)	8,023	6,591
14063	Fredonia	(716)	10,436	11,126	*10551	Mount Vernon	(914)	67,153	66,713
11520	Freeport	(516)	39,894	38,272	12590	Myers Corner(u)	(914)	5,599	5,180
13069	Fulton	(315)	12,929	13,312	10954	Nanuet(u)	(914)	14,065	12,578
*11530	Garden City	(516)	21,675	22,927	11767	Nesconset(u)	(516)	10,712	10,706
11040	Garden City Park(u)	(516)	7,437	7,712	14513	Newark	(315)	9,849	10,017
14624	Gates-North Gates(u)	(716)	14,995	15,244	*12550	Newburgh	(914)	26,454	23,438
14454	Geneseo	(716)	7,187	6,746	11590	New Cassel(u)	(516)	10,257	9,635
14456	Geneva	(315)	14,143	15,133	10956	New City(u)	(914)	33,673	35,859
11542	Glen Cove	(516)	24,149	24,618	*11040	New Hyde Park	(516)	9,728	9,801
12801	Glens Falls	(518)	15,023	15,897	12561	New Paltz	(914)	5,470	4,938
12801	Glens Falls North(u)	(518)	7,978	6,956	*10802	New Rochelle	(914)	67,265	70,794
12078	Gloversville	(518)	16,656	17,836	*12550	New Windsor Center(u)	(914)	8,898	7,812
10924	Goshen	(914)	5,255	4,874	*10001	New York	(212)/(718)	7,322,564	7,071,639
*11022	Great Neck	(516)	8,745	9,168	*14302	Niagara Falls	(716)	61,840	71,384
11020	Great Neck Plaza	(516)	5,897	5,604	11701	North Amityville(u)	(516)	13,849	13,140
14616	Greece(u)	(716)	15,632	16,177	11703	North Babylon(u)	(516)	18,081	19,019
11740	Greenlawn(u)	(516)	13,208	13,869	11706	North Bay Shore(u)	(516)	12,799	35,020
*10583	Greenville(Westchester)(u)	(914)	9,528	8,706	11710	North Bellmore(u)	(516)	19,707	20,630
14075	Hamburg	(716)	10,442	10,582	11713	North Bellport(u)	(516)	8,182	7,432
11946	Hampton Bays(u)	(516)	7,893	7,256	11757	North Lindenhurst(u)	(516)	10,563	11,511
10528	Harrison	(914)	23,308	23,046	11758	North Massapequa(u)	(516)	19,365	21,385
10530	Hartsdale(u)	(914)	9,587	10,216	11566	North Merrick(u)	(516)	12,113	12,848
10706	Hastings-on-Hudson	(914)	8,000	8,573	11040	North New Hyde Park(u)	(516)	14,359	15,114
*11787	Hauppauge(u)	(516)	19,750	20,960	11772	North Patchogue(u)	(516)	7,374	7,126
10927	Haverstraw	(914)	9,438	8,800	11768	Northport	(516)	7,572	7,651
*11551	Hempstead	(516)	47,982	40,404	13212	North Syracuse	(315)	7,363	7,970
13350	Herkimer	(315)	7,945	8,383	10591	North Tarrytown	(914)	8,152	7,994
11557	Hewlett(u)	(516)	6,620	6,986	14120	North Tonawanda	(716)	34,989	35,760
*11802	Hicksville(u)	(516)	40,174	43,245	11580	North Valley Stream(u)	(516)	14,574	14,530
10977	Hillcrest(u)	(914)	6,447	5,733	11793	North Wantagh(u)	(516)	12,276	12,677
14468	Hilton	(716)	5,216	4,151	13815	Norwich	(607)	7,613	8,082
11741	Holbrook(u)	(516)	25,273	24,382	10960	Nyack	(914)	6,558	6,428
11742	Holtsville(u)	(516)	14,972	13,515	11769	Oakdale(u)	(516)	7,875	8,090
14843	Hornell	(607)	9,877	10,234	11572	Oceanside(u)	(516)	32,423	33,639
*14845	Horseheads(u)	(607)	6,802	7,348	13669	Ogdensburg	(315)	13,521	12,375
12534	Hudson	(518)	8,034	7,986	11804	Old Bethpage(u)	(516)	5,610	6,215
12839	Hudson Falls	(518)	7,651	7,419	14760	Olean	(716)	16,946	18,207
11743	Huntington(u)	(516)	18,243	21,727	13421	Oneida	(315)	10,850	10,810
11746	Huntington Station(u)	(516)	28,247	28,769	13820	Oneonta	(607)	13,954	14,933
13357	Ilion	(315)	8,888	9,450	12550	Orange Lake(u)	(914)	5,196	5,120
11696	Inwood(u)	(516)	7,767	8,228	10562	Ossining	(914)	22,582	20,196
14617	Irondequoit(u)	(716)	52,322	57,648	13126	Oswego	(315)	19,195	19,793
10533	Irvington	(914)	6,348	5,774	11771	Oyster Bay(u)	(516)	6,687	6,497
11751	Islip(u)	(516)	18,924	13,438	11772	Patchogue	(516)	11,060	11,291
11752	Islip Terrace(u)	(516)	5,530	5,588	10965	Pearl River(u)	(914)	15,314	15,893
*14850	Ithaca	(607)	29,541	28,732	10566	Peekskill	(914)	19,536	18,236
*14702	Jamestown	(716)	34,681	35,775	10803	Pelham	(914)	6,413	6,848
10535	Jefferson Valley-Yorktown(u)	(914)	14,118	13,380	10803	Pelham Manor	(914)	5,443	6,130
11753	Jericho(Nassau)(u)	(516)	13,141	12,739	14527	Penn Yan	(315)	5,257	5,242
13790	Johnson City	(607)	16,578	17,126	11714	Plainedge(u)	(516)	8,739	9,629
12095	Johnstown	(518)	9,058	9,360	11803	Plainview(u)	(516)	26,207	28,037
14217	Kenmore	(716)	17,180	18,474	*12901	Plattsburgh	(518)	21,255	21,057
11754	Kings Park(u)	(516)	17,773	16,131	12903	Plattsburgh AFB(u)	(518)	5,483	5,905
12401	Kingston	(914)	23,095	24,481	10570	Pleasantville	(914)	6,592	6,749
10950	Kiryas Joel	(914)	7,437	2,088	10573	Port Chester	(914)	24,728	23,565
14218	Lackawanna	(716)	20,585	22,701	11777	Port Jefferson	(516)	7,455	6,731
10512	Lake Carmel(u)	(914)	8,489	7,295	11776	Port Jefferson Station(u)	(516)	7,232	17,009
11755	Lake Grove	(516)	9,612	9,692	12771	Port Jervis	(914)	9,060	8,699
11779	Lake Ronkonkoma(u)	(516)	18,997	38,336	11050	Port Washington(u)	(516)	15,387	14,521
11552	Lakeview(u)	(516)	5,476	5,276	13676	Potsdam	(315)	10,251	10,635
14086	Lancaster	(716)	11,940	13,056	*12601	Poughkeepsie	(914)	28,844	29,757
10538	Larchmont	(914)	6,181	6,308	12144	Rensselaer	(518)	8,255	9,047
12110	Latham(u)	(518)	10,131	11,182	11961	Ridge(u)	(516)	11,734	8,977
11559	Lawrence	(516)	6,513	6,175	11901	Riverhead(u)	(516)	8,814	6,339
11756	Levittown(u)	(516)	53,286	57,045	*14692	Rochester	(716)	230,356	241,741
11757	Lindenhurst	(516)	26,879	26,919	*11571	Rockville Centre	(516)	24,727	25,412
13365	Little Falls	(315)	5,829	6,156	11778	Rocky Point(u)	(516)	8,596	7,012
*14094	Lockport	(716)	24,426	24,844	12205	Roessleville(u)	(518)	10,753	11,685
11561	Long Beach	(516)	33,510	34,073	*13440	Rome	(315)	44,350	43,826
12211	Loudonville(u)	(518)	10,822	11,480	11779	Ronkonkoma(u)	(516)	20,391	....
11563	Lynbrook	(516)	19,208	20,424	11575	Roosevelt(u)	(516)	15,030	14,109
10541	Mahopac(u)	(914)	7,755	7,681	11577	Roslyn Heights(u)	(516)	6,405	6,546
12953	Malone	(518)	6,777	7,668	12303	Rotterdam(u)	(518)	21,228	22,933
11565	Malverne	(516)	9,054	9,262	10580	Rye	(914)	14,936	15,083
10543	Mamaroneck	(914)	17,325	17,616	10573	Rye Brook†	(914)	7,765	7,996
11030	Manhasset(u)	(516)	7,718	8,485	11780	Saint James(u)	(516)	12,703	12,122
11050	Manorhaven	(516)	5,672	5,384	14779	Salamanca	(716)	6,566	6,890
11949	Manorville(u)	(516)	6,198	....	13454	Salisbury(u)	(315)	12,226	9,732
11758	Massapequa(u)	(516)	22,018	24,454	12983	Saranac Lake	(518)	5,377	5,578
11762	Massapequa Park	(516)	18,044	19,779	12866	Saratoga Springs	(518)	25,001	23,906
13662	Massena	(315)	11,716	12,851	11782	Sayville(u)	(516)	16,550	12,013
11950	Mastic(u)	(516)	13,778	10,413	10583	Scarsdale	(914)	16,987	17,650
11951	Mastic Beach(u)	(516)	10,293	8,018	*12301	Schenectady	(518)	65,566	67,972
13211	Mattydale(u)	(315)	6,418	7,511	10940	Scotchtown(u)	(914)	8,765	7,352
12118	Mechanicville	(518)	5,249	5,500	12302	Scotia	(518)	7,359	7,280
11763	Medford(u)	(516)	21,274	20,418	11579	Sea Cliff	(516)	5,054	5,364
14103	Medina	(716)	6,686	6,392	11783	Seaford(u)	(516)	15,597	16,117
11746	Melville(u)	(516)	12,586	8,139	11507	Searingtown(u)	(516)	5,020	....
11566	Merrick(u)	(516)	23,042	24,478	11784	Selden(u)	(516)	20,608	17,259
11953	Middle Island(u)	(516)	7,848	5,703	13148	Seneca Falls	(315)	7,370	7,466
*10940	Middletown	(914)	24,160	21,454	11733	Setauket-East Setauket(u)	(516)	13,634	10,176
11764	Miller Place(u)	(516)	9,315	7,877	11967	Shirley(Suffolk)(u)	(516)	22,936	18,072
					11787	Smithtown(u)	(516)	25,638	30,906

ZIP	Place		1990	1980
13209	Solvay	(315)	6,717	7,140
11789	Sound Beach(u)	(516)	9,102	8,071
11735	South Farmingdale(u)	(516)	15,377	16,439
14850	South Hill(u)	(607)	5,423	5,276
11746	South Huntington(u)	(516)	9,624	14,854
14094	South Lockport(u)	(716)	7,112	3,366
11971	Southold(u)	(516)	5,192	4,770
14904	Southport(u)	(607)	7,753	8,329
11581	South Valley Stream(u)	(516)	5,328	5,462
10977	Spring Valley	(914)	21,802	20,537
11790	Stony Brook(u)	(516)	13,726	16,155
10980	Stony Point(u) (Rockland)	(914)	10,587	8,686
10901	Suffern	(914)	11,055	10,794
11791	Syosset(u)	(516)	18,967	9,818
*13220	Syracuse	(315)	163,860	170,105
10983	Tappan(u)	(914)	6,867	8,267
10591	Tarrytown	(914)	10,739	10,648
11776	Terryville	(516)	10,275	....
10984	Thiells	(914)	5,204	....
10594	Thornwood(u)	(914)	7,025	7,197
*14150	Tonawanda	(716)	17,284	18,693
*14150	Tonawanda(u)	(716)	65,284	72,795
*12180	Troy	(518)	54,269	56,638
10707	Tuckahoe	(914)	6,302	6,076
11553	Uniondale(u)	(516)	20,328	20,016
*13504	Utica	(315)	68,637	75,632
10989	Valley Cottage(u)	(914)	9,007	8,214
*11582	Valley Stream	(516)	33,946	35,769
11792	Wading River(u)	(516)	5,317	....
12586	Walden	(914)	5,836	5,659
11793	Wantagh(u)	(516)	18,567	19,817
10990	Warwick	(914)	5,984	4,320
13165	Waterloo	(315)	5,116	5,303
*13601	Watertown	(315)	29,429	27,861
12189	Watervliet	(518)	11,061	11,354
14580	Webster	(716)	5,464	5,499
14895	Wellsville	(716)	5,241	5,769
*11702	West Babylon(u)	(516)	42,410	41,699
11590	Westbury (Nassau)	(516)	13,060	13,871
14905	West Elmira(u)	(607)	5,218	5,485
12801	West Glens Falls(u)	(518)	5,964	5,331
10993	West Haverstraw	(914)	9,183	9,181
11552	West Hempstead(u)	(516)	17,689	18,536
11743	West Hills(u)	(516)	5,849	6,071
11795	West Islip(u)	(516)	28,419	29,533
12203	Westmere(u)	(518)	6,750	6,881
*10996	West Point(u)	(914)	8,024	8,105
14224	West Seneca(u)	(716)	47,866	51,210
13219	Westvale(u)	(315)	5,952	6,169
11798	Wheatley Heights(u)	(516)	5,027	....
*10602	White Plains	(914)	48,718	46,999
14221	Williamsville	(716)	5,583	6,017
11596	Williston Park	(516)	7,516	8,216
11797	Woodbury(u)	(516)	8,008	7,043
11598	Woodmere(u)	(516)	15,578	17,205
11798	Wyandach(u)	(516)	8,950	13,215
*10702	Yonkers	(914)	188,082	195,351
10598	Yorktown Heights(u)	(914)	7,690	7,696

ZIP	Place		1990	1980
*28603	Hickory	(704)	28,474	20,757
*27260	High Point	(910)	69,428	63,479
28348	Hope Mills	(919)	8,272	5,412
*28540	Jacksonville	(910)	30,398	18,237
*28081	Kannapolis†	(704)	29,709	30,303
*27284	Kernersville	(910)	10,899	5,875
28086	Kings Mountain	(704)	8,768	9,080
*28502	Kinston	(919)	25,295	25,234
*28352	Laurinburg	(919)	11,643	11,480
28645	Lenoir	(704)	14,223	13,748
*27292	Lexington	(704)	16,583	15,711
*28092	Lincolnton	(704)	6,955	4,879
*28358	Lumberton	(910)	18,656	18,241
28403	Masonboro(u)	(910)	7,010	3,729
*28105	Matthews	(704)	13,651	1,648
28227	Mint Hill	(704)	11,615	7,915
28110	Monroe	(704)	16,385	12,639
28115	Mooresville	(704)	9,317	8,575
28557	Morehead	(919)	6,046	4,359
*28655	Morganton	(704)	15,085	13,763
27030	Mount Airy	(910)	7,156	6,862
28120	Mount Holly	(704)	7,710	4,530
*28562	New Bern	(919)	17,363	14,557
27604	New Hope (Wake)(u)	(704)	5,694	6,745
28540	New River Station(u)	(919)	9,732	5,401
28658	Newton	(704)	9,077	7,624
27565	Oxford	(919)	7,965	7,709
28374	Pinehurst†	(919)	5,091	1,746
28399	Piney Green(u)	(919)	8,999	6,058
*27611	Raleigh	(919)	212,092	150,255
*27320	Reidsville	(910)	12,183	12,492
27870	Roanoke Rapids	(919)	15,722	14,702
28379	Rockingham	(910)	9,399	8,300
*27801	Rocky Mount	(919)	49,438	41,526
27573	Roxboro	(910)	7,332	7,532
28601	Saint Stephens(u)	(704)	8,734	10,797
*28144	Salisbury	(704)	23,626	22,677
*27330	Sanford	(919)	14,755	14,773
28403	Seagate(u)	(910)	5,444	3,421
*28150	Shelby	(704)	14,669	15,310
.....	Smith Creek(u)	(910)	7,461	6,562
27577	Smithfield	(919)	7,540	7,288
*28387	Southern Pines	(910)	9,213	8,620
28052	South Gastonia(u)	(704)	5,487	4,767
28390	Spring Lake	(919)	7,552	6,273
*28677	Statesville	(704)	17,567	18,622
27886	Tarboro	(919)	11,037	8,741
*27360	Thomasville	(910)	15,915	14,144
27370	Trinity(u)	(919)	5,469	6,887
*27587	Wake Forest	(919)	5,832	3,780
27889	Washington	(919)	9,160	8,418
28786	Waynesville	(704)	6,760	6,765
28472	Whiteville	(910)	5,078	5,565
27892	Williamston	(919)	5,503	6,159
*28402	Wilmington	(910)	55,530	44,000
*27893	Wilson	(919)	36,930	34,424
*27102	Winston-Salem	(910)	143,532	131,885

North Carolina

ZIP	Place		1990	1980
*28001	Albemarle	(704)	14,940	15,110
27263	Archdale	(919)	6,975	5,326
*27203	Asheboro	(910)	16,362	15,252
*28801	Asheville	(704)	61,855	54,022
28012	Belmont	(704)	8,434	4,607
28711	Black Mountain	(704)	5,533	4,083
28607	Boone	(704)	12,949	10,191
28712	Brevard	(704)	5,388	5,323
*27215	Burlington	(910)	39,498	37,266
28547	Camp Lejeune(u)	(919)	36,716	30,764
27510	Carrboro	(919)	12,134	7,336
*27511	Cary	(919)	44,397	21,763
*27514	Chapel Hill	(919)	38,711	32,421
*28204	Charlotte	(704)	395,925	315,474
27012	Clemmons†	(919)	5,982	4,842
28328	Clinton	(910)	8,385	7,552
*28025	Concord	(704)	27,601	16,942
28613	Conover	(704)	5,311	4,245
*28334	Dunn	(910)	8,556	8,962
*27701	Durham	(919)	136,612	101,149
*27288	Eden	(910)	15,238	15,672
27932	Edenton	(919)	5,268	5,357
*27909	Elizabeth City	(919)	14,292	14,004
*28302	Fayetteville	(910)	75,850	59,507
28043	Forest City	(704)	7,475	7,688
28307	Fort Bragg(u)	(919)	34,744	37,834
27529	Garner	(919)	14,716	10,073
*28052	Gastonia	(704)	54,725	47,218
*27530	Goldsboro	(919)	40,709	31,871
27253	Graham	(919)	10,368	8,674
*27420	Greensboro	(919)	183,894	155,642
*27834	Greenville	(919)	46,305	35,740
28540	Half Moon(u)	(910)	6,306	3,592
28345	Hamlet	(919)	6,324	4,720
28532	Havelock	(919)	20,300	17,718
27536	Henderson	(919)	15,655	13,522
*28739	Hendersonville	(704)	7,284	6,862

North Dakota (701)

ZIP	Place		1990	1980
*58501	Bismarck		49,272	44,485
58301	Devils Lake		7,782	7,442
*58601	Dickinson		16,097	15,924
*58102	Fargo		74,084	61,383
*58201	Grand Forks		49,417	43,765
58204	Grand Forks AFB(u)		9,343	9,390
*58401	Jamestown		15,571	16,280
58554	Mandan		15,177	15,513
*58701	Minot		34,544	32,843
*58704	Minot AFB(u)		9,095	9,880
58072	Valley City		7,163	7,774
*58075	Wahpeton		8,751	9,064
58078	West Fargo		12,287	10,099
*58801	Williston		13,136	13,336

Ohio

ZIP	Place		1990	1980
45810	Ada	(419)	5,428	5,669
*44309	Akron	(330)	223,019	237,177
44601	Alliance	(330)	23,376	24,315
44001	Amherst	(440)	10,332	10,638
44805	Ashland	(419)	20,079	20,326
*44004	Ashtabula	(440)	21,633	23,449
45701	Athens	(614)	21,265	19,743
44202	Aurora	(330)	9,192	8,177
44515	Austintown(u)	(330)	32,371	33,636
44011	Avon	(440)	7,337	7,241
44012	Avon Lake	(440)	15,066	13,222
44203	Barberton	(330)	27,623	29,751
44140	Bay Village	(440)	17,000	17,846
44122	Beachwood	(216)	10,644	9,983
45434	Beavercreek	(937)	33,626	31,589
44146	Bedford	(216)/(440)	14,822	15,056
44146	Bedford Heights	(216)/(440)	12,131	13,214
43906	Bellaire	(614)	6,028	8,241
45305	Bellbrook	(937)	6,511	5,174

ZIP	Place		1990	1980
43311	Bellefontaine	(937)	12,126	11,888
44811	Bellevue	(419)	8,157	8,187
45714	Belpre	(614)	6,796	7,193
44017	Berea	(440)	19,051	19,567
43209	Bexley	(614)	13,088	13,405
43004	Blacklick Estates(u)	(614)	10,080	11,223
45242	Blue Ash	(513)	11,923	9,510
44513	Boardman(u)	(330)	38,596	39,086
43402	Bowling Green	(419)	28,303	25,728
44141	Brecksville	(440)	11,818	10,132
45211	Bridgetown North(u)	(513)	11,748	11,460
44147	Broadview Heights	(440)	12,219	10,920
44144	Brooklyn	(216)	11,706	12,342
44142	Brook Park	(216)/(440)	22,865	26,195
44212	Brunswick	(330)	28,218	28,104
43506	Bryan	(419)	8,348	7,879
44820	Bucyrus	(419)	13,496	13,433
43725	Cambridge	(614)	11,748	13,573
44405	Campbell	(330)	10,038	11,619
44406	Canfield	(330)	5,409	5,535
*44711	Canton	(330)	84,161	93,077
45822	Celina	(419)	9,923	9,137
45459	Centerville (Montgomery)	(937)	21,082	18,886
45211	Cheviot	(513)	9,616	9,888
45601	Chillicothe	(614)	21,923	23,420
*45202	Cincinnati	(513)	364,114	385,409
43113	Circleville	(614)	11,666	11,700
*44101	Cleveland	(216)	505,616	573,822
44118	Cleveland Heights	(216)	54,052	56,438
43410	Clyde	(419)	5,776	5,489
*43216	Columbus	(614)	632,945	565,021
44030	Conneaut	(440)	13,241	13,835
44410	Cortland	(330)	5,652	5,011
43812	Coshocton	(614)	12,193	13,405
45238	Covedale(u)	(513)	6,669	5,830
*44222	Cuyahoga Falls	(330)	48,950	43,890
*45401	Dayton	(937)	182,005	193,536
45236	Deer Park	(513)	6,181	6,745
43512	Defiance	(419)	16,787	16,810
43015	Delaware	(614)	19,966	18,780
45833	Delphos	(419)	7,093	7,314
45247	Dent(u)	(513)	6,416	....
44622	Dover (Tuscarawas)	(330)	11,329	11,782
45427	Drexel(u)	(937)	5,143	....
45663	Dry Run(u)	(614)	5,389	....
43016	Dublin	(614)	16,366	3,855
44112	East Cleveland	(216)	33,096	36,957
44095	Eastlake	(440)	21,161	22,104
43920	East Liverpool	(330)	13,654	16,687
44413	East Palestine	(330)	5,168	5,306
45320	Eaton	(937)	7,396	6,839
44004	Edgewood(u)	(440)	5,189	3,099
*44035	Elyria	(440)	56,746	57,538
45322	Englewood	(937)	11,402	11,329
*44101	Euclid	(216)	54,875	59,999
45324	Fairborn	(937)	31,300	29,702
45014	Fairfield	(513)	39,709	30,777
44313	Fairlawn	(330)	5,779	6,100
44126	Fairview Park	(440)	18,028	19,311
*45839	Findlay	(419)	35,703	35,594
45224	Finneytown(u)	(513)	13,096	....
45405	Forest Park	(513)	18,621	18,566
45230	Forestville(u)	(513)	9,185	....
45426	Fort McKinley(u)	(937)	9,740	10,161
44830	Fostoria	(419)	14,971	15,743
45005	Franklin	(513)	11,026	10,711
43420	Fremont	(419)	17,619	17,834
43230	Gahanna	(614)	23,898	18,001
44833	Galion	(419)	11,859	12,391
44125	Garfield Heights	(216)	31,739	34,938
44041	Geneva	(440)	6,597	6,655
44420	Girard	(330)	11,304	12,517
43212	Grandview Heights	(614)	7,010	7,420
45123	Greenfield	(937)	5,172	5,150
45331	Greenville	(937)	12,863	12,999
45239	Groesbeck(u)	(513)	6,684	9,594
43123	Grove City	(614)	19,661	16,816
*45011	Hamilton	(513)	61,436	63,189
45030	Harrison	(513)	7,520	5,855
43056	Heath	(614)	7,231	6,969
44134	Highland Heights	(440)	6,249	5,739
43026	Hilliard	(614)	11,794	8,131
45133	Hillsboro	(937)	6,235	6,356
44484	Howland Center(u)	(330)	6,732	7,441
44425	Hubbard	(330)	8,248	9,245
45424	Huber Heights	(937)	38,696	35,480
43081	Huber Ridge(u)	(614)	5,255	5,835
44236	Hudson	(330)	5,159	4,615
44839	Huron	(419)	7,067	7,123
44131	Independence (Cuyahoga)	(216)/(440)	6,500	6,607
45638	Ironton	(614)	12,751	14,290
45640	Jackson	(614)	6,167	6,675
*44240	Kent	(330)	28,835	26,164
43326	Kenton	(419)	8,356	8,605
43606	Kenwood(u)	(513)	7,469	9,943
45429	Kettering	(937)	60,569	61,186
44094	Kirtland	(440)	5,881	5,969
43130	Lancaster	(614)	34,507	34,953
45039	Landen(u)	(513)	9,263	2,870
45036	Lebanon (Warren)	(513)	10,461	9,636
*45802	Lima	(419)	45,553	47,827
43228	Lincoln Village(u)	(614)	9,958	10,548
43138	Logan	(614)	6,725	6,557
43140	London	(614)	7,807	6,958
*44052	Lorain	(440)	71,245	75,416
44641	Louisville	(330)	8,087	7,996
45140	Loveland	(513)	10,122	9,106
44124	Lyndhurst	(216)/(440)	15,982	18,092
44056	Macedonia	(330)	7,509	6,571
.....	Mack South(u)		5,767	....
45243	Madeira	(513)	9,141	9,341
*44901	Mansfield	(419)	50,627	53,927
44137	Maple Heights	(216)	27,089	29,735
45750	Marietta	(614)	15,026	16,467
*43302	Marion	(614)	34,075	37,040
43935	Martins Ferry	(614)	8,003	9,331
43040	Marysville	(937)	9,656	7,414
45040	Mason	(513)	11,450	8,692
*44646	Massillon	(330)	30,969	30,557
43537	Maumee	(419)	15,561	15,747
44124	Mayfield Heights	(440)	19,847	21,550
*44256	Medina	(330)	19,231	15,268
*44060	Mentor	(440)	47,491	42,065
44060	Mentor-on-the-Lake	(216)	8,271	7,919
*45343	Miamisburg	(937)	17,834	15,304
44130	Middleburg Heights	(216)/(440)	14,702	16,218
*45042	Middletown	(513)	46,022	43,719
45150	Milford	(513)	5,660	5,232
45242	Montgomery	(513)	9,733	10,084
45439	Moraine	(937)	5,989	5,325
45231	Mount Healthy	(513)	7,580	7,562
43050	Mount Vernon	(614)	14,550	14,323
44262	Munroe Falls	(330)	5,359	4,731
43545	Napoleon	(419)	8,884	8,614
*43055	Newark	(614)	44,396	41,200
45344	New Carlisle	(937)	6,049	6,498
43764	New Lexington	(614)	5,117	5,179
44663	New Philadelphia	(330)	15,698	16,883
44446	Niles	(330)	21,128	23,088
45239	Northbrook(u)	(513)	11,471	8,357
44720	North Canton	(330)	14,904	14,228
45239	North College Hill	(513)	11,002	11,114
45251	Northgate(u)	(513)	7,864	....
44057	North Madison(u)	(440)	8,699	8,741
44070	North Olmsted	(440)	34,204	36,486
45502	Northridge(u) (Clark)	(937)	5,939	5,559
45414	Northridge(u) (Montgomery)	(937)	9,448	9,720
44039	North Ridgeville	(440)	21,564	21,522
44133	North Royalton	(440)	23,197	17,671
45322	Northview(u)	(937)	10,337	9,973
43619	Northwood	(419)	5,506	5,495
44203	Norton	(330)	11,477	12,242
44857	Norwalk	(419)	14,731	14,358
45212	Norwood	(513)	23,674	26,342
44146	Oakwood (Cuyahoga)	(440)	8,957	9,372
44074	Oberlin	(440)	8,191	8,660
44138	Olmsted Falls	(440)	6,741	5,868
*43601	Oregon	(419)	18,334	18,675
44667	Orrville	(330)	7,712	7,511
45431	Overlook-Page Manor(u)	(937)	13,242	14,825
45056	Oxford	(513)	18,937	17,655
44077	Painesville	(440)	15,769	16,391
44129	Parma	(216)/(440)	87,876	92,548
44130	Parma Heights	(216)/(440)	21,448	23,112
44124	Pepper Pike	(216)/(440)	6,185	6,177
44646	Perry Heights(u)	(330)	9,055	9,206
*43551	Perrysburg	(419)	12,551	10,215
43147	Pickerington	(614)	5,668	3,917
45356	Piqua	(937)	20,612	20,480
44319	Portage Lakes(u)	(330)	13,373	11,310
43452	Port Clinton	(419)	7,106	7,223
45662	Portsmouth	(614)	22,676	25,943
44266	Ravenna	(330)	12,069	11,987
45215	Reading	(513)	12,038	12,843
43068	Reynoldsburg	(614)	25,748	20,661
44143	Richmond Heights	(216)/(440)	9,611	10,095
44270	Rittman	(330)	6,147	6,063
44116	Rocky River	(440)	20,410	21,084
43460	Rossford	(419)	5,861	5,978
45217	Saint Bernard	(513)	5,344	5,396
43950	Saint Clairsville	(614)	5,136	5,452
45885	Saint Marys	(419)	8,441	8,414
44460	Salem	(330)	12,233	12,869
*44870	Sandusky	(419)	29,764	31,360
44870	Sandusky South(u)	(419)	6,336	6,548
44131	Seven Hills	(216)/(440)	12,339	13,650
44120	Shaker Heights	(216)	30,955	32,487
45241	Sharonville	(513)	13,121	10,108
44054	Sheffield Lake	(440)	9,025	10,484
44875	Shelby	(419)	9,610	9,703
44878	Shiloh(u)	(419)	11,607	11,735
45365	Sidney	(937)	18,710	17,657
45236	Silverton	(513)	5,859	6,172
44139	Solon	(440)	18,548	14,341

ZIP	Place		1990	1980
44121	South Euclid	(216)	23,866	25,713
45066	Springboro	(937)	6,574	4,962
45246	Springdale	(513)	10,621	10,111
*45501	Springfield	(937)	70,487	72,563
43952	Steubenville	(614)	22,125	26,400
44224	Stow	(330)	27,998	25,303
44241	Streetsboro	(330)	9,932	9,055
44136	Strongsville	(440)	35,308	28,577
44471	Struthers	(330)	12,284	13,624
43560	Sylvania	(419)	17,489	15,527
44278	Tallmadge	(330)	14,870	15,269
45243	The Village of Indian Hill	(513)	5,383	5,521
44883	Tiffin	(419)	18,604	19,549
45371	Tipp City	(937)	6,027	5,595
*43601	Toledo	(419)	332,943	354,635
43964	Toronto	(614)	6,127	6,934
45067	Trenton	(513)	6,189	6,401
45426	Trotwood	(937)	8,816	7,802
45373	Troy	(937)	19,478	19,086
44087	Twinsburg	(330)	9,606	7,632
44683	Uhrichsville	(614)	5,604	6,130
45322	Union	(937)	5,531	5,219
44118	University Heights	(216)	14,787	15,401
43221	Upper Arlington	(614)	34,128	35,648
43351	Upper Sandusky	(419)	5,906	5,967
43078	Urbana	(937)	11,353	10,762
45377	Vandalia	(937)	13,872	13,161
45891	Van Wert	(419)	10,922	11,035
44089	Vermilion	(440)	11,127	11,012
44281	Wadsworth	(330)	15,718	15,166
45895	Wapakoneta	(419)	9,214	8,402
*44481	Warren	(330)	50,793	56,629
44122	Warrensville Heights	(216)	15,745	16,565
43160	Washington Court House	(614)	13,080	12,682
43567	Wauseon	(419)	6,322	6,173
45692	Wellston	(614)	6,049	6,016
45449	West Carrollton City	(937)	14,403	13,148
*43081	Westerville	(614)	30,269	23,414
44145	Westlake	(440)	27,018	19,483
45694	Wheelersburg(u)	(614)	5,113	4,796
43213	Whitehall	(614)	20,572	21,299
45239	White Oak(u)	(513)	12,430	9,563
44092	Wickliffe	(440)	14,558	16,790
44890	Willard	(419)	6,210	5,720
*44094	Willoughby	(440)	20,510	19,329
44094	Willoughby Hills	(440)	8,427	8,612
44095	Willowick	(440)	15,269	17,834
45177	Wilmington	(937)	11,199	10,431
45459	Woodbourne-Hyde Park(u)	(937)	7,837	8,826
44691	Wooster	(330)	22,427	19,289
43085	Worthington	(614)	14,869	15,016
45431	Wright-Patterson AFB(u)	(937)	8,579	9,155
45215	Wyoming	(513)	8,128	8,282
45385	Xenia	(937)	24,836	24,653
*44501	Youngstown	(330)	95,732	115,511
*43701	Zanesville	(614)	26,778	28,655

Oklahoma

ZIP	Place		1990	1980
*74820	Ada	(405)	15,765	15,902
*73521	Altus	(405)	21,910	23,101
73717	Alva	(405)	5,495	6,416
73005	Anadarko	(405)	6,586	6,378
*73401	Ardmore	(405)	23,079	23,689
*74003	Bartlesville	(918)	34,256	34,568
73008	Bethany	(405)	20,075	22,038
74008	Bixby	(918)	9,502	6,969
74631	Blackwell	(405)	7,538	8,400
*74012	Broken Arrow	(918)	58,082	35,761
*73018	Chickasha	(405)	14,988	15,828
*73020	Choctaw	(405)	8,545	7,520
*74017	Claremore	(918)	13,280	12,085
73601	Clinton	(405)	9,298	8,796
74429	Coweta	(918)	6,159	4,554
74023	Cushing	(918)	7,218	7,720
73115	Del City	(405)	23,928	28,523
*73533	Duncan	(405)	21,732	22,517
*74701	Durant	(405)	12,929	11,972
*73034	Edmond	(405)	52,310	34,637
*73644	Elk City	(405)	10,428	9,579
73036	El Reno	(405)	15,414	15,486
*73701	Enid	(405)	45,309	50,363
73503	Fort Sill(u)	(405)	12,107	15,924
73542	Frederick	(405)	5,221	6,153
74033	Glenpool	(918)	6,688	2,706
73044	Guthrie	(405)	10,440	10,312
73942	Guymon	(405)	7,803	8,492
74437	Henryetta	(918)	5,872	6,432
74743	Hugo	(405)	5,978	7,172
74745	Idabel	(405)	6,957	7,622
74037	Jenks	(918)	7,484	5,876
*73501	Lawton	(405)	80,561	80,054
*74501	McAlester	(918)	16,739	17,255
*74354	Miami	(918)	13,142	14,237
73140	Midwest City	(405)	52,267	49,559
73153	Moore	(405)	40,318	35,063

ZIP	Place		1990	1980
*74401	Muskogee	(918)	37,708	40,011
73064	Mustang	(405)	10,434	7,496
*73069	Norman	(405)	80,071	68,020
*73125	Oklahoma City	(405)	444,724	404,014
74447	Okmulgee	(918)	13,441	16,263
74055	Owasso	(918)	11,151	6,149
73075	Pauls Valley	(405)	6,150	5,664
*74601	Ponca City	(405)	26,359	26,238
74953	Poteau	(918)	7,210	7,089
74361	Pryor Creek	(918)	8,327	8,483
74955	Sallisaw	(918)	7,122	6,403
74063	Sand Springs	(918)	15,339	13,121
*74066	Sapulpa	(918)	18,074	15,853
*74868	Seminole	(405)	7,071	8,590
*74801	Shawnee	(405)	26,017	26,506
*74074	Stillwater	(405)	36,676	38,268
*74464	Tahlequah	(918)	10,586	9,708
74873	Tecumseh	(405)	5,570	5,123
*74103	Tulsa	(918)	367,302	360,919
73156	Village	(405)	10,353	11,114
74301	Vinita	(918)	5,804	6,740
*74467	Wagoner	(918)	6,894	6,191
73132	Warr Acres	(405)	9,288	9,940
73096	Weatherford	(405)	10,124	9,640
*73801	Woodward	(405)	12,340	13,781
*73099	Yukon	(405)	20,935	17,112

Oregon

ZIP	Place		1990	1980
97321	Albany	(541)	29,540	26,511
97006	Aloha(u)	(503)	34,284	28,353
97601	Altamont(u)	(541)	18,591	19,805
97520	Ashland	(541)	16,252	14,943
97103	Astoria	(503)	10,069	9,998
97814	Baker City	(541)	9,140	9,471
*97005	Beaverton	(503)	53,307	31,962
*97701	Bend	(541)	20,447	17,263
97013	Canby	(503)	8,990	7,659
97225	Cedar Hills(u)	(503)	9,294	9,619
97291	Cedar Mill(u)†	(503)	9,697	22,118
97502	Central Point	(541)	7,512	6,357
97420	Coos Bay	(541)	15,076	14,424
97113	Cornelius	(503)	6,148	4,462
*97333	Corvallis	(541)	44,757	40,960
97424	Cottage Grove	(541)	7,403	7,148
97338	Dallas	(503)	9,422	8,530
*97401	Eugene	(541)	112,773	105,664
97439	Florence	(541)	5,171	4,411
97116	Forest Grove	(503)	13,559	11,499
97301	Four Corners(u)	(503)	12,156	11,316
97223	Garden Home-Whitford(u)	(503)	6,652	6,911
97027	Gladstone	(503)	10,152	9,500
*97526	Grants Pass	(541)	17,503	15,032
97470	Green(u)	(541)	5,076	3,897
*97030	Gresham	(503)	68,249	33,005
97303	Hayesville(u)	(503)	14,318	9,413
97230	Hazelwood(u)	(503)	11,480	25,541
97838	Hermiston	(541)	10,047	9,408
*97123	Hillsboro	(503)	37,598	27,664
97222	Jennings Lodge(u)	(503)	6,530	....
97303	Keizer†	(503)	21,884	19,785
*97601	Klamath Falls	(541)	17,737	16,661
97850	La Grande	(541)	11,766	11,354
*97034	Lake Oswego	(503)	30,576	22,527
97355	Lebanon	(541)	10,950	10,413
97367	Lincoln City	(541)	5,903	5,469
97128	McMinnville	(503)	17,894	14,080
*97501	Medford	(541)	47,021	39,746
97862	Milton-Freewater	(541)	5,533	5,086
97222	Milwaukie	(503)	18,670	17,931
97361	Monmouth	(503)	6,288	5,594
97132	Newberg	(503)	13,086	10,394
97365	Newport	(541)	8,437	7,519
97459	North Bend	(541)	9,614	9,779
97477	North Springfield(u)	(541)	5,451	6,140
97268	Oak Grove(u)	(503)	12,576	11,640
.....	Oak Hills(u)	....	6,450	....
.....	Oatfield(u)	....	15,348	....
97914	Ontario	(541)	9,394	8,814
97045	Oregon City	(503)	14,698	14,673
97801	Pendleton	(541)	15,142	14,521
*97208	Portland	(503)	438,802	368,148
97236	Powellhurst-Centennial(u)	(503)	28,756	20,122
97754	Prineville	(541)	5,355	5,276
97225	Raleigh Hills(u)	(503)	6,066	6,517
97756	Redmond	(541)	7,165	6,452
97404	River Road(u)	(541)	9,443	10,370
.....	Rockcreek(u)	....	8,282	....
97470	Roseburg	(541)	17,069	16,644
97470	Roseburg North(u)	(541)	6,831	....
97051	Saint Helens	(503)	7,535	7,064
*97301	Salem	(503)	107,793	89,091
97401	Santa Clara(u)	(541)	12,834	14,288
97138	Seaside	(503)	5,359	5,193
97381	Silverton	(503)	5,635	5,168
*97477	Springfield	(541)	44,664	41,621
97383	Stayton	(503)	5,011	4,396

ZIP	Place		1990	1980
97479	Sutherlin	(541)	5,020	4,560
97386	Sweet Home	(541)	6,850	6,921
97058	The Dalles, City of	(541)	11,021	10,820
97223	Tigard	(503)	29,435	14,799
97060	Troutdale	(503)	7,852	5,908
97062	Tualatin	(503)	14,664	7,483
97225	West Haven-Sylvan(u)	(503)	6,009	....
97068	West Linn	(503)	16,389	11,358
97225	West Slope(u)	(503)	7,959	5,364
97503	White City(u)	(541)	5,891	5,445
97070	Wilsonville	(503)	7,106	2,920
97071	Woodburn	(503)	13,404	11,196

Pennsylvania

ZIP	Place		1990	1980
15001	Aliquippa	(412)	13,374	17,094
*18105	Allentown (Lehigh)	(610)	105,301	103,758
*16603	Altoona	(814)	51,881	57,078
19002	Ambler	(215)/(610)	6,609	6,628
15003	Ambridge	(412)	8,133	9,575
18403	Archbald	(717)	6,291	6,295
19003	Ardmore(u)	(610)	12,646	....
15068	Arnold	(412)	6,113	6,853
19407	Audubon(u)†	(610)	6,328	6,853
15202	Avalon	(412)	5,784	6,240
15005	Baden	(412)	5,074	5,318
15234	Baldwin	(412)	21,923	24,714
18013	Bangor	(610)	5,383	5,006
15009	Beaver	(412)	5,028	5,441
15010	Beaver Falls	(412)	10,687	12,525
16823	Bellefonte	(814)	6,358	6,300
15202	Bellevue	(412)	9,126	10,128
18603	Berwick	(717)	10,976	11,850
15102	Bethel Park	(412)	33,823	34,755
*18016	Bethlehem	(610)	71,427	70,419
18447	Blakely	(717)	7,222	7,438
17815	Bloomsburg	(717)	12,439	11,717
19422	Blue Bell(u)	(215)/(610)	6,091	....
19061	Boothwyn(u)	(610)	5,069	....
16701	Bradford	(814)	9,625	11,211
15227	Brentwood	(412)	10,823	11,859
15017	Bridgeville	(412)	5,445	6,154
19007	Bristol	(215)	10,405	10,867
19015	Brookhaven	(610)	8,567	7,912
19008	Broomall(u)	(610)	10,930	....
*16001	Butler	(412)	15,714	17,026
15419	California	(412)	5,748	5,703
*17011	Camp Hill	(717)	7,831	8,422
15317	Canonsburg	(412)	9,200	10,459
18407	Carbondale	(717)	10,664	11,255
17013	Carlisle	(717)	18,419	18,314
15106	Carnegie	(412)	9,278	10,099
15108	Carnot-Moon(u)	(412)	10,187	11,102
15234	Castle Shannon	(412)	9,135	10,164
18032	Catasauqua	(610)	6,662	6,711
17201	Chambersburg	(717)	16,647	16,174
15022	Charleroi	(412)	5,014	5,717
*19013	Chester	(610)	41,856	45,794
19013	Chester Twp.(u)	(610)	5,399	5,687
15025	Clairton	(412)	9,656	12,188
16214	Clarion	(814)	6,457	6,198
18411	Clarks Summit	(717)	5,433	5,272
16830	Clearfield	(814)	6,633	7,580
19018	Clifton Heights	(610)	7,111	7,320
19320	Coatesville	(610)	11,038	10,698
19023	Collingdale	(610)	9,175	9,539
17109	Colonial Park(u) (Dauphin)	(717)	13,777	....
17512	Columbia	(717)	10,701	10,466
15425	Connellsville	(412)	9,229	10,319
19428	Conshohocken	(215)/(610)	8,064	8,591
15108	Coraopolis	(412)	6,747	7,308
16407	Corry	(814)	7,216	7,149
15205	Crafton	(412)	7,188	7,623
19021	Croydon(u)	(215)	9,967	....
17821	Danville	(717)	5,165	5,239
19023	Darby	(610)	11,140	11,513
19036	Darby Twp.(u)	(610)	10,955	12,264
19333	Devon-Berwyn(u)	(610)	5,019	5,246
18519	Dickson City	(717)	6,276	6,699
15033	Donora	(412)	5,928	7,524
15216	Dormont	(412)	9,772	11,275
19335	Downingtown	(610)	7,749	7,650
18901	Doylestown	(215)	8,575	8,717
19026	Drexel Hill(u)	(610)	29,744	....
15801	Du Bois	(814)	8,286	9,290
18512	Dunmore	(717)	15,403	16,781
15110	Duquesne	(412)	8,525	10,094
19401	East Norriton(u)	(215)/(610)	13,324	12,711
*18042	Easton	(610)	26,276	26,027
18301	East Stroudsburg	(717)	8,781	8,000
17405	East York(u)	(717)	8,487	....
15005	Economy	(412)	9,305	9,538
16412	Edinboro	(814)	7,736	6,324
18704	Edwardsville	(717)	5,399	5,729
17022	Elizabethtown	(717)	9,952	8,233
16117	Ellwood City	(412)	8,894	9,998
18049	Emmaus	(610)	11,157	11,001

ZIP	Place		1990	1980
17025	Enola(u)	(717)	5,961	....
17522	Ephrata	(717)	12,133	11,095
*16501	Erie	(814)	108,718	119,123
18643	Exeter	(717)	5,691	5,493
19030	Fairless Hills(u)	(215)	9,026	....
16121	Farrell	(412)	6,835	8,645
19053	Feasterville-Trevose(u)	(215)	6,696	....
16063	Fernway(u)	(412)	9,072	3,843
19032	Folcroft	(610)	7,506	8,231
19033	Folsom(u)	(610)	8,173	....
15221	Forest Hills	(412)	8,173	8,198
18704	Forty Fort	(717)	5,049	5,590
15238	Fox Chapel	(412)	5,319	5,049
16323	Franklin	(814)	7,329	8,146
15143	Franklin Park	(412)	10,109	6,135
18052	Fullerton(u)	(610)	13,127	8,055
17325	Gettysburg	(717)	7,025	7,194
15045	Glassport	(412)	5,582	6,242
19036	Glenolden	(610)	7,260	7,633
19038	Glenside(u)	(215)	8,704	....
15601	Greensburg	(412)	16,318	17,558
16125	Greenville	(412)	6,734	7,730
16127	Grove City	(412)	8,240	8,162
15101	Hampton Twp.(u) (Allegheny)	(412)	15,568	....
17331	Hanover	(717)	14,399	14,890
19438	Harleysville(u)	(215)/(610)	7,405	3,673
*17105	Harrisburg	(717)	52,376	53,264
15065	Harrison Twp.(u) (Allegheny)	(412)	11,763	....
19040	Hatboro	(215)	7,382	7,579
18201	Hazleton	(717)	24,730	27,318
18055	Hellertown	(610)	5,662	6,025
16148	Hermitage†	(412)	15,260	16,365
17033	Hershey(u)	(717)	11,860	13,249
16648	Hollidaysburg	(814)	5,624	5,892
16001	Homeacre-Lyndora(u)	(412)	7,511	8,333
19044	Horsham(u)	(215)	15,051	9,900
16652	Huntingdon	(814)	6,843	7,042
15701	Indiana	(412)	15,174	16,051
15644	Jeannette	(412)	11,221	13,106
15344	Jefferson	(412)	9,533	8,643
18229	Jim Thorpe	(717)	5,048	5,263
*15907	Johnstown	(814)	28,124	35,496
15108	Kennedy Twp.(u.)	(412)	7,152	7,159
19348	Kennett Square	(610)	5,218	4,715
19406	King of Prussia(u)	(215)/(610)	18,406	....
18704	Kingston	(717)	14,507	15,681
16201	Kittanning	(412)	5,120	5,432
19443	Kulpsville(u)	(215)	5,183	....
*17604	Lancaster	(717)	55,551	54,725
19446	Lansdale	(215)	16,362	16,526
19050	Lansdowne	(610)	11,712	11,891
15650	Latrobe	(412)	9,265	10,799
17540	Leacock-Leola-Bareville(u)	(717)	5,685	....
*17042	Lebanon	(717)	24,800	25,711
18235	Lehighton	(610)	5,914	5,826
*19055	Levittown(u)	(215)	55,362	....
17837	Lewisburg	(717)	5,785	5,407
17044	Lewistown (Mifflin)	(717)	9,341	9,830
17112	Linglestown(u)	(717)	5,862	....
19353	Lionville-Marchwood(u)	(610)	6,468	....
17543	Lititz	(717)	8,280	7,590
17745	Lock Haven	(717)	9,230	9,617
17011	Lower Allen(u)	(717)	6,329	....
15068	Lower Burrell	(412)	12,251	13,200
15237	McCandless Twp.(u)	(412)	28,781	26,191
*15134	McKeesport	(412)	26,016	31,012
15136	McKees Rocks	(412)	7,691	8,742
17948	Mahanoy City	(717)	5,209	6,167
17545	Manheim	(717)	5,011	5,015
19002	Maple Glen(u)	(215)	5,881	....
16335	Meadville	(814)	14,318	15,544
17055	Mechanicsburg	(717)	9,452	9,487
*19063	Media	(610)	5,957	6,119
17057	Middletown (Dauphin)	(717)	9,254	10,122
18017	Middletown (u) (Northampton)	(610)	6,866	5,801
17551	Millersville	(717)	8,099	7,668
17847	Milton	(717)	6,746	6,730
15061	Monaca	(412)	6,739	7,661
15062	Monessen	(412)	9,901	11,928
15146	Monroeville	(412)	29,169	30,977
18936	Montgomeryville(u)	(215)	9,114	....
18507	Moosic	(717)	5,397	6,068
19067	Morrisville (Bucks)	(215)	9,765	9,845
17851	Mount Carmel	(717)	7,196	8,190
17552	Mount Joy	(717)	6,398	5,680
15228	Mount Lebanon(u)	(412)	33,362	34,414
15120	Munhall	(412)	13,158	14,535
15668	Murrysville	(412)	17,240	16,036
18634	Nanticoke	(717)	12,267	13,044
18064	Nazareth	(610)	5,713	5,443
19086	Nether Providence Twp.(u)	(610)	13,229	12,730
15066	New Brighton	(412)	6,854	7,364
*16108	New Castle	(412)	28,334	33,621
17070	New Cumberland	(717)	7,665	8,051
15068	New Kensington	(412)	15,894	17,660
*19401	Norristown	(610)	30,754	34,684
18067	Northampton	(610)	8,717	8,240
15104	North Braddock	(412)	7,036	8,711
15137	North Versailles(u)	(412)	12,302	13,294

ZIP	Place		1990	1980
16421	Northwest Harborcreek(u)	(814)	6,662	7,485
19074	Norwood (Delaware)	(610)	6,162	6,647
15139	Oakmont (Allegheny)	(412)	6,961	7,039
15238	O'Hara(u)	(412)	9,096	....
16301	Oil City	(814)	11,949	13,881
18518	Old Forge	(717)	8,834	9,304
18447	Olyphant	(717)	5,222	5,204
19075	Oreland(u)	(215)	5,695	....
18071	Palmerton	(610)	5,394	5,455
17078	Palmyra	(717)	6,910	7,228
19301	Paoli(u)	(610)	5,603	5,277
16801	Park Forest Village(u)	(814)	6,703	....
17331	Parkville(u)	(717)	6,014	5,009
15235	Penn Hills(u)	(717)	51,430	57,632
19151	Penn Wynne(u)	(215)	5,807	....
18944	Perkasie	(215)	7,787	5,241
*19104	Philadelphia	(215)	1,585,577	1,688,210
19460	Phoenixville	(610)	15,066	14,165
*15233	Pittsburgh	(412)	369,879	423,959
*18640	Pittston	(717)	9,389	9,903
15236	Pleasant Hills	(412)	8,884	9,604
15239	Plum	(412)	25,609	25,390
18651	Plymouth	(717)	7,134	7,605
19462	Plymouth Meeting(u)	(215)/(610)	6,241	....
*19464	Pottstown	(610)	21,831	22,729
17901	Pottsville	(717)	16,603	18,195
17109	Progress(u)	(717)	9,654	....
19076	Prospect Park	(610)	6,764	6,593
15767	Punxsutawney	(814)	6,782	7,479
18951	Quakertown	(215)	8,982	8,867
19087	Radnor Twp.(u)	(610)	28,705	27,676
*19612	Reading	(610)	78,380	78,686
17356	Red Lion	(717)	6,130	5,824
18954	Richboro(u)	(215)	5,332	5,141
19078	Ridley Park	(610)	7,592	7,889
15136	Robinson (Allegheny)(u)	(412)	10,830	....
15237	Ross Twp.(u)	(412)	33,482	35,102
15857	Saint Marys	(814)	5,511	6,417
19464	Sanatoga(u)	(610)	5,534	3,723
18840	Sayre	(717)	5,791	6,951
17972	Schuylkill Haven	(717)	5,610	5,977
15683	Scottdale	(412)	5,184	5,833
15106	Scott Twp.(u)	(412)	17,118	20,413
*18505	Scranton	(717)	81,805	88,117
17870	Selinsgrove	(717)	5,384	5,227
15116	Shaler Twp.(u)	(412)	30,533	33,694
17872	Shamokin	(717)	9,184	10,357
16146	Sharon	(412)	17,533	19,057
19079	Sharon Hill	(610)	5,771	6,221
17976	Shenandoah	(717)	6,221	7,589
19607	Shillington	(610)	5,062	5,601
17404	Shiloh(u)	(717)	8,245	5,315
17257	Shippensburg	(717)	5,331	5,261
15501	Somerset	(814)	6,454	6,474
18964	Souderton	(215)	5,957	6,657
15129	South Park Twp.(u)	(814)	14,292	....
17701	South Williamsport	(717)	6,496	6,581
19064	Springfield (u) (Delaware)	(610)	24,160	25,326
*16804	State College	(814)	38,981	36,130
17113	Steelton	(717)	5,152	6,484
15136	Stowe Twp.(u)	(412)	7,681	9,202
18360	Stroudsburg	(717)	5,312	5,148
16323	Sugar Creek	(717)	5,532	5,954
17801	Sunbury	(717)	11,591	12,292
19081	Swarthmore	(610)	6,157	5,950
15218	Swissvale	(412)	10,637	11,345
18704	Swoyersville	(717)	5,630	5,795
18252	Tamaqua	(717)	7,943	8,843
15084	Tarentum	(412)	5,674	6,419
18517	Taylor	(717)	6,941	7,246
16354	Titusville	(814)	6,434	6,884
19401	Trooper(u)	(610)	5,137	7,370
15145	Turtle Creek	(412)	6,556	6,959
16686	Tyrone	(814)	5,743	6,346
15401	Uniontown (Fayette)	(412)	12,034	14,510
19063	Upper Providence Twp.(u)	(610)	9,727	9,477
15241	Upper Saint Clair(u)	(412)	19,692	19,023
15690	Vandergrift	(412)	5,904	6,823
19013	Village Green-Green Ridge(u)	(610)	9,026	....
16365	Warren	(814)	11,122	12,146
15301	Washington	(412)	15,864	18,363
17268	Waynesboro	(717)	9,578	9,726
17315	Weigelstown(u)	(717)	8,665	5,213
*19380	West Chester	(610)	18,041	17,435
19380	West Goshen(u)	(610)	8,948	7,998
*15122	West Mifflin	(412)	23,644	26,322
15905	Westmont	(814)	5,789	6,113
19401	West Norriton(u)	(610)	15,209	14,034
18643	West Pittston	(717)	5,590	5,980
15229	West View	(412)	7,734	7,648
15227	Whitehall (Allegheny)	(412)	14,451	15,143
15131	White Oak	(717)	8,761	9,480
*18703	Wilkes-Barre	(717)	47,523	51,551
15221	Wilkinsburg	(412)	21,080	23,669
15145	Wilkins Twp.(u)	(412)	7,487	8,472
*17701	Williamsport	(717)	31,933	33,401
19090	Willow Grove(u) (Montgomery)	(610)	16,325	....
17584	Willow Street(u)	(717)	5,817	....

ZIP	Place		1990	1980
15025	Wilson	(412)	7,830	7,564
19094	Woodlyn(u)	(610)	10,151	....
19118	Wyndmoor(u)	(215)	5,682	....
19610	Wyomissing	(610)	7,332	6,551
19050	Yeadon	(610)	11,980	11,727
*17405	York	(717)	42,192	44,619

Rhode Island (401)

See note on page 389

ZIP	Place	1990	1980
02806	Barrington(u)	15,849	16,174
02809	Bristol(u)	21,625	20,128
02830	Burrillville	16,230	13,164
02863	Central Falls	17,638	16,995
02813	Charlestown	6,478	4,800
02816	Coventry	31,083	27,065
*02910	Cranston	76,060	71,992
02864	Cumberland	29,038	27,069
02864	Cumberland Hill(u)	6,379	5,421
02818	East Greenwich	11,865	10,211
02914	East Providence	50,380	50,980
02822	Exeter	5,461	4,453
02814	Glocester	9,227	7,550
02828	Greenville(u)	8,303	7,576
02833	Hopkinton	6,873	6,406
02919	Johnston	26,542	24,907
02881	Kingston(u)	6,504	5,479
02865	Lincoln	18,045	16,949
02840	Middletown	19,460	17,216
02882	Narragansett	15,004	12,088
02840	Newport	28,227	29,259
02843	Newport East(u)	11,080	11,030
*02852	North Kingstown	23,786	21,938
02908	North Providence(u)	32,090	29,188
02876	North Smithfield	10,497	9,972
02859	Pascoag(u)	5,011	3,807
*02860	Pawtucket	72,644	71,204
02871	Portsmouth	16,857	14,257
*02904	Providence	160,728	156,804
02812	Richmond	5,351	4,018
02857	Scituate	9,796	8,405
02917	Smithfield	19,163	16,886
02879	South Kingstown	24,631	20,414
02878	Tiverton(u)	7,259	7,653
02878	Tiverton	14,312	13,526
02864	Valley Falls(u)	11,175	10,892
*02879	Wakefield-Peacedale(u)	7,134	6,474
02885	Warren	11,385	10,640
*02886	Warwick	85,427	87,123
02891	Westerly	21,605	18,580
02891	Westerly Center(u)	16,477	14,093
02893	West Warwick (u)	29,268	27,026
02895	Woonsocket	43,877	45,914

South Carolina

ZIP	Place		1990	1980
29620	Abbeville	(864)	5,778	5,833
*29801	Aiken	(803)	20,386	14,978
*29621	Anderson	(864)	26,385	27,546
29812	Barnwell	(803)	5,255	5,572
*29902	Beaufort	(803)	9,576	8,634
29841	Belvedere(u)	(803)	6,133	6,859
29512	Bennettsville	(803)	10,095	8,774
29611	Berea(u)	(864)	13,535	13,164
29115	Brookdale(u)	(803)	5,339	6,123
29902	Burton(u)	(803)	6,917	3,619
29020	Camden	(803)	6,696	7,462
29033	Cayce	(803)	10,824	11,701
*29402	Charleston	(803)	79,925	69,779
29520	Cheraw	(803)	5,553	5,654
29706	Chester	(803)	7,158	6,820
*29631	Clemson	(864)	11,145	8,118
29325	Clinton	(864)	9,603	8,596
*29201	Columbia	(803)	103,477	101,229
*29526	Conway	(803)	9,819	10,240
*29532	Darlington	(803)	7,310	7,989
29204	Dentsville(u)	(803)	11,839	13,579
29536	Dillon	(803)	6,829	7,060
*29640	Easley	(864)	15,179	14,264
*29501	Florence	(803)	29,913	29,842
29206	Forest Acres	(803)	7,181	6,062
*29341	Gaffney	(864)	13,149	13,453
29605	Gantt(u)	(864)	13,891	13,719
.....	Garden City(u)		6,305	....
*29440	Georgetown	(803)	9,517	10,144
29445	Goose Creek	(803)	24,692	17,811
*29602	Greenville	(864)	58,256	58,242
*29646	Greenwood	(864)	20,807	21,613
*29650	Greer	(864)	10,322	10,525
29406	Hanahan	(803)	13,176	13,224
*29550	Hartsville	(803)	8,372	7,631
*29928	Hilton Head Island†	(803)	23,694	11,239
29621	Homeland Park(u)	(864)	6,569	6,720
29063	Irmo	(803)	11,277	3,957
29456	Ladson(u)	(803)	13,540	13,246
29560	Lake City	(803)	7,153	6,731

ZIP	Place		1990	1980
*29720	Lancaster	(803)	8,914	9,703
29360	Laurens	(864)	9,694	10,587
29571	Marion	(803)	7,658	7,700
29662	Mauldin	(864)	11,662	8,143
29461	Moncks Corner	(803)	5,599	4,179
*29464	Mount Pleasant	(803)	30,108	14,464
29574	Mullins	(803)	5,910	6,068
*29577	Myrtle Beach	(803)	24,848	18,446
29108	Newberry	(803)	10,543	9,866
29841	North Augusta	(803)	15,684	13,593
29405	North Charleston	(803)	70,304	62,479
*29582	North Myrtle Beach	(803)	8,731	3,960
29565	Oak Grove(u)	(803)	7,173	7,092
*29115	Orangeburg	(803)	13,772	14,933
.....	Parker(u)		11,072	....
29905	Parris Island(u)	(803)	7,172	7,752
.....	Red Bank(u)		5,950	....
.....	Red Hill(u)	(803)	6,112	....
*29730	Rock Hill	(803)	41,610	35,327
29417	Saint Andrews(u)	(803)	25,692	20,245
29609	Sans Souci(u)	(864)	7,612	8,393
*29678	Seneca	(864)	7,726	7,436
29210	Seven Oaks(u)	(803)	15,722	16,604
*29681	Simpsonville	(864)	11,744	9,037
29577	Socastee(u)	(803)	10,426	1,082
*29306	Spartanburg	(864)	43,479	43,826
*29483	Summerville	(803)	22,519	6,492
*29150	Sumter	(803)	40,977	24,921
29687	Taylors(u)	(864)	19,619	15,801
29379	Union	(864)	9,840	10,523
29607	Wade Hampton(u)	(864)	20,014	20,180
29488	Walterboro	(803)	5,595	6,209
29611	Welcome(u)	(864)	6,560	6,922
*29169	West Columbia	(803)	10,974	10,409
29206	Woodfield(u)	(803)	8,862	9,588
29745	York	(803)	6,709	6,412

South Dakota (605)

ZIP	Place	1990	1980
*57401	Aberdeen	24,995	25,851
57006	Brookings	16,270	14,951
57706	Ellsworth AFB(u)	7,017	4,766
57350	Huron	12,448	13,000
57042	Madison	6,257	6,210
57301	Mitchell	13,798	13,916
57501	Pierre	12,906	11,973
*57701	Rapid City	54,523	46,492
57701	Rapid Valley(u)	5,968	3,265
*57101	Sioux Falls	100,836	81,343
57754	Spearfish Canyon	6,966	5,251
57785	Sturgis	5,330	5,184
57069	Vermillion	10,034	10,136
57201	Watertown	17,632	15,649
57078	Yankton	12,703	12,011

Tennessee

ZIP	Place		1990	1980
37701	Alcoa	(423)	6,400	6,870
*37303	Athens	(423)	12,054	12,080
38134	Bartlett	(901)	26,989	17,170
37660	Bloomingdale(u)	(423)	10,953	12,088
38008	Bolivar	(901)	5,969	6,597
*37027	Brentwood	(615)	16,392	9,431
*37621	Bristol	(423)	23,421	23,986
38012	Brownsville	(901)	10,017	9,307
*37401	Chattanooga	(423)	152,393	169,514
*37040	Clarksville	(615)	75,542	54,777
*37311	Cleveland	(423)	30,354	26,415
*37716	Clinton	(423)	8,960	5,245
37315	Collegedale	(423)	5,048	4,607
*38017	Collierville	(901)	14,501	7,839
37663	Colonial Heights(u)	(423)	6,716	6,744
*38401	Columbia	(615)	28,583	26,571
*38501	Cookeville	(615)	21,744	20,535
38019	Covington	(901)	7,487	6,065
*38555	Crossville	(615)	6,930	6,394
37321	Dayton	(423)	5,671	5,233
*37055	Dickson	(615)	8,783	7,040
*38024	Dyersburg	(901)	16,321	15,856
37801	Eagleton Village(u)	(423)	5,169	5,331
37411	East Brainerd(u)	(423)	11,594	....
37412	East Ridge	(423)	21,101	21,236
*37643	Elizabethton	(423)	11,931	12,431
37650	Erwin	(423)	5,017	4,739
37922	Farragut†	(423)	12,802	5,992
37334	Fayetteville	(615)	7,158	7,559
*37064	Franklin	(615)	20,098	12,407
37066	Gallatin	(615)	18,794	17,191
*38138	Germantown	(901)	32,016	21,467
*37072	Goodlettsville	(615)	11,219	8,327
*37743	Greeneville	(423)	13,532	14,097
37215	Green Hills(u)	(615)	6,763	....
38040	Halls(u)	(901)	6,450	10,363
37748	Harriman	(423)	7,119	8,303
37341	Harrison(u)	(423)	7,191	6,206
*37075	Hendersonville	(615)	32,188	26,561
38343	Humboldt	(901)	9,651	10,209

ZIP	Place		1990	1980
*38301	Jackson	(901)	49,145	49,258
37760	Jefferson City	(423)	5,522	5,612
*37601	Johnson City	(423)	49,479	39,753
*37662	Kingsport	(423)	36,353	32,027
*37950	Knoxville	(423)	165,039	175,045
37766	La Follette	(423)	7,201	8,198
37086	La Vergne	(615)	7,499	5,495
38464	Lawrenceburg	(615)	10,397	10,184
*37087	Lebanon	(615)	15,208	11,872
*37771	Lenoir City	(423)	6,147	5,180
37091	Lewisburg	(615)	9,879	8,760
38351	Lexington	(901)	5,810	5,934
38201	McKenzie	(901)	5,168	5,405
37110	McMinnville	(423)	11,194	10,683
37355	Manchester	(615)	7,709	7,250
38237	Martin	(901)	8,588	8,898
*37804	Maryville	(423)	19,208	17,480
*38101	Memphis	(901)	610,337	646,174
37343	Middle Valley(u)	(423)	12,255	11,420
38358	Milan	(901)	7,512	8,083
*38053	Millington	(901)	17,866	20,236
*37813	Morristown	(423)	21,316	19,570
37122	Mount Juliet	(615)	5,389	2,879
*37130	Murfreesboro	(615)	44,922	32,845
*37202	Nashville	(615)	488,374	455,651
37821	Newport	(423)	7,123	7,580
*37830	Oak Ridge	(423)	27,310	27,662
38242	Paris	(901)	9,332	10,728
37148	Portland	(615)	5,165	4,030
37849	Powell(u)	(423)	7,534	7,220
38478	Pulaski	(615)	7,916	7,184
37415	Red Bank	(423)	12,320	13,129
38063	Ripley	(901)	6,188	6,366
37854	Rockwood	(423)	5,348	5,687
38372	Savannah	(901)	6,547	6,992
*37862	Sevierville	(423)	7,178	4,556
37865	Seymour(u)	(423)	7,026	....
37160	Shelbyville	(615)	14,042	13,530
37377	Signal Mountain	(423)	7,034	5,818
37167	Smyrna	(615)	13,647	8,839
37379	Soddy-Daisy	(423)	8,240	8,388
37311	South Cleveland(u)	(423)	5,372	4,360
37172	Springfield	(615)	11,227	10,814
37874	Sweetwater	(423)	5,066	4,725
37388	Tullahoma	(423)	16,761	15,800
*38261	Union City	(901)	10,513	10,436
37398	Winchester	(615)	6,305	5,821

Texas

ZIP	Place		1990	1980
*79604	Abilene	(915)	106,707	98,315
75001	Addison	(972)	8,783	5,553
78516	Alamo	(956)	8,352	5,831
78209	Alamo Heights	(210)	6,502	6,252
77039	Aldine(u)	(281)	11,133	12,623
*78332	Alice	(512)	19,788	20,961
75002	Allen	(972)	19,315	8,314
*79830	Alpine	(915)	5,622	5,465
*77511	Alvin	(281)	19,220	16,515
*79105	Amarillo	(806)	157,571	149,230
78750	Anderson Mill(u)		9,468	....
79714	Andrews	(915)	10,678	11,061
*77515	Angleton	(409)	17,140	13,929
*78336	Aransas Pass	(512)	7,180	7,173
*76004	Arlington	(817)	261,717	160,113
75751	Athens	(903)	10,982	10,197
75551	Atlanta	(972)	6,118	6,272
*78767	Austin	(512)	465,648	345,890
*76020	Azle	(817)	8,868	5,822
77518	Bacliff(u)	(409)	5,549	4,851
75180	Balch Springs	(972)	17,406	13,746
*77414	Bay City	(409)	18,170	17,837
*77520	Baytown	(281)	63,843	56,923
*77707	Beaumont	(409)	114,323	118,102
*76021	Bedford	(817)	43,762	20,821
*78102	Beeville	(512)	13,547	14,574
*77401	Bellaire	(713)	13,844	14,950
76704	Bellmead	(254)	8,336	7,569
76513	Belton	(254)	12,463	10,660
76126	Benbrook	(817)	19,564	13,579
*79720	Big Spring	(915)	23,093	24,804
75418	Bonham	(903)	6,688	7,338
*79007	Borger	(806)	15,675	15,837
76825	Brady	(915)	5,946	5,969
76424	Breckenridge	(254)	5,665	6,921
*77833	Brenham	(409)	11,952	10,966
77611	Bridge City	(409)	8,010	7,667
79316	Brownfield	(806)	9,560	10,387
*78520	Brownsville	(956)	98,962	84,997
*76801	Brownwood	(915)	18,387	19,396
78717	Brushy Creek(u)	(903)	5,833	....
*77801	Bryan	(409)	55,002	44,337
76354	Burkburnett	(940)	10,145	10,668
*76028	Burleson	(817)	16,113	11,734
76520	Cameron	(254)	5,635	5,721
79015	Canyon	(806)	11,365	10,724
78130	Canyon Lake(u)	(830)	9,975	....
78834	Carrizo Springs	(830)	5,745	6,886

ZIP	Place		1990	1980
*75006	Carrolton	(972)	82,169	40,595
75633	Carthage	(903)	6,496	6,447
*75104	Cedar Hill	(972)	19,988	6,849
*78613	Cedar Park	(512)	5,121	3,474
77530	Channelview(u)	(281)	25,564	17,471
79201	Childress	(940)	5,055	5,817
*76031	Cleburne	(817)	22,205	19,218
*77327	Cleveland	(281)	7,124	5,977
77015	Cloverleaf(u)	(281)	18,230	17,317
77531	Clute	(409)	9,467	9,577
76834	Coleman	(915)	5,410	5,960
*77840	College Station	(409)	52,443	37,272
76034	Colleyville	(817)	12,724	6,700
*75428	Commerce	(903)	6,825	8,136
*77301	Conroe	(409)	27,675	18,034
78109	Converse	(512)	8,887	5,150
75019	Coppell	(972)	16,881	3,826
76522	Copperas Cove	(254)	24,079	19,469
*78469	Corpus Christi	(512)	257,428	232,134
*75110	Corsicana	(903)	22,911	21,712
75835	Crockett	(409)	7,024	7,405
76036	Crowley	(817)	6,974	5,852
78839	Crystal City	(830)	8,263	8,334
77954	Cuero	(512)	6,700	7,124
79022	Dalhart	(806)	6,246	6,854
75221	Dallas	(214)/(972)	1,007,618	904,599
77535	Dayton	(409)	5,042	4,908
77536	Deer Park	(281)	27,424	22,648
*78840	Del Rio	(830)	30,705	30,034
*75020	Denison	(903)	21,505	23,884
*76201	Denton	(940)	66,270	48,063
79323	Denver City	(512)	5,156	4,704
*75115	De Soto	(972)	30,544	15,538
77539	Dickinson	(281)	9,497	7,505
78537	Donna	(956)	12,652	9,952
79029	Dumas	(806)	12,871	12,194
*75138	Duncanville	(972)	35,008	27,781
76135	Eagle Mountain(u)	(817)	5,847	....
*78852	Eagle Pass	(830)	20,651	21,407
*78539	Edinburg	(956)	29,885	24,075
77957	Edna	(512)	5,343	5,650
77437	El Campo	(409)	10,511	10,462
*79910	El Paso	(915)	515,342	425,259
78543	Elsa	(956)	5,242	5,061
*75119	Ennis	(972)	13,869	12,110
*76039	Euless	(817)	38,149	24,002
76140	Everman	(817)	5,672	5,387
79838	Fabens(u)	(915)	5,599	4,285
78355	Falfurrias	(512)	5,788	6,103
75234	Farmers Branch	(972)	24,250	24,863
.....	First Colony(u)		18,327	....
78114	Floresville	(830)	5,247	4,381
75028	Flower Mound	(972)	15,527	4,402
76119	Forest Hill	(817)	11,482	11,684
79906	Fort Bliss(u)	(915)	13,915	12,687
76544	Fort Hood(u)	(254)	35,580	31,250
79735	Fort Stockton	(915)	8,524	8,688
*76161	Fort Worth	(817)	447,619	385,164
78624	Fredericksburg	(830)	6,934	6,412
77541	Freeport	(409)	11,389	13,444
77546	Friendswood	(281)	22,814	10,719
75034	Frisco	(972)	6,138	3,499
*76240	Gainesville	(940)	14,256	14,081
77547	Galena Park	(713)	10,033	9,879
*77550	Galveston	(409)	59,067	61,902
*75040	Garland	(972)	180,635	138,857
*76528	Gatesville	(254)	11,492	6,078
*78626	Georgetown	(512)	14,840	9,468
75647	Gladewater	(903)	6,027	6,548
78629	Gonzales	(830)	6,527	7,152
76450	Graham	(940)	8,986	9,170
*75051	Grand Prairie	(972)	99,606	71,462
*76051	Grapevine	(817)	29,198	11,801
*75401	Greenville	(903)	23,071	22,161
77619	Groves	(409)	16,744	17,090
76117	Haltom City	(817)	32,856	29,014
76543	Harker Heights	(254)	12,932	7,345
*78550	Harlingen	(956)	48,746	43,543
77859	Hearne	(409)	5,132	5,418
*75652	Henderson	(903)	11,139	11,473
79045	Hereford	(806)	14,745	15,853
76643	Hewitt	(254)	8,983	5,247
75205	Highland Park	(972)	8,739	8,909
*77562	Highlands(u)	(281)	6,632	6,467
75067	Highland Village	(972)	7,027	3,246
76645	Hillsboro	(254)	7,072	7,397
77563	Hitchcock	(409)	5,868	6,103
78861	Hondo	(830)	6,018	6,057
*77052	Houston	(281)/(713)	1,629,902	1,595,138
*77338	Humble	(281)	12,060	6,729
*77340	Huntsville	(409)	27,925	23,936
*76053	Hurst	(817)	33,574	31,420
78362	Ingleside	(512)	5,696	5,436
76367	Iowa Park	(940)	6,072	6,184
*75015	Irving	(972)	155,037	109,943
77029	Jacinto City	(713)	9,343	8,953
75766	Jacksonville	(972)	12,765	12,264
75951	Jasper	(409)	7,160	6,959
78729	Jollyville(u)	(512)	15,206	....
*77449	Katy	(281)	8,004	5,660

ZIP	Place		1990	1980
75142	Kaufman	(972)	5,251	4,658
*76248	Keller	(817)	13,683	4,156
79745	Kermit	(915)	6,875	8,015
*78028	Kerrville	(830)	17,384	15,276
*75662	Kilgore	(903)	11,066	11,331
*76540	Killeen	(254)	63,535	46,296
*78363	Kingsville	(512)	25,276	28,808
77325	Kingwood(u)	(281)	37,397	16,261
78219	Kirby	(210)	8,326	6,435
78236	Lackland AFB(u)	(210)	9,352	14,459
77566	Lake Jackson	(409)	22,771	19,102
77568	La Marque	(409)	14,120	15,372
79331	Lamesa	(806)	10,809	11,790
76550	Lampasas	(512)	6,382	6,165
*75146	Lancaster	(972)	22,117	14,807
*77571	La Porte	(281)	27,910	14,062
*78041	Laredo	(956)	122,893	91,449
*77573	League City	(281)	30,159	16,578
78268	Leon Valley	(210)	9,581	9,088
*79336	Levelland	(806)	13,986	13,809
*75067	Lewisville	(972)	46,521	24,273
77575	Liberty	(281)	7,690	7,945
79339	Littlefield	(806)	6,489	7,409
78233	Live Oak	(210)	10,023	8,183
77351	Livingston	(409)	5,019	4,928
78644	Lockhart	(512)	9,205	7,953
*75606	Longview	(903)	70,311	62,762
*79408	Lubbock	(806)	186,206	174,361
*79904	Lufkin	(409)	30,210	28,562
77657	Lumberton	(409)	6,640	2,480
*78501	McAllen	(956)	84,021	66,281
*75070	McKinney	(972)	21,283	16,256
76063	Mansfield	(817)	15,615	8,102
76661	Marlin	(254)	6,386	7,099
*75670	Marshall	(903)	23,682	24,921
78368	Mathis	(512)	5,423	5,667
78570	Mercedes	(956)	12,694	11,851
*75149	Mesquite	(972)	101,484	67,053
76667	Mexia	(254)	6,933	7,094
*79701	Midland	(915)	89,343	70,525
76065	Midlothian	(972)	5,040	3,219
*76067	Mineral Wells	(940)	14,935	14,468
*78572	Mission	(956)	28,653	22,653
.....	Mission Bend(u)		24,945	....
*77489	Missouri City	(281)	36,178	24,423
79756	Monahans	(915)	8,101	8,397
*75455	Mount Pleasant	(903)	12,291	11,003
*75961	Nacogdoches	(409)	30,872	27,149
77868	Navasota	(409)	6,296	5,971
77627	Nederland	(409)	16,192	16,855
75570	New Boston	(903)	5,057	4,628
*78130	New Braunfels	(830)	27,334	22,402
76118	North Richland Hills	(817)	45,895	30,592
*79761	Odessa	(915)	89,699	90,027
*77630	Orange	(409)	19,370	23,628
*75801	Palestine	(903)	18,042	15,948
*79065	Pampa	(806)	19,959	21,396
*75460	Paris	(903)	24,799	25,498
*77501	Pasadena	(281)/(713)	119,604	112,560
*77581	Pearland	(281)	18,927	13,248
78061	Pearsall	(830)	6,924	7,383
78721	Pecan Grove(u)		9,502	....
79772	Pecos	(915)	12,069	12,855
79070	Perryton	(806)	7,619	7,991
78577	Pharr	(956)	32,921	21,381
*79072	Plainview	(806)	21,698	22,187
*75074	Plano	(972)	127,885	72,331
78064	Pleasanton	(830)	7,678	6,346
*77640	Port Arthur	(409)	58,551	61,251
78374	Portland	(512)	12,224	12,023
77979	Port Lavaca	(512)	10,886	10,911
77651	Port Neches	(409)	12,908	13,944
78580	Raymondville	(956)	8,880	9,493
76028	Rendon(u)	(817)	7,658	....
*75080	Richardson	(972)	74,840	72,496
76118	Richland Hills	(817)	7,978	7,977
*77469	Richmond	(281)	10,042	9,692
78582	Rio Grande City(u)	(956)	9,891	8,930
77019	River Oaks	(817)	6,580	6,890
76701	Robinson	(254)	7,111	6,074
78380	Robstown	(512)	12,849	12,100
76567	Rockdale	(512)	5,235	5,611
75087	Rockwall	(972)	10,486	5,939
78584	Roma	(956)	8,059	3,384
77471	Rosenberg	(281)	20,183	17,840
*78681	Round Rock	(512)	30,923	12,740
*75088	Rowlett	(972)	23,260	7,522
75048	Sachse	(972)	5,346	1,640
76179	Saginaw	(817)	8,551	5,736
*76902	San Angelo	(915)	84,462	73,240
*78265	San Antonio	(210)	935,393	785,940
78586	San Benito	(956)	20,125	17,988
78589	San Juan	(956)	10,815	7,608
*78666	San Marcos	(512)	28,738	23,420
*77510	Santa Fe	(281)	8,429	6,172
78154	Schertz	(210)	10,597	7,262
77586	Seabrook	(281)	6,685	4,670
75159	Seagoville	(972)	8,969	7,304
*78155	Seguin	(830)	18,692	17,854
79360	Seminole	(915)	6,342	6,080

ZIP	Place		1990	1980
*75090	Sherman	(903)	31,584	30,413
77656	Silsbee	(409)	6,368	7,684
78387	Sinton	(512)	5,549	6,044
79364	Slaton	(806)	6,078	6,804
*79549	Snyder	(915)	12,195	12,705
79910	Socorro	(915)	22,995	12,341†
77587	South Houston	(713)	14,207	13,293
76092	Southlake	(817)	7,082	2,808
*77373	Spring(u)	(281)	33,111	
*77477	Stafford	(281)	8,395	4,755
76401	Stephenville	(254)	13,502	11,881
*77478	Sugar Land	(281)	24,549	8,826
*75482	Sulphur Springs	(903)	14,062	12,804
79556	Sweetwater	(915)	11,967	12,242
76574	Taylor	(512)	11,472	10,619
*76501	Temple	(254)	46,150	42,354
75160	Terrell	(972)	12,490	13,269
*75501	Texarkana	(903)	31,658	31,271
*77590	Texas City	(409)	40,822	41,201
75056	The Colony	(972)	22,113	11,586
77387	The Woodlands(u)	(281)	29,205	8,443
*77335	Tomball	(281)	6,370	3,996
.....	Town West(u)		6,166	....
*75702	Tyler	(903)	75,450	70,508
*78148	Universal City	(512)	13,057	10,720
76308	University Park	(972)	22,259	22,254
*78801	Uvalde	(830)	14,729	14,178
*76384	Vernon	(940)	12,001	12,695
*77901	Victoria	(512)	55,076	50,695
*77662	Vidor	(409)	10,935	11,834
*76702	Waco	(254)	103,590	101,261
76148	Watauga	(817)	20,009	10,284
75165	Waxahachie	(972)	17,984	14,624
*76086	Weatherford	(817)	14,804	12,049
78728	Wells Branch(u)		7,094	....
*78596	Weslaco	(956)	21,877	19,331
79764	West Odessa(u)	(915)	16,568	....
77005	West University Place	(713)	12,920	12,010
77488	Wharton	(409)	9,011	9,033
75693	White Oak	(903)	5,136	4,415
76108	White Settlement	(817)	15,472	13,508
*76307	Wichita Falls	(940)	96,259	94,201
78239	Windcrest	(210)	5,331	5,332
76712	Woodway	(254)	8,695	7,091
75098	Wylie	(972)	8,716	3,152
77995	Yoakum	(512)	5,611	6,148
78076	Zapata(u)	(956)	7,119	3,831

Utah

ZIP	Place		1990	1980
84003	American Fork	(801)	15,722	12,564
*84010	Bountiful	(801)	36,147	32,877
84302	Brigham City	(435)	15,644	15,596
84109	Canyon Rim(u)	(801)	10,527	....
*84720	Cedar City	(435)	13,443	10,972
84014	Centerville	(801)	11,500	8,069
*84015	Clearfield	(801)	21,435	17,982
84015	Clinton	(801)	7,945	5,777
84121	Cottonwood Heights(u)	(801)	28,766	22,665
84121	Cottonwood West(u)	(801)	17,476	11,117
84020	Draper	(801)	7,143	5,521
84109	East Millcreek(u)	(801)	21,184	24,150
84025	Farmington	(801)	9,049	4,691
84003	Highland	(801)	5,007	2,435
84117	Holladay-Cottonwood(u)†	(801)	14,095	22,189
84037	Kaysville	(801)	13,961	9,811
84118	Kearns(u)	(801)	28,374	21,353
*84041	Layton	(801)	41,784	22,862
84043	Lehi	(801)	8,475	6,848
.....	Little Cottonwood Creek Valley(u)	(801)	5,042	....
*84321	Logan	(435)	32,771	26,844
84044	Magna(u)	(801)	17,829	13,138
84047	Midvale	(801)	11,886	10,146
84109	Millcreek(u)	(801)	32,230	....
84117	Mount Olympus(u)	(801)	7,413	6,068
84107	Murray	(801)	31,274	25,750
84404	North Ogden	(801)	11,593	9,309
84054	North Salt Lake	(801)	6,464	5,548
*84401	Ogden	(801)	63,943	64,407
.....	Oquirrh(u)	(801)	7,593	....
*84057	Orem	(801)	67,561	52,399
84651	Payson	(801)	9,510	8,246
84062	Pleasant Grove	(801)	13,476	10,833
84501	Price	(435)	8,712	9,086
*84601	Provo	(801)	86,835	74,111
84701	Richfield	(435)	5,593	5,482
84403	Riverdale	(801)	6,419	6,031
84065	Riverton	(801)	11,261	7,032
84067	Roy	(801)	24,595	19,694
*84770	Saint George	(435)	28,572	11,350
*84101	Salt Lake City	(801)	159,928	163,034
*84070	Sandy	(801)	75,240	52,210
84335	Smithfield	(435)	5,566	4,993
84095	South Jordan	(801)	12,215	7,492
84403	South Ogden	(801)	12,105	11,366
84165	South Salt Lake	(801)	10,129	10,413
84660	Spanish Fork	(801)	11,272	9,825
84663	Springville	(801)	13,950	12,101

ZIP	Place		1990	1980
84015	Sunset	(801)	5,128	5,733
84107	Taylorsville-Bennion(u)†	(801)	52,351	17,448
84074	Tooele	(435)	13,887	14,335
84047	Union(u)	(801)	13,684	9,665
*84078	Vernal	(435)	6,640	6,600
84403	Washington Terrace	(801)	8,189	8,212
*84084	West Jordan	(801)	42,915	27,325
*84119	West Valley City†	(801)	86,969	72,509
84070	White City(u)	(801)	6,506	7,267
84087	Woods Cross	(801)	5,384	4,263

Vermont (802)

See note on page 389

ZIP	Place	1990	1980
05641	Barre	9,482	9,824
05641	*Barre*	7,411	7,090
05201	*Bennington*	16,451	15,815
05201	Bennington(u)	9,532	9,349
*05301	Brattleboro Center(u)	8,612	8,596
*05301	*Brattleboro*	12,241	11,886
*05401	Burlington	39,127	37,712
*05446	*Colchester*	14,731	12,629
05451	*Essex*	16,498	14,392
*05452	Essex Junction	8,396	7,033
05047	*Hartford*	9,404	7,963
05849	*Lyndon*	5,371	5,371
*05753	Middlebury	8,034	7,574
05468	*Milton*	8,404	6,829
*05602	Montpelier	8,247	8,241
05663	*Northfield*	5,610	5,435
05101	*Rockingham*	5,484	5,538
*05701	Rutland	18,230	18,436
05478	Saint Albans	7,339	7,308
05819	Saint Johnsbury(u)	7,608	6,424
05482	*Shelburne*	5,871	5,000
*05403	South Burlington	12,809	10,679
05156	*Springfield*	9,579	10,190
05488	Swanton	5,636	5,141
05404	Winooski	6,649	6,318

Virginia

ZIP	Place		1990	1980
*24210	Abingdon	(540)	7,003	4,318
*22313	Alexandria	(703)	111,182	103,217
22003	Annandale(u)	(540)	50,975	49,524
22554	Aquia Harbour(u)	(703)	6,308	2,870
*22210	Arlington(u)	(703)	170,936	152,599
23005	Ashland	(804)	5,864	4,640
22041	Bailey's Crossroads(u)	(703)	19,507	12,564
24523	Bedford	(540)	6,073	5,991
22306	Belle Haven(u)	(757)	6,427	6,520
23234	Bellwood(u)	(804)	6,178	6,439
23234	Bensley(u)	(804)	5,093	5,299
*24060	Blacksburg	(540)	34,590	30,638
24605	Bluefield	(540)	5,363	5,946
23235	Bon Air(u)	(804)	16,413	16,224
*24203	Bristol	(540)	18,426	19,042
24416	Buena Vista	(540)	6,406	6,717
.....	Bull Run(u)	(540)	5,525	....
*22015	Burke(u)	(703)	57,734	33,835
24018	Cave Spring(u)	(540)	24,053	21,682
22020	Centreville(u)	(703)	26,585	7,473
*22021	Chantilly(u)	(703)	29,337	12,259
*22906	Charlottesville	(804)	40,475	39,916
*23320	Chesapeake	(757)	151,982	114,486
23831	Chester(u)	(804)	14,986	11,728
*24073	Christiansburg	(540)	15,004	10,345
24078	Collinsville(u)	(540)	7,280	7,517
23834	Colonial Heights	(804)	16,064	16,509
22901	Commonwealth(u)	(804)	5,538	3,505
.....	Countryside(u)		8,349	....
24426	Covington	(540)	6,991	9,063
22701	Culpeper	(540)	8,581	6,621
22193	Dale City(u)	(540)	47,170	33,127
*24541	Danville	(804)	53,056	45,642
23228	Dumbarton(u)	(804)	8,526	8,149
22027	Dunn Loring(u)	(703)	6,509	6,077
23222	East Highland Park(u)	(804)	11,850	11,797
23847	Emporia	(804)	5,479	4,840
23803	Ettrick(u)	(804)	5,290	4,890
*22030	Fairfax	(703)	19,629	19,390
*22046	Falls Church	(703)	9,522	9,515
23901	Farmville	(804)	6,046	6,067
24551	Forest(u)	(804)	5,624	....
22060	Fort Belvoir(u)	(703)	8,590	7,726
22308	Fort Hunt(u)	(703)	12,989	14,294
23801	Fort Lee(u)	(804)	6,895	9,784
22310	Franconia(u)	(703)	19,882	8,476
23851	Franklin	(757)	7,864	7,308
*22404	Fredericksburg	(540)	19,027	15,322
*22630	Front Royal	(540)	11,880	11,126
24333	Galax	(540)	6,670	6,524
*23060	Glen Allen(u)	(804)	9,010	6,202
23062	Gloucester Point(u)	(804)	8,509	5,841
22066	Great Falls(u)	(703)	6,945	2,419
22306	Groveton(u)	(703)	19,997	18,860
*23670	Hampton	(757)	133,811	122,617

ZIP	Place		1990	1980
22801	Harrisonburg	(540)	30,707	19,671
*22070	Herndon	(703)	16,139	11,449
23075	Highland Springs(u)	(804)	13,823	12,146
24019	Hollins(u)	(540)	13,305	12,295
23860	Hopewell	(804)	23,101	23,397
22303	Huntington(u)	(703)	7,489	5,813
22306	Hybla Valley(u)	(703)	15,491	15,533
22043	Idylwood(u)	(703)	14,710	11,982
22042	Jefferson(u)	(703)	25,782	24,342
22041	Lake Barcroft(u)	(703)	8,686	8,725
22191	Lake Ridge(u)	(540)	23,862	11,072
23228	Lakeside(u)	(804)	12,081	12,289
23060	Laurel(u)	(804)	13,011	10,569
22075	Leesburg	(703)	16,202	8,357
24450	Lexington	(540)	6,959	7,292
22312	Lincolnia(u)	(703)	13,041	10,350
*22079	Lorton(u)	(703)	15,385	5,813
*24506	Lynchburg	(804)	66,049	66,743
*22101	McLean(u)	(703)	38,168	35,664
24572	Madison Heights(u)	(804)	11,700	14,146
*22110	Manassas	(703)	27,957	15,438
22110	Manassas Park	(703)	6,734	6,524
22030	Mantua(u)	(703)	6,804	6,523
24354	Marion	(540)	6,630	7,287
*24112	Martinsville	(540)	16,162	18,149
23111	Mechanicsville(u)	(804)	22,027	9,269
*22116	Merrifield(u)	(703)	8,399	7,525
.....	Montclair(u)		11,399	4,098
23231	Montrose(u)	(804)	6,405	5,349
22121	Mount Vernon(u)	(703)	27,485	24,058
22122	Newington(u)	(703)	17,965	8,313
*23607	Newport News	(757)	171,439	144,903
*23501	Norfolk	(757)	261,250	266,979
22151	North Springfield(u)	(703)	8,996	9,538
22124	Oakton(u)	(703)	24,610	19,150
*23804	Petersburg	(804)	37,027	41,055
22043	Pimmit Hills(u)	(703)	6,019	6,658
23662	Poquoson	(757)	11,005	8,726
*23705	Portsmouth	(757)	103,910	104,577
24301	Pulaski	(540)	9,985	10,106
22134	Quantico Station(u)	(703)	7,425	7,121
*24141	Radford	(540)	15,940	13,225
*22090	Reston(u)	(703)	48,556	36,407
*23232	Richmond	(804)	202,798	219,214
22901	Rio	(804)	5,133	2,851
*24022	Roanoke	(540)	96,509	100,220
24281	Rose Hill(u)	(540)	12,675	11,926
24153	Salem	(540)	23,797	23,958
22044	Seven Corners(u)	(703)	7,280	6,058
24592	South Boston	(804)	6,997	7,093
*22150	Springfield(u)	(703)	23,706	21,435
*24402	Staunton	(540)	24,461	21,857
*20164	Sterling(u)	(703)	20,512	16,080
24477	Stuarts Draft(u)	(540)	5,087	1,776
23162	Sudley(u)	(540)	7,321	4,674
*23434	Suffolk	(757)	52,143	47,621
22170	Sugarland Run(u)	(703)	9,357	6,258
24502	Timberlake(u)	(804)	10,314	9,697
23229	Tuckahoe(u)	(804)	42,629	39,868
22101	Tysons Corner(u)	(703)	13,124	10,065
22901	University Heights(u)	(804)	6,900	6,736
*22180	Vienna	(703)	14,852	15,469
24179	Vinton	(540)	7,643	8,027
*23458	Virginia Beach	(757)	393,089	262,199
22980	Waynesboro	(540)	18,549	15,329
22110	West Gate(u)	(703)	6,565	7,119
22152	West Springfield(u)	(703)	28,126	25,012
*23185	Williamsburg	(757)	11,409	9,870
*22601	Winchester	(540)	21,947	20,217
24592	Wolf Trap(u)	(703)	13,133	9,875
*22191	Woodbridge(u)	(540)	26,401	24,004
24382	Wytheville	(540)	8,036	7,135
22110	Yorkshire(u)	(703)	5,699	4,940

Washington

ZIP	Place		1990	1980
98520	Aberdeen	(360)	16,565	18,739
98036	Alderwood Manor-Bothell North(u)	(425)	22,945	16,524
98221	Anacortes	(360)	11,451	9,013
98335	Artondale(u)	(253)	7,141	....
*98002	Auburn	(253)	33,650	26,417
*98009	Bellevue	(425)	86,872	73,903
*98225	Bellingham	(360)	52,179	45,794
98390	Bonney Lake	(360)	7,494	5,328
*98011	Bothell	(425)	12,345	7,943
*98337	Bremerton	(360)	38,142	36,208
98036	Brier	(425)	5,633	2,915
98178	Bryn Mawr-Skyway(u)	(206)	12,514	11,754
98166	Burien(u)	(206)	25,089	23,189
98607	Camas	(360)	6,442	5,681
98055	Cascade-Fairwood(u)	(425)	30,107	16,939
98684	Cascade Park East(u)	(425)	6,996	....
98684	Cascade Park West(u)	(425)	6,656	....
98531	Centralia	(360)	12,101	11,555
98532	Chehalis	(360)	6,527	6,100
99004	Cheney	(509)	7,723	7,630
99403	Clarkston	(509)	6,753	6,903

ZIP	Place		1990	1980
99324	College Place	(509)	6,308	5,771
99218	Country Homes(u)	(509)	5,126	....
98042	Covington-Sawyer-Wilderness(u)		24,321	....
98198	Des Moines	(206)	17,283	7,378
99213	Dishman(u)	(509)	9,671	10,169
.....	East Hill-Meridian(u)		42,696	....
98366	East Port Orchard(u)	(360)	5,409	4,631
98056	East Renton Highlands(u)	(425)	13,218	11,695
98801	East Wenatchee Bench(u)	(509)	12,539	11,410
.....	Edgewood-North Hill(u)		9,120	....
*98020	Edmonds	(425)	30,743	27,679
98387	Elk Plain(u)		12,197	....
98926	Ellensburg	(509)	12,360	11,752
.....	Ellsworth North(u)		5,796	....
98022	Enumclaw	(360)	7,227	5,427
98823	Ephrata	(509)	5,349	5,359
99210	Esperance(u)	(509)	11,236	11,120
*98201	Everett	(425)	69,974	54,413
98411	Evergreen(u)		11,249	....
99218	Fairwood(u)	(509)	5,807	5,337
*98002	Federal Way	(253)	67,554	....
98248	Ferndale	(360)	5,398	3,855
98466	Fircrest	(253)	5,258	5,477
98597	Five Corners(u)		6,776	....
98433	Fort Lewis(u)	(253)	22,224	23,761
98930	Grandview	(509)	7,169	5,615
.....	Harbour Pointe(u)		9,107	....
98660	Hazel Dell North(u)†	(360)	6,924	15,386
98665	Hazel Dell South(u)	(360)	5,796	....
98550	Hoquiam	(360)	8,972	9,719
98011	Inglewood-Finn Hill(u)†	(425)	29,132	12,467
98027	Issaquah	(425)	7,786	5,536
98626	Kelso	(360)	11,767	11,129
98028	Kenmore(u)	(425)	8,917	7,281
*99336	Kennewick	(509)	42,148	34,397
*98031	Kent	(253)/(425)	37,960	22,961
98033	Kingsgate(u)	(425)	14,259	12,652
*98033	Kirkland	(425)	40,059	18,785
98503	Lacey	(360)	19,279	13,940
98155	Lake Forest North(u)	(206)	8,002	7,995
98002	Lakeland North(u)	(253)	14,402	11,648
98002	Lakeland South(u)	(253)	9,027	5,225
98036	Lake Serene-North Lynnwood(u)	(425)	14,290	....
98665	Lake Shore(u)	(360)	6,268	....
98259	Lakewood(u)	(253)	58,412	54,533
.....	Lea Hill(u)		6,876	....
98632	Longview	(360)	31,499	31,052
98264	Lynden	(360)	5,709	4,022
*98046	Lynnwood	(425)	28,637	22,641
98012	Martha Lake(u)	(425)	10,155	7,022
*98270	Marysville	(360)	10,328	5,080
98040	Mercer Island	(206)	20,816	21,522
98444	Midland(u)	(253)	5,587	....
98082	Mill Creek†	(425)	7,180	1,803
98661	Minnehaha(u)	(360)	9,661	....
98837	Moses Lake	(509)	11,235	10,629
98043	Mountlake Terrace	(425)	19,320	16,534
98273	Mount Vernon	(360)	17,647	13,009
98275	Mukilteo	(425)	6,982	1,426
98006	Newport Hills(u)	(425)	14,736	12,245
98166	Normandy Park	(206)	6,709	4,268
98155	North City-Ridgecrest(u)	(206)	13,832	13,551
.....	North Creek-Canyon Park(u)		23,236	....
98166	North Hill(u)	(206)	5,706	10,170
98270	North Marysville(u)	(425)	18,711	15,159
98277	Oak Harbor	(360)	17,176	12,271
*98501	Olympia	(360)	33,729	27,447
99214	Opportunity(u)	(509)	22,326	21,241
98662	Orchards North(u)†	(360)	6,479	8,828
98662	Orchards South(u)	(360)	12,956	....
99027	Otis Orchards-East Farms(u)	(360)	5,811	4,597
.....	Paine Field-Lake Stickney(u)		18,670	....
98444	Parkland(u)	(253)	20,882	23,355
98366	Parkwood(u)	(360)	6,853	4,599
*99301	Pasco	(509)	20,337	18,428
98027	Pine Lake(u)	(425)	13,940	....
98362	Port Angeles	(360)	17,710	17,311
98368	Port Townsend	(360)	7,001	6,067
98390	Prairie Ridge(u)		8,278	....
*99163	Pullman	(509)	23,478	23,579
*98371	Puyallup	(253)	23,878	18,251
*98052	Redmond	(425)	35,800	23,318
*98058	Renton	(425)	41,688	31,031
99352	Richland	(509)	32,315	33,578
98160	Richmond Beach-Innis Arden(u)	(206)	7,242	6,700
98113	Richmond Highlands(u)	(206)	26,037	24,463
98188	Riverton-Boulevard Park(u)†	(206)	15,337	14,182
.....	Sahalee(u)		13,951	....
98686	Salmon Creek(u)	(360)	11,989	....
*98148	Seatac	(206)	22,694	....
*98101	Seattle	(206)/(425)	516,259	493,846
98284	Sedro Woolley	(360)	6,333	6,110
98942	Selah	(509)	5,113	4,500
98584	Shelton	(360)	7,241	7,629
98155	Sheridan Beach(u)	(206)	6,518	6,873
*98383	Silverdale(u)	(360)	7,660	....
98201	Silver Lake-Fircrest(u)	(360)	24,474	10,299
*98290	Snohomish	(360)	6,499	5,294

ZIP	Place		1990	1980
98373	South Hill(u)		12,963	....
98387	Spanaway(u)	(253)	15,001	8,868
*99210	Spokane	(509)	177,165	171,300
98388	Steilacoom	(253)	5,728	4,886
*98371	Summit(u)	(253)	6,312	....
98390	Sumner	(253)	6,459	4,936
98944	Sunnyside	(509)	11,238	9,225
*98402	Tacoma	(253)	176,664	158,501
98501	Tanglewilde-Thompson Place(u)	(360)	6,061	5,910
98948	Toppenish	(509)	7,419	6,517
98138	Tukwila	(206)	11,874	3,578
98501	Tumwater	(360)	9,976	6,705
98464	University Place(u)	(253)	27,701	20,381
*98661	Vancouver	(360)	46,380	42,834
98662	Vancouver Mall(u)	(360)	6,938	....
99037	Veradale(u)	(509)	7,836	7,256
99362	Walla Walla	(509)	26,482	25,618
.....	Waller(u)	....	6,415	....
*98801	Wenatchee	(509)	21,746	17,257
.....	West Lake Sammamish(u)		6,087	....
98258	West Lake Stevens(u)	(425)	12,453	....
99301	West Pasco(u)	(509)	7,312	5,726
99181	West Valley(u)		6,594	....
98166	White Center-Shorewood(u)	(206)	20,531	19,362
98072	Woodinville(u)	(425)	23,654	....
98032	Woodmont Beach(u)	(253)	7,493	....
*98903	Yakima	(509)	54,843	49,826

West Virginia (304)

ZIP	Place	1990	1980
*25801	Beckley	18,274	20,492
24701	Bluefield	12,756	16,060
26330	Bridgeport	6,695	6,604
26201	Buckhannon	5,909	6,820
*25301	Charleston	57,287	63,968
*26301	Clarksburg	17,970	22,371
25301	Cross Lanes(u)	10,878	....
25064	Dunbar	8,697	9,285
26241	Elkins	7,494	8,536
*26554	Fairmont	20,210	23,863
26354	Grafton	5,524	6,845
*25704	Huntington	54,844	63,684
26726	Keyser	5,870	6,569
25401	Martinsburg	14,073	13,063
*26505	Morgantown	25,879	27,605
26041	Moundsville	10,753	12,419
26155	New Martinsville	6,705	7,109
25143	Nitro	6,851	8,074
25901	Oak Hill	6,812	7,120
*26101	Parkersburg	33,862	39,946
.....	Pea Ridge(u)	6,535	....
24740	Princeton	7,043	7,538
25177	Saint Albans	11,257	12,402
*25301	South Charleston	13,645	15,968
25569	Teays Valley(u)	8,436	....
26105	Vienna	10,862	11,618
26062	Weirton	22,124	25,371
26003	Wheeling	34,882	43,070

Wisconsin

See note on page 389

ZIP	Place		1990	1980
54301	Allouez†	(920)	14,431	14,882
54720	Altoona	(715)	5,889	4,393
54409	Antigo	(715)	8,284	8,653
*59411	Appleton	(920)	65,695	58,913
54806	Ashland	(715)	8,695	9,115
54304	Ashwaubenon	(920)	16,376	14,486
53913	Baraboo	(608)	9,203	8,081
53916	Beaver Dam	(920)	14,196	14,149
54311	Bellevue Town(u)	(920)	7,541	....
*53511	Beloit	(608)	35,571	35,207
54923	Berlin	(920)	5,371	5,478
*53045	Brookfield	(414)	35,184	34,035
53209	Brown Deer	(414)	12,236	12,921
53105	Burlington	(414)	8,855	8,385
53012	Cedarburg	(414)	10,086	9,005
54729	Chippewa Falls	(715)	12,727	12,270
53110	Cudahy	(414)	18,659	19,547
53018	Delafield	(414)	5,347	4,083
53115	Delavan	(414)	6,073	5,684
54115	De Pere	(920)	16,569	14,892
*54703	Eau Claire	(715)	56,806	51,509
53121	Elkhorn	(414)	5,337	4,605
53122	Elm Grove	(414)	6,261	6,735
53714	Fitchburg†	(608)	15,648	11,965
*54935	Fond du Lac	(920)	37,757	35,863
53538	Fort Atkinson	(920)	10,213	9,785
53217	Fox Point	(414)	7,238	7,649
53132	Franklin	(414)	21,855	16,871
53022	Germantown	(414)	13,658	10,729
53209	Glendale	(414)	14,088	13,882
53024	Grafton	(414)	9,340	8,381
*54303	Green Bay	(920)	96,466	87,899
53129	Greendale	(414)	15,128	16,928
53220	Greenfield	(414)	33,403	31,353

ZIP	Place		1990	1980
53130	Hales Corners	(414)	7,623	7,110
53027	Hartford	(414)	8,188	7,159
53029	Hartland	(414)	6,906	5,559
54303	Howard	(920)	9,874	8,240
54016	Hudson	(715)	6,378	5,434
*53545	Janesville	(608)	52,210	51,071
53549	Jefferson	(920)	6,078	5,647
54130	Kaukauna	(920)	11,982	11,310
*53140	Kenosha	(414)	80,426	77,685
54136	Kimberly	(414)	5,406	5,881
*54601	La Crosse	(608)	51,120	48,347
53147	Lake Geneva	(414)	5,979	5,612
54140	Little Chute	(920)	9,207	7,907
53558	McFarland	(608)	5,232	3,783
*53714	Madison	(608)	190,766	170,616
*54220	Manitowoc	(920)	32,521	32,547
54143	Marinette	(715)	11,843	11,965
54449	Marshfield	(715)	19,291	18,290
54952	Menasha	(920)	14,711	14,728
*53051	Menomonee Falls	(414)	26,840	27,845
54751	Menomonie	(715)	13,547	12,769
53097	Mequon	(414)	18,885	16,193
54452	Merrill	(715)	9,860	9,578
53562	Middleton	(608)	13,785	11,851
*53201	Milwaukee	(414)	628,088	636,297
53716	Monona	(608)	8,637	8,809
53566	Monroe	(608)	10,241	10,027
53150	Muskego	(414)	16,813	15,277
*54956	Neenah	(920)	23,219	22,432
*53151	New Berlin	(414)	33,592	30,529
54961	New London	(920)	6,658	6,210
54017	New Richmond	(715)	5,106	4,306
53154	Oak Creek	(414)	19,513	16,932
53066	Oconomowoc	(414)	10,993	9,909
54650	Onalaska	(608)	11,414	9,249
*54901	Oshkosh	(920)	55,006	49,620
53072	Pewaukee	(414)	5,287	4,637
53818	Platteville	(608)	9,862	9,580
53158	Pleasant Prairie†	(414)	12,037	12,176
54467	Plover	(715)	8,176	5,310
53073	Plymouth	(920)	6,769	6,027
53901	Portage	(608)	8,640	7,896
53074	Port Washington	(414)	9,338	8,612
53821	Prairie du Chien	(608)	5,657	5,859
*53401	Racine	(414)	84,298	85,725
53959	Reedsburg	(608)	5,834	5,038
54501	Rhinelander	(715)	7,382	7,873
54868	Rice Lake	(715)	7,998	7,691
53581	Richland Center	(608)	5,018	4,997
54971	Ripon	(920)	7,241	7,111
54022	River Falls	(715)	10,610	9,019
53207	Saint Francis	(414)	9,245	10,095
54166	Shawano	(715)	7,598	7,013
*53081	Sheboygan	(920)	49,587	48,085
53085	Sheboygan Falls	(920)	5,823	5,253
53211	Shorewood	(414)	14,116	14,327
53172	South Milwaukee	(414)	20,958	21,069
54656	Sparta	(608)	7,788	6,934
54481	Stevens Point	(715)	23,006	22,970
53589	Stoughton	(608)	8,786	7,589
54235	Sturgeon Bay	(920)	9,176	8,847
53590	Sun Prairie	(608)	15,333	12,931
54880	Superior	(715)	27,134	29,571
53089	Sussex	(414)	5,039	3,482
54660	Tomah	(608)	7,570	7,204
54241	Two Rivers	(920)	13,030	13,354
53593	Verona	(608)	5,374	3,336
*53094	Watertown	(920)	19,142	18,113
*53186	Waukesha	(414)	56,958	50,365
53597	Waunakee	(608)	5,897	3,866
53963	Waupun	(920)	8,844	8,132
*54403	Wausau	(715)	37,060	32,426
53213	Wauwatosa	(414)	49,366	51,308
53214	West Allis	(414)	63,221	63,982
53095	West Bend	(414)	24,470	21,484
54476	Weston(u)	(715)	9,714	8,775
53217	Whitefish Bay	(414)	14,272	14,930
53190	Whitewater	(414)	12,636	11,520
*54494	Wisconsin Rapids	(715)	18,245	17,995

Wyoming (307)

ZIP	Place	1990	1980
*82601	Casper	46,765	51,016
*82001	Cheyenne	50,008	47,283
82414	Cody	7,897	6,599
82633	Douglas	5,076	6,030
*82930	Evanston	10,904	6,265
*82716	Gillette	17,545	12,134
82935	Green River	12,711	12,807
82520	Landor	7,023	7,867
*82070	Laramie	26,607	24,410
82435	Powell	5,292	5,310
82301	Rawlins	9,380	11,547
82501	Riverton	9,202	9,562
*82901	Rock Springs	19,050	19,458
82801	Sheridan	13,904	15,146
82240	Torrington	5,651	5,441
82401	Worland	5,742	6,391

Populations and Areas of Counties and States

Source: U.S. Bureau of the Census, Dept. of Commerce; World Almanac research

State population figures below are estimates for July 1, 1996. For counties, July 1, 1996, population estimates and Apr. 1, 1990, decennial census figures are given. County areas may not add to total state areas because of rounding.

Alabama

(67 counties, 50,750 sq mi land; pop. 4,273,084)

County	County seat or courthouse	1996 Pop.	1990 Pop.	Land area sq mi
Autauga	Prattville	40,061	34,222	596
Baldwin	Bay Minette	123,023	98,280	1,597
Barbour	Clayton	26,475	25,417	885
Bibb	Centreville	18,142	16,576	622
Blount	Oneonta	43,392	39,248	646
Bullock	Union Springs	11,188	11,042	625
Butler	Greenville	21,530	21,892	777
Calhoun	Anniston	113,511	116,032	609
Chambers	Lafayette	36,748	36,876	597
Cherokee	Centre	21,170	19,543	553
Chilton	Clanton	35,323	32,458	694
Choctaw	Butler	15,714	16,018	914
Clarke	Grove Hill	27,982	27,240	1,239
Clay	Ashland	13,544	13,252	605
Cleburne	Heflin	13,445	12,730	560
Coffee	Elba	41,910	40,240	679
Colbert	Tuscumbia	52,490	51,666	595
Conecuh	Evergreen	14,112	14,054	851
Coosa	Rockford	11,444	11,063	653
Covington	Andalusia	37,263	36,478	1,035
Crenshaw	Luverne	13,514	13,635	610
Cullman	Cullman	73,274	67,613	739
Dale	Ozark	49,167	49,633	561
Dallas	Selma	47,362	48,130	981
De Kalb	Fort Payne	57,165	54,651	778
Elmore	Wetumpka	58,460	49,210	622
Escambia	Brewton	35,620	35,518	948
Etowah	Gadsden	102,129	99,840	535
Fayette	Fayette	17,944	17,962	628
Franklin	Russellville	29,253	27,814	636
Geneva	Geneva	24,618	23,647	576
Greene	Eutaw	9,947	10,153	646
Hale	Greensboro	16,288	15,498	644
Henry	Abbeville	15,232	15,374	562
Houston	Dothan	83,778	81,331	580
Jackson	Scottsboro	50,428	47,796	1,079
Jefferson	Birmingham	661,927	651,520	1,113
Lamar	Vernon	15,591	15,715	605
Lauderdale	Florence	83,593	79,661	670
Lawrence	Moulton	33,037	31,513	693
Lee	Opelika	95,038	87,146	609
Limestone	Athens	59,844	54,135	568
Lowndes	Hayneville	12,811	12,658	718
Macon	Tuskegee	23,563	24,928	611
Madison	Huntsville	270,309	238,912	805
Marengo	Linden	23,430	23,084	977
Marion	Hamilton	30,718	29,830	742
Marshall	Guntersville	79,159	70,832	567
Mobile	Mobile	395,952	378,643	1,233
Monroe	Monroeville	23,874	23,968	1,026
Montgomery	Montgomery	216,434	209,085	790
Morgan	Decatur	106,942	100,043	582
Perry	Marion	12,717	12,759	720
Pickens	Carrollton	20,864	20,699	882
Pike	Troy	28,464	27,595	671
Randolph	Wedowee	20,073	19,881	581
Russell	Phenix City	51,439	46,860	641
Saint Clair	Ashville & Pell City	59,218	49,811	634
Shelby	Columbiana	130,165	99,363	795
Sumter	Livingston	16,174	16,174	905
Talladega	Talladega	76,369	74,109	740
Tallapoosa	Dadeville	39,810	38,826	718
Tuscaloosa	Tuscaloosa	158,779	150,522	1,325
Walker	Jasper	69,686	67,670	795
Washington	Chatom	17,341	16,694	1,081
Wilcox	Camden	13,515	13,568	889
Winston	Double Springs	23,602	22,053	615

Alaska

(27 divisions, 570,374 sq mi land; pop. 607,007)

Census Division	1996 Pop.	1990 Pop.	Land area sq mi
Aleutians East Borough	2,304	2,464	6,985
Aleutians West Census Area	4,984	9,478	4,402
Anchorage Borough	250,505	226,338	1,698
Bethel Census Area	15,655	13,656	41,087
Bristol Bay Borough	1,322	1,410	519
Denali Borough	2,043	1,764	12,719
Dillingham Census Area	4,430	4,012	18,467
Fairbanks North Star Borough	84,061	77,720	7,362
Haines Borough	2,170	2,117	2,357
Juneau Borough	29,756	26,751	2,594
Kenai Peninsula Borough	47,131	40,802	16,079
Ketchikan Gateway Borough	14,517	13,828	1,220
Kodiak Island Borough	15,082	13,309	6,463
Lake and Peninsula Borough	1,701	1,668	23,632
Matanuska-Susitna Borough	52,500	39,683	24,694
Nome Census Area	8,908	8,288	23,013
North Slope Borough	7,110	5,979	87,861
Northwest Arctic Borough	6,552	6,113	35,863
Prince of Wales-Outer Ketchikan Census Area	7,187	6,278	7,325
Sitka Borough	8,510	8,588	2,882
Skagway-Hoonah-Angoon Census Area	3,941	3,680	8,012
Southeast Fairbanks Census Area	5,721	5,913	25,110
Valdez-Cordova Census Area	10,391	9,952	36,945
Wade Hampton Census Area	6,693	5,791	17,124
Wrangell-Petersburg Census Area	6,998	7,042	5,809
Yakutat Borough	827	705	4,865
Yukon-Koyukuk Census Area	6,008	6,714	145,287

Arizona

(15 counties, 113,642 sq mi land; pop. 4,428,068)

County	County seat or courthouse	1996 Pop.	1990 Pop.	Land area sq mi
Apache	Saint Johns	69,087	61,591	11,206
Cochise	Bisbee	110,358	97,624	6,170
Coconino	Flagstaff	112,260	96,591	18,619
Gila	Globe	47,338	40,216	4,768
Graham	Safford	30,780	26,554	4,630
Greenlee	Clifton	9,330	8,008	1,847
La Paz	Parker	14,497	13,844	4,500
Maricopa	Phoenix	2,611,327	2,122,101	9,204
Mohave	Kingman	126,294	93,497	13,312
Navajo	Holbrook	92,086	77,674	9,954
Pima	Tucson	767,873	666,957	9,187
Pinal	Florence	135,376	116,397	5,370
Santa Cruz	Nogales	36,952	29,676	1,238
Yavapai	Prescott	139,368	107,714	8,124
Yuma	Yuma	125,142	106,895	5,514

Arkansas

(75 counties, 52,075 sq mi land; pop. 2,509,793)

County	County seat or courthouse	1996 Pop.	1990 Pop.	Land area sq mi
Arkansas	DeWitt & Stuttgart	21,046	21,653	989
Ashley	Hamburg	24,543	24,319	921
Baxter	Mountain Home	36,382	31,186	554
Benton	Bentonville	125,956	97,499	843
Boone	Harrison	31,906	28,297	591
Bradley	Warren	11,617	11,793	651
Calhoun	Hampton	5,714	5,826	628
Carroll	Berryville & Eureka Springs	22,492	18,654	634
Chicot	Lake Village	15,130	15,713	644
Clark	Arkadelphia	22,087	21,437	866
Clay	Corning & Piggott	17,588	18,107	639
Cleburne	Heber Springs	22,447	19,411	553
Cleveland	Rison	8,337	7,781	598
Columbia	Magnolia	25,469	25,691	766
Conway	Morrilton	19,885	19,151	556
Craighead	Jonesboro & Lake City	76,155	68,956	711
Crawford	Van Buren	49,074	42493	596
Crittenden	Marion	49,604	49,939	611
Cross	Wynne	19,363	19,225	616
Dallas	Fordyce	9,335	9,614	668
Desha	Arkansas City	15,513	16,798	765
Drew	Monticello	17,863	17,369	828
Faulkner	Conway	73,909	60,006	647
Franklin	Charleston & Ozark	16,453	14,897	610
Fulton	Salem	10,708	10,037	618
Garland	Hot Springs	82,038	73,397	678
Grant	Sheridan	15,463	13,948	632
Greene	Paragould	35,037	31,804	578
Hempstead	Hope	22,064	21,621	729
Hot Spring	Malvern	28,242	26,115	615
Howard	Nashville	13,882	13,569	588
Independence	Batesville	33,003	31,192	764
Izard	Melbourne	12,794	11,364	581
Jackson	Newport	18,485	18,944	634
Jefferson	Pine Bluff	83,007	85,487	885
Johnson	Clarksville	20,898	18,221	662
Lafayette	Lewisville	9,231	9,643	527
Lawrence	Walnut Ridge	17,436	17,455	587
Lee	Marianna	12,802	13,053	602
Lincoln	Star City	14,309	13,690	561
Little River	Ashdown	13,333	13,966	532
Logan	Booneville & Paris	21,188	20,557	710
Lonoke	Lonoke	47,583	39,268	766
Madison	Huntsville	13,094	11,618	837

County	County seat or courthouse	1996 Pop.	1990 Pop.	Land area sq mi
Marion	Yellville	14,298	12,001	598
Miller	Texarkana	38,950	38,467	624
Mississippi	Blytheville & Osceola	50,606	57,525	898
Monroe	Clarendon	10,381	11,333	607
Montgomery	Mount Ida	8,448	7,841	781
Nevada	Prescott	10,067	10,101	620
Newton	Jasper	7,966	7,666	823
Ouachita	Camden	28,374	30,574	733
Perry	Perryville	9,312	7,969	551
Phillips	Helena	27,906	28,830	693
Pike	Murfreesboro	10,485	10,086	603
Poinsett	Harrisburg	24,720	24,664	758
Polk	Mena	19,336	17,347	860
Pope	Russellville	51,326	45,883	812
Prairie	Des Arc & De Valls Bluff	9,273	9,518	646
Pulaski	Little Rock	352,305	349,569	771
Randolph	Pocahontas	17,742	16,558	652
Saint Francis	Forrest City	28,348	28,497	634
Saline	Benton	74,555	64,183	725
Scott	Waldron	10,775	10,205	894
Searcy	Marshall	7,728	7,841	667
Sebastian	Fort Smith & Greenwood	105,827	99,590	536
Sevier	De Queen	14,754	13,637	564
Sharp	Ash Flat	16,467	14,109	604
Stone	Mountain View	10,877	9,775	607
Union	El Dorado	46,036	46,719	1,039
Van Buren	Clinton	15,325	14,008	712
Washington	Fayetteville	134,984	113,409	950
White	Searcy	61,954	54,676	1,034
Woodruff	Augusta	9,203	9,520	587
Yell	Danville & Dardanelle	19,000	17,759	928

California
(58 counties, 155,973 sq mi land; pop. 31,878,234)

County	County seat or courthouse	1996 Pop.	1990 Pop.	Land area sq mi
Alameda	Oakland	1,328,139	1,276,702	738
Alpine	Markleeville	1,232	1,113	739
Amador	Jackson	33,315	30,039	593
Butte	Oroville	192,507	182,120	1,640
Calaveras	San Andreas	38,437	31,998	1,020
Colusa	Colusa	18,223	16,275	1,151
Contra Costa	Martinez	881,490	803,732	720
Del Norte	Crescent City	26,947	23,460	1,008
El Dorado	Placerville	151,706	125,995	1,712
Fresno	Fresno	751,272	667,490	5,963
Glenn	Willows	26,202	24,798	1,315
Humboldt	Eureka	123,023	119,118	3,573
Imperial	El Centro	142,651	109,303	4,175
Inyo	Independence	18,433	18,281	10,192
Kern	Bakersfield	622,729	544,981	8,142
Kings	Hanford	113,351	101,469	1,390
Lake	Lakeport	55,261	50,631	1,259
Lassen	Susanville	31,431	27,598	4,558
Los Angeles	Los Angeles	9,127,751	8,863,052	4,060
Madera	Madera	110,481	88,090	2,138
Marin	San Rafael	233,230	230,096	520
Mariposa	Mariposa	15,869	14,302	1,451
Mendocino	Ukiah	83,298	80,345	3,509
Merced	Merced	192,311	178,403	1,929
Modoc	Alturas	9,693	9,678	3,944
Mono	Bridgeport	10,497	9,956	3,045
Monterey	Salinas	339,047	355,660	3,322
Napa	Napa	116,512	110,765	754
Nevada	Nevada City	89,016	78,510	958
Orange	Santa Ana	2,636,888	2,410,668	790
Placer	Auburn	213,227	172,796	1,404
Plumas	Quincy	20,597	19,739	2,554
Riverside	Riverside	1,417,425	1,170,413	7,208
Sacramento	Sacramento	1,117,275	1,041,219	966
San Benito	Hollister	44,503	36,697	1,389
San Bernardino	San Bernardino	1,598,358	1,418,380	20,062
San Diego	San Diego	2,655,463	2,498,016	4,205
San Francisco	San Francisco	735,315	723,959	47
San Joaquin	Stockton	533,392	480,628	1,399
San Luis Obispo	San Luis Obispo	229,437	217,162	3,305
San Mateo	Redwood City	686,909	649,623	449
Santa Barbara	Santa Barbara	385,573	369,608	2,739
Santa Clara	San Jose	1,599,604	1,497,577	1,291
Santa Cruz	Santa Cruz	237,821	229,734	446
Shasta	Redding	161,740	147,036	3,786
Sierra	Downieville	3,409	3,318	953
Siskiyou	Yreka	44,193	43,531	6,287
Solano	Fairfield	365,536	339,471	828
Sonoma	Santa Rosa	420,872	388,222	1,576
Stanislaus	Modesto	415,786	370,522	1,495
Sutter	Yuba City	75,650	64,415	603
Tehama	Red Bluff	54,108	49,625	2,951
Trinity	Weaverville	13,418	13,063	3,179
Tulare	Visalia	349,922	311,921	4,824
Tuolumne	Sonora	52,196	48,456	2,236
Ventura	Ventura	714,733	669,016	1,846

County	County seat or courthouse	1996 Pop.	1990 Pop.	Land area sq mi
Yolo	Woodland	149,925	141,210	1,012
Yuba	Marysville	60,905	58,228	631

Colorado
(63 counties, 103,729 sq mi land; pop. 3,822,676)

County	County seat or courthouse	1996 Pop.	1990 Pop.	Land area sq mi
Adams	Brighton	309,928	265,038	1,192
Alamosa	Alamosa	14,300	13,617	723
Arapahoe	Littleton	455,035	391,511	803
Archuleta	Pagosa Springs	7,953	5,345	1,349
Baca	Springfield	4,491	4,556	2,556
Bent	Las Animas	5,478	5,048	1,514
Boulder	Boulder	258,234	225,339	743
Chaffee	Salida	14,672	12,684	1,014
Cheyenne	Cheyenne Wells	2,323	2,397	1,782
Clear Creek	Georgetown	8,448	7,619	396
Conejos	Conejos	7,869	7,453	1,287
Costilla	San Luis	3,567	3,190	1,227
Crowley	Ordway	4,200	3,946	789
Custer	Westcliffe	3,062	1,926	739
Delta	Delta	25,563	20,980	1,142
Denver	Denver	497,840	467,610	153
Dolores	Dove Creek	1,677	1,504	1,067
Douglas	Castle Rock	111,647	60,391	840
Eagle	Eagle	30,525	21,928	1,688
Elbert	Kiowa	16,209	9,646	1,851
El Paso	Colorado Springs	472,924	397,014	2,127
Fremont	Canon City	41,694	32,273	1,533
Garfield	Glenwood Springs	36,499	29,974	2,948
Gilpin	Central City	3,725	3,070	150
Grand	Hot Sulphur Springs	9,536	7,966	1,850
Gunnison	Gunnison	12,148	10,273	3,239
Hinsdale	Lake City	666	467	1,118
Huerfano	Walsenburg	6,564	6,009	1,591
Jackson	Walden	1,521	1,605	1,613
Jefferson	Golden	492,528	438,430	772
Kiowa	Eads	1,646	1,688	1,771
Kit Carson	Burlington	7,218	7,140	2,161
Lake	Leadville	6,212	6,007	377
La Plata	Durango	39,453	32,284	1,692
Larimer	Fort Collins	221,725	186,136	2,601
Las Animas	Trinidad	14,485	13,765	4,773
Lincoln	Hugo	5,578	4,529	2,586
Logan	Sterling	18,021	17,567	1,839
Mesa	Grand Junction	108,371	93,145	3,328
Mineral	Creede	681	558	876
Moffat	Craig	12,086	11,357	4,743
Montezuma	Cortez	21,999	18,672	2,037
Montrose	Montrose	29,601	24,423	2,241
Morgan	Fort Morgan	24,788	21,939	1,286
Otero	La Junta	20,901	20,185	1,263
Ouray	Ouray	3,140	2,295	542
Park	Fairplay	11,602	7,174	2,201
Phillips	Holyoke	4,340	4,189	688
Pitkin	Aspen	13,489	12,661	970
Prowers	Lamar	13,689	13,347	1,641
Pueblo	Pueblo	131,217	123,051	2,389
Rio Blanco	Meeker	6,348	6,051	3,221
Rio Grande	Del Norte	11,319	10,770	913
Routt	Steamboat Springs	16,975	14,088	2,362
Saguache	Saguache	5,784	4,619	3,169
San Juan	Silverton	564	745	388
San Miguel	Telluride	5,208	3,653	1,287
Sedgwick	Julesburg	2,651	2,690	548
Summit	Breckenridge	17,896	12,881	608
Teller	Cripple Creek	18,717	12,468	557
Washington	Akron	4,673	4,812	2,521
Weld	Greeley	152,189	131,821	3,993
Yuma	Wray	9,284	8,954	2,366

Connecticut
(8 counties, 4,845 sq mi land; pop. 3,274,238)

County	County seat or courthouse	1996 Pop.	1990 Pop.	Land area sq mi
Fairfield	Bridgeport	833,761	827,645	626
Hartford	Hartford	831,694	851,783	736
Litchfield	Litchfield	180,339	174,092	920
Middlesex	Middletown	148,143	143,196	369
New Haven	New Haven	794,672	804,219	606
New London	Norwich	250,735	254,957	666
Tolland	Rockville	130,265	128,699	410
Windham	Putnam	104,629	102,525	513

Delaware
(3 counties, 1,955 sq mi land; pop. 724,842)

County	County seat or courthouse	1996 Pop.	1990 Pop.	Land area sq mi
Kent	Dover	122,244	110,993	591
New Castle	Wilmington	471,417	441,946	426
Sussex	Georgetown	131,181	113,229	938

District of Columbia

(61 sq mi land; pop. 543,213)

Florida

(67 counties, 53,937 sq mi land; pop. 14,399,985)

County	County seat or courthouse	1996 Pop.	1990 Pop.	Land area sq mi
Alachua	Gainesville	196,525	181,596	874
Baker	Macclenny	20,556	18,486	585
Bay	Panama City	144,637	126,994	764
Bradford	Starke	24,130	22515	293
Brevard	Titusville	453,998	398,978	1,019
Broward	Fort Lauderdale	1,438,228	1,255,531	1,209
Calhoun	Blountstown	12,217	11,011	567
Charlotte	Punta Gorda	130,426	110,975	694
Citrus	Inverness	109,389	93,513	584
Clay	Green Cove Springs	128,912	105,986	601
Collier	Naples	188,187	152,099	2,026
Columbia	Lake City	49,291	42,613	797
Dade	Miami	2,076,175	1,937,194	1,945
De Soto	Arcadia	25,253	23,865	637
Dixie	Cross City	12,352	10,585	704
Duval	Jacksonville	721,139	672,971	774
Escambia	Pensacola	277,634	262,798	664
Flagler	Bunnell	42,142	28,701	485
Franklin	Apalachicola	10,271	8,967	534
Gadsden	Quincy	43,787	41,116	516
Gilchrist	Trenton	12,871	9,667	349
Glades	Moore Haven	7,851	7,591	774
Gulf	Port Saint Joe	13,327	11,504	565
Hamilton	Jasper	12,288	10,930	515
Hardee	Wauchula	20,130	19,499	637
Hendry	La Belle	29,821	25,773	1,153
Hernando	Brooksville	121,266	101,115	478
Highlands	Sebring	74,836	68,432	1,029
Hillsborough	Tampa	897,522	834,054	1,051
Holmes	Bonifay	18,174	15,778	483
Indian River	Vero Beach	96,490	90,208	503
Jackson	Marianna	44,728	41,375	916
Jefferson	Monticello	13,260	11,296	598
Lafayette	Mayo	6,237	5,578	543
Lake	Tavares	186,631	152,104	953
Lee	Fort Myers	380,001	335,113	804
Leon	Tallahassee	215,593	192,493	667
Levy	Bronson	30,296	25,912	1,118
Liberty	Bristol	6,542	5,569	836
Madison	Madison	17,513	16,569	692
Manatee	Bradenton	232,285	211,707	741
Marion	Ocala	230,068	194,835	1,579
Martin	Stuart	112,527	100,900	556
Monroe	Key West	80,730	78,024	997
Nassau	Fernandina Beach	52,079	43,941	652
Okaloosa	Crestview	165,873	143,777	936
Okeechobee	Okeechobee	30,894	29,627	774
Orange	Orlando	758,980	677,491	908
Osceola	Kissimmee	135,812	107,728	1,322
Palm Beach	West Palm Beach	992,840	863,503	1,974
Pasco	New Port Richey	311,556	281,131	745
Pinellas	Clearwater	868,887	851,659	280
Polk	Bartow	440,954	405,382	1,875
Putnam	Palatka	69,704	65,070	722
Saint Johns	Saint Augustine	106,503	83,829	609
Saint Lucie	Fort Pierce	174,728	150,171	573
Santa Rosa	Milton	108,186	81,608	1,016
Sarasota	Sarasota	296,518	277,776	572
Seminole	Sanford	335,868	287,521	308
Sumter	Bushnell	35,948	31,577	546
Suwannee	Live Oak	30,901	26,780	688
Taylor	Perry	18,173	17,111	1,042
Union	Lake Butler	12,451	10,252	240
Volusia	De Land	414,322	370,737	1,106
Wakulla	Crawfordville	18,105	14,202	607
Walton	De Funiak Springs	35,255	27,759	1,058
Washington	Chipley	19,212	16,919	580

Georgia

(159 counties, 57,919 sq mi land; pop. 7,353,225)

County	County seat or courthouse	1996 Pop.	1990 Pop.	Land area sq mi
Appling	Baxley	16,333	15,744	509
Atkinson	Pearson	7,022	6,213	338
Bacon	Alma	10,344	9,566	285
Baker	Newton	3,686	3,615	343
Baldwin	Milledgeville	41,947	39,530	259
Banks	Homer	11,918	10,308	234
Barrow	Winder	37,407	29,721	162
Bartow	Cartersville	66,293	55,915	460
Ben Hill	Fitzgerald	17,322	16,245	252
Berrien	Nashville	15,784	14,153	453
Bibb	Macon	155,573	150,137	250
Bleckley	Cochran	10,930	10,430	217
Brantley	Nahunta	13,048	11,077	444
Brooks	Quitman	15,820	15,398	494
Bryan	Pembroke	22,286	15,438	442
Bulloch	Statesboro	49,328	43,125	683
Burke	Waynesboro	21,542	20,579	831
Butts	Jackson	16,583	15,326	187
Calhoun	Morgan	4,844	5,013	280
Camden	Woodbine	42,798	30,167	630
Candler	Metter	8,676	7,744	247
Carroll	Carrollton	79,307	71,422	499
Catoosa	Ringgold	48,541	42,464	162
Charlton	Folkston	9,293	8,496	781
Chatham	Savannah	226,961	216,774	440
Chattahoochee	Cusseta	16,137	16,934	249
Chattooga	Summerville	22,953	22,242	314
Cherokee	Canton	121,496	90,204	424
Clarke	Athens	90,602	87,594	121
Clay	Fort Gaines	3,360	3,364	195
Clayton	Jonesboro	202,427	181,436	143
Clinch	Homerville	6,582	6,160	809
Cobb	Marietta	538,832	447,745	340
Coffee	Douglas	33,188	29,592	599
Colquitt	Moultrie	38,960	36,645	552
Columbia	Appling	86,173	66,031	290
Cook	Adel	14,351	13,456	229
Coweta	Newnan	76,295	53,853	443
Crawford	Knoxville	10,514	8,991	325
Crisp	Cordele	20,643	20,011	274
Dade	Trenton	14,486	13,147	174
Dawson	Dawsonville	13,016	9,429	211
Decatur	Bainbridge	26,529	25,517	597
De Kalb	Decatur	589,796	546,171	268
Dodge	Eastman	17,936	17,607	501
Dooly	Vienna	10,416	9,901	393
Dougherty	Albany	96,581	96,321	330
Douglas	Douglasville	84,463	71,120	199
Early	Blakely	12,149	11,854	511
Echols	Statenville	2,325	2,334	404
Effingham	Springfield	33,363	25,687	480
Elbert	Elberton	19,286	18,949	369
Emanuel	Swainsboro	21,030	20,546	686
Evans	Claxton	9,519	8,724	185
Fannin	Blue Ridge	17,745	15,992	386
Fayette	Fayetteville	81,891	62,415	197
Floyd	Rome	84,422	81,251	513
Forsyth	Cumming	69,127	44,083	226
Franklin	Carnesville	18,184	16,650	263
Fulton	Atlanta	718,336	648,779	529
Gilmer	Ellijay	16,868	13,368	427
Glascock	Gibson	2,429	2,357	144
Glynn	Brunswick	65,608	62,496	422
Gordon	Calhoun	39,369	35,067	355
Grady	Cairo	21,454	20,279	458
Greene	Greensboro	13,010	11,793	388
Gwinnett	Lawrenceville	478,001	352,910	433
Habersham	Clarkesville	30,794	27,622	278
Hall	Gainesville	113,033	95,434	394
Hancock	Sparta	9,023	8,908	473
Haralson	Buchanan	23,871	21,966	282
Harris	Hamilton	21,303	17,788	464
Hart	Hartwell	21,005	19,712	232
Heard	Franklin	9,855	8,628	296
Henry	McDonough	90,969	58,741	323
Houston	Perry	101,384	89,208	377
Irwin	Ocilla	8,871	8,649	357
Jackson	Jefferson	35,230	30,005	342
Jasper	Monticello	9,556	8,453	371
Jeff Davis	Hazlehurst	12,612	12,032	333
Jefferson	Louisville	17,860	17,408	528
Jenkins	Millen	8,471	8,247	350
Johnson	Wrightsville	8,252	8,329	304
Jones	Gray	22,330	20,739	394
Lamar	Barnesville	14,029	13,038	185
Lanier	Lakeland	6,610	5,531	187
Laurens	Dublin	43,342	39,988	813
Lee	Leesburg	20,705	16,250	356
Liberty	Hinesville	59,063	52,745	519
Lincoln	Lincolnton	8,026	7,442	211
Long	Ludowici	8,151	6,202	401
Lowndes	Valdosta	83,982	75,981	504
Lumpkin	Dahlonega	17,286	14,573	285
McDuffie	Thomson	21,474	20,119	260
McIntosh	Darien	9,592	8,634	434
Macon	Oglethorpe	13,141	13,114	403
Madison	Danielsville	24,192	21,050	284
Marion	Buena Vista	6,345	5,590	367
Meriwether	Greenville	22,944	22,411	503
Miller	Colquitt	6,144	6,280	283
Mitchell	Camilla	20,990	20,275	512
Monroe	Forsyth	19,368	17,113	396
Montgomery	Mount Vernon	7,700	7,379	245
Morgan	Madison	14,171	12,883	350
Murray	Chatsworth	30,777	26,147	344
Muscogee	Columbus	183,394	179,280	216
Newton	Covington	52,709	41,808	276
Oconee	Watkinsville	22,410	17,618	186
Oglethorpe	Lexington	10,899	9,763	441
Paulding	Dallas	64,072	41,611	314
Peach	Fort Valley	23,529	21,189	151

County	County seat or courthouse	1996 Pop.	1990 Pop.	Land area sq mi
Pickens	Jasper	17,570	14,432	232
Pierce	Blackshear	15,270	13,328	343
Pike	Zebulon	11,702	10,224	218
Polk	Cedartown	35,370	33,815	311
Pulaski	Hawkinsville	8,268	8,108	247
Putnam	Eatonton	16,511	14,137	345
Quitman	Georgetown	2,463	2,210	152
Rabun	Clayton	13,013	11,648	371
Randolph	Cuthbert	7,989	8,023	429
Richmond	Augusta	193,784	189,719	324
Rockdale	Conyers	65,219	54,091	131
Schley	Ellaville	3,763	3,590	168
Screven	Sylvania	14,286	13,842	649
Seminole	Donalsonville	9,252	9,010	238
Spalding	Griffin	57,713	54,457	198
Stephens	Toccoa	25,246	23,436	179
Stewart	Lumpkin	5,532	5,654	459
Sumter	Americus	30,668	30,232	485
Talbot	Talbotton	6,865	6,524	393
Taliaferro	Crawfordville	1,861	1,915	195
Tattnall	Reidsville	18,728	17,722	484
Taylor	Butler	8,189	7,642	378
Telfair	MacRae	11,662	11,000	441
Terrell	Dawson	11,092	10,653	336
Thomas	Thomasville	41,908	38,943	548
Tift	Tifton	36,850	34,998	265
Toombs	Lyons	25,463	24,072	367
Towns	Hiawassee	7,990	6,754	167
Treutlen	Soperton	5,903	5,994	201
Troup	La Grange	58,568	55,532	414
Turner	Ashburn	9,003	8,703	286
Twiggs	Jeffersonville	9,873	9,806	360
Union	Blairsville	14,923	11,993	323
Upson	Thomaston	26,923	26,300	326
Walker	La Fayette	61,163	58,340	446
Walton	Monroe	49,307	38,586	329
Ware	Waycross	35,568	35,471	903
Warren	Warrenton	6,001	6,078	286
Washington	Sandersville	19,910	19,112	681
Wayne	Jesup	24,636	22,356	645
Webster	Preston	2,242	2,263	210
Wheeler	Alamo	4,933	4,903	298
White	Cleveland	16,140	13,006	242
Whitfield	Dalton	80,296	72,462	290
Wilcox	Abbeville	7,320	7,008	380
Wilkes	Washington	10,583	10,597	471
Wilkinson	Irwinton	10,801	10,228	447
Worth	Sylvester	22,003	19,744	570

Hawaii

(5 counties, 6,423 sq mi land; pop. 1,183,723)

County	County seat or courthouse	1996 Pop.	1990 Pop.	Land area sq mi
Hawaii	Hilo	138,422	120,317	4,028
Honolulu	Honolulu	871,766	836,231	600
Kalawao[1]		87	130	13
Kauai	Lihue	56,435	51,177	623
Maui	Wailuku	117,013	100,374	1,159

(1) Administered by state government.

Idaho

(44 counties, 82,751 sq mi land; pop. 1,189,251)

County	County seat or courthouse	1996 Pop.	1990 Pop.	Land area sq mi
Ada	Boise	260,057	205,775	1,055
Adams	Council	3,891	3,254	1,365
Bannock	Pocatello	73,608	66,026	1,113
Bear Lake	Paris	6,534	6,084	971
Benewah	Saint Maries	8,982	7,937	776
Bingham	Blackfoot	41,366	37,583	2,095
Blaine	Hailey	16,975	13,552	2,645
Boise	Idaho City	4,864	3,509	1,903
Bonner	Sandpoint	33,976	26,622	1,738
Bonneville	Idaho Falls	79,670	72,207	1,869
Boundary	Bonners Ferry	9,823	8,332	1,269
Butte	Arco	3,126	2,918	2,233
Camas	Fairfield	860	727	1,075
Canyon	Caldwell	112,530	90,076	590
Caribou	Soda Springs	7,398	6,963	1,766
Cassia	Burley	21,482	19,532	2,567
Clark	Dubois	830	762	1,765
Clearwater	Orofino	9,373	8,505	2,462
Custer	Challis	4,311	4,133	4,926
Elmore	Mountain Home	23,894	21,205	3,078
Franklin	Preston	10,615	9,232	666
Fremont	Saint Anthony	11,594	10,937	1,867
Gem	Emmett	14,129	11,844	563
Gooding	Gooding	13,335	11,633	731
Idaho	Grangeville	14,924	13,768	8,485
Jefferson	Rigby	18,903	16,543	1,095
Jerome	Jerome	17,339	15,138	600
Kootenai	Coeur d'Alene	95,535	69,795	1,245
Latah	Moscow	33,173	30,617	1,077

County	County seat or courthouse	1996 Pop.	1990 Pop.	Land area sq mi
Lemhi	Salmon	8,098	6,899	4,564
Lewis	Nez Perce	4,002	3,516	479
Lincoln	Shoshone	3,777	3,308	1,206
Madison	Rexberg	23,458	23,674	472
Minidoka	Rupert	20,756	19,361	760
Nez Perce	Lewiston	36,670	33,754	849
Oneida	Malad City	3,871	3,492	1,200
Owyhee	Murphy	10,012	8,392	7,678
Payette	Payette	19,957	16,434	408
Power	American Falls	8,234	7,086	1,406
Shoshone	Wallace	14,024	13,931	2,634
Teton	Driggs	5,168	3,439	450
Twin Falls	Twin Falls	60,403	53,580	1,925
Valley	Cascade	7,988	6,109	3,678
Washington	Weiser	9,836	8,550	1,456

Illinois

(102 counties, 55,593 sq mi land; pop. 11,846,544)

County	County seat or courthouse	1996 Pop.	1990 Pop.	Land area sq mi
Adams	Quincy	67,816	66,090	857
Alexander	Cairo	10,228	10,626	236
Bond	Greenville	17,069	14,991	380
Boone	Belvidere	37,389	30,806	281
Brown	Mount Sterling	6,400	5,836	306
Bureau	Princeton	35,739	35,688	869
Calhoun	Hardin	5,011	5,322	254
Carroll	Mount Carroll	16,907	16,805	444
Cass	Virginia	13,284	13,437	376
Champaign	Urbana	167,392	173,025	997
Christian	Taylorville	34,730	34,418	709
Clark	Marshall	17,571	15,921	502
Clay	Louisville	14,397	14,460	469
Clinton	Carlyle	35,368	33,944	474
Coles	Charleston	51,186	51,644	508
Cook	Chicago	5,096,540	5,105,044	946
Crawford	Robinson	21,071	19,464	444
Cumberland	Toledo	11,169	10,670	346
DeKalb	Sycamore	82,703	77,932	634
De Witt	Clinton	16,795	16,516	398
Douglas	Tuscola	19,799	19,464	417
Du Page	Wheaton	859,310	781,689	334
Edgar	Paris	20,106	19,595	624
Edwards	Albion	7,129	7,440	222
Effingham	Effingham	33,337	31,704	479
Fayette	Vandalia	21,362	20,893	717
Ford	Paxton	14,164	14,275	486
Franklin	Benton	40,948	40,319	412
Fulton	Lewiston	38,650	38,080	866
Gallatin	Shawneetown	6,753	6,909	324
Greene	Carrollton	15,733	15,317	543
Grundy	Morris	35,712	32,337	420
Hamilton	McLeansboro	8,622	8,499	435
Hancock	Carthage	21,205	21,373	795
Hardin	Elizabethtown	5,068	5,189	178
Henderson	Oquawka	8,526	8,096	379
Henry	Cambridge	51,807	51,159	823
Iroquois	Watseka	31,625	30,787	1,117
Jackson	Murphysboro	61,154	61,067	588
Jasper	Newton	10,635	10,609	494
Jefferson	Mount Vernon	39,090	37,020	571
Jersey	Jerseyville	21,308	20,539	369
Jo Daviess	Galena	21,783	21,821	601
Johnson	Vienna	12,954	11,347	346
Kane	Geneva	370,361	317,471	521
Kankakee	Kankakee	101,949	96,255	678
Kendall	Yorkville	47,894	39,413	321
Knox	Galesburg	55,936	56,393	716
Lake	Waukegan	582,983	516,418	448
La Salle	Ottawa	109,462	106,913	1,135
Lawrence	Lawrenceville	15,865	15,972	372
Lee	Dixon	35,959	34,392	725
Livingston	Pontiac	40,597	39,301	1,044
Logan	Lincoln	31,499	30,798	618
McDonough	Macomb	34,152	35,244	589
McHenry	Woodstock	230,555	183,241	604
McLean	Bloomington	139,133	129,180	1,184
Macon	Decatur	115,416	117,206	581
Macoupin	Carlinville	48,994	47,679	864
Madison	Edwardsville	256,007	249,238	725
Marion	Salem	42,295	41,561	572
Marshall	Lacon	12,789	12,846	386
Mason	Havana	16,820	16,269	539
Massac	Metropolis	15,336	14,752	239
Menard	Petersburg	12,359	11,164	314
Mercer	Aledo	17,605	17,290	561
Monroe	Waterloo	25,358	22,422	388
Montgomery	Hillsboro	31,059	30,728	704
Morgan	Jacksonville	36,052	36,397	569
Moultrie	Sullivan	14,319	13,930	336
Ogle	Oregon	50,107	45,957	759
Peoria	Peoria	183,337	182,827	620
Perry	Pinckneyville	21,498	21,412	441
Piatt	Monticello	16,357	15,548	440
Pike	Pittsfield	17,251	17,577	830

County	County seat or courthouse	1996 Pop.	1990 Pop.	Land area sq mi
Pope	Golconda	4,735	4,373	371
Pulaski	Mound City	7,348	7,523	201
Putnam	Hennepin	5,715	5,730	160
Randolph	Chester	34,240	34,583	578
Richland	Olney	16,747	16,545	360
Rock Island	Rock Island	148,640	148,723	427
Saint Clair	Belleville	264,419	262,852	664
Saline	Harrisburg	26,476	26,551	383
Sangamon	Springfield	191,771	178,386	868
Schuyler	Rushville	7,702	7,498	437
Scott	Winchester	5,615	5,644	251
Shelby	Shelbyville	22,660	22,261	759
Stark	Toulon	6,402	6,534	288
Stephenson	Freeport	49,167	48,052	564
Tazewell	Pekin	128,366	123,692	649
Union	Jonesboro	18,079	17,619	416
Vermilion	Danville	85,260	88,257	899
Wabash	Mount Carmel	12,681	13,111	224
Warren	Monmouth	18,901	19,181	543
Washington	Nashville	15,204	14,965	563
Wayne	Fairfield	17,049	17,241	714
White	Carmi	15,840	16,522	495
Whiteside	Morrison	60,225	60,186	685
Will	Joliet	427,818	357,313	837
Williamson	Marion	60,764	57,733	424
Winnebago	Rockford	264,873	252,913	514
Woodford	Eureka	34,798	32,653	528

Indiana

(92 counties, 35,870 sq mi land; pop. 5,840,528)

County	County seat or courthouse	1996 Pop.	1990 Pop.	Land area sq mi
Adams	Decatur	32,686	31,095	339
Allen	Fort Wayne	310,803	300,836	657
Bartholomew	Columbus	68,441	63,657	407
Benton	Fowler	9,669	9,441	406
Blackford	Hartford City	14,134	14,067	165
Boone	Lebanon	42,453	38,147	423
Brown	Nashville	15,485	14,080	312
Carroll	Delphi	19,643	18,809	372
Cass	Logansport	38,829	38,413	413
Clark	Jeffersonville	92,530	87,774	375
Clay	Brazil	26,491	24,705	358
Clinton	Frankfort	32,876	30,974	405
Crawford	English	10,559	9,914	306
Daviess	Washington	28,760	27,533	431
Dearborn	Lawrenceburg	45,236	38,835	305
Decatur	Greensburg	25,105	23,645	373
DeKalb	Auburn	38,272	35,324	363
Delaware	Muncie	118,600	119,659	393
Dubois	Jasper	39,088	36,616	430
Elkhart	Goshen	168,941	156,198	464
Fayette	Connersville	26,237	26,015	215
Floyd	New Albany	70,746	64,404	148
Fountain	Covington	18,207	17,808	396
Franklin	Brookville	21,530	19,580	386
Fulton	Rochester	20,223	18,840	369
Gibson	Princeton	32,058	31,913	489
Grant	Marion	73,469	74,169	414
Greene	Bloomfield	32,942	30,410	542
Hamilton	Noblesville	147,719	108,936	398
Hancock	Greenfield	52,000	45,527	306
Harrison	Corydon	33,349	29,890	485
Hendricks	Danville	89,343	75,717	408
Henry	New Castle	49,135	48,139	393
Howard	Kokomo	84,126	80,827	293
Huntington	Huntington	37,024	35,427	383
Jackson	Brownstown	40,467	37,730	509
Jasper	Rensselaer	28,368	24,960	560
Jay	Portland	21,733	21,512	384
Jefferson	Madison	31,039	29,797	361
Jennings	Vernon	26,747	23,661	377
Johnson	Franklin	104,280	88,109	320
Knox	Vincennes	39,667	39,884	516
Kosciusko	Warsaw	69,932	65,294	538
Lagrange	Lagrange	32,103	29,477	380
Lake	Crown Point	479,940	475,594	497
La Porte	La Porte	109,604	107,066	598
Lawrence	Bedford	45,361	42,836	449
Madison	Anderson	132,782	130,669	452
Marion	Indianapolis	817,525	797,159	396
Marshall	Plymouth	45,173	42,182	444
Martin	Shoals	10,581	10,369	336
Miami	Peru	32,686	36,897	376
Monroe	Bloomington	116,176	108,978	394
Montgomery	Crawfordsville	36,349	34,436	505
Morgan	Martinsville	63,244	55,920	407
Newton	Kentland	14,611	13,551	402
Noble	Albion	41,449	37,877	411
Ohio	Rising Sun	5,490	5,315	87
Orange	Paoli	19,221	18,409	400
Owen	Spencer	20,158	17,281	385
Parke	Rockville	16,339	15,410	445
Perry	Cannelton	19,210	19,107	381
Pike	Petersburg	12,569	12,509	336
Porter	Valparaiso	142,363	128,932	418
Posey	Mount Vernon	26,505	25,968	409
Pulaski	Winamac	13,103	12,643	434
Putnam	Greencastle	33,451	30,315	480
Randolph	Winchester	27,530	27,148	453
Ripley	Versailles	26,932	24,616	446
Rush	Rushville	18,285	18,129	408
Saint Joseph	South Bend	257,740	247,052	457
Scott	Scottsburg	22,652	20,991	190
Shelby	Shelbyville	42,951	40,307	413
Spencer	Rockport	20,540	19,490	399
Starke	Knox	23,399	22,747	309
Steuben	Angola	30,831	27,446	309
Sullivan	Sullivan	20,115	18,993	447
Switzerland	Vevay	8,380	7,738	221
Tippecanoe	Lafayette	138,324	130,598	500
Tipton	Tipton	16,453	16,119	260
Union	Liberty	7,345	6,976	162
Vanderburgh	Evansville	167,716	165,058	235
Vermillion	Newport	16,791	16,773	257
Vigo	Terre Haute	106,389	106,107	403
Wabash	Wabash	34,661	35,069	413
Warren	Williamsport	8,188	8,176	365
Warrick	Boonville	50,070	44,920	384
Washington	Salem	26,689	23,717	515
Wayne	Richmond	72,017	71,951	404
Wells	Bluffton	26,651	25,948	370
White	Monticello	25,081	23,265	505
Whitley	Columbia City	29,863	27,651	336

Iowa

(99 counties, 55,875 sq mi land; pop. 2,851,792)

County	County seat or courthouse	1996 Pop.	1990 Pop.	Land area sq mi
Adair	Greenfield	8,224	8,409	569
Adams	Corning	4,494	4,866	424
Allamakee	Waukon	14,002	13,855	640
Appanoose	Centerville	13,616	13,743	496
Audubon	Audubon	6,894	7,334	443
Benton	Vinton	24,510	22,429	717
Black Hawk	Waterloo	122,806	123,798	567
Boone	Boone	25,875	25,186	572
Bremer	Waverly	23,280	22,813	438
Buchanan	Independence	21,175	20,844	571
Buena Vista	Storm Lake	19,862	19,965	575
Butler	Allison	15,781	15,731	580
Calhoun	Rockwell City	11,478	11,508	570
Carroll	Carroll	21,536	21,423	569
Cass	Atlantic	14,930	15,128	564
Cedar	Tipton	17,809	17,444	580
Cerro Gordo	Mason City	46,584	46,733	568
Cherokee	Cherokee	13,477	14,098	577
Chickasaw	New Hampton	13,493	13,295	505
Clarke	Osceola	8,255	8,287	431
Clay	Spencer	17,598	17,585	569
Clayton	Elkader	18,893	19,054	779
Clinton	Clinton	50,471	51,040	695
Crawford	Denison	16,503	16,775	714
Dallas	Adel	33,900	29,755	587
Davis	Bloomfield	8,447	8,312	503
Decatur	Leon	8,232	8,338	532
Delaware	Manchester	18,506	18,035	578
Des Moines	Burlington	42,564	42,614	416
Dickinson	Spirit Lake	15,725	14,909	381
Dubuque	Dubuque	88,201	86,403	608
Emmet	Estherville	11,114	11,569	396
Fayette	West Union	22,061	21,843	731
Floyd	Charles City	16,538	17,058	501
Franklin	Hampton	11,017	11,364	583
Fremont	Sidney	7,918	8,226	511
Greene	Jefferson	10,120	10,045	568
Grundy	Grundy Center	12,340	12,029	503
Guthrie	Guthrie Center	11,420	10,935	591
Hamilton	Webster City	16,102	16,071	577
Hancock	Garner	12,152	12,638	571
Hardin	Eldora	18,682	19,094	569
Harrison	Logan	15,230	14,730	697
Henry	Mount Pleasant	19,867	19,226	435
Howard	Cresco	9,766	9,809	473
Humboldt	Dakota City	10,431	10,756	434
Ida	Ida Grove	8,109	8,365	432
Iowa	Marengo	15,381	14,630	587
Jackson	Maquoketa	20,057	19,950	636
Jasper	Newton	35,470	34,795	730
Jefferson	Fairfield	16,901	16,310	435
Johnson	Iowa City	101,609	96,119	615
Jones	Anamosa	20,593	19,444	575
Keokuk	Sigourney	11,594	11,624	579
Kossuth	Algona	18,021	18,591	973
Lee	Fort Madison & Keokuk	38,879	38,687	517
Linn	Cedar Rapids	179,411	168,767	718
Louisa	Wapello	12,017	11,592	402
Lucas	Chariton	9,054	9,070	431

County	County seat or courthouse	1996 Pop.	1990 Pop.	Land area sq mi
Lyon	Rock Rapids	11,962	11,952	588
Madison	Winterset	13,663	12,483	561
Mahaska	Oskaloosa	21,757	21,532	571
Marion	Knoxville	31,359	30,001	554
Marshall	Marshalltown	38,868	38,276	572
Mills	Glenwood	14,054	13,202	437
Mitchell	Osage	11,130	10,928	469
Monona	Onawa	9,981	10,034	693
Monroe	Albia	8,113	8,114	433
Montgomery	Red Oak	11,908	12,076	424
Muscatine	Muscatine	41,158	39,907	439
O'Brien	Primghar	15,030	15,444	573
Osceola	Sibley	7,095	7,267	399
Page	Clarinda	16,784	16,870	535
Palo Alto	Emmetsburg	10,136	10,669	564
Plymouth	Le Mars	24,482	23,388	864
Pocahontas	Pocahontas	9,001	9,525	578
Polk	Des Moines	354,150	327,140	570
Pottawattamie	Council Bluffs	84,939	82,628	954
Poweshiek	Montezuma	18,975	19,033	585
Ringgold	Mount Ayr	5,345	5,420	538
Sac	Sac City	11,986	12,324	576
Scott	Davenport	157,353	150,973	458
Shelby	Harlan	13,065	13,230	591
Sioux	Orange City	31,191	29,903	768
Story	Nevada	74,610	74,252	573
Tama	Toledo	17,678	17,419	721
Taylor	Bedford	7,186	7,114	534
Union	Creston	12,613	12,750	424
Van Buren	Keosauqua	7,807	7,676	485
Wapello	Ottumwa	35,766	35,696	432
Warren	Indianola	39,386	36,033	572
Washington	Washington	20,706	19,612	569
Wayne	Corydon	6,847	7,067	526
Webster	Fort Dodge	39,014	40,342	715
Winnebago	Forest City	11,984	12,122	401
Winneshiek	Decorah	20,963	20,847	690
Woodbury	Sioux City	102,580	98,276	873
Worth	Northwood	7,865	7,991	400
Wright	Clarion	14,327	14,269	581

Kansas

(105 counties, 81,823 sq mi land; pop. 2,572,150)

County	County seat or courthouse	1996 Pop.	1990 Pop.	Land area sq mi
Allen	Iola	14,645	14,638	503
Anderson	Garnett	8,054	7,803	583
Atchison	Atchison	16,234	16,932	432
Barber	Medicine Lodge	5,484	5,874	1,134
Barton	Great Bend	28,097	29,382	894
Bourbon	Fort Scott	15,159	14,966	637
Brown	Hiawatha	10,965	11,128	571
Butler	El Dorado	59,226	50,580	1,428
Chase	Cottonwood Falls	2,886	3,021	776
Chautauqua	Sedan	4,379	4,407	642
Cherokee	Columbus	22,505	21,374	587
Cheyenne	Saint Francis	3,220	3,243	1,020
Clark	Ashland	2,382	2,418	975
Clay	Clay Center	9,319	9,158	644
Cloud	Concordia	10,247	11,023	716
Coffey	Burlington	8,743	8,404	630
Comanche	Coldwater	2,072	2,313	788
Cowley	Winfield	37,055	36,915	1,126
Crawford	Girard	36,337	35,582	593
Decatur	Oberlin	3,521	4,021	894
Dickinson	Abilene	19,856	18,958	848
Doniphan	Troy	7,766	8,134	392
Douglas	Lawrence	89,899	81,798	457
Edwards	Kinsley	3,471	3,787	622
Elk	Howard	3,393	3,327	648
Ellis	Hays	26,186	26,004	900
Ellsworth	Ellsworth	6,372	6,586	716
Finney	Garden City	35,545	33,070	1,300
Ford	Dodge City	29,309	27,463	1,099
Franklin	Ottawa	23,565	21,994	574
Geary	Junction City	26,341	30,453	384
Gove	Gove	3,089	3,231	1,072
Graham	Hill City	3,260	3,543	898
Grant	Ulysses	7,697	7,159	575
Gray	Cimarron	5,527	5,396	869
Greeley	Tribune	1,754	1,774	778
Greenwood	Eureka	8,090	7,847	1,140
Hamilton	Syracuse	2,296	2,388	997
Harper	Anthony	6,524	7,124	802
Harvey	Newton	31,302	31,028	539
Haskell	Sublette	3,922	3,886	577
Hodgeman	Jetmore	2,231	2,177	860
Jackson	Holton	11,978	11,525	657
Jefferson	Oskaloosa	17,514	15,905	526
Jewell	Mankato	4,011	4,251	909
Johnson	Olathe	408,341	355,021	477
Kearny	Lakin	4,216	4,027	870
Kingman	Kingman	8,545	8,292	864
Kiowa	Greensburg	3,571	3,660	722
Labette	Oswego	22,869	23,693	649
Lane	Dighton	2,211	2,375	717

County	County seat or courthouse	1996 Pop.	1990 Pop.	Land area sq mi
Leavenworth	Leavenworth	69,904	64,371	463
Lincoln	Lincoln	3,388	3,653	719
Linn	Mound City	8,974	8,254	599
Logan	Oakley	3,113	3,081	1,073
Lyon	Emporia	34,384	34,732	851
McPherson	McPherson	27,548	27,268	900
Marion	Marion	12,898	12,888	943
Marshall	Marysville	11,286	11,705	903
Meade	Meade	4,436	4,247	979
Miami	Paola	25,933	23,466	577
Mitchell	Beloit	7,096	7,203	700
Montgomery	Independence	37,414	38,816	645
Morris	Council Grove	6,340	6,198	697
Morton	Elkhart	3,315	3,480	730
Nemaha	Seneca	10,389	10,446	719
Neosho	Erie	16,893	17,035	572
Ness	Ness City	3,663	4,033	1,075
Norton	Norton	5,762	5,947	878
Osage	Lyndon	16,726	15,248	704
Osborne	Osborne	4,606	4,867	893
Ottawa	Minneapolis	5,815	5,634	721
Pawnee	Larned	7,470	7,555	754
Phillips	Phillipsburg	6,194	6,590	886
Pottawatomie	Westmoreland	17,908	16,128	844
Pratt	Pratt	9,746	9,702	735
Rawlins	Atwood	3,249	3,404	1,070
Reno	Hutchinson	62,901	62,389	1,255
Republic	Belleville	6,253	6,482	717
Rice	Lyons	10,044	10,610	727
Riley	Manhattan	64,716	67,139	610
Rooks	Stockton	5,849	6,039	888
Rush	LaCrosse	3,537	3,842	718
Russell	Russell	7,658	7,835	885
Saline	Salina	51,782	49,301	720
Scott	Scott City	5,029	5,289	718
Sedgwick	Wichita	422,437	403,662	1,000
Seward	Liberal	20,002	18,743	640
Shawnee	Topeka	164,938	160,976	550
Sheridan	Hoxie	2,760	3,043	896
Sherman	Goodland	6,733	6,926	1,056
Smith	Smith Center	4,741	5,078	896
Stafford	Saint John	5,129	5,365	792
Stanton	Johnson	2,297	2,333	680
Stevens	Hugoton	5,347	5,048	728
Sumner	Wellington	26,901	25,841	1,182
Thomas	Colby	8,326	8,258	1,075
Trego	WaKeeney	3,440	3,694	888
Wabaunsee	Alma	6,664	6,603	798
Wallace	Sharon Springs	1,812	1,821	914
Washington	Washington	6,738	7,073	899
Wichita	Leoti	2,725	2,758	719
Wilson	Fredonia	10,353	10,289	574
Woodson	Yates Center	3,980	4,116	501
Wyandotte	Kansas City	153,427	162,026	151

Kentucky

(120 counties, 39,732 sq mi land; pop. 3,883,723)

County	County seat or courthouse	1996 Pop.	1990 Pop.	Land area sq mi
Adair	Columbia	16,460	15,360	407
Allen	Scottsville	15,844	14,628	346
Anderson	Lawrenceburg	17,734	14,571	203
Ballard	Wickliffe	8,252	7,902	251
Barren	Glasgow	36,255	34,001	491
Bath	Owingsville	10,143	9,692	279
Bell	Pineville	30,193	31,506	361
Boone	Burlington	72,926	57,589	246
Bourbon	Paris	19,199	19,236	291
Boyd	Catlettsburg	50,263	51,150	160
Boyle	Danville	26,945	25,641	182
Bracken	Brooksville	8,237	7,766	203
Breathitt	Jackson	15,640	15,703	495
Breckinridge	Hardinsburg	16,901	16,312	572
Bullitt	Shepherdsville	57,161	47,567	299
Butler	Morgantown	11,701	11,245	428
Caldwell	Princeton	13,290	13,232	347
Calloway	Murray	32,579	30,735	386
Campbell	Newport	87,233	83,866	152
Carlisle	Bardwell	5,309	5,238	193
Carroll	Carrollton	9,516	9,292	130
Carter	Grayson	26,328	24,340	411
Casey	Liberty	14,512	14,211	446
Christian	Hopkinsville	65,445	68,941	721
Clark	Winchester	31,604	29,496	254
Clay	Manchester	22,736	21,746	471
Clinton	Albany	9,269	9,135	198
Crittenden	Marion	9,400	9,196	362
Cumberland	Burkesville	6,077	6,784	306
Daviess	Owensboro	90,818	87,189	462
Edmonson	Brownsville	11,076	10,357	303
Elliott	Sandy Hook	6,584	6,455	234
Estill	Irvine	15,494	14,614	254
Fayette	Lexington	239,942	225,366	285
Fleming	Flemingsburg	13,161	12,292	351
Floyd	Prestonsburg	43,744	43,586	394

County	County seat or courthouse	1996 Pop.	1990 Pop.	Land area sq mi
Franklin	Frankfort	46,410	44,143	211
Fulton	Hickman	7,794	8,271	209
Gallatin	Warsaw	6,409	5,393	99
Garrard	Lancaster	13,251	11,579	231
Grant	Williamstown	19,269	15,737	260
Graves	Mayfield	35,601	33,550	556
Grayson	Leitchfield	22,910	21,050	504
Green	Greensburg	10,582	10,371	289
Greenup	Greenup	37,183	36,742	346
Hancock	Hawesville	8,750	7,864	189
Hardin	Elizabethtown	89,404	89,240	628
Harlan	Harlan	35,411	36,574	467
Harrison	Cynthiana	17,170	16,248	310
Hart	Munfordville	16,328	14,890	416
Henderson	Henderson	44,444	43,044	440
Henry	New Castle	14,581	12,823	289
Hickman	Clinton	5,306	5,566	245
Hopkins	Madisonville	46,545	46,126	551
Jackson	McKee	12,832	11,955	346
Jefferson	Louisville	673,040	665,123	385
Jessamine	Nicholasville	35,426	30,508	173
Johnson	Paintsville	24,147	23,248	262
Kenton	Covington	145,597	142,031	163
Knott	Hindman	18,214	17,906	352
Knox	Barbourville	31,514	29,676	388
Larue	Hodgenville	12,760	11,679	263
Laurel	London	49,185	43,438	436
Lawrence	Louisa	15,468	13,998	419
Lee	Beattyville	7,906	7,422	210
Leslie	Hyden	13,523	13,642	404
Letcher	Whitesburg	26,744	27,000	339
Lewis	Vanceburg	13,516	13,029	485
Lincoln	Stanford	21,781	20,045	337
Livingston	Smithland	9,290	9,062	316
Logan	Russellville	25,902	24,416	556
Lyon	Eddyville	7,849	6,624	216
McCracken	Paducah	64,940	62,879	251
McCreary	Whitley City	16,583	15,603	428
McLean	Calhoun	9,756	9,628	254
Madison	Richmond	64,297	57,508	441
Magoffin	Salyersville	13,804	13,077	310
Marion	Lebanon	17,001	16,499	347
Marshall	Benton	29,683	27,205	305
Martin	Inez	12,658	12,526	231
Mason	Maysville	16,891	16,666	241
Meade	Brandenburg	27,522	24,170	309
Menifee	Frenchburg	5,483	5,092	204
Mercer	Harrodsburg	20,412	19,148	251
Metcalfe	Edmonton	9,369	8,963	291
Monroe	Tompkinsville	11,314	11,401	331
Montgomery	Mount Sterling	20,492	19,561	199
Morgan	West Liberty	13,420	11,648	381
Muhlenberg	Greenville	31,857	31,318	475
Nelson	Bardstown	34,332	29,710	423
Nicholas	Carlisle	6,942	6,725	197
Ohio	Hartford	21,826	21,105	594
Oldham	La Grange	42,287	33,263	189
Owen	Owenton	9,905	9,035	352
Owsley	Booneville	5,481	5,036	198
Pendleton	Falmouth	13,757	12,036	280
Perry	Hazard	31,199	30,283	342
Pike	Pikeville	73,389	72,584	788
Powell	Stanton	12,409	11,686	180
Pulaski	Somerset	55,065	49,489	662
Robertson	Mount Olivet	2,209	2,124	100
Rockcastle	Mount Vernon	15,627	14,803	318
Rowan	Morehead	21,768	20,353	281
Russell	Jamestown	16,401	14,716	254
Scott	Georgetown	28,565	23,867	285
Shelby	Shelbyville	28,227	24,824	384
Simpson	Franklin	16,084	15,145	236
Spencer	Taylorsville	8,649	6,801	186
Taylor	Campbellsville	22,712	21,146	270
Todd	Elkton	11,225	10,940	376
Trigg	Cadiz	11,857	10,361	443
Trimble	Bedford	7,246	6,090	149
Union	Morganfield	16,508	16,557	345
Warren	Bowling Green	85,545	77,720	545
Washington	Springfield	10,815	10,441	301
Wayne	Monticello	18,703	17,468	459
Webster	Dixon	13,524	13,955	335
Whitley	Williamsburg	35,668	33,326	440
Wolfe	Campton	7,363	6,503	223
Woodford	Versailles	22,040	19,955	191

Louisiana

(64 parishes, 43,566 sq mi land; pop. 4,350,579)

Parish	Parish seat or courthouse	1996 Pop.	1990 Pop.	Land area sq mi
Acadia	Crowley	57,590	55,882	655
Allen	Oberlin	23,892	21,226	765
Ascension	Donaldsonville	67,958	58,214	292
Assumption	Napoleonville	22,681	22,753	339
Avoyelles	Marksville	40,433	39,159	833
Beauregard	De Ridder	31,771	30,083	1,160

Parish	Parish seat or courthouse	1996 Pop.	1990 Pop.	Land area sq mi
Bienville	Arcadia	16,676	15,979	811
Bossier	Benton	91,811	86,088	839
Caddo	Shreveport	245,095	248,253	882
Calcasieu	Lake Charles	178,881	168,134	1,071
Caldwell	Columbia	10,189	9,806	530
Cameron	Cameron	8,733	9,260	1,313
Catahoula	Harrisonburg	11,155	11,065	704
Claiborne	Homer	17,185	17,405	755
Concordia	Vidalia	20,854	20,828	696
De Soto	Mansfield	23,428	25,346	877
East Baton Rouge	Baton Rouge	395,914	380,105	456
East Carroll	Lake Providence	9,154	9,709	422
East Feliciana	Clinton	20,833	19,211	453
Evangeline	Ville Platte	34,281	33,274	664
Franklin	Winnsboro	22,078	22,387	623
Grant	Colfax	18,591	17,526	645
Iberia	New Iberia	71,685	68,297	575
Iberville	Plaquemine	30,929	31,049	619
Jackson	Jonesboro	15,492	15,705	570
Jefferson	Gretna	455,043	448,306	306
Jefferson Davis	Jennings	31,753	30,722	652
Lafayette	Lafayette	181,851	164,762	270
Lafourche	Thibodaux	87,772	85,860	1,085
La Salle	Jena	13,840	13,662	624
Lincoln	Ruston	42,302	41,745	471
Livingston	Livingston	82,900	70,523	648
Madison	Tallulah	12,997	12,463	624
Morehouse	Bastrop	31,969	31,938	794
Natchitoches	Natchitoches	38,173	36,689	1,256
Orleans	New Orleans	476,625	496,938	181
Ouachita	Monroe	147,302	142,191	611
Plaquemines	Pointe a la Hache	25,848	25,575	845
Pointe Coupee	New Roads	23,200	22,540	557
Rapides	Alexandria	126,290	131,556	1,323
Red River	Coushatta	9,746	9,387	389
Richland	Rayville	20,892	20,629	559
Sabine	Many	23,741	22,646	865
Saint Bernard	Chalmette	66,641	66,631	465
Saint Charles	Hahnville	47,031	42,437	284
Saint Helena	Greensburg	9,748	9,874	408
Saint James	Convent	20,959	20,879	246
Saint John the Baptist	Edgard	42,260	39,996	219
Saint Landry	Opelousas	82,955	80,312	929
Saint Martin	Saint Martinville	46,239	44,097	740
Saint Mary	Franklin	57,425	58,086	613
Saint Tammany	Covington	178,483	144,500	854
Tangipahoa	Amite	94,273	85,709	790
Tensas	Saint Joseph	6,883	7,103	603
Terrebonne	Houma	102,097	96,982	1,255
Union	Farmerville	21,607	20,796	878
Vermilion	Abbeville	51,299	50,055	1,174
Vernon	Leesville	54,546	61,961	1,329
Washington	Franklinton	43,315	43,185	670
Webster	Minden	42,690	41,989	596
West Baton Rouge	Port Allen	20,616	19,419	191
West Carroll	Oak Grove	12,191	12,093	359
West Feliciana	Saint Francisville	12,964	12,915	406
Winn	Winnfield	16,824	16,269	951

Maine

(16 counties, 30,865 sq mi land; pop. 1,243,316)

County	County seat or courthouse	1996 Pop.	1990 Pop.	Land area sq mi
Androscoggin	Auburn	101,754	105,259	470
Aroostook	Houlton	78,113	86,936	6,672
Cumberland	Portland	251,087	243,135	836
Franklin	Farmington	29,200	29,008	1,698
Hancock	Ellsworth	49,500	46,948	1,589
Kennebec	Augusta	116,214	115,904	868
Knox	Rockland	37,487	36,310	366
Lincoln	Wiscasset	31,303	30,357	456
Oxford	South Paris	53,797	52,602	2,078
Penobscot	Bangor	144,989	146,601	3,396
Piscataquis	Dover-Foxcroft	18,329	18,653	3,967
Sagadahoc	Bath	35,508	33,535	254
Somerset	Skowhegan	52,507	49,767	3,927
Waldo	Belfast	35,822	33,018	730
Washington	Machias	36,224	35,308	2,569
York	Alfred	171,482	164,587	991

Maryland

(23 counties, 1 ind. city, 9,775 sq mi land; pop. 5,071,604)

County	County seat or courthouse	1996 Pop.	1990 Pop.	Land area sq mi
Allegany	Cumberland	73,037	74,946	425
Anne Arundel	Annapolis	465,582	427,239	416
Baltimore	Towson	717,765	692,134	599
Calvert	Prince Frederick	66,779	51,372	215
Caroline	Denton	29,189	27,035	320
Carroll	Westminster	143,648	123,372	449

County	County seat or courthouse	1996 Pop.	1990 Pop.	Land area sq mi
Cecil	Elkton	79,475	71,347	348
Charles	La Plata	113,557	101,154	461
Dorchester	Cambridge	29,988	30,236	558
Frederick	Frederick	179,327	150,208	663
Garrett	Oakland	29,445	28,138	648
Harford	Bel Air	209,121	182,132	440
Howard	Ellicott City	224,483	187,328	252
Kent	Chestertown	18,889	17,842	279
Montgomery	Rockville	816,999	757,027	495
Prince George's	Upper Marlboro	773,810	728,553	486
Queen Anne's	Centreville	38,024	33,953	372
Saint Mary's	Leonardtown	82,655	75,974	361
Somerset	Princess Anne	24,266	23,440	327
Talbot	Easton	32,381	30,549	269
Washington	Hagerstown	127,278	121,393	458
Wicomico	Salisbury	79,253	74,339	377
Worcester	Snow Hill	41,158	35,028	473
Independent City				
Baltimore		675,401	736,014	81

Massachusetts

(14 counties, 7,838 sq mi land; pop. 6,092,352)

County	County seat or courthouse	1996 Pop.	1990 Pop.	Land area sq mi
Barnstable	Barnstable	201,970	186,605	396
Berkshire	Pittsfield	134,788	139,352	931
Bristol	Taunton	513,899	506,325	556
Dukes	Edgartown	13,259	11,639	104
Essex	Salem	686,774	670,080	498
Franklin	Greenfield	71,209	70,092	702
Hampden	Springfield	442,194	456,310	619
Hampshire	Northampton	149,610	146,568	529
Middlesex	East Cambridge	1412,561	1,398,468	824
Nantucket	Nantucket	7,267	6,012	48
Norfolk	Dedham	637,388	616,087	400
Plymouth	Plymouth	456,820	435,276	661
Suffolk	Boston	645,068	663,906	59
Worcester	Worcester	719,545	709,705	1,513

Michigan

(83 counties, 56,809 sq mi land; pop. 9,594,350)

County	County seat or courthouse	1996 Pop.	1990 Pop.	Land area sq mi
Alcona	Harrisville	10,799	10,145	675
Alger	Munising	9,971	8,972	918
Allegan	Allegan	99,019	90,509	828
Alpena	Alpena	30,746	30,605	574
Antrim	Bellaire	20,595	18,185	477
Arenac	Standish	16,268	14,906	367
Baraga	L'Anse	8,472	7,954	904
Barry	Hastings	53,145	50,057	556
Bay	Bay City	110,824	111,723	444
Benzie	Beulah	14,037	12,200	321
Berrien	Saint Joseph	161,434	161,378	571
Branch	Coldwater	42,991	41,502	507
Calhoun	Marshall	140,112	135,982	709
Cass	Cassopolis	50,050	49,477	492
Charlevoix	Charlevoix	23,503	21,468	417
Cheboygan	Cheboygan	22,993	21,398	716
Chippewa	Sault Sainte Marie	37,289	34,604	1,561
Clare	Harrison	28,618	24,952	567
Clinton	Saint Johns	62,239	57,893	572
Crawford	Grayling	13,671	12,260	558
Delta	Escanaba	39,047	37,780	1,170
Dickinson	Iron Mountain	27,285	26,831	766
Eaton	Charlotte	99,562	92,879	577
Emmet	Petoskey	27,870	25,040	468
Genesee	Flint	436,128	430,459	640
Gladwin	Gladwin	24,615	21,896	507
Gogebic	Bessemer	17,704	18,052	1,102
Grand Traverse	Traverse City	72,072	64,273	465
Gratiot	Ithaca	39,978	38,982	570
Hillsdale	Hillsdale	45,887	43,431	599
Houghton	Houghton	36,230	35,446	1,012
Huron	Bad Axe	35,281	34,951	837
Ingham	Mason	285,737	281,912	559
Ionia	Ionia	60,378	57,024	573
Iosco	Tawas City	24,761	30,209	549
Iron	Crystal Falls	13,121	13,175	1,167
Isabella	Mount Pleasant	57,118	54,624	574
Jackson	Jackson	154,563	149,756	707
Kalamazoo	Kalamazoo	229,008	223,411	562
Kalkaska	Kalkaska	15,325	13,497	561
Kent	Grand Rapids	536,103	500,631	856
Keweenaw	Eagle River	2,010	1,701	541
Lake	Baldwin	9,874	8,583	568
Lapeer	Lapeer	85,479	74,768	654
Leelanau	Leland	18,430	16,527	349
Lenawee	Adrian	97,133	91,476	751
Livingston	Howell	137,616	115,645	568
Luce	Newberry	6,180	5,763	903
Mackinac	Saint Ignace	11,096	10,674	1,022
Macomb	Mount Clemens	734,625	717,400	480
Manistee	Manistee	22,902	21,265	544

County	County seat or courthouse	1996 Pop.	1990 Pop.	Land area sq mi
Marquette	Marquette	62,017	70,887	1,821
Mason	Ludington	27,725	25,537	495
Mecosta	Big Rapids	38,460	37,308	556
Menominee	Menominee	24,551	24,920	1,044
Midland	Midland	80,669	75,651	521
Missaukee	Lake City	13,607	12,147	567
Monroe	Monroe	140,488	133,600	551
Montcalm	Stanton	58,969	53,059	708
Montmorency	Atlanta	9,868	8,936	548
Muskegon	Muskegon	164,913	158,983	509
Newaygo	White Cloud	44,285	38,206	842
Oakland	Pontiac	1,162,098	1,083,592	873
Oceana	Hart	24,397	22,455	541
Ogemaw	West Branch	20,790	18,681	564
Ontonagon	Ontonagon	8,405	8,854	1,312
Osceola	Reed City	22,047	20,146	566
Oscoda	Mio	8,775	7,842	565
Otsego	Gaylord	21,343	17,957	515
Ottawa	Grand Haven	215,064	187,768	566
Presque Isle	Rogers City	14,407	13,743	660
Roscommon	Roscommon	22,847	19,776	521
Saginaw	Saginaw	211,808	211,946	809
Saint Clair	Port Huron	155,636	145,607	725
Saint Joseph	Centreville	60,977	58,913	504
Sanilac	Sandusky	42,440	39,928	964
Schoolcraft	Manistique	8,653	8,302	1,178
Shiawassee	Corunna	72,333	69,770	539
Tuscola	Caro	57,837	55,498	813
Van Buren	Paw Paw	75,308	70,060	611
Washtenaw	Ann Arbor	295,149	282,937	710
Wayne	Detroit	2,039,819	2,111,687	614
Wexford	Cadillac	28,789	26,360	566

Minnesota

(87 counties, 79,617 sq mi land; pop. 4,657,758)

County	County seat or courthouse	1996 Pop.	1990 Pop.	Land area sq mi
Aitkin	Aitkin	13,715	12,425	1,819
Anoka	Anoka	282,139	243,641	424
Becker	Detroit Lakes	29,161	27,881	1,311
Beltrami	Bemidji	38,274	34,384	2,505
Benton	Foley	33,336	30,185	408
Big Stone	Ortonville	5,839	6,285	497
Blue Earth	Mankato	54,199	54,044	752
Brown	New Ulm	27,262	26,984	611
Carlton	Carlton	30,426	29,259	860
Carver	Chaska	61,415	47,915	357
Cass	Walker	25,329	21,791	2,018
Chippewa	Montevideo	13,132	13,228	583
Chisago	Center City	38,123	30,521	418
Clay	Moorhead	51,848	50,422	1,045
Clearwater	Bagley	8,254	8,309	995
Cook	Grand Marais	4,688	3,868	1,451
Cottonwood	Windom	12,321	12,694	640
Crow Wing	Brainerd	50,634	44,249	997
Dakota	Hastings	326,016	275,189	570
Dodge	Mantorville	16,855	15,731	440
Douglas	Alexandria	30,459	28,674	634
Faribault	Blue Earth	16,405	16,937	714
Fillmore	Preston	20,860	20,777	861
Freeborn	Albert Lea	31,972	33,060	708
Goodhue	Red Wing	42,366	40,690	759
Grant	Elbow Lake	6,154	6,246	547
Hennepin	Minneapolis	1,058,746	1,032,431	557
Houston	Caledonia	19,226	18,497	558
Hubbard	Park Rapids	16,406	14,939	923
Isanti	Cambridge	29,017	25,921	439
Itasca	Grand Rapids	43,392	40,863	2,665
Jackson	Jackson	11,718	11,677	702
Kanabec	Mora	13,838	12,802	525
Kandiyohi	Willmar	41,324	38,761	796
Kittson	Hallock	5,419	5,767	1,097
Koochiching	International Falls	15,858	16,299	3,102
Lac qui Parle	Madison	8,228	8,924	765
Lake	Two Harbors	10,707	10,415	2,099
Lake of the Woods	Baudette	4,598	4,076	1,297
Le Sueur	Le Center	24,715	23,239	449
Lincoln	Ivanhoe	6,687	6,890	537
Lyon	Marshall	24,791	24,789	714
McLeod	Glencoe	33,636	32,030	492
Mahnomen	Mahnomen	5,144	5,044	556
Marshall	Warren	10,563	10,993	1,772
Martin	Fairmont	22,462	22,914	709
Meeker	Litchfield	21,463	20,846	609
Mille Lacs	Milaca	20,312	18,670	575
Morrison	Little Falls	30,528	29,604	1,125
Mower	Austin	37,151	37,385	712
Murray	Slayton	9,609	9,660	705
Nicollet	Saint Peter	29,846	28,076	452
Nobles	Worthington	20,060	20,098	716
Norman	Ada	7,753	7,975	876
Olmsted	Rochester	113,182	106,470	653
Otter Tail	Fergus Falls	53,889	50,714	1,980
Pennington	Thief River Falls	13,564	13,306	617

County	County seat or courthouse	1996 Pop.	1990 Pop.	Land area sq mi
Pine	Pine City	23,331	21,264	1,411
Pipestone	Pipestone	10,124	10,491	466
Polk	Crookston	32,433	32,589	1,971
Pope	Glenwood	11,051	10,745	670
Ramsey	Saint Paul	484,484	485,783	156
Red Lake	Red Lake Falls	4,342	4,525	432
Redwood	Redwood Falls	16,878	17,254	880
Renville	Olivia	17,075	17,673	983
Rice	Faribault	52,888	49,183	498
Rock	Luverne	9,948	9,806	483
Roseau	Roseau	16,215	15,026	1,663
Saint Louis	Duluth	196,414	198,213	6,226
Scott	Shakopee	72,813	57,846	357
Sherburne	Elk River	55,401	41,945	437
Sibley	Gaylord	14,652	14,366	589
Stearns	Saint Cloud	126,990	119,324	1,345
Steele	Owatonna	31,567	30,729	430
Stevens	Morris	10,197	10,634	562
Swift	Benson	10,857	10,724	744
Todd	Long Prairie	24,128	23,363	942
Traverse	Wheaton	4,298	4,463	574
Wabasha	Wabasha	20,752	19,744	525
Wadena	Wadena	13,126	13,154	536
Waseca	Waseca	17,998	18,079	423
Washington	Stillwater	185,074	145,858	392
Watonwan	Saint James	11,600	11,682	435
Wilkin	Breckenridge	7,381	7,516	752
Winona	Winona	48,411	47,828	626
Wright	Buffalo	80,757	68,710	661
Yellow Medicine	Granite Falls	11,559	11,684	758

Mississippi

(82 counties, 46,914 sq mi land; pop. 2,716,115)

County	County seat or courthouse	1996 Pop.	1990 Pop.	Land area sq mi
Adams	Natchez	34,726	35,356	460
Alcorn	Corinth	32,755	31,722	400
Amite	Liberty	13,564	13,328	730
Attala	Kosciusko	18,437	18,481	735
Benton	Ashland	8,025	8,046	407
Bolivar	Cleveland & Rosedale	41,113	41,875	876
Calhoun	Pittsboro	14,997	14,908	587
Carroll	Carrollton & Vaiden	10,009	9,237	628
Chickasaw	Houston & Okolona	18,320	18,085	502
Choctaw	Ackerman	9,285	9,071	419
Claiborne	Port Gibson	11,521	11,370	487
Clarke	Quitman	17,860	17,313	691
Clay	West Point	21,746	21,120	409
Coahoma	Clarksdale	31,645	31,665	554
Copiah	Hazlehurst	28,558	27,592	777
Covington	Collins	17,441	16,527	414
De Soto	Hernando	87,823	67,910	478
Forrest	Hattiesburg	73,054	68,314	467
Franklin	Meadville	8,270	8,377	565
George	Lucedale	18,599	16,673	478
Greene	Leakesville	11,797	10,220	713
Grenada	Grenada	22,455	21,555	422
Hancock	Bay Saint Louis	38,304	31,760	477
Harrison	Gulfport	176,613	165,365	581
Hinds	Jackson & Raymond	250,381	254,441	869
Holmes	Lexington	21,408	21,604	756
Humphreys	Belzoni	11,445	12,134	418
Issaquena	Mayersville	1,664	1,909	413
Itawamba	Fulton	21,076	20,017	532
Jackson	Pascagoula	128,267	115,243	727
Jasper	Bay Springs & Paulding	17,410	17,114	676
Jefferson	Fayette	8,545	8,653	519
Jefferson Davis	Prentiss	13,949	14,051	408
Jones	Ellisville & Laurel	63,447	62,031	694
Kemper	De Kalb	10,378	10,356	766
Lafayette	Oxford	33,515	31,826	631
Lamar	Purvis	34,843	30,424	497
Lauderdale	Meridian	76,987	75,555	704
Lawrence	Monticello	12,873	12,458	431
Leake	Carthage	19,403	18,436	583
Lee	Tupelo	73,357	65,579	450
Leflore	Greenwood	36,907	37,341	592
Lincoln	Brookhaven	31,490	30,278	586
Lowndes	Columbus	61,203	59,308	502
Madison	Canton	68,273	53,794	719
Marion	Columbia	26,093	25,544	542
Marshall	Holly Springs	32,233	30,361	706
Monroe	Aberdeen	37,922	36,582	764
Montgomery	Winona	12,413	12,387	407
Neshoba	Philadelphia	27,043	24,800	570
Newton	Decatur	21,455	20,291	578
Noxubee	Macon	12,414	12,604	695
Oktibbeha	Starkville	39,303	38,375	458
Panola	Batesville & Sardis	32,615	29,996	684
Pearl River	Poplarville	44,359	38,714	812
Perry	New Augusta	11,874	10,865	647
Pike	Magnolia	38,093	36,882	409
Pontotoc	Pontotoc	24,518	22,237	497

County	County seat or courthouse	1996 Pop.	1990 Pop.	Land area sq mi
Prentiss	Booneville	24,011	23,278	415
Quitman	Marks	9,888	10,490	405
Rankin	Brandon	102,414	87,161	775
Scott	Forest	25,194	24,137	609
Sharkey	Rolling Fork	6,814	7,066	428
Simpson	Mendenhall	25,221	23,953	589
Smith	Raleigh	15,069	14,798	636
Stone	Wiggins	12,670	10,750	445
Sunflower	Indianola	36,266	35,129	694
Tallahatchie	Charleston & Sumner	15,033	15,210	644
Tate	Senatobia	22,842	21,432	405
Tippah	Ripley	20,751	19,523	458
Tishomingo	Iuka	18,430	17,683	424
Tunica	Tunica	8,043	8,164	455
Union	New Albany	23,117	22,085	416
Walthall	Tylertown	14,414	14,352	404
Warren	Vicksburg	49,047	47,880	587
Washington	Greenville	66,115	67,935	724
Wayne	Waynesboro	20,003	19,517	810
Webster	Walthall	10,437	10,222	423
Wilkinson	Woodville	9,294	9,678	677
Winston	Louisville	19,442	19,433	607
Yalobusha	Coffeeville & Water Valley	12,212	12,033	467
Yazoo	Yazoo City	25,295	25,506	920

Missouri

(114 cos., 1 ind. city, 68,898 sq mi land; pop. 5,358,692)

County	County seat or courthouse	1996 Pop.	1990 Pop.	Land area sq mi
Adair	Kirksville	24,501	24,577	568
Andrew	Savannah	15,270	14,632	435
Atchison	Rockport	7,291	7,457	545
Audrain	Mexico	23,385	23,599	693
Barry	Cassville	32,325	27,547	779
Barton	Lamar	11,829	11,312	594
Bates	Butler	15,608	15,025	849
Benton	Warsaw	16,050	13,859	706
Bollinger	Marble Hill	11,361	10,619	621
Boone	Columbia	125,676	112,379	685
Buchanan	Saint Joseph	82,066	83,083	410
Butler	Poplar Buff	40,217	38,765	698
Caldwell	Kingston	8,589	8,380	429
Callaway	Fulton	36,036	32,809	839
Camden	Camdenton	32,552	27,495	655
Cape Girardeau	Jackson	65,719	61,633	579
Carroll	Carrollton	10,273	10,748	695
Carter	Van Buren	6,187	5,515	508
Cass	Harrisonville	75,665	63,808	699
Cedar	Stockton	13,012	12,093	476
Chariton	Keytesville	8,818	9,202	756
Christian	Ozark	44,871	32,644	563
Clark	Kahoka	7,499	7,547	507
Clay	Liberty	170,447	153,411	397
Clinton	Plattsburg	18,115	16,595	419
Cole	Jefferson City	68,185	63,579	392
Cooper	Boonville	15,947	14,835	565
Crawford	Steelville	21,754	19,173	743
Dade	Greenfield	7,919	7,449	490
Dallas	Buffalo	14,728	12,646	542
Daviess	Gallatin	7,814	7,865	567
De Kalb	Maysville	11,037	9,967	424
Dent	Salem	14,054	13,702	754
Douglas	Ava	12,235	11,876	815
Dunklin	Kennett	32,991	33,112	546
Franklin	Union	89,485	80,603	922
Gasconade	Hermann	14,615	14,006	520
Gentry	Albany	6,887	6,854	492
Greene	Springfield	223,873	207,949	675
Grundy	Trenton	10,238	10,536	436
Harrison	Bethany	8,317	8,469	725
Henry	Clinton	21,051	20,044	703
Hickory	Hermitage	8,493	7,335	399
Holt	Oregon	5,658	6,034	462
Howard	Fayette	9,708	9,631	466
Howell	West Plains	34,972	31,447	928
Iron	Ironton	10,931	10,726	551
Jackson	Kansas City	646,341	633,234	605
Jasper	Carthage	97,965	90,465	640
Jefferson	Hillsboro	188,863	171,380	657
Johnson	Warrensburg	46,491	42,514	831
Knox	Edina	4,309	4,482	506
Laclede	Lebanon	29,804	27,158	766
Lafayette	Lexington	32,259	31,107	629
Lawrence	Mount Vernon	32,396	30,236	613
Lewis	Monticello	10,121	10,233	505
Lincoln	Troy	34,119	28,892	631
Linn	Linneus	14,007	13,885	620
Livingston	Chillicothe	14,306	14,592	535
McDonald	Pineville	19,030	16,938	540
Macon	Macon	15,159	15,345	804
Madison	Fredericktown	11,379	11,127	497
Maries	Vienna	8,208	7,976	528
Marion	Palmyra	27,841	27,682	438
Mercer	Princeton	4,004	3,723	455

County	County seat or courthouse	1996 Pop.	1990 Pop.	Land area sq mi
Miller	Tuscumbia	22,321	20,700	592
Mississippi	Charleston	13,629	14,442	413
Moniteau	California	13,047	12,298	417
Monroe	Paris	8,872	9,104	646
Montgomery	Montgomery City	11,825	11,355	539
Morgan	Versailles	17,592	15,574	598
New Madrid	New Madrid	20,611	20,928	678
Newton	Neosho	47,751	44,445	627
Nodaway	Maryville	21,030	21,709	877
Oregon	Alton	10,095	9,470	792
Osage	Linn	12,396	12,018	606
Ozark	Gainesville	9,629	8,598	747
Pemiscot	Caruthersville	21,666	21,921	493
Perry	Perryville	17,433	16,648	475
Pettis	Sedalia	36,767	35,437	685
Phelps	Rolla	37,848	35,248	673
Pike	Bowling Green	16,169	15,969	673
Platte	Platte City	67,251	57,867	420
Polk	Bolivar	25,148	21,826	637
Pulaski	Waynesville	34,334	41,307	547
Putnam	Unionville	5,049	5,079	518
Ralls	New London	8,905	8,476	471
Randolph	Huntsville	23,793	24,370	482
Ray	Richmond	22,660	21,968	570
Reynolds	Centerville	6,699	6,661	811
Ripley	Doniphan	13,626	12,303	630
Saint Charles	Saint Charles	255,066	212,751	561
Saint Clair	Osceola	9,100	8,457	677
Sainte Genevieve	Sainte Genevieve	16,853	16,037	502
Saint Francois	Farmington	53,843	48,904	450
Saint Louis	Clayton	1,003,807	993,508	508
Saline	Marshall	22,922	23,523	756
Schuyler	Lancaster	4,376	4,236	308
Scotland	Memphis	4,800	4,822	439
Scott	Benton	40,241	39,376	421
Shannon	Eminence	7,976	7,613	1,004
Shelby	Shelbyville	6,845	6,942	501
Stoddard	Bloomfield	29,625	28,895	827
Stone	Galena	25,875	19,078	463
Sullivan	Milan	6,648	6,326	651
Taney	Forsyth	33,271	25,561	632
Texas	Houston	22,385	21,476	1,179
Vernon	Nevada	19,285	19,041	834
Warren	Warrenton	22,873	19,534	432
Washington	Potosi	22,315	20,380	760
Wayne	Greenville	12,842	11,543	761
Webster	Marshfield	27,601	23,753	593
Worth	Grant City	2,335	2,440	267
Wright	Hartville	19,241	16,758	682
Independent City				
Saint Louis		351,565	396,685	62

Montana

(56 counties, 145,556 sq mi land; pop. 879,372)

County	County seat or courthouse	1996 Pop.	1990 Pop.	Land area sq mi
Beaverhead	Dillon	9,144	8,424	5,543
Big Horn	Hardin	12,308	11,337	4,995
Blaine	Chinook	7,114	6,728	4,226
Broadwater	Townsend	4,012	3,318	1,192
Carbon	Red Lodge	9,248	8,080	2,048
Carter	Ekalaka	1,489	1,503	3,340
Cascade	Great Falls	81,087	77,691	2,698
Chouteau	Fort Benton	5,361	5,452	3,973
Custer	Miles City	12,285	11,697	3,783
Daniels	Scobey	2,136	2,266	1,426
Dawson	Glendive	9,085	9,505	2,373
Deer Lodge	Anaconda	10,093	10,356	737
Fallon	Baker	2,992	3,103	1,620
Fergus	Lewistown	12,697	12,083	4,339
Flathead	Kalispell	71,253	59,218	5,099
Gallatin	Bozeman	60,565	50,463	2,507
Garfield	Jordan	1,410	1,589	4,668
Glacier	Cut Bank	12,675	12,121	2,995
Golden Valley	Ryegete	984	912	1,175
Granite	Philipsburg	2,585	2,548	1,728
Hill	Havre	17,730	17,654	2,896
Jefferson	Boulder	9,668	7,939	1,657
Judith Basin	Stanford	2,278	2,282	1,870
Lake	Polson	24,921	21,041	1,494
Lewis & Clark	Helena	53,345	47,495	3,461
Liberty	Chester	2,311	2,295	1,430
Lincoln	Libby	18,833	17,481	3,613
McCone	Circle	2,055	2,276	2,643
Madison	Virginia City	6,773	5,989	3,587
Meagher	White Sulphur Springs	1,798	1,819	2,392
Mineral	Superior	3,719	3,315	1,220
Missoula	Missoula	88,523	78,007	2,598
Musselshell	Roundup	4,675	4,106	1,867
Park	Livingston	16,143	14,484	2,656
Petroleum	Winnett	533	519	1,654
Phillips	Malta	5,025	5,163	5,140
Pondera	Conrad	6,344	6,433	1,625
Powder River	Broadus	1,930	2,090	3,297
Powell	Deer Lodge	7,115	6,620	2,326
Prairie	Terry	1,392	1,383	1,737
Ravalli	Hamilton	33,586	25,010	2,394
Richland	Sidney	10,313	10,716	2,084
Roosevelt	Wolf Point	11,065	10,999	2,356
Rosebud	Forsyth	10,457	10,505	5,012
Sanders	Thompson Falls	10,140	8,669	2,762
Sheridan	Plentywood	4,363	4,732	1,677
Silver Bow	Butte	34,634	33,941	718
Stillwater	Columbus	7,653	6,536	1,795
Sweet Grass	Big Timber	3,437	3,154	1,855
Teton	Choteau	6,371	6,271	2,273
Toole	Shelby	4,918	5,046	1,911
Treasure	Hysham	866	874	979
Valley	Glasgow	8,363	8,239	4,921
Wheatland	Harlowton	2,420	2,246	1,423
Wibaux	Wibaux	1,146	1,191	889
Yellowstone	Billings	125,966	113,419	2,635
Yellowstone National Park[1]	NA	40	52	245

NA=Not applicable. (1) The area of Yellowstone National Park in Montana is not included in any county.

Nebraska

(93 counties, 76,878 sq mi land; pop. 1,652,093)

County	County seat or courthouse	1996 Pop.	1990 Pop.	Land area sq mi
Adams	Hastings	29,698	29,625	563
Antelope	Neligh	7,453	7,965	857
Arthur	Arthur	428	462	715
Banner	Harrisburg	859	852	746
Blaine	Brewster	651	675	711
Boone	Albion	6,536	6,667	687
Box Butte	Alliance	12,984	13,130	1,075
Boyd	Butte	2,746	2,835	540
Brown	Ainsworth	3,637	3,657	1,221
Buffalo	Kearney	40,037	37,447	968
Burt	Tekamah	7,944	7,868	493
Butler	David City	8,623	8,601	584
Cass	Plattsmouth	23,478	21,318	559
Cedar	Hartington	9,936	10,131	740
Chase	Imperial	4,265	4,381	895
Cherry	Valentine	6,433	6,307	5,961
Cheyenne	Sidney	9,690	9,494	1,196
Clay	Clay Center	7,209	7,123	573
Colfax	Schuyler	10,388	9,139	413
Cuming	West Point	10,126	10,117	572
Custer	Broken Bow	12,228	12,270	2,576
Dakota	Dakota City	18,528	16,742	264
Dawes	Chadron	9,086	9,021	1,396
Dawson	Lexington	23,126	19,940	1,013
Deuel	Chappell	2,068	2,237	440
Dixon	Ponca	6,337	6,143	476
Dodge	Fremont	35,022	34,500	535
Douglas	Omaha	438,835	416,444	331
Dundy	Benkelman	2,387	2,582	920
Fillmore	Geneva	6,871	7,103	577
Franklin	Franklin	3,868	3,938	576
Frontier	Stockville	3,220	3,101	975
Furnas	Beaver City	5,556	5,553	718
Gage	Beatrice	22,903	22,794	855
Garden	Oshkosh	2,242	2,460	1,705
Garfield	Burwell	2,081	2,141	570
Gosper	Elwood	2,256	1,928	458
Grant	Hyannis	749	769	776
Greeley	Greeley	2,969	3,006	570
Hall	Grand Island	51,485	48,925	546
Hamilton	Aurora	9,245	8,862	544
Harlan	Alma	3,755	3,810	553
Hayes	Hayes Center	1,136	1,222	713
Hitchcock	Trenton	3,401	3,750	710
Holt	O'Neill	12,163	12,599	2,413
Hooker	Mullen	707	793	721
Howard	Saint Paul	6,444	6,057	570
Jefferson	Fairbury	8,454	8,759	573
Johnson	Tecumseh	4,604	4,673	376
Kearney	Minden	6,648	6,629	516
Keith	Ogallala	8,643	8,584	1,061
Keya Paha	Springview	1,002	1,029	773
Kimball	Kimball	4,056	4,108	952
Knox	Center	9,387	9,564	1,108
Lancaster	Lincoln	231,765	213,641	839
Lincoln	North Platte	33,619	32,508	2,564
Logan	Stapleton	894	878	571
Loup	Taylor	698	683	570
McPherson	Tryon	565	546	859
Madison	Madison	34,702	32,655	573
Merrick	Central City	8,149	8,049	485
Morrill	Bridgeport	5,376	5,423	1,424
Nance	Fullerton	4,293	4,275	441
Nemaha	Auburn	7,878	7,980	409
Nuckolls	Nelson	5,376	5,786	575
Otoe	Nebraska City	14,515	14,252	616
Pawnee	Pawnee City	3,261	3,317	432

County	County seat or courthouse	1996 Pop.	1990 Pop.	Land area sq ml
Perkins	Grant	3,250	3,367	883
Phelps	Holdrege	9,995	9,715	540
Pierce	Pierce	7,945	7,827	574
Platte	Columbus	30,755	29,820	678
Polk	Osceola	5,581	5,668	439
Red Willow	McCook	11,448	11,705	717
Richardson	Falls City	9,689	9,937	554
Rock	Bassett	1,807	2,019	1,009
Saline	Wilber	12,988	12,715	575
Sarpy	Papillion	116,271	102,583	241
Saunders	Wahoo	19,135	18,285	754
Scotts Bluff	Gering	36,679	36,025	739
Seward	Seward	16,194	15,450	575
Sheridan	Rushville	6,645	6,750	2,441
Sherman	Loup City	3,574	3,718	566
Sioux	Harrison	1,509	1,549	2,067
Stanton	Stanton	6,195	6,244	430
Thayer	Hebron	6,418	6,635	575
Thomas	Thedford	824	851	713
Thurston	Pender	7,274	6,936	394
Valley	Ord	4,850	5,169	568
Washington	Blair	18,175	16,607	391
Wayne	Wayne	9,517	9,364	444
Webster	Red Cloud	4,037	4,279	575
Wheeler	Bartlett	957	948	575
York	York	14,707	14,428	576

Nevada

(16 counties, 1 ind. city, 109,806 sq mi land; pop. 1,603,163)

County	County seat or courthouse	1996 Pop.	1990 Pop.	Land area sq ml
Churchill	Fallon	21,792	17,938	4,929
Clark	Las Vegas	1,048,717	741,368	7,911
Douglas	Minden	35,745	27,637	710
Elko	Elko	43,567	33,463	17,182
Esmeralda	Goldfield	1,180	1,344	3,589
Eureka	Eureka	1,577	1,547	4,176
Humboldt	Winnemucca	16,453	12,844	9,648
Lander	Battle Mountain	6,815	6,266	5,494
Lincoln	Pioche	3,903	3,775	10,635
Lyon	Yerington	27,357	20,001	1,994
Mineral	Hawthorne	6,064	6,475	3,757
Nye	Tonopah	26,062	17,781	18,147
Pershing	Lovelock	4,708	4,336	6,009
Storey	Virginia City	2,917	2,526	264
Washoe	Reno	298,787	254,667	6,343
White Pine	Ely	10,282	9,264	8,877
Independent City				
Carson City	Carson City	47,237	40,443	144

New Hampshire

(10 counties, 8,969 sq mi land; pop. 1,162,481)

County	County seat or courthouse	1996 Pop.	1990 Pop.	Land area sq ml
Belknap	Laconia	51,466	49,216	401
Carroll	Ossipee	38,240	35,410	934
Cheshire	Keene	71,531	70,121	708
Coos	Lancaster	33,531	34,828	1,801
Grafton	Woodsville	78,329	74,929	1,714
Hillsborough	Nashua	354,196	335,838	877
Merrimack	Concord	125,085	120,240	935
Rockingham	Exeter	262,893	245,845	695
Strafford	Dover	107,344	104,233	369
Sullivan	Newport	39,866	38,592	537

New Jersey

(21 counties, 7,419 sq mi land; pop. 7,987,933)

County	County seat or courthouse	1996 Pop.	1990 Pop.	Land area sq ml
Atlantic	Mays Landing	235,447	224,327	561
Bergen	Hackensack	846,498	825,380	234
Burlington	Mount Holly	410,931	395,066	805
Camden	Camden	506,420	502,824	222
Cape May	Cape May Courthouse	98,252	95,089	255
Cumberland	Bridgeton	135,943	138,053	489
Essex	Newark	755,089	777,964	126
Gloucester	Woodbury	244,203	230,082	325
Hudson	Jersey City	550,789	553,099	47
Hunterdon	Flemington	118,737	107,802	430
Mercer	Trenton	330,226	325,824	226
Middlesex	New Brunswick	702,458	671,811	311
Monmouth	Freehold	591,182	553,093	472
Morris	Morristown	449,218	421,361	469
Ocean	Toms River	474,102	433,203	636
Passaic	Paterson	464,833	453,302	185
Salem	Salem	67,540	65,294	338
Somerset	Somerville	269,902	240,245	305
Sussex	Newton	141,308	130,943	521
Union	Elizabeth	497,281	493,819	103
Warren	Belvidere	97,574	91,607	358

New Mexico

(33 counties, 121,364 sq mi land; pop. 1,713,407)

County	County seat or courthouse	1996 Pop.	1990 Pop.	Land area sq ml
Bernalillo	Albuquerque	526,614	480,577	1,166
Catron	Reserve	2,657	2,563	6,928
Chaves	Roswell	62,564	57,849	6,071
Cibola	Grants	25,473	23,794	4,540
Colfax	Raton	13,867	12,925	3,757
Curry	Clovis	47,753	42,207	1,406
DeBaca	Fort Sumner	2,358	2,252	2,325
Dona Ana	Las Cruces	163,849	135,510	3,807
Eddy	Carlsbad	53,358	48,605	4,182
Grant	Silver City	30,700	27,676	3,966
Guadalupe	Santa Rosa	4,195	4,156	3,031
Harding	Mosquero	946	987	2,126
Hidalgo	Lordsburg	6,328	5,958	3,446
Lea	Lovington	56,634	55,765	4,393
Lincoln	Carrizozo	15,362	12,219	4,831
Los Alamos	Los Alamos	18,212	18,115	109
Luna	Deming	23,089	18,110	2,965
McKinley	Gallup	67,754	60,686	5,449
Mora	Mora	4,798	4,264	1,931
Otero	Alamogordo	55,881	51,928	6,627
Quay	Tucumcari	10,291	10,823	2,875
Rio Arriba	Tierra Amarilla	37,580	34,365	5,858
Roosevelt	Portales	18,700	16,702	2,449
Sandoval	Bernalillo	83,264	63,319	3,710
San Juan	Aztec	102,508	91,605	5,514
San Miguel	Las Vegas	28,703	25,743	4,717
Santa Fe	Santa Fe	119,011	98,928	1,909
Sierra	Truth or Consequences	10,953	9,912	4,181
Socorro	Socorro	16,155	14,764	6,647
Taos	Taos	25,985	23,118	2,203
Torrance	Estancia	13,584	10,285	3,345
Union	Clayton	4,067	4,124	3,830
Valencia	Los Lunas	60,214	45,235	1,068

New York

(62 counties, 47,224 sq mi land; pop. 18,184,774)

County	County seat or courthouse	1996 Pop.	1990 Pop.	Land area sq ml
Albany	Albany	296,087	292,793	524
Allegany	Belmont	51,282	50,470	1,030
Bronx[1]	Bronx	1,193,775	1,203,789	42
Broome	Binghamton	201,533	212,160	707
Cattaraugus	Little Valley	85,680	84,234	1,310
Cayuga	Auburn	82,062	82,313	693
Chautauqua	Mayville	140,800	141,895	1,062
Chemung	Elmira	93,282	95,195	408
Chenango	Norwich	52,121	51,768	894
Clinton	Plattsburgh	80,537	85,969	1,039
Columbia	Hudson	63,613	62,982	636
Cortland	Cortland	48,573	48,963	500
Delaware	Delhi	47,287	47,225	1,446
Dutchess	Poughkeepsie	262,675	259,462	802
Erie	Buffalo	954,021	968,584	1,045
Essex	Elizabethtown	37,789	37,152	1,797
Franklin	Malone	49,335	46,540	1,632
Fulton	Johnstown	53,965	54,191	496
Genesee	Batavia	61,206	60,060	494
Greene	Catskill	47,291	44,739	648
Hamilton	Lake Pleasant	5,232	5,279	1,721
Herkimer	Herkimer	65,968	65,809	1,412
Jefferson	Watertown	113,844	110,943	1,272
Kings[1]	Brooklyn	2,273,966	2,300,664	71
Lewis	Lowville	27,799	26,796	1,276
Livingston	Geneseo	65,898	62,372	632
Madison	Wampsville	71,508	69,166	656
Monroe	Rochester	721,996	713,968	659
Montgomery	Fonda	51,894	51,981	405
Nassau	Mineola	1,303,389	1,287,444	287
New York[1]	New York	1,533,774	1,487,536	28
Niagara	Lockport	221,219	220,756	523
Oneida	Utica	236,437	250,836	1,213
Onondaga	Syracuse	466,675	468,973	780
Ontario	Canandaigua	99,634	95,101	644
Orange	Goshen	324,422	307,647	816
Orleans	Albion	44,979	41,846	391
Oswego	Oswego	125,446	121,785	953
Otsego	Cooperstown	61,470	60,517	1,003
Putnam	Carmel	90,983	83,941	232
Queens[1]	Jamaica	1,980,643	1,951,598	109
Rensselaer	Troy	155,098	154,429	654
Richmond[1]	Saint George	398,748	378,977	59
Rockland	New City	278,136	265,475	174
Saint Lawrence	Canton	114,759	111,974	2,686
Saratoga	Ballston Spa	194,837	181,276	812
Schenectady	Schenectady	147,599	149,285	206
Schoharie	Schoharie	33,012	31,859	622
Schuyler	Watkins Glen	19,108	18,662	329
Seneca	Ovid & Waterloo	32,530	33,683	325
Steuben	Bath	99,201	99,088	1,393

County	County seat or courthouse	1996 Pop.	1990 Pop.	Land area sq mi
Suffolk	Riverhead	1,356,896	1,321,768	911
Sullivan	Monticello	70,346	69,277	970
Tioga	Owego	52,520	52,337	519
Tompkins	Ithaca	96,152	94,097	476
Ulster	Kingston	167,082	165,304	1,127
Warren	Lake George	61,490	59,209	870
Washington	Hudson Falls	60,777	59,330	836
Wayne	Lyons	94,324	89,123	604
Westchester	White Plains	893,412	874,866	433
Wyoming	Warsaw	44,357	42,507	593
Yates	Penn Yan	24,300	22,810	338

(1) New York City consists of 5 counties: Bronx, Kings (Brooklyn), New York (Manhattan), Queens, and Richmond (Staten Island).

North Carolina

(100 counties, 48,718 sq mi land; pop. 7,322,870)

County	County seat or courthouse	1996 Pop.	1990 Pop.	Land area sq mi
Alamance	Graham	116,514	108,213	431
Alexander	Taylorsville	30,192	27,544	260
Alleghany	Sparta	9,849	9,590	235
Anson	Wadesboro	24,302	23,474	532
Ashe	Jefferson	23,792	22,209	426
Avery	Newland	15,626	14,867	247
Beaufort	Washington	44,027	42,283	828
Bertie	Windsor	20,722	20,388	699
Bladen	Elizabethtown	30,330	28,663	875
Brunswick	Bolivia	63,225	50,985	855
Buncombe	Asheville	191,800	174,819	656
Burke	Morganton	80,986	75,740	507
Cabarrus	Concord	113,165	98,935	364
Caldwell	Lenoir	74,683	70,709	472
Camden	Camden	6,523	5,904	241
Carteret	Beaufort	58,773	52,553	531
Caswell	Yanceyville	21,585	20,693	426
Catawba	Newton	129,104	118,412	400
Chatham	Pittsboro	43,870	38,759	683
Cherokee	Murphy	21,934	20,170	455
Chowan	Edenton	14,099	13,506	173
Clay	Hayesville	8,132	7,155	215
Cleveland	Shelby	91,381	84,713	464
Columbus	Whiteville	51,975	49,587	937
Craven	New Bern	86,352	81,613	696
Cumberland	Fayetteville	284,800	274,713	653
Currituck	Currituck	16,766	13,736	262
Dare	Manteo	26,803	22,746	382
Davidson	Lexington	137,395	126,677	552
Davie	Mocksville	30,243	27,859	265
Duplin	Kenansville	42,802	39,995	818
Durham	Durham	197,352	181,855	291
Edgecombe	Tarboro	56,166	56,692	505
Forsyth	Winston-Salem	284,207	265,878	410
Franklin	Louisburg	42,872	36,414	492
Gaston	Gastonia	182,623	175,093	357
Gates	Gatesville	9,911	9,305	341
Graham	Robbinsville	7,616	7,196	292
Granville	Oxford	41,622	38,341	531
Greene	Snow Hill	17,660	15,384	265
Guilford	Greensboro	379,201	347,420	650
Halifax	Halifax	57,183	55,516	725
Harnett	Lillington	79,052	67,833	595
Haywood	Waynesville	50,387	46,942	554
Henderson	Hendersonville	77,940	69,285	374
Hertford	Winton	22,447	22,523	354
Hoke	Raeford	28,471	22,856	391
Hyde	Swan Quarter	5,413	5,411	613
Iredell	Statesville	106,383	92,935	574
Jackson	Sylva	29,668	26,846	491
Johnston	Smithfield	98,289	81,306	792
Jones	Trenton	9,501	9,414	473
Lee	Sanford	47,483	41,370	257
Lenoir	Kinston	59,355	57,274	400
Lincoln	Lincolnton	56,235	50,319	299
McDowell	Marion	38,057	35,681	442
Macon	Franklin	27,114	23,499	517
Madison	Marshall	18,242	16,953	449
Martin	Williamston	26,438	25,078	463
Mecklenburg	Charlotte	597,589	511,481	527
Mitchell	Bakersville	14,719	14,433	222
Montgomery	Troy	24,144	23,352	491
Moore	Carthage	68,483	59,000	699
Nash	Nashville	87,991	76,677	540
New Hanover	Wilmington	143,513	120,284	199
Northampton	Jackson	21,180	20,798	536
Onslow	Jacksonville	144,533	149,838	767
Orange	Hillsborough	108,795	93,851	400
Pamlico	Bayboro	12,188	11,368	337
Pasquotank	Elizabeth City	34,058	31,009	227
Pender	Burgaw	36,601	28,855	871
Perquimans	Hertford	10,913	10,447	247
Person	Roxboro	32,793	30,180	392
Pitt	Greenville	119,064	108,480	652
Polk	Columbus	16,226	14,416	238
Randolph	Asheboro	117,455	106,546	788
Richmond	Rockingham	45,665	44,518	474

County	County seat or courthouse	1996 Pop.	1990 Pop.	Land area sq mi
Robeson	Lumberton	113,169	105,170	949
Rockingham	Wentworth	89,575	86,064	567
Rowan	Salisbury	121,785	110,605	511
Rutherford	Rutherfordton	59,723	56,919	564
Sampson	Clinton	50,675	47,297	946
Scotland	Laurinburg	35,404	33,763	319
Stanly	Albemarle	54,850	51,765	395
Stokes	Danbury	42,062	37,223	452
Surry	Dobson	65,848	61,704	537
Swain	Bryson City	12,008	11,268	528
Transylvania	Brevard	27,499	25,520	378
Tyrrell	Columbia	3,820	3,856	390
Union	Monroe	102,372	84,210	637
Vance	Henderson	41,312	38,892	254
Wake	Raleigh	534,075	426,300	834
Warren	Warrenton	18,039	17,265	429
Washington	Plymouth	13,956	13,997	348
Watauga	Boone	40,357	36,952	313
Wayne	Goldsboro	111,581	104,666	553
Wilkes	Wilkesboro	61,884	59,393	757
Wilson	Wilson	67,809	66,061	371
Yadkin	Yadkinville	34,161	30,488	336
Yancey	Burnsville	16,380	15,419	312

North Dakota

(53 counties, 68,994 sq mi land; pop. 643,539)

County	County seat or courthouse	1996 Pop.	1990 Pop.	Land area sq mi
Adams	Hettinger	2,841	3,174	988
Barnes	Valley City	12,114	12,545	1,492
Benson	Minnewaukan	6,905	7,198	1,389
Billings	Medora	1,129	1,108	1,152
Bottineau	Bottineau	7,538	8,011	1,669
Bowman	Bowman	3,303	3,596	1,162
Burke	Bowbells	2,469	3,002	1,104
Burleigh	Bismarck	65,681	60,131	1,633
Cass	Fargo	113,343	102,874	1,766
Cavalier	Langdon	5,270	6,064	1,489
Dickey	Ellendale	5,676	6,107	1,131
Divide	Crosby	2,523	2,899	1,259
Dunn	Manning	3,751	4,005	2,010
Eddy	New Rockford	2,876	2,951	632
Emmons	Linton	4,443	4,830	1,510
Foster	Carrington	3,866	3,983	635
Golden Valley	Beach	1,932	2,108	1,002
Grand Forks	Grand Forks	71,450	70,683	1,438
Grant	Carson	3,114	3,549	1,660
Griggs	Cooperstown	2,984	3,303	709
Hettinger	Mott	2,982	3,445	1,132
Kidder	Steele	2,997	3,332	1,352
La Moure	La Moure	4,970	5,383	1,147
Logan	Napoleon	2,443	2,847	993
McHenry	Towner	6,161	6,528	1,874
McIntosh	Ashley	3,642	4,021	975
McKenzie	Watford City	5,851	6,383	2,742
McLean	Washburn	9,897	10,457	2,110
Mercer	Stanton	9,548	9,808	1,045
Morton	Mandan	24,422	23,700	1,926
Mountrail	Stanley	6,753	7,021	1,824
Nelson	Lakota	3,905	4,410	982
Oliver	Center	2,234	2,381	724
Pembina	Cavalier	8,741	9,238	1,119
Pierce	Rugby	4,718	5,052	1,018
Ramsey	Devils Lake	12,455	12,681	1,186
Ransom	Lisbon	5,794	5,921	863
Renville	Mohall	2,843	3,160	875
Richland	Wahpeton	18,162	18,148	1,437
Rolette	Rolla	14,029	12,772	903
Sargent	Forman	4,441	4,549	859
Sheridan	McClusky	1,859	2,148	972
Sioux	Fort Yates	4,095	3,761	1,094
Slope	Amidon	827	907	1,218
Stark	Dickinson	22,694	22,832	1,338
Steele	Finley	2,277	2,420	712
Stutsman	Jamestown	21,338	22,241	2,222
Towner	Cando	3,209	3,627	1,025
Traill	Hillsboro	8,706	8,752	862
Walsh	Grafton	12,799	13,840	1,282
Ward	Minot	59,734	57,921	2,013
Wells	Fessenden	5,271	5,864	1,271
Williams	Williston	20,534	21,129	2,071

Ohio

(88 counties, 40,953 sq mi land; pop. 11,172,782)

County	County seat or courthouse	1996 Pop.	1990 Pop.	Land area sq mi
Adams	West Union	28,093	25,371	584
Allen	Lima	108,440	109,755	405
Ashland	Ashland	51,372	47,507	424
Ashtabula	Jefferson	102,207	99,821	703
Athens	Athens	61,162	59,549	507
Auglaize	Wapakoneta	47,059	44,585	401

County	County seat or courthouse	1996 Pop.	1990 Pop.	Land area sq mi
Belmont	Saint Clairsville	70,022	71,074	537
Brown	Georgetown	39,358	34,966	492
Butler	Hamilton	323,579	291,479	467
Carroll	Carrollton	28,522	26,521	395
Champaign	Urbana	37,910	36,019	429
Clark	Springfield	147,472	147,548	400
Clermont	Batavia	169,670	150,167	452
Clinton	Wilmington	38,645	35,417	411
Columbiana	Lisbon	111,406	108,276	533
Coshocton	Coshocton	36,131	35,427	564
Crawford	Bucyrus	47,290	47,870	402
Cuyahoga	Cleveland	1,401,552	1,412,140	458
Darke	Greenville	54,259	53,619	600
Defiance	Defiance	40,059	39,350	411
Delaware	Delaware	83,245	66,929	443
Erie	Sandusky	78,913	76,779	255
Fairfield	Lancaster	119,182	103,472	506
Fayette	Washington Courthouse	28,395	27,466	407
Franklin	Columbus	1,013,724	961,437	540
Fulton	Wauseon	41,180	38,498	407
Gallia	Gallipolis	32,820	30,954	469
Geauga	Chardon	86,054	81,129	404
Greene	Xenia	139,936	136,731	415
Guernsey	Cambridge	40,509	39,024	522
Hamilton	Cincinnati	857,616	866,228	407
Hancock	Findlay	68,562	65,536	531
Hardin	Kenton	31,629	31,111	470
Harrison	Cadiz	16,001	16,085	404
Henry	Napoleon	29,901	29,108	417
Highland	Hillsboro	39,388	35,728	553
Hocking	Logan	28,413	25,533	423
Holmes	Millersburg	36,786	32,849	423
Huron	Norwalk	59,563	56,240	493
Jackson	Jackson	32,352	30,230	420
Jefferson	Steubenville	77,037	80,298	410
Knox	Mount Vernon	51,702	47,473	527
Lake	Painesville	223,301	215,499	228
Lawrence	Ironton	64,258	61,834	455
Licking	Newark	137,584	128,300	687
Logan	Bellefontaine	45,606	42,310	459
Lorain	Elyria	281,231	271,126	493
Lucas	Toledo	452,691	462,361	340
Madison	London	41,184	37,068	465
Mahoning	Youngstown	260,107	264,806	415
Marion	Marion	65,323	64,274	404
Medina	Medina	138,943	122,354	422
Meigs	Pomeroy	23,938	22,987	430
Mercer	Celina	40,890	39,443	463
Miami	Troy	96,941	93,182	407
Monroe	Woodsfield	15,268	15,497	456
Montgomery	Dayton	566,312	573,809	462
Morgan	McConnelsville	14,599	14,194	418
Morrow	Mount Gilead	30,481	27,749	406
Muskingum	Zanesville	84,349	82,068	665
Noble	Caldwell	12,134	11,336	399
Ottawa	Port Clinton	40,535	40,029	255
Paulding	Paulding	20,344	20,488	416
Perry	New Lexington	33,834	31,557	410
Pickaway	Circleville	52,727	48,244	502
Pike	Waverly	27,156	24,249	442
Portage	Ravenna	149,571	142,585	492
Preble	Eaton	42,633	40,113	425
Putnam	Ottawa	35,199	33,819	484
Richland	Mansfield	128,151	126,137	497
Ross	Chillicothe	74,407	69,330	689
Sandusky	Fremont	62,732	61,963	409
Scioto	Portsmouth	80,905	80,327	612
Seneca	Tiffin	60,368	59,733	551
Shelby	Sidney	46,837	44,915	409
Stark	Canton	374,406	367,585	576
Summit	Akron	530,571	514,990	413
Trumbull	Warren	227,069	227,813	616
Tuscarawas	New Philadelphia	87,803	84,090	568
Union	Marysville	37,396	31,969	437
Van Wert	Van Wert	30,426	30,464	410
Vinton	McArthur	12,068	11,098	414
Warren	Lebanon	134,791	113,927	400
Washington	Marietta	63,827	62,254	635
Wayne	Wooster	108,556	101,461	555
Williams	Bryan	37,950	36,956	422
Wood	Bowling Green	117,546	113,269	617
Wyandot	Upper Sandusky	22,718	22,254	406

Oklahoma

(77 counties, 68,679 sq mi land; pop. 3,300,902)

County	County seat or courthouse	1996 Pop.	1990 Pop.	Land area sq mi
Adair	Stillwell	19,914	18,421	576
Alfalfa	Cherokee	6,155	6,416	867
Atoka	Atoka	13,250	12,778	978
Beaver	Beaver	6,013	6,023	1,815
Beckham	Sayre	18,552	18,812	902
Blaine	Watonga	10,748	11,470	929
Bryan	Durant	33,920	32,089	909
Caddo	Anadarko	30,663	29,550	1,278
Canadian	El Reno	83,342	74,409	900
Carter	Ardmore	44,280	42,919	824
Cherokee	Tahlequah	37,879	34,049	751
Choctaw	Hugo	15,250	15,302	774
Cimarron	Boise City	3,087	3,301	1,835
Cleveland	Norman	194,687	174,253	536
Coal	Coalgate	6,162	5,780	518
Comanche	Lawton	111,171	111,486	1,069
Cotton	Walters	6,879	6,651	637
Craig	Vinita	14,440	14,104	761
Creek	Sapulpa	65,469	60,915	956
Custer	Arapaho	25,937	26,897	987
Delaware	Jay	33,141	28,070	741
Dewey	Taloga	5,112	5,551	1,000
Ellis	Arnett	4,185	4,497	1,229
Garfield	Enid	57,312	56,735	1,059
Garvin	Pauls Valley	26,733	26,605	809
Grady	Chickasha	44,896	41,747	1,101
Grant	Medford	5,546	5,689	1,001
Greer	Mangum	6,750	6,559	639
Harmon	Hollis	3,592	3,793	538
Harper	Buffalo	3,781	4,063	1,039
Haskell	Stigler	11,283	10,940	577
Hughes	Holdenville	13,077	13,014	807
Jackson	Altus	29,990	28,764	803
Jefferson	Waurika	6,724	7,010	759
Johnston	Tishomingo	10,458	10,032	645
Kay	Newkirk	47,285	48,056	919
Kingfisher	Kingfisher	13,471	13,212	903
Kiowa	Hobart	10,859	11,347	1,015
Latimer	Wilburton	10,235	10,333	722
Le Flore	Poteau	46,037	43,270	1,586
Lincoln	Chandler	30,945	29,216	959
Logan	Guthrie	30,940	29,011	745
Love	Marietta	8,637	7,788	515
McClain	Purcell	25,475	22,795	570
McCurtain	Idabel	34,754	33,433	1,852
McIntosh	Eufaula	18,556	16,779	620
Major	Fairview	7,758	8,055	957
Marshall	Madill	11,869	10,829	371
Mayes	Pryor	36,565	33,366	656
Murray	Sulphur	12,400	12,042	418
Muskogee	Muskogee	69,298	68,078	814
Noble	Perry	11,239	11,045	732
Nowata	Nowata	9,846	9,992	565
Okfuskee	Okemah	11,358	11,551	625
Oklahoma	Oklahoma City	630,531	599,611	709
Okmulgee	Okmulgee	37,821	36,490	697
Osage	Pawhuska	42,503	41,645	2,251
Ottawa	Miami	30,310	30,561	471
Pawnee	Pawnee	16,043	15,575	570
Payne	Stillwater	64,219	61,507	686
Pittsburg	McAlester	43,101	40,950	1,306
Pontotoc	Ada	34,822	34,119	720
Pottawatomie	Shawnee	61,682	58,760	788
Pushmataha	Antlers	11,586	10,997	1,397
Roger Mills	Cheyenne	3,721	4,147	1,142
Rogers	Claremore	63,536	55,170	675
Seminole	Wewoka	24,960	25,412	633
Sequoyah	Sallisaw	36,581	33,828	674
Stephens	Duncan	43,336	42,299	877
Texas	Guymon	17,322	16,419	2,037
Tillman	Frederick	9,634	10,384	872
Tulsa	Tulsa	531,596	503,341	570
Wagoner	Wagoner	53,389	47,883	563
Washington	Bartlesville	47,423	48,066	417
Washita	Cordell	11,698	11,441	1,004
Woods	Alva	8,516	9,103	1,287
Woodward	Woodward	18,667	18,976	1,242

Oregon

(36 counties, 96,002 sq mi land; pop. 3,203,735)

County	County seat or courthouse	1996 Pop.	1990 Pop.	Land area sq mi
Baker	Baker City	16,410	15,317	3,068
Benton	Corvallis	75,926	70,811	677
Clackamas	Oregon City	324,043	278,850	1,868
Clatsop	Astoria	35,132	33,301	827
Columbia	Saint Helens	42,969	37,557	657
Coos	Coquille	63,036	60,273	1,601
Crook	Prineville	16,615	14,111	2,980
Curry	Gold Beach	21,038	19,327	1,627
Deschutes	Bend	98,524	74,976	3,018
Douglas	Roseburg	101,076	94,649	5,037
Gilliam	Condon	1,948	1,717	1,204
Grant	Canyon City	7,973	7,853	4,529
Harney	Burns	7,075	7,060	10,135
Hood River	Hood River	19,338	16,903	522
Jackson	Medford	168,609	146,387	2,785
Jefferson	Madras	16,360	13,676	1,781
Josephine	Grants Pass	72,182	62,649	1,640

County	County seat or courthouse	1996 Pop.	1990 Pop.	Land area sq mi
Klamath	Klamath Falls	62,502	57,702	5,945
Lake	Lakeview	7,303	7,186	8,136
Lane	Eugene	306,862	282,912	4,554
Lincoln	Newport	45,041	38,889	980
Linn	Albany	102,217	91,227	2,291
Malheur	Vale	28,425	26,038	9,888
Marion	Salem	260,919	228,483	1,185
Morrow	Heppner	9,229	7,625	2,033
Multnomah	Portland	624,903	583,887	435
Polk	Dallas	58,501	49,541	741
Sherman	Moro	1,825	1,918	823
Tillamook	Tillamook	24,098	21,570	1,102
Umatilla	Pendleton	64,547	59,249	3,215
Union	La Grande	25,012	23,598	2,037
Wallowa	Enterprise	7,495	6,911	3,145
Wasco	The Dalles	23,093	21,683	2,381
Washington	Hillsboro	383,603	311,554	724
Wheeler	Fossil	1,658	1,396	1,715
Yamhill	McMinnville	78,248	65,551	716

Pennsylvania

(67 counties, 44,820 sq mi land; pop. 12,056,112)

County	County seat or courthouse	1996 Pop.	1990 Pop.	Land area sq mi
Adams	Gettysburg	84,921	78,274	520
Allegheny	Pittsburgh	1,296,037	1,336,449	730
Armstrong	Kittanning	73,872	73,478	654
Beaver	Beaver	187,009	186,093	435
Bedford	Bedford	49,322	47,919	1,015
Berks	Reading	352,353	336,523	859
Blair	Hollidaysburg	131,450	130,542	526
Bradford	Towanda	62,352	60,967	1,151
Bucks	Doylestown	578,715	541,174	608
Butler	Butler	167,732	152,013	789
Cambria	Ebensburg	158,500	163,062	688
Cameron	Emporium	5,745	5,913	397
Carbon	Jim Thorpe	58,783	56,846	383
Centre	Bellefonte	131,489	124,812	1,108
Chester	West Chester	410,744	376,396	756
Clarion	Clarion	42,205	41,699	603
Clearfield	Clearfield	79,640	78,097	1,147
Clinton	Lock Haven	37,130	37,182	891
Columbia	Bloomsburg	64,079	63,202	486
Crawford	Meadville	89,175	86,170	1,013
Cumberland	Carlisle	207,042	195,257	550
Dauphin	Harrisburg	246,807	237,813	525
Delaware	Media	547,592	547,651	184
Elk	Ridgway	35,141	34,878	829
Erie	Erie	280,570	275,572	802
Fayette	Uniontown	145,628	145,351	790
Forest	Tionesta	4,942	4,802	428
Franklin	Chambersburg	127,035	121,082	772
Fulton	McConnellsburg	14,435	13,837	438
Greene	Waynesburg	42,054	39,550	576
Huntingdon	Huntingdon	44,977	44,164	875
Indiana	Indiana	90,073	89,994	830
Jefferson	Brookville	46,624	46,083	656
Juniata	Mifflintown	21,793	20,625	392
Lackawanna	Scranton	213,323	219,097	459
Lancaster	Lancaster	450,834	422,822	949
Lawrence	New Castle	95,780	96,246	361
Lebanon	Lebanon	117,179	113,744	362
Lehigh	Allentown	297,802	291,130	347
Luzerne	Wilkes-Barre	321,309	328,149	891
Lycoming	Williamsport	119,083	118,710	1,235
McKean	Smethport	48,156	47,131	982
Mercer	Mercer	122,155	121,003	672
Mifflin	Lewistown	47,006	46,197	411
Monroe	Stroudsburg	119,581	95,709	607
Montgomery	Norristown	708,782	678,193	483
Montour	Danville	18,044	17,735	131
Northampton	Easton	257,719	247,105	374
Northumberland	Sunbury	95,897	96,771	460
Perry	New Bloomfield	43,727	41,172	554
Philadelphia	Philadelphia	1,478,002	1,585,577	135
Pike	Milford	38,139	27,966	547
Potter	Coudersport	17,103	16,717	1,081
Schuylkill	Pottsville	152,630	152,585	779
Snyder	Middleburg	38,034	36,680	331
Somerset	Somerset	80,517	78,218	1,075
Sullivan	Laporte	6,145	6,104	450
Susquehanna	Montrose	42,002	40,380	823
Tioga	Wellsboro	41,510	41,126	1,134
Union	Lewisburg	40,826	36,176	317
Venango	Franklin	58,820	59,381	675
Warren	Warren	44,624	45,049	884
Washington	Washington	206,708	204,584	857
Wayne	Honesdale	44,718	39,944	729
Westmoreland	Greensburg	376,297	370,321	1,023
Wyoming	Tunkhannock	29,362	28,076	397
York	York	368,332	339,574	905

Rhode Island

(5 counties, 1,045 sq mi land; pop. 990,225)

County	County seat or courthouse	1996 Pop.	1990 Pop.	Land area sq mi
Bristol	Bristol	49,213	48,859	25
Kent	East Greenwich	162,185	161,135	170
Newport	Newport	82,746	87,194	104
Providence	Providence	577,906	596,270	413
Washington	West Kingston	118,175	110,006	333

South Carolina

(46 counties, 30,111 sq mi land; pop. 3,698,746)

County	County seat or courthouse	1996 Pop.	1990 Pop.	Land area sq mi
Abbeville	Abbeville	24,275	23,862	508
Aiken	Aiken	133,130	120,991	1,073
Allendale	Allendale	11,471	11,722	408
Anderson	Anderson	156,558	145,177	718
Bamberg	Bamberg	16,702	16,902	393
Barnwell	Barnwell	21,640	20,293	549
Beaufort	Beaufort	102,735	86,425	587
Berkeley	Moncks Corner	132,502	128,776	1,100
Calhoun	Saint Matthews	13,724	12,753	380
Charleston	Charleston	277,721	295,041	917
Cherokee	Gaffney	48,003	44,506	393
Chester	Chester	33,488	32,170	581
Chesterfield	Chesterfield	39,794	38,575	799
Clarendon	Manning	29,406	28,450	607
Colleton	Walterboro	36,893	34,377	1,057
Darlington	Darlington	65,319	61,851	562
Dillon	Dillon	29,574	29,114	405
Dorchester	Saint George	84,920	83,060	575
Edgefield	Edgefield	19,051	18,360	502
Fairfield	Winnsboro	22,305	22,295	687
Florence	Florence	123,365	114,344	799
Georgetown	Georgetown	51,555	46,302	815
Greenville	Greenville	345,173	320,167	792
Greenwood	Greenwood	62,789	59,567	456
Hampton	Hampton	19,098	18,191	560
Horry	Conway	163,856	144,053	1,134
Jasper	Ridgeland	16,365	15,487	654
Kershaw	Camden	47,279	43,599	726
Lancaster	Lancaster	57,164	54,516	549
Laurens	Laurens	61,614	58,092	713
Lee	Bishopville	18,537	18,437	410
Lexington	Lexington	195,606	167,611	701
McCormick	McCormick	9,432	8,868	360
Marion	Marion	34,895	33,899	489
Marlboro	Bennettsville	29,770	29,716	480
Newberry	Newberry	34,268	33,172	631
Oconee	Walhalla	62,643	57,494	625
Orangeburg	Orangeburg	87,324	84,803	1,106
Pickens	Pickens	103,983	93,896	497
Richland	Columbia	292,601	286,321	757
Saluda	Saluda	16,843	16,357	451
Spartanburg	Spartanburg	242,962	226,793	811
Sumter	Sumter	107,161	101,276	666
Union	Union	30,709	30,337	514
Williamsburg	Kingstree	37,244	36,815	934
York	York	147,299	131,497	683

South Dakota

(66 counties, 75,896 sq mi land; pop. 732,405)

County	County seat or courthouse	1996 Pop.	1990 Pop.	Land area sq mi
Aurora	Plankinton	3,038	3,135	708
Beadle	Huron	18,149	18,253	1,259
Bennett	Martin	3,379	3,206	1,185
Bon Homme	Tyndall	7,032	7,089	563
Brookings	Brookings	26,394	25,207	795
Brown	Aberdeen	35,829	35,580	1,713
Brule	Chamberlain	5,541	5,485	819
Buffalo	Gannvalley	1,805	1,759	471
Butte	Belle Fourche	9,039	7,914	2,249
Campbell	Mound City	1,893	1,965	736
Charles Mix	Lake Andes	9,395	9,131	1,098
Clark	Clark	4,373	4,403	958
Clay	Vermillion	13,639	13,186	412
Codington	Watertown	25,099	22,698	688
Corson	McIntosh	4,269	4,195	2,473
Custer	Custer	6,828	6,179	1,558
Davison	Mitchell	17,769	17,503	436
Day	Webster	6,567	6,978	1,029
Deuel	Clear Lake	4,578	4,522	624
Dewey	Timber Lake	5,772	5,523	2,303
Douglas	Armour	3,577	3,746	434
Edmunds	Ipswich	4,334	4,050	1,146
Fall River	Hot Springs	7,164	7,353	1,740
Faulk	Faulkton	2,581	2,744	1,000
Grant	Milbank	8,054	8,372	683
Gregory	Burke	5,125	5,359	1,016
Haakon	Philip	2,514	2,624	1,813
Hamlin	Hayti	5,359	4,974	511

County	County seat or courthouse	1996 Pop.	1990 Pop.	Land area sq mi
Hand	Miller	4,143	4,272	1,437
Hanson	Alexandria	2,942	2,994	435
Harding	Buffalo	1,559	1,669	2,671
Hughes	Pierre	15,531	14,817	741
Hutchinson	Olivet	8,129	8,262	813
Hyde	Highmore	1,648	1,696	861
Jackson	Kadoka	2,909	2,811	1,869
Jerauld	Wessington Springs	2,310	2,425	530
Jones	Murdo	1,262	1,324	971
Kingsbury	De Smet	5,877	5,925	838
Lake	Madison	10,656	10,550	563
Lawrence	Deadwood	22,371	20,655	800
Lincoln	Canton	18,377	15,427	578
Lyman	Kennebec	3,849	3,638	1,640
McCook	Salem	5,808	5,688	575
McPherson	Leola	2,950	3,228	1,137
Marshall	Britton	4,699	4,844	839
Meade	Sturgis	22,592	21,878	3,471
Mellette	White River	2,023	2,137	1,307
Miner	Howard	3,014	3,272	570
Minnehaha	Sioux Falls	138,221	123,809	809
Moody	Flandreau	6,608	6,507	520
Pennington	Rapid City	87,145	81,343	2,776
Perkins	Bison	3,647	3,932	2,872
Potter	Gettysburg	2,983	3,190	867
Roberts	Sisseton	9,857	9,914	1,101
Sanborn	Woonsocket	2,759	2,833	569
Shannon	(Attached to Fall River)	11,837	9,902	2,094
Spink	Redfield	7,746	7,981	1,504
Stanley	Fort Pierre	2,961	2,453	1,443
Sully	Onida	1,593	1,589	1,007
Todd	(Attached to Tripp)	9,246	8,352	1,388
Tripp	Winner	6,861	6,924	1,614
Turner	Parker	8,630	8,576	617
Union	Elk Point	11,644	10,189	460
Walworth	Selby	5,784	6,087	708
Yankton	Yankton	20,848	19,252	522
Ziebach	Dupree	2,230	2,220	1,963

Tennessee
(95 counties, 41,219 sq mi land; pop. 5,319,654)

County	County seat or courthouse	1996 Pop.	1990 Pop.	Land area sq mi
Anderson	Clinton	71,587	68,250	338
Bedford	Shelbyville	33,856	30,411	474
Benton	Camden	16,014	14,524	395
Bledsoe	Pikeville	10,386	9,669	406
Blount	Maryville	99,010	85,969	559
Bradley	Cleveland	80,133	73,712	329
Campbell	Jacksboro	37,340	35,079	480
Cannon	Woodbury	11,722	10,467	266
Carroll	Huntingdon	28,836	27,514	599
Carter	Elizabethton	53,193	51,505	341
Cheatham	Ashland City	33,175	27,140	303
Chester	Henderson	14,099	12,819	289
Claiborne	Tazewell	28,828	26,137	434
Clay	Celina	7,323	7,238	236
Cocke	Newport	31,495	29,141	434
Coffee	Manchester	44,780	40,339	429
Crockett	Alamo	13,686	13,378	265
Cumberland	Crossville	42,048	34,736	682
Davidson	Nashville	535,036	510,786	502
Decatur	Decaturville	10,731	10,472	334
De Kalb	Smithville	15,474	14,360	305
Dickson	Charlotte	39,666	35,061	490
Dyer	Dyersburg	36,193	34,854	511
Fayette	Somerville	28,309	25,559	705
Fentress	Jamestown	15,714	14,669	499
Franklin	Winchester	36,850	34,725	553
Gibson	Trenton	47,657	46,315	603
Giles	Pulaski	28,430	25,741	611
Grainger	Rutledge	19,107	17,095	280
Greene	Greeneville	58,613	55,853	622
Grundy	Altamont	13,859	13,362	361
Hamblen	Morristown	53,321	50,480	161
Hamilton	Chattanooga	295,373	285,536	543
Hancock	Sneedville	6,879	6,739	222
Hardeman	Bolivar	24,228	23,377	668
Hardin	Savannah	24,566	22,633	578
Hawkins	Rogersville	48,388	44,565	487
Haywood	Brownsville	19,764	19,437	533
Henderson	Lexington	23,451	21,844	520
Henry	Paris	29,736	27,888	562
Hickman	Centerville	19,430	16,754	613
Houston	Erin	7,782	7,018	200
Humphreys	Waverly	16,675	15,813	532
Jackson	Gainesboro	9,409	9,297	309
Jefferson	Dandridge	40,268	33,016	274
Johnson	Mountain City	16,485	13,766	299
Knox	Knoxville	364,566	335,749	509
Lake	Tiptonville	8,331	7,129	163
Lauderdale	Ripley	23,972	23,491	471
Lawrence	Lawrenceburg	38,785	35,303	617
Lewis	Hohenwald	10,548	9,247	282
Lincoln	Fayetteville	28,756	28,157	570

County	County seat or courthouse	1996 Pop.	1990 Pop.	Land area sq mi
Loudon	Loudon	37,240	31,255	229
McMinn	Athens	45,706	42,383	430
McNairy	Selmer	23,679	22,422	560
Macon	Lafayette	17,373	15,906	307
Madison	Jackson	84,390	77,982	557
Marion	Jasper	26,533	24,860	500
Marshall	Lewisburg	25,173	21,539	375
Maury	Columbia	66,683	54,812	613
Meigs	Decatur	9,289	8,033	195
Monroe	Madisonville	33,289	30,541	635
Montgomery	Clarksville	120,923	100,498	539
Moore	Lynchburg	5,241	4,721	129
Morgan	Wartburg	18,280	17,300	522
Obion	Union City	32,053	31,717	545
Overton	Livingston	18,654	17,636	433
Perry	Linden	7,217	6,612	415
Pickett	Byrdstown	4,633	4,548	163
Polk	Benton	14,421	13,643	435
Putnam	Cookeville	57,928	51,373	401
Rhea	Dayton	27,214	24,344	316
Roane	Kingston	49,859	47,227	361
Robertson	Springfield	49,672	41,492	477
Rutherford	Murfreesboro	154,333	118,570	619
Scott	Huntsville	19,575	18,358	532
Sequatchie	Dunlap	9,994	8,863	266
Sevier	Sevierville	61,335	51,043	592
Shelby	Memphis	867,409	826,330	755
Smith	Carthage	15,663	14,143	314
Stewart	Dover	11,009	9,479	458
Sullivan	Blountville	149,844	143,596	413
Sumner	Gallatin	119,675	103,281	529
Tipton	Covington	45,006	37,568	459
Trousdale	Hartsville	6,588	5,920	114
Unicoi	Erwin	17,135	16,549	186
Union	Maynardville	15,539	13,694	224
Van Buren	Spencer	5,046	4,846	274
Warren	McMinnville	35,556	32,992	433
Washington	Jonesboro	100,265	92,315	326
Wayne	Waynesboro	16,308	13,935	734
Weakley	Dresden	32,568	31,972	580
White	Sparta	21,872	20,090	377
Williamson	Franklin	106,119	81,021	583
Wilson	Lebanon	79,502	67,675	571

Texas
(254 counties, 261,914 sq mi land; pop. 19,128,261)

County	County seat or courthouse	1996 Pop.	1990 Pop.	Land area sq mi
Anderson	Palestine	52,174	48,024	1,071
Andrews	Andrews	14,087	14,338	1,501
Angelina	Lufkin	76,069	69,884	802
Aransas	Rockport	21,803	17,892	252
Archer	Archer City	8,247	7,973	910
Armstrong	Claude	2,162	2,021	914
Atascosa	Jourdanton	35,044	30,533	1,232
Austin	Bellville	22,768	19,832	653
Bailey	Muleshoe	6,789	7,064	827
Bandera	Bandera	14,287	10,562	792
Bastrop	Bastrop	46,819	38,263	889
Baylor	Seymour	4,153	4,385	871
Bee	Beeville	27,833	25,135	880
Bell	Belton	222,450	191,073	1,059
Bexar	San Antonio	1,318,322	1,185,394	1,247
Blanco	Johnson City	7,774	5,972	711
Borden	Gail	807	799	899
Bosque	Meridian	16,756	15,125	989
Bowie	Boston	84,969	81,665	888
Brazoria	Angleton	220,854	191,707	1,387
Brazos	Bryan	131,904	121,862	586
Brewster	Alpine	9,221	8,653	6,193
Briscoe	Silverton	1,917	1,971	900
Brooks	Falfurrias	8,493	8,204	943
Brown	Brownwood	36,746	34,371	944
Burleson	Caldwell	15,288	13,625	666
Burnet	Burnet	29,753	22,677	995
Caldwell	Lockhart	30,514	26,392	546
Calhoun	Port Lavaca	20,711	19,053	512
Callahan	Baird	12,580	11,859	899
Cameron	Brownsville	315,015	260,120	906
Camp	Pittsburg	10,913	9,904	198
Carson	Panhandle	6,714	6,576	923
Cass	Linden	30,621	29,982	938
Castro	Dimmitt	8,535	9,070	898
Chambers	Anahuac	22,789	20,088	599
Cherokee	Rusk	42,484	41,049	1,052
Childress	Childress	7,580	5,953	710
Clay	Henrietta	10,450	10,024	1,098
Cochran	Morton	4,083	4,377	775
Coke	Robert Lee	3,437	3,424	899
Coleman	Coleman	9,700	9,710	1,273
Collin	McKinney	372,445	264,036	848
Collingsworth	Wellington	3,269	3,573	919
Colorado	Columbus	18,757	18,383	963
Comal	New Braunfels	67,687	51,832	562
Comanche	Comanche	13,645	13,381	938
Concho	Paint Rock	3,186	3,044	992

County	County seat or courthouse	1996 Pop.	1990 Pop.	Land area sq mi	County	County seat or courthouse	1996 Pop.	1990 Pop.	Land area sq mi
Cooke	Gainesville	32,254	30,777	874	Liberty	Liberty	63,294	52,726	1,160
Coryell	Gatesville	74,446	64,226	1,052	Limestone	Groesbeck	20,829	20,946	909
Cottle	Paducah	1,975	2,247	901	Lipscomb	Lipscomb	3,081	3,143	932
Crane	Crane	4,514	4,652	786	Live Oak	George West	10,195	9,556	1,036
Crockett	Ozona	4,372	4,078	2,808	Llano	Llano	12,861	11,631	935
Crosby	Crosbyton	7,349	7,304	900	Loving	Mentone	141	107	673
Culberson	Van Horn	3,210	3,407	3,813	Lubbock	Lubbock	232,035	222,636	900
Dallam	Dalhart	6,269	5,461	1,505	Lynn	Tahoka	6,588	6,758	892
Dallas	Dallas	2,000,192	1,852,810	880	McCulloch	Brady	8,694	8,778	1,069
Dawson	Lamesa	15,172	14,349	902	McLennan	Waco	201,775	189,123	1,042
Deaf Smith	Hereford	19,519	19,153	1,497	McMullen	Tilden	799	817	1,113
Delta	Cooper	4,923	4,857	277	Madison	Madisonville	11,984	10,931	470
Denton	Denton	348,453	273,525	889	Marion	Jefferson	10,430	9,984	381
DeWitt	Cuero	19,657	18,840	909	Martin	Stanton	4,957	4,956	915
Dickens	Dickens	2,317	2,571	904	Mason	Mason	3,598	3,423	932
Dimmit	Carrizo Springs	10,475	10,433	1,331	Matagorda	Bay City	38,192	36,928	1,115
Donley	Clarendon	3,863	3,696	930	Maverick	Eagle Pass	46,563	36,378	1,280
Duval	San Diego	13,383	12,918	1,793	Medina	Hondo	35,363	27,312	1,328
Eastland	Eastland	18,064	18,488	926	Menard	Menard	2,361	2,252	902
Ector	Odessa	123,398	118,934	901	Midland	Midland	116,016	106,611	900
Edwards	Rocksprings	3,374	2,266	2,120	Milam	Cameron	23,972	22,946	1,017
Ellis	Waxahachie	97,054	85,167	940	Mills	Goldthwaite	4,767	4,531	748
El Paso	El Paso	684,446	591,610	1,013	Mitchell	Colorado City	9,002	8,016	910
Erath	Stephenville	30,815	27,991	1,086	Montague	Montague	18,030	17,274	931
Falls	Marlin	17,727	17,712	769	Montgomery	Conroe	245,845	182,201	1,044
Fannin	Bonham	27,614	24,804	892	Moore	Dumas	19,427	17,865	900
Fayette	La Grange	21,185	20,095	950	Morris	Daingerfield	13,262	13,200	255
Fisher	Roby	4,449	4,842	901	Motley	Matador	1,330	1,532	989
Floyd	Floydada	8,334	8,497	992	Nacogdoches	Nacogdoches	56,533	54,753	947
Foard	Crowell	1,719	1,794	707	Navarro	Corsicana	41,290	39,926	1,071
Fort Bend	Richmond	306,832	225,421	875	Newton	Newton	14,259	13,569	933
Franklin	Mount Vernon	9,320	7,802	286	Nolan	Sweetwater	16,370	16,594	912
Freestone	Fairfield	17,476	15,818	885	Nueces	Corpus Christi	315,722	291,145	836
Frio	Pearsall	15,824	13,472	1,133	Ochiltree	Perryton	8,791	9,128	918
Gaines	Seminole	14,719	14,123	1,502	Oldham	Vega	2,270	2,278	1,501
Galveston	Galveston	240,653	217,396	399	Orange	Orange	84,488	80,509	356
Garza	Post	4,729	5,143	896	Palo Pinto	Palo Pinto	25,463	25,055	953
Gillespie	Fredericksburg	19,635	17,204	1,061	Panola	Carthage	22,899	22,035	801
Glasscock	Garden City	1,407	1,447	901	Parker	Weatherford	76,073	64,785	904
Goliad	Goliad	6,586	5,980	854	Parmer	Farwell	10,403	9,863	882
Gonzales	Gonzales	17,608	17,205	1,068	Pecos	Fort Stockton	16,349	14,675	4,764
Gray	Pampa	23,335	23,967	928	Polk	Livingston	44,906	30,687	1,057
Grayson	Sherman	100,589	95,019	934	Potter	Amarillo	108,636	97,841	909
Gregg	Longview	112,138	104,948	274	Presidio	Marfa	7,966	6,637	3,856
Grimes	Anderson	22,192	18,828	794	Rains	Emory	7,869	6,715	232
Guadalupe	Seguin	75,235	64,873	711	Randall	Canyon	97,379	89,673	915
Hale	Plainview	36,548	34,671	1,005	Reagan	Big Lake	4,254	4,514	1,175
Hall	Memphis	3,750	3,905	903	Real	Leakey	2,724	2,412	700
Hamilton	Hamilton	7,570	7,733	836	Red River	Clarksville	13,959	14,317	1,050
Hansford	Spearman	5,372	5,848	920	Reeves	Pecos	14,993	15,852	2,636
Hardeman	Quanah	4,808	5,283	695	Refugio	Refugio	7,903	7,976	770
Hardin	Kountze	47,544	41,320	894	Roberts	Miami	988	1,025	924
Harris	Houston	3,126,966	2,818,101	1,729	Robertson	Franklin	15,522	15,511	855
Harrison	Marshall	59,685	57,483	899	Rockwall	Rockwall	34,153	25,604	129
Hartley	Channing	5,210	3,634	1,462	Runnels	Ballinger	11,410	11,294	1,055
Haskell	Haskell	6,247	6,820	903	Rusk	Henderson	45,596	43,735	924
Hays	San Marcos	81,744	65,614	678	Sabine	Hemphill	10,443	9,586	490
Hemphill	Canadian	3,648	3,720	910	San Augustine	San Augustine	8,051	7,999	528
Henderson	Athens	65,664	58,543	874	San Jacinto	Coldspring	19,957	16,372	571
Hidalgo	Edinburg	495,594	383,545	1,569	San Patricio	Sinton	68,334	58,749	692
Hill	Hillsboro	29,698	27,146	962	San Saba	San Saba	6,024	5,401	1,135
Hockley	Levelland	23,931	24,199	908	Schleicher	Eldorado	3,088	2,990	1,311
Hood	Granbury	34,976	28,981	422	Scurry	Snyder	18,248	18,634	903
Hopkins	Sulphur Springs	30,455	28,833	785	Shackelford	Albany	3,296	3,316	914
Houston	Crockett	21,962	21,375	1,231	Shelby	Center	22,677	22,034	794
Howard	Big Spring	32,836	32,343	903	Sherman	Stratford	2,818	2,858	923
Hudspeth	Sierra Blanca	3,265	2,915	4,571	Smith	Tyler	165,002	151,309	929
Hunt	Greenville	67,906	64,343	841	Somervell	Glen Rose	5,986	5,360	187
Hutchinson	Stinnett	24,425	25,689	887	Starr	Rio Grande City	53,974	40,518	1,223
Irion	Mertzon	1,718	1,629	1,052	Stephens	Breckenridge	9,798	9,010	895
Jack	Jacksboro	7,285	6,981	917	Sterling	Sterling City	1,411	1,438	923
Jackson	Edna	13,687	13,039	830	Stonewall	Aspermont	1,813	2,013	919
Jasper	Jasper	32,954	31,102	938	Sutton	Sonora	4,449	4,135	1,454
Jeff Davis	Fort Davis	2,155	1,946	2,265	Swisher	Tulia	8,495	8,133	901
Jefferson	Beaumont	243,733	239,389	904	Tarrant	Fort Worth	1,305,185	1,170,103	864
Jim Hogg	Hebbronville	5,036	5,109	1,136	Taylor	Abilene	122,130	119,655	916
Jim Wells	Alice	39,725	37,679	865	Terrell	Sanderson	1,237	1,410	2,358
Johnson	Cleburne	110,344	97,165	729	Terry	Brownfield	13,093	13,218	890
Jones	Anson	18,692	16,490	931	Throckmorton	Throckmorton	1,797	1,880	912
Karnes	Karnes City	12,567	12,455	750	Titus	Mount Pleasant	24,909	24,009	411
Kaufman	Kaufman	62,116	52,220	786	Tom Green	San Angelo	102,580	98,458	1,522
Kendall	Boerne	19,639	14,589	663	Travis	Austin	683,967	576,407	989
Kenedy	Sarita	438	460	1,457	Trinity	Groveton	12,454	11,445	693
Kent	Jayton	864	1,010	902	Tyler	Woodville	20,283	16,646	923
Kerr	Kerrville	41,406	36,304	1,106	Upshur	Gilmer	34,909	31,370	588
Kimble	Junction	4,215	4,122	1,251	Upton	Rankin	3,816	4,447	1,242
King	Guthrie	336	354	912	Uvalde	Uvalde	25,343	23,340	1,557
Kinney	Brackettville	3,402	3,119	1,364	Val Verde	Del Rio	43,131	38,721	3,171
Kleberg	Kingsville	30,325	30,274	871	Van Zandt	Canton	42,579	37,944	849
Knox	Benjamin	4,413	1,007	954	Victoria	Victoria	81,541	74,361	883
Lamar	Paris	45,255	43,949	917	Walker	Huntsville	54,417	50,017	799
Lamb	Littlefield	14,989	15,072	1,016	Waller	Hempstead	26,195	23,389	514
Lampasas	Lampasas	17,163	13,521	712	Ward	Monahans	11,994	13,115	836
La Salle	Cotulla	6,063	5,254	1,489	Washington	Brenham	28,610	26,154	609
Lavaca	Hallettsville	18,872	18,690	970	Webb	Laredo	176,792	133,239	3,357
Lee	Giddings	14,442	12,854	629	Wharton	Wharton	40,224	39,955	1,090
Leon	Centerville	14,190	12,665	1,072	Wheeler	Wheeler	5,344	5,879	914

County	County seat or courthouse	1996 Pop.	1990 Pop.	Land area sq mi
Wichita	Wichita Falls	128,064	122,378	628
Wilbarger	Vernon	14,308	15,121	971
Willacy	Raymondville	19,419	17,705	597
Williamson	Georgetown	198,286	139,551	1,124
Wilson	Floresville	28,867	22,650	807
Winkler	Kermit	8,043	8,626	841
Wise	Decatur	40,451	34,679	905
Wood	Quitman	33,321	29,380	650
Yoakum	Plains	8,325	8,786	800
Young	Graham	17,528	18,126	922
Zapata	Zapata	11,100	9,279	997
Zavala	Crystal City	12,322	12,162	1,299

Utah

(29 counties, 82,168 sq mi land; pop. 2,000,494)

County	County seat or courthouse	1996 Pop.	1990 Pop.	Land area sq mi
Beaver	Beaver	5,591	4,765	2,590
Box Elder	Brigham City	39,177	36,485	5,724
Cache	Logan	83,710	70,183	1,165
Carbon	Price	20,437	20,228	1,479
Daggett	Manila	752	690	698
Davis	Farmington	214,990	187,941	305
Duchesne	Duchesne	13,778	12,645	3,238
Emery	Castle Dale	10,402	10,332	4,452
Garfield	Panguitch	4,076	3,980	5,175
Grand	Moab	7,826	6,620	3,682
Iron	Parowan	26,875	20,789	3,299
Juab	Nephi	6,845	5,817	3,392
Kane	Kanab	5,751	5,169	3,992
Millard	Fillmore	12,019	11,333	6,590
Morgan	Morgan	6,660	5,528	609
Piute	Junction	1,404	1,277	758
Rich	Randolph	1,799	1,725	1,029
Salt Lake	Salt Lake City	827,818	725,956	737
San Juan	Monticello	13,221	12,621	7,821
Sanpete	Manti	19,883	16,259	1,588
Sevier	Richfield	17,156	15,431	1,910
Summit	Coalville	23,988	15,518	1,871
Tooele	Tooele	29,558	26,601	6,946
Uintah	Vernal	24,472	22,211	4,477
Utah	Provo	319,694	263,590	1,998
Wasatch	Heber City	12,046	10,089	1,181
Washington	Saint George	73,161	48,560	2,427
Wayne	Loa	2,371	2,177	2,461
Weber	Ogden	175,034	158,330	576

Vermont

(14 counties, 9,249 sq mi land; pop. 588,654)

County	County seat or courthouse	1996 Pop.	1990 Pop.	Land area sq mi
Addison	Middlebury	35,079	32,953	770
Bennington	Bennington	36,357	35,845	676
Caledonia	Saint Johnsbury	28,800	27,846	651
Chittenden	Burlington	141,115	131,761	539
Essex	Guildhall	6,511	6,405	665
Franklin	Saint Albans	43,465	39,980	637
Grand Isle	North Hero	5,968	5,318	83
Lamoille	Hyde Park	21,373	19,735	461
Orange	Chelsea	27,562	26,149	689
Orleans	Newport	25,117	24,053	697
Rutland	Rutland	62,757	62,142	932
Washington	Montpelier	56,437	54,928	690
Windham	Newfane	42,923	41,588	789
Windsor	Woodstock	55,190	54,055	971

Virginia

(95 cos., 40 ind. cities, 39,598 sq mi land; pop. 6,675,451)

County	County seat or courthouse	1996 Pop.	1990 Pop.	Land area sq mi
Accomack	Accomac	32,065	31,703	455
Albemarle	Charlottesville	74,189	68,172	723
Alleghany	Covington	12,586	12,969	446
Amelia	Amelia Courthouse	9,912	8,787	357
Amherst	Amherst	30,065	28,578	475
Appomattox	Appomattox	12,879	12,298	334
Arlington	Arlington	175,334	170,897	26
Augusta	Staunton	59,515	54,677	972
Bath	Warm Springs	4,959	4,799	532
Bedford	Bedford	52,768	45,552	755
Bland	Bland	6,834	6,514	359
Botetourt	Fincastle	27,813	24,992	543
Brunswick	Lawrenceville	16,458	15,987	566
Buchanan	Grundy	30,033	31,333	504
Buckingham	Buckingham	14,388	12,873	581
Campbell	Rustburg	48,946	47,572	505
Caroline	Bowling Green	21,399	19,217	533
Carroll	Hillsville	27,703	26,565	477
Charles City	Charles City	6,887	6,282	183
Charlotte	Charlotte Courthouse	12,218	11,688	475
Chesterfield	Chesterfield	242,686	209,564	426
Clarke	Berryville	12,543	12,101	177

County	County seat or courthouse	1996 Pop.	1990 Pop.	Land area sq mi
Craig	New Castle	4,839	4,372	330
Culpeper	Culpeper	31,981	27,791	381
Cumberland	Cumberland	7,845	7,825	299
Dickenson	Clintwood	17,381	17,620	333
Dinwiddie	Dinwiddie	22,961	22,319	504
Essex	Tappahannock	9,373	8,689	258
Fairfax	Fairfax	902,492	818,358	396
Fauquier	Warrenton	51,765	48,860	650
Floyd	Floyd	12,832	11,965	382
Fluvanna	Palmyra	16,887	12,429	287
Franklin	Rocky Mount	43,574	39,549	692
Frederick	Winchester	52,459	45,723	415
Giles	Pearisburg	16,349	16,366	358
Gloucester	Gloucester	33,659	30,131	217
Goochland	Goochland	16,586	14,163	285
Grayson	Independence	16,420	16,278	443
Greene	Stanardsville	12,972	10,297	157
Greensville	Emporia	10,954	8,630	296
Halifax	Halifax	37,581	36,030	820
Hanover	Hanover	76,781	63,306	473
Henrico	Henrico	232,810	217,849	238
Henry	Martinsville	56,326	56,942	382
Highland	Monterey	2,543	2,635	416
Isle of Wight	Isle of Wight	28,391	25,053	316
James City	Williamsburg	41,370	34,970	143
King and Queen	King and Queen Courthouse	6,390	6,289	316
King George	King George	16,379	13,527	180
King William	King William	12,333	10,913	275
Lancaster	Lancaster	11,418	10,896	133
Lee	Jonesville	24,257	24,496	437
Loudoun	Leesburg	123,333	86,129	520
Louisa	Louisa	23,321	20,325	498
Lunenburg	Lunenburg	11,104	11,419	432
Madison	Madison	12,405	11,949	322
Mathews	Mathews	8,967	8,348	86
Mecklenburg	Boydton	30,946	29,241	624
Middlesex	Saluda	9,396	8,653	130
Montgomery	Christiansburg	75,443	73,913	388
Nelson	Lovingston	13,529	12,778	472
New Kent	New Kent	12,047	10,445	210
Northampton	Eastville	12,908	13,061	207
Northumberland	Heathsville	11,226	10,524	192
Nottoway	Nottoway	15,230	14,993	315
Orange	Orange	24,512	21,421	342
Page	Luray	22,891	21,690	311
Patrick	Stuart	18,075	17,473	483
Pittsylvania	Chatham	55,774	55,672	971
Powhatan	Powhatan	19,794	15,328	261
Prince Edward	Farmville	18,751	17,320	353
Prince George	Prince George	28,401	27,394	266
Prince William	Manassas	249,278	215,677	338
Pulaski	Pulaski	34,290	34,496	321
Rappahannock	Washington	7,206	6,622	267
Richmond	Warsaw	8,496	7,273	192
Roanoke	Salem	81,585	79,294	251
Rockbridge	Lexington	19,006	18,350	600
Rockingham	Harrisonburg	62,432	57,482	851
Russell	Lebanon	29,134	28,667	475
Scott	Gate City	22,949	23,204	537
Shenandoah	Woodstock	33,612	31,636	512
Smyth	Marion	33,076	32,370	452
Southampton	Courtland	17,682	17,550	600
Spotsylvania	Spotsylvania	74,106	57,403	401
Stafford	Stafford	82,488	61,236	270
Surry	Surry	6,406	6,145	279
Sussex	Sussex	10,088	10,248	491
Tazewell	Tazewell	47,070	45,960	520
Warren	Front Royal	29,879	26,142	214
Washington	Abingdon	48,498	45,887	564
Westmoreland	Montross	16,549	15,480	229
Wise	Wise	39,494	39,573	403
Wythe	Wytheville	26,357	25,471	463
York	Yorktown	55,010	42,434	106
Independent Cities				
Alexandria		117,586	111,182	15
Bedford		6,530	6,177	7
Bristol		17,957	18,426	12
Buena Vista		6,368	6,406	7
Charlottesville		40,767	40,475	10
Chesapeake		192,342	151,982	341
Clifton Forge		4,457	4,679	3
Colonial Heights		17,154	16,064	8
Covington		6,781	7,198	4
Danville		53,472	53,056	43
Emporia		5,831	5,479	7
Fairfax		20,990	19,894	6
Falls Church		9,781	9,522	2
Franklin		8,586	7,864	8
Fredericksburg		22,586	19,027	11
Galax		6,649	6,699	8
Hampton		138,757	133,811	52
Harrisonburg		33,446	30,707	18
Hopewell		22,566	23,101	10
Lexington		7,164	6,959	3
Lynchburg		67,250	66,049	49

Independent Cities

County	County seat or courthouse	1996 Pop.	1990 Pop.	Land area sq mi
Manassas		33,200	27,957	10
Manassas Park		7,541	6,734	2
Martinsville		15,850	16,162	11
Newport News		176,122	171,439	68
Norfolk		233,430	261,250	54
Norton		4,288	4,247	7
Petersburg		38,234	37,027	23
Poquoson		11,922	11,005	16
Portsmouth		101,308	103,910	33
Radford		16,145	15,940	10
Richmond		198,267	202,798	60
Roanoke		95,548	96,509	43
Salem		24,159	23,797	15
Staunton		24,800	24,461	20
Suffolk		58,901	52,143	400
Virginia Beach		430,385	393,089	248
Waynesboro		18,928	18,549	14
Williamsburg		12,922	11,409	9
Winchester		23,649	21,947	9

Washington

(39 counties, 66,581 sq mi land; pop. 5,532,939)

County	County seat or courthouse	1996 Pop.	1990 Pop.	Land area sq mi
Adams	Ritzville	15,254	13,603	1,925
Asotin	Asotin	20,761	17,605	636
Benton	Prosser	134,359	112,560	1,703
Chelan	Wenatchee	59,532	52,250	2,922
Clallam	Port Angeles	63,419	56,210	1,745
Clark	Vancouver	305,171	238,053	628
Columbia	Dayton	4,265	4,024	869
Cowlitz	Kelso	89,984	82,119	1,139
Douglas	Waterville	32,689	26,205	1,821
Ferry	Republic	7,195	6,295	2,204
Franklin	Pasco	45,590	37,473	1,242
Garfield	Pomeroy	2,306	2,248	711
Grant	Ephrata	67,597	54,798	2,676
Grays Harbor	Montesano	67,923	64,175	1,917
Island	Coupeville	69,194	60,195	209
Jefferson	Port Townsend	25,477	20,406	1,809
King	Seattle	1,619,411	1,507,305	2,126
Kitsap	Port Orchard	231,741	189,731	396
Kittitas	Ellensburg	30,846	26,725	2,297
Klickitat	Goldendale	18,526	16,616	1,873
Lewis	Chehalis	66,848	59,358	2,408
Lincoln	Davenport	9,594	8,864	2,311
Mason	Shelton	48,577	38,341	961
Okanogan	Okanogan	38,005	33,350	5,268
Pacific	South Bend	21,067	18,882	975
Pend Oreille	Newport	11,141	8,915	1,401
Pierce	Tacoma	657,272	586,203	1,676
San Juan	Friday Harbor	12,061	10,035	175
Skagit	Mount Vernon	95,543	79,545	1,735
Skamania	Stevenson	9,371	8,289	1,657
Snohomish	Everett	546,102	465,628	2,090
Spokane	Spokane	404,920	361,333	1,764
Stevens	Colville	38,624	30,948	2,478
Thurston	Olympia	197,109	161,238	727
Wahkiakum	Cathlamet	3,775	3,327	264
Walla Walla	Walla Walla	53,488	48,439	1,271
Whatcom	Bellingham	152,512	127,780	2,120
Whitman	Colfax	39,456	38,775	2,159
Yakima	Yakima	216,234	188,823	4,296

West Virginia

(55 counties, 24,087 sq mi land; pop. 1,825,754)

County	County seat or courthouse	1996 Pop.	1990 Pop.	Land area sq mi
Barbour	Philippi	16,360	15,699	341
Berkeley	Martinsburg	68,197	59,253	321
Boone	Madison	26,403	25,870	503
Braxton	Sutton	13,449	12,998	514
Brooke	Wellsburg	26,573	26,992	89
Cabell	Huntington	96,178	96,827	282
Calhoun	Grantsville	7,982	7,885	281
Clay	Clay	10,412	9,983	342
Doddridge	West Union	7,235	6,994	321
Fayette	Fayetteville	48,908	47,952	664
Gilmer	Glenville	7,184	7,669	340
Grant	Petersburg	11,172	10,428	477
Greenbrier	Lewisburg	35,734	34,693	1,021
Hampshire	Romney	18,808	16,498	642
Hancock	New Cumberland	34,705	35,233	83
Hardy	Moorefield	11,723	10,977	583
Harrison	Clarksburg	71,143	69,371	416
Jackson	Ripley	27,399	25,900	100
Jefferson	Charles Town	39,979	35,926	210
Kanawha	Charleston	204,968	207,619	903
Lewis	Weston	17,642	17,223	389
Lincoln	Hamlin	22,150	21,382	438
Logan	Logan	41,839	43,032	454
McDowell	Welch	31,524	35,233	535
Marion	Fairmont	57,571	57,249	310
Marshall	Moundsville	36,284	37,356	307
Mason	Point Pleasant	25,838	25,178	432
Mercer	Princeton	64,521	64,980	421
Mineral	Keyser	27,563	26,697	328
Mingo	Williamson	32,986	33,739	423
Monongalia	Morgantown	78,234	75,509	361
Monroe	Union	13,015	12,406	473
Morgan	Berkeley Springs	13,520	12,128	229
Nicholas	Summersville	27,604	26,775	649
Ohio	Wheeling	49,502	50,871	106
Pendleton	Franklin	8,112	8,054	698
Pleasants	St. Marys	7,484	7,546	131
Pocahontas	Marlinton	9,086	9,008	940
Preston	Kingwood	29,903	29,037	648
Putnam	Winfield	49,607	42,835	346
Raleigh	Beckley	78,963	76,819	607
Randolph	Elkins	28,999	27,803	1,040
Ritchie	Harrisville	10,286	10,233	454
Roane	Spencer	15,400	15,120	484
Summers	Hinton	13,909	14,204	361
Taylor	Grafton	15,387	15,144	173
Tucker	Parsons	7,787	7,728	419
Tyler	Middlebourne	9,995	9,796	258
Upshur	Buckhannon	23,640	22,867	355
Wayne	Wayne	42,431	41,636	506
Webster	Webster Springs	10,420	10,729	556
Wetzel	New Martinsville	18,688	19,258	359
Wirt	Elizabeth	5,589	5,192	233
Wood	Parkersburg	87,770	86,915	367
Wyoming	Pineville	27,993	28,990	501

Wisconsin

(72 counties, 54,314 sq mi land; pop. 5,159,795)

County	County seat or courthouse	1996 Pop.	1990 Pop.	Land area sq mi
Adams	Friendship	17,836	15,682	648
Ashland	Ashland	16,569	16,307	1,044
Barron	Barron	43,451	40,750	863
Bayfield	Washburn	15,059	14,008	1,476
Brown	Green Bay	213,072	194,594	529
Buffalo	Alma	14,215	13,584	685
Burnett	Siren	14,383	13,084	822
Calumet	Chilton	37,762	34,291	320
Chippewa	Chippewa Falls	54,348	52,360	1,011
Clark	Neillsville	32,866	31,647	1,216
Columbia	Portage	49,914	45,088	774
Crawford	Prairie du Chien	16,479	15,940	573
Dane	Madison	395,366	367,085	1,202
Dodge	Juneau	81,750	76,559	882
Door	Sturgeon Bay	26,934	25,690	483
Douglas	Superior	43,051	41,758	1,309
Dunn	Menomonie	38,494	35,909	852
Eau Claire	Eau Claire	88,897	85,183	638
Florence	Florence	5,230	4,590	488
Fond du Lac	Fond du Lac	94,400	90,083	723
Forest	Crandon	9,588	8,776	1,014
Grant	Lancaster	49,531	49,266	1,148
Green	Monroe	32,755	30,339	584
Green Lake	Green Lake	19,414	18,651	354
Iowa	Dodgeville	21,862	20,150	763
Iron	Hurley	6,520	6,153	757
Jackson	Black River Falls	17,325	16,588	987
Jefferson	Jefferson	73,042	67,783	557
Juneau	Mauston	23,753	21,650	768
Kenosha	Kenosha	141,646	128,181	273
Kewaunee	Kewaunee	19,661	18,878	343
La Crosse	La Crosse	102,318	97,904	453
Lafayette	Darlington	16,568	16,074	634
Langlade	Antigo	20,535	19,505	873
Lincoln	Merrill	29,395	26,993	883
Manitowoc	Manitowoc	82,588	80,421	592
Marathon	Wausau	121,791	115,400	1,545
Marinette	Marinette	42,751	40,548	1,402
Marquette	Montello	14,566	12,321	456
Menominee	Keshena	4,609	3,890	358
Milwaukee	Milwaukee	922,243	959,275	242
Monroe	Sparta	39,044	36,633	901
Oconto	Oconto	32,795	30,226	998
Oneida	Rhinelander	35,516	31,679	1,125
Outagamie	Appleton	153,099	140,510	640
Ozaukee	Port Washington	80,257	72,831	232
Pepin	Durand	7,130	7,107	232
Pierce	Ellsworth	34,994	32,765	577
Polk	Balsam Lake	37,761	34,773	917
Portage	Stevens Point	65,146	61,405	806
Price	Phillips	15,910	15,600	1,253
Racine	Racine	185,003	175,034	333
Richland	Richland Center	17,958	17,521	586
Rock	Janesville	150,584	139,510	721
Rusk	Ladysmith	15,460	15,070	913
Saint Croix	Hudson	56,137	50,251	722
Sauk	Baraboo	52,164	46,975	838
Sawyer	Hayward	15,985	14,181	1,257
Shawano	Shawano	38,487	37,157	893
Sheboygan	Sheboygan	109,705	103,877	514
Taylor	Medford	19,264	18,901	975

County	County seat or courthouse	1996 Pop.	1990 Pop.	Land area sq mi
Trempealeau	Whitehall	26,191	25,263	734
Vernon	Viroqua	27,279	25,617	795
Vilas	Eagle River	20,769	17,707	873
Walworth	Elkhorn	83,355	75,000	555
Washburn	Shell Lake	15,132	13,772	810
Washington	West Bend	111,358	95,328	431
Waukesha	Waukesha	343,797	304,715	556
Waupaca	Waupaca	49,811	46,104	751
Waushara	Wautoma	21,272	19,385	626
Winnebago	Oshkosh	149,703	140,320	439
Wood	Wisconsin Rapids	76,219	73,605	793

Wyoming
(23 counties, 97,105 sq mi land; pop. 481,400)

County	County seat or courthouse	1996 Pop.	1990 Pop.	Land area sq mi
Albany	Laramie	30,831	30,797	4,274
Big Horn	Basin	11,276	10,525	3,137
Campbell	Gillette	32,012	29,370	4,797
Carbon	Rawlins	15,855	16,659	7,897
Converse	Douglas	11,989	11,128	4,255
Crook	Sundance	5,763	5,294	2,859
Fremont	Lander	35,940	33,662	9,183
Goshen	Torrington	12,731	12,373	2,226
Hot Springs	Thermopolis	4,627	4,809	2,004
Johnson	Buffalo	6,690	6,145	4,166
Laramie	Cheyenne	79,175	73,142	2,686
Lincoln	Kemmerer	13,971	12,625	4,069
Natrona	Casper	63,875	61,226	5,340
Niobrara	Lusk	2,637	2,499	2,626
Park	Cody	25,373	23,178	6,943
Platte	Wheatland	8,425	8,145	2,085
Sheridan	Sheridan	25,318	23,562	2,523
Sublette	Pinedale	5,577	4,843	4,882
Sweetwater	Green River	40,322	38,823	10,426
Teton	Jackson	13,587	11,173	4,008
Unita	Evanston	20,255	18,705	2,082
Washakie	Worland	8,617	8,388	2,240
Weston	Newcastle	6,554	6,518	2,398

Population of Outlying Areas

Source: Bureau of the Census, U.S. Dept. of Commerce; World Almanac research

Population estimates for July 1, 1996, are given for Puerto Rican municipios; all other population counts and all land area figures are from the U.S. census conducted on Apr. 1, 1990. Because only selected areas are shown, the population and land area figures may not equal the total reported. ZIP codes with an asterisk (*) are general delivery ZIP codes. Consult the local postmaster for more specific delivery information. Wake Atoll, Johnston Atoll, and Midway Atoll receive mail through APO and FPO addresses. U.S. outlying areas that are not listed in this table may not receive U.S. mail delivery.

Commonwealth of Puerto Rico

ZIP code	Municipio	1996 Pop.	Land area sq mi
*00601	Adjuntas	19,592	67
00602	Aguada	37,651	31
*00605	Aguadilla	65,207	37
00703	Aguas Buenas	30,062	31
00705	Aibonito	27,863	31
00610	Añasco	27,007	39
*00612	Arecibo	100,755	126
00714	Arroyo	19,549	15
00617	Barceloneta	26,480	23
00794	Barranquitas	28,702	34
*00958	Bayamón	231,845	44
00623	Cabo Rojo	47,365	70
*00726	Caguas	140,114	59
00627	Camuy	32,438	46
00729	Canóvanas	50,666	33
*00984	Carolina	188,427	45
*00962	Cataño	32,391	5
*00737	Cayey	50,728	52
00735	Ceiba	17,715	29
00638	Ciales	19,447	67
00739	Cidra	49,326	36
00769	Coamo	35,673	78
00782	Comerío	20,914	28
00783	Corozal	36,304	43
00775	Culebra	1,632	12
00646	Dorado	32,166	23
00738	Fajardo	38,383	30
00650	Florida	8,434	10
00653	Guánica	21,596	37
*00784	Guayama	41,994	65
00656	Guayanilla	27,316	42
*00970	Guaynabo	104,927	27
00778	Gurabo	32,003	28
00659	Hatillo	40,149	42
00660	Hormigueros	16,121	11
*00792	Humacao	57,643	45
00662	Isabela	41,156	55
00664	Jayuya	16,791	45
00795	Juana Díaz	49,693	60
00777	Juncos	41,424	27
00667	Lajas	26,704	60
00669	Lares	32,282	62
00670	Las Marías	9,923	46
00771	Las Piedras	30,111	34
00772	Loíza	27,904	19
00773	Luquillo	18,407	26
00674	Manatí	38,781	45
00606	Maricao	5,979	37
00707	Maunabo	13,503	21
*00681	Mayagüez	100,937	78
00676	Moca	37,154	50
00687	Morovis	33,388	39
00718	Naguabo	24,517	52
00719	Naranjito	29,016	27
00720	Orocovis	24,075	64
00723	Patillas	21,259	47
00624	Peñuelas	26,595	45
*00732	Ponce	189,988	116
00678	Quebradillas	26,008	23
00677	Rincón	13,589	14
00721	Río Grande	48,997	61
00637	Sabana Grande	23,244	36
00751	Salinas	29,962	69
00683	San Germán	36,925	55
*00936	San Juan	433,705	48
00754	San Lorenzo	36,435	53
00685	San Sebastián	42,573	70
00757	Santa Isabel	19,546	34
*00953	Toa Alta	58,240	27
*00951	Toa Baja	92,702	23
*00976	Trujillo Alto	74,644	21
00641	Utuado	35,212	114
00692	Vega Alta	35,828	28
*00693	Vega Baja	61,401	46
00765	Vieques	9,503	51
00766	Villalba	22,695	36
00767	Yabucoa	40,602	55
00698	Yauco	42,879	68
Total		**3,782,862**	**3,427**

Commonwealth of the Northern Mariana Islands

ZIP code	Municipality	1990 Pop.	Land area sq mi
96950	Northern Islands	36	60
96951	Rota	2,295	33
96950	Saipan	38,896	47
96952	Tinian	2,118	39
Total		**43,345**	**179**

Other U.S. External Territories

American Samoa

ZIP code	Location	1990 Pop.	Land area sq mi
96799	American Samoa	46,773	77

Guam

ZIP code	Location	1990 Pop.	Land area sq mi
96910	Agaña	1,139	1
96919	Agaña Hts.	3,646	1
*96928	Agat	4,960	10
96922	Asan	2,070	6
*96921	Barrigada	8,846	9
96924	Chalan-Pago-Ordot	4,451	6
96912	Dededo	31,728	30
96917	Inarajan	2,469	19
96923	Mangilao	10,483	10
96916	Merizo	1,742	6
96927	Mongmong-Toto-Maite	5,845	2
96925	Piti	1,827	7
96915	Santa Rita	11,857	17
96926	Sinajana	2,658	1
96930	Talofofo	2,310	17
*96931	Tamuning	16,673	6
96918	Umatac	897	6
96929	Yigo	14,213	35
96914	Yona	5,338	20
Total		**133,152**	**210**

Virgin Islands

ZIP code	Location	1990 Pop.	Land area sq mi
*00820	Saint Croix	50,139	83
*00820	Christiansted	2,555	
*00840	Frederiksted	1,064	
*00830	Saint John	3,504	20
*00801	Saint Thomas	48,166	31
00801	Charlotte Amalie	12,331	
Total		**101,809**	**134**

LANGUAGE

New Words in English*

The following words and definitions were provided by Merriam-Webster Inc., publishers of *Merriam-Webster's Collegiate Dictionary, Tenth Edition*. The words are among those that the Merriam-Webster editors decided had achieved enough currency in English to be entered in 1996 or 1997 copyright revisions of the dictionary.

blow off (1) to refuse to take notice of, honor, or deal with; ignore; (2) to fail to attend or show up for

brewpub a restaurant that sells beverages brewed on the premises

caffe latte espresso mixed with hot or steamed milk

channel surfing the act or practice of scanning through television programs usually by use of a remote control

chump change a relatively small or insignificant amount of money

cineplex a complex that houses several movie theaters

cocooning the practice of spending leisure time at home in preference to going out

ear candy music that is pleasing to listen to but lacks depth

Ebola virus an RNA-containing virus of African origin that causes an often fatal hemorrhagic fever

edutainment a form of entertainment (as a game, film, or show) that is designed to be educational

ethnic cleansing the expulsion, imprisonment, or killing of ethnic or racial minorities by a dominant majority group

gangsta rap rap music with lyrics explicitly relating to urban gangs, violence, drug use, and the degradation of women

gender bender a person who dresses and behaves like a member of the opposite sex

gigaflop a unit of measure for the speed of calculation of a computer equal to one billion floating-point operations per second

graphic novel a fictional story for adults that is presented in comic-strip format and published as a trade book

grunge (1) one that is grungy; (2) a style of popular music mixing elements of rock and roll, punk rock, and heavy metal; *also* the unkempt working-class fashions typical of fans of grunge

homeschool to teach school subjects to one's children at home

homosocial of, relating to, or involving social relationships between persons of the same sex and especially between men

maquiladora a foreign-owned factory in Mexico at which imported parts are assembled by lower-paid workers into products for export

masculinist an advocate of male superiority or dominance

minibar a small refrigerator in a hotel room that is stocked with especially alcoholic beverages and snacks for guests

morph to change the form or character of; transform

mosh to engage in uninhibited often frenzied activities (an intentional collision) with others near the stage at a rock concert

reality check something that clarifies reality, often by correcting a misconception

sport-utility vehicle a rugged automotive vehicle similar to a station wagon but built on a light-truck chassis

tapenade a seasoned spread made chiefly with mashed black olives, capers, and anchovies

tsuris *also* **tsouris** trouble, distress

telephone tag telephoning back and forth by parties trying to reach each other

victimology (1) the study of victims and victimization; (2) the claim that one's problems result from victimization

zone out to become oblivious to one's surroundings, especially in order to relax

* See also glossaries in the Computers and Economics chapters.

Eponyms
(words named for people)

Bloody Mary—a vodka and tomato juice drink; after the nickname of Mary I, Queen of England (1553-58), notorious for persecution of Protestants

bloomers—full, loose trousers gathered at the knee; after Amelia Bloomer, an American social reformer who advocated (1851) such clothing

bobbies—in Great Britain, police officers; after Sir Robert Peel, the statesman who organized the London police force, 1850

bowdlerize—to delete written matter considered indelicate; after Thomas Bowdler, English editor of an expurgated Shakespeare (1825)

boycott—to avoid trade or dealings with, as a protest; after Charles C. Boycott, an English land agent in County Mayo, Ireland, ostracized in 1880 for refusing to reduce rents

Braille—a system of writing for the blind; after Louis Braille, the French teacher of the blind who invented it (1853)

Casanova—a man who is a promiscuous and unscrupulous lover; after Giovanni Giacomo Casanova (1725-98), an Italian adventurer

chauvinist—excessively patriotic; after Nicolas Chauvin, a character in a 19th-cent. play who is devoted to Napoleon

derby—a stiff felt hat with a dome-shaped crown and rather narrow rolled brim; after Edward Stanley, 12th earl of Derby, who in 1780 founded the Derby horse race, to which these hats are worn

diesel—a type of internal combustion engine or a vehicle driven by it; after Rudolf Diesel (1858-1913), who built the first successful diesel engine

gerrymander—to draw an election district in such a way as to favor a political party; after Elbridge Gerry, who created (1812) just such an election district (shaped like a salamander) during his governorship of Massachusetts

guillotine—a machine for beheading; after Joseph Guillotin, a French physician who proposed its use in 1789 as more humane than hanging

leotard—a close-fitting garment for the torso, worn by dancers, acrobats, and the like; after Julius Leotard, a 19th-century French aerial gymnast

sandwich—2 or more slices of bread with a filling in between; after John Montagu, 4th earl of Sandwich (1718-92), who supposedly ate food in this form so that he would not have to leave the gaming table

silhouette—an outline image; from Étienne de Silhouette (1709-67), a close-fisted French finance minister

National Spelling Bee

The Scripps Howard National Spelling Bee, conducted by Scripps Howard Newspapers and other leading newspapers since 1939, was instituted by the Louisville (KY) *Courier-Journal* in 1925. Children under 16 years old and not beyond 8th grade are eligible to compete for cash prizes at the finals, held annually in Washington, DC. The 1997 winners were: 1st prize, Rebecca Sealfon, New York City; 2d prize, Prem Murthy Trivedi, Howell, NJ; 3d prize, Sudheer Potru, Beverly Hills, MI.

Here are the last words given, and spelled correctly, in each of the years 1974-97 at the national spelling bee.

1974 — hydrophyte	1980 — elucubrate	1986 — odontalgia	1992 — lyceum
1975 — incisor	1981 — sarcophagus	1987 — staphylococci	1993 — kamikaze
1976 — narcilepsy	1982 — psoriasis	1988 — elegiacal	1994 — antediluvian
1977 — cambist	1983 — purim	1989 — spoliator	1995 — xanthosis
1978 — deification	1984 — luge	1990 — fibranne	1996 — vivisepulture
1979 — maculature	1985 — milieu	1991 — antipyretic	1997 — euonym

Foreign Words and Phrases

(L=Latin; F=French; Y=Yiddish; R=Russian; G=Greek; I=Italian; S=Spanish)

ad hoc (L; ad HOK): for the end or purpose at hand

ad infinitum (L; ad in-fi-NITE-um): without end; forever

ad nauseam (L; ad NAWZ-ee-um): to a sickening degree

apropos (F; ap-ruh-POH): relevant

bête noire (F; BET NWAHR): a thing or person viewed with particular dislike

bon appétit (F; BOH nap-uh-teet): have a good meal!

bona fide (L; BOH nuh-feyed): genuine; in good faith

carte blanche (F; kahrt BLANNSH): full discretionary power

cause célèbre (F; kawz suh-LEB-ruh): a notorious incident

c'est la vie (F; se lah VEE): that's life

chutzpah (Y; KHOOT-spuh): nerve bordering on arrogance

coup de grâce (F; kooh duh GRAHS): the final blow

coup d'état (F; kooh day TAH): overthrow of an existing government by a small group

crème de la crème (F; KREM duh luh KREM): the best of the best

cum laude/magna cum laude/summa cum laude (L; KUHM loud-ay; MAGN-ya . . . ; SOO-ma . . .): with praise or honor/great praise or honor/highest praise or honor

de facto (L; di FAK-toh): in fact, though not by right

déjà vu (F; DAY-zhah VOOH): the sensation that something happening has happened before

de jure (L; dee JOOR-ee, day YOOR-ay): in accordance with right or law; officially

de rigueur (F; duh ree-GUR): necessary according to convention or etiquette

détente (F; day-TAHNT): an easing of strained relations

éminence grise (F; ay-meh-NAHNN-suh GREEZ): one who wields power behind the scenes

enfant terrible (F; ahnn-FAHNN te-REE-bluh): one whose unconventional behavior causes embarrassment

en masse (F; ahn MAHS): in a large body

ergo (L; ER-goh): therefore

esprit de corps (F; es-PREE duh KAWR): group spirit; feeling of camaraderie

ex post facto (L; eks pohst FAK-toh): retroactive(ly)

fait accompli (F; fayt uh-kom-PLEE): an accomplished fact

faux pas (F; fowe PAH): a social blunder

hoi polloi (G; hoy puh-LOY): the masses

in loco parentis (L; in LOH-koh puh-REN-tis): in place of a parent

in memoriam (L; in muh-MAWR-ee-uhm): in memory of

in situ (L; in SEYE-tyooh): in the original place or position

in toto (L; in TOH-toh): totally

je ne sais quoi (F; zhuh nuh say KWAH): I don't know what; the little something that eludes description

joie de vivre (F; zhwah duh VEEV-ruh): zest for life

mea culpa (L; MAY-uh CUL-puh): through my fault

modus operandi (L; MOH-duhs op-uh-RAN-dee): method of operation

noblesse oblige (F; noh-BLES uh-BLEEZH): the obligation of nobility to help the less fortunate

non compos mentis (L; non KOM-puhs MEN-tis): not of sound mind

nouveau riche (F; nooh-voh REESH): a person newly rich; perhaps one who spends money conspicuously

persona non grata (L; per-SOH-nah non GRAH-tah): unwelcome person

postmortem (L; pohst-MORE-tuhm): after death; autopsy; analysis after an event

prima donna (I; pree-muh DAH-nuh): a principal female opera singer; temperamental person

pro tempore (L; proh TEM-puh-ree): for the time being

que sera sera (S; keh sair-ah sair-AH): what will be will be

quid pro quo (L; kwid proh KWOH): something given or received for something else

raison d'être (F; RAY-zohnn DET-ruh): reason for being

savoir faire (F; sav-wahr-FAIR): dexterity in social affairs

schlemiel (Y; shleh-MEEL): an unlucky, bungling person

semper fidelis (L; SEM-puhr fee-DAY-lis): always faithful

status quo (L; STAY-tus QWOH): existing order of things

terra firma (L; TER-uh FUR-muh): solid ground

tour de force (F; TOOR duh FAWRS): feat accomplished through great skill

verbatim (L; ver-BAY-tuhm): word for word

vis-à-vis (F; vee-ZUH-VEE): compared with; with regard to; with respect to

Some Common Abbreviations and Acronyms

Acronyms are pronounceable words formed from first letters (or syllables) of other words. Many of the abbreviations below (e.g., AIDS, NATO) are thus acronyms. Some acronyms are words coined as abbreviations and written in lower case (e.g., *radar, yuppie);* these are among abbreviations that may be more familiar than the terms they stand for. Acronyms do not have periods; usage for other abbreviations varies, but periods have become less common. Capitalization usage also may often vary from what is shown here. Italicized words preceding parenthetical definitions below are Latin unless otherwise noted. *See also* other chapters, including Computers and Weights and Measures.

AA=Alcoholics Anonymous

AAA=American Automobile Association

AARP=American Association of Retired Persons

ABA=American Bar Association

AC=alternating current

AD=*anno Domini* (in the year of the Lord)

AFL-CIO=American Federation of Labor and Congress of Industrial Organizations

AIDS=acquired immune deficiency syndrome

AM=*ante meridiem* (before noon)

AMA=American Medical Association

anon=anonymous

ASAP=as soon as possible

ASCAP=American Society of Composers, Authors, and Publishers

ASPCA=American Society for Prevention of Cruelty to Animals

ATM=automated teller machine

Ave.=Avenue

AWOL=absent without leave

BA=Bachelor of Arts

bbl=barrel(s)

BC=before Christ

BCE=before Common Era

bpd=barrels per day

BS=Bachelor of Science

Btu=British thermal unit(s)

bu=bushel(s)

C= Celsius, centigrade

c=*circa* (about), copyright

Capt.=Captain

CE=Common Era

CEO=chief executive officer

CFO=chief financial officer

CIA=Central Intelligence Agency

cm=centimeter(s)

Col.=Colonel

COD=cash (or collect) on delivery

COLA=cost of living allowance

CPA=certified public accountant

Cpl.=Corporal

CPR=cardiopulmonary resuscitation

DA=district attorney

DAR=Daughters of the American Revolution

DC=direct current

DD=Doctor of Divinity

DDS=Doctor of Dental Science (or Surgery)

DNA=deoxyribonucleic acid

DNR=do not resuscitate

DOA=dead on arrival

DWI=driving while intoxicated

ed.=edited, edition, editor

e.g.=*exempli gratia* (for example)

EKG=electrocardiogram

EPA=Environmental Protection Agency
ESP=extrasensory perception
esp.=especially
et al.=*et alii* (and others)
etc.=*et cetera* (and so forth)
EU=European Union
F=Fahrenheit
FBI=Federal Bureau of Investigation
FICA=Federal Insurance Contributions Act (Social Security)
FOB=free on board
ft=foot, feet
FY=fiscal year
FYI=for your information
gal=gallon(s)
GB=gigabyte(s)
GDP=gross domestic product
Gen.=General
GIGO=garbage in, garbage out
GNP=gross national product
GOP=Grand Old Party (Republican Party)
Hon.=the Honorable
hr=hour(s)
ht=height
HVAC=heating, ventilating, and air-conditioning
i.e.=*id est* (that is)
in.=inch(es)
IQ=intelligence quotient
IMF=International Monetary Fund
IRA=individual retirement account, Irish Republican Army
IRS=Internal Revenue Service
ISBN=International Standard Book Number
JD=*Juris Doctor* (doctor of laws)
JP=Justice of the Peace
K=Kelvin
k=karat
KB=kilobyte(s)
kg=kilogram(s)
km=kilometer(s)
kw=kilowatt(s)
kwh=kilowatt-hour(s)
l=liter(s)
lb=*libra* (pound or pounds)
Lieut. or Lt.=Lieutenant

LLB=*Legum Baccalaureus* (bachelor of laws)
m=meter(s)
MA=Master of Arts
Maj.=Major
MB=megabyte(s)
MD=*Medicinae Doctor* (doctor of medicine)
MFN=most favored nation
mi=mile(s)
MIA=missing in action
min=minute(s)
ml=milliliter(s)
mm=millimeter(s)
mph=miles per hour
MS=Master of Science
MSG=monosodium glutamate
Msgr.=Monsignor
MVP=most valuable player
NASA=National Aeronautics and Space Administration
NAFTA=North American Free Trade Agreement
NATO=North Atlantic Treaty Organization
NAACP=National Association for the Advancement of Colored People
NB=*nota bene* (note carefully)
NCAA=National Collegiate Athletic Association
no=*numero* (number)
NOW=National Organization for Women
op=*opus* (work)
OPEC=Organization of Petroleum Exporting Countries
oz=ounce(s)
p, pp=page(s)
PAC=political action committee
PC=personal computer
PhD=*Philosophiae Doctor* (doctor of philosophy)
PIN=Personal Identification Number
PM=*post meridiem* (afternoon)
POW=prisoner of war
PS=*post scriptum* (postscript)
pt=part(s), pint(s), point(s)

Pvt.=Private
qt=quart(s)
q.v.=quod vide (which see)
radar=radio detecting and ranging
REM=rapid eye movement
Rev.=Reverend
RFD=rural free delivery
RIP=*requiescat in pace* (May he/she rest in peace)
RN=registered nurse
RNA=ribonucleic acid
ROTC=Reserve Officers' Training Corps
rpm=revolutions per minute
RR=railroad
RSVP=*répondez s'il vous plaît* (Fr.) (Please reply)
SASE=self-addressed stamped envelope
sec=second(s)
Sgt.=Sergeant
SIDS=sudden infant death syndrome
S.J.=Society of Jesus (Jesuits)
SRO=standing room only
St.=Saint, Street
TGIF=Thank God it's Friday
UFO=unidentified flying object
UHF=ultrahigh frequency
UNESCO=United Nations Educational, Social, and Cultural Organization
UNICEF=United Nations (International) Children's (Emergency) Fund
USS=United States ship
v (or vs)=*versus* (against)
VCR=videocassette recorder
VHF=very high frequency
VISTA=Volunteers in Service to America
W=watt(s)
Wasp=white Anglo-Saxon Protestant
WHO=World Health Organization
yd=yard(s)
yuppie=young urban professional
ZIP=zone improvement plan (U.S. Postal Service)

Names of the Days

English	Russian	Hebrew	French	Italian	Spanish	German	Japanese
Sunday	Voskresenje	Yom rishon	Dimanche	Domenica	Domingo	Sonntag	Nichiyo\bi
Monday	Ponedeljnic	Yom sheni	Lundi	Lunedì	Lunes	Montag	Getsuyo\bi
Tuesday	Vtornik	Yom shlishi	Mardi	Martedì	Martes	Dienstag	Kayo\bi
Wednesday	Sreda	Yom ravii	Mercredi	Mercoledì	Miércoles	Mittwoch	Suiyo\bi
Thursday	Chetverg	Yom hamishi	Jeudi	Giovedì	Jueves	Donnerstag	Mokuyo\bi
Friday	Pjatnitsa	Yom shishi	Vendredi	Venerdì	Viernes	Freitag	Kin-yo\bi
Saturday	Subbota	Shabbat	Samedi	Sabato	Sábado	Samstag	Doyo\bi

Names for Young of Animals

The young of many animals have come to be called by special names. Many of these are listed below.

bunny: rabbit
calf: cattle, elephant, antelope, rhino, hippo, whale, others
cheeper: grouse, partridge, quail
chick, chicken: fowl
cockerel: rooster
codling, sprag: codfish
colt: horse (male)
cub: lion, bear, shark, fox, others
cygnet: swan

duckling: duck
eaglet: eagle
elver: eel
eyas: hawk, others
fawn: deer
filly: horse (female)
fingerling: fish generally
flapper: wild fowl
fledgling: birds generally
foal: horse, zebra, others
fry: fish generally
gosling: goose
heifer: cow

joey: kangaroo, others
kid: goat
kit: fox, beaver, rabbit, cat
kitten, kitty, catling: cats, other small mammals
lamb, lambkin, cosset, hog: sheep
leveret: hare
nestling: birds generally
owlet: owl
parr, smolt, grilse: salmon
piglet, shoat, farrow, suckling: pig

polliwog, tadpole: frog
poult: turkey
pullet: hen
pup: dog, seal, sea lion, fox
puss, pussy: cat
spike, blinker, tinker: mackerel
squab: pigeon
squeaker: pigeon, others
whelp: dog, tiger, beasts of prey
yearling: cattle, sheep, horse, others

A Collection of Animal Collectives

The English language boasts an exotic abundance of different names to denote groups of animals. Many are listed below.

bale of turtles
band of gorillas
bed of clams, oysters
bevy of quail, swans
brace of ducks
brood of chicks
cast of hawks
cete of badgers
charm of goldfinches
cloud of gnats
clowder of cats
clutch of chicks
clutter of cats
congregation of plovers
covey of quail, partridge

crash of rhinoceri
cry of hounds
down of hares
drift of swine
drove of cattle, sheep
exaltation of larks
flight of birds
gaggle of geese
gam of whales
gang of elks
grist of bees
herd of elephants
horde of gnats
husk of hares
kindle or **kendle** of kittens

knot of toads
leap of leopards
leash of greyhounds, foxes
litter of pigs
mob of kangaroos
murder of crows
muster of peacocks
mute of hounds
nest of vipers
nest, nide of pheasants
pack of hounds, wolves
pod of whales, seals
pride of lions
school of fish
sedge or **siege** of cranes

shoal of fish, pilchàrds
skein of geese
skulk of foxes
sleuth of bears
sounder of boars, swine
span of mules
spring of teals
team of ducks, horses
tribe or **trip** of goats
troop of kangaroos, monkeys
volery of birds
watch of nightingales
wing of plovers
yoke of oxen

Idioms: Their Meaning and Derivation

dyed in the wool: deeply ingrained as a trait; from the fact that if wool is dyed before being made into yarn, or while still raw wool, the color is more firmly fixed.

feet of clay: a blemish in the character of one previously held above reproach; from Daniel's interpretation of Nebuchadnezzar's dream in the Old Testament. The king dreamed of an image made of precious metals, except for feet made of clay and iron; Daniel said that the feet symbolized human vulnerability to weakness and destruction.

hands down: effortlessly; incontestably; from the way a jockey, sure of victory, loosens grip on the reins.

in seventh heaven: in a state of bliss; especially in Islamic beliefs, heaven of heavens, home of God and highest angels.

kiss of death: something that seems good but is in reality the instrument of one's downfall; from the earlier phrase "Judas kiss," betrayal of Jesus to the authorities.

mad as a hatter: crazy; from mercury's use in the making of felt hats; hatters often were afflicted with a violent twitching of the muscles as a result of its effects.

red herring: a herring cured by smoke; a false lead, or irrelevant argument meant to mislead; from the use of a strong-smelling herring, trailed over the ground, for inducing a dog to follow this scent over any other.

red-letter day: a memorable day; from the custom of using red or purple colors to mark holy days on the calendar.

to bark up the wrong tree: to pursue a false lead; derived from hunting, some say specifically nocturnal racoon hunting, in which dogs often lost track of their quarry.

to buckle down: to adopt an attitude of effort and determination; probably from act of buckling on armor before battle.

to go at it with hammer and tongs: to proceed with no restraint; from the blacksmith who, with his tongs (long-handled pincers) took a piece of red-hot metal from the forge, laid it on the anvil, and beat it into shape with a hammer.

to hold water: to pass a test for soundness; from testing a pitcher by filling it with water.

to knuckle under: to submit to another; as when one knelt before a conqueror putting "knuckles" of the knees (rounded part of the bone where the joint is bent) on the ground.

to make hay while the sun shines: to seize the opportunity; from the production of hay, or mown grass dried for fodder, from exposure to the sun when available.

to strike while the iron is hot: to seize the opportunity; from the blacksmith's need to swing the hammer while the metal on the anvil is glowing, to avoid having to start up the forge again and reheat the iron.

Commonly Confused English Words

adverse: unfavorable
averse: opposed

affect: to influence
effect: to cause

aggravate: to make worse
annoy: to irritate

allusion: an indirect reference
illusion: an unreal impression

appraise: to set a value on
apprise: to inform

capital: the seat of government
capitol: building where a legislature meets

complement: to make complete; something that completes
compliment: to praise; praise

denote: to mean
connote: to suggest beyond the explicit meaning

discreet: prudent
discrete: separate

disinterested: impartial
uninterested: without interest

elicit: to draw or bring out
illicit: illegal

emigrate: to leave for another place of residence
immigrate: to come to another place of residence

flaunt: to display ostentatiously
flout: to treat with contemptuous disregard

grisly: inspiring horror or great fear
grizzly: sprinkled or streaked with gray

historic: important in history
historical: relating to history

imminent: ready to take place
eminent: standing out

imply: to suggest but not explicitly; to entail
infer: to assume or understand information not relayed explicitly

include: used when the items following are part of a whole
comprise: used when the items following are all of a whole

incredible: unbelievable
incredulous: skeptical

ingenious: clever
ingenuous: innocent

insidious: intended to trick
invidious: detrimental to reputation

oral: spoken, as opposed to written
verbal: relating to language

pestilence: epidemic disease
petulance: rudeness

prostrate: stretched out face down
prostate: relating to prostate gland

Commonly Misspelled English Words

accidentally	conscious	fluorine	license	performance
accommodate	convenience	foreign	lightning	permanent
acknowledgment	deceive	forty	liquefy	perseverance
acquainted	defendant	government	maintenance	privilege
all right	describe	grammar	marriage	receive
already	description	harass	miniature	receipt
amateur	desirable	humorous	misspelled	rhythm
appearance	despair	hurrying	mysterious	ridiculous
appropriate	desperate	incidentally	necessary	separate
bureau	eliminate	independent	noticeable	seize
business	embarrass	indispensable	occasionally	similar
character	environment	inoculate	occurrence	sincerely
commitment	existence	irresistible	opportunity	supersede
committee	fascinating	judgment	optimistic	transferred
conscientious	finally	laboratory	parallel	weird

Forms of Address

Addressee	Address	Salutation
Government		
President of the U.S.	The President, The White House, Washington, DC 20500; also, The President and Mrs. ____ or The President and Mr. ____	Dear Sir or Madam; Mr. President or Madam President; Dear Mr. President or Dear Madam President
U.S. Vice President	The Vice President, The White House, Washington, DC 20500; also, The Vice President and Mrs. ____ or The Vice President and Mr. ____	Dear Sir or Madam; Mr. Vice President or Madam Vice President; Dear Mr. Vice President or Dear Madam Vice President
Chief Justice	The Hon. *Firstname Surname*, Chief Justice of the U.S., The Supreme Court, Washington, DC 20543	Dear Sir or Madam; Dear Mr. or Madam Chief Justice
Associate Justice	The Hon. Justice *Firstname Surname,* The Supreme Court, Washington, DC 20543	Dear Sir or Madam; Dear Justice *Surname*
Judge	The Hon. *Firstname Surname*, Associate Judge, U.S. District Court	Dear Judge *Surname*
Attorney General	The Hon. *Firstname Surname,* Attorney General, Dept. of Justice, Constitution Ave. & 10th St. NW, Washington, DC 20530	Dear Sir or Madam; Dear Mr. or Ms. Attorney General
Cabinet Officer	The Hon. *Firstname Surname*, Secretary of ____	Dear Mr. or Madam Secretary; or Dear Mr. or Ms. *Surname*
Senator	The Hon. or Sen. *Firstname Surname*, U.S. Senate, Washington, DC 20510	Dear Mr. or Madam Senator, or Dear Mr. or Ms. *Surname*
Representative	The Hon. or Rep. *Firstname Surname*, House of Representatives, Washington, DC 20515	Dear Mr. or Madam *Surname*
Speaker of the House	The Hon. Speaker of the House of Representatives, House of Representatives, Washington, DC 20515	Dear Mr. or Madam Speaker
Ambassador, U.S.	The Hon. *Firstname Surname*, American Ambassador[1]	Sir or Madam; Dear Mr. or Madam Ambassador
Ambassador, Foreign	His or Her Excellency[2] *Firstname Surname*, Ambassador of _____	Excellency;[2] Dear Mr. or Madam Ambassador
Governor	The Hon. *Firstname Surname*, Governor of *State*; or in some states, His or Her Excellency, the Governor of *State*	Sir or Madam; Dear Governor *Surname*
Mayor	The Hon. *Firstname Surname*, Mayor of *City*	Sir or Madam; Dear Mayor *Surname*
Military Personnel		
All Titles	Full or abbreviated rank + full name + comma + abbreviation for branch of service. *Example*: Adm. John Smith, USN	Dear *Rank Surname*
Religious		
Clergy, Protestant	The Reverend *Firstname Surname*[3]	Dear Ms. or Mr. *Surname*
Pope	His Holiness Pope *Name* or His Holiness the Pope	Your Holiness or Most Holy Father
Priest	The Reverend *Firstname Surname* or The Reverend Father *Surname*	Reverend Father, Dear Father *Surname*, or Dear Father
Rabbi	Rabbi *Firstname Surname*	Dear Rabbi *Surname*
Royalty and Nobility,		
King/Queen	His or Her Majesty, King or Queen of *Country*	Sir or Madam, or May it please Your Majesty

(1) If in Canada or Latin America, The Ambassador of the United States of America. (2) An American ambassador is not to be addressed as His or Her Excellency. (3) A member of the Protestant clergy who has a doctorate may be so addressed; for example, The Reverend Firstname Surname, DD, and Dear Dr. Surname.

Pen Names

Shalom Aleichem (Solomon J. Rabinowitz)
Woody Allen (Allen Stewart Konigsberg)
Currer, Ellis, and Acton Bell (Charlotte, Emily, and Anne Brontë)
John le Carré (David John Moore Cornwell)
Lewis Carroll (Charles Lutwidge Dodgson)
Colette (Sidonie Gabrielle Colette)
Isak Dinesen (Karen Blixen)
Dorothy Dix (Elizabeth Gilmer)

Elia (Charles Lamb)
George Eliot (Mary Ann or Marian Evans)
Maksim Gorky (Aleksey Maksimovich Peshkov)
O. Henry (William Sydney Porter)
James Herriot (James Alfred Wight)
P. D. James (Phyllis Dorothy James White)
[John] Ross Macdonald (Kenneth Millar)
André Maurois (Émile Herzog)
Molière (Jean Baptiste Poquelin)
George Orwell (Eric Arthur Blair)

Ellery Queen (Frederic Dannay and Manfred B. Lee)
Mary Renault (Mary Challans)
Françoise Sagan (Françoise Quoirez)
Saki (Hector Hugh Munro)
George Sand (Amandine Lucie Aurore Dupin)
Dr. Seuss (Theodor Seuss Geisel)
Stendhal (Marie Henri Beyle)
Mark Twain (Samuel Clemens)
Voltaire (François Marie Arouet)
Artemus Ward (Charles Farrar Browne)
Tom Wolfe (Thomas Kennerly Jr.)

The Principal Languages of the World

Source: Prof. Sidney Culbert, 351525, University of Washington, Seattle, WA 98195; data as of mid-1997

Languages Spoken by the Most People

	Speakers (millions) Native[1]	Total		Speakers (millions) Native[1]	Total		Speakers (millions) Native[1]	Total
Mandarin	863	1,025	Bengali	200	207	Japanese	125	126
Hindi	357	476	Arabic	200	235	German	99	126
Spanish	352	409	Portuguese	173	187	French	75	127
English	335	497	Russian	168	279	Malay-Indonesian	57	170

(1) A native speaker is one for whom the language is his or her first language.

Languages Spoken by at Least 1 Million People

Total number of speakers (native plus nonnative) of languages spoken by at least 1 million speakers. A native speaker is one for whom the language is his or her first language. Locations in parentheses are principal areas where the language is spoken.

Note: Languages are distinguished here according to consistent criteria commonly accepted by linguists and may sometimes be more narrowly defined than others may suppose. For example, Neapolitan, Piedmontese, Sardinian, Sicilian, and Venetian, all spoken in Italy, are here regarded as distinct languages, so their speakers are not counted as Italian speakers. In some cases nonlinguistic criteria supervene, as in the case of Arabic here, where speakers of many variants are, according to custom, included under one broad term, "Arabic."

Achinese (N Sumatra, Indonesia)	3	Dyerma (SW Niger)	2	Javanese (Java, Indonesia)	64
Afghan (see Pashtu)		Edo (Bendel, S Nigeria)	1	Kabyle (W Kabylia, N Algeria)	3
Afrikaans (S Africa)	9	Efik (incl. Ibibio) (SE Nigeria)	6	Kamba (E Kenya)	3
Akan (or Twi-Fanti) (Ghana)	8	English (see also above)	497	Kannada (S India)	46
Albanian (Albania; Kosovo, Yugoslavia)	5	Esperanto	2	Kanuri (Nigeria; Niger; Chad; Cameroon)	4
Amharic (Ethiopia)	21	Estonian (Estonia)	1	Karen (see Sgaw)	
Arabic (see also above)	235	Ewe (SE Ghana; S Togo)	3	Karo-Dairi (N Sumatra, Indonesia)	1
Armenian (Armenia)	6	Fang-Bulu (dialects of Beti, q. v.)		Kashmiri[1] (N India; NE Pakistan)	4
Assamese[1] (India; Bangladesh)	10	Farsi (see Persian)		Kazak (Kazakstan)	8
Aymara (Bolivia; Peru)	2	Finnish (Finland; Sweden)	6	Khalka (see Mongolian)	
Azeri (Azerbaijan)	11	Fon (SC Benin; S Togo)	1	Khmer (Cambodia; Vietnam; Thai.)	7
Balinese (Bali, Indonesia)	4	French (see also above)	127	Khmer, Northern (Thailand)	1
Baluchi (Baluchistan, in SW Pakistan and SE Iran)	5	Fula (or Peulh) (Cameroon; Nigeria)	13	Kikuyu (or Gekoyo) (WC Kenya)	6
Bashkir (Bashkortostan, Russia)	1	Fulakunda (Senegal; Gambia; Guinea-Bissau)	3	Kituba (Bas-Congo, Bandundu, Congo)	5
Batak Toba (Indonesia)	3	Futa Jalon (Guinea; Sierra Leone)	3	Kongo (W Congo; S Congo Rep.[5]; NW Angola)	3
Baule (Côte d'Ivoire)	2	Galician (Galicia, NW Spain)	4	Konkani (Maharashtra and SW India)	2
Beja (Spoken Arabic dialect group)	5	Galla (see Oromo)		Korean (Korea; China; Japan)	77
Bemba (Zambia)	2	Ganda (or Luganda) (S Uganda)	3	Kurdish (Iran; Iraq; Turkey)	11
Bengali[1] (see also above)	207	Georgian (Georgia)	4	Kurukh (or Oraon) (C and E India)	2
Berber[2]		German (see also above)	126	Kyrgyz (Kyrgyzstan)	3
Beti (Cameroon; Gabon; Eq. Guinea)	2	Gilaki (Gilan, NW Iran)	3	Lampung (Sumatra, Indonesia)	2
Bhili (India)	6	Gogo (Riff Valley, Tanzania)	1	Lao[6] (Laos)	4
Bikol (SE Luzon, Philippines)	4	Gondi (Central India)	3	Latvian (Latvia)	2
Brahui (Pakistan)	2	Greek (Greece)	12	Lingala (incl. Bangala) (Congo[5])	8
Bugis (Indonesia; Malaysia)	4	Guarani (Paraguay)	5	Lithuanian (Lithuania)	4
Bulgarian (Bulgaria)	9	Gujarati[1] (WC India; S Pakistan)	44	Luba-Lulua (or Chiluba) (Congo[5])	7
Burmese (Myanmar)	32	Gusii (Kisii District, Nyanza, Kenya)	2	Luba-Shaba (Shaba, Congo[5])	2
Buyi (S Guizhou, S China)	2	Gypsy (see Romany)		Luhya (W Kenya)	3
Byelorussian (Belarus)	10	Hadiyya (Arusi, Ethiopia)	1	Luo (Kenya; Nyanza, Tanzania)	4
Cantonese (China, incl. Hong Kong)	71	Hakka (or Kejia) (SE China)	34	Luri (SW Iran; Iraq)	4
Catalan (NE Spain; Balearic Is.; S France; Andorra)	10	Hausa (N Nigeria; Niger; Cameroon)	39	Lwena (E Angola; W Zambia)	1
Cebuano (Bohol Sea, Philippines)	13	Haya (Kagera, NW Tanzania)	1	Macedonian (Macedonia)	2
Chagga (Kilimanjaro area, Tanzania)	1	Hebrew (Israel)	5	Madurese (Madura, Indonesia)	10
Chiga (Uganda)	1	Hindi[1,4] (see also above)	476	Magindanaon (S Philippines)	1
Chinese[3]		Hmong (S China; SE Asia)	6	Makassar (S Sulawesi, Indonesia)	2
Chuvash (Chuvash, Russia)	2	Ho (Bihar and Orissa States, India)	1	Makua (S Tanzania; N Mozambique)	2
Czech (Czech Republic)	12	Hungarian (or Magyar) (Hungary)	14	Malagasy (Madagascar)	1
Danish (Denmark)	5	Iban (Indonesia; Malaysia)	1	Malay-Indonesian (see also above)	170
Dimli (EC Turkey)	1	Ibibio (see Efik)		Malay, Pattani (SE Thailand)	2
Dogri (Jammu-Kashmir, CE India)	1	Igbo (or Ibo) (lower Niger, Nigeria)	18	Malayalam[1] (Kerala, S India)	36
Dong (SC China)	2	Ijaw (Niger River delta, Nigeria)	2	Malinke-Bambara-Dyula (W Africa)	9
Dutch-Flemish (Netherlands; Belg.; NE France)	21	Ilocano (NW Luzon, Philippines)	8		
		Indonesian (see Malay-Indonesian)			
		Italian (Italy)	62		
		Japanese (see also above)	126		

Mandarin (China; Taiwan; see also above)	1,025	Romanian (Romania; Moldova)	26	Tausug (Philippines; Malaysia)	1
Marathi[1] (Maharashtra, India)	71	Romany[7]	2	Telugu[1] (Andhra Pradesh, SE India)	75
Mazandarani (N Iran)	3	Ruanda (Rwanda; Uganda; Congo[5])	6	Temne (central Sierra Leone)	2
Mbundu (Benguela, Angola)	4	Rundi (Burundi)	6	Thai[6] (Thailand)	52
Mbundu (Luanda, Angola)	3	Russian (see also above)	279	Tho (N Vietnam; S China)	2
Meithei (NE India; Bangladesh)	1	Samar-Leyte (Central E Philippines)	3	Thonga (Mozambique; So. Africa)	3
Mende (Sierra Leone)	2	Sango (central African Republic)	5	Tibetan (SW China; N India; Nepal)	4
Meru (Eastern Province, central Tanzania)	1	Santali (E India; Nepal)	6	Tigrinya (S Eritrea; Tigre, Ethiopia)	5
Mien (China; Viet.; Laos; Thailand)	1	Sasak (Lombok, Alas Strait, Indon.)	2	Tiv (SE Nigeria; Cameroon)	2
Min (SE China; Taiwan; Malaysia)	50	Serbo-Croatian (Croatia; Serbia; and other former Yugoslav republics and autonomous regions)	21	Tong (see Dong)	
Minangkabau (W Sumatra, Indon.)	6			Tonga (SW Zambia; NW Zimbabwe)	2
Moldavian (incl. with Romanian)		Sgaw (SW Myanmar)	2	Tswana (Botswana; South Africa)	4
Mongolian (Mongolia; NE China)	6	Shan (E Myanmar)	3	Tulu (S India)	2
Moré (central Burkina Faso)	5	Shilha (W Algeria; S Morocco)	2	Tumbuka (N Malawi; NE Zambia)	2
Nepali (Nepal; NE India; Bhutan)	16	Shona (Zimbabwe)	7	Turkish (Turkey)	61
Ngulu (Mozambique; Malawi)	3	Sidamo (Sidamo, S Ethiopia)	2	Turkmen (Turkmenistan; Afghanistan)	5
Nkole (Western Prov., Uganda)	2	Sindhi[1] (SE Pakistan; W India)	19	Twi-Fante (see Akan)	
Norwegian (Norway)	5	Sinhalese (Sri Lanka)	13	Uighur (Xinjiang, NW China)	8
Nung (NE of Hanoi, Vietnam; China)	1	Slovak (Slovakia)	6	Ukrainian (Ukraine; Russia; Poland)	47
Nupe (Kwara, Niger States, Nigeria)	1	Slovene (Slovenia)	2	Urdu[1,4] (Pakistan; India)	104
Nyamwezi-Sukuma (NW Tanzania)	6	Soga (Busoga, Uganda)	1	Uzbek (Uzbekistan)	18
Nyanja (Malawi; Zambia; Zimbabwe)	10	Somali (Som.; Eth.; Ken.; Djibouti)	5	Vietnamese (Vietnam)	68
Oriya[1] (central and E India)	31	Songye (Kasai Or., NW Shaba, Congo[5])	1	Wolaytta (SE Ethiopia)	2
Oromo (West Ethiopia; N Kenya)	10	Soninke (Mali; countries to W S E)	1	Wolof (Senegal)	7
Pampangan (NW of Manila, Philip.)	2	Sotho, Northern (So. Africa)	4	Wu (Shanghai region, China)	70
Panay-Hiligaynon (Philippines)	7	Sotho, Southern (So. Afr.; Lesotho)	4	Xhosa (SW Cape Prov., South Africa)	8
Pangasinan (Lingayen G., Philip.)	2	Spanish (see also above)	409	Yao (see Mien)	
Pashtu (Pakistan; Afghanistan; Iran)	19	Sundanese (Sunda Strait, Indonesia)	26	Yao (Malawi; Tanzania; Mozambique)	2
Pedi (see Sotho, Northern)		Swahili (Kenya; Tanzania; Congo[5]; Uganda)	49	Yi (S and SW China)	7
Persian (Iran; Afghanistan)	35	Swati (Swaziland; South Africa)	2	Yiddish[8]	3
Polish (Poland)	44	Swedish (Sweden; Finland)	9	Yoruba (SW Nigeria; Zou, Benin)	22
Portuguese (see also above)	187	Sylhetti (Bangladesh)	5	Zande (NE Congo[5]; SW Sudan)	1
Provençal (S France)	3	Tagalog (Philippines)	57	Zhuang (S China)	4
Punjabi[1] (Punjab, Pakistan; India)	94	Tajiki (Tajikistan; Uzbek.; Kyrgyz.)	5	Zulu (N. Natal, South Africa; Lesotho)	9
Pushto (see Pashtu)		Tamazight (N Morocco; W Algeria)	3		
Quechua A (Peru; Boliv.; Ecuad.; Arg.)	8	Tamil[1] (Tamil Nadu, India; Sri Lanka)	74		
Rejang (SW Sumatra, Indonesia)	1	Tartar (Tartarstan, Russia)	8		
Riff (N Morocco; Algerian coast)	2				

(1) One of the 15 languages under the constitution of India. (2) See Kabyle, Riff, Shilha, and Tamazight. (3) See Mandarin, Cantonese, Wu, Min, and Hakka. The "common speech" (Putonghua) or the "national language" (Guoyu) is a standardized form of Mandarin as spoken in the area of Beijing. (4) Hindi and Urdu are essentially the same language, Hindustani. As the official language of Pakistan, it is written in a modified Arabic script and called Urdu. As the official language of India, it is written in the Devanagari script and called Hindi. (5) Congo refers to the Democratic Republic of the Congo (formerly Zaire), as distinct from the smaller Congo Republic. (6) The distinctions between some Thai dialects and Lao are political rather than linguistic. (7) Mainly in central, E, and SE Europe and Turkey; some in the U.S. (8) Yiddish is usually considered a variant of German, but it has its own standard grammar and dictionaries, has a highly developed literature, and is written in Hebrew characters.

American Manual Alphabet

In the American Manual Alphabet, each letter of the alphabet is represented by a position of the fingers. This system was originally developed in France by Abbe Charles Michel De I'Epee in the late 1700s. It was brought to the U.S. by Laurent Clerce (1785-1869), a Frenchman who taught deaf or hearing-impaired people.

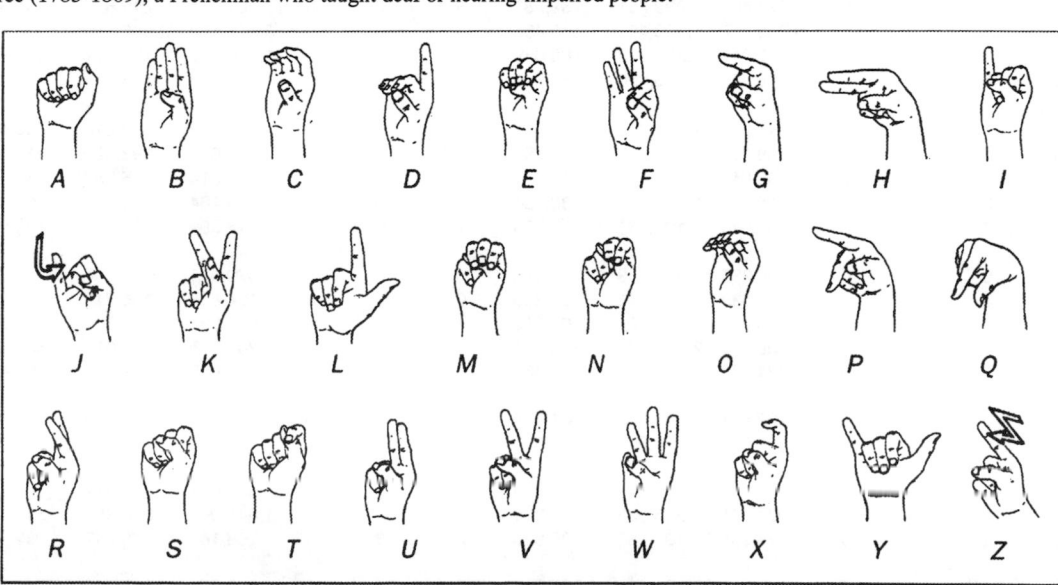

© National Association of the Deaf

PRESIDENTIAL ELECTIONS
Popular and Electoral Vote, 1992 and 1996

Source: Voter News Service; Federal Election Commission; totals are official.

	1996						1992					
	Electoral Vote			Democrat	Republican	Reform	Electoral Vote			Democrat	Republican	Independent
State	Clinton	Dole	Perot	Clinton	Dole	Perot	Clinton	Bush	Perot	Clinton	Bush	Perot
AL	0	9	0	662,165	769,044	92,149	0	9	0	690,080	804,283	183,109
AK	0	3	0	80,380	122,746	26,333	0	3	0	78,294	102,000	73,481
AZ	8	0	0	653,288	622,073	112,072	0	8	0	543,050	572,086	353,741
AR	6	0	0	475,171	325,416	69,884	6	0	0	505,823	337,324	99,132
CA	54	0	0	5,119,835	3,828,380	697,847	54	0	0	5,121,325	3,630,574	2,296,006
CO	0	8	0	671,152	691,848	99,629	8	0	0	629,681	562,850	366,010
CT	8	0	0	735,740	483,109	139,523	8	0	0	682,318	578,313	348,771
DE	3	0	0	140,355	99,062	28,719	3	0	0	126,054	102,313	59,213
DC	3	0	0	158,220	17,339	3,611	3	0	0	192,619	20,698	9,681
FL	25	0	0	2,545,968	2,243,324	483,776	0	25	0	2,071,651	2,171,781	1,052,481
GA	0	13	0	1,053,849	1,080,843	146,337	13	0	0	1,008,966	995,252	309,657
HI	4	0	0	205,012	113,943	27,358	4	0	0	179,310	136,822	53,003
ID	0	4	0	165,443	256,595	62,518	0	4	0	137,013	202,645	130,395
IL	22	0	0	2,341,744	1,587,021	346,408	22	0	0	2,453,350	1,734,096	840,515
IN	0	12	0	887,424	1,006,693	224,299	0	12	0	848,420	989,375	455,934
IA	7	0	0	620,258	492,644	105,159	7	0	0	586,353	504,891	253,468
KS	0	6	0	387,659	583,245	92,639	0	6	0	390,434	449,951	312,358
KY	8	0	0	636,614	623,283	120,396	8	0	0	665,104	617,178	203,944
LA	9	0	0	927,837	712,586	123,293	9	0	0	815,971	733,386	211,478
ME	4	0	0	312,788	186,378	85,970	4	0	0	263,420	206,504	206,820
MD	10	0	0	966,207	681,530	115,812	10	0	0	988,571	707,094	281,414
MA	12	0	0	1,571,509	718,058	227,206	12	0	0	1,318,639	805,039	630,731
MI	18	0	0	1,989,653	1,481,212	336,670	18	0	0	1,871,182	1,554,940	824,813
MN	10	0	0	1,120,438	766,476	257,704	10	0	0	1,020,997	747,841	562,506
MS	0	7	0	394,022	439,838	52,222	0	7	0	400,258	487,793	85,626
MO	11	0	0	1,025,935	890,016	217,188	11	0	0	1,053,873	811,159	518,741
MT	0	3	0	167,922	179,652	55,229	3	0	0	154,507	144,207	107,225
NE	0	5	0	236,761	363,467	71,278	0	5	0	216,864	343,678	174,104
NV	4	0	0	203,974	199,244	43,986	4	0	0	189,148	175,828	132,580
NH	4	0	0	246,166	196,486	48,387	4	0	0	209,040	202,484	121,337
NJ	15	0	0	1,652,361	1,103,099	262,134	15	0	0	1,436,206	1,356,865	521,829
NM	5	0	0	273,495	232,751	32,257	5	0	0	261,617	212,824	91,895
NY	33	0	0	3,756,177	1,933,492	503,458	33	0	0	3,444,450	2,346,649	1,090,721
NC	0	14	0	1,107,849	1,225,938	168,059	0	14	0	1,114,042	1,134,661	357,864
ND	0	3	0	106,905	125,050	32,515	0	3	0	99,168	136,244	71,084
OH	21	0	0	2,148,222	1,859,883	483,207	21	0	0	1,984,942	1,894,310	1,036,426
OK	0	8	0	488,105	582,315	130,788	0	8	0	473,066	592,929	319,878
OR	7	0	0	649,641	538,152	121,221	7	0	0	621,314	475,757	354,091
PA	23	0	0	2,215,819	1,801,169	430,984	23	0	0	2,239,164	1,791,841	902,667
RI	4	0	0	233,050	104,683	43,723	4	0	0	213,299	131,601	105,045
SC	0	8	0	506,283	573,458	64,386	0	8	0	479,514	577,507	138,872
SD	0	3	0	139,333	150,543	31,250	0	3	0	124,888	136,718	73,295
TN	11	0	0	909,146	863,530	105,918	11	0	0	933,521	841,300	199,968
TX	0	32	0	2,459,683	2,736,167	378,537	0	32	0	2,281,815	2,496,071	1,354,781
UT	0	5	0	221,633	361,911	66,461	0	5	0	183,429	322,632	203,400
VT	3	0	0	137,894	80,352	31,024	3	0	0	133,590	88,122	65,985
VA	0	13	0	1,091,060	1,138,350	159,861	0	13	0	1,038,650	1,150,517	348,639
WA	11	0	0	1,123,323	840,712	201,003	11	0	0	993,037	731,234	541,780
WV	5	0	0	327,812	233,946	71,639	5	0	0	331,001	241,974	108,829
WI	11	0	0	1,071,971	845,029	227,339	11	0	0	1,041,066	930,855	544,479
WY	0	3	0	77,934	105,388	25,928	0	3	0	68,160	79,347	51,263
Total	379	159	0	47,401,185	39,197,469	8,085,294	370	168	0	44,908,254	39,102,343	19,741,065

PRESIDENTIAL ELECTION RETURNS BY COUNTIES

All 1996 results are official. Results for New England states are for selected cities or towns because county results are not available. Totals are always statewide. D-Democrat; R-Republican; RF-Reform; I-Independent. (In 1996, Ross Perot was listed on the ballot in some states as "Independent.")

Source: Voter News Service; Federal Election Commission; Alaska Division of Elections

Alabama

County	1996 Clinton (D)	1996 Dole (R)	1996 Perot (RF)	1992 Clinton (D)	1992 Bush (R)	1992 Perot (I)
Autauga . . .	5,015	9,509	813	4,819	8,715	1,916
Baldwin . . .	12,776	29,487	4,520	12,195	26,270	7,656
Barbour . . .	4,787	3,627	515	4,836	4,475	1,020
Bibb	2,775	3,037	455	2,900	3,124	686
Blount	5,061	9,056	985	5,433	8,882	1,949
Bullock . . .	3,078	1,154	111	3,259	1,253	266
Butler	3,828	3,352	538	4,021	3,494	867
Calhoun . .	15,725	18,088	2,613	16,453	20,623	4,717
Chambers . .	5,515	4,707	812	5,938	5,682	1,427
Cherokee . .	4,399	3,048	899	4,222	2,745	846
Chilton . .	5,354	7,910	929	4,946	8,126	1,363
Choctaw . .	4,074	2,623	413	3,941	3,069	489
Clarke . . .	4,831	4,785	478	5,023	5,495	872
Clay	2,306	2,694	538	2,073	2,859	652
Cleburne . .	1,737	2,063	385	2,144	2,425	630
Coffee	5,168	7,805	1,042	5,776	7,591	2,021
Colbert . . .	10,226	8,305	1,696	12,206	8,073	2,098
Conecuh . .	2,903	2,093	445	3,155	2,463	552
Coosa . . .	2,121	1,721	262	2,330	1,973	476
Covington .	4,543	6,035	1,098	5,004	6,840	1,880
Crenshaw . .	2,172	1,939	317	2,404	2,339	485
Cullman . . .	9,544	14,308	2,440	10,451	14,411	4,113
Dale	4,732	8,288	1,216	5,098	8,123	2,423
Dallas	10,507	6,612	477	11,053	7,394	1,110
DeKalb . . .	6,544	9,823	1,609	8,245	10,519	2,741
Elmore . . .	6,530	12,937	1,368	6,223	11,356	2,765
Escambia . .	4,651	5,214	867	4,809	5,955	1,616
Etowah . . .	17,976	16,835	2,529	20,558	17,467	4,277
Fayette . . .	3,381	3,191	590	3,830	3,604	1,012
Franklin . . .	5,028	4,449	966	5,953	4,794	1,075
Geneva . . .	3,174	4,725	857	3,622	4,843	1,323
Greene . . .	3,526	796	55	3,865	805	194
Hale	3,372	1,893	190	3,481	2,001	486
Henry	3,019	3,082	515	2,804	2,970	667
Houston . . .	8,791	17,476	1,653	8,857	17,360	3,492
Jackson . . .	8,204	5,650	1,573	10,628	5,711	2,462
Jefferson . .	120,208	130,980	7,997	125,889	149,832	22,191
Lamar	2,843	2,955	597	2,849	3,262	763
Lauderdale .	13,619	14,058	2,574	15,936	13,728	4,009
Lawrence . .	5,254	3,893	964	6,364	3,576	1,624
Lee	12,919	17,985	1,949	13,770	16,885	4,572
Limestone .	8,045	10,862	1,659	8,087	9,862	3,584
Lowndes . .	3,970	1,369	72	3,500	1,328	284
Macon	7,018	987	150	7,253	1,134	283
Madison . . .	42,259	50,390	7,437	38,974	51,444	16,989
Marengo . .	4,899	4,013	337	5,632	4,470	919
Marion . . .	5,049	4,742	979	6,167	5,692	1,389
Marshall . . .	8,722	12,323	2,150	10,421	12,249	3,795
Mobile	54,749	66,775	7,555	54,962	72,935	15,105
Monroe . . .	3,815	4,382	486	3,872	4,919	759
Montgomery	38,382	37,784	2,036	37,342	40,742	7,647
Morgan . . .	14,616	21,765	3,348	15,091	21,073	7,683
Perry	4,053	1,703	119	3,712	1,829	213
Pickens . . .	4,018	3,322	403	3,783	3,634	690
Pike	4,514	5,281	503	4,688	5,423	1,024
Randolph . .	3,023	3,304	603	3,318	3,813	919
Russell . . .	7,834	5,025	792	8,647	5,587	1,360
St. Clair . . .	6,187	12,762	1,417	6,517	12,447	2,614
Shelby . . .	11,280	37,090	2,035	10,317	32,736	5,022
Sumter . . .	4,706	1,561	172	4,810	1,807	388
Talladega . .	10,385	10,931	1,335	10,695	12,661	2,629
Tallapoosa	6,071	7,627	1,038	5,703	8,140	1,562
Tuscaloosa	23,067	27,939	3,048	23,495	27,454	7,011
Walker . . .	12,929	9,837	2,012	14,831	11,301	3,344
Washington	3,935	2,900	819	4,046	3,270	829
Wilcox	3,303	1,454	71	3,439	1,671	174
Winston . . .	3,120	4,728	723	3,415	5,550	1,110
Totals	662,165	769,044	92,149	690,080	804,283	183,109

Alabama Vote Since 1948

1948, Thurmond, States' Rights, 171,443; Dewey, Rep., 40,930; Wallace, Prog., 1,522; Watson, Proh., 1,085.

1952, Eisenhower, Rep., 149,231; Stevenson, Dem., 275,075; Hamblen, Proh., 1,814.

1956, Stevenson, Dem., 290,844; Eisenhower, Rep., 195,694; Independent electors, 20,323.

1960, Kennedy, Dem., 324,050; Nixon, Rep., 237,981; Faubus, States' Rights, 4,367; Decker, Proh., 2,106; King, Afro-Americans, 1,485; scattering, 236.

1964, Dem. (electors unpledged), 209,848; Goldwater, Rep., 479,085; scattering, 105.

1968, Nixon, Rep., 146,923; Humphrey, Dem., 196,579; Wallace, 3d Party, 691,425; Munn, Proh., 4,022.

1972, Nixon, Rep., 728,701; McGovern, Dem., 219,108 plus 37,815 Natl. Demo. Party of Alabama; Schmitz, Conservative, 11,918; Munn., Proh., 8,551.

1976, Carter, Dem., 659,170; Ford, Rep., 504,070; Maddox, Amer. Ind., 9,198; Bubar, Proh., 6,669; Hall, Com., 1,954; MacBride, Libertarian, 1,481.

1980, Reagan, Rep., 654,192; Carter, Dem., 636,730; Anderson, Independent, 16,481; Rarick, Amer. Ind., 15,010; Clark, Libertarian, 13,318; Bubar, Statesman, 1,743; Hall, Com., 1,629; DeBerry, Soc. Workers, 1,303; McReynolds, Socialist, 1,006; Commoner, Citizens, 517.

1984, Reagan, Rep., 872,849; Mondale, Dem., 551,899; Bergland, Libertarian, 9,504.

1988, Bush, Rep., 815,576; Dukakis, Dem., 549,506; Paul, Lib., 8,460; Fulani, Ind., 3,311.

1992, Bush, Rep., 804,283; Clinton, Dem., 690,080; Perot, Ind., 183,109; Marrou, Libertarian, 5,737; Fulani, New Alliance, 2,161.

1996, Dole, Rep., 769,044; Clinton, Dem., 662,165; Perot, Ind. (Ref.), 92,149; Browne, Libertarian, 5,290; Phillips, Ind., 2,365; Hagelin, Natural Law, 1,697; Harris, Ind., 516.

Alaska

Election District[1]	1996 Clinton (D)	1996 Dole (R)	1996 Perot (RF)	1992 Clinton (D)	1992 Bush (R)	1992 Perot (I)
No. 1 . . .	1,480	4,209	696	2,055	2,495	2,120
No. 2 . . .	2,563	3,247	912	2,565	2,916	2,137
No. 3 . . .	3,724	2,671	654	4,064	2,447	1,424
No. 4 . . .	3,037	3,336	694	2,688	2,894	1,561
No. 5 . . .	2,148	2,564	826	2,095	1,844	1,684
No. 6 . . .	1,576	2,707	557	1,546	2,345	1,748
No. 7 . . .	2,177	3,517	907	2,088	2,173	2,244
No. 8 . . .	1,643	3,624	826	1,509	2,499	2,325
No. 9 . . .	1,334	3,459	727	1,540	2,349	2,368
No. 10. . . .	2,203	4,184	642	1,947	3,548	1,899
No. 11. . . .	1,946	3,073	603	2,009	2,730	2,081
No. 12. . . .	1,825	3,568	543	1,831	2,999	2,039
No. 13. . . .	2,780	3,270	608	3,001	2,963	1,907
No. 14. . . .	1,471	3,005	458	1,423	3,013	1,599
No. 15. . . .	2,178	1,974	552	2,389	1,842	1,591
No. 16. . . .	1,629	1,328	414	1,814	1,375	1,320
No. 17. . . .	1,868	3,284	633	1,749	2,623	1,958
No. 18. . . .	2,708	4,245	694	2,483	3,629	2,134
No. 19. . . .	2,014	3,159	636	1,931	2,539	1,840
No. 20. . . .	2,144	3,025	545	2,383	2,914	1,823
No. 21. . . .	2,228	2,553	557	2,386	2,437	1,693
No. 22. . . .	2,511	3,887	624	2,253	3,164	1,713
No. 23. . . .	1,071	2,127	388	1,139	2,127	1,217
No. 24. . . .	1,914	3,653	548	1,876	3,441	1,930
No. 25. . . .	1,629	4,099	691	1,513	3,197	2,122
No. 26. . . .	1,519	3,913	883	1,439	2,675	2,419
No. 27. . . .	1,887	4,384	1,122	1,625	2,757	2,401
No. 28. . . .	1,645	4,202	1,333	1,522	2,459	2,825
No. 29. . . .	3,023	3,012	658	3,216	2,205	2,026
No. 30. . . .	1,794	2,785	601	1,860	2,434	1,912
No. 31. . . .	1,903	2,721	684	1,969	2,223	1,992
No. 32. . . .	1,275	2,736	675	1,150	2,339	1,724
No. 33. . . .	1,852	4,089	759	1,712	3,100	2,278
No. 34. . . .	1,388	3,677	734	1,455	3,408	2,201
No. 35. . . .	1,447	3,016	875	1,572	2,525	2,139
No. 36. . . .	2,321	1,992	453	1,748	2,081	1,322
No. 37. . . .	2,134	1,835	456	1,822	1,689	925
No. 38. . . .	2,436	1,716	393	1,897	2,011	850
No. 39. . . .	2,692	1,618	404	1,797	1,777	860
No. 40. . . .	1,260	1,280	368	1,211	1,786	1,122
Totals. . . .	80,377	122,744	26,333	78,294	102,000	73,481

(1) 1992 and 1996 results are not comparable because of a 1994 reapportionment of districts.

Alaska Vote Since 1960

1960, Kennedy, Dem., 29,809; Nixon, Rep., 30,953.

1964, Johnson, Dem., 44,329; Goldwater, Rep., 22,930.

1968, Nixon, Rep., 37,600; Humphrey, Dem., 35,411; Wallace, 3d Party, 10,024.

1972, Nixon, Rep., 55,349; McGovern, Dem., 32,967; Schmitz, Amer., 6,903.

1976, Carter, Dem., 44,058; Ford, Rep., 71,555; MacBride, Libertarian, 6,785.

1980, Reagan, Rep., 86,112, Carter, Dem., 41,842; Clark, Libertarian, 18,479; Anderson, Ind., 11,155; write-in, 857.

1984, Reagan, Rep., 138,377; Mondale, Dem., 62,007; Bergland, Libertarian, 6,378.

1988, Bush, Rep., 119,251; Dukakis, Dem., 72,584; Paul, Lib., 5,484; Fulani, New Alliance, 1,024.

1992, Bush, Rep., 102,000; Clinton, Dem., 78,294; Perot, Ind., 73,481; Gritz, Populist/America First, 1,379; Marrou, Libertarian, 1,378.

1996, Dole, Rep., 122,746; Clinton, Dem., 80,380; Perot, Ref., 26,333; Nader, Green, 7,597; Browne, Libertarian, 2,276; Phillips, Taxpayers, 925; Hagelin, Natural Law, 729.

Arizona

County	1996 Clinton (D)	Dole (R)	Perot (RF)	1992 Clinton (D)	Bush (R)	Perot (I)
Apache	12,394	4,761	1,296	11,218	4,588	1,979
Cochise	13,782	14,365	3,346	12,701	12,202	7,857
Coconino	20,475	13,638	3,666	18,888	13,769	9,363
Gila	8,577	6,407	2,211	7,571	5,781	4,694
Graham	3,938	4,222	1,034	3,391	4,169	1,860
Greenlee	1,755	1,159	426	1,695	1,451	794
La Paz	1,964	1,902	597	1,808	1,599	1,488
Maricopa	363,991	386,015	58,479	285,457	360,049	221,475
Mohave	16,629	17,997	6,369	13,255	13,684	12,706
Navajo	12,912	9,262	2,461	10,882	7,994	4,787
Pima	137,983	104,121	18,809	128,569	97,036	53,925
Pinal	19,579	13,034	3,972	15,468	11,669	9,231
Santa Cruz	5,241	2,256	600	3,512	3,024	1,447
Yavapai	21,801	29,921	6,649	18,268	23,419	16,409
Yuma	12,267	13,013	2,157	10,367	11,652	5,726
Totals	653,288	622,073	112,072	543,050	572,086	353,741

Arizona Vote Since 1948

1948, Truman, Dem., 95,251; Dewey, Rep., 77,597; Wallace, Prog., 3,310; Watson, Proh., 786; Teichert, Soc. Labor, 121.

1952, Eisenhower, Rep., 152,042; Stevenson, Dem., 108,528.

1956, Eisenhower, Rep., 176,990; Stevenson, Dem., 112,880; Andrews, Ind. 303.

1960, Kennedy, Dem., 176,781; Nixon, Rep., 221,241; Hass, Soc. Labor, 469.

1964, Johnson, Dem., 237,753; Goldwater, Rep., 242,535; Hass, Soc. Labor, 482.

1968, Nixon, Rep., 266,721; Humphrey, Dem., 170,514; Wallace, 3d Party, 46,573; McCarthy, New Party, 2,751; Halstead, Soc. Workers, 85; Cleaver, Peace and Freedom, 217; Blomen, Soc. Labor, 75.

1972, Nixon, Rep., 402,812; McGovern, Dem., 198,540; Schmitz, Amer., 21,208; Soc. Workers, 30,945. Because of ballot peculiarities in 3 counties (particularly Pima), thousands of voters cast ballots for the Soc. Workers Party *and* one of the major candidates. Court ordered both votes counted as official.

1976, Carter, Dem., 295,602; Ford, Rep., 418,642; McCarthy, Ind., 19,229; MacBride, Libertarian, 7,647; Camejo, Soc. Workers, 928; Anderson, Amer., 564; Maddox, Amer. Ind., 85.

1980, Reagan, Rep., 529,688; Carter, Dem., 246,843; Anderson, Ind., 76,952; Clark, Libertarian, 18,784; De Berry, Soc. Workers, 1,100; Commoner, Citizens, 551; Hall, Com., 25; Griswold, Workers World, 2.

1984, Reagan, Rep., 681,416; Mondale, Dem., 333,854; Bergland, Libertarian, 10,585.

1988, Bush, Rep., 702,541; Dukakis, Dem., 454,029; Paul, Lib., 13,351; Fulani, New Alliance, 1,662.

1992, Bush, Rep., 572,086; Clinton, Dem., 543,050; Perot, Ind., 353,741; Gritz, Populist/America First, 8,141; Marrou, Libertarian, 6,759; Hagelin, Natural Law, 2,267.

1996, Clinton, Dem., 653,288; Dole, Rep., 622,073; Perot, Ref., 112,072; Browne, Libertarian, 14,358.

Arkansas

County	1996 Clinton (D)	Dole (R)	Perot (RF)	1992 Clinton (D)	Bush (R)	Perot (I)
Arkansas	4,220	1,910	463	4,709	2,594	639
Ashley	5,011	2,428	704	5,876	2,686	931
Baxter	6,703	6,877	1,572	6,991	5,640	2,938
Benton	17,205	23,748	4,147	15,774	21,126	6,128
Boone	5,745	6,093	1,132	6,128	6,094	2,079
Bradley	2,566	1,146	221	2,954	1,482	391
Calhoun	1,306	727	237	1,389	1,047	257
Carroll	3,689	3,957	986	3,769	3,535	1,500
Chicot	3,090	1,056	233	3,504	1,242	347
Clark	5,281	2,112	567	5,767	2,403	714
Clay	3,848	1,512	464	4,848	1,647	568
Cleburne	4,475	3,807	1,021	5,090	3,580	1,263
Cleveland	1,741	990	268	1,893	1,127	337
Columbia	4,730	3,376	678	4,747	3,702	1,090
Conway	4,055	2,307	746	4,898	2,719	803
Craighead	13,284	9,210	1,778	13,931	9,104	2,274
Crawford	6,749	7,182	1,683	6,656	6,882	2,442
Crittenden	8,415	4,673	554	9,683	5,910	848
Cross	3,631	2,000	466	4,058	2,303	602
Dallas	2,118	1,041	236	2,107	1,458	345
Desha	3,230	978	247	3,815	1,279	392
Drew	3,570	1,657	395	3,748	1,938	596
Faulkner	12,032	10,178	1,528	13,000	9,491	2,437
Franklin	3,269	2,246	626	3,217	2,495	987
Fulton	2,361	1,351	455	2,827	1,258	631
Garland	19,211	13,662	2,769	18,811	12,886	3,475
Grant	2,948	1,925	557	3,190	2,272	702
Greene	6,622	3,757	1,014	7,541	3,510	1,213
Hempstead	4,983	2,021	501	5,476	2,387	1,022
Hot Spring	6,002	2,864	1,123	6,308	3,036	1,209
Howard	2,741	1,478	369	2,764	1,728	466
Independence	6,240	4,021	1,126	7,083	4,232	1,444
Izard	2,818	1,678	541	3,419	1,532	606
Jackson	4,304	1,525	611	4,944	1,864	673
Jefferson	19,701	6,330	1,284	21,819	7,525	2,067
Johnson	3,585	2,367	757	3,951	2,563	1,013
Lafayette	2,466	971	374	2,273	1,188	504
Lawrence	3,652	1,823	609	4,146	2,124	636
Lee	3,267	1,013	257	3,436	1,293	308
Lincoln	2,517	907	221	2,805	1,142	390
Little River	3,183	1,409	480	3,327	1,483	890
Logan	3,832	2,966	1,048	3,995	3,408	1,220
Lonoke	8,049	6,414	1,369	7,963	6,253	1,554
Madison	2,504	2,303	461	2,415	2,238	598
Marion	2,735	2,312	764	2,757	2,023	1,327
Miller	6,469	4,874	1,043	7,050	5,273	2,249
Mississippi	8,301	3,919	1,016	10,046	4,697	981
Monroe	2,247	973	202	2,578	1,324	355
Montgomery	1,830	1,137	427	1,904	1,205	576
Nevada	2,279	976	345	2,242	1,217	455
Newton	1,631	1,927	498	1,765	1,730	608
Ouachita	6,635	3,136	733	7,411	3,711	1,238
Perry	1,873	1,143	395	1,906	1,162	412
Phillips	5,715	2,205	461	6,456	2,695	634
Pike	2,362	1,401	441	2,168	1,577	472
Poinsett	4,686	2,034	647	5,341	2,425	761
Polk	2,824	2,852	876	3,162	2,757	1,225
Pope	8,433	8,243	1,891	7,704	8,056	1,989
Prairie	2,211	1,025	305	2,366	1,154	434
Pulaski	75,084	44,780	6,014	79,482	47,789	8,751
Randolph	3,213	1,789	561	3,921	1,766	578
St. Francis	5,562	2,523	506	6,548	3,289	766
Saline	14,027	11,695	2,612	12,671	10,105	2,751
Scott	2,259	1,426	513	2,228	1,695	610
Searcy	1,669	1,786	381	1,679	1,772	503
Sebastian	15,514	16,482	2,899	16,570	16,817	6,023
Sevier	2,553	1,379	446	2,558	1,592	643
Sharp	3,573	2,635	687	3,761	2,486	921
Stone	2,227	1,526	579	2,622	1,672	697
Union	8,373	6,053	1,073	8,786	7,305	1,919
Van Buren	3,521	2,345	830	3,819	2,612	888
Washington	20,419	19,476	3,133	22,029	20,292	5,304
White	10,204	8,659	1,828	10,494	8,538	2,366
Woodruff	2,044	598	186	2,589	676	227
Yell	3,749	2,111	714	4,165	2,506	940
Totals	475,171	325,416	69,884	505,823	337,324	99,132

Arkansas Vote Since 1948

1948, Truman, Dem., 149,659; Dewey, Rep., 50,959; Thurmond, States' Rights, 40,068; Thomas, Soc., 1,037; Wallace, Prog., 751; Watson, Proh., 1.

1952, Eisenhower, Rep., 177,155; Stevenson, Dem., 226,300; Hamblen, Proh., 886; MacArthur, Christian Nationalist, 458; Hass, Soc. Labor, 1.

1956, Stevenson, Dem., 213,277; Eisenhower, Rep., 186,287; Andrews, Ind., 7,008.

1960, Kennedy, Dem., 215,049; Nixon, Rep., 184,508; Natl. States' Rights, 28,952.

1964, Johnson, Dem., 314,197; Goldwater, Rep., 243,264; Kasper, Natl. States' Rights, 2,965.

1968, Nixon, Rep., 189,062; Humphrey, Dem., 184,901; Wallace, 3d Party, 235,627.

1972, Nixon, Rep., 445,751; McGovern, Dem., 198,899; Schmitz, Amer., 3,016.

1976, Carter, Dem., 498,604; Ford, Rep., 267,903; McCarthy, Ind., 639; Anderson, Amer., 389.

1980, Reagan, Rep., 403,164; Carter, Dem., 398,041; Anderson, Ind., 22,468; Clark, Libertarian, 8,970; Commoner, Citizens, 2,345; Bubar, Statesman, 1,350; Hall, Com., 1,244.

1984, Reagan, Rep., 534,774; Mondale, Dem., 338,646; Bergland, Libertarian, 2,220.

1988, Bush, Rep., 466,578; Dukakis, Dem., 349,237; Duke, Chr. Pop., 5,146; Paul, Lib., 3,297.

1992, Clinton, Dem., 505,823; Bush, Rep., 337,324; Perot, Ind., 99,132; Phillips, U.S. Taxpayers, 1,437; Marrou, Libertarian, 1,261; Fulani, New Alliance, 1,022.

1996, Clinton, Dem., 475,171; Dole, Rep., 325,416; Perot, Ref., 69,884; Nader, Ind., 3,649; Browne, Ind., 3,076; Phillips, Ind., 2,065; Forbes, Ind., 932; Collins, Ind., 823; Masters, Ind., 749; Hagelin, Ind., 729; Moorehead, Ind., 747; Hollis, Ind., 538; Dodge, Ind., 483.

California

County	1996 Clinton (D)	Dole (R)	Perot (RF)	1992 Clinton (D)	Bush (R)	Perot (I)
Alameda	303,903	106,581	24,270	334,224	109,292	81,643
Alpine	258	264	63	215	222	186

County	1996 Clinton (D)	Dole (R)	Perot (RF)	1992 Clinton (D)	Bush (R)	Perot (I)
Amador . . .	5,868	6,870	1,267	5,286	5,477	4,553
Butte	30,651	38,961	6,393	32,489	31,608	20,231
Calaveras. .	6,646	8,279	1,612	5,989	6,006	4,848
Colusa. . . .	2,054	3,047	404	1,798	2,589	1,206
Contra Costa	196,512	123,954	20,416	194,960	112,965	72,518
Del Norte . .	3,652	3,670	1,225	3,639	3,083	2,575
El Dorado . .	22,957	32,759	5,077	21,012	25,906	17,503
Fresno . . .	94,448	98,813	10,962	92,418	89,137	36,299
Glenn	2,841	5,041	788	2,666	3,812	2,278
Humboldt . .	24,628	19,803	5,811	28,854	18,299	12,340
Imperial . .	14,591	9,705	1,778	11,109	9,759	4,247
Inyo.	2,601	3,924	811	2,695	3,689	1,999
Kern	62,658	92,151	13,452	60,510	80,762	36,891
Kings.	11,254	12,368	1,745	9,982	10,673	4,899
Lake	10,432	7,458	2,539	10,548	6,678	5,797
Lassen. . . .	3,318	5,194	1,080	3,388	3,836	3,004
Los Angeles.	1,430,629	746,544	157,752	1,446,529	799,607	488,624
Madera . . .	11,254	16,510	2,192	10,863	13,066	6,156
Marin.	67,406	32,714	6,559	76,158	30,479	22,986
Mariposa . .	2,920	3,976	729	3,023	2,982	2,211
Mendocino .	14,952	9,765	3,685	18,344	7,958	9,753
Merced . . .	21,786	20,847	3,427	20,133	17,981	10,914
Modoc	1,368	2,285	528	1,489	1,803	1,269
Mono	1,580	1,882	447	1,489	1,570	1,248
Monterey . .	57,700	39,794	7,240	54,861	36,461	24,472
Napa	24,588	17,439	4,254	24,215	15,662	13,150
Nevada . . .	15,369	21,784	3,330	15,433	17,343	11,072
Orange . . .	327,485	446,717	66,195	306,930	426,613	232,394
Placer	34,981	49,808	6,542	30,783	38,298	21,741
Plumas . . .	3,540	4,905	919	3,742	3,599	2,551
Riverside . .	168,579	178,611	35,481	166,241	159,457	102,233
Sacramento	203,019	166,049	23,856	197,540	160,366	91,412
San Benito .	7,030	5,384	1,044	5,354	4,112	3,182
San Bernardino	183,372	180,135	39,330	183,634	176,563	109,183
San Diego .	389,964	402,876	63,037	367,397	352,125	259,249
San Francisco	209,777	45,479	9,659	233,263	57,352	29,018
San Joaquin	67,253	65,131	9,692	63,655	58,355	31,205
San Luis Obispo . . .	40,395	46,733	8,204	40,136	36,384	27,314
San Mateo .	152,304	73,508	15,047	149,232	75,080	50,465
Santa Barbara	70,650	63,915	9,457	69,215	57,375	35,105
Santa Clara	297,635	168,291	34,908	296,265	170,870	128,895
Santa Cruz .	58,250	27,766	6,555	66,183	24,916	21,615
Shasta. . . .	20,848	34,736	5,875	21,605	28,190	17,990
Sierra	573	877	170	653	691	519
Siskiyou . . .	7,022	8,653	1,879	8,254	6,660	5,567
Solano	64,644	40,742	8,682	64,320	38,883	27,851
Sonoma . . .	100,738	53,555	13,862	104,334	47,619	43,859
Stanislaus .	53,738	52,403	8,360	52,415	47,275	27,651
Sutter	8,504	14,264	1,533	7,883	12,956	4,881
Tehama . . .	7,290	10,292	2,325	7,508	7,419	5,884
Trinity	2,203	2,530	856	1,967	1,886	2,092
Tulare	32,666	46,272	5,106	31,188	40,482	16,430
Tuolumne . .	8,950	10,386	1,925	9,216	8,525	6,294
Ventura . . .	110,772	109,202	23,054	99,011	94,911	71,844
Yolo	33,033	18,807	3,150	33,297	17,574	11,073
Yuba	5,789	7,971	1,308	5,785	7,333	3,637
Totals . . .	5,119,835	3,828,380	697,847	5,121,325	3,630,574	2,296,006

California Vote Since 1948

1948, Truman, Dem., 1,913,134; Dewey, Rep., 1,895,269; Wallace, Prog., 190,381; Watson, Proh., 16,926; Thomas, Soc., 3,459; Thurmond, States' Rights, 1,228; Teichert, Soc. Labor, 195; Dobbs, Soc. Workers, 133.

1952, Eisenhower, Rep., 2,897,310; Stevenson, Dem., 2,197,548; Hallinan, Prog., 24,106; Hamblen, Proh., 15,653; MacArthur, (Tenny Ticket) 3,326; (Kellems Ticket) 178; Hass, Soc. Labor, 273; Hoopes, Soc., 206; scattered, 3,249.

1956, Eisenhower, Rep., 3,027,668; Stevenson, Dem., 2,420,136; Holtwick, Proh., 11,119; Andrews, Constitution, 6,087; Hass, Soc. Labor, 300; Hoopes, Soc., 123; Dobbs, Soc. Workers, 96; Smith, Christian Natl., 8.

1960, Kennedy, Dem., 3,224,099; Nixon, Rep., 3,259,722; Decker, Proh., 21,706; Hass, Soc. Labor, 1,051.

1964, Johnson, Dem., 4,171,877; Goldwater, Rep., 2,879,108; Hass, Soc. Labor, 489; DeBerry, Soc. Workers, 378; Munn, Proh., 305; Hensley, Universal, 19.

1968, Nixon, Rep., 3,467,664; Humphrey, Dem., 3,244,318; Wallace, 3d Party, 487,270; Peace and Freedom, 27,707; McCarthy, Alternative, 20,721; Gregory, write-in, 3,230; Mitchell, Com., 260; Munn, Proh., 59; Blomen, Soc. Labor, 341; Soeters, Defense, 17.

1972, Nixon, Rep., 4,602,096; McGovern, Dem., 3,475,847; Schmitz, Amer., 232,554; Spock, Peace and Freedom, 55,167; Hall, Com., 373; Hospers, Libertarian, 900; Munn, Proh., 53; Fisher, Soc. Labor, 197; Jenness, Soc. Workers, 574; Green, Universal, 21.

1976, Carter, Dem., 3,742,284; Ford, Rep., 3,882,244; MacBride, Libertarian, 56,388; Maddox, Amer. Ind., 51,098; Wright, People's, 41,731; Camejo, Soc. Workers, 17,259; Hall, Com., 12,766; write-in, McCarthy, 58,412; other write-in, 4,935.

1980, Reagan, Rep. 4,524,858; Carter, Dem., 3,083,661; Anderson, Ind., 739,833; Clark, Libertarian, 148,434; Commoner, Ind., 61,063; Smith, Peace and Freedom, 18,116; Rarick, Amer. Ind., 9,856.

1984, Reagan, Rep. 5,305,410; Mondale, Dem., 3,815,947; Bergland, Libertarian, 48,400.

1988, Bush, Rep., 5,054,917; Dukakis, Dem., 4,702,233; Paul, Lib., 70,105; Fulani, Ind., 31,181.

1992, Clinton, Dem., 5,121,325; Bush, Rep., 3,630,575; Perot, Ind., 2,296,006; Marrou, Libertarian, 48,139; Daniels, Ind., 18,597; Phillips, U.S. Taxpayers, 12,711.

1996, Clinton, Dem., 5,119,835; Dole, Rep., 3,828,380; Perot, Ref., 697,847; Nader, Green, 237,016; Browne, Libertarian, 73,600; Feinland, Peace & Freedom, 25,332; Phillips, Amer. Ind., 21,202; Hagelin, Natural Law, 15,403.

Colorado

County	1996 Clinton (D)	Dole (R)	Perot (RF)	1992 Clinton (D)	Bush (R)	Perot (I)
Adams. . . .	48,314	36,666	7,206	45,357	30,856	26,379
Alamosa. . .	2,330	2,038	437	1,928	1,572	1,089
Arapahoe. .	68,306	82,778	8,476	66,607	72,221	44,363
Archuleta . .	997	1,963	360	819	1,242	741
Baca	659	1,321	203	726	1,240	647
Bent	1,046	917	209	985	759	506
Boulder . . .	63,316	41,922	6,840	64,567	33,553	27,762
Chaffee . . .	2,768	3,052	538	2,284	2,419	1,549
Cheyenne. .	328	739	91	301	615	292
Clear Creek	1,863	1,746	365	1,744	1,356	1,308
Conejos . . .	1,726	1,149	245	1,705	1,160	578
Costilla . . .	1,168	333	112	1,180	366	199
Crowley . . .	559	680	114	570	602	276
Custer	412	920	164	343	651	368
Delta	3,584	6,047	1,060	3,624	4,359	2,627
Denver	120,312	58,529	8,777	121,961	55,418	37,298
Dolores . . .	276	417	95	242	315	285
Douglas . . .	16,232	32,120	2,662	9,991	18,592	11,329
Eagle.	5,094	4,637	1,193	3,870	3,100	3,821
Elbert	1,894	4,125	507	1,237	2,205	1,567
El Paso . . .	55,822	102,403	11,175	45,827	86,044	34,346
Fremont . . .	5,344	7,437	1,438	5,356	5,961	3,709
Garfield . . .	5,722	6,281	1,562	5,082	4,404	4,408
Gilpin.	799	682	184	726	462	545
Grand	2,012	2,264	473	1,678	1,763	1,454
Gunnison . .	2,812	2,230	570	2,389	1,662	1,671
Hinsdale. . .	185	289	56	151	188	136
Huerfano . .	1,483	996	210	1,224	685	385
Jackson . . .	222	486	107	216	422	326
Jefferson . .	89,494	101,517	12,967	80,834	82,705	58,404
Kiowa	246	549	74	290	472	267
Kit Carson .	1,073	2,068	235	925	1,801	919
Lake	1,338	728	274	1,426	605	863
La Plata . . .	6,509	8,057	1,403	5,913	5,522	4,083
Larimer . . .	40,965	45,935	6,823	38,232	35,995	24,879
Las Animas.	3,611	1,905	427	3,847	1,739	953
Lincoln . . .	729	1,272	164	640	1,079	581
Logan	2,765	4,032	609	2,718	3,420	2,184
Mesa	17,114	24,761	3,707	15,162	18,169	10,474
Mineral . . .	192	179	69	171	159	117
Moffat	1,635	2,466	649	1,386	1,809	1,875
Montezuma .	2,578	4,175	827	2,270	3,124	2,205
Montrose . .	4,019	6,730	1,187	3,713	4,847	3,093
Morgan . . .	3,347	4,557	687	2,985	3,724	2,175
Otero.	3,386	3,356	581	3,485	3,120	1,590
Ouray	569	984	167	461	653	466
Park	1,844	2,661	534	1,307	1,530	1,396
Philips	706	1,284	156	692	1,075	525
Pitkin	3,949	1,969	535	3,820	1,686	1,907
Prowers . . .	1,745	2,504	342	1,770	2,371	1,184
Pueblo	28,791	17,402	3,374	30,261	16,120	9,841
Rio Blanco .	731	1,697	243	778	1,231	794
Rio Grande .	1,720	2,129	379	1,541	1,927	1,043
Routt	3,660	3,019	859	3,188	2,358	2,564
Saguache . .	969	712	160	1,011	675	471
San Juan . .	133	153	50	147	118	183
San Miguel .	1,535	773	231	1,380	628	634
Sedgwick . .	519	715	101	397	447	295
Summit . . .	3,970	3,261	823	3,344	2,256	2,715
Teller	2,312	4,458	707	1,873	3,050	1,927
Washington	649	1,566	190	660	1,266	671
Weld	21,325	26,518	4,347	19,295	20,958	13,571
Yuma	1,439	2,589	319	1,269	2,019	1,197
Totals	671,152	691,848	99,629	629,681	562,850	366,010

Colorado Vote Since 1948

1948, Truman, Dem., 267,288; Dewey, Rep., 239,714; Wallace, Prog., 6,115; Thomas, Soc., 1,678; Dobbs, Soc. Workers, 228; Teichert, Soc. Labor, 214.

1952, Eisenhower, Rep., 379,782; Stevenson, Dem., 245,504; MacArthur, Constitution, 2,181; Hallinan, Prog., 1,919; Hoopes, Soc., 365; Hass, Soc. Labor, 352.

1956, Eisenhower, Rep., 394,479; Stevenson, Dem., 263,997; Hass, Soc. Lab., 3,308; Andrews, Ind., 759; Hoopes, Soc., 531.

1960, Kennedy, Dem., 330,629; Nixon, Rep., 402,242; Hass, Soc. Labor, 2,803; Dobbs, Soc. Workers, 572.

1964, Johnson, Dem., 476,024; Goldwater, Rep., 296,767; Hass, Soc. Labor, 302; DeBerry, Soc. Workers, 2,537; Munn, Proh., 1,356.

1968, Nixon, Rep., 409,345; Humphrey, Dem., 335,174; Wallace, 3d Party, 60,813; Blomen, Soc. Labor, 3,016; Gregory, New-party, 1,393; Munn, Proh., 275; Halstead, Soc. Workers, 235.

1972, Nixon, Rep., 597,189; McGovern, Dem., 329,980; Fisher, Soc. Labor, 4,361; Hospers, Libertarian, 1,111; Hall, Com., 432; Jenness, Soc. Workers, 555; Munn, Proh., 467; Schmitz, Amer., 17,269; Spock, Peoples, 2,403.

1976, Carter, Dem., 460,353; Ford, Rep., 584,367; McCarthy, Ind., 26,107; MacBride, Libertarian, 5,330; Bubar, Proh., 2,882.

1980, Reagan, Rep., 652,264; Carter, Dem., 367,973; Anderson, Ind., 130,633; Clark, Libertarian, 25,744; Commoner, Citizens, 5,614; Bubar, Statesman, 1,180; Pulley, Socialist, 520; Hall, Com., 487.

1984, Reagan, Rep., 821,817; Mondale, Dem., 454,975; Bergland, Libertarian, 11,257.

1988, Bush, Rep., 728,177; Dukakis, Dem., 621,453; Paul, Lib., 15,482; Dodge, Proh., 4,604.

1992, Clinton, Dem., 629,681; Bush, Rep., 562,850; Perot, Ind., 366,010; Marrou, Libertarian, 8,669; Fulani, New Alliance, 1,608.

1996, Dole, Rep., 691,848; Clinton, Dem., 671,152; Perot, Ref., 99,629; Nader, Green, 25,070; Browne, Libertarian, 12,392; Collins, Ind., 2,809; Phillips, Amer. Constitution, 2,813; Hagelin, Natural Law, 2,547; Hollis, Soc., 669; Moorehead, Workers World, 599; Templin, Amer., 557; Dodge, Proh., 375; Harris, Soc. Workers, 244.

Connecticut

City	1996 Clinton (D)	Dole (R)	Perot (RF)	1992 Clinton (D)	Bush (R)	Perot (I)
Bridgeport .	22,883	6,785	2,367	22,321	13,149	6,263
Bristol	13,616	6,560	3,049	11,872	8,407	7,890
Danbury . . .	12,102	7,965	2,158	9,909	10,310	5,517
Fairfield . . .	12,639	12,314	2,092	12,099	13,968	5,941
Greenwich .	11,622	14,308	1,437	11,893	15,885	4,584
Hartford . . .	22,929	3,082	1,010	26,971	6,180	3,390
New Britain .	14,322	4,911	1,717	14,159	7,040	4,983
New Haven .	26,161	4,822	1,555	29,774	8,931	4,130
Norwalk . . .	17,354	10,800	2,237	16,488	14,743	6,046
Stamford . .	25,005	14,696	2,595	23,185	19,809	6,763
Waterbury .	18,901	12,075	3,169	16,366	16,155	9,188
West Hartford	19,037	10,781	1,890	19,623	12,266	5,017
Other.	519,169	374,010	114,247	467,658	431,470	279,059
Totals	735,740	483,109	139,523	682,318	578,313	348,771

Connecticut Vote Since 1948

1948, Truman, Dem., 423,297; Dewey, Rep., 437,754; Wallace, Prog., 13,713; Thomas, Soc., 6,964; Teichert, Soc. Labor, 1,184; Dobbs, Soc. Workers, 606.

1952, Eisenhower, Rep., 611,012; Stevenson, Dem., 481,649; Hoopes, Soc., 2,244; Hallinan, Peoples, 1,466; Hass, Soc. Labor, 535; write-in, 5.

1956, Eisenhower, Rep., 711,837; Stevenson, Dem., 405,079; scattered, 205.

1960, Kennedy, Dem., 657,055; Nixon, Rep., 565,813.

1964, Johnson, Dem., 826,269; Goldwater, Rep., 390,996; scattered, 1,313.

1968, Nixon, Rep., 556,721; Humphrey, Dem., 621,561; Wallace, 3d Party, 76,650; scattered, 1,300.

1972, Nixon, Rep., 810,763; McGovern, Dem., 555,498; Schmitz, Amer., 17,239; scattered, 777.

1976, Carter, Dem., 647,895; Ford, Rep., 719,261; Maddox, George Wallace Party, 7,101; LaRouche, U.S. Labor, 1,789.

1980, Reagan, Rep., 677,210; Carter, Dem., 541,732; Anderson, Ind., 171,807; Clark, Libertarian, 8,570; Commoner, Citizens, 6,130; scattered, 836.

1984, Reagan, Rep., 890,877; Mondale, Dem., 569,597.

1988, Bush, Rep., 750,241; Dukakis, Dem., 676,584; Paul, Lib., 14,071; Fulani, New Alliance, 2,491.

1992, Clinton, Dem., 682,318; Bush, Rep., 578,313; Perot, Ind., 348,771; Marrou, Libertarian, 5,391; Fulani, New Alliance, 1,363.

1996, Clinton, Dem., 735,740; Dole, Rep., 483,109; Perot, Ref., 139,523; Nader, Green, 24,321; Browne, Libertarian, 5,788; Phillips, Concerned Citizens, 2,425; Hagelin, Natural Law, 1,703.

Delaware

County	1996 Clinton (D)	Dole (R)	Perot (RF)	1992 Clinton (D)	Bush (R)	Perot (I)
Kent	18,327	15,932	4,705	15,364	15,562	8,916
New Castle.	98,837	60,943	17,748	91,516	66,311	37,581
Sussex. . . .	23,191	22,187	6,266	19,174	20,440	12,716
Totals	140,355	99,062	28,719	126,054	102,313	59,213

Delaware Vote Since 1948

1948, Truman, Dem., 67,813; Dewey, Rep., 69,688; Wallace, Prog., 1,050; Watson, Proh., 343; Thomas, Soc., 250; Teichert, Soc. Labor, 29.

1952, Eisenhower, Rep., 90,059; Stevenson, Dem., 83,315; Hass, Soc. Labor, 242; Hamblen, Proh., 234; Hallinan, Prog., 155; Hoopes, Soc., 20.

1956, Eisenhower, Rep., 98,057; Stevenson, Dem., 79,421; Oltwick, Proh., 400; Hass, Soc. Labor, 110.

1960, Kennedy, Dem., 99,590; Nixon, Rep., 96,373; Faubus, States' Rights, 354; Decker, Proh., 284; Hass, Soc. Labor, 82.

1964, Johnson, Dem., 122,704; Goldwater, Rep., 78,078; Hass, Soc. Labor, 113; Munn, Proh., 425.

1968, Nixon, Rep., 96,714; Humphrey, Dem., 89,194; Wallace, 3d Party, 28,459.

1972, Nixon, Rep., 140,357; McGovern, Dem., 92,283; Schmitz, Amer., 2,638; Munn, Proh., 238.

1976, Carter, Dem., 122,596; Ford, Rep., 109,831; McCarthy, non-partisan, 2,437; Anderson, Amer., 645; LaRouche, U.S. Labor, 136; Bubar, Proh., 103; Levin, Soc. Labor, 86.

1980, Reagan, Rep., 111,252; Carter, Dem., 105,754; Anderson, Ind., 16,288; Clark, Libertarian, 1,974; Greaves, Amer., 400.

1984, Reagan, Rep., 152,190; Mondale, Dem., 101,656; Bergland, Libertarian, 268.

1988, Bush, Rep., 139,639; Dukakis, Dem., 108,647; Paul, Lib., 1,162; Fulani, New Alliance, 443.

1992, Clinton, Dem., 126,054; Bush, Rep., 102,313; Perot, Ind., 59,213; Fulani, New Alliance, 1,105.

1996, Clinton, Dem., 140,355; Dole, Rep., 99,062; Perot, Ind. (Ref.), 28,719; Browne, Libertarian, 2,052; Phillips, Taxpayers, 348; Hagelin, Natural Law, 274.

District of Columbia

	1996 Clinton (D)	Dole (R)	Perot (RF)	1992 Clinton (D)	Bush (R)	Perot (I)
Totals	158,220	17,339	3,611	192,619	20,698	9,681

District of Columbia Vote Since 1964

1964, Johnson, Dem., 169,796; Goldwater, Rep., 28,801.

1968, Nixon, Rep., 31,012; Humphrey, Dem., 139, 566.

1972, Nixon, Rep., 35,226; McGovern, Dem., 127,627; Reed, Soc. Workers, 316; Hall, Com., 252.

1976, Carter, Dem., 137,818; Ford, Rep., 27,873; Camejo, Soc. Workers, 545; MacBride, Libertarian, 274; Hall, Com., 219; LaRouche, U.S. Labor, 157.

1980, Reagan, Rep., 23,313; Carter, Dem., 130,231; Anderson, Ind., 16,131; Commoner, Citizens, 1,826; Clark, Libertarian, 1,104; Hall, Com., 369; DeBerry, Soc. Workers, 173; Griswold, Workers World, 52; write-ins, 690.

1984, Mondale, Dem., 180,408; Reagan, Rep., 29,009; Bergland, Libertarian, 279.

1988, Bush, Rep., 27,590; Dukakis, Dem., 159,407; Fulani, New Alliance, 2,901; Paul, Lib., 554.

1992, Clinton, Dem., 192,619; Bush, Rep., 20,698; Perot, Ind., 9,681; Fulani, New Alliance, 1,459; Daniels, Ind., 1,186.

1996, Clinton, Dem., 158,220; Dole, Rep., 17,339; Perot, Ref., 3,611; Nader, Green, 4,780; Browne, Libertarian, 588; Hagelin, Natural Law, 283; Harris, Soc. Workers, 257.

Florida

County	1996 Clinton (D)	Dole (R)	Perot (RF)	1992 Clinton (D)	Bush (R)	Perot (I)
Alachua . . .	40,144	25,303	8,072	37,876	22,806	15,293
Baker	2,273	3,684	667	1,974	3,417	1,315
Bay.	17,020	28,290	5,922	12,830	22,820	9,702
Bradford . .	3,356	4,038	819	3,040	3,671	1,572
Brevard . . .	80,416	87,980	25,249	61,070	84,545	49,491
Broward . . .	320,736	142,834	38,964	276,309	164,782	90,923
Calhoun . . .	1,794	1,717	630	1,665	1,721	1,176
Charlotte . .	27,121	27,836	7,783	22,904	24,302	14,711
Citrus	22,042	20,114	7,244	15,935	16,402	12,310
Clay	13,246	30,332	3,281	10,597	26,313	8,414
Collier	23,182	42,590	6,320	18,794	38,447	14,514
Columbia . .	6,691	7,588	1,970	5,526	6,489	2,906
Dade	317,378	209,634	24,722	254,444	235,149	53,957
De Soto . . .	3,219	3,272	965	2,646	3,070	1,687
Dixie	1,731	1,398	652	1,855	1,401	1,094
Duval.	112,258	126,857	13,844	92,010	123,480	33,335
Escambia . .	37,768	60,839	8,587	32,018	52,775	19,868
Flagler. . . .	9,583	8,232	2,185	6,692	6,241	3,387
Franklin . . .	2,095	1,563	878	1,534	1,660	1,143
Gadsden . .	9,405	3,813	938	8,478	3,975	1,871
Gilchrist . . .	1,985	1,939	841	1,511	1,395	1,090
Glades. . . .	1,530	1,361	521	1,305	1,185	878

County	1996 Clinton (D)	Dole (R)	Perot (RF)	1992 Clinton (D)	Bush (R)	Perot (I)
Gulf	2,480	2,424	1,054	1,938	2,650	1,245
Hamilton	1,734	1,518	406	1,622	1,402	695
Hardee	2,417	2,926	851	2,017	2,898	1,498
Hendry	3,882	3,855	1,135	2,690	3,279	2,032
Hernando	28,520	22,039	7,272	19,171	17,896	11,845
Highlands	14,244	15,608	3,739	11,234	14,497	6,592
Hillsborough	144,223	136,621	25,154	115,261	130,611	63,037
Holmes	2,310	3,248	1,208	1,877	3,196	1,426
Indian River	16,373	22,709	4,635	12,359	19,137	12,375
Jackson	6,665	7,187	1,602	5,481	6,720	2,447
Jefferson	2,543	1,851	393	2,270	1,506	894
Lafayette	829	1,166	316	866	1,037	612
Lake	29,750	35,089	8,813	23,199	30,818	15,606
Lee	65,692	80,882	18,389	53,656	73,423	38,446
Leon	50,058	33,914	6,672	47,770	31,964	17,207
Levy	4,938	4,299	1,774	4,330	3,796	2,784
Liberty	868	913	376	820	1,126	617
Madison	2,791	2,195	578	2,644	2,006	1,174
Manatee	41,835	44,059	10,360	33,826	42,708	23,282
Marion	37,033	41,397	11,340	30,823	35,438	20,524
Martin	20,851	28,516	5,005	14,778	24,768	13,433
Monroe	15,219	12,021	4,817	10,435	9,891	8,306
Nassau	7,276	12,134	1,657	5,497	9,364	3,251
Okaloosa	16,434	40,631	5,432	12,003	32,755	16,649
Okeechobee	4,824	3,415	1,666	3,418	3,298	2,645
Orange	105,513	106,026	18,191	82,656	108,738	44,827
Osceola	21,870	18,335	6,091	15,009	19,139	11,021
Palm Beach	230,621	133,762	30,739	187,840	140,317	76,223
Pasco	66,472	48,346	18,011	53,125	47,721	34,650
Pinellas	184,728	152,125	36,990	160,217	158,733	101,150
Polk	66,735	67,943	14,991	51,442	65,952	28,198
Putnam	12,008	9,781	3,272	10,707	8,909	5,975
St. Johns	16,713	27,311	4,205	12,284	20,173	7,397
St. Lucie	36,168	28,892	8,482	23,873	24,397	19,813
Santa Rosa	10,923	26,244	4,957	6,526	17,229	8,735
Sarasota	63,648	69,198	14,939	54,536	66,831	34,281
Seminole	45,051	59,778	9,357	35,649	57,085	24,477
Sumter	7,014	5,960	2,375	5,027	4,366	2,901
Suwannee	4,479	5,742	1,874	3,985	4,571	2,790
Taylor	3,583	3,188	1,140	2,568	2,693	1,929
Union	1,388	1,636	425	1,247	1,543	770
Volusia	78,905	63,067	17,319	65,213	59,155	30,813
Wakulla	3,054	2,931	1,091	2,319	2,586	1,790
Walton	5,341	7,706	2,342	3,886	5,719	3,886
Washington	2,992	3,522	1,287	2,544	3,694	1,596
Totals	2,545,968	2,243,324	483,776	2,071,651	2,171,781	1,052,481

Florida Vote Since 1948

1948, Truman, Dem., 281,988; Dewey, Rep., 194,280; Thurmond, States' Rights, 89,755; Wallace, Prog., 11,620.

1952, Eisenhower, Rep., 544,036; Stevenson, Dem., 444,950; scattered, 351.

1956, Eisenhower, Rep., 643,849; Stevenson, Dem., 480,371.

1960, Kennedy, Dem., 748,700; Nixon, Rep., 795,476.

1964, Johnson, Dem., 948,540; Goldwater, Rep., 905,941.

1968, Nixon, Rep., 886,804; Humphrey, Dem., 676,794; Wallace, 3d Party, 624,207.

1972, Nixon, Rep., 1,857,759; McGovern, Dem., 718,117; scattered, 7,407.

1976, Carter, Dem., 1,636,000; Ford, Rep., 1,469,531; McCarthy, Ind., 23,643; Anderson, Amer., 21,325.

1980, Reagan, Rep., 2,046,951; Carter, Dem., 1,419,475; Anderson, Ind., 189,692; Clark, Libertarian, 30,524; write-ins, 285.

1984, Reagan, Rep., 2,728,775; Mondale, Dem., 1,448,344.

1988, Bush, Rep., 2,616,597; Dukakis, Dem., 1,655,851; Paul, Lib., 19,796; Fulani, New Alliance, 6,655.

1992, Bush, Rep., 2,171,781; Clinton, Dem., 2,071,651; Perot, Ind., 1,052,481; Marrou, Libertarian, 15,068.

1996, Clinton, Dem., 2,545,968; Dole, Rep., 2,243,324; Perot, Ref., 483,776; Browne, Libertarian, 23,312.

Georgia

County	1996 Clinton (D)	Dole (R)	Perot (RF)	1992 Clinton (D)	Bush (R)	Perot (I)
Appling	2,070	2,572	446	2,455	2,514	1,047
Atkinson	823	784	215	1,056	779	342
Bacon	1,360	1,580	402	1,423	1,301	604
Baker	955	408	105	864	391	210
Baldwin	5,740	4,570	849	5,813	4,262	1,679
Banks	1,536	1,925	595	1,530	1,551	583
Barrow	3,928	5,342	942	3,991	4,328	1,633
Bartow	6,853	9,250	1,770	6,675	7,742	2,500
Ben Hill	2,198	1,516	358	2,348	1,476	619
Berrien	2,066	1,950	525	2,103	1,637	750
Bibb	26,727	20,778	2,268	28,070	19,847	6,021
Bleckley	1,365	1,632	300	1,710	1,570	662
Brantley	1,494	1,738	386	1,883	1,541	840
Brooks	1,977	1,738	314	1,895	1,779	630
Bryan	2,152	3,577	513	2,031	2,789	1,095
Bulloch	5,396	6,646	939	4,903	5,690	2,020
Burke	3,915	2,590	389	3,647	2,390	807
Butts	2,271	2,027	416	2,448	1,768	619
Calhoun	1,217	541	106	1,301	464	248
Camden	3,644	4,222	572	2,952	3,517	1,077
Candler	1,097	1,131	264	1,192	1,014	541
Carroll	8,438	11,157	2,002	8,404	10,750	3,358
Catoosa	5,185	8,237	1,257	4,817	7,599	2,290
Charlton	1,368	1,374	280	1,127	1,333	427
Chatham	35,781	31,987	3,028	31,533	31,925	8,269
Chattahoochee	565	398	115	604	413	177
Chattooga	3,003	2,513	796	2,976	2,439	965
Cherokee	10,802	24,527	2,872	8,113	16,054	4,950
Clarke	15,206	10,504	1,201	15,403	10,459	2,987
Clay	787	293	62	778	264	155
Clayton	30,687	20,625	3,494	25,890	23,965	7,942
Clinch	973	789	182	759	790	286
Cobb	73,750	114,188	10,438	63,960	103,734	28,747
Coffee	3,407	3,934	711	3,275	3,778	1,256
Colquitt	4,135	4,847	977	3,891	4,680	1,682
Columbia	8,601	21,291	1,709	7,115	16,657	4,379
Cook	1,780	1,354	267	1,731	1,318	537
Coweta	7,794	13,058	1,949	7,093	9,814	3,587
Crawford	1,534	1,290	270	1,648	974	549
Crisp	2,504	2,321	445	2,610	2,253	823
Dade	1,737	2,295	618	1,782	2,191	823
Dawson	1,434	2,343	473	1,399	1,696	790
Decatur	3,245	3,035	497	3,198	3,142	1,068
DeKalb	137,903	60,255	6,742	124,559	70,282	19,741
Dodge	2,696	2,478	587	3,002	2,287	978
Dooly	1,951	990	207	1,993	1,034	350
Dougherty	15,600	11,144	1,072	15,236	12,455	3,178
Douglas	9,631	14,495	2,109	8,869	13,349	4,362
Early	1,648	1,374	246	1,970	1,457	652
Echols	308	335	97	312	361	238
Effingham	3,031	5,022	769	2,690	3,814	1,443
Elbert	2,900	2,393	552	3,025	2,372	757
Emanuel	2,947	2,451	450	2,951	2,662	755
Evans	1,117	1,206	204	1,230	1,244	480
Fannin	2,741	3,373	782	2,902	3,255	1,028
Fayette	9,875	21,005	2,016	8,430	17,576	5,598
Floyd	10,464	12,426	2,345	11,614	12,378	3,779
Forsyth	5,957	15,013	1,889	4,936	8,652	3,453
Franklin	2,338	2,364	665	2,505	2,391	1,014
Fulton	143,306	89,809	7,720	147,459	85,451	23,578
Gilmer	2,464	3,121	725	2,311	2,661	879
Glascock	348	532	128	316	516	180
Glynn	8,058	12,305	1,137	8,581	11,242	3,053
Gordon	4,239	5,232	1,284	4,103	5,265	1,818
Grady	2,862	2,674	633	2,520	2,370	1,126
Greene	2,115	1,702	173	2,259	1,307	483
Gwinnett	53,819	96,610	10,236	44,253	81,822	23,926
Habersham	3,170	4,730	1,149	3,098	4,569	1,444
Hall	10,362	19,280	2,321	11,214	16,108	5,043
Hancock	2,135	438	71	2,461	506	189
Haralson	2,850	3,260	808	3,281	3,142	1,167
Harris	2,779	3,829	489	2,679	3,316	954
Hart	3,486	2,884	767	3,614	2,607	1,376
Heard	1,248	1,170	406	1,456	1,190	617
Henry	9,498	16,968	2,320	7,817	12,634	3,769
Houston	12,760	17,050	2,730	12,270	14,119	6,263
Irwin	1,225	1,085	224	1,366	973	465
Jackson	3,746	4,782	899	3,792	3,976	1,381
Jasper	1,553	1,423	243	1,485	1,153	373
Jeff Davis	1,576	1,796	428	2,031	1,947	958
Jefferson	3,404	2,077	298	3,220	2,077	685
Jenkins	1,336	955	166	1,401	929	394
Johnson	1,194	815	242	1,473	1,314	502
Jones	3,195	3,272	497	3,338	2,770	1,159
Lamar	2,125	1,988	409	2,065	1,707	600
Lanier	818	519	160	811	600	298
Laurens	5,792	6,118	818	6,184	6,146	1,602
Lee	2,005	3,983	506	1,811	3,061	1,024
Liberty	4,462	3,042	580	3,853	2,832	1,176
Lincoln	1,334	1,391	208	1,327	1,149	479
Long	936	791	236	874	719	355
Lowndes	9,470	10,578	1,518	9,019	10,276	2,864
Lumpkin	1,949	2,576	588	2,010	1,972	1,035
McDuffie	2,725	3,254	395	2,640	2,955	860
McIntosh	1,927	1,219	293	1,925	1,027	550
Macon	2,618	1,006	159	2,491	944	363
Madison	2,571	3,992	868	2,393	3,351	1,129
Marion	977	678	159	1,145	711	198
Meriwether	3,492	2,259	480	4,002	2,364	942
Miller	909	847	235	934	826	455
Mitchell	3,165	2,033	372	3,052	1,917	818
Monroe	2,768	3,054	488	2,774	2,423	949
Montgomery	1,233	1,163	284	1,185	1,009	416
Morgan	2,111	2,118	364	2,057	1,797	596
Murray	2,861	3,289	938	2,764	3,256	1,186
Muscogee	24,867	19,360	1,891	25,476	21,386	4,327
Newton	6,759	7,274	1,258	5,811	5,804	1,998
Oconee	2,002	5,110	915	2,715	4,106	1,190
Oglethorpe	1,570	1,826	369	1,491	1,590	620
Paulding	5,699	10,152	1,603	5,212	7,180	2,654
Peach	3,582	2,676	471	3,677	2,327	947
Pickens	2,693	3,041	783	2,359	2,332	1,037
Pierce	1,420	2,319	333	1,852	1,899	708
Pike	1,474	2,054	357	1,651	1,822	623

County	1996 Clinton (D)	Dole (R)	Perot (RF)	1992 Clinton (D)	Bush (R)	Perot (I)
Polk.	4,298	4,130	1,076	4,872	4,158	1,598
Pulaski. . . .	1,554	1,196	268	1,756	1,075	614
Putnam . . .	2,340	2,306	474	2,149	1,756	775
Quitman. . .	514	224	59	523	284	113
Rabun	1,943	2,213	585	1,878	1,902	825
Randolph . .	1,438	816	126	1,756	887	315
Richmond. .	30,738	23,670	2,310	28,910	24,227	6,290
Rockdale . .	7,656	13,006	1,750	7,003	11,945	3,664
Schley	576	470	123	601	511	180
Screven . . .	2,087	1,862	263	1,940	1,705	709
Seminole . .	1,265	1,003	250	1,193	850	468
Spalding. . .	6,017	7,376	1,059	6,392	7,262	2,044
Stephens . .	3,072	3,890	979	2,976	4,047	1,448
Stewart . . .	1,537	525	152	1,540	1,186	175
Sumter. . . .	4,239	3,358	451	4,489	3,616	1,046
Talbot	1,579	652	111	1,768	671	238
Taliaferro . .	615	235	36	755	269	80
Tattnall. . . .	2,369	2,518	541	2,360	2,566	996
Taylor	1,450	1,002	195	1,508	1,078	281
Telfair	1,856	1,143	322	2,238	1,324	613
Terrell	1,509	1,111	129	1,942	1,143	384
Thomas . . .	5,183	5,649	667	4,841	5,500	1,591
Tift	4,198	5,613	728	3,930	4,485	1,139
Toombs . . .	2,763	3,646	602	2,648	3,609	1,210
Towns	1,664	2,030	459	1,487	1,674	537
Treutlen . . .	912	723	122	1,116	898	318
Troup.	5,940	8,716	1,090	6,412	8,118	2,488
Turner	1,272	924	246	1,669	936	370
Twiggs. . . .	1,927	958	210	2,097	853	432
Union	2,175	2,685	622	2,304	2,533	804
Upson	3,491	3,783	731	3,740	4,053	1,186
Walker. . . .	6,743	8,817	1,969	6,217	8,489	2,748
Walton. . . .	5,618	7,934	1,323	4,821	5,619	1,923
Ware.	4,171	4,746	636	4,573	4,573	1,263
Warren. . . .	1,230	735	83	1,239	751	180
Washington	4,057	2,348	488	3,508	2,384	820
Wayne. . . .	2,734	3,709	665	3,052	3,381	1,107
Webster. . .	529	235	59	600	208	103
Wheeler. . .	751	460	141	880	601	214
White.	1,864	2,959	556	1,756	2,477	981
Whitfield. . .	7,720	12,368	1,637	7,335	12,003	2,866
Wilcox	1,067	882	171	1,365	916	433
Wilkes	1,971	1,417	184	1,955	1,535	464
Wilkinson . .	2,278	1,332	287	2,286	1,232	520
Worth	2,300	2,752	521	2,578	2,344	905
Totals	1,053,849	1,080,843	146,337	1,008,966	995,252	309,657

Georgia Vote Since 1948

1948, Truman, Dem., 254,646; Dewey, Rep., 76,691; Thurmond, States' Rights, 85,055; Wallace, Prog., 1,636; Watson, Proh., 732.

1952, Eisenhower, Rep., 198,979; Stevenson, Dem., 456,823; Liberty Party, 1.

1956, Stevenson, Dem., 444,388; Eisenhower, Rep., 222,778; Andrews, Ind., write-in, 1,754.

1960, Kennedy, Dem., 458,638; Nixon, Rep., 274,472; write-in, 239.

1964, Johnson, Dem., 522,557; Goldwater, Rep., 616,600.

1968, Nixon, Rep., 380,111; Humphrey, Dem., 334,440; Wallace, 3d Party, 535,550; write-in, 162.

1972, Nixon, Rep., 881,496; McGovern, Dem., 289,529; scattered, 2,935; Schmitz, Amer., 812.

1976, Carter, Dem., 979,409; Ford, Rep., 483,743; write-in, 4,306.

1980, Reagan, Rep., 654,168; Carter, Dem., 890,955; Anderson, Ind., 36,055; Clark, Libertarian, 15,627.

1984, Reagan, Rep., 1,068,722; Mondale, Dem., 706,628.

1988, Bush, Rep., 1,081,331; Dukakis, Dem., 714,792; Paul, Lib., 8,435; Fulani, New Alliance, 5,099.

1992, Clinton, Dem., 1,008,966; Bush, Rep., 995,252; Perot, Ind., 309,657; Marrou, Libertarian, 7,110.

1996, Dole, Rep., 1,080,843; Clinton, Dem., 1,053,849; Perot, Ref., 146,337; Browne, Libertarian, 17,870.

Hawaii

County	1996 Clinton (D)	Dole (R)	Perot (RF)	1992 Clinton (D)	Bush (R)	Perot (I)
Hawaii. . . .	27,262	13,516	5,137	25,725	15,460	8,889
Honolulu . .	143,793	85,779	17,389	123,908	103,937	35,728
Kauai	13,357	5,325	1,568	10,715	6,274	1,756
Maui	20,600	9,323	3,264	18,962	11,151	6,630
Totals. . . .	205,012	113,943	27,358	179,310	136,822	53,003

Hawaii Vote Since 1960

1960, Kennedy, Dem., 92,410; Nixon, Rep., 92,295.

1964, Johnson, Dem., 163,249; Goldwater, Rep., 44,022.

1968, Nixon, Rep., 91,425; Humphrey, Dem., 141,324; Wallace, 3d Party, 3,469.

1972, Nixon, Rep., 168,865; McGovern, Dem., 101,409.

1976, Carter, Dem., 147,375; Ford, Rep., 140,003; MacBride, Libertarian, 3,923.

1980, Reagan, Rep., 130,112; Carter, Dem., 135,879; Anderson, Ind., 32,021; Clark, Libertarian, 3,269; Commoner, Citizens, 1,548; Hall, Com., 458.

1984, Reagan, Rep., 184,934; Mondale, Dem., 147,098; Bergland, Libertarian, 2,167.

1988, Bush, Rep., 158,625; Dukakis, Dem., 192,364; Paul, Lib., 1,999; Fulani, New Alliance, 1,003.

1992, Clinton, Dem., 179,310; Bush, Rep., 136,822; Perot, Ind., 53,003; Gritz, Populist/America First, 1,452; Marrou, Libertarian, 1,119.

1996, Clinton, Dem., 205,012; Dole, Rep., 113,943; Perot, Ref., 27,358; Nader, Green, 10,386; Browne, Libertarian, 2,493; Hagelin, Natural Law, 570; Phillips, Taxpayers, 358.

Idaho

County	1996 Clinton (D)	Dole (R)	Perot (RF)	1992 Clinton (D)	Bush (R)	Perot (I)
Ada.	43,040	61,811	11,171	31,941	49,000	28,192
Adams . . .	537	1,053	311	457	754	695
Bannock. . .	12,806	14,058	4,158	11,091	12,016	8,116
Bear Lake .	805	1,583	396	562	1,419	684
Benewah . .	1,488	1,667	701	1,270	1,223	1,165
Bingham . .	4,304	8,391	2,021	3,565	7,333	4,144
Blaine	3,840	3,003	1,193	2,865	2,243	2,831
Boise	879	1,576	440	623	912	754
Bonner. . . .	5,294	6,207	2,669	4,995	3,937	4,645
Bonneville .	9,013	19,977	3,921	7,014	16,557	10,241
Boundary . .	1,194	1,937	626	1,095	1,479	1,136
Butte	507	741	233	433	602	392
Camas . . .	156	283	95	134	202	145
Canyon . . .	11,800	23,988	3,956	9,095	19,220	8,974
Caribou . . .	841	1,740	501	562	1,350	1,088
Cassia . . .	1,596	4,663	976	1,351	4,052	1,785
Clark	117	266	45	95	195	119
Clearwater .	1,507	1,658	650	1,433	1,152	1,098
Custer	635	1,249	400	564	829	729
Elmore. . . .	2,324	3,668	845	1,858	3,087	1,867
Franklin . . .	807	2,435	589	524	2,115	890
Fremont . . .	1,114	3,042	630	903	2,333	1,349
Gem	1,968	3,362	833	1,609	2,455	1,555
Gooding . . .	1,503	2,637	980	1,530	2,178	1,591
Idaho.	1,979	3,871	1,083	1,974	2,709	1,900
Jefferson . .	1,427	4,925	994	978	3,471	2,164
Jerome . . .	1,679	3,358	1,014	1,739	2,972	1,768
Kootenai . .	13,627	18,740	6,083	11,553	13,065	11,261
Latah.	7,741	6,311	1,828	7,233	5,353	3,602
Lemhi	1,015	2,334	461	996	1,540	1,175
Lewis	674	861	316	674	593	491
Lincoln . . .	478	744	319	514	656	441
Madison . .	1,216	5,706	744	741	4,591	1,920
Minidoka . .	1,977	4,008	977	1,815	3,304	1,875
Nez Perce .	7,491	6,675	2,385	7,069	5,431	4,363
Oneida . . .	429	993	285	351	713	590
Owyhee . . .	895	2,033	354	686	1,469	862
Payette . . .	2,119	3,901	906	1,656	2,895	2,055
Power	1,070	1,501	344	837	1,352	697
Shoshone. .	2,981	1,588	1,283	3,182	1,441	1,878
Teton	866	1,251	326	472	762	608
Twin Falls. .	6,826	12,393	3,383	6,593	10,335	6,043
Valley	1,564	2,089	568	1,259	1,548	1,313
Washington	1,314	2,318	525	1,122	1,802	1,204
Totals	165,443	256,595	62,518	137,013	202,645	130,395

Idaho Vote Since 1948

1948, Truman, Dem., 107,370; Dewey, Rep., 101,514; Wallace, Prog., 4,972; Watson, Proh., 628; Thomas, Soc., 332.

1952, Eisenhower, Rep., 180,707; Stevenson, Dem., 95,081; Hallinan, Prog., 443; write-in, 23.

1956, Eisenhower, Rep., 166,979; Stevenson, Dem., 105,868; Andrews, Ind., 126; write-in, 16.

1960, Kennedy, Dem., 138,853; Nixon, Rep., 161,597.

1964, Johnson, Dem., 148,920; Goldwater, Rep., 143,557.

1968, Nixon, Rep., 165,369; Humphrey, Dem., 89,273; Wallace, 3d Party, 36,541.

1972, Nixon, Rep., 199,384; McGovern, Dem., 80,826; Schmitz, Amer., 28,869; Spock, Peoples, 903.

1976, Carter, Dem., 126,549; Ford, Rep., 204,151; Maddox, Amer., 5,935; MacBride, Libertarian, 3,558; LaRouche, U.S. Labor, 739.

1980, Reagan, Rep., 290,699; Carter, Dem., 110,192; Anderson, Ind., 27,058; Clark, Libertarian, 8,425; Rarick, Amer., 1,057.

1984, Reagan, Rep., 297,523; Mondale, Dem., 108,510; Bergland, Libertarian, 2,823.

1988, Bush, Rep., 253,881; Dukakis, Dem., 147,272; Paul, Lib., 5,313; Fulani, Ind., 2,502.

1992, Clinton, Dem., 137,013; Bush, Rep., 202,645; Perot, Ind., 130,395; Gritz, Populist/America First, 10,281; Marrou, Libertarian, 1,167.

1996, Dole, Rep., 256,595; Clinton, Dem., 165,443; Perot, Ref., 62,518; Browne, Libertarian, 3,325; Phillips, Taxpayers, 2,230; Hagelin, Natural Law, 1,600.

Illinois

County	1996 Clinton (D)	Dole (R)	Perot (RF)	1992 Clinton (D)	Bush (R)	Perot (I)
Adams . . .	11,336	13,836	3,069	11,748	13,529	6,157
Alexander .	2,753	1,212	321	2,566	1,301	474
Bond	3,213	3,018	685	3,428	2,715	1,373
Boone . . .	5,345	6,181	1,377	5,114	5,589	2,880
Brown . . .	997	1,053	237	1,146	1,029	504
Bureau . . .	7,651	6,528	1,798	7,551	6,836	3,465
Calhoun . .	1,676	941	363	1,519	745	532
Carroll . . .	2,926	3,029	792	2,854	3,297	1,502
Cass	2,834	2,214	589	3,200	2,162	1,072
Champaign	32,454	28,232	4,806	35,003	27,096	13,571
Christian . .	7,431	5,563	1,727	9,042	5,087	3,401
Clark	2,995	3,409	781	3,338	3,175	1,450
Clay	2,750	2,703	719	2,962	2,471	1,193
Clinton . . .	6,104	6,065	1,580	6,686	5,771	3,315
Coles	8,950	8,038	2,137	9,402	8,098	4,707
Cook . . .	1,153,289	461,557	96,633	1,249,533	605,300	281,999
Crawford . .	3,627	3,965	1,057	3,964	3,606	2,062
Cumberland	1,776	2,002	657	2,111	1,860	1,209
DeKalb . . .	12,715	12,380	3,009	13,744	12,655	7,680
DeWitt . . .	2,878	2,978	694	3,009	3,164	1,543
Douglas . .	2,955	3,272	740	3,341	3,309	1,600
DuPage . .	129,709	164,630	27,419	114,564	178,271	76,839
Edgar	3,552	3,746	935	4,014	3,790	1,930
Edwards . .	1,089	1,613	384	1,299	1,601	634
Effingham .	4,825	7,696	1,555	5,221	6,329	3,354
Fayette . . .	3,887	3,881	964	4,833	3,508	1,730
Ford	2,065	3,077	590	2,175	3,046	1,222
Franklin . .	9,814	5,354	2,096	12,744	5,504	3,180
Fulton . . .	8,857	5,155	1,610	9,725	5,062	2,874
Gallatin . .	2,113	856	527	2,371	990	568
Greene . . .	2,734	2,245	903	3,164	2,391	1,461
Grundy . . .	6,759	6,177	1,860	6,122	6,346	3,724
Hamilton . .	2,242	1,677	560	2,582	1,521	862
Hancock . .	4,001	3,961	1,148	4,213	3,714	2,091
Hardin . . .	1,323	790	485	1,665	985	515
Henderson	1,953	1,233	408	2,013	1,310	715
Henry . . .	11,201	8,393	2,194	11,077	8,989	4,231
Iroquois . .	4,559	6,564	1,522	4,440	6,948	3,073
Jackson . .	12,214	7,422	2,082	13,373	6,899	3,995
Jasper . . .	2,038	2,234	641	2,284	1,996	1,160
Jefferson . .	7,263	5,937	1,647	8,665	5,497	3,403
Jersey . . .	4,275	3,211	1,186	4,749	2,933	2,363
Jo Daviess	4,171	3,915	1,131	4,044	4,249	2,102
Johnson . .	2,009	2,241	640	2,299	2,124	944
Kane	47,902	54,375	11,270	44,568	55,684	27,179
Kankakee .	16,820	14,595	3,574	17,229	15,411	7,264
Kendall . . .	6,499	8,958	2,055	5,423	8,521	4,394
Knox	12,487	7,822	2,096	12,524	8,331	4,357
Lake	93,315	93,149	16,640	81,693	99,000	42,384
LaSalle . . .	21,643	15,299	5,259	23,276	16,078	10,434
Lawrence .	2,871	2,568	916	3,270	2,681	1,498
Lee	5,895	6,677	1,520	5,530	6,652	3,191
Livingston .	5,641	7,653	1,409	6,007	8,004	3,029
Logan	4,618	6,518	1,141	5,169	6,567	2,420
McDonough	5,632	5,049	1,217	5,814	5,297	2,770
McHenry .	31,240	41,136	10,082	24,783	41,356	21,817
McLean . .	22,708	26,428	3,816	23,090	25,726	10,282
Macon . . .	24,256	18,161	4,540	27,449	18,684	9,236
Macoupin .	11,107	7,235	2,532	12,050	6,518	5,018
Madison . .	53,568	35,758	10,121	58,484	32,167	23,110
Marion . . .	7,792	5,999	1,825	9,669	5,764	3,407
Marshall . .	2,640	2,453	586	2,819	2,491	1,169
Mason . . .	3,385	2,430	600	3,969	2,473	1,245
Massac . .	2,841	2,507	675	3,347	2,754	892
Menard . .	2,204	3,106	534	2,264	2,834	1,179
Mercer . . .	4,278	2,688	889	3,990	2,983	1,535
Monroe . .	4,798	5,350	1,276	4,894	4,807	2,813
Montgomery	6,338	4,770	1,436	7,424	4,407	2,956
Morgan . .	6,150	6,352	1,633	6,351	6,566	3,317
Moultrie . .	2,629	2,199	596	3,056	2,065	1,322
Ogle	6,765	9,558	1,876	6,512	9,008	4,455
Peoria . . .	37,383	30,990	5,220	38,099	30,718	12,195
Perry	5,347	3,237	1,262	6,009	3,105	1,955
Piatt	3,274	3,265	818	3,520	3,076	1,822
Pike	3,604	3,225	1,039	4,016	3,342	1,643
Pope	915	850	277	1,063	951	391
Pulaski . . .	1,524	1,036	235	1,987	1,169	379
Putnam . .	1,425	987	322	1,574	969	752
Randolph .	7,419	5,422	1,698	8,529	4,899	3,092
Richland . .	2,679	3,137	927	3,286	3,053	1,689
Rock Island	34,822	20,626	5,135	37,412	23,212	10,416
St. Clair . .	53,405	33,066	7,027	57,625	31,951	17,592
Saline . . .	6,150	3,693	1,752	7,258	3,667	2,302
Sangamon	38,902	42,174	6,446	40,052	39,641	16,861
Schuyler . .	1,636	1,597	483	1,650	1,912	813
Scott	1,012	1,112	396	1,057	1,132	588
Shelby . . .	4,249	4,215	1,262	5,101	3,631	2,401
Stark	1,262	1,278	312	1,336	1,384	625
Stephenson	7,145	8,871	1,940	7,899	9,005	4,677
Tazewell . .	24,139	24,395	4,814	26,428	23,469	9,927
Union	4,252	3,147	832	4,681	3,003	1,373

County	1996 Clinton (D)	Dole (R)	Perot (RF)	1992 Clinton (D)	Bush (R)	Perot (I)
Vermilion .	15,525	12,015	3,577	18,383	11,703	8,162
Wabash . .	2,177	2,381	683	2,436	2,485	1,302
Warren . . .	3,500	2,974	742	3,661	3,325	1,436
Washington	2,744	3,339	790	2,986	3,003	1,542
Wayne . . .	3,054	4,029	999	3,332	3,809	1,702
White	3,553	2,878	888	4,308	3,057	1,428
Whiteside .	11,913	8,859	2,436	12,329	10,146	4,589
Will	69,354	62,506	15,485	59,633	58,337	32,788
Williamson .	12,510	9,734	2,877	14,361	9,462	4,779
Winnebago	46,264	44,479	8,192	48,298	42,221	21,227
Woodford .	5,270	8,527	1,170	5,490	8,032	2,733
Totals . . .	2,341,744	1,587,021	346,408	2,453,350	1,734,096	840,515

Illinois Vote Since 1948

1948, Truman, Dem., 1,994,715; Dewey, Rep., 1,961,103; Watson, Proh., 11,959; Thomas, Soc., 11,522; Teichert, Soc. Labor, 3,118.

1952, Eisenhower, Rep., 2,457,327; Stevenson, Dem., 2,013,920; Hass, Soc. Labor, 9,363; write-in, 448.

1956, Eisenhower, Rep., 2,623,327; Stevenson, Dem., 1,775,682; Hass, Soc. Labor, 8,342; write-in, 56.

1960, Kennedy, Dem., 2,377,846; Nixon, Rep., 2,368,988; Hass, Soc. Labor, 10,560; write-in, 15.

1964, Johnson, Dem., 2,796,833; Goldwater, Rep., 1,905,946; write-in, 62.

1968, Nixon, Rep., 2,174,774; Humphrey, Dem., 2,039,814; Wallace, 3d Party, 390,958; Blomen, Soc. Labor, 13,878; write-in, 325.

1972, Nixon, Rep. 2,788,179; McGovern, Dem., 1,913,472; Fisher, Soc. Labor, 12,344; Schmitz, Amer., 2,471; Hall, Com., 4,541; others, 2,229.

1976, Carter, Dem., 2,271,295; Ford, Rep., 2,364,269; McCarthy, Ind., 55,939; Hall, Com., 9,250; MacBride, Libertarian, 8,057; Camejo, Soc. Workers, 3,615; Levin, Soc. Labor, 2,422; LaRouche, U.S. Labor, 2,018; write-in, 1,968.

1980, Reagan, Rep., 2,358,049; Carter, Dem., 1,981,413; Anderson, Ind., 346,754; Clark, Libertarian, 38,939; Commoner, Citizens, 10,692; Hall, Com., 9,711; Griswold, Workers World, 2,257; DeBerry, Soc. Workers, 1,302; write-ins, 604.

1984, Reagan, Rep., 2,707,103; Mondale, Dem., 2,086,499; Bergland, Libertarian, 10,086.

1988, Bush, Rep., 2,310,939; Dukakis, Dem., 2,215,940; Paul, Lib., 14,944; Fulani, Solid., 10,276.

1992, Clinton, Dem., 2,453,350; Bush, Rep., 1,734,096; Perot, Ind., 840,515; Marrou, Libertarian, 9,218; Fulani, New Alliance, 5,267; Gritz, Populist/America First, 3,577; Hagelin, Natural Law, 2,751; Warren, Soc. Workers, 1,361.

1996, Clinton, Dem., 2,341,744; Dole, Rep., 1,587,021; Perot, Ref., 346,408; Browne, Libertarian, 22,548; Phillips, Taxpayers, 7,606; Hagelin, Natural Law, 4,606.

Indiana

County	1996 Clinton (D)	Dole (R)	Perot (RF)	1992 Clinton (D)	Bush (R)	Perot (I)
Adams	4,247	6,960	1,346	3,708	6,078	2,865
Allen	41,450	59,255	8,808	39,629	55,003	25,809
Bartholomew	9,301	13,188	2,815	8,284	13,146	5,882
Benton . . .	1,311	1,947	609	1,221	2,030	1,056
Blackford . .	2,335	2,070	681	2,088	2,347	1,319
Boone	4,625	11,338	1,498	3,982	9,485	3,826
Brown	2,413	2,988	802	2,029	2,633	1,635
Carroll	2,747	4,062	1,171	2,561	3,800	2,173
Cass	5,419	8,020	2,029	4,757	7,421	3,944
Clark	17,799	14,396	3,578	17,460	13,333	5,653
Clay	3,605	4,858	1,406	3,306	4,696	2,134
Clinton	3,949	6,156	1,355	3,490	6,141	2,535
Crawford . .	2,324	1,759	700	2,260	1,903	819
Daviess . . .	3,230	5,531	994	3,201	5,591	1,695
Dearborn . .	6,269	8,318	1,731	5,116	6,974	3,384
Decatur . . .	3,190	4,782	1,389	2,774	5,195	2,299
Dekalb	4,840	6,851	1,534	4,652	6,682	3,554
Delaware . .	20,385	18,126	6,042	19,556	20,473	10,453
Dubois	6,499	6,840	1,777	5,878	6,785	3,195
Elkhart	16,598	28,770	5,133	14,660	27,920	9,450
Fayette	3,822	4,091	1,137	3,969	4,376	2,299
Floyd	13,814	12,473	2,609	13,166	11,932	4,421
Fountain . . .	2,327	3,984	1,033	2,829	3,391	2,162
Franklin . . .	2,808	4,167	943	2,456	3,831	1,858
Fulton	2,956	3,934	1,143	2,552	3,982	1,963
Gibson	6,488	5,392	1,585	6,909	5,172	2,680
Grant	9,818	13,443	3,008	9,211	13,806	5,597
Greene . . .	5,077	5,746	1,690	5,431	5,410	2,610
Hamilton . .	14,153	42,792	4,234	10,215	34,622	10,365
Hancock . .	6,123	12,907	2,258	4,752	11,072	4,752
Harrison . .	5,900	6,073	1,839	5,768	5,403	2,469
Hendricks . .	9,392	22,293	3,405	7,071	18,373	7,519
Henry	7,667	8,537	2,381	6,794	8,720	4,416
Howard . . .	11,999	16,771	4,172	10,288	15,306	8,575

County	1996 Clinton (D)	Dole (R)	Perot (RF)	1992 Clinton (D)	Bush (R)	Perot (I)
Huntington	4,287	8,275	1,400	3,855	9,093	2,967
Jackson	5,150	5,883	1,590	5,663	7,246	3,148
Jasper	3,554	5,173	1,271	3,033	4,809	2,019
Jay	3,356	3,584	1,022	3,208	3,609	1,994
Jefferson	5,441	4,827	1,438	5,510	4,937	2,565
Jennings	4,223	4,461	1,629	3,471	4,392	2,370
Johnson	11,278	23,733	3,975	8,712	20,353	8,246
Knox	7,003	6,395	2,022	6,718	6,683	3,719
Kosciusko	6,166	15,084	2,531	5,307	14,179	5,115
LaGrange	2,704	4,033	949	2,093	3,584	1,736
Lake	100,198	47,873	15,051	102,778	53,867	28,635
LaPorte	19,879	14,106	5,133	17,717	14,962	9,641
Lawrence	5,703	8,107	2,063	5,557	7,712	3,452
Madison	23,772	23,151	6,447	22,276	23,479	13,100
Marion	124,448	133,329	21,358	122,234	141,369	57,878
Marshall	5,486	8,158	1,698	4,912	8,048	3,522
Martin	1,848	2,281	485	2,018	2,523	883
Miami	4,260	6,719	1,657	3,967	6,416	3,428
Monroe	18,531	16,744	3,179	19,712	16,661	6,943
Montgomery	3,825	7,705	1,766	3,371	7,602	3,511
Morgan	5,812	12,872	2,755	4,690	10,939	5,375
Newton	1,897	2,075	801	1,757	2,295	1,274
Noble	5,101	6,782	1,521	4,411	5,883	3,328
Ohio	1,083	1,098	281	970	1,009	527
Orange	3,016	3,355	938	2,948	3,738	1,296
Owen	2,244	3,056	874	2,207	2,753	1,563
Parke	2,453	3,151	981	2,429	2,953	1,696
Perry	4,427	2,554	913	4,829	2,973	1,560
Pike	2,780	2,174	884	2,960	2,156	1,238
Porter	24,044	22,931	7,169	21,022	22,644	13,096
Posey	4,965	4,638	1,304	4,632	4,435	2,357
Pulaski	2,010	2,693	634	1,950	2,712	1,214
Putnam	3,962	5,958	1,619	3,487	5,341	3,174
Randolph	4,087	4,708	1,557	3,870	4,937	2,939
Ripley	4,097	5,303	1,216	3,480	5,033	2,406
Rush	2,578	3,827	973	2,168	3,873	1,948
St. Joseph	45,704	38,281	8,379	46,203	38,934	18,828
Scott	3,798	2,620	760	4,085	2,649	1,092
Shelby	5,374	7,778	1,874	4,560	8,075	3,521
Spencer	4,058	3,770	739	4,301	3,789	1,464
Starke	3,854	3,108	1,096	3,695	3,100	1,885
Steuben	4,124	5,513	1,390	3,630	4,868	2,896
Sullivan	4,076	3,207	1,178	4,211	3,052	1,857
Switzerland	1,496	1,266	403	1,535	1,211	636
Tippecanoe	17,232	22,556	5,394	17,343	23,050	9,684
Tipton	2,478	3,980	861	2,125	3,906	1,816
Union	1,019	1,334	364	898	1,394	664
Vanderburgh	30,934	28,509	6,132	33,799	30,271	12,513
Vermillion	3,251	2,334	1,029	3,652	2,360	1,794
Vigo	17,974	15,751	4,508	18,050	15,834	8,141
Wabash	4,577	6,990	1,294	4,518	7,062	3,424
Warren	1,394	1,678	560	1,367	1,601	1,020
Warrick	9,285	9,221	2,471	8,612	8,087	3,862
Washington	3,819	4,066	1,264	4,092	4,043	1,846
Wayne	10,905	12,188	2,525	9,960	12,221	5,095
Wells	3,752	6,322	1,157	3,282	5,799	2,890
White	3,396	4,642	1,610	2,988	4,622	2,582
Whitley	4,176	5,965	1,392	3,569	5,217	3,195
Totals	887,424	1,006,693	224,299	848,420	989,375	455,934

Indiana Vote Since 1948

1948, Truman, Dem., 807,833; Dewey, Rep., 821,079; Watson, Proh., 14,711; Wallace, Prog., 9,649; Thomas, Soc., 2,179; Teichert, Soc. Labor, 763.

1952, Eisenhower, Rep., 1,136,259; Stevenson, Dem., 801,530; Hamblen, Proh., 15,335; Hallinan, Prog., 1,222; Hass, Soc. Labor, 979.

1956, Eisenhower, Rep., 1,182,811; Stevenson, Dem., 783,908; Holtwick, Proh., 6,554; Hass, Soc. Labor, 1,334.

1960, Kennedy, Dem., 952,358; Nixon, Rep., 1,175,120; Decker, Proh., 6,746; Hass, Soc. Labor, 1,136.

1964, Johnson, Dem., 1,170,848; Goldwater, Rep., 911,118; Munn, Proh., 8,266; Hass, Soc. Labor, 1,374.

1968, Nixon, Rep., 1,067,885; Humphrey, Dem., 806,659; Wallace, 3d Party, 243,108; Munn, Proh., 4,616; Halstead, Soc. Workers, 1,293; Gregory, write-in, 36.

1972, Nixon, Rep., 1,405,154; McGovern, Dem., 708,568; Reed, Soc. Workers, 5,575; Fisher, Soc. Labor, 1,688; Spock, Peace and Freedom, 4,544.

1976, Carter, Dem., 1,014,714; Ford, Rep., 1,185,958; Anderson, Amer., 14,048; Camejo, Soc. Workers, 5,695; LaRouche, U.S. Labor, 1,947.

1980, Reagan, Rep., 1,255,656; Carter, Dem., 844,197; Anderson, Ind., 111,639; Clark, Libertarian, 19,627; Commoner, Citizens, 4,852; Greaves, Amer., 4,750; Hall, Com., 702; DeBerry, Soc., 610.

1984, Reagan, Rep., 1,377,230; Mondale, Dem., 841,481; Bergland, Libertarian, 6,741.

1988, Bush, Rep., 1,297,763; Dukakis, Dem., 860,643; Fulani, New Alliance, 10,215.

1992, Bush, Rep., 989,375; Clinton, Dem., 848,420; Perot, Ind., 455,934; Marrou, Libertarian, 7,936; Fulani, New Alliance, 2,583.

1996, Dole, Rep., 1,006,693; Clinton, Dem., 887,424; Perot, Ref., 224,299; Browne, Libertarian, 15,632.

Iowa

County	1996 Clinton (D)	Dole (R)	Perot (RF)	1992 Clinton (D)	Bush (R)	Perot (I)
Adair	1,802	1,655	458	1,655	1,713	814
Adams	1,070	920	320	1,034	863	679
Allamakee	2,551	2,457	680	2,362	2,627	1,543
Appanoose	2,747	2,233	554	2,810	2,346	1,161
Audubon	1,827	1,314	314	1,589	1,373	887
Benton	5,546	3,835	846	4,467	3,469	2,454
Black Hawk	29,651	19,322	3,623	29,584	21,398	10,182
Boone	6,446	4,293	987	5,913	4,148	2,070
Bremer	5,023	4,213	862	4,774	4,482	2,338
Buchanan	4,997	3,043	836	4,166	3,313	2,126
Buena Vista	3,420	3,636	831	3,374	3,863	1,955
Butler	3,061	3,036	489	2,548	3,209	1,333
Calhoun	2,193	2,077	462	2,140	2,169	946
Carroll	4,333	3,392	998	3,800	3,439	2,192
Cass	2,616	3,384	809	2,231	3,176	1,608
Cedar	3,856	2,966	756	3,296	2,965	1,945
Cerro Gordo	11,943	7,427	1,689	11,415	8,250	4,498
Cherokee	2,853	2,629	834	2,590	2,768	1,503
Chickasaw	3,355	2,191	759	2,913	2,129	1,566
Clarke	2,053	1,401	440	1,921	1,417	899
Clay	3,659	3,129	802	3,346	3,011	1,964
Clayton	4,284	2,944	912	3,742	3,044	2,309
Clinton	11,481	7,624	2,300	11,683	8,746	4,414
Crawford	3,140	2,686	847	3,004	2,693	1,905
Dallas	8,017	6,647	1,198	6,554	5,587	2,665
Davis	1,894	1,445	382	1,962	1,344	718
Decatur	1,846	1,287	452	1,866	1,316	786
Delaware	3,704	3,065	679	3,093	3,195	2,144
Des Moines	10,761	5,778	1,792	11,309	6,378	3,386
Dickinson	3,562	3,129	901	3,106	3,196	1,974
Dubuque	20,839	13,391	3,304	20,539	14,007	8,208
Emmet	2,270	1,641	470	2,239	1,749	1,010
Fayette	4,832	3,848	890	4,412	3,879	2,493
Floyd	3,769	2,379	689	3,688	2,404	1,611
Franklin	2,232	2,054	417	2,049	2,137	1,045
Fremont	1,481	1,576	480	1,422	1,459	1,003
Greene	2,519	1,861	396	2,422	1,952	956
Grundy	2,322	2,928	401	1,895	3,160	1,069
Guthrie	2,552	2,034	515	2,234	1,962	1,216
Hamilton	3,455	3,109	661	3,262	3,031	1,348
Hancock	2,399	2,353	529	2,175	2,428	1,170
Hardin	4,053	3,505	713	3,792	3,590	1,547
Harrison	2,576	3,070	820	2,349	2,763	1,691
Henry	3,798	3,478	914	3,544	3,435	1,522
Howard	2,303	1,528	555	2,099	1,516	1,193
Humboldt	2,080	2,236	590	1,765	2,299	1,093
Ida	1,589	1,684	436	1,449	1,714	1,061
Iowa	3,354	3,042	575	2,560	2,656	1,709
Jackson	4,609	2,827	936	4,421	2,673	2,096
Jasper	8,776	6,414	1,263	8,120	6,866	2,972
Jefferson	2,597	2,541	571	2,562	2,541	1,241
Johnson	27,888	13,402	2,313	28,656	14,041	8,625
Jones	4,668	3,083	765	3,508	3,071	2,306
Keokuk	2,545	2,080	432	2,329	1,981	1,238
Kossuth	4,031	3,477	932	3,660	3,464	1,906
Lee	8,831	4,932	1,734	9,366	4,777	2,920
Linn	45,497	30,958	5,607	38,567	30,215	19,643
Louisa	2,081	1,565	590	2,091	1,691	1,044
Lucas	2,168	1,586	433	2,072	1,734	848
Lyon	1,489	3,396	422	1,331	3,272	1,068
Madison	3,070	2,550	654	2,525	2,421	1,168
Mahaska	3,737	4,473	656	3,714	4,953	1,508
Marion	5,978	6,100	871	5,531	6,062	1,896
Marshall	8,669	7,017	1,455	8,303	6,784	3,100
Mills	2,068	2,958	683	1,798	2,699	1,638
Mitchell	2,596	1,877	563	2,177	1,933	1,199
Monona	1,952	1,674	580	1,939	1,660	1,231
Monroe	1,884	1,272	329	1,829	1,323	612
Montgomery	1,912	2,583	663	1,599	2,404	1,341
Muscatine	7,674	5,858	1,705	7,089	6,087	3,583
O'Brien	2,236	3,877	578	2,122	3,869	1,557
Osceola	1,010	1,736	274	990	1,756	813
Page	2,220	4,032	753	1,951	3,670	1,669
Palo Alto	2,371	1,817	477	2,374	1,789	1,186
Plymouth	3,745	5,117	997	3,171	5,196	2,039
Pocahontas	1,981	1,707	478	1,919	1,743	942
Polk	83,877	60,884	9,516	78,585	63,708	24,155
Pottawattamie	13,276	15,648	3,534	13,228	15,671	8,035
Poweshiek	4,183	3,221	681	4,056	3,245	1,680
Ringgold	1,439	967	310	1,341	967	551
Sac	2,170	2,209	579	1,896	2,138	1,157
Scott	32,694	26,751	4,991	33,765	28,844	11,423
Shelby	2,176	3,056	652	2,094	2,809	1,614
Sioux	2,392	10,864	718	2,226	10,637	1,771
Story	17,234	12,468	2,091	17,118	12,702	6,275
Tama	3,994	2,986	713	3,573	2,948	1,748
Taylor	1,458	1,419	379	1,430	1,200	910
Union	2,787	2,156	660	2,565	2,224	1,280
Van Buren	1,536	1,460	347	1,464	1,418	811
Wapello	8,437	4,828	1,376	8,670	4,852	2,513

County	1996 Clinton (D)	Dole (R)	Perot (RF)	1992 Clinton (D)	Bush (R)	Perot (I)
Warren....	9,120	6,905	1,267	8,612	7,242	3,217
Washington.	3,828	3,600	636	3,384	3,576	1,994
Wayne....	1,650	1,295	310	1,632	1,299	642
Webster...	8,380	6,275	1,580	8,562	6,992	3,272
Winnebago.	2,679	2,211	590	2,322	2,407	1,329
Winneshiek.	4,122	3,532	973	3,791	3,331	2,416
Woodbury..	17,224	16,368	3,436	17,398	18,148	7,182
Worth	2,293	1,284	403	2,009	1,382	1,044
Wright	2,912	2,473	536	2,776	2,708	1,151
Totals	**620,258**	**492,644**	**105,159**	**586,353**	**504,891**	**253,468**

Iowa Vote Since 1948

1948, Truman, Dem., 522,380; Dewey, Rep., 494,018; Wallace, Prog., 12,125; Teichert, Soc. Labor, 4,274; Watson, Proh., 3,382; Thomas, Soc., 1,829; Dobbs, Soc. Workers, 26.

1952, Eisenhower, Rep., 808,906; Stevenson, Dem., 451,513; Hallinan, Prog., 5,085; Hamblen, Proh., 2,882; Hoopes, Soc., 219; Hass, Soc. Labor, 139; scattering, 29.

1956, Eisenhower, Rep., 729,187; Stevenson, Dem., 501,858; Andrews (A.C.P. of Iowa), 3,202; Hoopes, Soc., 192; Hass, Soc. Labor, 125.

1960, Kennedy, Dem., 550,565; Nixon, Rep., 722,381; Hass, Soc. Labor, 230; write-in, 634.

1964, Johnson, Dem., 733,030; Goldwater, Rep., 449,148; Hass, Soc. Labor, 182; DeBerry, Soc. Workers, 159; Munn, Proh., 1,902.

1968, Nixon, Rep., 619,106; Humphrey, Dem., 476,699; Wallace, 3d Party, 66,422; Munn, Proh., 362; Halstead, Soc. Workers, 3,377; Cleaver, Peace and Freedom, 1,332; Blomen, Soc. Labor, 241.

1972, Nixon, Rep., 706,207; McGovern, Dem., 496,206; Schmitz, Amer., 22,056; Jenness, Soc. Workers, 488; Fisher, Soc. Labor, 195; Hall, Com., 272; Green, Universal, 199; scattered, 321.

1976, Carter, Dem., 619,931; Ford, Rep., 632,863; McCarthy, Ind., 20,051; Anderson, Amer., 3,040; MacBride, Libertarian, 1,452.

1980, Reagan, Rep., 676,026; Carter, Dem., 508,672; Anderson, Ind., 115,633; Clark, Libertarian, 13,123; Commoner, Citizens, 2,273; McReynolds, Socialist, 534; Hall, Com., 298; DeBerry, Soc. Workers, 244; Greaves, Amer., 189; Bubar, Statesman, 150; scattering, 519.

1984, Reagan, Rep., 703,088; Mondale, Dem., 605,620; Bergland, Libertarian, 1,844.

1988, Bush, Rep., 545,355; Dukakis, Dem., 670,557; LaRouche, Ind., 3,526; Paul, Lib., 2,494.

1992, Clinton, Dem., 586,353; Bush, Rep., 504,891; Perot, Ind., 253,468; Hagelin, Natural Law, 3,079; Gritz, Populist/America First, 1,177; Marrou, Libertarian, 1,076.

1996, Clinton, Dem., 620,258; Dole, Rep., 492,644; Perot, Ref., 105,159; Nader, Green, 6,550; Hagelin, Natural Law, 3,349; Browne, Libertarian, 2,315; Phillips, Taxpayers, 2,229; Harris, Soc. Workers, 331.

Kansas

County	1996 Clinton (D)	Dole (R)	Perot (RF)	1992 Clinton (D)	Bush (R)	Perot (I)
Allen	2,299	2,797	793	2,312	2,351	1,746
Anderson ..	1,367	1,636	449	1,178	1,218	1,282
Atchison..	2,926	2,828	727	2,959	2,521	2,020
Barber	730	1,696	279	759	1,225	893
Barton	3,121	7,855	1,004	3,846	5,113	4,574
Bourbon ...	2,491	3,318	760	2,509	2,876	1,763
Brown	1,529	2,688	497	1,476	2,203	1,603
Butler.....	7,294	13,979	2,274	7,029	9,166	7,355
Chase	496	778	259	470	610	600
Chautauqua	568	1,142	222	598	853	607
Cherokee ..	3,771	4,138	1,072	4,083	3,589	2,067
Cheyenne .	422	1,211	174	407	863	477
Clark	334	855	109	293	676	341
Clay	963	2,793	389	947	2,198	1,434
Cloud....	1,615	2,743	609	1,720	2,131	1,578
Coffey	1,118	2,369	572	1,021	1,824	1,443
Comanche .	298	691	133	325	636	324
Cowley....	5,588	7,872	1,904	5,405	5,422	4,911
Crawford ..	7,504	6,447	1,785	7,366	5,468	3,706
Decatur ...	417	1,255	156	576	940	565
Dickinson ..	2,423	5,174	888	2,518	3,851	2,833
Doniphan ..	1,050	1,962	0	1,177	1,579	1,200
Douglas ...	18,116	16,116	2,030	15,453	12,540	6,000
Edwards ..	539	1,088	180	567	769	584
Elk	488	933	206	485	748	503
Ellis	4,142	6,809	894	4,544	3,985	3,887
Ellsworth ..	899	2,078	245	1,010	1,197	1,020
Finney	2,420	6,188	805	2,612	5,278	3,011
Ford	2,628	5,681	914	2,635	4,342	3,341

County	1996 Clinton (D)	Dole (R)	Perot (RF)	1992 Clinton (D)	Bush (R)	Perot (I)
Franklin ...	3,552	5,007	1,184	2,968	3,699	3,184
Geary	2,444	3,686	618	2,559	2,928	2,057
Gove	351	1,123	141	379	792	532
Graham ...	432	1,031	152	554	752	603
Grant	633	1,772	250	619	1,561	835
Gray	404	1,457	164	443	1,039	686
Greeley ...	161	567	47	191	504	175
Greenwood.	1,108	1,932	552	1,262	1,411	1,167
Hamilton ..	342	811	84	386	716	271
Harper	836	1,941	355	845	1,371	1,151
Harvey....	4,918	8,382	1,023	5,047	6,259	3,653
Haskell ...	304	1,143	96	336	1,023	462
Hodgeman .	251	808	99	258	625	343
Jackson ...	1,983	2,682	735	1,639	1,970	1,927
Jefferson ..	2,757	3,781	1,030	2,538	2,569	2,642
Jewell	417	1,374	188	546	1,050	698
Johnson ...	68,129	110,368	10,425	59,573	85,418	49,136
Kearny ...	335	1,041	106	384	943	376
Kingman ..	1,006	2,659	409	1,100	1,680	1,370
Kiowa	331	1,264	170	355	1,057	475
Labette ...	3,931	4,283	1,091	4,196	3,368	2,577
Lane	271	865	86	265	674	356
Leavenworth	9,098	10,778	2,419	8,077	7,738	7,306
Lincoln ...	528	1,372	212	612	893	657
Linn.....	1,590	2,077	535	1,353	1,413	1,358
Logan	296	1,155	112	355	905	446
Lyon	4,884	6,612	1,584	4,811	5,090	4,717
McPherson .	3,536	8,142	1,115	3,645	5,745	3,561
Marion....	1,673	4,173	492	1,627	3,142	1,557
Marshall...	1,932	2,811	713	2,022	2,030	1,786
Meade	426	1,443	173	430	1,135	592
Miami	4,237	5,256	1,339	3,835	3,528	3,701
Mitchell ...	833	2,435	246	938	1,601	1,098
Montgomery.	5,269	7,428	1,528	5,453	6,848	3,570
Morris	965	1,553	451	957	1,071	1,071
Morton	376	1,073	124	398	915	350
Nemaha...	1,648	3,014	676	1,580	2,220	1,804
Neosho ...	2,527	3,409	907	2,799	2,926	2,136
Ness	428	1,336	186	565	967	678
Norton ...	640	1,814	265	779	1,469	815
Osage	2,502	3,487	1,101	2,297	2,561	2,532
Osborne ...	608	1,582	191	779	1,003	819
Ottawa ...	752	1,846	261	764	1,284	762
Pawnee ...	932	1,927	275	1,118	1,357	1,097
Phillips ...	758	2,005	242	843	1,579	955
Pottawatomie	1,997	4,504	1,035	2,099	3,106	2,759
Pratt	1,367	2,591	408	1,466	1,779	1,528
Rawlins ...	335	1,393	146	393	1,023	517
Reno	9,108	14,275	2,661	9,257	11,377	7,636
Republic ..	688	2,283	268	939	1,767	1,084
Rice	1,434	2,842	482	1,555	2,158	1,543
Riley	6,746	11,113	1,478	7,933	8,394	5,387
Rooks	650	1,864	251	771	1,249	1,063
Rush	547	1,239	185	689	756	665
Russell	705	3,347	164	1,178	1,434	1,395
Saline	7,728	12,475	2,192	7,890	8,565	7,108
Scott	458	1,750	160	480	1,426	621
Sedgwick ..	59,643	93,397	11,875	62,670	75,577	47,238
Seward ...	1,309	3,812	396	1,488	3,477	1,818
Shawnee ..	32,803	34,845	7,304	31,972	29,344	20,653
Sheridan ..	264	1,053	95	347	739	546
Sherman ..	736	2,110	220	810	1,630	828
Smith	638	1,628	213	789	1,236	816
Stafford ...	651	1,604	276	777	1,064	910
Stanton ...	189	628	60	224	556	214
Stevens ...	405	1,548	213	390	1,408	674
Sumner ...	3,638	5,952	1,260	3,564	4,087	3,887
Thomas ...	866	2,725	295	932	1,849	1,129
Trego	548	1,205	209	608	727	574
Wabaunsee	966	1,884	479	851	1,254	1,258
Wallace ...	160	738	65	164	679	219
Washington	804	2,397	326	893	1,740	1,054
Wichita ...	239	796	80	241	681	303
Wilson ...	1,297	2,458	562	1,331	1,925	1,365
Woodson ..	598	953	269	590	662	604
Wyandotte.	31,252	14,011	3,931	34,397	12,872	13,620
Totals	**387,659**	**583,245**	**92,639**	**390,434**	**449,951**	**312,358**

Kansas Vote Since 1948

1948, Truman, Dem., 351,902; Dewey, Rep., 423,039; Watson, Proh., 6,468; Wallace, Prog., 4,603; Thomas, Soc., 2,807.

1952, Eisenhower, Rep., 616,302; Stevenson, Dem., 273,296; Hamblen, Proh., 6,038; Hoopes, Soc., 530.

1956, Eisenhower, Rep., 566,878; Stevenson. Dem., 296,317; Holtwick, Proh., 3,048.

1960, Kennedy, Dem., 363,213; Nixon, Rep., 561,474; Decker, Proh., 4,138.

1964, Johnson, Dem., 464,028; Goldwater, Rep., 386,579; Munn, Proh., 5,393; Hass, Soc. Labor, 1,901.

1968, Nixon, Rep., 478,674; Humphrey, Dem., 302,996; Wallace, 3d Party, 88,921; Munn, Proh., 2,192.

1972, Nixon, Rep., 619,812; McGovern, Dem., 270,287; Schmitz, Conservative, 21,808; Munn, Proh., 4,188.

1976, Carter, Dem., 430,421; Ford, Rep., 502,752; McCarthy, Ind., 13,185; Anderson, Amer., 4,724; MacBride, Libertarian, 3,242; Maddox, Conservative, 2,118; Bubar, Proh., 1,403.

1980, Reagan, Rep., 566,812; Carter, Dem., 326,150; Anderson, Ind., 68,231; Clark, Libertarian, 14,470; Shelton, Amer., 1,555; Hall, Com., 967; Bubar, Statesman, 821; Rarick, Conservative, 789.

1984, Reagan, Rep., 674,646; Mondale, Dem., 332,471; Bergland, Libertarian, 3,585.

1988, Bush, Rep., 554,049; Dukakis, Dem., 422,636; Paul, Ind., 12,553; Fulani, Ind., 3,806.

1992, Clinton, Dem., 390,434; Bush, Rep., 449,951; Perot, Ind., 312,358; Marrou, Libertarian, 4,314.

1996, Dole, Rep., 583,245; Clinton, Dem., 387,659; Perot, Ref., 92,639; Browne, Libertarian, 4,557; Phillips, Ind., 3,519; Hagelin, Ind., 1,655.

Kentucky

County	Clinton (D) 1996	Dole (R) 1996	Perot (RF) 1996	Clinton (D) 1992	Bush (R) 1992	Perot (I) 1992
Adair	1,821	3,876	790	2,044	3,740	617
Allen	1,781	3,032	393	2,040	2,747	606
Anderson	2,898	2,972	751	2,491	2,731	1,219
Ballard	2,255	1,064	411	2,268	1,108	500
Barren	5,044	5,700	1,065	5,688	5,467	1,778
Bath	1,886	1,229	428	2,229	1,259	694
Bell	5,058	3,917	940	5,745	4,501	1,193
Boone	8,379	15,085	1,900	6,514	12,306	4,676
Bourbon	3,030	2,592	603	2,895	2,707	1,290
Boyd	9,668	7,054	2,070	10,496	7,387	3,195
Boyle	3,877	4,157	709	3,894	4,019	1,335
Bracken	1,055	1,371	271	1,259	1,162	500
Breathitt	3,106	1,058	397	3,496	1,303	515
Breckinridge	2,956	3,151	670	3,113	2,941	945
Bullitt	7,651	8,697	1,973	7,830	7,745	3,333
Butler	1,260	2,531	348	1,468	2,729	596
Caldwell	2,434	2,067	637	3,000	1,966	670
Calloway	5,281	4,989	1,223	6,181	4,654	1,853
Campbell	11,957	16,640	2,312	10,673	16,382	5,659
Carlisle	1,355	816	245	1,383	844	309
Carroll	1,689	1,170	351	2,119	1,046	566
Carter	3,728	3,240	781	4,224	3,305	989
Casey	1,106	3,187	525	1,409	3,317	542
Christian	6,843	8,285	1,064	6,709	7,737	1,789
Clark	4,987	4,739	1,095	4,892	4,625	1,955
Clay	2,135	3,716	478	2,012	4,747	648
Clinton	1,072	2,521	350	1,241	2,830	348
Crittenden	1,480	1,509	400	1,740	1,576	495
Cumberland	753	1,654	227	917	1,866	268
Daviess	15,366	15,844	3,344	16,592	14,936	5,112
Edmonson	1,595	2,619	298	1,653	2,486	438
Elliott	1,298	421	284	1,796	444	273
Estill	1,724	2,220	479	1,837	2,453	736
Fayette	43,632	42,930	5,345	38,306	41,908	14,215
Fleming	1,913	2,313	522	2,257	2,045	815
Floyd	9,655	3,139	1,518	13,351	3,540	1,723
Franklin	11,251	7,132	1,873	9,896	7,591	3,340
Fulton	1,614	863	223	1,813	1,073	306
Gallatin	1,189	838	299	1,171	699	445
Garrard	1,486	2,540	337	1,730	2,359	697
Grant	2,541	2,697	661	2,097	2,128	1,149
Graves	6,991	5,130	1,596	8,001	5,311	1,943
Grayson	2,716	4,249	677	2,909	4,533	993
Green	1,285	2,763	475	1,760	2,709	500
Greenup	6,883	5,370	1,627	7,214	4,975	2,188
Hancock	1,547	1,356	418	1,714	1,261	551
Hardin	11,031	12,642	2,815	9,417	12,299	4,026
Harlan	5,874	3,337	884	6,796	3,970	1,391
Harrison	2,934	2,433	801	2,795	2,148	1,225
Hart	2,527	2,701	501	2,852	2,401	579
Henderson	8,051	5,092	1,556	8,270	5,125	2,678
Henry	2,324	2,110	564	2,838	1,640	720
Hickman	1,220	695	247	1,296	861	294
Hopkins	7,239	6,363	1,512	8,881	6,032	2,565
Jackson	960	3,045	299	776	3,398	341
Jefferson	144,207	114,860	19,413	152,728	116,566	39,822
Jessamine	4,428	6,686	1,040	3,764	6,474	2,059
Johnson	3,348	3,262	1,010	3,669	3,614	1,118
Kenton	19,407	28,579	3,680	16,344	27,261	9,336
Knott	4,842	1,201	517	5,500	1,243	560
Knox	3,736	4,502	811	3,787	5,011	972
Larue	2,040	2,140	469	2,190	2,154	582
Laurel	4,306	9,454	1,211	4,560	8,583	1,859
Lawrence	2,195	1,812	481	2,400	2,084	557
Lee	1,023	1,302	181	1,170	1,617	356
Leslie	1,466	2,296	304	1,591	2,879	450
Letcher	4,160	2,222	782	5,817	3,011	1,206
Lewis	1,415	2,365	561	1,713	2,493	673
Lincoln	2,550	3,006	526	2,532	2,624	762
Livingston	2,228	1,258	449	2,386	1,339	578
Logan	4,181	3,888	704	4,064	3,710	1,043
Lyon	1,641	999	284	1,583	820	293
McCracken	12,670	10,221	2,268	13,341	10,657	3,077
McCreary	1,710	2,527	488	1,934	3,588	624
McLean	1,834	1,368	385	2,223	1,355	529
Madison	8,142	9,212	1,613	8,005	8,719	3,038
Magoffin	2,249	1,434	337	3,261	1,992	440
Marion	2,922	2,013	757	3,403	2,091	805
Marshall	6,054	4,579	1,391	6,576	4,368	1,773
Martin	1,807	1,612	401	1,715	1,961	393
Mason	2,444	2,588	484	2,657	2,432	916
Meade	3,653	2,855	912	3,387	2,641	1,298
Menifee	979	608	179	1,311	557	254
Mercer	3,179	3,264	738	3,010	3,211	1,298
Metcalfe	1,349	1,651	355	1,703	1,683	409
Monroe	1,114	3,300	415	1,515	3,776	480
Montgomery	3,372	2,681	705	3,686	2,590	1,308
Morgan	1,843	1,439	380	2,655	1,239	498
Muhlenberg	6,564	3,569	1,218	7,901	3,551	1,624
Nelson	5,392	4,645	1,067	5,437	4,495	1,638
Nicholas	1,092	950	265	1,341	894	513
Ohio	3,487	3,475	1,076	4,022	3,385	1,423
Oldham	6,202	10,477	1,521	5,457	8,263	2,855
Owen	1,603	1,709	454	1,830	1,108	613
Owsley	647	920	153	678	1,437	209
Pendleton	1,926	2,177	462	1,740	1,810	1,086
Perry	6,015	3,382	894	6,619	4,128	1,308
Pike	14,126	7,160	2,148	17,358	8,212	2,444
Powell	2,156	1,526	523	2,323	1,809	874
Pulaski	5,340	11,945	1,420	5,465	11,423	2,449
Robertson	360	368	117	439	329	170
Rockcastle	1,160	3,106	338	1,144	3,287	446
Rowan	3,215	2,309	724	3,558	2,469	1,212
Russell	1,582	4,017	837	1,950	4,641	673
Scott	4,258	4,349	977	3,639	3,810	1,800
Shelby	4,629	5,307	780	4,398	4,550	1,451
Simpson	2,749	2,186	401	2,834	2,280	708
Spencer	1,404	1,614	341	1,383	1,305	466
Taylor	2,897	4,573	829	3,518	4,319	1,044
Todd	1,744	1,912	424	1,858	1,691	612
Trigg	2,087	1,975	394	2,438	1,820	573
Trimble	1,245	999	308	1,413	789	413
Union	2,913	1,554	598	3,325	1,605	794
Warren	11,642	15,784	1,835	11,529	14,748	3,533
Washington	1,639	2,116	383	2,008	2,098	542
Wayne	2,422	3,122	481	2,516	3,412	560
Webster	2,852	1,568	660	3,380	1,408	854
Whitley	4,174	5,402	1,027	4,600	5,998	1,533
Wolfe	1,297	772	202	1,674	697	297
Woodford	3,910	4,270	746	3,161	3,992	1,535
Totals	636,614	623,283	120,396	665,104	617,178	203,944

Kentucky Vote Since 1948

1948, Truman, Dem., 466,756; Dewey, Rep., 341,210; Thurmond, States' Rights, 10,411; Wallace, Prog., 1,567; Thomas, Soc., 1,284; Watson, Proh., 1,245; Teichert, Soc. Labor, 185.

1952, Eisenhower, Rep., 495,029; Stevenson, Dem., 495,729; Hamblen, Proh., 1,161; Hass, Soc. Labor, 893; Hallinan, Proh., 336.

1956, Eisenhower, Rep., 572,192; Stevenson, Dem., 476,453; Byrd, States' Rights, 2,657; Holtwick, Proh., 2,145; Hass, Soc. Labor, 358.

1960, Kennedy, Dem., 521,855; Nixon, Rep., 602,607.

1964, Johnson, Dem., 669,659; Goldwater, Rep., 372,977; Kasper, Natl. States Rights, 3,469.

1968, Nixon, Rep., 462,411; Humphrey, Dem., 397,547; Wallace, 3d Party, 193,098; Halstead, Soc. Workers, 2,843.

1972, Nixon, Rep., 676,446; McGovern, Dem., 371,159; Schmitz, Amer., 17,627; Jenness, Soc. Workers, 685; Hall, Com., 464; Spock, Peoples, 1,118.

1976, Carter, Dem., 615,717; Ford, Rep., 531,852; Anderson, Amer., 8,308; McCarthy, Ind., 6,837; Maddox, Amer. Ind., 2,328; MacBride, Libertarian, 814.

1980, Reagan, Rep., 635,274; Carter, Dem., 616,417; Anderson, Ind., 31,127; Clark, Libertarian, 5,531; McCormack, Respect For Life, 4,233; Commoner, Citizens, 1,304; Pulley, Socialist, 393; Hall, Com., 348.

1984, Reagan, Rep., 815,345; Mondale, Dem., 536,756.

1988, Bush, Rep., 734,281; Dukakis, Dem., 580,368; Duke, Pop., 4,494; Paul, Lib., 2,118.

1992, Clinton, Dem., 665,104; Bush, Rep., 617,178; Perot, Ind., 203,944; Marrou, Libertarian, 4,513.

1996, Clinton, Dem., 636,614; Dole, Rep., 623,283; Perot, Ref., 120,396; Browne, Libertarian, 4,009; Phillips, Taxpayers, 2,204; Hagelin, Natural Law, 1,493.

Louisiana

Parish	Clinton (D) 1996	Dole (R) 1996	Perot (RF) 1996	Clinton (D) 1992	Bush (R) 1992	Perot (I) 1992
Acadia . . .	12,300	9,246	2,234	12,276	9,017	3,145
Allen	4,930	2,589	1,187	5,626	3,069	1,245
Ascension	15,263	10,885	3,027	13,036	10,275	4,295
Assumption	6,416	2,698	904	5,639	2,928	1,358
Avoyelles .	9,689	4,433	1,937	8,696	4,851	2,139
Beauregard	4,925	5,526	1,834	5,037	5,119	2,103
Bienville . .	4,335	2,402	457	3,899	2,412	832
Bossier . .	15,504	16,852	2,660	11,313	15,628	4,863
Caddo . . .	55,543	38,445	4,821	47,733	42,665	11,830
Calcasieu .	38,238	26,494	8,281	33,570	24,847	10,980
Caldwell . .	2,117	1,842	514	2,061	1,752	653
Cameron . .	2,103	1,365	594	1,985	1,329	995
Catahoula.	2,692	1,770	615	2,570	1,976	773
Claiborne .	3,609	2,500	530	3,263	2,599	926
Concordia.	4,565	3,134	855	4,283	3,223	1,317
DeSoto . .	6,221	3,526	646	5,671	3,643	1,358
E. Baton Rouge . .	83,493	77,811	7,990	68,622	81,072	16,102
East Carroll	2,149	1,008	186	1,835	1,142	283
East Feliciana	4,714	2,949	660	4,093	2,813	932
Evangeline	7,847	5,278	1,447	8,564	5,147	2,124
Franklin . .	4,076	3,961	814	4,127	3,889	1,311
Grant	2,980	3,117	1,055	3,122	3,214	1,174
Iberia	15,087	12,014	2,448	13,040	11,905	4,337
Iberville . .	9,553	4,031	1,076	8,218	5,211	1,543
Jackson . .	3,368	3,030	571	3,370	3,072	882
Jefferson .	80,407	92,820	9,667	64,302	100,493	21,278
Jefferson Davis . . .	6,897	4,311	1,543	7,022	4,513	2,221
Lafayette .	32,504	36,419	4,631	28,583	32,406	9,124
Lafourche .	18,810	12,105	2,984	16,182	12,744	5,077
LaSalle . .	2,543	2,925	947	2,389	3,068	993
Lincoln . . .	7,903	6,973	761	7,205	7,220	1,751
Livingston .	13,276	16,159	4,150	11,499	14,808	4,971
Madison . .	3,085	1,591	315	2,773	1,702	469
Morehouse	6,160	5,193	963	6,013	5,364	1,727
Natchitoches	8,296	5,471	1,053	6,974	5,694	1,606
Orleans . .	144,720	39,576	3,805	133,261	52,019	10,889
Ouachita .	24,525	28,559	3,586	20,835	27,600	6,612
Plaquemines	5,348	4,493	856	4,467	5,018	1,729
Pointe Coupee .	6,835	3,545	845	6,512	3,563	1,157
Rapides . .	23,004	21,548	4,670	20,873	22,783	6,599
Red River .	2,641	1,344	268	2,360	1,649	566
Richland. .	4,143	3,765	645	3,706	3,808	1,054
Sabine . .	4,263	3,043	1,043	4,173	3,586	1,219
St. Bernard	14,312	13,549	2,664	12,305	16,131	4,308
St. Charles	10,612	9,316	1,307	8,810	9,158	2,593
St. Helena	3,692	1,455	417	3,416	1,515	589
St. James .	7,247	2,832	608	6,609	3,339	993
St. John the Baptist . . .	9,937	6,025	966	8,977	6,730	1,922
St. Landry.	20,636	12,273	2,311	20,383	11,882	4,266
St. Martin .	12,492	6,296	1,607	11,252	5,909	2,573
St. Mary . .	12,402	8,018	1,850	10,648	8,792	3,257
St. Tammany	24,281	44,761	4,741	19,735	37,839	9,005
Tangipahoa	18,617	15,517	3,144	15,194	14,128	4,612
Tensas. . .	1,882	1,000	176	1,666	1,153	353
Terrebonne	18,550	13,944	3,359	13,325	14,662	5,505
Union. . . .	4,260	4,418	696	4,005	4,434	1,209
Vermilion .	12,609	7,653	1,954	12,324	7,062	3,127
Vernon. . .	6,195	5,449	2,068	6,005	5,912	2,313
Washington	9,603	6,642	1,643	9,095	7,227	2,303
Webster . .	9,688	6,153	1,324	8,380	6,640	2,629
W. Baton Rouge . .	5,697	3,254	799	5,131	3,522	1,249
West Carroll	1,853	2,366	461	2,068	2,082	771
W. Feliciana	2,416	1,616	388	2,328	1,501	516
Winn	3,779	2,803	735	3,537	2,932	843
Totals . . .	**927,837**	**712,586**	**123,293**	**815,971**	**733,386**	**211,478**

Louisiana Vote Since 1948

1948, Thurmond, States' Rights, 204,290; Truman, Dem., 136,344; Dewey, Rep., 72,657; Wallace, Prog., 3,035.

1952, Eisenhower, Rep., 306,925; Stevenson, Dem., 345,027.

1956, Eisenhower, Rep., 329,047; Stevenson, Dem., 243,977; Andrews, States' Rights, 44,520.

1960, Kennedy, Dem., 407,339; Nixon, Rep., 230,890; States' Rights (unpledged), 169,572.

1964, Johnson, Dem., 387,068; Goldwater, Rep., 509,225.

1968, Nixon, Rep., 257,535; Humphrey, Dem., 309,615; Wallace, 3d Party, 530,300.

1972, Nixon, Rep., 686,852; McGovern, Dem., 298,142; Schmitz, Amer., 52,099; Jenness, Soc. Workers, 14,398.

1976, Carter, Dem., 661,365; Ford, Rep., 507,446, Maddox, Amer., 10,058; Hall, Com., 7,417; McCarthy, Ind., 6,588; MacBride, Libertarian, 3,325.

1980, Reagan, Rep., 792,853; Carter, Dem., 708,453; Anderson, Ind., 26,345; Rarick, Amer. Ind., 10,333; Clark, Libertarian, 8,240; Commoner, Citizens, 1,584; DeBerry, Soc. Work., 783.

1984, Reagan, Rep., 1,037,299; Mondale, Dem., 651,586; Bergland, Libertarian, 1,876.

1988, Bush, Rep., 883,702; Dukakis, Dem., 717,460; Duke, Pop., 18,612; Paul, Lib., 4,115.

1992, Clinton, Dem., 815,971; Bush, Rep., 733,386; Perot, Ind., 211,478; Gritz, Populist/America First, 18,545; Marrou, Libertarian, 3,155; Daniels, Ind., 1,663; Phillips, U.S. Taxpayers, 1,552; Fulani, New Alliance, 1,434; LaRouche, Ind., 1,136.

1996, Clinton, Dem., 927,837; Dole, Rep., 712,586; Perot, Ref., 123,293; Browne, Libertarian, 7,499; Nader, Liberty, Ecology, Community, 4,719; Phillips, Taxpayers, 3,366; Hagelin, Natural Law, 2,981; Moorehead, Workers World, 1,678.

Maine

City	Clinton (D) 1996	Dole (R) 1996	Perot (RF) 1996	Clinton (D) 1992	Bush (R) 1992	Perot (I) 1992
Auburn. . . .	5,750	3,060	1,484	5,025	3,653	3,964
Augusta . .	5,307	2,353	1,100	4,657	3,003	3,002
Bangor. . . .	7,609	4,476	1,399	6,826	5,185	4,689
Biddeford . .	5,653	1,768	1,019	4,945	2,533	2,717
Brunswick .	5,258	2,850	841	4,686	3,058	2,282
Gorham . . .	2,990	2,269	710	2,516	2,422	2,015
Lewiston . .	10,275	3,182	2,113	9,265	4,372	6,180
Orono	2,748	1,106	369	2,813	1,336	1,502
Portland . . .	19,755	7,178	2,255	19,510	8,660	6,910
Presque Isle	2,015	1,491	594	1,750	1,709	1,318
Saco	4,506	2,140	834	4,000	2,769	2,303
Sanford . . .	4,368	2,239	1,524	3,854	3,030	3,215
Scarborough	3,906	3,214	805	2,941	3,235	2,033
S. Portland	6,777	3,241	906	5,933	3,999	2,734
Waterville .	4,219	1,478	750	3,868	1,832	2,257
Westbrook .	4,373	2,186	864	3,665	2,904	2,512
Windham . .	3,251	2,396	898	2,444	2,603	2,250
York	2,970	2,525	649	2,445	2,740	1,648
Other.	211,058	137,226	66,856	172,277	147,461	153,289
Totals	**312,788**	**186,378**	**85,970**	**263,420**	**206,504**	**206,820**

Maine Vote Since 1948

1948, Truman, Dem., 111,916; Dewey, Rep., 150,234; Wallace, Prog., 1,884; Thomas, Soc., 547; Teichert, Soc. Labor, 206.

1952, Eisenhower, Rep., 232,353; Stevenson, Dem., 118,806; Hallinan, Prog., 332; Hass, Soc. Labor, 156; Hoopes, Soc., 138; scattered, 1.

1956, Eisenhower, Rep., 249,238; Stevenson, Dem., 102,468.

1960, Kennedy, Dem., 181,159; Nixon, Rep., 240,608.

1964, Johnson, Dem., 262,264; Goldwater, Rep., 118,701.

1968, Nixon, Rep., 169,254; Humphrey, Dem., 217,312; Wallace, 3d Party, 6,370.

1972, Nixon, Rep., 256,458; McGovern, Dem., 160,584; scattered, 229.

1976, Carter, Dem., 232,279; Ford, Rep., 236,320; McCarthy, Ind., 10,874; Bubar, Proh., 3,495.

1980, Reagan, Rep., 238,522; Carter, Dem., 220,974; Anderson, Ind., 53,327; Clark, Libertarian, 5,119; Commoner, Citizens, 4,394; Hall, Com., 591; write-ins, 84.

1984, Reagan, Rep., 336,500; Mondale, Dem., 214,515.

1988, Bush, Rep., 307,131; Dukakis, Dem., 243,569; Paul, Lib., 2,700; Fulani, New Alliance, 1,405.

1992, Clinton, Dem., 263,420; Perot, Ind., 206,820; Bush, Rep., 206,504; Marrou, Libertarian, 1,681.

1996, Clinton, Dem., 312,788; Dole, Rep., 186,378; Perot, Ref., 85,970; Nader, Green, 15,279; Browne, Libertarian, 2,996; Phillips, Taxpayers, 1,517; Hagelin, Natural Law, 825.

Maryland

County	Clinton (D) 1996	Dole (R) 1996	Perot (RF) 1996	Clinton (D) 1992	Bush (R) 1992	Perot (I) 1992
Allegany. . .	11,025	12,136	2,652	11,501	13,862	5,081
Anne Arundel	72,147	83,574	14,287	68,629	81,467	35,191
Baltimore . .	132,599	114,449	20,393	143,498	126,728	51,757
Calvert. . . .	10,008	11,509	1,932	8,619	10,026	4,499
Caroline . . .	3,251	3,874	947	2,822	3,856	1,729
Carroll	17,122	30,316	4,873	15,447	28,405	10,965
Cecil	10,144	10,885	3,124	10,232	10,784	6,115
Charles . . .	15,890	17,432	2,333	14,498	17,293	6,501
Dorchester .	4,613	4,337	1,008	3,933	4,934	2,010
Frederick . .	25,081	34,494	4,989	21,848	31,290	11,373
Garrett. . . .	3,121	5,400	1,200	2,856	5,714	1,987
Harford . . .	29,779	39,686	7,939	27,164	36,350	17,002
Howard . . .	47,569	40,849	6,011	44,763	38,594	16,182
Kent	2,207	3,065	676	3,093	3,094	1,411
Montgomery	198,807	117,730	14,450	199,757	119,705	41,971
Prince George's . .	176,612	52,697	9,153	168,691	62,955	23,355
Queen Anne's	5,054	7,147	1,312	4,668	6,829	2,958
St. Mary's. .	9,988	11,835	1,827	8,931	11,485	4,550
Somerset . .	3,557	2,919	613	3,210	3,450	1,230

County	1996 Clinton (D)	Dole (R)	Perot (RF)	1992 Clinton (D)	Bush (R)	Perot (I)
Talbot ...	4,821	6,997	914	4,642	6,774	2,233
Washington	16,481	21,434	3,934	16,495	21,977	7,537
Wicomico .	12,303	12,687	2,160	11,481	13,560	5,140
Worcester.	7,587	7,621	1,612	6,040	7,237	3,256
City						
Baltimore ..	145,441	28,467	7,473	185,753	40,725	17,381
Totals	966,207	681,530	115,812	988,571	707,094	281,414

Maryland Vote Since 1948

1948, Truman, Dem., 286,521; Dewey, Rep., 294,814; Wallace, Prog., 9,983; Thomas, Soc., 2,941; Thurmond, States' Rights, 2,476; Wright, write-in, 2,294.

1952, Eisenhower, Rep., 499,424; Stevenson, Dem., 395,337; Hallinan, Prog., 7,313.

1956, Eisenhower, Rep., 559,738; Stevenson, Dem., 372,613.

1960, Kennedy, Dem., 565,800; Nixon, Rep., 489,538.

1964, Johnson, Dem., 730,912; Goldwater, Rep., 385,495; write-in, 50.

1968, Nixon, Rep., 517,995; Humphrey, Dem., 538,310; Wallace, 3d Party, 178,734.

1972, Nixon, Rep., 829,305; McGovern, Dem., 505,781; Schmitz, Amer., 18,726.

1976, Carter, Dem., 759,612; Ford, Rep., 672,661.

1980, Reagan, Rep., 680,606; Carter, Dem., 726,161; Anderson, Ind., 119,537; Clark, Libertarian, 14,192.

1984, Reagan, Rep., 879,918; Mondale, Dem., 787,935; Bergland, Libertarian, 5,721.

1988, Bush, Rep., 876,167; Dukakis, Dem., 826,304; Paul, Lib., 6,748; Fulani, New Alliance, 5,115.

1992, Clinton, Dem., 988,571; Bush, Rep., 707,094; Perot, Ind., 281,414; Marrou, Libertarian, 4,715; Fulani, New Alliance, 2,786.

1996, Clinton, Dem., 966,207; Dole, Rep., 681,530; Perot, Ref., 115,812; Browne, Libertarian, 8,765; Phillips, Taxpayers, 3,402; Hagelin, Natural Law, 2,517.

Massachusetts

City	1996 Clinton (D)	Dole (R)	Perot (RF)	1992 Clinton (D)	Bush (R)	Perot (I)
Boston . . .	125,529	33,366	8,428	114,260	41,868	25,189
Brockton..	16,361	6,972	2,738	13,209	8,863	7,579
Brookline .	18,812	4,579	799	19,848	4,892	2,629
Cambridge	29,913	4,976	1,415	30,737	5,847	4,106
Chicopee .	14,203	5,188	2,495	11,433	6,138	6,452
Fall River .	22,796	4,287	2,612	18,652	5,456	6,922
Framingham	16,836	6,669	1,700	15,165	8,114	6,089
Lawrence .	8,615	2,804	1,096	7,698	5,079	3,245
Lowell . . .	16,912	5,896	2,911	14,492	8,467	8,893
Lynn	18,370	5,634	2,726	15,275	7,350	7,665
Medford . .	16,639	5,844	1,741	14,690	7,690	5,480
New Bedford	23,620	4,151	2,547	20,880	5,255	6,965
Newton. . .	30,005	8,499	1,674	29,136	9,623	5,685
Quincy . . .	23,182	9,824	3,066	18,891	12,306	9,068
Somerville.	20,206	3,983	1,455	19,792	5,883	4,416
Springfield	31,266	9,110	3,407	27,302	12,200	10,361
Waltham..	13,607	5,830	1,663	11,333	7,365	5,092
Weymouth	13,536	6,904	2,181	10,762	7,849	6,552
Worcester .	35,607	12,879	3,925	32,326	17,228	10,488
Other	1,075,494	570,663	178,627	872,758	617,566	487,855
Totals . . .	1,571,509	718,058	227,206	1,318,639	805,039	630,731

Massachusetts Vote Since 1948

1948, Truman, Dem., 1,151,788; Dewey, Rep., 909,370; Wallace, Prog., 38,157; Teichert, Soc. Labor, 5,535; Watson, Proh., 1,663.

1952, Eisenhower, Rep., 1,292,325; Stevenson, Dem., 1,083,525; Hallinan, Prog., 4,636; Hass, Soc. Labor, 1,957; Hamblen, Proh., 886; scattered, 69; blanks, 41,150.

1956, Eisenhower, Rep., 1,393,197; Stevenson, Dem., 948,190; Hass, Soc. Labor, 5,573; Holtwick, Proh., 1,205; others, 341.

1960, Kennedy, Dem., 1,487,174; Nixon, Rep., 976,750; Hass, Soc. Labor, 3,892; Decker, Proh., 1,633; others, 31; blank and void, 26,024.

1964, Johnson, Dem., 1,786,422; Goldwater, Rep., 549,727; Hass, Soc. Labor, 4,755; Munn, Proh., 3,735; scattered, 159; blank, 48,104.

1968, Nixon, Rep., 766,844; Humphrey, Dem., 1,469,218; Wallace, 3d Party, 87,088; Blomen, Soc. Labor, 6,180; Munn, Proh., 2,369; scattered, 53; blanks, 25,394.

1972, Nixon, Rep., 1,112,078; McGovern, Dem., 1,332,540; Jenness, Soc. Workers, 10,600; Fisher, Soc. Labor, 129; Schmitz, Amer., 2,877; Spock, Peoples, 101; Hall, Com., 46; Hospers, Libertarian, 43; scattered, 342.

1976, Carter, Dem., 1,429,475; Ford, Rep., 1,030,276; McCarthy, Ind., 65,637; Camejo, Soc. Workers, 8,138; Anderson, Amer., 7,555; La Rouche, U.S. Labor, 4,922; MacBride, Libertarian, 135.

1980, Reagan, Rep., 1,057,631; Carter, Dem., 1,053,802; Anderson, Ind., 382,539; Clark, Libertarian, 22,038; DeBerry, Soc. Workers, 3,735; Commoner, Citizens, 2,056; McReynolds, Soc., 62; Bubar, Statesman, 34; Griswold, Workers World, 19; scattered, 2,382.

1984, Reagan, Rep., 1,310,936; Mondale, Dem., 1,239,606.

1988, Bush, Rep., 1,194,635; Dukakis, Dem., 1,401,415; Paul, Lib., 24,251; Fulani, New Alliance, 9,561.

1992, Clinton, Dem., 1,318,639; Bush, Rep., 805,039; Perot, Ind., 630,731; Marrou, Libertarian, 9,021; Fulani, New Alliance, 3,172; Phillips, U.S. Taxpayers, 2,218; Hagelin, Natural Law, 1,812; LaRouche, Ind., 1,027.

1996, Clinton, Dem., 1,571,509; Dole, Rep., 718,058; Perot, Ref., 227,206; Browne, Libertarian, 20,424; Hagelin, Natural Law, 5,183; Moorehead, Workers World, 3,276.

Michigan

County	1996 Clinton (D)	Dole (R)	Perot (RF)	1992 Clinton (D)	Bush (R)	Perot (I)
Alcona	2,619	2,227	669	2,383	2,247	1,117
Alger	2,229	1,429	537	2,144	1,471	941
Allegan . . .	14,361	20,859	3,269	12,823	19,077	8,742
Alpena . . .	7,114	4,525	1,730	6,894	4,878	3,236
Antrim	4,226	4,630	1,129	3,431	3,984	2,528
Arenac . . .	3,472	2,247	844	3,244	2,330	1,608
Baraga. . . .	1,601	1,209	460	1,695	1,160	754
Barry.	9,467	11,139	2,282	8,652	9,489	6,303
Bay	27,835	16,038	5,410	26,492	16,383	11,258
Benzie	3,081	2,856	763	2,715	2,438	1,657
Berrien . . .	24,614	28,254	5,958	25,840	29,252	14,056
Branch. . . .	6,567	6,321	1,779	5,850	5,976	4,683
Calhoun . .	26,287	20,953	4,765	25,542	19,791	13,058
Cass	8,207	7,373	2,241	8,047	7,391	4,756
Charlevoix .	4,689	4,864	1,303	4,063	4,017	3,360
Cheboygan .	5,018	4,244	1,462	4,459	3,864	2,495
Chippewa..	6,532	5,137	1,453	5,434	5,462	2,706
Clare	6,311	3,742	1,531	5,346	3,916	2,812
Clinton	11,945	13,694	2,698	10,116	12,216	7,877
Crawford . .	2,666	2,157	840	2,252	2,193	1,442
Delta	8,561	5,925	1,543	8,387	6,027	3,485
Dickinson ..	5,614	4,408	1,478	5,689	4,273	3,022
Eaton.	19,781	20,092	4,378	16,752	18,669	12,208
Emmet. . . .	4,892	6,002	1,512	4,245	5,312	3,576
Genesee . .	106,065	49,332	17,671	105,156	47,834	46,259
Gladwin . . .	5,494	3,670	1,466	4,457	3,616	2,649
Gogebic . . .	4,436	2,769	917	4,792	2,838	1,543
Grand Traverse..	12,987	16,355	3,527	11,148	13,629	9,495
Gratiot	6,793	6,214	1,762	5,678	6,280	3,866
Hillsdale . . .	5,955	7,947	2,262	5,244	7,579	4,968
Houghton . .	5,957	5,941	1,584	6,558	5,575	2,945
Huron	6,827	6,126	1,811	6,023	6,491	4,064
Ingham . . .	63,584	43,096	8,640	61,596	43,926	27,683
Ionia	9,261	9,574	2,354	8,370	9,135	6,211
Iosco	6,240	4,410	1,710	5,369	4,912	3,131
Iron	3,232	2,014	755	3,648	1,971	1,344
Isabella . . .	9,635	7,460	2,069	8,784	7,706	5,434
Jackson . . .	24,633	24,987	5,968	23,686	25,424	15,194
Kalamazoo .	45,644	40,703	5,867	43,568	38,035	21,666
Kalkaska . .	2,666	2,455	922	2,297	2,173	1,915
Kent	85,912	121,335	14,120	82,305	115,285	43,707
Keweenaw .	572	491	169	582	378	212
Lake	2,606	1,213	552	2,351	1,194	981
Lapeer. . . .	14,308	13,369	4,793	11,982	12,326	10,541
Leelanau . .	4,019	5,155	924	3,445	3,993	2,685
Lenawee . .	16,924	14,168	4,167	15,399	14,297	9,517
Livingston. .	22,517	30,598	6,337	17,851	27,539	15,971
Luce	1,107	964	366	972	958	660
Mackinac . .	2,700	2,281	742	2,293	2,278	1,379
Macomb. . .	151,430	120,616	29,859	130,732	147,795	67,954
Manistee . .	5,383	3,807	1,230	5,193	3,491	2,923
Marquette. .	15,168	8,805	2,492	16,038	9,665	5,768
Mason	5,597	5,066	1,525	4,829	5,102	3,096
Mecosta . .	6,370	5,289	1,373	6,097	6,047	3,612
Menominee .	4,880	4,038	1,205	4,559	3,995	2,487
Midland . . .	15,177	16,547	3,964	13,382	16,149	8,945
Missaukee .	2,256	3,012	719	1,893	2,829	1,306
Monroe . . .	26,072	19,678	6,315	24,957	20,250	13,551
Montcalm . .	10,053	8,679	2,530	8,730	8,420	5,504
Montmorency.	2,120	1,760	682	1,903	1,794	1,077
Muskegon .	35,328	21,873	5,794	32,515	23,769	15,268
Newaygo . .	7,614	7,868	2,047	6,455	7,333	4,056
Oakland . . .	241,884	219,855	36,709	214,733	242,160	94,911
Oceana . . .	4,419	3,947	1,286	3,846	3,944	2,713
Ogemaw . .	4,725	2,904	1,369	4,016	2,936	2,122
Ontonagon .	2,080	1,523	604	2,451	1,463	805
Osceola . . .	4,085	3,855	1,068	3,529	3,606	2,199
Oscoda . . .	1,652	1,545	503	1,471	1,583	755
Otsego. . . .	3,351	3,638	1,280	3,129	3,393	2,635
Ottawa	27,024	61,436	6,275	22,180	56,862	16,855
Presque Isle	3,449	2,463	932	3,308	2,398	1,612
Roscommon .	6,092	4,135	1,539	5,243	4,170	2,551
Saginaw. . .	47,579	31,577	8,081	43,819	32,103	20,523
St. Clair . . .	28,881	22,495	8,134	23,385	24,508	18,523
St. Joseph .	8,529	9,764	2,319	7,817	9,836	6,209

County	1996 Clinton (D)	Dole (R)	Perot (RF)	1992 Clinton (D)	Bush (R)	Perot (I)
Sanilac...	7,092	7,821	2,265	5,868	7,891	4,894
Schoolcraft	2,187	1,200	460	2,139	1,253	721
Shiawassee	14,662	11,714	3,703	12,629	10,930	8,632
Tuscola..	10,314	9,154	3,013	9,138	8,636	6,765
Van Buren	13,355	11,347	2,946	12,466	10,357	7,255
Washtenaw	73,106	40,097	8,020	73,325	41,386	21,889
Wayne...	504,466	175,886	43,554	508,464	227,002	102,074
Wexford..	5,510	4,866	1,386	4,894	4,696	2,923
Totals...	1,989,653	1,481,212	336,670	1,871,182	1,554,940	824,813

Michigan Vote Since 1948

1948, Truman, Dem., 1,003,448; Dewey, Rep., 1,038,595; Wallace, Prog., 46,515; Watson, Proh., 13,052; Thomas, Soc., 6,063; Teichert, Soc. Labor, 1,263; Dobbs, Soc. Workers, 672.

1952, Eisenhower, Rep., 1,551,529; Stevenson, Dem., 1,230,657; Hamblen, Proh., 10,331; Hallinan, Prog., 3,922; Hass, Soc. Labor, 1,495; Dobbs, Soc. Workers, 655; scattered, 3.

1956, Eisenhower, Rep., 1,713,647; Stevenson, Dem., 1,359,898; Holtwick, Proh., 6,923.

1960, Kennedy, Dem., 1,687,269; Nixon, Rep., 1,620,428; Dobbs, Soc. Workers, 4,347; Decker, Proh., 2,029; Daly, Tax Cut, 1,767; Hass, Soc. Labor, 1,718; Ind. Amer., 539.

1964, Johnson, Dem., 2,136,615; Goldwater, Rep., 1,060,152; DeBerry, Soc. Workers, 3,817; Hass, Soc. Labor, 1,704; Proh. (no candidate listed), 699; scattering, 145.

1968, Nixon, Rep., 1,370,665; Humphrey, Dem., 1,593,082; Wallace, 3d Party, 331,968; Halstead, Soc. Workers, 4,099; Blomen, Soc. Labor, 1,762; Cleaver, New Politics, 4,585; Munn, Proh., 60; scattering, 29.

1972, Nixon, Rep., 1,961,721; McGovern, Dem., 1,459,435; Schmitz, Amer., 63,321; Fisher, Soc. Labor, 2,437; Jenness, Soc. Workers, 1,603; Hall, Com., 1,210.

1976, Carter, Dem., 1,696,714; Ford, Rep., 1,893,742; McCarthy, Ind., 47,905; MacBride, Libertarian, 5,406; Wright, People's, 3,504; Camejo, Soc. Workers, 1,804; LaRouche, U.S. Labor, 1,366; Levin, Soc. Labor, 1,148; scattering, 2,160.

1980, Reagan, Rep., 1,915,225; Carter, Dem., 1,661,532; Anderson, Ind., 275,223; Clark, Libertarian, 41,597; Commoner, Citizens, 11,930; Hall, Com., 3,262; Griswold, Workers World, 30; Greaves, Amer., 21; Bubar, Statesman, 9.

1984, Reagan, Rep., 2,251,571; Mondale, Dem., 1,529,638; Bergland, Libertarian, 10,055.

1988, Bush, Rep., 1,965,486; Dukakis, Dem., 1,675,783; Paul, Lib., 18,336; Fulani, Ind., 2,513.

1992, Clinton, Dem., 1,871,182; Bush, Rep., 1,554,940; Perot, Ind., 824,813; Marrou, Libertarian, 10,175; Phillips, U.S. Taxpayers, 8,263; Hagelin, Natural Law, 2,954.

1996, Clinton, Dem., 1,989,653; Dole, Rep., 1,481,212; Perot, Ref., 336,670; Browne, Libertarian, 27,670; Hagelin, Natural Law, 4,254; Moorehead, Workers World, 3,153; White, Soc. Equality, 1,554.

Minnesota

County	1996 Clinton (D)	Dole (R)	Perot (RF)	1992 Clinton (D)	Bush (R)	Perot (I)
Aitkin....	3,810	2,327	1,155	3,400	2,151	1,951
Anoka....	63,756	41,745	16,448	54,621	39,458	35,140
Becker...	5,911	5,461	1,813	4,958	5,430	3,238
Beltrami..	8,006	5,806	1,635	7,210	5,204	3,473
Benton...	6,006	4,835	2,133	5,156	5,053	4,048
Big Stone.	1,619	990	368	1,610	1,052	740
Blue Earth.	12,420	9,082	3,324	11,531	8,813	7,299
Brown ...	4,864	5,580	1,786	4,278	5,390	3,845
Carlton...	8,052	4,034	1,591	7,736	3,922	3,005
Carver ..	11,554	12,380	3,781	8,349	10,201	7,942
Cass	5,437	4,791	1,620	4,901	4,276	2,939
Chippewa.	3,178	2,119	782	2,929	2,143	1,505
Chisago ..	8,611	5,984	2,812	7,077	4,813	5,098
Clay.....	10,476	8,764	1,733	9,845	9,666	3,835
Clearwater	1,578	1,423	471	1,587	1,315	841
Cook	1,169	1,010	246	1,005	878	704
Cottonwood	2,737	2,633	741	2,382	2,481	1,749
Crow Wing	11,156	10,095	3,423	8,896	9,112	6,367
Dakota...	77,297	57,244	17,095	63,660	52,312	40,244
Dodge ...	3,233	2,888	1,223	2,620	3,049	2,231
Douglas ..	6,450	6,747	2,093	5,252	6,356	4,138
Faribault..	3,817	3,272	1,103	3,339	3,439	2,322
Fillmore ..	4,732	3,466	1,575	3,977	3,583	3,011
Freeborn..	8,458	5,166	2,220	7,733	5,000	1,070
Goodhue ..	9,931	7,293	2,806	7,916	7,321	5,790
Grant....	1,806	1,284	434	1,561	1,201	885
Hennepin..	285,126	173,887	47,663	278,648	179,581	123,659
Houston ..	4,153	3,674	1,439	3,744	3,853	2,697
Hubbard ..	3,802	3,593	1,141	3,362	3,227	1,949
Isanti....	6,041	4,450	2,242	5,386	3,988	3,898

County	1996 Clinton (D)	Dole (R)	Perot (RF)	1992 Clinton (D)	Bush (R)	Perot (I)
Itasca....	10,706	6,506	2,889	9,621	5,952	5,147
Jackson...	2,727	2,153	908	2,481	1,824	1,918
Kanabec..	2,927	1,924	996	2,532	1,876	1,836
Kandiyohi.	9,009	7,119	2,229	7,914	6,784	4,869
Kittson...	1,394	1,055	270	1,307	1,098	558
Koochiching	3,472	2,080	1,098	3,474	1,954	1,993
LacQuiParle	2,420	1,447	561	2,342	1,435	1,163
Lake	3,388	1,684	752	3,415	1,465	1,437
Lake of the Woods ..	888	814	287	794	762	629
Le Sueur ..	5,457	3,902	1,699	4,662	3,858	3,363
Lincoln...	1,641	1,199	504	1,555	1,084	967
Lyon	5,062	4,932	1,351	4,481	4,591	3,180
McLeod ..	6,027	5,474	2,402	4,919	5,422	4,933
Mahnomen	1,026	877	270	1,035	854	483
Marshall..	2,333	2,068	710	2,309	2,136	1,306
Martin ...	4,718	4,303	1,405	4,019	4,438	3,089
Meeker...	4,531	3,428	1,571	3,861	3,497	3,120
Mille Lacs.	4,336	2,948	1,467	3,648	2,814	2,615
Morrison..	5,728	5,054	2,310	5,588	5,038	3,710
Mower ...	10,413	4,994	2,464	9,935	5,147	5,001
Murray ...	2,173	1,907	753	1,993	1,609	1,588
Nicollet...	6,772	5,057	1,737	6,055	5,091	3,799
Nobles ...	4,106	3,769	1,132	3,756	3,548	2,586
Norman ..	1,875	1,392	425	1,584	1,541	776
Olmsted ..	22,857	22,860	5,640	19,039	23,404	13,806
Otter Tail.	10,519	11,808	3,191	9,176	11,074	6,274
Pennington	2,814	2,129	910	2,578	2,155	1,598
Pine.....	5,432	3,080	1,597	4,929	2,841	2,952
Pipestone .	1,999	2,096	599	1,773	1,953	1,429
Polk.....	6,369	5,563	1,502	5,850	5,817	3,176
Pope	2,803	1,992	665	2,619	1,886	1,390
Ramsey ..	133,878	66,954	20,351	130,932	68,206	50,757
Red Lake .	1,053	695	334	1,020	691	472
Redwood .	2,997	3,700	1,053	2,740	3,408	2,710
Renville ..	3,956	2,887	1,311	3,414	2,852	2,598
Rice.....	12,821	7,016	2,872	10,908	7,015	6,057
Rock	2,142	2,169	554	2,006	2,065	1,244
Roseau ..	2,759	2,988	1,081	2,346	2,785	2,099
St. Louis..	60,736	25,553	11,308	61,813	24,579	21,714
Scott	14,657	12,734	4,886	11,225	10,936	9,881
Sherburne.	10,551	8,699	3,665	7,843	7,339	6,534
Sibley ...	2,769	2,590	1,226	2,421	2,315	2,407
Stearns ..	24,238	21,474	8,150	21,451	22,502	14,834
Steele ...	6,974	5,617	2,197	5,152	5,964	4,542
Stevens ...	2,741	2,141	467	2,466	2,229	1,086
Swift	3,054	1,541	690	2,980	1,603	1,359
Todd	4,520	4,078	1,958	4,059	3,990	2,976
Traverse..	1,135	775	295	1,053	841	582
Wabasha .	4,523	3,452	1,474	3,736	3,397	3,012
Wadena ..	2,480	2,696	801	2,340	2,492	1,535
Waseca ..	3,819	3,171	1,385	3,146	3,118	2,621
Washington	45,119	31,219	10,106	35,820	26,568	22,585
Watonwan	2,534	1,997	711	2,100	1,871	1,574
Wilkin....	1,319	1,508	358	1,122	1,626	748
Winona ..	10,272	7,955	2,907	9,707	8,585	5,993
Wright ...	15,542	13,224	5,550	12,465	11,650	10,829
Yellow Medicine	2,741	2,006	818	2,593	1,909	1,645
Totals...	1,120,438	766,476	257,704	1,020,997	747,841	562,506

Minnesota Vote Since 1948

1948, Truman, Dem., 692,966; Dewey, Rep., 483,617; Wallace, Prog., 27,866; Thomas, Soc., 4,646; Teichert, Soc. Labor, 2,525; Dobbs, Soc. Workers, 606.

1952, Eisenhower, Rep., 763,211; Stevenson, Dem., 608,458; Hallinan, Prog., 2,666; Hass, Soc. Labor, 2,383; Hamblen, Proh., 2,147; Dobbs, Soc. Workers, 618.

1956, Eisenhower, Rep., 719,302; Stevenson, Dem., 617,525; Hass, Soc. Labor (Ind. Gov.), 2,080; Dobbs, Soc. Workers, 1,098.

1960, Kennedy, Dem., 779,933; Nixon, Rep., 757,915; Dobbs, Soc. Workers, 3,077; Industrial Gov., 962.

1964, Johnson, Dem., 991,117; Goldwater, Rep., 559,624; DeBerry, Soc. Workers, 1,177; Hass, Industrial Gov., 2,544.

1968, Nixon, Rep., 658,643; Humphrey, Dem., 857,738; Wallace, 3d Party, 68,931; scattered, 2,443; Halstead, Soc. Workers, 808; Blomen, Ind. Gov't., 285; Mitchell, Com., 415; Cleaver, Peace, 935; McCarthy, write-in, 585; scattered, 170.

1972, Nixon, Rep., 898,269; McGovern, Dem., 802,346; Schmitz, Amer., 31,407; Spock, Peoples, 2,805; Fisher, Soc. Labor, 4,261; Jenness, Soc. Workers, 940; Hall, Com., 662; scattered, 962.

1976, Carter, Dem., 1,070,440; Ford, Rep., 819,395; McCarthy, Ind., 35,490; Anderson, Amer., 13,592; Camejo, Soc. Workers, 4,149; MacBride, Libertarian, 3,529; Hall, Com., 1,092.

1980, Reagan, Rep., 873,268; Carter, Dem., 954,173; Anderson, Ind., 174,997; Clark, Libertarian, 31,593; Commoner, Citizens, 8,406; Hall, Com., 1,117; DeBerry, Soc. Workers, 711; Griswold, Workers World, 698; McReynolds, Soc., 536; write-ins, 281.

1984, Reagan, Rep., 1,032,603; Mondale, Dem., 1,036,364; Bergland, Libertarian, 2,996.

1988, Bush, Rep., 962,337; Dukakis, Dem., 1,109,471; McCarthy, Minn. Prog., 5,403; Paul, Lib., 5,109.

1992, Clinton, Dem., 1,020,997; Bush, Rep., 747,841; Perot, Ind., 562,506; Marrou, Libertarian, 3,373; Gritz, Populist/America First, 3,363; Hagelin, Natural Law, 1,406.

1996, Clinton, Dem., 1,120,438; Dole, Rep., 766,476; Perot, Ref., 257,704; Nader, Green, 24,908; Browne, Libertarian, 8,271; Peron, Grass Roots, 4,898; Phillips, Taxpayers, 3,416; Hagelin, Natural Law, 1,808; Birrenbach, Ind. Grass Roots, 787; Harris, Soc. Workers, 684; White, Soc. Equality, 347.

Mississippi

County	1996 Clinton (D)	Dole (R)	Perot (RF)	1992 Clinton (D)	Bush (R)	Perot (I)
Adams...	8,218	5,378	779	8,255	5,831	1,753
Alcorn...	4,964	4,960	929	6,373	6,249	1,349
Amite...	2,824	2,521	351	2,608	2,561	498
Attala...	3,092	3,130	383	3,015	3,520	529
Benton...	1,944	993	209	2,402	1,253	293
Bolivar...	8,670	4,027	320	8,801	4,752	593
Calhoun..	2,178	2,470	351	2,462	3,191	607
Carroll...	2,041	2,629	245	1,182	1,695	200
Chickasaw	2,971	2,535	401	3,220	3,150	629
Choctaw..	1,247	1,715	247	1,435	2,026	298
Claiborne.	3,739	784	103	3,302	935	161
Clarke...	2,337	3,470	366	2,259	4,207	450
Clay....	4,267	2,948	337	4,620	3,297	626
Coahoma.	5,776	3,441	256	6,409	4,120	518
Copiah...	4,415	4,138	375	4,397	4,600	409
Covington.	2,628	3,219	417	2,775	3,525	654
DeSoto...	10,282	18,135	2,399	8,833	16,104	2,569
Forrest...	7,965	11,278	1,094	8,333	12,432	1,909
Franklin..	1,381	1,586	329	1,587	1,942	393
George...	1,888	3,311	710	2,650	4,141	1,335
Greene..	1,347	1,947	322	1,664	2,406	559
Grenada.	4,402	4,527	470	4,203	4,721	609
Hancock..	4,303	5,820	1,143	4,651	6,422	2,302
Harrison..	18,775	25,486	3,726	15,268	25,049	6,855
Hinds...	45,410	35,653	2,929	43,434	45,031	5,341
Holmes..	4,720	1,536	140	4,092	1,694	203
Humphreys	2,305	1,382	110	2,696	1,721	258
Issaquena.	546	269	42	550	298	79
Itawamba.	2,987	3,490	732	3,635	4,142	918
Jackson..	13,598	24,918	2,947	13,017	25,321	6,484
Jasper...	3,170	2,615	353	3,059	2,789	568
Jefferson.	2,531	489	89	2,796	562	156
Jefferson Davis...	2,663	1,890	264	2,991	2,228	382
Jones...	7,360	13,020	1,362	8,035	13,824	2,523
Kemper..	2,048	1,439	188	2,243	1,830	278
Lafayette.	4,646	4,753	580	5,224	5,251	861
Lamar...	3,169	8,609	925	3,208	8,259	1,543
Lauderdale	8,668	15,055	1,036	8,489	17,098	1,659
Lawrence.	2,481	2,392	471	2,582	2,689	765
Leake...	2,902	3,017	406	3,333	3,943	497
Lee....	8,438	11,815	1,361	7,710	12,231	2,041
Leflore..	6,853	4,456	240	6,374	5,298	611
Lincoln...	4,294	5,960	778	4,744	7,040	1,281
Lowndes.	6,220	9,169	750	6,552	10,509	1,716
Madison..	9,354	14,467	759	9,386	12,810	1,478
Marion...	4,334	5,023	585	4,654	5,776	1,162
Marshall..	7,521	3,272	482	7,913	3,847	689
Monroe..	5,184	5,206	889	4,933	5,994	1,255
Montgomery	1,970	1,943	197	2,076	2,324	370
Neshoba.	2,646	4,545	560	3,090	6,135	794
Newton..	2,163	4,223	464	2,146	5,128	494
Noxubee.	2,801	1,287	119	3,188	1,623	203
Oktibbeha.	5,923	6,142	395	5,726	6,381	984
Panola...	5,408	3,701	513	6,066	4,644	729
Pearl River	4,892	8,212	1,190	4,683	7,726	2,352
Perry...	1,413	2,178	450	1,490	2,538	462
Pike....	6,302	5,403	683	6,279	6,005	1,380
Pontotoc.	2,597	4,289	774	2,965	4,595	777
Prentiss..	3,053	3,473	574	3,385	4,317	781
Quitman..	2,186	1,121	126	2,422	1,451	210
Rankin..	8,614	24,585	2,093	8,155	24,537	3,454
Scott....	3,163	4,018	466	3,349	5,268	691
Sharkey..	1,566	906	70	1,526	1,008	145
Simpson..	2,851	4,455	525	3,213	5,358	726
Smith....	1,858	3,371	522	1,968	4,106	680
Stone....	1,551	2,288	417	1,447	2,295	447
Sunflower.	4,960	2,926	290	5,050	3,726	600
Tallahatchie	2,990	1,676	251	2,902	2,213	380
Tate....	3,195	3,694	406	3,519	4,196	634
Tippah...	2,992	3,249	661	3,475	4,444	802
Tishomingo	2,709	2,766	609	3,910	3,393	751
Tunica...	1,263	557	55	1,451	693	96
Union....	3,316	4,375	788	3,714	5,173	816
Walthall..	2,240	2,239	444	2,476	2,728	711
Warren...	8,774	9,261	1,259	8,175	10,209	2,146
Washington	10,053	6,762	437	10,588	7,598	795
Wayne...	2,652	3,219	595	3,064	3,874	824
Webster..	1,379	2,254	255	1,746	2,791	444
Wilkinson.	2,807	1,016	226	3,210	1,399	307
Winston..	3,488	3,498	434	3,953	4,311	688
Yalobusha.	2,437	1,711	332	2,617	2,179	438
Yazoo....	4,754	4,152	362	4,880	5,113	669
Totals....	394,022	439,838	52,222	400,258	487,793	85,626

Mississippi Vote Since 1948

1948, Thurmond, States' Rights, 167,538; Truman, Dem., 19,384; Dewey, Rep., 5,043; Wallace, Prog., 225.

1952, Eisenhower, Ind. vote pledged to Rep. candidate, 112,966; Stevenson, Dem., 172,566.

1956, Eisenhower, Rep., 56,372; Stevenson, Dem., 144,498; Black and Tan Grand Old Party, 4,313; total, 60,685; Byrd, Ind., 42,966.

1960, Kennedy, Dem., 108,362; Democratic unpledged electors, 116,248; Nixon, Rep., 73,561. Mississippi's victorious slate of 8 unpledged Democratic electors cast their votes for Sen. Harry F. Byrd (D, VA).

1964, Johnson, Dem., 52,618; Goldwater, Rep., 356,528.

1968, Nixon, Rep., 88,516; Humphrey, Dem., 150,644; Wallace, 3d Party, 415,349.

1972, Nixon, Rep., 505,125; McGovern, Dem., 126,782; Schmitz, Amer., 11,598; Jenness, Soc. Workers, 2,458.

1976, Carter, Dem., 381,309; Ford, Rep., 366,846; Anderson, Amer., 6,678; McCarthy, Ind., 4,074; Maddox, Ind., 4,049; Camejo, Soc. Workers, 2,805; MacBride, Libertarian, 2,609.

1980, Reagan, Rep., 441,089; Carter, Dem., 429,281; Anderson, Ind., 12,036; Clark, Libertarian, 5,465; Griswold, Workers World, 2,402; Pulley, Soc. Workers, 2,347.

1984, Reagan, Rep., 582,377; Mondale, Dem., 352,192; Bergland, Libertarian, 2,336.

1988, Bush, Rep., 557,890; Dukakis, Dem., 363,921; Duke, Ind., 4,232; Paul, Lib., 3,329.

1992, Bush, Rep., 487,793; Clinton, Dem., 400,258; Perot, Ind., 85,626; Fulani, New Alliance, 2,625; Marrou, Libertarian, 2,154; Phillips, U.S. Taxpayers, 1,652; Hagelin, Natural Law, 1,140.

1996, Dole, Rep., 439,838; Clinton, Dem., 394,022; Perot, Ind. (Ref.), 52,222; Browne, Libertarian, 2,809; Phillips, Taxpayers, 2,314; Hagelin, Natural Law, 1,447; Collins, Ind., 1,205.

Missouri

County	1996 Clinton (D)	Dole (R)	Perot (RF)	1992 Clinton (D)	Bush (R)	Perot (I)
Adair.....	4,441	4,656	1,170	4,232	4,141	2,224
Andrew...	2,807	3,281	964	2,675	2,652	2,151
Atchison..	1,266	1,327	367	1,208	1,140	840
Audrain...	4,690	3,955	1,046	4,731	3,798	2,099
Barry.....	4,352	5,855	1,494	4,791	5,565	2,381
Barton....	1,625	2,812	563	1,433	2,775	971
Bates.....	3,224	2,904	949	2,993	2,499	2,225
Benton....	2,996	2,895	764	3,195	2,511	1,551
Bollinger...	2,044	2,420	506	2,150	2,289	909
Boone....	24,984	22,047	4,083	26,176	19,405	12,040
Buchanan.	15,848	12,610	4,248	16,570	11,275	9,404
Butler	5,780	6,996	1,414	6,602	6,450	2,189
Caldwell..	1,487	1,464	468	1,456	1,295	1,283
Callaway..	5,880	5,567	1,530	5,799	4,880	3,266
Camden...	5,566	7,190	1,809	5,140	5,554	3,891
Cape Girardeau.	9,957	15,557	1,861	9,605	13,464	5,199
Carroll	2,080	1,839	580	2,100	1,774	1,495
Carter	1,172	1,180	301	1,169	1,101	405
Cass	11,743	13,495	3,474	10,246	10,349	9,216
Cedar	2,027	2,484	658	2,064	2,085	1,173
Chariton...	2,072	1,508	423	2,141	1,378	1,067
Christian ..	6,627	9,477	2,301	6,242	7,422	3,422
Clark	1,749	1,081	458	1,815	1,039	725
Clay	32,603	28,935	7,048	30,565	23,798	20,951
Clinton....	3,445	2,780	848	3,400	2,391	2,423
Cole	10,857	16,140	2,121	10,201	15,270	5,770
Cooper ...	2,753	2,900	891	2,709	2,867	1,735
Crawford ..	3,349	2,990	1,223	3,515	2,831	2,002
Dade	1,243	1,822	447	1,332	1,577	834
Dallas	2,277	2,554	787	2,533	2,116	1,392
Daviess ...	1,534	1,321	466	1,477	1,107	1,143
DeKalb ...	1,679	1,627	492	1,630	1,318	1,207
Dent	2,234	2,542	693	2,689	2,125	1,049
Douglas ...	1,744	2,601	775	2,126	2,569	1,081
Dunklin ...	5,428	3,766	934	6,277	4,024	1,166
Franklin ...	13,908	13,715	5,517	13,431	11,477	11,043
Gasconade.	2,104	2,997	820	1,952	2,690	1,672
Gentry ...	1,493	1,361	416	1,519	1,272	921
Greene ...	39,300	48,193	8,569	41,137	46,457	17,770
Grundy ...	2,073	1,883	631	1,968	1,749	1,372
Harrison...	1,628	1,737	484	1,590	1,563	1,059
Henry	4,579	3,260	1,231	4,232	2,681	2,807
Hickory ...	1,858	1,491	531	1,929	1,259	864
Holt......	1,144	1,323	314	1,050	1,202	781
Howard ...	2,014	1,545	568	2,085	1,253	1,090
Howell....	5,261	5,991	2,066	5,492	5,360	2,650

County	1996 Clinton (D)	Dole (R)	Perot (RF)	1992 Clinton (D)	Bush (R)	Perot (I)
Iron	2,221	1,328	568	2,507	1,276	841
Jackson . .	140,317	85,534	21,047	145,999	78,611	66,142
Jasper . . .	11,462	18,361	3,545	11,727	17,592	6,440
Jefferson .	32,073	23,877	8,893	32,569	20,637	20,057
Johnson . .	6,220	6,276	1,911	5,546	5,032	4,578
Knox	891	862	254	1,010	724	523
Laclede . .	4,047	5,887	1,459	4,179	5,176	2,852
Lafayette .	6,118	5,489	1,516	5,213	4,651	3,561
Lawrence .	4,465	6,099	1,613	4,666	5,608	2,570
Lewis . . .	2,050	1,453	644	2,196	1,461	892
Lincoln. . .	5,644	4,897	1,881	5,453	3,718	3,572
Linn	2,967	2,097	781	2,916	1,967	1,524
Livingston.	2,913	2,384	777	2,505	2,370	1,976
McDonald.	1,980	3,008	923	2,281	3,010	1,551
Macon . . .	2,937	2,634	848	3,194	2,256	1,697
Madison . .	2,351	1,595	625	2,501	1,673	899
Maries . . .	1,540	1,560	516	1,732	1,356	915
Marion . . .	4,924	4,653	1,082	5,156	4,762	1,841
Mercer. . .	700	660	208	843	626	378
Miller. . . .	3,110	4,387	1,185	2,905	4,175	2,391
Mississippi	3,235	1,595	380	3,226	1,675	776
Moniteau .	2,129	2,603	693	2,018	2,566	1,499
Monroe . .	1,938	1,333	532	2,060	1,153	969
Montgomery	2,277	2,124	772	2,063	1,974	1,266
Morgan . .	3,006	3,059	1,006	2,906	2,819	2,028
New Madrid	4,451	2,417	663	4,883	2,431	962
Newton . .	5,840	10,067	1,995	5,987	8,804	3,567
Nodaway . .	3,966	3,362	1,043	3,723	3,147	2,484
Oregon . . .	1,795	1,502	475	2,258	1,402	564
Osage . . .	2,045	2,890	608	1,860	2,784	1,423
Ozark . . .	1,445	1,882	595	1,581	1,772	906
Pemiscot .	3,371	1,820	458	3,924	2,161	670
Perry	2,517	3,427	777	2,525	3,205	1,498
Pettis. . . .	6,057	7,336	1,716	5,314	6,823	4,278
Phelps . . .	6,405	6,990	1,703	6,852	6,040	3,774
Pike.	3,495	2,209	916	3,609	2,255	1,464
Platte. . . .	12,705	13,332	3,035	10,920	9,380	9,062
Polk.	3,307	4,521	1,169	3,316	3,465	1,879
Pulaski. . .	3,783	4,089	1,141	4,113	3,793	2,057
Putnam . .	857	1,091	276	838	1,143	522
Ralls	1,998	1,513	520	2,158	1,349	880
Randolph .	4,502	3,274	1,130	4,951	3,025	2,212
Ray	4,714	2,884	1,113	4,457	2,563	2,567
Reynolds .	1,631	903	386	2,014	776	532
Ripley . . .	2,081	1,988	530	2,300	1,814	739
St. Charles	41,369	47,705	11,591	37,263	38,673	30,351
St. Clair . .	1,974	1,815	650	1,965	1,555	1,083
St. Francois	9,034	6,200	2,266	9,367	5,889	3,635
St. Louis. .	225,524	196,096	34,850	235,760	188,285	109,099
Ste. Genevieve	3,597	2,078	942	3,795	1,780	1,547
Saline . . .	4,765	2,931	1,090	4,643	2,688	2,815
Schuyler. .	857	777	287	936	742	487
Scotland. .	990	773	326	1,070	798	617
Scott	7,011	6,641	1,483	7,452	6,265	2,763
Shannon . .	1,882	1,339	524	2,135	1,224	579
Shelby . . .	1,410	1,213	413	1,435	1,169	786
Stoddard .	4,883	5,020	1,185	5,720	4,608	1,977
Stone. . . .	3,497	5,223	1,353	3,256	4,035	1,884
Sullivan . .	1,402	1,275	340	1,510	1,326	596
Taney . . .	4,623	6,844	1,580	4,682	6,081	2,395
Texas . . .	3,897	4,065	1,335	4,597	3,470	1,900
Vernon. . .	3,363	3,123	1,135	3,546	2,851	1,890
Warren. . .	3,443	3,768	1,254	3,213	2,953	2,471
Washington	4,315	2,259	1,169	4,211	2,157	1,618
Wayne. . .	2,754	2,172	674	3,073	2,101	837
Webster. .	3,855	4,958	1,214	4,149	4,361	2,108
Worth . . .	572	540	150	599	483	328
Wright . . .	2,280	3,754	890	2,814	3,427	1,425
City						
St. Louis .	91,233	22,121	7,276	102,356	25,441	18,864
Totals . . .	**1,025,935**	**890,016**	**217,188**	**1,053,873**	**811,159**	**518,741**

Missouri Vote Since 1948

1948, Truman, Dem., 917,315; Dewey, Rep., 655,039; Wallace, Prog., 3,998; Thomas, Soc., 2,222.

1952, Eisenhower, Rep., 959,429; Stevenson, Dem., 929,830; Hallinan, Prog., 987; Hamblen, Proh., 885; MacArthur, Christian Nationalist, 302; America First, 233; Hoopes, Soc., 227; Hass, Soc. Labor, 169.

1956, Stevenson, Dem., 918,273; Eisenhower, Rep., 914,299.

1960, Kennedy, Dem., 972,201; Nixon, Rep., 962,221.

1964, Johnson, Dem., 1,164,344; Goldwater, Rep., 653,535.

1968, Nixon, Rep., 811,932; Humphrey, Dem., 791,444; Wallace, 3d Party, 206,126.

1972, Nixon, Rep., 1,154,058; McGovern, Dem., 698,531.

1976, Carter, Dem., 999,163; Ford, Rep., 928,808; McCarthy, Ind., 24,329.

1980, Reagan, Rep., 1,074,181; Carter, Dem., 931,182; Anderson, Ind., 77,920; Clark, Libertarian, 14,422; DeBerry, Soc. Workers, 1,515; Commoner, Citizens, 573; write-ins, 31.

1984, Reagan, Rep., 1,274,188; Mondale, Dem., 848,583.

1988, Bush, Rep., 1,084,953; Dukakis, Dem., 1,001,619; Fulani, New Alliance, 6,656; Paul, write-in, 434.

1992, Clinton, Dem., 1,053,873; Bush, Rep., 811,159; Perot, Ind., 518,741; Marrou, Libertarian, 7,497.

1996, Clinton, Dem., 1,025,935; Dole, Rep., 890,016; Perot, Ref., 217,188; Phillips, Taxpayers, 11,521; Browne, Libertarian, 10,522; Hagelin, Natural Law, 2,287.

Montana

County	1996 Clinton (D)	Dole (R)	Perot (RF)	1992 Clinton (D)	Bush (R)	Perot (I)
Beaverhead.	1,164	2,414	412	1,098	1,746	1,202
Big Horn. . .	2,453	1,336	424	2,154	1,377	840
Blaine . . .	1,316	1,127	435	1,355	971	699
Broadwater.	603	1,029	318	491	830	505
Carbon . . .	1,854	2,147	713	1,549	1,562	1,482
Carter	150	522	89	154	497	220
Cascade . .	15,707	14,291	4,749	14,719	12,494	9,151
Chouteau . .	1,039	1,660	434	959	1,380	870
Custer	2,115	2,467	695	1,968	2,105	1,505
Daniels . . .	510	558	240	457	496	402
Dawson . . .	1,903	1,890	842	1,785	1,679	1,370
Deer Lodge.	3,331	883	772	3,174	832	1,207
Fallon	452	778	276	446	731	427
Fergus	1,866	3,671	605	1,615	2,736	1,934
Flathead. . .	10,452	16,542	4,786	9,746	11,699	9,109
Gallatin . . .	10,972	14,559	3,146	9,535	11,109	7,711
Garfield . . .	107	562	69	125	403	281
Glacier . . .	2,292	1,270	491	2,076	1,222	997
Golden Valley	128	284	73	142	192	157
Granite . . .	429	733	228	358	556	386
Hill	3,517	2,601	950	3,618	2,408	2,017
Jefferson . .	1,775	2,248	729	1,415	1,541	1,172
Judith Basin.	452	753	126	409	610	415
Lake	4,195	4,723	1,804	3,938	3,596	2,878
Lewis & Clark .	11,535	11,665	3,140	11,117	9,351	5,560
Liberty	379	634	144	321	512	363
Lincoln. . . .	2,705	3,552	1,425	2,765	2,799	2,637
McCone. . .	390	615	244	424	528	395
Madison . . .	955	1,984	516	779	1,415	1,043
Meagher . .	281	505	142	260	422	310
Mineral . . .	658	549	383	664	403	543
Missoula . .	21,874	16,034	5,586	20,347	12,898	9,735
Musselshell.	652	1,121	291	648	876	691
Park	2,564	3,837	959	2,258	2,846	2,182
Petroleum. .	62	186	36	61	135	95
Phillips. . . .	705	1,392	401	634	1,026	949
Pondera. . .	1,123	1,438	383	1,046	1,252	855
Powder River	236	663	137	258	547	340
Powell	952	1,274	531	989	1,058	872
Prairie	259	417	99	260	412	179
Ravalli	5,200	8,138	2,731	4,644	5,392	4,573
Richland. . .	1,614	2,021	906	1,440	1,760	1,525
Roosevelt. .	2,118	1,209	645	1,827	1,212	1,089
Rosebud . . .	1,681	1,413	547	1,669	1,130	1,099
Sanders . . .	1,573	2,043	990	1,689	1,361	1,378
Sheridan . .	1,187	832	408	1,077	795	782
Silver Bow .	11,199	3,909	2,447	9,960	3,491	4,570
Stillwater . .	1,282	1,871	618	1,178	1,390	1,056
Sweet Grass	469	1,109	186	395	880	507
Teton	1,188	1,701	416	1,043	1,364	969
Toole.	874	1,203	386	854	943	903
Treasure . .	171	237	87	157	206	178
Valley	1,674	1,838	645	1,715	1,497	1,320
Wheatland .	391	563	127	384	478	264
Wibaux . . .	197	284	128	195	234	173
Yellowstone.	22,992	26,367	6,139	20,163	22,822	13,133
Totals	**167,922**	**179,652**	**55,229**	**154,507**	**144,207**	**107,225**

Montana Vote Since 1948

1948, Truman, Dem., 119,071; Dewey, Rep., 96,770; Wallace, Prog., 7,313; Thomas, Soc., 695; Watson, Proh., 429.

1952, Eisenhower, Rep., 157,394; Stevenson, Dem., 106,213; Hallinan, Prog., 723; Hamblen, Proh., 548; Hoopes, Soc., 159.

1956, Eisenhower, Rep., 154,933; Stevenson, Dem., 116,238.

1960, Kennedy, Dem., 134,891; Nixon, Rep., 141,841; Decker, Proh., 456; Dobbs, Soc. Workers, 391.

1964, Johnson, Dem., 164,246; Goldwater, Rep., 113,032; Kasper, Natl. States' Rights, 519; Munn, Proh., 499; DeBerry, Soc. Workers, 332.

1968, Nixon, Rep., 138,835; Humphrey, Dem., 114,117; Wallace, 3d Party, 20,015; Halstead, Soc. Workers, 457; Munn, Proh., 510; Caton, New Reform, 470.

1972, Nixon, Rep., 183,976; McGovern, Dem., 120,197; Schmitz, Amer., 13,430.

1976, Carter, Dem., 149,259; Ford, Rep., 173,703; Anderson, Amer., 5,772.

1980, Reagan, Rep., 206,814; Carter, Dem., 118,032; Anderson, Ind., 29,281; Clark, Libertarian, 9,825.

1984, Reagan, Rep., 232,450; Mondale, Dem., 146,742; Bergland, Libertarian, 5,185.

1988, Bush, Rep., 190,412; Dukakis, Dem., 168,936; Paul, Lib., 5,047; Fulani, New Alliance, 1,279.

1992, Clinton, Dem., 154,507; Bush, Rep., 144,207; Perot, Ind., 107,225; Gritz, Populist/America First, 3,658.

1996, Dole, Rep., 179,652; Clinton, Dem., 167,922; Perot, Ref., 55,229; Browne, Libertarian, 2,526; Hagelin, Natural Law, 1,754.

Nebraska

County	Clinton (D)	1996 Dole (R)	Perot (RF)	Clinton (D)	1992 Bush (R)	Perot (I)
Adams . . .	3,935	6,924	1,513	3,445	6,346	3,273
Antelope. .	884	2,005	457	650	1,979	1,134
Arthur . . .	25	187	46	18	148	97
Banner. . .	62	309	30	68	284	128
Blaine . . .	53	284	39	64	256	130
Boone . . .	806	1,695	424	604	1,588	956
Box Butte .	1,782	2,458	695	1,935	2,198	1,508
Boyd . . .	372	778	181	353	744	468
Brown . . .	359	1,105	289	311	999	525
Buffalo . . .	4,277	10,004	1,484	3,742	9,708	4,083
Burt.	1,237	1,707	497	1,224	1,667	1,009
Butler. . . .	1,099	2,042	512	1,087	1,881	1,157
Cass	3,477	4,878	1,239	2,949	4,314	2,657
Cedar . . .	1,218	2,171	739	1,007	1,981	1,507
Chase . . .	365	1,277	197	398	1,000	674
Cherry . . .	551	1,905	332	563	1,707	730
Cheyenne. .	1,059	2,571	287	967	2,197	1,061
Clay	880	1,982	425	802	1,818	952
Colfax . . .	1,065	1,954	492	1,011	1,915	1,197
Cuming . . .	1,033	2,520	503	835	2,711	1,192
Custer . . .	1,293	3,453	615	1,126	3,180	1,492
Dakota. . .	2,632	2,592	721	2,322	2,771	1,307
Dawes . . .	1,108	1,991	442	987	1,961	1,103
Dawson . .	2,180	4,794	1,044	1,739	4,710	2,305
Deuel. . . .	245	629	111	232	558	327
Dixon. . . .	931	1,478	414	830	1,484	726
Dodge . . .	5,181	7,484	1,894	4,665	7,269	4,432
Douglas . .	70,708	92,334	14,863	67,003	93,421	38,641
Dundy . . .	224	752	112	244	664	332
Fillmore . .	1,058	1,696	321	988	1,495	993
Franklin . .	483	1,013	215	477	967	527
Frontier . .	310	901	169	302	785	479
Furnas . . .	663	1,475	207	624	1,365	804
Gage	4,008	4,413	1,346	3,309	3,995	2,726
Garden . .	279	851	155	212	697	385
Garfield . .	249	625	111	221	595	270
Gosper. . .	275	609	150	254	492	297
Grant. . . .	84	258	55	75	247	124
Greeley . .	472	642	155	435	587	395
Hall	6,708	10,183	2,403	5,519	9,264	5,822
Hamilton. .	1,172	2,623	457	992	2,379	1,213
Harlan . . .	520	1,120	203	488	991	623
Hayes . . .	87	439	39	85	362	207
Hitchcock. .	409	977	173	359	824	540
Holt	1,107	3,436	677	835	3,131	1,714
Hooker. . .	115	308	83	70	283	102
Howard . .	853	1,294	417	778	1,138	940
Jefferson .	1,520	1,979	495	1,506	1,783	1,177
Johnson. .	770	1,009	309	822	885	642
Kearney. .	782	1,953	296	644	1,751	844
Keith	830	2,504	460	731	2,019	1,130
Keya Paha	94	385	47	105	368	158
Kimball. . .	527	1,011	212	408	931	440
Knox	1,266	2,123	531	968	2,112	1,166
Lancaster. .	43,339	44,812	8,595	41,207	41,400	21,783
Lincoln. . .	5,165	7,482	2,043	5,142	7,025	3,384
Logan . . .	79	294	72	80	271	98
Loup	74	229	28	58	233	96
McPherson	50	233	33	49	217	62
Madison. .	3,047	7,965	1,554	2,352	7,851	3,486
Merrick . .	997	2,084	449	864	1,854	1,072
Morrill . . .	620	1,296	262	577	1,184	752
Nance . . .	585	892	238	559	851	569
Nemaha. .	1,232	1,888	485	1,110	1,696	1,020
Nuckolls. .	757	1,383	306	834	1,277	825
Otoe	2,279	3,290	877	2,038	2,960	1,800
Pawnee . .	580	766	207	566	670	565
Perkins . .	352	1,018	163	300	842	522
Phelps . . .	1,071	3,015	465	829	2,748	1,298
Pierce . . .	697	1,923	446	611	1,853	1,084
Platte. . . .	3,010	7,948	1,353	2,409	7,712	3,656
Polk.	750	1,504	268	661	1,435	812
Red Willow	1,365	3,112	499	1,164	2,488	1,660
Richardson	1,517	2,089	633	1,513	2,050	1,356
Rock	180	564	135	162	588	233
Saline . . .	2,523	1,945	689	2,425	1,740	1,576
Sarpy. . . .	12,806	23,023	3,722	10,720	20,482	9,270
Saunders .	2,777	4,514	1,223	2,509	4,037	2,567
Scotts Bluff	4,547	7,641	1,251	4,173	7,213	3,514
Seward . .	2,432	3,479	745	2,118	3,044	1,722
Sheridan . .	573	1,834	289	535	1,698	751
Sherman . .	567	822	266	568	736	582
Sioux. . . .	138	551	75	148	445	206
Stanton . .	577	1,457	386	496	1,274	786
Thayer. . .	933	1,698	334	923	1,387	1,077
Thomas . .	64	303	62	69	283	115
Thurston. .	962	835	293	865	898	487

County	Clinton (D)	1996 Dole (R)	Perot (RF)	Clinton (D)	1992 Bush (R)	Perot (I)
Valley	758	1,346	274	716	1,173	693
Washington. .	2,248	4,391	971	2,108	4,035	2,148
Wayne. . . .	1,048	2,150	440	921	2,122	1,047
Webster. . .	621	1,094	236	624	972	657
Wheeler. . .	106	241	69	88	246	127
York	1,653	4,266	559	1,385	3,783	1,825
Totals	236,761	363,467	71,278	216,864	343,678	174,104

Nebraska Vote Since 1948

1948, Truman, Dem., 224,165; Dewey, Rep., 264,774.

1952, Eisenhower, Rep., 421,603; Stevenson, Dem., 188,057.

1956, Eisenhower, Rep., 378,108; Stevenson, Dem., 199,029.

1960, Kennedy, Dem., 232,542; Nixon, Rep., 380,553.

1964, Johnson, Dem., 307,307; Goldwater, Rep., 276,847.

1968, Nixon, Rep., 321,163; Humphrey, Dem., 170,784; Wallace, 3d Party, 44,904.

1972, Nixon, Rep., 406,298; McGovern, Dem., 169,991; scattered, 817.

1976, Carter, Dem., 233,287; Ford, Rep., 359,219; McCarthy, Ind., 9,383; Maddox, Amer. Ind., 3,378; MacBride, Libertarian, 1,476.

1980, Reagan, Rep., 419,214; Carter, Dem., 166,424; Anderson, Ind., 44,854; Clark, Libertarian, 9,041.

1984, Reagan, Rep., 459,135; Mondale, Dem., 187,475; Bergland, Libertarian, 2,075.

1988, Bush, Rep., 397,956; Dukakis, Dem., 259,235; Paul, Lib., 2,534; Fulani, New Alliance, 1,740.

1992, Bush, Rep., 343,678; Clinton, Dem., 216,864; Perot, Ind., 174,104; Marrou, Libertarian, 1,340.

1996, Dole, Rep., 363,467; Clinton, Dem., 236,761; Perot, Ref., 71,278; Browne, Libertarian, 2,792; Phillips, Ind., 1,928; Hagelin, Natural Law, 1,189.

Nevada

County	Clinton (D)	1996 Dole (R)	Perot (RF)	Clinton (D)	1992 Bush (R)	Perot (I)
Churchill. . .	2,282	4,369	821	1,770	3,789	1,964
Clark	127,963	103,431	23,177	124,586	97,403	75,364
Douglas . . .	5,109	8,828	1,486	3,928	6,182	4,814
Elko.	3,149	6,512	1,539	2,782	5,208	3,628
Esmeralda .	140	277	91	118	221	220
Eureka. . . .	158	412	90	129	330	214
Humboldt . .	1,467	2,334	603	810	1,505	1,149
Lander. . . .	660	1,107	361	423	885	652
Lincoln. . . .	499	936	255	511	890	394
Lyon	3,419	4,753	1,104	2,777	3,509	2,716
Mineral . . .	1,068	814	361	909	918	746
Nye.	3,300	3,979	1,544	2,561	2,743	2,501
Pershing . .	565	743	203	467	643	429
Storey	614	705	244	488	458	550
Washoe . . .	44,915	49,477	9,970	39,500	42,636	30,974
White Pine .	1,397	1,399	546	1,354	1,206	1,070
City						
Carson City	7,269	9,168	1,591	6,035	7,302	5,195
Totals	203,974	199,244	43,986	189,148	175,828	132,580

Nevada Vote Since 1948

1948, Truman, Dem., 31,291; Dewey, Rep., 29,357; Wallace, Prog., 1,469.

1952, Eisenhower, Rep., 50,502; Stevenson, Dem., 31,688.

1956, Eisenhower, Rep., 56,049; Stevenson, Dem., 40,640.

1960, Kennedy, Dem., 54,880; Nixon, Rep., 52,387.

1964, Johnson, Dem., 79,339; Goldwater, Rep., 56,094.

1968, Nixon, Rep., 73,188; Humphrey, Dem., 60,598; Wallace, 3d Party, 20,432.

1972, Nixon, Rep., 115,750; McGovern, Dem., 66,016.

1976, Carter, Dem., 92,479; Ford, Rep., 101,273; MacBride, Libertarian, 1,519; Maddox, Amer. Ind., 1,497; scattered, 5,108.

1980, Reagan, Rep., 155,017; Carter, Dem., 66,666; Anderson, Ind., 17,651; Clark, Libertarian, 4,358.

1984, Reagan, Rep., 188,770; Mondale, Dem., 91,655; Bergland, Libertarian, 2,292.

1988, Bush, Rep., 206,040; Dukakis, Dem., 132,738; Paul, Lib., 3,520; Fulani, New Alliance, 835.

1992, Clinton, Dem., 189,148; Bush, Rep., 175,828; Perot, Ind., 132,580; Gritz, Populist/America First, 2,892; Marrou, Libertarian, 1,835.

1996, Clinton, Dem., 203,974; Dole, Rep., 199,244; Perot, Ref., 43,986; "None of These Candidates," 5,608; Nader, Green, 4,730; Browne, Libertarian, 4,460; Phillips, Ind. Amer., 1,732; Hagelin, Natural Law, 545.

New Hampshire

City	1996 Clinton (D)	Dole (R)	Perot (RF)	1992 Clinton (D)	Bush (R)	Perot (I)
Concord ..	9,719	5,082	1,164	8,325	5,651	2,843
Derry	4,814	4,503	1,083	3,962	4,750	3,363
Dover ...	6,332	3,752	930	5,449	4,197	2,246
Hudson ...	3,841	3,167	976	3,053	3,315	2,774
Keene ...	5,401	2,910	621	5,210	3,257	1,736
Laconia ..	2,865	2,842	508	2,390	3,033	1,496
Londonderry	3,666	4,076	838	2,915	3,960	2,532
Manchester	20,185	14,704	3,053	16,627	16,298	7,441
Merrimack..	4,934	4,499	949	3,764	4,410	2,787
Nashua ..	16,584	11,479	2,858	14,777	12,514	8,306
Portsmouth	6,343	3,014	661	6,132	3,563	2,088
Rochester.	5,489	3,650	1,108	4,588	4,272	2,541
Salem ...	5,164	4,257	1,241	4,184	4,864	3,382
Other....	150,829	128,551	32,397	127,664	128,400	77,802
Totals ...	**246,166**	**196,486**	**48,387**	**209,040**	**202,484**	**121,337**

New Hampshire Vote Since 1948

1948, Truman, Dem., 107,995; Dewey, Rep., 121,299; Wallace, Prog., 1,970; Thomas, Soc., 86; Teichert, Soc. Labor, 83; Thurmond, States' Rights, 7.

1952, Eisenhower, Rep., 166,287; Stevenson, Dem., 106,663.

1956, Eisenhower, Rep., 176,519; Stevenson, Dem., 90,364; Andrews, Const., 111.

1960, Kennedy, Dem., 137,772; Nixon, Rep., 157,989.

1964, Johnson, Dem., 182,065; Goldwater, Rep., 104,029.

1968, Nixon, Rep., 154,903; Humphrey, Dem., 130,589; Wallace, 3d Party, 11,173; New Party, 421; Halstead, Soc. Workers, 104.

1972, Nixon, Rep., 213,724; McGovern, Dem., 116,435; Schmitz, Amer., 3,386; Jenness, Soc. Workers, 368; scattered, 142.

1976, Carter, Dem., 147,645; Ford, Rep., 185,935; McCarthy, Ind., 4,095; MacBride, Libertarian, 936; Reagan, write-in, 388; La Rouche, U.S. Labor, 186; Camejo, Soc. Workers, 161; Levin, Soc. Labor, 66; scattered, 215.

1980, Reagan, Rep., 221,705; Carter, Dem., 108,864; Anderson, Ind., 49,693; Clark, Libertarian, 2,067; Commoner, Citizens, 1,325; Hall, Com., 129; Griswold, Workers World, 76; DeBerry, Soc. Workers, 72; scattered, 68.

1984, Reagan, Rep., 267,051; Mondale, Dem., 120,377; Bergland, Libertarian, 735.

1988, Bush, Rep., 281,537; Dukakis, Dem., 163,696; Paul, Lib., 4,502; Fulani, New Alliance, 790.

1992, Clinton, Dem., 209,040; Bush, Rep., 202,484; Perot, Ind., 121,337; Marrou, Libertarian, 3,548.

1996, Clinton, Dem., 246,166; Dole, Rep., 196,486; Perot, Ref., 48,387; Browne, Libertarian, 4,214; Phillips, Taxpayers, 1,344.

New Jersey

County	1996 Clinton (D)	Dole (R)	Perot (RF)	1992 Clinton (D)	Bush (R)	Perot (I)
Atlantic...	44,434	29,538	8,261	39,633	34,279	15,890
Bergen...	191,085	141,164	25,512	171,104	178,223	52,082
Burlington	85,086	57,337	18,407	72,845	63,709	35,322
Camden ..	114,962	52,791	17,433	104,915	67,205	37,144
Cape May.	19,849	19,357	4,978	17,324	21,502	9,798
Cumberland	25,444	14,744	5,348	22,220	19,253	9,901
Essex ...	175,387	65,172	9,513	158,130	89,146	26,961
Gloucester	51,928	32,138	14,361	42,425	37,335	24,132
Hudson ...	116,121	38,288	8,965	99,799	66,505	14,569
Hunterdon	18,446	26,379	5,686	15,423	25,130	12,736
Mercer...	77,641	40,559	10,536	71,383	50,473	22,503
Middlesex.	145,201	82,433	24,643	128,824	108,701	45,055
Monmouth	120,414	99,975	22,754	101,593	117,715	45,445
Morris ...	81,092	95,830	15,289	67,593	108,431	32,447
Ocean ...	94,243	82,830	22,864	75,431	95,984	41,668
Passaic ..	85,879	53,584	10,944	70,030	71,147	21,494
Salem ...	12,044	9,294	4,124	10,062	10,363	7,274
Somerset..	50,673	51,868	8,377	42,867	56,044	21,014
Sussex...	19,525	26,746	6,705	14,775	29,510	12,537
Union....	108,102	65,912	12,432	96,671	87,742	23,991
Warren...	14,805	17,160	4,992	13,002	18,468	9,866
Totals ...	**1,652,361**	**1,103,099**	**262,134**	**1,436,206**	**1,356,865**	**521,829**

New Jersey Vote Since 1948

1948, Truman, Dem., 895,455; Dewey, Rep., 981,124; Wallace, Prog., 42,683; Watson, Proh., 10,593; Thomas, Soc., 10,521; Dobbs, Soc. Workers, 5,825; Teichert, Soc. Labor, 3,354.

1952, Eisenhower, Rep., 1,373,613; Stevenson, Dem., 1,015,902; Hoopes, Soc., 8,593; Hass, Soc. Labor, 5,815; Hallinan, Prog., 5,589; Krajewski, Poor Man's, 4,203; Dobbs, Soc. Workers, 3,850; Hamblen, Proh., 989.

1956, Eisenhower, Rep., 1,606,942; Stevenson Dem., 850,337; Holtwick, Proh., 9,147; Hass, Soc. Labor, 6,736; Andrews,

Cons., 5,317; Dobbs, Soc. Workers, 4,004; Krajewski, Amer. Third Party, 1,829.

1960, Kennedy, Dem., 1,385,415; Nixon, Rep., 1,363,324; Dobbs, Soc. Workers, 11,402; Lee, Cons., 8,708; Hass, Soc. Labor, 4,262.

1964, Johnson, Dem., 1,867,671; Goldwater, Rep., 963,843; DeBerry, Soc. Workers, 8,181; Hass, Soc. Labor, 7,075.

1968, Nixon, Rep., 1,325,467; Humphrey, Dem., 1,264,206; Wallace, 3d Party, 262,187; Halstead, Soc. Workers, 8,667; Gregory, Peace and Freedom, 8,084; Blomen, Soc. Labor, 6,784.

1972, Nixon, Rep., 1,845,502; McGovern, Dem., 1,102,211; Schmitz, Amer., 34,378; Spock, Peoples, 5,355; Fisher, Soc. Labor, 4,544; Jenness, Soc. Workers, 2,233; Mahalchik, Amer. First, 1,743; Hall, Com., 1,263.

1976, Carter, Dem., 1,444,653; Ford, Rep., 1,509,688; McCarthy, Ind., 32,717; MacBride, Libertarian, 9,449; Maddox, Amer., 7,716; Levin, Soc. Labor, 3,686; Hall, Com., 1,662; LaRouche, U.S. Labor, 1,650; Camejo, Soc. Workers, 1,184; Wright, People's, 1,044; Bubar, Proh., 554; Zeidler, Soc., 469.

1980, Reagan, Rep., 1,546,557; Carter, Dem., 1,147,364; Anderson, Ind., 234,632; Clark, Libertarian, 20,652; Commoner, Citizens, 8,203; McCormack, Right to Life, 3,927; Lynen, Middle Class, 3,694; Hall, Com., 2,555; Pulley, Soc. Workers, 2,198; McReynolds, Soc., 1,973; Gahres, Down With Lawyers, 1,718; Griswold, Workers World, 1,288; Wendelken, Ind., 923.

1984, Reagan, Rep., 1,933,630; Mondale, Dem., 1,261,323; Bergland, Libertarian, 6,416.

1988, Bush, Rep., 1,740,604; Dukakis, Dem., 1,317,541; Lewin, Peace and Freedom, 9,953; Paul, Lib., 8,421.

1992, Clinton, Dem., 1,436,206; Bush, Rep., 1,356,865; Perot, Ind., 521,829; Marrou, Libertarian, 6,822; Fulani, New Alliance, 3,513; Phillips, U.S. Taxpayers, 2,670; LaRouche, Ind., 2,095; Warren, Soc. Workers, 2,011; Daniels, Ind., 1,996; Gritz, Populist/America First, 1,867; Hagelin, Natural Law, 1,353.

1996, Clinton, Dem., 1,652,361; Dole, Rep., 1,103,099; Perot, Ref., 262,134; Nader, Green, 32,465; Browne, Libertarian, 14,763; Hagelin, Natural Law, 3,887; Phillips, Taxpayers, 3,440; Harris, Soc. Workers, 1,837; Moorehead, Workers World, 1,337; White, Soc. Equality, 537.

New Mexico

County	1996 Clinton (D)	Dole (R)	Perot (RF)	1992 Clinton (D)	Bush (R)	Perot (I)
Bernalillo ..	88,140	78,832	8,708	90,863	77,304	31,241
Catron ...	423	923	114	465	771	289
Chaves ...	7,014	9,991	1,271	6,360	8,872	3,590
Cibola	4,030	2,245	488	3,334	2,051	847
Colfax	2,659	1,975	411	2,607	1,730	871
Curry.....	4,116	7,378	842	3,699	6,831	2,056
De Baca...	509	489	86	451	526	204
Dona Ana..	22,766	17,541	2,269	19,894	16,308	7,682
Eddy	8,959	8,534	1,297	7,409	7,313	3,430
Grant.....	5,860	3,993	778	5,603	2,917	1,685
Guadalupe .	1,208	436	79	1,225	691	173
Harding ...	264	321	28	268	312	98
Hidalgo ...	943	789	209	995	871	442
Lea	5,393	7,661	1,465	5,047	7,921	3,233
Lincoln....	2,209	3,396	666	1,730	2,669	1,431
Los Alamos.	3,983	4,999	560	3,897	4,320	2,339
Luna	3,001	2,616	598	2,637	2,166	1,445
McKinley ..	10,124	4,470	650	9,405	4,720	1,304
Mora	1,646	561	131	1,555	668	188
Otero.....	5,938	9,065	1,096	5,377	7,481	3,257
Quay.....	1,830	1,943	377	1,758	1,759	755
Rio Arriba..	7,965	2,551	469	7,832	2,680	984
Roosevelt..	2,097	3,245	467	2,172	3,215	1,085
Sandoval ..	13,081	11,015	1,482	10,951	8,491	3,954
San Juan..	12,070	17,478	2,355	11,302	13,415	5,351
San Miguel.	6,995	1,938	405	6,186	2,183	965
Santa Fe ..	26,349	10,857	1,846	27,189	9,684	5,656
Sierra	2,154	2,140	431	1,771	1,562	1,055
Socorro ...	3,374	2,315	455	2,908	2,186	918
Taos	6,635	2,126	545	7,051	2,260	1,300
Torrance ..	2,072	2,154	332	1,662	1,667	810
Union.....	519	995	125	519	975	355
Valencia...	9,169	7,779	1,222	7,495	6,305	2,902
Totals	**273,495**	**232,751**	**32,257**	**261,617**	**212,824**	**91,895**

New Mexico Vote Since 1948

1948, Truman, Dem., 105,464; Dewey, Rep., 80,303; Wallace, Prog., 1,037; Watson, Proh., 127; Thomas, Soc., 83; Teichert, Soc. Labor, 49.

1952, Eisenhower, Rep., 132,170; Stevenson, Dem., 105,661; Hamblen, Proh., 297; Hallinan, Ind. Prog., 225; MacArthur, Christian National, 220; Hass, Soc. Labor, 35.

1956, Eisenhower, Rep., 146,788; Stevenson, Dem., 106,098; Holtwick, Proh., 607; Andrews, Ind., 364; Hass, Soc. Labor, 69.

1960, Kennedy, Dem., 156,027; Nixon, Rep., 153,733; Decker, Proh., 777; Hass, Soc. Labor, 570.

1964, Johnson, Dem., 194,017; Goldwater, Rep., 131,838; Hass, Soc. Labor, 1,217; Munn, Proh., 543.

1968, Nixon, Rep., 169,692; Humphrey, Dem., 130,081; Wallace, 3d Party, 25,737; Chavez, 1,519; Halstead, Soc. Workers, 252.

1972, Nixon, Rep., 235,606; McGovern, Dem., 141,084; Schmitz, Amer., 8,767; Jenness, Soc. Workers, 474.

1976, Carter, Dem., 201,148; Ford, Rep., 211,419; Camejo, Soc. Workers, 2,462; MacBride, Libertarian, 1,110; Zeidler, Soc., 240; Bubar, Proh., 211.

1980, Reagan, Rep., 250,779; Carter, Dem., 167,826; Anderson, Ind., 29,459; Clark, Libertarian, 4,365; Commoner, Citizens, 2,202; Bubar, Statesman, 1,281; Pulley, Soc. Workers, 325.

1984, Reagan, Rep., 307,101; Mondale, Dem., 201,769; Bergland, Libertarian, 4,459.

1988, Bush, Rep., 270,341; Dukakis, Dem., 244,497; Paul, Lib., 3,268; Fulani, New Alliance, 2,237.

1992, Clinton, Dem., 261,617; Bush, Rep., 212,824; Perot, Ind., 91,895; Marrou, Libertarian, 1,615.

1996, Clinton, Dem., 273,495; Dole, Rep., 232,751; Perot, Ref., 32,257; Nader, Green, 13,218; Browne, Libertarian, 2,996; Phillips, Taxpayers, 713; Hagelin, Natural Law, 644.

New York

County	1996 Clinton (D)	Dole (R)	Perot (RF)	1992 Clinton (D)	Bush (R)	Perot (I)
Albany . . .	85,993	39,785	11,957	80,641	49,452	24,064
Allegany . .	6,621	8,107	2,730	4,848	8,976	4,703
Bronx. . .	248,276	30,435	7,186	225,038	63,310	15,115
Broome . .	44,407	31,327	9,114	43,444	34,653	21,280
Cattaraugus	13,029	12,971	5,151	10,150	13,944	10,662
Cayuga . .	15,879	11,093	4,420	13,088	12,065	10,279
Chautauqua	26,831	21,261	7,484	22,645	21,222	18,455
Chemung . .	16,977	14,287	3,967	15,099	16,088	7,493
Chenango .	8,797	7,319	2,822	8,017	8,114	5,356
Clinton . . .	15,386	9,759	3,488	12,881	13,455	5,389
Columbia .	12,910	10,324	3,466	11,368	11,568	5,829
Cortland . .	9,130	7,606	2,398	7,815	7,782	5,098
Delaware .	8,724	7,684	2,601	7,152	8,829	4,404
Dutchess .	47,339	41,929	12,294	41,655	46,709	26,320
Erie	224,554	132,343	45,679	196,233	129,444	123,358
Essex . . .	7,893	6,379	2,363	6,717	8,278	3,784
Franklin . .	8,494	5,072	2,499	7,654	6,635	3,857
Fulton . . .	9,779	7,881	3,214	8,400	9,137	5,120
Genesee .	10,074	10,821	2,996	8,071	11,663	6,192
Greene . .	8,251	8,712	2,790	6,924	9,390	4,689
Hamilton. .	1,228	1,841	492	963	2,038	793
Herkimer .	11,910	10,085	4,235	10,880	12,052	6,866
Jefferson .	16,783	12,362	4,561	13,380	14,227	9,461
Kings. . . .	432,232	81,406	15,031	411,183	133,344	33,014
Lewis. . . .	4,402	3,965	1,669	3,676	4,101	3,164
Livingston.	10,868	10,981	2,889	8,648	12,122	5,775
Madison. .	11,832	11,324	3,379	10,099	11,293	7,391
Monroe . .	164,858	115,694	23,936	141,502	134,021	63,229
Montgomery	10,485	7,172	3,253	9,509	8,802	5,020
Nassau . .	303,587	196,820	36,122	282,593	246,881	77,097
New York .	394,131	67,839	11,144	416,142	84,501	27,689
Niagara . .	44,203	31,438	12,564	35,649	30,401	30,126
Oneida. . .	44,399	37,996	11,296	40,966	43,806	22,717
Onondaga	100,190	73,771	17,602	90,645	77,642	45,175
Ontario. . .	19,156	17,237	4,391	16,064	18,995	9,571
Orange . .	54,995	45,956	11,778	45,946	53,493	22,499
Orleans . .	6,233	6,865	1,986	4,927	7,468	4,275
Oswego . .	20,440	17,159	7,499	16,990	18,530	14,853
Otsego. . .	11,470	8,774	3,217	10,471	10,141	5,841
Putnam . .	16,173	17,452	4,032	14,048	18,934	8,011
Queens . .	372,925	107,650	22,288	349,520	157,561	46,014
Rensselaer	34,273	23,482	8,405	29,793	28,937	15,198
Richmond. .	64,684	52,207	8,968	56,901	70,707	19,678
Rockland .	63,127	40,395	6,798	56,759	49,608	15,026
St. Lawrence	21,798	10,827	5,309	18,197	13,901	9,758
Saratoga .	39,832	34,337	10,141	33,011	36,917	19,091
Schenectady	35,404	22,106	7,865	32,335	26,258	14,838
Schoharie.	5,902	5,353	1,796	4,997	5,678	3,327
Schuyler. .	3,303	3,134	1,037	2,859	3,226	2,051
Seneca . .	6,825	5,004	1,889	5,810	5,432	3,660
Steuben . .	14,481	17,710	5,496	12,043	19,761	9,378
Suffolk . . .	261,828	182,510	52,209	220,811	229,467	112,973
Sullivan . .	15,052	9,321	3,453	13,717	11,396	6,336
Tioga. . . .	8,769	9,416	2,721	7,791	9,287	5,867
Tompkins .	20,772	11,532	2,623	23,197	11,520	6,704
Ulster. . . .	35,852	26,212	9,246	32,886	29,223	17,952
Warren . . .	11,603	11,152	3,623	9,820	12,260	6,401
Washington	9,572	8,954	3,648	8,429	10,305	6,143
Wayne. . . .	15,145	15,837	4,619	11,866	18,019	9,188
Westchester.	196,310	123,719	18,028	184,300	151,990	39,933
Wyoming .	5,735	7,477	2,411	4,045	7,324	4,837
Yates. . . .	4,066	3,925	1,190	3,242	4,366	2,354
Totals . . .	**3,756,177**	**1,933,492**	**503,458**	**3,444,450**	**2,346,649**	**1,090,721**

New York Vote Since 1948

1948, Truman, Dem., 2,557,642; Liberal, 222,562; total, 2,780,204; Dewey, Rep., 2,841,163; Wallace, Amer. Lab., 509,559; Thomas, Soc., 40,879; Teichert, Ind. Gov't., 2,729; Dobbs, Soc. Workers, 2,675.

1952, Eisenhower, Rep., 3,952,815; Stevenson, Dem., 2,687,890; Liberal, 416,711; total, 3,104,601; Hallinan, Amer. Lab., 64,211; Hoopes, Soc., 2,664; Dobbs, Soc. Workers, 2,212; Hass, Ind. Gov't., 1,560; scattering, 178; blank and void, 87,813.

1956, Eisenhower, Rep., 4,340,340; Stevenson, Dem., 2,458,212; Liberal, 292,557; total, 2,750,769; write-in votes for Andrews, 1,027; Werdel, 492; Hass, 150; Hoopes, 82; others, 476.

1960, Kennedy, Dem., 3,423,909; Liberal, 406,176; total, 3,830,085; Nixon, Rep., 3,446,419; Dobbs, Soc. Workers, 14,319; scattering, 256; blank and void, 88,896.

1964, Johnson, Dem., 4,913,156; Goldwater, Rep., 2,243,559; Hass, Soc. Labor, 6,085; DeBerry, Soc. Workers, 3,215; scattering, 188; blank and void, 151,383.

1968, Nixon, Rep., 3,007,932; Humphrey, Dem., 3,378,470; Wallace, 3d Party, 358,864; Blomen, Soc. Labor, 8,432; Halstead, Soc. Workers, 11,851; Gregory, Freedom and Peace, 24,517; blank, void, and scattering, 171,624.

1972, Nixon, Rep., 3,824,642; Cons., 368,136; McGovern, Dem., 2,767,956; Liberal, 183,128; Reed, Soc. Workers, 7,797; Fisher, Soc. Labor, 4,530; Hall, Com., 5,641; blank, void, or scattered, 161,641.

1976, Carter, Dem., 3,389,558; Ford, Rep., 3,100,791; MacBride, Libertarian, 12,197; Hall, Com., 10,270; Camejo, Soc. Workers, 6,996; LaRouche, U.S. Labor, 5,413; blank, void, or scattered, 143,037.

1980, Reagan, Rep., 2,893,831; Carter, Dem., 2,728,372; Anderson, Ind., 467,801; Clark, Libertarian, 52,648; McCormack, Right To Life, 24,159; Commoner, Citizens, 23,186; Hall, Com., 7,414; DeBerry, Soc. Workers, 2,068; Griswold, Workers World, 1,416; scattering, 1,064.

1984, Reagan, Rep., 3,664,763; Mondale, Dem., 3,119,609; Bergland, Libertarian, 11,949.

1988, Bush, Rep., 3,081,871; Dukakis, Dem., 3,347,882; Marra, Right to Life, 20,497; Fulani, New Alliance, 15,845.

1992, Clinton, Dem., 3,444,450; Bush, Rep., 2,346,649; Perot, Ind., 1,090,721; Warren, Soc. Workers, 15,472; Marrou, Libertarian, 13,451; Fulani, New Alliance, 11,318; Hagelin, Natural Law, 4,420.

1996, Clinton, Dem., 3,756,177; Dole, Rep., 1,933,492; Perot, Ind. (Ref.), 503,458; Nader, Green, 75,956; Phillips, Right to Life, 23,580; Browne, Libertarian, 12,220; Hagelin, Natural Law, 5,011; Harris, Soc. Workers, 2,762; Moorehead, Workers World, 3,473.

North Carolina

County	1996 Clinton (D)	Dole (R)	Perot (RF)	1992 Clinton (D)	Bush (R)	Perot (I)
Alamance. .	15,814	22,461	3,395	15,521	20,637	6,444
Alexander. .	3,955	6,748	1,004	4,849	6,764	2,002
Alleghany . .	1,801	1,936	458	2,271	1,853	600
Anson	4,890	2,193	512	5,269	2,334	921
Ashe	3,825	5,203	865	4,624	5,200	1,220
Avery.	1,586	3,870	655	1,755	3,895	1,123
Beaufort. . .	6,172	8,154	834	6,445	7,337	2,174
Bertie	4,202	1,745	316	4,382	1,756	600
Bladen . . .	4,952	3,335	655	5,700	3,214	1,248
Brunswick .	10,041	10,065	1,815	10,177	8,833	3,349
Buncombe .	31,658	30,518	6,254	32,955	30,892	11,481
Burke	11,678	13,853	2,654	12,565	13,397	4,124
Cabarrus . .	14,447	23,035	3,626	13,513	21,281	6,251
Caldwell. . .	8,050	12,653	2,099	9,033	12,543	3,965
Camden. . .	1,186	1,074	293	1,153	1,039	479
Carteret . . .	7,566	11,721	1,467	8,028	10,334	3,401
Caswell . . .	4,312	3,310	510	4,725	2,793	827
Catawba . .	15,601	26,898	3,629	16,334	25,466	7,523
Chatham . .	9,353	7,731	1,113	9,520	6,568	2,425
Cherokee . .	3,129	3,883	785	3,686	4,021	1,040
Chowan . . .	2,239	1,659	359	2,136	1,661	700
Clay	1,462	1,769	387	1,600	1,890	465
Cleveland. .	12,728	13,474	1,931	13,037	13,650	3,784
Columbus. .	9,019	6,017	1,170	11,469	5,462	1,963
Craven. . . .	10,317	13,264	1,528	9,998	11,575	3,679
Cumberland .	32,739	29,804	3,776	30,291	27,139	6,792
Currituck . .	2,277	2,569	770	1,935	2,188	1,163
Dare	4,522	4,977	1,258	3,925	4,357	2,388
Davidson . .	13,593	24,797	3,698	16,462	24,869	8,324
Davie	3,525	8,141	915	3,675	6,796	1,903
Duplin	6,179	5,432	766	6,816	5,286	1,636
Durham . . .	49,186	27,825	3,122	47,331	27,581	7,504
Edgecombe .	10,568	6,010	660	11,174	6,275	2,175
Forsyth . . .	46,543	59,160	5,747	49,006	52,787	14,262

County	1996 Clinton (D)	Dole (R)	Perot (RF)	1992 Clinton (D)	Bush (R)	Perot (I)
Franklin ..	6,448	5,648	891	6,517	4,669	2,062
Gaston...	19,458	33,149	3,921	19,121	34,714	7,490
Gates ...	2,155	1,072	307	2,206	1,158	466
Graham ..	1,210	1,801	270	1,551	1,919	403
Granville..	6,747	5,498	432	6,178	4,538	1,321
Greene..	2,224	2,689	280	2,768	2,180	780
Guilford ..	69,208	67,727	9,739	66,319	60,140	19,601
Halifax ..	9,551	5,700	816	9,960	5,769	2,047
Harnett...	8,767	11,596	1,287	8,473	9,751	2,684
Haywood .	9,350	7,995	2,594	10,385	7,292	3,303
Henderson	10,626	19,182	2,679	10,747	17,010	5,260
Hertford ..	4,856	1,823	356	4,609	2,208	846
Hoke	3,510	1,914	481	3,730	1,711	887
Hyde	1,109	782	143	1,206	740	340
Iredell ...	13,102	21,163	2,970	13,263	19,411	6,204
Jackson ...	5,211	4,244	970	5,753	4,275	1,516
Johnston .	11,175	18,704	2,163	11,284	15,418	4,939
Jones ...	1,829	1,682	197	1,962	1,438	444
Lee.....	6,290	7,321	980	5,852	6,658	2,125
Lenoir..	8,635	9,433	822	8,793	8,932	2,107
Lincoln...	7,721	11,439	1,619	8,150	11,018	3,142
McDowell.	4,553	6,407	1,275	5,309	6,090	1,881
Macon..	4,209	5,267	1,121	4,624	4,797	1,829
Madison..	3,333	3,110	538	3,980	3,121	857
Martin..	4,500	3,590	445	4,069	2,958	981
Mecklenburg	103,429	97,719	10,473	97,065	99,496	31,283
Mitchell ..	1,496	3,874	549	1,727	4,405	877
Montgomery.	3,856	3,379	587	4,422	3,543	1,185
Moore..	9,847	14,760	1,761	9,649	12,448	4,448
Nash	11,142	15,309	1,751	10,809	14,446	4,544
New Hanover	22,839	27,889	3,615	20,291	24,338	7,401
Northampton	5,207	1,881	402	5,195	1,845	916
Onslow ..	8,685	13,396	1,857	8,045	11,842	4,387
Orange ..	28,674	15,053	1,534	28,595	13,009	5,535
Pamlico ..	2,204	2,270	297	2,229	1,929	809
Pasquotank	4,233	2,999	565	4,709	3,419	1,434
Pender..	5,409	5,538	945	5,825	4,857	1,725
Perquimans	2,069	1,561	369	1,818	1,429	624
Person...	4,540	4,883	591	4,323	4,460	1,431
Pitt....	17,555	18,227	2,037	17,959	16,609	5,262
Polk.....	2,704	3,516	493	2,939	3,448	1,134
Randolph..	10,783	23,030	3,593	11,274	20,697	6,870
Richmond.	7,564	3,973	1,230	9,163	4,356	2,015
Robeson .	17,361	8,146	2,105	19,378	7,777	3,277
Rockingham	12,096	14,255	2,528	13,880	12,678	4,671
Rowan...	13,461	22,754	2,902	14,308	21,297	7,053
Rutherford	7,162	9,792	1,585	7,855	9,748	2,695
Sampson..	8,150	8,241	825	8,698	8,007	1,852
Scotland..	4,870	2,858	548	5,175	2,980	1,196
Stanly ...	7,131	11,446	1,690	7,735	11,030	2,855
Stokes ...	4,769	9,471	1,025	6,463	7,979	2,183
Surry	7,303	11,117	1,538	9,392	10,866	3,164
Swain..	1,869	1,444	401	2,117	1,640	568
Transylvania	4,842	6,734	1,183	5,120	5,984	2,006
Tyrrell ...	908	488	112	928	553	189
Union....	11,525	18,802	2,477	10,789	16,542	4,601
Vance..	6,385	4,651	575	6,598	4,747	1,444
Wake....	103,574	108,780	11,811	88,979	86,798	31,140
Warren...	4,141	1,861	319	4,656	1,767	693
Washington	2,790	1,562	171	2,902	1,780	563
Watauga .	7,349	8,146	1,415	8,262	7,899	3,007
Wayne...	11,580	16,588	1,178	10,307	14,397	2,798
Wilkes..	6,793	12,395	1,967	7,991	12,547	3,307
Wilson...	9,779	10,518	1,100	10,105	10,176	2,630
Yadkin...	2,927	8,439	913	3,913	7,311	1,725
Yancey ..	3,956	3,973	720	4,285	3,994	917
Totals...	1,107,849	1,225,938	168,059	1,114,042	1,134,661	357,864

North Carolina Vote Since 1948

1948, Truman, Dem., 459,070; Dewey, Rep., 258,572; Thurmond, States' Rights, 69,652; Wallace, Prog., 3,915.

1952, Eisenhower, Rep., 558,107; Stevenson, Dem., 652,803.

1956, Eisenhower, Rep., 575,062; Stevenson, Dem., 590,530.

1960, Kennedy, Dem., 713,136; Nixon, Rep., 655,420.

1964, Johnson, Dem., 800,139; Goldwater, Rep., 624,844.

1968, Nixon, Rep., 627,192; Humphrey, Dem., 464,113; Wallace, 3d Party, 496,188.

1972, Nixon, Rep., 1,054,889; McGovern, Dem., 438,705; Schmitz, Amer., 25,018.

1976, Carter, Dem., 927,365; Ford, Rep., 741,960; Anderson, Amer., 5,607; MacBride, Libertarian, 2,219; LaRouche, U.S. Labor, 755.

1980, Reagan, Rep., 915,018; Carter, Dem., 875,635; Anderson, Ind., 52,800; Clark, Libertarian, 9,677; Commoner, Citizens, 2,287; DeBerry, Soc. Workers, 416.

1984, Reagan, Rep., 1,346,481; Mondale, Dem., 824,287; Bergland, Libertarian, 3,794.

1988, Bush, Rep., 1,237,258; Dukakis, Dem., 890,167; Fulani, New Alliance, 5,682; Paul, write-in, 1,263.

1992, Clinton, Dem., 1,114,042; Bush, Rep., 1,134,661; Perot, Ind., 357,864; Marrou, Libertarian, 5,171.

1996, Dole, Rep., 1,225,938; Clinton, Dem., 1,107,849; Perot, Ref., 168,059; Browne, Libertarian, 8,740; Hagelin, Natural Law, 2,771.

North Dakota

County	1996 Clinton (D)	Dole (R)	Perot (RF)	1992 Clinton (D)	Bush (R)	Perot (I)
Adams....	366	575	200	469	647	499
Barnes....	2,317	2,449	666	2,124	2,728	1,568
Benson ...	1,059	850	252	1,126	874	610
Billings...	116	281	107	123	279	270
Bottineau..	1,280	1,682	536	1,266	1,787	1,036
Bowman..	489	710	261	506	712	678
Burke...	416	483	176	458	551	506
Burleigh...	10,679	15,464	3,535	8,940	16,484	6,780
Cass.....	21,693	24,238	4,116	18,077	25,312	9,513
Cavalier..	941	1,188	326	866	1,527	723
Dickey....	953	1,418	276	918	1,514	616
Divide	637	488	209	634	515	456
Dunn	587	830	304	667	784	637
Eddy	553	517	201	575	591	432
Emmons..	544	1,148	441	595	1,047	774
Foster....	664	801	265	565	803	556
Golden Valley	235	520	163	255	503	352
Grand Forks	11,376	11,606	2,663	10,930	13,705	6,349
Grant....	300	760	295	415	900	629
Griggs....	670	731	162	647	773	330
Hettinger..	418	765	238	465	854	500
Kidder....	434	691	242	468	739	489
La Moure..	880	1,220	276	797	1,270	679
Logan....	360	705	254	383	703	390
McHenry..	1,096	1,187	453	1,173	1,321	886
McIntosh..	470	1,005	295	450	1,134	454
McKenzie..	928	1,338	428	787	1,324	969
McLean...	1,759	1,988	618	1,808	2,124	1,330
Mercer....	1,300	1,953	764	1,323	2,274	1,378
Morton....	3,745	4,699	1,566	3,594	5,042	2,787
Mountrail ..	1,277	965	360	1,393	1,017	861
Nelson....	827	745	206	841	864	486
Oliver....	333	499	183	306	503	407
Pembina ..	1,191	1,678	400	1,186	1,917	991
Pierce....	671	1,017	270	761	1,099	554
Ramsey ...	2,123	2,077	549	2,008	2,516	1,507
Ransom...	1,199	920	303	1,166	1,102	625
Renville..	562	576	210	580	655	429
Richland..	2,890	3,345	782	2,688	3,873	1,698
Rolette....	2,299	823	448	2,002	895	660
Sargent ...	1,003	814	241	961	816	463
Sheridan..	252	566	121	276	589	304
Sioux.....	393	207	82	463	264	244
Slope.....	123	260	60	145	226	162
Stark....	3,095	4,086	1,456	3,003	4,491	3,123
Steele....	620	486	115	598	503	267
Stutsman..	3,589	3,784	1,141	3,313	4,039	2,580
Towner ...	649	542	187	748	600	402
Traill	1,822	1,820	380	1,638	2,019	875
Walsh....	2,082	2,222	599	1,936	2,544	1,384
Ward....	8,660	10,546	2,587	7,856	12,056	5,856
Wells....	962	1,192	373	888	1,171	850
Williams...	3,018	3,590	1,174	3,008	3,664	3,180
Totals	106,905	125,050	32,515	99,168	136,244	71,084

North Dakota Vote Since 1948

1948, Truman, Dem., 95,812; Dewey, Rep., 115,139; Wallace, Prog., 8,391; Thomas, Soc., 1,000; Thurmond, States' Rights, 374.

1952, Eisenhower, Rep., 191,712; Stevenson, Dem., 76,694; MacArthur, Christian Nationalist, 1,075; Hallinan, Prog., 344; Hamblen, Proh., 302.

1956, Eisenhower, Rep., 156,766; Stevenson, Dem., 96,742; Andrews, Amer., 483.

1960, Kennedy, Dem., 123,963; Nixon, Rep., 154,310; Dobbs, Soc. Workers, 158.

1964, Johnson, Dem., 149,784; Goldwater, Rep., 108,207; DeBerry, Soc. Workers, 224; Munn, Proh., 174.

1968, Nixon, Rep., 138,669; Humphrey, Dem., 94,769; Wallace, 3d Party, 14,244; Halstead, Soc. Workers, 128; Munn, Prohibition, 38; Troxell, Ind., 34.

1972, Nixon, Rep., 174,109; McGovern, Dem., 100,384; Jenness, Soc. Workers, 288; Hall, Com., 87; Schmitz, Amer., 5,646.

1976, Carter, Dem., 136,078; Ford, Rep., 153,470; Anderson, Amer., 3,698; McCarthy, Ind., 2,952; Maddox, Amer. Ind., 269; MacBride, Libertarian, 256; scattering, 371.

1980, Reagan, Rep., 193,695; Carter, Dem., 79,189; Anderson, Ind., 23,640; Clark, Libertarian, 3,743; Commoner, Libertarian, 429; McLain, Natl. People's League, 296; Greaves, Amer., 235; Hall, Com., 93; DeBerry, Soc. Workers, 89; McReynolds, Soc., 82; Bubar, Statesman, 54.

1984, Reagan, Rep., 200,336; Mondale, Dem., 104,429; Bergland, Libertarian, 703.

1988, Bush, Rep., 166,559; Dukakis, Dem., 127,739; Paul, Lib., 1,315; LaRouche, Natl. Econ. Recovery, 905.

1992, Clinton, Dem., 99,168; Bush, Rep., 136,244; Perot, Ind., 71,084.

1996, Dole, Rep., 125,050; Clinton, Dem., 106,905; Perot, Ref., 32,515; Browne, Libertarian, 847; Phillips, Ind., 745; Hagelin, Natural Law, 349.

Ohio

County	1996 Clinton (D)	Dole (R)	Perot (RF)	1992 Clinton (D)	Bush (R)	Perot (I)
Adams...	4,317	4,763	1,223	3,998	4,722	1,993
Allen...	15,529	24,325	3,799	13,777	25,322	8,131
Ashland..	6,573	10,402	2,630	5,985	9,864	4,950
Ashtabula.	19,341	13,287	5,700	18,843	13,254	10,765
Athens...	13,418	7,154	2,777	13,423	7,184	5,074
Auglaize..	6,652	10,169	2,641	4,960	10,455	4,840
Belmont..	17,705	8,213	4,452	18,527	8,614	6,142
Brown...	6,318	6,970	1,941	5,540	5,912	3,676
Butler....	43,690	67,023	10,540	39,682	63,375	27,527
Carroll...	4,792	4,449	2,445	4,731	4,224	3,434
Champaign	5,990	6,568	2,219	5,201	7,004	3,992
Clark....	27,890	22,297	7,083	26,692	24,011	12,571
Clermont.	21,329	36,457	5,795	17,558	32,065	14,279
Clinton...	5,303	7,504	1,588	4,638	7,290	3,402
Columbiana	20,716	15,386	7,127	19,765	15,016	12,611
Coshocton	6,005	6,018	2,183	6,212	5,705	4,081
Crawford .	7,449	8,730	3,072	6,351	8,618	5,764
Cuyahoga.	341,357	163,770	50,691	337,548	187,186	112,352
Darke...	8,871	10,798	3,168	7,016	11,098	6,217
Defiance..	6,343	7,469	1,929	5,735	7,195	4,187
Delaware .	13,463	24,123	3,471	9,263	18,225	9,244
Erie.....	16,730	12,204	4,225	14,531	12,459	8,720
Fairfield .	18,821	26,850	4,660	14,249	24,125	12,246
Fayette ..	3,665	4,831	1,047	2,976	4,916	2,162
Franklin .	192,795	178,412	25,400	176,656	186,324	79,049
Fulton ...	6,662	8,703	2,412	5,576	8,358	4,798
Gallia....	5,386	5,135	1,839	5,350	5,776	2,549
Geauga ..	14,143	19,662	4,848	11,466	18,200	10,577
Greene ..	25,082	30,677	5,246	20,139	27,651	11,459
Guernsey.	6,731	5,970	2,251	6,428	5,749	4,103
Hamilton..	160,458	186,493	21,335	148,409	192,447	60,145
Hancock..	9,334	17,252	2,904	7,944	16,821	7,002
Hardin ...	4,930	5,506	1,365	4,364	5,851	2,867
Harrison..	3,721	2,310	1,302	3,830	2,289	1,679
Henry ...	4,762	6,385	1,550	3,933	6,196	3,178
Highland..	5,837	7,102	1,629	4,866	7,020	3,315
Hocking ..	4,646	4,017	1,564	3,935	3,761	2,831
Holmes ..	2,531	5,213	1,276	1,969	5,079	1,945
Huron ...	8,858	8,750	3,338	7,930	9,480	6,751
Jackson..	5,538	4,922	1,529	5,016	5,422	2,389
Jefferson .	19,402	10,212	4,748	20,978	10,764	6,910
Knox....	7,562	10,159	2,138	7,259	9,044	5,282
Lake....	43,186	40,974	12,507	37,682	40,766	26,878
Lawrence .	11,595	8,832	3,232	12,325	10,044	4,536
Licking...	22,624	28,276	6,516	18,898	26,918	13,806
Logan ...	6,397	8,325	2,264	4,889	9,364	4,472
Lorain ...	55,744	34,937	14,889	50,962	36,803	30,425
Lucas ...	104,911	58,120	17,282	99,989	63,297	38,108
Madison..	5,072	6,871	1,386	3,998	6,865	3,170
Mahoning .	72,716	31,397	13,213	64,731	31,191	29,417
Marion ...	10,482	11,112	2,897	9,444	11,675	6,471
Medina...	23,727	26,120	8,700	18,995	24,090	17,290
Meigs...	4,275	3,622	1,453	4,226	3,916	2,098
Mercer...	6,300	8,832	2,361	4,883	8,683	4,913
Miami ...	15,540	19,509	4,599	12,547	19,741	10,544
Monroe ..	3,914	1,856	1,128	4,235	1,823	1,505
Montgomery	115,469	95,391	18,298	108,017	104,751	47,854
Morgan ..	2,385	2,566	922	2,402	2,719	1,551
Morrow ..	4,627	5,655	1,745	3,907	5,208	3,623
Muskingum	13,813	13,861	4,880	11,670	14,168	8,731
Noble....	2,366	2,183	899	2,201	2,223	1,429
Ottawa ..	9,321	6,991	2,438	8,128	6,782	4,832
Paulding..	3,449	3,760	1,292	3,293	3,652	2,510
Perry ...	5,819	4,606	1,854	4,972	4,712	3,810
Pickaway .	7,042	8,666	1,702	5,765	8,690	4,319
Pike.....	5,542	3,759	1,402	5,057	4,094	2,192
Portage ..	29,441	18,939	9,178	26,325	18,447	17,065
Preble ...	6,611	8,139	2,235	5,557	8,023	4,460
Putnam ..	4,972	9,294	1,767	3,962	9,338	3,648
Richland..	20,832	23,697	6,613	19,606	23,532	13,370
Ross	12,649	10,286	2,648	10,452	10,825	5,616
Sandusky.	11,547	10,033	3,617	9,878	10,772	6,682
Scioto ...	15,041	11,679	4,418	14,715	11,931	6,860
Seneca ..	10,044	9,713	3,498	9,280	9,763	6,967
Shelby ..	6,729	8,773	2,686	5,262	8,854	5,835
Stark	73,437	60,212	23,004	70,064	61,863	42,413
Summit ..	112,050	73,555	27,723	107,881	77,530	55,151
Trumbull..	55,604	24,811	13,563	54,591	25,831	26,791
Tuscarawas.	15,244	13,388	5,682	14,787	13,179	8,785
Union....	4,989	8,290	1,596	3,465	7,818	3,433
Van Wert ..	4,453	6,999	1,487	3,822	7,227	3,102
Vinton	2,350	1,673	728	2,308	1,975	1,050
Warren ...	17,089	33,210	4,689	13,542	27,998	11,115
Washington.	10,945	11,965	2,832	10,380	12,204	5,415
Wayne....	14,850	19,628	5,771	13,953	18,350	9,482
Williams...	5,524	7,747	2,121	4,862	7,614	4,902
Wood.....	23,183	20,518	5,065	20,754	20,579	11,682
Wyandot .	3,677	4,473	1,347	3,031	4,411	2,929
Totals ...	2,148,222	1,859,883	483,207	1,984,942	1,894,310	1,036,426

Ohio Vote Since 1948

1948, Truman, Dem., 1,452,791; Dewey, Rep., 1,445,684; Wallace, Prog., 37,596.

1952, Eisenhower, Rep., 2,100,391; Stevenson, Dem., 1,600,367.

1956, Eisenhower, Rep., 2,262,610; Stevenson, Dem., 1,439,655.

1960, Kennedy, Dem., 1,944,248; Nixon, Rep., 2,217,611.

1964, Johnson, Dem., 2,498,331; Goldwater, Rep., 1,470,865.

1968, Nixon, Rep., 1,791,014; Humphrey, Dem., 1,700,586; Wallace, 3d Party, 467,495; Gregory, 372; Munn, Proh., 19; Blomen, Soc. Labor, 120; Halstead, Soc. Workers, 69; Mitchell, Com., 23.

1972, Nixon, Rep., 2,441,827; McGovern, Dem., 1,558,889; Fisher, Soc. Labor, 7,107; Hall, Com., 6,437; Schmitz, Amer., 80,067; Wallace, Ind., 460.

1976, Carter, Dem., 2,011,621; Ford, Rep., 2,000,505; McCarthy, Ind., 58,258; Maddox, Amer. Ind., 15,529; MacBride, Libertarian, 8,961; Hall, Com., 7,817; Camejo, Soc. Workers, 4,717; LaRouche, U.S. Labor, 4,335; scattered, 130.

1980, Reagan, Rep., 2,206,545; Carter, Dem., 1,752,414; Anderson, Ind., 254,472; Clark, Libertarian, 49,033; Commoner, Citizens, 8,564; Hall, Com., 4,729; Congress, Ind., 4,029; Griswold, Workers World, 3,790; Bubar, Statesman, 27.

1984, Reagan, Rep., 2,678,559; Mondale, Dem., 1,825,440; Bergland, Libertarian, 5,886.

1988, Bush, Rep., 2,416,549; Dukakis, Dem., 1,939,629; Fulani, Ind., 12,017; Paul, Ind., 11,926.

1992, Clinton, Dem., 1,984,942; Bush, Rep., 1,894,310; Perot, Ind., 1,036,426; Marrou, Libertarian, 7,252; Fulani, New Alliance, 6,413; Gritz, Populist/America First, 4,699; Hagelin, Natural Law, 3,437; LaRouche, Ind., 2,446.

1996, Clinton, Dem., 2,148,222; Dole, Rep., 1,859,883; Perot, Ref., 483,207; Browne, Ind., 12,851; Moorehead, Ind., 10,813; Hagelin, Natural Law, 9,120; Phillips, Ind., 7,361.

Oklahoma

County	1996 Clinton (D)	Dole (R)	Perot (RF)	1992 Clinton (D)	Bush (R)	Perot (I)
Adair.....	2,792	2,956	751	2,645	2,994	914
Alfalfa	796	1,504	348	741	1,567	722
Atoka....	2,281	1,542	532	2,336	1,561	1,255
Beaver....	515	1,893	199	580	1,699	565
Beckham .	2,797	2,912	817	2,947	2,913	1,929
Blaine ...	1,832	2,127	563	1,564	2,209	1,258
Bryan	5,962	3,943	1,396	6,259	3,452	3,713
Caddo ...	4,844	3,422	1,358	4,861	3,664	2,911
Canadian ..	8,977	18,139	3,297	7,215	16,756	8,985
Carter ...	6,979	6,769	1,997	7,171	5,947	5,188
Cherokee..	6,817	5,046	1,777	6,794	4,977	3,297
Choctaw...	3,198	1,580	589	3,413	1,641	1,298
Cimarron ..	361	986	102	395	965	254
Cleveland..	26,038	36,457	6,785	24,404	35,561	20,352
Coal	1,205	734	323	1,448	714	618
Comanche .	12,841	14,461	2,819	12,237	15,704	7,463
Cotton ...	1,258	1,042	381	1,314	910	853
Craig.....	2,649	2,058	758	2,780	2,106	1,316
Creek	9,674	9,861	2,837	9,118	10,055	5,984
Custer	4,027	4,723	1,101	3,540	5,362	2,741
Delaware .	5,094	5,230	1,573	4,842	4,840	2,689
Dewey....	816	1,179	292	845	1,244	684
Ellis......	619	1,090	279	594	1,072	632
Garfield ..	7,504	11,712	2,523	6,720	13,095	5,559
Garvin ...	4,639	3,745	1,345	4,811	3,983	3,014
Grady	6,256	7,228	2,048	6,177	6,997	4,528
Grant....	867	1,382	384	864	1,311	871
Greer.....	1,240	905	361	1,162	964	640
Harmon...	729	448	143	783	496	326
Harper....	511	1,036	219	486	1,038	501
Haskell ...	2,762	1,442	590	3,069	1,461	995
Hughes ...	2,748	1,510	730	2,850	1,522	1,158
Jackson...	3,245	4,422	892	3,273	3,893	2,227
Jefferson ..	1,430	865	337	1,580	671	758
Johnston ..	1,998	1,229	532	2,096	1,191	1,040
Kay......	6,882	9,741	2,785	6,643	9,115	6,984
Kingfisher..	1,626	3,423	621	1,379	3,479	1,534

County	1996 Clinton (D)	Dole (R)	Perot (RF)	1992 Clinton (D)	Bush (R)	Perot (I)
Kiowa	1,973	1,638	510	2,143	1,635	1,114
Latimer	2,222	1,189	578	2,606	1,212	1,049
Le Flore	6,831	5,689	1,721	7,843	5,850	3,021
Lincoln	4,332	5,243	1,500	3,904	5,315	3,160
Logan	4,854	5,949	1,410	4,453	6,071	3,239
Love	1,675	1,224	385	1,708	922	1,033
McClain	3,753	4,363	1,289	3,378	4,377	2,996
McCurtain	4,350	3,892	1,483	5,082	3,519	2,852
McIntosh	4,219	2,400	1,044	4,184	2,225	1,469
Major	900	2,188	410	731	2,154	857
Marshall	2,624	1,605	663	2,519	1,478	1,486
Mayes	6,377	5,268	1,617	6,432	5,445	3,235
Murray	2,620	1,712	723	2,594	1,536	1,447
Muskogee	12,963	8,974	3,163	13,619	8,782	5,454
Noble	1,756	2,318	694	1,333	2,474	1,449
Nowata	1,788	1,457	586	1,912	1,531	1,063
Okfuskee	2,074	1,380	536	2,141	1,580	889
Oklahoma	80,438	120,429	18,411	76,271	126,788	56,139
Okmulgee	7,555	4,246	1,487	7,767	4,586	3,013
Osage	7,342	5,827	1,938	6,894	5,891	4,477
Ottawa	5,844	4,127	1,496	6,304	4,141	2,721
Pawnee	2,663	2,560	756	2,612	2,675	1,656
Payne	9,985	11,686	2,472	9,886	13,032	7,852
Pittsburg	8,475	5,966	2,217	8,523	5,659	4,594
Pontotoc	6,470	5,366	1,712	6,350	5,206	3,916
Pottawatomie	9,141	9,802	2,724	8,616	10,350	6,520
Pushmataha	2,270	1,458	588	2,553	1,319	1,000
Roger Mills	733	959	233	767	890	505
Rogers	9,544	12,883	3,022	8,257	12,455	7,101
Seminole	4,225	2,935	1,041	4,624	3,253	2,330
Sequoyah	5,665	4,733	1,673	6,092	4,925	2,486
Stephens	7,248	8,144	2,312	7,644	7,085	5,692
Texas	1,408	4,139	518	1,487	4,059	1,417
Tillman	1,827	1,346	471	1,749	1,377	1,039
Tulsa	76,924	111,243	18,201	71,165	117,465	49,760
Wagoner	7,749	9,392	2,357	7,041	9,053	5,381
Washington	6,732	11,605	2,255	6,593	11,342	5,664
Washita	1,913	1,994	748	1,929	1,912	1,468
Woods	1,431	2,151	497	1,361	2,225	1,167
Woodward	2,403	4,093	963	2,063	4,006	2,411
Totals	488,105	582,315	130,788	473,066	592,929	319,878

Oklahoma Vote Since 1948

1948, Truman, Dem., 452,782; Dewey, Rep., 268,817.

1952, Eisenhower, Rep., 518,045; Stevenson, Dem., 430,939.

1956, Eisenhower, Rep., 473,769; Stevenson, Dem., 385,581.

1960, Kennedy, Dem., 370,111; Nixon, Rep., 533,039.

1964, Johnson, Dem., 519,834; Goldwater, Rep., 412,665.

1968, Nixon, Rep., 449,697; Humphrey, Dem., 301,658; Wallace, 3d Party, 191,731.

1972, Nixon, Rep., 759,025; McGovern, Dem., 247,147; Schmitz, Amer., 23,728.

1976, Carter, Dem., 532,442; Ford, Rep., 545,708; McCarthy, Ind., 14,101.

1980, Reagan, Rep., 695,570; Carter, Dem., 402,026; Anderson, Ind., 38,284; Clark, Libertarian, 13,828.

1984, Reagan, Rep., 861,530; Mondale, Dem., 385,080; Bergland, Libertarian, 9,066.

1988, Bush, Rep., 678,367; Dukakis, Dem., 483,423; Paul, Lib., 6,261; Fulani, New Alliance, 2,985.

1992, Clinton, Dem., 473,066; Bush, Rep., 592,929; Perot, Ind., 319,878; Marrou, Libertarian, 4,486.

1996, Dole, Rep., 582,315; Clinton, Dem., 488,105; Perot, Ref., 130,788; Browne, Libertarian, 5,505.

Oregon

County	1996 Clinton (D)	Dole (R)	Perot (RF)	1992 Clinton (D)	Bush (R)	Perot (I)
Baker	2,547	3,975	900	2,395	2,862	2,191
Benton	17,211	12,450	2,445	17,966	11,550	8,103
Clackamas	67,709	59,443	12,304	60,310	53,724	39,776
Clatsop	7,732	5,334	1,582	7,700	4,683	4,316
Columbia	9,275	6,205	2,330	8,298	5,227	5,670
Coos	12,171	10,886	3,460	12,072	9,284	7,989
Crook	2,607	3,250	948	2,508	2,703	2,024
Curry	4,202	4,790	1,560	3,841	3,809	3,310
Deschutes	17,151	21,135	5,306	15,693	15,655	12,293
Douglas	15,250	21,855	4,465	14,137	19,011	12,377
Gilliam	485	398	143	374	377	283
Grant	1,180	2,110	432	1,135	1,496	1,302
Harney	980	1,948	506	973	1,350	1,024
Hood River	3,654	2,794	721	3,100	3,005	2,005
Jackson	29,230	33,771	7,470	29,146	28,704	18,633
Jefferson	2,555	2,634	813	2,161	1,962	1,741
Josephine	11,113	16,048	3,546	11,007	13,003	8,426
Klamath	7,207	12,116	2,538	7,918	11,864	6,636
Lake	962	2,239	385	1,019	1,791	980
Lane	69,461	48,253	11,498	74,083	41,789	34,906

County	1996 Clinton (D)	Dole (R)	Perot (RF)	1992 Clinton (D)	Bush (R)	Perot (I)
Lincoln	10,552	6,717	2,269	9,603	5,716	6,127
Linn	17,041	18,331	4,773	15,399	16,461	13,256
Malheur	2,827	6,045	844	2,539	5,374	2,654
Marion	48,637	46,415	8,802	41,137	42,145	26,156
Morrow	1,426	1,381	455	1,174	1,187	1,089
Multnomah	159,878	71,094	17,536	165,081	72,326	58,236
Polk	10,942	11,478	2,093	9,551	10,082	5,818
Sherman	444	476	126	362	424	326
Tillamook	5,775	3,884	1,263	5,040	3,359	2,997
Umatilla	8,774	9,703	2,500	6,787	7,095	5,581
Union	4,379	5,414	1,241	3,990	4,223	3,305
Wallowa	1,321	2,379	483	1,203	1,630	1,209
Wasco	4,967	3,662	1,004	4,663	3,242	3,008
Washington	76,619	65,221	11,446	67,528	57,146	41,575
Wheeler	299	418	121	267	357	227
Yamhill	13,078	13,900	2,913	11,148	11,693	8,312
Totals	649,641	538,152	121,221	621,314	475,757	354,091

Oregon Vote Since 1948

1948, Truman, Dem., 243,147; Dewey, Rep., 260,904; Wallace, Prog., 14,978; Thomas, Soc., 5,051.

1952, Eisenhower, Rep., 420,815; Stevenson, Dem., 270,579; Hallinan, Ind., 3,665.

1956, Eisenhower, Rep., 406,393; Stevenson, Dem., 329,204.

1960, Kennedy, Dem., 367,402; Nixon, Rep., 408,060.

1964, Johnson, Dem., 501,017; Goldwater, Rep., 282,779; write-in, 2,509.

1968, Nixon, Rep., 408,433; Humphrey, Dem., 358,866; Wallace, 3d Party, 49,683; write-in, McCarthy, 1,496; N. Rockefeller, 69; others, 1,075.

1972, Nixon, Rep., 486,686; McGovern, Dem., 392,760; Schmitz, Amer., 46,211; write-in, 2,289.

1976, Carter, Dem., 490,407; Ford, Rep., 492,120; McCarthy, Ind., 40,207; write-in, 7,142.

1980, Reagan, Rep., 571,044; Carter, Dem., 456,890; Anderson, Ind., 112,389; Clark, Libertarian, 25,838; Commoner, Citizens, 13,642; scattered, 1,713.

1984, Reagan, Rep., 658,700; Mondale, Dem., 536,479.

1988, Bush, Rep., 560,126; Dukakis, Dem., 616,206; Paul, Lib., 14,811; Fulani, Ind., 6,487.

1992, Clinton, Dem., 621,314; Bush, Rep., 475,757; Perot, Ind., 354,091; Marrou, Libertarian, 4,277; Fulani, New Alliance, 3,030.

1996, Clinton, Dem., 649,641; Dole, Rep., 538,152; Perot, Ref., 121,221; Nader, Pacific, 49,415; Browne, Libertarian, 8,903; Phillips, Taxpayers, 3,379; Hagelin, Natural Law, 2,798; Hollis, Soc., 1,922.

Pennsylvania

County	1996 Clinton (D)	Dole (R)	Perot (RF)	1992 Clinton (D)	Bush (R)	Perot (I)
Adams	10,774	15,338	3,186	9,576	13,552	6,313
Allegheny	284,480	204,067	42,309	324,004	183,035	103,470
Armstrong	11,130	11,052	3,452	12,995	9,122	6,166
Beaver	39,578	26,048	8,276	44,887	21,361	15,954
Bedford	5,954	10,064	2,041	5,840	9,216	3,731
Berks	49,887	56,289	13,788	46,031	52,939	31,663
Blair	15,036	21,282	4,014	14,857	21,447	8,284
Bradford	7,736	10,393	2,712	6,903	10,221	5,452
Bucks	103,313	94,899	24,544	97,902	94,584	53,931
Butler	21,990	32,038	6,145	22,303	23,656	15,013
Cambria	30,391	20,341	7,837	34,334	20,770	11,070
Cameron	822	1,113	283	824	1,173	676
Carbon	9,457	7,193	2,992	9,072	7,243	5,222
Centre	21,145	20,935	4,173	21,177	20,478	9,356
Chester	64,783	77,029	14,067	59,643	74,002	34,536
Clarion	5,954	6,916	2,064	5,584	6,477	3,619
Clearfield	11,991	12,987	3,758	12,247	11,553	6,989
Clinton	5,658	4,293	1,424	5,397	4,471	2,654
Columbia	8,379	8,234	3,654	8,261	9,742	5,683
Crawford	12,943	14,659	3,519	12,813	14,112	7,392
Cumberland	28,749	43,943	5,669	26,635	43,447	14,344
Dauphin	40,936	44,417	6,967	36,990	45,479	16,063
Delaware	115,946	92,628	21,883	111,210	108,587	43,728
Elk	5,749	4,889	2,293	5,016	4,908	3,885
Erie	57,508	39,884	10,386	56,381	39,283	21,510
Fayette	26,359	14,019	5,722	30,577	12,820	10,162
Forest	964	902	325	890	801	448
Franklin	14,980	25,392	4,127	13,440	23,387	6,941
Fulton	1,620	2,665	554	1,588	2,558	869
Greene	7,620	4,002	2,052	8,438	3,482	3,186
Huntingdon	5,285	7,324	1,813	5,153	7,249	3,273
Indiana	10,929	12,974	3,674	15,194	10,966	7,089
Jefferson	5,846	8,156	2,322	5,998	7,271	4,403
Juniata	2,896	4,128	911	2,601	3,980	1,819
Lackawanna	46,377	26,930	8,189	45,054	33,443	15,667
Lancaster	49,120	92,875	11,601	44,255	88,447	26,807
Lawrence	18,993	13,088	4,002	20,830	12,359	7,950
Lebanon	14,187	21,885	4,235	12,350	21,512	9,005

County	1996 Clinton (D)	Dole (R)	Perot (RF)	1992 Clinton (D)	Bush (R)	Perot (I)
Lehigh . . .	48,568	45,103	10,947	46,711	42,631	24,853
Luzerne . .	60,174	43,577	12,424	56,623	49,285	21,007
Lycoming .	13,516	21,535	3,855	13,315	20,536	9,170
McKean . .	5,509	6,838	2,350	5,331	6,965	4,019
Mercer . .	23,003	17,213	5,108	23,264	16,081	10,277
Mifflin. . . .	5,327	6,888	1,392	4,946	6,300	3,382
Monroe . .	16,547	17,326	4,650	13,468	14,557	9,257
Montgomery	143,664	121,047	24,392	136,572	125,704	53,738
Montour . .	2,183	2,785	784	2,150	3,096	1,373
Northampton	43,959	35,726	9,848	42,203	34,429	20,234
Northumberland	13,418	13,551	5,173	12,814	15,057	7,782
Perry	4,611	8,156	1,609	4,086	7,871	3,334
Philadelphia	412,988	85,345	29,329	434,904	133,328	65,455
Pike. . . .	5,509	6,697	1,873	4,382	6,084	3,019
Potter . . .	2,146	3,714	925	1,892	3,452	1,687
Schuylkill .	24,860	22,920	8,471	23,679	25,780	13,398
Snyder . . .	3,405	6,742	1,451	2,952	6,934	2,686
Somerset .	12,719	14,735	3,968	12,493	13,858	6,333
Sullivan . .	1,071	1,352	418	1,030	1,340	731
Susquehanna.	5,912	7,354	2,266	5,368	7,356	3,946
Tioga	4,961	7,382	1,993	4,868	7,823	3,804
Union. . . .	3,658	6,570	1,431	3,623	6,362	2,255
Venango .	8,205	8,398	2,777	8,230	8,545	4,695
Warren . . .	7,291	7,056	2,504	6,972	6,585	4,795
Washington	40,952	27,777	8,661	46,143	21,977	16,083
Wayne . . .	5,928	8,077	2,126	4,817	8,318	3,727
Westmoreland	63,686	62,058	16,230	69,817	47,315	37,036
Wyoming .	4,049	4,888	1,414	3,158	5,143	2,525
York	49,596	65,188	11,652	46,113	60,130	27,743
Totals . . .	2,215,819	1,801,169	430,984	2,239,164	1,791,841	902,667

Pennsylvania Vote Since 1948

1948, Truman, Dem., 1,752,426; Dewey, Rep., 1,902,197; Wallace, Prog., 55,161; Thomas, Soc., 11,325; Watson, Proh., 10,338; Dobbs, Militant Workers, 2,133; Teichert, Ind. Gov., 1,461.

1952, Eisenhower, Rep., 2,415,789; Stevenson, Dem., 2,146,269; Hamblen, Proh., 8,771; Hallinan, Prog., 4,200; Hoopes, Soc., 2,684; Dobbs, Militant Workers, 1,502; Hass, Ind. Gov., 1,347; scattered, 155.

1956, Eisenhower, Rep., 2,585,252; Stevenson, Dem., 1,981,769; Hass, Soc. Labor, 7,447; Dobbs, Militant Workers, 2,035.

1960, Kennedy, Dem., 2,556,282; Nixon, Rep., 2,439,956; Hass, Soc. Labor, 7,185; Dobbs, Soc. Workers, 2,678; scattering, 440.

1964, Johnson, Dem., 3,130,954; Goldwater, Rep., 1,673,657; DeBerry, Soc. Workers, 10,456; Hass, Soc. Labor, 5,092; scattering, 2,531.

1968, Nixon, Rep., 2,090,017; Humphrey, Dem., 2,259,405; Wallace, 3d Party, 378,582; Blomen, Soc. Labor, 4,977; Halstead, Soc. Workers, 4,862; Gregory, Peace and Freedom, 7,821; others, 2,264.

1972, Nixon, Rep., 2,714,521; McGovern, Dem., 1,796,951; Schmitz, Amer., 70,593; Jenness, Soc. Workers, 4,639; Hall, Com., 2,686; others, 2,715.

1976, Carter, Dem., 2,328,677; Ford, Rep., 2,205,604; McCarthy, Ind., 50,584; Maddox, Constitution, 25,344; Camejo, Soc. Workers, 3,009; LaRouche, U.S. Labor, 2,744; Hall, Com., 1,891; others, 2,934.

1980, Reagan, Rep., 2,261,872; Carter, Dem., 1,937,540; Anderson, Ind., 292,921; Clark, Libertarian, 33,263; DeBerry, Soc. Workers, 20,291; Commoner, Consumer, 10,430; Hall, Com., 5,184.

1984, Reagan, Rep., 2,584,323; Mondale, Dem., 2,228,131; Bergland, Libertarian, 6,982.

1988, Bush, Rep., 2,300,087; Dukakis, Dem., 2,194,944; McCarthy, Consumer, 19,158; Paul, Lib., 12,051.

1992, Clinton, Dem., 2,239,164; Bush, Rep., 1,791,841; Perot, Ind., 902,667; Marrou, Libertarian, 21,477; Fulani, New Alliance, 4,661.

1996, Clinton, Dem., 2,215,819; Dole, Rep., 1,801,169; Perot, Ref., 430,984; Browne, Libertarian, 28,000; Phillips, Constitutional, 19,552; Hagelin, Natural Law, 5,783.

Rhode Island

City	1996 Clinton (D)	Dole (R)	Perot (RF)	1992 Clinton (D)	Bush (R)	Perot (I)
Cranston . .	20,901	9,098	3,457	18,589	12,450	8,331
East Providence. . . .	12,846	4,199	1,971	11,701	5,843	4,661
Pawtucket .	14,719	3,877	2,508	14,177	6,322	6,244
Providence.	29,450	7,068	2,733	32,536	11,519	7,816
Warwick . .	23,152	10,414	4,541	20,504	13,348	10,526
Other	131,982	70,027	28,513	115,792	82,119	67,467
Totals. . . .	233,050	104,683	43,723	213,299	131,601	105,045

Rhode Island Vote Since 1948

1948, Truman, Dem., 188,736; Dewey, Rep., 135,787; Wallace, Prog., 2,619; Thomas, Soc., 429; Teichert, Soc. Labor, 131.

1952, Eisenhower, Rep., 210,935; Stevenson, Dem., 203,293; Hallinan, Prog., 187; Hass, Soc. Labor, 83.

1956, Eisenhower, Rep., 225,819; Stevenson, Dem., 161,790.

1960, Kennedy, Dem., 258,032; Nixon, Rep., 147,502.

1964, Johnson, Dem., 315,463; Goldwater, Rep., 74,615.

1968, Nixon, Rep., 122,359; Humphrey, Dem., 246,518; Wallace, 3d Party, 15,678; Halstead, Soc. Workers, 383.

1972, Nixon, Rep., 220,383; McGovern, Dem., 194,645; Jenness, Soc. Workers, 729.

1976, Carter, Dem., 227,636; Ford, Rep., 181,249; MacBride, Libertarian, 715; Camejo, Soc. Workers, 462; Hall, Com., 334; Levin, Soc. Labor, 188.

1980, Reagan, Rep., 154,793; Carter, Dem., 198,342; Anderson, Ind., 59,819; Clark, Libertarian, 2,458; Hall, Com., 218; McReynolds, Soc., 170; DeBerry, Soc. Workers, 90; Griswold, Workers World, 77.

1984, Reagan, Rep., 212,080; Mondale, Dem., 197,106; Bergland, Libertarian, 277.

1988, Bush, Rep., 177,761; Dukakis, Dem., 225,123; Paul, Lib., 825; Fulani, New Alliance, 280.

1992, Clinton, Dem., 213,299; Bush, Rep., 131,601; Perot, Ind., 105,045; Fulani, New Alliance, 1,878.

1996, Clinton, Dem., 233,050; Dole, Rep., 104,683; Perot, Ref., 43,723; Nader, Green, 6,040; Browne, Libertarian, 1,109; Phillips, Taxpayers, 1,021; Hagelin, Natural Law, 435; Moorehead, Workers World, 186.

South Carolina

County	1996 Clinton (D)	Dole (R)	Perot (RF)	1992 Clinton (D)	Bush (R)	Perot (I)
Abbeville . .	3,493	3,054	537	3,968	3,317	1,036
Aiken.	14,314	26,539	1,984	14,802	25,731	6,056
Allendale . .	2,222	941	87	2,159	1,049	212
Anderson . .	17,460	24,137	3,896	16,072	24,793	6,966
Bamberg . .	3,380	1,715	192	3,426	1,906	360
Barnwell. . .	3,620	3,808	310	3,344	4,026	752
Beaufort. . .	15,764	17,575	1,838	11,466	14,735	4,966
Berkeley. . .	13,358	17,691	1,922	12,533	18,048	4,632
Calhoun . . .	2,716	2,520	316	2,770	2,418	564
Charleston .	43,571	48,675	3,514	40,095	47,403	10,354
Cherokee .	5,821	6,689	1,064	5,453	6,887	2,186
Chester . . .	5,108	3,157	758	5,458	3,451	1,350
Chesterfield.	5,734	4,028	768	5,691	4,183	1,315
Clarendon .	5,930	3,841	395	6,033	4,147	744
Colleton . . .	5,329	4,462	550	5,455	4,545	1,245
Darlington. .	8,943	8,220	898	9,090	8,912	1,863
Dillon.	3,992	2,774	275	4,953	3,575	831
Dorchester .	9,931	15,283	1,591	9,160	15,004	3,648
Edgefield . .	3,576	3,640	244	3,433	3,339	596
Fairfield . . .	4,719	2,414	284	4,867	2,518	652
Florence. . .	15,804	18,490	1,563	15,569	19,802	3,499
Georgetown.	8,298	7,023	950	7,494	6,870	1,840
Greenville. .	41,605	71,210	6,761	34,651	65,066	13,699
Greenwood.	8,193	8,865	985	7,621	9,079	2,101
Hampton . .	4,828	2,111	344	4,332	2,402	564
Horry.	23,722	26,159	4,446	18,896	23,489	8,472
Jasper. . . .	4,053	2,024	348	3,453	1,725	549
Kershaw. . .	6,764	8,513	996	6,585	8,499	2,150
Lancaster. .	8,752	7,544	1,598	8,307	7,757	2,563
Laurens. . .	7,055	8,057	1,341	6,638	8,347	2,157
Lee	3,588	1,973	320	4,454	2,730	611
Lexington. .	18,907	39,658	3,703	18,312	41,759	8,652
McCormick .	1,858	1,104	148	1,846	899	295
Marion	6,359	3,595	356	5,843	3,647	822
Marlboro . .	5,348	2,148	494	5,111	2,526	895
Newberry . .	4,804	5,670	682	4,896	5,980	1,393
Oconee . . .	7,398	10,503	1,961	6,617	10,379	3,405
Orangeburg.	18,610	10,494	1,112	18,440	11,328	2,383
Pickens . . .	8,369	17,151	2,211	8,275	17,008	4,128
Richland. . .	52,222	39,092	3,158	53,648	43,744	7,918
Saluda. . . .	2,486	2,825	371	2,393	2,968	833
Spartanburg.	26,814	35,972	3,885	25,488	37,707	8,900
Sumter. . . .	12,198	12,080	933	11,852	12,576	2,062
Union.	5,407	3,855	749	4,644	4,647	1,371
Williamsburg	6,987	3,957	375	8,077	5,289	864
York	16,873	22,222	3,173	15,844	21,297	6,418
Totals	506,283	573,458	64,386	479,514	577,507	138,872

South Carolina Vote Since 1948

1948, Thurmond, States' Rights, 102,607; Truman, Dem., 34,423; Dewey, Rep., 5,386; Wallace, Prog., 154; Thomas, Soc., 1.

1952, Eisenhower ran on two tickets. Under state law vote cast for two Eisenhower slates of electors could not be combined. Eisenhower, Ind., 158,289; Rep., 9,793; total, 168,082; Stevenson, Dem., 173,004; Hamblen, Proh., 1.

1956, Eisenhower, Rep., 75,700; Stevenson, Dem., 136,372; Byrd, Ind., 88,509; Andrews, Ind., 2.

1960, Kennedy, Dem., 198,129; Nixon, Rep., 188,558; write-in, 1.

1964, Johnson, Dem., 215,700; Goldwater, Rep., 309,048; write-ins: Nixon, 1, Wallace, 5; Powell, 1; Thurmond, 1.

1968, Nixon, Rep., 254,062; Humphrey, Dem., 197,486; Wallace, 3d Party, 215,430.

1972, Nixon, Rep., 477,044; McGovern, Dem., 184,559; United Citizens, 2,265; Schmitz, Amer., 10,075; write-in, 17.

1976, Carter, Dem., 450,807; Ford, Rep., 346,149; Anderson, Amer., 2,996; Maddox, Amer. Ind., 1,950; write-in, 681.

1980, Reagan, Rep., 439,277; Carter, Dem., 428,220; Anderson, Ind., 13,868; Clark, Libertarian, 4,807; Rarick, Amer. Ind., 2,086.

1984, Reagan, Rep., 615,539; Mondale, Dem., 344,459; Bergland, Libertarian, 4,359.

1988, Bush, Rep., 606,443; Dukakis, Dem., 370,554; Paul, Lib., 4,935; Fulani, United Citizens, 4,077.

1992, Clinton, Dem., 479,514; Bush, Rep., 577,507; Perot, Ind., 138,872; Marrou, Libertarian, 2,719; Phillips, U.S. Taxpayers, 2,680; Fulani, New Alliance, 1,235.

1996, Dole, Rep., 573,458; Clinton, Dem., 506,283; Perot, Ref./Patriot, 64,386; Browne, Libertarian, 4,271; Phillips, Taxpayers, 2,043; Hagelin, Natural Law, 1,248.

County	1996 Clinton (D)	Dole (R)	Perot (RF)	1992 Clinton (D)	Bush (R)	Perot (I)
Spink	1,636	1,651	360	1,732	1,527	839
Stanley	454	795	121	427	719	240
Sully	321	592	106	273	565	167
Todd	1,380	482	108	915	456	246
Tripp	1,088	1,680	337	1,046	1,459	848
Turner	1,682	1,970	385	1,507	1,906	867
Union	2,378	2,234	555	2,210	1,784	1,085
Walworth	939	1,461	366	829	1,439	628
Yankton	3,775	3,885	1,073	3,404	3,430	2,511
Ziebach	483	375	62	280	328	117
Totals	139,333	150,543	31,250	124,888	136,718	73,295

South Dakota Vote Since 1948

1948, Truman, Dem., 117,653; Dewey, Rep., 129,651; Wallace, Prog., 2,801.

1952, Eisenhower, Rep., 203,857; Stevenson, Dem., 90,426.

1956, Eisenhower, Rep., 171,569; Stevenson, Dem., 122,288.

1960, Kennedy, Dem., 128,070; Nixon, Rep., 178,417.

1964, Johnson, Dem., 163,010; Goldwater, Rep., 130,108.

1968, Nixon, Rep., 149,841; Humphrey, Dem., 118,023; Wallace, 3d Party, 13,400.

1972, Nixon, Rep., 166,476; McGovern, Dem., 139,945; Jenness, Soc. Workers, 994.

1976, Carter, Dem., 147,068; Ford, Rep., 151,505; MacBride, Libertarian, 1,619; Hall, Com., 318; Camejo, Soc. Workers, 168.

1980, Reagan, Rep., 198,343; Carter, Dem., 103,855; Anderson, Ind., 21,431; Clark, Libertarian, 3,824; Pulley, Soc. Workers, 250.

1984, Reagan, Rep., 200,267; Mondale, Dem., 116,113.

1988, Bush, Rep., 165,415; Dukakis, Dem., 145,560; Paul, Lib., 1,060; Fulani, New Alliance, 730.

1992, Clinton, Dem., 124,888; Bush, Rep., 136,718; Perot, Ind., 73,295.

1996, Dole, Rep., 150,543; Clinton, Dem., 139,333; Perot, Ref., 31,250; Browne, Libertarian, 1,472; Phillips, Taxpayers, 912; Hagelin, Natural Law, 316.

South Dakota

County	1996 Clinton (D)	Dole (R)	Perot (RF)	1992 Clinton (D)	Bush (R)	Perot (I)
Aurora	664	709	199	680	594	435
Beadle	3,984	3,670	842	3,925	3,363	1,819
Bennett	507	539	93	413	556	221
Bon Homme	1,569	1,428	391	1,294	1,212	836
Brookings	5,105	5,112	979	4,645	4,698	2,614
Brown	7,913	6,801	1,622	7,521	6,665	3,812
Brule	1,091	981	281	1,060	908	687
Buffalo	465	134	35	282	137	72
Butte	1,132	1,947	541	973	1,674	1,039
Campbell	202	623	140	222	574	252
Chas. Mix.	1,913	1,711	390	1,639	1,570	886
Clark	956	998	272	799	803	761
Clay	2,980	2,008	505	2,826	1,869	1,303
Codington	4,722	4,995	1,239	3,701	3,943	3,262
Corson	539	533	216	444	483	321
Custer	1,122	1,740	418	1,078	1,422	845
Davison	3,364	3,371	737	3,285	3,111	1,706
Day	1,840	1,282	395	1,578	1,161	973
Deuel	1,090	955	275	880	778	761
Dewey	1,114	657	195	766	642	340
Douglas	524	1,210	161	481	1,175	403
Edmunds	973	1,055	263	894	944	415
Fall River	1,357	1,636	417	1,416	1,533	792
Faulk	493	726	165	488	658	281
Grant	1,805	1,782	471	1,484	1,595	1,018
Gregory	923	1,208	286	879	1,027	688
Haakon	284	887	110	209	860	245
Hamlin	1,101	1,352	285	826	1,133	774
Hand	803	1,187	250	785	1,130	624
Hanson	541	801	170	566	522	341
Harding	151	537	90	139	515	225
Hughes	2,788	4,469	531	2,578	4,325	1,160
Hutchinson	1,285	2,177	409	1,211	2,002	920
Hyde	309	493	95	301	440	211
Jackson/Washabaugh	423	646	88	351	627	184
Jerauld	656	530	151	600	518	346
Jones	184	463	75	166	454	154
Kingsbury	1,357	1,297	320	1,267	1,113	744
Lake	2,526	1,966	593	2,388	1,890	1,299
Lawrence	3,568	4,430	1,308	3,157	3,770	2,673
Lincoln	3,643	4,201	682	2,943	3,365	1,593
Lyman	646	726	130	486	669	311
McCook	1,166	1,292	245	1,167	1,177	617
McPherson	463	1,080	182	478	945	322
Marshall	1,185	861	189	1,056	810	427
Meade	2,960	4,984	1,133	2,694	4,724	2,611
Mellette	302	417	67	277	417	140
Miner	739	571	170	698	543	332
Minnehaha	29,790	27,432	4,425	27,016	25,081	11,496
Moody	1,443	1,024	294	1,473	898	719
Pennington	12,784	19,293	3,149	11,106	18,052	8,358
Perkins	460	983	225	566	872	541
Potter	534	979	181	493	901	375
Roberts	2,186	1,646	474	1,716	1,437	954
Sanborn	647	630	151	632	595	376
Shannon	1,926	253	87	1,267	225	137

Tennessee

County	1996 Clinton (D)	Dole (R)	Perot (RF)	1992 Clinton (D)	Bush (R)	Perot (I)
Anderson	13,457	11,943	1,817	13,482	11,838	3,149
Bedford	5,735	4,634	823	5,978	3,836	1,541
Benton	4,341	2,395	663	3,896	1,625	559
Bledsoe	1,621	1,626	251	1,884	1,776	352
Blount	14,687	19,310	2,556	14,655	18,415	4,468
Bradley	9,095	15,478	1,856	9,889	16,528	3,212
Campbell	6,122	4,393	785	6,756	4,897	1,240
Cannon	2,318	1,468	361	2,593	1,229	495
Carroll	4,912	4,206	697	5,741	4,842	1,139
Carter	6,218	10,540	1,383	6,502	10,712	1,898
Cheatham	4,883	4,283	705	4,817	3,496	1,433
Chester	1,922	2,746	203	2,317	2,834	439
Claiborne	3,861	4,023	727	4,509	4,065	860
Clay	1,559	1,108	316	1,922	1,072	223
Cocke	3,326	4,481	798	3,495	5,298	1,124
Coffee	7,951	7,038	1,205	8,534	6,047	2,420
Crockett	2,256	1,872	201	2,657	2,180	507
Cumberland	6,676	8,096	1,399	6,393	7,116	2,200
Davidson	110,865	78,453	9,018	106,355	76,567	20,184
Decatur	2,262	1,712	229	2,633	1,667	351
De Kalb	3,213	1,696	342	4,382	1,714	608
Dickson	7,458	5,283	996	7,863	4,450	1,730
Dyer	5,602	5,059	676	5,845	5,668	1,241
Fayette	4,655	4,406	416	4,211	3,713	657
Fentress	2,332	2,307	386	2,730	2,391	606
Franklin	6,929	5,296	1,057	7,773	4,507	1,837
Gibson	8,851	6,614	891	9,555	7,161	1,536
Giles	4,948	3,269	733	5,601	2,827	1,309
Grainger	2,162	2,875	382	2,242	2,772	513
Greene	6,885	9,779	1,604	7,857	9,912	2,930
Grundy	2,596	1,094	326	2,997	1,004	366
Hamblen	7,006	9,797	1,106	7,114	8,898	1,760
Hamilton	48,008	55,205	6,699	46,770	53,476	14,400
Hancock	760	1,259	116	1,000	1,274	151
Hardeman	4,859	2,961	346	4,832	3,122	594
Hardin	3,508	3,980	594	3,922	3,875	734
Hawkins	6,367	8,164	1,282	6,623	7,758	1,847
Haywood	3,565	2,293	154	3,511	2,518	331
Henderson	2,841	4,002	408	3,502	4,719	785
Henry	6,153	4,272	992	6,797	3,661	1,588
Hickman	3,917	2,002	460	4,093	1,820	795
Houston	1,868	742	182	2,012	648	280
Humphreys	3,675	1,892	423	3,875	1,641	609
Jackson	2,000	811	000	2,009	709	222
Jefferson	4,688	6,446	882	4,740	6,184	1,385
Johnson	1,698	3,137	489	1,781	3,170	574
Knox	61,158	70,761	6,402	59,702	66,607	15,669
Lake	1,273	589	110	1,449	680	151
Lauderdale	4,349	2,481	308	4,452	2,928	561
Lawrence	6,188	6,115	973	6,816	5,608	1,403

County	Clinton (D)	1996 Dole (R)	Perot (RF)	Clinton (D)	1992 Bush (R)	Perot (I)
Lewis....	1,971	1,298	316	2,491	1,218	434
Lincoln...	4,361	4,551	761	5,063	3,814	1,371
Loudon...	5,552	7,097	889	5,414	6,444	1,602
McMinn..	5,987	7,655	1,033	6,682	7,453	1,812
McNairy..	4,050	3,960	519	4,691	4,093	774
Macon...	2,240	2,481	421	2,961	2,299	443
Madison..	13,577	14,908	968	13,629	14,869	2,634
Marion...	5,194	3,166	768	5,589	3,262	1,186
Marshall..	4,447	2,781	603	4,491	2,516	1,050
Maury...	10,367	8,737	1,366	9,997	7,440	2,821
Meigs...	1,476	1,228	245	1,673	1,355	453
Monroe...	4,872	5,257	713	5,384	6,025	936
Montgomery	16,498	15,133	1,781	14,507	13,011	3,753
Moore...	935	846	177	1,151	661	327
Morgan...	2,767	2,070	446	3,190	2,306	658
Obion...	6,226	4,310	932	6,497	4,812	1,494
Overton...	3,800	1,756	431	4,489	1,657	468
Perry....	1,444	747	178	1,889	708	317
Pickett...	901	1,046	116	1,144	1,094	121
Polk.....	2,450	1,910	377	2,583	1,584	419
Putnam...	10,047	9,093	1,487	10,858	7,998	2,473
Rhea....	3,969	4,476	694	4,289	4,860	1,163
Roane...	9,744	9,044	1,438	9,812	8,719	2,396
Robertson.	8,465	6,685	993	8,498	5,271	1,978
Rutherford	22,815	24,565	3,787	21,084	18,877	7,005
Scott....	2,506	2,646	431	2,730	3,011	643
Sequatchie	1,598	1,391	288	1,754	1,381	405
Sevier...	7,136	11,847	1,650	6,719	11,714	2,760
Shelby...	179,663	136,315	8,307	191,322	153,310	20,223
Smith....	3,812	1,857	346	5,061	1,482	486
Stewart...	2,962	1,306	386	2,779	1,046	487
Sullivan...	20,571	29,296	3,555	20,935	28,801	6,730
Sumner...	19,205	20,863	2,783	19,387	17,401	5,177
Tipton...	6,596	7,585	799	5,652	6,757	1,279
Trousdale.	1,615	683	190	1,846	565	243
Unicoi...	2,131	3,122	447	2,375	3,344	709
Union....	2,421	2,253	385	2,478	2,274	580
Van Buren	1,010	504	128	1,329	555	191
Warren...	6,389	4,226	917	7,189	3,704	1,415
Washington	13,259	18,960	2,237	13,071	18,206	4,002
Wayne...	1,574	2,715	323	1,868	2,955	424
Weakley..	5,657	4,622	873	5,691	4,800	1,355
White...	3,592	2,498	505	4,102	2,118	821
Williamson	15,231	27,699	2,071	13,053	22,015	5,026
Wilson...	13,655	13,817	1,841	13,861	12,061	3,848
Totals...	909,146	863,530	105,918	933,521	841,300	199,968

Tennessee Vote Since 1948

1948, Truman, Dem., 270,402; Dewey, Rep., 202,914; Thurmond, States' Rights, 73,815; Wallace, Prog., 1,864; Thomas, Soc., 1,288.

1952, Eisenhower, Rep., 446,147; Stevenson, Dem., 443,710; Hamblen, Proh., 1,432; Hallinan, Prog., 885; MacArthur, Christian Nationalist, 379.

1956, Eisenhower, Rep., 462,288; Stevenson, Dem., 456,507; Andrews, Ind., 19,820; Holtwick, Proh., 789.

1960, Kennedy, Dem., 481,453; Nixon, Rep., 556,577; Faubus, States' Rights, 11,304; Decker, Proh., 2,458.

1964, Johnson, Dem., 635,047; Goldwater, Rep., 508,965; write-in, 34.

1968, Nixon, Rep., 472,592; Humphrey, Dem., 351,233; Wallace, 3d Party, 424,792.

1972, Nixon, Rep., 813,147; McGovern, Dem., 357,293; Schmitz, Amer., 30,373; write-in, 369.

1976, Carter, Dem., 825,879; Ford, Rep., 633,969; Anderson, Amer., 5,769; McCarthy, Ind., 5,004; Maddox, Amer. Ind., 2,303; MacBride, Libertarian, 1,375; Hall, Com., 547; LaRouche, U.S. Labor, 512; Bubar, Proh., 442; Miller, Ind., 316; write-in, 230.

1980, Reagan, Rep., 787,761; Carter, Dem., 783,051; Anderson, Ind., 35,991; Clark, Libertarian, 7,116; Commoner, Citizens, 1,112; Bubar, Statesman, 521; McReynolds, Soc., 519; Hall, Com., 503; DeBerry, Soc. Workers, 490; Griswold, Workers World, 400; write-ins, 152.

1984, Reagan, Rep., 990,212; Mondale, Dem., 711,714; Bergland, Libertarian, 3,072.

1988, Bush, Rep., 947,233; Dukakis, Dem., 679,794; Paul, Ind., 2,041; Duke, Ind., 1,807.

1992, Clinton, Dem., 933,521; Bush, Rep., 841,300; Perot, Ind., 199,968; Marrou, Libertarian, 1,847.

1996, Clinton, Dem., 909,146; Dole, Rep., 863,530; Perot, Ind. (Ref.), 105,918; Nader, Ind., 6,427; Browne, Ind., 5,020; Phillips, Ind., 1,818; Collins, Ind., 688; Hagelin, Ind., 636; Michael, Ind., 408; Dodge, Ind., 324.

Texas

County	Clinton (D)	1996 Dole (R)	Perot (RF)	Clinton (D)	1992 Bush (R)	Perot (I)
Anderson..	5,693	6,458	1,170	5,322	5,598	3,519
Andrews..	1,181	2,360	431	1,081	2,266	875
Angelina..	11,346	11,789	2,160	10,318	9,722	6,204
Aransas..	2,964	3,769	655	2,246	2,826	1,676
Archer....	1,235	1,974	437	1,284	1,560	1,106
Armstrong.	272	582	75	278	561	187
Atascosa..	4,259	4,102	813	3,766	3,806	2,035
Austin...	2,719	4,669	577	2,278	4,015	1,585
Bailey....	706	1,246	109	677	1,308	376
Bandera..	1,383	3,700	520	1,059	2,674	1,537
Bastrop...	6,773	6,323	1,342	6,252	4,980	3,240
Baylor....	955	860	262	990	611	529
Bee....	4,561	3,611	539	4,083	3,633	1,367
Bell....	22,638	30,348	3,666	18,684	24,936	11,026
Bexar...	180,308	161,619	17,822	172,513	168,816	72,110
Blanco....	1,028	1,919	330	891	1,370	830
Borden...	93	194	45	106	184	87
Bosque...	2,427	2,840	739	2,173	2,300	1,999
Bowie....	13,657	12,750	2,760	11,825	11,776	6,659
Brazoria..	22,959	36,392	5,869	21,861	30,384	18,954
Brazos...	13,968	22,082	2,215	14,819	23,943	10,372
Brewster..	1,643	1,438	299	1,383	1,127	712
Briscoe...	408	416	65	430	360	164
Brooks....	2,945	413	108	2,856	585	318
Brown...	4,138	6,524	1,081	4,264	5,313	3,034
Burleson..	2,419	2,174	347	2,511	2,013	1,179
Burnet....	4,123	5,744	1,108	3,638	4,272	2,865
Caldwell..	3,961	3,239	545	3,794	2,749	1,776
Calhoun..	2,753	2,832	507	2,550	2,640	1,579
Callahan..	1,666	2,480	534	1,694	2,134	1,452
Cameron..	34,891	18,434	2,760	29,435	20,123	9,286
Camp....	1,912	1,488	252	1,938	1,219	821
Carson...	742	1,742	227	825	1,647	578
Cass....	5,691	4,066	1,038	5,476	3,999	2,168
Castro....	1,107	1,231	144	1,113	1,307	485
Chambers..	2,876	4,101	818	2,832	3,398	2,122
Cherokee..	5,185	6,483	971	5,003	5,847	3,273
Childress..	719	1,072	165	881	1,033	421
Clay.....	1,690	1,997	465	1,919	1,586	1,397
Cochran..	541	667	127	454	750	255
Coke.....	595	790	157	580	640	393
Coleman..	1,488	1,793	349	1,579	1,462	1,095
Collin.....	37,854	83,750	10,443	24,508	60,514	43,287
Collingsworth	581	729	118	635	697	265
Colorado..	2,795	3,381	574	2,442	3,286	1,421
Comal...	7,132	16,763	1,903	6,312	12,651	5,841
Comanche..	2,138	2,123	511	2,296	1,666	1,281
Concho...	434	488	107	489	414	329
Cooke....	3,782	7,320	1,150	3,105	5,299	4,658
Coryell...	5,300	7,143	1,443	4,157	6,144	3,974
Cottle....	404	331	77	542	245	235
Crane....	616	984	201	514	918	412
Crockett...	684	714	147	653	623	368
Crosby...	1,122	968	189	1,010	1,006	313
Culberson.	804	329	99	424	251	171
Dallam....	483	970	170	434	922	325
Dallas...	255,766	260,058	36,759	231,412	256,007	170,571
Dawson...	1,612	2,319	232	1,639	2,691	518
Deaf Smith.	1,655	3,051	310	1,642	3,137	772
Delta.....	849	744	146	864	599	551
Denton...	36,138	65,313	9,294	27,891	48,492	39,653
DeWitt....	2,074	3,577	483	2,127	3,238	1,346
Dickens...	509	421	117	536	373	250
Dimmit....	2,242	604	128	3,172	844	361
Donley....	495	988	97	578	893	260
Duval....	3,958	543	136	4,006	698	326
Eastland..	2,594	3,272	705	2,738	2,830	1,698
Ector.....	12,017	17,746	2,511	11,130	18,161	6,668
Edwards...	437	511	60	254	460	171
Ellis.....	10,832	16,046	2,750	9,537	13,564	10,303
El Paso...	83,964	43,255	6,300	67,715	47,224	19,738
Erath.....	3,664	4,750	1,134	3,531	3,835	3,046
Falls.....	3,256	2,260	479	2,761	1,826	1,185
Fannin...	4,276	3,495	980	4,164	2,510	2,919
Fayette...	3,119	4,195	708	2,923	3,789	2,088
Fisher....	1,142	537	170	1,242	539	442
Floyd....	986	1,530	126	947	1,676	385
Foard....	355	166	52	435	207	152
Fort Bend..	38,163	49,945	4,363	29,992	41,039	16,853
Franklin...	1,484	1,575	386	1,338	1,058	942
Freestone.	2,630	2,888	568	2,445	2,316	1,596
Frio.....	2,593	1,225	253	2,377	1,275	654
Gaines....	1,012	1,812	353	1,095	2,138	696
Galveston.	38,458	35,251	5,897	38,623	31,303	20,103
Garza....	703	946	103	558	982	345
Gillespie..	1,655	5,867	542	1,600	4,712	2,018
Glasscock..	70	382	30	100	379	93
Goliad....	1,135	1,335	148	1,069	1,236	521
Gonzales..	2,110	2,687	354	2,006	2,502	1,018
Gray.....	2,114	6,102	568	2,426	6,105	1,810
Grayson...	14,338	17,169	3,745	12,547	12,322	13,327
Gregg....	13,659	21,611	2,079	12,797	20,542	8,437
Grimes...	2,584	2,564	538	2,594	2,402	1,213
Guadalupe.	8,079	14,254	1,811	6,567	10,818	5,618
Hale....	3,204	5,905	605	2,761	6,098	1,357
Hall.....	750	626	94	819	631	263
Hamilton..	1,200	1,493	323	1,100	1,232	921
Hansford..	343	1,493	105	345	1,660	398

County	1996 Clinton (D)	Dole (R)	Perot (RF)	1992 Clinton (D)	Bush (R)	Perot (I)
Hardeman .	750	610	168	954	614	362
Hardin	7,179	8,529	2,112	6,753	5,885	4,129
Harris ...	386,726	421,462	42,364	360,171	406,778	172,922
Harrison..	10,307	9,835	1,427	9,538	8,733	4,371
Hartley...	463	1,242	101	406	1,081	308
Haskell ...	1,374	966	225	1,438	852	562
Hays	11,580	12,865	1,990	10,842	10,008	6,252
Hemphill .	344	986	104	479	989	232
Henderson .	10,085	10,345	2,274	9,105	8,368	6,746
Hidalgo ...	56,335	24,437	3,536	51,205	26,976	9,757
Hill	3,988	4,401	1,052	3,929	3,669	2,752
Hockley...	2,170	4,230	519	2,301	4,261	1,291
Hood	5,459	7,575	1,445	4,359	5,313	4,457
Hopkins ...	4,522	4,341	1,034	4,085	3,398	3,147
Houston...	3,383	3,443	585	3,250	3,067	1,690
Howard ...	3,732	5,007	1,037	3,735	5,129	1,984
Hudspeth ..	427	367	92	364	325	178
Hunt	8,801	10,746	2,225	7,452	9,739	7,387
Hutchinson.	2,553	6,350	864	2,833	6,034	1,993
Irion	213	386	86	256	283	290
Jack	1,019	1,162	301	1,254	1,041	1,045
Jackson...	1,785	2,533	309	1,722	2,451	976
Jasper	5,039	4,523	1,041	5,658	3,870	2,539
Jeff Davis.	370	482	99	321	360	187
Jefferson ..	45,854	32,821	5,314	48,405	29,622	17,242
Jim Hogg ..	1,437	307	64	1,520	478	107
Jim Wells.	7,116	2,989	430	7,812	3,311	1,413
Johnson...	12,817	16,246	3,250	12,030	13,473	11,573
Jones	2,422	2,351	614	2,400	2,088	1,436
Karnes....	2,154	1,869	291	1,897	1,990	802
Kaufman ..	7,383	8,697	1,831	6,498	6,578	5,913
Kendall ...	2,092	5,940	620	1,374	4,162	1,773
Kenedy ...	133	71	4	87	69	18
Kent	260	187	67	271	175	163
Kerr......	4,192	11,173	1,236	3,707	8,787	3,790
Kimble....	521	898	131	467	790	354
King	46	97	29	54	79	56
Kinney....	503	650	97	598	634	299
Kleberg ...	5,136	3,391	431	5,109	3,897	1,470
Knox	785	599	149	854	521	438
Lamar	6,075	6,393	1,198	6,328	5,778	4,093
Lamb.....	1,683	2,593	283	1,737	2,998	709
Lampasas .	1,819	3,008	509	1,508	2,233	1,432
LaSalle ...	1,522	570	85	1,522	586	211
Lavaca ...	2,575	3,697	551	2,700	3,362	1,696
Lee	2,008	2,354	421	1,847	2,108	1,088
Leon	2,217	2,839	499	2,042	2,212	1,251
Liberty....	6,877	7,784	2,011	7,036	6,959	4,311
Limestone .	3,236	2,691	693	3,188	2,358	1,505
Lipscomb..	357	869	115	338	839	270
Live Oak ..	1,372	1,929	292	1,345	1,805	806
Llano	2,633	4,290	762	2,409	3,056	1,799
Loving	14	48	15	20	31	45
Lubbock...	22,786	47,304	3,996	22,240	48,847	11,618
Lynn	903	1,151	136	902	1,233	291
McCulloch .	1,231	1,465	296	1,393	1,108	986
McLennan .	27,050	30,666	5,131	25,903	28,473	15,505
McMullen .	117	274	35	78	274	89
Madison...	1,470	1,576	293	1,553	1,544	778
Marion....	2,028	1,260	353	2,156	1,245	882
Martin	643	973	140	641	986	356
Mason	618	949	151	570	776	364
Matagorda .	5,374	5,876	1,190	4,759	5,328	3,045
Maverick ..	5,307	1,050	202	4,540	2,002	771
Medina ...	3,880	5,710	715	3,650	4,912	2,167
Menard ...	490	443	102	553	354	367
Midland ...	9,513	25,382	2,079	9,160	24,143	7,880
Milam	3,869	3,019	657	3,542	2,414	1,495
Mills	748	1,044	230	753	702	530
Mitchell ...	1,213	949	232	1,353	1,128	604
Montague..	2,718	3,029	842	2,885	2,304	2,330
Montgomery	20,722	51,011	6,065	18,551	39,976	19,203
Moore	1,358	3,353	359	1,361	3,147	976
Morris	2,973	1,449	402	3,028	1,400	1,138
Motley	164	380	56	256	446	117
Nacogdoches	7,641	10,361	1,352	6,937	9,864	4,803
Navarro ...	6,078	5,236	1,140	6,006	4,897	3,800
Newton ...	2,554	1,409	474	3,249	1,212	1,032
Nolan	2,582	2,166	613	2,490	1,993	1,455
Nueces ...	50,009	37,470	5,103	46,317	36,781	17,374
Ochiltree ..	467	2,448	167	557	2,419	576
Oldham ...	213	583	77	225	583	177
Orange ...	13,741	12,560	2,836	15,305	9,793	7,321
Palo Pinto .	3,938	3,666	1,011	3,392	2,852	3,010
Panola....	4,168	4,008	777	3,950	3,473	1,906
Parker	9,447	14,580	2,703	7,934	10,321	9,148
Parmer ...	676	2,042	160	637	1,829	564
Pecos	1,816	1,730	369	1,778	1,836	895
Polk	6,360	6,473	1,347	5,942	5,390	2,884
Potter	9,273	14,995	1,799	9,527	13,510	4,655
Presidio ...	1,205	383	111	1,105	400	200
Rains.....	1,265	1,123	335	1,108	975	890
Randall ...	9,177	28,266	1,985	9,119	24,971	6,340
Reagan ...	407	645	101	337	651	259
Real	414	845	178	463	787	386
Red River .	2,339	1,783	433	2,686	1,735	1,228
Reeves ...	2,279	1,007	245	2,569	1,244	734
Refugio ...	1,635	1,376	222	1,531	1,469	716
Roberts ...	122	421	40	126	391	99
Robertson .	2,912	1,944	315	2,927	1,707	963
Rockwall ..	3,289	8,319	1,121	2,397	6,427	4,393
Runnels...	1,417	1,941	396	1,401	1,653	1,279
Rusk.....	5,988	8,423	1,072	5,391	7,560	3,575
Sabine....	1,913	1,660	334	2,288	1,490	894
San Augustine	1,924	1,296	324	1,737	1,243	667
San Jacinto.	2,771	2,878	810	2,846	2,494	1,653
San Patricio.	8,132	7,678	1,085	8,202	7,456	3,178
San Saba..	726	991	194	716	723	660
Schleicher .	505	587	111	420	452	355
Scurry	2,099	2,929	813	1,609	2,670	1,826
Shackelford.	502	792	169	484	623	422
Shelby....	3,720	3,482	815	3,986	3,217	1,487
Sherman ..	243	809	89	261	851	256
Smith	18,265	32,171	2,933	17,514	27,753	13,569
Somervell..	993	1,099	273	782	872	903
Starr.....	6,312	756	157	7,668	1,209	345
Stephens ..	1,218	1,714	336	1,115	1,573	1,062
Sterling ...	186	394	86	127	322	182
Stonewall..	487	323	105	561	242	322
Sutton	508	688	102	524	687	387
Swisher ...	1,224	1,159	195	1,413	989	541
Tarrant ...	170,431	208,312	28,715	156,230	183,387	129,998
Taylor	13,213	23,682	2,912	12,382	22,614	10,331
Terrell	278	185	47	325	176	128
Terry.....	1,272	2,013	269	1,461	2,309	619
Throckmorton	285	360	90	401	389	228
Titus	3,725	3,438	744	3,625	3,024	2,146
Tom Green.	11,782	18,112	2,757	11,437	14,989	10,244
Travis	128,970	98,454	14,008	130,546	88,105	56,158
Trinity	2,774	2,058	460	2,784	1,988	1,133
Tyler	3,340	2,804	645	3,465	2,357	1,529
Upshur ...	5,032	5,174	1,086	4,776	4,511	2,896
Upton	424	685	88	489	908	313
Uvalde....	3,397	3,494	403	3,482	3,635	1,387
Val Verde..	5,623	4,357	548	4,748	4,102	2,093
Van Zandt .	5,752	7,453	1,756	5,310	5,810	5,239
Victoria ...	8,238	14,457	1,197	7,604	13,086	5,136
Walker....	6,088	7,177	1,186	5,619	6,662	3,619
Waller	4,535	3,559	499	4,270	3,065	1,692
Ward	1,644	1,620	446	1,695	1,769	948
Washington.	3,460	6,319	601	3,283	5,817	1,738
Webb	18,997	4,712	936	14,509	7,789	2,517
Wharton...	5,176	6,163	871	4,643	5,503	2,624
Wheeler...	750	1,355	174	938	1,458	367
Wichita ...	15,775	20,495	3,371	17,021	17,956	11,478
Wilbarger..	1,730	2,037	465	1,924	1,959	1,453
Willacy....	3,789	1,332	241	3,359	1,490	652
Williamson .	24,175	36,836	4,931	19,437	26,208	15,415
Wilson	3,713	4,530	760	3,711	3,766	2,105
Winkler ...	872	1,009	218	942	1,173	582
Wise	5,056	6,330	1,516	4,478	4,555	4,485
Wood	4,711	6,228	1,184	4,084	4,708	3,494
Yoakum...	738	1,485	218	595	1,486	484
Young	2,394	3,647	639	2,464	2,894	2,302
Zapata....	1,786	521	131	2,052	866	326
Zavala....	2,629	463	91	3,058	571	237
Totals....	2,459,683	2,736,167	378,537	2,281,815	2,496,071	1,354,781

Texas Vote Since 1948

1948, Truman, Dem., 750,700; Dewey, Rep., 282,240; Thurmond, States' Rights, 106,909; Wallace, Prog., 3,764; Watson, Proh., 2,758; Thomas, Soc., 874.

1952, Eisenhower, Rep., 1,102,878; Stevenson, Dem., 969,228; Hamblen, Proh., 1,983; MacArthur, Christian Nationalist, 833; MacArthur, Constitution, 730; Hallinan, Prog., 294.

1956, Eisenhower, Rep., 1,080,619; Stevenson, Dem., 859,958; Andrews, Ind., 14,591.

1960, Kennedy, Dem., 1,167,932; Nixon, Rep., 1,121,699; Sullivan, Constitution, 18,169; Decker, Proh., 3,870; write-in, 15.

1964, Johnson, Dem., 1,663,185; Goldwater, Rep., 958,566; Lightburn, Constitution, 5,060.

1968, Nixon, Rep., 1,227,844; Humphrey, Dem., 1,266,804; Wallace, 3d Party, 584,269; write-in, 489.

1972, Nixon, Rep., 2,298,896; McGovern, Dem., 1,154,289; Schmitz, Amer., 6,039; Jenness, Soc. Workers, 8,664; others, 3,393.

1976, Carter, Dem., 2,082,319; Ford, Rep., 1,953,300; McCarthy, Ind., 20,118; Anderson, Amer., 11,442; Camejo, Soc. Workers, 1,723; write-in, 2,982.

1980, Reagan, Rep., 2,510,705; Carter, Dem., 1,881,147; Anderson, Ind., 111,613; Clark, Libertarian, 37,643; write-in, 528.

1984, Reagan, Rep., 3,433,428; Mondale, Dem., 1,949,276.

1988, Bush, Rep., 3,036,829; Dukakis, Dem., 2,352,748; Paul, Lib., 30,355; Fulani, New Alliance, 7,208.

1992, Clinton, Dem., 2,281,815; Bush, Rep., 2,496,071; Perot, Ind., 1,354,781; Marrou, Libertarian, 19,699.

1996, Dole, Rep., 2,736,167; Clinton, Dem., 2,459,683; Perot, Ind. (Ref.), 378,537; Browne, Libertarian, 20,256; Phillips, Taxpayers, 7,472; Hagelin, Natural Law, 4,422.

Utah

County	Clinton 1996 (D)	Dole (R)	Perot (RF)	Clinton 1992 (D)	Bush (R)	Perot (I)
Beaver...	687	1,164	217	668	1,040	330
Box Elder.	3,170	8,373	1,578	2,186	7,712	4,507
Cache ...	6,595	16,832	2,399	4,973	15,971	8,032
Carbon...	4,172	2,343	952	4,480	2,038	2,002
Daggett ..	131	237	55	122	172	117
Davis....	19,301	42,768	7,495	14,924	39,087	24,105
Duchesne.	892	2,648	566	772	1,983	1,229
Emery ...	1,371	2,033	663	1,349	1,643	1,138
Garfield ..	283	1,330	222	309	1,235	355
Grand ...	1,199	1,384	432	1,160	1,100	991
Iron	1,887	6,550	716	1,537	5,616	1,693
Juab	928	1,290	353	823	1,237	616
Kane	304	1,682	290	295	1,241	534
Millard ...	945	2,681	505	742	2,496	1,064
Morgan ..	859	1,659	337	520	1,339	851
Piute	176	475	59	169	429	146
Rich	179	523	88	154	525	187
Salt Lake .	117,951	127,951	27,620	100,082	117,247	91,968
San Juan .	1,675	2,139	271	1,639	2,004	576
Sanpete..	1,568	3,631	801	1,302	2,995	1,742
Sevier ...	1,327	4,031	670	1,039	3,160	1,671
Summit ..	4,177	3,867	971	3,013	3,133	3,060
Tooele ..	3,992	3,881	1,244	3,270	3,676	3,011
Uintah ...	1,714	4,743	899	1,374	3,505	2,250
Utah	18,291	69,653	8,106	14,090	61,398	24,558
Wasatch..	1,374	2,222	558	1,042	1,822	1,234
Washington	4,816	17,637	2,069	3,364	11,310	4,623
Wayne...	265	741	121	236	706	251
Weber ...	21,404	27,443	6,204	17,795	26,812	20,559
Totals ...	221,633	361,911	66,461	183,429	322,632	203,400

Utah Vote Since 1948

1948, Truman, Dem., 149,151; Dewey, Rep., 124,402; Wallace, Prog., 2,679; Dobbs, Soc. Workers, 73.

1952, Eisenhower, Rep., 194,190; Stevenson, Dem., 135,364.

1956, Eisenhower, Rep., 215,631; Stevenson, Dem., 118,364.

1960, Kennedy, Dem., 169,248; Nixon, Rep., 205,361; Dobbs, Soc. Workers, 100.

1964, Johnson, Dem., 219,628; Goldwater, Rep., 181,785.

1968, Nixon, Rep., 238,728; Humphrey, Dem., 156,665; Wallace, 3d Party, 26,906; Halstead, Soc. Workers, 89; Peace and Freedom, 180.

1972, Nixon, Rep., 323,643; McGovern, Dem., 126,284; Schmitz, Amer., 28,549.

1976, Carter, Dem., 182,110; Ford, Rep., 337,908; Anderson, Amer., 13,304; McCarthy, Ind., 3,907; MacBride, Libertarian, 2,438; Maddox, Amer. Ind., 1,162; Camejo, Soc. Workers, 268; Hall, Com., 121.

1980, Reagan, Rep., 439,687; Carter, Dem., 124,266; Anderson, Ind., 30,284; Clark, Libertarian, 7,226; Commoner, Citizens, 1,009; Greaves, Amer., 965; Rarick, Amer. Ind., 522; Hall, Com., 139; DeBerry, Soc. Workers, 124.

1984, Reagan, Rep., 469,105; Mondale, Dem., 155,369; Bergland, Libertarian, 2,447.

1988, Bush, Rep., 428,442; Dukakis, Dem., 207,352; Paul, Lib., 7,473; Dennis, Amer., 2,158.

1992, Clinton, Dem., 183,429; Bush, Rep., 322,632; Perot, Ind., 203,400; Gritz, Populist/America First, 28,602; Marrou, Libertarian, 1,900; Hagelin, Natural Law, 1,319; LaRouche, Ind., 1,089.

1996, Dole, Rep., 361,911; Clinton, Dem., 221,633; Perot, Ref., 66,461; Nader, Green, 4,615; Browne, Libertarian, 4,129; Phillips, Taxpayers, 2,601; Templin, Ind. Amer., 1,290; Crane, Ind., 1,101; Hagelin, Natural Law, 1,085; Moorehead, Workers World, 298; Harris, Soc. Workers, 235; Dodge, Proh., 111.

Vermont

City	Clinton 1996 (D)	Dole (R)	Perot (RF)	Clinton 1992 (D)	Bush (R)	Perot (I)
Barre City..	1,890	1,107	376	1,807	1,508	1,035
Bennington.	3,454	1,654	960	3,646	2,151	1,536
Brattleboro.	3,016	1,195	395	3,519	1,447	847
Burlington..	11,600	3,762	1,309	12,508	4,462	3,241
Colchester .	3,314	2,035	769	2,966	1,997	1,739
Essex	4,063	2,944	796	3,825	2,960	2,302
Hartford ...	2,106	1,290	400	2,034	1,564	793
Montpelier .	2,458	1,118	269	2,490	1,407	657
Rutland City.	3,817	2,320	741	3,888	2,915	1,722
S. Burlington	3,929	2,274	548	3,730	2,131	1,359
Springfield .	2,267	1,189	561	2,179	1,468	1,091
Other.....	95,980	59,464	23,900	90,998	64,112	49,663
Totals	137,894	80,352	31,024	133,590	88,122	65,985

Vermont Vote Since 1948

1948, Truman, Dem., 45,557; Dewey, Rep., 75,926; Wallace, Prog., 1,279; Thomas, Soc., 585.

1952, Eisenhower, Rep., 109,717; Stevenson, Dem., 43,355; Hallinan, Prog., 282; Hoopes, Soc., 185.

1956, Eisenhower, Rep., 110,390; Stevenson, Dem., 42,549; scattered, 39.

1960, Kennedy, Dem., 69,186; Nixon, Rep., 98,131.

1964, Johnson, Dem., 107,674; Goldwater, Rep., 54,868.

1968, Nixon, Rep., 85,142; Humphrey, Dem., 70,255; Wallace, 3d Party, 5,104; Halstead, Soc. Workers, 295; Gregory, New Party, 579.

1972, Nixon, Rep., 117,149; McGovern, Dem., 68,174; Spock, Liberty Union, 1,010; Jenness, Soc. Workers, 296; scattered, 318.

1976, Carter, Dem., 77,798; Carter, Ind. Vermonter, 991; Ford, Rep., 100,387; McCarthy, Ind., 4,001; Camejo, Soc. Workers, 430; LaRouche, U.S. Labor, 196; scattered, 99.

1980, Reagan, Rep., 94,598; Carter, Dem., 81,891; Anderson, Ind., 31,760; Commoner, Citizens, 2,316; Clark, Libertarian, 1,900; McReynolds, Liberty Union, 136; Hall, Com., 118; DeBerry, Soc. Workers, 75; scattering, 413.

1984, Reagan, Rep., 135,865; Mondale, Dem., 95,730; Bergland, Libertarian, 1,002.

1988, Bush, Rep., 124,331; Dukakis, Dem., 115,775; Paul, Lib., 1,000; LaRouche, Ind., 275.

1992, Clinton, Dem., 133,590; Bush, Rep., 88,122; Perot, Ind., 65,985.

1996, Clinton, Dem., 137,894; Dole, Rep., 80,352; Perot, Ref., 31,024; Nader, Green, 5,585; Browne, Libertarian, 1,183; Hagelin, Natural Law, 498; Peron, Grass Roots, 480; Phillips, Taxpayers, 382; Hollis, Liberty Union, 292; Harris, Soc. Workers, 199.

Virginia

County	Clinton 1996 (D)	Dole (R)	Perot (RF)	Clinton 1992 (D)	Bush (R)	Perot (I)
Accomack.	5,220	5,013	1,218	4,950	5,666	2,304
Albemarle.	14,089	15,243	1,533	13,886	13,894	3,855
Alleghany .	2,398	2,015	607	2,396	2,294	926
Amelia ..	1,625	2,119	323	1,534	2,062	574
Amherst ..	4,864	5,094	835	4,101	5,482	1,268
Appomattox	2,239	2,625	510	1,919	2,830	801
Arlington..	45,573	26,106	2,782	47,756	26,376	7,992
Augusta ..	5,965	13,458	1,916	5,190	12,896	3,397
Bath	922	847	247	855	1,075	354
Bedford ..	7,786	11,955	1,976	6,792	10,496	3,251
Bland....	939	1,167	385	1,001	1,368	408
Botetourt .	4,576	6,404	1,138	4,349	5,904	1,819
Brunswick.	3,442	2,059	340	3,687	2,480	479
Buchanan .	6,551	2,785	858	7,405	3,297	815
Buckingham	2,374	1,974	392	2,193	2,368	459
Campbell .	6,788	10,273	1,505	5,999	10,931	2,553
Caroline ..	3,897	2,816	521	3,770	2,947	965
Carroll ...	3,611	5,088	1,158	3,790	5,664	1,388
Charles City	1,842	729	178	2,010	729	251
Charlotte .	2,007	2,103	431	2,098	2,293	640
Chesterfield	30,220	56,650	6,004	28,028	56,626	16,898
Clarke ...	1,906	2,201	379	1,811	1,994	802
Craig	895	979	262	965	1,008	304
Culpeper .	3,907	5,688	787	3,444	5,226	1,640
Cumberland	1,303	1,544	275	1,284	1,643	372
Dickenson .	3,913	2,229	660	4,839	2,574	660
Dinwiddie .	3,871	3,503	666	3,624	3,648	1,198
Essex	1,668	1,627	188	1,583	1,897	382
Fairfax ...	170,150	176,033	16,134	160,186	170,488	53,012
Fauquier..	6,759	11,063	1,287	6,600	10,497	3,464
Floyd....	1,909	2,374	545	2,026	2,575	672
Fluvanna .	2,676	3,442	457	2,134	2,811	871
Franklin ..	7,300	7,382	2,015	6,590	6,724	2,232
Frederick ..	5,976	10,608	1,599	4,942	9,425	2,981
Giles	3,196	2,566	841	3,346	3,023	1,142
Gloucester .	4,710	6,447	1,266	4,058	6,461	2,640
Goochland .	2,784	4,119	424	2,589	3,834	994
Grayson ..	2,661	3,004	675	2,615	3,378	860
Greene...	1,440	2,351	346	1,353	2,265	627
Greensville	2,381	1,176	263	2,237	1,335	360
Halifax ...	5,599	6,490	876	4,752	5,199	1,140
Hanover..	9,880	22,086	2,447	8,021	20,336	5,674
Henrico ..	41,121	54,430	5,920	36,807	56,910	14,720
Henry....	9,061	9,110	2,370	9,296	9,005	3,212
Highland..	446	631	134	494	686	212
Isle of Wight	4,952	5,416	893	4,380	5,370	1,536
James City	7,247	10,120	1,116	6,536	8,781	2,675
King and Queen ..	1,393	1,073	213	1,811	2,570	918
King George	1,875	2,597	341	1,363	1,206	323
King William	1,765	2,346	339	1,822	2,591	758
Lancaster .	1,844	2,709	324	1,812	2,841	739
Lee	4,444	3,225	822	5,215	3,504	1,002
Loudoun..	19,942	25,715	3,082	14,462	19,290	7,391

County	Clinton (D)	1996 Dole (R)	Perot (RF)	Clinton (D)	1992 Bush (R)	Perot (I)
Louisa . . .	3,761	3,768	693	3,399	3,461	1,381
Lunenburg	1,995	2,063	299	2,082	2,227	505
Madison . .	1,734	2,296	360	1,700	2,341	653
Mathews. .	1,602	2,206	403	1,402	2,179	884
Mecklenburg	4,408	4,933	789	4,273	5,401	1,128
Middlesex. .	1,704	2,141	350	1,597	2,224	768
Montgomery	10,867	10,517	2,594	10,658	10,606	3,449
Nelson . . .	2,782	1,988	411	2,586	2,159	748
New Kent .	1,859	2,852	520	1,738	2,708	1,017
Northampton	2,569	1,763	522	2,568	2,088	844
Northumberland .	1,957	2,605	375	1,862	2,667	729
Nottoway .	2,327	2,416	346	2,411	2,610	606
Orange. . .	3,590	4,435	750	3,348	4,092	1,425
Page . . .	2,868	3,876	640	3,010	4,203	1,163
Patrick . . .	2,301	3,547	719	2,465	3,521	1,026
Pittsylvania	7,681	12,127	1,469	7,675	11,467	2,296
Powhatan .	2,254	4,679	626	1,950	3,832	1,232
Prince Edward . .	2,678	2,530	403	2,775	2,858	635
Prince George . .	3,498	5,216	698	3,087	4,799	1,459
Prince William . .	33,462	39,292	4,881	26,486	35,432	13,190
Pulaski. . .	5,333	5,387	1,399	5,633	6,148	2,066
Rappahannock. . . .	1,405	1,505	213	1,273	1,410	487
Richmond .	1,101	1,424	201	1,034	1,609	366
Roanoke. .	15,387	20,700	2,934	14,704	20,667	5,477
Rockbridge	3,116	3,274	760	2,908	3,228	1,254
Rockingham	5,867	14,035	1,318	5,407	13,016	2,839
Russell. . .	5,437	3,706	862	6,480	3,891	958
Scott	3,449	4,086	798	3,979	4,515	957
Shenandoah	4,224	7,440	1,353	3,956	7,746	2,063
Smyth . . .	4,990	4,966	1,407	4,924	6,128	1,618
Southampton	3,454	2,275	564	3,199	2,844	754
Spotsylvania	10,342	13,786	1,860	8,133	11,829	3,918
Stafford . .	9,902	14,098	1,856	7,718	12,528	4,481
Surry	1,753	944	181	1,823	1,046	364
Sussex . . .	2,089	1,378	256	2,193	1,527	446
Tazewell. .	7,500	6,131	1,554	8,586	6,375	1,872
Warren . . .	3,814	4,657	904	3,554	4,319	1,650
Washington	6,939	9,098	1,654	7,269	9,150	2,288
Westmoreland	2,949	2,333	427	2,758	2,554	818
Wise	6,712	4,660	1,478	7,681	5,144	1,835
Wythe . . .	3,275	4,274	955	3,616	5,121	1,557
York.	7,731	11,396	1,469	6,218	10,197	3,426
Cities						
Alexandria	27,968	15,554	1,472	30,784	16,700	4,934
Bedford . .	1,065	990	212	963	1,091	313
Bristol . . .	2,586	2,983	429	2,948	3,616	851
Buena Vista	1,090	713	216	1,023	849	291
Charlottesville	7,916	4,091	565	8,685	4,705	1,397
Chesapeake	28,713	29,251	4,456	23,495	28,909	9,237
Clifton Forge	974	486	147	958	632	251
Colonial Heights . .	1,782	4,632	518	1,721	5,298	1,312
Covington .	1,394	763	255	1,442	995	402
Danville . .	8,168	9,254	762	8,134	9,584	1,679
Emporia . .	1,103	835	98	1,048	1,094	157
Fairfax . . .	3,909	4,319	422	3,884	4,333	1,439
Falls Church	2,375	1,644	202	2,864	1,912	599
Franklin . .	1,962	1,200	201	1,696	1,347	272
Fredericksburg	3,215	2,579	300	3,266	2,819	738
Galax	1,033	910	221	957	1,087	276
Hampton. .	24,493	16,596	2,783	23,395	19,219	6,581
Harrisonburg	3,346	4,945	434	3,414	4,935	1,162
Hopewell .	2,868	3,493	550	2,863	3,818	1,227
Lexington .	1,059	850	112	1,128	894	228
Lynchburg.	10,281	11,441	1,155	9,587	12,518	2,545
Manassas.	4,378	5,799	670	3,647	5,453	1,971
Manassas Park	748	916	151	567	792	356
Martinsville	2,941	2,446	387	3,073	2,690	748
Newport News . . .	27,678	23,072	3,090	25,743	26,779	8,217
Norfolk. . .	37,655	18,693	3,435	37,602	22,362	8,732
Norton . . .	802	416	138	871	472	182
Petersburg	8,105	2,261	423	8,671	3,125	834
Poquoson .	1,409	3,422	400	1,086	3,354	960
Portsmouth	22,150	10,686	2,238	20,416	12,575	4,360
Radford . .	2,113	1,742	381	2,183	1,996	582
Richmond.	42,273	20,993	2,762	47,642	24,341	6,992
Roanoke. .	17,282	12,283	2,169	17,724	13,443	3,753
Salem . . .	4,282	4,936	796	4,028	5,143	1,430
S. Boston[1] .	—	—	—	1,051	1,435	252
Staunton. .	3,162	4,526	605	2,851	4,989	1,146
Suffolk . . .	10,827	8,572	1,266	9,196	8,697	2,150
Virginia Beach. . .	52,142	63,741	9,328	44,294	68,938	24,087
Waynesboro	2,398	3,466	462	2,302	3,758	961
Williamsburg	1,820	1,560	162	1,856	1,349	445
Winchester	3,027	3,681	434	2,768	3,833	1,048
Totals . . .	**1,091,060**	**1,138,350**	**159,861**	**1,038,650**	**1,150,517**	**348,639**

(1) South Boston merged with Halifax County in July 1996.

Virginia Vote Since 1948

1948, Truman, Dem., 200,786; Dewey, Rep., 172,070; Thurmond, States' Rights, 43,393; Wallace, Prog., 2,047; Thomas, Soc., 726; Teichert, Soc. Labor, 234.

1952, Eisenhower, Rep., 349,037; Stevenson, Dem., 268,677; Hass, Soc. Labor, 1,160; Hoopes, Soc. Dem., 504; Hallinan, Prog., 311.

1956, Eisenhower, Rep., 386,459; Stevenson, Dem., 267,760; Andrews, States' Rights, 42,964; Hoopes, Soc. Dem., 444; Hass, Soc. Labor, 351.

1960, Kennedy, Dem., 362,327; Nixon, Rep., 404,521; Coiner, Cons., 4,204; Hass, Soc. Labor, 397.

1964, Johnson, Dem., 558,038; Goldwater, Rep., 481,334; Hass, Soc. Labor, 2,895.

1968, Nixon, Rep., 590,319; Humphrey, Dem., 442,387; Wallace, 3d Party, *320,272; Blomen, Soc. Labor, 4,671; Munn, Proh., 601; Gregory, Peace and Freedom, 1,680.

*10,561 votes for Wallace were omitted in the count.

1972, Nixon, Rep., 988,493; McGovern, Dem., 438,887; Schmitz, Amer., 19,721; Fisher, Soc. Labor, 9,918.

1976, Carter, Dem., 813,896; Ford, Rep., 836,554; Camejo, Soc. Workers, 17,802; Anderson, Amer., 16,686; LaRouche, U.S. Labor, 7,508; MacBride, Libertarian, 4,648.

1980, Reagan, Rep., 989,609; Carter, Dem., 752,174; Anderson, Ind., 95,418; Commoner, Citizens, 14,024; Clark, Libertarian, 12,821; DeBerry, Soc. Workers, 1,986.

1984, Reagan, Rep., 1,337,078; Mondale, Dem., 796,250.

1988, Bush, Rep., 1,309,162; Dukakis, Dem., 859,799; Fulani, Ind., 14,312; Paul, Lib., 8,336.

1992, Clinton, Dem., 1,038,650; Bush, Rep., 1,150,517; Perot, Ind., 348,639; LaRouche, Ind., 11,937; Marrou, Libertarian, 5,730; Fulani, New Alliance, 3,192.

1996, Dole, Rep., 1,138,350; Clinton, Dem., 1,091,060; Perot, Ref., 159,861; Phillips, Taxpayers, 13,687; Browne, Libertarian, 9,174; Hagelin, Natural Law, 4,510.

Washington

County	Clinton (D)	1996 Dole (R)	Perot (RF)	Clinton (D)	1992 Bush (R)	Perot (I)
Adams. . . .	1,740	2,356	448	1,449	2,087	1,010
Asotin	3,349	2,860	936	3,239	2,425	1,849
Benton. . . .	20,783	26,664	5,311	16,459	22,883	12,878
Chelan. . . .	8,595	12,363	2,332	7,860	10,716	4,606
Clallam . . .	12,585	12,432	3,187	10,820	9,765	7,775
Clark	52,254	46,794	9,663	42,648	36,906	26,163
Columbia . .	743	948	228	668	761	466
Cowlitz. . . .	18,054	11,221	3,441	15,052	10,000	9,246
Douglas . . .	3,913	5,682	1,132	3,731	4,920	2,315
Ferry	1,197	1,091	408	963	773	762
Franklin . . .	4,961	5,946	992	3,743	4,486	2,597
Garfield . . .	497	623	117	473	620	222
Grant.	8,065	10,895	2,496	7,278	9,503	4,898
Grays Harbor	14,082	7,635	3,757	12,599	6,904	7,460
Island	12,157	12,387	2,787	9,555	9,526	7,889
Jefferson . .	7,145	4,607	1,385	6,148	3,467	3,168
King	417,846	232,811	51,309	391,050	212,986	167,216
Kitsap	44,167	35,304	8,769	34,442	29,340	23,873
Kittitas . . .	5,707	5,224	1,214	5,432	4,078	2,778
Klickitat . . .	3,214	2,662	875	2,758	2,085	1,938
Lewis	10,331	13,238	3,373	7,810	12,316	6,684
Lincoln. . . .	1,806	2,587	518	1,653	2,152	1,098
Mason	10,088	7,149	2,816	8,076	5,776	5,577
Okanogan .	4,810	5,890	1,797	5,015	4,265	3,541
Pacific. . . .	5,095	2,598	1,131	4,587	2,243	2,351
Pend Oreille	2,126	2,012	709	1,798	1,528	1,340
Pierce	120,893	89,295	22,051	102,243	77,410	59,523
San Juan . .	3,663	2,523	508	3,353	1,901	1,776
Skagit	18,295	16,397	4,818	15,936	13,388	10,973
Skamania. .	1,724	1,387	450	1,474	1,102	1,050
Snohomish .	109,649	81,885	22,731	88,643	69,137	65,838
Spokane . .	71,727	66,628	16,532	69,526	59,984	38,251
Stevens . . .	5,591	7,524	2,158	4,960	5,706	3,769
Thurston . .	45,522	29,835	7,622	38,293	25,643	19,551
Wahkiakum.	924	619	215	696	488	584
Walla Walla.	8,038	9,085	1,894	7,325	7,894	4,507
Whatcom . .	29,074	27,153	4,854	26,619	23,801	12,455
Whitman . .	7,262	6,734	1,315	7,637	6,428	3,220
Yakima . . .	25,676	27,648	4,724	21,026	25,841	10,583
Totals	**1,123,323**	**840,712**	**201,003**	**993,037**	**731,234**	**541,780**

Washington Vote Since 1948

1948, Truman, Dem., 476,165; Dewey, Rep., 386,315; Wallace, Prog., 31,692; Watson, Proh., 6,117; Thomas, Soc., 3,534; Teichert, Soc. Labor, 1,133; Dobbs, Soc. Workers, 103.

1952, Eisenhower, Rep., 599,107; Stevenson, Dem., 492,845; MacArthur, Christian Nationalist, 7,290; Hallinan, Prog., 2,460; Hass, Soc. Labor, 633; Hoopes, Soc., 254; Dobbs, Soc. Workers, 119.

1956, Eisenhower, Rep., 620,430; Stevenson, Dem., 523,002; Hass, Soc. Labor, 7,457.

1960, Kennedy, Dem., 599,298; Nixon, Rep., 629,273; Hass, Soc. Labor, 10,895; Curtis, Constitution, 1,401; Dobbs, Soc. Workers, 705.

1964, Johnson, Dem., 779,699; Goldwater, Rep., 470,366; Hass, Soc. Labor, 7,772; DeBerry, Freedom Soc., 537.

1968, Nixon, Rep., 588,510; Humphrey, Dem., 616,037; Wallace, 3d Party, 96,990; Blomen, Soc. Labor, 488; Cleaver, Peace and Freedom, 1,609; Halstead, Soc. Workers, 270; Mitchell, Free Ballot, 377.

1972, Nixon, Rep., 837,135; McGovern, Dem., 568,334; Schmitz, Amer., 58,906; Spock, Ind., 2,644; Fisher, Soc. Labor, 1,102; Jenness, Soc. Workers, 623; Hall, Com., 566; Hospers, Libertarian, 1,537.

1976, Carter, Dem., 717,323; Ford, Rep., 777,732; McCarthy, Ind., 36,986; Maddox, Amer. Ind., 8,585; Anderson, Amer., 5,046; MacBride, Libertarian, 5,042; Wright, People's, 1,124; Camejo, Soc. Workers, 905; LaRouche, U.S. Labor, 903; Hall, Com., 817; Levin, Soc. Labor, 712; Zeidler, Soc., 358.

1980, Reagan, Rep., 865,244; Carter, Dem., 650,193; Anderson, Ind., 185,073; Clark, Libertarian, 29,213; Commoner, Citizens, 9,403; DeBerry, Soc. Workers, 1,137; McReynolds, Soc., 956; Hall, Com., 834; Griswold, Workers World, 341.

1984, Reagan, Rep., 1,051,670; Mondale, Dem., 798,352; Bergland, Libertarian, 8,844.

1988, Bush, Rep., 903,835; Dukakis, Dem., 933,516; Paul, Lib., 17,240; LaRouche, Ind., 4,412.

1992, Clinton, Dem., 993,037; Bush, Rep., 731,234; Perot, Ind., 541,780; Marrou, Libertarian, 7,533; Gritz, Populist/America First, 4,854; Hagelin, Natural Law, 2,456; Phillips, U.S. Taxpayers, 2,354; Fulani, New Alliance, 1,776; Daniels, Ind., 1,171.

1996, Clinton, Dem., 1,123,323; Dole, Rep., 840,712; Perot, Ref., 201,003; Nader, Ind., 60,322; Browne, Libertarian, 12,522; Hagelin, Natural Law, 6,076; Phillips, Taxpayers, 4,578; Collins, Ind., 2,374; Moorehead, Workers World, 2,189; Harris, Soc. Workers, 738.

West Virginia

County	1996 Clinton (D)	Dole (R)	Perot (RF)	1992 Clinton (D)	Bush (R)	Perot (I)
Barbour..	3,076	2,155	784	3,467	2,322	1,153
Berkeley..	8,321	9,859	2,291	7,159	9,134	3,645
Boone...	6,048	1,917	927	6,576	2,021	1,037
Braxton..	3,001	1,441	527	3,396	1,535	823
Brooke...	5,338	2,741	1,375	5,693	2,582	2,103
Cabell...	16,277	13,179	2,968	15,111	13,203	5,311
Calhoun..	1,402	1,000	307	1,627	1,095	537
Clay....	2,074	1,137	355	1,928	1,255	462
Doddridge.	865	1,335	382	968	1,500	515
Fayette..	9,471	3,669	1,552	9,574	3,991	2,002
Gilmer..	1,390	933	316	1,576	1,085	484
Grant....	1,206	2,599	481	1,011	2,762	519
Greenbrier	6,286	4,434	1,418	5,784	4,442	1,898
Hampshire	2,335	2,814	605	2,365	2,767	1,022
Hancock..	7,521	4,268	2,158	7,830	3,897	3,267
Hardy...	1,911	1,895	438	1,917	2,144	602
Harrison..	14,746	8,857	3,135	15,480	9,687	5,131
Jackson..	4,882	4,235	1,295	5,102	4,192	1,908
Jefferson..	6,361	5,287	1,307	5,363	4,656	2,114
Kanawha.	40,357	29,311	6,412	38,315	31,358	11,778
Lewis....	2,868	2,285	974	2,931	2,413	1,197
Lincoln..	4,994	2,530	696	4,502	2,637	787
Logan...	10,840	2,627	1,532	11,095	3,336	1,835
McDowell.	5,989	1,550	655	7,019	1,941	803
Marion..	12,994	6,160	2,881	14,042	6,380	4,736
Marshall..	7,045	4,460	2,202	7,298	4,463	3,402
Mason...	5,284	3,581	1,533	5,331	3,808	2,045
Mercer...	8,721	7,768	2,141	9,511	7,888	2,817
Mineral..	3,487	4,380	1,170	3,992	4,837	1,884
Mingo...	7,584	2,229	1,020	7,342	2,584	915
Monongalia	13,406	10,189	3,040	14,142	9,831	4,576
Monroe..	2,382	2,131	559	2,418	2,311	685
Morgan..	1,929	2,599	513	1,854	2,585	886
Nicholas..	4,769	2,649	1,071	5,042	2,959	1,495
Ohio....	8,781	7,267	2,065	9,522	7,421	3,632
Pendleton.	1,591	1,431	276	1,626	1,589	362
Pleasants..	1,478	1,265	416	1,387	1,248	731
Pocahontas	1,796	1,242	426	1,741	1,401	627
Preston..	4,237	4,257	1,760	3,933	4,429	2,109
Putnam..	8,029	8,803	1,901	6,817	7,653	2,910
Raleigh..	12,547	8,628	2,355	13,171	8,700	3,247
Randolph..	5,469	3,348	1,184	5,097	3,496	1,582
Ritchie..	1,385	1,906	522	1,474	2,184	745
Roane...	2,572	2,069	622	2,607	2,207	1,009
Summers..	2,397	1,505	438	2,650	1,652	565
Taylor...	2,692	1,977	844	2,843	2,022	1,242
Tucker..	1,649	1,217	424	1,805	1,261	550
Tyler....	1,459	734	563	1,587	1,593	1,013

County	1996 Clinton (D)	Dole (R)	Perot (RF)	1992 Clinton (D)	Bush (R)	Perot (I)
Upshur....	3,052	3,325	1,031	3,161	3,505	1,558
Wayne....	8,300	5,492	1,633	8,392	5,729	2,199
Webster..	2,292	654	369	2,320	811	436
Wetzel....	3,209	2,037	1,004	3,753	2,271	1,550
Wirt....	906	928	280	1,043	939	394
Wood.....	13,261	15,502	3,694	13,529	15,441	6,998
Wyoming..	5,550	2,155	812	5,782	2,821	996
Totals	**327,812**	**233,946**	**71,639**	**331,001**	**241,974**	**108,829**

West Virginia Vote Since 1948

1948, Truman, Dem., 429,188; Dewey, Rep., 316,251; Wallace, Prog., 3,311.

1952, Eisenhower, Rep., 419,970; Stevenson, Dem., 453,578.

1956, Eisenhower, Rep., 449,297; Stevenson, Dem., 381,534.

1960, Kennedy, Dem., 441,786; Nixon, Rep., 395,995.

1964, Johnson, Dem., 538,087; Goldwater, Rep., 253,953.

1968, Nixon, Rep., 307,555; Humphrey, Dem., 374,091; Wallace, 3d Party, 72,560.

1972, Nixon, Rep., 484,964; McGovern, Dem., 277,435.

1976, Carter, Dem., 435,864; Ford, Rep., 314,726.

1980, Reagan, Rep., 334,206; Carter, Dem., 367,462; Anderson, Ind., 31,691; Clark, Libertarian, 4,356.

1984, Reagan, Rep., 405,483; Mondale, Dem., 328,125.

1988, Bush, Rep., 310,065; Dukakis, Dem., 341,016; Fulani, New Alliance, 2,230.

1992, Clinton, Dem., 331,001; Bush, Rep., 241,974; Perot, Ind., 108,829; Marrou, Libertarian, 1,873.

1996, Clinton, Dem., 327,812; Dole, Rep., 233,946; Perot, Ref., 71,639; Browne, Libertarian, 3,062.

Wisconsin

County	1996 Clinton (D)	Dole (R)	Perot (RF)	1992 Clinton (D)	Bush (R)	Perot (I)
Adams...	4,119	2,450	1,122	3,539	2,465	2,003
Ashland..	3,808	1,863	861	4,213	2,372	1,746
Barron...	8,025	6,158	2,692	8,063	6,572	5,479
Bayfield..	3,895	2,250	899	3,873	2,393	1,786
Brown...	42,823	38,563	8,036	37,513	42,352	22,395
Buffalo...	2,681	1,800	972	2,996	2,029	1,889
Burnet...	3,625	2,452	962	3,172	2,340	1,855
Calumet..	6,940	7,049	2,112	5,701	7,541	5,055
Chippewa.	9,647	7,520	3,567	10,487	8,215	6,408
Clark....	5,540	4,622	2,486	5,540	4,977	4,284
Columbia.	10,336	8,377	2,377	9,348	9,099	5,439
Crawford.	3,658	2,149	1,060	3,540	2,390	1,797
Dane....	109,347	59,487	12,436	114,724	61,957	31,874
Dodge...	12,625	12,890	3,322	11,438	14,971	9,136
Door....	5,590	4,948	1,475	4,735	5,468	3,506
Douglas..	10,976	5,167	2,001	12,319	5,679	4,150
Dunn....	7,536	4,917	2,555	7,965	5,283	4,809
Eau Claire	20,298	13,900	5,160	21,221	15,915	9,783
Florence..	869	927	316	978	942	719
Fond du Lac.	15,542	16,488	4,204	13,757	19,785	10,660
Forest...	2,092	1,166	678	1,904	1,393	1,062
Grant....	9,203	7,021	2,648	8,914	7,678	6,405
Green...	6,136	4,697	1,534	5,467	4,887	3,735
Green Lake	3,152	3,565	1,025	2,772	3,897	2,827
Iowa	4,690	2,866	1,071	4,467	3,288	2,341
Iron	1,725	1,260	469	1,762	1,273	835
Jackson..	3,705	2,262	1,163	3,681	2,644	2,040
Jefferson..	13,188	12,681	3,177	11,593	13,072	7,960
Juneau...	4,331	3,226	1,393	4,177	4,051	2,670
Kenosha..	27,964	18,296	6,507	27,341	19,854	14,232
Kewaunee	4,311	3,431	1,161	4,050	3,570	2,700
La Crosse.	23,647	16,482	4,844	22,838	18,891	10,224
La Fayette	3,261	2,172	944	3,143	2,582	2,079
Langlade.	4,074	3,206	1,249	3,630	3,890	2,444
Lincoln...	6,166	4,076	1,800	5,297	4,321	3,605
Manitowoc	16,750	13,239	3,941	15,903	14,008	11,179
Marathon.	24,012	19,874	6,749	21,482	20,948	14,600
Marinette.	8,413	7,231	2,367	7,626	7,984	5,412
Marquette.	2,859	2,208	915	2,533	2,322	1,818
Menominee	992	230	107	691	244	221
Milwaukee	216,620	119,407	26,027	235,521	151,314	76,039
Monroe..	6,924	5,299	2,081	6,427	6,118	4,183
Oconto...	6,723	5,389	1,655	5,898	5,720	4,405
Oneida..	7,619	6,339	2,604	7,160	6,725	4,782
Outagamie	28,815	27,758	7,235	23,735	30,370	18,479
Ozaukee..	13,269	22,078	2,774	11,879	22,805	8,002
Pepin....	1,585	1,007	456	1,673	1,098	781
Pierce...	7,970	4,599	2,074	7,824	4,844	4,492
Polk....	8,334	5,387	2,369	7,746	5,446	4,753
Portage..	15,901	9,631	3,410	15,553	10,914	7,083
Price....	3,523	2,545	1,218	3,575	2,654	2,286
Racine...	38,567	30,105	7,611	34,875	32,310	20,227
Richland..	3,502	2,642	901	3,458	3,144	1,899
Rock....	32,450	20,096	6,800	31,154	21,942	15,700
Rusk....	2,941	2,219	1,331	3,376	2,430	2,085
St. Croix..	11,384	8,253	3,180	10,281	8,114	7,125
Sauk	9,889	7,448	2,448	9,128	8,886	5,280

County	1996 Clinton (D)	Dole (R)	Perot (RF)	1992 Clinton (D)	Bush (R)	Perot (I)
Sawyer...	2,773	2,603	962	2,796	2,658	1,861
Shawano.	6,850	6,396	2,071	6,062	7,253	4,540
Sheboygan	22,022	20,067	4,157	20,568	22,526	11,295
Taylor ...	3,253	3,108	1,457	3,305	3,415	2,590
Trempealeau	5,848	3,035	1,688	6,218	3,577	3,160
Vernon....	5,572	3,796	1,523	5,673	4,072	2,890
Vilas	4,226	4,496	1,548	3,764	4,616	2,827
Walworth.	13,283	15,099	3,729	11,825	15,727	9,029
Washburn.	3,231	2,703	920	3,080	2,586	1,978
Washington	17,154	25,829	4,786	13,339	22,739	13,045
Waukesha	57,354	91,729	13,109	50,270	91,461	36,622
Waupaca.	7,800	8,679	2,464	6,666	10,252	6,088
Waushara.	3,824	3,573	1,264	3,402	4,045	2,829
Winnebago	29,564	27,880	6,531	27,234	33,709	16,140
Wood....	14,650	12,666	4,599	13,208	13,843	8,822
Totals ...	1,071,971	845,029	227,339	1,041,066	930,855	544,479

Wisconsin Vote Since 1948

1948, Truman, Dem., 647,310; Dewey, Rep., 590,959; Wallace, Prog., 25,282; Thomas, Soc., 12,547; Teichert, Soc. Labor, 399; Dobbs, Soc. Workers, 303.

1952, Eisenhower, Rep., 979,744; Stevenson, Dem., 622,175; Hallinan, Ind., 2,174; Dobbs, Ind., 1,350; Hoopes, Ind., 1,157; Hass, Ind., 770.

1956, Eisenhower, Rep., 954,844; Stevenson, Dem., 586,768; Andrews, Ind., 6,918; Hoopes, Soc., 754; Hass, Soc. Labor, 710; Dobbs, Soc. Workers, 564.

1960, Kennedy, Dem., 830,805; Nixon, Rep., 895,175; Dobbs, Soc. Workers, 1,792; Hass, Soc. Labor, 1,310.

1964, Johnson, Dem., 1,050,424; Goldwater, Rep., 638,495; DeBerry, Soc. Workers, 1,692; Hass, Soc. Labor, 1,204.

1968, Nixon, Rep., 809,997; Humphrey, Dem., 748,804; Wallace, 3d Party, 127,835; Blomen, Soc. Labor, 1,338; Halstead, Soc. Workers, 1,222; scattered, 2,342.

1972 Nixon, Rep., 989,430; McGovern, Dem., 810,174; Schmitz, Amer., 47,525; Spock, Ind., 2,701; Fisher, Soc. Labor, 998; Hall, Com., 663; Reed, Ind., 506; scattered, 893.

1976, Carter, Dem., 1,040,232; Ford, Rep., 1,004,987; McCarthy, Ind., 34,943; Maddox, Amer. Ind., 8,552; Zeidler, Soc., 4,298; MacBride, Libertarian, 3,814; Camejo, Soc. Workers, 1,691; Wright, People's, 943; Hall, Com., 749; LaRouche, U.S. Lab., 738; Levin, Soc. Labor, 389; scattered, 2,839.

1980, Reagan, Rep., 1,088,845; Carter, Dem., 981,584; Anderson, Ind., 160,657; Clark, Libertarian, 29,135; Commoner, Citizens, 7,767; Rarick, Constitution, 1,519; McReynolds, Soc., 808; Hall, Com., 772; Griswold, Workers World, 414; DeBerry, Soc. Workers, 383; scattering, 1,337.

1984, Reagan, Rep., 1,198,584; Mondale, Dem., 995,740; Bergland, Libertarian, 4,883.

1988, Bush, Rep., 1,047,499; Dukakis, Dem., 1,126,794; Paul, Lib., 5,157; Duke, Pop., 3,056.

1992, Clinton, Dem., 1,041,066; Bush, Rep., 930,855; Perot, Ind., 544,479; Marrou, Libertarian, 2,877; Gritz, Populist/America First, 2,311; Daniels, Ind., 1,883; Phillips, U.S. Taxpayers, 1,772; Hagelin, Natural Law, 1,070.

1996, Clinton, Dem., 1,071,971; Dole, Rep., 845,029; Perot, Ref., 227,339; Nader, Green, 28,723; Phillips, Taxpayers, 8,811; Browne, Libertarian, 7,929; Hagelin, Natural Law, 1,379; Moorehead, Workers World, 1,333; Hollis, Soc., 848; Harris, Soc. Workers, 483.

Wyoming

County	1996 Clinton (D)	Dole (R)	Perot (RF)	1992 Clinton (D)	Bush (R)	Perot (I)
Albany....	6,399	5,967	1,333	5,713	4,176	2,862
Big Horn...	1,438	2,821	545	1,216	2,216	1,236
Campbell ..	3,468	6,382	1,954	2,709	5,315	3,133
Carbon ...	2,690	2,930	855	2,737	2,320	1,579
Converse ..	1,520	2,702	639	1,307	2,159	1,260
Crook	651	1,698	394	568	1,377	718
Fremont...	5,445	7,554	1,840	4,765	5,387	3,594
Goshen ...	1,923	2,989	547	1,754	2,395	1,144
Hot Springs.	779	1,348	287	740	978	652
Johnson...	815	2,071	378	656	1,614	844
Laramie ...	13,676	16,924	2,958	12,177	12,890	6,607
Lincoln....	1,803	3,764	906	1,430	2,595	1,495
Natrona ...	11,240	13,182	3,524	9,817	9,717	7,647
Niobrara...	325	757	209	298	635	355
Park	3,240	7,430	1,318	2,771	5,218	3,145
Platte.....	1,631	2,155	579	1,398	1,668	956
Sheridan ..	4,594	5,892	1,414	4,139	4,303	3,035
Sublette ...	677	1,829	401	536	1,168	828
Sweetwater.	7,088	5,591	2,792	6,417	4,476	3,879
Teton.....	4,042	3,918	839	3,120	2,854	2,340
Uinta	2,414	3,471	1,242	2,047	2,701	2,041
Washakie..	1,205	2,250	470	1,118	1,720	1,084
Weston ...	871	1,763	504	727	1,465	829
Totals....	77,934	105,388	25,928	68,160	79,347	51,263

Wyoming Vote Since 1948

1948, Truman, Dem., 52,354; Dewey, Rep., 47,947; Wallace, Prog., 931; Thomas, Soc., 137; Teichert, Soc. Labor, 56.

1952, Eisenhower, Rep., 81,047; Stevenson, Dem., 47,934; Hamblen, Proh., 194; Hoopes, Soc., 40; Haas, Soc. Labor, 36.

1956, Eisenhower, Rep., 74,573; Stevenson, Dem., 49,554.

1960, Kennedy, Dem., 63,331; Nixon, Rep., 77,451.

1964, Johnson, Dem., 80,718; Goldwater, Rep., 61,998.

1968, Nixon, Rep., 70,927; Humphrey, Dem., 45,173; Wallace, 3d Party, 11,105.

1972, Nixon, Rep., 100,464; McGovern, Dem., 44,358; Schmitz, Amer., 748.

1976, Carter, Dem., 62,239; Ford, Rep., 92,717; McCarthy, Ind., 624; Reagan, Ind., 307; Anderson, Amer., 290; MacBride, Libertarian, 89; Brown, Ind., 47; Maddox, Amer. Ind., 30.

1980, Reagan, Rep., 110,700; Carter, Dem., 49,427; Anderson, Ind., 12,072; Clark, Libertarian, 4,514.

1984, Reagan, Rep., 133,241; Mondale, Dem., 53,370; Bergland, Libertarian, 2,357.

1988, Bush, Rep., 106,867; Dukakis, Dem., 67,113; Paul, Lib., 2,026; Fulani, New Alliance, 545.

1992, Clinton, Dem., 68,160; Bush, Rep., 79,347; Perot, Ind., 51,263.

1996, Dole, Rep., 105,388; Clinton, Dem., 77,934; Perot, Ind. (Ref.), 25,928; Browne, Libertarian, 1,739; Hagelin, Natural Law, 582.

1996 Official Presidential General Election Results

Source: Voter News Service; *Congressional Quarterly*

Candidate (Party)	Popular Vote	Percent of Popular Vote
Bill Clinton (Democrat)	47,401,185	49.25
Bob Dole (Republican)	39,197,469	40.73
Ross Perot (Reform)	8,085,294	8.40
Ralph Nader (Green)	651,771	.68
Harry Browne (Libertarian)	485,120	.50
Howard Phillips (U.S. Taxpayers)	182,924	.19
John Hagelin (Natural Law)	112,978	.12
Monica Moorehead (Workers World)	29,082	.03
Marsha Feinland (Peace & Freedom)	25,332	.03
James Harris (Socialist Workers)	8,286	.01
Charles Collins (Independent)	7,899	.01
Dennis Peron (Grass Roots)	5,378	.01
Mary Cal Hollis (Socialist)	4,269	.00
Jerome White (Socialist Equality)	2,438	.00
Diane Beall Templin (American)	1,847	.00
Earl Dodge (Prohibition)	1,293	.00
A. Peter Crane (Independent)	1,101	.00
Ralph Forbes (Independent)	932	.00
John Birrenbach (Independent Grass Roots)	787	.00
Isabell Masters (Independent)	749	.00
Steve Michael (Independent)	408	.00
Write-in	24,475	.03
None of These Candidates (Nevada)	5,608	.01
Total	96,236,625	100

Note: Party designations may vary from one state to another.

Voter Turnout in Presidential Elections, 1932-96

Source: Federal Election Commission; Commission for Study of American Electorate; *Congressional Quarterly*

	Candidates	Voter Participation (% of voting-age population)		Candidates	Voter Participation (% of voting-age population)
1932	Roosevelt-Hoover	52.4	1968	Humphrey-Nixon	60.9
1936	Roosevelt-Landon	56.0	1972	McGovern-Nixon	55.2(1)
1940	Roosevelt-Willkie	58.9	1976	Carter-Ford	53.5
1944	Roosevelt-Dewey	56.0	1980	Carter-Reagan	54.0
1948	Truman-Dewey	51.1	1984	Mondale-Reagan	53.1
1952	Stevenson-Eisenhower	61.6	1988	Dukakis-Bush	50.2
1956	Stevenson-Eisenhower	59.3	1992	Clinton-Bush-Perot	55.9
1960	Kennedy-Nixon	62.8	1996	Clinton-Dole-Perot	49.0
1964	Johnson-Goldwater	61.9			

(1) The sharp drop in 1972 reflects the expansion of eligibility with the enfranchisement of 18- to 21-year olds.

Electoral Votes for President

(based on 1990 Census)

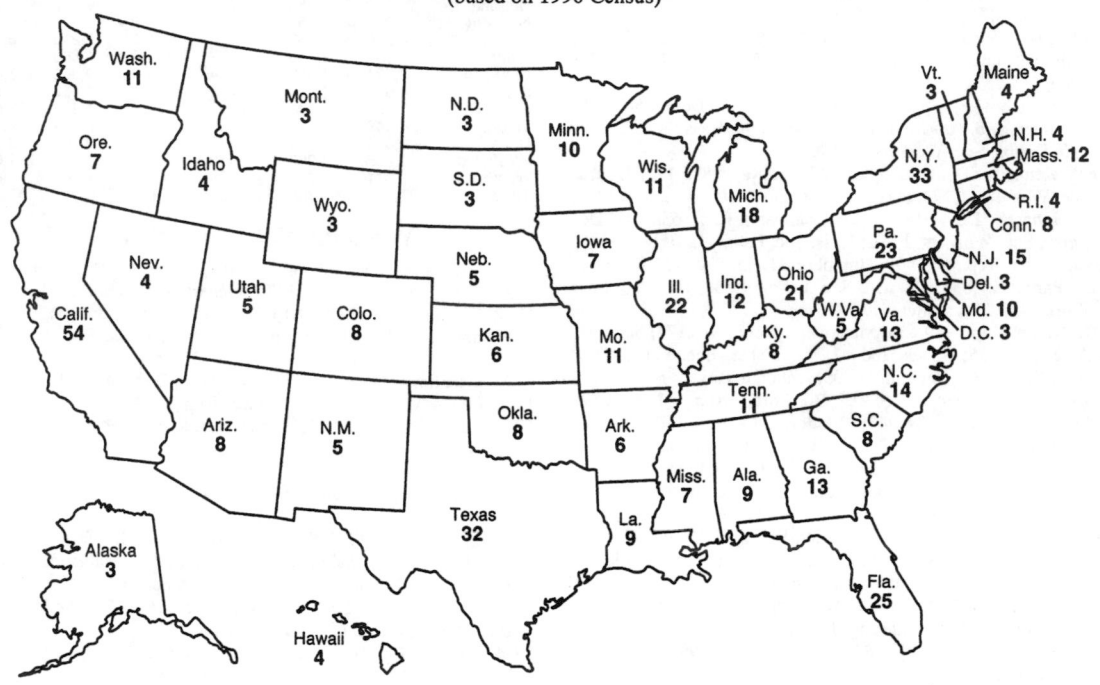

The Electoral College

The president and the vice president are the only elective federal officials not chosen by direct vote of the people. They are elected by the members of the Electoral College, an institution provided for in the U.S. Constitution.

On presidential election day, the first Tuesday after the first Monday in Nov. of every 4th year, each state chooses as many electors as it has senators and representatives in Congress. In 1964, for the first time, as provided by the 23d Amendment to the Constitution, the District of Columbia voted for 3 electors. Thus, with 100 senators and 435 representatives, there are 538 members of the Electoral College, with a majority of 270 electoral votes needed to elect the president and vice president.

Although political parties were not part of the original plan created by the Founding Fathers, today political parties customarily nominate their lists of electors at their respective state conventions. Some states print the names of the candidates for president and vice president at the top of the Nov. ballot; others list only the names of the electors. In either case, the electors of the party receiving the highest vote are elected.

The electors meet on the first Monday after the 2d Wednesday in Dec. in their respective state capitals or in some other place prescribed by state legislatures. By long-established custom, they vote for their party nominees, although this is not required by law.

The Constitution requires electors to cast a ballot for at least one person who is not an inhabitant of that elector's home state. This ensures that presidential and vice presidential candidates from the same party will not be from the same state. Also, an elector cannot be a member of Congress or hold federal office.

Certified and sealed lists of the votes of the electors in each state are sent to the president of the U.S. Senate, who then opens them in the presence of the members of the Senate and House of Representatives in a joint session held in early Jan., and the electoral votes of all the states are then officially counted. (The count was made on Jan. 9 in 1997.)

If no candidate for president has a majority, the House of Representatives chooses a president from among the 3 highest candidates, with all representatives from each state combining to cast one vote for that state. The House decided the outcome of the presidential elections of 1800 and 1824. If no candidate for vice president has a majority, the Senate chooses from the top 2, with the senators voting as individuals. The Senate chose the vice president following the 1836 election.

Under the electoral college system, a candidate who fails to be the top vote getter in the popular vote may still win a majority of electoral votes. This happened in the elections of 1876 and 1888.

In the 1996 election, Bill Clinton won 379 electoral votes, and Bob Dole won 159.

Third-Party and Independent Presidential Candidates

Although many "third party" candidates or independents have pursued the presidency, only 9 of these have polled more than a million votes. In most elections since 1860, fewer than one vote in 20 has been cast for a third-party candidate. In only 5 presidential elections since then have all non-major-party candidates combined polled more than 10% of the vote. The major vote getters in those elections were James B. Weaver (People's Party), 1892; former President Theodore Roosevelt (Progressive Party), 1912; Robert M. La Follette (Progressive Party), 1924; George C. Wallace (American Independent Party), 1968; and H. Ross Perot, an independent in 1992.

Roosevelt outpolled the Republican candidate, William Howard Taft, in 1912, capturing 28% of the popular vote

and 88 electoral votes. In 1948, Strom Thurmond was able to capture 39 electoral votes (from 5 Southern states); however, all third parties received only 5.75% of the popular vote in the election. Twenty years later, George Wallace's popularity in the same region allowed him to get 46 electoral votes and 13.5% of the popular vote. In 1992 Perot was able to capture 19% of the popular vote; however, he did not win a single state. In 1996, Perot (as the candidate of his newly formed Reform Party) won 8% of the vote; all third-party candidates combined won 10%.

Despite the difficulty in winning the presidency, independent and third-party candidates sometimes succeed in winning other offices and often bring the attention of all presidential candidates combined to particular issues.

Notable Third Party and Independent Campaigns by Year

Party	Presidential nominee	Year	Issues	Strength in . . .
Anti-Masonic	William Wirt	1832	Against secret societies and oaths	PA, VT
Liberty	James G. Birney	1844	Anti-slavery	North
Free Soil	Martin Van Buren	1848	Anti-slavery	NY, OH
American (Know-Nothing)	Millard Fillmore	1856	Anti-immigrant	Northeast, South
Greenback	Peter Cooper	1876	For "cheap money," labor rights	National
Greenback	James B. Weaver	1880	For "cheap money," labor rights	National
Prohibition	John P. St. John	1884	Anti-liquor	National
People's (Populists)	James B. Weaver	1892	For "cheap money," end of national banks	South, West
Socialist	Eugene V. Debs	1900-12; 1920	For public ownership	National
Progressive (Bull Moose)	Theodore Roosevelt	1912	Against high tariffs	Midwest, West
Progressive	Robert M. La Follette	1924	Farmer and labor rights	Midwest, West
Socialist	Norman Thomas	1928-48	Liberal reforms	National
Union	William Lemke	1936	Anti-New Deal	National
States' Rights (Dixiecrats)	Strom Thurmond	1948	For states' rights	South
Progressive	Henry A. Wallace	1948	Anti-cold war	NY, CA
American Independent	George C. Wallace	1968	For states' rights	South
American	John G. Schmitz	1972	For "law and order"	Far West, OH, LA
None (Independent)	John B. Anderson	1980	A 3d choice	National
None (Independent)	H. Ross Perot	1992	Federal budget deficit	National
Reform	H. Ross Perot	1996	Deficit; campaign finance	National

Major-Party Nominees for President and Vice President
Asterisk (*) denotes winning ticket

Year	Democratic President	Vice President	Republican President	Vice President
1856	James Buchanan*	John Breckinridge	John Frémont	William Dayton
1860	Stephen A. Douglas(1)	Herschel V. Johnson	Abraham Lincoln*	Hannibal Hamlin
1864	George McClellan	G.H. Pendleton	Abraham Lincoln*	Andrew Johnson
1868	Horatio Seymour	Francis Blair	Ulysses S. Grant*	Schuyler Colfax
1872	Horace Greeley	B. Gratz Brown	Ulysses S. Grant*	Henry Wilson
1876	Samuel J. Tilden	Thomas Hendricks	Rutherford B. Hayes*	William Wheeler
1880	Winfield Hancock	William English	James A. Garfield*	Chester A. Arthur
1884	Grover Cleveland*	Thomas Hendricks	James Blaine	John Logan
1888	Grover Cleveland	A.G. Thurman	Benjamin Harrison*	Levi Morton
1892	Grover Cleveland*	Adlai Stevenson	Benjamin Harrison	Whitelaw Reid
1896	William J. Bryan	Arthur Sewall	William McKinley*	Garret Hobart
1900	William J. Bryan	Adlai Stevenson	William McKinley*	Theodore Roosevelt
1904	Alton Parker	Henry Davis	Theodore Roosevelt*	Charles Fairbanks
1908	William J. Bryan	John Kern	William H. Taft*	James Sherman
1912	Woodrow Wilson*	Thomas Marshall	William H. Taft	James Sherman(2)
1916	Woodrow Wilson*	Thomas Marshall	Charles Hughes	Charles Fairbanks
1920	James M. Cox	Franklin D. Roosevelt	Warren G. Harding*	Calvin Coolidge
1924	John W. Davis	Charles W. Bryan	Calvin Coolidge*	Charles G. Dawes
1928	Alfred E. Smith	Joseph T. Robinson	Herbert Hoover*	Charles Curtis
1932	Franklin D. Roosevelt*	John N. Garner	Herbert Hoover	Charles Curtis
1936	Franklin D. Roosevelt*	John N. Garner	Alfred M. Landon	Frank Knox
1940	Franklin D. Roosevelt*	Henry A. Wallace	Wendell L. Willkie	Charles McNary
1944	Franklin D. Roosevelt*	Harry S. Truman	Thomas E. Dewey	John W. Bricker
1948	Harry S. Truman*	Alben W. Barkley	Thomas E. Dewey	Earl Warren
1952	Adlai E. Stevenson	John J. Sparkman	Dwight D. Eisenhower*	Richard M. Nixon
1956	Adlai E. Stevenson	Estes Kefauver	Dwight D. Eisenhower*	Richard M. Nixon
1960	John F. Kennedy*	Lyndon B. Johnson	Richard M. Nixon	Henry Cabot Lodge
1964	Lyndon B. Johnson*	Hubert H. Humphrey	Barry M. Goldwater	William E. Miller
1968	Hubert H. Humphrey	Edmund S. Muskie	Richard M. Nixon*	Spiro T. Agnew
1972	George S. McGovern	R. Sargent Shriver Jr.	Richard M. Nixon*	Spiro T. Agnew
1976	Jimmy Carter*	Walter F. Mondale	Gerald R. Ford	Bob Dole
1980	Jimmy Carter	Walter F. Mondale	Ronald Reagan*	George Bush
1984	Walter F. Mondale	Geraldine Ferraro	Ronald Reagan*	George Bush
1988	Michael S. Dukakis	Lloyd Bentsen	George Bush*	Dan Quayle
1992	Bill Clinton*	Al Gore	George Bush	Dan Quayle
1996	Bill Clinton*	Al Gore	Bob Dole	Jack Kemp

(1) Douglas and Johnson were nominated at the Baltimore convention. An earlier convention in Charleston, SC, failed to reach a consensus and resulted in a split in the party. The Southern faction of the Democrats nominated John Breckinridge for president and Joseph Lane for vice president. (2) Died Oct. 30; replaced on ballot by Nicholas Butler.

Popular and Electoral Vote for President

(D) Democrat; (DR) Democratic Republican; (F) Federalist; (LR) Liberal Republican; (NR) National Republican; (P) People's; (PR) Progressive; (R) Republican; (RF) Reform; (SR) States' Rights; (W) Whig; Asterisk (*)—See notes.

Year	President elected	Popular	Elec.	Major losing candidate(s)	Popular	Elec.
1789	George Washington (F)	Unknown	69	No opposition	—	—
1792	George Washington (F)	Unknown	132	No opposition		
1796	John Adams (F)	Unknown	71	Thomas Jefferson (DR)	Unknown	68
1800*	Thomas Jefferson (DR)	Unknown	73	Aaron Burr (DR)	Unknown	73
1804	Thomas Jefferson (DR)	Unknown	162	Charles Pinckney (F)	Unknown	14
1808	James Madison (DR)	Unknown	122	Charles Pinckney (F)	Unknown	47
1812	James Madison (DR)	Unknown	128	DeWitt Clinton (F)	Unknown	89
1816	James Monroe (DR)	Unknown	183	Rufus King (F)	Unknown	34
1820	James Monroe (DR)	Unknown	231	John Quincy Adams (DR)	Unknown	1
1824*	John Quincy Adams (DR)	105,321	84	Andrew Jackson (DR)	155,872	99
				Henry Clay (DR)	46,587	37
				William H. Crawford (DR)	44,282	41
1828	Andrew Jackson (D)	647,231	178	John Quincy Adams (NR)	509,097	83
1832	Andrew Jackson (D)	687,502	219	Henry Clay (NR)	530,189	49
1836	Martin Van Buren (D)	762,678	170	William H. Harrison (W)	548,007	73
1840	William H. Harrison (W)	1,275,017	234	Martin Van Buren (D)	1,128,702	60
1844	James K. Polk (D)	1,337,243	170	Henry Clay (W)	1,299,068	105
1848	Zachary Taylor (W)	1,360,101	163	Lewis Cass (D)	1,220,544	127
				Martin Van Buren (Free Soil)	291,501	—
1852	Franklin Pierce (D)	1,601,474	254	Winfield Scott (W)	1,386,578	42
1856	James Buchanan (D)	1,927,995	174	John C. Fremont (R)	1,391,555	114
				Millard Fillmore (American)	873,053	8
1860	Abraham Lincoln (R)	1,866,352	180	Stephen A. Douglas (D)	1,375,157	12
				John C. Breckinridge (D)	845,763	72
				John Bell (Const. Union)	589,581	39
1864	Abraham Lincoln (R)	2,216,067	212	George McClellan (D)	1,808,725	21
1868	Ulysses S. Grant (R)	3,015,071	214	Horatio Seymour (D)	2,709,615	80
1872*	Ulysses S. Grant (R)	3,597,070	286	Horace Greeley (D-LR)*	2,834,079	—
1876*	Rutherford B. Hayes (R)	4,033,950	185	Samuel J. Tilden (D)	4,284,757	184
1880	James A. Garfield (R)	4,449,053	214	Winfield S. Hancock (D)	4,442,030	155
1884	Grover Cleveland (D)	4,911,017	219	James G. Blaine (R)	4,848,334	182
1888*	Benjamin Harrison (R)	5,444,337	233	Grover Cleveland (D)	5,540,050	168
1892	Grover Cleveland (D)	5,554,414	277	Benjamin Harrison (R)	5,190,802	145
				James Weaver (P)	1,027,329	22
1896	William McKinley (R)	7,035,638	271	William J. Bryan (D-P)	6,467,946	176
1900	William McKinley (R)	7,219,530	292	William J. Bryan (D)	6,358,071	155
1904	Theodore Roosevelt (R)	7,628,834	336	Alton B. Parker (D)	5,084,491	140
1908	William H. Taft (R)	7,679,006	321	William J. Bryan (D)	6,409,106	162
1912	Woodrow Wilson (D)	6,286,214	435	Theodore Roosevelt (PR)	4,216,020	88
				William H. Taft (R)	3,483,922	8
1916	Woodrow Wilson (D)	9,129,606	277	Charles E. Hughes (R)	8,538,221	254
1920	Warren G. Harding (R)	16,152,200	404	James M. Cox (D)	9,147,353	127
1924	Calvin Coolidge (R)	15,725,016	382	John W. Davis (D)	8,385,586	136
				Robert M. La Follette (PR)	4,822,856	13
1928	Herbert Hoover (R)	21,392,190	444	Alfred E. Smith (D)	15,016,443	87
1932	Franklin D. Roosevelt (D)	22,821,857	472	Herbert Hoover (R)	15,761,841	59
1936	Franklin D. Roosevelt (D)	27,751,597	523	Alfred Landon (R)	16,679,583	8
1940	Franklin D. Roosevelt (D)	27,243,466	449	Wendell Willkie (R)	22,304,755	82
1944	Franklin D. Roosevelt (D)	25,602,505	432	Thomas E. Dewey (R)	22,006,278	99
1948	Harry S. Truman (D)	24,105,812	303	Thomas E. Dewey (R)	21,970,065	189
				Strom Thurmond (SR)	1,169,021	39
				Henry A. Wallace (PR)	1,157,172	—
1952	Dwight D. Eisenhower (R)	33,936,252	442	Adlai E. Stevenson (D)	27,314,992	89
1956*	Dwight D. Eisenhower (R)	35,585,316	457	Adlai E. Stevenson (D)	26,031,322	73
1960*	John F. Kennedy (D)	34,227,096	303	Richard M. Nixon (R)	34,108,546	219
1964	Lyndon B. Johnson (D)	43,126,506	486	Barry M. Goldwater (R)	27,176,799	52
1968	Richard M. Nixon (R)	31,785,480	301	Hubert H. Humphrey (D)	31,275,166	191
				George C. Wallace (3d party)	9,906,473	46
1972*	Richard M. Nixon (R)	47,165,234	520	George S. McGovern (D)	29,170,774	17
1976*	Jimmy Carter (D)	40,828,929	297	Gerald R. Ford (R)	39,148,940	240
1980	Ronald Reagan (R)	43,899,248	489	Jimmy Carter (D)	35,481,435	49
				John B. Anderson (independent)	5,719,437	—
1984	Ronald Reagan (R)	54,281,858	525	Walter F. Mondale (D)	37,457,215	13
1988*	George Bush (R)	48,881,221	426	Michael S. Dukakis (D)	41,805,422	111
1992	Bill Clinton (D)	44,908,254	370	George Bush (R)	39,102,343	168
				H. Ross Perot (independent)	19,741,065	—
1996	Bill Clinton (D)	47,401,185	379	Bob Dole (R)	39,197,469	159
				H. Ross Perot (RF)	8,085,294	—

1800—Elected by House of Representatives because of tied electoral vote. **1824**—Elected by House of Representatives because no candidate had polled a majority. By 1824, the Democratic Republicans had become a loose coalition of competing political groups. By 1828, the supporters of Jackson were known as Democrats, and the John Q. Adams and Henry Clay supporters as National Republicans. **1872**—Greeley died Nov. 29, 1872. His electoral votes were split among 4 individuals. **1876**—FL, LA, OR, and SC election returns were disputed. Congress in joint session (Mar. 2, 1877) declared Hayes and Wheeler elected president and vice president. **1888**—Cleveland had more popular votes than Harrison, but since Harrison won 233 electoral votes as against 168 for Cleveland, Harrison won the presidency. **1956**—Democrats elected 74 electors, but one from Alabama refused to vote for Stevenson. **1960**—Sen. Harry F. Byrd (D, VA) received 15 electoral votes. **1972**—John Hospers of California received one vote from an elector of Virginia. **1976**—Ronald Reagan of CA received one vote from an elector of Washington. **1988**—Sen. Lloyd Bentsen (D, TX) received 1 vote from an elector of West Virginia.

Presidents of the U.S.

No.	Name	Politics	Born	in	Inaug.	at age	Died	at age
1	George Washington	Fed.	1732, Feb. 22	VA	1789	57	1799, Dec. 14	67
2	John Adams	Fed.	1735, Oct. 30	MA	1797	61	1826, July 4	90
3	Thomas Jefferson	Dem.-Rep.	1743, Apr. 13	VA	1801	57	1826, July 4	83
4	James Madison	Dem.-Rep.	1751, Mar. 16	VA	1809	57	1836, June 28	85
5	James Monroe	Dem.-Rep.	1758, Apr. 28	VA	1817	58	1831, July 4	73
6	John Quincy Adams	Dem.-Rep.	1767, July 11	MA	1825	57	1848, Feb. 23	80
7	Andrew Jackson	Dem.	1767, Mar. 15	SC	1829	61	1845, June 8	78
8	Martin Van Buren	Dem.	1782, Dec. 5	NY	1837	54	1862, July 24	79
9	William Henry Harrison	Whig	1773, Feb. 9	VA	1841	68	1841, Apr. 4	68
10	John Tyler	Whig	1790, Mar. 29	VA	1841	51	1862, Jan. 18	71
11	James Knox Polk	Dem.	1795, Nov. 2	NC	1845	49	1849, June 15	53
12	Zachary Taylor	Whig	1784, Nov. 24	VA	1849	64	1850, July 9	65
13	Millard Fillmore	Whig	1800, Jan. 7	NY	1850	50	1874, Mar. 8	74
14	Franklin Pierce	Dem.	1804, Nov. 23	NH	1853	48	1869, Oct. 8	64
15	James Buchanan	Dem.	1791, Apr. 23	PA	1857	65	1868, June 1	77
16	Abraham Lincoln	Rep.	1809, Feb. 12	KY	1861	52	1865, Apr. 15	56
17	Andrew Johnson	(1)	1808, Dec. 29	NC	1865	56	1875, July 31	66
18	Ulysses Simpson Grant	Rep.	1822, Apr. 27	OH	1869	46	1885, July 23	63
19	Rutherford Birchard Hayes	Rep.	1822, Oct. 4	OH	1877	54	1893, Jan. 17	70
20	James Abram Garfield	Rep.	1831, Nov. 19	OH	1881	49	1881, Sept. 19	49
21	Chester Alan Arthur	Rep.	1830, Oct. 5	VT	1881	50	1886, Nov. 18	56
22	Grover Cleveland	Dem.	1837, Mar. 18	NJ	1885	47	1908, June 24	71
23	Benjamin Harrison	Rep.	1833, Aug. 20	OH	1889	55	1901, Mar. 13	67
24	Grover Cleveland	Dem.	1837, Mar. 18	NJ	1893	55	1908, June 24	71
25	William McKinley	Rep.	1843, Jan. 29	OH	1897	54	1901, Sept. 14	58
26	Theodore Roosevelt	Rep.	1858, Oct. 27	NY	1901	42	1919, Jan. 6	60
27	William Howard Taft	Rep.	1857, Sept. 15	OH	1909	51	1930, Mar. 8	72
28	Woodrow Wilson	Dem.	1856, Dec. 28	VA	1913	56	1924, Feb. 3	67
29	Warren Gamaliel Harding	Rep.	1865, Nov. 2	OH	1921	55	1923, Aug. 2	57
30	Calvin Coolidge	Rep.	1872, July 4	VT	1923	51	1933, Jan. 5	60
31	Herbert Clark Hoover	Rep.	1874, Aug. 10	IA	1929	54	1964, Oct. 20	90
32	Franklin Delano Roosevelt	Dem.	1882, Jan. 30	NY	1933	51	1945, Apr. 12	63
33	Harry S. Truman	Dem.	1884, May 8	MO	1945	60	1972, Dec. 26	88
34	Dwight David Eisenhower	Rep.	1890, Oct. 14	TX	1953	62	1969, Mar. 28	78
35	John Fitzgerald Kennedy	Dem.	1917, May 29	MA	1961	43	1963, Nov. 22	46
36	Lyndon Baines Johnson	Dem.	1908, Aug. 27	TX	1963	55	1973, Jan. 22	64
37	Richard Milhous Nixon (2)	Rep.	1913, Jan. 9	CA	1969	56	1994, Apr. 22	81
38	Gerald Rudolph Ford	Rep.	1913, July 14	NE	1974	61		
39	Jimmy Carter	Dem.	1924, Oct. 1	GA	1977	52		
40	Ronald Reagan	Rep.	1911, Feb. 6	IL	1981	69		
41	George Bush	Rep.	1924, June 12	MA	1989	64		
42	Bill Clinton	Dem.	1946, Aug. 19	AR	1993	46		

(1) Andrew Johnson was a Democrat, nominated vice president by Republicans, and elected with Lincoln on National Union ticket.
(2) Resigned Aug. 9, 1974.

U.S. Presidents, Vice Presidents, Congresses

	President	Service		Vice President	Congress
1	George Washington	Apr. 30, 1789—Mar. 3, 1797	1	John Adams	1, 2, 3, 4
2	John Adams	Mar. 4, 1797—Mar. 3, 1801	2	Thomas Jefferson	5, 6
3	Thomas Jefferson	Mar. 4, 1801—Mar. 3, 1805	3	Aaron Burr	7, 8
"	"	Mar. 4, 1805—Mar. 3, 1809	4	George Clinton	9, 10
4	James Madison	Mar. 4, 1809—Mar. 3, 1813		" (1)	11, 12
"	"	Mar. 4, 1813—Mar. 3, 1817	5	Elbridge Gerry(2)	13, 14
5	James Monroe	Mar. 4, 1817—Mar. 3, 1825	6	Daniel D. Tompkins	15, 16, 17, 18
6	John Quincy Adams	Mar. 4, 1825—Mar. 3, 1829	7	John C. Calhoun	19, 20
7	Andrew Jackson	Mar. 4, 1829—Mar. 3, 1833		" (3)	21, 22
"	"	Mar. 4, 1833—Mar. 3, 1837	8	Martin Van Buren	23, 24
8	Martin Van Buren	Mar. 4, 1837—Mar. 3, 1841	9	Richard M. Johnson	25, 26
9	William Henry Harrison(4)	Mar. 4, 1841—Apr. 4, 1841	10	John Tyler	27
10	John Tyler	Apr. 6, 1841—Mar. 3, 1845			27, 28
11	James K. Polk	Mar. 4, 1845—Mar. 3, 1849	11	George M. Dallas	29, 30
12	Zachary Taylor(4)	Mar. 5, 1849—July 9, 1850	12	Millard Fillmore	31
13	Millard Fillmore	July 10, 1850—Mar. 3, 1853			31, 32
14	Franklin Pierce	Mar. 4, 1853—Mar. 3, 1857	13	William R. King(5)	33, 34
15	James Buchanan	Mar. 4, 1857—Mar. 3, 1861	14	John C. Breckinridge	35, 36
16	Abraham Lincoln	Mar. 4, 1861—Mar. 3, 1865	15	Hannibal Hamlin	37, 38
" (4)	"	Mar. 4, 1865—Apr. 15, 1865	16	Andrew Johnson	39
17	Andrew Johnson	Apr. 15, 1865—Mar. 3, 1869			39, 40
18	Ulysses S. Grant	Mar. 4, 1869—Mar. 3, 1873	17	Schuyler Colfax	41, 42
"	"	Mar. 4, 1873—Mar. 3, 1877	18	Henry Wilson(6)	43, 44
19	Rutherford B. Hayes	Mar. 4, 1877—Mar. 3, 1881	19	William A. Wheeler	45, 46
20	James A. Garfield(4)	Mar. 4, 1881—Sept. 19, 1881	20	Chester A. Arthur	47
21	Chester A. Arthur	Sept. 20, 1881—Mar. 3, 1885			47, 48
22	Grover Cleveland(7)	Mar. 4, 1885—Mar. 3, 1889	21	Thomas A. Hendricks(8)	49, 50
23	Benjamin Harrison	Mar. 4, 1889—Mar. 3, 1893	22	Levi P. Morton	51, 52
24	Grover Cleveland(7)	Mar. 4, 1893—Mar. 3, 1897	23	Adlai E. Stevenson	53, 54
25	William McKinley	Mar. 4, 1897—Mar. 3, 1901	24	Garret A. Hobart(9)	55, 56
" (4)	"	Mar. 4, 1901—Sept. 14, 1901	25	Theodore Roosevelt	57
26	Theodore Roosevelt	Sept. 14, 1901—Mar. 3, 1905			57, 58
"	"	Mar. 4, 1905—Mar. 3, 1909	26	Charles W. Fairbanks	59, 60
27	William H. Taft	Mar. 4, 1909—Mar. 3, 1913	27	James S. Sherman(10)	61, 62
28	Woodrow Wilson	Mar. 4, 1913—Mar. 3, 1921	28	Thomas R. Marshall	63, 64, 65, 66

(continued)

U.S. Presidents, Vice Presidents, Congresses (continued)

	President	Service		Vice President	Congress
29	Warren G. Harding(4)	Mar. 4, 1921—Aug. 2, 1923	29	Calvin Coolidge	67
30	Calvin Coolidge	Aug. 3, 1923—Mar. 3, 1925			68
	"	Mar. 4, 1925—Mar. 3, 1929			69, 70
31	Herbert C. Hoover	Mar. 4, 1929—Mar. 3, 1933	30	Charles G. Dawes	71, 72
32	Franklin D. Roosevelt(11)	Mar. 4, 1933—Jan. 20, 1941	31	Charles Curtis	73, 74, 75, 76
	"	Jan. 20, 1941—Jan. 20, 1945	32	John N. Garner	77, 78
	" (4)	Jan. 20, 1945—Apr. 12, 1945	33	Henry A. Wallace	79
33	Harry S. Truman	Apr. 12, 1945—Jan. 20, 1949	34	Harry S. Truman	79, 80
	"	Jan. 20, 1949—Jan. 20, 1953	35	Alben W. Barkley	81, 82
34	Dwight D. Eisenhower	Jan. 20, 1953—Jan. 20, 1961	36	Richard M. Nixon	83, 84, 85, 86
35	John F. Kennedy(4)	Jan. 20, 1961—Nov. 22, 1963	37	Lyndon B. Johnson	87, 88
36	Lyndon B. Johnson	Nov. 22, 1963—Jan. 20, 1965			88
	"	Jan. 20, 1965—Jan. 20, 1969	38	Hubert H. Humphrey	89, 90
37	Richard M. Nixon	Jan. 20, 1969—Jan. 20, 1973	39	Spiro T. Agnew(12)	91, 92, 93
	" (13)	Jan. 20, 1973—Aug. 9, 1974	40	Gerald R. Ford(14)	93
38	Gerald R. Ford(15)	Aug. 9, 1974—Jan. 20, 1977	41	Nelson A. Rockefeller(16)	93, 94
39	Jimmy (James Earl) Carter	Jan. 20, 1977—Jan. 20, 1981	42	Walter F. Mondale	95, 96
40	Ronald Reagan	Jan. 20, 1981—Jan. 20, 1989	43	George Bush	97, 98, 99, 100
41	George Bush	Jan. 20, 1989—Jan. 20, 1993	44	Dan Quayle	101, 102
42	Bill Clinton	Jan. 20, 1993—	45	Al Gore	103, 104, 105

(1) Died Apr. 20, 1812. (2) Died Nov. 23, 1814. (3) Resigned Dec. 28, 1832, to become U.S. senator. (4) Died in office. (5) Died Apr. 18, 1853. (6) Died Nov. 22, 1875. (7) Terms not consecutive. (8) Died Nov. 25, 1885. (9) Died Nov. 21, 1899. (10) Died Oct. 30, 1912. (11) First president to be inaugurated under 20th Amendment, Jan. 20, 1937. (12) Resigned Oct. 10, 1973. (13) Resigned Aug. 9, 1974. (14) First nonelected vice president, chosen under 25th Amendment procedure. (15) First nonelected president. (16) Second nonelected vice president, chosen under 25th Amendment procedure.

Vice Presidents of the U.S.

The numerals given vice presidents do not coincide with those given presidents, because some presidents had none and some had more than one.

	Name	Birthplace	Year	Home	Inaug.	Politics	Place of death	Year	Age
1	John Adams	Quincy, MA	1735	MA	1789	Fed.	Quincy, MA	1826	90
2	Thomas Jefferson	Shadwell, VA	1743	VA	1797	Dem.-Rep.	Monticello, VA	1826	83
3	Aaron Burr	Newark, NJ	1756	NY	1801	Dem.-Rep.	Staten Island, NY	1836	80
4	George Clinton	Ulster Co., NY	1739	NY	1805	Dem.-Rep.	Washington, DC	1812	73
5	Elbridge Gerry	Marblehead, MA	1744	MA	1813	Dem.-Rep.	Washington, DC	1814	70
6	Daniel D. Tompkins	Scarsdale, NY	1774	NY	1817	Dem.-Rep.	Staten Island, NY	1825	51
7	John C. Calhoun(1)	Abbeville, SC	1782	SC	1825	Dem.-Rep.	Washington, DC	1850	68
8	Martin Van Buren	Kinderhook, NY	1782	NY	1833	Dem.	Kinderhook, NY	1862	79
9	Richard M. Johnson(2)	Louisville, KY	1780	KY	1837	Dem.	Frankfort, KY	1850	70
10	John Tyler	Greenway, VA	1790	VA	1841	Whig	Richmond, VA	1862	71
11	George M. Dallas	Philadelphia, PA	1792	PA	1845	Dem.	Philadelphia, PA	1864	72
12	Millard Fillmore	Summerhill, NY	1800	NY	1849	Whig	Buffalo, NY	1874	74
13	William R. King	Sampson Co., NC	1786	AL	1853	Dem.	Dallas Co., AL	1853	67
14	John C. Breckinridge	Lexington, KY	1821	KY	1857	Dem.	Lexington, KY	1875	54
15	Hannibal Hamlin	Paris, ME	1809	ME	1861	Rep.	Bangor, ME	1891	81
16	Andrew Johnson	Raleigh, NC	1808	TN	1865	(3)	Carter Co., TN	1875	66
17	Schuyler Colfax	New York, NY	1823	IN	1869	Rep.	Mankato, MN	1885	62
18	Henry Wilson	Farmington, NH	1812	MA	1873	Rep.	Washington, DC	1875	63
19	William A. Wheeler	Malone, NY	1819	NY	1877	Rep.	Malone, NY	1887	68
20	Chester A. Arthur	Fairfield, VT	1830	NY	1881	Rep.	New York, NY	1886	57
21	Thomas A. Hendricks	Muskingum Co., OH	1819	IN	1885	Dem.	Indianapolis, IN	1885	66
22	Levi P. Morton	Shoreham, VT	1824	NY	1889	Rep.	Rhinebeck, NY	1920	96
23	Adlai E. Stevenson(4)	Christian Co., KY	1835	IL	1893	Dem.	Chicago, IL	1914	78
24	Garret A. Hobart	Long Branch, NJ	1844	NJ	1897	Rep.	Paterson, NJ	1899	55
25	Theodore Roosevelt	New York, NY	1858	NY	1901	Rep.	Oyster Bay, NY	1919	60
26	Charles W. Fairbanks	Unionville Centre, OH	1852	IN	1905	Rep.	Indianapolis, IN	1918	66
27	James S. Sherman	Utica, NY	1855	NY	1909	Rep.	Utica, NY	1912	57
28	Thomas R. Marshall	N. Manchester, IN	1854	IN	1913	Dem.	Washington, DC	1925	71
29	Calvin Coolidge	Plymouth, VT	1872	MA	1921	Rep.	Northampton, MA	1933	60
30	Charles G. Dawes	Marietta, OH	1865	IL	1925	Rep.	Evanston, IL	1951	85
31	Charles Curtis	Topeka, KS	1860	KS	1929	Rep.	Washington, DC	1936	76
32	John Nance Garner	Red River Co., TX	1868	TX	1933	Dem.	Uvalde, TX	1967	98
33	Henry Agard Wallace	Adair County, IA	1888	IA	1941	Dem.	Danbury, CT	1965	77
34	Harry S. Truman	Lamar, MO	1884	MO	1945	Dem.	Kansas City, MO	1972	88
35	Alben W. Barkley	Graves County, KY	1877	KY	1949	Dem.	Lexington, VA	1956	78
36	Richard M. Nixon	Yorba Linda, CA	1913	CA	1953	Rep.	New York, NY	1994	81
37	Lyndon B. Johnson	Johnson City, TX	1908	TX	1961	Dem.	San Antonio, TX	1973	64
38	Hubert H. Humphrey	Wallace, SD	1911	MN	1965	Dem.	Waverly, MN	1978	66
39	Spiro T. Agnew(5)	Baltimore, MD	1918	MD	1969	Rep.	Berlin, MD	1996	77
40	Gerald R. Ford(6)	Omaha, NE	1913	MI	1973	Rep.			
41	Nelson A. Rockefeller(7)	Bar Harbor, ME	1908	NY	1974	Rep.	New York, NY	1979	70
42	Walter F. Mondale	Ceylon, MN	1928	MN	1977	Dem.			
43	George Bush	Milton, MA	1924	TX	1981	Rep.			
44	Dan Quayle	Indianapolis, IN	1947	IN	1989	Rep.			
45	Al Gore	Washington, DC	1948	TN	1993	Dem.			

(1) John C. Calhoun resigned Dec. 28, 1832, having been elected to the Senate to fill a vacancy. (2) Richard M. Johnson was the only vice president to be chosen by the Senate because of a tied vote in the Electoral College. (3) Andrew Johnson was a Democrat, nominated vice president by Republicans, and elected with Lincoln on the National Union Ticket. (4) Adlai E. Stevenson, 23d vice president, was grandfather of Democratic candidate for president in 1952 and 1956. (5) Resigned Oct. 10, 1973. (6) First nonelected vice president, chosen under the 25th Amendment procedure. (7) Second nonelected vice president, chosen under the 25th Amendment procedure.

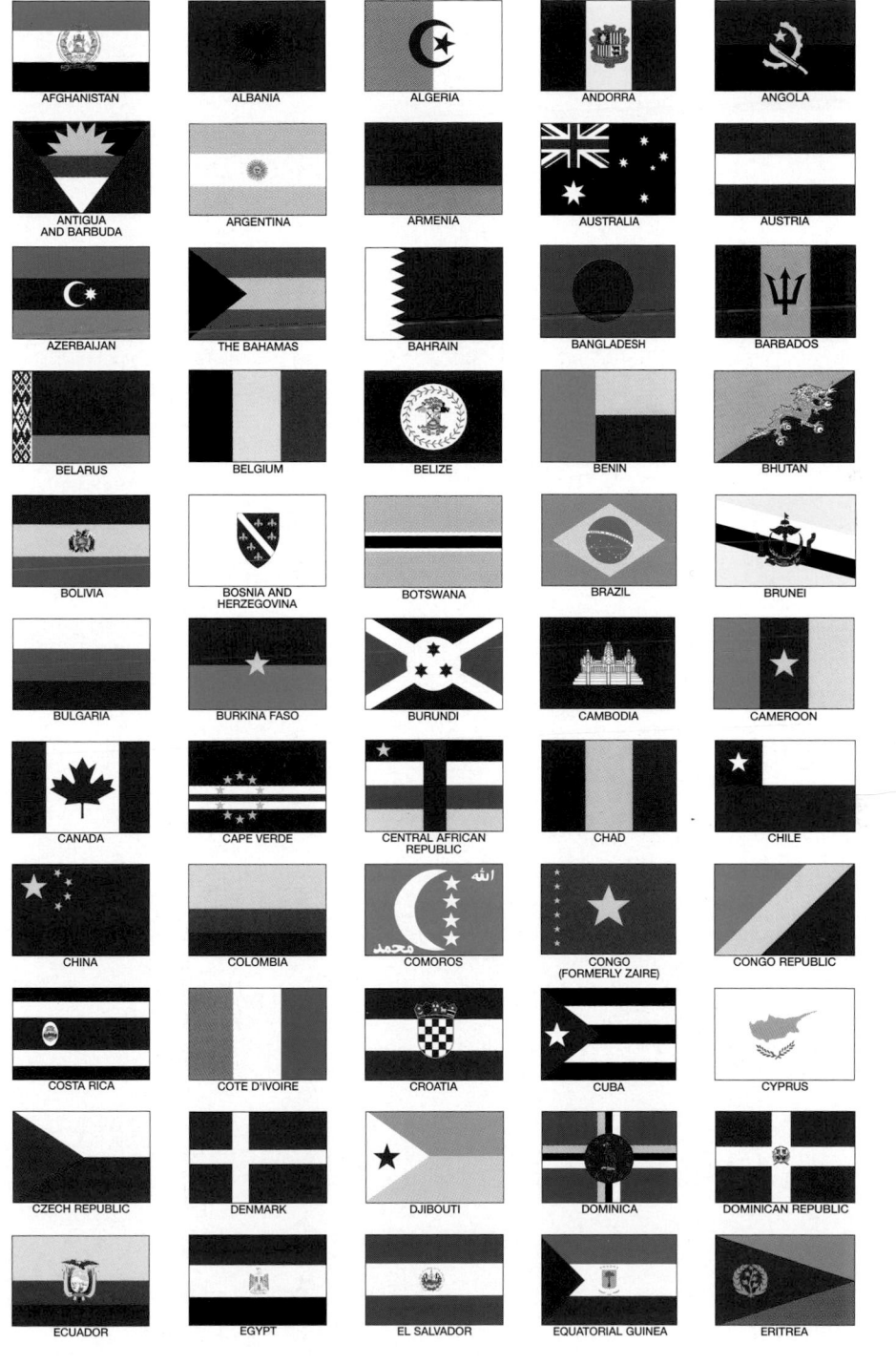

AFGHANISTAN	ALBANIA	ALGERIA	ANDORRA	ANGOLA
ANTIGUA AND BARBUDA	ARGENTINA	ARMENIA	AUSTRALIA	AUSTRIA
AZERBAIJAN	THE BAHAMAS	BAHRAIN	BANGLADESH	BARBADOS
BELARUS	BELGIUM	BELIZE	BENIN	BHUTAN
BOLIVIA	BOSNIA AND HERZEGOVINA	BOTSWANA	BRAZIL	BRUNEI
BULGARIA	BURKINA FASO	BURUNDI	CAMBODIA	CAMEROON
CANADA	CAPE VERDE	CENTRAL AFRICAN REPUBLIC	CHAD	CHILE
CHINA	COLOMBIA	COMOROS	CONGO (FORMERLY ZAIRE)	CONGO REPUBLIC
COSTA RICA	COTE D'IVOIRE	CROATIA	CUBA	CYPRUS
CZECH REPUBLIC	DENMARK	DJIBOUTI	DOMINICA	DOMINICAN REPUBLIC
ECUADOR	EGYPT	EL SALVADOR	EQUATORIAL GUINEA	ERITREA

ESTONIA ETHIOPIA FIJI FINLAND FRANCE

GABON THE GAMBIA GEORGIA GERMANY GHANA

GREECE GRENADA GUATEMALA GUINEA GUINEA-BISSAU

GUYANA HAITI HONDURAS HUNGARY ICELAND

INDIA INDONESIA IRAN IRAQ IRELAND

ISRAEL ITALY JAMAICA JAPAN JORDAN

KAZAKHSTAN KENYA KIRIBATI NORTH KOREA SOUTH KOREA

KUWAIT KYRGYZSTAN LAOS LATVIA LEBANON

LESOTHO LIBERIA LIBYA LIECHTENSTEIN LITHUANIA

LUXEMBOURG MACEDONIA MADAGASCAR MALAWI MALAYSIA

MALDIVES MALI MALTA MARSHALL ISLANDS MAURITANIA

MAURITIUS	MEXICO	MICRONESIA	MOLDOVA	MONACO
MONGOLIA	MOROCCO	MOZAMBIQUE	MYANMAR (BURMA)	NAMIBIA
NAURU	NEPAL	NETHERLANDS	NEW ZEALAND	NICARAGUA
NIGER	NIGERIA	NORWAY	OMAN	PAKISTAN
PALAU	PANAMA	PAPUA NEW GUINEA	PARAGUAY	PERU
PHILIPPINES	POLAND	PORTUGAL	QATAR	ROMANIA
RUSSIA	RWANDA	ST. KITTS AND NEVIS	ST. LUCIA	ST. VINCENT AND THE GRENADINES
SAMOA	SAN MARINO	SAO TOME AND PRINCIPE	SAUDI ARABIA	SENEGAL
SEYCHELLES	SIERRA LEONE	SINGAPORE	SLOVAKIA	SLOVENIA
SOLOMON ISLANDS	SOMALIA	SOUTH AFRICA	SPAIN	SRI LANKA
SUDAN	SURINAME	SWAZILAND	SWEDEN	SWITZERLAND

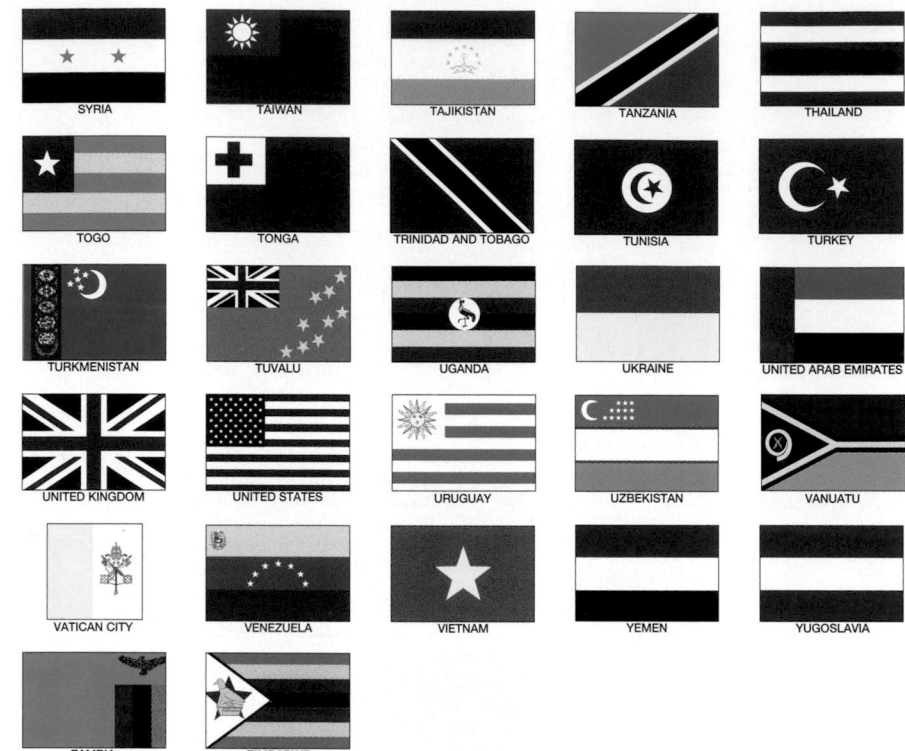

SYRIA TAIWAN TAJIKISTAN TANZANIA THAILAND

TOGO TONGA TRINIDAD AND TOBAGO TUNISIA TURKEY

TURKMENISTAN TUVALU UGANDA UKRAINE UNITED ARAB EMIRATES

UNITED KINGDOM UNITED STATES URUGUAY UZBEKISTAN VANUATU

VATICAN CITY VENEZUELA VIETNAM YEMEN YUGOSLAVIA

ZAMBIA ZIMBABWE

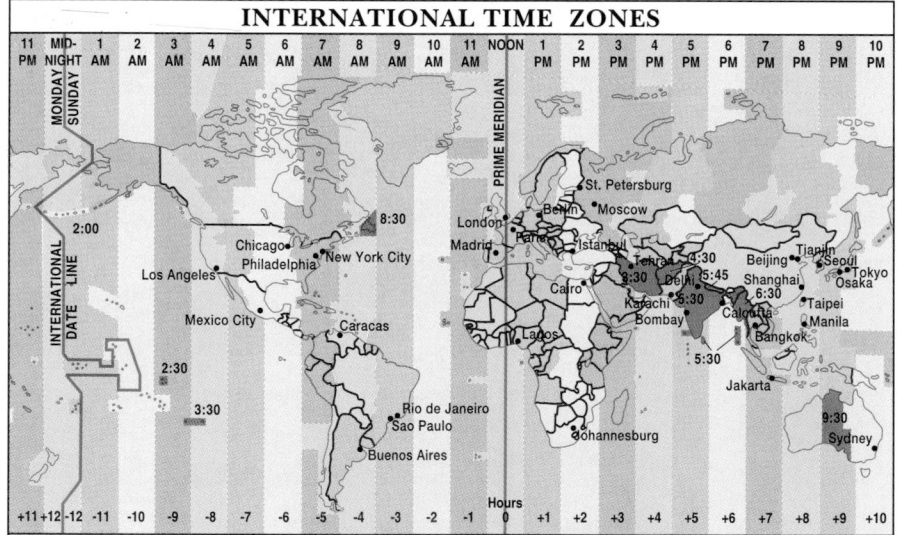

INTERNATIONAL TIME ZONES

The world is divided into 24 time zones, each 15° longitude wide. The longitudinal meridian passing through Greenwich, England, is the starting point, and is called the *prime meridian*. The 12th zone is divided by the 180th meridian (International Date Line). When the line is crossed going west, the date is advanced one day; when crossed going east, the date becomes a day earlier.

© The World Almanac and Book of Facts

484

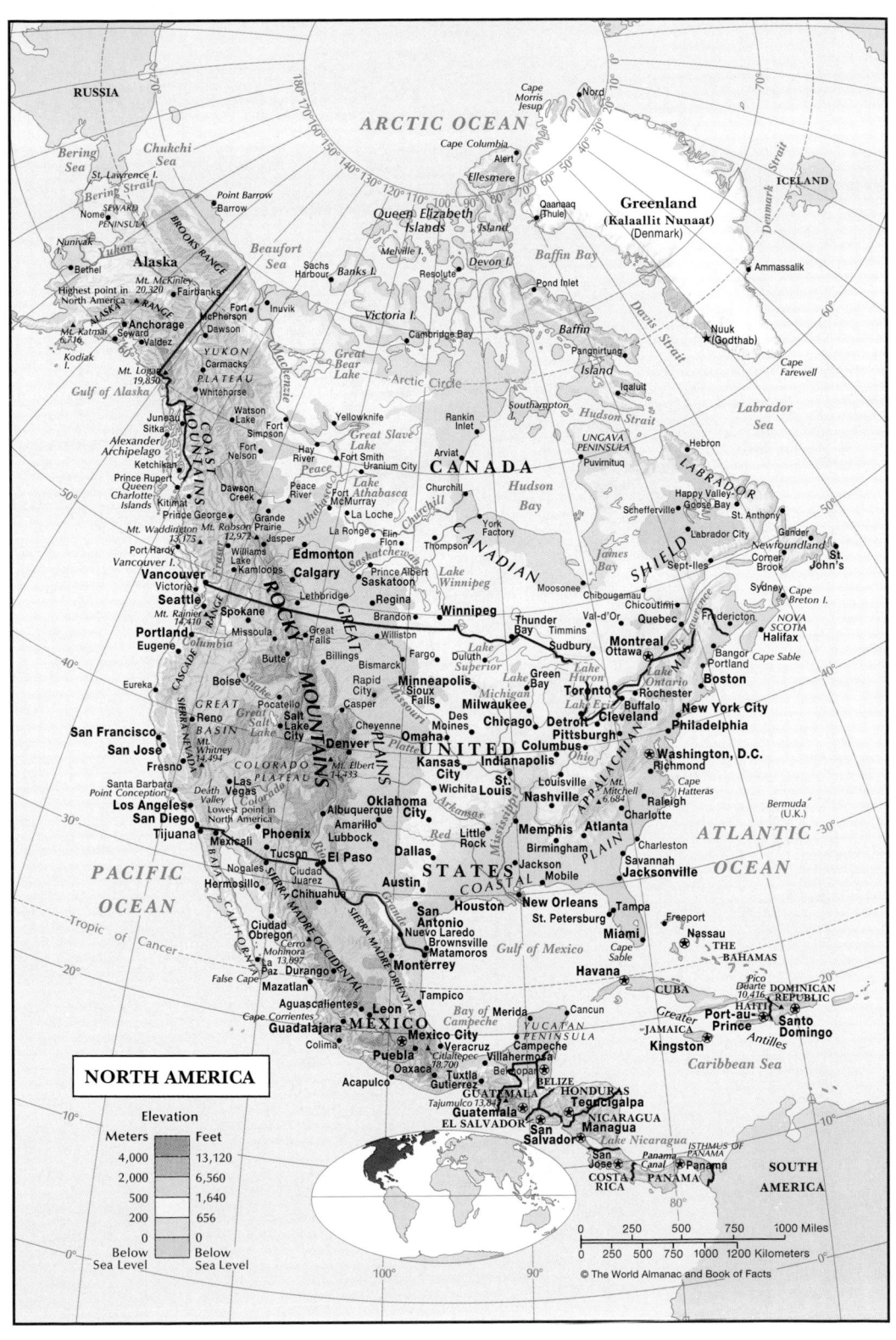

NORTH AMERICA

Elevation

Meters	Feet
4,000	13,120
2,000	6,560
500	1,640
200	656
0	0
Below Sea Level	Below Sea Level

0   250   500   750   1000 Miles

0   250   500   750   1000   1200 Kilometers

© The World Almanac and Book of Facts

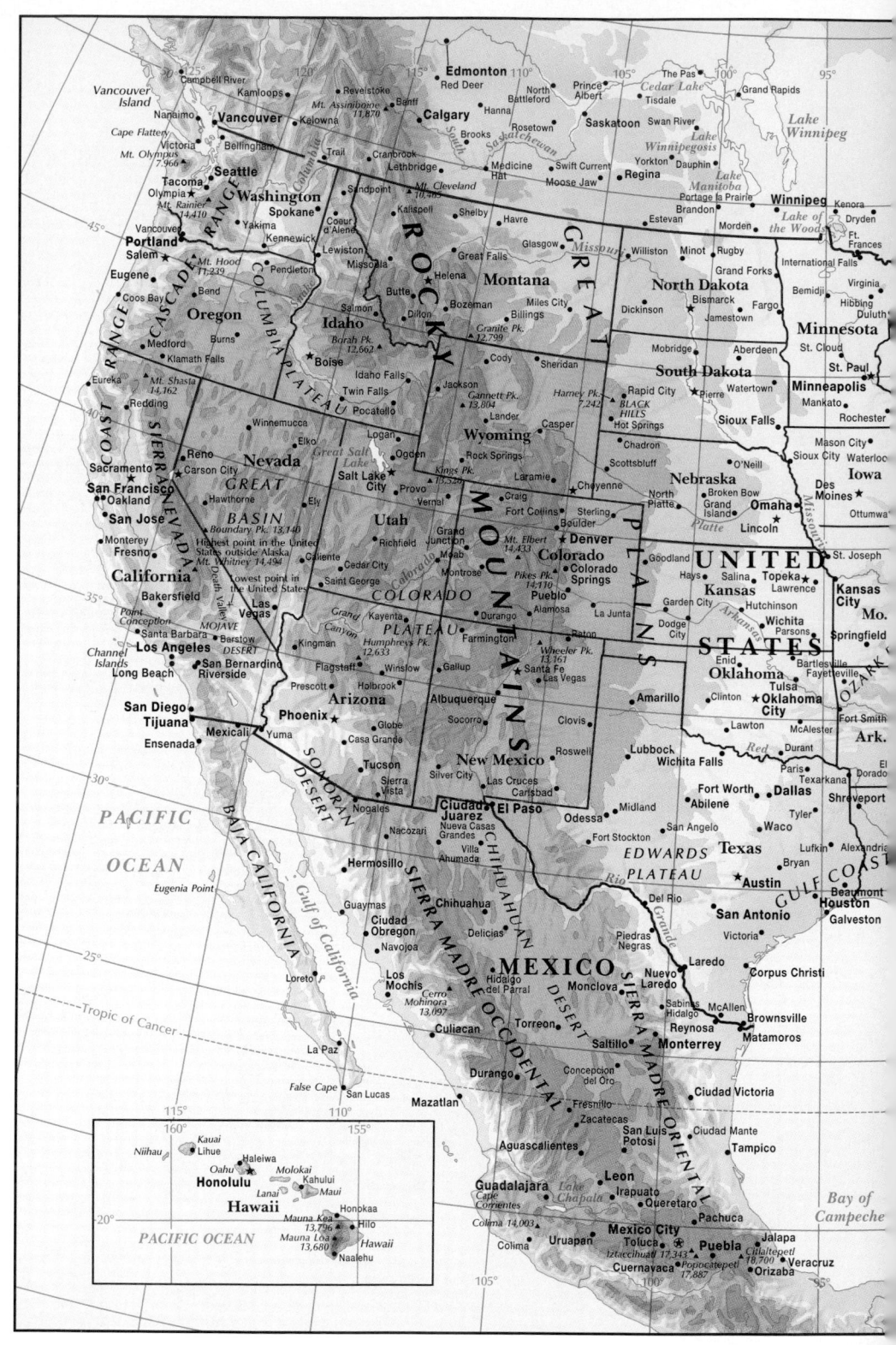

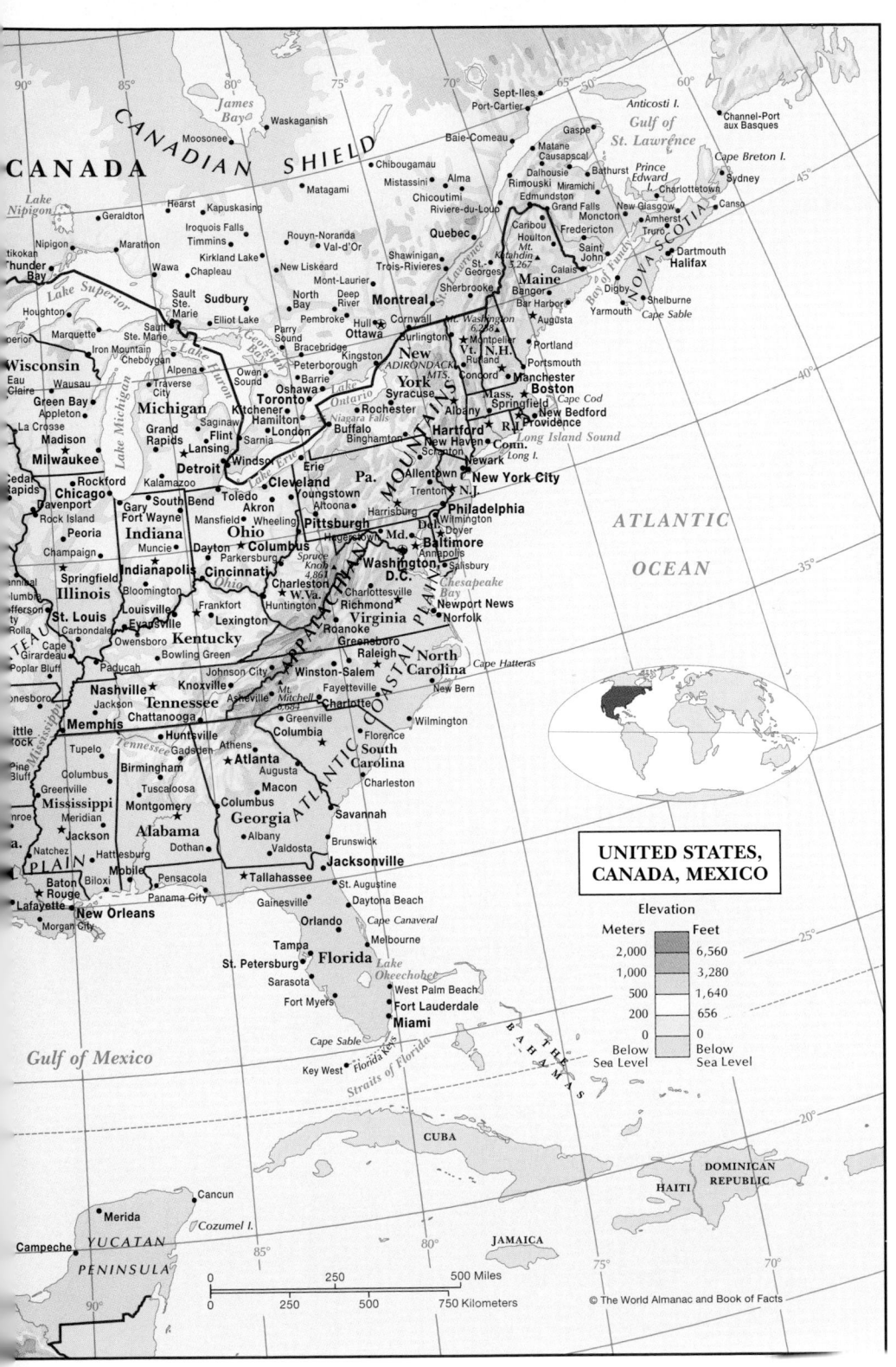

United States, Canada, Mexico (eastern)

90° 85° 80° 75° 70° 65° 50° 60° 45° 40° 35° 25° 20°

CANADA

CANADIAN SHIELD

James Bay

Lake Nipigon

Lake Superior

Lake Michigan

Lake Huron

Lake Erie

Lake Ontario

Moosonee
Waskaganish
Chibougamau
Matagami
Mistassini
Alma

Geraldton
Hearst
Kapuskasing
Iroquois Falls
Timmins
Rouyn-Noranda
Val-d'Or
Shawinigan
Trois-Rivieres

Nipigon
Marathon
Thunder Bay
Wawa
Chapleau
Kirkland Lake
New Liskeard
Mont-Laurier

tikokan
Houghton
Superior
Marquette
Iron Mountain
Cheboygan

Wisconsin
Eau Claire
Wausau
Green Bay
Appleton
La Crosse
Madison
Milwaukee

Sault Ste. Marie
Sault Ste. Marie
Elliot Lake
Sudbury
North Bay
Deep River
Pembroke
Parry Sound
Bracebridge
Peterborough
Owen Sound
Barrie

Alpena
Traverse City

Michigan
Grand Rapids
Saginaw
Flint
Lansing
London
Sarnia
Windsor

Toronto
Kitchener
Hamilton
Oshawa
Rochester
Niagara Falls
Buffalo
Binghamton

Ottawa
Kingston

New York
ADIRONDACK MTS.

Syracuse
Albany

Montreal

Quebec

Rimouski
Riviere-du-Loup
St. Georges
Sherbrooke

Caribou
Houlton
Grand Falls
Edmundston
Fredericton
Saint John

Maine
Bangor
Augusta
Bar Harbor

Mt. Washington
6,288
Montpelier
Vt. N.H.
Concord
Manchester

Sept-Iles
Port-Cartier
Baie-Comeau
Gaspe
Matane
Causapscal
Dalhousie
Bathurst
Miramichi
Moncton
New Glasgow
Amherst
Truro

Anticosti I.

Gulf of St. Lawrence

Channel-Port aux Basques

Cape Breton I.
Sydney
Canso

Prince Edward I.
Charlottetown

NOVA SCOTIA
Dartmouth
Halifax
Digby
Shelburne
Yarmouth
Cape Sable

Bay of Fundy

Cornwall
Burlington

Mass.
Springfield
New Bedford

Boston

Portland
Portsmouth

Cape Cod

Hartford
New Haven
Providence
Conn. R.I.

Long Island Sound
Long I.

ATLANTIC
OCEAN

Cedar Rapids
Rockford
Chicago
Davenport
Rock Island
Peoria
Champaign

Gary
Fort Wayne
South Bend
Toledo
Mansfield
Wheeling

Indiana
Muncie
Dayton

Detroit
Cleveland
Akron
Youngstown
Altoona

Erie

Pa.
Pittsburgh

Allentown
Trenton
N.J.

New York City

Philadelphia

nnual
lumbia
ty
Jefferson
Rolla

Springfield
Bloomington

Illinois
St. Louis
Evansville

Indianapolis
Cincinnati

Columbus
Ohio

Parkersburg

Spruce Knob
4,861

Del.
Wilmington
Dover
Hagerstown
Md.
Baltimore
Annapolis
Washington, D.C.
Salisbury

Chesapeake Bay

Cape Girardeau
Poplar Bluff

Paducah

Frankfort
Louisville
Owensboro
Bowling Green

Lexington

Kentucky

Charleston
W.Va.
Huntington

Richmond

Virginia
Charlottesville
Newport News
Norfolk
Roanoke
Greensboro
Raleigh

Cape Hatteras

onesboro

ittle Rock

Nashville
Memphis

Johnson City
Knoxville
Asheville

Mt. Mitchell
6,684

North Carolina
Winston-Salem
Fayetteville
Charlotte

New Bern

Tupelo
Columbus
Greenville

Tennessee
Chattanooga
Jackson
Huntsville
Gadsden
Athens

Greenville
Columbia

Florence

Wilmington

Pine Bluff

Columbus
Greenville

Birmingham
Tuscaloosa

Mississippi
Meridian
Jackson

Montgomery

Columbus

Atlanta
Augusta
Macon

South Carolina
Charleston

a.
Natchez
Hattiesburg

Alabama
Dothan

Georgia
Albany
Valdosta

Savannah
Brunswick

PLAIN
Mobile
Pensacola
Biloxi
Baton Rouge
New Orleans
Lafayette
Morgan City

Tallahassee
Panama City

Jacksonville
St. Augustine

Daytona Beach
Gainesville

Orlando
Melbourne
Cape Canaveral

Tampa
St. Petersburg
Sarasota
Fort Myers

Florida

Lake Okeechobee

West Palm Beach
Fort Lauderdale
Miami

Cape Sable

APPALACHIAN MOUNTAINS

ATLANTIC COASTAL PLAIN

Mississippi

Tennessee

Ohio

Gulf of Mexico

Key West
Florida Keys
Straits of Florida

BAHAMAS

CUBA

HAITI
DOMINICAN REPUBLIC

JAMAICA

Merida
Cancun
Cozumel I.

Campeche
YUCATAN PENINSULA

UNITED STATES,
CANADA, MEXICO

Elevation

Meters		Feet
2,000		6,560
1,000		3,280
500		1,640
200		656
0		0
Below Sea Level		Below Sea Level

0   250   500 Miles

0 250 500 750 Kilometers

© The World Almanac and Book of Facts

487

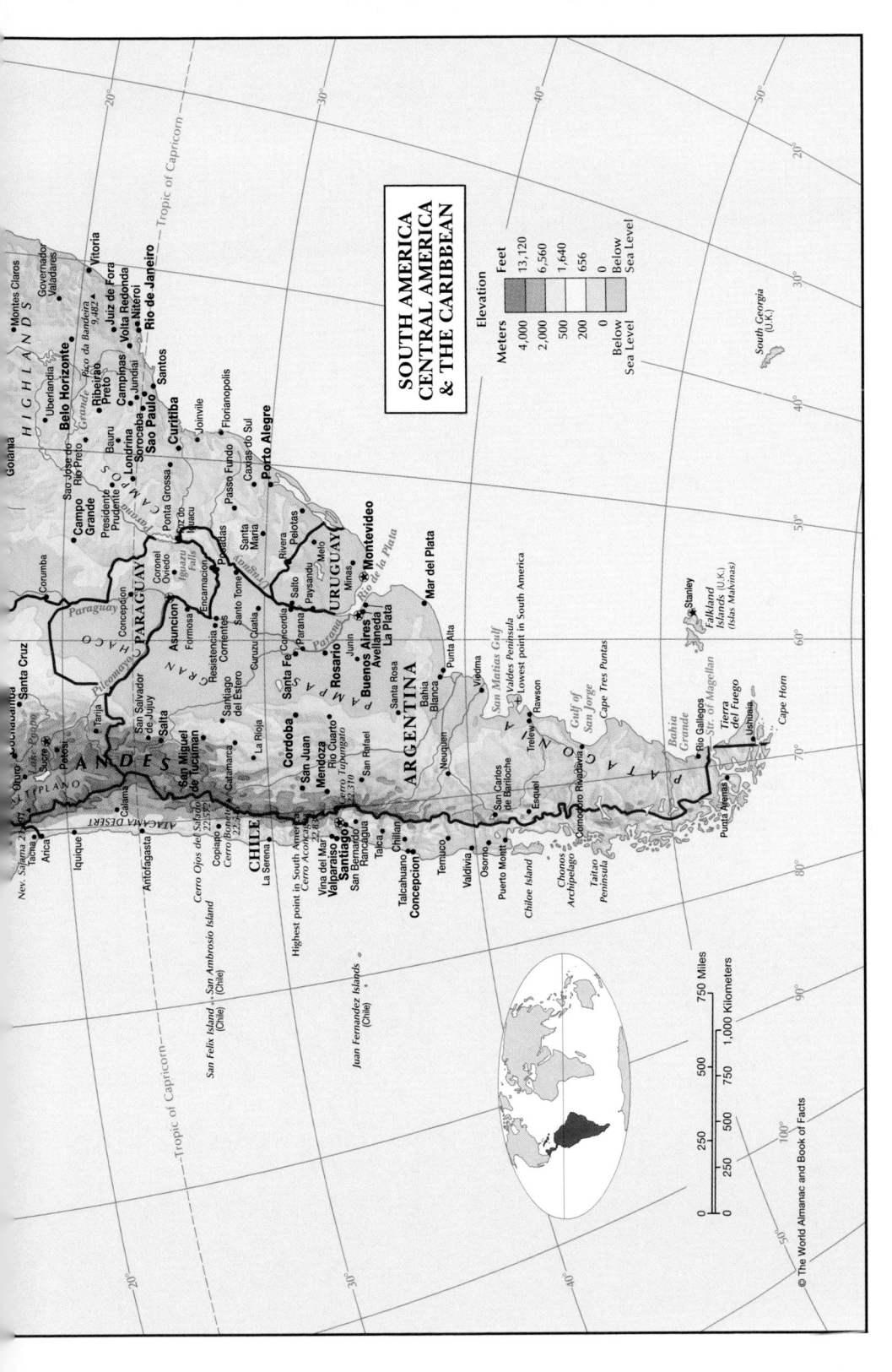

SOUTH AMERICA
CENTRAL AMERICA
& THE CARIBBEAN

Elevation

Meters	Feet	
4,000	13,120	
2,000	6,560	
500	1,640	
200	656	
0	0	
Below Sea Level	Below Sea Level	

Montes Claros
Governador
Valadares
Goiânia
Vitória
Uberlândia
Belo Horizonte
Juiz de Fora
Volta Redonda
Campinas
Rio de Janeiro
Jundiaí
Niterói
Paço da Bandeira
9,482 ▲
São José do Rio Preto
Ribeirão Preto
São Paulo
Santos
Corumbá
Campo Grande
Presidente Prudente
Londrina
Sorocaba
Curitiba
Joinville
Bauru
Ponta Grossa
Florianópolis
Passo Fundo
Caxias do Sul
Porto Alegre

H I G H L A N D S
CAMPOS

Santa Cruz
Tarija
Concepción
PARAGUAY
Asunción
Coronel Oviedo
Iguaçu Falls
Encarnación
Posadas
Pelotas
Santa Maria
Rivera
Melo
URUGUAY
Montevideo

CHACO
GRAN
Formosa
Resistencia
Corrientes
Santo Tomé
Curuzú Cuatiá
Santa Fe
Concordia
Paraná
Salto
Paysandú
Minas
Mar del Plata

Paraguay River
Pilcomayo
Paraná River
Río de la Plata

San Salvador de Jujuy
Salta
San Miguel de Tucumán
Catamarca
Santiago del Estero
La Rioja
Córdoba
Rosario
Buenos Aires
Avellaneda
La Plata

ANDES
San Juan
Mendoza
Río Cuarto
Cerro Aconcagua 22,835
Cerro Tupungato 22,310
San Rafael
Santa Rosa
Junín

PAMPAS
Bahía Blanca
Punta Alta
Viedma
Lowest point in South America
Valdés Peninsula

Nev. Sajama 21,463
Oruro
Sucre
Potosí
ALTIPLANO
Lake Poopó
Arica
Tacna
Calama
ATACAMA DESERT
Iquique
Antofagasta
Cerro Ojos del Salado 22,572
Cerro Bonete 22,546
Copiapó
La Serena
Highest point in South America
CHILE
Valparaíso
Viña del Mar
Santiago
San Bernardo
Rancagua
Talca
Chillán
Talcahuano
Concepción
Temuco
Valdivia
Osorno
Puerto Montt

San Felix Island (Chile)
San Ambrosio Island (Chile)

Juan Fernandez Islands (Chile)

ARGENTINA
Neuquén
San Carlos de Bariloche
Esquel
Trelew
Rawson
Comodoro Rivadavia
San Matías Gulf
Gulf of San Jorge
Cape Tres Puntas

PATAGONIA
Chonos Archipelago
Chiloé Island
Taitao Peninsula

Río Gallegos
Punta Arenas
Str. of Magellan
Tierra del Fuego
Ushuaia
Cape Horn
Bahía Grande

Stanley
Falkland Islands (U.K.) (Islas Malvinas)

South Georgia (U.K.)

Tropic of Capricorn
Tropic of Capricorn

0	250	500	750 Miles
0	250	500	750	1,000 Kilometers

© The World Almanac and Book of Facts

20°
30°
40°
50°
20°
30°
40°
50°
60°
70°
80°
90°
100°

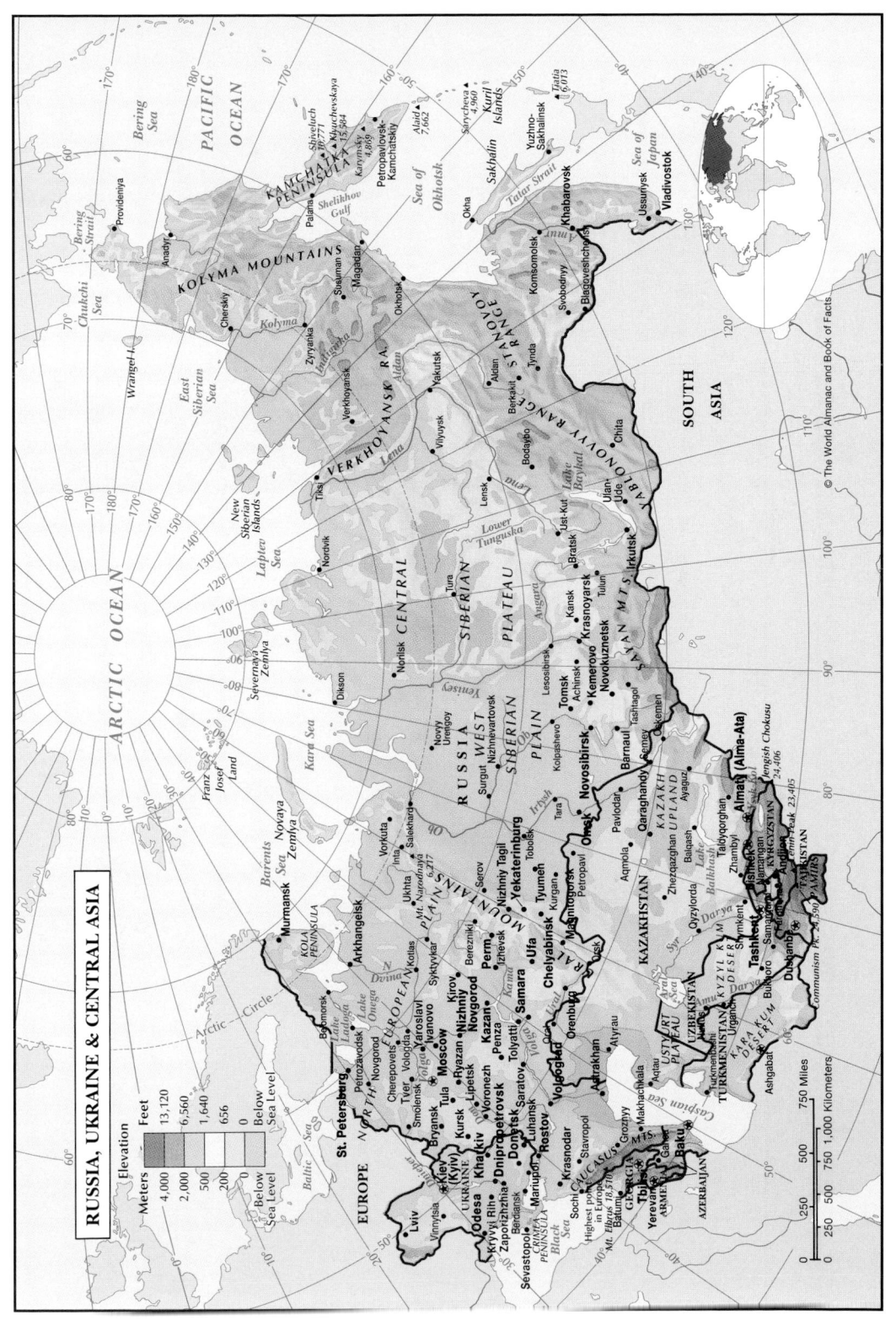

RUSSIA, UKRAINE & CENTRAL ASIA

SOUTH ASIA

Elevation

Meters		Feet
4,000		13,120
2,000		6,560
500		1,640
200		656
0		0
Below Sea Level		Below Sea Level

0   250   500   750   1,000 Miles
0   250   500   750   1,000   1,250 Kilometers

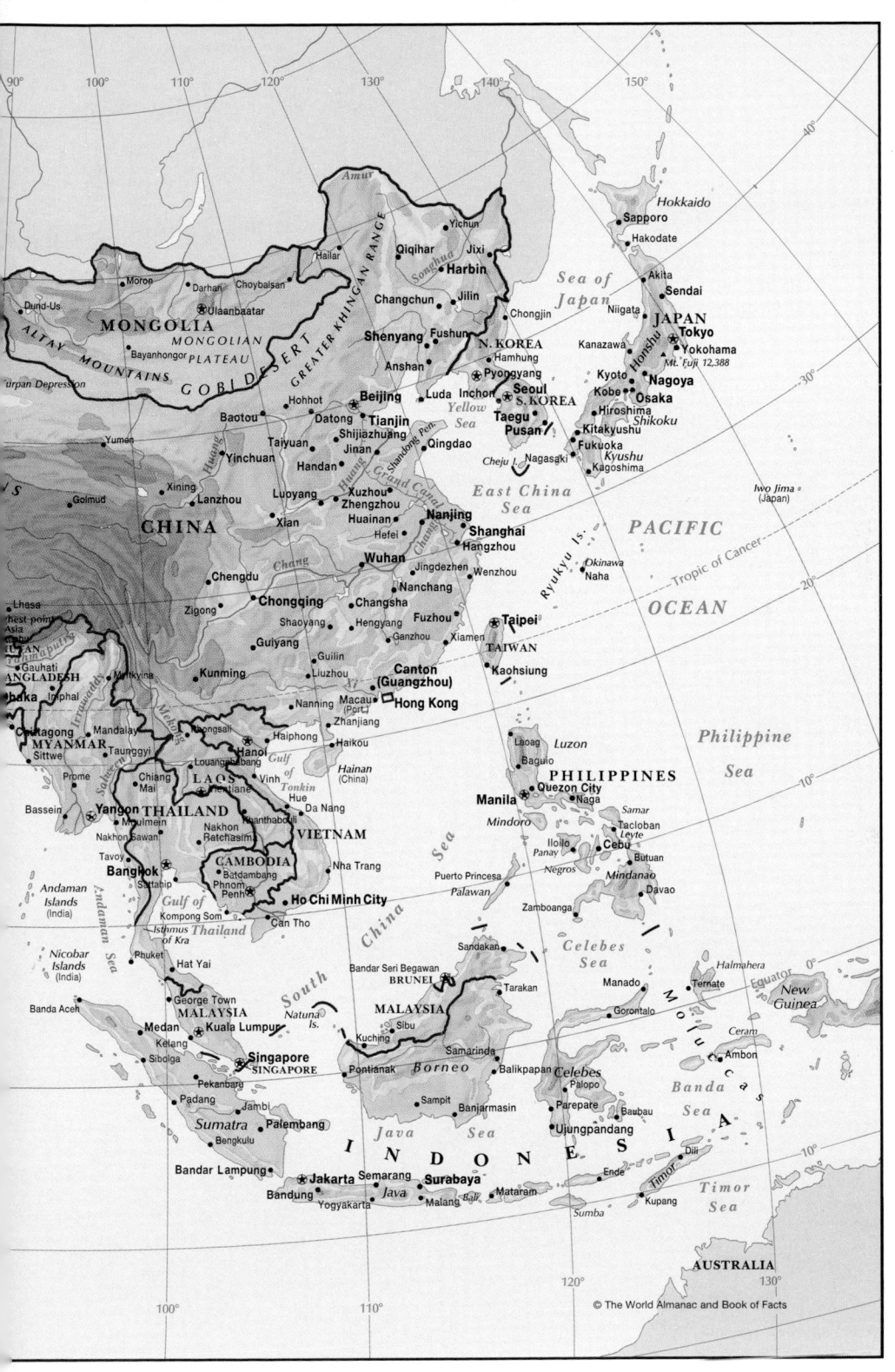

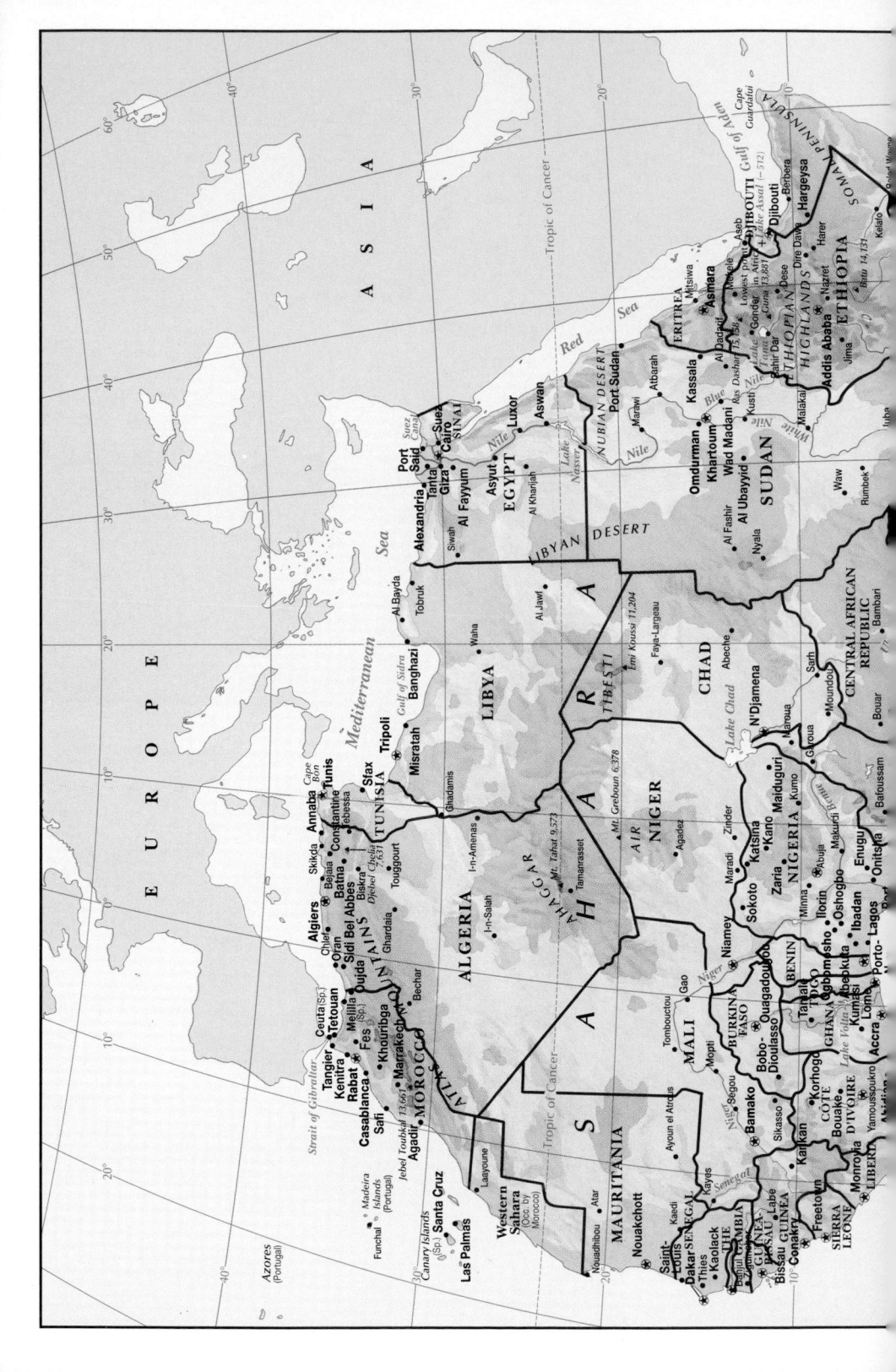

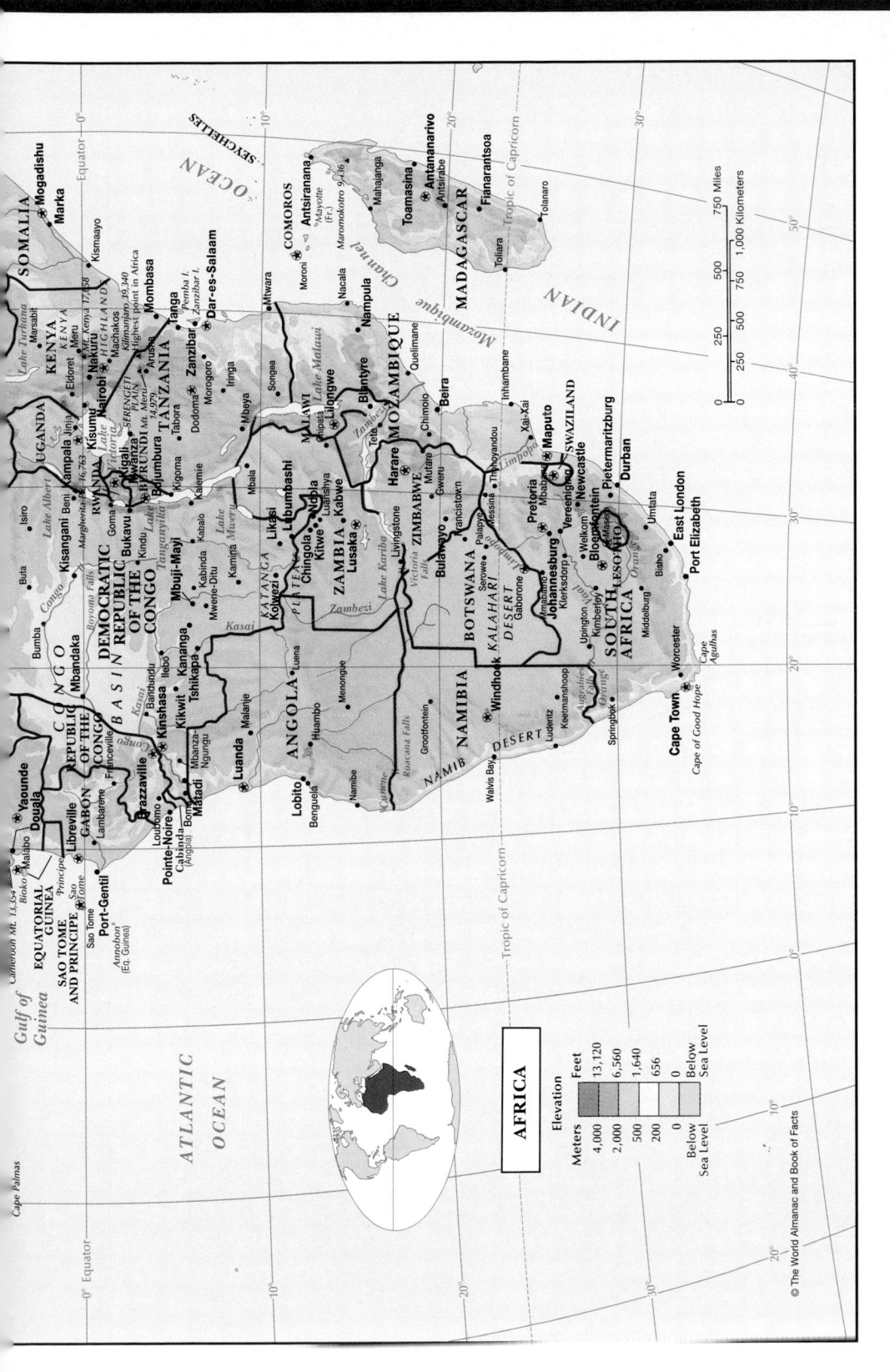

AFRICA

Elevation

Meters	Feet
4,000	13,120
2,000	6,560
500	1,640
200	656
0	0
Below Sea Level	Below Sea Level

© The World Almanac and Book of Facts

SOMALIA
- Mogadishu
- Marka

KENYA
- Marsabit
- Meru
- Eldoret
- Nairobi
- Nakuru
- Machakos
- Kismaayo
- Mt. Kenya 17,058
- Highest point in Africa
- Mt. Elgon 14,178

Lake Turkana

UGANDA
- Kampala
- Jinja
- Beni

Lake Albert

SEYCHELLES

COMOROS
- Moroni
- Antsiranana
- Mayotte (Fr.)
- Maromokotro 9,436

MADAGASCAR
- Mahajanga
- Toamasina
- Antananarivo
- Antsirabe
- Fianarantsoa
- Toliara
- Tolanaro

Tropic of Capricorn

INDIAN OCEAN

Mozambique Channel

TANZANIA
- Mombasa
- Tanga
- Zanzibar
- Pemba I.
- Zanzibar I.
- Dar-es-Salaam
- Dodoma
- Morogoro
- Iringa
- Tabora
- Kilimanjaro 19,340
- Kigali
- Kilimanjaro Highest point in Africa
- Arusha
- Mwanza
- Mbeya
- Mt. Meru 14,979
- SERENGETI PLAIN
- Songea

RWANDA
- Kigali

BURUNDI
- Bujumbura

Lake Victoria

KENYA HIGHLAND

MALAWI
- Lilongwe
- Blantyre
- Mzuzu
- Lake Malawi

MOZAMBIQUE
- Nampula
- Quelimane
- Nacala
- Mtwara
- Beira
- Chimoio
- Inhambane
- Xai-Xai
- Maputo
- Tete

ZIMBABWE
- Harare
- Mutare
- Gweru
- Bulawayo
- Francistown

SWAZILAND
- Mbabane

ZAMBIA
- Lusaka
- Kabwe
- Kitwe
- Ndola
- Chingola
- Kabcompo
- Livingstone
- Victoria Falls

DEMOCRATIC REPUBLIC OF THE CONGO
- Kisangani
- Bukavu
- Goma
- Kindu
- Kalemie
- Kabalo
- Kananga
- Mbuji-Mayi
- Kikwit
- Kinshasa
- Mbandaka
- Bumba
- Buta
- Isiro
- Kananga
- Tshikapa
- Likasi
- Lubumbashi
- Kolwezi
- Kamina
- Mwene-Ditu
- KATANGA PLATEAU

Lake Tanganyika

Lake Kivu

Lake Mweru

Congo

Kasai

Zambezi

Lake Kariba

ANGOLA
- Luanda
- Lobito
- Benguela
- Huambo
- Malanje
- Menongue
- Namibe

REPUBLIC OF THE CONGO
- Brazzaville
- Pointe-Noire
- Loubomo
- Cabinda (Angola)

GABON
- Libreville
- Port-Gentil
- Lambaréné
- Franceville

CAMEROON
- Yaoundé
- Douala

EQUATORIAL GUINEA
- Malabo
- Bioko

SAO TOME AND PRINCIPE
- Sao Tome
- Principe
- Annobon (Eq. Guinea)
- Cameroon Mt. 13,354

Gulf of Guinea

ATLANTIC OCEAN

Cape Palmas

NAMIBIA
- Windhoek
- Grootfontein
- Walvis Bay
- Lüderitz
- Keetmanshoop
- Ruacana Falls
- NAMIB DESERT
- Orange
- Cunene

BOTSWANA
- Gaborone
- Serowe
- KALAHARI DESERT

SOUTH AFRICA
- Pretoria
- Johannesburg
- Vereeniging
- Klerksdorp
- Kimberley
- Bloemfontein
- Welkom
- Upington
- Springbok
- Worcester
- Cape Town
- Cape of Good Hope
- Cape Agulhas
- Port Elizabeth
- East London
- Umtata
- Bisho
- Durban
- Pietermaritzburg
- Newcastle
- Middelburg
- Messina
- Polokwane

LESOTHO
- Maseru

Limpopo

Orange

Tropic of Capricorn

Equator 0°

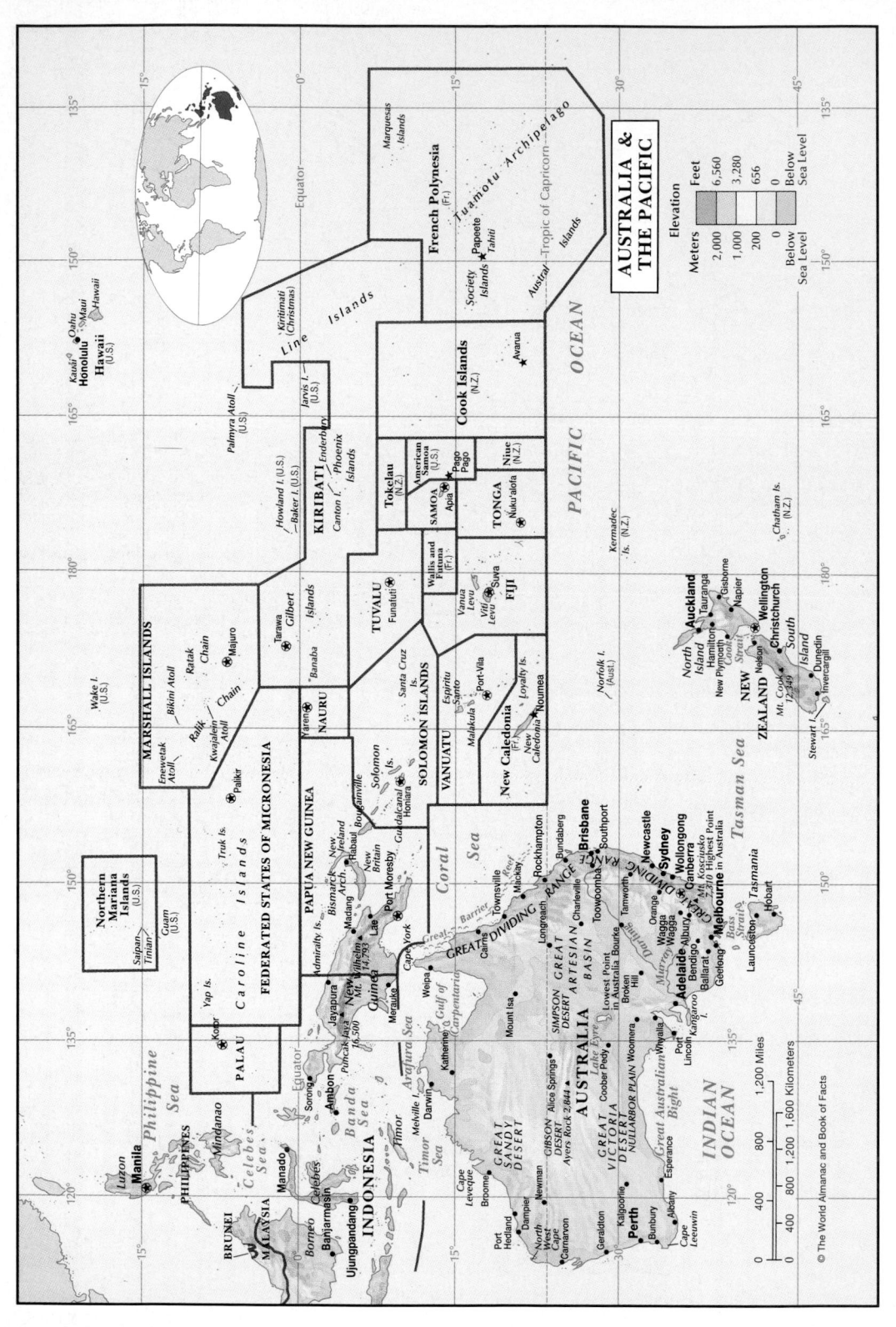

AUSTRALIA &
THE PACIFIC

Elevation

Meters		Feet
2,000		6,560
1,000		3,280
200		656
0		0
Below Sea Level		Below Sea Level

PACIFIC OCEAN

Marquesas Islands

French Polynesia

Tuamotu Archipelago

Society Islands   Papeete Tahiti

Austral - Tropic of Capricorn Islands

Cook Islands (N.Z.)

Avarua

Line Islands

Kiritimati (Christmas)

Palmyra Atoll (U.S.)

Jarvis I. (U.S.)

Kaua'i Oahu Maui
Honolulu Hawaii (U.S.)

Howland I. (U.S.)
Baker I. (U.S.)

KIRIBATI Enderbury

Canton I. Phoenix Islands

Tokelau (N.Z.)

American Samoa (U.S.) Pago Pago

Niue (N.Z.)

SAMOA Apia

TONGA Nuku'alofa

Kermadec Is. (N.Z.)

Chatham Is. (N.Z.)

Wake I. (U.S.)

Bikini Atoll

MARSHALL ISLANDS

Enewetak Atoll

Ralik Chain Ratak Chain

Kwajalein Atoll

Majuro

Tarawa Gilbert Islands

Banaba

TUVALU Funafuti

Wallis and Futuna (Fr.)

Vanua Levu

Viti Levu Suva FIJI

Santa Cruz Is.

Espiritu Santo

VANUATU Port-Vila

Loyalty Is.

New Caledonia (Fr.) Noumea

Norfolk I. (Aust.)

North Island

Auckland

Hamilton Tauranga
New Plymouth Gisborne
Napier
Wellington

NEW ZEALAND

Nelson Christchurch

Mt. Cook South Island
12,349

Dunedin

Stewart I. Invercargill

Northern Mariana Islands (U.S.)

Saipan
Tinian
Guam (U.S.)

Truk Is.

Caroline Islands

FEDERATED STATES OF MICRONESIA

Yap Is.

PALAU Koror

Palikir

Yaren NAURU

SOLOMON ISLANDS

Solomon Is.

Bougainville

Rabaul New Ireland

New Britain

Bismarck Arch.

Admiralty Is.

Madang Lae PAPUA NEW GUINEA

Port Moresby

Mt. Wilhelm
14,793

Cape York

Malakula

Guadalcanal Honiara

Coral Sea

Great Barrier Reef

Cairns

Townsville

Mackay

Rockhampton

Bundaberg

Brisbane
Southport

Newcastle
Sydney
Wollongong

Canberra
GREAT DIVIDING RANGE
Mt. Kosciusko 7,310 Highest Point in Australia

Tamworth

Toowoomba

Charleville

Longreach

GREAT DIVIDING RANGE

GREAT ARTESIAN BASIN

Orange
Wagga Wagga
Albury
Bendigo

Melbourne
Geelong

Bass Strait

Launceston

Tasmania

Hobart

Tasman Sea

Philippine Sea

Luzon Manila

PHILIPPINES

Mindanao

Celebes Sea

Manado

Celebes

BRUNEI

Borneo Banjarmasin

MALAYSIA

Ujungpandang

INDONESIA

Sorong

Ambon

Banda Sea

Jayapura Pulau Jaya
16,500

New Guinea

Merauke

Timor

Timor Sea

Melville I.
Darwin

Katherine

Gulf of Carpentaria

Weipa

Cape York

Arafura Sea

AUSTRALIA

GREAT SANDY DESERT

Broome

Port Hedland

Newman

North West Cape

Dampier

Cape Leveque

Geraldton

Carnarvon

GIBSON DESERT

Alice Springs
Ayers Rock 2,844

SIMPSON DESERT

GREAT VICTORIA DESERT

Mount Isa

Lowest Point in Australia
Lake Eyre

Coober Pedy

Woomera

Port Augusta

Whyalla

Port Lincoln

Kangaroo I.

Adelaide

Broken Hill

Bourke

Darling

Murray

Great Australian Bight

NULLARBOR PLAIN

Esperance

Kalgoorlie

Albany

Cape Leeuwin

Bunbury

Perth

INDIAN OCEAN

0	400	800	1,200 Miles	
0	400	800	1,200	1,600 Kilometers

© The World Almanac and Book of Facts

UNITED STATES HISTORY

1492
Christopher Columbus and crew sighted land **Oct. 12** in the present-day Bahamas.

1497
John Cabot explored northeast coast to Delaware.

1513
Juan Ponce de León explored Florida coast.

1524
Giovanni da Verrazano led French expedition along coast from Carolina north to Nova Scotia; entered New York harbor.

1539
Hernando de Soto landed in Florida **May 28**; crossed Mississippi River, **1541.**

1540
Francisco Vásquez de Coronado explored Southwest north of Rio Grande. Hernando de Alarcón reached Colorado River; Don Garcia Lopez de Cardenas reached Grand Canyon. Others explored California coast.

1565
St. Augustine, FL, founded **Sept. 8** by Pedro Menéndez. Razed by Francis Drake **1586.**

1579
Francis Drake entered San Francisco Bay and claimed region for Britain.

1607
Capt. John Smith and 105 cavaliers in 3 ships landed on Virginia coast, started first permanent English settlement in New World at **Jamestown** in **May.**

1609
Henry Hudson, English explorer of Northwest Passage, employed by Dutch, sailed into New York harbor in **Sept.,** and up Hudson to Albany. **Samuel de Champlain** explored Lake Champlain, just to the north.

Spaniards settled **Santa Fe, NM.**

1619
House of Burgesses, first representative assembly in New World, elected **July 30** at Jamestown, VA.

First black laborers—indentured servants—in English N. American colonies, landed by Dutch at Jamestown in **Aug.** Chattel slavery legally recognized, **1650.**

1620
Plymouth Pilgrims, Puritan separatists, left Plymouth, England, **Sept. 16** on *Mayflower.* They reached Cape Cod **Nov. 19,** explored coast; 103 passengers landed **Dec. 26** at Plymouth. **Mayflower Compact** was agreement to form a government and abide by its laws. Half of colony died during harsh winter.

1624
Dutch colonies started in Albany and in New York area, where **New Netherland** was established in **May.**

1626
Peter Minuit bought Manhattan for Dutch from Man-a-hat-a Indians during summer for goods valued at $24; named island **New Amsterdam.**

1630
Settlement of **Boston** established by Massachusetts colonists led by John Winthrop.

1634
Maryland, founded as a Catholic colony, under a charter granted to Lord Baltimore. Religious toleration granted **1649.**

1636
Roger Williams founded Providence, RI, **June,** as a democratically ruled colony with separation of church and state. Charter granted, **1644.**

Harvard College founded **Oct. 28,** now oldest in U.S.; grammar school, compulsory education established at Boston.

1640
First book was printed in America, the so-called Bay Psalm Book.

1647
Liberal constitution drafted in Rhode Island.

1660
British Parliament passed First **Navigation Act Dec. 1,** regulating colonial commerce to suit English needs.

1664
British troops Sept. 8 seized **New Netherland** from Dutch. Charles II granted New Netherland and city of New Amsterdam to brother, Duke of York; both renamed **New York.** Dutch recaptured colony **1673,** but ceded it to Britain **Nov. 10, 1674.**

1673
Jacques **Marquette** and Louis **Joliet** reached the upper **Mississippi** and traveled down it.

1676
Nathaniel Bacon led planters against autocratic British Gov. Sir William Berkeley, burned Jamestown, VA, **Sept. 19.** Rebellion collapsed when Bacon died; 23 followers executed.

Bloody **Indian war** in New England ended **Aug. 12.** King Philip, Wampanoag chief, and Narragansett Indians killed.

1682
Robert Cavelier, Sieur de La Salle, claimed lower Mississippi River country for France, called it Louisiana **Apr. 9.** Had French outposts built in Illinois and Texas, **1684.** Killed during mutiny **Mar. 19, 1687.**

William Penn arrived in **Pennsylvania.**

1683
William Penn signed treaty with Delaware Indians and made payment for Pennsylvania lands.

1692
Witchcraft delusion at Salem, MA; 20 alleged witches executed by special court.

1696
Capt. William Kidd settled in America, was hired by British to fight pirates and take booty, but himself became one. Arrested and sent to England; hanged **1701.**

1699
French settlements made in Mississippi, Louisiana.

1704
Indians attacked Deerfield, MA, **Feb. 28-29;** killed 40, carried off 100.

Boston News Letter, **first regular newspaper,** started by John Campbell, postmaster. (An earlier paper, *Publick Occurences,* was suppressed after one issue **1690.**)

1709
British-Colonial troops captured French fort, Port Royal, Nova Scotia, in **Queen Anne's War 1701-13.** France yielded Nova Scotia by treaty **1713.**

1712
Slaves revolted in New York **Apr. 6.** Six committed suicide; 21 were executed. Second rising, **1741;** 13 slaves hanged, 13 burned, 71 deported.

1716
First theater in colonies opened in Williamsburg, VA.

1726
Poor people **rioted** in Philadelphia.

Great Awakening religious revival began.

1732
Benjamin Franklin published the first *Poor Richard's Almanac;* published annually to **1757.**

Last of the 13 colonies, **Georgia,** chartered.

1735
Editor **John Peter Zenger acquitted** in New York of libeling British governor by criticizing his conduct in office.

1740-41
Capt. Vitus Bering reached Alaska.

1744
King George's War pitted British and colonials vs. French. Colonials captured Louisburg, Cape Breton Is., **June 17, 1745.** Returned to France **1748** by Treaty of Aix-la-Chapelle.

1752
Benjamin Franklin, flying kite in thunderstorm, proved lightning is electricity **June 15;** invented lightning rod.

1754
French and Indian War began when French occupied Ft. Duquesne (Pittsburgh). British moved Acadian French from Nova Scotia to Louisiana **Oct. 8, 1755.** British captured Québec **Sept. 18, 1759,** in battles in which French Gen. Joseph de Montcalm and British Gen. James Wolfe were killed. Peace pact signed **Feb. 10, 1763.** French lost Canada and Midwest.

1764
Sugar Act, placed duties on lumber, foodstuffs, molasses, and rum in colonies, to pay French and Indian War debts.

1765
Stamp Act, enacted by Parliament **Mar. 22,** required revenue stamps to help fund royal troops. Nine colonies, at **Stamp Act Congress** in New York **Oct. 7-25,** adopted Declaration of Rights. Stamp Act **repealed Mar 17, 1766.**

1767
Townshend Acts levied taxes on glass, painter's lead, paper, and tea. In **1770** all duties except on tea were repealed.

1770

British troops fired **Mar. 5** into Boston mob, killed 5 including **Crispus Attucks,** a black man, reportedly leader of group; later called **Boston Massacre.**

1773

East India Co. tea ships turned back at Boston, New York, and Philadelphia in **May.** Cargo ship burned at Annapolis **Oct. 14;** cargo thrown overboard at **Boston Tea Party Dec. 16,** to protest the tea tax.

1774

"Intolerable Acts" of Parliament curtailed Massachusetts self-rule; barred use of Boston harbor till tea was paid for.

First Continental Congress held in Philadelphia **Sept. 5-Oct. 26;** called for civil disobedience against British.

Rhode Island abolished slavery.

1775

Patrick Henry addressed Virginia convention, **Mar. 23,** said "Give me liberty or give me death."

Paul Revere and William Dawes on night of **Apr. 18** rode to alert Patriots that British were on their way to Concord to destroy arms. At Lexington, MA, **Apr. 19,** Minutemen lost 8. On return from Concord, British took 273 casualties.

Col. Ethan Allen (joined by Col. Benedict Arnold) captured **Ft. Ticonderoga, NY, May 10;** also Crown Point. Colonials headed for **Bunker Hill,** fortified Breed's Hill, Charlestown, MA. Repulsed British under Gen. William Howe twice before retreating **June 17;** called Battle of Bunker Hill.

Continental Congress **June 15** named **George Washington** commander in chief.

1776

France and Spain each agreed **May 2** to provide arms.

In Continental Congress **June 7,** Richard Henry Lee (VA) moved "that these united colonies are and of right ought to be free and independent states." Resolution adopted July 2. **Declaration of Independence** approved **July 4.**

Col. William Moultrie's batteries at **Charleston, SC,** repulsed British sea attack **June 28.** Washington, with 10,000 men, lost **Battle of Long Island Aug. 27;** evacuated New York.

Nathan Hale executed as spy by British **Sept. 22.**

Brig. Gen. Arnold's **Lake Champlain** fleet was defeated at Valcour **Oct. 11,** but British returned to Canada. Howe failed to destroy Washington's army at **White Plains Oct. 28.** Hessians captured Ft. Washington, Manhattan, and 3,000 men **Nov. 16;** captured Ft. Lee, NJ, **Nov. 18.**

Washington in Pennsylvania, recrossed **Delaware River Dec. 25-26,** defeated Hessians at Trenton, NJ, **Dec. 26.**

1777

Washington defeated Lord Cornwallis at **Princeton Jan. 3.** Continental Congress adopted Stars and Stripes.

Maj. Gen. John Burgoyne, force of 8,000 from Canada, captured **Ft. Ticonderoga July 6.** Americans beat back Burgoyne at Bemis Heights **Oct. 7,** cut off British escape route. Burgoyne surrendered 5,000 men at **Saratoga, NY, Oct. 17.**

Articles of Confederation adopted by Continental Congress **Nov. 15;** ratified **Mar. 1,** by last state, Maryland.

France recognized independence of 13 colonies **Dec. 17.**

1778

France signed treaty of aid with U.S. **Feb. 6.** Sent fleet; British evacuated Philadelphia in consequence **June 18.**

1779

John Paul Jones on the *Bonhomme Richard* defeated *Serapis* in British North Sea waters **Sept. 23.**

1780

Charleston, SC, fell to the British **May 12,** but a British force was defeated near **Kings Mountain, NC, Oct. 7** by militiamen.

Benedict Arnold found to be a traitor **Sept. 23.** Arnold escaped, made brigadier general in British army.

1781

Bank of North America incorporated **May 26.**

Cornwallis, sapped by Patriot victories, retired to **Yorktown, VA.** Adm. Francois Joseph de Grasse landed 3,000 French and stopped British fleet in Hampton Roads. Washington and Jean Baptiste de Rochambeau joined forces, arrived near Williamsburg **Sept. 26.** Siege of Cornwallis began **Oct. 6; Cornwallis surrendered Oct. 19.**

1782

New **British** cabinet agreed **in March** to **recognize U.S.** independence. Preliminary agreement signed in Paris **Nov. 30.**

1783

Massachusetts Supreme Court declared **slavery** illegal in that state.

Britain, U.S. signed Paris **peace treaty Sept. 3** recognizing American independence (Congress ratified it **Jan. 14, 1784**).

Washington ordered army disbanded Nov. 3, bade farewell to his officers at Fraunces Tavern, New York City, **Dec. 4.**

Noah Webster published *American Spelling Book.*

1784

Thomas Jefferson's proposal to **ban slavery** in new territory after 1802 was narrowly defeated **Mar. 1.**

First successful daily newspaper, *Pennsylvania Packet & General Advertiser,* published **Sept. 21.**

1786

Delegates from 5 states at **Annapolis, MD, Sept. 11-14** asked Congress to call convention in Philadelphia to write practical constitution for the 13 states.

1787

Shays's Rebellion of debt-ridden farmers in Massachusetts failed **Jan. 25.**

Northwest Ordinance adopted **July 13** by Continental Congress for Northwest Territory, N of Ohio River, W of New York; made rules for statehood. Guaranteed freedom of religion, support for schools, no slavery.

Constitutional convention opened at Philadelphia **May 25** with Washington presiding. Constitution accepted by delegates **Sept. 17;** ratification by 9th state, New Hampshire, **June 21, 1788,** meant adoption; declared in effect **Mar. 4, 1789.**

1789

George Washington chosen president by all electors voting (73 eligible, 69 voting, 4 absent); John Adams, vice president, got 34 votes. First Congress met at Federal Hall, New York City, **Mar. 4.** Washington inaugurated there **Apr. 30.** Supreme Court created by Federal Judiciary Act **Sept. 24.** Congress submitted Bill of Rights to states **Sept. 25.**

1790

Congress, **Mar. 1,** authorized decennial U.S. **census; Naturalization Act** (2-year residency) passed **Mar. 26.**

Congress met in Philadelphia, new temporary capital, **Dec. 6.**

1791

Bill of Rights went into effect **Dec. 15.**

1792

Coinage Act established **U.S. Mint** in Philadelphia **Apr. 2.**

Gen. **"Mad" Anthony Wayne** made commander in Ohio-Indiana area, trained "American Legion," established string of forts. Routed Indians at Fallen Timbers on Maumee River **Aug. 20, 1794,** checked British at Fort Miami, OH.

White House cornerstone laid **Oct. 13.**

1793

Eli Whitney invented **cotton gin,** reviving Southern slavery.

1794

Whiskey Rebellion, W Pennsylvania farmers protesting liquor tax of **1791,** was suppressed by federal militia **Sept. 1794.**

1795

U.S. bought peace from **Algerian pirates** by paying $1 mil ransom for 115 seamen **Sept. 5,** followed by annual tributes.

Gen. Wayne signed peace with Indians at Fort Greenville.

University of North Carolina became first operating state university.

1796

Washington's Farewell Address as president delivered **Sept. 19.** Gave strong warnings against permanent alliances with foreign powers, big public debt, large military establishment, and devices of "small, artful, enterprising minority."

1797

U.S. **frigate** *United States* launched at Philadelphia **July 10;** *Constellation* at Baltimore **Sept. 7;** *Constitution* (Old Ironsides) at Boston **Sept. 20.**

1798

Alien & Sedition Acts passed by Federalists **June-July;** intended to silence political opposition.

War with France threatened over French raids on U.S. shipping and rejection of U.S. diplomats. Navy (45 ships) and 365 privateers captured 84 French ships. *USS Constellation* took French warship *Insurgente* **1799.** Napoleon stopped French raids after becoming First Consul.

1800

Federal government moved to **Washington, DC.**

1801

John Marshall named Supreme Court chief justice, **Jan. 20.**

Tripoli declared war June 10 against U.S., which refused added tribute to commerce-raiding Arab corsairs. Land and naval campaigns forced Tripoli to negotiate **peace June 4, 1805.**

1803

Supreme Court, in **Marbury v Madison** case, for the first time overturned a U.S. law **Feb. 24.**

Napoleon sold all of **Louisiana,** stretching to Canadian border, to U.S., for $11,250,000 in bonds, plus $3,750,000 indemnities to American citizens with claims against France. U.S. took title **Dec. 20.** Purchases doubled U.S. area.

1804

Lewis and Clark expedition ordered by Pres. Thomas Jefferson to explore what is now northwest U.S. Started from St. Louis **May 14;** ended **Sept. 23, 1806.**

Vice Pres. **Aaron Burr shot Alexander Hamilton** in a duel **July 11** in Weehawken, NJ; Hamilton died the next day.

1807

Robert Fulton made first practical steamboat trip; left New York City **Aug. 17,** reached Albany, 150 mi, in 32 hr.

Embargo Act banned all trade with foreign countries, forbidding ships to set sail for foreign ports **Dec. 22.**

1808

Slave importation outlawed. Some 250,000 slaves were illegally imported **1808-60.**

1811

William Henry Harrison, governor of Indiana, defeated Indians under the Prophet, in battle of **Tippecanoe Nov. 7.**

Cumberland Road begun at Cumberland, MD; became important route to West.

1812

War of 1812 had 3 main causes: Britain seized U.S. ships trading with France; Britain seized 4,000 naturalized U.S. sailors by **1810;** Britain armed Indians who raided western border. U.S. stopped trade with Europe **1807** and **1809.** Trade with Britain only was stopped **1810.**

Unaware that Britain had raised the blockade against France 2 days before, **Congress declared war June 18.**

USS Essex captured *Alert* **Aug. 13;** *USS Constitution* destroyed *Guerriere* **Aug. 19;** *USS Wasp* took *Frolic* **Oct. 18;** *USS United States* defeated *Macedonian* off Azores **Oct. 25;** *Constitution* beat *Java* **Dec. 29.** British took Detroit **Aug. 16.**

1813

Oliver H. Perry defeated British fleet at Battle of Lake Erie, **Sept. 10.** U.S. won Battle of the Thames, Ontario, **Oct. 5,** but failed in Canadian invasion attempts. York (Toronto) and Buffalo were burned.

1814

British landed in Maryland in Aug., defeated U.S. force **Aug. 24, burned Capitol and White House.** Maryland militia stopped British advance **Sept. 12.** Bombardment of Ft. McHenry, Baltimore, for 25 hours, **Sept. 13-14,** by British fleet failed; Francis Scott Key wrote words to **"Star Spangled Banner."**

U.S. won naval Battle of **Lake Champlain Sept. 11.** Peace treaty signed at Ghent **Dec. 24.**

1815

Some 5,300 British, unaware of peace treaty, attacked U.S. entrenchments near **New Orleans, Jan. 8.** British had more than 2,000 casualties; Americans lost 71.

U.S. flotilla finally ended piracy by **Algiers, Tunis, Tripoli** by **Aug. 6.**

1816

Second **Bank of the U.S.** chartered.

1817

Rush-Bagot treaty signed **Apr. 28-29;** limited U.S., British armaments on the Great Lakes.

William Cullen Bryant's poem "Thanatopsis" published.

1819

Spain ceded **Florida** to U.S. **Feb. 22.**

American steamship *Savannah* made first part-steam-powered, part-sail-powered crossing of Atlantic, Savannah, GA, to Liverpool, England, 29 days.

1820

First organized **immigration of blacks to Africa** from U.S. began with 86 free blacks sailing **Feb.** to Sierra Leone.

Henry Clay's **Missouri Compromise** bill passed by Congress **Mar. 3.** Slavery was allowed in Missouri, but not elsewhere west of the Mississippi River north of 36° 30′ latitude (the southern line of Missouri). Repealed **1854.**

1821

Emma Willard founded Troy Female Seminary, first U.S. women's college.

1823

Monroe Doctrine, opposing European intervention in the Americas, enunciated by Pres. James Monroe **Dec. 2.**

1824

Pawtucket, RI, **weavers strike** marked the first such action by women.

1825

After a deadlocked election, John Quincy Adams was elected president by the U.S. House, **Feb. 9.**

Erie Canal opened; first boat left Buffalo **Oct. 26,** reached New York City **Nov. 4.** Canal cost $7 mil but opened Great Lakes area, made New York City chief Atlantic port.

John Stevens, of Hoboken, NJ, built and operated first experimental **steam locomotive** in U.S.

1826

Thomas Jefferson and John Adams both died **July 4.**

1828

South Carolina **Dec. 19** declared the right of state **nullification of federal laws,** opposing the "Tariff of Abominations."

Noah Webster published his *American Dictionary of the English Language.*

Baltimore & Ohio, 1st U.S. passenger railroad, was begun **July 4.**

1829

Andrew Jackson inaugurated as president, **Mar. 4.**

1830

Mormon church organized by Joseph Smith in Fayette, NY, **Apr. 6.**

1831

William Lloyd Garrison began abolitionist newspaper *The Liberator,* **Jan. 1.**

Nat Turner, black slave in Virginia, led local slave rebellion, starting **Aug. 21;** 57 whites killed. Troops called in, 100 slaves killed, Turner captured, tried, and hanged **Nov. 11.**

1832

Black Hawk War (IL-WI) **Apr.-Sept.** pushed Sauk and Fox Indians west across Mississippi.

South Carolina convention passed **Ordinance of Nullification Nov.** 24 against permanent tariff, threatening to withdraw from Union. Congress **Feb. 1833** passed compromise tariff act, whereupon South Carolina repealed its act.

1833

Oberlin College became first in U.S. to adopt coeducation.

1835

Seminole Indians in Florida under Osceola began attacks **Nov. 1,** protesting forced removal. The unpopular 8-year war ended **Aug. 14, 1842;** Indians were sent to Oklahoma.

Texas proclaimed right to secede from Mexico; Sam Houston put in command of Texas army, **Nov. 2-4.**

Gold discovered on **Cherokee land** in Georgia. Indians forced to cede lands **Dec. 20** and to cross Mississippi.

Halley's Comet passed by the Earth.

1836

Texans besieged in Alamo in San Antonio by Mexicans under Santa Anna **Feb. 23-Mar. 6;** entire garrison killed. Texas independence declared, **Mar. 2.** At San Jacinto **Apr. 21,** Sam Houston and Texans defeated Mexicans.

Marcus Whitman, H. H. Spaulding, and wives reached Fort Walla Walla on Columbia River, OR. **First white women to cross plains.**

1838

Cherokee Indians made "Trail of Tears," removed from Georgia to Oklahoma starting **Oct.**

1841

First emigrant **wagon train for California,** 47 persons, left Independence, MO, **May 1,** reached California **Nov. 4.**

Brook Farm commune set up by New England Transcendentalist intellectuals. Lasted to **1846.**

1842

Webster-Ashburton Treaty signed **Aug. 9,** fixing the U.S.-Canada border in Maine and Minnesota.

First use of **anesthetic** (sulphuric ether gas).

Settlement of Oregon began via **Oregon Trail.**

1843

More than 1,000 settlers left Independence, MO, for Oregon **May 22,** arrived **Oct.**

1844

First message over first **telegraph line** sent **May 24** by inventor Samuel F.B. Morse from Washington to Baltimore: "What hath God wrought!"

1845

Texas Congress **voted for annexation** by U.S. **July 4.** U.S. Congress admitted Texas to Union **Dec. 29.**

Edgar Allan Poe's poem "The Raven" published.

1846

Mexican War began after Pres. James K. Polk ordered Gen. Zachary Taylor to seize disputed Texan land settled by Mexicans. After border clash, U.S. declared war **May 13;** Mexico **May 23.**

Bear flag of Republic of California raised by American settlers at Sonoma **June 14.**

About 12,000 U.S. troops took Vera Cruz **Mar. 27, 1847,** and Mexico City **Sept. 14, 1847.** By **treaty,** signed **Feb. 2, 1848,** war was ended, and Mexico ceded claims to Texas, California, and other territory.

Treaty with Britain **June 15** set **boundary in Oregon** territory at 49th parallel (extension of existing line). Expansionists had used slogan "54° 40´ or fight."

Mormons, after violent clashes with settlers over polygamy, left Nauvoo, IL, for West under Brigham Young; settled **July 1847** at **Salt Lake City, UT.**

Elias Howe invented **sewing machine.**

1847

First **adhesive U.S. postage stamps** on sale **July 1;** Benjamin Franklin 5¢, Washington 10¢.

Ralph Waldo Emerson published first book of poems; **Henry Wadsworth Longfellow** published *Evangeline.*

1848

Gold discovered Jan. 24 in California; 80,000 prospectors emigrated in **1849.**

Lucretia Mott and Elizabeth Cady Stanton led **Seneca Falls, NY, Women's Rights Convention July 19-20.**

1850

Sen. Henry Clay's **Compromise of 1850** admitted California as 31st state **Sept. 9,** with slavery forbidden; made Utah and New Mexico territories; made Fugitive Slave Law more harsh; ended District of Columbia slave trade.

Nathaniel Hawthorne's *The Scarlet Letter* published.

1851

Herman Melville's *Moby-Dick* published.

1852

Uncle Tom's Cabin, by **Harriet Beecher Stowe,** published.

1853

Comm. **Matthew C. Perry,** U.S.N., received by Japan, **July 14; negotiated treaty to open Japan** to U.S. ships.

1854

Republican Party formed at Ripon, WI, **Feb. 28.** Opposed Kansas-Nebraska Act (became law **May 30**), which left issue of slavery to vote of settlers.

Henry David Thoreau published *Walden.*

1855

Walt Whitman published *Leaves of Grass.*

First railroad train crossed Mississippi on the river's first bridge, Rock Island, IL, Davenport, IA, **Apr. 21.**

1856

Republican Party's first nominee for president, **John C. Fremont,** defeated. Abraham Lincoln made 50 speeches for him.

Lawrence, KS, sacked **May 21** by proslavery group; abolitionist **John Brown** led antislavery men against Missourians at **Osawatomie, KS, Aug. 30.**

1857

Dred Scott decision by Supreme Court **Mar. 6** held that slaves did not become free in a free state, Congress could not bar slavery from a territory, and blacks could not be citizens.

1858

First **Atlantic cable** completed by Cyrus W. Field **Aug. 5.**

Lincoln-Douglas debates in Illinois **Aug. 21-Oct. 15.**

1859

First commercially productive **oil well,** drilled near Titusville, PA, by Edwin L. Drake **Aug. 27.**

Abolitionist **John Brown,** with 21 men, seized U.S. Armory at **Harpers Ferry Oct. 16.** U.S. Marines captured raiders, killing several. Brown was hanged for treason **Dec. 2.**

1860

Approximately 20,000 **New England shoe workers** went on strike **Feb. 22** and won higher wages.

Abraham Lincoln, Republican, elected president **Nov. 6** in 4-way race.

First **Pony Express** between Sacramento, CA, and St. Joseph, MO, started **Apr. 3;** service ended **Oct. 24, 1861,** when first transcontinental telegraph line was completed.

1861

Seven southern states set up **Confederate States of America Feb. 8,** with Jefferson Davis as president, captured federal arsenals and forts. **Civil War** began as Confederates fired on **Ft. Sumter** in Charleston, SC, **Apr. 12,** capturing it **Apr. 14.**

Pres. **Lincoln called for 75,000 volunteers Apr. 15.** By **May,** 11 states had seceded. Lincoln blockaded Southern ports **Apr. 19,** cutting off vital exports, aid.

Confederates repelled Union forces at first **Battle of Bull Run July 21.**

First **transcontinental telegraph** was put in operation.

1862

Homestead Act approved **May 20;** it granted free family farms to settlers.

Land Grant Act approved **July 7,** providing for public land sale to benefit agricultural education; eventually led to establishment of state university systems.

Union forces were victorious in Western campaigns, took **New Orleans May 1.** Battles in East were inconclusive.

1863

Pres. Lincoln issued **Emancipation Proclamation Jan. 1,** freeing "all slaves in areas still in rebellion."

Entire **Mississippi River** was in Union hands by **July 4.** Union forces won a major victory at **Gettysburg, PA, July 1-3.** Lincoln read his **Gettysburg Address Nov. 19.**

In **draft riots** in New York City about 1,000 were killed or wounded; some blacks were hanged by mobs **July 13-16.**

1864

Gen. William Tecumseh **Sherman marched through Georgia,** taking Atlanta **Sept. 1,** Savannah **Dec. 22.**

Sand Creek massacre of Cheyenne and Arapaho Indians **Nov. 29.** Cavalry attacked Indians awaiting surrender terms.

1865

Gen. **Robert E. Lee surrendered** 27,800 Confederate troops to Gen. Ulysses S. Grant at Appomattox Court House, VA, **Apr. 9.** J. E. Johnston surrendered 31,200 to Sherman at Durham Station, NC, **Apr. 18.** Last rebel troops surrendered **May 26.**

Pres. **Lincoln was shot Apr. 14** by John Wilkes Booth in Ford's Theater, Washington, DC; died the following morning. Vice Pres. **Andrew Johnson** was sworn in as president. Booth was hunted down; fatally wounded, perhaps by his own hand, **Apr. 26.** Four co-conspirators were hanged **July 7.**

13th Amendment, abolishing slavery, ratified **Dec. 6.**

1866

Ku Klux Klan formed secretly in South to terrorize blacks who voted. Disbanded **1869-71.** A 2d Klan organized **1915.**

Congress took control of Southern Reconstruction, backed freedmen's rights.

1867

Alaska sold to U.S. by Russia for $7.2 mil **Mar. 30** through efforts of Sec. of State William H. Seward.

Horatio Alger published first book, *Ragged Dick.*

The **Grange** was organized **Dec. 4,** to protect farmer interests.

1868

The World Almanac, a publication of the *New York World,* appeared for the first time.

Pres. **Johnson** tried to remove Edwin M. Stanton, secretary of war; was impeached by House **Feb. 24** for violation of Tenure of Office Act; acquitted by Senate **Mar.-May.**

1869

Financial **"Black Friday"** in New York **Sept. 24;** caused by attempt to "corner" gold.

Transcontinental railroad completed; golden spike driven at Promontory, UT, **May 10,** marking the junction of Central Pacific and Union Pacific.

Knights of Labor formed in Philadelphia. By **1886,** this labor union had 700,000 members nationally.

Woman suffrage law passed in Wyoming Territory **Dec. 10.**

1871

Great fire destroyed **Chicago Oct. 8-11.**

1872

Amnesty Act restored civil rights to citizens of the South **May 22** except for 500 Confederate leaders.

Congress founded first national park—**Yellowstone.**

1873

First U.S. **postal card** issued **May 1.**

Banks failed, panic began in **Sept.** Depression lasted 5 years.

"Boss" William Tweed of New York City convicted **Nov. 19** of stealing public funds. He died in jail in **1878.**

New York's Bellevue Hospital started **first nursing school.**

1875

Congress passed **Civil Rights Act Mar. 1,** giving equal rights to blacks in public accommodations and jury duty. Act invalidated in **1883** by Supreme Court.

First **Kentucky Derby** held **May 17.**

1876

Samuel J. Tilden, Democrat, received majority of popular votes for president over **Rutherford B. Hayes,** Republican, but 22 electoral votes were in dispute; issue left to Congress. Hayes given presidency in **Feb. 1877** after Republicans agreed to end Reconstruction of South.

Col. **George A. Custer** and 264 soldiers of the 7th Cavalry killed **June 25** in "last stand," Battle of the Little Big Horn, MT, in Sioux Indian War.

1877

Molly Maguires, Irish terrorist society in Scranton, PA, mining areas, broken up by hanging **June 21,** of 11 leaders for murders of mine officials and police.

Pres. Rutherford B. Hayes sent troops in violent national **railroad strike.**

1878

First commercial **telephone** exchange opened, New Haven, CT, **Jan. 28.**

Thomas A. Edison founded **Edison Electric Light Co.** on **Oct. 15.**

1879

F. W. Woolworth opened his first five-and-ten store, in Utica, NY, **Feb. 22.**

Henry George published *Progress & Poverty,* advocating single tax on land.

1881

Pres. **James A. Garfield shot** in Washington, DC, **July 2;** died **Sept. 19.**

Booker T. Washington founded Tuskegee Institute for blacks.

Helen Hunt Jackson published *A Century of Dishonor,* about mistreatment of Indians.

1883

Pendleton Act passed **Jan. 16,** reformed civil service.

Brooklyn Bridge opened **May 24.**

1884

Mark Twain's masterpiece, *The Adventures of Huckleberry Finn,* appeared.

1886

Haymarket riot and bombing, **May 4,** followed bitter labor battles for 8-hour day in Chicago; 7 police and 4 workers died. Eight anarchists found guilty **Aug. 20,** 4 hanged **Nov. 11.**

Geronimo, Apache Indian, finally surrendered **Sept. 4.**

Statue of Liberty dedicated **Oct. 28.**

American Federation of Labor (AFL) formed **Dec. 8** by 25 craft unions.

1888

Great blizzard struck eastern U.S. **Mar. 11-14,** causing about 400 deaths.

1889

U.S. opened Oklahoma to white settlement **Apr. 22;** within 24 hours **claims for 2 mil acres** were staked by 50,000 settlers.

Johnstown, PA, flood May 31; 2,200 lives lost.

1890

Battle of **Wounded Knee, SD, Dec. 29,** the last major conflict between Indians and U.S. troops. About 200 Indian men, women, and children and 29 soldiers were killed.

Sherman Antitrust Act passed **July 2,** began federal effort to curb monopolies.

Jacob Riis published How the Other Half Lives, about city slums.

Poems of **Emily Dickinson** published posthumously.

1891

Forest Reserve Act Mar. 3 let president close public forest land to settlement for establishment of national parks.

1892

Ellis Island, in New York Bay, opened **Jan. 1** to receive immigrants.

Homestead, PA, strike at Carnegie steel mills; 7 guards and 11 strikers and spectators shot to death **July 6;** setback for unions. **Ellis Island** opened as New York immigration depot.

1893

Financial panic began, led to 4-year depression.

1894

Thomas A. **Edison's kinetoscope** (motion pictures) (invented **1887**) given first public showing **Apr. 14.**

The **Pullman strike** began **May 11** at a railroad car plant in Chicago.

Jacob S. Coxey led army of unemployed from the Midwest, reaching Washington, DC, **Apr. 30.** Coxey arrested **May 1** for trespassing on Capitol grounds; his army disbanded.

1896

William Jennings Bryan delivered "Cross of Gold" speech **July 8;** won Democratic Party nomination.

Supreme Court, in **Plessy v. Ferguson,** approved racial segregation under the "separate but equal" doctrine.

1898

U.S. **battleship** *Maine* blown up **Feb. 15** at Havana; 260 killed.

U.S. **blockaded Cuba Apr. 22** in aid of independence forces. U.S. declared war on Spain, **Apr. 24,** destroyed Spanish fleet in Philippines **May 1,** took Guam **June 20.**

Puerto Rico taken by U.S. **July 25-Aug. 12.** Spain agreed **Dec. 10** to cede Philippines, Puerto Rico, and Guam, and approved independence for Cuba.

Annexation of **Hawaii** signed by Pres. William McKinley, **July 7.**

1899

Filipino insurgents, unable to get recognition of independence from U.S., started guerrilla war **Feb. 4.** Their leader, Emilio Aguinaldo, captured **May 23, 1901.** Philippine Insurrection ended **1902.**

U.S. declared **Open Door Policy** to make China an open international market and to preserve its integrity as a nation.

John Dewey published *School and Society,* advocating "progressive education."

1900

Carry Nation, Kansas antisaloon agitator, began raiding with hatchet.

U.S. helped suppress **"Boxers"** in Beijing.

International Ladies' Garment Workers Union was founded in New York City in **Nov.**

1901

Texas had first significant **oil strike, Jan. 10.**

Pres. **McKinley was shot Sept. 6** in Buffalo, NY, by an anarchist, Leon Czolgosz; died **Sept. 14.**

1903

Treaty between U.S. and Colombia to have U.S. dig **Panama Canal** signed **Jan. 22,** rejected by Colombia. Panama declared independence from Columbia with U.S. support **Nov. 3;** recognized by Pres. Theodore Roosevelt **Nov. 6.** U.S., Panama signed canal treaty **Nov. 18.**

Wisconsin set first **direct primary** voting system **May 23.**

First successful flight in heavier-than-air mechanically propelled airplane by **Orville Wright Dec. 17** near Kitty Hawk, NC, 120 ft in 12 secs. Fourth flight same day by **Wilbur Wright,** 852 ft in 59 secs. Improved plane patented, **1906.**

Jack London published *Call of the Wild.*

Great Train Robbery, pioneering film, produced.

1904

Ida Tarbell published muckraking *History of Standard Oil.*

1905

First **Rotary Club** founded in Chicago in Dec.

1906

San Francisco earthquake and fire **Apr. 18-19** left 503 dead, $350 mil damages.

Pure Food and Drug Act and Meat Inspection Act both passed **June 30.**

1907

Financial panic and depression started **Mar. 13.**

First round-world cruise of U.S. **"Great White Fleet";** 16 battleships, 12,000 men.

1908

Henry Ford introduced **Model T** car, priced at $850, **Oct. 1.**

1909

Adm. Robert E. Peary claimed to have reached **North Pole Apr. 6** on 6th attempt, accompanied by Matthew Henson, a black man, and 4 Eskimos; may have fallen short.

National Conference on the Negro convened **May 30,** leading to founding of National Association for the Advancement of Colored People.

1910

Boy Scouts of America founded **Feb. 8.**

1911

Supreme Court dissolved **Standard Oil Co. May 15.**

Building holding New York City's **Triangle Shirtwaist Co.** factory caught fire **Mar. 25;** 146 died.

First **transcontinental airplane flight** (with numerous stops) by C. P. Rodgers, New York to Pasadena, CA, **Sept. 17-Nov. 5;** time in air 82 hr, 4 min.

1912

American Girl Guides founded **Mar. 12;** name changed in **1913** to **Girl Scouts.**

U.S. sent Marines **Aug. 14** to **Nicaragua,** which was in default of loans to U.S. and Europe.

1913

NY Armory Show brought modern art to U.S. **Feb. 17.**

U.S. blockaded Mexico in support of revolutionaries.

Charles Beard published his *Economic Interpretation of the Constitution.*

Federal Reserve System was authorized **Dec. 23,** in a major reform of U.S. banking and finance.

1914

Ford Motor Co. raised basic wage rates from $2.40 for 9-hr day to $5 for 8-hr day **Jan. 5.**

When U.S. sailors were arrested at Tampico, Mexico, **Apr. 9,** Atlantic fleet was sent to **Veracruz,** occupied city.

Pres. Woodrow Wilson proclaimed **U.S. neutrality** in the European war **Aug. 4.**

Panama Canal was officially opened **Aug. 15.**

The **Clayton Antitrust Act** was passed **Oct. 15,** strengthening federal antimonopoly powers.

1915

First transcontinental **telephone call,** New York to San Francisco, **Jan. 25,** by Alexander Graham Bell and Thomas A. Watson.

British ship *Lusitania* sunk **May 7** by German submarine; 128 American passengers lost (Germany had warned passengers in advance). As a result of U.S. campaign, Germany issued apology and promise of payments **Oct. 5.** Pres. Wilson asked for a military fund increase **Dec. 7.**

U.S. troops landed in **Haiti July 28.** Haiti became a virtual U.S. protectorate under **Sept. 16** treaty.

1916

Gen. John J. **Pershing entered Mexico** to pursue Francisco (Pancho) Villa, who had raided U.S. border areas. Forces withdrawn **Feb. 5, 1917.**

Rural Credits Act passed **July 17,** followed by Warehouse Act **Aug. 11;** both provided financial aid to farmers.

Bomb exploded during **San Francisco** Preparedness Day parade **July 22,** killed 10. Thomas J. Mooney, labor organizer, and Warren K. Billings, shoe worker, were convicted **1917;** both later pardoned.

U.S. bought **Virgin Islands** from Denmark **Aug. 4.**

Jeannette Rankin elected as **first** U.S. congresswoman (R, MT).

U.S. established military government in the **Dominican Republic Nov. 29.**

Trade and loans to **European allies** soared during the year.

Carl Sandburg published *Chicago Poems.*

1917

Germany, suffering from British blockade, declared almost unrestricted **submarine warfare Jan. 31.** U.S. cut diplomatic ties with Germany **Feb. 3,** and formally declared war **Apr. 6.**

Conscription law was passed **May 18.** First U.S. troops arrived in Europe **June 26.**

18th **(Prohibition)** Amendment to the Constitution was submitted to the states by Congress **Dec. 18.** On **Jan. 16, 1919,** the 36th state (Nevada) ratified it.

1918

Pres. Wilson set out his **14 Points** as basis for peace **Jan. 8.**

More than 1 mil **American troops** were in Europe by **July.** Allied counteroffensive launched at Château-Thierry **July 18.** War ended with signing of armistice **Nov. 11.**

Influenza epidemic killed an estimated 20 mil worldwide, 548,000 in U.S.

1919

First **transatlantic flight,** by U.S. Navy seaplane, left Rockaway, NY, **May 8,** stopped at Newfoundland, Azores, Lisbon **May 27.**

Boston police strike Sept. 9; National Guard breaks strike.

Sherwood Anderson published *Winesburg, Ohio.*

About 250 **alien radicals** were deported **Dec. 22.**

1920

In national **Red Scare,** some 2,700 Communists, anarchists, and other radicals were arrested **Jan.-May.**

Senate refused **Mar. 19** to ratify the **League of Nations Covenant.**

Radicals Nicola **Sacco** and Bartolomeo **Vanzetti** accused of killing 2 men in Massachusetts payroll holdup **Apr. 15.** Found guilty **1921.** A 6-year campaign for their release failed, and both were executed **Aug. 23, 1927.** Controversial verdict repudiated **1977,** by proclamation of Massachusetts Gov. Michael Dukakis.

First regular licensed **radio broadcasting** begun **Aug. 20.**

19th Amendment ratified **Aug. 18,** giving women right to vote.

League of Women Voters founded.

Wall St., New York City, **bomb** explosion killed 30, injured 100, did $2 mil damage **Sept. 16.**

Sinclair Lewis's *Main Street,* F. Scott Fitzgerald's *This Side of Paradise* published.

1921

Congress sharply curbed **immigration,** set national quota system **May 19.**

Joint congressional resolution declaring **peace with Germany, Austria, and Hungary** signed **July 2** by Pres. Warren G. Harding; treaties were signed in **Aug.**

Limitation of Armaments Conference met in Washington, DC, **Nov. 12-Feb. 6, 1922.** Major powers agreed to curtail naval construction, outlaw poison gas, restrict submarine attacks on merchant vessels, respect integrity of China.

Ku Klux Klan began revival with violence against Catholics in North, South, and Midwest.

1922

Violence during **coal-mine strike** at Herrin, IL, **June 22-23** cost 36 lives, including those of 21 nonunion miners.

Reader's Digest founded.

1923

First **sound-on-film motion picture**, *Phonofilm*, shown at Rivoli Theater, New York City, beginning in **April.**

1924

Law approved by Congress **June 15** making all **Indians citizens.**

Nellie Tayloe Ross elected governor of Wyoming **Nov. 9** as nation's first woman governor. **Miriam (Ma) Ferguson** elected governor of Texas **Nov. 9**; installed **Jan. 20, 1925.**

George Gershwin wrote *Rhapsody in Blue.*

1925

John T. Scopes found guilty of having taught **evolution** in Dayton, TN, high school, fined $100 and costs **July 24.**

1926

Dr. **Robert H. Goddard** demonstrated practicality of **rockets Mar. 16** at Auburn, MA, with first liquid-fuel rocket; rocket traveled 184 ft in 2.5 sec.

Congress established **Army Air Corps July 2.**

Air Commerce Act passed **Nov. 2**, providing federal aid for airlines and airports.

Ernest Hemingway's *The Sun Also Rises* published.

1927

About 1,000 **marines landed in China Mar. 5** to protect property in civil war.

Capt. **Charles A. Lindbergh** left Roosevelt Field, NY, **May 20** alone in plane *Spirit of St. Louis* on first New York-Paris nonstop flight. Reached Le Bourget airfield **May 21**, 3,610 mi in 33½ hours.

The Jazz Singer, with **Al Jolson**, demonstrated part-talking pictures in New York City **Oct. 6.**

Show Boat opened in New York **Dec. 27.**

O. E. Rolvaag published *Giants in the Earth.*

1928

Herbert Hoover elected president, defeating New York Gov. **Alfred E. Smith**, a Catholic.

Amelia Earhart became first woman to fly the Atlantic, **June 17.**

1929

"St. Valentine's Day massacre" in Chicago **Feb. 14**; gangsters killed 7 rivals.

Farm price stability aided by **Agricultural Marketing Act,** passed **June 15.**

Albert B. Fall, former secretary of the interior, was convicted of accepting bribe of $100,000 in the leasing of the **Elk Hills (Teapot Dome)** naval oil reserve; sentenced **Nov. 1** to a year in prison and fined $100,000.

Stock market crash Oct. 29 marked end of past prosperity as stock prices plummeted. Stock losses for 1929-31 estimated at $50 bil; worst American depression began.

Thomas Wolfe published *Look Homeward, Angel.* **William Faulkner** published *The Sound and the Fury.*

1930

London **Naval Reduction Treaty** signed by U.S., Britain, Italy, France, and Japan **Apr. 22**; in effect **Jan. 1, 1931;** expired **Dec. 31, 1936.**

Hawley-Smoot Tariff signed; rate hikes slash world trade.

1931

Empire State Building opened in New York City **May 1.**

Al Capone was convicted of tax evasion **Oct. 17.**

Pearl Buck published *The Good Earth.*

1932

Reconstruction Finance Corp. established **Jan. 22** to stimulate banking and business. Unemployment at 12 mil.

19-month-old **Charles Lindbergh Jr. was kidnapped Mar. 1**; found dead **May 12.** Bruno Hauptmann found guilty in trial **Jan-Feb. 1935**; executed **Apr. 3, 1936.**

Bonus March on Washington, DC, launched **May 29** by World War I veterans demanding Congress pay their bonus in full.

Franklin D. Roosevelt elected president for the first time.

1933

Pres. Roosevelt named **Frances Perkins** U.S. secretary of labor; first woman in U.S. cabinet.

All **banks in the U.S. were ordered closed** by Pres. Roosevelt **Mar. 6.**

In a "100 days" special session, **Mar. 9-June 16**, Congress passed **New Deal** social and economic measures, including measures to regulate banks, distribute funds to the jobless, create jobs, raise agricultural prices, and set wage and production standards for industry.

Tennessee Valley Authority created by act of Congress, **May 18.**

Gold standard dropped by U.S.; announced by Pres. Roosevelt **Apr. 19**, ratified by Congress **June 5.**

Prohibition ended in the U.S. as 36th state ratified 21st Amendment **Dec. 5.**

U.S. foreswore armed intervention in **western hemisphere** nations **Dec. 26.**

1934

U.S. troops pulled out of **Haiti Aug. 6.**

1935

Works Progress Administration (**WPA**) instituted **May 6.** Rural Electrification Administration created **May 11.** National Industrial Recovery Act struck down by Supreme Court **May 27.**

Comedian **Will Rogers** and aviator **Wiley Post killed Aug. 15** in Alaska plane crash.

Social Security Act passed by Congress **Aug. 14.**

Huey Long, senator from Louisiana and national political leader, **assassinated Sept. 8.**

Porgy and Bess opened **Oct. 10** in New York.

Committee for Industrial Organization (CIO; later Congress of Industrial Organizations) formed to expand industrial unionism **Nov. 9.**

1936

Boulder Dam completed.

Margaret Mitchell published *Gone With the Wind.*

1937

Joe Louis knocked out James J. Braddock, became world heavyweight champ **June 22.**

Amelia Earhart, aviator, and copilot Fred Noonan lost **July 2** near Howland Island, in the Pacific.

Pres. Roosevelt asked for 6 additional Supreme Court justices; **"packing" plan** defeated.

Auto, steel labor unions won first big contracts.

1938

Naval Expansion Act passed **May 17.**

National minimum wage enacted **June 25.**

Orson Welles radio dramatization of **Martian invasion**, *War of the Worlds,* caused nationwide scare **Oct. 30.**

1939

Pres. Roosevelt asked for **defense budget hike Jan. 5, 12.**

New York World's Fair opened **Apr. 30**, closed **Oct. 31;** reopened **May 11, 1940,** and finally closed **Oct. 21.**

Albert Einstein alerted Pres. Roosevelt to **A-bomb** opportunity in **Aug. 2** letter.

U.S. declared its neutrality in European war **Sept. 5.**

Roosevelt proclaimed a limited **national emergency Sept. 8**, an unlimited emergency **May 27, 1941.** Both ended by Pres. Harry Truman **Apr. 28, 1952.**

John Steinbeck published *Grapes of Wrath.*

Gone With the Wind and *The Wizard of Oz* appeared on screen.

1940

U.S. okayed sale of **surplus war material** to Britain **June 3;** announced transfer of 50 overaged destroyers **Sept. 3.**

First **peacetime draft** approved **Sept. 14.**

Richard Wright published *Native Son.*

1941

Four Freedoms termed essential by Pres. Roosevelt in speech to Congress **Jan. 6:** freedom of speech and religion, freedom from want and fear.

Lend-Lease Act signed **Mar. 11** provided $7 bil in military credits for Britain. Lend-Lease for USSR approved in **Nov.**

U.S. occupied **Iceland July 7.**

The **Atlantic Charter**, 8-point declaration of principles, issued by Roosevelt and British Prime Min. Winston Churchill **Aug. 14.**

Japan attacked **Pearl Harbor**, Hawaii, 7:55 AM Hawaiian time, **Dec. 7;** 19 ships sunk or damaged, 2,300 dead. U.S. declared war on Japan **Dec. 8**, on Germany and Italy **Dec. 11** after those countries declared war.

1942

Japanese troops took Bataan peninsula **Apr. 8,** Corregidor **May 6.**

Federal government forcibly moved 110,000 **Japanese-Americans** from West Coast to detention camps. Exclusion lasted 3 years.

Battle of **Midway June 4-7** was Japan's first major defeat.

Marines landed on **Guadalcanal Aug. 7;** last Japanese not expelled until **Feb. 9, 1943.**

U.S., Britain invaded North Africa **Nov. 8.**

First **nuclear chain reaction** (fission of uranium isotope U-235) produced at University of Chicago, under physicists Arthur Compton, Enrico Fermi, others **Dec. 2.**

1943

Oklahoma! opened **Mar. 31** on Broadway.

All war contractors barred from **racial discrimination, May 27.**

Pres. Roosevelt signed **June 10** pay-as-you-go income tax bill. Starting **July 1** wage and salary earners were subject to a **paycheck withholding** tax.

Race riot in Detroit June 21; 34 dead, 700 injured. Riot in Harlem section of New York City; 6 killed.

U.S., Britain invaded **Sicily July 9,** Italian **mainland Sept. 3.**

Marines advanced on **Gilbert Island in Nov.**

1944

U.S., Allied forces invaded Europe at **Normandy June 6** in greatest amphibious landing in history.

GI Bill of Rights signed **June 22,** providing veterans' benefits.

U.S. forces landed on **Leyte,** Philippines, **Oct. 20.**

1945

Yalta Conference met in the Crimea, USSR, **Feb. 4-11.** Roosevelt, Churchill, and Soviet leader Joseph Stalin agreed that their 3 countries, plus France, would occupy Germany and that the Soviet Union would enter war against Japan.

Marines landed on **Iwo Jima Feb. 19,** won, Iwo Jima **Mar. 16** after heavy casualties. U.S. forces invaded **Okinawa Apr. 1,** captured Okinawa **June 21.**

Pres. Roosevelt, 63, died in Warm Springs, GA, **Apr. 12;** Vice Pres. **Harry S. Truman** became president.

Germany surrendered May 7; May 8 proclaimed V-E Day.

First **atomic bomb,** produced at Los Alamos, NM, exploded at Alamogordo, NM, **July 16.** Bomb dropped on **Hiroshima Aug. 6,** with about 75,000 people killed; bomb dropped on **Nagasaki Aug. 9,** killing about 40,000. Japan agreed to surrender, **Aug. 14;** formally surrendered **Sept. 2.**

At **Potsdam Conference, July 17-Aug. 2,** leaders of U.S., USSR, and Britain agreed on disarmament of Germany, occupation zones, war crimes trials.

U.S. forces entered **Korea** south of 38th parallel to displace Japanese **Sept. 8.**

Gen. Douglas MacArthur took over supervision of Japan **Sept. 9.**

1946

Strike by 400,000 **mine workers** began **Apr. 1;** other industries followed.

Philippines given independence by U.S. **July 4.**

1947

Pres. Truman asked Congress to aid Greece and Turkey to combat Communist terrorism **(Truman Doctrine) Mar. 12.** Approved **May 15.**

UN Security Council voted unanimously **Apr. 2** to place under **U.S. trusteeship** the Pacific islands formerly mandated to Japan.

Jackie Robinson joined the Brooklyn Dodgers **Apr. 11,** breaking the color barrier in major league baseball.

Taft-Hartley Labor Act curbing strikes was vetoed by Truman **June 20;** Congress overrode the veto.

Proposals known as the **Marshall Plan,** under which the U.S. would extend aid to European countries, were made by Sec. of State George C. Marshall **June 5.** Congress authorized some $12 bil in next 4 years.

1948

USSR halted all surface traffic into W. Berlin, **July 23;** in response, U.S. and British troops launched an airlift. Soviet blockade halted **May 12, 1949;** airlift ended **Sept. 30.**

Organization of American States founded **Apr. 30.**

Alger Hiss indicted **Dec. 15** for perjury, after denying he had passed secret documents to Whittaker Chambers for transmission to a Communist spy ring. Convicted **Jan. 21, 1950.**

Pres. Truman reelected Nov. 2, defeating Gov. Thomas E. Dewey in a historic upset.

Kinsey Report on sexuality in the human male published.

1949

U.S. troops withdrawn from **Korea June 29.**

NATO established **Aug. 24** by U.S., Canada, and 10 Western European nations, agreeing that an armed attack against one or more would be considered an attack against all.

Mrs. I. Toguri D'Aquino **(Tokyo Rose** of Japanese wartime broadcasts) was sentenced **Oct. 7** to 10 years in prison for treason. Paroled **1956,** pardoned **1977.**

Eleven leaders of **U.S. Communist Party** convicted **Oct. 14** of advocating violent overthrow of U.S. government; sentenced to prison. Supreme Court upheld convictions **1951.**

1950

Masked bandits robbed **Brink's, Inc.,** Boston express office, **Jan. 17** of $2.8 mil, of which $1.2 mil was in cash. Case solved **1956;** 8 sentenced to life.

Pres. Truman authorized production of **H-bomb Jan. 31.**

North Korea forces invaded **South Korea June 25.** UN asked for troops to restore peace.

Truman ordered Air Force and Navy to Korea **June 27.** Truman approved ground forces, air strikes against North Korea **June 30.**

U.S. sent 35 military advisers to **South Vietnam June 27,** and agreed to provide military and economic aid to anti-Communist government.

Army seized all railroads Aug. 27 on Truman's order to prevent a general strike; returned to owners in **1952.**

U.S. forces landed at Inchon Sept. 15; UN force took Pyongyang **Oct. 20,** reached China border **Nov. 20;** China sent troops across border **Nov. 26.**

Two members of **Puerto Rican nationalist** movement tried to kill Pres. Truman **Nov. 1.**

U.S. **Dec. 8** banned shipments to **Communist China** and to Asiatic ports trading with it.

1951

Sen. Estes Kefauver led Senate investigation into organized crime.

Julius Rosenberg, his wife, Ethel, and Morton Sobell found guilty **Mar. 29** of conspiracy to commit wartime espionage. Rosenbergs executed **June 19, 1953.** Sobell sentenced to 30 years; released **1969.**

Gen. Douglas MacArthur removed from Korea command **Apr. 11** by Pres. Truman for unauthorized policy statements.

Korea cease-fire talks began in July; lasted 2 years. **Fighting ended July 27, 1953.**

Tariff concessions by the U.S. to the Soviet Union, Communist China, and all Communist-dominated lands were suspended **Aug. 1.**

The **U.S., Australia,** and **New Zealand** signed a mutual security pact **Sept. 1.**

Transcontinental television inaugurated **Sept. 4** with Pres. Truman's address at the Japanese Peace Treaty Conference in San Francisco.

Japanese peace treaty signed in San Francisco **Sept. 8** by U.S., Japan, and 47 other nations.

J. D. Salinger published *Catcher in the Rye.*

1952

U.S. **seizure of nation's steel mills** was ordered by Pres. Truman **Apr. 8** to avert a strike. Ruled illegal by Supreme Court **June 2.**

Peace contract between West Germany, U.S., Great Britain, and France was signed **May 26.**

The last racial and ethnic barriers to naturalization removed, **June 26-27,** with passage of **Immigration and Naturalization Act of 1952.**

First **hydrogen device** explosion **Nov. 1** at Eniwetok Atoll in Pacific.

1953

Pres. Dwight D. Eisenhower announced **May 8** that U.S. had given France $60 mil for **Indochina War.** More aid was announced in **Sept.**

Korean War armistice signed **July 27.**

1954

Nautilus, first atomic-powered submarine, was launched at Groton, CT, **Jan. 21.**

Five members of Congress were wounded in the House **Mar. 1** by 4 **Puerto Rican independence supporters** who fired at random from a spectators' gallery.

Sen. Joseph McCarthy (R, WI) led televised hearings **Apr. 22-June 17** into alleged Communist influence in the Army.

Racial segregation in public schools unanimously ruled unconstitutional by Supreme Court May 17, in Brown v. Board of Education of Topeka.

Southeast Asia Treaty Organization (SEATO) formed by defense pact signed in Manila Sept. 8 by U.S., Britain, France, Australia, New Zealand, Philippines, Pakistan, and Thailand.

Condemnation of Sen. McCarthy voted by Senate, 67-22, Dec. 2 for contempt of Senate subcommittee, abuse of its members, insults to Senate during Army investigation hearings.

1955

U.S. agreed Feb. 12 to help train South Vietnamese army.

Supreme Court ordered "all deliberate speed" in integration of public schools May 31.

A summit meeting of leaders of U.S., Britain, France, and USSR took place July 18-23 in Geneva, Switzerland.

Rosa Parks refused Dec. 1 to give her seat to a white man on a bus in Montgomery, AL. Bus segregation ordinance declared unconstitutional by a federal court following boycott and NAACP protest.

America's 2 largest labor organizations merged Dec. 5 under the name American Federation of Labor and Congress of Industrial Organizations.

1956

Massive resistance to Supreme Court desegregation rulings was called for Mar. 12 by 101 Southern congressmen.

Federal-Aid Highway Act signed June 29, inaugurating interstate highway system.

First transatlantic telephone cable activated Sept. 25.

1957

Congress approved first civil rights bill for blacks since Reconstruction Apr. 29, to protect voting rights.

National Guardsmen, called out by Arkansas Gov. Orval Faubus Sept. 4, barred 9 black students from entering all-white high school in Little Rock. Faubus complied Sept. 21 with federal court order to remove Guardsmen, but the blacks were ordered to withdraw by local authorities. Pres. Eisenhower sent federal troops Sept. 24 to enforce court order.

Jack Kerouac published On the Road.

1958

First U.S. earth satellite to go into orbit, Explorer I, launched by Army Jan. 31 at Cape Canaveral, FL; discovered Van Allen radiation belt.

U.S. Marines sent to Lebanon to protect elected government from threatened overthrow July-Oct.

First domestic jet airline passenger service in U.S. opened by National Airlines Dec. 10 between New York and Miami.

1959

Alaska admitted as 49th state Jan. 3; Hawaii admitted as 50th Aug. 21.

St. Lawrence Seaway opened Apr. 25.

Soviet Premier Nikita Khrushchev paid unprecedented visit to U.S. Sept. 15-27, made transcontinental tour.

1960

Sit-ins began Feb. 1 when 4 black college students in Greensboro, NC, refused to move from a Woolworth lunch counter when denied service. By Sept. 1961 more than 70,000 students, whites and blacks, had participated in sit-ins.

Congress approved a strong voting rights act Apr. 21.

A U.S. U-2 reconnaissance plane was shot down in the Soviet Union May 1; pilot Gary Powers captured. The incident led to cancellation of an imminent Paris summit conference.

Vice Pres. Richard Nixon and Sen. John F. Kennedy faced each other, Sept. 26, in the first in a series of televised campaign debates. Kennedy defeated Nixon to win the presidency, Nov. 8.

U.S. announced Dec. 15 it backed rightist group in Laos, which took power the next day.

1961

U.S. severed diplomatic and consular relations with Cuba Jan. 3, after disputes over nationalizations of U.S. firms, U.S. military presence at Guantanamo base.

Invasion of Cuba's "Bay of Pigs" Apr. 17 by Cuban exiles trained, armed, and directed by U.S., attempted to overthrow the regime of Premier Fidel Castro, unsuccessfully.

Peace Corps created by executive order, Mar. 1.

Commander Alan B. Shepard Jr. was rocketed from Cape Canaveral, FL, 116.5 mi above the earth in a Mercury capsule May 5, in first U.S.-crewed suborbital space flight.

"Freedom Rides" from Washington, DC, across deep South were launched in May to protest segregation in interstate transportation.

1962

Lt. Col. John H. Glenn Jr. became first American in orbit Feb. 20 when he circled the earth 3 times in the Mercury capsule Friendship 7.

Pres. John F. Kennedy said Feb. 14 U.S. military advisers in Vietnam would fire if fired upon.

Supreme Court Mar. 26 backed "one-man one-vote" apportionment of seats in state legislatures.

James Meredith became first black student at University of Mississippi Oct. 1 after 3,000 troops put down riots.

A Soviet offensive missile buildup in Cuba was revealed Oct. 22 by Pres. Kennedy, who ordered a naval and air quarantine on shipment of offensive military equipment to the island. He and Soviet Premier Khrushchev agreed Oct. 28 on a formula to end the crisis. Kennedy announced Nov. 2 that Soviet missile bases in Cuba were being dismantled.

Rachel Carson's Silent Spring launched environmentalist movement.

1963

Supreme Court ruled Mar. 18 that all criminal defendants must have counsel and that illegally acquired evidence was inadmissible in state as well as federal courts.

University of Alabama desegregated after Gov. George Wallace stepped aside when confronted by federally deployed National Guard troops, June 11.

Civil rights leader Medgar Evers assassinated June 12.

Supreme Court ruled, 8-1, June 17 that laws requiring recitation of the Lord's Prayer or Bible verses in public schools were unconstitutional.

A limited nuclear test-ban treaty was agreed upon July 25 by the U.S., the Soviet Union, and Britain.

March on Washington by 200,000 persons Aug. 28 in support of black demands for equal rights. Highlight was "I have a dream" speech by Dr. Martin Luther King Jr.

Baptist church in Birmingham, AL, bombed Sept. 15 in racial violence; 4 black girls killed.

South Vietnam Pres. Ngo Dinh Diem assassinated Nov. 2; U.S. had earlier withdrawn support.

Pres. Kennedy shot and fatally wounded Nov. 22 as he rode in a motorcade through downtown Dallas, TX. Vice Pres. Lyndon B. Johnson sworn in as president shortly afterward. Lee Harvey Oswald arrested and charged with the murder; he was shot and fatally wounded Nov. 24. Jack Ruby, a nightclub owner, was convicted of Oswald's murder; he died in 1967, while awaiting retrial following reversal of his conviction.

Betty Friedan's Feminine Mystique ignited the women's movement.

1964

Panama suspended relations with U.S. Jan. 9 after riots. U.S. offered Dec. 18 to negotiate a new canal treaty.

Supreme Court ordered Feb. 17 that congressional districts have equal populations.

U.S. reported May 27 it was sending military planes to Laos.

Omnibus civil rights bill cleared by Congress July 2, signed same day by Pres. Johnson, banning discrimination in voting, jobs, public accommodations.

Three civil rights workers were reported missing in Mississippi June 22; found buried Aug. 4. Twenty-one white men were arrested. On Oct. 20, 1967, an all-white federal jury convicted 7 of conspiracy in the slayings.

Bill establishing Medicare, government health insurance program for persons over 65, signed July 30.

U.S. Congress Aug. 7 passed Tonkin Gulf Resolution, authorizing presidential action in Vietnam, after N Vietnamese boats reportedly attacked 2 U.S. destroyers Aug. 2.

Congress approved War on Poverty bill Aug. 11, providing for a domestic Peace Corps (VISTA), a Job Corps, and antipoverty funding.

The Warren Commission released Sept. 27 a report concluding that Lee Harvey Oswald was solely responsible for the Kennedy assassination.

Pres. **Johnson was elected** to a full term, **Nov. 3,** defeating Republican **Sen. Barry Goldwater** (AZ) in a landslide.

1965

Pres. Johnson in **Feb.** ordered continuous **bombing of North Vietnam** below 20th parallel.

Malcolm X assassinated **Feb. 21** at New York City rally.

Some 14,000 U.S. troops sent to **Dominican Republic** during civil war **Apr. 28.** All troops withdrawn by next year.

March from Selma to Montgomery, AL, begun **Mar. 21** by Rev. Martin Luther King Jr. to demand federal protection of **blacks' voting rights.** New **Voting Rights Act** signed **Aug. 6.**

Los Angeles riot by blacks living in **Watts** area resulted in death of 34 persons and property damage estimated at $200 mil **Aug. 11-16.**

National origins quota system of **immigration** abolished **Oct. 3.**

Electric power failure blacked out most of northeastern U.S., parts of 2 Canadian provinces the night of **Nov. 9-10.**

U.S. forces in **S. Vietnam** reached 184,300 by year-end.

1966

U.S. forces began firing into **Cambodia May 1.**

Bombing of Hanoi area of N Vietnam by U.S. planes began **June 29.** By **Dec. 31,** 385,300 U.S. troops were stationed in S Vietnam, plus 60,000 offshore and 33,000 in Thailand.

Medicare began **July 1.**

Edward Brooke (R, MA) elected **Nov. 8** as first black U.S. senator in 85 years.

1967

Black U.S. Rep. **Adam Clayton Powell** (D, NY) was denied **Mar. 1** his seat because of charges he misused government funds. Reelected in **1968,** he was seated, but fined $25,000 and stripped of his seniority.

Pres. Johnson and Soviet Premier Aleksei Kosygin met **June 23 and 25** at **Glassboro State College** in NJ; agreed not to let any crisis push them into war.

The **25th Amendment,** providing for **presidential succession,** was ratified **Feb. 10.**

USS Liberty, an intelligence ship, was torpedoed by Israel in the Mediterranean, apparently by accident **June 8**; 34 killed.

Riots by blacks in **Newark, NJ, July 12-17** killed 26, injured 1,500; more than 1,000 arrested. In **Detroit, MI, July 23-30,** more than 40 died; 2,000 injured, 5,000 left homeless by rioting, looting, burning in city's black ghetto.

Thurgood Marshall was sworn in **Oct. 2** as first black U.S. Supreme Court Justice. **Carl B. Stokes** (D, Cleveland) and **Richard G. Hatcher** (D, Gary, IN) were elected first black mayors of major U.S. cities **Nov. 7.**

1968

USS Pueblo and 83-man crew seized in Sea of Japan **Jan. 23** by North Koreans; 82 men released **Dec. 22.**

"Tet offensive": Communist troops attacked Saigon, 30 province capitals **Jan. 30,** suffered heavy casualties.

Pres. Johnson **curbed bombing** of North Vietnam **Mar. 31.** Peace talks began in Paris **May 10.** All bombing of North halted **Oct. 31.**

Martin Luther King Jr., 39, assassinated **Apr. 4** in Memphis, TN. **James Earl Ray,** an escaped convict, pleaded guilty to the slaying, was sentenced to 99 years.

Sen. Robert F. Kennedy (D, NY), 42, **shot June 5** in Hotel Ambassador, Los Angeles, after celebrating presidential primary victories. Died **June 6.** Sirhan Bishara Sirhan, convicted of murder **1969**; death sentence commuted to life in prison, **1972.**

Vice Pres. **Hubert Humphrey nominated** for president by Democrats **at national convention in Chicago,** marked by clash between police and **antiwar protesters, Aug. 26-29.**

The Republican nominee, **Richard Nixon, won the presidency,** defeating Hubert Humphrey in a close race **Nov. 5.**

Rep. Shirley Chisholm (D, NY) became the first black woman elected to Congress.

1969

Expanded 4-party **Vietnam peace talks** began **Jan. 18.** U.S. force peaked at 543,400 in April. Withdrawal started **July 8.** Pres. Nixon set Vietnamization policy **Nov. 3.**

U.S. astronaut **Neil Armstrong,** commander of the Apollo 11 mission, became the first person to **set foot on the moon, July 20;** followed by astronaut **Edwin Aldrin;** astronaut **Michael Collins** remained aboard command module.

Woodstock music festival near Bethel, NY, drew 300,000-500,000 people, **Aug. 15-17.**

Anti-Vietnam War **demonstrations reached peak** in U.S.; some 250,000 marched in Washington, DC, **Nov. 15.**

Massacre of hundreds of civilians at **Mylai, South Vietnam,** in 1968 incident reported **Nov. 16.**

1970

United Mine Workers official **Joseph A. Yablonski,** his wife, and their daughter found shot to death **Jan. 5;** UMW chief W. A. (Tony) Boyle later convicted of the killing.

A federal jury **Feb. 18** found the **"Chicago 7"** antiwar activists innocent of conspiring to incite riots during the 1968 **Democratic National Convention.** However, 5 were convicted of crossing state lines with intent to incite riots.

Millions of Americans participated in antipollution demonstrations **Apr. 22** to mark the **first Earth Day.**

U.S. and South Vietnamese forces crossed **Cambodian** borders **Apr. 30** to get at enemy bases. Four students were killed **May 4** at **Kent State** University in Ohio by National Guardsmen during a protest against the war.

Two **women generals,** the first in U.S. history, were named by Pres. Nixon **May 15.**

A **postal reform** measure was signed **Aug. 12,** creating an independent U.S. Postal Service.

1971

Charles Manson and 3 of his cult followers were found guilty **Jan. 25** of first-degree murder in **1969** slaying of actress Sharon Tate and 6 others.

The 26th Amendment, lowering the **voting age to 18** in all elections, was ratified **June 20.**

A court-martial jury **Mar. 29,** convicted **Lt. William L. Calley Jr.** of premeditated murder of 22 South Vietnamese at Mylai on **Mar. 16, 1968.** He was sentenced to life imprisonment **Mar. 31.** Sentence was reduced to 20 years **Aug. 20.**

Publication of classified **Pentagon papers** on U.S. involvement in Vietnam was begun **June 13** by the *New York Times.* In a 6-3 vote, U.S. Supreme Court **June 30** upheld the right of the *Times* and the *Washington Post* to publish the documents.

U.S. bombers struck massively in North Vietnam for 5 days starting **Dec. 26,** in retaliation for alleged violations of agreements reached prior to the 1968 bombing halt.

1972

Pres. Nixon arrived in **Beijing Feb. 21** for an 8-day visit to China, which he called a "journey for peace."

By a vote of 84 to 8, the Senate approved **Mar. 22** banning **discrimination** on the basis of sex, and sent the measure to the states for ratification.

North Vietnamese forces launched the biggest attacks in 4 years across the demilitarized zone **Mar. 30.** The U.S. responded **Apr. 15** by resumption of bombing of Hanoi and Haiphong after a 4-year lull.

Pres. Nixon announced **May 8** the mining of **North Vietnam ports.** Last U.S. combat troops left **Aug. 11.**

Alabama Gov. **George C. Wallace,** campaigning for the presidency at a Laurel, MD, shopping center **May 15, was shot** and seriously wounded. Arthur H. Bremer, was **convicted Aug. 4,** sentenced to 63 years for shooting Wallace and 3 bystanders.

In **first visit of a U.S. president to Moscow,** Pres. Nixon arrived **May 22** for a week of summit talks with Kremlin leaders that culminated in a landmark **strategic arms pact.**

Five men were arrested **June 17** for breaking into the offices of the Democratic National Committee in the **Watergate** office complex in Washington, DC.

Pres. Nixon reelected **Nov. 7** in a landslide, defeating Democratic Sen. George McGovern (SD).

The Dow Jones industrial average closed above 1,000 for the first time, **Nov. 14.**

Full-scale **bombing of North Vietnam** resumed after Paris peace negotiations reached an impasse **Dec. 18.**

1973

Five of 7 defendants in **Watergate** break-in trial pleaded guilty **Jan. 11 and 15;** the other 2 were convicted **Jan. 30.**

In *Roe* v. *Wade,* Supreme Court ruled, 7-2, **Jan. 22,** that states may not prohibit **abortions** during **first 3 months of pregnancy** and may regulate but not prohibit abortions during 2d trimester.

Four-party **Vietnam peace pacts** were signed in Paris **Jan. 27,** and North Vietnam released some 590 U.S. prisoners by **Apr. 1.** Last U.S. troops left **Mar. 29.**

End of the military draft announced **Jan. 27.**

Top **Nixon aides** H. R. Haldeman, John D. Ehrlichman, and John Dean and Attorney Gen. Richard Kleindienst **resigned Apr. 30** amid charges of White House efforts to obstruct justice in the Watergate case.

John Dean, former Nixon counsel, told Senate hearings **June 25** that Nixon, his staff and campaign aides, and the Justice Department had conspired to cover up Watergate facts.

The U.S. officially ceased bombing in **Cambodia** at midnight **Aug. 14** in accord with a June congressional action.

Vice Pres. Spiro T. Agnew Oct. 10 resigned and pleaded no contest to a charge of tax evasion on payments made to him by contractors when he was governor of Maryland. **Gerald R. Ford Oct. 12** became **first appointed vice president** under the 25th Amendment; sworn in **Dec. 6.**

A total ban on **oil exports** to the U.S. was imposed by Arab oil-producing nations **Oct. 19-21** after the outbreak of an Arab-Israeli war. The ban was lifted **Mar. 18, 1974.**

Attorney Gen. Elliot Richardson resigned, and his deputy William D. Ruckelshaus and **Watergate Special Prosecutor Archibald Cox** were **fired** by Pres. Nixon **Oct. 20,** when Cox threatened to secure a judicial ruling that Nixon was violating a court order to turn tapes over to Judge John Sirica.

Leon Jaworski named **Nov. 1** by the Nixon administration to be special prosecutor, succeeding Archibald Cox.

Congress overrode **Nov. 7** Pres. Nixon's veto of the **war powers** bill, which curbed president's power to commit armed forces to hostilities abroad without congressional approval.

1974

Impeachment hearings opened **May 9** against Pres. Nixon by the House Judiciary Committee.

John D. Ehrlichman and 3 **White House "plumbers"** found guilty **July 12** of conspiring to violate the civil rights of Pentagon Papers leaker Daniel Ellsberg's psychiatrist by breaking into his office.

U.S. Supreme Court ruled, 8-0, **July 24** that Nixon had to turn over **64 tapes** of White House conversations.

House Judiciary Committee, in televised hearings **July 24-30,** recommended 3 **articles of impeachment** against Pres. Nixon. The first, voted 27-11 **July 27,** charged conspiracy to obstruct justice in the Watergate cover-up. The 2d, voted 28-10 **July 29,** charged abuses of power. The 3d, voted 21-17 **July 30,** charged defiance of committee subpoenas. The House voted **Aug. 20,** 412-3, to accept the committee report, which included the impeachment articles.

Pres. Nixon announced his resignation, Aug. 8, and resigned Aug. 9; his support in Congress had begun to collapse **Aug. 5,** after release of tapes implicating him in Watergate cover-up. **Vice Pres. Gerald R. Ford was sworn in Aug. 9** as 38th U.S. president.

An **unconditional pardon** to ex-Pres. Nixon for any federal crimes he committed while president was issued by Pres. Ford **Sept. 8.**

1975

Found guilty of Watergate cover-up charges Jan. 1 were ex-Atty. Gen. John Mitchell, ex-presidential advisers H. R. Haldeman and John Ehrlichman.

U.S. launched **evacuation of American and some South Vietnamese from Saigon Apr. 29** as Communist forces completed takeover of South Vietnam; **South Vietnamese** government officially **surrendered Apr. 30.**

U.S. merchant ship *Mayaguez* and its crew of 39 were seized by Cambodian forces in Gulf of Siam **May 12.** In rescue operation, U.S. Marines attacked Tang Island, planes bombed air base; Cambodia surrendered ship and crew.

Congress voted $405 mil for **South Vietnam refugees May 16;** 140,000 were flown to the U.S.

Illegal CIA operations, including records on 300,000 persons and groups, and infiltration of agents into black, antiwar, and political movements, were described by a "blue-ribbon" panel headed by Vice Pres. **Nelson Rockefeller June 10.**

FBI agents captured publishing heiress **Patricia (Patty) Hearst,** kidnapped **Feb. 4, 1974,** by "Symbionese Liberation Army" militants in San Francisco **Sept. 18** with others. She was convicted **Mar. 20, 1976,** of bank robbery.

1976

U.S. celebrated **200th anniversary of independence July 4,** with festivals, parades, and New York City's Operation Sail, a gathering of tall ships from around the world.

"Legionnaire's disease" killed 29 persons who attended an American Legion convention **July 21-24** in Philadelphia.

Viking II set down on **Mars'** Utopia Plains **Sept. 3,** following the successful landing by *Viking I* **July 20.**

1977

Pres. Jimmy Carter **Jan. 21** pardoned most Vietnam War **draft evaders,** who numbered some 10,000.

Convicted murderer **Gary Gilmore executed** by a Utah firing squad **Jan. 17,** in the first exercise of capital punishment in the U.S. since **1967.**

Pres. Carter signed an act **Aug. 4** creating a new cabinet-level **Energy Department.**

1978

U.S. Senate voted **Apr. 18** to turn over **Panama Canal** to Panama Dec. 31, 1999; **Mar. 16** vote had given approval to a treaty guaranteeing the area's neutrality after the year 2000.

Californians, **June 6,** approved **Proposition 13,** a state constitutional amendment slashing property taxes.

U.S. Supreme Court, **June 28,** ruled against **racial quotas** in *Bakke* v. *University of California.*

1979

Partial meltdown released radioactive material **Mar. 28,** at nuclear reactor on **Three Mile Island** near Middletown, PA.

Federal government announced, **Nov. 1,** a $1.5 bil loan-guarantee plan to aid the ailing **Chrysler Corp.**

Some 90 people, including 63 Americans, **taken hostage, Nov. 4,** at **American embassy in Tehran,** Iran, by militant followers of Ayatollah Khomeini. He demanded return of former Shah Muhammad Reza Pahlavi, who was undergoing medical treatment in New York City.

1980

Pres. Carter announced, **Jan. 4, sanctions against the USSR,** including an embargo on sales of grain and high technology, in retaliation for Soviet invasion of Afghanistan. At Carter's request, **U.S. Olympic Committee** voted, **Apr. 12,** against U.S. participation in Moscow Summer Olympics.

Eight Americans killed and 5 wounded, **Apr. 24, in ill-fated** attempt to **rescue hostages** held by Iranian militants.

Mt. St. Helens, in Washington state, erupted, May 18. The blast, with others **May 25** and **June 12,** left 57 dead.

In a sweeping victory, **Nov. 4, Ronald Reagan** was elected 40th president. Republicans gained control of the Senate, defeating incumbent Pres. Carter.

Former Beatle **John Lennon** was shot and killed, **Dec. 8,** in New York City.

1981

Minutes after **Reagan's inauguration Jan. 20,** the **52 Americans** held **hostage in Iran** for 444 days were freed.

Pres. Reagan was **shot and seriously wounded, Mar. 30,** in Washington, DC; also seriously wounded were a Secret Service agent, a policeman, and Press Sec. **James Brady. John W. Hinckley Jr.** arrested, found not guilty by reason of insanity in **1982** committed to mental institution.

World's first reusable spacecraft, the **space shuttle** *Columbia,* was sent into space, **Apr. 12.**

Congress passed, **July 29,** Pres. Reagan's **tax-cut legislation,** expected to save taxpayers $750 bil over the next 5 years.

Federal air traffic controllers, Aug. 3, began an illegal **nationwide strike.** Most defied a back-to-work order and were dismissed by Reagan **Aug. 5.**

In a 99-0 vote, the Senate confirmed, **Sept. 21,** appointment of **Sandra Day O'Connor** as an **associate justice of U.S. Supreme Court.** She was the first woman appointed to that body.

1982

The 13-year-old lawsuit against **AT&T** by the **Justice Dept.** was settled **Jan. 8.** AT&T agreed to give up the 22 Bell System companies and was allowed to expand business.

The **Equal Rights Amendment was defeated** after a 10-year struggle for ratification.

In Dec., **unemployment hit** 10.8%, highest rate since 1940.

A retired dentist, **Dr. Barney B. Clark,** 61, became first recipient of a **permanent artificial heart, Dec. 2.**

1983

On **Apr. 20, Pres. Reagan** signed a compromise bipartisan bill designed to rescue **Social Security** from bankruptcy.

Sally Ride became the first American **woman** to travel in **space, June 18,** when the **space shuttle** *Challenger* was launched from Cape Canaveral, FL.

On **Sept. 1, a South Korean passenger jet** infringing on Soviet air space was **shot down;** 269 people killed.

On **Oct. 23,** 241 **U.S. Marines and sailors,** members of the multinational **peacekeeping force** in **Lebanon,** were killed when a TNT-laden suicide bomb blew up Marine headquarters at **Beirut** International Airport.

U.S. troops, with a small force from 6 **Caribbean** nations invaded **Grenada Oct. 25,** in response to a request from the Organization of Eastern Caribbean States. After a few days, Grenadian militia and Cuban "construction workers" were overcome, U.S. citizens evacuated safely, and the **Marxist regime deposed.** U.S. Congress applied the War Powers Resolution, requiring U.S. troops to leave Grenada by **Dec. 24.**

1984

The space shuttle *Challenger* was launched on its 4th trip into space, **Feb. 3.** On **Feb. 7,** Navy Capt. Bruce McCandless, followed by Army Lt. Colonel Robert Stewart, **became first humans to fly free of a spacecraft.**

On **May 7,** American **Vietnam war** veterans reached an **out-of-court settlement with 7 chemical companies** in their class-action suit regarding the herbicide **Agent Orange.**

Former Vice Pres. **Walter Mondale** won the **Democratic presidential nomination, June 6;** chose a woman, Rep. **Geraldine Ferraro** (D, NY), as candidate for **vice president.**

Ronald Reagan was reelected U.S. president **Nov. 6** in the greatest Republican **landslide** in history, carrying 49 states.

1985

"Live Aid," a 17-hour rock concert broadcast around the world **July 13,** raised $70 mil for starving peoples of Africa.

On **June 14** a **TWA jet was seized** by terrorists after takeoff from Athens; 153 passengers and crew held hostage for 17 days; 1 U.S. serviceman killed.

On **Oct. 7, 4 Palestinian hijackers seized** Italian cruise ship, **Achille Lauro** at sea as it approached Port Said, Egypt. More than 400 passengers and crew were held hostage for 2 days; one American, Leon Klinghoffer, was killed.

1986

On **Jan. 20,** for the first time, the U.S. officially observed **Martin Luther King Jr. Day.**

Moments after liftoff, **Jan. 28,** the **space shuttle Challenger exploded, killing 6 astronauts and Christa McAuliffe,** a New Hampshire teacher, on board. Later investigations found NASA had taken inadequate safety precautions.

U.S., via Congress's **Sept.** override of Pres. Reagan's veto, joined other nations in imposing **economic sanctions on South Africa,** pressuring the government to end apartheid.

U.S. Senate confirmed, **Sept. 17,** Pres. Reagan's nomination of **William Rehnquist** as chief justice and **Antonin Scalia** as associate justice of the Supreme Court.

Congress passed, in late **Sept.,** a major **tax reform law.**

In **congressional races, Nov. 4, Democrats won a 55-45 Senate majority,** after 6 years of Republican majority, and **enlarged their House majority** by 5, to 258-177.

Press reports in early **Nov.** broke first news of the **Iran-contra scandal,** involving secret U.S. sale of arms to Iran.

The most scandalous year in Wall Street history climaxed when **Ivan Boesky agreed, Nov. 14,** to **plead guilty** to an unspecified criminal count, pay a $100 mil fine, and return profits; he was barred for life from trading securities.

1987

Pres. Reagan produced the nation's first **trillion-dollar budget, Jan. 5.**

The stock market continued a phenomenal rise, with the **Dow closing** at 2002.25, **Jan. 8,** its **first finish above 2000.**

An **Iraqi warplane missile killed 37 sailors** on the frigate USS *Stark* in the Persian Gulf, **May 17.** Iraq called it an accident. The *Stark's* officers were found negligent.

Public hearings by Senate and House committees investigating the **Iran-contra affair** were held **May-Aug.** Lt. Col. **Oliver North** said he had believed all his activities were authorized by his superiors. Pres. Reagan, **Aug. 12,** denied knowing of the funds' diversion to the contras.

Wall Street crashed, Oct. 19, with the Dow plummeting a record 508 points.

Pres. Reagan and Soviet leader **Mikhail Gorbachev, Dec. 8,** signed a **pact to dismantle** all 1,752 **U.S. and** 859 **Soviet missiles** with a 300- to 3,400-mi. range.

1988

Nearly **1.4 mil illegal aliens** met **May 4** deadline for applying for **amnesty** under a new federal policy.

Much of the U.S. suffered the worst **drought** in more than 50 years. By **June 23,** half the nation's agricultural counties had been designated disaster areas.

A missile, fired from the **U.S. Navy warship** *Vincennes,* in the Persian Gulf, mistakenly struck and **destroyed a commercial Iranian airliner, July 3,** killing all 290 passengers.

George Bush, vice president under Reagan, **elected** 41st U.S. **president, Nov. 8.** Bush decisively defeated the Democratic nominee, Gov. **Michael Dukakis** (MA).

Drexel Burnham Lambert agreed, **Dec. 21, to plead guilty to 6 violations of federal law,** including insider trading, stock manipulation, and falsified records, and **pay penalties of $650 mil,** the largest such settlement ever.

1989

One of the **largest oil spills in U.S. history** occurred after the *Exxon Valdez* struck Bligh Reef in Alaska's Prince William Sound, **Mar. 24.**

Former National Security Council staff member **Oliver North** became the first person, **May 4, convicted in a jury trial** in connection with the **Iran-contra** scandal. Conviction thrown out on appeal in **1991.**

Legislation to **rescue the savings and loan industry** was signed into law, **Aug. 9,** by Pres. Bush.

Army Gen. **Colin Powell** was nominated **Aug. 10** by Pres. Bush, as **chairman of the Joint Chiefs of Staff;** he became the first black to hold the post.

Just before a World Series game, **Oct. 17,** an **earthquake struck the San Francisco Bay area,** causing 62 deaths.

L. Douglas Wilder (D) was elected governor of Virginia, the **first U.S. black governor** since Reconstruction.

U.S. troops invaded Panama, Dec. 20, overthrowing the government of **Manuel Noriega.** Noriega, wanted by U.S. authorities on drug charges, took refuge in the Vatican mission; he surrendered to the U.S. **Jan. 3, 1990.**

1990

Pres. Bush signed **Americans With Disabilities Act** on **July 26,** barring discrimination against handicapped.

Justice **William Brennan** announced, **July 20,** his resignation from the U.S. Supreme Court; in his place, Bush nominated **Judge David Souter,** who was confirmed **Sept. 27.**

Operation Desert Shield forces left for **Saudi Arabia, Aug. 7,** to defend that country following the **invasion** of its neighbor **Kuwait by Iraq,** Aug. 2.

Pres. Bush signed, **Nov. 5,** a bill to **reduce budget deficits** $500 bil over 5 years, by spending curbs and tax hikes.

1991

The **U.S. and its allies defeated Iraq** in the **Persian Gulf War** and liberated Kuwait, which Iraq had overrun in Aug. 1990. On **Jan. 17,** the allies launched a devastating **attack on Iraq from the air.** In a **ground war** starting **Feb. 24,** that lasted just 100 hours, the U.S.-led attackers killed or captured many thousands of Iraqi soldiers and sent the rest into retreat before Pres. Bush ordered a cease-fire **Feb. 27.**

The **Dow Jones industrial average** finished above 3,000 for the first time, **Apr. 17,** closing at 3004.46.

U.S. **House bank** ordered closed **Oct. 3** after revelations House members had written 8,331 bad checks.

The **Senate approved, Oct. 15, nomination of Clarence Thomas** to the Supreme Court, despite allegations of sexual harassment against him by **Anita Hill,** a former aide. He became the 2d African-American to serve on the Court, replacing retiring Justice **Thurgood Marshall,** the 1st black to do so.

Charles Keating convicted of securities fraud **Dec. 4.**

1992

Riots swept South-Central Los Angeles Apr. 29, after jury **acquitted 4 white policemen** on all but one count in the videotaped 1991 beating of black motorist **Rodney King.** The death toll in the L.A. violence was put at 52.

Democrats nominated **Gov. Bill Clinton** for president, and **Sen. Al Gore Jr.** for vice president, **July 15-16. Ross Perot,** an independent, announced, **July 16,** he would not run for president, but returned to the race **Oct. 1.** Republicans renominated **Pres. Bush** and **Vice Pres. Dan Quayle** in early **Aug.**

Bill Clinton was **elected** 42d president, **Nov. 3.**

A UN-sanctioned military force, led by U.S. troops, arrived in **Somalia Dec. 9.**

1993

A powerful bomb exploded in a parking garage beneath the **World Trade Center** in New York City, **Feb. 26,** killing 6 people. More than 1,000 people suffered injuries.

Janet Reno became the first woman U.S. attorney general **Mar. 12.**

Four federal agents were killed, Feb. 28, during an unsuccessful raid on the **Branch Davidian compound near Waco, TX.** A 51-day siege of the compound by federal agents ended **Apr. 19,** when armored vehicles pumped tear gas into it; those inside responded with gunfire. The compound then **burned down,** leaving more than 70 cult members dead.

A federal jury, **Apr. 17, found 2 Los Angeles police officers guilty** and 2 not guilty of violating the civil rights of motorist **Rodney King** in 1991 beating incident.

Pres. Clinton **July 2** approved recommendation to close 33 major military installations

"The Great Flood of 1993" inundated 8 mil acres in 9 Midwestern states in summer, leaving 50 dead.

Pres. Clinton, **July 19,** announced a "don't ask, don't tell, don't pursue" policy for **homosexuals** in the U.S. military.

Vincent Foster, deputy White House counsel, was found shot to death in a N Virginia park, an apparent suicide.

Judge Ruth Bader Ginsburg was sworn in, **Aug. 10,** as **107th justice of the U.S. Supreme Court,** replacing Associate Justice Byron White, who retired.

Pres. Clinton, **Aug. 10,** signed a compromise bill designed to **cut federal budget deficits** $496 bil over 5 years, through spending cuts and new taxes.

The **"Brady Bill,"** a major gun-control measure, was signed into law by Pres. Clinton **Nov. 30.**

1994

North American Free Trade Agreement took effect **Jan. 1.**

A predawn **earthquake struck the Los Angeles area,** Jan. 17, claiming 61 lives and causing heavy damage.

Attorney Gen. Janet Reno **Jan. 20** appointed Robert Fiske independent counsel to investigate the **Whitewater affair;** under a court ruling he was **replaced Aug. 5 by Kenneth Starr,** who was named by 3-judge panel. Senate and House committees, late July, began hearings into Whitewater.

Byron De La Beckwith convicted Feb. 5 of the 1963 murder of **civil rights leader Medgar Evers.**

Longtime CIA officer **Aldrich Ames,** and his wife were **charged Feb. 21 with spying.** Under a plea bargain, he received life in prison, while she was sentenced to 63 months.

Eleven **Branch Davidian cult** members were acquitted **Feb. 26,** of charges in the deaths of 4 federal agents in a 1993 shootout at the cult's compound near Waco, TX.

Four men were found guilty, **Mar. 4,** in the 1993 bombing at the **World Trade Center** in New York City.

A former Arkansas state employee, **Paula Jones, filed a suit, May 6,** that accused Pres. Clinton of sexual harassment while governor of Arkansas.

Former football star **O. J. Simpson was charged, June 17,** with **murders of** former wife **Nicole Brown Simpson and** her friend **Ronald Goldman.** The trial began **Sept. 26.**

Major league **baseball players went on strike,** following **Aug. 11** games; strike ended **Apr. 25, 1995.**

Senate Majority Leader George Mitchell (D, ME), **Sept. 26,** dropped efforts to pass Clinton's **health-care reform** package.

On **Nov. 3, Susan Smith,** a South Carolina mother, was **charged with murdering her 2 young sons,** by allowing her car to roll into a lake with them inside; she was convicted, sentenced to life, **July 1995.**

Republicans won control of Congress in **Nov. 8** elections.

Pres. Clinton, **Dec. 8,** approved tariff-cutting provisions of the Uruguay Round of the General Agreement on Tariffs and Trade (GATT; renamed **World Trade Organization [WTO]).**

1995

When the 104th Congress opened, **Jan. 4, Sen. Bob Dole** (R, KS) became **Senate majority leader** and **Rep. Newt Gingrich** (R, GA) was elected **House Speaker.** A bill to end Congress's exemption from federal labor laws, first in a series of measures in Republicans' **"Contract With America,"** cleared Congress **Jan. 17;** signed into law **Jan. 23.**

Clinton invoked emergency powers, **Jan. 31,** to extend a **$20 bil loan to help Mexico** avert financial collapse.

A bill making it more difficult for Congress to approve **"unfunded mandates"**—measures requiring but not funding actions by states—was signed by Pres. Clinton **Mar. 22.** A proposed constitutional **amendment mandating a balanced budget** passed the House **Jan. 26** but failed in the Senate **Mar. 2.** A proposed constitutional **amendment limiting terms** in Congress failed in the House, **Mar. 29.**

The Dow Jones industrial average passed 4,000 **Feb 23.**

The last UN peacekeeping troops withdrew from **Somalia Feb. 28-Mar. 3,** with the aid of U.S. Marines. In **Haiti,** peacekeeping responsibilities were transferred from U.S. to UN forces **Mar. 31,** with the U.S. providing 2,400 soldiers.

A truck bomb exploded outside a federal office building in Oklahoma City Apr. 19, killing 168 people in all. Timothy McVeigh was charged in the crime **Apr. 21.**

Webster Hubbell, a close friend of the Clintons and former associate U.S. attorney general, was **sentenced June 28** to 21 months in prison for tax evasion and mail fraud.

The U.S. space shuttle *Atlantis* made the first in a series of planned **dockings with the Russian space station** *Mir,* **June 29-July 4.**

A U.S. **F-16 fighter jet** piloted by Air Force Capt. **Scott O'Grady was shot down over Bosnia and Herzegovina June 2;** O'Grady was **rescued** by U.S. Marines 6 days later.

At least **800 people died** in the Middle West and Northeast from a **heat wave** July 12-17.

In his **first veto,** Clinton, **June 7,** struck down a bill cutting $16.4 bil from spending appropriated by Congress. On **July 27,** however, he signed a revised bill cutting $16.3 bil.

The U.S. announced on **July 11** that it was reestablishing **diplomatic relations with Vietnam.**

Whitewater hearings opened in the Senate **July 18** and the House **Aug. 7.**

Shannon Faulkner won her legal fight to gain **admission** to the previously all-male cadet corps of **The Citadel, Aug. 11,** but dropped out after a few days of training.

Sen. Bob Packwood (R, OR) announced **Sept. 7** that he would **resign,** after a Senate committee recommend his expulsion for sexual misconduct and other charges.

Ten Muslim militants were **convicted in New York, Oct. 1,** on conspiracy charges stemming from a failed terrorist **plot.**

After a televised trial, **O. J. Simpson** was found **not guilty** Oct. 3 of the murders of his former wife, Nicole Brown Simpson, and her friend Ronald Goldman.

Hundreds of thousands of African-American men participated in **"Million Man March"** and rally in Washington, DC, **Oct. 16,** organized by Rev. Louis Farrakhan.

Gen. Colin Powell (ret.) announced, **Nov. 8,** that he **would not seek the GOP nomination** for president in 1996.

Billy Dale, discharged head of the White House travel office, was **acquitted of embezzlement** Nov. 16.

The federal **55-mile-per-hour speed limit** was **repealed** by a measure signed **Nov. 28.**

After talks outside Dayton, OH, **warring parties in Bosnia and Herzegovina reached agreement Nov. 21** to end their conflict; treaty was signed **Dec. 14,** after which first of some 20,000 **U.S. peacekeeping troops arrived in Bosnia.**

Five Americans were among 7 **killed, Nov. 13,** when 2 **bombs exploded** at a military post **in Riyadh, Saudi Arabia.** Four Saudis confessed and were executed.

A budget impasse between Congress and Pres. Clinton led to a **partial government shutdown,** Nov. 14. Operations resumed Nov. 20 under continuing resolutions. On **Dec. 6, Clinton vetoed a budget reconciliation bill** including tax cuts and cuts in projected Medicare spending; the continuing resolution expired **Dec. 16** and a longer shutdown began.

House Ethics Committee voted unanimously **Dec. 6** to have an **independent counsel** investigate charges that Speaker **Newt Gingrich** had violated tax laws.

The **Dow Jones** industrial average, which passed 5,000 **Nov. 21,** closed **Dec. 29** at 5117.12, up 33.5% for the year.

1996

Long-sought records released by White House **Jan. 5** showed **Hillary Rodham Clinton** did 60 hours of work for an S&L linked to **Whitewater** scandal. Responding to a subpoena, she testified **Jan. 26** before a grand jury.

A **blizzard** swept the Northeast **Jan. 7-8.**

Senate, **Jan. 26,** approved, 87–4, the Second Strategic Arms Reduction Treaty, signed by Pres. Boris Yeltsin of Russia and Pres. Bush in **Jan. 1993.**

On **Feb. 24 Cuban jets shot down 2 unarmed planes** owned by a Cuban exile organization; all 4 persons on the planes were presumed killed. Pres. Clinton, **Mar. 12,** signed a bill strengthening U.S. economic embargo against Cuba.

On **Mar. 8** the **Dow Jones** industrial average fell by 171.24 points, the biggest one-day drop since 1991.

John Salvi was found guilty, **Mar. 18,** in the **1994 murder** of receptionists **at 2 abortion clinics** in Brookline, MA.

Congress, in late **Mar.,** approved a **"line item veto"** bill, allowing the president to veto parts of a spending bill while approving the rest, and a bill sharply curtailing the **farm subsidy** program. Pres. Clinton signed both.

U.S. Commerce Sec. **Ron Brown** was killed **Apr. 3** in a plane crash in Croatia.

On **Apr. 3, Theodore Kaczynski** was arrested in Montana; later charged with being the notorious **Unabomber** who had killed 3 people in a series of bombings.

On **Apr. 10,** Pres. Clinton vetoed a bill that would have banned so-called **partial-birth abortions.**

Pres. Clinton testified on videotape Apr. 28 in the trial of Arkansas Gov. Jim Guy Tucker and James and Susan McDougal; denied pressing for a fraudulent loan to Susan McDougal.

Jessica Dubroff, 7, was killed **Apr. 11,** with her father and her flight instructor, in a **plane crash** near Cheyenne, WY, while trying to become youngest to pilot a plane across U.S.

An auction, **Apr. 23–26** of items owned by former First Lady **Jacqueline Kennedy Onassis** brought in $34 mil.

A **Valu-Jet airliner crashed** in the Florida Everglades **May 11,** killing all 110 aboard. A fire in the cargo hold was blamed.

James and Susan McDougal were convicted **May 28** of fraud and conspiracy. Arkansas Gov. **Jim Guy Tucker** was convicted of similar charges by the same jury.

Attorney Gen. Janet Reno, **June 20,** asked that Whitewater independent counsel **Kenneth Starr** be authorized to investigate the acquisition of FBI files by the Clinton White House; a panel of 3 federal judges granted the request, **June 21.** Congress, on **June 19,** opened hearings on **"Filegate."**

The antitax group known as the **Freemen** surrendered to federal authorities **June 13** after an 81-day standoff at their remote ranch near Jordan, MT.

Sen. **Robert Dole,** prospective GOP presidential nominee, resigned from Senate, **June 11.** Republicans **June 12** chose Sen. **Trent Lott** (MS) as new majority leader.

The Republican majority and Democratic minority on the **Senate Whitewater Committee** issued separate final reports, **June 18,** based on their investigations.

A **bomb** exploded at a military complex near Dhahran, **Saudi Arabia, June 25,** killing 19 American servicemen.

TWA Flight 800, bound from New York to Paris, **crashed** into the Atlantic shortly after takeoff **July 17,** killing 230.

On **July 27 a pipe bomb exploded** in a downtown Atlanta park filled with people attending the **Olympics;** one person was directly killed.

The Senate, **July 30,** 78–21, and House, **July 31,** 328–101, approved a wide-ranging **welfare reform bill** which provided for welfare through block grants to states and ended federal guarantee of subsidies to poor people with children. Pres. Clinton signed it **Aug. 22,** though opposing some provisions.

Scientific evidence pointing to the possible existence of **life beyond Earth** was announced **Aug. 6** by NASA.

Dole proposed, **Aug. 5,** an across-the-board **tax cut** totaling 15%, and announced, **Aug. 10,** choice of former U.S. Rep. **Jack Kemp** for running mate. Delegates to GOP National Convention in San Diego nominated Dole **Aug. 14.**

Texas billionaire **Ross Perot** was declared, **Aug. 17,** to have won the presidential nomination of his new Reform Party.

The Citadel, a military academy in Charleston, SC, on **Aug. 24 admitted 4 women** to its formerly all-male student body. On **June 26,** the U.S. Supreme Court had ordered **Virginia Military Institute,** another all-male school supported by the state, **to admit women.**

Pres. Clinton nominated for 2d term at Democratic National Convention in Chicago, **Aug. 29.** The same day, Clinton adviser **Dick Morris resigned,** as it emerged that he had been seeing a prostitute.

Susan McDougal was sent to jail **Sept. 9** for contempt, after refusing to testify about Whitewater.

Shannon Lucid, Sept. 26, completed a space voyage of 188 days, a record for women and for U.S. astronauts.

Pres. Clinton and Republican nominee **Bob Dole** held campaign debates **Oct. 6** in Hartford, CT, and **Oct. 16** in San Diego, CA; the vice-presidential candidates debated **Oct. 9** in St. Petersburg, FL.

Democratic National Committee **Oct. 18** suspended the fund-raising activities of **John Huang,** who had solicited an illegal contribution of $250,000 from a South Korean conglomerate. Huang also organized a **fund-raising event at a Buddhist temple,** which brought in $140,000, some of it ostensibly from monks who had taken vows of poverty.

On **Oct. 14,** the **Dow Jones** industrial average closed above **6,000** for the first time—at 6,010.

Archer Daniels Midland Co. announced, **Oct. 14,** it had agreed to pay a fine of $100 mil for price fixing.

Mark Fuhrman, a retired Los Angeles detective, pleaded no contest, **Oct. 2,** to a **perjury charge** in connection with his testimony at O. J. Simpson's criminal trial.

Pres. Clinton reelected to 2d term, **Nov. 5,** carrying 31 states and District of Columbia.

Pres. Clinton announced **Nov. 8-9** his choice of **Erskine Bowles** as White House chief of staff, **Madeleine Albright** as secretary of state, and Sen. **William Cohen** (ME), a Republican, as secretary of defense. Albright became highest-ranking female U.S. government official ever.

Pres. Clinton announced, **Nov. 15,** that 8,500 U.S. troops would **remain in Bosnia** after the end of 1996.

Trustees for a trust fund set up in **1994** to help the Clintons pay legal costs announced, **Dec. 16,** that $639,000 in questionable donations had been returned.

A House Subcommittee said, **Dec. 21,** that House Speaker **Gingrich** had violated House ethics rules in use of tax-exempt funds to support a course he taught.

On **Dec. 20, O. J. Simpson** won custody of his 2 children by his murdered 2d wife, Nicole Brown Simpson.

On **Dec. 31,** the **Dow Jones** industrial average closed at 6448.27, a 26% advance for 1996.

The Mayflower Compact

The threat of James I to "harry them out of the land" sent a little band of religious dissenters from England to Holland in 1608. They were known as Separatists because they wished to cut all ties with the established church. In 1620, some of them, known now as the Pilgrims, joined with a larger group in England to set sail on the *Mayflower* for the New World. A joint stock company financed their venture.

In November, they sighted Cape Cod and decided to land an exploring party at Plymouth Harbor. A rebellious group picked up at Southampton and London troubled the Pilgrim leaders, however, and to control their actions 41 Pilgrims drew up the Mayflower Compact and signed it before going ashore. The voluntary agreement to govern themselves was America's first written constitution. It reads as follows:

In the name of God, Amen. We, whose names are underwritten, the Loyal Subjects of our dread Sovereign Lord, King *James,* by the Grace of God, of *Great Britain, France and Ireland,* King, *Defender of the Faith,* etc.

Having undertaken for the Glory of God, and Advancement of the Christian Faith, and the Honour of our King and Country, a voyage to plant the first colony in the northern Parts of Virginia; do by these Presents, solemnly and mutually in the Presence of God and one of another, covenant and combine ourselves together into a civil Body Politick, for our better Ordering and Preservation, and Furtherance of the Ends aforesaid; And by Virtue hereof to enact, constitute, and frame, such just and equal Laws, Ordinances, Acts, Constitutions and Offices, from time to time, as shall be thought most meet and convenient for the General good of the Colony; unto which we promise all due Submission and Obedience.

In Witness whereof we have hereunto subscribed our names at *Cape Cod* the eleventh of *November,* in the Reign of our Sovereign Lord, King *James* of *England, France* and *Ireland,* the eighteenth, and of *Scotland* the fifty-fourth. *Anno Domini, 1620.*

The Continental Congress: Meetings, Presidents

Meeting places	Dates of meetings	Congress presidents	Date elected
Philadelphia, PA	Sept. 5 to Oct. 26, 1774	Peyton Randolph, VA (1)	Sept. 5, 1774
"	"	Henry Middleton, SC	Oct. 22, 1774
Philadelphia, PA	May 10, 1775 to Dec. 12, 1776	Peyton Randolph, VA.	May 10, 1775
"	"	John Hancock, MA	May 24, 1775
Baltimore, MD	Dec. 20, 1776 to Mar. 4, 1777		
Philadelphia, PA	Mar. 5 to Sept. 18, 1777	"	
Lancaster, PA	Sept. 27, 1777 (one day)		
York, PA	Sept. 30, 1777 to June 27, 1778	Henry Laurens, SC	Nov. 1, 1777(4)
Philadelphia, PA	July 2, 1778 to June 21, 1783	John Jay, NY	Dec. 10, 1778
"	"	Samuel Huntington, CT	Sept. 28, 1779
"	"	Thomas McKean, DE	July 10, 1781
"	"	John Hanson, MD (2)	Nov. 5, 1781
"	"	Elias Boudinot, NJ	Nov. 4, 1782
Princeton, NJ	June 30 to Nov. 4, 1783	Thomas Mifflin, PA.	Nov. 3, 1783
Annapolis, MD	Nov. 26, 1783 to June 3, 1784		
Trenton, NJ	Nov. 1 to Dec. 24, 1784	Richard Henry Lee, VA	Nov. 30, 1784
New York City, MNY	Jan. 11 to Nov. 4, 1785		
"	Nov. 7, 1785 to Nov. 3, 1786	John Hancock, MA (3)	Nov. 23, 1785
"		Nathaniel Gorham, MA.	June 6, 1786
"	Nov. 6, 1786 to Oct. 30, 1787	Arthur St. Clair, PA	Feb. 2, 1787
"	Nov. 5, 1787 to Oct. 21, 1788	Cyrus Griffin, VA	Jan. 22, 1788
"	Nov. 3, 1788 to Mar. 2, 1789	"	

(1) Resigned Oct. 22, 1774. (2) Titled "President of the United States in Congress Assembled," John Hanson is considered by some the first U.S. president because he was the first to serve under the Articles of Confederation. He was, however, little more than presiding officer of the Congress, which retained full executive power. He could be considered the head of government, but not head of state. (3) Resigned May 29, 1786, without serving, because of illness. (4) Articles of Confederation agreed upon, Nov. 15, 1777; last ratification from Maryland, Mar. 1, 1781.

Patrick Henry's Speech to the Virginia Convention

The following is an excerpt from Patrick Henry's speech to the Virginia Convention on Mar. 23, 1775:

Gentlemen may cry, peace, peace—but there is no peace. The war is actually begun! The next gale that sweeps from the north will bring to our ears the clash of resounding arms! Our brethren are already in the field! Why stand we here idle? What is it that gentlemen wish? What would they have? Is life so dear, or peace so sweet, as to be purchased at the price of chains and slavery? Forbid it, Almighty God! I know not what course others may take; but as for me, give me liberty, or give me death!

MILLENNIUM FACT BOX

The Growth of Democracy

Democracy, or government by the people, originated in ancient times—5th cent. B.C. in Greece—but developed and spread through much of the world in the 2nd millennium. Greek democracy was direct (decisions were made by the people themselves in assembly) but restricted (slaves, women, or the foreign-born were excluded). Movement toward modern democracy found partial expression in the **Magna Carta**, signed by the English King John in 1215 under duress, which restricted royal power and laid down rights of due process for freemen. Contention over royal power in England led to civil war and, eventually, to parliamentary supremacy after the **Glorious Revolution** (1688); the English **Bill of Rights** (1689) and legislative reforms followed. Ideals of self-government, embodied in the Pilgrims' **Mayflower Compact** (1620), and respect for individual rights found expression in America in the **Declaration of Independence** (1776) and **Bill of Rights** (1791). The **U.S. Constitution**, effective in 1789, established an indirect, or representative, democracy (decisions to be made by elected representatives), which developed further in U.S. history, such as through abolition of slavery and extension of suffrage to all adults. Influenced also by the **French Revolution** (1789), democracy developed in much of Western Europe; in Canada, Australia, and New Zealand; and later in India, Japan, and many other nations—including Third World countries and, recently, the former Soviet Union and Eastern Europe.

How the Declaration of Independence Was Adopted

On June 7, 1776, Richard Henry Lee, who had issued the first call for a congress of the colonies, introduced in the Continental Congress at Philadelphia a resolution declaring "that these United Colonies are, and of right ought to be, free and independent states, that they are absolved from all allegiance to the British Crown, and that all political connection between them and the state of Great Britain is, and ought to be, totally dissolved."

The resolution, seconded by John Adams on behalf of the Massachusetts delegation, came up again on June 10 when a committee of 5, headed by Thomas Jefferson, was appointed to express the purpose of the resolution in a declaration of independence. The others on the committee were John Adams, Benjamin Franklin, Robert R. Livingston, and Roger Sherman.

Drafting the Declaration was assigned to Jefferson, who worked on a portable desk of his own construction in a room at Market and 7th Sts. The committee reported the result on June 28, 1776. The members of the Congress suggested a number of changes, which Jefferson called "deplorable." They didn't approve Jefferson's arraignment of the British people and King George III for encouraging and fostering the slave trade, which Jefferson called "an execrable commerce." They made 86 changes, eliminating 480 words and leaving 1,337. In the final form, capitalization was erratic. Jefferson had written that men were endowed with "inalienable" rights; in the final copy it came out as "unalienable" and has been thus ever since.

The Lee-Adams resolution of independence was adopted by 12 yeas on July 2—the actual date of the act of independence. The Declaration, which explains the act, was adopted July 4, in the evening.

After the Declaration was adopted, July 4, 1776, it was turned over to John Dunlap, printer, to be printed on broadsides. The original copy was lost and one of his broadsides was attached to a page in the journal of the Congress. It was read aloud July 8 in Philadelphia, PA, Easton, PA, and Trenton, NJ. On July 9 at 6 PM it was read by order of Gen. George Washington to the troops assembled on the Common in New York City (City Hall Park).

The Continental Congress of July 19, 1776, adopted the following resolution:

"Resolved, That the Declaration passed on the 4th, be fairly engrossed on parchment with the title and stile of 'The Unanimous Declaration of the thirteen United States of America' and that the same, when engrossed, be signed by every member of Congress."

Not all delegates who signed the engrossed Declaration were present on July 4. Robert Morris (PA), William Williams (CT), and Samuel Chase (MD) signed on Aug. 2; Oliver Wolcott (CT), George Wythe (VA), Richard Henry Lee (VA), and Elbridge Gerry (MA) signed in August and September; Matthew Thornton (NH) joined the Congress Nov. 4 and signed later. Thomas McKean (DE) rejoined Washington's army before signing and said later that he signed in 1781.

Charles Carroll of Carrollton was appointed a delegate by Maryland on July 4, 1776, presented his credentials July 18, and signed the engrossed Declaration on Aug. 2. Born Sept. 19, 1737, he was 95 years old and the last surviving signer when he died on Nov. 14, 1832.

Two Pennsylvania delegates who did not support the Declaration on July 4 were replaced.

The 4 New York delegates did not have authority from their state to vote on July 4. On July 9, the New York state convention authorized its delegates to approve the Declaration, and the Congress was so notified on July 15, 1776. The 4 signed the Declaration on Aug. 2.

The original engrossed Declaration is preserved in the National Archives Building in Washington.

Declaration of Independence

The Declaration of Independence was adopted by the Continental Congress in Philadelphia on July 4, 1776. John Hancock was president of the Congress, and Charles Thomson was secretary. A copy of the Declaration, engrossed on parchment, was signed by members of Congress on and after Aug. 2, 1776. On Jan. 18, 1777, Congress ordered that "an authenticated copy, with the names of the members of Congress subscribing the same, be sent to each of the United States, and that they be desired to have the same put upon record." Authenticated copies were printed in broadside form in Baltimore, where the Continental Congress was then in session. The following text is that of the original printed by John Dunlap at Philadelphia for the Continental Congress.

IN CONGRESS, July 4, 1776.

A DECLARATION

By the REPRESENTATIVES of the

UNITED STATES OF AMERICA,

In GENERAL CONGRESS assembled

When in the Course of human Events, it becomes necessary for one People to dissolve the Political Bands which have connected them with another, and to assume among the Powers of the Earth, the separate and equal Station to which the Laws of Nature and of Nature's God entitle them, a decent Respect to the Opinions of Mankind requires that they should declare the causes which impel them to the Separation.

We hold these Truths to be self-evident, that all Men are created equal, that they are endowed by their Creator with certain unalienable Rights, that among these are Life, Liberty, and the Pursuit of Happiness—That to secure these Rights, Governments are instituted among Men, deriving their just Powers from the Consent of the Governed, that whenever any Form of Government becomes destructive of these Ends, it is the Right of the People to alter or to abolish it, and to institute new Government, laying its Foundation on such Principles, and organizing its Powers in such Form, as to them shall seem most likely to effect their Safety and Happiness. Prudence, indeed, will dictate that Governments long established should not be changed for light and transient Causes; and accordingly all Experience hath shewn, that Mankind are more disposed to suffer, while Evils are sufferable, than to right themselves by abolishing the Forms to which they are accustomed. But when a long Train of Abuses and Usurpations, pursuing invariably the same Object, evinces a Design to reduce them under absolute Despotism, it is their Right, it is their Duty, to throw off such Government, and to provide new Guards for their future Security. Such has been the patient Sufferance of these Colonies; and such is now the Necessity which constrains them to alter their former Systems of Government. The History of the present King of Great-Britain is a History of repeated Injuries and Usurpations, all having in direct Object the Establishment of an absolute Tyranny over these States. To prove this, let Facts be submitted to a candid World.

He has refused his Assent to Laws, the most wholesome and necessary for the public Good.

He has forbidden his Governors to pass Laws of immediate and pressing Importance, unless suspended in their Operation till his Assent should be obtained; and when so suspended, he has utterly neglected to attend to them.

He has refused to pass other Laws for the Accommodation of large Districts of People, unless those People would relinquish the Right of Representation in the Legislature, a Right inestimable to them, and formidable to Tyrants only.

He has called together Legislative Bodies at Places unusual, uncomfortable, and distant from the Depository of their Public Records, for the sole Purpose of fatiguing them into Compliance with his Measures.

He has dissolved Representative Houses repeatedly, for opposing with manly Firmness his Invasions on the Rights of the People.

He has refused for a long Time, after such Dissolutions, to cause others to be elected; whereby the Legislative Powers, incapable of Annihilation, have returned to the People at large for their exercise; the State remaining in the mean time exposed to all the Dangers of Invasion from without, and Convulsions within.

He has endeavoured to prevent the Population of these States; for that Purpose obstructing the Laws for Naturalization of Foreigners; refusing to pass others to encourage their Migrations hither, and raising the Conditions of new Appropriations of Lands.

He has obstructed the Administration of Justice, by refusing his Assent to Laws for establishing Judiciary Powers.

He has made Judges dependent on his Will alone, for the Tenure of their Offices, and the Amount and payment of their Salaries.

He has erected a Multitude of new Offices, and sent hither Swarms of Officers to harrass our People, and eat out their Substance.

He has kept among us, in Times of Peace, Standing Armies, without the consent of our Legislatures.

He has affected to render the Military independent of, and superior to the Civil Power.

He has combined with others to subject us to a Jurisdiction foreign to our Constitution, and unacknowledged by our Laws; giving his Assent to their Acts of pretended Legislation:

For quartering large Bodies of Armed Troops among us:

For protecting them, by a mock Trial, from Punishment for any Murders which they should commit on the Inhabitants of these States:

For cutting off our Trade with all Parts of the World:

For imposing Taxes on us without our Consent:

For depriving us, in many Cases, of the Benefits of Trial by Jury:

For transporting us beyond Seas to be tried for pretended Offences:

For abolishing the free System of English Laws in a neighbouring Province, establishing therein an arbitrary Government, and enlarging its Boundaries, so as to render it at once an Example and fit Instrument for introducing the same absolute Rule into these Colonies:

For taking away our Charters, abolishing our most valuable Laws, and altering fundamentally the Forms of our Governments:

For suspending our own Legislatures, and declaring themselves invested with Power to legislate for us in all Cases whatsoever.

He has abdicated Government here, by declaring us out of his Protection and waging War against us.

He has plundered our Seas, ravaged our Coasts, burnt our towns, and destroyed the Lives of our People.

He is, at this Time, transporting large Armies of foreign Mercenaries to complete the works of Death, Desolation, and Tyranny, already begun with circumstances of Cruelty and Perfidy, scarcely paralleled in the most barbarous Ages, and totally unworthy the Head of a civilized Nation.

He has constrained our fellow Citizens taken Captive on the high Seas to bear Arms against their Country, to become the Executioners of their Friends and Brethren, or to fall themselves by their Hands.

He has excited domestic Insurrections amongst us, and has endeavoured to bring on the Inhabitants of our Frontiers, the merciless Indian Savages, whose known Rule of Warfare, is an undistinguished Destruction, of all Ages, Sexes and Conditions.

In every stage of these Oppressions we have Petitioned for Redress in the most humble Terms: Our repeated Petitions have been answered only by repeated Injury. A Prince, whose Character is thus marked by every act which may define a Tyrant, is unfit to be the Ruler of a free People.

Nor have we been wanting in Attentions to our British Brethren. We have warned them from Time to Time of Attempts by their Legislature to extend an unwarrantable Jurisdiction over us. We have reminded them of the Circumstances of our Emigration and Settlement here. We have appealed to their native Justice and Magnanimity, and we have conjured them by the Ties of our common Kindred to disavow these Usurpations, which, would inevitably interrupt our Connections and Correspondence. They too have been deaf to the Voice of Justice and of Consanguinity. We must, therefore, acquiesce in the Necessity, which denounces our Separation, and hold them, as we hold the rest of Mankind, Enemies in War, in Peace, Friends.

We, therefore, the Representatives of the UNITED STATES OF AMERICA, in General Congress, Assembled, appealing to the Supreme Judge of the World for the Rectitude of our Intentions, do, in the Name, and by Authority of the good People of these Colonies, solemnly Publish and Declare, That these United Colonies are, and of Right ought to be, Free and Independent States; that they are absolved from all Allegiance to the British Crown, and that all political Connection between them and the State of Great-Britain, is and ought to be totally dissolved; and that as Free and Independent States, they have full Power to levy War, conclude Peace, contract Alliances, establish Commerce, and to do all other Acts and Things which Independent States may of right do. And for the support of this declaration, with a firm Reliance on the Protection of Divine Providence, we mutually pledge to each other our lives, our Fortunes, and our sacred Honor.

JOHN HANCOCK, President

Attest.
CHARLES THOMSON, Secretary.

Signers of the Declaration of Independence

Delegate (state)	Occupation	Birthplace	Born	Died
Adams, John (MA)	Lawyer	Braintree (Quincy), MA	Oct. 30, 1735	July 4, 1826
Adams, Samuel (MA)	Political leader	Boston, MA	Sept. 27, 1722	Oct. 2, 1803
Bartlett, Josiah (NH)	Physician, judge	Amesbury, MA	Nov. 21, 1729	May 19, 1795
Braxton, Carter (VA)	Farmer	Newington Plantation, VA	Sept. 10, 1736	Oct. 10, 1797
Carroll, Chas. of Carrollton (MD)	Lawyer	Annapolis, MD	Sept. 19, 1737	Nov. 14, 1832
Chase, Samuel (MD)	Judge	Princess Anne, MD	Apr. 17, 1741	June 19, 1811
Clark, Abraham (NJ)	Surveyor	Roselle, NJ	Feb. 15, 1726	Sept. 15, 1794
Clymer, George (PA)	Merchant	Philadelphia, PA	Mar. 16, 1739	Jan. 23, 1813
Ellery, William (RI)	Lawyer	Newport, RI	Dec. 22, 1727	Feb. 15, 1820
Floyd, William (NY)	Soldier	Brookhaven, NY	Dec. 17, 1734	Aug. 4, 1821
Franklin, Benjamin (PA)	Printer, publisher	Boston, MA	Jan. 17, 1706	Apr. 17, 1790
Gerry, Elbridge (MA)	Merchant	Marblehead, MA	July 17, 1744	Nov. 23, 1814
Gwinnett, Button (GA)	Merchant	Down Hatherly, England	c. 1735	May 19, 1777
Hall, Lyman (GA)	Physician	Wallingford, CT	Apr. 12, 1724	Oct. 19, 1790
Hancock, John (MA)	Merchant	Braintree (Quincy), MA	Jan. 12, 1737	Oct. 8, 1793

Delegate (state)	Occupation	Birthplace	Born	Died
Harrison, Benjamin (VA)	Farmer	Berkeley, VA	Apr. 5, 1726	Apr. 24, 1791
Hart, John (NJ)	Farmer	Stonington, CT	c. 1711	May 11, 1779
Hewes, Joseph (NC)	Merchant	Princeton, NJ	Jan. 23, 1730	Nov. 10, 1779
Heyward, Thos. Jr. (SC)	Lawyer, farmer	St. Luke's Parish, SC.	July 28, 1746	Mar. 6, 1809
Hooper, William (NC)	Lawyer	Boston, MA	June 28, 1742	Oct. 14, 1790
Hopkins, Stephen (RI)	Judge, educator	Providence, RI	Mar. 7, 1707	July 13, 1785
Hopkinson, Francis (NJ)	Judge, author	Philadelphia, PA	Sept. 21, 1737	May 9, 1791
Huntington, Samuel (CT)	Judge	Windham County, CT	July 3, 1731	Jan. 5, 1796
Jefferson, Thomas (VA)	Lawyer	Shadwell, VA	Apr. 13, 1743	July 4, 1826
Lee, Francis Lightfoot (VA)	Farmer	Westmoreland County, VA	Oct. 14, 1734	Jan. 11, 1797
Lee, Richard Henry (VA)	Farmer	Westmoreland County, VA	Jan. 20, 1732	June 19, 1794
Lewis, Francis (NY)	Merchant	Llandaff, Wales	Mar., 1713	Dec. 31, 1802
Livingston, Philip (NY)	Merchant	Albany, NY	Jan. 15, 1716	June 12, 1778
Lynch, Thomas Jr. (SC)	Farmer	Winyah, SC	Aug. 5, 1749	(at sea) 1779
McKean, Thomas (DE)	Lawyer	New London, PA	Mar. 19, 1734	June 24, 1817
Middleton, Arthur (SC)	Farmer	Charleston, SC	June 26, 1742	Jan. 1, 1787
Morris, Lewis (NY)	Farmer	Morrisania (Bronx County), NY.	Apr. 8, 1726	Jan. 22, 1798
Morris, Robert (PA)	Merchant	Liverpool, England	Jan. 20, 1734	May 9, 1806
Morton, John (PA)	Judge	Ridley, PA	1724	Apr., 1777
Nelson, Thos. Jr. (VA)	Farmer	Yorktown, VA	Dec. 26, 1738	Jan. 4, 1789
Paca, William (MD)	Judge	Abingdon, MD	Oct. 31, 1740	Oct. 23, 1799
Paine, Robert Treat (MA)	Judge	Boston, MA	Mar. 11, 1731	May 12, 1814
Penn, John (NC)	Lawyer	Near Port Royal, VA	May 17, 1741	Sept. 14, 1788
Read, George (DE)	Judge	Near North East, MD.	Sept. 18, 1733	Sept. 21, 1798
Rodney, Caesar (DE)	Judge	Dover, DE	Oct. 7, 1728	June 29, 1784
Ross, George (PA)	Judge	New Castle, DE	May 10, 1730	July 14, 1779
Rush, Benjamin (PA)	Physician	Byberry, PA (Philadelphia)	Dec. 24, 1745	Apr. 19, 1813
Rutledge, Edward (SC)	Lawyer	Charleston, SC	Nov. 23, 1749	Jan. 23, 1800
Sherman, Roger (CT)	Lawyer	Newton, MA	Apr. 19, 1721	July 23, 1793
Smith, James (PA)	Lawyer	Dublin, Ireland	c. 1719	July 11, 1806
Stockton, Richard (NJ)	Lawyer	Near Princeton, NJ	Oct. 1, 1730	Feb. 28, 1781
Stone, Thomas (MD)	Lawyer	Charles County, MD	1743	Oct. 5, 1787
Taylor, George (PA)	Ironmaster	Ireland	1716	Feb. 23, 1781
Thornton, Matthew (NH)	Physician	Ireland	1714	June 24, 1803
Walton, George (GA)	Judge	Prince Edward County, VA	1741	Feb. 2, 1804
Whipple, William (NH)	Merchant, judge	Kittery, ME.	Jan. 14, 1730	Nov. 28, 1785
Williams, William (CT)	Merchant	Lebanon, CT	Apr. 23, 1731	Aug. 2, 1811
Wilson, James (PA)	Judge	Carskerdo, Scotland.	Sept. 14, 1742	Aug. 28, 1798
Witherspoon, John (NJ)	Clergyman, educator	Gifford, Scotland	Feb. 5, 1723	Nov. 15, 1794
Wolcott, Oliver (CT)	Judge	Windsor, CT	Dec. 1, 1726	Dec. 1, 1797
Wythe, George (VA)	Lawyer	Elizabeth City Co. (Hampton), VA	1726	June 8, 1806

Origin of the Constitution

The War of Independence was conducted by delegates from the original 13 states, called the Congress of the United States of America and known as the Continental Congress. In 1777 the Congress submitted to the legislatures of the states the Articles of Confederation and Perpetual Union, which were ratified by New Hampshire, Massachusetts, Rhode Island, Connecticut, New York, New Jersey, Pennsylvania, Delaware, Virginia, North Carolina, South Carolina, and Georgia and finally, in 1781, by Maryland.

The first article read: "The stile of this confederacy shall be the United States of America." This did not signify a sovereign nation, because the states delegated only those powers they could not handle individually, such as to wage war, make treaties, and contract debts for general expenses (e.g. paying the army). Taxes for payment of such debts were levied by the individual states. The president signed himself "President of the United States in Congress assembled," but here the United States were considered in the plural, a cooperating group.

When the war was won, it became evident that a stronger federal union was needed. The Congress left the initiative to the legislatures. Virginia in Jan. 1786 appointed commissioners to meet with representatives of other states; delegates from Virginia, Delaware, New York, New Jersey, and Pennsylvania met at Annapolis. Alexander Hamilton prepared their call asking delegates from all states to meet in Philadelphia in May 1787 "to render the Constitution of the federal government adequate to the exigencies of the union." Congress endorsed the plan on Feb. 21, 1787. Delegates were appointed by all states except Rhode Island.

The convention met on May 14, 1787. George Washington was chosen president (presiding officer). The states certified 65 delegates, but 10 did not attend. The work was done by 55, not all of whom were present at all sessions. Of the 55 attending delegates, 16 failed to sign, and 39 actually signed Sept. 17, 1787, some with reservations. Some historians have said 74 delegates (9 more than the 65 actually certified) were named and 19 failed to attend. These 9 additional persons refused the appointment, were never delegates, and never counted as absentees. Washington sent the Constitution to Congress, and that body, Sept. 28, 1787, ordered it sent to the legislatures, "in order to be submitted to a convention of delegates chosen in each state by the people thereof."

The Constitution was ratified by votes of state conventions as follows: Delaware, Dec. 7, 1787, unanimous; Pennsylvania, Dec. 12, 1787, 43 to 23; New Jersey, Dec. 18, 1787, unanimous; Georgia, Jan. 2, 1788, unanimous; Connecticut, Jan. 9, 1788, 128 to 40; Massachusetts, Feb. 6, 1788, 187 to 168; Maryland, Apr. 28, 1788, 63 to 11; South Carolina, May 23, 1788, 149 to 73; New Hampshire, June 21, 1788, 57 to 46; Virginia, June 25, 1788, 89 to 79; New York, July 26, 1788, 30 to 27. Nine states were needed to establish the operation of the Constitution "between the states so ratifying the same," and New Hampshire was the 9th state. The government did not declare the Constitution in effect until the first Wednesday in Mar. 1789, which was Mar. 4. After that, North Carolina ratified it on Nov. 21, 1789, 194 to 77; and Rhode Island, May 29, 1790, 34 to 32. Vermont in convention ratified it on Jan. 10, 1791, and by act of Congress approved on Feb. 18, 1791, was admitted into the Union as the 14th state, Mar. 4, 1791.

Constitution of the United States
The Original 7 Articles

The text of the Constitution below (with the exception of Amendment XXVII) is taken from the pocket-size edition of the Constitution published by the U.S. Government Printing Office as a result of a U.S. House and Senate resolution to print the Constitution in its original form as amended through July 5, 1971. Text in **boldface** summarizes an article or amendment and was added by *The World Almanac*. Text in *italic* indicates that an item has been superseded or amended, or provides background information on amendments.

PREAMBLE

We, the People of the United States, in Order to form a more perfect Union, establish Justice, insure domestic Tranquility, provide for the common defence, promote the general Welfare, and secure the Blessings of Liberty to ourselves and our Posterity, do ordain and establish this Constitution for the United States of America.

ARTICLE I.

Section 1—Legislative powers; in whom vested:

All legislative Powers herein granted shall be vested in a Congress of the United States, which shall consist of a Senate and House of Representatives.

Section 2—House of Representatives, how and by whom chosen. Qualifications of a Representative. Representatives and direct taxes, how apportioned. Enumeration. Vacancies to be filled. Power of choosing officers, and of impeachment.

The House of Representatives shall be composed of Members chosen every second Year by the People of the several States, and the Electors in each State shall have the Qualifications requisite for Electors of the most numerous Branch of the State Legislature.

No person shall be a Representative who shall not have attained to the Age of twenty-five Years, and been seven Years a Citizen of the United States, and who shall not, when elected, be an Inhabitant of that State in which he shall be chosen.

(Representatives and direct taxes shall be apportioned among the several States which may be included within this Union, according to their respective Numbers, which shall be determined by adding to the whole Number of free Persons, including those bound to Service for a Term of Years, and excluding Indians not taxed, three-fifths of all other persons.) (The previous sentence was superseded by Amendment XIV, section 2.) The actual Enumeration shall be made within three Years after the first Meeting of the Congress of the United States, and within every subsequent Term of ten Years, in such Manner as they shall by Law direct. The Number of Representatives shall not exceed one for every thirty Thousand, but each State shall have at Least one Representative; and until such enumeration shall be made, the State of New Hampshire shall be entitled to chuse three, Massachusetts eight, Rhode-Island and Providence Plantations one, Connecticut five, New-York six, New Jersey four, Pennsylvania eight, Delaware one, Maryland six, Virginia ten, North Carolina five, South Carolina five, and Georgia three.

When vacancies happen in the Representation from any State, the Executive Authority thereof shall issue Writs of Election to fill such Vacancies.

The House of Representatives shall chuse their Speaker and other Officers; and shall have the sole Power of Impeachment.

Section 3—Senators, how and by whom chosen. How classified. Qualifications of a Senator. President of the Senate, his right to vote. President pro tem., and other officers of the Senate, how chosen. Power to try impeachments. When President is tried, Chief Justice to preside. Sentence.

The Senate of the United States shall be composed of two Senators from each State, *(chosen by the Legislature thereof)*, *(The preceding five words were superseded by Amendment XVII, section 1.)* for six Years; and each Senator shall have one Vote.

Immediately after they shall be assembled in Consequence of the first Election, they shall be divided as equally as may be into three Classes. The Seats of the Senators of the first Class shall be vacated at the Expiration of the second Year, of the second Class at the Expiration of the fourth Year, and of the third Class at the Expiration of the Sixth year, so that one-third may be chosen every second Year; *(and if Vacancies happen by Resignation, or otherwise, during the Recess of the Legislature of any State, the Executive thereof may make temporary Appointments until the next Meeting of the Legislature,*

which shall then fill such Vacancies.) (The words in parentheses were superseded by Amendment XVII, section 2.)

No person shall be a Senator who shall not have attained to the Age of thirty Years, and been nine Years a Citizen of the United States, and who shall not, when elected, be an Inhabitant of that State for which he shall be chosen.

The Vice President of the United States shall be President of the Senate, but shall have no Vote, unless they be equally divided.

The Senate shall chuse their other Officers, and also a President pro tempore, in the absence of the Vice President, or when he shall exercise the Office of President of the United States.

The Senate shall have the sole Power to try all Impeachments. When sitting for that Purpose, they shall be on Oath or Affirmation. When the President of the United States is tried, the Chief Justice shall preside: And no Person shall be convicted without the Concurrence of two thirds of the Members present.

Judgment in Cases of Impeachment shall not extend further than to removal from Office, and disqualification to hold and enjoy any Office of honor, Trust or Profit under the United States: but the Party convicted shall nevertheless be liable and subject to Indictment, Trial, Judgment and Punishment, according to Law.

Section 4—Times, etc., of holding elections, how prescribed. One session each year.

The Times, Places and Manner of holding Elections for Senators and Representatives, shall be prescribed in each State by the Legislature thereof; but the Congress may at any time by Law make or alter such Regulations, except as to the Place of Chusing Senators.

The Congress shall assemble at least once in every Year, and such Meeting shall *(be on the first Monday in December,) (The words in parentheses were superseded by Amendment XX, section 2.)* unless they shall by Law appoint a different Day.

Section 5—Membership, quorum, adjournments, rules. Power to punish or expel. Journal. Time of adjournments, how limited, etc.

Each House shall be the Judge of the Elections, Returns and Qualifications of its own Members, and a Majority of each shall constitute a Quorum to do Business; but a smaller number may adjourn from day to day, and may be authorized to compel the Attendance of absent Members, in such manner, and under such Penalties as each House may provide.

Each House may determine the Rules of its Proceedings, punish its members for disorderly Behavior, and, with the Concurrence of two thirds, expel a Member.

Each House shall keep a Journal of its Proceedings, and from time to time publish the same, excepting such Parts as may in their Judgment require Secrecy; and the Yeas and Nays of the Members of either House on any question shall, at the Desire of one fifth of those Present, be entered on the Journal.

Neither House, during the Session of Congress, shall, without the Consent of the other, adjourn for more than three days, nor to any other Place than that in which the two Houses shall be sitting.

Section 6—Compensation, privileges, disqualifications in certain cases.

The Senators and Representatives shall receive a Compensation for their Services, to be ascertained by Law, and paid out of the Treasury of the United States. They shall in all Cases, except Treason, Felony and Breach of the Peace, be privileged from Arrest during their Attendance at the Session of their respective Houses, and in going to and returning from the same; and for any Speech or Debate in either House, they shall not be questioned in any other Place.

No Senator or Representative shall, during the Time for which he was elected, be appointed to any civil Office under the Authority of the United States, which shall have been created, or the Emoluments whereof shall have been encreased during such time; and no Person holding any Office under the United States, shall be a Member of either House during his Continuance in Office.

Section 7—House to originate all revenue bills. Veto. Bill may be passed by two-thirds of each House, notwithstanding, etc. Bill, not returned in ten days, to become a law. Provisions as to orders, concurrent resolutions, etc.

All bills for raising Revenue shall originate in the House of Representatives; but the Senate may propose or concur with Amendments as on other Bills.

Every Bill which shall have passed the House of Representatives and the Senate, shall, before it become a Law, be presented to the President of the United States; If he approve he shall sign it, but if not he shall return it, with his Objections to that House in which it shall have originated, who shall enter the Objections at large on their Journal, and proceed to reconsider it. If after such Reconsideration two thirds of that House shall agree to pass the Bill, it shall be sent, together with the Objections, to the other House, by which it shall likewise be reconsidered, and if approved by two thirds of that House, it shall become a Law. But in all such Cases the Votes of both Houses shall be determined by Yeas and Nays, and the Names of the Persons voting for and against the Bill shall be entered on the Journal of each House respectively. If any Bill shall not be returned by the President within ten Days (Sundays excepted) after it shall have been presented to him, the Same shall be a Law, in like Manner as if he had signed it, unless the Congress by their Adjournment prevent its Return, in which Case it shall not be a Law.

Every order, Resolution, or Vote to which the Concurrence of the Senate and House of Representatives may be necessary (except on a question of Adjournment) shall be presented to the President of the United States; and before the Same shall take Effect, shall be approved by him, or being disapproved by him, shall be repassed by two thirds of the Senate and House of Representatives, according to the Rules and Limitations prescribed in the Case of a Bill.

Section 8—Powers of Congress.

The Congress shall have Power To lay and collect Taxes, Duties, Imposts and Excises, to pay the Debts and provide for the common Defence and general Welfare of the United States; but all Duties, Imposts and Excises shall be uniform throughout the United States;

To borrow money on the credit of the United States;

To regulate Commerce with foreign Nations, and among the several States, and with the Indian Tribes;

To establish an uniform Rule of Naturalization, and uniform Laws on the subject of Bankruptcies throughout the United States;

To coin Money, regulate the Value thereof, and of foreign Coin, and fix the Standard of Weights and Measures;

To provide for the Punishment of counterfeiting the Securities and current Coin of the United States;

To establish Post Offices and post Roads;

To promote the Progress of Science and useful Arts, by securing for limited Times to Authors and Inventors the exclusive Right to their respective Writings and Discoveries;

To constitute Tribunals inferior to the supreme Court;

To define and punish Piracies and Felonies committed on the high Seas, and Offenses against the Law of Nations;

To declare War, grant Letters of Marque and Reprisal, and make Rules concerning Captures on Land and Water;

To raise and support Armies, but no Appropriation of Money to that Use shall be for a longer Term than two Years;

To provide and maintain a Navy;

To make Rules for the Government and Regulation of the land and naval Forces;

To provide for calling forth the Militia to execute the Laws of the Union, suppress Insurrections and repel Invasions;

To provide for organizing, arming, and disciplining the Militia, and for governing such Part of them as may be employed in the Service of the United States, reserving to the States respectively, the Appointment of the Officers, and the Authority of training the Militia according to the discipline prescribed by Congress;

To exercise exclusive Legislation in all Cases whatsoever, over such District (not exceeding ten Miles square) as may, by Cession of particular States, and the acceptance of Congress, become the Seat of the Government of the United States, and to exercise like Authority over all Places purchased by the Consent of the Legislature of the State in which the Same shall be, for the Erection of Forts, Magazines, Arsenals, dock-Yards, and other needful Buildings;—And

To make all Laws which shall be necessary and proper for carrying into Execution the foregoing Powers, and all other Powers vested by this Constitution in the Government of the United States, or in any Department or Officer thereof.

Section 9—Provision as to migration or importation of certain persons. Habeas corpus, bills of attainder, etc. Taxes, how apportioned. No export duty. No commercial preference. Money, how drawn from Treasury, etc. No titular nobility. Officers not to receive presents, etc.

The Migration or Importation of such Persons as any of the States now existing shall think proper to admit, shall not be prohibited by the Congress prior to the Year one thousand eight hundred and eight, but a tax or duty may be imposed on such Importation, not exceeding ten dollars for each Person.

The privilege of the Writ of Habeas Corpus shall not be suspended, unless when in Cases of Rebellion or Invasion the public Safety may require it.

No Bill of Attainder or ex post facto Law shall be passed.

No capitation, or other direct, Tax shall be laid, unless in Proportion to the Census or Enumeration herein before directed to be taken. *(Modified by Amendment XVI.)*

No Tax or Duty shall be laid on Articles exported from any State.

No Preference shall be given by any Regulation of Commerce or Revenue to the Ports of one State over those of another: nor shall Vessels bound to, or from, one State, be obliged to enter, clear, or pay Duties in another.

No Money shall be drawn from the Treasury, but in Consequence of Appropriations made by Law; and a regular Statement and Account of the Receipts and Expenditures of all public Money shall be published from time to time.

No Title of Nobility shall be granted by the United States: and no Person holding any Office of Profit or Trust under them, shall, without the Consent of the Congress, accept of any present, Emolument, Office, or Title, of any kind whatever, from any King, Prince, or foreign State.

Section 10—States prohibited from the exercise of certain powers.

No State shall enter into any Treaty, Alliance, or Confederation; grant Letters of Marque and Reprisal; coin Money; emit Bills of Credit; make any Thing but gold and silver Coin a Tender in Payment of Debts; pass any Bill of Attainder, ex post facto Law, or Law impairing the Obligation of Contracts, or grant any Title of Nobility.

No State shall, without the Consent of the Congress, lay any Imposts or Duties on Imports or Exports, except what may be absolutely necessary for executing its inspection Laws: and the net Produce of all Duties and Imposts, laid by any State on Imports or Exports, shall be for the Use of the Treasury of the United States; and all such Laws shall be subject to the Revision and Control of the Congress.

No State shall, without the Consent of Congress, lay any duty of Tonnage, keep Troops, or Ships of War in time of Peace, enter into any Agreement or Compact with another State, or with a foreign Power, or engage in War, unless actually invaded, or in such imminent Danger as will not admit of delay.

ARTICLE II.

Section 1—President: his term of office. Electors of President; number and how appointed. Electors to vote on same day. Qualification of President. On whom his duties devolve in case of his removal, death, etc. President's compensation. His oath of office.

The executive Power shall be vested in a President of the United States of America. He shall hold his Office during the Term of four Years, and, together with the Vice President, chosen for the same Term, be elected, as follows:

Each State shall appoint, in such Manner as the Legislature thereof may direct, a Number of Electors, equal to the whole Number of Senators and Representatives to which the State may be entitled in the Congress: but no Senator or Representative, or Person holding an Office of Trust or Profit under the United States, shall be appointed an Elector.

(The Electors shall meet in their respective States, and vote by Ballot for two persons, of whom one at least shall not be an Inhabitant of the same State with themselves. And they shall make a List of all the Persons voted for, and of the Number of Votes for each; which List they shall sign and certify, and transmit sealed to the Seat of the Government of the United States, directed to the President of the Senate. The President of the Senate shall, in the Presence of the Senate and House of Representatives, open all the Certificates, and the Votes shall then be counted. The Person having the greatest Number of Votes shall be the President, if such Number be a Majority of the whole Number of Electors appointed; and if there be more than one who have such Majority, and have an equal Number of Votes, then the House of Representatives shall immediately chuse by Ballot one of them for President; and if no Person have a Majority, then from the five highest on the List the said House shall in like Manner chuse the President. But in chusing the President, the Votes shall be taken by States, the Representation from each State having one Vote; a quorum for this Purpose shall consist of a Member or Members from two thirds of the States, and a Majority of all the States shall be necessary to a Choice. In every Case, after the Choice of the President, the Person having the greatest Number of Votes of the Electors shall be the Vice President. But if there should remain two or more who have equal Votes, the Senate shall chuse from them by Ballot the Vice-President.)

(This clause was superseded by Amendment XII.)

The Congress may detemine the Time of chusing the Electors, and the Day on which they shall give their Votes; which Day shall be the same throughout the United States.

No person except a natural born Citizen, or a Citizen of the United States, at the time of the Adoption of this Constitution, shall be eligible to the Office of President; neither shall any Person be eligible to that Office who shall not have attained to the Age of thirty-five Years, and been fourteen Years a Resident within the United States.

(For qualification of the Vice President, see Amendment XII.)

In Case of the Removal of the President from Office, or of his Death, Resignation, or Inability to discharge the Powers and Duties of the said Office, the same shall devolve on the Vice President, and the Congress may by Law, provide for the Case of Removal, Death, Resignation or Inability, both of the President and Vice President, declaring what Officer shall then act as President, and such Officer shall act accordingly, until the Disability be removed, or a President shall be elected.

(This clause has been modified by Amendments XX and XXV.)

The President shall, at stated Times, receive for his Services, a Compensation, which shall neither be encreased nor diminished during the Period for which he shall have been elected, and he shall not receive within that Period any other Emolument from the United States, or any of them.

Before he enter on the Execution of his Office, he shall take the following Oath or Affirmation:–"I do solemnly swear (or affirm) that I will faithfully execute the Office of President of the United States, and will to the best of my Ability, preserve, protect and defend the Constitution of the United States."

Section 2—President to be Commander-in-Chief. He may require opinions of cabinet officers, etc., may pardon. Treaty-making power. Nomination of certain officers. When President may fill vacancies.

The President shall be Commander in Chief of the Army and Navy of the United States, and of the Militia of the

several States, when called into the actual Service of the United States; he may require the Opinion in writing, of the principal Officer in each of the executive Departments, upon any subject relating to the Duties of their respective Offices, and he shall have Power to Grant Reprieves and Pardons for Offenses against the United States, except in Cases of Impeachment.

He shall have Power, by and with the Advice and Consent of the Senate, to make Treaties, provided two-thirds of the Senators present concur; and he shall nominate, and by and with the Advice and Consent of the Senate, shall appoint Ambassadors, other public Ministers and Consuls, Judges of the supreme Court, and all other Officers of the United States, whose Appointments are not herein otherwise provided for, and which shall be established by Law: but the Congress may by Law vest the Appointment of such inferior Officers, as they think proper, in the President alone, in the Courts of Law, or in the Heads of Departments.

The President shall have Power to fill up all Vacancies that may happen during the Recess of the Senate, by granting Commissions which shall expire at the End of their next Session.

Section 3—President shall communicate to Congress. He may convene and adjourn Congress, in case of disagreement, etc. Shall receive ambassadors, execute laws, and commission officers.

He shall from time to time give to the Congress Information of the State of the Union, and recommend to their Consideration such Measures as he shall judge necessary and expedient; he may, on extraordinary Occasions, convene both Houses, or either of them, and in Case of Disagreement between them, with Respect to the Time of Adjournment, he may adjourn them to such Time as he shall think proper; he shall receive Ambassadors and other public Ministers; he shall take Care that the Laws be faithfully executed, and shall Commission all the Officers of the United States.

Section 4—All civil offices forfeited for certain crimes.

The President, Vice President and all civil Officers of the United States, shall be removed from Office on Impeachment for, and Conviction of, Treason, Bribery, or other high Crimes and Misdemeanors.

ARTICLE III.
Section 1—Judicial powers, Tenure. Compensation.

The judicial Power of the United States, shall be vested in one supreme Court, and in such inferior Courts as the Congress may from time to time ordain and establish. The Judges, both of the supreme and inferior Courts, shall hold their Offices during good Behaviour, and shall, at stated Times, receive for their Services, a Compensation, which shall not be diminished during their Continuance in Office.

Section 2—Judicial power; to what cases it extends. Original jurisdiction of Supreme Court; appellate jurisdiction. Trial by jury, etc. Trial, where.

The judicial Power shall extend to all Cases, in Law and Equity, arising under this Constitution, the Laws of the United States, and Treaties made, or which shall be made, under their Authority;–to all Cases affecting Ambassadors, other public Ministers and Consuls;–to all Cases of admiralty and maritime Jurisdiction;–to Controversies to which the United States shall be a Party;–to Controversies between two or more States;–between a State and Citizens of another State;–between Citizens of different States;–between Citizens of the same State claiming Lands under Grants of different States, and between a State, or the Citizens thereof, and foreign States, Citizens or Subjects.

(This section is modified by Amendment XI.)

In all Cases affecting Ambassadors, other public Ministers and Consuls, and those in which a State shall be Party, the supreme Court shall have original Jurisdiction. In all the other Cases before mentioned, the supreme Court shall have appellate Jurisdiction, both as to Law and Fact, with such Exceptions, and under such Regulations as the Congress shall make.

The trial of all Crimes, except in Cases of Impeachment, shall be by Jury; and such Trial shall be held in the State where the said Crimes shall have been committed; but when not committed within any State, the Trial shall be at such Place or Places as the Congress may by Law have directed.

Section 3—Treason Defined, Proof of, Punishment of.

Treason against the United States, shall consist only in levying War against them, or in adhering to their Enemies, giving them Aid and Comfort. No Person shall be convicted of Treason unless on the Testimony of two Witnesses to the same overt Act, or on Confession in open Court.

The Congress shall have Power to declare the Punishment of Treason, but no Attainder of Treason shall work Corruption of Blood, or Forfeiture except during the Life of the Person attainted.

ARTICLE IV.

Section 1—Each State to give credit to the public acts, etc., of every other State.

Full Faith and Credit shall be given in each State to the public Acts, Records, and judicial Proceedings of every other State. And the Congress may by general Laws prescribe the Manner in which such Acts, Records and Proceedings shall be proved, and the Effect thereof.

Section 2—Privileges of citizens of each State. Fugitives from justice to be delivered up. Persons held to service having escaped, to be delivered up.

The Citizens of each State shall be entitled to all Privileges and Immunities of Citizens in the several States.

A Person charged in any State with Treason, Felony, or other Crime, who shall flee from Justice, and be found in another State, shall on demand of the executive Authority of the State from which he fled, be delivered up, to be removed to the State having Jurisdiction of the Crime.

(No Person held to Service or Labour in one State, under the Laws thereof, escaping into another, shall, in Consequence of any Law or Regulation therein, be discharged from such Service or Labour, but shall be delivered up on Claim of the Party to whom such Service or Labour may be due.) (This clause was superseded by Amendment XIII.)

Section 3—Admission of new States. Power of Congress over territory and other property.

New States may be admitted by the Congress into this Union; but no new State shall be formed or erected within the Jurisdiction of any other State; nor any State be formed by the Junction of two or more States, or parts of States, without the Consent of the Legislatures of the States concerned as well as of the Congress.

The Congress shall have Power to dispose of and make all needful Rules and Regulations respecting the Territory or other Property belonging to the United States; and nothing in this Constitution shall be so construed as to Prejudice any Claims of the United States, or of any particular State.

Section 4—Republican form of government guaranteed. Each state to be protected.

The United States shall guarantee to every State in this Union a Republican Form of Government, and shall protect each of them against Invasion; and on Application of the Legislature, or of the Executive (when the Legislature cannot be convened) against domestic Violence.

ARTICLE V.

Constitution: how amended; proviso.

The Congress, whenever two-thirds of both Houses shall deem it necessary, shall propose Amendments to this Constitution, or, on the Application of the Legislatures of two-thirds of the several States, shall call a Convention for proposing Amendments, which, in either Case, shall be valid to all Intents and Purposes, as part of this Constitution, when ratified by the Legislatures of three-fourths of the several States, or by Conventions in three-fourths thereof, as the one or the other Mode of Ratification may be proposed by the Congress: Provided that no Amendment which may be made prior to the Year One thousand eight hundred and eight shall in any Manner affect the first and fourth Clauses in the Ninth Section of the first Article; and that no State, without its Consent, shall be deprived of its equal Suffrage in the Senate.

ARTICLE VI.

Certain debts, etc., declared valid. Supremacy of Constitution, treaties, and laws of the United States. Oath to support Constitution, by whom taken. No religious test.

All Debts contracted and Engagements entered into, before the Adoption of this Constitution, shall be as valid against the United States under this Constitution, as under the Confederation.

This Constitution, and the Laws of the United States which shall be made in Pursuance thereof; and all Treaties made, or which shall be made, under the Authority of the United States, shall be the supreme Law of the Land; and the Judges in every State shall be bound thereby, any Thing in the Constitution or Laws of any State to the Contrary notwithstanding.

The Senators and Representatives before mentioned, and the Members of the several State Legislatures, and all executive and judicial Officers, both of the United States and of the several States, shall be bound by Oath or Affirmation, to support this Constitution; but no religious Test shall ever be required as a Qualification to any Office or public Trust under the United States.

ARTICLE VII.

What ratification shall establish Constitution.

The Ratification of the Conventions of nine States shall be sufficient for the Establishment of this Constitution between the States so ratifying the Same.

Done in Convention by the Unanimous Consent of the States present the Seventeenth Day of September in the Year of our Lord one thousand seven hundred and Eighty seven and of the Independence of the United States of America the Twelfth.

In Witness whereof We have hereunto subscribed our Names.

Go WASHINGTON, Presidt and deputy from Virginia

New Hampshire—John Langdon, Nicholas Gilman

Massachusetts—Nathaniel Gorham, Rufus King

Connecticut—Wm Saml Johnson, Roger Sherman

New York—Alexander Hamilton

New Jersey—Wil: Livingston, David Brearley, Wm Paterson, Jona: Dayton

Pennsylvania—B Franklin, Thomas Mifflin, Robt. Morris, Geo. Clymer, Thos. FitzSimons, Jared Ingersoll, James Wilson, Gouv Morris

Delaware—Geo: Read, Gunning Bedford jun, John Dickinson, Richard Bassett, Jaco: Broom

Maryland—James McHenry, Dan: of St Thos Jenifer, Danl Carrol

Virginia—John Blair, James Madison Jr.

North Carolina—Wm Blount, Richd. Dobbs Spaight, Hu Williamson

South Carolina—J. Rutledge, Charles Cotesworth Pinckney, Charles Pinckney, Pierce Butler

Georgia—William Few, Abr Baldwin

Attest: William Jackson, Secretary.

Ten Original Amendments: The Bill of Rights

In force Dec. 15, 1791

(The First Congress, at its first session in the City of New York, Sept. 25, 1789, submitted to the states 12 amendments to clarify certain individual and state rights not named in the Constitution. They are generally called the Bill of Rights.

(Influential in framing these amendments was the Declaration of Rights of Virginia, written by George Mason (1725-1792) in 1776. Mason, a Virginia delegate to the Constitutional Convention, did not sign the Constitution and opposed its ratification on the ground that it did not sufficiently oppose slavery or safeguard individual rights.

(In the preamble to the resolution offering the proposed amendments, Congress said: "The conventions of a number of the States having at the time of their adopting the Constitution, expressed a desire, in order to prevent misconstruction or abuse of its powers, that further declaratory and restrictive clauses should be added, as extending the ground of public confidence in the government will best insure the beneficent ends of its institution, be it resolved," etc.

(Ten of these amendments, now commonly known as one to 10 inclusive, but originally 3 to 12 inclusive, were ratified by the states as follows: New Jersey, Nov. 20, 1789; Maryland, Dec. 19, 1789; North Carolina, Dec. 22, 1789; South Carolina, Jan. 19, 1790; New Hampshire, Jan. 25, 1790; Delaware, Jan. 28, 1790; New York, Feb. 27, 1790; Pennsylvania, Mar. 10, 1790; Rhode Island, June 7, 1790; Vermont, Nov. 3, 1791; Virginia, Dec. 15, 1791; Massachusetts, Mar. 2, 1939; Georgia, Mar. 18, 1939; Connecticut, Apr. 19, 1939. These original 10 ratified amendments follow as Amendments I to X inclusive.

(Of the two original proposed amendments that were not ratified promptly by the necessary number of states, the first related to apportionment of Representatives; the second, relating to compensation of members of Congress, was ratified in 1992 and became Amendment 27.)

AMENDMENT I.

Religious establishment prohibited. Freedom of speech, of press, right to assemble and to petition.

Congress shall make no law respecting an establishment of religion, or prohibiting the free exercise thereof; or abridging the freedom of speech, or of the press; or the right of the people peaceably to assemble, and to petition the Government for a redress of grievances.

AMENDMENT II.

Right to keep and bear arms.

A well regulated Militia, being necessary to the security of a free State, the right of the people to keep and bear Arms, shall not be infringed.

AMENDMENT III.

Conditions for quarters for soldiers.

No Soldier shall, in time of peace be quartered in any house, without the consent of the Owner, nor in time of war, but in a manner to be prescribed by law.

AMENDMENT IV.

Protection from unreasonable search and seizure.

The right of the people to be secure in their persons, houses, papers, and effects, against unreasonable searches and seizures, shall not be violated, and no Warrants shall issue, but upon probable cause, supported by Oath or affirmation, and particularly describing the place to be searched, and the persons or things to be seized.

AMENDMENT V.

Provisions concerning prosecution and due process of law. Double jeopardy restriction. Private property not to be taken without compensation.

No person shall be held to answer for a capital, or otherwise infamous crime, unless on a presentment or indictment of a Grand Jury, except in cases arising in the land or naval forces, or in the Militia, when in actual service in time of War or public danger; nor shall any person be subject for the same offence to be twice put in jeopardy of life or limb;

nor shall be compelled in any criminal case to be a witness against himself, nor be deprived of life, liberty, or property, without due process of law; nor shall private property be taken for public use, without just compensation.

AMENDMENT VI.

Right to speedy trial, witnesses, etc.

In all criminal prosecutions, the accused shall enjoy the right to a speedy and public trial, by an impartial jury of the State and district wherein the crime shall have been committed, which district shall have been previously ascertained by law, and to be informed of the nature and cause of the accusation; to be confronted with the witnesses against him; to have compulsory process for obtaining witnesses in his favor, and to have the Assistance of Counsel for his defence.

AMENDMENT VII.

Right of trial by jury.

In suits at common law, where the value in controversy shall exceed twenty dollars, the right of trial by jury shall be preserved, and no fact tried by a jury, shall be otherwise reexamined in any Court of the United States, than according to the rules of the common law.

AMENDMENT VIII.

Excessive bail or fines; cruel and unusual punishment.

Excessive bail shall not be required, nor excessive fines imposed, nor cruel and unusual punishments inflicted.

AMENDMENT IX.

Rule of construction of Constitution.

The enumeration in the Constitution, of certain rights, shall not be construed to deny or disparage others retained by the people.

AMENDMENT X.

Rights of States under Constitution.

The powers not delegated to the United States by the Constitution, nor prohibited by it to the States, are reserved to the States respectively, or to the people.

Amendments Since the Bill of Rights

AMENDMENT XI.

Judicial powers construed.

The Judicial power of the United States shall not be construed to extend to any suit in law or equity, commenced or prosecuted against one of the United States by Citizens of another State, or by Citizens or Subjects of any Foreign State.

(This amendment was proposed to the Legislatures of the several States by the Third Congress on March 4, 1794, and was declared to have been ratified in a message from the President to Congress, dated Jan. 8, 1798.

(It was on Jan. 5, 1798, that Secretary of State Pickering received from 12 of the States authenticated ratifications, and informed President John Adams of that fact.

(As a result of later research in the Department of State, it is now established that Amendment XI became part of the Constitution on Feb. 7, 1795, for on that date it had been ratified by 12 States as follows:

(1. New York, Mar. 27, 1794. 2. Rhode Island, Mar. 31, 1794. 3. Connecticut, May 8, 1794. 4. New Hampshire, June 16, 1794. 5. Massachusetts, June 26, 1794. 6. Vermont, between Oct. 9, 1794, and Nov. 9, 1794. 7. Virginia, Nov. 18,

1794. 8. Georgia, Nov. 29, 1794. 9. Kentucky, Dec. 7, 1794. 10. Maryland, Dec. 26, 1794. 11. Delaware, Jan. 23, 1795. 12. North Carolina, Feb. 7, 1795.

(On June 1, 1796, more than a year after Amendment XI had become a part of the Constitution—but before anyone was officially aware of this—Tennessee had been admitted as a State; but not until Oct. 16, 1797, was a certified copy of the resolution of Congress proposing the amendment sent to the Governor of Tennessee, John Sevier, by Secretary of State Pickering, whose office was then at Trenton, New Jersey, because of the epidemic of yellow fever at Philadelphia; it seems, however, that the Legislature of Tennessee took no action on Amendment XI, owing doubtless to the fact that public announcement of its adoption was made soon thereafter.

(Besides the necessary 12 States, one other, South Carolina, ratified Amendment XI, but this action was not taken until Dec. 4, 1797; the two remaining States, New Jersey and Pennsylvania, failed to ratify.)

AMENDMENT XII.
Manner of choosing President and Vice-President.

(Proposed by Congress Dec. 9, 1803; ratified June 15, 1804.)

The Electors shall meet in their respective states and vote by ballot for President and Vice-President, one of whom, at least, shall not be an inhabitant of the same state with themselves; they shall name in their ballots the person voted for as President, and in distinct ballots the person voted for as Vice-President, and they shall make distinct lists of all persons voted for as President, and of all persons voted for as Vice-President, and of the number of votes for each, which lists they shall sign and certify, and transmit sealed to the seat of the government of the United States, directed to the President of the Senate;—The President of the Senate shall, in presence of the Senate and House of Representatives, open all the certificates and the votes shall then be counted;—The person having the greatest number of votes for President, shall be the President, if such number be a majority of the whole number of Electors appointed; and if no person have such majority, then from the persons having the highest numbers not exceeding three on the list of those voted for as President, the House of Representatives shall choose immediately, by ballot, the President. But in choosing the President, the votes shall be taken by states, the representation from each state having one vote; a quorum for this purpose shall consist of a member or members from two-thirds of the states, and a majority of all the states shall be necessary to a choice. *(And if the House of Representatives shall not choose a President whenever the right of choice shall devolve upon them, before the fourth day of March next following, then the Vice-President shall act as President, as in the case of the death or other constitutional disability of the President.) (The words in parentheses were superseded by Amendment XX, section 3.)* The person having the greatest number of votes as Vice-President, shall be the Vice-President, if such number be a majority of the whole number of Electors appointed, and if no person have a majority, then from the two highest numbers on the list, the Senate shall choose the Vice-President; a quorum for the purpose shall consist of two-thirds of the whole number of Senators, and a majority of the whole number shall be necessary to a choice. But no person constitutionally ineligible to the office of President shall be eligible to that of Vice-President of the United States.

THE RECONSTRUCTION AMENDMENTS

(Amendments XIII, XIV, and XV are commonly known as the Reconstruction Amendments, inasmuch as they followed the Civil War, and were drafted by Republicans who were bent on imposing their own policy of reconstruction on the South. Post-bellum legislatures there— Mississippi, South Carolina, Georgia, for example—had set up laws which, it was charged, were contrived to perpetuate Negro slavery under other names.)

AMENDMENT XIII.
Slavery abolished.

(Proposed by Congress Jan. 31, 1865; ratified Dec. 6, 1865. The amendment, when first proposed by a resolution

in Congress, was passed by the Senate, 38 to 6, on Apr. 8, 1864, but was defeated in the House, 95 to 66 on June 15, 1864. On reconsideration by the House, on Jan. 31, 1865, the resolution passed, 119 to 56. It was approved by President Lincoln on Feb. 1, 1865, although the Supreme Court had decided in 1798 that the President has nothing to do with the proposing of amendments to the Constitution, or their adoption.)*

1. Neither slavery nor involuntary servitude, except as a punishment for crime whereof the party shall have been duly convicted, shall exist within the United States, or any place subject to their jurisdiction.

2. Congress shall have power to enforce this article by appropriate legislation.

AMENDMENT XIV.
Citizenship rights not to be abridged.

(The following amendment was proposed to the Legislatures of the several states by the 39th Congress, June 13, 1866, ratified July 9, 1868, and declared to have been ratified in a proclamation by the Secretary of State, July 28, 1868.

(The 14th amendment was adopted only by virtue of ratification subsequent to earlier rejections. Newly constituted legislatures in both North Carolina and South Carolina (respectively July 4 and 9, 1868), ratified the proposed amendment, although earlier legislatures had rejected the proposal. The Secretary of State issued a proclamation, which, though doubtful as to the effect of attempted withdrawals by Ohio and New Jersey, entertained no doubt as to the validity of the ratification by North and South Carolina. The following day (July 21, 1868), Congress passed a resolution which declared the 14th Amendment to be a part of the Constitution and directed the Secretary of State so to promulgate it. The Secretary waited, however, until the newly constituted Legislature of Georgia had ratified the amendment, subsequent to an earlier rejection, before the promulgation of the ratification of the new amendment.)

1. All persons born or naturalized in the United States, and subject to the jurisdiction thereof, are citizens of the United States and of the State wherein they reside. No State shall make or enforce any law which shall abridge the privileges or immunities of citizens of the United States; nor shall any State deprive any person of life, liberty, or property, without due process of law; nor deny to any person within its jurisdiction the equal protection of the laws.

2. Representatives shall be apportioned among the several States according to their respective numbers, counting the whole number of persons in each State, excluding Indians not taxed. But when the right to vote at any election for the choice of electors for President and Vice-President of the United States, Representatives in Congress, the Executive and Judicial officers of a State, or the members of the Legislature thereof, is denied to any of the male inhabitants of such State, being twenty-one years of age, and citizens of the United States, or in any way abridged, except for participation in rebellion, or other crime, the basis of representation therein shall be reduced in the proportion which the number of such male citizens shall bear to the whole number of male citizens twenty-one years of age in such State.

3. No person shall be a Senator or Representative in Congress, or elector of President and Vice-President, or hold any office, civil or military, under the United States, or under any State, who, having previously taken an oath, as a member of Congress, or as an officer of the United States, or as a member of any State legislature, or as an executive or judicial officer of any State, to support the Constitution of the United States, shall have engaged in insurrection or rebellion against the same, or given aid or comfort to the enemies thereof. But Congress may by a vote of two-thirds of each House, remove such disability.

4. The validity of the public debt of the United States, authorized by law, including debts incurred for payment of pensions and bounties for services in suppressing insurrection or rebellion, shall not be questioned. But neither the United States nor any State shall assume or pay any debt or obligation incurred in aid of insurrection or rebellion against the United

States, or any claim for the loss or emancipation of any slave; but all such debts, obligations and claims shall be held illegal and void.

The Congress shall have power to enforce, by appropriate legislation, the provisions of this article.

AMENDMENT XV.

Race no bar to voting rights.

(The following amendment was proposed to the legislatures of the several States by the 40th Congress, Feb. 26, 1869, and ratified Feb. 8, 1870.)

1. The right of citizens of the United States to vote shall not be denied or abridged by the United States or by any State on account of race, color, or previous condition of servitude–

2. The Congress shall have power to enforce this article by appropriate legislation.

AMENDMENT XVI.

Income taxes authorized.

(Proposed by Congress July 12, 1909; ratified Feb. 3, 1913.)

The Congress shall have power to lay and collect taxes on incomes, from whatever source derived, without apportionment among the several States, and without regard to any census or enumeration.

AMENDMENT XVII.

United States Senators to be elected by direct popular vote.

(Proposed by Congress May 13, 1912; ratified Apr. 8, 1913.)

The Senate of the United States shall be composed of two Senators from each State, elected by the people thereof, for six years; and each Senator shall have one vote. The electors in each State shall have the qualifications requisite for electors of the most numerous branch of the State legislatures.

When vacancies happen in the representation of any State in the Senate, the executive authority of such State shall issue writs of election to fill such vacancies: *Provided,* That the legislature of any State may empower the executive thereof to make temporary appointments until the people fill the vacancies by election as the legislature may direct.

This amendment shall not be so construed as to affect the election or term of any Senator chosen before it becomes valid as part of the Constitution.

AMENDMENT XVIII.

Liquor prohibition amendment.

(Proposed by Congress Dec. 18, 1917; ratified Jan. 16, 1919. Repealed by Amendment XXI, effective Dec. 5, 1933.)

1. After one year from the ratification of this article the manufacture, sale, or transportation of intoxicating liquors within, the importation thereof into, or the exportation thereof from the United States and all territory subject to the jurisdiction thereof for beverage purposes is hereby prohibited.

2. The Congress and the several States shall have concurrent power to enforce this article by appropriate legislation.

3. This article shall be inoperative unless it shall have been ratified as an amendment to the Constitution by the legislatures of the several States as provided in the Constitution, within seven years from the date of the submission hereof to the States by the Congress.

(The total vote in the Senates of the various States was 1,310 for, 237 against 81.6% dry. In the lower houses of the States the vote was 3,782 for, 1,035 against—78.5% dry.

(The amendment ultimately was adopted by all the States except Connecticut and Rhode Island.)

AMENDMENT XIX.

Giving nationwide suffrage to women.

(Proposed by Congress June 4, 1919; ratified Aug. 18, 1920.)

The right of citizens of the United States to vote shall not be denied or abridged by the United States or by any State on account of sex.

Congress shall have power to enforce this Article by appropriate legislation.

AMENDMENT XX.

Terms of President and Vice President to begin on Jan. 20; those of Senators, Representatives, Jan. 3.

(Proposed by Congress Mar. 2, 1932; ratified Jan. 23, 1933.)

1. The terms of the President and Vice President shall end at noon on the 20th day of January, and the terms of Senators and Representatives at noon on the 3d day of January, of the years in which such terms would have ended if this article had not been ratified; and the terms of their successors shall then begin.

2. The Congress shall assemble at least once in every year, and such meeting shall begin at noon on the 3d day of January, unless they shall by law appoint a different day.

3. If, at the time fixed for the beginning of the term of the President, the President elect shall have died, the Vice President elect shall become President. If a President shall not have been chosen before the time fixed for the beginning of his term, or if the President elect shall have failed to qualify, then the Vice President elect shall act as President until a President shall have qualified; and the Congress may by law provide for the case wherein neither a President elect nor a Vice President elect shall have qualified, declaring who shall then act as President, or the manner in which one who is to act shall be selected, and such person shall act accordingly until a President or Vice President shall have qualified.

4. The Congress may by law provide for the case of the death of any of the persons from whom the House of Representatives may choose a President whenever the right of choice shall have devolved upon them, and for the case of the death of any of the persons from whom the Senate may choose a Vice President whenever the right of choice shall have devolved upon them.

5. Sections 1 and 2 shall take effect on the 15th day of October following the ratification of this article (Oct. 1933).

6. This article shall be inoperative unless it shall have been ratified as an amendment to the Constitution by the legislatures of three-fourths of the several States within seven years from the date of its submission.

AMENDMENT XXI.

Repeal of Amendment XVIII.

(Proposed by Congress Feb. 20, 1933; ratified Dec. 5, 1933.)

1. The eighteenth article of amendment to the Constitution of the United States is hereby repealed.

2. The transportation or importation into any State, Territory, or possession of the United States for delivery or use therein of intoxicating liquors, in violation of the laws thereof, is hereby prohibited.

3. This article shall be inoperative unless it shall have been ratified as an amendment to the Constitution by conventions in the several States, as provided in the Constitution, within seven years from the date of the submission hereof to the States by the Congress.

AMENDMENT XXII.

Limiting Presidential terms of office.

(Proposed by Congress Mar. 24, 1947; ratified Feb. 27, 1951.)

1. No person shall be elected to the office of the President more than twice, and no person who has held the office of President, or acted as President, for more than two years of a term to which some other person was elected President shall be elected to the office of the President more than once. But this Article shall not apply to any person holding the office of

President when this Article was proposed by the Congress, and shall not prevent any person who may be holding the office of President, or acting as President, during the term within which this Article becomes operative from holding the office of President or acting as President during the remainder of such term.

2. This article shall be inoperative unless it shall have been ratified as an amendment to the Constitution by the legislatures of three-fourths of the several States within seven years from the date of its submission to the States by the Congress.

AMENDMENT XXIII.

Presidential vote for District of Columbia.

(Proposed by Congress June 16, 1960; ratified Mar. 29, 1961.)

1. The District constituting the seat of Government of the United States shall appoint in such manner as the Congress may direct:

A number of electors of President and Vice President equal to the whole number of Senators and Representatives in Congress to which the District would be entitled if it were a State, but in no event more than the least populous State; they shall be in addition to those appointed by the States, but they shall be considered, for the purposes of the election of President and Vice President, to be electors appointed by a State; and they shall meet in the District and perform such duties as provided by the twelfth article of amendment.

2. The Congress shall have power to enforce this article by appropriate legislation.

AMENDMENT XXIV.

Barring poll tax in federal elections.

(Proposed by Congress Aug. 27, 1962; ratified Jan. 23, 1964.)

1. The right of citizens of the United States to vote in any primary or other election for President or Vice President, for electors for President or Vice President, or for Senator or Representative in Congress, shall not be denied or abridged by the United States or any State by reason of failure to pay any poll tax or other tax.

2. The Congress shall have power to enforce this article by appropriate legislation.

AMENDMENT XXV.

Presidential disability and succession.

(Proposed by Congress July 6, 1965; ratified Feb. 10, 1967.)

1. In case of the removal of the President from office or of his death or resignation, the Vice President shall become President.

2. Whenever there is a vacancy in the office of the Vice President, the President shall nominate a Vice President who shall take office upon confirmation by a majority vote of both houses of Congress.

3. Whenever the President transmits to the President pro tempore of the Senate and the Speaker of the House of Representatives his written declaration that he is unable to discharge the powers and duties of his office, and until he transmits to them a written declaration to the contrary, such powers and duties shall be discharged by the Vice President as Acting President.

4. Whenever the Vice President and a majority of either the principal officers of the executive departments or of such other body as Congress may by law provide, transmit to the President pro tempore of the Senate and the Speaker of the House of Representatives their written declaration that the President is unable to discharge the powers and duties of his office, the Vice President shall immediately assume the powers and duties of the office as Acting President.

Thereafter, when the President transmits to the President pro tempore of the Senate and the Speaker of the House of Representatives his written declaration that no inability exists, he shall resume the powers and duties of his office unless the Vice President and a majority of either the principal officers of the executive department or of such other body as Congress may by law provide, transmit within four days to the President pro tempore of the Senate and the Speaker of the House of Representatives their written declaration that the President is unable to discharge the powers and duties of his office. Thereupon Congress shall decide the issue, assembling within forty-eight hours for that purpose if not in session. If the Congress, within twenty-one days after receipt of the latter written declaration, or, if Congress is not in session, within twenty-one days after Congress is required to assemble, determines by two-thirds vote of both Houses that the President is unable to discharge the powers and duties of his office, the Vice President shall continue to discharge the same as Acting President; otherwise, the President shall resume the powers and duties of his office.

AMENDMENT XXVI.

Lowering voting age to 18 years.

(Proposed by Congress Mar. 23, 1971; ratified July 1, 1971.)

1. The right of citizens of the United States, who are eighteen years of age or older, to vote shall not be denied or abridged by the United States or by any State on account of age.

2. The Congress shall have the power to enforce this article by appropriate legislation.

AMENDMENT XXVII.

Congressional pay.

(Proposed by Congress Sept. 25, 1789; ratified May 7, 1992.)

No law, varying the compensation for the services of the Senators and Representatives, shall take effect, until an election of Representatives shall have intervened.

How a Bill Becomes a Law

1. A senator or representative introduces a bill by sending it to the clerk of the House or the Senate, who assigns it a number and title. This procedure is termed the first reading. The clerk then refers the bill to the appropriate Senate or House committee.

2. If the committee opposes the bill, it will table, or kill, it. Otherwise, the committee holds hearings to listen to opinions and facts offered by members and other interested people. The committee then debates the bill and possibly offers amendments. A vote is taken, and if favorable, the bill is sent back to the clerk of the House or Senate.

3. The clerk reads the bill to the house—the second reading. Members may then debate the bill and suggest amendments.

4. After debate and possibly amendment, the bill is given a third reading, simply of the title, and put to a voice or roll-call vote.

5. If passed, the bill goes to the other house, where it may be defeated or passed, with or without amendments. If defeated, the bill dies. If passed with amendments, a conference committee made up of members of both houses works out the differences and arrives at a compromise.

6. After passage of the final version by both houses, the bill is sent to the president. If the president signs it, the bill becomes a law. The president may, however, veto the bill by refusing to sign it and sending it back to the house where it originated, with reasons for the veto.

7. The president's objections are then read and debated, and a roll-call vote is taken. If the bill receives less than a two-thirds majority, it is defeated. If it receives at least two-thirds, it is sent to the other house. If that house also passes it by at least a two-thirds majority, the veto is overridden, and the bill becomes a law.

8. If the president neither signs nor vetoes the bill within 10 days—not including Sundays—it automatically becomes a law even without the president's signature. However, if Congress has adjourned within those 10 days, the bill is automatically killed; this indirect rejection is termed a pocket veto.

Note: Under "line-item veto" legislation effective Jan. 1, 1997, the president could also, under certain circumstances, eliminate a tax cut or expenditure (not including entitlements such as Medicare or Social Security) in a bill without vetoing the whole bill.

Confederate States and Secession

The American Civil War (1861-65) grew out of sectional disputes over the continued existence of slavery in the South and the contention of Southern legislators that the states retained many rights, including the right to secede.

The war was not fought by state against state but by one federal regime against another, the Confederate government in Richmond assuming control over the economic, political, and military life of the South, under protest from Georgia and South Carolina.

South Carolina voted an ordinance of secession from the Union, repealing its 1788 ratification of the U.S. Constitution on Dec. 20, 1860, to take effect on Dec. 24. Other states seceded in 1861. Their votes in conventions were: Mississippi, Jan. 9, 84-15; Florida, Jan. 10, 62-7; Alabama, Jan. 11, 61-39; Georgia, Jan. 19, 208-89; Louisiana, Jan. 26, 113-17; Texas, Feb. 1, 166-7, ratified by popular vote on Feb. 23 (for 34,794, against 11,325); Virginia, Apr. 17, 88-55, ratified by popular vote on May 23 (for 128,884; against 32,134); Arkansas, May 6, 69-1; Tennessee, May 7,

ratified by popular vote on June 8 (for 104,019, against 47,238); North Carolina, May 21.

Missouri Unionists stopped secession in conventions Feb. 28 and Mar. 9. The legislature condemned secession Mar. 7. Under the protection of Confederate troops, secessionist members of the legislature adopted a resolution of secession at Neosho, Oct. 31. The Confederate Congress seated the secessionists' representatives.

Kentucky did not secede, and its government remained Unionist. In a part of the state occupied by Confederate troops, Kentuckians approved secession, and the Confederate Congress admitted their representatives.

The Maryland legislature voted against secession Apr. 27, 53-13. Delaware did not secede. Western Virginia held conventions at Wheeling, named a pro-Union governor on June 11, 1861, and was admitted to the Union as West Virginia on June 20, 1863. Its constitution provided for gradual abolition of slavery.

Confederate Government

Forty-two delegates from South Carolina, Georgia, Alabama, Mississippi, Louisiana, and Florida met in convention at Montgomery, AL, on Feb. 4, 1861. They adopted a provisional constitution of the Confederate States of America and elected Jefferson Davis (MS) as provisional president and Alexander H. Stephens (GA) as provisional vice president.

A permanent constitution was adopted Mar. 11. It abolished the African slave trade, but it did not bar interstate

commerce in slaves. On July 20 the Congress moved to Richmond, VA. Davis was elected president in October and was inaugurated on Feb. 22, 1862.

The Congress adopted a flag, consisting of a red field with a white stripe, and a blue jack with a circle of white stars. Later the more popular flag was the red field with blue diagonal crossbars that held 13 white stars, for the 11 states in the Confederacy plus Kentucky and Missouri.

Lincoln's Address at Gettysburg, 1863

Fourscore and seven years ago our fathers brought forth on this continent a new nation, conceived in liberty and dedicated to the proposition that all men are created equal.

Now we are engaged in a great civil war, testing whether that nation or any nation so conceived and so dedicated can long endure. We are met on a great battle field of that war. We have come to dedicate a portion of that field, as a final resting-place for those who here gave their lives that that nation might live. It is altogether fitting and proper that we should do this.

But, in a larger sense, we can not dedicate—we can not consecrate—we can not hallow—this ground. The brave men, living and dead, who struggled here, have consecrated

it, far above our poor power to add or detract. The world will little note, nor long remember, what we say here, but it can never forget what they did here. It is for us the living, rather, to be dedicated here to the unfinished work which they who fought here have thus far so nobly advanced. It is rather for us to be here dedicated to the great task remaining before us—that from these honored dead we take increased devotion to that cause for which they gave the last full measure of devotion—that we here highly resolve that these dead shall not have died in vain—that this nation, under God, shall have a new birth of freedom—and that government of the people, by the people, for the people, shall not perish from the earth.

Selected Landmark Decisions of the U.S. Supreme Court

1803: Marbury v. Madison. The Court ruled that Congress exceeded its power in the Judiciary Act of 1789; the Court thus established its power to review acts of Congress and declare invalid those it found in conflict with the Constitution.

1819: McCulloch v. Maryland. The Court ruled that Congress had the authority to charter a national bank, under the Constitution's granting of the power to enact all laws "necessary and proper" to responsibilities of government.

1819: Trustees of Dartmouth College v. Woodward. The Court ruled that a state could not arbitrarily alter the terms of a college's contract. (In later years the Court used a similar principle to limit the states' ability to interfere with business contracts.)

1857: Dred Scott v. Sanford. The Court declared unconstitutional the already-repealed Missouri Compromise of 1820 because it deprived a person of his or her property—a slave—without due process of law. The Court also ruled that slaves were not citizens of any state nor of the U.S. (The latter part of the decision was overturned by ratification of the 14th Amendment in 1868.)

1896: Plessy v. Ferguson. The Court ruled that a state law requiring federal railroad trains to provide separate but equal facilities for black and white passengers neither in-

fringed upon federal authority to regulate interstate commerce nor violated the 13th and 14th Amendments. (The "separate but equal" doctrine remained effective until the 1954 **Brown** v. **Board of Education** decision.)

1904: Northern Securities Co. v. U.S. The Court ruled that a holding company formed solely to eliminate competition between two railroad lines was a combination in restraint of trade, violating the federal antitrust act.

1908: Muller v. Oregon. The Court upheld a state law limiting the working hours of women. (Instead of presenting legal arguments, Louis D. Brandeis, counsel for the state, brought forth evidence from social workers, physicians, and factory inspectors that the number of hours women worked affected their health and morals.)

1911: Standard Oil Co. of New Jersey et al. v. U.S. The Court ruled that the Standard Oil Trust must be dissolved because of its unreasonable restraint of trade.

1919: Schenck v. U.S. The Court sustained the Espionage Act of 1917, maintaining that freedom of speech and press could be constrained if "the words used . . . create a clear and present danger. . ."

1925: Gitlow v. New York. The Court ruled that the First Amendment prohibition against government abridgment of the freedom of speech applied to the states as well as to the federal government. The decision was the first of a number of rulings holding that the 14th Amendment extended the guarantees of the Bill of Rights to state action.

1935: Schechter Poultry Corp. v. U.S. The Court ruled that Congress exceeded its authority to delegate legislative powers and to regulate interstate commerce when it enacted the National Industrial Recovery Act, which afforded the U.S. president too much discretionary power.

1951: Dennis et al. v. U.S. The Court upheld convictions under the Smith Act of 1940 for speaking about Communist theory that advocated the forcible overthrow of the government. (In the **1957 Yates v. U.S.** decision, the Court moderated this ruling by allowing such advocacy in the abstract, if not connected to action to achieve the goal.)

1954: Brown v. Board of Education of Topeka. The Court ruled that separate public schools for black and white students were inherently unequal, so that state-sanctioned segregation in public schools violated the equal protection guarantee of the 14th Amendment. And in **Bolling v. Sharpe** the Court ruled that the congressionally mandated segregated public school system in the District of Columbia violated the 5th Amendment's due process guarantee of personal liberty. (The Brown ruling also led to abolition of state-sponsored segregation in other public facilities.)

1957: Roth v. U.S., Alberts v. California. The Court ruled obscene material was not protected by First Amendment guarantees of freedom of speech and press, defining obscene as "utterly without redeeming social value" and appealing to "prurient interests" in the view of the average person. This definition was modified in later decisions, and the "average person" standard was replaced by the "local community" standard in **Miller v. California (1973).**

1961: Mapp v. Ohio. The Court ruled that evidence obtained in violation of the 4th Amendment guarantee against unreasonable search and seizure must be excluded from use at state as well as federal trials.

1962: Engel v. Vitale. The Court ruled that public school officials could not require pupils to recite a state-composed prayer at the start of each school day, even if the prayer was nondenominational and voluntary, because such official state sanction of religious utterances was an unconstitutional attempt to establish religion.

1962: Baker v. Carr. The Court held that the constitutional challenges to the unequal distribution of voters among legislative districts could be resolved by federal courts, rejecting its own **1946** precedent.

1963: Gideon v. Wainwright. The Court ruled that the due process clause of the 14th Amendment extended to state as well as federal defendants, so that all persons charged with serious crimes have access to an attorney, and at state expense if necessary.

1964: New York Times Co. v. Sullivan. The Court ruled that the First Amendment guarantee of freedom of the press protected the press from libel suits for defamatory reports on public officials unless it was proved that the reports were made from malice. The Court defined malice as "with knowledge that [the defamatory statement] was false or with reckless disregard of whether it was false or not."

1965: Griswold v. Conn. The Court ruled that a state unconstitutionally interfered with personal privacy in the marriage relationship when it prohibited anyone, including married couples, from using contraceptives.

1966: Miranda v. Arizona. The Court ruled that the guarantee of due process required that before questioning of suspects in police custody, suspects must be informed that they have the right to remain silent, that anything they say may be used against them, and that they have the right to counsel.

1973: Roe v. Wade, Doe v. Bolton. The Court ruled that the fetus was not a "person" with constitutional rights and that a right to privacy inherent in the 14th Amendment's due process guarantee of personal liberty protected a woman's decision to have an abortion. During the first tri-mester of pregnancy, the Court maintained, the decision should be left entirely to a woman and her physician. Some regulation of abortion procedures was allowed in the 2d trimester, and some restriction of abortion in the 3d.

1974: U.S. v. Nixon. The Court ruled that neither the separation of powers nor the need to preserve the confidentiality of presidential communications could alone justify an absolute executive privilege of immunity from judicial demands for evidence to be used in a criminal trial.

1976: Gregg v. Georgia, Profitt v. Fla., Jurek v. Texas. The Court held that death, as a punishment for persons convicted of first degree murder, was not in and of itself cruel and unusual punishment in violation of the 8th Amendment. But the Court ruled that the sentencing judge and jury must consider the individual character of the offender and the circumstances of the particular crime. In the associated **Woodson v. N.C., Roberts v. La.,** the Court ruled that states could not make death a mandatory penalty regardless of circumstances.

1978: Regents of Univ. of Calif. v. Bakke. The Court ruled that a special admissions program for a state medical school, under which a set number of places were reserved for minorities only, violated Title XIV of the 1964 Civil Rights Act, which forbids the exclusion of anyone, because of race, from a federally funded program. However, the Court ruled that admissions programs that considered race as one of a complex of factors involved were not unconstitutional.

1986: Bowers v. Hardwick. The Court refused to extend any constitutional right of privacy to homosexual activity, upholding a Georgia law that in effect made such activity a crime. (Although the Georgia law specifically prohibited sodomy, whether heterosexual or homosexual, enforcement had been confined to homosexual sodomy.) In **Romer v. Evans (1996),** however, the Court struck down a Colorado constitutional provision that barred legislation protecting homosexuals from discrimination.

1990: Cruzan v. Missouri. The Court ruled that a person had the right to refuse life-sustaining medical treatment. However, the Court also ruled that, before treatment could be withheld from a comatose patient, a state could require "clear and convincing evidence" that the patient would not have wanted to live. And in 2 **1997** rulings, **Washington v. Glucksberg** and **Vacco v. Quill,** the Court ruled that states could ban doctor-assisted suicide.

1995: Adarand Constructors v. Peña. The Court held that federal programs that classify people by race, unless "narrowly tailored" to accomplish a "compelling governmental interest," may deny individuals the right to equal protection. Such federal programs, the Court maintained, must adhere to the same strict standards required of state-run affirmative action programs.

1995: U.S. Term Limits Inc. v. Thorton. The Court ruled that it is unconstitutional for either the states or Congress to limit the terms of members of Congress, since the Constitution reserves to the people the right to choose federal lawmakers.

1997: Clinton v. Jones. Rejecting an appeal by Pres. Clinton in a sexual harassment suit, the Court ruled that a sitting president did not have temporary immunity from facing a civil lawsuit for actions outside the realm of official duties.

1997: City of Boerne v. Flores. The Court overturned the 1993 Religious Freedom Restoration Act, portions of which banned enforcement of laws that "substantially burden" religious practice unless there is a "compelling need" to do so. The Court held that the act was both an unwarranted intrusion by Congress on the traditional prerogatives of the states and an infringement of the judiciary's power to interpret the Constitution.

1997: Reno v. ACLU. Citing the right to free expression, the Court overturned a provision in a 1996 federal law making it a crime to display or distribute "indecent" or "patently offensive" material on the Internet.

Presidential Oath of Office

The Constitution (Article II) directs that the president shall take the following oath or affirmation: "I do solemnly swear (affirm) that I will faithfully execute the office of President of the United States, and will, to the best of my ability, preserve, protect, and defend the Constitution of the United States." (Custom decrees the use of the words "So help me God" at the end of the oath when taken by the president-elect, his or her left hand on the Bible for the duration of the oath, with his or her right hand slightly raised.)

Law on Succession to the Presidency

If by reason of death, resignation, removal from office, inability, or failure to qualify there is neither a president nor vice president to discharge the powers and duties of the office of president, then the speaker of the House of Representatives shall upon his resignation as speaker and as representative, act as president. The same rule shall apply in the case of the death, resignation, removal from office, or inability of an individual acting as president.

If at the time when a speaker is to begin the discharge of the powers and duties of the office of president there is no speaker, or the speaker fails to qualify as acting president, then the president pro tempore of the Senate, upon his resignation as president pro tempore and as senator, shall act as president.

An individual acting as president shall continue to act until the expiration of the then current presidential term, except that (1) if his discharge of the powers and duties of the office is founded in whole or in part in the failure of both the president-elect and the vice president-elect to

qualify, then he shall act only until a president or vice president qualifies, and (2) if his discharge of the powers and duties of the office is founded in whole or in part on the inability of the president or vice president, then he shall act only until the removal of the disability of one of such individuals.

If, by reason of death, resignation, removal from office, or failure to qualify, there is no president pro tempore to act as president, then the officer of the United States who is highest on the following list, and who is not under any disability to discharge the powers and duties of president shall act as president; the secretaries of state, treasury, defense, attorney general; secretaries of interior, agriculture, commerce, labor, health and human services, housing and urban development, transportation, energy, education, veterans affairs.

(Legislation approved July 18, 1947; amended Sept. 9, 1965, Oct. 15, 1966, Aug. 4, 1977, and Sept. 27, 1979. See also Constitutional Amendment XXV.)

Origin of the United States National Motto

In God We Trust, designated as the U.S. National Motto by Congress in 1956, originated during the Civil War as an inscription for U. S. coins, although it was used by Francis Scott Key in a slightly different form when he wrote "The Star-Spangled Banner" in 1814. On Nov. 13, 1861, when Union morale had been shaken by battlefield defeats, the Rev. M. R. Watkinson, of Ridleyville, PA, wrote to Secy. of the Treasury Salmon P. Chase. "From my heart I have felt our national shame in disowning God

as not the least of our present national disasters," the minister wrote, suggesting "recognition of the Almighty God in some form on our coins." Secy. Chase ordered designs prepared with the inscription *In God We Trust* and backed coinage legislation that authorized use of this slogan. It first appeared on some U.S. coins in 1864, disappeared and reappeared on various coins until 1955, when Congress ordered it placed on all paper money and all coins.

The Great Seal of the U.S.

On July 4, 1776, the Continental Congress appointed a committee consisting of Benjamin Franklin, John Adams, and Thomas Jefferson "to bring in a device for a seal of the United States of America." The designs submitted by this and a subsequent committee were considered unacceptable. After many delays, a third committee, appointed early in 1782, presented a design prepared by William Barton. Charles Thomson, the secretary of

Congress, suggested certain changes, and Congress finally approved the design on June 20, 1782. The obverse side of the seal shows an American bald eagle. In its mouth is a ribbon bearing the motto *e pluribus unum* (one out of many). In the eagle's talons are the arrows of war and an olive branch of peace. The reverse side shows an unfinished pyramid with an eye (the eye of Providence) above it.

The American's Creed

William Tyler Page, Clerk of the U.S. House of Representatives, wrote "The American's Creed" in 1917. It was accepted by the House on behalf of the American people on April 3, 1918.

"I believe in the United States of America as a government of the people, by the people, for the people; whose just powers are derived from the consent of the governed; a democracy in a republic; a sovereign Nation of many sovereign States; a perfect union, one and inseparable; established upon those

principles of freedom, equality, justice, and humanity for which American patriots sacrificed their lives and fortunes.

"I therefore believe it is my duty to my country to love it, to support its Constitution, to obey its laws, to respect its flag, and to defend it against all enemies."

The Flag of the U.S.—The Stars and Stripes

The 50-star flag of the United States was raised for the first time officially at 12:01 AM on July 4, 1960, at Fort McHenry National Monument in Baltimore, MD. The 50th star had been added for Hawaii; a year earlier the 49th, for Alaska. Before that, no star had been added since 1912, when New Mexico and Arizona were admitted to the Union.

The true history of the Stars and Stripes has become so cluttered by myth and tradition that the facts are difficult, and in some cases impossible, to establish. For example, it is not certain who designed the Stars and Stripes, who made the first such flag, or even whether it ever flew in any sea fight or land battle of the American Revolution.

All agree, however, that the Stars and Stripes originated as the result of a resolution offered by the Marine Commit-

tee of the Second Continental Congress at Philadelphia and adopted on June 14, 1777. It read:

Resolved: that the flag of the United States be thirteen stripes, alternate red and white; that the union be thirteen stars, white in a blue field, representing a new constellation.

Congress gave no hint as to the designer of the flag, no instructions as to the arrangement of the stars, and no information on its appropriate uses. Historians have been unable to find the original flag law.

The resolution establishing the flag was not even published until Sept. 2, 1777. Despite repeated requests, Washington did not get the flags until 1783, after the American Revolution was over. And there is no certainty that they were the Stars and Stripes.

Early Flags

Many historians consider the first flag of the U.S. to have been the Grand Union (sometimes called Great Union) flag, although the Continental Congress never officially adopted it. This flag was a modification of the British Meteor flag, which had the red cross of St. George and the white cross of St. Andrew combined in the blue canton. For the Grand Union flag, 6 horizontal stripes were imposed on the red field, dividing it into 13 alternating red and white stripes. On Jan. 1, 1776, when the Continental Army came into formal existence, this flag was unfurled on Prospect Hill, Somerville, MA. Washington wrote that "we hoisted the Union Flag in compliment to the United Colonies."

One of several flags about which controversy has raged for years is at Easton, PA. Containing the devices of the national flag in reversed order, this flag has been in the public library at Easton for more than 150 years. Some contend that this flag was actually the first Stars and Stripes, first displayed on July 8, 1776. This flag has 13 red and white stripes in the canton, 13 white stars centered in a blue field.

A flag was hastily improvised from garments by the defenders of Fort Schuyler at Rome, NY, Aug. 3-22, 1777. Historians believe it was the Grand Union Flag.

The Sons of Liberty had a flag of 9 red and white stripes, to signify 9 colonies, when they met in New York in 1765 to oppose the Stamp Tax. By 1775, the flag had grown to 13 red and white stripes, with a rattlesnake on it.

At Concord, Apr. 19, 1775, the minutemen from Bedford, MA, are said to have carried a flag having a silver arm with sword on a red field. At Cambridge, MA, the Sons of Liberty used a plain red flag with a green pine tree on it.

In June 1775, Washington went from Philadelphia to Boston to take command of the army, escorted to New York by the Philadelphia Light Horse Troop. It carried a yellow flag that had an elaborate coat of arms—the shield charged with 13 knots, the motto "For These We Strive"—and a canton of 13 blue and silver stripes.

In Feb. 1776, Col. Christopher Gadsden, a member of the Continental Congress, gave the South Carolina Provincial Congress a flag "such as is to be used by the commander-in-chief of the American Navy." It had a yellow field, with a rattlesnake about to strike and the words "Don't Tread on Me."

At the Battle of Bennington, Aug. 16, 1777, patriots used a flag of 7 white and 6 red stripes with a blue canton extending down 9 stripes and showing an arch of 11 white stars over the figure 76 and a star in each of the upper corners. The stars are 7-pointed. This flag is preserved in the Historical Museum at Bennington, VT.

At the Battle of Cowpens, Jan. 17, 1781, the 3d Maryland Regiment is said to have carried a flag of 13 red and white stripes, with a blue canton containing 12 stars in a circle around one star.

Who Designed the Flag? No one knows for certain. Francis Hopkinson, designer of a naval flag, declared he also had designed the flag and in 1781 asked Congress to reimburse him for his services. Congress did not do so. Dumas Malone of Columbia University wrote: "This talented man . . . designed the American flag."

Who Called the Flag "Old Glory"? The flag is said to have been named Old Glory by William Driver, a sea captain of Salem, MA. One legend has it that when he raised the flag on his brig, the *Charles Doggett*, in 1824, he said: "I name thee Old Glory." But his daughter, who presented the flag to the Smithsonian Institution, said he named it at his 21st birthday celebration on Mar. 17, 1824, when his mother presented the homemade flag to him.

The Betsy Ross Legend. The widely publicized legend that Mrs. Betsy Ross made the first Stars and Stripes in June 1776, at the request of a committee composed of George Washington, Robert Morris, and George Ross, an uncle, was first made public in 1870, by a grandson of Mrs. Ross. Historians have been unable to find a historical record of such a meeting or committee.

Adding New Stars

The flag of 1777 was used until 1795. Then, on the admission of Vermont and Kentucky to the Union, Congress passed and Pres. Washington signed an act that after May 1, 1795, the flag should have 15 stripes, alternating red and white, and 15 white stars on a blue field.

When new states were admitted, it became evident that the flag would become burdened with stripes. Congress thereupon ordered that after July 4, 1818, the flag should have 13 stripes, symbolizing the 13 original states; that the union have 20 stars, and that whenever a new state was admitted a new star should be added on the July 4 following admission. No law designates the permanent arrangement of the stars. However, since 1912, when a new state has been admitted, the new design has been announced by executive order. No star is specifically identified with any state.

Code of Etiquette for Display and Use of the U.S. Flag

Reviewed by National Flag Foundation

Although the Stars and Stripes originated in 1777, it was not until 146 years later that there was a serious attempt to establish a uniform code of etiquette for the U.S. flag. On Feb. 15, 1923, the War Department issued a circular on the rules of flag usage. These rules were adopted almost in their entirety June 14, 1923, by a conference of 68 patriotic organizations in Washington. Finally, on June 22, 1942, a joint resolution of Congress, amended by Public Law 94-344 July 7, 1976, codified "existing rules and customs pertaining to the display and use of the flag . . ."

When to Display the Flag—The flag should be displayed on all days, especially on legal holidays and other special occasions, on official buildings when in use, in or near polling places on election days, and in or near schools when in session. Citizens may fly the flag at any time. It is customary to display the flag only from sunrise to sunset on buildings and on stationary flagstaffs in the open. It may be displayed at night, however, on special occasions, preferably lighted. In Washington, the flag now flies over the White House both day and night. It flies over the Senate wing of the Capitol when the Senate is in session and over the House wing when that body is in session. It flies day and night over the east and west fronts of the Capitol, without floodlights at night but receiving light from the illuminated Capitol Dome. It flies 24 hours a day at several other places, including the Fort McHenry National Monument in Baltimore, where it inspired Francis Scott Key to write "The Star Spangled Banner." The flag also flies 24 hours a day, properly illuminated, at U.S. Customs ports of entry.

Flying the Flag at Half-Staff—Flying the flag at half-staff, that is, halfway up the staff, is a signal of mourning. The flag should be hoisted to the top of the staff for an instant before being lowered to half-staff. It should be hoisted to the peak again before being lowered for the day or night.

As provided by presidential proclamation, the flag should fly at half-staff for 30 days from the day of death of a president or former president; for 10 days from the day of death of a vice president, chief justice or retired chief justice of the U.S., or speaker of the House of Representatives; from day of death until burial of an associate justice of the Supreme Court, cabinet member, former vice president, Senate president pro tempore, or majority or minority Senate or House leader; for a U.S. senator, representative, territorial delegate, or the resident commissioner of Puerto Rico, on day of death and the following day within the metropolitan area of the District of Columbia and from day of death until burial within the decedent's state, congressional district, territory or commonwealth; and for the death of the governor of a state, territory, or possession of the U.S., from day of death until burial.

On Memorial Day, the flag should fly at half-staff until noon and then be raised to the peak. The flag should also fly at half-staff on Korean War Veterans Armistice Day (July 27), National Pearl Harbor Remembrance Day (Dec. 7), and Peace Officers Memorial Day (May 15).

How to Fly the Flag—The flag should be hoisted briskly and lowered ceremoniously and should never be allowed to touch the ground or the floor. When the flag is hung over a sidewalk from a rope extending from a building to a pole, the union should be away from the building. When the flag is hung over the center of a street the union should be to the north in an east-west street and to the east in a north-south street. No other flag may be flown above or, if on the same level, to the right of the U.S. flag, except that at the United Nations Headquarters the UN flag may be placed above flags of all member nations and other national flags may be flown with equal prominence or honor with the flag of the U.S. At services by Navy chaplains at sea, the church pennant may be flown above the flag.

When 2 flags are placed against a wall with crossed staffs, the U.S. flag should be at right—its own right, and its staff should be in front of the staff of the other flag; when a number of flags are grouped and displayed from staffs, it should be at the center and highest point of the group.

Church and Platform Use—In an auditorium, the flag may be displayed flat, above and behind the speaker. When displayed from a staff in a church or in a public auditorium, the flag should hold the position of superior prominence, in advance of the audience, and in the position of honor at the speaker's right as she or he faces the audience. Any other flag so displayed should be placed on the left of the speaker or to the right of the audience.

When the flag is displayed horizontally or vertically against a wall, the stars should be uppermost and at the observer's left.

When used to cover a casket, the flag should be placed so that the union is at the head and over the left shoulder. It should not be lowered into the grave nor touch the ground.

How to Dispose of Worn Flags—When the flag is in such condition that it is no longer a fitting emblem for display, it should be destroyed in a dignified way, preferably by burning.

When to Salute the Flag—All persons present should face the flag, stand at attention, and salute on the following occasions: (1) when the flag is passing in a parade or in a review, (2) during the ceremony of hoisting or lowering, (3) when the national anthem is played, and (4) during the Pledge of Allegiance. Those present in uniform should render the military salute. Those not in uniform should place the right hand over the heart. A man wearing a hat should remove it with his right hand and hold it to his left shoulder during the salute.

Prohibited Uses of the Flag—The flag should not be dipped to any person or thing. (An exception—customarily, ships salute by dipping their colors.) It should never be displayed with the union down save as a distress signal. It should never be carried flat or horizontally, but always aloft and free.

It should not be displayed on a float, an automobile, or a boat except from a staff. It should never be used as a covering for a ceiling, nor have placed on it any word, design, or drawing. It should never be used as a receptacle for carrying anything. It should not be used to cover a statue or a monument.

The flag should never be used for advertising purposes, nor be embroidered on such articles as cushions or handkerchiefs, printed or otherwise impressed on boxes or anything that is designed for temporary use and discard; or used as a costume or athletic uniform. Advertising signs should not be fastened to its staff or halyard.

The flag should never be used as drapery of any sort, never festooned, drawn back, nor up, in folds, but always allowed to fall free. Bunting of blue, white, and red, always arranged with the blue above and the white in the middle, should be used for covering a speaker's desk, draping the front of a platform, and for decoration in general.

An act of Congress approved on Feb. 8, 1917, provided certain penalties for the desecration, mutilation, or improper use of the flag within the District of Columbia. A 1968 federal law provided penalties of as much as a year's imprisonment or a $1,000 fine or both for publicly burning or otherwise desecrating any U.S. flag. In addition, many states have laws against flag desecration. In 1989, the Supreme Court ruled that no laws could prohibit political protesters from burning the flag. The decision had the effect of declaring unconstitutional the flag desecration laws of 48 states, as well as a similar federal statute, in cases of peaceful political expression.

The Supreme Court, June 1990, declared that a new federal law making it a crime to burn or deface the American flag violates the free-speech guarantee of the First Amendment. The 5-4 decision led to renewed calls in Congress for a constitutional amendment to make it possible to prosecute flag burners.

Pledge of Allegiance to the Flag

I pledge allegiance to the flag of the United States of America and to the republic for which it stands, one nation under God, indivisible, with liberty and justice for all.

This, the current official version of the Pledge of Allegiance, has developed from the original pledge, which was first published in the Sept. 8, 1892, issue of *Youth's Companion*, a weekly magazine published in Boston. The original pledge contained the phrase "my flag," which was changed more than 30 years later to "flag of the United States of America." A 1954 act of Congress added the words "under God."

The authorship of the pledge had been in dispute for many years. The *Youth's Companion* stated in 1917 that the original draft was written by James B. Upham, an executive of the magazine who died in 1910. A leaflet circulated by the magazine later named Upham as the originator of the draft "afterwards condensed and perfected by him and his associates of the Companion force."

Francis Bellamy, a former member of *Youth's Companion* editorial staff, publicly claimed authorship of the pledge in 1923. The United States Flag Association, acting on the advice of a committee named to study the controversy, upheld in 1939 the claim of Bellamy, who had died 8 years earlier. The Library of Congress issued in 1957 a report attributing the authorship to Bellamy.

The History of the National Anthem

"The Star-Spangled Banner" was ordered played by the military and naval services by President Woodrow Wilson in 1916. It was designated the national anthem by Act of Congress, Mar. 3, 1931. It was written by Francis Scott Key, of Georgetown, MD, during the bombardment of Fort McHenry, Baltimore, MD, Sept. 13-14, 1814. Key was a lawyer, a graduate of St. John's College, Annapolis, and a volunteer in a light artillery company. When a friend, Dr. Beanes, a physician of Upper Marlborough, MD, was taken aboard Admiral Cockburn's British squadron for interfering with ground troops, Key and J. S. Skinner, carrying a note from President Madison, went to the fleet under a flag of truce on a cartel ship to ask Beanes's release. Cockburn consented, but as the fleet was about to sail up the Patapsco to bombard Fort McHenry, he detained them, first on HMS *Surprise* and then on a supply ship.

Key witnessed the bombardment from his own vessel. It began at 7 AM, Sept. 13, 1814, and lasted, with intermissions, for 25 hr. The British fired more than 1,500 shells, each weighing as much as 220 lb. They were unable to approach closely because the U.S. had sunk 22 vessels. Only 4 Americans were killed and 24 wounded. A British bomb-ship was disabled.

During the bombardment, Key wrote a stanza on the back of an envelope. Next day at Indian Queen Inn, Baltimore, he wrote out the poem and gave it to his brother-in-law, Judge J. H. Nicholson. Nicholson suggested the tune, Anacreon in Heaven, and had the poem printed on broadsides, of which 2 survive. On Sept. 20 it appeared in the *Baltimore American*. Later Key made 3 copies; one is in the Library of Congress, and one is in the Pennsylvania Historical Society.

The copy that Key wrote in his hotel on Sept. 14, 1814, remained in the Nicholson family for 93 years. In 1907 it was sold to Henry Walters of Baltimore. In 1934 it was bought at auction in New York from the Walters estate by the Walters Art Gallery, Baltimore, for $26,400. The Walters Gallery in 1953 sold the manuscript to the Maryland Historical Society for the same price.

The flag that Key saw during the bombardment is preserved in the Smithsonian Institution, Washington, DC. It is 30 by 42 ft and has 15 alternating red and white stripes and 15 stars, for the original 13 states plus Kentucky and Vermont. It was made by Mary Young Pickersgill. The Baltimore Flag House, a museum, occupies her premises, which were restored in 1953.

The Star-Spangled Banner

I

Oh, say can you see by the dawn's early light
  What so proudly we hailed at the twilight's last gleaming?
Whose broad stripes and bright stars thru the perilous fight,
  O'er the ramparts we watched were so gallantly streaming?
And the rocket's red glare, the bombs bursting in air,
  Gave proof through the night that our flag was still there.
Oh, say does that star-spangled banner yet wave
  O'er the land of the free and the home of the brave?

II

On the shore, dimly seen through the mists of the deep,
  Where the foe's haughty host in dread silence reposes,
What is that which the breeze, o'er the towering steep,
  As it fitfully blows, half conceals, half discloses?
Now it catches the gleam of the morning's first beam,
  In full glory reflected now shines in the stream:
'Tis the star-spangled banner! Oh long may it wave
  O'er the land of the free and the home of the brave!

III

And where is that band who so vauntingly swore
  That the havoc of war and the battle's confusion,
A home and a country should leave us no more!
  Their blood has washed out their foul footsteps' pollution.
No refuge could save the hireling and slave
  From the terror of flight, or the gloom of the grave:
And the star-spangled banner in triumph doth wave
  O'er the land of the free and the home of the brave!

IV

Oh! thus be it ever, when freemen shall stand
  Between their loved home and the war's desolation!
Blest with victory and peace, may the heav'n rescued land
  Praise the Power that hath made and preserved us a nation.
Then conquer we must, when our cause it is just,
  And this be our motto: "In God is our trust."
And the star-spangled banner in triumph shall wave
  O'er the land of the free and the home of the brave!

America
(My Country 'Tis of Thee)

First sung in public on July 4, 1831, at a service in the Park Street Church, Boston, the words were written by Rev. Samuel Francis Smith, a Baptist clergyman, who set them to a melody he found in a German songbook, unaware that it was the tune for the British anthem, "God Save the King/Queen."

My country, 'tis of thee,
Sweet land of liberty, Of thee I sing.
Land where my fathers died!
Land of the Pilgrims' pride!
From ev'ry mountainside,
Let freedom ring!

My native country, thee,
Land of the noble free,
Thy name I love.
I love thy rocks and rills,
Thy woods and templed hills;
My heart with rapture thrills
Like that above.

Let music swell the breeze,
And ring from all the trees
Sweet freedom's song.
Let mortal tongues awake;
Let all that breathe partake;
Let rocks their silence break,
The sound prolong.

Our fathers' God, to Thee,
Author of liberty,
To Thee we sing.
Long may our land be bright
With freedom's holy light;
Protect us by Thy might,
Great God, our King!

America, the Beautiful

Composed by Katharine Lee Bates, a Massachusetts educator and author, in 1893. It was inspired by the view Bates experienced atop Pikes Peak. Its final form was established in 1911 and is set to the music of Samuel A. Ward's "Materna."

O beautiful for spacious skies,
For amber waves of grain,
For purple mountain majesties
Above the fruited plain.
America! America!
God shed His grace on thee,
And crown thy good with brotherhood
From sea to shining sea.

O beautiful for pilgrim feet
Whose stern impassion'd stress
A thorough-fare for freedom beat
Across the wilderness.
America! America!
God mend thine ev'ry flaw,
Confirm thy soul in self control,
Thy liberty in law.

O beautiful for heroes prov'd
In liberating strife,
Who more than self their country lov'd
And mercy more than life.
America! America!
May God thy gold refine
Till all success be nobleness,
And ev'ry gain divine.

O beautiful for patriot dream
That sees beyond the years,
Thine alabaster cities gleam,
Undimmed by human tears.
America! America!
God shed His grace on thee,
And crown thy good with brotherhood
From sea to shining sea.

The Liberty Bell: Its History and Significance

The Liberty Bell, in Independence National Historical Park, Philadelphia, is an object of great reverence to Americans because of its association with the historic events of the American Revolution.

The original Province bell was ordered by Assembly Speaker and Chairman of the State House Superintendents Isaac Norris and was ordered from Thomas Lester, Whitechapel Foundry, London. It reached Philadelphia at the end of August 1752. It bore an inscription from Leviticus 25:10: "PROCLAIM LIBERTY THROUGHOUT ALL THE LAND UNTO ALL THE INHABITANTS THEREOF."

The bell was cracked by a stroke of its clapper in Sept. 1752 while it hung on a truss in the State House yard for testing. Pass & Stow, Philadelphia founders, recast the bell, adding 1½ ounces of copper to a pound of the original "Whitechapel" metal to reduce its high tone and brittleness. It was found that the bell contained too much copper, injuring its tone, so Pass & Stow recast it again, this time successfully.

In June 1753 the bell was hung in the old wooden steeple of the State House, erected on top of the brick tower. In use while the Continental Congress was in session in the State House, it rang out in defiance of British tax and trade restrictions, and it proclaimed the Boston Tea Party and the first public reading of the Declaration of Independence.

On Sept. 18, 1777, when the British Army was about to occupy Philadelphia, the bell was moved in a baggage train of the American Army to Allentown, PA, where it was hidden in the Zion Reformed Church until June 27, 1778. It was moved back to Philadelphia after the British left.

In July 1781 the wooden steeple became insecure and had to be taken down. The bell was lowered into the brick section of the tower, where it remained until 1828. Between 1828 and 1844 the old State House bell continued to ring during special occasions. It rang for the last time on Feb. 23, 1846. In 1852 it was placed on exhibition in the Declaration Chamber of Independence Hall.

In 1876, when many thousands of Americans visited Philadelphia for the Centennial Exposition, the bell was placed in its old wooden support in the tower hallway. In 1877 it was hung from the ceiling of the tower by a chain of 13 links. It was returned again to the Declaration Chamber and in 1896 taken back to the tower hall, where it occupied a glass case. In 1915 the case was removed so that the public might touch it. On Jan. 1, 1976, just after midnight to mark the opening of the Bicentennial Year, the bell was moved to a new glass and steel pavilion behind Independence Hall for easier viewing by the larger number of visitors expected during the year.

The measurements of the bell are: circumference around the lip, 12 ft ½ in; circumference around the crown, 6 ft 11¼ in; lip to the crown, 3 ft; height over the crown, 2 ft 3 in; thickness at lip, 3 in; thickness at crown, 1¼ in; weight, 2,080 lb; length of clapper, 3 ft 2 in; cost, £60 14s 5d.

The specific source of the crack in the bell is unknown.

Statue of Liberty National Monument

Since 1886, the Statue of Liberty Enlightening the World has stood as a symbol of freedom in New York harbor. It also commemorates French-American friendship, for it was given by the people of France and designed by French sculptor Frederic Auguste Bartholdi (1834-1904).

Edouard de Laboulaye, French historian and admirer of American political institutions, suggested that the French present a monument to the U.S., the latter to provide pedestal and site. Bartholdi visualized a colossal statue at the entrance of New York harbor, welcoming the peoples of the world with the torch of liberty.

On Washington's Birthday, Feb. 22, 1877, Congress approved the use of a site on Bedloe's Island suggested by Bartholdi. This island of 12 acres had been owned in the 17th century by a Walloon named Isaac Bedloe. It was called Bedloe's until Aug. 3, 1956, when Pres. Eisenhower approved a resolution of Congress changing the name to Liberty Island.

The statue was finished on May 21, 1884, and formally presented to the U.S. minister to France, Levi Parsons Morton, July 4, 1884, by Ferdinand de Lesseps, head of the Franco-American Union, promoter of the Panama Canal, and builder of the Suez Canal.

On Aug. 5, 1884, the Americans laid the cornerstone for the pedestal. This was to be built on the foundations of Fort Wood, which had been erected by the government in 1811. The American committee had raised $125,000, but this was found to be inadequate. Joseph Pulitzer, owner of the *New York World,* appealed on Mar. 16, 1885, for general donations. By Aug. 11, 1885, he had raised $100,000.

The statue arrived dismantled, in 214 packing cases, from Rouen, France, in June 1885. The last rivet of the statue was driven on Oct. 28, 1886, when Pres. Grover Cleveland dedicated the monument.

The statue weighs 450,000 lb, or 225 tons. The copper sheeting weighs 200,000 lb. There are 167 steps from the land level to the top of the pedestal, 168 steps inside the statue to the head, and 54 rungs on the ladder leading to the arm that holds the torch.

A $2.5 million building housing the American Museum of Immigration was opened by Pres. Richard Nixon on Sept. 26, 1972, at the base of the statue. It houses a permanent exhibition of photos, posters, and artifacts tracing the history of American immigration. The Statue of Liberty National Monument is administered by the National Park Service.

Two years of restoration work was completed before the statue's centennial celebration on July 4, 1986. Among other repairs, the multimillion dollar project included replacing the 1,600 wrought iron bands that hold the statue's copper skin to its frame, replacing its torch, and installing an elevator.

A 4-day extravaganza of concerts, tall ships, ethnic festivals, and fireworks celebrated the 100th anniversary. The festivities included Chief Justice Warren E. Burger's swearing-in of 5,000 new citizens on Ellis Island, while 20,000 others across the country were simultaneously sworn in through a satellite telecast.

The ceremonies were followed by others on Oct. 28, 1986, the statue's 100th birthday.

Dimensions of the Statue	Ft.	In.
Height from base to torch (45.3 meters)	151	1
Foundation of pedestal to torch (91.5 meters) . . .	305	1
Heel to top of head	111	1
Length of hand	16	5
Index finger	8	0
Circumference at second joint	3	6
Size of finger nail . . . . 13x10 in.		
Head from chin to cranium	17	3
Head thickness from ear to ear	10	0
Distance across the eye	2	6
Length of nose	4	6
Right arm, length	42	0
Right arm, greatest thickness.	12	0
Thickness of waist.	35	0
Width of mouth	3	0
Tablet, length	23	7
Tablet, width.	13	7
Tablet, thickness.	2	0

Emma Lazarus's Famous Poem

A poem by Emma Lazarus is graven on a tablet within the pedestal on which the Statue of Liberty stands.

The New Colossus
Not like the brazen giant of Greek fame,
With conquering limbs astride from land to land;
Here at our sea-washed, sunset gates shall stand
A mighty woman with a torch, whose flame
Is the imprisoned lightning, and her name
Mother of Exiles. From her beacon-hand
Glows world-wide welcome; her mild eyes command
The air-bridged harbor that twin cities frame.
"Keep ancient lands, your storied pomp!" cries she
With silent lips. "Give me your tired, your poor,
Your huddled masses yearning to breathe free,
The wretched refuse of your teeming shore.
Send these, the homeless, tempest-tost to me,
I lift my lamp beside the golden door!"

Ellis Island

Ellis Island was the gateway to America for more than 12 million immigrants between 1892 and 1924. In the late 18th century, Samuel Ellis, a New York City merchant, purchased the island and gave it his name. From Ellis, it passed to New York State, and the U.S. government bought it in 1808. In 1892 the government opened an immigration center on the island. The 27½-acre site eventually supported more than 35 buildings, including the Main Building with its Great Hall, in which as many as 5,000 people a day were processed during peak periods. Closed as an immigration station in 1954, Ellis Island was proclaimed part of the National Monument in 1965 by Pres. Lyndon B. Johnson. After an 8-year privately funded $156 million restoration project, Ellis Island was reopened as a museum in 1990. Artifacts, historic photographs and documents, oral histories, and ethnic music depicting 400 years of American immigration are housed in the museum. The museum also includes the American Immigrant Wall of Honor, inscribed with more than 520,000 names.

BIOGRAPHIES OF U.S. PRESIDENTS

George Washington (1789-97)

George Washington, first president, Federalist, was born on Feb. 22, 1732, in Wakefield on Pope's Creek, Westmoreland Co., VA, the son of Augustine and Mary Ball Washington. He spent his early childhood on a farm near Fredericksburg. His father died when George was 11. He studied mathematics and surveying, and when he was 16, he went to live with his elder half brother, Lawrence, who built and named Mount Vernon. George surveyed the lands of Thomas Fairfax in the Shenandoah Valley, keeping a diary. He accompanied Lawrence to Barbados, West Indies, where he contracted smallpox and was deeply scarred. Lawrence died in 1752, and George inherited his property. He valued land, and when he died, he owned 70,000 acres in Virginia and 40,000 acres in what is now West Virginia.

Washington's military service began in 1753, when Lt. Gov. Robert Dinwiddie of Virginia sent him on missions deep into Ohio country. He clashed with the French and had to surrender Fort Necessity on July 3, 1754. He was an aide to the British general Edward Braddock and was at his side when the army was ambushed and defeated (July 9, 1755) on a march to Fort Duquesne. He helped take Fort Duquesne from the French in 1758.

After Washington's marriage to Martha Dandridge Custis, a widow, in 1759, he managed his family estate at Mount Vernon. Although not at first for independence, he opposed the repressive measures of the British crown and took charge of the Virginia troops before war broke out. He was made commander of the newly created Continental Army by the Continental Congress on June 15, 1775.

The American victory was due largely to Washington's leadership. He was resourceful, a stern disciplinarian, and the one strong, dependable force for unity. Washington favored a federal government. He became chairman of the Constitutional Convention of 1787 and helped get the Constitution ratified. Unanimously elected president by the Electoral College, he was inaugurated Apr. 30, 1789, on the balcony of New York's Federal Hall.

He was reelected in 1792. Washington made an effort to avoid partisan politics as president.

Refusing to consider a 3d term, he retired to Mount Vernon in March 1797. He suffered acute laryngitis after a ride in snow and rain around his estate, was bled profusely, and died Dec. 14, 1799.

John Adams (1797-1801)

John Adams, 2d president, Federalist, was born on Oct. 30, 1735, in Braintree (now Quincy), MA, the son of John and Susanna Boylston Adams. He was a great-grandson of Henry Adams, who came from England in 1636. He graduated from Harvard in 1755 and then taught school and studied law. He married Abigail Smith in 1764. In 1765 he argued against taxation without representation before the royal governor. In 1770 he successfully defended in court the British soldiers who fired on civilians in the Boston Massacre. He was a delegate to the Continental Congress and a signer of the Declaration of Independence. In 1778, Congress sent Adams and John Jay to join Benjamin Franklin as diplomatic representatives in Europe. Because he ran second to Washington in Electoral College balloting in February 1789, Adams became the nation's first vice president; he was reelected in 1792.

In 1796 Adams was chosen president by the electors. His administration was marked by rivalry with Alexander Hamilton and a crisis in U.S.-French relations. He was extraordinarily unpopular for securing passage of the Alien and Sedition Acts in 1798. His foreign policy contributed significantly to the election of Thomas Jefferson in 1800.

Adams lived for a quarter century after he left office, during which time he wrote extensively. He died July 4, 1826, on the same day as Thomas Jefferson (the 50th anniversary of the Declaration of Independence).

Thomas Jefferson (1801-9)

Thomas Jefferson, 3d president, Democratic-Republican, was born on Apr. 13, 1743, in Shadwell in Goochland (now Albemarle) Co., VA, the son of Peter and Jane Randolph Jefferson. Peter died when Thomas was 14, leaving him 2,750 acres and his slaves. Jefferson attended (1760-62) the College of William and Mary, read Greek and Latin classics, and played the violin. In 1769 he was elected to the Virginia House of Burgesses. In 1770 he began building his home, Monticello, and in 1772 he married Martha Wayles Skelton, a wealthy widow. Jefferson helped establish the Virginia Committee of Correspondence. As a member of the Second Continental Congress he drafted the Declaration of Independence in late June 1776. He also was a member of the Virginia House of Delegates (1776-79) and was first elected governor of Virginia in 1779, succeeding Patrick Henry. He was reelected governor in 1780 but resigned in June 1781 after British troops invaded Virginia. During his term he wrote the statute on religious freedom. After his wife's death in 1782, Jefferson again became a delegate to the Congress, and in 1784 he drafted the report that was the basis for the Ordinances of 1784, 1785, and 1787. He was minister to France from 1785 to 1789, when George Washington appointed him secretary of state.

Jefferson's strong faith in the consent of the governed conflicted with the emphasis on executive control, favored by Alexander Hamilton, secretary of the Treasury, and Jefferson resigned on Dec. 31, 1793. In the 1796 election Jefferson was the Democratic-Republican candidate for president; John Adams won the election, and Jefferson became vice president. In 1800, Jefferson and Aaron Burr received equal Electoral College votes. The House of Representatives elected Jefferson president. Major events of his first term were the Louisiana Purchase (1803) and the Lewis and Clark Expedition. An important development during his second term was passage of the Embargo Act, barring U.S. ships from setting sail to foreign ports. Jefferson established the University of Virginia and designed its buildings. He died July 4, 1826, on the same day as John Adams (the 50th anniversary of the Declaration of Independence).

James Madison (1809-17)

James Madison, 4th president, Democratic-Republican, was born on Mar. 16, 1751, in Port Conway, King George Co., VA, the son of James and Eleanor Rose Conway Madison. Madison graduated from Princeton in 1771. He served in the Virginia Constitutional Convention (1776), and, in 1780, became a delegate to the Second Continental Congress. He was chief recorder at the Constitutional Convention in 1787 and supported ratification in the *Federalist Papers*, written with Alexander Hamilton and John Jay. In 1789, Madison was elected to the House of Representatives, where he helped frame the Bill of Rights and fought against passage of the Alien and Sedition Acts. In the 1790s, he helped found the Democratic-Republican Party, which ultimately became the Democratic Party. He became Jefferson's secretary of state in 1801.

Madison was elected president in 1808. His first term was marked by tensions with Great Britain, and his conduct of foreign policy was criticized by the Federalists and by his own party. Nevertheless, he was reelected in 1812, the year war was declared on Great Britain. The war that many considered a second American revolution ended with a treaty that settled none of the issues. Madison's most important action after the war was demilitarizing the U.S.-Canadian border.

In 1817, Madison retired to his estate, Montpelier, where he served as an elder statesman, "the last of the fathers." He edited his famous papers on the Constitutional Convention and helped found the University of Virginia, of which he became rector in 1826. He died June 28, 1836.

James Monroe (1817-25)

James Monroe, 5th president, Democratic-Republican, was born on Apr. 28, 1758, in Westmoreland Co., VA, the son of Spence and Eliza Jones Monroe. He entered the College of William and Mary in 1774 but left to serve in the 3d Virginia Regiment during the American Revolution. After the war, he studied law with Thomas Jefferson. In 1782 he was elected to the Virginia House of Delegates, and he served (1783-86) as a delegate to the Confederation Congress. He opposed ratification of the Constitution because it lacked a bill of rights. Monroe was elected to the U.S. Senate in 1790. In 1794 President George Washington appointed Monroe minister to France. He served twice as governor of Virginia (1799-1802, 1811). President Jefferson also sent him to France as minister (1803), and from 1803 to 1807 he served as minister to Great Britain.

In 1816 Monroe was elected president; he was reelected in 1820 with all but one Electoral College vote. His administration became known as the Era of Good Feeling. He obtained Florida from Spain, settled boundary disputes with Britain over Canada, and eliminated border forts. He supported the antislavery position that led to the Missouri Compromise. His most significant contribution was the Monroe Doctrine, which opposed European intervention in the Western Hemisphere and became a cornerstone of U.S. foreign policy.

Although Monroe retired to Oak Hill, VA, financial problems forced him to sell his property and move to New York City. He died there on July 4, 1831.

John Quincy Adams (1825-29)

John Quincy Adams, 6th president, independent Federalist, later Democratic-Republican, was born on July 11, 1767, in Braintree (now Quincy), MA, the son of John and Abigail Adams. His father was the 2d president. He studied abroad and at Harvard University from which he graduated in 1787. In 1803, he was elected to the U.S. Senate. President Monroe chose him as his secretary of state in 1817. In this capacity he negotiated the cession of the Floridas from Spain, supported exclusion of slavery in the Missouri Compromise, and helped formulate the Monroe Doctrine.

In 1824 Adams was elected president by the House of Representatives after he failed to win an Electoral College majority. His expansion of executive powers was strongly opposed, and in the 1828 election he lost to Andrew Jackson. In 1831 he entered the House of Representatives and served 17 years with distinction. He opposed slavery, the annexation of Texas, and the Mexican War. He helped establish the Smithsonian Institution. He suffered a stroke in the House and died in the Speaker's Room on Feb. 23, 1848.

Andrew Jackson (1829-37)

Andrew Jackson, 7th president, Democratic-Republican, later a Democrat, was born on Mar. 15, 1767, in the Waxhaw district, on the border of North Carolina and South Carolina, the son of Andrew and Elizabeth Hutchinson Jackson. At the age of 13, he joined the militia to fight in the American Revolution and was captured. Orphaned at the age of 14, Jackson was brought up by a well-to-do uncle. By age 20, he was practicing law, and he later served as prosecuting attorney in Nashville, TN. In 1796 he helped draft the constitution of Tennessee, and for a year he occupied its one seat in the House of Representatives. The next year he served in the U.S. Senate.

In the War of 1812, Jackson crushed (1814) the Creek Indians at Horseshoe Bend, AL, and, with an army consisting chiefly of backwoodsmen, defeated (1815) General Edward Pakenham's British troops at the Battle of New Orleans. In 1818 he briefly invaded Spanish Florida to quell Seminoles and outlaws who harassed frontier settlements. In 1824 he ran for president against John Quincy Adams. Although he won the most popular and electoral votes, he did not have a majority. The House of Representatives decided the election and chose Adams. In the 1828 election, however, Jackson defeated Adams, carrying the West and the South.

As president, Jackson introduced what became known as the spoils system—rewarding party members with government posts. Perhaps his most controversial act, however, was depositing federal funds in so-called pet banks, those directed by Democratic bankers, rather than in the Bank of the United States. "Let the people rule" was his slogan. In 1832, Jackson killed the congressional caucus for nominating presidential candidates and substituted the national convention. When South Carolina refused to collect imports under his protective tariff, he ordered army and naval forces to Charleston. After leaving office in 1837, he retired to the Hermitage, outside Nashville, where he died on June 8, 1845.

Martin Van Buren (1837-41)

Martin Van Buren, 8th president, Democrat, was born on Dec. 5, 1782, in Kinderhook, NY, the son of Abraham and Maria Hoes Van Buren. After attending local schools, he studied law and became a lawyer at the age of 20. A consummate politician, Van Buren began his career in the New York state senate and then served as state attorney general from 1816 to 1819. He was elected to the U.S. Senate in 1821. He helped swing eastern support to Andrew Jackson in the 1828 election and then served as Jackson's secretary of state from 1829 to 1831. In 1832 he was elected vice president. Known as the Little Magician, Van Buren was extremely influential in Jackson's administration. In the election of 1836 he defeated William Henry Harrison for president and took office as the financial panic of 1837 initiated a nationwide depression. Although he instituted the independent treasury system, his refusal to spend land revenues led to his defeat by William Henry Harrison in the election of 1840. In 1844 he lost the Democratic nomination to James Knox Polk. In 1848 he again ran for president on the Free Soil ticket but lost. He died in Kinderhook on July 24, 1862.

William Henry Harrison (1841)

William Henry Harrison, 9th president, Whig, who served only 31 days, was born on Feb. 9, 1773, in Berkeley, Charles City Co., VA, the son of Benjamin Harrison, a signer of the Declaration of Independence, and of Elizabeth Bassett Harrison. He attended Hampden-Sydney College. Harrison served as secretary of the Northwest Territory in 1798 and was its delegate to the House of Representatives in 1799. He was the first governor of the Indiana Territory and served as superintendent of Indian affairs. With 900 men he put down a Shawnee uprising at Tippecanoe, IN, on Nov. 7, 1811. A generation later, in 1840, he waged a rousing presidential campaign, using the slogan "Tippecanoe and Tyler too." The Tyler of the slogan was his running mate, John Tyler. Although born to one of the wealthiest, most prestigious, and most influential families in Virginia, Harrison was elected president with a "log cabin and hard cider" slogan. He caught pneumonia during the inauguration and died Apr. 4, 1841.

John Tyler (1841-45)

John Tyler, 10th president, independent Whig, was born on Mar. 29, 1790, in Greenway, Charles City Co., VA, the son of John and Mary Armistead Tyler. His father was governor of Virginia (1808-11). Tyler graduated from the College of William and Mary in 1807 and in 1811 was elected to the Virginia legislature. In 1816 he was chosen for the U.S. House of Representatives. He served in the Virginia legislature again from 1823 to 1825, when he was elected governor of Virginia. After a stint in the U.S. Senate (1827-36), he was elected vice president (1840). When William Henry Harrison died only a month after taking office, Tyler succeeded him. Because he was the first person to occupy the presidency without having been elected to that office, he was referred to as "His Accidency." Tyler gained passage of the Preemption Act of 1841, which gave squatters on government land the right to buy 160 acres at the minimum auction price. His last act as president was to sign the resolution annexing Texas. Tyler accepted renomination in 1844 from some Democrats but withdrew in favor of the official party candidate, James K. Polk. He died in Richmond, VA, on Jan. 18, 1862.

James Knox Polk (1845-49)

James Knox Polk, 11th president, Democrat, was born on Nov. 2, 1795, in Mecklenburg Co., NC, the son of Samuel and Jane Knox Polk. He graduated from the University of North Carolina in 1818 and served in the Tennessee state legislature from 1823 to 1825. He served in the U.S. House of Representatives from 1825 to 1839, the last 4 years as Speaker. He was governor of Tennessee from 1839 to 1841. In 1844, after the Democratic National Convention became deadlocked, it nominated Polk, who thus became the nation's first "dark horse" candidate for president. He was nominated primarily because he was known to favor annexation of Texas. As president, Polk reestablished the independent treasury system originated by Van Buren. He was so intent on acquiring California from Mexico that he sent troops under Zachary Taylor to the Mexican border and, when Mexicans attacked, declared that a state of war existed. The Mexican War ended with the annexation of California and much of the Southwest as part of America's "manifest destiny." Polk compromised on the Oregon boundary ("54-40 or fight!") by accepting the 49th parallel and yielding Vancouver Island to the British. A few weeks after leaving office, Polk died in Nashville, TN, on June 15, 1849.

Zachary Taylor (1849-50)

Zachary Taylor, 12th president, Whig, who served only 16 months, was born on Nov. 24, 1784, in Orange Co., VA, the son of Richard and Sarah Strother Taylor. He grew up on his father's plantation near Louisville, KY, where he was educated by private tutors. In 1808 Taylor joined the regular army and was commissioned first lieutenant. He fought in the War of 1812, the Black Hawk War (1832), and the second Seminole War (beginning in 1837). He was called "Old Rough and Ready." In 1846 President Polk sent him with an army to the Rio Grande. When the Mexicans attacked him, Polk declared war. Outnumbered 4-1, Taylor defeated (1847) Santa Anna at Buena Vista. A national hero, he received the Whig nomination in 1848 and was elected president, even though he had never bothered to vote. He resumed the spoils system and, though a slaveholder, worked to admit California as a free state. He fell ill and died in office on July 9, 1850.

Millard Fillmore (1850-53)

Millard Fillmore, 13th president, Whig, was born on Jan. 7, 1800, in Cayuga Co., NY, the son of Nathaniel and Phoebe Millard Fillmore. Although he had little schooling, he became a law clerk at the age of 22 and a year later was admitted to the bar. He was elected to the New York state assembly in 1828 and served until 1831. From 1833 until 1835 and again from 1837 to 1843, he represented his district in the U.S. House of Representatives. He opposed the entrance of Texas as a slave territory and voted for a protective tariff. In 1844 he was defeated for governor of New York. In 1848 he was elected vice president, and he succeeded as president after Taylor's death. Fillmore favored the Compromise of 1850 and signed the Fugitive Slave Law. His policies pleased neither expansionists nor slaveholders, and he was not renominated in 1852. In 1856 he was nominated by the American (Know-Nothing) Party, but despite the support of the Whigs, he was defeated by James Buchanan. He died in Buffalo, NY, on Mar. 8, 1874.

Franklin Pierce (1853-57)

Franklin Pierce, 14th president, Democrat, was born on Nov. 23, 1804, in Hillsboro, NH, the son of Benjamin Pierce, an American Revolutionary War general and governor of New Hampshire, and Anna Kendrick. He graduated from Bowdoin College in 1824 and was admitted to the bar in 1827. He was elected to the New Hampshire state legislature in 1829 and was chosen Speaker in 1831. He went to the U.S. House of Representatives in 1833 and was elected a U.S. senator in 1837. He enlisted in the Mexican War and became brigadier general under Gen. Winfield Scott. In 1852 Pierce was nominated as the Democratic presidential candidate on the 49th ballot. He decisively defeated Gen. Scott, his Whig opponent, in the election. Although against slavery, Pierce was influenced by pro-slavery Southerners. He supported the controversial Kansas-Nebraska Act, which left the question of slavery in the new territories of Kansas and Nebraska to popular vote. Pierce signed a reciprocity treaty with Canada and approved the Gadsden Purchase, a border area on a proposed railroad route, from Mexico. Denied renomination by the Democrats, he spent most of his remaining years in Concord, NH, where he died on Oct. 8, 1869.

James Buchanan (1857-61)

James Buchanan, 15th president, Federalist, later Democrat, was born on Apr. 23, 1791, near Mercersburg, PA, the son of James and Elizabeth Speer Buchanan. He graduated from Dickinson College in 1809 and was admitted to the bar in 1812. He fought in the War of 1812 as a volunteer. He was twice elected to the Pennsylvania general assembly, and in 1821 he entered the U.S. House of Representatives. After briefly serving (1832-33) as minister to Russia, he was elected U.S. senator from Pennsylvania. As Polk's secretary of state

(1845-49), he ended the Oregon dispute with Britain and supported the Mexican War and annexation of Texas. As minister to Great Britain, he signed the Ostend Manifesto (1854), declaring a U.S. right to take Cuba by force should efforts to purchase it fail. Nominated by Democrats, Buchanan was elected president in 1856. On slavery he favored popular sovereignty and choice by state constitutions but did not consistently uphold this position. He denied the right of states to secede but opposed coercion and attempted to keep peace by not provoking secessionists. Buchanan left office having failed to deal decisively with the situation. He died at Wheatland, his estate, near Lancaster, PA, on June 1, 1868.

Abraham Lincoln (1861-65)

Abraham Lincoln, 16th president, Republican, was born on Feb. 12, 1809, in a log cabin on a farm then in Hardin Co., KY, now in Larue, the son of Thomas and Nancy Hanks Lincoln. The Lincolns moved to Spencer Co., IN, near Gentryville, when Abe was 7. After Abe's mother died, his father married (1819) Mrs. Sarah Bush Johnston. In 1830 the family moved to Macon Co., IL.

Defeated in 1832 in a race for the state legislature, Lincoln was elected on the Whig ticket 2 years later and served in the lower house from 1834 to 1842. In 1837 Lincoln was admitted to the bar and became partner in a Springfield, IL, law office. He soon won recognition as an effective and resourceful attorney. In 1846, he was elected to the House of Representatives, where he attracted attention during a single term for his opposition to the Mexican War and his position on slavery. In 1856 he campaigned for the newly founded Republican Party, and in 1858 he became its senatorial candidate against Stephen A. Douglas. Although he lost the election, Lincoln gained national recognition from his debates with Douglas.

In 1860, Lincoln was nominated for president by the Republican Party on a platform of restricting slavery. He ran against Douglas, a northern Democrat; John C. Breckinridge, a Southern proslavery Democrat; and John Bell, of the Constitutional Union Party. As a result of Lincoln's winning the election, South Carolina seceded from the Union on Dec. 20, 1860, followed in 1861 by 10 other Southern states.

The Civil War erupted when Fort Sumter, which Lincoln decided to resupply, was attacked by Confederate forces on Apr. 12, 1861. Lincoln called successfully for recruits from the North. On Sept. 22, 1862, 5 days after the Battle of Antietam, Lincoln announced that slaves in territory then in rebellion would be free Jan. 1, 1863, the date of the Emancipation Proclamation. His speeches, including his Gettysburg and Inaugural addresses, are remembered for their eloquence.

Lincoln was reelected, in 1864, over Gen. George B. McClellan, Democrat. Lee surrendered on Apr. 9, 1865. On Apr. 14, Lincoln was shot by actor John Wilkes Booth in Ford's Theater, in Washington, DC. He died the next day.

Andrew Johnson (1865-69)

Andrew Johnson, 17th president, Democrat, was born on Dec. 29, 1808, in Raleigh, NC, the son of Jacob and Mary McDonough Johnson. He was apprenticed to a tailor as a youth, but ran away after two years and eventually settled in Greeneville, TN. He became popular with the townspeople and in 1829 was elected councilman and later mayor. In 1835 he was sent to the state general assembly. In 1843 he was elected to the U.S. House of Representatives, where he served for 10 years. Johnson was governor of Tennessee from 1853 to 1857, when he was elected to the U.S. Senate. He supported John C. Breckinridge against Lincoln in the 1860 election. Although Johnson had held slaves, he opposed secession and tried to prevent Tennessee from seceding. In Mar. 1862, Lincoln appointed him military governor of occupied Tennessee.

In 1864, in order to balance Lincoln's ticket with a Southern Democrat, the Republicans nominated Johnson for vice president. He was elected vice president with Lincoln and then succeeded to the presidency upon Lincoln's death. Soon afterward, in a controversy with Congress over the president's power over the South, he proclaimed an amnesty to all Confederates, except certain leaders, if they would ratify the 13th Amendment abolishing slavery. States doing so added anti-

Negro provisions that enraged Congress, which restored military control over the South. When Johnson removed Edwin M. Stanton, secretary of war, without notifying the Senate, the House, in Feb. 1868, impeached him. Ostensibly charging him with thereby having violated the Tenure of Office Act, the House was actually responding to his opposition to harsh congressional Reconstruction, expressed in repeated vetoes. He was tried by the Senate, and in May, in two separate votes on different counts, was acquitted, both times by only one vote. Johnson was denied renomination but remained politically active. He was re-elected to the Senate in 1874. Johnson died July 31, 1875, at Carter Station, TN.

Ulysses Simpson Grant (1869-77)

Ulysses S. Grant, 18th president, Republican, was born on Apr. 27, 1822, in Point Pleasant, OH, the son of Jesse R. and Hannah Simpson Grant. The next year the family moved to Georgetown, OH. Grant was named Hiram Ulysses, but on entering West Point in 1839, his name was put down as Ulysses Simpson, and he adopted it. He graduated in 1843. During the Mexican War, Grant served under both Gen. Zachary Taylor and Gen. Winfield Scott. In 1854, he resigned his commission because of loneliness and drinking problems, and in the following years he engaged in generally unsuccessful farming and business ventures. With the start of the Civil War, he was named colonel and then brigadier general of the Illinois Volunteers. He took Forts Henry and Donelson and fought at Shiloh. His brilliant campaign against Vicksburg and his victory at Chattanooga made him so prominent that Lincoln placed him in command of all Union armies. Grant accepted Lee's surrender at Appomattox Court House on Apr. 9, 1865. President Johnson appointed Grant secretary of war when he suspended Stanton, but Grant was not confirmed. He was nominated for president by the Republicans in 1868 and elected over Horatio Seymour, Democrat. The 15th Amendment, amnesty bill, and the peaceful settlement of disputes with Great Britain were events of his administration. The Liberal Republicans and Democrats opposed him with Horace Greeley in the 1872 election, but Grant was reelected. His second administration was marked by many scandals, including widespread corruption in the Treasury Department and the Indian Service. An attempt by the Stalwarts (Old Guard Republicans) to nominate him in 1880 failed. In 1884 the collapse of Grant & Ward, an investment firm in which he was a partner, left him penniless. He wrote his personal memoirs while ill with cancer and completed them shortly before his death at Mt. McGregor, NY, on July 23, 1885.

Rutherford Birchard Hayes (1877-81)

Rutherford B. Hayes, 19th president, Republican, was born on Oct. 4, 1822, in Delaware, OH, the son of Rutherford and Sophia Birchard Hayes. He was reared by his uncle, Sardis Birchard. Hayes graduated from Kenyon College in 1842 and from Harvard Law School in 1845. He practiced law in Lower Sandusky (now Fremont), OH, and was city solicitor of Cincinnati from 1858 to 1861. During the Civil War, he was major of the 23d Ohio Volunteers. He was wounded several times, and by the end of the war he had risen to the rank of brevet major general. While serving (1865-67) in the U.S. House of Representatives, Hayes supported Reconstruction and Johnson's impeachment. He was twice elected governor of Ohio (1867, 1869). After losing a race for the U.S. House in 1872, he was reelected governor of Ohio in 1875. In 1876 he was nominated for president and believed he had lost the election to Samuel J. Tilden, Democrat. But a few Southern states submitted 2 sets of electoral votes, and the result was in dispute. An electoral commission, appointed by Congress and consisting of 8 Republicans and 7 Democrats, awarded all disputed votes to Hayes, allowing him to become president by one electoral vote. Hayes, keeping a promise to southerners, withdrew troops from areas still occupied in the South, ending the era of Reconstruction. He proposed civil service reforms, alienating those favoring the spoils system, and advocated repeal of the Tenure of Office Act restricting presidential power to dismiss officials. He supported sound money and specie payments. Hayes died in Fremont, OH, on Jan. 17, 1893.

James Abram Garfield (1881)

James A. Garfield, 20th president, Republican, was born on Nov. 19, 1831, in Orange, Cuyahoga Co., OH, the son of Abram and Eliza Ballou Garfield. His father died in 1833, and he was reared in poverty by his mother. He worked as a canal bargeman, a farmer, and a carpenter and managed to secure a college education. He taught at Hiram College and later became principal. In 1859 he was elected to the Ohio legislature. Antislavery and antisecession, he volunteered for military service in the Civil War, becoming colonel of the 42d Ohio Infantry and brigadier in 1862. He fought at Shiloh, was chief of staff for Gen. William Starke Rosecrans, and was made major general for gallantry at Chickamauga. He entered Congress as a radical Republican in 1863, calling for execution or exile of Confederate leaders, but he moderated his views after the Civil War. On the electoral commission in 1877 he voted for Hayes against Tilden on strict party lines. He was a senator-elect in 1880 when he became the Republican nominee for president. He was chosen as a compromise over Gen. Grant, James G. Blaine, and John Sherman, and won election despite some bitterness among Grant's supporters. On July 2, 1881, Garfield was shot and seriously wounded by a mentally disturbed office-seeker, Charles J. Guiteau, while entering a railroad station in Washington, DC. He died on Sept. 19, 1881, in Elberon, NJ.

Chester Alan Arthur (1881-85)

Chester A. Arthur, 21st president, Republican, was born on Oct. 5, 1829, in Fairfield, VT, the son of William and Malvina Stone Arthur. He graduated from Union College in 1848, taught school in Vermont, then studied law and opened a practice in New York City. In 1853 he argued in a fugitive slave case that slaves transported through New York state were thereby freed. In 1871, he was appointed to the lucrative post of collector of the Port of New York. President Hayes, an opponent of the spoils system, forced Arthur to resign in 1878. This made the New York machine strong enemies of Hayes. Arthur and the Stalwarts (Old Guard Republicans) tried to nominate Grant for a 3d term in 1880. When Garfield was nominated, Arthur received 2d place in the interests of harmony. Upon Garfield's assassination, Arthur became president. Despite his past connections, he signed civil service reform legislation. Arthur tried to dissuade Congress from enacting the high protective tariff of 1883. He was defeated for renomination in 1884 by James G. Blaine. He died in New York City on Nov. 18, 1886.

Grover Cleveland (1885-89; 1893-97)

(According to a ruling of the State Dept., Grover Cleveland should be counted as both the 22d and the 24th president, because his 2 terms were not consecutive.)

Grover Cleveland, Democrat, was born Stephen Grover Cleveland on Mar. 18, 1837, in Caldwell, NJ, the son of Richard F. and Ann Neal Cleveland. When he was a small boy, his family moved to New York. Prevented by his father's death from attending college, he studied by himself and was admitted to the bar in Buffalo, NY, in 1859. In succession he became assistant district attorney (1863), sheriff (1871), mayor (1881), and governor of New York (1882). He was an independent, honest administrator who hated corruption. He was nominated for president over Tammany Hall opposition in 1884 and defeated Republican James G. Blaine. As president, he enlarged the civil service and vetoed many pension raids on the Treasury. In the 1888 election he was defeated by Benjamin Harrison, although his popular vote was larger. Reelected over Harrison in 1892, he faced a money crisis brought about by a lowered gold reserve, circulation of paper, and exorbitant silver purchases under the Sherman Silver Purchase Act. He obtained a repeal of the Sherman Act, but was unable to secure effective tariff reform. A severe economic depression and labor troubles racked his administration, but he refused to interfere in business matters and rejected Jacob Coxey's demand for unemployment relief. In 1894, he broke the Pullman strike. In 1896, the Democrats repudiated his administration and chose silverite William Jennings Bryan as their candidate. Cleveland died in Princeton, NJ, on June 24, 1908.

Benjamin Harrison (1889-93)

Benjamin Harrison, 23d president, Republican, was born on Aug. 20, 1833, in North Bend, OH, the son of John Scott and Elizabeth Irwin Harrison. His great-grandfather, Benjamin Harrison, was a signer of the Declaration of Independence; his grandfather, William Henry Harrison, was 9th president; his father was a member of Congress. He attended school on his father's farm and graduated from Miami University in Oxford, OH, in 1852. He was admitted to the bar in 1854 and practiced in Indianapolis. During the Civil War, he rose to the rank of brevet brigadier general and fought at Kennesaw Mountain, at Peachtree Creek, at Nashville, and in the Atlanta campaign. He lost the 1876 gubernatorial election in Indiana but succeeded in becoming a U.S. senator in 1881. In 1888 he defeated Cleveland for president despite receiving fewer popular votes. As president, he expanded the pension list and signed the McKinley high tariff bill, the Sherman Antitrust Act, and the Sherman Silver Purchase Act. During his administration, 6 states were admitted to the Union. He was defeated for reelection in 1892. He died in Indianapolis on Mar. 13, 1901.

William McKinley (1897-1901)

William McKinley, 25th president, Republican, was born on Jan. 29, 1843, in Niles, OH, the son of William and Nancy Allison McKinley. McKinley briefly attended Allegheny College. When the Civil War broke out in 1861, he enlisted and served for the duration. He rose to captain and in 1865 was made brevet major. After studying law in Albany, NY, he opened (1867) a law office in Canton, OH. He served twice in the U.S. House of Representatives (1877-83; 1885-91) and led the fight there for the McKinley Tariff, which was passed in 1890. However, he was not reelected to the House as a result. He served two terms (1892-96) as governor of Ohio. In 1896 he was elected president as a proponent of a protective tariff and sound money (gold standard), over William Jennings Bryan, the Democrat and a proponent of free silver. McKinley was reluctant to intervene in Cuba, but the loss of the battleship *Maine* at Havana crystallized opinion. He demanded Spain's withdrawal from Cuba; Spain made some concessions, but Congress announced a state of war as of Apr. 21, 1898. He was reelected in the 1900 campaign, defeating Bryan's anti-imperialist arguments with the promise of a "full dinner pail." McKinley was respected for his conciliatory nature and for his conservative stance on business issues. On Sept. 6, 1901, while welcoming citizens at the Pan-American Exposition, in Buffalo, NY, he was shot by Leon Czolgosz, an anarchist. He died Sept. 14.

Theodore Roosevelt (1901-9)

Theodore Roosevelt, 26th president, Republican, was born on Oct. 27, 1858, in New York City, the son of Theodore and Martha Bulloch Roosevelt. He was a 5th cousin of Franklin D. Roosevelt and an uncle of Eleanor Roosevelt. Roosevelt graduated from Harvard University in 1880. He attended Columbia Law School briefly but abandoned the study of law to enter politics. He was elected to the New York state assembly in 1881 and served until 1884. He spent the next 2 years ranching and hunting in the Dakota Territory. Back in politics in 1886, he ran unsuccessfully for mayor of New York City. He was Civil Service commissioner in Washington, DC, from 1889 to 1895. From 1895 to 1897, he served as New York City's police commissioner. He was assistant secretary of the navy under McKinley. The Spanish-American War made Roosevelt a nationally known figure. He organized the 1st U.S. Volunteer Cavalry (Rough Riders) and, as lieutenant colonel, led the charge up Kettle Hill in San Juan. Elected New York governor in 1898, he fought the spoils system and achieved taxation of corporation franchises.

Nominated for vice president in 1900, he became the nation's youngest president when McKinley was assassinated. He was reelected in 1904. As president he fought corruption of politics by big business, dissolved the Northern Securities Co. and others for violating antitrust laws, intervened in the 1902 coal strike on behalf of the public, obtained the Elkins Law (1903) forbidding rebates to favored corporations, and helped pass the Hepburn Railway Rate Act of 1906 (extending jurisdiction of the Interstate Commerce Commission). He helped obtain passage of the Pure Food and Drug Act (1906), and employers' liability laws. Roosevelt vigorously organized conservation efforts. He mediated (1905) the peace between Japan and Russia, for which he won the Nobel Peace Prize. He abetted the 1903 revolution in Panama that led to U.S. acquisition of territory for the U.S. Panama Canal.

In 1908 Roosevelt obtained the nomination of William H. Taft, who was elected. Feeling that Taft had abandoned his policies, Roosevelt unsuccessfully sought the nomination in 1912. He bolted the party and ran on the Progressive "Bull Moose" ticket against Taft and Woodrow Wilson, splitting the Republicans and ensuring Wilson's election. He was shot during the campaign but recovered. In 1916, after unsuccessfully seeking the presidential nomination for himself, Roosevelt supported the Republican candidate, Charles E. Hughes. A strong friend of Britain, he fought for American intervention in World War I. He wrote some 40 books on many topics; his book *The Winning of the West* is perhaps best known. He died Jan. 6, 1919, at Sagamore Hill, Oyster Bay, NY.

William Howard Taft (1909-13)

William Howard Taft, 27th president, Republican, and 10th chief justice of the U.S., was born on Sept. 15, 1857, in Cincinnati, OH, the son of Alphonso and Louisa Maria Torrey Taft. His father was secretary of war and attorney general in Grant's cabinet and minister to Austria and Russia under Arthur. Taft graduated from Yale in 1878 and from Cincinnati Law School in 1880. After working as a law reporter for Cincinnati newspapers, he served as assistant prosecuting attorney (1881-82), assistant county solicitor (1885), judge, superior court (1887), U.S. solicitor-general (1890), and federal circuit judge (1892). In 1900 he became head of the U.S. Philippines Commission and was the first civil governor of the Philippines (1901-4). In 1904 he served as secretary of war, and in 1906 he was sent to Cuba to help avert a threatened revolution. He was groomed for the presidency by Theodore Roosevelt and elected over William Jennings Bryan in 1908. Taft vigorously continued Roosevelt's trust-busting, instituted the Department of Labor, and drafted the amendments calling for direct election of senators and the income tax. His tariff and conservation policies angered progressives. Although renominated in 1912, he was opposed by Roosevelt, who ran on the Progressive Party ticket; the result was Democrat Woodrow Wilson's election. Taft, with some reservations, supported the League of Nations. After leaving office, he was professor of constitutional law at Yale (1913-21) and chief justice of the U.S. (1921-30). Taft was the only person in U.S. history to have been both president and chief justice. Illness forced him to resign from the Court in Feb. 1930, and he died in Washington, DC, on Mar. 8, 1930.

Woodrow Wilson (1913-21)

Thomas Woodrow Wilson, 28th president, Democrat, was born on Dec. 28, 1856, in Staunton, VA, the son of Joseph Ruggles and Janet (Jessie) Woodrow Wilson. He grew up in Georgia and South Carolina. He attended Davidson College in North Carolina before graduating from Princeton University in 1879. He studied law at the University of Virginia and then studied political science at Johns Hopkins University, where he received his PhD in 1886. He taught at Bryn Mawr (1885-88) and then at Wesleyan (1888-90) before joining the faculty at Princeton. He was president of Princeton from 1902 until 1910, when he was elected governor of New Jersey. In 1912 he was nominated for president with the aid of William Jennings Bryan, who sought to block James "Champ" Clark and Tammany Hall. Wilson won the election because the Republican vote for Taft was split by the Progressives.

As president, Wilson protected American interests in revolutionary Mexico and fought for American rights on the high seas. He oversaw the creation of the Federal Reserve system, cut the tariff, and developed a reputation as a reformer. His sharp warnings to Germany led to the resignation of his secretary of state, Bryan, a pacifist. In 1916 he was reelected by a slim margin with the slogan, "He kept us out of war," although his attempts to mediate in the war failed. After several American ships had been sunk by the Germans, he secured a declaration of war against Germany on Apr. 6, 1917.

Wilson outlined his peace program on Jan. 8, 1918, in the Fourteen Points, a state paper that had worldwide influence. He enunciated a doctrine of self-determination for the settlement of territorial disputes. The Germans accepted his terms and an armistice on Nov. 11, 1918.

Wilson went to Paris to help negotiate the peace treaty, the crux of which he considered the League of Nations. The Senate demanded reservations that would not make the U.S. subordinate to the votes of other nations in case of war. Wilson refused to consider any reservations and toured the country to get support. He suffered a stroke in Oct. 1919. An invalid for months, he clung to his executive powers while his wife and doctors effectively functioned as president.

Wilson was awarded the 1919 Nobel Peace Prize, but the treaty embodying the League of Nations was ultimately rejected by the Senate in 1920. He left the White House in Mar. 1921. He died in Washington, DC, on Feb. 3, 1924.

Warren Gamaliel Harding (1921-23)

Warren Gamaliel Harding, 29th president, Republican, was born on Nov. 2, 1865, near Corsica (now Blooming Grove), OH, the son of George Tyron and Phoebe Elizabeth Dickerson Harding. He attended Ohio Central College, studied law, and became editor and publisher of a county newspaper. He entered the political arena as state senator (1901-4) and then served as lieutenant governor (1904-6). In 1910 he ran unsuccessfully for governor of Ohio; then in 1914 he was elected to the U.S. Senate. In the Senate he voted for antistrike legislation, woman suffrage, and the Volstead Prohibition Enforcement Act over President Wilson's veto. He opposed the League of Nations. In 1920 he was nominated for president and defeated James M. Cox in the election. The Republicans capitalized on war weariness and fear that Wilson's League of Nations would curtail U.S. sovereignty. Harding stressed a return to "normalcy" and worked for tariff revision and the repeal of excess profits law and high income taxes. His secretary of interior, Albert B. Fall, became involved in the Teapot Dome scandal. As rumors began to circulate about the corruption in his administration, Harding became ill while returning from a trip to Alaska, and he died in San Francisco on Aug. 2, 1923.

Calvin Coolidge (1923-29)

John Calvin Coolidge, 30th president, Republican, was born on July 4, 1872, in Plymouth, VT, the son of John Calvin and Victoria J. Moor Coolidge. Coolidge graduated from Amherst College in 1895. He entered Republican state politics and served as mayor of Northampton, MA, as state senator, as lieutenant governor, and, in 1919, as governor. In Sept. 1919, Coolidge attained national prominence by calling out the state guard in the Boston police strike. He declared: "There is no right to strike against the public safety by anybody, anywhere, anytime." This brought his name before the Republican convention of 1920, where he was nominated for vice president. He succeeded to the presidency on Harding's death. As president, he opposed the League of Nations and the soldiers' bonus bill, which was passed over his veto. In 1924 he was elected by a huge majority. He substantially reduced the national debt. He twice vetoed the McNary-Haugen farm bill, which would have provided relief to financially hard-pressed farmers. With Republicans eager to renominate him, Coolidge simply announced, Aug. 2, 1927: "I do not choose to run for president in 1928." He died in Northampton, MA, on Jan. 5, 1933.

Herbert Clark Hoover (1929-33)

Herbert Hoover, 31st president, Republican, was born on Aug. 10, 1874, in West Branch, IA, the son of Jesse Clark and Hulda Randall Minthorn Hoover. Hoover grew up in Indian Territory (now Oklahoma) and Oregon and graduated from Stanford University with a degree in engineering in 1895. He worked briefly with the U.S. Geological Survey and then managed mines in Australia, Asia, Europe, and Africa. While chief engineer of imperial mines in China, he directed food relief for victims of the Boxer Rebellion. He gained a reputation not only as an engineer but as a humanitarian as he directed the American Relief Committee, London (1914-15) and the U.S. Commission for Relief in Belgium (1915-19). He was U.S. Food Administrator (1917-19), American Relief Administrator (1918-23), and in charge of Russian Relief (1918-23). He served as secretary of commerce under both Harding and Coolidge. Some historians believe that he was the most effective secretary of commerce ever to hold that office.

In 1928 Hoover was elected president over Alfred E. Smith. In 1929 the stock market crashed, and the economy collapsed. During the depression, Hoover inaugurated some government assistance programs, but he was opposed to administration of aid through a federal bureaucracy. As the effects of the depression continued, he was defeated in the 1932 election by Franklin D. Roosevelt. President Truman named him coordinator of the European Food Program (1946) and chairman of the Commission on Organization of the Executive Branch (1947-49; 1953-55). Hoover died in New York City on Oct. 20, 1964.

Franklin Delano Roosevelt (1933-45)

Franklin D. Roosevelt, 32d president, Democrat, was born on Jan. 30, 1882, near Hyde Park, NY, the son of James and Sara Delano Roosevelt. He graduated from Harvard University in 1904. He attended Columbia University Law School without taking a degree and was admitted to the New York state bar in 1907. His political career began when he was elected to the New York state senate in 1910. In 1913 President Wilson appointed him assistant secretary of the navy, a post he held during World War I.

In 1920 Roosevelt ran for vice president with James Cox and was defeated. From 1921 to 1928 he worked in his New York law office and was also vice president of Fidelity & Deposit Co. of Maryland. In Aug. 1921, he was stricken with poliomyelitis, which left his legs paralyzed. As a result of therapy he was able to stand, or walk a few steps, with the aid of leg braces.

Roosevelt served 2 terms as governor of New York (1929-33). In 1932, W. G. McAdoo, pledged to John N. Garner, threw his votes to Roosevelt, who was nominated for president. The depression and the promise to repeal Prohibition ensured his election. He asked for emergency powers, proclaimed the New Deal, and put into effect a vast number of administrative changes. Foremost was the use of public funds for relief and public works, resulting in deficit financing. He greatly expanded the federal government's regulation of business and by an excess profits tax and progressive income taxes produced a redistribution of earnings on an unprecedented scale. The Wagner Act gave labor many advantages in organizing and collective bargaining. He promoted legislation establishing the Social Security system. He was the last president inaugurated on Mar. 4 (1933) and the first inaugurated on Jan. 20 (1937).

Roosevelt was the first president to use radio for "fireside chats." When the Supreme Court nullified some New Deal laws, he sought power to "pack" the court with additional justices, but Congress refused to give him the authority. He was the first president to break the "no 3d term" tradition (1940) and was elected to a 4th term in 1944, despite failing health. Roosevelt was openly hostile to fascist governments before World War II and launched a lend-lease program on behalf of the Allies. With British Prime Min. Winston Churchill he wrote a declaration of principles to be followed after Nazi defeat (the Atlantic Charter of Aug. 14, 1941) and urged the Four Freedoms (freedom of speech, of worship, from want, from fear) Jan. 6, 1941. When Japan attacked Pearl Harbor on Dec. 7, 1941, the U.S. entered the war. Roosevelt conferred with allied heads of state at Casablanca (Jan. 1943), Quebec (Aug. 1943), Teheran (Nov.-Dec. 1943), Cairo (Nov. and Dec. 1943), and Yalta (Feb. 1945). He did not, however, see the end of the war. He died of a cerebral hemorrhage in Warm Springs, GA, on Apr. 12, 1945.

Harry S. Truman (1945-53)

Harry S. Truman, 33d president, Democrat, was born on May 8, 1884, in Lamar, MO, the son of John Anderson and Martha Ellen Young Truman. A family disagreement on whether his middle name should be Shippe or Solomon, after names of 2 grandfathers, resulted in his using only the middle initial S. After graduating from high school in Independence, MO, he worked (1901) for the *Kansas City Star*, as a railroad timekeeper, and as a clerk in Kansas City banks until about 1905. He ran his family's farm from 1906 to 1917. He served in France during World War I. After the war he opened a haberdashery shop, was a judge on the Jackson Co. Court (1922-24), and attended Kansas City School of Law (1923-25).

Truman was elected to the U.S. Senate in 1934 and re-elected in 1940. In 1944, with Roosevelt's backing, he was nominated for vice president and elected. On Roosevelt's death in 1945, Truman became president. In 1948, in a famous upset victory, he defeated Republican Thomas E. Dewey to win election to a new term.

Truman authorized the first uses of the atomic bomb (Hiroshima and Nagasaki, Aug. 6 and 9, 1945), bringing World War II to a rapid end. He was responsible for what came to be called the Truman Doctrine (to aid nations such as Greece and Turkey, threatened by Communist takeover), and his strong commitment to NATO and to the Marshall Plan helped bring them about. In 1948-49, he broke a Soviet blockade of West Berlin with a massive airlift. When Communist North Korea invaded South Korea (June 1950), he won UN approval for a "police action" and sent in forces under Gen. Douglas MacArthur. When MacArthur opposed his policy of limited objectives, Truman removed him.

Truman was responsible for a higher minimum-wage, increased Social Security, and aid-for-housing laws. He died in Kansas City, MO, on Dec. 26, 1972.

Dwight David Eisenhower (1953-61)

Dwight D. Eisenhower, 34th president, Republican, was born on Oct. 14, 1890, in Denison, TX, the son of David Jacob and Ida Elizabeth Stover Eisenhower. He grew up on a small farm in Abilene, KS, and graduated from West Point in 1915. He was on the staff of Gen. Douglas MacArthur in the Philippines from 1935 to 1939. In 1942, he was made commander of Allied forces landing in North Africa; the next year he was made full general. He became supreme Allied commander in Europe that same year and as such led the Normandy invasion (June 6, 1944). He was given the rank of general of the army on Dec. 20, 1944, which was made permanent in 1946. On May 7, 1945, he received the surrender of Germany at Rheims. He returned to the U.S. to serve as chief of staff (1945-48). His war memoir, *Crusade in Europe (1948)*, was a best-seller. In 1948 he became president of Columbia University; in 1950 he became Commander of NATO forces.

Eisenhower resigned from the army and was nominated for president by the Republicans in 1952. He defeated Adlai E. Stevenson in the 1952 election and again in 1956. He called himself a moderate; favored the "free market system" vs. government price and wage controls; kept government out of labor disputes; reorganized the defense establishment; and promoted missile programs. He continued foreign aid; sped the end of the Korean War; endorsed Taiwan and SE Asia defense treaties; backed the UN in condemning the Anglo-French raid on Egypt; and advocated the "open skies" policy of mutual inspection with the USSR. He sent U.S. troops into Little Rock, AR, in Sept. 1957, during the segregation crisis.

Eisenhower died on Mar. 28, 1969, in Washington, DC.

John Fitzgerald Kennedy (1961-63)

John F. Kennedy, 35th president, Democrat, was born on May 29, 1917, in Brookline, MA, the son of Joseph P. and Rose Fitzgerald Kennedy. He graduated from Harvard University in 1940. While serving in the navy (1941-45), he commanded a PT boat in the Solomons and won the Navy and Marine Corps Medal. In 1956, while recovering from spinal surgery, he wrote *Profiles in Courage*, which won a Pulitzer Prize in 1957. He served in the House of Representatives from 1947 to 1953 and was elected to the Senate in 1952 and again in 1958. In 1960, Kennedy won the Democratic nomination for president and narrowly defeated Republican Vice Pres. Richard M. Nixon Kennedy was the youngest president ever elected and the first Roman Catholic.

In Apr. 1961, the new Kennedy administration suffered a severe setback when an invasion force of anti-Castro Cubans, trained and directed by the U.S. Central Intelligence Agency, failed to establish a beachhead at the Bay of Pigs in Cuba. By the same token, one of Kennedy's most important acts as president was his successful demand on Oct. 22, 1962, that the Soviet Union dismantle its missile bases in Cuba. Kennedy also defied Soviet attempts to force the Allies out of Berlin. He backed civil rights and expanded medical care for the aged. Space exploration was greatly developed during his administration.

On Nov. 22, 1963, Kennedy was assassinated while riding in a motorcade in Dallas, TX.

Lyndon Baines Johnson (1963-69)

Lyndon B. Johnson, 36th president, Democrat, was born on Aug. 27, 1908, near Stonewall, TX, the son of Sam Ealy and Rebekah Baines Johnson. He graduated from Southwest Texas State Teachers College in 1930 and attended Georgetown University Law School. He taught public speaking in Houston (1930-31) and then served as secretary to Rep. R. M. Kleberg (1931-35). In 1937 Johnson won an election to fill the vacancy caused by the death of a U.S. representative and in 1938 was elected to the full term, after which he returned for 4 terms. During 1941 and 1942 he also served in the Navy in the Pacific, earning a Silver Star for bravery. He was elected U.S. senator in 1948 and reelected in 1954. He became Democratic leader of the Senate in 1953. Johnson had strong support for the Democratic presidential nomination at the 1960 convention, where the nominee, John F. Kennedy, asked him to run for vice president. His campaigning helped overcome religious bias against Kennedy in the South.

Johnson became president when Kennedy was assassinated. He was elected to a full term in 1964. Johnson's domestic program was of considerable importance. He won passage of major civil rights, anti-poverty, aid to education, and health-care (Medicare, Medicaid) legislation—the "Great Society" program. However, his escalation of the war in Vietnam came to overshadow the achievements of his administration. In the face of increasing division in the nation and in his own party over his handling of the war, Johnson declined to seek another term.

Johnson died on Jan. 22, 1973, in San Antonio, TX.

Richard Milhous Nixon (1969-74)

Richard M. Nixon, 37th president, Republican, was born on Jan. 9, 1913, in Yorba Linda, CA, the son of Francis Anthony and Hannah Milhous Nixon. He graduated from Whittier College in 1934 and from Duke University Law School in 1937. After practicing law in Whittier and serving briefly in the Office of Price Administration in 1942, he entered the navy and served in the South Pacific. Nixon was elected to the House of Representatives in 1946 and 1948. He achieved prominence as the House Un-American Activities Committee member who forced the showdown leading to the Alger Hiss perjury conviction. In 1950 he was elected to the Senate.

Nixon was elected vice president in the Eisenhower landslides of 1952 and 1956. He won the Republican nomination for president in 1960 but was narrowly defeated by John F. Kennedy. He ran unsuccessfully for governor of California in 1962. In 1968 he again won the GOP presidential nomination, then defeated Hubert Humphrey for the presidency.

Nixon appointed 4 Supreme Court justices, including the chief justice, moving the court to the right, and as a "new federalist" sought to shift responsibility to state and local governments. He dramatically altered relations with China, which he visited in 1972—the first president to do so. With foreign affairs adviser Henry Kissinger he pursued détente with the Soviet Union. He began a gradual withdrawal from Vietnam, but U.S. troops remained there through his first term. He ordered an incursion into Cambodia (1970) and the bombing of Hanoi and mining of Haiphong Harbor (1972). Reelected by a large majority in Nov. 1972, he secured a Vietnam cease-fire.

Nixon's 2d term was cut short by scandal, after disclosures relating to a June 1972 burglary of Democratic Party headquarters in the Watergate office complex. After it emerged that most of Nixon's office conversations and calls had been taped, the courts and Congress sought the tapes for criminal proceedings against former White House aides and for a House inquiry into possible impeachment. Nixon claimed executive privilege to keep the tapes secret, but the Supreme Court ruled against him. In late July the House Judiciary Committee recommended adoption of 3 impeachment articles charging him with obstruction of justice, abuse of power, and contempt of Congress. On Aug. 5, he released transcripts of conversations that linked him to cover-up activities. He resigned on Aug. 9, becoming the first president ever to do so. In later years, Nixon emerged as an elder statesman

Nixon died Apr. 22, 1994, in New York City.

Gerald Rudolph Ford (1974-77)

Gerald R. Ford, 38th president, Republican, was born on July 14, 1913, in Omaha, NE, the son of Leslie and Dorothy Gardner King, and was named Leslie Jr. When he was 2, his parents were divorced, and his mother moved with the boy to Grand Rapids, MI. There she met and married Gerald R. Ford, who formally adopted him and gave him his own name. Ford graduated from the University of Michigan in 1935 and from Yale Law School in 1941. He began practicing law in Grand Rapids, but in 1942 joined the navy and served in the Pacific, leaving the service in 1946 as a lieutenant commander. He entered the House of Representatives in 1949 and spent 25 years in the House, 8 of them as Republican leader.

On Oct. 12, 1973, after Vice President Spiro T. Agnew resigned, Ford was nominated by President Nixon to replace him. It was the first use of the procedures set out in the 25th Amendment. When Nixon resigned, Aug. 9, 1974, Ford became president; he was the only president who was never elected either to the presidency or to the vice presidency. On Sept. 8, in a controversial move, he pardoned Nixon for any federal crimes he might have committed as president. Ford vetoed 48 bills in his first 21 months in office, mostly in the interest of fighting high inflation; he was less successful in curbing high unemployment. In foreign policy, Ford continued to pursue détente. He was narrowly defeated in the 1976 election by Democrat Jimmy Carter.

Jimmy (James Earl) Carter (1977-81)

Jimmy (James Earl) Carter, 39th president, Democrat, was the first president from the Deep South since before the Civil War. He was born on Oct. 1, 1924, in Plains, GA, the son of James and Lillian Gordy Carter.

Carter graduated from the U.S. Naval Academy in 1946 and in 1952 entered the navy's nuclear submarine program as an aide to Capt. (later Adm.) Hyman Rickover. He studied nuclear physics at Union College. Carter's father died in 1953, and he left the navy to take over the family businesses. He served in the Georgia state senate (1963-67) and as governor of Georgia (1971-75). In 1976, Carter won the Democratic nomination and defeated President Gerald R. Ford.

On his first full day in office, Carter pardoned all Vietnam draft evaders. He played a major role in the peace negotiations between Israel and Egypt. However, Carter was widely criticized for the poor state of the economy and was viewed by many as weak in his handling of foreign policy. In Nov. 1979, Iranian student militants attacked the U.S. embassy in Tehran and held members of the embassy staff hostage. Efforts to obtain release of the hostages were a major preoccupation during the rest of his term. He reacted to the Soviet invasion of Afghanistan by imposing a grain embargo and boycotting the Moscow Olympic Games.

Carter was defeated by Ronald Reagan in the 1980 election. Carter administration efforts finally resulted in the release of the hostages on Inauguration Day, 1981, just after Reagan officially became president. After leaving office, Carter was hailed for his humanitarian efforts and took a prominent role in mediating international disputes.

Ronald Wilson Reagan (1981-89)

Ronald Wilson Reagan, 40th president, Republican, was born on Feb. 6, 1911, in Tampico, IL, the son of John Edward and Nellie Wilson Reagan. Reagan graduated from Eureka College in 1932, after which he worked as a sports announcer in Des Moines, IA. He began a successful career as an actor in 1937, starring in numerous movies, and later in television, until the 1960s. He served as president of the Screen Actors Guild from 1947 to 1952 and in 1959-60. Reagan was elected governor of California in 1966 and reelected in 1970.

In 1980, Reagan gained the Republican presidential nomination and won a landslide victory over Jimmy Carter. He was easily reelected in 1984. Reagan successfully forged a bipartisan coalition in Congress, which led to enactment of his program of large-scale tax cuts, cutbacks in many government programs, and a major defense buildup. He signed a Social Security reform bill designed to provide for the long-term solvency of the system. In 1986, he signed into law a major tax-reform bill. He was shot and wounded in an assassination attempt in 1981.

In 1982, the U.S. joined France and Italy in maintaining a peacekeeping force in Beirut, Lebanon, and the next year Reagan sent a task force to invade the island of Grenada after 2 Marxist coups there. Reagan's opposition to international terrorism led to the U.S. bombing of Libyan military installations in 1986. He strongly supported El Salvador, the Nicaraguan contras, and other anti-communist governments and forces throughout the world. He also held 4 summit meetings with Soviet leader Mikhail Gorbachev. At the 1987 meeting in Washington, DC, a historic treaty eliminating short- and medium-range missiles from Europe was signed.

Reagan faced a crisis in 1986-87, when it was revealed that the U.S. had sold weapons to Iran in exchange for release of U.S. hostages being held in Lebanon and that subsequently some of the money was diverted to the Nicaraguan contras (Congress had barred aid to the contras). The scandal led to the resignation of leading White House aides. As Reagan left office in Jan. 1989, the nation was experiencing its 6th consecutive year of economic prosperity. Reagan, however, was unable to control the high budget deficits that plagued him throughout his administration.

In 1994, in a letter to the American people, Reagan revealed that he was suffering from Alzheimer's disease.

George Herbert Walker Bush (1989-93)

George Herbert Walker Bush, 41st president, Republican, was born on June 12, 1924, in Milton, MA, the son of Prescott and Dorothy Walker Bush. He served as a U.S. Navy pilot in World War II. After graduating from Yale University in 1948, he settled in Texas, where, in 1953, he helped found an oil company. After losing a bid for a U.S. Senate seat in Texas in 1964, he was elected to the House of Representatives in 1966 and 1968. He lost a 2d U.S. Senate race in 1970. Subsequently he served as U.S. ambassador to the United Nations (1971-73), headed the U.S. Liaison Office in Beijing (1974-75), and was director of central intelligence (1976-77).

Following an unsuccessful bid for the 1980 Republican presidential nomination, Bush was chosen by Ronald Reagan as his vice presidential running mate. He served as U.S. vice president from 1981 to 1989.

In 1988, Bush gained the Republican presidential nomination and defeated Democrat Michael Dukakis in the November elections. Bush took office faced with the ongoing U.S. budget and trade deficits as well as the rescue of insolvent U.S. savings and loan institutions. He faced a severe budget deficit annually, struggled with military cutbacks in light of reduced cold war tensions, and vetoed abortion-rights legislation. In 1990 he agreed to a budget deficit-reduction plan that included tax hikes.

Bush supported Soviet reforms and Eastern Europe democratization. He was criticized by some for keeping U.S. policy tied closely to Mikhail Gorbachev as the Soviet leader lost power and for underreaction to China's violent repression of pro-democracy demonstrators in 1989. In Dec. 1989, Bush sent troops to Panama; they overthrew the government and captured strongman Gen. Manuel Noriega.

Bush reacted to Iraq's Aug. 1990 invasion of Kuwait by sending U.S. forces to the Persian Gulf area and assembling a UN-backed coalition, including NATO and Arab League members. After a month-long air war, in Feb. 1991, Allied forces retook Kuwait in a 4-day ground assault. The quick victory, with light casualties, gave Bush one of the highest presidential approval ratings in history. His popularity plummeted by the end of 1991, however, as the economy struggled through a prolonged recession. He was defeated by his Democratic opponent, Bill Clinton, in the 1992 election.

Bill (William Jefferson) Clinton (1993-)

Bill Clinton, 42d president, Democrat, was born on Aug. 19, 1946, in Hope, AR, son of William Blythe and Virginia Cassidy Blythe, and was named William Jefferson Blythe IV. Blythe died in an automobile accident before his son was born. His widow married Roger Clinton, and at the age of 16, William Jefferson Blythe IV changed his name to Bill Clinton. Clinton graduated from Georgetown University in 1968, attended Oxford University as a Rhodes scholar, and earned a degree from Yale Law School in 1973.

Clinton worked on George McGovern's 1972 presidential campaign. He taught at the University of Arkansas from 1973 to 1976, when he was elected state attorney general. In 1978, he was elected governor, becoming the nation's youngest. Defeated for reelection in 1980, he was returned to office in 1982, 1984, 1986, and 1990. He married Hillary Rodham in 1975.

Despite attacks on his character, Clinton won most of the 1992 presidential primaries, moving the Democratic Party toward the center as he tried to broaden his appeal; he became the party's presidential nominee and defeated Pres. George Bush in November.

In 1993, Clinton narrowly won passage of $500 billion in taxes and spending cuts to reduce the federal budget deficit, and won congressional approval of the North American Free Trade Agreement. He proposed major health-care reform legislation, but his plan died in Congress. Following 1994 midterm elections, Clinton faced Republican majorities in both houses of Congress. He pursued a centrist course, winning passage of an anti-crime bill in 1995 and supporting, in 1996 (with reservations), a measure to overhaul the welfare system and end federal guarantees of support. In foreign policy, Clinton pursued peace efforts in the Middle East, sent U.S. troops to Bosnia to help implement a peace settlement, and cultivated relations with Russia and China.

Despite controversy over his involvement while governor in an Arkansas real estate venture (Whitewater) and over the White House's obtaining of FBI files of Republicans, Clinton easily won reelection in 1996. In 1997 he reached agreement with Congress on legislation to balance the federal budget by 2002. A strong economy and growing disunity in GOP ranks strengthened his position in 1997, in spite of controversy over Democratic fund-raising practices.

Wives and Children of the Presidents

(listed in order of presidential administrations)

Name (Born–died, married)	State	Sons/ daughters	Name (Born–died, married)	State	Sons/ daughters
Martha Dandridge Custis Washington (1731-1802, 1759)	VA	None	Frances Folsom Cleveland (1864-1947, 1886)	NY	2/3
Abigail Smith Adams (1744-1818, 1764)	MA	3/2	Caroline Lavinia Scott Harrison (1832-92, 1853)	OH	1/1
Martha Wayles Skelton Jefferson (1748-82, 1772)	VA	1/5	Mary Scott Lord Dimmick Harrison (1858-1948, 1896)	PA	.../1
Dorothea "Dolley" Payne Todd Madison (1768-1849, 1794)	NC	None	Ida Saxton McKinley (1847-1907, 1871)	OH	.../2
Elizabeth Kortright Monroe (1768-1830, 1786)	NY	.../2 (A)	Alice Hathaway Lee Roosevelt (1861-84, 1880)	MA	.../1
Louisa Catherine Johnson Adams (1775-1852, 1797)	MD(B)	3/1	Edith Kermit Carow Roosevelt (1861-1948, 1886)	CT	4/1
Rachel Donelson Robards Jackson (1767-1828, 1791)	VA	None	Helen Herron Taft (1861-1943, 1886)	OH	2/1
Hannah Hoes Van Buren (1783-1819, 1807)	NY	4/...	Ellen Louise Axson Wilson (1860-1914, 1885)	GA	.../3
Anna Tuthill Symmes Harrison (1775-1864, 1795)	NJ	6/4	Edith Bolling Galt Wilson (1872-1961, 1915)	VA	None
Letitia Christian Tyler (1790-1842, 1813)	VA	3/4 (A)	Florence Kling De Wolfe Harding (1860-1924, 1891)	OH	None
Julia Gardiner Tyler (1820-89, 1844)	NY	5/2	Grace Anna Goodhue Coolidge (1879-1957, 1905)	VT	2/...
Sarah Childress Polk (1803-91, 1824)	TN	None	Lou Henry Hoover (1875-1944, 1899)	IA	2/...
Margaret Mackall Smith Taylor (1788-1852, 1810)	MD	1/5	Anna Eleanor Roosevelt Roosevelt (1884-1962, 1905)	NY	4/1 (A)
Abigail Powers Fillmore (1798-1853, 1826)	NY	1/1	Elizabeth Virginia "Bess" Wallace Truman (1885-1982, 1919)	MO	.../1
Caroline Carmichael McIntosh Fillmore (1813-81, 1858)	NJ	None	Mamie Geneva Doud Eisenhower (1896-1979, 1916)	IA	1/... (A)
Jane Means Appleton Pierce (1806-63, 1834)	NH	3/...	Jacqueline Lee Bouvier Kennedy (1929-94, 1953)	NY	1/1 (A)
Mary Todd Lincoln (1818-82, 1842)	KY	4/...	Claudia "Lady Bird" Alta Taylor Johnson (b 1912, 1934)	TX	.../2
Eliza McCardle Johnson (1810-76, 1827)	TN	3/2	Thelma Catherine Patricia Ryan Nixon (1912-1993, 1940)	NV	.../2
Julia Boggs Dent Grant (1826-1902, 1848)	MO	3/1	Elizabeth Bloomer Warren Ford (b 1918, 1948)	IL	3/1
Lucy Ware Webb Hayes (1831-89, 1852)	OH	7/1	Rosalynn Smith Carter (b 1927, 1946)	GA	3/1
Lucretia Rudolph Garfield (1832-1918, 1858)	OH	4/1	Anne Frances "Nancy" Robbins Davis Reagan (b 1921, 1952)	NY	1/1 (C)
Ellen Lewis Herndon Arthur (1837-80, 1859)	VA	2/1	Barbara Pierce Bush (b 1925, 1945)	NY	4/2
			Hillary Rodham Clinton (b 1947, 1975)	IL	.../1

James Buchanan, 15th president, was unmarried. (A) plus one infant, deceased. (B) Born London, father a MD citizen. (C) President Reagan married and divorced Jane Wyman; they had a daughter who died in infancy, and a son and daughter lived past infancy.

First Lady Hillary Rodham Clinton

Hillary Rodham Clinton was born in Chicago, Ill., Oct. 26, 1947, the daughter of Hugh and Dorothy Rodham. She graduated from Wellesley College and Yale Law School. She married Bill Clinton in 1975, and a daughter, Chelsea, was born in 1980. From 1977 to 1992, she was a partner in the Rose law firm in Little Rock, AR, and in 1988 and 1991, she was voted one of the "100 Most Influential Lawyers in America" by the *National Law Journal*.

Public reaction to the first lady tended to polarize along party lines. Soon after becoming first lady she played a leading role in an unsuccessful effort to reform the U.S. healthcare system. Subsequently, she avoided public involvement in policy initiatives. In 1995 her book *It Takes a Village*, about the needs of children, was published; her recording of the text won a Grammy in 1997.

Presidential Facts

- **Oldest president**: Ronald Reagan, who was 77 when he left office
- **Youngest president**: Theodore Roosevelt, who was 42 when sworn in after McKinley's death
- **Only president to serve more than 2 terms**: Franklin D. Roosevelt
- **Only president to serve 2 terms that were not back to back**: Grover Cleveland, who was both the 22d and the 24th president
- **President who served the shortest term**: William Henry Harrison, who died of pneumonia 31 days after being inaugurated
- **Only president to also serve as chief justice of the U.S.**: William Howard Taft
- **Only president to resign**: Richard Nixon, after a House committee recommended impeachment for Watergate scandal

- **State where the greatest number of presidents were born**: Virginia (8)
- **First president to live in the White House**: John Adams
- **Only president who was never married**: James Buchanan. His niece acted as White House hostess.
- **Only president to serve without having been elected vice president or president in a national election**: Gerald Ford
- **Presidents who died on July 4**: John Adams, Thomas Jefferson, and James Monroe
- **Presidents who died in office**: Eight presidents have died in office. Four of them were assassinated: Abraham Lincoln, James Garfield, William McKinley, and John F. Kennedy. The other four were William Henry Harrison, Zachary Taylor, Warren G. Harding, and Franklin Delano Roosevelt.

Burial Places of the Presidents

President	Burial Place	President	Burial Place	President	Burial Place
Washington	Mt. Vernon, VA	Fillmore....	Buffalo, NY	T. Roosevelt	Oyster Bay, NY
J. Adams...	Quincy, MA	Pierce.....	Concord, NH	Taft	Arlington Natl. Cem.
Jefferson..	Charlottesville, VA	Buchanan..	Lancaster, PA	Wilson....	Wash. Natl. Cathedral
Madison...	Montpelier Station, VA	Lincoln	Springfield, IL	Harding ...	Marion, OH
Monroe ...	Richmond, VA	A. Johnson .	Greeneville, TN	Coolidge ..	Plymouth, VT
J. Q. Adams	Quincy, MA	Grant	New York, NY	Hoover....	West Branch, IA
Jackson...	Nashville, TN	Hayes	Fremont, OH	F. Roosevelt	Hyde Park, NY
Van Buren .	Kinderhook, NY	Garfield....	Cleveland, OH	Truman ...	Independence, MO
W. H. Harrison	North Bend, OH	Arthur	Albany, NY	Eisenhower	Abilene, KS
Tyler	Richmond, VA	Cleveland..	Princeton, NJ	Kennedy ..	Arlington Natl. Cem.
Polk......	Nashville, TN	B. Harrison .	Indianapolis, IN	L. B. Johnson	Johnson City, TX
Taylor	Louisville, KY	McKinley...	Canton, OH	Nixon	Yorba Linda, CA

Presidential Libraries

The libraries listed below, except for that of Richard Nixon (which is a private institution), are coordinated by the National Archives and Records Administration in Washington, DC. The newest of these, the Bush presidential library, was scheduled to be dedicated Nov. 6, 1997. Further information is available at the NARA Web site (see http://www.nara.gov/nara/president/overview.html). NARA also has custody of the Nixon presidential historical materials. Materials for presidents prior to Herbert Hoover are held by private institutions.

Herbert Hoover Library
211 Parkside Dr., PO Box 488
West Branch, IA 52358-0488
PHONE: 319-643-5301
FAX: 319-643-5825
E-MAIL:library@hoover.nara.gov
Franklin D. Roosevelt Library
511 Albany Post Rd.
Hyde Park, NY 12538-1999
PHONE: 914-229-8114
FAX: 914-229-0872
E-MAIL: library@roosevelt.nara.gov
Harry S. Truman Library
500 West U.S. Hwy. 24
Independence, MO 64050-1798
PHONE: 816-833-1400
FAX: 816-833-4368
E-MAIL: library@truman.nara.gov
Dwight D. Eisenhower Library
200 S.E. 4th St.
Abilene, KS 67410-2900
PHONE: 785-263-4751
FAX: 785-263-4218
E-MAIL: library@eisenhower.nara.gov

John Fitzgerald Kennedy Library
Columbia Pt.
Boston, MA 02125-3398
PHONE: 617-929-4500
FAX: 617-929-4538
E-MAIL: library@kennedy.nara.gov
Lyndon Baines Johnson Library
2313 Red River St.
Austin, TX 78705-5702
PHONE: 512-916-5137
FAX: 512-478-9104
E-MAIL: library@johnson.nara.gov
Richard Nixon Library & Birthplace
18001 Yorba Linda Blvd.
Yorba Linda, CA 92886
PHONE: 714-993-3393
FAX: 714-528-0544
WEB SITE:http://www.chapman.edu/nixon
E-MAIL:stedman@chapman.edu

Gerald R. Ford Library
1000 Beal Ave.
Ann Arbor, MI 48109-2114
PHONE: 313-741-2218
FAX: 313-741-2341
E-MAIL: library@fordlib.nara.gov
Jimmy Carter Library
1 Copenhill Ave., N.E.
Atlanta, GA 30307-1406
PHONE: 404-331-3942
FAX: 404-730-2215
E-MAIL: library@carter.nara.gov
Ronald Reagan Library
40 Presidential Dr.
Simi Valley, CA 93065-0666
PHONE: 805-522-8444
FAX: 805-522-9621
E-MAIL: library@reagan.nara.gov
George Bush Library
PO Box 10410
College Station, TX 77482-0410
PHONE: 409-260-9552
FAX: 409-260-9537
E-MAIL: library@bush.nara.gov

UNITED STATES FACTS
Superlative U.S. Statistics[1]

Source: U.S. Geological Survey, Dept. of the Interior; U.S. Bureau of the Census, Dept. of Commerce; World Almanac research

Area for 50 states and Washington, DC	Total	3,787,319 sq mi
	Land, 3,536,278 sq mi; Water, 251,041 sq mi	
Largest state	Alaska	656,424 sq mi
Smallest state	Rhode Island	1,545 sq mi
Largest county (excludes Alaska)	San Bernardino County, CA	20,061 sq mi
Smallest county	Kalawao, HI	13 sq mi
Largest incorporated city	Sitka, AK	2,881 sq mi
Northernmost city	Barrow, AK	71°17′ N
Northernmost point	Point Barrow, AK	71°23′ N
Southernmost city	Hilo, HI	19°44′ N
Southernmost settlement	Naalehu, HI	19°03′ N
Southernmost point	Ka Lae (South Cape), Island of Hawaii	18°55′ N(155°41′ W)
Easternmost city	Eastport, ME	66°59′ 05″W
Easternmost settlement[2]	Amchitka Isl., AK	179°15′ E
Easternmost point[2]	Pochnoi Point, on Semisopochnoi Isl., AK	179°46′ E
Westernmost city	Atka, AK	174°20′ W
Westernmost settlement	Adak Station, AK	176°39′ W
Westernmost point	Amatignak Isl., AK	179°06′ W
Highest settlement	Climax, CO	11,360 ft
Lowest settlement	Calipatria, CA	−184 ft
Highest point on Atlantic coast	Cadillac Mountain, Mount Desert Isl., ME	1,530 ft
Oldest national park	Yellowstone National Park (1872), WY, MT, ID	2,219,791 acres
Largest national park	Wrangell-St. Elias, AK	8,323,618 acres
Highest waterfall	Yosemite Falls—Total in 3 sections	2,425 ft
	Upper Yosemite Fall	1,430 ft
	Cascades in middle section	675 ft
	Lower Yosemite Fall	320 ft
Longest river	Mississippi-Missouri-Red Rock	3,710 mi
Highest mountain	Mount McKinley, AK	20,320 ft
Lowest point	Death Valley, CA	−282 ft
Deepest lake	Crater Lake, OR	1,932 ft
Rainiest spot	Mount Waialeale, HI	Annual avg rainfall 460 in
Largest gorge	Grand Canyon, Colorado River, AZ	277 mi long, 600 ft
		to 18 mi wide, 1 mi deep
Deepest gorge	Hells Canyon, Snake River, OR-ID	7,900 ft
Strongest surface wind	Mount Washington, NH, recorded 1934	231 mph
Largest dam	New Cornelia Tailings, Ten Mile Wash, AZ[3]	274,026,000 cu yds material used
Tallest building	Sears Tower, Chicago, IL	1,450 ft
Largest building	Boeing 747 Manufacturing Plant, Everett, WA	205,600,000 cu ft; covers 47 acres
Tallest structure	TV tower, Blanchard, ND	2,063 ft
Longest bridge span	Verrazano-Narrows, NY	4,260 ft
Highest bridge	Royal Gorge, CO	1,053 ft above water
Deepest well	Gas well, Washita County, OK	31,441 ft

The 48 Contiguous States

Area for 48 states and Washington, DC	Total	3,119,963 sq mi[4]
	Land, 2,959,481 sq mi; Water, 160,483 sq mi	
Largest state	Texas	268,601 sq mi
Northernmost city	Bellingham, WA	48°46′ N
Northernmost settlement	Angle Inlet, MN	49°21′ N
Northernmost point	Northwest Angle, MN	49°23′ N
Southernmost city	Key West, FL	24°33′ N
Southernmost mainland city	Florida City, FL	25°27′ N
Southernmost point	Key West, FL	24°33′ N
Easternmost settlement	Lubec, ME	66°58′49″ W
Easternmost point	West Quoddy Head, ME	66°57′ W
Westernmost town	La Push, WA	124°38′ W
Westernmost point	Cape Alava, WA	124°44′ W
Highest mountain	Mount Whitney, CA	14,494 ft

(1) All areas are total area, including water, unless otherwise noted. (2) Alaska's Aleutian Islands extend into the eastern hemisphere and therefore technically contain the easternmost point and settlement in the U.S. (3) The New Cornelia Tailings Dam is a privately owned industrial dam composed of tailings, which are remnants of a mining process that once occurred on this site. (4) Does not add, because of rounding.

Geodetic Datum of North America

In July 1986, the National Oceanic and Atmospheric Administration's National Geodetic Survey (NGS), in cooperation with Canada and Mexico, completed the readjustment and redefinition of the system of latitudes and longitudes. Known as the North American Datum of 1983 (NAD 83), it replaces the North American Datum of 1927, as well as local reference systems for the Hawaiian Islands (the Old Hawaiian Datum) and Puerto Rico and the Virgin Islands (the Puerto Rico Datum). The change was prompted by an increased need for accurate coordinate information. To facilitate the use of satellite surveying and navigation systems, such as the Global Positioning System (GPS), the new datum was redefined using the Geodetic Reference System 1980 as the reference ellipsoid because this model more closely approximates the true size and shape of the earth. In addition, the origin of the coordinate system is referenced to the mass center of the earth to coincide with the orbital orientation of the GPS satellites. Positional changes resulting from the datum redefinition can be as much as 330 ft in the continental U.S., Canada, and Mexico. Changes that exceed 660 ft can be expected in Alaska, Puerto Rico, and the Virgin Islands. Hawaii's coordinates changed approximately 1,300 ft.

Additional Statistical Information About the U.S.

The annual *Statistical Abstract of the United States,* published by U.S. Dept. of Commerce, contains additional social, political, and economic data about the U.S. Information concerning these and other publications may be obtained by writing New Orders, Supt. of Documents, PO Box 371954, Pittsburgh, PA 15250-7954, or by phoning the Census Customer Services Dept. at (301) 457-4100. Selected parts of *The Statistical Abstract* can be viewed on the Internet. For this and other Internet addresses see Directory of Internet Sites in the Computer chapter.

Highest and Lowest Altitudes in U.S. States and Territories

Source: U.S. Geological Survey, Dept. of the Interior

(Minus sign means below sea level.)

State/Terr.	Highest Point Name	County	Elev. (ft)	Lowest Point Name	County	Elev. (ft)
Alabama	Cheaha Mountain	Cleburne	2,405	Gulf of Mexico		Sea level
Alaska	Mount McKinley	Denali	20,320	Pacific Ocean		Sea level
Arizona	Humphreys Peak	Coconino	12,633	Colorado R	Yuma	70
Arkansas	Magazine Mountain	Logan	2,753	Ouachita R	Ashley-Union	55
California	Mount Whitney	Inyo-Tulare	14,494	Death Valley	Inyo	−282
Colorado	Mount Elbert	Lake	14,433	Arkansas R	Prowers	3,350
Connecticut	Mount Frissell	Litchfield	2,380	Long Island Sound		Sea level
Delaware	On Ebright Road	New Castle	448	Atlantic Ocean		Sea level
Dist. of Col.	Tenleytown	N W part	410	Potomac R		1
Florida	Sec. 30, T6N, R20W[1]	Walton	345	Atlantic Ocean		Sea level
Georgia	Brasstown Bald	Towns-Union	4,784	Atlantic Ocean		Sea level
Guam	Mount Lamlam	Agat District	1,332	Pacific Ocean		Sea level
Hawaii	Mauna Kea	Hawaii	13,796	Pacific Ocean		Sea level
Idaho	Borah Peak	Custer	12,662	Snake R	Nez Perce	710
Illinois	Charles Mound	Jo Daviess	1,235	Mississippi R	Alexander	279
Indiana	Franklin Township	Wayne	1,257	Ohio R	Posey	320
Iowa	Sec. 29, T100N, R41W[1]	Osceola	1,670	Mississippi R	Lee	480
Kansas	Mount Sunflower	Wallace	4,039	Verdigris R	Montgomery	679
Kentucky	Black Mountain	Harlan	4,139	Mississippi R	Fulton	257
Louisiana	Driskill Mountain	Bienville	535	New Orleans	Orleans	−8
Maine	Mount Katahdin	Piscataquis	5,267	Atlantic Ocean		Sea level
Maryland	Backbone Mountain	Garrett	3,360	Atlantic Ocean		Sea level
Massachusetts	Mount Greylock	Berkshire	3,487	Atlantic Ocean		Sea level
Michigan	Mount Arvon	Baraga	1,979	Lake Erie	Monroe	571
Minnesota	Eagle Mountain	Cook	2,301	Lake Superior		600
Mississippi	Woodall Mountain	Tishomingo	806	Gulf of Mexico		Sea level
Missouri	Taum Sauk Mt.	Iron	1,772	St. Francis R	Dunklin	230
Montana	Granite Peak	Park	12,799	Kootenai R	Lincoln	1,800
Nebraska	Johnson Township	Kimball	5,424	Missouri R	Richardson	840
Nevada	Boundary Peak	Esmeralda	13,140	Colorado R	Clark	479
New Hamp.	Mt. Washington	Coos	6,288	Atlantic Ocean	Rockingham	Sea level
New Jersey	High Point	Sussex	1,803	Atlantic Ocean		Sea level
New Mexico	Wheeler Peak	Taos	13,161	Red Bluff Res.	Eddy	2,842
New York	Mount Marcy	Essex	5,344	Atlantic Ocean		Sea level
North Carolina	Mount Mitchell	Yancey	6,684	Atlantic Ocean		Sea level
North Dakota	White Butte	Slope	3,506	Red R	Pembina	750
Ohio	Campbell Hill	Logan	1,549	Ohio R	Hamilton	455
Oklahoma	Black Mesa	Cimarron	4,973	Little R	McCurtain	289
Oregon	Mount Hood	Clackamas-Hood R.	11,239	Pacific Ocean		Sea level
Pennsylvania	Mt. Davis	Somerset	3,213	Delaware R	Delaware	Sea level
Puerto Rico	Cerro de Punta	Ponce District	4,390	Atlantic Ocean		Sea level
Rhode Island	Jerimoth Hill	Providence	812	Atlantic Ocean		Sea level
Samoa	Lata Mountain	Tau Island	3,160	Pacific Ocean		Sea level
South Carolina	Sassafras Mountain	Pickens	3,560	Atlantic Ocean		Sea level
South Dakota	Harney Peak	Pennington	7,242	Big Stone Lake	Roberts	966
Tennessee	Clingmans Dome	Sevier	6,643	Mississippi R	Shelby	178
Texas	Guadalupe Peak	Culberson	8,749	Gulf of Mexico		Sea level
Utah	Kings Peak	Duchesne	13,528	Beaverdam Wash	Washington	2,000
Vermont	Mount Mansfield	Lamoille	4,393	Lake Champlain		95
Virginia	Mount Rogers	Grayson-Smyth	5,729	Atlantic Ocean		Sea level
Virgin Islands	Crown Mountain	St. Thomas Island	1,556	Atlantic Ocean		Sea level
Washington	Mount Rainier	Pierce	14,410	Pacific Ocean		Sea level
West Virginia	Spruce Knob	Pendleton	4,861	Potomac R	Jefferson	240
Wisconsin	Timms Hill	Price	1,951	Lake Michigan		579
Wyoming	Gannett Peak	Fremont	13,804	Belle Fourche R	Crook	3,099

(1) Sec.=section; T=township; R=range; N=north; W=west.

U.S. Coastline by States

Source: National Oceanic and Atmospheric Administration, U.S. Dept. of Commerce

(in statute miles)

State	Coastline[1]	Shoreline[2]	State	Coastline[1]	Shoreline[2]
Atlantic coast	**2,069**	**28,673**	**Gulf coast**	**1,631**	**17,141**
Connecticut	0	618	Alabama	53	607
Delaware	28	381	Florida	770	5,095
Florida	580	3,331	Louisiana	397	7,721
Georgia	100	2,344	Mississippi	44	359
Maine	228	3,478	Texas	367	3,359
Maryland	31	3,190			
Massachusetts	192	1,519	**Pacific coast**	**7,623**	**40,298**
New Hampshire	13	131	Alaska	5,580	31,383
New Jersey	130	1,792	California	840	3,427
New York	127	1,850	Hawaii	750	1,052
North Carolina	301	3,375	Oregon	296	1,410
Pennsylvania	0	89	Washington	157	3,026
Rhode Island	40	384			
South Carolina	187	2,876	**Arctic coast, Alaska**	**1,060**	**2,521**
Virginia	112	3,315	**United States**	**12,383**	**88,633**

(1) Figures are lengths of general outline of seacoast. Measurements were made with a unit measure of 30 minutes of latitude on charts as near the scale of 1:1,200,000 as possible. Coastline of sounds and bays is included to a point where they narrow to width of unit measure, and includes the distance across at such point. (2) Figures obtained in 1939-40 with a recording instrument on the largest-scale charts and maps then available. Shoreline of outer coast, offshore islands, sounds, bays, rivers, and creeks is included to the head of tidewater or to a point where tidal waters narrow to a width of 100 ft.

States: Settled, Capitals, Entry Into Union, Area, Rank

The 13 colonies that seceded from Great Britain and fought the War of Independence (American Revolution) became the 13 original states. They were (in the order in which they ratified the Constitution): Delaware, Pennsylvania, New Jersey, Georgia, Connecticut, Massachusetts, Maryland, South Carolina, New Hampshire, Virginia, New York, North Carolina, and Rhode Island.

State	Set-tled[1]	Capital	Entered Union Date	Order	Extent in miles Long (approx. mean)	Wide	Area in sq. mi Land	Inland Water	Total	Rank in area[2]
AL....	1702	....Montgomery.....	Dec. 14, 1819	22	330	190	50,750	1,673	52,423	30
AK....	1784	....Juneau	Jan. 3, 1959	49	1,480[3]	810[3]	570,374	86,050	656,424	1
AZ....	1776	....Phoenix........	Feb. 14, 1912	48	400	310	113,642	364	114,006	6
AR....	1686	....Little Rock	June 15, 1836	25	260	240	52,075	1,107	53,182	29
CA....	1769	....Sacramento	Sept. 9, 1850	31	770	250	155,973	7,734	163,707	3
CO....	1858	....Denver.........	Aug. 1, 1876	38	380	280	103,729	371	104,100	8
CT....	1634	....Hartford........	Jan. 9, 1788	5	110	70	4,845	698	5,544	48
DE....	1638	....Dover.........	Dec. 7, 1787	1	100	30	1,955	535	2,489	49
DC....	NA	....Washington	NA	NA	...	...	61	7	68	51
FL....	1565	....Tallahassee	Mar. 3, 1845	27	500	160	53,937	11,821	65,756	22
GA....	1733	....Atlanta........	Jan. 2, 1788	4	300	230	57,919	1,522	59,441	24
HI....	1820	....Honolulu	Aug. 21, 1959	50	...	...	6,423	4,508	10,932	43
ID....	1842	....Boise..........	July 3, 1890	43	570	300	82,751	823	83,574	14
IL....	1720	....Springfield	Dec. 3, 1818	21	390	210	55,593	2,325	57,918	25
IN....	1733	....Indianapolis	Dec. 11, 1816	19	270	140	35,870	550	36,420	38
IA....	1788	....Des Moines	Dec. 28, 1846	29	310	200	55,875	401	56,276	26
KS....	1727	....Topeka	Jan. 29, 1861	34	400	210	81,823	459	82,282	15
KY....	1774	....Frankfort	June 1, 1792	15	380	140	39,732	679	40,411	37
LA....	1699	....Baton Rouge	Apr. 30, 1812	18	380	130	43,566	8,277	51,843	31
ME....	1624	....Augusta........	Mar. 15, 1820	23	320	190	30,865	4,523	35,387	39
MD....	1634	....Annapolis.......	Apr. 28, 1788	7	250	90	9,775	2,632	12,407	42
MA....	1620	....Boston........	Feb. 6, 1788	6	190	50	7,838	2,717	10,555	44
MI....	1668	....Lansing	Jan. 26, 1837	26	490	240	56,809	39,896	96,705	11
MN....	1805	....St. Paul	May 11, 1858	32	400	250	79,617	7,326	86,943	12
MS....	1699	....Jackson........	Dec. 10, 1817	20	340	170	46,914	1,520	48,434	32
MO....	1735	....Jefferson City....	Aug. 10, 1821	24	300	240	68,898	811	69,709	21
MT....	1809	....Helena.........	Nov. 8, 1889	41	630	280	145,556	1,490	147,046	4
NE....	1823	....Lincoln........	Mar. 1, 1867	37	430	210	76,878	481	77,358	16
NV....	1849	....Carson City	Oct. 31, 1864	36	490	320	109,806	761	110,567	7
NH....	1623	....Concord........	June 21, 1788	9	190	70	8,969	382	9,351	46
NJ....	1660	....Trenton........	Dec. 18, 1787	3	150	70	7,419	1,303	8,722	47
NM....	1610	....Santa Fe	Jan. 6, 1912	47	370	343	121,364	234	121,598	5
NY....	1614	....Albany.........	July 26, 1788	11	330	283	47,224	7,247	54,471	27
NC....	1660	....Raleigh	Nov. 21, 1789	12	500	150	48,718	5,103	53,821	28
ND....	1812	....Bismarck	Nov. 2, 1889	39	340	211	68,994	1,710	70,704	19
OH....	1788	....Columbus	Mar. 1, 1803	17	220	220	40,953	3,875	44,828	34
OK....	1889	....Oklahoma City ...	Nov. 16, 1907	46	400	220	68,679	1,224	69,903	20
OR....	1811	....Salem	Feb. 14, 1859	33	360	261	96,002	2,383	98,386	9
PA....	1682	....Harrisburg	Dec. 12, 1787	2	283	160	44,820	1,239	46,058	33
RI....	1636	....Providence......	May 29, 1790	13	40	30	1,045	500	1,545	50
SC....	1670	....Columbia.......	May 23, 1788	8	260	200	30,111	1,897	32,008	40
SD....	1859	....Pierre.........	Nov. 2, 1889	40	380	210	75,896	1,225	77,121	17
TN....	1769	....Nashville	June 1, 1796	16	440	120	41,219	926	42,146	36
TX....	1682	....Austin	Dec. 29, 1845	28	790	660	261,914	6,687	268,601	2
UT....	1847	....Salt Lake City....	Jan. 4, 1896	45	350	270	82,168	2,736	84,904	13
VT....	1724	....Montpelier	Mar. 4, 1791	14	160	80	9,249	366	9,615	45
VA....	1607	....Richmond	June 25, 1788	10	430	200	39,598	3,179	42,777	35
WA....	1811	....Olympia........	Nov. 11, 1889	42	360	240	66,581	4,721	71,302	18
WV....	1727	....Charleston	June 20, 1863	35	240	130	24,087	145	24,231	41
WI....	1766	....Madison........	May 29, 1848	30	310	260	54,314	11,186	65,499	23
WY....	1834	....Cheyenne	July 10, 1890	44	360	280	97,105	714	97,818	10

NA=Not applicable. (1) First permanent European settlement. (2) Rank is based on total area, including inland and coastal waters. (3) Aleutian Islands and Alexander Archipelago are not considered in these measurements.

The Continental Divide of the U.S.

The Continental Divide of the U.S., also known as the Great Divide, is located at the watershed created by the mountain ranges, or tablelands, of the Rocky Mountains. This watershed separates the waters that drain easterly into the Atlantic Ocean and its marginal seas, such as the Gulf of Mexico, from those that drain westerly into the Pacific Ocean. The majority of easterly flowing water drains into the Gulf of Mexico before reaching the Atlantic Ocean. The majority of westerly flowing water, before reaching the Pacific Ocean, either drains through the Columbia R. or through the Colorado R., which flows into the Gulf of California before reaching the Pacific Ocean.

The location and route of the Continental Divide across the U.S. can briefly be described as follows:

Beginning at point of crossing the U.S.-Mexican boundary, near long. 108°45′ W, the Divide, in a northerly direction, crosses New Mexico along the western edge of the Rio Grande drainage basin, entering Colorado near long. 106°41′ W.

From there by a very irregular route north across Colorado along the W summits of the Rio Grande and of the Arkansas, the South Platte, and the North Platte river basins, and across Rocky Mountain National Park, entering Wyoming near long. 106°52′ W.

From there in a northwesterly direction, forming the W rims of the North Platte, the Big Horn, and the Yellowstone river basins, crossing the SW portion of Yellowstone National Park.

From there in a westerly and then a northerly direction forming the common boundary of Idaho and Montana, to a point on said boundary near long. 114°00′ W.

From there northeasterly and northwesterly through Montana and the Glacier National Park, entering Canada near long. 114°04′ W.

Chronological List of Territories, With State Admissions to Union

Source: National Archives and Records Service

Name of territory	Date of Organic Act creating territory	Organic Act effective	Admission as state	Yrs. terr.
Northwest Territory[1]	July 13, 1787	No fixed date	Mar. 1, 1803[2]	16
Territory southwest of River Ohio	May 26, 1790	No fixed date	June 1, 1796[3]	6
Mississippi	Apr. 7, 1798	When president acted	Dec. 10, 1817	19
Indiana	May 7, 1800	July 4, 1800	Dec. 11, 1816	16
Orleans	Mar. 26, 1804	Oct. 1, 1804	Apr. 30, 1812[4]	7
Michigan	Jan. 11, 1805	June 30, 1805	Jan. 26, 1837	31
Louisiana-Missouri[5]	Mar. 3, 1805	July 4, 1805	Aug. 10, 1821	16
Illinois	Feb. 3, 1809	Mar. 1, 1809	Dec. 3, 1818	9
Alabama	Mar. 3, 1817	When MS became a state	Dec. 14, 1819	2
Arkansas	Mar. 2, 1819	July 4, 1819	June 15, 1836	17
Florida	Mar. 30, 1822	No fixed date	Mar. 3, 1845	23
Wisconsin	Apr. 20, 1836	July 3, 1836	May 29, 1848	12
Iowa	June 12, 1838	July 3, 1838	Dec. 28, 1846	8
Oregon	Aug. 14, 1848	Date of act	Feb. 14, 1859	10
Minnesota	Mar. 3, 1849	Date of act	May 11, 1858	9
New Mexico	Sept. 9, 1850	On president's proclamation	Jan. 6, 1912	61
Utah	Sept. 9, 1850	Date of act	Jan. 4, 1896	46
Washington	Mar. 2, 1853	Date of act	Nov. 11, 1889	36
Nebraska	May 30, 1854	Date of act	Mar. 1, 1867	12
Kansas	May 30, 1854	Date of act	Jan. 29, 1861	6
Colorado	Feb. 28, 1861	Date of act	Aug. 1, 1876	15
Nevada	Mar. 2, 1861	Date of act	Oct. 31, 1864	3
Dakota	Mar. 2, 1861	Date of act	Nov. 2, 1889	28
Arizona	Feb. 24, 1863	Date of act	Feb. 14, 1912	49
Idaho	Mar. 3, 1863	Date of act	July 3, 1890	27
Montana	May 26, 1864	Date of act	Nov. 8, 1889	25
Wyoming	July 25, 1868	When officers were qualified	July 10, 1890	22
Alaska[6]	May 17, 1884	No fixed date	Jan. 3, 1959	75
Oklahoma	May 2, 1890	Date of act	Nov. 16, 1907	17
Hawaii	Apr. 30, 1900	June 14, 1900	Aug. 21, 1959	59

(1) Included what is now Ohio, Indiana, Illinois, Michigan, Wisconsin, eastern Minnesota. (2) Whole territory admitted as the state of Ohio. (3) Admitted as the state of Tennessee. (4) Admitted as the state of Louisiana. (5) The organic act for Missouri Territory of June 4, 1812, became effective Dec. 7, 1812. (6) Although the May 17, 1884, act actually constituted Alaska as a district, it was often referred to as a territory, and unofficially administered as such. The Territory of Alaska was legally and formally organized by an act of Aug. 24, 1912.

Geographic Centers, U.S. and Each State

Source: U.S. Geological Survey, Dept. of the Interior

There is no generally accepted definition of geographic center and no uniform method for determining it. Following the U.S. Geological Survey, the geographic center of an area is defined here as the center of gravity of the surface, or that point on which the surface would balance if it were a plane of uniform thickness. All locations in the following list are approximate.

No marked or monumented point has been established by any government agency as the geographic center of the 50 states, the conterminous U.S. (48 states), or the North American continent. However, a group of citizens erected a monument in Lebanon, KS, marking it as geographic center of the conterminous U.S., and a cairn in Rugby, ND, designates that location as the center of the North American continent.

United States, including Alaska and Hawaii—W of Castle Rock, Butte County, South Dakota; lat. 44°59′N, long. 103°38′W
Conterminous U.S. (48 states)—Near Lebanon, Smith Co., Kansas, lat. 39°50′N, long. 98°35′W
North American continent—6 mi W of Balta, Pierce County, North Dakota; lat. 48°10′N, long. 100°10′W

State—county, locality of center

Alabama—Chilton, 12 mi SW of Clanton
Alaska—lat. 63°50′N, long. 152°W; approx. 60 mi NW of Mt. McKinley
Arizona—Yavapai, 55 mi E-SE of Prescott
Arkansas—Pulaski, 12 mi NW of Little Rock
California—Madera, 38 mi E of Madera
Colorado—Park, 30 mi NW of Pikes Peak
Connecticut—Hartford, at East Berlin
Delaware—Kent, 11 mi S of Dover
District of Columbia—Near 4th and L Sts. NW
Florida—Hernando, 12 mi N-NW of Brooksville
Georgia—Twiggs, 18 mi SE of Macon
Hawaii—Hawaii, lat. 20°15′N, long. 156°20′W, off Maui Isl.
Idaho—Custer, SW of Challis
Illinois—Logan, 28 mi NE of Springfield
Indiana—Boone, 14 mi N-NW of Indianapolis
Iowa—Story, 5 mi NE of Ames
Kansas—Barton, 15 mi NE of Great Bend
Kentucky—Marion, 3 mi N-NW of Lebanon
Louisiana—Avoyelles, 3 mi SE of Marksville
Maine—Piscataquis, 18 mi N of Dover
Maryland—Prince George's, 4.5 mi NW of Davidsonville
Massachusetts—Worcester, N part of city

Michigan—Wexford, 5 mi N-NW of Cadillac
Minnesota—Crow Wing, 10 mi SW of Brainerd
Mississippi—Leake, 9 mi W-NW of Carthage
Missouri—Miller, 20 mi SW of Jefferson City
Montana—Fergus, 11 mi W of Lewistown
Nebraska—Custer, 10 mi NW of Broken Bow
Nevada—Lander, 26 mi SE of Austin
New Hampshire—Belknap, 3 mi E of Ashland
New Jersey—Mercer, 5 mi SE of Trenton
New Mexico—Torrance, 12 mi S-SW of Willard
New York—Madison, 12 mi S of Oneida and 26 mi SW of Utica
North Carolina—Chatham, 10 mi NW of Sanford
North Dakota—Sheridan, 5 mi SW of McClusky
Ohio—Delaware, 25 mi N-NE of Columbus
Oklahoma—Oklahoma, 8 mi N of Oklahoma City
Oregon—Crook, 25 mi S-SE of Prineville
Pennsylvania—Centre, 2.5 mi SW of Bellefonte
Rhode Island—Kent, 1 mi S-SW of Crompton
South Carolina—Richland, 13 mi SE of Columbia
South Dakota—Hughes, 8 mi NE of Pierre
Tennessee—Rutherford, 5 mi NE of Murfreesboro
Texas—McCulloch, 15 mi NE of Brady
Utah—Sanpete, 3 mi N of Manti
Vermont—Washington, 3 mi E of Roxbury
Virginia—Buckingham, 5 mi SW of Buckingham
Washington—Chelan, 10 mi W-SW of Wenatchee
West Virginia—Braxton, 4 mi E of Sutton
Wisconsin—Wood, 9 mi SE of Marshfield
Wyoming—Fremont, 58 mi E-NE of Lander

International Boundary Lines of the U.S.

The length of the N boundary of the conterminous U.S.—the U.S.-Canadian border, excluding Alaska—is 3,987 mi according to the U.S. Geological Survey, Dept. of the Interior. The length of the Alaskan-Canadian border is 1,538 mi. The length of the U.S.-Mexican border, from the Gulf of Mexico to the Pacific Ocean, is approximately 1,933 mi (1963 boundary agreement).

Origins of the Names of U.S. States

Source: State officials, Smithsonian Institution, and Topographic Division, U.S. Geological Survey, Dept. of the Interior

Alabama—Indian for tribal town, later a tribe (Alabamas or Alibamons) of the Creek confederacy.

Alaska—Russian version of Aleutian (Eskimo) word, *alakshak*, for "peninsula," "great lands," or "land that is not an island."

Arizona—Spanish version of Pima Indian word for "little spring place," or Aztec *arizuma*, meaning "silver-bearing."

Arkansas—French name for Quapaw ("downstream people"), a Siouan people.

California—Bestowed by the Spanish conquistadors (possibly by Cortez). It was the name of an imaginary island, an earthly paradise, in *Las Serges de Esplandian*, a Spanish romance written by Montalvo in 1510. *Baja California* (Lower California, in Mexico) was first visited by Spanish in 1533. The present U.S. state was called *Alta* (Upper) *California*.

Colorado—From Spanish for "red," first applied to Colorado River.

Connecticut—From Mohican and other Algonquin words meaning "long river place."

Delaware—Named for Lord De La Warr, early governor of Virginia; first applied to river, then to Indian tribe (Lenni-Lenape), and the state.

District of Columbia—For Christopher Columbus, 1791.

Florida—Named by Ponce de Leon *Pascua Florida*, "Flowery Easter," on Easter Sunday, 1513.

Georgia—For King George II of England, by James Oglethorpe, colonial administrator, 1732.

Hawaii—Possibly derived from native word for homeland, *Hawaiki* or *Owhyhee*.

Idaho—Said to be a coined name with an invented meaning: "gem of the mountains"; originally suggested for the Pikes Peak mining territory (Colorado), then applied to the new mining territory of the Pacific Northwest. Another theory suggests *Idaho* may be a Kiowa Apache term for the Comanche.

Illinois—French for *Illini* or "land of *Illini*," Algonquin word meaning "men" or "warriors."

Indiana—Means "land of the Indians."

Iowa— Indian word variously translated as "here I rest" or "beautiful land." Named for the Iowa R., which was named for the Iowa Indians.

Kansas—Sioux word for "south wind people."

Kentucky—Indian word that is variously translated as "dark and bloody ground," "meadowland," and "land of tomorrow."

Louisiana—Part of territory called Louisiana by Sieur de La Salle for French King Louis XIV.

Maine—From Maine, ancient French province. Also: descriptive, referring to the mainland as distinct from the many coastal islands.

Maryland—For Queen Henrietta Maria, wife of Charles I of England.

Massachusetts—From Indian tribe named after "large hill place" identified by Capt. John Smith as being near Milton, MA.

Michigan—From Chippewa words, *mici gama*, meaning "great water," after the lake of the same name.

Minnesota—From Dakota Sioux word meaning "cloudy water" or "sky-tinted water" of the Minnesota River.

Mississippi—Probably Chippewa; *mici zibi*, "great river" or "gathering-in of all the waters." Also: Algonquin word, *messipi*.

Missouri—An Algonquin Indian term meaning "river of the big canoes."

Montana—Latin or Spanish for "mountainous."

Nebraska—From Omaha or Otos Indian word meaning "broad water" or "flat river," describing the Platte River.

Nevada—Spanish, meaning "snow-clad."

New Hampshire—Named, 1629, by Capt. John Mason of Plymouth Council for his home county in England.

New Jersey—The Duke of York, 1664, gave a patent to John Berkeley and Sir George Carteret to be called Nova Caesaria, or New Jersey, after England's Isle of Jersey.

New Mexico—Spaniards in Mexico applied term to land north and west of Rio Grande in the 16th century.

New York—For Duke of York and Albany, who received patent to New Netherland from his brother Charles II and sent an expedition to capture it, 1664.

North Carolina—In 1619 Charles I gave a large patent to Sir Robert Heath to be called Province of Carolana, from *Carolus*, Latin name for Charles. A new patent was granted by Charles II to Earl of Clarendon and others. Divided into North and South Carolina, 1710.

North Dakota—*Dakota* is Sioux for "friend" or "ally."

Ohio—Iroquois word for "fine or good river."

Oklahoma—Choctaw word meaning "red man," proposed by Rev. Allen Wright, Choctaw-speaking Indian.

Oregon—Origin unknown. One theory holds that the name may have been derived from that of the Wisconsin River, shown on a 1715 French map as "Ouaricon-sint."

Pennsylvania—William Penn, the Quaker who was made full proprietor of this area by King Charles II in 1681, suggested "Sylvania," or "woodland," for his tract. The king's government owed Penn's father, Admiral William Penn, £16,000, and the land was granted as partial settlement. Charles II added the "Penn" to Sylvania, against the desires of the modest proprietor, in honor of the admiral.

Puerto Rico—Spanish for "rich port."

Rhode Island—Exact origin is unknown. One theory notes that Giovanni de Verrazano recorded an island about the size of Rhodes in the Mediterranean in 1524, but others believe the state was named *Roode Eylandt* by Adriaen Block, Dutch explorer, because of its red clay.

South Carolina—See North Carolina.

South Dakota—See North Dakota.

Tennessee—*Tanasi* was the name of Cherokee villages on the Little Tennessee River. From 1784 to 1788 this was the State of Franklin, or Frankland.

Texas—Variant of word used by Caddo and other Indians meaning "friends" or "allies," and applied to them by the Spanish in eastern Texas. Also written *Texias*, *Tejas*, *Teysas*.

Utah—From a Navajo word meaning "upper," or "higher up," as applied to a Shoshone tribe called Ute. Spanish form is *Yutta*. The English is *Uta* or *Utah*. Proposed name *Deseret*, "land of honeybees," from Book of Mormon, was rejected by Congress.

Vermont—From French words *vert* (green) and *mont* (mountain). The Green Mountains were said to have been named by Samuel de Champlain. When the state was formed, 1777, Dr. Thomas Young suggested combining *vert* and *mont* into Vermont.

Virginia—Named by Sir Walter Raleigh, who fitted out the expedition of 1584, in honor of Queen Elizabeth, the Virgin Queen of England.

Washington—Named after George Washington. When the bill creating the Territory of Columbia was introduced in the 32d Congress, the name was changed to Washington because of the existence of the District of Columbia.

West Virginia—So named when western counties of Virginia refused to secede from the U.S. in 1863.

Wisconsin—An Indian name, spelled *Ouisconsin* and *Mesconsing* by early chroniclers. Believed to mean "grassy place" in Chippewa. Congress made it *Wisconsin*.

Wyoming—From the Algonquin words for "large prairie place," "at the big plains," or "on the great plain."

Territorial Sea of the U.S.

According to a Dec. 27, 1988, proclamation by Pres. Ronald Reagan: "The territorial sea of the United States henceforth extends to 12 nautical miles from the baselines of the United States determined in accordance with international law. In accordance with international law, as reflected in the applicable provisions of the 1982 United Nations Convention on the Law of the Sea, within the territorial sea of the United States, the ships of all countries enjoy the right of innocent passage and the ships and aircraft of all countries enjoy the right of transit passage through international straits."

Accession of Territory by the U.S.

Source: U.S. Dept. of the Interior; Bureau of the Census, U.S. Dept. of Commerce

	Acquisi-tion date	Land area (sq mi)[1]		Acquisi-tion date	Land area (sq mi)[1]		Acquisi-tion date	Land area (sq mi)[1]
Total U.S.[2]	NA	3,540,305	Texas	1845	388,687	*Other areas:*		
50 states and			Oregon Territory . . .	1846	286,541	Puerto Rico[5]	1899	3,427
Washington, DC . .	NA	3,536,278	Mexican Cession . . .	1848	529,189	Guam[6]	1899	210
Territory in 1790[3] . . .	NA	895,415	Gadsden Purchase .	1853	29,670	American Samoa[7] . .	1900	77
Louisiana Purchase[4] .	1803	909,380	Alaska	1867	570,374	U.S. Virgin Islands . .	1917	134
Purchase of Florida. .	1819	58,666	Hawaii	1898	6,423	N Mariana Islands[8] . .	1986	179
						All other[9]	NA	16

NA=not applicable. (1) Area figures from the Bureau of the Census, Apr. 1, 1990. As a result of independent rounding, the sum of these figures does not equal the total. (2) Includes outlying areas. (3) Includes that part of a drainage basin of Red River of the North, S of 49th parallel, sometimes considered part of Louisiana Purchase. (4) Also acquired areas W of the Mississippi River amounting to 22,834 sq mi, but relinquished to Spain 97,150 sq mi, or a net loss of 15,650 sq mi. (5) Ceded by Spain in 1898, ratified in 1899, and became the Commonwealth of Puerto Rico by Act of Congress on July 25, 1952. (6) Acquired 1898; ratified 1899. (7) Acquired 1899; ratified 1900. (8) Acquired 1986. (9) Consisting of the following islands, with gross areas as indicated in sq mi: Midway (2), Wake (3), Palmyra (2), Navassa (3), Baker, Howland, and Jarvis (combined area, 3), Johnston Atoll (combined area, less than 1), and Kingman Reef (less than 0.5).

Federally Owned Land, by State, 1995

Source: Bureau of Land Management, U.S. Dept. of the Interior; as of Sept. 30, 1995

State	Federal acreage[1]	Total acreage of state[2]	Percentage of federally-owned acreage[1]	State	Federal acreage[1]	Total acreage of state[2]	Percentage of federally-owned acreage[1]
AL	1,072,188.6	32,678,400	3.281	MT	25,688,895.2	93,271,040	27.542
AK	166,513,594.0	365,481,600	45.560	NE	582,497.0	49,031,680	1.188
AZ	30,190,227.2	72,688,000	41.534	NV	54,159,457.7	70,264,320	77.080
AR	2,777,281.6	33,599,360	8.266	NH	736,023.3	5,768,960	12.758
CA	44,689,648.1	100,206,720	44.598	NJ	160,399.1	4,813,440	3.332
CO	23,904,445.1	66,485,760	35.954	NM	26,325,860.4	77,766,400	33.853
CT	7,475.6	3,135,360	0.238	NY	210,372.6	30,680,960	0.686
DE	28,085.3	1,265,920	2.219	NC	2,157,303.3	31,402,880	6.870
DC	9,170.0	39,040	23.489	ND	1,789,136.2	44,452,480	4.025
FL	2,625,499.1	34,721,280	7.562	OH	280,638.1	26,222,080	1.070
GA	1,451,561.1	37,295,360	3.892	OK	640,797.6	44,087,680	1.454
HI	350,932.7	4,105,600	8.548	OR	31,930,737.6	61,598,720	51.837
ID	32,071,047.6	52,933,120	60.588	PA	635,088.5	28,804,480	2.205
IL	453,261.8	35,795,200	1.266	RI	4,611.1	677,120	0.681
IN	399,428.3	23,158,400	1.725	SC	732,670.0	19,374,080	3.782
IA	66,910.2	35,860,480	0.187	SD	2,682,085.8	48,881,920	5.487
KS	282,912.3	52,510,720	0.539	TN	1,534,313.7	26,727,680	5.741
KY	1,073,040.0	25,512,320	4.206	TX	2,346,012.2	168,217,600	1.395
LA	795,853.7	28,867,840	2.757	UT	33,258,252.5	52,696,960	63.112
ME	186,886.2	19,847,680	0.942	VT	380,359.8	5,936,640	6.407
MD	198,354.1	6,319,360	3.139	VA	2,394,064.6	25,496,320	9.390
MA	60,427.8	5,034,880	1.200	WA	10,272,658.0	42,693,760	24.061
MI	3,680,355.2	36,492,160	10.085	WV	1,079,865.2	15,410,560	7.007
MN	1,564,392.2	51,205,760	3.055	WI	1,852,539.5	35,011,200	5.291
MS	1,295,325.1	30,222,720	4.286	WY	30,206,194.2	62,343,040	48.452
MO	1,684,786.9	44,248,320	3.808	**Total. . . . .**	**549,473,923.0**	**2,271,343,360**	**24.192**

Note: Totals do not include inland water. (1) Excludes trust properties. (2) Bureau of the Census, U.S. Dept. of Commerce figures.

Special Recreation Areas Administered by the U.S. Forest Service, 1996

Source: U.S. Forest Service, Dept. of Agriculture

Area name	Location	Estab.	Acres	Area name	Location	Estab.	Acres
Admiralty Island	AK	1980	978,881	Mount Pleasant	VA	1994	7,580
Allegheny	PA	1984	23,063	Mount Rogers	VA	1966	114,520
Arapaho	CO	1978	30,690	Mount St. Helens	WA	1989	112,593
Beech Creek	OK	1988	7,500	Newberry	OR	1990	54,822
Cascade Head	OR	1974	6,630	North Cascades	WA	1984	87,600
Columbia River Gorge	OR-WA . .	1986	63,150	Oregon Dunes	OR	1972	27,212
Coosa Bald	GA	1991	7,100	Pine Ridge	NE	1986	6,600
Ed Jenkins	GA	1991	23,166	Rattlesnake	MT	1980	59,119
Flaming Gorge.	WY-UT . .	1968	189,825	Sawtooth	ID	1972	729,322
Grand Island	MI	1990	12,961	Smith River	CA	1990	305,169
Hells Canyon	ID-OR . . .	1975	536,648	Spring Mt.	NV	1993	312,683
Indian Nations	OK	1988	40,051	Spruce Knob-Seneca Rocks	WV	1965	57,237
Jemez.	NM	1993	57,000	Whiskeytown-Shasta-			
Misty Fiords.	AK	1980	2,293,428	Trinity.	CA	1965	176,367
Mono Basin	CA	1984	115,600	White Rocks	VT	1984	36,400
Mount Baker	WA	1984	8,473	Winding Stair Mt.	OK	1988	25,890

National Parks, Other Areas Administered by National Park Service

Dates that the sites were authorized for initial protection by Congress or by presidential proclamation are given in parenthesis. If different, the date the area was given its current designation, or was transferred to the National Park Service, follows. Gross area in acres, as of Dec. 31, 1996, follows date(s). More than 83 mil acres of federal land are now administered by the National Park Service.

National Parks

Acadia, ME (1916/1929) 46,998. Includes Mount Desert Island, half of Isle au Haut, Schoodic Peninsula on mainland. Highest elevation on Eastern seaboard.

American Samoa, AS (1988) 9,000. Features a paleotropical rain forest and a coral reef. No federal facilities.

Arches, UT (1929/1971) 73,379. Contains giant red sandstone arches and other products of erosion.

Badlands, SD (1929/1978) 242,756; prairie with bison, bighorn, and antelope. Contains animal fossils from 26 to 37 mil years ago.

Big Bend, TX (1935) 801,163. Rio Grande, Chisos Mts.

Biscayne, FL (1968/1980) 172,924. Aquatic park encompassing chain of islands south of Miami.

Bryce Canyon, UT (1923/1928) 35,835. Spectacularly colorful and unusual display of erosion effects.

Canyonlands, UT (1964) 337,570. At junction of Colorado and Green rivers; extensive evidence of prehistoric Indians.

Capitol Reef, UT (1937/1971) 241,904. A 70-mi uplift of sandstone cliffs dissected by high-walled gorges.

Carlsbad Caverns, NM (1923/1930) 46,766. Largest known caverns; not yet fully explored.

Channel Islands, CA (1938/1980) 249,354. Sea lion breeding place, nesting sea birds, unique plants.

Crater Lake, OR (1902) 183,224. Extraordinary blue lake in the crater of Mt. Mazama, a volcano that erupted about 7,700 years ago; deepest U.S. lake.

Death Valley, CA-NV (1933/1994) 3,367,628. Large desert area. Includes the lowest point in the Western Hemisphere; also includes Scottys Castle.

Denali, AK (1917/1980) 4,741,800. Name changed from Mt. McKinley NP. Contains highest mountain in U.S.; wildlife.

Dry Tortugas, FL (1935/1992) 64,700. Formerly Ft. Jefferson National Monument.

Everglades, FL (1934) 1,507,850. Largest remaining subtropical wilderness in continental U.S.

Gates of the Arctic, AK (1978/1984) 7,523,898. Vast wilderness in north central region. Limited federal facilities.

Glacier, MT (1910) 1,013,572. Superb Rocky Mt. scenery, numerous glaciers and glacial lakes. Part of Waterton-Glacier Intl. Peace Park established by U.S. and Canada in 1932.

Glacier Bay, AK (1925/1980) 3,224,794. Great tidewater glaciers that move down mountainsides and break up into the sea; much wildlife.

Grand Canyon, AZ (1893/1919) 1,217,158. Most spectacular part of Colorado River's greatest canyon.

Grand Teton, WY (1929) 309,995. Most impressive part of the Teton Mountains, winter feeding ground of largest American elk herd.

Great Basin, NV (1922/1986) 77,180. Includes Wheeler Pk., Lexington Arch, and Lehman Caves.

Great Smoky Mountains, NC-TN (1926/1934) 521,621. Largest Eastern mountain range, magnificent forests.

Guadalupe Mountains, TX (1966) 86,416. Extensive Permian limestone fossil reef; tremendous earth fault.

Haleakala, HI (1916/1960) 28,091. Dormant volcano on Maui with large colorful craters.

Hawaii Volcanoes, HI (1916/1961) 209,695. Contains Kilauea and Mauna Loa, active volcanoes.

Hot Springs, AR (1832/1921) 5,549. Bathhouses are furnished with thermal waters from the park's 47 hot springs; these waters are used for bathing and drinking.

Isle Royale, MI (1931) 571,790. Largest island in Lake Superior, noted for its wilderness area and wildlife.

Joshua Tree, CA (1936/1994) 792,750. Desert region includes Joshua trees and other plant and animal life.

Katmai, AK (1918/1980) 3,674,541. "Valley of Ten Thousand Smokes," scene of 1912 volcanic eruption.

Kenai Fjords, AK (1978/1980) 670,643. Abundant marine mammals, birdlife; the Harding Icefield, one of the 4 major icecaps in U.S.

Kings Canyon, CA (1890/1940) 461,901. Mountain wilderness, dominated by Kings River Canyons and High Sierra; contains giant sequoias.

Kobuk Valley, AK (1978/1980) 1,750,737. Contains geological and recreational sites. Limited federal facilities.

Lake Clark, AK (1978/1980) 2,619,859. Across Cook Inlet from Anchorage. A scenic wilderness rich in fish and wildlife. Limited federal facilities.

Lassen Volcanic, CA (1907/1916) 106,372. Contains Lassen Peak, recently active volcano, and other volcanic phenomena.

Mammoth Cave, KY (1926/1941) 52,830. 144 mi of surveyed underground passages, beautiful natural formations, river 300 ft below surface.

Mesa Verde, CO (1906) 52,122. Most notable and best preserved prehistoric cliff dwellings in the U.S.

Mount Rainier, WA (1899) 235,613. Greatest single-peak glacial system in the U.S.

North Cascades, WA (1968) 504,781. Spectacular mountainous region with many glaciers, lakes.

Olympic, WA (1909/1938) 922,651. Mountain wilderness containing finest remnant of Pacific Northwest rain forest, active glaciers, Pacific shoreline, rare elk.

Petrified Forest, AZ (1906/1962) 93,533. Extensive petrified wood and Indian artifacts. Contains part of Painted Desert.

Redwood, CA (1968) 110,232. 40 mi of Pacific coastline, groves of ancient redwoods and world's tallest trees.

Rocky Mountain, CO (1915) 265,727. On the Continental Divide; includes peaks over 14,000 ft.

Saguaro, AZ (1933/1994) 91,453. Part of the Sonoran Desert; includes the giant saguaro cacti, unique to the region.

Sequoia, CA (1890) 402,482. Groves of giant sequoias, highest mountain in conterminous U.S.—Mt. Whitney (14,494 ft). World's largest tree.

Shenandoah, VA (1926) 197,389. Portion of the Blue Ridge Mts.; overlooks Shenandoah Valley; Skyline Drive.

Theodore Roosevelt, ND (1947/1978) 70,447. Contains part of T.R.'s ranch and scenic badlands.

Virgin Islands, VI (1956) 14,689. Authorized to cover 75% of St. John Isl. and Hassel Isl.; lush growth, lovely beaches, Carib Indian petroglyphs, evidence of colonial Danes.

Voyageurs, MN (1971) 218,035. Abundant lakes, forests, wildlife, canoeing, boating.

Wind Cave, SD (1903) 28,295. Limestone caverns in Black Hills. Extensive wildlife includes a herd of bison.

Wrangell-St. Elias, AK (1978/1980) 8,323,618. Largest area in park system; most peaks over 16,000 ft, abundant wildlife; day's drive east of Anchorage. Limited federal facilities.

Yellowstone, ID-MT-WY (1872) 2,219,791. World's first national park. World's greatest geyser area has about 10,000 geysers and hot springs; spectacular falls and impressive canyons of the Yellowstone River; grizzly bear, moose, and bison.

Yosemite, CA (1890) 761,236. Yosemite Valley, the nation's highest waterfall, grove of sequoias, and mountains.

Zion, UT (1909/1919) 146,598. Unusual shapes and landscapes have resulted from erosion and faulting; evidence of past volcanic acitivity; Zion Canyon, with sheer walls ranging up to 2,640 ft, is readily accessible.

National Historical Parks

Appomattox Court House, VA (1930/1954) 1,775. Where Lee surrendered to Grant.

Boston, MA (1974) 41. Includes Faneuil Hall, Old North Church, Bunker Hill, Paul Revere House.

Cane River Creole, LA (1994) 207. Preserves the Creole culture as it developed along the Cane R.

Chaco Culture, NM (1907/1980) 33,974. Ruins of pueblos built by prehistoric Indians.

Chesapeake and Ohio Canal, MD-DC-WV (1938/1971) 19,237. 184-mi historic canal; DC to Cumberland, MD.

Colonial, VA (1930/1936) 9,353. Includes most of Jamestown Island, site of first successful English colony; Yorktown, site of Cornwallis's surrender to George Washington; and the Colonial Parkway.

Cumberland Gap, KY-TN-VA (1940) 20,454. Mountain pass of the Wilderness Road, which carried the first great migration of pioneers into America's interior.

Dayton Aviation Heritage, OH (1992) 86. Commemorates the area's aviation heritage.

George Rogers Clark, Vincennes, IN (1966) 26. Commemorates American defeat of British in West during Revolution.

Harpers Ferry, MD-VA-WV (1944/1963) 2,287. At the confluence of the Shenandoah and Potomac rivers, the site of John Brown's 1859 raid on the Army arsenal.

Hopewell Culture, OH (1923/1992) 1,134. Formerly Mound City Group National Monument.

Independence, PA (1948) 45. Contains several properties in Philadelphia associated with the American Revolution and the founding of the U.S. Includes Independence Hall.

Jean Laffite (and preserve), LA (1907/1978) 20,020. Includes Chalmette, site of 1815 Battle of New Orleans; French Quarter.

Kalaupapa, HI (1980) 10,779. Molokai's former leper colony site and other historic areas.

Kaloko-Honokohau, HI (1978) 1,161. Preserves the native culture of Hawaii. No federal facilities.

Keweenaw, MI (1992) 1,870. Site of first significant copper mine in U.S. Federal facilities are under development.

Klondike Gold Rush, AK-WA (1976) 13,191. Alaskan Trails in 1898 Gold Rush. Museum in Seattle.

Lowell, MA (1978) 137. Textile mills, canal, 19th-cent. structures; park shows planned city of Industrial Revolution.

Lyndon B. Johnson, TX (1969/1980) 1,570. President's birthplace, boyhood home, ranch.

Marsh-Billings, VT (1992) 643. Boyhood home of pioneer conservationist George Perkins Marsh. No federal facilities.

Minute Man, MA (1959) 936. Where the colonial Minute Men battled the British, Apr. 19, 1775. Also contains Nathaniel Hawthorne's home.

Morristown, NJ (1933) 1,684. Sites of important military encampments during the American Revolution; Washington's headquarters, 1777, 1779-80.

Natchez, MS (1988) 108. Mansions, townhouses, and villas related to history of Natchez, MS.

New Bedford Whaling, MA (1996) 20. Preserves structures and relics associated with the city's 19th-century whaling industry.

New Orleans Jazz, LA (1994) Acreage undetermined. Preserves, educates, and interprets jazz as it has evolved in New Orleans.

Nez Perce, ID (1965) 2,123. Illustrates the history and culture of the Nez Perce Indian country (38 separate sites).

Pecos, NM (1965/1990) 6,671. Ruins of ancient Pueblo of Pecos, archaeological sites, and 2 associated Spanish colonial missions from the 17th and 18th centuries.

Pu'uhonua o Honaunau, HI (1955/1978) 182. Until 1819, a sanctuary for Hawaiians vanquished in battle and for those guilty of crimes or breaking taboos.

Salt River Bay (ecological preserve), St. Croix, VI (1992) 945. The only site known where, 500 years ago, members of a Columbus party landed on what is now territory of the U.S.

San Antonio Missions, TX (1978) 819. Four of finest Spanish missions in U.S., 18th-cent. irrigation system.

San Francisco Maritime, CA (1988) 31. Artifacts, photographs, and historic vessels related to the development of the Pacific Coast.

San Juan Island, WA (1966) 1,752. Commemorates peaceful relations between the U.S., Canada, and Great Britain since the 1872 boundary disputes.

Saratoga, NY (1938) 3,392. Scene of a major battle that became a turning point in the American Revolution.

Sitka, AK (1910/1972) 107. Scene of last major resistance of the Tlingit Indians to the Russians, 1804.

Tumacacori, AZ (1908/1990) 47. Historic Spanish Catholic mission building stands near the site first visited by Jesuit Father Kino in 1691.

Valley Forge, PA (1976) 3,466. Continental Army campsite in 1777-78 winter.

War in the Pacific, GU (1978) 1,960. Seven distinct units illustrating the Pacific theater of WWII. Limited federal facilities.

Women's Rights, NY (1980) 7. Seneca Falls site where Susan B. Anthony, Elizabeth Cady Stanton began rights movement in 1848.

National Battlefields

Antietam, MD (1890/1978) 3,256. Battle here ended first Confederate invasion of North, Sept. 17, 1862.

Big Hole, MT (1910/1963) 656. Site of major battle with Nez Perce Indians.

Cowpens, SC (1929/1972) 842. American Revolution battlefield.

Fort Donelson, TN (1928/1985) 552. Site of first major Union victory.

Fort Necessity, PA (1931/1961) 903. Some of first battle of French and Indian War.

Monocacy, MD (1934/1976) 1,647. Civil War battle in defense of Washington, DC, fought here, July 9, 1864.

Moores Creek, NC (1926/1980) 87. 1776 battle between Patriots and Loyalists commemorated here.

Petersburg, VA (1926/1962) 2,744. Scene of 10-month Union campaigns 1864-65.

Stones River, TN (1927/1960) 708. Scene of battle that began federal offensive to trisect the Confederacy.

Tupelo, MS (1929/1961) 1. Site of crucial battle over Sherman's supply line.

Wilson's Creek, MO (1960/1970) 1,750. Scene of Civil War battle for control of Missouri.

National Battlefield Parks

Kennesaw Mountain, GA (1917/1935) 2,884. Site of two major battles of Atlanta campaign in Civil War.

Manassas, VA (1940) 5,072. Scene of two battles in Civil War, 1861 and 1862.

Richmond, VA (1936) 821. Site of battles defending Confederate capital.

National Battlefield Site

Brices Cross Roads, MS (1929) 1. Civil War battlefield.

National Military Parks

Chickamauga and Chattanooga, GA-TN (1890) 8,119. Site of major Confederate victory, 1863.

Fredericksburg and Spotsylvania County, VA (1927/1933) 7,787. Sites of several major Civil War battles and campaigns.

Gettysburg, PA (1895/1933) 5,906. Site of decisive Confederate defeat in North and Gettysburg Address.

Guilford Courthouse, NC (1917/1933) 220. American Revolution battle site.

Horseshoe Bend, AL (1956) 2,040. On Tallapoosa River, where Gen. Andrew Jackson's forces broke the power of the Upper Creek Indian Confederacy.

Kings Mountain, SC (1931/1933) 3,945. Site of American Revolution battle.

Pea Ridge, AR (1956) 4,300. Scene of Civil War battle.

Shiloh, TN (1894/1933) 3,973. Major Civil War battlesite; includes some well-preserved Indian burial mounds.

Vicksburg, MS-LA (1899/1933) 1,736. Union victory gave North control of the Mississippi and split the Confederate forces.

National Memorials

Arkansas Post, AR (1960) 389. First permanent French settlement in the lower Mississippi River valley.

Arlington House, the Robert E. Lee Memorial, VA (1925/1972) 28. Lee's home overlooking the Potomac.

Chamizal, El Paso, TX (1966/1974) 55. Commemorates 1963 settlement of 99-year border dispute with Mexico.

Coronado, AZ (1941/1952) 4,750. Commemorates first European exploration of the Southwest.

DeSoto, FL (1948) 27. Commemorates 16th-cent. Spanish explorations.

Federal Hall, NY (1939/1955) 0.45. First seat of U.S. government under the Constitution.

Fort Caroline, FL (1950) 138. On St. Johns River, overlooks site of a French Huguenot colony.

Fort Clatsop, OR (1958) 125. Lewis and Clark encampment, 1805-6.

Franklin Delano Roosevelt, DC (1982) 7.5. Statues of Pres. Roosevelt and Eleanor Roosevelt, as well as waterfalls and gardens. Dedicated May 2, 1997.

General Grant, NY (1958) 0.76. Tomb of Grant and wife.

Hamilton Grange, NY (1962) 0.11. Home of Alexander Hamilton.

Jefferson National Expansion Memorial, St. Louis, MO (1935) 91. Commemorates westward expansion.

Johnstown Flood, PA (1964) 164. Commemorates tragic flood of 1889.

Korean War Veterans, DC (1986) 2. Dedicated in 1995; honors those who served in the Korean War.

Lincoln Boyhood, IN (1962) 200. Lincoln grew up here.

Lincoln Memorial, DC (1911/1933) 107. Marble statue of the 16th U.S. president.

Lyndon B. Johnson Grove on the Potomac, DC (1973) 17. Overlooks the Potomac R.; vista of the Capital.

Mount Rushmore, SD (1925) 1,278. World-famous sculpture of 4 presidents.

Perry's Victory and International Peace Memorial, Put-in-Bay, OH (1936/1972) 25. The world's most massive Doric column, constructed 1912-15, promotes pursuit of international peace through arbitration and disarmament.

Roger Williams, Providence, RI (1965) 5. Memorial to founder of Rhode Island.

Thaddeus Kosciuszko, PA (1972) 0.02. Memorial to Polish hero of American Revolution.

Theodore Roosevelt Island, DC (1932/1933) 89. Statue of Roosevelt in wooded island sanctuary.

Thomas Jefferson Memorial, DC (1934) 18. Statue of Jefferson in an inscribed circular, colonnaded structure.

USS Arizona, HI (1980). 11. Memorializes American losses at Pearl Harbor.

Vietnam Veterans, DC (1980) 2. Black granite wall inscribed with names of those missing or killed in action in the Vietnam War.

Washington Monument, DC (1848/1933) 106. Obelisk honoring the first U.S. president.

Wright Brothers, NC (1927/1953) 428. Site of first powered flight.

National Historic Sites

Abraham Lincoln Birthplace, Hodgenville, KY (1916/1959) 117. Early 17th-cent. cabin.

Adams, Quincy, MA (1946/1952) 14. Home of Presidents John Adams, John Quincy Adams, and celebrated descendants.

Allegheny Portage Railroad, PA (1964) 1,249. Linked the Pennsylvania Canal system and the West.

Andersonville, Andersonville, GA (1970) 495. Noted Civil War prisoner-of-war camp.

Andrew Johnson, Greeneville, TN (1935/1963) 17. Two homes and the tailor shop of the 17th U.S. president.

Bent's Old Fort, CO (1960) 800. Reconstruction of S Plains outpost.

Boston African American, MA (1980) Acreage undetermined. Pre-Civil War black history structures.

Brown v. Board of Education, KS (1992) 2. Commemorates the landmark 1954 U.S. Supreme Court decision.

Carl Sandburg Home, Flat Rock, NC (1968) 264. Poet's home.

Charles Pinckney, SC (1988) 28. Statesman's farm.

Christiansted, St. Croix, VI (1952/1961) 27. Commemorates Danish colony.

Clara Barton, MD (1974) 9. Home of founder of American Red Cross.

Edgar Allan Poe, PA (1978/1980) 0.52. U.S. writer's home.

Edison, West Orange, NJ (1955/1962) 21. Inventor's home and laboratory.

Eisenhower, Gettysburg, PA (1967) 690. Home of 34th president.

Eleanor Roosevelt, Hyde Park, NY (1977) 181. Personal retreat.

Eugene O'Neill, Danville, CA (1976) 13. Playwright's home.

Ford's Theatre, DC (1866/1970) 0.29. Includes theater, now restored, where Lincoln was assassinated, house where he died, and Lincoln Museum.

Fort Bowie, AZ (1964) 1,000. Focal point of operations against Geronimo and the Apaches.

Fort Davis, TX (1961) 460. Key frontier outpost in West Texas.

Fort Laramie, WY (1938/1960) 833. Military post on Oregon Trail.

Fort Larned, KS (1964/1966) 718. Military post on Santa Fe Trail.

Fort Point, San Francisco, CA (1970) 29. West Coast fortification.

Fort Raleigh, NC (1941) 513. First attempted English settlement in North America.

Fort Scott, KS (1965/1978) 17. Commemorates U.S. frontier of 1840s and '50s.

Fort Smith, AR-OK (1961) 75. Active post during 1817-90.

Fort Union Trading Post, MT-ND (1966) 444. Principal fur-trading post on upper Missouri, 1829-67.

Fort Vancouver, WA (1948/1961) 209. Headquarters for Hudson's Bay Company in 1825. Early political seat.

Frederick Douglass, DC (1962/1988) 9. Home of famous black abolitionist, writer, and orator.

Frederick Law Olmsted, MA (1979) 2. Home of famous city planner.

Friendship Hill, PA (1978) 675. Home of Albert Gallatin, Jefferson's and Madison's secretary of treasury.

Golden Spike, UT (1957) 2,735. Commemorates completion of first transcontinental railroad in 1869.

Grant-Kohrs Ranch, MT (1972) 1,498. Ranch house and part of 19th-cent. ranch.

Hampton, MD (1948) 62. 18th-cent. Georgian mansion.

Harry S. Truman, MO (1983) 7. Home of Pres. Truman after 1919.

Herbert Hoover, West Branch, IA (1965) 187. Birthplace and boyhood home of 31st president.

Home of Franklin D. Roosevelt, Hyde Park, NY (1944) 290. FDR's birthplace, home, and "summer White House."

Hopewell Furnace, PA (1938/1985) 848. 19th-cent. iron-making village.

Hubbell Trading Post, AZ (1965) 160. Still-active trading post.

James A. Garfield, Mentor, OH (1980) 8. Home of 20th president.

Jimmy Carter, GA (1987) 71. Birthplace and home of 39th president.

John Fitzgerald Kennedy, Brookline, MA (1967) 0.09. Birthplace and childhood home of 35th president.

John Muir, Martinez, CA (1964) 345. Home of early conservationist and writer.

Knife River Indian Villages, ND (1974) 1,758. Remnants of villages last occupied by Hidatsa and Mandan Indians.

Lincoln Home, Springfield, IL (1971) 12. Lincoln's residence at the time he was elected 16th president, 1860.

Longfellow, Cambridge, MA (1972) 2. Longfellow's home, 1837-82, and Washington's headquarters during Boston Siege, 1775-76.

Maggie L. Walker, VA (1978) 1. Richmond home of black leader and bank president, daughter of an ex-slave.

Manzanar, Lone Pine, CA (1992) 800. Commemorates Manzanar War Relocation Ctr., a Japanese-American internment camp during WWII. No federal facilities.

Martin Luther King, Jr., Atlanta, GA (1980) 37. Birthplace, grave, and church of the civil rights leader. Limited federal facilities.

Martin Van Buren, NY (1974) 40. Lindenwald, home of 8th president, near Kinderhook.

Mary McLeod Bethune Council House, DC (1982/1991) 0.07. Commemorates Bethune's leadership in the black women's movement.

Nicodemus, KS (1996) 161. Only remaining western town established by African-Americans during Reconstruction.

Ninety Six, SC (1976) 989. Colonial trading village.

Palo Alto Battlefield, TX (1978) 3,357. Scene of first battle of the Mexican War.

Pennsylvania Avenue, DC (1965) Acreage undetermined. Also includes area adjacent to the road between Capitol and White House, encompassing Ford's Theatre and a number of other federal structures.

Puukohola Heiau, HI (1972) 86. Ruins of temple built by King Kamehameha.

Sagamore Hill, Oyster Bay, NY (1962) 83. Home of President Theodore Roosevelt from 1885 until his death in 1919.

Saint-Gaudens, Cornish, NH (1964) 148. Home, studio, and gardens of American sculptor Augustus Saint-Gaudens.

Saint Paul's Church, NY (1943) 6. 18th-cent. site associated with John Peter Zenger's "freedom of press" trial.

Salem Maritime, MA (1938) 9. Only port never seized from the patriots by the British. Major fishing and whaling port.

San Juan, PR (1949) 75. 16th-cent. Span. fortifications.

Saugus Iron Works, MA (1974) 9. Reconstructed 17th-cent. colonial ironworks.

Springfield Armory, MA (1974) 55. Small-arms manufacturing center for nearly 200 years.

Steamtown, PA (1986) 62. Railyard, roadhouse, and repair shops of former Delaware, Lackawanna, and Western Railroad.

Theodore Roosevelt Birthplace, New York, NY (1962) 0.11. Reconstructed brownstone.

Theodore Roosevelt Inaugural, Buffalo, NY (1966) 1. Wilcox House where he took oath of office, 1901.

Thomas Stone, MD (1978) 328. Home of signer of Declaration of Independence, built in 1771.

Tuskegee Institute, AL (1974) 58. College founded by Booker T. Washington in 1881 for blacks.

Ulysses S. Grant, St. Louis Co., MO (1989) 10. Home of Grant during pre-Civil War years.

Vanderbilt Mansion, Hyde Park, NY (1940) 212. Mansion of 19th-cent. financier.

Washita Battlefield, OK (1996) 330. Scene of Nov. 27, 1868, battle between Plains tribes and the U.S. army.

Weir Farm, Wilton, CT (1990) 61. Home and studio of American impressionist painter J. Alden Weir.

Whitman Mission, WA (1936/1963) 98. Site where Dr. and Mrs. Marcus Whitman ministered to the Indians until slain by them in 1847.

William Howard Taft, Cincinnati, OH (1969) 3. Birthplace and early home of the 27th president.

National Monuments

Name	State	Year[1]	Acreage
Agate Fossil Beds	NE	1965	3,055
Alibates Flint Quarries	NM-TX	1965	1,371
Aniakchak**	AK	1978	137,176
Aztec Ruins	NM	1923	320
Bandelier	NM	1916	32,737
Black Canyon of the Gunnison	CO	1933	20,766
Booker T. Washington	VA	1956	224
Buck Island Reef	VI	1961	880
Cabrillo	CA	1913	137
Canyon de Chelly	AZ	1931	83,840
Cape Krusenstern†	AK	1978	650,000
Capulin Volcano	NM	1916	793
Casa Grande Ruins	AZ	1889	473
Castillo de San Marcos	FL	1924	21
Castle Clinton	NY	1946	1
Cedar Breaks	UT	1933	6,155
Chiricahua	AZ	1924	11,985
Colorado	CO	1911	20,454
Congaree Swamp	SC	1976	22,200
Craters of the Moon	ID	1924	53,440
Devils Postpile	CA	1911	798
Devils Tower	WY	1906	1,347
Dinosaur	CO-UT	1915	210,844
Effigy Mounds	IA	1949	1,481
El Malpais	NM	1987	114,277
El Morro	NM	1906	1,279
Florissant Fossil Beds	CO	1969	5,998
Fort Frederica	GA	1936	241
Fort Matanzas	FL	1924	228
Fort McHenry National Monument and Historic Shrine	MD	1925	43
Fort Pulaski	GA	1924	5,623
Fort Stanwix	NY	1935	16
Fort Sumter	SC	1948	195
Fort Union	NM	1954	721
Fossil Butte	WY	1972	8,198
G. Washington Birthplace	VA	1930	550
George Washington Carver	MO	1943	210
Gila Cliff Dwellings	NM	1907	533
Grand Portage	MN	1951	710
Grand Staircase-Escalante[2]	UT	1996	1,700,000
Great Sand Dunes	CO	1932	38,662
Hagerman Fossil Beds†	ID	1988	4,346
Hohokam Pima*	AZ	1972	1,690
Homestead Natl. Monument of America	NE	1936	195
Hovenweep	CO-UT	1923	785
Jewel Cave	SD	1908	1,274
John Day Fossil Beds	OR	1974	14,015
Lava Beds	CA	1925	46,560
Little Big Horn Battlefield	MT	1879	765

Name	State	Year[1]	Acreage
Montezuma Castle	AZ	1906	858
Muir Woods	CA	1908	554
Natural Bridges	UT	1908	7,636
Navajo	AZ	1909	360
Ocmulgee	GA	1934	702
Oregon Caves	OR	1909	488
Organ Pipe Cactus	AZ	1937	330,689
Petroglyph	NM	1990	7,240
Pinnacles	CA	1908	16,265
Pipe Spring	AZ	1923	40
Pipestone	MN	1937	282
Poverty Point**	LA	1988	911
Rainbow Bridge†	UT	1910	160
Russell Cave	AL	1961	310
Salinas Pueblo Missions	NM	1909	1,071
Scotts Bluff	NE	1919	3,003
Statue of Liberty	NJ-NY	1924	58
Sunset Crater Volcano	AZ	1930	3,040
Timpanogos Cave	UT	1922	250
Tonto	AZ	1907	1,120
Tuzigoot	AZ	1939	801
Walnut Canyon	AZ	1915	3,541
White Sands	NM	1933	143,733
Wupatki	AZ	1924	35,422
Yucca House*	CO	1919	34

National Preserves

Name	State	Year[1]	Acreage
Aniakchak	AK	1978	465,603
Bering Land Bridge†	AK	1978	2,698,000
Big Cypress	FL	1974	716,000
Big Thicket	TX	1974	96,680
Denali	AK	1917	1,334,200
Gates of the Arctic	AK	1978	948,629
Glacier Bay	AK	1925	58,406
Katmai	AK	1918	418,699
Lake Clark	AK	1978	1,410,642
Little River Canyon**	AL	1992	13,669
Mojave	CA	1994	1,450,000
Noatak†	AK	1978	6,570,000
Tallgrass Prairie	KS	1996	10,894
Timucuan Ecological & Historic Preserve†	FL	1988	46,000
Wrangell-St. Elias	AK	1978	4,852,773
Yukon-Charley Rivers†	AK	1978	2,526,509

National Seashores

Name	State	Year[1]	Acreage
Assateague Island	MD-VA	1965	39,722
Canaveral	FL	1975	57,662
Cape Cod	MA	1961	43,569
Cape Hatteras	NC	1937	30,319
Cape Lookout	NC	1966	28,243
Cumberland Island	GA	1972	36,415
Fire Island	NY	1964	19,579
Gulf Islands	FL-MS	1971	135,607
Padre Island	TX	1962	130,434
Point Reyes	CA	1962	71,057

National Parkways

Name	State	Year[1]	Acreage
Blue Ridge	NC-VA	1933	87,992
George Washington Memorial	VA-MD-DC	1930	7,248
John D. Rockefeller Jr. Mem.	WY	1972	23,777
Natchez Trace	MS-AL-TN	1938	51,748

National Lakeshores

Name	State	Year[1]	Acreage
Apostle Islands	WI	1970	69,372
Indiana Dunes	IN	1966	15,139
Pictured Rocks	MI	1966	73,236
Sleeping Bear Dunes	MI	1970	71,189

National Reserves

Name	State	Year[1]	Acreage
City of Rocks†	ID	1988	14,407
Ebey's Landing†	WA	1978	19,000

National Rivers

Name	State	Year[1]	Acreage
Big South Fork Natl. R and Recreation Area	KY-TN	1976	125,000
Buffalo	AR	1972	94,309
Mississippi Natl. R and Recreation Area	MN	1988	53,775
Missouri	NE-SD	1991	NA
New River Gorge	WV	1978	70,912
Ozark	MO	1964	80,790

National Wild and Scenic Rivers

Name	State	Year[1]	Acreage
Alagnak	AK	1980	30,800
Bluestone**	WV	1978	4,310
Delaware	NY-NJ-PA	1978	1,973
Great Egg Harbor	NJ	1992	NA
Niobrara	NE-SD	1991	NA
Obed	TN	1976	5,122
Rio Grande**	TX	1978	9,600
Saint Croix	MN-WI	1968	67,456
Upper Delaware	NY-PA	1978	75,000

National Recreation Areas

Name	State	Year[1]	Acreage
Amistad	TX	1965	58,500
Bighorn Canyon	MT-WY	1966	120,296
Boston Harbor Islands	MA	1996	1,482
Chattahoochee R.	GA	1978	9,239
Chickasaw	OK	1902	9,889
Coulee Dam	WA	1946	100,390
Curecanti	CO	1965	41,972
Cuyahoga Valley	OH	1974	32,525
Delaware Water Gap	NJ-PA	1965	67,192
Gateway	NJ-NY	1972	26,601
Gauley R.†	WV	1988	11,145
Glen Canyon	AZ-UT	1958	1,236,880
Golden Gate	CA	1972	74,441
Lake Chelan	WA	1968	61,887
Lake Mead	AZ-NV	1936	1,495,666
Lake Meredith	TX	1965	44,978
Ross Lake	WA	1968	117,575
Santa Monica Mts.†	CA	1978	150,050
Whiskeytown	CA	1965	42,503

National Scenic Trails

Name	State	Year[1]	Acreage
Appalachian	ME to GA	1968	172,110
Natchez Trace	MS-AL-TN	1983	10,995
Potomac Heritage	MD-DC-VA-PA	1983	NA

Parks (no other classification)

Name	State	Year[1]	Acreage
Catoctin Mountain	MD	1954	5,770
Constitution Gardens	DC	1974	52
Fort Washington	MD	1930	341
Greenbelt	MD	1950	1,176
National Capital	DC	1933	6,547
National Mall	DC	1933	146
Piscataway	MD	1961	4,441
Prince William Forest	VA	1948	18,572
Rock Creek	DC	1890	1,754
White House	DC	1933	18
Wolf Trap Farm Park for the Performing Arts	VA	1966	130

International Historic Site

Name	State	Year[1]	Acreage
Saint Croix Island†	ME	1949	35

NA=Not available. *Not open to the public. **No federal facilities. † Limited federal facilities. (1) First designated. (2) Administered by Bureau of Land Management; acreage is estimated.

20 Most-Visited Sites in the National Park System, 1996

Source: National Park Service, Dept. of the Interior

Attendance at all areas administered by the National Park Service in 1996 totaled 265,796,163 recreation visits.

Site (location)	Recreation visits
Blue Ridge Parkway (NC, VA)	17,169,062
Golden Gate National Recreation Area (CA)	14,043,984
Lake Mead National Recreation Area (AZ, NV)	9,350,847
Great Smoky Mountains National Park (TN, NC)	9,265,667
Gateway National Recreation Area (NY, NJ)	6,381,502
George Washington Memorial National Parkway (VA, MD, DC)	6,126,490
National Capital Parks (DC)	6,094,875
Natchez Trace National Parkway (MS, AL, TN)	6,088,610
Cape Cod National Seashore (MA)	4,901,782
Delaware Water Gap National Recreation Area (PA, NJ)	4,657,735
Grand Canyon National Park (AZ)	4,537,703
Statue of Liberty National Monument (NY, NJ)	4,494,076
Yosemite National Park (CA)	4,046,207
Castle Clinton National Monument (NY)	3,753,944
San Francisco Maritime National Historical Park (CA)	3,670,972
Jefferson National Expansion Memorial (MO)	3,649,308
Chattahoochee River National Recreation Area (GA)	3,540,375
Cuyahoga Valley National Recreation Area (OH)	3,455,878
Olympic National Park (WA)	3,348,723
Colonial National Historical Park (VA)	3,145,039

Federal Indian Reservations and Trust Lands[1]

Source: Tiller Research, Inc., Albuquerque, NM

State	No. of reser.	Tribally owned acreage[2]	Individually owned acreage[2]	No. of persons[2]	Major tribes and/or nations
Alabama	1	230	0	16,506	Poarch Creek
Alaska	1[4]	86,773	1,265,432	85,698	Aleut, Eskimo, Athabascan,[5] Haida, Tlingit, Tsimpshian
Arizona	23	19,775,959	311,579	203,527	Navajo, Apache, Papago, Hopi, Yavapai, Pima
California	96	520,049	66,769	242,164	Hoopa, Paiute, Yurok, Karok, Cherokee
Colorado	2	764,120	2,805	27,776	Ute
Connecticut	1	1,638	0	6,654	Mashantucket Pequot
Florida	4	153,874	0	36,335	Seminole, Miccosukee, Cherokee
Idaho	4	609,622	327,301	13,780	Shoshone, Bannock, Nez Perce
Iowa	1	3,550	0	7,349	Sac and Fox
Kansas	4	7,219	23,763	21,965	Potawatomi, Kickapoo, Iowa
Louisiana	3	415	0	18,541	Chitimacha, Coushatta, Tunica-Biloxi
Maine	3	191,511	0	5,998	Passamaquoddy, Penobscot, Maliseet
Massachusetts	1	157	0	12,241	Wampanoag
Michigan	8	14,411	9,276	55,638	Chippewa, Potawatomi, Ottawa, Cherokee
Minnesota	14	779,138	50,338	49,909	Chippewa, Sioux
Mississippi	1	20,486	0	8,525	Choctaw
Montana	7	2,663,385	2,911,450	47,679	Blackfoot, Crow, Sioux, Assiniboine, Cheyenne
Nebraska	3	23,792	43,208	12,410	Omaha, Winnebago, Santee Sioux
Nevada	19	1,147,088	78,529	19,637	Paiute, Shoshone, Washoe
New Mexico	25	7,252,326	630,293	134,355	Apache, Navajo, Pueblo
New York	8	118,199	0	62,651	Seneca, Mohawk, Onondaga, Oneida
North Carolina	1	56,509	0	80,155	Cherokee, Lumbee
North Dakota	3	214,006	627,289	25,917	Sioux, Chippewa, Mandan, Arikara, Hidatsa
Oklahoma	36[6]	96,839	1,000,165	252,420	Cherokee, Creek, Choctaw, Chickasaw, Osage, Cheyenne, Arapahoe, Kiowa, Comanche
Oregon	7	660,367	135,053	38,496	Warm Springs, Wasco, Paiute, Umatilla, Siletz
Rhode Island	1	1,800	0	4,071	Narragansett
South Carolina	1	639	0	8,246	Catawba
South Dakota	9	2,399,531	2,121,188	50,575	Sioux
Texas	3	4,726	0	65,877	Alabama-Coushatta, Tiwa, Kickapoo
Utah	4	2,286,448	32,838	24,283	Ute, Goshute, Southern Paiute, Navajo
Washington	27	2,250,731	467,785	81,483	Yakama, Lummi, Quinault
Wisconsin	11	338,097	80,345	39,387	Chippewa, Oneida, Winnebago
Wyoming	1	1,958,095	101,537	9,479	Shoshone, Arapahoe

(1) In Oct. 1993, the Bureau of Indian Affairs of the U.S. Dept. of the Interior published in the *Federal Register* (vol. 58, no. 202, pp. 54364-69) a comprehensive listing of 552 "Indian Entities Recognized and Eligible to Receive Services From the United States Bureau of Indian Affairs" (328 in the conterminous 48 states, 224 in Alaska). The term *Indian entities* includes Indian tribes, bands, villages, groups, and pueblos; also included are Eskimo and Aleut villages and tribes. All such entities have a government-to-government relationship with the U.S. Some reservation boundaries transcend state boundaries (e.g., Navajo, which is in Arizona, New Mexico, and Utah). For the purpose of "Number of Reservations," such reservations are counted in the state where their population is predominant and/or tribal headquarters are located. (2) Information provided by the Bureau of Indian Affairs; data current as of 1990. Acreages refer only to lands that are either owned by the tribes and individual members or are held in trust by the U.S. government. Many of these parcels are located off reservations. Not all lands within reservation boundaries are necessarily trust lands. Many are privately owned by tribes, tribal members, or non-Indians; others are the property of various governmental agencies. (3) Total Native American (Indian, Eskimo, or Aleut) population in each state with reservation/trust lands, including those persons living outside the Bureau of Indian Affairs service area. Populations as of 1990. (4) The only federally recognized reservation in Alaska is the Annette Island Reserve. In all other cases, the U.S. government's relationship to Native Americans in Alaska is set out by the Alaska Native Claims Settlement Act of 1971. The act provided for the establishment of regional and village corporations to conduct business for profit and nonprofit purposes; these corporations are also landowners. There are 12 regional corporations, each with organized village corporations, plus one regional corporation for Alaska Natives outside the state. (5) Aleuts and Eskimos are racially and linguistically related. Athabascans are related to the Navajo and Apache Indians. (6) There are 36 tribal entities in Oklahoma, each of which owns land in the state. Because of the way in which the state was formed out of the Oklahoma and Indian territories, the reservation status of land in the state is frequently disputed in both civil and criminal proceedings.

Largest American Indian Tribes

Source: Bureau of the Census, U.S. Dept. of Commerce, as of 1990 census

Tribe	Number	Percent	Tribe	Number	Percent
All American Indians	**1,937,391**	**100.0**	Chickasaw	21,522	1.1
Cherokee	369,035	19.0	Tohono O'Odham	16,876	0.9
Navajo	225,298	11.6	Potawatomi	16,719	0.9
Sioux	107,321[1]	5.5	Seminole	15,564	0.8
Chippewa	105,988	5.5	Pima	15,074	0.8
Choctaw	86,231	4.5	Tlingit	14,417	0.7
Pueblo	55,330	2.9	Alaskan Athabaskans	14,198	0.7
Apache	53,330	2.8	Cheyenne	11,809	0.6
Iroquois[2]	52,557	2.7	Comanche	11,437	0.6
Lumbee	50,888	2.6	Paiute	11,369	0.6
Creek	45,872	2.4	Osage	10,430	0.5
Blackfoot	37,992	2.0	Puget Sound Salish	10,384	0.5
Canadian and Latin American	27,179	1.4	Yaqui	9,838	0.5

(1) Any entry from NC with the spelling "Siouan" in the 1990 census was miscoded to count as Sioux. (2) Reporting and/or processing problems in the 1990 census have affected accuracy of the data for this tribe.

WORLD HISTORY

Prehistory: Our Ancestors Emerge

Revised by Susan Skomal, Ph.D., Editor, Anthropology Newsletter, *American Anthropological Association*

Homo sapiens. The precise origins of *Homo sapiens,* the species to which all humans belong, are subject to broad speculation based on a small, but increasing, number of fossils, on genetic and anatomical studies, and on interpretation of the geological record. Most scientists at least agree that humans evolved from apelike primate ancestors in a process that began millions of years ago.

Current theories trace the first hominid (humanlike primate) to Africa, where at least 2 lines of hominids appeared 5 to 7 million years before the present (BP). In one line was *Australopithecus,* a social animal that lived from perhaps 5 million to 3 million years BP, then apparently died out. In the other, human line was *Homo habilis,* a large-brained specimen that walked upright and had a dextrous hand. *Homo habilis* appeared some 2.5 million years BP, lived in semipermanent camps, had a food-gathering economy, and probably produced stone tools.

Homo erectus, the nearest ancestor to humans, appeared in Africa perhaps 2 million years BP and began spreading into Asia and Europe soon after. It had a fairly large brain and a skeletal structure similar to that of modern humans. *Homo erectus* hunted, learned to control fire, and may have had some primitive language skills. Brain development to *Homo sapiens,* then to the subspecies *Homo sapiens sapiens,* occurred between 500,000 and 50,000 years BP in Africa. All modern humans are members of the subspecies *Homo sapiens sapiens.*

Humans have roamed widely over the globe throughout their development. There is increasing evidence that migration from Asia to Australia via the Timor Straits took place as early as 100,000 BP. Evidence of hominids in Siberia dates as early as 300,000 BP. First confirmed evidence for the crossing from Asia to the Americas, by land bridge, dates to the end of the last Ice Age, at 12,500 BP.

Earliest cultures. A variety of cultural modes—in toolmaking, diet, shelter, and possibly social arrangements and spiritual expression—arose as humans adapted to different geographic and climatic zones and the database of knowledge grew. Sites from all over the world show seasonal migration patterns and efficient exploitation of a wide range of plant and animal foods.

Archaeologists recognize 5 basic toolmaking traditions as arising and often coexisting from more than 2.5 million years ago to the near past: (1) the *chopper tradition*—also known as the Oldowan—found in Africa, producing crude chopping tools and simple flake tools; (2) the *biface* or handaxe tradition, found in Africa, W and S Europe, and S Asia, producing pointed hand axes chipped on both faces for cutting; (3) the *flake tradition,* found in Africa and Europe, producing small cutting and flaking tools; (4) the *blade tradition,* a more efficient technology characteristic of the Upper Paleolithic, found across Eurasia to Siberia and N Africa, producing many usable blades from a single stone; and (5) the *microlith tradition,* found throughout the inhabited world, producing specialized small tools for use as projectile points, in carving softer materials, and in making more complex tools.

Sketchy evidence remains for the stages in increasing control over the environment. Fire was used for heating and cooking by 465,000 BP in W France. Fire-hardened wooden spears, weighted and set with small stone blades, were fashioned by big-game hunters 400,000 years ago in Germany. Scraping tools found at certain sites (200,000-30,000 BP in Europe, N Africa, the Middle East, and Cen. Asia) suggest the treatment of skins for clothing. By the time Australia was settled, human ancestors had learned to navigate in boats over open water. The earliest bone tools found to date were developed 80,000 years ago in the Congo basin by fishermen, who created sophisticated fishing tackle to catch giant catfish.

Early human ancestors included artists and musicians. About 60,000 years ago the earliest immigrants to Australia carved and painted abstract designs on rocks. Painting and decoration flourished, along with stone and ivory sculpture, from 30,000 BP in Europe; more than 200 caves, mainly in S France and N Spain, show remarkable examples of naturalistic wall painting. Other examples have been found in Africa. Proto-religious rites are suggested by these works, and by evidence of ritual burial. A variety of musical instruments, including bone flutes with precisely bored holes, have been found in Paleolithic (early Stone Age) sites going back as far as 40,000-80,000 years BP.

Neolithic advances. Some time after 10,000 BC, among widely separated communities, a series of dramatic technological and social changes occurred, marking the Neolithic, or New Stone, Age. As the world climate became drier and warmer, humans learned to cultivate plants. This in turn encouraged growth of permanent settlements. Animals were domesticated. Manufacture of pottery and cloth began. These techniques permitted a dramatic increase in world population and social complexity, and accelerated humankind's ability to manipulate the environment.

Sites in N, Cen., and S America, SE Europe, and the Middle East show roughly contemporaneous (10,000-8000 BC) evidence of one or more Neolithic traits. Dates near 6000-3000 BC have been given for E and S Asian, W European, and sub-Saharan African Neolithic remains. The variety of crops—field grains, rice, maize, and roots—and varying mix of other characteristics suggest that this adaptation occurred independently in all these regions.

History Begins: 4000-1000 BC

Near Eastern cradle. If history began with writing, the first chapter opened in Mesopotamia, the Tigris-Euphrates river valley. The Sumerians used clay tablets with pictographs to keep records after 4000 BC. A **cuneiform** (wedge-shaped) script evolved by 3000 BC as a full syllabic alphabet. Neighboring peoples adapted the script to their own language.

Sumerian life centered, from 4000 BC, on large cities (Eridu, Ur, Uruk, Nippur, Kish, and Lagash) organized around temples and priestly bureaucracies, with surrounding plains watered by vast irrigation works and worked with traction plows. Sailboats, wheeled vehicles, potter's wheels, and kilns were used. Copper was smelted and tempered from c 4000 BC; bronze was produced not long after. Ores, as well as precious stones and metals, were obtained through long-distance ship and caravan trade. Iron was used from c 2000 BC. Improved ironworking, developed partly by the Hittites, became widespread by 1200 BC.

Sumerian political primacy passed among cities and their kingly dynasties. Semitic-speaking peoples, with cultures derived from the Sumerian, founded a succession of dynasties that ruled in Mesopotamia and neighboring areas for most of 1,800 years; among them were the **Akkadians** (first under Sargon I, c 2350 BC), the Amorites (whose laws, codified by **Hammurabi,** c 1792-1750 BC, have biblical parallels), and the Assyrians, with interludes of rule by the Hittites, Kassites, and Mitanni.

Mesopotamian learning, maintained by scribes and preserved in vast libraries, was practically oriented. Advances in mathematics related to construction, commerce, and administration. Lists of astronomical phenomena, plants, animals, and stones were kept; medical texts listed ailments and herbal cures. The Sumerians worshiped anthropomorphic gods representing natural forces, such as Anu, god of heaven, and Enlil (Ea), god of water. Sacrifices were made at **ziggurats**—huge stepped temples.

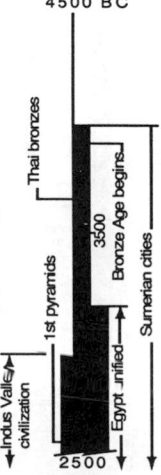

2500 BC
Ebla civilization
Bronze-age Minoan civilization emerges on Crete
Egyptian literature begins
Peruvian neolithic ceremonial centers
Phonetic alphabet invented before 1600
Hammurabi
1750
Aryans invade India
Chinese Shang dynasty
Mt. Sinai revelations to Moses
Mexican Olmec civilization established
1000 BC

The Syria-Palestine area, site of some of the earliest urban remains (Jericho, 7000 BC), and of the recently uncovered **Ebla** civilization (fl 2500 BC), experienced Egyptian cultural and political influence along with Mesopotamian. The **Phoenician** coast was an active commercial center. A phonetic alphabet was invented here before 1600 BC. It became the ancestor of many other alphabets.

Egypt. Agricultural villages along the Nile were united by 3300 BC into 2 kingdoms, Upper and Lower Egypt, which were unified (c 3100 BC) under the pharaoh Menes. A bureaucracy supervised construction of canals and monuments (**pyramids** starting 2700 BC). Control over Nubia to the S was asserted from 2600 BC. Brilliant Old Kingdom Period achievements in architecture, sculpture, and painting, which reached their height during the 3d and 4th Dynasties, set the standards for subsequent Egyptian civilization. **Hieroglyphic writing** appeared by 3200 BC, recording a sophisticated literature that included religious writings, philosophies, history, and science. An ordered hierarchy of gods, including totemistic animal elements, was served by a powerful priesthood in Memphis. The pharaoh was identified with the falcon god Horus. Other trends included belief in an afterlife and short-lived quasi-monotheistic reforms introduced by the pharaoh **Akhenaton** (c 1379-1362 BC).

After a period of dominance by Semitic Hyksos from Asia (c 1700-1550 BC), the New Kingdom established an empire in Syria. Egypt became increasingly embroiled in Asiatic wars and diplomacy. Conquered by Persia in 525 BC, it eventually faded away as an independent culture.

India. An urban civilization with a so-far-undeciphered writing system stretched across the Indus Valley and along the Arabian Sea c 3000-1500 BC. Major sites are Harappa and **Mohenjo-Daro** in Pakistan, well-planned geometric cities with underground sewers and vast granaries. The entire region (600,000 sq mi) may have been ruled as a single state. Bronze was used, and arts and crafts were well developed. Religious life apparently took the form of fertility cults. Indus civilization was probably in decline when it was destroyed by **Aryan invaders** from the NW, speaking an Indo-European language from which most languages of Pakistan, N India, and Bangladesh descend. Led by a warrior aristocracy whose legendary deeds are in the **Rig Veda**, the Aryans spread E and S, bringing their sky gods, elaborate priestly (Brahman) ritual, and the beginnings of the caste system; local customs and beliefs were assimilated by the conquerors.

Europe. On Crete, the Bronze Age **Minoan civilization** emerged c 2500 BC. A prosperous economy and richly decorative art was supported by seaborne commerce. Mycenae and other cities in mainland Greece and Asia Minor (e.g., **Troy**) preserved elements of the culture until c 1200 BC. Cretan Linear A script (c 2000-1700 BC) remains undeciphered; Linear B script (c 1300-1200 BC) records an early Greek dialect. Unclear is the possible connection between Mycenaean monumental stonework and the great megalithic monuments of W Europe, Iberia, and Malta (c 4000-1500 BC).

China. Proto-Chinese neolithic cultures had long covered N and SE China when the first large political state was organized in the N by the **Shang dynasty** (c 1523 BC). Shang kings called themselves Sons of Heaven, and they presided over a cult of human and animal sacrifice to ancestors and nature gods. The Chou dynasty, starting c 1027 BC, expanded the area of the Son of Heaven's dominion, but feudal states exercised most temporal power. A writing system with 2,000 characters was already in use under the Shang, with **pictographs** later supplemented by phonetic characters. Many of its principles and symbols, despite changes in spoken Chinese, were preserved in later writing systems. Technical advances allowed urban specialists to create fine ceramic and jade products, and bronze casting after 1500 BC was the most advanced in the world. Bronze artifacts have recently been discovered in N Thailand dating from 3600 BC, hundreds of years before similar Middle Eastern finds.

Americas. Olmecs settled (1500 BC) on the Gulf coast of Mexico and soon developed the first civilization in the western hemisphere. Temple cities and huge stone sculpture date from 1200 BC. A rudimentary calendar and writing system existed. Olmec religion, centering on a jaguar god, and Olmec art forms influenced all later Meso-American cultures.

Classical Era of Old World Civilizations: 1000 BC - 400 BC

Greece. After a period of decline during the Dorian Greek invasions (1200-1000 BC), Greece and the Aegean area developed a unique civilization. Drawing upon Mycenaean traditions, Mesopotamian learning (weights and measures, lunisolar calendar, astronomy, musical scales), the Phoenician alphabet (modified for Greek), and Egyptian art, the revived **Greek city-states** saw a rich elaboration of intellectual life. Homer's epics, the *Iliad* and the *Odyssey,* were probably composed around the 8th cent. BC. Long-range commerce was aided by metal coinage (introduced by the Lydians in Asia Minor before 700 BC); colonies were founded around the Mediterranean (Cumae in Italy in 760 BC; Massalia in France c 600 BC) and Black Sea shores.

Philosophy, starting with Ionian speculation on the nature of matter (Thales, c 634-546 BC), continued by other "Pre-Socratics" (e.g., Heraclitus, c 535-415 BC), reached a high point in Athens in the rationalist idealism of **Plato** (c 428-347 BC), a disciple of **Socrates** (c 469-399 BC; executed for alleged impiety), and in **Aristotle** (384-322 BC), a pioneer in many fields, from natural sciences to logic, ethics, and metaphysics. The **arts** were highly valued. Architecture culminated in the **Parthenon** (438 BC) by Phidias (fl 490-430 BC). Poetry (Sappho, c 610-580 BC; Pindar, c 518-438 BC) and **drama** (Aeschylus, 525-456 BC; Sophocles, c 496-406 BC; Euripides, c 484-406 BC) thrived. Male beauty and strength, a chief artistic theme, were enhanced at the gymnasium and celebrated at the national games at Olympia. Ruled by local tyrants or **oligarchies**, the Greeks were not politically united, but managed to resist inclusion in the Persian Empire—Persian king Darius was defeated at Marathon(490 BC), his son Xerxes at Salamis (480 BC), and the Persian army at Plataea (479 BC). Local warfare was common; the **Peloponnesian Wars** (431-404 BC) ended in Sparta's victory over Athens. Greek political power waned, but Greek cultural forms spread throughout the ancient world.

Hebrews. Nomadic Hebrew tribes entered Canaan before 1200 BC, settling among other Semitic peoples speaking the same language. They brought from the desert a **monotheistic** faith said to have been revealed to Abraham in Canaan c 1800 BC and Moses at Mt. Sinai c 1250 BC, after the Hebrews' escape from bondage in Egypt. David (r 1000-961 BC) and Solomon (r 961-922 BC) united them in a kingdom that briefly dominated the area. **Phoenicians** to the N founded Mediterranean colonies (Carthage, c 814 BC) and sailed into the Atlantic.

(continues on p. 554)

Paleontology: The History of Life

All dates are approximate, and are subject to change based on new fossil finds or new dating techniques, but the sequence of events is generally accepted. Dates are in years before the present.

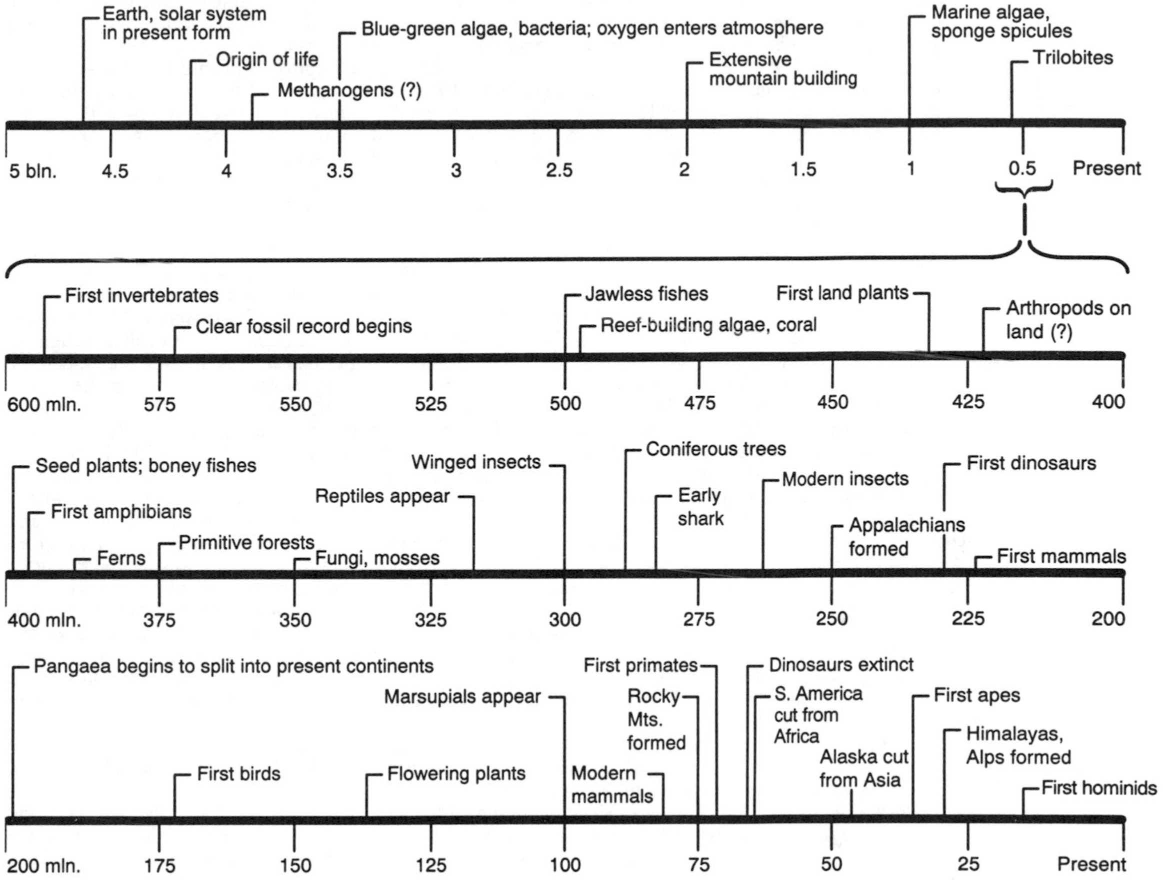

Earth, solar system in present form — Blue-green algae, bacteria; oxygen enters atmosphere — Marine algae, sponge spicules

Origin of life — Extensive mountain building — Trilobites

Methanogens (?)

| 5 bln. | 4.5 | 4 | 3.5 | 3 | 2.5 | 2 | 1.5 | 1 | 0.5 | Present |

First invertebrates — Jawless fishes — First land plants

Clear fossil record begins — Reef-building algae, coral — Arthropods on land (?)

| 600 mln. | 575 | 550 | 525 | 500 | 475 | 450 | 425 | 400 |

Seed plants; boney fishes — Winged insects — Coniferous trees — First dinosaurs

First amphibians — Reptiles appear — Early shark — Modern insects

Ferns — Primitive forests — Appalachians formed

Fungi, mosses — First mammals

| 400 mln. | 375 | 350 | 325 | 300 | 275 | 250 | 225 | 200 |

Pangaea begins to split into present continents — First primates — Dinosaurs extinct

Marsupials appear — Rocky Mts. formed — S. America cut from Africa — First apes

First birds — Flowering plants — Modern mammals — Alaska cut from Asia — Himalayas, Alps formed

First hominids

| 200 mln. | 175 | 150 | 125 | 100 | 75 | 50 | 25 | Present |

World Population Growth: AD 1 to 1997

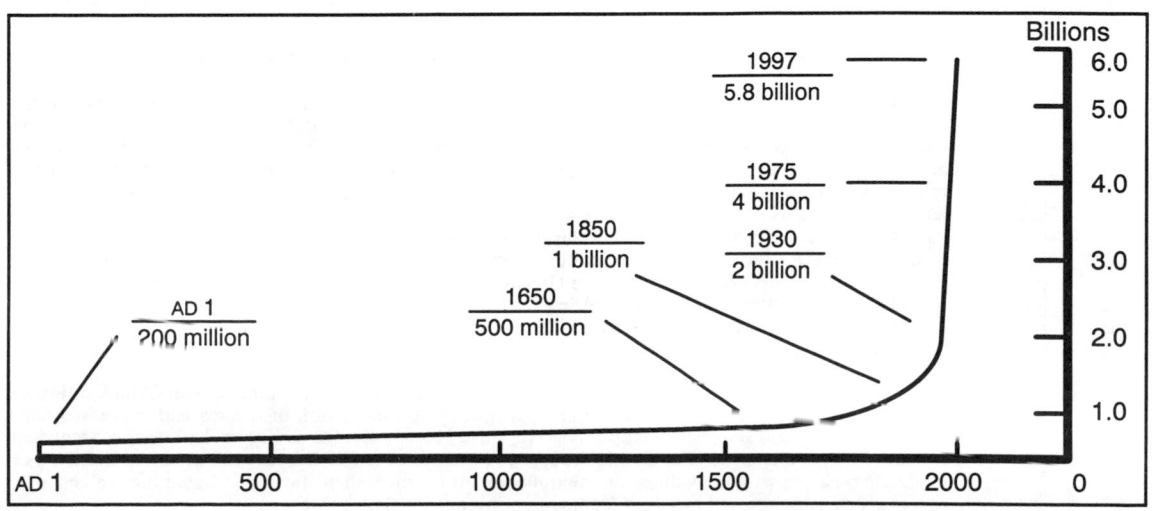

1997 — 5.8 billion

1975 — 4 billion

1850 — 1 billion

1930 — 2 billion

1650 — 500 million

AD 1 — 200 million

| AD 1 | 500 | 1000 | 1500 | 2000 | 0 |

Billions: 6.0, 5.0, 4.0, 3.0, 2.0, 1.0

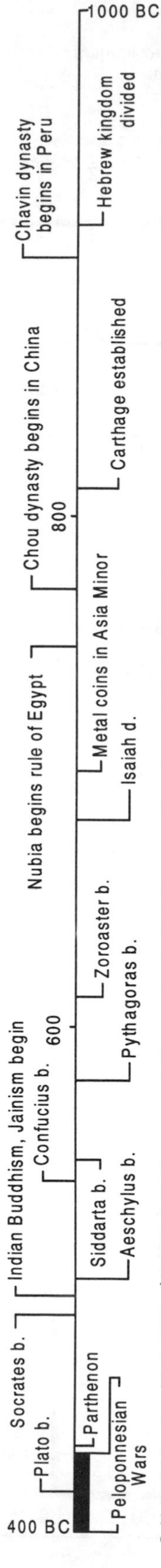

1000 BC A temple in Jerusalem became the national religious center, with sacrifices performed by a hereditary priesthood. Polytheistic influences, especially of the fertility cult of Baal, were opposed by **prophets** (Elijah, Amos, Isaiah).

Divided into **two kingdoms** after Solomon, the Hebrews were unable to resist the revived Assyrian empire, which conquered Israel, the N kingdom, in 722 BC. Judah, the S kingdom, was conquered in 586 BC by the Babylonians under Nebuchadnezzar II. But with the fixing of most of the biblical canon by the mid-4th cent. BC and the emergence of rabbis, Judaism successfully survived the loss of Hebrew autonomy. A Jewish kingdom was revived under the Hasmoneans (168-42 BC).

China. During the **Eastern Chou** dynasty (770-256 BC), Chinese culture spread E to the sea and S to the Yangtze R. Large feudal states on the periphery of the empire contended for preeminence, but continued to recognize the Son of Heaven (king), who retained a purely ritual role enriched with courtly music and dance. In the Age of Warring States (403-221 BC), when the first sections of the **Great Wall** were built, the Ch'in state in the W gained supremacy and finally united all of China.

Iron tools entered China c 500 BC, and casting techniques were advanced, aiding agriculture. Peasants owned their land and owed civil and military service to nobles. Cities grew in number and size, although barter remained the chief trade medium.

Intellectual ferment among noble scribes and officials produced the Classical Age of Chinese literature and philosophy. **Confucius** (551-479 BC) urged a restoration of a supposedly harmonious social order of the past through proper conduct in accordance with one's station and through filial and ceremonial piety. The *Analects* attributed to him are revered throughout E Asia. **Mencius** (d 289 BC) added the view that the Mandate of Heaven can be removed from an unjust dynasty. The Legalists sought to curb the supposed natural wickedness of people through new institutions and harsh laws; they aided the Ch'in rise to power. The Naturalists emphasized the balance of opposites—yin, yang—in the world. **Taoists** sought mystical knowledge through meditation and disengagement.

India. The political and cultural center of India shifted from the Indus to the Ganges River Valley. Buddhism, Jainism, and mystical revisions of orthodox Vedism all developed c 500-300 BC. The *Upanishads,* last part of the *Veda,* urged escape from the physical world. Vedism remained the preserve of the Brahman caste. In contrast, **Buddhism**, founded by Siddarta Gautama (c 563-c 483 BC)—Buddha ("Enlightened One")—appealed to merchants in the urban centers and took hold at first (and most lastingly) on the geographic fringes of Indian civilization. The classic Indian epics were composed in this era: the **Ramayana** perhaps c 300 BC, the **Mahabharata** over a period starting 400 BC.

N India was divided into a large number of monarchies and aristocratic republics, probably derived from tribal groupings, when the Magadha kingdom was formed in Bihar c 542 BC. It soon became the dominant power. The **Maurya dynasty**, founded by Chandragupta c 321 BC, expanded the kingdom, uniting most of N India in a centralized bureaucratic empire. The third Mauryan king, **Asoka** (reigned c 274-236 BC), conquered most of the subcontinent. He converted to Buddhism and inscribed its tenets on pillars throughout India. He downplayed the caste system and tried to end expensive sacrificial rites.

Before its final decline in India, Buddhism developed into a popular worship of heavenly Bodhisattvas ("enlightened beings"); and produced a refined architecture (the Great Stupa [shrine] at Sanchi, AD 100) and sculpture (Gandhara reliefs, AD 1-400).

Persia. Aryan peoples (Persians, Medes) dominated the area of present Iran by the beginning of the 1st millennium BC. The prophet **Zoroaster** (born c 628 BC) introduced a dualistic religion in which the forces of good (Ahura Mazda, "Lord of Wisdom") and evil (Ahriam) battle for dominance; individuals are judged by their actions and earn damnation or salvation. Zoroaster's hymns (*Gathas*) are included in the *Avesta*, the Zoroastrian scriptures. A version of this faith became the established religion of the Persian Empire and probably influenced later monotheistic religions.

Africa. Nubia, periodically occupied by Egypt since about 2600 BC, ruled Egypt c 750-661 BC and survived as an independent Egyptianized kingdom (**Kush;** capital Meroe) for 1,000 years. The Iron Age Nok culture flourished c 500 BC- AD 200 on the Benue Plateau of **Nigeria**.

Americas. The Chavin culture controlled N Peru from 900 BC to 200 BC. Its ceremonial centers, featuring the jaguar god, survived long after. Chavin architecture, ceramics, and textiles influenced other Peruvian cultures. **Mayan civilization** began to develop in Central America as early as 1500 BC.

Great Empires Unite the Civilized World: 400 BC - AD 400

Persia and Alexander the Great. **Cyrus,** ruler of a small kingdom in Persia from 559 BC, united the Persians and Medes within 10 years and conquered Asia Minor and Babylonia in another 10. His son Cambyses followed by **Darius** (r 522-486 BC) added vast lands to the E and N as far as the Indus Valley and Central Asia, as well as Egypt and Thrace. The whole empire was ruled by an international bureaucracy and army, with Persians holding the chief positions. The resources and styles of all the subject civilizations were exploited to create a rich syncretic art.

The kingdom of Macedon, which under Philip II dominated the Greek world and Egypt, passed to his son **Alexander** in 336 BC. Within 13 years, Alexander had conquered all the Persian dominions. Imbued by his tutor Aristotle with Greek ideals, Alexander encouraged Greek colonization, and Greek-style cities were founded. After his death in 323 BC, wars of succession divided the empire into 3 parts—**Macedon,** Egypt (ruled by the **Ptolemies**), and the **Seleucid** Empire.

In the ensuing 300 years (the **Hellenistic Era**), a cosmopolitan Greek-oriented culture permeated the ancient world from W Europe to the borders of India, absorbing native elites everywhere.

Hellenistic philosophy stressed the private individual's search for happiness. The Cynics followed Diogenes (c 372-287 BC), who stressed self-sufficiency and restriction of desires and expressed contempt for luxury and social convention. Zeno (c 335-c 263 BC) and the **Stoics** exalted reason, identified it with virtue, and counseled an ascetic disregard for misfortune. The **Epicureans** tried to build lives of moderate pleasure without political or emotional involvement. Hellenistic arts imitated life realistically, especially in sculpture and literature (comedies of Menander, 342-292 BC).

(continues on p. 556)

Timeline (left margin):
- Chavin dynasty begins in Peru
- Hebrew kingdom divided
- Chou dynasty begins in China
- Carthage established
- **800**
- Nubia begins rule of Egypt
- Metal coins in Asia Minor
- Isaiah d.
- Zoroaster b.
- Pythagoras b.
- Indian Buddhism, Jainism begin
- Confucius b.
- **600**
- Siddarta b.
- Aeschylus b.
- Socrates b.
- Plato b.
- Parthenon
- Peloponnesian Wars
- **400 BC**

Major Gods & Goddesses of the Classical World

Greek	Roman	Relations	Sphere or Position
Aphrodite	Venus	Daughter of Zeus & Dione	Love
Apollo	—	Son of Zeus & Leto	Healing, poetry, light
Ares	Mars	Son of Zeus & Hera	War
Artemis	Diana	Daughter of Zeus & Leto	Hunting, chastity
Athena	Minerva	Daughter of Zeus & Metis	Wisdom, crafts, war
Cronus	Saturn	Father of Zeus	Titans' ruler
Demeter	Ceres	Sister of Zeus	Agriculture, fertility
Dionysus	Bacchus	Son of Zeus & Semele	Wine, fertility, ecstasy
Eros	Cupid	Son of Ares & Aphrodite	Love
Hades	Pluto	Brother of Zeus	The underworld, death
Hephaestus	Vulcan	Son of Zeus & Hera	Fire
Hera	Juno	Wife & sister of Zeus	Earth
Hermes	Mercury	Son of Zeus & Maia	Travel, commerce, gods' messenger
Hestia	Vesta	Sister of Zeus	The hearth
Pan	—	Son of Hermes & a wood nymph	Forests, flocks, shepherds
Persephone	Proserpina	Daughter of Zeus & Demeter	Grain
Poseidon	Neptune	Brother of Zeus	The sea
Rhea	Ops	Mother of Zeus	The earth
Uranus	Uranus	Father of Titans (elder gods)	The heavens
Zeus	Jupiter	Son of Cronus & Rhea	Ruler of the gods

The Seven Wonders of the Ancient World

These ancient works of art and architecture were considered awe-inspiring in splendor and/or size by the Greek and Roman world of the Alexandrian epoch. Later classical writers disagreed as to which works made up the list of Wonders, but the following were usually included:

The Pyramids of Egypt: The only surviving ancient Wonder, these monumental structures of masonry, located at Giza on the W bank of the Nile R above Cairo, were built from c 2700 to 2500 BC as royal tombs. Three—Khufu (Cheops), Khafra (Chephren), and Menkaura (Mycerimus)— were often grouped as the first Wonder of the World. The largest, the Great Pyramid of Khufu, is a solid mass of limestone blocks covering 13 acres. It is estimated to contain 2.3 million blocks of stone, the stones themselves averaging 2½ tons and some weighing 30 tons. Its construction reputedly took 100,000 laborers 20 years.

The Hanging Gardens of Babylon: These gardens were laid out on a brick terrace about 400 ft square and 75 ft above the ground. To irrigate the trees, shrubs, and flowers, screws were turned to lift water from the Euphrates R. The gardens were probably built by King Nebuchadnezzar II about 600 BC. The Walls of Babylon, long, thick, and made of colorfully glazed brick, were considered by some among the Seven Wonders.

The Statue of Zeus (Jupiter) at Olympia: This statue of the king of the gods showed him seated on a throne. His flesh was made of ivory, his robe and ornaments of gold. Reputedly 40 ft high, the statue was made by Phidias and was placed in the great temple of Zeus in the sacred grove of Olympia about 457 BC.

The Colossus of Rhodes: A bronze statue of the sun god Helios, the Colossus was worked on for 12 years in the third cent. BC by the sculptor Chares. It was probably 120 ft high. A symbol of the city of Rhodes at its height, the statue stood on a promontory overlooking the harbor.

The Temple of Artemis (Diana) at Ephesus: This largest and most complex temple of ancient times was built about 550 BC and was made of marble except for its tile-covered wooden roof. It was begun in honor of a non-Hellenic goddess who later became identified with the Greek goddess of the same name. Ephesus was one of the greatest of the Ionian cities.

The Mausoleum at Halicarnassus: The source of our word *mausoleum*, this marble tomb was built in what is now SE Turkey by Artemisia for her husband Mausolus, king of Caria in Asia Minor, who died in 353 BC. About 135 ft high, the tomb was adorned with the works of 4 sculptors.

The Pharos (Lighthouse) of Alexandria: This structure was designed about 270 BC, during the reign of Ptolemy II, by the Greek architect Sostratos. Estimates of its height range from 200 to 600 ft.

The Seven Wonders of the Middle Ages

These sites and structures were considered significant by the people of the Middle Ages (from c 5th cent. to c 15th cent.).

The Colosseum of Rome: Erected by the Roman emperor Vespasian, this amphitheater was dedicated by his son and successor, Titus, in AD 80. It could seat about 50,000 persons and was used for Roman spectacles and contests. It is now in ruins.

The Catacombs of Alexandria, Egypt: This network of subterranean chambers and galleries was used for burial purposes by peoples of the ancient world and as refuge for early Christians.

The Great Wall of China: Begun c 221 BC and completed c 204 BC, this fortification finally reached a length of about 1500 mi. It is built of earth and stone and is faced with brick in the E parts. On average, it is about 20 ft thick at the base and tapers to some 12 ft at the top. The height averages 25 ft, exclusive of the crenellated parapets. Several hundred miles of the Great Wall in the E reaches still are intact.

Stonehenge: This prehistoric ritual monument is situated on Salisbury Plain, N of Salisbury, England, and dates from the late Stone and early Bronze ages (c. 3000-1000 BC). The monument itself consists of 4 concentric ranges of stones. Grouped around the main structure are a number of barrows, some of which contain chips of a blue stone similar to that found in the concentric ranges. In 1964, an American astronomer, Gerald S. Hawkins, concluded that Stonehenge functioned as a means of predicting the positions of the sun and moon relative to the earth, and thereby the seasons, and perhaps also as a simple daily calendar.

The Leaning Tower of Pisa (Italy): Construction on this bell tower began in 1174 but was suspended when the builders became aware that the shallow foundation would be inadequate in the soft soil. The structure was nevertheless complete by the late 14th cent. The Leaning Tower is cylindrical in shape, with 8 arcaded stories, and today slants more than 14 ft from the perpendicular.

The Porcelain Tower of Nanking: This tower in China was built to a height of 260 ft during the 15th cent. and was destroyed in 1853.

The Mosque of Hagia Sophia: Built in the 6th cent., this imposing structure was originally a church (Holy Wisdom). It was converted to a mosque in the 15th cent. and is now a museum.

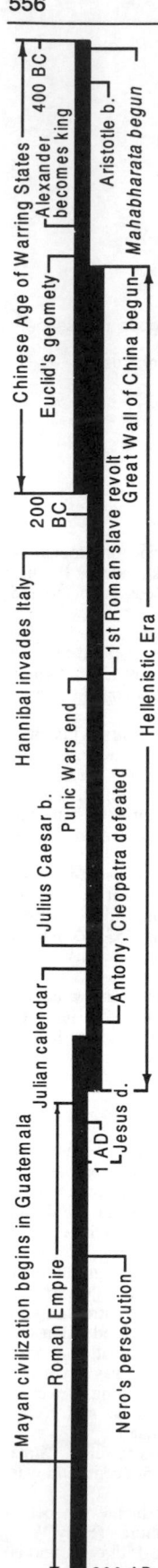

The sciences thrived, especially at Alexandria, where the Ptolemies financed a great library and museum. Fields of study included mathematics (**Euclid's** geometry, c 300 BC); astronomy (heliocentric theory of Aristarchus, 310-230 BC; Julian calendar, 45 BC; Ptolemy's *Almagest*, c AD 150); geography (world map of Eratosthenes, 276-194 BC); hydraulics (**Archimedes**, 287-212 BC); medicine (Galen, AD 130-200); and chemistry. Inventors refined uses for siphons, valves, gears, springs, screws, levers, cams, and pulleys.

A restored Persian empire under the **Parthians** (N Iranian tribesmen) controlled the eastern Hellenistic world from 250 BC to AD 229. The Parthians and the succeeding Sassanian dynasty (c AD 224-651) fought with Rome periodically. The **Sassanians** revived Zoroastrianism as a state religion and patronized a nationalistic artistic and scholarly renaissance.

Rome. The city of Rome was founded, according to legend, by Romulus in 753 BC. Through military expansion and colonization, and by granting citizenship to conquered tribes, the city annexed all of Italy S of the Po in the 100-year period before 268 BC. The Latin and other Italic tribes were annexed first, followed by the **Etruscans** (founders of a great civilization, N of Rome) and the Greek colonies in the S. With a large standing army and reserve forces of several hundred thousand, Rome was able to defeat **Carthage** in the 3 **Punic Wars** (264-241, 218-201, 149-146 BC), despite the invasion of Italy (218 BC) by **Hannibal,** thus gaining Sicily and territory in Spain and N Africa.

New provinces were added in the E, as Rome exploited local disputes to conquer Greece and Asia Minor in the 2d cent. BC, and Egypt in the 1st (after the defeat and suicide of **Antony and Cleopatra,** 30 BC). All the Mediterranean civilized world up to the disputed Parthian border was now Roman and remained so for 500 years. Less civilized regions were added to the Empire: Gaul (conquered by **Julius Caesar,** 58-51 BC), Britain (AD 43), and Dacia NE of the Danube (AD 107).

The original aristocratic republican government, with democratic features added in the 5th and 4th cent. BC, deteriorated under the pressures of empire and class conflict (**Gracchus** brothers, social reformers, murdered in 133 BC and 121 BC; slave revolts in 135 BC and 73 BC). After a series of civil wars (Marius vs. Sulla 88-82 BC, Caesar vs. **Pompey** 49-45 BC, triumvirate vs. Caesar's assassins 44-43 BC, Antony vs. Octavian 32-30 BC), the empire came under the rule of a deified monarch (first emperor, **Augustus,** 27 BC- AD 14). Provincials (nearly all granted citizenship by Caracalla, AD 212) came to dominate the army and civil service. Traditional Roman law, systematized and interpreted by independent jurists, and local self-rule in provincial cities were supplanted by a vast tax-collecting bureaucracy in the 3d and 4th cent. The legal rights of women, children, and slaves were strengthened.

Roman innovations in **civil engineering** included water mills, windmills, and rotary mills and use of cement that hardened under water. Monumental architecture (baths, theaters, temples) relied on the arch and the dome. The network of roads (some still standing) stretched 53,000 mi, passing through mountain tunnels as long as 3.5 mi. Aqueducts brought water to cities; underground sewers removed waste.

Roman art and literature were to a large extent derivative of Greek models. Innovations were made in sculpture (naturalistic busts and equestrian statues), decorative wall painting (as at Pompeii), satire (Juvenal, AD 60-127), history (Tacitus, AD 56-120), prose romance (Petronius, d AD 66). Gladiatorial contests dominated mass public amusements, which were supported by the state.

India. The **Gupta** monarchs reunited N India c AD 320. Their peaceful and prosperous reign saw a revival of Hindu religious thought and Brahman power. The old Vedic traditions were combined with devotion to many indigenous deities (who were seen as manifestations of Vedic gods). **Caste lines** were reinforced, and Buddhism gradually disappeared. The art (often erotic), architecture, and literature of the period, patronized by the Gupta court, are considered among India's finest achievements (Kalidasa, poet and dramatist, fl. c AD 400). Mathematical innovations included use of the zero and decimal numbers. Invasions by White Huns from the NW destroyed the empire c 550. Rich cultures also developed in S India in this era. Emotional Tamil religious poetry aided the Hindu revival. The Pallava kingdom controlled much of S India c 350-880 and helped spread Indian civilization to SE Asia.

China. The Ch'in ruler Shih Huang Ti (r 221-210 BC), known as the First Emperor, centralized political authority in China, standardized the written language, laws, weights, measures, and coinage, and conducted a census, but tried to destroy most philosophical texts. The **Han dynasty** (202 BC-AD 220) instituted the Mandarin bureaucracy, which lasted for 2,000 years. Local officials were selected by examination in the Confucian classics and trained at the imperial university and at provincial schools. The invention of **paper** facilitated this bureaucratic system. Agriculture was promoted, but the peasants bore most of the tax burden. Irrigation was improved, water clocks and sundials were used, astronomy and mathematics thrived, and landscape painting was perfected.

With the expansion S and W (to nearly the present borders of today's China), trade was opened with India, SE Asia, and the Middle East, over sea and caravan routes. Indian missionaries brought Mahayana Buddhism to China by the 1st cent. AD and spawned a variety of sects. Taoism was revived and merged with popular superstitions. Taoist and Buddhist monasteries and convents multiplied in the turbulent centuries after the collapse of the Han dynasty.

Monotheism Emerges: AD 1-750

Roman Empire. Polytheism was practiced in the Roman Empire, and religions indigenous to particular Middle Eastern nations became international. Roman citizens worshiped **Isis** of Egypt, **Mithras** of Persia, **Demeter** of Greece, and the great mother **Cybele** of Phrygia. Their cults centered on mysteries (secret ceremonies) and the promise of an afterlife, symbolized by the death and rebirth of the god. The Jews living in the empire preserved their monotheistic religion—Judaism, the world's oldest (c 1200 BC) continuous religion. Its teachings are contained in the Bible (the Old Testament). First-cent. Judaism embraced several sects, including the **Sadducees,** mostly drawn from the Temple priesthood, who were culturally Hellenized; the **Pharisees,** who upheld the full range of traditional customs and practices as of equal weight to literal scriptural law and elaborated synagogue worship; and the **Essenes,** an ascetic, millennarian sect. Messianic fervor led to repeated, unsuccessful rebellions against Rome (66-70, 135). As a result, the Temple in Jerusalem was destroyed and the population decimated; this event marked the beginning of the Diaspora (living in exile). To avoid dissolution of the faith, a program of codification of law was begun at the academy of Yavneh. The work continued for some 500 years in Palestine and in Babylonia, ending in the final redaction (c 600) of the **Talmud**, a huge collection of legal and moral debates, rulings, liturgy, biblical exegesis, and legendary materials.

Christianity, which emerged as a distinct sect by the second half of the 1st cent., is based on the teachings of **Jesus**, whom believers considered the Savior (Messiah or Christ) and the son of God. The missionary activities of the Apostles and such early leaders as **Paul of Tarsus** spread the faith. Intermittent persecution, as in Rome under Nero in AD 64, on grounds of suspected disloyalty, failed to disrupt the Christian communities. Each congregation, generally urban and of plebeian character, was tightly organized under a leader (bishop), elders (presbyters or priests), and assistants (deacons). The four **Gospels** (accounts of the life and teachings of Jesus) and the Acts of the Apostles were written down in the late 1st and early 2d cent. and circulated along with letters of Paul and other Christian leaders. An authoritative canon of these writings was not fixed until the 4th cent.

A school for priests was established at Alexandria in the 2d cent. Its teachers (**Origen** c 182-251) helped define doctrine and promote the faith in Greek-style philosophical works. Neoplatonism was given Christian coloration in the writings of Church Fathers such as **Augustine** (354-430). Christian hermits began to associate in monasteries, first in Egypt (St. Pachomius c 290-345), then in other eastern lands, then in the W (**St. Benedict's rule**, 529). Popular devotion to saints, especially Mary, mother of Jesus, spread. Under **Constantine** (r 306-37), Christianity became in effect the established religion of the Empire. Pagan temples were expropriated, state funds were used to build large churches and support the hierarchy, and laws were adjusted in accordance with Christian ideas. Pagan worship was banned by the end of the 4th cent., and severe restrictions were placed on Judaism.

The newly established church was rocked by doctrinal disputes, often exacerbated by regional rivalries both within and outside the Empire. Chief heresies (as defined by church councils, backed by imperial authority) were **Arianism**, which denied the divinity of Jesus; the **Monophysite** position denying the human nature of Christ; **Donatism**, which regarded as invalid any sacraments administered by sinful clergy; and **Pelagianism,** which denied the necessity of unmerited divine aid (grace) for salvation.

Islam. The earliest Arab civilization emerged by the end of the 2d millennium BC in the watered highlands of Yemen. Seaborne and caravan trade in frankincense and myrrh connected the area with the Nile and Fertile Crescent. The Minaean, Sabean (Sheba), and Himyarite states successively held sway. By Muhammad's time (7th cent. AD), the region was a province of Sassanian Persia. In the N, the Nabataean kingdom at Petra and the kingdom of Palmyra were Aramaicized, Romanized, and finally absorbed, as neighboring Judea had been, into the Roman Empire. Nomads shared the central region with a few trading towns and oases. Wars between tribes and raids on communities were common and were celebrated in a poetic tradition that by the 6th cent. helped establish a classic literary Arabic.

About 610, **Muhammad**, a 40-year-old Arab of Mecca, emerged as a prophet to his people. He proclaimed a revelation from the one true God, calling on contemporaries to abandon idolatry and restore the faith of Abraham. He introduced his religion as "Islam," meaning "submission" to the one God, Allah, as a continuation of the biblical faith of Abraham, Moses, and Jesus, all respected as prophets in this system. His teachings, recorded in the **Koran** (al-Qur'an in Arabic) in many ways were inclusive of Abrahamic monotheistic ideas known to the Jews and Christians in Arabia. A key aspect of the Abrahamic connection was insistence on justice in society, which led to severe opposition among the aristocrats in Mecca. As conditions worsened for Muhammad and his followers, he decided in 622 to make a ***hijra*** (emigration) to Medina, 200 mi. to the N. This event marks the beginning of the Muslim lunar calendar. Hostilities between Mecca and Medina increased, and in 629 Muhammad conquered Mecca. By his death in 632, nearly all the Arabian peninsula accepted his political and religious leadership.

After his death the majority of Muslims recognized the leadership of the **caliph** ("successor") Abu Bakr (632-34), followed by Umar (634-44), Uthman (644-56), and Ali (656-60). A minority, the **Shiites**, insisted instead on the leadership of Ali, Muhammad's cousin and son-in-law. By 644 **Muslim rule** over Arabia was confirmed. Muslim armies had threatened the Byzantine and Persian empires, which were weakened by wars and disaffection among subject peoples (including Coptic and Syriac Christians opposed to the Byzantine Orthodox establishment). Syria, Palestine, Egypt, Iraq, and Persia fell to Muslim armies. The new administration assimilated existing systems in the region; hence the conquered peoples participated in running of the empire. The Koran recognized the Peoples of the Book, i.e., Christians, Jews, and Zoroastrians, as tolerated monotheists, and Muslim policy was relatively tolerant to minorities living as "protected" peoples. An expanded tax system, based on conquests of the Persian and Byzantine empires, provided revenue to organize campaigns against neighboring non-Muslim regions.

Disputes over succession, and pious opposition to injustices in society, led to a number of oppositional movements, which also led to the factionalization of Muslim community. The **Shiites** supported leadership candidates descended from Muhammad, believing them to be carriers of some kind of divine authority. The **Kharijites** supported an egalitarian system derived from the Koran, opposing and even engaging in battle against those who did not agree with them.

Under the **Umayyads** (661-750) and **Abbasids** (750-1256), territorial expansion led Muslim armies across N Africa and into Spain (711). Muslim armies in the W were stopped at Tours (France) in 732 by the Frankish ruler **Charles Martel**. Asia Minor, the Indus Valley, and Transoxiana were conquered in the E. The conversion of conquered peoples to Islam was gradual. In many places the official Arabic language supplanted the local tongues. But in the eastern regions the Arab rulers and their armies adopted Persian cultures and language as part of their Muslim identity.

New Peoples Enter World History: 400-900

Barbarian invasions. Germanic tribes infiltrated S and E from their Baltic homeland during the 1st millennium BC, reaching S Germany by 100 BC and the Black Sea by AD 214. Organized into large federated tribes under elected kings, most resisted Roman domination and raided the empire in time of civil war (Goths took Dacia in 214, raided Thrace in 251-69). Germanic troops and commanders dominated the Roman armies by the end of the 4th cent. **Huns**, invaders from Asia, entered Europe in 372, driving more Germans into the W empire. Emperor Valens allowed Visigoths to cross the Danube

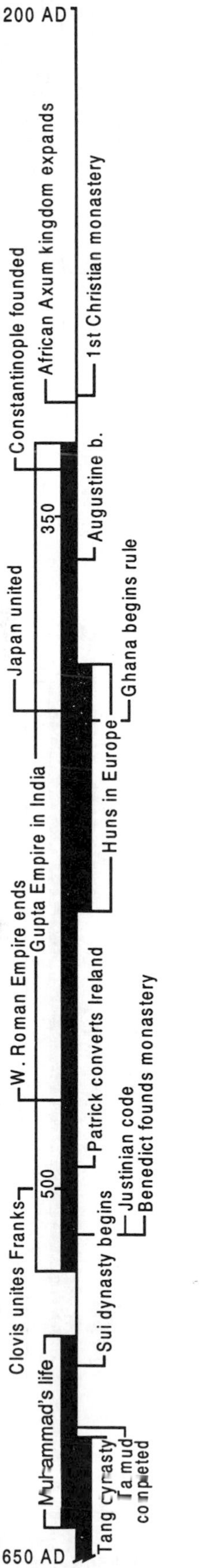
200 AD
350
500
650 AD
Constantinople founded
African Axum kingdom expands
1st Christian monastery
Augustine b.
Japan united
Ghana begins rule
Huns in Europe
Gupta Empire in India
W. Roman Empire ends
Patrick converts Ireland
Justinian code
Benedict founds monastery
Clovis unites Franks
Sui dynasty begins
Muhammad's life
Tang dynasty
Talmud completed

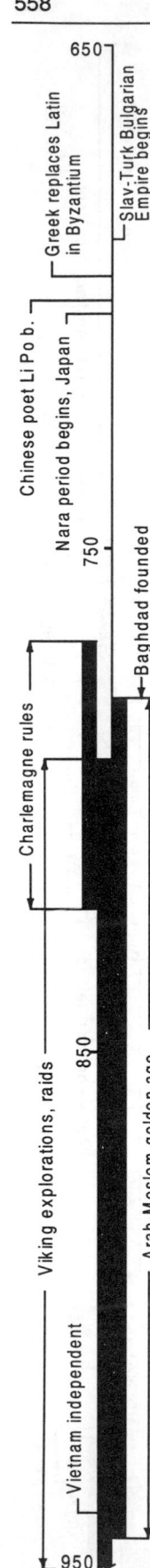

in 376. Huns under Attila (d 453) raided Gaul, Italy, and the Balkans. The W empire, weakened by overtaxation and social stagnation, was overrun in the 5th cent. Gaul was effectively lost in 406-7, Spain in 409, Britain in 410, Africa in 429-39. Rome was sacked in 410 by Visigoths under Alaric and in 455 by Vandals. The last western emperor, Romulus Augustulus, was deposed in 476 by the Germanic chief Odovacar.

Celts. Celtic cultures, which in pre-Roman times covered most of W Europe, were confined almost entirely to the British Isles after the Germanic invasions. **St. Patrick** completed (c 457-92) the conversion of Ireland. A strong monastic tradition took hold. Irish monastic missionaries in Scotland, England, and the continent (Columba c 521-97; Columban c 543-615) helped restore Christianity after the Germanic invasions. Monasteries became centers of classic and Christian learning and presided over the recording of a Christianized Celtic mythology, elaborated by secular writers and bards. An intricate decorative art style developed, especially in book illumination (Lindisfarne Gospels, c 700; Book of Kells, 8th cent.).

Successor states. The Visigothic kingdom in Spain (from 419) and much of France (to 507) saw continuation of Roman administration, language, and law (Breviary of Alaric, 506) until its destruction by the Muslims (711). The Vandal kingdom in Africa (from 429) was conquered by the Byzantines in 533. Italy was ruled successively by an Ostrogothic kingdom under Byzantine suzerainty (489-554), direct Byzantine government, and German Lombards (568-774). The Lombards divided the peninsula with the Byzantines and papacy under the dynamic reformer **Pope Gregory the Great** (590-604) and successors.

King Clovis (r 481-511) united the Franks on both sides of the Rhine and, after his conversion to Christianity, defeated the Arian heretics, Burgundians (after 500), and Visigoths (507) with the support of native clergy and the papacy. Under the **Merovingian** kings, a feudal system emerged: Power was fragmented among hierarchies of military landowners. Social stratification, which in late Roman times had acquired legal, hereditary sanction, was reinforced. The Carolingians (747-987) expanded the kingdom and restored central power. **Charlemagne** (r 768-814) conquered nearly all the Germanic lands, including Lombard Italy, and was crowned Emperor by Pope Leo III in Rome in 800. A centuries-long decline in commerce and arts was reversed under Charlemagne's patronage. He welcomed Jews to his kingdom, which became a center of Jewish learning (Rashi, 1040-1105). He sponsored the Carolingian Renaissance of learning under the Anglo-Latin scholar Alcuin (c 732-804), who reformed church liturgy.

Byzantine Empire. Under **Diocletian** (r 284-305) the empire had been divided into 2 parts to facilitate administration and defense. **Constantine** founded (330) **Constantinople** (at old Byzantium) as a fully Christian city. Commerce and taxation financed a sumptuous, orientalized court, a class of hereditary bureaucratic families, and magnificent urban construction (Hagia Sophia, 532-37). The city's fortifications and naval innovations (Greek fire) repelled assaults by Goths, Huns, Slavs, Bulgars, Avars, Arabs, and Scandinavians. Greek replaced Latin as the official language by c 700. Byzantine art, a solemn, sacral, and stylized variation of late classical styles (mosaics at the Church of San Vitale, Ravenna, Italy 526-48), was a starting point for medieval art in E and W Europe.

Justinian (r 527-65) reconquered parts of Spain, N Africa, and Italy, codified Roman law (Codex Justinianus [529] was medieval Europe's chief legal text), closed the Platonic Academy at Athens, and ordered all pagans to convert. Lombards in Italy and Arabs in Africa retook most of his conquests. The Isaurian dynasty from Anatolia (from 717) and the Macedonian dynasty (867-1054) restored military and commercial power. The Iconoclast controversy (726-843) over the permissibility of images helped alienate the Eastern Church from the papacy.

Abbasid Empire. Baghdad (est. 762), became seat of the **Abbasid dynasty** (est 750), while Ummayads continued to rule in Spain. A brilliant cosmopolitan civilization emerged, inaugurating a Muslim-Arab golden age. Arabic was the lingua franca of the empire; intellectual sources from Persian, Sanskrit, Greek, and Syriac were rendered into Arabic. Christians and Jews equally participated in this translation movement, which also involved interaction between Jewish legal thought and Islamic law, as much as between Christian theology and Muslim scholasticism. Persian-style court life, with art and music, flourished at the court of **Harun al-Rashid** (786-809), celebrated in the masterpiece known to English readers as *The Arabian Nights*. The sciences, medicine, and mathematics were pursued at Baghdad, Cordova, and Cairo (est 969). The culmination of this intellectual synthesis in Islamic civilization came with the scientific and philosophical works of **Avicenna** (980-1037), **Averroes** (1126-98), and **Maimonides** (1135-1204), a Jew who wrote in Arabic. This intellectual tradition was translated into Latin and opened a new period in Christian thought.

The decentralization of the Abbasid empire, from 874, led to establishment of various Muslim dynasties under different ethnic groups. Persians, Berbers, and Turks ruled different regions, retaining connection with the Abbasid caliph at the religious level. The Abbasid period also saw various religious movements against the orthodox position held by governing authorities. This situation in religion led to establishment of different legal, theological, and mystical schools of thought. The most influential mass movement was Sufism, which aimed at the reaching out of the average individual in quest of a spiritual path. Al-Ghazali (1058-1111) is credited with reconciling personal Sufism with orthodox Sunni tradition.

Africa. Immigrants from Saba in S Arabia helped set up the **Axum** kingdom in Ethiopia in the 1st cent. (their language, Ge'ez, is preserved by the Ethiopian Church). In the 3d cent., when the kingdom became Christianized, it defeated Kushite Meroe and expanded its influence into Yemen. Axum was the center of a vast ivory trade and controlled the Red Sea coast until c 1100. Arab conquest in Egypt cut Axum's political and economic ties with Byzantium.

The Iron Age entered W Africa by the end of the 1st millennium BC. **Ghana**, the first known sub-Saharan state, ruled in the upper Senegal-Niger region c 400-1240, controlling the trade of gold from mines in the S to trans-Sahara caravan routes to the N. The **Bantu** peoples, probably of W African origin, began to spread E and S perhaps 2,000 years ago, displacing the Pygmies and Bushmen of central and S Africa during a 1,500-year period.

Japan. The advanced Neolithic Yayoi period, when irrigation, rice farming, and iron and bronze casting techniques were introduced from China or Korea, persisted to c AD 400. The myriad Japanese states were then united by the **Yamato** clan, under an emperor who acted as chief priest of the animistic Shinto cult. Japanese political and military intervention by the 6th cent. in Korea, then under strong Chinese influence, quickened a Chinese cultural invasion of Japan, bringing Buddhism, the Chinese language (which long remained a literary and governmental medium), Chinese ideographs, and Buddhist styles in painting, sculpture, literature, and architecture (7th cent., Horyu-ji temple at Nara). The Taika Reforms (646) tried unsuccessfully to centralize Japan according to Chinese bureaucratic and Buddhist philosophical values. A nativist reaction against the Buddhist **Nara period** (710-94) ushered in the **Heian period** (794-1185) centered at the new capital, Kyoto. Japanese elegance and simplicity modified Chinese styles in architecture, scroll painting, and literature; the writing system was also simplified. The courtly novel *Tale of Genji* (1010-20) testifies to the enhanced role of women.

Southeast Asia. The historic peoples of SE Asia began arriving some 2,500 years ago from China and Tibet, displacing scattered aborigines. Their agriculture relied on rice and yams, which they may have introduced to Africa. Indian cultural influences were strongest; literacy and Hindu and Buddhist ideas followed the S India-China trade route. From the S tip of Indochina, the kingdom of **Funan** (1st-7th cent.) traded as far W as Persia. It was absorbed by Chenla, itself conquered by the **Khmer Empire** (600-1300). The Khmers, under Hindu god-kings (Suryavarman II, 1113-c 1150) built the monumental Angkor Wat temple center for the royal phallic cult. The **Nam-Viet** kingdom in Annam, dominated by China and Chinese culture for 1,000 years, emerged in the 10th cent., growing at the expense of the Khmers, who also lost ground in the NW to the new, highly organized **Thai** kingdom. On Sumatra, the **Srivijaya** Empire controlled vital sea lanes (7th to 10th cent.). A Buddhist dynasty, the Sailendras, ruled central **Java** (8th-9th cent.), building at Borobudur one of the largest stupas in the world.

China. The Sui dynasty (581-618) ushered in a period of commercial, artistic, and scientific achievement in China, continuing under the **Tang** dynasty (618-906). Inventions like the magnetic compass, gunpowder, the abacus, and printing were introduced or perfected. Medical innovations included cataract surgery. The state, from its cosmopolitan capital, Chang-an, supervised foreign trade, which exchanged Chinese silks, porcelains, and art for spices, ivory, etc., over Central Asian caravan routes and sea routes reaching Africa. A golden age of poetry bequeathed valuable works to later generations (Tu Fu, 712-70; Li Po, 701-62). Landscape painting flourished. Commercial and industrial expansion continued under the **Northern Sung** dynasty (960-1126), facilitated by paper money and credit notes. But commerce never achieved respectability; government monopolies expropriated successful merchants. The population, long stable at 50 million, doubled in 200 years with the introduction of early-ripening rice and the double harvest. In art, native Chinese styles were revived.

Americas. From 300 to 600 a Native American empire stretched from the Valley of Mexico to Guatemala, centering on the huge city **Teotihuacán** (founded 100 BC). To the S, in Guatemala, a high **Mayan** civilization developed (150-900) around hundreds of rural ceremonial centers. The Mayans improved on Olmec writing and the calendar and pursued astronomy and mathematics (using the idea of zero). In South America, a widespread pre-Inca culture grew from **Tiahuanacu,** Bolivia, near Lake Titicaca (Gateway of the Sun, c 700).

Christian Europe Regroups and Expands: 900-1300

Scandinavians. Pagan Danish and Norse (Viking) adventurers, traders, and pirates raided the coasts of the British Isles (Dublin, est. c 831), France, and even the Mediterranean for over 200 years beginning in the late 8th cent. Inland settlement in the W was limited to Great Britain (King Canute, 994-1035) and Normandy, settled (911) under Rollo, as a fief of France. Vikings also reached Iceland (874), Greenland (c 986), and North America (**Leif Eriksson,** c 1000). Norse traders (**Varangians**) developed Russian river commerce from the 8th to the 11th cent. and helped set up a state at Kiev in the late 9th cent.. Conversion to Christianity occurred in 10th cent., reaching Sweden 100 years later. In the 11th cent. Norman bands conquered S Italy and Sicily, and Duke **William of Normandy** conquered (1066) England, bringing feudalism and the French language, essential elements in later English civilization.

Central and East Europe. Slavs began to expand from about AD 150 in all directions in Europe, and by the 7th cent. they reached as far S as the Adriatic and Aegean seas. In the Balkan Peninsula they dislocated Romanized local populations or assimilated newcomers (Bulgarians, a Turkic people). The first Slavic states were Moravia (628) in Central Europe and the Bulgarian state (680) in the Balkans. Missions of St. Methodius and Cyril (whose Greek-based cyrillic alphabet is still used by some S and E Slavs) converted (863) Moravia. The Eastern Slavs, part-civilized under the overlordship of the Turkish-Jewish **Khazar** trading empire (7th-10th cent.), gravitated toward Constantinople by the 9th cent.. The **Kievan state** adopted (989) Eastern Christianity under Prince Vladimir. King Boleslav I (992-1025) began **Poland's** long history of eastern conquest. The Magyars (**Hungarians**), in present-day Hungary since 896, accepted (1001) Latin Christianity.

Germany. The German kingdom that emerged after the breakup of Charlemagne's W Empire remained a confederation of largely autonomous states. Otto I, a Saxon who was king from 936, established the **Holy Roman Empire**—a union of Germany and N Italy—in alliance with Pope John XII, who crowned (962) him emperor; he defeated (955) the Magyars. Imperial power was greatest under the **Hohenstaufens** (1138-1254); despite the growing opposition of the papacy, which ruled central Italy, and the Lombard League cities. Frederick II (1194-1250) improved administration and patronized the arts; after his death, German influence was removed from Italy.

Christian Spain. From its N mountain redoubts, Christian rule slowly migrated S through the 11th cent., when Muslim unity collapsed. After the capture (1085) of **Toledo,** the kingdoms of Portugal, Castile, and Aragon undertook repeated crusades of reconquest, finally completed in 1492. Elements of Islamic civilization persisted in recaptured areas, influencing all Western Europe.

Crusades. Pope Urban II called (1095) for a crusade to restore Asia Minor to Byzantium and to regain the Holy Land from the Turks. Some 10 crusades (to 1291) succeeded only in founding 4 temporary Frankish states in the Levant. The 4th crusade sacked (1204) Constantinople. In Rhineland (1096), England (1290), and France (1306), Jews were massacred or expelled, and wars were launched against Christian heretics (**Albigensian** crusade in France, 1229). Trade in eastern luxuries expanded, led by the Venetian naval empire.

Economy. The agricultural base of European life benefited from improvements in **plow design** (c 1000) and by draining of lowlands and clearing of forests, leading to a rural population increase. Towns grew in N Italy, Flanders, and N Germany (Hanseatic League). Improvements in **loom design** permitted

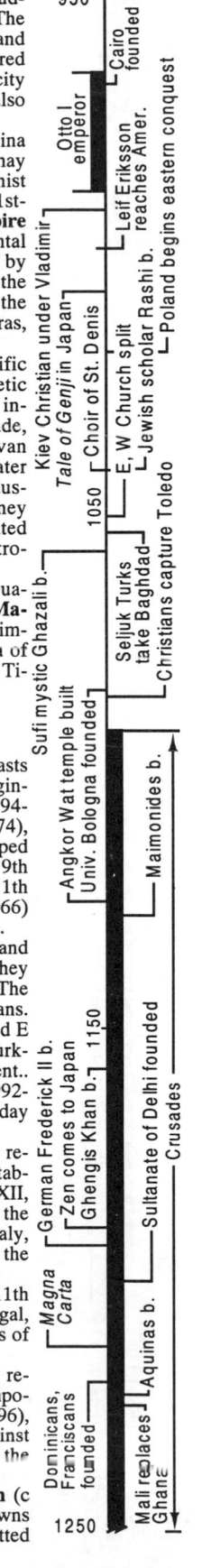

950 — Otto I emperor — Cairo founded — Leif Eriksson reaches Amer. — Poland begins eastern conquest — Kiev Christian under Vladimir — *Tale of Genji* in Japan — Choir of St. Denis — E, W Church split — Jewish scholar Rashi b. — Sufi mystic Ghazali b. — 1050 — Seljuk Turks take Baghdad — Christians capture Toledo — Angkor Wat temple built — Univ. Bologna founded — Maimonides b. — German Frederick II b. — Zen comes to Japan — Ghengis Khan b. — 1150 — Sultanate of Delhi founded — Crusades — *Magna Carta* — Aquinas b. — Dominicans, Franciscans founded — Mali replaces Ghana — 1250

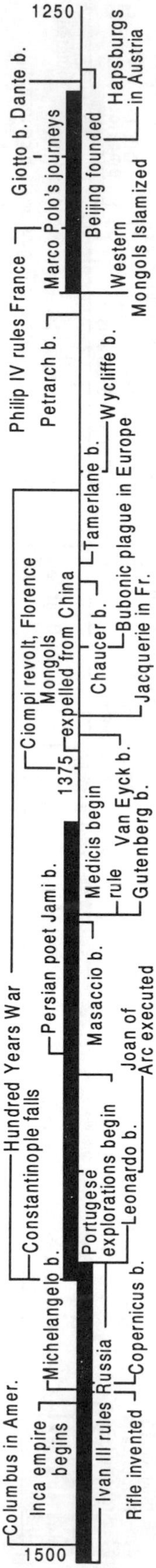

Timeline (left margin, 1250–1500):

- 1250
- Giotto b. Dante b.
- Hapsburgs founded in Austria
- Philip IV rules France
- Marco Polo's journeys
- Beijing founded
- Petrarch b.
- Wycliffe b.
- Western Mongols Islamized
- Tamerlane b.
- Bubonic plague in Europe
- Ciompi revolt, Florence Mongols expelled from China
- Chaucer b.
- Jacquerie in Fr.
- 1375
- Medicis begin rule
- Van Eyck b.
- Gutenberg b.
- Persian poet Jami b.
- Hundred Years War
- Masaccio b.
- Joan of Arc executed
- Constantinople falls
- Portugese explorations begin
- Leonardo b.
- Michelangelo b.
- Ivan III rules Russia
- Rifle invented
- Copernicus b.
- Columbus in Amer.
- Inca empire begins
- 1500

factory textile production. **Guilds** dominated urban trades from the 12th cent. Banking (centered in Italy, 12th-15th cent.) facilitated long-distance trade.

The Church. The split between the Eastern and Western churches was formalized in 1054. Western and Central Europe was divided into 500 bishoprics under one united hierarchy, but conflicts between secular and church authorities were frequent (German **Investiture Controversy**, 1075-1122). Clerical power was first strengthened through the international monastic reform begun at Cluny in 910. Popular religious enthusiasm often expressed itself in heretical movements (Waldensians from 1173), but was channelled by the **Dominican** (1215) and **Franciscan** (1223) friars into the religious mainstream.

Arts. Romanesque architecture (11th-12th century) expanded on late Roman models, using the rounded arch and massed stone to support enlarged basilicas. Painting and sculpture followed Byzantine models. The literature of **chivalry** was exemplified by the epic (*Chanson de Roland*, c 1100) and by courtly love poems of the troubadours of Provence and minnesingers of Germany. **Gothic** architecture emerged in France (choir of St. Denis, c 1040) and spread as French cultural influence predominated in Europe. Rib vaulting and pointed arches were used to combine soaring heights with delicacy, and they freed walls for display of stained glass. Exteriors were covered with painted relief sculpture and elaborate architectural detail.

Learning. Law, medicine, and philosophy were advanced at independent **universities** (Bologna, late 11th cent.), originally corporations of students and masters. Twelfth-cent. translations of Greek classics, especially Aristotle, encouraged an analytic approach. Scholastic philosophy, from Anselm (1033-1109) to **Aquinas** (1225-74), attempted to understand revelation through reason.

Apogee of Central Asian Power; Islam Grows: 1250-1500

Turks. Turkic peoples, of Central Asian ancestry, were a military threat to the Byzantine and Persian Empires from the 6th cent.. After several waves of invasions, during which most of the Turks adopted Islam, the **Seljuk Turks** took (1055) Baghdad. They ruled Persia, Iraq and, after 1071, Asia Minor, where massive numbers of Turks settled. The empire was divided in the 12th cent. into smaller states ruled by Seljuks, Kurds (**Saladin**, c 1137-93), and Mamluks (a military caste of former Turk, Kurd, and Circassian slaves), which governed Egypt and the Middle East until the Ottoman era (c 1290-1922).

Osman I (r c 1290-1326) and succeeding sultans united Anatolian Turkish warriors in a militaristic state that waged holy war against Byzantium and Balkan Christians. Most of the Balkans had been subdued, and Anatolia united, when Constantinople fell (1453). By the mid-16th cent., Hungary, the Middle East, and N Africa had been conquered. The Turkish advance was stopped at Vienna (1529) and at the naval battle of Lepanto (1571) by Spain, Venice, and the papacy.

The Ottoman state was governed in accordance with orthodox Muslim law. Greek, Armenian, and Jewish communities were segregated and were ruled by religious leaders responsible for taxation; they dominated trade. State offices and most army ranks were filled by slaves through a system of child conscription among Christians.

India. Mahmud of Ghazni (971-1030) led repeated Turkish raids into N India. Turkish power was consolidated in 1206 with the start of the **Sultanate at Delhi**. Centralization of state power under the early Delhi sultans went far beyond traditional Indian practice. Muslim rule of most of the subcontinent lasted until the British conquest some 600 years later.

Mongols. Genghis Khan (c 1167-1227) first united the feuding Mongol tribes, and built their armies into an effective offensive force around a core of highly mobile cavalry. He and his immediate successors created the largest land empire in history; by 1279 it stretched from the E coast of Asia to the Danube, from the Siberian steppes to the Arabian Sea. East-West trade and contacts were facilitated (Marco Polo, c 1254-1324). The W Mongols were Islamized by 1295; successor states soon lost their Mongol character by assimilation. They were briefly reunited under the Turk Tamerlane (1336-1405).

Kublai Khan ruled China from his new capital Beijing (est c 1264). Naval campaigns against Japan (1274, 1281) and Java (1293) were defeated, the latter by the Hindu-Buddhist maritime kingdom of Majapahit. The **Yuan** dynasty used Mongols and other foreigners (including Europeans) in official posts and tolerated the return of Nestorian Christianity (suppressed 841-45) and the spread of Islam in the S and W. A native reaction expelled the Mongols in 1367-68.

Russia. The Kievan state in Russia, weakened by the decline of Byzantium and the rise of the Catholic Polish-Lithuanian state, was overrun (1238-40) by the Mongols. Only the N trading republic of Novgorod remained independent. The grand dukes of Moscow emerged as leaders of a coalition of princes that eventually (by 1481) defeated the Mongols. With the fall of Constantinople, the **Tsars** (Caesars) at Moscow (from Ivan III, r 1462-1505) set up an independent Russian Orthodox Church. Commerce failed to revive. The isolated Russian state remained agrarian, with the peasant class falling into serfdom.

Persia. A revival of Persian literature, using the Arab alphabet and literary forms, began in the 10th cent. (epic of Firdausi, 935-1020). An art revival, influenced by Chinese styles introduced after the Mongols came to power in Iran, began in the 13th. Persian cultural and political forms, and often the Persian language, were used for centuries by Turkish and Mongol elites from the Balkans to India. Persian mystics from Rumi (1207-73) to Jami (1414-92) promoted **Sufism** in their poetry.

Africa. Two militant Islamic Berber dynasties emerged from the Sahara to carve out empires from the Sahel to central Spain—the **Almoravids** (c 1050-1140) and the fanatical **Almohads** (c 1125-1269). The Ghanaian empire was replaced in the upper Niger by Mali (c 1230-c 1340), whose Muslim rulers imported Egyptians to help make **Timbuktu** a center of commerce (in gold, leather, and slaves) and learning. The Songhay empire (to 1590) replaced Mali. To the S, forest kingdoms produced refined artworks (Ife terra cotta, **Benin** bronzes). Other Muslim states in Nigeria (Hausas) and Chad originated in the 11th cent. and continued in some form until the 19th-cent. European conquest. Less-developed Bantu kingdoms existed across central Africa.

Some 40 Muslim Arab-Persian trading colonies and city-states were established all along the E African coast from the 10th cent. (Kilwa, Mogadishu). The interchange with Bantu peoples produced the **Swahili** language and culture. Gold, palm oil, and slaves were brought from the interior, stimulating the growth of the Monamatapa kingdom of the Zambezi (15th cent.). The Christian Ethiopian empire (from 13th cent.) continued the traditions of Axum.

Southeast Asia. Islam was introduced into Malaya and the Indonesian islands by Arab, Persian, and Indian traders. Coastal Muslim cities and states (starting before 1300) soon dominated the interior. Chief among these was the **Malacca** state (c 1400-1511), on the Malay peninsula.

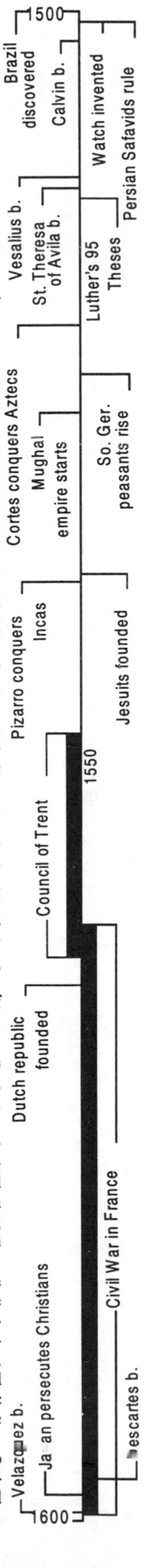

Arts and Statecraft Thrive in Europe: 1350-1600

Italian Renaissance and Humanism. Distinctive Italian achievements in the arts in the late Middle Ages (**Dante,** 1265-1321; Giotto, 1276-1337) led to the vigorous new styles of the Renaissance (14th-16th cent.). Patronized by the rulers of the quarreling petty states of Italy (**Medicis** in Florence and the papacy, c 1400-1737), the plastic arts perfected realistic techniques, including **perspective** (Masaccio, 1401-28, **Leonardo,** 1452-1519). Classical motifs were used in architecture, and increased talent and expense were put into secular buildings. The Florentine dialect was refined as a national literary language (**Petrarch,** 1304-74). Greek refugees from the E strengthened the respect of humanist scholars for the classic sources (Bruni, 1370-1444). Soon an international movement aided by the spread of **printing** (Gutenberg, c 1400-68), **humanism** was optimistic about the power of human reason (Erasmus of Rotterdam, 1466-1536, Thomas **More's** *Utopia*, 1516) and valued individual effort in the arts and in politics (**Machiavelli,** 1469-1527).

France. The French monarchy, strengthened in its repeated struggles with powerful nobles (Burgundy, Flanders, Aquitaine) by alliances with the growing commercial towns, consolidated bureaucratic control under Philip IV (r 1285-1314) and extended French influence into Germany and Italy (popes at Avignon, France, 1309-1417). The **Hundred Years War** (1337-1453) ended English dynastic claims in France (battles of Crécy, 1346, and Poitiers, 1356; Joan of Arc executed, 1431). A French Renaissance, dating from royal invasions (1494, 1499) of Italy, was encouraged at the court of Francis I (r 1515-47), who centralized taxation and law. French vernacular literature consciously asserted its independence (La Pléiade, 1549).

England. The evolution of England's unique political institutions began with the **Magna Carta** (1215), by which King John guaranteed the privileges of nobles and church against the monarchy and assured jury trial. After the **Wars of the Roses** (1455-85), the **Tudor dynasty** reasserted royal prerogatives (Henry VIII, r 1509-47), but the trend toward independent departments and ministerial government also continued. English trade (wool exports from c 1340) was protected by the nation's growing maritime power (**Spanish Armada** destroyed, 1588).

English replaced French and Latin in the late 14th cent. in law and literature (**Chaucer,** c 1340-1400) and English translation of the Bible began (Wycliffe, 1380s). **Elizabeth I** (r 1558-1603) presided over a confident flowering of poetry (Spenser, 1552-99), drama (**Shakespeare,** 1564-1616), and music.

German Empire. From among a welter of minor feudal states, church lands, and independent cities, the **Hapsburgs** assembled a far-flung territorial domain, based in Austria from 1276. The family held the title Holy Roman Emperor from 1438 to the Empire's dissolution in 1806, but failed to centralize its domains, leaving Germany disunited for centuries. Resistance to Turkish expansion brought Hungary under Austrian control from the 16th cent. The Netherlands, Luxembourg, and Burgundy were added in 1477, curbing French expansion.

The Flemish painting tradition of naturalism, technical proficiency, and bourgeois subject matter began in the 15th cent. (Jan **Van Eyck,** c 1390-1441), the earliest northern manifestation of the Renaissance. **Dürer** (1471-1528) typified the merging of late Gothic and Italian trends in 16th-cent. German art. Imposing civic architecture flourished in the prosperous commercial cities.

Spain. Despite the unification of Castile and Aragon in 1479, the 2 countries retained separate governments, and the nobility, especially in Aragon and Catalonia, retained many privileges. Spanish lands in Italy (Naples, Sicily) and the Netherlands entangled the country in European wars through the mid-17th cent., while explorers, traders, and conquerors built up a Spanish empire in the Americas and the Philippines.

From the late 15th cent., a **golden age** of literature and art produced works of social satire (plays of Lope de Vega, 1562-1635; **Cervantes,** 1547-1616), as well as spiritual intensity (**El Greco,** 1541-1614; **Velazquez,** 1599-1660).

Black Death. The bubonic plague reached Europe from the E in 1348, killing as much as half the population by 1350. Labor scarcity forced a rise in wages and brought greater freedom to the peasantry, making possible **peasant uprisings** (Jacquerie in France, 1358; Wat Tyler's rebellion in England, 1381). In the *ciompi* revolt (1378), Florentine wage earners demanded a say in economic and political power.

Explorations. Organized European maritime exploration began, seeking to evade the Venice-Ottoman monopoly of E trade and to promote Christianity. Beginning in 1418, expeditions from Portugal explored the W coast of Africa, until **Vasco da Gama** rounded the Cape of Good Hope in 1497 and reached India. A Portuguese trading empire was consolidated by the seizure of Goa (1510) and Malacca (1551). Japan was reached in 1542. The voyages of **Columbus** (1492-1504) uncovered a new world, which Spain hastened to subdue. Navigation schools in Spain and Portugal, the development of large sailing ships (carracks), and the invention (c 1475) of the rifle aided European penetration.

Mughals and Safavids. E of the Ottoman Empire, 2 Muslim dynasties ruled unchallenged in the 16th and 17th cent.. The Mughal dynasty of India, founded by Persianized Turkish invaders from the NW under Babur, dates from their 1526 conquest of the Delhi Sultanate. The dynasty ruled most of India for more than 200 years, surviving nominally until 1857. **Akbar** (r 1556-1605) consolidated administration at his glorious court, where the Urdu language (Persian-influenced Hindi) developed. Trade relations with Europe increased. Under Shah Jahan (1629-58), a secularized art fusing Hindu and Muslim element flourished in miniature painting and in architecture (**Taj Mahal**). **Sikhism** (founded c 1519) combined elements of both faiths. Suppression of Hindus and Shi'ite Muslims in S India in the late 17th cent. weakened the empire.

Fanatical devotion to the Shi'ite sect characterized the Safavids (1502-1736) of Persia and led to hostilities with the Sunni Ottomans for more than a century. The prosperity and the strength of the empire are evidenced by the mosques at its capital city, **Isfahan.** The Safavids enhanced Iranian national consciousness.

Timeline (right margin, top to bottom):
1500 — Brazil discovered — Calvin b. — Watch invented — Persian Safavids rule — Vesalius b. — St. Theresa of Avila b. — Luther's 95 Theses — Cortes conquers Aztecs — Mughal empire starts — So. Ger. peasants rise — Pizarro conquers Incas — Jesuits founded — 1550 — Council of Trent — Dutch republic founded — Civil War in France — Ja... an persecutes Christians — Velazquez b. — Descartes b. — 1600

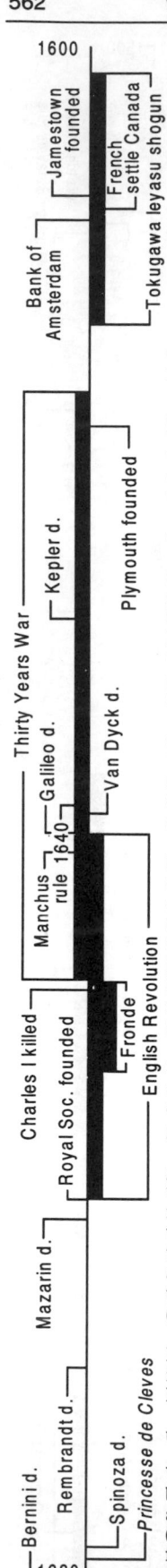

China. The **Ming** emperors (1368-1644), the last native dynasty in China, wielded unprecedented personal power, while the Confucian bureaucracy began to suffer from inertia. European trade (Portuguese monopoly through **Macao** from 1557) was strictly controlled. Jesuit scholars and scientists (Matteo Ricci, 1552-1610) introduced some Western science; their writings familiarized the West with China. Chinese technological inventiveness declined from this era, but the arts thrived, especially painting and ceramics.

Japan. After the decline of the first hereditary shogunate (chief generalship) at **Kamakura** (1185-1333), fragmentation of power accelerated, as did the consequent social mobility. Under Kamakura and the Ashikaga shogunate (1338-1573), the daimyos (lords) and samurai (warriors) grew more powerful and promoted a martial ideology. Japanese pirates and traders plied the China coast. Popular Buddhist movements included the nationalist Nichiren sect (from c 1250) and **Zen** (brought from China, 1191), which stressed meditation and a disciplined esthetic (tea ceremony, gardening, martial arts, No drama).

Reformed Europe Expands Overseas: 1500-1700

Reformation begun. Theological debate and protests against real and perceived clerical corruption existed in the medieval Christian world, expressed by such dissenters as **Wycliffe** (c 1320-84) and his followers, the Lollards, in England, and **Huss** (burned as a heretic, 1415) in Bohemia.

Luther (1483-1546) preached that faith alone leads to salvation, without the mediation of clergy or good works. He attacked the authority of the pope, rejected priestly celibacy, and recommended individual study of the Bible (which he translated c 1525). His 95 Theses (1517) led to his excommunication (1521). **Calvin** (1509-64) said that God's elect were predestined for salvation and that good conduct and success were signs of election. Calvin in Geneva and Knox (1505-72) in Scotland established theocratic states.

Henry VIII asserted English national authority and secular power by breaking away (1534) from the Catholic Church. Monastic property was confiscated, and some Protestant doctrines given official sanction.

Religious wars. A century and a half of religious wars began with a S German peasant uprising (1524), repressed with Luther's support. Radical sects—democratic, pacifist, millennarian—arose (Anabaptists ruled Münster in 1534-35) and were suppressed violently. Civil war in France from 1562 between **Huguenots** (Protestant nobles and merchants) and Catholics ended with the 1598 **Edict of Nantes** tolerating Protestants (revoked 1685). Hapsburg attempts to restore Catholicism in Germany were resisted in 25 years of fighting; the 1555 Peace of Augsburg guarantee of religious independence to local princes and cities was confirmed only after the **Thirty Years War** (1618-48), when much of Germany was devastated by local and foreign armies (Sweden, France).

A Catholic Reformation, or **Counter Reformation**, met the Protestant challenge, clearly defining an official theology at the Council of Trent (1545-63). The **Jesuit** order (Society of Jesus), founded in 1534 by Loyola (1491-1556), helped reconvert large areas of Poland, Hungary, and S Germany and sent missionaries to the New World, India, and China, while the Inquisition helped suppress heresy in Catholic countries. A revival of piety appeared in the devotional literature (Theresa of Avila, 1515-82) and the grandiose Baroque art (Bernini, 1598-1680) of Roman Catholic countries.

Scientific Revolution. The late nominalist thinkers (Ockham, c 1300-49) of Paris and Oxford challenged Aristotelian orthodoxy, allowing for a freer scientific approach. But metaphysical values, such as the Neoplatonic faith in an orderly, mathematical cosmos, still motivated and directed subsequent inquiry. **Copernicus** (1473-1543) promoted the heliocentric theory, which was confirmed when Kepler (1571-1630) discovered the mathematical laws describing the orbits of the planets. The traditional Christian-Aristotelian belief that heavens and earth were fundamentally different collapsed when **Galileo** (1564-1642) discovered moving sunspots, irregular moon topography, and moons around Jupiter. He and **Newton** (1642-1727) developed a mechanics that unified cosmic and earthly phenomena. To meet the needs of the new physics, Newton and Leibnitz (1646-1716) invented calculus, and Descartes (1596-1650) invented analytic geometry.

An explosion of **observational science** included the discovery of blood circulation (Harvey, 1578-1657) and microscopic life (Leeuwenhoek, 1632-1723) and advances in anatomy (Vesalius, 1514-64, dissected corpses) and chemistry (Boyle, 1627-91). Scientific research institutes were founded: Florence (1657), London (**Royal Society**, 1660), Paris (1666). Inventions proliferated (Savery's steam engine, 1696).

Arts. Mannerist trends of the High Renaissance (**Michelangelo**, 1475-1564) exploited virtuosity, grace, novelty, and exotic subjects and poses. The notion of artistic genius was promoted, in contrast to the anonymous medieval artisan. Private connoisseurs entered the art market. These trends were elaborated in the 17th cent. **Baroque** era on a grander scale. Dynamic movement in painting and sculpture was emphasized by sharp lighting effects, use of rich materials (colored marble, gilt), and realistic details. Curved facades, broken lines, rich, deep-cut detail, and ceiling decoration characterized Baroque architecture, especially in Germany. Monarchs, princes, and prelates, usually Catholic, used Baroque art to enhance and embellish their authority, as in royal portraits by Velazquez (1599-1660) and Van Dyck (1599-1641).

National styles emerged. In France, a taste for rectilinear order and serenity (Poussin, 1594-1665), linked to the new rational philosophy, was expressed in classical forms. The influence of **classical values** in French literature (tragedies of **Racine**, 1639-99) gave rise to the "battle of the Ancients and Moderns." New forms included the essay (**Montaigne**, 1533-92) and novel (*Princesse de Cleves*, La Fayette, 1678).

Dutch painting of the 17th cent. was unique in its wide social distribution. The Flemish tradition of undemonstrative realism reached its peak in **Rembrandt** (1606-69) and Vermeer (1632-75).

Economy. European economic expansion was stimulated by the new trade with the East, by New World gold and silver, and by a doubling of population (50 million in 1450, 100 million in 1600). New business and financial techniques were developed and refined, such as joint-stock companies, insurance, and letters of credit and exchange. The Bank of Amsterdam (1609) and the Bank of England (1694) broke the old monopoly of private banking families. The rise of a business mentality was typified by the spread of clock towers in cities in the 14th cent. By the mid-15th cent., portable clocks were available; the first watch was invented in 1502.

By 1650, most governments had adopted the **mercantile system**, in which they sought to amass metallic wealth by protecting their merchants' foreign and colonial trade monopolies. The rise in prices and the new coin-based economy undermined the craft guild and feudal manorial systems. Expanding industries, such as clothweaving and mining, benefited from technical advances. Coal replaced disappearing wood as the chief fuel; it was used to fuel new 16th-cent. blast furnaces making cast iron.

New World. The **Aztecs** united much of the Meso-American culture area in a militarist empire by 1519, from their capital, Tenochtitlán (pop. 300,000), which was the center of a cult requiring enormous levels of ritual human sacrifice. Most of the civilized areas of South America were ruled by the centralized Inca Empire (1476-1534), stretching 2,000 mi from Ecuador to NW Argentina. Lavish and sophisticated traditions in pottery, weaving, sculpture, and architecture were maintained in both regions.

These empires, beset by revolts, fell in 2 short campaigns to gold-seeking Spanish forces based in the Antilles and Panama. **Cortes** took Mexico (1519-21); **Pizarro,** Peru (1532-35). From these centers, land and sea expeditions claimed most of North and South America for Spain. The Indian high cultures did not survive the impact of Christian missionaries and the new upper class of whites and mestizos. In turn, New World silver and such Indian products as potatoes, tobacco, corn, peanuts, chocolate, and rubber exercised a major economic influence on Europe. Although the Spanish administration intermittently concerned itself with the welfare of Indians, the population remained impoverished at most levels, despite the growth of a distinct South American civilization. European diseases reduced the native population.

Brazil, which the Portuguese reached in 1500 and settled after 1530, and the Caribbean colonies of several European nations developed a plantation economy where sugarcane, tobacco, cotton, coffee, rice, indigo, and lumber were grown commercially by slaves. From the early 16th to the late 19th cent., some 10 million Africans were transported to **slavery** in the New World.

Netherlands. The urban, Calvinist N provinces of the Netherlands rebelled (1568) against Hapsburg Spain and founded an oligarchic mercantile republic. Their strategic control of the Baltic grain market enabled them to exploit Mediterranean food shortages. Religious refugees—French and Belgian Protestants, Iberian Jews—added to the cosmopolitan commercial talent pool. After Spain absorbed Portugal in 1580, the Dutch seized Portuguese possessions and created a vast, though generally short-lived commercial empire in Brazil, the Antilles, Africa, India, Ceylon, Malacca, Indonesia, and Taiwan and challenged or supplanted Portuguese traders in China and Japan. Revolution in 1640 restored Portuguese independence.

England. Anglicanism became firmly established under Elizabeth I after a brief Catholic interlude under "Bloody Mary" (1553-58). But religious and political conflicts led to a rebellion (1642) by Parliament. Roundheads (Puritans) defeated Cavaliers (Royalists); Charles I was beheaded (1649). The new **Commonwealth** was ruled as a military dictatorship by Cromwell, who also brutally crushed (1649-51) an Irish rebellion. Conflicts within the Puritan camp (democratic Levelers defeated 1649) aided the Stuart restoration (1660), but Parliament was permanently strengthened and the peaceful **"Glorious Revolution"** (1688) advanced political and religious liberties (writings of **Locke,** 1632-1704). British privateers (Drake, 1540-96) challenged Spanish control of the New World and penetrated Asian trade routes (Madras taken, 1639). North American colonies (Jamestown, 1607; Plymouth, 1620) provided an outlet for religious dissenters from Europe.

France. Emerging from the religious civil wars in 1628, France regained military and commercial great power status under the ministries of **Richelieu** (1624-42), Mazarin (1643-61), and Colbert (1662-83). Under **Louis XIV** (reigned 1643-1715) royal absolutism triumphed over nobles and local *parlements* (defeat of Fronde, 1648-53). Permanent colonies were founded in Canada (1608), the Caribbean (1626), and India (1674).

Sweden. Sweden seceded from the Scandinavian Union in 1523. The thinly populated agrarian state (with copper, iron, and timber exports) was united by the Vasa kings, whose conquests by the mid-17th cent. made Sweden the dominant Baltic power. The empire collapsed in the Great Northern War (1700-21).

Poland. After the union with Lithuania in 1447, Poland ruled vast territories from the Baltic to the Black Sea, resisting German and Turkish incursions. Catholic nobles failed to gain the loyalty of their Orthodox Christian subjects in the E; commerce and trades were practiced by German and Jewish immigrants. The bloody 1648-49 Cossack uprising began the kingdom's dismemberment.

China. A new dynasty, the **Manchus,** invaded from the NE, seized power in 1644, and expanded Chinese control to its greatest extent in Central and SE Asia. Trade and diplomatic contact with Europe grew, carefully controlled by China. New crops (sweet potato, maize, peanut) allowed an economic and population growth (pop. 300 million, in 1800). Traditional arts and literature were pursued with increased sophistication (*Dream of the Red Chamber*, novel, mid-18th cent.).

Japan. Tokugawa Ieyasu, shogun from 1603, finally unified and pacified feudal Japan. Hereditary daimyos and samurai monopolized government office and the professions. An urban merchant class grew, literacy spread, and a cultural renaissance occurred (**haiku**, a verse innovation of the poet Basho, 1644-94). Fear of European domination led to persecution of Christian converts from 1597 and to stringent isolation from outside contact from 1640.

Philosophy, Industry, and Revolution: 1700-1800

Science and Reason. Greater faith in human reason and empirical observation as a source of truth and a means to improve the physical and social environment, espoused since the Renaissance (Francis Bacon, 1561-1626), was bolstered by scientific discoveries in spite of theological opposition (Galileo's forced retraction, 1633). **Descartes** used a rationalistic approach modeled on geometry to discover "self-evident" truths as a foundation of knowledge. **Newton** emphasized induction from experimental observation. **Spinoza** (1632-77), who called for political and intellectual freedom, developed a systematic rationalistic philosophy in his classic work *Ethics*.

French philosophers assumed leadership of the **Enlightenment** in the 18th cent. Montesquieu (1689-1755) used British history to support his notions of limited government. **Voltaire's** (1694-1778) diaries and novels of exotic travel illustrated the intellectual trends toward secular ethics and relativism. Rousseau's (1712-1778) radical concepts of the **social contract** and of the inherent goodness of the common

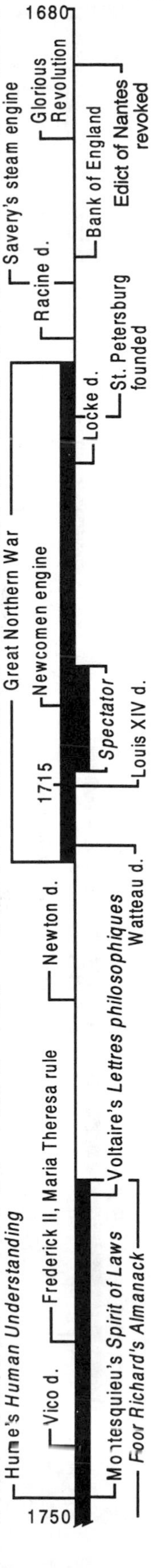

Timeline (right margin):
1680
Glorious Revolution
Bank of England
Edict of Nantes revoked
Savery's steam engine
Racine d.
Locke d.
St. Petersburg founded
Great Northern War
Newcomen engine
Spectator
Louis XIV d.
1715
Newton d.
Voltaire's *Lettres philosophiques*
Watteau d.
Frederick II, Maria Theresa rule
Montesquieu's *Spirit of Laws*
Poor Richard's Almanack
Vico d.
Hume's *Human Understanding*
1750

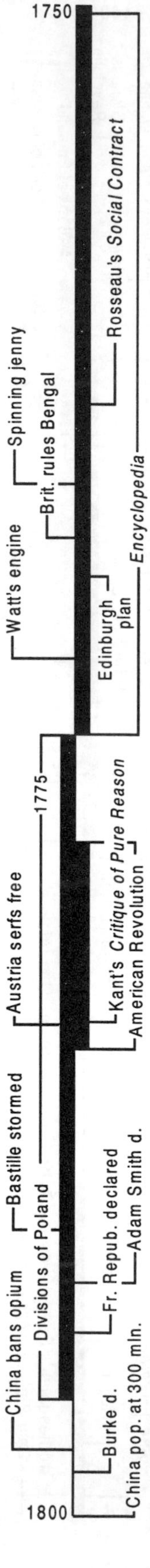
1750
1775
1800
Rosseau's *Social Contract*
Spinning jenny
Brit. rules Bengal
Encyclopedia
Watt's engine
Edinburgh plan
Kant's *Critique of Pure Reason*
American Revolution
Austria serfs free
Bastille stormed
Divisions of Poland
Fr. Repub. declared
Adam Smith d.
China bans opium
Burke d.
China pop. at 300 mln.

man gave impetus to antimonarchical republicanism. The *Encyclopedia* (1751-72), edited by Diderot and d'Alembert and designed as a monument to reason, was largely devoted to practical technology.

In England, ideals of political and religious liberty were connected with empiricist philosophy and science in the followers of Locke. But British empiricism, especially as developed by the skeptical **Hume** (1711-76), radically reduced the role of reason in philosophy, as did the evolutionary approach to law and politics of Burke (1729-97) and the utilitarian ethics of Bentham (1748-1832). Adam Smith (1723-90) and other **physiocrats** called for a rationalization of economic activity by removing artificial barriers to a supposedly natural free exchange of goods.

German writers participated in the new philosophical trends popularized by Wolff (1679-1754). **Kant's** (1724-1804) transcendental idealism, unifying an empirical epistemology with a priori moral and logical concepts, directed German thought away from skepticism. Italian contributions included work on electricity by Galvani (1737-98) and Volta (1745-1827), the pioneer **historiography of Vico** (1668-1744), and writings on penal reform by Beccaria (1738-94). Benjamin Franklin (1706-90) was celebrated in Europe for his varied achievements.

The growth of the **press** (*Spectator*, 1711-12) and the wide distribution of realistic but sentimental **novels** attested to the increase of a large bourgeois public.

Arts. Rococo art, characterized by extravagant decorative effects, asymmetries copied from organic models, and artificial pastoral subjects, was favored by the continental aristocracy for most of the cent. (Watteau, 1684-1721) and had musical analogies in the ornamentalized polyphony of late Baroque. The **Neoclassical** art after 1750, associated with the new scientific archaeology, was more streamlined and was infused with the supposed moral and geometric rectitude of the Roman Republic (David, 1748-1825). In England, **town planning** on a grand scale began.

Industrial Revolution in England. Agricultural improvements, such as the sowing drill (1701) and livestock breeding, were implemented on the large fields provided by enclosure of common lands by private owners. Profits from agriculture and from colonial and foreign trade (1800 volume, £54 million) were channeled through hundreds of banks and the **Stock Exchange** (est 1773) into new industrial processes.

The Newcomen steam pump (1712) aided coal mining. Coal fueled the new efficient steam engines patented by Watt in 1769, and coke-smelting produced cheap, sturdy iron for machinery by the 1730s. The **flying shuttle** (1733) and **spinning jenny** (c 1764) were used in the large new cotton textile factories, where women and children were much of the work force. Goods were transported cheaply over **canals** (2,000 mi; built 1760-1800).

American Revolution. The British colonies in North America attracted a mass immigration of religious dissenters and poor people throughout the 17th and 18th cent., coming from the British Isles, Germany, the Netherlands, and other countries. The population reached 3 million non-natives by the 1770s. The small native population was greatly reduced by European diseases and by wars with and between the various colonies. British attempts to control colonial trade and to tax the colonists to pay for the costs of colonial administration and defense clashed with traditions of local self-government and eventually provoked the colonies to rebellion.

Central and East Europe. The monarchs of the three states that dominated E Europe—Austria, Prussia, and Russia—accepted the advice and legitimation of philosophes in creating more modern, centralized institutions in their kingdoms, enlarged by the division (1772-95) of Poland.

Under **Frederick II** (r 1740-86) Prussia, with its efficient modern army, doubled in size. State monopolies and tariff protection fostered industry, and some legal reforms were introduced. Austria's heterogeneous realms were unified under **Maria Theresa** (r 1740-80) and **Joseph II** (r 1780-90). Reforms in education, law, and religion were enacted, and the Austrian serfs were freed (1781). With its defeat in the Seven Years' War in 1763, Austria failed to regain Silesia, which had been seized by Prussia, but it was compensated by expansion to the E and S (Hungary, Slavonia, 1699; Galicia, 1772).

Russia, whose borders continued to expand in all directions, adopted some Western bureaucratic and economic policies under **Peter I** (r 1682-1725) and **Catherine II** (r 1762-96). Trade and cultural contacts with the West multiplied from the new Baltic Sea capital, **St. Petersburg** (est 1703).

French Revolution. The growing French middle class lacked political power and resented aristocratic tax privileges, especially in light of the successful American Revolution. Peasants lacked adequate land and were burdened with feudal obligations to nobles. War with Britain led to the loss of French Canada and drained the treasury, finally forcing the king to call the **Estates-General** in 1789 (first time since 1614), in an atmosphere of food riots (poor crop in 1788).

Aristocratic resistance to absolutism was soon overshadowed by the reformist Third Estate (middle class), which proclaimed itself the **National Constituent Assembly** June 17 and took the "Tennis Court oath" on June 20 to secure a constitution. The storming of the **Bastille** on July 14 by Parisian artisans was followed by looting and seizure of aristocratic property throughout France. Assembly reforms included abolition of class and regional privileges, a Declaration of Rights, suffrage by taxpayers (75% of males), and the **Civil Constitution of the Clergy** providing for election and loyalty oaths for priests. A republic was declared Sept. 22, 1792, in spite of royalist pressure from Austria and Prussia, which had declared war in April (joined by Britain the next year). Louis XVI was beheaded Jan. 21, 1793, Queen Marie Antoinette was beheaded Oct. 16, 1793.

Royalist uprisings in La Vendée and military reverses led to a **reign of terror** in which tens of thousands of opponents of the Revolution and criminals were executed. Radical reforms in the **Convention** period (Sept. 1793-Oct. 1795) included the abolition of colonial slavery, economic measures to aid the poor, support of public education, and a short-lived de-Christianization.

Division among radicals (execution of Hebert, Danton, and Robespierre, 1794) aided the ascendance of a moderate **Directory**, which consolidated military victories. **Napoleon Bonaparte** (1769-1821), a popular young general, exploited political divisions and participated in a coup Nov. 9, 1799, making himself first consul (dictator).

India. Sikh and Hindu rebels (Rajputs, Marathas) and Afghans destroyed the power of the Mughals during the 18th cent. After France's defeat (1763) in the Seven Years' War, Britain was the primary European trade power in India. Its control of inland **Bengal and Bihar** was recognized (1765) by the Mughal shah, who granted the **British East India Co.** (under Clive, 1725-74) the right to collect land revenue there. Despite objections from Parliament (1784 India Act), the company's involvement in local wars and politics led to repeated acquisitions of new territory. The company exported Indian textiles, sugar, and indigo.

Change Gathers Steam: 1800-40

French ideals and empire spread. Inspired by the ideals of the French Revolution, and supported by the expanding French armies, new republican regimes arose near France: the **Batavian** Republic in the Netherlands (1795-1806), the **Helvetic** Republic in Switzerland (1798-1803), the **Cisalpine** Republic in N Italy (1797-1805), the **Ligurian** Republic in Genoa (1797-1805), and the **Parthenopean** Republic in S Italy (1799). A Roman Republic existed briefly in 1798 after Pope Pius VI was arrested by French troops. In Italy and Germany, new nationalist sentiments were stimulated both in imitation of and in reaction to developments in France (anti-French and anti-Jacobin peasant uprisings in Italy, 1796-99).

From 1804, when Napoleon declared himself emperor, to 1812, a succession of military victories (Austerlitz, 1805; Jena, 1806) extended his control over most of Europe, through puppet states (**Confederation of the Rhine** united W German states for the first time and **Grand Duchy of Warsaw** revived Polish national hopes), expansion of the empire, and alliances.

Among the lasting reforms initiated under Napoleon's absolutist reign were: establishment of the Bank of France, centralization of tax collection, codification of law along Roman models (Code Napoléon), and reform and extension of secondary and university education. In an 1801 concordat, the papacy recognized the effective autonomy of the French Catholic Church. Some 400,000 French soldiers were killed in the Napoleonic Wars, along with 600,000 foreign troops.

Last gasp of old regime. France's coastal blockade of Europe (**Continental System**) failed to neutralize Britain. The disastrous 1812 invasion of Russia exposed Napoleon's overextension. After Napoleon's 1814 exile at Elba, his armies were defeated (1815) at **Waterloo**, by British and Prussian troops.

At the **Congress of Vienna**, the monarchs and princes of Europe redrew their boundaries, to the advantage of Prussia (in Saxony and the Ruhr), Austria (in Illyria and Venetia), and Russia (in Poland and Finland). British conquest of Dutch and French colonies (S Africa, Ceylon, Mauritius) was recognized, and France, under the restored Bourbons, retained its expanded 1792 borders. The settlement brought 50 years of international peace to Europe.

But the Congress was unable to check the advance of liberal ideals and of nationalism among the smaller European nations. The 1825 **Decembrist uprising** by liberal officers in Russia was easily suppressed. But an independence movement in **Greece**, stirred by commercial prosperity and a cultural revival, succeeded in expelling Ottoman rule by 1831, with the aid of Britain, France, and Russia.

A constitutional monarchy was secured in France by the **1830 Revolution**; Louis Philippe became king. The revolutionary contagion spread to **Belgium**, which gained its independence (1830) from the Dutch monarchy, to **Poland**, whose rebellion was defeated (1830-31) by Russia, and to Germany.

Romanticism. A new style in intellectual and artistic life began to replace Neoclassicism and Rococo after the mid-18th cent. By the early 19th cent., this style, Romanticism, had prevailed in the European world.

Rousseau had begun the reaction against rationalism; in education (*Émile*, 1762) he stressed subjective spontaneity over regularized instruction. In Germany, Lessing (1729-81) and Herder (1744-1803) favorably compared the German folk song to classical forms and began a cult of Shakespeare, whose passion and "natural" wisdom was a model for the romantic *Sturm und Drang* (Storm and Stress) movement. **Goethe's** *Sorrows of Young Werther* (1774) set the model for the tragic, passionate genius.

A new interest in **Gothic architecture** in England after 1760 (Walpole, 1717-97) spread through Europe, associated with an aesthetic Christian and mystic revival (**Blake,** 1757-1827). Celtic, Norse, and German mythology and folk tales were revived or imitated (Macpherson's Ossian translation, 1762; Grimm's Fairy Tales, 1812-22). The medieval revival (Scott's *Ivanhoe*, 1819) led to a new interest in history, stressing national differences and organic growth (**Carlyle**, 1795-1881; Michelet, 1798-1874), corresponding to theories of natural evolution (Lamarck's *Philosophie Zoologique*, 1809; Lyell's *Geology*, 1830-33). A reaction against classicism characterized the English **romantic poets**, beginning with **Wordsworth** (1770-1850). Revolution and war fed an emphasis on freedom and conflict, expressed by both poets (**Byron**, 1788-1824; **Hugo**, 1802-85) and philosophers (**Hegel**, 1770-1831).

Wild gardens replaced the formal French variety, and painters favored rural, stormy, and mountainous landscapes (**Turner**, 1775-1851; **Constable**, 1776-1837). Clothing became freer, with wigs, hoops, and ruffles discarded. Originality and genius were expected in the life as well as the work of inspired artists (Murger's *Scenes from Bohemian Life*, 1847-49). Exotic locales and themes (as in Gothic horror stories) were used in art and literature (Delacroix, 1798-1863; **Poe**, 1809-49).

Music exhibited the new dramatic style and a breakdown of classical forms (**Beethoven,** 1770-1827). The use of folk melodies and modes aided the growth of distinct national traditions (Glinka in Russia, 1804-57).

Latin America. Francois **Toussaint L'Ouverture** led a successful slave revolt in Haiti, which subsequently became the first Latin American state to achieve independence (1804). The mainland Spanish colonies won their independence (1810-24), under such leaders as **Bolivar** (1783-1830). Brazil became an independent empire (1822) under the Portuguese prince regent. A new class of military officers divided power with large landholders and the church.

United States. Heavy immigration and exploitation of ample natural resources fueled rapid economic growth. The spread of the franchise, public education, and antislavery sentiment were signs of a widespread democratic ethic.

China. Failure to keep pace with Western arms technology exposed China to greater European influence and hampered efforts to bar imports of opium, which had damaged Chinese society and drained wealth overseas. In the **Opium War** (1839-42), Britain forced China to expand trade opportunities and to cede Hong Kong.

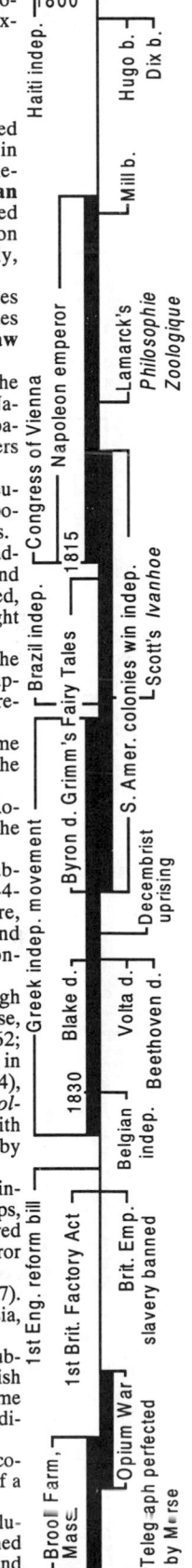

Timeline (1800–1845):
- 1800
- Haiti indep.
- Hugo b. / Dix b.
- Mill b.
- Congress of Vienna / Napoleon emperor
- Lamarck's *Philosophie Zoologique*
- 1815
- Brazil indep.
- S. Amer. colonies win indep. / Scott's *Ivanhoe*
- Byron d. / Grimm's Fairy Tales
- Decembrist uprising
- Greek indep. movement
- 1830
- Blake d.
- Volta d. / Beethoven d.
- Belgian indep.
- 1st Eng. reform bill
- 1st Brit. Factory Act
- Brit. Emp. slavery banned
- Brook Farm, Mass.
- Opium War
- Telegraph perfected by Morse
- 1845

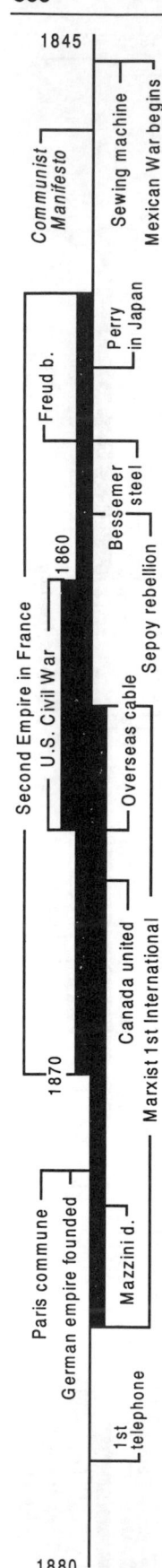

1845

Communist Manifesto

Freud b.

Second Empire in France

U.S. Civil War

1860

Paris commune

German empire founded

1870

Sewing machine

Mexican War begins

Perry in Japan

Bessemer steel

Sepoy rebellion

Overseas cable

Canada united

Marxist 1st International

Mazzini d.

1st telephone

1880

Triumph of Progress: 1840-80

Idea of Progress. As a result of the cumulative scientific, economic, and political changes of the preceding eras, the idea took hold among literate people in the West that continuing growth and improvement was the usual state of human and natural life.

Darwin's statement of the **theory of evolution** and survival of the fittest (*Origin of Species*, 1859), defended by intellectuals and scientists against theological objections, was taken as confirmation that progress was the natural direction of life. The controversy helped define popular ideas of the dedicated scientist and ever-expanding human knowledge of and control over the world (Foucault's demonstration of earth's rotation, 1851; **Pasteur's** germ theory, 1861).

Liberals following Ricardo (1772-1823) in their faith that unrestrained competition would bring continuous economic expansion sought to adjust political life to the new social realities and believed that unregulated competition of ideas would yield truth (**Mill**, 1806-73). In England, successive reform bills (1832, 1867, 1884) gave representation to the new industrial towns and extended the franchise to the middle and lower classes and to Catholics, Dissenters, and Jews. On both sides of the Atlantic, reformists tried to improve conditions for the mentally ill (**Dix**, 1802-87), women (Anthony, 1820-1906), and prisoners. Slavery was barred in the British Empire (1833); the U.S. (1865); and Brazil (1888).

Socialist theories based on ideas of human perfectibility or historical progress were widely disseminated. Utopian socialists such as Saint-Simon (1760-1825) envisaged an orderly, just society directed by a technocratic elite. A model factory town, New Lanark, Scotland, was set up by utopian Robert Owen (1771-1858), and utopian communal experiments were tried in the U.S. (Brook Farm, Mass., 1841-47). Bakunin's (1814-76) anarchism represented the opposite utopian extreme of total freedom. **Marx** (1818-83) posited the inevitable triumph of socialism in the industrial countries through a historical process of class conflict.

Spread of industry. The technical processes and managerial innovations of the English industrial revolution spread to Europe (especially Germany) and the U.S., causing an explosion of industrial production, demand for raw materials, and competition for markets. Inventors, both trained and self-educated, provided the means for larger-scale production (Bessemer steel, 1856; sewing machine, 1846). Many inventions were shown at the 1851 London Great Exhibition at the **Crystal Palace,** the theme of which was universal prosperity.

Local specialization and long-distance trade were aided by a revolution in transportation and communication. Railroads were first introduced in the 1820s in England and the U.S. More than 150,000 mi of track had been laid worldwide by 1880, with another 100,000 mi laid in the next decade. Steamships were improved (*Savannah* crossed Atlantic, 1819). The telegraph, perfected by 1844 (Morse), connected the Old and New Worlds by cable in 1866 and quickened the pace of international commerce and politics. The first commercial telephone exchange went into operation in the U.S. in 1878.

The new class of industrial workers, uprooted from their rural homes, lacked job security and suffered from dangerous overcrowded conditions at work and at home. Many responded by organizing **trade unions** (legalized in England, 1824; France, 1884). The U.S. Knights of Labor had 700,000 members by 1886. The First International (1864-76) tried to unite workers internationally around a Marxist program. The quasi-Socialist Paris Commune uprising (1871) was violently suppressed. Factory Acts to reduce child labor and regulate conditions were passed (1833-50 in England). Social security measures were introduced by the Bismarck regime (1883-89) in Germany.

Revolutions of 1848. Among the causes of the continent-wide revolutions were an international collapse of credit and resulting unemployment, bad harvests in 1845-47, and a cholera epidemic. The new urban proletariat and expanding bourgeoisie demanded a greater political role. Republics were proclaimed in France, Rome, and Venice. Nationalist feelings reached fever pitch in the Hapsburg empire, as Hungary declared independence under Kossuth, as a Slav Congress demanded equality, and as Piedmont tried to drive Austria from Lombardy. A national liberal assembly at Frankfurt called for German unification.

But riots fueled bourgeois fears of socialism (**Marx and Engels,** *Communist Manifesto*, 1848), and peasants remained conservative. The old establishment—the Papacy, the Hapsburgs with the help of the Czarist Russian army —was able to rout the revolutionaries by 1849. The French Republic succumbed to a renewed monarchy by 1852 (Emperor Napoleon III).

Great nations unified. Using the "blood and iron" tactics of Bismarck from 1862, Prussia controlled N Germany by 1867 (war with Denmark, 1864; Austria, 1866). After defeating France in 1870 (annexation of Alsace-Lorraine), it won the allegiance of S German states. A new **German Empire** was proclaimed (1871). **Italy,** inspired by Mazzini (1805-72) and Garibaldi (1807-82), was unified by the reformed Piedmont kingdom through uprisings, plebiscites, and war.

The U.S., its area expanded after the 1846-48 Mexican War, defeated (1861-65) a secession attempt by slave states. The Canadian provinces were united in an autonomous **Dominion of Canada** (1867). Control in **India** was removed from the East India Co. and centralized under British administration after the 1857-58 Sepoy rebellion, laying the groundwork for the modern Indian State. Queen Victoria was named Empress of India (1876).

Europe dominates Asia. The Ottoman Empire began to collapse in the face of Balkan nationalisms and European imperial incursions in N Africa (Suez Canal, 1869). The Turks had lost control of most of both regions by 1882. Russia completed its expansion S by 1884 (despite the temporary setback of the Crimean War with Turkey, Britain, and France, 1853-56), taking Turkestan, all the Caucasus, and Chinese areas in the E and sponsoring Balkan Slavs against the Turks. A succession of reformist and reactionary regimes presided over a slow modernization (serfs freed, 1861). Persian independence suffered as Russia and British India competed for influence.

China was forced to sign a series of unequal treaties with European powers and Japan. Overpopulation and an inefficient dynasty brought misery and caused rebellions (Taiping, Muslims) leaving tens of millions dead. Japan was forced by the U.S. (Commodore Perry's visits, 1853-54) and Europe to end its isolation. The Meiji restoration (1868) gave power to a Westernizing oligarchy. Intensified empire-building gave Burma to Britain (1824-85) and Indochina to France (1862-95). Christian missionary activity followed imperial and trade expansion in Asia.

Respectability. The fine arts were expected to reflect and encourage the progress of morals and manners among the Victorians. Prudery, exaggerated delicacy, and familial piety were heralded by **Bowdler's** expurgated edition (1818) of Shakespeare. Government-supported mass education inculcated a work ethic as a means to escape poverty (Horatio Alger, 1832-99).

The official **Beaux Arts** school in Paris set an international style of imposing public buildings (Paris Opera, 1861-74; Vienna Opera, 1861-69) and uplifting statues (Bartholdi's *Statue of Liberty*, 1884). Realist painting, influenced by photography (Daguerre, 1837), appealed to a new mass audience with social or historical narrative (Wilkie, 1785-1841; Poynter, 1836-1919) or with serious religious, moral, or social messages (pre-Raphaelites, Millet's *Angelus*, 1858) often drawn from ordinary life. The **Impressionists** (Monet, 1840-1926; Pissarro, 1830-1903; Renoir, 1841-1919) rejected the formalism, sentimentality, and precise techniques of academic art in favor of a spontaneous, undetailed rendering of the world through careful representation of the effect of natural light on objects.

Realistic **novelists** presented the full panorama of social classes and personalities, but retained sentimentality and moral judgment (**Dickens**, 1812-70; **Eliot**, 1819-80; **Tolstoy**, 1828-1910; **Balzac**, 1799-1850).

Veneer of Stability: 1880-1900

Imperialism triumphant. The vast **African** interior, visited by European explorers (Barth, 1821-65; Livingstone, 1813-73), was conquered by the European powers in rapid, competitive thrusts from their coastal bases after 1880, mostly for domestic political and international strategic reasons. W African Muslim kingdoms (Fulani), Arab slave traders (Zanzibar), and Bantu military confederations (Zulu) were alike subdued. Only Christian Ethiopia (defeat of Italy, 1896) and Liberia resisted successfully. France (W Africa) and Britain ("Cape to Cairo," **Boer War,** 1899-1902) were the major beneficiaries. The ideology of "the white man's burden" (Kipling, *Barrack Room Ballads*, 1892) or of a "civilizing mission" (France) justified the conquests.

W European foreign capital investment soared to nearly $40 billion by 1914, but most was in E Europe (France, Germany), the Americas (Britain), and the Europeans' colonies. The foundation of the modern interdependent world economy was laid, with cartels dominating raw material trade.

An industrious world. Industrial and technological proficiency characterized the 2 new great powers—Germany and the U.S. Coal and iron deposits enabled Germany to reach 2d or 3d place status in iron, steel, and shipbuilding by the 1900s. German electrical and chemical industries were world leaders. The U.S. post-Civil War boom (interrupted by "panics"—1884, 1893, 1896) was shaped by massive immigration from S and E Europe from 1880, government subsidy of railroads, and huge private monopolies (Standard Oil, 1870; U.S. Steel, 1901). The **Spanish-American War**, 1898 (Philippine Insurrection, 1899-1902), and the Open Door policy in China (1899) made the U.S. a world power.

England led in **urbanization** (72% by 1890), with **London** the world capital of finance, insurance, and shipping. Sewer systems (Paris, 1850s), electric subways (London, 1890), parks, and bargain department stores helped improve living standards for most of the urban population of the industrial world.

Westernization of Asia. Asian reaction to European economic, military, and religious incursions took the form of imitation of Western techniques and adoption of Western ideas of progress and freedom. The Chinese "self-strengthening" movement of the 1860s and '70s included rail, port, and arsenal improvements and metal and textile mills. Reformers such as **K'ang Yu-wei** (1858-1927) won liberalizing reforms in 1898, right after the European and Japanese "scramble for concessions."

A universal education system in Japan and importation of foreign industrial, scientific, and military experts aided Japan's unprecedented rapid modernization after 1868, under the authoritarian Meiji regime. Japan's victory in the **Sino-Japanese War** (1894-95) put Formosa and Korea in its power.

In India, the British alliance with the remaining princely states masked reform sentiment among the Westernized urban elite; higher education had been conducted largely in English for 50 years. The **Indian National Congress**, founded in 1885, demanded a larger government role for Indians.

Fin-de-siècle **sophistication**. **Naturalist** writers pushed realism to its extreme limits, adopting a quasi-scientific attitude and writing about formerly taboo subjects such as sex, crime, extreme poverty, and corruption (Flaubert, 1821-80; Zola, 1840-1902; Hardy, 1840-1928). Unseen or repressed psychological motivations were explored in the clinical and theoretical works of **Freud** (1856-1939) and in the fiction of **Dostoyevsky** (1821-81), James (1843-1916), Schnitzler (1862-1931), and others.

A contempt for bourgeois life or a desire to shock a complacent audience was shared by the French **symbolist** poets (Verlaine, 1844-96; Rimbaud, 1854-91), by neopagan English writers (Swinburne, 1837-1909), by continental dramatists (**Ibsen,** 1828-1906), and by satirists (Wilde, 1854-1900). **Nietzsche** (1844-1900) was influential in his elitism and pessimism.

Postimpressionist art neglected long-cherished conventions of representation (Cezanne, 1839-1906) and showed a willingness to learn from primitive and non-European art (Gauguin, 1848-1903; Japanese prints).

Racism. Gobineau (1816-82) gave a pseudobiological foundation to modern racist theories, which spread in the latter 19th cent., along with **Social Darwinism**, the belief that societies are and should be organized as a struggle for survival of the fittest. The medieval period was interpreted as an era of natural Germanic rule (Chamberlain, 1855-1927), and notions of superiority were associated with German national aspirations (Treitschke, 1834-96). **Anti-Semitism**, with a new racist rationale, became a significant political force in Germany (Anti-Semitic Petition, 1880), Austria (Lueger, 1844-1910), and France (Dreyfus case, 1894-1906).

Last Respite: 1900-9

Alliances. While the peace of Europe (and its dependencies) continued to hold (1907 **Hague Conference** extended the rules of war and international arbitration procedures), imperial rivalries, protectionist trade practices (in Germany and France), and the escalating arms race (British *Dreadnought* battleship launched; Germany widens Kiel canal, 1906) exacerbated minor disputes (German-French Moroccan "crises," 1905, 1911).

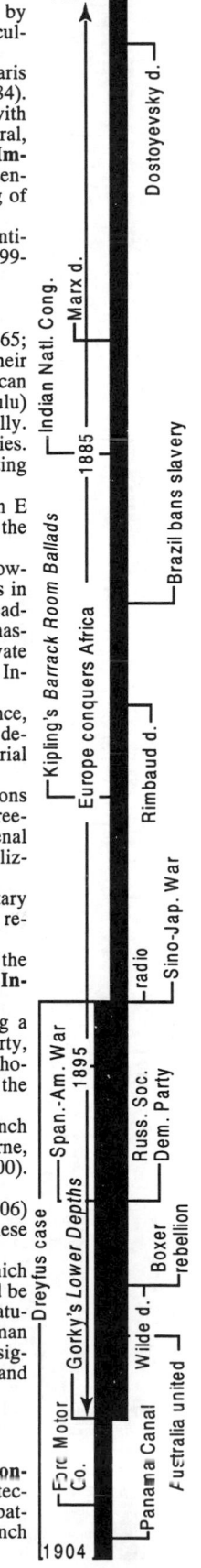

1904

Pure Food & Drug Act

Rev. in Russia

Russo-Jap. War

Labour Party

Ibsen d.

Dreadnought launched

Hague Conf.

Young Turks rev.

Robie House

Futurist Manifesto

Japan annexes Korea

Mex. rev. starts

Portugal rev. starts

1910

2d Morocco crisis

Diaz Mex. rule ends

Chinese repub.

Ottomans lose Europe

Theory of Relativity

Maugham's Of Human Bondage

World War I

1916

Security was sought through alliances: **Triple Alliance** (Germany, Austria-Hungary, Italy; renewed in 1902 and 1907); Anglo-Japanese Alliance (1902), Franco-Russian Alliance (1899), **Entente Cordiale** (Britain, France, 1904), Anglo-Russian Treaty (1907), German-Ottoman friendship.

Ottomans decline. The inefficient, corrupt Ottoman government was unable to resist further loss of territory. Nearly all European lands were lost in 1912 to Serbia, Greece, Montenegro, and Bulgaria. Italy took Libya and the Dodecanese islands the same year, and Britain took Kuwait (1899) and the Sinai (1906). The **Young Turk** revolution in 1908 forced the sultan to restore a constitution, and it introduced some social reform, industrialization, and secularization.

British Empire. British trade and cultural influence remained dominant in the empire, but constitutional reforms presaged its eventual dissolution: The colonies of **Australia** were united in 1901 under a self-governing commonwealth. **New Zealand** acquired dominion status in 1907. The old Boer republics joined Cape Colony and Natal in the self-governing **Union of South Africa** in 1910.

The 1909 Indian Councils Act enhanced the role of elected province legislatures in **India**. The Muslim League (founded 1906) sought separate communal representation.

East Asia. Japan exploited its growing industrial power to expand its empire. Victory in the 1904-5 war against Russia (naval battle of Tsushima, 1905) assured Japan's domination of **Korea** (annexed 1910) and Manchuria (Port Arthur taken, 1905).

In China, central authority began to crumble (empress died, 1908). Reforms (Confucian exam system ended 1905, modernization of the army, building of railroads) were inadequate, and secret societies of reformers and nationalists, inspired by the Westernized **Sun Yat-sen** (1866-1925) fomented periodic uprisings in the S.

Siam, whose independence had been guaranteed by Britain and France in 1896, was split into spheres of influence by those countries in 1907.

Russia. The population of the Russian Empire approached 150 million in 1900. Reforms in education, in law, and in local institutions (*zemstvos*) and an industrial boom starting in the 1880s (oil, railroads) created the beginnings of a modern state, despite the autocratic tsarist regime. Liberals (1903 Union of Liberation), Socialists (Social Democrats founded 1898, Bolsheviks split off 1903), and populists (Social Revolutionaries founded 1901) were periodically repressed, and national minorities were persecuted (anti-Jewish pogroms, 1903, 1905-6).

An industrial crisis after 1900 and harvest failures aggravated poverty among urban workers, and the 1904-5 defeat by Japan (which checked Russia's Asian expansion) sparked **the Revolution of 1905-6.** A **Duma** (parliament) was created, and an agricultural reform (under Stolypin, prime minister 1906-11) created a large class of landowning peasants (kulaks).

The world shrinks. Developments in transportation and communication and mass population movements helped create an awareness of an interdependent world. Early **automobiles** (Daimler, Benz, 1885) were experimental or were designed as luxuries. Assembly-line mass production (Ford Motor Co., 1903) made the invention practicable, and by 1910 nearly 500,000 motor vehicles were registered in the U.S. alone. **Heavier-than-air flights** began in 1903 in the U.S. (Wright brothers), preceded by glider, balloon, and model plane advances in several countries. Trade was advanced by improvements in **ship design** (gyrocompass, 1910), speed (*Lusitania* crossed Atlantic in 5 days, 1907), and reach (Panama Canal begun, 1904).

The first transatlantic **radio** telegraphic transmission occurred in 1901, 6 years after Marconi discovered radio. Radio transmission of human speech had been made in 1900. Telegraphic transmission of photos was achieved in 1904, lending immediacy to news reports. **Phonographs**, popularized by Caruso's recordings (starting 1902), made for quick international spread of musical styles (ragtime). **Motion pictures**, perfected in the 1890s (Dickson, Lumière brothers), became a popular and artistic medium after 1900; newsreels appeared in 1909.

Emigration from crowded European centers soared in the decade: 9 million migrated to the U.S., and millions more went to Siberia, Canada, Argentina, Australia, South Africa, and Algeria. Some 70 million Europeans emigrated in the cent. before 1914. Several million Chinese, Indians, and Japanese migrated to SE Asia, where their urban skills often enabled them to take a predominant economic role.

Social reform. The social and economic problems of the poor were kept in the public eye by realist fiction writers (Dreiser's *Sister Carrie*, 1900; Gorky's *Lower Depths*, 1902; Sinclair's *Jungle*, 1906), journalists (U.S. **muckrakers**—Steffens, Tarbell), and artists (Ashcan school). Frequent labor strikes and occasional assassinations by anarchists or radicals (Empress Elizabeth of Austria, 1898; King Umberto I of Italy, 1900; U.S. Pres. McKinley, 1901; Russian Interior Minister Plehve, 1904; Portugal's King Carlos, 1908) added to social tension and fear of revolution.

But democratic reformism prevailed. In Germany, Bernstein's (1850-1932) **revisionist Marxism**, downgrading revolution, was accepted by the powerful Social Democrats and trade unions. The British Fabian Society (the Webbs, Shaw) and the Labour Party (founded 1906) worked for reforms such as Social Security and union rights (1906), while woman suffragists grew more militant. U.S. **progressives** fought big business (Pure Food and Drug Act, 1906). In France, the 10-hour work day (1904) and separation of church and state (1905) were reform victories, as was universal suffrage in Austria (1907).

Arts. An unprecedented period of experimentation, centered in France, produced several new **painting** styles: Fauvism exploited bold color areas (Matisse, *Woman with Hat*, 1905); expressionism reflected powerful inner emotions (the Brücke group, 1905); cubism combined several views of an object on one flat surface (Picasso's *Demoiselles*, 1906-7); futurism tried to depict speed and motion (Italian Futurist Manifesto, 1910). **Architects** explored new uses of steel structures, with facades either neoclassical (Adler and Sullivan in U.S.); curvilinear Art Nouveau (Gaudi's Casa Mila, 1905-10); or functionally streamlined (Wright's Robie House, 1909).

Music and dance shared the experimental spirit. Ruth St. Denis (1877-1968) and Isadora Duncan (1878-1927) pioneered modern dance, while Diaghilev in Paris revitalized classic ballet from 1909. Composers explored atonal music (Debussy, 1862-1918) and dissonance (Schoenberg, 1874-1951) or revolutionized classical forms (Stravinsky, 1882-1971), often showing jazz or folk music influences.

War and Revolution: 1910-19

War threatens. Germany under Wilhelm II sought a political and imperial role consonant with its industrial strength, challenging Britain's world supremacy and threatening France, which was still resenting the loss (1871) of Alsace-Lorraine. Austria wanted to curb an expanded Serbia (after 1912) and the threat it posed to its own Slav lands. Russia feared Austrian and German political and economic aims in the Balkans and Turkey. An accelerated arms race resulted: The German standing army rose to more than 2 million men by 1914. Russia and France had more than a million each, and Austria and the British Empire nearly a million each. Dozens of enormous battleships were built by the powers after 1906.

The **assassination of Austrian Archduke Franz Ferdinand** by a Serbian, June 28, 1914, was the pretext for war. The system of alliances made the conflict Europe-wide; Germany's invasion of Belgium to outflank France forced Britain to enter the war. Patriotic fervor was nearly unanimous among all classes in most countries.

World War I. German forces were stopped in France in one month. The rival armies dug **trench networks.** Artillery and improved machine guns prevented either side from any lasting advance despite repeated assaults (600,000 dead at **Verdun,** Feb.-July 1916). Poison gas, used by Germany in 1915, proved ineffective. More than 1 million U.S. troops tipped the balance after mid-1917, forcing Germany to sue for peace the next year. The formal armistice was signed at 5 AM, Nov. 11, 1918.

In the E, the Russian armies were thrown back (battle of **Tannenberg,** Aug. 20, 1914), and the war grew unpopular in Russia. An allied attempt to relieve Russia through Turkey failed (**Gallipoli,** 1915). The **Russian Revolution** (1917) abolished the monarchy. The new Bolshevik regime signed the capitulatory Brest-Litovsk peace in March 1918. Italy entered the war on the allied side in May 1915 but was pushed back by Oct. 1917. A renewed offensive with Allied aid in Oct.-Nov. 1918 forced Austria to surrender.

The British Navy successfully blockaded Germany, which responded with submarine U-boat attacks; **unrestricted submarine warfare** against neutrals after Jan. 1917 helped bring the U.S. into the war. Other battlefields included Palestine and Mesopotamia, both of which Britain wrested from the Turks in 1917, and the African and Pacific colonies of Germany, most of which fell to Britain, France, Australia, Japan, and South Africa.

From 1916, the civilian populations and economies of both sides were mobilized to an unprecedented degree. Hardships intensified among fighting nations in 1917 (French mutiny crushed in May). More than 10 million soldiers died in the war.

Settlement. At the **Paris Peace Conference** (Jan.-June 1919), concluded by the **Treaty of Versailles,** and in subsequent negotiations and local wars (Russian-Polish War, 1920), the map of Europe was redrawn with a nod to U.S. Pres. Wilson's principle of self-determination. Austria and Hungary were separated, and much of their land was given to Yugoslavia (formerly Serbia), Romania, Italy, and the newly independent Poland and Czechoslovakia. Germany lost territory in the W, N, and E, while Finland and the Baltic states were detached from Russia. Turkey lost nearly all its Arab lands to British-sponsored Arab states or to direct French and British rule. Belgium's sovereignty was recognized.

A huge **reparations** burden and partial demilitarization were imposed on Germany. Pres. Wilson obtained approval for a League of Nations, but the U.S. Senate refused to allow the U.S. to join.

Russian revolution. Military defeats and high casualties caused a contagious lack of confidence in Tsar Nicholas, who was forced to abdicate Mar. 1917. A liberal provisional government failed to end the war, and massive desertions, riots, and fighting between factions followed. A moderate socialist government under Aleksandr Kerensky was overthrown (Nov. 1917) in a violent coup by the **Bolsheviks** in Petrograd under **Lenin,** who later disbanded the elected Constituent Assembly.

The Bolsheviks brutally suppressed all opposition and ended the war with Germany in Mar. 1918. **Civil war** broke out in the summer between the Red Army, including the Bolsheviks and their supporters, and monarchists, anarchists, nationalities (Ukrainians, Georgians, Poles), and others. Small U.S., British, French, and Japanese units also opposed the Bolsheviks (1918-19; Japan in Vladivostok to 1922). The civil war, anarchy, and pogroms devastated the country until the 1920 Red Army victory. The wartime total monopoly of political, economic, and police power by the Communist Party leadership was retained.

Other European revolutions. An unpopular monarchy in **Portugal** was overthrown in 1910. The new republic took severe anticlerical measures in 1911.

After a century of Home Rule agitation, during which **Ireland** was devastated by famine (1 million dead, 1846-47) and emigration, republican militants staged an unsuccessful uprising in Dublin during Easter 1916. The execution of the leaders and mass arrests by the British won popular support for the rebels. The Irish Free State, comprising all but the 6 N counties, achieved dominion status in 1922.

In the aftermath of the world war, radical revolutions were attempted in Germany (**Spartacist** uprising, Jan. 1919), **Hungary** (Kun regime, 1919), and elsewhere. All were suppressed or failed for lack of support.

Chinese revolution. The Manchu Dynasty was overthrown and a republic proclaimed in Oct. 1911. First Pres. Sun Yat-sen resigned in favor of strongman Yuan Shih-k'ai. Sun organized the parliamentarian **Kuomintang** party.

Students launched protests on May 4, 1919, against League of Nations concessions in China to Japan. Nationalist, liberal, and socialist ideas and political groups spread. The **Communist Party** was founded in 1921. A Communist regime took power in Mongolia with Soviet support in 1921.

India restive. Indian objections to British rule erupted in nationalist riots as well as in the nonviolent tactics of Gandhi (1869-1948). Nearly 400 unarmed demonstrators were shot at **Amritsar** in Apr. 1919. Britain approved limited self-rule that year.

Mexican revolution. Under the long Diaz dictatorship (1877-1911) the economy advanced, but Indian and mestizo lands were confiscated, and concessions to foreigners (mostly U.S.) damaged the middle class. A **revolution in 1910** led to civil wars and U.S. intervention (1914, 1916-17). Land reform and a more democratic constitution (1917) were achieved.

Timeline (1916–1928):

- Dada movement
- Bolshevik coup
- World War I
- China May 4 protest
- Russian Civil War
- Amritsar riots
- U.S. prohibition
- Iraq, Transjordan
- Russia's NEP
- Rathenau killed
- U.S. women's vote
- Reza Khan in Persia
- 1922
- Ulysses
- Irish Free State
- Fasc. March on Rome
- Lenin d.
- Kafka's Trial
- Eng. Labour govt.
- Portugal coup
- Kellogg-Briand Pact
- Threepenny Opera

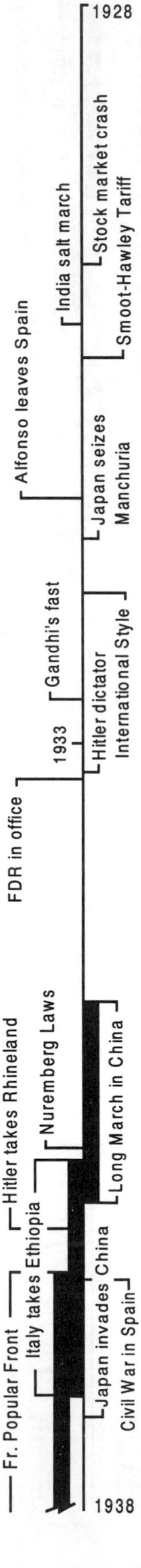
1928
India salt march
Stock market crash
Smoot-Hawley Tariff
Alfonso leaves Spain
Japan seizes Manchuria
Gandhi's fast
Hitler dictator
International Style
1933
FDR in office
Hitler takes Rhineland
Nuremberg Laws
Long March in China
Italy takes Ethiopia
Japan invades China
Civil War in Spain
Fr. Popular Front
1938

The Aftermath of War: 1920-29

U.S. Easy credit, technological ingenuity, and war-related industrial decline in Europe caused a long economic boom, in which ownership of the new products—**autos, phones, radios**—became democratized. Prosperity, an increase in women workers, woman suffrage (1920), and drastic change in fashion (flappers, mannish bob for women, clean-shaven men) created a wide perception of social change, despite prohibition of alcoholic beverages (1919-33). Union membership and strikes increased. Fear of radicals led to Palmer raids (1919-20) and the Sacco/Vanzetti case (1921-27).

Europe sorts itself out. Germany's liberal **Weimar constitution** (1919) could not guarantee a stable government in the face of rightist violence (Rathenau assassinated, 1922) and Communist refusal to cooperate with Socialists. Reparations and Allied occupation of the Rhineland caused staggering inflation that destroyed middle-class savings, but economic expansion resumed after mid-decade, aided by U.S. loans. A sophisticated, **innovative culture** developed in architecture and design (Bauhaus, 1919-28), film (Lang, *M*, 1931), painting (Grosz), music (Weill, *Threepenny Opera*, 1928), theater (Brecht, *A Man's a Man*, 1926), criticism (Benjamin), philosophy (Jung), and fashion. This culture was considered decadent and socially disruptive by rightists.

England elected its first Labour governments (Jan. 1924, June 1929). A 10-day general strike in support of coal miners failed in May 1926. In **Italy**, strikes, political chaos, and violence by small Fascist bands culminated in the Oct. 1922 Fascist March on Rome, which established Mussolini's dictatorship. Strikes were outlawed (1926), and Italian influence was pressed in the Balkans (Albania a protectorate, 1926). A conservative dictatorship was also established in **Portugal** in a 1926 military coup.

Czechoslovakia, the only stable democracy to emerge from the war in Central or East Europe, faced opposition from Germans (in the Sudetenland), Ruthenians, and some Slovaks. As the industrial heartland of the old Hapsburg empire, it remained fairly prosperous. With French backing, it formed the Little Entente with Yugoslavia (1920) and **Romania** (1921) to block Austrian or Hungarian irredentism. Hungary remained dominated by the landholding classes and expansionist feeling. Croats and Slovenes in **Yugoslavia** demanded a federal state until King Alexander I proclaimed (1929) a royal dictatorship. Poland faced nationality problems as well (Germans, Ukrainians, Jews); Pilsudski ruled as dictator from 1926. The Baltic states were threatened by traditionally dominant ethnic Germans and by Soviet-supported Communists.

An economic collapse and famine in **Russia** (1921-22) claimed 5 million lives. The New Economic Policy (1921) allowed landownership by peasants and some private commerce and industry. Stalin was absolute ruler within 4 years of Lenin's death (1924). He inaugurated a brutal collectivization program (1929-32) and used foreign Communist parties for Soviet state advantage.

Internationalism. Revulsion against World War I led to pacifist agitation, to the Kellogg-Briand Pact renouncing aggressive war (1928), and to **naval disarmament** pacts (Washington, 1922; London, 1930). But the League of Nations was able to arbitrate only minor disputes (Greece-Bulgaria, 1925).

Middle East. Mustafa Kemal (Ataturk) led **Turkish** nationalists in resisting Italian, French, and Greek military advances (1919-23). The sultanate was abolished (1922), and elaborate reforms were passed, including secularization of law and adoption of the Latin alphabet. Ethnic conflict led to persecution of **Armenians** (more than 1 million dead in 1915, 1 million expelled), Greeks (forced Greek-Turk population exchange, 1923), and Kurds (1925 uprising).

With evacuation of the Turks from **Arab** lands, the puritanical Wahabi dynasty of E Arabia conquered (1919-25) what is now Saudi Arabia. British, French, and Arab dynastic and nationalist maneuvering resulted in the creation of 2 more Arab monarchies in 1921—Iraq and Transjordan (both under British control)—and 2 French mandates—Syria and Lebanon. Jewish immigration into British-mandated **Palestine**, inspired by the Zionist movement, was resisted by Arabs, at times violently (1921, 1929 massacres).

Reza Khan ruled **Persia** after his 1921 coup (shah from 1925), centralized control, and created the trappings of a modern state.

China. The Kuomintang under **Chiang Kai-shek** (1887-1975) subdued the warlords by 1928. The Communists were brutally suppressed after their alliance with the Kuomintang was broken in 1927. Relative peace thereafter allowed for industrial and financial improvements, with some Russian, British, and U.S. cooperation.

Arts. Nearly all bounds of subject matter, style, and attitude were broken in the arts of the period. **Abstract** art first took inspiration from natural forms or narrative themes (Kandinsky from 1911) and then worked free of any representational aims (Malevich's suprematism, 1915-19; Mondrian's geometric style from 1917). The **Dada** movement (from 1916) mocked artistic pretension with absurd collages and constructions (Arp, Tzara, from 1916). Paradox, illusion, and psychological taboos were exploited by **surrealists** by the latter 1920s (Dali, Magritte). Architectural schools celebrated industrial values, whether vigorous abstract constructivism (Tatlin, *Monument to 3rd International*, 1919) or the machined, streamlined **Bauhaus** style, which was extended to many design fields (Helvetica typeface).

Prose writers explored revolutionary narrative modes related to dreams (Kafka's *Trial*, 1925), internal monologue (Joyce's **Ulysses**, 1922), and word play (Stein's *Making of Americans*, 1925). Poets and novelists wrote of modern alienation (Eliot's ***Waste Land***, 1922) and aimlessness (Lost Generation).

Sciences. Scientific specialization prevailed by the 20th cent. Advances in knowledge and technological aptitude increased with the geometric rise in the number of practitioners. Physicists challenged common-sense views of causality, observation, and a mechanistic universe, putting science further beyond popular grasp (**Einstein's** general theory of relativity, 1915; Bohr's quantum mechanics, 1913; Heisenberg's uncertainty principle, 1927).

Rise of Totalitarians: 1930-39

Depression. A worldwide financial panic and economic depression began with the Oct. 1929 U.S. stock market crash and the May 1931 failure of the Austrian Credit-Anstalt. A credit crunch caused international bankruptcies and **unemployment**: 12 million jobless by 1932 in the U.S., 5.6 million in Germany, 2.7 million in England. Governments responded with **tariff restrictions** (Smoot-Hawley Act,

1930; Ottawa Imperial Conference, 1932), which dried up world trade. Government public works programs were vitiated by deflationary budget balancing.

Germany. Years of agitation by violent extremists were brought to a head by the Depression. Nazi leader **Hitler** was named chancellor by Pres. Hindenburg in Jan. 1933 and given dictatorial power by the Reichstag in March. Opposition parties were disbanded, strikes banned, and all aspects of economic, cultural, and religious life were brought under central government and Nazi party control and manipulated by sophisticated propaganda. Severe persecution of Jews began (**Nuremberg Laws,** Sept. 1935). Many Jews, political opponents, and others were sent to concentration camps (Dachau, 1933), where thousands died or were killed. Public works, renewed conscription (1935), arms production, and a 4-year plan (1936) all but ended unemployment.

Hitler's expansionism started with reincorporation of the Saar (1935), occupation of the **Rhineland** (Mar. 1936), and annexation of Austria (Mar. 1938). At **Munich** (Sept. 1938) an indecisive Britain and France sanctioned German dismemberment of Czechoslovakia.

Russia. Urbanization and education advanced. Rapid industrialization was achieved through successive **5-year-plans** starting in 1928, using severe labor discipline and mass forced labor. Industry was financed by a decline in living standards and exploitation of agriculture, which was almost totally collectivized by the early 1930s (*kolkhoz*, collective farm; *sovkhoz*, state farm, often in newly worked lands). Successive **purges** increased the role of professionals and management at the expense of workers. Millions perished in a series of manufactured disasters: extermination (1929-34) of kulaks (peasant landowners), severe famine (1932-33), party purges and show trials (Great Purge, 1936-38), suppression of nationalities, and poor conditions in labor camps.

Spain. An industrial revolution during World War I created an urban proletariat, which was attracted to socialism and anarchism; Catalan nationalists challenged central authority. The 5 years after King Alfonso left Spain in Apr. 1931 were dominated by tension between intermittent leftist and anticlerical governments and clericals, monarchists, and other rightists. Anarchist and Communist rebellions were crushed, but a July 1936 extreme right rebellion led by Gen. Francisco Franco and aided by Nazi Germany and Fascist Italy succeeded, after a 3-year **civil war** (more than 1 million dead in battles and atrocities). The war polarized international public opinion.

Italy. Despite propaganda for the ideal of the Corporate State, few domestic reforms were attempted. An entente with Hungary and Austria (Mar. 1934), a pact with Germany and Japan (Nov. 1937), and intervention by 50,000-75,000 troops in Spain (1936-39) sealed Italy's identification with the fascist bloc (anti-Semitic laws after Mar. 1938). Ethiopia was conquered (1935-36), and **Albania** annexed (Jan. 1939) in conscious imitation of ancient Rome.

East Europe. Repressive regimes fought for power against an active opposition (liberals, socialists, Communists, peasants, Nazis). Minority groups and Jews were restricted within national boundaries that did not coincide with ethnic population patterns. In the destruction of **Czechoslovakia, Hungary** occupied S Slovakia (Nov. 1938) and Ruthenia (Mar. 1939), and a pro-Nazi regime took power in the rest of Slovakia. Other boundary disputes (e.g., Poland-Lithuania, Yugoslavia-Bulgaria, Romania-Hungary) doomed attempts to build joint fronts against Germany or Russia. Economic depression was severe.

East Asia. After a period of liberalism in **Japan,** nativist militarists dominated the government with peasant support. Manchuria was seized (Sept. 1931-Feb. 1932), and a puppet state was set up (Manchukuo). Adjacent Jehol (Inner Mongolia) was occupied in 1933. China proper was invaded in July 1937; large areas were conquered by Oct. 1938.

In **China** Communist forces left Kuomintang-besieged strongholds in the S in a Long March (1934-35) to the N. The Kuomintang-Communist civil war was suspended in Jan. 1937 in the face of threatening Japan.

The democracies. The Roosevelt Administration, in office Mar. 1933, embarked on an extensive program of **New Deal** social reform and economic stimulation, including protection for labor unions (heavy industries organized), Social Security, public works, wage-and-hour laws, and assistance to farmers. Isolationist sentiment (1937 Neutrality Act) prevented U.S. intervention in Europe, but military expenditures were increased in 1939.

French political instability and polarization prevented resolution of economic and international security questions. The **Popular Front** government under Blum (June 1936-Apr. 1938) passed social reforms (40-hour week) and raised arms spending. National coalition governments, which ruled Britain from Aug. 1931, brought some economic recovery but failed to define a consistent international policy until Chamberlain's government (from May 1937), which practiced deliberate **appeasement** of Germany and Italy.

India. Twenty years of agitation for autonomy and then for independence (Gandhi's **salt march,** 1930) achieved some constitutional reform (extended provincial powers, 1935) despite Muslim-Hindu strife. Social issues assumed prominence with peasant uprisings (1921), strikes (1928), Gandhi's efforts for untouchables (1932 "fast unto death"), and social and agrarian reform by the provinces after 1937.

Arts. The streamlined, geometric design motifs of Art Deco (from 1925) prevailed through the 1930s. **Abstract art** flourished (Moore sculptures from 1931) alongside a new **realism** related to social and political concerns (Socialist Realism, the official Soviet style from 1934; Mexican muralist Rivera, 1886-1957; and Orozco, 1883-1949), which were also expressed in fiction and poetry (Steinbeck's *Grapes of Wrath*, 1939; Sandburg's *The People, Yes*, 1936). Modern architecture (International Style, 1932) was unchallenged in its use of artificial materials (concrete, glass), lack of decoration, and monumentality (Rockefeller Center, 1929-40). U.S.-made films captured a worldwide audience with their larger-than-life fantasies *(Gone With the Wind,* 1939).

War, Hot and Cold; 1940-49

War in Europe. The Nazi-Soviet nonaggression pact (Aug. 1939) freed Germany to attack Poland (Sept.). Britain and France, who had guaranteed Polish independence, declared war on Germany. Russia seized E Poland (Sept.), attacked Finland (Nov.), and took the Baltic states (July 1940). Mobile German forces staged *blitzkrieg* attacks during Apr.-June 1940, conquering neutral Denmark, Norway, and the Low Countries and defeating France; 350,000 British and French troops were evacuated at **Dunkirk**

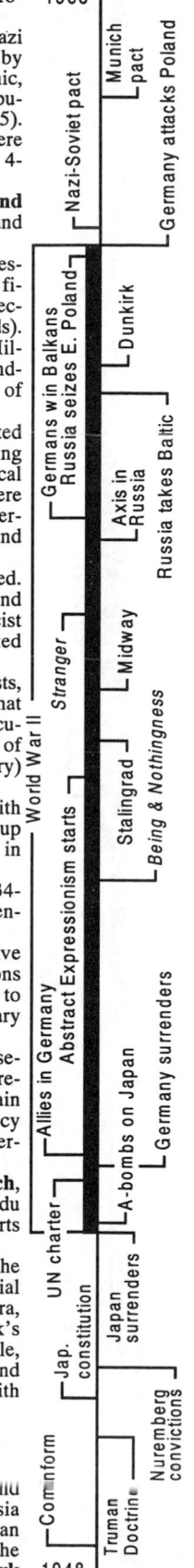

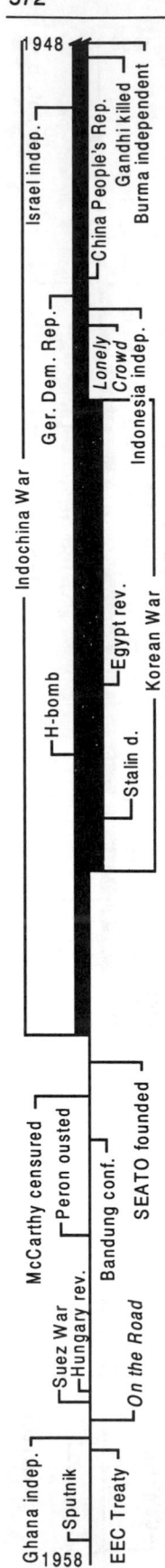

(May). The **Battle of Britain** (June-Dec. 1940) denied Germany air superiority. German-Italian campaigns won the Balkans by Apr. 1941. Three million Axis troops **invaded Russia** in June 1941, marching through Ukraine to the Caucasus, and through White Russia and the Baltic republics to Moscow and Leningrad.

Russian winter counterthrusts (1941-42 and 1942-43) stopped the German advance (**Stalingrad,** Sept. 1942-Feb. 1943). With British and U.S. Lend-Lease aid and sustaining great casualties, the Russians drove the Axis from all E Europe and the Balkans in the next 2 years. Invasions of N Africa (Nov. 1942), Italy (Sept. 1943), and **Normandy** (launched on D-Day, June 6, 1944) brought U.S., British, Free French, and allied troops to Germany by spring 1945. Germany surrendered May 7, 1945.

War in Asia-Pacific. Japan occupied Indochina in Sept. 1940, dominated Thailand in Dec. 1941, and attacked Hawaii, the Philippines, Hong Kong, Malaya on Dec. 7, 1941. Indonesia was attacked in Jan. 1942, and Burma was conquered in Mar. 1942. The Battle of **Midway** (June 1942) turned back the Japanese advance. "Island-hopping" battles (**Guadalcanal,** Aug. 1942-Jan. 1943; **Leyte Gulf,** Oct. 1944; **Iwo Jima,** Feb.-Mar. 1945; **Okinawa,** Apr. 1945) and massive bombing raids on Japan from June 1944 wore out Japanese defenses. U.S. atom bombs, dropped Aug. 6 and 9 on **Hiroshima** and Nagasaki, forced Japan to agree, on Aug. 14, to surrender; formal surrender was on Sept. 2, 1945.

Atrocities. The war brought 20th-cent. cruelty to its peak. The Nazi regime systematically killed an estimated 5-6 million Jews, including some 3 million who died in death camps (e.g., **Auschwitz**). Gypsies, political opponents, sick and retarded people, and others deemed undesirable were also murdered by the Nazis, as were vast numbers of Slavs, especially peasants.

Civilian deaths. German bombs killed 70,000 British civilians. Some 100,000 Chinese civilians were killed by Japanese forces in the capture of Nanking. Severe retaliation by the Soviet army, E European partisans, Free French, and others took a heavy toll. U.S. and British bombing of Germany killed hundreds of thousands, as did U.S. bombing of Japan (80,000-200,000 at Hiroshima alone). Some 45 million people lost their lives in the war.

Settlement. The **United Nations** charter was signed in San Francisco on June 26, 1945, by 50 nations. The International Tribunal at **Nuremberg** convicted 22 German leaders for war crimes in Sept. 1946; 23 Japanese leaders were convicted in Nov. 1948. Postwar border changes included large gains in territory for the USSR, losses for Germany, a shift to the W in Polish borders, and minor losses for Italy. Communist regimes, supported by Soviet troops, took power in most of E Europe, including Soviet-occupied Germany (GDR proclaimed Oct. 1949). Japan lost all overseas lands.

Recovery. Basic political and social changes were imposed on Japan and W Germany by the western allies (Japan constitution adopted, Nov. 1946; W German basic law, May 1949). U.S. **Marshall Plan** aid ($12 billion, 1947-51) spurred W European economic recovery after a period of severe inflation and strikes in Europe and the U.S. The British Labour Party introduced a national health service and nationalized basic industries in 1946.

Cold War. Western fears of further Soviet advances (Cominform formed in Oct. 1947; Czechoslovakia coup, Feb. 1948; Berlin blockade, Apr. 1948-Sept. 1949) led to the formation of **NATO.** Civil War in Greece and Soviet pressure on Turkey led to U.S. aid under the **Truman Doctrine** (Mar. 1947). Other anti-Communist security pacts were the Organization of American States (Apr. 1948) and the SE Asia Treaty Organization (Sept. 1954). A new wave of **Soviet purges** and repression intensified in the last years of Stalin's rule, extending to E Europe (Slansky trial in Czechoslovakia, 1951). Only Yugoslavia resisted Soviet control (expelled by Cominform, June 1948; U.S. aid, June 1949).

China, Korea. Communist forces emerged from World War II strengthened by the Soviet takeover of industrial Manchuria. In 4 years of fighting, the Kuomintang was driven from the mainland; the People's Republic was proclaimed Oct. 1, 1949. Korea was divided by USSR and U.S. occupation forces. Separate republics were proclaimed in the 2 zones in Aug.-Sept. 1948.

India. India and Pakistan became independent dominions on Aug. 15, 1947. Millions of Hindu and Muslim refugees were created by the partition; riots (1946-47) took hundreds of thousands of lives; **Gandhi** was assassinated in Jan. 1948. Burma became completely independent in Jan. 1948; Ceylon took dominion status in Feb.

Middle East. The UN approved partition of Palestine into Jewish and Arab states. **Israel** was proclaimed a state, May 14, 1948. Arabs rejected partition, but failed to defeat Israel in war (May 1948-July 1949). Immigration from Europe and the Middle East swelled Israel's Jewish population. British and French forces left Lebanon and Syria in 1946. Transjordan occupied most of Arab Palestine.

Southeast Asia. Communists and others fought against restoration of French rule in Indochina from 1946; a non-Communist government was recognized by France in Mar. 1949, but fighting continued. Both Indonesia and the Philippines became independent; the former in 1949 after 4 years of war with Netherlands, the latter in 1946. Philippine economic and military ties with the U.S. remained strong; a Communist-led peasant rising was checked in 1948.

Arts. New York became the center of the world art market; **abstract expressionism** was the chief mode (Pollock from 1943, de Kooning from 1947). Literature and philosophy explored **existentialism** (Camus's *Stranger*, 1942; Sartre's *Being and Nothingness*, 1943). Non-Western attempts to revive or create regional styles (Senghor's Négritude, Mishima's novels) only confirmed the emergence of a universal culture. Radio and phonograph records spread American popular music (swing, bebop) around the world.

The American Decade: 1950-59

Polite decolonization. The peaceful decline of European political and military power in Asia and Africa accelerated in the 1950s. Nearly all of N Africa was freed by 1956, but France fought a bitter war to retain Algeria, with its large European minority, until 1962. **Ghana,** independent in 1957, led a parade of new black African nations (more than 2 dozen by 1962), which altered the political character of the UN. Ethnic disputes often exploded in the new nations after decolonization (UN troops in Cyprus, 1964; **Nigeria** civil war, 1967-70). Leaders of the new states, mostly sharing socialist ideologies, tried to create an Afro-Asian bloc (Bandung Conference, 1955), but Western economic influence and U.S. political ties remained strong (Baghdad Pact, 1955).

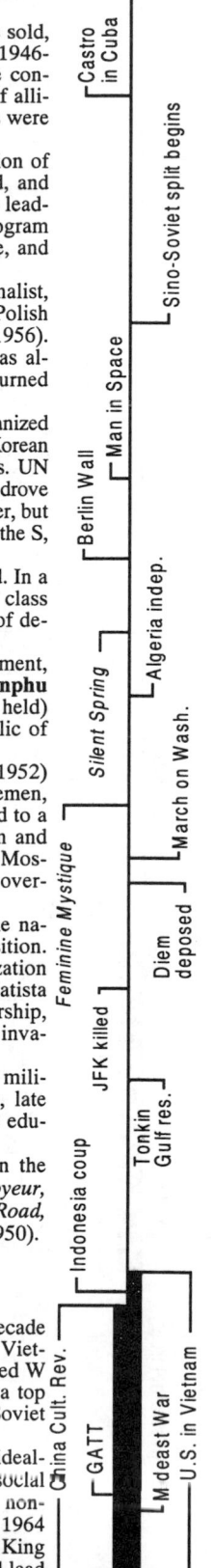

Trade. World trade volume soared, in an atmosphere of monetary stability assured by international accords (**Bretton Woods,** 1944). In Europe, economic integration advanced (**European Economic Community,** 1957; European Free Trade Association, 1960). Comecon (1949) coordinated the economies of Soviet-bloc countries.

U.S. Economic growth produced an abundance of consumer goods (9.3 million motor vehicles sold, 1955). Suburban housing tracts changed life patterns for middle and working classes (Levittown, 1946-51). **Eisenhower's** landslide election victories (1952, 1956) reflected consensus politics. Senate condemnation of **McCarthy** (Dec. 1954) curbed the political abuse of anti-Communism. A system of alliances and military bases bolstered U.S. influence on all continents. Trade and payments surpluses were balanced by overseas investments and foreign aid ($50 billion, 1950-59).

USSR. In the "thaw" after Stalin's death in 1953, relations with the West improved (evacuation of Vienna, Geneva summit conference, both 1955). Repression of scientific and cultural life eased, and many prisoners were freed or rehabilitated culminating in **de-Stalinization** (1956). **Khrushchev's** leadership aimed at consumer sector growth, but farm production lagged, despite the virgin lands program (from 1954). Soviet crushing of the 1956 Hungarian revolution, the 1960 U-2 spy plane episode, and other incidents renewed East-West tension and domestic curbs.

East Europe. Resentment of Russian domination and Stalinist repression combined with nationalist, economic, and religious factors to produce periodic violence. E Berlin workers rioted (1953), Polish workers rioted in Poznan (June 1956), and a broad-based revolution broke out in Hungary (Oct. 1956). All were suppressed by Soviet force or threats (at least 7,000 dead in Hungary). But Poland was allowed to restore private ownership of farms, and a degree of personal and economic freedom returned to Hungary. Yugoslavia experimented with worker self-management and a market economy.

Korea. The 1945 division of Korea along the 38th parallel left industry in the N, which was organized into a militant regime and armed by the USSR. The S was politically disunited. More than 60,000 N Korean troops invaded the S on June 25, 1950. The U.S., backed by the UN Security Council, sent troops. UN troops reached the Chinese border in Nov. Some 200,000 Chinese troops crossed the Yalu R. and drove back UN forces. By spring 1951 battle lines had become stabilized near the original 38th parallel border, but heavy fighting continued. Finally, an armistice was signed on July 27, 1953. U.S. troops remained in the S, and U.S. economic and military aid continued. The war stimulated rapid economic recovery in Japan.

China. Starting in 1952, industry, agriculture, and social institutions were forcibly collectivized. In a massive purge, as many as several million people were executed as Kuomintang supporters or as class and political enemies. The Great Leap Forward (1958-60) unsuccessfully tried to force the pace of development by substituting labor for investment.

Indochina. Ho Chi Minh's forces, aided by the USSR and the new Chinese Communist government, fought French and pro-French Vietnamese forces to a standstill and captured the strategic **Dienbienphu** camp in May 1954. The Geneva Agreements divided Vietnam in half pending elections (never held) and recognized Laos and Cambodia as independent. The U.S. aided the anti-Communist Republic of Vietnam in the S.

Middle East. Arab revolutions placed leftist, militantly nationalist regimes in power in Egypt (1952) and Iraq (1958). But Arab unity attempts failed (United Arab Republic joined Egypt, Syria, Yemen, 1958-61). Arab refusal to recognize Israel (Arab League economic blockade began Sept. 1951) led to a permanent state of war, with repeated incidents (Gaza, 1955). Israel occupied Sinai, and Britain and France took (Oct. 1956) the Suez Canal, but were replaced by the UN Emergency Force. The Mossadegh government in Iran nationalized (May 1951) the British-owned oil industry May, but was overthrown (Aug. 1953) in a U.S.-aided coup.

Latin America. Argentinian Dictator Juan **Perón,** in office 1946, enforced land reform, some nationalization, welfare state measures, and curbs on the Roman Catholic Church, and crushed opposition. A Sept. 1955 coup deposed Perón. The 1952 revolution in Bolivia brought land reform, nationalization of tin mines, and improvement in the status of Indians, who nevertheless remained poor. The Batista regime in Cuba was overthrown (Jan. 1959) by Fidel **Castro,** who imposed a Communist dictatorship, aligned Cuba with the USSR, but improved education and health care. A U.S.-backed anti-Castro invasion (Bay of Pigs, Apr. 1961) was crushed. Self-government advanced in the British Caribbean.

Technology. Large outlays on research and development in the U.S. and the USSR focused on military applications (H-bomb in U.S., 1952; USSR, 1953; Britain, 1957; intercontinental missiles, late 1950s). Soviet launching of the **Sputnik** satellite (Oct. 4, 1957) spurred increases in U.S. science education funds (National Defense Education Act).

Literature and film. Alienation from social and literary conventions reached an extreme in the theater of the absurd (Beckett's *Waiting for Godot,* 1952), the "new novel" (Robbe-Grillet's *Voyeur,* 1955), and avant-garde film (Antonioni's *L'Avventura,* 1960). U.S. beatniks (Kerouac's *On the Road,* 1957) and others rejected the supposed conformism of Americans (Riesman's *The Lonely Crowd,* 1950).

Rising Expectations: 1960-69

Economic boom. The longest sustained economic boom on record spanned almost the entire decade in the capitalist world; the closely watched GNP figure doubled (1960-70) in the U.S., fueled by Vietnam War–related budget deficits. The **General Agreement on Tariffs and Trade** (1967) stimulated W European prosperity, which spread to peripheral areas (Spain, Italy, E Germany). Japan became a top economic power. Foreign investment aided the industrialization of Brazil. There were limited Soviet economic reform attempts

Reform and radicalization. Pres. John F. Kennedy, inaugurated 1961, emphasized youthful idealism and vigor; his assassination Nov. 22, 1963, was a national trauma. A series of political and social reform movements took root in the U.S., later spreading to other countries. Blacks demonstrated nonviolently and with partial success against segregation and poverty (1963 March on Washington; 1964 **Civil Rights Act**), but some urban ghettos erupted in extensive riots (Watts, 1965; Detroit, 1967; King assassination, Apr. 4, 1968). New concern for the poor (Harrington's *Other America,* 1963) helped lead to Pres. Johnson's **"Great Society"** programs (Medicare, Water Quality Act, Higher Education Act, all

Timeline (left margin):

1968

- Sino-Soviet fighting
- Pentagon Papers published
- First Earth Day
- Woodstock festival
- Men on moon
- Roe v. Wade abortion ruling
- U.S. SST barred
- Bangladesh indep.
- Nixon in Peking
- Arab-Israel Yom Kippur War
- Worldwide recession
- Nixon resigns
- Indochina War ends
- Mao d.
- 1 mln. die in Cambodia
- Franco d.
- U.S. hostages taken in Iran
- Khomeini gvt. in Iran
- Egypt-Israel treaty
- 3 Mile Island
- USSR invades Afghanistan
- 18% inflation rate in U.S.

1980

1965). Concern with the **environment** surged (Carson's *Silent Spring*, 1962). **Feminism** revived as a cultural and political movement (Friedan's *Feminine Mystique*, 1963; National Organization for Women founded 1966), and a movement for homosexual rights emerged (Stonewall riot in NYC, 1969). Pope John XXIII called the Second Vatican Council (1962-65), which liberalized Roman Catholic liturgy and some other aspects of Catholicism.

Opposition to U.S. involvement in Vietnam, especially among university students (**Moratorium** protest, Nov. 1969), turned violent (Weatherman Chicago riots, Oct. 1969). **New Left** and Marxist theories became popular, and membership in radical groups (Students for a Democratic Society, Black Panthers) increased. Maoist groups, especially in Europe, called for total transformation of society. In France, students sparked a nationwide strike affecting 10 million workers in May-June 1968, but an electoral reaction barred revolutionary change.

Arts and styles. The boundary between fine and popular arts was blurred to some extent by Pop Art (Warhol) and rock musicals (*Hair*, 1968). Informality and exaggeration prevailed in fashion (beards, miniskirts). A nonpolitical "counterculture" developed, rejecting traditional bourgeois life goals and personal habits, and use of marijuana and hallucinogens spread (**Woodstock** festival, Aug. 1969). Indian influence was felt in religion (Ram Dass) and fashion, and The **Beatles,** who brought unprecedented sophistication to rock music, became for many a symbol of the decade.

Science. Achievements in space (**humans on the moon,** July 1969) and electronics (lasers, integrated circuits) encouraged a faith in scientific solutions to problems in agriculture ("green revolution"), medicine (heart transplants, 1967), and other areas. Harmful technology, it was believed, could be controlled (1963 nuclear weapon test ban treaty, 1968 nonproliferation treaty).

China. Mao's revolutionary militancy caused disputes with the USSR under "revisionist" Khrushchev, starting in 1960. The 2 powers exchanged fire in 1969 border disputes. China used force to capture (1962) areas disputed with India. The **"Great Proletarian Cultural Revolution"** tried to impose a utopian egalitarian program in China and spread revolution abroad; political struggle, often violent, convulsed China in 1965-68.

Indochina. Communist-led guerrillas aided by N Vietnam fought from 1960 against the S Vietnam government of Ngo Dinh Diem (killed 1963). The U.S. military role increased after the 1964 **Tonkin Gulf** incident. U.S. forces peaked at 543,400 in Apr. 1969. Massive numbers of N Vietnamese troops also fought. Laotian and Cambodian neutrality were threatened by Communist insurgencies, with N Vietnamese aid, and U.S. intrigues.

Third World. A bloc of authoritarian leftist regimes among the newly independent nations emerged in political opposition to the U.S.-led Western alliance and came to dominate the conference of nonaligned nations (Belgrade, 1961; Cairo, 1964; Lusaka, 1970). Soviet political ties and military bases were established in Cuba, Egypt, Algeria, Guinea, and other countries whose leaders were regarded as revolutionary heroes by opposition groups in pro-Western or colonial countries. Some leaders were ousted in coups by pro-Western groups—Zaire's Lumumba (killed 1961), Ghana's Nkrumah (exiled 1966), and Indonesia's Sukarno (effectively ousted in 1965 after a Communist coup failed).

Middle East. Arab-Israeli tension erupted into a brief war June 1967. Israel emerged as a major regional power. Military shipments before and after the war brought much of the Arab world into the Soviet political sphere. Most Arab states broke U.S. diplomatic ties, while Communist countries cut their ties to Israel. Intra-Arab disputes continued: Egypt and Saudi Arabia supported rival factions in a bloody Yemen civil war 1962-70; Lebanese troops fought Palestinian commandos 1969.

East Europe. To stop the large-scale exodus of citizens, E German authorities built (Aug. 1961) a **fortified wall across Berlin.** Soviet sway in the Balkans was weakened by Albania's support of China (USSR broke ties in Dec. 1961) and Romania's assertion (1964) of industrial and foreign policy autonomy. Liberalization (spring 1968) in Czechoslovakia was crushed with massive force by troops of 5 Warsaw Pact countries. W German treaties (1970) with the USSR and Poland facilitated the transfer of German technology and confirmed postwar boundaries.

Disillusionment: 1970-79

U.S.: Caution and neoconservatism. A relatively sluggish economy, energy and resource shortages (natural gas crunch, 1975; gasoline shortage, 1979), and environmental problems contributed to a **"limits of growth"** philosophy. Suspicion of science and technology killed or delayed major projects (supersonic transport dropped, 1971; Seabrook nuclear power plant protests, 1977-78) and was fed by the Three Mile Island nuclear reactor accident (Mar. 1979).

There were signs of growing mistrust of big government and weakened support for government reform plans. School busing and racial quotas were opposed (Bakke decision, June 1978); the Equal Rights Amendment for women languished; civil rights for homosexuals were opposed (Dade County referendum, June 1977).

Completion of Communist forces' takeover of **S Vietnam** (evacuation of U.S. civilians, Apr. 1975), revelations of Central Intelligence Agency misdeeds (Rockefeller Commission report, June 1975), and **Watergate** scandals (Nixon resigned in Aug. 1974) reduced faith in U.S. moral and material capacity to influence world affairs. Revelations of Soviet crimes (Solzhenitsyn's *Gulag Archipelago,* 1974) and Russian intervention in Africa aided a revival of anti-Communist sentiment.

Economy sluggish. The 1960s boom faltered in the 1970s; a severe recession in the U.S. and Europe (1974-75) followed a huge oil price hike (Dec. 1973). Monetary instability (U.S. cut ties to gold in Aug. 1971), the decline of the dollar, and **protectionist** moves by industrial countries (1977-78) threatened trade. Business investment and spending for research declined. Severe inflation plagued many countries (25% in Britain, 1975; 18% in U.S., 1979).

China picks up pieces. After the 1976 deaths of Mao and Zhou, a power struggle for the leadership succession was won by pragmatists. A nationwide purge of orthodox Maoists was carried out, and the **Gang of Four,** led by Mao's widow, Chiang Ching, were arrested.

The new leaders freed more than 100,000 political prisoners and reduced public adulation of Mao. Political and trade ties were expanded with Japan, Europe, and the U.S. in the late 1970s, as relations worsened with the USSR, Cuba, and Vietnam (4-week invasion by China, 1979). Ideological guidelines in industry, science, education, and the armed forces, which the ruling faction said had caused chaos and decline, were reversed (bonuses to workers, Dec. 1977; exams for college entrance, Oct. 1977). Severe restrictions on cultural expression were eased (Beethoven ban lifted, Mar. 1977).

Europe. European unity moves (EEC-EFTA trade accord, 1972) faltered as economic problems appeared (Britain floated pound, 1972; France floated franc, 1974). Germany and Switzerland curbed guest workers from S Europe. Greece and Turkey quarreled over Cyprus and Aegean oil rights.

All non-Communist Europe was under democratic rule after free elections were held (June 1976) in **Spain** 7 months after the death of Franco. The conservative, colonialist regime in **Portugal** was overthrown in Apr. 1974. In **Greece** the 7-year-old military dictatorship yielded power in 1974. N Europe, though ruled mostly by Socialists (**Swedish** Socialists unseated in 1976 after 44 years in power), turned more conservative. The **British** Labour government imposed (1975) wage curbs and suspended nationalization schemes. Terrorism in **Germany** (1972 Munich Olympics killings) led to laws curbing some civil liberties. **French** "new philosophers" rejected leftist ideologies, and the shaky Socialist-Communist coalition lost a 1978 election bid.

Religion back in politics. The improvement in **Muslim** countries' political fortunes by the 1950s (with the exception of Central Asia under Soviet and Chinese rule) and the growth of Arab oil wealth were followed by a resurgence of traditional piety. Libyan dictator Qaddafi mixed Islamic laws with socialism and called for Muslim return to Spain and Sicily. The illegal Muslim Brotherhood in **Egypt** was accused of violence, while extreme groups bombed (1977) theaters to protest secular values.

In **Turkey**, the National Salvation Party was the first Islamic group to share (1974) power since secularization in the 1920s. Religious authorities, such as Ayatollah Ruhollah Khomeini, led the **Iranian** revolution, and religiously motivated Muslims took part in the insurrection in Saudi Arabia that briefly seized (1979) the Grand Mosque in Mecca. Muslim puritan opposition to **Pakistan** Pres. Bhutto helped lead to his overthrow in July 1977. Muslim solidarity, however, could not prevent Pakistan's E province (**Bangladesh**) from declaring (Dec. 1971) independence after a bloody civil war.

Muslim and Hindu resentment of coerced sterilization in **India** helped defeat the Gandhi government, which was replaced (Mar. 1977) by a coalition including religious Hindu parties and led by devout Hindu Desai. Muslims in the S **Philippines**, aided by Libya, rebelled against central rule from 1973.

Evangelical Protestant groups grew in numbers and prosperity in the U.S. A revival of interest in Orthodox Christianity occurred among **Russian** intellectuals (Solzhenitsyn). The secularist **Israeli** Labor party, after decades of rule, was ousted in 1977 by conservatives led by Begin, an observant Jew; religious militants founded settlements on the disputed West Bank, part of biblically promised Israel. U.S. Reform Judaism revived many previously discarded traditional practices.

The Buddhist Soka Gakkai movement launched (1964) the Komeito party in Japan, which became a major opposition party in 1972 and 1976 elections.

Old-fashioned religious wars raged intermittently in **N Ireland** (Catholic vs. Protestant, 1969-) and **Lebanon** (Christian vs. Muslim, 1975-), while religious militancy complicated the Israel-Arab dispute (1973 Israel-Arab war). Despite a **1979 peace treaty between Egypt and Israel,** increased religious militancy on the West Bank prevented a quick resolution.

Latin America. Repressive conservative regimes strengthened their hold on most of the continent, with the violent coup against the elected (Sept. 1973) Allende government in **Chile,** the 1976 military coup in **Argentina,** and coups against reformist regimes in **Bolivia** (1971, 1979) and **Peru** (1976). In Central America increasing liberal and leftist militancy led to the ouster (1979) of the Somoza regime of Nicaragua and to civil conflict in El Salvador.

Indochina. Communist victories in Vietnam, Cambodia, and Laos by May 1975 did not bring peace. The **Pol Pot regime** ordered millions of city-dwellers to resettle in rural areas, in a program of forced labor, combined with terrorism, that cost as many as 2 million lives (1975-79) and caused hundreds of thousands of ethnic Chinese and others to flee Vietnam ("boat people," 1979). The Vietnamese invasion of Cambodia swelled the refugee population and contributed to widespread starvation in that devastated country.

Russian expansion. Soviet influence, checked in some countries (troops ousted by Egypt, 1972), was projected further afield, often with the use of Cuban troops (Angola, 1975-89; Ethiopia, 1977-88) and aided by a growing navy, a merchant fleet, and international banking ability. Détente with the West —1972 Berlin pact, 1972 strategic arms pact (**SALT**)—gave way to a more antagonistic relationship in the late 1970s, exacerbated by the Soviet invasion (1979) of Afghanistan.

Africa. The last remaining European colonies were granted independence (**Spanish Sahara,** 1976; **Djibouti,** 1977) and, after 10 years of civil war and many negotiation sessions, a black government took over (1979) in Zimbabwe (Rhodesia); white domination remained in S **Africa.** Great power involvement in local wars (Russia in **Angola, Ethiopia;** France in **Chad, Zaire, Mauritania**) and the use of tens of thousands of Cuban troops were denounced by some African leaders as neocolonialism. Ethnic or tribal clashes made Africa the chief locus of sustained warfare during the late 1970s.

Arts. Traditional modes in painting, architecture, and music, pursued in relative obscurity for much of the 20th cent., received increased popular and critical attention in the 1970s. The pictorial emphasis in neorealist and photorealist painting, the return of many architects to detail, decoration, and natural materials, and the concern with ordered structure in musical composition were, ironically, novel experiences for artistic consumers after the exhaustion of experimental possibilities. These more conservative styles, however, coexisted with modernist works in an atmosphere of variety and tolerance.

Revitalization of Capitalism, Demand for Democracy: 1980-89

USSR, Eastern Europe. A troublesome 1980-85 for the USSR was followed by 5 years of astonishing change: the surrender of the Communist monopoly, remaking of the Soviet state, and disintegration of the Soviet empire. After the deaths of Brezhnev (1982), Andropov (1984), and Chernenko (1985); the harsh treatment of dissent and restriction of emigration; and the Soviet invasion (Dec. 1979) of Afghanistan, Gen. Sec. Mikhail **Gorbachev** (in office 1985-1991) promoted *glasnost* and *perestroika*—economic, political, and social reform. Supported by the Communist Party (July 1988), he signed (Dec. 1987) the INF disarmament treaty, and he pledged (1988) to cut the military budget. Military withdrawal from Afghanistan was completed in Feb. 1989, democratization was not hindered in Poland and

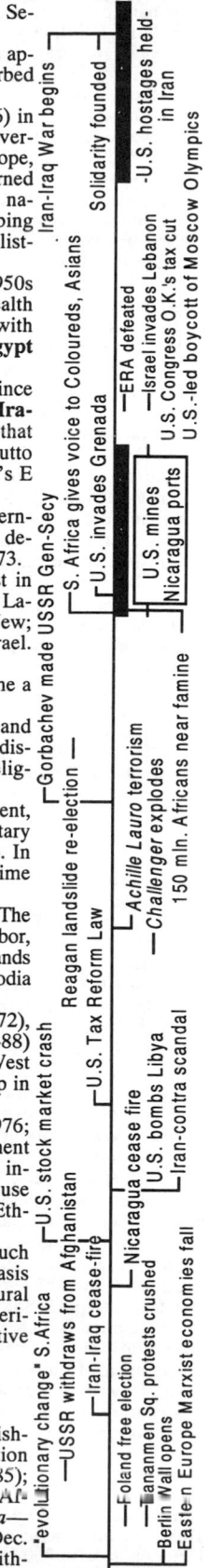

1980

Iran-Iraq War begins
Solidarity founded
-U.S. hostages held-in Iran
-U.S.-led boycott of Moscow Olympics
—ERA defeated
—Israel invades Lebanon
U.S. Congress O.K.'s tax cut
U.S. mines Nicaragua ports
U.S. invades Grenada
S. Africa gives voice to Coloureds, Asians
Gorbachev made USSR Gen-Secy
150 mln. Africans near famine
—Achille Lauro terrorism
—Challenger explodes
Reagan landslide re-election
—U.S. Tax Reform Law
—U.S. stock market crash
Nicaragua cease fire
U.S. bombs Libya
Iran-contra scandal
"revolutionary change" S. Africa
USSR withdraws from Afghanistan
Iran-Iraq cease-fire
Poland free election
Tiananmen Sq. protests crushed
Berlin Wall opens
Eastern Europe Marxist economies fall

1990

Hungary, and the Soviet people chose (Mar. 1989) part of the new Congress from competing candidates. By 1989 the **Cold War** had apparently ended, with much of the credit given to Gorbachev.

Poland. Solidarity, the labor union founded (1980) by **Lech Walesa**, was outlawed in 1982 and then legalized in 1988, after years of unrest. Poland's first free election since the Communist takeover brought Solidarity victory (June 1989); Tadeusz Mazowiecki, a Walesa adviser, became (Aug. 1989) prime minister in a government with the Communists.

In the fall of 1989 the failure of Marxist economies in **Hungary, E Germany, Czechoslovakia, Bulgaria, and Romania** brought the collapse of the Communist monopoly and a demand for democracy. In a historic step, the **Berlin Wall** was opened in Nov. 1989.

U.S. "The Reagan Years" (1981-88) brought the **longest economic boom** yet in U.S. history via budget and tax cuts, deregulation, "junk bond" financing, leveraged buyouts, and mergers and takeovers, as well as a **strong anti-Communist stance**, via increased defense spending, aid to anti-Communists in Central America, invasion of Cuba-threatened Grenada, and championing of the MX missile system and "Star Wars" missile defense program. The Republican Party, and conservatism, appeared to strengthen. Four Reagan-Gorbachev summits (1985-88) climaxed in the INF treaty (1987). The Iran-contra affair (North's TV testimony, July 1987) was a major political scandal. There were also significant financial scandals (E. F. Hutton, 1985; Ivan Boesky, 1986). The stock market crashed (Oct. 1987), and the U.S. trade imbalance grew (especially with Japan). The federal budget deficit soared. Homelessness and drug abuse (esp. "crack") were growing social problems. In 1988, Vice Pres. Bush was elected to succeed Reagan as president.

Middle East. The Middle East remained militarily unstable, with sharp divisions along economic, political, racial, and religious lines. In **Iran**, an Islamic revolution (1979-80) and violent political upheavals afterward, brought a strong anti-U.S. stance. In Sept. 1980, **Iraq** repudiated its border agreement with Iran and began major hostilities that led to an 8-year war in which millions were killed.

Libya's support for international terrorism induced the U.S. to close (May 1981) its diplomatic mission there and embargo (Mar. 1982) Libyan oil. The U.S. accused Libyan leader Qaddafi of aiding (Dec. 1985) terrorists in Rome and of Vienna airport attacks, and retaliated by bombing (Apr. 1986) Libya.

Israel affirmed (July 1980) all Jerusalem as its capital, destroyed (1981) an Iraqi atomic reactor, and invaded (1982) Lebanon, forcing the PLO to agree to withdraw. A **Palestinian uprising**, including women and children hurling rocks and bottles at troops, began (Dec. 1987) in Israeli-occupied Gaza and spread to the West Bank; troops responded with force, killing 300 by the end of 1988, with 6,000 more in detention camps.

Israeli withdrawal from **Lebanon** began in Feb. 1985 and ended in June 1985, as Lebanon continued torn by military and political conflict. Premier Karami was assassinated in June 1987. Artillery duels (Mar.-Apr. 1989) between Christian East Beirut and Muslim W Beirut left 200 dead and 700 wounded. At decade's end, violence still dominated.

Central America. In **Nicaragua**, the leftist Sandinista National Liberation Front, in power after the 1979 civil war, faced problems as a result of Nicaragua's military aid to leftist guerrillas in El Salvador and U.S. backing of antigovernment contras. The U.S. CIA admitted (1984) having directed the mining of Nicaraguan ports, and the U.S. sent humanitarian (1985) and military (1986) aid. Profits from secret arms sales to Iran were found (1987) diverted to contras. Cease-fire talks between the Sandinista government and contras came in 1988, and elections were held in Feb. 1990.

In **El Salvador**, a military coup (Oct. 1979) failed to halt extreme right-wing violence and left-wing terrorism. Archbishop Oscar Romero was assassinated in Mar. 1980; from Jan. to June some 4,000 civilians reportedly were killed in the civil unrest. In 1984, newly elected Pres. Duarte worked to stem human rights abuses. Leftist guerrillas continued their offensive in 1989.

Africa. 1980-85 marked a rapid decline in the economies of virtually all African countries, a result of accelerating desertification, the world economic recession, heavy indebtedness to overseas creditors, rapid population growth, and political instability. Some 60 million Africans faced prolonged hunger in 1981; much of Africa had one of the worst droughts ever in 1983, and by year's end **150 million faced near-famine**. "Live Aid," a marathon rock concert, was presented in July 1985, and the U.S. and Western nations sent aid in Sept. 1985. Economic hardship fueled political unrest and coups. Wars in Ethiopia and Sudan and military strife in several other nations continued through 1989. AIDS took a heavy toll.

South Africa. Antiapartheid sentiment gathered force; demonstrations and violent police response grew. South African white voters approved (Nov. 1983) the first constitution to give Coloureds and Asians a voice, while still excluding blacks (70% of the population). The U.S. imposed economic sanctions in Aug. 1985, and 11 Western nations followed in Sept. **P. W. Botha**, 1980s president, was succeeded by **F. W. de Klerk**, in Sept. 1989, who promised "evolutionary" change via negotiation with the black population.

China. From 1980 through mid-1989 the Communist government and paramount leader **Deng Xiaoping** pursued **far-reaching changes**, expanding commercial and technical ties to the industrialized world and increasing the role of market forces in stimulating urban economic development. Apr. 1989 brought new demands for democratization: student demonstrators camped out in Tiananmen Sq., Beijing, in a massive peaceful protest. Some 100,000 students and workers marched, and at least 20 other cities saw protests. In response, martial law was imposed; army troops crushed the demonstration in Tiananmen Sq. on June 3-4, with death toll estimates at 500-7,000, as many as 10,000 injured, as many as 10,000 dissidents arrested, and 31 people tried and executed. The conciliatory Communist Party chief was ousted; the Politburo adopted (July) reforms against official corruption.

Japan. Japan's relations with other nations, especially the U.S., were dominated (1980-89) by **trade imbalances favoring Japan**. In 1985 the U.S. trade deficit with Japan was $49.7 billion, one-third of the total U.S. trade deficit. After Japan was found (Apr. 1986) to sell semiconductors and computer memory chips below cost, the U.S. was assured a "fair share" of the market, but charged (Mar. 1987) Japan with failing to live up to the agreement. The **Omnibus Trade Bill** (Aug. 1988) provided for retaliation.

European Community. With the addition of Greece, Portugal, and Spain, the EC became a **common market of more than 300 million people**, the West's largest trading entity. **Margaret Thatcher** became the first British prime minister in this century to win 3 consecutive terms (1987). France elected (1981) its first socialist president, **François Mitterrand**, who was reelected in 1988. Italy elected (1983) its first socialist premier, **Bettino Craxi**.

International Terrorism. With the 1979 overthrow of the Shah of Iran, terrorism became a prominent political tactic. It increased through the '80s, but with fewer high-profile attacks after 1985. In 1979-81, Iranian militants held 52 Americans hostage in Iran for 444 days; in 1983 a TNT-laden suicide terrorist blew up U.S. Marine headquarters in Beirut, killing 241 Americans, and a truck bomb blew up a French paratroop barracks, killing 58. The *Achille Lauro* cruise ship was hijacked in 1986, and an American passenger killed; the U.S. subsequently intercepted the Egyptian plane flying the terrorists to safety. Incidents rose to 700 in 1985, and to 1,000 in 1988. **Assassinated leaders** included Egypt's Pres. **Anwar al-Sadat** (1981), India's Prime Min. **Indira Gandhi** (1984), and Lebanese Premier **Rashid Karami** (1987).

HISTORICAL FIGURES

Ancient Greeks and Latins

Greeks

Aeschines, orator, 389-314BC.
Aeschylus, dramatist, 525-456BC.
Aesop, fableist, c620-c560BC.
Alcibiades, politician, 450-404BC.
Anacreon, poet, c582-c485BC.
Anaxagoras, philosopher, c500-428BC.
Anaximander, philosopher, 611-546BC.
Anaximenes, philosopher, c570-500BC.
Antiphon, speechwriter, c480-411BC.
Apollonius, mathematician, c265-170BC.
Archimedes, math. 287-212BC.
Aristophanes, dramatist, c448-380BC.
Aristotle, philosopher, 384-322BC.
Athenaeus, scholar, fl. c200.
Callicrates, architect, fl. 5th cent.BC.
Callimachus, poet, c305-240BC.
Cratinus, comic dramatist, 520-421BC.
Democritus, philosopher, c460-370BC.
Demosthenes, orator, 384-322BC.
Diodorus, historian, fl. 20BC.

Diogenes, philosopher, 372-c287BC.
Dionysius, historian, d. c7BC.
Empedocles, philosopher, c490-430BC.
Epicharmus, dramatist, c530-440BC.
Epictetus, philosopher, c55-c135.
Epicurus, philosopher, 341-270BC.
Eratosthenes, scientist, 276-194BC.
Euclid, mathematician, fl. c300BC.
Euripides, dramatist, c484-406BC.
Galen, physician, 130-200.
Heraclitus, philosopher, c540-c475BC.
Herodotus, historian, c484-420BC.
Hesiod, poet, 8th cent. BC.
Hippocrates, physician, c460-377BC.
Homer, poet, fl. c700BC(?).
Isocrates, orator, 436-338BC.
Menander, dramatist, 342-292BC.
Parmenides, philosopher, b c515BC.
Pericles, statesman, c495-429BC.
Phidias, sculptor, c500-435BC.

Pindar, poet, c518-c438BC.
Plato, philosopher, c428-347BC.
Plutarch, biographer, c46-120.
Polybius, historian, c200-c118BC.
Praxiteles, sculptor, 400-330BC.
Pythagoras, phil., math., c580-c500BC.
Sappho, poet, c610-c580BC.
Simonides, poet, 556-c468BC.
Socrates, philosopher, 469-399BC.
Solon, statesman, 640-560BC.
Sophocles, dramatist, c496-406BC.
Strabo, geographer, c63BC-AD24.
Thales, philosopher, c634-546BC.
Themistocles, politician, c524-c460BC.
Theocritus, poet, c310-250BC.
Theophrastus, phil., c372-c287BC.
Thucydides, historian, fl. 5th cent.BC.
Timon, philosopher, c320-c230BC.
Xenophon, historian, c434-c355BC.
Zeno, philosopher, c495-c430BC.

Latins

Ammianus, historian, c330-395.
Apuleius, satirist, c124-c170.
Boethius, scholar, c480-524.
Caesar, Julius, leader, 100-44BC.
Catilina, politician, c108-62BC.
Cato (Elder), statesman, 234-149BC.
Catullus, poet, c84-54BC.
Cicero, orator, 106-43BC.
Claudian, poet, c370-c404.
Ennius, poet, 239-170BC.
Gellius, author, c130-c165.
Horace, poet, 65-8BC.

Juvenal, satirist, 60-127.
Livy, historian, 59BC-AD17.
Lucan, poet, 39-65.
Lucilius, poet, c180-c102BC.
Lucretius, poet, c99-c55BC.
Martial, epigrammatist, c38-c103.
Nepos, historian, c100-c25BC.
Ovid, poet, 43BC-AD17.
Persius, satirist, 34-62.
Plautus, dramatist, c254-c184BC.
Pliny the Elder, scholar, 23-79.
Pliny the Younger, author, 62-113.

Quintilian, rhetorician, c35-c97.
Sallust, historian, 86-34BC.
Seneca, philosopher, 4BC-AD65.
Silius, poet, c25-101.
Statius, poet, c45-c96.
Suetonius, biographer, c69-c122.
Tacitus, historian, 56-120.
Terence, dramatist, 185-c159BC.
Tibullus, poet, c55-c19BC.
Virgil, poet, 70-19BC.
Vitruvius, architect, fl. 1st cent.BC.

Rulers of England and Great Britain

England

Name		Began	Died	Age	Rgd
	Saxons and Danes				
Egbert	King of Wessex, won allegiance of all English	829	839	—	10
Ethelwulf	Son, King of Wessex, Sussex, Kent, Essex	839	858	—	19
Ethelbald	Son of Ethelwulf, displaced father in Wessex	858	860	—	2
Ethelbert	2d son of Ethelwulf, united Kent and Wessex	860	866	—	6
Ethelred I	3d son, King of Wessex, fought Danes	866	871	—	5
Alfred	The Great, 4th son, defeated Danes, fortified London	871	899	52	28
Edward	The Elder, Alfred's son, united English, claimed Scotland	899	924	55	25
Athelstan	The Glorious, Edward's son, King of Mercia, Wessex	924	940	45	16
Edmund	3d son of Edward, King of Wessex, Mercia	940	946	25	6
Edred	4th son of Edward	946	955	32	9
Edwy	The Fair, eldest son of Edmund, King of Wessex	955	959	18	3
Edgar	The Peaceful, 2d son of Edmund, ruled all English	959	975	32	17
Edward	The Martyr, eldest son of Edgar, murdered by stepmother	975	978	17	4
Ethelred II	The Unready, 2d son of Edgar, married Emma of Normandy	978	1016	48	37
Edmund II	Ironside, son of Ethelred II, King of London	1016	1016	27	0
Canute	The Dane, gave Wessex to Edmund, married Emma	1016	1035	40	19
Harold I	Harefoot, natural son of Canute	1035	1040	—	5
Hardecanute	Son of Canute by Emma, Danish King	1040	1042	24	2
Edward	The Confessor, son of Ethelred II (canonized 1161)	1042	1066	62	24
Harold II	Edward's brother-in-law, last Saxon King	1066	1066	44	0
	House of Normandy				
William I	The Conqueror, defeated Harold at Hastings	1066	1087	60	21
William II	Rufus, 3d son of William I, killed by arrow	1087	1100	43	13
Henry I	Beauclerc, youngest son of William I	1100	1135	67	35
	House of Blois				
Stephen	Son of Adela, daughter of William I, and Count of Blois	1135	1154	50	19
	House of Plantagenet				
Henry II	Son of Geoffrey Plantagenet (Angevin) by Matilda, daughter of Henry I	1154	1189	56	35
Richard I	Coeur de Lion, son of Henry II, crusader	1189	1199	42	10
John	Lackland, son of Henry II, signed Magna Carta, 1215	1199	1216	50	17
Henry III	Son of John, acceded at 9, under regency until 1227	1216	1272	65	56
Edward I	Longshanks, son of Henry III	1272	1307	68	35
Edward II	Son of Edward I, deposed by Parliament, 1327	1307	1327	43	20
Edward III	Of Windsor, son of Edward II	1327	1377	65	50
Richard II	Grandson of Edward III, minor until 1389, deposed 1399	1377	1400	33	22
	House of Lancaster				
Henry IV	Son of John of Gaunt, Duke of Lancaster, son of Edward III	1399	1413	47	13
Henry V	Son of Henry IV, victor of Agincourt	1413	1422	34	9
Henry VI	Son of Henry V, deposed 1461, died in Tower	1422	1471	49	39

(continued)

Rulers of England (continued)

Name		Began	Died	Age	Rgd
House of York					
Edward IV	Great-great-grandson of Edward III, son of Duke of York	1461	1483	40	22
Edward V	Son of Edward IV, murdered in Tower of London	1483	1483	13	0
Richard III	Crookback, brother of Edward IV, fell at Bosworth Field	1483	1485	32	2
House of Tudor					
Henry VII	Son of Edmund Tudor, Earl of Richmond, whose father had married the widow of Henry V; descended from Edward III through his mother, Margaret Beaufort via John of Gaunt. By marriage with daughter of Edward IV he united Lancaster and York	1485	1509	53	24
Henry VIII	Son of Henry VII by Elizabeth, dau. of Edward IV	1509	1547	56	38
Edward VI	Son of Henry VIII, by Jane Seymour, his 3d queen. Ruled under regents. Was forced to name Lady Jane Grey his successor. Council of State proclaimed her queen July 10, 1553. Mary Tudor won Council, was proclaimed queen July 19, 1553. Mary had Lady Jane Grey beheaded for treason, Feb., 1554	1547	1553	16	6
Mary I	Daughter of Henry VIII, by Catherine of Aragon.	1553	1558	43	5
Elizabeth I	Daughter of Henry VIII, by Anne Boleyn	1558	1603	69	44

Great Britain

House of Stuart

		Began	Died	Age	Rgd
James I	James VI of Scotland, son of Mary, Queen of Scots. *First to call himself King of Great Britain. This became official with the Act of Union, 1707.*	1603	1625	59	22
Charles I	Only surviving son of James I; beheaded Jan. 30, 1649.	1625	1649	48	24

Commonwealth, 1649-1660
Council of State, 1649; Protectorate, 1653

		Began	Died	Age	Rgd
The Cromwells. .	Oliver Cromwell, Lord Protector	1653	1658	59	—
	Richard Cromwell, son, Lord Protector, resigned May 25, 1659	1658	1712	86	—

House of Stuart (Restored)

		Began	Died	Age	Rgd
Charles II	Eldest son of Charles I, died without issue	1660	1685	55	25
James II	2d son of Charles I. Deposed 1688. Interregnum Dec. 11, 1688, to Feb. 13, 1689	1685	1701	68	3
William III	Son of William, Prince of Orange, by Mary, daughter of Charles I	1689	1702	51	13
and Mary II	Eldest daughter of James II and wife of William III		1694	33	6
Anne	2d daughter of James II.	1702	1714	49	12

House of Hanover

		Began	Died	Age	Rgd
George I.	Son of Elector of Hanover, by Sophia, granddaughter of James I	1714	1727	67	13
George II	Only son of George I, married Caroline of Brandenburg	1727	1760	77	33
George III	Grandson of George II, married Charlotte of Mecklenburg	1760	1820	81	59
George IV	Eldest son of George III, Prince Regent, from Feb. 1811	1820	1830	67	10
William IV	3d son of George III, married Adelaide of Saxe-Meiningen	1830	1837	71	7
Victoria	Daughter of Edward, 4th son of George III; married (1840) Prince Albert of Saxe-Coburg and Gotha, who became Prince Consort.	1837	1901	81	63

House of Saxe-Coburg and Gotha

		Began	Died	Age	Rgd
Edward VII	Eldest son of Victoria, married Alexandra, Princess of Denmark	1901	1910	68	9

House of Windsor
Name Adopted July 17, 1917

		Began	Died	Age	Rgd
George V	2d son of Edward VII, married Princess Mary of Teck	1910	1936	70	25
Edward VIII	Eldest son of George V; acceded Jan. 20, 1936, abdicated Dec. 11 . . .	1936	1972	77	1
George VI	2d son of George V; married Lady Elizabeth Bowes-Lyon	1936	1952	56	15
Elizabeth II	Elder daughter of George VI, acceded Feb. 6, 1952	1952	—	—	—

Rulers of Scotland

Kenneth I MacAlpin was the first Scot to rule both Scots and Picts, AD 846.

Duncan I was the first general ruler, 1034. Macbeth seized the kingdom 1040, was slain by Duncan's son, Malcolm III MacDuncan (Canmore), 1057.

Malcolm married Margaret, Saxon princess who had fled from the Normans. Queen Margaret introduced English language and English monastic customs. She was canonized, 1250. Her son Edgar, 1097, moved the court to Edinburgh. His brothers Alexander I and David I succeeded. Malcolm IV, the Maiden, 1153, grandson of David I, was followed by his brother, William the Lion, 1165, whose son was Alexander II, 1214. The latter's son, Alexander III, 1249, defeated the Norse and regained the Hebrides. When he died, 1286, his granddaughter, Margaret, child of Eric of Norway and grandniece of Edward I of England, known as the Maid of Norway, was chosen ruler, but died 1290, aged 8.

John Baliol, 1292-1296. (Interregnum, 10 years.)

Robert Bruce (The Bruce), 1306-1329, victor at Bannockburn, 1314.

David II, only son of Robert Bruce, ruled 1329-1371.

Robert II, 1371-1390, grandson of Robert Bruce, son of Walter, the Steward of Scotland, was called The Steward, first of the so-called Stuart line.

Robert III, son of Robert II, 1390-1406.

James I, son of Robert III, 1406-1437.

James II, son of James I, 1437-1460.

James III, eldest son of James II, 1460-1488.

James IV, eldest son of James III, 1488-1513.

James V, eldest son of James IV, 1513-1542.

Mary, daughter of James V, born 1542, became queen when one week old; was crowned 1543. Married, 1558, Francis, son of Henry II of France, who became king 1559, died 1560. Mary ruled Scots 1561 until abdication, 1567. She also married Henry Stewart, Lord Darnley (1565), and James, Earl of Bothwell (1567). Imprisoned by Elizabeth I, Mary was beheaded 1587.

James VI, 1566-1625, son of Mary and Lord Darnley, became King of England on death of Elizabeth in 1603. Although the thrones were thus united, the legislative union of Scotland and England was not effected until the Act of Union, May 1, 1707.

Prime Ministers of Great Britain

Designations in parentheses describe each government;
W=Whig; T=Tory; L=Liberal; C=Conservative; La=Labour; Cl=Coalition; P=Peelite.

Sir Robert Walpole (W)	1721-1742	Earl Grey (W)	1830-1834	Herbert H. Asquith (Coal)	1915-1916
Earl of Wilmington (W)	1742-1743	Viscount Melbourne (W)	1834	David Lloyd George (Coal)	1916-1922
Henry Pelham (W)	1743-1754	Sir Robert Peel (T)	1834-1835	Andrew Bonar Law (C)	1922-1923
Duke of Newcastle (W)	1754-1756	Viscount Melbourne (W)	1835-1841	Stanley Baldwin (C)	1923-1924
Duke of Devonshire (W)	1756-1757	Sir Robert Peel (T)	1841-1846	James Ramsay MacDonald	
Duke of Newcastle (W)	1757-1762	Lord (later Earl) John		(La)	1924
Earl of Bute (T)	1762-1763	Russell (W)	1846-1852	Stanley Baldwin (C)	1924-1929
George Grenville (W)	1763-1765	Earl of Derby (T)	1852	James Ramsay MacDonald	
Marquess of Rockingham (W)	1765-1766	Earl of Aberdeen (P)	1852-1855	(La)	1929-1931
William Pitt the Elder(Earl		Viscount Palmerston (Li)	1855-1858	James Ramsay MacDonald	
of Chatham) (W)	1766-1768	Earl of Derby (C)	1858-1859	(Coal)	1931-1935
Duke of Grafton (W)	1768-1770	Viscount Palmerston (Li)	1859-1865	Stanley Baldwin (Coal)	1935-1937
Frederick North (Lord		Earl Russell (Li)	1865-1866	Neville Chamberlain (Coal)	1937-1940
North) (T)	1770-1782	Earl of Derby (C)	1866-1868	Winston Churchill (Coal)	1940-1945
Marquess of Rockingham (W)	1782	Benjamin Disraeli (C)	1868	Winston Churchill (C)	1945
Earl of Shelburne (W)	1782-1783	William E. Gladstone (Li)	1868-1874	Clement Attlee (La)	1945-1951
Duke of Portland (Coal)	1783	Benjamin Disraeli (C)	1874-1880	Sir Winston Churchill (C)	1951-1955
William Pitt the Younger (T)	1783-1801	William E. Gladstone (Li)	1880-1885	Sir Anthony Eden (C)	1955-1957
Henry Addington (T)	1801-1804	Marquess of Salisbury (C)	1885-1886	Harold Macmillan (C)	1957-1963
William Pitt the Younger (T)	1804-1806	William E. Gladstone (Li)	1886	Sir Alec Douglas-Home (C)	1963-1964
William Wyndham Grenville,		Marquess of Salisbury (C)	1886-1892	Harold Wilson (La)	1964-1970
Baron Grenville (W)	1806-1807	William E. Gladstone (Li)	1892-1894	Edward Heath (C)	1970-1974
Duke of Portland (T)	1807-1809	Earl of Rosebery (Li)	1894-1895	Harold Wilson (La)	1974-1976
Spencer Perceval (T)	1809-1812	Marquess of Salisbury (C)	1895-1902	James Callaghan (La)	1976-1979
Earl of Liverpool (T)	1812-1827	Arthur J. Balfour (C)	1902-1905	Margaret Thatcher (C)	1979-1990
George Canning (T)	1827	Sir Henry Campbell-		John Major (C)	1990-1997
Viscount Goderich (T)	1827-1828	Bannerman (Li)	1905-1908	Tony Blair (La)	1997-
Duke of Wellington (T)	1828-1830	Herbert H. Asquith (Li)	1908-1915		

Historical Periods of Japan

Yamato	c. 300-592	Conquest of Yamato plain c. AD 300.	**Ashikaga**	1338-1573	Ashikaga Takauji becomes shogun, 1338.
Asuka	592-710	Accession of Empress Suiko, 592.	**Muromachi**	1392-1573	Unification of Southern and Northern Courts, 1392.
Nara	710-794	Completion of Heijo (Nara), 710; the capital moves to Nagaoka, 784.	**Sengoku**	1467-1600	Beginning of the Onin war, 1467.
			Momoyama	1573-1603	Oda Nobunaga enters Kyoto, 1568; Nobunaga deposes last Ashikaga shogun, 1573; Tokugawa Ieyasu victor at Sekigahara, 1600.
Heian	794-1185	Completion of Heian (Kyoto), 794.			
Fujiwara	858-1160	Fujiwara-no-Yoshifusa becomes regent, 858.			
			Edo	1603-1867	Ieyasu becomes shogun, 1603.
Taira	1160-1185	Taira-no-Kiyomori assumes control, 1160; Minamoto-no-Yoritomo victor over Taira, 1185.	**Meiji**	1868-1912	Enthronement of Emperor Mutsuhito (Meiji), 1867; Meiji Restoration and Charter Oath, 1868.
Kamakura	1192-1333	Yoritomo becomes shogun, 1192.	**Taisho**	1912-1926	Accession of Emperor Yoshihito, 1912.
Namboku	1334-1392	Restoration of Emperor Godaigo, 1334; Southern Court established by Godaigo at Yoshino, 1336.	**Showa**	1926-1989	Accession of Emperor Hirohito, 1926.
			Heisei	1989-	Accession of Emperor Akihito, 1989.

Rulers of France: Kings, Queens, Presidents

Caesar to Charlemagne

Julius Caesar subdued the Gauls, native tribes of Gaul (France), 58 to 51 BC. The Romans ruled 500 years. The Franks, a Teutonic tribe, reached the Somme from the East c. AD 250. By the 5th century the Merovingian Franks ousted the Romans. In 451, with the help of Visigoths, Burgundians and others, they defeated Attila and the Huns at Chalons-sur-Marne.

Childeric I became leader of the Merovingians 458. His son Clovis I (Chlodwig, Ludwig, Louis), crowned 481, founded the dynasty. After defeating the Alemanni (Germans) 496, he was baptized a Christian and made Paris his capital. His line ruled until Childeric III was deposed, 751.

The West Merovingians were called Neustrians, the eastern Austrasians. Pepin of Herstal (687-714), major domus, or head of the palace, of Austrasia, took over Neustria as dux (leader) of the Franks. Pepin's son, Charles, called Martel (the Hammer), defeated the Saracens at Tours-Poitiers, 732; was succeeded by his son, Pepin the Short, 741, who deposed Childeric III and ruled as king until 768.

His son, Charlemagne, or Charles the Great (742-814), became king of the Franks, 768, with his brother Carloman, who died 771. Charlemagne ruled France, Germany, parts of Italy, Spain, Austria, and enforced Christianity. Crowned Emperor of the Romans by Pope Leo III in St. Peter's, Rome, Dec. 25, 800. Succeeded by son, Louis I the Pious, 814. At death, 840, Louis left empire to sons, Lothair (Roman emperor); Pepin I (king of Aquitaine); Louis II (of Germany); Charles the Bald (France). They quarreled and, by the peace of Verdun, 843, divided the empire.

Date in bold is year of accession.

The Carolingians

843 Charles I (the Bald); Roman Emperor, 875
877 Louis II (the Stammerer), son
879 Louis III (died 882) and Carloman, brothers
885 Charles II (the Fat); Roman Emperor, 881
888 Eudes (Odo), elected by nobles
898 Charles III (the Simple), son of Louis II, defeated by
922 Robert, brother of Eudes, killed in war
923 Rudolph (Raoul), Duke of Burgundy
936 Louis IV, son of Charles III
954 Lothair, son, aged 13, defeated by Capet
986 Louis V (the Sluggard), left no heirs

The Capets

987 Hugh Capet, son of Hugh the Great
996 Robert II (the Wise), his son
1031 Henry I, his son
1060 Philip I (the Fair), son
1108 Louis VI (the Fat), son
1137 Louis VII (the Younger), son
1180 Philip II (Augustus), son, crowned at Reims
1223 Louis VIII (the Lion), son
1226 Louis IX, son, crusader; Louis IX (1214-1270) reigned 44 years, arbitrated disputes with English King Henry III; led crusades, 1248 (captured in Egypt 1250) and 1270, when he died of plague in Tunis. Canonized 1297 as St. Louis.
1270 Philip III (the Hardy), son
1285 Philip IV (the Fair), son, king at 17
1314 Louis X (the Headstrong), son. His posthumous son, John I, lived only 7 days
1316 Philip V (the Tall), brother of Louis X
1322 Charles IV (the Fair), brother of Louis X

House of Valois

1328 Philip VI (of Valois), grandson of Philip III
1350 John II (the Good), his son, retired to England
1364 Charles V (the Wise), son
1380 Charles VI (the Beloved), son
1422 Charles VII (the Victorious), son. In 1429 Joan of Arc (Jeanne d'Arc) promised Charles to oust the English, who occupied northern France. Joan won at Orleans and Patay and had Charles crowned at Reims, July 17, 1429. Joan was captured May 24, 1430, and executed May 30, 1431, at Rouen for heresy. Charles ordered her rehabilitation, effected 1455.
1461 Louis XI (the Cruel), son, civil reformer
1483 Charles VIII (the Affable), son
1498 Louis XII, great-grandson of Charles V
1515 Francis I, of Angouleme, nephew, son-in-law. Francis I (1494-1547) reigned 32 years, fought 4 big wars, was patron of the arts, aided Cellini, del Sarto, Leonardo da Vinci, Rabelais, embellished Fontainebleau.
1547 Henry II, son, killed at a joust in a tournament. He was the husband of Catherine de Medicis (1519-1589) and the lover of Diane de Poitiers (1499-1566). Catherine was born in Florence, daughter of Lorenzo de Medici. By her marriage to Henry II she became the mother of Francis II, Charles IX, Henry III and Queen Margaret (Reine Margot), wife of Henry IV. She persuaded Charles IX to order the massacre of Huguenots on the Feast of St. Bartholomew, Aug. 24, 1572, the day her daughter was married to Henry of Navarre.
1559 Francis II, son. In 1548, Mary, Queen of Scots since infancy, was betrothed when 6 to Francis, aged 4. They were married 1558. Francis died 1560, aged 16; Mary ruled Scotland, abdicated 1567.
1560 Charles IX, brother
1574 Henry III, brother, assassinated

House of Bourbon

1589 Henry IV, of Navarre, assassinated. Henry IV made enemies when he gave tolerance to Protestants by Edict of Nantes, 1598. He was grandson of Queen Margaret of Navarre, literary patron. He married Margaret of Valois, daughter of Henry II and Catherine de Medicis; was divorced; in 1600 married Marie de Medicis, who became Regent of France, 1610-1617, for her son, Louis XIII, but was exiled by Richelieu, 1631.
1610 Louis XIII (the Just), son. Louis XIII (1601-1643) married Anne of Austria. His ministers were Cardinals Richelieu and Mazarin.

1643 Louis XIV (The Grand Monarch), son. Louis XIV was king 72 years. He exhausted a prosperous country in wars for thrones and territory. By revoking the Edict of Nantes (1685) he caused the emigration of the Huguenots. He said: "I am the state."
1715 Louis XV, great-grandson. Louis XV married a Polish princess; lost Canada to the English. His favorites, Mme. Pompadour and Mme. Du Barry, influenced policies. Noted for saying "After me, the deluge."
1774 Louis XVI, grandson; married Marie Antoinette, daughter of Empress Maria Therese of Austria. King and queen beheaded by Revolution, 1793. Their son, called Louis XVII, died in prison, never ruled.

First Republic

1792 National Convention of the French Revolution
1795 Directory, under Barras and others
1799 Consulate, Napoleon Bonaparte, first consul. Elected consul for life, 1802.

First Empire

1804 Napoleon I (Napoleon Bonaparte), emperor. Josephine (de Beauharnais), empress, 1804-1809; Marie Louise, empress, 1810-1814. Her son, Francois (1811-1832), titular King of Rome, later Duke de Reichstadt and "Napoleon II," never ruled. Napoleon abdicated 1814, died 1821.

Bourbons Restored

1814 Louis XVIII, king; brother of Louis XVI
1824 Charles X, brother; reactionary; deposed by the July Revolution, 1830

House of Orleans

1830 Louis-Philippe, the "citizen king"

Second Republic

1848 Louis Napoleon Bonaparte, president, nephew of Napoleon I.

Second Empire

1852 Napoleon III (Louis Napoleon Bonaparte), emperor; Eugenie (de Montijo), empress. Lost Franco-Prussian war, deposed 1870. Son, Prince Imperial (1856-1879), died in Zulu War. Eugenie died 1920.

Third Republic—Presidents

1871 Thiers, Louis Adolphe (1797-1877)
1873 MacMahon, Marshal Patrice M. de (1808-1893)
1879 Grevy, Paul J. (1807-1891)
1887 Sadi-Carnot, M. (1837-1894), assassinated
1894 Casimir-Perier, Jean P. P. (1847-1907)
1895 Faure, François Felix (1841-1899)
1899 Loubet, Emile (1838-1929)
1906 Fallieres, C. Armand (1841-1931)
1913 Poincare, Raymond (1860-1934)
1920 Deschanel, Paul (1856-1922)
1920 Millerand, Alexandre (1859-1943)
1924 Doumergue, Gaston (1863-1937)
1931 Doumer, Paul (1857-1932), assassinated
1932 Lebrun, Albert (1871-1950), resigned 1940
1940 Vichy govt. under German armistice: Henri Philippe Petain (1856-1951), Chief of State, 1940-1944. Provisional govt. after liberation: Charles de Gaulle (1890-1970), Oct. 1944-Jan. 21, 1946; Felix Gouin (1884-1977), Jan. 23, 1946; Georges Bidault (1899-1983), June 24, 1946.

Fourth Republic—Presidents

1947 Auriol, Vincent (1884-1966)
1954 Coty, Rene (1882-1962)

Fifth Republic—Presidents

1959 De Gaulle, Charles Andre J. M. (1890-1970)
1969 Pompidou, Georges (1911-1974)
1974 Giscard d'Estaing, Valery (1926-   )
1981 Mitterrand, François (1916-1996)
1995 Chirac, Jacques (1932-   )

Rulers of Middle Europe; Rise and Fall of Dynasties; Rulers of Germany

Carolingian Dynasty

Charles the Great, or Charlemagne, ruled France, Italy, and Middle Europe; established Ostmark (later Austria); crowned Roman emperor by pope in Rome, AD 800; died 814.

Louis I (Ludwig) the Pious, son; crowned by Charlemagne 814; died 840.

Louis II, the German, son; succeeded to East Francia (Germany) 843-876.

Charles the Fat, son; inherited East Francia and West Francia (France) 876, reunited empire, crowned emperor by pope 881, deposed 887.

Arnulf, nephew, 887-899. Partition of empire.

Louis the Child, 899-911, last direct descendant of Charlemagne.

Conrad I, duke of Franconia, first elected German king, 911-918, founded House of Franconia.

Saxon Dynasty; First Reich

Henry I, the Fowler, duke of Saxony, 919-936.

Otto I, the Great, 936-973, son; crowned Holy Roman Emperor by pope, 962.

Otto II, 973-983, son; failed to oust Greeks and Arabs from Sicily.

Otto III, 983-1002, son; crowned emperor at 16.

Henry II, the Saint, duke of Bavaria, 1002-1024, great-grandson of Otto the Great.

House of Franconia

Conrad II, 1024-1039, elected king of Germany.

Henry III, the Black, 1039-1056, son; deposed 3 popes; annexed Burgundy.

Henry IV, 1056-1106, son; regency by his mother, Agnes of Poitou. Banned by Pope Gregory VII, he did penance at Canossa.

Henry V, 1106-1125, son; last of Salic House.

Lothair, duke of Saxony, 1125-1137. Crowned emperor in Rome, 1134.

House of Hohenstaufen

Conrad III, duke of Swabia, 1138-1152. In 2d Crusade.

Frederick I, Barbarossa, 1152-1190; Conrad's nephew.

Henry VI, 1190-1196, took lower Italy from Normans. Son became king of Sicily.

Philip of Swabia, 1197-1208, brother.

Otto IV, of House of Welf, 1198-1215; deposed.

Frederick II, 1215-1250, son of Henry VI; king of Sicily; crowned king of Jerusalem in 5th Crusade.

Conrad IV, 1250-1254, son; lost lower Italy to Charles of Anjou.

Conradin, 1252-1268, son, king of Jerusalem and Sicily, beheaded. Last Hohenstaufen.

Interregnum, 1254-1273, Rise of the Electors.

Transition

Rudolph I of Hapsburg, 1273-1291, defeated King Ottocar II of Bohemia. Bequeathed duchy of Austria to eldest son, Albert.

Adolph of Nassau, 1292-1298, killed in war with Albert of Austria.

Albert I, king of Germany, 1298-1308, son of Rudolph.

Henry VII, of Luxemburg, 1308-1313, crowned emperor in Rome. Seized Bohemia, 1310.

Louis IV of Bavaria (Wittelsbach), 1314-1347. Also elected was Frederick of Austria, 1314-1330 (Hapsburg). Abolition of papal sanction for election of Holy Roman Emperor.

Charles IV, of Luxemburg, 1347-1378, grandson of Henry VII, German emperor and king of Bohemia, Lombardy, Burgundy; took Mark of Brandenburg.

Wenceslaus, 1378-1400, deposed.

Rupert, Duke of Palatine, 1400-1410.

Sigismund, 1411-1437.

Hungary

Stephen I, house of Arpad, 997-1038. Crowned king 1000; converted Magyars; canonized 1083. After several centuries of feuds Charles Robert of Anjou became Charles I, 1308-1342.

Louis I, the Great, son, 1342-1382; joint ruler of Poland with Casimir III, 1370. Defeated Turks.

Mary, daughter, 1382-1395, ruled with husband. Sigismund of Luxemburg, 1387-1437, also king of Bohemia. As bro. of Wenceslaus he succeeded Rupert as Holy Roman Emperor, 1410.

Albert, 1438-1439, son-in-law of Sigismund; also Roman emperor as Albert II (see under Hapsburg).

Ulaszlo I of Poland, 1440-1444.

Ladislaus V, posthumous son of Albert II, 1444-1457. John Hunyadi (Hunyadi Janos), governor (1446-1452), fought Turks, Czechs; died 1456.

Matthias I (Corvinus), son of Hunyadi, 1458-1490. Shared rule of Bohemia, captured Vienna, 1106, annexed Austria, Styria, Carinthia.

Ulaszlo II (king of Bohemia), 1490-1516.

Louis II, son, aged 10, 1516-1526. Wars with Suleiman, Turk. In 1527 Hungary split between Ferdinand I, Archduke of Austria, bro.-in-law of Louis II, and John Zapolya of Transylvania. After Turkish invasion, 1547, Hungary split between Ferdinand, Prince John Sigismund (Transylvania), and the Turks.

House of Hapsburg

Albert V of Austria, Hapsburg, crowned king of Hungary, Jan. 1438, Roman emperor, March 1438, as Albert II; died 1439.

Frederick III, cousin, 1440-1493. Fought Turks.

Maximilian I, son, 1493-1519. Assumed title of Holy Roman Emperor (German), 1493.

Charles V, grandson, 1519-1556. King of Spain with mother co-regent; crowned Roman emperor at Aix, 1520. Confronted Luther at Worms; attempted church reform and religious conciliation; abdicated 1556.

Ferdinand I, king of Bohemia, 1526, of Hungary, 1527; disputed. German king, 1531. Crowned Roman emperor on abdication of brother Charles V, 1556.

Maximilian II, son, 1564-1576.

Rudolph II, son, 1576-1612.

Matthias, brother, 1612-1619, king of Bohemia and Hungary.

Ferdinand II of Styria, king of Bohemia, 1617, of Hungary, 1618, Roman emperor, 1619. Bohemian Protestants deposed him, elected Frederick V of Palatine, starting Thirty Years War.

Ferdinand III, son, king of Hungary, 1625, Bohemia, 1627, Roman emperor, 1637. Peace of Westphalia, 1648, ended war. Leopold I, 1658-1705; Joseph I, 1705-1711; Charles VI, 1711-1740.

Maria Theresa, daughter, 1740-1780, Archduchess of Austria, queen of Hungary; ousted pretender, Charles VII, crowned 1742; in 1745 obtained election of her husband Francis I as Roman emperor and co-regent (d. 1765). Fought Seven Years' War with Frederick II of Prussia. Mother of Marie Antoinette.

Joseph II, son, 1765-1790, Roman emperor, reformer; powers restricted by Empress Maria Theresa until her death, 1780. First partition of Poland. Leopold II, 1790-1792.

Francis II, son, 1792-1835. Fought Napoleon. Proclaimed first hereditary emperor of Austria, 1804. Forced to abdicate as Roman emperor, 1806; last use of title. Ferdinand I, son, 1835-1848, abdicated during revolution.

Austro-Hungarian Monarchy

Francis Joseph I, nephew, 1848-1916, emperor of Austria, king of Hungary. Dual monarchy of Austria-Hungary formed, 1867. After assassination of heir, Archduke Francis Ferdinand, June 28, 1914, Austrian diplomacy precipitated World War I.

Charles I, grand-nephew, 1916-1918, last emperor of Austria and king of Hungary. Abdicated Nov. 11-13, 1918, died 1922.

Rulers of Prussia

Nucleus of Prussia was the Mark of Brandenburg. First margrave Albert the Bear (Albrecht), 1134-1170. First Hohenzollern margrave was Frederick, burgrave of Nuremberg, 1417-1440.

Frederick William, 1640-1688, the Great Elector. Son, Frederick III, 1688-1713, crowned King Frederick of Prussia, 1701.

Frederick William I, son, 1713-1740.

Frederick II, the Great, son, 1740-1786, annexed Silesia, part of Austria.

Frederick William II, nephew, 1786-1797.

Frederick William III, son, 1797-1840. Napoleonic wars.

Frederick William IV, son, 1840-1861. Uprising of 1848 and first parliament and constitution.

Second and Third Reich

William I, 1861-1888, brother. Annexation of Schleswig and Hanover; Franco-Prussian war, 1870-1871, proclamation of German Reich, Jan. 18, 1871, at Versailles; William, German emperor (Deutscher Kaiser), Bismarck, chancellor.

Frederick III, son, 1888.

William II, son, 1888-1918. Led Germany in World War I, abdicated as German emperor and king of Prussia, Nov. 9, 1918. Died in exile in Netherlands, June 4, 1941. Minor rulers of Bavaria, Saxony, Wurttemberg also abdicated.

Germany proclaimed republic at Weimar, July 1, 1919. Presidents included: Frederick Ebert, 1919-1925; Paul von Hindenburg-Beneckendorff, 1925, reelected 1932, d. Aug. 2, 1934. Adolf Hitler, chancellor, chosen successor as Leader-Chancellor (Fuehrer-Reichskanzler) of Third Reich. Annexed Austria, Mar. 1938. Precipitated World War II, 1939-1945. Suicide Apr. 30, 1945.

Germany After 1945

Following World War II, Germany was split between democratic West and Soviet-dominated East. West German chancellors: Konrad Adenauer, 1949-1963; Ludwig Erhard, 1963-1966; Kurt Georg Kiesinger, 1966-1969; Willy Brandt, 1969-1974; Helmut Schmidt, 1974-1982; Helmut Kohl, 1982-1990. East German Communist party leaders: Walter Ulbricht, 1946-1971; Erich Honecker, 1971-1989; Egon Krenz, 1989-1990.

Germany was reunited Oct. 3, 1990. First post-reunification chancellor: Helmut Kohl, 1990- .

Rulers of Poland

House of Piasts

Miesko I, 962?-992; Poland Christianized 966. Expansion under 3 Boleslavs: I, 992-1025, son, crowned king 1024; II, 1058-1079, great-grandson, exiled after killing bishop Stanislav who became chief patron saint of Poland; III, 1106-1138, nephew, divided Poland among 4 sons, eldest suzerain.

1138-1306, feudal division. 1226 founding in Prussia of military order Teutonic Knights. 1226 invasion by Tartars/Mongols.

Vladislav I, 1306-1333, reunited most Polish territories, crowned king 1320. Casimir III the Great, 1333-1370, son, developed economic, cultural life, foreign policy.

House of Anjou

Louis I, 1370-1382, nephew/was also Louis I of Hungary.

Jadwiga, 1384-1399, daughter, married 1386 Jagiello, Grand Duke of Lithuania.

House of Jagiellonians

Vladislav II, 1386-1434, Christianized Lithuania, founded personal union between Poland & Lithuania. Defeated 1410 Teutonic Knights at Grunwald.

Vladislav III, 1434-1444, son, simultaneously king of Hungary. Fought Turks, killed 1444 in battle of Varna.

Casimir IV, 1446-1492, brother, competed with Hapsburgs, put son Vladislav on throne of Bohemia, later also of Hungary (Ulaszlo II).

Sigismund I, 1506-1548, son, patronized science and arts, his and son's reign "Golden Age."

Sigismund II, 1548-1572, son, established 1569 real union of Poland and Lithuania (lasted until 1795).

Elective Kings

Polish nobles in 1572 proclaimed Poland a republic headed by king to be elected by whole nobility.

Stephen Batory, 1576-1586, duke of Transylvania, married Ann, sister of Sigismund II August. Fought Russians.

Sigismund III Vasa, 1587-1632, nephew of Sigismund II. 1592-1598 also king of Sweden. His generals fought Russians, Turks.

Vladislav II Vasa, 1632-1648, son. Fought Russians.

John II Casimir Vasa, 1648-1668, brother. Fought Cossacks, Swedes, Russians, Turks, Tatars (the "Deluge"). Abdicated 1668.

John III Sobieski, 1674-1696. Won Vienna from besieging Turks, 1683.

Stanislav II, 1764-1795, last king. Encouraged reforms; 1791 1st modern Constitution in Europe. 1772, 1793, 1795 Poland partitioned among Russia, Prussia, Austria. Unsuccessful insurrection against foreign invasion 1794 under Kosciuszko, American-Polish general.

1795-1918: Poland Under Foreign Rule

1807-1815 Grand Duchy of Warsaw created by Napoleon I, Frederick August of Saxony grand duke.

1815 Congress of Vienna proclaimed part of Poland "Kingdom" in personal union with Russia.

Polish uprisings: 1830 against Russia; 1846, 1848 against Austria; 1863 against Russia—all repressed.

1918-1939: Second Republic

1918-1922 Head of State Jozef Pilsudski. Presidents: Gabriel Narutowicz 1922, assassinated; Stanislav Wojciechowski 1922-1926, had to abdicate after Pilsudski's coup d'état; Ignacy Moscicki, 1926-1939, ruled (with Pilsudski until his death, 1935) as virtual dictator.

1939-1945: Poland Under Foreign Occupation

Nazi aggression Sept. 1939. Polish government-in-exile, first in France, then in England. Vladislav Raczkiewicz president; Gen. Vladislav Sikorski, then Stanislav Mikolajczyk, prime ministers. Soviet-sponsored Polish Committee of National Liberation proclaimed at Lublin July 1944, transformed into government Jan. 1, 1945.

Poland After 1945

In the late 1940s, Poland came increasingly under Soviet control. Communist party ruled in Poland until Aug. 1989, when democratic Solidarity party gained control of government. Solidarity leader Lech Walesa was elected president, Nov. 1990; succeeded by former Communist Aleksander Kwasniewski, Nov. 1995.

Rulers of Denmark, Sweden, Norway

Denmark

Earliest rulers invaded Britain; King Canute, who ruled in London 1016-1035, was most famous. The Valdemars furnished kings until the 15th century. In 1282 the Danes won the first national assembly, Danehof, from King Erik V.

Most redoubtable medieval character was Margaret, daughter of Valdemar IV, born 1353, married at 10 to King Haakon VI of Norway. In 1376 she had her first infant son Olaf made king of Denmark. After his death, 1387, she was regent of Denmark and Norway. In 1388 Sweden accepted her as sovereign. In 1389 she made her grand-nephew, Duke Erik of Pomerania, titular king of Denmark, Sweden, and Norway, with herself as regent. In 1397 she effected the Union of Kalmar of the three kingdoms and had Erik VII crowned. In 1439 the three kingdoms deposed him and elected, 1440, Christopher of Bavaria king (Christopher III). On his death, 1448, the union broke up.

Succeeding rulers were unable to enforce their claims as rulers of Sweden until 1520, when Christian II conquered Sweden. He was thrown out 1522, and in 1523 Gustavus Vasa united Sweden. Denmark continued to dominate Norway until the Napoleonic wars, when Frederick VI, 1808-1839, joined the Napoleonic cause after Britain had destroyed the Danish fleet, 1807. In 1814 he was forced to cede Norway to Sweden and Helgoland to Britain, receiving Lauenburg. Successors Christian VIII, 1839; Frederick VII, 1848; Christian IX, 1863; Frederick VIII, 1906; Christian X, 1912; Frederick IX, 1947; Margrethe II, 1972.

Sweden

Early kings ruled at Uppsala, but did not dominate the country. Sverker, c1130-c1156, united the Swedes and Goths. In 1435 Sweden obtained the Riksdag, or parliament. After the Union of Kalmar, 1397, the Danes either ruled or harried the country until Christian II of Denmark conquered it anew, 1520. This led to a rising under Gustavus Vasa, who ruled Sweden 1523-1560, and established an independent kingdom. Charles IX, 1599-1611, crowned 1604, conquered Moscow. Gustavus II Adolphus, 1611-1632, was called the Lion of the North. Later rulers: Christina, 1632; Charles X Gustavus, 1654; Charles XI, 1660; Charles XII (invader of Russia and Poland, defeated at Poltava, June 28, 1709), 1697; Ulrika Eleanora, sister, elected queen 1718; Frederick I (of Hesse), her husband, 1720; Adolphus Frederick, 1751; Gustavus III, 1771; Gustavus IV Adolphus, 1792; Charles XIII, 1809. (Union with Norway began 1814.) Charles XIV John, 1818 (he was Jean Bernadotte, Napoleon's Prince of Ponte Corvo, elected 1810 to succeed Charles XIII); he founded the present dynasty: Oscar I, 1844; Charles XV, 1859; Oscar II, 1872; Gustavus V, 1907; Gustav VI Adolf, 1950; Carl XVI Gustaf, 1973.

Norway

Overcoming many rivals, Harald Haarfager, 872-930, conquered Norway, Orkneys, and Shetlands; Olaf I, great-grandson, 995-1000, brought Christianity into Norway, Iceland, and Greenland. In 1035 Magnus the Good also became king of Denmark. Haakon V, 1299-1319, had married his daughter to Erik of Sweden. Their son, Magnus, became ruler of Norway and Sweden at 6. His son, Haakon VI, married Margaret of Denmark; their son Olaf IV became king of Norway and Denmark, followed by Margaret's regency and the Union of Kalmar, 1397.

In 1450 Norway became subservient to Denmark. Christian IV, 1588-1648, founded Christiania, now Oslo. After Napoleonic wars, when Denmark ceded Norway to Sweden, a strong nationalist movement forced recognition of Norway as an independent kingdom united with Sweden under the Swedish kings, 1814-1905. In 1905 the union was dissolved and Prince Charles of Denmark became Haakon VII. He died Sept. 21, 1957; succeeded by son, Olav V. Olav V died Jan. 17, 1991; succeeded by son, Harald V.

Rulers of the Netherlands and Belgium

The Netherlands (Holland)

William Frederick, Prince of Orange, led a revolt against French rule, 1813; crowned king, 1815. Belgium seceded Oct. 4, 1830, after a revolt. The secession was ratified by the two kingdoms by treaty, Apr. 19, 1839.

Succession: William II, son, 1840; William III, son, 1849; Wilhelmina, daughter of William III and his 2d wife Princess Emma of Waldeck, 1890; Wilhelmina abdicated, Sept. 4, 1948, in favor of daughter, Juliana. Juliana abdicated, Apr. 30, 1980, in favor of daughter, Beatrix.

Belgium

A national congress elected Prince Leopold of Saxe-Coburg as king; he took the throne July 21, 1831, as Leopold I. Succession: Leopold II, son, 1865; Albert I, nephew of Leopold II, 1909; Leopold III, son of Albert, 1934; Prince Charles, Regent 1944; Leopold returned 1950, yielded powers to son Baudouin, Prince Royal, Aug. 6, 1950, abdicated July 16, 1951. Baudouin I took throne July 17, 1951, died July 31, 1993; succeeded by brother, Albert II.

Roman Rulers

Listed up to the end of the Empire in the West. Rulers in the East sat in Constantinople and, briefly, in Nicaea, until the capture of Constantinople by the Turks in 1453, when Byzantium was succeeded by the Ottoman Empire.

BC — The Kingdom
753 Romulus (Quirinus)
716 Numa Pompilius
673 Tullus Hostilius
640 Ancus Marcius
616 L. Tarquinius Priscus
578 Servius Tullius
534 L. Tarquinius Superbus

The Republic
509 Consulate established
509 Quaestorship instituted
498 Dictatorship introduced
494 Plebeian Tribunate created
494 Plebeian Aedileship created
444 Consular Tribunate organized
435 Censorship instituted
366 Praetorship established
366 Curule Aedileship created
362 Military Tribunate elected
326 Proconsulate introduced
311 Naval Duumvirate elected
217 Dictatorship of Fabius Maximus
133 Tribunate of Tiberius Gracchus
123 Tribunate of Gaius Gracchus
82 Dictatorship of Sulla
60 First Triumvirate formed (Caesar, Pompeius, Crassus)
46 Dictatorship of Caesar
43 Second Triumvirate formed (Octavianus, Antonius, Lepidus)

The Empire
27 Augustus (Gaius Julius Caesar Octavianus)

AD
14 Tiberius I
37 Gaius Caesar (Caligula)
41 Claudius I
54 Nero
68 Galba
69 Galba; Otho, Vitellius
69 Vespasianus
79 Titus

81 Domitianus
96 Nerva
98 Trajanus
117 Hadrianus
138 Antoninus Pius
161 Marcus Aurelius and Lucius Verus
169 Marcus Aurelius (alone)
180 Commodus
193 Pertinax; Julianus I
193 Septimius Severus
211 Caracalla and Geta
212 Caracalla (alone)
217 Macrinus
218 Elagabalus (Heliogabalus)
222 Alexander Severus
235 Maximinus I (the Thracian)
238 Gordianus I and Gordianus II; Pupienus and Balbinus
238 Gordianus III
244 Philippus (the Arabian)
249 Decius
251 Gallus and Volusianus
253 Aemilianus
253 Valerianus and Gallienus
258 Gallienus (alone)
268 Claudius Gothicus
270 Quintillus
270 Aurelianus
275 Tacitus
276 Florianus
276 Probus
282 Carus
283 Carinus and Numerianus
284 Diocletianus
286 Diocletianus and Maximianus
305 Galerius and Constantius I
306 Galerius, Maximinus II, Severus I
307 Galerius, Maximinus II, Constantinus I, Licinius, Maxentius
311 Maximinus II, Constantinus I, Licinius, Maxentius
314 Maximinus II, Constantinus I, Licinius
314 Constantinus I and Licinius

324 Constantinus I (the Great)
337 Constantinus II, Constans I, Constantius II
340 Constantius II and Constans I
350 Constantius II
361 Julianus II (the Apostate)
363 Jovianus

West (Rome) and East (Constantinople)
364 Valentinianus I (West) and Valens (East)
367 Valentinianus I with Gratianus (West) and Valens (East)
375 Gratianus with Valentinianus II (West) and Valens (East)
378 Gratianus with Valentinianus II (West), Theodosius I (East)
383 Valentinianus II (West) and Theodosius I (East)
394 Theodosius I (the Great)
395 Honorius (West) and Arcadius (East)
408 Honorius (West) and Theodosius II (East)
423 Valentinianus III (West) and Theodosius II (East)
450 Valentinianus III (West) and Marcianus (East)
455 Maximus (West), Avitus (West); Marcianus (East)
456 Avitus (West), Marcianus (East)
457 Majorianus (West), Leo I (East)
461 Severus II (West), Leo I (East)
467 Anthemius (West), Leo I (East)
472 Olybrius (West), Leo I (East)
473 Glycerius (West), Leo I (East)
474 Julius Nepos (West), Leo II (East)
475 Romulus Augustulus (West) and Zeno (East)
476 End of Empire in West; Odovacar, King, drops title of Emperor; murdered by King Theodoric of Ostrogoths, 493

MILLENNIUM FACT BOX

World Leaders in AD 1000 and in 1997

Around the beginning of the current millennium, many nations familiar today existed in some form, ruled by figures now almost forgotten. Here is a list of monarchs and major political leaders of selected countries in AD 1000 and today.[1]

Nation/Region	1000	1997 (as of Sept.)
China	Emperor Chen Tsung	President Jiang Zemin
Denmark	King Sweyn I	Queen Margrethe II; Prime Min. Poul Nyrup Rasmussen
Egypt	Caliph Al-Hakim (Fatimid Caliphate)	President Hosni Mubarak
France	King Robert II	President Jacques Chirac
Germany	Emperor Otto III (Holy Roman Empire[2])	Chancellor Helmut Kohl
Great Britain	King Ethelred II (the Unready) (England)	Queen Elizabeth II; Prime Min. Tony Blair
Japan	Emperor Ichijo; (Regent) Fujiwara Michinaga	Emperor Akihito; Prime Min. Hashimoto Ryutaro
Norway	King Olaf I	King Harald V; Prime Min. Thorbjorn Jagland
Poland	Prince (later King) Boleslav I	President Aleksander Kwasniewski
Russia	Grand Prince Vladimir I (Kievan Rus)	President Boris Yeltsin
Sweden	King Olof	King Carl XVI Gustaf; Prime Min. Goran Persson

[1]Regions in 1000 and today not always coextensive. [2]At this time an unstable union that included Germany and northern Italy.

Rulers of Modern Italy

After the fall of Napoleon in 1814, the Congress of Vienna, 1815, restored Italy as a political patchwork, comprising the Kingdom of Naples and Sicily, the Papal States, and smaller units. Piedmont and Genoa were awarded to Sardinia, ruled by King Victor Emmanuel I of Savoy.

United Italy emerged under the leadership of Camillo, Count di Cavour (1810-1861), Sardinian prime minister. Agitation was led by Giuseppe Mazzini (1805-1872) and Giuseppe Garibaldi (1807-1882), soldier; Victor Emmanuel I abdicated 1821. After a brief regency for a brother, Charles Albert was king 1831-1849, abdicating when defeated by the Austrians at Novara. Succeeded by Victor Emmanuel II, 1849-1861.

In 1859 France forced Austria to cede Lombardy to Sardinia, which gave rights to Savoy and Nice to France. In 1860 Garibaldi led 1,000 volunteers in a spectacular campaign, took Sicily and expelled the King of Naples. In 1860 the House of Savoy annexed Tuscany, Parma, Modena, Romagna, the Two Sicilies, the Marches, and Umbria. Victor Emmanuel assumed the title of King of Italy at Turin Mar. 17, 1861. In 1866 he allied with Prussia in the Austro-Prussian War, with Prussia's victory received Venetia. On Sept. 20, 1870, his troops under Gen. Raffaele entered Rome and took over the Papal States, ending the temporal power of the Roman Catholic Church.

Succession: Umberto I, 1878, assassinated 1900; Victor Emmanuel III, 1900, abdicated 1946, died 1947; Humbert II, 1946, ruled a month. In 1921 Benito Mussolini (1883-1945) formed the Fascist party; he became prime minister Oct. 31, 1922. He entered World War II as an ally of Hitler. He was deposed July 25, 1943.

At a plebiscite June 2, 1946, Italy voted for a republic; Premier Alcide de Gasperi became chief of state June 13, 1946. On June 28, 1946, the Constituent Assembly elected Enrico de Nicola, Liberal, provisional president. Successive presidents: Luigi Einaudi, elected May 11, 1948; Giovanni Gronchi, Apr. 29, 1955; Antonio Segni, May 6, 1962; Giuseppe Saragat, Dec. 28, 1964; Giovanni Leone, Dec. 29, 1971; Alessandro Pertini, July 9, 1978; Francesco Cossiga, July 9, 1985; Oscar Luigi Scalfaro, May 28, 1992.

Rulers of Spain

From 8th to 11th centuries Spain was dominated by the Moors (Arabs and Berbers). The Christian reconquest established small kingdoms (Asturias, Aragon, Castile, Catalonia, Leon, Navarre, and Valencia). In 1474 Isabella, b. 1451, became Queen of Castile & Leon. Her husband, Ferdinand, b. 1452, inherited Aragon 1479, with Catalonia, Valencia, and the Balearic Islands, became Ferdinand V of Castile. By Isabella's request Pope Sixtus IV established the Inquisition, 1478. Last Moorish kingdom, Granada, fell 1492. Columbus opened New World of colonies, 1492. Isabella died 1504, succeeded by her daughter, Juana "the Mad," but Ferdinand ruled until his death 1516.

Charles I, b. 1500, son of Juana, grandson of Ferdinand and Isabella, and of Maximilian I of Hapsburg; succeeded later as Holy Roman Emperor, Charles V, 1520; abdicated 1556. Philip II, son, 1556-1598, inherited only Spanish throne; conquered Portugal, fought Turks, sent Armada vs. England. Married to Mary I of England, 1554-1558. Succession: Philip III, 1598-1621; Philip IV, 1621-1665; Charles II, 1665-1700, left Spain to Philip of Anjou, grandson of Louis XIV, who as Philip V, 1700-1746, founded Bourbon dynasty; Ferdinand VI, 1746-1759; Charles III, 1759-1788; Charles IV, 1788-1808, abdicated.

Napoleon now dominated politics and made his brother Joseph King of Spain 1808, but the Spanish ousted him in 1813. Ferdinand VII, 1808, 1814-1833, lost American colonies; succeeded by daughter Isabella II, aged 3, with wife Maria Christina of Naples regent until 1843. Isabella deposed by revolution 1868. Elected king by the Cortes, Amadeo of Savoy, 1870; abdicated 1873. First republic, 1873-74. Alphonso XII, son of Isabella, 1875-85. His posthumous son was Alphonso XIII, with his mother, Queen Maria Christina regent; Spanish-American war, Spain lost Cuba, gave up Puerto Rico, Philippines, Sulu Is., Marianas. Alphonso took throne 1902, aged 16, married British Princess Victoria Eugenia of Battenberg. Dictatorship of Primo de Rivera, 1923-30, precipitated revolution of 1931. Alphonso agreed to leave without formal abdication. Monarchy abolished; the second republic established, with socialist backing. Niceto Alcala Zamora was president until 1936, when Manuel Azaña was chosen.

In July 1936, the army in Morocco revolted against the government and General Francisco Franco led the troops into Spain. The revolution succeeded by Feb. 1939, when Azaña resigned. Franco became chief of state.

Alphonso XIII died in Rome Feb. 28, 1941, aged 54. His property and citizenship had been restored.

A law restoring the monarchy was approved in a 1947 referendum. Prince Juan Carlos, b. 1938, grandson of Alphonso XIII, was designated by Franco and the Cortes (Parliament) in 1969 as future king and chief of state. Franco died Nov. 20, 1975; Juan Carlos proclaimed king, Nov. 22.

Leaders in the South American Wars of Liberation

Here are some of the heroes in the early 19th century struggles of South American nations for independence:

Francisco Antonio Gabriel Miranda (1750-1816), Venezuelan. Served with the French in the American Revolution, commanded parts of French Revolutionary armies in the Netherlands. In 1806 attempted to start a revolt in Venezuela and failed. In 1810 became dictator until Britain and U.S. withdrew support. Overthrown, died 1816 in a Spanish prison.

Jose Francisco de San Martin (1778-1850), born in Argentina. Served in Spanish campaigns in Europe and Africa, 1789-1811. Joined Argentina's independence movement, 1812; invaded Chile, 1817; with Gen. Bernardo O'Higgins (1778-1842) defeated the Spaniards at Chacabuco, 1817. O'Higgins was named Liberator, became first director of Chile, 1817-23. In 1821 San Martin occupied Lima and Callao, Peru, and became protector of Peru.

Simon Bolivar (1783-1830), greatest leader of South American liberation from Spain, born to an aristocratic family in Venezuela. First served under Miranda, 1812; captured Caracas, named Liberator, 1813. Forced out by civil strife, led campaign that captured Bogota, 1814. In 1817 was again in control of Venezuela, named dictator. Organized Nueva Granada with help of Gen. Francisco de Paula Santander (1792-1840). By joining Nueva Granada, Venezuela, and the area that is now Panama and Ecuador, the republic of Colombia was formed, with Bolivar president. After numerous setbacks he decisively defeated the Spaniards, June 24, 1821. In May 1822, Gen. Antonio Jose de Sucre (1795-1830), Bolivar's lieutenant, took Quito. Bolivar conferred with San Martin, who resigned as protector of Peru and withdrew from politics. With a new army of Colombians and Peruvians Bolivar defeated the Spaniards in 1824 and cleared Peru. De Sucre organized Charcas (Upper Peru) as Republica Bolivar (now Bolivia), acted as president in place of Bolivar, who wrote its constitution. De Sucre defeated the Spanish faction of Peru at Ayacucho, Dec. 19, 1824. Continued civil strife led to the breakup of the Colombian federation. Santander turned against Bolivar, but was defeated and banished. In 1828 Bolivar gave up the presidency he had held precariously for 14 years. He became ill from tuberculosis and died Dec. 17, 1830.

Rulers of Russia; Leaders of the USSR and Russian Federation

First ruler to consolidate Slavic tribes was Rurik, leader of the Russians who established himself at Novgorod, AD 862. He and his immediate successors had Scandinavian affiliations. They moved to Kiev after 972 and ruled as Dukes of Kiev. In 988 Vladimir was converted and adopted the Byzantine Greek Orthodox service, later modified by Slav influences. Important as organizer and lawgiver was Yaroslav, 1019-1054, whose daughters married kings of Norway, Hungary, and France. His grandson, Vladimir II (Monomakh), 1113-1125, was progenitor of several rulers, but in 1169 Andrew Bogolubski overthrew Kiev and began the line known as Grand Dukes of Vladimir.

Of the Grand Dukes of Vladimir, Alexander Nevsky, 1246-1263, had a son, Daniel, first to be called Duke of Muscovy (Moscow), who ruled 1294-1303. His successors became Grand Dukes of Muscovy. After Dmitri III Donskoi defeated the Tatars in 1380, they also became Grand Dukes of all Russia. Independence of the Tatars and considerable territorial expansion were achieved under Ivan III, 1462-1505.

Tsars of Muscovy—Ivan III was referred to in church ritual as Tsar. He married Sofia, niece of the last Byzantine emperor. His successor, Basil III, died in 1533 when Basil's son Ivan was only 3. He became Ivan IV, "the Terrible"; crowned 1547 as Tsar of all the Russias, ruled until 1584. Under the weak rule of his son, Feodor I, 1584-1598, Boris Godunov had control. The dynasty died, and after years of tribal strife and intervention by Polish and Swedish armies, the Russians united under 17-year-old Michael Romanov, distantly related to the first wife of Ivan IV. He ruled 1613-1645 and established the Romanov line. Fourth ruler after Michael was Peter I.

Tsars, or Emperors, of Russia (Romanovs)—Peter I, 1682-1725, known as Peter the Great, took title of Emperor in 1721. His successors and dates of accession were: Catherine, his widow, 1725; Peter II, his grandson, 1727; Anne, Duchess of Courland, 1730, daughter of Peter the Great's brother, Tsar Ivan V; Ivan VI, 1740, great-grandson of Ivan V, child, kept in prison and murdered 1764; Elizabeth, daughter of Peter I, 1741; Peter III, grandson of Peter I, 1761, deposed 1762 for his consort, Catherine II, former princess of Anhalt Zerbst (Germany) who is known as Catherine the Great; Paul I, her son, 1796, killed 1801; Alexander I, son of Paul, 1801, defeated Napoleon; Nicholas I, his brother, 1825; Alexander II, son of Nicholas, 1855, assassinated 1881 by terrorists; Alex-

ander III, son, 1881. Nicholas II, son, 1894-1917, last Tsar of Russia, was forced to abdicate by the Revolution that followed losses to Germany in WWI. The Tsar, the Empress, the Tsarevich (Crown Prince), and the Tsar's 4 daughters were murdered by the Bolsheviks in Yekaterinburg, July 16, 1918.

Provisional Government—Prince Georgi Lvov and Alexander Kerensky, premiers, 1917.

Union of Soviet Socialist Republics

Bolshevik Revolution, Nov. 7, 1917, displaced Kerensky; council of People's Commissars formed, Lenin (Vladimir Ilyich Ulyanov), premier. Lenin died Jan. 21, 1924. Aleksei Rykov (executed 1938) and V. M. Molotov held the office, but actual ruler was Joseph Stalin (Joseph Vissarionovich Djugashvili), general secretary of the Central Committee of the Communist Party. Stalin became president of the Council of Ministers (premier) May 7, 1941, died Mar. 5, 1953. Succeeded by Georgi M. Malenkov, as head of the Council and premier, and Nikita S. Khrushchev, first secretary of the Central Committee. Malenkov resigned Feb. 8, 1955, became deputy premier, was dropped July 3, 1957. Marshal Nikolai A. Bulganin became premier Feb. 8, 1955; was demoted and Khrushchev became premier Mar. 27, 1958.

Khrushchev was ousted Oct. 14-15, 1964, replaced by Leonid I. Brezhnev as first secretary of the party and by Aleksei N. Kosygin as premier. On June 16, 1977, Brezhnev also took office as president. He died Nov. 10, 1982; 2 days later the Central Committee elected former KGB head Yuri V. Andropov president. Andropov died Feb. 9, 1984; on Feb. 13, Konstantin U. Chernenko chosen by Central Committee as its general secretary. Chernenko died Mar. 10, 1985; on Mar. 11, he was succeeded as general secretary by Mikhail Gorbachev, who replaced Andrei Gromyko as president on Oct. 1, 1988. Gorbachev resigned Dec. 25, 1991, and the Soviet Union officially disbanded the next day. A loose Commonwealth of Independent States, made up of most of the 15 former Soviet constituent republics, was created.

Post-Soviet Russia

After adopting a degree of sovereignty, the Russian Republic had held elections in June 1991. Boris Yeltsin was sworn in, July 10, 1991, as Russia's first elected president. After the Dec. 1991 dissolution of the Soviet Union, Yeltsin remained as president of Russia (officially Russian Federation).

Governments of China

(Until 221 BC and frequently thereafter, China was not a unified state. Where dynastic dates overlap, the rulers or events referred to appeared in different areas of China.)

Hsia	c1994 BC	-	c1523 BC	Tang (a golden age of Chinese culture;	
Shang	c1523	-	c1028	capital: Xian) . . . 618 - 906	
Western Chou	c1027	-	770	Five Dynasties (Yellow River basin) . . . 902 - 960	
Eastern Chou	770	-	256	Ten Kingdoms (southern China) . . . 907 - 979	
Warring States	403	-	222	Liao (Khitan Mongols; capital at site of	
Ch'in (first unified empire)	221	-	206	Beijing) . . . 947 - 1125	
Han	202 BC	-	AD 220	Sung . . . 960 - 1279	
Western Han (expanded Chinese state				Northern Sung (reunified central and	
beyond the Yellow and Yangtze River				southern China) . . . 960 - 1126	
valleys)	202 BC	-	AD 9	Western Hsai (non-Chinese rulers in	
Hsin (Wang Mang, usurper)	AD 9	-	AD 23	northwest) . . . 990 - 1227	
Eastern Han (expanded Chinese state				Chin (Tatars; drove Sung out of central	
into Indochina and Turkestan)	25	-	220	China) . . . 1115 - 1234	
Three Kingdoms (Wei, Shu, Wu)	220	-	265	Yuan (Mongols; Kublai Khan est. capital	
Chin (western)	265	-	317	at site of Beijing, c. 1264) . . . 1271 - 1368	
(eastern)	317	-	420	Ming (China reunified under Chinese rule;	
Northern Dynasties (followed several short-				capital: Nanjing, then Beijing in 1420) . . 1368 - 1644	
lived governments by Turks, Mongols, etc.)	386	-	581	Ch'ing (Manchus, descendents of Tatars) 1644 - 1911	
Southern Dynasties (capital: Nanjing)	420	-	589	Republic (disunity; provincial rulers, warlords) 1912 - 1949	
Sui (reunified China)	581	-	618	People's Republic of China . . . 1949 - —	

Leaders of China Since 1949

Mao Zedong	Chairman, Central People's Administrative Council, Communist Party (CPC), 1949-1976	Zhao Ziyang	Premier, 1980-1988; CPC General Secretary, 1987-1989
Zhou Enlai	Premier, foreign minister, 1949-1976	Hu Yaobang	CPC Chairman, 1981-1982; CPC General Secretary 1982-1987
Deng Xiaoping	Vice Premier, 1952-1966, 1973-1976, 1977-1980; "paramount leader," 1978-1997	Li Xiannian	President, 1983-1988
Liu Shaoqi	President, 1959-1969	Yang Shangkun	President, 1988-1993
Hua Guofeng	Premier, 1976-1980; CPC Chairman, 1976-1981	Li Peng	Premier, 1988-
		Jiang Zemin	CPC General Secretary, 1989- ; President, 1993-

WORLD EXPLORATION AND GEOGRAPHY

Early Explorers of the Western Hemisphere

Source: Reviewed by Paul B. Frederic, PhD, prof. of Geography, Univ. of Maine at Farmington; Susan Skomal, PhD, editor, *Anthropology Newsletter*, American Anthropological Assn.

The first people to discover the New World, or western hemisphere, are believed to have traveled across a "land bridge" from Siberia to Alaska, an isthmus since broken by the Bering Strait. From Alaska, these early Native Americans could then have spread through North, Central, and South America. This theory is supported by archaeological and genetic evidence; a theory that the first Americans came by sea, landing in S. America, is no longer seriously considered by archaeologists, partly because of a lack of evidence of such early habitation in Polynesia.

In 1997, archaeologists confirmed evidence of human habitation in the Americas at least 12,500 years ago at a site in Chile known as Monte Verde. This site predates a previously discovered site in Clovis, NM, by over 1,000 years. The findings raise questions concerning the migratory path of these peoples, since a glacier covered most of N. America for a period between 20,000 years ago and some time after 13,000 years ago. The migration may have taken place in an ice-free corridor or along the west coast, perhaps in vessels along the water. An alternative possibility is that people had spread to S. America before the coming of the ice.

At first, these early Americans were hunters, using flint weapons and tools. In Mexico, about 7000-6000 BC, they founded farming cultures and developed crops, such as corn and squash. Eventually they created complex civilizations—the Olmec, Toltec, Aztec, Maya, and, in S. America, the Inca. Carbon-14 tests show that humans lived about 8000 BC near what are now Front Royal, VA; Kanawha, WV; and Dutchess Quarry, NY. The Hopewell Culture, based on farming, flourished about 1000 BC; remains of it are seen today in large mounds in Ohio and other states.

Norsemen (Norwegian Vikings sailing out of Iceland and Greenland), led by Leif Ericson, are credited by most scholars with having been the first Europeans to reach America, with at least 5 voyages occurring about AD 1000 to areas they called Helluland, Markland, and Vinland—possibly what are known today as Labrador, Nova Scotia or Newfoundland, and New England. L'Anse aux Meadows, on the northern tip of Newfoundland, is the only documented settlement.

Sustained contact between the hemispheres began with the first voyage of Christopher Columbus (born Cristoforo Colombo, c 1451, in or near Genoa, Italy). Columbus made trips to the New World while sailing for the Spanish.

His earliest voyage began when he left Palos, Spain, Aug. 3, 1492, with 88 (est.) men and landed at San Salvador (Watling Islands, Bahamas) on Oct. 12, 1492. His fleet consisted of 3 vessels—the *Niña*, *Pinta*, and *Santa María*. Stops were also made on Cuba and Hispaniola. A 2d expedition left Cadiz, Spain, Sept. 25, 1493, with 17 ships and 1,500 men, and reached the Lesser Antilles Nov. 3.

His 3d voyage brought him from Sanlucar, Spain (May 30, 1498, with 6 ships), to the north coast of S. America. A few years later a 4th voyage reached the mainland of Central America, after leaving Cadiz, Spain, May 9, 1502. Columbus died in 1506 convinced he had reached Asia by sailing west from Europe.

In N. America, John and Sebastian Cabot, Italian explorers sailing for the English, reached Newfoundland and possibly Nova Scotia in 1497. John's 2d voyage (1498), intended to produce a new trade route to Asia, resulted in the loss of his entire fleet.

During this period exploration in the western hemisphere was dominated by Spain and Portugal. In 1497 and 1499 Amerigo Vespucci (whom the Americas are named for), an Italian explorer sailing for the Spanish, passed along the N and E coasts of S America. He was the first to argue that the newly discovered lands were a continent other than Asia. The basic geography of the hemisphere became well understood by the early 1800s, as explorers from many countries helped fill in the map.

Year	Explorer	Nationality (employer, if different)	Area reached or explored
c1000	Leif Ericson	Norse	Newfoundland
1492-1502	Christopher Columbus	Italian (Spanish)	West Indies, S. and C. America
1497	John and Sebastian Cabot	Italian (English)	Atlantic Canada
1497-99	Amerigo Vespucci	Italian (Spanish)	E and N Coast of S. America
1499	Alonso de Ojeda	Spanish	N South American coast, Venezuela
1500, Feb.	Vicente Yañez Pinzon	Spanish	S. American coast, Amazon R.
1500, Apr.	Pedro Alvarez Cabral	Portuguese	Brazil
1500-02	Gaspar Corte-Real	Portuguese	Labrador
1501	Rodrigo de Bastidas	Spanish	Central America
1513	Vasco Nunez de Balboa	Spanish	Panama, Pacific Ocean
1513	Juan Ponce de Leon	Spanish	Florida, Yucatán Peninsula
1515	Juan de Solis	Spanish	Río de la Plata
1519	Alonso de Pineda	Spanish	Mouth of Mississippi R.
1519	Hernando Cortes	Spanish	Mexico
1519-20	Ferdinand Magellan	Portuguese (Spanish)	Straits of Magellan, Tierra del Fuego
1524	Giovanni da Verrazano	Italian (French)	Atlantic coast, inc. New York harbor
1528	Cabeza de Vaca	Spanish	Texas coast and interior
1532	Francisco Pizarro	Spanish	Peru
1534	Jacques Cartier	French	Canada, Gulf of St. Lawrence
1536	Pedro de Mendoza	Spanish	Buenos Aires
1539	Francisco de Ulloa	Spanish	California coast
1539-41	Hernando de Soto	Spanish	Mississippi R., near Memphis
1539	Marcos de Niza	Italian (Spanish)	SW United States
1540	Francisco de Coronado	Spanish	SW United States
1540	Hernando Alarcon	Spanish	Colorado R.
1540	Garcia de L. Cardenas	Spanish	Colorado, Grand Canyon
1541	Francisco de Orellana	Spanish	Amazon R.
1542	Juan Rodriguez Cabrillo	Portuguese (Spanish)	W Mexico, San Diego harbor
1565	Pedro Menéndez de Aviles	Spanish	St. Augustine, FL
1576	Sir Martin Frobisher	English	Frobisher's Bay, Canada
1577-80	Sir Francis Drake	English	California coast
1582	Antonio de Espejo	Spanish	Southwest U.S. (New Mexico)
1584	Amadas & Barlow (for Raleigh)	English	Virginia
1585-87	Sir Walter Raleigh's men	English	Roanoke Isl., NC
1595	Sir Walter Raleigh	English	Orinoco R.
1603-09	Samuel de Champlain	French	Canadian interior, Lake Champlain
1607	Capt. John Smith	English	Atlantic coast
1609-10	Henry Hudson	English (Dutch)	Hudson R., Hudson Bay
1634	Jean Nicolet	French	Lake Michigan, Wisconsin
1673	Jacques Marquette, Louis Jolliet	French	Mississippi R., S to Arkansas
1682	Robert Cavelier, sieur de La Salle	French	Mississippi R., S to Gulf of Mexico
1727-29	Vitus Bering	Danish (Russian)	Bering Strait and Alaska
1789	Sir Alexander Mackenzie	Canadian	NW Canada
1804-06	Meriwether Lewis and William Clark	American	Missouri R., Rocky Mts., Columbia R.

Arctic Exploration

Early Explorers

1587 — John Davis (Eng.). Davis Strait to Sanderson's Hope, 72°12′ N.

1596 — Willem Barents and Jacob van Heemskerck (Holland). Discovered Bear Isl., touched NW tip of Spitsbergen, 79°49′ N, rounded Novaya Zemlya, wintered at Ice Haven.

1607 — Henry Hudson (Eng.). North along Greenland's E coast to Cape Hold-with-Hope, 73°30′, then N of Spitsbergen to 80°23′. Returning he explored Hudson's Touches (Jan Mayen).

1616 — William Baffin and Robert Bylot (Eng.). Baffin Bay to Smith Sound.

1728 — Vitus Bering (Russ.). Proved Asia and America are separated, by sailing through strait that now bears his name.

1733-40 — Great Northern Expedition (Russ.). Surveyed Siberian Arctic coast.

1741 — Vitus Bering (Russ.). Sighted Alaska from sea, named Mount St. Elias. His lieutenant, Chirikof, explored coast.

1771 — Samuel Hearne (Hudson's Bay Co.). Overland from Prince of Wales Fort (Churchill) on Hudson Bay to mouth of Coppermine R.

1778 — James Cook (Brit.). Through Bering Strait to Icy Cape, AK, and North Cape, Siberia.

1789 — Alexander Mackenzie (North West Co., Brit.). Montreal to mouth of Mackenzie River.

1806 — William Scoresby (Brit.). N of Spitsbergen to 81°30′.

1820-23 — Ferdinand von Wrangel (Russ.). Completed a survey of Siberian Arctic coast. His exploration joined that of James Cook at North Cape, confirming separation of the continents.

1878-79 — (Nils) Adolf Erik Nordenskjöld (Swed.). The first to navigate the Northeast Passage—an ocean route connecting Europe's North Sea, along the Arctic coast of Asia and through the Bering Sea, to the Pacific Ocean.

1881 — The U.S. steamer *Jeannette*, led by Lt. Cmdr. George W. DeLong, was trapped in ice and crushed, June 1881. DeLong and 11 others died; 12 survived.

1888 — Fridtjof Nansen (Nor.) crossed Greenland's icecap.

1893-96 — Nansen in *Fram* drifted from New Siberian Isls. to Spitsbergen; tried polar dash in 1895, reached Franz Josef Land, 86°14′ N.

1897 — Salomon A. Andrée (Switz.) and 2 others started in balloon from Spitsbergen, July 11, to drift across pole to U.S., and disappeared. More than 33 yrs. later, Aug. 6, 1930, their frozen bodies were found on White Isl., 82°57′ N, 29°52′ E.

1903-6 — Roald Amundsen (Nor.) first sailed the Northwest Passage—an ocean route linking the Atlantic Ocean to the Pacific via Canada's marine waterways.

North Pole Exploration

Robert E. Peary explored Greenland's coast, 1891-92; tried for North Pole, 1893. In 1900 he reached N limit of Greenland and 83°50′ N; in 1902 he reached 84°06′ N; in 1906 he went from Ellesmere Isl. to 87°06′ N. He sailed in the *Roosevelt*, July 1908, to winter off Cape Sheridan, Grant Land. The dash for the North Pole began Mar. 1 from Cape Columbia, Ellesmere Isl. Peary reportedly reached the pole, 90° N, Apr. 6, 1909; however, subsequent research suggests that he may have miscalculated and fallen short of his goal by c. 30-60 mi. Peary had several supporting groups carrying supplies until the last group turned back at 87°47′ N. Peary, Matthew Henson, and 4 Eskimos proceeded with dog teams and sleds. They were said to have crossed the pole several times, then built an igloo there and remained 36 hours. Started south, Apr. 7 at 4 PM, for Cape Columbia.

1914 — Donald MacMillan (U.S.). Northwest, 200 mi, from Axel Heiberg Isl. to seek Peary's Crocker Land.

1915-17 — Vihjalmur Stefansson (Can.). Discovered Borden, Brock, Meighen, and Lougheed Isls.

1918-20 — Amundsen sailed the Northeast Passage.

1925 — Amundsen and Lincoln Ellsworth (U.S.) reached 87°44′ N in attempt to fly to North Pole from Spitsbergen.

1926 — Richard E. Byrd and Floyd Bennett (U.S.) reputedly flew over North Pole, May 9. (Claim to have reached the Pole is in dispute, however.)

1926 — Amundsen, Ellsworth, and Umberto Nobile (It.) flew from Spitsbergen over North Pole May 12, to Teller, AK, in dirigible *Norge*.

1928 — Nobile crossed North Pole in airship, May 24; crashed, May 25. Amundsen died attempting a rescue.

North Pole Exploration Records

On Aug. 3, 1958, the *Nautilus,* under Comdr. William R. Anderson, became the first ship to cross the North Pole beneath the Arctic ice.

In Aug. 1960, the nuclear-powered U.S. submarine *Seadragon* (Comdr. George P. Steele 2d) made the first E-W underwater transit through the Northwest Passage. Traveling submerged for the most part, it took 6 days to make the 850-mi trek from Baffin Bay to the Beaufort Sea.

On Aug. 16, 1977, the Soviet nuclear icebreaker *Arktika* reached the North Pole, becoming the first surface ship to break through the Arctic ice pack.

On Apr. 30, 1978, Naomi Uemura (Jap.) became the first person to reach the North Pole alone. Traveling by dog sled during the 54-day, 600-mi trek over the frozen Arctic, Uemura survived attacks by a marauding polar bear.

In Apr. 1982, Sir Ranulph Fiennes and Charles Burton, Brit. explorers, reached the North Pole and became the first to circle the earth from pole to pole. They had reached the South Pole 16 months earlier. The 52,000-mi trek took 3 years, involved 23 people, and cost an estimated $18 mil. The expedition was also the first to travel down the Scott Glacier and the first to journey up the Yukon and through the Northwest Passage in a single season.

On May 2, 1986, 6 Amer. and Can. explorers reached the North Pole assisted only by dogs. They became the first to reach the pole without aerial logistics support since Robert E. Peary planted a flag there in 1909. The explorers, Amer. Will Steger, Paul Schurke, Anne Bancroft, and Geoff Carroll, and Can. Brent Boddy and Richard Weber, completed the 500-mi journey in 56 days.

On June 15, 1995, Weber and Russ. Mikhail Malakhov became the first pair to make it to the pole and back without any mechanical assistance. The 940-mi trip, made entirely on skis, took 121 days.

Antarctic Exploration

Antarctica has been approached since 1773-75, when Capt. James Cook (Brit.) reached 71° 10′ S. Many sea and landmarks bear names of early explorers. Fabian von Bellingshausen (Russ.) discovered Peter I and Alexander I Isls., 1819-21. Nathaniel Palmer (U.S.) traveled throughout Palmer Peninsula, 60° W, 1820, without realizing that this was a continent. Capt. John Davis (U.S.) made the first known landing on the continent on Feb. 7, 1821. Later, in 1823, James Weddell (Brit.) found Weddell Sea, 74° 15′ S, the southernmost point that had been reached.

First to announce existence of the continent of Antarctica was Charles Wilkes (U.S.), who followed the coast for 1,500 mi, 1840. Adelie Coast, 140° E, was found by Dumont d'Urville (Fr.), 1840. Ross Ice Shelf was found by James Clark Ross (Brit.), 1841-42.

1895 — Leonard Kristensen (Nor.) landed a party on the coast of Victoria Land. They were the first ashore on the main continental mass. C. E. Borchgrevink, a member of that party, returned in 1899 with a Brit. expedition, first to winter on Antarctica.

1902-4 — Robert F. Scott (Brit.) explored Edward VII Peninsula. He reached 82° 17′ S, 146° 33′ E from McMurdo Sound.

1908-9 — Ernest Shackleton (Brit.) introduced the use of Manchurian ponies in Antarctic sledging. He reached 88° 23′ S, discovering a route on to the plateau by way of the Beardmore Glacier and pioneering the way to the pole.

1911 — Roald Amundsen (Nor.) with 4 men and dog teams reached the South Pole, Dec. 14.

(continued)

Antarctic Exploration (continued)

1912 — Scott reached the pole from Ross Isl., Jan. 18, with 4 companions. None of Scott's party survived. Their bodies and expedition notes were found, Nov. 12.

1928 — First person to use an airplane over Antarctica was Sir George Hubert Wilkins (Austral.).

1929 — Richard E. Byrd (U.S.) established Little America on Bay of Whales. On 1,600-mi airplane flight begun Nov. 28, he crossed South Pole, Nov. 29, with 3 others.

1934-35 — Byrd led 2d expedition to Little America, explored 450,000 sq mi, wintered alone at weather station, 80°08′ S.

1934-37 — John Rymill led British Graham Land expedition; discovered Palmer Penin. is part of mainland.

1935 — Lincoln Ellsworth (U.S.) flew S along E Coast of Palmer Penin., then crossed continent to Little America, making 4 landings on unprepared terrain in bad weather.

1939-41 — U.S. Antarctic Service Expedition built West Base on Ross Ice Shelf under Paul Siple, and East Base on Palmer Peninsula under Richard Black. U.S. Navy plane flights discovered about 150,000 sq mi of new land.

1940 — Byrd charted most of coast between Ross Sea and Palmer Penin.

1946-47 — U.S. Navy undertook Operation Highjump, commanded by Byrd, included 13 ships and 4,000 men. Airplanes photomapped coastline and penetrated beyond pole.

1946-48 — Ronne Antarctic Research Expedition Comdr., Finn Ronne, USNR, determined the Antarctic to be only one continent with no strait between Weddell Sea and Ross Sea; explored 250,000 sq mi of land by flights to 79° S. Mrs. Ronne and Mrs. H. Darlington were the first women to winter on Antarctica.

1955-57 — U.S. Navy's Operation Deep Freeze led by Adm. Byrd. Supporting U.S. scientific efforts for the International Geophysical Year (IGY), the operation was commanded by Rear Adm. George Dufek. It established 5 coastal stations fronting the Indian, Pacific, and Atlantic oceans and also 3 interior stations; explored more than 1,000,000 sq mi in Wilkes Land.

1957-58 — During the IGY, July 1957 through Dec. 1958, scientists from 12 countries conducted ambitious programs of Antarctic research at a network of some 60 stations on the continent.

Dr. Vivian E. Fuchs led a 12-person Trans-Antarctic Expedition on the first land crossing of Antarctica. Starting from the Weddell Sea, they reached Scott Station, Mar. 2, 1958, after traveling 2,158 mi in 98 days.

1958 — A group of 5 U.S. scientists led by Edward C. Thiel, seismologist, moving by tractor from Ellsworth Station on Weddell Sea, identified a huge mountain range, 5,000 ft above the ice sheet and 9,000 ft above sea level. The range, originally seen by a Navy plane, was named the Dufek Massif, for Rear Adm. George Dufek.

1959 — 12 nations — Argentina, Australia, Belgium, Chile, France, Japan, New Zealand, Norway, South Africa, the Soviet Union, the United Kingdom, and the U.S. — signed a treaty suspending any territorial claims for 30 yrs. and reserving the continent, S of 60° S, for research.

1961-62 — Scientists discovered the Bentley Trench, running from Ross Ice Shelf into Marie Byrd Land, near the end of the Ellsworth Mts., toward the Weddell Sea.

1962 — First nuclear power plant began operation at McMurdo Sound.

1963 — On Feb. 22, a U.S. plane made the longest nonstop flight ever in the South Pole area, covering 3,600 mi in 10 hr. The flight was from McMurdo Station S past the pole to Shackleton Mts., SE to the "Area of Inaccessibility," and back to McMurdo Station.

1964 — A Brit. survey team was landed by helicopter on Cook Island, the first recorded visit since 1775.

1964 — New Zealanders mapped the mountain area from Cape Adare W some 400 mi to Pennell Glacier.

1985 — Igor A. Zotikov, a Russian researcher, discovered sediments in the Ross Ice Shelf that seem to support the continental drift theory. Research by the Ocean Drilling Project off the Queen Maud Land coast indicated that the ice sheets of E Antarctica are 37 million yrs. old.

1989 — Victoria Murden and Shirley Metz became both the first women and the first Americans to reach the South Pole overland when they arrived with 9 others on Jan. 17, 1989. The 51-day trek on skis covered 740 mi.

1991 — 24 nations approved a protocol to the 1959 Antarctica Treaty, Oct. 4. New conservation provisions, including banning oil and other mineral exploration for 50 yrs.

1995 — On Dec. 22, a Norwegian, Borge Ousland, reached the South Pole in the fastest time on skis: 44 days.

1996-97 — Ousland became 1st person to traverse Antarctica alone; reached South Pole Dec. 19, 1996; traveled 1,675 mi in 64 days, ending Jan. 18, 1997.

Volcanoes

Sources: *Volcanoes of the World*, Geoscience Press; Global Volcanism Network, Smithsonian Institution

Nearly 75% of the world's approximately 540 historically active volcanoes—those that were active and could become active again—lie within the Ring of Fire, a zone running along the W coast of the Americas from Chile to Alaska, down the E coast of Asia from Siberia to New Guinea, and continuing to New Zealand. About 20% of these volcanoes are in Indonesia. Other prominent groupings are in Japan, the Aleutian Islands, and Central America. Almost all active regions are at the boundaries of the large moving plates that constitute the earth's surface. The Ring of Fire marks the boundary between the plates underlying the Pacific Ocean and those underlying the surrounding continents. Other active regions, such as the Mediterranean and Iceland, are on plate boundaries.

Notable Volcanic Eruptions

Approximately 7,000 years ago, Mazama, a 9,900-ft volcano in S Oregon, erupted violently, ejecting ash and lava. The ash spread over the entire northwestern U.S. and as far away as Saskatchewan, Can. During the eruption, the top of the mountain collapsed, leaving a caldera 6 mi across and about a half mile deep, which filled with rainwater to form what is now called Crater Lake.

In AD 79, Vesuvio, or Vesuvius, a 4,190-ft volcano overlooking Naples Bay, became active after several centuries of apparent quiescence. On Aug. 24 of that year, a heated mud and ash flow swept down the mountain, engulfing the cities of Pompeii, Herculaneum, and Stabiae with debris more than 60 ft deep. About 10% of the population of the 3 towns were killed.

Some of the largest eruptions in recent centuries have been in Indonesia. In 1883, an eruption similar to the Mazama eruption occurred on the island of Krakatau. At least 2,000 people died in pyroclastic flows on Aug. 26. The next day, the 2,640-ft peak of the volcano collapsed to 1,000 ft below sea level, leaving only a small portion of the island standing above the sea and killing more than 3,000 people. A tsunami (tidal wave) generated by the collapse then killed more than 31,000 people in nearby Java and Sumatra and eventually reached England. Ash from the eruption colored sunsets around the world for 2 years. A similar, but even more powerful, eruption had taken place 68 years earlier at Mt. Tambora on the Indonesian island of Sumbawa.

The Soufriere Hills volcano on the Caribbean Island of Montserrat began a series of eruptions in July 1995. Eruptions continued during 1997, with much of the island evacuated. At least 19 people were killed in an eruption on June 25, 1997.

Date	Volcano	Estimated Deaths	Date	Volcano	Estimated Deaths
Aug. 24, AD 79	Mt. Vesuvius, Italy	16,000	May 21, 1792	Mt. Unzen, Japan	14,500
1586	Kelut, Java, Indon.	10,000	Apr. 10-12, 1815	Mt. Tambora, Sumbawa, Indon.	92,000[1]
Dec. 15, 1631	Mt. Vesuvius, Italy	4,000	Aug. 26-28, 1883	Krakatau, Indon.	36,000
Aug. 12, 1772	Mt. Papandayan, Java, Indon.	3,000	Apr. 24, 1902	Santa María, Guatemala	1,000[2]
June 8, 1783	Laki, Iceland	9,350	May 8, 1902	Mt. Pelée, Martinique	28,000

Date	Volcano	Estimated Deaths
Jan. 30, 1911	Mt. Taal, Phil.	1,400
May 19, 1919	Mt. Kelud, Java, Indon.	5,000
Jan. 17-21, 1951	Mt. Lamington, New Guinea	3,000
May 18, 1980	Mt. St. Helens, U.S.	57

Date	Volcano	Estimated Deaths
Mar. 28, 1982	El Chichon, Mex.	1,880
Nov. 13, 1985	Nevado del Ruiz, Colombia	23,000
Aug. 21, 1986	Lake Nyos, Cameroon	1,700
June 15, 1991	Mt. Pinatubo, Luzon, Phil.	800

(1) Of these, 10,000 were directly related to the eruption; an additional 82,000 were the result of starvation and disease brought on by the event. (2) An additional 3,000 deaths due to a malaria outbreak are sometimes attributed to the eruption.

Notable Active Volcanoes

Active volcanoes display a wide range of activity. In this table, years are given for last display of eruptive activity, as of June 1997. An eruption may be defined as the explosive ejection of new or old fragmental material, escape of liquid lava, or both. Volcanoes are listed by height; however, height does not reflect magnitude of a volcano's force.

Name (latest eruption)	Location	Height (ft)
Africa		
Mt. Cameroon (1982)	Cameroon	13,435
Nyiragogo (1994)	Congo	11,400
Nyamuragira (1994)	Congo	10,028
Ol Doinyo Lengai (1996)	Tanzania	9,469
Karthala (1991)	Comoros	8,000
Piton de la Fournaise (1992)	Réunion Isl.	5,981
Lake Nyos (1986)	Cameroon	3,011
Erta-Ale (1995)	Ethiopia	1,650
Antarctica		
Erebus (1995)	Ross Isl.	12,450
Deception Island (1970)	S. Shetland Isl.	1,890
Asia-Oceania		
Kliuchevskoi (1997)	Kamchatka, Russia	15,863
Kerinci (1970)	Sumatra, Indon.	12,467
Fuji (1708)	Honshu, Japan	12,388
Tolbachik (1876)	Kamchatka, Russia	12,080
Semeru (1997)	Java, Indon.	12,060
Slamet (1989)	Java, Indon.	11,247
Raung (1997)	Java, Indon.	10,932
Sheveluch (1997)	Kamchatka, Russia	10,771
On-take (1980)	Honshu, Japan	10,049
Mayon (1993)	Luzon, Phil.	9,991
Merapi (1997)	Java, Indon.	9,550
Bezymianny (1997)	Kamchatka, Russia	9,455
Ruapehu (1995)	New Zealand	9,175
Baitoushan (1702)	China/Korea	9,003
Asama (1990)	Honshu, Japan	8,300
Niigata Yake-yama (1989)	Honshu, Japan	8,111
Canlaon (1993)	Negros, Phil.	8,070
Alaid (1986)	Kuril Isl., Russia	7,662
Ulawun (1993)	Papua New Guinea	7,532
Ngauruhoe (1977)	New Zealand	7,515
Chokai (1974)	Honshu, Japan	7,300
Galunggung (1984)	Java, Indon.	7,113
Azuma (1977)	Honshu, Japan	6,700
Bagana (1993)	Papua New Guinea	6,558
Sangeang Api (1988)	Lesser Sunda Isl., Indon.	6,351
Nasu (1963)	Honshu, Japan	6,210
Tiatia (1981)	Kuril Isl., Russia	6,013
Soputan (1996)	Celebes, Indon.	5,994
Bandai (1888)	Honshu, Japan	5,968
Manam (1997)	Papua New Guinea	5,928
Karangetang (1995)	Sangihe, Indon.	5,853
Kelud (1990)	Java, Indon.	5,679
Gamalama (1993)	Halmahera, Indon.	5,627
Kirishima (1992)	Kyushu, Japan	5,577
Akita Komaga-take (1996)	Honshu, Japan	5,449
Gamkonora (1987)	Halmahera, Indon.	5,364
Pinatubo (1995)	Luzon, Phil.	5,249
Aso (1995)	Kyushu, Japan	5,223
Lokon-Empung (1992)	Celebes, Indon.	5,187
Bulusan (1995)	Luzon, Phil.	5,115
Sarychev Peak (1989)	Kuril Isl., Russia	4,960
Karkar (1979)	Papua New Guinea	4,920
Me-Akan (1997)	Hokkaido, Japan	4,918
Karymsky (1996)	Kamchatka, Russia	4,875
Lopevi (1982)	Vanuatu	4,755
Akita-Yakeyama (1997)	Japan	4,482
Unzen (1996)	Kyushu, Japan	4,462
Ambrym (1991)	Vanuatu	4,376
Langila (1997)	Papua New Guinea	4,363
Awu (1992)	Sangihe Isl., Indon.	4,350
Sakura-jima (1997)	Kyushu, Japan	3,665
Krakatau (1995)	Indonesia	2,667
Suwanose-jima (1997)	Kyushu, Japan	2,621
Oshima (1990)	Izu Isl., Japan	2,550
Usu (1982)	Hokkaido, Japan	2,400
Rabaul (1997)	Papua New Guinea	2,257
Pagan (1993)	N. Mariana Isl.	1,870
Yasur (1997)	Tanna Island, Vanuatu	1,184
White Island (1995)	New Zealand	1,053
Taal (1977)	Luzon, Phil.	984

Name (latest eruption)	Location	Height (ft)
Central America—Caribbean		
Acatenango (1972)	Guatemala	12,992
Fuego (1987)	Guatemala	12,582
Tacana (1986)	Guatemala	12,400
Santa María (1993)	Guatemala	12,375
Irazú (1965)	Costa Rica	11,260
Turrialba (1866)	Costa Rica	10,958
Póas (1994)	Costa Rica	8,884
Pacaya (1996)	Guatemala	8,373
San Miguel (1986)	El Salvador	6,994
Rincón de la Vieja (1995)	Costa Rica	6,286
San Cristobal (1997)	Nicaragua	5,725
Arenal (1997)	Costa Rica	5,436
Concepcion (1986)	Nicaragua	5,106
Pelee (1932)	Martinique	4,583
Momotombo (1905)	Nicaragua	4,199
Soufrière St. Vincent (1979)	St. Vincent	4,048
Soufriere Hills (1997)	Montserrat	3,091
Masaya (1996)	Nicaragua	2,083
South America		
Llullaillaco (1877)	Chile	22,057
Guallatiri (1960)	Chile	19,882
Láscar (1995)	Chile	19,652
Cotopaxi (1940)	Ecuador	19,347
El Misti (1870?)	Peru	19,101
Tupungatito (1986)	Chile	18,504
Ruiz (1991)	Colombia	17,716
Sangay (1996)	Ecuador	17,159
Irruptuncu (1995)	Chile	16,939
Guagua Pichincha (1993)	Ecuador	15,696
Purace (1977)	Colombia	15,601
Galeras (1993)	Colombia	14,028
Llaima (1995)	Chile	10,253
Villarrica (1997)	Chile	9,340
Cerro Hudson (1991)	Chile	8,580
Fernandina (1995)	Galapagos Isls., Ecuador	4,905
Mid-Pacific		
Mauna Loa (1984)	Hawaii, HI	13,680
Kilauea (1997)	Hawaii, HI	4,009
Mid-Atlantic Ridge		
Beerenberg (1985)	Jan Mayen Isl., Norway	7,470
Hekla (1991)	Iceland	4,892
Krafla (1984)	Iceland	2,145
Grímsvötn (1996)	Iceland	1,725
Europe		
Etna (1997)	Italy	10,990
Stromboli (1997)	Italy	3,038
Santorini (1950)	Greece	1,850
North America		
Citlaltepetl (Orizaba) (1687)	Mexico	18,700
Popocatépetl (1997)	Mexico	17,930
Rainier (1894?)	Washington	14,410
Wrangell (1907?)	Alaska	14,163
Shasta (1786)	California	14,162
Colima (1994)	Mexico	14,003
Redoubt (1990)	Alaska	10,197
Iliamna (1953)	Alaska	10,016
Shishaldin (1995)	Aleutian Isl., AK	9,387
Pavlof (1997)	Alaska	8,264
St. Helens (1991)	Washington	8,363
Veniaminof (1995)	Alaska	8,225
El Chichon (1982)	Mexico	7,300
Novarupta (Katmai) (1912)	Alaska	6,715
Makushin (1987)	Aleutian Isl., AK	6,680
Great Sitkin (1974)	Aleutian Isl., AK	5,710
Cleveland (1994)	Aleutian Isl., AK	5,675
Gareloi (1989)	Aleutian Isl., AK	5,334
Korovin (1987)	Aleutian Isl., AK	4,852
Akutan (1992)	Aleutian Isl., AK	4,275
Kiska (1990)	Aleutian Isl., AK	4,275
Augustine (1986)	Alaska	3,999
Okmok (1997)	Aleutian Isl., AK	3,520
Seguam (1993)	Aleutian Isl., AK	3,458

Mountains

Height of Mount Everest

Mt. Everest was considered 29,002 ft when Edmund Hillary and Tenzing Norgay scaled it in 1953. This triangulation figure had been accepted since 1850. In 1954 the Surveyor General of the Republic of India set the height at 29,028 ft, plus or minus 10 ft because of snow; this figure is used below. The National Geographic Society accepts it, but many mountaineering groups still use 29,002 ft.

In 1987, new calculations based on satellite measurements suggested that the Himalayan peak K-2 rose 29,064 ft above sea level and that Mt. Everest is 800 ft higher. The National Geographic Society kept to the figure of 29,028 ft.

United States, Canada, Mexico

Name	Place	Height (ft)	Name	Place	Height (ft)	Name	Place	Height (ft)
McKinley	AK	20,320	Alverstone	AK-Yukon	14,565	Shavano	CO	14,229
Logan	Yukon	19,850	Browne Tower	AK	14,530	Belford	CO	14,197
Citlaltepetl (Orizaba)	Mexico	18,700	Whitney	CA	14,494	Princeton	CO	14,197
St. Elias	AK-Yukon	18,008	Elbert	CO	14,433	Crestone Needle	CO	14,197
Popocatépetl	Mexico	17,930	Massive	CO	14,421	Yale	CO	14,196
Foraker	AK	17,400	Harvard	CO	14,420	Bross	CO	14,172
Iztaccihuatl	Mexico	17,343	Rainier	WA	14,410	Kit Carson	CO	14,165
Lucania	Yukon	17,147	University Peak	AK	14,410	Wrangell	AK	14,163
King	Yukon	16,971	Williamson	CA	14,375	Shasta	CA	14,162
Steele	Yukon	16,644	La Plata Peak	CO	14,361	El Diente Peak	CO	14,159
Bona	AK	16,550	Blanca Peak	CO	14,345	Point Success	WA	14,158
Blackburn	AK	16,390	Uncompahgre Peak	CO	14,309	Maroon Peak	CO	14,156
Kennedy	AK	16,286	Crestone Peak	CO	14,294	Tabeguache	CO	14,155
Sanford	AK	16,237	Lincoln	CO	14,286	Oxford	CO	14,153
Vancouver	AK-Yukon	15,979	Grays Peak	CO	14,270	Sill	CA	14,153
South Buttress	AK	15,885	Antero	CO	14,269	Sneffels	CO	14,150
Wood	Yukon	15,885	Torreys Peak	CO	14,267	Democrat	CO	14,148
Churchill	AK	15,638	Castle Peak	CO	14,265	Capitol Peak	CO	14,130
Fairweather	AK-BC	15,300	Quandary Peak	CO	14,265	Liberty Cap	WA	14,112
Zinantecatl (Toluca)	Mexico	15,016	Evans	CO	14,264	Pikes Peak	CO	14,110
Hubbard	AK-Yukon	15,015	Longs Peak	CO	14,255	Snowmass	CO	14,092
Bear	AK	14,831	McArthur	Yukon	14,253	Russell	CA	14,088
Walsh	Yukon	14,780	Wilson	CO	14,246	Eolus	CO	14,083
East Buttress	AK	14,730	White Mt. Peak	CA	14,246	Windom	CO	14,082
Matlalcueyetl	Mexico	14,636	North Palisade	CA	14,242	Columbia	CO	14,073
Hunter	AK	14,573	Cameron	CO	14,238	Augusta	AK	14,070

South America

Peak, country	Height (ft)	Peak, country	Height (ft)	Peak, country	Height (ft)
Aconcagua, Argentina	22,834	Coropuna, Peru	21,083	Solo, Argentina	20,492
Ojos del Salado, Arg.-Chile	22,572	Laudo, Argentina	20,997	Polleras, Argentina	20,456
Bonete, Argentina	22,546	Ancohuma, Bolivia	20,958	Pular, Chile	20,423
Tupungato, Argentina-Chile	22,310	Ausangate, Peru	20,945	Chani, Argentina	20,341
Pissis, Argentina	22,241	Toro, Argentina-Chile	20,932	Aucanquilcha, Chile	20,295
Mercedario, Argentina	22,211	Illampu, Bolivia	20,873	Juncal, Argentina-Chile	20,276
Huascaran, Peru	22,205	Tres Cruces, Argentina-Chile	20,853	Negro, Argentina	20,184
Llullaillaco, Argentina-Chile	22,057	Huandoy, Peru	20,852	Quela, Argentina	20,128
El Libertador, Argentina	22,047	Parinacota, Bolivia-Chile	20,768	Condoriri, Bolivia	20,095
Cachi, Argentina	22,047	Tortolas, Argentina-Chile	20,745	Palermo, Argentina	20,079
Incahuasi, Argentina-Chile	21,720	Ampato, Peru	20,702	Solimana, Peru	20,068
Yerupaja, Peru	21,709	El Condor, Argentina	20,669	San Juan, Argentina-Chile	20,049
Galan, Argentina	21,654	Salcantay, Peru	20,574	Sierra Nevada, Arg.-Chile	20,023
El Muerto, Argentina-Chile	21,457	Chimborazo, Ecuador	20,561	Antofalla, Argentina	20,013
Sajama, Bolivia	21,391	Huancarhuas, Peru	20,531	Marmolejo, Argentina-Chile	20,013
Nacimiento, Argentina	21,302	Famatina, Argentina	20,505	Chachani, Peru	19,931
Illimani, Bolivia	21,201	Pumasillo, Peru	20,492		

The highest point in the West Indies is in the Dominican Republic, Pico Duarte (10,417 ft).

Africa

Peak, country/island	Height (ft)	Peak, country/island	Height (ft)	Peak, country/island	Height (ft)
Kilimanjaro, Tanzania	19,340	Meru, Tanzania	14,979	Guna, Ethiopia	13,881
Kenya, Kenya	17,058	Karisimbi, Congo-Rwanda	14,787	Gughe, Ethiopia	13,780
Margherita Pk., Uganda-Congo	16,763	Elgon, Kenya-Uganda	14,178	Toubkal, Morocco	13,661
Ras Dashan, Ethiopia	15,158	Batu, Ethiopia	14,131	Cameroon, Cameroon	13,435

Australia, New Zealand, SE Asian Islands

Peak, country/island	Height (ft)	Peak, country/island	Height (ft)	Peak, country/island	Height (ft)
Jaya, New Guinea	16,500	Kinabalu, Malaysia	13,455	Teide, Canary Isls.	12,198
Trikora, New Guinea	15,585	Kerinci, Sumatra, Indon.	12,467	Semeru, Java, Indon.	12,060
Mandala, New Guinea	15,420				
Wilhelm, New Guinea	14,793	Cook, New Zealand	12,349	Kosciusko, Australia	7,310

Europe

Alps

Peak, country	Height (ft)
Mont Blanc, Fr.-It.	15,771
Monte Rosa (highest peak of group), Switz.	15,203
Dom, Switz.	14,911
Liskamm, It., Switz.	14,852
Weisshorn, Switz.	14,780
Taschhorn, Switz.	14,733
Matterhorn, It., Switz.	14,690
Dent Blanche, Switz.	14,293
Nadelhorn, Switz.	14,196
Grand Combin, Switz.	14,154
Lenzpitze, Switz.	14,088
Finsteraarhorn, Switz.	14,022
Castor, Switz.	13,865
Zinalrothorn, Switz.	13,849
Hohberghorn, Switz.	13,842
Alphubel, Switz.	13,799
Rimpfischhom, Switz.	13,776
Aletschorn, Switz.	13,763
Strahlhorn, Switz.	13,747
Dent D'Herens, Switz.	13,686
Breithorn, It., Switz.	13,665
Bishorn, Switz.	13,645
Jungfrau, Switz.	13,642
Ecrins, Fr.	13,461
Monch, Switz.	13,448
Pollux, Switz.	13,422
Schreckhorn, Switz.	13,379
Ober Gabelhorn, Switz.	13,330
Gran Paradiso, It.	13,323
Bernina, It., Switz.	13,284
Fiescherhorn, Switz.	13,283
Grunhorn, Switz.	13,266
Lauteraarhorn, Switz.	13,261
Durrenhorn, Switz.	13,238
Allalinhorn, Switz.	13,213
Weissmies, Switz.	13,199
Lagginhorn, Switz.	13,156
Zupo, Switz.	13,120
Fletschhorn, Switz.	13,110
Adlerhorn, Switz.	13,081
Gletscherhorn, Switz.	13,068
Schalihorn, Switz.	13,040
Scerscen, Switz.	13,028
Eiger, Switz.	13,025
Jagerhorn, Switz.	13,024
Rottalhorn, Switz.	13,022

Pyrenees

Peak, country	Height (ft)
Aneto, Sp.	11,168
Posets, Sp.	11,073
Perdido, Sp.	11,007
Vignemale, Fr.-Sp.	10,820
Long, Sp.	10,479
Estats, Sp.	10,304
Montcalm, Sp.	10,105

Caucasus (Europe-Asia)

Peak, country	Height (ft)
Elbrus, Russia	18,841
Shkhara, Georgia	17,064
Dykh Tau, Russia	17,054
Kashtan Tau, Russia	16,877
Janqi, Georgia	16,565
Kazbek, Georgia	16,558

Asia (Mainland)

Peak	Place	Height (ft)
Everest	Nepal-Tibet	29,028
K2 (Godwin Austen)	Kashmir	28,250
Kanchenjunga	India-Nepal	28,208
Lhotse I (Everest)	Nepal-Tibet	27,923
Makalu I	Nepal-Tibet	27,824
Lhotse II (Everest)	Nepal-Tibet	27,560
Dhaulagiri	Nepal	26,810
Manaslu I	Nepal	26,760
Cho Oyu	Nepal-Tibet	26,750
Nanga Parbat	Kashmir	26,660
Annapurna I	Nepal	26,504
Gasherbrum	Kashmir	26,470
Broad	Kashmir	26,400
Gosainthan	Tibet	26,287
Annapurna II	Nepal	26,041
Gyachung Kang	Nepal-Tibet	25,910
Disteghil Sar	Kashmir	25,868
Himalchuli	Nepal	25,801
Nuptse (Everest)	Nepal-Tibet	25,726
Masherbrum	Kashmir	25,660
Nanda Devi	India	25,645
Rakaposhi	Kashmir	25,550
Kamet	India-Tibet	25,447
Namcha Barwa	Tibet	25,445
Gurla Mandhata	Tibet	25,355
Ulugh Muz Tagh	Xinjiang-Tibet	25,340
Kungur	Xinjiang	25,325
Tirich Mir	Pakistan	25,230
Makalu II	Nepal-Tibet	25,120
Minya Konka	China	24,900
Kula Gangri	Bhutan-Tibet	24,784
Changtzu (Everest)	Nepal-Tibet	24,780
Muz Tagh Ata	Xinjiang	24,757
Skyang Kangri	Kashmir	24,750
Communism Peak	Tajikistan	24,590
Jongsang Peak	India-Nepal	24,472
Jengish Chokusu	Xinjiang-Kyrgyzstan	24,406
Sia Kangri	Kashmir	24,350
Haramosh Peak	Pakistan	24,270
Istoro Nal	Pakistan	24,240
Tent Peak	India-Nepal	24,165
Chomo Lhari	Bhutan-Tibet	24,040
Chamlang	Nepal	24,012
Kabru	India-Nepal	24,002
Alung Gangri	Tibet	24,000
Baltoro Kangri	Kashmir	23,990
Mussu Shan	Xinjiang	23,890
Mana	India	23,860
Baruntse	Nepal	23,688
Nepal Peak	India-Nepal	23,500
Amne Machin	China	23,490
Gauri Sankar	Nepal-Tibet	23,440
Badrinath	India	23,420
Nunkun	Kashmir	23,410
Lenin Peak	Tajikistan	23,405
Pyramid	India-Nepal	23,400
Api	Nepal	23,399
Pauhunri	India-Tibet	23,385
Trisul	India	23,360
Kangto	India-Tibet	23,260
Nyenchhe Thanglha	Tibet	23,255
Trisuli	India	23,210
Pumori	Nepal-Tibet	23,190
Dunagiri	India	23,184
Lombo Kangra	Tibet	23,165
Saipal	Nepal	23,100
Macha Pucchare	Nepal	22,958
Numbar	Nepal	22,817
Kanjiroba	Nepal	22,580
Ama Dablam	Nepal	22,350
Cho Polu	Nepal	22,093
Lingtren	Nepal-Tibet	21,972
Khumbutse	Nepal-Tibet	21,785
Hlako Gangri	Tibet	21,266
Mt. Grosvenor	China	21,190
Thagchhab Gangri	Tibet	20,970
Damavand	Iran	18,606
Ararat	Turkey	16,804

Antarctica

Peak	Height (ft)
Vinson Massif	16,864
Tyree	16,290
Shinn	15,750
Gardner	15,375
Epperly	15,100
Kirkpatrick	14,855
Elizabeth	14,698
Markham	14,290
Bell	14,117
Mackellar	14,098
Anderson	13,957
Bentley	13,934
Kaplan	13,878
Andrew Jackson	13,750
Sidley	13,720
Ostenso	13,710
Minto	13,668
Miller	13,650
Long Gables	13,620
Dickerson	13,517
Giovinetto	13,412
Wade	13,400
Fisher	13,386
Fridtjof Nansen	13,350
Wexler	13,202
Lister	13,200
Shear	13,100
Odishaw	13,008
Donaldson	12,894
Ray	12,808
Sellery	12,779
Waterman	12,730
Anne	12,703
Press	12,566
Falla	12,549
Rucker	12,520
Goldthwait	12,510
Morris	12,500
Erebus	12,450
Campbell	12,434
Don Pedro Christophersen	12,355
Lysaght	12,326
Huggins	12,247
Sabine	12,200
Astor	12,175
Mohl	12,172
Frankes	12,064
Jones	12,040
Gjelsvik	12,008
Coman	12,000

Some Notable U.S. Mountains

Name	Place	Height (ft)
Gannett Peak	WY	13,804
Grand Teton	WY	13,766
Kings	UT	13,528
Cloud	WY	13,175
Wheeler	NM	13,161
Boundary	NV	13,140
Granite	MT	12,799
Borah	ID	12,662
Humphreys	AZ	12,633
Adams	WA	12,307
San Gorgonio	CA	11,502
Hood	OR	11,239
Lassen	CA	10,457
Granite	CA	10,321
Guadalupe	TX	8,749
Olympus	WA	7,965
Harney	SD	7,242
Mitchell	NC	6,684
Clingmans Dome	NC-TN	6,643
Washington	NH	6,288
Rogers	VA	5,729
Marcy	NY	5,344
Katahdin	ME	5,268
Spruce Knob	WV	4,862
Mansfield	VT	4,393
Black Mountain	KY	4,145

Important Islands and Their Areas

Source: Bureau of the Census, U.S. Dept. of Commerce; National Atlas Information Services, Natural Resources Canada; World Almanac research

Figure in parentheses shows rank among the world's 10 largest individual islands. Because some islands have not been surveyed accurately, some areas shown are estimates. Figures are for total land area in square miles. Some "islands" listed are island groups.

Arctic Ocean

Canadian

Axel Heiberg	16,671
Baffin (5)	195,928
Banks	27,038
Bathurst	6,194
Devon	21,331
Ellesmere (10)	75,767
Melville	16,274
Prince of Wales	12,872
Somerset	9,570
Southampton	15,913
Victoria (9)	83,897

Norwegian

Svalbard	23,957
Nordaustlandet	5,410
Spitsbergen	15,060

Russian

Franz Josef Land	8,000
Novaya Zemlya (2 isls.)	31,730
Wrangel	2,800

Atlantic Ocean

Anticosti, Canada	3,066
Ascension, UK.	34
Azores, Portugal	868
Faial	67
Sao Miguel	291
Bahamas	5,382
Bermuda Isls., UK	20
Bioko Isl., Equatorial Guinea	785
Block Isl., RI	10
Canary Isls., Spain	2,807
Fuerteventura	668
Gran Canaria	592
Tenerife	795
Cape Breton, Canada	3,981
Cape Verde Isls.	1,557
Faroe Isls., Denmark	540
Falkland Isls., UK.	4,700
Fernando de Noronha Archipelago, Brazil	7
Greenland, Denmark (1).	840,000
Iceland	39,699
Long Island, NY.	1,320
Madeira Isls. , Portugal.	306
Marajo, Brazil	15,444
Martha's Vineyard, MA.	89
Mount Desert, ME	104
Nantucket, MA.	45
Newfoundland, Canada	42,031
Prince Edward, Canada	2,185
St. Helena, UK.	47
South Georgia, UK.	1,450
Tierra del Fuego, Chile and Argentina	18,800
Tristan da Cunha, UK.	40

British Isles

Great Britain, mainland (8)	84,200
Channel Isls.	75
Guernsey	24
Jersey	45
Sark	2
Hebrides	2,744
Ireland	32,589
Irish Republic	27,137
Northern Ireland	5,452
Isle of Man	227
Orkney Isls.	390
Scilly Isls.	6
Shetland Isls.	567
Skye	670
Wight	147

Baltic Sea

Aland Isls., Finland	590
Bornholm, Denmark	227
Gotland, Sweden	1,159

Caribbean Sea

Antigua	108
Aruba, Netherlands	75
Barbados	166
Cuba	42,804
Isle of Youth	926
Curaçao, Netherlands	171
Dominica	290
Guadeloupe, France	687
Hispaniola, Haiti and Dominican Republic	29,389
Jamaica	4,244
Martinique, France	436
Puerto Rico, U.S.	3,339
Tobago	116
Trinidad	1,864
Virgin Isls., UK.	59
Virgin Isls., U.S.	134

Indian Ocean

Andaman Isls., India	2,500
Madagascar (4)	226,658
Mauritius	720
Pemba, Tanzania	380
Réunion, France	970
Seychelles	176
Sri Lanka	25,332
Zanzibar, Tanzania	640

Persian Gulf

Bahrain	217

Mediterranean Sea

Balearic Isls., Spain	1,927
Corfu, Greece	229
Corsica, France	3,369
Crete, Greece	3,189
Cyprus	3,572
Elba, Italy	86
Euboea, Greece	1,411
Malta	95
Rhodes, Greece	540
Sardinia, Italy	9,301
Sicily, Italy	9,926

Pacific Ocean

Aleutian Isls., AK.	6,912
Adak	275
Amchitka	116
Attu	350
Kanaga	142
Kiska	106
Tanaga	195
Umnak	686
Unalaska	1,051
Unimak	1,571
Canton, Kiribati*	4
Christmas, Kiribati*	94
Clipperton, France	2
Diomede, Big, Russia.	11
Diomede, Little, U.S.	3
Easter Isl., Chile	69
Fiji	7,056
Vanua Levu	2,242
Viti Levu	4,109
Funafuti, Tuvalu*	2
Galapagos Isls., Ecuador	3,043
Guadalcanal, Solomon Isls.	2,180
Guam, U.S.	210
Hainan, China	13,000
Hawaiian Isls., HI	6,423
Hawaii	4,028
Oahu	600
Hong Kong, China	31
Japan	145,850
Hokkaido	30,144
Honshu (7)	87,805
Iwo Jima	8
Kyushu	14,114
Okinawa	459
Shikoku	7,049
Kodiak, AK	3,465
Marquesas Isls., France	492
Marshall Isls.	70
Bikini*	2
Micronesia	271
Nauru	8
New Caledonia, France	6,530
New Zealand	104,454
Chatham Isls.	372
North	44,702
South	58,384
Stewart	674
Northern Mariana Isls., U.S.	179
Palau	188
Philippines	115,860
Leyte	2,787
Luzon	40,880
Mindanao	36,775
Mindoro	3,790
Negros	4,907
Palawan	4,554
Panay	4,446
Samar	5,050
Sakhalin, Russia	29,500
Samoa Isls.	1,177
American Samoa, U.S.	77
Tutuila	55
Samoa	1,093
Savaii	659
Upolu	432
Santa Catalina, CA	75
Tahiti, France	402
Taiwan	13,969
Quemoy	56
Tasmania, Australia	26,178
Tonga Isls.	290
Vancouver, Canada	12,079
Vanuatu	4,707

East Indies

Bali, Indonesia	2,171
Borneo, Indonesia-Malaysia-Brunei (3)	280,100
Celebes, Indonesia	69,000
Java, Indonesia	48,900
Madura, Indonesia	2,113
Moluccas, Indonesia	32,307
New Britain, Papua New Guinea	14,093
New Guinea, Indonesia-Papua New Guinea (2)	306,000
New Ireland, Papua New Guinea	3,707
Sumatra, Indonesia (6)	165,000
Timor, Indonesia	13,094

* Atolls: Bikini (lagoon area, 230 sq mi; land area, 2 sq mi); Canton (lagoon, 20 sq mi; land, 4 sq mi), Kiribati; Christmas (lagoon, 140 sq mi; land, 94 sq mi), Kiribati; Funafuti (lagoon, 84 sq mi; land, 2 sq mi), Tuvalu.

Australia, sometimes called an island, is classified as a continent.

Islands in minor waters: Manhattan (22 sq mi), Staten (59 sq mi), and Governors (173 acres), all in New York Harbor, U.S.; Isle Royale (209 sq mi), Lake Superior, U.S.; Manitoulin (1,068 sq mi), Lake Huron, Canada; Pinang (110 sq mi), Strait of Malacca, Malaysia; Singapore (239 sq mi), Singapore Strait, Singapore.

Areas and Average Depths of Oceans, Seas, and Gulfs

Geographers and mapmakers recognize 4 major bodies of water: the Pacific, the Atlantic, the Indian, and the Arctic oceans. The Atlantic and Pacific oceans are considered divided at the equator into the N and S Atlantic and the N and S Pacific. The Arctic Ocean is the name for waters N of the continental landmasses in the region of the Arctic Circle.

	Area (sq mi)	Avg. depth (ft)		Area (sq mi)	Avg. depth (ft)
Pacific Ocean	64,186,300	12,925	Hudson Bay	281,900	305
Atlantic Ocean	33,420,000	11,730	East China Sea	256,600	620
Indian Ocean	28,350,500	12,598	Andaman Sea	218,100	3,667
Arctic Ocean	5,105,700	3,407	Black Sea	196,100	3,906
South China Sea	1,148,500	4,802	Red Sea	174,900	1,764
Caribbean Sea	971,400	8,448	North Sea	164,900	308
Mediterranean Sea	969,100	4,926	Baltic Sea	147,500	180
Bering Sea	873,000	4,893	Yellow Sea	113,500	121
Gulf of Mexico	582,100	5,297	Persian Gulf	88,800	328
Sea of Okhotsk	537,500	3,192	Gulf of California	59,100	2,375
Sea of Japan	391,100	5,468			

Principal Ocean Depths

Source: Defense Mapping Agency, Hydrographic/Topographic Center, U.S. Dept. of Defense

Name of area	Location (lat.)	Location (long.)	Depth (meters)	Depth (fathoms)	Depth (ft)
Pacific Ocean					
Mariana Trench	11°22′ N	142°36′ E	10,924	5,973	35,840
Tonga Trench	23°16′ S	174°44′ W	10,800	5,906	35,433
Philippine Trench	10°38′ N	126°36′ E	10,057	5,499	32,995
Kermadec Trench	31°53′ S	177°21′ W	10,047	5,494	32,963
Bonin Trench	24°30′ N	143°24′ E	9,994	5,464	32,788
Kuril Trench	44°15′ N	150°34′ E	9,750	5,331	31,988
Izu Trench	31°05′ N	142°10′ E	9,695	5,301	31,808
New Britain Trench	06°19′ S	153°45′ E	8,940	4,888	29,331
Yap Trench	08°33′ N	138°02′ E	8,527	4,663	27,976
Japan Trench	36°08′ N	142°43′ E	8,412	4,600	27,599
Peru-Chile Trench	23°18′ S	71°14′ W	8,064	4,409	26,457
Palau Trench	07°52′ N	134°56′ E	8,054	4,404	26,424
Aleutian Trench	50°51′ N	177°11′ E	7,679	4,199	25,194
New Hebrides Trench	20°36′ S	168°37′ E	7,570	4,139	24,836
North Ryukyu Trench	24°00′ N	126°48′ E	7,181	3,927	23,560
Mid. America Trench	14°02′ N	93°39′ W	6,662	3,643	21,857
Atlantic Ocean					
Puerto Rico Trench	19°55′ N	65°27′ W	8,605	4,705	28,232
S Sandwich Trench	55°42′ S	25°56′ E	8,325	4,552	27,313
Romanche Gap	0°13′ S	18°26′ W	7,728	4,226	25,354
Cayman Trench	19°12′ N	80°00′ W	7,535	4,120	24,721
Brazil Basin	09°10′ S	23°02′ W	6,119	3,346	20,076
Indian Ocean					
Java Trench	10°19′ S	109°58′ E	7,125	3,896	23,376
Ob' Trench	09°45′ S	67°18′ E	6,874	3,759	22,553
Diamantina Trench	35°50′ S	105°14′ E	6,602	3,610	21,660
Vema Trench	09°08′ S	67°15′ E	6,402	3,501	21,004
Agulhas Basin	45°20′ S	26°50′ E	6,195	3,387	20,325
Arctic Ocean					
Eurasia Basin	82°23′ N	19°31′ E	5,450	2,980	17,881
Mediterranean Sea					
Ionian Basin	36°32′ N	21°06′ E	5,150	2,816	16,896

Note: Greater depths have been reported in some areas but are not officially confirmed by research vessels.

Latitude, Longitude, and Altitude of World Cities

Source: Defense Mapping Agency, Hydrographic/Topographic Center, U.S. Dept. of Defense

City	Lat. °	′	Long. °	′	Alt. (ft)	City	Lat. °	′	Long. °	′	Alt. (ft)
Athens, Greece	37	59 N	23	44 E	300	Mexico City, Mexico	19	24 N	99	09 W	7,347
Bangkok, Thailand	13	45 N	100	31 E	0	Moscow, Russia	55	45 N	37	35 E	394
Beijing, China	39	56 N	116	24 E	600	New Delhi, India	28	36 N	77	12 E	770
Berlin, Germany	52	31 N	13	25 E	110	Panama City, Panama	08	58 N	79	32 W	0
Bogotá, Colombia	04	36 N	74	05 W	8,660	Paris, France	48	52 N	02	20 E	300
Bombay (Mumbai), India	18	58 N	72	50 E	27	Quito, Ecuador	00	13 S	78	30 W	9,222
Buenos Aires, Argentina	34	36 S	58	28 W	0	Rio de Janeiro, Brazil	22	43 S	43	13 W	30
Cairo, Egypt	30	03 N	31	15 E	381	Rome, Italy	41	53 N	12	30 E	95
Jakarta, Indonesia	06	10 S	106	48 E	26	Santiago, Chile	33	27 S	70	40 W	4,921
Jerusalem, Israel	31	46 N	35	14 E	2,500	Seoul, South Korea	37	34 N	127	00 E	34
Johannesburg, So. Afr.	26	12 S	28	05 E	5,740	Sydney, Australia	33	53 S	151	12 E	25
Kathmandu, Nepal	27	43 N	85	19 E	4,500	Tehran, Iran	35	40 N	51	26 E	3,937
Kiev, Ukraine	50	26 N	30	31 E	587	Tokyo, Japan	35	42 N	139	46 E	30
London, UK (Greenwich)	51	30 N	00	00	245	Tripoli, Libya	32	54 N	13	11 E	0
Manila, Philippines	14	35 N	120	00 E	0	Warsaw, Poland	52	15 N	21	00 E	360
Mecca, Saudi Arabia	21	27 N	39	49 E	6,562	Wellington, New Zealand	41	18 S	174	47 E	0

Latitude, Longitude, and Altitude of U.S. and Canadian Cities

Source: U.S. geographic positions were provided by National Oceanic Atmospheric Administration, U.S. Dept. of Commerce. U.S. altitudes were provided by Geological Survey, U.S. Dept. of the Interior. Canadian geographic positions were provided by the Geodetic Survey of Canada, Natural Resources Canada. Canadian altitudes were provided by National Atlas Information Service, Natural Resources Canada.

Altitudes are measured in feet at the downtown business areas of U.S. cities or at the city hall of Canadian cities, except where (a) indicates that measurements were made at the tower of a major airport located within the city.

City	Lat. N °	'	"	Long. W °	'	"	Alt. (ft)
Abilene, TX	32	27	05	99	43	51	1,710
Akron, OH	41	05	00	81	30	44	874
Albany, NY	42	39	01	73	45	01	20
Albuquerque, NM	35	05	01	106	39	05	4,945
Alert, N.W.T.	82	29	50	62	21	15	95
Allentown, PA	40	36	11	75	28	06	255
Amarillo, TX	35	12	27	101	50	04	3,685
Anchorage, AK	61	10	00	149	59	00	118
Ann Arbor, MI	42	16	59	83	44	52	880
Asheville, NC	35	35	42	82	33	26	1,985
Ashland, KY	38	28	36	82	38	23	536
Atlanta, GA	33	45	10	84	23	37	1,050
Atlantic City, NJ	39	21	32	74	25	53	10
Augusta, GA	33	28	20	81	58	00	143
Augusta, ME	44	18	53	69	46	29	45
Austin, TX	30	16	09	97	44	37	505
Bakersfield, CA	35	22	31	119	01	18	400
Baltimore, MD	39	17	26	76	36	45	20
Bangor, ME	44	48	13	68	46	18	20
Baton Rouge, LA	30	26	58	91	11	00	57
Battle Creek, MI	42	18	58	85	10	48	820
Bay City, MI	43	36	04	83	53	15	595
Beaumont, TX	30	05	20	94	06	09	20
Belleville, Ont.	44	09	42	77	23	11	257
Bellingham, WA	48	45	34	122	28	36	60
Berkeley, CA	37	52	10	122	16	17	40
Billings, MT	45	47	00	108	30	04	3,120
Biloxi, MS	30	23	48	88	53	00	20
Binghamton, NY	42	06	03	75	54	47	865
Birmingham, AL	33	31	01	86	48	36	600
Bismarck, ND	46	48	23	100	47	17	1,674
Bloomington, IL	40	28	58	88	59	36	800
Boise, ID	43	37	07	116	11	58	2,704
Boston, MA	42	21	24	71	03	25	21
Bowling Green, KY	36	59	41	86	26	33	510
Brandon, Man.	49	51	00	99	57	00	1,343(a)
Brantford, Ont.	43	08	34	80	15	39	705(a)
Brattleboro, VT	42	51	06	72	33	48	300
Bridgeport, CT	41	10	49	73	11	22	10
Brockton, MA	42	05	02	71	01	25	130
Buffalo, NY	42	52	52	78	52	21	585
Burlington, Ont.	43	19	33	79	47	57	284
Burlington, VT	44	28	34	73	12	46	110
Butte, MT	46	01	06	112	32	11	5,765
Calgary, Alta.	51	02	46	114	03	24	3,427
Cambridge, MA	42	22	01	71	06	22	20
Canton, OH	40	47	50	81	22	37	1,030
Carson City, NV	39	10	00	119	46	00	4,680
Cedar Rapids, IA	41	58	01	91	39	53	730
Central Islip, NY	40	47	24	73	12	00	80
Champaign, IL	40	07	05	88	14	48	740
Charleston, SC	32	46	35	79	55	53	9
Charleston, WV	38	21	01	81	37	52	601
Charlotte, NC	35	13	44	80	50	45	720
Charlottetown, P.E.I.	46	14	07	63	07	49	31
Chattanooga, TN	35	02	41	85	18	32	675
Cheyenne, WY	41	08	09	104	49	07	6,100
Chicago, IL	41	52	28	87	38	22	595
Churchill, Man.	58	45	15	94	10	00	94(a)
Cincinnati, OH	39	06	07	84	30	35	550
Cleveland, OH	41	29	51	81	41	50	660
Colorado Springs, CO	38	50	07	104	49	16	5,980
Columbia, MO	38	57	03	92	19	46	730
Columbia, SC	34	00	02	81	02	00	190
Columbus, GA	32	28	07	84	59	24	265
Columbus, OH	39	57	47	83	00	17	780
Concord, NH	43	12	22	71	32	25	290
Corpus Christi, TX	27	47	51	97	23	45	35
Dallas, TX	32	47	09	96	47	37	435
Dartmouth, N.S.	44	39	50	63	34	08	24
Dawson, Yukon	64	03	30	139	26	00	1,050
Dayton, OH	39	45	32	84	11	43	574
Daytona Beach, FL	29	12	44	81	01	10	7
Decatur, IL	39	50	42	88	56	47	682
Denver, CO	39	44	58	104	59	22	5,280
Des Moines, IA	41	35	14	93	37	00	803
Detroit, MI	42	19	48	83	02	57	585

City	Lat. N °	'	"	Long. W °	'	"	Alt. (ft)
Dodge City, KS	37	45	17	100	01	09	2,480
Dubuque, IA	42	29	55	90	40	08	620
Duluth, MN	46	46	56	92	06	24	610
Durham, NC	36	00	00	78	54	45	405
Eau Claire, WI	44	48	31	91	29	49	790
Edmonton, Alta.	53	32	43	113	29	21	2,186
Elizabeth, NJ	40	39	43	74	12	59	21
El Paso, TX	31	45	36	106	29	11	3,695
Enid, OK	36	23	40	97	52	35	1,240
Erie, PA	42	07	15	80	04	57	685
Eugene, OR	44	03	16	123	05	30	422
Eureka, CA	40	48	08	124	09	46	45
Evansville, IN	37	58	20	87	34	21	385
Fairbanks, AK	64	48	00	147	51	00	448
Fall River, MA	41	42	06	71	09	18	40
Fargo, ND	46	52	30	96	47	18	900
Flagstaff, AZ	35	11	36	111	39	06	6,900
Flint, MI	43	00	50	83	41	33	750
Ft. Smith, AR	35	23	10	94	25	36	440
Ft. Wayne, IN	41	04	21	85	08	26	790
Ft. Worth, TX	32	44	55	97	19	44	670
Fredericton, N.B.	45	57	47	66	38	38	29
Fresno, CA	36	44	12	119	47	11	285
Gadsden, AL	34	00	57	86	00	41	555
Gainesville, FL	29	38	56	82	19	19	175
Gallup, NM	35	31	30	108	44	30	6,540
Galveston, TX	29	18	10	94	47	43	5
Gary, IN	41	36	12	87	20	19	590
Grand Junction, CO	39	04	06	108	33	54	4,590
Grand Rapids, MI	42	58	03	85	40	13	610
Great Falls, MT	47	29	33	111	18	23	3,340
Green Bay, WI	44	30	48	88	00	50	590
Greensboro, NC	36	04	17	79	47	25	839
Greenville, SC	34	50	50	82	24	01	966
Guelph, Ont.	43	32	35	80	14	54	1,065
Gulfport, MS	30	22	04	89	05	36	20
Halifax, N.S.	44	38	54	63	34	30	60
Hamilton, OH	39	23	59	84	33	47	600
Hamilton, Ont.	43	15	20	79	52	30	329
Harrisburg, PA	40	15	43	76	52	59	365
Hartford, CT	41	46	12	72	40	49	40
Helena, MT	46	35	33	112	02	24	4,155
Hilo, HI	19	43	30	155	05	24	40
Honolulu, HI	21	18	22	157	51	35	21
Houston, TX	29	45	26	95	21	37	40
Hull, Que.	45	25	42	75	42	41	185
Huntsville, AL	34	44	18	86	35	19	640
Indianapolis, IN	39	46	07	86	09	46	710
Iowa City, IA	41	39	37	91	31	53	685
Jackson, MI	42	14	43	84	24	22	940
Jackson, MS	32	17	56	90	11	06	298
Jacksonville, FL	30	19	44	81	39	42	20
Jersey City, NJ	40	43	50	74	03	56	20
Johnstown, PA	40	19	35	78	55	03	1,185
Joplin, MO	37	05	26	94	30	00	990
Juneau, AK	58	18	12	134	24	30	50
Kalamazoo, MI	42	17	29	85	35	14	755
Kansas City, KS	39	07	04	94	38	24	750
Kansas City, MO	39	04	56	94	35	20	750
Kenosha, WI	42	35	43	87	50	11	610
Key West, FL	24	33	30	81	48	12	5
Kingston, Ont.	44	13	53	76	28	48	264
Kitchener, Ont.	43	26	58	80	29	12	1,100
Knoxville, TN	35	57	39	83	55	07	890
Lafayette, IN	40	25	11	86	53	39	550
Lancaster, PA	40	02	25	76	18	29	355
Lansing, MI	42	44	01	84	33	15	830
Laredo, TX	27	30	22	99	30	30	440
La Salle, Que.	45	25	30	73	39	30	110
Las Vegas, NV	36	10	20	115	08	37	2,030
Laval, Que.	45	33	05	73	44	42	142
Lawrence, MA	42	42	16	71	10	08	65
Lethbridge, Alta.	49	41	38	112	49	58	2,985

City	Lat. N °	′	″	Long. W °	′	″	Alt. (ft)
Lexington, KY	38	02	50	84	29	46	955
Lihue, HI	21	58	48	159	22	30	210
Lima, OH	40	44	35	84	06	20	865
Lincoln, NE	40	48	59	96	42	15	1,150
Little Rock, AR	34	44	42	92	16	37	286
London, Ont.	42	59	17	81	14	03	822
Los Angeles, CA	34	03	15	118	14	28	340
Louisville, KY	38	14	47	85	45	49	450
Lowell, MA	42	38	25	71	19	14	100
Lubbock, TX	33	35	05	101	50	33	3,195
Macon, GA	32	50	12	83	37	36	335
Madison, WI	43	04	23	89	22	55	860
Manchester, NH	42	59	28	71	27	41	175
Marshall, TX	32	33	00	94	23	00	410
Memphis, TN	35	08	46	90	03	13	275
Meriden, CT	41	32	06	72	47	30	190
Miami, FL	25	46	37	80	11	32	10
Milwaukee, WI	43	02	19	87	54	15	635
Minneapolis, MN	44	58	57	93	15	43	815
Minot, ND	48	14	09	101	17	38	1,550
Mississauga, Ont.	43	33	00	79	35	00	510
Mobile, AL	30	41	36	88	02	33	5
Moncton, N.B.	46	05	18	64	46	41	38
Montgomery, AL	32	22	33	86	18	31	160
Montpelier, VT	44	15	36	72	34	41	485
Montréal, Que.	45	30	33	73	33	14	90
Moose Jaw, Sask.	50	23	34	105	32	04	1,784
Muncie, IN	40	11	28	85	23	16	950
Nashville, TN	36	09	33	86	46	55	450
Natchez, MS	31	33	48	91	23	30	210
Newark, NJ	40	44	14	74	10	19	55
New Britain, CT	41	40	08	72	46	59	200
New Haven, CT	41	18	25	72	55	30	40
New Orleans, LA	29	56	53	90	04	10	5
New York, NY	40	45	06	73	59	39	55
Niagara Falls, Ont.	43	06	22	79	03	51	590
Nome, AK	64	30	00	165	25	00	25
Norfolk, VA	36	51	10	76	17	21	10
North Bay, Ont.	46	18	35	79	27	45	670
Oakland, CA	37	48	03	122	15	54	25
Ogden, UT	41	13	31	111	58	21	4,295
Oklahoma City, OK	35	28	26	97	31	04	1,195
Omaha, NE	41	15	42	95	56	14	1,040
Orlando, FL	28	32	42	81	22	38	70
Ottawa, Ont.	45	26	24	75	41	42	185
Paducah, KY	37	05	13	88	35	56	345
Pasadena, CA	34	08	44	118	08	41	830
Paterson, NJ	40	55	01	74	10	21	100
Pensacola, FL	30	24	51	87	12	56	15
Peoria, IL	40	41	42	89	35	33	470
Peterborough, Ont.	44	18	32	78	19	13	673
Philadelphia, PA	39	56	58	75	09	21	100
Phoenix, AZ	33	27	12	112	04	28	1,090
Pierre, SD	44	22	18	100	20	54	1,480
Pittsburgh, PA	40	26	19	80	00	00	745
Pittsfield, MA	42	26	53	73	15	14	1,015
Pocatello, ID	42	51	38	112	27	01	4,460
Pt. Arthur, TX	29	52	30	93	56	15	10
Portland, ME	43	39	33	70	15	19	25
Portland, OR	45	31	06	122	40	35	77
Portsmouth, NH	43	04	30	70	45	24	20
Portsmouth, VA	36	50	07	76	18	14	10
Prince Rupert, B.C.	54	19	00	130	19	00	125(a)
Providence, RI	41	49	32	71	24	41	80
Provo, UT	40	14	06	111	39	24	4,550
Pueblo, CO	38	16	17	104	36	33	4,690
Québec City, Que.	46	48	51	71	12	30	163
Racine, WI	42	43	49	87	47	12	630
Raleigh, NC	35	46	38	78	38	21	365
Rapid City, SD	44	04	52	103	13	11	3,230
Reading, PA	40	20	09	75	55	40	265
Regina, Sask.	50	26	55	104	36	50	1,894(a)
Reno, NV	39	31	27	119	48	40	4,490
Richmond, VA	37	32	15	77	26	09	160
Roanoke, VA	37	16	13	79	56	44	905
Rochester, MN	44	01	21	92	28	03	990
Rochester, NY	43	09	41	77	06	21	515
Rockford, IL	42	16	07	89	05	48	715
Sacramento, CA	38	34	57	121	29	41	30
Saginaw, MI	43	25	52	83	56	05	595
St. Catharines, Ont.	43	09	33	79	14	50	362(a)
St. Cloud, MN	45	34	00	94	10	24	1,040
St. John, N.B.	45	16	22	66	03	48	27
St. John's, Nfld.	47	33	42	52	42	48	200(a)
St. Joseph, MO	39	45	57	94	51	02	850
St. Louis, MO	38	37	45	90	12	22	455
St. Paul, MN	44	57	19	93	06	07	780
St. Petersburg, FL	27	46	18	82	38	19	20
Salem, OR	44	56	24	123	01	59	155
Salina, KS	38	50	36	97	36	46	1,229
Salt Lake City, UT	40	45	23	111	53	26	4,390
San Antonio, TX	29	25	37	98	29	06	650
San Bernardino, CA	34	06	30	117	17	28	1,080
San Diego, CA	32	42	53	117	09	21	20
San Francisco, CA	37	46	39	122	24	40	65
San Jose, CA	37	20	16	121	53	24	90
San Juan, P.R.	18	27	00	66	04	15	35
Santa Barbara, CA	34	25	18	119	41	55	100
Santa Cruz, CA	36	58	18	122	01	18	20
Santa Fe, NM	35	41	11	105	56	10	6,950
Sarasota, FL	27	20	05	82	32	30	20
Saskatoon, Sask.	52	07	49	106	39	35	1,587
Sault Ste. Marie, Ont.	46	30	24	84	20	04	589
Savannah, GA	32	04	42	81	05	37	20
Schenectady, NY	42	48	42	73	55	42	245
Seattle, WA	47	36	32	122	20	12	10
Sheboygan, WI	43	45	03	87	42	52	630
Sherbrooke, Que.	45	24	27	71	51	07	627
Sheridan, WY	44	47	55	106	57	10	3,740
Shreveport, LA	32	30	46	93	44	58	204
Sioux City, IA	42	29	46	96	24	30	1,110
Sioux Falls, SD	43	32	35	96	43	35	1,395
South Bend, IN	41	40	33	86	15	01	710
Spartanburg, SC	34	57	03	81	56	06	875
Spokane, WA	47	39	32	117	25	33	1,890
Springfield, IL	39	47	58	89	38	51	610
Springfield, MA	42	06	21	72	35	32	85
Springfield, MO	37	13	03	93	17	32	1,300
Springfield, OH	39	55	38	83	48	29	980
Stamford, CT	41	03	09	73	32	24	35
Steubenville, OH	40	21	42	80	36	53	660
Stockton, CA	37	57	30	121	17	16	20
Sudbury, Ont.	46	29	24	80	59	24	879
Superior, WI	46	43	14	92	06	07	630
Sydney, N.S.	46	08	15	60	11	48	25
Syracuse, NY	43	03	04	76	09	14	400
Tacoma, WA	47	14	59	122	26	15	110
Tallahassee, FL	30	26	30	84	16	56	150
Tampa, FL	27	56	58	82	27	25	15
Terre Haute, IN	39	28	03	87	24	26	496
Texarkana, TX	33	25	48	94	02	30	324
Thunder Bay, Ont.	48	22	54	89	14	42	616
Toledo, OH	41	39	14	83	32	39	585
Topeka, KS	39	03	16	95	40	23	930
Toronto, Ont.	43	39	10	79	23	00	300
Trenton, NJ	40	13	14	74	46	13	35
Trois-Rivières, Que.	46	20	36	72	32	37	115(a)
Troy, NY	42	43	45	73	40	58	35
Tucson, AZ	32	13	15	110	58	08	2,390
Tulsa, OK	36	09	12	95	59	34	804
Urbana, IL	40	06	42	88	12	06	725
Utica, NY	43	06	12	75	13	33	415
Vancouver, B.C.	49	18	56	123	04	44	141
Victoria, B.C.	48	25	43	123	21	49	57
Waco, TX	31	33	12	97	08	00	405
Walla Walla, WA	46	04	08	118	20	24	936
Washington, DC	38	53	51	77	00	33	25
Waterloo, IA	42	29	40	92	20	20	850
West Palm Beach, FL	26	42	36	80	03	07	15
Wheeling, WV	40	04	03	80	43	20	650
Whitehorse, Yukon	60	43	17	135	03	03	2,050
White Plains, NY	41	02	00	73	45	48	220
Wichita, KS	37	41	30	97	20	16	1,290
Wilkes-Barre, PA	41	14	32	75	53	17	640
Wilmington, DE	39	44	46	75	32	51	135
Wilmington, NC	34	14	14	77	56	58	35
Windsor, Ont.	42	18	56	83	02	10	603
Winnipeg, Man.	49	53	56	97	08	23	762
Winston-Salem, NC	36	05	52	80	14	42	860
Worcester, MA	42	15	37	71	48	17	475
Yakima, WA	46	36	05	120	00	00	1,060
Yellowknife, N.W.T.	62	27	16	114	22	33	674
Youngstown, OH	41	05	57	80	39	02	840
Yuma, AZ	32	42	54	114	37	24	160
Zanesville, OH	39	56	18	82	00	30	720

Principal World Rivers

Source: Geological Survey, U.S. Dept. of the Interior

River	Outflow	Length (mi)
Albany	James Bay	610
Amazon	Atlantic Ocean	4,000
Amu	Aral Sea	1,578
Amur	Tatar Strait	2,744
Angara	Yenisey River	1,151
Arkansas	Mississippi R.	1,459
Back, N.W.T.	Arctic Ocean	605
Brahmaputra	Bay of Bengal	1,800
Bug, Southern	Dnieper River	532
Bug, Western	Wisla River	481
Canadian	Arkansas River	906
Chang	E China Sea	3,964
Churchill, Man.	Hudson Bay	1,000
Churchill, Que.	Atlantic Ocean	532
Colorado, AZ	Gulf of Calif.	1,450
Columbia	Pacific Ocean	1,243
Congo	Atlantic Ocean	2,718
Danube	Black Sea	1,776
Dnieper	Black Sea	1,420
Dniester	Black Sea	877
Don	Sea of Azov	1,224
Drava	Danube River	447
Dvina, North	White Sea	824
Dvina, West	Gulf of Riga	634
Ebro	Mediterranean	565
Elbe	North Sea	724
Euphrates	Shatt al-Arab	1,700
Fraser	Str. of Georgia	850
Gambia	Atlantic Ocean	700
Ganges	Bay of Bengal	1,560
Garonne	Bay of Biscay	357
Huang	Yellow Sea	3,395
Indus	Arabian Sea	1,800
Irrawaddy	Bay of Bengal	1,337
Japura	Amazon River	1,750
Jordan	Dead Sea	200
Kootenay	Columbia R.	485
Lena	Laptev Sea	2,734
Loire	Bay of Biscay	634
Mackenzie	Arctic Ocean	1,025
Madeira	Amazon River	2,013
Magdalena	Caribbean Sea	956
Marne	Seine River	326
Mekong	S China Sea	2,600
Meuse	North Sea	580
Mississippi	Southwest Pass	2,340
Missouri	Mississippi R.	2,315
Murray-Darling	Indian Ocean	2,310
Negro	Amazon	1,400
Nelson	Hudson Bay	410
Niger	Gulf of Guinea	2,590
Nile	Mediterranean	4,160
Ob-Irtysh	Gulf of Ob	3,362
Oder	Baltic Sea	567
Ohio	Mississippi	981
Orange	Atlantic Ocean	1,300
Orinoco	Atantic Ocean	1,600
Ottawa	St. Lawrence R.	790
Paraguay	Parana River	1,584
Parana	Rio de la Plata	2,485
Peace	Slave River	1,210
Pilcomayo	Paraguay River	1,000
Po	Adriatic Sea	405
Purus	Amazon River	2,100
Red	Atchafalaya R.	1,290
Red River of N.	Lake Winnipeg	545
Rhine	North Sea	820
Rhone	Gulf of Lions	505
Rio de la Plata	Atlantic Ocean	150
Rio Grande	Gulf of Mexico	1,900
Rio Roosevelt	Aripuana	400
Saguenay	St. Lawrence R.	434
St. John	Bay of Fundy	418
St. Lawrence	Gulf of St. Law.	800
Salween	Andaman Sea	1,500
Sao Francisco	Atlantic Ocean	1,988
Seine	English Chan.	496
Shannon	Atlantic Ocean	230
Snake	Columbia River	1,038
Songhua	Amur River	1,150
Syr	Aral Sea	1,370
Tajo, Tagus	Atlantic Ocean	626
Tennessee	Ohio River	652
Thames	North Sea	210
Tiber	Tyrrhenian Sea	252
Tigris	Shatt al-Arab	1,180
Tisza	Danube River	600
Tocantins	Para River	1,677
Ural	Caspian Sea	1,575
Uruguay	Rio de la Plata	1,000
Volga	Caspian Sea	2,290
Weser	North Sea	454
Wisla	Bay of Danzig	675
Xi	S. China Sea	1,200
Yangtze. See Chang		
Yellow. See Huang		
Yenisey	Kara Sea	2,543
Yukon	Bering Sea	1,979
Zambezi	Indian Ocean	1,700

Major Rivers in North America

Source: Geological Survey, U.S. Dept. of the Interior

River	Source or upper limit of length	Outflow	Length (mi)
Alabama	Gilmer County, GA	Mobile River	729
Albany	Lake St. Joseph, Ontario	James Bay	610
Allegheny	Potter County, PA	Ohio River	325
Altamaha-Ocmulgee	Junction of Yellow and South Rivers, Newton County, GA	Atlantic Ocean	392
Apalachicola-Chattahoochee	Towns County, GA	Gulf of Mexico	524
Arkansas	Lake County, CO	Mississippi River	1,459
Assiniboine	Eastern Saskatchewan	Red River	450
Attawapiskat	Attawapiskat, Ontario	James Bay	465
Back (N.W.T.)	Contwoyto Lake	Chantrey Inlet, Arctic Ocean	605
Big Black (MS)	Webster County, MS	Mississippi River	330
Brazos	Junction of Salt and Double Mountain Forks, Stonewall County, TX	Gulf of Mexico	923
Canadian	Las Animas County, CO	Arkansas River	906
Cedar (IA)	Dodge County, MN	Iowa River	329
Cheyenne	Junction of Antelope Creek and Dry Fork, Converse County, WY	Missouri River	290
Churchill, Man.	Methy Lake, Saskatchewan	Hudson Bay	1,000
Cimarron	Colfax County, NM	Arkansas River	600
Colorado (AZ)	Rocky Mountain Natl. Park, CO (90 mi in Mexico)	Gulf of California	1,450
Colorado (TX)	West Texas	Matagorda Bay	862
Columbia	Columbia Lake, British Columbia	Pacific Ocean, bet. OR and WA	1,243
Columbia, Upper	Columbia Lake, British Columbia	To mouth of Snake River	890
Connecticut	Third Connecticut Lake, NH	Long Island Sound, CT	407
Coppermine (N.W.T.)	Lac de Gras	Coronation Gulf (Arctic Ocean)	525
Cumberland	Letcher County, KY	Ohio River	720
Delaware	Schoharie County, NY	Liston Point, Delaware Bay	390
Fraser	Near Mount Robson (on Continental Divide)	Strait of Georgia	850
Gila	Catron County, NM	Colorado River	649
Green (UT-WY)	Junction of Wells and Trail Creeks, Sublette County, WY	Colorado River	730
Hamilton (Lab.)	Lake Ashuanipi	Atlantic Ocean	532
Hudson	Henderson Lake, Essex County, NY	Upper NY Bay	306
Illinois	St. Joseph County, IN	Mississippi River	420
James (ND-SD)	Wells County, ND	Missouri River	710
James (VA)	Junction of Jackson and Cowpasture Rivers, Botetourt County, VA	Hampton Roads	340
Kanawha-New	Junction of North and South Forks of New River, NC	Ohio River	352
Kentucky	Junction of North and Middle Forks, Lee County, KY	Ohio River	259
Klamath	Lake Ewauna, Klamath Falls, OR	Pacific Ocean	250
Koyukuk	Endicott Mountains, AK	Yukon River	470
Kuskokwim	Alaska Range	Kuskokwim Bay	724
Liard	Southern Yukon, Alaska	Mackenzie River	693
Little Missouri	Crook County, WY	Missouri River	560
Mackenzie	Great Slave Lake, N.W.T.	Arctic Ocean	1,025

River	Source or upper limit of length	Outflow	Length (mi)
Milk	Junction of North and South Forks, Alberta	Missouri River	625
Minnesota	Big Stone Lake, MN	Mississippi River	332
Mississippi	Lake Itasca, MN	Mouth of Southwest Pass	2,340
Mississippi, Upper	Lake Itasca, MN	To mouth of Missouri River	1,171
Mississippi-Missouri-Red Rock	Source of Red Rock, Beaverhead Co., MT	Mouth of Southwest Pass	3,710
Missouri	Junction of Jefferson, Madison, and Gallatin rivers, Madison County, MT	Mississippi River	2,315
Missouri-Red Rock	Source of Red Rock, Beaverhead Co., MT	Mississippi River	2,540
Mobile-Alabama-Coosa	Gilmer County, GA	Mobile Bay	774
Nelson (Man.)	Lake Winnipeg	Hudson Bay	410
Neosho	Morris County, KS	Arkansas River, OK	460
Niobrara	Niobrara County, WY	Missouri River, NE	431
North Canadian	Union County, NM	Canadian River, OK	800
North Platte	Junction of Grizzly and Little Grizzly creeks, Jackson County, CO	Platte River, NE	618
Ohio	Junction of Allegheny and Monongahela rivers, Pittsburgh, PA	Mississippi River	981
Ohio-Allegheny	Potter County, PA	Mississippi River	1,310
Osage	East-central Kansas	Missouri River	500
Ottawa	Lake Capimitchigama	St. Lawrence River	790
Ouachita	Polk County, AR	Black River	605
Peace	Stikine Mountains, B.C.	Slave River	1,210
Pearl	Neshoba County, MS	Gulf of Mexico	411
Pecos	Mora County, NM	Rio Grande	926
Pee Dee-Yadkin	Watauga County, NC	Winyah Bay	435
Pend Oreille-Clark Fork	Near Butte, MT	Columbia River	531
Platte	Junction of North and South Platte Rivers, NE	Missouri River	310
Porcupine	Ogilvie Mountains, AK	Yukon River, Alaska	569
Potomac	Garrett County, MD	Chesapeake Bay	383
Powder	Junction of South and Middle Forks, WY	Yellowstone River	375
Red (OK-TX-LA)	Curry County, NM	Atchafalaya River	1,290
Red River of the North	Junction of Otter Tail and Bois de Sioux Rivers, Wilkin County, MN	Lake Winnipeg	545
Republican	Junction of North Fork and Arikaree River, NE	Kansas River	445
Rio Grande	San Juan County, CO	Gulf of Mexico	1,900
Roanoke	Junction of North and South Forks, Montgomery County, VA	Albemarle Sound	380
Rock (IL-WI)	Dodge County, WI	Mississippi River	300
Sabine	Junction of South and Caddo Forks, Hunt County, TX	Sabine Lake	380
Sacramento	Siskiyou County, CA	Suisun Bay	377
St. Francis	Iron County, MO	Mississippi River	425
St. Lawrence	Lake Ontario	Gulf of St. Lawrence (Atlantic Ocean)	800
Salmon (ID)	Custer County, ID	Snake River	420
San Joaquin	Junction of South and Middle Forks, Madera County, CA	Suisun Bay	350
San Juan	Silver Lake, Archuleta County, CO	Colorado River	360
Santee-Wateree-Catawba	McDowell County, NC	Atlantic Ocean	538
Saskatchewan, North	Rocky Mountains	Saskatchewan R.	800
Saskatchewan, South	Rocky Mountains	Saskatchewan R.	865
Savannah	Junction of Seneca and Tugaloo rivers, Anderson County, SC	Atlantic Ocean, GA-SC	314
Severn (Ont.)	Sandy Lake	Hudson Bay	610
Smoky Hill	Cheyenne County, CO	Kansas River, KS	540
Snake	Teton County, WY	Columbia River, WA	1,038
South Platte	Junction of South and Middle Forks, Park County, CO	Platte River	424
Susitna	Alaska Range	Cook Inlet	313
Susquehanna	Huyden Creek, Otsego County, NY	Chesapeake Bay	447
Tallahatchie	Tippah County, MS	Yazoo River	301
Tanana	Wrangell Mountains, AK	Yukon River	659
Tennessee	Junction of French Broad and Holston Rivers	Ohio River	652
Tennessee-French Broad	Courthouse Creek, Transylvania County, NC	Ohio River	886
Tombigbee	Prentiss County, MS	Mobile River	525
Trinity	North of Dallas, TX	Galveston Bay	360
Wabash	Darke County, OH	Ohio River	512
Washita	Hemphill County, TX	Red River, OK	500
White (AR-MO)	Madison County, AR	Mississippi River	722
Willamette	Douglas County, OR	Columbia River	309
Wind-Bighorn	Junction of Wind and Little Wind Rivers, Fremont Co., WY (Source of Wind R. is Togwotee Pass, Teton Co., WY)	Yellowstone River	336
Wisconsin	Lac Vieux Desert, Vilas County, WI	Mississippi River	430
Yellowstone	Park County, WY	Missouri River	692
Yukon	McNeil R., Yukon Territory	Bering Sea	1,979

Highest and Lowest Continental Altitudes

Source: National Geographic Society

Continent	Highest point	Elevation (ft)	Lowest point	ft below sea level
Asia	Mount Everest, Nepal-Tibet	29,028	Dead Sea, Israel-Jordan	1,312
South America	Mount Aconcagua, Argentina	22,834	Valdes Peninsula, Argentina	131
North America	Mount McKinley, AK	20,320	Death Valley, California	282
Africa	Kilimanjaro, Tanzania	19,340	Lake Assal, Djibouti	512
Europe	Mount Elbrus, Russia	18,510	Caspian Sea, Russia, Azerbaijan	92
Antarctica	Vinson Massif	16,864	Bentley Subglacial Trench	8,327[1]
Australia	Mount Kosciusko, New South Wales	7,310	Lake Eyre, South Australia	52

(1) Estimated level of the continental floor. Lower points that have yet to be discovered may exist further beneath the ice.

Major Natural Lakes of the World

Source: Geological Survey, U.S. Dept. of the Interior

A lake is generally defined as a body of water surrounded by land. By this definition some bodies of water that are called seas, such as the Caspian Sea and the Aral Sea, are really lakes. The word *lake* is omitted when part of name.

Name	Continent	Area (sq mi)	Length (mi)	Maximum depth (ft)	Elevation (ft)
Caspian Sea	Asia-Europe	143,244	760	3,363	-92
Superior	North America	31,700	350	1,330	600
Victoria	Africa	26,828	250	270	3,720
Aral Sea	Asia	24,904[1]	280	220	174
Huron	North America	23,000	206	750	579
Michigan	North America	22,300	307	923	579
Tanganyika	Africa	12,700	420	4,823	2,534
Baykal	Asia	12,162	395	5,315	1,493
Great Bear	North America	12,096	192	1,463	512
Nyasa (Malawi)	Africa	11,150	360	2,280	1,550
Great Slave	North America	11,031	298	2,015	513
Erie	North America	9,910	241	210	570
Winnipeg	North America	9,417	266	60	713
Ontario	North America	7,340	193	802	245
Balkhash	Asia	7,115	376	85	1,115
Ladoga	Europe	6,835	124	738	13
Chad	Africa	6,300	175	24	787
Maracaibo	South America	5,217	133	115	sea level
Onega	Europe	3,710	145	328	108
Eyre	Australia	3,600[2]	90	4	-52
Volta	Africa	3,276	250	....	....
Titicaca	South America	3,200	122	922	12,500
Nicaragua	Central America	3,100	102	230	102
Athabasca	North America	3,064	208	407	700
Reindeer	North America	2,568	143	720	1,106
Turkana (Rudolf)	Africa	2,473	154	240	1,230
Issyk Kul	Asia	2,355	115	2,303	5,279
Torrens	Australia	2,230	130	....	92
Vanern	Europe	2,156	91	328	144
Nettilling	North America	2,140	67	....	95
Winnipegosis	North America	2,075	141	38	830
Albert	Africa	2,075	100	168	2,030
Kariba	Africa	2,050	175	390	1,590
Nipigon	North America	1,872	72	540	1,050
Gairdner	Australia	1,840	90	....	112
Urmia	Asia	1,815	90	49	4,180
Manitoba	North America	1,799	140	12	813

(1) Probably less because of the diversion of feeder rivers. (2) Approximate figure, subject to great seasonal variation.

The Great Lakes

Source: National Ocean Service, U.S. Dept. of Commerce

The Great Lakes form the world's largest body of fresh water and with their connecting waterways are the largest inland water transportation unit. Draining the great North Central basin of the U.S., they enable shipping to reach the Atlantic via their outlet, the St. Lawrence R., and to reach the Gulf of Mexico via the Illinois Waterway, from Lake Michigan to the Mississippi R. A 3d outlet connects with the Hudson R. and then the Atlantic via the New York State Barge Canal System. Traffic on the Illinois Waterway and the N.Y. State Barge Canal System is limited to recreational boating and small shipping vessels.

Only one of the lakes, Lake Michigan, is wholly in the U.S.; the others are shared with Canada. Ships move from the shores of Lake Superior to Whitefish Bay at the E end of the lake, then through the Soo (Sault Ste. Marie) locks, through the St. Mary's R. and into Lake Huron. To reach Gary and the Port of Indiana and South Chicago, IL, ships move W from Lake Huron to Lake Michigan through the Straits of Mackinac. Lake Superior is 600 ft above mean water level at Point-au-Pere, Quebec, on the International Great Lakes Datum (1955). From Duluth, MN, to the E end of Lake Ontario is 1,156 mi.

	Superior	Michigan	Huron	Erie	Ontario
Length in mi	350	307	206	241	193
Breadth in mi	160	118	183	57	53
Deepest soundings in ft	1,333	923	750	210	802
Volume of water in cu mi	2,935	1,180	850	116	393
Area (sq mi) water surface—U.S.	20,600	22,300	9,100	4,980	3,460
Canada	11,100	.....	13,900	4,930	3,880
Area (sq mi) entire drainage basin—U.S.	16,900	45,600	16,200	18,000	15,200
Canada	32,400	.....	35,500	4,720	12,100
Total area (sq mi) U.S. and Canada	**81,000**	**67,900**	**74,700**	**32,630**	**34,850**
Mean surface above mean water level at Point-au-Pere, Quebec, avg. level in ft (1900-88)	600.61	578.34	578.34	570.53	244.74
Latitude, N	46° 25′	41° 37′	43° 00′	41° 23′	43° 11′
	49° 00′	46° 06′	46° 17′	42° 52′	44° 15′
Longitude, W	84° 22′	84° 45′	79° 43′	78° 51′	76° 03′
	92° 06′	88° 02′	84° 45′	83° 29′	79° 53′
National boundary line in mi	282.8	None	260.8	251.5	174.6
United States shoreline (mainland only) mi	863	1,400	580	431	300

Famous Waterfalls

Source: National Geographic Society

The earth has thousands of waterfalls, some of considerable magnitude. Their importance is determined not only by height but by volume of flow, steadiness of flow, crest width, whether the water drops sheerly or over a sloping surface, and whether it descends in one leap or a succession of leaps. A series of low falls flowing over a considerable distance is known as a cascade.

Estimated mean annual flow, in cubic feet per second, of major waterfalls are as follows: Niagara, 212,200; Paulo Afonso, 100,000; Urubupunga, 97,000; Iguazu, 61,000; Patos-Maribondo, 53,000; Victoria, 35,400; and Kaieteur, 23,400.

Elevation = total drop in feet in one or more leaps. †= falls of more than one leap; *= falls that diminish greatly seasonally; **= falls that reduce to a trickle or are dry for part of each year. If river names not shown, they are the same as the falls. R. = river; L. = lake; (C) = cascade type.

Africa

Name and location	Elevation (ft)
Angola	
Ruacana, Cuene R.	406
Ethiopia	
Fincha	508
Lesotho	
Maletsunyane*	630
Zimbabwe-Zambia	
Victoria, Zambezi R.*	343
South Africa	
Augrabies, Orange R.*	480
Tugela†	2,014
Tanzania-Zambia	
Kalambo*	726

Asia

Name and location	Elevation (ft)
India—Cauvery*	330
Jog (Gersoppa), Sharavathi R.*	830
Japan	
Kegon, Daiya R.*	330

Australia

Name and location	Elevation (ft)
Australia	
New South Wales	
Wentworth	614
Wollomombi	1,100
Queensland	
Tully	885
Wallaman, Stony Cr.†	1,137
New Zealand	
Helena	890
Sutherland, Arthur R.†	1,904

Europe

Name and location	Elevation (ft)
Austria—Gastein†	492
Krimml†	1,312
France—Gavarnie*	1,385
Great Britain	
Scotland	
Glomach	370
Wales	
Rhaiadr	240

Name and location	Elevation (ft)
Italy—Frua, Toce R. (C)	470
Norway	
Mardalsfossen (Northern)	1,535
Mardalsfossen (Southern)†	2,149
Skjeggedal, Nybuai R.†**	1,378
Skykje**	984
Vetti, Morka-Koldedola R.	900
Sweden	
Handol†	427
Switzerland	
Giessbach (C)	984
Reichenbach†	656
Simmen†	459
Staubbach	984
Trummelbach†	1,312

North America

Name and location	Elevation (ft)
Canada	
Alberta	
Panther, Nigel Cr.	600
British Columbia	
Della†	1,443
Takakkaw, Daly Glacier†	1,200
Quebec	
Montmorency	274
Canada—United States	
Niagara: American	182
Horseshoe	173
United States	
California	
Feather, Fall R. *	640
Yosemite National Park	
Bridalveil*	620
Illilouette*	370
Nevada, Merced R.*	594
Ribbon**	1,612
Silver Strand, Meadow Br.**	1,170
Vernal, Merced R. *	317
Yosemite†**	2,425
Colorado	
Seven, South Cheyenne Cr.†	300
Hawaii	
Akaka, Kolekole Str.	442
Idaho	
Shoshone, Snake R.**	212

Name and location	Elevation (ft)
Kentucky	
Cumberland	68
Maryland	
Great, Potomac R. (C) *	71
Minnesota	
Minnehaha**	53
New Jersey	
Passaic	70
New York	
Taughannock*	215
Oregon	
Multnomah†	620
Tennessee	
Fall Creek	256
Washington	
Mt. Rainier Natl. Park	
Sluiskin, Paradise R.	300
Snoqualmie**	268
Wisconsin	
Big Manitou, Black R. (C)*	165
Wyoming	
Yellowstone Natl. Pk. Tower	132
Yellowstone (upper)*	109
Yellowstone (lower)*	308
Mexico	
El Salto	218

South America

Name and location	Elevation (ft)
Argentina-Brazil	
Iguazu	230
Brazil	
Glass	1,325
Patos-Maribondo, Grande R.	115
Paulo Afonso, Sao Francisco R.	275
Urubupunga, Parana R.	39
Colombia	
Catarata de Candelas, Cusiana R.	984
Tequendama, Bogota R. *	427
Ecuador	
Agoyan, Pastaza R. *	200
Guyana	
Kaieteur, Potaro R.	741
Great, Kamarang R.	1,600
Marina, Ipobe R. †	500
Venezuela	
Angel†*	3,212
Cuquenan	2,000

Notable Deserts of the World

Arabian (Eastern), 70,000 sq mi in Egypt between the Nile R and Red Sea, extending southward into Sudan

Atacama, 600-mi-long area rich in nitrate and copper deposits in N Chile

Chihuahuan, 140,000 sq mi in TX, NM, AZ, and Mexico

Dasht-e Kauir, approx. 300 mi long by approx. 100 mi wide in N central Iran

Dasht-e Lut, 20,000 sq mi in E Iran

Death Valley, 3,300 sq mi in CA and NV

Gibson, 120,000 sq mi in the interior of W Australia

Gobi, 500,000 sq mi in Mongolia and China

Great Sandy, 150,000 sq mi in W Australia

Great Victoria, 150,000 sq mi in SW Australia

Kalahari, 225,000 sq mi in S Africa

Kara Kum, 120,000 sq mi in Turkmenistan

Kyzyl Kum, 100,000 sq mi in Kazakhstan and Uzbekistan

Libyan, 450,000 sq mi in the Sahara, extending from Libya through SW Egypt into Sudan

Mojave, 15,000 sq mi in southern CA

Namib, long narrow area (varies from 30-100 mi wide) extending 800 mi along SW coast of Africa

Nubian, 100,000 sq mi in the Sahara in NE Sudan

Patagonia, 300,000 sq mi in S Argentina

Painted Desert, section of high plateau in northern AZ extending 150 mi

Rub al-Khali (Empty Quarter), 250,000 sq mi in the S Arabian Peninsula

Sahara, 3,500,000 sq mi in N Africa, extending westward to the Atlantic. Largest desert in the world

Sonoran, 70,000 sq mi in southwestern AZ and southeastern CA extending into NW Mexico

Syrian, 100,000-sq-mi arid wasteland extending over much of N Saudi Arabia, E Jordan, S Syria, and W Iraq

Taklimakan, 140,000 sq mi in Xinjiang Prov., China

Thar (Great Indian), 100,000-sq-mi arid area extending 400 mi along India-Pakistan border

WEIGHTS AND MEASURES

Source: National Institute of Standards and Technology, U.S. Dept. of Commerce

The International System of Units (SI)

Two systems of weights and measures coexist in the U.S. today: the U.S. Customary System and the International System of Units (SI, after the initials of Système International). SI, commonly identified with the metric system, is actually a more complete, coherent version of it. Throughout U.S. history, the Customary System (inherited from, but now different from, the British Imperial System) has been generally used; federal and state legislation has given it, through implication, standing as the primary weights and measures system. The metric system, however, is the only system that Congress has ever specifically sanctioned. An 1866 law reads:

> It shall be lawful throughout the United States of America to employ the weights and measures of the metric system; and no contract or dealing, or pleading in any court, shall be deemed invalid or liable to objection because the weights or measures expressed or referred to therein are weights or measures of the metric system.

Since that time, use of the metric system in the U.S. has slowly and steadily increased, particularly in the scientific community, in the pharmaceutical industry, and in the manufacturing sector—the last motivated by the practice in international commerce, in which the metric system is now predominantly used.

On Feb. 10, 1964, the National Bureau of Standards (now known as the National Institute of Standards and Technology) issued the following statement:

> Henceforth it shall be the policy of the National Bureau of Standards to use the units of the International System (SI), as adopted by the 11th General Conference on Weights and Measures (October 1960), except when the use of these units would obviously impair communication or reduce the usefulness of a report.

On Dec. 23, 1975, Pres. Gerald R. Ford signed the Metric Conversion Act of 1975. It defines the metric system as being the International System of Units as interpreted in the U.S. by the secretary of commerce. The Trade Act of 1988 and other legislation declare the metric system the preferred system of weights and measures for U.S. trade and commerce, call for the federal government to adopt metric specifications, and mandate the Commerce Dept. to oversee the program. However, the metric system has still not become the system of choice for most Americans' daily use.

The following 7 units serve as the base units for the International System: **length**—meter; **mass**—kilogram; **time**—second; **electric current**—ampere; **thermodynamic temperature**—kelvin; **amount of substance**—mole; and **luminous intensity**—candela.

Prefixes

The following prefixes, in combination with the basic unit names, provide the multiples and submultiples in the International System. For example, the unit name *meter*, with the prefix *kilo* added, produces *kilometer*, meaning "1,000 meters."

Prefix	Symbol	Multiples	Equivalent	Prefix	Symbol	Submultiples	Equivalent
yotta	Y	10^{24}	septillionfold	deci	d	10^{-1}	tenth part
zetta	Z	10^{21}	sextillionfold	centi	c	10^{-2}	hundredth part
exa	E	10^{18}	quintillionfold	milli	m	10^{-3}	thousandth part
peta	P	10^{15}	quadrillionfold	micro	μ	10^{-6}	millionth part
tera	T	10^{12}	trillionfold	nano	n	10^{-9}	billionth part
giga	G	10^{9}	billionfold	pico	p	10^{-12}	trillionth part
mega	M	10^{6}	millionfold	femto	f	10^{-15}	quadrillionth part
kilo	k	10^{3}	thousandfold	atto	a	10^{-18}	quintillionth part
hecto	h	10^{2}	hundredfold	zepto	z	10^{-21}	sextillionth part
deka	da	10	tenfold	yocto	y	10^{-24}	septillionth part

Tables of Metric Weights and Measures

(Note: The SI generally uses the term *mass* instead of *weight*. Mass is a measure of an object's inertial property, or the amount of matter it contains. Weight is a measure of the force exerted on an object by gravity or the force needed to support it. Also, the SI does not make a distinction between "dry volume" and "liquid volume.")

Length

10 millimeters (mm)	= 1 centimeter (cm)
10 centimeters.	= 1 decimeter (dm) = 100 millimeters
10 decimeters	= 1 meter (m) = 1,000 millimeters
10 meters	= 1 dekameter (dam)
10 dekameters.	= 1 hectometer (hm) = 100 meters
10 hectometers	= 1 kilometer (km) = 1,000 meters

Area

100 square millimeters (mm²)	= 1 square centimeter (cm²)
10,000 square centimeters	= 1 square meter (m²) = 1,000,000 square millimeters
100 square meters	= 1 are (a)
100 ares	= 1 hectare (ha) = 10,000 square meters
100 hectares	= 1 square kilometer (km²) = 1,000,000 square meters

Volume

10 milliliters (mL).	= 1 centiliter (cL)
10 centiliters.	= 1 deciliter (dL) = 100 milliliters
10 deciliters	= 1 liter (L) = 1,000 milliliters
10 liters.	= 1 dekaliter (daL)
10 dekaliters	= 1 hectoliter (hL) = 100 liters
10 hectoliters	= 1 kiloliter (kL) = 1,000 liters

Volume (Cubic Measure)

1,000 cubic millimeters (mm³)	= 1 cubic centimeter (cm³)
1,000 cubic centimeters. .	= 1 cubic decimeter (dm³) = 1,000,000 cubic millimeters
1,000 cubic decimeters . .	= 1 cubic meter (m³) = 1 stere = 1,000,000 cubic centimeters = 1,000,000,000 cubic millimeters

Weight (Mass)

10 milligrams (mg).	= 1 centigram (cg)
10 centigrams.	= 1 decigram (dg) = 100 milligrams
10 decigrams	= 1 gram (g) = 1,000 milligrams
10 grams	= 1 dekagram (dag)
10 dekagrams.	= 1 hectogram (hg) = 100 grams
10 hectograms	= 1 kilogram (kg) = 1,000 grams
1,000 kilograms	= 1 metric ton (t)

Table of U.S. Customary Weights and Measures

Length

12 inches (in)	= 1 foot (ft)
3 feet	= 1 yard (yd)
5 ½ yards	= 1 rod (rd), pole, or perch (16 ½ feet)
40 rods	= 1 furlong (fur)=220 yards= 660 feet
8 furlongs	= 1 statute mile (mi) = 1,760 yards = 5,280 feet
3 miles.	= 1 league = 5,280 yards = 15,840 feet
6076.11549 feet . . .	= 1 international nautical mile

Volume (Liquid Measure)

When necessary to distinguish the liquid pint or quart from the dry pint or quart, the word *liquid* or the abbreviation *liq* is used in combination with the name or abbreviation of the liquid unit.

4 gills (gi)	= 1 pint (pt) = 28.875 cubic inches
2 pints	= 1 quart (qt) = 57.75 cubic inches
4 quarts	= 1 gallon (gal) = 231 cubic inches = 8 pints = 32 gills

Volume (Dry Measure)

When necessary to distinguish the dry pint or quart from the liquid pint or quart, the word *dry* is used in combination with the name or abbreviation of the dry unit.

2 pints (pt)	= 1 quart (qt) = 67.2006 cubic inches
8 quarts	= 1 peck (pk) = 537.605 cubic inches = 16 pints
4 pecks	= 1 bushel (bu) = 2,150.42 cubic inches = 32 quarts

Area

Squares and cubes of units are sometimes abbreviated by using superscripts. For example, ft^2 means square foot, and ft^3 means cubic foot.

144 square inches	= 1 square foot (ft²)
9 square feet	= 1 square yard (yd²) = 1,296 square inches
30 ¼ square yards	= 1 square rod (rd²) = 272 ¼ square feet
160 square rods	= 1 acre = 4,840 square yards = 43,560 square feet
640 acres	= 1 square mile (mi²)
1 mile square	= 1 section (of land)
6 miles square	= 1 township = 36 sections = 36 square miles

Cubic Measure

1 cubic foot (ft³)	= 1,728 cubic inches (in³)
27 cubic feet	= 1 cubic yard (yd³)

Gunter's, or Surveyor's, Chain Measure

7.92 inches (in)	= 1 link
100 links	= 1 chain (ch) = 4 rods = 66 feet
80 chains	= 1 statute mile (mi) = 320 rods = 5,280 feet

Avoirdupois Weight

When necessary to distinguish the avoirdupois ounce or pound from the troy ounce or pound, the word *avoirdupois* or the abbreviation *avdp* is used in combination with the name or abbreviation of the avoirdupois unit. The *grain* is the same in avoirdupois and troy weight.

27 11/32 grains	= 1 dram (dr)
16 drams	= 1 ounce (oz) = 437 ½ grains
16 ounces	= 1 pound (lb) = 256 drams = 7,000 grains
100 pounds	= 1 hundredweight (cwt)°
20 hundredweights	= 1 ton = 2,000 pounds°

In *gross* or *long* measure, the following values are recognized.

112 pounds	= 1 gross or long hundredweight°
20 gross or long hundredweights	= 1 gross or long ton = 2,240 pounds°

°When the terms *hundredweight* and *ton* are used unmodified, they are commonly understood to mean the 100-pound hundredweight and the 2,000-pound ton, respectively; these units may be designated *net* or *short* when necessary to distinguish them from the corresponding units in gross or long measure.

Troy Weight

24 grains	= 1 pennyweight (dwt)
20 pennyweights . . .	= 1 ounce troy (oz t) = 480 grains
12 ounces troy	= 1 pound troy (lb t) = 240 pennyweights = 5,760 grains

Tables of Equivalents

In this table it is necessary to distinguish between the *international* and the *survey* foot. The international foot, defined in 1959 as exactly equal to 0.3048 meter, is shorter than the old survey foot by exactly 2 parts in one million. The survey foot is still used in data expressed in feet in geodetic surveys within the U.S. In this table the survey foot is italicized.

When the name of a unit is enclosed in brackets, e.g., [1 hand], either (1) the unit is not in general current use in the U.S. or (2) the unit is believed to be based on custom and usage rather than on formal definition.

Equivalents involving decimals are, in most instances, rounded to the 3d decimal place; exact equivalents are so designated.

Lengths

1 angstrom (Å)	= 0.1 nanometer (exactly)
	= 0.000 1 micrometer (exactly)
	= 0.000 000 1 millimeter (exactly)
	= 0.000 000 004 inch
1 cable's length	= 120 fathoms (exactly)
	= 720 *feet* (exactly)
	= 219 meters
1 centimeter (cm)	= 0.3937 inch
1 chain (ch) (Gunter's or surveyor's)	= 66 *feet* (exactly)
	= 20.1168 meters
1 chain (engineer's)	= 100 feet
	= 30.48 meters (exactly)
1 decimeter (dm)	= 3.937 inches
1 degree (geographical)	= 364,566.929 feet
	= 69.047 miles (avg.)
	= 111.123 kilometers (avg.)
-of latitude	= 68.708 miles at equator
	= 69.403 miles at poles
-of longitude	= 69.171 miles at equator
1 dekameter (dam)	= 32.808 feet
1 fathom	= 6 *feet* (exactly)
	= 1.8288 meters
1 foot (ft)	= 0.3048 meters (exactly)
1 furlong (fur)	= 10 chains (surveyors) (exactly)
	= 660 *feet* (exactly)
	= ¹/₈ statute mile (exactly)
	= 201.168 meters
[1 hand] (height measure for horses from ground to top of shoulders) .	= 4 inches
1 inch (in)	= 2.54 centimeters (exactly)
1 kilometer (km)	= 0.621 mile
	= 3,280.8 feet

1 league (land)	= 3 statute miles (exactly)
	= 4.828 kilometers
1 link (Gunter's or surveyor's)	= 7.92 inches (exactly)
	= 0.201 meter
1 link (engineer's)	= 1 foot
	= 0.305 meter
1 meter (m)	= 39.37 inches
	= 1.094 yards
1 micrometer (μm) [the Greek letter mu]	= 0.001 millimeter (exactly)
	= 0.000 039 37 inch
1 mil	= 0.001 inch (exactly)
	= 0.025 4 millimeter (exactly)
1 mile (mi) (statute or land)	= 5,280 *feet* (exactly)
	= 1.609 kilometers
1 international nautical mile (nmi)	= 1.852 kilometers (exactly)
	= 1.150779 statute miles
	= 6,076.11549 feet
1 millimeter (mm)	= 0.039 37 inch
1 nanometer (nm)	= 0.001 micrometer (exactly)
	= 0.000 000 039 37 inch
1 pica (typography)	= 12 points
1 point (typography)	= 0.013 837 inch (exactly)
	= 0.351 millimeter
1 rod (rd), pole, or perch	= 16½ *feet* (exactly)
	= 5.029 meters
1 yard (yd)	= 0.9144 meter (exactly)

Areas or Surfaces

1 acre	= 43,560 square *feet* (exactly)
	= 4,840 square yards
	= 0.405 hectare
1 are (a)	= 119.599 square yards
	= 0.025 acre

1 bolt (cloth measure):
length. . . . . = 100 yards (on modern looms)
width . . . . = 45 or 60 inches
1 hectare (ha) . . . . = 2.471 acres
[1 square (building)] . . . . = 100 square feet
1 square centimeter (cm²) . . . . . . = 0.155 square inch
1 square decimeter (dm²) . . . . . . = 15.500 square inches
1 square foot (ft²) . . . . = 929.030 square centimeters
1 square inch (in²) . . . . = 6.4516 square centimeters
                                        (exactly)
1 square kilometer (km²). . . . . . . = 247.104 acres
                                        = 0.386 square mile
1 square meter (m²) . . . . = 1.196 square yards
                                        = 10.764 square feet
1 square mile (mi²). . . . . = 258.999 hectares
1 square millimeter (mm²). . . . . . = 0.002 square inch
1 square rod (rd²), sq. pole, or
   sq. perch . . . . = 25.293 square meters
1 square yard (yd²). . . . . = 0.836 square meter

Capacities or Volumes

1 barrel (bbl), liquid . . . . = 31 to 42 gallons°

°There are a variety of "barrels" established by law or usage. For example: federal taxes on fermented liquors are based on a barrel of 31 gallons; many state laws fix the "barrel for liquids" as 31½ gallons; one state fixes a 36-gallon barrel for cistern measurement; federal law recognizes a 40-gallon barrel for "proof spirits"; by custom, 42 gallons constitute a barrel of crude oil or petroleum products for statistical purposes, and this equivalent is recognized "for liquids" by 4 states.

1 barrel (bbl), standard for fruits,
   vegetables, and other dry com-
   modities except dry cranberries = 7,056 cubic inches
                                        = 105 dry quarts
                                        = 3.281 bushels, struck measure
1 barrel (bbl), standard, cranberry = 5,826 cubic inches
                                        = 86 ⁴⁵/₆₄ dry quarts
                                        = 2.709 bushels, struck measure
1 board foot (lumber measure) . . = a foot-square board 1 inch thick
1 bushel (bu) (U.S.)
   (struck measure) . . . . = 2,150.42 cubic inches (exactly)
                                        = 35.239 liters
[1 bushel, heaped (U.S.)] . . . . . = 2,747.715 cubic inches
                                        = 1.278 bushels, struck measure°
°Frequently recognized as 1¼ bushels, struck measure.
[1 bushel (bu) (British Imperial)
   (struck measure)]. . . . . = 1.032 U.S. bushels, struck
                                        measure
                                        = 2,219.36 cubic inches
1 cord (cd) firewood . . . . = 128 cubic feet (exactly)
1 cubic centimeter (cm³). . . . . . = 0.061 cubic inch
1 cubic decimeter (dm³) . . . . . . = 61.024 cubic inches
1 cubic inch (in³) . . . . = 0.554 fluid ounce
                                        = 4.433 fluid drams
                                        = 16.387 cubic centimeters
1 cubic foot (ft³) . . . . = 7.481 gallons
                                        = 28.317 cubic decimeters
1 cubic meter (m³) . . . . = 1.308 cubic yards
1 cubic yard (yd³) . . . . = 0.765 cubic meter
1 cup, measuring . . . . = 8 fluid ounces (exactly)
                                        = ½ liquid pint (exactly)
[1 drachm, fluid (fl dr) (British)] = 0.961 U.S. fluid dram
                                        = 0.217 cubic inch
                                        = 3.552 milliliters
1 dekaliter (daL) . . . . = 2.642 gallons
                                        = 1.135 pecks
1 gallon (gal) (U.S.) . . . . = 231 cubic inches (exactly)
                                        = 3.785 liters
                                        = 0.833 British gallon
                                        = 128 U.S. fluid ounces (exactly)
[1 gallon (gal) British Imperial]. . = 277.42 cubic inches
                                        = 1.201 U.S. gallons
                                        = 4.546 liters
                                        = 160 British fluid ounces (exactly)
1 gill (gi) . . . . = 7.219 cubic inches
                                        = 4 fluid ounces (exactly)
                                        = 0.118 liter
1 hectoliter (hL) . . . . = 26.418 gallons
                                        = 2.838 bushels
1 liter (L) (1 cubic decimeter
   exactly) . . . . = 1.057 liquid quarts
                                        = 0.908 dry quart
                                        = 61.024 cubic inches
1 milliliter (mL) (1 cu cm exactly) = 0.271 fluid dram
                                        = 16.231 minims
                                        = 0.061 cubic inch

1 ounce, liquid (U.S.) . . . . = 1.805 cubic inches
                                        = 29.574 milliliters
                                        = 1.041 British fluid ounces
[1 ounce, fluid (fl oz) (British)] . . = 0.961 U.S. fluid ounce
                                        = 1.734 cubic inches
                                        = 28.412 milliliters
1 peck (pk) . . . . = 8.810 liters
1 pint (pt), dry . . . . = 33.600 cubic inches
                                        = 0.551 liter
1 pint (pt), liquid . . . . = 28.875 cubic inches (exactly)
                                        = 0.473 liter
1 quart (qt), dry (U.S.) . . . . = 67.201 cubic inches
                                        = 1.101 liters
                                        = 0.969 British quart
1 quart (qt), liquid (U.S.) . . . . . . = 57.75 cubic in (exactly)
                                        = 0.946 liter
                                        = 0.833 British quart
[1 quart (qt) (British)] . . . . = 69.354 cubic inches
                                        = 1.032 U.S. dry quarts
                                        = 1.201 U.S. liquid quarts
1 tablespoon. . . . . = 3 teaspoons°(exactly)
                                        = 4 fluid drams
                                        = ½ fluid ounce (exactly)
1 teaspoon . . . . = ⅓ tablespoon°(exactly)
                                        = 1⅓ fluid drams°

°The equivalent "1 teaspoon=1⅓ fluid drams" has been found to correspond more closely with the actual capacities of teaspoons in use than the equivalent "1 teaspoon=1 fluid dram" which is given by many dictionaries.

Weights or Masses

1 assay ton°° (AT) . . . . = 29.167 grams

°°Used in assaying. The assay ton bears the same relation to the milligram that a ton of 2,000 pounds avoirdupois bears to the ounce troy; hence, the weight in milligrams of precious metal obtained from one assay ton of ore gives directly the number of troy ounces to the net ton.

1 bale (cotton measure) . . . . = 500 pounds in U.S.
                                        = 750 pounds in Egypt
1 carat (c) . . . . = 200 milligrams (exactly)
                                        = 3.086 grains
1 dram avoirdupois (dr avdp) . . . . = 27 ¹¹/₃₂(=27.344) grains
                                        = 1.772 grams
1 gamma (γ). . . . . = 1 microgram (exactly), see
                                        below
1 grain. . . . . = 64.799 milligrams
1 gram. . . . . = 15.432 grains
                                        = 0.035 ounce, avoirdupois
1 hundredweight, gross or
   long°°° (gross cwt) . . . . = 112 pounds (exactly)
                                        = 50.802 kilograms
1 hundredweight, net or short
   (cwt or net cwt). . . . . = 100 pounds (exactly)
                                        = 45.359 kilograms
1 kilogram (kg). . . . . = 2.205 pounds
1 microgram (μg [the Greek
   letter mu in combination with
   the letter g]). . . . . = 0.000001 gram (exactly)
1 milligram (mg). . . . . = 0.015 grain
1 ounce, avoirdupois (oz avdp). . = 437.5 grains (exactly)
                                        = 0.911 troy ounce
                                        = 28.350 grams
1 ounce, troy (oz t) . . . . = 480 grains (exactly)
                                        = 1.097 avoirdupois ounces
                                        = 31.103 grams
1 pennyweight (dwt) . . . . = 1.555 grams
1 pound, avoirdupois (lb avdp). . = 7,000 grains (exactly)
                                        = 1.215 troy pounds
                                        = 453.592 37 grams (exactly)
1 pound, troy (lb t) . . . . = 5,760 grains (exactly)
                                        = 0.823 avoirdupois pound
                                        = 373.242 grams
1 ton, gross or long°°° (gross ton) = 2,240 pounds (exactly)
                                        = 1.12 net tons (exactly)
                                        = 1.016 metric tons

°°°The gross or long ton and hundredweight are used commercially in the U.S. to only a limited extent, usually in restricted industrial fields. These units are the same as the British ton and hundredweight.

1 ton, metric (t) . . . . = 2,204.623 pounds
                                        = 0.984 gross ton
                                        = 1.102 net tons
                                        = 2,000 pounds (exactly)
1 ton, net or short (sh ton) . . . . . = 0.893 gross ton
                                        = 0.907 metric ton

Tables of Interrelation of Units of Measurement

Units of length and area of the international and survey measures are included in the following tables. Units unique to the survey measure are *italicized*. See Tables of Equivalents, 1st paragraph.

1 international foot	= 0.999 998 survey foot (exactly)
1 survey foot	= 1200/3937 meter (exactly)
1 international foot	= 12 × 0.0254 meter (exactly)

Boldface type indicates exact values.

Units of Length

Units	Inches	*Links*	Feet	Yards	*Rods*	*Chains*	Miles	Cm	Meters
1 inch=	1	0.126 263	0.083 333	0.027 778	0.005 051	0.001 263	0.000 016	**2.54**	**0.025 4**
1 *link*=	7.92	1	**0.66**	0.22	0.04	0.01	0.000 125	20.117	0.201 168
1 foot=	**12**	1.515 152	1	0.333 333	0.060 606	0.015 152	0.000 189	**30.48**	**0.304 8**
1 yard=	**36**	4.545 45	**3**	1	0.181 818	0.045 455	0.000 568	**91.44**	**0.914 4**
1 *rod*=	**198**	**25**	**16.5**	**5.5**	1	**0.25**	0.003 125	502.92	5.029 2
1 *chain*=	**792**	**100**	**66**	**22**	**4**	1	**0.012 5**	2011.68	20.116 8
1 mile=	**63 360**	**8000**	**5280**	**1760**	**320**	**80**	1	160 934.4	1609.344
1 cm=	0.3937	0.049 710	0.032 808	0.010 936	0.001 988	0.000 497	0.000 006	1	**0.01**
1 meter=	39.37	4.970 960	3.280 840	1.093 613	0.198 838	0.049 710	0.000 621	**100**	1

Units of Area

Units	Sq. Inches	*Sq. links*	Sq. feet	Sq. yards	*Sq. rods*	*Sq. chains*
1 sq. inch=	1	0.015 942 3	0.006 944	0.000 771 605	0.000 025 5	0.000 001 594
1 sq. *link*=	62.726 4	1	**0.435 6**	**0.0484**	**0.0016**	0.000 1
1 sq. foot=	**144**	2.295 684	1	0.111 111 1	0.003 673 09	0.000 229 568
1 sq. yard=	**1296**	20.661 16	**9**	1	0.033 057 85	0.002 066 12
1 sq. *rod*=	**39 204**	**625**	**272.25**	**30.25**	1	**0.062 5**
1 sq. *chain*=	**627 264**	**10 000**	**4356**	**484**	**16**	1
1 acre=	**6 272 640**	**100 000**	**43 560**	**4840**	**160**	**10**
1 sq. mile=	**4 014 489 600**	**64 000 000**	**27 878 400**	**3 097 600**	**102 400**	**6400**
1 sq. cm=	0.155 000 3	0.002 471 05	0.001 076	0.000 119 599	0.000 003 954	0.000 000 247
1 sq. meter=	1550.003	24.710 44	10.763 91	1.195 990	0.039 536 70	0.002 471 044
1 *hectare*=	15 500 031	247 104	107 639.1	11 959.90	395.367 0	**24.710 44**

Units	*Acres*	Sq. miles	Sq. cm	Sq. meters	*Hectares*
1 sq. inch=	0.000 000 159 423	0.000 000 000 249 10	**6.451 6**	**0.000 645 16**	0.000 000 065
1 sq. *link*=	**0.000 01**	0.000 000 015 625	404.685 642 24	0.040 468 56	0.000 004 047
1 sq. foot=	0.000 022 956 84	0.000 000 035 870 06	929.034 1	0.092 903 41	0.000 009 290
1 sq. yard=	0.000 206 611 6	0.000 000 322 830 6	**8361.273 6**	0.836 127 36	0.000 083 613
1 sq. *rod*=	**0.006 25**	0.000 000 009 765 625	252 929.5	25.292 95	0.002 529 295
1 sq. *chain*=	**0.1**	0.000 156 25	4 046 873	404.687 3	0.040 468 73
1 acre=	1	0.001 562 5	40 468 730	4046.873	0.404 687 3
1 sq. mile=	**640**	1	25 899 881 103	2 589 988.11	258.998 811 034
1 sq. cm=	0.000 000 024 711	0.000 000 000 038 610	1	**0.000 1**	0.000 000 01
1 sq. meter=	0.000 247 104 4	0.000 000 386 102 2	10 000	1	**0.0001**
1 *hectare*=	2.471 044	0.003 861 006	100 000 000	10 000	1

Units of Weight or Mass Not Greater Than Pounds and Kilograms

Units	Grains	Pennyweights	Avdp drams	Avdp ounces
1 grain=	1	0.041 666 67	0.036 571 43	0.002 285 71
1 pennyweight=	**24**	1	0.877 714 3	0.054 857 14
1 dram avdp=	**27.343 75**	1.139 323	1	**0.062 5**
1 ounce avdp=	**437.5**	18.229 17	**16**	1
1 ounce troy=	**480**	**20**	17.554 29	1.097 143
1 pound troy=	**5760**	**240**	210.651 4	13.165 71
1 pound avdp=	**7000**	291.666 7	**256**	**16**
1 milligram=	0.015 432	0.000 643 015	0.000 564 383	0.000 035 274
1 gram=	15.432 36	0.643 014 9	0.564 383 4	0.035 273 96
1 kilogram=	15 432.36	643.014 9	564.383 4	35.273 96

Units	Troy ounces	Troy pounds	Avdp pounds	Milligrams	Grams	Kilograms
1 grain=	0.002 083 33	0.000 173 611	0.000 142 857	**64.798 91**	**0.064 798 91**	0.000 064 799
1 pennywt.=	0.05	0.004 166 667	0.003 428 571	**1555.173 84**	**1.555 173 84**	0.001 555 174
1 dram avdp=	0.056 966 15	0.004 747 179	0.003 906 25	1771.845 195	1.771 845 195	0.001 771 845
1 oz avdp=	0.911 458 3	0.075 954 86	**0.062 5**	**28 349.523 125**	**28.349 523 125**	0.028 349 52
1 oz troy=	1	0.083 333 333	0.068 571 43	**31 103.476 8**	**31.103 476 8**	0.031 103 48
1 lb troy=	**12**	1	0.822 857 1	**373 241.721 6**	**373.241 721 6**	0.373 241 722
1 lb avdp=	14.583 33	1.215 278	1	**453 592.37**	**453.592 37**	0.453 592 37
1 milligram=	0.000 032 151	0.000 002 679	0.000 002 205	1	**0.001**	0.000 001
1 gram=	0.032 150 75	0.002 679 229	0.002 204 623	**1000**	1	**0.001**
1 kilogram=	32.150 75	2.679 229	2.204 623	**1 000 000**	**1000**	1

Units of Weight or Mass Not Less Than Avoirdupois Ounces

Units	Avdp oz	Avdp lb	Short cwt	Short tons	Long tons	Kilograms	Metric tons
1 oz avdp=	1	**0.0625**	**0.000 625**	**0.000 031 25**	0.000 027 902	0.028 349 523	0.000 028 350
1 lb avdp=	**16**	1	**0.01**	**0.000 5**	0.000 446 429	0.453 592 37	0.000 453 592
1 sh cwt=	**1600**	**100**	1	**0.05**	0.044 642 86	45.359 237	0.045 359 237
1 sh ton=	**32 000**	**2000**	**20**	1	0.892 857 1	907.184 74	0.907 184 74
1 long ton=	**35 840**	**2240**	**22.4**	**1.12**	1	1 016.046 908 8	1.016 046 909
1 kg=	35.273 96	2.204 623	0.022 046 23	0.001 102 311	0.000 984 207	1	**0.001**
1 metric ton=	35 273.96	2204.623	22.046 23	1.102 311	0.984 206 5	**1000**	1

Units of Volume

Units	Cubic inches	Cubic feet	Cubic yards	Cubic cm	Cubic dm	Cubic meters
1 cubic inch=	1	0.000 578 704	0.000 021 433	16.387 064	0.016 387	0.000 016 387
1 cubic foot=	1728	1	0.037 037 04	28 316.846 592	28.316 847	0.028 316 847
1 cubic yard=	46 656	27	1	764 554.857 984	764.554 858	0.764 554 858
1 cubic cm=	0.061 023 74	0.000 035 315	0.000 001 308	1	0.001	0.000 001
1 cubic dm=	61.023 74	0.035 314 67	0.001 307 951	1000	1	0.001
1 cubic meter=	61 023.74	35.314 67	1.307 951	1 000 000	1000	1

Units of Capacity (Liquid Measure)

Units	Minims	Fluid drams	Fluid ounces	Gills	Liquid pint
1 minim=	1	0.016 666 7	0.002 083 33	0.000 520 833	0.000 130 208
1 fluid dram=	60	1	0.125	0.031 25	0.007 812 5
1 fluid ounce=	480	8	1	0.25	0.062 5
1 gill=	1920	32	4	1	0.25
1 liquid pint=	7680	128	16	4	1
1 liquid quart=	15 360	256	32	8	2
1 gallon=	61 440	1024	128	32	8
1 cubic inch=	265.974	4.432 900	0.554 112 6	0.138 528 1	0.034 632 03
1 cubic foot=	459 603.1	7660.052	957.506 5	239.376 6	59.844 16
1 liter=	16 230.73	270.512 18	33.814 02	8.453 506	2.113 376

Units	Liquid quarts	Gallons	Cubic inches	Cubic feet	Liters
1 minim=	0.000 065 104 17	0.000 016 276 04	0.003 759 766	0.000 002 175 790	0.000 061 611 52
1 flu. dram=	0.003 906 25	0.000 976 562 5	0.225 585 9	0.000 130 547 4	0.003 696 691
1 fluid oz=	0.031 25	0.007 812 5	1.804 687 5	0.001 044 379	0.029 573 53
1 gill=	0.125	0.031 25	7.218 75	0.004 177 517	0.118 294 118
1 liquid pt=	0.5	0.125	28.875	0.016 710 07	0.473 176 473
1 liquid qt=	1	0.25	57.75	0.033 420 14	0.946 352 946
1 gallon=	4	1	231	0.133 680 6	3.785 411 784
1 cubic inch=	0.017 316 02	0.004 329 004	1	0.000 578 703 7	0.016 387 064
1 cubic foot=	29.922 08	7.480 519	1728	1	28.316 846 592
1 liter=	1.056 688	0.264 172 05	61.023 74	0.035 314 67	1

Units of Capacity (Dry Measure)

Units	Dry pints	Dry quarts	Pecks	Bushels	Cubic in.	Liters
1 dry pint=	1	0.5	0.062 5	0.015 625	33.600 312 5	0.550 610 47
1 dry quart=	2	1	0.125	0.031 25	67.200 625	1.101 220 9
1 peck=	16	8	1	0.25	537.605	8.809 767 5
1 bushel=	64	32	4	1	2150.42	35.239 07
1 cubic inch=	0.029 761 6	0.014 880 8	0.001 860 10	0.000 465 025	1	0.016 387 06
1 liter=	1.816 166	0.908 083	0.113 510 37	0.028 377 59	61.023 74	1

Miscellaneous Measures

Caliber—the diameter of a gun bore. In the U.S., caliber is traditionally expressed in hundredths of inches, e.g., .22 or .30. In Britain, caliber is often expressed in thousandths of inches, e.g., .270 or .465. Now it is commonly expressed in millimeters, e.g., the 5.56 mm M16 rifle. Heavier weapons' caliber has long been expressed in millimeters, e.g., the 81 mm mortar, the 105 mm howitzer (light), the 155 mm howitzer (medium or heavy).

Naval guns' caliber refers to the barrel length as a multiple of the bore diameter. A 5-inch, 50-caliber naval gun has a 5-inch bore and a barrel length of 250 inches.

Karat or carat—a measure of fineness for gold equal to 1/24 part of pure gold in an alloy. Thus 24-karat gold is pure; 18-karat gold is 1/4 alloy. (A *carat* is also a unit of weight for precious stones, equal to 200 milligrams.)

Decibel (dB)—a measure of the relative loudness or intensity of sound. A 20-decibel sound is 10 times louder than a 10-decibel sound; 30 decibels is 100 times louder; 40 decibels is 1,000 times louder, etc. One decibel is the smallest difference between sounds detectable by the human ear. A 120-decibel sound is painful.

10 decibels	– a light whisper
20	– quiet conversation
30	– normal conversation
40	– light traffic
50	– typewriter, loud conversation
60	– noisy office
70	– normal traffic, quiet train
80	– rock music, subway
90	– heavy traffic, thunder
100	– jet plane at takeoff

Em—a printer's measure designating the square width of any given type size. Thus, an em of 10-point type is 10 points. An en is half an em.

Gauge—a measure of shotgun bore diameter. Gauge numbers originally referred to the number of lead balls just fitting the gun barrel diameter required to make a pound. Thus, a 16-gauge shotgun's bore was smaller than a 12-gauge shotgun's. Today, an international agreement assigns millimeter measures to each gauge, e.g.:

Gauge	Bore diameter (in mm)
6	23.34
10	19.67
12	18.52
14	17.60
16	16.81
20	15.90

Horsepower—the power needed to lift 550 pounds 1 foot in 1 second or to lift 33,000 pounds 1 foot in 1 minute. Equivalent to 746 watts or 2,546.0756 Btu/h.

Knot—a measure of the speed of ships. A knot equals 1 nautical mile per hour.

Quire—25 sheets of paper

Ream—500 sheets of paper

Electrical Units

The **watt** is the unit of power (electrical, mechanical, thermal, etc.). Electrical power is given by the product of the voltage and the current.

Energy is sold by the **joule,** but in common practice the billing of electrical energy is expressed in terms of the **kilowatt-hour,** which is 3,600,000 joules or 3.6 megajoules.

The **horsepower** is a nonmetric unit sometimes used in mechanics. It is equal to 746 watts.

The **ohm** is the unit of electrical resistance and represents the physical property of a conductor that offers a resistance to the flow of electricity, permitting just 1 ampere to flow at 1 volt of pressure.

Ancient Measures

Biblical			Greek			Roman		
Cubit	=	21.8 inches	Cubit	=	18.3 inches	Cubit		= 17.5 inches
Omer	=	0.45 peck	Stadion	=	607.2 or 622 feet	Stadium		= 202 yards
	=	3.964 liters	Obolos	=	715.38 milligrams	As, libra,		
Ephah	=	10 omers	Drachma	=	4.2923 grams	pondus		= 325.971 grams
Shekel	=	0.497 ounce	Mina	=	0.9463 pound			= 0.71864 pound
	=	14.1 grams	Talent	=	60 mina			

Weight or Mass of Water

Weight, at 20°C

1	cubic inch	0.0360 pound
12	cubic inches	0.433 pound
1	cubic foot	62.4 pounds
1	cubic foot	7.48052 U.S. gal
1.8	cubic feet	112.0 pounds
35.96	cubic feet	2240.0 pounds

1	U.S. gallon	8.33 pounds
13.45	U.S. gallons	112.0 pounds
269.0	U.S. gallons	2240.0 pounds

Mass, at 4°C (Maximum Density)

1	cubic centimeter	1 gram
1	liter	1 kilogram
1	cubic meter	1 metric ton

Density of Gases and Vapors

at 0°C and 760 mmHg; kilograms per cubic meter

Gas	Mass	Gas	Mass	Gas	Mass
Acetylene.	1.171	Ethylene.	1.260	Methyl fluoride	1.545
Air	1.293	Fluorine	1.696	Mono methylamine	1.38
Ammonia	0.759	Helium	0.178	Neon	0.900
Argon.	1.784	Hydrogen	0.090	Nitric oxide	1.341
Arsine	3.48	Hydrogen bromide.	3.50	Nitrogen	1.250
Butane-iso	2.60	Hydrogen chloride.	1.639	Nitrosyl chloride	2.99
Butane-n	2.519	Hydrogen iodide	5.724	Nitrous oxide	1.997
Carbon dioxide	1.977	Hydrogen selenide	3.66	Oxygen	1.429
Carbon monoxide	1.250	Hydrogen sulfide.	1.539	Phosphine	1.48
Carbon oxysulfide	2.72	Krypton	3.745	Propane.	2.020
Chlorine	3.214	Methane.	0.717	Silicon tetrafluoride	4.67
Chlorine monoxide	3.89	Methyl chloride	2.25	Sulfur dioxide	2.927
Ethane.	1.356	Methyl ether	2.091	Xenon	5.897

Temperature Conversion Table

The numbers in **boldface type** refer to the temperatures either in degrees Celsius or Fahrenheit that are to be converted. If converting from degrees Fahrenheit to Celsius, refer to the column on the left; if converting from degrees Celsius to Fahrenheit, consult the column on the right.

For temperatures not shown. To convert Fahrenheit to Celsius by formula, subtract 32 degrees and divide by 1.8; to convert Celsius to Fahrenheit, multiply by 1.8 and add 32 degrees.

Note: Although the term *centigrade* is still frequently used, the International Committee on Weights and Measures and the National Institute of Standards and Technology have recommended since 1948 that this scale be called Celsius.

Celsius		Fahrenheit	Celsius		Fahrenheit	Celsius		Fahrenheit
−273.2	**−459.7**	. . . . . .	−17.8	**0**	32	35.0	**95**	203
−184	**−300**	. . . . . .	−12.2	**10**	50	36.7	**98**	208.4
−169	**−273**	− 459.4	− 6.67	**20**	68	37.8	**100**	212
−157	**−250**	− 418	− 1.11	**30**	86	43	**110**	230
−129	**−200**	− 328	4.44	**40**	104	49	**120**	248
−101	**−150**	− 238	10.0	**50**	122	54	**130**	266
− 73.3	**−100**	− 148	15.6	**60**	140	60	**140**	284
− 45.6	**− 50**	− 58	21.1	**70**	158	66	**150**	302
− 40.0	**− 40**	− 40	23.9	**75**	167	93	**200**	392
− 34.4	**− 30**	− 22	26.7	**80**	176	121	**250**	482
− 28.9	**− 20**	− 4	29.4	**85**	185	149	**300**	572
− 23.3	**− 10**	14	32.2	**90**	194			

Boiling and Freezing Points

Water boils at 212°F at sea level. For every 550 feet above sea level, boiling point of water is lower by about 1°F. Methyl alcohol boils at 148°F. Average human oral temperature, 98.6°F. Water freezes at 32°F.

Compound Interest

Compounded Annually

Principal	Period	4%	5%	6%	7%	8%	9%	10%	12%	14%	16%
$100	1 day	0.011	0.014	0.016	0.019	0.022	0.025	0.027	0.033	0.038	0.044
	1 week	0.077	0.096	0.115	0.134	0.153	0.173	0.192	0.230	0.268	0.307
	6 mos.	2.00	2.50	3.00	3.50	4.00	4.50	5.00	6.00	7.00	8.00
	1 year	4.00	5.00	6.00	7.00	8.00	9.00	10.00	12.00	14.00	16.00
	2 years	8.16	10.25	12.36	14.49	16.64	18.81	21.00	25.44	29.96	34.56
	3 years	12.49	15.76	19.10	22.50	25.97	29.50	33.10	40.49	48.15	56.09
	4 years	16.99	21.55	26.25	31.08	36.05	41.16	46.41	57.35	68.90	81.06
	5 years	21.67	27.63	33.82	40.26	46.93	53.86	61.05	76.23	92.54	110.03
	6 years	26.53	34.01	41.85	50.07	58.69	67.71	77.16	97.38	119.50	143.64
	7 years	31.59	40.71	50.36	60.58	71.38	82.80	94.87	121.07	150.22	192.62
	8 years	36.86	47.75	59.38	71.82	85.09	99.26	114.36	147.60	185.26	227.84
	9 years	42.33	55.13	68.95	83.85	99.90	117.19	135.79	177.31	225.19	280.30
	10 years	48.02	62.89	79.08	96.72	115.89	136.74	159.37	210.58	270.72	341.14
	12 years	60.10	79.59	101.22	125.22	151.82	181.27	213.84	289.60	381.79	493.60
	15 years	80.09	107.89	139.66	175.90	217.22	264.25	317.72	447.36	613.79	826.55
	20 years	119.11	165.33	220.71	286.97	366.10	460.44	572.75	864.63	1,274.35	1,846.08

Breaking the Sound Barrier; Speed of Sound

The prefix Mach is used to describe supersonic speed. It was named for Ernst Mach (1838-1916), a Czech-born Austrian physicist, who contributed to the study of sound. When a plane moves at the speed of sound, it is Mach 1. When moving at twice the speed of sound, it is Mach 2. When it is below the speed of sound, the speed can be designated accordingly—for example, Mach 0.90. Mach is defined as "the ratio of the velocity of a rocket or a jet to the velocity of sound in the medium being considered."

When a plane passes the sound barrier—flying faster than sound travels—listeners in the area hear thunderclaps, but the pilot of the plane does not hear them.

Sound is produced by vibrations of an object and is transmitted by alternate increase and decrease in pressures that radiate outward through a material media of molecules—somewhat like waves spreading out on a pond after a rock has been tossed into it.

The frequency of sound is determined by the number of times the vibrating waves undulate per second and is measured in cycles per second. The slower the cycle of waves, the lower the frequency. As frequencies increase, the sound is higher in pitch.

Sound is audible to human beings only if the frequency falls within a certain range. The human ear is usually not sensitive to frequencies of fewer than 20 vibrations per second or greater than about 20,000 vibrations per second—although this range varies among individuals. Any sound at a pitch higher than the human ear can hear is termed ultrasonic.

Intensity, or loudness, is the strength of the pressure of these radiating waves and is measured in decibels. The human ear responds to intensity in a range from zero to 120 decibels. Any sound with a pressure of more than 120 decibels is painful to the human ear.

The speed of sound is generally defined as 1,088 feet per second at sea level at 32°F. It varies in other temperatures and in different media. Sound travels faster in water than in air, and even faster in iron and steel. It takes 5 seconds to travel a mile in air, and 1 second to move a mile under water, and sound travels through iron in 1/3 second. It travels through ice-cold vapor at approximately 4,708 feet per second; ice-cold water, 4,938; granite, 12,960; hardwood, 12,620; brick, 11,960; glass, 16,410 to 19,690; silver, 8,658; gold, 5,717.

Colors of the Spectrum

Color, an electromagnetic wave phenomenon, is a sensation produced through the excitation of the retina of the eye by rays of light. The colors of the spectrum may be produced by viewing a light beam refracted by passage through a prism, which breaks the light into its wavelengths.

Customarily, the primary colors of the spectrum are taken to be the 6 monochromatic colors that occupy relatively large areas of the spectrum: red, orange, yellow, green, blue, and violet. However, Sir Isaac Newton named a 7th, indigo, situated between blue and violet on the spectrum. Aubert estimated (1865) the solar spectrum to contain approximately 1,000 distinguishable hues; of the hues, according to Rood (1881), 2 million tints and shades can be distinguished. Luckiesh stated (1915) that 55 distinctly different hues have been seen in a single spectrum.

Many physicists recognize only 3 primary colors: red, yellow, and blue (Mayer, 1775); red, green, and violet (Thomas Young, 1801); or red, green, and blue (Clerk Maxwell, 1860).

The color sensation of black is due to complete lack of stimulation of the retina, that of white to complete stimulation. The infrared and ultraviolet rays, below the red (long) end of the spectrum and above the violet (short) end respectively, are invisible to the naked eye. Heat is the principal effect of the infrared rays, and chemical action that of the ultraviolet rays.

Common Fractions Reduced to Decimals

8ths	16ths	32ds	64ths		8ths	16ths	32ds	64ths		8ths	16ths	32ds	64ths	
			1	= 0.015625				23	= 0.359375			11	22	44	= 0.6875
		1	2	= 0.03125	3	6	12	24	= 0.375				45	= 0.703125
			3	= 0.046875				25	= 0.390625				23	46	= 0.71875
	1	2	4	= 0.0625				13	26	= 0.40625				47	= 0.734375
			5	= 0.078125				27	= 0.421875	6	12	24	48	= 0.75
		3	6	= 0.09375		7	14	28	= 0.4375				49	= 0.765625
			7	= 0.109375				29	= 0.453125				25	50	= 0.78125
1	2	4	8	= 0.125				15	30	= 0.46875				51	= 0.796875
			9	= 0.140625				31	= 0.484375		13	26	52	= 0.8125
		5	10	= 0.15625	4	8	16	32	= 0.5				53	= 0.828125
			11	= 0.171875				33	= 0.515625			27	54	= 0.84375
	3	6	12	= 0.1875			17	34	= 0.53125				55	= 0.859375
			13	= 0.203125				35	= 0.546875	7	14	28	56	= 0.875
		7	14	= 0.21875			18	36	= 0.5625				57	= 0.890625
			15	= 0.234375				37	= 0.578125			29	58	= 0.90625
2	4	8	16	= 0.25			19	38	= 0.59375				59	= 0.921875
			17	= 0.265625				39	= 0.609375		15	30	60	= 0.9375
		9	18	= 0.28125	5	10	20	40	= 0.625				61	= 0.953125
			19	= 0.296875				41	= 0.640625			31	62	= 0.96875
	5	10	20	= 0.3125			21	42	= 0.65625				63	= 0.984375
			21	= 0.328125				43	= 0.671875	8	16	32	64	= 1.0
		11	22	= 0.34375										

Spirits Measures

Pony . . . . = 0.5 jigger
Shot . . . . = 0.666 jigger
        = 1.0 ounce
Jigger . . . . = 1.5 shots
Pint . . . . = 16 shots
        = 0.625 fifth
Fifth . . . . = 25.6 shots
        = 1.6 pints
        = 0.8 quart
        = 0.75706 liter

Quart . . . . = 32 shots
        = 1.25 fifths
Magnum . . . . = 2 quarts
        = 2.49797 bottles
         (wine)

For champagne and brandy only:

Jeroboam . . . . = 6.4 pints
        = 1.6 magnum
        = 0.8 gallon

For champagne only:

Rehoboam . . . . = 3 magnums
Methuselah . . . . . . = 4 magnums
Salmanazar . . . . . . = 6 magnums
Balthazar . . . . = 8 magnums
Nebuchadnezzar . . . = 10 magnums

Wine bottle (standard) = 0.800633 quart
           = 0.7576778 liter

Measures of Force and Pressure

Dyne = force necessary to accelerate a 1-gram mass 1 centimeter per second squared = 0.000072 poundal
Poundal = force necessary to accelerate a 1-pound mass 1 foot per second squared = 13,825.5 dynes = 0.138255 newtons
Newton = force needed to accelerate a 1-kilogram mass 1 meter per second squared

Pascal (pressure) = 1 newton per square meter = 0.020885 pound per square foot
Atmosphere (air pressure at sea level) = 2,116.102 pounds per square foot = 14.6952 pounds per square inch = 1.0332 kilograms per square centimeter = 101,323 newtons per square meter

Mathematical Formulas

Note: The value of π (the Greek letter pi) is approximately 3.14159265 (equal to the ratio of the circumference of a circle to the diameter), typically rounded further to 3.1416 or 3.14.

To find the CIRCUMFERENCE of a:

Circle — Multiply the diameter by π.

To find the AREA of a:

Circle — Multiply the square of the radius (equal to ½ the diameter) by π.
Rectangle — Multiply the length of the base by the height.
Sphere (surface) — Multiply the square of the radius by π and multiply by 4.

Square — Square the length of one side.
Trapezoid — Add the two parallel sides, multiply by the height, and divide by 2.
Triangle — Multiply the base by the height, divide by 2.

To find the VOLUME of a:

Cone — Multiply the square of the radius of the base by π, multiply by the height, and divide by 3.
Cube — Cube the length of one edge.
Cylinder — Multiply the square of the radius of the base by π and multiply by the height.

Pyramid — Multiply the area of the base by the height and divide by 3.
Rectangular Prism — Multiply the length by the width by the height.
Sphere — Multiply the cube of the radius by π, multiply by 4, and divide by 3.

Playing Cards and Dice Chances

5-Card Poker Hands

Hand	Number possible	Odds against
Royal flush	4	649,739 to 1
Other straight flush	36	72,192 to 1
Four of a kind	624	4,164 to 1
Full house	3,744	693 to 1
Flush	5,108	508 to 1
Straight	10,200	254 to 1
Three of a kind	54,912	46 to 1
Two pairs	123,552	20 to 1
One pair	1,098,240	4 to 3 (1.37 to 1)
Nothing	1,302,540	1 to 1
Total	**2,598,960**	

Dice
(probabilities of consecutive winning plays)

No. consecutive wins	By 7,11, or point	No. consecutive wins	By 7, 11, or point
1	244 in 495	6	1 in 70
2	6 in 25	7	1 in 141
3	3 in 25	8	1 in 287
4	1 in 17	9	1 in 582
5	1 in 34		

Dice
(probabilities on 2 dice)

Total	Odds against (single toss)	Total	Odds against (single toss)
2	35 to 1	8	31 to 5
3	17 to 1	9	8 to 1
4	11 to 1	10	11 to 1
5	8 to 1	11	17 to 1
6	31 to 5	12	35 to 1
7	5 to 1		

Pinochle Auction
(odds against finding in "widow" of 3 cards)

Open places	Odds	Open places	Odds
1	5 to 1 against	4	1½ to 1 for
2	2 to 1 against	5	2 to 1 for
3	Even	6	3 to 1 for

Bridge

The odds—against suit distribution in a hand of 4-4-3-2 are about 4 to 1, against 5-4-2-2 about 8 to 1, against 6-4-2-1 about 20 to 1, against 7-4-1-1 about 254 to 1, against 8-4-1-0 about 2,211 to 1, and against 13-0-0-0 about 158,753,389,899 to 1.

Large Numbers

U.S.	Number of zeros	British[1], French, German	U.S.	Number of zeros	British[1], French, German
million	6	million	tredecillion	42	septillion
billion	9	milliard	quattuordecillion	45	1,000 septillion
trillion	12	billion	quindecillion	48	octillion
quadrillion	15	1,000 billion	sexdecillion	51	1,000 octillion
quintillion	18	trillion	septendecillion	54	nonillion
sextillion	21	1,000 trillion	octodecillion	57	1,000 nonillion
septillion	24	quadrillion	novemdecillion	60	decillion
octillion	27	1,000 quadrillion	vigintillion	63	1,000 decillion
nonillion	30	quintillion	googol	100	googol
decillion	33	1,000 quintillion	centillion	303	—
undecillion	36	sextillion	—	600	centillion
duodecillion	39	1,000 sextillion	googolplex	googol	googolplex

(1) In recent years, it has become more common in Britain to use American terminology for large numbers.

Roman Numerals

I	—	1	VI	—	6	XI	—	11	L	—	50	C̄Ð	—	400	X̄	—	10,000
II	—	2	VII	—	7	XIX	—	19	LX	—	60	D	—	500	L̄	—	50,000
III	—	3	VIII	—	8	XX	—	20	XC	—	90	CM	—	900	C̄	—	100,000
IV	—	4	IX	—	9	XXX	—	30	C	—	100	M	—	1,000	D̄	—	500,000
V	—	5	X	—	10	XL	—	40	CC	—	200	V̄	—	5,000	M̄	—	1,000,000

HEALTH
Basic First Aid

First aid experts stress that knowing what to do for an injured victim until a doctor or other trained person gets to the accident scene can save a life, especially in cases of stoppage of breathing, severe bleeding, and shock.

People with special medical problems, such as diabetes, cardiovascular disease, epilepsy, or allergy, are urged to wear some sort of emblem identifying the problem, as a safeguard against administration of medication that might be injurious or even fatal. Emblems may be obtained from Medic Alert Foundation, 2323 Colorado Ave., Turlock, CA 95382; 800-344-3226.

It is important to get medical assistance as soon as possible.

Animal bite — Wash wound with soap under running water and apply antibiotic ointment and dressing. When possible, the animal should be caught alive for rabies testing.

Asphyxiation — Start rescue breathing immediately after getting patient to fresh air.

Bleeding — Elevate the wound above the heart if possible. Press hard on wound with sterile compress until bleeding stops. Send for doctor if bleeding is severe.

Burn — If mild, with skin unbroken and no blisters, put into ice water until pain subsides. Apply a dry dressing if necessary. If severe, send for doctor. Apply sterile compresses and keep patient comfortably warm until doctor's arrival. Do not try to clean burn or break blisters.

Chemical in eye — With patient lying down, pour cupfuls of water immediately into corner of eye, letting it run to other side to remove chemicals thoroughly. Cover with sterile compress. Get medical attention immediately.

Choking — See **Abdominal Thrust**.

Convulsions — Place person on back on bed or rug. Loosen clothing. Turn head to side. Do not place a blunt object between the patient's teeth. If convulsions do not stop, get medical attention immediately.

Cut (minor) — Apply mild antiseptic and sterile compress after washing with soap under warm running water.

Fainting — If victim feels faint, lower head to knees. Lay patient down on back with head turned to side if he or she becomes unconscious. Elevate the legs 8 to 10 inches. Loosen clothing and open windows. Keep patient lying quietly for at least 15 minutes after he or she regains consciousness. Call doctor if faint lasts for more than a few minutes.

Foreign body in eye — Touch object with moistened corner of handkerchief if it can be seen. If it cannot be seen or does not come out after a few attempts, take patient to doctor. Do not rub the eye.

Frostbite — Handle frostbitten area gently. Do not rub. Soak affected area in water no warmer than 105°F. Do not allow frostbitten area to touch the container. Soak until frostbitten part looks red and feels warm. Loosely bandage. If fingers or toes are frostbitten, put gauze between them.

Heat Stroke and Heat Exhaustion — Remove the patient from the heat. Loosen any tight clothing and apply cool, wet cloths to the skin. Give the victim cool water, to drink slowly. Call an ambulance if the victim refuses water, vomits, or experiences changes in consciousness.

Hypothermia — Move victim to a warm place. Remove wet clothing and dry victim, if necessary. Warm patient gradually by wrapping the person in warm blankets or clothing. Apply heat pads or other heat sources if available, but not directly to the body. Give the victim warm liquids. Call an ambulance if breathing is slowed or stopped or if the pulse is slow or irregular.

Loss of Limb — If a limb is severed, it is important to properly protect the limb so that it can possibly be reattached. After the patient is cared for, the limb should be wrapped in a sterile gauze or clean material and placed in a clean plastic bag, garbage can, or other suitable container. Pack ice around the limb on the OUTSIDE of the bag to keep the limb cold. Call ahead to the hospital to alert staff there of the situation.

Poisoning — Call doctor. Use antidote listed on label if container is found. Call local Poison Control Center if possible. Do not give the victim any food or drink or induce vomiting, unless specified on the label or by a medical professional.

Shock (injury-related) — Keep the victim lying down; if uncertain as to his or her injuries, keep the patient flat on the back. Maintain normal body temperature; if the weather is cold or damp, place blankets or extra clothing over and under the victim; if weather is hot, provide shade.

Snakebite — Wash the injury. Keep the area still and at a lower level than the heart. Keep the victim quiet. Use a snakebite kit if available.

Sprains and fractures — Apply ice to reduce swelling and pain. Do not try to straighten or move broken limbs. Apply a splint to immobilize the injured area if the victim must be transported.

Sting from insect — If possible, remove stinger. Wash the area with soap and water; cover it to keep it clean. Apply a cold pack to reduce pain and swelling. Call physician immediately if body swells or patient collapses.

Unconsciousness — Send for doctor and place person on his or her back. Start rescue breathing if victim stops breathing. Never give food or liquids.

Abdominal Thrust (Heimlich Maneuver)

The American Red Cross and the American Heart Association both agree that the recommended first aid for choking victims is the abdominal thrust, also known as the Heimlich maneuver, after its creator, Dr. Henry Heimlich. Slaps on the back are no longer advised and may even prove detrimental in an attempt to assist a choking victim.

- Get behind the victim and wrap your arms around him or her above the waist.
- Make a fist with one hand and place it, with the thumb knuckle pressing inward, just below the point of the "v" of the rib cage.
- Grasp the wrist with the other hand and give one or more upward thrusts or hugs.
- Start rescue breathing if breathing stops.

Rescue Breathing

Stressing that your breath can save a life, the American Red Cross gives the following directions for rescue breathing if the victim is not breathing:

- Determine consciousness by tapping the victim on the shoulder and asking loudly, "Are you okay?"
- Tilt the victim's head back so that the chin is pointing upward. Do not press on the soft tissue under the chin, as this might obstruct the airway. If you suspect that an accident victim might have neck or back injuries, open the airway by placing the tips of your index and middle fingers on the corners of the person's jaw to lift it forward without tilting the head.
- Place your cheek and ear close to the victim's mouth and nose. Look at the chest to see if it rises and falls. Listen and feel for air to be exhaled for about 5 seconds.
- If there is no breathing, pinch the victim's nostrils shut with the thumb and index finger of your hand that is pressing on the victim's forehead. Another way to prevent leakage of air when the lungs are inflated is to press your cheek against the victim's nose.
- Blow air into the mouth by taking a deep breath and then sealing your mouth tightly around the victim's mouth. Initially, give 2, quick (approx. 1.5 seconds each), full breaths without allowing the lungs to deflate completely between each breath.
- Watch the patient's chest to see if it rises.
- Stop when the chest is expanded. Raise your mouth; turn your head to the side and listen for exhalation.
- Watch the chest to see if it falls.
- Repeat the blowing cycle until the victim starts breathing.

Note: Infants (up to 1 year) and children (1 to 8 years) should be administered rescue breathing as described above, except for the following:

- Do not tilt the head as far back as an adult's head.
- Both the mouth and nose of an infant should be sealed by the mouth.
- Give breaths to a child once every 3 seconds.
- Blow into the infant's mouth and nose once every 3 seconds with less pressure and volume than for a child.

Food and Nutrition

The U.S. Dept. of Health and Human Services and the Dept. of Agriculture reissued dietary guidelines Jan. 2, 1996, that offered dietary and exercise advice for children age 2 and over, as well as for adults. Recommended were: (1) no more than 30 percent of calories from fat, or about 65 grams of fat in a 2,000-calorie daily diet; and no more than 10 percent of calories, or 20 grams of fat, from saturated fats; (2) maximum alcohol consumption of about 1 drink a day for women, 2 for men; (3) daily consumption of vegetables of 3-5 servings; fruits, 2-4; pastas, cereals, or breads, 6-11; milk, 2-3; meat, poultry, fish, beans, and eggs, 2-3. (For vegetables, 1 serving equals about 1 cup raw leafy greens or one-half cup other kinds; fruit, 1 medium apple, banana, or orange, or ¾ cup of fruit juice; grains, 1 slice of bread, ½ cup of pasta, or 1 oz. cereal; milk, 1 cup or 1.5 oz. of cheese; meat and poultry, 2-3 oz. cooked lean beef or chicken without skin; cooked dry beans, ½ cup.)

Protein

Proteins, composed of amino acids, are essential to good nutrition. They build, maintain, and repair the body. Best sources: eggs, milk, fish, meat, poultry, soybeans, nuts. High-quality proteins such as eggs, meat, or fish supply all 8 amino acids needed in the diet. Plant foods can be combined to meet protein needs as well: whole grain breads and cereals, rice, oats, soybeans, other beans, split peas, and nuts.

Fats

Fats provide energy by furnishing calories to the body, and they also carry vitamins A, D, E, and K. They are the most concentrated source of energy in the diet. Best sources of polyunsaturated and monounsaturated fats: margarine, vegetable/plant oils, nuts. Meats, cheeses, butter, cream, egg yolks, lard are concentrated sources of saturated fats.

Carbohydrates

Carbohydrates provide energy for body function and activity by supplying immediate calories. The carbohydrate group includes sugars, starches, fiber, and starchy vegetables. Best sources: grains, legumes, potatoes, vegetables, fruits.

Fiber

The portion of plant foods that our bodies cannot digest is known as fiber. There are 2 basic types: insoluble ("roughage") and soluble. Insoluble fibers help move food materials through the digestive tract, whereas soluble fibers tend to slow it down. Both types absorb water, enabling them to prevent and treat constipation by softening and increasing the bulk of the undigested food components that pass through the digestive tract. Soluble fibers have also been reported to be helpful in reducing blood cholesterol levels. Best sources: beans, bran, fruits, whole grains, vegetables.

Water

Water dissolves and transports other nutrients throughout the body, aiding the processes of digestion, absorption, circulation, and excretion. It helps regulate body temperature.

Vitamins

Vitamin A—promotes good eyesight and helps keep the skin and mucous membranes resistant to infection. Best sources: liver, sweet potatoes, carrots, kale, cantaloupe, turnip greens, collard greens, broccoli, fortified milk.

Vitamin B_1 (thiamine)—prevents beriberi. Essential to carbohydrate metabolism and health of nervous system. Best sources: pork, enriched cereals, grains, soybeans, and nuts.

Vitamin B_2 (riboflavin)—protects skin, mouth, eyes, eyelids, and mucous membranes. Essential to protein and energy metabolism. Best sources: milk, meat, poultry, cheese, broccoli, spinach.

Vitamin B_6 (pyridoxine)—important in the regulation of the central nervous system and in protein metabolism. Best sources: whole grains, meats, fish, poultry, nuts, brewers' yeast.

Vitamin B_{12} (cobalamin)—needed to form red blood cells. Best sources: meat, fish, poultry, eggs, dairy products.

Niacin—maintains health of skin, tongue, digestive system. Best sources: poultry, peanuts, fish, enriched flour and bread.

Folic acid (folacin)—required for normal blood cell formation, growth, and reproduction and for important chemical reactions in body cells. Best sources: yeast, orange juice, green leafy vegetables, wheat germ, asparagus, broccoli, nuts.

Other B vitamins—biotin, pantothenic acid.

Vitamin C (ascorbic acid)—maintains collagen, a protein necessary for the formation of skin, ligaments, and bones. It helps heal wounds and mend fractures and aids in resisting some types of viral and bacterial infections. Best sources: citrus fruits and juices, cantaloupe, broccoli, brussels sprouts, potatoes and sweet potatoes, tomatoes, cabbage.

Vitamin D—important for bone development. Best sources: sunlight, fortified milk and milk products, fish-liver oils, egg yolks.

Vitamin E (tocopherol)—helps protect red blood cells. Best sources: vegetable oils, wheat germ, whole grains, eggs, peanuts, margarine, green leafy vegetables.

Vitamin K—necessary for formation of prothrombin, which helps blood to clot. Also made by intestinal bacteria. Best dietary sources: green leafy vegetables, tomatoes.

Minerals

Calcium—works with phosphorus in building and maintaining bones and teeth. Best sources: milk and milk products, cheese, blackstrap molasses, some types of tofu.

Phosphorus—performs more functions than any other mineral, and plays a part in nearly every chemical reaction in the body. Best sources: cheese, milk, meats, poultry, fish, tofu.

Iron—Necessary for the formation of myoglobin, which is a reservoir of oxygen for muscle tissue, and hemoglobin, which transports oxygen in the blood. Best sources: lean meats, beans, green leafy vegetables, shellfish, enriched breads and cereals, whole grains.

Other minerals—chromium, cobalt, copper, fluorine, iodine, magnesium, manganese, molybdenum, potassium, selenium, sodium, sulfur, and zinc.

Understanding Food Label Claims

Source: Food Labeling Education Information Center, Beltville, Md.

The federal Nutrition Labeling and Education Act of 1990 requires that manufacturers can make certain claims on processed food labels only if they meet the definitions specified here:

Sugar

Sugar free: less than 0.5 g per serving

No added sugar; Without added sugar; No sugar added:

- No sugars added during processing or packing, including ingredients that contain sugars (for example, fruit juices, applesauce, or dried fruit).
- Processing does not increase the sugar content above the amount naturally present in the ingredients. (A functionally insignificant increase in sugars is acceptable from processes used for purposes other than increasing sugar content.)
- The food for which it substitutes normally contains added sugars.

Reduced sugar: at least 25% less sugar than reference food

Calories

Calorie free: fewer than 5 calories per serving

Low calorie: 40 calories or less per serving; if the serving is 30 g or less or 2 tablespoons or less, 40 calories or less per 50 g of food

Reduced or Fewer calories: at least 25% fewer calories than reference food

Fat

Fat free: less than 0.5 g of fat per serving

Saturated fat free: less than 0.5 g of saturated fat per serving, and the level of trans fatty acids does not exceed 1% of total fat

Low fat: 3 g or less per serving and, if the serving is 30 g or less or 2 tbs or less, per 50 g of the food

Low saturated fat: 1 g or less per serving and not more than 15% of calories from saturated fatty acids

Reduced or Less fat: at least 25% less per serving than reference food

Cholesterol

Cholesterol free: less than 2 mg of cholesterol and 2 g or less of saturated fat per serving

Low cholesterol: 20 mg or less and 2 g or less of saturated fat per serving and, if the serving is 30 g or less or 2 tbs or less, per 50 g of the food

Reduced or Less cholesterol: at least 25% less than reference food

Sodium

Sodium free: less than 5 mg per serving

Low sodium: 140 mg or less per serving and, if the serving is 30 g or less or 2 tbs or less, per 50 g of the food

Very low sodium: 35 mg or less per serving and, if the serving is 30 g or less or 2 tbs or less, per 50 g of the food

Reduced or Less sodium: at least 25% less per serving than reference food

Fiber

High fiber: 5 g or more per serving. (Also, must meet low-fat definition, or must state level of total fat.)

Good source of fiber: 2.5 g to 4.9 g per serving

More or Added fiber: at least 2.5 g more per serving than reference food

Nutritive Value of Food (Calories, Proteins, etc.)

Source: *Home and Garden Bulletin No. 72;* U.S. Dept. of Agriculture

Food	Measure	Grams	Food Energy (calories)	Protein (grams)	Fat (grams)	Saturated fats (grams)	Carbohydrate (grams)	Calcium (milligrams)	Iron (milligrams)	Sodium (milligrams)	Vitamin A (I.U.)	Ascorbic Acid (milligrams)
Dairy products												
Cheese, cheddar, cut pieces	1 oz.	28	115	7	9	6.0	T	204	0.2	176	300	0
Cheese, cottage, small curd	1 cup	210	215	26	9	6.0	6	126	0.3	850	340	T
Cheese, cream.	1 oz.	28	100	2	10	6.2	1	23	0.3	84	400	0
Cheese, Swiss	1 oz.	28	95	7	7	4.5	1	219	0.2	388	230	0
Half-and-half	1 tbsp.	15	20	T	2	1.1	1	16	T	6	70	T
Cream, sour	1 tbsp.	12	25	T	3	1.6	1	14	T	6	90	T
Milk, whole	1 cup	244	150	8	8	5.1	11	291	0.1	120	310	2
Milk, nonfat (skim)	1 cup	245	85	8	T	0.3	12	302	0.1	126	500	2
Milkshake, chocolate.	10 oz.	283	355	9	8	4.8	60	374	0.9	314	240	0
Ice cream, hardened	1 cup	133	270	5	14	8.9	32	176	0.1	116	540	1
Sherbet.	1 cup	193	270	2	4	2.4	59	103	0.3	88	190	4
Yogurt, fruit-flavored	8 oz.	227	230	10	2	1.6	43	345	0.2	133	100	1
Eggs												
Fried in margarine	1	46	90	6	7	1.9	1	25	0.7	162	390	0
Hard-cooked	1	50	75	6	5	1.6	1	25	0.6	62	280	0
Scrambled (milk added) in margarine	1	61	100	7	7	2.2	1	44	0.7	171	420	T
Fats & oils												
Butter, salted	1 tbsp.	14	100	T	11	7.1	T	3	T	116	430	0
Margarine, salted	1 tbsp.	14	100	T	11	2.2	T	4	T	132	460	0
Olive oil	1 tbsp.	14	125	0	14	1.9	0	0	0	0	0	0
Salad dressing, blue cheese.	1 tbsp.	15	75	1	8	1.5	1	12	T	164	30	T
Salad dressing, French, regular.	1 tbsp.	16	85	T	9	1.4	1	2	T	188	T	T
Salad dressing, French, low calorie	1 tbsp.	16	25	T	2	0.2	2	6	T	306	T	T
Salad dressing, Italian	1 tbsp.	15	80	T	9	1.3	1	1	T	162	30	T
Mayonnaise.	1 tbsp.	14	100	T	11	1.7	T	3	0.1	80	40	0
Fish, meat, poultry												
Clams, raw, meat only	3 oz.	85	65	11	1	0.3	2	59	2.6	102	90	9
Crabmeat, canned	1 cup	135	135	23	3	0.5	1	61	1.1	1,350	50	0
Fish sticks, frozen, reheated	1 fish stick	28	70	6	3	0.8	4	11	0.3	53	20	0
Salmon canned (pink), solids and liquid . . .	3 oz.	85	120	17	5	0.9	0	167	0.7	443	60	0
Sardines, Atlantic, canned in oil, drained solids	3 oz.	85	175	20	9	2.1	0	371	2.6	425	190	0
Shrimp, French fried	3 oz.	85	200	16	10	2.5	11	61	2.0	384	90	0
Trout, broiled, with butter and lemon juice . .	3 oz.	85	175	21	9	4.1	T	26	1.0	122	230	1
Tuna, canned in oil	3 oz.	85	165	24	7	1.4	0	7	1.6	303	70	0
Bacon, broiled or fried crisp	3 slices	19	110	6	9	3.3	T	2	0.3	303	0	6
Ground beef, broiled, regular	3 oz.	85	245	20	18	6.9	0	9	2.1	70	T	0
Roast beef, relatively lean (lean only)	2.6 oz.	75	135	22	5	1.9	0	3	1.5	46	T	0
Beef steak, lean and fat	3 oz.	85	240	23	15	6.4	0	9	2.6	53	T	0
Beef & vegetable stew	1 cup	245	220	16	11	4.4	15	29	2.9	292	5,690	17
Lamb, chop, broiled loin, lean and fat	2.8 oz.	80	235	22	16	7.3	0	16	1.4	62	T	0
Liver, beef, fried	3 oz.	85	185	23	7	2.5	7	9	5.3	90	30,690	23
Ham, light cure, roasted, lean and fat	3 oz.	85	205	18	14	5.1	0	6	0.7	1,009	0	0
Pork, chop, broiled, lean and fat	3.1 oz.	87	275	24	19	7.0	0	3	0.7	61	10	T
Bologna	2 slices	57	180	7	16	6.1	2	7	0.9	581	0	12
Frankfurter, pork, cooked.	1	45	145	5	13	4.8	1	5	0.5	504	0	12
Sausage, pork link, cooked.	1 link	13	50	3	4	1.4	T	4	0.2	168	0	T
Veal, cutlet, braised or broiled.	3 oz.	85	185	23	9	4.1	0	9	0.8	56	T	0
Chicken, drumstick, fried, bones removed . .	2.5 oz.	72	195	16	11	3.0	6	12	1.0	194	60	0
Chicken, roasted, half breast, without skin. .	3 oz.	86	140	27	3	0.9	0	13	0.9	64	20	0
Turkey, roasted, chopped light and dark meat	1 cup	140	240	41	7	2.3	0	35	2.5	98	0	0
Frankfurter, chicken, cooked.	1	45	115	6	9	2.5	3	43	0.9	616	60	0
Fruits & fruit products												
Apple, raw, 2-3/4 in. diam.	1	138	80	T	T	0.1	21	10	0.2	T	70	8
Apple juice	1 cup	248	115	T	T	T	29	17	0.9	7	T	2
Apricots, raw	3	106	50	1	T	T	12	15	0.6	1	2,770	11
Banana, raw	1	114	105	1	1	0.2	27	7	0.4	1	90	10
Cherries, sweet, raw	10	68	50	1	1	0.1	11	10	0.3	T	150	5
Cranberry juice cocktail, sweetened.	1 cup	253	145	T	T	T	38	8	0.4	10	10	108
Fruit cocktail, canned, in heavy syrup	1 cup	255	185	1	T	T	48	15	0.7	15	520	5
Grapefruit, raw, medium, white	1/2	120	40	1	T	T	10	14	0.1	T	10	41
Grapes, Thompson seedless	10	50	35	T	T	0.1	9	6	0.1	1	40	5
Lemonade, frozen, unsweetened.	6 oz.	244	55	1	T	0.1	16	20	0.3	2	30	77
Cantaloupe, 5-in. diam.	1/2	267	95	2	1	0.1	22	29	0.6	24	8,610	113
Orange, 2-5/8 in. diam.	1	131	60	1	T	T	15	52	0.1	T	270	70
Orange juice, frozen, diluted	1 cup	249	110	2	T	T	27	22	0.2	2	190	97
Peach, 2-1/2 in. diam.	1	87	35	1	T	T	10	4	0.1	T	470	6
Raisins, seedless	1 cup	145	435	5	1	0.2	115	71	3.0	17	10	5
Strawberries, whole	1 cup	149	45	1	1	T	10	21	0.6	1	40	84
Watermelon, 4 by 8 in. wedge	1 piece	482	155	3	2	0.3	35	39	0.8	10	1,760	46
Grain products												
Bagel, plain	1	68	200	7	2	0.3	38	29	1.8	245	0	0
Biscuit, 2 in. diam., from home recipe.	1	28	100	2	5	1.2	13	47	0.7	195	10	T
Bread, pita, enriched, white, 6-1/2 in. diam .	1 pita	60	165	6	1	0.1	12	15	0.7	124	0	0
Bread, white, enriched.	1 slice	25	65	2	1	0.3	12	32	0.7	129	T	T
Bread, whole-wheat	1 slice	28	70	3	1	0.4	13	20	1.0	180	T	T
Oatmeal or rolled oats, without added salt. .	1 cup	234	145	6	2	0.4	25	19	1.6	2	40	0
Bran flakes (40% bran), added sugar, salt, iron, vitamins	1 oz.	28	90	4	1	0.1	22	14	8.1	264	1,250	0
Corn flakes, added sugar, salt, iron, vitamins	1 oz.	28	110	2	T	T	24	1	1.8	351	1,250	15
Rice, puffed, added iron, thiamine, niacin . .	1 oz.	28	110	2	T	T	25	4	1.8	340	1,250	15
Wheat, shredded, plain, 1 biscuit or 2/3 cup	1 oz.	28	100	3	1	0.1	23	11	1.2	3	0	0
Bulgur, uncooked.	1 cup	170	600	19	3	1.2	129	49	9.5	7	0	0
Cake, angel food, 1/12 of cake	1	53	125	3	T	T	29	44	0.2	269	0	0
Cupcake, 2-1/2 in. diam., with chocolate icing	1	35	120	2	4	1.8	20	21	0.7	92	50	T

Food	Measure	Grams	Food Energy (calories)	Protein (grams)	Fat (grams)	Saturated fats (grams)	Carbohydrate (grams)	Calcium (milligrams)	Iron (milligrams)	Sodium (milligrams)	Vitamin A (I.U.)	Ascorbic Acid (milligrams)
Plain sheet cake with white, uncooked frosting, 1/9 of cake	1	121	445	4	14	4.6	77	61	1.2	275	240	T
Fruitcake, dark, 1/32 of loaf	1	43	165	2	7	1.5	25	41	1.2	67	50	16
Cake, pound, 1/17 of loaf	1	29	110	2	5	3.0	15	8	0.5	108	160	0
Cheesecake, 1/12 of 9-in. diam. cake	1	92	280	5	18	9.9	26	52	0.4	204	230	5
Brownies, with nuts, from commercial recipe	1	25	100	1	4	1.6	16	13	0.6	59	70	T
Cookies, chocolate chip, from home recipe	4	40	185	2	11	3.9	26	13	1.0	82	20	0
Crackers, graham, 2-1/2 in. squares	2	14	60	1	1	0.4	11	6	0.4	86	0	0
Crackers, saltines	4	12	50	1	1	0.5	9	3	0.5	165	0	0
Danish pastry, round piece	1	57	220	4	12	3.6	26	60	1.1	218	60	T
Doughnut, cake type	1	50	210	3	12	2.8	24	22	1.0	192	20	T
Macaroni, firm stage (hot)	1 cup	130	190	7	1	0.1	39	14	2.1	1	0	0
Muffin, bran, commercial mix	1	45	140	3	4	1.3	24	27	1.7	385	100	0
Muffin, corn, from home recipe	1	45	145	3	5	1.5	21	66	0.9	169	80	T
Noodles, enriched, cooked	1 cup	160	200	7	2	0.5	37	16	2.6	3	110	0
Pie, apple, 1/6 of pie	1	158	405	3	18	4.6	60	13	1.6	476	50	2
Pie, cherry, 1/6 of pie	1	158	410	4	18	4.7	61	22	1.6	480	700	0
Pie, lemon meringue, 1/6 of pie	1	140	355	5	14	4.3	53	20	1.4	395	240	4
Pie, pecan, 1/6 of pie	1	138	575	7	32	4.7	71	65	4.6	305	220	0
Popcorn, air-popped, plain	1 cup	8	30	1	T	T	6	1	0.2	T	10	0
Pretzels, stick	10	3	10	T	T	T	2	1	0.1	48	0	0
Rolls, enriched, brown & serve	1	28	85	2	2	0.5	14	33	0.8	155	T	T
Rolls, frankfurter & hamburger	1	40	115	3	2	0.5	20	54	1.2	241	T	T
Tortillas, corn	1	30	65	2	1	0.1	13	42	0.6	1	80	0
Legumes, nuts, seeds												
Beans, Black	1 cup	171	225	15	1	0.1	41	47	2.9	1	T	0
Beans, Great Northern, cooked	1 cup	180	210	14	1	0.1	38	90	4.9	13	0	0
Peanuts, roasted in oil, salted	1 cup	145	840	39	71	9.9	27	125	2.8	626	0	0
Peanut butter	1 tbsp.	16	95	5	8	1.4	3	5	0.3	75	0	0
Refried beans, canned	1 cup	290	295	18	3	0.4	51	141	5.1	1,228	0	17
Tofu	1 piece	120	85	9	5	0.7	3	108	2.3	8	0	0
Sunflower seeds, hulled	1 oz.	28	160	6	14	1.5	5	33	1.9	1	10	T
Mixed foods												
Chop suey with beef and pork, home recipe	1 cup	250	300	26	17	4.3	13	60	4.8	1,053	600	33
Enchilada	1	230	235	20	16	7.7	24	97	3.3	1,332	2,720	T
Pizza, cheese, 1/8 of 15 in.-diam. pie	1	120	290	15	9	4.1	39	220	1.6	699	750	2
Spaghetti with meatballs & tomato sauce	1 cup	248	330	19	12	3.9	39	124	3.7	1,009	1,590	22
Sugars & sweets												
Candy, caramels	1 oz.	28	115	1	3	2.2	22	42	0.4	64	T	T
Candy, milk chocolate	1 oz.	28	145	2	9	5.4	16	50	0.4	23	30	T
Fudge, chocolate	1 oz.	28	115	1	3	2.1	21	22	0.3	54	T	T
Gelatin dessert, from prepared powder	1/2 cup	120	70	2	0	0.0	17	2	T	55	0	0
Candy, hard	1 oz.	28	110	0	0	0.0	28	T	0.1	7	0	0
Honey	1 tbsp.	21	65	T	0	0.0	17	1	0.1	1	0	T
Jams & Preserves	1 tbsp.	20	55	T	T	0.0	14	4	0.2	2	T	T
Popsicle, 3 fl. oz.	1	95	70	0	0	0.0	18	0	T	11	0	0
Sugar, white, granulated	1 tbsp.	12	45	0	0	0.0	12	T	T	T	0	0
Vegetables												
Asparagus, spears, cooked from raw	4 spears	60	15	2	T	T	3	14	0.4	2	500	16
Beans, green, from frozen, cuts	1 cup	135	35	2	T	T	8	61	1.1	18	710	11
Broccoli, cooked from raw	1 spear	180	50	5	1	0.1	10	82	2.1	20	2,540	113
Cabbage, raw, coarsely shredded or sliced	1 cup	70	15	1	T	T	4	33	0.4	13	90	33
Carrots, raw, 7-1/2 by 1-1/8 in.	1	72	30	1	T	T	7	19	0.4	25	20,250	7
Cauliflower, cooked, drained, from raw	1 cup	125	30	2	T	T	6	34	0.5	8	20	69
Celery, raw	1 stalk	40	5	T	T	T	1	14	0.2	35	50	3
Collards, cooked from raw	1 cup	190	25	2	T	0.1	5	148	0.8	36	4,220	19
Corn, sweet, yellow, cooked from raw	1 ear	77	85	3	1	0.2	19	2	0.5	13	170	5
Eggplant, cooked, steamed	1 cup	96	25	1	T	T	6	6	0.3	3	60	1
Lettuce, iceberg, chopped	1 cup	55	5	1	T	T	1	10	0.3	5	180	2
Lettuce, looseleaf (such as romaine)	1 cup	56	10	1	T	T	2	38	0.8	5	1,060	10
Mushrooms, raw	1 cup	70	20	1	T	T	3	4	0.9	3	0	2
Onions, raw, chopped	1 cup	160	55	2	T	0.1	12	40	0.6	3	0	13
Peas, green, frozen, cooked	1 cup	160	125	8	T	0.1	23	38	2.5	139	1,070	16
Potatoes, baked, peeled	1	156	145	3	T	T	34	8	0.5	8	0	20
Potatoes, frozen, French fried (oven-heated)	10	50	110	2	4	2.1	17	5	0.7	16	0	5
Potatoes, mashed, milk added	1 cup	210	160	4	1	0.7	37	55	0.6	636	40	14
Potato chips	10	20	105	1	7	1.8	10	5	0.2	94	0	8
Potato salad	1 cup	250	360	7	21	3.6	28	48	1.6	1,323	520	25
Spinach, drained, cooked from raw	1 cup	180	40	5	T	0.1	7	245	6.4	126	14,740	18
Sweet potatoes, baked in skin, peeled	1	114	115	2	T	T	28	32	0.5	11	24,880	28
Tomatoes, raw	1	123	25	1	T	T	5	9	0.6	10	1,390	22
Vegetable juice cocktail, canned	1 cup	242	45	2	T	T	11	27	1.0	883	2,830	67
Miscellaneous												
Beer, regular	12 fl. oz.	360	150	1	0	0.0	13	14	0.1	18	0	0
Gin, rum, vodka, whisky, 86 proof	1-1/2 fl. oz.	42	105	0	0	0.0	T	T	T	T	0	0
Wine, table, white	3-1/2 fl. oz.	102	80	T	0	0.0	3	9	0.3	5	(¹)	0
Cola-type beverage	12 fl. oz.	369	160	0	0	0.0	41	11	0.2	18	0	0
Ginger ale	12 fl. oz.	366	125	0	0	0.0	32	11	0.1	29	0	0
Coffee, brewed	6 fl. oz.	180	T	T	T	T	T	4	T	2	0	0
Tea, brewed	8 fl. oz.	240	T	T	T	T	T	0	T	1	0	0
Catsup	1 tbsp.	15	15	T	T	T	4	3	0.1	156	210	2
Mustard, prepared, yellow	1 tsp.	5	5	T	T	T	T	4	0.1	63	0	T
Olives, canned, green	4 medium	13	15	T	2	0.2	T	8	0.2	312	40	0
Pickles, dill, whole	1	65	5	T	T	T	1	17	0.7	928	70	4
Relish, finely chopped, sweet	1 tbsp.	15	20	T	T	T	5	3	0.1	107	20	1
Soup, tomato, prepared with milk	1 cup	248	160	6	6	2.9	22	160	1.8	932	850	68
Soup, chicken noodle, prepared with water	1 cup	241	75	4	2	0.7	9	17	0.8	1,106	710	T
Soup, green pea, prepared with water	1 cup	250	165	9	3	1.4	27	28	2.0	988	200	2
Soup, vegetarian, prepared with water	1 cup	241	70	2	2	0.3	12	22	1.1	822	3,010	1

T — Indicates trace (¹) — Value not determined. **Note:** Values shown here for these foods may be from several different manufacturers and, therefore, may differ somewhat from the values provided by one source.

Dietary Requirements

In Aug. 1997, the Institute of Medicine released a report on Dietary Reference Intakes (DRIs), which updated and expanded dietary requirements set by the National Academy of Sciences for calcium, phosphorus, magnesium, vitamin D, and fluoride. The new values are based on the latest knowledge relevant to optimizing individuals' health at all stages of life and not simply protecting against nutritional deficiencies. Reports on other nutrients are under development. In the meantime, the previously established Recommended Dietary Allowances (RDAs) for these nutrients apply.

Dietary Reference Intakes (DRIs) for 5 Nutrients

The new DRIs include 4 categories for daily consumption: **RDA**—the intake that meets the nutrient requirements of almost all healthy individuals in a specified group; **Estimated Average Requirement (EAR)**—the intake that meets the estimated nutrient need of half the individuals in a specified group; **Adequate Intake (AI)**—the intake used when sufficient broad scientific evidence is not available to calculate an EAR; and **Tolerable Upper Intake Level (UL)**—the maximum intake that is unlikely to pose risks of adverse health effects in almost all healthy individuals in a specified group. The UL is not recommended as a goal.

Source: *Dietary Reference Intakes for Calcium, Phosphorus, Magnesium, Vitamin D, and Fluoride,* Institute of Medicine, 1997

Group	Calcium AI[1]	Calcium UL[2]	Phosphorus EAR[1]	Phosphorus RDA[1]	Phosphorus AI[1]	Phosphorus UL[2]	Magnesium EAR[1] m	Magnesium EAR[1] f	Magnesium RDA[1] m	Magnesium RDA[1] f	Magnesium AI[1] m	Magnesium AI[1] f	Magnesium UL[1,3]	Vitamin D AI[4,5]	Vitamin D UL[4]	Fluoride AI[1] m	Fluoride AI[1] f	Fluoride UL[1]
0-6 mos ...	210	ND	—	—	100	ND	—	—	—	—	30	30	ND	5	25	0.01	0.01	0.7
6-12 mos ...	270	ND	—	—	275	ND	—	—	—	—	75	75	ND	5	25	0.50	0.50	0.9
1-3 yrs	500	2.5	380	460	—	3.0	65	65	80	80	—	—	65	5	50	0.70	0.70	1.3
4-8 yrs	800	2.5	405	500	—	3.0	110	110	130	130	—	—	110	5	50	1.10	1.10	2.2
9-13 yrs	1,300	2.5	1,055	1,250	—	4.0	200	200	240	240	—	—	350	5	50	2.00	2.00	10.0
14-18 yrs ...	1,300	2.5	1,055	1,250	—	4.0	340	300	410	360	—	—	350	5	50	3.20	2.90	10.0
19-30 yrs ...	1,000	2.5	580	700	—	3.0	330	255	400	310	—	—	350	5	50	3.80	3.10	10.0
31-50 yrs ...	1,000	2.5	580	700	—	3.0	350	265	420	320	—	—	350	5	50	3.80	3.10	10.0
51-70 yrs ...	1,200	2.5	580	700	—	3.0	350	265	420	320	—	—	350	10	50	3.80	3.10	10.0
over 70 yrs ..	1,200	2.5	580	700	—	3.0	350	265	420	320	—	—	350	15	50	3.80	3.10	10.0
Pregnant																		
18 yrs or less	1,300	2.5	1,055	1,250	—	3.5	—	335	—	400	—	—	350	5	50	—	2.90	10.0
19-50 yrs ..	1,000	2.5	580	700	—	3.5	—	290	—	350	—	—	350	—	50	—	3.10	10.0
Lactating																		
18 yrs or less	1,300	2.5	1,055	1,250	—	4.0	—	300	—	360	—	—	350	5	50	—	2.90	10.0
19-50 yrs ..	1,000	2.5	580	700	—	4.0	—	255	—	310	—	—	350	—	50	—	3.10	10.0

m=male. f=female. ND=Not determinable, because of a lack of data on adverse effects in this age group and a concern over body's lack of ability to handle excess amounts. Source of intake in this case should be from food only. (1) mg/day. (2) g/day. (3) The UL for magnesium represents intake from a pharmacological agent only and does not include intake from food and water. (4) μg/day (microgram/day). (5) In the absence of adequate exposure to sunlight.

Recommended Dietary Allowances (RDAs)

Source: Food and Nutrition Board of the Institute of Medicine, Natl. Academy of Sciences, 1989

Age (years) and sex group	Weight (lbs.)	Protein (grams)	Fat soluble vitamins Vitamin A*	Fat soluble vitamins Vitamin E†	Fat soluble vitamins Vitamin K (micrograms)	Water soluble vitamins Vitamin C (mg.)	Water soluble vitamins Thiamine (mg.)	Water soluble vitamins Riboflavin (mg.)	Water soluble vitamins Niacin (mg.)‡	Water soluble vitamins Vitamin B6 (mg.)	Water soluble vitamins Folate (micrograms)	Water soluble vitamins Vitamin B12 (micrograms)	Minerals Iron (mg.)	Minerals Zinc (mg.)	Minerals Iodine (micrograms)	Minerals Selenium (micrograms)
Infants ... to 5 mos.	13	13	375	3	5	30	0.3	0.4	5	0.3	25	0.3	6	5	40	10
to 1 yr.	20	14	375	4	10	35	0.4	0.5	6	0.6	35	0.5	10	5	50	15
Children .. 1-3	29	16	400	6	15	40	0.7	0.8	9	1.0	50	0.7	10	10	70	20
4-6	44	24	500	7	20	45	0.9	1.1	12	1.1	75	1.0	10	10	90	20
7-10.	62	28	700	7	30	45	1.0	1.2	13	1.4	100	1.4	10	10	120	30
Males .... 11-14.	99	45	1000	10	45	50	1.3	1.5	17	1.7	150	2.0	12	15	150	40
15-18.	145	59	1000	10	65	60	1.5	1.8	20	2.0	200	2.0	12	15	150	50
19-24.	160	58	1000	10	70	60	1.5	1.7	19	2.0	200	2.0	10	15	150	70
25-50.	174	63	1000	10	80	60	1.5	1.7	19	2.0	200	2.0	10	15	150	70
51+	170	63	1000	10	80	60	1.2	1.4	15	2.0	200	2.0	10	15	150	70
Females .. 11-14.	101	46	800	8	45	50	1.1	1.3	15	1.4	150	2.0	15	12	150	45
15-18.	120	44	800	8	55	60	1.1	1.3	15	1.5	180	2.0	15	12	150	50
19-24.	128	46	800	8	60	60	1.1	1.3	15	1.6	180	2.0	15	12	150	55
25-50.	138	50	800	8	65	60	1.1	1.3	15	1.6	180	2.0	15	12	150	55
51+	143	50	800	8	65	60	1.0	1.2	13	1.6	180	2.0	10	12	150	55

* Retinol equivalents. † Milligrams alpha-tocopherol equivalents. ‡ Niacin equivalents.

Weight Ranges for Adults

Source: U.S. Department of Agriculture; U.S. Department of Health and Human Services

Weight in lbs., without clothes. Height without shoes.

Height	Healthy weight	Moderately overweight	Severely overweight[1]	Height	Healthy weight	Moderately overweight	Severely overweight[1]
4'10"	91-118	119-137	138	5'9"	129-168	169-195	196
4'11"	94-123	124-143	144	5'10"	132-173	174-201	202
5'0"	97-127	128-147	148	5'11"	136-178	179-206	207
5'1"	101-131	132-152	153	6'0"	140-183	184-212	213
5'2"	104-136	137-157	158	6'1"	144-188	189-218	219
5'3"	107-140	141-162	163	6'2"	148-194	195-224	225
5'4"	111-145	146-168	169	6'3"	152-199	200-231	232
5'5"	114-149	150-173	174	6'4"	156-204	205-237	238
5'6"	118-154	155-178	179	6'5"	160-210	211-243	244
5'7"	121-159	160-184	185	6'6"	164-215	216-249	250
5'8"	125-163	164-189	190				

Note: The higher weights apply to people with more muscle and bone, such as many men. You ordinarily do not need to lose weight if you have gained less than 10 lb. since reaching your adult height, are within the "healthy" weight range for your height and volume of muscle and bone, and are otherwise healthy. (1) Number given is low end of range.

U.S. Recommended Childhood Immunization Schedule

Source: Advisory Committee on Immunization Practices (ACIP), Amer. Acad. of Pediatrics, and Amer. Acad. of Family Physicians (AAFP), 1997

Vaccines are listed under the routinely recommended ages[1]. Bars indicate range of acceptable ages for vaccination. Bars with dotted rules indicate *catch-up vaccination:* at 11-12 years of age, hepatitis B vaccine should be administered to children not previously vaccinated, and Varicella vaccine should be administered to children not previously vaccinated who lack a reliable history of chickenpox (the chickenpox vaccine has been approved for use in the U.S. only since 1995).

Age → Vaccine ↘	Birth	1 mo	2 mos	4 mos	6 mos	12 mos	15 mos	18 mos	4-6 yrs	11-12 yrs	14-16 yrs
Hepatitis B [2,3]	Hep B-1										
		Hep B-2			Hep B-3					Hep B [3]	
Diphtheria, Tetanus, Pertussis (whooping cough) [4]			DTaP or DTP	DTaP or DTP	DTaP or DTP		DTaP or DTP [4]		DTaP or DTP	Td	
H. influenzae type b [5]			Hib	Hib	Hib [5]	Hib [5]					
Polio			Polio [6]	Polio		Polio [6]			Polio		
Measles, Mumps, Rubella (German measles) [7]						MMR			MMR [7] or	MMR [7]	
Varicella [8] (chickenpox)						Var				Var [8]	

(1) This schedule indicates the recommended age for routine administration of currently licensed childhood vaccines. Some combination vaccines are available and may be used whenever administration of all components of the vaccine is indicated.

(2) Infants born to HBsAg(hepatits B)-negative mothers should receive 2.5 μg (micrograms) of Merck vaccine (Recombivax HB) or 10 μg of Smithkline Beecham (SB) vaccine (Engerix-B). The 2d dose should be administered at least 1 mo after the 1st dose. Infants born to HBsAg-positive mothers should receive 0.5 mL (milliliter) hepatitis B immune globulin (HBIG) within 12 hrs of birth, and either 5 μg of Merck vaccine (Recombivax HB) or 10 μg of SB vaccine (Engerix-B) at a separate site. The 2d dose is recommended at 1-2 mos of age and the 3d dose at 6 mos of age. Infants born to mothers whose HBsAg status is unknown should receive either 5 μg of Merck vaccine (Recombivax HB) or 10 μg of SB vaccine (Engerix-B) within 12 hrs of birth. The 2d dose of vaccine is recommended at 1 mo of age and the 3d dose at 6 mos of age. Blood should be drawn at the time of delivery to determine the mother's HBsAg status; if it is positive, the infant should receive HBIG as soon as possible (no later than 1 wk of age). The dosage and timing of subsequent vaccine doses should be based upon the mother's HBsAg status.

(3) Children and adolescents who have not been vaccinated against hepatitis B in infancy may begin the series during any childhood visit. Those who have not previously received 3 doses of hepatitis B vaccine should initiate or complete the series during the 11-12-year-old visit. The 2d dose should be administered at least 1 mo after the 1st dose, and the 3d dose should be administered at least 4 mos after the 1st dose and at least 2 mos after the 2d dose.

(4) DTaP (diphtheria and tetanus toxoids and acellular pertussis vaccine) is the preferred vaccine for all doses in the vaccination series, including completion of the series in children who have received at least 1 dose of whole-cell DTP vaccine. Whole-cell DTP is an acceptable alternative to DTaP. The 4th dose of DTaP may be administered as early as 12 months of age, provided 8 months have elapsed since the 3d dose, and if the child is considered unlikely to return at 15-18 mos of age. Td (tetanus and diphtheria toxoids, absorbed, for adult use) is recommended at 11-12 years of age if at least 5 years have elapsed since the last dose of DTP, DTaP, or DT. Subsequent routine Td boosters are recommended every 10 years.

(5) *Haemophilus influenzae* type b is a bacterium that can cause such serious infectious diseases as meningitis and pneumonia. Three *H. influenzae* type b (Hib) conjugate vaccines are licensed for infant use. If PRP-OMP (PedvaxHIB [Merck]) is administered at 2 and 4 mos of age, a dose at 6 mos is not required. After completing the primary series, any Hib conjugate vaccine may be used as a booster.

(6) Two poliovirus vaccines are currently licensed in the US: inactivated poliovirus vaccine (IPV) and oral poliovirus vaccine (OPV). The following schedules are all acceptable by the ACIP, the AAP, and the AAFP, and parents and providers may choose among them:

    1. IPV at 2 and 4 mos; OPV at 12-18 mos and 4-8 yrs
    2. IPV at 2, 4, 12-18 mos, and 4-6 yrs
    3. OPV at 2, 4, 6-18 mos, and 4-6 yrs

The ACIP routinely recommends schedule 1. IPV is the only poliovirus vaccine recommended for immunocompromised persons and their household contacts.

(7) The 2d dose of MMR is routinely recommended at 4-6 yrs or 11-12 yrs of age, but may be administered during any visit, provided at least 1 mo has elapsed since receipt of the 1st dose and both doses are administered at or after 12 mos of age.

(8) Susceptible children may receive Varicella vaccine (Var) at any visit after the 1st birthday, and those who lack a reliable history of chickenpox should be immunized during the 11-12-year-old visit. Children 13 years of age or older should receive 2 doses, at least 1 mo apart.

Allergies and Asthma

Source: Asthma and Allergy Foundation of America, Washington, DC

One out of every five Americans suffers from allergies. People with allergies have extra-sensitive immune systems which react to normally harmless substances. Allergens that sometimes produce this reaction include plant pollen, dust mites, or animal dander; plants such as poison ivy; certain drugs, such as penicillin; and certain foods such as eggs, milk, nuts, or seafood.

The tendency to develop a particular kind of allergy is inherited, and allergies usually begin to appear in childhood, but they can show up at any age. Common allergies for infants include food allergies and eczema (patches of dry skin). Older children and adults may often develop allergic rhinitis (hay fever), a reaction to an inhaled allergen; common symptoms include nasal congestion, runny nose, and sneezing.

It is best to avoid contact with the allergen, if feasible. In some cases, drugs such as antihistamines are used to decrease the reaction, and there are treatments aimed at gradually desensitizing the patient. Other effective allergy treatments include decongestants, eye drops, and ointments.

Some people with allergies also have asthma, and allergens are a common asthma trigger. Asthma is a disease of chronic inflammation, affecting the passages that carry air into and out of the lungs. It is most often seen in children, but can develop at any age.

People with asthma have inflamed, supersensitive airways that tighten and become filled with mucus during an asthma episode. Wheezing, difficulty in breathing, painless tightening of the chest, and coughing are common symptoms. Asthma can progress through stages to become life-threatening if not controlled. Emergency symptoms of asthma include a bluish cast to the face and lips, severe anxiety, increased pulse rate, and sweating.

Besides common allergens, tobacco smoke, cold air, and air pollutants can trigger an asthma attack, as can respiratory infections or physical exercise that taxes the breathing. Of course, an accurate diagnosis by a physician is important. Besides avoidance of triggers, treatment for asthma includes preventive drugs and allergy immunotherapy, as well as bronchodilators and anti-inflammatory agents to better control the breathing.

Cancer Prevention

Source: American Cancer Society, 1599 Clifton Road NE, Atlanta, GA 30329-4251; phone: (800) 227-2345

PRIMARY PREVENTION: Modifiable determinants of cancer risk.

Smoking	Lung cancer mortality rates are 23 times higher for current male smokers and 13 times higher for current female smokers, than for those who have never smoked. Smoking accounts for about 29% of all cancer deaths and about 20% of all deaths in the U.S. Smoking is associated with cancer of the lungs, mouth, pharynx, larynx, esophagus, pancreas, uterine cervix, kidney, and bladder.
Nutrition and Diet	Risk for colon, rectum, breast (among postmenopausal women), kidney, prostate, and endometrial cancers increases in obese people. High-fat diets may contribute to the development of certain cancers, particularly those of the colon, rectum, endometrium, and prostate. High-fiber foods may help reduce risk of colon cancer. Eating 5 or more servings of fruits and vegetables each day, and eating other foods from plant sources (especially grains and beans) may reduce risk for many cancers. Physical activity can help protect against some cancers.
Sunlight	Almost all of the more than 1,000,000 skin cancer cases diagnosed each year in the U.S. are sun-related. Epidemiological evidence shows that sun exposure is a major factor in the development of melanoma, and the incidence increases for those living near the equator.
Alcohol	Oral cancer and cancers of the larynx, throat, esophagus, breast, and liver occur more frequently among heavy drinkers of alcohol, especially when accompanied by cigarette smoking or use of chewing tobacco. Studies have also noted an association between alcohol consumption and an increased risk of breast cancer.
Smokeless Tobacco	Use of chewing tobacco or snuff increases risk of cancers of the mouth, larynx, throat, and esophagus. The excess risk of cancer of the cheek and gum may reach nearly 50-fold among long-term snuff users.
Estrogen	Estrogen treatment to control menopausal symptoms can increase risk of endometrial cancer. However, including progesterone in estrogen replacement therapy helps to minimize this risk. Use of estrogen by menopausal women needs careful discussion by the woman and her physician, while research continues.
Radiation	Excessive exposure to ionizing radiation can increase cancer risk. Medical and dental X rays are adjusted to deliver the lowest dose possible without sacrificing image quality. Excessive radon exposure in the home may increase lung cancer risk, especially in cigarette smokers. If levels are found to be too high, remedial actions should be taken.
Environmental Hazards	Exposure to various chemicals (including benzene, asbestos, vinyl chloride, arsenic, and aflatoxin) increases risk of various cancers. Risk of lung cancer from asbestos is greatly increased when combined with smoking. Pesticides, low-frequency radiation, toxic wastes, and proximity to nuclear power plants have not been proven to cause cancer.

SECONDARY PREVENTION: Steps to diagnose a cancer or precursor as early as possible after it has developed.

CANCER-DETECTION GUIDELINES

A cancer-related checkup is recommended every 3 years for people aged 20-40 and every year for people 40 years of age and older. This exam should include health counseling and, depending on a person's age, might include examinations for cancers of the thyroid, oral cavity, skin, limph nodes, testes, prostate, and ovaries, as well as for some nonmalignant diseases. Special tests for certain cancer sites are recommended as outlined below:

Breast Cancer	• Breast self-exam monthly, beginning at age 20. • Breast clinical physical examination for women aged 20-40, every 3 years; over 40, every year. • Mammography for women aged 40 and over, every year.
Cervical Cancer	Annual Pap test and pelvic exam for women who are or have been sexually active or have reached age 18. After 3 or more consecutive satisfactory normal annual exams, the Pap test may be performed less frequently at the discretion of the physician.
Colorectal Cancer	Beginning at age 50, both men and women should follow this testing schedule: • Yearly fecal occult blood test, plus flexible sigmoidoscopy and digital rectal examination every 5 years, or • Colonoscopy and digital rectal examination every 10 years, or • Double-contrast barium enema and digital rectal examination every 5-10 years.
Endometrial Cancer	Sampling of asymptomatic women at high risk of developing endometrial cancer should begin at menopause and may be indicated at various intervals thereafter, depending on the degree of risk and other factors determined by the physician. Factors that contribute to increased endometrial cancer risk include history of infertility, obesity, previous abnormal uterine bleeding, estrogen therapy opposed by progestin intake, and tamoxifen therapy.
Oral Cancer	Oral exam for men and women every year.
Prostate Cancer	Both Prostate-Specific Antigen (PSA) and Digital Rectal Examination (DRE) should be offered annually, beginning at age 50, to men who have at least a 10-year life expectancy, and should be offered to younger men who are at high risk. Information should be provided to patients regarding potential risks and benefits of intervention. • Men who choose to undergo screening should begin at age 50. However, men in high-risk groups, such as those with a strong familial predisposition (e.g., 2 or more affected first-degree relatives) or African Americans may begin at a younger age (e.g. 45 years). More data on the precise age to start prostate cancer screening are needed for men at high risk. • Screening for prostate cancer in asymptomatic men can detect tumors at a more favorable stage (anatomic extent of disease). There has been a reduction in mortality from prostate cancer, but it has not been established that this is a direct result of screening. • An abnormal PSA test result has been defined as a value of above 4.0 ng (nanogram)/ml. Some elevations in PSA may be due to benign conditions of the prostate. • The DRE of the prostate should be performed by health care workers skilled in recognizing subtle prostate abnormalities, including those of symmetry and consistency, as well as the more classic findings of marked induration or nodules. DRE is less effective in detecting prostate cancer than is PSA.
Skin Cancer	Skin exam for men and women over 20, every 3 years; for men and women over 40, every year.

Trends in Daily Use of Cigarettes, for 8th, 10th, and 12th Graders

Source: *Monitoring the Future*, Univ. of Michigan Inst. for Social Research and National Inst. on Drug Abuse

(percent who smoked daily in last 30 days)

	8th grade						10th grade						12th grade					
	1991	1992	1993	1994	1995	'94-'95 change	1991	1992	1993	1994	1995	'94-'95 change	1991	1992	1993	1994	1995	'94-'95 change
Total......	7.2	7.0	8.3	8.8	9.3	+0.5	12.6	12.3	14.2	14.6	16.3	+1.7	18.5	17.2	19.0	19.4	21.6	+2.2
Sex																		
Male	8.1	6.9	8.8	9.5	9.2	–0.3	12.4	12.1	13.8	15.2	16.3	+1.1	18.8	17.2	19.4	20.4	21.7	+1.3
Female ...	6.2	7.2	7.8	8.0	9.2	+1.2	12.5	12.4	14.3	13.7	16.1	+2.4	17.9	16.7	18.2	18.1	20.8	+2.7
College plans																		
None or under 4 yrs.	18.5	20.1	21.5	22.6	22.5	–0.1	25.7	25.5	28.9	28.9	32.7	+3.8	28.4	28.1	27.8	29.8	33.7	+3.9
Complete 4 yrs. ...	5.3	5.1	6.4	6.8	7.5	+0.7	9.6	9.5	11.0	11.5	13.3	+1.8	14.1	12.9	15.9	15.7	17.4	+1.7
Region																		
Northeast..	7.2	7.1	7.1	8.6	9.2	+0.6	14.3	13.1	16.3	14.1	15.8	+1.7	20.9	19.4	23.5	21.3	22.5	+1.2
North central	7.8	7.6	8.5	9.4	11.0	+1.6	14.3	14.3	15.1	16.9	17.6	+0.7	23.0	19.0	21.3	23.8	25.7	+1.9
South	7.9	7.8	9.3	9.4	9.4	0.0	12.8	11.4	13.9	15.5	19.3	+3.8	16.4	16.7	18.5	19.3	21.7	+2.4
West	4.6	4.8	7.4	7.4	7.0	–0.4	9.1	10.7	10.9	9.7	9.4	–0.3	13.9	13.3	13.0	12.4	14.5	+2.1
Parental education																		
1.0-2.0 (low)	15.9	11.9	127	13.0	15.8	–2.8	16.0	17.8	19.3	15.5	20.0	+4.5	21.2	16.5	17.6	16.9	21.3	+4.4
2.5-3.0....	8.6	8.4	9.7	11.3	11.3	0.0	15.5	13.9	16.9	17.6	21.6	+4.0	19.8	20.4	20.2	22.4	24.6	+2.2
3.5-4.0....	6.5	6.9	8.5	8.9	9.4	+0.5	12.0	11.8	13.6	15.9	17.0	+1.1	18.5	16.9	18.9	18.9	21.6	+2.7
4.5-5.0....	4.0	5.2	5.9	6.1	7.2	+1.1	10.6	10.5	10.7	11.5	12.6	+1.1	16.2	15.0	18.9	18.7	19.7	+1.0
5.5-6.0 (high)	4.9	4.2	6.3	5.8	5.7	–0.1	9.6	9.0	10.5	9.6	10.3	+0.7	16.1	12.8	16.6	17.3	18.5	+1.2
Race[1]																		
White.....	—	7.7	8.8	9.7	10.5	+0.8	—	14.5	15.3	16.5	17.6	+1.1	21.5	20.5	21.4	22.9	23.9	+1.0
Black.....	—	1.4	1.8	2.6	2.8	+0.2	—	2.8	3.1	3.8	4.7	+0.9	5.1	4.2	4.1	4.9	6.1	+1.2
Hispanic ..	—	7.3	7.2	9.0	9.2	+0.2	—	8.4	8.9	8.1	9.9	+1.8	11.5	12.5	11.8	10.6	11.6	+1.0

— = data not available. (1) For each racial group, data for the specified year and previous year have been combined to increase subgroup sample size and thus provide a more reliable estimate.

Some Benefits of Quitting Smoking

Source: American Cancer Society, phone: (800) 227-2345; U.S. Centers for Disease Control and Prevention

Within 20 Minutes
- Blood pressure drops to normal
- Pulse rate drops to normal
- Body temperature of hands and feet increases to normal

Within 8 Hours
- Carbon monoxide level in blood drops to normal
- Oxygen level in blood increases to normal

Within 24 Hours
- Chance of heart attack decreases

Within 48 Hours
- Nerve endings start regrowing
- Ability to smell and taste is enhanced

Within 2 Weeks to 3 Months
- Circulation improves
- Walking becomes easier
- Lung function increases up to 30%

Within 1 to 9 Months
- Coughing, sinus congestion, fatigue, and shortness of breath decrease

- Cilia regrow in lungs, increasing ability to handle mucus, clean the lungs, reduce infection
- Body's overall energy increases

Within 1 Year
- Excess risk of coronary heart disease is cut by half

Within 5 Years
- Lung cancer death rate for average former smoker (one pack a day) decreases by almost half
- Stroke risk is reduced to that of a nonsmoker 5-15 years after quitting
- Risk of cancer of the mouth, throat, and esophagus is half that of a smoker's

Within 10 Years
- Lung cancer death rate similar to that of nonsmokers
- Precancerous cells are replaced
- Risk of cancer of the mouth, throat, esophagus, bladder, kidney, and pancreas decreases

Within 15 Years
- Risk of coronary heart disease is that of a nonsmoker

MILLENNIUM FACT BOX

Death Rates for Selected Causes, 1900-96

(per 100,000 population)

	1900	1910	1920	1930	1940	1950	1960	1970	1980	1990	1996[1]
Cardiovascular disease.....	345.2	371.9	364.9	414.4	485.7	510.8	521.8	496.0	436.4	368.3	358.6
Diphtheria	40.3	21.1	15.3	4.9	1.1	0.3	z	z	z	z	z
Influenza & pneumonia ..	202.2	155.9	207.3	102.5	70.3	31.3	37.3	30.9	24.1	32.0	31.1
Cancer.......	64.0	76.2	83.4	97.4	120.3	139.8	149.2	162.8	183.9	203.2	205.2
Measles......	13.3	12.4	8.8	3.2	0.5	0.3	0.2	z	z	z	z
Scarlet fever ..	9.6	11.4	4.6	1.9	0.5	0.2	0.1	z	z	z	z
Tuberculosis ..	194.4	153.8	113.1	71.1	45.0	22.5	6.1	2.6	0.9	0.7	0.5
Typhoid	31.3	22.5	7.6	4.8	1.1	0.1	z	z	z	z	z
Whooping cough	12.2	11.6	12.5	4.8	2.2	0.7	0.1	z	z	z	z

z = Less than 0.05. (1) Data are preliminary.

Diabetes

Source: American Diabetes Association, 1660 Duke St., Alexandria, VA 22314; phone: (800) 342-2383

Diabetes is a chronic disease in which the body does not produce or properly use insulin, a hormone needed to convert sugar, starches, and other foods into energy necessary for daily life. Both genetics and environment appear to play roles in the onset of diabetes. This disease, which has no cure, is the 4th-leading cause of death by disease in the U.S. In 1996, more than 178,000 Americans were expected to die from the disease and its complications.

In 1997, the American Diabetes Association issued new guidelines for diagnosing diabetes. The new recommendations include: lowering the acceptable level of blood sugar from 140 mg of glucose/deciliter of blood to 126 mg/deciliter, possibly identifying 2 million more people with the disease; testing all adults 45 years and older, and

then every 3 years if normal; and testing at a younger age, or more frequently, in high-risk individuals. The American Diabetes Association believes that detection at an earlier stage will help prevent or delay complications of diabetes.

There are 2 major types of diabetes:

• **Type 1 (formerly known as insulin dependent)**—The body produces very little or no insulin; disease most often begins in childhood or early adulthood. People with type I diabetes must take daily insulin injections to stay alive.

• **Type 2 (formerly known as non-insulin dependent)**—The body does not produce enough or cannot properly use insulin. It is the most common form of the disease (90-95% of cases in people over age 20) and often begins later in life.

Warning Signs of Diabetes

Type 1 Diabetes (usually occurs suddenly):

- frequent urination
- unusual thirst
- extreme hunger
- unusual weight loss
- extreme fatigue
- irritability

Type 2 Diabetes (occurs less suddenly):

- any type 1 symptoms
- frequent infections
- blurred vision
- cuts/bruises slow to heal
- tingling/numbness in hands or feet
- recurring skin, gum, or bladder infections

Complications of Diabetes

More than half of all individuals with diabetes do not know that they have the disease until one of its life-threatening complications occurs. Potential complications include:

Blindness. Diabetes is the leading cause of blindness in people ages 20-74. Each year, from 12,000 to 24,000 people lose their sight because of diabetes.

Kidney disease. 10% to 21% of all people with diabetes develop kidney disease. In 1992, more than 19,800 people initiated treatment for end-stage renal disease (kidney failure) because of diabetes.

Amputations. Diabetes is the most frequent cause of nontraumatic lower limb amputations. The risk of a leg

amputation is 15 to 40 times greater for a person with diabetes than for the average American. Each year, 54,000 people lose a foot or leg to complications brought on by diabetes.

Heart disease and stroke. People with diabetes are 2 to 4 times more likely to have heart disease (more than 77,000 deaths due to heart disease annually). And they are 2 to 4 times more likely to suffer a stroke (more than 11,000 diabetes-related stroke deaths each year).

Health-care and related costs for the treatment of the disease, as well as the cost of lost productivity, total nearly $92 billion annually in the U.S.

Alzheimer's Disease

Source: Alzheimer's Association, 919 N Michigan Ave., Suite 1000, Chicago, IL 60611-1676; phone: (800) 272-3900

Alzheimer's disease is a progressive, degenerative disease of the brain in which brain cells die and are not replaced. It results in impaired memory, thinking, and behavior, and is the most common form of dementing illness. The debilitating nature of the disease renders patients susceptible to infections (such as pneumonia and urinary tract infections) as they become emaciated, incontinent, immobile, or enter a persistent vegetative state.

Alzheimer's disease afflicts an estimated 4 million Americans, striking equally among men and women of all races. Although most people diagnosed with Alzheimer's are older than age 60, the disease can occur in people in their 40s and 50s. Ten percent of those 65 years of age or older, and almost half of those over age 85, have the disease. It is estimated that the cost of diagnosis, treatment, and long-term care for patients with the disease costs American society $100 billion per year.

The rate of the progression of Alzheimer's disease from the onset of symptoms until death ranges from 3 to 20 years; the average is 8 years. Eventually, patients become totally incapable of caring for themselves.

Diagnosis is complicated by the lack of a single, simple test to identify the disease. Through a series of diagnostic

tests by a qualified physician, possible causes of symptoms, such as depression, drug interactions, nutrient imbalances, or other forms of dementia, such as those associated with stroke, Huntington's disease, Parkinson's disease, Pick's disease, and infections (AIDS, meningitis, syphilis) are ruled out, yielding a diagnosis of Alzheimer's disease that is 80-90% accurate. A definitive diagnosis is possible only with a brain biopsy or an autopsy.

No treatment has proven successful in reversing the course of the disease, and providing care for patients with Alzheimer's disease is very physically and psychologically demanding. Nearly 70% of those afflicted with Alzheimer's disease live at home and are cared for by family and friends. In the last stages of the disease, it is often necessary for those afflicted to be cared for in a nursing home. Nearly half of all nursing home patients in the United States suffer from Alzheimer's disease.

People with Alzheimer's disease need a safe, stable environment and a regular daily schedule. Physical exercise and social activity are important, as is proper nutrition. A bracelet identifying the person's name and condition may be helpful in case the person wanders away.

The causes of Alzheimer's disease are unknown.

Warning Signs

- Recent memory loss that affects job performance
- Inability to learn new information
- Difficulty with everyday tasks such as cooking or dressing oneself
- Inability to remember simple words
- Use of inappropriate words when communicating
- Disorientation of time and place
- Poor or decreased judgment
- Problems with abstract thinking
- Misplacing objects in inappropriate places
- Rapid changes in mood or behavior
- Increased irritability, anxiety, depression, confusion, and restlessness
- Prolonged loss of initiative

Heart and Blood Vessel Disease

Source: American Heart Association, 7272 Greenville Ave., Dallas, TX 75231-4596; phone: (800) 242-8721

Warning Signs

Of Heart Attack

- Uncomfortable pressure, fullness, squeezing, or pain in the center of the chest lasting 2 minutes or longer
- Pain may radiate to the shoulder, arm, neck, or jaw
- Sweating may accompany pain or discomfort
- Nausea and vomiting may also occur
- Shortness of breath, dizziness, or fainting may accompany other signs

The American Heart Association advises immediate action at the onset of these symptoms. The association points out that more than half of heart attack victims die within 1 hour of the onset of symptoms and before they have reached the hospital.

Of Stroke

- Sudden temporary weakness or numbness of face or limbs on one side of the body
- Temporary loss of speech, or trouble speaking or understanding speech
- Temporary dim or lost vision, especially in one eye
- Unexplained dizziness, unsteadiness, or sudden falls

Some Major Risk Factors

Blood pressure—High blood pressure increases the risk of stroke, heart attack, kidney failure, and congestive heart failure. **Cholesterol**—A blood cholesterol level over 240 mg/dl (milligrams of cholesterol per deciliter of blood) approximately doubles the risk of coronary heart disease; about 20% of the U.S. adult population (37.7 mil) falls into this category. Blood cholesterol levels between 200 and 240 mg/dl are in a zone of moderate and increasing risk. An estimated 6.5 mil (10.8% of) youths age 4-19 have levels of 200 mg/dl or higher.

Cigarettes—Cigarette smokers have more than twice the risk of heart attack and 2-4 times the risk of sudden cardiac death as nonsmokers. Young smokers have a higher risk for early death from stroke.

Obesity—More than 65 mil adults are 20% or more over their desirable weight.

Understanding Blood Pressure

High blood pressure, or hypertension, affects people of all races, sexes, ethnic origins, and ages. Various causes can trigger this often symptomless disease. Since hypertension can increase one's risk for stroke, heart attack, kidney failure, and congestive heart failure, it is recommended that individuals have a blood pressure reading at least once every 2 years (more often if advised by a physician).

A blood pressure reading is really two measurements in one, with one written over the other, such as 122/78. The **upper number (systolic pressure)** represents the amount of pressure in the blood vessels when the heart contracts (beats) and pushes blood through the circulatory system. The **lower number (diastolic pressure)** represents the pressure in the blood vessels between beats, when the heart is resting. According to National Institutes of Health guidelines, normal blood pressure is below 130/85 and "high normal" is between 130/85 and 139/89. High blood pressure is divided into 4 stages, based on severity:

- **Stage 1 (mild)** high blood pressure ranges from 140/90 to 159/99
- **Stage 2 (moderate)** is from 160/100 to 179/109
- **Stage 3 (severe)** is from 180/110 to 209/119
- **Stage 4 (very severe)** is 210/120 and up

The diagnosis of hypertension can be based on either the systolic or the diastolic reading.

High blood pressure usually cannot be cured, but it can be controlled in a variety of ways, including lifestyle modifications and medication. Treatment should be at the direction and under the supervision of a physician.

Examples of Moderate[1] Amounts of Exercise

Source: *Physical Activity and Health: A Report of the Surgeon General*, U.S. Dept. of Health and Human Services, 1996

Activity	Duration[2] (min)	Activity	Duration[2] (min)
Washing and waxing a car	45-60	Raking leaves	30
Washing windows or floors	45-60	Walking 2 mi (15 min/mi)	30
Playing touch football	30-45	Swimming laps	20
Wheeling self in wheelchair	30-40	Basketball (playing a game)	15-20
Walking 1¾ mi (20 min/mi)	35	Bicycling 4 mi	15
Basketball (shooting baskets)	30	Jumping rope	15
Bicycling 5 mi	30	Running 1½ mi (10 min/mi)	15
Dancing fast (social)	30	Shoveling snow	15

Note: The activities are arranged from less vigorous, and using more time, to more vigorous, and using less time. (1) A "moderate" amount of physical activity uses c. 150 calories (kcal), or 1,000 if done daily for a week. (2) Some activities can be performed at various intensities; the suggested durations are based on the expected intensity of effort.

Finding Your Target Heart Rate

Source: Carole Casten, EdD, *Aerobics Today;* Peg Jordan, RN, Aerobics and Fitness Assoc. of America

The target heart rate is the heartbeat rate a person should have during aerobic exercise (such as running, fast walking, cycling, or cross-country skiing) to get the full benefit of the exercise for cardiovascular conditioning.

First, determine the intensity level at which one would like to exercise. A sedentary person may want to begin an exercise regimen at the 60% level and work up gradually to the 70% level. Athletes and highly fit individuals must work at the 85-95% level to receive benefits.

Second, calculate the target heart rate. One common way of doing this is by using the American College of Sports Medicine Method.

To obtain cardiovascular fitness benefits from aerobic exercise, it is recommended that an individual participate in an aerobic activity at least 3-5 times a week for 20-30 minutes per session, although cardiac patients and very sedentary individuals can obtain benefits with shorter periods (15-20 minutes). Generally, training changes occur in 4-6 weeks, but they can occur in as little as 2 weeks.

The American College of Sports Medicine Method

Using the American College of Sports Medicine Method to calculate one's target heart rate, an individual should subtract his or her age from 220, then multiply by the desired intensity level of the workout. Then divide the answer by 6 for a 10-second pulse count. (The 10-second pulse count is useful for checking whether the target heart rate is being achieved during the workout. One can easily check one's pulse—at the wrist or side of the neck—counting the number of beats in 10 seconds.)

For example, a 20-year-old wishing to exercise at 70% intensity, would employ the following steps:

Maximum Heart Rate	$220 - 20 = 200$
Target Heart Rate	$200 \times .70 = 110$
10-second Pulse Count	$140 \div 6 = 23$

To work at the desired level of intensity, this 20-year-old would strive for a target heart rate of 140 beats per minute, or a 10-second pulse count of 23.

Where to Get Help

Source: Based on Health & Medical Year Book.
Copyright © by Collier Newfield, Inc.

Listed here are some of the major U.S. and Canadian organizations providing information about good health practices generally, or about specific conditions and how to deal with them. (Canadian sources are identified as such.) Where a toll-free number is not available, an address is given when possible.

Some entries conclude with an e-mail address for the organization and/or an address for its Internet site, where you can also obtain useful information. When inputting an e-mail or Internet address, be certain to type it exactly as it appears, including capital and lowercase letters, nonalphanumeric characters, and spaces (generally none). In addition to these selected sites, there is a vast array of medical information on the Internet; however, it is very important to be certain that the source of information is reliable and accurate. Always check with a physician before embarking on any new health-related ventures.

General Sources

Centers for Disease Control and Prevention Voice Information System
404-332-4555
Recorded information about public health topics, such as AIDS and Lyme disease. Also, you can request to talk with a CDC expert or have information faxed to you.
Web site: http://www.cdc.gov
National Health Information Center
800-336-4797; in Maryland, 301-565-4167
Phone numbers for more than 1,000 health-related organizations in the United States and offers printed materials.
E-mail: nhicinfo@health.org
National Institutes of Health
Bethesda, MD 20892
301-496-4000
Free information, including the latest research findings, on many diseases.
Web site: http://www.nih.gov
Tel-Med
Check the phone book for local listings or call Tel-Med at 909-825-6034
Recorded information on over 600 health topics. Sponsored by local medical societies, health organizations, or hospitals.

Aging

National Association of Area Agencies on Aging's Eldercare Locator Line
800-677-1116
Information and assistance on a wide range of services and programs including adult day-care and respite services, consumer fraud, hospital and nursing home information, legal services, elder abuse/protective services, Medicaid/Medigap information, tax assistance, and transportation.
National Institute on Aging
800-222-2225
Information and publications about disabling conditions, support groups, and community resources.
E-mail: niainfo@access.digex.net
Web site: http://www.nih.gov/nia

AIDS

AIDS Clinical Trials Information Service
800-874-2572;
for the hearing impaired, 800-243-7012
Information on federally and privately sponsored clinical trials for patients with AIDS or HIV.
E-mail: actis@cdcnac.org
Canadian AIDS Society
800-499-1986
Written materials and referrals in the Toronto area.
Centers for Disease Control and Prevention National AIDS/HIV Hotline
800-342-AIDS 24 hours;
in Spanish, 800-344-SIDA;
for the hearing impaired, 800-AIDS-TTY
Information on the prevention and spread of AIDS, along with referrals.
HIV-AIDS Treatment Information Service
800-HIV-0440
Treatment information to people with AIDS, their families, and health care providers.

Alcoholism and Drug Abuse

Alcohol and Drug Helpline
800-821-4357
Referrals to local facilities (24 hours).

Alcoholics Anonymous
212-870-3400
Worldwide support groups for alcoholics. Check phone book for local chapters.
American Council on Alcoholism
800-527-5344
Treatment referrals and counseling for recovering alcoholics.
National Clearinghouse for Alcohol and Drug Information
800-729-6686
Provides written materials on alcohol and drug-related subjects.
Web site: http://www.health.org
National Council on Alcoholism and Drug Dependence Hopeline
800-622-2255
An answering machine for callers to request information.
National Health Lines
800-262-2463
Answers questions on substance abuse and provides referrals to treatment centers. Operates 24 hours.

Alzheimer's Disease

Alzheimer's Association
800-272-3900
Referrals to local chapters and support groups; offers information on publications available from the association.
E-mail: info@alz.org
Web site: http://www.alz.org
Alzheimer's Society of Canada
1320 Yonge Street, Suite 201
Toronto, ON M4T 1X2
416-925-3552
Phone numbers for local support chapters. Publishes support materials.
E-mail: alzca@istar.ca

Amyotrophic Lateral Sclerosis

ALS Association
800-782-4747; in the San Fernando Valley, 818-340-7500
Information about ALS (Lou Gehrig's Disease) and referrals to ALS specialists, local chapters and support groups.
Web site: http://www.alsa.org

Arthritis

Arthritis Foundation
800-283-7800
Information, publications, and referrals to local groups.
Web site: http://www.arthritis.org
Arthritis Society (Canada)
250 Bloor Street East, Suite 901
Toronto, ON M4W 3P2
416-967-1414; in Ontario only, 800-321-1433
Phone numbers for local chapters.
Web site: http://www.arthritis.ca
National Arthritis and Musculoskeletal and Skin Diseases Information Clearinghouse
301-495-4484
Subject searches and resource referrals.
Web site: http://www.nih.gov/niams

Asthma and Allergies
See also *Lung Diseases*

Asthma and Allergy Foundation Information Clearinghouse
800-7-ASTHMA
Written information.
American Academy of Allergy, Asthma, and Immunology Referral Line
800-822-ASMA

Written materials on asthma and allergies. Operates 24 hours.
Web site: http://www.aaaai.org

Blindness and Eye Care

Canadian National Institute for the Blind
1929 Bayview Avenue
Toronto, ON M4G 3E8
416-480-7595 or contact your local chapter
National office offers training and library with braille books and audiotapes. Local chapters provide core services: orientation in mobility, sight enhancement, counseling, referrals, career aid.
Web site: http://www.cnib.ca
Foundation Fighting Blindness
800-683-5555; in Maryland, 410-785-1414; for the hearing impaired, 800-683-5551
Answers questions about retinal degenerative diseases; written materials.
Web site: http://www.blindness.org
Library of Congress National Service for the Blind and Physically Handicapped
800-424-9100; in Spanish, 800-345-8901; in Washington, DC, 202-707-5100
Information on libraries that offer talking books and books in braille.
Web site: http://lcweb.loc.gov/nls/nls.html
National Association for Parents of the Visually Impaired
800-562-6265
Support and information for parents of individuals who are visually impaired.

Blood Disorders

Cooley's Anemia Foundation
800-522-7222
Information on patient care and support groups; makes referrals to local chapters.
E-mail: ncaf@aol.com
Sickle Cell Disease Association of America
800-421-8453; in California, 310-216-6363
Genetic counseling and information packet.

Burns

Phoenix Society
800-888-2876
Counseling for burn victims and information on self-help services for burn victims and their families.

Cancer

American Cancer Society
800-ACS-2345
Publications and information about cancer and coping with cancer; makes referrals to local chapters for support services.
Web site: http://www.cancer.org
Canadian Cancer Information Service
800-263-6750
Written materials, videos, support services, and referrals.
National Cancer Institute's Cancer Information Service
800-4-CANCER
Information about clinical trials, treatments, and success rates for any type of cancer.
Web site: http://wwwicic.nci.nih.gov/occdocs/cis/cis.html
Y-Me Breast Cancer Support Program
800-221-2141, 24 hours; in Illinois, 312-986-8228
Information and literature on breast cancer, counseling, and referrals.
Web site: http://www.y-me.org

Cerebral Palsy

Ontario Federation for Cerebral Palsy
1630 Lawrence Avenue West
Toronto, ON M6L 1C5
416-244-8003
Canada does not have a national cerebral palsy organization, but the provincial organizations offer information on housing, services, and coping with life, and each one will provide contact numbers for the others.
United Cerebral Palsy Associations
800-USA-5UCP;
in Washington, DC, 202-776-0406
Written materials.
Web site: http://www.ucpa.org

Children

American Academy of Pediatrics
847-228-5005
Child-care publications and materials; referrals to pediatricians.
Web site: http://www.aap.org
Childhelp's USA National Child Abuse Hotline
800-4-A-CHILD
Crisis intervention, professional counseling, referrals to local groups and to shelters for runaways, and literature. Operates 24 hrs.
National Center for Missing and Exploited Children
800-843-5678; for the hearing impaired, 800-826-7653
Hotline for reporting missing children and sightings of missing children.

Chronic Fatigue Syndrome

CFIDS Association of America
800-442-3437
Literature and a list of support groups.
E-mail: info@cfids.org
Web site: http://www.cfids.org

Crisis

National Runaway Switchboard
800-621-4000
Crisis intervention and referrals for runaways. Runaways can leave messages for parents, and vice versa. Operates 24 hours.

Cystic Fibrosis

Canadian Cystic Fibrosis Foundation
416-485-9149; for long distance in Canada, 800-378-2233
Information and brochures; makes referrals to local chapters.
Cystic Fibrosis Foundation
800-FIGHT-CF
Answers questions and offers literature and referrals to local clinics.
Web site: http://www.cff.org

Diabetes

American Diabetes Association
800-ADA-DISC; in Virginia and Washington, DC, 703-549-1500
Information about diabetes, nutrition, exercise, and treatment and offers referrals to diabetes specialists.
Web site: http://www.diabetes.org
Canadian Diabetes Association
15 Toronto Street, Suite 800, Toronto, ON M5C 2E3
416-363-3373; in Ontario only, 800-361-1306
Information and publications.
Web site: http://www.diabetes.ca
Juvenile Diabetes Foundation Hotline
800-223-1138 or 800-533-2873
Answers questions, provides literature (some in Spanish), and offers referrals to local chapters, physicians, and clinics.
Web site: http://www.jdfcure.com

Digestive Diseases

Crohn's and Colitis Foundation of America
800-932-2423; in New York, 212-685-3440
Educational materials; offers referrals to local chapters, which can provide referrals to support groups and physicians.
Web site: http://www.ccfa.org
Crohn's Colitis Foundation of Canada
21 St. Clair Avenue E, Suite 301,
Toronto, ON M4T 1L9
416-920-5035; in Canada only, 800-387-1479
Will send educational materials on request.
Web site: http://www.ccfc.ca

Disabilities

National Information Clearinghouse for Infants With Life-Threatening Conditions and Severe Disabilities
800-922-9234
Referrals to support groups and to sources of financial, medical, and legal aid for developmentally disabled and chronically ill children, aged up to 3, and disabled children of Vietnam veterans.

Domestic Violence

National Council on Child Abuse and Family Violence
800-222-2000;
in Washington, DC, 202-429-6695
A recording provides toll-free numbers to call for information or referrals.

Down Syndrome

National Down Syndrome Congress
800-232-6372; in Georgia, 404-633-1555
Answers questions on all aspects of Down syndrome; referrals.
E-mail: ndsc@charitiesusa.com
National Down Syndrome Society
800-221-4602; in New York City, 212-460-9330
Information; referrals to local programs for newborns.
Web site: http://www.ndss.org

Drug Abuse

See Alcoholism and Drug Abuse

Dyslexia

Orton Dyslexia Society
800-ABCD-123; in Maryland, 410-296-0232
Information on testing, tutoring, and computers used to aid people with dyslexia and related disorders.
E-mail: info@ods.org

Eating Disorders

National Association of Anorexia Nervosa and Associated Disorders
Box 7, Highland Park, IL 60035
847-831-3438
Written materials, referrals, and telephone counseling.

Endometriosis

Endometriosis Association
800-992-ENDO; in Canada, 800-426-2END
An answering machine for callers to request information.

Epilepsy

Epilepsy and Seizure Disorder Service at the Epilepsy Foundation of America
800-332-1000
Information and referrals to local chapters.
Web site: http://www.efa.org

Food Safety and Nutrition

Meat and Poultry Hotline of the U.S. Department of Agriculture's Food, Safety, and Inspection Service
800-535-4555
Information on proper handling, preparation, storage, and cooking of meat, poultry, and eggs.
FDA Center for Food Safety and Applied Nutrition
800-FDA-4010;
in Washington, DC, 202-205-4314
Information on how to buy and use seafood products and on their proper handling and storage. Callers may speak to food specialists, Mon. through Fri., 12 noon to 4 PM (EST).
Web site: http://www.cfsan.fda.gov

Headaches

National Headache Foundation
800-843-2256
Literature on headaches and treatment.

Heart Disease and Stroke

American Heart Association
800-242-8721
Information, publications, and referrals to organizations.
Web site: http://www.amhrt.org

National Institute of Neurological Disorders and Stroke

800-352-9424
Literature and information.
Web site: http://www.ninds.nih.gov
National Stroke Association
800-787-6537
Information on support networks for stroke victims and their families; referrals to local support groups.
Web site: http://www.stroke.org

Hospices

Children's Hospice International
800-242-4453; in Virginia, 703-684-0330
Information; referrals to children's hospices.
Hospice Education Institute Hospicelink
800-331-1620
General information about hospice care and referrals to local programs.
E-mail: hospiceall@aol.com

Huntington's Disease

Huntington's Disease Society of America
800-345-4372; in New York, 212-242-1968
Information and referrals to physicians and support groups.
Web site: http://neuro-www2.mgh.harvard.edu/hdsa/hdsamain.nclk
Huntington Society of Canada
P.O. Box 1269,13 Water Street North, Suite 3, Cambridge, ON N1R 7G6
519-622-1002
Information, including telephone numbers of local services, and publications and referrals.

Impotence

Impotence Information Center
800-843-4315
Information on the causes and treatment of impotence, incontinence, and prostate problems.
Impotence World Association Hotline
800-669-1603
Written materials, physician referrals, and telephone phone numbers of local Impotents Anonymous chapters.

Kidney Diseases

Kidney Foundation of Canada
800-361-7494; in Ontario, 514-369-4806
Educational materials and general information.
E-mail: kidney-f-c@vir.com
Web site: http://www.kidney.ca
National Kidney and Urologic Diseases Information Clearinghouse
3 Information Way
Bethesda, MD 20892-3580
301-654-4415
Information about kidney and urologic diseases and referrals to organizations.
Web site: http://www.niddk.nih.gov
National Kidney Foundation
800-622-9010
Information and referrals.
Web site: http://www.kidney.org

Lead Exposure

National Lead Information Center
800-LEAD-FYI
Recommendations (in English and Spanish) for reducing a child's exposure to lead. Referrals to state and local agencies.
Web site: http://www.nsc.org/ehc/lead.htm

Liver Diseases

American Liver Foundation
800-223-0179; in New Jersey, 201-256-2550
Information on hepatitis, liver disease, and gallbladder disease.
Web site: http://sadieo.ucsf.edu/alf/alffinal/homepagealf.html

Lung Diseases

See also Asthma and Allergies

American Lung Association
Check the phone book for local listings or call the national office at 800-LUNG-USA for automatic connection to the office nearest you. Answers questions about asthma and lung diseases; publications and referrals.
(continued)

Lung Line Information Service at the National Jewish Medical and Research Center
800-222-LUNG; in Denver, 303-355-LUNG
Answers questions on asthma, emphysema, allergies, smoking, and other respiratory and immune system disorders.
Web site:
http://www.njc.org/Markethtml/Lungline.html

Lupus
American Lupus Society
800-331-1802
Sends information to those who leave name and address on answering machine.
Lupus Foundation of America
800-558-0121
Sends information to those who leave name and address on answering machine.

Lyme Disease
Lyme Disease Foundation
800-886-LYME
Written information; doctor referrals (24 hours).

Mental Health
National Clearinghouse on Family Support and Children's Mental Health
800-628-1696
Publications, computerized databank, and state-by-state resource file (24 hours).
National Depressive and Manic Depressive Association
800-826-3632
Support for patients and families, answers questions, provides publications, and makes referrals to affiliated organizations.
Web site: http://www.ndmda.org
National Foundation for Depressive Illness
800-248-4344
Recorded message describing the symptoms of depression and offering an address for more information and physician referral (24 hours).
National Institute of Mental Health
5600 Fisher's Lane, Room 7C02
Rockville, MD 20857
301-443-4513
Information on a range of topics, from children's mental disorders to schizophrenia, depression, eating disorders, and others.
Web site: http://www.nimh.nih.gov
National Mental Health Association
800-969-6642
Referrals to mental health groups.

Multiple Sclerosis
Multiple Sclerosis Society of Canada
800-268-7582
Counseling, literature, and referrals to local chapters.
National Multiple Sclerosis Society
800-344-4867
Information about local chapters.
Web site: http://www.nmss.org

Muscular Dystrophy
Muscular Dystrophy Association
800-572-1717
Written materials on 40 neuromuscular diseases, including muscular dystrophy. Will give information over the phone about such matters as MDA clinics, support groups, summer camps, and wheelchair purchase assistance.
E-mail: mda@mdausa.org

Nutrition
See *Food Safety and Nutrition*

Organ Donation
Living Bank
800-528-2971
A registry and referral service for people wanting to commit organs to transplantation or research. Operates 24 hours.

Osteoporosis
National Osteoporosis Foundation
800-223-9994
Information packet available on request.
Web site: http://www.nof.org

Pain
National Chronic Pain Outreach Association
540-997-5004
Information packet available on request.

Parkinson's Disease
National Parkinson Foundation
800-327-4545; in Florida, 800-433-7022; in Miami, 305-547-6666
Answers questions, makes physician referrals, and provides written information in English and Spanish.
E-mail: mailbox@npf.med.miami.edu
Web site: http://www.parkinson.org
Parkinson Foundation of Canada
800-565-3000
Information; referrals to support groups.

Plastic Surgery
Plastic Surgery Information Service
800-635-0635
Referrals to board-certified plastic surgeons in the U.S. and Canada; general information.
Web site: http://www.plasticsurgery.org

Polio
International Polio Network
4207 Lindell Blvd., #110
St. Louis, MO 63108
314-534-0475
Information on coping with the late effects of polio; referrals to other organizations.
E-mail: gini_intl@msn.com

Prostate Problems
Prostate Information Line
800-543-9632
Advice on treatment.

Rare Disorders
National Organization for Rare Disorders
800-999-6673
Information on diseases and networking programs; referrals to organizations for specific disorders.
Web site: http://199.249.196.59/nord

Rehabilitation
National Rehabilitation Information Center
800-34-NARIC; in Maryland, 301-588-9284
Research referrals and information on rehabilitation issues.
Web site: http://www.cais.net/naric

Scleroderma
United Scleroderma Foundation
800-722-4673; in California, 408-728-2202
Referrals to local support groups and treatment centers, as well as information on scleroderma and related skin disorders.
E-mail: outreach@scleroderma.com
Web site: http://www.scleroderma.com

Sexually Transmitted Diseases
See also *AIDS*
National STD Hotline
800-227-8922
Information; confidential referrals.

Sjogren's Syndrome
Sjogren's Syndrome Foundation
800-4-SJOGREN
Provides an answering machine for callers to request treatment literature.

Skin Problems
National Psoriasis Foundation
800-723-9166
Information and referrals.
Web site: http://www.psoriasis.org

Speech and Hearing
American Speech-Language-Hearing Association Helpline
800-638-8255 (also TTY); in Maryland, 301-897-8628
Materials on speech and language disorders and hearing impairment; referrals.
Web site: http://www.asha.org

Canadian Hard of Hearing Association
2435 Holly Lane, Suite 205
Ottawa, ON K1V 7P2
613-526-1584; TTY 613-526-2692; fax 613-526-4718
Publications; answers general questions.
E-mail: chhanational@cyberuf.ca
Dial a Hearing Screening Test
800-222-EARS
Answers questions on hearing problems. Makes referrals to local telephone numbers for a two-minute hearing test. Also to ear, nose, and throat specialists and to organizations that can provide specialized ear and hearing aid information.
E-mail: dabiddle@aol.com
International Hearing Aid Helpline
800-521-5247
Information and distributes a directory of hearing aid specialists certified by the International Hearing Society.
National Center for Stuttering
800-221-2483
in New York State, 212-532-1460
Information on stuttering in all age groups.
Web site: http://www.stuttering.com
Stuttering Foundation of America
800-992-9392
Referrals to speech pathologists, resource lists, and other publications.
E-mail: stutterssa@aol.com

Spinal Injuries
National Spinal Cord Injury Association
800-962-9629;
in Maryland, 301-588-6959
Peer counseling; referrals to local chapters and other organizations.
Web site: http://www.spinalcord.org
National Spinal Cord Injury Hotline
800-526-3456
Written materials on spinal cord injuries; referrals to organizations and support groups.
Web site: http://members.aol.com/scihotline

Stroke
See *Heart Disease and Stroke*

Sudden Infant Death Syndrome
American Sudden Infant Death Syndrome Institute
800-232-SIDS; in Georgia, 800-847-7437
Answers questions; literature; referrals to other organizations.
National SIDS Foundation
800-221-SIDS; in Maryland, 410-653-8226
Literature on medical information, referrals, and support groups.

Tourette Syndrome
Tourette Syndrome Association
800-237-0717; in New York, 718-224-2999
Printed information.
E-mail: tourette@ix.netcom.com

Urinary Incontinence
National Association for Continence
800-BLADDER
Information on bladder control, services available for incontinence, and assistive devices.
Web site: http://www.nafc.org
Simon Foundation
800-23-SIMON
Support and literature on incontinence.

Women's Health
National Women's Health Network
514 10th Street NW, Suite 400
Washington, DC 20004
202-347-1140
Information and referrals on more than 70 women's health concerns.
National Women's Health Resource Center
2425 L Street NW, Third Floor
Washington, DC 20037
202-293-6045
A national clearinghouse for women's health information.

ASSOCIATIONS AND SOCIETIES

Source: World Almanac questionnaire

Selected list, by first key word in each title. Founding year in parentheses; last figure after ZIP code = membership as reported by organization. See also Directory of Sports Organizations, under Sports; Where to Get Help directory, under Health; Labor Union Directory, under Employment; lists of religious grous' headquarters (for U.S. and for Canada), under Religion.

Aaron Burr Assn. (1946), 4520 King Edward Ct., Annandale, VA 22003; 220.

Abortion Federation, Natl. (1977), 1436 U St. NW, Ste. 103, Wash., DC 20009; 350 organizations.

Accountants, American Institute of Certified Public (1887), 1211 Ave. of the Americas, New York, NY 10036; 330,000.

Accountants, Natl. Assn. of Enrolled Federal Tax (1960), PO Box 59-009, Chicago, IL 60659.

Accountants for Cooperatives, Natl. Soc. of (1936), 6320 Augusta Dr., Ste. 800, Springfield, VA 22150; 2,000.

Acoustical Society of America (1929), 500 Sunnyside Blvd., Woodbury, NY 11797; 6,800.

Actors Guild, Screen (1933), 5757 Wilshire Blvd., Los Angeles, CA 90036; 90,000.

Actuaries, Society of (1949), 475 N. Martingale Rd., Ste. 800, Schaumburg, IL 60173; 16,500.

Advertisers, Assn. of Natl. (1910), 155 E. 44th St., New York, NY 10017; 5,300.

Advertising Agencies, American Assn. of (1917), 405 Lexington Ave., New York, NY 10174; 600 agencies.

Aeronautic Assn., Natl. (1911), 1815 N. Fort Myer Dr., Ste. 700, Arlington, VA 22209; 8,000.

Aerospace Industries Assn. of America (1919), 1250 Eye St. NW, Wash., DC 20005; 50 cos.

African Violet Soc. of America (1946), 2375 North, Beaumont, TX 77702; 12,000.

Afro-American Life and History, Assn. for the Study of (1915), 1407 14th St. NW, Wash., DC 20005; 1,400.

AFS Intl. Intercultural Programs (1947), 220 E. 42d St., New York, NY 10017; 475,000.

Aging Assn., American (1970), 2129 Providence Ave., Chester, PA 19013; 400.

Agricultural Economics Assn., American (1910), 1110 Buckeye Ave., Ames, IA 50010; 3,516.

Agricultural Engineers, American Soc. of (ASAE) (1907), 2950 Niles Rd., St. Joseph, MI 49085; 7,500.

Agricultural History Society (1919), 1301 New York Ave. NW, Ste. 928, Wash., DC 20005; 1,500.

Agronomy, American Society of (1907), 677 S. Segoe Rd., Madison, WI 53711; 12,000.

Aircraft Owners and Pilots Assn. (1939), 421 Aviation Way, Frederick, MD 21701; 340,000.

Air Force Assn. (1946), 1501 Lee Hwy., Arlington, VA 22209; 176,000.

Air Force Gunners Assn. (1986), 453 Plaza Circle, Bossier City, LA 71111; 1,700.

Air & Waste Management Assn. (1907), One Gateway Center, 3d Fl., Pittsburgh, PA 15222; 16,000.

Al-Anon Family Groups (1951), 1600 Corporate Landing Pkwy., Virginia Beach, VA 23454; 500,000 worldwide.

Alcoholics Anonymous (1935), 475 Riverside Dr., New York, NY 10115; 2 mil+.

Alcoholism and Drug Dependence, Inc., Natl. Council on (1944), 12 W. 21st St., New York, NY 10010.

Alcohol Problems, American Council on (1895), 3426 Bridgeland Dr., Bridgeton, MO 63044; 36 state affiliates.

Allergy, Asthma, and Immunology, American Academy of (1943), 611 E. Wells St., Milwaukee, WI 53202; 5,000.

Alpha Delta Kappa Intl. (1947), 1615 West 92d St., Kansas City, MO 64114; 56,000.

Alpine Club, American (1902), 710 Tenth St., Ste. 100, Golden, CO 80401; 3,750.

Alzheimer's Assn. (1980), 919 Michigan Ave., Chicago, IL 60611.

American Indian Affairs, Inc., Assn. on (1922), PO Box 268, Sisseton, SD 57262; 25,000.

American Indians, Natl. Congress of (1944), 2010 Massachusetts Ave. NW, Wash., DC 20036; 3,000.

American Legion (1919), 700 N. Pennsylvania Ave., Indianapolis, IN 46204; 2.9 mil.

American Legion Auxiliary (1921), 777 N. Meridian St., Indianapolis, IN 46204; 975,000.

American Veterans (AMVETS) (1947); **AMVETS Natl. Auxiliary** (1946), 4647 Forbes Blvd., Lanham, MD 20706; 175,000+.

Americares Foundation (1982), 161 Cherry St., New Canaan, CT 06840.

Amnesty Intl. USA (1961), 322 8th Ave., New York, NY 10001.

Amputation Foundation, Natl. (1919), 38-40 Church St., Malverne, NY 11565; 2,000.

Amusement Parks and Attractions, Intl. Assn. of (1918), 1448 Duke St., Alexandria, VA 22314; 5,000.

Animals, American Society for Prevention of Cruelty to (ASPCA) (1866), 424 E. 92d St., New York, NY 10128; 299,000.

Animal Protection Institute (1968), PO Box 22505, Sacramento, CA 95822; 75,000.

Animal Welfare Institute (1951), PO Box 3650, Wash., DC 20007; 4,500

Anthropological Assn., American (1902), 4350 N. Fairfax Dr., Ste. 640, Arlington, VA 22203; 10,000.

Antiquarian Society, American (1812), 185 Salisbury St., Worcester, MA 01609; 642.

Appalachian Mountain Club (1876), 5 Joy St., Boston, MA 02108; 72,000.

Appalachian Trail Conference (1925), Washington & Jackson Sts., Harpers Ferry, WV 25425; 23,000.

Appraisers, American Society of (1936), 555 Herndon Pkwy., Ste. 125, Herndon, VA 22070; 6,500.

Arab Americans, Natl. Assn. of (1972), 1212 New York Ave. NW, Wash., DC 20005.

Arbitration Assn., American (1926), 140 W. 51st St., New York, NY 10020; 10,000.

Arc, The (1950), 500 E. Border St., Ste. 300, Arlington, TX 76010; 140,000.

Archaeological Institute of America (1879), 656 Beacon St., Boston, MA 02215; 11,000.

Archery Assn. of the U.S., Natl. (1879), One Olympic Plaza, Colorado Springs, CO 80909; 5,720.

Architects, American Institute of (1857), 1735 New York Ave. NW, Wash., DC 20006; 55,000.

Architectural Historians, Society of (1940), 1365 North Astor St., Chicago, IL 60610; 4,000.

Armed Forces Communications and Electronics Assn. (1946), 4400 Fair Lakes Ct., Fairfax, VA 22033; 40,000.

Army, Assn. of the United States (1950), 2425 Wilson Blvd., Arlington, VA 22201; 117,000.

Arthritis Foundation (1948), 1330 W. Peachtree St., Atlanta, GA 30309; 500,000.

Arts, American Council for the (1960), One E. 53d St., New York, NY 10022; 1,500.

Arts, American Federation of (1909), 41 E. 65th St., New York, NY 10021; 520+ museums/inst.

Arts, Americans for the (1996), 1000 Vermont Ave., 12th Fl., Wash., DC 20005; 2,500.

Arts and Letters, American Academy of (1898), 633 W. 155 St., New York, NY 10032; 250.

Arts and Letters, Natl. Society of (1944), 655 15th St. NW, Wash., DC 20005; 1,600.

Arts and Sciences, American Academy of (1780), Norton's Woods, 136 Irving St., Cambridge, MA 02138; 633.

Associated Press (1848), 50 Rockefeller Plaza, New York, NY 10020; 1,554 newspapers & 6,000 broadcast stations.

Association Executives, American Society of (1925), 1575 Eye St. NW, Wash., DC 20005; 23,400.

Astrologers, Inc., American Federation of (1938), PO Box 22040, Tempe, AZ 85285; 3,500.

Astronautical Society, American (1954), 6352 Rolling Mill Pl., Ste. 102, Springfield, VA 22152; 1,400.

Astronomical Society, American (1899), 2000 Florida Ave. NW, Ste. 400, Wash., DC 20009; 6,000.

Ataxia Foundation, Natl. (1957), 15500 Wayzata Blvd., Ste. 750, Wayzata, MN 55391; 9,068.

Atheists, Inc., American (1964), PO Box 140195, Austin, TX 78714; 2,400.

Athletic Assns., Natl. Federation of State H. S. (1920), 11724 Plaza Circle, Box 20626, Kansas City, MO 64195.

Athletics, Natl. Assn. of Intercollegiate (1940), 6120 S. Yale Ave., Ste. 1450, Tulsa, OK 74136; 362 schools.

Auctioneers Assn., Natl. (1949), 8880 Ballentine, Overland Park, KS 66214; 5,532.

Audubon Society, Natl. (1905), 700 Broadway, New York, NY 10003; 550,000.

Authors Guild, Inc., The (1919), 330 W. 42d St., New York, NY 10036; 7,054.

Authors League of America (1912), 234 W. 44th St., New York, NY 10036; 15,000.

Authors Registry, The (1995), 330 W. 42d St., 29th Fl., New York, NY 10036; representing approx. 50,000 authors.

Autism Society of America (1965), 7910 Woodmont Ave., Ste. 650, Bethesda, MD 20814; 24,000+.

Autograph Collectors Club, Universal (1965), PO Box 6181, Wash., DC 20044; 1,800.

Automobile Assn., American (1902), 1000 AAA Dr., Heathrow, FL 32746; 40 mil.

Automobile Club of America, Antique (1935), 501 W. Governor Rd., Hershey, PA 17033; 53,000.

Automobile Dealers Assn., Natl. (1917), 8400 Westpark Dr., McLean, VA 22102; 19,500.

Automobile License Plate Collectors Assn. (1954), PO Box 7, Horner, WV 26372; 2,500.

Automotive Hall of Fame (1939), PO Box 1727, Midland, MI 48641; 1,500.

Badminton Assn., U.S. (1936), One Olympic Plaza, Colorado Springs, CO 80909; 2,500+.

Baker Street Irregulars (1934), PO Box 2189, Easton, MD 21601; 300.

Bald-Headed Men of America (1972), 102 Bald Dr., Morehead City, NC 28557; approx. 36,000.

Ball Players of America, Assn. of Prof. (1924), 12062 Valley View St., Ste. 211, Garden Grove, CA 92845; 25,000.

Band Directors Hall of Fame, Natl. High School (1985), 519 N. Halifax Ave., Daytona Beach, FL 32118; 3,624.

Bankers Assn., American (1875), 1120 Connecticut Ave. NW, Wash., DC 20036.

Bankers Assn. of America, Independent (1930), One Thomas Circle NW, Ste. 950, Wash., DC 20005; 5,800 banks.

Bar Assn., Federal (1920), 1815 H St. NW, Ste. 408, Wash., DC 20006; 15,000.

Barber Shop Quartet Singing in America, Inc., Soc. for the Preservation & Encouragement of (1938), 6315 Third Ave., Kenosha, WI 53143; 34,400.

Baseball Congress, American Amateur (1935), 118 Redfield Plaza, Marshall, MI 49068; 14,500 teams.

Baseball Congress, Natl. (1931), Lawrence-Dumont Stadium, 300 S. Sycamore, Wichita, KS 67213.

Baseball Players of America, Assn. of Prof. (1924), 12062 Valley View St., Ste. 211, Garden Grove, CA 92845; 16,000+.

Baseball Research, Society for American (1971), PO Box 93183, Cleveland, OH 44101; 6,500.

Battleship Assn., American (1964), PO Box 711247, San Diego, CA 92171; 2,210.

Beer Can Collectors of America (1970), 747 Merus Ct., Fenton, MO 63026; 4,100.

Beta Gamma Sigma, Inc. (1913), 11701 Borman Dr., Ste. 320, St. Louis, MO 63146; 388,000.

Beta Sigma Phi (1931), 1800 W. 91st Pl., Kansas City, MO 64114; 200,000.

Better Business Bureaus, Council of (1970), 4200 Wilson Blvd., Ste. 800, Arlington, VA 22203; 138 bureaus.

Bible Society, American (1816), 1865 Broadway, New York, NY 10023; 280,000.

Biblical Literature, Society of (1880), 1549 Clairmont Rd., Ste. 204, Decatur, GA 30033; 6,000+.

Bibliographical Society of America (1904), PO Box 397, Grand Central Station, New York, NY 10163; 1,200.

Big Brothers/Big Sisters of America (1902), 230 N. 13th St., Philadelphia, PA 19107; 494 agencies.

Biochemistry and Molecular Biology, American Society for (1906), 9650 Rockville Pike, Bethesda, MD 20814; 9,300.

Biological Sciences, American Institute of (1947), 730 11th St. NW, Wash., DC 20001; 5,000.

Biology, Society for Integrative and Comparative (1890), 401 N. Michigan Ave. Chicago, IL 60611; 2,200.

Black History Honors & Awards, Contemporary & (1990), 6514 Georgia Rd., Birmingham, AL 35212; 152.

Blind, American Council of the (1961), 1155 15th St. NW, Ste. 720, Wash., DC 20005; 40,000.

Blind, Natl. Federation of the (1940), 1800 Johnson St., Baltimore, MD 21230; 60,000.

Blinded Veterans Assn. (1945), 477 H St. NW, Wash., DC 20001; 7,900.

Blindness America, Prevent (1908), 500 E. Remington Rd., Schaumburg, IL 60173.

Blueberry Council, North American (1965), 4995 Golden Foothill Pkwy., Ste. 2, El Dorado Hills, CA 95762.

B'nai B'rith Intl. (1853), 1640 Rhode Island Ave. NW, Wash., DC 20036; 150,000.

Boat Owners Assn. of the U.S. (1966), 880 S. Pickett St., Alexandria, VA 22304; 500,000.

Bookplate Collectors and Designers, American Soc. of (1922), 605 N. Stoneman Ave., #F, Alhambra, CA 91801; 200.

Booksellers Assn., American (1900), 828 S. Broadway, Tarrytown, NY 10591; 8,000.

Bowling Congress, American (1895), 5301 S. 76th St., Greendale, WI 53129; 4.7 mil.

Boy Scouts of America (1910), 1325 Walnut Hill Lane, Irving, TX 75015; 5.6 mil.

Boys & Girls Clubs of America (1906), 1230 W. Peachtree St. NW, Atlanta, GA 30309; 2.6 mil.

Bread for the World, Inc. (1974), 1100 Wayne Ave., Ste. 1000, Silver Spring, MD 20910; 44,000.

Bridge League, American Contract (1937), 2990 Airways Blvd., Memphis, TN 38116; 170,000.

Bridge, Tunnel & Turnpike Assn., Intl. (1932), 2120 L St. NW, Ste. 305, Wash., DC 20037; 250 organizations.

Brith Sholom (1905), 3939 Conshohocken Ave., Philadelphia, PA 19131; 6,000.

Broadcasters, Natl. Assn. of (1922-23), 1771 N St. NW, Wash., DC 20036.

Burroughs Bibliophiles, The (1960), 454 Elaine Dr., Pittsburgh, PA 15236; 786.

Business Clubs, Inc., Natl. American (AMBUCS) (1922), 3315 N. Main St., High Point, NC 27265; 6,320.

Business Communicators, Intl. Assn. of (1970), One Hallidie Plaza, Ste. 600, San Francisco, CA 94102; 12,500.

Business Education Assn., Natl. (1946), 1906 Association Dr., Reston, VA 22091; 18,000.

Business Women's Assn., American (1949), 9100 Ward Pkwy., PO Box 8728, Kansas City, MO 64114; 80,000.

Button Society, Natl. (1938), 2733 Juno Pl., Akron, OH 44333; 4,500+.

Byron Society, The (1971 in Eng., 1973 in U.S.), Dept. of English, Univ. of Delaware, Newark, DE 19716; 300 individuals and libraries.

Camp Fire Boys & Girls (1910), 4601 Madison, Kansas City, MO 64112; 700,000.

Camping Assn., American (1910), 5000 State Rd. 67 N., Martinsville, IN 46131; 5,400.

Cancer Society, American (1913), 1599 Clifton Rd. NE, Atlanta, GA 30329.

Carnegie Hero Fund Commission (1904), 2307 Oliver Bldg., Pittsburgh, PA 15222; 21 members.

Cartoonists Society, Natl. (1946), Columbus Circle Station, PO Box 20267, New York, NY 10023; 630.

Cat Fanciers' Assn. (1906), 1805 Atlantic Ave., Manasquan, NJ 08736; 650 clubs.

Cat Writers' Assn. (1992), 1759 Lake Cypress Dr., Safety Harbor, FL 34695; 225.

Catholic Bishops, U.S. Natl. Conference of (1917), 3211 4th St. NE, Wash., DC 20017; 402 members, 350 staff.

Catholic Church Extension Society (1905), 35 E. Wacker Dr., #400, Chicago, IL 60601; 90,000.

Catholic Daughters of the Americas (1903), 10 W. 71st St., New York, NY 10023; 125,000.

Catholic Educational Assn., Natl. (1904), 1077 30th St. NW, Ste. 100, Wash., DC 20007; 18,353.

Catholic Historical Soc., American (1884), 263 S. Fourth St., PO Box 84, Philadelphia, PA 19105; 750.

Catholic Library Association (1921), 100 North St., Ste. 224, Pittsfield, MA 01201; 1,000.

Catholic Rural Life Conference, Natl. (1923), 4625 Beaver Ave., Des Moines, IA 50310; 4,000+.

Catholic War Veterans of the U.S.A., Inc. (1935), 419 N. Lee St., Alexandria, VA 22314; 25,000.

Cemetery Assn., American (1887), 1895 Preston White Dr., #220, Reston, VA 22091; 2,200.

Ceramic Society, American (1898), 735 Ceramic Place, Westerville, OH 43081; 12,000.

Cerebral Palsy Assns., United (1949), 1660 L St. NW, Ste. 700, Wash., DC 20036.

Chamber of Commerce of the U.S.A. (1912), 1615 H St. NW, Wash., DC 20062; 215,000.

Chamber Music Players, Inc., Amateur (1947), 1123 Broadway, New York, NY 10010; 4,300.

Chartered Life Underwriters, American Soc. of (1927), 270 Bryn Mawr Ave., Bryn Mawr, PA 19010; 30,000.

Checker Federation, American (1948), 220 Lynn Ray Rd., PO Box 365, Petal, MS 39465; 1,000.

Chemical Engineers, American Inst. of (1908), 345 E. 47th St., New York, NY 10017; 60,000.

Chemical Manufacturers Assn. (1872), 1300 Wilson Blvd., Arlington, VA 22209; 190 cos.

Chemical Society, American (1876), 1155 16th St. NW, Wash., DC 20036; 151,000.

Chemists, American Assn. of Cereal (1914), 3340 Pilot Knob Rd., St. Paul, MN 55121; 4,000.

Chess Federation, U.S. (1949), 186 Rt. 9W, New Windsor, NY 12553; 84,327.

Chess League of American, Correspondence (1897), PO Box 3481, Barrington, IL 60011; 1,200.

Childhood Education Intl., Assn. for (1892), 11501 Georgia Ave., Ste. 315, Wheaton, MD 20902; 10,000.

Children, Natl. Center for Missing and Exploited (1984), 2101 Wilson Blvd., #550, Arlington, VA 22201.

Children of the American Revolution, Natl. Society of the (1895), 1776 D St. NW, Wash., DC 20006.

Children's Aid Society (1853), 105 E. 22d St., New York, NY 10010; 1,207.

Children's Book Council (1945), 568 Broadway, Ste. 404, New York, NY 10012; 80 publishing houses.

Child Welfare League of America (1920), 440 First St. NW, Ste. 310, Wash., DC 20001; 900+ agencies.

Chiropractic Assn., American (1963), 1701 Clarendon Blvd., Arlington, VA 22209; 19,000.

Chris Craft Antique Boat Club, Inc. (1973), 217 S. Adams St., Tallahassee, FL 32301; 2,800.

Christian Endeavor Union, World's (1895), 3575 Valley Rd., PO Box 820, Liberty Corner, NJ 07938.

Christian Laity Counseling Board, Inc. (1970), 5901 Plainfield Dr., Charlotte, NC 28215; 52.5 mil.

Christians and Jews, Natl. Conference of (1927), 71 Fifth Ave., Ste. 1100, New York, NY 10003.

Church Women United (1941), 475 Riverside Dr., Ste. 500, New York, NY 10115.

Cincinnati, Society of the (1783), 2118 Massachusetts Ave. NW, Wash., DC 20008; 3,300.

Cities, Natl. League of (1924), 1301 Pennsylvania Ave. NW, Wash., DC 20004; 1,450 cities.

City/County Management Assn., Intl. (1914), 777 N. Capitol St. NE, Ste. 500, Wash., DC 20002.

Civic League, Natl. (1894), 1445 Market St., Ste. 300, Denver, CO 80202; 1,100.

Civil Air Patrol (1941), HQ CAP-USAF, Maxwell AFB, AL 36112; 63,000.

Civil Engineers, American Society of (1852), 345 E. 47th St., New York, NY 10017; 104,000.

Civil Liberties Union, American (ACLU) (1920), 132 W. 43d St., New York, NY 10036; 250,000.

Civitan International (1920), One Civitan Pl., Birmingham, AL 35213; 55,000.

Classical League, American (1919), Miami Univ., Oxford, OH 45056; 3,604.

Clean Energy Research Institute (1974), Univ. of Miami, Coral Gables, FL, 33124; 120.

CLU & ChFC, American Soc. of (1928), 270 S. Bryn Mawr Ave., Bryn Mawr, PA 19010; 34,000.

Coal Assn., Natl. (1917), 1130 17th St. NW, Wash., DC 20036; 150 corporate members.

Coaster Enthusiasts, American (1978), PO Box 8226, Chicago, IL 60680; 4,700+.

Coast Guard Combat Veterans Assn. (1986), 17728 Striley Dr., Ashton, MD 20861; 1,800.

Codependents Anonymous (1986), 5150 N. 16th St., Phoenix, AZ 85016.

College Admission Counseling, Natl. Assn. for (1937), 1631 Prince St., Alexandria, VA 22314; 6,300.

College Board, The (1900), 45 Columbus Ave., New York, NY 10023; 2,900 institutions.

College English Assn. (1934), English Dept., Winthrop Univ., Rock Hill, SC 29733; 1,200.

College Music Society (1958), 202 W. Spruce St., Missoula, MT 59802; 5,500.

Colleges and Employers, Natl. Assn. of (1956), 62 Highland Ave., Bethlehem, PA 18017; 2,920.

Colleges and Universities, Assn. of American (1915), 1818 R St. NW, Wash., DC 20009; 680 institutions.

Collegiate Schools of Business, American Assembly of (1916), 600 Emerson Rd. Ste. 300, St. Louis, MO 63141; 850 inst.

Colonial Dames XVII Century, Natl. Society of (1915), 1300 New Hampshire Ave. NW, Wash., DC 20036; 14,000.

Commerce, U.S. Junior Chamber of (1915), 4 W. 21st St., Tulsa, OK 74114; 200,000.

Commercial Collectors Assn., Int'l. (1971), 4040 W. 70th St., Minneapolis, MN 55435; 360.

Commercial Law League of America (1895), 150 N. Michigan, Ste. 600, Chicago, IL 60601; 4,800.

Common Cause (1970), 2030 M St. NW, Wash., DC 20036.

Communication, Intl. Training in (1938), 2519 Woodland Dr., Anaheim, CA 92801; 15,000.

Communication Industry Assn., Personal (1949), 500 Montgomery St., Ste. 700, Alexandria, VA 22314; 1,400.

Community Cultural Center Assn., American (1985), 149 Cannongate III, Nashua, NH 03063.

Community Colleges, American Assn. of (1920), One Dupont Circle NW, Ste. 410, Wash., DC 20036; 1,113 inst.

Composers, Authors & Publishers, American Soc. of (ASCAP) (1914), One Lincoln Plaza, New York, NY 10023; 24,000.

Composers/USA, Natl. Assn. of (NACUSA) (1932), PO Box 49256, Barrington Sta., Los Angeles, CA 90049; 600.

Computing Machinery, Assn. for (1947), 1515 Broadway, 17th Fl., New York, NY 10036; 85,000.

Computing Professionals, Inst. for Certification of (1973), 2200 E. Devon Ave., Ste. 247, Des Plaines, IL 60018; 50,000+.

Concerned Women for America (1979), 370 L'Enfant Promenade SW, Ste. 800, Wash., DC 20024; 500,000.

Concrete Institute, American (1904), 22400 W. Seven Mile Rd., Detroit, MI 48219; 20,000.

Congress of Racial Equality (CORE) (1942), 30 Cooper Square, 9th Fl., New York, NY 10003.

Conscientious Objectors, Central Committee for (1948), 1515 Cherry St., Philadelphia, PA 19102.

Conservation Engineers, Assn. of (1961), 64 N. Union St., Rm. 479, Montgomery, AL 36104; 295

Constantian Society (1970), 840 Old Washington Rd., McMurray, PA 15317; 560.

Construction Industry Manufacturers Assn. (1911), 111 E. Wisconsin Ave., Ste. 1000, Milwaukee, WI 53202; 410 cos.

Construction Specifications Institute (1948), 601 Madison St., Alexandria, VA 22314; 17,000.

Consulting Organizations, Council of (1989), 521 5th Ave., New York, NY 10175.

Consumer Credit Assn., Intl. (1912), 243 N. Lindbergh Blvd., St. Louis, MO 63141; 20,000.

Consumer Federation of America (1968), 1424 16th St. NW, Ste. 604, Wash., DC 20036; 250 organizations.

Consumer Interests, American Council on (1953), 1416 Longwell Dr., Columbia, MO 65211; 1,200.

Consumer Protection Institute (1970), 5901 Plainfield Dr., Charlotte, NC 28215.

Consumers Union of the U.S. (1936), 101 Truman Ave., Yonkers, NY 10703; 405,990.

Contractors of America, General (1919), 1957 E St. NW, Wash., DC 20006; 32,000.

Co-op America (1982), 1612 K St. NW, Ste. 600, Wash., DC 20006; 48,000 individuals, 2,000 businesses.

Cooperative Business Assn., Natl. (1916), 1401 New York Ave. NW, Ste. 1100, Wash., DC 20005; 540.

Cooperative League of the U.S.A. (1916), 1401 New York Ave. NW, Ste. 1100, Wash., DC 20005; 285 co-ops.

Correctional Assn., American (1870), 4380 Forbes Blvd., Lanham, MD 20706; 20,000+.

Correctional Officers, Intl. Assn. of (1977), 8600 Glenarden Pkwy., Glenarden, MD 20706.

Cosmetology Assn., Natl. (1921), 3510 Olive St., St. Louis, MO 63103; 32,000.

Cotton Council of America, Natl. (1938), 1918 N. Pkwy., Memphis, TN 38112.

Counseling Assn., American (1952), 5999 Stevenson Ave., Alexandria, VA 22304; 55,738.

Count Dracula Society (1962), 334 W. 54th St., Los Angeles, CA 90037; 500.

Country Music Assn. (1958), One Music Circle S, Nashville, TN 37203; 6,588.

Crafts & Creative Industries, Assn. of (ACCI) (1976), 1100-H Brandywine Blvd., PO Box 2188, Zanesville, OH 43702; 6,000.

Creative Children and Adults, Natl. Assn. for (1974), 8080 Springvalley Dr., Cincinnati, OH 45236; 6,000.

Credit Assn., Intl. (1912), 243 N. Lindbergh Blvd., St. Louis, MO 63141; 7,300.

Credit Union Natl. Assn. & Affiliates (1934), 5710 Mineral Point Rd., Madison, WI 53705; 51 credit union leagues.

Cribbage Congress, American (1979), PO Box 10486, Napa, CA 94581; 6,800.

Crime and Delinquency, Natl. Council on (1907), 685 Market St., Ste. 620, San Francisco, CA 94105; 500.

Criminology, American Society of (1941), 1314 Kinnear Rd., Ste. 212, Columbus, OH 43212; 2,600.

Crop Protection Assn., American (1933), 1156 15th St. NW, Ste. 900, Wash., DC 20005; 80 cos.

Crop Science Society of America (1955), 677 S. Segoe Rd., Madison, WI 53711; 4,450.

Cryogenic Soc. of America, Inc. (1964), 1033 South Blvd., Ste. 13, Oak Park, IL 60302; 500.

Cystic Fibrosis Foundation (1955), 6931 Arlington Rd., Bethesda, MD 20814.

Dairy Council, Natl. (1915), 6300 N. River Rd., Rosemont, IL 60018.

Dairy and Food Industries Supply Assn. (1917), 6245 Executive Blvd., Rockville, MD 20852; 800 cos.

Dairy Goat Assn., American (1904), 209 W. Main St., Spindale, NC 28160; 13,000.

Daughters of the American Revolution, Natl. Society (1890), 1776 D St. NW, Wash., DC 20006; 190,000.

Daughters of the British Empire (1920), 800 Carrington Dr., Raleigh, NC 27615; 4,769.

Daughters of the Confederacy, United (1894), 328 North Blvd., Richmond, VA 23220; 24,000.

Daughters of the Republic of Texas (1891), 510 E. Anderson Ln., Austin, TX 78752; 7,400.

Daughters of Union Veterans of the Civil War (1885), 503 S. Walnut St., Springfield, IL 62704; 3,700

Deaf, Alexander Graham Bell Assn. for the (1890), 3417 Volta Pl. NW, Wash., DC 20007.

Deaf, Natl. Assn. of the (1880), 814 Thayer Ave., Silver Spring, MD 20910; 26,000.

Defense Preparedness Assn., American (1919), 2101 Wilson Blvd., Ste. 400, Arlington, VA 22201; 28,000.

Delta Kappa Gamma Society Intl. (1929), 416 W. 12th St., Austin, TX 78701; 165,000.

Delta Mu Delta (1913), PO Box 46935, 11707 Borman Dr., Ste. 320, St. Louis, MO 63146; 80,000.

Deltiologists of America (1960), PO Box 8, Norwood, PA 19074; 725.

Democratic Natl. Committee (1848), 430 S. Capitol St. SE, Wash., DC 20003; 432 elected members.

DeMolay International (1919), 10200 N. Executive Hills Blvd., Kansas City, MO 64153; 30,000.

Dental Assn., American (1859), 211 E. Chicago Ave., Chicago, IL 60611; 140,000.

Descendants of the Colonial Clergy, Society of the (1933), 17 Lowell Mason Rd., Medfield, MA 02052; 1,300.

Descendants of Washington's Army at Valley Forge, Society of (1976), PO Box 915, Valley Forge, PA 19482; 982.

Desert Protective Council (1954), PO Box 2312, Valley Center, CA 92082; 400+.

Destroyer-Escort Sailors Assn., Inc. (1975), PO Box 469, Allenhurst, NJ 07711; 11,500.

Diabetes Assn., American (1940), 1660 Duke St., Alexandria, VA 22314; 300,000.

Dialect Society, American (1889), c/o Allan Metcalf, English Dept., MacMurray College, Jacksonville, IL 62650; 550.

Digital Printing & Imaging Assn. (1992), 10015 Main St., Fairfax, VA 22031; 750 cos.

Directors Guild of America (1936), 7920 Sunset Blvd., Los Angeles, CA 90046; 9,700.

Disabled American Veterans (1920), 3725 Alexandria Pike, Cold Spring, KY 41076; 1,077,276.

Disabled Collectors' Correspondence Club (1991), PO Box 3113, Fremont, CA 94539.

Disabled Sports USA (1967), 451 Hungerford Dr., Ste. 100, Rockville, MD 20850; 20,000.

Dogs International, Inc., Therapy (1976), 6 Hilltop Rd., Mendham, NJ 07945; 4,000+

Dogs on Stamps Study Unit (1979), 202A Newport Rd., Cranbury, NJ 08512; 400.

Dozenal Society of America (1944), Math Dept., Nassau Community College, Garden City, NY 11530; 144.

Drug, Chemical, and Allied Trades Assn. (1890), 2 Roosevelt Ave., Syosset, NY 11791; 2,018.

Ducks Unlimited (1937), One Waterfowl Way, Memphis, TN 38120; 500,000+.

Eaglehunters Intl. (1994), PO Box 1599, Hernando, FL 34442; 600.

Eagles, Fraternal Order of (1898), 12660 W. Capitol Dr., Brookfield, WI 53055; 1.1 mil.

Easter Seal Society, Natl. (1919), 230 W. Monroe, Ste. 1800, Chicago, IL 60606.

Eastern Airline Retirees Assn. (1985), 700 S. Royal Poinciana Blvd., Miami, FL 33166; 9,960.

Eastern Star, General Grand Chapter, Order of the (1876), 1618 New Hampshire Ave. NW, Wash., DC 20009; 1.5 mil.

Economic Assn., American (1885), 2014 Broadway, Ste. 305, Nashville, TN 37203; 20,000.

Ecumenical Church Federation (1982), 13014-270 N. Dalemabry, Tampa, FL 33618.

Edsel Club, Intl. (1969), PO Box 371, Sully, IA 50251; 1,090.

Education, American Council on (1918), One Dupont Circle NW, #800, Wash., DC 20036; 1,800.

Education, Council for Advancement & Support of (1974), 11 Dupont Circle NW, Wash., DC 20036; 2,950 schools.

Education, Natl. Assn. for Family and Community (1936), 5963 Jefferson St., Burlington, KY 41005; 45,000.

Educational Research Assn., American (1916), 1230 17th St. NW, Wash., DC 20036; 22,300.

Education of Young Children, Natl. Assn. for the (1926), 1509 16th St. NW, Wash., DC 20036; 95,000.

Educators for World Peace, Natl. Assn. of (1969), PO Box 3282, Mastin Lake Station, Huntsville, AL 35810; 25,500.

Egalitarian Communities, Federation of (1976), E. Wind, Rt. 3, Box 6B2, Tecumseh, MO 65760; 250+.

8th Air Force Historical Society (1975), PO Box 7215, St. Paul, MN 55107; 18,500.

88th Infantry Division Assn., Inc. (1948), PO Box 925, Havertown, PA 19083; 5,600.

82d Airborne Division Assn., Inc. (1946), NFCS, PO Box 9308, Fayetteville, NC 28311; 23,000 +.

Electrical and Electronics Engineers, Institute of (1884), 345 E. 47th St., New York, NY 10017; 320,000.

Electrical Manufacturers Assn., Natl. (1926), 2101 L St. NW, Wash., DC 20037; 560 cos.

Electrochemical Society, Inc. (1902), 10 S. Main St., Pennington, NJ 08534; 7,000.

Electronic Circuits, The Institute for Interconnecting & Packaging (1957), 2215 Sanders Blvd., Northbrook, IL 60062; 2,000 cos.

Electronic Industries Assn. (1924), 2001 Pennsylvania Ave., Wash., DC 20006; 1,058 cos.

Electronics Technicians, Intl. Society of Certified (1970), 2708 W. Berry, Ft. Worth, TX 76109; 2,000.

Electroplaters' and Surface Finishers' Society, American (1909), 12644 Research Pkwy., Orlando, FL 32826; 7,300.

Elks of the U.S.A., Benevolent and Protective Order of (1868), 2750 N. Lakeview Ave., Chicago, IL 60614; 1.5 mil.

Elvis Presley Burning Love Fan Club (1983), 1904 Williamsburg Dr., Streamwood, IL 60107; 1,500+.

Energy Engineers, Assn. of (1977), 4025 Pleasantdale Rd., Ste. 420, Atlanta, GA 30340; 8,500.

Engineering, Natl. Academy of (1964), 2101 Constitution Ave. NW, Wash., DC 20418; 1,893.

Engineering in Agricultural, Food, and Biological Systems, Society for (1907), 2950 Niles Rd., St. Joseph, MI 49085; 8,000.

Engineers, Natl. Society of Professional (1934), 1420 King St., Alexandria, VA 22314; 65,000.

English, U.S. (1983), 1747 Pennsylvania Ave. NW, Ste. 1100, Wash., DC 20006; Approx. 1,000,000.

English-Speaking Union of the U.S. (1920), 16 E. 69th St., New York, NY 10021; 18,000.

Entomological Society of America (1889), 9301 Annapolis Rd., Lanham, MD 20706; 6,500.

Environmental Health Assn., Natl. (1937), 720 S. Colorado Blvd., Ste. 970 South, Denver, CO 80222; 5,100.

Environmental Information Assn. (1983), 4915 Auburn Ave., Ste. 303, Bethesda, MD 20814; 1,000.

Environmental Medicine, American Academy of (1965), PO Box CN 1001-8001, New Hope, PA 18938; 500.

Epigraphic Society, Inc., The (1974), 2443 Filmore St., Ste. 328, San Francisco, CA 94115.

Esperanto League for North America (1953), PO Box 1129, El Cerrito, CA 94530; 1,000+.

Evangelism Crusades, Intl. (1959), 14617 Victory Blvd., Van Nuys, CA 91411; 500.

Exchange Club, Natl. (1911), 3050 Central Ave., Toledo, OH 43606; 33,000.

Experimental Aircraft Assn. (1953), PO Box 3086, Oshkosh, WI 54903; 166,000.

Exploration Geophysicists, Society of (1930), PO Box 702740, Tulsa, OK 74170; 14,500.

Fairs & Expositions, Intl. Assn. of (1919), PO Box 985, Springfield, MO 65809; 2,500.

Family Campers and RVers (1949), 4804 Transit Rd., Bldg. 2, Depew, NY 14043; 56,000 families.

Family Relations, Natl. Council on (1938), 3989 Central Ave. NE, Ste. 550, Minneapolis, MN 55421; 4,000.

Family Service America (1911), 11700 W. Lake Park Dr., Milwaukee, WI 53224; 250 agencies.

Farm Bureau Federation, American (1919), 225 Touhy Ave., Park Ridge, IL 60068; 4 mil.

Farmers of America Org., Natl. Future (1928), 5632 Mt. Vernon Memorial Hwy., Alexandria, VA 22309; 294,000 families.

Farmers Educational & Co-operative Union of America (1902), 11900 E. Cornell Ave., Aurora, CO 80014; 250,000.

Farmers Union, Natl. (1902), Denver, CO 80251; 250,000.

Fat Acceptance, Natl. Assn. to Advance (NAAFA) (1969), PO Box 188620, Sacramento, CA 95818; 5,000.

Feminists for Life of America (1972), 733 15th St. NW, Ste. 1100, Wash., DC 20005; 5,000.

Financial Analysts Federation (1945), 5 Boar's Head Lane, Charlottesville, VA 22903; 22,700.

Financial Executives Institute (1938), 10 Madison Ave., PO Box 1938, Morristown, NJ 07962; 14,000.

Financial Women Intl. (1921), 200 North Glebe Rd., Ste. 814, Arlington, VA 22203; 10,000.

Financiers, Intl. Society of (1979), PO Box 18508, Asheville, NC 28814; 300.

Fire Chiefs, Intl. Assn. of (1873), 4025 Fair Ridge Dr., Fairfax, VA 22033; 10,000+.

Fire Protection Assn., Natl. (1896), One Batterymarch Park, Quincy, MA 02269; 65,000.

Fire Protection Engineers, Soc. of (1972), One Liberty Sq., 5th Fl., Boston, MA 02109; 4,500.

First Amendment Studies, Institute for (1984), 187 Main St., Great Barrington, MA 01230; 10,000.

Fisheries Soc., American (1870), 5410 Grosvenor Lane, Ste. 110, Bethesda, MD 20814; 10,000.

Fishes, Soc. for the Protection of Old (1967), School of Fisheries, 357980, Univ. of Washington, Seattle, WA 98195.

Flag Research Center, The (1962), Box 580, Winchester, MA 01890; 1,300.

Fly Fishers, Fed. of (1965), 502 S. 19th, Ste. 1, Bozeman, MT 59715; 11,000.

Flying Disc Federation, World (1985), Gnejsvägen 24, 85357, Sundsvall, Sweden; 15,000.

Food Institute, American Frozen (1942), 2000 Corporate Ridge, Ste. 1000, McLean, VA 22102; 540 firms.

Food Technologists, Institute of (1939), 221 N. LaSalle, Ste. 300, Chicago, IL 60601; 28,000.

Footwear Industries Assn., American (1869), 1420 K St. NW, Ste. 600, Wash., DC 20005; 160 cos.

Foreign Student Affairs, Natl. Assn. for (1948), 1875 Connecticut Ave., Ste. 1000, Wash., DC 20009; 6,800.

Foreign Study, American Institute for (1964), 102 Greenwich Ave., Greenwich, CT 06830; 300,000.

Foreign Trade Council, Inc., Natl. (1914), 1270 Avenue of the Americas, #206, New York, NY; 556 cos.

Forensic Sciences, American Academy of (1948), 410 N. 21st St., Ste. 203, Colorado Springs, CO 80901; 4,500.

Foresters, Society of American (1900), 5400 Grosvenor La., Bethesda, MD 20814; 18,800.

Forest History Society (1946), 701 Vickers Ave., Durham, NC 27701; 1,200.

Forest & Paper Assn., American (1993), 1111 19th St. NW, Wash., DC 20036; 400 cos.

Forest Products Society (1947), 2801 Marshall Ct., Madison, WI 53705; 2,500.

Forestry Assn., American (1875), 1516 P St. NW, Wash., DC 20005; 150,000.

Forests, American (1875), 910 17th St., Ste. 600, Wash., DC 20013; 137,000.

Forrestal **CVA/CV/AVT-59 Assn., Inc., USS** (1991), 300 Cassady Ave., Virginia Beach, VA 23452; 1,229.

Fortean Organization, Intl. (1965), PO Box 367, Arlington, VA 22210; 800.

Founders and Patriots of America, Order of the (1896), 3892 College Ave., Ellicott City, MD 21043; 1,250.

Foundrymen's Society, American (1896), 505 State St., Des Plaines, IL 60016; 13,000.

4-H Clubs (1914), 1400 Independence Ave., U.S. Dept of Agriculture, Wash., DC 20250; 5.5 mil.

Frederick A. Cook Society, (1940), PO Box 11421, Pittsburgh, PA 15238; 178.

Freedom From Religion Foundation (1978), PO Box 750, Madison, WI 53701; 3,500.

Freedom of Information Center (1958), 127 Neff Annex, Univ. of Missouri, Columbia, MO 65211.

Freedoms Foundation at Valley Forge (1949), 1601 Valley Forge Rd., PO Box 706, Valley Forge, PA 19482; 5,000.

French Institute/Alliance Française (1898), 22 E. 60th St., New York, NY 10022; 6,500.

Friendship and Good Will, Intl. Soc. of (1978), 412 Cherry Hills Dr., Bakersfield, CA 93309; 4,117.

Funeral & Memorial Societies of America (1963), PO Box 10, Hinesburg, VT 05461; 500,000.

Galactic Society Intl. (1986), Box 326, Rock Hill, SC 29731; 300.

Gamblers Anonymous (1957), PO Box 17173, Los Angeles, CA 90017.

Garden Club of American (1913), 598 Madison Ave., New York, NY 10022; 15,000.

Garden Clubs, Natl. Council of State (1929), 4401 Magnolia Ave., St. Louis, MO 63110; 308,623.

Gas Appliance Manufacturers Assn. (1935), 1901 N. Moore St., Arlington, VA 22209; 205 cos.

Gas Assn., American (1918), 1515 Wilson Blvd., Arlington, VA 22209; 229 cos.; 3,000.

Gay and Lesbian Task Force, Natl. (1973), 2320 17th St. NW, Wash., DC 20009; 35,000.

Genealogical Society, Natl. (1903), 4527 17th St. NW, Arlington, VA 22207; 15,000.

Genetic Assn., American (1905), PO Box 257, Buckeystown, MD 21717; 850.

Geographers, Assn. of American (1904), 1710 16th St. NW, Wash., DC 20009; 7,200.

Geographical Society, American (1851), 120 Wall St., Ste. 100, New York, NY 10010; approx. 2,500.

Geographic Education, Natl. Council for (1915), 16A Leonard Hall, IUP, Indiana, PA 15705; 3,800.

Geographic Society, Natl. (1888), 1145 17th St. NW, Wash., DC 20036; 9.7 mil.

Geological Society of America (1888), 3300 Penrose Pl., PO Box 9140, Boulder, CO 80301; 14,400.

George S. Patton, Jr. Historical Society (1970), 3116 Thorn St., San Diego, CA 92104; 75.

Geriatrics Society, American (1942), 770 Lexington Ave., Ste. 300, New York, NY 10021; 6,500.

Gideons Intl. (1899), 2900 Lebanon Rd., Nashville, TN 37214; 131,000.

Gifted Children, Natl. Assn. for (1954), 1707 L St. NW, Ste. 550, Wash., DC 20036; 7,500.

Girl Scouts of the U.S.A. (1912), 420 5th Ave., New York, NY 10018; 3.5 mil.

Girls Incorporated (1945), 30 E. 33d St., New York, NY 10016.

Glenn Miller Birthplace Society (1976), 107 East Main St., PO Box 61, Clarinda, IA 51632; 1,400.

Golf Assn., U.S. (1894), Golf House, PO Box 708, Far Hills, NJ 07931; 8,631 clubs.

Gospel Music Assn. (1964), 1205 Division St., Nashville, TN 37203; 5,500.

Governing Boards of Universities & Colleges, Assn. of (1921), One Dupont Circle NW, Ste. 400, Wash., DC 20036.

Government Finance Officers Assn. (1906), 180 N. Michigan Ave., Ste. 800, Chicago, IL 60601; 13,600.

Governors' Assn., Natl. (1908), Hall of the States, 444 N. Capitol #267, Wash., DC 20001; 55 govs.

Graduate Schools, Council of (1960), One Dupont Circle NW, #430 Wash., DC 20036; 415 institutions.

Grand Encampment Knights Templar U.S.A. (1816), 5097 N. Elston, Ste. 101, Chicago, IL 60630.

Grandmother Clubs of America, Natl. Federation of (1938), 313 E. Liberty St., Wauconda, IL 60084; 5000.

Graphic Arts, American Institute of (1914), 164 5th Ave., New York, NY 10010; 9,000.

Gray Panthers (1970), PO Box 21477, Wash., DC 20009; 50,000.

Great Council of the U.S., Improved Order of Red Men (1765), 4521 Speight Ave., Waco, TX 76711; 28,000.

Green Mountain Club (1910), Rt. 100, RR1, Box 650, Waterbury Ctr., VT 05677; 7,000+.

Grocers Assn., Nat'l. (1982), 1825 Samuel Morse Dr., Reston, VA 22190; 2,500.

Grocery Manufacturers of America (1908), 1010 Wisconsin Ave., Ste. 800, Wash., DC 20007; 140 cos.

Ground Water Assn., Natl. (1948), 6375 Riverside Dr., Dublin, OH 43017; 24,500.

Group Against Smokers' Pollution, Inc. (GASP) (1971), PO Box 632, College Park, MD 20741; 10,000+.

Guide Dog Foundation for the Blind, Inc. (1946), 371 E. Jericho Tpk., Smithtown, NY 11787.

Gyro Intl. (1912), 1096 Mentor Ave., Painesville, OH 44077; 4,600.

Hadassah, the Women's Zionist Organization of America (1912), 50 W. 58th St., New York, NY 10019; 385,000.

Hairdressers and Cosmetologists Assn., Natl. (1921), 3510 Olive St., St. Louis, MO 63103; 50,406.

Handball Assn., U.S. (1951), 2333 N. Tucson Blvd., Tucson, AZ 85716; 9,000.

Handicapped, Federation of the (1935), 211 W. 14th St., New York, NY 10011; 650.

Handicapped, Natl. Assn. of the Physically (1958), NAPH Business Office, Bethesda Scarlet Oaks, 440 Lafayette Ave., #GA4, Cincinnati, OH 45220; approx. 650.

Health, Physical Education, Recreation and Dance, American Alliance for (1885), 1900 Association Dr., Reston, VA 22091.

Health Council, Natl. (1920), 1730 M St. NW, Ste. 500, Wash., DC 20036.

Health Info. Management Assn., American (1928), 919 N. Michigan Ave., #1400, Chicago, IL 60611; 35,000.

Healthcare Strategy and Market Development of the American Hospital Assn., Soc. for (1996), One N. Franklin, Chicago, IL 60606; 5,000.

Hearing Society, Intl. (1951), 20361 Middlebelt Rd., Livonia, MI 48152; 3,000.

Hearing and Speech Action, Natl. Assn. for (1910), 10801 Rockville Pike, Rockville, MD 20852.

Heart Assn., American (1924), 7272 Greenville Ave., Dallas, TX 75231.

Heating, Refrigerating & Air Conditioning Engineers, Inc., American Soc. of (1894), 1791 Tullie Cir. NE, Atlanta, GA 30329; 50,000.

Hebrew Immigrant Aid Society (HIAS) (1880), 333 7th Ave., New York, NY 10001.

Helicopter Assn. Intl. (1948), 1635 Prince St., Alexandria, VA 22314; 3,000.

Helicopter Society, American (1943), 217 N. Washington St., Alexandria, VA 22314; 6,140.

Hemispheric Affairs, Council on (1975), 724 9th St. NW, Ste. 401, Wash., DC 20001; 1,750.

Hibernians in America, Ancient Order of (1845), 9240 Milford Dr., Northfield, OH 44067; 7,500.

Highpointers Club (1987), PO Box 70, Arcadia, MO 63621; 1,212.

High School Assns., Natl. Federation of State (1920), PO Box 20626, Kansas City, MO 64195; 51 state assns.

High Twelve International (1921), 3633 Lindell Blvd., St. Louis, MO 63108; 20,000.

Hiking Society, American (1976), PO Box 20160, Wash., DC 20041; 5,500.

Historians, Organization of American (1907), 112 N. Bryan St., Bloomington, IN 47408; 12,000.

Historical Assn., American (1884), 400 A St. SE, Wash., DC 20003; 16,000.

Historical Review, Institute for (1978), PO Box 2739, Newport Beach, CA 92659.

Historic Preservation, Natl. Trust for (1949), 1785 Massachusetts Ave. NW, Wash., DC 20036; 250,000.

History, American Assn. for State & Local (1944), 530 Church St., Ste. 600, Nashville, TN 37219; 5,000.

Hockey, U.S.A. (1937), 4965 N. 30th St., Colorado Springs, CO 80919; 300,000.

Home Builders, Natl. Assn. of (1942), 1201 15th St. NW, Wash., DC 20005; 157,000.

Home Economics Assn., American (1909), 1555 King St., Alexandria, VA 22314; 20,000.

Homeless, Natl. Coalition for the (1984), 1612 K St. NW, Wash., DC 20006; 1,388.

Homemakers of America, Future (1945), 1910 Association Dr., Reston, VA 22091; 281,000+.

Honor Society, Natl. (1921), 1904 Association Dr., Reston, VA 22091; 21,000.

Horatio Alger Soc. (1961), PO Box 70361, Richmond, VA 23255; 250.

Horse Council, American (1969), 1700 K St. NW, #300, Wash., DC 20006; 2,000 members, 191 org.

Horse Protection Assn., American (1966), 1000 29th St. NW, Ste. T-100, Wash., DC 20007; 8,000.

Horse Shows Assn., Inc., American (1917), 220 E. 42d St., New York, NY 10017; 65,000.

Hospital Assn., American (1899), 1 N. Franklin, Chicago, IL 60606; 5,100 hospitals.

Hospital Marketing and Public Relations, American Society for (1964), 840 N. Lake Shore Dr., Chicago, IL 60611; 3,167.

Hostelling Intl., American Youth Hostels (1934), 733 15th Street NW, Ste. 840, Wash., DC 20005; 125,000.

Hotel & Motel Assn., American (1910), 1201 New York Ave. NW, Wash., DC 20005; 10,000+.

Hot Rod Assn., Natl. (1951), 2035 Financial Way, Glendora, CA 91741; 85,000.

Hudson-Essex Terraplane Club (1959), 100 E. Cross St., Ypsilanti, MI 48198; 3,200.

Humane Society of the U.S. (1954), 2100 L St. NW, Wash., DC 20037; 650,000.

Human Resource Management, Society for (1948), 1800 Duke St., Alexandria, VA 22314; 80,000+.

Husbandry, Natl. Grange of the Order of Patrons of (1867), 1616 H St. NW, Wash., DC 20006; 28,000.

Hybrid & Alternative Vehicle Society (1994), 3301 N. Belaire Dr., Altadena, CA 91001; 5,000.

Hydrogen Energy, Intl. Assn. for (1975), PO Box 248266, Coral Gables, FL 33124; 2,500.

Idaho **Assn., U.S.S.**(1957), PO Box 711247, San Diego, CA 92171; 488.

Identification, Intl. Assn. for (1915), PO Box 2423, Alameda, CA 94501; 4,100.

Illuminating Engineering Society of N. America (1906), 120 Wall St., 17th Fl., New York, NY 10005; 10,000.

Illustrators, Society of (1901), 128 E. 63d St., New York, NY 10021; 950.

Immigration Reform, Federation for American (1979), 1666 Connecticut Ave. NW, #400, Wash., DC; 70,000

Impotence Inst. of America (1983), 2020 Pennsylvania Ave. NW, Ste. 292, Wash., DC 20006.

Independent Airmen, Assn. of (1989), 1625 Massachusetts Ave. NW, Wash., DC 20036; 3,000.

Indoor Sports Club (1930), 1145 Highland St., Napoleon, OH 43545; 950.

Industrial Designers Society of America (1965), 1142-E Walker Rd., Great Falls, VA 22066; 2,350.

Industrial Engineers, Institute of (1948), 25 Technology Park, Norcross, GA 30092; 24,000.

Industrial Health Foundation (1935), 34 Penn Circle W, Pittsburgh, PA 15206; 170 cos.

Industrial Security, American Soc. for (1955), 1655 N. Ft. Myer Dr., Ste. 1200, Arlington, VA 22209; 28,000.

Information and Image Management, Assn. for (1943), 1100 Wayne Ave., Ste. 1100, Silver Spring, MD 20910; 11,000.

Information Industry Assn. (1968), 1625 Massachusetts Ave. NW, Ste. 700, Wash., DC 20036; 550 cos.

Insurance Assn., American (1964), 1130 Connecticut Ave. NW, Ste. 1000, Wash., DC 20036; 250+ cos.

Insurance Society, Inc., Intl. (1965), Univ. of Alabama, Rm. 445, Alston Hall, Tuscaloosa, AL 35487; 1,200.

Intellectual Property Owners (1972), 1255 23d St. NW, #850, Wash., DC 20037; 725.

Intelligence Officers, Assn. of Former (1975), 6723 Whittier Ave., Ste. 303A, McLean, VA 22101; 2,700.

Interior Designers, American Society of (1975), 608 Massachusetts Ave. NE, Wash., DC 20002; 30,500.

Intl. Colleges and Universities, Assn. of (1973), 1301 S. Noland Rd., Independence, MO 64055; 8,729 ind., 26 inst.

Intl. Education, Institute of (1919), 809 United Nations Plaza, New York, NY 10017; 650 U.S. colleges and universities.

Intl. Educational Exchange, Council on (1947), 205 E. 42d St., New York, NY 10017; 240 organizations.

Intl. Educators, Assn. of (NAFSA) (1948), 1875 Connecticut Ave., Ste. 1000, Wash., DC 20009; 7,500.

Inventors, American Assn. of (1891), 2020 Pennsylvania Ave. NW, Wash., DC 20006; 5,727.

Investment Clubs, Natl. Assn. of (1951), 1515 E. Eleven Mile Rd., Royal Oak, MI 48067; 140,000.

Investment Management and Research, Assn. for (1990), 5 Boar's Head La., Charlottesville, VA 22901; 29,000.

Investors Corp., Natl. Assn. of (1951), 711 W. Thirteen Mile Rd., Madison Heights, MI 48701 530,000.

Irish-American Cultural Inst. (1962), 1 Lackawanna Pl., Morristown, NJ 07960; 7,000.

Irish Historical Society, American (1897), 991 5th Ave., New York, NY 10028; 800.

Iron Castings Society (1897), 455 State St., Des Plaines, IL 60016; 200 firms.

Iron and Steel Engineers, Assn. of (1907), Three Gateway Center, Ste. 2350, Pittsburgh, PA 15222; 10,000.

Iron and Steel Institute, American (1855), 1101 17th St. NW, Ste. 1300, Wash., DC 20036; 1,100.

Islamic Relations, Council on American- (1994), 1050 17th St. NW, Ste. 490, Wash., DC 20036.

Italian Historical Society of America (1949), 111 Columbia Heights, Brooklyn, NY 11201.

Izaak Walton League of America (1922), IWLA Conservation Ctr. 707 Coservation La. Gaithersburg, MD 20878;

Jail Assn., American (1981), 2053 Day Rd., Ste. 100, Hagerstown, MD 21740; 4,700.

Jane Austen Society of North America (1979), 254 E. 68th St., #21D, New York, NY 10021; 3,700.

Japanese American Citizens League (1929), 1765 Sutter St., San Francisco, CA 94115; 23,900.

Jewish Book Council (1946), 15 E. 26th St., New York, NY 10010.

Jewish Committee, American (1906), 165 E. 56th St., New York, NY 10022; 50,000.

Jewish Community Centers Assn. (1917), 15 E. 26th St., New York, NY 10010.

Jewish Congress, American (1918), 15 E. 84th St., New York, NY 10028; 50,000.

Jewish Federations, Council of (1932), 730 Broadway, New York, NY 10003; 200 agencies.

Jewish Historical Society, American (1892), 2 Thornton Rd., Waltham, MA 02154; 3,500.

Jewish War Veterans of the U.S.A. (1896), 1811 R St. NW, Wash., DC 20009; 100,000.

Jewish Women, Natl. Council of (1893), 53 W. 23d St., 6th Fl., New York, NY 10010; 90,000.

Job's Daughters, Intl. Order of (1920), 233 W. 6th St., Papillion, NE 68046; 21,000.

Jockey Club (1894), 40 E. 52d St., New York, NY 10022; 93.

John Birch Society (1958), 770 Westhill Blvd, PO Box 8040, Appleton, WI 54913; nearly 100,000.

Joseph Diseases Foundation, Intl. (1977), 4047 First St., Ste. 107, Livermore, CA 94550; 2,950.

Journalists, Society of Professional (1909), PO Box 77, Greencastle, IN 46135; 13,500.

Journalists and Authors, American Society of (1948), 1501 Broadway, Ste. 302, New York, NY 10036; 900.

Judaism, American Council for (1943), PO Box 9009, Alexandria, VA 22304.

Judicature Society, American (1913), 180 N. Michigan Ave., Ste. 600, Chicago, IL 60601; 10,000.

Jugglers Assn., Intl. (1947), PO Box 218, Montague, MA 01351; 4,000.

Junior Achievement (1919), One Education Way, Colorado Springs, CO 80906; 300,000.

Junior Auxiliaries, Natl. Assn. of (1941), 845 S. Main St., Greenville, MS 38701; 11,500.

Junior College Athletic Assn., Natl. (1938), PO Box 7305, Colorado Springs, CO 80933; 530.

Junior Leagues, Assn. of (1921), 660 First Ave., New York, NY 10016; 195,000.

Kennel Club, American (1884), 51 Madison Ave., New York, NY 10010; 500+ clubs.

Kidney Fund, American (1971), 6110 Executive Blvd., Ste. 1010, Rockville, MD 20852.

Kiwanis International (1915), 3636 Woodview Trace, Indianapolis, IN 46268; 325,000.

Knights of Columbus (1882), One Columbus Plaza, New Haven, CT 06510; 1,560,633.

Knights of Pythias (1864), 1495 Hancock St., Quincy, MA 02169.

Krishna Consciousness, Intl. Soc. for (ISKON) (1966), 3764 Watseka Ave., Los Angeles, CA 92109; 300 temples.

La Leche League Intl. (1956), 1400 N. Meacham Rd., Schaumburg, IL 60173; 50,000+

Labor Party of America (1996), 295 Auburn Pkwy., Athens, GA 30606; 51.

Lambs, The (1874), 3 W. 51st St., New York, NY 10019; 170.

Landscape Architects, American Society of (1899), 4401 Connecticut Ave. NW, Wash., DC 20008; 11,500.

Language Assn. of America, Modern (1883), 10 Astor Pl., New York, NY 10003; 31,000.

Language Teachers Assns., Natl. Federation of Modern (1916), Gannon Univ., Erie, PA 16541; 7,200.

Law, American Society of Intl. (1906), 2223 Massachusetts Ave. NW, Wash., DC 20008; 4,400.

Law Libraries, American Assn. of (1906), 53 W. Jackson Blvd., #940, Chicago, IL 60604; 5,000.

LCI **Natl. Assn., U.S.S.** (1991), 134 Lancaster Ave., Columbia, PA 17512; 2,880.

Learned Societies, American Council of (1919), 228 E. 45th St., New York, NY 10017; 56 societies.

Lefthanders Intl. (1974), PO Box 8249, Topeka, KS 66608; 50,000.

Legal Administrators, Assn. of (1971), 175 E. Hawthorn Pkwy., Ste. 325, Vernon Hills, IL 60061; 8,055.

Legal Secretaries, Natl. Assn. of (1950), 2448 E. 81st St., Ste. 3400, Tulsa, OK 74137; 7,400.

Legion of Valor of the U.S.A. (1890), 92 Oak Leaf Lane, Chapel Hill, NC 27516; 800.

Leif Ericson Society (1962), 128 Asbury Ave., Ste. 103, Evanston, IL 60202; 999.

Leprosy Missions, American (1906), One Alm Way, Greenville, SC 29601.

Leukemia Society of America (1949), 600 Third Ave., New York, NY 10016; approx. 1 mil. volunteers.

Lewis and Clark Trail Heritage Foundation, Inc. (1969), PO Box 3434, Great Falls, MT 59403; 1,600.

Lewis Carroll Society of North America (1974), 1655 34th St. NW, Wash., DC 20007; 370.

Libertarian Party (1971), 2600 Virginia Ave. NW, Ste. 100, Wash., DC 20037; 123,000.

Liberty Library (1955), 300 Independence Ave. SE, Wash., DC 20003; 20,000.

Libraries Assn., Special (1909), 1700 18th St. NW, Wash., DC 20009; 15,000.

Library Assn., American (1876), 50 E. Huron St., Chicago, IL 60611; 57,000.

Life Insurance, American Council of (1976), 1001 Pennsylvania Ave. NW, Wash., DC 20004; 616 firms.

Lighter Than Air Society (1952), 1436 Triplett Blvd., Akron, OH 44306; 1,600.

Lions Clubs, Intl. (1917), 300 22d St., Oak Brook, IL 60521; 1,430,000.

Liquid Crystal Soc., Intl. (1965), Liquid Crystal Institute, Kent State Univ., Kent, OH 44242; 1,000.

Linguistic Society of America (1924), Archibald A. Hill Suite, 1325 18th St. NW, Ste. 211, Wash., DC 20036; 5,000.

Literacy Volunteers of America (1962), 635 James St., Syracuse, NY 13203; 111,319.

Little People of America (1957), PO Box 9897, Wash., DC 20016; 5,000.

Logistics Engineers, Soc. of (1966), 8100 Professional Place, Ste. 211, New Carrollton, MD 20785; 5,200.

London Club (1975), Rt. 1, Lecompton, KS 66050; 100+.

Lung Assn., American (1904), 1740 Broadway, New York, NY 10019.

Lutheran Education Assn. (1942), 7400 Augusta St., River Forest, IL 60305; 3,800.

Magazine Publishers of America (1919), 919 Third Ave., New York, NY 10022; 1,200 titles.

Magicians, Intl. Brotherhood of (1922), 11137C S. Towne Sq., St. Louis, MO 63123; 14,000.

Magicians, Society of American (1902), PO Box 510260, St. Louis, MO 63151; 5,500.

Management Accountants, Institute of (1919), 10 Paragon Dr., Montvale, NJ 07015; 90,000.

Management Assn., American (1923), 1601 Broadway, New York, NY 10019; 70,000.

Management Consulting Firms, Assn. of (1929), 521 5th Ave., 35th Fl., New York, NY 10175; 50 firms.

Management Education, Intl. Society for (1916), 600 Emerson Rd., Ste. 300, St. Louis, MO 63141; 847.

Manufacturing Engineers, Soc. of (1932), One SME Dr., Dearborn, MI 48121; 70,000.

Manufacturers, Natl. Assn. of (1895), 1331 Pennsylvania Ave. NW, Ste. 1500 N. Tower, Wash., DC 20004; 14,000 cos.

Manufacturers' Agents Natl. Assn. (1947), 23016 Mill Creek Rd., Laguna Hills, CA 92654; 7,000.

March of Dimes (1938), 1275 Mamaroneck Ave., White Plains, NY 10605.

Marine Corps League (1937), PO Box 3070, Merrifield, VA 22116; 42,000.

Marine Manufacturers Assn., Natl. (1904), 401 N. Michigan Ave., Chicago, IL 60611; 1,650 cos.

Marketing Assn., American (1937), 250 S. Wacker Dr., Chicago, IL 60606; 41,000.

Marketing Assn., Inc., Direct (1917), 1120 Ave. of the Americas, New York, NY 10036; 3,500.

Masonic Relief Assn. of U.S. and Canada (1889), 3827 Canal St., New Orleans, LA 70119.

Masons, Royal Arch, General Grand Chapter (1797), PO Box 489, Danville, KY 40423; 220,000.

Masons, Supreme Council 33, Ancient and Accepted Scottish Rite, Northern Masonic Jurisdiction (1813), PO Box 519, 33 Marrett Rd., Lexington, MA 02173; 345,257; **Southern Jurisdiction** (1801), PO Box 3467, 1733 16th St. NW, Wash., DC 20009; 478,747.

Mathematical Society, American (1888), 201 Charles St., Providence, RI 02904; 30,000.

Mathematical Statistics, Institute of (1935), 3401 Investment Blvd., Ste. 7, Hayward, CA 94545; 4,000.

Mathematics, Society for Industrial and Applied (1952), 3600 Univ. Science Ctr., Philadelphia, PA 19104; 9,300.

Material & Process Engineering, Soc. for the Advancement of (1944), PO Box 2459, Covina, CA 91722; 6,000.

Mayflower Descendants, General Society of (1897), 4 Winslow St., PO Box 3297, Plymouth, MA 02361; 30,000+.

Mayors, U.S. Conference of (1932), 1620 Eye St. NW, Wash., DC 20006.

Mechanical Engineers, American Soc. of (1881), 345 E. 47th St., New York, NY 10017; 120,000.

Mechanics, American Academy of (1969), Dept. of Civil Engineering, Northwestern Univ., Evanston, IL 60201; 1,200.

Medical Assn., Aerospace (1929), 320 S. Henry St., Alexandria, VA 22314; 3,600.

Medical Assn., American (1847), 515 N. State St., Chicago, IL 60610; 300,000.

Medical Assn., Natl. (1895), 1012 Tenth St. NW, Wash., DC 20001; 22,000.

Medical Library Assn. (1898), 6 N. Michigan Ave., Ste. 300, Chicago, IL 60602; 3,800.

Medical Record Assn., American (1928), 919 N. Michigan Ave., Chicago, IL 60611; 31,000.

Medieval Academy of America (1925), Ste. 313, 1430 Massachusetts Ave., Cambridge, MA 02138; 3,973.

Meeting Planners, Intl. Society of (1989), 8383 E. Evans Rd., Scottsdale, AZ 85260; 1,800.

Men, Natl. Coalition of Free (1977), PO Box 129, Manhasset, NY 11030.

Mended Hearts (1951), 7320 Greenville Ave., Dallas, TX 75231; 20,000.

Mensa (1960), 201 Main St., Ste. 1101, Fort Worth, TX 76102; 45,000.

Mental Health Assn., Natl. (1909), 1021 Prince St., Alexandria, VA 22314; 325 affiliates.

Mental Health Program Directors, Natl. Assn. of State (1959), 66 Canal Ctr. Plaza, Ste. 302, Alexandria, VA 22314; 55.

Mentally Ill, Natl. Alliance for the (1980), 200 North Glebe Rd., Arlington, VA 22203; 140,000.

Merchant Marine Veterans of WWII, U.S. (1945), PO Box 629, San Pedro, CA 90733; 7,612.

Merrill's Marauders Assn. (1947), 11244 N. 33d St., Phoenix, AZ 85028; 1,300.

Metallurgy Institute Intl., American Powder (1959), 105 College Rd. East, Princeton, NJ 08540; 2,800.

Metal Powder Industries Federation (1944), 105 College Rd. East, Princeton, NJ 08540; 285 cos.

Metals Intl. (ASM), American Society for (1913), 9639 Kinsman Rd., Materials Park, OH 44073; 47,000.

Meteorological Society, American (1919), 45 Beacon St., Boston, MA 02108; 11,000.

Metric Assn., Inc., U.S. (1916), 10245 Andasol Ave., Northridge, CA 91325; 900.

Microbiology, American Society for (1899), 1325 Massachusetts Ave. NW, Wash., DC 20005; 45,000.

Mideast Educational & Training Services, American (1951), 1730 M St. NW, Ste. 1100, Wash., DC 20036; 190 inst.

Military Order of the Loyal Legion of the U.S. (1865), 1805 Pine St., Philadelphia, PA 19103; 930.

Military Order of the Purple Heart of the USA (1958), 5413-B Backlick Rd., Springfield, VA 22151; 32,000.

Military Order of the World Wars (1920), 435 N. Lee St., Alexandria, VA 22314; 13,000.

Military Surgeons of the U.S., Assn. of (1897), 9320 Old Georgetown Rd., Bethesda, MD 20814; 12,000.

Miniatures Industry Assn. of America (MIAA) (1979), 1100-H Brandywine Blvd., PO Box 2188, Zanesville, OH 43702; 365.

Mining Engineers, Society of (1871), 8307 Shaffer Pkwy., Littleton, CO 80127; 23,058.

Mining, Metallurgy and Exploration, Inc., Society for (1871), PO Box 625002, Littleton, CO 80162; 17,000.

Mining, Metallurgical and Petroleum Engineers, American Institute of (1871), 345 E. 47th St., 14th Fl., New York, NY 10017; 100,000.

Ministerial Assn., American (1929), 2210 Wilshire Blvd., Ste. 582, Santa Monica, CA 90403; 1,000+.

Model Railroad Assn., Natl. (1935), 4121 Cromwell Rd., Chattanooga, TN 37421; 24,500.

Moose Intl., Inc. (1988), Mooseheart, IL 60539; 1.8 mil.

Mothers, Inc.®, American (1935), 301 Park Ave., New York, NY 10022; 8,000+.

Mothers, American Gold Star (1928), 2128 Leroy Place NW, Wash., DC 20008; 2,000.

Mothers, American War (1925), 2615 Woodley Pl. NW, Wash., DC 20008; 1,000.

Mothers of Twins Clubs, Natl. Organization of (1960), PO Box 23188, Albuquerque, NM 87192; 14,000.

Motion Picture Arts & Sciences, Academy of (1927), 8949 Wilshire Blvd., Beverly Hills, CA 90211; 5,900.

Motion Pictures, Natl. Board of Review of (1909), PO Box 589, Lenox Hill Sta., New York, NY 10021.

Motion Picture & Television Engineers, Soc. of (1916), 595 W. Hartsdale Ave., White Plains, NY 10607; 9,000+.

Motorcyclist Assn., American (1924), 33 Collegeview Rd., Westerville, OH 43081; 200,000.

Motor Fire Apparatus in America, Soc. for the Preservation & Appreciation of Antique (1958), PO Box 2005, Syracuse, NY 13220; 3,000.

Motor Vehicle Manufacturers Assn. (1903), 7430 Second Ave., Ste. 300, Detroit, MI 48202; 7 cos.

Multiple Sclerosis Society, Natl. (1945), 733 Third Ave., New York, NY 10017; 518,567.

Muscular Dystrophy Assn. (1950), 3300 E. Sunrise Dr., Tucson, AZ 85718.

Museums, American Assn. of (1906), 1575 Eye St. NW, Ste. 400, Wash., DC 20005; 15,000.

Music Center, American (1939), 30 W. 26th St., New York, NY 10010.

Music Educators Natl. Conference (1907), 1806 Robert Fulton Dr., Reston, VA 22091; 65,000+.

Musicological Society, American (1934), 201 S. 34th St., Philadelphia, PA 19104; 3,500.

Music Scholarship Assn., American (1956), The Carew Tower, 441 Vine St., Ste. 1030, Cincinnati, OH 45202.

Music Teachers Natl. Assn. (1876), 505 Carew Tower, 441 Vine St., Ste. 505, Cincinnati, OH 45202; 23,000.

Muzzle Loading Rifle Assn., Natl. (1933), PO Box 67, Friendship, IN 47021; 24,000.

Myasthenia Gravis Foundation of America (1952), 222 S. Riverside Plaza, Ste. 1540, Chicago, IL 60606; 30,000.

Mystery Writers of America (1945), 17 E. 47th St., 6th Fl., New York, NY 10017; 2,600.

NA'AMAT USA (1925), 200 Madison Ave., New York, NY 10016; 50,000.

Narcotics Anonymous (1953), PO Box 9999, Van Nuys, CA 91409; 270,000.

Natl. Assn. for the Advancement of Colored People (NAACP) (1909), 4805 Mt. Hope Dr., Baltimore, MD 21215.

National Guard Assn. of the U.S. (1878), One Massachusetts Ave. NW, Wash., DC 20001; 56,000.

National Party for America (1996), 10799 Sherman Grove Ave., # 18, Sunland, CA; 91040; 5,200.

National Press Club (1908), 529 14th St. NW, Wash., DC 20045; 4,800.

Nature Conservancy (1951), 1815 N. Lynn St., Arlington, VA 22209; 900,000.

Naturist Society, The (1980), 454 N. Main St., Oshkosh, WI 54901; 20,000.

Nautical Archaeology, Institute of (1972), PO Drawer HG, College Station, TX 77841; 1,150.

Naval Architects & Marine Engineers, Society of (1893), 601 Pavonia Ave., Ste. 400, Jersey City, NJ 07306; 10,000.

Naval Engineers, American Soc. of (1888), 1452 Duke St., Alexandria, VA 22314; 5,600.

Naval Institute, U.S. (1873), 118 Maryland Ave., Annapolis, MD 21402; 80,000.

Naval Reserve Assn. (1954), 1619 King St., Alexandria, VA 22314; 22,000.

Navigation, Institute of (1945), 1800 Diagonal Rd., Ste. 480, Alexandria, VA 22314.

Navy League of the U.S. (1902), 2300 Wilson Blvd., Arlington, VA 22201; 71,308.

Needlework Guild of America (1885), 1007-B Street Rd., Southampton, PA 18966; 75,000.

Negro College Fund, United (1944), 500 E. 62d St., New York, NY 10021; 41 institutions.

Neurofibromatosis Foundation, Inc., Natl. (1978), 95 Pine St., 16th Fl., New York, NY 10005; 38,000.

New Age Walkers (1982), 3301 Bellaire Dr., Altadena, CA 91001; 4,700.

Newspaper Assn. of America (NAA) (1992), The Newspaper Center, 11600 Sunrise Valley Dr., Reston, VA 22091; 1,800.

Newspaper Marketing Assn., Intl. (1930), 11600 Sunrise Valley Dr., Reston, VA 22071; 1,532.

Newswomen's Club of New York, Inc. (1922), 15 Gramercy Park S., New York, NY 10011; 230.

Ninety-Nines (Intl. Organization of Women Pilots) (1929), Box 965, Will Rogers Airport, Oklahoma City, OK 73159; 6,400.

Nobel Center, American (1942), 45 Southport Woods Dr. Southport, CT 06490; 800.

Non-Commissioned Officers Assn. (1960), 10635 IH 35 North, San Antonio, TX 78233; 160,000.

Northern Cross Society (1986), Rt. One, Big Springs, KS 66050; 100+.

Notaries, American Society of (1965), PO Box 5707, Tallahassee, FL 32314; 19,000+.

Nuclear Society, American (1954), 555 N. Kensington Ave., La Grange Park, IL 60525; 16,000.

Nude Recreation, American Assn. for (1931), 1703 N. Main St., Kissimmee, FL 34744; 45,000.

Numismatic Assn., American (1891), 818 N. Cascade Ave., Colorado Springs, CO 80903; 31,000.

Numismatic Society, American (1858), Broadway at 155th St., New York, NY 10032; 2,000.

Nursing, Natl. League for (1952), 350 Hudson St., New York, NY 10014; 16,000.

Nutritional Sciences, American Society for (1928), 9650 Rockville Pike, Bethesda, MD 20814; 3,400.

Odd Fellows, Independent Order of (1819), 422 Trade St., Winston-Salem, NC 27101; 415,000.

Old Crows, Assn. of (1964), 1000 N. Payne St., Alexandria, VA 22314; 25,000.

Olympic Committee, U.S. (1921), One Olympic Plaza, Colorado Springs, CO 80909.

Opthalmology, American Academy of (1979), 655 Beach St., San Francisco, CA 94109; 21,000.

Optical Society of America (1917), 2010 Massachusetts Ave. NW, Wash., DC 20036; 11,000.

Optimist Intl. (1917), 4494 Lindell Blvd., St. Louis, MO 63108; 150,000.

Optometric Assn., American (1898), 243 N. Lindbergh Blvd., St. Louis, MO 63141; 31,000+.

Organists, American Guild of (1896), 475 Riverside Dr., Ste. 1260, New York, NY 10115; 20,200.

Oriental Society, American (1842), Univ. of Michigan, Hatcher Graduate Library, 110D, Ann Arbor, MI 48109; 1,350.

ORT Federation, American (Org. for Rehabilitation Through Training) (1924), 817 Broadway, 10th Fl., New York, NY 10003; 20,000.

Ornithologists' Union, American (1883), c/o Division of Birds, MRC-116, Smithsonian Institution, Wash., DC 20560; 5,000.

Osteopathic Assn., American (1887), 212 E. Ohio St., Chicago, IL 60611; 23,292.

Ostomy Assn., United (1962), 36 Executive Park, Ste. 120, Irving, CA 92714, 35,500.

Outlaw and Lawman History,Inc., Natl. Assn. for (NOLA) (1974), 1201 Holly Ct., Harker Heights, TX 76548; 475.

Paralyzed Veterans of America (1946), 801 18th St. NW, Wash., DC 20006; 16,984.

Parametric Analysts, Intl. Soc. of (1978), PO Box 6402, Chesterfield, MO 63006; 300+.

Parents Without Partners (1957), 401 N. Michigan Ave., Chicago, IL 60611; 70,000.

Parkinson's Disease Foundation, Inc. (1957), 710 W. 168th St., New York, NY 10032; 95,000.

Parliamentarians, Natl. Assn. of (1930), 213 S. Main St., Independence, MO 64050; 4,292.

Parliamentary Law, Intl. Organization of Professionals in (1975), 3611 Victoria Ave., Los Angeles, CA 90016; 250.

Pasta Assn., Natl. (1904), 2101 Wilson Blvd., Ste. 920, Arlington, VA 22201; 80 cos.

Pathologists, American Assn. of (1976), 9650 Rockville Pike, Bethesda, MD 20814; 2,000.

Pathologists, American Society of Clinical (1922), 2100 W. Harrison St., Chicago, IL 60612; approx. 78,000.

Pathology, Inc., American Soc. for Investigative (1900), 9650 Rockville Pike, Bethesda, MD 20814; 2,300.

Pearl Harbor History Associates, Inc. (1985), PO Box 25432, Seattle, WA 98125; 295.

PEN American Center, Inc. (1922), 568 Broadway, Rm. 401, New York, NY 10012; 2,800.

Pen Friends, Intl. (1967), PO Box 65, Brooklyn, NY 11229; 300,000.

Pen Women, Natl. League of American (1897), 1300 17th St. NW, Wash., DC 20036; 4,010.

P.E.O. (Philanthropic Educational Organization) Sisterhood (1869), 3700 Grand Ave., Des Moines, IA 50312; 242,000.

People for the Ethical Treatment of Animals (PETA) (1980), 501 Front St., Norfolk, VA 23510; 500,000.

Performance Improvement, Intl. Society for (1962), 1300 L St. NW, #1250, Wash., DC 20005; 6,000.

Personnel Administration, American Society for (1948), 606 N. Washington St., Alexandria, VA 22314; 40,000.

Petroleum Equipment Inst. (1951), 6514 E. 69 St., Tulsa, OK 74133; 1,755 cos.

Petroleum Geologists, American Assn. of (1917), PO Box 979, 1444 S. Boulder, Tulsa, OK 74101.

Petroleum Institute, American (1919), 1220 L St. NW, Wash., DC 20005; 350 companies.

Pharmaceutical Assn., American (1852), 2215 Constitution Ave. NW, Wash., DC 20037; 50,000.

Phi Beta Kappa (1776), 1811 Q St. NW, Wash., DC 20009; c500,000.

Phi Delta Kappa (1906), 408 N. Union, PO Box 789, Bloomington, IN 47402; 172,000.

Philatelic Golf Society (1987), PO Box 2183, Norfolk, VA 23501; 240.

Philatelic Pages & Panels, American Soc. for (1984), 4116 Kilmer Ave., Allentown, PA 18104; 950.

Philatelic Society, American (1886), 100 Oakwood Ave., PO Box 8000, State College, PA 16803; 56,000.

Philological Assn., American (1869), Dept. of Classics, College of the Holy Cross, Worcester, MA 01610; 3,300.

Philosophical Assn., American (1900), Univ. of Delaware, Newark, DE 19716; 10,000.

Philosophical Enquiry, Intl. Soc. For (1974), 5409 Pipers Gap Dr., Memphis, TN 38134; 700+.

Philosophical Society, American (1743), 104 S. 5th St., Philadelphia, PA 19106; 690.

Photogrammetry and Remote Sensing, American Society of (1934), 5410 Grosvenor Ln., Ste. 210, Bethesda, MD 20814; 7,880.

Photographers of America, Inc., Professional (1880), 57 Forsyth St. NW, Ste. 1600, Atlanta, GA 30303; 14,000.

Photographic Society of America, Inc. (1934), 3000 United Founders Blvd., Ste. 103, Oklahoma City, OK 73112; 6,500.

Physical Therapy Assn., American (1921), 1111 N. Fairfax St., Alexandria, VA 22314; 70,000.

Physicians, American Academy of Family (1947), 8880 Ward Pkwy., Kansas City, MO 64114; 84,000.

Physics, American Inst. of (1931), One Physics Ellipse, College Park, MD 20740; 100,000.

Physiological Society, American (1887), 9650 Rockville Pike, Bethesda, MD 20814; 8,300.

Phytopathological Society, American (1908), 3340 Pilot Knob Rd., St. Paul, MN 55121; 5,000.

Pilgrim Society (1820), 75 Court St., Plymouth, MA 02360; 900.

Pilot Intl. & Pilot Intl. Foundation (1921, 1975), PO Box 4844, 244 College St., Macon, GA 31208; 26,000.

Planetary Society (1979), 65 N. Catalina Ave., Pasadena, CA 91106; 100,000.

Planned Parenthood Federation of America (1916), 810 Seventh Ave., New York, NY 10019; 187 affiliates.

Plastic Modelers Society, Intl. (1963), PO Box 6138, Warner Robins, GA 31095; 4,750.

Plastics Engineers, Society of (1942), 14 Fairfield Dr., Brookfield, CT 06804; 37,000.

Plastics Industry, Inc., Society of the (1937), 1801 K St., NW, Ste. 800K, Wash., DC 20006; 2,000.

Platform Assn., Intl. (1835), Box 250, Winnetka II. 60093; 5,000.

Poetry Day Committee, Natl. (1947), 1110 N. Venetian Dr., Miami, FL 33139; 17,500.

Poetry Society of America (1910), 15 Gramercy Park, New York, NY 10003; 2,500.

Poets, Academy of American (1934), 584 Broadway, Ste. 1208, New York, NY 10012; 4,220.

Police, Intl. Assn. of Chiefs of (1893), 515 N. Washington St., #400, Alexandria, VA 22314; 13,920.

Polish Army Veterans Assn. of America (1921), 155 Noble St., Brooklyn, NY 11222; 3,500.

Polish Cultural Society of America, Inc. (1940), PO Box 31, Wall St., New York, NY 10005; 101,352.

Political Items Collectors, American (1945), PO Box 340339, San Antonio, TX 78234; 3,200.

Political Science, Academy of (1880), 475 Riverside Dr., Ste. 1274, New York, NY 10115; 6,489.

Political Science Assn., American (1903), 1527 New Hampshire Ave. NW, Wash., DC 20036; 16,200.

Political & Social Science, American Academy of (1889), 3937 Chestnut St., Philadelphia, PA 19104; 3,200.

Polo Assn., U.S. (1890), 4059 Iron Works Pike, Lexington, KY, 40511; 3,000.

Population Assn. of America (1931), 721 Ellsworth Dr., Ste. 303, Silver Spring, MD 20910; 3,000.

Portuguese-American Federation, Inc. (1974), PO Box 694, Bristol, RI 02809; 250.

Portuguese Continental Union of the U.S.A. (1925), 899 Boylston St., Boston, MA 02115; 6,428.

Postal Stationary Society, United (1945), PO Box 48, Redlands, CA 92373; 1,200.

Postmasters of the U.S., Natl. Assn. of (1898), 8 Herbert St., Arlington, VA 22305; 43,000.

Postmasters, Natl. League of (1904), 1023 N. Royal St., Alexandria, VA 22314; 28,000.

Poultry Science Assn. (1908), 1111 N. Dunlap Ave. Savoy, IL 61874; 2,100.

Power Boat Assn., American (1903), PO Box 377, Eastpointe, MI 48021; 6,000.

Precancel Collectors, Inc., Natl. Assn. of (1950), 84 W National Dr., Newark, OH 43055; 7,700+.

Press and Radio Club (1948), 29 Bradley Dr., Montgomery, AL 36109; 772.

Printing Industries of America (1887), 100 Dangerfield Rd., Alexandria, VA 22314; 14,000.

Prisoners of War, American Ex- (1942), 3201 E. Pioneer Pkwy., #40, Arlington, TX 76010; 31,000.

Procrastinators Club of America (1956), Box 712, Bryn Athyn, PA 19009; 16,000.

Production and Inventory Control Soc., American (1957), 500 W. Annandale Rd., Falls Church, VA 22046; 69,114.

Psoriasis Foundation, Natl. (1968), 6600 SW 92d Ave., Ste. 300, Portland, OR 97223; 40,000.

Psychiatric Assn., American (1844), 1400 K St. NW, Wash., DC 20005; 40,453.

Psychical Research, American Society for (1885), 5 W. 73d St., New York, NY 10023.

Psychoanalytic Assn., American (1911), 309 E. 49th St., New York, NY 10017; 3,000.

Psychological Assn., American (1892), 750 1st St. NE, Wash., DC 20002; 142,000.

Psychological Assn. for Psychoanalysis, Inc., Natl. (1948), 150 W. 13th St., New York, NY 10011; 358.

PTA, Natl. (Natl. Congress of Parents and Teachers) (1897), 330 N. Wabash, Chicago, IL 60611; 6,487,791

Public Administration, American Soc. for (1939), 1120 G St. NW, Wash., DC 20005; 11,000+.

Public Health Assn., World Fed. of (1967), 1015 15th St. NW, Wash., DC 20005; 48 natl. assn.

Public Relations Soc. of America, Inc. (1947), 33 Irving Pl., 3d Fl., New York, NY 10003; 17,383.

Publishers, Assn. of America (1970), 71 5th Ave., New York, NY 10003; 180 cos.

Pulp and Paper Industry, Technical Assn. of the (TAPPI) (1915), 15 Technology Pkwy. S., Norcross, GA 30092; 33,000.

Puppeteers of America (1936), 5 Cricklewood Path, Pasadena, CA 91107; 2,400.

Puzzle Buffs Intl. (1979), 1772 State Rd., Cuyahoga Falls, OH 44223; 65,000.

Quality Control, American Society for (ASQC) (1946), 611 E. Wisconsin Ave., Milwaukee, WI 53201; 140,000.

Quota International, Inc. (1919), 1420 21st St. NW, Wash., DC 20036; 11,000+.

Rabbis, Central Conference of American (1889), 192 Lexington Ave., New York, NY 10016; 1,540.

Racquetball Assn., American Amateur (1968), 815 N. Weber, Colorado Springs, CO.

Racquetball Assn., U.S. (1969), 1685 W, Vintah, Colorado Springs, CO 80904; 25,000.

Radio, Natl. Assn. of Business and Educational (1965), 1501 Duke St., Alexandria, VA 22314; 2,400.

Radio Relay League, American (1914), 225 Main St., Newington, CT 06111; 172,000.

Radio and Television Society Foundation, Intl. (1962), 420 Lexington Ave., Ste. 1714, New York, NY 10170; 1,100.

Radio Union, Intl. Amateur (1925), PO Box 310905, Newington, CT 06131; 150 organizations.

Railsplitter Society, Inc., 84th Infantry Div. (1945), PO Box 827, Sioux Falls, SD 57101; 3,000.

Railway Historical Society, Natl. (1935), PO Box 58153, Philadelphia, PA 19102; 21,000+.

Railway Progress Institute (1908), 700 N. Fairfax St., Ste. 601, Alexandria, VA 22314; 100.

Range Management, Society for (1948), 1839 York St., Denver, CO 80206; 5,000.

Reading Assn., Intl. (1956), 800 Barksdale Rd., PO Box 8139, Newark, DE 19714; 95,000.

Real Estate Institute, Intl. (1972), 8383 E. Evans Rd., Scottsdale, AZ 85260; 2,846.

Rebekah Assemblies, Intl. Assn. of (1922), 422 N. Trade St., Winston-Salem, NC 27101; 136,994.

Reconciliation, Fellowship of (1915), PO Box 271, Nyack, NY 10960; 15,000.

Records Managers & Administrators, Assn. of (1975), 4200 Somerset Dr., Ste. 215, Prairie Village, KS 66208; 10,600.

Recreation and Park Assn., Natl. (1965), 2775 S. Quincy St., Ste. 300, Arlington, VA 22206; 23,533.

Recycling Coalition, Natl. (1979), 1727 King St., Ste. 105, Alexandria, VA 22514; 3,500.

Red Cross, American (1881), 8111 Gatehouse Rd., Falls Church, VA 22042; 1.44 mil volunteers.

Redwoods League, Save-the- (1917), 114 Sansome St., Ste. 605, San Francisco, CA 94040; 45,000.

Rehabilitation Assn., Natl. (1925), 633 S. Washington St., Alexandria, VA 22314; 14,000.

Religion, American Academy of (1909), 1703 Clifton Rd. Ste. G5, Atlanta, GA 30329; 8,000.

Renaissance Society of America (1954), 24 W. 12th St., 3d Fl., New York, NY 10011; 3,700.

Republican National Committee (1856), 310 1st St. SE, Wash., DC 20003.

Reserve Officers Assn. of the U.S. (1922), One Constitution Ave. NE, Wash., DC 20003; 95,000.

Restaurant Assn., Natl. (1919), 1200 17th St. NW, Wash., DC 20036; 33,000.

Retail Federation, Natl. (1918), 100 W. 31st St., New York, NY 10001; 50,000.

Retired Credit Union People, Natl. Assn. for (1978), PO Box 391, 5910 Mineral Pt. Rd., Madison, WI 53705; 81,180.

Retired Federal Employees, Natl. Assn. of (1921), 1533 New Hampshire Ave. NW, Wash., DC 20036; 500,000.

Retired Officers Assn. (1929), 201 N. Washington St., Alexandria, VA 22314; approx. 400,000.

Retired Persons, American Assn. of (1958), 601 E St. NW, Wash., DC 20049; 32 mil.

Retired Teachers Assn., Natl. (1947), 1909 K St. NW, Wash., DC 20049; 540,000.

Revolver Assn., U.S. (1900), 40 Larchmont Ave., Taunton, MA 02780; 1,450.

Reye's Syndrome Foundation, Natl. (1974), 426 N. Lewis, PO Box 829, Bryan, OH 43506; 5,000.

Richard III Society (1969), PO Box 13786, New Orleans, LA 70185; 700.

Rifle Assn., Natl. (1871), 11250 Waples Mill Rd., Fairfax, VA 22030; 3.4 mil.

Road & Transportation Builders' Assn., American (1902), 1010 Massachusetts Ave. NW, Wash., DC 20001; 3,985.

Roller Skating, U.S. Amateur Confederation of (1937), 4730 South St., PO Box 6579, Lincoln, NE 68506; 34,000.

Rose Society, American (1892), PO Box 30,000, Shreveport, LA 71130; 23,000.

Rotary Intl. (1905), 1560 Sherman Ave., Evanston, IL 60201; 1,203,726.

Running and Fitness Assn., American (1968), 4405 East West Highway, Ste. 405, Bethesda, MD 20877; 15,000.

Ruritan Natl., Inc. (1928), PO Box 487, Dublin, VA 24084; 35,000.

Safety Council, Natl. (1913), 1121 Spring Lake Dr., Itasca, IL 60143; 18,000.

Safety Engineers, American Soc. of (1911), 1800 E. Oakton St., Des Plaines, IL 60018; 32,000.

Safety and Fairness Everywhere, Nat'l. Organization Taunting (NOT-SAFE) (1982), PO Box 5743-WA, Montecito, CA 93108; 1,471.

St. Andrew, Brotherhood of (1883), 1109 Merchant St., PO Box 632, Ambridge, PA 15003; 5,000.

St. Paul, Natl. Guild of (1937), 601 Hill 'n Dale, Lexington, KY 40503; 13,652.

Salespersons, Natl. Assn. of Professional (1970), PO Box 76461, Atlanta, GA 30358; 35,000.

Salt Institute (1914), 700 N. Fairfax St., Ste. 600, Alexandria, VA, 22314; 8 cos.

Sand Castle Builders, Intl. Society of (1988), 172 N. Pershing Ave., Akron, OH 44313; 200.

School Administrators, American Assn. of (1865), 1801 N. Moore St., Arlington, VA 22209; 16,409.

School Boards Assn., Natl. (1940), 1680 Duke St., Alexandria, VA 22314.

School Counselor Assn., American (1953), 5999 Stevenson Ave., Alexandria, VA 22304; 13,000.

Schools of Art, Natl. Assn. of (1944), 11250 Roger Bacon Dr., Reston, VA 22090; 553 institutions.

Schools & Colleges, American Council on (1927), 13014-363 Dale Mabry Hwy., Carrollwood, FL 33618; 186.

Science, American Assn. for the Advancement of (1848), 1200 New York Ave. NW, Wash., DC 20005; 144,000.

Science Fiction Society, World (1939), PO Box 1270, Kendall Sq. Sta., Cambridge, MA 02142; 5,000.

Science Service (1922), 1719 N St. NW, Wash., DC 20036; 200,000.

Sciences, Natl. Academy of (1863), 2101 Constitution Ave. NW, Wash., DC 20418; 4,000+.

Science Teachers Assn., Natl. (1944), 1840 Wilson Blvd., Arlington, VA 22201; 53,000.

Science Writers, Natl. Assn. of (1934), PO Box 294, Greenlawn, NY 11740; 1,801.

Scrabble® Assn., Natl. (1980), PO Box 700, 120 Front St., Greenport, NY 11944; 10,000.

Screenprinting & Graphic Imaging Assn. Intl. (1948), 10015 Main St., Fairfax, VA 22031; 3,200 cos.

Screen Printing Technical Foundation (1985), 10015 Main St., Fairfax, VA 22031; 3,300.

Sculpture Soc., Natl. (1893), 1177 Ave. of the Americas, New York, NY 10036; 4,000.

Seamen's Service, United, (1942,), One World Trade Center, Ste. 2161, New York, NY 11743.

2d Air Division Assn. (1947), 06-410 Delaire Landing. Rd., Philadelphia, PA 19114; 7,852.

Secondary School Principals, Natl. Assn. of (1916), 1904 Association Dr., Reston, VA 22091; 42,000.

Secretaries Intl.®, Professional/The Assn. for Office Professionals™ (1942), 10502 N.W. Ambassador Dr., Kansas City, MO 64195; 40,000.

Secular Humanism, Council for (1980), PO Box 664, Buffalo, NY 14226; 3,500.

Securities Industry Assn. (1972), 120 Broadway, New York, NY 10271; 715 firms.

Separation of Church & State, Americans United for (1947), 1816 Jefferson Place NW, Wash., DC 20036; 50,000.

Sertoma International (1912), 1912 E. Meyer Blvd., Kansas City, MO 64132; 25,000.

Sexuality Information & Education Council of the U.S. (SIECUS) (1964), 130 W. 42d St., Ste. 350, New York, NY 10036.

Sharkhunters (1983), PO Box 1539, Hernando, FL 34442; 5,300.

Shipbuilders Council of America (1921), 901 Washington St., Ste. 204, Alexandria, VA 22314; 50 organizations.

Ships-in-Bottles Assn. of American (1983), PO Box 180550, Coronado, CA 92178; 400.

Shore & Beach Preservation Assn., American (1926), PO Box 279, Middletown, CA 95461; 900.

Shrine of North America (1872), 2900 N. Rocky Point Dr., Tampa, FL 33607; 591,924.

Sierra Club (1892), 85 2d St., 2d Fl., San Francisco, CA 94105; 550,000.

Sigma Beta Delta (1994), PO Box 46935, 11701 Borman Dr., Ste. 320, St. Louis, MO 63146; 6,000.

Skeet Shooting Assn., Natl. (1946), PO Box 680007, San Antonio, TX 78268; 15,800.

Ski Team Foundation, U.S. (1964), 1500 Kearns Blvd., Park City, UT 84060; 60,000.

Small Business United, Natl. (1937), 1156 15th St. NW, Ste. 1100, Wash., DC 20005; 65,000+.

Smoking & Health, Natl. Clearinghouse for (1965), Center for Disease Control, 1600 Clifton Rd. NE, Atlanta, GA 30333.

Social Sciences, Natl. Institute of (1865), 1192 Park Ave., 15B, New York, NY 10128; 315.

Social Work Education, Council on (1952), 1600 Duke St., Alexandria, VA 22314; 4,000.

Sociological Assn., American (1905), 1722 N St. NW, Wash., DC 20036; 13,000.

Softball Assn., Amateur (1933), 2801 N.E. 50th St., Oklahoma City, OK 73111; 5 mil+.

Soft Drink Assn., Natl. (1921), 1101 16th St. NW, Wash., DC 20036; 1,700.

Soil Science Society of America (1936), 677 S. Segoe Rd., Madison, WI 53711; 5,800.

Soil & Water Conservation Society of America (1949), 7515 N.E. Ankeny Rd., Ankeny, IA 50021; 10,000.

Songwriters Guild of America (1933), 1500 Harbor Blvd., Weehawken, NJ 07087; 5,000+.

Sons of the American Legion (1932), Box 1055, Indianapolis, IN 46206; 161,376.

Sons of the American Revolution, Natl. Society of (1889), 1000 S. Fourth St., Louisville, KY 40203; 27,000.

Sons of Confederate Veterans (1896), 740 Mooresville Pike, Columbia, TN 38401; 26,000.

Sons of the Desert (1965), c/o Lori Jones, PO Box 8341, Universal City, CA 91608; 15,000.

Sons of Italy in America, Order of (1905), 219 E St. NE, Wash. DC 20002; 500,000.

Sons of Norway (1895), 1455 W. Lake St., Minneapolis, MN 55408; 70,000.

Sons of the Republic of Texas (1922), 1717 8th St., Bay City, TX 77414; 3,500.

Sons of St. Patrick, Society of the Friendly (1784), 80 Wall St., New York, NY 10005; 1,500.

Sons of Sherman's March to the Sea (1966), 1725 Farmer Ave., Tempe, AZ 85281; 790.

Sons of Union Veterans of the Civil War (1881), 7017 Granada Lane, Flint, MI 48532; 5,000.

Soroptimist Intl. of the Americas (1921), Two Penn Center Plaza, Ste. 1000, Philadelphia, PA 19102; 48,000.

Southern Christian Leadership Conference (1957), 334 Auburn Ave. NE, Atlanta, GA 30303; 1 mil.

Space Education Assn., U.S. (1973), 231 School Lane, Rheems, PA 17570; 1,500.

Space Society, Natl. (1974), 600 Pennsylvania Ave SE, Ste. 201, Wash., DC 20003; 25,000.

Special Olympics Intl. (1968), 1325 G St. NW, Wash., DC 20005.

Speech Communication Assn. (1914), 5105 Backlick Rd., Bldg. E, Annandale, VA 22003; 7,000.

Speech-Language-Hearing Assn., American (1925), 10801 Rockville Pike, Rockville, MD 20852; 84,000.

Speedskating Union of the U.S., Amateur (1927), 1033 Shady Lane, Glen Ellyn, IL 60137; 3,000.

Speleological Society, Natl. (1941), 2813 Cave Ave., Huntsville, AL 35810; 12,000.

Spiritual Awareness and Holistic Principles of Body, Mind and Spirit, Inc., Assn. for (1986), PO Box 41, Clifton Hill, MO 65244; 5,500.

Sports Car Club of America (1944), 9033 E. Eastern Pl., Englewood, CO 80112; 50,000+.

Sportscasters Assn., American (1980), 5 Beekman St., New York, NY 10038; 500+.

State Governments, Council of (1933), PO Box 11910, Lexington, KY 40517; 50 states, 4 territories.

Statistical Assn., American (1839), 1429 Duke St., Alexandria, VA 22314; 18,000.

Steamship Historical Society of America, Inc. (1940), PO Box 2394, Providence, RI 02906; 3,400.

Steel Construction, American Institute of (1921), 1 E. Wacker Dr., Ste. 3100, Chicago, IL 60601; 2,770.

Stock Exchange, American (1911), 86 Trinity Pl., New York, NY 10006; 871.

Stock Exchange, New York (1792); 11 Wall St., New York, NY 10005.

Stock Exchange, Philadelphia (1790), 1900 Market St., Philadelphia, PA 19103; 504.

Student Councils, Natl. Assn. of (1931), 1904 Association Dr., Reston, VA 22091; 9,000 schools.

Stuttering Project, Natl. (1977), 5100 E. LaPalma Ave., #208, Anaheim Hills, CA 92807; 2,900.

Submarine Veterans of WWII, U.S. (1955), 317 N. Palm Ave., Frostproof, FL 33843; 8,250.

Surgeons, American College of (1913), 55 E. Erie St., Chicago, IL 60611; 50,000.

Surveying & Mapping, American Congress on (1941), 5410 Grosvenor Ln., Ste. 100, Bethesda, MD 20814; 8,000.

Symphony Orchestra League, American (1942), 1156 Fifteenth St. NW, Ste. 800, Wash., DC 20005; 840.

Systems Management, Assn. for (1947), PO Box 38370, Cleveland, OH 44138; 5,100.

Table Tennis Assn., U.S. (1933), One Olympic Plaza, Colorado Springs, CO 80909; 7,754.

Tailhook Assn. (1956), 9696 Businese Park Ave., PO Box 26700, San Diego, CA 92131; 11,800.

Tall Buildings and Urban Habitat, Council on (1969), Lehigh Univ., 13 E. Packer Ave., Bethlehem, PA 18015; 3,000.

Tax Administrators, Federation of (1937), 444 N. Capitol St. NW, Ste. 348, Wash., DC 20001.

Tax Foundation, Inc. (1937), 1250 H St. NW, Ste. 750, Wash., DC 20005; 50 U.S. states.

Taxpayers Union, Natl. (1969), 108 N. Alfred St., Alexandria, VA 22314; 300,000.

Tea Assn. of the U.S.A., Inc. (1899), 230 Park Ave., Ste. 1460, New York, NY 10169.

Teachers of English, Natl. Council of (1911), 1111 W. Kenyon Rd., Urbana, IL 61801; 68,000.

Teachers of English to Speakers of Other Languages (1966), 1600 Cameron St., Ste. 300, Alexandria, VA 22314; 18,000.

Teachers of French, American Assn. of (1927), 57 E. Armory Ave., Champaign, IL 61820; 10,500.

Teachers of Mathematics, Natl. Council of (1920), 1906 Association Dr., Reston, VA 22091; 120,000.

Teachers of Singing, Natl. Assn. of (1944), 2800 Univ. Blvd. N., J.U. Sta., Jacksonville, FL 32211; 5,174.

Teachers of Spanish & Portuguese, American Assn. of (1917), 8 Frasier Hall, Univ. of Northern Colorado, Greeley, CO 80939; 13,000.

Technology Honor Society, American (ATHS) (1995), 1905 Association Dr., Reston, VA 22091; 125 chapts.

Telephone Pioneers of America (1911), 930 15th St., 12th Fl., Denver, CO 80202; 875,000.

Television Arts & Sciences, Natl. Academy of (1947), 111 W. 57th St., Ste. 1020, New York, NY 10019; 12,000.

Television Bureau of Advertising (1954), 850 3d Ave., 10th Fl., New York, NY 10022.

Tesla Memorial Soc., Inc. (1979), 453 Martin Rd., Buffalo, NY 14218; 1,700.

Testing & Materials, American Society for (1898), 100 Barr Harbor Dr., West Conshohocken, PA 19428; 35,000.

Textile Manufacturers Institute, American (1949), 1130 Connecticut Ave., Ste 1200, Wash., DC 20036; 118 cos.

Theodore Roosevelt Assn. (1919), Nassau Hall, 1864 Muttantown Rd., Syosset, NY 11791; 1,400.

Theological Library Assn., American (1947), 820 Church St., Ste. 300, Evanston, IL 60201; 188 libraries.

Theological Schools in the U.S. and Canada, Assn. of (1918), 10 Summit Park Dr., Pittsburgh, PA 15275; 232.

Theosophical Society in America, (1875), 1926 N. Main St., Wheaton, IL 60187; 4,200.

Thoreau Society, Inc. (1941), 44 Baker Farm, Lincoln, MA 01773; 1,500.

Thoroughbred Racing Assns. (1942), 420 Fair Hill Dr., Ste. 1, Elkton, MD 21921; 41 racing associations.

Tin Can Sailors (1976), PO Box 100, Somerset, MA 02726; 17,000.

Titanic Historical Society, Inc. (1963), 208 Main St., PO Box 51053, Indian Orchard, MA 01151; 5,110.

Toastmasters Intl. (1924), 23182 Arroyo Vista, Rancho Santa Margarite, CA 92688; 170,000.

Topical Assn., American (1949), PO Box 65749, Tucson, AZ 85728; 5,400.

Toy Manufacturers of America (1916), 200 Fifth Ave., New York, NY 10010; 265.

Trade Assn., Intl. (1990), 8383 E. Evans Rd., Scottsdale, AZ 85260; 1,000.

Trademark Assn., Intl. (1878), 1133 Avenue of the Americas, New York, NY 10036; 2,800.

Trail Assn., North Country (1980), 49 Monroe Center NW, Ste. 200B, Grand Rapids, MI 49503; 750.

Transit Assn., American Public (1974), 1201 New York Ave. NW, Wash., DC 20005; 1,100 organizations.

Translators Assn., American (1959), 1800 Diagonal Rd., Ste. 220, Alexandria, VA 22314; 6,000.

Transportation Engineers, Inst. of (1930), 525 School St. SW, Ste. 410, Wash., DC 20024; 12,800.

Trapshooting Assn., Amateur (1923), 601 W. National Rd., Vandalia, OH 45377; 102,360.

Travel Agents, American Society of (1931), 1101 King St., Ste. 200, Alexandria, VA 22314; 27,000.

Travelers of America, Order of United Commercial (1888), 632 N. Park St., Columbus, OH 43215; 135,000.

Travelers Protective Assn. of America (1890), 3755 Lindell Blvd., St. Louis, MO 63108; 137,979.

Treasury Management Assn. (1979), 7315 Wisconsin Ave., Ste. 600W, Bethesda, MD 20814; 10,000.

Trilateral Commission (1973), 345 E. 46th St., New York, NY 10017; 335.

Truck Historical Soc., American (1971), 300 Office Park Dr., Ste. 120, Birmingham, AL 35223; 19,474.

Trucking Assn., American (1933), 2200 Mill Rd., Alexandria, VA 22314; 4,500 cos.

True Sisters, Inc., United Order (1846), 212 Fifth Ave., Rm. 1407, New York, NY 10010; 8,000.

T. S. Eliot Society (1980), 709 S. Skinker Blvd. #401, St. Louis, MO 63105; 165.

Tuberous Sclerosis Assn., Natl. (1974), 8181 Professional Place, Ste. 110, Landover, MD 20785.

UFO Society of America (1997), 10799 Sherman Grove Ave, #18, Sunland, CA 91040; 520.

UFOs, Natl. Investigation Committee on (1967), 14617 Victory Blvd., Van Nuys, CA 91411; 1000.

UNICEF, U.S. Committee for (1947), 333 E. 38th St., New York, NY 10016.

Underwriters, Natl. Assn. of Life (1890), 1922 F St. NW, Wash., DC 20006; 143,000.

Underwriters (CPCU), Soc. of Chartered Property and Casualty (1944), Kahler Hall, 720 Providence Rd., Malvern, PA 19355; 28,000.

Uniformed Services, Natl. Assn. for (1968), 5535 Hempstead Way, Springfield, VA 22151; 160,000.

United Nations Assn. of the U.S.A. (1923, as League of Nations Assn.), 485 Fifth Ave., New York, NY 10017; 30,000.

United Press Intl. (1907), 1400 Eye St. NW, Wash., DC 20005.

United Way of America (1932), 701 N. Fairfax St., Alexandria, VA 22314-2045; 1,353.

Universities, Assn. of American (1914), One Dupont Circle, Ste. 730, Wash., DC 20036; 59 institutions.

University Continuing Education Assn., (1915), One Dupont Circle, Ste. 615, Wash., DC 20036; 2,100.

University Extension Assn., Natl. (1915), One Dupont Circle NW, Ste. 400, Wash., DC 20036; 1,100.

University Foundation, Intl. (1973), 1301 S. Noland Rd., Independence, MO 64055; 62,311.

University Women, American Assn. of (1881), 1111 16th St. NW, Wash., DC 20036; 150,000.

Urban League, Natl. (1910), 500 E. 62d St., New York, NY 10020.

Useless Skills, Institute of Totally (1987), Box 181, Temple, NH 03084; 457.

USO, Inc. (United Service Organizations) (1941), Washington Navy Yard, 901 M St. SE, Bldg. 198, Wash., DC 20374-5096.

Utility Commissioners, Natl. Assn. of Regulatory (NARUC) (1889), PO Box 684, Wash., DC 20044; 100 agencies.

Vampire Research Center (1972), PO Box 5442, Babylon, NY 11707; 1,174.

Variety Clubs Intl. (1928), 1560 Broadway, New York, NY 10036; 15,000.

Ventriloquists, North American Assn. of (1944), Box 420, Littleton, CO 80160; 1,700.

Veterans of Foreign Wars of the U.S. (1899), 406 W. 34th St., Kansas City, MO 64111.

Veterans of Foreign Wars of the U.S, Ladies Auxiliary to the (1914), 406 W. 34th St., Kansas City, MO 64111; 765,283.

Veterans of Underage Military Service (1991), 100 Village Lane, Philadelphia, PA 19154; 874.

Veterans of the Vietnam War, Inc. (1980), 760 Jumper Rd., Wilkes-Barre, PA 18702; 25,000.

Veterans of World War I of the USA, Inc. (1958), PO Box 8027, Alexandria, VA 22306; 7,900.

Veterinary Medical Assn., American (1863), 1931 N. Meacham Rd., Schaumburg, IL 60173; 59,263.

Victorian Society in America (1966), 219 S. Sixth St., Philadelphia, PA 19106.

Viewers for Quality Television, Inc. (1987), PO Box 195, Fairfax Station, VA 22039; 3,000.

Virgil Fox Society (1977), 88 Chestnut St., Brooklyn, NY 11208; 400.

Volleyball, U.S.A. (1928), 3595 E. Fountain Blvd., Ste. I-2, Colorado Springs, CO 80910; 110,000.

Warrant and Warrant Officers' Assn., Chief U.S. Coast Guard (1929), c/o Fort McNair Yacht Basin, 200 V St. SW, Wash., DC 20024; 3,346.

Watch & Clock Collectors, Natl. Assn. of (1943), 514 Poplar St., Columbia, PA 17512; 35,000+.

Watercolor Society, American (1866), 47 5th Ave., New York, NY 10003; 500+.

Water Environment Federation (1928), 601 Wythe St., Alexandria, VA 22314; 40,000.

Water Pollution Control Administration, Assn. of State and Interstate (1961), 750 First St. NE, Ste. 910, Wash., DC 20002; 85.

Water Pollution Control Federation (1928), 601 Wythe St., Alexandria, VA 22314; 32,000.

Water Ski Assn., American (1939), 799 Overlook Dr. SE, Winter Haven, FL 33830; 30,000.

Water Works Assn., American (1881), 6666 W. Quincy Ave., Denver, CO 80235; 55,000.

Welding Society, American (1919), 550 N.W. LeJeune Rd., Miami, FL 33126; 47,500.

Wheelchair Sports, USA (1956), 3595 E. Fountain Blvd., Ste. L-1, Colorado Springs, CO 80910; 4,600.

Widows, Society of Military (1968), 5535 Hempstead Way, Springfield, VA 22151; 2,000.

Wilderness Society (1935), 900 17th St. NW, Wash., DC 20006; 271,268.

Wildflower Research Center, Natl. (1982), 4801 La Crosse Ave., Austin, TX 78739; 20,000.

Wildlife, Defenders of (1947), 1244 19th St. NW, Wash., DC 20036; 80,000.

Wildlife Federation, Natl. (1936), 1400 16th St. NW, Wash., DC 20036-2266; 4.7 mil.

Wildlife Management Institute (1911), 1101 14th St. NW, Ste. 801, Wash., DC 20005; 400.

William Penn Assn. (1886), 709 Brighton Rd., Pittsburgh, PA 15233; 90,000.

Wireless Pioneers, Society of (1968), PO Box 86, Geyserville, CA 95441; 1,500.

Wizard of Oz Club, Intl. (1957), PO Box 266, Kalamazoo, MI 49004; 2,000.

Women, Natl. Organization for (NOW) (1966), 1000 16th St. NW, Ste. 700, Wash., DC 20036; 250,000.

Women Artists, Natl. Assn. of (1889), 41 Union Sq. W, #906, New York, NY 10003; 925.

Women in Communications Foundation (1968), 6900 Newman Rd., Clifton, VA 20124.

Women Engineers, Society of (1950), 120 Wall St., 11th Fl., New York, NY 10005; 16,500.

Women in Radio and TV, Inc., American (1950), 1650 Tyson's Blvd., Ste. 200, McLean, VA 22102; 1,500.

Women World War Veterans (1919), 237 Madison Ave., New York, NY 10016; 35,000.

Women's Army Corps Veterans Assn. (1946), PO Box 5577, Ft. McClellan, AL 36205; 4,500.

Women's Christian Temperance Union, Natl. (1874), 1730 Chicago Ave., Evanston, IL 60201; 12,594.

Women's Clubs, General Federation of (1890), 1734 N St. NW, Wash., DC 20036; 300,000 U.S.

Women's Clubs, Natl. Fed. of Business & Prof. (1919), 2012 Massachusetts Ave. NW, Wash., DC 20036; 70,000.

Women's Intl. League for Peace & Freedom (1915), 1213 Race St., Philadelphia, PA 19107; 8,000.

Women's Legal Defense Fund (1971), 1875 Connecticut Ave. NW, Ste. 710, Wash., DC 20009; 2,500.

Women's Overseas Service League (1921), PO Box 39058, Friendship Station, Wash., DC 20016; 1,164.

Women Strike for Peace (1961), 110 Maryland Ave. NE, Ste. 102, Wash., DC 20002; 10,000.

Women of the U.S., Inc., Natl. Council of (1888), 777 UN Plaza, 7th Fl., New York, NY 10017; 500 members, 33 affiliate org.

Women Voters of the U.S., League of (1920), 1730 M St. NW, Wash., DC 20036; 100,000.

Woodmen of America, Modern (1883), 1701 1st Ave., Rock Island, IL 61201; 750,000.

Woodmen of the World Life Insurance Soc. (1890), 1700 Farnam St., Omaha, NE 68102; 850,000.

Workmen's Circle (1900), 45 E. 33d St., New York, NY 10016; 35,000.

World Council of Churches, U.S. Conference for the (1948), 475 Riverside Dr., New York, NY 10115; 317 denominations.

World Federalist Assn. (1975), 418 7th St. SE, Wash., DC 20003; 9,000.

World Future Society (1966), 7910 Woodmont Ave., Ste. 450, Bethesda, MD 20814; 30,000.

World Learning Inc. (1932), Kipling Rd., PO Box 676, Brattleboro, VT 05153; 2,500.

World Wildlife Fund (1961), 1250 24th St. NW, Wash., DC 20037; 1.25 mil.

World's Fair Collectors Soc., Inc. (1968), PO Box 20806, Sarasota, FL 34276-3806; 510.

Writers Guild of America, West (1933), 7000 W. Third St., Los Angeles, CA 90048; 8,000.

Yachting Assn., Southern California (1921), 5855 Naples Plaza, Ste. 211, Long Beach, CA 90803; 21,500 families.

Young America's Foundation (1969), 110 Elden St., Herndon, VA 22170.

Young Men's Christian Assns. of the U.S.A. (1864), 101 N. Wacker Dr., Chicago, IL 60606.

Young Women's Christian Assn. of the U.S.A. (1906), 726 Broadway, New York, NY 10003.

Zero Population Growth (1968), 1400 16th St. NW, Ste. 320, Wash., DC 20036; 45,000.

Zionist Organization of America (1897), 4 E. 34th St., New York, NY 10016; 110,000.

Zoo and Aquarium Assn., American (1924), 7970-D Old Georgetown Rd., Bethesda, MD 20814; 6,500.

POSTAL INFORMATION

U.S. Postal Service

The Postal Reorganization Act, creating a government-owned postal service under the executive branch and replacing the old Post Office Department, was signed into law by Pres. Richard Nixon Aug. 12, 1970. The service officially came into being on July 1, 1971.

The U.S. Postal Service is governed by an 11-person Board of Governors. Nine members are appointed to 9-year terms by the president with Senate approval. These 9, in turn, choose a postmaster general. The board and the postmaster general choose the 11th member, who serves as deputy postmaster general. An independent Postal Rate Commission of 5 members, appointed by the president, reviews and rules on proposed postal rate increases submitted by the Board of Governors.

As of June 20, 1997, there were 27,973 post offices throughout the U.S.

U.S. Domestic Rates

The postal rates and fees shown here all remained in effect as of Sept. 1997. Domestic rates apply to the U.S., to its territories and possessions, and to APOs and FPOs.

First Class

First Class includes written matter such as letters, postal cards, and postcards (private mailing cards) plus all other matter wholly or partly in writing, whether sealed or unsealed, except manuscripts for books, periodical articles and music, manuscript copy accompanying proofsheets or corrected proofsheets of the same, and the writing authorized by law on matter of other classes. Also included: matter sealed or closed against inspection, bills, and statements of accounts.

Mailing written letters and matter sealed against inspection costs 32¢ for first ounce or fraction, 23¢ for each additional ounce or fraction up to and including 11 oz.

U.S. Postal Service cards and private postcards alike cost 20¢ single, 40¢ double.

Express Mail

Express Mail Service is available for any mailable article up to 70 lb, and guarantees delivery between major U.S. cities within a specified time frame or your money back. Articles received by the acceptance time authorized by the postmaster at a postal facility offering Express Mail are delivered by 3 PM the next day to some locations or by noon the next day to other destinations. Or, if you prefer, you can pick up the package yourself, as early as 10 AM the next business day. Second-day service is available to locations not on the Next Day Delivery Network. Rates include insurance, shipment receipt, and record of delivery at the destination post office.

The rate for Express Mail weighing up to 8 oz is $10.75. Consult postmaster for other Express Mail Services and rates. The Postal Service will refund, upon application to originating office, the postage for any Express Mail shipments not meeting the service standard, except for those delayed by strike or work stoppage, delay or cancellation of flights, or government action beyond the control of the Postal Service.

Periodicals

Periodicals include newspapers and magazines.

For the general public, the applicable Standard Mail postage is paid for this type of mail.

For publishers, rates vary according to (1) whether the item is delivered in the county in which it is mailed, (2) the percentage of reading and advertising matter, (3) the item's weight, and (4) the distance it must travel.

Standard Mail (A)

Standard Mail (A) is any piece of mail weighing less than 16 oz that is not included in First Class or Periodicals.

For single-piece mailing of publications, small parcels, printed matter, booklets, and catalogs, first ounce or fraction is 32¢; each additional ounce or fraction up to 11 oz is 23¢; the flat fee for pieces over 11 oz up to 13 oz is $2.90 and for pieces over 13 oz up to 16 oz is $2.95.

For mailing Standard Mail (A) in bulk (at least 200 pieces or 50 lb of such items as solicitations, newsletters, advertising materials, books, and cassettes, each item of which individually weighs less than 1 lb.), the minimum rate per piece, basic, non-letter, is $0.306 for pieces weighing 3.3087 oz or less; for pieces weighing more than 3.3087 oz, the rate is $0.166 per piece plus $0.677 per pound. Contact your post office for the discounts offered for presorted, letter-shaped, destination entry, and automation-compatible mail.

Separate rates are available for some nonprofit organizations provided they apply to the postmaster for a permit. The permit requires a one-time imprint fee of $85 plus an annual (calendar year) fee of $85.

Parcel Post—Standard Mail (B)

Any matter that weighs 16 oz or more and is not included in First Class or Periodicals goes as Parcel Post, or Standard Mail (B). The post office determines Parcel Post charges according to the weight of the package in pounds and the zone distance it is being shipped. All fractions of a pound are counted as a full pound.

Forwarding Addresses

To obtain a forwarding address, the mailer must write on the envelope or cover the words "Address Correction Requested." The destination post office then will determine whether a forwarding address has been left on file and provide it for a fee of 50¢ per manual correction and 20¢ per automated correction.

Priority Mail Flat Rate

The most expeditious handling and transportation available will be used for fast delivery by "Priority Mail." If the item fits into a special Postal Service flat-rate envelope, the rate is $3.00 regardless of weight.

Pickup service for Priority Mail is available for $4.95 per stop (not per package) by the Postal Service.

Priority Mail by Weight

Priority Mail may include packages weighing up to 70 lb and not exceeding 108 in. in length and girth combined, whether sealed or unsealed, including written and other First Class material. Fractions of a pound are rounded up to the rate for the next full pound.

Up to 2 lb	3 lb	4 lb	5 lb
$3.00	$4.00	$5.00	$6.00

For parcels over 5 lb, rates by zone apply within and between the U.S. and Puerto Rico and the Virgin Islands. The mileage between the specific geographic locations of 3-digit ZIP codes determines the zone number to be used. The mileage range represented by the zone number is: Zone 1—up to 50 mi; 2—51 to 150 mi; 3—151 to 300 mi; 4—301 to 600 mi; 5—601 to 1,000 mi; 6—1,001 to 1,400 mi; 7—1,401 to 1,800 mi; 8—over 1,800 mi. Consult postmaster for details.

Parcels weighing less than 15 lb and measuring over 84 in. in length or girth, but not exceeding 108 in. in length and girth combined, cost the same as a 15-lb parcel mailed to the same zone.

Special Handling

Standard Mail and Parcel Post parcels can be given special, expedited handling upon payment of the following surcharge: up to 10 lb, $5.40; over 10 lb, $7.50. Such parcels must be marked for "Special Handling."

Bound Printed Matter Rates

(single-piece zone rate)

Weight				Zones				
lb	Local	1&2	3	4	5	6	7	8
1.5	$1.11	$1.49	$1.52	$1.58	$1.66	$1.74	$1.84	$1.93
2	1.12	1.52	1.56	1.63	1.74	1.85	1.99	2.10
2.5	1.14	1.55	1.60	1.69	1.82	1.96	2.13	2.28
3	1.15	1.57	1.64	1.74	1.90	2.07	2.27	2.45
3.5	1.17	1.60	1.67	1.80	1.98	2.18	2.42	2.62
4	1.18	1.63	1.71	1.85	2.07	2.29	2.56	2.79
4.5	1.20	1.65	1.75	1.91	2.15	2.40	2.71	2.97
5	1.22	1.68	1.79	1.96	2.23	2.51	2.85	3.14
6	1.25	1.73	1.86	2.07	2.39	2.73	3.14	3.49
7	1.28	1.79	1.94	2.18	2.56	2.95	3.43	3.83
8	1.31	1.84	2.01	2.29	2.72	3.17	3.71	4.18
9	1.34	1.90	2.09	2.40	2.89	3.39	4.00	4.52
10	1.37	1.95	2.16	2.51	3.05	3.61	4.29	4.87

(Includes both catalogs and similar bound printed matter.)

(Bound printed matter must weigh at least 1 lb and not more than 10 lb. Bound printed matter includes catalogs, directories, and books not eligible for special Parcel Post rates.)

Domestic Mail Special Services

Registry—Only matter prepaid with postage at First Class postage rates may be registered. Stamps or meter stamps must be attached. The face of the article must be at least 5″ long, 3½″ high. The mailer is required to declare the value of mail presented for registration.

Registered Mail

Declared Value	Fee[1]
$0.00 to $100	$4.85[2]
$0.00 to $100	4.95
$100.01 to $500	5.40
$500.01 to $1,000	5.85
$1,000.01 to $2,000	6.30
$2,000.01 to $3,000	6.75
$3,000.01 to $4,000	7.20
$4,000.01 to $5,000	7.65
$5,000.01 to $6,000	8.10
$6,000.01 to $7,000	8.55
$7,000.01 to $8,000	9.00
$8,000.01 to $9,000	9.45
$9,000.01 to $10,000	9.90

Consult postmaster for registry rates above $10,000.
(1) Fee for articles with declared value over $100 includes insurance; fee is in addition to postage. (2) Without insurance.

C.O.D.: Unregistered: Applicable to First Class, Standard Mail, and Express Mail matter. Such mail must be sent as bona fide orders or be in conformity with agreements between senders and addressees. **Registered:** For details, consult postmaster.

Insurance: Applicable to Standard Mail matter. Matter for sale addressed to prospective purchasers who have not ordered it or authorized its sending cannot be insured.

Insured Mail Rates

Declared Value	Fee
$0.01 to $50	$0.75
50.01 to $100	1.60
100.01 to $200	2.50
200.01 to $300	3.40
300.01 to $400	4.30
400.01 to $500	5.20
500.01 to $600	6.10

Liability for insured mail is limited to $600.

Certified mail: This service is available for any matter having no intrinsic value on which First Class or Air Mail postage is paid. Receipt is furnished at time of mailing, and evidence of delivery is obtained. The basic fee is $1.35 in addition to postage. Return receipt, restricted delivery, and special delivery are available upon payment of additional fees. No indemnity.

Special Standard Mail

(limit 70 lb)

Applies to only the following specific articles: Books of at least 8 printed pages consisting wholly of reading matter or scholarly bibliography, or reading matter with incidental blank spaces for notations and containing no advertising matter other than incidental announcements of books; 16-mm or narrower-width films in final form and catalogs of such films of 24 pages or more (at least 22 of which are printed) except films and film catalogs sent to or from commercial theaters; printed music in bound or sheet form; printed objective test materials; sound recordings, playscripts, and manuscripts for books, periodicals, and music; printed educational reference charts; loose-leaf pages and binders consisting of medical information for distribution to doctors, hospitals, medical schools, and medical students; computer-readable media containing prerecorded information and guides for use with such media. Package must be marked "Special Standard Class Rate" and must state what it contains. The rates are: first pound or fraction, $1.24 (70¢ if 500 pieces or more of special rate matter are presorted to 5-digit ZIP code, or $1.04 if 500 pieces or more are presorted to Bulk Mail Centers); each additional pound or fraction through 7 lb, 50¢; each additional pound, 31¢.

Library Mail

(limit 70 lb)

Library Mail includes the following: books when loaned or exchanged between and sent to or from schools, colleges, public libraries, and certain nonprofit organizations; books, printed music, bound academic theses, periodicals, sound recordings, other library materials, museum materials (specimens, collections), scientific or mathematical kits, instruments or other devices; also catalogs, guides, or scripts for some of these materials. Also qualifying for library rate are books mailed from publishers or distributors to schools, libraries, colleges, or universities or to bookstores owned, operated, and controlled by schools, colleges, or universities. All such packages must be marked "Library Mail." The rate is: first pound, $1.12; each additional pound through 7 lb, 41¢; each additional pound, 22¢.

Parcel Post Rate Schedule

(Inter BMC/ASF ZIP codes only, machinable parcels, no discount, no surcharge)

Weight up to but not exceeding—(pounds)	Local	1 and 2	3	Zones 4	5	6	7	8
2	$2.56	$2.63	$2.79	$2.87	$2.95	$2.95	$2.95	$2.95
3	2.63	2.76	3.00	3.34	3.68	3.95	3.95	3.95
4	2.71	2.87	3.20	3.78	4.68	4.95	4.95	4.95
5	2.77	2.97	3.38	4.10	5.19	5.56	5.95	5.95
6	2.84	3.07	3.55	4.39	5.67	6.90	7.75	7.95
7	2.90	3.16	3.71	4.67	6.11	7.51	9.15	9.75
8	2.96	3.26	3.85	4.91	6.53	8.08	9.94	11.55
9	3.01	3.33	3.99	5.16	6.92	8.62	10.65	12.95
10	3.07	3.42	4.12	5.38	7.29	9.12	11.31	14.00
11	3.12	3.49	4.25	5.59	7.63	9.59	11.93	15.05
12	3.17	3.57	4.37	5.79	7.96	10.03	12.52	16.10
13	3.23	3.64	4.47	5.98	8.26	10.45	13.07	17.15
14	3.27	3.71	4.59	6.16	8.55	10.84	13.59	18.20
15	3.32	3.77	4.69	6.34	8.82	11.22	14.08	19.25
16	3.37	3.83	4.79	6.50	9.09	11.58	14.55	20.30
17	3.41	3.90	4.88	6.66	9.33	11.92	15.00	21.35

Weight up to but not exceeding—(pounds)	Local	1 and 2	3	Zones 4	5	6	7	8
18	$3.45	$3.95	$4.97	$6.81	$9.58	$12.24	$15.42	$22.40
19	3.49	4.02	5.06	6.95	9.80	12.55	15.83	23.25
20	3.54	4.07	5.14	7.08	10.01	12.84	16.21	23.84
21	3.57	4.12	5.23	7.21	10.23	13.12	16.59	24.41
22	3.61	4.18	5.30	7.34	10.43	13.39	16.94	24.96
23	3.65	4.23	5.39	7.47	10.62	13.66	17.28	25.47
24	3.69	4.27	5.46	7.58	10.80	13.90	17.60	25.97
25	3.73	4.32	5.53	7.70	10.98	14.14	17.91	26.45

Postal Union Mail Special Services

Registration: Available to practically all countries. Fee $4.85. The maximum indemnity payable—generally only in case of complete loss (of both contents and wrapper)—is $42.30. To Canada only, the fee is $4.95, providing indemnity for loss up to $100, $5.40 for loss up to $500, and $5.85 for loss up to $1,000.

Return receipt: Shows to whom and date delivered, $1.10.

Special delivery: As of June 8, 1997, this service was no longer available.

Marking: An article that is intended for special delivery service must have affixed to the cover near the name of the country of destination "EXPRES" (special delivery) label, obtainable at the post office, or the word "EXPRES" (special delivery) may be marked on the cover boldly in red letters.

Special handling: Entitles AO surface packages to priority handling between mailing point and U.S. point of dispatch. Fees: $5.40 for packages to 10 lb, and $7.50 for packages over 10 lb.

Air mail: Daily air service is available to practically all countries.

Prepayment of replies from other countries: A mailer who wishes to prepay a reply by letter from another country may do so by sending one or more international reply coupons, available at U.S. post offices. These should be accepted in any country in exchange for stamps to prepay an air mail letter of the first unit of weight to the U.S.

Additional international special services: Insurance: Available to many countries for loss of or damage to items paid at parcel post rate. Consult postmaster for indemnity limits for individual countries.

Limit of indemnity Not over	Fees Canada[1]	All other countries[1]
$50	$0.75	$1.60
100	1.60	2.45
200	2.50	3.35
300	3.40	4.25
400	4.30	5.15
500	5.20	6.05
600	6.10	6.95
700		7.40
800		7.85
900		8.30
1,000		8.75
1,100		9.20
1,200		9.65

(1) Not all countries insure items up to the amounts listed in the table. Canada does not insure items for more than $600.

Restricted delivery: Available to many countries for registered mail; limits who may receive an item. Fee: $2.75.

Post Office-Authorized 2-Letter State Abbreviations

The abbreviations below are approved by the U.S. Postal Service for use in addresses for the 50 states, the District of Columbia, Puerto Rico, the U.S. Virgin Islands, American Samoa, Guam, and certain other areas in the Pacific.

Alabama	AL	Hawaii	HI	Missouri	MO	Pennsylvania	PA
Alaska	AK	Idaho	ID	Montana	MT	Puerto Rico	PR
American Samoa	AS	Illinois	IL	Nebraska	NE	Rhode Island	RI
Arizona	AZ	Indiana	IN	Nevada	NV	South Carolina	SC
Arkansas	AR	Iowa	IA	New Hampshire	NH	South Dakota	SD
California	CA	Kansas	KS	New Jersey	NJ	Tennessee	TN
Colorado	CO	Kentucky	KY	New Mexico	NM	Texas	TX
Connecticut	CT	Louisiana	LA	New York	NY	Utah	UT
Delaware	DE	Maine	ME	North Carolina	NC	Vermont	VT
Dist. of Col.	DC	Marshall Islands[1]	MH	North Dakota	ND	Virginia	VA
Federated States		Maryland	MD	Northern Mariana Is.	MP	Virgin Islands	VI
of Micronesia[1]	FM	Massachusetts	MA	Ohio	OH	Washington	WA
Florida	FL	Michigan	MI	Oklahoma	OK	West Virginia	WV
Georgia	GA	Minnesota	MN	Oregon	OR	Wisconsin	WI
Guam	GU	Mississippi	MS	Palau[1]	PW	Wyoming	WY

(1) Although an independent nation, this country is currently subject to domestic rates and fees.

Canadian Province and Territory Postal Codes

Alberta	AB	Northwest Territories	NT
British Columbia	BC	Ontario	ON
Manitoba	MB	Prince Edward Island	PE
New Brunswick	NB	Quebec	QC
Newfoundland and Labrador	NF	Saskatchewan	SK
Nova Scotia	NS	Yukon Territory	YT

MILLENNIUM FACT BOX

First Class Stamp Rates in the 20th Century

At the beginning of the 20th century the cost to send a letter that weighed 1 oz or less was 2 cents. The following table shows the rising rates for first class stamps and the date on which each new rate became effective.

Date	Year	Cost	Date	Year	Cost	Date	Year	Cost	Date	Year	Cost
Nov. 2	1917	$0.03	Jan. 7	1963	$0.05	Dec. 31	1975	$0.13	Feb. 17	1985	$0.22
July 1	1919	0.02	Jan. 7	1968	0.06	May 29	1978	0.15	Apr. 3	1988	0.25
July 6	1932	0.03	May 16	1971	0.08	Mar. 22	1981	0.18	Feb. 3	1991	0.29
Aug. 1	1958	0.04	Mar. 2	1974	0.10	Nov. 1	1981	0.20	Jan. 1	1995	0.32

International Air Mail Rates

Aerogrammes — 50¢ from U.S. to all countries.
Air mail postcards (single) — 50¢ to all countries except Canada (40¢ each) and Mexico (35¢ each).
International letters and letter packages: to Canada and Mexico (by air mail; there are no surface rates to these countries)—weight not over 0.5 oz, 46¢ to Canada, 40¢ to Mexico; not over 1.0 oz, 52¢ to Canada, 46¢ to Mexico; not over 2 oz, 72¢ to Canada, 86¢ to Mexico; not over 3 oz, 95¢ to Canada, $1.26 to Mexico.

Air Mail, Letter, and Letter Package Rates to Countries Other Than Canada and Mexico

(weight limit: 64 oz [4 lb])

Weight not over	Rate	Weight not over	Rate	Weight not over	Rate	Weight not over	Rate
0.5 oz	$0.60	12.5 oz	$10.20	24.5 oz	$19.80	41 oz	$29.40
1.0	1.00	13.0	10.60	25.0	20.20	42	29.80
1.5	1.40	13.5	11.00	25.5	20.60	43	30.20
2.0	1.80	14.0	11.40	26.0	21.00	44	30.60
2.5	2.20	14.5	11.80	26.5	21.40	45	31.00
3.0	2.60	15.0	12.20	27.0	21.80	46	31.40
3.5	3.00	15.5	12.60	27.5	22.20	47	31.80
4.0	3.40	16.0	13.00	28.0	22.60	48	32.20
4.5	3.80	16.5	13.40	28.5	23.00	49	32.60
5.0	4.20	17.0	13.80	29.0	23.40	50	33.00
5.5	4.60	17.5	14.20	29.5	23.80	51	33.40
6.0	5.00	18.0	14.60	30.0	24.20	52	33.80
6.5	5.40	18.5	15.00	30.5	24.60	53	34.20
7.0	5.80	19.0	15.40	31.0	25.00	54	34.60
7.5	6.20	19.5	15.80	31.5	25.40	55	35.00
8.0	6.60	20.0	16.20	32.0	25.80	56	35.40
8.5	7.00	20.5	16.60	33.0	26.20	57	35.80
9.0	7.40	21.0	17.00	34.0	26.60	58	36.20
9.5	7.80	21.5	17.40	35.0	27.00	59	36.60
10.0	8.20	22.0	17.80	36.0	27.40	60	37.00
10.5	8.60	22.5	18.20	37.0	27.80	61	37.40
11.0	9.00	23.0	18.60	38.0	28.20	62	37.80
11.5	9.40	23.5	19.00	39.0	28.60	63	38.20
12.0	9.80	24.0	19.40	40.0	29.00	64	38.60

Air Mail Parcel Post Rates

Weight	Canada	Mexico	A	B	C	D	E
			Cost, depending on country's rate group				
First pound	$7.00[1]	$6.50[2]	$6.50	$8.25	$9.75	$11.20	$12.80
Each additional pound or fraction up to 5 lb	1.28	2.56	3.36	4.00	5.28	5.76	6.40
Each additional pound or fraction up to 10 lb	1.20	2.24	2.88	3.20	4.32	5.28	5.44
Each additional pound or fraction up to 20 lb	1.12	1.92	2.72	2.88	4.00	4.32	4.48
Each additional pound or fraction up to 30 lb	1.12	1.60	2.24	2.56	3.84	4.16	4.32
Each additional pound or fraction over 30 lb	1.12	1.60	1.92	2.24	3.68	4.00	4.16

(1) Fee up to 2 lbs. is $7.00. (2) Rate for each additional pound or fraction up to 3 lb is $3.20.

Country Rate Groups

(For further information, consult your local post office.)

Country or territory	Rate group	Maximum weight limit (lbs)	Country or territory	Rate group	Maximum weight limit (lbs)
Afghanistan[1]	D	44	Brunei	D	44
Albania	C	44	Bulgaria	D	44
Algeria	D	66	Burkina Faso	D	44
Andorra	B	44	Burma	see Myanmar	
Angola	E	22	Burundi	E	44
Anguilla	A	22	Cambodia[2]	E	44 (air only)
Antigua & Barbuda	A	22	Cameroon	D	44
Argentina	D	44	Cape Verde	D	44
Armenia	E	44	Cayman Islands	A	44
Aruba	A	44	Central African Republic	E	44
Ascension	no air service	44 (surface)	Chad[3]	D	44 (air only)
Australia	D	44	Chile	D	44
Austria	B	44	China (People's Republic of)	D	44
Azerbaijan	E	22	Colombia	B	44
Azores	C	44	Comoros	E	44
Bahamas	A	44	Congo, Dem. Rep. of (Zaire)	E	44
Bahrain	D	44	Congo Republic	D	44
Bangladesh	E	22	Corsica	E	44
Barbados	B	44	Costa Rica	A	44
Belarus	E	44	Côte d'Ivoire	D	44
Belgium	D	44	Croatia	C	44
Belize	A	44	Cuba[2]	no parcel post service	
Benin	C	44	Cyprus	C	44
Bermuda	A	44	Czech Republic	C	33
Bhutan	E	44	Denmark	C	66
Bolivia	B	44	Djibouti	D	44
Bosnia and Herzegovina	C	33	Dominica	A	44
Botswana	E	44	Dominican Republic	A	44
Brazil	E	44			
British Virgin Islands	A	44			

Country or territory	Rate group	Maximum weight limit (lbs)
East Timor	see Indonesia	
Ecuador	C	44
Egypt	D	44
El Salvador	B	44
Equatorial Guinea	D	44
Eritrea	D	44
Estonia	E	44
Ethiopia	D	44
Faroe Islands	C	66
Falkland Islands[2]	no air PP	44 (surface)
Fiji	B	44
Finland	D	44
France	E	44
French Guiana	C	44
French Polynesia	D	44
Gabon[3]	D	44
Gambia, The	B	22
Georgia, Republic of	E	22
Germany	B	44
Ghana	D	44
Gibraltar	C	44
Great Britain and Northern Ireland	C	66
Greece	C	44
Greenland	D	66
Grenada	A	44
Guadeloupe	A	44
Guatemala	A	44
Guinea	B	44
Guinea-Bissau	B	22
Guyana	B	44
Haiti	A	44
Honduras	B	44
Hungary	C	44
Iceland	C	44
India	D	44
Indonesia[4]	E	44
Iran	D	44
Iraq[2]	D	44
Ireland	C	66
Israel[5]	C	44
Italy	C	44
Ivory Coast	see Côte d'Ivoire	
Jamaica	A	22
Japan	E	44
Jordan	C	44
Kazakhstan	E	44
Kenya	D	44
Kiribati	B	44
Korea, Democratic People's Rep. of (North)[2]	no parcel post service	
Korea, Republic of (South)	C	44
Kuwait[3]	C	44 (air only)
Kyrgyzstan	E	22
Laos	E	44
Latvia	E	44
Lebanon[2,3]	C	11 (air only)
Lesotho	E	44
Liberia[3]	C	44
Libya[2]	D	44
Liechtenstein	B	66
Lithuania	E	44
Luxembourg	B	44
Macao	C	44
Macedonia	C	33
Madagascar	E	44
Madeira Islands	B	44
Malawi	D	44
Malaysia	D	22
Maldives	D	22
Mali	C	44
Malta	C	22
Martinique	A	44
Mauritania	D	44
Mauritius	E	22
Moldova	E	44
Monaco	E	44
Mongolia	no parcel post service	
Montserrat	A	44
Morocco	C	44
Mozambique	E	44
Myanmar	D	22
Namibia	D	44
Nauru	C	44
Nepal	D	44 (surface) 11 (air)
Netherlands	C	44
Netherlands Antilles	A	44
New Caledonia	D	44
New Zealand	D	44
Nicaragua	B	44
Niger	D	44
Nigeria	C	44
Norway	D	44
Oman	D	44
Pakistan	D	44
Panama	A	44
Papua New Guinea[2]	D	44
Paraguay	D	44
Peru	B	44
Philippines	D	44
Pitcairn Island	B	22
Poland	B	33
Portugal	C	44
Qatar	E	44
Reunion	E	44
Romania	C	44
Russia	E	22
Rwanda[2]	D	44
Saint Helena	C	44
Saint Kitts & Nevis	A	44
Saint Lucia	A	44
Saint Pierre & Miquelon	A	44
Saint Vincent & the Grenadines	A	22
Samoa	B	44
San Marino	C	44
São Tomé & Príncipe	D	44
Saudi Arabia	D	44
Senegal	D	44
Seychelles	D	44
Sierra Leone	D	44
Singapore	D	44
Slovakia	C	33
Slovenia	C	33
Solomon Islands	C	44
Somalia[1]	D	44
South Africa	D	44
Spain	C	44
Sri Lanka	D	44
Sudan	D	44
Suriname	B	44
Swaziland	D	44
Sweden	D	44
Switzerland	B	66
Syria	C	44
Taiwan	C	44
Tajikistan	E	22
Tanzania	E	44
Thailand	D	44
Togo	D	44
Tonga	B	44
Trinidad & Tobago	B	22
Tristan da Cunha	E	22
Tunisia	C	44
Turkey	C	44
Turkmenistan	E	22
Turks and Caicos Islands	A	22
Tuvalu	B	44
Uganda	D	44
Ukraine	E	44
United Arab Emirates	D	44
United Kingdom	C	66
Uruguay	B	44
Uzbekistan	E	22
Vanuatu	B	44
Vatican City	C	44
Venezuela	B	44
Vietnam	E	44
Wallis & Futuna Islands	D	44
Yemen	E	44
Yugoslavia[2]	C	00
Zambia	E	44
Zimbabwe	E	44

(1) All mail service suspended. (2) Mail service restrictions apply. (3) Surface mail service suspended. (4) Includes East Timor. (5) West Bank and Gaza Strip are same rate group as Israel.

SCIENCE AND TECHNOLOGY
Inventions

Inventions	Date	Inventor	Nationality
Adding machine	1642	Pascal	French
Adding machine	1885	Burroughs	U.S.
Aerosol spray	1926	Rotheim	Norwegian
Air brake	1868	Westinghouse	U.S.
Air conditioning	1911	Carrier	U.S.
Air pump	1654	Guericke	German
Airplane, automatic pilot	1912	Sperry	U.S.
Airplane, experimental	1896	Langley	U.S.
Airplane jet engine	1939	Ohain	German
Airplane with motor	1903	Wright bros	U.S.
Airplane, hydro	1911	Curtiss	U.S.
Airship	1852	Giffard	French
Airship, rigid dirigible	1900	Zeppelin	German
Arc welder	1919	Thomson	U.S.
Aspartame	1965	Schlatter	U.S.
Autogyro	1920	de la Cierva	Spanish
Automobile, differential gear	1885	Benz	German
Automobile, electric	1892	Morrison	U.S.
Automobile, exp'mtl	1864	Marcus	Austrian
Automobile, gasoline	1889	Daimler	German
Automobile, gasoline	1892	Duryea	U.S.
Automobile magneto	1897	Bosch	German
Automobile muffler	1904	Pope	U.S.
Automobile self-starter	1911	Kettering	U.S.
Babbitt metal	1839	Babbitt	U.S.
Bakelite	1907	Baekeland	Belg., U.S.
Balloon	1783	Montgolfier	French
Barometer	1643	Torricelli	Italian
Bicycle, modern	1885	Starley	English
Bifocal lens	1780	Franklin	U.S.
Block signals, railway	1867	Hall	U.S.
Bomb, depth	1916	Tait	U.S.
Bottle machine	1895	Owens	U.S.
Braille printing	1829	Braille	French
Burner, gas	1855	Bunsen	German
Calculating machine	1833	Babbage	English
Calculator, electronic pocket	1972	Merryman, Van Tassel	U.S.
Camera, Kodak	1888	Eastman, Walker	U.S
Camera, Polaroid Land	1948	Land	U.S.
Car coupler	1873	Janney	U.S.
Carburetor, gasoline	1893	Maybach	German
Card time recorder	1894	Cooper	U.S.
Carding machine	1797	Whittemore	U.S.
Carpet sweeper	1876	Bissell	U.S.
Cash register	1879	Ritty	U.S.
Cassette, audio	1963	Philips Co	Dutch
Cassette, videotape	1969	Sony	Japanese
Cathode ray oscilloscope	1897	Braun	German
Cathode ray tube	1878	Crookes	English
CAT, or CT, scan	1973	Hounsfield	English
Cellophane	1908	Brandenberger	Swiss
Celluloid	1870	Hyatt	U.S.
Cement, Portland	1824	Aspdln	English
Chronometer	1761	Harrison	English
Circuit breaker	1925	Hilliard	U.S.
Circuit, integrated	1959	Kilby, Noyce, Texas Instr.	U.S.

Inventions	Date	Inventor	Nationality
Clock, pendulum	1657	Huygens	Dutch
Coaxial cable system	1929	Affel, Espensched	U.S.
Coke oven	1893	Hoffman	Austrian
Compressed air rock drill	1871	Ingersoll	U.S.
Comptometer	1887	Felt	U.S.
Computer, automatic sequence	1944	Aiken, et al.	U.S.
Computer, electronic	1942	Atanasoff, Berry	U.S.
Computer, mini	1960	Digital Corp	U.S.
Condenser microphone (telephone)	1916	Wente	U.S.
Contraceptive, oral	1954	Pincus, Rock	U.S.
Corn, hybrid	1917	Jones	U.S.
Cotton gin	1793	Whitney	U.S.
Cream separator	1878	DeLaval	Swedish
Cultivator, disc	1878	Mallon	U.S.
Cystoscope	1878	Nitze	German
Diesel engine	1895	Diesel	German
Disc, compact	1972	RCA	U.S.
Disk, floppy	1970	IBM	U.S.
Disc player, compact	1979	Sony, Philips Co.	Japan., Dutch
Disk, video	1972	Philips Co.	Dutch
Dynamite	1866	Nobel	Swedish
Dynamo, continuous current	1871	Gramme	Belgian
Dynamo, hydrogen cooled	1915	Schuler	U.S.
Electric battery	1800	Volta	Italian
Electric fan	1882	Wheeler	U.S.
Electrocardiograph	1903	Einthoven	Dutch
Electroencephalograph	1929	Berger	German
Electromagnet	1824	Sturgeon	English
Electron spectrometer	1944	Deutsch, Elliott, Evans	U.S.
Electron tube multigrid	1913	Langmuir	U.S.
Electroplating	1805	Brugnatelli	Italian
Electrostatic generator	1929	Van de Graaff	U.S.
Elevator brake	1852	Otis	U.S.
Elevator, push button	1922	Larson	U.S.
Engine, automatic transmission	1910	Fottinger	German
Engine, coal-gas 4-cycle	1876	Otto	German
Engine, compression ignition	1883	Daimler	German
Engine, electric ignition	1883	Benz	German
Engine, gas, compound	1926	Eickemeyer	U.S.

Inventions	Date	Inventor	Nationality
Engine, gasoline	1872	Brayton, Geo.	U.S.
Engine, gasoline	1889	Daimler	German
Engine, jet	1930	Whittle	English
Engine, steam, piston	1705	Newcomen	English
Engine, steam, piston	1769	Watt	Scottish
Engraving, half-tone	1852	Talbot	U.S.
Fiberglass	1938	Owens-Corning	U.S.
Fiber optics	1955	Kapany	English
Filament, tungsten	1913	Coolidge	U.S.
Flanged rail	1831	Stevens	U.S.
Flatiron, electric	1882	Seely	U.S.
Food, frozen	1924	Birdseye	U.S.
Freon	1930	Midgley, et al.	U.S.
Furnace (for steel)	1858	Siemens	German
Galvanometer	1820	Sweigger	German
Gas discharge tube	1922	Hull	U.S.
Gas lighting	1792	Murdoch	Scottish
Gas mantle	1885	Welsbach	Austrian
Gasoline (lead ethyl)	1922	Midgley	U.S.
Gasoline, cracked	1913	Burton	U.S.
Gasoline, high octane	1930	Ipatieff	Russian
Geiger counter	1913	Geiger	German
Glass, laminated safety	1909	Benedictus	French
Glider	1853	Cayley	English
Gun, breechloader	1811	Thornton	U.S.
Gun, Browning	1897	Browning	U.S.
Gun, magazine	1875	Hotchkiss	U.S.
Gun, silencer	1908	Maxim, H.P.	U.S.
Guncotton	1847	Schoenbein	German
Gyrocompass	1911	Sperry	U.S.
Gyroscope	1852	Foucault	French
Harvester-thresher	1818	Lane	U.S.
Heart, artificial	1982	Jarvik	U.S.
Helicopter	1939	Sikorsky	U.S.
Hydrometer	1768	Baume	French
Iron lung	1928	Drinker, Slaw	U.S.
Kaleidoscope	1817	Brewster	Scottish
Kinetoscope	1889	Edison	U.S.
Lacquer, nitrocellulose	1921	Flaherty	U.S.
Lamp, arc	1847	Staite	English
Lamp, fluorescent	1938	GE, Westinghouse	U.S.
Lamp, incandescent	1879	Edison	U.S.
Lamp, incand. frosted	1924	Pipkin	U.S.
Lamp, incand., gas	1913	Langmuir	U.S.
Lamp, klieg	1911	Kliegl, A. & J.	U.S.
Lamp, mercury vapor	1912	Hewitt	U.S.
Lamp, miner's safety	1816	Davy	English
Lamp, neon	1909	Claude	French
Lathe, turret	1845	Fitch	U.S.
Launderette	1934	Cantrell	U.S.
Lens, achromatic	1758	Dollond	English
Lens, fused bifocal	1908	Borsch	U.S.
Leyden jar (condenser)	1745	von Kleist	German
Lightning rod	1752	Franklin	U.S.
Linoleum	1860	Walton	English
Linotype	1884	Mergenthaler	U.S.
Lock, cylinder	1851	Yale	U.S.
Locomotive, electric	1851	Vail	U.S.
Locomotive, exp'mtl	1802	Trevithick	English
Locomotive, exp'mtl	1812	Fenton, et al.	English
Locomotive, exp'mtl	1813	Hedley	English
Locomotive, exp'mtl	1814	Stephenson	English
Locomotive, practical	1829	Stephenson	English
Locomotive, 1st U.S.	1830	Cooper, P.	U.S.
Loom, power	1785	Cartwright	English
Loudspeaker, dynamic	1924	Rice, Kellogg	U.S.
Machine gun	1861	Gatling	U.S.
Machine gun, improved	1872	Hotchkiss	U.S.
Machine gun (Maxim)	1883	Maxim, H.S.	U.S., Eng.
Magnet, electro	1828	Henry	U.S.
Mantle, gas	1885	Welsbach	Austrian
Mason jar	1858	Mason, J.	U.S.
Match, friction	1827	John Walker	English
Mercerized textiles	1843	Mercer, J.	English
Meter, induction	1888	Shallenberg	U.S.
Metronome	1816	Malezel	German
Microcomputer	1973	Truong, et al.	French
Micrometer	1636	Gascoigne	English
Microphone	1877	Berliner	U.S.
Microprocessor	1971	Intel Corp.	U.S.
Microscope, compound	1590	Janssen	Dutch
Microscope, electronic	1931	Knoll, Ruska	German
Microscope, field ion	1951	Mueller	German
Monitor, warship	1861	Ericsson	U.S.
Monotype	1887	Lanston	U.S.
Motor, AC	1892	Tesla	U.S.
Motor, DC	1837	Davenport	U.S.
Motor, induction	1887	Tesla	U.S.
Motorcycle	1885	Daimler	German
Movie machine	1894	Jenkins	U.S.
Movie, panoramic	1952	Waller	U.S.
Movie, talking	1927	Warner Bros.	U.S.
Mower, lawn	1831	Budding, Ferrabee	English
Mowing machine	1822	Bailey	U.S.
Neoprene	1930	Carothers	U.S.
Nylon synthetic	1930	Carothers	U.S.
Nylon	1937	Du Pont lab	U.S.
Oil cracking furnace	1891	Gavrilov	Russian
Oil filled power cable	1921	Emanueli	Italian

Inventions	Date	Inventor	Nationality
Oleomargarine	1869	Mege-Mouries	French
Ophthalmoscope	1851	Helmholtz	German
Paper	105	Ts'ai	Chinese
Paper machine	1809	Dickinson	U.S.
Parachute	1785	Blanchard	French
Pen, ballpoint	1888	Loud	U.S.
Pen, fountain	1884	Waterman	U.S.
Pen, steel	1780	Harrison	English
Pendulum	1583	Galileo	Italian
Percussion cap	1807	Forsythe	Scottish
Phonograph	1877	Edison	U.S.
Photo, color	1892	Ives	U.S.
Photo film, celluloid	1893	Reichenbach	U.S.
Photo film, transparent	1884	Eastman, Goodwin	U.S.
Photoelectric cell	1895	Elster	German
Photographic paper	1835	Talbot	English
Photography	1835	Talbot	English
Photography	1835	Daguerre	French
Photography	1816	Niepce	French
Photophone	1880	Bell	U.S.-Scot.
Phototelegraphy	1925	Bell Labs	U.S.
Piano	1709	Cristofori	Italian
Piano, player	1863	Fourneaux	French
Pin, safety	1849	Hunt	U.S.
Pistol (revolver)	1836	Colt	U.S.
Plow, cast iron	1785	Ransome	English
Plow, disc	1896	Hardy	U.S.
Pneumatic hammer	1890	King	U.S.
Powder, smokeless	1884	Vieille	French
Printing press, rotary	1845	Hoe	U.S.
Printing press, web	1865	Bullock	U.S.
Propeller, screw	1804	Stevens	U.S.
Propeller, screw	1837	Ericsson	Swedish
Pulsars	1967	Bell	English
Punch card accounting	1889	Hollerith	U.S.
Quasars	1963	Schmidt	U.S.
Radar	1940	Watson-Watt	Scottish
Radio amplifier	1906	De Forest	U.S.
Radio beacon	1928	Donovan	U.S.
Radio crystal oscillator	1918	Nicolson	U.S.
Radio receiver, cascade tuning	1913	Alexanderson	U.S.
Radio receiver, heterodyne	1913	Fessenden	U.S.
Radio transmitter triode modulation	1914	Alexanderson	U.S.
Radio tube diode	1905	Fleming	English
Radio tube oscillator	1915	De Forest	U.S.
Radio tube triode	1906	De Forest	U.S.
Radio, signals	1895	Marconi	Italian
Radio, magnetic detector	1902	Marconi	Italian
Radio FM, 2-path	1933	Armstrong	U.S.
Rayon (acetate)	1895	Cross	English
Rayon (cuprammonium)	1890	Despeissis	French
Rayon (nitrocellulose)	1884	Chardonnet	French
Razor, electric	1917	Schick	U.S.
Razor, safety	1895	Gillette	U.S.
Reaper	1834	McCormick	U.S.
Record, cylinder	1887	Bell, Tainter	U.S.
Record, disc	1887	Berliner	U.S.
Record, long playing	1947	Goldmark	U.S.
Record, wax cylinder	1888	Edison	U.S.
Refrigerator car	1868	David	U.S.
Resin, synthetic	1931	Hill	English
Richter scale	1935	Richter	U.S.
Rifle, repeating	1860	Spencer	U.S.
Rocket engine	1926	Goddard	U.S.
Rubber, vulcanized	1839	Goodyear	U.S.
Saccharin	1879	Remsen, Fahlberg	U.S.
Saw, band	1808	Newberry	English
Saw, circular	1777	Miller	English
Sewing machine	1846	Howe	U.S.
Shoe-lasting maching	1883	Matzeliger	U.S.
Shoe-sewing machine	1860	McKay	U.S.
Shrapnel shell	1784	Shrapnel	English
Shuttle, flying	1733	Kay	English
Sleeping-car	1865	Pullman	U.S.
Slide rule	1620	Oughtred	English
Soap, hardwater	1928	Bertsch	German
Spectroscope	1859	Kirchoff, Bunsen	German
Spectroscope (mass)	1918	Dempster	U.S.
Spinning jenny	c.1764	Hargreaves	English
Spinning mule	1779	Crompton	English
Steamboat, exp'mtl	1778	Jouffroy	French
Steamboat, exp'mtl	1785	Fitch	U.S.
Steamboat, exp'mtl	1787	Rumsey	U.S.
Steamboat, exp'mtl	1788	Miller	Scottish
Steamboat, exp'mtl	1803	Fulton	U.S.
Steamboat, exp'mtl	1804	Stevens	U.S.
Steamboat, practical	1802	Symington	Scottish
Steamboat, practical	1807	Fulton	U.S.
Steam car	1770	Cugnot	French
Steam turbine	1884	Parsons	English
Steel (converter)	1856	Bessemer	English
Steel alloy	1891	Harvey	U.S.
Steel alloy, high-speed	1901	Taylor, White	U.S.
Steel, electric	1900	Heroult	French
Steel, manganese	1884	Hadfield	English
Steel, stainless	1916	Brearley	English
Stereoscope	1838	Wheatstone	English
Stethoscope	1819	Laennec	French
Stethoscope, binaural	1840	Cammann	U.S.
Stock ticker	1870	Edison	U.S.
Storage battery, rechargeable	1859	Plante	French
Stove, electric	1896	Hadaway	U.S.
Submarine	1891	Holland	U.S.
Submarine, even keel	1894	Lake	U.S.
Submarine, torpedo	1776	Bushnell	U.S.
Superconductivity	1957	Bardeen, Cooper, Schreiffer	U.S.
Synthesizer	1964	Moog	U.S.
Tank, military	1914	Swinton	English
Tape recorder, magnetic	1899	Poulsen	Danish
Teflon	1938	Du Pont	U.S.
Telegraph, magnetic	1837	Morse	U.S.
Telegraph, quadruplex	1864	Edison	U.S.
Telegraph, railroad	1887	Woods	U.S.
Telegraph, wireless high frequency	1895	Marconi	Italian
Telephone	1876	Bell	U.S.-Scot.
Telephone amplifier	1912	De Forest	U.S.
Telephone, automatic	1891	Stowger	U.S.
Telephone, radio	1900	Poulsen, Fessenden	Danish
Telephone, radio	1906	De Forest	U.S.
Telephone, radio, l. d.	1915	AT&T	U.S.
Telephone, recording	1898	Poulsen	Danish
Telephone, wireless	1899	Collins	U.S.
Telescope	1608	Lippershey	Neth.
Telescope	1609	Galileo	Italian
Telescope, astronomical	1611	Kepler	German
Teletype	1928	Morkrum, Kleinschmidt	U.S.
Television, color	1928	Baird	Scottish
Television, iconoscope	1923	Zworykin	U.S.
Television, electronic	1927	Farnsworth	U.S.
Television, mech. scanner	1923	Baird	Scottish
Thermometer	1593	Galileo	Italian
Thermometer	1730	Reaumur	French
Thermometer, mercury	1714	Fahrenheit	German
Time recorder	1890	Bundy	U.S.
Time, self-regulator	1918	Bryce	U.S.
Tire, double-tube	1845	Thomson	Scottish
Tire, pneumatic	1888	Dunlop	Scottish
Toaster, automatic	1918	Strite	U.S.
Toilet, flush	1589	Harington	English
Tool, pneumatic	1865	Law	English
Torpedo, marine	1804	Fulton	U.S.
Tractor, crawler	1904	Holt	U.S.
Transformer, AC	1885	Stanley	U.S.
Transistor	1947	Shockley, Brattain, Bardeen	U.S.
Trolley car, electric	1884-87	Van DePoele, Sprague	U.S.
Tungsten, ductile	1912	Coolidge	U.S.
Tupperware	1945	Tupper	U.S.
Turbine, gas	1849	Bourdin	French
Turbine, hydraulic	1849	Francis	U.S.
Turbine, steam	1884	Parsons	English
Type, movable	1447	Gutenberg	German
Typewriter	1867	Sholes, Soule, Glidden	U.S.
Vacuum cleaner, electric	1907	Spangler	U.S.
Vacuum evaporating pan	1846	Rillieux	U.S.
Velcro	1948	de Mestral	Swiss
Video game ("Pong")	1972	Buschnel	U.S.
Video home system (VHS)	1975	Matsushita, JVC	Japan.
Washer, electric	1901	Fisher	U.S.
Welding, atomic hydrogen	1924	Langmuir, Palmer	U.S.
Welding, electric	1877	Thomson	U.S.
Wind tunnel	1912	Eiffel	French
Wire, barbed	1874	Glidden	U.S.
Wire, barbed	1875	Haisn	U.S.
Wrench, double-acting	1913	Owen	U.S.
X-ray tube	1913	Coolidge	U.S.

MILLENNIUM FACT BOX

An Era of Inventions

From the magnetic compass and movable type to the telephone, televisions, and computers, most of the inventions and devices we depend on today were developed in the 2d millennium. One of the most prolific and successful inventors of the whole era was Thomas Alva Edison (1847-1931), who patented 1,093 devices, including 389 related to electric light and power, 195 for the phonograph, 150 for the telegraph, 141 for the storage battery, and 34 for the telephone. Among his inventions: the quadruplex telegraph (1864), stock ticker (1870), mimeograph (1877), phonograph (1877), incandescent lamp (1879), talking doll (1880), wax cylinder record (1888), and kinetoscope (1889).

Discoveries and Innovations: Chemistry, Physics, Biology, Medicine

	Date	Discoverer	Nationality
Acetylene gas	1862	Berthelot	French
ACTH	1927	Evans, Long	U.S.
Adrenalin	1901	Takamine	Japanese
Aluminum, electrolytic process	1886	Hall	U.S.
Aluminum, isolated	1825	Oersted	Danish
Anesthesia, ether	1842	Long	U.S.
Anesthesia, local	1885	Koller	Austrian
Anesthesia, spinal	1898	Bier	German
Aniline dye	1856	Perkin	English
Anti-rabies	1885	Pasteur	French
Antiseptic surgery	1867	Lister	English
Antitoxin, diphtheria	1891	Von Behring	German
Argyrol	1897	Bayer	German
Arsphenamine	1910	Ehrlich	German
Aspirin	1889	Dresser	German
Atabrine	1932	Mietzsch, et al.	German
Atomic numbers	1913	Moseley	English
Atomic theory	1803	Dalton	English
Atomic time clock	1948	Lyons	U.S.
Atomic time clock, cesium beam	1948	Essen	English
Atom-smashing theory	1919	Rutherford	English
Bacitracin	1945	Johnson, et al.	U.S.
Bacteria, description	1676	Leeuwenhoek	Dutch
Barbital	1903	Fischer	German
Bleaching powder	1798	Tennant	English
Blood, circulation	1628	Harvey	English
Blood plasma storage (blood banks)	1940	Drew	U.S.
Bordeaux mixture	1885	Millardet	French
Bromie from sea	1924	Edgar Kramer	U.S.
Calcium carbide	1888	Wilson	U.S.
Calculus	1670	Newton	English
Camphor synthetic	1896	Haller	French
Canning (food)	1804	Appert	French
Carbomycin	1952	Tanner	U.S.
Carbon oxides	1925	Fisher	German
Chloamphenicol	1947	Burkholder	U.S.
Chlorine	1774	Scheele	Swedish
Chloroform	1831	Guthrie, S.	U.S.
Chlortetracycline	1948	Duggen	U.S.
Classification of plants and animals	1735	Linnaeus	Swedish
Cloning, mammal	1996	Wilmut et. al.	Scottish
Cocaine	1860	Niermann	German
Combustion explained	1777	Lavoisier	French
Conditioned reflex	1914	Pavlov	Russian
Cortisone	1936	Kendall	U.S.
Cortisone, synthesis	1946	Sarett	U.S.
Cosmic rays	1910	Gockel	Swiss
Cyanamide	1905	Frank, Caro	German
Cyclotron	1930	Lawrence	U.S.
DDT (not applied as insecticide until 1939)	1874	Zeidler	German
Deuterium	1932	Urey, Brickwedde, Murphy	U.S.
DNA (structure)	1951	Crick	English
		Watson	U.S.
		Wilkins	English
Electric resistance, law of	1827	Ohm	German
Electric waves	1888	Hertz	German
Electrolysis	1852	Faraday	English
Electromagnetism	1819	Oersted	Danish
Electron	1897	Thomson, J.	English
Electron diffraction	1936	Thomson, G.	English
		Davisson	U.S.
Electroshock treatment	1938	Cerletti, Bini	Italian
Erythromycin	1952	McGuire	U.S.
Evolution, natural selection	1858	Darwin	English
Falling bodies, law of	1590	Galileo	Italian
Gases, law of combining volumes	1808	Gay-Lussac	French
Geometry, analytic	1619	Descartes	French
Gold, cyanide process for extraction	1887	MacArthur, Forest	British
Gravitation, law	1687	Newton	English
Holograph	1948	Gabor	British
Human heart transplant	1967	Barnard	S. African
Human immunodeficiency virus identified	1984	Gallo, Montagnier	French, U.S.
Indigo, synthesis of	1880	Baeyer	German
Induction, electric	1830	Henry	U.S.
Insulin	1922	Banting, Best, Macleod	Canadian, Scottish
Intelligence testing	1905	Binet, Simon	French
In vitro fertilization	1978	Steptoe, Edwards	English
Isoniazid	1952	Hoffmann-La-Roche	U.S.
		Domagk	German
Isotopes, theory	1912	Soddy	English

	Date	Discoverer	Nationality
Laser (light amplification by stimulated emission of radiation)	1957	Gould	U.S.
Light, velocity	1675	Roemer	Danish
Light, wave theory	1690	Huygens	Dutch
Lithography	1796	Senefelder	Bohemian
Logarithms	1614	Napier	Scottish
Lobotomy	1935	Egas Moniz	Portuguese
LSD-25	1943	Hoffman	Swiss
Mendelian laws	1866	Mendel	Austrian
Mercator projection (map)	1568	Mercator (Kremer)	Flemish
Methanol	1661	Boyle	Irish
Milk condensation	1853	Borden	U.S.
Molecular hypothesis	1811	Avogadro	Italian
Motion, laws of	1687	Newton	English
Neomycin	1949	Waksman, Lechevalier	U.S.
Neutron	1932	Chadwick	English
Nitric acid	1648	Glauber	German
Nitric oxide	1772	Priestley	English
Nitroglycerin	1846	Sobrero	Italian
Oil cracking process	1891	Dewar	U.S.
Oxygen	1774	Priestley	English
Oxytetracycline	1950	Finlay, et al.	U.S.
Ozone	1840	Schonbein	German
Paper, sulfite process	1867	Tilghman	U.S.
Paper, wood pulp, sulfate process	1884	Dahl	German
Penicillin	1929	Fleming	Scottish
practical use	1941	Florey, Chain	English
Periodic law and table of elements	1869	Mendeleyev	Russian
Physostigmine synthesis	1935	Julian	U.S.
Planetary motion, laws	1609	Kepler	German
Plutonium fission	1940	Kennedy, Wahl, Seaborg, Segre	U.S.
Polymyxin	1947	Ainsworth	English
Positron	1932	Anderson	U.S.
Proton	1919	Rutherford	N. Zealand
Psychoanalysis	1900	Freud	Austrian
Quantum theory	1900	Planck	German
Quasars	1963	Matthews, Sandage	U.S.
Quinine synthetic	1946	Woodward, Doering	U.S.
Radioactivity	1896	Becquerel	French
Radiocarbon dating	1947	Libby	U.S.
Radium	1898	Curie, Pierre	French
		Curie, Marie	Pol.-Fr.
Relativity theory	1905	Einstein	German
Reserpine	1949	Jal Vaikl	Indian
Schick test	1913	Schick	U.S.
Silicon	1823	Berzelius	Swedish
Smallpox eradication	1979	World Health Organization	UN
Streptomycin	1945	Schatz, Waksman	U.S.
Sulfanilamide	1935	Bovet, Trefouel	French
Sulfanilamide theory	1908	Gelmo	German
Sulfapyridine	1938	Ewins, Phelps	English
Sulfathiazole	1939	Fosbinder, Walter	U.S.
Sulfuric acid	1831	Phillips	English
Sulfuric acid, lead	1746	Roebuck	English
Syphilis test	1906	Wassermann	German
Thiacetazone	1950	Belmisch, Mietzsch, Domagk	German
Tuberculin	1890	Koch	German
Uranium fission theory	1939	Hahn, Meitner, Strassmann	German
		Bohr	Danish
		Fermi	Italian
		Einstein, Pegram, Wheeler	U.S.
Uranium fission, atomic reactor	1942	Fermi, Szilard	U.S.
Vaccine, measles	1954	Enders, Peebles	U.S.
Vaccine, meningitis (first conjugate)	1987	Gordon, et. al., Connaught Lab.	U.S.
Vaccine, polio	1955	Salk	U.S.
Vaccine, polio, oral	1955	Sabin	U.S.
Vaccine, rabies	1885	Pasteur	French
Vaccine, smallpox	1796	Jenner	English
Vaccine, typhus	1909	Nicolle	French
Vaccine, varicella	1974	Takahashi	Japan
Van Allen belts, radiation	1958	Van Allen	U.S.
Vitamin A	1913	McCollum, Davis	U.S.
Vitamin B	1916	McCollum	U.S.
Vitamin C	1928	Szent-Gyorgyi, King	U.S.
Vitamin D	1922	McCollum	U.S.
Vitamin K	1935	Dam, Doisy	U.S.
Xerography	1938	Carlson	U.S.
X ray	1895	Roentgen	German

Top 20 Corporations Receiving U.S. Patents in 1996

Source: *Technology Assessment and Forecast Report,* U.S. Patent and Trademark Office, U.S. Department of Commerce

Rank	Company	Number of patents	Rank	Company	Number of patents
1.	International Business Machines Corp.	1,867	11.	General Electric Company	819
2.	Canon K. K.	1,541	12.	Eastman Kodak Company	768
3.	Motorola, Inc.	1,064	13.	Xerox Corp.	703
4.	NEC Corp.	1,043	14.	Texas Instruments, Inc.	600
5.	Hitachi, Ltd.	963	15.	Minnesota Mining & Manufacturing Co.	537
6.	Mitsubishi Denki K. K.	934	16.	AT&T Corp.	510
7.	Toshiba Corp.	914	16.	Fuji Photo Film Co., Ltd.	510
8.	Fujitsu, Ltd.	869	18.	Hewlett-Packard Company	501
9.	Sony Corp.	855	19.	Samsung Electronics Co., Ltd.	482
10.	Matsushita Electric Industrial Co., Ltd.	841	20.	U.S. Philips Corp.	477

Chemical Elements, Atomic Weights, Discoverers

Source: Glenn T. Seaborg, Ph.D., Ernest Orlando Lawrence Berkeley National Laboratory, Berkeley, CA

Atomic weights, based on the exact number 12 as the assigned atomic mass of the principal isotope of carbon, carbon 12, are provided through the courtesy of the International Union of Pure and Applied Chemistry and Butterworth Scientific Publications. For the radioactive elements, with the exception of uranium and thorium, the mass number of either the isotope of longest half-life (*) or the better known isotope (**) is given.

Chemical element	Symbol	Atomic number	Atomic weight	Year discov.	Discoverer
Actinium	Ac	89	227*	1899	Debierne
Aluminum	Al	13	26.9815	1825	Oersted
Americium	Am	95	243*	1944	Seaborg, et al.
Antimony	Sb	51	121.75	1450	Valentine
Argon	Ar	18	39.948	1894	Rayleigh, Ramsay
Arsenic	As	33	74.9216	13th c.	Albertus Magnus
Astatine	At	85	210*	1940	Corson, et al.
Barium	Ba	56	137.34	1808	Davy
Berkelium	Bk	97	249**	1949	Thompson, Ghiorso, Seaborg
Beryllium	Be	4	9.0122	1798	Vauquelin
Bismuth	Bi	83	208.980	15th c.	Valentine
Bohrium	Bh	107	262*	1981	Münzenberg, et al.
Boron	B	5	10.811[a]	1808	Gay-Lussac, Thenard
Bromine	Br	35	79.904[b]	1826	Balard
Cadmium	Cd	48	112.40	1817	Stromeyer
Calcium	Ca	20	40.08	1808	Davy
Californium	Cf	98	251*	1950	Thompson, et al.
Carbon	C	6	12.01115[a]	BC	unknown
Cerium	Ce	58	140.12	1803	Klaproth
Cesium	Cs	55	132.905	1860	Bunsen, Kirchhoff
Chlorine	Cl	17	35.453[b]	1774	Scheele
Chromium	Cr	24	51.996[b]	1797	Vauquelin
Cobalt	Co	27	58.9332	1735	Brandt
Copper	Cu	29	63.546[b]	BC	unknown
Curium	Cm	96	247*	1944	Seaborg, James, Ghiorso
Dubnium	Db	105	262*	1970	Ghiorso, et al.
Dysprosium	Dy	66	162.50*	1886	Boisbaudran
Einsteinium	Es	99	254**	1952	Ghiorso, et al.
Erbium	Er	68	167.26	1843	Mosander
Europium	Eu	63	151.96	1901	Demarcay
Fermium	Fm	100	257*	1953	Ghiorso, et al.
Fluorine	F	9	18.9984	1771	Scheele
Francium	Fr	87	223*	1939	Perey
Gadolinium	Gd	64	157.25	1886	Marignac
Gallium	Ga	31	69.72	1875	Boisbaudran
Germanium	Ge	32	72.59	1886	Winkler
Gold	Au	79	196.967	BC	unknown
Hafnium	Hf	72	178.49	1923	Coster, Hevesy
Hassium	Hs	108	269*	1984	Münzenberg, et al.
Helium	He	2	4.0026	1868	Janssen, Lockyer
Holmium	Ho	67	164.930	1878	Soret, Delafontaine
Hydrogen	H	1	1.00797[a]	1766	Cavendish
Indium	In	49	114.82	1863	Reich, Richter
Iodine	I	53	126.9044	1811	Courtois
Iridium	Ir	77	192.2	1804	Tennant

(continued)

Chemical Elements *(continued)*

Chemical element	Symbol	Atomic number	Atomic weight	Year discov.	Discoverer
Iron	Fe	26	55.847[b]	BC	unknown
Krypton	Kr	36	83.80	1898	Ramsay, Travers
Lanthanum	La	57	138.91	1839	Mosander
Lawrencium	Lr	103	262*	1961	Ghiorso, T. Sikkeland, A.E. Larsh, and R.M. Latimer
Lead	Pb	82	207.19	BC	unknown
Lithium	Li	3	6.939	1817	Arfvedson
Lutetium	Lu	71	174.97	1907	Welsbach, Urbain
Magnesium	Mg	12	24.312	1829	Bussy
Manganese	Mn	25	54.9380	1774	Gahn
Meitnerium	Mt	109	266*	1982	Münzenberg, et al.
Mendelevium	Md	101	258*	1955	Ghiorso, et al.
Mercury	Hg	80	200.59	BC	unknown
Molybdenum	Mo	42	95.94	1782	Hjelm
Neodymium	Nd	60	144.24	1885	Welsbach
Neon	Ne	10	20.183	1898	Ramsay, Travers
Neptunium	Np	93	237*	1940	McMillan, Abelson
Nickel	Ni	28	58.71	1751	Cronstedt
Niobium[1]	Nb	41	92.906	1801	Hatchett
Nitrogen	N	7	14.0067	1772	Rutherford
Nobelium	No	102	259*	1958	Ghiorso, et al.
Osmium	Os	76	190.2	1804	Tennant
Oxygen	O	8	15.9994[a]	1774	Priestley, Scheele
Palladium	Pd	46	106.4	1803	Wollaston
Phosphorus	P	15	30.9738	1669	Brand
Platinum	Pt	78	195.09	1735	Ulloa
Plutonium	Pu	94	242**	1940	Seaborg, et al.
Polonium	Po	84	210**	1898	P. and M. Curie
Potassium	K	19	39.102	1807	Davy
Praseodymium	Pr	59	140.907	1885	Welsbach
Promethium	Pm	61	147**	1945	Glendenin, Marinsky, Coryell
Protactinium	Pa	91	231*	1917	Hahn, Meitner
Radium	Ra	88	226*	1898	P. and M. Curie, Bemont
Radon	Rn	86	222*	1900	Dorn
Rhenium	Re	75	186.2	1925	Noddack, Tacke, Berg
Rhodium	Rh	45	102.905	1803	Wollaston
Rubidium	Rb	37	85.47	1861	Bunsen, Kirchhoff
Ruthenium	Ru	44	101.07	1845	Klaus
Rutherfordium	Rf	104	261*	1969	Ghiorso, et al.
Samarium	Sm	62	150.35	1879	Boisbaudran
Scandium	Sc	21	44.956	1879	Nilson
Seaborgium	Sg	106	266*	1974	Ghiorso, et al.
Selenium	Se	34	78.96	1817	Berzelius
Silicon	Si	14	28.086[a]	1823	Berzelius
Silver	Ag	47	107.868[b]	BC	unknown
Sodium	Na	11	22.9898	1807	Davy
Strontium	Sr	38	87.62	1790	Crawford
Sulfur	S	16	32.064[a]	BC	unknown
Tantalum	Ta	73	180.948	1802	Ekeberg
Technetium	Tc	43	99**	1937	Perrier and Segre
Tellurium	Te	52	127.60	1782	Von Reichenstein
Terbium	Tb	65	158.924	1843	Mosander
Thallium	Tl	81	204.37	1861	Crookes
Thorium	Th	90	232.038	1828	Berzelius
Thulium	Tm	69	168.934	1879	Cleve
Tin	Sn	50	118.69	BC	unknown
Titanium	Ti	22	47.90	1791	Gregor
Tungsten (Wolfram)	W	74	183.85	1783	d'Elhujar
Uranium	U	92	238.03	1789	Klaproth
Vanadium	V	23	50.942	1830	Sefstrom
Xenon	Xe	54	131.30	1898	Ramsay, Travers
Ytterbium	Yb	70	173.04	1878	Marignac
Yttrium	Y	39	88.905	1794	Gadolin
Zinc	Zn	30	65.37	BC	unknown
Zirconium	Zr	40	91.22	1789	Klaproth

Note: 109 elements are listed here. In addition, elements 110-112 were discovered recently at the Gesellschaft für Schwerionenforschung (GSI) at Darmstadt, Germany, by a team led by Dr. Sigurd Hofmann; these elements have not yet been named. Elements 110 and 111, discovered in 1994, have atomic weights 271 and 272, respectively; element 112, discovered in 1996, has atomic weight 277. (1) Formerly Columbium. (a) Atomic weights so designated are known to be variable because of natural variations in isotopic composition. The observed ranges are: hydrogen±0.0001; boron±0.003; carbon±0.005; oxygen±0.0001; silicon±0.001; sulfur±0.003. (b) Atomic weights so designated are believed to have the following experimental uncertainties: chlorine±0.001; chromium±0.001; iron±0.003; copper±0.001; bromine±0.001; silver±0.001.

COMPUTERS

The Internet

See also Glossary of Computer and Internet Terms, pages 647-49.

What Is the Internet?

The **Internet,** sometimes called the "information super-highway" is a vast computer network of computer networks. It is estimated that there are some 30 million Internet users in the United States and that, by the year 2000, half of all U.S. households will be online.

Some other facts about the Internet:

- The Internet is accessible in more than 100 countries, and there are more than 1 million Web servers worldwide.

- An average World Wide Web page contains about 500 words, and experts put the number of Web pages at somewhere between 30 million and 50 million.

- The average Web user is 35.2 years old and accesses the Web primarily from home.

The Internet is *not* owned or funded by any one institution, organization, or government. It does not have a CEO and is not a commercial service. The Internet is, however, directed by the Internet Society (ISOC), composed of volunteers. The ISOC appoints a subcouncil, the Internet Architecture Board (IAB), which works out issues of standards, network resources, network addresses, and so on. Another volunteer group, the Internet Engineering Task Force (IETF), handles day-to-day issues of Internet operation.

Practically speaking, the Internet is composed of people, hardware, and software. With the proper equipment on both ends, you can sit at your computer and communicate with someone any place in the world. You can also use the Internet to access vast amounts of information, including text, graphics, sound, and video. From your computer, you can send e-mail, "chat" with others on another continent, work with others on an electronic whiteboard, and, with the appropriate equipment, video-conference.

How Did It Originate?

The Internet grew out of a series of developments in the academic, governmental, and information technology communities. Listed below are some of the major milestones:

- In 1969, ARPAnet, an experimental 4-computer network, was established by the Advanced Research Projects Agency (ARPA) of the U.S. Department of Defense so that research scientists could communicate.

- By 1971, ARPAnet linked almost 2 dozen sites, including MIT and Harvard. By 1974, there were over 200 sites.

- During the 1980s, more and more computers using different operating systems were connected. In 1983, the military portion of ARPAnet was moved onto the MILnet, and ARPAnet was officially disbanded in 1990.

- In the late 1980s, the National Science Foundation's NSFnet began its own network and allowed everyone to access it. It was, however, primarily the domain of "techies," computer-science graduates, and university professors.

- In 1991, Al Gore, then a U.S. senator, proposed widening the NSFnet to include more schools and colleges. Resulting legislation expanded NSFnet, renamed it NREN (National Research and Educational Network), and allowed businesses to purchase part of the network for commercial uses. The mass commercialization of today's Internet is a result of this legislation.

- In 1992, the World Wide Web system and software were released, and in 1993, the National Center for Supercomputing Applications released versions of Mosaic (first graphical Web browser) for Microsoft Windows, for Unix systems running the X Window System, and for the Apple Macintosh.

- In 1994, Netscape Communications released the Netscape Navigator browser, and in 1995, Microsoft released Internet Explorer. By mid-1997, these browsers were in head-to-head competition for a place on each Internet user's computer.

How Can You Get There?

First, you need the equipment. You can get basic Internet access with any computer that has a modem connected to a phone line. However, to take full advantage of all the Internet has to offer, you need either a Macintosh that has a 68040 or higher CPU or a PC that has an 80486 or higher CPU. With either system, you also need the following:

- At least 4 megabytes of RAM (8 is recommended)
- A 250-megabyte hard drive
- A 14.4-bps modem (28.8 or faster is even better)

An **Internet service provider** is a company that provides access to the Internet; some also provide content and e-mail. The best-known ISPs are the commercial online services such as America Online, CompuServe, Prodigy, and MSN (The Microsoft Network), but many national companies (for example, MCI and AT&T) and local and regional companies also provide Internet access. ISPs generally charge a monthly subscription rate. Some may charge additionally for connect time beyond that included in the monthly rate, but in 1997 it became increasingly common to charge a set monthly fee for unlimited access, including e-mail and access to a news server.

Internet Resources

What you can do on the Internet depends on which resource you access.

E-mail. Electronic mail is probably the most popular and widely used resource on the Internet. To use it you must know and accurately input the recipient's address. An e-mail address consists of a **username,** a **service,** and a **domain.** For example, in `Walmanac@aol.com` (The World Almanac's e-mail address), `Walmanac` is the username, `aol` is the service (in this case, America Online), and `com` the domain (in this case, a commercial organization). Domains are identified in the Domain Name Service, also known as the Domain Name System. A consortium between AT&T and Network Solutions, called InterNIC (Internet Network Information Center), manages the task of registering addresses, or domain names. In mid-1997 `com`, `org`, and `net` domain names cost $100 for 2 years (and $50 per year thereafter).

Domain names can be applied for online through `http://rs.internic.net` or by contacting Network Solutions, InterNIC Registration Services, 505 Huntmar Park Dr., Herndon, VA 20170.

Here are the most familiar domains:

Domain	What It Is
com	a commercial organization, business, or company
edu	an educational institution
gov	a nonmilitary government entity
int	an international organization
mil	a military organization
net	a network administration
org	some other organization

Outside the U.S., the final part of a domain name represents the name of the country where the site is located—for example, `jp` for Japan, `uk` for Great Britain, and `ru` for Russia.

FAQs. Frequently Asked Questions documents contain the answers to common Internet questions. Reading some of these documents should help Internet newcomers.

FTP. File Transfer Protocol is a method of transferring files on the Internet and a type of Internet site. Using FTP, you log on to a remote site, usually a server, view the available files, and copy them to your computer. The address for an FPT site begins with `ftp:`

Gopher. Developed at the University of Minnesota, home of the Golden Gophers, Gopher is a hierarchy of menus you can use to browse the Internet or search for a specific file. These menus are available on numerous Gopher servers on the Internet. Any Internet address that begins with gopher points to a location on a Gopher server.

Newsgroups. Newsgroups, a classic institution of the Internet, are found on the part of the Internet called Usenet. In a newsgroup, messages concerning a particular topic are posted in a public forum. You can simply read the postings, or you can post an article yourself.

The World Wide Web. The Web may be the most complete realization of the Internet to date. It was developed in the early 1990s at the European Center for Nuclear Research as an environment in which scientists in Geneva, Switzerland, could share information. It has evolved into a medium that consists of text, graphics, audio, animation, and video. The address of a **Web site** usually begins with http://www. The World Wide Web is a graphical environment that can be navigated through hyperlinks. From one site you click on hyperlinks to go to any number of related sites.

How the World Wide Web Works

The Internet involves 3 fundamental elements: server, client, and network. A **server** is a computer program that makes data available to other programs on the same or other computers—it "serves" them. A **client** is a computer that requests data from a server. A **network** is an interconnected system in which multiple computers can communicate. The communication may be via copper wire, coaxial cable, fiber-optic cable, satellite transmission, etc. The software by which you access Internet resources is the **browser.** When you go to a site on the World Wide Web, you access the site's files.

Here are the steps in opening and accessing a file:

- In the browser, specify the address, or **URL,** of the Web site.
- The browser sends your request to the Internet service provider's server.
- That server sends the request to the server at the specified URL.
- The file is sent to the Internet service provider's server, which sends the file back to the browser, which displays the file.

Safety and Security on the Internet

The Internet has no governing body through which laws and policies are enforced, and its original inhabitants were known for their opposition to censorship. When President Bill Clinton on Feb. 8, 1996, signed into law the Communications Decency Act (CDA), a broad coalition of free speech and computer industry groups immediately filed a lawsuit. Under the CDA, anyone who made "indecent" or "patently offensive" material available to a minor through an "interactive computer service" would be subject to a $250,000 fine and 2 years in jail. In June 1996, 3 federal district and appellate court judges blocked the bill, calling the restrictions a "profound and repugnant" violation of First Amendment rights and arguing that the Internet must have the broadest possible protection against government intrusion. In July 1997, the U.S. Supreme Court ruled 7-2 that the CDA was a violation of the First Amendment and thus unconstitutional.

The Supreme Court adopted the view of Internet advocates that there is no way to screen material from children without censoring the source of the material. Thus, the responsibility for safety and security on the Internet rests with those who use it. Common sense dictates some basic rules of conduct:

- If you encounter an area that you find offensive—for example, a newsgroup or a chat room—remove that area from your list of places to visit.
- If you feel someone is being threatening or dangerous, inform your Internet service provider, which can issue a warning or can even withdraw entirely the person's online privileges.
- Be conscious of your privacy needs, as you would in any other situation where you interact with strangers. Children, especially, should not give out their phone number, address, or other personal information.
- Be extremely careful about giving out credit card numbers. They will not be 100% secure.

The two major browsers, Netscape Navigator and Internet Explorer, both contain features that let you filter the content that can be viewed on your computer. Among other blocking devices are the following:

- Cyber Patrol (Microsystems Software, 800-828-2608), which lets parents select categories to block (pornography, etc.) and blocks transmission of personal data.
- CYBERsitter (Solid Oak Software, 800-388-2761), which lets you customize a list of sites and categories to block.
- Microsoft Plus! for Kids (Microsoft), which includes password-protected controls and other security features.
- Net Nanny (Net Nanny Ltd., 800-340-7177), which can log visited sites and shut down the computer if inappropriate sites are accessed.
- Rated-PG (PC DataPower, 800-404-9913), which allows parents to block Web sites and unapproved CD-ROMs and diskettes.
- SurfWatch (Spyglass, 800-458-6600), which screens Web sites, newsgroups, and other areas.

Netparents.org is an association devoted to providing information about such resources. Check out its Web site at http://www.netparents.org

Searching the Internet

A **search engine** is a special Web site you can use to locate Web sites based on specific keywords. Many of the newer search engines actively search the Web, checking that existing URLs in their giant databases still work and adding information about new sites. The programs that do this are called **Web crawlers,** spiders, or bots (short for robots). Some search engines store only the title and URL of sites; others index every word of a site's content. Some of the most popular are described below.

AltaVista, sponsored by Digital Equipment Corp., processes more than 2.5 million search requests every day. It has catalogued more than 15 billion words on some 30 million Web pages, as well as all 13,000 Usenet newsgroups. It collects Web pages at the rate of 2.5 million a day. Find AltaVista at http://www.altavista.digital.com

Excite lets you search more than 50 million Web pages, 140,000 Web site listings, and thousands of Usenet postings. You can search either by keyword or by concept. Find Excite at http://www.excite.com

HotBot features a menu-driven search engine. You can search by file type, date, geographic location and domain, and Web site, as well as by categories such as Dictionaries, Atlases, Web tools, etc. You can access HotBot at http://www.hotbot.com

InfoSeek is a full-text search system that calls itself the "Web's largest directory." You can use it to find e-mail addresses, street maps, and investing opportunities. Enter a word or a question, or choose from a category to search. Access InfoSeek at http://www2.infoseek.com

Lycos is a search service and more. Use it to find personal home pages, to locate the best Web sites in a particular country, and to track UPS packages. Find Lycos at http://www.lycos.com

Open Text Index is a very powerful, multilingual search engine with which you can do a weighted search and receive information ranked by relevancy. You can find Open Text at http://www.opentext.com

WebCrawler is also much more than a search service. In addition to searching the Web, you can get free e-mail and browse or submit free classified ads. Access WebCrawler at http://webcrawler.com

Yahoo is perhaps the best known and most often used of all the search services. In addition to the standard search options, it now includes Yellow Pages, maps, classified ads, and stock quotes, as well as sports scores. Find Yahoo at http://www.yahoo.com

Internet Lingo

The following abbreviations are commonly used in Internet documents and in e-mail.

BTW	By the way	**HHOS**	Ha, ha—only serious
F2F	Face to face, a personal meeting	**IMHO**	In my humble opinion
FCOL	For crying out loud	**IMO**	In my opinion
FWIW	For what it's worth	**LOL**	Laughing out loud
FYI	For your information	**OTOH**	On the other hand
GOK	God only knows	**ROFL** or **ROTFL**	Rolling on the floor laughing
HHOK	Ha, ha—only kidding	**TAFN**	That's all for now

Emoticons, or **smileys**, are a series of typed characters that, when turned sideways, resemble a face and express an emotion. Here are some smileys that are often encountered on the Internet.

:-)	Smile	:-(	Unhappy	=:o	Argh!
;-)	Wink	:-o	Shouting	{*}	A hug and a kiss
:-*	Kiss	:-b...	Drooling	:p	Raz

Internet Directory to Selected Sites

The e-mail and site addresses listed are but a small sampling of what is available on the Internet. For some other web sites, see the Where to Get Help directory in the Health chapter, the Directory of Sports Organizations, and chapters on U.S. cities and U.S. states. Sites or products are not endorsed by *The World Almanac*.

When you enter an address, you must type it exactly as written, including capital and lowercase letters, any nonalphanumeric characters, and spaces. You may be unable to connect to a site for the following reasons: (1) You have mistyped the address; (2) the site is busy; (3) as often happens, the site has moved or no longer exists.

Online Service Providers

America Online
http://www.aol.com
CompuServe
http://www.compuserve.com
The Microsoft Network
http://www.msn.com
Prodigy
http://www.prodigy.com
Internet Service Providers
http://thelist.internet.com

Introduction to the World Wide Web
The World Wide Web Consortium
http://www.w3.org
The World Wide Web Frequently Asked Questions List
http://www.boutell.com/faq

Security Information
The National Fraud Information Center
http://www.fraud.org
The Secure Electronic Transaction Standard (general
information about electronic commerce)
http://www.visa.com/cgi-bin/
vee/sf/standard.html?2+0

Directory Services
(Online directories that contain names, addresses,
phone numbers, and e-mail addresses)
Bigfoot (e-mail addresses and white page listings)
http://www.bigfoot.com
Four11, the Internet White Pages
http://www.four11.com
InfoSpace, the Ultimate Directory
http://www.infospace.com
People Search
http://www.yahoo.com/search/people
Switchboard, the People and Business Directory
http://www.switchboard.com
WhoWhere?
http://www.whowhere.com

Bookstores
Amazon.com Inc (a completely Web-based bookstore
that has a database of 1.1 million titles)
http://www.amazon.com
Barnes and Noble
http://www.barnesandnoble.com
Book Stacks Unlimited, Inc.
http://www.books.com/scripts/news.exe

Borders Books, Music, Cafe
http://www.borders.com
The Complete Guide to Online Bookstores
http://www.paperz.com/bookstores.html
Crown Books
http://crownbooks.com
Ingram Book Group
http://ingrambook.com

U.S. Government
To send e-mail to the president, the vice president, or the
first lady, use the following addresses:
president@whitehouse.gov
vice.president@whitehouse.gov
first.lady@whitehouse.gov

To take a virtual tour of the White House, connect to the
following site:
http://www.whitehouse.gov

The White House FAQ is at the following address:
http://www.whitehouse.gov/WH/html/faq.html

To access the complete text of the U.S. Constitution, go to:
http://www.house.gov/Constitution/
Constitution.html

For a complete list of links to all U.S. government servers
and an e-mail address for each one, go to:
http://www.sbaonline.sba.gov/world/
federal-servers.html

To get a complete listing of the e-mail addresses and Web
sites of members of Congress, connect to:
www.yahoo.com/Government/
Legislative_Branch/Congressional_E_Mail_
Addresses

U.S. House of Representatives
http://www.house.gov
U.S. Senate
http://www.senate.gov
U.S. Supreme Court
http://supct.law.cornell.edu/supct

Department of Agriculture
http://www.usda.gov
Department of Commerce
http://www.doc.gov
Department of Defense
http://www.dtic.dla.mil/defenselink

Department of Education
http://www.ed.gov
Department of Energy
http://www.doe.gov
Department of Health and Human Services
http://www.os.dhhs.gov
Department of Housing and Urban Development
http://www.hud.gov
Department of the Interior
http://www.doi.gov
Department of Justice
http://www.usdoj.gov
Department of Labor
http://www.dol.gov
Department of State
http://www.state.gov/html/
Department_of_State.html
Department of Transportation
http://www.dot.gov
Department of the Treasury
http://www.ustreas.gov
Department of Veterans Affairs
http://www.va.gov

Census Bureau
http://www.census.gov
Central Intelligence Agency
http://www.odci.gov/cia
Environmental Protection Agency
http://www.epa.gov
Federal Bureau of Investigation
http://www.fbi.gov
Federal Emergency Management Agency
http://www.fema.gov
Federal Trade Commisssion
http://www.ftc.gov
Library of Congress
http://www.loc.gov
NASA
http://www.nasa.gov
National Institutes of Health
http://www.nih.gov
National Weather Service
http://www.nws.noaa.gov
Postal Service
http://www.usps.gov
Social Security Administration
http://www.ssa.gov
THOMAS: Legislative Information
http://thomas.loc.gov

Economic Data

Bureau of Economic Analysis
http://www.bea.doc.gov
Bureau of Labor Statistics
http://www.bls.gov
Economics Statistics Briefing Room
http://www.whitehouse.gov/fsbr/
prices.html
Economy at a Glance
http://stats.bls.gov/eag.table.html
Government Information Sharing Project
http://govinfo.kerr.orst.edu
Office of Management and Budget
http://www.access.gpo.gov/omb/omb003.html
Statistical Abstract of the United States (a sampling
of selective data)
http://www.census.gov:80/stat_abstract
STAT-USA/Internet (a subscription-based government
service)
http://www.stat-usa.gov/stat-usa.html

Travel

Best Fares Magazine
http://www.bestfares.com
City.Net
http://www.city.net

Cruises of Value
http://cruisesofvalue.com
The Lonely Planet Guide
http://www.lonely planet.com/lp.htm
MapQuest
http://www.mapquest.com
National Geographic
http://www.nationalgeographic.com
The Virtual Tourist
http://www.vtourist.com

Sites for Kids

Little League Baseball
http://www.littleleague.org
Major League Baseball
http://www.majorleaguebaseball.com
National Basketball Association
http://www.nba.com
National Football League
http://www.nfl.com
National Hockey League
http://www.nhl.com
Major League Soccer
http://www.mlsnet.com
Rock and Roll Hall of Fame and Museum
http://www.rockhall.com
Special Olympics
http://www.specialolympics.org
SuperSite for Kids
http://www.bonus.com
Vividus
http://www.vividus.com
White House for Kids
http://www.whitehouse.gov/WH/kids/html/
home.html
Yahooligans (guide to homework help sites)
http://www.yahooligans.com

Resources for Families

Family.Com
http://www.family.com
Family Internet
http://www.familyinternet.com
Kidshop Online
http://www.kidshoponline.com
KidSource Online
http://www.kidsource.com
ParenthoodWeb
http://www.parenthoodweb.com
Parent Soup
http://www.parentsoup.com
ParentsPlace.com
http://parentsplace.com
ParentTime
http://parenttime.com
Screen It!
http://www.screenit.com

Reference

BookWire—The First Place to Look for Book Information
http://www.bookwire.com
Internet Search Tools, The Library of Congress
http://lcweb.loc.gov/global/search.html
Libweb—Library Servers via WWW
http://sunsite.berkeley.edu/Libweb
Liszt, the Mailing List Directory
http://www.liszt.com
On-line Dictionaries, A Web of
http://www.bucknell.edu/~rbeard/
diction.html
Reference Reviews Europe
http://www.library.upenn.edu/ifba
WWWebster Dictionary
http://www.m-w.com/mw
The WWW Virtual Library
http://celtic.stanford.edu/vlib/
overview.html

Glossary of Computer and Internet Terms

Source: *Microsoft Press® Computer Dictionary, Third Edition.* Copyright 1997 by Microsoft Press. Reproduced by permission of Microsoft Press.

application   A program designed to assist in the performance of a specific task, such as word processing, accounting, or inventory management.

Archie   An Internet utility for finding files in public archives obtainable by anonymous FTP. Archie is a shortened form of *archive. See* **FTP.**

artificial intelligence (AI)   The branch of computer science concerned with enabling computers to simulate such aspects of human intelligence as speech recognition, deduction, inference, creative response, and the ability to learn from experience.

ASCII   Pronounced "askee." An acronym for American Standard Code for Information Interchange, a coding scheme using 7 or 8 bits that assigns numeric values to up to 256 characters, including letters, numerals, punctuation marks, control characters, and other symbols.

backup (noun); back up (verb)   As a noun, a duplicate copy of a program, a disk, or data. As a verb, to make a duplicate copy of a program, a disk or data.

bandwidth   Data transfer capacity of a digital communications system.

baud rate   Speed at which a modem can transmit data.

BBS   An abbreviation for bulletin board system, a computer system equipped with one or more modems or other means of network access that serves as an information and message-passing center for remote users.

bit   Short for binary digit; the smallest unit of information handled by a computer. One bit expresses a 1 or a 0 in a binary numeral, or a true or a false logical condition, and is represented physically by an element such as a high or low voltage at one point in a circuit or a small spot on a disk magnetized one way or the other.

boot   The process of starting or resetting a computer.

broadband network   A local area network on which transmissions travel as radio-frequency signals over separate inbound and outbound channels. Stations on that network are connected by coaxial or fiber-optic cable which can carry data, voice, and video simultaneously.

browser   *See* **Web browser.**

bug   An error in coding or logic that causes a program to malfunction or to produce incorrect results. Also, a recurring physical problem that prevents a system or set of components from working together properly.

bulletin board system   *See* **BBS.**

byte   Short for binary term. A unit of data, today almost always consisting of 8 bits. A byte can represent a single character, such as a letter, a digit, or a punctuation mark.

CD-ROM   Acronym for compact disc read-only memory, a form of storage characterized by high capacity (roughly 650 megabytes) and the use of laser optics rather than magnetic means for reading data.

central processing unit (CPU)   The computational and control unit of a computer; the device that interprets and executes instructions.

chat   Real-time conversation via computer. Also, an Internet utility program that supports chat.

chip   *See* **integrated circuit.**

client   On a local area network, a computer that accesses shared network resources provided by another computer (called a server). *See also* **server.**

computer   Any machine that does three things: accepts structured input, processes it according to prescribed rules, and produces the results as output.

copy protection   A software "lock" placed on a computer program by its developer to prevent the product from being copied and distributed without authorization.

CPU   *See* **central processing unit.**

cracker   A person who overcomes the security measures of a computer system and gains unauthorized access. *See also* **hacker.**

crash   The failure of either a program or a disk drive. A program crash results in the loss of all unsaved data and can leave the operating system unstable enough to require restarting the computer.

cursor   A special on-screen indicator, such as a blinking underline or rectangle, that marks the place at which keystrokes will appear when typed.

cyberspace   The universe of environments, such as the Internet, in which persons interact by means of connected computers.

database   A file composed of records, each of which contains fields, together with a set of operations for searching, sorting, recombining, and other functions.

data compression   A means of reducing the space or bandwidth needed to store or transmit a block of data.

debug   To detect, locate, and correct logical or syntactical errors in a program or malfunctions in hardware.

desktop publishing   The use of a computer and specialized software to combine text and graphics to create a document that can be printed on either a laser printer or a typesetting machine.

dial-up access   Connection to a data communications network through the public switched telecommunication network.

directory service   A service on a network that returns mail addresses of other users or enables a user to locate hosts and services.

disk   A round, flat piece of flexible plastic (floppy disk) or inflexible metal (hard disk) coated with a magnetic material that can be electrically influenced to hold information recorded in digital (binary) format.

disk drive   An electromechanical device that reads from and writes to disks.

disk operating system   Abbreviated DOS. A generic term describing any operating system that is loaded from disk devices when the system is started or rebooted.

document   Any self-contained piece of work created with an application program and, if saved on disk, given a unique filename by which it can be retrieved.

DOS   *See* **disk operating system.**

download   In communications, to transfer a copy of a file from a remote computer to the requesting computer by means of a modem or network. *See also* **upload.**

FAQ   An abbreviation for Frequently Asked Questions, a document listing common questions and answers on a particular subject. FAQs are often posted on Internet newsgroups where new participants ask the same questions that regular readers have answered many times.

field   A location in a record in which a particular type of data is stored.

file   A complete, named collection of information, such as a program, a set of data used by a program, or a user-created document.

file server   A file-storage device on a local area network that is accessible to all users on the network. A file server not only stores files but manages them and maintains order as network users request files and make changes to them.

filename   The set of letters, numbers, and allowable symbols assigned to a file to distinguish it from other files.

firewall   A security system intended to protect an organization's network against external threats, such as hackers, from another network. *See also* **proxy server.**

flame   An abusive or personally insulting e-mail message or newsgroup posting.

format   In general, the structure or appearance of a unit of data. As a verb, to change the appearance of selected text or the contents of a selected cell in a spreadsheet.

forum   A medium provided by an online service or BBS for users to carry on written discussions of a topic by posting messages and replying to them.

FTP   An abbreviation for File Transfer Protocol, the protocol used for copying files to and from remote computer systems on a network using TCP/IP such as the Internet.

gigabyte   Abbreviated GB; 1024 megabytes. *See* **megabyte.**

Gopher   An Internet utility for finding textual information and presenting it to the user in the form of hierarchical menus, from which the user selects submenus or files that can be downloaded and displayed. Gopher is being superseded by the World Wide Web.

graphical user interface   Abbreviated GUI (pronounced "gooey"). A type of environment that represents programs, files, and options by means of icons, menus, and dialog boxes on the screen. The user can select and activate these options by pointing and clicking with a mouse or, often, with the keyboard. *See also* **icon.**

hacker   A computerphile—a person who is engrossed in computer technology and programming or who likes to examine the code of operating systems and other programs to see how they work. Also, a person who uses computer expertise for illicit ends, such as for gaining access to computer systems without permission and tampering with programs and data. *See also* **cracker.**

hard copy   Printed output on paper, film, or other permanent medium. *See* **soft copy.**

home page   A document intended to serve as a starting point in a hypertext system, especially the World Wide Web. Also, an entry page for a set of Web pages and other files in a Web site.

host   The main computer in a system of computers or terminals connected by communications links.

HTML   An abbreviation for HyperText Markup Language, the markup language used for documents on the Web.

HTTP   An abbreviation for HyperText Transfer Protocol, the client/server protocol used to access information on the Web.

hyperlink   A connection between an element in a hypertext document, such as a word, phrase, symbol, or image, and a different element in the document, another hypertext document, a file, or a script. The user activates the link by clicking on the linked element, which is usually highlighted in some way.

hypermedia   The integration of any combination of text, graphics, sound, and video into a primarily associative system of information storage and retrieval in which users jump from subject to related subject.

hypertext   Text linked together in a complex, nonsequential web of associations in which the user can browse through related topics.

icon   A small image displayed on the screen to represent an object that can be manipulated by the user.

import   To bring information from one system or program into another.

integrated circuit   Also called a chip. A device consisting of a number of connected circuit elements, such as transistors and resistors, fabricated on a single chip of silicon crystal or other semiconductor material.

interactive   Characterized by conversational exchange of input and output, as when a user enters a question or command the system immediately responds.

Internet   The worldwide collection of networks and gateways that use the TCP/IP suite of protocols to communicate with each other. At the heart of the Internet is a backbone of high-speed data communication lines between major nodes or host computers, consisting of thousands of commercial, government, educational, and other computer systems, that route data and messages.

intranet   A TCP/IP network designed for information processing within a company or organization. It usually employs Web pages for information dissemination and Internet applications, such as Web browsers.

IP address   Short for Internet Protocol address, a 32-bit (4-byte) binary number that uniquely identifies a host (computer) connected to the Internet to other Internet hosts, for the purposes of communication through the transfer of packets.

Java   An object-oriented programming language, developed by Sun Microsystems, Inc. Similar to C++, Java is smaller, more portable, and easier to use than C++ because there are fewer concepts to learn and it manages memory on its own. Java can be run on any platform.

kilobyte   Abbreviated K, KB, or Kbyte; 1,024 bytes.

kludge   Pronounced "klooj." A short-term or makeshift hardware construction. Also, a program characterized by a lack of design or forethought, as if written in a hurry to satisfy an immediate need. A kludge basically operates properly, but lacks elegance or logical efficiency.

LAN   Rhymes with "can." Acronym for local area network, a group of computers and other devices dispersed over a limited area and connected by a communications link that enables any device to interact with any other on the network.

laptop   A small, portable computer that runs on either batteries or AC power, designed for use during travel. Laptops have flat LCD or plasma screens and small keyboards. Some weigh as little as 5 pounds.

legacy system   A computer, software program, network, or other computer equipment that remains in use after a business or organization installs new systems.

link   *See* **hyperlink.**

logon   The process of identifying oneself to a computer after connecting to it over a communications line. Also called *login.*

lurk   To receive and read articles or messages in a newsgroup or other online conference without contributing anything to the ongoing conversation.

mailing list   A list of names and e-mail addresses that are grouped under a single name. When a user places the name of the mailing list in a mail client's To: field, the client automatically sends the same message to the machine where the mailing list resides, and that machine sends the message to all the addresses on the list.

mainframe computer   A high-level computer designed for the most intensive computational tasks.

megabyte   Abbreviated MB. Usually 1,048,576 bytes (2^{20}); sometimes interpreted as 1 million bytes.

memory   Circuitry that allows information to be stored and retrieved. In common usage it refers to the fast semiconductor storage (RAM) directly connected to the processor. *See also* **RAM.**

menu   A list of options from which a program user can make a selection in order to perform a desired action, such as choosing a command or applying a format.

microcomputer   A computer built around a single-chip microprocessor.

microprocessor   A central processing unit (CPU) on a single chip. *See also* **integrated circuit.**

minicomputer   A mid-level computer built to perform complex computations while dealing efficiently with a high level of input and output from users connected via terminals.

modem   A communications device that enables a computer to transmit information over a standard telephone line.

monitor   The device on which images generated by the computer's video adapter are displayed.

Mosaic   The first popular graphical World Wide Web browser; released on the Internet in early 1993.

motherboard   The main circuit board containing the primary components of a computer system.

mouse   A common pointing device. It has a flat-bottomed casing designed to be gripped by one hand; one or more buttons on the top; a multidirectional detection device (usually a ball) on the bottom; and a cable connecting the mouse to the computer. To select items or choose commands on the screen, the user presses one of the mouse's buttons, producing a "mouse click."

multitasking   A mode of operation offered by an operating system in which a computer works on more than one task at a time.

Net   Short for Internet.

netiquette   Short for network etiquette.

netizen A person who participates in online communication through the Internet and other networks, especially conference and chat services.

network A group of computers and associated devices that are connected by communications facilities.

newbie An inexperienced user on the Internet.

newsgroup A forum on the Internet for threaded discussions on a specified range of subjects. A newsgroup consists of articles and follow-up posts. *See* **posting, thread.**

online Activated and ready for operating; capable of communicating with or being controlled by a computer.

operating system The software that controls the allocation and usage of hardware resources such as memory, CPU time, disk space, and peripheral devices.

optical fiber A thin strand of transparent material used to carry optical signals.

optical scanner An input device that uses light-sensing equipment to scan paper or another medium, translating the pattern of light and dark or color into a digital signal that can be manipulated by either optical character recognition software or graphics software.

packet A unit of information transmitted as a whole from one device to another on a network.

password A unique string of characters that a user types in as an identification code.

PC Abbreviation for personal computer, a microcomputer that conforms to the standard developed by IBM for personal computers, which uses an Intel microprocessor (or one that is compatible).

Pentium A microprocessor introduced by Intel Corporation in March 1993 as the successor to the 80486.

peripheral A device, such as a disk drive, printer, modem, or joystick, that is connected to a computer and is controlled by the computer's microprocessor.

pixel Short for picture element; also called *pel*. One spot in a rectilinear grid of thousands of such spots that are individually "painted" to form an image produced on the screen by a computer or on paper by a printer.

post To submit an article in a newsgroup or other online conference. *See* **thread.**

printer A computer peripheral that puts text or a computer-generated image on paper or on another medium, such as a transparency.

program A sequence of instructions that can be executed by a computer.

protocol A set of rules or standards designed to enable computers to communicate with one another and to exchange information with as little error as possible.

proxy server A firewall component that manages Internet traffic to and from a local area network and can provide other features, such as document caching and access control.

push In networks and the Internet, to send data or a program from a server to a client at the instigation of the server.

RAM Pronounced "ram." An acronym for random access memory. Semiconductor-based memory that can be read and written by the CPU or other hardware devices.

search engine On the Internet, a program that searches for keywords in files and documents from the World Wide Web, newsgroups, Gopher menus, and FTP archives.

server On a local area network (LAN), a computer running administrative software that controls access to the network and its resources, such as printers and disk drives. On the Internet or other network, a computer or program that responds to commands from a client. *See* **client, LAN.**

shell account A computer service that permits a user to enter operating-system commands on the service provider's system through a command-line interface (usually one of the Unix shells) rather than to access the Internet through a graphical interface.

snail mail A phrase popular on the Internet for referring to mail services provided by the United States Postal Service and similar agencies in other countries.

soft copy The temporary images presented on a computer display screen. *See* **hard copy.**

software Computer programs; instructions that make hardware work.

spam An unsolicited e-mail message sent to many recipients at one time, or a news article posted simultaneously to many newsgroups. Electronic junk mail.

spreadsheet program An application commonly used for budgets, forecasting, and other finance-related tasks that organizes data values using cells, where the relationships between cells are defined by formulas.

supercomputer A large, extremely fast, and expensive computer used for complex or sophisticated calculations.

system administrator The person responsible for administering use of a multiuser computer system, communications system, or both.

TCP/IP An abbreviation for Transmission Control Protocol/Internet Protocol, a protocol developed by the Department of Defense for communications between computers. It has become the de facto standard for data transmission over networks, including the Internet.

telecommute To work in one location (often, at home) and communicate with a main office at a different location through a personal computer.

teleconferencing The use of audio, video, or computer equipment linked through a communications system to enable geographically separated individuals to participate in a meeting or discussion.

thread In electronic mail and Internet newsgroups, a series of messages and replies related to a specific topic.

Unix Pronounced "ewe-niks." A multiuser, multitasking operating system that was originally developed by Ken Thompson and Dennis Ritchie at AT&T Bell Laboratories in 1969 for use on minicomputers.

upload In communications, the process of transferring a copy of a file from a local computer to a remote computer by means of a modem or network.

URL An abbreviation for Uniform Resource Locator, an address for a resource on the Internet.

Usenet A worldwide network of Unix systems that has a decentralized administration and is used as a bulletin board system by special-interest discussion groups.

user interface The portion of a program with which a user interacts.

user-friendly Easy to learn and easy to use.

username The name by which a user is identified to a computer system or network.

virus An intrusive program that infects computer files by inserting in those files copies of itself.

Web *See* **World Wide Web.**

Web browser A client application that enables a user to view HTML documents, follow the hyperlinks among them, transfer files, and execute some programs.

webmaster The person or persons responsible for creating and maintaining a World Wide Web site.

Web site A group of related HTML documents and associated files, scripts, and databases that is served up by an HTTP server on the World Wide Web.

wide area network (WAN) A communications network that connects geographically separated areas.

window In applications and graphical interfaces, a portion of the screen that can contain its own document or message.

word processor A program for manipulating text-based documents; the electronic equivalent of paper, pen, typewriter, eraser, and, most likely, dictionary and thesaurus.

workstation A combination of input, output, and computing hardware used for work by an individual.

World Wide Web (WWW) The total set of interlinked hypertext documents residing on Web, or HTTP, servers all around the world.

WYSIWYG Pronounced "wizzywig." An acronym for "What you see is what you get." A display method that shows documents and graphics characters on the screen as they will appear when printed.

Yahoo The first major online Web-based directory and search engine for Internet resources.

Top-Selling Software, 1997

Source: PC Data, Reston, VA

(based on average U.S. sales, Jan.-June 1997)

CD-ROM, All Categories
1. Microsoft Windows 95 Upgrade, Microsoft
2. TurboTax Deluxe, Intuit
3. Diablo, CUC Software
4. Myst, Brøderbund
5. Quicken Deluxe, Intuit
6. Microsoft Flight Simulator, Microsoft
7. Command & Conquer Red Alert, Virgin
8. Microsoft Office Pro 97 Upgrade, Microsoft
9. Viruscan, McAfee
10. Print Shop Deluxe III, Brøderbund

Windows 95 Software
1. Microsoft Windows 95 Upgrade, Microsoft
2. Viruscan, McAfee
3. Diablo, CUC Software
4. Norton Antivirus, Symantec
5. Microsoft Flight Simulator, Microsoft
6. Command & Conquer Red Alert, Virgin
7. Microsoft Office Pro 97 Upgrade, Microsoft
8. Print Shop Deluxe III, Brøderbund
9. First Aid Deluxe 97, Cybermedia
10. NASCAR II, CUC Software

PC Games (MS-DOS/Windows/Win95)
1. Diablo, CUC Software
2. Myst, Brøderbund
3. Microsoft Flight Simulator, Microsoft
4. Command & Conquer Red Alert, Virgin
5. NASCAR II, CUC Software
6. X-Wing vs Tie Fighter, LucasArts
7. Monopoloy Game CD-ROM, Hasbro Interactive
8. Quake, GT Interactive
9. Barbie Fashion Designer, Mattel
10. Warcraft Battle Chest, CUC Software

Games (Macintosh)
1. Archives II: Star Wars Collection, LucasArts
2. Myst, Brøderbund
3. Command & Conquer, Virgin
4. Archives I, LucasArts
5. Links Pro, Access
6. Warcraft II, CUC Software
7. Mac Attack Pack, Aztech New Media
8. FA-18 Hornet, Graphic Simulations
9. Dark Forces, LucasArts
10. Mac Cube, Aztech New Media

Home Education (MS-DOS/Windows/Win95)
1. 101 Dalmatians Storybook, Disney
2. Jumpstart First Grade, CUC Software
3. Jumpstart Kindergarten, CUC Software
4. Mavis Beacon Teaches Typing, Mindscape
5. Toy Story Activity Center, Disney
6. Where In The World Is Carmen Sandiego?, Brøderbund
7. Math Blaster 1: In Search of Spot, CUC Software
8. Jumpstart Preschool, CUC Software
9. Jumpstart Toddlers, CUC Software
10. Toy Story Animated Storybook, Disney

Home Education (Macintosh)
1. Mavis Beacon Teaches Typing, Mindscape
2. Winnie The Pooh Animated Storybook, Disney
3. Lion King Activity Center, Disney
4. Aladdin Activity Center, Disney
5. Pocahontas Animated Storybook, Disney

6. A.D.A.M. Inside Story, Mindscape
7. Kids Mac Pack, Palladium Interactive
8. Treasure Mountain, Learning Co.
9. Guitar Method, Emedia
10. Correct Grammar, Learning Co.

Reference Software
1. Microsoft Encarta Encyclopedia Deluxe, Microsoft
2. Microsoft Encarta Encyclopedia, Microsoft
3. World Book Encyclopedia, IBM
4. 130 Million American Directory, American Business Info.
5. Compton's Interactive Encyclopedia 97, Learning Company

Personal Productivity (MS-DOS/Windows/Win95)
1. TurboTax, Intuit
2. TurboTax Deluxe, Intuit
3. Taxcut, Block Financial
4. Quicken, Intuit
5. Quicken Deluxe, Intuit
6. Print Shop Deluxe III, Brøderbund
7. Microsoft Greetings Workshop, Microsoft
8. Print Shop Ensemble III, Brøderbund
9. Microsoft Publisher, Microsoft
10. Printmaster Gold Publisher Suite, Mindscape

Personal Productivity (Macintosh)
1. Macintax Deluxe, Intuit
2. Quicken Deluxe, Intuit
3. Macintax Final, Intuit
4. Quicken, Intuit
5. State Macintax CA, Intuit

Business Software (MS-DOS/OS/2)
1. System Commander, V Communications
2. MS-DOS 6.x Upgrade, Microsoft
3. Art Explosion 40,000 Images, Nova Development
4. MBA Box Set, SofSource
5. Complete Red Hat Linux, Simon & Schuster
6. Viruscan, McAfee
7. Check It Diagnostic Kit, Touchstone
8. PC DOS 7.x, IBM
9. Project Manager Pro, Learning Company
10. Day-Timer Address Book, Day-Timer

Business Software (Windows/Win95/NT)
1. Microsoft Windows 95 Upgrade, Microsoft
2. Viruscan, McAfee
3. Norton Antivirus, Symantec
4. First Aid Deluxe 97, Cybermedia
5. Netscape Navigator Personal Edition 3.0, Netscape
6. Corel WordPerfect Suite Upgrade, Corel
7. CleanSweep III, Quarterdeck
8. Microsoft Plus, Microsoft
9. Norton Utilities, Symantec
10. First Aid 97, Cybermedia

Business Software (Macintosh)
1. System 7.x Upgrade, Apple
2. System 7.x, Apple
3. Adobe Photoshop Upgrade, Adobe
4. Norton Utilities, Symantec
5. Norton Utilities Upgrade, Symantec
6. Pagemaker Upgrade, Adobe
7. Symantec SAM, Symantec
8. Ram Doubler, Connectix
9. Spring Cleaning, Aladdin
10. Adobe Illustrator Upgrade, Adobe

U.S. Computer Sales and Ownership, 1984-97

Source: Electronic Industries Association, Arlington, VA

(U.S. sales through retail consumer channels)

Year	Unit sales to dealers (thousands)	Dollar sales to dealers (millions)	Percentage of house-holds with owners	Year	Unit sales to dealers (thousands)	Dollar sales to dealers (millions)	Percentage of house-holds with owners
1984	3,975	$ 2,385	13	1991	3,900	$ 4,287	25
1985	3,200	2,175	15	1992	4,875	6,825	27
1986	2,950	3,060	16	1993	5,850	8,190	30
1987	3,125	3,100	18	1994	6,725	10,088	33
1988	3,500	3,340	20	1995	8,400	12,600	37
1989	3,900	3,711	21	1996	9,400	15,040	40
1990	4,000	4,187	22	1997[1]	10,700	16,585	41[2]

(1) Estimated figures. Sales and households with owners estimated through the end of the calendar year. (2) As of June 1997, an estimated 23% of households had computers with CD-ROM drives, and 21% had modems.

RELIGIOUS INFORMATION
Membership of Religious Groups in the U.S.

Source: *1997 Yearbook of American & Canadian Churches,* © *National Council of the Churches of Christ in the USA;* World Almanac research

These membership figures generally are based on reports made by officials of each group, and not on any religious census. Figures from other sources may vary. Many groups keep careful records; others only estimate. Not all groups report annually. Christian church membership figures reported in this table are inclusive and refer to all "members," not simply full communicants or confirmed members. Definitions of "member," however, vary from one denomination to another. Only data reported within the past 10 years are included.

The number of houses of worship appears in parentheses. * Indicates that the group declines to make membership figures public. Groups reporting fewer than 5,000 members are not included; if membership numbers are not given, only those churches with 50 or more houses of worship are listed.

Religious Group	Members
Adventist churches:	
Advent Christian Ch. (317)	27,100
Ch. of God Gen. Conf. (Oregon, IL; Morrow, GA) (88).	5,040
Seventh-day Adventist Ch. (4,297)	790,731
American Rescue Workers (15)	**8,000**
Apostolic Christian Churches of America (80)	**11,450**
Baha'i Faith	**130,000[1]**
Baptist churches:	
American Baptist Assn. (1,705)	250,000
American Baptist Chs. in the U.S.A. (5,823)	1,517,400
Baptist Bible Fellowship Intl. (3,600)	1,500,000
Baptist General Conference (857)	135,008
Baptist Missionary Assn. of America (1,355)	231,191
Conservative Baptist Assn. of America (1,084)	200,000
Free Will Baptists, Natl. Assn. of (2,491)	213,716
General Assn. of General Baptists (876)	74,156
General Assn. of Regular Baptist Chs. (1,458)	136,380
Natl. Baptist Convention of America (2,500)	3,500,000
Natl. Baptist Convention, U.S.A. (33,000)	8,200,000
Natl. Missionary Baptist Convention of America (*)	2,500,000
North American Baptist Conference (263)	43,928
Progressive National Baptist Convention (2,000)	2,500,000
Separate Baptists in Christ (100)	8,000
Southern Baptist Convention (40,039)	15,663,296
Brethren in Christ Church (200)	**18,529**
Brethren (German Baptists):	
Brethren Ch. (Ashland, OH) (121)	13,578
Church of the Brethren (1,114)	143,121
Grace Brethren Chs.,Fellowship of (273)	39,511
Old German Baptist Brethren (57)	5,623
Buddhist Churches of America	**780,000[1]**
Christian Brethren (Plymouth Brethren) (1,150)	**98,000**
Christian Church (Disciples of Christ) (4,036)	**929,725**
Christian Churches and Churches of Christ (5,579)	**1,070,616**
Christian Congregation (1,431)	**113,259**
Christian and Missionary Alliance (1,957)	**307,366**
Christian Union, Churches of Christ in (240)	**10,400**
Church of Christ, Scientist (2,400)	*
Church of the United Brethren in Christ (234)	**24,095**
Churches of Christ (13,020)	**1,655,500**
Churches of God:	
Chs. of God, General Conference (349)	31,745
Ch. of God (Anderson, IN) (2,307)	224,061
Ch. of God (Seventh Day), Denver, CO (161)	6,000
Ch. of God by Faith (145)	8,235
Ch. of God, Mountain Assembly (118)	6,140
Church of the Living God (170)	**42,000**
Church of the Nazarene (5,135)	**601,900**
Community Churches, Intl. Council of (517)	**250,000**
Congregational Christian Chs., Nat'l Assoc. of (426)	**70,000**
Conservative Congregational Christian Conference (201)	**36,864**
Eastern Orthodox churches:	
American Carpatho-Russian Orthodox Greek Catholic Ch. (78)	12,541
Antiochian Orthodox Christian Archdiocese of North America (184)	300,000
Apostolic Catholic Assyrian Ch. of the East, N.A. Diocese (22)	120,000
Armenian Apostolic Ch. of America (28)	180,000
Armenian Church of Amer., Diocese of the (72)	414,000
Coptic Orthodox Ch. (85)	180,000
Greek Orthodox Archdiocese of North and South America (approx. 500)	*
Orthodox Ch. in America (600)	2,000,000
Romanian Orthodox Episcopate of America (37)	65,000
Russian Orthodox Ch. in U.S.A. Patriarchal Parishes (38)	9,780
Russian Orthodox Church Outside of Russia (147)	*
Serbian Orthodox Ch. in U.S.A. & Canada (68)	67,000
Syrian Orthodox Ch. of Antioch (17)	32,500
Ukrainian Orthodox Church of America (27)	5,000

Religious Group	Members
Episcopal Church (7,415)	**2,536,550**
Evangelical Church (132)	**12,444**
Evangelical Congregational Church (150)	**23,422**
Evangelical Covenant Church (*)	**91,458**
Evangelical Free Church of America (1,224)	**242,619**
Friends:	
Evangelical Friends Intl.-North American Region (92)	8,666
Friends General Conference (602)	31,415
Friends United Meeting (503)	43,680
Full Gospel Fellowship of Churches and Ministers Intl. (650)	**195,000**
General Church of the New Jerusalem (34)	**5,587**
Grace Gospel Fellowship (128)	**60,000**
Hindu	**910,000[1]**
Independent Fundamental Churches of America (670)	**69,857**
Islam	**5,100,000[1]**
Jehovah's Witnesses (10,541)	**966,243**
Jewish organizations:	
Union of American Hebrew Congregations (Reform) (876)	1,300,000[1]
Union of Orthodox Jewish Congregations of America (1,200)	1,000,000[1]
United Synagogues of Conservative Judaism, The (800)	2,000,000[1]
Latter-day Saints:	
The Ch. of Jesus Christ of Latter-day Saints (Mormon) (10,417)	4,711,500
Reorganized Ch. of Jesus Christ of Latter-day Saints (1,160)	177,779
Lutheran churches:	
Apostolic Lutheran Ch. of America (60)	7,700
Ch. of the Lutheran Brethren of America (118)	24,906
Ch. of the Lutheran Confession (70)	8,783
Evangelical Lutheran Ch. in America (10,955)	5,190,489
Evangelical Lutheran Synod (135)	22,371
Free Lutheran Congregations, Assn. of (230)	30,769
Latvian Evangelical Lutheran Church in America (57)	12,097
Lutheran Ch.—Missouri Synod (6,154)	2,594,555
Lutheran Chs., American Assn. of (91)	17,973
Wisconsin Evangelical Lutheran Synod (1,252)	412,478
Mennonite churches:	
Beachy Amish Mennonite Chs. (95)	6,968
Church of God in Christ (Mennonite) (96)	11,037
Hutterian Brethren (398)	41,600
Mennonite Brethren Chs., The Conf. of (147)	19,218
Mennonite Church (986)	90,812
Mennonite Ch., The General Conference (268)	35,852
Old Order Amish Ch. (898)	80,820
Methodist churches:	
African Methodist Episcopal Ch. (8,000)	3,500,000
African Methodist Episcopal Zion Ch. (3,098)	1,230,842
Evangelical Methodist Ch. (132)	8,500
Free Methodist Ch. of North America (1,068)	74,707
Primitive Methodist Ch., U.S.A. (78)	7,234
Southern Methodist Ch. (127)	7,669
United Methodist Ch. (36,361)	8,538,662
The Wesleyan Church (U.S.A.) (1,624)	115,867
Metropolitan Community Churches, Universal Fellowship of (291)	**30,000**
Missionary Church (315)	**29,542**
Moravian churches:	
Moravian Ch. in America, Northern Prov. (95)	27,656
Moravian Ch. in America, Southern Prov. (56)	21,513
Natl. Organization of the New Apostolic Ch. of North America (554)	**41,863**
Pentecostal churches:	
Apostolic Faith Mission Ch. of God (20)	11,450
Apostolic Overcoming Holy Church of God (162)	12,390
Assemblies of God (11,823)	2,387,982
Bible Church of Christ (6)	6,850

(continued)

Religious Group	Members	Religious Group	Members
Church of God (Cleveland, TN) (6,060)	753,230	Evangelical Presbyterian Ch. (177)	56,499
Church of God in Christ (15,300)	5,499,875	Korean Presbyterian Church in America (203)	26,988
Church of God of Prophecy (1,961)	72,859	Orthodox Presbyterian Ch. (189)	21,131
Elim Fellowship (170)	21,038	Presbyterian Ch. in America (1,299)	267,764
Intl. Ch. of the Foursquare Gospel (1,742)	227,307	Presbyterian Ch. (U.S.A.) (11,361)	3,669,489
Intl. Pentecostal Church of Christ (73)	5,411	Reformed Presbyterian Ch. of N. America (70)	5,657
Intl. Pentecostal Holiness Church (1,653)	157,163	**Reformed churches:**	
Open Bible Standard Chs. (361)	45,988	Christian Reformed Ch. in N. America (716)	206,789
Pentecostal Assemblies of the World (1,760)	1,000,000	Hungarian Reformed Ch. in America (27)	9,780
Pentecostal Church of God (1,224)	119,200	Protestant Reformed Churches in America (27)	6,318
Pentecostal Free Will Baptist Ch. (149)	12,640	Reformed Ch. in America (908)	306,312
United Pentecostal Ch. Intl. (3,790)	*	United Church of Christ (6,145)	1,472,213
Polish National Catholic Church (143)	**50,000**	**Reformed Episcopal Church (102)**	**6,084**
Presbyterian churches:		**Roman Catholic Church (19,726)**	**60,280,454**
Associate Reformed Presbyterian Ch.		**Salvation Army (1,264)**	**453,150**
(General Synod) (207)	38,996	**Unitarian Universalist Assn. of N. America (1,039)**	**209,129**
Cumberland Presbyterian Ch. (783)	87,896	**United Brethren in Christ (239)**	**24,671**

(1) Based on reliable estimates; figures from other sources may vary.

Headquarters of Selected Religious Groups in the U.S.

Source: *1997 Yearbook of American & Canadian Churches*, © *National Council of the Churches of Christ in the USA;* World Almanac research

Year organized in parentheses

African Methodist Episcopal Church, (1787), 1134 11th St. NW, Washington, DC 20001; Senior Bishop, Bishop John H. Adams

African Methodist Episcopal Zion Church (1796), PO Box 32843, Charlotte, NC 28232; Pres., Bishop Richard K. Thompson

American Baptist Churches in the U.S.A. (1907), PO Box 851, Valley Forge, PA 19482; Pres., G. Elaine Smith

American Rescue Workers (1890), 643 Elmira St., Williamsport, PA 17701; Commander-in-Chief & Pres., Gen. Claude S. Astin Jr., Rev.

Antiochian Orthodox Christian Archdiocese of North America (1895), 358 Mountain Rd., Englewood, NJ 07631; Primate, Metropolitan Philip Saliba

Armenian Apostolic Church of America (1887), **Eastern Prelacy**: 138 E. 39th St., New York, NY 10016; Prelate, Archbishop Mesrob Ashjian; **Western Prelacy**: 4401 Russel Ave, Los Angeles, CA 90027; Prelate, Very Rev. Moushegh Maedizossian

Assemblies of God (1914), 1445 Boonville Ave., Springfield, MO 65802; General Supt., Thomas E. Trask

Baha'l Faith, 536 Sheridan Rd., Wilmette, IL 60091

Baptist Convention, U.S.A., National 1700 Baptist World Center Dr., Nashville, TN 37207; Pres., Dr. Henry J. Lyons

Baptist Convention of America, Inc., National (1880), 777 S. R. L. Thornton Freeway, Ste. 205, Dallas, TX 75203; Pres., Dr. E. Edward Jones

Baptist Convention of America, Natl. Missionary (1988), 1404 E. Firestone, Los Angeles, CA 90001; Pres., Dr. W. T. Snead Sr.

Baptist Bible Fellowship Intl. (1950), Baptist Bible Fellowship Missions Bldg., 720 E. Kearney St., Springfield, MO 65803; Pres., Sam Davison

Baptist General Conference (1852), 2002 S. Arlington Heights Rd., Arlington Heights, IL 60005; Pres., Dr. Robert S. Ricker

Baptist Convention, Progressive Natl. (1961), 601 50th St., NE, Washington, DC 20019; Pres., Dr. Bennett W. Smith Sr.

Baptist Convention, Southern (1845), 901 Commerce St., Ste. 750, Nashville, TN 37203; Pres., Tom Elliff

Brethren in Christ Church (1778), PO Box 290, Grantham, PA 17027; Moderator, Rev. Harvey R. Sider

Buddhist Churches of America (1899), 1710 Octavia St., San Francisco, CA 94109

Christian Church (Disciples of Christ) (1809), 130 E. Washington St., PO Box 1986, Indianapolis, IN 46206; Gen. Minister and Pres., Richard L. Hamm

Christian Churches and Churches of Christ, 4210 Bridgetown Rd., Box 11326, Cincinnati, OH 45211

Christian Congregation, Inc. (1887), 804 W. Hemlock St., LaFollette, TN 37766; General Supt., Rev. Ora W. Eads, D.D.

Christian Methodist Episcopal Church (1870), 4466 Elvis Presley Blvd., Memphis, TN 38116; Executive Secretary, Dr. W. Clyde Williams

Christian and Missionary Alliance (1897), PO Box 35000, Colorado Springs, CO 80935; Pres., Rev. P. F. Bubna, DD

Christian Reformed Church in North America (1857), 2850 Kalamazoo Ave. SE, Grand Rapids, MI 49560; Gen. Secretary, Dr. David H. Engelhard

Church of the Brethren (1708) 1451 Dundee Ave., Elgin, IL; Moderator, David M. Wine

Church of Christ (1830), PO Box 472, Independence, MO 64051; Council of Apostles Sec., Apostle Smith N. Brickhouse

Church of Christ, Scientist (1879), 175 Huntington Ave., Boston, MA 01945; Pres., Juan Carlos Lavigne

Church of God (Anderson, IN) (1881), Box 2420, Anderson, IN 46018; General Sec., Edward L. Foggs

Church of God (Cleveland, TN) (1886), PO Box 2430, Cleveland, TN 37320; Gen. Overseer, Paul L. Walker

Church of God in Christ (1907), Mason Temple, 939 Mason St., Memphis, TN 38126; Presiding Bishop, Bishop Chandler D. Owens

Church of Jesus Christ (Bickertonites) (1862), 6th & Lincoln Sts., Monongahela, PA 15063; Pres., Dominic Thomas

The Church of Jesus Christ of Latter-day Saints (Mormon) (1830), 50 E. North Temple St., Salt Lake City, UT 84150; Pres., Gordon B. Hinckley

Church of the Nazarene (1907), 6401 The Paseo, Kansas City, MO 64131; General Sec., Jack Stone

Community Churches, International Council of (1950), 21116 Washington Pkwy., Frankfort, IL 60423; Pres., J. Ronald Miller

Conservative Judaism, United Synagogues of 155 5ths Ave., New York, NY 10010; Pres., Alan Tichnor

Coptic Orthodox Church, 427 West Side Ave., Jersey City, NJ 07304

Cumberland Presbyterian Church (1810), 1978 Union Ave., Memphis, TN 38104; Moderator, Rev. Merlyn Alexander

Episcopal Church (1789), 815 Second Ave., New York, NY 10017; Presiding Bishop, Most Rev. Edmond L. Browning

Evangelical Free Church of America (1884), 901 E. 78th St., Minneapolis, MN 55420; Pres., Rev. William Hamel

Evangelical Lutheran Church in America (1987), 8765 W. Higgins Rd., Chicago, IL 60631; Bishop, Rev. Dr. H. George Anderson

Fellowship of Grace Brethren Churches (1882), PO Box 386, Winona Lake, IN 46590; Moderator, Wayne Hannah

Free Methodist Church of North America (1860), World Ministries Center, 770 N. High School Rd., Indianapolis, IN 46214

Friends General Conference (1900), 1216 Arch St. 2B, Philadelphia, PA 19107; Gen. Sec., Bruce Birchard

Greek Orthodox Archdiocese of America (1864), 8-10 E. 79th St., New York, NY 10021; Primate of the Archdiocese of North and South America, Archbishop Spyridon

Hebrew Congregations, Union of American (Reform), 838 5th Ave., New York, NY; Pres., Rabbi Alexander M. Schindler

International Church of the Foursquare Gospel (1927), 1910 W. Sunset Blvd., Ste. 200, PO Box 26902, Los Angeles, CA 90026; Pres., Dr. John R. Holland

Islamic Associations in the U.S. and Canada, Federation of, 25351 Five Mile Rd., Redford Township, MI 48239; Sec., Nihad Hamed

Jehovah's Witnesses, 25 Columbia Heights, Brooklyn, NY 11201; Pres., Milton G. Henschel

Lutheran Church—Missouri Synod (1847), 1333 S. Kirkwood Rd., St. Louis, MO 63122; Pres., Dr. A. L. Barry

Mennonite Brethren Churches, General Conference of (1860), 4812 E. Butler Ave., Fresno CA 93727; Moderator, Ed Boschman

Mennonite Church (1893), 421 S. Second St., Ste. 600, Elkhart, IN 46516; Moderator, Owen E. Burkholder

Mennonite Church, The General Conference (1860), 722 Main, P.O. Box 347, Newton, KS 67114; Moderator, Darrell Fast

Moravian Church in America (1735), **Northern Prov.:** 1021 Center St., PO Box 1245, Bethlehem, PA 18016; Pres., Rev. Dr. Gordon L. Sommers; **Southern Prov.:** 459 S. Church St., Winston-Salem, NC 27101; Pres., Rev. Dr. Robert E. Sawyer; **Alaska Prov.:** PO Box 545, Bethel, AK 99559; Pres., Rev. Frank Chingliak

Orthodox Church in America (1794), PO Box 675, Syosset, NY 11791; Primate, Most Blessed Theodosius

Orthodox Jewish Congregations in America, Union of 333 7th Ave., New York, NY 10001; Exec.V.P., Rabbi Pinchas Stolper

Pentecostal Assemblies of the World (c 1900), 3939 Meadows Dr., Indianapolis, IN 46205; Presiding Bishop, Paul A. Bowers

Presbyterian Church in America (1973), 1852 Century Pl., Atlanta, GA 30345; Moderator, Rev. Charles E. McGowan

Presbyterian Church (USA), (1983), 100 Witherspoon St., Louisville, KY 40202; Moderator, John M. Buchanan

Reformed Church in America (1628), 475 Riverside Dr., New York, NY 10115; Pres., Anthony Vis

Restoration Church of Jesus Christ of Latter-day Saints (1830), 801 W. 23rd St., Independence, MO 64055; Pres. Marcus L. Juby

Roman Catholic Church (1634), National Conference of Catholic Bishops, 3211 Fourth St., Washington, DC 20017; Pres.,Anthony M. Pilla

Romanian Orthodox Episcopate of America (1929), PO Box 309, Grass Lake, MI 49240; Ruling Bishop, His Grace Bishop Nathaniel Popp

Salvation Army (1865), 615 Slaters Lane, Alexandria, VA 22313; National Comdr., Commissioner Robert A. Watson

Seventh-Day Adventist Ch. (1863), 12501 Old Columbia Pike, Silver Spring, MD 20904; Pres., Robert S. Folkenberg

Swedenborgian Church (1792), 48 Sargent St., Newton, MA 02158; Pres., Rev. Edwin G. Capon

Unitarian Universalist Association of North America (1793), 25 Beacon St., Boston, MA 02108

United Church of Christ (1957), 700 Prospect Ave., Cleveland, OH 44115; Pres., Rev. Paul H. Sherry

United Methodist Church (1968), PO Box 320, Nashville, TN 37202; Pres., Bishop Roy A. Sano

United Pentecostal Church Intl. (1925), 8855 Dunn Rd., Hazelwood, MO 63042; General Superintendent, The Rev. Nathaniel A. Urshan

Vedanta Societies (1893), 34 W. 71st St., New York, NY 10023

Volunteers of America (1896), 110 S. Union St., Alexandria, VA 22314; Chairperson,Jean Galloway

Wesleyan Church (1968), PO Box 50434, Indianapolis, IN 46250; General Supts., Dr. Earle L. Wilson; Dr. Lee H. Haines; Dr. Harry F. Wood

Membership of Religious Groups in Canada

Source: *1997 Yearbook of American and Canadian Churches*; World Almanac research

Figures are generally based on reports of all-inclusive number of "members" by officials of each group; some groups keep careful records, while others only estimate. Not all groups report annually.

The number of houses of worship appears in parentheses. * Indicates that the group declines to make membership figures public.

Groups reporting fewer than 5,000 members are not included; if membership numbers are not given, only those churches with 50 or more houses of worship are listed.

Religious Group	Members
Anglican Church of Canada (1,740)	780,897
Antiochian Orthodox Christian Archdiocese of North America (16)	50,000
Apostolic Church of Pentecost of Canada Inc. (160)	13,500
Armenian Holy Apostolic Church (Canadian Diocese) (10)	75,000
Associated Gospel Churches (126)	9,284
Baha'i Faith[1]	25,000
Baptist Conference, North American (122)	17,613
Baptist Convention of Ontario and Quebec (372)	44,713
Baptist General Conference of Canada (70)	6,066
Baptist Ministries, Canadian (1,150)	130,000
Baptist Union of Western Canada (161)	20,006
Christian and Missionary Alliance in Canada (376)	87,197
Christian Brethren (also known as Plymouth Brethren) (60)	*
Christian Churches and Churches of Christ in Canada (140)	7,500
Christian Reformed Church in North America (226)	83,054
Church of God (Cleveland, TN) (115)	8,908
Church of Jesus Christ of Latter-day Saints in Canada (391)	130,000
Church of the Nazarene (166)	11,725
Churches of Christ in Canada (145)	6,950
Estonian Evangelical Lutheran Church (12)	6,159
Evangelical Baptist Churches in Canada, Fellowship of (506)	*
Evangelical Free Church of Canada (137)	*
Evangelical Lutheran Church in Canada (650)	100,761
Evangelical Mennonite Conference of Canada (52)	6,758
Evangelical Missionary Church of Canada (145)	12,217
Free Methodist Church in Canada (146)	7,186
Hindu[1]	90,000
Islam[1]	120,000
Jehovah's Witnesses (1,366)	112,960
Jewish congregations[1] (250+)	350,000
Lutheran Church–Canada (329)	79,844
Mennonite Brethren Churches, Canadian Conference of (207)	30,281
Mennonite Church (115)	90,812
Mennonites in Canada, Conference of (223)	35,995
Old Order Amish Church (930)	*
Orthodox Church in America (Canada Section) (606)	1,000,000
Pentecostal Assemblies of Canada (1,100)	218,782
Pentecostal Assemblies of Newfoundland (157)	30,992
Presbyterian Church in Canada (1,004)	227,814
Reformed Church in Canada (41)	6,490
Reformed Churches, Canadian and American (46)	14,407
Reorganized Church of Jesus Christ of Latter Day Saints (75)	11,264
Roman Catholic Church in Canada (5,706)	12,498,605
Romanian Orthodox Episcopate of America (Jackson, MI) (13)	8,600
Salvation Army in Canada (370)	95,763
Seventh-day Adventist Church in Canada (331)	45,129
Southern Baptists, Canadian Convention of (134)	7,818
Ukrainian Orthodox Church of Canada (258)	120,000
United Baptist Convention of the Atlantic Provinces (546)	63,788
United Church of Canada (3,909)	1,867,500
United Pentecostal Church in Canada (196)	*
Wesleyan Church of Canada (82)	5,256

(1) Based on reliable estimates; figures from other sources may vary.

Headquarters of Selected Religious Groups in Canada

Source: *1997 Yearbook of American & Canadian Churches, © National Council of the Churches of Christ in the USA;* World Almanac research

(Year organized in parentheses)

Anglican Church of Canada (1700), Church House, 600 Jarvis St., Toronto, ON M4Y 2J6; Primate, Most Rev. Michael G. Peers

Bahá'í National Centre of Canada, 7200 Leslie St., Thornhill, ON L3T 6L8

Baptist Ministries, Canadian, 7185 Millcreek Dr., Mississauga, ON L5N 5R4; Pres., Dr. Bruce Milne

Buddhist Churches, 4860 Garry St., Richmond, BC V7E 2V2

Christian and Missionary Alliance in Canada (1887), #510-105 Gordon Baker Rd., North York, ON M2H 3P8; Pres., Dr. Arnold Cook

The Church of Jesus Christ of Latter-day Saints (Mormon) (1830), 50 E. North Temple St., Salt Lake City, UT 84150

Church of the Nazarene (1902), 20 Regan Rd. Unit 9, Brampton, ON L7A 1C3; Natl. Dir., Dr. William E. Stewart

Evangelical Baptist Churches in Canada, Fellowship of (1953), 679 Southgate Dr., Guelph, ON N1G 4S2; Pres., Rev. Terry D. Cuthbert

Evangelical Lutheran Church in Canada (1985), 1512 St. James St., Winnipeg, MB R3H OL2; Bishop, Rev. Telmor G. Sartison

Evangelical Missionary Church in Canada, #550 1212 31st Ave. NE, Calgary, AB T2E 7S8; Pres., Rev. David Crouse

Greek Orthodox Diocese of Toronto, 27 Teddington Park Ave., Toronto, ON M4N 2C4; Primate of the Archdiocese of North and South America, Archbishop Spyridon

Jehovah's Witnesses (1879), Canadian office: Box 4100, Halton Hills, ON L7G 4Y4; Pres., Milton Henschel

Jewish Congress, Canadian (1919), 1590 Ave. Docteur Penfield, Montreal, Que. H3G 1C5. Nat. Exec. Dir., Jack Silverstone. (Nonreligious umbrella organization of Jewish groups)

Lutheran Church—Canada (1959), 3074 Portage Ave., Winnipeg, MB R3K OY2; Pres., Ralph Mayan

Mennonite Church (1898), 421 S. Second St., Ste. 600, Elkhart, IN 46516; Mod., Owen E. Burkholder

Muslim Communities in Canada, Council of 1250 Ramsey View Ct., Ste. 504, Sudbury, ON P3E 2E7; Dir., Mir Iqbal Ali

North American Shi'a Muslim Communities Organization (NASIMCO), Super Center Postal Outlet, Box 76559, Markham, ON L3R ON5; Pres., Ahmad Bhalloo

Pentecostal Assemblies of Canada (1919), 6745 Century Ave., Mississauga, ON L5N 6P7; General Supt., Rev. William D. Morrow

Presbyterian Church (1925), 50 Wynford Dr., North York, ON M3C 1J7; Moderator, Tameko Nakamura Corbett

Roman Catholic Church, Canadian Conference of Catholic Bishops, 90 Parent Ave., Ottawa, ON K1N 7B1; Pres., Most Rev. Francis J. Spence

Salvation Army (1865), 2 Overlea Blvd., Toronto, ON M4H 1P4; Territorial Cmdr., Commissioner Donald O. Kerr

Seventh-Day Adventist Church, 1148 King St., Oshawa, ON L1H 1H8; Pres., Orville Parchment

Ukranian Orthodox Church (1918), Consistory of the Ukrainian Orthodox Church of Canada, 9 St. John's Ave., Winnipeg, MB R2W; Primate, Most Rev. Metropolitan Wasyly

United Brethren Church (1767) 302 Lake St., Huntington, IN 46750; Pres. Rev. Brian Magnus

United Church of Canada (1925), The United Church House, 3250 Bloor St. W., Etobicoke, ON M8X 2Y4; Moderator, Marion S. Best

Wesleyan Church (1889), The Wesleyan Church Intl. Center, PO Box 50434, Indianapolis, IN 46250-0434

Adherents of All Religions by Six Continental Areas, Mid-1996

Source: *1997 Encyclopædia Britannica Book of the Year*

	Africa	Asia	Europe	Latin America	Northern America	Oceania	World
Atheists	440,000	175,450,000	40,845,000	3,010,000	1,850,000	600,000	1,782,809,000
Baha'is	1,923,000	3,230,000	95,000	722,00	357,000	77,000	6,404,000
Buddhists	38,000	321,985,000	1,563,000	569,000	920,000	200,000	325,275,000
Chinese folk religionists	13,000	220,653,000	120,000	68,000	100,000	17,000	220,971,000
Christians	360,874,000	303,127,000	555,614,000	455,819,000	255,542,000	24,253,000	1,955,229,000
Roman Catholics	125,376,000	94,250,000	269,021,000	408,968,000	75,398,000	8,452,000	981,465,000
Protestants	114,726,000	45,326,000	79,534,000	34,816,000	121,361,000	8,257,000	404,020,000
Orthodox	25,215,000	13,970,000	171,665,000	460,000	6,390,000	650,000	218,350,000
Anglicans	27,200,000	650,000	28,357,000	1,089,000	6,300,000	5,540,000	69,136,000
Other Christians	68,357,000	148,931,000	7,037,000	10,486,000	46,093,000	1,354,000	282,258,000
Confucians	1,000	5,050,000	4,500	2,500	27,000	1,000	5,086,000
Ethnic religionists	70,250,000	30,350,000	1,150,000	1,042,000	45,000	108,000	102,945,000
Hindus	1,986,000	786,991,000	1,650,000	760,000	1,365,000	323,000	793,075,000
Jains	59,000	4,835,000	16,000	4,500	4,500	1,000	4,920,000
Jews	165,000	4,257,000	2,432,000	1,084,000	5,836,000	92,000	13,866,000
Mandeans	0	45,000	0	0	0	0	45,000
Muslims	308,660,000	778,362,000	32,032,000	1,356,000	5,530,000	385,000	1,126,325,000
New-Religionists	21,000	103,361,000	803,000	919,000	900,000	11,000	106,015,000
Nonreligious	3,567,000	752,759,000	90,389,500	16,053,000	21,315,000	2,845,000	886,928,500
Parsees	1,500	185,000	1,000	1,000	1,000	1,000	190,500
Sikhs	37,000	18,465,000	494,000	9,000	496,000	7,000	19,508,000
Shintoists	0	2,893,000	1,000	1,000	1,500	1,000	2,897,500
Spiritists	4,500	1,120,000	18,000	8,834,000	315,000	1,000	10,292,500
Other religionists	90,000	100,000	450,000	190,000	1,072,000	50,000	1,952,000
Non-Christians	387,256,000	3,210,091,000	172,678,000	34,625,000	40,135,000	4,720,000	3,848,891,000
Total Population	748,130,000	3,513,218,000	727,678,000	490,444,000	295,677,000	28,973,000	5,804,120,000

Continents. These follow current UN demographic practice, which divides the world into the 6 major areas shown above and 21 regions. "Asia" now includes the former USSR Central Asian republics. "Europe" extends eastward to Vladivostok, the Sea of Japan, and the Bering Strait.

Adherents. As defined and enumerated in *World Christian Encyclopedia* (1982), projected to mid-1996, adjusted for recent data.

Christians. Followers of Jesus Christ affiliated with churches (church members, including children: 1,782,809,000) plus persons professing in censuses or polls though not so affiliated.

Other Christians. Catholics (non-Roman), marginal Protestants, crypto-Christians, and adherents of African, Asian, black, and Latin-American indigenous churches.

Atheists. Persons professing atheism, skepticism, disbelief, or irreligion, including antireligious (opposed to all religion).

Buddhists. 56% Mahayana, 38% Theravada (Hinayana), 6% Tantrayana (Lamaism).

Chinese folk religionists. Followers of traditional Chinese religion (local deities, ancestor veneration, Confucian ethics, Taoism, universism, divination, some Buddhist elements).

Confucians. Non-Chinese followers of Confucius and Confucianism, mostly Koreans in Korea.

Hindus. 70% Vaishnavites, 25% Shaivites, 2% neo-Hindus and reform Hindus.

Jews. Adherents of Judaism. For detailed data on "core" Jewish population, see "World Jewish Populations" in the American Jewish Committee's *American Jewish Year Book.*

Muslims. 83% Sunni Muslims, 16% Shia Muslims (Shi'ites), 1% other schools.

New-Religionists. Followers of Asian 20th-cent. New Religions, New Religious movements, radical new crisis religions, and non-Christian syncretistic mass religions, all founded since 1800 and most since 1945.

Nonreligious. Persons professing no religion, nonbelievers, agnostics, freethinkers, dereligionized secularists indifferent to all religion.

Other religionists. Including 70 minor world religions and a large number of spiritist religions, New Age religions, quasi-religions, pseudo-religions, parareligions, religious or mystic systems, and religious and semireligious brotherhoods of numerous varieties.

Total Population. UN medium variant figures for mid-1996, as given in *World Population Prospects: The 1994 Revision* (1995).

Episcopal Church Liturgical Colors and Calendar

Source: The Episcopal Church Center, New York City

The liturgical colors in the Episcopla Church are as follows: **White**—from Christmas Day through the First Sunday after Epiphany; Maundy Thursday (as an alternative to crimson at the Eucharist); from the Vigil of Easter to the Day of Pentecost (Whitsunday); Trinity Sunday; Feasts of the Lord (except Holy Cross Day); the Confession of St. Peter; the Conversion of St. Paul; St. Joseph; St. Mary Magdalene; St. Mary the Virgin; St. Michael and All Angels; All Saints' Day; St. John the Evangelist; memorials of other saints who were not martyred; Independence Day and Thanksgiving Day; weddings and funerals. **Red**—the Day of Pentecost; Holy Cross Day; feasts of apostles and evangelists (except those listed above); feasts and memorials of martyrs (including Holy Innocents' Day). **Violet**—Advent and Lent. **Crimson** (dark red)—Holy Week. **Green**—the seasons after Epiphany and after Pentecost. **Black**—optional alternative for funerals. Alternative colors used in some churches: **Blue**—Advent; **Lenten White**—Ash Wednesday to Palm Sunday.

In the Episcopal Church the days of fasting are Ash Wednesday and Good Friday. Other days of special devotion (penitence) are the 40 days of Lent and all Fridays of the year, except those in Christmas and Easter seasons and any Feasts of the Lord that occur on a Friday or during Lent. Ember Days (optional) are days of prayer for the church's ministry. They fall on the Wednesday, Friday, and Saturday after the first Sunday in Lent, the Day of Pentecost, Holy Cross Day, and the Third Sunday of Advent. Rogation Days (also optional), the 3 days before Ascension Day, are days of prayer for God's blessing on the crops, on commerce and industry, and for conservation of the earth's resources.

Days, etc.	1997	1998	1999	2000	2001
Golden Number	3	4	5	6	7
Sunday Letter	E	D	C	b & a	g
Sundays after Epiphany	5	7	6	9	8
Ash Wednesday	Feb. 12	Feb. 25	Feb. 17	Mar. 8	Feb. 28
First Sunday in Lent	Feb. 16	Mar. 1	Feb. 21	Mar. 12	March 4
Passion/Palm Sunday	Mar. 23	Apr. 5	Mar. 28	Apr. 16	April 8
Good Friday	Mar. 28	Apr. 10	Apr. 2	Apr. 21	April 13
Easter Day	Mar. 30	Apr. 12	Apr. 4	Apr. 23	April 15
Ascension Day	May 8	May 21	May 13	June 1	May 24
The Day of Pentecost	May 18	May 31	May 23	June 11	June 3
Trinity Sunday	May 25	June 7	May 30	June 18	June 10
Numbered Proper of 2 Pentecost	#4	#6	#5	#7	#6
First Sunday of Advent	Nov. 30	Nov. 29	Nov. 28	Dec. 3	Dec. 2

Greek Orthodox Movable Ecclesiastical Dates, 1997-2001

This 5-year chart has the dates of feast days and fasting days, which are determined annually on the basis of the date of Holy Pascha (Easter). This ecclesiastical cycle begins with the first day of the Triodion and ends with the Sunday of All Saints, a total of 18 weeks.

	1997	1998	1999	2000	2001
Triodion begins	Feb. 16	Feb. 8	Jan. 31	Feb. 20	Feb. 4
Sat. of Souls	Mar. 1	Feb. 21	Feb. 13	Mar. 4	Feb. 17
Meat Fare	Mar. 2	Feb. 22	Feb. 14	Mar. 5	Feb. 18
2d Sat. of Souls	Mar. 8	Feb. 28	Feb. 20	Mar 11	Feb. 24
Lent Begins	Mar. 10	Mar. 2	Feb. 22	Mar. 13	Feb. 26
St. Theodore—3d Sat. of Souls	Mar. 15	Mar. 7	Feb. 27	Mar. 18	Mar. 3
Sunday of Orthodoxy	Mar. 16	Mar. 8	Feb. 28	Mar. 19	Mar. 4
Sat. of Lazarus	Apr. 19	Apr. 11	Apr. 3	Apr. 22	Apr. 7
Palm Sunday	Apr. 20	Apr. 12	Apr. 4	Apr. 23	Apr. 8
Holy (Good) Friday	Apr. 25	Apr. 17	Apr. 9	Apr. 28	Apr. 13
Western Easter	Mar. 30	Apr. 12	Apr. 4	Apr. 23	Apr. 15
Orthodox Easter	Apr. 27	Apr. 19	Apr. 11	Apr. 30	Apr. 15
Ascension	June 5	May 28	May 20	June 8	May 24
Sat. of Souls	June 14	June 6	May 29	June 17	June 2
Pentecost	June 15	June 7	May 30	June 18	June 3
All Saints	June 22	June 14	June 6	June 25	June 10

Important Islamic Dates, 1996-2001 (1417-21)

The Islamic calendar is a lunar reckoning from the year of the hijra, AD 622, when Muhammad moved from Mecca to Medina. It runs in cycles of 30 years, of which the 2d, 5th, 7th, 10th, 13th, 16th, 18th, 21st, 24th, 26th, and 29th are leap years; 1417 is the 7th year of the cycle. Common years have 354 days, leap years 355, the extra day being added to the last month, Dhû al-Hijjah. Except for this case, the 12 months beginning with Muharram have alternately 30 and 29 days.

Actual western-hemisphere moon sightings may occur a day later, but never earlier, than these dates reflect.

	1996-97 (1417)	1997-98 (1418)	1998-99 (1419)	1999-2000 (1420)	2000-01 (1421)
New Year's Day (Muharram 1)	May 18, 1996	May 8, 1997	Apr. 07, 1998	Apr. 17, 1999	Apr. 6, 2000
Ashura (Muharram 10)	May 27, 1996	May 17, 1997	May 6, 1998	Apr. 26, 1999	Apr 15, 2000
Mawlid (Rabi'l 12)	July 28, 1996	July 17, 1997	July 6, 1998	June 26, 1999	June 14, 2000
Ramadan 1	Jan. 10, 1997	Dec. 31, 1997	Dec. 20, 1998	Dec. 9, 1999	Nov. 27, 2000
Id al-Fitr (Shawwal 1)	Feb. 8, 1997	Jan. 29, 1998	Jan. 19, 1999	Jan. 8, 2000	Dec. 27, 2000
Id al-Adha (Dhû al-Hijjah 10)	Apr. 17, 1997	Apr. 7, 1998	Mar. 28, 1999	Mar. 16, 2000	Mar. 5, 2001

Jewish Holy Days, Festivals, and Fasts, 1997-2001

	1997 (5757-58)		1998 (5758-59)		1999 (5759-60)		2000 (5760-61)		2001 (5761-62)	
Tu B'Shvat	Jan. 23	Thu.	Feb. 11	Wed.	Feb. 1	Mon.	Jan. 22	Sat.	Feb. 8	Thu.
Ta'anis Esther (Fast of Esther) . . .	Mar. 20	Thu.*	Mar. 11	Wed.	Mar. 1	Mon.	Mar. 20	Mon.	March 8	Thu.
Purim	Mar. 23	Sun.	Mar. 12	Thu.	Mar. 2	Tue.	Mar. 21	Tue.	March 9	Fri.
Pesach (Passover)	Apr. 22	Tue.	Apr. 11	Sat.	Apr. 1	Thu.	Apr. 20	Thu.	April 8	Sun.
	Apr. 29	Tue.	Apr. 18	Sat.	Apr. 8	Thu.	Apr. 27	Thu.	April 15	Sun.
Lag B'Omer	May 25	Sun.	May 14	Thu.	May 4	Tue.	May 23	Tue.	May 11	Fri.
Shavuot (Pentecost)	June 11	Wed..	May 31	Sun.	May 21	Fri.	June 9	Fri.	May 28	Mon.
	June 12	Thu.	June 1	Mon.	May 22	Sat.	June 10	Sat.	May 29	Tue.
Fast of the 17th Day of Tammuz	July 22	Tue.	July 12	Sun.*	July 1	Thu.	July 20	Thu.	July 8	Sun.
Fast of the 9th Day of Av	Aug. 12	Tue.	Aug. 2	Sun.*	July 22	Thu.	Aug. 10	Thu.	July 29	Sun.
Rosh Hashanah (Jewish New Year)	Oct. 2	Thu.	Sept. 21	Mon.	Sept. 11	Sat.	Sept. 30	Sat.	Sept. 18	Tue.
	Oct. 3	Fri.	Sept. 22	Tue.	Sept. 12	Sun.	Oct. 1	Sun.	Sept. 19	Wed.
Fast of Gedalya	Oct. 5	Sun.*	Sept. 23	Wed.	Sept. 13	Mon.	Oct. 2	Mon.	Sept. 20	Thu.
Yom Kippur (Day of Atonement) . .	Oct. 11	Sat.	Sept. 30	Wed.	Sept. 20	Mon.	Oct. 9	Mon.	Sept. 27	Thu.
Sukkot	Oct. 16	Thu.	Oct. 5	Mon.	Sept. 25	Sat.	Oct. 14	Sat.	Oct. 2	Tue.
	Oct. 22	Wed.	Oct. 11	Sun.	Oct. 1	Fri.	Oct. 20	Fri.	Oct. 8	Mon.
Shmini Atzeret	Oct. 23	Thu.	Oct. 12	Mon.	Oct. 2	Sat.	Oct. 21	Sat.	Oct. 9	Tue.
	Oct. 24	Fri.	Oct. 13	Tue.	Oct. 3	Sun.	Oct. 22	Sun.	Oct. 10	Wed.
Hanukkah	Dec. 24	Wed.	Dec. 14	Mon.	Dec. 4	Sat.	Dec. 22	Fri.	Dec. 10	Mon.
	Dec. 31	Wed.	Dec. 21	Mon.	Dec. 11	Sat.	Dec. 29	Fri.	Dec. 17	Mon.
Fast of the 10th of Tevet	Jan. 8	Thu.	Dec. 29	Tue.	Dec. 19	Sun.	Jan. 5	Fri.	Dec. 25	Tue.

The months of the Jewish year are: 1) Tishri; 2) Cheshvan (also Marcheshvan); 3) Kislev; 4) Tebet (also Tebeth); 5) Shebat (also Shebhat); 6) Adar; 6a) Adar Sheni (II) added in leap years; 7) Nisan; 8) Iyar; 9) Sivan; 10) Tammuz; 11) Av (also Abh); 12) Elul. All Jewish holy days, etc., begin at sunset on the previous day. *Date changed to avoid Sabbath.

Ash Wednesday and Easter Sunday (Western churches)

Year	Ash Wed.	Easter Sunday	Year	Ash Wed.	Easter Sunday	Year	Ash Wed.	Easter Sunday	Year	Ash Wed.	Easter Sunday
1901 . . .	Feb. 20	Apr. 7	1951 . . .	Feb. 7	Mar. 25	2001 . . .	Feb. 28	Apr. 15	2051 . . .	Feb. 15	Apr. 2
1902 . . .	Feb. 12	Mar. 30	1952 . . .	Feb. 27	Apr. 13	2002 . . .	Feb. 13	Mar. 31	2052 . . .	Mar. 6	Apr. 21
1903 . . .	Feb. 25	Apr. 12	1953 . . .	Feb. 18	Apr. 5	2003 . . .	Mar. 5	Apr. 20	2053 . . .	Feb. 19	Apr. 6
1904 . . .	Feb. 17	Apr. 3	1954 . . .	Mar. 3	Apr. 18	2004 . . .	Feb. 25	Apr. 11	2054 . . .	Feb. 11	Mar. 29
1905 . . .	Mar. 8	Apr. 23	1955 . . .	Feb. 23	Apr. 10	2005 . . .	Feb. 9	Mar. 27	2055 . . .	Mar. 3	Apr. 18
1906 . . .	Feb. 28	Apr. 15	1956 . . .	Feb. 15	Apr. 1	2006 . . .	Mar. 1	Apr. 16	2056 . . .	Feb. 16	Apr. 2
1907 . . .	Feb. 13	Mar. 31	1957 . . .	Mar. 6	Apr. 21	2007 . . .	Feb. 21	Apr. 8	2057 . . .	Mar. 7	Apr. 22
1908 . . .	Mar. 4	Apr. 19	1958 . . .	Feb. 19	Apr. 6	2008 . . .	Feb. 6	Mar. 23	2058 . . .	Feb. 27	Apr. 14
1909 . . .	Feb. 24	Apr. 11	1959 . . .	Feb. 11	Mar. 29	2009 . . .	Feb. 25	Apr. 12	2059 . . .	Feb. 12	Mar. 30
1910 . . .	Feb. 9	Mar. 27	1960 . . .	Mar. 2	Apr. 17	2010 . . .	Feb. 17	Apr. 4	2060 . . .	Mar. 3	Apr. 18
1911 . . .	Mar. 1	Apr. 16	1961 . . .	Feb. 15	Apr. 2	2011 . . .	Mar. 9	Apr. 24	2061 . . .	Feb. 23	Apr. 10
1912 . . .	Feb. 21	Apr. 7	1962 . . .	Mar. 7	Apr. 22	2012 . . .	Feb. 22	Apr. 8	2062 . . .	Feb. 8	Mar. 26
1913 . . .	Feb. 5	Mar. 23	1963 . . .	Feb. 27	Apr. 14	2013 . . .	Feb. 13	Mar. 31	2063 . . .	Feb. 28	Apr. 15
1914 . . .	Feb. 25	Apr. 12	1964 . . .	Feb. 12	Mar. 29	2014 . . .	Mar. 5	Apr. 20	2064 . . .	Feb. 20	Apr. 6
1915 . . .	Feb. 17	Apr. 4	1965 . . .	Mar. 3	Apr. 18	2015 . . .	Feb. 18	Apr. 5	2065 . . .	Feb. 11	Mar. 29
1916 . . .	Mar. 8	Apr. 23	1966 . . .	Feb. 23	Apr. 10	2016 . . .	Feb. 10	Mar. 27	2066 . . .	Feb. 24	Apr. 11
1917 . . .	Feb. 21	Apr. 8	1967 . . .	Feb. 8	Mar. 26	2017 . . .	Mar. 1	Apr. 16	2067 . . .	Feb. 16	Apr. 3
1918 . . .	Feb. 13	Mar. 31	1968 . . .	Feb. 28	Apr. 14	2018 . . .	Feb. 14	Apr. 1	2068 . . .	Mar. 7	Apr. 22
1919 . . .	Mar. 5	Apr. 20	1969 . . .	Feb. 19	Apr. 6	2019 . . .	Mar. 6	Apr. 21	2069 . . .	Feb. 27	Apr. 14
1920 . . .	Feb. 18	Apr. 4	1970 . . .	Feb. 11	Mar. 29	2020 . . .	Feb. 26	Apr. 12	2070 . . .	Feb. 12	Mar. 30
1921 . . .	Feb. 9	Mar. 27	1971 . . .	Feb. 24	Apr. 11	2021 . . .	Feb. 17	Apr. 4	2071 . . .	Mar. 4	Apr. 19
1922 . . .	Mar. 1	Apr. 16	1972 . . .	Feb. 16	Apr. 2	2022 . . .	Mar. 2	Apr. 17	2072 . . .	Feb. 24	Apr. 10
1923 . . .	Feb. 14	Apr. 1	1973 . . .	Mar. 7	Apr. 22	2023 . . .	Feb. 22	Apr. 9	2073 . . .	Feb. 8	Mar. 26
1924 . . .	Mar. 5	Apr. 20	1974 . . .	Feb. 27	Apr. 14	2024 . . .	Feb. 14	Mar. 31	2074 . . .	Feb. 28	Apr. 15
1925 . . .	Feb. 25	Apr. 12	1975 . . .	Feb. 12	Mar. 30	2025 . . .	Mar. 5	Apr. 20	2075 . . .	Feb. 20	Apr. 7
1926 . . .	Feb. 17	Apr. 4	1976 . . .	Mar. 3	Apr. 18	2026 . . .	Feb. 18	Apr. 5	2076 . . .	Mar. 4	Apr. 19
1927 . . .	Mar. 2	Apr. 17	1977 . . .	Feb. 23	Apr. 10	2027 . . .	Feb. 10	Mar. 28	2077 . . .	Feb. 24	Apr. 11
1928 . . .	Feb. 22	Apr. 8	1978 . . .	Feb. 8	Mar. 26	2028 . . .	Mar. 1	Apr. 16	2078 . . .	Feb. 16	Apr. 3
1929 . . .	Feb. 13	Mar. 31	1979 . . .	Feb. 28	Apr. 15	2029 . . .	Feb. 14	Apr. 1	2079 . . .	Mar. 8	Apr. 23
1930 . . .	Mar. 5	Apr. 20	1980 . . .	Feb. 20	Apr. 6	2030 . . .	Mar. 6	Apr. 21	2080 . . .	Feb. 21	Apr. 7
1931 . . .	Feb. 18	Apr. 5	1981 . . .	Mar. 4	Apr. 19	2031 . . .	Feb. 26	Apr. 13	2081 . . .	Feb. 12	Mar. 30
1932 . . .	Feb. 10	Mar. 27	1982 . . .	Feb. 24	Apr. 11	2032 . . .	Feb. 11	Mar. 28	2082 . . .	Mar. 4	Apr. 19
1933 . . .	Mar. 1	Apr. 16	1983 . . .	Feb. 16	Apr. 3	2033 . . .	Mar. 2	Apr. 17	2083 . . .	Feb. 17	Apr. 4
1934 . . .	Feb. 14	Apr. 1	1984 . . .	Mar. 7	Apr. 22	2034 . . .	Feb. 22	Apr. 9	2084 . . .	Feb. 9	Mar. 26
1935 . . .	Mar. 6	Apr. 21	1985 . . .	Feb. 20	Apr. 7	2035 . . .	Feb. 7	Mar. 25	2085 . . .	Feb. 28	Apr. 15
1936 . . .	Feb. 26	Apr. 12	1986 . . .	Feb. 12	Mar. 30	2036 . . .	Feb. 27	Apr. 13	2086 . . .	Feb. 13	Mar. 31
1937 . . .	Feb. 10	Mar. 28	1987 . . .	Mar. 4	Apr. 19	2037 . . .	Feb. 18	Apr. 5	2087 . . .	Mar. 5	Apr. 20
1938 . . .	Mar. 2	Apr. 17	1988 . . .	Feb. 17	Apr. 3	2038 . . .	Mar. 10	Apr. 25	2088 . . .	Feb. 25	Apr. 11
1939 . . .	Feb. 22	Apr. 9	1989 . . .	Feb. 8	Mar. 26	2039 . . .	Feb. 23	Apr. 10	2089 . . .	Feb. 16	Apr. 3
1940 . . .	Feb. 7	Mar. 24	1990 . . .	Feb. 28	Apr. 15	2040 . . .	Feb. 15	Apr. 1	2090 . . .	Mar. 1	Apr. 16
1941 . . .	Feb. 26	Apr. 13	1991 . . .	Feb. 13	Mar. 31	2041 . . .	Mar. 6	Apr. 21	2091 . . .	Feb. 21	Apr. 8
1942 . . .	Feb. 18	Apr. 5	1992 . . .	Mar. 4	Apr. 19	2042 . . .	Feb. 19	Apr. 6	2092 . . .	Feb. 13	Mar. 30
1943 . . .	Mar. 10	Apr. 25	1993 . . .	Feb. 24	Apr. 11	2043 . . .	Feb. 11	Mar. 29	2093 . . .	Feb. 25	Apr. 12
1944 . . .	Feb. 23	Apr. 9	1994 . . .	Feb. 16	Apr. 3	2044 . . .	Mar. 2	Apr. 17	2094 . . .	Feb. 17	Apr. 4
1945 . . .	Feb. 14	Apr. 1	1995 . . .	Mar. 1	Apr. 16	2045 . . .	Feb. 22	Apr. 9	2095 . . .	Mar. 9	Apr. 24
1946 . . .	Mar. 6	Apr. 21	1996 . . .	Feb. 21	Apr. 7	2046 . . .	Feb. 7	Mar. 25	2096 . . .	Feb. 29	Apr. 15
1947 . . .	Feb. 19	Apr. 6	1997 . . .	Feb. 12	Mar. 30	2047 . . .	Feb. 27	Apr. 14	2097 . . .	Feb. 13	Mar. 31
1948 . . .	Feb. 11	Mar. 28	1998 . . .	Feb. 25	Apr. 12	2048 . . .	Feb. 19	Apr. 5	2098 . . .	Mar. 5	Apr. 20
1949 . . .	Mar. 2	Apr. 17	1999 . . .	Feb. 17	Apr. 4	2049 . . .	Mar. 3	Apr. 18	2099 . . .	Feb. 25	Apr. 12
1950 . . .	Feb. 22	Apr. 9	2000 . . .	Mar. 8	Apr. 23	2050 . . .	Feb. 23	Apr. 10	2100 . . .	Feb. 10	Mar. 28

The Ten Commandments

According to Judeo-Christian tradition, as related in the Bible, the Ten Commandments were revealed by God to Moses and form the basic moral component of God's covenant with Israel. The Ten Commandments appear in 2 places in the Old Testament—Exodus 20:1-17 and Deuteronomy 5:6-21; the phrasing is similar but not identical.

Following is abridged text of the Ten Commandments in Exodus 20:1-17:

I. I am the Lord your God, who brought you out of the land of Egypt, out of the house of bondage. You shall have no other gods before me.

II. You shall not make for yourself a graven image. You shall not bow down to them or serve them.

III. You shall not take the name of the Lord your God in vain.

IV. Remember the sabbath day, to keep it holy.

V. Honor your father and your mother.

VI. You shall not kill.

VII. You shall not commit adultery.

VIII. You shall not steal.

IX. You shall not bear false witness against your neighbor.

X. You shall not covet.

Most Protestant, Anglican, and Orthodox Christians follow Jewish tradition, which considers the introduction ("I am the Lord...") the first commandment and makes the prohibition against idolatry the second. Roman Catholic and Lutheran traditions follow a division used by St. Augustine, which combines I and II and splits the last commandment into 2 that separately prohibit coveting of a neighbor's wife and a neighbor's goods. This arrangement alters the numbering of the other commandments by one.

Books of the Bible

Old Testament—Standard Protestant List

Genesis	II Chronicles	Daniel
Exodus	Ezra	Hosea
Leviticus	Nehemiah	Joel
Numbers	Esther	Amos
Deuteronomy	Job	Obadiah
Joshua	Psalms	Jonah
Judges	Proverbs	Micah
Ruth	Ecclesiastes	Nahum
I Samuel	Song of Solomon	Habakkuk
II Samuel	Isaiah	Zephaniah
I Kings	Jeremiah	Haggai
II Kings	Lamentations	Zechariah
I Chronicles	Ezekiel	Malachi

New Testament List

Matthew	Ephesians	Hebrews
Mark	Phillippians	James
Luke	Colossians	I Peter
John	I Thessalonians	II Peter
Acts	II Thessalonians	I John
Romans	I Timothy	II John
I Corinthians	II Timothy	III John
II Corinthians	Titus	Jude
Galatians	Philemon	Revelation

The standard Protestant Old Testament consists of the same 39 books as in the Bible of Judaism, but the latter is organized differently. The Old Testament used by Roman Catholics has 7 additional "deuterocanonical" books, plus some additional parts of books. The 7 are: **Tobit, Judith, Wisdom, Sirach (Ecclesiasticus), Baruch, I Maccabees,** and **II Maccabees.** Both Catholic and Protestant versions of the New Testament have 27 books, with the same names.

Roman Catholic Hierarchy

Source: U.S. Catholic Conference; as of mid-1997

Supreme Pontiff

At the head of the Roman Catholic Church is the supreme pontiff, Pope John Paul II, Karol Wojtyla, born at Wadowice (Kraków), Poland, May 18, 1920; ordained priest Nov. 1, 1946; appointed bishop July 4, 1958; promoted to archbishop of Kraków Jan. 13, 1964; proclaimed cardinal June 26, 1967; elected pope as successor of Pope John Paul I Oct. 16, 1978; installed as pope Oct. 22, 1978.

College of Cardinals

Members of the Sacred College of Cardinals are chosen by the pope to be his chief assistants and advisers in the administration of the church. Among their duties is the election of the pope when the Holy See becomes vacant.

In its present form, the College of Cardinals dates from the 12th century. The first cardinals, from about the 6th century, were deacons and priests of the leading churches of Rome and were bishops of neighboring dioceses. The title of cardinal was limited to members of the college in 1567. The number of cardinals was set at 70 in 1586 by Pope Sixtus V. From 1959 Pope John XXIII began to increase the number; however, the number of cardinals eligible to participate in papal elections was limited to 120. There were lay cardinals until 1918, when the Code of Canon Law specified that all cardinals must be priests. Pope John XXIII in 1962 established that all cardinals must be bishops. The first age limits were set in 1971 by Pope Paul VI, who decreed that at age 80 cardinals must retire from curial departments and offices and from participation in papal elections.

North American Cardinals

Name	Office	Born	Named Cardinal
Luis Apone Martinez	Archbishop of San Juan	1922	1973
William W. Baum	Major Penitentiary of Apostolic Penitentiary, the Vatican	1926	1976
Anthony J. Bevilacqua	Archbishop of Philadelphia	1923	1991
John J. Carberry[1]	Archbishop emeritus of St. Louis	1904	1969
G. Emmett Carter[1]	Archbishop emeritus of Toronto	1912	1979
Ernesto Corripio Ahumada	Archbishop emeritus of Mexico	1919	1979
Edouard Gagnon	Pres. of Pontifical Commission of Intl. Eucharistic Congresses	1918	1985
James A. Hickey	Archbishop of Washington, DC	1920	1988
William Henry Keeler	Archbishop of Baltimore	1931	1994
Bernard F. Law	Archbishop of Boston	1931	1985
Adam Joseph Maida	Archbishop of Detroit	1930	1994
Roger Mahony	Archbishop of Los Angeles	1936	1991
John J. O'Connor	Archbishop of New York	1920	1985
Juan Sandoval Iniquez	Archbishop of Guadalajara	1933	1994
Adolfo Antonio Suarez Rivera	Archbishop of Monterrey	1007	1994
Edmund C. Szoka	Pres. of Prefecture of Economic Affairs of Holy See, the Vatican	1927	1988
Jean-Claude Turcotte	Archbishop of Montreal	1936	1994
Louis-Albert Vachon[1]	Archbishop emeritus of Quebec	1912	1985

(1) Ineligible to take part in papal elections.

Chronological List of Popes

Source: Annuario Pontificio. Table lists year of accession of each pope.

The Roman Catholic Church names the Apostle Peter as founder of the church in Rome and the first pope. He arrived there c 42, was martyred there c 67, and was ultimately canonized as a saint.

The pope's temporal title is: Sovereign of the State of Vatican City. **The pope's spiritual titles are:** Bishop of Rome, Vicar of Jesus Christ, Successor of St. Peter, Prince of the Apostles, Supreme Pontiff of the Universal Church, Patriarch of the West, Primate of Italy, Archbishop and Metropolitan of the Roman Province.

The names of antipopes are in *italics*. Antipopes were illegitimate claimants of or pretenders to the papal throne.

Year	Pope	Year	Pope	Year	Pope	Year	Pope
	St. Peter	615	St. Deusdedit	974	Benedict VII	1305	Clement V
67	St. Linus		or Adeodatus	983	John XIV	1316	John XXII
76	St. Anacletus	619	Boniface V	985	John XV	*1328*	*Nicholas V*
	or Cletus	625	Honorius I	996	Gregory V	1334	Benedict XII
88	St. Clement I	640	Severinus	*997*	*John XVI*	1342	Clement VI
97	St. Evaristus	640	John IV	999	Sylvester II	1352	Innocent VI
105	St. Alexander I	642	Theodore I	1003	John XVII	1362	Bl. Urban V
115	St. Sixtus I	649	St. Martin I, Martyr	1004	John XVIII	1370	Gregory XI
125	St. Telesphorus	654	St. Eugene I	1009	Sergius IV	1378	Urban VI
136	St. Hyginus	657	St. Vitalian	1012	Benedict VIII	*1378*	*Clement VII*
140	St. Pius I	672	Adeodatus II	*1012*	*Gregory*	1389	Boniface IX
155	St. Anicetus	676	Donus	1024	John XIX	*1394*	*Benedict XIII*
166	St. Soter	678	St. Agatho	1032	Benedict IX	1404	Innocent VII
175	St. Eleutherius	682	St. Leo II	1045	Sylvester III	1406	Gregory XII
189	St. Victor I	684	St. Benedict II	1045	Benedict IX	*1409*	*Alexander V*
199	St. Zephyrinus	685	John V	1045	Gregory VI	*1410*	*John XXIII*
217	St. Callistus I	686	Conon	1046	Clement II	1417	Martin V
217	*St. Hippolytus*	*687*	*Theodore*	1047	Benedict IX	1431	Eugene IV
222	St. Urban I	*687*	*Paschal*	1048	Damasus II	*1439*	*Felix V*
230	St. Pontian	687	St. Sergius I	1049	St. Leo IX	1447	Nicholas V
235	St. Anterus	701	John VI	1055	Victor II	1455	Callistus III
236	St. Fabian	705	John VII	1057	Stephen IX (X)	1458	Pius II
251	St. Cornelius	708	Sisinnius	*1058*	*Benedict X*	1464	Paul II
251	*Novatian*	708	Constantine	1059	Nicholas II	1471	Sixtus IV
253	St. Lucius I	715	St. Gregory II	1061	Alexander II	1484	Innocent VIII
254	St. Stephen I	731	St. Gregory III	*1061*	*Honorius II*	1492	Alexander VI
257	St. Sixtus II	741	St. Zachary	1073	St. Gregory VII	1503	Pius III
259	St. Dionysius	752	Stephen II (III)	*1080*	*Clement III*	1503	Julius II
269	St. Felix I	757	St. Paul I	1086	Bl. Victor III	1513	Leo X
275	St. Eutychian	*767*	*Constantine*	1088	Bl. Urban II	1522	Adrian VI
283	St. Caius	*768*	*Philip*	1099	Paschal II	1523	Clement VII
296	St. Marcellinus	768	Stephen III (IV)	*1100*	*Theodoric*	1534	Paul III
308	St. Marcellus I	772	Adrian I	*1102*	*Albert*	1550	Julius III
309	St. Eusebius	795	St. Leo III	*1105*	*Sylvester IV*	1555	Marcellus II
311	St. Melchiades	816	Stephen IV (V)	1118	Gelasius II	1555	Paul IV
314	St. Sylvester I	817	St. Paschal I	*1118*	*Gregory VIII*	1559	Pius IV
336	St. Marcus	824	Eugene II	1119	Callistus II	1566	St. Pius V
337	St. Julius I	827	Valentine	1124	Honorius II	1572	Gregory XIII
352	Liberius	827	Gregory IV	*1124*	*Celestine II*	1585	Sixtus V
355	*Felix II*	*844*	*John*	1130	Innocent II	1590	Urban VII
366	St. Damasus I	844	Sergius II	*1130*	*Anacletus II*	1590	Gregory XIV
366	*Ursinus*	847	St. Leo IV	*1138*	*Victor IV*	1591	Innocent IX
384	St. Siricius	855	Benedict III	1143	Celestine II	1592	Clement VIII
399	St. Anastasius I	*855*	*Anastasius*	1144	Lucius II	1605	Leo XI
401	St. Innocent I	858	St. Nicholas I	1145	Bl. Eugene III	1605	Paul V
417	St. Zosimus	867	Adrian II	1153	Anastasius IV	1621	Gregory XV
418	St. Boniface I	872	John VIII	1154	Adrian IV	1623	Urban VIII
418	*Eulalius*	882	Marinus I	1159	Alexander III	1644	Innocent X
422	St. Celestine I	884	St. Adrian III	*1159*	*Victor IV*	1655	Alexander VII
432	St. Sixtus III	885	Stephen V (VI)	*1164*	*Paschal III*	1667	Clement IX
440	St. Leo I	891	Formosus	*1168*	*Callistus III*	1670	Clement X
461	St. Hilary	896	Boniface VI	*1179*	*Innocent III*	1676	Bl. Innocent XI
468	St. Simplicius	896	Stephen VI (VII)	1181	Lucius III	1689	Alexander VIII
483	St. Felix III (II)	897	Romanus	1185	Urban III	1691	Innocent XII
492	St. Gelasius I	897	Theodore II	1187	Gregory VIII	1700	Clement XI
496	Anastasius II	898	John IX	1187	Gregory VIII	1721	Innocent XIII
498	St. Symmachus	900	Benedict IV	1191	Celestine III	1724	Benedict XIII
498	*Lawrence*	903	Leo V	1198	Innocent III	1730	Clement XII
	(501-505)	*903*	*Christopher*	1216	Honorius III	1740	Benedict XIV
514	St. Hormisdas	904	Sergius III	1227	Gregory IX	1758	Clement XIII
523	St. John I, Martyr	911	Anastasius III	1241	Celestine IV	1769	Clement XIV
526	St. Felix IV (III)	913	Landus	1243	Innocent IV	1775	Pius VI
530	Boniface II	914	John X	1254	Alexander IV	1800	Pius VII
530	*Dioscorus*	928	Leo VI	1261	Urban IV	1823	Leo XII
533	John II	928	Stephen VII (VIII)	1265	Clement IV	1829	Pius VIII
535	St. Agapitus I	931	John XI	1271	Bl. Gregory X	1831	Gregory XVI
536	St. Silverius, Martyr	936	Leo VII	1276	Bl. Innocent V	1846	Pius IX
537	Vigilius	939	Stephen VIII (IX)	1276	Adrian V	1878	Leo XIII
556	Pelagius I	942	Marinus II	1276	John XXI	1903	St. Pius X
561	John III	946	Agapitus II	1277	Nicholas III	1914	Benedict XV
575	Benedict I	955	John XII	1281	Martin IV	1922	Pius XI
579	Pelagius II	963	Leo VIII	1285	Honorius IV	1939	Pius XII
590	St. Gregory I	964	Benedict V	1288	Nicholas IV	1958	John XXIII
604	Sabinian	965	John XIII	1294	St. Celestine V	1963	Paul VI
607	Boniface III	973	Benedict VI	1294	Boniface VIII	1978	John Paul I
608	St. Boniface IV	*974*	*Boniface VII*	1303	Bl. Benedict XI	1978	John Paul II

Major Non-Christian World Religions

Source: Reviewed by Anthony Padovano, PhD, STD; prof. of literature & relig. studies, Ramapo College, NJ; adj. prof. of theol., Fordham U., NYC, and (Islam) by Abdulaziz Sachedina, PhD, prof. of Islamic studies, Univ. of Virginia

Buddhism

Founded: About 525 BC, reportedly near Benares, India.

Founder: Gautama Siddhartha (c 563-483 BC), the Buddha, who achieved enlightenment through intense meditation.

Sacred Texts: The *Tripitaka*, a collection of the Buddha's teachings, rules of monastic life, and philosophical commentaries on the teachings; also a vast body of Buddhist teachings and commentaries, many of which are called *sutras.*

Organization: The basic institution is the *sangha*, or monastic order, through which the traditions are passed to from generation to generation. Monastic life tends to be democratic and anti-authoritarian. Large lay organizations have developed in some sects.

Practice: Varies widely according to the sect, and ranges from austere meditation to magical chanting and elaborate temple rites. Many practices, such as exorcism of devils, reflect pre-Buddhist beliefs.

Divisions: A variety of sects grouped into 3 primary branches: Theravada (sole survivor of the ancient Hinayana schools), which emphasizes the importance of pure thought and deed; Mahayana (includes Zen and Soka-gakkai), which ranges from philosophical schools to belief in the saving grace of higher beings or ritual practices and to practical meditative disciplines; and Tantrism, a combination of belief in ritual magic and sophisticated philosophy.

Location: Throughout Asia, from Sri Lanka to Japan. Zen and Soka-gakkai have several thousand adherents in the U.S.

Beliefs: Life is misery and decay, and there is no ultimate reality in it or behind it. The cycle of endless birth and rebirth continues because of desire and attachment to the unreal "self." Right meditation and deeds will end the cycle and achieve Nirvana, the Void, nothingness.

Hinduism

Founded: About 500 BC by Aryan invaders of India where their Vedic religion intermixed with the practices and beliefs of the natives.

Sacred texts: The *Veda,* including the *Upanishads,* a collection of rituals and mythological and philosophical commentaries; a vast number of epic stories about gods, heroes, and saints, including the *Bhagavadgita,* a part of the *Mahabharata,* and the *Ramayana;* and a great variety of other literature.

Organization: None, strictly speaking. Generally, rituals should be performed or assisted by Brahmins, the priestly caste, but in practice, simpler rituals can be performed by anyone. Brahmins are the final judges of ritual purity, the vital element in Hindu life. Temples and religious organizations are usually presided over by Brahmins.

Practice: A variety of private rituals, primarily passage rites (e.g., initiation, marriage, death, etc.) and daily devotions, and a similar variety of public rites in temples. Of the public rites, the *puja,* a ceremonial dinner for a god, is the most common.

Divisions: There is no concept of orthodoxy in Hinduism, which presents a variety of sects, most of them devoted to the worship of one of the many gods. The 3 major living traditions are those devoted to the gods Vishnu and Shiva and to the goddess Shakti; each is divided into further subsects. Numerous folk beliefs and practices, often in amalgamation with the above groups, exist side by side with sophisticated philosophical schools and exotic cults.

Location: Mainly India, Nepal, Malaysia, Guyana, Suriname, and Sri Lanka.

Beliefs: There is only one divine principle; the many gods are only aspects of that unity. Life in all its forms is an aspect of the divine, but it appears as a separation from the divine, a meaningless cycle of birth and rebirth (*samsara*) determined by the purity or impurity of past deeds (*karma*). To improve one's *karma* or escape *samsara* by pure acts, thought, and/or devotion is the aim of every Hindu.

Islam

Founded: About AD 622 in Mecca, Arabian Peninsula.

Founder: Muhammad (c 570-632), the Prophet.

Sacred texts: The *Koran* (al-Qur'an), the Word of God; *Sunna*, collections of *adth*, describing what Muhammad said or did.

Organization: Since the founder was both a prophet and a statesman, Muslim leadership has combined the civil and moral function of a state. Within the larger community, there are cultural and national groups, held together by a common religious law, the *Shari'a*, enforced uniformly in matters of religion only. In social transactions the community has often departed from traditional formulations. Although Islam is basically egalitarian and suspicious of authoritarianism, Muslim culture tends to be dominated by the conservative spirit of its religious establishment, the *ulema*.

Practice: Besides the general moral guidance that determines everyday life, there are "Five Pillars of Islam": profession of faith (oneness of God and prophethood of Muhammad); prayer 5 times a day; alms *(zakat)* from one's savings and estate; dawn-to-dusk fasting in the month of Ramadan; and once in a lifetime, pilgrimage to Mecca, if possible.

Divisions: There are 2 major groups: the majority known as Sunni and the minority Shiites. Shiites believe in Twelve Imams (perfect teachers) after the Prophet, of whom the last Imam has lived an invisible existence since 874, continuing to guide his community. Sunni Muslims believe in God's overpowering will over their affairs and tend to be predestinarian; Shiites believe in free will and give a substantial role to human reason in daily life. Sufism (mystical dimension of Islam) is prevalent among both Sunni and Shiites. Sufis emphasize personal relation to God and obedience informed by love of God.

Location: W Africa to Philippines, across band including E Africa, Central Asia and W China, India, Malaysia, Indonesia. Islam has several million adherents in North America.

Beliefs: Strictly monotheistic. God is creator of the universe, omnipotent, omniscient, just, forgiving, and merciful. The human is God's highest creation, but weak and egocentric, prone to forget the goal of life, constantly tempted by the Satan, an evil being. God revealed the Koran to Muhammad to guide humanity to truth and justice. Those who repent and sincerely "submit" (literal meaning of "islam") to God attain salvation. The forgiven enter the Paradise, and the wicked burn in Hell.

Judaism

Founded: About 1300 BC.

Founder: Abraham is regarded as the founding patriarch, but the Torah of Moses is the basic source of the teachings.

Sacred Texts: The 5 books of Moses constitute the written Torah. Special sanctity is also assigned other writings of the Hebrew Bible—the teachings of oral Torah are recorded in the Talmud, in the Midrash, and in various commentaries.

Organization: Originally theocratic, Judaism has evolved a congregational polity. The basic institution is the local synagogue, operated by the congregation and led by a rabbi of their choice. Chief rabbis in France and Great Britain have authority only over those who accept it; in Israel, the 2 chief rabbis have civil authority in family law.

Practice: Among traditional practicioners, almost all areas of life are governed by strict religious discipline. Sabbath and holidays are marked by special observances, and attendance at public worship is considered especially important then. Chief annual observances are Passover, celebrating liberation of the Israelites from Egypt and marked by the Seder meal in homes, and the 10 days from Rosh Hashana (New Year) to Yom Kippur (Day of Atonement), a period of fasting and penitence.

Divisions: Judaism is an unbroken spectrum from ultraconservative to ultraliberal, largely reflecting different points of view regarding the binding character of the prohibitions and duties—particularly the dietary and Sabbath observations—traditionally prescribed for the daily life of the Jew.

Location: Almost worldwide, with concentrations in Israel and the U.S.

Beliefs: Strictly monotheistic. God is the creator and absolute ruler of the universe. Men and women are free to choose to rebel against God's rule. God established a particular relationship with the Hebrew people: by obeying a divine law God gave them, they would be a special witness to God's mercy and justice. Judaism stresses ethical behavior (and, among the traditional, careful ritual obedience) as true worship of God.

Major Christian Denominations:

Italics indicate some features that tend to

Denomination	Origins	Organization	Authority	Special rites
Baptists	In radical Reformation, objections to infant baptism, demands for church and state separation; John Smyth, English Separatist, in 1609; Roger Williams, 1638, Providence, RI.	Congregational; each local church is autonomous.	Scripture; some Baptists, particularly in the South, interpret the Bible literally.	*Baptism, usually early teen years and after, by total immersion; Lord's Supper.*
Church of Christ (Disciples)	Among evangelical Presbyterians in KY (1804) and PA (1809), in distress over Protestant factionalism and decline of fervor; organized in 1832.	Congregational.	*"Where the Scriptures speak, we speak; where the Scriptures are silent, we are silent."*	Adult baptism; Lord's Supper (weekly).
Episcopalians	Henry VIII separated English Catholic Church from Rome, 1534, for political reasons; Protestant Episcopal Church in U.S. founded in 1789.	*Diocesan bishops, in apostolic succession, are elected by parish representatives; the national Church is headed by General Convention and Presiding Bishop; part of the Anglican Communion.*	Scripture as interpreted by tradition, especially *39 Articles*(1563); not dogmatic; tri-annual convention of bishops, priests, and laypeople.	Infant baptism, Eucharist, and other sacraments; sacrament taken to be symbolic, but as having real spiritual effect.
Jehovah's Witnesses	Founded 1870 in PA by Charles Taze Russell; incorporated as Watch Tower Bible and Tract Society of PA, 1884; name Jehovah's Witnesses adopted in 1931.	A governing body located in NY coordinates worldwide activities; each congregation cared for by a body of elders; each Witness considered a minister.	The Bible.	Baptism by immersion; annual Lord's Meal ceremony.
Latter-day Saints (Mormons)	In a vision of the Father and the Son reported by Joseph Smith (1820s) in NY. Smith also reported receiving new scripture on golden tablets: The Book of Mormon.	Theocratic; 1st Presidency (church president, 2 counselors), 12 Apostles preside over international church. Local congregations headed by lay priesthood leaders.	Revelation to living prophet (church president). The Bible, Book of Mormon, and other revelations to Smith and his successors.	Baptism, at age 8; laying on of hands (which confers the gift of the Holy Ghost); Lord's Supper; temple rites: baptism for the dead, marriage for eternity, others.
Lutherans	Begun by Martin Luther in Wittenberg, Germany in 1517; objection to Catholic doctrine of salvation and sale of indulgences; break complete, 1519.	Varies from congregational to episcopal; in U.S. a combination of regional synods and congregational polities is most common.	Scripture alone. The Book of Concord (1580), which includes the three Ecumenical Creeds, is subscribed to as a correct exposition of Scripture.	Infant baptism; Lord's Supper; Christ's true body and blood present "in, with, and under the bread and wine."
Methodists	Rev. John Wesley began movement in 1738, within Church of England; first U.S. denomination, Baltimore (1784).	Conference and superintendent system; *in United Methodist Church, general superintendents are bishops—not a priestly order, only an office—who are elected for life.*	Scripture as interpreted by tradition, reason, and experience.	Baptism of infants or adults; Lord's Supper commanded; other rites include marriage, ordination, solemnization of personal commitments.
Orthodox	Developed in original Christian proselytizing; broke with Rome in 1054, after centuries of doctrinal disputes and diverging traditions	Synods of bishops in autonomous, usually national, churches elect a patriarch, archbishop, or metropolitan; these men, as a group, are the heads of the church.	Scripture, tradition, and the first 7 church councils up to Nicaea II in 787; bishops in council have authority in doctrine and policy.	Seven sacraments: infant baptism and anointing, Eucharist, ordination, penance, and marriage.
Pentecostal	In Topeka, KS (1901) and Los Angeles (1906), in reaction to perceived loss of evangelical fervor among Methodists and others.	Originally a movement, not a formal organization, Pentecostalism now has a variety of organized forms and continues also as a movement.	Scripture; individual charismatic leaders, the teachings of the Holy Spirit.	*Spirit baptism, especially as shown in "speaking in tongues"; healing and sometimes exorcism; adult baptism; Lord's Supper.*
Presbyterians	In 16th-cent. Calvinist Reformation; differed with Lutherans over sacraments, church government; John Knox founded Scotch Presbyterian church about 1560.	*Highly structured representational system of ministers and laypersons (presbyters) in local, regional, and national bodies (synods).*	Scripture.	Infant baptism; Lord's Supper; bread and wine symbolize Christ's spiritual presence.
Roman Catholics	Traditionally, founded by Jesus who named St. Peter the 1st vicar; developed in early Christian proselytizing, especially after the conversion of imperial Rome in the 4th cent.	Hierarchy with supreme power vested in pope elected by cardinals; councils of bishops advise on matters of doctrine and policy.	*The pope, when speaking for the whole church in matters of faith and morals; and tradition (which is partly recorded in Scripture and expressed in church councils)*	Mass; 7 sacraments: baptism, reconciliation, Eucharist, confirmation, marriage, ordination, and anointing of the sick (unction).
United Church of Christ	*By ecumenical union, in 1957, of Congregationalists and Evangelical & Reformed, representing both Calvinist and Lutheran traditions.*	Congregational; a General Synod, representative of all congregations, sets general policy.	Scripture.	Infant baptism; Lord's Supper.

How Do They Differ?

distinguish a denomination sharply from others.

Practice	Ethics	Doctrine	Other	Denom ination
Worship style varies from staid to evangelistic; extensive missionary activity.	Usually opposed to alcohol and tobacco; some tendency toward a perfectionist ethical standard.	*No creed; true church is of believers only, who are all equal.*	Believing no authority can stand between the believer and God, the Baptists are strong supporters of church and state separation.	**Bap- tists**
Tries to avoid any rite not considered part of the 1st-century church; some congregations may reject instrumental music.	Some tendency toward perfectionism; increasing interest in social action programs.	Simple New Testament faith; avoids any elaboration not firmly based on Scripture.	Highly tolerant in doctrinal and religious matters; strongly supportive of scholarly education.	**Church of Christ (Dis- ciples)**
Formal, based on *Book of Common Prayer,* updated 1979; services range from austerely simple to highly liturgical.	Tolerant, sometimes permissive; some social action programs.	Scripture; the "historic creeds," which include the Apostles, Nicene, and Athanasian, and the *Book of Common Prayer*; ranges from Anglo-Catholic to low church, with Calvinist influences.	Strongly ecumenical, holding talks with many branches of Christendom.	**Episco- palians**
Meetings are held in Kingdom Halls and members' homes for study and worship; extensive door-to-door visitations.	High moral code; stress on marital fidelity and family values; avoidance of tobacco and blood transfusions.	*God, by his first creation, Christ, will soon destroy all wickedness; 144,000 faithful ones will rule in heaven with Christ over others on a paradise earth.*	Total allegiance proclaimed only to God's kingdom or heavenly govern- ment by Christ; politically neutral; main periodical, *The Watchtower* is printed in 115 languages.	**Jeho- vah's Wit- nesses**
Simple service with prayers, hymns, sermon; private temple ceremonies may be more elaborate.	Temperance; strict moral code; tithing; a strong work ethic with communal self- reliance; strong missionary activity; strong family emphasis.	Jesus Christ is the Son of God, the Eternal Father. Jesus' atonement saves all humans; those who are obedient to God's laws may become joint- heirs with Christ in God's kingdom.	Mormons believe theirs is the true church of Jesus Christ, restored by God through Joseph Smith. Official name: The Church of Jesus Christ of Latter-day Saints.	**Latter- day Saints (Mor- mons)**
Relatively simple, formal liturgy with emphasis on the sermon.	Generally conservative in personal and social ethics; doctrine of "2 kingdoms" (worldly and holy) supports conservatism in secular affairs.	Salvation by grace alone through faith; Lutheranism has made major contributions to Protestant theology.	Though still somewhat divided along ethnic lines (German, Swedish, etc.), main divisions are between fundamentalists and liberals.	**Luther- ans**
Worship style varies widely by denomination, local church, geography.	Originally pietist and perfectionist; always strong social activist elements.	No distinctive theological development; 25 Articles abridged from Church of England's 39, not binding.	In 1968, The United Methodist Church was formed by the union of The Methodist Church and The Evangelical United Brethren Church.	**Meth- odists**
Elaborate liturgy, usually in the vernacular, though extremely traditional; the liturgy is the essence of Orthodoxy; veneration of icons.	Tolerant; little stress on social action; divorce, remarriage permitted in some cases; bishops are celibate; priests need not be.	Emphasis on Christ's resurrection, rather than crucifixion; the Holy Spirit proceeds from God the Father only.	Orthodox Church in America originally under Patriarch of Moscow, was granted autonomy in 1970; Greek Orthodox do not recognize this autonomy.	**Ortho- dox**
Loosely structured service with rousing hymns and sermons, culminating in spirit baptism.	Usually, emphasis on per- fectionism with varying degrees of tolerance.	Simple traditional beliefs, usually Protestant, with emphasis on the immediate presence of God in the Holy Spirit.	Once confined to lower-class "holy rollers," Pentecostalism now appears in mainline churches and has established middle-class congregations.	**Pente- costal**
A simple, sober service in which the sermon is central.	Traditionally, a tendency toward strictness with firm church- and self-discipline; otherwise tolerant.	Emphasizes the sovereignty and justice of God; no longer dogmatic.	Although traces of belief in pre- destination (that God has fore- ordained salvation for the "elect") remain, this idea is no longer a central element in Presbyterianism.	**Presby- terians**
Relatively elaborate ritual centered on the Mass; also rosary recitation, novenas, etc.	Traditionally strict, but increasingly tolerant in practice; divorce and remarriage not accepted, but annulments sometimes granted; celibate clergy, except in Eastern rite.	Highly elaborated; salvation by merit gained through grace; dogmatic; special veneration of Mary, the mother of Jesus	Relatively rapid change followed Vatican Council II; Mass now in vernacular; more stress on social action, tolerance, ecumenism.	**Roman Catho- lics**
Usually simple services with emphasis on the sermon.	Tolerant; some social action emphasis.	Standard Protestant; *Statement of Faith* (1959) is not binding.	The 2 main churches in the 1957 union represented earlier unions with small groups of almost every Protestant denomination.	**United Church of Christ**

STATES AND OTHER AREAS OF THE U.S.

Sources: Population: Commerce Dept., Bureau of the Census (July 1996 est., including armed forces personnel in each state but excluding such personnel stationed overseas); area: Bureau of the Census, Geography Division; forested land: Agriculture Dept., Forest Service; lumber production: Bureau of the Census, Industry Division; mineral production: Dept. of Interior, Office of Mineral Information; commercial fishing: Commerce Dept., Natl. Marine Fisheries Service; value of construction: McGraw-Hill Information Systems Co., F.W. Dodge Division; personal per capita income: Commerce Dept., Bureau of Economic Analysis; unemployment: Labor Dept., Bureau of Labor Statistics; finance: Federal Deposit Insurance Corp.; federal employees: Labor Dept., Office of Personnel Management; energy: Energy Dept., Energy Information Administration; education: Education Dept., National Education Assn. Other information from sources in individual states, usually Commerce Dept.

Note: Categories under racial/ethnic distrib. do not necessarily converge or add to 100%. Famous Persons lists include nonnatives associated with the state as well as persons born there. Web site addresses listed (at the end of each state entry) may not be official state sites; all are subject to change.

Alabama

Heart of Dixie, Camellia State

People. Population (1996): 4,273,084; rank: 23; **Net change** (1990-96): 5.8%. **Pop. density:** (1990) 79.6 per sq mi. **Racial/ethnic distrib.** (1990): 73.6% white; 25.3% black; 0.6% Hispanic.

Geography. Total area: 52,423 sq mi; rank: 30. **Land area:** 50,750 sq mi; rank: 28. **Acres forested land:** 21,974,000. **Location:** East South Central state extending N-S from Tenn. to the Gulf of Mexico; east of the Mississippi River. **Climate:** long, hot summers; mild winters; generally abundant rainfall. **Topography:** coastal plains, including Prairie Black Belt, give way to hills, broken terrain; highest elevation, 2,407 ft. **Capital:** Montgomery.

Economy. Principal industries: pulp and paper, chemicals, electronics, apparel, textiles, primary metals, lumber and wood products, food processing, fabricated metals, automotive tires, oil and gas exploration. **Principal manufactured goods:** electronics, cast iron and plastic pipe, fabricated steel products, ships, paper products, chemicals, steel, mobile homes, fabrics, poultry processing, soft drinks, furniture, tires. **Chief crops:** cotton, greenhouse & nursery, peanuts, pecans, sweet potatoes, potatoes and other vegetables. **Livestock** (1997): 1.6 mil cattle; (1996) 200,000 hogs/pigs; 873 mil broilers; 10.6 mil hens and pullets. **Timber/lumber** (1996): pine, hardwoods; 2.5 bil bd. ft. **Nonfuel minerals** (est. 1996): $735 mil; crushed stone, portland cement, lime, sand & gravel. **Commercial fishing** (1996): $38 mil. **Chief port:** Mobile. **Value of construction** (1996): $4.8 bil. **Employment distribution** (1995): 21.7% mfg.; 22.8% trade; 21.9% serv; 19% govt. **Per capita personal income** (1996): $20,055. **Unemployment** (1996): 5.1%. **Tourism** (1991): $4.5 bil.

Finance. FDIC-insured commercial banks & trust companies (1996): 183. **Deposits:** $45.5 bil. **FDIC-insured savings institutions** (1996): 14. **Assets:** $2.0 bil.

Federal government. No. federal civilian employees (Mar. 1996): 39,459. **Avg. salary:** $41,623. **Notable federal facilities:** George C. Marshall NASA Space Center; Gunter Annex & Maxwell AFB; Ft. Rucker; Ft. McClellan; Natl. Fertilizer Development Center; Navy Station & U.S. Corps of Engineers; Redstone Arsenal.

Energy. Electricity production (1996, kWh, by source): Coal: 73.6 bil; Petroleum: 156 mil; Gas: 550 mil; Hydroelectric: 11.1 bil; Nuclear: 29.7 bil.

Public education. Student-teacher ratio (1995): 16.9. **Avg. teachers' salary** (1996-97): $32,549.

State data. Motto: We dare defend our rights. **Flower:** Camellia. **Bird:** Yellowhammer. **Tree:** Southern pine. **Song:** Alabama. **Entered union** Dec. 14, 1819; rank, 22d. **State fair:** Regional and county fairs held in Sept. and Oct.; no state fair.

History. Alabama was inhabited by the Creek, Cherokee, Chickasaw, Alabama, and Choctaw peoples when the Europeans arrived. The first Europeans were Spanish explorers in the early 1500s. The French made the first permanent settlement on Mobile Bay, 1702. France later gave up the entire region to England under the terms of the Treaty of Paris, 1763. Spanish forces took control of the Mobile Bay area, 1780, and it remained Spanish until U.S. troops seized the area, 1813. Most of present-day Alabama was held by the Creeks until Gen. Andrew Jackson broke their power, 1814, and they were removed to Oklahoma Territory. The state seceded, 1861, and the Confederate states were organized Feb. 4, at Montgomery, the first capital; it was readmitted 1868.

Tourist attractions. First White House of the Confederacy, Civil Rights Memorial, Alabama Shakespeare Festival, all Montgomery; Ivy Green, Helen Keller's birthplace, Tuscumbia; Civil Rights Museum, statue of Vulcan, Birmingham; Carver Museum, Tuskegee; W. C. Handy Home & Museum, Florence; Alabama Space and Rocket Center, Huntsville; Moundville State Monument, Moundville; Pike Pioneer Museum, Troy; USS *Alabama* Memorial Park, Mobile; Russell Cave Natl. Monument, near Bridgeport: a detailed record of occupancy by humans from about 10,000 BC to AD 1650.

Famous Alabamians. Hank Aaron, Tallulah Bankhead, Hugo L. Black, Paul "Bear" Bryant, George Washington Carver, Nat King Cole, William C. Handy, Bo Jackson, Helen Keller, Harper Lee, Joe Louis, Willie Mays, John Hunt Morgan, Jesse Owens, George Wallace, Booker T. Washington, Hank Williams.

Tourist information. Business Council of Alabama, PO Box 76, Montgomery, AL 36101.

Toll-free travel information. 1-800-ALABAMA out of state.

Web site. http://alaweb.asc.edu

Alaska

The Last Frontier (unofficial)

People. Population (1996): 607,007; rank: 48; **Net change** (1990-96): 10.4%. **Pop. density:** (1990) 1.0 per sq mi. **Racial/ethnic distrib.** (1990): 75.5% white; 4.1% black; 15.6% Amer. Indian, Eskimo or Aleut; 3.6% Asian or Pacific Is.; 3.2% Hispanic.

Geography. Total area: 656,424 sq mi; rank: 1. **Land area:** 570,374 sq mi; rank: 1. **Acres forested land:** 129,131,000. **Location:** NW corner of North America, bordered on east by Canada. **Climate:** SE, SW, and central regions, moist and mild; far north extremely dry. Extended summer days, winter nights, throughout. **Topography:** includes Pacific and Arctic mountain systems, central plateau, and Arctic slope. Mt. McKinley, 20,320 ft, is the highest point in North America. **Capital:** Juneau.

Economy. Principal industries: petroleum, tourism, fishing, mining, forestry, transportation, aerospace. **Principal manufactured goods:** fish products, lumber and pulp, furs. **Agriculture:** Chief crops: barley, oats, hay, silage, potatoes, lettuce. **Livestock** (1996): 10,200 cattle; (1995) 30,000 reindeer; 2,000 hogs. **Timber/lumber** (1996): spruce, yellow cedar, hemlock. **Nonfuel minerals** (est. 1996): $523 mil; zinc, gold, silver, tin, lead, sand & gravel, crushed stone. **Commercial fishing** (1996): $1.2 bil. **Chief ports:** Anchorage, Dutch Harbor, Kodiak, Seward, Skagway, Juneau, Sitka, Valdez, Wrangell. **International airports at:** Anchorage, Fairbanks, Juneau. **Value of construction** (1996): $1.0 bil. **Employment distribution** (1996): 27.7% govt.; 23.7% serv.; 20.7% trade. **Per capita personal income** (1996): $24,558. **Unemployment** (1996): 7.8%. **Tourism** (1994): $863 mil.

Finance. FDIC-insured commercial banks & trust companies (1996): 8. **Deposits:** $4.2 bil. **FDIC-insured savings institutions** (1996): 2. **Assets:** $243 mil.

Federal government. No. federal civilian employees (Mar. 1996): 11,611. **Avg. salary:** $41,541.

Energy. Electricity production (1996, kWh, by source): Coal: 229 mil; Petroleum: 1.5 bil; Gas: 2.9 bil; Hydroelectric: 1.2 bil.

Education. Pupil-teacher ratio (1995): 17.3. **Avg. teachers' salary** (1996-97): $50,647.

State data. Motto: North to the future. **Flower:** Forget-Me-Not. **Bird:** Willow ptarmigan. **Tree:** Sitka spruce. **Song:**

Alaska's Flag. **Entered union** Jan. 3, 1959; rank, 49th.
State fair at Palmer; late Aug.-early Sept.

History. Early inhabitants were the Tlingit-Haida people and tribes of the Athabascan family. The Aleut and Inuit (Eskimo), who arrived about 4,000 years ago from Siberia, lived in the coastal areas. Vitus Bering, a Danish explorer working for Russia, was the first European to land in Alaska, 1741. The first permanent Russian settlement was established on Kodiak Island, 1784. In 1799, the Russian-American Co. controlled the region, and the first chief manager, Aleksandr Baranov, set up headquarters at Archangel, near present-day Sitka. Sec. of State William H. Seward bought Alaska from Russia for $7.2 mil in 1867, a bargain some called "Seward's Folly." In 1896, gold was discovered in the Klondike region, and the famed gold rush began. Alaska became a territory in 1912.

Tourist attractions. Inside Passage; Portage Glacier; Mendenhall Glacier; Ketchikan Totems; Glacier Bay Natl. Park and Preserve; Denali Natl. Park, one of N. America's great wildlife sanctuaries, surrounding Mt. McKinley, N. America's highest peak; Mt. Roberts Tramway, Juneau; Pribilof Islands fur seal rookeries; restored St. Michael's Russian Orthodox Cathedral, Sitka; Katmai Natl. Park & Preserve.

Famous Alaskans. Tom Bodett, Susan Butcher, Ernest Gruening, Gov. Tony Knowles, Sydney Laurence, Libby Riddles, Jefferson "Soapy" Smith.

Tourist information. Alaska Division of Tourism, PO Box 110801, Juneau, AK 99811-0801; 1-907-465-2010.

Web site. http://www.state.ak.us

Arizona
Grand Canyon State

People. Population (1996): 4,428,068; rank: 21; **Net change** (1990-96): 20.8.1%. **Pop. density:** (1990) 32.3 per sq mi. **Racial/ethnic distrib.** (1990): 80.8% white; 3.0% black; 5.6% American Indian; 18.8% Hispanic.

Geography. Total area: 114,006 sq mi; rank: 6. **Land area:** 113,642 sq mi; rank: 6. **Acres forested land:** 19,596,000. **Location:** in the southwestern U.S. **Climate:** clear and dry in the southern regions and northern plateau; high central areas have heavy winter snows. **Topography:** Colorado plateau in the N, containing the Grand Canyon; Mexican Highlands running diagonally NW to SE; Sonoran Desert in the SW. **Capital:** Phoenix.

Economy. Principal industries: manufacturing, construction, tourism, mining, agriculture. **Principal manufactured goods:** electronics, printing and publishing, foods, primary and fabricated metals, aircraft and missiles, apparel. **Chief crops:** cotton, lettuce, cauliflower, broccoli, sorghum, barley, corn, wheat, citrus fruits. **Livestock** (1996): 790,000 cattle; 150,000 hogs/pigs; 125,000 sheep. **Timber/lumber** (1996): pine, fir, spruce; 121 mil bd. ft. **Nonfuel minerals** (est. 1996): $3.53 bil; copper, sand and gravel, cement, gold, molybdenum, silver, perlite. **International airports at:** Phoenix, Tucson, Yuma. **Value of construction** (1996): $9.8 bil. **Employment distribution** (1996): 29.6% services; 24.6% trade; 16.9% govt.; 10.5% mfg. **Per capita personal income** (1996): $20,989. **Unemployment** (1996): 5.5%. **Tourism** (1994): $10.5 bil.

Finance. FDIC-insured commercial banks & trust companies (1996): 35. **Deposits:** $28.2 bil. **FDIC-insured savings institutions** (1996): 2. **Assets:** $515 mil.

Federal government. No. federal civilian employees (Mar. 1996): 27,703. **Avg. salary:** $37,639. **Notable federal facilities:** Luke, Davis-Monthan AF bases; Ft. Huachuca Army Base; Yuma Proving Grounds.

Energy. Electricity production (1996, kWh, by source): Coal: 30.8 bil; Petroleum: 65 mil; Gas: 1.7 bil; Hydroelectric: 9.5 bil; Nuclear: 28.8 bil.

Public education. Student-teacher ratio (1995): 19.6. **Avg. teachers' salary** (1996-97): $33,350.

State data. Motto: Ditat Deus (God enriches). **Flower:** Blossom of the Saguaro cactus. **Bird:** Cactus wren. **Tree:** Paloverde. **Song:** Arizona. **Entered union** Feb. 14, 1912; rank, 48th. **State fair** at Phoenix, late Oct.-early Nov.

History. Anasazi, Mogollon, and Hohokam civilizations inhabited the area c 300 BC-AD 1300, later Pueblo peoples, with the Navajo and Apache arriving c 15th cent. Marcos de Niza, a Franciscan, and Estevanico, a former black slave, explored the area, 1539; Spanish explorer Francisco

Vásquez de Coronado visited, 1540. Eusebio Francisco Kino, a Jesuit missionary, taught the Indians Christianity and farming, 1692-1711, and left a chain of missions. Tubac, a Spanish fort, became the first European settlement, 1752. Spain ceded Arizona to Mexico, 1821. The U.S. took over, 1848, after the Mexican War. The area below the Gila River was obtained from Mexico in the Gadsden Purchase, 1853. Arizona became a territory in 1863. Apache wars ended with Geronimo's surrender in 1886.

Tourist attractions. The Grand Canyon of the Colorado; Painted Desert; Petrified Forest Natl. Park; Canyon de Chelly; Meteor Crater; London Bridge, Lake Havasu City; Biosphere 2, Oracle; Navajo Natl. Monument; Sedona.

Famous Arizonans. Bruce Babbitt, Cochise, Geronimo, Barry Goldwater, Zane Grey, Carl Hayden, George W. P. Hunt, Helen Jacobs, Percival Lowell, William H. Pickering, John J. Rhodes, Morris Udall, Stewart Udall, Frank Lloyd Wright.

Tourist information. Phoenix & Valley of the Sun Visitor and Convention Bureau, 1-602-254-6500.

Web site. http://www.state.az.us

Arkansas
The Natural State, The Razorback State

People. Population (1996): 2,509,793; rank: 33; **Net change** (1990-96): 6.8%. **Pop. density:** (1990) 45.1 per sq mi. **Racial/ethnic distrib.** (1990): 82.7% white; 15.9% black; 0.8% Hispanic.

Geography. Total area: 53,182 sq mi; rank: 29. **Land area:** 52,075 sq mi; rank: 27. **Acres forested land:** 17,864,000. **Location:** in the west south-central U.S. **Climate:** long, hot summers, mild winters; generally abundant rainfall. **Topography:** eastern delta and prairie, southern lowland forests, and the northwestern highlands, which include the Ozark Plateaus. **Capital:** Little Rock.

Economy. Principal industries: manufacturing, agriculture, tourism, forestry. **Principal manufactured goods:** food products, chemicals, lumber, paper, plastics, electric motors, furniture, auto components, airplane parts, apparel, machinery, steel. **Chief crops:** soybeans, rice, cotton, tomatoes, grapes, apples, vegetables, peaches, wheat. **Livestock** (1995): 1.9 mil cattle; 770,000 hogs/pigs; 1.1 mil broilers. **Timber/lumber** (1996): oak, hickory, gum, cypress, pine; 2.3 bil bd. ft. **Nonfuel minerals** (est. 1996): $453 mil; crushed stone, bromine, cement, sand & gravel. **Chief ports:** Little Rock, Pine Bluff, Osceola, Helena, Fort Smith, Van Buren, Camden, Dardanelle, North Little Rock, West Memphis, Crossett, McGehee, Morrilton. **Value of construction** (1996): $2.8 bil. **Employment distribution** (1996): 23.4% mfg.; 22.8% trade; 22.7% serv.; 16.7% govt. **Per capita personal income** (1996): $18,928. **Unemployment** (1996): 5.4%. **Tourism** (1995): $3.1 bil.

Finance. FDIC-insured commercial banks & trust companies (1996): 233. **Deposits:** $26.5 bil. **FDIC-insured savings institutions** (1996): 16. **Assets:** $3.4 bil.

Federal government. No. federal civilian employees (Mar. 1996): 11,066. **Avg. salary:** $36,237. **Notable federal facilities:** Nat'l. Center for Toxicological Research, Jefferson; Pine Bluff Arsenal, Little Rock AFB.

Energy. Electricity production (1996, kWh, by source): Coal: 24.3 bil; Petroleum: 98 mil; Gas: 3.1 bil; Hydroelectric: 2.1 bil; Nuclear: 13.4 bil.

Public education. Student-teacher ratio (1995): 17.1. **Avg. teachers' salary** (1996-97): $29,975.

State data. Motto: Regnat Populus (The people rule). **Flower:** Apple blossom. **Bird:** Mockingbird. **Tree:** Pine. **Song:** Arkansas. **Entered union** June 15, 1836; rank, 25th. **State fair** at Little Rock; late Sept.-early Oct.

History. Quapaw, Caddo, Osage, Cherokee, and Choctaw peoples lived in the area at the time of European contact. The first European explorers were de Soto, 1541; Marquette and Jolliet, 1673; and La Salle, 1682. The first settlement was by the French under Henri de Tony, 1686, at Arkansas Post. In 1762, the area was ceded by France to Spain, then given back again, 1800, and was part of the Louisiana Purchase, 1803. It was made a territory, 1819. Arkansas seceded from the Union in 1861, only after the Civil War began; more than 10,000 Arkansans fought on the Union side.

Tourist attractions. Hot Springs Natl. Park; Eureka Springs; Ozark Folk Center, Blanchard Caverns, both Mountain View; Crater of Diamonds, only U.S. diamond mine, near Murfreesboro; Toltec Mounds Archeological State Park, Little Rock.

Famous Arkansans. Daisy Bates, Dee Brown, Paul "Bear" Bryant, Glen Campbell, Johnny Cash, Hattie Caraway, Bill Clinton, "Dizzy" Dean, Orval Faubus, James W. Fulbright, John H. Johnson, John Grisham, Douglas MacArthur, John L. McClellan, James S. McDonnel, Scottie Pipen, Dick Powell, Winthrop Rockefeller, Mary Steenburgen, Edward Durell Stone, Archibald Yell.

Chamber of Commerce. 410 South Cross, Little Rock, AR 72201. (Phone): 501-374-9225

Toll-free travel information. 1-800-NATURAL.

Web site. http://www.state.ar.us

California
Golden State

People. Population (1996): 31,878,234; rank: 1; **Net change** (1990-96): 7.1%. **Pop. density:** (1990) 190.8 per sq mi. **Racial/ethnic distrib.** (1990): 69.0% white; 7.4% black; 9.6% Asian; 25.8% Hispanic.

Geography. Total area: 163,707 sq mi; rank: 3. **Land area:** 155,973 sq mi; rank: 3. **Acres forested land:** 37,263,000. **Location:** on western coast of the U.S. **Climate:** moderate temperatures and rainfall along the coast; extremes in the interior. **Topography:** long mountainous coastline; central valley; Sierra Nevada on the east; desert basins of the southern interior; rugged mountains of the north. **Capital:** Sacramento.

Economy. Principal industries: agriculture, tourism, apparel, electronics, telecommunications, entertainment. **Principal manufactured goods:** electronic and electrical equip., computers, industrial machinery, transportation equip. and instruments, food. **Chief farm products:** milk and cream, grapes, cotton, flowers, oranges, nursery products, hay, tomatoes, lettuce, strawberries, almonds, asparagus. **Livestock** (1996): 4.7 mil. cattle and calves; 255,000 hogs/pigs; 520,000 sheep and lambs; 31.5 mil chickens exc. broilers. **Timber/lumber** (1996): fir, pine, redwood, oak; 3.3 bil bd. ft. **Nonfuel Minerals:** (1995): $2.84 bil; portland cement, sand & gravel, boron, dimension stone, diatomite, gold, silver, tungsten, copper, asbestos. **Commercial fishing** (1996): $187 mil. **Chief ports:** Long Beach, Los Angeles, San Diego, Oakland, San Francisco, Sacramento, Stockton. **International airports at:** Fresno, Los Angeles, Sacramento, San Francisco, San Jose, San Diego. **Value of construction** (1996): $31.7 bil. **Employment distribution** (1996): 30.7% serv.; 23.3% trade; 14.5% mfg.; 16.6% govt. **Per capita personal income** (1996): $25,144. **Unemployment** (1996): 7.2%. **Tourism** (1996): $58.3 bil.

Finance. FDIC-insured commercial banks & trust companies (1996): 360. **Deposits:** $321.5 bil. **FDIC-insured savings institutions** (1996): 66. **Assets:** $248.0 bil.

Federal government. No. federal civilian employees (Mar. 1996): 169,396. **Avg. salary:** $41,773. **Notable federal facilities:** Vandenberg, Beale, Travis, McClellan AF bases; San Francisco Mint.

Energy. Electricity production (1996, kWh, by source): Petroleum: 675 mil; Gas: 30.8 bil; Hydroelectric: 44.2 bil; Nuclear: 34.1 bil.

Public education. Student-teacher ratio (1995): 24.0. **Avg. teachers' salary** (1996-97): $43,474.

State data. Motto: Eureka (I have found it). **Flower:** Golden poppy. **Bird:** California valley quail. **Tree:** California redwood. **Song:** I Love You, California. **Entered union** Sept. 9, 1850; rank, 31st. **State fair** at Sacramento; late Aug.-early Sept.

History. Early inhabitants included more than 100 different Native American tribes with multiple dialects. The first European explorers were Cabrillo, 1542, and Drake, 1579. The first settlement was the Spanish Alto California mission at San Diego, 1769, first in a string founded by Franciscan Father Junípero Serra. U.S. traders and settlers arrived in the 19th cent. and staged the Bear Flag revolt, 1846, in protest against Mexican rule; later that year U.S. forces occupied California. At the end of the Mexican War, Mexico ceded the territory to the U.S., 1848; that same year gold was discovered by James Marshall, and the famed gold rush began.

Tourist attractions. RMS *Queen Mary*, Long Beach; Palomar Observatory; Disneyland, Anaheim; J. Paul Getty Museum, Malibu; Tournament of Roses and Rose Bowl, Pasadena; Universal Studios, Hollywood; Los Angeles County Art Museum; San Diego Zoo; Yosemite Valley; Lassen and Sequoia-Kings Canyon natl. parks; Lake Tahoe; Mojave and Colorado deserts; San Francisco Bay; Napa Valley; Monterey Peninsula; oldest living things on earth believed to be a stand of Bristlecone pines in the Inyo National Forest, est. 4,700 years old; world's tallest tree, 365-ft "National Geographic Society" coast redwood, in Humboldt Redwoods State Park.

Famous Californians. Edmund G. (Pat) Brown, Jerry Brown, Luther Burbank, Ted Danson, John C. Fremont, Tom Hanks, Bret Harte, William Randolph Hearst, Jack Kemp, Jack London, Aimee Semple McPherson, John Muir, Richard M. Nixon, George S. Patton Jr., Sally Ride, William Saroyan, Father Junípero Serra, Leland Stanford, John Steinbeck, Shirley Temple, Earl Warren.

California Division of Tourism. 801 K St., Ste. 1600, Sacramento, CA 95814.

Toll-free travel information. 1-800-862-2543.

Web site. http://www.ca.gov/s/

Colorado
Centennial State

People. Population (1996): 3,822,676; rank: 25; **Net change** (1990-96): 16.0%. **Pop. density:** (1990) 31.8 per sq mi. **Racial/ethnic distrib.** (1990): 88.2% white; 4.0% black; 12.9% Hispanic.

Geography. Total area: 104,100 sq mi; rank: 8. **Land area:** 103,729 sq mi; rank: 8. **Acres forested land:** 21,338,000. **Location:** in west central U.S. **Climate:** low relative humidity, abundant sunshine, wide daily, seasonal temperatures ranges; alpine conditions in the high mountains. **Topography:** eastern dry high plains; hilly to mountainous central plateau; western Rocky Mountains of high ranges alternating with broad valleys and deep, narrow canyons. **Capital:** Denver.

Economy. Principal industries: manufacturing, construction, government, tourism, agriculture, aerospace, electronics equipment. **Principal manufactured goods:** computer equipment and instruments, foods, machinery, aerospace products. **Chief crops:** corn, wheat, hay, sugar beets, barley, potatoes, apples, peaches, pears, dry edible beans, sorghum, onions, oats sunflowers, vegetables. **Livestock** (1997): 3.2 mil cattle; (1996) 630,000 hogs/pigs; 4.1 mil poultry. **Timber/lumber** (1996): oak, ponderosa pine, Douglas fir; 113 mil bd. ft. **Nonfuel minerals** (est. 1996): $528 mil; construction sand & gravel, portland cement, crushed stone, gold, lead, zinc, molybdenum. **International airport at:** Denver. **Value of construction** (1996): $8.0 bil. **Employment distribution** (1996): 29.8% serv.; 24.5% trade; 16.3% govt.; 10.3% mfg. **Per capita personal income** (1996): $25,084. **Unemployment** (1996) 4.2%. **Tourism** (1992): $6.4 bil.

Finance. FDIC-insured commercial banks & trust companies (1996): 223. **Deposits:** $34.3 bil. **FDIC-insured savings institutions** (1996): 15. **Assets:** $2.5 bil.

Federal government. No. federal civilian employees (Mar. 1996): 35,403. **Avg. salary:** $42,324. **Notable federal facilities:** U.S. Air Force Academy; U.S. Mint; Ft. Carson; Natl. Renewable Energy Labs; U.S. Rail Transportation Test Center; N. American Aerospace Defense Command; Consolidated Space Operations Ctr.; Denver Federal Center; Natl. Center for Atmospheric Research; Natl. Instit. for Standards in Technology; Natl. Oceanic and Atmospheric Administration.

Energy. Electricity production (1996, kWh, by source): Coal: 32.0 bil; Petroleum: 14 mil; Gas: 351 mil; Hydroelectric: 1.6 bil.

Public education. Student-teacher ratio (1995): 18.5. **Avg. teachers' salary** (1996-97): $36,175.

State data. Motto: Nil Sine Numine (Nothing Without Providence). **Flower:** Rocky Mountain columbine. **Bird:** Lark bunting. **Tree:** Colorado blue spruce. **Song:** Where the Columbines Grow. **Entered union** Aug. 1, 1876; rank 38th. **State fair** at Pueblo; Aug. 16- Sept. 1, 1997.

History. Early civilization centered around the Mesa Verde c 2,000 years ago, later, Ute, Pueblo, Cheyenne, and Arapaho peoples lived in the area. The region was claimed by Spain, but passed to France. The U.S. acquired eastern Colorado in the Louisiana Purchase, 1803. Lt. Zebulon M. Pike explored the area, 1806, discovering the peak that bears his name. After the Mexican War, 1846-48, U.S. immigrants settled in the east, former Mexicans in the south. Gold was discovered in 1858, causing a population boom. Displaced Native Americans protested, resulting in the so-called Sand Creek Massacre, 1864, where more than 200 Cheyenne and Arapaho were killed. All Native Americans were later removed to Oklahoma Territory.

Tourist attractions. Rocky Mountain Natl. Park; Aspen Ski Resort; Garden of the Gods, Colorado Springs; Great Sand Dunes, Dinosaur, Black Canyon of the Gunnison, and Colorado natl. monuments; Pikes Peak and Mt. Evans highways; Mesa Verde Natl. Park (ancient Anasazi Indian cliff dwellings); Grand Mesa Natl. Forest; mining towns of Central City, Silverton, Cripple Creek; Burlington's Old Town; Bent's Fort, outside La Junta; Georgetown Loop Historic Mining Railroad Park, Cumbres & Toltec Scenic Railroad; limited stakes gaming in Central City, Blackhawk, Cripple Creek, Ignacio, and Towaoe.

Famous Coloradans. Frederick Bonfils, Henry Brown, Molly Brown, William N. Byers, M. Scott Carpenter, Jack Dempsey, Mamie Eisenhower, Douglas Fairbanks, Barney Ford, Scott Hamilton, Chief Ourey, "Baby Doe" Tabor, Lowell Thomas, Byron R. White, Paul Whiteman.

State Chamber of Commerce. 1776 Lincoln, Ste. 1200, Denver, CO 80203. Phone:: 303-831-7411

Tourist information. Colorado Travel and Tourism Authority, P. O. Box 3524, Englewood, CO 80155.

Toll-free travel information. 1-800-265-6723.

Web site. http://www.state.co.us

Connecticut
Constitution State, Nutmeg State

People. Population (1996): 3,274,238; rank: 28; **Net change** (1990-96): -0.4%. **Pop. density:** (1990) 678.4 per sq mi. **Racial/ethnic distrib.** (1990): 87.0% white; 8.3% black; 6.5% Hispanic.

Geography. Total area: 5,544 sq mi; rank: 48. **Land area:** 4,845 sq mi; rank: 48. **Acres forested land:** 1,819,000. **Location:** New England state in NE corner of the U.S. **Climate:** moderate; winters avg. slightly below freezing; warm, humid summers. **Topography:** western upland, the Berkshires, in the NW, highest elevations; narrow central lowland N-S; hilly eastern upland drained by rivers. **Capital:** Hartford.

Economy. Principal industries: manufacturing, retail trade, government, services, finances, insurance, real estate. **Principal manufactured goods:** aircraft engines and parts, submarines, helicopters, machinery and computer equipment, electronics and electrical equipment, medical instruments, pharmaceuticals. **Chief crops:** nursery stock, Christmas trees, mushrooms, vegetables, sweet corn, tobacco, apples. **Livestock** (1996): 70,000 cattle; 5,000 hogs/pigs; 7,000 sheep; 4.4 mil poultry. **Timber/lumber** (1996): oak, birch, beech, maple; 40 mil bd. ft. **Nonfuel minerals** (est. 1996): $103 mil; crushed stone, construction sand & gravel. **Commercial fishing** (1996): $48 mil. **Chief ports:** New Haven, Bridgeport, New London. **International airport at:** Windsor Locks. **Value of construction** (1996): $3.4 bil. **Employment distribution** (1996): 17.4% mfg.; 30.4% serv.; 22% trade; 14.1% govt. **Per capita personal income** (1996): $33,189. **Unemployment** (1996): 5.7%. **Tourism** (1993): $3.9 bil.

Finance. FDIC-insured commercial banks & trust companies (1996): 28. **Deposits:** $8.6 bil. **FDIC-insured savings institutions** (1996): 57. **Assets:** $40.0 bil.

Federal government. No. federal civilian employees (Mar. 1996): 9,322. **Avg. salary:** $43,544. **Notable federal facilities:** U.S. Coast Guard Academy; U.S. Navy Submarine Base.

Energy. Electricity production (1996, kWh, by source): Coal: 2.4 bil; Petroleum: 5.3 bil; Gas: 959 mil; Hydroelectric: 524 mil; Nuclear: 6.2 bil.

Public education. Student-teacher ratio (1995): 14.4. **Avg. teachers' salary** (1996-97): $50,426.

State data. Motto: Qui Transtulit Sustinet (He who transplanted still sustains). **Flower:** Mountain laurel. **Bird:** American robin. **Tree:** White oak. **Song:** Yankee Doodle. **Fifth** of the 13 original states to ratify the Constitution, Jan. 9, 1788. **State Fair** at Topsfield; early Oct.

History. At the time of European contact, inhabitants of the area were Algonquian peoples, including the Mohegan and Pequot. Dutch explorer Adriaen Block was the first European visitor, 1614. By 1634, settlers from Plymouth Bay had started colonies along the Connecticut River in 1637; they defeated the Pequots. The Colony of Connecticut was chartered by England, 1662, adding New Haven, 1665. In the American Revolution, Connecticut Patriots fought in most major campaigns, while Connecticut privateers captured British merchant ships.

Tourist attractions. Mark Twain House, Hartford; Yale University's Art Gallery, Peabody Museum, both in New Haven; Mystic Seaport; Mystic Marine Life Aquarium; P. T. Barnum Museum, Bridgeport; Gillette Castle, Hadlyme; U.S.S. *Nautilus* Memorial, Groton (1st nuclear-powered submarine); Foxwoods Casino, Ledyard.

Famous "Nutmeggers." Ethan Allen, Phineas T. Barnum, Samuel Colt, Jonathan Edwards, Nathan Hale, Katharine Hepburn, Isaac Hull, Robert Mitchum, J. Pierpont Morgan, Israel Putnam, Wallace Stevens, Harriet Beecher Stowe, Mark Twain, Noah Webster, Eli Whitney.

Tourist information. Dept. of Economic and Community Development, 865 Brook St., Rocky Hill, CT 06067.

Toll-free travel information. 1-800-CTBOUND

Web site. http://www.state.ct.us

Delaware
First State, Diamond State

People. Population (1996): 724,842; rank: 46; **Net change** (1990-96): 8.8%. **Pop. density:** (1990) 340.8 per sq mi. **Racial/ethnic distrib.** (1990): 80.3% white; 16.9% black; 2.4% Hispanic.

Geography. Total area: 2,489 sq mi; rank: 49. **Land area:** 1,955 sq mi; rank: 49. **Acres forested land:** 398,000. **Location:** occupies the Delmarva Peninsula on the Atlantic coastal plain. **Climate:** moderate. **Topography:** Piedmont plateau to the N, sloping to a near sea-level plain. **Capital:** Dover.

Economy. Principal industries: chemicals, agriculture, finance, poultry, shellfish, tourism, auto assembly, food processing, transportation equipment. **Principal manufactured goods:** nylon, apparel, luggage, foods, autos, processed meats and vegetables, railroad and aircraft equipment. **Chief crops:** soybeans, potatoes, corn, mushrooms, lima beans, green peas, barley, cucumbers, wheat, corn, grain sorghum, greenhouse and nursery. **Livestock** (1996): 31,000 cattle, 33,000 hogs, 257.6 mil broilers. **Timber/lumber** (1996): hardwoods and softwoods (except for soutern yellow pine); 15 mil bd. ft. **Nonfuel minerals** (est. 1996): $10.7 mil; construction sand & gravel. **Commercial fishing** (1996): $4.4 mil. **Chief ports:** Wilmington. **International airport at:** Philadelphia/Wilmington. **Value of construction** (1996): $800 mil. **Employment distribution** (1996): 85.2% nonmanufacturing; 14.8% mfg. **Per capita personal income** (1996): $27,622. **Unemployment** (1996): 5.2%. **Tourism** (1995): $836 mil.

Finance. FDIC-insured commercial banks & trust companies (1996): 39. **Deposits:** $40.1 bil. **FDIC-insured savings institutions** (1996): 5. **Assets:** $2.2 bil.

Federal government. No. federal civilian employees (Mar. 1996): 2,769. **Avg. salary:** $38,477. **Notable federal facilities:** Dover Air Force Base, Federal Wildlife Refuge, Bombay Hook.

Energy. Electricity production (1996, kWh, by source): Coal: 4.2 bil; Petroleum: 1.2 bil; Gas: 2.7 bil.

Public education. Student-teacher ratio (1995): 16.8. **Avg. teachers' salary** (1996-97): $41,436.

State data. Motto: Liberty and independence. **Flower:** Peach blossom. **Bird:** Blue hen chicken. **Tree:** American holly. **Song:** Our Delaware. **First** of original 13 states to ratify the Constitution, Dec. 7, 1787. **State fair** at Harrington; end of July.

History. The Lenni Lenape (Delaware) people lived in the region at the time of European contact. Explorer Henry Hudson located the Delaware R., 1609, and in 1610,

English explorer Samuel Argall entered Delaware Bay, naming the area after Virginia's governor, Lord De La Warr. The Dutch first settled near present Lewes, 1631, but the colony was destroyed by Indians. Swedes settled at Fort Christina (now Wilmington), 1638. Dutch settled anew, 1651, near New Castle and seized the Swedish settlement, 1655, only to lose all Delaware and New Netherland to the British, 1664. After 1682, Delaware became part of Pennsylvania and in 1704, was granted its own assembly. In 1776, it adopted a constitution as the state of Delaware. Although it remained in the Union during the Civil War, Delaware retained slavery until it was abolished by the 13th Amendment in 1865.

Tourist attractions. Ft. Christina Monument, site of founding of New Sweden, Holy Trinity (Old Swedes) Church, erected 1698, the oldest Protestant church in the U.S. still in use, Wilmington; Hagley Museum, Winterthur Museum and Gardens, both near Wilmington; historic district, New Castle; John Dickinson "Penman of the Revolution" home, Dover; Rehoboth Beach, "nation's summer capital," Rehoboth; Dover Downs Intl. Speedway.

Famous Delawareans. Thomas F. Bayard, Henry Seidel Canby, E. I. du Pont, John P. Marquand, Howard Pyle, Caesar Rodney.

Chamber of Commerce. 1200 N. Orange St., Ste. 200, Wilmington, DE 19899-0671.

Toll-free travel information. 1-800-441-8846.

Web site. http://www.state.de.us

Florida
Sunshine State

People. Population (1996): 14,399,985; rank: 4; **Net change** (1990-96): 11.3%. **Pop. density:** (1990) 239.6 per sq mi. **Racial/ethnic distrib.** (1990): 83.1% white; 13.6% black; 12.2% Hispanic.

Geography. Total area: 65,756 sq mi; rank: 22. **Land area:** 53,937 sq mi; rank: 26. **Acres forested land:** 16,549,000. **Location:** peninsula jutting southward 500 mi between the Atlantic and the Gulf of Mexico. **Climate:** subtropical N of Bradenton-Lake Okeechobee-Vero Beach line; tropical S of line. **Topography:** land is flat or rolling; highest point is 345 ft in the NW. **Capital:** Tallahassee.

Economy. Principal industries: tourism, agriculture, manufacturing, construction, services, international trade. **Principal manufactured goods:** electric & electronic equipment, transportation equipment, food, printing & publishing, chemicals, instruments. **Chief crops:** citrus fruits, greenhouse and nursery products, vegetables, potatoes, melons, strawberries, sugarcane. **Livestock** (1996): 2 mil cattle, including 156,000 milk cows; 65,000 hogs/pigs; 131 mil broilers; 2.3 bil eggs. **Timber/lumber** (1996): pine, cypress, cedar; 773 mil bd. ft. **Nonfuel minerals** (est. 1996): $1.54 bil; mostly phosphate, cement, sand and gravel, peat, titanium concentrates, crushed stone. **Commercial fishing** (1996): $205 mil. **Chief ports:** Pensacola, Tampa, Manatee, Miami, Port Everglades, Jacksonville, St. Petersburg, Canaveral. **International airports at:** Ft. Lauderdale/Hollywood, Daytona Beach, Ft. Myers, Key West, Jacksonville, Miami, Orlando, St. Petersburg/Clearwater, Panama City, Tampa, Sarasota/Bradenton, West Palm Beach. **Value of construction** (1996): $22.3 bil. **Employment distribution** (1996): 34.3% services, 26% trade, 15% govt., 8% mfg. **Per capita personal income** (1996): $24,104. **Unemployment** (1996): 5.1% **Tourism** (1994): $33.39 bil.

Finance. FDIC-insured commercial banks & trust companies (1996): 289. **Deposits:** $130.5 bil. **FDIC-insured savings institutions** (1996): 57. **Assets:** $16.8 bil.

Federal government. No. federal civilian employees (Mar. 1996): 61,983. **Avg. salary:** $40,531. **Notable federal facilities:** John F. Kennedy Space Center, NASA-Kennedy Space Center's Spaceport USA; Eglin Air Force Base.

Energy. Electricity production (1996, kWh, by source): Coal: 65.4 bil; Petroleum: 22.9 bil; Gas: 30.8 bil; Hydroelectric: 208 mil; Nuclear: 25.5 bil.

Public education. Student-teacher ratio (1995): 18.9. **Avg. teachers' salary** (1996-97): $33,881.

State data. Motto: In God we trust. **Flower:** Orange blossom. **Bird:** Mockingbird. **Tree:** Sabal palmetto palm. **Song:** Old Folks at Home. **Entered union** Mar. 3, 1845; rank, 27th. **State fair** at Tampa; early Feb.

History. The original inhabitants of Florida included the Timucua, Apalachee, and Calusa peoples. Later the Seminole migrated from Georgia to Florida, becoming dominant there in the early 18th cent. The first European to see Florida was Ponce de León, 1513. France established a colony, Fort Caroline, on the St. John River, 1564. Spain settled St. Augustine, 1565, and Spanish troops massacred most of the French. Britain's Sir Francis Drake burned St. Augustine, 1586. In 1763, Spain ceded Florida to Great Britain, which held the area briefly, 1763-83, before returning it to Spain. After Andrew Jackson led a U.S. invasion, 1818, Spain ceded Florida to the U.S., 1819. The Seminole War, 1835-42, resulted in removal of most Native Americans to Oklahoma Territory. Florida seceded from the Union, 1861, and was readmitted in 1868.

Tourist attractions. Miami Beach; St. Augustine, oldest permanent European settlement in U.S.; Castillo de San Marcos, St. Augustine; Walt Disney World's Magic Kingdom, EPCOT Center, and Disney-MGM Studios, all near Orlando; Sea World, Universal Studios, near Orlando; Spaceport USA, Kennedy Space Center; Everglades Natl. Park; Ringling Museum of Art, Ringling Museum of the Circus, both in Sarasota; Cypress Gardens, Winter Haven; Busch Gardens, Tampa.

Famous Floridians. Henry M. Flagler, James Weldon Johnson, MacKinlay Kantor, Henry B. Plant, A. Philip Randolph, Marjorie Kinnan Rawlings, Joseph W. Stilwell, Charles P. Summerall.

Tourist information. Florida Division of Tourism, 126 Van Buren St., Tallahassee, FL 32399-2000, 1-904-487-1462.

Web site. http://www.state.fl.us

Georgia
Empire State of the South, Peach State

People. Population (1996): 7,353,225; rank: 10; **Net change** (1990-96): 13.5%. **Pop. density:** (1990) 111.9 per sq mi. **Racial/ethnic distrib.** (1990): 71.0% white; 27.0% black; 1.7% Hispanic.

Geography. Total area: 59,441 sq mi; rank: 24. **Land area:** 57,919 sq mi; rank: 21. **Acres forested land:** 24,137,000. **Location:** South Atlantic state. **Climate:** maritime tropical air masses dominate in summer; polar air masses in winter; E central area drier. **Topography:** most southerly of the Blue Ridge Mts. cover NE and N central; central Piedmont extends to the fall line of rivers; coastal plain levels to the coast flatlands. **Capital:** Atlanta.

Economy. Principal industries: services, manufacturing, retail trade. **Principal manufactured goods:** textiles, apparel, food, and kindred products, pulp and paper products. **Chief crops:** peanuts, cotton, corn, tobacco, hay, soybeans. **Livestock** (1996): 1.5 mil cattle; 800,000 hogs/pigs; 27.7 mil poultry. **Timber/lumber** (1996): pine, hardwood; 3 bil bd. ft. **Nonfuel minerals** (est. 1996): $1.72 bil; mostly kaolin and other clays, crushed stone. **Commercial fishing** (1996): $21 mil. **Chief ports:** Savannah, Brunswick. **International airports at:** Atlanta. **Value of construction** (1996): $12.3 bil. **Employment distribution** (1995): 23% services; 18% mfg.; 19% retail trade; 17% govt. **Per capita personal income** (1996): $22,709. **Unemployment** (1996): 4.6%. **Tourism** (1995): $13.5 bil.

Finance. FDIC-insured commercial banks & trust companies (1996): 354. **Deposits:** $101.6 bil. **FDIC-insured savings institutions** (1996): 35. **Assets:** $5.8 bil.

Federal government. No. federal civilian employees (Mar. 1996): 64,292. **Avg. salary:** $39,018. **Notable federal facilities:** Dobbins AFB; Fts. Benning, Gordon, McPherson; Fed. Law Enforcement Training Ctr., Glynco, Warner Robins AFB; Centers for Disease Control.

Energy. Electricity production (1996, kWh, by source): Coal: 63.2 bil; Petroleum: 292 mil; Gas: 343 mil; Hydroelectric: 4.9 bil; Nuclear: 29.9 bil.

Public education. Student-teacher ratio (1995): 16.5. **Avg. teachers' salary** (1996-97): $36,042.

State data. Motto: Wisdom, justice and moderation. **Flower:** Cherokee rose. **Bird:** Brown thrasher. **Tree:** Live oak. **Song:** Georgia On My Mind. **Fourth** of the 13 original states to ratify the Constitution, Jan. 2, 1788. **State fair** at Perry, Oct.

History. Creek and Cherokee peoples were early inhabitants of the region. The earliest known European settlement was the Spanish mission of Santa Catalina, 1566, on Saint Catherines Island. Gen. James Oglethorpe established a colony at Savannah, 1733, for the poor and religiously persecuted. Oglethorpe defeated a Spanish army from Florida at Bloody Marsh, 1742. In the American Revolution, Georgians seized the Savannah armory, 1775, and sent the munitions to the Continental Army. They fought seesaw campaigns with Cornwallis's British troops, twice liberating Augusta and forcing final evacuation by the British from Savannah, 1782. The Cherokee were removed to Oklahoma Territory, 1832-38, and thousands died on the long march, known as the Trail of Tears. Georgia seceded from the Union, 1861, and was invaded by Union forces, 1864, under Gen. William T. Sherman, who took Atlanta, Sept. 2, and proceeded on his famous "march to the sea," ending in Dec., in Savannah. Georgia was readmitted, 1870.

Tourist attractions. State Capitol, Stone Mt. Park, Six Flags Over Georgia, Kennesaw Mt. Natl. Battlefield Park, Martin Luther King Jr. Natl. Historic Site, Underground Atlanta, Jimmy Carter Library & Museum, all Atlanta; Chickamauga and Chattanooga Natl. Military Park, near Dalton; Chattahoochee Natl. Forest; alpine village of Helen; Dahlonega, site of America's first gold rush; Brasstown Bald Mt.; Lake Lanier; Franklin D. Roosevelt's Little White House, Warm Springs; Callaway Gardens, Pine Mt.; Andersonville Natl. Historic Site; Okefenokee Swamp, near Waycross; Jekyll Island; St. Simons Island; Cumberland Island Natl. Seashore; historic riverfront district, Savannah.

Famous Georgians. Griffin Bell, James Bowie, James Brown, Erskine Caldwell, Jimmy Carter, Ray Charles, Lucius D. Clay, Ty Cobb, James Dickey, John C. Fremont, Newt Gingrich, Joel Chandler Harris, Martin Luther King Jr., Gladys Knight, Sidney Lanier, Juliette Gordon Low, Margaret Mitchell, Flannery O'Connor, Otis Redding, Jackie Robinson, Alice Walker, Joseph Wheeler, Joanne Woodward, Andrew Young.

Chamber of Commerce. 235 International Blvd., Atlanta, GA 30303; (404) 880-9000.

Toll-free travel information. 1-800-VISITGA.

Web site. http://www.state.ga.us

Hawai'i
Aloha State

People. Population (1996): 1,183,723; rank: 41; **Net change** (1990-96): 6.8%. **Pop. density:** (1990) 172.5 per sq mi. **Racial/ethnic distrib.** (1990): 33.4% white; 2.5% black; 61.8% Asian or Pacific Is.; 7.3% Hispanic.

Geography. Total area: 10,932 sq mi; rank: 43. **Land area:** 6,423 sq mi; rank: 47. **Acres forested land:** 1,748,000. **Location:** Hawaiian Islands lie in the North Pacific, 2,397 mi SW from San Francisco. **Climate:** subtropical, with wide variations in rainfall; Waialeale, on Kaua'i, wettest spot in U.S. (annual rainfall 460 in.) **Topography:** islands are tops of a chain of submerged volcanic mountains; active volcanoes: Mauna Loa, Kilauea. **Capital:** Honolulu.

Economy. Principal industries: tourism, defense, sugar, pineapples. **Principal manufactured goods:** processed sugar, canned pineapple, clothing, foods, printing and publishing. **Chief crops:** sugar, pineapples, macadamia nuts, fruits, coffee, vegetables, floriculture. **Livestock** (1996): 171,000 cattle and calves; 28,000 hogs/pigs; 870,000 chickens. **Nonfuel minerals** (est. 1996): $112 mil; mostly crushed stone, cement. **Commercial fishing** (1996): $64 mil. **Chief ports:** Honolulu, Nawiliwili, Barbers Point, Kahului, Hilo. **International airport at:** Honolulu. **Value of construction** (1996): $1.8 bil. **Employment distribution** (1995): 25.4% trade; 3.2% mfg.; 36.9% serv.; 20.1% govt. **Per capita personal income** (1996): $25,159. **Unemployment** (1996): 6.4%. **Tourism** (1995): $11.6 bil.

Finance. FDIC-insured commercial banks & trust companies (1996): 14. **Deposits:** $15.2 bil. **FDIC-insured savings institutions** (1996): 5. **Assets:** $6.6 bil.

Federal government. No. federal civilian employees (Mar. 1996): 20,539. **Avg. salary:** $38,814. **Notable federal facilities:** Pearl Harbor Naval Shipyard; Hickam AFB; Schofield Barracks; Ft. Shafter; Marine Corps Base-Kaneohe Bay; Barbers Point NAS; Wheeler AFB; Prince Kuhio Federal Building.

Energy. Electricity production (1996, kWh, by source): Petroleum: 6.4 bil; Hydroelectric: 18 mil.

Public education. Student-teacher ratio (1995): 17.8. **Avg. teachers' salary** (1996-97): $35,842.

State data. Motto: The life of the land is perpetuated in righteousness. **Flower:** Yellow hibiscus. **Bird:** Hawaiian goose. **Tree:** Kukui (Candlenut). **Song:** Hawai'i Pono'i. **Entered union** Aug. 21, 1959; rank, 50th. **State fair:** State Fair in June and State Farm Fair in July.

History. Polynesians from islands 2,000 mi to the south settled the Hawaiian Islands, probably between AD 300 and AD 600. The first European visitor was British captain James Cook, 1778. Between 1790 and 1810, the islands were united politically under the leadership of a native king, Kamehameha I, whose five successors—all bearing the name Kamehameha—ruled the kingdom from his death, 1819, until the end of the dynasty, 1872. Missionaries arrived, 1820, bringing Western culture. King Kamehameha III and his chiefs created the first constitution and a legislature that set up a public school system. Sugar production began, 1835, and it became the dominant industry. In 1893, Queen Liliuokalani was deposed, and a republic was instituted, 1894, headed by Sanford B. Dole. Annexation by the U.S. came in 1898. The Japanese attack on Pearl Harbor, Dec. 7, 1941, brought the U.S. into World War II.

Tourist attractions. Hawaii Volcanoes, Haleakala natl. parks; Natl. Memorial Cemetery of the Pacific, Waikiki Beach, Diamond Head, Honolulu; U.S.S. *Arizona* Memorial, Pearl Harbor; Hanauma Bay; Polynesian Cultural Center, Laie; Nu'uanu Pali; Waimea Canyon; Wailoa and Wailuku River state parks.

Famous islanders. Bernice Pauahi Bishop, Tia Carrera, Father Damien de Veuster, Don Ho, Duke Kahanamoku, King Kamehameha, Brook Mahealani Lee, Daniel K. Inouye, Jason Scott Lee, Queen Liliuokalani, Bette Midler, Ellison Onizuka.

Chamber of Commerce of Hawaii. 1132 Bishop St., Suite 200, Honolulu, HI 96813.

Toll free travel information. 1-800-464-2924.

Web site. http://www.hawaii.gov

Idaho
Gem State

People. Population (1996): 1,189,251; rank: 40; **Net change** (1990-96): 18.1%. **Pop. density:** (1990) 12.2 per sq mi. **Racial/ethnic distrib.** (1990): 94.4% white; 0.3% black; 5.3% Hispanic.

Geography. Total area: 83,574 sq mi; rank: 14. **Land area:** 82,751 sq mi; rank: 11. **Acres forested land:** 21,621,000. **Location:** northwestern Mountain state bordering on British Columbia. **Climate:** tempered by Pacific westerly winds; drier, colder, continental climate in SE; altitude an important factor. **Topography:** Snake R. plains in the S; central region of mountains, canyons, gorges (Hells Canyon, 7,900 ft, deepest in N. America); subalpine northern region. **Capital:** Boise.

Economy. Principal industries: agriculture, manufacturing, tourism, lumber, mining, electronics. **Principal manufactured goods:** processed foods, lumber and wood products, chemical products, primary metals, fabricated metal products, machinery, electronic components, computer equipment. **Chief crops:** potatoes, peas, dry beans, sugar beets, alfalfa seed, lentils, wheat, hops, barley, plums and prunes, mint, onions, corn, cherries, apples, hay. **Livestock** (1996): 1.75 mil cattle; 285,000 sheep & lambs; 33,000 hogs; 1.3 mil poultry. **Timber/lumber** (1996): yellow, white pine; Douglas fir; white spruce; 1.8 bil bd. ft. **Nonfuel minerals** (est. 1996): $411 mil; phosphate rock, sand & gravel, gold, molybdenum, silver, lead. **Chief port:** Lewiston. **Value of construction** (1996) $1.9 bil. **Employment distribution** (1994): 24% trade; 21.2% serv., 14.9% mfg.; 6% constr. **Per capita personal income** (1996): $19,539. **Unemployment** (1996): 5.2%. **Tourism** (1994): $1.4 bil.

Finance. FDIC-insured commercial banks & trust companies (1996): 15. **Deposits:** $5.3 bil. **FDIC-insured savings institutions** (1996): 4. **Assets:** $589 mil.

Federal government. No. federal civilian employees (Mar. 1996): 7,687. **Avg. salary:** $38,823. **Notable federal facilities:** Idaho Natl. Engineering Lab; Mt. Home Air Force Base.

Energy. Electricity production (1996, kWh, by source): Hydroelectric: 12.3 bil.

Education: Student-teacher ratio (1995): 19.0. **Avg. teachers' salary** (1996-97): $31,818.

State data. Motto: Esto Perpetua (It is perpetual). **Flower:** Syringa. **Bird:** Mountain bluebird. **Tree:** White pine. **Song:** Here We Have Idaho. **Entered union** July 3, 1890; rank, 43d. **State fair** at Boise, late Aug.; at Blackfoot, early Sept.

History. Early inhabitants were Shoshone, Northern Paiute, Bannock, and Nez Percé peoples. White exploration of the region began with Lewis and Clark, 1805-6. Next came fur traders, setting up posts, 1809-34, and missionaries, 1830s-50s. Mormons made their first permanent settlement at Franklin, 1860. Idaho's gold rush began the same year and brought thousands of permanent settlers. Most remarkable of the Indian wars was the 1,700-mi trek, 1877, of Chief Joseph and the Nez Percé, pursued by U.S. troops through 3 states and finally caught just short of the Canadian border. The Idaho territory was organized, 1863. Idaho adopted a progressive constitution and became a state, 1890.

Tourist attractions. Hells Canyon, deepest gorge in N. America; World Center for Birds of Prey; Craters of the Moon; Sun Valley, in Sawtooth Mts.; Crystal Falls Cave; Shoshone Falls; Lava Hot Springs; Lake Pend Oreille; Lake Coeur d'Alene; Sawtooth Natl. Recreation Area; River of No Return Wilderness Area; Redfish Lake.

Famous Idahoans. William E. Borah, Frank Church, Fred T. Dubois, Ezra Pound, Chief Joseph, Sacagawea.

Tourist information. Department of Commerce, 700 W. State St., Boise, ID 83720.

Toll-free travel information. 1-800-VISIT-ID.

Web site. http://www.state.id.us

Illinois

Prairie State

People. Population (1996): 11,846,544; rank: 6; **Net change** (1990-96): 3.6%. **Pop. density:** (1990) 205.6 per sq mi. **Racial/ethnic distrib.** (1990): 78.3% white; 14.8% black; 7.9% Hispanic.

Geography. Total area: 57,918 sq mi; rank: 25. **Land area:** 55,593 sq mi; rank: 24. **Acres forested land:** 4,266,000. **Location:** East North Central state; western, southern, and eastern boundaries formed by Mississippi, Ohio, and Wabash rivers, respectively. **Climate:** temperate; typically cold, snowy winters, hot summers. **Topography:** prairie and fertile plains throughout; open hills in the southern region. **Capital:** Springfield.

Economy. Principal industries: services, manufacturing, travel, wholesale and retail trade, finance, insurance, real estate, construction, health care, agriculture. **Principal manufactured goods:** machinery, electric and electronic equipment, primary and fabricated metals, chemical products, printing and publishing, food and kindred products. **Chief crops:** corn, soybeans, wheat, sorghum, hay. **Livestock** (1996): 1.68 mil cattle; 4.4 mil hogs/pigs; 79,000 sheep; 3.5 mil poultry. **Timber/lumber** (1996): oak, hickory, maple, cottonwood; 85 mil bd. ft. **Nonfuel minerals** (est. 1996): $817 mil; mostly crushed stone, cement, construction & industrial sand & gravel, lime, zinc. **Commercial fishing** (1996): $415,000. **Chief ports:** Chicago. **International airport at:** Chicago. **Value of construction** (1996): $12.6 bil. **Employment distribution** (1996): 28.9% serv.; 23% trade; 17.1% mfg. **Per capita personal income** (1996): $26,598. **Unemployment** (1996): 5.3%. **Tourism** (1995): $17 bil.

Finance. FDIC-insured commercial banks & trust companies (1996): 833. **Deposits:** $181.4 bil. **FDIC-insured savings institutions** (1996): 141. **Assets:** $49.8 bil.

Federal government. No. federal civilian employees (Mar. 1996): 47,140. **Avg. salary:** $43,069. **Notable federal facilities:** Fermi Natl. Accelerator Lab; Argonne Natl. Lab; Rock Island Arsenal; Great Lakes, Naval Training Station, Scott AFB.

Energy. Electricity production (1996, kWh, by source): Coal: 71.5 bil; Petroleum: 797 mil; Gas: 1.9 bil; Hydroelectric: 30 mil; Nuclear: 69.8 bil.

Public education. Student-teacher ratio (1995): 17.1. **Avg. teachers' salary** (1996-97): $42,679.

State data. Motto: State sovereignty—national union. **Flower:** Native violet. **Bird:** Cardinal. **Tree:** White oak. **Song:** Illinois. **Entered union** Dec. 3, 1818; rank, 21st. **State fair** at Springfield, mid-Aug.; DuQuoin, late Aug.

History. Seminomadic Algonquian peoples, including the Peoria, Illinois, Kaskaskia, and Tamaroa, lived in the region at the time of European contact. Fur traders were the first Europeans in Illinois, followed shortly by Jolliet and Marquette, 1673, and La Salle, 1680, who built a fort near present-day Peoria. The first settlements were French, at Cahokia, near present-day St. Louis, 1699, and Kaskaskia, 1703. France ceded the area to Britain, 1763, and in 1778, American Gen. George Rogers Clark took Kaskaskia from the British without a shot. Defeat of Native American tribes in Black Hawk War, 1832, and growth of railroads brought change to the area. In 1787, it became part of the Northwest Territory. Post-Civil War Illinois became a center for the labor movement as bitter strikes, such as the Haymarket Square riot, occurred in 1885-86.

Tourist attractions. Chicago museums and parks; Lincoln shrines at Springfield, New Salem, Sangamon County; Cahokia Mounds, Collinsville; Starved Rock State Park; Crab Orchard Wildlife Refuge; Mormon settlement at Nauvoo; Fts. Kaskaskia, Chartres, Massac (parks); Shawnee Natl. Forest, Southern Illinois; Illinois State Museum, Springfield; Dickson Mounds Museum, between Havana and Lewistown.

Famous Illinoisans. Jane Addams, Saul Bellow, Jack Benny, Ray Bradbury, Gwendolyn Brooks, William Jennings Bryan, St. Frances Xavier Cabrini, Hillary Rodham Clinton, Clarence Darrow, John Deere, Stephen A. Douglas, James T. Farrell, George W. Ferris, Marshall Field, Betty Friedan, Benny Goodman, Ulysses S. Grant, Ernest Hemingway, Wild Bill Hickok, Abraham Lincoln, Vachel Lindsay, Edgar Lee Masters, Oscar Mayer, Cyrus McCormick, Ronald Reagan, Carl Sandburg, Adlai Stevenson, Frank Lloyd Wright, Philip Wrigley.

Tourist Information. Illinois Dept. of Commerce and Community Affairs, 620 E. Adams St., Springfield, IL 62701.

Toll-free travel information: 1-800-223-0121.

Web site. http://www.state.il.us

Indiana

Hoosier State

People. Population (1996): 5,840,528; rank: 14; **Net change** (1990-96): 5.3%. **Pop. density:** (1990) 154.6 per sq mi. **Racial/ethnic distrib.** (1990): 90.6% white; 7.8% black; 1.8% Hispanic.

Geography. Total area: 36,420 sq mi; rank: 38. **Land area:** 35,870 sq mi; rank: 38. **Acres forested land:** 4,439,000. **Location:** East North Central state; Lake Michigan on northern border. **Climate:** 4 distinct seasons with a temperate climate. **Topography:** hilly southern region; fertile rolling plains of central region; flat, heavily glaciated north; dunes along Lake Michigan shore. **Capital:** Indianapolis.

Economy: Principal industries: manufacturing, services, agriculture, government, wholesale and retail trade, transportation and public utilities. **Principal manufactured goods:** primary metals, transportation equipment, motor vehicles and equipment, industrial machinery and equipment, electronic and electric equipment. **Chief crops:** corn, soybeans, wheat, nursery and greenhouse products, vegetables, popcorn, fruit, hay, tobacco, mint. **Livestock** (1996): 1.15 mil cattle; 3.75 mil hogs/pigs; 67,000 sheep; 25.4 mil chickens; 14 mil turkeys; 20.8 mil laying chickens. **Timber/lumber** (1996): oak, tulip, beech, sycamore; 356 mil bd. ft. **Nonfuel minerals** (est. 1996): $617 mil; mostly crushed stone, cement, construction sand & gravel. **Commercial fishing** (1996): $736,000 **Chief ports:** Burns Harbor, Portage; Southwind Maritime, Mt. Vernon; Clark Maritime, Jeffersonville. **International airports at:** Indianapolis, Ft. Wayne. **Value of construction** (1996): $8.9 bil. **Employment distribution** (1996): 24% mfg.; 24.2% trade; 23.2% serv; 14% govt. **Per capita personal income** (1996): $22,440. **Unemployment** (1996): 4.1%. **Tourism** (1993): $4.4 bil.

Finance. FDIC-insured commercial banks & trust companies (1996): 204. **Deposits:** $52.1 bil. **FDIC-insured savings institutions** (1996): 76. **Assets:** $15.3 bil.

Federal government. No. federal civilian employees (Mar. 1996): 21,912. **Avg. salary:** $39,862. **Notable federal facilities:** Naval Air Warfare Center; Ft. Benjamin Harrison; Del. Grissom AFB; Naval Surface Warfare Center.

Energy. Electricity production (1996, kWh, by source): Coal: 104.4 bil; Petroleum: 321 mil; Gas: 373 mil; Hydroelectric: 448 mil.

Public education. Student-teacher ratio (1995): 17.5. **Avg. teachers' salary** (1996-97): $38,575.

State data. Motto: Crossroads of America. **Flower:** Peony. **Bird:** Cardinal. **Tree:** Tulip poplar. **Song:** On the Banks of the Wabash, Far Away. **Entered union** Dec. 11, 1816; rank, 19th. **State fair** at Indianapolis; mid-Aug.

History. When the Europeans arrived, Miami, Potawatomi, Kickapoo, Piankashaw, Wea, and Shawnee peoples inhabited the area. A French trading post was built, 1731-32, at Vincennes. La Salle visited the present South Bend area, 1679 and 1681. The first French fort was built near present-day Lafayette, 1717. France ceded the area to Britain, 1763. During the American Revolution, American Gen. George Rogers Clark captured Vincennes, 1778, and defeated British forces, 1779. At war's end, Britain ceded the area to the U.S. Miami Indians defeated U.S. troops twice, 1790, but were beaten, 1794, at Fallen Timbers by Gen. Anthony Wayne. At Tippecanoe, 1811, Gen. William H. Harrison defeated Tecumseh's Indian confederation. The Delaware, Potawatomi, and Miami were moved farther west, 1820-1850.

Tourist attractions. Lincoln Log Cabin Historic Site, near Charleston; George Rogers Clark Park, Vincennes; Wyandotte Cave; Tippecanoe Battlefield Memorial Park; Benjamin Harrison home; Indianapolis 500 raceway and museum, all Indianapolis; Indiana Dunes, near Chesterton; National College Football Hall of Fame, South Bend; Hoosier Nat'l. Forest, south/central Indiana.

Famous "Hoosiers." Larry Bird, Ambrose Burnside, Hoagy Carmichael, Jim Davis, James Dean, Eugene V. Debs, Theodore Dreiser, Paul Dresser, Gil Hodges, David Letterman, Jane Pauley, Cole Porter, Dan Quayle, Gene Stratton Porter, Ernie Pyle, James Whitcomb Riley, Oscar Robertson, Red Skelton, Booth Tarkington, Kurt Vonnegut, Lew Wallace, Wendell L. Willkie, Wilbur Wright.

Chamber of Commerce. One North Capital, Suite 200, Indianapolis, IN 46204.

Toll-free travel information. 1-800-289-6646.

Web site. http://www.ai.org

Iowa
Hawkeye State

People. Population (1996): 2,851,792; rank: 30; **Net change** (1990-96): 2.7%. **Pop. density:** (1990) 49.7 per sq mi. **Racial/ethnic distrib.** (1990) 96.6% white; 1.7% black; 1.2% Hispanic.

Geography. Total area: 56,276 sq mi; rank: 26. **Land area:** 55,875 sq mi; rank: 23. **Acres forested land:** 2,050,000. **Location:** West North Central state bordered by Mississippi R. on the E and Missouri R. on the W. **Climate:** humid, continental. **Topography:** Watershed from NW to SE; soil especially rich and land level in the N central counties. **Capital:** Des Moines.

Economy. Principal industries: agriculture, communications, construction, finance, insurance, trade, services, manufacturing. **Principal manufactured goods:** processed food products, tires, farm machinery, electronic products, appliances, household furniture, chemicals, fertilizers, auto accessories. **Chief crops:** silage and grain corn, soybeans, oats, hay. **Livestock** (1996): 3.95 mil cattle; 13.3 mil hogs/pigs; 345,000 sheep and lambs; (1995): 8 mil turkeys. **Timber/lumber** (1996): red cedar; 73 mil bd. ft. **Nonfuel minerals** (est. 1996): $486 mil; mostly crushed stone, portland cement, construction sand and gravel, gypsum. **International airport at:** Des Moines. **Value of construction** (1996): 2.8 bil. **Employment distribution** (1996): 24.7% trade; 26% serv.; 17.9% mfg.; 16.8% govt. **Per capita personal income** (1996): $22,560. **Unemployment** (1996): 3.8%. **Tourism** (1995): $2.3 bil.

Finance. FDIC-insured commercial banks & trust companies (1996): 467. **Deposits:** $35.0 bil. **FDIC-insured savings institutions** (1996): 30. **Assets:** $5.9 bil.

Federal government. No. federal civilian employees (Mar. 1996): 7,372. **Avg. salary:** $37,880.

Energy. Electricity production (1996, kWh, by source): Coal: 28.3 bil; Petroleum: 73 mil; Gas: 211 mil; Hydroelectric: 929 mil; Nuclear: 3.9 bil.

Public education. Student-teacher ratio (1995): 15.5. **Avg. teachers' salary** (1996-97): $33,275.

State data. Motto: Our liberties we prize, and our rights we will maintain. **Flower:** Wild rose. **Bird:** Eastern goldfinch. **Tree:** Oak. **Rock:** Geode. **Entered union** Dec. 28, 1846; rank, 29th. **State fair** at Des Moines; mid-Aug.

History. Early inhabitants were Mound Builders who dwelt on Iowa's fertile plains. Later, Woodland tribes including the Iowa and Yankton Sioux lived in the area. The first Europeans, Marquette and Jolliet, gave France its claim to the area, 1673. In 1762, France ceded the region to Spain, but Napoleon took it back, 1800. It became part of the U.S. through the Louisiana Purchase, 1803. Native American Sauk and Fox tribes moved into the area from states farther east but relinquished their land in defeat, after the 1832 uprising led by the Sauk chieftain Black Hawk. By mid-19th cent. they were forced to move on to Kansas. Iowa became a territory in 1838, and entered as a free state, 1846, strongly supporting the Union.

Tourist attractions. Herbert Hoover birthplace and library, West Branch; Effigy Mounds Natl. Monument, prehistoric Indian burial site, Marquette; Amana Colonies; Grant Wood's paintings and memorabilia, Davenport Municipal Art Gallery; Living History Farms, Des Moines; Adventureland, Altoona; Boone & Scenic Valley Railroad, Boone; Greyhound Parks, in Dubuque and Council Bluffs; Prairie Meadows horse racing, Altoona; riverboat cruises and casino gambling, Mississippi and Missouri Rivers; Iowa Great Lakes, Okoboji.

Famous Iowans. Tom Arnold, Johnny Carson, Marquis Childs, Buffalo Bill Cody, Mamie Dowd Eisenhower, George Gallup, Susan Glaspell, James Norman Hall, Harry Hansen, Herbert Hoover, Glenn Miller, Lillian Russell, Billy Sunday, James A. Van Allen, Carl Van Vechten, Henry Wallace, John Wayne, Meredith Willson, Grant Wood.

Tourist information. Division of Tourism, Iowa Dept. of Economic Development, 200 E. Grand Ave., Des Moines, IA 50309.

Toll-free travel information. 1-800-345-IOWA.

Web site. http://www.state.ia.us

Kansas
Sunflower State

People. Population (1996): 2,572,150; rank: 32; **Net change** (1990-96): 3.8%. **Pop. density:** (1990) 30.3 per sq mi. **Racial/ethnic distrib.** (1990): 90.1% white; 5.8% black; 3.8% Hispanic.

Geography. Total area: 82,282 sq mi; rank: 15. **Land area:** 81,823 sq mi; rank: 13. **Acres forested land:** 1,359,000. **Location:** West North Central state, with Missouri R. on E. **Climate:** temperate but continental, with great extremes between summer and winter. **Topography:** hilly Osage Plains in the E; central region level prairie and hills; high plains in the W. **Capital:** Topeka.

Economy. Principal industries: manufacturing, finance, insurance, real estate, services. **Principal manufactured goods:** transportation equipment, machinery and computer equipment, food and kindred products, printing and publishing. **Chief crops:** wheat, sorghum, corn, hay, soybeans, sunflowers. **Chief products:** wheat flour, beef, sorghum silage, sunflowers, soybean oil, soybean meal. **Livestock** (1995): 4.9 mil cattle; 1.25 mil hogs/pigs; 170,000 sheep & lambs; 2 mil poultry. **Timber/lumber:** (1996) oak, walnut; 10 mil bd. ft. **Nonfuel minerals** (est. 1996): $524 mil; salt, helium, cement, crushed stone, sand & gravel. **Chief ports:** Kansas City. **International airports at:** Wichita. **Value of construction** (1996): $3.8 bil. **Employment distribution** (1994): 24.2% trade; 23.7% serv.; 20% govt.; 16.1% mfg. **Per capita personal income** (1996): $23,281. **Unemployment** (1996): 4.5%. **Tourism** (1993): $2.5 bil.

Finance. FDIC-insured commercial banks & trust companies (1996): 416. **Deposits:** $24.5 bil. **FDIC-insured savings institutions** (1996): 22. **Assets:** $7.8 bil.

Federal government. No. federal civilian employees (Mar. 1996): 15,457. **Avg. salary:** $38,240. **Notable federal facilities:** Fts. Riley, Leavenworth; Leavenworth Federal Penitentiary; Colmery-O'Neal Veterans Hospital.

Energy. Electricity production (1996, kWh, by source): Coal: 29.7 bil; Petroleum: 154 mil; Gas: 1.8 bil; Nuclear: 8.2 bil.

Public education. Student-teacher ratio (1995): 15.1. **Avg. teachers' salary** (1996-97): $35,837.

State data. Motto: Ad Astra per Aspera (To the stars through difficulties). **Flower:** Native sunflower. **Bird:** Western meadowlark. **Tree:** Cottonwood. **Song:** Home on the Range. **Entered union** Jan. 29, 1861; rank, 34th. **State fair** at Hutchinson; begins Friday after Labor Day.

History. When Coronado first explored the area, Wichita, Pawnee, Kansa, and Osage peoples lived there. These Native Americans—hunters who also farmed—were joined on the Plains by the nomadic Cheyenne, Arapaho, Comanche, and Kiowa about 1800. French explorers established trading between 1682 and 1739, and the U.S. took over most of the area in the Louisiana Purchase, 1803. After 1830, thousands of eastern Native Americans were removed to Kansas. Kansas became a territory, 1854. Disputes over whether Kansas would enter the Union as a free or slave state continued until 1858. Violent incidents between pro- and antislavery settlers, caused the territory to be known as "Bleeding Kansas." It eventually entered as a free state, 1861. Railroad construction after the war made Abilene and Dodge City terminals of large cattle drives from Texas.

Tourist attractions. Eisenhower Center, Abilene; Agricultural Hall of Fame and Natl. Center, Bonner Springs; Dodge City-Boot Hill & Frontier Town; Old Cowtown Museum, Wichita; Ft. Scott and Ft. Larned, restored 1800s cavalry forts; Kansas Cosmosphere and Space Center, Hutchinson; Woodlands Racetrack, Kansas City; U.S. Cavalry Museum, Ft. Riley; NCAA Visitors Center, Shawnee; Heartland Park Raceway, Topeka.

Famous Kansans. Ed Asner, Thomas Hart Benton, John Brown, Walter P. Chrysler, Glen Cunningham, John Stuart Curry, Robert Dole, Amelia Earhart, Dwight D. Eisenhower, Ron Evans, Wild Bill Hickok, Cyrus Holliday, Dennis Hopper, William Inge, Walter Johnson, Nancy Landon Kassebaum, Buster Keaton, Emmett Kelly, Alf Landon, Edgar Lee Masters, Hattie McDaniel, Oscar Micheaux, Carrie Nation, Georgia Neese-Gray, Gordon Parks, Jim Ryun, Barry Sanders, Vivian Vance, William Allen White, Jess Willard.

Tourist information. Kansas Dept. of Commerce & Housing, Travel and Tourism Div., 700 SW Harrison, Suite 1300, Topeka, KS 66601; 1-913-296-2009.

Toll-free travel information. 1-800-2KANSAS.

Web site. http://www.ink.org

Kentucky
Bluegrass State

People. Population (1996): 3,883,723; rank: 24; **Net change** (1990-96): 5.3%. **Pop. density:** (1990) 92.8 per sq mi. **Racial/ethnic distrib.** (1990): 92.0% white; 7.1% black; 0.6% Hispanic.

Geography. Total area: 40,411 sq mi; rank: 37. **Land area:** 39,732 sq mi; rank: 36. **Acres forested land:** 12,714,000. **Location:** East South Central state, bordered on N by Illinois, Indiana, Ohio; on E by West Virginia and Virginia; on S by Tennessee; on W by Missouri. **Climate:** moderate, with plentiful rainfall. **Topography:** mountainous in E; rounded hills of the Knobs in the N; Bluegrass, heart of state; wooded rocky hillsides of the Pennyroyal; Western Coal Field; the fertile Purchase in the SW. **Capital:** Frankfort.

Economy. Principal industries: manufacturing, services, finance, insurance and real estate, retail trade. **Principal manufactured goods:** industrial machinery, transportation equipment, apparel, printing and publishing, food products, rubber and plastic products. **Chief crops:** tobacco, corn, soybeans. **Livestock** (1996): 2.7 mil cattle; 800,000 hogs/pigs; 20,000 sheep; 3.6 mil chickens; (1995) horse & mule sales, $559 mil. **Timber/lumber** (1996): hardwoods, pines; 744 mil bd. ft. **Nonfuel minerals** (est. 1996): $453 mil; mostly crushed stone, lime, cement, sand & gravel. **Chief ports:** Paducah, Louisville, Covington, Owensboro, Ashland, Henderson County, Lyon County, Hickman-Fulton County. **International airports at:** Covington and Louisville. **Value of construction** (1996): $4.7 bil. **Employment distribution** (1996): 23.2% serv.; 22.8% trade; 17.7% mfg.;

16.4% govt. **Per capita personal income** (1996): $19,687. **Unemployment** (1996): 5.6%. **Tourism** (1996): $7.1 bil.

Finance. FDIC-insured commercial banks & trust companies (1996): 275. **Deposits:** $39.8 bil. **FDIC-insured savings institutions** (1996): 46. **Assets:** $7.0 bil.

Federal government. No. federal civilian employees (Mar. 1996): 24,457. **Avg. salary:** $34,339. **Notable federal facilities:** U.S. Gold Bullion Depository, Fort Knox; Federal Correctional Institution, Lexington.

Energy. Electricity production (1996, kWh, by source): Coal: 84.7 bil; Petroleum: 135 mil; Gas: 146 mil; Hydroelectric: 3.8 bil.

Public education. Student-teacher ratio (1995): 16.9. **Avg. teachers' salary** (1996-97): $33,950.

State data. Motto: United we stand, divided we fall. **Flower:** Goldenrod. **Bird:** Cardinal. **Tree:** Tulip Popular. **Song:** My Old Kentucky Home. **Entered union** June 1, 1792; rank, 15th. **State fair** at Louisville, late Aug.

History. The area was predominantly hunting grounds for Shawnee, Wyandot, Delaware, and Cherokee peoples. Explored by Americans Thomas Walker and Christopher Gist, 1750-51, Kentucky was the first area west of the Alleghenies settled by American pioneers. The first permanent settlement was Harrodsburg, 1744. Daniel Boone blazed the Wilderness Trail through the Cumberland Gap and founded Ft. Boonesborough, 1775. Conflicts with Native Americans, spurred by the British, were unceasing until, during the American Revolution, Gen. George Rogers Clark captured British forts in Indiana and Illinois, 1778. In 1792, Virginia dropped its claims to the region, and it became the 15th state. Although officially a Union state, Kentuckians had divided loyalties during the Civil War and were forced to choose sides; its slaves were freed only after the adoption of the 13th Amendment to the U.S. Constitution, 1865.

Tourist attractions. Kentucky Derby; Louisville; Land Between the Lakes Natl. Recreation Area, Kentucky Lake and Lake Barkley; Mammoth Cave Natl. Park; Echo River, 360 ft below ground; Lake Cumberland; Lincoln's birthplace, Hodgenville; My Old Kentucky Home State Park, Bardstown; Cumberland Gap Natl. Historical Park, Middlesboro; Kentucky Horse Park, Lexington; Shaker Village, Pleasant Hill.

Famous Kentuckians. Muhammad Ali, John James Audubon, Alben W. Barkley, Daniel Boone, Louis D. Brandeis, John C. Breckinridge, Kit Carson, Albert B. "Happy" Chandler, Henry Clay, Jefferson Davis, D. W. Griffith, "Casey" Jones, Abraham Lincoln, Mary Todd Lincoln, Thomas Hunt Morgan, Carrie Nation, Col. Harland Sanders, Diane Sawyer, Jesse Stuart, Adlai Stevenson, Zachary Taylor, Robert Penn Warren, Whitney Young Jr.

Chamber of Commerce. 464 Chenault Rd., PO Box 817, Frankfort, KY 40602.

Toll-free travel information. 1-800-225-TRIP, ext. 67.

Web site. http://www.state.ky.us

Louisiana
Pelican State

People. Population (1996): 4,350,579; rank: 22; **Net change** (1990-96): 3.1%. **Pop. density:** (1990) 96.9 per sq mi. **Racial/ethnic distrib.** (1990): 67.3% white; 30.8% black; 2.2% Hispanic.

Geography. Total area: 51,843 sq mi; rank: 31. **Land area:** 43,566 sq mi; rank: 33. **Acres forested land:** 13,864,000. **Location:** West South Central state on the Gulf Coast. **Climate:** subtropical, affected by continental weather patterns. **Topography:** lowlands of marshes and Mississippi R. flood plain; Red R. Valley lowlands; upland hills in the Florida Parishes; average elevation, 100 ft **Capital:** Baton Rouge.

Economy. Principal industries: wholesale and retail trade, tourism, manufacturing, construction, transportation, communication, public utilities, finance, insurance, real estate, mining. **Principal manufactured goods:** chemical products, foods, transportation equipment, electronic equipment, petroleum products, lumber, wood, and paper. **Chief crops:** soybeans, sugarcane, rice, corn, cotton, sweet potatoes, pecans, sorghum, aquaculture. **Livestock** (1996): 1.02 mil cattle; 40,000 hogs/pigs; 16,000 sheep; 2.6 mil poultry. **Timber/lumber** (1996): pines, hardwoods, oak; 1.3 bil bd. ft. **Nonfuel minerals** (est. 1996): $428 mil; mostly salt, construction sand & gravel, sulfur. **Commercial fishing** (1996):

$267 mil. **Chief ports:** New Orleans, Baton Rouge, Lake Charles, Port of S. Louisiana (La Place), Shreveport, Plaquemine, St. Bernard, Alexandria.. **International airports at:** New Orleans, Alexandria. **Value of construction** (1996): $4.9 bil. **Employment distribution** (1996): 23.3% trade; 26.8% service; 20.0% govt.; 10.4% mfg. **Per capita personal income** (1996): $19,824. **Unemployment** (1996): 6.7%. **Tourism** (1995): $6.6 bil.

Finance. FDIC-insured commercial banks & trust companies (1996): 172. **Deposits:** $38.2 bil. **FDIC-insured savings institutions** (1996): 38. **Assets:** $5.0 bil.

Federal government. No. federal civilian employees (Mar. 1996): 20,693. **Avg. salary:** $37,586. **Notable federal facilities:** Strategic Petroleum Reserve, Michoud Assembly Plant, Southeast U.S. Agricultural Research Ctr., U.S Army Corps of Engineers, all New Orleans; Ft. Polk military bases, Barksdale; U.S. Public Service Hospital, Carville; Naval Air Station, Chalmette; V.A. Hospital, Pineville.

Energy. Electricity production (1996, kWh, by source): Coal: 18.6 bil; Petroleum: 273 mil; Gas: 24.2 bil; Nuclear: 15.8 bil.

Public education. Student-teacher ratio (1995): 17.0. **Avg. teachers' salary** (1996-97): $28,347.

State data. Motto: Union, justice, and confidence. **Flower:** Magnolia. **Bird:** Eastern brown pelican. **Tree:** Cypress. **Song:** Give Me Louisiana. **Entered union** Apr. 30, 1812; rank, 18th. **State fair** at Shreveport; Oct.

History. Caddo, Tunica, Choctaw, Chitimacha, and Chawash peoples lived in the region at the time of European contact. Europeans Cabeza de Vaca and Panfilo de Narvaez first visited, 1530. The region was claimed for France by La Salle, 1682. The first permanent settlement was by the French at Biloxi, now in Mississippi, 1699. France ceded the region to Spain, 1762, took it back, 1800, and sold it to the U.S., 1803, in the Louisiana Purchase. During the American Revolution, Spanish Louisiana aided the Americans. Admitted as a state in 1812, Louisiana was the scene of the Battle of New Orleans, 1815.

Louisiana Creoles are descendants of early French and/or Spanish settlers. About 4,000 Acadians, French settlers in Nova Scotia, Canada, were forcibly transported by the British to Louisiana in 1755 (an event commemorated in Longfellow's "Evangeline") and settled near Bayou Teche; their descendants became known as Cajuns. Another group, the Islenos, were descendants of Canary Islanders brought to Louisiana by a Spanish governor in 1770. Traces of Spanish and French survive in local dialects.

Tourist attractions. Mardi Gras, French Quarter, Superdome, Dixieland jazz, Aquarium of the Americas, Audobon Zoo & Gardens, all New Orleans; Battle of New Orleans site; Longfellow-Evangeline Memorial Park, St. Martinville; Kent House Museum, Alexandria; Hodges Gardens, Natchitoches, USS Kidd Memorial, Baton Rouge.

Famous Louisianans. Louis Armstrong, Pierre Beauregard, Judah P. Benjamin, Braxton Bragg, Kate Chopin, Lillian Hellman, Grace King, Huey Long, Leonidas K. Polk, Winton Marsalis, Anne Rice, Henry Miller Shreve, Edward D. White Jr.

Tourist information. State Dept. of Culture, Recreation & Tourism, PO Box 94291, Baton Rouge, LA 70804-9291.

Toll-free travel information. 1-800-33GUMBO.

Web site. http://www.state.la.us

Maine

Pine Tree State

People. Population (1996): 1,243,316; rank: 39; **Net change** (1990-96): 1.3%. **Pop. density:** (1990) 39.8 per sq mi. **Racial/ethnic distrib.** (1990): 98.4% white; 0.4% black; 0.6% Hispanic.

Geography. Total area: 35,387 sq mi; rank: 39. **Land area:** 30,865 sq mi; rank: 39. **Acres forested land:** 17,533,000. **Location:** New England state at northeastern tip of U.S. **Climate:** Southern interior and coastal, influenced by air masses from the S and W; northern clime harsher, avg. over 100 in. snow in winter. **Topography:** Appalachian Mts. extend through state; western borders have rugged terrain; long sand beaches on southern coast; northern coast mainly rocky promontories, peninsulas, fjords. **Capital:** Augusta.

Economy. Principal industries: manufacturing, agriculture, fishing, services, trade, government, finance, insurance, real estate, construction. **Principal manufactured goods:** paper and wood products, transportation equipment. **Principal crops:** potatoes, aquaculture products. **Livestock** (1995): 117,000 cattle; 11,000 sheep; 6.7 mil poultry. **Timber/lumber** (1996): pine, spruce, fir; 1.1 bil bd. ft. **Nonfuel minerals** (est. 1996): $73.1 mil; cement, construction sand & gravel, crushed stone. **Commercial fishing** (1996): $201 mil. **Chief ports:** Searsport, Portland, Eastport. **International airports at:** Portland, Bangor. **Value of construction** (1996): $983 mil. **Employment distribution** (1994): 24.3% serv.; 19.4% trade; 15.4% govt.; 23.3% mfg. **Per capita personal income** (1996): $20,826. **Unemployment** (1996): 5.1%. **Tourism** (1995): $3 bil.

Finance. FDIC-insured commercial banks & trust companies (1996): 20. **Deposits:** $6.5 bil. **FDIC-insured savings institutions** (1996): 28. **Assets:** $7.6 bil.

Federal government. No. federal civilian employees (Mar. 1996): 8,034. **Avg. salary:** $38,828. **Notable federal facilities:** Kittery Naval Shipyard; Brunswick Naval Air Station.

Energy. Electricity production (1996, kWh, by source): Petroleum: 619 mil; Hydroelectric: 2.1 bil; Nuclear: 5.1 bil.

Public education. Student-teacher ratio (1995): 13.9. **Avg. teachers' salary** (1996-97): $33,800.

State data. Motto: Dirigo (I direct). **Flower:** White pine cone and tassel. **Bird:** Chickadee. **Tree:** Eastern white pine. **Song:** State of Maine Song. **Entered union** Mar. 15, 1820; rank, 23d. **State fair:** at Bangor, July-Aug. 3; at Skowhegan, mid-Aug.

History. When the Europeans arrived, Maine was inhabited by Algonquian peoples including the Abnaki, Penobscot, and Passamaquoddy. Maine's rocky coast was believed to have been explored by the Cabots, 1498-99. French settlers arrived, 1604, at the St. Croix River, English, c 1607, on the Kennebec; both settlements failed. Maine was made part of Massachusetts, 1691. In the American Revolution, a Maine regiment fought at Bunker Hill. A British fleet destroyed Falmouth (now Portland), 1775, but the British ship *Margaretta* was captured near Machiasport. In 1820, Maine broke off from Massachusetts and became a separate state.

Tourist attractions. Acadia Natl. Park, Bar Harbor, on Mt. Desert Island; Old Orchard Beach; Portland's Old Port; Kennebunkport; Common Ground Country Fair; Portland Headlight; Baxter State Pk.; Freeport/L. L. Bean.

Famous "Down Easters." James G. Blaine, Cyrus H. K. Curtis, Hannibal Hamlin, Sarah Jewett, Stephen King, Henry Wadsworth Longfellow, Sir Hiram and Hudson Maxim, Edna St. Vincent Millay, Edmund Muskie, Edwin Arlington Robinson, Kate Douglas Wiggin, Ben Ames Williams.

Chamber of Commerce and Industry. Maine Chamber & Business Alliance, 7 Community Dr., Augusta, ME 04330.

Toll-free travel information. 1-800-533-9595, out of state only (not applicable to Canada).

Web site. http://www.state.me.us

Maryland

Old Line State, Free State

People. Population (1996): 5,071,604; rank: 19; **Net change** (1990-96): 6.1%. **Pop. density:** (1990) 489.2 per sq mi. **Racial/ethnic distrib.** (1990): 71.0% white; 24.9% black; 2.9% Asian; 2.6% Hispanic.

Geography. Total area: 12,407 sq mi; rank: 42. **Land area:** 9,775 sq mi; rank: 42. **Acres forested land:** 2,700,000. **Location:** South Atlantic state stretching from the Ocean to the Allegheny Mts. **Climate:** continental in the west; humid subtropical in the east. **Topography:** Eastern Shore of coastal plain and Maryland Main of coastal plain, piedmont plateau, and the Blue Ridge, separated by the Chesapeake Bay. **Capital:** Annapolis.

Economy. Principal industries: manufacturing, biotechnology and information technology, services, tourism. **Principal manufactured goods:** electric and electronic equipment; food and kindred products, chemicals and allied products, printed materials. **Chief crops:** greenhouse and nursery products, soybeans, corn. **Livestock** (1996): 270,000 cattle; 64,000 hogs/pigs; 32,000 sheep/lambs; 3.6 mil layers; 294.8 mil broilers. **Tim-**

ber/lumber: (1996) hardwoods; 241 mil bd. ft. **Nonfuel minerals** (est. 1996): $324 mil; crushed stone, sand & gravel, portland cement. **Commercial fishing** (1996): $53 mil. **Chief port:** Baltimore. **International airport at:** Baltimore-Washington Intl. **Value of construction** (1996): $6.5 bil. **Employment distribution** (1995): 16.4% mfg.; 19.4% serv.; 20.6% trade; 25% govt. **Per capita personal income** (1996): $27,221. **Unemployment** (1996): 4.9%. **Tourism** (1995): $5.8 bil.

Finance. FDIC-insured commercial banks & trust companies (1996): 90. **Deposits:** $30.2 bil. **FDIC-insured savings institutions** (1996): 71. **Assets:** $9.8 bil.

Federal government. No. federal civilian employees (Mar. 1996): 102,009. **Avg. salary:** $48,242. **Notable federal facilities:** U.S. Naval Academy; Natl. Agriculture Research Center; Ft. George G. Meade, Aberdeen Proving Ground; Goddard Space Flight Center; Natl. Institutes of Health; Natl. Institute of Standards & Technology; Food & Drug Administration; Bureau of the Census.

Energy. Electricity production (1996, kWh, by source): Coal: 27.8 bil; Petroleum: 1.4 bil; Gas: 649 mil; Hydroelectric: 2.5 bil; Nuclear: 12.1 bil.

Public education. Student-teacher ratio (1995): 16.8. **Avg. teachers' salary** (1996-97): $41,148.

State data. Motto: Fatti Maschii, Parole Femine (Manly deeds, womanly words). **Flower:** Black-eyed susan. **Bird:** Baltimore oriole. **Tree:** White oak. **Song:** Maryland, My Maryland. **Seventh** of the original 13 states to ratify Constitution, Apr. 28, 1788. **State fair** at Timonium; late Aug.-early Sept.

History. Europeans encountered Algonquian-speaking Nanticoke and Piscataway and Iroquios-speaking Susquehannock when they first visited the area. Italian explorer Verrazano visited the Chesapeake region in the early 16th cent. English Capt. John Smith explored and mapped the area, 1608. William Claiborne set up a trading post on Kent Island in Chesapeake Bay, 1631. British King Charles I granted land to Cecilius Calvert, Lord Baltimore, 1632; Calvert's brother Leonard, with about 200 settlers, founded St. Marys, 1634. The bravery of Maryland troops in the American Revolution, as at the Battle of Long Island, won the state its nickname "The Old Line State." In the War of 1812, when a British fleet tried to take Ft. McHenry, Marylander Francis Scott Key wrote "The Star Spangled Banner," 1814. Although a slave-holding state, Maryland remained with the Union during the Civil War and was the site of the battle of Antietam, 1862, which halted Gen. Robert E. Lee's march north.

Tourist attractions. The Preakness and Maryland Million, both at Pimlico track, Baltimore, and the International, at Laurel Race Course; Ocean City; restored Ft. McHenry, near which Francis Scott Key wrote "The Star-Spangled Banner"; Edgar Allan Poe house, Ravens Football at Memorial Stadium, Camden Yards, Natl. Aquarium, Harborplace, all Baltimore; Antietam Battlefield, near Hagerstown; South Mountain Battlefield; U.S. Naval Academy, Annapolis; Maryland State House, Annapolis, 1772, the oldest still in use in the U.S.

Famous Marylanders. John Astin, Benjamin Banneker, Tom Clancy, Jonathan Demme, Francis Scott Key, H. L. Mencken, Charles Willson Peale, William Pinkney, Edgar Allan Poe, Upton Sinclair, Roger B. Taney.

Maryland Dept. of Business & Economic Development. 217 E. Redwood St., Baltimore, MD 21202; (410) 767-6870.

Toll-free travel information. 1-800-543-1036.

Web site. http://www.state.md.us

Massachusetts

Bay State, Old Colony

People. Population (1996): 6,092,352; rank: 13; **Net change** (1990-96): 1.3%. **Pop. density:** (1990) 767.6 per sq mi. **Racial/ethnic distrib.** (1990): 89.8% white; 5.0% black; 2.4% Asian; 4.8% Hispanic.

Geography. Total area: 10,555 sq mi; rank: 44. **Land area:** 7,838 sq mi; rank: 45. **Acres forested land:** 3,203,000. **Location:** New England state along Atlantic

seaboard. **Climate:** temperate, with colder and drier clime in western region. **Topography:** jagged indented coast from Rhode Island around Cape Cod; flat land yields to stony upland pastures near central region and gentle hilly country in west; except in west, land is rocky, sandy, and not fertile. **Capital:** Boston.

Economy. Principal industries: services, trade, manufacturing. **Principal manufactured goods:** electric and electronic equipment, instruments, industrial machinery and equipment, printing and publishing, fabricated metal products. **Chief crops:** cranberries, greenhouse, nursery, vegetables. **Livestock** (1994): 68,000 cattle; 32,200 hogs/pigs; 11,500 sheep; 646,000 chickens, 140,000 turkeys. **Timber/lumber** white pine, oak, other hard woods. **Nonfuel minerals** (est. 1996): $191 mil; mostly crushed stone, construction sand & gravel. **Commercial fishing** (1996): $231 mil. **Chief ports:** Boston, Fall River, New Bedford, Salem, Gloucester, Plymouth. **International airport at:** Boston. **Value of construction** (1996): $7.7 bil. **Employment distribution** (1996): 22.9% trade; 35% serv.; 14.6% mfg.; 13.2% govt. **Per capita personal income** (1996): $29,439. **Unemployment** (1996): 4.3%. **Tourism** (1994): $9.2 bil.

Finance. FDIC-insured commercial banks & trust companies (1996): 50. **Deposits:** $106.6 bil. **FDIC-insured savings institutions** (1996): 208. **Assets:** $53.4 bil.

Federal government. No. federal civilian employees (Mar. 1996): 27,666. **Avg. salary:** $43,009. **Notable federal facilities:** Thomas P. O'Neill Jr. Federal Bldg., J.W. McCormack Bldg., John Fitzgerald Kennedy Federal Bldg., Q.M. Laboratory, Natick.

Energy. Electricity production (1996, kWh, by source): Coal: 11.5 bil; Petroleum: 5.9 bil; Gas: 4.4 bil; Hydroelectric: 263; Nuclear: 5.3 bil.

Public education. Student-teacher ratio (1995): 14.6. **Avg. teachers' salary** (1996-97): $43,806.

State data. Motto: Ense Petit Placidam Sub Libertate Quietem (By the sword we seek peace, but peace only under liberty). **Flower:** Mayflower. **Bird:** Chickadee. **Tree:** American elm. **Song:** All Hail to Massachusetts. **Sixth** of the original 13 states to ratify Constitution, Feb. 6, 1788. **State Fair** at Topsfield, early Oct.

History. Early inhabitants were the Algonquian Nauset, Wampanoag, Massachuset, Pennacook, Nipmuc, and Pocumtuc peoples. Pilgrims settled in Plymouth, 1620, giving thanks for their survival with the first Thanksgiving Day, 1621. About 20,000 new settlers arrived, 1630-40. Native American relations with the colonists deteriorated leading to King Philip's War, 1675-76, which the colonists won, ending Native American resistance. Demonstrations against British restrictions set off the Boston Massacre, 1770, and the Boston Tea Party, 1773. The first bloodshed of American Revolution was at Lexington, 1775.

Tourist attractions. Provincetown artists' colony; Cape Cod; Plymouth Rock, Plymouth Plantation, Mayflower II, all Plymouth; Freedom Trail, Museum of Fine Arts, Children's Museum, Museum of Science, New England Aquarium, JFK Library, Boston Ballet, Boston Pops, Boston Symphony Orchestra, all Boston; Tanglewood, Jacob's Pillow Dance Festival, Hancock Shaker Village Berkshire Railway Museum, all in the Berkshires; Salem; Old Sturbridge Village; Deerfield Historic District; Walden Pond; Naismith Memorial Basketball Hall of Fame, Springfield.

Famous "Bay Staters." John Adams, John Quincy Adams, Samuel Adams, Louisa May Alcott, Horatio Alger, Susan B. Anthony, Crispus Attucks, Clara Barton, Alexander Graham Bell, Stephen Breyer, George Bush, John Cheever, E. E. Cummings, Emily Dickinson, Charles Eliot, Ralph Waldo Emerson, William Lloyd Garrison, Edward Everett Hale, John Hancock, Nathaniel Hawthorne, Oliver Wendell Holmes, Winslow Homer, Elias Howe, John F. Kennedy, James Russell Lowell, Cotton Mather, Samuel F. B. Morse, Edgar Allan Poe, Paul Revere, Dr. Seuss, Henry David Thoreau, James McNeil Whistler, John Greenleaf Whittier.

Tourist information. Massachusetts Office of Travel & Tourism, 100 Cambridge St., 13th Floor, Boston, MA 02202.

Toll-free travel information. 1-800-447-MASS.

Web site. http://www.state.ma.us

Michigan
Great Lakes State, Wolverine State

People. Population (1996): 9,594,350; rank: 8; **Net change** (1990-96): 3.2%. **Pop. density:** (1990) 163.6 per sq mi. **Racial/ethnic distrib.** (1990): 83.4% white; 13.9% black; 2.2% Hispanic.

Geography. Total area: 96,705 sq mi; rank: 11. **Land area:** 56,809 sq mi; rank: 22. **Acres forested land:** 18,253,000. **Location:** East North Central state bordering on 4 of the 5 Great Lakes, divided into an Upper and Lower Peninsula by the Straits of Mackinac, which link lakes Michigan and Huron. **Climate:** well-defined seasons tempered by the Great Lakes. **Topography:** low rolling hills give way to northern tableland of hilly belts in Lower Peninsula; Upper Peninsula is level in the east, with swampy areas; western region is higher and more rugged. **Capital:** Lansing.

Economy. Principal industries: manufacturing, services, tourism, agriculture, forestry/lumber. **Principal manufactured goods:** automobiles, transportation equipment, machinery, fabricated metals, food products, plastics, office furniture. **Chief crops:** corn, wheat, soybeans, dry beans, hay, potatoes, sweet corn, apples, cherries, sugar beets, blueberries, cucumbers. **Livestock** (1996): 1.2 mil cattle; 1.1 mil hogs/pigs; 93,000 sheep; 6.5 mil poultry. **Timber/lumber** (1996): maple, oak, aspen; 652 mil bd. ft. **Nonfuel minerals** (est. 1996): $1.51 bil; iron ore, magnesium compounds, portland cement, sand & gravel, crushed stone. **Commercial fishing** (1996): $9 mil. **Chief ports:** Detroit, Saginaw River, Escanaba, Muskegon, Sault Ste. Marie, Port Huron, Marine City. **International airports at:** Detroit, Grand Rapids, Flint, Kalamazoo, Lansing, Saginaw. **Value of construction** (1996): $10.8 bil. **Employment distribution** (1996): 22.2% mfg.; 23.7% trade; 26.7% service; 14.7% govt. **Per capita personal income** (1996): $24,810. **Unemployment** (1996): 4.9%. **Tourism** (1995): $8 bil.

Finance. FDIC-insured commercial banks & trust companies (1996): 176. **Deposits:** $84.2 bil. **FDIC-insured savings institutions** (1996): 26. **Assets:** $26.5 bil.

Federal government. No. federal civilian employees (Mar. 1996): 23,009. **Avg. salary:** $42,477. **Notable federal facilities:** Isle Royal, Sleeping Bear Dunes national parks.

Energy. Electricity production (1996, kWh, by source): Coal: 66.1 bil; Petroleum: 652 mil; Gas: 771 mil; Hydroelectric: 858 mil; Nuclear: 26.8 bil.

Public education. Student-teacher ratio (1995): 19.7. **Avg. teachers' salary** (1996-97): $44,251.

State data. Motto: Si Quaeris Peninsulam Amoenam, Circumspice (If you seek a pleasant peninsula, look about you). **Flower:** Apple blossom. **Bird:** Robin. **Tree:** White pine. **Song:** Michigan, My Michigan. **Entered union** Jan. 26, 1837; rank, 26th. **State fair** at Detroit, late Aug.-early Sept.; Upper Peninsula (Escanaba), mid-Aug; Michigan Festival, mid-Aug.

History. Early inhabitants were the Ojibwa, Ottawa, Miami, Potawatomi, and Huron. French fur traders and missionaries visited the region, 1616, set up a mission at Sault Ste. Marie, 1641, and a settlement there, 1668. French settlements were taken over, 1763, by the British, who crushed a Native American uprising led by Ottawa chieftain Pontiac that same year. Treaty of Paris ceded territory to U.S., 1783, but British remained until 1796. The British seized Ft. Mackinac and Detroit, 1812. After Oliver H. Perry's Lake Erie victory and William H. Harrison's victory near the Thames River, 1813, the British retreated to Canada. The opening of the Erie Canal, 1825, and new land laws and additional Native American cessions led the way for a flood of settlers.

Tourist attractions. Henry Ford Museum, Greenfield Village, both in Dearborn; Michigan Space Center, Jackson; Tahquamenon (*Hiawatha*) Falls; DeZwaan windmill and Tulip Festival, Holland; Soo Locks," Ot. Mary's Falls Ship Canal, Sault Ste. Marie, Kalamazoo Aviation History Museum; Mackinac Island.

Michigan's Famous People. Ralph Bunche, Paul de Kruif, Thomas A. Edison, Edna Ferber, Gerald R. Ford, Henry Ford, Aretha Franklin, Edgar Guest, Lee Iacocca, Robert Ingersoll, Magic Johnson, Will Kellogg, Ring Lardner, Elmore Leonard, Charles Lindbergh, Joe Louis, Madonna, Jack Paar, Pontiac, Diana Ross, Tom Selleck, John Smoltz, Lily Tomlin, Stewart Edward White, Malcolm X.

State Chamber of Commerce. 600 S. Walnut, Lansing, MI 48933. Phone: 517-371-2100

Toll-free travel information. 1-888-784-7328.

Web site. http://www.migov.state.mi.us

Minnesota
North Star State, Gopher State

People. Population (1996): 4,657,758; rank: 20; **Net change** (1990-96): 6.4%. **Pop. density:** (1990) 55.0 per sq mi. **Racial/ethnic distrib.** (1990): 94.4% white; 2.2% black; 1.8% Asian; 1.2% Hispanic.

Geography. Total area: 86,943 sq mi; rank: 12. **Land area:** 79,617 sq mi; rank: 14. **Acres forested land:** 16,718,000. **Location:** West North Central state bounded on the E by Wisconsin and Lake Superior, on the N by Canada, on the W by the Dakotas, and on the S by Iowa. **Climate:** northern part of state lies in the moist Great Lakes storm belt; the western border lies at the edge of the semi-arid Great Plains. **Topography:** central hill and lake region covering approx. half the state; to the NE, rocky ridges and deep lakes; to the NW, flat plain; to the S, rolling plains and deep river valleys. **Capital:** St. Paul.

Economy. Principal industries: agribusiness, forest products, mining, manufacturing, tourism. **Principal manufactured goods:** food, chemical and paper products, industrial machinery, electric and electronic equipment, computers, printing and publishing, scientific and medical instruments, fabricated metal products, forest products. **Chief crops:** corn, soybeans, wheat, sugar beets, hay, barley, potatoes, sunflowers. **Livestock** (1995): 2.80 mil cattle; 4.85 mil hogs/pigs; 190,000 sheep; 14.2 mil chickens; 41.5 mil turkeys. **Timber/lumber** (1996): needle-leaves and hardwoods; 313 mil bd. ft. **Nonfuel minerals** (est. 1996): $1.8 bil; mostly iron ore, construction sand & gravel, crushed stone. **Commercial fishing** (1996): $221,000. **Chief ports:** Duluth, St. Paul, Minneapolis. **International airport at:** Minneapolis-St. Paul. **Value of construction** (1996): $5.4 bil. **Employment distribution** (1995): 24.3% trade; 27.1% serv.; 17.9% mfg.; 16% govt. **Per capita personal income** (1996): $25,580. **Unemployment** (1996): 4.0%. **Tourism** (1994): $7 bil.

Finance. FDIC-insured commercial banks & trust companies (1996): 519. **Deposits:** $53.9 bil. **FDIC-insured savings institutions** (1996): 23. **Assets:** $6.1 bil.

Federal government. No. federal civilian employees (Mar. 1996): 13,638. **Avg. salary:** $41,118.

Energy. Electricity production (1996, kWh, by source): Coal: 27.3 bil; Petroleum: 639 mil; Gas: 468 mil; Hydroelectric: 843 mil; Nuclear: 12.1 bil.

Public education. Student-teacher ratio (1995): 17.8. **Avg. teachers' salary** (1996-97): $37,975.

State data. Motto: L'Etoile du Nord (The star of the north). **Flower:** Pink and white lady's-slipper. **Bird:** Common loon. **Tree:** Red pine. **Song:** Hail! Minnesota. **Entered union** May 11, 1858; rank, 32d. **State fair** at Saint Paul; late Aug.-early Sept.

History. Dakota Sioux were early inhabitants of the area, and in the 16th cent., the Ojibwa began moving in from the east. French fur traders Médard Chouart and Pierre Esprit Radisson entered the region in the mid-17th cent. In 1679, French explorer Daniel Greysolon, sieur Duluth, claimed the entire region in the name of France. Britain took the area east of the Mississippi, 1763. The U.S. took over that portion after the American Revolution and in 1803, gained the western area in the Louisiana Purchase. The U.S. built Ft. St. Anthony (now Ft. Snelling), 1819, and in 1837, bought Native American lands, spurring an influx of settlers from the east. In 1849, the Territory of Minnesota was created. Sioux Indians staged a bloody uprising, the Battle of Woods Lake, 1862, and were driven from the state.

Tourist attractions. Minneapolis Institute of Arts, Walker Art Center, Minneapolis Sculpture Garden, Minnehaha Falls, inspiration for Longfellow's *Hiawatha*, Guthrie Theater, Minneapolis; Ordway Theater, St. Paul; Voyageurs Natl. Park, a water wilderness along the Canadian border; Mayo Clinic, Rochester; St. Paul Winter Carnival; North Shore (of Lake Superior).

Famous Minnesotans. Warren Burger, William O. Douglas, Bob Dylan, F. Scott Fitzgerald, Judy Garland, Cass Gilbert, Hubert Humphrey, Garrison Keillor, Sister Elizabeth Kenny, Sinclair Lewis, Paul Manship, E. G. Marshall, William and Charles Mayo, Eugene McCarthy, Walter F. Mondale, Charles Schulz, Harold Stassen, Thorstein Veblen.

Tourist information. Minnesota Office of Tourism, 500 Metro Square, 121 7th Place East, St. Paul, MN 55101.

Toll-free travel information. 1-800-657-3700.

Web site. http://www.state.mn.us

Mississippi
Magnolia State

People. Population (1996): 2,716,115; rank: 31; **Net change** (1990-96): 5.5%. **Pop. density:** (1990) 54.9 per sq mi. **Racial/ethnic distrib.** (1990): 63.5% white; 35.6% black; 0.6% Hispanic.

Geography. Total area: 48,434 sq mi; rank: 32. **Land area:** 46,914 sq mi; rank: 31. **Acres forested land:** 17,000,000. **Location:** East South Central state bordered on the W by the Mississippi R. and on the S by the Gulf of Mexico. **Climate:** semi-tropical, with abundant rainfall, long growing season, and extreme temperatures unusual. **Topography:** low, fertile delta between the Yazoo and Mississippi rivers; loess bluffs stretching around delta border; sandy gulf coastal terraces followed by piney woods and prairie; rugged, high sandy hills in extreme NE followed by Black Prairie Belt, Pontotoc Ridge, and flatwoods into the north central highlands. **Capital:** Jackson.

Economy. Principal industries: services, manufacturing, government, wholesale and retail trade. **Principal manufactured goods:** apparel, food & kindred products, furniture, lumber and wood products, electrical machinery, transportation equipment. **Chief crops:** cotton, rice, soybeans. **Livestock** (1997): 1.34 mil cattle; (1996) 240,000 hogs/pigs; 10.7 mil chickens excl. broilers; 1.7 mil hogs/pigs; 676 mil broilers. **Timber/lumber** (1996): pine, oak, hardwoods; 2.8 bil bd. ft. **Nonfuel minerals** (est. 1996): $140 mil; mostly crushed stone, construction sand & gravel. **Commercial fishing** (1996): $33 mil. **Chief ports:** Pascagoula, Vicksburg, Gulfport, Natchez, Greenville. **Value of construction** (1996): $3.6 bil. **Employment distribution** (1996): 22.5% mfg.; 20% govt.; 21% trade; 22.6% serv. **Per capita personal income** (1996): $17,471. **Unemployment** (1996): 6.1%. **Tourism** (1996): 4.4 bil.

Finance. FDIC-insured commercial banks & trust companies (1996): 111. **Deposits:** $23.4 bil. **FDIC-insured savings institutions** (1996): 14. **Assets:** $2.6 bil.

Federal government. No. federal civilian employees (Mar. 1996): 17,284. **Avg. salary:** $38,010. **Notable federal facilities:** Columbus, Keesler AF bases; Meridian Naval Air Station, John C. Stennis Space Center; U.S. Army Corps of Engineers Waterway Experiment Station.

Energy. Electricity production (1996, kWh, by source): Coal: 12.0 bil; Petroleum: 1.2 bil; Gas: 6.4 bil; Nuclear: 9.2 bil.

Public education. Student-teacher ratio (1995): 17.5. **Avg. teachers' salary** (1995): $27,720.

State data. Motto: Virtute et Armis (By valor and arms). **Flower:** Magnolia. **Bird:** Mockingbird. **Tree:** Magnolia. **Song:** Go, Mississippi! **Entered union** Dec. 10, 1817; rank, 20th. **State fair** at Jackson; early Oct.

History. Early inhabitants of the region were Choctaw, Chickasaw, and Natchez peoples. Hernando de Soto explored the area, 1540, and sighted the Mississippi River, 1541. Robert La Salle traced the river from Illinois to its mouth and claimed the entire valley for France, 1682. The first settlement was the French Ft. Maurepas, near Ocean Springs, 1699. The area was ceded to Britain, 1763; American settlers followed. During the American Revolution, Spain seized part of the area and refused to leave even after the U.S. acquired title at the end of the conflict; Spain finally moved out, 1798. The Territory of Mississippi was formed, 1798. Mississippi seceded, 1861. Union forces captured Corinth and Vicksburg and destroyed Jackson and much of Meridian. Mississippi was readmitted to the Union in 1870.

Tourist attractions. Vicksburg Natl. Military Park and Cemetery, other Civil War sites; Hattiesburg; Natchez Trace; Indian mounds; Antebellum homes; pilgrimages in

Natchez and some 25 other cities; Smith Robertson Museum, Mynelle Gardens, both Jackson; Mardi Gras and Shrimp Festival, both in Biloxi; Gulf Islands Natl. Seashore; Casinos on the Mississippi River.

Famous Mississippians. Dana Andrews, Margaret Walker Alexander, Jimmy Buffett, Hodding Carter III, Bo Diddley, William Faulkner, Brett Favre, Shelby Foote, Morgan Freeman, John Grisham, Fannie Lou Hamer, Jim Henson, Robert Johnson, James Earl Jones, B. B. King, L. Q. C. Lamar, Gerald McRaney, Willie Morris, Walter Payton, Elvis Presley, Leontyne Price, Charlie Pride, LeAnn Rimes, Muddy Waters, Eudora Welty, Tennessee Williams, Oprah Winfrey, Johnny Winter, Richard Wright, Tammy Wynette.

Dept. of Economic & Community Development. PO Box 849, Jackson, MS 39205-0849.

Toll-free travel information. 1-800-WARMEST.

Web site. http://www.state.ms.us

Missouri
Show Me State

People. Population (1996): 5,358,692; rank: 16; **Net change** (1990-96): 4.7%. **Pop. density:** (1990) 74.3 per sq mi. **Racial/ethnic distrib.** (1990): 87.7% white; 10.7% black; 1.2% Hispanic.

Geography. Total area: 69,709 sq mi; rank: 21. **Land area:** 68,898 sq mi; rank: 18. **Acres forested land:** 14,007,000. **Location:** West North Central state near the geographic center of the conterminous U.S.; bordered on the E by the Mississippi R., on the NW by the Missouri R. **Climate:** continental, susceptible to cold Canadian air, moist, warm gulf air, and drier SW air. **Topography:** rolling hills, open, fertile plains, and well-watered prairie N of the Missouri R.; south of the river land is rough and hilly with deep, narrow valleys; alluvial plain in the SE; low elevation in the west. **Capital:** Jefferson City.

Economy. Principal industries: agriculture, manufacturing, aerospace, tourism. **Principal manufactured goods:** transportation equipment, food and related products, electrical and electronic equipment, chemicals. **Chief crops:** soybeans, corn, wheat, hay. **Livestock** (1995): 4.65 mil cattle; 3.55 mil hogs/pigs; 73,000 sheep; 8.4 mil chickens, 1.7 mil eggs, 22.5 mil turkeys. **Timber/lumber** (1996): oak, hickory; 546 mil bd. ft. **Nonfuel minerals** (est. 1996): $1.25 bil; mostly lead, portland cement, crushed stone. **Chief ports:** St. Louis, Kansas City. **International airports at:** St. Louis, Kansas City. **Value of construction** (1996): $6.0 bil. **Employment distribution** (1995): 27% services; 24% trade; 17% mfg.; 15% govt. **Per capita personal income** (1996): $22,864. **Unemployment** (1996): 4.6%. **Tourism** (1993): $5 bil.

Finance. FDIC-insured commercial banks & trust companies (1996): 430. **Deposits:** $70.6 bil. **FDIC-insured savings institutions** (1996): 49. **Assets:** $15.3.7bil.

Federal government. No. federal civilian employees (Mar. 1996): 39,490. **Avg. salary:** $38,743. **Notable federal facilities:** Federal Reserve banks; Ft. Leonard Wood; Jefferson Barracks; Whiteman AFB.

Energy. Electricity production (1996 kWh, by source): Coal: 57.2 bil; Petroleum: 97 mil; Gas: 404 mil; Hydroelectric: 1.2 bil; Nuclear: 8.9 bil.

Public education. Student-teacher ratio (1995): 15.4. **Avg. teachers' salary** (1996-97): $34,342.

State data. Motto: Salus Populi Suprema Lex Esto (The welfare of the people shall be the supreme law). **Flower:** Hawthorn. **Bird:** Bluebird. **Tree:** Dogwood. **Song:** Missouri Waltz. **Entered union** Aug. 10, 1821; rank, 24th. **State fair** at Sedalia; 3d week in Aug.

History. Early inhabitants of the region were Algonquian Sauk, Fox, and Illinois and Siouan Osage, Missouri, Iowa, and Kansa peoples. Hernando de Soto visited the area, 1541. French hunters and lead miners made the first settlement c 1735, at Ste. Genevieve. The territory was ceded to Spain by the French, 1763, then returned to France, 1800. The U.S. acquired Missouri as part of the Louisiana Purchase, 1803. The influx of white settlers drove Native American tribes to the Kansas and Oklahoma territories; most were gone by 1836. The fur trade and the Santa Fe Trail provided prosperity; St. Louis became the gateway for pioneers heading West. Missouri entered the Union as a slave state, 1821. Though it remained with the Union, pro- and antislavery forces battled there during the Civil War.

Tourist attractions. Silver Dollar City, Branson; Mark Twain Area, Hannibal; Pony Express Museum, St. Joseph; Harry S. Truman Library, Independence; Gateway Arch, St. Louis; Worlds of Fun, Kansas City; Lake of the Ozarks; Churchill Mem., Fulton; State Capitol, Jefferson City.

Famous Missourians. Maya Angelou, Robert Altman, Burt Bacharach, Josephine Baker, Scot Bakula, Thomas Hart Benton, Tom Berenger, Chuck Berry, George Caleb Bingham, Daniel Boone, Omar Bradley, Kate Capshaw, Dale Carnegie, George Washington Carver, Bob Costas, Walter Cronkite, Walt Disney, T. S. Eliot, John Goodman, Betty Grable, Edwin Hubbles, Jesse James, Marianne Moore, Reinhold Niebuhr, J. C. Penney, John J. Pershing, Brad Pitt, Joseph Pulitzer, Ginger Rogers, Bess Truman, Harry S. Truman, Kathleen Turner, Tina Turner, Mark Twain, Dick Van Dyke, Tennessee Williams, Lanford Wilson, Shelly Winters, Jane Wyman.

Chamber of Commerce. 428 E. Capitol, Jefferson City, MO 65101.

Toll-free travel information. 1-800-877-1234.

Web site. http://www.ecodev.state.mo.us

Montana
Treasure State

People. Population (1996): 879,372; rank: 44; **Net change** (1990-96): 10.1%. **Pop. density:** (1990) 5.5 per sq mi. **Racial/ethnic distrib.** (1990) 92.7% white; 0.3% black; 6.0% Amer. Indian; 1.5% Hispanic.

Geography. Total area: 147,046 sq mi; rank: 4. **Land area:** 145,556 sq mi; rank: 4. **Acres forested land:** 22,512,000. **Location:** Mountain state bounded on the E by the Dakotas, on the S by Wyoming, on the SSW by Idaho, and on the N by Canada. **Climate:** colder, continental climate with low humidity. **Topography:** Rocky Mts. in western third of the state; eastern two-thirds gently rolling northern Great Plains. **Capital:** Helena.

Economy. Principal industries: agriculture, timber, mining, tourism, oil and gas. **Principal manufactured goods:** food products, wood and paper products, primary metals, printing and publishing, petroleum and coal products. **Chief crops:** wheat, barley, sugar beets, hay, oats. **Livestock** (1995): 2.8 mil cattle; 180,000 hogs/pigs; 430,000 sheep; 540,000 chickens. **Timber/lumber** (1996) Douglas fir, pines, larch; 1.3 bil bd. ft. **Nonfuel minerals** (est. 1996): $523 mil; platinum, palladium, talc and pyrophylite, copper, gold, zinc, phosphate rock, portland cement. **International airports at:** Great Falls, Billings, Kalispell, Missoula. **Value of construction** (1996): $916 mil. **Employment distribution** (1995): 29.0% serv.; 23.3% trade; 16.6% govt.; 5.6% mfg. **Per capita personal income** (1996): $19,047. **Unemployment** (1996): 5.3%. **Tourism** (1996): $1.3 bil.

Finance. FDIC-insured commercial banks & trust companies (1996): 100. **Deposits:** $7.3 bil. **FDIC-insured savings institutions** (1996): 10. **Assets:** $1.8 bil.

Federal government. No. federal civilian employees (Mar. 1996): 8,046. **Avg. salary:** $37,911. **Notable federal facilities:** Malmstrom AFB; Ft. Peck, Hungry Horse, Libby, Yellowtail dams; numerous missile silos.

Energy. Electricity production (1996, kWh, by source): Coal: 12.2 bil; Petroleum: 18 mil; Gas: 38 mil; Hydroelectric: 13.7 bil.

Public education. Student-teacher ratio (1995): 16.4. **Avg. teachers' salary** (1996-97): $29,950.

State data. Motto: Oro y Plata (Gold and silver). **Flower:** Bitterroot. **Bird:** Western meadowlark. **Tree:** Ponderosa pine. **Song:** Montana. **Entered union** Nov. 8, 1889; rank, 41st. **State fair** at Great Falls; late July-early Aug.

History. Cheyenne, Blackfoot, Crow, Assiniboin, Salish (Flatheads), Kootenai, and Kalispel peoples were early inhabitants of the area. French explorers visited the region, 1742. The U.S. acquired the area partly through the Louisiana Purchase, 1803, and partly through the explorations of Lewis and Clark, 1805-6. Fur traders and missionaries established posts in the early 19th cent. Gold was discovered, 1863, and the Montana territory was established, 1864. Indian uprisings reached their peak with the Battle of Little

Bighorn, 1876. Chief Joseph and the Nez Percé tribe surrendered here, 1877, after long trek across the state. Mining activity and the coming of the Northern Pacific Railway, 1883, brought population growth. Copper wealth from the Butte pits resulted in the turn of the century "War of Copper Kings" as factions fought for control of "the richest hill on earth."

Tourist attractions. Glacier Natl. Park; Yellowstone Natl. Park; Museum of the Rockies, Bozeman; Museum of the Plains Indian, Blackfeet Reservation, near Browning; Little Bighorn Battlefield Natl. Monument and Custer Natl. Cemetery; Flathead Lake; Helena; Lewis and Clark Caverns State Park, near Whitehall.

Famous Montanans. Gary Cooper, Marcus Daly, Chet Huntley, Will James, Myrna Loy, Mike Mansfield, Brent Musburger, Jeannette Rankin, Charles M. Russell, Lester Thurow.

Chamber of Commerce. 2030 11th Ave., PO Box 1730, Helena, MT 59624.

Toll-free travel information. 1-800-VISITMT.

Web site. http://www.mt.gov

Nebraska
Cornhusker State

People. Population (1996): 1,652,093; rank: 37; **Net change** (1990-96): 4.7%. **Pop. density:** (1990) 20.5 per sq mi. **Racial/ethnic distrib.** (1990): 93.8% white; 3.6% black; 2.3% Hispanic.

Geography. Total area: 77,358 sq mi; rank: 16. **Land area:** 76,878 sq mi; rank: 15. **Acres forested land:** 722,000. **Location:** West North Central state with the Missouri R. for a NE and E border. **Climate:** continental semi-arid. **Topography:** till plains of the central lowland in the eastern third rising to the Great Plains and hill country of the north central and NW. **Capital:** Lincoln.

Economy. Principal industries: agriculture, manufacturing. **Principal manufactured goods:** processed foods, industrial machinery, printed materials, electric and electronic equipment, primary and fabricated metal products, transportation equipment. **Chief crops:** corn, sorghum, soybeans, hay, wheat, dry beans, oats, potatoes, sugar beets. **Livestock** (1996): 7.3 mil cattle; 3.6 mil hogs/pigs; 95,000 sheep and lambs; 11.5 mil chickens, 3.5 mil turkeys. **Timber/lumber** (1996): oak, hickory, and elm; 25 mil bd. ft. **Nonfuel minerals** (est. 1996): $147 mil; mostly construction sand & gravel, portland cement, crushed stone. **Chief ports:** Omaha, Sioux City, Brownville, Blair, Plattsmouth, Nebraska City. **Value of construction** (1996): $1.9 bil. **Employment distribution** (1996): 24.9% trade; 26.4% serv.; 18.2% govt.; 13.6% mfg. **Per capita personal income** (1996): $23,047. **Unemployment** (1996): 2.9%. **Tourism** (1995): $2 bil.

Finance. FDIC-insured commercial banks & trust companies (1996): 329. **Deposits:** $23.3 bil. **FDIC-insured savings institutions** (1996): 13. **Assets:** $8.7 bil.

Federal government. No. federal civilian employees (Mar. 1996): 8,183. **Avg. salary:** $38,550. **Notable federal facilities:** Offutt AFB.

Energy. Electricity production (1996, kWh, by source): Coal: 16.0 bil; Petroleum: 20 mil; Gas: 193 mil; Hydroelectric: 1.6 mil; Nuclear: 9.5 bil.

Public education. Student-teacher ratio (1995): 14.5. **Avg. teachers' salary** (1996-97): $31,768.

State data. Motto: Equality before the law. **Flower:** Goldenrod. **Bird:** Western meadowlark. **Tree:** Cottonwood. **Song:** Beautiful Nebraska. **Entered union** Mar. 1, 1867; rank, 37th. **State fair** at Lincoln; Aug.- Sept.

History. When the Europeans first arrived, Pawnee, Ponca, Omaha, and Oto peoples lived in the region. Spanish and French explorers and fur traders visited the area prior to its acquisition in the Louisiana Purchase, 1803. Lewis and Clark passed through, 1804-6. The first permanent settlement was Bellevue, near Omaha, 1823. The region was settled gradually despite the 1834 Indian Intercourse Act, which declared Nebraska part of Indian country and excluded white settlement. Conflicts with settlers eventually forced Native Americans to give up their land and move on to reservations. Many Civil War veterans settled under free land terms of the 1862 Homestead Act; as agriculture grew, struggles followed between homesteaders and ranchers.

Tourist attractions. State Museum (Elephant Hall), State Capitol, both Lincoln; Stuhr Museum of the Prairie Pioneer, Grand Island; Museum of the Fur Trade, Chadron; Henry Doorly Zoo, Joslyn Art Museum, both Omaha; Strategic Air Command Museum, Bellevue; Boys Town, west of Omaha; Arbor Lodge State Park, Nebraska City; Buffalo Bill Ranch State Hist. Park, North Platte; Pioneer Village, Minden; Oregon Trail landmarks; Scotts Bluff Natl. Monument; Chimney Rock Historic Site; Ft. Robinson; Hastings Museum, McDonald Planetarium, Hastings.

Famous Nebraskans. Fred Astaire, Marlon Brando, Charles W. Bryan, William Jennings Bryan, Johnny Carson, Willa Cather, Dick Cavett, William F. "Buffalo Bill" Cody, Loren Eiseley, Rev. Edward J. Flanagan, Henry Fonda, Gerald R. Ford, Rollin Kirby, Swoosie Kurtz, Harold Lloyd, Malcolm X, J. Sterling Morton, John Neihardt, Nick Nolte, George Norris, John J. Pershing, Roscoe Pound, Chief Red Cloud, Mari Sandoz, Robert Taylor, Daryl F. Zannuck.

Chamber of Commerce and Industry. 1320 Lincoln Mall, Ste. 201, Lincoln, NE 68508; 402-474-4422

Toll-free travel information. 1-800-228-4307.

Web site. http://www.state.ne.us

Nevada
Sagebrush State, Battle Born State, Silver State

People. Population (1996): 1,603,163; rank: 38; **Net change** (1990-96): 33.4%. **Pop. density:** (1990) 10.9 per sq mi. **Racial/ethnic distrib.** (1990): 84.3% white; 6.6% black; 3.2% Asian; 10.4% Hispanic.

Geography. Total area: 110,567 sq mi; rank: 7. **Land area:** 109,806 sq mi; rank: 7. **Acres forested land:** 8,938,000. **Location:** Mountain state bordered on N by Oregon and Idaho, on E by Utah and Arizona, on SE by Arizona, and on SW and W by California. **Climate:** semi-arid and arid. **Topography:** rugged N-S mountain ranges; highest elevation, Boundary Peak, 13,140 ft; southern area is within the Mojave Desert; lowest elevation, Colorado River at southern tip of state, 479 ft. **Capital:** Carson City.

Economy. Principal industries: gaming, tourism, mining, manufacturing, government, retailing, warehousing, trucking. **Principal manufactured goods:** food products, plastics, chemicals, aerospace products, lawn and garden irrigation equipment, seismic and machinery-monitoring devices. **Chief crops:** hay, alfalfa seed, potatoes, onions, garlic, barley, wheat. **Livestock** (1996): 520,000 cattle; 8,000 hogs/pigs; 85,000 sheep. **Timber/lumber:** piñon, juniper, other pines. **Nonfuel minerals** (est. 1996): $3.23 bil; mostly gold, silver, construction sand & gravel. **International airports at:** Las Vegas, Reno. **Value of construction** (1996): $7.0 bil. **Employment distribution** (1996): 43.1% serv.; 20.1% trade; 12% govt. **Per capita personal income** (1996): $25,451. **Unemployment** (1996): 5.4%. **Tourism** (1996): $27.5 bil.

Finance. FDIC-insured commercial banks & trust companies (1996): 26. **Deposits:** $9.7 bil. **FDIC-insured savings institutions** (1996): 1. **Assets:** $2.8 bil.

Federal government. No. federal civilian employees (Mar. 1996): 7,189. **Avg. salary:** $41,501. **Notable federal facilities:** Nevada Test Site; Hawthorne Army Ammunition Plant, Nellis Air Force Base and Gunnery Range; Fallon Naval Air Station; Palomino Valley Wild Horse and Burro Placement Center.

Energy. Electricity production (1996, kWh, by source): Coal: 14.7 bil; Petroleum: 94 mil; Gas: 4.5 bil; Hydroelectric: 2.1 bil.

Public education. Student-teacher ratio (1995): 19.1. **Avg. teachers' salary** (1996-97): $37,340.

State data. Motto: All for our country. **Flower:** Sagebrush. **Bird:** Mountain bluebird. **Trees:** Single-leaf piñon and bristlecone pine. **Song:** Home Means Nevada. **Entered union** Oct. 31, 1864; rank, 36th. **State fair** at Reno; late Aug.

History. Shoshone, Paiute, Bannock, and Washoe peoples lived in the area at the time of European contact. Nevada was first explored by Spaniards, 1776. Hudson's Bay Co. trappers explored the north and central region, 1825; trader Jedediah Smith crossed the state, 1826-27. The area was acquired by the U.S., 1848, at the end of the Mexican War. The first settlement, Mormon Station, now Genoa, was established, 1849. Discovery of the Comstock Lode, rich in gold and silver, 1859, spurred a population boom. In the early

20th cent., Nevada adopted progressive measures such as the initiative, referendum, recall, and woman suffrage.

Tourist attractions. Legalized gambling at: Lake Tahoe, Reno, Las Vegas, Laughlin, Elko County, and elsewhere. Hoover Dam; Lake Mead; Great Basin Natl. Park; Valley of Fire State Park; Virginia City; Red Rock Canyon Natl. Conservation Area; Liberace Museum, the Las Vegas Strip, Guinness World of Records Museum, Lost City Museum, Overton, Lamoille Canyon, Pyramid Lake, all Las Vegas; Skiing near Lake Tahoe.

Famous Nevadans. Walter Van Tilburg Clark, George Ferris, Sarah Winnemucca Hopkins, Paul Laxalt, Dat So La Lee, John William Mackay, Anne Martin, Pat McCarran, Key Pittman, William Morris Stewart.

Tourist information. Commission on Tourism, 5151 S. Carson St., Carson City, NV 89701.

Toll-free travel information. 1-800-638-2328.

Web site. http://www.state.nv.us

New Hampshire
Granite State

People. Population (1996): 1,162,481; rank: 42; **Net change** (1990-96): 4.8%. **Pop. density:** (1990) 123.7 per sq mi. **Racial/ethnic distrib.** (1990): 98.0% white; 0.6% black; 1.0% Hispanic.

Geography. Total area: 9,351 sq mi; rank: 46. **Land area:** 8,969 sq mi; rank: 44. **Acres forested land:** 4,981,000. **Location:** New England state bounded on S by Massachusetts, on W by Vermont, on N and NW by Canada, on E by Maine and the Atlantic Ocean. **Climate:** highly varied, due to its nearness to high mountains and ocean. **Topography:** low, rolling coast followed by countless hills and mountains rising out of a central plateau. **Capital:** Concord.

Economy. Principal industries: tourism, manufacturing, agriculture, trade, mining. **Principal manufactured goods:** machinery, electrical and electronic products, plastics, fabricated metal products. **Chief crops:** dairy products, nursery and greenhouse products, hay, vegetables, fruit, maple syrup & sugar products. **Livestock** (1995): 48,000 cattle; 3,000 hogs/pigs; 275,000 poultry (1996) 7,500 sheep. **Timber/lumber** (1996): white pine, hemlock, oak, birch; 275 mil bd. ft. **Nonfuel minerals** (est. 1996): $43.9 mil; mostly construction sand & gravel, crushed and dimension stone. **Commercial fishing** (1996): $14 mil. **Chief ports:** Portsmouth, Hampton, Rye. **Value of construction** (1996): $1.2 bil. **Employment distribution** (1995): 19.4% mfg.; 28.7% trade; 26.1% serv.; 13.2% govt. **Per capita personal income** (1996): $26,520. **Unemployment** (1996): 4.2%. **Tourism** (1996): $2.7 bil.

Finance. FDIC-insured commercial banks & trust companies (1996): 20. **Deposits:** $9.0 bil. **FDIC-insured savings institutions** (1996): 25. **Assets:** $9.3 bil.

Federal government. No. federal civilian employees (Mar. 1996): 3,493. **Avg. salary:** $45,512.

Energy. Electricity production (1996, kWh, by source): Coal: 3.3 bil; Petroleum: 938 mil; Hydroelectric: 1.4 bil; Nuclear: 9.8 bil.

Public education. Student-teacher ratio (1995): 15.7. **Avg. teachers' salary** (1996-97): $36,867.

State data. Motto: Live free or die. **Flower:** Purple lilac. **Bird:** Purple finch. **Tree:** White birch. **Song:** Old New Hampshire. **Ninth** of the original 13 states to ratify the Constitution, June 21, 1788. **State Fair:** Many agricultural fairs statewide, July through Sept.; no State fair

History. Algonquian-speaking peoples, including the Pennacook, lived in the region when the European arrived. The first explorers to visit the area were England's Martin Pring, 1603, and France's Champlain, 1605. The first settlement was Odiorne's Point (now port of Rye), 1623. Native American conflicts were ended, 1759, by Robert Rogers' Rangers. Before the American Revolution, New Hampshire residents seized a British fort at Portsmouth, 1774, and drove the royal governor out, 1775. New Hampshire became the first colony to adopt its own constitution, 1776. Three regiments served in the Continental Army, and scores of privateers raided British shipping.

Tourist attractions. Mt. Washington, highest peak in Northeast; Lake Winnipesaukee; White Mt. National Forest; Crawford, Franconia—famous for the Old Man of the Mountain, described by Hawthorne as the Great Stone Face, Pinkham notches, all White Mt. region; the Flume, a spectacular gorge; the aerial tramway, Cannon Mt.; Strawbery Banke, Portsmouth; Shaker Village, Canterbury; Saint-Gaudens, natl. historic site, Cornish; Mt. Monadnock.

Famous New Hampshirites. Salmon P. Chase, Ralph Adams Cram, Mary Baker Eddy, Daniel Chester French, Robert Frost, Horace Greeley, Sarah Buell Hale, Franklin Pierce, Augustus Saint-Gaudens, David H. Souter, Daniel Webster.

Tourist information. Department of Resources and Economic Development, Division of Travel & Tourism Development, PO Box 1856, Concord, NH 03302-1856; 603-271-2343.

Toll-free travel information. 1-800-386-4664.

Web site. http://www.state.nh.us

New Jersey
Garden State

People. Population (1995): 7,987,933; rank: 9; **Net change** (1990-96): 3.3%. **Pop. density:** (1990) 1,042.0 per sq mi. **Racial/ethnic distrib.** (1990): 79.3% white; 13.4% black; 3.5% Asian; 9.6% Hispanic.

Geography. Total area: 8,722 sq mi; rank: 47. **Land area:** 7,419 sq mi; rank: 46. **Acres forested land:** 2,007,000. **Location:** Middle Atlantic state bounded on the N and E by New York and the Atlantic Ocean, on the S and W by Delaware and Pennsylvania. **Climate:** moderate, with marked difference bet. NW and SE extremities. **Topography:** Appalachian Valley in the NW also has highest elevation, High Pt., 1,801 ft; Appalachian Highlands, flat-topped NE-SW mountain ranges; Piedmont Plateau, low plains broken by high ridges (Palisades) rising 400-500 ft; Coastal Plain, covering three-fifths of state in SE, gradually rises from sea level to gentle slopes. **Capital:** Trenton.

Economy. Principal industries: services, trade, manufacturing, printing and publishing, food. **Principal manufactured goods:** chemicals, electronic and electrical equipment, non-electrical machinery, fabricated metals. **Chief crops:** nursery and greenhouse, tomatoes, blueberries, peaches, peppers, cranberries, soybeans. **Livestock** (1996): 68,000 cattle; 34,000 hogs/pigs; 18,500 sheep; 1.9 mil poultry. **Timber/lumber** (1996) pine, cedar, mixed hardwoods; 8 mil bd. ft. **Nonfuel minerals** (est. 1996): $222 mil; mostly crushed stone, construction sand & gravel. **Commercial fishing** (1996): $94 mil. **Chief ports:** Newark, Elizabeth, Hoboken, Camden. **International airport at:** Newark. **Value of construction** (1996): $7.1 bil. **Employment distribution** (1996): 31% serv.; 23.5% trade; 13.3% mfg.; 15.6% govt. **Per capita personal income** (1996): $31,053. **Unemployment** (1996): 6.2%. **Tourism** (1996): $24.6 bil.

Finance. FDIC-insured commercial banks & trust companies (1996): 66. **Deposits:** $59.3 bil. **FDIC-insured savings institutions** (1996): 92. **Assets:** $48.6 bil.

Federal government. No. federal civilian employees (Mar. 1996): 32,466. **Avg. salary:** $44,516. **Notable federal facilities:** McGuire AFB; Fort Dix; Fort Monmouth; Picatinny Arsenal; Lakehurst Naval Air Engineering Center.

Energy. Electricity production (1996, kWh, by source): Coal: 5.8 bil; Petroleum: 611 mil; Gas: 2.4 bil; Nuclear: 11.1 bil.

Public education. Student-teacher ratio (1995): 13.8. **Avg. teachers' salary** (1996-97): $49,349.

State data. Motto: Liberty and prosperity. **Flower:** Purple violet. **Bird:** Eastern goldfinch. **Tree:** Red oak. **Third** of the original 13 states to ratify the Constitution, Dec. 18, 1787. **State fair** at Camden; Aug.

History. The Lenni Lenape (Delaware) peoples lived in the region and had mostly peaceful relations with European colonists, who arrived after the explorers Verrazano, 1524, and Hudson, 1609. The first permanent European settlement was Dutch, at Bergen (now Jersey City), 1660. When the British took New Netherland, 1664, the area between the Delaware and Hudson Rivers was given to Lord John Berkeley and Sir George Carteret. During the American Revolution, New Jersey was the scene of nearly 100 battles, large and small, including Trenton, 1776; Princeton, 1777; Monmouth, 1778.

Tourist attractions. 127 mi of beaches; Miss America Pageant, Atlantic City; Grover Cleveland birthplace, Cald-

well; Cape May Historic District; Edison Natl. Historic Site, W. Orange; Six Flags Great Adventure, Jackson; Liberty State Park, Jersey City; Meadowlands Sports Complex, E. Rutherford; Pine Barrens wilderness area; Princeton University; numerous Revolutionary War historical sites; State Aquarium, Camden.

Famous New Jerseyans. Count Basie, Judy Blume, Bill Bradley, Jon Bon Jovi, Aaron Burr, Grover Cleveland, James Fenimore Cooper, Stephen Crane, Thomas Edison, Albert Einstein, Allen Ginsberg, Alexander Hamilton, Whitney Houston, Buster Keaton, Joyce Kilmer, George McClellan, Thomas Paine, Dorothy Parker, Molly Pitcher, Paul Robeson, Philip Roth, Wally Schirra, Frank Sinatra, Bruce Springsteen, Martha Stewart, Meryl Streep, Walt Whitman, William Carlos Williams, Woodrow Wilson.

Chamber of Commerce. 50 W. State St., Trenton, NJ 08608.

Toll-free travel information. 1-800-JERSEY7.

Web site. http://www.state.nj.us

New Mexico
Land of Enchantment

People. Population (1996): 1,713,407; rank: 36; **Net change** (1990-96): 13.1%. **Pop. density:** (1990) 12.5 per sq mi. **Racial/ethnic distrib.** (1990): 75.6% white; 2.0% black; 8.9% Amer. Indian; 38.2% Hispanic.

Geography. Total area: 121,598 sq mi; rank: 5. **Land area:** 121,364 sq mi rank: 5. **Acres forested land:** 15,296,000. **Location:** southwestern state bounded by Colorado on the N, Oklahoma, Texas, and Mexico on the E and S, and Arizona on the W. **Climate:** dry, with temperatures rising or falling 5° F with every 1,000 ft elevation. **Topography:** eastern third, Great Plains; central third, Rocky Mts. (85% of the state is over 4,000-ft elevation); western third, high plateau. **Capital:** Santa Fe.

Economy. Principal industries: government, services, trade. **Principal manufactured goods:** foods, machinery, apparel, lumber, printing, transportation equipment, electronics, semiconductors. **Chief crops:** hay, pecans, onions, chiles, greenhouse nursery, corn, cotton. **Livestock** (1996): 1.52 mil cattle; 5,000 hogs; 265,000 sheep; 1.4 mil poultry. **Timber/lumber** (1996): ponderosa pine, Douglas fir; 90 mil bd. ft. **Nonfuel minerals** (est. 1996): $963 mil; copper, potash, construction sand & gravel. **International airports at:** Albuquerque. **Value of construction** (1996): $2.2 bil. **Employment distribution** (1996): 27.7% serv.; 24.6% govt. 23.6% trade; 6.6% Mfg. **Per capita personal income** (1996): $18,770. **Unemployment** (1996): 8.1%. **Tourism** (1994): $2.75 bil.

Finance. FDIC-insured commercial banks & trust companies (1996): 69. **Deposits:** $12.0 bil. **FDIC-insured savings institutions** (1996): 10. **Assets:** $1.4 bil.

Federal government. No. federal civilian employees (Mar. 1996): 21,947. **Avg. salary:** $39,159. **Notable federal facilities:** Kirtland, Cannon, Holloman AF bases; Los Alamos Scientific Laboratory; White Sands Missile Range; Natl. Solar Observatory; Natl. Radio Astronomy Observatory, Sandia National Laboratories.

Energy. Electricity production (1996, kWh, by source): Coal: 26.5 bil; Petroleum: 22 mil; Gas: 2.8 bil; Hydroelectric: 211 mil.

Public education. Student-teacher ratio (1995): 17.0. **Avg. teachers' salary** (1996-97): $29,715.

State data. Motto: Crescit Eundo (It grows as it goes). **Flower:** Yucca. **Bird:** Roadrunner. **Tree:** Piñon. **Song:** O, Fair New Mexico; Asi Es Nuevo Mexico. **Entered union** Jan. 6, 1912; rank, 47th. **State fair** at Albuquerque; mid-Sept.

History. Early inhabitants were peoples of the Mogollon and Anasazi civilizations, followed by the Pueblo peoples, Anasazi descendants. The nomadic Navajo and Apache tribes arrived c 15th cent. Franciscan Marcos de Niza and a former black slave Estevanico explored the area, 1539, seeking gold. First settlements were at San Juan Pueblo, 1598, and Santa Fe, 1610. Settlers alternately traded and fought with the Apache, Comanche, and Navajo. Trade on the Santa Fe Trail to Missouri started, 1821. The Mexican War was declared in May 1846; Gen. Stephen Kearny took Santa Fe without firing a shot, Aug. 18, 1846, declaring New Mexico part of the

U.S. All Hispanic New Mexicans and Pueblo became U.S. citizens by terms of the 1848 treaty ending the war, but Congress denied the area statehood and created the territory of New Mexico, 1850. Pancho Villa raided Columbus, 1916, and U.S. troops were sent to the area. The world's first atomic bomb was exploded near Alamogordo, south of Santa Fe, 1945.

Tourist attractions. Carlsbad Caverns Natl. Park, with the largest natural underground chamber in the world; White Sands Natl. Monument, the largest gypsum deposit in the world; Pueblo Bonito Ruins, Chaco Canyon; Acoma Pueblo, the "sky city," built atop a 357-ft mesa; Taos; Ute Lake State Park; Shiprock.

Famous New Mexicans. Billy (the Kid) Bonney, Kit Carson, Peter Hurd, Archbishop Jean Baptiste Lamy, Nancy Lopez, Bill Mauldin, Georgia O'Keeffe, Kim Stanley, Al Unser, Bobby Unser, Lew Wallace.

Tourist Information. New Mexico Dept. of Tourism, PO Box 20002, Santa Fe, NM 87503.

Toll-free travel information. 1-800-733-6396.

Web site. http://www.state.nm.us

New York
Empire State

People. Population (1996): 18,184,774; rank: 3; **Net change** (1990-96): 1.1%. **Pop. density:** (1990) 381.0 per sq mi. **Racial/ethnic distrib.** (1990): 74.4% white; 15.9% black; 3.9% Asian; 12.3% Hispanic.

Geography. Total area: 54,471 sq mi; rank: 27. **Land area:** 47,224 sq mi; rank: 30. **Acres forested land:** 18,713,000. **Location:** Middle Atlantic state, bordered by the New England states, Atlantic Ocean, New Jersey and Pennsylvania, Lakes Ontario and Erie, and Canada. **Climate:** variable; the SE region moderated by the ocean. **Topography:** highest and most rugged mountains in the NE Adirondack upland; St. Lawrence-Champlain lowlands extend from Lake Ontario NE along the Canadian border; Hudson-Mohawk lowland follows the flows of the rivers N and W, 10-30 mi wide; Atlantic coastal plain in the SE; Appalachian Highlands, covering half the state westward from the Hudson Valley, include the Catskill Mts., Finger Lakes; plateau of Erie-Ontario lowlands. **Capital:** Albany.

Economy. Principal industries: manufacturing, finance, communications, tourism, transportation, services. **Principal manufactured goods:** books and periodicals, clothing and apparel, pharmaceuticals, machinery, instruments, toys and sporting goods, electronic equipment, automotive and aircraft components. **Chief crops:** apples, grapes, strawberries, cherries, pears, onions, potatoes, cabbage, sweet corn, green beans, cauliflower, field corn, hay, wheat, oats, dry beans. **Products:** milk, cheese, maple syrup, wine. **Livestock** (1997): 1.5 mil cattle; 70,000 hogs/pigs; 60,000 sheep; 8.7 mil poultry. **Timber/lumber** (1996): birch, sugar and red maple, basswood, hemlock, pine, oak, ash; 534 mil bd. ft. **Nonfuel minerals** (est. 1996): $891 mil; mostly salt, crushed stone, construction sand & gravel, portland cement. **Commercial fishing** (1996): $84 mil. **Chief ports:** New York, Buffalo, Albany. **International airports at:** New York, Buffalo, Syracuse, Massena, Ogdensburg, Watertown, Niagara Falls, Newburgh. **Value of construction** (1996): $13.9 bil. **Employment distribution** (1996): 33% serv.; 21% trade; 17% govt.; 11% mfg. **Per capita personal income** (1996): $28,782. **Unemployment** (1996): 6.2%. **Tourism** (1995): $24.3 bil.

Finance. FDIC-insured commercial banks & trust companies (1996): 159. **Deposits:** $602.5 bil. **FDIC-insured savings institutions** (1996): 105. **Assets:** $121.3 bil.

Federal government. No. federal civilian employees (Mar. 1996): 61,958. **Avg. salary:** $41,257. **Notable federal facilities:** West Point Military Academy; Merchant Marine Academy; Ft. Drum; Rome Labs.; Watervliet Arsenal.

Energy. Electricity production (1996, kWh, by source): Coal: 20.4 bil; Petroleum: 9.3 bil; Gas: 13.4 bil; Hydroelectric: 26.1 bil; Nuclear: 35.2 bil.

Public education. Student-teacher ratio (1995): 15.5. **Avg. teachers' salary** (1996-97): $49,560.

State data. Motto: Excelsior (Ever upward). **Flower:** Rose. **Bird:** Bluebird. **Tree:** Sugar maple. **Song:** I Love New York. **Eleventh** of the original 13 states to ratify the Constitution, July 26, 1788. **State fair** at Syracuse; late Aug.-early Sept.

History. Algonquians including the Mahican, Wappinger, and Lenni Lenape inhabited the region, as did the Iroquoian Mohawk, Oneida, Onondaga, Cayuga, and Seneca tribes, who established the League of the Five Nations. In 1609, Henry Hudson visited the river that bears his name, and Champlain explored the lake that was named for him. The first permanent settlement was Dutch, near present-day Albany, 1624. New Amsterdam was settled, 1626, at the southern tip of Manhattan Island. A British fleet seized New Netherland, 1664. Ninety-two of the 300 or more engagements of the American Revolution were fought in New York, including the Battle of Bemis Heights-Saratoga, 1777, a turning point of the war. Completion of Erie Canal, 1825, established the state as a gateway to the West. The first woman's rights convention was held in Seneca Falls, 1848.

Tourist attractions. New York City; Adirondack and Catskill Mts.; Finger Lakes; Great Lakes; Thousand Islands; Niagara Falls; Saratoga Springs; Philipsburg Manor, Sunnyside (Washington Irving's home), the Dutch Church of Sleepy Hollow, all in Tarrytown area; Corning Glass Center and Steuben factory, Corning; Fenimore House, Natl. Baseball Hall of Fame and Museum, both in Cooperstown; Ft. Ticonderoga overlooking Lakes George and Champlain; Empire State Plaza, Albany; Lake Placid; Franklin D. Roosevelt Natl. Historic Site, including the Roosevelt Library, Hyde Park; Long Island beaches; Theodore Roosevelt estate, Sagamore Hill, Oyster Bay; Turning Stone Casino.

Famous New Yorkers. Woody Allen, Susan B. Anthony, Lucille Ball, James Baldwin, Benjamin Cardozo, De Witt Clinton, Peter Cooper, Aaron Copland, George Eastman, Millard Fillmore, George and Ira Gershwin, Ruth Bader Ginsberg, Julia Ward Howe, Charles Evans Hughes, Washington Irving, Henry and William James, John Jay, Fiorello La Guardia, Herman Melville, J. Pierpont Morgan Jr., Joyce Carol Oates, Eugene O'Neill, Colin Powell, Nancy Reagan, John D. Rockefeller, Nelson Rockefeller, Eleanor Roosevelt, Franklin D. Roosevelt, Theodore Roosevelt, J. D. Salinger, Jerry Seinfeld, Paul Simon, Alfred E. Smith, Elizabeth Cady Stanton, William (Boss) Tweed, Martin Van Buren, Gore Vidal, Edith Wharton, Walt Whitman.

Tourist information. N.Y. State Dept. of Economic Development, 1 Commerce Plaza, Albany, NY 12245.

Toll-free travel information. 1-800-CALLNYS from 50 states and U.S. territories; 1-518-474-4116 from other areas and Canada.

Web site. http://www.state.ny.us

North Carolina
Tar Heel State, Old North State

People. Population (1996): 7,322,870; rank: 11; **Net change** (1990-96): 10.4%. **Pop. density:** (1990) 136.1 per sq mi. **Racial/ethnic distrib.** (1990): 75.6% white; 22.0% black; 1.2% Amer. Indian; 1.2% Hispanic.

Geography. Total area: 53,821 sq mi; rank: 28. **Land area:** 48,718 sq mi; rank: 29. **Acres forested land:** 19,278,000. **Location:** South Atlantic state bounded by Virginia, South Carolina, Georgia, Tennessee, and the Atlantic Ocean **Climate:** sub-tropical in SE, medium-continental in mountain region; tempered by the Gulf Stream and the mountains in W. **Topography:** coastal plain and tidewater, two-fifths of state, extending to the fall line of the rivers; piedmont plateau, another two-fifths, 200 mi wide of gentle to rugged hills; southern Appalachian Mts. contains the Blue Ridge and Great Smoky Mts. **Capital:** Raleigh.

Economy. Principal industries: manufacturing, agriculture, tourism. **Principal manufactured goods:** food products, textiles, industrial machinery and equipment, electrical and electronic equipment, furniture, tobacco products, apparel. **Chief crops:** tobacco, cotton, soybeans, corn, food grains, wheat, peanuts, sweet potatoes. **Livestock** (1995): 1.2 mil cattle; 8.3 mil hogs/pigs; 18.8 mil chickens, 61.2 mil turkeys. **Timber/lumber** (1996): yellow pine, oak, hickory, poplar, maple; 2.2 bil bd. ft. **Nonfuel minerals** (est. 1996): $731 mil; mostly, construction sand & gravel, crushed stone, dimension stone, phosphate rock, lithium. **Commercial fishing** (1996): $110 mil. **International airports at:**

Charlotte/Douglas, Raleigh/Durham. **Chief ports:** Morehead City, Wilmington. **Value of construction** (1996): $12.4 bil. **Employment distribution** (1996): 24% mfg.; 23.1% trade; 21.7% serv.; 15.4% govt. **Per capita personal income** (1996): $22,010. **Unemployment** (1996): 4.3%. **Tourism** (1996): $9.8 bil.

Finance. FDIC-insured commercial banks & trust companies (1996): 56. **Deposits:** $121.4 bil. **FDIC-insured savings institutions** (1996): 60. **Assets:** $7.7 bil.

Federal government. No. federal civilian employees (Mar. 1996): 31,590. **Avg. salary:** $36,882. **Notable federal facilities:** Ft. Bragg; Camp LeJeune Marine Base; U.S. EPA Research and Development Labs, Cherry Point Marine Corps Air Station; Natl. Humanities Center; Natl. Inst. of Environmental Health Science; Natl. Center for Health Statistics Lab, Research Triangle Park.

Energy. Electricity production (1996, kWh, by source): Coal: 64.1 bil; Petroleum: 259 mil; Gas: 195 mil; Hydroelectric: 4.5 bil; Nuclear: 33.7 bil.

Public education. Student-teacher ratio (1995): 16.2. **Avg. teachers' salary** (1996-97): $31,225.

State data. Motto: Esse Quam Videri (To be rather than to seem). **Flower:** Dogwood. **Bird:** Cardinal. **Tree:** Pine. **Song:** The Old North State. **Twelfth** of the original 13 states to ratify the Constitution, Nov. 21, 1789. **State fair** at Raleigh; mid-Oct.

History. Algonquian, Siouan, and Iroquoian peoples lived in the region at the time of European contact. The first English colony in America was the first of 2 established by Sir Walter Raleigh on Roanoke Island, 1585 and 1587. The first group returned to England; the second, the "Lost Colony," disappeared without a trace. Permanent settlers came from Virginia, c 1660. Roused by British repression, the colonists drove out the royal governor, 1775. The province's congress was the first to vote for independence; ten regiments were furnished to the Continental Army. Cornwallis's forces were defeated at Kings Mountain, 1780, and forced out after Guilford Courthouse, 1781. The state seceded in 1861, and provided more troops to the Confederacy than any other state; it was readmitted in 1868.

Tourist attractions. Cape Hatteras and Cape Lookout natl. seashores; Great Smoky Mts.; Guilford Courthouse and Moore's Creek parks; 66 American Revolution battle sites; Bennett Place, near Durham, where Gen. Joseph Johnston surrendered the last Confederate army to Gen. William Sherman; Ft. Raleigh, Roanoke Island, where Virginia Dare, first child of English parents in the New World, was born Aug. 18, 1587; Wright Brothers Natl. Memorial, Kitty Hawk; Battleship *North Carolina*, Wilmington; NC Zoo, Asheboro; NC Symphony, NC Museum, Raleigh; Carl Sandburg Home, Hendersonville, Biltmore House & Gardens, Asheville.

Famous North Carolinians. David Brinkley, Elizabeth Dole, Richard J. Gatling, Billy Graham, Andy Griffith, O. Henry, Andrew Jackson, Andrew Johnson, Michael Jordan, Wm. Rufus King, Charles Kuralt, Dolley Madison, Edward R. Murrow, James K. Polk, Carl Sandburg, Enos Slaughter, Dean Smith, Thomas Wolfe, Orville and Wilbur Wright.

Tourist information. Travel & Tourism Division, 301 N. Wilmington St., Raleigh, NC 27601.

Toll-free travel information. 1-800-VISITNC.

Web site. http://www.state.nc.us

North Dakota
Peace Garden State

People. Population (1996): 643,539; rank: 47; **Net change** (1990-96): 0.7%. **Pop. density:** (1990) 9.3 per sq mi. **Racial/ethnic distrib.** (1990): 94.6% white; 0.6% black; 4.1% Amer. Indian; 0.7% Hispanic.

Geography. Total area: 70,704 sq mi; rank: 19. **Land area:** 68,994 sq mi; rank: 17. **Acres forested land:** 462,000. **Location.** West North Central state, situated exactly in the middle of North America, bounded on the N by Canada, on the E by Minnesota, on the S by South Dakota, on the W by Montana. **Climate:** continental, with a wide range of temperature and moderate rainfall. **Topography:** Central Lowland in the E comprises the flat Red River Valley and the Rolling Drift Prairie; Missouri Plateau of the Great Plains on the W. **Capital:** Bismarck.

Economy. Principal industries: agriculture, mining, tourism, manufacturing, telecommunications, energy, food processing. **Principal manufactured goods:** farm equipment, processed foods, fabricated metal, high-tech. electronics. **Chief crops:** spring wheat, durum, barley, flaxseed, oats, potatoes, dry edible beans, honey, soybeans, sugar beets, sunflowers, hay. **Livestock** (1997): 1.9 mil cattle; 135,000 sheep; (1996): 200,000 hogs/pigs; 245,000 chickens; 2.1 million turkeys. **Timber/lumber:** (1996) oak, ash, cottonwood, aspen; 3 mil bd. ft. **Nonfuel minerals** (est. 1996): $30.3 mil; mostly construction sand & gravel, lime. **International airports at:** Fargo, Grand Forks, Bismarck, Minot, Pembina, Dunseith. **Value of construction** (1996): $656 mil. **Employment distribution** (1996): 26% trade; 27.4% serv.; 23% govt.; 7% mfg. **Per capita personal income** (1996): $20,710. **Unemployment** (1996): 3.1%. **Tourism** (1992): $826 mil.

Finance. FDIC-insured commercial banks & trust companies (1996): 123. **Deposits:** $7.3 bil. **FDIC-insured savings institutions** (1996): 3. **Assets:** $5.6 bil.

Federal government. No. federal civilian employees (Mar. 1996): 4,984. **Avg. salary:** $36,352. **Notable federal facilities:** Strategic Air Command Base; Northern Prairie Wildlife Research Center; Garrison Dam; Theodore Roosevelt Natl. Park; Grand Forks Energy Research Center; Ft. Union Natl. Historic Site.

Energy. Electricity production (1996, kWh, by source): Coal: 27.5 bil; Petroleum: 89 mil; Hydroelectric: 3.2 bil.

Public education. Student-teacher ratio (1995): 15.9. **Avg. teachers' salary** (1996-97): $27,711.

State data. Motto: Liberty and union, now and forever, one and inseparable. **Flower:** Wild prairie rose. **Bird:** Western meadowlark. **Tree:** American elm. **Song:** North Dakota Hymn. **Entered union** Nov. 2, 1889; rank, 39th. **State fair** at Minot; July.

History. At the time of European contact, the Ojibwa, Yanktonai and Teton Sioux, Mandan, Arikara, and Hidatsa peoples lived in the region. Pierre de Varennes was the first French fur trader in the area, 1738, followed later by the English. The U.S. acquired half the territory in the Louisiana Purchase, 1803. Lewis and Clark built Ft. Mandan, near present-day Stanton, 1804-5, and wintered there. In 1818, American ownership of the other half was confirmed by agreement with Britain. The first permanent settlement was at Pembina, 1812. Missouri River steamboats reached the area, 1832, the first railroad, 1873, bringing many homesteaders. The "bonanza farm" craze of the 1870s-80s attracted many settlers. The state was first to hold a national Pres.ial primary, 1912.

Tourist attractions. North Dakota Heritage Center, Bismarck; Bonanzaville, Fargo; Ft. Union Trading Post Natl. Historic Site; Lake Sakakawea; Intl. Peace Garden; Theodore Roosevelt Natl. Park, including Elkhorn Ranch, Badlands; Ft. Abraham Lincoln State Park and Museum, near Mandan; Dakota Dinosaur Museum, Dickinson.

Famous North Dakotans. Maxwell Anderson, Angie Dickinson, John Bernard Flannagan, Phil Jackson, Louis L'Amour, Peggy Lee, Eric Sevareid, Vilhjalmur Stefansson, Lawrence Welk.

Chamber of Commerce. PO Box 2639, 2000 Schafer St., Bismarck, ND 58501.

Toll-free travel information. 1-800-HELLO-ND

Web site. http://www.state.nd.us

Ohio
Buckeye State

People. Population (1996): 11,172,782; rank: 7; **Net change** (1990-96): 3.0%. **Pop. density:** (1990) 264.9 per sq mi. **Racial/ethnic distrib.** (1990): 87.8% white; 10.6% black; 1.3% Hispanic.

Geography. Total area: 44,828 sq mi; rank: 34. **Land area:** 40,953 sq mi; rank: 35. **Acres forested land:** 7,863,000. **Location.** East North Central state bounded on the N by Michigan and Lake Erie; on the E and S by Pennsylvania, West Virginia, and Kentucky; on the W by Indiana. **Climate:** temperate but variable; weather subject to much precipitation. **Topography:** generally rolling plain; Allegheny plateau in E; Lake Erie plains extend southward; central plains in the W. **Capital:** Columbus.

Economy. Principal industries: manufacturing, trade, services. **Principal manufactured goods:** transportation equipment, machinery, primary and fabricated metal products. **Chief crops:** corn, hay, winter wheat, oats, soybeans. **Livestock** (1997): 1.54 mil cattle; 130,000 sheep and lambs; (1996) 1.8 mil hogs/pigs; 48.6 mil broilers, 30.8 mil layers; 1.7 mil hogs/pigs; 6.8 mil turkeys. **Timber/lumber** (1996): oak, ash, maple, walnut, beech; 383 mil bd. ft. **Nonfuel minerals** (est. 1996): $935 mil; mostly crushed stone, construction sand & gravel, salt, lime. **Commercial fishing** (1996): $2 mil. **Chief ports:** Toledo, Conneaut, Cleveland, Ashtabula. **International airports at:** Cleveland, Cincinnati, Columbus, Dayton. **Value of construction** (1996): $14.0 bil. **Employment distribution** (1996): 20.7% mfg.; 19.2% trade; 26.7% serv.; 14.2% govt. **Per capita personal income** (1996): $23,537. **Unemployment** (1996): 4.9%. **Tourism** (1992): $8.8 bil.

Finance. FDIC-insured commercial banks & trust companies (1996): 257. **Deposits:** $117.0 bil. **FDIC-insured savings institutions** (1996): 159. **Assets:** $51.9 bil.

Federal government. No. federal civilian employees (Mar. 1996): 49,119. **Avg. salary:** $42,842. **Notable federal facilities:** Wright Patterson AFB; Defense Construction Supply Center; Lewis Research Ctr.; Portsmouth Gaseous Diffusion Plant.

Energy. Electricity production (1996, kWh, by source): Coal: 128.1 bil; Petroleum: 267 mil; Gas: 193 mil; Hydroelectric: 392 mil; Nuclear: 13.9 mil.

Public education. Student-teacher ratio (1995): 17.1. **Avg. teachers' salary** (1996-97): $38,831.6

State data. Motto: With God, all things are possible. **Flower:** Scarlet carnation. **Bird:** Cardinal. **Tree:** Buckeye. **Song:** Beautiful Ohio. **Entered union** Mar. 1, 1803; rank, 17th. **State fair** at Columbus; Aug.

History. Wyandot, Delaware, Miami, and Shawnee peoples sparsely occupied the area when the first Europeans arrived. La Salle visited the region, 1669, and France claimed the area, 1682. Around 1730, traders from Pennsylvania and Virginia entered the area; the French and their Native American allies sought to drive them out. France ceded its claim, 1763, to Britain. During the American Revolution, George Rogers Clark seized British posts and held the region, until Britain gave up its claim, 1883, in the Treaty of Paris. The region became U.S. territory after the American Revolution. First organized settlement was at Marietta, 1788. Indian warfare ended with Anthony Wayne's victory at Fallen Timbers, 1794. In the War of 1812, Oliver Hazard Perry's victory on Lake Erie and William Henry Harrison's invasion of Canada, 1813, ended British incursions.

Tourist attractions. Mound City Group Natl. Monuments, a group of 24 prehistoric Indian burial mounds; Neil Armstrong Air and Space Museum, Wapakoneta; Air Force Museum, Dayton; Pro Football Hall of Fame, Canton; King's Island amusement park, Mason; Lake Erie Islands, Cedar Point amusement park, both Sandusky; birthplaces, homes of, and memorials to U.S. Pres.s W. H. Harrison, Grant, Garfield, Hayes, McKinley, Harding, Taft, Benjamin Harrison; Amish Region, Tuscarawas/Holmes counties; German Village, Columbus; Sea World, Aurora; Jack Nicklaus Sports Center, Mason; Bob Evans Farm, Rio Grande; Rock and Roll Hall of Fame and Museum, Cleveland.

Famous Ohioans. Sherwood Anderson, Neil Armstrong, George Bellows, Ambrose Bierce, Erma Bombeck, Hart Crane, George Coster, Clarence Darrow, Paul Laurence Dunbar, Thomas Edison, Clark Gable, John Glenn, Bob Hope, William Dean Howells, Toni Morrison, Jack Nicklaus, Jesse Owens, Pontiac, Eddie Rickenbacker, John D. Rockefeller Sr. and Jr., Pete Rose, Gen. William Sherman, Gloria Steinem, Harriet Beecher Stowe, Charles Taft, Robert A. Taft, William H. Taft, Tecumseh, James Thurber, Orville and Wilbur Wright.

Chamber of Commerce. PO Box 15159. 230 E. Town St., Columbus, OH 43215-0159.

Toll-free travel information. 1-800-BUCKEYE.

Web site. http://www.state.oh.us

Oklahoma
Sooner State

People. Population (1996): 3,300,902; rank: 27; **Net change** (1990-96): 4.9%. **Pop. density:** (1990) 45.8 per sq mi. **Racial/ethnic distrib.** (1990): 82.1% white; 7.4% black; 8.0% Amer. Indian; 2.7% Hispanic.

Geography. Total area: 69,903 sq mi; rank: 20. **Land area:** 68,679 sq mi; rank: 19. **Acres forested land:** 7,539,000. **Location:** West South Central state bounded on the N by Colorado and Kansas; on the E by Missouri and Arkansas; on the S and W by Texas and New Mexico. **Climate:** temperate; southern humid belt merging with colder northern continental; humid eastern and dry western zones. **Topography:** high plains predominate in the W, hills and small mountains in the E; the east central region is dominated by the Arkansas R. Basin, and the Red R. Plains, in the S. **Capital:** Oklahoma City.

Economy. Principal industries: manufacturing, mineral and energy exploration and production, agriculture, services. **Principal manufactured goods:** nonelectrical machinery, transportation equipment, food products, fabricated metal products. **Chief crops:** wheat, cotton, hay, peanuts, grain sorghum, soybeans, corn, pecans. **Livestock** (1995): 5.7 mil cattle; 1 mil hogs/pigs; 96,000 sheep; 5.1 mil poultry. **Timber/lumber** (1996): pine, oak, hickory. **Nonfuel minerals** (est. 1996): $372 mil; mostly crushed stone, portland cement, sand & gravel, gypsum, iodine. **Chief ports:** Catoosa, Muskogee. **International airports at:** Oklahoma City, Tulsa. **Value of construction** (1996): $3.2 bil. **Employment distribution** (1996): 26.9% serv.; 23.5% trade; 20% govt.; 12.8% mfg. **Per capita personal income** (1996): $19,350. **Unemployment** (1996): 4.1%. **Tourism** (1995): $3 bil.

Finance. FDIC-insured commercial banks & trust companies (1996): 332. **Deposits:** $30.1 bil. **FDIC-insured savings institutions** (1996): 13. **Assets:** $6.2 bil.

Federal government. No. federal civilian employees (Mar. 1996): 30,480. **Avg. salary:** $38,025. **Notable federal facilities:** Federal Aviation Agency and Tinker AFB; Ft. Sill, Lawton; Altus AFB; Vance AFB.

Energy. Electricity production (1996, kWh, by source): Coal: 31.9 bil; Petroleum: 125 mil; Gas: 13.5 bil; Hydroelectric: 2.1 bil.

Public education. Student-teacher ratio (1995): 15.7. **Avg. teachers' salary** (1996-97): $29,270.

State data. Motto: Labor Omnia Vincit (Labor conquers all things). **Flower:** Mistletoe. **Bird:** Scissor-tailed flycatcher. **Tree:** Redbud. **Song:** Oklahoma! **Entered union** Nov. 16, 1907; rank, 46th. **State fair** at Oklahoma City; last 2 full weeks of Sept.

History. The region was sparsely inhabited by a few scattered Native American tribes when Coronado, the first European to enter Oklahoma, arrived in 1541; in the 16th and 17th cent., French traders visited the region. Part of the Louisiana Purchase, 1803, Oklahoma was established as Indian Territory (but was not given territorial government). It became home to the "Five Civilized Tribes"—Cherokee, Choctaw, Chickasaw, Creek, and Seminole—after the forced removal of Native Americans from the eastern U.S., 1828-46. The land was also used by Comanche, Osage, and other Plains Indians. As white settlers pressed west, land was opened for homesteading by runs and lottery, the first run taking place on Apr. 22, 1889. The most famous run was to the Cherokee Outlet, 1893.

Tourist attractions. Cherokee Heritage Center, Tahlequah; White Water Bay and Frontier City theme pks., both Oklahoma City; Will Rogers Memorial, Claremore; Natl. Cowboy Hall of Fame and Remington Park Race Track, both Oklahoma City; Ft. Gibson Stockade, near Muskogee; Ouachita Natl. Forest; Tulsa's art deco district; Wichita Mts. Wildlife Refuge, Lawton; Woolaroc Museum & Wildlife Preserve, Bartlesville; Sequoyah's Home Site, near Sallisaw; Philbrook Museum of Art, Tulsa.

Famous Oklahomans. Troy Aikman, Carl Albert, Gene Autry, Johnny Bench, Garth Brooks, William "Hopalong Cassidy" Boyd, Lon Chaney, Walter Conkite, L. Gordon Cooper, Jerome "Dizzy" Dean, Ralph Ellison, John Hope Franklin, James Garner, Geronimo, Woody Guthrie, Paul Harvey, Ron Howard, Gen. Patrick J. Hurley, Jeane Kirkpatrick, Louis L'Amour, Shannon Lucid, Mickey Mantle, Reba McEntire, Wiley Post, Tony Randall, Oral Roberts, Will Rogers, Maria Tallchief, Jim Thorpe.

Chamber of Commerce. Chamber of Commerce, 330 NE 10th, Oklahoma City, OK 73104.

Tourism Dept. PO Box 60789, Oklahoma City, OK 73146-0789.
Toll-free travel information. 1-800-652-6552.
Web site. http://www.state.ok.us

Oregon
Beaver State

People. Population (1996): 3,203,735; rank: 29; **Net change** (1990-96): 12.7%. **Pop. density:** (1990) 29.6 per sq mi. **Racial/ethnic distrib.** (1990): 92.8% white; 1.6% black; 4.0% Hispanic.

Geography. Total area: 98,386 sq mi; rank: 9. **Land area:** 96,002 sq mi; rank: 10. **Acres forested land:** 27,997,000. **Location:** Pacific state, bounded on N by Washington; on E by Idaho; on S by Nevada and California; on W by the Pacific. **Climate:** coastal mild and humid climate; continental dryness and extreme temperatures in the interior. **Topography:** Coast Range of rugged mountains; fertile Willamette R. Valley to E and S; Cascade Mt. Range of volcanic peaks E of the valley; plateau E of Cascades, remaining two-thirds of state. **Capital:** Salem.

Economy. Principal industries: aerospace, forestry, agriculture, biotechnology, environmental technology, fiseries, film and video. **Principal manufactured goods:** lumber and wood products, computer equipment, foods, machinery, fabricated metals, paper, primary metals. **Chief crops:** greenhouse, hay, wheat, grass seed, potatoes, onions, Christmas trees, pears, mint. **Livestock** (1997): 1.45 mil cattle; 304,000 sheep; (1996): 45,000 hogs/pigs; 21.09 mil poultry. **Timber/lumber** (1996): Douglas fir, hemlock, ponderosa pine; 5.3 bil bd. ft. **Nonfuel minerals** (est. 1996): $251 mil; mostly crushed stone, construction sand & gravel, portland cement. **Commercial fishing** (1996): $84 mil. **Chief ports:** Portland, Astoria, Coos Bay. **International airports at:** Portland, Klamath Falls. **Value of construction** (1996): $5.4 bil. **Employment distribution** (1995): 25.3% trade; 25.7% serv.; 16.1% mfg.; 16.8% govt. **Per capita personal income** (1996): $22,668. **Unemployment** (1996): 5.9%. **Tourism** (1995): $4.1 bil.

Finance. FDIC-insured commercial banks & trust companies (1996): 43. **Deposits:** $16.1 bil. **FDIC-insured savings institutions** (1996): 9. **Assets:** $14.3 bil.

Federal government. No. federal civilian employees (Mar. 1996): 18,568. **Avg. salary:** $40,123. **Notable federal facilities:** Bonneville Power Administration.

Energy. Electricity production (1996, kWh, by source): Coal: 1.7 bil; Petroleum: 7 mil; Gas: 1.6 bil; Hydroelectric: 44.6 bil.

Public education. Student-teacher ratio (1995): 19.8. **Avg. teachers' salary** (1995-96): $40,900.

State data. Motto: She flies with her own wings. **Flower:** Oregon grape. **Bird:** Western meadowlark. **Tree:** Douglas fir. **Song:** Oregon, My Oregon. **Entered union** Feb. 14, 1859; rank, 33d. **State fair** at Salem; 12 days ending with Labor Day.

History. More than 100 Native American tribes inhabited the area at the time of European contact, including the Chinook, Yakima, Cayuse, Modoc, and Nez Percé. Capt. Robert Gray sighted and sailed into the Columbia River, 1792; Lewis and Clark, traveling overland, wintered at its mouth, 1805-6; John Jacob Astor established a trading post in the Columbia River region, 1811. Settlers arrived in the Willamette Valley, 1834. In 1843, the first large wave of settlers arrived via the Oregon Trail. Early in the 20th cent., the "Oregon System"—political reforms that included the initiative, referendum, recall, direct primary, and woman suffrage—was adopted.

Tourist attractions. John Day Fossil Beds Natl. Monument; Columbia River Gorge; Timberline Lodge, Mt. Hood Natl. Forest; Crater Lake Natl. Park; Oregon Dunes Natl. Recreation Area; Ft. Clatsop Natl. Memorial; Oregon Caves Natl. Monument; Oregon Museum of Science and Industry, Portland; Shakespearean Festival, Ashland; High Desert Museum, Bend; Multnomah Falls; Diamond Lake.

Famous Oregonians. Ernest Bloch, Raymond Carver, Ernest Haycox, Chief Joseph, Edwin Markham, Tom McCall, Dr. John McLoughlin, Joaquin Miller, Linus Pauling, John Reed, Alberto Salazar, Mary Decker Slaney, William Simon U'Ren.

Tourist information. Economic Development Department, 775 Summer St. NE, Salem, OR 97310.
Toll-free travel information. 1-800-547-7842.
Web site. http://www.state.or.us

Pennsylvania
Keystone State

People. Population (1996): 12,056,112; rank: 5; **Net change** (1990-96): 1.5%. **Pop. density:** (1990) 265.1 per sq mi. **Racial/ethnic distrib.** (1990): 88.5% white; 9.2% black; 2.0% Hispanic.

Geography. Total area: 46,058 sq mi; rank: 33. **Land area:** 44,820 sq mi; rank: 32. **Acres forested land:** 16,969,000. **Location:** Middle Atlantic state, bordered on the E by the Delaware R.; on the S by the Mason-Dixon Line; on the W by West Virginia and Ohio; on the N/NE by Lake Erie and New York. **Climate:** continental with wide fluctuations in seasonal temperatures. **Topography:** Allegheny Mts. run SW to NE, with Piedmont and Coast Plain in the SE triangle; Allegheny Front a diagonal spine across the state's center; N and W rugged plateau falls to Lake Erie Lowland. **Capital:** Harrisburg.

Economy. Principal industries: steel, travel and tourism, biotechnology, apparel, advanced materials, agribusiness. **Principal manufactured goods:** primary metals; foods; fabricated metal products; nonelectrical machinery; electrical machinery; printing and publishing; stone, clay, and glass products. **Chief crops:** corn, hay, mushrooms, apples, potatoes, winter wheat, oats, vegetables, tobacco, grapes. **Livestock** (1997): 1.8 mil cattle; 950,000 hogs/pigs; 94,000 sheep; 21.3 mil poultry. **Timber/lumber** (1996): pine, oak, maple; 1.0 bil bd. ft. **Nonfuel minerals** (est. 1996): $1.04 bil; mostly crushed stone, portland cement, lime, construction sand & gravel. **Commercial fishing** (1996): $274,000. **Chief ports:** Philadelphia, Pittsburgh, Erie. **International airports at** Allentown, Erie, Harrisburg, Philadelphia, Pittsburgh, Wilkes-Barre/Scranton. **Value of construction** (1996): $9.4 bil. **Employment distribution** (1996): 31.1% serv.; 22.7% trade; 17.5% mfg.; 13.6% govt. **Per capita personal income** (1996): $24,668. **Unemployment** (1996): 5.3%. **Tourism** (1996): $14.2 bil.

Finance. FDIC-insured commercial banks & trust companies (1996): 217. **Deposits:** $184.3 bil. **FDIC-insured savings institutions** (1996): 122. **Assets:** $45.2 bil.

Federal government. No. federal civilian employees (Mar. 1996): 69,390. **Avg. salary:** $38,479. **Notable federal facilities:** Army War College, Ships Control Ctr.; New Cumberland Army Depot; Indiantown Gap; Letterkenny Army Depot; Charles E. Kelly Spt Fac; Tobyhanna Army Depot; Naval Air Development Center; NAS Grove; Greater Pittsburgh IAP AGS; Willow Grove ARS; Harrisburg Olmsred IAP AGS.

Energy. Electricity production (1996, kWh, by source): Coal: 100.9 bil; Petroleum: 3.2 bil; Gas: 641 mil; Hydroelectric: 1.6 bil; Nuclear: 68.7 bil.

Public education. Student-teacher ratio (1995): 17.0. **Avg. teachers' salary** (1995-96): $47,429.

State data. Motto: Virtue, liberty and independence. **Flower:** Mountain laurel. **Bird:** Ruffed grouse. **Tree:** Hemlock. **Second** of the original 13 states to ratify the Constitution, Dec. 12, 1787. **State fair** at Harrisburg; 2d week in Jan. at State Farm Show Building.

History. At the time of European contact, Lenni Lenape (Delaware), Shawnee and Iroquoian Susquehannocks, Erie, and Seneca occupied the region. Swedish explorers established the first permanent settlement, 1643, on Tinicum Island. In 1655, the Dutch seized the settlement but lost it to the British, 1664. The region was given by Charles II to William Penn, 1681. Philadelphia ("brotherly love") was the capital of the colonies during most of the American Revolution, and of the U.S., 1790-1800. Philadelphia was taken by the British, 1777; Washington's troops encamped at Valley Forge in the bitter winter of 1777-78. The Declaration of Independence, 1776, and the Constitution, 1787, were signed in Philadelphia. The three-day Civil War battle of Gettysburg, July 1-3, 1863, marked a turning point, favoring Union forces.

Tourist attractions. Independence Natl. Historic Park, Franklin Institute Science Museum, Philadelphia Museum of Art, all in Philadelphia; Valley Forge Natl. Historic Park;

Gettysburg Natl. Military Park; Pennsylvania Dutch Country; Hershey; Duquesne Incline, Carnegie Institute, Heinz Hall, all in Pittsburgh; Pocono Mts.; Pennsylvania's Grand Canyon, Tioga County; Allegheny Natl. Forest; Laurel Highlands; Presque Isle State Park; Fallingwater, Ligonier; Johnstown; SteamTown U.S.A., Scranton; State Flagship Niagara, Erie; Oil Heritage Region, Northwest PA.

Famous Pennsylvanians. Marian Anderson, Maxwell Anderson, James Buchanan, Andrew Carnegie, Rachel Carson, Thomas Eakins, Stephen Foster, Benjamin Franklin, Robert Fulton, Martha Graham, Milton Hershey, Gene Kelly, Grace Kelly (Princess Grace of Monaco), George C. Marshall, John J. McCloy, Margaret Mead, Andrew W. Mellon, Robert E. Peary, John O'Hara, Mary Roberts Rinehart, Betsy Ross, Will Smith, Jimmy Stewart, Jim Thorpe, John Updike, Benjamin West.

Chamber of Business and Industry. 417 Walnut St., Harrisburg, PA 17120; 717-255-3252.

Toll-free travel information. 1-800-VISITPA.

Web site. http://www.state.pa.us

Rhode Island
Little Rhody, Ocean State

People. Population (1996): 990,225; rank: 43; **Net change** (1990-96): -1.3%. **Pop. density:** (1990) 960.3 per sq mi. **Racial/ethnic distrib.** (1990): 91.4% white; 3.9% black; 4.6% Hispanic.

Geography. Total area: 1,545 sq mi; rank: 50. **Land area:** 1,045 sq mi; rank: 50. **Acres forested land:** 401,000. **Location:** New England state. **Climate:** invigorating and changeable. **Topography:** eastern lowlands of Narragansett Basin; western uplands of flat and rolling hills. **Capital:** Providence.

Economy. Principal industries: services, manufacturing. **Principal manufactured goods:** costume jewelry, toys, machinery, textiles, electronics. **Chief crops:** nursery products, turf, potatoes, apples. **Timber/lumber:** (1996) oak; 11 mil bd. ft. **Nonfuel minerals** (est. 1996): $31.9 mil; construction sand & gravel, crushed stone. **Commercial fishing** (1996): $70 mil. **Chief ports:** Providence, Quonset Point, Newport. **Value of construction** (1996): $658 mil. **Employment distribution** (1996): 33% services; 19% mfg.; 22% trade. **Per capita personal income** (1996): $24,765. **Unemployment** (1996): 5.1%. **Tourism** (1995): $1.6 bil.

Finance. FDIC-insured commercial banks & trust companies (1996): 8. **Deposits:** $5.0 bil. **FDIC-insured savings institutions** (1996): 6. **Assets:** $5.6 bil.

Federal government. No. federal civilian employees (Mar. 1996): 5,594. **Avg. salary:** $42,699. **Notable federal facilities:** Naval War College; Naval Underwater Warfare Center; Natl. Marine Fisheries Laboratory; EPA Environmental Research Laboratory.

Energy. Electricity production (1996, kWh, by source): Petroleum: 73 mil; Gas: 3.2 bil.

Public education. Student-teacher ratio (1995): 14.3. **Avg. teachers' salary** (1996-97): $43,019.

State data. Motto: Hope. **Flower:** Violet. **Bird:** Rhode Island red. **Tree:** Red maple. **Song:** Rhode Island. **Thirteenth** of original 13 states to ratify the Constitution, May 29, 1790. **State fair** at Richmond; mid-Aug.

History. When the Europeans arrived Narragansett, Niantic, Nipmuc, and Wampanoag peoples lived in the region. Verrazano visited the area, 1524. The first permanent settlement was founded at Providence, 1636, by Roger Williams, who was exiled from the Massachusetts Bay Colony; Anne Hutchinson, also exiled, settled Portsmouth, 1638. Quaker and Jewish immigrants seeking freedom of worship began arriving, 1650s-60s. The colonists broke the power of the Narragansett in the Great Swamp Fight, 1675, the decisive battle in King Philip's War. British trade restrictions angered colonists, and they burned the British customs vessel *Gaspee*, 1772. The colony became the first to formally renounce all allegiance to King George III, May 4, 1776. Initially opposed to joining the Union, Rhode Island was the last of the original 13 colonies to ratify the Constitution, 1790.

Tourist attractions. Newport mansions; yachting races including Newport to Bermuda; Block Island; Touro Synagogue, oldest in U.S., Newport; first Baptist Church in America, Providence; Slater Mill Historic Site, Pawtucket; Gilbert Stuart birthplace, Saunderstown.

Famous Rhode Islanders. Ambrose Burnside, George M. Cohan, Nelson Eddy, Jabez Gorham, Nathanael Greene, Christopher and Oliver La Farge, Matthew C. and Oliver Hazard Perry, Gilbert Stuart.

Chamber of Commerce. 30 Exchange Terr., Providence, RI 02908.

Toll-free travel information. 1-800-556-2484.

Web site. http://www.state.ri.us

South Carolina
Palmetto State

People. Population (1996): 3,698,746; rank: 26; **Net change** (1990-96): 6.1%. **Pop. density:** (1990) 115.8 per sq mi. **Racial/ethnic distrib.** (1990): 69.0% white; 29.8% black; 0.9% Hispanic.

Geography. Total area: 32,008 sq mi; rank: 40. **Land area:** 30,111 sq mi; rank: 40. **Acres forested land:** 12,257,000. **Location:** South Atlantic state, bordered by North Carolina on the N; Georgia on the SW and W; the Atlantic Ocean on the E, SE, and S. **Climate:** humid subtropical. **Topography:** Blue Ridge province in NW has highest peaks; piedmont lies between the mountains and the fall line; coastal plain covers two-thirds of the state. **Capital:** Columbia.

Economy. Principal industries: tourism, agriculture, manufacturing. **Principal manufactured goods:** textiles, chemicals and allied products, machinery and fabricated metal products, apparel and related products. **Chief crops:** tobacco, soybeans, corn, cotton, peaches, hay. **Livestock** (1994): 500,000 cattle; 350,000 hogs/pigs; 6.3 mil chickens, excluding broilers. **Timber/lumber** (1996): pine, oak; 1.4 bil bd. ft. **Nonfuel minerals** (est. 1996): $495 mil; mostly portland cement, crushed stone, construction and masonary sand & gravel. **Commercial fishing** (1996): $24 mil. **Chief ports:** Charleston, Georgetown, Beaufort/ Port Royal. **International airport at:** Charleston. **Value of construction** (1996): $5.4 bil. **Employment distribution** (1996): 21.8% mfg.; 22.3% serv.; 23.7% trade; 6.1% govt. **Per capita personal income** (1996): $19,755. **Unemployment** (1996): 6.0%. **Tourism** (1996): $13.1 bil.

Finance. FDIC-insured commercial banks & trust companies (1996): 79. **Deposits:** $21.3 bil. **FDIC-insured savings institutions** (1996): 34. **Assets:** $7.7 bil.

Federal government. No. federal civilian employees (Mar. 1996): 17,346. **Avg. salary:** $36,924. **Notable federal facilities:** Polaris Submarine Base; Barnwell Nuclear Power Plant; Ft. Jackson; Parris Island; Savannah River Plant.

Energy. Electricity production (1996, kWh, by source): Coal: 29.0 bil.; Petroleum: 118 mil; Gas: 91 mil; Hydroelectric: 2.2 bil; Nuclear: 43.6 bil.

Public education. Student-teacher ratio (1995): 16.2. **Avg. teachers' salary** (1996-97): $32,659.

State data. Motto: Dum Spiro Spero (While I breathe, I hope). **Flower:** Yellow jessamine. **Bird:** Carolina wren. **Tree:** Palmetto. **Song:** Carolina. **Eighth** of the original 13 states to ratify the Constitution, May 23, 1788. **State fair** at Columbia; mid-Oct.

History. At the time of European settlement, Cherokee, Catawba, and Muskogean peoples lived in the area. The first English colonists settled near the Ashley River, 1670, and moved to the site of Charleston, 1680. The colonists seized the government, 1775, and the royal governor fled. The British took Charleston, 1780, but were defeated at Kings Mountain that same year, and at Cowpens and Eutaw Springs, 1781. In the 1830s, South Carolinians, angered by federal protective tariffs, adopted the Nullification Doctrine, holding that a state can void an act of Congress. The state was the first to secede from the Union, 1861, and Confederate troops fired on and forced the surrender of U.S. troops at Ft. Sumter, in Charleston Harbor, launching the Civil War. South Carolina was readmitted,1868.

Tourist attractions. Historic Charleston; Ft. Sumter Natl. Monument, in Charleston Harbor; Charleston Museum, est. 1773, oldest museum in U.S.; Middleton Place, Magnolia Plantation, Cypress Gardens, Drayton Hall, all near Charleston; other gardens at Brookgreen, Edisto, Glencairn;

Myrtle Beach; Hilton Head Island; American Revolution War battle sites; Andrew Jackson State Park & Museum; South Carolina State Museum, Columbia; Riverbanks Zoo, Columbia.

Famous South Carolinians. Charles Bolden, James F. Byrnes, John C. Calhoun, DuBose Heyward, Ernest F. Hollings, Andrew Jackson, Jesse Jackson, James Longstreet, Francis Marion, Ronald McNair, Charles Pinckney, John Rutledge, Thomas Sumter, Strom Thurmond, John B. Watson.

Tourist information. S. Carolina Dept. of Parks, Recreation, & Tourism; 803-734-0122.

Toll-free travel information. 1-800-346-3634.

Web site. http://www.state.sc.us

South Dakota
Coyote State, Mount Rushmore State

People. Population (1996): 732,405; rank: 45; **Net change** (1990-96): 5.2%. **Pop. density:** (1990) 9.2 per sq mi. **Racial/ethnic distrib.** (1990): 91.6% white; 0.5% black; 7.3% Amer. Indian; 0.8% Hispanic.

Geography. Total area: 77,121 sq mi; rank: 17. **Land area:** 75,896 sq mi; rank: 16. **Acres forested land:** 1,690,000. **Location:** West North Central state bounded on the N by North Dakota; on the E by Minnesota and Iowa; on the S by Nebraska; on the W by Wyoming and Montana. **Climate:** characterized by extremes of temperature, persistent winds, low precipitation and humidity. **Topography:** Prairie Plains in the E; rolling hills of the Great Plains in the W; the Black Hills, rising 3,500 ft, in the SW corner. **Capital:** Pierre.

Economy. Principal industries: agriculture, services, manufacturing. **Principal manufactured goods:** food and kindred products, machinery, electric and electronic equipment. **Chief crops:** corn, oats, wheat, sunflowers, soybeans, sorghum. **Livestock** (1997): 3.8 mil cattle; 450,000 sheep (1996) 1.2 mil hogs/pigs. **Timber/lumber** ponderosa pine. **Nonfuel minerals** (est. 1996): $353 mil; mostly gold, portland cement, construction sand & gravel. **Value of construction** (1996): $814 mil. **Employment distribution** (1996): 26% serv.; 14% mfg. **Per capita personal income** (1996): $21,516. **Unemployment** (1996): 3.2%. **Tourism** (1995): $1.25 bil.

Finance. FDIC-insured commercial banks & trust companies (1996): 117. **Deposits:** $13.2 bil. **FDIC-insured savings institutions** (1996): 5. **Assets:** $844 mil.

Federal government. No. federal civilian employees (Mar. 1996): 6,851. **Avg. salary:** $35,428. **Notable federal facilities:** Ellsworth AFB, Corp of Engineers, Nat'l Park Service.

Energy. Electricity production (1996, kWh, by source): Coal: 2.0 bil; Petroleum: 9 mil; Gas: 50 mil; Hydroelectric: 8.0 bil.

Public education. Student-teacher ratio (1995): 15.0. **Avg. teachers' salary** (1996-97): $26,764.

State data. Motto: Under God, the people rule. **Flower:** Pasqueflower. **Bird:** Chinese ring-necked pheasant. **Tree:** Black Hills spruce. **Song:** Hail, South Dakota. **Entered union** Nov. 2, 1889; rank, 40th. **State fair** at Huron; late Aug.-early Sept.

History. At the time of first European contact, Mandan, Hidatsa, Arikara and Sioux lived in the area. The French Verendrye brothers explored the region, 1742-43. The U.S. acquired the area, 1803, in the Louisiana Purchase. Lewis and Clark passed through the area, 1804-6. In 1817 a trading post was opened at Fort Pierre, which later became the site of the first European settlement in South Dakota. Gold was discovered, 1874, in the Black Hills on the great Sioux reservation; the "Great Dakota Boom" began in 1879. Conflicts with Native Americans led to the Great Sioux Agreement, 1889, which established reservations and opened up more land for white settlement. The massacre of Native American families at Wounded Knee, 1890, ended Sioux resistance.

Tourist attractions. Black Hills; Mt. Rushmore; Needles Highway; Harney Peak, tallest E. of Rockies; Deadwood, 1876 Gold Rush town; Custer State Park; Jewel Cave Natl. Monument; Badlands Natl. Park "moonscape"; "Great Lakes of S. Dakota"; Ft. Sisseton; Great Plains Zoo & Museum, Sioux Falls; Corn Palace, Mitchell; Wind Cave Natl. Park; Crazy Horse Memorial, mountain carving in progress.

Famous South Dakotans. Sparky Anderson, Tom Brokaw, Crazy Horse, Thomas Daschle, Myron Floren, Mary Hart, Cheryl Ladd, Dr. Ernest O. Lawrence, George McGovern, Billy Mills, Allen Neuharth, Pat O'Brien, Sitting Bull.

Tourist information. South Dakota Tourism, 711 E. Wells Ave., Pierre, SD 57501-3369.

Toll-free travel information. 1-800-SDAKOTA.

Web site. http://www.state.sd.us

Tennessee
Volunteer State

People. Population (1996): 5,319,654; rank: 17; **Net change** (1990-96): 9.1%. **Pop. density:** (1990) 118.3 per sq mi. **Racial/ethnic distrib.** (1990): 83.0% white; 16.0% black; 0.7% Hispanic.

Geography. Total area: 42,146 sq mi; rank: 36. **Land area:** 41,219 sq mi; rank: 34. **Acres forested land:** 13,612,000. **Location:** East South Central state bounded on the N by Kentucky and Virginia; on the E by North Carolina; on the S by Georgia, Alabama, and Mississippi; on the W by Arkansas and Missouri. **Climate:** humid continental to the N; humid subtropical to the S. **Topography:** rugged country in the E; the Great Smoky Mts. of the Unakas; low ridges of the Appalachian Valley; the flat Cumberland Plateau; slightly rolling terrain and knobs of the Interior Low Plateau, the largest region; Eastern Gulf Coastal Plain to the W, laced with streams; Mississippi Alluvial Plain, a narrow strip of swamp and flood plain in the extreme W. **Capital:** Nashville.

Economy. Principal industries: manufacturing, trade, services, tourism, finance, insurance, real estate. **Principal manufactured goods:** chemicals, food, transportation equipment, industrial machinery and equipment, fabricated metal products, rubber/plastic products, paper and allied products, printing and publishing. **Chief crops:** tobacco, cotton, lint, soybeans, grain, corn. **Livestock** (1995): 2.7 mil cattle; 560,000 hogs/pigs; 1.64 mil poultry. **Timber/lumber** (1996): red oak, white oak, yellow poplar, hickory; 911 mil bd. ft. **Nonfuel minerals** (est. 1996): $651 mil; mostly crushed stone, sand & gravel, zinc, cement. **Chief ports:** Memphis, Nashville, Chattanooga, Knoxville. **International airports at:** Memphis, Nashville. **Value of construction** (1996): $8.3 bil. **Employment distribution** (1996): 20.6% mfg.; 23.5% trade; 25.9% serv.; 15.1% govt. **Per capita personal income** (1996): $21,764. **Unemployment** (1996): 5.2%. **Tourism** (1995): $7.7 bil.

Finance. FDIC-insured commercial banks & trust companies (1996): 238. **Deposit:** $57.2 bil. **FDIC-insured savings institutions** (1996): 24. **Assets:** $4.0 bil.

Federal government. No. federal civilian employees (Mar. 1996): 33,622. **Avg. salary:** $40,859. **Notable federal facilities:** Tennessee Valley Authority; Oak Ridge Nat'l. Laboratories; Arnold Engineering Development Center; Ft. Campbell Army Base; Millington Naval Station.

Energy. Electricity production (1996, kWh, by source): Coal: 55.5 bil; Petroleum: 258 mil; Gas: 61 mil; Hydroelectric: 9.9 bil; Nuclear: 22.9 bil.

Public education. Student-teacher ratio (1995): 16.7. **Avg. teachers' salary** (1996-97): $33,789.

State data. Motto: Agriculture and commerce. **Flower:** Iris. **Bird:** Mockingbird. **Tree:** Tulip poplar. **Song:** The Tennessee Waltz. **Entered union** June 1, 1796; rank, 16th. **State fair** at Nashville; mid-Sept.

History. When the first European explorers arrived, Creek and Yuchi peoples lived in the area; the Cherokee moved into the region in the early 18th cent. Spanish explorers first visited the area, 1541. English traders crossed the Great Smokies from the east while France's Marquette and Jolliet sailed down the Mississippi on the west, 1673. The first permanent settlement was by Virginians on the Watauga River, 1769. During the American Revolution, the colonists helped win the Battle of Kings Mountain (NC), 1780, and joined other eastern campaigns. The state seceded from the Union, 1861, and saw many Civil War engagements, but 30,000 soldiers fought for the Union. Tennessee was re-admitted in 1866, the only former Confederate state not to have a postwar military government.

Tourist attractions. Reelfoot Lake; Lookout Mountain, Chattanooga; Fall Creek Falls; Great Smoky Mountains

Natl. Park; Lost Sea, Sweetwater; Cherokee Natl. Forest; Cumberland Gap Natl. Park; Andrew Jackson's home, the Hermitage, near Nashville; homes of Pres.s Polk and Andrew Johnson; American Museum of Science and Energy, Oak Ridge; Parthenon, Grand Old Opry, Opryland USA, all Nashville; Dollywood theme park, Pigeon Forge; Tennessee Aquarium, Chattanooga; Graceland, home of Elvis Presley, Memphis; Alex Haley Home and Museum, Henning; Casey Jones Home and Museum, Jackson.

Famous Tennesseans. Roy Acuff, Davy Crockett, David Farragut, Ernie Ford, Aretha Franklin, Al Gore Jr., Alex Haley, William C. Handy, Sam Houston, Cordell Hull, Andrew Jackson, Andrew Johnson, Casey Jones, Estes Kefaurer, Grace Moore, Dolly Parton, Minnie Pearl, James Polk, Elvis Presley, Dinah Shore, Bessie Smith, Alvin York.

Tourist information. Dept. of Tourist Development, 5th Floor, Rachel Jackson Bldg., 320 6th Ave. N., Nashville, TN 37202.

Toll-free travel information. 1-800-TENN200.

Web site. http://www.state.tn.us

Texas
Lone Star State

People. Population (1996): 19,128,261; rank: 2; **Net change** (1990-96): 12.6%. **Pop. density:** (1990) 64.9 per sq mi. **Racial/ethnic distrib.** (1990): 75.2% white; 11.9% black; 25.5% Hispanic.

Geography. Total area: 268,601 sq mi; rank: 2. **Land area:** 261,914 sq mi; rank: 2. **Acres forested land:** 19,193,000. **Location:** Southwestern state, bounded on the SE by the Gulf of Mexico; on the SW by Mexico, separated by the Rio Grande; surrounding states are Louisiana, Arkansas, Oklahoma, New Mexico. **Climate:** extremely varied; driest region is the Trans-Pecos; wettest is the NE. **Topography:** Gulf Coast Plain in the S and SE; North Central Plains slope upward with some hills; the Great Plains extend over the Panhandle, are broken by low mountains; the Trans-Pecos is the southern extension of the Rockies. **Capital:** Austin.

Economy. Principal industries: manufacturing, trade, oil and gas extraction, services. **Principal manufactured goods:** industrial machinery and equipment, foods, electrical and electronic products, chemicals and allied products, apparel. **Chief crops:** cotton, grain sorghum, grains, vegetables, citrus and other fruits, pecans, peanuts. **Livestock** (1996): 15 mil cattle; 500,000 hogs/pigs; 1.7 mil sheep; 19.3 mil poultry. **Timber/lumber** (1996): pine, cypress; 1.5 bil bd. ft. **Nonfuel minerals** (est. 1996): $1.78 bil; mostly portland cement, crushed stone, magnesium, gypsum, construction sand and gravel, lime, salt. **Commercial fishing** (1996): $191 mil. **Chief ports:** Houston, Galveston, Brownsville, Beaumont, Port Arthur, Corpus Christi. **Major international airports at:** Houston, Dallas/Ft. Worth, San Antonio. **Value of construction** (1996): $25.0 bil. **Employment distribution** (1996): 24.1% trade; 26.9% serv.; 17.6% govt.; 12.8% mfg. **Per capita personal income** (1996): $22,045. **Unemployment** (1996): 5.6%. **Tourism** (1994): $24.6 bil.

Finance. FDIC-insured commercial banks & trust companies (1996): 877. **Deposits:** $168.2 bil. **FDIC-insured savings institutions** (1996): 52. **Assets:** $62.3 bil.

Federal government. No. federal civilian employees (Mar. 1996): 111,902. **Avg. salary:** $38,610. **Notable federal facilities:** Fort Hood, Kelly AFB, and Ft. Sam Houston.

Energy. Electricity production (1996, kWh, by source): Coal: 133.3 bil; Petroleum: 556 mil; Gas: 102.0 bil; Hydroelectric: 930 mil; Nuclear: 35.8 bil.

Public education. Student-teacher ratio (1995): 15.6. **Avg. teachers' salary** (1996-97): $32,644.6

State data. Motto: Friendship. **Flower:** Bluebonnet. **Bird:** Mockingbird. **Tree:** Pecan. **Song:** Texas, Our Texas. **Entered union** Dec. 29, 1845; rank, 28th. **State fair** at Dallas; mid-Oct.

History. At the time of European contact, Native American tribes in the region were numerous and diverse in culture. Coahuiltecan, Karankawa, Caddo, Jumano, and Tonkawa peoples lived in the area, and during the 19th cent., the Apache, Comanche, Cherokee, and Wichita arrived. Spanish explorer Pineda sailed along the Texas coast, 1519; Cabeza de Vaca and Coronado visited the interior, 1541. Spaniards made the first settlement at Ysleta,

near El Paso, 1682. Americans moved into the land early in the 19th cent. Mexico, of which Texas was a part, won independence from Spain, 1821; Santa Anna became dictator in 1835; Texans rebelled. Santa Anna wiped out defenders of the Alamo, 1836; Sam Houston's Texans defeated Santa Anna at San Jacinto, and independence was proclaimed that same year. The Republic of Texas, with Sam Houston as its first Pres., functioned as a nation until 1845, when it was admitted to the Union.

Tourist attractions. Padre Island Natl. Seashore; Big Bend, Guadalupe Mts. natl. parks; The Alamo; Ft. Davis; Six Flags Amusement Park; Sea World and Fiesta Texas, both in San Antonio; San Antonio Missions Natl. Park; Cowgirl Hall of Fame, Fort Worth; Lyndon B. Johnson Natl. Park, marking his birthplace, boyhood home, and ranch, near Johnson City; Lyndon B. Johnson Library and Museum, Austin; Texas State Aquarium, Corpus Christi; Kimball Art Museum, Fort Worth; George Bush Library, College Station.

Famous Texans. Stephen F. Austin, Lloyd Bentsen, James Bowie, Carol Burnett, George Bush, J. Frank Dobie, Dwight D. Eisenhower, Farrah Fawcett, Sam Houston, Howard Hughes, Lyndon B. Johnson, Tommy Lee Jones, Janis Joplin, Mary Martin, Chester Nimitz, Sandra Day O'Connor, H. Ross Perot, Katharine Ann Porter, Dan Rather, Sam Rayburn, Sissy Spacek, George Strait.

Chamber of Commerce. 900 Congress, Suite 501, Austin, TX 78701.

Toll-free travel information. 1-800-8888TEX.

Web site. http://www.state.tx.us

Utah
Beehive State

People. Population (1996): 2,000,494; rank: 34; **Net change** (1990-96): 16.1%. **Pop. density:** (1990) 21.0 per sq mi. **Racial/ethnic distrib.** (1990): 93.8% white; 0.7% black; 4.9% Hispanic.

Geography. Total area: 84,904 sq mi; rank: 13. **Land area:** 82,168 sq mi; rank: 12. **Acres forested land:** 16,234,000. **Location:** Middle Rocky Mountain state; its southeastern corner touches Colorado, New Mexico, and Arizona, and is the only spot in the U.S. where 4 states join. **Climate:** arid; ranging from warm desert in SW to alpine in NE. **Topography:** high Colorado plateau is cut by brilliantly colored canyons of the SE; broad, flat, desert-like Great Basin of the W; the Great Salt Lake and Bonneville Salt Flats to the NW; Middle Rockies in the NE run E-W; valleys and plateaus of the Wasatch Front. **Capital:** Salt Lake City.

Economy. Principal industries: services, trade, manufacturing, government, transportation, utilities. **Principal manufactured goods:** medical instruments, electronic components, food products, fabricated metals, transportation equipment, steel and copper. **Chief crops:** hay, corn, wheat, barley, apples, potatoes, cherries, onions, peaches, pears. **Livestock:** (1996) 930,000 cattle; 90,000 milking cows; 163,000 hogs/pigs; 375,000 sheep; turkeys and mink. **Timber/lumber:** (1996) aspen, spruce, pine; 36 mil bd. ft. **Nonfuel minerals** (est. 1996): $1.56 bil; copper, potash, gold, molybdenum, iron ore, magnesium, phosphate rock, salt. **International airports at:** Salt Lake City. **Value of construction** (1996): $3.7 bil. **Employment distribution** (1995): 35.7% serv.; 24.2% trade; 7.0% govt; 13.6% mfg. **Per capita personal income** (1996): $19,156. **Unemployment** (1996): 3.5%. **Tourism** (1995): $3.6 bil.

Finance. FDIC-insured commercial banks & trust companies (1996): 48. **Deposits:** $18.9 bil. **FDIC-insured savings institutions** (1996): 2. **Assets:** $571 mil.

Federal government. No. federal civilian employees (Mar. 1996): 24,343. **Avg. salary:** $36,278. **Notable federal facilities:** Hill AFB; Tooele Army Depot; IRS Western Service Center.

Energy. Electricity production (1996, kWh, by source): Coal: 30.7 bil; Petroleum: 29 mil; Gas: 242 mil; Hydroelectric: 1.1 bil.

Public education. Student-teacher ratio (1995): 23.8. **Avg. teachers' salary** (1996-97): $31,750.

State data. Motto: Industry. **Flower:** Sego lily. **Bird:** Seagull. **Tree:** Blue spruce. **Song:** Utah, We Love Thee.

Entered union Jan. 4, 1896; rank, 45th. **State fair** at Salt Lake City; Sept.

History. Ute, Gosiute, Southern Paiute, and Navajo peoples lived in the region at the time of European contact. Spanish Franciscans visited the area, 1776, the first white men to do so. American fur traders followed. Permanent settlement began with the arrival of the Mormons, 1847; they made the arid land bloom and created a prosperous economy. The State of Deseret was organized in 1849, and asked admission to the Union. In 1850, Congress established the region as the territory of Utah, and Brigham Young was appointed governor. The Union and Pacific Railroads met near Promontory, May 10, 1869, creating the first transcontinental railroad. Statehood was not achieved until 1896, after a long period of controversy over the Mormon Church's doctrine of polygamy, which it discontinued in 1890.

Tourist attractions. Temple Square, Mormon Church headquarters, Salt Lake City; Great Salt Lake; Natural Zion, Canyonlands, Bryce Canyon, Arches, and Capitol Reef natl. parks; Dinosaur, Rainbow Bridge, Timpanogos Cave, and Natural Bridges natl. monuments; Lake Powell; Flaming Gorge Natl. Recreation Area.

Famous Utahans. Maude Adams, Ezra Taft Benson, John Moses Browning, Mariner Eccles, Philo Farnsworth, James Fletcher, David M. Kennedy, J. Willard Marriott, Merlin Olsen, Osmond family, Ivy Baker Priest, George Romney, Brigham Young, Loretta Young.

Tourist information. Utah Travel Council, Council Hall, Salt Lake City, UT 84114; 801-538-1030.

Toll-free travel information. 1-800-200-1160

Web site. http://www.state.ut.us

Vermont
Green Mountain State

People. Population (1996): 588,654; rank: 49; **Net change** (1990-96): 4.6%. **Pop. density:** (1990) 60.8 per sq mi. **Racial/ethnic distrib.** (1990): 98.6% white; 0.3% black; 0.6% Asian; 0.7% Hispanic.

Geography. Total area: 9,615 sq mi; rank: 45. **Land area:** 9,249 sq mi; rank: 43. **Acres forested land:** 4,538,000. **Location:** northern New England state. **Climate:** temperate, with considerable temperature extremes; heavy snowfall in mountains. **Topography:** Green Mts. N-S backbone 20-36 mi wide; avg. altitude 1,000 ft. **Capital:** Montpelier.

Economy. Principal industries: manufacturing, tourism, agriculture, trade, finance, insurance, real estate, government. **Principal manufactured goods:** machine tools, furniture, scales, books, computer components, speciality foods. **Chief crops:** dairy products, apples, maple syrup, greenhouse/nursery, vegetables and small fruits. **Livestock** (1996): 300,000 cattle/cows; 1,600 hogs/pigs; 15,000 sheep/lambs; 31,000 turkeys. **Timber/lumber** (1996): pine, spruce, fir, hemlock; 228 mil bd. ft. **Nonfuel minerals** (est. 1996): $66.8 mil; mostly dimension stone, crushed stone, construction sand & gravel, asbestos. **International airport at:** Burlington. **Value of construction** (1996): $592 mil. **Employment distribution** (1997): 28.8% serv.; 23.7% trade; 16.8% mfg 17% govt. **Per capita personal income** (1996): $22,124. **Unemployment** (1996): 4.6%. **Tourism** (1995): $2.2 bil.

Finance. FDIC-insured commercial banks & trust companies (1996): 22. **Deposits:** $5.2 bil. **FDIC-insured savings institutions** (1996): 7. **Assets:** $2.4 bil.

Federal government. No. federal civilian employees (Mar. 1996): 2,754. **Avg. salary:** $37,890.

Energy. Electricity production (1996, kWh, by source): Petroleum: 4 mil; Hydroelectric: 1.1 bil; Nuclear: 3.8 bil.

Public education. Student-teacher ratio (1995): 13.8. **Avg. teachers' salary** (1996-97): $37,200.

State data. Motto: Freedom and unity. **Flower:** Red clover. **Bird:** Hermit thrush. **Tree:** Sugar maple. **Song:** Hail, Vermont. **Entered union** Mar. 4, 1791; rank, 14th. **State fair** at Rutland; early Sept.

History. Before the arrival of the Europeans, Abnaki and Mahican peoples lived in the region. Champlain explored the lake that bears his name, 1609. The first American settlement was Ft. Dummer, 1724, near Brattleboro. During the American Revolution, Ethan Allen and the Green Mountain Boys captured Ft. Ticonderoga (NY), 1775; John Stark defeated part of Burgoyne's forces near Bennington, 1777. In the War of 1812, Thomas MacDonough defeated a British fleet on Lake Champlain off Plattsburgh (NY), 1814.

Tourist attractions. Shelburne Museum; Rock of Ages Quarry, Graniteville; Vermont Marble Exhibit, Proctor; Bennington Battle Monument; Pres. Calvin Coolidge homestead, Plymouth; Maple Grove Maple Museum, St. Johnsbury; Ben & Jerry's Factory, Waterbury.

Famous Vermonters. Ethan Allen, Chester A. Arthur, Calvin Coolidge, George Dewey, John Dewey, Stephen A. Douglas, Dorothy Canfield Fisher, James Fisk.

Chamber of Commerce. PO Box 37, Montpelier, VT 05601.

Tourist information. Vermont Dept. of Tourism and Marketing, 134 State St., Montpelier, VT 05602; 802-828-3237 .

Toll-free travel information. 1-800-VERMONT

Web site. http://www.state.vt.us

Virginia
Old Dominion

People. Population (1996): 6,675,451; rank: 12; **Net change** (1990-96): 7.9%. **Pop. density:** (1990) 156.3 per sq mi. **Racial/ethnic distrib.** (1990): 77.4% white; 18.8% black; 2.6% Asian; 2.6% Hispanic.

Geography. Total area: 42,777 sq mi; rank: 35. **Land area:** 39,598 sq mi; rank: 37. **Acres forested land:** 15,858,000. **Location:** South Atlantic state bounded by the Atlantic Ocean on the E and surrounded by North Carolina, Tennessee, Kentucky, West Virginia, and Maryland. **Climate:** mild and equable. **Topography:** mountain and valley region in the W, including the Blue Ridge Mts.; rolling piedmont plateau; tidewater, or coastal plain, including the eastern shore. **Capital:** Richmond.

Economy. Principal industries: services, trade, government, manufacturing, tourism, agriculture. **Principal manufactured goods:** textiles, transportation equipment, electric and electronic equipment, food processing, chemicals, printing lumber and wood products, apparel. **Chief crops:** soy-beans, grain corn tobacco, peanuts, corn, far grain. **Livestock** (1995): 1.8 mil cattle; 380,000 hogs/pigs; 84,000 sheep; 282.3 mil broilers, 23.5 mil turkeys. **Timber/lumber** (1996): pine and hardwoods; 1.3 bil bd. ft. **Nonfuel minerals** (est. 1996): $529 mil; mostly crushed stone, lime, construction sand & gravel. **Commercial fishing** (1996): $106 mil. **Chief ports:** Hampton Roads, Richmond, Alexandria. **International airports at:** Norfolk, Dulles, Richmond, Newport News. **Value of construction** (1996): $9.2 bil. **Employment distribution** (1995): 28.4% serv.; 22.8% trade; 19.5% govt.; 13.1% mfg. **Per capita personal income** (1996): $24,925. **Unemployment** (1996): 4.4%. **Tourism** (1994): $9.4 bil.

Finance. FDIC-insured commercial banks & trust companies (1996): 154. **Deposits:** $64.9 bil. **FDIC-insured savings institutions** (1996): 31. **Assets:** $15.5 bil.

Federal government. No. federal civilian employees (Mar. 1996): 125,937. **Avg. salary:** $46,547. **Notable federal facilities:** Pentagon; Norfolk Naval Station, Norfolk Naval Air Station; Naval Shipyard; Marine Corps Base; Langley AFB; NASA at Langley.

Energy. Electricity production (1996, kWh, by source): Coal: 27.9 bil; Petroleum: 683 mil; Gas: 1.1 bil; Hydroelectric: 556 mil; Nuclear: 26.3 bil.

Public education. Student-teacher ratio (1995): 14.4. **Avg. teachers' salary** (1996-97): $35,837.

State data. Motto: Sic Semper Tyrannis (Thus always to tyrants). **Flower:** Dogwood. **Bird:** Cardinal. **Tree:** Dogwood. **Song Emeritus:** Carry Me Back to Old Virginia. **Tenth** of the original 13 states to ratify the Constitution, June 25, 1788. **State fair** at Richmond; late Sept.-early Oct.

History. Living in the area at the time of European contact were the Cherokee and Susquehanna and the Algonquians of the Powhatan Confederacy. English settlers founded Jamestown, 1607. Virginians took over much of the government from royal governor Dunmore, 1775, forcing him to flee. Virginians under George Rogers Clark freed the Ohio-Indiana-Illinois area of British forces. Benedict Arnold burned Richmond and Petersburg for the British, 1781. That same year, Britain's Cornwallis was trapped at Yorktown and surrendered, ending the American Revolution. Virginia seceded from the Union, 1861, and Richmond became the capital of the Confederacy. Hampton Roads, off the Virginia coast, was the site of the famous naval battle of the USS *Monitor* and CSS *Virginia* (Merrimac), 1862. Virginia was readmitted, 1870.

Tourist attractions. Colonial Williamsburg; Busch Gardens, Williamsburg; Wolf Trap Farm, near Falls Church; Arlington Natl. Cemetery; Mt. Vernon, home of George Washington; Jamestown Festival Park; Yorktown; Jefferson's Monticello, Charlottesville; Robert E. Lee's birthplace, Stratford Hall, and grave, Lexington; Appomattox; Shenandoah Natl. Park; Blue Ridge Parkway; Virginia Beach; Paramount's King's Dominion, near Richmond.

Famous Virginians. Richard E. Byrd, James B. Cabell, Henry Clay, Jerry Falwell, William Henry Harrison, Patrick Henry, Thomas Jefferson, Joseph E. Johnston, Robert E. Lee, Meriwether Lewis and William Clark, James Madison, John Marshall, George Mason, James Monroe, Pocahontas, Edgar Allan Poe, John Randolph, Walter Reed, John Smith, William Styron, Zachary Taylor, John Tyler, Maggie Walker, Booker T. Washington, George Washington, Woodrow Wilson.

Chamber of Commerce. 9 South Fifth St., Richmond, VA 23219.

Toll-free travel information. 1-800-VISITVA.

Web site. http://www.state.va.us

Washington
Evergreen State

People. Population (1996): 5,532,939; rank: 15; **Net change** (1990-96): 13.7%. **Pop. density:** (1990) 73.1 per sq mi. **Racial/ethnic distrib.** (1990): 88.5% white; 3.1% black; 4.3% Asian; 4.4% Hispanic.

Geography. Total area: 71,302 sq mi; rank: 18. **Land area:** 66,581 sq mi; rank: 20. **Acres forested land:** 20,483,000. **Location:** Pacific state bordered by Canada on the N; Idaho on the E; Oregon on the S; and the Pacific Ocean on the W. **Climate:** mild, dominated by the Pacific Ocean and protected by the Rockies. **Topography:** Olympic Mts. on NW peninsula; open land along coast to Columbia R.; flat terrain of Puget Sound Lowland; Cascade Mts. region's high peaks to the E; Columbia Basin in central portion; highlands to the NE; mountains to the SE. **Capital:** Olympia.

Economy. Principal industries: forestry, aerospace, manufacturing, agriculture. **Principal manufactured goods:** aircraft, pulp and paper, lumber and plywood, aluminum, processed fruits and vegetables, machinery, electronics, computer software. **Chief crops:** apples, potatoes, hay, farm forest products. **Livestock** (1996): 1.3 mil cattle; 60,000 sheep/lamb (1995): 51,000 hogs/pigs; 7.0 mil poultry. **Timber/lumber** (1996): Douglas fir, hemlock, cedar, pine; 4.1 bil bd. ft. **Nonfuel minerals** (est. 1996): $626 mil; mostly construction sand & gravel, crushed stone, magnesium metal, portland cement. **Commercial fishing** (1996): $148 mil. **Chief ports:** Seattle, Tacoma, Vancouver, Kelso-Longview. **International airports at:** Seattle/Tacoma, Spokane, Boeing Field. **Value of construction** (1996): $8.4 bil. **Employment distribution** (1995): 24.8% trade; 26.5% serv.; 18.9% govt.; 14.1% mfg. **Per capita personal income** (1996): $24,838. **Unemployment** (1996): 6.5%. **Tourism** (1994): $7.5 bil.

Finance. FDIC-insured commercial banks & trust companies (1996): 84. **Deposits:** $35.5 bil. **FDIC-insured savings institutions** (1996): 21. **Assets:** $36.7 bil.

Federal government. No. federal civilian employees (Mar. 1996): 45,112. **Avg. salary:** $41,360. **Notable federal facilities:** Bonneville Power Admin.; Ft. Lewis; McChord AFB; Hanford Nuclear Reservation; Bremerton Naval Shipyards.

Energy. Electricity production (1996, kWh, by source): Coal: 8.0 bil; Petroleum: 8 mil; Gas: 529 mil; Hydroelectric: 98.1 bil; Nuclear: 5.6 bil.

Public education. Student-teacher ratio (1995): 20.4. **Avg. teachers' salary** (1996-97): $37,860.

State data. Motto: Alki (By and by). **Flower:** Western rhododendron. **Bird:** Willow goldfinch. **Tree:** Western hem-

lock. **Song:** Washington, My Home. **Entered union** Nov. 11, 1889; rank, 42d. **State fairs:** various county fairs, mostly in Aug. or Sept.; no State fair.

History. At the time of European contact, many Native American tribes lived in the area, including the Nez Percé, Spokan, Yakima, Cayuse, Okanogan, Walla Walla, and Colville peoples, who lived in the interior region, and the Nooksak, Chinook, Nisqually, Clallam, Makah, Quinault, and Puyallup peoples, who inhabited the coastal area. Spain's Bruno Hezeta sailed the coast, 1775. In 1792, British naval officer George Vancouver mapped Puget Sound area, and that same year, American Capt. Robert Gray sailed up the Columbia River. Canadian fur traders set up Spokane House, 1810. Americans under John Jacob Astor established a post at Ft. Okanogan, 1811, and missionary Marcus Whitman settled near Walla Walla, 1836. Final agreement on the border of Washington and Canada was made with Britain, 1846, and Washington became part of the Oregon Territory, 1848. Gold was discovered, 1855.

Tourist attractions. Seattle Waterfront, Seattle Center and Space Needle, Museum of Flight, all Seattle; Mt. Rainier, Olympic, and North Cascades natl. parks; Mt. St. Helens; Puget Sound; San Juan Islands; Grand Coulee Dam; Columbia R. Gorge Natl. Scenic Area; Spokane's Riverfront Park.

Famous Washingtonians. Bing Crosby, William O. Douglas, Bill Gates, Henry M. Jackson, Gary Larson, Mary McCarthy, Robert Motherwell, Edward R. Murrow, Theodore Roethke, Marcus Whitman, Minoru Yamasaki.

Tourist information. WA State Tourism Division, PO Box 42500, Olympia, WA 98504-2500.

Toll-free travel information. 1-800-544-1800. ext. 101

Web site. http://www.wa.gov

West Virginia
Mountain State

People. Population (1996): 1,825,754; rank: 35; **Net change** (1990-96): 1.8%. **Pop. density:** (1990) 74.5 per sq mi. **Racial/ethnic distrib.** (1990): 96.2% white; 3.1% black; 0.5% Hispanic.

Geography. Total area: 24,231 sq mi; rank: 41. **Land area:** 24,087 sq mi; rank: 41. **Acres forested land:** 12,128,000. **Location:** South Atlantic state bounded on the N by Ohio, Pennsylvania, Maryland; on the S and W by Virginia, Kentucky, Ohio; on the E by Maryland and Virginia. **Climate:** humid continental climate except for marine modification in the lower panhandle. **Topography:** ranging from hilly to mountainous; Allegheny Plateau in the W, covers two-thirds of the state; mountains here are the highest in the state, over 4,000 ft. **Capital:** Charleston.

Economy. Principal industries: manufacturing, services, mining, tourism. **Principal manufactured goods:** machinery, plastic and hardwood products, fabricated metals, chemicals, aluminum, automotive parts, steel. **Chief crops:** apples, peaches, hay, tobacco, corn, wheat, oats. **Chief products:** dairy products, eggs. **Livestock** (1996): 450,000 cattle; 19,000 hogs/pigs; 50,000 sheep; 1.8 mil chickens. **Timber/lumber** (1996): oak, yellow poplar, hickory, walnut, cherry; 653 mil bd. ft. **Nonfuel minerals** (est. 1996): $191 mil; mostly crushed stone, portland cement, salt. **Chief port:** Huntington. **Value of construction** (1996): $1.2 bil. **Employment distribution** (1996): 22.9% trade; 19.8% govt.; 27.4% serv.; 11.7% mfg. **Per capita personal income** (1996): $18,444. **Unemployment** (1996): 7.5%. **Tourism** (1996): $4.03 bil.

Finance. FDIC-insured commercial banks & trust companies (1996): 113. **Deposits:** $18.0 bil. **FDIC-insured savings institutions** (1996): 9. **Assets:** $1.1 bil.

Federal government. No. federal civilian employees (Mar. 1996): 11,364. **Avg. salary:** $38,227. **Notable federal facilities:** National Radio Astronomy Observatory; Bureau of Public Debt Bldg.; Harpers Ferry Natl. Park; Correctional Institution for Women; FBI Identification Center.

Energy. Electricity production (1996, kWh, by source): Coal: 83.3 bil; Petroleum: 204 mil; Gas: 20 mil; Hydroelectric: 497 mil.

Public education. Student-teacher ratio (1995): 14.6. **Avg. teachers' salary** (1996-97): $33,159.

State data. Motto: Montani Semper Liberi (Mountaineers are always free). **Flower:** Big rhododendron. **Bird:** Cardinal.

Tree: Sugar maple. **Songs:** The West Virginia Hills; This Is My West Virginia; West Virginia, My Home, Sweet Home. **Entered union** June 20, 1863; rank, 35th. **State fair** at Lewisburg (Fairlea); late Aug.

History. Sparsely inhabited at the time of European contact, the area was primarily Native American hunting grounds. British explorers Thomas Batts and Robert Fallam reached the New River, 1671. Early American explorers included George Washington, 1753, and Daniel Boone. The area became part of Virginia and often objected to rule by the eastern part of the state. When Virginia seceded in 1861, the Wheeling Convention repudiated the act and created a new state, Kanawha, subsequently changed to West Virginia. It was admitted to the Union as such, 1863.

Tourist attractions. Harpers Ferry Natl. Historic Park; Science and Cultural Center, Charleston; White Sulphur and Berkeley Springs mineral water spas; New River Gorge, Fayetteville; Exhibition Coal Mine, Beckley; Monongahela Natl. Forest; Fenton Glass, Williamstown, Viking Glass, New Martinsville; Blenko Glass, Milton; Sternwheel Regatta, Charleston; Mountain State Forest Festival; Snowshoe Ski Resort, Slaty Fork; Canaan State Park, Davis; Mountain State Arts & Crafts Fair, Ripley.

Famous West Virginians. Newton D. Baker, Pearl Buck, John W. Davis, Thomas "Stonewall" Jackson, Don Knotts, Dwight Whitney Morrow, Michael Owens, Walter Reuther, Cyrus Vance, Charles "Chuck" Yeager.

Tourist information. Dept. of Commerce, West Virginia Division of Tourism, State Capitol, Charleston WV 25305.

Toll-free travel information. 1-800-CALLWVA.

Web site. http://www.state.wv.us

Wisconsin
Badger State

People. Population (1996): 5,159,795; rank: 18; **Net change** (1990-96): 5.5%. **Pop. density:** (1990) 90.1 per sq mi. **Racial/ethnic distrib.** (1990): 92.2% white; 5.0% black; 1.9% Hispanic.

Geography. Total area: 65,499 sq mi; rank: 23. **Land area:** 54,314 sq mi; rank: 25. **Acres forested land:** 15,513,000. **Location:** East North Central state, bounded on the N by Lake Superior and Upper Michigan; on the E by Lake Michigan; on the S by Illinois; on the W by the St. Croix and Mississippi rivers. **Climate:** long, cold winters and short, warm summers tempered by the Great Lakes. **Topography:** narrow Lake Superior Lowland plain met by Northern Highland, which slopes gently to the sandy crescent Central Plain; Western Upland in the SW; 3 broad parallel limestone ridges running N-S are separated by wide and shallow lowlands in the SE. **Capital:** Madison.

Economy. Principal industries: services, manufacturing, trade, government, agriculture, tourism. **Principal manufactured goods:** food products, motor vehicles and equipment, paper products, medical instruments and supplies, printing, plastics. **Chief crops:** corn, soybeans, peas, hay, oats, potatoes, sweet corn, snap beans, cranberries. **Chief products:** milk, butter, cheese, canned and frozen vegetables. **Livestock** (1996): 3.8 mil cattle; 1.4 mil milk cows; 800,000 hogs; 4.7 mil poultry; .79,000 sheep. **Timber/lumber** (1996): maple, birch, oak, evergreens; 617 mil bd. ft. **Nonfuel minerals** (est. 1996): $399 mil; mostly crushed stone, construction and industrial sand & gravel, lime. **Commercial fishing** (1996): $4 mil. **Chief ports:** Superior, Ashland, Milwaukee, Green Bay, Kewaunee, Pt. Washington, Manitowoc, Sheboygan, Marinette, Kenosha. **International airports at:** Milwaukee. **Value of construction** (1996): $6.0 bil. **Employment distribution** (1996): 23.7% trade; 24.1% mfg.; 23.7% serv.; 13.4% govt. **Per capita personal income** (1996): $23,269. **Unemployment** (1996): 3.5%. **Tourism** (1995): $6.1 bil.

Finance. FDIC-insured commercial banks & trust companies (1996): 365. **Deposits:** $51.1 bil. **FDIC-insured savings institutions** (1996): 51. **Assets:** $25.2 bil.

Federal government. No. federal civilian employees (Mar. 1996): 11,983. **Avg. salary:** $37,757. **Notable federal facilities:** Ft. McCoy.

Energy. Electricity production (1996, kWh, by source): Coal: 38.1 bil; Petroleum: 132 mil; Gas: 540 mil; Hydroelectric: 2.4 bil; Nuclear: 10.1 bil.

Public education. Student-teacher ratio (1995): 15.8. **Avg. teachers' salary** (1996-97): $38,950.

State data. Motto: Forward. **Flower:** Wood violet. **Bird:** Robin. **Tree:** Sugar maple. **Song:** On, Wisconsin! **Entered union** May 29, 1848; rank, 30th. **State fair** at West Allis; July-Aug.

History. At the time of European contact, Ojibwa, Menominee, Winnebago, Kickapoo, Sauk, Fox, and Potawatomi peoples inhabited the region. Jean Nicolet was the first European to see the Wisconsin area, arriving in Green Bay, 1634; French missionaries and fur traders followed. The British took over, 1763. The U.S. won the land after the American Revolution, but the British were not ousted until after the War of 1812. Lead miners came next, then farmers. In 1816, the U.S. government built a fort at Prairie du Chien on Wisconsin's border with Iowa. Native Americans in the area rebelled against the seizure of their tribal lands in the Black Hawk War of 1832, but a series of treaties from 1829 to 1848, effectively transferred all land titles in Wisconsin to the U.S. government. Railroads were started in 1851, serving growing wheat harvests and iron mines. Some 96,000 soldiers served the Union cause during the Civil War.

Tourist attractions. Old Wade House and Carriage Museum, Greenbush; Villa Louis, Prairie du Chien; Circus World Museum, Baraboo; Wisconsin Dells; Old World Wisconsin, Eagle; Door County peninsula; Chequamegon and Nicolet national forests; Lake Winnebago; House on the Rock, Dodgeville; Monona Terrace, Madison.

Famous Wisconsinites. Carrie Chapman Catt, Edna Ferber, King Camp Gillette, Harry Houdini, Robert La Follette, Alfred Lunt, Pat O'Brien, Georgia O'Keeffe, William H. Rehnquist, John Ringling, Donald K. "Deke" Slayton, Spencer Tracy, Thorstein Veblen, Orson Welles, Laura Ingalls Wilder, Thornton Wilder, Frank Lloyd Wright.

Tourist information. Carrie Chapman Catt, Wisconsin Dept. of Tourism, 123 W. Washington Ave., PO Box 7606, Madison, WI 53707.

Toll-free travel information. 1-800-432-8747.

Web site. http://www.state.wi.us

Wyoming
Equality State

People. Population (1996): 481,400; rank: 50; **Net change** (1990-96): 6.1%. **Pop. density:** (1990) 4.7 per sq mi. **Racial/ethnic distrib.** (1990): 94.2% white; 0.8% black; 2.1% Amer. Indian; 5.7% Hispanic.

Geography. Total area: 97,818 sq mi; rank: 10. **Land area:** 97,105 sq mi; rank: 9. **Acres forested land:** 9,966,000. **Location:** Mountain state lying in the high western plateaus of the Great Plains. **Climate:** semi-desert conditions throughout; true desert in the Big Horn and Great Divide basins. **Topography:** the eastern Great Plains rise to the foothills of the Rocky Mts.; the Continental Divide crosses the state from the NW to the SE. **Capital:** Cheyenne.

Economy. Principal industries: mineral extraction, oil, natural gas, tourism and recreation, agriculture. **Principal manufactured goods:** refined petroleum, wood, stone, clay products, foods electronic devices, sporting apparel, and aircraft. **Chief crops:** wheat, beans, barley, oats, sugar beets, hay. **Livestock** (Jan. 1, 1997): 1.5 mil cattle/calves; 720,000 sheep/lambs; (Dec. 1, 1996) 82,000 hogs/pigs. **Timber/lumber** (1996): ponderosa & lodgepole pine, Douglas fir, Engelmann spruce; 227 mil bd. ft. **Nonfuel minerals** (est. 1996): $918 mil; mostly soda ash, clays, helium, gypsum, portland cement, crushed stone. **International airports at:** Casper. **Value of construction** (1996): $642 mil. **Employment distribution** (1997): 23.2% trade; 21.5% services; 27.4% govt, 6.7% mining. **Per capita personal income** (1996): $21,245. **Unemployment** (1996): 5.0%. **Tourism** (1992): $1.5 bil.

Finance. FDIC-insured commercial banks & trust companies (1996): 54. **Deposits:** $7.0 bil. **FDIC-insured savings institutions** (1996): 4. **Assets:** $340 mil.

Federal government. No. federal civilian employees (Mar. 1996): 4,581. **Avg. salary:** $37,233. **Notable federal facilities:** Warren AFB.

Energy. Electricity production (1996, kWh, by source): Coal: 39.6 bil; Petroleum: 59 mil; Gas: 9 mil; Hydroelectric: 1.2 bil.

Public education. Student-teacher ratio (1995): 14.8. **Avg. teachers' salary** (1996-97): $31,721.

State data. Motto: Equal Rights. **Flower:** Indian paintbrush. **Bird:** Meadowlark. **Tree:** Cottonwood. **Song:** Wyoming. **Entered union** July 10, 1890; rank, 44th. **State fair** at Douglas; late Aug.

History. Shoshone, Crow, Cheyenne, Oglala, and Arapaho peoples lived in the area at the time of European contact. Frances François and Louis La Verendrye were the first Europeans to see the region, 1743. John Colter, an American, was first to traverse Yellowstone park, 1807-8. Trappers and fur traders followed in the 1820s. Forts Laramie and Bridger became important stops on the pioneer trail to the West Coast. Population grew after the Union Pacific crossed the state, 1869. Women won the vote, for the first time in the U.S., from the Territorial Legislature, 1869. Disputes between large land owners and small ranchers culminated in the Johnson County Cattle War, 1892; federal troops were called in to restore order.

Tourist attractions. Yellowstone Natl. Park, the oldest U.S. national park, est. 1872; Grand Teton Natl. Park; Natl. Elk Refuge; Devils Tower; Fort Laramie and surrounding areas of pioneer trails; Buffalo Bill Museum, Cody; Cheyenne Frontier Days Celebration.

Famous Wyomingites. James Bridger, Buffalo Bill Cody, Esther Hobart Morris, Nellie Tayloe Ross.

Tourist information. Division of Tourism & State Marketing, I-25 at College Dr., Cheyenne, WY 82002.

Toll-free travel information. 1-800-CALLWYO.

Web site. http://www.state.wy.us

District of Columbia

People. Population (1996): 543,213; **Net change** (1990-96): -10.5%. **Pop. Density:** (1990): 9,882.8 per sq mi.

Geography. Total area: 68 sq mi; rank: 51. **Land area:** 61 sq mi; rank: 51. **Location:** at the confluence of the Potomac and Anacostia rivers, flanked by Maryland on the N, E, and SE and by Virginia on the SW. **Climate:** hot humid summers, mild winters. **Topography:** low hills rise toward the N away from the Potomac R. and slope to the S; highest elevation, 410 ft, lowest Potomac R., 1 ft.

Economy. Principal Industries: government, service, tourism. **Value of construction** (1996): $1.2 bil. **Employment distribution** (1995) 39.5% govt., 8% trade, 41% service. **Per capita personal income** (1996): $34,932; **Unemployment** (1996): 8.5%.

Finance. FDIC-Insured commercial banks & trust companies (1996): 8 **Deposits:** $2.6 bil. **FDIC-Insured savings institutions** (1996): 1. **Assets:** $261 mil.

Federal Government. No. of federal employees (Mar. 1996): 152,185; **Avg. salary:** $54,206.

Energy. Electricity production (1996, kWh, by source): Petroleum: 110 mil.

Public education. Student-teacher ratio (1995): 15.0. **Avg. teachers' salary** (1996-97): $45,012.

District Data. Motto: Justitia omnibus (Justice for all). **Flower:** American beauty rose. **Tree:** Scarlet oak. **Bird:** Wood thrush.

History. The District of Columbia, coextensive with the city of Washington, is the seat of the U.S. federal government. It lies on the west central edge of Maryland on the Potomac River, opposite Virginia. Its area was originally 100 sq mi taken from the sovereignty of Maryland and Virginia. Virginia's portion south of the Potomac was given back to that state in 1846.

The 23d Amendment, ratified in 1961, granted residents the right to vote for Pres. and vice Pres. for the first time since 1800 and gave them 3 members in the Electoral College. The first such votes were cast in Nov. 1964.

Congress, which has legislative authority over the District under the Constitution, established in 1874 a government of 3 commissioners appointed by the Pres.. The Reorganization Plan of 1967 substituted a single appointive commissioner (also called mayor), assistant, and 9-member City Council. Funds were still appropriated by Congress; residents had no vote in local government, except to elect school board members.

In Sept. 1970, Congress approved legislation giving the District one delegate to the House of Representatives, who can vote in committee but not on the House floor. The first such delegate was elected 1971.

In May 1974 voters approved a congressionally drafted charter giving them the right to elect their own mayor and a 13-member city council; the first took office Jan. 2, 1975. The district won the right to levy its own taxes, but Congress retained power to veto council actions and approve the city budget.

Proposals for a "federal town" for the deliberations of the Continental Congress were made in 1783, 4 years before the adoption of the Constitution. Rivalry between Northern and Southern delegates over the site appeared in the First Congress, 1789. John Adams, presiding officer of the Senate, cast the deciding vote of that body for Germantown, PA. In 1790 Congress compromised by making Philadelphia the temporary capital for 10 years. The Virginia members of the House wanted a permanent capital on the eastern bank of the Potomac, while the Southerners opposed having the nation assume the war debts of the 13 original states as provided under the Assumption Bill, fathered by Alexander Hamilton. Hamilton and Jefferson arranged a compromise: the Virginia men voted for the Assumption Bill, and the Northerners conceded the capital to the Potomac. Pres. Washington chose the site in Oct. 1790 and persuaded landowners to sell their holdings to the government. The capital was named Washington.

Washington appointed Pierre Charles L'Enfant, a Frenchman, to plan the capital on an area not more than 10 mi square. The L'Enfant plan, for streets 100 to 110 ft. wide and one avenue 400 ft. wide and a mile long, seemed grandiose and foolhardy, but Washington endorsed it. When L'Enfant ordered a wealthy landowner to remove his new manor house because it obstructed a vista, and demolished it when the owner refused, Washington stepped in and dismissed the architect. Andrew Ellicott, who was working on surveying the area, finished the official map and design of the city. Ellicott was assisted by Benjamin Banneker, a distinguished black architect and astronomer.

On Sept. 18, 1793, Pres. Washington laid the cornerstone of the north wing of the Capitol. On June 3, 1800, Pres. John Adams moved to Washington, and on June 10, Philadelphia ceased to be the temporary capital. The City of Washington was incorporated in 1802; the District of Columbia was created as a municipal corporation in 1874, embracing Washington, Georgetown, and Washington County.

Tourist attraction: See Washington, DC, Capital of the U.S. (after Outlying Areas section).

Tourist information. 202-789-7000.

Web site. http://dcpages.ari.net

OUTLYING U.S. AREAS

American Samoa

People. Population: (1996 est.) 59,566. **Population growth rate** (1994 est.) -0.52%. **Land area:** 77 sq. mi. **Total area:** 90 sq mi. **Capital:** Pago Pago, Island of Tutuila. **Motto:** Samoa Muamua le Atua (In Samoa, God Is First). **Song:** Amerika Samoa. **Flower:** Paogo (Ula-fala). **Plant:** Ava.

Public education. Student-teacher ratio (1995): 20.0.

Boasting spectacular scenery and delightful South Seas climate, American Samoa is the most southerly of all lands under U.S. sovereignty. It is an unincorporated territory consisting of 7 small islands of the Samoan group: **Tutuila, Aunu'u, Manu'a Group (Ta'u, Olosega, Ofu), Rose,** and **Swains Island.** The islands are 2,300 mi SW of Honolulu.

Economy. Principal industries: trade, services and tourism. **Agriculture. Chief crops:** vegetables, nuts, melons and other fruits. **Livestock:** (1990) 179 cattle; 7,580 hogs/pigs; 27,401 chickens.

Finance. FDIC-Insured commercial banks & trust companies (1996): 1. **Deposits:** $4.7 mil.

A tripartite agreement between Great Britain, Germany, and the U.S. in 1899 gave the U.S. sovereignty over the eastern islands of the Samoan group; these islands became American Samoa. Local chiefs officially ceded Tutuila and Aunu'u to the U.S. in Apr. 1900, and the Manu'a group and Rose in July 1904; Swains Island was annexed in 1925.

Samoa (Western), comprising the larger islands of the Samoan group, was a New Zealand mandate and UN Trusteeship until it became an independent nation Jan. 1, 1962 (now called Samoa).

Tutuila and Aunu'u have an area of 53 sq mi. Ta'u has an area of 17 sq mi, and the islets of Ofu and Olosega, 5 sq mi with a population of a few thousand. Swains Island has nearly 2 sq mi and a population of about 100.

About 70% of the land is bush and mountains. Chief products and exports are fish products. Taro, breadfruit, yams, coconuts, pineapples, oranges, and bananas are also produced.

From 1900 to 1951, American Samoa was under the jurisdiction of the U.S. Navy. Since 1951, it has been under the Interior Dept. On Jan. 3, 1978, the first popularly elected Samoan governor and lieutenant governor were inaugurated. Previously, the governor was appointed by the Secretary of the Interior. American Samoa has a bicameral legislature and elects a delegate to the House of Representatives, who has a voice but no vote, except in committees.

The American Samoans are of Polynesian origin. They are nationals of the U.S.; approximately 20,000 live in Hawaii, 65,000 in California and Washington.

Guam
Where America's Day Begins

People. Population (1996 est.): 156,974. **Population growth rate** (1994): 2.48%. **Pop. density:** (1990) 631.6 per sq mi. **Ethnic distribution** (1994 est.): Chamorro 47%, Filipino 25%, Caucasian 10%, Chinese, Japanese, Korean, and other 18%. Native Guamanians, ethnically Chamorros, are basically of Indonesian stock, with a mixture of Spanish and Filipino; in addition to the offical language, they speak the native Chamorro. **Migration** (1990): About 52% of population were born elsewhere; of these, 48% in Asia, 40% in U.S.

Geography. Total area: 217 sq mi. **Land area:** 210 sq. mi. **Location:** largest and southernmost of the Mariana Islands in the West Pacific, 3,700 mi W of Hawaii. **Climate:** tropical, with temperatures from 70° to 90° F; avg. annual rainfall, about 70 in. **Topography:** coralline limestone plateau in the N; southern chain of low volcanic mountains sloping gently to the W, more steeply to coastal cliffs on the E; general elevation, 500 ft; highest point, Mt. Lamlam, 1,334 ft. **Capital:** Agaña.

Economy. Principal industries: tourism, U.S. military, construction, banking, printing and publishing. **Principal manufactured goods:** textiles, foods. **Chief crops:** cabbages, eggplants, cucumber, long beans, tomatoes, bananas, coconuts, watermelon, yams, canteloupe, papayas, maize, sweet potatoes. **Livestock** (1992): 388 cattle; 2,038 hogs/pigs; 12,206 chickens. **Chief port:** Apra Harbor. **International airport at:** Agaña. **Value of construction** (1994): $614.3 mil. **Employment distribution** (1994): 19.5% service; 20.2% trade; 64.9% govt. **Per capita income** (1992): $10,834. **Median household income** (1992): $44,369. **Unemployment** (1994): 6.7%. **Tourism** (1992): visitors' receipts $1.5 bil.

Finance. Notable industries: insurance, real estate, finance. **FDIC-insured commercial banks & trust companies** (1996): 2. **Deposits:** $658 mil. **FDIC-insured savings institutions** (1996): 2. **Assets:** $261 mil.

Federal government. No. federal employees (1990): 7,200. **Notable federal facilities:** Anderson AFB; naval, air, and port bases.

Public education. Student-teacher ratio (1995): 18.3.

Misc. data. Flower: Puti Tai Nobio (Bougainvillea). **Bird:** Toto (Fruit dove). **Tree:** Ifit (Intsiabijuga). **Song:** Stand Ye Guamanians.

History. Guam was probably settled by voyagers from the Indonesian-Philippine archipelago by at least the 3d cent. BC. Pottery, rice cultivation, and megalithic technology show strong East Asian cultural influence. Centralized, village clan-based communities engaged in agriculture and offshore fishing. The estimated population by the early 16th cent. was between 50,000 and 75,000 inhabitants. Magellan arrived in the Marianas Mar. 6, 1521. They were colonized in 1668 by Spanish missionaries, who named them the Mariana Islands in honor of Maria Anna, queen of Spain. When Spain ceded Guam to the U.S., it sold the other Marianas to Germany. Japan obtained a League of Nations mandate over the German islands in 1919; in Dec. 1941 it seized Guam, the island was retaken by the U.S. in July and August 1944.

Guam is a self-governing organized unincorporated U.S. territory. The Organic Act of 1950 provided for a governor, elected to a 4-year term, and a 21-member unicameral legislature, elected biennially by the residents, who are American citizens. In 1970, the first governor was elected.

In 1972, a U.S. law gave Guam one delegate to the U.S. House of Representatives who has a voice but no vote, except in committees.

Guam's quest to change its status to a U.S. Commonwealth began in the late 1970s. The Guam Commission on Self-Determination, created in 1984, developed a draft Commonwealth Act. After consultations with a U.S. government representative in late 1993, it was decided that legislation proposing a change of status would be submitted to the U.S. Congress.

In 1994, the U.S. Congress passed legislation transferring 3,200 acres of land on Guam from federal to local control.

Tourist attractions. Tropical climate, oceanic marine environment; annual mid-Aug. Merizo Water Festival; Tarzan Falls; beaches; water sports; duty-free port shopping.

Commonwealth of the Northern Mariana Islands

People. Population (1996 est.): 52,284. **Total area:** 189 sq. mi. **Land area:** 179 sq. mi. Located in the perpetually warm climes between Guam and the Tropic of Cancer, the 14 islands of the Northern Marianas form a 300-mile-long archipelago. The indigenous population in 1990 was concentrated on the 3 largest of the 6 inhabited islands: **Saipan,** the seat of government and commerce (38,896), **Rota** (2,295), and **Tinian** (2,118).

Economy. Principal industries: trade, services, and tourism **Principal manufactured goods:** apparel, stone, clay and glass products. **Chief crops:** melons, vegetables, horticulture, fruits and nuts. **Livestock:** (1990) 4,513 cattle; 1,260 hogs/pigs; 9,580. **Employment distribution** (1992): 53% trade; 8% const.; 6% manuf.; 33% serv.

Education. Pupil-teacher ratio (1995): 20.9.

The people of the Northern Marianas are predominantly of Chamorro cultural extraction, although Carolinians and immigrants from other areas of E. Asia and Micronesia have also settled in the islands. English is among the several languages commonly spoken. Pursuant to the Covenant of 1976, which established the Northern Marianas as a commonwealth in political union with the U.S., most of the indigenous population and many domiciliaries of these islands achieved U.S. citizenship on Nov. 3, 1986, when the U.S. terminated its administration of the UN trusteeship as it affected the Northern Marianas. From July 18, 1947, the U.S. had administered the Northern Marianas under a trusteeship agreement with the UN Security Council.

The Northern Mariana Islands has been self-governing since 1978, when a constitution drafted and adopted by the people became effective and a popularly elected bicameral legislature (2-year term), with offices of governor (4-year term) and lieut. governor, was inaugurated.

Commonwealth of Puerto Rico
(Estado Libre Asociado de Puerto Rico)

People. Population (1996 est): 3,782,862 (about 2.7 mil more Puerto Ricans reside in the mainland U.S.). **Net change** (1990-96): 7.4% **Pop. density:** (1990) 1,035 per sq mi. **Urban** (1990): 66.8%. **Ethnic distribution** (1990): 99.9% Hispanic. **Language:** On Jan. 28, 1993, the government of Puerto Rico declared Spanish and English joint official languages.

Geography. Total area: 3,508 sq. mi. **Land area:** 3,427 sq mi. **Location:** island lying between the Atlantic to the N and the Caribbean to the S; it is easternmost of the West Indies group called the Greater Antilles, of which Cuba, Hispaniola, and Jamaica are the larger islands. **Climate:** mild, with a mean temperature of 77° F. **Topography:** mountainous throughout three-fourths of its rectangular area, surrounded by a broken coastal plain; highest peak is Cerro de Punto, 4,390 ft. **Capital:** San Juan.

Economy. Principal industries: manufacturing, service. **Principal manufactured goods:** pharmaceuticals, appael, electronics and other electric equipment, industrial machinery. **Gross Domestic Product:** (1995) $28.4 bil. **Chief crops:** coffee, plantains, pineapples, tomatoes, sugarcane, bananas, mangoes, ornamental plants **Livestock** (1996): 370,655 cattle; 182,247 hogs; 12.6 mil poultry. **Nonfuel minerals** (1996): $31.1 mil, mostly portland cement, crushed stone. **Commercial fishing** (1996): $15.7 mil. **Chief ports/river shipping:** San Juan, Ponce, Mayagüez. **Major airports at:** San Juan, Ponce, Mayagüez, Aguadilla. **Value of construction** (1996): $4.1 bil. **Employment distribution** (1996): 23.1% serv. 32.6% public admin., 19.9% trade, 16.3% mfg. **Per capita income** (1996): $7,882. **Unemployment** (1996): 13.4%. **Tourism** (1996): $1.9 mil.

Finance. FDIC-insured commercial banks & trust companies (1996): 14. **Deposits:** $21.3 bil. **FDIC-insured savings institutions** (1996): 2. **Assets:** $310 mil.

Federal government. No. federal civilian employees (1997): 13,874. **Notable federal facilities:** U.S. Naval Station at Roosevelt Roads; P.R. National Guard Training Area at Camp Santiago, and at Ft. Allen, Juana Diaz; Sabana SECA Communications Center (U.S. Navy); U.S. Army Station at Ft. Buchanan.

Energy. Electicity production (1996): 15.9 bil kWh.

Public education. Student-teacher ratio (1995): 16.0. **Min. teachers' salary** (1997): $1,500 monthly.

Misc. data. Motto: Joannes Est Nomen Eius (John is his name). **Flower:** Maga. **Bird:** Reinita. **Tree:** Ceiba. **National anthem:** La Borinqueña.

History. Puerto Rico (or Borinquen, after the original Arawak Indian name, Boriquen) was visited by Columbus on his second voyage, Nov. 19, 1493. In 1508, the Spanish arrived.

Sugarcane was introduced, 1515, and slaves were imported 3 years later. Gold mining petered out, 1570. Spaniards fought off a series of British and Dutch attacks; slavery was abolished, 1873. Under the treaty of Paris, Puerto Rico was ceded to the U.S. after the Spanish-American War, 1898. In 1952 the people voted in favor of Commonwealth status.

The Commonwealth of Puerto Rico is a self-governing part of the U.S. with a primarily Hispanic culture. The current commonwealth political status of Puerto Rico gives the island's citizens virtually the same control over their internal affairs as the 50 states of the U.S. However, they do not vote in national general elections, although they do vote in national primaries.

Puerto Rico is represented in the U.S. House of Representatives by a delegate who has a voice but no vote, except in committees.

No federal income tax is collected from residents on income earned from local sources in Puerto Rico. Nevertheless, as part of the U.S. legal system, Puerto Rico is subject to the provisions of the U.S. Constitution; most federal laws apply as they do in the 50 states.

Puerto Rico's famous "Operation Bootstrap," begun in the late 1940s, succeeded in changing the island from "The Poorhouse of the Caribbean" to an area with the highest per capita income in Latin America. This program encouraged manufacturing and the development of the tourist trade by selective tax exemption, low-interest loans, and other incentives. Despite the marked success of Puerto Rico's development efforts over an extended period of time, per capita income in Puerto Rico is low in comparison to that of the U.S.

Tourist attractions. Ponce Museum of Art; Forts El Morro and San Cristobal; Old Walled City of San Juan; Arecibo Observatory; Cordillera Central and state parks; El Yunque Rain Forest; San Juan Cathedral; Porta Coeli Chapel and Museum of Religious Art, Interamerican Univ., San Germán; Condado Convention Center; Casa Blanca, Ponce de León family home, Puerto Rican Family Museum of 16th and 17th centuries, and Fine Arts Center all in San Juan.

Cultural facilities and events. Festival Casals classical music concerts, mid-June; Puerto Rico Symphony Orchestra at Music Conservatory; Botanical Garden and Museum of Anthropology, Art, and History at the University of Puerto Rico; Institute of Puerto Rican Culture, at the Dominican Convent; and many popular festivals throughout the island.

Famous Puerto Ricans. Julia de Burgos, Marta Casals Istomin, Pablo Casals, José Celso Barbosa, Orlando Cepeda, Roberto Clemente, Rafael Hernández Colón, José de Diego, José Feliciano, Doña Felisa Rincón de Gautier, Luis A. Ferré, José Ferrer, Commodore Diégo E. Hernández, Miguel Hernández Agosto, Rafael Hernández (El Jibarito), Raúl Julía, René Marqués, Concha Meléndez, Rita Moreno, Luis Muñoz Marín, Luis Palés Matos, Adm. Horacio Rivero.

Chamber of Commerce. 100 Tetuán, PO Box S-3789, San Juan, PR 00902.

Web site. http://fortaleza.govpr.org

Virgin Islands

St. John, St. Croix, St. Thomas

People. Population (1996 est.): 97,120. **Population growth rate** (1994 est.): –0.52% **Racial distribution**

(1980): 85% black, 15% white. **Major ethnic groups:** West Indian, French, Hispanic.

Geography. Total area: 171 sq mi. **Land area:** 134 sq mi. **Location:** 3 larger and 50 smaller islands and cays in the S and W of the V.I. group (British V.I. colony to the N and E), which is situated 70 mi E of Puerto Rico, located W of the Anegada Passage, a major channel connecting the Atlantic Ocean and the Caribbean Sea. **Climate:** subtropical; the sun tempered by gentle trade winds; humidity is low; average temperature, 78° F. **Topography:** St. Thomas is mainly a ridge of hills running E and W, and has little tillable land; St. Croix rises abruptly in the N but slopes to the S to flatlands and lagoons; St. John has steep, lofty hills and valleys with little level tillable land. **Capital:** Charlotte Amalie, St. Thomas.

Economy. Principal industries: tourism, rum, alumina, petroleum refining, watches, textiles, electronics, printing and publishing. **Principal manufactured goods:** rum, textiles, pharmaceuticals, perfumes, stone, glass and clay products. **Gross domestic product** (1987): $1.246 bil. **Chief crops:** vegetables, horticulture, fruits and nuts. **Livestock** (1992): 7,132 cattle; 1,311 hogs/pigs; 9,087 chickens. **Minerals:** sand, gravel. **Chief ports:** Cruz Bay, St. John; Frederiksted and Christiansted, St. Croix; Charlotte Amalie, St. Thomas. **International airports on:** St. Thomas, St. Croix. **Value of construction** (1992): $168.9 mil. **Employment distribution** (1992): 50% trade; 43% serv. **Per capita income** (1989): $11,052. **Unemployment** (1992): 2.8%. **Tourism** (1992): $792 mil.

Finance. FDIC-insured savings institutions (1996): 2. **Deposits:** $7.3 mil. **FDIC-insured savings institutions** (1996): 1. **Assets:** 57 mil.

Energy. Electicity production (1992): 565 mil kWh.

Public education. Student-teacher ratio (1995): 14.0.

Misc. data. Flower: Yellow elder or yellow trumpet, local designation Ginger Thomas. **Bird:** Yellow breast. **Song:** Virgin Islands March.

History. The islands were visited by Columbus in 1493. Spanish forces, 1555, defeated the Caribes and claimed the territory; by 1596 the native population was annihilated. First permanent settlement in the U.S. territory, 1672, by the Danes; U.S. purchased the islands, 1917, for defense purposes.

The Virgin Islands has a republican form of government, headed by a governor and lieut. governor elected, since 1970, by popular vote for 4-year terms. There is a 15-member unicameral legislature, elected by popular vote for a 2-year term. Residents of the V.I. have been U.S. citizens since 1927. Since 1973 they have elected a delegate to the U.S. House of Representatives, who has a voice but no vote, except in committees.

Tourist attractions. Magens Bay, St. Thomas; duty-free shopping; Virgin Islands Natl. Park, beaches, Indian relics, and evidence of colonial Danes.

Tourist information. Dept. of Economic Development & Agriculture: St. Thomas, PO Box 6400, St. Thomas, VI 00801; St. Croix, PO Box 4535, Christiansted, St. Croix 00820.

Other Islands

Navassa lies between Jamaica and Haiti, 100 mi south of Guantanamo Bay, Cuba, in the Caribbean; it covers about 3 sq mi, is reserved by the U.S. for a lighthouse, and is uninhabited. It is administered by the U.S. Coast Guard.

Wake Atoll, and its neighboring atolls, **Wilkes** and **Peale,** lie in the Pacific Ocean on the direct route from Hawaii to Hong Kong, about 2,300 mi W of Honolulu and 1,290 mi E of Guam. The group is 4.5 mi long, 1.5 mi wide, and totals less than 3 sq mi. The U.S. flag was hoisted over Wake Atoll, July 4, 1898, formal possession taken Jan. 17, 1899; Wake was administered by the U.S. Air Force, 1972-94. The population consists of about 200 persons.

Midway Atoll, acquired in 1867, consist of 2 atolls, **Sand** and **Eastern,** in N Pacific 1,150 mi. NW of Honolulu, with an area of about 3 sq mi, administered by the U.S. Navy. There is no indigenous population; total pop. is about 450.

Johnston Atoll, 717 mi WSW of Honolulu, area 1 sq mi, is operated by the Defense Nuclear Agency, and the Fish and Wildlife Service, U.S. Dept. of the Interior; its population is about 1,200. **Kingman Reef,** 920 mi S of Hawaii, is under Navy control.

Howland, Jarvis, and **Baker Islands,** 1,400-1,650 mi SW of Honolulu, uninhabited since World War II, are under the Interior Dept.

Palmyra is an atoll about 1,000 mi south of Hawaii, 2 sq mi. Privately owned, it is under the Interior Dept.

Washington, DC, Capital of the U.S.

Tourism information available from the Washington, DC, Convention and Visitors Association; Phone:: 202-789-7000.

Bureau of Engraving and Printing

The **Bureau of Engraving and Printing** is the headquarters for the making of U.S. paper money. 25-minute self-guided tours Mon.-Fri., 9 AM-2 PM year-round, and extended hours Apr.-Sept., 3:30 PM-7:30 PM. Closed federal holidays and Dec. 24-Jan. 3. 14th and C Sts. SW. Phone: 202-874-3019.

Capitol

The **United States Capitol** was originally designed by Dr. William Thornton, an amateur architect, who submitted a plan in 1793 that won him $500 and a city lot.

The south, or House, wing was completed in 1807 under the direction of Benjamin H. Latrobe.

The present Senate and House wings and the iron dome were designed and constructed by Thomas U. Walter, the 4th architect of the Capitol, between 1851 and 1863.

The present cast iron dome at its greatest exterior measures 135 ft 5 in., and it is topped by the bronze Statue of Freedom that stands 19½ ft and weighs 14,985 lb. On its base are the words *E Pluribus Unum* (Out of Many, One).

The Capitol is normally open from 9 AM to 4:30 PM, and to 10 PM June to Labor Day. It is closed on Dec. 25, Jan. 1, and Thanksgiving Day. Tours through the Capitol, including the House and Senate galleries, are conducted from 9 AM to 3:45 PM; there is no charge.

To observe the debate in the House or Senate while Congress is in session, individuals living in the U.S. may obtain tickets to the visitor's galleries from their congressperson or senator. Visitors from other countries may obtain passes at the Capitol. Between Constitution & Independence Ave., at Pennsylvania Ave. Phone: 202-225-6827.

Federal Bureau of Investigation

The **Federal Bureau of Investigation** offers a tour of its headquarters, beginning with a videotape presentation. Visitors learn about the history of the FBI and see such things as the weapons confiscated from famous gangsters, photos of the most-wanted fugitives, the DNA laboratory, goods forfeited and seized in narcotics operations, and a sharpshooting demonstration.

Tours are conducted Mon.-Fri., 8:45 AM-4:15 PM, except Jan. 1, Dec. 25, and other federal holidays. Tickets may be obtained at the FBI on the day of the tour or through a congressperson or senator. Admission is free. J. Edgar Hoover Bldg., Pennsylvania Ave., between 9th and 10th Sts. NW. Phone: 202-324-3447.

Folger Shakespeare Library

The **Folger Shakespeare Library,** on Capitol Hill, is a research institution holding rare books and manuscripts of the Renaissance period and the largest collection of Shakespearean materials in the world, including 79 copies of the First Folio. The library's museum and performing arts programs are presented in the Elizabethan Theatre, which resembles an innyard theater of Shakespeare's day.

Exhibit may be visited Mon.-Sat., 10 AM-4 PM. 201 E. Capitol St., SE , Phone: 202-544-4600.

Holocaust Memorial Museum

The **U.S. Holocaust Memorial Museum** opened on Apr. 21, 1993. The museum documents, through permanent and temporary displays, interactive videos, and special lectures, the events of the Holocaust beginning in 1933 and continuing World War II. The permanent exhibition is not recommended for children under the age of 11.

The museum is open daily, 10 AM-5:30 PM, except Yom Kippur and Dec. 25. A limited number of free tickets are available on the day of visit; advance tickets may be ordered for a small fee. 100 Raoul Wallenberg Pl. SW (formerly 15th St. SW), near Independence Ave. Phone: 202-488-0400.

Jefferson Memorial

Dedicated in 1943, the **Thomas Jefferson Memorial** stands on the south shore of the Tidal Basin in West Poto-

mac Park. It is a circular stone structure, with Vermont marble on the exterior and Georgia white marble inside, and combines architectural elements of the dome of the Pantheon in Rome and the rotunda designed by Jefferson for the University of Virginia.

The memorial, which is located on the South edge of the Tidal Basin, is open daily, 8 AM-midnight. An elevator and curb ramps for the handicapped are in service. Phone: 202-426-6841.

John F. Kennedy Center

The **John F. Kennedy Center for the Performing Arts,** designated by Congress as the National Cultural Center and the official memorial in Washington, DC, to Pres. John F. Kennedy, opened Sept. 8, 1971. Designed by Edward Durell Stone, the center includes an opera house, a concert hall, several theaters, 2 restaurants, and a library.

Free tours are available daily, 10 AM-1 PM. New Hampshire Ave. at F St. NW. Phone: 202-416-8340.

Korean War Memorial

Dedicated on July 27, 1995, the **Korean War Memorial** honors all Americans who served in the Korean War. Situated at the west end of the Mall, just across the reflecting pool from the Vietnam Memorial, the triangular-shaped stone and steel memorial features a multiservice formation of 19 troops clad in ponchos with the wind at their back, ready for combat. A granite wall, exhibiting real-life images of the men and women who served, juts into a pool of water, the Pool of Remembrance, and is inscribed with the words *Freedom Is Not Free*.

The $18 mil memorial, which was funded by private donations, is open 24 hr daily. Phone: 202-619-7222.

Library of Congress

Established by and for Congress in 1800, the **Library of Congress** has extended its services over the years to other government agencies and other libraries, to scholars, and to the general public, and it now serves as the national library. It contains more than 80 million items in 470 languages.

The library's exhibit halls are open to the public Mon.-Fri., 8:30 AM-9:30 PM; Sat., 8:30 AM-6 PM. The library is closed Jan. 1 and Dec. 25. 101 Independence Ave., SE. Phone: 202-707-8000.

Lincoln Memorial

Designed by Henry Bacon, the **Lincoln Memorial** in West Potomac Park, on the axis of the Capitol and the Washington Monument, consists of a large marble hall enclosing a heroic statue of Abraham Lincoln in meditation sitting on a large armchair. The memorial was dedicated on Memorial Day, May 30, 1922. The statue of Lincoln was designed by Daniel Chester French and sculpted by French and the Piccirilli brothers. Murals and ornamentation on the bronze ceiling beams are by Jules Guerin. The text of the Gettysburg Address is in the south chamber, and that of Lincoln's Second Inaugural speech is in the north chamber. Each is engraved on a stone tablet.

The memorial is open 24 hr daily. An elevator for the handicapped is in service. Phone: 202-619-7222.

National Archives

Original copies of the Declaration of Independence, the Constitution, and the Bill of Rights are on permanent display in the **National Archives** Exhibition Hall. The National Archives also holds other valuable U.S. government records and historic maps, photographs, and manuscripts.

Central Research and Microfilm Research Rooms are also available to the public for genealogical research.

The Exhibition Hall is open daily, 10 AM-9 PM; closed Jan. 1 and Dec. 25. Pennsylvania Ave. between 7th & 9th Sts. NW. Phone: 202-501-5000.

(continued)

National Gallery of Art

The **National Gallery of Art**, situated on the north side of the Mall facing Constitution Avenue, was established by Joint Resolution of Congress Mar. 24, 1937, and opened Mar. 17, 1941. The original West building was designed by John Russell Pope. The East building, opened in 1978, was designed by I. M. Pei. The National Gallery is separate from, but maintains a relationship with, the Smithsonian Institution.

Normally open daily, 10 AM-5 PM; Sunday, 11 AM-5:30 PM. Closed Jan. 1 and Dec. 25. Constitution Ave. between 3d & 7th Sts. Phone: 202-737-4215.

Franklin Delano Roosevelt Memorial

Opened, in a ceremony on May 2, 1997, by Pres. Bill Clinton, the **FDR Memorial** features 9 bronze sculptural ensembles depicting FDR, Eleanor Roosevelt (the first First Lady to be honored in a national memorial), and events from the Great Depression and World War II. This 7.5-acre Memorial is located near the Tidal Basin in a park-like setting and includes waterfalls, quiet pools, and reddish Dakota granite upon which some of Pres. Roosevelt's well-known words are carved. The monument is the first of its kind designed to be totally wheelchair accessible.

Grounds are staffed daily from 8 AM to 12 midnight, except Dec. 25. For more information call the West Potomac Park public inquiry line at (202) 619-7222.

Smithsonian Institution

The **Smithsonian Institution,** established in 1846, is the world's largest museum complex and consists of 14 museums and the National Zoo. It holds some 100 million artifacts and specimens in its trust "for the increase and diffusion of knowledge among men." Nine museums are on the National Mall between the Washington Monument and the Capitol; 5 other museums and the zoo are elsewhere in Washington (the Cooper-Hewitt Museum and the National Museum of the American Indian, also administered by the Smithsonian, are in New York City). Most visitors begin their trip with a visit to the **Smithsonian Information Center**, located in "the Castle" on the Mall. Also on the Mall are the **National Museum of American History,** the **National Museum of Natural History,** the **National Air and Space Museum,** the **Hirshhorn Museum and Sculpture Garden,** the **Arthur M. Sackler Gallery,** the **National Museum of African Art,** the **Freer Gallery of Art,** and the **Arts and Industries Building.** Near the Sackler Gallery is the **Enid A. Haupt Garden.** Located nearby are the **National Postal Museum,** the **National Museum of American Art,** the **National Portrait Gallery,** and the **Renwick Gallery.** Farther away, at 1901 Fort Place SE, is the **Anacostia Museum.**

Most museums are open daily, except Dec. 25, 10 AM-5:30 PM. Phone: 202-357-2700.

Vietnam Veterans Memorial

Originally dedicated on Nov. 13, 1982, the **Vietnam Veterans Memorial** is a recognition of the men and women who served in the armed forces in the Vietnam War. On a V-shaped black-granite wall, designed by Maya Ying Lin, are inscribed the names of the more than 58,000 Americans who lost their lives or remain missing.

Since 1982, 2 additions have been made to the Memorial. The 1st, dedicated on Nov. 11, 1984, is the Frederick Hart sculpture *Three Servicemen.* On Nov. 11, 1993, the Vietnam Women's Memorial was dedicated, honoring the more than 11,500 women who served in Vietnam. The bronze sculpture, portraying 3 women helping a wounded male soldier, was designed by Glenna Goodacre.

The memorial is open 24 hr daily. Phone: 202-426-6841.

Washington Monument

The **Washington Monument,** dedicated in 1885, is a tapering shaft, or obelisk, of white marble, 555 ft, 5⅛ inches in height and 55 ft, 1½ in. square at base. Eight small windows, 2 on each side, are located at the 500-ft level, where points of interest are indicated.

Open daily except Dec. 25, 9 AM-4:30 PM; 8 AM-midnight, Apr.-Labor Day. Phone: 202-426-6841.

White House

The **White House,** the Pres.'s residence, stands on 18 acres on the south side of Pennsylvania Ave., between the Treasury and the old Executive Office Building. The walls are of sandstone, quarried at Aquia Creek, VA. The exterior walls were painted, causing the building to be termed the "White House." On Aug. 24, 1814, during Madison's administration, the house was burned by the British. James Hoban rebuilt it by Oct. 1817.

The White House is normally open for free self-guided tours Tues.-Sat., 10 AM-12 noon (passes, necessary Apr. 1-Labor Day, are available at White House Visitor's Center, open 7:30 AM- 4:30 PM, located at 1450 Pennsylvania Ave., NW) Only the public rooms on the ground floor and state floor may be visited. Free reserved tickets for guided tours can be obtained 8 to 10 weeks in advance from your local congressperson or senator. 1600 Pennsylvania Ave. Phone: 202-456-7041.

Attractions Near Washington, DC

Arlington National Cemetery

Arlington National Cemetery, on the former Custis estate in Arlington, VA, is the site of the **Tomb of the Unknowns** and is the final resting place of John Fitzgerald Kennedy, 35th Pres. of the U.S., who was buried there on Nov. 25, 1963. His wife, Jacqueline Bouvier Kennedy Onassis, was buried at the same site on May 23, 1994. An eternal flame burns over the grave site. In an adjacent area is the grave of Pres. Kennedy's brother Sen. Robert F. Kennedy (NY), interred on June 8, 1968. Many other famous Americans are also buried at Arlington, as well as more than 200,000 American soldiers from every major war.

North of the National Cemetery, approximately 350 yd, stands the **U.S. Marine Corps War Memorial,** also known as Iwo Jima. The memorial is a bronze statue of the raising of the U.S. flag on Mt. Suribachi, Feb. 23, 1945, during World War II, executed by Felix de Weldon from the photograph by Joe Rosenthal, and presented to the nation by members and friends of the U.S. Marine Corps.

Open daily, 8 AM-5 PM (8 AM-7 PM., Apr.- Sept.), Arlington, VA. Phone: 703-697-2131.

Mount Vernon

Mount Vernon, George Washington's estate, is on the south bank of the Potomac R., 16 mi below Washington, DC, in northern Virginia.

The present house is an enlargement of one apparently built on the site by Augustine Washington, who lived there 1735-38. His son Lawrence came there in 1743, when he renamed the plantation Mount Vernon in honor of Admiral Vernon, under whom he had served in the West Indies. Lawrence Washington died in 1752 and was succeeded as proprietor of Mount Vernon by his half-brother, George Washington.

The estate has been restored to its 18th-century appearance and includes many original furnishings. Washington and his wife, Martha, are buried on the grounds.

Open 365 days, Apr.-Aug., 8 AM-5 PM; Sept.-Mar., 9 AM-5 PM (Nov.-Feb. closes at 4 PM). Phone: 703-780-2000.

The Pentagon

The **Pentagon,** headquarters of the Department of Defense, is one of the world's largest office buildings. Situated in Arlington, VA, it houses more than 23,000 employees in offices that occupy 3,707,745 sq ft.

Free tours are available Mon.-Fri. (excluding federal holidays), 9:30 AM-3:30 PM. Arlington, VA (I-395 South to Boundary Channel Drive exit); 703-695-1776.

CITIES OF THE U.S.

Sources: Bureau of the Census: population, with rank in parentheses; estimated as of July 1994; population growth (1990-94). Geography Division, Bureau of the Census: population density (1994 est.); area (1990). Bureau of Labor Statistics: employment (1996 averages for city proper only). Bureau of Economic Analysis: per capita personal income (Metropolitan Statistical Area, 1995).

Included here are the 100 most populous cities, based on July 1994 Census Bureau estimates (inc.=incorporated; est.=established).
Note: Official city web sites are listed first, where available.

Akron, Ohio

Population: 221,886 (75); **Pop. density:** 3,567 per sq. mi; **Pop. growth:** -0.5%. **Area:** 62.2 sq. mi. **Employment:** 105,401 employed, 6.5% unemployed. **Per capita income:** $23,103; % increase 1990-95: 26.0.
History: settled 1825; inc. as city 1865; located on Ohio-Erie Canal and is a port of entry; since 1870, rubber capital of U.S.
Transportation: 1 airport; major trucking industry; Conrail; metro transit system. **Communications:** 4 TV, 7 radio stations. **Medical facilities:** 4 hosp.; specialized children's treatment center. **Educational facilities:** 2 univ. and colleges; 68 pub. schools. **Further information:** Akron Regional Development Board, Cascade Plaza, Akron, OH 44308.
Web sites: http://204.210.221.2/City_of_Akron
http://www.ardb.org

Albuquerque, New Mexico

Population: 411,994 (36); **Pop. density:** 3,116 per sq. mi; **Pop. growth:** 7.1%. **Area:** 132.2 sq. mi. **Employment:** 219,712 employed, 5.2% unemployed. **Per capita income:** $21,452; % increase 1990-95: 28.8.
History: founded 1706 by the Spanish; inc. 1890.
Transportation: 1 intl. airport; 1 railroad; 1 bus line. **Communications:** 8 TV, 38 radio stations. **Medical facilities:** 6 major hosp. **Educational facilities:** 1 univ., 13 colleges. **Further information:** Convention & Visitors Bureau, PO Box 26866, Albuquerque, NM 87125-6866.
Web sites: http://www.abqcvb.org
http://www.cabq.org
http://www.technet.nm.org/gacc

Anaheim, California

Population: 282,133 (58); **Pop. density:** 6,369 per sq. mi; **Pop. growth:** 5.9%. **Area:** 44.3 sq. mi. **Employment:** 141,542 employed, 4.8% unemployed. **Per capita income:** $27,420; % increase 1990-95: 8.8.
History: founded 1857; inc. 1870; now known as home of Disneyland and the Mighty Ducks of Anaheim.
Transportation: 3 municipal airports; 4 railroads; Greyhound buses (MSA). **Communications:** 12 TV, 4 radio stations (MSA). **Medical facilities:** 5 hosp.; 4 medical centers (MSA). **Educational facilities:** 13 univ. and colleges; 47 elem., 10 junior high, 11 high schools (MSA). **Further information:** Chamber of Commerce, 100 South Anaheim Blvd., Ste. 300, Anaheim, CA 92805.
Web site: http://www.anaheim.net

Anchorage, Alaska

Population: 253,649 (64); **Pop. density:** 149 per sq. mi; **Pop. growth:** 12.1%. **Area:** 1,697.6 sq. mi. **Employment:** 130,557 employed, 5.5% unemployed. **Per capita income:** $27,914; % increase 1990-95: 14.0.
History: founded 1914 as a construction camp for railroad; HQ of Alaska Defense Command, WWII; severely damaged in earthquake 1964.
Transportation: 1 intl. airport, 3 other airports; railroad; transit system. **Communications:** 9 TV, 22 radio stations. **Medical facilities:** 4 hosp. **Educational facilities:** 4 univ., 3 colleges. **Further information:** Chamber of Commerce, 441 W. 5th Ave., Ste. 300, Anchorage, AK 99501-2309.
Web sites: http://www.ci.anchorage.ak.us
http://www.anchoragechamber.org

Arlington, Texas

Population: 286,922 (56); **Pop. density:** 3,085 per sq. mi; **Pop. growth:** 9.6%. **Area:** 93 sq. mi. **Employment:** 171,706 employed, 3.4% unemployed. **Per capita income:** $22,665; % increase 1990-95: 20.2.
History: settled in 1840s between Dallas and Ft. Worth; inc. 1884.
Transportation: Dallas/Ft. Worth airport is 20 min away; 11 railway lines; intercity transport system in planning stage. **Communications:** 11 TV, 44 radio stations. **Medical facilities:** 2 hosp. **Educational facilities:** 1 univ., 1 junior college; 54 pub. schools. **Further information:** The Arlington Chamber, 316 W. Main St., Arlington, TX 76010.
Web sites: http://www.ci.arlington.tx.us
http://www.chamber.arlingtontx.com

Atlanta, Georgia

Population: 396,052 (37); **Pop. density:** 3,005 per sq. mi; **Pop. growth:** 0.5%. **Area:** 131.8 sq. mi. **Employment:** 197,531 employed, 6.7% unemployed. **Per capita income:** $25,563; % increase 1990-95: 23.2.
History: founded as "Terminus" 1837; renamed Atlanta 1845; inc. 1847; played major role in Civil War; became permanent state capital 1877; birthplace of civil rights movement; host to 1996 Centennial Olympic Games.
Transportation: 1 intl. airport; 3 railroad lines; MARTA bus and rapid rail service. **Communications:** 11 TV, 49 radio stations; 26 cable TV cos.. **Medical facilities:** 61 hosp.; VA hosp.; U.S. Centers for Disease Control and Prevention; American Cancer Society. **Educational facilities:** 60+ colleges, univ., seminaries, junior colleges. **Further information:** Metro Atlanta Chamber of Commerce, 235 Intl. Blvd. NW, Atlanta, GA 30303.
Web sites: http://www.atlanta.org
http://www.metroatlantachamber.com

Aurora, Colorado

Population: 250,717 (65); **Pop. density:** 1,892 per sq. mi; **Pop. growth:** 12.9%. **Area:** 132.5 sq. mi. **Employment:** 143,954 employed, 3.5% unemployed. **Per capita income:** $27,069; % increase 1990-95: 25.3.
History: located 5 mi east of Denver; early growth stimulated by presence of military bases; fast-growing trade center.
Transportation: adjacent to new Denver Intl. Airport; 1 airport; 4 railroads; bus system. **Communications:** 1 TV station. **Medical facilities:** 2 private hosp.; 1 pub. hosp. **Educational facilities:** 1 univ., 1 community college, 2 technical colleges. **Further information:** Aurora Planning Dept., 1470 S. Havana St., Rm. 608, Aurora, CO 80012.
Web sites: http://www.ci.aurora.co.us
http://www.mktplace.net/aurora/chamber

Austin, Texas

Population: 514,013 (23); **Pop. density:** 2,360 per sq. mi; **Pop. growth:** 10.4%. **Area:** 217.8 sq. mi. **Employment:** 339,462 employed, 3.4% unemployed. **Per capita income:** $22,185; % increase 1990-95: 26.6.
History: first permanent settlement 1835; capital of Rep. of Texas 1838; named after Stephen Austin; inc. 1840.
Transportation: 1 intl. airport; 4 railroads. **Communications:** 7 TV, 20 radio stations. **Medical facilities:** 11 hosp. **Educational facilities:** 8 univ. and colleges. **Further information:** Chamber of Commerce, PO Box 1967, Austin, TX 78767.
Web sites: http://www.ci.austin.tx.us
http://www.austin-chamber.org

Bakersfield, California

Population: 191,060 (89); **Pop. density:** 2,081 per sq. mi; **Pop. growth:** 9.2%. **Area:** 91.8 sq. mi. **Employment:** 88,046 employed, 9.4% unemployed. **Per capita income:** $17,625; % increase 1990-95: 11.1.
History: named after Col. Thomas Baker, an early settler; inc. 1898.
Transportation: 1 airport; 3 railroads; Amtrak; Greyhound buses; local bus system. **Communications:** 5 TV, 34 radio stations. **Medical facilities:** 6 major hosp.; 9 convalescent, 1 psychiatric, 3 physical rehab., 5 urgent care facilities; 3 clinics. **Educational facilities:** 1 univ., 1 community college; 9 vocational schools; 1 adult school; 1 college of law. **Further information:** Greater Bakersfield Chamber of Commerce, 1033 Truxtun Avenue, PO Box 1947, Bakersfield, CA 93303.
Web site: http://www.bakersfield.org/chamber

Baltimore, Maryland

Population: 702,979 (14); **Pop. density:** 8,700 per sq. mi; **Pop. growth:** -4.5%. **Area:** 80.8 sq. mi. **Employment:** 252,537 employed, 8.1% unemployed. **Per capita income:** $25,347; % increase 1990-95: 17.8.
History: founded by Maryland legislature 1729; inc. 1797; bombing of Ft. McHenry 1814 inspired Francis Scott Key to write "Star-Spangled Banner"; birthplace of America's railroads 1828; rebuilt after fire 1904; site of National Aquarium 1981.

Transportation: 1 major airport; 3 railroads; bus system; subway system; light rail system; Inner Harbor water taxi system; 2 underwater tunnels. **Communications:** 6 TV, 33 radio stations. **Medical facilities:** 29 hosp.; 2 major medical centers. **Educational facilities:** over 30 univ. and colleges; 177 pub. schools. **Further Information:** Greater Baltimore Committee, 111 S. Calvert St., Ste. 1500, Baltimore, MD 21202-6180.

Web sites: http://www.ci.baltimore.md.us
http://www.gbc.org

Baton Rouge, Louisiana

Population: 227,482 (72); **Pop. density:** 3,078 per sq. mi; **Pop. growth:** 3.6%. **Area:** 73.9 sq. mi. **Employment:** 109,104 employed, 6.1% unemployed. **Per capita income:** $21,159; % increase 1990-95: 27.9.

History: claimed by Spain at time of La. Purchase 1803; est. independence by rebellion 1810; inc. as town 1817; became state capital 1849; Union-held during most of Civil War.

Transportation: 1 airport, 5 airlines; 1 bus line; 3 railroad trunk lines. **Communications:** 5 TV, 19 radio stations. **Medical facilities:** 5 hosp. **Educational facilities:** 2 univ.; 92 pub., 39 private schools. **Further Information:** Chamber of Commerce, PO Box 3217, Baton Rouge, LA 70821.

Web sites: http://www.intersurf.com/~aevinc/aev2gbr.htm
http://www.brchamber.org

Birmingham, Alabama

Population: 264,527 (61); **Pop. density:** 1,781 per sq. mi; **Pop. growth:** −0.3%. **Area:** 148.5 sq. mi. **Employment:** 120,993 employed, 4.9% unemployed. **Per capita income:** $22,830; % increase 1990-95: 26.3.

History: settled as a result of discovery of elements needed for steel production; inc. 1871; named after Great Britain's steel-making center.

Transportation: 1 airport; 4 major rail freight lines, Amtrak; 1 bus line; 75 truck line terminals; 4 interstate highways. **Communications:** 5 TV, 27 radio stations; 1 educational TV, 1 educational radio station. **Medical facilities:** Univ. of Alabama at Birmingham Medical Center; VA hosp. with organ transplant program; 15 other hosp. **Educational facilities:** 1 univ., 2 colleges, 2 junior colleges. **Further Information:** Chamber of Commerce, 2027 First Ave. N, Birmingham, AL 35202.

Web sites: http://www.birmingham.org/thechamber
http://www2.bham.net/bhamcity.html

Boston, Massachusetts

Population: 547,725 (21); **Pop. density:** 11,317 per sq. mi; **Pop. growth:** −4.6%. **Area:** 48.4 sq. mi. **Employment:** 275,388 employed, 4.5% unemployed. **Per capita income:** $28,564; % increase 1990-95: 21.5.

History: settled 1630 by John Winthrop; capital of Mass. Bay Colony; figured strongly in Am. Revolution, earning distinction as the "Cradle of Liberty"; inc. 1822.

Transportation: 1 major airport; 2 railroads; city rail and subway system; 3 underwater tunnels; port. **Communications:** 9 TV, 21 radio stations. **Medical facilities:** 13 hosp.; 8 major medical research centers. **Educational facilities:** 30 univ. and colleges. **Further Information:** Greater Boston Chamber of Commerce, 1 Beacon St., 4th fl., Boston, MA 02108-3114.

Web sites: http://www.ci.boston.ma.us
http://www.gbcc.org

Buffalo, New York

Population: 312,965 (53); **Pop. density:** 7,708 per sq. mi; **Pop. growth:** −4.6%. **Area:** 40.6 sq. mi. **Employment:** 130,780 employed, 8.2% unemployed. **Per capita income:** $22,645; % increase 1990-95: 22.1.

History: founded 1790 by the Dutch; raided twice by British, War of 1812; served as western terminus for Erie Canal, became a center for trade and manufacturing; inc. 1832; last stop on the Underground Railroad; key point for Canada-U.S. political, trade, and social relations.

Transportation: 1 intl. airport; 6 major railroads; metro rail system; water service to Great Lakes-St. Lawrence Seaway system, and Atlantic seaboard. **Communications:** 7 TV, 18 radio stations. **Medical facilities:** 14 hosp., 37 research centers. **Educational facilities:** 12 colleges and univ.; 111 pub. and private schools. **Further information:** Greater Buffalo Partnership, 300 Main Place Tower, Buffalo, NY 14202-3797.

Web sites: http://www.ci.buffalo.ny.us
http://www.gbpartnership.org

Charlotte, North Carolina

Population: 437,797 (32); **Pop. density:** 2,512 per sq. mi; **Pop. growth:** 10.6%. **Area:** 174.3 sq. mi. **Employment:** 254,915 employed, 3.2% unemployed. **Per capita income:** $24,022; % increase 1990-95: 25.8.

History: settled by Scotch-Irish immigrants 1740s; inc. 1768 and named after Queen Charlotte, George III's wife; scene of first major U.S. gold discovery 1799.

Transportation: 1 airport; 2 major railway lines; 2 bus lines; 238 trucking firms. **Communications:** 7 TV, 26 radio stations. **Medical facilities:** 12 hosp., 1 medical center. **Educational facilities:** 3 univ., 5 colleges. **Further Information:** Chamber of Commerce, PO Box 32785, Charlotte, NC 28232.

Web sites: http://www.charlottechamber.org
http://www.charweb.org

Chesapeake, Virginia

Population: 180,577 (98); **Pop. density:** 530 per sq. mi; **Pop. growth:** 18.8%. **Area:** 340.7 sq. mi. **Employment:** 92,735 employed, 3.9% unemployed. **Per capita income:** $20,332; % increase 1990-95: 18.4.

History: Battle of Great Bridge fought here 1775; inc. as a city 1963.

Transportation: Amtrak; bus service; deepwater ports. **Communications:** 6 TV, 29 radio stations. **Medical facilities:** 1 hosp. **Educational facilities:** 1 college; 41 pub. schools. **Further Information:** Hampton Roads Chamber of Commerce, 420 Bank St., PO Box 327, Norfolk, VA 23501.

Web site: http://www.chesapeake.va.us

Chicago, Illinois

Population: 2,731,743 (3); **Pop. density:** 12,024 per sq. mi; **Pop. growth:** −1.9%. **Area:** 227.2 sq. mi. **Employment:** 1,204,185 employed, 6.7% unemployed. **Per capita income:** $28,177; % increase 1990-95: 24.8.

History: site acquired from Indians 1795; significant white settlement began with opening of Erie Canal 1825; chartered as city 1837; boomed with arrival of railroads from east and canal to Mississippi R.; about one-third of city destroyed by fire 1871; major grain & livestock market.

Transportation: 3 airports; major railroad system; major trucking industry. **Communications:** 9 TV, 31 radio stations. **Medical facilities:** over 123 hosp. **Educational facilities:** 95 institutions of higher learning. **Further Information:** Chicagoland Chamber of Commerce, 1 IBM Plaza, Ste. 2800, Chicago, IL 60611.

Web sites: http://www.ci.chi.il.us
http://www.chicagolandchamber.org

Cincinnati, Ohio

Population: 358,170 (46); **Pop. density:** 4,640 per sq. mi; **Pop. growth:** −1.6%. **Area:** 77.2 sq. mi. **Employment:** 165,033 employed, 5.8% unemployed. **Per capita income:** $24,199; % increase 1990-95: 23.5.

History: founded 1788 and named after the Society of Cincinnati, an organization of Revolutionary War officers; chartered as village 1802; inc. as city 1819.

Transportation: 1 intl. airport; 3 railroads; 1 bus system. **Communications:** 9 TV, 27 radio stations. **Medical facilities:** 32 hosp.; Children's Hosp. Medical Center; VA hosp. **Educational facilities:** 4 univ.; 11 colleges, 8 technical & 2-year colleges. **Further Information:** Chamber of Commerce, 300 Carew Tower, 441 Vine St., Cincinnati, OH 45202.

Web sites: http://www.gccc.com
http://www.cincinnatigov.com

Cleveland, Ohio

Population: 492,901 (26); **Pop. density:** 6,401 per sq. mi; **Pop. growth:** −2.5%. **Area:** 77 sq. mi. **Employment:** 186,358 employed, 9.8% unemployed. **Per capita income:** $25,303; % increase 1990-95: 22.1.

History: surveyed in 1796; given recognition as village 1815, inc. as city 1836; annexed Ohio City 1854.

Transportation: 1 intl. airport; rail service; major port; rapid transit system. **Communications:** 9 TV, 21 radio stations. **Medical facilities:** 14 hosp. **Educational facilities:** 8 univ. and colleges; 127 pub. schools. **Further Information:** Greater Cleveland Growth Assn., 200 Tower City Center, 50 Pub. Square, Cleveland, OH 44113-2291.

Web site: http://www.cleveland.oh.us

Colorado Springs, Colorado

Population: 316,480 (51); **Pop. density:** 1,728 per sq. mi. **Pop. growth:** 12.9%. **Area:** 183.2 sq. mi. **Employment:** 169,107 employed, 4.7% unemployed. **Per capita income:** $20,770; % increase 1990-95: 22.1.

History: founded 1871 at the foot of Pikes Peak; inc. 1872.

Transportation: 1 municipal airport; 2 railroads; bus line. **Communications:** 9 TV, 28 radio stations. **Medical facilities:** 7 hosp. **Educational facilities:** 11 univ., 12 colleges. **Further Information:** Chamber of Commerce, PO Box B, Colorado Springs, CO 80901.

Web sites: http://www.coloradosprings-travel.com/ cscvb
http://www.cscc.org

Columbus, Georgia

Population: 186,470 (92); **Pop. density:** 863 per sq. mi. **Pop. growth:** 4.4%. **Area:** 216.1 sq. mi. **Employment:** 75,668 employed, 5.4% unemployed. **Per capita income:** $18,616; % increase 1990-95: 25.6.

History: settled and inc. 1828; port city on Chattahoochee R.

Transportation: 1 airport; Metra bus system; bus line; 2 railroads. **Communications:** 5 TV, 11 radio stations. **Medical facilities:** 5 hosp. **Educational facilities:** 4 colleges; 48 pub., 1 technical, 13 private schools. **Further Information:** Chamber of Commerce, PO Box 1200, Columbus, GA 31902.

Web site: http://www.columbusga.com

Columbus, Ohio

Population: 635,913 (16); **Pop. density:** 3,331 per sq. mi. **Pop. growth:** 0.5%. **Area:** 190.9 sq. mi. **Employment:** 364,997 employed, 3.4% unemployed. **Per capita income:** $24,132; % increase 1990-95: 27.9.

History: first settlement 1797; laid out as new capital 1812 with current name; became city 1834.

Transportation: 6 airports; 3 railroads; 4 intercity bus lines. **Communications:** 8 TV, 25 radio stations. **Medical facilities:** 18 hosp. **Educational facilities:** 11 univ. and colleges; 8 technical/2-year schools. **Further Information:** Chamber of Commerce, 37 N. High St., Columbus, OH 43215.

Web site: http://www.columbus.org

Corpus Christi, Texas

Population: 275,419 (59); **Pop. density:** 2,040 per sq. mi. **Pop. growth:** 7.0%. **Area:** 135 sq. mi. **Employment:** 123,586 employed, 8.3% unemployed. **Per capita income:** $17,984; % increase 1990-95: 21.3.

History: settled 1839 and inc. 1852.

Transportation: 1 intl. airport; 2 bus lines, metro bus system; 3 freight railroads. **Communications:** 6 TV, 17 radio stations. **Medical facilities:** 14 hosp. including a children's center. **Educational facilities:** 1 univ., 1 college. **Further Information:** Greater Corpus Christi Business Alliance, PO Box 640, Corpus Christi, TX 78403.

Web site: http://www.cctexas.org

Dallas, Texas

Population: 1,022,830 (8); **Pop. density:** 2,987 per sq. mi. **Pop. growth:** 1.5%. **Area:** 342.4 sq. mi. **Employment:** 600,378 employed, 5.2% unemployed. **Per capita income:** $26,803; % increase 1990-95: 25.1.

History: first settled 1841; platted 1846; inc. 1871; developed as the financial and commercial center of Southwest; major center for distribution and high-tech manufacturing.

Transportation: 1 intl. airport, 1 regional airport; Amtrak; transit system. **Communications:** 8 TV, 27 radio stations. **Medical facilities:** 14 general hosp.; major medical center. **Educational facilities:** 11 univ. and colleges, 3 community college campuses. **Further Information:** Greater Dallas Chamber, Information Services, 1201 Elm, Ste. 2000, Dallas, TX 75270.

Web sites: http://www.gdc.org
http://www.ci.dallas.tx.us

Dayton, Ohio

Population: 178,540 (100); **Pop. density:** 3,246 per sq. mi. **Pop. growth:** −1.9%. **Area:** 55 sq. mi. **Employment:** 72,000 employed, 7.6% unemployed. **Per capita income:** $23,238; % increase 1990-95: 27.3.

History: settled 1796; inc. 1805; disastrous flood 1913; site where Wright Bros. invented first airplane to sustain flight 1903; cenetr for automobile manufacturing, information systems, software development.

Transportation: 1 intl. airport, 16 airlines; 3 railroads; 2 bus lines; countywide Miami Valley Regional Transit Authority. **Communications:** 5 TV, 26 radio stations. **Medical facilities:** 14 hosp. including VA facility. **Educational facilities:** 26 colleges and univ. in area. **Further Information:** Dayton Area Chamber of Commerce, 1 Chamber Plaza, Dayton, OH 45402.

Web sites: http://www.dayton.net/dayton
http://www.ci.dayton.oh.us
http://www.daytonchamber.org

Denver, Colorado

Population: 493,559 (25); **Pop. density:** 3,220 per sq. mi. **Pop. growth:** 5.5%. **Area:** 153.3 sq. mi. **Employment:** 260,526 employed, 4.9% unemployed. **Per capita income:** $27,069; % increase 1990-95: 25.3.

History: settled 1858 by gold prospectors and miners; inc. 1861; became territorial capital 1867; growth spurred by gold and silver boom; financial, industrial, cultural center of Rocky Mt. region.

Transportation: 1 intl. airport, 3 corporate reliever airports; 5 rail freight lines, Amtrak; 1 bus line. **Communications:** 14 TV, 29 radio stations. **Medical facilities:** 20 hosp. **Educational facilities:** 13 univ. and colleges; 8 two-yr. and community colleges. **Further Information:** Denver Metro Chamber of Commerce, 1445 Market St., Denver, CO 80202-1729.

Web site: http://www.den-chamber.org

Des Moines, Iowa

Population: 193,965 (86); **Pop. density:** 2,576 per sq. mi. **Pop. growth:** 0.4%. **Area:** 75.3 sq. mi. **Employment:** 118,175 employed, 3.7% unemployed. **Per capita income:** $25,331; % increase 1990-95: 25.7.

History: Fort Des Moines built 1843; settled and inc. 1851; chartered as city 1857.

Transportation: 1 intl. airport; 4 bus lines; 4 railroads; metro bus system. **Communications:** 5 TV, 17 radio stations. **Medical facilities:** 8 hosp. **Educational facilities:** 2 univ., 5 colleges. **Further Information:** Greater Des Moines Chamber of Commerce Federation, 601 Locust St., Ste. 100, Des Moines, IA 50309.

Web sites: http://www.dmchamber.com
http://www.ci.des-moines.ia.us

Detroit, Michigan

Population: 992,038 (10); **Pop. density:** 7,152 per sq. mi. **Pop. growth:** −3.5%. **Area:** 138.7 sq. mi. **Employment:** 345,324 employed, 9.1% unemployed. **Per capita income:** $26,889; % increase 1990-95: 27.8.

History: founded by French 1701; controlled by British 1760; acquired by U.S. 1796; destroyed by fire 1805; inc. as city 1824; capital of state 1837-47; auto manufacturing began 1899.

Transportation: 1 intl. airport; 10 railroads; major intl. port; pub. transit system. **Communications:** 9 TV, 37 radio stations. **Medical facilities:** 28 hosp.; major medical center. **Educational facilities:** 18 univ. and colleges. **Further Information:** Greater Detroit Chamber of Commerce, 600 W. Lafayette Blvd., PO Box 33840, Detroit, MI 48232-0840.

Web sites: http://www.detroitchamber.com
http://detroit.freenet.org

El Paso, Texas

Population: 579,307 (19); **Pop. density:** 2,361 per sq. mi. **Pop. growth:** 12.4%. **Area:** 245.4 sq. mi. **Employment:** 231,609 employed, 11.1% unemployed. **Per capita income:** $13,702; % increase 1990-95: 15.8.

History: first settled 1827; inc. 1873; arrival of railroad 1881 boosted city's population and industries.

Transportation: 1 intl. airport; 5 major rail lines; 8 bus lines; 5 major highways; gateway to Mexico. **Communications:** 12 TV, 24 radio stations. **Medical facilities:** 8 hosp.; 2 cancer treatment, 2 rehabilitation, 5 specialty centers. **Educational facilities:** 2 univ., 3 colleges (1 grad. only). **Further Information:** Greater El Paso Chamber of Commerce, 10 Civic Center Plaza, El Paso, TX 79901.

Web sites: http://www.elpaso.org
http://cs.utep.edu/elpaso

Fort Wayne, Indiana

Population: 183,359 (95); **Pop. density:** 2,921 per sq. mi. **Pop. growth:** −0.5%. **Area:** 62.7 sq. mi. **Employment:** 93,540 employed, 4.4% unemployed. **Per capita income:** $23,048; % increase 1990-95: 25.3.

History: French fort 1680; U.S. fort 1794; settled by 1832; inc. 1840 prior to Wabash-Erie canal completion 1843.

Transportation: 2 airports; 3 railroads; 6 bus lines. **Communications:** 5 TV, 13 radio stations. **Medical facilities:** 3 regional hosp.; VA hosp. **Educational facilities:** 4 univ., 5 colleges, 2 bus. schools; 82 pub. schools. **Further information:** Chamber of Commerce, 826 Ewing Street, Fort Wayne, IN 46802-2182.
Web sites: http://www.ft-wayne.in.us
http://www.fwchamber.org

Fort Worth, Texas

Population: 451,814 (29); **Pop. density:** 1,607 per sq. mi; **Pop. growth:** 0.9%. **Area:** 281.1 sq. mi. **Employment:** 242,864 employed, 5.1% unemployed. **Per capita income:** $22,665; % increase 1990-95: 20.2.
History: est. as military post 1849; inc. 1873; oil discovered 1917.
Transportation: 1 intl. airport; 9 major railroads, Amtrak; local bus service; 2 transcontinental, 2 intrastate bus lines. **Communications:** 14 TV, 11 local radio stations. **Medical facilities:** 25 hosp.; 1 children's hosp.; 4 government hosp. **Educational facilities:** 8 univ. and colleges. **Further information:** Chamber of Commerce, 777 Taylor St. #900, Fort Worth, TX 76102.
Web site: http://www.fortworth.acn.net

Fremont, California

Population: 183,575 (93); **Pop. density:** 2,384 per sq. mi; **Pop. growth:** 5.9%. **Area:** 77 sq. mi. **Employment:** 98,521 employed, 3.4% unemployed. **Per capita income:** $28,729; % increase 1990-95: 19.7.
History: area first settled by Spanish 1769; inc. 1956 with the consolidation of 5 communities.
Transportation: intracity bus line; Bay Area Rapid Transit System (southern terminal). **Communications:** 1 radio station. **Medical facilities:** 2 hosp. **Educational facilities:** 1 junior college; 43 pub. schools. **Further information:** Chamber of Commerce, 2201 Walnut Ave., Ste. 110, Fremont, CA 94538.
Web sites: http://www.infolane.com/fremont
http://www.fremontbusiness.com

Fresno, California

Population: 386,551 (38); **Pop. density:** 3,901 per sq. mi; **Pop. growth:** 9.2%. **Area:** 99.1 sq. mi. **Employment:** 168,838 employed, 11.6% unemployed. **Per capita income:** $18,014; % increase 1990-95: 11.3.
History: founded 1872; inc. as city 1885.
Transportation: municipal airport; Amtrak; 1 bus line; intracity bus system. **Communications:** 11 TV, 30 radio stations. **Medical facilities:** 7 general hosp. **Educational facilities:** 9 colleges; 102 pub. schools. **Further information:** Chamber of Commerce, 2331 Fresno St., Fresno, CA 93721.
Web sites: http://fresno-online.com/cvb
http://www.fresnochamber.com

Garland, Texas

Population: 194,218 (84); **Pop. density:** 3,389 per sq. mi; **Pop. growth:** 7.5%. **Area:** 57.3 sq. mi. **Employment:** 114,049 employed, 3.4% unemployed. **Per capita income:** $26,803; % increase 1990-95: 25.1.
History: settled 1850s; inc. 1891.
Transportation: 25 min. from Dallas/Ft. Worth Intl. Airport; 2 railroads. **Communications:** 14 local TV (Dallas/Ft. Worth), 25+ radio stations. **Medical facilities:** 2 hosp.; 329 beds. **Educational facilities:** 1 univ., 2 community colleges; 59 pub. schools. **Further information:** Chamber of Commerce, 914 S. Garland Ave., Garland, TX 75040.
Web sites: http://www.ci.garland.tx.us
http://www.garlandtx.com

Grand Rapids, Michigan

Population: 190,395 (90); **Pop. density:** 4,298 per sq. mi; **Pop. growth:** 0.7%. **Area:** 44.3 sq. mi. **Employment:** 99,983 employed, 5.6% unemployed. **Per capita income:** $23,174; % increase 1990-95: 30.0.
History: originally site of Ottawa Indian village; trading post 1826; became lumbering center and chartered as town 1850.
Transportation: 1 intl. airport; 3 rail carriers; 5 bus lines; transit bus system. **Communications:** 7 TV, 34 radio stations. **Medical facilities:** 10 hosp. **Educational facilities:** 8 colleges; 64 pub. schools. **Further information:** Chamber of Commerce, 111 Pearl St., NW, Grand Rapids, MI 49503.
Web sites: http://www.grcvb.org;
http://www.grand-rapids.mi.us

Greensboro, North Carolina

Population: 196,167 (80); **Pop. density:** 2,458 per sq. mi; **Pop. growth:** 6.7%. **Area:** 79.8 sq. mi. **Employment:** 110,236 employed, 3.6% unemployed. **Per capita income:** $23,428; % increase 1990-95: 23.7.
History: settled 1749; site of Revolutionary War conflict 1781 between Nathanael Greene and Cornwallis; inc. 1807.
Transportation: 1 regional airport; 2 railroads; Trailways/Greyhound bus service. **Communications:** all cable TV stations; 11 radio stations. **Medical facilities:** 4 hosp. **Educational facilities:** 2 univ., 3 colleges; 56 pub. schools. **Further information:** Chamber of Commerce, P.O. Box 3246, Greensboro, NC 27402.
Web sites: http://www.ci.greensboro.nc.us
http://www.greensboro.org

Hialeah, Florida

Population: 194,120 (85); **Pop. density:** 10,110 per sq. mi; **Pop. growth:** 3.3%. **Area:** 19.2 sq. mi. **Employment:** 95,071 employed, 7.6% unemployed. **Per capita income:** $21,058; % increase 1990-95: 18.0.
History: founded 1917, inc. 1925; industrial and residential city NW of Miami; Hialeah Park Horse Racing Track.
Transportation: 5 mi from Miami Intl. Airport; access to Port of Miami; Amtrak; 2 rail freight lines; Metrorail, Metrobus systems. **Communications:** 5 TV, 7 radio stations. **Medical facilities:** 4 hosp. (30 more in the area). **Educational facilities:** 7 univ. and colleges. **Further information:** Hialeah-Dade Development, Inc., 501 Palm Ave., Hialeah, FL 33010-4720.
Web site: http://www.hialeahchamber.com

Honolulu, Hawaii

Population: 385,881 (39); **Pop. density:** 4,660 per sq. mi; **Pop. growth:** 2.3%. **Area:** 82.8 sq. mi. **Employment (MSA):** 404,739 employed, 5.3% unemployed. **Per capita income:** $26,300; % increase 1990-95: 16.8.
History: harbor entered by Europeans 1794; declared capital of kingdom by King Kamehameha III 1850; Pearl Harbor naval base attacked by Japanese Dec. 7, 1941.
Transportation: 1 major airport; large, active port for passengers and cargo. **Communications:** 10 TV, 30 radio stations. **Medical facilities:** 13 major medical centers. **Educational facilities:** 4 univ., 5 colleges; 246 pub. schools, 98 private schools. **Further information:** Hawaii Visitors and Convention Bureau, 2270 Kalakaua Avenue, Honolulu, HI 96815.
Web sites: http://www.co.honolulu.hi.us
http://www.gohawaii.com

Houston, Texas

Population: 1,702,086 (4); **Pop. density:** 3,153 per sq. mi; **Pop. growth:** 4.4%. **Area:** 539.9 sq. mi. **Employment:** 916,238 employed, 6.4% unemployed. **Per capita income:** $25,449; % increase 1990-95: 22.8.
History: founded 1836; inc. 1837; capital of Repub. of Texas 1837-39; developed rapidly after construction of channel to Gulf of Mexico 1914; world center of oil and natural gas technology.
Transportation: 3 commercial airports; 4 mainline railroads; major bus transit system; major intl. port. **Communications:** 14 TV, 54 radio stations. **Medical facilities:** 53 hosp.; major medical center. **Educational facilities:** 23 univ. and colleges. **Further information:** Greater Houston Partnership, 1200 Smith St., Houston, TX 77002.
Web sites: http://www.houston.org
http://www.ci.houston.tx.us

Huntington Beach, California

Population: 189,220 (91); **Pop. density:** 7,167 per sq. **Pop. growth:** 4.2%. **Area:** 26.4 sq. mi. **Employment:** 108,110 employed, 3.1% unemployed. **Per capita income:** $23,501; % increase 1990-95: 9.6.
History: settled in early 1880s; inc. 1909; oil discovered 1920, led to city's development.
Transportation: 1 railroad; 2 bus lines. **Communications:** 2 TV stations. **Medical facilities:** 2 hosp. **Educational facilities:** 1 community college; 34 pub. schools. **Further information:** Chamber of Commerce, Seacliff Office Park, 2100 Main St., #200, Huntington Beach, CA 92648.
Web sites: http://www.thebeach.com/cities/hb
http://www.hbchamber.org

Indianapolis, Indiana

Population: 752,279 (12); **Pop. density:** 2,080 per sq. mi; **Pop. growth:** 2.9%. **Area:** 361.7 sq. mi. **Employment:** 400,623 employed, 3.7% unemployed. **Per capita income:** $24,664; % increase 1990-95: 25.5.
History: settled 1820; became capital 1825.
Transportation: 1 intl. airport; 5 railroads; 3 interstate bus lines. **Communications:** 10 TV, 27 radio stations. **Medical facilities:** 17 hosp.; 1 major medical and research center. **Educational facilities:** 8 univ. and colleges; major pub. library system. **Further Information:** Chamber of Commerce, 320 N. Meridian St., Indianapolis, IN 46204.
Web sites: http://www.ci.indianapolis.in.us; http://www.indychamber.com

Jackson, Mississippi

Population: 193,097 (87); **Pop. density:** 1,772 per sq. mi; **Pop. growth:** −1.8%. **Area:** 109 sq. mi. **Employment:** 96,357 employed, 4.4% unemployed. **Per capita income:** $20,646; % increase 1990-95: 32.3.
History: originally known as Le Fleur's Bluff; selected as capital 1822 and named for Andrew Jackson; inc. 1823; scene of secession convention 1861; captured by Sherman 1863.
Transportation: 9 airlines; 1 bus line; 2 railroads; 5 freight carriers. **Communications:** 5 TV, 20 radio stations. **Medical facilities:** 9 hosp. incl. a VA facility. **Educational facilities:** 2 univ., 4 colleges; 1 pub. school district. **Further Information:** Metro Jackson Chamber of Commerce, PO Box 22548, Jackson, MS 39225-2548.
Web site: http://www.visitjackson.com

Jacksonville, Florida

Population: 665,070 (15); **Pop. density:** 877 per sq. mi; **Pop. growth:** 4.7%. **Area:** 758.7 sq. mi. **Employment:** 332,307 employed, 3.8% unemployed. **Per capita income:** $22,617; % increase 1990-95: 23.2.
History: settled 1816 as Cowford; renamed after Andrew Jackson 1822; inc. 1832; rechartered 1851; scene of conflicts in Seminole and Civil wars.
Transportation: 1 intl. airport; 3 railroads; 2 interstate bus lines. **Communications:** 6 TV, 34 radio stations. **Medical facilities:** 11 hosp. **Educational facilities:** 3 univ., 4 colleges. **Further Information:** Chamber of Commerce, 3 Independent Drive, Jacksonville, FL 32202-5092.
Web sites: http://www.jacksonvillechamber.org http://www.ci.jax.fl.us

Jersey City, New Jersey

Population: 226,022 (73); **Pop. density:** 15,169 per sq. mi; **Pop. growth:** −1.1%. **Area:** 14.9 sq. mi. **Employment:** 101,564 employed, 11.3% unemployed. **Per capita income:** $23,561; % increase 1990-95: 19.3.
History: site bought from Indians 1630; chartered as town by British 1668; scene of Revolutionary War conflict 1779; chartered under present name 1838; important station on Underground Railroad.
Transportation: bus and subway system. **Communications:** see New York City. **Medical facilities:** 4 hosp. **Educational facilities:** 3 colleges. **Further Information:** Hudson County Chamber of Commerce, 574 Summit Ave., Ste. 404, Jersey City, NJ 07306.
Web site: http://www.jerseycitynet.com

Kansas City, Missouri

Population: 443,878 (31); **Pop. density:** 1,425 per sq. mi; **Pop. growth:** 2.1%. **Area:** 311.5 sq. mi. **Employment:** 243,353 employed, 4.9% unemployed. **Per capita income:** $24,576; % increase 1990-95: 25.5.
History: settled by 1838 at confluence of the Missouri and Kansas rivers; inc. 1851.
Transportation: 1 intl. airport; a major rail center; 191 trunk lines; several barge cos.. **Communications:** 7 TV, 29 radio stations. **Medical facilities:** 14 hosp.; VA facility. **Educational facilities:** 9 univ. and colleges. **Further Information:** Greater Kansas City Chamber of Commerce, 911 Main St., Ste. 2600, Kansas City, MO 64105,
Web sites: http://www.kansascity.com http://www.kcity.com http://www.kcmo.org

Las Vegas, Nevada

Population: 327,878 (49); **Pop. density:** 3,936 per sq. mi; **Pop. growth:** 27.0%. **Area:** 83.3 sq. mi. **Employment:**
187,024 employed, 5.3% unemployed. **Per capita income:** $22,927; % increase 1990-95: 21.1.
History: occupied by Mormons 1855-57; bought by railroad 1903; city of Las Vegas inc. 1911; gambling legalized 1931.
Transportation: 1 intl. airport; 2 railroads; bus system. **Communications:** 9 TV, 30 radio stations. **Medical facilities:** 11 hosp. **Educational facilities:** 1 univ., 4 colleges; 205 pub. schools in area. **Further Information:** Chamber of Commerce, 3720 Howard Hughes Parkway, Las Vegas, NV 89109.
Web sites: http://www.vegas.com http://www.lvchamber.com

Lexington, Kentucky

Population: 237,612 (69); **Pop. density:** 835 per sq. mi; **Pop. growth:** 5.4%. **Area:** 284.5 sq. mi. **Employment:** 133,345 employed, 2.5% unemployed. **Per capita income:** $22,394; % increase 1990-95: 23.4.
History: site was founded and named 1775 by hunters who heard of the Revolutionary War battle at Lexington, Mass.; settled 1779; chartered 1782; inc. as a city 1832.
Transportation: 7 commercial airlines; 2 railroads; city buses; trolley. **Communications:** 5 TV, 14 radio stations. **Medical facilities:** 5 general, 5 specialized hosp. **Educational facilities:** 2 univ., 4 colleges. **Further Information:** Greater Lexington Chamber of Commerce, 330 E. Main St., Lexington, KY 40507.
Web site: http://www.lexchamber.com

Lincoln, Nebraska

Population: 203,076 (77); **Pop. density:** 3,208 per sq. mi; **Pop. growth:** 5.8%. **Area:** 63.3 sq. mi. **Employment:** 122,454 employed, 2.7% unemployed. **Per capita income:** $22,446; % increase 1990-95: 27.1.
History: originally called Lancaster; chosen state capital 1867, renamed after Abraham Lincoln; inc. 1869.
Transportation: 1 airport; Greyhound; Amtrak, 2 railroads. **Communications:** 2 TV, 13 radio stations. **Medical facilities:** 5 hosp. including VA, rehabilitation facilities. **Educational facilities:** 3 univ., 3 voc.-tech./business colleges; 48 pub., 15 private schools. **Further Information:** Chamber of Commerce, PO Box 83006, Lincoln, NE 68501.
Web sites: http://www.lincoln.org http://www.lcoc.com

Long Beach, California

Population: 433,852 (34); **Pop. density:** 8,677 per sq. mi; **Pop. growth:** 1.1%. **Area:** 50 sq. mi. **Employment:** 190,027 employed, 7.7% unemployed. **Per capita income:** $23,501; % increase 1990-95: 9.6.
History: settled as early as 1784 by Spanish; by 1884 present site developed on harbor; inc. 1888; oil discovered 1921.
Transportation: 1 airport; 3 railroads; major intl. port; 4 bus co. with 40 bus lines, light rail service. **Communications:** 1 radio station, 1 CATV franchise. **Medical facilities:** 10 hosp. **Educational facilities:** 1 univ., 1 community college (2 campuses); 85 pub. schools in district. **Further Information:** Long Beach City Hall, 333 W. Ocean Blvd., Long Beach, CA 90802
Web sites: http://www.ci.long-beach.ca.us http://www.lbchamber.com

Los Angeles, California

Population: 3,448,613 (2); **Pop. density:** 7,348 per sq. mi; **Pop. growth:** −1.1%. **Area:** 469.3 sq. mi. **Employment:** 1,610,392 employed, 9.3% unemployed. **Per capita income:** $23,501; % increase 1990-95: 9.6.
History: founded by Spanish 1781; captured by U.S. 1846; inc. 1850; Hollywood a district of L.A.
Transportation: 1 intl. airport; 3 railroads; major freeway system; intracity transit system. **Communications:** 21 TV, 70 radio stations. **Medical facilities:** 822 hosp. and clinics in metropolitan area. **Educational facilities:** 192 univ. and colleges (incl. junior, community, and other); 1,678 pub. schools; 1,470 private schools. **Further Information:** Chamber of Commerce, 350 S. Bixel St., PO Box 3696, Los Angeles, CA 90051-1696.
Web sites: http://www.ci.la.ca.us http://www.lachamber.com

Louisville, Kentucky

Population: 270,308 (60); **Pop. density:** 4,353 per sq. mi; **Pop. growth:** 0.3%. **Area:** 62.1 sq. mi. **Employment:** 125,346 employed, 5.0% unemployed. **Per capita income:** $23,552; % increase 1990-95: 26.4.

History: settled 1778; named for Louis XVI of France; inc. 1828; base for Union forces in Civil War.
Transportation: 2 municipal airports; 1 terminal, 4 trunk-line railroads; metro bus line, Greyhound station; 5 barge lines. **Communications:** 5 TV, 21 radio stations, 2 educational. **Medical facilities:** 23 hosp. **Educational facilities:** 10 univ. and colleges, 9 business colleges and technical schools. **Further Information:** Louisville Area Chamber of Commerce, 600 W. Main St., Louisville, KY 40202.
Web sites: http://www.louisville.com
http://www.lacc.org
http://www.louisville.ky.us/louisvil.htm

Lubbock, Texas

Population: 194,467 (83); **Pop. density:** 1,868 per sq. mi; **Pop. growth:** 4.4%. **Area:** 104.1 sq. mi. **Employment:** 99,127 employed, 4.0% unemployed. **Per capita income:** $19,783; % increase 1990-95: 23.3.
History: settled 1879; laid out 1891; inc. 1909 through merger of two towns.
Transportation: 1 intl. airport; 2 railroads, bus line. **Communications:** 5 TV, 18 radio stations. **Medical facilities:** 7 hosp. **Educational facilities:** 3 univ., 1 junior college; 51 pub. schools. **Further Information:** Chamber of Commerce, P.O. Box 561, Lubbock, TX 79408.
Web sites: http://www.ci.lubbock.tx.us
http://interoz.com/lubbock/llubbock.htm

Madison, Wisconsin

Population: 194,586 (82); **Pop. density:** 3,367 per sq. mi; **Pop. growth:** 2.0%. **Area:** 57.8 sq. mi. **Employment:** 127,485 employed, 1.8% unemployed. **Per capita income:** $26,449; % increase 1990-95: 29.3.
History: first white settlement 1832; selected as site for state capital and named after James Madison, 1836; chartered 1856.
Transportation: 1 airport, 9 airlines; 1 intracity, 3 intercity bus systems; 3 freight rail lines. **Communications:** 5 TV, 23 radio stations. **Medical facilities:** 4 hosp. **Educational facilities:** 7 colleges and univ., including main branch of Univ. of Wisconsin; 43 pub. schools. **Further Information:** Greater Madison Chamber of Commerce, PO Box 71, Madison, WI 53701-0071.
Web sites: http://www.ci.madison.wi.us
http://www.greatermadisonchamber.com

Memphis, Tennessee

Population: 614,289 (18); **Pop. density:** 2,400 per sq. mi; **Pop. growth:** –0.7%. **Area:** 256 sq. mi. **Employment:** 295,304 employed, 5.3% unemployed. **Per capita income:** $23,640; % increase 1990-95: 29.7.
History: French, Spanish, and U.S. forts by 1797; settled by 1819; inc. as town 1826, as city 1840; surrendered charter to state 1879 after yellow fever epidemics; rechartered as city 1893.
Transportation: 1 intl. airport; 6 railroads; bus system. **Communications:** 6 TV, 29 radio stations. **Medical facilities:** 21 hosp. **Educational facilities:** 12 univ. and colleges; 206 pub., 76 private schools. **Further Information:** Memphis Area Chamber of Commerce, 22 N. Front St., Ste. 200, PO Box 224, Memphis, TN 38101-0224.
Web sites: http://www.memphis.acn.net
http://www.ci.memphis.tn.us
http://www.memphischamber.com

Mesa, Arizona

Population: 313,649 (52); **Pop. density:** 2,888 per sq. mi; **Pop. growth:** 8.5%. **Area:** 108.6 sq. mi. **Employment:** 182,167 employed, 3.1% unemployed. **Per capita income:** $21,839; % increase 1990-95: 20.1.
History: founded by Mormons 1878; inc. 1883; 13 mi. from Phoenix; population boomed fivefold 1960-80.
Transportation: near Sky Harbor Intl. Airport in Phoenix; 2 railroads; bus line. **Medical facilities:** 4 major hosp. **Educational facilities:** 1 univ., 3 colleges; 70 pub. schools. **Further Information:** Convention and Visitor's Bureau, 120 N. Center, Mesa, AZ 85201.
Web site: http://www.ci.mesa.az.us

Miami, Florida

Population: 373,024 (42); **Pop. density:** 10,478 per sq. mi; **Pop. growth:** 4.0%. **Area:** 35.6 sq. mi. **Employment:** 160,410 employed, 10.5% unemployed. **Per capita income:** $21,058; % increase 1990-95: 18.0.
History: site of fort 1836; settlement began 1870; inc. 1896; modern city developed into resort and recreation center; land speculation in 1920s added to city's growth, as did Cuban, Central and South American, and Haitian immigration since 1960.
Transportation: 1 intl. airport; seaport; Amtrak, transit rail system; 2 bus lines; 65 truck lines. **Communications:** 9 commercial, 2 educational TV stations; 41 radio stations. **Medical facilities:** 36 hosp.; VA hosp. **Educational facilities:** 6 univ. and colleges. **Further Information:** Metro-Dade Dept. of Planning, Development, and Regulation, Research Div., 111 NW 1st St., Ste. 1220, Miami, FL 33128.
Web sites: http://ci.miami.fl.us
http://www.greatermiami.com
http://www.metro-dade.com

Milwaukee, Wisconsin

Population: 617,044 (17); **Pop. density:** 6,421 per sq. mi; **Pop. growth:** –1.8%. **Area:** 96.1 sq. mi. **Employment:** 286,640 employed, 5.1% unemployed. **Per capita income:** $25,906; % increase 1990-95: 27.3.
History: Indian trading post by 1674; settlement began 1835; inc. as city 1848; famous beer industry.
Transportation: 1 intl. airport; 2 railroads; major port; 4 bus lines. **Communications:** 12 TV, 37 radio stations. **Medical facilities:** 21 hosp.; major medical center. **Educational facilities:** 15 univ. and colleges. **Further Information:** Metropolitan Milwaukee Association of Commerce, 756 N. Milwaukee Street, Milwaukee, WI 53202.
Web sites: http://www.ci.mil.wi.us
http://www.milwaukee.org

Minneapolis, Minnesota

Population: 354,590 (47); **Pop. density:** 6,459 per sq. mi; **Pop. growth:** –3.7%. **Area:** 54.9 sq. mi. **Employment:** 197,972 employed, 4.0% unemployed. **Per capita income:** $27,436; % increase 1990-95: 24.0.
History: site visited by Hennepin 1680; included in area of military reservations 1819; inc. 1867.
Transportation: 1 intl. airport; 5 railroads; mass transit systems; 24-36 barge lines per year come into city. **Communications:** 7 TV, 25 radio stations. **Medical facilities:** 7 hosp., including leading heart hosp. at Univ. of Minnesota. **Educational facilities:** 10 univ. and colleges; 80 pub., 38 private schools. **Further Information:** City of Minneapolis Office of Pub. Affairs, 323M City Hall, 350 S. 5th St., Minneapolis, MN 55415.
Web sites: http://www.ci.minneapolis.mn.us
http://www.tc-chamber.org

Mobile, Alabama

Population: 204,490 (76); **Pop. density:** 1,733 per sq. mi; **Pop. growth:** 4.2%. **Area:** 118 sq. mi. **Employment:** 97,112 employed, 5.9% unemployed. **Per capita income:** $18,429; % increase 1990-95: 27.1.
History: settled by French 1711; occupied by U.S. 1813; inc. as town 1814, as city 1819; only seaport of Alabama.
Transportation: 4 rail freight lines, Amtrak; 4 airlines; 65 truck lines; leading river system. **Communications:** 7 TV, 21 radio stations. **Medical facilities:** 9 hosp. **Educational facilities:** 3 univ., 3 colleges. **Further Information:** Chamber of Commerce, PO Box 2187, Mobile, AL 36652.
Web sites: http://www.ci.mobile.al.us
http://www.mobcham.org

Montgomery, Alabama

Population: 195,471 (81); **Pop. density:** 1,448 per sq. mi; **Pop. growth:** 4.2%. **Area:** 135 sq. mi. **Employment:** 93,766 employed, 4.2% unemployed. **Per capita income:** $21,000; % increase 1990-95: 25.0.
History: inc. as town 1819, as city 1837; became state capital 1846; first capital of Confederacy 1861.
Transportation: 4 airlines; 2 railroads; 2 bus lines; Alabama River is navigable to Gulf of Mexico. **Communications:** 5 TV, 2 CATV, 15 radio stations. **Medical facilities:** 4 major hosp.; VA and 32 clinics. **Educational facilities:** 5 univ.; 49 pub., 28 private schools. **Further Information:** Montgomery Area Chamber of Commerce, PO Box 79, Montgomery, AL 36101.
Web sites: http://www.montgomery.al.us
http://www.montgomery-al.com

Nashville, Tennessee

Population: 504,505 (24); **Pop. density:** 1,066 per sq. mi; **Pop. growth:** 3.3%. **Area:** 473.3 sq. mi. **Employment:** 283,247 employed, 3.2% unemployed. **Per capita income:** $25,077; % increase 1990-95: 33.5.

History: settled 1779; first chartered 1806; became permanent state capital 1843; home of Grand Ole Opry.

Transportation: 1 airport; 1 railroad; bus line; transit system of buses and trolleys. **Communications:** 11 TV, 34 radio stations. **Medical facilities:** 14 hosp.; VA and speech-hearing center. **Educational facilities:** 16 universities and colleges. **Further information:** Chamber of Commerce, 161 4th Ave., Nashville, TN 37219.

Web site: http://www.nashville.org

Newark, New Jersey

Population: 258,751 (63); **Pop. density:** 10,872 per sq. mi; **Pop. growth:** –6.0%. **Area:** 23.8 sq. mi. **Employment:** 99,757 employed, 13.0% unemployed. **Per capita income:** $32,346; % increase 1990-95: 22.8.

History: settled by Puritans 1666; used as supply base by Washington 1776; inc. as town 1833, as city 1836.

Transportation: 1 intl. airport; 2 railroads; bus system; 2 subways. **Communications:** 3 TV, 5 radio stations within city limits. **Medical facilities:** 6 hosp. **Educational facilities:** 5 univ. and colleges; 71 pub. schools. **Further Information:** Regional Business Partnership, 1 Newark Center, 22d fl., Newark, NJ 07102-5265.

Web sites: http://www.ci.newark.nj.us
http://www.rbp.org

New Orleans, Louisiana

Population: 484,149 (27); **Pop. density:** 2,681 per sq. mi; **Pop. growth:** –2.6%. **Area:** 180.6 sq. mi. **Employment:** 188,917 employed, 7.8% unemployed. **Per capita income:** $21,374; % increase 1990-95: 25.8.

History: founded by French 1718; became major seaport on Mississippi R.; acquired by U.S. as part of La. Purchase 1803; inc. as city 1805; Battle of New Orleans was last battle of War of 1812.

Transportation: 2 airports; major railroad center; major intl. port. **Communications:** 7 TV, 18 radio stations. **Medical facilities:** numerous hosp.; major research center. **Educational facilities:** 13 univ. and colleges. **Further information:** New Orleans Metropolitan Convention & Visitors Bureau, Inc., 1520 Sugar Bowl Dr., New Orleans, LA 70112.

Web site: http://www.neworleanscvb.com

Newport News, Virginia

Population: 179,127 (99); **Pop. density:** 2,623 per sq. mi; **Pop. growth:** 4.5%. **Area:** 68.3 sq. mi. **Employment:** 78,766 employed, 5.2% unemployed. **Per capita income:** $20,332; % increase 1990-95: 18.4.

History: inc. 1896; the cities of Warwick and Newport News consolidated in 1958 into the larger city of Newport News; one of the world's major shipbuilding centers.

Transportation: 1 intl. airport; 2 railroads; Greyhound buses; local bus system. **Communications:** 8 TV, 29 radio stations received in area. **Medical facilities:** 3 hosp.; adolescent psychiatry hosp. **Educational facilities:** 33 pub. schools. **Further information:** Virginia Peninsula Chamber of Commerce, 6 Manhattan Square, PO Box 7269, Hampton, VA 23666.

Web site: http://www.newport-news.va.us

New York City, New York

Population: 7,333,253 (1); **Pop. density:** 23,740 per sq. mi; **Pop. growth:** 0.1%. **Area:** 308.9 sq. mi. **Employment:** 3,004,195 employed, 8.8% unemployed. **Per capita income:** $30,896; % increase 1990-95: 21.0.

History: trading post established by H. Hudson 1609; British took control from Dutch 1664 and named New York; briefly U.S. capital; Washington inaugurated as president 1789; under new charter, 1898, city expanded to include 5 boroughs: The Bronx, Brooklyn, Queens, Staten Island, as well as Manhattan.

Transportation: 3 airports serve area; 2 rail terminals; major subway network; ferry system; 4 underwater tunnels. **Communications:** 13 TV, 117 radio stations. **Medical facilities:** 81 hosp.; 5 academic medical centers. **Educational facilities:** 92 univ. and colleges; 1,095 pub. schools, 914 private schools. **Further information:** Convention and Visitors Bureau, 2 Columbus Circle, New York, NY 10019.

Web sites: http://www.ci.nyc.ny.us
http://www.nycvisit.com

Norfolk, Virginia

Population: 241,426 (67); **Pop. density:** 4,487 per sq. mi; **Pop. growth:** –7.6%. **Area:** 53.8 sq. mi. **Employment:** 81,749 employed, 6.6% unemployed. **Per capita income:** $20,332; % increase 1990-95: 18.4.

History: founded 1682; burned by patriots to prevent capture by British during Revolutionary War; rebuilt and inc. as town 1805, as city 1845; site of world's largest naval base.

Transportation: 1 intl. airport; 2 railroads; Amtrak; bus system. **Communications:** 6 TV, 29 radio stations. **Medical facilities:** 6 hosp. **Educational facilities:** 2 univ., 1 college, 1 medical school; 48 pub. schools. **Further information:** Hampton Roads Chamber of Commerce, 420 Bank St., PO Box 327, Norfolk, VA 23501.

Web site: http://www.norfolk.va.us

Oakland, California

Population: 366,926 (44); **Pop. density:** 6,541 per sq. mi; **Pop. growth:** –1.4%. **Area:** 56.1 sq. mi. **Employment:** 166,301 employed, 7.8% unemployed. **Per capita income:** $28,729; % increase 1990-95: 19.7.

History: area settled by Spanish 1820; inc. as city under present name 1854.

Transportation: 1 intl. airport; western terminus for 3 railroads; underground, underwater 75-mi subway. **Communications:** 1 TV, 3 radio stations in city. **Medical facilities:** 10 hosp. in MSA, including Children's Hosp. Oakland, VA center. **Educational facilities:** 8 East Bay colleges and univ.; 94 pub. schools. **Further information:** Oakland Metropolitan Chamber of Commerce, 475 14th St., Oakland, CA 94612-1903.

Web sites: http://oakweb.ci.oakland.ca.us
http://www.oaklandchamber.com

Oklahoma City, Oklahoma

Population: 463,201 (28); **Pop. density:** 762 per sq. mi; **Pop. growth:** 4.2%. **Area:** 608.2 sq. mi. **Employment:** 230,680 employed, 3.7% unemployed. **Per capita income:** $20,139; % increase 1990-95: 19.7.

History: settled during land rush in Midwest 1889; inc. 1890; became capital 1910; oil discovered 1928.

Transportation: 1 intl. airport; 3 railroads; pub. transit system; 5 major bus lines. **Communications:** 8 TV, 24 radio stations. **Medical facilities:** 20 hosp. **Educational facilities:** 17 univ. and colleges; 83 pub., 37 private schools. **Further information:** Chamber of Commerce, Economic Development Division, 123 Park Ave., Oklahoma City, OK 73102.

Web sites: http://www.ionet.net/~okcpio
http://www.ci.okc.ok.us
http://www.soonernet.com/okccoc

Omaha, Nebraska

Population: 345,033 (48); **Pop. density:** 3,430 per sq. mi; **Pop. growth:** 2.8%. **Area:** 100.6 sq. mi. **Employment:** 192,131 employed, 3.4% unemployed. **Per capita income:** $24,002; % increase 1990-95: 28.1.

History: founded 1854; inc. 1857; large food-processing, telecommunications, information-processing center; home of more than 20 insurance cos..

Transportation: 12 major airlines; 4 major railroads; intercity bus line. **Communications:** 8 TV, 22 radio stations. **Medical facilities:** 16 hosp.; institute for cancer research. **Educational facilities:** 5 univ., 4 colleges; 243 pub., 78 private schools. **Further Information:** Greater Omaha Chamber of Commerce, 1301 Harney St., Omaha, NE 68102.

Web sites: http://www.ci.omaha.ne.us
http://www.accessomaha.com

Philadelphia, Pennsylvania

Population: 1,524,249 (5); **Pop. density:** 11,282 per sq. mi; **Pop. growth:** –3.9%. **Area:** 135.1 sq. mi. **Employment:** 606,938 employed, 6.9% unemployed. **Per capita income:** $26,959; % increase 1990-95: 22.1.

History: first settled by Swedes 1638; Swedes surrendered to Dutch 1654; settled by English & Scottish Quakers 1678; named Philadelphia 1682; chartered 1701; Continental Congresses convened 1774, 1775; Declaration of Independence signed here 1776; national capital 1790-1800; state capital 1683-1799.

Transportation: 1 major airport; 3 railroads; major freshwater port; subway, el, rail commuter, bus, and streetcar system. **Communications:** 11 TV, 44 radio stations. **Medical facilities:** 47 hosp. **Educational facilities:** 25 degree-granting institutions;

10 community college campuses. **Further Information:** Office of City Representative and City Commerce Director, 1600 Arch St., 13th fl., Philadelphia, PA 19103.
Web site: http://www.phila.gov

Phoenix, Arizona

Population: 1,048,949 (7); **Pop. density:** 2,498 per sq. mi; **Pop. growth:** 6.6%. **Area:** 419.9 sq. mi. **Employment:** 646,442 employed, 4.0% unemployed. **Per capita Income:** $21,839; % increase 1990-95: 20.1.
History: settled 1870; inc. as city 1881; became territorial capital 1889.
Transportation: 1 intl. airport; 5 railroads; transcontinental bus line; pub. transit system. **Communications:** 13 TV, 45 radio stations. **Medical facilities:** 20 hosp., 1 medical research center. **Educational facilities:** 12 institutions of higher learning; 217 pub. schools. **Further Information:** Chamber of Commerce, 201 N. Central Ave., 27th fl., Phoenix, AZ 85073.
Web sites: http://www.ci.phoenix.az.us
http://www.phoenixchamber.com

Pittsburgh, Pennsylvania

Population: 358,883 (45); **Pop. density:** 6,455 per sq. mi; **Pop. growth:** −3.0%. **Area:** 55.6 sq. mi. **Employment:** 155,080 employed, 5.3% unemployed. **Per capita Income:** $24,071; % increase 1990-95: 24.3.
History: settled around Ft. Pitt 1758; inc. as city 1816; has one of the largest inland ports; by Civil War, already a center for iron production.
Transportation: 1 intl. airport; 20 railroads; 2 bus lines; trolley/subway system. **Communications:** 6 TV, 26 radio stations. **Medical facilities:** 35 hosp.; VA installation. **Educational facilities:** 3 univ., 6 colleges; 86 pub. schools. **Further Information:** Greater Pittsburgh Convention & Visitors Bureau, 4 Gateway Ctr., Pittsburgh, PA 15222.
Web sites: http://www.pittsburgh.net
http://www.pittsburgh-cvb.org

Portland, Oregon

Population: 450,777 (30); **Pop. density:** 3,615 per sq. mi; **Pop. growth:** 2.7%. **Area:** 124.7 sq. mi. **Employment:** 259,525 employed, 5.5% unemployed. **Per capita Income:** $24,553; % increase 1990-95: 25.5.
History: settled by pioneers 1845; developed as trading center, aided by California Gold Rush 1849; city chartered 1851.
Transportation: 1 intl. airport; 2 major rail freight lines, Amtrak; 2 intercity bus lines; 27-mi. frontage freshwater port; mass transit bus and rail system. **Communications:** 7 TV, 37 radio stations. **Medical facilities:** 16 hosp.; VA hosp. **Educational facilities:** 26 univ. and colleges, 1 community college. **Further Information:** Portland Metropolitan Chamber of Commerce, 221 N.W. 2d Ave., Portland, OR 97209-3999.
Web sites: http://www.ci.portland.or.us
http://www.pdxchamber.org

Raleigh, North Carolina

Population: 236,707 (70); **Pop. density:** 2,687 per sq. mi; **Pop. growth:** 11.6%. **Area:** 88.1 sq. mi. **Employment:** 147,946 employed, 2.5% unemployed. **Per capita income:** $24,675; % increase 1990-95: 24.3.
History: named after Sir Walter Raleigh; site chosen for capital 1788; laid out 1792; inc. 1795; occupied by Gen. Sherman 1865.
Transportation: 1 intl. airport, 10 airlines, 5 commuter airlines; 3 railroads; 2 bus lines. **Communications:** 8 TV, 30 radio stations. **Medical facilities:** 6 hosp. **Educational facilities:** 6 univ. and colleges; 1 community college; 105 pub. schools (county). **Further Information:** Chamber of Commerce, 800 S. Salisbury St., PO Box 2978, Raleigh, NC 27602.
Web sites: http://www.raleigh.acn.net
http://www.raleighchamber.org

Richmond, Virginia

Population: 201,108 (78); **Pop. density:** 3,346 per sq. mi; **Pop. growth:** −0.8%. **Area:** 60.1 sq. mi. **Employment:** 92,964 employed, 5.3% unemployed. **Per capita income:** $25,851; % increase 1990-95: 19.3.
History: first settled 1607; became capital of Commonwealth of Virginia, 1779; attacked by British under Benedict Arnold 1781; inc. as city 1782; capital of Confederate States of America, 1861-65.
Transportation: 1 intl. airport; 4 railroads; 3 intracity bus lines; deepwater terminal accessible to oceangoing ships.

Communications: 6 TV, 26 radio stations. **Medical facilities:** Medical Coll. of Virginia renowned for heart and kidney transplants; 19 other hosp. incl. VA facility. **Educational facilities:** 9 univ. and colleges; 173 pub., 45 private schools. **Further Information:** Chamber of Commerce, PO Box 12280, Richmond, VA 23241-2280.
Web sites: http://www.ci.richmond.va.us
http://www.grcc.com

Riverside, California

Population: 241,644 (66); **Pop. density:** 3,110 per sq. mi; **Pop. growth:** 6.7%. **Area:** 77.7 sq. mi. **Employment:** 120,708 employed, 8.1% unemployed. **Per capita income:** $18,685; % increase 1990-95: 6.8.
History: founded 1870; inc. 1886; known for its citrus industry; home of the parent navel orange.
Transportation: municipal airport, intl. airport nearby; rail freight lines, commuter line; trolley/bus system. **Communications:** 5 TV, 47 radio stations. **Medical facilities:** 4 hosp.; many clinics. **Educational facilities:** 3 univ., 1 community college. **Further Information:** Chamber of Commerce, 3685 Main St., Ste. 350, Riverside, CA 92501.
Web sites: http://www.ci.riverside.ca.us
http://www.riverside-chamber.com

Rochester, New York

Population: 231,170 (71); **Pop. density:** 6,457 per sq. mi; **Pop. growth:** 0.4%. **Area:** 35.8 sq. mi. **Employment:** 105,976 employed, 6.2% unemployed. **Per capita income:** $24,566; % increase 1990-95: 18.1.
History: first permanent white settlement 1812; inc. as village 1817, as city 1834; developed as Erie Canal town.
Transportation: 1 intl. airport; Amtrak; 3 bus lines; intracity transit service; Port of Rochester. **Communications:** 6 TV, 18 radio stations. **Medical facilities:** 8 general hosp. **Educational facilities:** 10 colleges, 3 community colleges. **Further Information:** Chamber of Commerce, 55 St. Paul St., Rochester, NY 14604-1391.
Web sites: http://www.rochester.lib.ny.us/cityhall
http://www.rnychamber.com

Sacramento, California

Population: 373,964 (41); **Pop. density:** 3,883 per sq. mi; **Pop. growth:** 1.2%. **Area:** 96.3 sq. mi. **Employment:** 171,419 employed, 7.4% unemployed. **Per capita income:** $23,459; % increase 1990-95: 17.6.
History: settled 1839; important trading center during California Gold Rush 1840s; became state capital 1854.
Transportation: metropolitan, executive, and cargo airports; 2 mainline transcontinental rail carriers; bus and light rail system; Port of Sacramento. **Communications:** 7 TV, 25 radio stations; 3 cable TV cos. **Medical facilities:** 8 hosp. **Educational facilities:** 2 univ., 4 community colleges. **Further Information:** Chamber of Commerce, 917 7th St., Sacramento, CA 95814.
Web sites: http://www.ci.sacramento.ca.us
http://www.metrochamber.org

St. Louis, Missouri

Population: 368,215 (43); **Pop. density:** 5,948 per sq. mi; **Pop. growth:** −7.2%. **Area:** 61.9 sq. mi. **Employment:** 159,307 employed, 7.5% unemployed. **Per capita income:** $25,170; % increase 1990-95: 23.1.
History: founded 1764 as a fur trading post by French; acquired by U.S. 1803; chartered as city 1822; lies on Mississippi R., near confluence with Missouri R.
Transportation: 1 intl. airport; major rail center, 17 trunk-line railroads; major inland port; 14 bus lines; 14 barge lines. **Communications:** 7 TV, 35 radio stations. **Medical facilities:** 65 hosp. **Educational facilities:** 6 univ., 25 colleges and seminaries. **Further Information:** St. Louis Community Development Agency, 1015 Locust St., Ste. 1200, St. Louis, MO 63101.
Web sites: http://www.st-louis.mo.us
http://stlouis.missouri.org

St. Paul, Minnesota

Population: 262,071 (62); **Pop. density:** 4,963 per sq. mi; **Pop. growth:** −3.7%. **Area:** 52.8 sq. mi. **Employment:** 136,648 employed, 3.9% unemployed. **Per capita income:** $27,436; % increase 1990-95: 24.0.
History: founded in early 1840s as "Pig's Eye Landing"; became capital of the Minnesota territory 1849 and chartered as St. Paul 1854.

Transportation: 1 intl., 1 business airport; 6 major rail lines; 3 interstate bus lines; pub. transit system. **Communications:** 6 TV, 35 radio stations. **Medical facilities:** 7 hosp. **Educational facilities:** 3 univ., 4 colleges; 1 technical, 3 first professional colleges. **Further information:** St. Paul Area Chamber of Commerce, 332 Minnesota St., Ste. N-205, St. Paul, MN 55101.
Web site: http://www.ci.stpaul.mn.us

St. Petersburg, Florida

Population: 238,585 (68); **Pop. density:** 4,030 per sq. mi; **Pop. growth:** −0.7%. **Area:** 59.2 sq. mi. **Employment:** 122,015 employed, 4.3% unemployed. **Per capita income:** $22,646; % increase 1990-95: 23.7.
History: founded 1888; inc. 1892.
Transportation: 2 airports (1 intl.); Amtrak; bus system; 1 full-service port. **Communications:** 12 TV, 22 radio stations. **Medical facilities:** 4 major hosp.; VA hosp. **Educational facilities:** 1 univ., 1 college, 1 law school, 1 junior college; 119 pub. schools. **Further information:** St. Petersburg Area Chamber of Commerce, PO Box 1371, St. Petersburg, FL 33731.
Web site: http://www.stpete.com

San Antonio, Texas

Population: 998,905 (9); **Pop. density:** 3,000 per sq. mi; **Pop. growth:** 6.8%. **Area:** 333 sq. mi. **Employment:** 484,106 employed, 4.9% unemployed. **Per capita income:** $20,034; % increase 1990-95: 26.2.
History: first Spanish garrison 1718; Battle at the Alamo fought here 1836; city subsequently captured by Texans; inc. 1837.
Transportation: 1 intl., 1 municipal airport; 4 railroads; 4 bus lines; pub. transit system; 25 common-carrier truck lines. **Communications:** 9 TV, 34 radio stations. **Medical facilities:** 38 hosp.; major medical center. **Educational facilities:** 17 univ. and colleges; 16 pub. school districts. **Further information:** Chamber of Commerce, 602 E. Commerce, P.O. Box 1628, San Antonio, TX 78296.
Web sites: http://www.tristero.com/usa/tx/
http://www.ci.sat.tx.us
http://www.sachamber.org

San Bernardino, California

Population: 181,718 (97); **Pop. density:** 3,298 per sq. mi; **Pop. growth:** 10.7%. **Area:** 55.1 sq. mi. **Employment:** 66,912 employed, 10.4% unemployed. **Per capita income:** $18,685; % increase 1990-95: 6.8.
History: Spanish missionaries arrived here 1810; Mormons est. first permanent settlement 1851; inc. 1854.
Transportation: 1 intl. airport nearby; Amtrak; rail transit system; bus systems. **Communications:** 5 TV, 22 radio stations. **Medical facilities:** 17 hosp. (county). **Educational facilities:** 1 univ., 2 community colleges; 51 pub. schools. **Further information:** San Bernardino Area Chamber of Commerce, 546 W. 6th St., PO Box 658, San Bernardino, CA 92402.
Web site: http://www.co.san-bernardino.ca.us/cities/
sanberna.htm

San Diego, California

Population: 1,151,977 (6); **Pop. density:** 3,555 per sq. mi; **Pop. growth:** 3.7%. **Area:** 324 sq. mi. **Employment:** 536,491 employed, 5.4% unemployed. **Per capita income:** $23,263; % increase 1990-95: 15.4.
History: claimed by the Spanish 1542; first mission est. 1769; scene of conflict during Mexican-American War 1846; inc. 1850.
Transportation: 1 major airport; 1 railroad; major freeway system; bus system; trolley system. **Communications:** 8 TV, 22 radio stations. **Medical facilities:** 28 hosp. **Educational facilities:** 5 univ., 7 colleges. **Further information:** Greater San Diego Chamber of Commerce, 402 W. Broadway, Ste. 1000, San Diego, CA 92101-3585.
Web sites: http://www.sannet.gov
http://www.sdchamber.org

San Francisco, California

Population: 734,676 (13); **Pop. density:** 15,732 per sq. mi; **Pop. growth:** 1.5%. **Area:** 46.7 sq. mi. **Employment:** 384,055 employed, 4.7% unemployed. **Per capita income:** $36,989; % increase 1990-95: 20.8.

History: nearby Farallon Islands sighted by Spanish 1542; city settled by 1776; claimed by U.S. 1846; became a major city during California Gold Rush 1849; inc. as city 1850; earthquake devastated city 1906.
Transportation: 1 major airport; intracity railway system; 2 railway transit systems; bus and railroad service; ferry system; 1 underwater tunnel. **Communications:** 14 TV; 35 radio stations. **Medical facilities:** 4 medical centers; 3 hosp. **Educational facilities:** 18 univ. and colleges; 2 fashion institutes. **Further information:** Convention & Visitors Bureau, 201 3d St., Ste. 900, San Francisco, CA 94103.
Web sites: http://www.ci.sf.ca.us
http://www.sfchamber.com

San Jose, California

Population: 816,884 (11); **Pop. density:** 4,769 per sq. mi; **Pop. growth:** 4.4%. **Area:** 171.3 sq. mi. **Employment:** 436,870 employed, 4.2% unemployed. **Per capita income:** $31,487; % increase 1990-95: 23.0.
History: founded by the Spanish 1777 between San Francisco and Monterey; state cap. 1849-51; inc. 1850.
Transportation: 1 intl. airport; 2 railroads; bus system. **Communications:** 4 TV, 14 radio stations. **Medical facilities:** 6 hosp. **Educational facilities:** 3 univ. and colleges. **Further information:** Chamber of Commerce, 180 S. Market St., San Jose, CA 95113.
Web sites: http://www.ipac.net/csj
http://www.sjchamber.com

Santa Ana, California

Population: 290,827 (55); **Pop. density:** 10,732 per sq. mi; **Pop. growth:** −1.0%. **Area:** 27.1 sq. mi. **Employment:** 140,409 employed, 7.3% unemployed. **Per capita income:** $27,420; % increase 1990-95: 8.3.
History: founded 1869; inc. as city 1886.
Transportation: 1 airport; 5 major freeways including main Los Angeles-San Diego artery; Amtrak. **Communications:** 14 TV, 28 radio stations. **Medical facilities:** 4 hosp. **Educational facilities:** 1 community college. **Further information:** Chamber of Commerce, 856 N. Ross St., PO Box 205, Santa Ana, CA 92701.
Web site: http://www.ci.santa-ana.ca.us

Seattle, Washington

Population: 520,947 (22); **Pop. density:** 6,209 per sq. mi; **Pop. growth:** 0.9%. **Area:** 83.9 sq. mi. **Employment:** 314,713 employed, 5.7% unemployed. **Per capita income:** $28,773; % increase 1990-95: 22.9.
History: settled 1851; inc. 1869; suffered severe fire 1889; played prominent role during Alaska Gold Rush 1897; growth followed opening of Panama Canal 1914; center of aircraft industry WWII.
Transportation: 1 intl. airport; 2 railroads; ferries serve Puget Sound, Alaska; Canada. **Communications:** 7 TV, 39 radio stations. **Medical facilities:** 40 hosp. **Educational facilities:** 7 univ., 6 colleges, 11 community colleges. **Further information:** Greater Seattle Chamber of Commerce, 1301 5th Ave., Ste. 2400, Seattle, WA 98101-2603.
Web sites: http://www.ci.seattle.wa.us
http://www.seattlechamber.com

Shreveport, Louisiana

Population: 196,982 (79); **Pop. density:** 1,998 per sq. mi; **Pop. growth:** −0.8%. **Area:** 98.6 sq. mi. **Employment:** 88,537 employed, 7.3% unemployed. **Per capita income:** $20,228; % increase 1990-95: 30.7.
History: founded 1833 near site of a 160-mi logjam cleared by Capt. Henry Shreve; inc. 1839; oil discovered 1906.
Transportation: 2 airports; 1 bus line. **Communications:** 6 TV, 16 radio stations. **Medical facilities:** 16 hosp. **Educational facilities:** 4 univ., 3 colleges. **Further information:** Chamber of Commerce, PO Box 20074, Shreveport, LA 71120.
Web sites: http://www.shreveport.
http://www.ci.shreveport.la.us
http://www.shreveportchamber.org

Spokane, Washington

Population: 182,701 (00); **Pop. density:** 3,449 per sq. mi; **Pop. growth:** 8.8%. **Area:** 55.9 sq. mi. **Employment:** 90,779 employed, 6.6% unemployed. **Per capita income:** $20,575; % increase 1990-95: 23.8.
History: settled 1872; inc. as village of Spokane Falls 1881; destroyed in fire 1889; reinc. as city of Spokane 1891.

Transportation: 1 intl. airport; 2 railroads; bus system. **Communications:** 5 TV, 25 radio stations. **Medical facilities:** 6 major hosp. **Educational facilities:** 8 univ. and colleges; 14 pub. school districts, 11 high schools. **Further information:** Chamber of Commerce, W. 1020 Riverside Ave., PO Box 2147, Spokane, WA 99210.
Web site: http://www.spokanecity.org
http://www.spokane.org/chamber

Stockton, California

Population: 222,633 (74); **Pop. density:** 4,233 per sq. mi; **Pop. growth:** 5.5%. **Area:** 52.6 sq. mi. **Employment:** 86,554 employed, 13.1% unemployed. **Per capita income:** $18,874; % increase 1990-95: 14.4.
History: site purchased 1842; settled 1847; inc. 1850; chief distributing point for agric. products of San Joaquin Valley.
Transportation: 1 airport; deepwater inland seaport; 7 railroads; 2 bus lines, county bus system. **Communications:** 5 TV stations. **Medical facilities:** 4 hosp.; regional burn, cancer, heart centers. **Educational facilities:** 6 univ. and colleges; 54 pub. schools. **Further information:** Chamber of Commerce, 445 W. Weber Ave., Ste. 220, Stockton, CA 95203.
Web sites: http://www.ci.stockton.ca.us
http://www.stocktonchamber.org

Tacoma, Washington

Population: 183,060 (96); **Pop. density:** 3,814 per sq. mi; **Pop. growth:** 3.6%. **Area:** 48 sq. mi. **Employment:** 88,907 employed, 7.2% unemployed. **Per capita income:** $20,945; % increase 1990-95: 20.8.
History: first European explorer of area was British Capt. George Vancouver 1792; colonized by Hudson's Bay Co. at Ft. Nisqually 1833; inc. 1884.
Transportation: 1 intl. airport; 2 railroads; transit system; Port of Tacoma. **Communications:** 6 TV stations. **Medical facilities:** 7 hosp.; Army Medical Center; VA facility. **Educational facilities:** 3 univ., 4 colleges. **Further information:** Chamber of Commerce, PO Box 1933, Tacoma, WA 98401.
Web sites: http://www.ci.tacoma.wa.us
http://www.tpchamber.org

Tampa, Florida

Population: 285,523 (57); **Pop. density:** 2,627 per sq. mi; **Pop. growth:** 2.0%. **Area:** 108.7 sq. mi. **Employment:** 149,932 employed, 4.8% unemployed. **Per capita income:** $22,646; % increase 1990-95: 23.7.
History: U.S. army fort on site 1824; inc. 1855.
Transportation: 1 intl. airport; Port of Tampa; CSX rail, bus system. **Communications:** 12 TV, 30 radio stations. **Medical facilities:** 17 hosp. **Educational facilities:** 3 univ. and colleges; 183 pub. schools. **Further information:** Chamber of Commerce, 401 E. Jackson St., PO Box 420, Tampa, FL 33601-0420.
Web site: http://www.ci.tampa.fl.us

Toledo, Ohio

Population: 322,550 (50); **Pop. density:** 4,002 per sq. mi; **Pop. growth:** –3.1%. **Area:** 80.6 sq. mi. **Employment:** 148,782 employed, 6.0% unemployed. **Per capita income:** $22,971; % increase 1990-95: 26.0.
History: site of Ft. Industry 1794; Battles of Ft. Meigs and Ft. Timbers 1812; figured in "Toledo War" 1835-36 between Ohio and Michigan over their borders; inc. 1837.
Transportation: 6 major airlines; 5 railroads; 98 motor freight lines; 2 interstate bus lines. **Communications:** 7 TV, 19 radio stations. **Medical facilities:** 8 major hosp. complexes. **Educational facilities:** 6 univ. and colleges. **Further information:** Toledo Area Chamber of Commerce, 300 Madison Ave., Ste. 200, Toledo, OH 43604.
Web site: http://www.toledochamber.com

Tucson, Arizona

Population: 434,726 (33); **Pop. density:** 2,781 per sq. mi; **Pop. growth:** 6.4%. **Area:** 156.3 sq. mi. **Employment:** 227,882 employed, 4.1% unemployed. **Per capita income:** $19,556; % increase 1990-95: 24.8.
History: settled 1775 by Spanish as a presidio; acquired by U.S. in Gadsden Purchase 1853; inc. 1877.
Transportation: 1 intl. airport; 2 railroads; bus system. **Communications:** 9 TV, 27 radio stations. **Medical facilities:** 12 hosp. **Educational facilities:** 3 univ., 1 college; 165 pub. schools. **Further information:** Chamber of Commerce, PO Box 991, Tucson, AZ 85702.
Web sites: http://www.ci.tucson.az.us
http://www.tucsonchamber.org

Tulsa, Oklahoma

Population: 374,851 (40); **Pop. density:** 2,043 per sq. mi; **Pop. growth:** 2.1%. **Area:** 183.5 sq. mi. **Employment:** 197,851 employed, 3.4% unemployed. **Per capita income:** $21,789; % increase 1990-95: 19.7.
History: settled in 1830s by Creek Indians; modern town founded 1882 and inc. 1898; oil discovered early 20th century.
Transportation: 1 intl. airport; 5 rail lines; 2 bus lines; transit bus system. **Communications:** 43 TV, 27 radio stations. **Medical facilities:** 10 hosp. **Educational facilities:** 8 univ. and colleges; 78 pub., 40 private schools. **Further information:** Metropolitan Tulsa Chamber of Commerce, 616 S. Boston Ave., Ste. 100, Tulsa, OK 74119-1298.
Web site: http://www.tulsachamber.com

Virginia Beach, Virginia

Population: 430,295 (35); **Pop. density:** 1,733 per sq. mi; **Pop. growth:** 9.5%. **Area:** 248.3 sq. mi. **Employment:** 198,521 employed, 4.1% unemployed. **Per capita income:** $20,332; % increase 1990-95: 18.4.
History: area founded by Capt. John Smith 1607; formed by merger with Princess Anne Co. 1963.
Transportation: 1 airport; 2 railroads; 2 bus lines; pub. transit system. **Communications:** 6 TV, 41 radio stations. **Medical facilities:** 2 hosp. **Educational facilities:** 1 univ., 2 colleges; 83 pub. schools. **Further information:** Virginia Beach Dept. of Economic Development, One Columbus Center, Ste. 300, Virginia Beach, VA 23462.
Web site: http://www.virginia-beach.va.us

Washington, District of Columbia

Population: 567,094 (20); **Pop. density:** 9,236 per sq. mi; **Pop. growth:** –6.6%. **Area:** 61.4 sq. mi. **Employment:** 248,963 employed, 8.5% unemployed. **Per capita income:** $30,824; % increase 1990-95: 19.1.
History: U.S. capital; site at Potomac R. chosen by George Washington 1790 on land ceded from VA and MD (portion S of Potomac returned to VA 1846); Congress first met 1800; inc. 1802; sacked by British, War of 1812.
Transportation: 3 intl. airports in area; Amtrak, 6 other passenger & cargo rail lines; Metrobus/Metrorail transit system; bus line. **Communications:** 5 TV, 61 radio stations. **Medical facilities:** 16 hosp. **Educational facilities:** 10 univ. and colleges. **Further information:** DC Chamber of Commerce, 1301 Pennsylvania Ave. NW, Ste. 309, Washington, DC 20004.
Web sites: http://www.ci. washington.dc.us
http://www.dcchamber.org

Wichita, Kansas

Population: 310,236 (54); **Pop. density:** 2,695 per sq. mi; **Pop. growth:** 2.0%. **Area:** 115.1 sq. mi. **Employment:** 160,027 employed, 4.8% unemployed. **Per capita income:** $22,823; % increase 1990-95: 20.4.
History: founded 1864; inc. 1871.
Transportation: 2 airports; 3 major rail freight lines; 2 bus lines. **Communications:** 5 TV, 26 radio stations. **Medical facilities:** 7 hosp., 2 psychiatric rehab. centers. **Educational facilities:** 2 univ., 1 college, 1 medical school; 96 pub. schools. **Further information:** Chamber of Commerce, 350 W. Douglas Ave., Wichita, KS 67202.
Web sites: http://www.ci.wichita.ks.us
http://www.southwind.net/ict
http://www.southwind.net/ict/wacc.html

Yonkers, New York

Population: 183,490 (94); **Pop. density:** 10,138 per sq. mi; **Pop. growth:** –2.4%. **Area:** 18.1 sq. mi. **Employment:** 84,856 employed, 5.5% unemployed. **Per capita income:** $30,896; % increase 1990-95: 21.0.
History: founded 1641 by the Dutch; inc. as town 1855; chartered as city 1872; directly north of NYC.
Transportation: intracity bus system; rail service. **Communications:** see New York City. **Medical facilities:** 3 hosp. **Educational facilities:** 1 college; 32 pub. schools. **Further information:** Chamber of Commerce, 20 S. Broadway, 12th fl., Yonkers, NY 10701.
Web sites: http://www.ci.yonkers.ny.us
http://www.yonkerschamber.com

BUILDINGS, BRIDGES, AND TUNNELS
Notable Tall Buildings in North American Cities
Source: Council on Tall Buildings and Urban Habitat; World Almanac Research; Sept. 1997

Lists include some structures that do not have stories and are not technically considered "buildings." Height is generally measured from sidewalk to roof, including penthouse and tower if enclosed as integral part of structure; stories generally counted from street level. Asterisk (*) denotes building still under construction. Year in parentheses is date of completion.

Albany, NY

Building	Ht. (ft.)	Stories
Office Tower, South Mall (1973)	589	44
State Office Bldg. (1930)	388	34

Atlanta, GA

Building	Ht. (ft.)	Stories
NationsBank Plaza (1992)	1,023	55
Sun Trust Bank Tower (1992)	880	63
One Peachtree Center (1992)	867	60
One Atlantic Center (1988)	820	50
Georgia-Pacific Corporation (1982)	754	52
191 Peachtree (1992)	740	50
Peachtree Plaza Hotel (1975)	723	70
Promenade Two (1989)	691	40
Bell South Telephone (1980)	677	47
GLG Grand (1993)	609	53
Concourse Tower #5 (1988)	570	32
First National Bank (1967)	562	44
State of Georgia Tower (1968)	556	44
Marriott Marquis (1985)	554	52
Concourse Tower #6 (1991)	553	32
Equitable Bldg. (1969)	453	34
101 Marietta Tower (1975)	446	36
Ravinia #3 (1991)	444	34
National Bank of Georgia (1961)	439	32
AT&T Long Line Bldg. (1975)	433	NA
Bell South Enterprises (1990)	428	28
Atlanta Plaza I (1986)	425	32
Park Place, 2660 Peachtree (1986)	420	40
Club Towers Apts. (1989)	410	38
One Park Tower (1961)	409	32
Peachtree Summit Number 1 (1976)	406	31
North Avenue Tower (1979)	403	26
Tower Place (1975)	401	29
First Union Bank (1987)	396	30
Atlanta Federal Center (1996)	388	25
*Monarch Plaza (1997)	387	24
Atlanta Hilton Hotel (1976)	383	32
Richard R. Russell, Federal Bldg. (1979)	383	26
Peachtree Center, Harris Bldg. (1976)	382	31
Hewlett-Packard Bldg. (1995)	381	27
Marquis One (1985)	378	30
Marquis Two (1987)	378	30
Trust Company Bank (1968)	377	28
Coastal State Insurance (1971)	377	27
Peachtree Center Cain Bldg. (1972)	376	30

Austin, TX

Building	Ht. (ft.)	Stories
One American Center (1982)	395	32
One Congress Plaza (1987)	391	30

Baltimore, MD

Building	Ht. (ft.)	Stories
U.S. Fidelity & Guaranty Co. (1973)	529	40
Maryland National Bank (1929)	509	34
William Donald Schaefer Tower	493	29
Commerce Place	454	30
World Trade Center Bldg. (1977)	405	32

Birmingham, AL

Building	Ht. (ft.)	Stories
Southtrust Tower (1986)	454	34
AmSouth/Harbert Plaza (1989)	390	30
AmSouth/Sonat Tower (1972)	390	30
South Central Bell Headquarters. Bldg.	390	30
First National Southern Natural	390	30

Boston, MA

Building	Ht. (ft.)	Stories
John Hancock Tower (1976)	788	60
Prudential Center (1964)	750	52
Federal Reserve Bldg. (1977)	604	32
Boston Company County Bldg.(1970)	601	41
One International Place	600	46
One Financial Center	598	47
First National Bank of Boston	591	37
Exchange Place, 53 State Street	554	40
John Hancock Bldg.	528	36
One Post Office Square	525	40
Shawmut Bank Bldg.	520	38
Sixty State Bldg.	509	38
Employers' Commercial Uniom Company	507	40
New England Merchant Bank Bldg.	500	40
U.S. Custom House, State Street	496	32
John Hancock Bldg. (1973)	495	26
State Street Bank Bldg.	477	34
100 Summer Street	450	33
Two International Place	433	33
McCormack Bldg.	401	22
Keystone Custodian Funds Bldg. (1971)	400	32
Harbor Towers (2 bldgs.) (1972) 85 E. India	400	40
65 E. India	396	40
125 High St. (1990)	399	30
One Devonshire Place	396	40
Saltonstall Office Bldg.	396	22
Westin Hotel, Copley Place	395	36
Federal Center (1988)	393	28
75 State St. (1988)	390	31
John F. Kennedy Bldg.	387	24
Marriott Hotel, Copley Place	382	38
One Beacon Street	380	38
Longfellow Towers, 80 Staniford St.	380	37

Buffalo, NY

Building	Ht. (ft.)	Stories
Marine Midland Center (1970)	529	40
City Hall	378	32

Calgary, Alberta

Building	Ht. (ft.)	Stories
Petro-Canada I (1984)	689	52
Bankers Hall (1989)	645	50
Calgary Tower (1988)	626	–
Canterra Tower (1988)	580	46
First Canadian Place (1982)	530	41
Calgary Eatons Centre	530	40
Norcen Tower (1976)	508	33
Western Canadian Place (1983)	507	41
Scotia Centre (1975)	504	38
Nova Bldg., 801 7th Ave. SW	500	37
Petro-Canada Centre, E. Tower (1984)	469	33
Two Bow Valley Square (1974)	468	39
Toronto Dominion Square- North (1976)	463	34
Canada Trust Tower (1991)	462	40
Shell Tower (1977)	460	34
Petro-Canada II (1983)	455	32
Toronto Dominion Square- South (1976)	449	33
Three Bow Valley Square (1979)	432	35
Fifth & Fifth Bldg. (1980)	410	34
Esso Plaza (twin towers)	435	34
Sovereign Life Bldg.	410	33
Pan Canadian Bldg.	410	28
Norcen Tower	408	33
Alberta Stock Exchange Bldg.	407	33
Sun Oil Bldg. (1975)	397	34
Amoco Centre (1988)	396	30
Western Canadian Place, South Tower (1983)	392	31
Western Centre (1971)	385	40
Calgary Place	385	30
Two Bow Valley Square (1975)	378	39
Monenco Place (1983)	378	28

Charlotte, NC

Building	Ht. (ft.)	Stories
NationsBank Corporate Center (1992)	871	60
One First Union Center (1988)	588	42
North Carolina NationsBank Plaza (1974)	503	40
Interstate Tower (1990)	459	32
Jefferson First Union Tower (1971)	433	32
Wachovia Center (1974)	420	32
Carillon (1991)	394	24
Charlotte Plaza (1982)	388	27

Chicago, IL

Building	Ht. (ft.)	Stories
Sears Tower (1974)	1,450	110
Amoco Bldg. (1973)	1,136	80
John Hancock Center (1969)	1,127	100
AT&T Corporate Center (1989)	1,007	60
Two Prudential Plaza (1990)	978	64
311 South Wacker Drive (1990)	959	65
900 North Michigan Ave. (1989)	871	66
Water Tower Place (1976)	859	74
One First National Plaza (1969)	850	60

(continued)

Chicago, IL (continued)

Building	Ht. (ft.)	Stories
Three First National Plaza (1981)	753	57
Chicago Title and Trust (1992)	742	51
Olympia Centre (1981)	725	63
One IBM Plaza (1973)	695	52
181 West Madison Street (1990)	680	50
77 West Wacker Drive (1992)	668	50
One Magnificent Mile (1983)	660	58
Civic Center (1965)	648	31
Lake Point Tower (1968)	645	70
1000 Lake Shore Plaza (1964)	640	55
Leo Burnett Bldg. (1989)	635	46
NBC Chicago Cityfront Center (1989)	627	34
Chicago Place (1990)	605	43
Prudential Plaza Bldg. (1955)	601	41
Heller International Tower (1992)	600	45
Marina City Twin Towers (1962)	588	61
Mid-Continental Plaza (1972)	582	50
North Pier Apartments (1990)	581	61
55 East Monroe Street	580	50
Madison Plaza (1983)	580	41
One Park Place (1984)	576	38
Stone Container Bldg. (1984)	575	40
190 South LaSalle Street (1986)	573	42
Onterie Center (1985)	570	58
Palmolive Bldg. (1929)	565	37
Morton International Bldg. (1990)	560	36
C. N. A. Towers (1972)	560	40
Newberry Plaza (1972)	560	56
Huron Plaza Apartments (1983)	560	54
Harbor Point (1975)	558	59
Pittsfield Bldg. (1927)	557	38
Chicago Temple (1923)	556	21
Kemper Bldg. (1929)	555	45
Civic Opera Bldg. (1929)	554	45
75 East Wacker Drive (1928)	554	42
30 North LaSalle Street (1975)	553	43
Boulevard Towers South (1985)	553	44
Brunswick Bldg. (1965)	550	38
Xerox Center (1979)	550	45
Two First National Bank (1972)	550	40
Kluczynski Bldg. (1971)	547	42
One South Wacker Dr. (1983)	540	40
LaSalle Natl. Bank (1934)	535	44
Frontier Towers (1973)	533	55
10 & 30 South Wacker Drive (1988)	525	38
River Plaza (1978)	524	56
Chicago Board of Trade Bldg. (1930)	524	45
Pure Oil Bldg. (1978)	523	40
35 East Wacker Drive (1926)	523	40
Parkshore Tower (1991)	523	61
United Insurance Company (1978)	522	41
111 East Chestnut Street (1972)	520	57
175 North Harbor Drive (1991)	520	55
Northwestern Atrium Center (1987)	516	40
One Financial Place (1984)	515	40
Hotel Inter-Continental Chicago (1929)	513	42
Quaker Tower (1987)	510	35
200 South Wacker Drive (1981)	505	38
Carbide & Carbon Bldg. (1929)	503	37
LaSalle-Wacker (1934)	491	41
American National Bank (1929)	479	40
Park Tower (1974)	476	54
Bankers Bldg. (1927)	476	41
American Furniture Mart (1926)	476	24
310 Center (1924)	475	37
333 West Wacker Drive (1983)	475	36
Continental Companies	475	45
Sheraton Hotel (1961)	474	42
666 North Lake Shore Drive (1923)	474	30
City Place (1990)	470	40
Harris Bank III (1976)	470	35
919 North Michigan Ave. (1929)	468	37
188 Randolph Tower	465	45
Tribune Tower (1925)	462	36
Chicago Marriott Hotel (1981)	460	45
Olympic Towers (1984)	460	45
Equitable Life Bldg. (1964)	457	35
Roanoke Bldg.	452	37
Gateway Center III (1972)	450	35

Cincinnati, OH

Building	Ht. (ft.)	Stories
Carew Tower (1930)	574	49
First National Bank Center	545	28
Central Trust Tower (1913)	495	34
312 Walnut Street (1990)	468	36
Fifth Third Center (1970)	460	31
Atrium Two (1984)	428	30
DuBois Tower	423	32

Building	Ht. (ft.)	Stories
Chemed Center (1990)	410	32
Central Trust Tower (1913)	408	28
Cincinnati Commerce Center (1984)	402	29

Cleveland, OH

Building	Ht. (ft.)	Stories
Society Center (1991)	950	57
Terminal Tower (1930)	708	52
BP America (1986)	658	45
Erieview Plaza Tower (1964)	529	40
*Federal Courthouse (2000)	460	25
One Cleveland Center (1983)	450	31
Bank One Center (1991)	446	28
A. J. Celebreeze Federal Bldg. (1968)	440	32
Justice Center (1976)	420	26
*Federal Bldg.	419	32
National City Center (1980)	410	35
900 Euclid (1971)	383	29
Cleveland Trust Tower I	383	29

Columbus, OH

Building	Ht. (ft.)	Stories
Rhodes Office Bldg. (1973)	624	41
State Office Bldg. (1973)	592	41
LeVeque Tower	555	47
Ohio Bureau of Worker's Compensation & Ind. Comm. (1990)	530	33
Huntington Center	512	37
Verne-Riffe State Office Tower	503	33
Nationwide Plaza	485	40
Franklin County Courthouse	464	27
One Riverside Plaza	456	31
Borden Bldg. (1974)	438	34
Three Nationwide Plaza (1989)	408	27

Dallas, TX

Building	Ht. (ft.)	Stories
NationsBank Plaza (1985)	921	72
Renaissance Tower (1975)	886	56
Bank One Center (1987)	787	60
Texas Commerce Tower (1987)	738	55
Fountain Place (1986)	721	60
First Interstate Bank (1986)	716	62
L T V Center (1985)	686	54
Trammell Crow Center (1987)	686	49
First City Center (1982)	655	50
Thanksgiving Tower (1982)	645	50
Arco Tower (1983)	629	49
First National Bank (1964)	625	52
Elm Place (1965)	625	50
Republic Bank Tower (1964)	598	50
Republic Bank Tower 2 (1980)	598	50
Lincoln Plaza (1984)	579	45
One Lincoln Plaza	574	45
Harwood @Bryan Corp. Center (1982)	562	36
Cityplace Center (1989)	560	42
Southland Life Insurance Bldg. (1958)	550	41
Maxus Energy Tower (1980)	550	34
2001 Bryan Street Tower (1972)	512	40
Olympia & York Tower (1982)	483	36
San Jacinto Tower (1982)	456	33
Republic Bank Bldg. (1954)	452	36
M-Bank Bldg. (1943)	452	31
Stouffer Hotel	451	29
One Dallas Centre (1979)	448	30
One Main Place (1968)	445	34
1600 Pacific Bldg. (1964)	434	32
L T V Tower (1964)	434	32
Mobil Bldg. (1921)	430	31
Mercantile National Bank (1937)	430	31
Magnolia Bldg. (1923)	430	27
Fidelity Union Tower (1959)	400	33

Dayton, OH

Building	Ht. (ft.)	Stories
Kettering Tower (1970)	405	30
Winters Bank Bldg. (1970)	404	30

Denver, CO

Building	Ht. (ft.)	Stories
Republic Plaza (1984)	714	56
City Center 4 (1982)	709	54
One Norwest Center (1983)	698	52
Colombia Plaza	600	50
Anaconda Bldg. (1978)	580	40
1999 Broadway (1985)	544	43
MCI Tower (1982)	527	42
Brooks Tower (1965)	504	42
Amoco Bldg (1980)	450	36
17th Street Plaza (1982)	438	32
First of Denver (1974)	431	32
One Denver Place (1983)	428	34

Building	Ht. (ft.)	Stories
One Tabor Center (1984)	408	30
Energy Center I.	405	29
Manville Plaza (1989)	404	29
Colorado National. Bank (1982)	389	26
First National Bank (1982)	385	28
Security Life Bldg. (1967)	384	32
1616 Glenarm Bldg. (1981)	384	31

Des Moines, IA

Building	Ht. (ft.)	Stories
Principal Financial Group Bldg. (1990) . .	630	44

Detroit, MI

Building	Ht. (ft.)	Stories
The Westin (1977)	739	73
Renaissance Center. Complex (1977) . . .	739	73
One Detroit Center (1990)	620	43
City National Bank Bldg. (1928)	562	47
Penobscot Bldg. (1928)	557	46
Renaissance Center II-V(4 bldgs.) (1976)	534	40
Guardian (1928)	485	40
Book Tower (1925)	472	35
Madden Bldg. (1988	470	26
Prudential 3000 Town Center	448	32
Cadillac Tower (1928)	437	40
David Stott (1930)	436	38
Consolidated Gas Co.	430	32
ANR Bldg. (1962) 1 Woodward.	430	30
Isher (1928)	420	28
Town Center (1975).	405	32
McNamara Federal Office Bldg. (1974) . .	393	27
2000 Prudential Town Ctr.	392	28

Edmonton, Alberta

Building	Ht. (ft.)	Stories
Manulife Place (1983)	479	36
AGT Tower (1971).	441	33
Canada Trust Tower (1982)	440	31
Commerce Place (1990)	409	30
Toronto Dominion Bank Tower (1976) . . .	400	30
Metropolitan Place (1980)	397	31
Oxford Tower (1978)	390	27
TD Tower (1975)	386	27

Fort Worth, TX

Building	Ht. (ft.)	Stories
City Center Tower II (1984)	546	38
Burnett Plaza (1983)	538	40
Continental Plaza (1982)	520	40
Texas Commerce Tower(1982)	475	33
Bank One Tower (1975)	457	35
Fort Worth National Bank.	454	37
Texas Bldg. (1955)	420	30
Continental National Bldg.	380	30

Hartford, CT

Building	Ht. (ft.)	Stories
City Place (1983).	535	38
Travelers Ins. Co. Bldg. (1919)	527	34
Goodwin Square (1990)	522	30
Hartford Plaza (1967)	420	22

Honolulu, HI

Building	Ht. (ft.)	Stories
First Hawaiian Bank (1995)	430	27
Waterfront Towers (1990)	400	46
Nauru Tower (1991).	400	45
Imperial Plaza (1992).	400	40
Ala Moana Hotel	396	38

Houston, TX

Building	Ht. (ft.)	Stories
Texas Commerce Tower (1982)	1,000	75
First Interstate Plaza (1983)	972	71
Transco Tower (1983)	901	64
NationsBank Center (1984)	780	56
Heritage Plaza, (1987)	762	53
1100 Louisiana Bldg. (1980).	748	55
InterFirst Plaza (1980)	744	55
Houston Industries Plaza	741	53
1600 Smith Street (1984)	732	55
Gulf Tower (1982)	725	52
One Shell Plaza (1971)		
(not incl. 285-ft. TV tower)	714	50
Enron Bldg. (1983)	692	50
Four Allen Center (1304)	691	50
Three Allen Center (1980)	686	50
One Houston Center (1978)	682	46
First City Tower (1981)	663	49
First City, Tex. Financial Center (1984) . .	662	47
Brookhollow Central Two	656	15

Building	Ht. (ft.)	Stories
1100 Milam Bldg. (1974)	651	47
San Felipe Plaza (1984)	625	45
Exxon Bldg. (1964)	606	44
The America Tower (1983)	590	42
Two Houston Center (1974)	581	40
Marathon Oil Tower (1983)	562	41
1200 Milam Bldg.	558	NA
United Bank Plaza (1984)	550	45
1415 Louisiana Tower (1983)	550	44
Dresser Tower (1974).	550	40
MW Kellogg Tower (1973)	550	40
Pennzoil Place (1976) (2 bldgs.)	522	36
Two Allen Center (1978)	521	36
Entex Bldg. (1971)	518	35
1201 Louisiana (1971)	518	35
The Huntington (1982)	503	34
Tenneco Bldg. (1963)	500	32
Conoco Bldg. (1973).	465	32
One Allen Center (1973)	452	34

Indianapolis, IN

Building	Ht. (ft.)	Stories
Bank One Center (1989)	700	51
AUL Tower (1981)	533	38
Market Tower (1988)	515	32
National Bank Tower (1971)	504	37
Riley Towers (1963) (2 bldgs.)	427	30
300 North Meridian Bldg. (1988)	408	28

Jacksonville, FL

Building	Ht. (ft.)	Stories
Barnett Center (1990)	617	42
Independent Life and Accident Insur. (1974)	535	37
Southern Bell (1983).	447	32
Gulf Life Tower (1967)	433	27

Kansas City, MO

Building	Ht. (ft.)	Stories
One Kansas City Place (1988)	626	42
AT&T Town Pavilion (1986).	590	38
Hyatt Regency (1980)	504	40
Kansas City Power and Light Bldg (1931).	476	33
City Hall (1936)	443	29
Fidelity Bank and Trust Bldg. (1931)	426	35
1201 Walnut (1991)	425	30
Federal Office Bldg (1946).	417	36
Commerce Tower (1963)	407	31
City Center Square (1977).	402	30
Southwestern Bell Bldg. (1913)	379	28

Las Vegas, NV

Building	Ht. (ft.)	Stories
*Stratosphere Tower (1997)	1,049	114
New York- New York Hotel and Casino (1997)	525	48
Sahara Hotel	376	37
Las Vegas Hilton (1995)	375	30

Little Rock, AR

Building	Ht. (ft.)	Stories
TCBY Towers (1986)	546	40
First National Bank (1975).	454	33
Worthen Bank & Trust (1969)	375	24

Los Angeles, CA

Building	Ht. (ft.)	Stories
First Interstate World Center (1989)	1,018	75
First Interstate Tower (1974)	858	62
Two California Plaza (1992)	750	52
Gas Company Tower (1991)	749	50
333 South Hope Bldg. (1975)	743	55
Wells Fargo Tower (1983)	740	54
777 Tower	725	52
Sanwa Bank Plaza (1990)	717	53
Atlantic Richfield Tower.	699	52
Bank of America Tower.	699	52
444 South Flower Street	625	48
Crocker Citizens Tower (1969)	620	42
Jay Square	597	48
One California Plaza.	578	42
Theme Towers (1974) (2 bldgs.)	576	43
Century Plaza Towers (2 bldgs.)	571	44
IBM Tower.	560	45
Citicorp Plaza.	534	42
1999 Ave. of the Stars (1989)	533	39
Manulife Tower (1990)	517	37
Union Bank Plaza (1966)	512	41
MCA-Getty.	500	36
WTC Bldg.	496	36
Fox Plaza	492	34
ARCO Center.	462	32
Equitable Life (1969).	454	34

(continued)

Los Angeles, CA *(continued)*

Building	Ht. (ft.)	Stories
City Hall (1927)	454	29
Occidental Life (1965)	452	32
Mutual Benefit Life Bldg. (1970)	435	31
Warner Center Plaza III	415	25
Broadway Plaza (1973)	414	32
1900 Ave. of Stars	398	27
One Wilshire (1968)	395	28
The Evian	390	31
400 S. Hope Street	375	26

Louisville, KY

Building	Ht. (ft.)	Stories
Providian Center (1992)	549	35
First National Bank	512	40
National City Tower (1972)	495	40
Citizens Fidelity Bank (1972)	420	30
Humana Bldg (1985)	417	30

Memphis, TN

Building	Ht. (ft.)	Stories
100 N. Main Bldg.	430	37
Commerce Square	396	31

Mexico City, Mexico

Building	Ht. (ft.)	Stories
Petrolaos Mexicanos (1984)	702	52
Latin American Tower (1956)	668	55
Hotel de Mexico (1972)	573	48
Nonoalco Tlateloco Tower (1962)	417	25

Miami, FL

Building	Ht. (ft.)	Stories
Southeast Financial Center (1983)	738	55
International Place (1987)	562	35
Metro-Dade Administration Bldg.	510	30
Florida National Tower (1986)	484	35
One Biscayne Corporation.	456	40
Barnett Tower (1986)	450	33
Courthouse Center (1986)	405	30
First Federal Savings and Loan	375	32
Sunbank International Center (1973)	375	31

Milwaukee, WI

Building	Ht. (ft.)	Stories
First Wisconsin Bank (1973)	625	42
Faison Bldg., 100 East (1989)	549	37
Milwaukee Center (1987)	426	29
411 Bldg., 411 East Wisconsin (1983)	408	30
Northwestern Mutual Tower (1989)	395	19

Minneapolis, MN

Building	Ht. (ft.)	Stories
IDS Center (1972)	775	57
Norwest (1988)	774	57
First Bank Place (1992)	774	53
Multifoods Tower (1983)	608	51
Piper Jaffray Tower (1984)	627	42
Dain Bosworth Plaza	539	40
Pillsbury Bldg.(1981)	529	40
150 South Fifth	498	36
Metropolitan Center (1987)	496	31
Plaza VII, 45 South 7th (1987)	468	36
Foshay Tower (1929) (not incl. 160-ft. antenna tower)	447	32
Hennepin County Convention Center (1974)	403	24
Marriott Hotel (1983)	379	33

Montreal, Quebec

Building	Ht. (ft.)	Stories
1100 Rue de la Gauchetiere	669	45
1250 Boulevard Rene Levesque	640	45
Place Ville Marie (1962)	630	47
Place Victoria (1964)	624	47
Royal Bank Bldg. (1961)	612	54
Canadian Imperial Bank of Commerce (1962)	590	45
Place Desjardins (1976) (3 bldgs.)		
La Tour du Sud	498	40
La Tour du L'Est.	428	32
La Tour du Nord	355	27
Le Chateau Champlain (1967)	480	38
Les Cooperants (1987)	479	34
CIL House (1962)	450	33
Holiday Inn Hotel (1977)	450	38
Place Montreal Trust (1988)	449	32
Le Port Royal (1964)	425	33
Le Cartier Apts. (1964).	425	32
Tour Terminal (1966)	400	30
Royal Bank	397	22
Banque Canadienne National	390	32
Sun Life Bldg.	390	26
Place International de L'Aviation (1975)	380	28

Nashville, TN

Building	Ht. (ft.)	Stories
South Central Bell Bldg.	617	33
Third National Financial Center	490	30
National Life and Accident Insur. Co.	452	31
Landmark Center	409	30
Nashville City Center (1987)	402	27
James K. Polk State Office Bldg.	392	32
Stouffer Hotel (1987)	385	35

Newark, NJ

Building	Ht. (ft.)	Stories
Natl. Newark & Essex Bank.	465	36
Raymond-Commerce Bldg.	448	36
Park Plaza Bldg..	400	26

New Orleans, LA

Building	Ht. (ft.)	Stories
One Shell Square (1972)	697	51
Place St. Charles (1985)	645	53
Plaza Tower (1970)	531	45
Energy Centre (1984)	530	39
LL&E Tower (1987)	481	36
Sheraton Hotel (1985)	478	47
Marriott Hotel (1974)	450	42
Texaco Bldg. (1983)	442	33
Canal Place One (1979)	439	32
Bank of New Orleans (1970)	438	31
International Trade Mart (1967).	407	33

New York, NY

Building	Ht. (ft.)	Stories
One World Trade Center (1972)	1,368	110
Two World Trade Center (1973)	1,362	110
Empire State Bldg. (1931)	1,250	102
(incl. 164-ft. TV tower)	1,414	–
Chrysler Bldg. (1930)	1,046	77
American International Bldg.(1932)	950	66
40 Wall Street (1930)	927	70
Citicorp Center (1977)	915	59
G.E. Bldg. (1933)	850	70
Cityspire (1989)	814	72
One Chase Manhattan Plaza (1961)	813	60
Met Life (1963).	808	59
Woolworth Bldg. (1913)	792	57
One Worldwide Plaza (1989)	778	47
Carnegie Hall Tower (1991)	757	60
Equitable Tower (1985)	752	51
One Penn Plaza (1972)	750	57
1251 Ave. of Americas (1972)	750	54
J. P. Morgan Headquarters (1989)	745	50
One Liberty Plaza (1973)	743	54
20 Exchange Place (Citibank) (1931)	741	55
World Financial Center (1984)	739	53
One Astor Plaza (1972)	730	54
Solow Bldg. (1979)	725	50
Metropolitan Life Insurance Tower (1909)	720	52
Metropolitan Tower (1985)	716	68
Union Carbide Bldg. (1960)	707	52
General Motors Bldg. (1968)	705	50
500 5th Ave. (1930)	700	60
Nine West 57th Street (1974)	689	50
Marine Midland Bldg. (1966)	688	52
55 Water Street (1972)	687	53
Chemical Bank World Headquarters (1963)	685	50
Iris Bldg. (1972)	685	50
Four Seasons Hotel (1993)	682	52
Chanin Bldg.(1929).	680	55
Trump International Hotel and Tower (1970)	679	52
Lincoln (1939)	673	53
Citicorp (Queens) (1990)	673	50
McGraw Hill (1972.	670	51
1633 Broadway (1972)	670	48
Trump Tower (1982)	664	58
599 Lexington Ave. (1988)	653	47
Museum Tower Apts. (1985)	650	58
712 5th Ave. (1990)	650	56
550 Madison Ave. (1983)	648	37
American Brands Bldg. (1967)	647	47
AT&T Headquarters (1932)	647	27
Irving Trust (1931)	645	50
World Financial Center Tower B (1986)	645	50
RCA Bldg. (1931)	642	51
345 Park Ave. (1968).	634	44
One New York Plaza (1969)	630	50
Grace Plaza (1972).	630	50
Home Insurance Co. Bldg. (1966)	630	45
New York Telephone.(1975)	630	40
Central Park Place (1988)	628	56
One Dag Hammarskjold Plaza (1972)	628	50
888 7th Ave. (1971)	628	45
Burlington House (1969)	625	50

Building	Ht. (ft.)	Stories
Waldorf-Astoria (1931).	623	47
Olympic Tower (1976).	620	51
10 East 40th Street (1929)	620	48
101 Park Ave. (1982).	618	46
General Electric Bldg. (1930)	616	50
New York Life (1928).	615	33
750 7th Ave.	615	35
Rihga Royal Hotel	610	54
17 State Street	610	41
Penney Bldg. (1964)..	609	46
IBM Headquarters (1983)	603	43
780 3d Ave.	600	50
Jacob K. Javits Federal Bldg. (1960). . . .	593	45
Celanese Bldg. (1973).	592	45
U.S. Court House (1976)	590	37
Kalikow Hotel	588	58
Time & Life Bldg. (1959)	587	48
Federal Office Bldg. (1968)	587	41
Stevens Tower	580	42
Cooper Bregstein Bldg. (1969).	580	38
Municipal Bldg. (1914)	580	34
Millennium (1995)	580	46
1185 Avenue of the Americas (1971) . . .	580	42
520 Madison Ave. (1983)	577	42
One Madison Square Plaza (1973)	576	42
Park Ave. Plaza (1981)	575	44
World Financial Center Tower A (1986). .	575	42
One Financial Square (1987)	575	37
Marriott Marquis Hotel (1985)	574	50
Westvaco Bldg. (1967).	574	42
Socony Mobil Bldg. (1956)	572	42
780 3d Ave. (1983)	570	49
Sperry Rand Bldg. (1963).	570	43
600 3d Ave. (1971).	570	42
One Bankers Trust Plaza (1974)	565	40
New York General (1965)	565	35
Hemsley Palace Hotel (1980)	563	51
30 Broad Street (1932).	562	48
Park Ave. Tower (1986)	561	36
Sherry-Netherland Bldg. (1927).	560	40
Continental Can Company (1962).	557	41
Three Park Ave. (1975)	556	42
Continental Corp	555	41
Sperry & Hutchinson (1964)	555	41
Galleria (1975), 117 East 57th Street . . .	552	57
Interchem Bldg..	552	45
919 3d Ave.	550	47
NYNEX (1979)	550	45
Burroughs Bldg. (1963)	550	44
151 East 44th Street	550	44
Bankers Trust Bldg. (1912)	547	37
Transportation Bldg. (1928)	546	44
Equitable Bldg. (1915)	542	36
1166 Ave. of Americas (1974)	540	44
Equitable Life (1959)	540	42
One Brooklyn Bridge Plaza (1976)	540	42
Paine Webber Bldg. (1961)	540	42
Ritz Tower, Park Ave. & 57th Street	540	41
Bankers Trust, 6 Wall Street.	540	39
1700 Broadway (1969).	533	42
Downtown Athletic Club	530	45

Oakland, CA

Building	Ht. (ft.)	Stories
Ordway Bldg.(1985).	404	28
Kaiser Bldg. (1958)	390	28

Oklahoma City, OK

Building	Ht. (ft.)	Stories
Liberty Tower (1971)	500	36
First National Bank (1974)	493	33
City National Bank Tower (1985)	440	32
First Oklahoma Tower (1982)	434	31
Kerr-McGee Center (1973).	393	30

Omaha, NE

Building	Ht. (ft.)	Stories
Woodmen Tower (1970)	440	30
Enron Bldg. (1960)	400	18

Orlando, FL

Building	Ht. (ft.)	Stories
Sun Bank Center Tower (1988)	441	35
Orange County Courthouse (1997).	416	24
Barnett Bank Center (1988)	404	28

Philadelphia, PA

Building	Ht. (ft.)	Stories
One Liberty Place (1987)	945	61
Two Liberty Place (1990)	848	58
Mellon Bank Center (1990).	792	54

Building	Ht. (ft.)	Stories
Bell Atlantic Tower (1991)	739	53
Blue Cross Tower (1990)	700	50
Commerce Sq., #1 (1990)	572	40
Commerce Sq., #2 (1992)	572	40
City Hall Tower (1901), (incl. 37-ft. statue of William Penn.).	548	7
1818 Market St. (1974)	500	40
Phila. Saving Fund Society (1932)	492	39
Fidelity Mutual Life Bldg. (1971).	492	38
Meridan Bank (1972)	492	38
PSFS Bldg. (1932)	491	NA
Provident Mutual Life (1983)	491	40
Central Penn Natl. Bank (1970)	490	36
Centre Square (2 towers) (1973)	490/416	38/32
5 Penncenter (1970).	488	36
Industrial Valley Bank Bldg. (1969)	482	32
Philadelphia National Bank (1930)	475	25
Two Mellon Plaza (1930).	450	30
Two Logan Square (1987).	435	34
2000 Market Street (1973).	435	29
Two Girard Plaza (1930)	412	30
Fidelity Bank (1927)	405	30
Two Girard Plaza	404	30
Lewis Tower (1929)	400	33
One Logan Square (1982)	400	32
1500 Locust Street (1973).	390	44
Philadelphia Electric Co. (1970).	384	27
I. N. A. Annex.	383	27
Academy House.	377	37
The Drake (1928)	375	33
Penn Mutual Life (1931)	375	20

Phoenix, AZ

Building	Ht. (ft.)	Stories
Valley Bank Center (1972)	483	40
Arizona Bank Downtown (1976).	407	31
Phoenix Plaza I (1989)	397	20
Phoenix Plaza II(1990).	397	20

Pittsburgh, PA

Building	Ht. (ft.)	Stories
USX Tower (1970)	841	64
One Mellon Bank Center (1983)	725	54
One PPG Place	635	40
Fifth Avenue Place (1987).	616	31
One Oxford Centre	615	45
Gulf Bldg.	582	38
University of Pittsburgh (1936).	535	42
Mellon Bank Bldg. (1951)	520	41
One Oliver Plaza (1968)	511	40
Grant (1928).	485	40
Koppers (1929)	475	34
Two PNC Plaza	445	34
Equibank Bldg. (1975)	442	34
CNG Tower (1987)	430	32
Pittsburgh National Bldg. (1972)	428	30
One PNC Plaza	424	30
Alcoa Bldg. (1953)	410	30

Portland, OR

Building	Ht. (ft.)	Stories
Wells Fargo Tower	546	40
First National Bank of Oregon (1973)	536	40
Koin Tower Plaza	509	35

Providence, RI

Building	Ht. (ft.)	Stories
Industrial Trust Bldg. (1927)	428	26
Rhode Island Hospital Trust Co. (1973) . .	394	28

Raleigh, NC

Building	Ht. (ft.)	Stories
BB & T/2 Hanover Square (1991)	431	29
First Union Capitol Center (1991)	390	29

Richmond, VA

Building	Ht. (ft.)	Stories
James Monroe Bldg..	450	29
City Hall (incl. penthouse)	425	17
Crestar Bank HQ. Bldg..	400	24
Federal Reserve Bank	393	26
Medical College of Virginia Univ. Hospital.	376	12

Rochester, NY

Building	Ht. (ft.)	Stories
Xerox Tower (1967)	443	30
Lincoln First Tower (1973).	392	27

Sacramento, CA

Building	Ht. (ft.)	Stories
Wells Fargo Center.	402	30

St. Louis, MO

Building	Ht. (ft.)	Stories
Gateway Arch (1965)	630	–
Metropolitan Square Tower (1988)	593	42
One Bell Center (1984)	588	44
Mercantile Trust Bldg. (1975)	485	35
Laclede Gas. Bldg. (1969)	400	34
Boatmen's Plaza (1982)	420	30
Bell Telephone Bldg. (1926)	398	33
Civil Courts Bldg. (1929)	387	13
One City Center (1986)	375	25

St. Paul, MN

Building	Ht. (ft.)	Stories
Minnesota World Trade Center	471	36
Galtier Plaza's Jackson Tower	440	46
First Natl. Bank Bldg.	417	32

Salt Lake City, UT

Building	Ht. (ft.)	Stories
L.D.S. Church Office Bldg.	420	30

San Antonio, TX

Building	Ht. (ft.)	Stories
Tower of the Americas (1968)	622	–
Marriott Rivercenter (1988)	546	38
Weston Centre (1988)	444	32
Tower Life (1929)	404	30
NationsBank Plaza (1983)	387	28
NIX Professional Bldg. (1931)	375	23

San Diego, CA

Building	Ht. (ft.)	Stories
One American Plaza (1991)	500	34
Symphony Tower (1989)	499	34
Hyatt Regency San Diego (1992)	495	39
Emerald-Shapery Center (1991)	450	30
One Harbor Drive (1992)	424	41
First Interstate Bank (1985)	398	23
Meridian Condominiums (1985)	395	27
Union Bank (1969)	388	27
California First Bank (1966)	388	25
Columbia Centre (1982)	379	27

San Francisco, CA

Building	Ht. (ft.)	Stories
Transamerica Pyramid (1972)	853	48
Bank of America (1969)	779	52
345 California Bldg.	615	48
101 California Street (1986)	600	48
California Center (1983)	600	47
Pacific Gas and Electric Bldg. (1970)	598	35
Embarcadero Center, No. 4 (1982)	570	45
Security Pacific Bank (1970)	569	45
One Market Plaza, Spear Street (1976)	565	43
Southern Pacific (1975)	564	43
Wells Fargo Bldg. (1966)	561	43
Standard Oil Bldg. (1948)	551	37
One Sansome-Citicorp.	550	39
Shaklee Bldg. (1981)	537	38
Crocker Plaza (1967)	532	38
AETNA Bldg. (1969)	529	38
525 Market Street (1973)	529	38
First and Market Bldg.	529	38
Metropolitan Life Bldg. (1973)	524	38
Crocker National Bank	500	38
333 Bush Street	495	40
Hilton Hotel (1971)	493	46
Pacific Gas & Electric (1970)	492	34
Union Bank Bldg. (1972)	490	37
Pacific Insurance Co. Bldg. (1972)	476	34
Bechtel Bldg. (1977)	475	33
333 Market Bldg. (1979)	474	33
Hartford Insurance (1965)	446	33
Mutual Benefit Life (1969)	438	32
Russ Bldg. (1928)	435	31
Telephone Bldg. (1925)	435	26
Pacific Gateway (1983)	416	30
Levi Strauss Bldg. (1974)	412	31
Embarcadero Center Complex III (1976)	412	31
101 Montgomery Street	405	28
California State Automobile Assn. (1974)	399	29
Alcoa Bldg. (1967)	398	27
St. Francis Hotel (1970)	395	32
Shell Bldg. (1928)	386	29
St Francis Hotel Addition (1972)	378	32
Del Monte Bldg.	378	28
Mills Tower (1970)	376	22

Seattle, WA

Building	Ht. (ft.)	Stories
Columbia Seafirst Center (1985)	943	76
Two Union Square (1989)	740	56
Washington Mutual Tower (1988)	735	55
AT&T Gateway Tower (1989)	722	62
Key Tower	722	62
Seattle First National Bank (1969)	609	50
Space Needle (1962)	605	–
Pacific First Center (1989)	580	44
First Interstate Center (1983)	574	48
Rainier National Bank (1976)	569	51
Bank of California (1974)	543	43
Seafirst 5th Ave. Plaza (1981)	543	42
L. C. Smith Tower (1925)	520	42
Security Pacific Bank Tower (1977)	514	42
Henry M. Jackson Federal Bldg. (1974)	514	34
Federal Office Bldg. (1973)	499	38
520 Pike Tower (1984)	498	29
Key Tower (1986)	493	40
Federal Office Bldg.	487	37
1600 Bell Plaza	480	33
US West Communications	466	33
One Union Square (1981)	456	38
1111 3d Ave. Bldg. (1980)	454	38
Westin Bldg. (1981)	409	34
Westin Hotel (1969)	397	40
Unigard Financial Center (1973)	389	27
Washington Plaza Hotel (1969)	380	40
Century Square (1986)	379	30

Tampa, FL

Building	Ht. (ft.)	Stories
100 N. Tampa (1992)	579	42
Barnett Plaza (1986)	577	42
One Tampa Center (1981)	537	39
SunTrust Financial Centre (1992)	525	36
First Financial Tower (1973)	458	36
NationsBank Plaza (1988)	454	33

Toledo, OH

Building	Ht. (ft.)	Stories
One SeaGate. (1962)	404	30
Owens Illinois Headquarters Bldg. (1982)	404	30
Owens-Corning Fiberglas Tower (1970)	400	30

Toronto, Ontario

Building	Ht. (ft.)	Stories
CN Tower (1975) (world's tallest self-supporting structure)	1,821	–
First Canadian Place (1975)	952	72
Scotia Plaza (1989)	902	68
Canada Trust Tower (1990)	863	51
Commerce Court West (1973)	784	57
Toronto-Dominion Bank Tower (1967)	731	56
Bay-Wellington Tower (1990)	705	47
Royal Trust Tower (1969)	609	46
Royal Bank Plaza(1976)	567	41
Manu-Life Centre (1975)	525	51
Eaton Centre (1990)	494	34
AETNA Life Bldg. (1986)	489	36
Workers' Compensation Bldg. (1995)	487	33
Two Bloor Street West (1974)	480	34
Old Bank Of Commerce (1930)	477	34
Exchange Tower (1981)	475	36
Cadillac/Fairview Tower (1982)	466	36
Continental Bank (1980)	465	35
Commerce Court North- C.I.B.C. (1930)	464	34
Cadillac- Fairview Tower (1982)	460	36
Palace Place (1992)	455	46
Palace Pier (1978)	453	46
Richmond Adelaide Centre (1980)	450	35
Sheraton Centre (1972)	443	43
Hudson's Bay Centre (1974)	442	35
Two Bloor Street East (1974)	442	34
Royal York Hotel (1929)	439	26
Harbour Castle Hotel	438	38
Ernst & Yonge Tower (TD Centre) (1990)	438	31
Four Seasons Sheraton Hotel (1972)	428	43
Leaside Towers (2 bldgs.) (1970)	423	44
Commercial Union Tower (TD Centre) (1974)	420	32
Metro Hall (1991)	420	27
Commercial Union Tower (1974)	419	32
Hotel Plaza II	415	41
Leaside Towers (1970)	410	43
Young-Eglinton Centre-Triathlon Tower	408	30
Harbour Square Apts.	403	34
390 Bay Street (1973)	394	33

Tulsa, OK

Building	Ht. (ft.)	Stories
Bank of Oklahoma Tower	667	52
Cityplex Towers	640	60
First National Tower	516	41
Mid-Continent Tower	513	36

Tulsa, OK *(continued)*

Building	Ht. (ft.)	Stories
Fourth National Bank of Tulsa	412	21
National Bank of Tulsa.	400	24
Cities Service Bldg.	388	28
University Club Tower	377	32

Vancouver, British Columbia

Building	Ht. (ft.)	Stories
Harbour Centre (1976).	479	28
Royal Bank Tower (1973).	468	37
Granville Square	466	28
Vancouver Center (1977).	462	36
Scotiabank Tower	451	36
Bentall IV (1981)	450	35
Park Place (1984)	450	35
Toronto Dominion Bank	440	30

Building	Ht. (ft.)	Stories
Harbour Centre (1977)	426	21
200 Granville Square	403	30
Bentall III (1974)	400	31
Sheraton Landmark Hotel	394	41
First Bank Tower	386	30

Winnipeg, Manitoba

Building	Ht. (ft.)	Stories
Trizec (1980)	494	32
Toronto Dominion Centre (1989)	413	33
Richardson Bldg. (1969)	439	34
Commodity Exchange Tower (1980)	384	31

Winston-Salem, NC

Building	Ht. (ft.)	Stories
Wachovia Bldg. (1995).	460	28
Wachovia Bldg. (1965)	410	27

Some Other Notable Tall Buildings in North American Cities

Building	City	Ht. (ft.)	Stories
One Canada Square	London, Ont.	777	50
Skylon	Niagara Falls, Ont.	774	–
Vehicle Assembly Bldg.	Cape Canaveral, FL	552	40
State Capitol (1932)	Baton Rouge, LA	460	34
One Summit Square	Fort Wayne, IN	442	26
State Capitol	Lincoln, NE	432	40
Taj Mahal	Atlantic City, NJ	429	51

Building	City	Ht. (ft.)	Stories
First Natl. Bank	Mobile, AL	420	33
Century Twenty One	Hamilton, Ont.	418	43
Complex G (1972)	Quebec City, Que.	415	33
Lexington Financial Ctr.	Lexington, KY	410	30
United American Bank.	Knoxville, TN	400	30
Kanawha Valley Bldg.	Charleson, WV	384	20
Otis Research Tower (1986)	Bristol, CT	383	29

Notable International Buildings

Source: Council on Tall Buildings and Urban Habitat, Lehigh Univ.; as of Sept. 1997

List includes some structures that do not have stories and are not technically considered buildings.

Building (year completed or to be completed)	Ht. (ft.)	Stories
Oriental Pearl Television Tower (1995), Shanghai, China.	1,535	–
Petronas Tower I (1997), Kuala Lumpur, Malaysia	1,483	88
Petronas Tower II (1997), Kuala Lumpur, Malaysia	1,483	88
*Jin Mao Bldg. (1998), Shanghai, China.	1,379	88
*Plaza Rakyat (1998), Kuala Lumpur, Malaysia	1,254	77
Central Plaza (1992), Hong Kong, China	1,227	78
Bank of China Tower (1989), Hong Kong, China	1,209	70
*T & C Tower (1997), Kaoshiung, Taiwan.	1,140	85
Shun Hing Square (1996), Shenzen, China	1,066	81
Sky Central Plaza (1997), Guangzhou, China.	1,056	80
*Chicago Beach Tower Hotel (1998), Dubai,UAE	1,053	60
Baiyoke Tower II (1997), Bangkok, Thailand.	1,050	90
*BDNI Center-TowerA (1999), Jakarta, Indonesia	1,040	62
Eiffel Tower (1889), Paris, France	984	–
**Ryugyong Hotel (1995), Pyongyang, N. Korea	984	105
Landmark Tower (1993), Yokohama, Japan.	971	70
*Jubilee St./Queen's Rd. Central (1998), Hong Kong, China.	958	69
Overseas Union Bank Centre(1986), Singapore	919	66
United Overseas Bank Plaza (1992), Singapore	919	66
Republic Plaza (1995), Singapore	919	66
Commerzbank Tower (1997), Frankfurt, Germany.	850	60

Building (year completed or to be completed)	Ht. (ft.)	Stories
Messeturm. Bldg. (1990), Frankfurt, Germany	843	63
Gate Tower (1996), Osaka, Japan.	833	56
World Trade Center (1995), Osaka, Japan.	827	55
BNI City Tower (1995), Jakarta, Indonesia.	820	46
Korea Life Ins. Co. (1985), Seoul, S. Korea	817	60
Kompleks Tun Abdul Razak Bldg. (1985), Penang, Malaysia	804	65
Shin Kong Life Tower (1993), Taipei, Taiwan.	801	51
Malayan Bank(1988), Kuala Lumpur, Malaysia	799	50
Metropolitan Gov't Bldg. (1991), Tokyo, Japan.	797	48
Rialto Tower (1985), Melbourne, Australia.	794	56
*BDNI Center-Tower B (1999), Jakarta, Indonesia.	788	45
*JR Central Towers (1999), Nagoya, Jpn.	787	53
*Graha Kuningan (1998), Jakarta, Indonesia.	784	52
Moscow State Univ. (1953), Moscow, Russia.	784	26
Empire Tower (1994), Kuala Lumpur, Malaysia	781	62
Singapore Treasury Bldg. (1986), Singapore	771	52
Opera City Tower (1997), Tokyo, Japan	768	54
Shinjuku Park Tower (1994), Tokyo, Japan.	764	52
Palace of Culture & Science (1955), Warsaw, Poland	758	42
MLC Centre (1978), Sydney, Australia	748	65

* construction not completed. ** not yet certified as safe for occupancy.

Notable Bridges in North America

Source: Federal Highway Administration, Bridge Division, U.S. Dept. of Transportation;World Almanac Research

Asterisk (*) designates railroad bridge. Double asterisk (**) designates bridge under construction.
Span of a bridge is the distance between its supports.

Suspension

Year	Bridge	Location	Main span (ft.)
1964	Verrazano-Narrows	New York, NY.	4,260
1937	Golden Gate	San Fran. Bay, CA	4,200
1957	Mackinac Straits	Sts. of Mackinac, MI	3,800
1931	Geo. Washington.	Hudson R., NY–NJ.	3,500
1950	Tacoma Narrows.	Tacoma, WA.	2,800
1936	San. Fran.-Oakland Bay[1]	San Fran. Bay, CA	2,310
1939	Bronx-Whitestone	East R., NY	2,300
1970	Pierre Laporte	Quebec, Canada.	2,190
1960	Seaway Skyway	Ogdensburg, NY.	2,150
1968	Del. Memorial	Wilmington, DE.	2,150
1957	Walt Whitman	Philadelphia, PA.	2,000
1929	Ambassador	Detroit, MI–Can.	1,850
1961	Throgs Neck	Long Is. Sound, NY.	1,800
1917	Quebec.	Quebec, Canada.	1,800
1926	Benjamin Franklin	Philadelphia, PA.	1,750
1924	Bear Mt.	Hudson R., NY.	1,632
1952	Wm. Preston La. Mem.[2]	Sandy Point, MD.	1,600
1952	Chesapeake Bay	Sandy Point, MD.	1,600
1903	Williamsburg	East R., NY.	1,600

Year	Bridge	Location	Main span (ft.)
1969	Newport.	Narragansett Bay, RI	1,600
1883	Brooklyn	East R., NY.	1,595
1939	Lion's Gate	Burrard Inlet, B.C.	1,550
1930	Mid-Hudson	Poughkeepsie, NY.	1,500
1963	Vincent Thomas	L. A. Harbor, CA.	1,500
1909	Manhattan	East R., NY.	1,470
1955	MacDonald Bridge	Halifax, Nova Scotia.	1,447
1970	A. Murray Mackay.	Halifax, Nova Scotia.	1,400
1936	Triborough	East R., NY.	1,380
1931	St. Johns	Portland, OR	1,207
1929	Mount Hope	RI	1,200
1960	Ogdensburg	St. Lawrence R., NY.	1,150
1965	Bidwell Bar Bridge	Oroville, CA.	1,108
1964	Middle Fork Feather	CA	1,105
1939	Deer Isle	ME	1,080
1931	Oiman Kenton Memorial	Ohio R., KY	1,060
1936	Ile d'Orleans	St. Lawrence R., Quebec	1,059
1867	John A. Roebling	Ohio R., KY.	1,057
1971	Dent	Clearwater Co., ID.	1,050
1900	Miampimi	Mexico	1,030
1849	Wheeling	Ohio R., WV.	1,010

Cantilever

Year	Bridge	Location	Main span (ft.)
1917	Québec Bridge	St. Lawrence R., Quebec	1,800
1974	Commodore Barry	Chester, PA	1,622
1988	Mississippi R.	New Orleans, LA	1,575
1995	Mississippi R.	Gramercy, LA	1,460
1936	Transbay	San Fran. Bay, CA	1,400
1968	Mississippi R.	Baton Rouge, LA	1,235
1955	Tappan Zee	Hudson R., NY	1,212
1930	Lewis and Clark	Longview, WA–OR	1,200
1976	Patapsco River	Baltimore, MD	1,200
1909	Queensboro	East R., N.Y.	1,182
1927	Carquinez Strait	CA	1,100
1958	Parallel Span	CA	1,100
1930	Jacques Cartier	Montreal, Canada	1,097
1968	Isaiah D. Hart	Jacksonville, FL	1,088
1956	Richmond[3]	San Fran. Bay, CA	1,070
1929	Grace Memorial	Charleston, SC	1,050
1980	Newburgh-Beacon	Hudson R., NY	1,000
1949	Martin Luther King	St. Louis, MO	963
1975	Caruthersville	Mississippi R., MO–TN	920
1977	Saint Marys	Saint Marys, WV–OH	900
1969	Silver Memorial	Pt. Pleasant, WV–OH	900
1981	Ravenswood	WV	900
1987	Carl Perkins	Ohio R., KY	900
1988	Mississippi R.	Natchez, MS	875
1938	Blue Water	Pt. Huron, MI	871
1972	Mississippi R.	Vicksburg, MS	870
1972	N. Fork American R.	Auburn, CA	862
1940	*Baton Rouge	Mississippi R., LA.	848
1899	*Cornwall	St. Lawrence R.	843
1961	Mississippi R.	Greenville, MS	840
1940	Rte. 82	Mississippi R., AR	840
1961	Rte. 49	Mississippi R., AR	840
1963	Brent Spence	KY–OH	830
1963	Mississippi R.	Donaldsonville, LA	825
1940	Mississippi R.	Vicksburg, MS	825
1929	Clark Memorial	Ohio R., KY	820
1961	Campbellton-Cross Pt.	New Brunswick, Can.	815
1935	Rip Van Winkle	Catskill, NY.	800
1938	Cairo	Ohio R., IL–KY	800
1932	Washington Mem.	Seattle, WA	800
1936	McCullough	Coos Bay, OR.	793
1935	Huey P. Long[4]	New Orleans, LA.	790
1892	Memphis	Mississippi R., TN	790
1949	Rte. 55	Mississippi R, AR–TN	790
1910	*P&LE RR Bridge	Ohio R., PA	750
1932	Bi-State Vietnam Gold Star	Henderson, KY.	720
1904	*Norfolk Southern RR	Ohio R., OH.	700
1943	*Pit River	Redding, CA.	620
1941	Columbia R.	Kettle Falls, WA	600
1954	Columbia R.	Umatilla, OR.	600
1954	Columbia R.	The Dalles, OR.	576
1968	W. 17th St.	Huntington, WV.	562

Simple Truss

Year	Bridge	Location	Main span (ft.)
1976	Chester	Chester, WV.	745
1929	Irvin S. Cobb	Ohio R.,IL–KY.	716
1922	*Tanana R.	Nenana, AK	700
1967	I-77, Ohio R.	Williamstown, WV	650
1917	MacArthur[4]	St. Louis, IL–MO	647
1992	St. Charles	Missouri R, MO.	625
1933	Atchafalaya	Morgan City, LA	608
1924	*Castleton	Hudson R., NY.	598
1937	Delaware R.	Easton, PA	550
1930	Swindell Bridge	Pittsburgh, PA.	545
1952	Allegheny R. Tpk.	Pittsburgh, PA.	534
1930	*Martinez	Martinez, CA.	528
1951	Rankin	Pittsburgh, PA.	525
1914	Old Brownsville	Brownsville, PA.	520
1906	Donora-Webster	Donora-Webster, PA	515
1909	Hulton	Pittsburgh, PA.	505
1967	Tanana R.	AK	500

Steel Truss

Year	Bridge	Location	Main span (ft.)
1988	Glade Creek	Raleigh Co., WV	784
1973	Atchafalaya R.	Krotz Springs, LA	780
1972	Piscataqua R.	NH–ME	756
1972	Atchafalaya R.	Simmesport, LA	720
1957	SR-3, Rappahannock R.	Middlesex Co., VA.	648
1978	Atchafalaya R.	Morgan City, LA	607
1959	Summit	Summit, DE.	600
1969	Reedy Point	Delaware City, DE.	600
1938	US-22	Delaware R., NJ	540
1955	Interstate (I-5)	Columbia R., OR–WA	531
1910	McKinley, St. Louis[4]	Mississippi R., MO.	517
1972	Mississippi R.	Muscatine, IA	512
1896	Newport	Ohio R., KY	511

Year	Bridge	Location	Main span (ft.)
1989	US 190, Atchafalaya R.	Krotz Springs, LA.	506
1970	Lake Koocanusa	Lincoln Co., MT	500
1931	Lucy Jefferson Lewis	Cumberland R., KY	500
1958	Lake Oahe	Gettysburg, SD	500
1958	Lake Oahe	Mobridge, SD.	500

Continuous Truss

Year	Bridge	Location	Main span (ft.)
1966	Columbia R. (Astoria)	OR–WA.	1,232
1977	Francis Scott Key	Baltimore, MD.	1,200
1995	**Central	Ohio R., KY–OH	850
1943	Dubuque	Mississippi R., IA	845
1966	Charles Braga	Fall River, MA	840
1956	Earl C. Clements[5]	Ohio R., IL–KY	825
1929	U.S. 31	Ohio R., IN–KY	820
1953	John E. Mathews	Jacksonville, FL	810
1950	Maurice J. Tobin	Boston, MA.	801
1940	Gov. Nice Memorial	Potomac River, MD	800
1957	Kingston-Rhinecliff	Hudson R., NY.	800
1992	Mark Clark Expwy. I-526	Cooper R., Charleston,SC	800
1986	Rochester-Monaca	Rochester-Monaca,PA	780
1940	U.S. 231	Ohio R., IN	750
1974	Carroll L. Cropper	Ohio R., IN–KY	750
1981	Sewickley	Sewickley, PA	750
1984	13th St. Bridge, Ohio R.	Ashland, KY.	740
1959	Monaca-E. Rochester	Monaca-E. Rochester, PA.	730
1976	Betsy Ross	Philadelphia, PA	729
1929	U.S. 421	Ohio R., IN–KY	727
1967	Matthew E. Welsh[6]	Mauckport, IN	725
1994	6th St.	Huntington, WV	720
1962	U.S. 41	Ohio R., IN–KY.	720
1970	Vanport	Vanport, PA.	715
1962	Champlain	Montreal, Que.	707
1962	John F. Kennedy[7]	Ohio R., IN–KY	701
1973	Girard Point	Philadelphia, PA	700
1954	PA Tpk., Delaware R.	Philadelphia, PA	682
1949	George Platt	Philadelphia, PA	680
1938	Port Arthur-Orange	TX	680
1926	Cape Girardeau	Mississippi R., MO	677
1929	*Cincinnati	Ohio R., OH.	675
1946	Chester	Mississippi R, IL.	670
1970	Gulfgate	Port Arthur, TX.	664
1994	Williamstown-Marietta	Williamstown, WV	650
1955	Jefferson City	Missouri R., MO.	640
1930	Quincy	Mississippi R., IL	628
1961	Shippingport	Shippingport, PA	620
1959	US 181, over harbor	Corpus Christi, TX	620
1935	Bourne-Sagamore	Cape Cod Canal, MA	616
1965	Clarion R. (I-80)	Clarion, PA.	612
1975	Donora-Monessen	Donora-Monessen, PA	608
1991	Hoffstadt Creek	Mt. St. Helens, WA.	600
1957	Blatnik	Duluth, MN	600
1965	Rio Grande Gorge	Taos, NM	600
1991	Jefferson City	Missouri R., MO.	596
1962	W. Branch Feather R.	Oroville, CA.	576
1967	Glenwood	Pittsburgh, PA	567
1936	Mark Twain Mem.	Hannibal, MO.	562
1957	Mackinac	Mackinac Straits, MI.	560
1932	Pulaski Skyway	Passaic R.-Hackensack R., NJ	550
1973	Gold Star Memorial	New London, CT	540
1966	Emlenton	Emlenton, PA.	540
1936	Homestead High Level	Pittsburgh, PA	534
1959	Martinez	Benicia-Martinez, CA	528
1960	Brownsville High Level	Brownsville, PA	518
1971	Grandad	Elk River, ID	504
1945	Mansfield-Dravosburg	Pittsburgh, PA.	500

Continuous Box and Plate Girder

Year	Bridge	Location	Main span (ft.)
1982	Houston Ship Chan.	Houston, TX.	750
1967	San Mateo-Hayward #2	San Fran. Bay, CA.	750
1977	Intracoastal Canal	Gibbstown, LA.	750
1976	Intracoastal Canal	Forked Is., LA	750
1969	San Diego-Coronado[8]	San Diego Bay, CA	660
1987	Umatilla, Columbia R.	OR–WA.	660
1994	Acosta	Jacksonville, FL	630
1981	Douglas	Juneau, AK	620
1976	Wax L. Outlet	Calumet, LA.	618
1981	Glenn Jackson (I-205)	Columbia R., OR–WA	600
1963	Poplar St.	St. Louis, MO.	600
1976	Stanislaus River	Sonora, CA	580
1982	Illinois R.	Pekin, IL	550
1982	I-440	Arkansas R., AR.	540
1980	US-64, Tennessee R.	Savannah, TN	525
1988	Mon City	Monongahela, PA	520
1965	McDonald-Cartier	Ottawa, Canada.	520
1984	Columbia R.	Richland, WA.	450
1986	Veterans	Pittsburgh, PA.	440
1987	SR 76, Cumberland R.	Dover, TN	440

Year	Bridge	Location	Main span (ft.)
1987	SR 20, Tennessee R...	Perryville, TN	440
1970	Willamette R., I-205	West Linn, OR	430
1974	I-430.	Arkansas R., AR.	430
1984	FAU 3456, TN R.	Chattanooga, TN.	420
1965	I-24, Tennessee R.	Marion Co., TN	420
1978	Snake R.	Clarkston, WA.	420
1975	36th St.	Charleston, WV.	420
1974	Dunbar-S. Charleston	S. Charleston, WV.	420

Continuous Plate

Year	Bridge	Location	Main span (ft.)
1973	Ship Channel (I-610)	Houston, TX	630
1971	W. Atchafalaya	Henderson, LA	573
1992	State Route 76	Paris, TN	525
1981	Illinois 23	Illinois R., IL	510
1968	Trinity R.	Dallas, TX	480
1978	San Joaquin R.	Antioch, CA	460
1977	Thomas Johnson Mem.	Solomons, MD	451
1992	Cuba Landing Bridge	Tennessee R., TN	450
1979	Lewis	St. Louis, MO	450
1975	I-129.	Missouri R., IA–NE	450
1967	Mississippi R.	La Crosse, WI.	450
1972	Whiskey Bay Pilot	Ramah, LA	425
1966	I-480.	Missouri R., IA–NE	425
1972	I-80	Missouri R., IA–NE	425
1987	I-435.	Missouri R., KS–MO	425
1983	US-36.	Missouri R., KS–MO	425
1972	I-635, Kansas City	Missouri R., KS–MO	425
1978	I-24	Cumberland R., KY	420

Cable-Stayed

Year	Bridge	Location	Main span (ft.)
1986	Annacis (Alex Fraser)	Vancouver, BC	1,526
1993	Quetzalapa Bridge	Quetzalapa, Mexico	1,391
1988	Dames Point	Jacksonville, FL	1,300
1995	Houston Ship Channel	Baytown, TX	1,250
1983	Hale Boggs Memorial	Luling, LA	1,222
1987	Sunshine Skyway	Tampa Bay, FL	1,200
1988	Tampico/Panuco R.	Mexico	1,181
1988	ALRT Fraser River Bridge	Vancouver, BC	1,115
1990	Talmadge Mem.	Savannah, GA	1,100
1993	Mezcala	Mex. City/Acapulco. Hwy.	1,024
1978	Pasco-Kennewick	Columbia R., WA	981
1984	Coatzacoalcos R.	Mexico	919
1985	E. Huntington	E. Huntington, WV.	900
1987	Bayview Bridge	Quincy, IL.	900
1970	Burton Bridge	New Brunswick, Canada	850
1990	Weirton-Steubenville	WV–OH	820
1969	Papineau-Leblanc	Montreal, PQ	790
1991	Cochrane	Mobile, AL	780
1994	Clark Bridge	Alton, IL	756
1995	Chesapeake & Delaware Canal Bridge	Dover-Wilmington, DE	750
1966	Longs Creek	New Brunswick, Canada	713
1967	Hawkshaw	New Brunswick, Canada	713
1993	Quetzalapa Bridge	Quetzalapa, Mexico	699
1993	Burlington Bridge	Burlington, IA	660
1991	Neches R.	Port Arthur-Orange, TX	640
1989	James River Bridge.	Richmond., VA	630

I-Beam Girder

Year	Bridge	Location	Main span (ft.)
1980	Interstate 20	Shreveport, LA	438
1988	Route 18.	Weston's Mill Pond, NJ	276

Steel Arch

Year	Bridge	Location	Main span (ft.)
1977	New River Gorge	Fayetteville, WV	1,700
1931	Bayonne (Kill Van Kull)	Bayonne, NJ.	1,652
1973	Fremont	Portland, OR.	1,255
1964	Port Mann.	Vancouver, BC	1,200
1967	Trois-Rivieres	St. Lawrence R., Que.	1,100
1967	Lavioleete	Three Rivers, Canada	1,100
1992	Roosevelt Lake	Roosevelt Lake, AZ	1,080
1959	Glen Canyon.	Page., AZ	1,028
1962	Lewiston-Queenston	Niagara R., Ont.	1,000
1976	Perrine	Twin Falls, ID	993
1941	Rainbow Bridge.	Niagara Falls, NY	984
1917	*Hell Gate	East R., N.Y.	977
1977	Moundsville.	Ohio R., WV	912
1992	I-255, Miss. R.	St. Louis, MO	909
1972	I-40, Miss. R.[9]	AR–TN	900
1936	Henry Hudson	Harlem R., N.Y.	840
1967	Lincoln Trail Bridge	Ohio R., IN–KY	825
1929	I-57, Miss. R.	Cairo, IL	821
1980	I-65, Mobile R.	Mobile, AL	800
1961	I-64, Ohio R.	IN	800
1978	I-470 Bridge, Ohio R.	Wheeling, WV.	780
1930	West End	Pittsburgh, PA.	780
1996	Navajo Bridge	Glen Canyon, AZ	726

Concrete Arch

Year	Bridge	Location	Main span (ft.)
1993	Natchez Trace Pkwy.	Franklin, TN.	582
1993	Lake Street Bridge	St. Paul, MN	556
1971	Selah Creek (twin)	Selah, WA.	549
1968	Cowlitz R.	Mossyrock, WA	520
1931	Westinghouse	Pittsburgh, PA	460
1923	Cappelen	Minneapolis, MN	435
1930	Jack's Run	Pittsburgh, PA.	400

Segmental Concrete

Year	Bridge	Location	Main span (ft.)
1997	Confederation Bridge	Prince Edward Isl., NB	820
1982	Jesse H, Jones Memorial	Houston, TX	750
1978	Shubenacadie River	S. Maitland, Nova Scotia	790
1992	Narragansett Bay Crossing	Jamestown, RI	674
1986	WB I-82 (Columbia R.)	Umatilla, OR	660
1976	Stanislaus River	Parrets Ferry. CA	640
1992	Jamestown-Verranzzano	Jamestown, RI	636
1981	Gastineau Channel Br.	Juneau, AK	620
1991	Veterans Memorial Centennial Bridge.	Coeur d'Alene, ID.	520
1974	Pine Valley Creek.	Pine Valley, CA	450
1988	Zilwaukee Bridge (twin)	Zilwaukee, MI	392
1985	Red River Bridge	Boyce, LA	370

Twin Concrete Trestle [10]

Year	Bridge	Location	Total length
1979	I-55/I-10.	Manchac, LA.	181,157
1969	L. Pontchartrain Cswy.	Mandeville, LA.	126,720
1972	Atchafalaya Flwy.	Baton Rouge, LA.	93,984
1963	L. Pontchartrain	Slidell, LA.	28,547
1983	Interstate 310.	Kenner, LA	25,925

Concrete Slab Dam [10]

Year	Bridge	Location	Total length
1927	Conowingo Dam.	MD	4,611
1952	SR-4, Roanoke R.	Mecklenburg Co., VA	2,785
1936	Hoover Dam.	Lake Mead, NV	1,324

Drawbridges

Vertical Lift

Year	Bridge	Location	Main span (ft.)
1959	*Arthur Kill	NY–NJ	558
1965	Pennsylvania Railroad	Kirkwood-Mt. Pleasant, DE	548
1935	*Cape Cod Canal	Cape Cod, MA.	544
1961	*Delair	Delaware R., NJ.	542
1937	Marine Parkway	Jamaica Bay, N.Y.	540
1931	Burlington-Bristol	Delaware R., NJ–PA.	540
1908	*Willamette R.	Portland, OR	521
1968	Second Narrows	Vancouver, B.C.	493
1912	*A-S-B Fratt	Kansas City, MO	428
1945	*Harry S Truman	Kansas City, MO	427
1955	Roosevelt Island	East R., N.Y.	418
1980	US-17, James R.	Isle of Wight, Co., VA	415
1932	*M-K-T R.R.	Missouri R., MO	414
1969	Cape Fear Mem.	Wilmington, NC	408
1930	Aerial.	Duluth, MN	386
1962	Burlington	Ontario, Can.	370
1941	Main Street	Jacksonville, FL.	365
1922	*Cincinnati	Ohio R., OH.	365
1967	SR-156, James R.	Prince George Co., VA	364
1957	Industrial Canal	New Orleans, LA	360
1950	Red R.	Moncla, LA	360
1936	Tribo	Harlem R., N.Y.	344
1961	Corpus Christi Harbor[4]	Corpus Christi, TX.	344
1939	U.S. 1&9, Passaic R.	Newark, NJ	333
1930	*Martinez	Martinez, CA	328
1960	St. Andrews Bay.	Panama City, FL	327
1929	*Penn-Lehigh	Newark Bay, PA.	322
1987	Industrial Canal	New Orleans, LA	320
1920	*Chattanooga	Tennessee R., TN	310

Bascule

Year	Bridge	Location	Main span (ft.)
1940	Lorain	Black R., OH	333
1917	SR-8, Tennessee R.	Chattanooga, TN	306
1956	Duwamish R.	Seattle, WA	300
1955	Chehalis R.	Aberdeen, WA	288
1968	Elizabeth R.	Chesapeake, VA	280
1913	Broadway	Portland, OR	278
1954	Fuller Warren	Jacksonville, FL.	267

Swing Bridges

Year	Bridge	Location	Main span (ft.)
1927	Fort Madison[4]	Mississippi R., IA	545
1991	SW. Spokane St.	Seattle, WA.	480
1930	Rigolets Pass.	New Orleans, LA	400

(continued)

Swing Bridges (continued)

Year	Bridge	Location	Main span (ft.)
1950	Douglass Memorial ...	Washington, DC ...	386
1945	Lord Delaware.......	Mattaponi R., VA...	252

Swing Span

Year	Bridge	Location	Main span (ft.)
1952	US-17.............	York R., VA	500
1897	*Duluth..........	St. Louis Bay, MN ..	486
1899	*C.M.&N.R.R.......	Chicago, IL.......	474

Year	Bridge	Location	Main span (ft.)
1913	Rt. 82, Conn.-R.	E. Haddam, CT	465
1914	*Coos Bay	OR	458

Floating Pontoon

Year	Bridge	Location	Floating length
1963	Evergreen Pt.......	Seattle, WA.....	7,578
1961	Hood Canal	Pt. Gamble, WA....	6,521
1993	Lacey V. Murrow[11] ..	Seattle, WA.....	6,620
1989	Third Lake Washington	Seattle, WA.....	5,811

(1) Swing span bridge with 2 spans of 2,310 ft. each. (2) A second bridge in parallel was completed in 1973. (3) The Richmond Bridge has twin spans 1,070 ft. each. (4) Railroad and vehicular bridge. (5) Two spans each 825 ft. (6) Two spans each 707 ft. (7) Two spans each 700 ft. (8) Two spans each 660 ft. (9) Two spans each 900 ft. (10) Length listed is total length of bridge (11) Replaces the original Lacey V. Murrow bridge, which opened in 1940 and sank in 1990.

Oldest U.S. Bridge in Continuous Use

Built in 1697, the stone-arch Frankford Ave. Bridge crosses Pennypack Creek in Philadelphia, PA. A 3-span bridge with a total length of 75 ft., it was constructed as part of the King's Road, which eventually connected Philadelphia to New York.

Oldest U.S. Covered Bridge in Continuous Use

Completed in 1827, the double-span, 278-ft. Haverhill Bath Bridge spans the Ammonoosuc River, between the towns of Bath and Haverhill, NH.

Some Notable International Bridges

Span of bridge is the distance between its supports. Asterisk (*) designates under construction as of Sept. 1997.

Suspension

Year	Bridge	Location	Main span (ft.)
1998*	Akashi Kaikyo	Japan........	6,529
1998*	Storebælt (East Bridge)	Denmark	5,328
1981	Humber.........	England	4,626
1999*	Jiangyin Yangtze	China........	4,544
1997	Tsing Ma[1]	China........	4,518
1997*	Hoga Kusten	Sweden	3,970
1988	Minami Bisan-Seto ..	Japan........	3,609
1988	Bosphorus II	Turkey	3,576
1973	Bosphorus I	Turkey	3,524
1999*	Kurushima III	Japan........	3,379
1999*	Kurushima II.....	Japan........	3,346
1966	Tagus River[2]	Portugal	3,323
1964	Forth Road	Scotland	3,300
1988	Kita Bisan-Seto......	Japan........	3,248
1966	Severn	England	3,241
1988	Shimotsui Strait	Japan........	3,084

Cantilever

Year	Bridge	Location	Main span (ft.)
1890	Forth[3] (rail)	Scotland	1,710
1974	Nanko	Japan	1,673

Steel Arch

Year	Bridge	Location	Main span (ft.)
1932	Sydney Harbour	Australia	1,650
1967	Zdakov	Czech Republic ...	1,244
1962	Thatcher	Panama Canal Zone	1,128
1961	Runcorn-Widnes....	England	1,082
1935	Birchenough	Zimbabwe	1,080

(1) Double-decked road and rail bridge. (2) Railroad and highway bridge. (3) Two spans of 1,710 ft. each.

Concrete Arch

Year	Bridge	Location	Main span (ft.)
1980	Krk I	Croatia.	1,280
1964	Gladesville	Australia	1,000
1964	Amizade	Brazil	951
1963	Arrabida.	Portugal	886
1943	Sando.	Sweden	866

Steel Plate and Box Girder

Year	Bridge	Location	Main span (ft.)
1974	President Costa e Silva	Brazil	984
1956	Sava I.	Yugoslavia	856
1966	Zoobrüke	Germany	850

Cable-Stayed

Year	Bridge	Location	Main span (ft.)
1999*	Tatara	Japan.........	2,920
1995	Pont de Normandie ..	France	2,808
1996	Quingzhou Minjang ..	China	1,985
1993	Yangpu.	China	1,975
1997*	Xupu	China	1,936
1998*	Meiko Chuo	Japan.........	1,936
1991	Skarnsundet.	Norway	1,739
1995	Tsurumi Tsubasa.	Japan.........	1,673
2000*	Oresund.	Denmark/Sweden .	1,614
1991	Ikuchi	Japan.........	1,608
1994	Higashi Kobe	Japan.........	1,591
1997*	Ting Kau	China	1,558

Underwater Vehicular Tunnels in North America

(more than 5,000 ft. in length; year in parentheses is date of completion)

Name	Location	Waterway	Feet
Brooklyn-Battery (1950) (twin)	New York, NY............	East River	9,117
Holland Tunnel (1927) (twin)	New York, NY............	Hudson River.	8,557
Ted Williams Tunnel (1995)	Boston, MA...........	Boston Harbor	8,448
Lincoln Tunnel (1937, 1945, 1957) (3 tubes)	New York, NY.......	Hudson River.	8,216
Thimble Shoal Channel (1964)	Northampton Co., VA....	Chesapeake Bay	8,187
Chesapeake Channel (1964)	Northampton Co., VA....	Chesapeake Bay	7,941
Fort McHenry Tunnel (1985) (twin)	Baltimore, MD.......	Baltimore Harbor	7,920
Hampton Roads (1957) (twin)	Hampton, VA.......	Hampton Roads.	7,479
Baltimore Harbor Tunnel (1957) (twin)	Baltimore, MD.......	Patapsco River	7,392
Queens Midtown (1940) (twin)	New York, NY.......	East River	6,414
Sumner Tunnel (1934).	Boston, MA...........	Boston Harbor	5,653
Louis-Hippolyte Lafontaine Tunnel	Montreal, Que.	St. Lawrence R.	5,280
Detroit-Windsor (1930).	Detroit, MI...........	Detroit River	5,160
Callahan Tunnel (1961)	Boston, MA...........	Boston Harbor	5,070

Land Vehicular Tunnels in the U.S.

(more than 3,000 ft. in length)

Name	Location	Feet	Name	Location	Feet
E. Johnson Memorial	I-70, CO.	8,959	Zion Natl. Park	Rte. 9, UT	5,766
Eisenhower Memorial....	I-70, CO.	8,941	East River Mt. (twin)....	VA—WV	5,412
Allegheny (twin)........	PA Turnpike	6,072	Tuscarora (twin)	PA Turnpike.	5,400
Liberty Tubes	Pittsburgh, PA	5,920	Tetsuo Harano (twin)	H-3, HI	5,165

Name	Location	Feet
Kittatinny (twin)	PA Turnpike	4,660
Cumberland Gap (twin)	KY–TN	4,600
Blue Mountain (twin)	PA Turnpike	4,435
Lehigh (twin)	PA Turnpike	4,379
Wawona	Yosemite Natl. Park, CA.	4,233
Big Walker Mt.	Bland Co., VA	4,229
Squirrel Hill	Pittsburgh, PA	4,225
Hanging Lake (twin)	Glenwood Canyon, CO.	4,000
Caldecott (3 tubes)	Oakland, CA	3,616
Fort Pitt (twin)	Pittsburgh, PA	3,560
Dingess Tunnel	Mingo Co., WV	3,400
Mall Tunnel	Dist. of Columbia	3,400
Cody No. 1	U.S. 14, 16, 20, WY	3,202

World's Longest Railway Tunnels

Source: Railway Directory & Year Book.

Tunnel	Date	Miles	Operating railway	Country
Seikan	1985	33.50	Japanese Railway.	Japan
English Channel Tunnel	1994	31.04	Eurotunnel.	UK-France
Dai-shimizu	1979	14.00	Japanese Railway.	Japan
Simplon No. 1 and 2	1906, 1922	12.00	Swiss Fed. & Italian St.	Switz.-Italy
Kanmon	1975	12.00	Japanese Railway.	Japan
Apennine	1934	11.00	Italian State	Italy
Rokko	1972	10.00	Japanese Railway.	Japan
Mt. MacDonald	1989	9.10	Canadian Pacific.	Canada
Gotthard	1882	9.00	Swiss Federal.	Switz.
Lotschberg	1913	9.00	Bern-Lotschberg-Simplon	Switz.
Hokuriku	1962	9.00	Japanese Railway.	Japan
Mont Cenis (Frejus)	1871	8.00	Italian State	France-It.
Shin-Shimizu	1961	8.00	Japanese Railway.	Japan
Aki	1975	8.00	Japanese Railway.	Japan
Cascade	1929	8.00	Burlington Northern.	U.S.
Flathead	1970	8.00	Burlington Northern.	U.S.

World's Largest-Capacity Hydro Plants

Source: U.S. Committee on Large Dams of the Intl. Commission on Large Dams, 1997

Rank order	Name	Country	Rated capacity now (MW)	Rated capacity planned (MW)	Rank order	Name	Country	Rated capacity now (MW)	Rated capacity planned (MW)
1	Turukhansk (Lower Tungu-ska)*	Russia	–	20,000	12	Xingo	Brazil	3,012	5,020
2	Three Gorges Dam*	China	–	18,200	13	Tarbela	Pakistan	1,750	4,678
3	Itaipu	Brazil/Paraguay	7,400	13,320	14	Bratsk	Russia	4,500	4,500
4	Grand Coulee	U.S.	6,495	10,830	14	Ust-Ilim	Russia	3,675	4,500
5	Guri (Raúl Leoni)	Venezuela	10,300	10,300	16	Cabora Bassa	Mozambique	2,425	4,150
6	Tucuruí	Brazil	2,640	7,260	17	Boguchany*	Russia	–	4,000
7	Sayano Shushensk*	Russia	6,400	6,400	18	Rogun*	Tajikistan	3,600	3,600
8	Corpus Posadas	Argentina/Paraguay	4,700	6,000	20	Paulo Afonso I	Brazil	1,524	3,409
8	Krasnoyarsk	Russia	6,000	6,000	18	Oak Creek	U.S.	3,600	3,600
10	La Grande 2	Canada	5,328	5,328	21	Pati*	Argentina	–	3,300
11	Churchill Falls	Canada	5,225	5,225	22	Ilha Solteira	Brazil	3,200	3,200
					24	Chapetón*	Argentina	–	3,000
					22	Brumley Gap*	U.S.	3,200	3,200
					25	Gezhouba	China	2,715	2,715

*Planned or under construction.

Major Dams of the World

Source: U.S. Committee on Large Dams of the Intl. Commission on Large Dams, 1997

World's Highest Dams

Rank order	Name	Country	Height above lowest formation (m)	Rank order	Name	Country	Height above lowest formation (m)
1	Rogun*	Tajikistan	335	11	Mica	Canada	242
2	Nurek	Tajikistan	300	12	Mauvoisin	Switzerland	237
3	Grand Dixence	Switzerland	285	13	Chivor	Colombia	237
4	Inguri	Georgia	272	14	El Cajón	Honduras	234
5	Chicoasén	Mexico	261	15	Chirkei	Russia	233
6	Tehri*	India	261	16	Oroville	U.S.	230
7	Kishau*	India	253	17	Bhakra	India	226
8	Ertan	China	245	18	Hoover	U.S.	221
8	Sayano-Shushensk*	Russia	245	19	Contra	Switzerland	220
10	Guavio*	Colombia	243	20	Mratinje	Yugoslavia	220

*Under construction.

World's Largest-Volume Embankment Dams

Rank order	Name	Country	Volume cubic meters × 1000	Rank order	Name	Country	Volume cubic meters × 1000
1	Tarbela	Pakistan	148,500	11	Gardiner	Canada	65,000
2	Fort Peck	U.S.	96,050	12	Afsluitdijk	Netherlands	63,400
3	Tucurui	Brazil	85,200	13	Mangla	Pakistan	63,379
4	Ataturk*	Turkey	85,000	14	Oroville	U.S.	59,635
5	Yacireta*	Argentina	81,000	15	San Luis	U.S.	59,559
6	Rogun*	Tajikistan	75,500	16	Nurek	Tajikistan	58,000
7	Oahe	U.S.	70,339	17	Tanda	Pakistan	57,250
8	Guri	Venezuela	70,000	18	Garrison	U.S.	50,843
9	Parambikulam	India	69,165	19	Cochiti	U.S.	50,228
10	High Island West	China	67,000	20	Oosterschelde	Netherlands	50,000

*Under construction.

World's Largest-Capacity Reservoirs

Source: U.S. Committee on Large Dams of the Intl. Commission on Large Dams, 1997

Rank order	Name	Country	Capacity cubic meters × 1,000,000	Rank order	Name	Country	Capacity cubic meters × 1,000,000
1	Owen Falls	Uganda	204,800	11	Cabora Bassa	Mozambique	63,000
2	Bratsk	Russia	169,000	12	La Grande 2	Canada	61,715
3	Aswan (High)	Egypt	162,000	13	La Grande 3	Canada	60,020
4	Kariba	Zimbabwe/Zambia	160,368	14	Ust-Ilim	Russia	59,300
5	Akosombo	Ghana	147,960	15	Boguchany*	Russia	58,200
6	Daniel Johnson	Canada	141,851	16	Kuibyshev	Russia	58,000
7	Guri	Venezuela	135,000	17	Serra de Mesa	Brazil	54,400
8	Krasnoyarsk	Russia	73,300	18	Caniapiscau Barrage KA 3	Canada	53,790
9	W A C Bennett (Portage Mt.)	Canada	70,309	19	Bukhtarma	Kazakhstan	49,800
10	Zeya	Russia	68,400	20	Ataturk	Turkey	48,700

*Under construction.

Major U.S. Dams and Reservoirs

Source: Committee on Register of Dams, Corps of Engineers, U.S. Army, 1997

Highest U.S. Dams

Order	Dam name	River	State	Type	Height Feet	Height Meters	Year completed
1	Oroville	Feather	California	E	754	230	1968
2	Hoover	Colorado	Nevada	A	725	221	1936
3	Dworshak	N. Fork Clearwater	Idaho	G	718	219	1973
4	Glen Canyon	Colorado	Arizona	A	708	216	1966
5	New Bullards Bar	North Yuba	California	A	636	194	1970
6	New Melones	Stanislaus	California	R	626	191	1979
7	Swift	Lewis	Washington	E	610	186	1958
8	Mossyrock	Cowlitz	Washington	A	607	185	1968
9	Shasta	Sacramento	California	G	600	183	1945
10	Hungry Horse	S. Fork Flathead	Montana	A	564	172	1953
11	Grand Coulee	Columbia	Washington	G	551	168	1942
12	Ross	Skagit	Washington	A	541	165	1949

E= Embankment, Earthfill; R= Embankment, Rockfill; G= Gravity; A= Arch.

Largest U.S. Embankment Dams

Order	Dam name	River	State	Type	Volume Cubic yards × 1000	Volume Cubic meters × 1000	Year completed
1	Fort Peck	Missouri	Montana	E	125,624	96,050	1937
2	Oahe	Missouri	South Dakota	E	91,996	70,339	1958
3	Oroville	Feather	California	E	77,997	59,635	1968
4	San Luis	San Luis Creek	California	E	77,897	59,559	1967
5	Garrison	Missouri	North Dakota	E	66,498	50,843	1953
6	Cochiti	Rio Grande	New Mexico	E	65,693	50,228	1975
7	Fort Randall	Missouri	South Dakota	E	49,962	38,200	1952
8	Castaic	Castaic Creek	California	E	43,998	33,640	1973
9	Ludington P/S	Lake Michigan	Michigan	E	37,699	28,824	1973
10	Kingsley	N. Platte	Nebraska	E	31,999	24,466	1941
11	Warm Springs	Dry Creek	California	E	29,977	22,920	1982
12	Trinity	Trinity	California	E	29,251	22,486	1962

E= Embankment, Earthfill; G= Gravity.

Largest U.S. Reservoirs

Ord.	Dam name, location	Reservoir name	Location	Reservoir capacity Acre-Feet	Reservoir capacity Cubic meters × 1000	Year completed
1	Hoover, NV	Lake Mead	AZ/NV	28,253,000	34,850,000	1936
2	Glen Canyon, AZ	Lake Powell	AZ/UT	26,997,000	33,300,000	1966
3	Garrison, ND	Lake Sakakawea	ND	22,635,000	27,920,000	1953
4	Oahe, SD	Lake Oahe	ND/SD	22,238,000	27,430,000	1958
5	Fort Peck, MT	Fort Peck Lake	MT	17,933,000	22,120,000	1937
6	Grand Coulee, WA	F. D. Roosevelt Lake	WA	9,558,000	11,790,000	1942
7	Libby, MT	Lake Koocanusa	MT/B.C.	5,813,000	7,170,000	1973
8	Fort Randall, SD	Lake Francis Case	SD	4,621,000	5,700,000	1952
9	Shasta, CA	Lake Shasta	CA	4,548,000	5,610,000	1945
10	Toledo Bend, LA	Toledo Bend Lake	LA/TX	4,475,000	5,520,000	1968
11	Wolf Creek, KY	Cumberland Lake	KY	3,997,000	4,930,000	1951
12	Flaming Gorge, UT	Flaming Gorge Reservoir	UT/WY	3,786,000	4,670,000	1964

1 acre-foot = 1 acre of water, 1 foot deep

SOCIAL SECURITY

Social Security Programs

Source: Social Security Administration, U.S. Dept. of Health and Human Services; data as of Aug. 1997

Old-Age, Survivors, and Disability Insurance; Medicare; Supplemental Security Income

Social Security Benefits

Social Security benefits are based on a worker's primary insurance amount (PIA), which is related by law to the average indexed monthly earnings (AIME) on which Social Security contributions have been paid. The full PIA is payable to a retired worker who becomes entitled to benefits at age 65 and to an entitled disabled worker at any age. Spouses and children of retired or disabled workers and survivors of deceased workers receive set proportions of the PIA subject to a family maximum amount. The PIA is calculated by applying varying percentages to succeeding parts of the AIME. The formula is adjusted annually to reflect changes in average annual wages.

Automatic increases in Social Security benefits are initiated for Dec. of each year, assuming the Consumer Price Index (CPI) of the Bureau of Labor Statistics for the 3d calendar quarter of the year increased relative to the base quarter, which is either the 3d calendar quarter of the preceding year or the quarter in which an increase legislated by Congress became effective. The size of the benefit increase is determined by the actual percentage rise of the CPI between the quarters measured.

The average monthly benefit payable to all retired workers was $745.00 in Dec. 1996. The average amount for disabled workers in that month was $704.00.

Minimum and maximum monthly retired-worker benefits payable to individuals who retired at age 65[1]

	Minimum benefit[2]		Maximum benefit[2]			
Year of attain- ment of age 65	Payable at time of re- tirement	Payable effective Dec. 1994	Payable at time of retirement		Payable effective Dec. 1994	
			Men	Women[3]	Men	Women[3]
1970 . . .	$64.00	$275.10	$189.80	$196.40	$815.60	$844.60
1980 . . .	133.90	275.10	572.00	—	1,176.50	—
1990 . . .	(4)	(4)	975.00	—	1,157.50	—
1993 . . .	(4)	(4)	1,128.80	—	1,190.50	—
1994 . . .	(4)	(4)	1,147.50	—	1,179.60	—
1995 . . .	(4)	(4)	1,199.10	—	—	—
1996 . . .	(4)	(4)	1,248.90	—	—	—

(1) Assumes retirement at beginning of year. (2) The final benefit amount payable is rounded to next lower $1 (if not already a multiple of $1). (3) Benefits for women are the same as for men except where women's benefit appears separately. (4) Minimum eliminated for workers who reach age 62 after 1981.

Amount of Work Required

To qualify for benefits, the worker must have worked in covered employment long enough to become insured. Just how long depends on when the worker reaches age 62 or, if earlier, when he or she dies or becomes disabled.

A person is fully insured if he or she has 1 quarter of coverage for every year after 1950 (or year age 21 is reached, if later) up to but not including the year when the worker reaches age 62, dies, or becomes disabled. In 1997, a person earns 1 quarter of coverage for each $670.00 of annual earnings in covered employment, up to a maximum of 4 quarters per year.

The law permits special monthly payments under the Social Security program to certain very old persons who are not eligible for regular Social Security benefits since they had little or no opportunity to earn Social Security work credits during their working lifetime (so-called special age-72 beneficiaries).

To receive disability benefits, the worker, in addition to being fully insured, must generally have credit for 20 quarters of coverage out of the 40 calendar quarters before he or she became disabled. A disabled blind worker need meet only the fully insured requirement. Persons disabled before age 31 can qualify with a briefer period of coverage. Certain survivor benefits are payable if the deceased worker had 6 quarters of coverage in the 13 quarters preceding death.

Work credit for fully insured status for benefits

Born after 1929; die, become disabled, or reach age 62 in — **Years needed**

1983	8
1984	8¼
1985	8½
1986	8¾
1987	9
1988	9¼
1989	9½
1990	9¾
1991 and after	10

Contribution and benefit base

Calendar year	OASDI[1] Base	HI[2] Base
1988.	$45,000	$45,000
1989.	48,000	48,000
1990.	51,300	51,300
1991.	53,400	125,000
1992.	55,500	130,200
1993.	57,600	135,000
1994.	60,600	no limit
1995.	61,200	no limit
1996.	62,700	no limit
1997.	65,400	no limit
1998.	68,100	no limit

(1) Old-Age, Survivors, and Disability Insurance. (2) Hospital Insurance.

Tax-rate schedule
(percentage of covered earnings)

Year	Total	OASDI	HI
	(for employees and employers, each)		
1979-80.	6.13	5.08	1.05
1981.	6.65	5.35	1.30
1982-83.	6.70	5.40	1.30
1984	7.00	5.70	1.30
1985	7.05	5.70	1.35
1986-87.	7.15	5.70	1.45
1988-89.	7.51	6.06	1.45
1990 and after	7.65	6.20	1.45
For self-employed			
1979-80.	8.10	7.05	1.05
1981	9.30	8.00	1.30
1982-83.	9.35	8.05	1.30
1984	14.00	11.40	2.60
1985	14.10	11.40	2.70
1986-87.	14.30	11.40	2.90
1988-89.	15.02	12.12	2.90
1990 and after	15.30	12.40	2.90

What Aged Workers Receive

When a person has enough work in covered employment and reaches retirement age (currently age 65 for full benefit, age 62 for reduced benefit), he or she may retire and receive monthly old-age benefits. The age when unreduced benefits become payable will be increased gradually from 65 to 67 over a 21-year period beginning with workers age 62 in the year 2000 (reduced benefits will still be available as early as age 62, but with a larger reduction at that age). If a person age 65-69 continues to work and has earnings of more than $13,500 in 1997, $1 in benefits will be withheld for every $3 above $13,500. For those under 65, the annual exempt amount is $8,640 in 1997, and $1 in benefits is withheld for every $2 in earnings above the exempt amount for them. However, the eligible worker who is age 70 or over receives the full benefit regardless of earnings. The annual exempt amount has been raised automatically as the general earnings level rises. However, legislation enacted in 1996 (PL 104-121) provided for more sizable increases in the annual exempt amount for persons aged 65-69, rising to $13,500 in 1997 and to $30,000 by 2002. After the year 2002, the annual exempt amount for those aged 65-69 will be raised automatically as general earnings levels rise.

For workers who reached age 65 between 1982 and 1989, Social Security benefits are raised by 3% for each year for which the worker between ages 65 and 70 (72 before 1984) failed to receive benefits, whether because of earnings from work or because the worker had not applied for benefits. The delayed retirement credit is 1% per year for workers who reached age 65 before 1982. The delayed retirement credit will gradually rise to 8% per year by 2008. The rate for workers who reached age 65 in 1996-97 is 5%. The rate for reaching age 65 in 1998-99 will be 5.5%.

Effective Dec. 1996, the special benefit for persons aged 72 or over who do not meet the regular coverage requirements became $199.00 a month. Like other monthly benefits, these payments are subject to cost-of-living increases. They are not made to persons on the public assistance or supplemental security income rolls.

Workers retiring before age 65 have their benefits permanently reduced by $5/9$ of 1% for each month they receive benefits before that age. Thus, workers entitled to benefits in the month they reach age 62 receive 80% of the PIA, while a worker retiring at age 65 receives a benefit equal to 100% of the PIA. The nearer to age 65 the worker is when he or she begins collecting a benefit, the larger the benefit will be.

Benefits for Worker's Spouse

The spouse of a worker who is getting Social Security retirement or disability payments may become entitled to an insurance benefit of one-half of the worker's PIA, when he or she reaches 65. Reduced spouse's benefits are available at age 62 ($25/36$ of 1% reduction for each month of entitlement before age 65). Benefits are also payable to the aged divorced spouse of an insured worker if he or she was married to the worker for at least 10 years.

Benefits for Children of Retired or Disabled Workers

If a retired or disabled worker has a child under age 18, the child will get a benefit equal to half of the worker's unreduced benefit. So will the worker's spouse, even if under age 62, if he or she is caring for an entitled child of the worker who is under 16 or became disabled before age 22. Total benefits paid on a worker's earnings record are subject to a maximum; if the total that would be paid to a family exceeds that maximum, the dependents' benefits are adjusted downward. (Total monthly benefits paid to the family of a worker who retired in Jan. 1997 at age 65 and always had the maximum earnings creditable under Social Security can not exceed $2,321.50.)

When entitled children reach age 18, their benefits will generally stop, except that a child disabled before age 22 may get a benefit as long as the disability meets the definition in the law. Additionally, benefits will be paid to a child until age 19 if the child is in full-time attendance at an elementary or secondary school.

Benefits may also be paid to a grandchild or step-grandchild of a worker or of his or her spouse, in special circumstances.

OASDI	May 1997	May 1996	May 1995
Monthly beneficiaries, total			
(in thousands)[1]	43,796	43,463	43,068
Aged 65 and over, total	31,641	31,401	31,137
Retired workers	24,498	24,226	23,943
Survivors and dependents. . .	7,143	7,174	7,193
Special age-72 beneficiaries .	1	1	1
Under age 65, total	12,155	12,062	11,931
Retired workers	2,457	2,459	2,508
Disabled workers	4,407	4,273	4,049
Survivors and dependents. . .	5,291	5,330	5,374
Total monthly benefits (in			
millions)	**$29,542**	**$28,275**	**$27,086**

(1) Totals may not add because of rounding.

What Disabled Workers Receive

A worker who becomes so disabled as to be unable to work may be eligible for a monthly disability benefit. Benefits continue until it is determined that the individual is no longer disabled. Eligibility is reviewed periodically. When a disabled-worker beneficiary reaches age 65, the disability benefit becomes a retired-worker benefit.

Benefits generally like those for dependents of retired-worker beneficiaries may be paid to dependents of disabled beneficiaries. However, the maximum family benefit in disability cases is generally lower than in retirement cases.

Survivor Benefits

If an insured worker should die, one or more types of benefits may be payable to survivors, again subject to a maximum family benefit as described above.

1. If claiming benefits at age 65, the surviving spouse will receive a benefit equal to 100% of the deceased worker's PIA. The surviving spouse may choose to get the benefit as early as age 60, but it is then reduced by $19/40$ of 1% for each month it is paid before age 65. However, for those whose spouses claimed their benefits before age 65, these are limited to the reduced amount the worker would be getting if alive, but not less than $82 1/2$% of the worker's PIA. Marriage after the worker's death ends the surviving spouse's benefit rights. However, if the widow(er) marries and the marriage is ended, he or she regains benefit rights. (A marriage after age 60, age 50 if disabled, is deemed not to have occurred for benefit purposes.) Survivor benefits may also be paid to a divorced spouse if the marriage lasted for at least 10 years.

Disabled widows and widowers may under certain circumstances qualify for benefits after attaining age 50 at the rate of 71.5% of the deceased worker's PIA. The widow or widower must have become totally disabled before or within 7 years after the spouse's death or the last month in which he or she received mother's or father's insurance benefits.

2. There is a benefit for each child until the child reaches age 18. The monthly benefit for each child of a deceased worker is three-quarters of the amount the worker would have received if he or she had lived and drawn full retirement benefits. A child with a disability that began before age 22 may also receive benefits. Also, a child may receive benefits until reaching age 19 if he or she is in full-time attendance at an elementary or secondary school.

3. There is a mother's or father's benefit for the widow(er) if children of the worker under age 16 are in his or her care. The benefit is 75% of the PIA, and it continues until the youngest child reaches age 16, at which time payments stop even if the child's benefit continues. However, if the widow(er) has a disabled child beneficiary age 16 or over in care, benefits may continue.

4. Dependent parents may be eligible for benefits if they have been receiving at least half their support from the worker before his or her death, have reached age 62, and (except in certain circumstances) have not remarried since the worker's death. Each parent gets 75% of the worker's PIA; if only one parent survives, the benefit is $82 1/2$%.

5. A lump sum cash payment of $255 is made when there is a spouse who was living with the worker or a spouse or child who is eligible for immediate monthly survivor benefits.

Self-Employed Workers

A self-employed person who has net earnings of $400 or more in a year must report such earnings for Social Security tax and credit purposes. The person reports net returns from the business. Income from real estate, savings, dividends, loans, pensions, or insurance policies are not included unless it is part of the business.

A self-employed person receives 1 quarter of coverage for each $670.00 (for 1997), up to a maximum of 4 quarters of coverage.

The nonfarm self-employed have the option of reporting their earnings as $2/3$ of their gross income from self-employment, but not more than $1,600 a year and not less than their actual net earnings. This option can be used only if actual net earnings from self-employment income are less than $1,600, and may be used only 5 times. Also, the self-employed person must have actual net earnings of $400 or more in 2 of the 3 taxable years immediately preceding the year in which he or she uses the option.

When a person has both taxable wages and earnings derived from self-employment, the wages are credited for Social Security purposes first; only as much of the self-employment income as will bring total earnings up to the current taxable maximum becomes subject to the self-employment tax.

Farm Owners and Workers

Self-employed farmers whose gross annual earnings from farming are $2,400 or less may report ²/₃ of their gross earnings instead of net earnings for Social Security purposes. Farmers whose gross income is over $2,400 and whose net earnings are less than $1,600 can report $1,600. Cash or crop shares received from a tenant or share farmer count if the owner participated materially in production or management. The self-employed farmer pays contributions at the same rate as other self-employed persons.

Agricultural employees. A worker's earnings from farm work count toward benefits (1) if the employer pays the worker $150 or more in cash during the year; or (2) if the employer spends $2,500 or more in the year for agricultural labor. Under these rules a person gets credit for 1 calendar quarter for each $670.00 in cash pay in 1997 up to 4 quarters.

Foreign farm workers admitted to the U.S. on a temporary basis are not covered.

Household Workers

Anyone 18 or older employed as maid, cook, laundry worker, nurse, babysitter, chauffeur, gardener, or other worker in the house of another is covered by Social Security if paid $1,000 or more in cash in a calendar year by any one employer. Room and board do not count, but transportation costs count if paid in cash. The job need not be regular or full-time. The employee should get a Social Security card at the Social Security office and show it to the employer.

The employer deducts the amount of the employee's Social Security tax from the worker's pay, adds an identical amount as the employer's Social Security tax, and sends the total amount to the federal government, with the employee's Social Security number.

Medicare Coverage

The Medicare health insurance program provides acute-care coverage for Social Security and Railroad Retirement beneficiaries age 65 and over, for persons entitled for 24 months to receive Social Security or Railroad Retirement disability benefits, and for certain persons with end-stage kidney disease.

Persons eligible for Medicare may choose to have their covered services provided through a health maintenance organization (HMO).

Hospital insurance. The hospital insurance program pays covered services for hospital and posthospital care as follows:

- All necessary inpatient hospital care for the first 60 days of each benefit period, except for a deductible ($760 in 1997). For days 61-90, Medicare pays for services over and above a coinsurance amount ($190 per day in 1997). After 90 days, the beneficiary has 60 reserve days for which Medicare helps pay. The coinsurance amount for reserve days was $380 in 1997.
- Up to 100 days' care in a skilled-nursing facility in each benefit period. Hospital insurance pays for all covered services for the first 20 days; for the 21-100th day, the beneficiary pays coinsurance ($95 a day in 1997).
- Visits by nurses or other health workers (not doctors) from a home health agency.
- Hospice care for terminally ill individuals.

Medical insurance. Aged persons can receive benefits under this supplementary program only if they sign up for them and agree to a monthly premium ($43.50 in 1997). The federal government pays the rest of the cost.

The medical insurance program usually pays 80% of the approved amount (after the first $100 in each calendar year) for the following services:

- Covered services received from a doctor in his or her office, in a hospital, in a skilled-nursing facility, at home, or in other locations.
- Medical and surgical services, including anesthesia.
- Diagnostic tests and procedures that are part of the patient's treatment.
- Radiology and pathology services by doctors while the individual is a hospital inpatient or outpatient.

- Treatment of mental illness. Medicare payments are limited; services may be obtained from doctors, comprehensive outpatient rehabilitation facilities (CORFs), physician assistants, psychologists, and clinical social workers.

Note: The services for nonhospital treatment of a mental illness are subject to a special payment rule. In effect, once the annual deductible is met, Medicare pays only 50% (not 80%) of approved charges. On assigned claims (those in which the service provider agrees to the fee set by Medicare), beneficiaries are responsible for paying the remaining 50%. For unassigned claims, beneficiaries may have to pay more.

Partial hospitalization services for treatment of mental illness are not subject to this special payment rule. Also, brief office visits for the sole purpose of monitoring or changing drug prescriptions used in the treatment of mental illness are not subject to this special payment rule.

Other services such as X-rays, services of a doctor's office nurse, drugs and biologicals that cannot be self-administered, transfusions of blood and blood components, medical supplies, physical/occupational therapy and speech pathology services.

To get medical insurance protection, persons approaching age 65 may enroll in the 7-month period that includes 3 months before the 65th birthday, the month of the birthday, and 3 months after the birthday, but if they wish coverage to begin in the month they reach age 65, they must enroll in the 3 months before their birthday. Persons not enrolling within their first enrollment period may enroll later, during the first 3 months of each year (coverage begins July 1), but their premium may be 10% higher for each 12-month period elapsed since they first could have enrolled.

The monthly premium is deducted from the cash benefit for persons receiving Social Security, Railroad Retirement, or Civil Service retirement benefits. Income from the medical premiums and the federal matching payments are put in a Supplementary Medical Insurance Trust Fund, from which benefits and administrative expenses are paid.

Medicare card. Persons qualifying for hospital insurance under Social Security receive a health insurance card similar to cards now used by Blue Cross and other health insurers. The card indicates whether the individual has taken out medical insurance protection. It is to be shown to the hospital, skilled-nursing facility, home health agency, doctor, or whoever provides the covered services.

Payments are made only in the 50 states, Puerto Rico, the Virgin Islands, Guam, and American Samoa, except that, in rare cases, inpatient hospital services may be provided in Canada and Mexico.

Social Security Financing

Social Security is paid for by a tax on certain earnings (for 1997, on earnings up to $65,400) for Old Age, Survivors, and Disability Insurance and on all earnings (no upper limit) for Hospital Insurance with the Medicare Program; the taxable earnings base for OASDI has been adjusted annually to reflect increases in average wages. The employed worker and his or her employer share Social Security taxes equally.

Employers remit amounts withheld from employee wages for Social Security and income taxes to the Internal Revenue Service; employer Social Security taxes are also payable at the same time. (Self-employed workers pay Social Security taxes when filing their regular income tax forms.) The Social Security taxes (along with revenues arising from partial taxation of the Social Security benefits of certain high-income people) are transferred to the Social Security Trust Funds—the Federal Old-Age and Survivors Insurance (OASI) Trust Fund, the Federal Disability Insurance (DI) Trust Fund, and the Federal Hospital Insurance (HI) Trust Fund; they can be used only to pay benefits, the cost of rehabilitation services, and administrative expenses. Money not immediately needed for these purposes is by law invested in obligations of the federal government, which must pay interest on the money borrowed and must repay the principal when the obligations are redeemed or mature.

Supplemental Security Income

On Jan. 1, 1974, the Supplemental Security Income (SSI) program established by the 1972 Social Security Act amendments replaced the former federal grants to states for aid to the needy aged, blind, and disabled in the 50 states and the District of Columbia. The program provides both for federal payments, based on uniform national standards and eligibility requirements, and for state supplementary payments varying from state to state. The Social Security Administration administers the federal payments financed from general funds of the Treasury—and the state supplements as well, if the state elects to have its supplementary program federally administered. The states may supplement the federal payment for all recipients and must supplement it for persons otherwise adversely affected by the transition from the former public assistance programs. In May 1997, the number of persons receiving federal payments and federally administered state payments was 6,554,645, and the amount of these payments totaled $2.4 billion.

The maximum monthly federal SSI payment for individuals with no other countable income, living in their own household, was $484.00 in 1997. For couples it was $726.00.

Obtaining Earnings and Benefits Statements

To obtain Personal Earnings and Benefit Estimates Statements (PEBES) from the Social Security Administration (SSA) through the mail, call 1-800-772-1213 and request a PEBES form. On Mar. 5, 1997, the SSA began a test to provide PEBES information online via its Internet home page. The agency suspended this service on Apr. 9, 1997, for privacy and security reasons. There were plans to restore this service with additional safeguards by early 1998. For more information on services and data available from the SSA, visit its web site at http://www.ssa.gov

Examples of Monthly Benefits Available

Description of benefit or beneficiary	For low earnings ($12,028 in 1997)[1]	For avg. earnings ($26,731 in 1997)[2]	For max. earnings ($65,400 in 1997)
Primary insurance amount (worker retiring at 65)	$566.00	$933.00	$1,326.00
Maximum family benefit (worker retiring at 65)	849.20	1,703.50	2,322.10
Maximum family disability benefit (worker disabled at 55; in 1996)*	757.30	1,331.50	1,946.70
Disabled worker: (worker disabled at 55)			
Worker alone	560.20	922.00	1,363.00
Worker, spouse, and 1 child	786.00	1,382.00	2,043.00
Retired worker claiming benefits at age 62:			
Worker alone[3]	452.00	746.00	1,060.00
Worker with spouse claiming benefits at—			
Age 65 or over	735.00	1,212.00	1,723.00
Age 62[3]	664.00	1,095.00	1,557.00
Widow or widower claiming benefits at—			
Age 65 or over[4]	566.00	933.00	1,326.00
Age 60 (spouse died at 65 without receiving reduced benefits)	404.00	667.00	948.00
Disabled widow or widower claiming benefits at age 50-59[5]	404.00	667.00	948.00
1 surviving child	424.00	699.00	994.00
Widow or widower age 65 or over and 1 child[6]	848.00	1,632.00	2,320.00
Widowed mother or father and 1 child[6]	848.00	1,348.00	1,988.00
Widowed mother or father and 2 children[6]	849.00	1,701.00	2,322.00

Effective Jan. 1997, for beneficiaries with first entitlement in 1977. Assumes work beginning at age 22. (1) 45% of average. (2) Estimate. (3) Assumes maximum reduction. (4) A widow(er)'s benefit amount is limited to the amount the spouse would have been receiving if still living, but not less than 82.5 % of the PIA. (5) Effective Jan. 1984, disabled widow(er)s claiming a benefit at ages 50-59 receive a benefit equal to 71.5 % of the PIA (based on 1983 Social Security Amendment provision). (6) Based on worker dying at age 65.

Social Security Trust Funds
Old-Age and Survivors Insurance Trust Fund, 1940-96
(in millions)

Fiscal year[1]	Income					Disbursements						
	Total	Net contributions[2]	Income from taxation of benefits	Payments from the general fund of the Treasury[3]	Net interest[4]	Total	Benefit payments[5]	Administrative expenses	Transfers to Railroad Retirement program	Interfund borrowing transfers[6]	Net increase in fund	Fund at end of period
1940	$592	$550	—	—	$42	$28	$16	$12	—	—	$564	$1,745
1950	2,367	2,106	—	$4	257	784	727	57	—	—	1,583	12,893
1960	10,360	9,843	—	—	517	11,073	10,270	202	$600	—	−713	20,829
1970	31,746	29,955	—	442	1,350	27,321	26,268	474	579	—	4,425	32,616
1980	100,051	97,608	—	557	1,886	103,228	100,626	1,160	1,442	—	−3,177	24,566
1985	179,881	175,305	$3,151	105	1,321	169,210	165,310	1,589	2,310	−$4,364	6,308	33,877
1990	278,607	261,506	2,924	34	14,143	223,481	218,948	1,564	2,969	—	55,126	203,445
1991	293,288	270,841	5,790	−2,089	18,746	241,316	236,195	1,746	3,375	—	51,972	255,417
1992	307,102	278,506	6,019	19	22,557	256,239	251,268	1,823	3,148	—	50,862	306,280
1993	319,298	287,569	5,893	14	25,822	269,934	264,561	2,021	3,353	—	49,364	355,644
1994	342,263	308,397	5,351	10	28,505	281,572	276,278	1,874	3,420	—	50,691	415,335
1995	326,067	289,529	5,114	7	31,417	294,456	288,607	1,797	4,052	—	31,611	447,946
1996	356,843	317,157	5,785	−124	34,026	305,311	299,968	1,788	3,554	—	51,533	499,479

(1) Under the Congressional Budget Act of 1974 (PL 93-344), fiscal years 1977 and later consist of the 12 months ending on Sept. 30 of each year. Fiscal years prior to 1977 consisted of the 12 months ending on June 30 of each year. (2) Beginning in 1983, includes transfers from general fund of Treasury representing contributions that would have been paid on deemed wage credits for military service in 1957 and later, if such credits were considered covered wages. (3) Includes payments (a) in 1947-52 and in 1967 and later, for costs of noncontributory wage credits for military service performed before 1957; (b) in 1972-83, for costs of deemed wage credits for military service performed after 1956; and (c) in 1969 and later, for costs of benefits to certain uninsured persons who attained age 72 before 1968. (4) Net interest includes net profits or losses on marketable investments. Beginning in 1967, administrative expenses were charged currently to the trust fund on an estimated basis, with a final adjustment, including interest, made in the following fiscal year. The amounts of these interest adjustments are included in net interest. For years prior to 1967, a description of the method of accounting for administrative expenses is contained in the 1970 Annual Report. Beginning in Oct. 1973, the figures shown include relatively small amounts of gifts to the fund. The figure shown for 1985 reflects payments from a borrowing trust fund to a lending trust fund for interest on amounts owed under the interfund borrowing provisions. During 1983-91, interest paid from the trust fund to the general fund on advance tax transfers is reflected. The amount shown for 1985 includes interest adjustments of $76.5 mil on unnegotiated checks issued before Apr. 1985. (5) Beginning in 1967, includes payments for vocational rehabilitation services furnished to disabled persons receiving benefits because of their disabilities. Beginning in 1983, amounts are reduced by amount of reimbursement for unnegotiated benefit checks. (6) Negative figures represent amounts repaid from the OASI Trust Fund to the DI and HI Trust Funds.

Disability Insurance Trust Fund, 1970-96
(in millions)

Fiscal year[1]		Income				Disbursements					
	Total	Net contribu-tions[2]	Income from taxation of benefits	Payments from the general fund of the Treasury[3]	Net interest[4]	Total	Benefit payments[5]	Adminis-trative expenses	Transfers to Railroad Retirement program	Net increase in fund	Fund at end of period
1970	$4,380	$4,141	—	$16	$223	$2,954	$2,795	$149	$10	$1,426	$5,104
1980	17,376	16,805	—	118	453	15,320	14,998	334	-12	2,056	7,680
1985	17,984	16,876	$217	—	891	19,294	18,648	603	43	1,230[6]	5,873[6]
1990	28,215	27,291	158	—	766	25,124	24,327	717	80	3,091	11,455
1991	29,322	28,953	131	-775	1,014	27,780	26,909	789	82	1,543	12,997
1992	31,168	29,871	218	—	1,080	31,285	30,382	845	58	-116	12,881
1993	32,056	30,822	268	—	966	34,632	33,615	935	83	-2,576	10,305
1994	34,044	33,041	305	—	699	37,979	36,851	1,022	106	-3,935	6,370
1995	70,209	67,987	335	—	1,888	41,374	40,234	1,072	68	28,835	35,206
1996	59,220	56,571	370	-203	2,482	44,343	43,266	1,074	2	14,877	50,083

(1) Under the Congressional Budget Act of 1974, fiscal years 1977 and later consist of the 12 months ending on Sept. 30 of each year. Fiscal years prior to 1977 consisted of the 12 months ending June 30 of each year. (2) Beginning in 1983, includes transfers from general fund of Treasury representing contributions that would have been paid on deemed wage credits for military service in 1957 and later, if such credits were considered to be covered wages. (3) Includes payments (a) for costs of noncontributory wage credits for military service performed before 1957; and (b) in 1972-83, for costs of deemed wage credits for military service performed after 1956. (4) Net interest includes net profits or losses on marketable investments. Administrative expenses are charged currently to the trust fund on an estimated basis, with a final adjustment, including interest, made in the following fiscal year. Figures shown include relatively small amounts of gifts to the trust fund. For 1983-86, these figures reflect payments from a borrowing trust fund to a lending trust fund for interest on amounts owed under the interfund borrowing provisions. During the years 1983-91, interest paid from the trust fund to the general fund on advance tax transfers is reflected. The amount shown for 1985 includes an interest adjustment of $14.8 mil on unnegotiated checks issued before Apr. 1985. (5) Includes payments for vocational rehabilitation services. Beginning in 1983, amounts are reduced by amount of reimbursement for unnegotiated benefit checks. (6) In fiscal year 1982, $5,081 mil was loaned to the Old-Age and Survivors Trust Fund under the interfund borrowing provisions of the Social Security Act. Repayments were made in 1985 and 1986. NOTE: Totals may not add because of rounding.

Supplementary Medical Insurance Trust Fund, 1975-96
(in millions)

Fiscal year[1]		Income			Disbursements			Balance in fund at end of year[5]
	Premium from participants	Government contribu-tions[2]	Interest and other income[3]	Total Income	Benefit payments[4]	Adminis-trative expenses	Total disburse-ments	
1975	$1,887	$2,330	$105	$4,322	$3,765	$405	$4,170	$1,424
1980	2,928	6,932	415	10,275	10,144	593	10,737	4,532
1985	5,524	17,898	1,155	24,577	21,808	922	22,730	10,646
1990	11,494[4]	33,210	1,434[5]	46,138[5]	41,498	1,524[5]	43,022[5]	14,527[5]
1991	11,807	34,730	1,629	48,166	45,514	1,505	47,019	15,675
1992	12,748	38,684	1,717	53,149	48,627	1,661	50,288	18,535
1993	14,683	44,227	1,889	60,799	54,214[6]	1,845	56,059	23,276
1994	16,895	38,355	2,118	57,368	58,006	1,718	59,724	20,919
1995	19,244	36,988	1,937	58,169	63,491	1,722	65,213	13,874
1996	18,931	61,702	1,392	82,025	67,176	1,771	68,946	26,953

(1) For 1975, the fiscal year covers the interval from July 1 through June 30; fiscal years 1980 and later cover the interval from Oct. 1 through Sept. 30. (2) General fund matching payments, plus certain interest-adjustment items. (3) Other income includes recoveries of amounts reimbursed from the trust fund that are not obligations of the trust fund and other miscellaneous income. (4) The financial status of the program depends on both the assets and the liabilities of the program. (5) Includes the impact of the Medicare Catastrophic Coverage Act of 1988 (PL 100-360). (6) Includes $1,805 mil transfer to the HI trust fund, as provided for by PL 102-394. NOTE: Totals may not add because of rounding.

Hospital Insurance Trust Fund, 1975-96
(in millions)

Fiscal year[1]			Income						Disbursements				
	Payroll taxes	Income from taxation of benefits	Transfers from railroad retirement acct.	Reimburse-ment for uninsured persons	Premiums from voluntary enrollees	Pymts. for military wage credits	Interest on investments and other income[2]	Total income	Benefit pymts.[3]	Adminis-trative expense[4]	Total disburse-ments	Net increase in fund	Fund at end of year
1975	$11,291	—	$132	$481	$6	$48	$609	$12,568	$10,353	$259	$10,612	$1,956	$9,870
1980	23,244	—	244	697	17	141	1,072	25,415	23,790	497	24,288	1,127	14,490
1985	46,490	—	371	766	38	86	3,182	50,933	47,841	813	48,654	4,103[5]	21,277[5]
1990	70,655	—	367	413	113	107	7,908	79,563	65,912	774	66,687	12,876	95,631
1991	74,655	—	352	605	367	-1,011[6]	8,969	83,938	68,705	934	69,638	14,299	109,930
1992	80,978	—	374	621	484	86	10,133	92,677	80,784	1,191	81,974	10,703	120,633
1993	83,147	—	400	367	622	81	12,484[7]	97,101	90,738	866	91,604	5,497	126,131
1994	92,028	$1,639	413	506	852	80	10,676	106,195	101,535	1,235	102,770	3,425	129,555
1995	98,053	3,913	396	462	998	61	10,963	114,847	113,583	1,300	114,883	-36	129,520
1996	106,934	4,069	401	419	1,107	-2,293[8]	10,496	121,135	124,088	1,229	125,317	-4,182	125,338

(1) Fiscal year 1975 consists of the 12 months ending on June 30 of each year; fiscal years 1980 and later consist of the 12 months ending on Sept. 30 of each year. (2) Other income includes recoveries of amounts reimbursed from the trust fund that are not obligations of the trust fund and a small amount of miscellaneous income. (3) Includes costs of Peer Review Organizations (beginning with the implementation of the Prospective Payment System on Oct. 1, 1983). (4) Includes costs of experiments and demonstration projects. (5) In fiscal year 1983, $12,437 mil was loaned to the Old-Age and Survivors Insurance Trust Fund under the interfund borrowing provisions of the Social Security Act. Repayments of $1,824 mil and $10,613 mil were made in fiscal years 1985 and 1986, respectively. (6) Includes the lump sum general revenue adjustment of $-1,100 mil, as provided for by section 151 of PL 98-21. (7) Includes $1,805 mil transfer from the SMI catastrophic coverage reserve fund, as provided for by PL 102-394. (8) Includes the lump-sum general revenue adjustment of $-2,366 mil, as provided for by section 151 of PL 98-21. NOTE: Totals do not necessarily equal the sum of rounded components.

CONSUMER INFORMATION

Consumer Information Catalog

Source: Consumer Information Center, U.S. General Services Administration

The *Consumer Information Catalog* is a free listing of more than 200 federal consumer publications. The topics of these booklets range from financial planning to planning a diet, from federal benefits to getting an education, from fixing a car to dealing effectively with consumer problems. Many of these booklets are available free.

The *Consumer Information Catalog* is published quarterly by the Consumer Information Center (CIC) of the U.S. General Services Administration. For a free copy of the most current *Consumer Information Catalog,* send your name and address to Consumer Information Catalog, Pueblo, CO 81009. You can also order a copy of the catalog by phone at 1-888-8PUEBLO. Educators, librarians, and members of nonprofit groups who are able to distribute 25 or more copies of the *Consumer Information Catalog* on a quarterly basis should write to the same address for an application to be placed on the mailing list. Costs prevent the Consumer Information Center from maintaining a mailing list for the use of individuals.

Publications listed in the *Consumer Information Catalog* are available online, along with other consumer news, updates, and information. Use your modem or Internet connection to access the Consumer Information Center electronically. Internet World Wide Web: http://www.pueblo.gsa.gov; Electronic BBS: 202-208-7679;

For detailed instructions on connecting to CIC, send e-mail to catalog.pueblo@gsa.gov with the words "SEND INFO" in the body of the message.

At-Home Shopping—Consumer Tips and Rights

Source: Consumer Information Catalog; U.S. Postal Service; U.S. Office of Consumer Affairs

Tips

• Deal only with reliable firms. Check with your local consumer protection agency or the Better Business Bureau (BBB) nearest the business.

• Review the advertising offer carefully.

• If not stated, inquire about warranty, refund, and exchange policies.

• Never send cash. Pay by money order, check, charge, or credit card so that you have a record of your purchase.

• Keep the ad you responded to and a copy of the order form. If there is no order form, record the company's name, address, phone number, date, the item you purchased, amount paid, and the promised delivery date.

• Never give your credit, debit, charge card or bank account number unless you have checked out the company or have done business with it before.

Rights

Late deliveries, delays, canceled orders. By federal law, a company must ship your order within 30 days, unless the advertisement promises a different shipping time. If the company cannot ship within 30 days or the promised time, it must give you an "Option Notice." You can choose to wait longer for your order or to cancel and get a prompt refund. If you cancel and if your order was paid by charge or credit card, the seller has one billing cycle to tell the card issuer to credit your account.

The following are exceptions to this rule:

(1) If a company does not promise a shipping time and if you are applying for credit to pay for your purchase, the company has 50 days after receiving your order to ship.

(2) Spaced deliveries, such as magazine subscriptions (except for 1st shipment), and items that continue until you cancel (for example, book or record clubs), cash on delivery (COD) orders, services, and seeds or growing plants.

Unordered merchandise. If you are shipped a product that you did not order, it's yours. It is illegal for a company to pressure you to pay for it or to return it.

Damaged or spoiled items. If damage is obvious, and if you decide not to accept the package, write "REFUSED" on the wrapper (at time of delivery) and return it unopened to the seller. No new postage is needed, unless the package came by insured, registered, certified, or COD mail and you signed for it.

Disputes or billing errors. If there is a problem with your order—you were billed the wrong amount, you never got the product, the goods arrived in damaged condition, or the merchandise or services were misrepresented—follow these steps:

(1) Write immediately to the company from whom you ordered, explaining the problem and asking for a specific resolution. Be sure to include your name, address, and daytime phone number, your order or invoice number, a copy of the canceled check, or any other helpful information about your purchase.

(2) If you charged your purchase to a charge or credit card account or if you arranged for the payment to be automatically withdrawn from a bank account, send a copy of your letter to the card issuer or bank.

You usually have 60 days after receiving a bill to dispute charges.

Postal regulations allow you to write a check payable to the sender, rather than the delivery company, on COD orders. If, after examining the merchandise, you feel there has been misrepresentation or fraud, you can stop payment on the check and file a complaint with the U.S. Postal Inspector's Office.

For other at-home shopping questions, contact: The Federal Trade Commission, Division of Enforcement, Washington, DC 20580; 202-326-3768.

Charitable Giving in the U.S., 1986-96, by Sources of Contributions

Source: American Assn. of Fund-Raising Counsel, Inc., AAFRC Trust for Philanthropy

(in billions of dollars)

Year	Corporations	Foundations	Bequests	Individuals	Total[1]
1986	$5.03	$5.43	$5.70	$67.63	$83.79
1987	5.21	5.88	6.58	72.32	89.99
1988	5.34	6.15	6.57	80.07	98.13
1989	5.46	6.55	6.97	87.75	108.73
1990	5.46	7.23	7.64	91.15	111.48
1991	5.62	7.72	7.78	96.10	117.22
1992	5.92	8.64	8.15	98.38	121.09
1993	6.26	9.53	8.54	102.13	126.46
1994	6.88	9.66	8.77	104.53	129.84
1995	7.40	10.44	9.77	116.23	143.84
1996	8.50	11.83	10.46	119.92	150.70

[1]Totals may not add exactly, because of independent rounding.

Business Directory

Listed below are major U.S. corporations whose operations—products and services—directly concern the American consumer. At the end of each listing is a **representative sample** of the company's products.

Company...Address...Telephone number...Top executive ...Business.

Abbott Laboratories...One Abbott Park Rd., North Chicago, IL 60064...(708) 937-6100...D. L. Burnham...health care prods. (Murine, Selsun Blue).

Aetna Inc....151 Farmington Ave., Hartford, CT 06156...(203) 273-0123...Ronald E. Compton...health insurance, financial services.

H. F. Ahmanson & Co....4900 Rivergrade Rd., Irwindale, CA 91706...(818) 814-7986...R. H. Deihl...largest thrift-holding co. in U.S. (Home Savings of America).

Alberto Culver Co....2525 Armitage Ave., Melrose Park, IL 60160...(708) 450-3000...Leonard H. Lavin...hair care, household products, beauty aids, grocery items.

Albertson's Inc....250 Parkcenter Blvd., Boise, ID 83726...(208) 395-6200...Gary Michael...supermarkets.

Allegheny Teledyne, Inc....1000 Six PPG Pl., Pittsburgh, PA 15222-5479...(412) 394-2800...Richard P. Simmons...electronics, aerospace, industrial, consumer prods. (Water Pik); specialty metals.

AlliedSignal...Morristown, NJ 07960...(201) 455-2000 ...Lawrence Bossidy...aerospace, engineered materials, automotive prods.

Allstate Corp....Allstate Plaza, Northbrook, IL 60062...(847) 402-5000...Jerry Choate...property/casualty, life insurance.

Aluminum Co. of America (Alcoa)...425 6th Ave., Pittsburgh, PA 15219...(412) 553-3042...Paul O'Neill...world's largest aluminum producer.

Amerada Hess Corp....1185 Ave. of the Americas, NY, NY 10036...(212) 997-8500...J. B. Hess...integrated petroleum co.

American Express Co....200 Vesey St., NY, NY 10285...(212) 640-2000...Harvey Golub...travelers checks, credit card services, insurance, investment services.

American Greetings Corp....1 American Rd., Cleveland, OH 44144...(216) 252-7300...Morry Weiss...greeting cards, stationery, gift items.

American Home Products Corp....5 Giralda Farms, Madison, NJ 07940...(201) 660-5000...John R. Stafford...prescription and over-the-counter drugs (Advil, Anacin, Robitussin), agricultural prods.

American Intl. Group...70 Pine St., NY, NY 10270...(212) 770-7000...Maurice R. Greenberg...insurance, financial services.

American Stores Co....709 E. South Temple, Salt Lake City, UT 84102...(801) 961-3000...Victor Lund...retail food markets, dept. & drug stores.

Ameritech...30 S. Wacker Dr., Chicago, IL 60606...(312) 750-5000...Richard C. Notebaert...communications services.

Amoco Corp....200 E. Randolph Dr., Chicago, IL 60601...(312) 856-6111...H. L. Fuller...integrated petroleum co.

AMP, Inc....Eisenhower Blvd., Harrisburg, PA 17105...(717) 564-0100...James E. Marley...designs, produces electronic connection devices.

AMR Corp....PO Box 619616, Dallas/Ft. Worth Airport, TX 75261...(817) 963-1234...Robert Crandall...air transportation (American Airlines).

Anheuser-Busch Cos., Inc....One Busch Place, St. Louis, MO 63118...(314) 577-2000...August A. Busch 3d...brewing (Budweiser, Michelob, Bud Light, Natural Light, Busch, O'Doul's), aluminum can manuf. & recycling, theme parks.

Apple Computer, Inc....1 Infinite Loop, Cupertino, CA 95014-2084...(408) 996-1010...Steve Jobs ...manuf. personal computers, software, peripherals.

Aramark Corp....1101 Market St., Philadelphia, PA 19107...(215) 238-3000...Joseph Neubauer...provides food, health, leisure, and other services.

Archer Daniels Midland Co....4666 Faires Pkwy., Decatur, IL 62526...(217) 424-5200...Dwayne O. Andreas...agricultural commodities, foods.

Armstrong World Industries, Inc....PO Box 3001, 313 W. Liberty St., Lancaster, PA 17604...(717) 397-0611...George A. Lorch...interior furnishings, specialty prods.

Arvin Industries, Inc....1531 13th St., Columbus, IN 47201...(812) 379-3000...Byron O. Pond...auto emission & ride control systems.

Ashland Inc....PO Box 391, Ashland, KY 41101...(606) 329-3333...Paul W. Chellgren...petroleum producer and refiner, chemicals, road construction.

Atlantic Richfield Co....515 S. Flower St., Los Angeles, CA 90071-2256...(213) 486-3511...M. R. Bowlin...integrated oil and gas producer.

AT&T Corp....32 Ave. of the Americas, NY, NY 10013-2412...(212) 387-5400...Robert E. Allen...communications, global information management, financial services.

Avon Products, Inc....9 West 57th St., NY, NY 10019...(212) 546-6015...James E. Preston...cosmetics, fragrances, toiletries, fashion jewelry, gift items, casual apparel, lingerie.

BankAmerica Corp....PO Box 37000, San Francisco, CA 94137...(415) 622-3456...R. M. Rosenberg...owns banks.

Bausch & Lomb...One Chase Square, Rochester, NY 14601...(716) 338-6000...William H. Waltrip...manuf. of vision-care products, accessories; health care products.

Baxter International Inc....One Baxter Pkwy., Deerfield, IL 60015...(847) 948-2000...Vernon R. Loucks Jr. ...health care prods. & services.

Bear Stearns Cos., Inc....245 Park Ave., NY, NY 10167...(212) 272-2000...Alan C. Greenberg...investment banking, securities trading, brokerage.

Becton, Dickinson & Co....One Becton Dr., Franklin Lakes, NJ 07417...(201) 847-6800...C. Castellini...medical, laboratory, diagnostic products.

Bell Atlantic Corp....1717 Arch St., Philadelphia, PA 19103...(215) 963-6000...Raymond W. Smith...telephone service in mid-Atlantic region.

BellSouth Corp....1155 Peachtree St. NE, Atlanta, GA 30367...(404) 249-2000...John L. Clendenin...provides telephone service in the southern U.S.

Best Buy Co., Inc....7075 Flying Cloud Dr., Eden Prairie, MN 55344...(612) 947-2000...R. M. Schulze...retailer of software, appliances, electronics, cameras, home office equipment.

Bethlehem Steel Corp....1170 8th Ave., Bethlehem, PA 18016...(610) 694-2424...Curtis H. Barnette...steel & steel prods.

Black & Decker Corp....701 E. Joppa Rd., Towson, MD 21204...(410) 716-3900...Nolan D. Archibald...manuf. power tools, household prods., small appliances.

H & R Block, Inc....4410 Main St., Kansas City, MO 64111...(816) 753-6900...Henry Bloch...tax preparation.

Boeing Co....7755 E. Marginal Way, Seattle, WA 98108...(206) 655-2121...Philip M. Condit...aerospace, aircraft manuf., defense systems. (Co. acquired McDonnell Douglas Corp. 8/1/97.)

Boise Cascade Corp....1111 W. Jefferson St., Boise, ID 83728...(208) 384-6161...George J. Harad...timber; paper, wood prods.

Borden, Inc....180 E. Broad St., Columbus OH 43215-3799...(614) 225-4000...C. Robert Kidder...food, cheese and cheese products, snacks (Wise), beverages, adhesives (Elmer's, Krazy Glue), pasta (Prince, Creamette, Goodman's), pasta sauce (Aunt Millie's, Classico).

Bristol-Myers Squibb Co....345 Park Ave., NY, NY 10022...(212) 546-4000...Charles A. Heimhold...toiletries (Ban antiperspirant), haircare items (Clairol), drugs (Bufferin, Comtrex, Excedrin), infant formula (Enfamil).

Brown-Forman Corp....PO Box 1080, Louisville, KY 40201-1080...(502) 585-1100...Owsley Brown 2d...distilled spirits (Jack Daniel's, Early Times), wines (Bolla, Fontina Candida, Korbel), liquor (Southern Comfort), Lenox china and crystal, luggage.

Brown Group, Inc....8300 Maryland Ave., St. Louis, MO 63166...(314) 854-4000...B. A. Bridgewater, Jr....manuf. & retailer of women's, men's, and children's shoes (Buster Brown, Naturalizer).

Brunswick Corp....One N. Field Ct., Lake Forest, IL 60045-4811...(847) 735-4700...P. N. Larson...marine, recreation, fitness equip., bowling centers & equip., fishing equip.

Burlington Northern Santa Fe Inc....2650 Lou Menk Dr., 2d Fl., Ft. Worth, TX 76131-2830...(847) 333-2000...Robert Krebs...one of the largest U.S. rail transportation cos.

Campbell Soup Co....Campbell Pl., Camden, NJ 08103...(609) 342-4800...David W. Johnson...canned soups, spaghetti (Franco-American), vegetable juice (V-8), pork and beans, pet foods, confections, Swanson frozen dinners, Prego spaghetti sauce, Mrs. Paul's frozen fish, Pepperidge Farm breads.

Carter-Wallace, Inc....1345 Ave. of the Americas, NY, NY 10105...(212) 339-5000...H. H. Hoyt...personal care items, antiperspirants (Arrid), shave lathers (Rise), tooth polish (Pearl Drops), condoms (Trojan), laxatives (Carter's Pills), hair removers (Nair), pet prods. (Victory flea collars).

Caterpillar Inc....100 N.E. Adams St., Peoria, IL 61629...(309) 675-1000...Donald Fites...heavy duty earth-moving equip.

Chase Manhattan Corp....270 Park Ave., NY, NY 10017 ...(212) 270-6000...Walter V. Shipley...largest U.S. banking company.

Chevron Corp....475 Market St., San Francisco, CA 94105 ...(415) 894-7700...Kenneth T. Derr...integrated oil co.

Chiquita Brands International, Inc....250 E. 5th St., Cincinnati, OH 45202...(513) 784-8000...Carl H. Lindner...bananas, other fruits, vegetables.

Chrysler Corp....1000 Chrysler Dr., Auburn Hills, MI 48288...(810) 576-5741...Robert J. Eaton...cars, trucks, auto parts.

Church & Dwight Co., Inc....469 N. Harrison St., Princeton, NJ 08543...(609) 683-5900...D. C. Minton...sodium bicarbonate, consumer prods. (Arm & Hammer).

CIGNA Corp....One Liberty Pl., Philadelphia, PA 19103...(215) 761-1000...Wilson H. Taylor...insurance holding co.

Circuit City Stores, Inc....9950 Maryland Dr., Richmond, VA 23233-1464...(804) 527-4000...Richard L. Sharp...retailer of electronic equip., consumer appliances; new and used-car stores.

Circus Circus Enterprises, Inc....2880 Las Vegas Blvd. S, Las Vegas, NV 89109...(702) 734-0410...Clyde Turner...casino operator.

Citicorp...399 Park Ave., NY, NY 10043...(212) 559-1000...J. S. Reed...one of the largest U.S. banking companies.

Clorox Co....1221 Broadway, Oakland, CA 94612...(510) 271-7000...G. Craig Sullivan...retail consumer prods. (Formula 409, Pine-Sol, Soft Scrub, Kingsford charcoal briquets, Combat and Black Flag insecticides, Hidden Valley Ranch dressing, Brita water systems).

Coastal Corp....9 Greenway Plaza, Houston, TX 77046...(713) 877-1400...David A. Arledge...oil refineries, natural gas pipeline systems.

Coca-Cola Co....One Coca-Cola Plaza, Atlanta, GA 30313...(404) 676-2121...Roberto C. Goizueta...soft drinks (Coca-Cola, Sprite, Nestea), syrups, citrus and fruit juices (Minute Maid, Hi-C).

Colgate-Palmolive Co....300 Park Ave., NY, NY 10022...(212) 310-2000...Reuben Mark...soap (Palmolive, Irish Spring), detergent (Fab, Ajax, Fresh Start), toothpaste (Colgate, Ultra Brite), household prods. (Handy Wipes, Curad bandages), pet food, crystal.

Columbia/HCA Healthcare Corp....One Park Plaza, Nashville, TN 37203...(615) 327-9551...R. L. Scott...largest hospital mgmt. co. in the U.S.

Compaq Computer Corp....20555 SH 249, Houston, TX 77070...(713) 370-0670...Benjamin M. Rosen...portable and desktop computers.

Comp USA, Inc....14951 N. Dallas Pkwy., Dallas, TX 75240...(972) 982-4000...G. H. Bateman...largest U.S. superstore retailer of microcomputers and peripherals.

Computer Sciences Corp....2100 E. Grand Ave., El Segundo, CA 90245...(310) 615-0311...Van B. Honeycutt...technology services.

ConAgra...One ConAgra Dr., Omaha, NE 68102...(402) 595-4000...Philip B. Fletcher...2d largest U.S. food processor.

Continental Airlines, Inc....2929 Allen Pkwy., Houston, TX 77019...(713) 834-2950...Gordon Bethune...air transportation.

Adolph Coors Co....Golden, CO 80401...(303) 279-6565...William K. Coors...brewer.

Corning, Inc....One Riverfront Plaza, Corning, NY 14831...(607) 974-9000...Roger G. Ackerman...specialty materials, optical fiber and cable.

Costco Cos., Inc....999 Lake Dr., Issaquah, WA 98027...(206) 313-8100...J. H. Brotman...wholesale warehouses.

CPC International, Inc....International Plaza, Englewood Cliffs, NJ 07632...(201) 894-4000...Charles Shoemate... branded food items (Hellmann's mayonnaise, Best Foods, Skippy peanut butter, Knorr soups, Thomas' English muffins, Mueller pasta prods., Freihofer's, Boboli, Arnold breads).

Crane Co....100 First Stamford Pl., Stamford, CT 06902...(203) 363-7300...R. S. Evans...manuf. fluid control devices, vending machines, fiberglass panels, aircraft brakes.

CVS Corp....One CVS Dr., Woonsocket, RI 02895...(401) 765-1500...Stanley P. Goldstein...largest U.S. drugstore chain.

A. T. Cross Co....One Albion Rd., Lincoln, RI 02865...(401) 333-1200...Bradford R. Boss...writing instruments.

Crown Cork & Seal Co....One Crown Way, Philadelphia, PA 19154-4599...(215) 698-5100...William J. Avery...metal & plastic containers, packaging machinery.

CSX Corp....901 E. Cary St., Richmond, VA 23219...(804) 782-1400...John W. Snow...rail, ocean, barge freight transport.

Culbro Corp....387 Park Ave. S, NY, NY 10016-8899...(212) 448-3800...E. M. Cullman...cigars (Macanudo, Robert Burns, White Owl, Tiparillo's); food, nursery prods., real estate.

Dana Corp....4500 Dorr St., Toledo, OH 43615...(419) 535-4500...Southwood J. Morcott...truck and auto parts, supplies.

Dayton Hudson Corp....777 Nicollet Mall, Minneapolis, MN 55402...(612) 370-6948...Robert J. Ulrich...department, specialty stores (Marshall Field's, Target).

Deere & Co....John Deere Rd., Moline, IL 61265...(309) 765-8000...Hans W. Becherer...farm, industrial, and outdoor power equip.

Dell Computer Corp....One Dell Way, Round Rock, TX 78682...(512) 338-4400...Michael S. Dell...portable and desktop computers.

Delta Air Lines, Inc....Hartsfield Atlanta International Airport, Atlanta, GA 30320...(404) 715-2600...Ronald W. Allen...air transportation.

Dial Corp....1850 N. Central Ave., Phoenix, AZ 85044...(602) 207-2800...Malcolm Jozoff...consumer prods. (Dial soap, Purex detergents, Armour Star meats, Renuzit air fresheners).

Diebold, Inc....PO Box 8230, Canton, OH 44711...(216) 489-4000...Robert W. Mahoney...manuf. automatic teller machines, security systems.

Digital Equipment Corp....111 Powdermill Rd., Maynard, MA 01754...(508) 493-5111...R. B. Palmer...supplies network computer systems and peripherals.

Dillard's...1600 Cantrell Rd., Little Rock, AR 72201...(501) 376-5200...William Dillard...large dept. store chain.

Walt Disney Co....500 S. Buena Vista St., Burbank, CA 91521-7320...(818) 560-1000...Michael D. Eisner...motion pictures, television (ESPN, ABC), radio stations, theme parks (Walt Disney World, Disneyland) and resorts, publishing, recordings, retailing (Disney Stores).

Dole Food Co. Inc....31365 Oak Crest Dr., Westlake Village, CA 91361...(818) 879-6600...David H. Murdock...food products, fresh fruits and vegetables.

R. R. Donnelley & Sons Co....77 W. Wacker Dr., Chicago, IL 60601-8375...(312) 326-8000...William L. Davis...largest commercial printer.

Dow Chemical Co....2030 Dow Center, Midland, MI 48674...(517) 636-1000...W. Stavrapoulos...chemicals, plastics, consumer prods. (Ziploc, Saran Wrap, Fantastik).

Dow Jones & Co., Inc....200 Liberty St., NY, NY 10281...(212) 416-2000...Peter R. Kann...financial news service, publishing (*Wall Street Journal*, *Barron's*, Ottaway Newspapers).

Dun & Bradstreet Corp....One Diamond Hill Rd., Murray Hill, NJ 07974...(908) 665-5000...Volney Taylor...business information, publishing (Moody's).

E. I. du Pont de Nemours & Co....1007 Market St., Wilmington, DE 19898...(302) 774-1000...Edgar Woolard Jr....largest U.S. chemical co.; petroleum, consumer prods.

Eastman Kodak Co....343 State St., Rochester, NY 14650...(716) 724-5492...G. Fisher...world's largest producer of photographic prods.

Eaton Corp....1111 Superior Ave., Cleveland, OH 44114...(216) 523-5000...Steven R. Hardis...manuf. of electronic, electrical prods., vehicle components.

Emerson Electric Co....8000 W. Florissant Ave., St. Louis, MO 63136...(314) 553-2000...C. F. Knight...electrical, electronics products & systems.

Exxon Corp....5959 Las Colinas Blvd., Irving, TX 75039-2298...(214) 444-1900...Lee R. Raymond...world's largest publicly owned integrated oil co.

Fabri-Centers of America, Inc....5555 Darrow Rd., Hudson, OH 44236...(216) 656-2600...Alan Rosskamm...specialty fabric stores.

Fedders Corp....PO Box 813, Liberty Corner, NJ 07938...(908) 604-8686...Salvatore Giordano...manuf. of room air conditioners, dehumidifiers.

Federal Express Corp....Box 727, Memphis, TN 38194...(901) 369-3600...F. W. Smith...express delivery service.

Federal Home Loan Mortgage Corp. (Freddie Mac)...8200 Jones Branch Dr., McLean, VA 22102...(703) 903-2000...Leland C. Brendsel...residential mortgage provider.

Federal National Mortgage Assn. (Fannie Mae)...3900 Wisconsin Ave. NW, Washington, DC 20016...(202) 752-7115...James A. Johnson...largest U.S. provider of residential mortgage funds.

Federated Dept. Stores...7 W. 7th St., Cincinnati, OH 45202...(513) 579-7000...James Zimmerman...Macy's, Bloomingdale's, Stern's dept. stores.

Fieldcrest Cannon, Inc....326 E. Stadium Dr., Eden, NC 27288...(910) 627-3117...James M. Fitzgibbons...household textile prods.

First Brands Corp....83 Wooster Hts. Rd., Danbury, CT 06813-1911...(203) 731-2300...William V. Stephenson...consumer prods. (Glad plastic bags, Scoop-Away cat litter, STP auto prods.).

First Data Corp....401 Hackensack Ave., Hackensack, NJ 07601...(201) 525-4702...Henry C. Duques...information retrieval, data processing.

Fleetwood Enterprises, Inc....3125 Myers St., Riverside, CA 92503-5527...(909) 351-3500...John C. Crean...manufactured homes, recreational vehicles.

Fleming Cos., Inc....6301 Waterford Blvd., PO Box 26647, Oklahoma City, OK 73126...(405) 840-7200...Robert E. Stauth...largest U.S. wholesale food distrib.

Fluor Corp....3353 Michelson Dr., Irvine, CA 92698...(714) 975-2000...L. G. McCraw...engineering and construction, mining.

Ford Motor Co....American Rd., Dearborn, MI 48121...(313) 845-8540...Alexander Trotman...motor vehicles (Ford Tractor, Lincoln-Mercury), rentals (Budget Rent A Car).

Fortune Brands, Inc....1700 E. Putnam Ave., Old Greenwich, CT 06870...(203) 698-5000...Thomas C. Hays... whiskey (Jim Beam), hardware, office prods., golf and leisure products (Titleist).

Fruit of the Loom, Inc....5000 Sears Tower, Chicago, IL 60606...(312) 876-1724...William Farley...manuf. of underwear, activewear.

Gannett Co., Inc....1100 Wilson Blvd., Arlington, VA 22234...(703) 284-6000...J. J. Curley...newspaper publishing (*USA Today*), network and cable TV, radio stations, home security systems.

The Gap, Inc....One Harrison, San Francisco, CA 94105...(415) 952-4400...Donald G. Fisher...casual and activewear retailer.

General Dynamics Corp....3190 Fairview Park Dr., Falls Church, VA 22042-4523...(703) 876-3000...J. R. Mellor...nuclear submarines, armored vehicles, warships.

General Electric Co....3135 Easton Tpke., Fairfield, CT 06431...(203) 373-2211...Nicholas D. Chabraja ...electrical, electronic equip., radio and television broadcasting (NBC), aircraft engines, power generation, appliances.

General Mills, Inc....PO Box 1113, Minneapolis, MN 55440...(612) 540-2444...S. W. Sanger...foods (Total, Bisquick, Wheaties, Cheerios, Chex, Hamburger Helper, Betty Crocker).

General Motors Corp....3044 W. Grand Blvd., Detroit, MI 48202-3091...(313) 556-5000...John F. Smith Jr. ...world's largest auto manuf. (Chevrolet, Pontiac, Cadillac, Buick).

Genuine Parts Co....2999 Circle 75 Pkwy., Atlanta, GA 30339...(404) 953-1700...Larry L. Prince...distributes auto replacement parts (NAPA).

Georgia-Pacific Corp....133 Peachtree St. NE, Atlanta, GA 30303...(404) 521-5210...A. D. Correll...one of world's largest manuf. of paper and wood prods.

Gillette Co....Prudential Tower Bldg., Boston, MA 02199...(617) 421-7000...Alfred Zeien...razors, pens (Paper Mate), toiletries (Right Guard deodorants, Foamy shaving cream), hair products (Adorn), household appliances (Braun), batteries (Duracell).

Goodyear Tire & Rubber Co....1144 E. Market St., Akron, OH 44316...(330) 796-8576...Samir F. Gibara...world's largest rubber manuf.; tires and other auto products.

W. R. Grace & Co....One Town Center Rd., Boca Raton, FL 33486...(561) 362-2000...Albert J. Costello...chemicals, packaging, construction prods.

Great Atlantic & Pacific Tea Co. (A&P)...2 Paragon Dr., Montvale, NJ 07645...(201) 573-9700...James Wood... supermarkets.

GTE Corp....One Stamford Forum, Stamford, CT 06904 ...(203) 965-2000...Charles R. Lee...large telecommunications co., cellular telephone provider.

Halliburton Co....500 N. Akard St., Dallas, TX 75201...(214) 978-2600...Richard Cheney...energy, engineering, and construction services.

Harley-Davidson, Inc....3700 W. Juneau Ave., Milwaukee, WI 53208...(414) 343-4680...R. F. Teerlink...manuf. of motorcycles, parts & accessories.

Harrah's Entertainment, Inc....1023 Cherry Rd., Memphis, TN 38117...(901) 762-8600...Philip G. Satre...casino-hotels.

Hartmarx...101 N. Wacker Dr., Chicago, IL 60606...(312) 372-6300...Elbert O. Hand...apparel manufacturer (Hickey Freeman, Hart Schaffner & Marx, Pierre Cardin, Perry Ellis).

Hasbro, Inc....1027 Newport Ave., Pawtucket, RI 02862 ...(401) 431-8697...A. G. Hassenfeld...toy and game manuf. & marketer (Milton Bradley, Playskool, G. I. Joe, Parker Bros., Play-Doh).

H. J. Heinz Co....PO Box 57, Pittsburgh, PA 15230...(412) 456-6014...Anthony J. F. O'Reilly...foods (Star-Kist, '57 Varieties), pet food (9 Lives), Weight Watchers.

Hershey Foods Corp....100 Crystal A Dr., Hershey, PA 17033...(717) 534-6799...Kenneth Wolfe...chocolate & confectionery prods. (Reese's, Kit Kat, Peter Paul Mounds, Almond Joy, Cadbury, Jolly Rancher, Milk Duds, Good 'n' Plenty), pasta (San Giorgio, Ronzoni).

Hewlett-Packard Co....3000 Hanover St., Palo Alto, CA 94304...(415) 857-1501...Lewis E. Platt...manuf. computers, electronic prods. and systems.

Hillenbrand Industries, Inc....700 State Rte. 46, Batesville, IN 47006...(812) 934-7000...D. A. Hillenbrand...manuf. caskets, electronically operated hospital beds, locks.

Hilton Hotels Corp....9336 Civic Center Dr., Beverly Hills, CA 90120...(310) 278-4321...Barron Hilton...casinos, hotels. (Co. announced 1/27/97 that it planned to acquire ITT Corp.)

Home Depot, Inc....2727 Paces Ferry Rd., Atlanta, GA 30339...(770) 433-8211...Bernard Marcus...retailer of building materials & home improvement prods.

Honeywell, Inc....Honeywell Plaza, Minneapolis, MN 55408...(612) 951-1000...Michael Bonsignore...industrial and home control systems, aerospace guidance systems, information systems.

Hormel Foods Corp....One Hormel Pl., Austin, MN 55912...(507) 437-5611...J. W. Johnson...meat packaging, pork and beef prods. (SPAM, Dinty Moore, Mary Kitchen).

Houghton Mifflin Co....222 Berkeley St., Boston, MA 02116...(617) 351-5000...Nader F. Darehshori...publisher of educational and reference books.

Huffy Corp....7701 Byers Rd., Miamisburg, OH 45342...(937) 866-6251...Richard L. Molen...bicycles, sports and hardware equip.

Humana, Inc....500 W. Main St., Louisville, KY 40201-1438...(502) 580-1000...David A. Jones...provides health care plans, financial services.

IBP, Inc....IBP Ave., PO Box 515, Dakota City, NE 68731...(402) 494-2061...Robert Peterson...world's largest processor of fresh beef and pork.

Ingersoll-Rand Co....Woodcliff Lake, NJ 07675...(201) 573-0123...J. E. Perella...industrial machinery.

Intel Corp....2200 Mission College Blvd., Santa Clara, CA 95052-8119...(408) 765-8080...A. S. Grove...manuf. integrated circuits (Pentium).

International Business Machines Corp. (IBM)...One Old Orchard Rd., Armonk, NY 10504...(914) 765-1900...Louis V. Gerstner Jr....information processing systems, equip., services.

International Paper Co....2 Manhattanville Rd., Purchase, NY 10577...(914) 397-1500...John T. Dillon...paper and wood prods., films, chemicals, minerals.

Interstate Bakeries Corp....12 E. Armour Blvd., Kansas City, MO 64111...(816) 502-4000...Charles A. Sullivan...baked goods wholesaler, distributor (Wonder, Hostess, Dolly Madison).

ITT Corp....1330 Ave. of the Americas, NY, NY 10022...(212) 258-1000...Rand V. Araskog...casinos and hotels (Caesars, Desert Inn, Sheraton), educational, informational services. (Co. announced 8/97 that it planned to split into 3 independent cos.)

Johnson Controls...5757 N. Green Bay Ave., Milwaukee, WI 53201...(414) 228-1200...James H. Keyes...fire protection services, auto seats and batteries.

Johnson & Johnson...501 George St., New Brunswick, NJ 08903...(908) 524-0400...Ralph S. Larsen...surgical dressings (Band-Aid), pharmaceuticals (Tylenol), toiletries.

Jostens, Inc....5501 Norman Center Dr., Minneapolis, MN 55437...(612) 830-3300...Robert P. Jensen...school rings, yearbooks, plaques, pictures.

Kellogg Co....One Kellogg Sq., Battle Creek, MI 49016...(616) 961-2000...Arnold G. Langbo...ready-to-eat cereals & other food prods. (Frosted Flakes, Rice Krispies, Froot Loops, Pop-Tarts, Nutri-Grain, Eggo, Lender's).

Kimberly-Clark Corp....PO Box 619100, Dallas, TX 75261-9100...(972) 281-1200...Wayne R. Sanders...paper and lumber prods., consumer prods. (Kleenex, Scott, Cottonelle, Huggies, Viva, Kotex).

King World Productions, Inc....1700 Broadway, NY, NY 10019...(212) 315-4000...Roger King...syndicator of TV programs (*Oprah Winfrey Show, Wheel of Fortune, Jeopardy!, Inside Edition*).

Kmart Corp....3100 W. Big Beaver Rd., Troy, MI 48084...(810) 643-1000...Floyd Hall...operates chain of discount stores, home improvement retail stores.

Knight-Ridder, Inc....One Herald Plaza, Miami, FL 33132...(305) 376-3800...P. A. Ridder...newspaper publishing.

Kroger Co....1014 Vine St., Cincinnati, OH 45202...(513) 762-4000...Joseph A. Pichler...largest U.S. grocery chain.

(Estee) Lauder Cos....767 5th Ave., NY, NY 10153...(212) 572-4200...Leonard A. Lauder...cosmetics, fragrance prods.

La-Z-Boy Chair Co....1284 N. Telegraph Rd., Monroe, MI 48161...(313) 242-1444...Charles T. Knabusch...reclining chairs, other furniture.

Leggett & Platt, Inc....No. 1 Leggett Rd., Carthage, MO 64836...(417) 358-8131...Harry M. Cornell Jr....furniture and related products.

Lehman Bros. Holdings, Inc....3 World Financial Ctr., NY, NY 10285...(212) 526-7000...Richard S. Fuld Jr....investment banker.

Levi Strauss Associates...1155 Battery St., San Francisco, CA 94111...(415) 544-6000...Robert D. Haas...blue jeans, casual apparel.

Eli Lilly & Company...Lilly Corporate Center, Indianapolis, IN 46285...(317) 276-2000...R. L. Tobias...manuf. pharmaceuticals (Prozac) and animal health products.

The Limited, Inc....3 Limited Pkwy., Columbus, OH 43216...(614) 479-7000...Leslie H. Wexner...women's apparel stores (Lane Bryant, Lerner, Victoria's Secret), Abercrombie & Fitch, other retailers.

Litton Industries, Inc....21240 Burbank Blvd., Woodland Hills, CA 91367...(818) 598-5000...John M. Leonis...industrial systems & services, advanced electronic systems, electronic & electrical prods., marine engineering.

Liz Claiborne, Inc....1441 Broadway, NY, NY 10018...(212) 354-4900...P. Charron...apparel, accessories, cosmetics.

Lockheed Martin Corp....6801 Rockledge Dr., Bethesda, MD 20817...(301) 897-6000...Norman Augustine...commercial and military aircraft, electronics, missiles (Co. announced 7/3/97 that it had agreed to acquire Northrop Grumman Corp.).

Loews Corp....667 Madison Ave., NY, NY 10021...(212) 545-2000...Laurence A. Tisch...tobacco prods. (Kent, Newport), watches (Bulova), hotels, insurance, offshore drilling.

Longs Drug Stores, Inc....141 North Civic Dr., Walnut Creek, CA 94596...(510) 937-1170...R. M. Long...drug store chain.

Lowe's Cos., Inc....Box 1111, N. Wilkesboro, NC 28656...(910) 651-4000...Robert L. Strickland...retailer of building materials & related prods.

Luby's Cafeterias, Inc....2211 Northeast Loop 410, San Antonio, TX 78217...(210) 654-9000...Barry J. C. Parker... operates cafeterias in south and southwest U.S.

Lucent Technologies, Inc....600 Mountain Ave., Murray Hill, NJ 07974...(908) 582-8500...Richard A. McGinn...leading developer, designer, and manuf. of telecommunications systems, software, and products.

Manpower Inc....5301 N. Ironwood Rd., Milwaukee, WI 53217 ...(414) 961-1000...Mitchell S. Fromstein...employment services.

Marriott International, Inc....Marriott Dr., Washington, DC 20058...(301) 380-9000...John Willard Marriott Jr....hotels, retirement communities, food service.

Masco Corp....21001 Van Born Rd., Taylor, MI 48180...(313) 274-7400...Richard A. Manoogian...manuf. kitchen, bathroom prods. (Delta faucets, Fieldstone cabinets).

Mattel, Inc....333 Continental Blvd., El Segundo, CA 90245...(213) 524-2000...Jill E. Barad...toy & hobby prods. (Barbie dolls, Fisher-Price, Hot Wheels).

May Department Stores Co....611 Olive St., St. Louis, MO 63101...(314) 342-6300...David Farrell...department stores (Hecht's, Lord & Taylor, Foley's).

Maytag Corp....Newton, IA 50208...(515) 792-8000...Leonard A. Hadley...manuf. home laundry equip., appliances (Magic Chef, Admiral, Hoover).

McDonald's Corp....One McDonald's Plaza, Oak Brook, IL 60521 ...(630) 623-7428...Michael R. Quinlan...fast-food restaurants.

McGraw-Hill Cos....1221 Ave. of the Americas, NY, NY 10020...(212) 512-2000...Joseph L. Dionne...book, magazine publishing (*Business Week*), information & financial services (Standard and Poor's), TV stations.

MCI Communications Corp....1801 Pennsylvania Ave., Washington, DC 20006...(202) 872-1600...Bert C. Roberts Jr....large long-distance telephone carrier. (As of Oct. 16, 1997, MCI had received merger or acquisition offers from 3 cos.)

McKesson Corp....One Post St., San Fransicso, CA 94104...(415) 983-8300...Alan Seelenfreund...drugs, toiletries, bottled water.

Mead Corporation...Courthouse Plaza NE, Dayton, OH 45463 ...(937) 495-6323...Steven C. Mason...printing and writing paper, paperboard, packaging, shipping containers.

Medtronic, Inc....7000 Central Ave. NE, Minneapolis, MN 55432...(612) 514-4000...W. W. George...manuf. prosthetic and pacemaker devices.

Merck & Co., Inc....PO Box 100, Whitehouse Station, NJ 08889-0100...(908) 423-1000...Raymond V. Gilmartin...human & animal health care prods.

Meredith Corp....1716 Locust St., Des Moines, IA 50336...(515) 284-3000...Jack D. Rehm...magazine publishing (*Better Homes and Gardens, Ladies Home Journal*), book publishing, broadcasting.

Merrill Lynch & Co., Inc....World Financial Ctr., N. Tower, NY, NY 10281-1332...(212) 449-1000...Daniel P. Tully ...securities broker, financial services.

Metropolitan Life Ins. Co....1 Madison Ave., NY, NY 10010-3690...(212) 578-2211...Harry P. Kamen...insurance, financial services.

Microsoft Corp....One Microsoft Way, Redmond, WA 98052-6399...(206) 882-8080...William H. Gates...largest independent software maker (Windows 95, Word, Excel).

Minnesota Mining & Manuf. Co....3M Center, St. Paul, MN 55144-1000...(612) 733-1110...L. D. DeSimone...abrasives, adhesives, recording materials; electrical, health care, cleaning (Scotch-Brite, O-Cel-O sponges), printing, consumer prods. (Scotch Tape, Post-It).

Mirage Resorts, Inc....3400 Las Vegas Blvd. S, Las Vegas, NV 89109...(702) 385-7111...Stephen A. Wynn...hotel-casino operator (Mirage, Treasure Island, Golden Nugget).

Mobil Corp....3225 Gallows Rd., Fairfax, VA 22037...(703) 846-3000...Lucio A. Noto...integrated international oil and petrochemical co.

Monsanto Company...800 N. Lindbergh Blvd., St. Louis, MO 63167...(314) 694-1000...Robert B. Shapiro...agricultural prods., pharmaceuticals, consumer prods. (NutraSweet, Equal).

J. P. Morgan & Co....60 Wall St., NY, NY 10260...(212) 483-2323...Douglas A. Warner...large bank.

Morgan Stanley, Dean Witter, Discover & Co....2 World Trade Ctr., NY, NY 10048...(212) 392-2222...Phillip J. Purcell...diversified financial services, largest U.S. credit-card issuer.

Motorola, Inc....1303 E. Algonquin Rd., Schaumburg, IL 60196...(847) 576-5000...G. L. Tooker...electronic equipment and components.

National Semiconductor Corp....2900 Semiconductor Dr., Santa Clara, CA 95052-8090...(408) 721-5000...B. Halla ...manuf. of semiconductors, integrated circuits.

NationsBank...NationsBank Corporate Center, Charlotte, NC 28255...(704) 386-5000...Hugh L. McColl Jr. ...commercial bank.

Navistar Intl. Corp....455 N. Cityfront Plaza Dr., Chicago, IL 60611...(312) 836-2000...John R. Horne...manuf. heavy-duty trucks, parts, school buses.

New York Times Co....229 W. 43d St., NY, NY 10036...(212) 556-3660...A. O. Sulzberger...newspapers, radio stations, TV stations, magazines (*Tennis, Golf Digest*).

Nike, Inc....One Bowerman Dr., Beaverton, OR 97005...(503) 671-6453...Philip Knight...athletic & leisure footware, apparel.

Nordstrom, Inc....1501 5th Ave., Seattle, WA 98101...(206) 628-2111...John J. Whitacre...upscale dept. store chain.

Norfolk Southern Corp....3 Commercial Pl., Norfolk, VA 23510...(757) 629-2640...David R. Goode...operates railways, freight carrier (North American Van Lines).

Northrop Grumman Corp....1840 Century Park East, Los Angeles, CA 90067...(310) 553-6262...Kent Kresa...aircraft, electronics, communications, missiles. (Co. announced 7/3/97 that it had agreed to be acquired by Lockheed Martin Corp.)

Northwest Airlines Corp....2700 Lone Oak Pkwy., Eagan, MN 55121...(612) 726-2111...John H. Dasburg...air transportation.

Occidental Petroleum Corp....10889 Wilshire Blvd., Los Angeles, CA 90024...(213) 879-1700...Ray R. Irani...oil, natural gas, chemicals, fertilizers.

Office Depot, Inc....2200 Old Germantown Rd., Delray Beach, FL 33445...(561) 278-4800...David Fuente...retail office supply stores.

Outboard Marine Corp....100 Sea-Horse Dr., Waukegan, IL 60085...(847) 689-6200...H. W. Bowman...outboard motors (Evinrude, Johnson), boats. (Co. announced 7/9/97 that it had agreed to be acquired by Detroit Diesel Corp.)

Owens Corning...One Owens Corning Pkwy., Toledo, OH 43659...(419) 248-8000...Glen H. Hiner...glass fiber and related prods., building materials.

Owens-Illinois...One SeaGate, Toledo, OH 43666...(419) 247-5000...J. H. Lemieux...manuf. glass and plastic containers.

Pacific Gas & Electric Corp. (PG&E)...77 Beale St., San Francisco, CA 94106...(800) 367-7731...Stanley T. Skinner...energy supplier.

PaineWebber Group, Inc....1285 Ave. of the Americas, NY, NY 10019-6028...Donald Marron...controls full-service securities firm.

J. C. Penney Co....6501 Legacy Dr., Plano, TX 75024...(214) 431-1000...James E. Oesterreicher...dept. stores, catalog sales, drug stores, insurance.

Pennzoil Co....PO Box 2967, Houston, TX 77252-8000...(713) 546-4000...J. L. Pate...integrated oil and gas co., franchises Jiffy Lube service centers. (Co. announced 6/23/97 that it had agreed to be acquired by Union Pacific Resources Grp.)

PepsiCo, Inc....700 Anderson Hill Rd., Purchase, NY 10577 ...(914) 253-2000...Roger A. Enrico...soft drinks (Pepsi-Cola, Mountain Dew, Slice), snacks (Ruffles, Lay's, Fritos, Doritos, Cracker Jack).

Pfizer, Inc....235 E. 42d St., NY, NY 10017...(212) 573-2323...W. C. Steere Jr....pharmaceutical, hospital, agricultural, chemical prods., consumer prods. (Visine eye drops, Ben-Gay pain relief).

Pharmacia & Upjohn, Inc....700 Portage Rd., Kalamazoo, MI 49001...(616) 323-4000...Jan Ekberg...pharmaceuticals (Motrin, Rogaine, Halcion, Xanax), chemicals, agricultural, health-care prods.

Philip Morris Cos., Inc....120 Park Ave., NY, NY 10017...(212) 880-5000...Geoffrey C. Bible...cigarettes (Marlboro, Virginia Slims), beer (Miller brands), packaged foods (Jell-O, Entenmann baked goods, Maxwell House coffee, Kool-Aid, Oscar Mayer meats, Tang, Kraft, Cheez Whiz & Velveeta cheese prods, Post cereals).

Phillips Petroleum Co....Bartlesville, OK 74004...(918) 661-6600...W. W. Allen...integrated oil and petrochemical co.

Pitney Bowes, Inc....Stamford, CT 06926...(203) 356-5000...Walter H. Wheeler Jr....postage meters, mail-handling equip.

Polaroid Corp....Technology Sq., Cambridge, MA 02139 ...(617) 386-2000...Gary T. DiCamillo...photographic equip., supplies, and optical goods.

PPG Industries, Inc....One PPG Place, Pittsburgh, PA 15272...(412) 434-3131...Jerry E. Dempsey...glass prods., fiberglass, paints, chemicals.

Premark Intl., Inc....1717 Deerfield Rd., Deerfield, IL 60015...(847) 405-6000...Warren L. Batts...food equip., home appliances, cookware.

Procter & Gamble Co....One Procter & Gamble Plaza, Cincinnati, OH 45202...(513) 983-1100...John Pepper...soaps & detergents (Ivory, Cheer, Tide, Mr. Clean, Comet, Spic and Span, Zest), toiletries (Crest toothpaste, Prell, Head and Shoulders shampoos, Noxzema, Oil of Olay, Old Spice), pharmaceuticals (Pepto-Bismol); Pampers disposable diapers, Folger's coffee, Hawaiian Punch, Charmin toilet tissues, Bounty towels, Vicks cough medicines, Crisco shortening, Duncan Hines cakes. (Co. announced 4/8/97 that it had agreed to acquire Tambrands.)

Prudential Ins. Co. of America...751 Broad St., Newark, NJ 07102-3777...(201) 802-6000...Arthur F. Ryan...insurance, financial services.

Quaker Oats Co....PO Box 049001, Chicago, IL 60604...(312) 222-7818...William D. Smithburg...cereal (Quaker Oat Bran, Life, Cap'n Crunch), foods (Aunt Jemima, Celeste pizza, Rice-A-Roni), beverages (Gatorade).

Quaker State Corp....255 E. John Carpenter Fwy., Irving, TX 75062...(972) 868-0438...Herbert M. Baum...marketing petroleum and car-care prods., quick-change oil centers.

Ralcorp Holdings, Inc....800 Market St., St. Louis, MO 63101...(314) 877-7000...Joe R. Micheletto...snack foods, baby food (Beech-Nut).

Ralston Purina Group...Checkerboard Sq., St. Louis, MO 63164...(314) 982-2161...W. P. Stiritz...pet and livestock food (Purina), batteries (Eveready, Energizer).

Raytheon Co....141 Spring St., Lexington, MA 02173...(617) 862-6600...Dennis J. Picard...electronics, aviation, appliances; Amana Refrigeration, Beech Aircraft.

Reader's Digest Assn., Inc....Pleasantville, NY 10570...(914) 238-1000...George Grune...magazines, books, home entertainment prods.

Reebok Intl., Ltd....100 Technology Ctr. Dr., Stoughton, MA 02072...(617) 341-5000...P. Fireman...athletic & casual footwear, sportswear.

Revlon Consumer Products Corp....625 Madison Ave., NY, NY 10022...(212) 527-4000...Jerry W. Levin...cosmetics, beauty aids, skin care.

Reynolds Metals Co....6601 W. Broad St., Richmond, VA 23230...(804) 281-2000...Richard G. Holder...aluminum prods.

Rite Aid Corp....30 Hunter Lane, Camp Hill, PA 17011-2404...(717) 761-2633...Martin Grass...discount drug stores.

RJR Nabisco Holdings Corp....1301 Ave. of the Americas, NY, NY 10019...(212) 258-5600...Steven F. Goldstone...cigarettes (Winston, Salem, Camel), foods (Oreo, Ritz, Grey Poupon, Cream of Wheat, A-1, Parkay).

Rockwell Intl. Corp....2201 Seal Beach Blvd., Seal Beach, CA 90740...(412) 565-2000...Donald R. Beall...diversified high-technology co.

Rubbermaid Inc....1147 Akron Rd., Wooster, OH 44691...(330) 264-6464...Wolfgang R. Schmitt...rubber and plastic consumer prods. (Little Tykes).

Ryder System, Inc....3600 NW 82d Ave., Miami, FL 33166...(305) 593-3726...M. Anthony Burns...truck-leasing service.

Safeway Inc....5918 Stoneridge Mall Rd., Pleasanton, CA 94588-3229...(510) 467-3000...Steven A. Burd...supermarkets.

Saloman Inc....7 World Trade Ctr., NY, NY 10048...(212) 783-7000...Robert E. Denham...investment banking, securities and commodities trading.

Sara Lee Corp....3 First National Plaza, Chicago, IL 60602...(312) 726-2600...John H. Bryan Jr....baked goods, fresh and processed meats (Ball Park, Jimmy Dean, Hillshire Farms), fresh and frozen fruits and vegetables and other packaged foods, beverages; hosiery, intimate apparel and knitwear (Hanes, L'eggs, Playtex, Champion).

SBC Communications, Inc....175 E. Houston, San Antonio, TX 78205...(210) 821-4105...Edward Whitacre Jr....telephone services.

Schering-Plough Corp....One Giralda Farms, Madison, NJ 07940...(201) 822-7000...R. P. Luciano...pharmaceuticals, consumer prods.

Seagate Technology...920 Disc Dr., Scotts Valley, CA 95066....(408) 438-6550....Alan F. Shugart manuf. disk drives.

Sears, Roebuck & Co....3333 Beverly Rd., Hoffman Estates, IL 60179...(847) 286-2500...Arthur Martinez...department, specialty stores.

Service Merchandise Co, Inc....PO Box 24600, Nashville, TN 37202-4600...(615) 660-6000...Raymond Zimmerman...operates catalog showrooms.

Shaw Industries, Inc....616 E. Walnut Ave., Dalton, GA 30720...(706) 278-3812...Robert E. Shaw...largest U.S. manuf. of carpeting (Armstrong, Magee, Philadelphia).

Sherwin-Williams Co....101 Prospect Ave. NW, Cleveland, OH 44115...(216) 566-2000...John G. Breen...largest North American paint producer (Dutch Boy, Kem-Tone).

J. M. Smucker Co....Strawberry Lane, Orrville, OH 44667 ...(216) 682-3000...T. P. Smucker...preserves, jams, jellies, toppings, syrups, juices.

Sprint Corp....PO Box 11315, Kansas City, MO 64112...(913) 624-3000...William T. Esrey...long-distance and local telecommunications.

Staples, Inc....One Research Dr., Westborough, MA 01581....(508) 370-8500....T. Stemberg....office-supply superstores.

State Farm Group...1 State Farm Plaza, Bloomington, IL 61710...(309) 766-2311...Edward B. Rust Jr....major insurance co.

Stone Container...150 N. Michigan Ave., Chicago, IL 60601...(312) 346-6600...R. W. Stone...corrugated containers, paper bags and sacks.

Stride Rite Corp....191 Spring St., Lexington, MA 02173...(617) 824-6000...Robert Siegel...adult's and children's footwear (Keds).

Sun Company, Inc....1801 Market St., Philadelphia, PA 19103-1000...(215) 977-3000 R. H. Campbell...energy resources co., markets Sunoco gasoline.

Sun Microsystems, Inc....2550 Garcia Ave., Mountain View, CA 94043...(415) 960-1300...Scott G. McNealy...supplier of network-based distributed computer systems (Java programming language).

SUPERVALU Inc....PO Box 990, Minneapolis, MN 55440...(612) 828-4000...Michael W. Wright...food wholesaler, retailer.

Sysco Corp....1390 Enclave Parkway, Houston, TX 77077-2099...(281) 584-1390...John F. Baugh...leading food distributor.

Tambrands Inc....777 Westchester Ave., White Plains, NY 10604...(914) 696-6000...E. Fogarty...feminine hygiene products (Tampax). (Co. announced 4/8/97 that it had agreed to be acquired by Procter & Gamble.)

Tandy Corp....1800 One Tandy Center, Fort Worth, TX 76102...(817) 390-3700...J. V. Roach...consumer electronics retailing (Computer City, Radio Shack).

Tenneco, Inc....1275 King St., Greenwich, CT 06831...(203) 863-1000...Dana G. Mead...packaging materials, (Hefty, Baggies), automotive parts (Monroe).

Texaco Inc....2000 Westchester Ave., White Plains, NY 10650...(914) 253-4000...P. I. Bijur...integrated international oil co.

Texas Instruments Inc....13500 N. Central Expressway, Dallas, TX 75265...(214) 995-3773...T. J. Engibous...electronics.

Textron, Inc....40 Westminster St., Providence, RI 02903...(401) 421-2800...J. F. Hardymon...aerospace, industrial, automotive prods., financial services.

Times Mirror Publishing Co....Times Mirror Sq., Los Angeles, CA 90053...(213) 237-3700...R. F. Erburu...newspapers, magazines (*Field & Stream, Popular Science*), books.

Time Warner Cos., Inc....75 Rockefeller Plaza, NY, NY 10020...(212) 522-1212...Gerald M. Levin...magazine publishing (Time, Sports Illustrated, Fortune, Money, People, DC Comics), TV and CATV (WB Network, HBO, Cinemax, CNN, TBS, TNT), book publishing (Little, Brown; Warner Books), motion pictures (Warner Bros.), recordings, Six Flags theme parks, sports teams, professional wrestling (Warner Bros. stores).

Tootsie Roll Industries, Inc....7401 S. Cicero Ave., Chicago, IL 60629...(773) 838-3400...M. J. Gordon...candy (Tootsie Roll, Mason Dots, Charms, Sugar Daddy, Charleston Chew).

Toro Co....8111 Lyndale Ave. S, Bloomington, MN 55420...(612) 888-8801...Kendrick B. Melrose...lawn and turf maintenance (Lawn-Boy), snow removal equipment, lightings and irrigation systems.

Toys "R" Us...461 From Rd., Paramus, NJ 07652...(201) 262-7800...Charles Lazarus...toy, clothing stores (Kids "R" Us).

Transamerica Corp....600 Montgomery St., San Francisco, CA 94111...(415) 983-4000...Frank C. Herringer...insurance, financial services.

Travelers Group, Inc....388 Greenwich St., NY, NY 10013...(212) 816-8000...Sanford I. Weill...insurance, financial services.

Triarc Cos., Inc....280 Park Ave., NY, NY 10017....(212) 451-3000...Nelson Peltz...fast-food restaurants (Arby's), beverages (Royal Crown, Mystic, Snapple, Stewart's), dyes and chemicals.

Tribune Co....435 N. Michigan Ave., Chicago, IL 60611...(312) 222-9100...J. W. Madigan...newspaper and book publishing, broadcasting, Chicago Cubs baseball team.

Tricon Global Restaurants, Inc....1441 Gardiner Lane, Louisville, KY 40213...(502) 456-8300...Andrall E. Pearson...restaurants (Pizza Hut, KFC, Taco Bell).

Trinity Industries, Inc....2525 Stemmons Freeway, Dallas, TX 75207...(214) 631-4420...W. Ray Wallace...manufactures metal products, rail and freight products.

TRW Inc....1900 Richmond Rd., Cleveland, OH 44124...(216) 291-7000...J. T. Gorman...car and truck operations, electronics, space and defense systems.

Tyco Intl., Ltd....One Tyco Pk., Exeter, NH 03833...(603) 778-9700...L. D. Kozlowski...fire protection systems, pipes, power cables, medical supplies, packaging.

Tyson Foods, Inc....2210 W. Oaklawn, Springdale, AR 72764...(501) 290-4000...Leland Tollett...fresh and processed poultry and seafood prods. (Holly Farms, Weaver).

UAL Corp....1200 E. Algonquin Rd., Elk Grove Township, IL 60007...(708) 952-4000...Gerald Greenwald...air transportation (United Airlines).

Union Carbide Corp....39 Old Ridgebury Rd., Danbury, CT 06817...(203) 794-2000...William H. Joyce...chemicals.

Union Pacific Corp....Martin Tower, 8th & Eaton Aves., Bethlehem, PA 18018...(610) 861-3200...Richard Davidson...railroad, trucking.

Unisys Corp....PO Box 500, Blue Bell, PA 19424-0001...(215) 986-4011...Lawrence A. Weinbach...designs, manuf. computer information systems and related products.

United HealthCare Corp....9900 Bren Rd. East, Minnetonka, MN 55343...(612) 936-1300...William W. McGuire...owns, manages health maintenance organizations.

United Parcel Service of America, Inc....55 Glenlake Pkwy. NE, Atlanta, GA 30328...(404) 828-6000...James P. Kelly...courier services, truck rentals.

United Technologies Corp....One Financial Plaza, Hartford, CT 06101...(860) 728-7000...George David... aerospace, industrial prods. & services (Carrier Corp., Otis Elevator, Pratt & Whitney, Sikorsky Aircraft).

Unocal Corp....2141 Rosencrans Ave., Ste. 400, El Segundo, CA 90245...(310) 726-7667...Roger Beach...oil, chemicals, geothermal energy.

US Airways Group, Inc....2345 Crystal Dr., Arlington, VA 22202...(703) 418-7000...Stephen M. Wolf...major domestic air carrier, other aviation subsidiaries.

UST Inc....100 W. Putnam Ave., Greenwich, CT 06830...(203) 661-1100...Vincent A. Gierer Jr. ...smokeless tobacco (Copenhagen, Skoal), pipe tobacco, wines.

USX-Marathon Group....600 Grant St., Pittsburgh, PA 15230...(412) 433-1121...Thomas J. Usher...integrated oil co.

V.F. Corp....1047 N. Park Rd., Wyomissing, PA 19610...(610) 378-1151...L. R. Pugh...apparel (Lee, Wrangler jeans, Vanity Fair, Jantzen).

Viacom, Inc....1515 Broadway, NY, NY 10036...(212) 258-6000...Sumner M. Redstone...TV broadcast stations and cable systems, channels (Showtime, MTV, VH-1, Nickelodeon); book publishing (Simon & Schuster, Macmillan, Prentice Hall); produces, distr. movies, TV shows (Paramount); video rental stores (Blockbuster), theme parks.

Walgreen Co....200 Wilmot Rd., Deerfield, IL 60015...(847) 914-2500...Charles R. Walgreen 3d...retail drug chain.

Wal-Mart Stores, Inc....Box 116, Bentonville, AR 72716...(501) 273-4000...S. Robson Walton...retail dept. and discount stores (Sam's Wholesale Clubs).

Warner-Lambert Co....201 Tabor Rd., Morris Plains, NJ 07950-2693...(201) 540-2000...M. R. Goodes...health care prods. (Benadryl), consumer prods. (Efferdent dental cleanser, Halls cough tablets, Schick razors, Certs mints, Listerine mouthwash, Trident, Chiclets, Dentyne gums).

Washington Post Co....1150 15th St. NW, Washington, DC 20071...(202) 334-6000...D. E. Graham...newspapers, *Newsweek* magazine, TV and CATV stations.

Waste Management, Inc....3003 Butterfield Rd., Oak Brook, IL 60521...(708) 572-8800...Ronald LeMay...solid waste collection and disposal.

Wells Fargo & Co....420 Montgomery St., San Francisco, CA 94163...(415) 396-3606...P. Hazen...banking.

Wendy's Intl., Inc....4288 W. Dublin-Granville Rd., Dublin, OH 43017...(614) 764-3100...Gordon F. Teter...quick-service restaurants.

Westinghouse Electric Corp....11 Stanwix St., Pittsburgh, PA 15222...(412) 244-2000...Michael H. Jordan...manuf. electrical, mechanical equip.; radio and television stations (CBS); power generation, energy services.

Weyerhaeuser Co....Tacoma, WA 98477...(206) 924-2345...George H. Weyerhaeuser...timber owner manuf., distrib. paper and wood prods.

Whirlpool Corp....Benton Harbor, MI 49022...(616) 923-5000...David Whitwam...major home appliances manuf. (KitchenAid, Kenmore).

Whitman Corp....3501 Algonquin Rd., Rolling Meadows, IL 60008...(708) 818-5000...Bruce S. Chelberg...beverage bottler.

Winn-Dixie Stores, Inc....5050 Edgewood Ct., Jacksonville, FL 32205...(904) 783-5000...A. Dano Davis....supermarkets.

Winnebago Industries, Inc....PO Box 152, Forest City, IA 50436...(515) 582-3535...Fred G. Dohrmann....manuf. and financing of motor homes, recreation vehicles.

Woolworth Corp....233 Broadway, NY, NY 10279...(212) 553-2000...Roger Farah...variety stores, shoes (Kinney), apparel, athletic footwear (Foot Locker).

Wm. Wrigley Jr. Co....410 N. Michigan Ave., Chicago, IL 60611...(312) 644-2121...William Wrigley...chewing gum.

Xerox Corp....PO Box 1600, Stamford, CT 06904...(203) 968-3000...Paul Allaire...copiers, printers, document pub. equip.

Zenith Electronics Corp....1000 Milwaukee Ave., Glenview, IL 60025...(708) 391-7000...H. J. Lee...televisions, other electronic products.

Who Owns What: Familiar Consumer Products

Listed below are consumer products and their parent companies. The parent company address can be found on pp. 721-26.

ABC broadcasting: Walt Disney
Abercrombie & Fitch: The Limited
Admiral appliances: Maytag
Advil: American Home Products
Ajax cleanser: Colgate-Palmolive
Anacin: American Home Products
Arm & Hammer: Church & Dwight
Arnold breads: CPC Intl.
Arrid antiperspirant: Carter-Wallace
Aunt Millie's pasta sauce: Borden
Baggies: Tenneco
Ban antiperspirant: Bristol-Myers
   Squibb
Banana Republic stores: The Gap
Barbie dolls: Mattell
Beech Aircraft: Raytheon
Beech-Nut baby food: Ralcorp
Ben-Gay: Pfizer
Betty Crocker products: General
   Mills
Black Flag insecticides: Clorox
Blockbuster video stores: Viacom
Bounce fabric softener: Procter &
   Gamble
Breck shampoo: Dial
Bubble Yum gum: RJR Nabisco
Budweiser beer: Anheuser-Busch
Bufferin: Bristol-Myers Squibb
Business Week magazine: McGraw-
   Hill
Buster Brown shoes: Brown Group
BVD underwear: Fruit of the Loom
Cadbury: Hershey
Cap'n Crunch cereal: Quaker Oats
Carrier air conditioners: United
   Technologies
CBS broadcasting: Westinghouse
Celeste Pizza: Quaker Oats
Charmin toilet tissue: Procter &
   Gamble
Cheer detergent: Procter & Gamble
Cheerios cereal: General Mills
Cheez Whiz: Philip Morris
Chef Boy-ar-dee products: American
   Home Products
Cinemax: Time Warner
Clairol hair prods.: Bristol-Myers
   Squibb
Clorets breath mints: Warner-Lambert
CNN: Time Warner
Combat insecticides: Clorox
Comet cleanser: Procter & Gamble
Coppertone sun care products:
   Schering-Plough
Cracker Jack: PepsiCo
Crest toothpaste: Procter & Gamble
Crisco shortening: Procter & Gamble
Doritos chips: PepsiCo
Dristan: American Home Products
Duncan Hines: Procter & Gamble
Dutch Boy paints: Sherwin-Williams
Efferdent dental cleanser: Warner-
   Lambert
Elmer's glue: Borden
Equal sweetener: Monsanto
ESPN: Walt Disney
Eveready batteries: Ralston Purina
Excedrin: Bristol-Myers Squibb
Fab detergent: Colgate-Palmolive
Fantastik spray cleaner: Dow
   Chemical
Foamy shaving cream: Gillette
Folger's coffee: Procter & Gamble
Formula 409 spray cleaner: Clorox
Franco-American foods: Campbell
   Soup

Frito-Lay snacks: PepsiCo
Fruitopia drinks: Coca-Cola
Gatorade: Quaker Oats
Glad plastic wrap: First Brands
Glass Plus cleaner: Dow Chemical
Godiva chocolate: Campbell Soup
Halcion: Pharmacia & Upjohn
Hamburger Helper: General Mills
Handy Wipes: Colgate-Palmolive
Hanes hosiery: Sara Lee
Hawaiian Punch: Procter & Gamble
HBO: Time Warner
Head and Shoulders shampoo:
   Procter & Gamble
Hellmann's mayonnaise: CPC Intl.
Hi-C fruit drinks: Coca-Cola
Hidden Valley Ranch dressing:
   Clorox
Hillshire Farms meats: Sara Lee
Hostess cakes: Interstate Bakeries
Huggies diapers: Kimberly-Clark
Hush Puppies shoes: Wolverine
   World Wide
Ivory soap: Procter & Gamble
Jack Daniel's bourbon: Brown-Forman
Java programming language: Sun
   Microsystems
Jell-O: Philip Morris
Jif peanut butter: Procter & Gamble
Jim Beam whiskey: Fortune
   Brands
Ken-L-Ration pet foods: H. J. Heinz
Kent cigarettes: Loews
KFC restaurants: Tricon
Kinney shoe stores: Woolworth
Kleenex: Kimberly-Clark
Knorr soups: CPC Intl.
Kool-Aid: Philip Morris
Krazy Glue: Borden
Ladies Home Journal magazine:
   Meredith
Lee jeans: V.F. Corp.
L'eggs hosiery: Sara Lee
Lender's bagels: Kellogg
Lenox china: Brown-Forman
Lerner stores: The Limited
Life Savers candy: RJR Nabisco
Listerine mouthwash: Warner-Lambert
Log Cabin syrup: Philip Morris
Lord & Taylor: May Dept. Stores
Marlboro cigarettes: Philip Morris
Maxwell House coffee: Philip Morris
Michelob beer: Anheuser-Busch
Miller beer: Philip Morris
Milton Bradley games: Hasbro
Minute Maid beverages: Coca-Cola
Monopoly: Hasbro
Mrs. Paul's frozen fish: Campbell
   Soup
MTV: Viacom
Nature Valley granola bars: General
   Mills
NBC broadcasting: General Electric
Neutrogena soap: Johnson & Johnson
Newsweek magazine: Washington
   Post
9 Lives cat food: H.J. Heinz
North American Van Lines: Norfolk
   Southern
NutraSweet: Monsanto
Old Spice: Procter & Gamble
Oreo cookies: RJR Nabisco
Oscar Mayer meats: Philip Morris
Pampers: Procter & Gamble
Paper Mate pens: Gillette
People magazine: Time Warner

Pepperidge Farm products: Camp-
   bell Soup
Pepto-Bismol: Procter & Gamble
Pine-Sol cleaner: Clorox
Pizza Hut restaurants: Tricon
Planters nuts: RJR Nabisco
Playskool toys: Hasbro
Playtex apparel: Sara Lee
Post-It stickers: Minn. Mining &
   Manufacturing
Prego pasta sauce: Campbell Soup
Prell shampoo: Procter & Gamble
Prentice Hall publishing: Viacom
Prozac: Eli Lilly
Purex detergent: Dial
Radio Shack retail outlets: Tandy
Reese's peanut butter cups: Hershey
Rice-A-Roni: Quaker Oats
Right Guard deodorant: Gillette
Ritz crackers: RJR Nabisco
Robitussin: American Home Products
Rogaine hair growth aide: Pharma-
   cia & Upjohn
Rolaids antacid: Warner-Lambert
Ronzoni pasta: Hershey
Ruffles chips: PepsiCo
San Giorgio pasta: Hershey
Saran Wrap: Dow Chemical
Schick razors: Warner-Lambert
Scholl's foot products: Schering-
   Plough
Scope mouthwash: Procter & Gam-
   ble
Scotch tape: Minn. Mining & Manuf.
Simon & Schuster publishing:
   Viacom
Skippy peanut butter: CPC Intl.
SnackWell's cookies: RJR Nabisco
Snapple beverages: Triarc
Southern Comfort liquor: Brown-
   Forman
SPAM meat: Hormel
Sports Illustrated magazine: Time
   Warner
Sprite soda: Coca-Cola
Star-Kist: H.J. Heinz
Sugar Twin: Alberto Culver
Swanson frozen dinners: Campbell
   Soup
Taco Bell restaurants: Tricon
Tampax tampons: Procter & Gamble
Thomas' English muffins: CPC Intl.
Tide detergent: Procter & Gamble
Titleist: Fortune Brands
Trojan condoms: Carter-Wallace
Tylenol: Johnson & Johnson
Ultra Brite toothpaste: Colgate-
   Palmolive
USA Today newspaper: Gannett
V-8 vegetable juice: Campbell Soup
Vanity Fair apparel: V.F. Corp.
Velveeta cheese prods.: Philip Morris
Vicks cough medicines: Procter &
   Gamble
Victoria's Secret stores: The Limited
Visine eye drops: Pfizer
Wall Street Journal: Dow Jones
Weight Watchers: H.J. Heinz
Wheaties cereal: General Mills
White Owl cigars: Culbro
Windows 95 software application:
   Microsoft
Wise snacks: Borden
Wonder bread: Interstate Bakeries
Zest soap: Procter & Gamble
Ziploc storage bags: Dow Chemical

Interest Laws and Consumer Finance Loan Rates

Source: Revised by Christian T. Jones, Editor, *Consumer Finance Law Bulletin*, Chicago, IL

All states have laws regulating interest rates. These laws fix a legal or conventional rate, which applies when there is no contract for interest. They also fix a general maximum contract rate, but there are so many exceptions that the general contract maximum actually applies to few cases. Also, federal law has preempted state limits on first home mortgages, subject to each state's right to reinstate its own law, and has given depository institutions parity with other state lenders.

Legal rate of interest. The legal or conventional rate of interest applies to money obligations when no interest rate is contracted for, and also to judgments. The rate is usually somewhat below the general contract interest rate.

General maximum contract rates. General interest laws in most states set the maximum contract rate between 8% and 16% per year. In Arkansas, the general maximum is fixed by the state constitution at 5% over the Federal Reserve discount rate. Loans to corporations are frequently exempted or subject to a higher maximum. In recent years, it has also been common to provide special rates for home mortgage loans and variable usury rates that are indexed to market rates.

Specific enabling acts. In many states special statutes permit industrial loan companies, second mortgage lenders, and banks to charge 1.5% a month or more. Laws regulating revolving loans, charge accounts, and credit cards generally limit rates to between 1.5% and 2% per month, plus annual fees for credit cards. Rates for installment sales contracts in most states are somewhat higher.

Credit unions may generally charge 1% to 1.5% a month. Pawnbrokers' rates vary widely. Savings and loan associations and loans insured by federal agencies are also specially regulated. A number of states allow regulated lenders to charge any rate agreed to with the customer either for all credit or for credit over a certain dollar amount.

Consumer finance loan statutes. Most consumer finance loan statutes are based on early models drafted by the Russell Sage Foundation (1916-42) to provide small loans to wage earners under license and other protective regulations. Since 1969, the model has frequently been the Uniform Consumer Credit Code, which applies to credit sales and loans for consumer purposes. In general, licensed lenders may charge 3% a month, with reduced rates for relatively high amounts. An add-on of 17% ($17 per $100) per year amounts to about 2.5% per month if paid in equal monthly installments (add-on rates are computed on the original principal, not taking into account reduced balances as payments are made). Discount rates are computed on the whole balance of the loan, including interest, to determine how much cash is paid out; thus, for a $1,000 loan at 10% interest the borrower would receive only $900. In the table below, unless otherwise stated, monthly and annual rates are based on reducing principal balances, annual add-on rates are based on the original principal for the full term, and 2 or more rates apply to different portions of the balance or original principal.

States (and Puerto Rico) With Consumer Finance Loan Laws and the Rates of Charge as of Aug. 1, 1997

Maximum monthly rates

AL. . . . . .Annual add-on: 15% to $750, 10% to $2,000 (min. 1.5% on unpaid balances). Higher rates for loans up to $749. Over $2,000, any agreed rate. Fee: 6% to $2,000; 5% real estate.

AK. . . . . .3% to $850, 2% to $10,000. Over $10,000, any agreed rate.

AZ. . . . . .To $1,000: 3%. Over $1,000: 3% to $500, 2% to $10,000. Over $10,000, any agreed rate. Fee: 4% for real estate credit.

CA . . . . .2.5% to $225, 2% to $900, 1.5% to $1,650, 1% to $2,500 (1.6% min.). Over $2,500, any agreed rate. 5% fee (max. $50-$75) to $5,000.

CO . . . . .36% per year to $630, 21% to $2,100, 15% to $25,000 (21% min.).

CT. . . . . .Annual add-on: 17% to $600, 11% to $5,000; 11% over $1,800 to $15,000 for certain secured loans. Any agreed rate for 2d mortgages; 8% fee.

DE . . . . .Any agreed rate; 10% fee.

DC . . . . .24% per year.

FL. . . . . .30% per year to $2,000, 24% to $3,000, 18% to $25,000; $10 fee.

GA . . . . .10% per year discount to 18 months, add-on to 36½ months; 8% fee to $600, 4% on excess plus $2 per month. Over $3,000, any agreed rate.

HI . . . . . .3.5% to $100, 2.5% to $300; 2% on entire balance over $300 or discount rates.

ID . . . . . .Any agreed rate.

IL . . . . . .Any agreed rate. Fee: 3% real estate.

IN . . . . . .36% per year to $900, 21% to $3,000, 15% to $25,000 (21% min.). Fee: 2% real estate.

IA . . . . . .3% to $1,000, 2% to $2,800, 1.5% to $10,000; or equivalent flat rate. Over $10,000, 21% per year.

KS. . . . . .36% per year to $780, 21% to $2,600, 14.45% to $25,000 (18% min.). Fee: 2% (max. $100); 3% real estate.

KY. . . . . .3% to $1,000, 2% to $3,000. Over $3,000, 2%.

LA. . . . . .36% per year to $1,400, 27% to $4,000, 24% to $7,000, 21% over $7,000, plus $25 fee.

ME . . . . .30% per year to $1,000, 21% to $2,800, 15% to $25,000 (18% min.).

MD . . . . .2.75% to $1,000, 2% to $2,000. Over $2,000, 2%.

MA . . . . .23% per year plus $20 annual fee to $6,000; any agreed rate over $6,000.

MI . . . . . .22% per year to $8,000; 18% for 2d mortgages, plus 2% fee (max. $200).

MN . . . . .33% per year to $750, 19% over $750 (21.75% min.) plus $25 fee to $4,230.

MS . . . . .36% per year to $1,000, 33% to $1,800, 24% to $5,000, 14% over $5,000. Over $25,000, 18%; 2% fee (max. $50).

MO. . . . .2.218% to $1,200, 1.67% over $1,200, plus 2% fee (max. $15); 1.67% plus 2% fee for 2d mortgages.

MT . . . . .Any agreed rate.

NE . . . . .24% per year to $1,000. 21% over $1,000, plus fee of 7% to $2,000 and 5% over $2,000 (max. $500). Any agreed rate for real estate loans of $7,500 or more or all loans over $25,000.

NV . . . . .Any agreed rate.

NH . . . . .2% to $600, 1.5% to $1,500; any agreed rate over $1,500 or for real estate mortgages.

NJ . . . . .30% per year to $5,000 or for 2d mortgages.

NM. . . . .Any agreed rate.

NY. . . . . .25% per year.

NC . . . . .2.5% to $1,000, 1.5% to $7,500; 1.5% on entire amount to $10,000. 1.5% or variable plus 2% fee for 2d mortgages.

ND . . . . .2.5% to $250, 2% to $500, 1.75% to $750, 1.5% to $1,000; any agreed rate over $1,000 to $35,000.

OH . . . . .28% per year to $1,000, 22% to $5,000; 25% on entire amount over $5,000; plus fee.

OK. . . . .30% per year to $990, 21% to $3,300, 15% to $45,000 (21% min.). Special rates to $660.

OR. . . . .Any agreed rate.

PA . . . . .9.5% per year discount to 48 months, 6% for remaining time plus 2% fee (max. $100); or 2% on unpaid balances. 1.85% for 2d mortgages over $5,000, plus 2% fee.

PR . . . . .21% per year to $2,000.

RI. . . . . .3% to $300, 2.5% for loans between $300 and $800; 2% for larger loans to $5,000. 1.75% over $5,000.

SC . . . . .Any agreed and posted rate.

SD . . . . .Any agreed rate.

TN . . . . .Over $100, 24% per year or discount rates plus fees.

TX . . . . .Annual add-on: 18% to $1,350, 8% to $11,250 or formula rate (18% to 24% per year on unpaid balances).

UT . . . . .Any agreed rate.

VT . . . . .2% to $1,000, 1% to $3,000 (min. 1.5%); 1.5% for 2d mortgages.

VA . . . . .3% to $2,500; any agreed rate to $6,000. Any agreed rate for 2d mortgages, plus 5% fee.

WA. . . . .25% per year plus fees.

WV. . . . .31% per year to $2,000, 27% per year to $10,000, 18% per year to $45,000; fees included in rates.

WI . . . . .Any agreed rate.

WY. . . . .36% per year to $1,000, 21% to $50,000. No limit over $50,000.

How to Check Your Credit File

Any individual can investigate the contents of his or her credit file by directly contacting one or more of the approximately 2,000 credit bureaus, or consumer credit clearinghouses, in the U.S. The nearest ones can be found by calling a local Better Business Bureau or by looking in the telephone Yellow Pages under "Credit Rating or Reporting Agencies."

Although the Fair Credit Reporting Act requires that a bureau give a person no more than an oral or written credit history review, many bureaus will go beyond the technical requirements of the law and furnish the same computer-generated compilation of facts that they give the banks, retailers, and other companies that subscribe to their service. An individual who has been denied credit on the basis of negative information from a credit bureau can obtain a review without charge (or sometimes for a small fee) within 30 days of the denial.

After inspecting this record of past credit behavior, a consumer can question any item believed to be inaccurate, misleading, or vague. The credit bureau must then investigate and remove any item that cannot be substantiated.

When a bureau affirms, rather than removes, a questionable item, an individual can present a 100-word explanation that must be placed in his or her file. And whenever an adverse item is deleted from the file or an explanatory statement is added to one, a consumer may request that the credit bureau inform every credit grantor who received a report within the previous 6 months.

Credit Card Rates

Source: Christian T. Jones, Editor, *Consumer Finance Law Bulletin*, Chicago, IL; as of Aug. 1, 1997

Nearly all states have special laws dealing with rates charged for credit cards issued by state banks and other financial institutions. Although some state laws apply only to banks, under federal parity law, the same charges can be made by other financial institutions. A bank can charge the highest rates and charges allowed for revolving credit extended by any other creditor for similar types of credit in the state where the bank is located. These rates and charges may also be charged to residents of any other state. Maximum rates and fees are shown below; rates are yearly unless otherwise stated.

AL . . No limit.
AK . . 17% plus fee.
AZ . . No limit.
AR . . 5% over FRB discount rate (max. 17%).
CA . . No limit.
CO . . 21%.
CT . . No limit.
DC . . 24%.
DE . . No limit.
FL . . No limit.
GA . . No limit on rate or fee.
HI . . 24%.
ID . . . No limit.
IL . . . No limit; plus fee.
IN . . . 36% to $900, 21% to $3,000, then 15%; or 21%.
IA . . . No limit.
KS . . 18% to $1,000 then 14.45%.
KY . . 21%; $20 annual fee.

LA . . 18%; 4% cash advance and $12 annual fee.
ME . . No limit; plus annual fee.
MD . . 24%; 2% fee.
MA . . 18% or formula rate.
MI . . No limit on rate or fee.
MN . . 18%; $50 annual fee.
MS . . 21%; or 18% plus $12 annual fee; no limit over $2,000.
MO . . 22 to $1,000, then 10%.
MT . . No limit.
NE . . No limit; plus fees.
NV . . No limit.
NH . . No limit.
NJ . . 30%; $15 annual fee or $50 over $5,000.
NM . . No limit.
NY . . 25% plus annual fee.
NC . . 18%; $24 annual fee.
ND . . No limit.

OH . . 25% plus fee.
OK . . 30% to $990, 21% to $3,300, then 15%; or 21%.
OR . . No limit.
PA . . Variable rate, plus fees.
PR . . 26% per year.
RI . . . No limit.
SC . . No limit.
SD . . No limit.
TN . . 24%.
TX . . Set by rule (max. 22%, min. 14%).
UT . . No limit.
VT . . No limit.
VA . . No limit.
WA . . 25% loan; no limit for purchases; fees.
WV . . 18%.
WI . . No limit.
WY . . 36% to $1,000, then 21%; no limit over $50,000.

Customs Exemptions and Advice to Travelers

Source: U.S. Dept. of the Treasury, U.S. Customs Service

U.S. residents returning after a stay abroad of at least 48 hours are usually granted customs exemptions of $400 each. The duty-free articles must accompany the traveler at the time of his or her return, be for personal or household use, have been acquired as an incident of the trip, and be properly declared to Customs. Not more than 1 liter of alcoholic beverages or more than 100 cigars and 200 cigarettes (1 carton) may be included in the $400 exemption. The exemption for alcoholic beverages is accorded only when the returning resident has attained 21 years of age at the time of arrival. Cuban cigars may be included only if purchased in Cuba.

If a U.S. resident arrives directly or indirectly from a U.S. insular possession — American Samoa, Guam, or the U.S. Virgin Islands — a customs exemption of $1,200 is allowed. Up to 1,000 cigarettes may be included, but only 200 of them may have been purchased elsewhere.

If a U.S. resident returns from any one of the following beneficiary places, the customs exemption is $600, based on fair market value: Antigua and Barbuda, Aruba, Bahamas, Barbados, Belize, British Virgin Islands, Costa Rica, Dominica, Dominican Republic, El Salvador, Grenada, Guatemala, Guyana, Haiti, Honduras, Jamaica, Montserrat, Netherlands Antilles, Nicaragua, Panama, St. Kitts and Nevis, St. Lucia, St. Vincent and the Grenadines, Trinidad and Tobago.

The $400, $600, or $1,200 exemption may be granted only if the exemption or any part of it has not been used within the preceding 30-day period and the stay abroad was for at least 48 hours. The 48-hr absence requirement does not apply to travelers returning from Mexico or the U.S. Virgin Islands. If you cannot claim the $400, $600, or $1,200 exemption because of the 30-day or 48-hr minimum limitations, you may bring in free of duty and tax articles acquired abroad for your personal or household use provided that the total fair retail value does not exceed $25.

Bona fide gifts of not more than $100 in fair retail value, when shipped, can be received by friends and relations in the U.S. free of duty and tax if the same person does not receive more than $100 in gift shipments in one day. The amount is increased to $200 if shipped from the U.S. Virgin Islands, American Samoa, or Guam. (Shipping of alcoholic beverages by mail is prohibited by U.S. postal laws. Alcoholic beverages include wine and beer, as well as distilled spirits.) These gifts are not declared by the traveler upon return to the U.S.

Goods shipped for personal use may be imported free of duty and tax if the total value is not more than $200. This exemption does not apply to perfume containing alcohol if it is valued at more than $5 retail, to alcoholic beverages, or to cigars and cigarettes. The $200 mail exemption does not apply to merchandise subject to absolute or tariff-rate quotas unless the item is for personal use. Tailor-made suits ordered from Hong Kong, however, are subject to quota/visa requirements even if imported for personal use.

The U.S. Customs Service booklet *Know Before You Go* answers frequently asked customs questions and is available free by writing U.S. Customs Services, KBYG, PO Box 7407, Washington, DC 20044. Online information can be obtained at the U.S. Customs web site— http://www.custom.ustreas.gov

Passport, Visa, and Health Requirements for Foreign Travel

Source: Bureau of Consular Affairs, U.S. Dept. of State, as of Sept. 1997

Passports are issued by the U.S. Department of State to citizens and nationals of the U.S. for the purpose of documenting them for foreign travel and identifying them as U.S. citizens. For U.S. citizens traveling on business or as tourists, especially in Europe, a U.S. passport is often sufficient to gain admission for a limited stay. For many countries, however, a visa must also be obtained before entering. It is the responsibility of the traveler to obtain any visas where required, from the appropriate embassy or nearest consulate of the country he or she is planning to visit.

How to Obtain a Passport

Applicants who have never been issued a passport in their own name must execute an application in person before (1) a passport agent; (2) a clerk of any federal court or state court of record or a judge or clerk of any probate court accepting applications; (3) a postal employee designated by the postmaster at a post office that has been selected to accept passport applications; or (4) a U.S. diplomatic or consular officer abroad. A DSP-11 is the correct form to use for applicants who must apply in person. All persons are required to obtain individual passports in their own name. An applicant who is 13 years of age or older is required to appear in person before the clerk or agent executing the application. A parent or legal guardian must execute the application for children under 13.

A full validity passport previously issued to the applicant or one in which he or she was included will be accepted as proof of U.S. citizenship. If the applicant has no prior passport and was born in the U.S., a certified copy of his/her birth certificate generally must be presented to the agent accepting the passport application. To be acceptable, the certificate must show the given name and surname, the date and place of birth, and that the birth record was filed shortly after birth. A delayed birth certificate (a record filed more than 1 year after the date of birth) is acceptable provided that it shows that acceptable secondary evidence was used for creating this record.

If a birth certificate is not obtainable, a notice from a state registrar must be submitted stating that no birth record exists. The notice must be accompanied by the best obtainable secondary evidence, such as a baptismal certificate or a hospital birth record.

A naturalized citizen with no previous passport must present a Certificate of Naturalization. A person born abroad claiming U.S. citizenship through either a native-born or naturalized citizen parent must normally submit a Certificate of Citizenship issued by the Immigration and Naturalization Service; or a Consular Report of Birth or Certification of Birth Abroad issued by the Dept. of State. If one of the above documents has not been obtained, evidence of citizenship of the parent(s) through whom citizenship is claimed and evidence that would establish the parent/child relationship must be submitted. Additionally, if citizenship is derived through birth to citizen parent(s), the following documents will be required: parents' marriage certificate plus an affidavit from parent(s) showing periods and places of residence or physical presence in the U.S. and abroad, specifying periods spent abroad in the employment of the U.S. government, including the armed forces, or with certain international organizations. If citizenship is derived through naturalization of parents, evidence of admission to the U.S. for permanent residence also will be required.

It is important to apply for a passport as far in advance as possible. Passport offices are busiest between March and September. It can take several weeks to receive your passport.

Persons who possess the most recent passport issued within the last 12 years and after their 18th birthday may be eligible to apply for a new passport by mail. The form DSP-82, *Application for Passport by Mail*, must be filled out and mailed to the address shown on the form, together with the previous passport, 2 recent identical photographs, and a fee of $55.00. The DSP-82 may not be used if the most recent passport has been altered or mutilated.

Photographs, Fees, and Identity

Photographs—Passport applicants must submit 2 identical photographs that are sufficiently recent (normally not more than 6 months old) and that are a good likeness of and satisfactorily identify the applicant. Photographs should be 2 × 2 in. in size. The image size measured from the bottom of the chin to the top of the head (including hair) should not be less than one inch or more than 1-3/8 in. Photographs should be portrait-type prints. They must be clear, front view, full face, with a plain white or off-white background. Photographs that depict the applicant as relaxed and smiling are encouraged.

Fees—For persons under 18 years of age, the fee for a passport is $30.00. These passports are valid for 5 years from the date of issue. The fee is $55.00 for passports issued to persons 18 and older. These passports are valid for 10 years from the date of issuance. To receive a passport within 10 days or less, a $30.00 expedite fee is required. An additional fee of $10.00 is charged for the execution of the application. There is no execution fee when using DSP-82, *Application for Passport by Mail*. Applicants eligible to use this form pay only the $55.00 passport fee.

Identity—Applicants must establish their identity to the satisfaction of the person accepting the application and to Passport Services. Generally acceptable documents of identity include a previous U.S. passport, a Certificate of Naturalization, a Certificate of Citizenship, a valid driver's license, or a government identification card. Applicants may not use a Social Security card, learner's or temporary driver's license, credit card, or expired identity card. Extremely old documents cannot be used by themselves.

Applicants unable to establish identity must present some documentation in their own name and must be accompanied by a person who has known the applicant for at least 2 years and who is a U.S. citizen or legal U.S. permanent resident alien. That person must sign an affidavit before the individual who executes the passport application. The witness will be required to establish his or her own identity.

The loss or theft of a valid passport is a serious matter and should be reported immediately in writing to Passport Services, 1111 19th St., NW, Dept. of State, Washington, DC 20524-1705, telephone: (202) 647-0518, or to the nearest passport agency or the nearest U.S. embassy or consulate when abroad.

Foreign Regulations

Each country has its own specific guidelines concerning length and purpose of visit, etc. Some may require visitors to display proof that they (1) have sufficient funds to stay for intended time period and (2) have onward/return tickets. Some countries, including Canada, Mexico, and some Caribbean islands, do not require a passport or a visa for limited stays. Such countries do require proof of U.S. citizenship, and may have other requirements that must be met. For further information, check with the embassy or nearest consulate of the country you plan to visit.

Under the International Health Regulations adopted by the World Health Organization, a country may require International Certificates of Vaccination against yellow fever. A cholera immunization may be required for travelers from infected areas. Check with health care providers or your records to ensure other immunizations (e.g. tetanus and polio) are up-to-date. Prophylactic medication for malaria and certain other preventive measures are advisable for travel to some countries. No immunizations are required to return to the U.S. An increasing number of countries have established regulations regarding AIDS testing, particularly for longtime visitors. Detailed health information is included in *Health Information for International Travel*, available from the U.S. Government Printing Office, Washington, DC 20402 for $14. Information may also be obtained from your local health department or physician, or by calling the Centers for Disease Control and Prevention at (404) 332-4559.

For more information, the booklets *Passports—Applying for the Easy Way* and *Foreign Entry Requiremensts* are available for 50¢ each from the Consumer Information Center, Pueblo, CO 81009. Online information can be obtained at the Consular Affairs web site— http://www.custom.ustreas.gov

Copyright Law of the United States

Source: Copyright Office, Library of Congress

What Copyright Is

Copyright is a form of protection provided by the laws of the U.S. (title 17, U.S. Code) to "original works of authorship," including literary, dramatic, musical, artistic, and certain other intellectual works. This protection is available to both published and unpublished works. Section 106 of the Copyright Act generally gives the owner of copyright the exclusive right to do and to authorize other parties to do the following:

Reproduce the copyrighted work in copies or phono records;

Prepare derivative works based upon the copyrighted work;

Distribute copies or phono records of the copyrighted work to the public by sale or other transfer of ownership, or by rental, lease, or lending;

Perform the copyrighted work publicly, in the case of literary, musical, dramatic, and choreographic works, pantomimes, and motion pictures and other audiovisual works; and

Display the copyrighted work publicly, in the case of literary, musical, dramatic, and choreographic works, pantomimes, and pictorial, graphic, or sculptural works, including individual images of a motion picture or other audiovisual work.

Perform the work publicly by means of a digital audio transmission, in the case of sound recordings.

It is illegal for anyone to violate any of the rights provided by the act to the owner of copyright. These rights, however, are not unlimited in scope. Sections 107 through 120 of the Copyright Act establish limitations on these rights. In some cases, these limitations are specified exemptions from copyright liability. One major limitation is the doctrine of "fair use," which is given a statutory basis by section 107 of the act. In other instances, the limitation takes the form of a "compulsory license," under which certain limited uses of copyrighted works are permitted upon payment of specified royalties and compliance with statutory conditions.

Copyright protection subsists from the time the work is created in fixed form. The copyright in the work of authorship *immediately* becomes the property of the author who created it. Only the author or those deriving their rights from the author can rightfully claim copyright.

In the case of works made for hire, the employer and not the employee is considered the author. Section 101 of the copyright statute defines a "work made for hire" as:

(1) a work prepared by an employee within the scope of his or her employment; or

(2) a work specially ordered or commissioned for use as a contribution to a collective work, as a part of a motion picture or other audiovisual work, as a translation, as a supplementary work, as a compilation, as an instructional text, as a test, as answer material for a test, or as an atlas, if the parties expressly agree in a written instrument signed by them that the work shall be considered a work made for hire.

The authors of a joint work are co-owners of the copyright in the work, unless there is an agreement to the contrary.

Copyright in each separate contribution to a periodical or other collective work is distinct from copyright in the collective work as a whole and vests initially with the author of the contribution.

Copyright protection is available for all unpublished works, regardless of the nationality or domicile of the author.

Published works are eligible for copyright protection in the U.S. if any one of the following conditions is met:

• On the date of first publication, one or more of the authors is a national or domiciliary of the U.S. or is a national, domiciliary, or sovereign authority of a foreign nation that is a party to a copyright treaty to which the U.S. is also a party, or is a stateless person wherever that person may be domiciled; or

• The work is first published in the U.S. or in a foreign nation that, on the date of first publication, is a party to the Universal Copyright Convention; or the work comes within the scope of a Presidential proclamation; or

• The work is first published on or after Mar. 1, 1989, in a foreign nation that on the date of first publication, is a party to the Berne Convention; or, if the work is *not* first published in a country party to the Berne Convention, it is published (on or after Mar. 1, 1989) within 30 days of first publication in a country that is party to the Berne Convention; or the work, first published on or after Mar. 1, 1989, is a pictorial, graphic, or sculptural work that is incorporated in a permanent structure located in the U.S.; or if the work, first published on or after Mar. 1, 1989, is a published audiovisual work, all the authors are legal entities with headquarters in the U.S.

• The work is a foreign work that was in the public domain in the U.S. prior to 1996 and its copyright was restored under the Uruguay Round Agreements Act (URAA). Request Circular 38b for further information.

Which Works Are Protected

Copyright protects "original works of authorship" that are fixed in a tangible form of expression. The fixation need not be directly perceptible, as long as it may be communicated with the aid of a machine or device. Copyrightable works include the following categories:

(1) literary works;

(2) musical works, including any accompanying words;

(3) dramatic works, including any accompanying music;

(4) pantomimes and choreographic works;

(5) pictorial, graphic, and sculptural works;

(6) motion pictures and other audiovisual works;

(7) sound recordings; and

(8) architectural works.

These categories should be viewed quite broadly: for example, computer programs and most "compilations" are registrable as "literary works"; maps and architectural plans are registrable as "pictorial, graphic, and sculptural works."

Which Works Are Not Protected

Several categories of material are generally not eligible for statutory copyright protection. These include among others:

• Works that have not been fixed in a tangible form of expression. For example: choreographic works that have not been notated or recorded, or improvisational speeches or performances that have not been written or recorded.

• Titles, names, short phrases, and slogans; familiar symbols or designs; mere variations of typographic ornamentation, lettering, or coloring; mere listings of ingredients or contents.

• Ideas, procedures, methods, systems, processes, concepts, principles, discoveries, or devices, as distinguished from a description, explanation, or illustration.

• Works consisting entirely of information that is common property and containing no original authorship. For example: standard calendars, height and weight charts, tape measures and rulers, and lists or tables taken from public documents.

Notice of Copyright

For works first published on or after Mar. 1, 1989, use of the copyright notice is optional, though highly recommended. Before Mar. 1, 1989, the use of the notice was mandatory on all published works, and any work first published before that date *must* bear a notice or risk loss of copyright protection.

Use of the notice is recommended because it informs the public that the work is protected by copyright, identifies the copyright owner, and shows the year of first publication. Furthermore, in the event that a work is infringed, if the work carries a proper notice, the court will not allow a defendant to claim "innocent infringement"—that is, that he or she did not realize that the work is protected. (A successful innocent infringement claim may result in a reduction in damages that the copyright owner would otherwise receive.)

The use of the copyright notice is the responsibility of the copyright owner and does not require advance permission from, or registration with, the Copyright Office.

For visually perceptible copies, the notice consists of the following: © (the letter C in a circle), the word "Copyright," or "Copr.," and the year of first publication, and the name of the owner of copyright in the work. Example: © 1997 Judy Smith. The notice must be affixed in such manner and location as to give reasonable notice of the claim of copyright.

The notice of copyright prescribed for all published phono records of sound recordings consists of the following: ℗ (the letter P in a circle), the year of first publication of the sound recording, and the name of the owner of copyright in the sound recording. Example: ℗ 1997 XYZ Records, Inc. The notice on phono records may appear on the surface of the phono record or on the phono record label or container, provided the manner of placement and location give reasonable notice of the claim.

How Long Copyright Protection Endures
Works Originally Created on or After Jan. 1, 1978

A work that is created (fixed in tangible form for the first time) on or after Jan. 1, 1978, is automatically protected from the moment of its creation and is ordinarily given a term enduring for the author's life, plus an additional 50 years after the author's death. In the case of "a joint work prepared by 2 or more authors who did not work for hire," the term lasts for 50 years after the last surviving author's death. For works made for hire and for anonymous and pseudonymous works (unless the author's identity is revealed in Copyright Office records) the duration of copyright is 75 years from publication or 100 years from creation, whichever is shorter.

Works that were created but not published or registered for copyright before Jan. 1, 1978, have been automatically brought under the statute and are now given Federal copyright protection. The duration of copyright in these works will generally be computed in the same way as for works created on or after Jan. 1, 1978: the life-plus-50 or 75/100-year terms will apply to them as well. The law provides that in no case will the term of copyright for works in this category expire before Dec. 31, 2002, and for works published on or before Dec. 31, 2002, the term of copyright will not expire before Dec. 31, 2027.

Works Created and Published or Registered Before Jan. 1, 1978

Under the law in effect before 1978, copyright was secured either on the date a work was published or on the date of registration if the work was registered in unpublished form. In either case, the copyright endured for a first term of 28 years from the date it was secured. During the last (28th) year of the first term, the copyright was eligible for renewal. The current copyright law has extended the renewal term from 28 to 47 years for copyrights that were subsisting on Jan. 1, 1978, making these works eligible for a total term of protection of 75 years. On June 26, 1992, Pres. George Bush signed Public Law 102-307, which amends the Copyright Law to extend automatically the term of copyrights secured between Jan. 1, 1964, and Dec. 31, 1977, to a further term of 47 years and increases the filing fee from $12.00 to $20.00. This fee increase applies to all renewal applications filed on or after June 29, 1992.

PL 102-307 makes renewal registration optional. An author need not file the renewal in order to extend the original 28-year copyright term to the full 75 years. It may be beneficial, however, to file a renewal registration during the 28th year of the original term. (For more information on copyright renewal, request Circular 15 from the Copyright Office.)

International Copyright Protection

There is no such thing as an "international copyright" that will in itself protect an author's writings throughout the world. Protection against unauthorized use in a particular country basically depends on the laws of that country. However, most countries do offer protection to foreign works under certain conditions which have been greatly simplified by international copyright treaties and conventions. There are two principal international copyright conventions, the Berne Union for the Protection of Literary and Artistic Property (Berne Convention) and the Universal Copyright Convention (UCC). The United States became a member of the Berne Convention on Mar. 1, 1989. It has been a member of the UCC since Sept. 16, 1955.

Generally, works of an author who is a national or domiciliary of a country subscribing to these treaties, or works first published in a member country, or works published in a Berne Union country within 30 days of first publication may claim protection. There are no formal requirements under the Berne Convention. Under the UCC, any formality in a national law may be satisfied by the use of a copyright notice in the form and position specified in the UCC. A UCC notice should consist of the symbol © accompanied by the year of first publication and the name of the copyright proprietor (example: © 1997 John Doe). This notice must be placed in such a manner and location as to give reasonable notice of the claim to copyright. Since the Berne Convention prohibits formal requirements that affect the "exercise and enjoyment" of the copyright, the U.S. changed its law on Mar. 1, 1989, to make the use of a copyright notice optional. However, U.S. law still provides certain advantages for use of a copyright notice; for example, its use can defeat a defense of "innocent infringement" brought by an alleged copyright violator.

Even if the work cannot be brought under an international convention, protection may be available in other countries by virtue of a bilateral agreement between the U.S. and other countries or under specific provision of a country's laws. (See Circular 38a, *International Copyright Relations of the United States*).

An author who wishes copyright protection for his or her work in a particular country should first determine the extent of protection available to works of foreign authors in that country. If possible, this should be done before the work is published anywhere, because protection may depend on the facts existing at the time of first publication.

There are some countries that offer little or no copyright protection to any foreign works. For current information on the requirements and protection provided by specific countries, it would be advisable to consult an expert familiar with foreign copyright laws.

Copyright Registration

Copyright registration is a legal formality intended to make a public record of the basic facts of a particular copyright. Except in specific situations, registration is not a condition for protection, but the copyright law provides several inducements or advantages to encourage copyright owners to register. Among these are the following:

- Registration establishes a public record of the copyright claim.
- Before an infringement suit may be filed in court, registration is necessary for works of U.S. origin and for foreign works not originating in a Berne Union country. (For more information on when a work is of U.S. origin, request Circular 93 from the Copyright Office.)
- If made before or within 5 years of publication, registration will establish prima facie evidence in court of the validity of the copyright and of the facts stated in the certificate.
- If registration is made within 3 months after publication of the work or prior to an infringement of the work, statutory damages and attorney's fees will be available to the copyright owner in court actions. Otherwise, only an award of actual damages and profits is available to the copyright owner.

Copyright registration allows the owner of the copyright to record the registration with the U.S. Customs Service for protection against the importation of infringing copies. For additional information, request Publication No. 563 from Commissioner of Customs, ATTN: IPR Branch, Rm 2104, U.S. Customs Service, 1301 Constitution Ave. NW, Washington, DC 20229.

Registration may be made at any time within the life of the copyright. When a work has been registered in unpublished form, making another registration when the work becomes published is unnecessary (although the copyright owner may register the published edition, if desired).

The process of registration is simple. Request an appropriate form from the Copyright Office and complete it. Returned it to the Copyright Office along with a $20 nonrefundable filing fee and the appropriate deposit(s) of the work for which registration is sought. In a common example—a published book—the deposit is 2 copies of the best edition of the book. The Copyright Office sends a certificate of registration when the paperwork is completed, a process that usually takes 12 to 16 weeks because of the large volume of registrations the Office must handle (over 500,000 annually).

Although a copyright registration is not required, the Copyright Act establishes a mandatory deposit requirement for works published in the U.S. In general, the owner of copyright or the owner of the exclusive right of publication in the work has a legal obligation to deposit in the Copyright Office, within 3 months of publication in the U.S., 2 copies (or, in the case of sound recordings, 2 phono records) for the use of the Library of Congress. Failure to deposit these copies can result in fines and other penalties but does not affect copyright protection. Certain categories of works are exempt entirely from the mandatory deposit requirements, and the obligation is reduced for certain other categories.

Information on registration and application forms may be obtained free of charge by writing the Copyright Office, Information Section, LM-401, Library of Congress, Washington, DC 20559. Registration application forms and circulars may be ordered on a 24-hr basis by calling (202) 707-9100. Request Circular 1 for additional general information on copyright, including a list of which application forms to use when registering specific types of works.

For more information on copyright laws, visit the Copyright Office web site— http://www.loc.gov/copyright

Median Price of Existing Single-Family Homes

Source: National Association of REALTORS®; data as of June 1997

City[1]	1995	1996	First Quarter 1997	City[1]	1995	1996	First Quarter 1997
Akron, OH	$ 92,100	$ 98,800	$ 99,000	Lincoln, NE	$ 82,500	$ 87,200	$ 89,300
Albany, NY	105,900	106,900	102,000	Little Rock, AR	79,000	83,700	87,000
Albuquerque, NM	117,000	122,300	131,700	Los Angeles, CA[2]	179,900	172,900	169,200
Amarillo, TX	71,000	73,700	75,000	Louisville, KY/IN	86,400	91,300	92,000
Anaheim/Santa Ana, CA[2]	208,800	213,900	215,300	Madison, WI	124,500	122,200	123,300
Atlanta, GA	97,500	100,700	105,100	Memphis, TN/AR/MS	86,500	96,100	99,400
Atlantic City, NJ	107,000	108,000	114,700	Miami, FL	107,100	113,200	116,100
Aurora, IL	131,600	137,000	147,100	Milwaukee, WI	114,700	119,400	121,700
Austin, TX	101,400	108,100	NA	Minneapolis, MN/WI	106,800	113,900	115,400
Baltimore, MD	111,300	113,000	115,300	Mobile, AL	75,100	83,200	89,400
Baton Rouge, LA	84,600	87,000	87,900	Montgomery, AL	85,800	90,100	89,800
Biloxi/Gulfport, MS	73,100	73,800	77,900	Nashville, TN	107,300	112,700	109,500
Birmingham, AL	103,600	114,100	115,400	New Haven, CT	135,100	133,300	126,300
Boise City, ID	98,900	101,200	NA	New Orleans, LA	78,000	87,000	90,400
Boston, MA	179,000	189,300	183,300	New York, NY	169,700	174,500	173,400
Bradenton, FL	91,000	95,100	86,500	Norfolk/Virginia Bch, VA	104,400	110,200	104,300
Buffalo/Niagara Falls, NY	81,300	82,900	80,900	Oklahoma City, OK	70,400	74,600	73,300
Canton, OH	84,000	89,300	87,500	Omaha, NE	83,000	88,300	88,600
Cedar Rapids, IA	86,200	91,200	88,800	Orlando, FL	89,200	92,400	94,100
Champaign, IL	79,400	79,800	76,500	Pensacola, FL	79,500	84,500	85,400
Charleston, SC	94,300	94,900	98,500	Peoria, IL	70,100	74,500	74,000
Charleston, WV	81,700	90,400	88,300	Philadelphia, PA/NJ	118,700	NA	NA
Charlotte, NC	107,800	116,800	117,200	Phoenix, AZ	96,800	105,300	109,500
Chattanooga, TN	82,800	89,500	88,600	Pittsburgh, PA	82,100	84,800	84,500
Chicago, IL	147,900	153,200	154,100	Portland, OR	128,400	141,500	147,500
Cincinnati, OH/KY/IN	100,400	104,800	106,600	Providence, RI	115,600	118,100	116,500
Cleveland, OH	104,700	111,900	112,900	Raleigh/Durham, NC	127,000	NA	NA
Colorado Springs, CO	114,700	126,600	128,500	Reno, NV	137,100	140,000	138,500
Columbia, SC	91,000	93,400	96,800	Richmond, VA	103,100	108,700	109,600
Columbus, OH	99,100	108,200	115,700	Riverside/San Bern.,CA[2]	120,900	115,200	111,200
Corpus Christi, TX	77,600	79,600	79,200	Rochester, NY	85,000	86,200	85,400
Dallas, TX	96,400	103,500	105,600	Rockford, IL	87,500	88,700	88,200
Davenport, IA/IL	66,200	69,400	70,500	Sacramento, CA[2]	120,200	115,200	113,300
Dayton/Springfield, OH	88,300	95,100	90,600	St. Louis, MO/IL	87,700	91,200	91,100
Daytona Beach, FL	69,600	73,300	72,500	Salt Lake City, UT	113,700	122,700	123,400
Denver, CO	127,300	133,400	136,200	San Antonio, TX	80,800	84,900	84,400
Des Moines, IA	87,000	92,400	93,600	San Diego, CA[2]	171,600	174,500	176,400
Detroit, MI	98,200	111,400	113,900	San Francisco, CA[2]	254,400	266,400	271,100
El Paso, TX	72,300	76,200	77,700	Sarasota, FL	104,500	107,700	108,500
Eugene, OR	104,900	116,200	117,300	Seattle, WA	159,000	164,600	167,600
Fargo, ND/MN	82,900	83,200	85,300	Shreveport, LA	72,500	77,600	75,100
Ft. Lauderdale, FL	105,900	112,300	122,100	Sioux Falls, SD	84,200	87,400	88,200
Ft. Myers, FL	77,700	78,700	82,600	South Bend, IN	69,300	76,700	71,100
Ft. Worth/Arlington, TX	83,700	86,500	88,500	Spokane, WA	98,400	101,200	99,700
Gainesville, FL	89,900	93,600	95,700	Springfield, IL	79,100	82,100	78,700
Gary/Hammond, IN	91,600	95,000	88,100	Springfield, MA	106,100	105,700	102,500
Grand Rapids, MI	80,600	87,200	91,200	Springfield, MO	78,300	79,200	80,900
Green Bay, WI	89,500	96,100	96,500	Syracuse, NY	81,200	79,100	77,300
Greensboro, NC	102,500	112,700	114,300	Tacoma, WA	121,400	125,400	127,300
Hartford, CT	133,400	139,200	133,400	Tallahassee, FL	99,800	109,800	105,400
Honolulu, HI	349,000	335,000	313,800	Tampa, FL	78,300	81,300	81,000
Houston, TX	79,200	84,700	87,600	Toledo, OH	77,600	84,200	82,900
Indianapolis, IN	94,600	98,000	106,000	Topeka, KS	68,200	73,900	74,400
Jacksonville, FL	83,100	88,400	86,200	Tucson, AZ	100,500	105,500	103,600
Kalamazoo, MI	82,200	90,000	88,800	Tulsa, OK	78,500	82,200	82,500
Kansas City, MO/KS	91,700	98,800	102,000	Washington, DC/MD/VA	156,500	160,700	158,800
Knoxville, TN	93,600	98,700	98,300	Waterloo/Cedar Falls,IA	56,500	60,600	62,600
Lake County, IL	136,200	144,700	147,000	W. Palm Beach, FL	121,300	126,600	128,000
Lansing, MI	79,800	84,700	82,800	Wichita, KS	76,500	80,700	80,100
Las Vegas, NV	113,500	118,500	119,800	Wilmington, DE/NJ/MD	123,600	NA	NA
Lexington/Fayette, KY	90,800	95,700	95,600	Worcester, MA	130,100	131,200	132,000

(1) All areas are metropolitan statistical areas (MSAs) as defined by the U.S. Office of Management and Budget. They include the named central city and surrounding areas. (2) Data provided by the California Association of REALTORS®. NA= not available.

Housing Affordability

Source: National Association of REALTORS®

Year	Median-priced existing home	Average mortgage rate[1]	Monthly principal and interest payment	Payment as percentage of median income	Year	Median-priced existing home	Average mortgage rate[1]	Monthly principal and interest payment	Payment as percentage of median income
1987	$85,600	9.28%	$565	21.9%	1993	$106,800	7.16%	$578	18.8%
1988	90,600	9.31	591	22.0	1994	109,900	7.47	613	19.0
1989	93,100	10.11	600	20.1	1995	113,100	7.85	661	19.7
1990	97,500	10.04	673	22.7	1996	118,200	7.71	675	19.1
1991	99,700	9.51	671	22.3	1997[2]	123,200	7.91	717	19.9
1992	103,700	8.11	615	20.0					

(1) The average mortgage rate is based on the effective rate on loans closed on existing homes monitored by the Federal Housing Finance Board. (2) Preliminary figures for May 1997.

Mortgage Payment Tables

Source: *The Mortgage Money Guide*, Federal Trade Commission

8% Annual Percentage Rate
Monthly payments (principal and interest)

Amount financed	10 Years	15 Years	20 Years	25 Years	30 Years
$ 50,000	$ 606.64	$ 477.83	$ 418.22	$ 385.91	$ 366.88
60,000	727.97	573.39	501.86	463.09	440.26
70,000	849.29	668.96	585.51	540.27	513.64
80,000	970.62	764.52	669.15	617.45	587.01
90,000	1091.95	860.09	752.80	694.63	660.39
100,000	1213.28	955.65	836.44	771.82	733.76
120,000	1455.94	1146.78	1003.72	926.18	880.52
140,000	1698.58	1337.92	1171.02	1080.54	1027.28
160,000	1941.24	1529.04	1338.30	1234.90	1174.02
180,000	2183.90	1720.18	1505.60	1389.26	1320.78
200,000	2426.56	1911.30	1672.88	1543.64	1467.52

10% Annual Percentage Rate
Monthly payments (principal and interest)

Amount financed	10 Years	15 Years	20 Years	25 Years	30 Years
$ 50,000	$ 660.75	$ 537.30	$ 482.51	$ 454.35	$ 438.79
60,000	792.90	644.76	579.01	545.22	526.54
70,000	925.06	752.22	675.52	636.09	614.30
80,000	1057.20	859.68	772.02	726.96	702.06
90,000	1189.36	967.14	868.52	817.83	789.81
100,000	1321.51	1074.61	965.02	908.70	877.57
120,000	1585.80	1289.52	1158.02	1090.44	1053.08
140,000	1850.12	1504.44	1351.04	1272.18	1228.60
160,000	2114.40	1719.36	1544.04	1453.92	1404.12
180,000	2378.72	1934.28	1737.04	1635.66	1579.62
200,000	2643.02	2149.22	1930.04	1817.40	1755.14

9% Annual Percentage Rate
Monthly payments (principal and interest)

Amount financed	10 Years	15 Years	20 Years	25 Years	30 Years
$ 50,000	$ 633.38	$ 507.13	$ 449.86	$ 419.60	$ 402.31
60,000	760.05	608.56	539.84	503.52	482.77
70,000	886.73	709.99	629.81	587.44	563.24
80,000	1013.41	811.41	719.78	671.36	643.70
90,000	1140.08	912.84	809.75	755.28	724.16
100,000	1266.76	1014.27	899.73	839.20	804.62
120,000	1520.10	1217.12	1079.68	1007.04	965.54
140,000	1773.46	1419.98	1259.62	1174.88	1126.48
160,000	2026.82	1622.82	1439.56	1342.72	1287.40
180,000	2280.16	1825.68	1619.50	1510.56	1448.32
200,000	2533.52	2028.54	1799.46	1678.40	1609.24

11% Annual Percentage Rate
Monthly payments (principal and interest)

Amount financed	10 Years	15 Years	20 Years	25 Years	30 Years
$ 50,000	$ 688.75	$ 568.30	$ 516.09	$ 490.06	$ 476.16
60,000	826.50	681.96	619.31	588.07	571.39
70,000	964.25	795.62	722.53	686.08	666.63
80,000	1102.00	909.28	825.75	784.09	761.86
90,000	1239.75	1022.94	928.97	882.10	857.09
100,000	1377.50	1136.60	1032.19	980.11	952.32
120,000	1653.00	1363.92	1238.62	1176.14	1142.78
140,000	1928.50	1591.24	1445.06	1372.16	1333.26
160,000	2204.00	1818.56	1651.50	1568.18	1523.72
180,000	2479.50	2045.88	1857.94	1764.20	1714.18
200,000	2755.00	2273.20	2064.38	1960.22	1904.64

How to Obtain Birth, Marriage, Death Records

The pamphlet *Where to Write for Vital Records: Births, Deaths, Marriages, and Divorces* (Stock # 017-022-01196-4) is available from the Superintendent of Documents, PO Box 371954, Pittsburgh, PA 15250-7954; advance payment of $2.25 is required. Orders can also be placed by calling (202) 512-1800 or via fax, (202) 512-2250, using a credit card.

Wedding Anniversaries

The traditional names for wedding anniversaries go back many years in social usage. As names like *wooden*, *crystal*, *silver*, and *golden* were applied to anniversary years, it was considered proper to present the married couple with gifts made of these products or of something related. The list of traditional products for gifts, with a few allowable revisions in parentheses, is presented below, with common modern gifts indicated in boldface.

1st	Paper, **clocks**	9th	Pottery (china), **leather goods**	25th	Silver, **sterling silver**
2d	Cotton, **china**	10th	Tin, aluminum, **diamond**	30th	Pearl, **diamond**
3d	Leather, **crystal, glass**	11th	Steel, **fashion jewelry**	35th	Coral (jade), **jade**
4th	Linen (silk), **appliances**	12th	Silk, **pearls, colored gems**	40th	Ruby, **ruby**
5th	Wood, **silverware**	13th	Lace, **textiles, furs**	45th	Sapphire, **sapphire**
6th	Iron, **wood objects**	14th	Ivory, **gold jewelry**	50th	Gold, **gold**
7th	Wool (copper), **desk sets**	15th	Crystal, **watches**	55th	Emerald, **emerald**
8th	Bronze, **linens, lace**	20th	China, **platinum**	60th	Diamond, **diamond**

Birthstones

Source: Jewelry Industry Council

Month	Ancient	Modern	Month	Ancient	Modern
January	Garnet	Garnet	**July**	Onyx	Ruby
February	Amethyst	Amethyst	**August**	Carnelian	Sardonyx or Peridot
March	Jasper	Bloodstone or Aquamarine	**September**	Chrysolite	Sapphire
April	Sapphire	Diamond	**October**	Aquamarine	Opal or Tourmaline
May	Agate	Emerald	**November**	Topaz	Topaz
June	Emerald	Pearl, Moonstone, or Alexandrite	**December**	Ruby	Turquoise or Zircon

The Cost of Raising a Child

Source: Family Economics Research Group, U.S. Dept. of Agriculture

Estimated annual expenditures in 1996 dollars for a child born in 1996, by income group. Estimates are for the younger child in a 2-parent family with 2 children, for the overall U.S.

Year	Age of child	Low	Middle	High	Year	Age of child	Low	Middle	High
1996	under 1	$5,670	$ 7,880	$11,680	2005	9	$ 9,370	$12,780	$18,610
1997	1	5,960	8,270	12,290	2006	10	9,860	13,450	19,570
1998	2	6,280	8,700	12,930	2007	11	10,370	14,150	20,590
1999	3	6,730	9,380	13,870	2008	12	12,380	16,220	23,190
2000	4	7,080	9,870	14,590	2009	13	13,030	17,070	24,390
2001	5	7,450	10,390	15,350	2010	14	13,710	17,950	25,660
2002	6	8,000	11,020	16,090	2011	15	14,230	19,170	27,660
2003	7	8,410	11,590	16,930	2012	16	14,960	20,160	29,100
2004	8	8,850	12,200	17,810	2013	17	15,740	21,210	30,610
					Total		**$178,080**	**$241,440**	**$350,920**

(1) In 1996, low income is less than $34,700 (average=$21,600); middle income is $34,700 to $58,300 (average=$46,800); high income is $58,300 or more (average=$87,300). The projected annual inflation rate is 5.2%.

Marriage Laws

Source: Gary N. Skoloff, Skoloff & Wolfe, Livingston, NJ; as of July 1997

State	Age with parental consent Male	Age with parental consent Female	Age without consent Male	Age without consent Female	Physical exam & blood test for male and female Max. period between exam and license	Scope of medical exam	Waiting period Before license	Waiting period After license issuance (expiration)
Alabama*	14a,t	14a,t	18	18	—	—	—	30 days
Alaska	16z	16z	18	18	—	—	3 days, w	—
Arizona	16z	16z	18	18	—	—	—	1 yr.
Arkansas	17c, z	16c, z	18	18	—	—	v	—
California	aa	aa	18	18	30 days, w, h	jj	—	90 days
Colorado*y	16z	16z	18	18	—	—	—	30 days
Connecticut	16z	16z	18	18	—	bb	4 days, w	65 days
Delaware	18c	16c	18	18	—	—	24 hr, e	30 days
Florida	16a, c	16a, c	18	18	—	—	—	—
Georgia*	aa, j	aa, j	16	16	—	bb	3 days, g	30 days
Hawaii	15j	15j	16	16	—	p	—	—
Idaho*	16z	16z	18	18	—	s, zzz	—	—
Illinois	16pp	16pp	18	18	30 days	n	1 day	60 days
Indiana	17c	17c	18	18	—	rr	72 hr, w	60 days
Iowa*	aa, j	aa, j	18	18	—	—	3 days	20 days
Kansas*y	aa, j	aa, j	18	18	—	—	3 days, w	—
Kentucky	aa, j	aa, j	18	18	—	—	—	—
Louisiana xx	18z	18z	18	18	10 days	—	72 hr, w	—
Maine	16z	16z	18	18	—	—	3 days, v, w	90 days
Maryland	16c, f	16c, f	18	18	—	—	48 hr, w	6 mo
Massachusetts	14j	12j	18	18	3-60 days, u	—	3 days, v	—
Michigan	16	16	18	18	—	—	3 days, w	—
Minnesota	16j	16j	18	18	—	—	5 days, w	—
Mississippi	aa, j	aa, j	17	15	30 days	b	3 days, w	—
Missouri	15d	15d	18	18	—	—	—	—
Montana*yy	16j	16j	18	18	—	b	—	180 days
Nebraska yy	17	17	19	19	—	bb	—	1 yr
Nevada	16z	16z	18	18	—	—	—	1 yr
New Hampshire	14k	13k	18	18	—	hh	3 days, v, w	90 days
New Jersey	16z, c	16z, c	18	18	30 days	b	72 hr, w	30 days
New Mexico	16d, c	16d, c	18	18	30 days	b	—	—
New York	16k	16k	18	18	—	nn	24 hr, ee	60 days
North Carolina	16c	16c	18	18	—	—	—	—
North Dakota	16	16	18	18	—	—	—	60 days
Ohio	aa, j	16c, z	18	18	30 days	b	5 days,w, r	60 days
Oklahoma*	16c, z	16c, z	18	18	30 days, w	b	ff	30 days
Oregon	17tt	17tt	18	18	—	—	3 days, w	—
Pennsylvania*	16d	16d	18	18	30 days	b	3 days, w	60 days
Rhode Island*	d	16d	18	18	—	rrr	—	—
South Carolina*	16c	14c	18	18	—	—	1 day	—
South Dakota	16c	16c	18	18	—	—	—	20 days
Tennesee	16d	16d	18	18	—	—	3 days, cc, w	30 days
Texas*y	14j, k	14j, k	18	18	—	—	zzzz	30 days
Utah*	14a	14a	18x	18x	—	—	—	30 days
Vermont	14j	14j	18	18	30 days, w	b	1 day, w	—
Virginia	16a, c	16a, c	18	18	—	zz	—	60 days
Washington	17d	17d	18	18	—	bbb	3 days	60 days
West Virginia	18c	18c	18	18	—	b	3 days, w	—
Wisconsin	16	16	18	18	—	zzz	5 days, w	30 days
Wyoming	16d	16d	18	18	—	bb	—	—
Dist. of Columbia*	16a	16a	18	18	30 days	b	3 days, w	—
Puerto Rico	18c, d, z	16c, d, z	21	21c	—	b	—	—

*Indicates common-law marriage recognized. (a)Parental consent not required if minor was previously married. (aa)No age limits. (b)Venereal diseases. In WV and OK, Circuit Court judge may waive requirement. (bb)Venereal diseases and rubella (for female). (bbb)No exam required, but parties must file affidavit of non-affliction with contagious venereal disease. (c)Younger parties may obtain license in case of pregnancy or birth of child. (cc)Unless parties are over 18 yr of age. (d)Younger parties may obtain license in special circumstances. (e)Residents, before expiration of 24-hr waiting period; non-residents, before expiration of 96-hr waiting period. (ee)License effective 1 day after issuance, unless court orders otherwise; valid for 60 days only. (f)If parties are at least 16 yr of age, proof of age and the consent of parents in person are required. If a parent is ill, an affidavit by the incapacitated parent and a physician's affidavit to that effect required. (ff)If one or both parties are below the age for marriage without parental consent, 3-day waiting period. (g)Unless parties are 18 yr of age or more, or female is pregnant, or applicants are the parents of a living child born out of wedlock. (h)When unmarried man and unmarried woman, not minors, have been living together as man and wife, they may, without health certificate, be married upon issuance of appropriate authorization. (hh)Parties must sign affidavit affirming that they have received and discussed brochure prepared by Division of Public Health Services, Dept. of Health and Human Services. (j)Parental consent and/or permission of judge required. (jj)Medical examination for syphilis (and for female, rubella), with required offer of HIV test. (k)Below age of consent parties need parental consent and permission of judge. (l)Medical examination not required but certificate evidencing HIV counseling required. (m)Mental incompetence, infectious tuberculosis, venereal diseases. (n)Venereal diseases; test for sickle cell anemia given at request of examining physician. (nn)Tests for sickle cell anemia may be required for certain applicants. (p)Rubella for female, except under limited circumstances. (pp)Judicial consent may be given when parents refuse to consent. (r)Applicants under age 18 must state that they have had marriage counseling. (rr)Any unsterilized female under 50 must submit with application for license a medical report stating whether she has immunological response to rubella, or a written record that the rubella vaccine was administered on or after her 1st birthday. Judge may by order dispense with these requirements. (rrr)Physical examination and blood test required; offer of HIV counseling required. (s)Rubella for female; there are certain exceptions, and district judge may waive medical examination on proof that emergency exists. (t)Other statutory requirements apply. (tt)If a party has no parent residing within state, and one party has residence within state for 6 mo, no permission required. (u)Doctor's certificate must be filed 30 days prior to notice of intention. (v)Parties must file notice of intention to marry with local clerk. (w)Waiting period may be avoided. (x)Authorizes counties to provide for premarital counseling as a requisite to issuance of license to persons under 19 and persons previously divorced. (xx)The "covenant marriage" bill, which went into effect Aug. 15, 1997, in Louisiana, provides for an optional, voluntary form of marriage that is more difficult to dissolve through divorce. The covenant marriage requires pre-marriage counseling and limits grounds for divorce to such issues as spousal or child abuse, imprisonment, or adultery. (y)Marriages by proxy are valid. (yy)Proxy marriages are valid under certain conditions. (z)Younger parties may marry with parental consent and/or permission of judge. In CT, judicial approval. (zz)Required offer of HIV test, and/or must be provided with information on AIDS and tests available. (zzz)Applicants must receive information on AIDS and certify having read it. (zzzz)72 hr waiting period following issuance of license.

Divorce Laws

Source: Gary N. Skoloff, Skoloff & Wolfe, Livingston, NJ; as of July 1996

Important: Almost all states also have other laws as well as qualifications of the laws shown below and have proposed divorce-reform laws pending. It would be wise to consult a lawyer in conjunction with the use of this chart.

Some Grounds for Absolute Divorce[1]

	Residence	Adultery	Mental or physical cruelty	Desertion	Alcoholism	Impotency	Non-support	Insanity	Bigamy	Felony conviction or imprisonment	Drug addiction	Fraud, force, duress
AL	6 mo*	Yes	Yes	1 yr	Yes	Yes	2 yr	5 yr	A	2 yr*	Yes	A
AK	*	Yes	Yes	1 yr	1 yr	Yes	No	18 mo	A	Yes	Yes	A
AZ	90 days	No	No	No	No	No	No	No	No	No	No	No
AR	60 days*	Yes	Yes	No	1 yr	Yes	Yes	3 yr	No	Yes	No	A
CA	6 mo*	No	No	No	No	A	No	Yes*	A	No	No	A
CO	90 days	No	No	No	No	A	No	No	A	No	No	A
CT	1 yr*	Yes	Yes	1 yr	Yes	No	Yes	5 yr	A	life*	No	Yes
DE	6 mo	Yes	Yes	Yes	Yes	A	No	Yes	Yes	Yes	Yes	A
FL	6 mo	No	No	No	No	No	No	3 yr	No	No	No	A
GA	6 mo	Yes	Yes	1 yr	Yes	Yes	No	2 yr	A	Yes*	Yes	Yes
HI	6 mo	No	No	No	No	No	No	No	A	No	No	A
ID	6 wk	Yes	Yes	Yes	No	A	No	3 yr	A	Yes	No	A
IL	90 days	Yes	Yes	1 yr	2 yr	Yes	No	No	Yes	Yes	2 yr	No
IN	6 mo*	No	No	No	No	Yes	No	2 yr	A	Yes	No	A
IA	1 yr*	No	No	No	No	A	No	A	A	No	No	No
KS	60 days	No	No	No	No	No	Yes	2 yr	A	No	No	A
KY	180 days	No	No	No	No	A	No	No	No	No	No	A
LA	6 mo*	Yes	No	No	No	No	No	No	A	Yes*	No	A
ME	6 mo*	Yes	Yes	3 yr	Yes	Yes	Yes	A	A	No	Yes	No
MD	*	Yes	†	1 yr†	No	No	No	3 yr	A	1 yr*	No	No
MA	1 yr*	Yes	Yes	1 yr	Yes	Yes	No†	A	A	5 yr*	Yes	No
MI	180 days*	No	No	No	No	No	No	No	No	No	No	A
MN	180 days	No	No	No	No	No	No	No	No	No	No	A
MS	6 mo	Yes	Yes	1 yr	Yes	Yes, A	No	3 yr, A	Yes	Yes	Yes	A
MO	90 days	No	No	No	No	No	No	No	A	No	No	A
MT	90 days	No	No	No	No	A	No	No	A	No	No	A
NE	1 yr*	No	No	No	No	A	No	A	A	No	No	A
NV	6 wk	No	No	No	No	No	No	2 yr	A	No	No	A
NH	1 yr*	Yes	Yes	2 yr	2 yr	Yes	2 yr	No	A	1 yr*	No	No
NJ	1 yr*	Yes	Yes	1 yr	1 yr	A	No	2 yr	A	18 mo	1 yr	A
NM	6 mo	Yes	Yes	Yes	No	No	No	No	No	No	No	No
NY	1 yr*	Yes†	Yes	1 yr†	No	No	†	A	A	3 yr†	No	A
NC	6 mo	No†	No†	No†	No†	A	No	3 yr	A	No	No†	No
ND	6 mo	Yes	Yes	1 yr	No	A	1 yr	5 yr	A	Yes	No	A
OH	6 mo	Yes†	Yes†	1 yr†	Yes†	No	Yes†	No	Yes†	Yes†	No	Yes†
OK	6 mo	Yes	Yes	1 yr	Yes	Yes	Yes	5 yr	Yes	Yes	No	Yes
OR	6 mo*	No	No	No	No	No	No	No	No	No	Yes	A
PA	6 mo	Yes	Yes	1 yr	No	No	No	18 mo*	Yes	Yes	No	No
RI	1 yr	Yes	Yes	5 yr*	Yes	Yes	1 yr	No	No	Yes	Yes	No
SC	1 yr*	Yes	Yes	1 yr	Yes	No	No	No	A	No	Yes	No
SD	*	Yes†	Yes†	1 yr†	1 yr†	A	1 yr†	5 yr†	A	Yes†	No	A
TN	6 mo*	Yes	Yes	1 yr	Yes	Yes	†	No	Yes	Yes	Yes	A
TX	6 mo*	Yes	Yes	1 yr	No	A	No	3 yr	No	1 yr	No	A
UT	3 mo*	Yes	Yes	1 yr	Yes	Yes	Yes	Yes*	A	Yes	No	No
VT	6 mo*	Yes	Yes	7 yr	No	No	Yes	5 yr†	A	3 yr	No	A
VA	6 mo*	Yes	Yes†	1 yr†	No	A	†	A	A	1 yr	No	A
WA	bona fide resident	No	No	No	No	No	No	No	A*	No	No	A
WV	1 yr*	Yes	Yes	6 mo	Yes	A	No	3 yr	A	Yes	Yes	No
WI	6 mo	No	No	No	No	A	No	No	A	No	No	A
WY	2 mo*	No	No	No	No	No	No	2 yr	A	No	No	A
DC	6 mo	No	No	No	No	A	No	A	A	No	No	A
PR	1 yr	Yes	Yes	1 yr	Yes	Yes	No	Yes	A	Yes*	Yes	No

(1)Almost all states have "no-fault" divorce laws. Conduct that constitutes "no-fault" divorce may vary from state to state. (*)Indicates qualification; check local statutes. (A)Indicates grounds for annulment. (†)Indicates grounds for divorce or legal separation.

NATIONS OF THE WORLD

As of mid-1997

The nations of the world are listed in alphabetical order. Initials in the following articles include UN (United Nations), OAS (Org. of American States), NATO (North Atlantic Treaty Org.), EU (European Union, or Common Market), OAU (Org. of African Unity), OECD (Org. for Economic Cooperation and Development), ILO (Intl. Labor Org.), FAO (Food & Agriculture Org.), WHO (World Health Org.), IMF (Intl. Monetary Fund), WTO (World Trade Organization, formerly GATT), CIS (Commonwealth of Independent States), FY (fiscal year). **Sources:** U.S. Census Bureau: Intl. Data Base*;* Central Intelligence Agency: *The World Factbook;* Encyclopaedia Britannica and Encyclopaedia Britannica Book of the Year; Intl. Monetary Fund; Intl. Institute for Strategic Studies: *The Military Balance;* Facts on File World News Digest; Keesing's Record of World Events; Current History; Collier's Encyclopedia and Collier's Year Book; Encyclopedia Americana Yearbook; Who's Who in the World; U.S. Dept. of State; American Automobile Manufacturers Assn.; U.S. Dept. of Energy; *World Urbanization Prospects,* UN Population Division; UN Statistical Yearbook; UN Demographic Yearbook; The Statesman's Year-Book; The Europa World Year Book; Funk & Wagnalls New Encyclopedia. Telephone data has been supplied by the Intl. Telecommunication Union, from the World Telecommunication Indicators database, copyright ITU. National population figures are mid-1997 estimates, unless otherwise noted. An * after city population figures indicates 1995 urban agglomeration. Gross Domestic Product/Gross National Product: Intl. GDP estimates are derived from purchasing power parity calculations, which involve use of intl. dollar price weights applied to the quantities of goods and services produced in a given economy; U.S. data is from U.S. Dept. of Commerce. *Note:* Because of rounding or incomplete enumeration, some percentages may not add to 100%. National Budget measures expenditures, unless otherwise noted. Tourism figures represent receipts from international tourism. Comm. (commercial) vehicles include trucks and buses. All embassy addresses are Wash., DC, area codes (202), unless otherwise noted. "Literacy" rates usually measure the percent of population able to read and write on a lower elementary school level. If literacy is defined as ability to read instructions necessary for a job or a license, illiteracy may be more common than these rates suggest. Per-person figures in communications section are post-1993 and in health section are post-1989.

See pages 481-96 for full-color maps and flags.

Afghanistan
Islamic State of Afghanistan
Dowlat-e Eslami-ye Afghanestan

People: Population: 23,738,085. **Age distrib.** (%): <15: 43; 65+: 3. **Pop. density:** 90 per sq. mi. **Urban:** 20%. **Ethnic groups:** Pashtun 38%, Tajik 25%, Hazara 19%, Uzbek 6%. **Principal languages:** Pashtu 35%, Dari Persian (spoken by Tajiks, Hazaras) 50% (both official), Turkic (incl. Uzbek, Turkmen) 11%. **Chief religions:** Sunni Muslim 84%, Shi'a Muslim 15%.

Geography: Area: 251,825 sq. mi. **Location:** In SW Asia, NW of the Indian subcontinent. **Neighbors:** Pakistan on E, S; Iran on W; Turkmenistan, Tajikistan, Uzbekistan on N. The NE tip touches China. **Topography:** The country is landlocked and mountainous, much of it over 4,000 ft. above sea level. The Hindu Kush Mts. tower 16,000 ft. above Kabul and reach a height of 25,000 ft. to the E. Trade with Pakistan flows through the 35-mile-long Khyber Pass. The climate is dry, with extreme temperatures, and there are large desert regions, though mountain rivers produce intermittent fertile valleys. **Capital:** Kabul: 2,029,000*.

Government: Type: In transition. **Local divisions:** 30 provinces. **Defense:** 15% of GNP (1990).

Economy: Industries: Textiles, soap, furniture, cement. **Chief crops:** Nuts, wheat, fruits. **Minerals:** Gas, oil, copper, coal, zinc, iron. **Other resources:** Wool, karakul pelts, mutton. **Arable land:** 12%. **Livestock** (1996): sheep: 14.3 mil; goats: 2.2 mil; cattle: 1.5 mil. **Electricity prod.** (1995): 655 mil kWh. **Labor force:** Agriculture supports about 68% of the population.

Finance: Monetary unit: Afghani (Aug. 1997: 55.00 = $1 US). **Gross domestic product** (1995 est.): $12.8 bil. **Per capita GDP:** $600. **Imports** (1994): $602 mil; partners: Japan 14%, EU 11%. **Exports** (1994): $296 mil; partners: EU 10%.

Transport: Railroad: Length: 15.3 mi. **Motor vehicles in use:** 34,000 passenger cars, 31,000 comm. vehicles. **Civil aviation:** 163.3 mil passenger-mi; 35 airports.

Communications: Television sets: 1 per 102 persons; **Radios:** 1 per 8.5 persons. **Telephones:** 1 per 694 persons. **Daily newspaper circ.:** 11 per 1,000 pop.

Health: Life expectancy at birth (1997): 46.9 male; 45.8 female. **Births** (per 1,000 pop.): 43. **Deaths** (per 1,000 pop.): 18. **Natural increase:** 2.5%. **Hospital beds:** 1 per 2,945 persons. **Physicians:** 1 per 6,690 persons. **Infant mortality** (per 1,000 live births 1997): 147.

Education: Over 88% of adults have no formal schooling. Compulsory: ages 7-13. **Literacy** (1995 est.): 31.5%.

Major International Organizations: UN (World Bank, IMF). **Embassy:** 2341 Wyoming Ave. NW 20008; 234-3770.

Afghanistan, occupying a favored invasion route since antiquity, has been variously known as Ariana or Bactria (in ancient times) and Khorasan (in the Middle Ages). Foreign empires alternated rule with local emirs and kings until the 18th century, when a unified kingdom was established. In 1973, a military coup ushered in a republic.

Pro-Soviet leftists took power in a bloody 1978 coup and concluded an economic and military treaty with the USSR. In Dec. 1979 the USSR began a massive airlift into Kabul and backed a new coup, leading to installation of a more pro-Soviet leader. Soviet troops fanned out over Afghanistan and waged a protracted guerrilla war with Muslim rebels, in which some 15,000 Soviet troops reportedly died.

A UN-mediated agreement was signed Apr. 14, 1988, providing for withdrawal of Soviet troops, a neutral Afghan state, and repatriation of refugees. Afghan rebels rejected the pact, vowing to continue fighting while "Soviets and their puppets" remained in Afghanistan. The Soviets completed their troop withdrawal Feb. 15, 1989; fighting between Afghan rebels and government forces ensued.

Communist Pres. Najibullah resigned Apr. 16, 1992, as competing guerrilla forces advanced on Kabul. The rebels achieved power Apr. 28, ending 14 years of Soviet-backed regimes. More than 2 million Afghans had been killed and 6 million had left the country since 1979.

Following the rebel victory there were clashes between moderates and Islamic fundamentalist forces. Burhanuddin Rabbani, a guerrilla leader, became president June 28, 1992, but fierce fighting continued around Kabul and elsewhere. The Taliban, an insurgent Islamic fundamentalist faction, gained increasing control and in Sept. 1996 captured Kabul and set up a government. The Taliban executed former President Najibullah and imposed strict Islamic rule. Rabbani and other ousted leaders fled to the north, where anti-Taliban forces launched a counteroffensive.

Albania
Republic of Albania
Republika e Shqipërisë

People: Population: 3,293,252. **Age distrib.** (%): <15: 33; 65+: 6. **Pop. density:** 297 per sq. mi. **Urban:** 38%. **Ethnic groups:** Albanians (Gegs in N, Tosks in S) 95%, Greeks 3%. **Principal languages:** Albanian (official; Tosk is the official dialect), Greek. **Chief religions:** Muslim 70%, Albanian Orthodox 20%, Roman Catholic 10%.

Geography: Area: 11,100 sq. mi. **Location:** SE Europe, on SE coast of Adriatic Sea. **Neighbors:** Greece on S, Yugoslavia on N, Macedonia on E. **Topography:** Apart from a narrow coastal plain, Albania consists of hills and mountains covered with scrub forest, cut by small E-W rivers. **Capital:** Tiranë. **Cities** (1993 met.): Tiranë 384,010; Elbasin 215,240; Durres 162,846.

Government: Type: Republic. **Head of state:** Pres. Rexhep Mejdani; in office: July 24, 1997. **Head of government:** Prem. Fatos Nano; b 1952; in office: July 25, 1997. **Local divisions:** 26 districts. **Defense:** 2.5% of GDP (1995). **Active troop strength:** 54,000.

Economy: Industries: Cement, textiles, food processing. **Chief crops:** Corn, wheat, potatoes, tobacco, fruits. **Minerals:** Chromium, coal, oil, gas. **Crude oil reserves** (1996): 165 mil bbls. **Other resources:** Timber. **Arable land:** 21%. **Livestock** (1996): sheep: 2.5 mil; goats: 1.9 mil; pigs: 1.1 mil; cattle: 850,000. **Electricity prod.** (1995): 4.4 bil kWh. **Labor force:** 49.5% agric.

Finance: Monetary unit: Lek (Aug. 1997: 156.5 = $1 US). **Gross domestic product** (1995 est.): $4.1 bil. **Per capita

GDP: $1,210. **Imports** (1994 est.): $601 mil; partners: Italy 35%, Greece 24%. **Exports** (1994 est.): $141 mil; partners: Italy 52%, U.S. 11%. **National budget** (1994): $550.4 mil. **International reserves less gold:** $271.63 mil. **Gold:** 120,000 oz t. **Consumer prices** (change in 1996): 12.7%.
Transport: Railroad: Length: 416.1 mi. **Chief ports:** Durres, Vlore, Sarande. **Civil aviation:** 1.2 mil passenger-mi.
Communications: Television sets: 1 per 11 persons. **Radios:** 1 per 5.3 persons. **Telephones:** 1 per 87 persons. **Daily newspaper circ.:** 54 per 1,000 pop.
Health: Life expectancy at birth (1997): 65.2 male; 71.6 female. **Births** (per 1,000 pop.): 22. **Deaths** (per 1,000 pop): 8. **Natural increase:** 1.4%. **Hospital beds:** 1 per 173 persons. **Physicians:** 1 per 585 persons. **Infant mortality** (per 1,000 live births 1997): 47.
Major International Organizations: UN (FAO, WHO, World Bank).
Education: Free and compulsory: ages 6-14. **Literacy** (1993): 100%.
Embassy: 1511 K St. NW 20005; 223-4942.

Ancient Illyria was conquered by Romans, Slavs, and Turks (15th century); the latter Islamized the population. Independent Albania was proclaimed in 1912, republic was formed in 1920. King Zog I ruled 1925-39, until Italy invaded.

Communist partisans took over in 1944, allied Albania with USSR, then broke with USSR in 1960 over de-Stalinization. Strong political alliance with China followed, leading to several billion dollars in aid, which was curtailed after 1974. China cut off aid in 1978 when Albania attacked its policies after the death of Chinese ruler Mao Zedong. Large-scale purges of officials occurred during the 1970s.

Enver Hoxha, the nation's ruler for 4 decades, died Apr. 11, 1985. Eventually the new regime introduced some liberalization, including measures in 1990 providing for freedom to travel abroad. Efforts were begun to improve ties with the outside world. Mar. 1991 elections left the former Communists in power, but a general strike and urban opposition led to the formation of a coalition cabinet including non-Communists.

Albania's former Communists were routed in elections Mar. 1992, amid economic collapse and social unrest. Sali Berisha was elected as the first non-Communist president since World War II. Berisha's party claimed a landslide victory in disputed parliamentary elections, May 26 and June 2, 1996. Public protests over the collapse of fraudulent investment schemes in Jan. 1997 led to armed rebellion and anarchy. The UN Security Council, Mar. 28, authorized a 7,000-member force to restore order. Socialists and their allies won parliamentary elections, June 29 and July 6, and international peacekeepers completed their pullout by Aug. 11.

Algeria
Democratic and Popular Republic of Algeria
Al Jumhuriyah al Jaza'iriyah ad Dimuqratiyah ash Shabiyah

People: Population: 29,830,370. **Age distrib.** (%): <15: 39; 65+: 4. **Pop. density:** 32 per sq. mi. **Urban:** 56%. **Ethnic groups:** Arab-Berber 99%. **Principal languages:** Arabic (official), French, Berber dialects. **Chief religions:** Sunni Muslim (state religion) 99%.
Geography: Area: 919,595 sq. mi. **Location:** In NW Africa, from Mediterranean Sea into Sahara Desert. **Neighbors:** Morocco on W; Mauritania, Mali, Niger on S; Libya, Tunisia on E. **Topography:** The Tell, located on the coast, comprises fertile plains 50-100 miles wide, with a moderate climate and adequate rain. Two major chains of the Atlas Mts., running roughly E-W and reaching 7,000 ft., enclose a dry plateau region. Below lies the Sahara, mostly desert with major mineral resources. **Capital:** Algiers (El Djazair): 3,705,000*.
Government: Type: Republic. **Head of state:** Pres. Liamine Zeroual; b July 3, 1941; in office: Jan. 31, 1994. **Head of government:** Prime Min. Ahmed Ouyahia; b July 2, 1952; in office: Dec. 31, 1995. **Local divisions:** 48 provinces. **Defense:** 2.7% of GDP (1994). **Active troop strength:** 123,700 est.
Economy: Industries: Oil, natural gas, light industries, food processing. **Chief crops:** Grains, grapes, citrus, olives. **Minerals:** Iron, phosphates, zinc, lead. **Crude oil reserves** (1996): 9.2 bil bbls. **Arable land:** 3%. **Livestock** (1996): sheep: 18.0 mil; goats: 2.55 mil; cattle: 1.5 mil. **Electricity prod.** (1995): 19.1 bil kWh. **Labor force:** 29% govt.; 27% ind., serv., commerce; 22% agric.
Finance: Monetary unit: Dinar (Aug. 1997: 59.64 = $1 US). **Gross domestic product** (1995 est.): $108.7 bil. **Per capita GDP:** $3,800. **Imports** (1995 est.): $10.6 bil; partners: France 29%, Italy 14%. **Exports** (1995 est.): $9.5 bil; partners: Italy 21%, France 16%. **National budget** (1995 est.):

$17.9 bil. **International reserves less gold** (June 1997): $6.4 bil. **Gold:** 5.6 mil oz t. **Consumer prices** (change in 1995): 32.2%.
Transport: Railroad: Length: 2,963.4 mi. **Motor vehicles in use:** 500,000 passenger cars, 420,000 comm. vehicles. **Civil aviation:** 1.7 bil passenger-mi.; 119 airports. **Chief ports:** Algiers, Oran.
Communications: Television sets: 1 per 13 persons. **Radios:** 1 per 4.2 persons. **Telephones:** 1 per 24 persons. **Daily newspaper circ.:** 46 per 1,000 pop.
Health: Life expectancy at birth (1997): 67.5 male; 69.8 female. **Births** (per 1,000 pop.): 28. **Deaths** (per 1,000 pop.): 6. **Natural increase:** 2.2%. **Hospital beds:** 1 per 455 persons. **Physicians:** 1 per 1,033 persons. **Infant mortality** (per 1,000 live births 1997): 47.
Education: Compulsory: ages 6-15. **Literacy** (1995 est.): 61.6%.
Major International Organizations: UN (WTO, World Bank, FAO, IMF, WHO), OAU, Arab League, OPEC.
Embassy: 2118 Kalorama Rd. NW 20008; 265-2800.

Earliest known inhabitants were ancestors of Berbers, followed by Phoenicians, Romans, Vandals, and, finally, Arabs. Turkey ruled 1518 to 1830, when France took control.

Large-scale European immigration and French cultural inroads did not prevent an Arab nationalist movement from launching guerrilla war. Peace, and French withdrawal, was negotiated with French Pres. Charles de Gaulle. One million Europeans left. Independence came July 5, 1962. Ahmed Ben Bella was the victor of infighting and ruled until 1965, when an army coup installed Col. Houari Boumedienne as leader; Boumedienne led until his death from a blood disease, 1978.

In 1967, Algeria declared war on Israel, broke ties with U.S., and moved toward eventual military and political ties with the USSR. Some 500 died in riots protesting economic hardship in 1988. In 1989, voters approved a new constitution, which cleared the way for a multiparty system.

The government canceled the Jan. 1992 elections that Islamic fundamentalists were expected to win, and banned all nonreligious activities at Algeria's 10,000 mosques. Pres. Mohammed Boudiaf was assassinated June 29, 1992. There were repeated attacks on high-ranking officials, security forces, foreigners, and others by militant Muslim fundamentalists over the next 5 years; pro-government death squads also were active. The overall estimated death toll exceeded 60,000 by mid-1997. In 2 large massacres, in Aug. and Sept. 1997, more than 140 people were killed.

Liamine Zeroual won the presidential election of Nov. 16, 1995. A new constitution banning Islamic political parties and increasing the powers of the president passed in a referendum on Nov. 28, 1996. Pro-government parties won the parliamentary election of June 6, 1997.

Andorra
Principality of Andorra
Principat d'Andorra

People: Population: 74,839. **Age distrib.** (%): <15: 16; 65+: 11. **Pop. density:** 413 per sq. mi. **Urban:** 95%. **Ethnic groups:** Spanish 61%, Andorran 30%, French 6%. **Principal languages:** Catalan (official), French, Castilian. **Chief religions:** Mostly Roman Catholic.
Geography: Area: 181 sq. mi. **Location:** SW Europe, in Pyrenees Mts. **Neighbors:** Spain on S, France on N. **Topography:** High mountains and narrow valleys cover the country. **Capital** (1993 est.): Andorra la Vella 22,387.
Government: Type: Parliamentary co-principality. **Heads of state:** President of France & Bishop of Urgel (Spain), as co-princes. **Head of government:** Marc Forné Molné; in office: Dec. 21, 1994. **Local divisions:** 7 parishes. **Defense:** Responsibility of France and Spain.
Economy: Industries: Tourism, sheep, tobacco products. **Minerals:** Iron, lead. **Arable land:** 2%.
Finance: Monetary unit: French Franc, Spanish Peseta. **Gross domestic product** (1993 est.): $1 bil. **Per capita GDP:** $16,200. **National budget** (1993): $177 mil.
Communications: Television sets: 1 per 2.7 persons. **Radios:** 1 per 4.7 persons. **Telephones:** 1 per 2.3 persons.
Health (1997): **Life expectancy at birth** (1996): 86 male; 95 female. **Births** (per 1,000 pop.): 10. **Deaths** (per 1,000 pop.): 3. **Natural increase:** 0.7%. **Hospital beds:** 1 per 556 persons. **Physicians:** 1 per 538 persons. **Infant mortality** (per 1,000 live births 1996): 2.
Education: Free and compulsory: ages 6-16. **Literacy** (1997): 100%.
Major International Organizations: UN.
Embassy: 2 UN Plaza, New York, NY 10017; (212) 750-6630.

Andorra was a co-principality, with joint sovereignty by France and the bishop of Urgel, from 1278 to 1993.

Tourism, especially skiing, is the economic mainstay. A free port, allowing for an active trading center, draws some 13 million tourists annually. Andorran voters chose to end a feudal system that had been in place for 715 years and adopt a parliamentary system of government Mar. 14, 1993.

Angola
Republic of Angola
República de Angola

People: Population: 10,623,994. **Age distrib.** (%): <15: 45; 65+: 3. **Pop. density:** 22 per sq. mi. **Urban:** 32%. **Ethnic groups:** Ovimbundu 37%, Kimbundu 25%, Bakongo 13%. **Principal languages:** Portuguese (official), various Bantu and other African languages. **Chief religions:** Roman Catholic 38%, Protestant 15%, indigenous beliefs 47%.

Geography: Area: 481,354 sq. mi. **Location:** In SW Africa on Atlantic coast. **Neighbors:** Namibia on S, Zambia on E, Congo-Kinshasa (formerly Zaire) on N; Cabinda, an enclave separated from rest of country by short Atlantic coast of Congo-Kinshasa, borders Congo-Brazzaville. **Topography:** Most of Angola consists of a plateau elevated 3,000 to 5,000 feet above sea level, rising from a narrow coastal strip. There is also a temperate highland area in the west-central region, a desert in the S, and a tropical rain forest covering Cabinda. **Capital:** Luanda: 2,081,000*.

Government: Type: Republic. **Head of state:** Pres. José Eduardo dos Santos; b Aug. 28, 1942; in office: Sept. 20, 1979. **Head of government:** Prime Min. Fernando Franca van Dunem; in office: June 8, 1996. **Local divisions:** 18 provinces. **Defense:** 31% of GDP (1993). **Active troop strength:** 97,000 est.

Economy: Industries: Food processing, textiles, mining, brewing, oil. **Chief crops:** Coffee, sugarcane, bananas. **Minerals:** Iron, diamonds (over 1 mil carats a year), gold, phosphates, oil. **Livestock** (1996): cattle: 3.3 mil; goats: 1.6 mil; pigs: 820,000. **Crude oil reserves** (1996): 5.4 bil bbls. **Arable land:** 2%. **Fish catch** (1993): 81,000 metric tons. **Electricity prod.** (1995): 1.9 bil. kWh. **Labor force:** 85% agric., 15% industry.

Finance: Monetary unit: Readjusted Kwanza (Aug. 1997: 265,000 = $1 US). **Gross domestic product** (1995 est.): $7.4 bil. **Per capita GDP:** $700. **Imports** (1994): $1.6 bil; partners: Portugal 30%, U.S. 11%, France 10%. **Exports** (1994): $3 bil; partners: U.S. 57%. **National budget** (1992 est.): $2.5 bil.

Transport: Railroad: Length: 1,833.2 mi. **Motor vehicles in use:** 120,000 passenger cars, 40,000 comm. vehicles. **Civil aviation:** 989.9 mil passenger-mi. **Chief ports:** Cabinda, Lobito, Luanda.

Communications: Television sets: 1 per 152 persons. **Radios:** 1 per 33 persons. **Telephones:** 1 per 180 persons. **Daily newspaper circ.:** 11 per 1,000 pop.

Health: Life expectancy at birth (1997): 45.1 male; 49.6 female. **Births** (per 1,000 pop.): 44. **Deaths** (per 1,000 pop.): 17. **Natural increase:** 2.7%. **Hospital beds:** 1 per 845 persons. **Physicians:** 1 per 15,136 persons. **Infant mortality** (per 1,000 live births 1997): 136.

Education: Free and compulsory: ages 7-15. **Literacy** (1992): 40%.

Major International Organizations: UN (WTO, FAO, IMF, World Bank, ILO, WHO), OAU.

Embassy: 1819 L St. NW 20036; 785-1156.

From the early centuries AD to 1500, Bantu tribes penetrated most of the region. Portuguese came in 1583, allied with the Bakongo kingdom in the north, and developed the slave trade. Large-scale colonization did not begin until the 20th century, when 400,000 Portuguese immigrated.

A guerrilla war begun in 1961 lasted until 1975, when Portugal granted independence. Fighting then erupted between three rival rebel groups—the National Front, based in Zaire (now Congo), the Soviet-backed Popular Movement for the Liberation of Angola (MPLA), and the National Union for the Total Independence of Angola (UNITA), aided by the U.S. and South Africa. The civil war killed thousands of blacks, drove most whites to emigrate, and completed economic ruin. Cuban troops and Soviet aid helped the MPLA win control of most of the country by 1976 and gain wide recognition as the government of Angola.

An agreement was signed in Dec. 1988 between Angola, Cuba, and South Africa on a timetable for withdrawal of Cuban troops, completed May 25, 1991. The 16-year war was officially ended May 1, 1991, as the government and UNITA signed a peace agreement.

Elections were held in Sept. 1992, but fighting again broke out, as UNITA rejected the presidential election results, and continued into 1993 and 1994, with UNITA forces holding most of the countryside. Large numbers of civilians died from war-related causes, especially starvation. UNITA signed a new peace treaty with the government, Nov. 20, 1994, but the rebels were slow to demobilize. The UN Security Council voted, Aug. 28, 1997, to impose sanctions on UNITA.

Antigua and Barbuda

People: Population: 66,175. **Age distrib.** (%): <15: 25; 65+: 6. **Pop. density:** 387 per sq. mi. **Urban:** 36%. **Ethnic groups:** Mostly black African. **Principal language:** English (official). **Chief religions:** Predominantly Anglican, other Christian.

Geography: Area: 171 sq. mi. **Location:** Eastern Caribbean. **Neighbors:** St. Kitts & Nevis to W, Guadeloupe (Fr.) to S. **Capital:** St. John's (1991): 35,635.

Government: Type: Constitutional monarchy with British-style parliament. **Head of state:** Queen Elizabeth II; represented by Gov.-Gen. James Carlisle; b Aug. 5, 1937; in office: June 10, 1993. **Head of government:** Prime Min. Lester Bird; b Feb. 21, 1938; in office: Mar. 9, 1994. **Defense:** 1% of GDP (FY 1990-91). **Active troop strength:** 150.

Economy: Industries: Tourism, manufacturing, construction. **Arable land:** 18%. **Electricity prod.** (1995): 95 mil kWh. **Labor force:** 82% commerce & serv.; 11% agric.; 7% ind.

Finance: Monetary unit: East Caribbean Dollar (Aug. 7 1996: 2.70 = $1 US). **Gross domestic product** (1994 est.): $425 mil. **Per capita GDP:** $6,600. **Tourism** (1994): $394 mil. **National budget** (1995): $135 mil.

Transport: Railroad: Length: 47.8 mi. **Civil aviation:** 149.0 mil passenger-mi.

Communications: Television sets: 1 per 2.7 persons. **Radios:** 1 per 2.3 persons.

Health (1997): **Births** (per 1,000 pop.): 17. **Deaths** (per 1,000 pop.): 5. **Natural increase:** 1.1%. **Hospital beds:** 1 per 173 persons. **Physicians:** 1 per 1,083 persons.

Education: Compulsory: ages 5-16. **Literacy** (1992): 90%.

Major International Organizations: UN, OAS, the Commonwealth.

Embassy: 3216 New Mexico Ave. NW 20016; 362-5211.

Columbus landed on Antigua in 1493. The British colonized it in 1632.

The British associated state of Antigua achieved independence as Antigua and Barbuda on Nov. 1, 1981. The government maintains close relations with the U.S., United Kingdom, and Venezuela. The country was hit hard by Hurricane Luis, Sept. 1995. About 3,000 refugees fleeing a volcanic eruption on Montserrat have settled in Antigua since 1995.

Argentina
Argentine Republic
República Argentina

People: Population: 35,797,536. **Age distrib.** (%): <15: 28; 65+: 10. **Pop. density:** 33 per sq. mi. **Urban:** 88%. **Ethnic groups:** White 85% (mostly Spanish, Italian), mestizo, Indian, nonwhite. **Principal languages:** Spanish (official), English, Italian. **Chief religions:** Nominally Roman Catholic 90%.

Geography: Area: 1,073,518 sq. mi., second largest country in South America. **Location:** Occupies most of S South America. **Neighbors:** Chile on W; Bolivia, Paraguay on N; Brazil, Uruguay on NE. **Topography:** Mountains in the W are: the Andean, Central, Misiones, and Southern. Aconcagua is the highest peak in the western hemisphere, alt. 22,834 ft. E of the Andes are heavily wooded plains, called the Gran Chaco in the N, and the fertile, treeless Pampas in the central region. Patagonia, in the S, is bleak and arid. Rio de la Plata, an estuary in the NE, 170 by 140 mi., is mostly fresh water, from 2,485-mi. Parana and 1,000-mi. Uruguay rivers. **Capital:** Buenos Aires (the Senate has approved moving the capital to the Patagonia Region). **Cities:** Buenos Aires 11,802,000; Cordoba 1,294,000; Rosario 1,155,000*.

Government: Type: Republic. **Head of state:** Pres. Carlos Saúl Menem; b July 2, 1930; in office: July 8, 1989. **Local divisions:** 23 provinces, 1 federal district. **Defense:** 1.5% of GDP (1995). **Active troop strength:** 72,500 est.

Economy: Industries: Food processing, autos, chemicals, textiles, printing. **Chief crops:** Grains, corn, sugar beets, sorghum, soybeans. **Minerals:** Oil, lead, zinc, iron, copper, tin, uranium. **Crude oil reserves** (1996): 2.4 bil bbls. **Arable land:** 9%. **Livestock** (1996): cattle: 54 mil; sheep: 18.0 mil; goats: 4.0 mil; pigs: 3.1 mil. **Fish catch** (1995): 1.15 mil metric tons. **Electricity prod.** (1995): 68.7 bil kWh. **Labor force:** 57% services; 31% ind.; 12% agric.

Finance: Monetary unit: Peso (June 1996: 1.00 = $1 US). **Gross domestic product** (1995 est.): $278.5 bil. **Per capita GDP:** $8,100. **Imports** (1995): $19.6 bil; partners: U.S. 23%, Brazil 20%, Germany 6%, Italy 7%. **Exports** (1995): $20.8 bil;

partners: Brazil; 23%, U.S. 11%. **Tourism** (1994): $4.0 bil. **National budget** (1994 est.): $46.5 bil. **International reserves less gold** (June 1997): $19.74 bil. **Gold:** 3.27 mil oz t. **Consumer prices** (change in 1996): 0.2%.
Transport: Railroad: Length: 23,542.1 mi. **Motor vehicles in use:** 4.7 mil passenger cars, 1.2 mil comm. vehicles. **Civil aviation:** 7.0 bil passenger-mi.; 1,253 airports. **Chief ports:** Buenos Aires, Bahia Blanca, La Plata.
Communications: Television sets: 1 per 4.6 persons. **Radios:** 1 per 1.5 persons. **Telephones:** 1 per 6.3 persons. **Daily newspaper circ.:** 138 per 1,000 pop.
Health: Life expectancy at birth (1997): 70.8 male; 78.1 female. **Births** (per 1,000 pop.): 20. **Deaths** (per 1,000 pop.): 8. **Natural increase:** 1.2%. **Hospital beds:** 1 per 227 persons. **Physicians:** 1 per 376 persons. **Infant mortality** (per 1,000 live births 1997): 19.
Education: Free and compulsory: ages 6-14. **Literacy** (1995 est.): 96%.
Major International Organizations: UN (World Bank, WTO, WHO, IMF, FAO), OAS.
Embassy: 1600 New Hampshire Ave. NW 20009; 939-6400.

Nomadic Indians roamed the Pampas when Spaniards arrived, 1515-16, led by Juan Diaz de Solis. Nearly all the Indians were killed by the late 19th century. The colonists won independence, 1816, and a long period of disorder ended in a strong centralized government.

Large-scale Italian, German, and Spanish immigration in the decades after 1880 spurred modernization. Social reforms were enacted in the 1920s, but military coups prevailed 1930-46, until the election of Gen. Juan Perón as president.

Perón, with his wife, Eva Duarte (d 1952), effected labor reforms, but also suppressed speech and press freedoms, closed religious schools, and ran the country into debt. A 1955 coup exiled Perón, who was followed by a series of military and civilian regimes. Perón returned in 1973, and was once more elected president. He died 10 months later, succeeded by his wife Isabel, who had been elected vice president, and who became the first woman head of state in the western hemisphere.

A military junta ousted Mrs. Perón in 1976 amid charges of corruption. Under a continuing state of siege, the army battled guerrillas and leftists, killed 5,000 people, and jailed and tortured others. On Dec. 9, 1985, after a trial of 5 months and nearly 1,000 witnesses, 5 former junta members were found guilty of murder and human rights abuses.

Argentine troops seized control of the British-held Falkland Islands on Apr. 2, 1982. Both countries had claimed sovereignty over the islands, located 250 miles off the Argentine coast, since 1833. The British dispatched a task force and declared a total air and sea blockade around the Falklands. Fighting began May 1; several hundred lost their lives as the result of the destruction of a British destroyer and the sinking of an Argentine cruiser.

British troops landed on East Falkland Island May 21 and eventually surrounded Stanley, the capital city and Argentine stronghold. The Argentine troops surrendered, June 14; Argentine Pres. Leopoldo Galtieri resigned June 17.

Democratic rule returned to Argentina in 1983 as Raul Alfonsín's Radical Civic Union gained an absolute majority in the presidential electoral college and Congress. By 1989 the nation was plagued by severe financial and political problems, as hyperinflation sparked looting and rioting in several cities. The government of Perónist Pres. Carlos Saúl Menem, installed 1989 and reelected 1995, introduced harsh economic measures to curtail inflation, control government spending, and restructure the foreign debt.

About 100 people were killed in the terrorist bombing of a Jewish cultural center in Buenos Aires, July 18, 1994.

Armenia
Republic of Armenia
Hayastani Hanrapetut'yun

People: Population: 3,465,611. **Age distrib.** (%): <15: 28; 65+: 8. **Pop. density:** 301 per sq. mi. **Urban:** 69%. **Ethnic groups:** Armenian 96%, Kurd 2%, Russian and other 2%. **Principal language:** Armenian (official) 96%. **Chief religions:** Armenian Orthodox 94%.
Geography: Area: 11,506 sq. mi. **Location:** SW Asia. **Neighbors:** Georgia on N, Azerbaijan on E, Iran on S, Turkey on W. **Topography:** Mountainous with many peaks above 10,000 ft. **Capital:** Yerevan; 1,278,000*.
Government: Type: Republic. **Head of state:** Pres. Levon Ter-Petrosyan; b Jan. 9, 1945; in office: Nov. 11, 1991. **Head of government:** Prime Min. Robert Kocharyan; b Aug. 31, 1954; in office: Mar. 20, 1997. **Local divisions:** 10 provinces, 1 capital. **Defense:** 0.9% of GNP (1994). **Active troop strength:** 57,400 est.

Economy: Industries: Manufacturing, machinery, chemicals. **Chief crops:** Vegetables, grapes, grain. **Minerals:** Copper, gold, zinc. **Arable land:** 17%. **Electricity prod.** (1995): 5.6 bil kWh.
Finance: Monetary unit: Dram (Aug. 1997: 497.00 = $1 US). **Gross domestic product** (1995 est.): $9.1 bil. **Per capita GDP:** $2,560. **Imports** (1995): $661 mil. **Exports** (1995): $248 mil.
Transport: Railroad: Length: 512.3 mi.
Communications: Television sets: 1 per 4.4 persons. **Radios:** 1 per 5.6 persons. **Telephones:** 1 per 6.5 persons. **Daily newspaper circ.:** 23 per 1,000 pop.
Health: Life expectancy at birth (1997): 64.6 male; 74.0 female. **Births** (per 1,000 pop.): 17. **Deaths** (per 1,000 pop.): 8. **Natural increase:** 0.9%. **Hospital beds:** 1 per 125 persons. **Physicians:** 1 per 288 persons. **Infant mortality** (per 1,000 live births 1996): 39.
Education: Free and compulsory: ages 6-17. **Literacy** (1989): 99%.
Major International Organizations: UN (IMF, FAO, WHO, World Bank), CIS.
Embassy: 1660 L St. NW 20036; 628-5766.

Ancient Armenia extended into parts of what are now Turkey and Iran. Present-day Armenia was set up as a Soviet republic Apr. 2, 1921. It joined Georgian and Azerbaijan SSRs Mar. 12, 1922, to form the Transcaucasian SFSR, which became part of the USSR Dec. 30, 1922. Armenia became a constituent republic of the USSR Dec. 5, 1936. An earthquake struck Armenia Dec. 7, 1988; more than 55,000 were killed and several cities and towns were left in ruins.

Armenia declared independence Sept. 23, 1991, and became an independent state when the USSR disbanded Dec. 26, 1991. Fighting between mostly Christian Armenia and mostly Muslim Azerbaijan escalated in 1992 and continued through 1993. Each country claimed Nagorno-Karabakh, an enclave in Azerbaijan that has a majority population of ethnic Armenians. A temporary cease-fire was announced in May 1994, with Armenian forces in control of the enclave. Voters approved, July 5, 1995, a new constitution strengthening presidential powers. Pres. Levon Ter-Petrosyan won reelection on Sept. 22, 1996, amid claims of fraud.

Australia
Commonwealth of Australia

People: Population: 18,438,824. **Age distrib.** (%): <15: 21; 65+: 12. **Pop. density:** 6 per sq. mi. **Urban:** 85%. **Ethnic groups:** Caucasian 95%, Asian 4%, aboriginal (including mixed) 1%. **Principal languages:** English (official), aboriginal languages. **Chief religions:** Anglican 26%, Roman Catholic 26%, other Christian 24%.
Geography: Area: 2,966,200 sq. mi. **Location:** SE of Asia, Indian O. is W and S, Pacific O. (Coral, Tasman seas) is E; they meet N of Australia in Timor and Arafura seas. Tasmania lies 150 mi. S of Victoria state, across Bass Strait. **Neighbors:** Nearest are Indonesia, Papua New Guinea on N; Solomons, Fiji, and New Zealand on E. **Topography:** An island continent. The Great Dividing Range along the E coast has Mt. Kosciusko, 7,310 ft. The W plateau rises to 2,000 ft., with arid areas in the Great Sandy and Great Victoria deserts. The NW part of Western Australia and Northern Terr. are arid and hot. The NE has heavy rainfall and Cape York Peninsula has jungles. The Murray R. rises in New South Wales and flows 1,600 mi. to the Indian O. **Capital:** Canberra. **Cities** (1995 est.): Sydney 3.8 mil; Melbourne 3.2 mil; Brisbane 1.5 mil; Perth 1.3 mil; Adelaide 1.1 mil.
Government: Type: Democratic, federal state system. **Head of state:** Queen Elizabeth II, represented by Gov.-Gen. Sir William Patrick Deane; b July 4, 1931; in office: Feb. 15, 1996. **Head of government:** Prime Min. John Howard; b July 26, 1939; in office: Mar. 8, 1996. **Local divisions:** 6 states, 2 territories. **Defense:** 2.0% of GDP (FY 1995-96). **Active troop strength:** 57,800.
Economy: Industries: Mining, steel, textiles, electrical equip., chemicals, autos, aircraft, ships, machinery. **Chief crops:** Wheat (a leading export), cotton, fruit, sugar. **Minerals:** Bauxite, coal, copper, iron, lead, tin, uranium, zinc. **Crude oil reserves** (1996): 1.8 bil bbls. **Other resources:** Wool (world's leading producer), beef. **Arable land:** 6%. **Livestock** (1996): sheep: 126 mil; cattle: 27 mil; pigs: 2.7 mil. **Fish catch** (1995): 218,489 metric tons. **Electricity prod.** (1995): 163.1 bil kWh. **Labor force:** 36% trade, manuf. & ind.; 34% finance & services; 6% agric.
Finance: Monetary unit: Dollar (Aug. 1997: 1.34 = $1 US). **Gross domestic product** (1995 est.): $405.4 bil. **Per capita income:** $22,100. **Imports** (1995): $57.4 bil; partners: U.S. 23%, Jap. 18%, UK 6%. **Exports** (1995): $51.6 bil; partners: Jap. 25%, U.S. 11%, S. Korea 6%. **Tourism** (1994): $7.3 bil. **National budget** (FY 1995-96): $95.2 bil. **International reserves less gold** (Mar. 1997): $14.37 bil. **Gold:** 7.90 mil oz t. **Consumer prices** (change in 1996): 2.6%.

Transport: Railroad: Length: 23,947.6 mi. **Motor vehicles in use:** 9.0 mil passenger cars, 2.2 mil comm. vehicles. **Civil aviation:** 38.0 bil passenger-mi.; 400 airports with scheduled flights. **Chief ports:** Sydney, Melbourne, Brisbane, Adelaide, Fremantle, Geelong.

Communications: Television sets: 1 per 2.0 persons. **Radios:** 1 per 0.8 persons. **Telephones:** 1 per 2.0 persons. **Daily newspaper circ.:** 258 per 1,000 pop.

Health: Life expectancy at birth (1997): 76.7 male; 82.7 female. **Births** (per 1,000 pop.): 14. **Deaths** (per 1,000 pop.): 7. **Natural increase:** 0.7%. **Hospital beds:** 1 per 226 persons. **Physicians:** 1 per 434 persons. **Infant mortality** (per 1,000 live births 1997): 5.

Education: Free and compulsory: ages 6-15. **Literacy** (1993): 100%.

Major International Organizations: UN and all its specialized agencies, OECD, the Commonwealth, APEC.

Embassy: 1601 Massachusetts Ave. NW 20036; 797-3000.

Australia harbors many plant and animal species not found elsewhere, including kangaroos, koalas, platypuses, dingos (wild dogs), Tasmanian devils (raccoon-like marsupials), wombats (bear-like marsupials), and barking and frilled lizards.

Capt. James Cook explored the E coast in 1770, when the continent was inhabited by a variety of different tribes. The first settlers, beginning in 1788, were mostly convicts, soldiers, and government officials. By 1830, Britain had claimed the entire continent, and the immigration of free settlers began to accelerate. The commonwealth was proclaimed Jan. 1, 1901. Northern Terr. was granted limited self-rule July 1, 1978.

State/Territory, Capital	Area (sq. mi.)	Population (1996 est.)
New South Wales, Sydney	309,500	6,190,000
Victoria, Melbourne	87,900	4,541,000
Queensland, Brisbane	666,990	3,355,000
Western Australia, Perth.	975,100	1,763,000
South Australia, Adelaide	379,900	1,479,000
Tasmania, Hobart	26,200	473,000
Australian Capital Terr., Canberra .	900	308,000
Northern Terr., Darwin	519,800	178,000

Racially discriminatory immigration policies were abandoned in 1973, after 3 million Europeans (half British) had entered since 1945. The 50,000 aborigines and 150,000 part-aborigines are mostly detribalized, but there are several preserves in the Northern Territory. They remain economically disadvantaged.

Australia's agricultural success makes the country among the top exporters of beef, lamb, wool, and wheat. Major mineral deposits have been developed, largely for export. Industrialization has been completed. The nation endured a deep recession 1990-93 but has rebounded strongly.

The Labor Party won a majority in Feb. 1983 general elections and was reelected in 1984, 1987, 1990, and 1993. After an election that focused mainly on economic issues, conservatives swept into power in elections Mar. 2, 1996.

Australian External Territories

Norfolk Isl., area 13.3 sq. mi., pop. (1996 est.) 2,209, was taken over, 1914. The soil is very fertile, suitable for citrus fruits, bananas, and coffee. Many of the inhabitants are descendants of the *Bounty* mutineers, moved to Norfolk 1856 from Pitcairn Isl. Australia offered the island limited home rule, 1978.

Coral Sea Isls. Territory, area 1 sq. mi., is administered from Norfolk I.

Territory of Ashmore and Cartier Isls., area 2 sq. mi., in the Indian O., came under Australian authority 1934 and are administered as part of Northern Territory. **Heard Isl. and McDonald Isls.,** area 159 sq. mi., are administered by the Dept. of Science.

Cocos (Keeling) Isls., 27 small coral islands in the Indian O. 1,750 mi. NW of Australia. Pop. (1996 est.) 609; area 5.5 sq. mi. The residents voted to become part of Australia, Apr. 1984.

Christmas Isl., area 52 sq. mi., pop. (1996 est.) 813; 230 mi. S of Java, was transferred by Britain in 1958. It has phosphate deposits.

Australian Antarctic Territory was claimed by Australia in 1933, including 2,362,000 sq. mi. of territory S of 60th parallel S Lat. and between 160th-45th meridians E Long. It does not include Adelie Coast.

Austria
Republic of Austria
Republik Österreich

People: Population: 8,054,078. **Age distrib.** (%): <15: 17; 65+: 15. **Pop. density:** 249 per sq. mi. **Urban:** 64%. **Ethnic**

groups: German 99%, Croatian, Slovene. **Principal language:** German (official). **Chief religions:** Roman Catholic 85%, Protestant 6%.

Geography: Area: 32,378 sq. mi. **Location:** In S Central Europe. **Neighbors:** Switzerland, Liechtenstein on W; Germany, Czech Rep. on N; Slovakia, Hungary on E; Slovenia, Italy on S. **Topography:** Austria is primarily mountainous, with the Alps and foothills covering the western and southern provinces. The eastern provinces and Vienna are located in the Danube River Basin. **Capital:** Vienna: 2,060,000*.

Government: Type: Parliamentary democracy. **Head of state:** Pres. Thomas Klestil; b Nov. 4, 1932; in office: July 8, 1992. **Head of government:** Chancellor Viktor Klima; b June 4, 1947; in office: Jan. 28, 1997. **Local divisions:** 9 bundeslaender (states), each with a legislature. **Defense:** 1.0% of GDP (1995). **Active troop strength:** 55,800 est.

Economy: Industries: Steel, machinery, autos, electrical equip., tourism, mining, paper, textiles, chemicals, cement. **Chief crops:** Grains, potatoes, sugar beets. **Minerals:** Iron ore, oil, magnesite. **Other resources:** Forests, hydropower. **Arable land:** 17%. **Livestock** (1996): pigs: 3.8 mil; cattle: 2.4 mil. **Electricity prod.** (1995): 53.9 bil kWh. **Labor force:** 8% agric.; 35% ind. & crafts; 57% services.

Finance: Monetary unit: Schilling (Aug. 1997: 12.73 = $1 US). **Gross domestic product** (1995 est.): $152 bil. **Per capita GDP:** $19,000. **Imports** (1994): $55.3 bil; partners: Germany 40%. **Exports** (1994): $45.2 bil; partners: Germany 38%. **Tourism** (1994): $13.2 bil. **National budget** (1995 est.): $75.8 bil. **International reserves less gold** (June 1997): $20.64 bil. **Gold:** 10.05 mil oz t. **Consumer prices** (change in 1996): 1.8%.

Transport: Railroad: Length: 3,492.5 mi. **Motor vehicles in use:** 3.6 mil passenger cars, 775,000 comm. vehicles. **Civil aviation:** 3.7 bil passenger-mi.; 6 airports with scheduled flights. **Chief ports:** Linz, Vienna.

Communications: Television sets: 1 per 2.1 persons. **Radios:** 1 per 1.6 persons. **Telephones:** 1 per 2.1 persons. **Daily newspaper circ.:** 472 per 1,000 pop.

Health: Life expectancy at birth (1997): 73.6 male; 80.0 female. **Births** (per 1,000 pop.): 11. **Deaths** (per 1,000 pop.): 10. **Natural increase:** 0.1%. **Hospital beds:** 1 per 113 persons. **Physicians:** 1 per 296 persons. **Infant mortality** (per 1,000 live births 1997): 6.

Education: Free and compulsory: ages 6-15. **Literacy** (1994): 100%.

Major International Organizations: UN and all of its specialized agencies, EU, OECD.

Embassy: 3524 International Ct. NW 20008; 895-6700.

Rome conquered Austrian lands from Celtic tribes around 15 BC. In 788 the territory was incorporated into Charlemagne's empire. By 1300, the House of Hapsburg had gained control; they added vast territories in all parts of Europe to their realm in the next few hundred years.

Austrian dominance of Germany was undermined in the 18th century and ended by Prussia by 1866. But the Congress of Vienna, 1815, confirmed Austrian control of a large empire in southeast Europe consisting of Germans, Hungarians, Slavs, Italians, and others. The dual Austro-Hungarian monarchy was established in 1867, giving autonomy to Hungary and almost 50 years of peace.

World War I, started after the June 28, 1914, assassination of Archduke Franz Ferdinand, the Hapsburg heir, by a Serbian nationalist, destroyed the empire. By 1918 Austria was reduced to a small republic, with the borders it has today.

Nazi Germany invaded Austria Mar. 13, 1938. The republic was reestablished in 1945, under Allied occupation. Full independence and neutrality were restored in 1955. Austria joined the European Union Jan. 1, 1995.

Azerbaijan
Azerbaijani Republic
Azarbaycan Respublikasi

People: Population: 7,735,918. **Age distrib.** (%): <15: 32; 65+: 6. **Pop. density:** 232 per sq. mi. **Urban:** 56%. **Ethnic groups:** Azeri 90%, Dagestani peoples 3%, Russian 2.5%, Armenian 2%. **Principal languages:** Azeri (official) 89%, Russian 3%, Armenian 2%. **Chief religions:** Muslim 93%, Orthodox 5%.

Geography: Area: 33,400 sq. mi. **Location:** SW Asia. **Neighbors:** Russia, Georgia on N; Iran on S; Armenia on W; Caspian Sea on E. **Capital:** Baku: 1,848,000*.

Government: Type: Republic. **Head of state:** Pres. Haydar A. Aliyev; b May 10, 1923; in office: June 30, 1993. **Head of government:** Prime Min. Artur Rasizade; in office: Nov. 26, 1996. **Defense:** 1.0% of GNP (1994). **Active troop strength:** 70,700.

Economy: Industries: Oil refining, mining, chemicals, textiles. **Chief crops:** Grain, cotton, grapes. **Minerals:** Oil, gas,

iron. **Arable land:** 18%. **Livestock** (1996): sheep: 4.4 mil; cattle: 1.7 mil. **Electricity prod.** (1995): 16.1 bil kWh.
Finance: Monetary unit: Manat (Aug. 1997: 3,945.00 = $1 US). **Gross Domestic Product** (1995 est.): $11.5 bil. **Per capita GDP:** $1,480. **Imports** (1995): $681.5 mil. **Exports** (1995): $549.9 mil. **National budget** (1995 est.): $488 mil.
Transport: Railroad: Length: 1,319.6 mi. **Motor vehicles in use:** 289,000 passenger cars; 89,000 comm. vehicles. **Civil aviation:** 1.1 bil passenger-mi. **Chief port:** Baku.
Communications: Daily newspaper circ.: 28 per 1,000 pop.
Health: Life expectancy at birth (1997): 60.3 male; 69.9 female. **Births** (per 1,000 pop.): 22. **Deaths** (per 1,000 pop.): 9. **Natural increase:** 1.3%. **Hospital beds:** 1 per 98 persons. **Physicians:** 1 per 251 persons. **Infant mortality** (per 1,000 live births 1997): 74.
Education: Compulsory: ages 6-14. **Literacy** (1989): 97%.
Major International Organizations: UN (ILO, IMF, WHO, CIS).
Embassy: 927 15th St. NW 20005; 842-0001.

Azerbaijan was the home of Scythian tribes and part of the Roman Empire. Overrun by Turks in the 11th century and conquered by Russia in 1806 and 1813, it joined the USSR Dec. 30, 1922, and became a constituent republic in 1936. Azerbaijan declared independence Aug. 30, 1991, and became an independent state when the Soviet Union disbanded Dec. 26, 1991.

Fighting between mostly Muslim Azerbaijan and mostly Christian Armenia escalated in 1992 and continued in 1993 and 1994. Each country claimed Nagorno-Karabakh, an enclave in Azerbaijan with a majority population of ethnic Armenians. A temporary cease-fire was announced in May 1994, with Armenian forces in control of the enclave.

A National Council ousted Communist Pres. Mutaibov and took power May 19, 1992. Abulfez Elchibey became the nation's first democratically elected president June 7, but was ousted from office by Surat Huseynov, commander of a private militia, June 30, 1993. Huseynov became prime minister, and Haydar Aliyev, a pro-Russian former Communist, became president. Huseynov fled the country after his supporters staged an unsuccessful coup attempt Oct. 1994. Voters approved a new constitution expanding presidential powers, Nov. 12, 1995.

The Bahamas
The Commonwealth of The Bahamas

People: Population: 262,034. **Age distrib.** (%): <15: 27; 65+: 6. **Pop. density:** 49 per sq. mi. **Urban:** 87%. **Ethnic groups:** Black 85%, white (British, Canadian, U.S.) 15%. **Principal languages:** English (official), Creole. **Chief religions:** Baptist 32%, Anglican 20%, Roman Catholic 19%, other Christian 24%.
Geography: Area: 5,382 sq. mi. **Location:** In Atlantic O., E of Florida. **Neighbors:** Nearest are U.S. on W, Cuba on S. **Topography:** Nearly 700 islands (29 inhabited) and over 2,000 islets in the W Atlantic O. extend 760 mi. NW to SE. **Capital:** Nassau. **Cities** (1990 est.): Nassau 172,196; Grand Bahama 40,898.
Government: Type: Independent commonwealth. **Head of state:** Queen Elizabeth II, represented by Gov.-Gen. Orville A Turnquest; b July 19, 1929; in office: Jan. 2, 1995. **Head of government:** Prime Min. Hubert Ingraham; b Aug. 4, 1947; in office: Aug. 21, 1992. **Local divisions:** 21 districts. **Defense:** 3.8% of GDP (FY 1995-96). **Security forces:** 3,160 incl. police.
Economy: Industries: Tourism (more than 50% of GDP), rum, cement, banking, pharmaceuticals. **Chief crops:** Citrus, vegetables. **Minerals:** Salt, aragonite. **Other resources:** Lobsters. **Arable land:** 1%. **Electricity prod.** (1995): 930 mil kWh. **Labor force:** 40% tourism; 30% govt.; 10% serv.; 5% agric.
Finance: Monetary unit: Dollar (Aug. 1997: 1.00 = $1 US). **Gross domestic product** (1995 est.): $4.8 bil. **Per capita GDP:** $18,700. **Imports** (1994): $1.1 bil; partners: U.S. 55%, Japan 17%, Nigeria 12%. **Exports** (1994): $224 mil; partners: U.S. 51%, UK 7%, Norway 7%. **Tourism** (1994): $1.3 bil. **National budget** (FY 1995-96): $725 mil. **International reserves less gold** (June 1997): $305.7 mil. **Consumer prices** (change in 1996): 1.4%.
Transport: Motor vehicles in use: 46,000 passenger cars, 12,000 comm. vehicles. **Civil aviation:** 118.6 mil passenger-mi. **Chief ports:** Nassau, Freeport.
Communications: Television sets: 1 per 4.4 persons. **Radios:** 1 per 1.4 persons. **Telephones:** 1 per 3.5 persons. **Daily newspaper circ.:** 129 per 1,000 pop.
Health: Life expectancy at birth (1997): 68.6 male; 77.4 female. **Births** (per 1,000 pop.): 18. **Deaths** (per 1,000 pop.): 6. **Natural increase:** 1.3%. **Hospital beds:** 1 per 249 persons. **Physicians:** 1 per 709 persons. **Infant mortality** (per 1,000 live births 1997): 22.
Education: Compulsory: ages 5-16. **Literacy** (1995): 98%.
Major International Organizations: UN (World Bank, FAO, IMF, WHO), OAS, the Commonwealth.
Embassy: 2220 Massachusetts Ave. NW 20008; 319-2660.

Christopher Columbus first set foot in the New World on San Salvador (Watling Isl.) in 1492, when Arawak Indians inhabited the islands. British settlement began in 1647; the islands became a British colony in 1783. Internal self-government was granted in 1964; full independence within the Commonwealth was attained July 10, 1973.

International banking and investment management have become major industries alongside tourism.

Bahrain
State of Bahrain
Dawlat al Bahrayn

People: Population: 603,318. **Age distrib.** (%): <15: 31; 65+: 3. **Pop. density:** 2,251 per sq. mi. **Urban:** 91%. **Ethnic groups:** Bahraini 63%, Asian 13%, other Arab 10%, Iranian 8%. **Principal languages:** Arabic (official), English, Farsi, Urdu. **Chief religions:** Shi'a Muslim 70%, Sunni Muslim 30%.
Geography: Area: 268 sq. mi. **Location:** SW Asia, in Persian Gulf. **Neighbors:** Nearest are Saudi Arabia on W, Qatar on E. **Topography:** Bahrain Island, and several adjacent, smaller islands, are flat, hot, and humid, with little rain. **Capital:** Manama (1992 est.): 140,000.
Government: Type: Traditional monarchy. **Head of state:** Emir Isa bin Sulman al-Khalifa; b July 3, 1933; in office: Nov. 2, 1961. **Head of government:** Prime Min. Kahlifa bin Sulman al-Khalifa; b 1935; in office: Jan. 19, 1970. **Local divisions:** 12 municipalities. **Defense:** 5.5% of GDP (1994). **Active troop strength:** 11,000.
Economy: Industries: Oil products, aluminum smelting. **Chief crops:** Fruits, vegetables. **Minerals:** Oil, gas. **Crude oil reserves** (1996): 210 mil bbls. **Arable land:** 2%. **Electricity prod.** (1995): 4.4 bil kWh. **Labor force:** 85% ind. and commerce; 5% agric.; 5% services; 3% govt.
Finance: Monetary unit: Dinar (Aug. 1997: 0.38 = $1 US). **Gross domestic product** (1995 est.): $7.3 bil. **Per capita income:** $12,000. **Imports** (1995 est.): $3.3 bil; partners: Saudi Arabia 37%, U.S. 12%, UK 6%. **Exports** (1995 est.): $3.2 bil; partners: India 20%, Japan 14%. **National budget** (1995 est.): $1.7 bil. **International reserves less gold** (June 1997): $1.44 bil. **Gold:** 150,000 oz t. **Consumer prices** (change in 1996): -0.3%.
Transport: Motor vehicles in use: 133,000 passenger cars, 29,000 comm. vehicles. **Civil aviation:** 1.5 bil passenger-mi. **Chief ports:** Manama, Sitrah.
Communications: Television sets: 1 per 2.3 persons. **Radios:** 1 per 1.8 persons. **Telephones:** 1 per 4.1 persons.
Health: Life expectancy at birth (1997): 72.1 male; 77.2 female. **Births** (per 1,000 pop.): 23. **Deaths** (per 1,000 pop.): 3. **Natural increase:** 2.0%. **Hospital beds:** 1 per 352 persons. **Physicians:** 1 per 1,115 persons. **Infant mortality** (per 1,000 live births 1997): 16.4.
Education: Free and compulsory: ages 6-17. **Literacy** (1995): 85%.
Major International Organizations: UN (WTO, IMF, FAO, World Bank, WHO), Arab League.
Embassy: 3502 International Dr. NW 20008; 342-0741.

Long ruled by the Khalifa family, Bahrain was a British protectorate from 1861 to Aug. 15, 1971, when it regained independence.

Pearls, shrimp, fruits, and vegetables were the mainstays of the economy until oil was discovered in 1932. By the 1970s, oil reserves were depleted; international banking thrived.

Bahrain took part in the 1973-74 Arab oil embargo against the U.S. and other nations. The government bought controlling interest in the oil industry in 1975. Violence in 1996 by Shiite dissidents brought a crackdown by the Sunni-led government.

Bangladesh
People's Republic of Bangladesh
Gana Prajatantri Bangladesh

People: Population: 125,340,261. **Age distrib.** (%): <15: 38; 65+: 3. **Pop. density:** 2,200 per sq. mi. **Urban:** 19%. **Ethnic groups:** Bengali 98%, Bihari, tribals. **Principal languages:** Bangla (official), English. **Chief religions:** Muslim 83%, Hindu 16%.
Geography: Area: 56,977 sq. mi. **Location:** In S Asia, on N bend of Bay of Bengal. **Neighbors:** India nearly surrounds country on W, N, E; Myanmar on SE. **Topography:** The country is mostly a low plain cut by the Ganges and Brahmaputra rivers and their delta. The land is alluvial and marshy along the coast, with hills only in the extreme SE and NE. A tropical monsoon climate prevails, among the rainiest in the world. **Capital:** Dhaka. **Cities:** Dhaka 8,545,000; Chittagong 2,477,000; Khulna 1,071,000*.

Government: Type: Parliamentary democracy. **Head of state:** Pres. Shahabuddin Ahmed; b 1930; in office: Oct. 9, 1996. **Head of government:** Prime Min. Hasina Wazed; b Sept. 27, 1947; in office: June 24, 1996. **Local divisions:** 4 divisions. **Defense:** 1.7% of GDP (FY 1995-96). **Active troop strength:** 117,500.

Economy: Industries: Food processing, jute, textiles, fertilizers, steel. **Chief crops:** Jute, rice, tea. **Minerals:** Natural gas. **Arable land:** 67%. **Livestock** (1996): goats: 30.3 mil; cattle: 24.3 mil. **Fish catch** (1995): 1,170,365 metric tons. **Electricity prod.** (1995): 10.5 bil kWh. **Labor force:** 65% agric.; 21% services; 14% ind. & mining.

Finance: Monetary unit: Taka (Aug. 1997: 44.65 = $1 US). **Gross domestic product** (1995 est.): $144.5 bil. **Per capita GDP:** $1,130. **Imports** (1995 est.): $4.7 bil; partners: Hong Kong 8%, Japan 7%. **Exports** (1995 est.): $2.7 bil; partners: U.S. 33%, Germany 8%. **Tourism** (1994): $19 mil. **National budget** (FY 1992-93): $4.1 bil. **International reserves less gold** (June 1997): $1.7 bil. **Gold:** 100,000 oz t. **Consumer prices** (change in 1996): 2.7%.

Transport: Railroad: Length: 1,795.9 mi. **Motor vehicles in use:** 150,000 passenger cars, 73,000 comm. vehicles. **Civil aviation:** 1.8 bil passenger-mi. **Chief ports:** Chittagong, Dhaka, Chalna.

Communications: Television sets: 1 per 172 persons. **Radios:** 1 per 21 persons. **Telephones:** 1 per 418 persons. **Daily newspaper circ.:** 6 per 1,000 pop.

Health: Life expectancy at birth (1997): 56.4 male; 56.2 female. **Births** (per 1,000 pop.): 30. **Deaths** (per 1,000 pop.): 11. **Natural increase:** 1.9%. **Hospital beds:** 1 per 3,218 persons. **Physicians:** 1 per 5,264 persons. **Infant mortality** (per 1,000 live births 1997): 100.

Education: Free and compulsory: ages 5-11. **Literacy** (1995 est.): 38%.

Major International Organizations: UN (WTO, FAO, World Bank, IMF, WHO), the Commonwealth.

Embassy: 2201 Wisconsin Ave. NW 20007; 342-8372.

Muslim invaders conquered the formerly Hindu area in the 12th century. British rule lasted from the 18th century to 1947, when East Bengal became part of Pakistan.

Charging West Pakistani domination, the Awami League, based in the East, won National Assembly control in 1971. Assembly sessions were postponed; riots broke out. Pakistani troops attacked Mar. 25; Bangladesh independence was proclaimed the next day. In the ensuing civil war, one million died and 10 million fled to India.

War between India and Pakistan broke out Dec. 3, 1971. Pakistan surrendered in the East on Dec. 16. Mujibur Rahman, known as Sheikh Mujib, became prime minister; he was killed in a coup, Aug. 15, 1975. During the 1970s the country moved into the Indian and Soviet orbits in response to U.S. support of Pakistan, and much of the economy was nationalized.

On May 30, 1981, Pres. Ziaur Rahman was killed in an unsuccessful coup attempt by army rivals. Vice President Abdus Sattar assumed the presidency but was ousted in a coup led by army chief of staff Gen. H. M. Ershad, Mar. 1982. Ershad declared Bangladesh an Islamic Republic in 1988. Bangladesh adopted a parliamentary system of government in 1991.

Bangladesh is subject to devastating storms and floods that kill thousands. A cyclone struck Apr. 1991, killing over 131,000 people and causing $2.7 billion in damages. Chronic destitution in the densely crowded population has been worsened by the decline of jute as a world commodity.

Political turmoil led to the resignation, Mar. 30, 1996, of Prime Minister Khaleda Zia, the widow of Ziaur Rahman. Sheikh Mujib's daughter, Hasina Wazed (known as Sheikh Hasina), led the country after the June 12, 1996 election. Bangladesh and India signed a treaty, Dec. 12, resolving their long-standing dispute over the use of water from the Ganges River. A cyclone in May 1997 left an estimated 800,000 people homeless.

Barbados

People: Population: 257,731. **Age distrib.** (%): <15: 23; 65+: 10. **Pop. density:** 1,553 per sq. mi. **Urban:** 48%. **Ethnic groups:** African 80%, European 4%, mixed and other 16%. **Principal language:** English (official). **Chief religions:** Protestant 67%, Roman Catholic 4%.

Geography: Area: 166 sq. mi. **Location:** In Atlantic O., farthest E of West Indies. **Neighbors:** Nearest are St. Lucia and St. Vincent & the Grenadines to the W. **Topography:** The island lies alone in the Atlantic almost completely surrounded by coral reefs. Highest point is Mt. Hillaby, 1,115 ft. **Capital:** Bridgetown (1990 met.): 97,516.

Government: Type: Parliamentary democracy. **Head of state:** Queen Elizabeth II, represented by Gov.-Gen. Sir Clifford Husbands; b Aug. 5, 1926; in office: June 1, 1996. **Head of government:** Prime Min. Owen Arthur; b Oct. 17, 1949; in office:

Sept. 7, 1994. **Local divisions:** 11 parishes and Bridgetown. **Defense: Active troop strength:** 610.

Economy: Industries: Sugar, tourism. **Chief crops:** Sugar, cotton. **Minerals:** Oil, gas. **Other resources:** Fish. **Arable land:** 77%. **Electricity prod.** (1995): 550 mil kWh. **Labor force:** 41% serv. & govt.; 18% manuf. & constr.; 15% commerce; 6% agric.

Finance: Monetary unit: Dollar (Aug. 1997: 2.00 = $1 US). **Gross domestic product** (1995 est.): $2.5 bil. **Per capita GDP:** $9,800. **Imports** (1995 est.): $693 mil; partners: U.S. 36%, UK 11%, Trin. & Tob. 11%. **Exports** (1995 est.): $158.6 mil; partners: U.S. 13%, UK 10%, Trin. & Tob. 9%. **Tourism** (1994): $598 mil. **National budget** (FY 1995-96 est.): $710 mil. **International reserves less gold** (Mar. 1997): $330.8 mil. **Consumer prices** (change in 1996): 2.4%.

Transport: Motor vehicles in use: 44,000 passenger cars; 9,100 comm. vehicles. **Civil aviation:** 204.9 mil passenger-mi. **Chief port:** Bridgetown.

Communications: Television sets: 1 per 3.6 persons. **Radios:** 1 per 1.1 persons. **Telephones:** 1 per 2.9 persons. **Daily newspaper circ.:** 159 per 1,000 pop.

Health: Life expectancy at birth (1997): 71.8 male; 77.4 female. **Births** (per 1,000 pop.): 15. **Deaths** (per 1,000 pop.): 8. **Natural increase:** 0.7%. **Hospital beds:** 1 per 134 persons. **Physicians:** 1 per 842 persons. **Infant mortality** (per 1,000 live births 1997): 18.

Education: Compulsory: ages 5-16. **Literacy** (1995 est.): 97%.

Major International Organizations: UN (FAO, WTO, World Bank, ILO, IMF, WHO), OAS, the Commonwealth.

Embassy: 2144 Wyoming Ave. NW 20008; 939-9218.

Barbados was probably named by Portuguese sailors in reference to bearded fig trees. An English ship visited in 1605, and British settlers arrived on the uninhabited island in 1627. Slaves worked the sugar plantations until slavery was abolished in 1834. Self-rule came gradually, with full independence proclaimed Nov. 30, 1966. British traditions have remained.

Belarus
Republic of Belarus
Respublika Byelarus

People: Population: 10,439,916. **Age distrib.** (%): <15: 21; 65+: 13. **Pop. density:** 130 per sq. mi. **Urban:** 72%. **Ethnic groups:** Belarussian 78%, Russian 13%, Polish 4%. **Principal languages:** Belarussian (official), Russian. **Chief religions:** Eastern Orthodox 60%, Roman Catholic, Muslim.

Geography: Area: 80,153 sq. mi. **Location:** E Europe. **Neighbors:** Poland on W; Latvia, Lithuania on N; Russia on E; Ukraine on S. **Capital:** Minsk. **Cities:** Minsk 1,784,000*.

Government: Republic. **Head of state:** Pres. Aleksandr Lukashenko; b Aug. 30, 1954; in office: July 1994. **Head of government:** Prime Min. Syarhei Linh; in office, Nov. 18, 1996. **Local divisions:** 6 voblastsi and 1 municipality. **Defense:** 1% of GDP (1995). **Active troop strength:** 85,500.

Economy: Industries: Manufacturing, chemical fibers, machine tools, agricultural & industrial machinery. **Chief crops:** Grain, vegetables, potatoes. **Arable land:** 29%. **Livestock** (1996): cattle: 5.0 mil; pigs: 3.9 mil. **Electricity prod.** (1995.): 24.9 bil kWh. **Labor force:** 40% ind. & const.; 21% agric. & forestry.

Finance: Monetary unit: Ruble (Aug. 1997: 27,200 = $1 US). **Gross domestic product** (1995 est.): $49.2 bil. **Per capita GDP:** $4,700. **Imports** (1995): $4.6 bil; partners: CIS 92%. **Exports** (1995): $4.2 bil; partners: CIS 83%. **National budget** (1996 est.): 5.5 bil. **Consumer prices** (change in 1996): 52.7%.

Transport: Railroads: Length: 3,408.0 mi. **Motor vehicles in use:** 842,500 passenger cars, 10,000 comm. vehicles. **Civil aviation:** 1.6 bil passenger-mi. **Chief port:** Mazyr.

Communications: Television sets: 1 per 4.4 persons. **Radios:** 1 per 3.5 persons. **Telephones:** 1 per 5.3 persons. **Daily newspaper circ.:** 187 per 1,000 pop.

Health: Life expectancy at birth (1997): 63.5 male; 74.3 female. **Births** (per 1,000 pop.): 13. **Deaths** (per 1,000 pop.): 13. **Natural increase:** –0.1%. **Hospital beds:** 1 per 82 persons. **Physicians:** 1 per 230 persons. **Infant mortality** (per 1,000 live births 1997): 13.

Education: Compulsory: ages 6-17. **Literacy** (1994) 98%.

Major International Organizations: UN, CIS.

Embassy: 1619 New Hampshire Ave. NW 20009; 986-1604.

The region was subject to Lithuanians and Poles in medieval times, and was a prize of war between Russia and Poland beginning in 1503. It became part of the USSR in 1922 although the western part of the region was controlled by Poland. Belarus was overrun by German armies in 1941; recovered by Soviet troops in 1944. Following World War II, Belarus increased in area through Soviet annexation of part of NE Poland. Belarus declared independence Aug. 25, 1991. It became an independent state when the Soviet Union disbanded Dec. 26, 1991.

A new constitution was adopted, Mar. 15, 1994, and a new president was chosen in elections concluding July 1. Russia and Belarus signed a pact Apr. 2, 1996, linking their political and economic systems. An authoritarian constitution enacted in Nov. gave Pres. Aleksandr Lukashenko vast new powers. Lukashenko's insistence on tightening ties with Russia resulted in the signing of new accords Apr. 2 and May 23, 1997.

Belgium
Kingdom of Belgium
Koninkrijk België (Dutch)
Royaume de Belgique (French)

People: Population: 10,203,683. **Age distrib.** (%): <15: 19; 65+: 16. **Pop. density:** 866 per sq. mi. **Urban:** 97%. **Ethnic groups:** Fleming 55%, Walloon 33%. **Principal languages:** Flemish (Dutch) 56%, French 32%, German 1% (all official). **Chief religions:** Roman Catholic 75%, Protestant & other 25%.

Geography: Area: 11,787 sq. mi. **Location:** In W Europe, on North Sea. **Neighbors:** France on W and S, Luxembourg on SE, Germany on E, Netherlands on N. **Topography:** Mostly flat, the country is trisected by the Scheldt and Meuse, major commercial rivers. The land becomes hilly and forested in the SE (Ardennes) region. **Capital:** Brussels. **Cities** (1995 met. est.): Antwerp 1,628,710; Ghent 1,349,382; Brussels 951,580.

Government: Type: Parliamentary democracy under a constitutional monarch. **Head of state:** King Albert II; b June 6, 1934; in office: Aug. 9, 1993. **Head of government:** Premier Jean-Luc Dehaene; b Aug. 7, 1940; in office: Mar. 7, 1992. **Local divisions:** 10 provinces. **Defense:** 1.7% of GDP (1995). **Active troop strength:** 46,300.

Economy: Industries: Metal products, glassware, autos, textiles, chemicals. **Chief crops:** Wheat, fruits, sugar beets, potatoes. **Minerals:** Coal, gas. **Arable land:** 24%. **Livestock** (1996): pigs: 6.9 mil; cattle: 3.4 mil. **Fish catch** (1993): 36,433 metric tons. **Electricity prod.** (1995): 70 bil kWh. **Labor force:** 64% services; 28% industry; 6% constr.; 2% agric.

Finance: Monetary unit: Franc (Aug. 1997: 37.37 = $1 US). **Gross domestic product** (1995 est.): $197 bil. **Per capita GDP** $19,500. *Note:* Import/Export data include Luxembourg. **Imports** (1994): $140 bil; partners: EU 68%, U.S. 9%. **Exports** (1994): $108 bil; partners: EU 67%, U.S. 6%. **Tourism** (1994): $5.2 bil. **National budget** (1994): $69.36 bil. **International reserves less gold** (May 1996): $16.76 bil. **Gold:** 15.32 mil oz t. **Consumer prices** (change in 1996): 2.1%.

Transport: Railroad: Length: 2,108.9 mi. **Motor vehicles in use:** 4.2 mil passenger cars, 515,000 comm. vehicles. **Civil aviation:** 4.7 bil passenger-mi.; 2 airports with scheduled flights. **Chief ports:** Antwerp, Zeebrugge, Ghent.

Communications: Television sets: 1 per 2.2 persons. **Radios:** 1 per 1.3 persons. **Telephones:** 1 per 2.2 persons. **Daily newspaper circ.:** 321 per 1,000 pop.

Health: Life expectancy at birth (1997): 74.0 male; 80.6 female. **Births** (per 1,000 pop.): 12. **Deaths** (per 1,000 pop.): 10. **Natural increase** 0.2%. **Hospital beds:** 1 per 124 persons. **Physicians:** 1 per 268 persons. **Infant mortality** (per 1,000 live births 1997): 6.

Education: Compulsory: ages 6-18. **Literacy** (1995): 99%.

Major International Organizations: UN and all of its specialized agencies, NATO, EU, OECD.

Embassy: 3330 Garfield St. NW 20008; 333-6900.

Belgium derives its name from the Belgae, the first recorded inhabitants, probably Celts. The land was conquered by Julius Caesar, and was ruled for 1800 years by conquerors, including Rome, the Franks, Burgundy, Spain, Austria, and France. After 1815, Belgium was made a part of the Netherlands, but it became an independent constitutional monarchy in 1830.

Belgian neutrality was violated by Germany in both world wars. King Leopold III surrendered to Germany, May 28, 1940. After the war, he was forced by political pressure to abdicate in favor of his son, King Baudouin. Baudouin was succeeded by his brother, Albert II, Aug. 9, 1993.

The Flemings of northern Belgium speak Dutch, while French is the language of the Walloons in the south. The language difference has been a perennial source of controversy and led to antagonism between the 2 groups. Parliament has passed measures aimed at transferring power from the central government to 3 regions—Wallonia, Flanders, and Brussels. Constitutional changes in 1993 made Belgium a federal state.

Belgium lives by its foreign trade; about 50% of its entire production is sold abroad.

Belize

People: Population: 224,663. **Age distrib.** (%): <15: 43; 65+: 4. **Pop. density:** 25 per sq. mi. **Urban:** 46%. **Ethnic** **groups:** Mestizo 44%, Creole 30%, Maya 11%, Garifuna 7%. **Principal languages:** English (official), Spanish, Maya, Garifuna (Carib). **Chief religions:** Roman Catholic 62%, Protestant 30%.

Geography: Area: 8,867 sq. mi. **Location:** Eastern coast of Central America. **Neighbors:** Mexico on N, Guatemala on W and S. **Capital:** Belmopan. **Cities** (1994 est.): Belize City 62,939.

Government: Type: Parliamentary democracy. **Head of state:** Queen Elizabeth II, represented by Gov.-Gen. Colville Young; b Nov. 20, 1932; in office: Nov. 17, 1993. **Head of government:** Prime Min. Manuel Esquivel; b May 2, 1940; in office: July 2, 1993. **Local divisions:** 6 districts. **Defense:** 1.7% of GNP (1994). **Active troop strength:** 1,050.

Economy: Industries: Garments, food processing, tourism. **Chief crops:** Sugar (main export), citrus, bananas. **Electricity prod.** (1995): 105 mil kWh. **Arable land:** 2%.

Finance: Monetary unit: Dollar (Aug. 1997: 2.00 = $1 US). **Gross domestic product** (1994 est.): $575 mil. **Per capita GDP:** $2,750. **Imports** (1993): $281 mil; partners: U.S. 53%. **Exports** (1993): $115 mil; partners: U.S. 38%. **National budget** (1991): $123.1 mil. **International reserves less gold** (June 1997): $59.56 mil. **Consumer prices** (change in 1996): 6.4%.

Communications: Television sets: 1 per 6.0 persons. **Radios:** 1 per 1.7 persons.

Health: Life expectancy at birth (1997): 66.8 male; 70.8 female. **Births** (per 1,000 pop.): 32. **Deaths** (per 1,000 pop.): 6. **Natural increase:** 2.6%. **Hospital beds:** 1 per 350 persons. **Physicians:** 1 per 1,708 persons. **Infant mortality** (per 1,000 live births 1997): 33.

Education: Compulsory: ages 5-14. **Literacy** (1993): 93%.

Major International Organizations: OAS, UN (IMF, FAO, WTO, WHO, World Bank), the Commonwealth.

Embassy: 2535 Massachusetts Ave. NW 20008; 332-9636.

Belize (formerly British Honduras) was Britain's last colony on the American mainland. The country achieved independence Sept. 21, 1981. Relations with neighboring Guatemala, initially tense, have improved in recent years. Belize has become a center for drug trafficking between Colombia and the U.S.

Benin
Republic of Benin
République du Bénin

People: Population: 5,902,178. **Age distrib.** (%): <15: 48; 65+: 2. **Pop. density:** 136 per sq. mi. **Urban:** 39%. **Ethnic groups:** African (Fon, Adja, Bariba, Yoruba) 99%. **Principal languages:** French (official), Fon, Yoruba. **Chief religions:** Indigenous beliefs 70%, Muslim 15%, Christian 15%.

Geography: Area: 43,500 sq. mi. **Location:** In W Africa on Gulf of Guinea. **Neighbors:** Togo on W; Burkina Faso, Niger on N; Nigeria on E. **Topography:** Most of Benin is flat and covered with dense vegetation. The coast is hot, humid, and rainy. **Capital:** Porto-Novo. **Cities** (1992 met.): Cotonou 1,060,310.

Government: Type: Republic. **Head of state:** Pres. Mathieu Kerekou; b Sept. 2, 1933; in office: Apr. 4, 1996. **Local divisions:** 6 provinces. **Defense:** 3.2% of GDP (1994). **Active troop strength:** 4,800 est.

Economy: Chief crops: Palm products, peanuts, cotton, corn, rice. **Minerals:** Oil, limestone. **Arable land:** 12%. **Livestock** (1996): cattle: 1.9 mil; goats: 1.0 mil; sheep: 601,000. **Fish catch** (1993): 40,983 metric tons. **Electricity prod.** (1995): 6 mil kWh. **Labor force:** 60% agric.; 38% transport, commerce, public services.

Finance: Monetary unit: CFA Franc (Aug. 1997: 610 = $1 US). **Gross domestic product** (1995 est.): $7.6 bil. **Per capita GDP:** $1,380. **Imports** (1994 est.): $439 mil; partners: France 24%. **Exports** (1994 est.): $310 mil. **National budget** (1993 est.): $375 bil. **International reserves less gold** (Mar. 1997): $255.2 mil. **Consumer prices** (change in 1996): 4.8%.

Transport: Railroads: Length: 358.9 mi. **Civil aviation:** 133.5 mil passenger-mi. **Chief port:** Cotonou.

Communications: Television sets: 1 per 182 persons. **Radios:** 1 per 11 persons. **Telephones:** 1 per 194 persons. **Daily newspaper circ.:** 2 per 1,000 pop.

Health: Life expectancy at birth (1997): 51.2 male; 55.2 female. **Births** (per 1,000 pop.): 46. **Deaths** (per 1,000 pop.): 13. **Natural increase:** 3.3%. **Infant mortality** (per 1,000 live births 1997): 103.

Education: Free and compulsory: ages 6-12. **Literacy** (1995 est.): 37%.

Major International Organizations: UN (FAO, WTO, World Bank, IMF, WHO), OAU.

Embassy: 2737 Cathedral Ave. NW 20008; 232-6656.

The Kingdom of Abomey, rising to power in wars with neighboring kingdoms in the 17th century, came under French domination in the late 19th century and was incorporated into French West Africa by 1904.

Under the name Dahomey, the country became independent Aug. 1, 1960. The name was changed to Benin in 1975. In the fifth coup since independence Col. Ahmed Kerekou took power in 1972; two years later he declared a socialist state with a "Marxist-Leninist" philosophy. In Dec. 1989, Kerekou announced that Marxism-Leninism would no longer be the state ideology.

In Mar. 1991, Kerekou lost to Nicéphore Soglo in Benin's first free presidential election in 30 years. Kerekou defeated Soglo in Mar. 1996 to reclaim the presidency.

Bhutan
Kingdom of Bhutan
Druk-Yul

People: Population: 1,865,191. **Age distrib.** (%): <15: 40; 65+: 4. **Pop. density:** 103 per sq. mi. **Urban:** 6%. **Ethnic groups:** Bhote 50%, Nepalese 35%. **Principal languages:** Dzongkha (official), Tibetan and Nepalese dialects. **Chief religions:** Lamaistic Buddhist (state religion) 75%, Hindu 25%.

Geography: Area: 18,150 sq. mi. **Location:** S Asia, in eastern Himalayan Mts. **Neighbors:** India on W (Sikkim) and S, China on N. **Topography:** Bhutan is comprised of very high mountains in the N, fertile valleys in the center, and thick forests in the Duar Plain in the S. **Capital:** Thimphu (1993 est.): 30,300.

Government: Type: Monarchy. **Head of state:** King Jigme Singye Wangchuk; b Nov. 11, 1955; in office: July 21, 1972. **Local divisions:** 18 districts.

Economy: Industries: Cement, wood products. **Chief crops:** Rice, corn, citrus. **Other resources:** Timber, hydropower. **Arable land:** 2%. **Electricity** (1995): 1.7 bil kWh. **Labor force:** 93% agric.; 5% services.

Finance: Monetary unit: Ngultrum (Aug. 1997: 36.47 = $1 US; Indian Rupee also used). **Gross domestic product** (1995 est.): $1.3 bil. **Per capita GDP:** $730. **Tourism** (1994): 4.0 mil. **Imports** (FY 1994-95 est.): $113.6 mil; partners: India 77%. **Exports** (FY 1994-95 est.): $70.9 mil; partners: India 94%. **National budget** (FY 1993-94): $150 mil. **International reserves less gold** (Mar. 1996): $164.49 mil.

Transport: Civil aviation: 3.1 mil passenger-mi.

Communications: Radios: 1 per 59 persons. **Telephones:** 1 per 160 persons.

Health: Life expectancy at birth (1997): 52.4 male; 51.4 female. **Births** (per 1,000 pop.): 38. **Deaths** (per 1,000 pop.): 15. **Natural increase:** 2.3%. **Hospital beds:** 1 per 822 persons. **Physicians:** 1 per 5,335 persons. **Infant mortality** (per 1,000 live births 1997): 114.

Education: Literacy (1995 est.): 42%.

Major International Organizations: UN (IMF, FAO, WHO, World Bank).

The region came under Tibetan rule in the 16th century. British influence grew in the 19th century. A monarchy, set up in 1907, became a British protectorate by a 1910 treaty. The country became independent in 1949, with India guiding foreign relations and supplying aid.

Links to India have been strengthened by airline service and a road network. Most of the population engages in subsistence agriculture.

Bolivia
Republic of Bolivia
República de Bolivia

People: Population: 7,669,868. **Age distrib.** (%): <15: 40; 65+: 5. **Pop. density:** 18 per sq. mi. **Urban:** 61%. **Ethnic groups:** Quechua 30%, mestizo 25-30%, Aymara 25%, European 5-15%. **Principal languages:** Spanish, Quechua, Aymara (all official). **Chief religions:** Roman Catholic 95%, Protestant.

Geography: Area: 424,164 sq. mi. **Location:** In W central South America, in the Andes Mts. (one of 2 landlocked countries in South America). **Neighbors:** Peru and Chile on W, Argentina and Paraguay on S, Brazil on E and N. **Topography:** The great central plateau, at an altitude of 12,000 ft., over 500 mi. long, lies between two great cordilleras having 3 of the highest peaks in South America. Lake Titicaca, on Peruvian border, is highest lake in world on which steamboats ply (12,506 ft.). The E central region has semitropical forests; the llanos, or Amazon-Chaco lowlands are in E. **Capitals:** La Paz (administrative), Sucre (judicial). **Cities:** La Paz 1,250,000; Santa Cruz 850,000*.

Government: Type: Republic. **Head of state:** Pres Hugo Banzer Suárez; b May 10, 1926; in office: Aug. 6, 1997. **Local divisions:** 9 departments. **Defense:** 1.9% of GDP (1996). **Active troop strength:** 33,500.

Economy: Industries: Mining, smelting, tobacco, handicrafts, clothing. **Chief crops:** Coffee, sugar, potatoes, soybeans, corn,

coca (sold for cocaine processing). **Minerals:** Antimony, tin, tungsten, silver, zinc, oil, gas, iron. **Crude oil reserves** (1996): 132 mil bbls. **Other resources:** Timber. **Arable land:** 3%. **Livestock** (1996): sheep: 8.0 mil; cattle: 6.2 mil; pigs: 2.5 mil; goats: 1.5 mil. **Electricity prod.** (1994): 2.9 bil kWh. **Labor force:** NA% agric.; 20% serv. & utilities; 7% manuf., mining, & constr.

Finance: Monetary unit: Boliviano (Aug. 1997: 5.27 = $1 US). **Gross domestic product** (1995 est.): $20 bil. **Per capita GDP:** $2,530. **Imports** (1994 est.): $1.21 bil; partners: U.S. 24%. **Exports** (1994 est.): $1.1 bil; partners: U.S. 26%. **National budget** (1995 est.): $3.75 bil. **International reserves less gold** (June 1997): $1.04 bil. **Gold:** 939,000 oz t. **Consumer prices** (change in 1996): 12.4%.

Transport: Railroad: Length: 2,292.1 mi. **Motor vehicles:** in use: 357,000 passenger cars, 190,000 comm. vehicles. **Civil aviation:** 707.3 mil passenger-mi.; 14 airports with scheduled flights.

Communications: Television sets: 1 per 8.8 persons. **Radios:** 1 per 1.5 persons. **Telephones:** 1 per 21 persons. **Daily newspaper circ.:** 69 per 1,000 pop.

Health: Life expectancy at birth (1997): 57.5 male; 63.4 female. **Births** (per 1,000 pop.): 32. **Deaths** (per 1,000 pop.): 10. **Natural increase:** 2.2%. **Hospital beds:** 1 per 1,005 persons. **Physicians:** 1 per 3,663 persons. **Infant mortality** (per 1,000 live births 1997): 66.

Education: Free and compulsory: ages 6-14. **Literacy** (1995 est.): 83%.

Major International Organizations: UN (IMF, FAO, WTO, World Bank, WHO), OAS.

Embassy: 3014 Massachusetts Ave. NW 20008; 483-4410.

The Incas conquered the region from earlier Indian inhabitants in the 13th century. Spanish rule began in the 1530s and lasted until Aug. 6, 1825. The country is named after Simon Bolivar, independence fighter.

In a series of wars, Bolivia lost its Pacific coast to Chile, the oil-bearing Chaco to Paraguay, and rubber-growing areas to Brazil, 1879-1935.

Economic unrest, especially among the militant mine workers, has contributed to continuing political instability. A reformist government under Victor Paz Estenssoro, 1951-64, nationalized tin mines and attempted to improve conditions for the Indian majority but was overthrown by a military junta. A series of coups and countercoups continued through 1981, until the military junta elected Gen. Celso Torrelio Villa as president.

In July 1982, the military junta assumed power amid a growing economic crisis and foreign debt difficulties. The junta resigned in Oct. and allowed the Congress, elected democratically in 1980, to take power. Gen. Hugo Banzer Suárez, who ruled as a dictator, 1971-78, led after presidential voting, June 1, 1997, and was elected by Congress, Aug. 5.

U.S. pressure on the government to reduce the country's output of coca, the raw material for cocaine, has led to clashes between police and coca growers and increased anti-U.S. feeling among Bolivians.

Bosnia and Herzegovina
Republic of Bosnia and Herzegovina
Republika Bosna i Hercegovina

People: Population: 2,607,734. **Age distrib.** (%): <15: 19; 65+: 13. **Pop. density:** 132 per sq. mi. **Urban:** 42%. **Ethnic groups:** Serbian 40%, Muslim 38%, Croatian 22%. **Principal languages:** Serbo-Croatian (official) 99%. **Chief religions:** Muslim 40%, Orthodox 31%, Catholic 15%.

Geography: Area: 19,741 sq. mi. **Location:** On Balkan Peninsula in SE Europe. **Neighbors:** Yugoslavia on E and SE, Croatia on N and W. **Topography:** Hilly with some mountains. About 36% of the land is forested. **Capital:** Sarajevo (1993 est.): 300,000.

Government: Type: Republic. **Heads of state:** Chairman, Collective Pres., Alija Izetbegovic (Muslim), b Aug. 8, 1925; members, Collective Pres., Momcilo Krajisnik (Serb), b 1945, and Kresimir Zubak (Croat), b Nov. 29, 1947; in office: Oct. 23, 1996. **Local divisions:** 109 districts. **Defense: Active troop strength:** 92,000 est.

Economy: Industries: Steel, mining, textiles, timber. **Chief crops:** Corn, wheat, berries, nuts. **Minerals:** Bauxite, iron, coal. **Arable land:** 20%. **Electricity prod.** (1995): 1.4 bil kWh.

Finance: Monetary unit: Yugoslav New Dinar (Aug. 1997: 5.71 = $1 US). **Gross domestic product** (1995 est.): $1 bil. **Per capita GDP:** $300.

Communications: Radios: 1 per 4.4 persons.

Transport: Railroad: Length: 634.0 mi. **Chief port:** Bosanski Brod.

Health: Life expectancy at birth (1997): 55.3 male; 64.9 female. **Births** (per 1,000 pop.): 6. **Deaths** (per 1,000 pop.): 15. **Natural increase:** -0.8%. **Hospital beds:** 1 per 217 persons.

Physicians: 1 per 711 persons. **Infant mortality** (per 1,000 live births 1997): 36.
Education: Free and compulsory: ages 7-15. **Literacy** (1991): 86%.
Major International Organizations: UN (ILO, FAO, WHO).
Embassy: 1707 L St. NW, Suite 760 20036; 833-3612.

Bosnia was ruled by Croatian kings c. AD 958, and by Hungary 1000-1200. It became organized c. 1200 and later took control of Herzegovina. The kingdom disintegrated from 1391, with the southern part becoming the independent duchy Herzegovina. It was conquered by Turks in 1463 and made a Turkish province. The area was placed under control of Austria-Hungary in 1878, and made part of the province of **Bosnia and Herzegovina,** which was formally annexed to Austria-Hungary 1908; Bosnia became a province of Yugoslavia in 1918. It was reunited with Herzegovina as a federated republic in the 1946 Yugoslavian constitution.

The Bosnia and Herzegovina parliament adopted a declaration of sovereignty Oct. 15, 1991. A referendum for independence was passed Feb. 29, 1992. Ethnic Serbs' opposition to the referendum spurred violent clashes and bombings. The U.S. and EU recognized the republic Apr. 7. Fierce three-way fighting continued between Bosnia's Serbs, Muslims, and Croats. Serb forces massacred thousands of Bosnian Muslims and engaged in "ethnic cleansing" (the expulsion of Muslims and other non-Serbs from areas under Bosnian Serb control). The capital, Sarajevo, was surrounded and besieged by Bosnian Serb forces. Muslims and Croats in Bosnia reached a cease fire Feb. 23, 1994, and signed an accord, Mar. 18, to create a Muslim-Croat confederation in Bosnia. However, by mid-1994, Bosnian Serbs controlled over 70% of the country.

As fighting continued in 1995, the balance of power began to shift toward the Muslim-Croat alliance. Massive NATO air strikes at Bosnian Serb targets beginning Aug. 30 triggered a new round of peace talks, and the siege of Sarajevo was lifted Sept. 15. The new talks produced an agreement in principle to create autonomous regions within Bosnia, with the Serb region constituting 49% of the country. A Croat-Muslim offensive in Sept. recaptured significant territory, leaving the Bosnian Serbs in control of approximately that percentage.

A peace agreement initialed in Dayton, Ohio, Nov. 21, 1995, was signed in Paris, Dec. 14, by leaders of Bosnia, Croatia, and Serbia. Some 60,000 NATO troops (about 20,000 from the U.S.) moved in to police the accord. Meanwhile, a UN tribunal began bringing charges against suspected war criminals. Bosnian Serb Pres. Radovan Karadzic was indicted for genocide July 24, 1995; under NATO pressure, he resigned June 30, 1996, and transferred his powers to a deputy, Biljana Plavsic, but he was not arrested.

Elections were held Sept. 14, 1996, for a 3-person collective presidency, for seats in a federal parliament, and for regional offices. In Dec. a revamped NATO "stabilization force" of some 30,000 members (more than 8,000 from the U.S.) received an 18-month mandate. A power struggle between Plavsic, backed by NATO, and Karadzic intensified during the summer of 1997.

Botswana
Republic of Botswana

People: Population: 1,500,765. **Age distrib.** (%): <15: 42; 65+: 4. **Pop. density:** 7 per sq. mi. **Urban:** 63%. **Ethnic groups:** Batswana 95%, Kalanga, Basarwa, Kgalagadi. **Principal languages:** English (official), Setswana. **Chief religions:** Indigenous beliefs 50%, Christian 50%.

Geography: Area: 224,607 sq. mi. **Location:** In southern Africa. **Neighbors:** Namibia on N and W, South Africa on S, Zimbabwe on NE; Botswana claims border with Zambia on N. **Topography:** The Kalahari Desert, supporting nomadic Bushmen and wildlife, spreads over SW; there are swamplands and farming areas in N, and rolling plains in E where livestock are grazed. **Capital:** Gaborone (1992 est.): 134,000.

Government: Type: Parliamentary republic. **Head of state:** Pres. Ketumile Masire; b July 23, 1925; in office: July 13, 1980. **Local divisions:** 10 districts and 4 town councils. **Defense:** 5.2% of GDP (FY 1993-94). **Active troop strength:** 7,500.

Economy: Industries: Livestock processing, mining, tourism. **Chief crops:** Corn, sorghum, millet, beans. **Minerals:** Copper, coal, nickel, diamonds. **Arable land:** 2%. **Livestock** (1996): cattle: 2.8 mil; goats: 1.9 mil. **Electricity prod.** (1995): 1 bil kWh. **Labor force:** 30% serv.; 23% agric.; 19% manuf. & constr.

Finance: Monetary unit: Pula (Aug. 1997: 3.70 = $1 US). **Gross domestic product** (1995 est.): $4.5 bil. **Per capita GDP:** $3,200. **Imports** (1992): $1.8 bil. **Exports** (1994): $1.8 bil. **Tourism** (1992): $65 mil. **National budget** (FY 1993-94): $1.99 bil. **International reserves less gold** (Mar. 1997): $5.37 bil. **Consumer prices** (change in 1996): 10.1%.

Transport: Railroads: Length: 603 mi. **Motor vehicles in use:** 73,000 passenger cars, 19,500 comm. vehicles. **Civil aviation:** 36.0 mil passenger-mi.
Communications: Television sets: 1 per 59 persons. **Radios:** 1 per 8.0 persons. **Telephones:** 1 per 25 persons. **Daily newspaper circ.:** 24 per 1,000 pop.
Health: Life expectancy at birth (1997): 43.5 male; 45.6 female. **Births** (1,000 pop.): 33. **Deaths** (per 1,000 pop.): 18. **Natural increase:** 1.5%. **Hospital beds:** 1 per 434 persons. **Physicians:** 1 per 4,395 persons. **Infant mortality** (per 1,000 live births 1997): 55.
Education: Literacy (1995 est.): 70%.
Major International Organizations: UN (WTO, IMF, FAO, World Bank, WHO), OAU, the Commonwealth.
Embassy: 3400 International Dr. NW 20008; 244-4990.

First inhabited by bushmen, then by Bantus, the region became the British protectorate of Bechuanaland in 1886, halting encroachment by Boers and Germans from the south and southwest. The country became fully independent Sept. 30, 1966, changing its name to Botswana. Cattle raising and mining (diamonds, copper, nickel) have contributed to economic growth. The economy is closely tied to South Africa.

Brazil
Federative Republic of Brazil
República Federativa do Brasil

People: Population: 164,511,366. **Age distrib.** (%): <15: 30; 65+: 5. **Pop. density:** 50 per sq. mi. **Urban:** 79%. **Ethnic groups:** White (incl. Portuguese, German, Italian, Spanish, Polish) 55%, mixed white & African 38%, African 6%. **Principal languages:** Portuguese (official), Spanish, English, French. **Chief religions:** Roman Catholic 70%.

Geography: Area: 3,300,171 sq. mi., largest country in South America. **Location:** Occupies E half of South America. **Neighbors:** French Guiana, Suriname, Guyana, Venezuela on N; Colombia, Peru, Bolivia, Paraguay, Argentina on W; Uruguay on S. **Topography:** Brazil's Atlantic coastline stretches 4,603 miles. In N is the heavily wooded Amazon basin covering half the country. Its network of rivers is navigable for 15,814 mi. The Amazon itself flows 2,093 miles in Brazil, all navigable. The NE region is semiarid scrubland, heavily settled and poor. The S central region, favored by climate and resources, has almost half of the population, produces 75% of farm goods and 80% of industrial output. The narrow coastal belt includes most of the major cities. Almost the entire country has a tropical or semitropical climate. **Capital:** Brasília. **Cities:** São Paulo 16,533,000; Rio de Janeiro 10,181,000; Belo Horizonte 3,775,000*.

Government: Type: Federal republic. **Head of state:** Pres. Fernando Henrique Cardoso; b June 18, 1931; in office: Jan. 1, 1995. **Local divisions:** 26 states, 1 federal district (Brasília). **Defense:** 1.1% of GDP (1994). **Active troop strength:** 295,000.

Economy: Industries: Steel, autos, textiles, shoes, chemicals, machinery. **Chief crops:** Coffee (largest grower), soybeans, sugar, cocoa, rice, corn, fruits, cotton. **Minerals:** Iron, manganese, phosphates, uranium, gold, nickel, tin, bauxite, oil. **Crude oil reserves** (1996): 4.8 bil bbls. **Arable land:** 7%. **Livestock** (1996): cattle: 165 mil; pigs: 36.6 mil; sheep: 18.0 mil; goats: 10.5 mil. **Fish catch** (1995): 800,000 metric tons. **Electricity prod.** (1995): 264.9 bil kWh. **Labor force:** 42% services; 31% agric.; 27% ind.

Finance: Monetary unit: Real (Aug. 1997: 1.09 = $1 US). **Gross domestic product** (1995 est.): $976.8 bil. **Per capita GDP:** $6,100. **Imports** (1995): $49.7 bil; partners: U.S. 23%, EU 22.5%. **Exports** (1995): $46.5 bil; partners: EU 28%, U.S. 17%. **Tourism** (1994): $1.4 bil. **National budget** (1994): $54.9 bil. **International reserves less gold** (Mar. 1997): $57.27 bil. **Gold:** 3.73 mil oz t. **Consumer prices** (change in 1996): 18.2%.

Transport: Railroad: Length: 17,026.6 mi. **Motor vehicles in use:** 12 mil passenger cars, 3.2 mil comm. vehicles. **Civil aviation:** 20.0 bil passenger-mi.; 139 airports with scheduled flights. **Chief ports:** Santos, Rio de Janeiro, Vitoria, Salvador, Rio Grande, Recife.
Communications: Television sets: 1 per 4.8 persons. **Radios:** 1 per 2.5 persons. **Telephones:** 1 per 13 persons. **Daily newspaper circ.:** 45 per 1,000 pop.
Health: Life expectancy at birth (1997): 56.8 male; 66.3 female. **Births** (per 1,000 pop.): 20. **Deaths** (per 1,000 pop.): 9. **Natural increase:** 1.1%. **Hospital beds:** 1 per 298 persons. **Physicians:** 1 per 681 persons. **Infant mortality** (per 1,000 live births 1997): 53.
Education: Free and compulsory: ages 7-14. **Literacy** (1995 est.): 83%.
Major International Organizations: UN and most of its specialized agencies, OAS.
Embassy: 3006 Massachusetts Ave. NW 20008; 745-2700.

Pedro Alvares Cabral, a Portuguese navigator, is generally credited as the first European to reach Brazil, in 1500. The country was thinly settled by various Indian tribes. Only a few have survived to the present, mostly in the Amazon basin.

In the next centuries, Portuguese colonists gradually pushed inland, bringing along large numbers of African slaves. (Slavery was not abolished until 1888.)

The King of Portugal, fleeing before Napoleon's army, moved the seat of government to Brazil in 1808. Brazil thereupon became a kingdom under Dom Joao VI. After his return to Portugal, his son Pedro proclaimed the independence of Brazil, Sept. 7, 1822, and was crowned emperor. The second emperor, Dom Pedro II, was deposed in 1889, and a republic proclaimed, called the United States of Brazil. In 1967 the country was renamed the Federative Republic of Brazil.

A military junta took control in 1930; dictatorial power was assumed by Getulio Vargas, until finally forced out by the military in 1945. A democratic regime prevailed 1945-64, during which time the capital was moved from Rio de Janeiro to Brasília.

In 1964, Pres. Joao Belchoir Marques Goulart instituted economic policies that aggravated Brazil's inflation; he was overthrown by an army revolt. The next 5 presidents were all military leaders. Censorship was imposed, and much of the opposition was suppressed amid charges of torture. In 1974 elections, the official opposition party made gains in the chamber of deputies; some relaxation of censorship occurred.

Since 1930, successive governments have pursued industrial and agricultural growth and the development of interior areas. Exploiting vast mineral resources, fertile soil in several regions, and a huge labor force, Brazil became the leading industrial power of Latin America by the 1970s, while agricultural output soared.

However, income maldistribution and inflation led to severe economic recession. Foreign debt is among the largest in the world. Brazil and its principal commercial bank lenders agreed to restructure the nation's $44 billion commercial debts, July 1992. The 1991 census revealed that population growth dipped below 2 percent for the first time in half a century.

Brazil unveiled a comprehensive environmental program for the Amazon region in 1989, amid an international outcry by environmentalists and others concerned about the ongoing destruction of the Amazon ecosystem. Brazil hosted delegates from 178 countries at the Earth Summit June 3-14, 1992.

Democratic presidential elections were held in 1985 as the nation returned to civilian rule. Fernando Collor de Mello was elected president in Dec. 1989. In Sept. 1992, Pres. Collor was impeached for corruption. He resigned on Dec. 29 as his trial was beginning, and Itamar Franco, who had been acting president, was sworn in as president. In elections held on Oct. 3, 1994, Fernando Henrique Cardoso was elected president.

Brunei
State of Brunei Darussalam
Negara Brunei Darussalam

People: Population: 307,616. **Age distrib.** (%): <15: 33; 65+: 4. **Pop. density:** 138 per sq. mi. **Urban:** 70%. **Ethnic groups:** Malay 64%, Chinese 20%. **Principal languages:** Malay (official), English, Chinese. **Chief religions:** Muslim (official) 63%, Buddhist 14%, Christian 8%.

Geography: Area: 2,226 sq. mi. **Location:** In SE Asia, on the N coast of the island of Borneo; it is surrounded on its landward side by the Malaysian state of Sarawak. **Capital:** Bandar Seri Begawan (1994 met. est.): 187,000.

Government: Type: Independent sultanate. **Head of government:** Sultan Sir Muda Hassanal Bolkiah Mu'izzadin Waddaulah; b July 15, 1946; in office: Jan. 1, 1984. **Local divisions:** 4 districts. **Defense:** 6.2% of GDP (1994). **Active troop strength:** 5,000.

Economy: Industries: Oil & gas (more than 40% of GDP is derived from oil and gas exports). **Chief crops:** Rice, bananas, cassava. **Crude oil reserves** (1996): 1.35 bil bbls. **Arable land:** 1%. **Electricity prod.** (1995): 1.3 bil kWh.

Finance: Monetary unit: Dollar (Aug. 1997: 1.48 = $1 US). **Gross domestic product** (1995 est.): $4.6 bil. **Per capita GDP:** $15,800. **Imports** (1994 est.): $1.8 bil. **Exports** (1994 est.): $2.4 bil.

Transport: Railroad: Length: 8.1 mi. **Motor vehicles in use:** 115,000 passenger cars, 13,000 commercial vehicles. **Civil aviation:** 1.3 bil passenger-mi.

Communications: Television sets: 1 per 4.1 persons. **Radios:** 1 per 3.7 persons. **Telephones:** 1 per 4.2 persons.

Health: Life expectancy at birth: (1997): 70.0 male; 73.2 female. **Births** (per 1,000 pop.): 25. **Deaths** (per 1,000 pop.): 5. **Natural increase:** 2.0%. **Hospital beds:** 1 per 285 persons. **Physicians:** 1 per 1,398 persons. **Infant mortality** (per 1,000 live births 1997): 24.

Education: Free and compulsory: ages 5-14. **Literacy** (1995 est.): 88%.

Major International Organizations: UN and some of its specialized agencies, ASEAN, APEC, the Commonwealth. **Embassy:** 2600 Virginia Ave. NW 20037; 342-0159.

The Sultanate of Brunei was a powerful state in the early 16th century, with authority over all of the island of Borneo as well as parts of the Sulu Islands and the Philippines. In 1888, a treaty placed the state under the protection of Great Britain.

Brunei became a fully sovereign and independent state on Jan. 1, 1984.

The Sultan of Brunei donated $10 million to the Nicaraguan *contras* in 1986; the subsequent misplacement of the funds generated much media attention in the U.S.

Bulgaria
Republic of Bulgaria
Republika Bulgaria

People: Population: 8,652,745. **Age distrib.** (%): <15: 17; 65+: 16. **Pop. density:** 202 per sq. mi. **Urban:** 69%. **Ethnic groups:** Bulgarian 85%, Turk 8.5%. **Principal languages:** Bulgarian (official), Turkish. **Chief religions:** Bulgarian Orthodox 85%, Muslim 13%.

Geography: Area: 42,855 sq. mi. **Location:** SE Europe, in E Balkan Peninsula on Black Sea. **Neighbors:** Romania on N; Yugoslavia, Macedonia on W; Greece, Turkey on S. **Topography:** The Stara Planina (Balkan) Mts. stretch E-W across the center of the country, with the Danubian plain on N, the Rhodope Mts. on SW, and Thracian Plain on SE. **Capital:** Sofia. **Cities** (1995 met. est.): Plovdiv 1,219,681; Sofia 973,870.

Government: Type: Republic. **Head of state:** Pres. Petar Stoyanov; b May 25, 1952; in office: Jan. 19, 1997. **Head of government:** Prime Min. Ivan Kostov; b Dec. 23, 1949; in office: May 21, 1997. **Local divisions:** 9 provinces. **Defense:** 2.5% of GDP (1995). **Active troop strength:** 103,500.

Economy: Industries: Chemicals, machinery, metals, textiles, food processing. **Chief crops:** Grains, fruit, oilseeds, tobacco. **Minerals:** Bauxite, copper, zinc, lead, coal. **Arable land:** 34%. **Livestock** (1996): sheep: 3.4 mil; pigs: 2.1 mil; goats: 757,000; cattle: 632,000. **Fish catch** (1993): 21,585 metric tons. **Electricity prod.** (1995): 41.4 bil kWh. **Labor force:** 41% ind.; 18% agric.

Finance: Monetary unit: Lev (Aug. 1997: 1785.00 = $1 US). **Gross domestic product** (1995 est.): $43.2 bil. **Per capita GDP:** $4,920. **Imports** (1994): $4 bil; partners: CIS 40%. **Exports** (1994): $4.2 bil; partners: CIS 3.6%. **Tourism** (1994): $358 mil. **National budget** (1994): $4.4 bil.

Transport: Railroads: Length: 2,665.3 mi. **Motor vehicles in use:** 1.6 mil passenger cars, 217,000 comm. vehicles. **Civil aviation:** 1.3 bil passenger-mi.; 3 airports with scheduled flights. **Chief ports:** Burgas, Varna.

Communications: Television sets: 1 per 2.8 persons. **Radios:** 1 per 2.2 persons. **Telephones:** 1 per 3.3 persons. **Daily newspaper circ.:** 209 per 1,000 pop.

Health: Life expectancy at birth (1997): 67.2 male; 75.3 female. **Births** (per 1,000 pop.): 8. **Deaths** (per 1,000 pop.): 14. **Natural increase:** –0.5%. **Hospital beds:** 1 per 95 persons. **Physicians:** 1 per 300 persons. **Infant mortality** (per 1,000 live births 1997): 15.

Education: Free and compulsory: ages 6-16. **Literacy** (1995): 98%.

Major International Organizations: UN (IMF, WHO). **Embassy:** 1621 22d St. NW 20008; 387-7969.

Bulgaria was settled by Slavs in the 6th century. Turkic Bulgars arrived in the 7th century, merged with the Slavs, became Christians by the 9th century, and set up powerful empires in the 10th and 12th centuries. The Ottomans prevailed in 1396 and remained for 500 years.

A revolt in 1876 led to an independent kingdom in 1908. Bulgaria expanded after the first Balkan War but lost its Aegean coastline in World War I, when it sided with Germany. Bulgaria joined the Axis in World War II but withdrew in 1944. Communists took power with Soviet aid; the monarchy was abolished Sept. 8, 1946.

On Nov. 10, 1989, Communist Party leader and head of state Todor Zhivkov, who had held power for 35 years, resigned. Zhivkov was imprisoned, Jan. 1990, and convicted, Sept. 1992, of corruption and abuse of power. In Jan. 1990, Parliament voted to revoke the constitutionally guaranteed dominant role of the Communist Party. A new constitution took effect July 13, 1991. An economic austerity program was launched in May 1996. Former Prime Min. Andrei Lukanov, a longtime Communist leader, was assassinated Oct. 2 in Sofia. Petar Stoyanov won a presidential runoff election Nov. 3. Bulgaria's deteriorating economy provoked nationwide strikes and demonstrations in Jan. 1997. The Union of Democratic Forces, an anti-Communist group, won parliamentary elections on Apr. 19.

Burkina Faso

People: Population: 10,891,159. **Age distrib.** (%): <15: 48; 65+ 3. **Pop. density:** 103 per sq. mi. **Urban:** 16%. **Ethnic groups:** Mossi, Gurunsi, Senufo, Lobi, Bobo, Mande, Fulani. **Principal languages:** French (official), Sudanic tribal languages. **Chief religions:** Muslim 50%, indigenous beliefs 40%, Christian (mostly Roman Catholic) 10%.

Geography: Area: 105,946 sq. mi. **Location:** In W Africa, S of the Sahara. **Neighbors:** Mali on NW; Niger on NE; Benin, Togo, Ghana, Côte d'Ivoire on S. **Topography:** Landlocked Burkina Faso is in the savanna region of W Africa. The N is arid, hot, and thinly populated. **Capital:** Ouagadougou. **Cities:** Ouagadougou 824,000*.

Government: Type: Republic. **Head of state:** Pres. Blaise Compaoré; b 1951; in office: Oct. 15, 1987. **Local divisions:** 30 provinces. **Defense:** 6.4% of GDP (1994). **Active troop strength:** 10,000.

Economy: Industries: Agricultural processing, textiles. **Chief crops:** Millet, sorghum, rice, peanuts, cotton. **Minerals:** Manganese, limestone, marble, gold. **Arable land:** 10%. **Livestock** (1996): goats: 7.2 mil; sheep: 5.8 mil; cattle: 4.35 mil. **Electricity prod.** (1995): 220 mil kWh. **Labor force:** 80% agric.; 15% ind.

Finance: Monetary unit: CFA Franc (Aug. 1997: 610 = $1 US). **Gross domestic product** (1995 est.): $7.4 bil. **Per capita GDP:** $700. **Imports** (1993): $636 mil; partners: France 24%, Côte d'Ivôire 19%. **Exports** (1993): $273 mil; partners: Japan 20%, France 13%. **National budget** (1992): $548 mil. **International reserves less gold** (Mar. 1997): $329.7 mil. **Gold:** 11,000 oz t. **Consumer prices** (change in 1996): 6.2%.

Transport: Railroad: Length: 386.3 mi. **Motor vehicles in use:** 12,000 passenger cars, 14,000 comm. vehicles. **Civil aviation:** 153.4 mil passenger-mi.

Communications: Television sets: 1 per 182 persons. **Radios:** 1 per 36 persons. **Telephones:** 1 per 347 persons.

Health: Life expectancy at birth (1997): 42.5 male; 42.1 female. **Births** (per 1,000 pop.): 46. **Deaths** (per 1,000 pop.): 20. **Natural increase:** 2.6%. **Hospital beds:** 1 per 1,837 persons. **Physicians:** 1 per 27,158 persons. **Infant mortality** (per 1,000 live births 1997): 117.

Education: Free and compulsory: ages 7-14. **Literacy** (1995 est.): 19%.

Major International Organizations: UN and many of its specialized agencies, OAU.

Embassy: 2340 Massachusetts Ave. NW 20008; 332-5577.

The Mossi tribe entered the area in the 11th to 13th centuries. Their kingdoms ruled until defeated by the Mali and Songhai empires.

French control came by 1896, but Upper Volta (renamed Burkina Faso on Aug. 4, 1984) was not established as a separate territory until 1947. Full independence came Aug. 5, 1960, and a pro-French government was elected. The military seized power in 1980. A 1987 coup established the current regime, which instituted a multiparty democracy in the early 1990s.

Several hundred thousand farm workers migrate each year to Côte d'Ivoire and Ghana. Burkina Faso is heavily dependent on foreign aid.

Burma

(See Myanmar)

Burundi
Republic of Burundi
Republika y'u Burundi

People: Population: 6,052,614. **Age distrib.** (%): <15: 37; 65+: 4. **Pop. density:** 564 per sq. mi. **Urban:** 8%. **Ethnic groups:** Hutu 85%, Tutsi 14%, Twa (Pygmy) 1%. **Principal languages:** Kirundi, French (both official), Swahili. **Chief religions:** Roman Catholic 62%, indigenous beliefs 32%, Protestant 5%.

Geography: Area: 10,740 sq. mi. **Location:** In central Africa. **Neighbors:** Rwanda on N, Congo-Kinshasa (formerly Zaire) on W, Tanzania on E and S. **Topography:** Much of the country is grassy highland, with mountains reaching 8,900 ft. The southernmost source of the White Nile is located in Burundi. Lake Tanganyika is the second deepest lake in the world. **Capital:** Bujumbura (1994 est.): 300,000.

Government: Type: In transition. **Head of state:** Pres. Pierre Buyoya; b 1949; in office: July 25, 1996. **Head of government:** Prime Min. Pascal Firmin Ndimira; in office: July 31, 1996. **Local divisions:** 15 provinces. **Defense:** 2.6% of GDP (1993). **Active troop strength:** 22,000 est.

Economy: Industries: Light consumer goods, food processing. **Chief crops:** Coffee (81% of exports), cotton, tea. **Minerals:** Nickel, uranium. **Arable land:** 43%. **Electricity prod.** (1995): 158 mil kWh. **Labor force:** 93% agric.

Finance: Monetary unit: Franc (Aug. 1997: 347.75 = $1 US). **Gross domestic product** (1995 est.): $4 bil. **Per capita GDP:** $600. **Imports** (1993): $203 mil; partners: EU 45%. **Exports** (1993): $68 mil; partners: EU 57%, U.S. 19%. **National budget** (1991 est.): $326 mil. **International reserves less gold** (June 1997): $141.8 mil. **Gold:** 17,000 oz t. **Consumer prices** (change in 1996): 26.4%.

Transport: Motor vehicles in use: 8,000 passenger cars, 11,000 comm. vehicles. **Civil aviation:** 1.2 mil passenger-mi. **Chief port:** Bujumbura.

Communications: Television sets: 1 per 667 persons. **Radios:** 1 per 16 persons. **Telephones:** 1 per 371 persons.

Health: Life expectancy at birth (1997): 47.9 male; 50.1 female. **Births** (per 1,000 pop.): 42. **Deaths** (per 1,000 pop.): 15. **Natural increase:** 2.7%. **Hospital beds:** 1 per 515 persons. **Physicians:** 1 per 31,777 persons. **Infant mortality** (per 1,000 live births 1997): 101.

Education: Free and compulsory: ages 7-13. **Literacy** (1995 est.): 35%.

Major International Organizations: UN (FAO, WTO, World Bank, ILO, IMF, WHO), OAU.

Embassy: 2233 Wisconsin Ave. NW 20007; 342-2574.

The pygmy Twa were the first inhabitants, followed by Bantu Hutus, who were conquered in the 16th century by the Tutsi (Watusi), probably from Ethiopia. Under German control in 1899, the area fell to Belgium in 1916, which exercised successively a League of Nations mandate and UN trusteeship over Ruanda-Urundi (now the two countries of Rwanda and Burundi).

Burundi became independent July 1, 1962.

An unsuccessful Hutu rebellion in 1972-73 left 10,000 Tutsi and 150,000 Hutu dead. Over 100,000 Hutu fled to Tanzania and Zaire (now Congo). In the 1980s, Burundi's Tutsi-dominated regime pledged itself to ethnic reconciliation and democratic reform. In the nation's first democratic presidential election, in June 1993, a Hutu, Melchior Ndadaye, was elected. He was killed in an attempted coup, Oct. 21, 1993. At least 150,000 Burundians died as a result of ethnic conflict during the next three years. Pres. Cyprien Ntaryamira, elected Jan. 1994, was killed with the president of Rwanda in a mysterious plane crash, Apr. 6. The incident sparked massive carnage in Rwanda; violence in Burundi, initially far more limited, intensified in 1995. Conditions continued to deteriorate after a military coup, July 25, 1996.

Cambodia
Kingdom of Cambodia
Preahreacheanachakr Kampuchea

People: Population: 11,163,861. **Age distrib.** (%): <15: 45; 65+: 3. **Pop. density:** 159 per sq. mi. **Urban:** 21%. **Ethnic groups:** Khmer 90%, Vietnamese 5%, Chinese 1%. **Principal languages:** Khmer (official), French. **Chief religions:** Theravada Buddhism 95%.

Geography: Area: 70,238 sq. mi. **Location:** SE Asia, on Indochina Peninsula. **Neighbors:** Thailand on W and N, Laos on NE, Vietnam on E. **Topography:** The central area, formed by the Mekong R. basin and Tonle Sap lake, is level. Hills and mountains are in SE, a long escarpment separates the country from Thailand on NW. 76% of the area is forested. **Capital:** Phnom Penh (1994 est.): 920,000.

Government: Type: Constitutional monarchy. **Head of state:** King Norodom Sihanouk; b Oct. 31, 1922; in office: Sept. 24, 1993. **Head of government:** Co-Prime Mins. Hun Sen; in office: Sept. 24, 1993; Ung Huot; in office: Aug. 6, 1997. **Local divisions:** 21 provinces. **Defense:** 1.4% of GDP (1995). **Active troop strength:** 87,700 est.

Economy: Industries: Rice milling, wood & wood products, fishing. **Chief crops:** Rice, corn, rubber. **Minerals:** Gemstones, phosphates, manganese. **Other resources:** Timber. **Arable land:** 16%. **Livestock** (1996): cattle: 2.8 mil; pigs: 2.05 mil. **Fish catch** (1994): 103,000 metric tons. **Electricity prod.** (1995): 190 mil kWh. **Labor force:** 69% agric.

Finance: Monetary unit: Riel (Aug. 1997: 2,940 = $1 US). **Gross domestic product** (1995 est.): $7 bil. **Per capita GDP:** $660. **Imports** (1994 est.): $630.5 mil. **Exports** (1994 est.): $240.7 mil. **National budget** (1994 est.): $346 mil. **International reserves less gold** (June 1997): $279.70 mil. **Consumer prices** (change in 1996): 10.1%.

Transport: Railroads: Length: 374.5 mi. **Motor vehicles in use:** 37,000 passenger cars, 11,000 comm. vehicles. **Chief port:** Kompong Som (Sihanoukville).

Communications: Television sets: 1 per 125 persons. **Radios:** 1 per 9.3 persons. **Telephones:** 1 per 1,890 persons.

Health: Life expectancy at birth (1997): 48.8 male; 51.8 female. Births (per 1,000 pop.): 43. Deaths (per 1,000 pop.): 15. Natural increase: 2.7%. Physicians: 1 per 7,900 persons. Infant mortality (per 1,000 live births 1997): 106.
Education: Compulsory: ages 6-12. Literacy (1993): 74%.
Major International Organizations: UN (IMF, WHO).
Embassy: 4500 16th St. NW 20011; 726-7742.

Early kingdoms dating from that of Funan in the 1st century AD culminated in the great Khmer empire that flourished from the 9th century to the 13th, encompassing present-day Thailand, Cambodia, Laos, and southern Vietnam. The peripheral areas were lost to invading Siamese and Vietnamese, and France established a protectorate in 1863. Independence came in 1953.

Prince Norodom Sihanouk, king 1941-1955 and head of state from 1960, tried to maintain neutrality. Relations with the U.S. were broken in 1965, after South Vietnam planes attacked Vietcong forces within Cambodia. Relations were restored in 1969, after Sihanouk charged Viet Communists with arming Cambodian insurgents.

In 1970, pro-U.S. Prem. Lon Nol seized power, demanding removal of 40,000 North Viet troops; the monarchy was abolished. Sihanouk formed a government-in-exile in Beijing, and open war began between the government and the Communist Khmer Rouge guerrillas. The U.S. provided heavy military and economic aid.

Khmer Rouge forces captured Phnom Penh Apr. 17, 1975. The new government evacuated all cities and towns, and shuffled the rural population, sending virtually the entire population to clear jungle, forest, and scrub. Over one million people were killed in executions and enforced hardships.

Severe border fighting broke out with Vietnam in 1978 and developed into a full-fledged Vietnamese invasion. Formation of a Vietnamese-backed government was announced, Jan. 8, 1979, one day after the Vietnamese capture of Phnom Penh. Thousands of refugees flowed into Thailand and widespread starvation was reported.

On Jan. 10, 1983, Vietnam launched an offensive against rebel forces in the west. They overran a refugee camp, Jan. 31, driving 30,000 residents into Thailand. In March, Vietnam launched a major offensive against camps on the Cambodian-Thailand border, engaged Khmer Rouge guerrillas, and crossed the border instigating clashes with Thai troops. Vietnam withdrew nearly all its troops by Sept. 1989.

Following UN-sponsored elections in Cambodia that ended May 28, 1993, the 2 leading parties agreed to share power in an interim government until a new constitution was adopted. On Sept. 21, a constitution reestablishing a monarchy was adopted by the National Assembly. It took effect Sept. 24, with Sihanouk as king. The Khmer Rouge, which had boycotted the elections, opposed the new government, and armed violence continued in the mid-1990s. Ieng Sary, a Khmer Rouge leader, broke with the guerrillas, formed a rival group, and announced his support for the monarchy in Aug. 1996, as Khmer Rouge strength rapidly diminished.

Co-Prime Min. Hun Sen staged a coup July 5, 1997, ousting his rival, Prince Norodom Ranariddh. Pol Pot, the Khmer Rouge leader who held power during the late 1970s, was denounced by his former comrades at a show trial, July 25, and sentenced to spend the rest of his life under house arrest.

Cameroon
Republic of Cameroon
République du Cameroun

People: Population: 14,677,510. Age distrib. (%): <15: 46; 65+: 3. Pop. density: 80 per sq. mi. Urban: 46%. Ethnic groups: Cameroon Highlander 31%, Equatorial Bantu 19%, Kirdi 11%, Fulani 10%, NW Bantu 8%. Principal languages: English, French (both official), numerous African groups. Chief religions: Indigenous beliefs 51%, Christian 33%, Muslim 16%.

Geography: Area: 183,569 sq. mi. Location: Between W and central Africa. Neighbors: Nigeria on NW; Chad, Central African Republic on E; Congo, Gabon, Equatorial Guinea on S. Topography: A low coastal plain with rain forests is in S; plateaus in center lead to forested mountains in W, including Mt. Cameroon, 13,350 ft.; grasslands in N lead to marshes around Lake Chad. Capital: Yaoundé. Cities: Douala 1,320,000; Yaoundé 1,119,000*.

Government: Type: Republic. Head of state: Pres. Paul Biya; b Feb. 13, 1933; in office: Nov. 6, 1982. Head of government: Prime Min. Peter Mafani Musonge; b Dec. 3, 1942; in office: Sept. 19, 1996. Local divisions: 10 provinces. Defense: 1.9% of GNP (1994). Active troop strength: 22,100 est.

Economy: Industries: Oil production and processing, food processing, light consumer goods. Chief crops: Cocoa, cof-

fee, cotton. Crude oil reserves (1996): 400 mil bbls. Minerals: Oil, bauxite, iron. Other resources: Timber. Arable land: 13%. Livestock (1996): cattle: 4.9 mil; sheep: 3.8 mil; goats: 3.8 mil; pigs: 1.4 mil. Fish catch (1993): 80,000 metric tons. Electricity prod. (1995): 2.7 bil kWh. Labor force: 74% agric.; 11% ind. & transport.

Finance: Monetary unit: CFA Franc (Aug. 1997: 610 = $1 US). Gross domestic product (1995 est.): $16.5 bil. Per capita GDP: $1,200. Imports (1994): $810 mil; partners: Fr. 38%. Exports (1994): $1.2 bil; partners: EU about 50%. National budget (FY 1992-93): $2.3 bil. International reserves less gold (Nov. 1996): $2.92 mil. Gold: 30,000 oz t. Consumer prices (change in 1996): 4.5%.

Transport: Railroad: Length: 685.6 mi. Motor vehicles in use: 90,000 passenger cars, 79,000 comm. vehicles. Civil aviation: 270.8 mil passenger-mi. Chief port: Douala.

Communications: Television sets: 1 per 42 persons. Radios: 1 per 6.8 persons. Telephones: 1 per 224 persons.

Health: Life expectancy at birth (1997): 51.2 male; 53.4 female. Births (per 1,000 pop.): 42. Deaths (per 1,000 pop.): 14. Natural increase: 2.9%. Infant mortality (per 1,000 live births 1997): 78.
Education: Compulsory: ages 6-12. Literacy (1995 est.): 63%.
Major International Organizations: UN, OAU, the Commonwealth.
Embassy: 2349 Massachusetts Ave. NW 20008; 265-8790.

Portuguese sailors were the first Europeans to reach Cameroon, in the 15th century. The European and American slave trade was very active in the area. German control lasted from 1884 to 1916, when France and Britain divided the territory, later receiving League of Nations mandates and UN trusteeships. French Cameroon became independent Jan. 1, 1960; one part of British Cameroon joined Nigeria in 1961, the other part joined Cameroon. Stability has allowed for development of roads, railways, agriculture, and petroleum production.

Pres. Paul Biya retained his office in Oct. 1992 elections, but the results were widely disputed. A new constitution won legislative approval in Dec. 1995. Fraud charges accompanied legislative elections, May 17, 1997, which Biya's party won.

Canada

People: Population: 29,123,194. Age distrib. (%): <15: 20; 65+: 13. Pop. density: 8 per sq. mi. Urban: 77%. Ethnic groups: British 40%, French 27%, other European 20%, indigenous Indian and Eskimo 1.5%, other (mostly Asian) 11.5%. Principal languages: English, French (both official). Chief religions: Roman Catholic 46%, United Church 12%, Anglican 8%.

Geography: Area: 3,849,674 sq. mi., the largest country in land size in the western hemisphere. Topography: Canada stretches 3,426 miles from east to west and extends southward from the North Pole to the U.S. border. Its seacoast includes 36,356 miles of mainland and 115,133 miles of islands, including the Arctic islands almost from Greenland to near the Alaskan border. Climate: While generally temperate, varies from freezing winter cold to blistering summer heat. Capital: Ottawa. Cities (met. 1996 cen.): Toronto 4.3 mil; Montreal 3.3 mil; Vancouver 1.8 mil; Ottawa-Hull 1.0 mil; Edmonton 862,600; Calgary 821,600; Quebec 671,900; Winnipeg 667,200.

Government: Type: Confederation with parliamentary democracy. Head of state: Queen Elizabeth II, represented by Gov.-Gen. Roméo A. LeBlanc; b Dec. 18, 1927; in office: Feb. 8, 1995. Head of government: Prime Min. Jean Chrétien; b Jan. 11, 1934; in office: Nov. 4, 1993. Local divisions: 10 provinces, 2 territories. Defense: 1.6% of GDP (FY 1995-96). Active troop strength: 70,500.

Economy: Industries: Mining, wood and food prods., transport equip., chemicals, oil & gas. Minerals: Nickel, zinc, copper, gold, lead, molybdenum, potash, silver. Crude oil reserves (1996): 4.9 bil barrels. Arable land: 9%. Livestock (1996): cattle: 13.4 mil; pigs: 12.0 mil; sheep: 677,000. Fish catch (1995): 801,225 metric tons. Electricity prod. (1995): 532.6 bil kWh. Labor force: 75% services, 14% manufacturing, 4% agric.

Finance: Monetary unit: Dollar (Aug. 1997: 1.39 = $1 US). Gross domestic product (1995 est.): $694 bil. Per capita GDP: $24,400. Imports (1995 est.): $166.7 bil; partners: U.S. 67%. Exports (1995 est.): $185 bil; partners: U.S. 80%. Tourism (1994): $6.3 bil. National budget (FY 1994-95 est.): $114.1 bil. International reserves less gold (June 1997): $21.1 bil. Gold: 3.09 mil oz t. Consumer prices (change in 1996): 1.6%.

Transport: Railroads: Length: 43,579.3 mi. Motor vehicles in use: 13.2 mil passenger cars, 3.5 mil comm. vehicles. Civil aviation: 27.0 bil passenger-mi.: 301 airports with scheduled flights. Chief ports: Halifax, Montreal, Quebec, Saint John, Toronto, Vancouver.

Communications: Television sets: 1 per 1.5 persons. **Radios:** 1 per 1.0 persons. **Telephones:** 1 per 1.7 persons. **Daily newspaper circ.:** 189 per 1,000 pop.

Health: Life expectancy at birth (1997): 75.9 male; 82.9 female. **Births** (per 1,000 pop.): 13. **Deaths** (per 1,000 pop.): 7. **Natural increase:** 0.6%. **Hospital beds:** 1 per 171 persons. **Physicians:** 1 per 464 persons. **Infant mortality** (per 1,000 live births 1997): 6.

Education: Compulsory primary education. **Literacy** (1994): 97%.

Major International Organizations: UN and all of its specialized agencies, NATO, OAS, APEC, OECD, the Commonwealth.

Embassy: 501 Pennsylvania Ave. NW 20001; 682-1740.

French explorer Jacques Cartier, who reached the Gulf of St. Lawrence in 1534, is generally regarded as Canada's founder. But English seaman John Cabot sighted Newfoundland in 1497, and Vikings are believed to have reached the Atlantic coast centuries before either explorer.

Canadian settlement was pioneered by the French who established Quebec City (1608) and Montreal (1642) and declared New France a colony in 1663.

Britain acquired Acadia (later Nova Scotia) in 1717 and, through military victory over French forces in Canada, captured Quebec (1759) and obtained control of the rest of New France in 1763. The French, through the Quebec Act of 1774, retained the rights to their own language, religion, and civil law. The British presence in Canada increased during the American Revolution when many colonials, proudly calling themselves United Empire Loyalists, moved north to Canada.

Fur traders and explorers led Canadians westward across the continent. Sir Alexander Mackenzie reached the Pacific in 1793 and scrawled on a rock by the ocean, "from Canada by land."

In Upper and Lower Canada (later called Ontario and Quebec) and in the Maritimes, legislative assemblies appeared in the 18th century and reformers called for responsible government. But the War of 1812 intervened. The war, a conflict between Great Britain and the United States fought mainly in Upper Canada, ended in a stalemate in 1814.

In 1837 political agitation for more democratic government culminated in rebellions in Upper and Lower Canada. Britain sent Lord Durham to investigate; in a famous report (1839), he recommended union of the 2 parts into one colony called Canada. The union lasted until Confederation, July 1, 1867, when proclamation of the British North America (BNA) Act (now known as the Constitution Act, 1867) launched the Dominion of Canada, consisting of Ontario, Quebec, and the former colonies of Nova Scotia and New Brunswick.

Since 1840 the Canadian colonies had held the right to internal self-government. The BNA Act, which was the basis for the country's written constitution, established a federal system of government on the model of a British parliament and cabinet structure under the crown. Canada was proclaimed a self-governing Dominion within the British Empire in 1931. With the ratification of the Constitution Act, 1982, Canada severed its last formal legislative link with Britain by obtaining the right to amend its constitution.

The so-called Meech Lake Agreement was signed (subject to provincial ratification) June 3, 1987. The accord would have assured constitutional protection for Quebec's efforts to preserve its French language and culture. Critics charged it did not make any provision for other minority groups and it gave Quebec too much power, which might enable Quebec to override the nation's 1982 Charter of Rights and Freedoms (an integral part of the constitution). The accord died June 22, 1990.

Its failure sparked a separatist revival in Quebec, which culminated in Aug. 1992 in the Charlottetown agreement. This called for changes to the constitution, such as recognition of Quebec as a "distinct society" within the Canadian confederation. It was defeated in a national referendum Oct. 26, 1992.

In May 1992 voters in the Northwest Territories approved the creation of a self-governing homeland for the 17,500 Inuit living in the territories. The area—to be known as Nunavut, "Our Land"—would cover an area of 136,493 sq. mi. and take effect by 1999.

Canada became the first nation to ratify the North American Free Trade Agreement between Canada, Mexico, and the U.S., June 23, 1993. It went into effect Jan. 1, 1994.

On Feb. 24, 1993, Brian Mulroney resigned as prime minister after more than 8 years in office; he was succeeded by Kim Campbell. In elections Oct. 25, 1993, the ruling Conservatives were defeated in a landslide that left them only 2 of the 295 seats in the House of Commons. Jean Chrétien became prime minister. In a Quebec referendum held Oct. 30, 1995, proponents of secession lost by a razor-thin margin. The elections of June 2, 1997, left the Liberals with a slim majority.

Provinces/Territories	Area (sq. mi.)	Population (1996 cen.)
Alberta	255,287	2,696,826
British Columbia	365,948	3,724,500
Manitoba	250,947	1,113,898
New Brunswick	28,355	738,133
Newfoundland	156,649	551,792
Nova Scotia	21,425	909,282
Ontario	412,581	10,753,573
Prince Edward Island	2,185	134,557
Quebec	594,860	7,138,795
Saskatchewan	251,866	990,237
Northwest Territories	1,322,910	64,402
Yukon Territory	186,661	30,766

Prime Ministers of Canada

Canada is a constitutional monarchy with a parliamentary system of government. It is also a federal state. Canada's official head of state, Queen Elizabeth II, is represented by a resident Governor-General. However, in practice the nation is governed by the Prime Minister, leader of the party that commands the support of a majority of the House of Commons, dominant chamber of Canada's bicameral Parliament.

Name	Party	Term	Name	Party	Term
Sir John A. MacDonald	Conservative	1867-1873	Richard Bedford Bennett	Conservative	1930-1935
Alexander Mackenzie	Liberal	1873-1878	W. L. Mackenzie King	Liberal	1935-1948
Sir John A. MacDonald	Conservative	1878-1891	Louis St. Laurent	Liberal	1948-1957
Sir John J. C. Abbott	Conservative	1891-1892	John G. Diefenbaker	Prog. Cons.	1957-1963
Sir John S. D. Thompson	Conservative	1892-1894	Lester Bowles Pearson	Liberal	1963-1968
Sir Mackenzie Bowell	Conservative	1894-1896	Pierre Elliott Trudeau	Liberal	1968-1979
Sir Charles Tupper	Conservative	1896[1]	Joe Clark	Prog. Cons.	1979-1980
Sir Wilfrid Laurier	Liberal	1896-1911	Pierre Elliott Trudeau	Liberal	1980-1984
Sir Robert Laird Borden	Cons./Union.[2]	1911-1920	John Napier Turner	Liberal	1984[4]
Arthur Meighen	Unionist	1920-1921	Brian Mulroney	Prog. Cons.	1984-1993
W. L. Mackenzie King	Liberal	1921-1926	Kim Campbell	Prog. Cons.	1993[5]
Arthur Meighen	Conservative	1926[3]	Jean Chrétien	Liberal	1993-
W. L. Mackenzie King	Liberal	1926-1930			

(1) May-July. (2) Conservative 1911-1917, Unionist 1917-1920. (3) June-Sept. (4) June-Sept. (5) June-Oct.

Cape Verde
Republic of Cape Verde
República de Cabo Verde

People: Population: 393,843. **Age distrib.** (%): <15: 46; 65+: 6. **Pop. density:** 253 per sq. mi. **Urban:** 56%. **Ethnic groups:** Creole (mulatto) 71%, African 28%, European 1%. **Principal languages:** Portuguese (official), Crioulo. **Chief religions:** Roman Catholic fused with indigenous beliefs.

Geography: Area: 1,557 sq. mi. **Location:** In Atlantic O., off W tip of Africa. **Neighbors:** Nearest are Mauritania, Senegal to E. **Topography:** Cape Verde Islands are 15 in number, volcanic in origin (active crater on Fogo). The landscape is eroded and stark, with vegetation mostly in interior valleys. **Capital:** Praia. **Cities** (1990 cen.): Praia 82,800; Mindelo 51,300.

Government: Type: Republic. **Head of state:** Pres. Antonio Mascarenhas Monteiro; b Feb. 16, 1944; in office: Mar. 22, 1991. **Head of government:** Prime Min. Carlos Veiga; b 1949; in office: Apr. 4, 1991. **Local divisions:** 14 administrative districts. **Defense:** 1.0% of GNP (1994). **Active troop strength:** 1,100 est.

Economy: Chief crops: Bananas, coffee, sweet potatoes, corn, beans. **Minerals:** Salt. **Other resources:** Fish. **Arable land:** 9%. **Electricity prod.** (1995): 40 mil kWh.

Finance: Monetary unit: Escudo (Aug. 1997: 96.59 = $1 US). **Gross domestic product** (1994 est.): $440 mil. **Per capita GDP:** $1,040. **Imports** (1992 est.): $173 mil; partners: Portugal 34%, Netherlands 9%. **Exports** (1992 est.): $4.4 mil; partners: Portugal 49%, Angola 16%. **National budget** (1993 est.): $235 mil.

Transport: Motor vehicles in use: 10,500 passenger cars, 5,500 comm. vehicles. **Civil aviation:** 107.4 mil passenger-mi. **Chief ports:** Mindelo, Praia.

Communications: Television sets: 1 per 313 persons. **Radios:** 1 per 6.8 persons. **Telephones:** 1 per 18 persons.

Health: Life expectancy at birth (1997): 66.8 male; 73.4 female. **Births** (per 1,000 pop.): 35. **Deaths** (per 1,000 pop.): 7. **Natural increase:** 2.8%. **Infant mortality** (per 1,000 live births 1997): 50.

Education: Compulsory: ages 7-11. **Literacy** (1995 est.): 72%.

Major International Organizations: UN (IMF, FAO, World Bank, WHO), OAU.

Embassy: 3415 Massachusetts Ave. NW 20007; 965-6820.

The uninhabited Cape Verdes were discovered by the Portuguese in 1456 or 1460. The first Portuguese colonists landed in 1462; African slaves were brought soon after, and most Cape Verdeans descend from both groups. Cape Verde independence came July 5, 1975. Antonio Mascarenhas Monteiro won the nation's first free presidential election Feb. 17, 1991; he was reelected without opposition five years later.

Central African Republic
République Centrafricaine

People: Population: 3,342,051. **Age distrib.** (%): <15: 44; 65+: 4. **Pop. density:** 14 per sq. mi. **Urban:** 40%. **Ethnic groups:** Baya 34%, Banda 27%, Mandjia 21%, Sara 10%. **Principal languages:** French (official), Sangho (national), Arabic, Hunsa, Swahili. **Chief religions:** Protestant 25%, Roman Catholic 25%, indigenous beliefs 24%, Muslim 15%.

Geography: Area: 240,324 sq. mi. **Location:** In central Africa. **Neighbors:** Chad on N, Cameroon on W, Congo-Brazzaville and Congo-Kinshasa (formerly Zaire) on S, Sudan on E. **Topography:** Mostly rolling plateau, average altitude 2,000 ft., with rivers draining S to the Congo and N to Lake Chad. Open, well-watered savanna covers most of the area, with an arid area in NE, and tropical rain forest in SW. **Capital:** Bangui (1994 est.): 524,000.

Government: Type: Republic. **Head of state:** Pres. Ange-Félix Patassé; b Jan. 25, 1937; in office: Oct. 22, 1993. **Head of government:** Prime Min. Michel Gbezera-Bria; b 1946; in office: Jan. 30, 1997. **Local divisions:** 16 prefectures and 1 commune. **Defense:** 2.3% of GDP (1994). **Active troop strength:** 4,950.

Economy: Industries: Textiles, breweries, sawmills, mining. **Chief crops:** Cotton, coffee, corn, cassava, yams. **Minerals:** Diamonds (chief export), uranium. **Other resources:** Timber. **Arable land:** 3%. **Livestock** (1996): cattle: 2.8 mil; goats: 1.35 mil. **Electricity prod.** (1995): 100 mil kWh. **Labor force:** 80% agric.

Finance: Monetary unit: CFA Franc (Aug. 1997: 610 = $1 US). **Gross domestic product** (1995 est.): $2.5 bil. **Per capita GDP:** $800. **Imports** (1994 est.): $215 mil; partners: France 12%.; Cameroon 4%. **Exports** (1994 est.): $154 mil; partners: Belg.-Lux. 61%. **National budget** (1991 est.): $312 mil. **International reserves less gold** (Nov. 1996): $236.34 mil. **Gold:** 11,000 oz t.

Transport: Motor vehicles in use: 9,500 passenger cars, 7,000 comm. vehicles. **Civil aviation:** 141.0 mil passenger-mi. **Chief port:** Bangui.

Communications: Television sets: 1 per 204 persons. **Radios:** 1 per 14 persons. **Telephones:** 1 per 428 persons.

Health: Life expectancy at birth (1997): 44.4 male; 46.1 female. **Births** (per 1,000 pop.): 40. **Deaths** (per 1,000 pop.): 18. **Natural increase:** 2.2%. **Hospital beds:** 1 per 672 persons. **Physicians:** 1 per 18,660 persons. **Infant mortality** (per 1,000 live births 1997): 110.

Education: Compulsory: ages 6-14. **Literacy** (1995 est.): 60%.

Major International Organizations: UN (WTO, IMF, FAO, World Bank, WHO), OAU.

Embassy: 1618 22d St. NW 20008; 483-7800.

Various Bantu tribes migrated through the region for centuries before French control was asserted in the late 19th century, when the region was named Ubangi-Shari. Complete independence was attained Aug. 13, 1960.

All political parties were dissolved in 1960, and the country became a center for Chinese political influence in Africa. Relations with China were severed after 1965. Pres. Jean-Bedel Bokassa, who seized power in a 1965 military coup, proclaimed himself constitutional emperor of the renamed Central African Empire Dec. 1976.

Bokassa's rule was characterized by ruthless and cruel authoritarianism and human rights violations. He was ousted in a bloodless coup aided by the French government, Sept. 20, 1979. In 1981, Gen. André Kolingba became head of state in another bloodless coup. Multiparty legislative and presidential elections were held in Oct. 1992 but were canceled by the government when Kolingba was losing. New elections were ultimately held in Aug. and Sept. 1993, leading to the installation of a civilian government. French troops intervened to suppress an army mutiny in May 1996. A month later, a 21-member government of national unity was formed. Another mutiny ended Jan. 25, 1997, after French intervention.

Chad
Republic of Chad
République du Tchad

People: Population: 7,166,023. **Age distrib.** (%): <15: 44; 65+: 3. **Pop. density:** 14 per sq. mi. **Urban:** 23%. **Ethnic groups:** 200 distinct groups. **Principal languages:** French, Arabic (both official), Sara, Sango, more than 100 other languages. **Chief religions:** Muslim 50%, Christian 25%, indigenous beliefs 25%.

Geography: Area: 495,755 sq. mi. **Location:** In central N Africa. **Neighbors:** Libya on N; Niger, Nigeria, Cameroon on W; Central African Republic on S; Sudan on E. **Topography:** Wooded savanna, steppe, and desert in the S; part of the Sahara in the N. Southern rivers flow N to Lake Chad, surrounded by marshland. **Capital:** N'Djamena 826,000*.

Government: Type: Republic. **Head of state:** Pres. Idriss Déby; in office: Dec. 4, 1990. **Head of government:** Prime Min. Nassour Guelengdoussia Ouaido; in office: May 17, 1997. **Local divisions:** 14 prefectures. **Defense:** 11.1% of GDP (1994). **Active troop strength:** 30,350 est.

Economy: Chief crops: Cotton, sorghum, millet. **Minerals:** Uranium. **Arable land:** 2%. **Livestock** (1996): cattle: 4.5 mil; goats: 3.3 mil; sheep: 2.2 mil. **Fish catch** (1993): 80,000 metric tons. **Electricity prod.** (1995): 80 mil kWh. **Labor force:** 85% agric.

Finance: Monetary unit: CFA Franc (Aug. 1997: 610 = $1 US). **Gross domestic product** (1995 est.): $3.3 bil. **Per capita GDP:** $600. **Imports** (1993): $201 mil; partners: U.S., France. **Exports** (1993): $132 mil; partners: France, Nigeria. **National budget** (1992 est.): $363 mil. **International reserves less gold** (Nov. 1996): $164.7 mil. **Gold:** 11,000 oz t.

Transport: Motor vehicles in use: 9,000 passenger cars, 12,000 comm. vehicles. **Civil aviation:** 137.9 mil passenger-mi.

Communications: Television sets: 1 per 714 persons. **Radios:** 1 per 4.1 persons. **Telephones:** 1 per 1,209 persons.

Health: Life expectancy at birth (1997): 45.5 male; 50.4 female. **Births** (per 1,000 pop.): 44. **Deaths** (per 1,000 pop.): 17. **Natural increase:** 2.7%. **Infant mortality** (per 1,000 live births 1997): 119.

Education: Compulsory: ages 6-14. **Literacy** (1995 est.): 48%.

Major International Organizations: UN (FAO, IMF, WTO, World Bank, WHO), OAU.

Embassy: 2002 R St. NW 20009; 462-4009.

Chad was the site of paleolithic and neolithic cultures before the Sahara Desert formed. A succession of kingdoms and Arab slave traders dominated Chad until France took control around 1900. Independence came Aug. 11, 1960.

Northern Muslim rebels have fought animist and Christian southern government and French troops from 1966, despite numerous cease-fires and peace pacts.

Libyan troops entered the country at the request of a pro-Libyan Chad government, Dec. 1980. The troops were withdrawn from Chad in Nov. 1981. Rebel forces, led by Hissène Habré, captured the capital and forced Pres. Goukouni Oueddei to flee the country in June 1982.

In 1983, France sent some 3,000 troops to Chad to assist Pres. Habré in opposing Libyan-backed rebels. France and

Libya agreed to a simultaneous withdrawal of troops from Chad in Sept. 1984, but Libyan forces remained in the north until Mar. 1987, when Chad forces drove them from their last major stronghold. In Dec. 1990, Habré was overthrown by a Libyan-supported insurgent group, the Patriotic Salvation Movement.

On Feb. 3, 1994, the World Court dismissed a long-standing territorial claim by Libya to the mineral-rich Aozou Strip, on the Libyan border. Libyan troops reportedly withdrew at the end of May. Following approval of a new constitution in March 1996, Chad's first multiparty presidential election was held in June and July.

Chile
Republic of Chile
República de Chile

People: Population: 14,508,168. **Age distrib.** (%): <15: 28; 65+: 7. **Pop. density:** 50 per sq. mi. **Urban:** 84%. **Ethnic groups:** European and European-Indian 95%, Indian 3%. **Principal language:** Spanish (official). **Chief religions:** Roman Catholic 89%, Protestant 11%.

Geography: Area: 292,135 sq. mi. **Location:** Occupies western coast of S South America. **Neighbors:** Peru on N, Bolivia on NE, Argentina on E. **Topography:** Andes Mts. are on E border including some of the world's highest peaks; on W is 2,650-mile Pacific coast. Width varies between 100 and 250 miles. In N is Atacama Desert, in center are agricultural regions, in S are forests and grazing lands. **Capital:** Santiago 4,891,000*.

Government: Type: Republic. **Head of state:** Pres. Eduardo Frei Ruiz-Tagle; b June 24, 1942; in office: Mar. 11, 1994. **Local divisions:** 13 regions. **Defense:** 2.0% of GDP (1994 est.). **Active troop strength:** 89,700 est.

Economy: Industries: Fish processing, wood products, iron, steel. **Chief crops:** Grain, grapes, beans, potatoes, sugar beets, fruits. **Minerals:** Copper (world's largest exporter and producer), molybdenum, nitrates, iodine, iron, coal, oil, gas, gold, manganese, salt, sulfur. **Crude oil reserves** (1996): 300 mil bbls. **Other resources:** Timber. **Arable land:** 7%. **Livestock** (1996): sheep: 4.3 mil; cattle: 3.9 mil; pigs: 1.5 mil. **Fish catch** (1995): 7.58 mil metric tons. **Electricity prod.** (1995): 24.5 bil kWh. **Labor force:** 38% serv.; 34% ind. & commerce; 19% agric., forestry, fishing.

Finance: Monetary unit: Peso (Aug. 1997: 413 = $1 US). **Gross domestic product** (1995 est.): $113.2 bil. **Per capita GDP:** $8,000. **Imports** (1995 est.): $14.3 bil; partners: U.S. 25%, EU 18%. **Exports** (1995 est.): $15.9 bil; partners: Asia 34%, EU 25%, U.S. 15%. **Tourism** (1994): $833 mil. **National budget** (1996 est.): $17 bil. **International reserves less gold** (May 1997): $16.51 bil. **Gold:** 1.86 mil oz. t. **Consumer prices** (change in 1996): 7.4%.

Transport: Railroad: Length: 4,211.6 mi. **Motor vehicles in use:** 889,000 passenger cars, 469,000 comm. vehicles. **Civil aviation:** 3.4 bil passenger-mi.; 18 airports with scheduled flights. **Chief ports:** Valparaiso, Arica, Antofagasta.

Communications: Television sets: 1 per 4.7 persons. **Radios:** 1 per 2.9 persons. **Telephones:** 1 per 7.6 persons. **Daily newspaper circ.:** 100 per 1,000 pop.

Health: Life expectancy at birth (1997): 71.5 male; 78.0 female. **Births** (per 1,000 pop.): 18. **Deaths** (per 1,000 pop.): 6. **Natural increase:** 1.2%. **Hospital beds:** 1 per 326 persons. **Physicians:** 1 per 875 persons. **Infant mortality** (per 1,000 live births 1997): 13.

Education: Free and compulsory, from age 6 or 7, for 8 years. **Literacy** (1995 est.): 95%.

Major International Organizations: UN and all of its specialized agencies, OAS, APEC.

Embassy: 1732 Massachusetts Ave. NW 20036; 785-1746.

Northern Chile was under Inca rule before the Spanish conquest, 1536-40. The southern Araucanian Indians resisted until the late 19th century. Independence was gained 1810-18, under José de San Martin and Bernardo O'Higgins; the latter, as supreme director 1817-23, sought social and economic reforms until deposed. Chile defeated Peru and Bolivia in 1836-39 and 1879-84, gaining mineral-rich northern land.

In 1970, Salvador Allende Gossens, a Marxist, became president with a third of the national vote. His government improved conditions for the poor, but illegal and violent actions by extremist supporters of the government, the regime's failure to attain majority support, and poorly planned socialist economic programs led to political and financial chaos.

A military junta seized power Sept. 11, 1973, and said Allende had killed himself. The junta, headed by Gen. Augusto Pinochet Ugarte, named a mostly military cabinet and announced plans to "exterminate Marxism." Repression continued during the 1980s with little sign of any political liberalization.

In a plebiscite held Oct. 5, 1988, voters rejected the incumbent president, Pinochet. He agreed to presidential elections. In Dec. 1989 voters elected a civilian president, although Pinochet continued to head the army. In Mar. 1994 a Chilean human rights group announced a revised estimate of more than 3,100 deaths from human rights violations during Pinochet's rule.

Tierra del Fuego is the largest (18,800 sq. mi.) island in the archipelago of the same name at the southern tip of South America, an area of majestic mountains, tortuous channels, and high winds. It was visited 1520 by Magellan and named the Land of Fire because of its many Indian bonfires. Part of the island is in Chile, part in Argentina. Punta Arenas, on a mainland peninsula, is a center of sheep raising and the world's southernmost city (pop. about 70,000); Puerto Williams is the southernmost settlement.

China
People's Republic of China
Zhonghua Renmin Gonghe Guo

(Statistical data on China do not include Hong Kong.)

People: Population: 1,210,004,956. **Age distrib.** (%): <15: 26; 65+: 6. **Pop. density:** 327 per sq. mi. **Urban:** 29%. **Ethnic groups:** Han Chinese 92%, Tibetan, Mongol, Korean, Manchu, others. **Principal languages:** Mandarin (official), Yue, Wu, Hakka, Xiang, Gan, Minbei, Minnan. **Chief religions:** Officially atheist; Buddhism, Taoism; some Muslims, Christians.

Geography: Area: 3,696,100 sq. mi. **Location:** Occupies most of the habitable mainland of E Asia. **Neighbors:** Mongolia on N; Russia on NE and NW; Afghanistan, Pakistan, Tajikistan, Kazakhstan on W; India, Nepal, Bhutan, Myanmar, Laos, Vietnam on S; North Korea on NE. **Topography:** Two-thirds of the vast territory is mountainous or desert; only one-tenth is cultivated. Rolling topography rises to high elevations in the N in the Daxinganlingshanmai separating Manchuria and Mongolia; the Tien Shan in Xinjiang; the Himalayan and Kunlunshanmai in the SW and in Tibet. Length is 1,860 mi. from N to S, width E to W is more than 2,000 mi. The eastern half of China is one of the world's best-watered lands. Three great river systems, the Chang (Yangtze), Huang (Yellow), and Xi, provide water for vast farmlands. **Capital:** Beijing. **Cities:** Shanghai 13,584,000; Beijing 11,299,000; Tianjin 9,415,000; Shenyang 5,116,000; Guangzhou 4,492,000*.

Government: Type: Communist Party-led state. **Head of state:** Pres. Jiang Zemin; b Aug. 17, 1926; in office: Mar. 27, 1993. **Head of government:** Premier Li Peng; b Oct. 1928; in office: Apr. 9, 1988. **Local divisions:** 23 provinces, 5 autonomous regions, and 3 municipalities, plus (as of July 1, 1997) the special administrative region of Hong Kong. **Defense:** 2.4% of GNP (1994). **Active troop strength:** 2.3 mil est.

Economy: Industries: Iron and steel, textiles and apparel, machine building, armaments. **Chief crops:** Grain, rice, cotton, potatoes, tea. **Minerals:** Tungsten, antimony, coal, oil, mercury, iron, lead, manganese, molybdenum, tin. **Crude oil reserves** (1995): 24 bil barrels. **Other resources:** Silk. **Arable land:** 10%. **Livestock** (1993): cattle: 83 mil; pigs: 394 mil; sheep: 110 mil. **Fish catch** (1995): 24.43 mil metric tons. **Electricity prod.** (1995): 887.4 bil kWh. **Labor force:** 60% agric. & forestry; 25% ind. & commerce.

Finance: Monetary unit: Renminbi (Yuan) (Aug. 1997: 8.28 = $1 US). **Gross domestic product** (1994 est.): $2.61 tril. **Per capita GDP:** $2,500. **Imports** (1994): $115.7 bil; partners: Japan 23%, Taiwan 12%, U.S. 12%. **Exports** (1994): $121 bil; partners: Hong Kong 27%, U.S. 18%, Japan 18%. **Tourism** (1994): $7.3 bil. **National budget** (1994): $13.7 bil deficit. **International reserves less gold** (June 1997): $122.83 bil. **Gold:** 12.7 mil oz t. **Consumer prices** (change in 1996): 8.3%.

Transport: Railroads: Length: 36,265.8 mi. **Motor vehicles:** in use: 2.9 mil passenger cars, 5.0 mil comm. vehicles. **Civil aviation:** 31.9 bil passenger-mi., 113 airports with scheduled flights. **Chief ports:** Shanghai, Qinhuangdao, Dalian, Canton (Guangzhou).

Communications: Television sets: 1 per 5.3 persons. **Radios:** 1 per 5.4 persons. **Telephones:** 1 per 30 persons. **Daily newsppare circ.:** 23 per 1,000 pop.

Health: Life expectancy at birth (1996): 68 male; 71 female. **Births** (per 1,000 pop.): 17. **Deaths** (per 1,000 pop.): 7. **Natural increase:** 1.0%. **Hospital beds:** 1 per 378 persons. **Physicians:** 1 per 630 persons. **Infant mortality** (per 1,000 live births 1996): 40.

Education: Compulsory 7-16. **Literacy** (1993): 82%.

Major International Organizations: UN (IMF, World Bank, FAO, WHO), APEC.

Embassy: 2300 Conn. Ave. NW 20008; 328-2500.

History. Remains of various humanlike creatures who lived as early as several hundred thousand years ago have been found in many parts of China. Neolithic agricultural settlements dotted the Huang (Yellow) R. basin from about 5000 BC. Their language, religion, and art were the sources of later Chinese civilization.

Bronze metallurgy reached a peak and Chinese pictographic writing, similar to today's, was in use in the more developed culture of the Shang Dynasty (c. 1500 BC-c. 1000 BC), which ruled much of North China.

A succession of dynasties and interdynastic warring kingdoms ruled China for the next 3,000 years. They expanded Chinese political and cultural domination to the south and west, and developed a brilliant technologically and a culturally advanced society. Rule by foreigners (Mongols in the Yuan Dynasty, 1271-1368, and Manchus in the Ch'ing Dynasty, 1644-1911) did not alter the underlying culture.

A period of relative stagnation left China vulnerable to internal and external pressures in the 19th century. Rebellions left tens of millions dead, and Russia, Japan, Britain, and other powers exercised political and economic control in large parts of the country. China became a republic Jan. 1, 1912, following the Wuchang Uprising inspired by Dr. Sun Yat-sen, founder of the Kuomintang (Nationalist) party. By 1928, the Kuomintang, led by Chiang Kai-shek, succeeded in nominal reunification of China. About the same time, a bloody purge of Communists from the ranks of the Kuomintang fomented hostilities between the two groups that would continue for decades.

For a period of 50 years, 1894-1945, China was involved in conflicts with Japan. In 1895, China ceded Korea, Taiwan, and other areas. On Sept. 18, 1931, Japan seized the Northeastern Provinces (Manchuria) and set up a puppet state called Manchukuo. The border province of Jehol was cut off as a buffer state in 1933. Japan invaded China proper July 7, 1937. After its defeat in World War II, Japan gave up all seized land.

Following World War II, internal conflicts involving the Kuomintang, Communists, and other factions resumed. China came under domination of Communist armies, 1949-1950. The Kuomintang government moved to Taiwan, 90 mi. off the mainland, Dec. 8, 1949.

The People's Republic of China was proclaimed in Beijing (Peking) Sept. 21, 1949, by the Chinese People's Political Consultative Conference under Mao Zedong. China and the USSR signed a 30-year treaty of "friendship, alliance and mutual assistance," Feb. 15, 1950. The U.S. refused recognition of the new regime. On Nov. 26, 1950, the People's Republic sent armies into Korea against U.S. troops and forced a stalemate in the Korean War.

After an initial period of consolidation, 1949-52, industry, agriculture, and social and economic institutions were forcibly molded according to Maoist ideals. However, frequent drastic changes in policy and violent factionalism interfered with economic development. In 1957, Mao admitted an estimated 800,000 people had been executed 1949-54; opponents claimed much higher figures.

The Great Leap Forward, 1958-60, tried to force the pace of economic development through intensive labor on huge new rural communes, and through emphasis on ideological purity. The program caused resistance and was largely abandoned.

By the 1960s, relations with the USSR deteriorated, with disagreements on borders, ideology, and leadership of world Communism. The USSR canceled aid accords, and China, with Albania, launched anti-Soviet propaganda drives.

The Great Proletarian Cultural Revolution, 1965, was an attempt to oppose pragmatism and bureaucratic power and instruct a new generation in revolutionary principles. Massive purges took place. A program of forcibly relocating millions of urban teenagers into the countryside was launched. By 1968 the movement had run its course; many purged officials returned to office in subsequent years, and reforms that had placed ideology above expertise were gradually weakened.

On Oct. 25, 1971, the UN General Assembly ousted the Taiwan government from the UN and seated the People's Republic in its place. The U.S. had supported the mainland's admission but opposed Taiwan's expulsion.

U.S. Pres. Richard Nixon visited China Feb. 21-28, 1972, on invitation from Premier Zhou Enlai, ending years of antipathy between the 2 nations. China and the U.S. opened liaison offices in each other's capitals, May-June 1973. The U.S., Dec. 15, 1978, formally recognized the People's Republic of China as the sole legal government of China; diplomatic relations between the 2 nations were established, Jan. 1, 1979.

Mao died Sept. 9, 1976. By 1978, Vice Premier Deng Xiaoping had consolidated his power, succeeding Mao as "paramount leader" of China. The new ruling group modified Maoist policies in education, culture, and industry, and sought better ties with non-Communist countries. During this "reassessment" of Mao's policies his widow, Jiang Qing, and other "Gang of Four" leftists were convicted of "committing crimes during the 'Cultural Revolution,'" Jan. 25, 1981.

By the mid-1980s, China had enacted far-reaching economic reforms, deemphasizing centralized planning and incorporating market-oriented incentives. Some 100,000 students and workers staged a march in Beijing to demand political reforms, May 4, 1989. The demonstrations continued during a visit to Beijing by Soviet leader Mikhail Gorbachev May 15-18; it was the first Sino-Soviet summit since 1959. As the unrest spread, martial law was imposed, May 20. Troops entered Beijing, June 3-4, and crushed the pro-democracy protests, as tanks and armored personnel carriers rolled through Tiananmen Square. It is estimated that 5,000 died, 10,000 were injured, and hundreds of students and workers were arrested.

China had one of the world's fastest-growing economies in the 1990s. Although human rights violations have persisted, the U.S. has continued to renew China's most-favored-nation trading status. Deng died Feb. 19, 1997, leaving his chosen successor, Jiang Zemin, firmly in control.

Under an agreement with Great Britain, Hong Kong reverted to Chinese sovereignty on July 1, 1997. Portugal has agreed to return Macau to China in 1999. Although China and Taiwan remain diplomatic rivals, they tightened economic ties in the 1990s.

Manchuria. Home of the Manchus, rulers of China 1644-1911, Manchuria has accommodated millions of Chinese settlers in the 20th century. Under Japanese rule 1931-45, the area became industrialized. The region is divided into the 3 NE provinces of Heilongjiang, Jilin, and Liaoning.

Guangxi is in SE China, bounded on N by Guizhou and Hunan provinces, E and S by Guangdong, on SW by Vietnam, and on W by Yunnan. It produces rice in the river valleys and has valuable forest products.

Inner Mongolia was organized by the People's Republic in 1947. Its boundaries have undergone frequent changes, reaching its greatest extent in 1956 (and restored in 1979), with an area of 454,600 sq. mi., allegedly in order to dilute the minority Mongol population. Chinese settlers outnumber the Mongols more than 10 to 1. Pop. (1995 est.): 22.6 mil. Capital: Hohhot.

Xinjiang, in Central Asia, is 635,900 sq. mi., pop. (1995 est.): 16.3 mil (75% Uygurs, a Turkic Muslim group, with a heavy Chinese increase in recent years). Capital: Urumqi. It is China's richest region in strategic minerals.

Tibet, 471,700 sq. mi., is a thinly populated region of high plateaus and massive mountains, the Himalayas on the S, the Kunluns on the N. High passes connect with India and Nepal; roads lead into China proper. Capital: Lhasa. Average altitude is 15,000 ft. Jiachan, 15,870 ft., is believed to be the highest inhabited town on earth. Agriculture is primitive. Pop. (1995 est.): 2.4 mil (of whom about 500,000 are Chinese). Another 4 million Tibetans form the majority of the population of vast adjacent areas that have long been incorporated into China.

China ruled all of Tibet from the 18th century, but independence came in 1911. China reasserted control in 1951, and a Communist government was installed in 1953, revising the theocratic Lamaist Buddhist rule. Serfdom was abolished, but all land remained collectivized.

A Tibetan uprising within China in 1956 spread to Tibet in 1959. The rebellion was crushed with Chinese troops, and Buddhism was almost totally suppressed. The Dalai Lama and 100,000 Tibetans fled to India.

Hong Kong

Hong Kong (Xianggang), located at the mouth of the Zhu Jiang (Pearl R.) in SE China, 90 mi. S of Canton (Guangzhou), was a British dependency from 1842 until July 1, 1997, when it became a Special Administrative Region of China. Its nucleus is Hong Kong Isl., 31 sq. mi., occupied by the British in 1841 and formally ceded to them in 1842, on which is located the seat of government. Opposite is Kowloon Peninsula, 3 sq. mi., and Stonecutters Isl., added to the territory in 1860. An additional 355 sq. mi. known as the New Territories, a mainland area and islands, were leased from China, 1898, for 99 years. Total area 415 sq. mi.; pop. (1997 est.) 6.4 million, including fewer than 20,000 British.

Hong Kong is a major center for trade and banking. Per capita GDP, $27,500 (1995 est.), is among the highest in the world. Principal industries are textiles and apparel; also tourism ($9.3 bil expenditures in 1995), electronics, shipbuilding, iron and steel, fishing, cement, and small manufactures. Hong Kong's spinning mills are among the best in the world.

Hong Kong harbor was long an important British naval station and one of the world's great transshipment ports. The colony was often a place of refuge for exiles from mainland China. It was occupied by Japan during World War II.

From 1949 to 1962 Hong Kong absorbed more than a million refugees fleeing communist China. Starting in the 1950s, cheap labor led to a boom in light manufacturing, while liberal tax policies attracted foreign investment; Hong Kong became one of the wealthiest and most productive areas in the Far East. Poor living and working conditions and low wages for many led to political unrest in the 1960s, but labor legislation and public works programs raised the standard of living by the 1970s.

With the end of the 99-year lease on the New Territories drawing near, Britain and China signed an agreement, Dec. 19, 1984, under which all of Hong Kong was to be returned to China in 1997; under this agreement Hong Kong was to be allowed to keep its capitalist system for 50 years. In Dec. 1996, an electoral college appointed by China chose a shipping magnate, Tung Chee-hwa, to be Hong Kong's chief executive when it reverted to Chinese control.

The July 1 transfer of government was marked by an elaborate ceremony. In the immediate wake of the changeover, Hong Kong retained its street names and its currency, the Hong Kong dollar (but without the queen's picture). Official languages remained Chinese (Cantonese dialect) and English. The Legislative Council was disbanded, and an appointed Provisional Legislature installed in its place. The new legislature imposed limits on opposition activities and approved a plan for 1998 legislative elections that sharply cut back the number of people eligible to vote.

Colombia
Republic of Colombia
República de Colombia

People: Population: 37,418,290. **Age distrib.** (%): <15: 31; 65+: 5. **Pop. density:** 85 per sq. mi. **Urban:** 73%. **Ethnic groups:** Mestizo 58%, white 20%, mulatto 14%, black 4%. **Principal language:** Spanish (official). **Chief religions:** Roman Catholic 95%.

Geography: Area: 440,762 sq. mi. **Location:** At the NW corner of South America. **Neighbors:** Panama on NW, Ecuador and Peru on S, Brazil and Venezuela on E. **Topography:** Three ranges of Andes—the Western, Central, and Eastern Cordilleras—run through the country from N to S. The eastern range consists mostly of high tablelands, densely populated. The Magdalena R. rises in Andes, flows N to Caribbean, through a rich alluvial plain. Sparsely settled plains in E are drained by Orinoco and Amazon systems. **Capital:** Bogotá. **Cities:** Bogotá 6,079,000; Medellín 3,291,000; Cali 1,870,000*.

Government: Type: Republic. **Head of state:** Pres. Ernesto Samper Pizano; b Aug. 3, 1950; in office: Aug. 7, 1994. **Local divisions:** 32 departments, capital district of Bogota. **Defense:** 2.8% of GDP (1995). **Active troop strength:** 146,300.

Economy: Industries: Textiles, food processing, metal products, cement, chemicals. **Chief crops:** Coffee (24% of exports), rice, bananas, oilseeds, corn, cotton, sugar, tobacco, coca. **Minerals:** Oil, gas, emeralds, gold, copper, coal, iron, nickel, salt. **Crude oil reserves** (1996): 2.8 bil bbls. **Other resources:** Forest products, cut flowers, hydropower. **Arable land:** 4%. **Livestock** (1996): cattle: 26.1 mil; pigs: 2.6 mil; sheep: 2.5 mil. **Fish catch** (1993): 146,407 metric tons. **Electricity prod.** (1995): 47 bil kWh. **Labor force:** 46% services; 30% agric.; 24% ind.

Finance: Monetary unit: Peso (Aug. 1997: 1,168 = $1 US). **Gross domestic product** (1995 est.): $192.5 bil. **Per capita GDP:** $5,300. **Imports** (1995 est.): $13.5 bil; partners: U.S. 36%, EU 18%. **Exports** (1995 est.): $10.5 bil; partners: U.S. 39%, EU 26%. **Tourism** (1994): $794 mil. **National budget** (1996 est.): $25 bil. **International reserves less gold** (June 1997): $9.94 bil. **Gold:** 354,000 oz t. **Consumer prices** (change in 1996): 20.2%.

Transport: Railroad: Length: 2,102.7 mi. **Motor vehicles in use:** 1.15 mil passenger cars, 550,000 comm. vehicles. **Civil aviation:** 3.5 bil passenger-mi.; 63 airports with scheduled flights. **Chief ports:** Buenaventura, Santa Marta, Barranquilla, Cartagena.

Communications: Television sets: 1 per 8.5 persons. **Radios:** 1 per 5.6 person. **Telephones:** 1 per 10 persons. **Daily newspaper circ.:** 64 per 1,000 pop.

Health: Life expectancy at birth (1997): 70.3 male; 76.1 female. **Births** (per 1,000 pop.): 21. **Deaths** (per 1,000 pop.): 5. **Natural increase:** 1.6%. **Hospital beds:** 1 per 693 persons. **Physicians:** 1 per 1,078 persons. **Infant mortality** (per 1,000 live births 1997): 25.

Education: Free and compulsory for 5 years between ages 6-12. **Literacy** (1995 est.): 91%.

Major International Organizations: UN (World Bank, FAO, IMF, WHO, WTO), OAS.

Embassy: 2118 Leroy Pl. NW 20008; 387-8338.

Spain subdued the local Indian kingdoms (Funza, Tunja) by the 1530s and ruled Colombia and neighboring areas as New Granada for 300 years. Independence was won by 1819. Venezuela and Ecuador broke away in 1829-30, and Panama withdrew in 1903.

One of the Latin American democracies, Colombia is plagued by rural and urban violence, though scaled down from "La Violencia" of 1948-58, which claimed 200,000 lives. Attempts at land and social reform and progress in industrialization have not succeeded in reducing massive social problems.

The government's increased activity against local drug traffickers sparked a series of retaliation killings. On Aug. 18, 1989, Luis Carlos Galán, the ruling party's presidential hopeful for the 1990 election, was assassinated. In 1990, 2 other presidential candidates were assassinated, as drug traffickers carried on a campaign of intimidation. Pablo Escobar, head of the Medellín drug cartel, escaped from prison in July 1992, allegedly with aid from military and prison officials. He was killed by government troops Dec. 1, 1993. Charges that Ernesto Samper Pizano's 1994 campaign received money from the Cali drug cartel engulfed his administration in scandal, although the legislature voted, June 12, 1996, not to impeach him.

Comoros
Federal Islamic Republic of the Comoros
Jumhuriyat al Qumur al Itthadiyah al Islamiyah

People: Population: 589,797. **Age. distrib.** (%): <15: 48; 65+: 3. **Pop. density:** 820 per sq. mi. **Urban:** 31%. **Ethnic groups:** Arab, African, Malay, Malagasy. **Principal languages:** Arabic, French, Comoran (all official). **Chief religions:** Sunni Muslim 86%, Roman Catholic 14%.

Geography: Area: 719 sq. mi. **Location:** 3 islands—Grande Comore (Njazidja), Anjouan (Nzwani), and Moheli (Mwali)—in the Mozambique Channel between NW Madagascar and SE Africa. **Neighbors:** Nearest are Mozambique on W, Madagascar on E. **Topography:** The islands are of volcanic origin, with an active volcano on Grande Comore. **Capital:** Moroni (1992 met. est.): 30,000.

Government: Type: In transition. **Head of state:** Pres. Mohamed Taki Abdul-Karim; in office: Mar. 1996. **Local divisions:** Each of the 3 main islands is a prefecture.

Economy: Industries: Perfume, textiles. **Chief crops:** Vanilla, copra, perfume plants, fruits. **Arable land:** 35%. **Electricity prod.** (1995): 17 mil kWh. **Labor force:** 80% agric.

Finance: Monetary unit: Franc (Aug. 1997: 452.61 = $1 US). **Gross domestic product** (1994 est.): $370 mil. **Per capita GDP:** $700. **Imports** (1993 est.): $40.9 mil; partners: France 34%. **Exports** (1993 est.): $13.7 mil; partners: U.S. 44%, France 40%. **National budget** (1992): $92 mil.

Transport: Civil aviation: 1.9 mil passenger-mi. **Chief ports:** Fomboni, Moroni, Mutsamudu.

Communications: Radios: 1 per 7.8 persons. **Telephones:** 1 per 111 persons.

Health: Life expectancy at birth (1997): 56.8 male; 61.5 female. **Births** (per 1,000 pop.): 45. **Deaths** (per 1,000 pop.): 10. **Natural increase:** 3.5%. **Infant mortality** (per 1,000 live births 1997): 73.

Education: Compulsory: ages 7-16. **Literacy** (1995 est.): 57%.

Major International Organizations: UN (IMF, FAO, WHO, World Bank), OAU, Arab League.

Embassy: 336 E. 45th St., 2d Fl., New York, NY 10017; (212) 972-8010.

The islands were controlled by Muslim sultans until the French acquired them 1841-1909. They became a French overseas territory in 1947. A 1974 referendum favored independence, with only the Christian island of Mayotte preferring association with France. The French National Assembly decided to allow each of the islands to decide its own fate. The Comore Chamber of Deputies declared independence July 6, 1975, with Ahmed Abdallah as president. In a referendum in 1976, Mayotte voted to remain French.

A leftist regime that seized power from Abdallah in 1975 was deposed in a pro-French 1978 coup in which he regained the presidency. In Nov. 1989, Pres. Abdallah was assassinated; soon after, a multiparty system was instituted. A Sept. 1995 military coup, assisted by French mercenaries, ousted Pres. Said Mohamed Djohar. French troops invaded, Oct. 4, and forced the surrender of coup leaders. Djohar returned from exile in Jan. 1996, and in Mar. a new presidential election was held. A hijacked Ethiopian Airlines Boeing 767 crashed offshore on Nov. 23, killing 123 of the 175 people on board. Seeking a resumption of ties with France, Anjouan seceded from the Comoros, Aug. 3, 1997. Comorian troops were unable to put down the rebellion, which was joined by Moheli.

Congo (*formerly* Zaire)

Democratic Republic of the Congo
République Democratique du Congo

(Congo, officially Democratic Republic of the Congo, is also known as Congo-Kinshasa. It should not be confused with Republic of the Congo, commonly called Congo Republic, and also known as Congo-Brazzaville.)

People: Population: 47,440,362. **Age distrib.** (%): <15: 48; 65+: 3. **Pop. density:** 52 per sq. mi. **Urban:** 29%. **Ethnic groups:** More than 200 tribes, mostly Bantu. **Principal languages:** French (official), more than 400 dialects. **Chief religions:** Christian 70%, Muslim 10%, Kimbanguist 10%.

Geography: Area: 905,354 sq. mi. **Location:** In central Africa. **Neighbors:** Congo-Brazzaville on W; Central African Republic, Sudan on N; Uganda, Rwanda, Burundi, Tanzania on E; Zambia, Angola on S. **Topography:** Congo includes the bulk of the Congo R. basin. The vast central region is a low-lying plateau covered by rain forest. Mountainous terraces in the W, savannas in the S and SE, grasslands toward the N, and the high Ruwenzori Mts. on the E surround the central region. A short strip of territory borders the Atlantic O. The Congo R. is 2,718 mi. long. **Capital:** Kinshasa. **Cities:** Kinshasa 4,241,000; Lubumbashi 810,000*.

Government: Type: Republic with strong presidential authority (in transition). **Head of state:** Pres. Laurent Kabila; b 1940; in office: May 29, 1997. **Local divisions:** 10 regions, Kinshasa. **Defense:** 1.5% of GDP (1990). **Active troop strength:** 49,100.

Economy: Industries: Mining, consumer prods., food processing. **Chief crops:** Sugar, rice, corn, bananas, plantains, cassava. **Minerals:** Cobalt (65% of world reserves), copper, cadmium, oil, diamonds, gold, silver, tin, germanium, zinc, iron, manganese, uranium, radium. **Crude oil reserves** (1996): 187 mil bbls. **Other resources:** Forests. **Arable land:** 3%. **Livestock** (1996): goats: 4.2 mil; cattle: 1.5 mil; pigs: 1.2 mil; sheep: 1.05 mil. **Fish catch** (1993): 147,250 metric tons. **Electricity prod.** (1995): 438 mil kWh. **Labor force:** 65% agric.; 19% services; 16% industry.

Finance: Monetary unit: Congolese franc (announced May 1997: 2.50 = $1). **Gross domestic product** (1995 est.): $16.5 bil. **Per capita GDP:** $400. **Imports** (1995): $870 mil; partners: Belg.-Lux. 15%, U.S. 7%. **Exports** (1995): $1.45 bil; partners: Belg.-Lux. 36%, U.S. 17%. **National budget** (1996 est.): $479 mil. **International reserves less gold** (Dec. 1996): $82.5 mil Consumer prices (change in 1996): 659%.

Transport: Railroads: Length: 3,190.7 mi. **Motor vehicles in use:** 300,000 passenger cars, 180,000 comm. vehicles. **Civil aviation:** 298.1 mil passenger-mi.; 12 airports with scheduled flights. **Chief ports:** Matadi, Boma, Kinshasa.

Communications: Television sets: 1 per 667 persons. **Radios:** 1 per 10 persons. **Telephones:** 1 per 1,219 persons. **Daily newspaper circ.:** 3 per 1,000 pop.

Health: Life expectancy at birth (1997): 45.2 male; 49.0 female. **Births** (per 1,000 pop.): 48. **Deaths** (per 1,000 pop.): 17. **Natural increase:** 3.1%. **Physicians:** 1 per 15,584 persons. **Infant mortality** (per 1,000 live births 1997): 106.

Education: Compulsory: ages 6-12. **Literacy** (1995): 77%.

Major International Organizations: UN and most of its specialized agencies, OAU.

Embassy: 1800 New Hampshire Ave. NW 20009; 234-7690.

The earliest inhabitants of Congo may have been the pygmies, followed by Bantus from the E and Nilotic tribes from the N. The large Bantu Bakongo kingdom ruled much of Congo and Angola when Portuguese explorers visited in the 15th century.

Leopold II, king of the Belgians, formed an international group to exploit the Congo region in 1876. In 1877 Henry M. Stanley explored the Congo, and in 1878 the king's group sent him back to organize the region and win over the native chiefs. The Conference of Berlin, 1884-85, organized the Congo Free State with Leopold as king and chief owner. Exploitation of native laborers on the rubber plantations caused international criticism and led to granting of a colonial charter, 1908; the colony became known as the Belgian Congo.

Belgian and Congolese leaders agreed Jan. 27, 1960, that the Congo would become independent in June. In the first general elections, May 31, the National Congolese movement of Patrice Lumumba won 35 of 137 seats in the National Assembly. He was appointed premier June 21, and formed a coalition cabinet. The Republic of the Congo was proclaimed on June 30.

Widespread violence caused Europeans and others to flee. The UN Security Council, Aug. 9, 1960, called on Belgium to withdraw its troops and sent a UN contingent. Pres. Joseph Kasavubu removed Lumumba as premier in Sept.; Lumumba was murdered in Feb. 1961.

The last UN troops left the Congo June 30, 1964, and Moise Tshombe became president.

On Sept. 7, 1964, leftist rebels set up a "People's Republic" in Stanleyville (now Kisangani). Tshombe hired foreign mercenaries and sought to rebuild the Congolese Army. In Nov. and Dec. 1964 rebels killed scores of white hostages and thousands of Congolese; Belgian paratroopers, dropped from U.S. transport planes, rescued hundreds. By July 1965 the rebels had lost their effectiveness.

In late 1965 Gen. Joseph D. Mobutu was named president. He later changed his name to Mobutu Sese Seko. In 1966 the country became the Democratic Republic of the Congo. The country was renamed the Republic of Zaire on Oct. 27, 1971.

Economic decline and government corruption plagued Zaire in the 1980s and worsened in the 1990s. In 1990, Pres. Mobutu announced an end to a 20-year ban on multiparty politics. He sought to retain power despite mounting international pressure and internal opposition.

During 1994, Zaire was inundated with refugees from the massive ethnic bloodshed in Rwanda. Ethnic violence spread to E Zaire in 1996. In Oct. militant Hutus, who dominated in the refugee camps, fought against rebels (mostly Tutsis) in Zaire, precipitating intervention by Zairean government troops. As a result of the fighting, Rwandan refugees abandoned the camps; hundreds of thousands returned to Rwanda, while hundreds of thousands more were dispersed throughout E Zaire. The rebels, led by Gen. Laurent Kabila—a former Marxist and longtime opponent of Mobutu—gained momentum and began to move W across Zaire. As turmoil engulfed his nation, Mobutu stayed in W Europe for most of the last 4 months of 1996, receiving treatment for prostate cancer.

With Mobutu out of the country, the poorly equipped, underpaid, and unmotivated Zairean army put up little resistance to the rebel charge. (The rebels were aided by several of Mobutu's enemies, including Rwanda, Uganda, and Angola.) Mobutu returned again to Zaire in March 1997, but attempts to negotiate with Kabila were ineffectual. On May 17, Kabila's troops entered Kinshasa and Mobutu went into exile. The country again assumed the name Democratic Republic of the Congo. Amid reports of rebel atrocities, UN aid workers feared for the safety of the Rwandan Hutus who remained in Congo. Mobutu died Sept. 7 in Rabat, Morocco.

Congo Republic

Republic of the Congo
République du Congo

(Congo Republic, officially Republic of the Congo, is also known as Congo and Congo-Brazzaville. It should not be confused with Democratic Republic of the Congo [formerly Zaire], now commonly called Congo, and also known as Congo-Kinshasa.)

People: Population: 2,583,198. **Age distrib.** (%): <15: 43; 65+: 3. **Pop. density:** 20 per sq. mi. **Urban:** 59%. **Ethnic groups:** Kongo 48%, Sangha 20%, Teke 17%, M'Bochi 12%. **Principal languages:** French (official); Lingala, Kikongo, other African languages. **Chief religions:** Christian 50% (mostly Roman Catholic), indigenous beliefs 48%, Muslim 2%.

Geography: Area: 132,047 sq. mi. **Location:** In W central Africa. **Neighbors:** Gabon and Cameroon on W, Central African Republic on N, Congo-Kinshasa (formerly Zaire) on E, Angola on SW. **Topography:** Much of the Congo is covered by thick forests. A coastal plain leads to the fertile Niari Valley. The center is a plateau; the Congo R. basin consists of flood plains in the lower and savanna in the upper portion. **Capital:** Brazzaville. **Cities:** Brazzaville 1,004,000*.

Government: Type: Republic. **Head of state:** Pres. Pascal Lissouba; b Nov. 15, 1931; in office: Aug. 20, 1992. **Head of government:** Prime Min. Bernard Kolelas; in office: Sept. 8, 1997. **Local divisions:** 9 regions and 1 commune. **Defense:** 3.8% of GDP (1993). **Active troop strength:** 10,000 est.

Economy: Industries: Oil, wood products, brewing. **Chief crops:** Cassava, palm kernels, sugar, cocoa, coffee. **Minerals:** Oil, potash, lead, copper, zinc. **Crude oil reserves** (1996): 1.5 bil bbls. **Arable land:** 2%. **Fish catch** (1995): 35,024 metric tons. **Electricity prod.** (1993): 400 mil kWh. **Labor force:** 75% agric., 25% comm., ind., govt.

Finance: Monetary unit: CFA Franc (Aug. 1997: 610 = $1 US). **Gross domestic product** (1995 est.): $7.7 bil. **Per capita GDP:** $3,100. **Imports** (1995): $600 mil; partners: France 32%. **Exports** (1995): $1 bil; partners: U.S. 23%, Italy 15%. **Tourism** (1994): $3 mil. **National budget** (1990): $952 mil. **In-**

ternational reserves less gold (Nov. 1996): $121.99 mil. Gold: 11,000 oz t.
Transport: Railroads: Length: 493.7 mi. **Motor vehicles in use:** 29,000 passenger cars, 17,000 comm. vehicles. **Civil aviation:** 163.9 mil passenger-mi. **Chief ports:** Pointe-Noire, Brazzaville.
Communications: Television sets: 1 per 143 persons. **Radios:** 1 per 8.7 persons. **Telephones:** 1 per 124 persons.
Health: Life expectancy at birth (1997): 44.2 male; 47.3 female. **Births** (per 1,000 pop.): 39. **Deaths** (per 1,000 pop.): 17. **Natural increase:** 2.1%. **Infant mortality** (per 1,000 live births 1997): 106.
Education: Compulsory: ages 6-16. **Literacy** (1995 est.): 75%.
Major International Organizations: UN (FAO, IMF, WTO, World Bank, WHO), OAU.
Embassy: 4891 Colorado Ave. NW 20011; 726-0825.

The Loango Kingdom flourished in the 15th century, as did the Anzico Kingdom of the Batekes; by the late 17th century they had become weakened. By 1885, France established control of the region, then called the Middle Congo. Republic of the Congo gained independence Aug. 15, 1960.

After a 1963 coup sparked by trade unions, the country adopted a Marxist-Leninist stance, with the USSR and China vying for influence. France remained a dominant trade partner and source of technical assistance, however, and French-owned private enterprise retained a major economic role. In 1970, the country was renamed People's Republic of the Congo.

In 1990, Marxism was renounced and opposition parties legalized. In 1991 the country's name was changed back to Republic of the Congo, and a new constitution was approved. A democratically elected government came into office in 1992; one of its key problems was a resurgence of ethnic and regional hostilities. Factional fighting broke out in Brazzaville, June 5, 1997, and intensified during the summer, devastating the capital and forcing international aid workers to flee.

Costa Rica
Republic of Costa Rica
República de Costa Rica

People: Population: 3,534,174. **Age distrib.** (%): <15: 34; 65+: 5. **Pop. density:** 179 per sq. mi. **Urban:** 50%. **Ethnic groups:** White and mestizo 96%. **Principal language:** Spanish (official). **Chief religions:** Roman Catholic 95%.
Geography: Area: 19,730 sq. mi. **Location:** In Central America. **Neighbors:** Nicaragua on N, Panama on S. **Topography:** Lowlands by the Caribbean are tropical. The interior plateau, with an altitude of about 4,000 ft., is temperate. **Capital:** San José: 920,000*.
Government: Type: Republic. **Head of state:** Pres. José María Figueres; b Dec. 24, 1954; in office: May 8, 1994. **Local divisions:** 7 provinces. **Defense:** 2.0% of GDP (1995). **Active troop strength:** 7,000.
Economy: Industries: Food processing, textiles, construction materials, fertilizer, plastics. **Chief crops:** Coffee (chief export), bananas, sugar, rice, potatoes. **Minerals:** Gold, limestone. **Other resources:** Fish, forests. **Arable land:** 6%. **Livestock** (1996): cattle: 1.6 mil. **Fish catch** (1992): 18,096 metric tons. **Electricity prod.** (1995): 4.5 bil kWh. **Labor force:** 23% serv. & govt.; 21% agric.
Finance: Monetary unit: Colon (Aug. 1997: 235.55 = $1 US). **Gross domestic product** (1995 est.): $18.4 bil. **Per capita GDP:** $5,400. **Imports** (1995 est.): $3 bil; partners: U.S. 43%, Japan 8%. **Exports** (1995 est.): $2.4 bil; partners: U.S. 42%, Germany 9%. **Tourism** (1994): $626 mil. **National budget** (1991 est.): $1.34 bil. **International reserves less gold** (June 1997): $1.14 bil. **Gold:** 2,000 oz t. **Consumer prices** (change in 1996): 17.5%.
Transport: Railroad: Length: 590.0 mi. **Motor vehicles in use:** 57,000 passenger cars, 73,000 comm. vehicles. **Civil aviation:** 1.0 mil passenger-mi.; 14 airports with scheduled flights. **Chief ports:** Limon, Puntarenas, Golfito.
Communications: Television sets: 1 per 7.0 persons. **Radios:** 1 per 3.8 persons. **Telephones:** 1 per 6.1 persons. **Daily newspaper circ.:** 99 per 1,000 pop.
Health: Life expectancy at birth (1997): 73.4 male; 78.4 female. **Births** (per 1,000 pop.): 23. **Deaths** (per 1,000 pop.): 4. **Natural increase:** 1.9%. **Hospital beds:** 1 per 564 persons. **Physicians:** 1 per 870 persons. **Infant mortality** (per 1,000 live births 1997): 13.
Education: Free and compulsory: ages 6-15. **Literacy** (1995 est.): 95%.
Major International Organizations: UN (FAO, WTO, World Bank, ILO, IMF, WHO), OAS.
Embassy: 2114 S St. NW 20008; 234-2945.

Guaymi Indians inhabited the area when Spaniards arrived, 1502. Independence came in 1821. Costa Rica seceded from the Central American Federation in 1838. Since the civil war of 1948-49, there has been little violent social conflict, and free political institutions have been preserved. During 1993 there was an unusual wave of kidnappings and hostage-taking, some of it related to the international cocaine trade.

Costa Rica, though still a largely agricultural country, has achieved a relatively high standard of living, and land ownership is widespread. Tourism is growing rapidly.

Côte d'Ivoire
Republic of Ivory Coast
République de Côte d'Ivoire

People: Population: 14,986,218. **Age distrib.** (%): <15: 47; 65+: 2. **Pop. density:** 120 per sq. mi. **Urban:** 44%. **Ethnic groups:** Baoule 23%, Bete 18%, Senoufou 15%, Malinke 11%, Agni, foreign Africans. **Principal languages:** French (official), Dioula and other native dialects. **Chief religions:** Muslim 60%, indigenous beliefs 25%, Christian 12%.
Geography: Area: 124,503 sq. mi. **Location:** On S coast of W Africa. **Neighbors:** Liberia, Guinea on W; Mali, Burkina Faso on N; Ghana on E. **Topography:** Forests cover the W half of the country, and range from a coastal strip to halfway to the N on the E. A sparse inland plain leads to low mountains in NW. **Capital:** Yamoussoukro (official); Abidjan (de facto). **Cities:** Abidjan 2,793,000*.
Government: Type: Republic. **Head of state:** Henri Konan Bédié; b 1934; in office: Dec. 7, 1993. **Head of government:** Prime Min. Daniel Kablan Duncan; in office: Dec. 1993. **Local divisions:** 50 departments. **Defense:** 1.4% of GDP (1993). **Active troop strength:** 13,900 est.
Economy: Industries: Food processing, vehicles, textiles. **Chief crops:** Coffee, cocoa, rubber, palm kernels. **Minerals:** Oil, diamonds, manganese. **Crude oil reserves** (1996): 100 mil bbls. **Other resources:** Timber. **Arable land:** 9%. **Livestock** (1996): sheep: 1.3 mil; cattle: 1.3 mil; goats: 1.0 mil. **Fish catch** (1993): 70,174 metric tons. **Electricity prod.** (1995): 1.9 bil kWh. **Labor force:** over 85% agric. & forestry.
Finance: Monetary unit: CFA Franc (Aug. 1997: 610 = $1 US). **Gross domestic product** (1995 est.): $21.9 bil. **Per capita GDP:** $1,500. **Imports** (1994 est.): $1.6 bil; partners: France 28%, Nigeria 27%. **Exports** (1994 est.): $2.7 bil; partners: France 16%, Germany 10%. **Tourism** (1994): $43 mil. **National budget** (1993): $3.4 bil. **International reserves less gold** (Mar. 1997): $876.9 mil. **Gold:** 45,000 oz t. **Consumer prices** (change in 1996): 2.5%.
Transport: Railroad: Length: 409.9 mi. **Motor vehicles in use:** 156,000 passenger cars, 91,000 comm. vehicles. **Civil aviation:** 175.1 mil passenger-mi. **Chief ports:** Abidjan, Dabou, San-Pédro.
Communications: Television sets: 1 per 17 persons. **Radios:** 1 per 7.0 persons. **Telephones:** 1 per 123 persons.
Health: Life expectancy at birth (1997): 43.6 male; 46.0 female. **Births** (per 1,000 pop.): 42. **Deaths** (per 1,000 pop.): 17. **Natural increase:** 2.5%. **Hospital beds:** 1 per 1,698 persons. **Physicians:** 1 per 11,745 persons. **Infant mortality** (per 1,000 live births 1997): 100.
Education: Free and compulsory: ages 7-13. **Literacy** (1995 est.): 40%.
Major International Organizations: UN and all of its specialized agencies, OAU.
Embassy: 2424 Massachusetts Ave. NW 20008; 797-0300.

A French protectorate from 1842, Côte d'Ivoire became independent in 1960. It is the most prosperous of all the tropical African nations, as a result of diversification of agriculture for export, close ties to France, and encouragement of foreign investment. About 20% of the population are workers from neighboring countries. Côte d'Ivoire officially changed its name from Ivory Coast in Oct. 1985.

Students and workers protested, Feb. 1990, demanding the ouster of longtime Pres. Félix Houphouët-Boigny and multiparty democracy. Côte d'Ivoire held its first multiparty presidential election Oct. 1990, and Houphouët-Boigny retained his office. He died Dec. 7, 1993. The National Assembly named a successor, Henri Konan Bédié, who was reelected Oct. 22, 1995.

Croatia
Republic of Croatia
Republika Hrvatska

People: Population: 5,026,995. **Age distrib.** (%): <15: 17; 65+: 14. **Pop. density:** 235 per sq. mi. **Urban:** 56%. **Ethnic groups:** Croat 78%, Serb 12%. **Principal language:** Croatian (official) 96%. **Chief religions:** Roman Catholic 76.5%, Orthodox 11%.

Geography: Area: 21,359 sq. mi. **Location:** SE Europe, on the Balkan Peninsula. **Neighbors:** Slovenia, Hungary on N; Bosnia and Herzegovina, Yugoslavia on E. **Topography:** Flat plains in NE; highlands, low mtns. along Adriatic coast. **Capital:** Zagreb: 981,000*.

Government: Type: Parliamentary democracy. **Head of state:** Pres. Franjo Tudjman; b May 14, 1922; in office: May 30, 1990. **Head of government:** Prime Min. Zlatko Matesa; b June 17, 1949; in office: Nov. 4, 1995. **Local divisions:** 21 counties. **Defense:** Active troop strength: 64,700 est.

Economy: Industries: Chemicals, plastics, machine tools, aluminum, steel, paper. **Chief crops:** Olives, wheat, corn, fruits. **Minerals:** Oil, bauxite, iron, coal. **Arable land:** 32%. **Electricity prod.** (1995): 7.2 bil kWh.

Finance: Monetary unit: Kuna (Aug. 1997: 6.30 = $1 US). **Gross domestic product** (1995 est.): $20.1 bil. **Per capita GDP:** $4,300. **Imports** (1994): $5.2 bil. **Exports** (1994): $4.3 bil. **Tourism** (1994): $1.4 bil. **National budget** (1994 est.): $3.7 bil. **International reserves less gold** (June 1997): 2.48 bil. **Consumer prices** (change in 1996): 4.3%.

Transport: Railroad: Length: 1,676.1 mi. **Motor vehicles in use:** 698,000 passenger cars, 54,000 comm. vehicles. **Civil aviation:** 251.5 mil passenger-mi. **Chief ports:** Rijeka, Split, Dubrovnik.

Communications: Television sets: 1 per 2.8 persons. **Radios:** 1 per 3.8 persons. **Telephones:** 1 per 3.7 persons. **Daily newspaper circ.:** 575 per 1,000 pop.

Health: Life expectancy at birth (1997): 69.2 male; 76.9 female. **Births** (per 1,000 pop.): 10. **Deaths** (per 1,000 pop.): 11. **Natural increase:** –0.2%. **Hospital beds:** 1 per 169 persons. **Physicians:** 1 per 524 persons. **Infant mortality** (per 1,000 live births 1997): 10.

Education: Free and compulsory: ages 6-15. **Literacy** (1993): 97%.

Major International Organizations: UN (IMF, ILO, FAO, World Bank, WHO).

Embassy: 2343 Massachusetts Ave. NW 20008; 588-5899.

From the 7th century the area was inhabited by Croats, a south Slavic people. It was formed into a kingdom under Tomislav in 924, and joined with Hungary in 1102. The Croats became westernized and separated from Slavs under Austro-Hungarian influence. The Croats retained autonomy under the Hungarian crown. Slavonia was taken by Turks in the 16th century; the northern part was restored by the Treaty of Karlowitz in 1699. Croatia helped Austria put down the Hungarian revolution 1848-49 and as a result was set up with Slavonia as the separate Austrian crownland of Croatia and Slavonia, which was reunited to Hungary as part of *Ausgleich* in 1867. It united with other Yugoslav areas to proclaim the Kingdom of Serbs, Croats, and Slovenes in 1918. At the reorganization of Yugoslavia in 1929, Croatia and Slavonia became Savska county, which in 1939 was united with Primorje county to form the county of Croatia. A nominally independent state between 1941 and 1945, it became a constituent republic in the 1946 constitution.

On June 25, 1991, Croatia declared independence from Yugoslavia. Fighting began between ethnic Serbs and Croats, with the former gaining control of about 30% of Croatian territory. A cease-fire was declared in Jan. 1992, but new hostilities broke out in 1993. A cease-fire with Serb rebels forming a self-declared republic of Krajina was agreed to Mar. 30, 1994. Croatian government troops recaptured most of the Serb-held territory Aug. 1995. Pres. Franjo Tudjman signed a peace accord with leaders of Bosnia and Serbia in Paris, Dec. 14. Tudjman won reelection June 15, 1997; international monitors called the vote "free but not fair."

Cuba

Republic of Cuba

República de Cuba

People: Population: 10,999,041. **Age distrib.** (%): <15: 22; 65+: 9. **Pop. density:** 257 per sq. mi. **Urban:** 76%. **Ethnic groups:** Mulatto 51%, white 37%, black 11%. **Principal language:** Spanish (official). **Religion:** Roman Catholic 85% prior to Castro.

Geography: Area: 42,804 sq. mi. **Location:** In the Caribbean, westernmost of West Indies. **Neighbors:** Bahamas and U.S. to N, Mexico to W, Jamaica to S, Haiti to E. **Topography:** The coastline is about 2,500 miles. The N coast is steep and rocky, the S coast low and marshy. Low hills and fertile valleys cover more than half the country. Sierra Maestra, in the E, is the highest of 3 mountain ranges. **Capital:** Havana. **Cities** (1994 est.): Havana 2,221,000*.

Government: Type: Communist state. **Head of state:** Pres. Fidel Castro Ruz; b Aug. 13, 1926; in office: Dec. 3, 1976 (formerly prime min. since Feb. 16, 1959). **Local divisions:** 14 provinces, 1 special municipality. **Defense:** 4% of GDP (1995 est.). **Active troop strength:** 100,000 est.

Economy: Industries: Oil, food and tobacco processing, sugar. **Chief crops:** Sugar, tobacco, rice, coffee, fruit. **Minerals:** Cobalt, nickel, iron, copper, manganese, salt. **Crude oil reserves** (1996): 100 mil bbls. **Other resources:** Timber. **Arable land:** 23%. **Livestock** (1996): cattle: 4.6 mil; pigs: 1.7 mil. **Fish catch** (1993): 93,435 metric tons. **Electricity prod.** (1995): 10.1 bil kWh. **Labor force:** 33% ind. & commerce; 30% services & govt.; 20% agric.

Finance: Monetary unit: Cuban Peso (Sept. 1996: 1.00 = $1 US). **Gross domestic product** (1995 est.): $14.7 bil. **Per capita GDP:** $1,300. **Imports** (1995 est.): $2.4 bil; partners: Spain 17%, Mexico 10%. **Exports** (1995 est.): $1.6 bil; partners: Canada 15%, China 15%, Russia 15%. **Tourism** (1994): $850 mil. **National budget** (1994 est.): $12.5 bil.

Transport: Railroads: Length: 2,904.4 mi. **Motor vehicles in use:** 241,000 passenger cars, 208,000 comm. vehicles. **Civil aviation:** 966.3 mil passenger-mi.; 14 airports with scheduled flights. **Chief ports:** Havana, Matanzas, Cienfuegos, Santiago de Cuba.

Communications: Television sets: 1 per 5.8 persons. **Radios:** 1 per 2.9 persons. **Telephones:** 1 per 31 persons. **Daily newspaper circ.:** 120 per 1,000 pop.

Health: Life expectancy at birth (1997): 72.8 male; 77.7 female. **Births** (per 1,000 pop.): 13. **Deaths** (per 1,000 pop.): 7. **Natural increase:** 0.6%. **Hospital beds:** 1 per 134 persons. **Physicians:** 1 per 231 persons. **Infant mortality** (per 1,000 live births 1997): 9.

Education: Free and compulsory: ages 6-11. **Literacy** (1995 est.): 96%.

Major International Organizations: UN (WTO, FAO, WHO).

Some 50,000 Indians lived in Cuba when it was reached by Columbus in 1492. Its name derives from the Indian Cubanacan. Except for British occupation of Havana, 1762-63, Cuba remained Spanish until 1898. A slave-based sugar plantation economy developed from the 18th century, aided by early mechanization of milling. Sugar remains the chief product and chief export despite government attempts to diversify.

A ten-year uprising ended in 1878 with guarantees of rights by Spain, which Spain failed to carry out. A full-scale movement under Jose Marti began Feb. 24, 1895.

The U.S. declared war on Spain in Apr. 1898, after the sinking of the USS *Maine* in Havana harbor, and defeated it in the Spanish-American War. Spain gave up all claims to Cuba. U.S. troops withdrew in 1902, but under 1903 and 1934 agreements, the U.S. leases a site at Guantánamo Bay in the SE as a naval base. U.S. and other foreign investments acquired a dominant role in the economy. In 1952, former Pres. Fulgencio Batista seized control and established a dictatorship, which grew increasingly harsh and corrupt. Fidel Castro assembled a rebel band in 1956; guerrilla fighting intensified in 1958. Batista fled Jan. 1, 1959, and in the resulting political vacuum Castro took power, becoming premier Feb. 16.

The government began a program of sweeping economic and social changes, without restoring promised liberties. Opponents were imprisoned, and some were executed. Some 700,000 Cubans emigrated in the first years after the Castro takeover, mostly to the U.S.

Cattle and tobacco lands were nationalized, while a system of cooperatives was instituted. By 1960 all banks and industrial companies had been nationalized, including over $1 billion worth of U.S.-owned properties, mostly without compensation.

Poor sugar crops resulted in farm collectivization, stringent labor controls, and rationing, despite continued aid from the USSR and other Communist countries. A U.S.-imposed export embargo in 1962 severely damaged the economy.

In 1961, some 1,400 Cubans, trained and backed by the U.S. Central Intelligence Agency, unsuccessfully tried to invade and overthrow the regime. In the fall of 1962, the U.S. learned the USSR had brought nuclear missiles to Cuba. After an Oct. 22 warning from Pres. John F. Kennedy, the missiles were removed.

In 1977, Cuba and the U.S. signed agreements to exchange diplomats, without restoring full ties, and to regulate offshore fishing. In 1978, and again in 1980, the U.S. agreed to accept political prisoners released by Cuba, some of whom were criminals and mental patients. A 1987 agreement provided for 20,000 Cubans to emigrate to the U.S. each year; Cuba agreed to take back some 2,500 jailed in the U.S. since 1980.

In 1975-78, Cuba sent troops to aid one faction in the Angola civil war; the last Cuban troops were withdrawn by May 1991. Cuba's involvement in Central America, Africa, and the Caribbean contributed to poor relations with the U.S.

Cuba's economy, formerly propped up by preferential trading status within the Communist bloc, was severely shaken by its collapse in the late 1980s. Stiffer trading sanctions enacted by the U.S. in 1992 made things worse. Antigovernment demonstrations in Aug. 1994 prompted Castro to loosen emigration restrictions. A new U.S.-Cuba emigration agreement in Sept. ended the exodus of "boat people" after more than 30,000 had left Cuba. In another policy shift, the U.S. announced May 2, 1995, that it would admit 20,000 Cuban refugees held at the Guantánamo base but would forcibly return further boat people to Cuba.

The U.S. imposed additional sanctions after Cuba, Feb. 24, 1996, shot down 2 aircraft operated by an anti-Castro exile group based in Miami. Cuba blamed exile groups for a wave of bombings at Havana tourist hotels during July-Sept. 1997.

Cyprus
Republic of Cyprus
Kypriaki Dimokratia (Greek)
Kibris Çumhuriyeti (Turkish)

(†Figures do not include Turkish-held area—Turkish Republic of Northern Cyprus)

People: Population: 752,808. **Age distrib.** (%): <15: 25; 65+: 10. **Pop. density:** 211 per sq. mi. **Urban:** 55%. **Ethnic groups:** Greeks 78%, Turks 18%. **Principal languages:** Greek, Turkish (both official), English. **Chief religions:** Greek Orthodox 78%, Muslim 18%.

Geography: Area: 3,572 sq. mi. **Location:** In eastern Mediterranean Sea, off Turkish coast. **Neighbors:** Nearest are Turkey on N, Syria and Lebanon on E. **Topography:** Two mountain ranges run E-W, separated by a wide, fertile plain. **Capital:** Nicosia (1994 est.): 186,400†.

Government: Type: Republic. **Head of state:** Pres. Glafcos Clerides; b Apr. 24, 1919; in office: Mar. 1, 1993. **Local divisions:** 6 districts. **Defense:** 5.6% of GDP (1995). **Active troop strength†:** 10,000.

Economy: Industries: Food, beverages, textiles. **Chief crops:** Barley, grapes, vegetables, citrus fruits, potatoes, olives. **Minerals:** Copper, pyrites, asbestos. **Arable land:** 40%. **Electricity prod.** (1995): 2.6 bil. kWh. **Labor force†:** 61.5% serv., 26% ind., 12.5% agric.

Finance: Monetary unit: Pound (Aug. 1997: 0.53 = $2.13 US). **Gross domestic product†** (1995 est.): $7.8 bil. **Per capita GDP†:** $13,000. **Imports†** (1994): $2.7 bil; partners: UK 12%, Italy 10%, Japan 9%. **Exports†** (1994): $968 mil; partners: UK 16%, Russia 12%, Lebanon 9%. **Tourism†** (1994): $1.7 bil. **National budget†** (1996 est.): $3.4 bil. **International reserves less gold** (May 1997): $1.25 bil. **Gold:** 461,000 oz t. **Consumer prices** (change in 1996): 3.0%.

Transport: Motor vehicles†: in use: 220,000 passenger cars, 104,000 comm. vehicles. **Civil aviation†:** 1.7 bil passenger-mi.; 2 airports. **Chief ports:** Famagusta, Limassol.

Communications: Television sets†: 1 per 3.1 persons. **Radios:** 1 per 3.3 persons. **Telephones†:** 1 per 2.1 persons. **Daily newspaper circ.†:** 110 per 1,000 pop.

Health: Life expectancy at birth (1997): 74.4 male; 78.8 female. **Births** (per 1,000 pop.): 15. **Deaths** (per 1,000 pop.): 8. **Natural increase:** 0.7%. **Hospital beds†:** 1 per 191 persons. **Physicians†:** 1 per 433 persons. **Infant mortality** (per 1,000 live births 1997): 8.

Education: Free and compulsory: ages 5½-15. **Literacy** (1994): 95%.

Major International Organizations: UN (IMF, FAO, WTO, World Bank, WHO), the Commonwealth.

Embassy: 2211 R St. NW 20008; 462-5772.

Agitation for enosis (union) with Greece increased after World War II, with the Turkish minority opposed, and broke into violence in 1955-56. In 1959, Britain, Greece, Turkey, and Cypriot leaders approved a plan for an independent republic, with constitutional guarantees for the Turkish minority and permanent division of offices on an ethnic basis. Greek and Turkish Communal Chambers dealt with religion, education, and other matters.

Archbishop Makarios III, formerly the leader of the enosis movement, was elected president, and full independence became final Aug. 16, 1960. Further communal strife led the United Nations to send a peacekeeping force in 1964; its mandate has been repeatedly renewed.

The Cypriot National Guard, led by officers from the army of Greece, seized the government July 15, 1974. On July 20, Turkey invaded the island; Greece mobilized its forces but did not intervene. A cease-fire was arranged but collapsed. By Aug. 16, Turkish forces had occupied the NE 40% of the island, despite the presence of UN peacekeeping forces.

Turkish Cypriots voted overwhelmingly, June 8, 1975, to form a separate Turkish Cypriot federated state. A president and assembly were elected in 1976. Some 200,000 Greeks have been expelled from the Turkish-controlled area, replaced by thousands of Turks, some from the mainland.

Turkish Republic of Northern Cyprus

A declaration of independence was announced by Turkish-Cypriot leader Rauf Denktash, Nov. 15, 1983. The state is not internationally recognized, although it does have trade relations with some countries. Area of TRNC: 1,295 sq mi.; pop. (1995 est.): 134,000, 99% Turkish; capital: Lefkosa (Nicosia).

Czech Republic
Ceská Republika

(Figures prior to 1993 are for Czechoslovakia)

People: Population: 10,318,958. **Age distrib.** (%): <15: 18; 65+: 14. **Pop. density:** 339 per sq. mi. **Urban:** 66%. **Ethnic groups:** Czech 94%, Slovak 3%. **Principal languages:** Czech (official), Slovak. **Chief religions:** Atheist 39.8%, Roman Catholic 39.2%, Protestant 4.6%, Orthodox 3%.

Geography: Area: 30,450 sq. mi. **Location:** In E central Europe. **Neighbors:** Poland on N, Germany on N and W, Austria on S, Slovakia on E and SE. **Topography:** Bohemia, in W, is a plateau surrounded by mountains; Moravia is hilly. **Capital:** Prague. **Cities** (1995 est.): Prague 1,213,299; Brno 389,576; Ostrava 325,827.

Government: Type: Republic. **Head of state:** Vaclav Havel; b Oct. 5, 1936; in office: Feb. 15, 1993. **Head of government:** Prime Min. Vaclav Klaus; b June 19, 1941; in office: July 1993. **Local divisions:** 8 regions. **Defense:** 2.5% of GDP (1995). **Active troop strength:** 70,000.

Economy: Industries: Machinery, oil products, iron and steel, glass, motor vehicles. **Chief crops:** Wheat, sugar beets, potatoes, rye, barley, hops, fruit. **Minerals:** Coal, kaolin. **Livestock:** (1996): pigs: 4.0 mil; cattle: 2.0 mil. **Electricity prod.** (1995): 53.3 bil kWh. **Labor force:** 38% ind.; 9% constr.; 8% agric.

Finance: Monetary unit: Koruna (Aug. 1997: 33.29 = $1 US). **Gross domestic product** (1995 est.): $106.2 bil. **Per capita GDP:** $10,200. **Imports** (1995 est.): $21.3 bil; partners: Germany 26%, Slovakia 13%, Russia 9%. **Exports** (1995 est.): $17.4 bil; partners: Germany 32%, Slovakia 16%, Austria 7%. **Tourism** (1994): $2.0 bil. **National budget** (1995 est.): $16.2 bil. **International reserves less gold** (Oct. 1996): $12.6 bil. **Gold:** 1.99 mil oz t. **Consumer prices** (change in 1996): 8.8%.

Transport: Railroads: Length: 5,845.5 mi. **Motor vehicles in use:** 3.0 mil passenger cars, 239,000 comm. vehicles. **Civil aviation:** 1.2 bil passenger-mi.; 2 airports with scheduled flights. **Chief ports:** Decin, Prague, Usti nad Labem.

Communications: Television sets: 1 per 2.1 persons. **Radios:** 1 per 1.6 persons. **Telephones:** 1 per 4.2 persons. **Daily newspaper circ.:** 219 per 1,000 pop.

Health: Life expectancy at birth (1997): 70.2 male; 77.8 female. **Births** (per 1,000 pop.): 11. **Deaths** (per 1,000 pop.): 11. **Natural increase:** –2.1. **Hospital beds:** 1 per 79 persons. **Physicians:** 1 per 272 persons. **Infant mortality** (per 1,000 live births 1997): 8.

Education: Compulsory: ages 6-16. **Literacy** (est.): 99%.

Major International Organizations: UN (WTO, FAO, World Bank, IMF, WHO), OECD.

Embassy: 3900 Spring of Freedom St. NW 20008; 363-6315.

Bohemia and Moravia were part of the Great Moravian Empire in the 9th century and later became part of the Holy Roman Empire. Under the kings of Bohemia, Prague in the 14th century was the cultural center of Central Europe. Bohemia and Hungary became part of Austria-Hungary.

In 1914-18 Thomas G. Masaryk and Eduard Benes formed a provisional government with the support of Slovak leaders including Milan Stefanik. They proclaimed the Republic of Czechoslovakia Oct. 28, 1918.

Czechoslovakia

By 1938 Nazi Germany had worked up disaffection among German-speaking citizens in Sudetenland and demanded its cession. British Prime Min. Neville Chamberlain, with the acquiescence of France, signed with Hitler at Munich, Sept. 30, 1938, an agreement to the cession, with a guarantee of peace by Hitler and Mussolini. Germany occupied Sudetenland Oct. 1-2.

Hitler on Mar. 15, 1939, dissolved Czechoslovakia, made protectorates of Bohemia and Moravia, and supported the autonomy of Slovakia, proclaimed independent Mar. 14, 1939.

Soviet troops with some Czechoslovak contingents entered eastern Czechoslovakia in 1944 and reached Prague in May 1945; Benes returned as president. In May 1946 elections, the Communist Party won 38% of the votes, and Benes accepted Klement Gottwald, a Communist, as prime minister.

In Feb. 1948, the Communists seized power in advance of scheduled elections. In May 1948 a new constitution was approved. Benes refused to sign it. On May 30 the voters were offered a one-slate ballot and the Communists won full control. Benes resigned June 7 and Gottwald became president. The country was renamed the Czechoslovak Socialist Republic. A harsh Stalinist period followed, with complete and violent suppression of all opposition.

In Jan. 1968 a liberalization movement spread explosively through Czechoslovakia. Antonin Novotny, long the Stalinist ruler of the nation, was deposed as party leader and succeeded by Alexander Dubcek, a Slovak, who supported democratic reforms. On Mar. 22 Novotny resigned as president and was succeeded by Gen. Ludvik Svoboda. On Apr. 6, Prem. Joseph Lenart resigned and was succeeded by Oldrich Cernik, a reformer.

In July 1968 the USSR and 4 Warsaw Pact nations demanded an end to liberalization. On Aug. 20, the Soviet, Polish, East German, Hungarian, and Bulgarian armies invaded Czechoslovakia. Despite demonstrations and riots by students and workers, press censorship was imposed, liberal leaders were ousted from office and promises of loyalty to Soviet policies were made by some old-line Communist Party leaders.

On Apr. 17, 1969, Dubcek resigned as leader of the Communist Party and was succeeded by Gustav Husak. In Jan. 1970, Cernik was ousted. Censorship was tightened, and the Communist Party expelled a third of its members. In 1973, amnesty was offered to some of the 40,000 who fled the country after the 1968 invasion, but repressive policies continued.

More than 700 leading Czechoslovak intellectuals and former party leaders signed a human rights manifesto in 1977, called Charter 77, prompting a renewed crackdown by the regime.

The police crushed the largest antigovernment protests since 1968, when tens of thousands took to the streets of Prague, Nov. 17, 1989. As protesters demanded free elections, the Communist Party leadership resigned Nov. 24; millions went on strike Nov. 27.

On Dec. 10, 1989, the first cabinet in 41 years without a Communist majority took power; Vaclav Havel, playwright and human rights campaigner, was chosen president, Dec. 29. In Mar. 1990 the country was officially renamed the Czech and Slovak Federal Republic. Havel failed to win reelection July 3, 1992; his bid was blocked by a Slovak-led coalition.

Slovakia declared sovereignty, July 17. Czech and Slovak leaders agreed, July 23, on a basic plan for a peaceful division of Czechoslovakia into 2 independent states.

Czech Republic

Czechoslovakia split into 2 separate states—the Czech Republic and Slovakia—on Jan. 1, 1993. Havel was elected president of the Czech Republic on Jan. 26. On July 8, 1997, NATO invited the Czech Republic to become a full member of the alliance within 2 years. Record floods in July caused more than $1.7 billion in damage.

Denmark
Kingdom of Denmark
Kongeriget Danmark

People: Population: 5,268,775. **Age distrib.** (%): <15: 18; 65+: 15. **Pop. density:** 317 per sq. mi. **Urban:** 85%. **Ethnic groups:** Scandinavian, Eskimo. **Principal languages:** Danish (official), Faroese. **Chief religions:** Evangelical Lutheran 91%.

Geography: Area: 16,639 sq. mi. **Location:** In N Europe, separating the North and Baltic seas. **Neighbors:** Germany on S, Norway on NW, Sweden on NE. **Topography:** Denmark consists of the Jutland Peninsula and about 500 islands, 100 inhabited. The land is flat or gently rolling and is almost all in productive use. **Capital:** Copenhagen: 1,326,000*.

Government: Type: Constitutional monarchy. **Head of state:** Queen Margrethe II; b Apr. 16, 1940; in office: Jan. 14, 1972. **Head of government:** Prime Min. Poul Nyrup Rasmussen; b June 15, 1943; in office: Jan. 25, 1993. **Local divisions:** 14 counties and 1 city (Copenhagen). **Defense:** 1.8% of GDP (1995). **Active troop strength:** 32,900.

Economy: Industries: Food processing, machinery, textiles, furniture, electronics. **Chief crops:** Grains, potatoes. **Minerals:** Oil, gas, salt. **Crude oil reserves** (1996): 957 mil bbls. **Arable land:** 61%. **Livestock** (1996): cattle: 10.7 mil; pigs: 2.1 mil. **Fish catch** (1995): 2.04 mil metric tons. **Electricity prod.** (1995): 34.2 bil kWh. **Labor force:** 67% serv. & govt.; 20% manuf. & mining; 6% constr.

Finance: Monetary unit: Krone (Aug. 1997: 6.89 = $1 US). **Gross domestic product** (1995 est.): $112.8 bil. **Per capita GDP:** $21,700. **Imports** (1994 est.): $34 bil; partners: EU 51%, Sweden 12%. **Exports** (1994): $39.6 bil; partners: EU 49%, Sweden 10%. **Tourism** (1994): $3.2 bil. **National budget** (1994 est.): $64.4 bil. **International reserves less gold** (June 1997): $16.6 bil. **Gold:** 2.0 mil oz t. **Consumer prices** (change in 1996): 2.1%.

Transport: Railroads: Length: 1,768.6 mi. **Motor vehicles in use:** 1.7 mil passenger cars, 342,000 comm. vehicles. **Civil aviation:** 3.2 bil passenger-mi.; 13 airports with scheduled flights. **Chief ports:** Copenhagen, Alborg, Arhus, Odense.

Communications: Television sets: 1 per 1.9 persons. **Radios:** 1 per 1.0 persons. **Telephones:** 1 per 1.6 persons. **Daily newspaper circ.:** 365 per 1,000 pop.

Health: Life expectancy at birth (1997): 73.9 male; 81.1 female. **Births** (per 1,000 pop.): 12. **Deaths** (per 1,000 pop.): 10. **Natural increase:** 0.1%. **Hospital beds:** 1 per 196 persons. **Physicians:** 1 per 358 persons. **Infant mortality** (per 1,000 live births 1997): 5.

Education: Compulsory: ages 7-16. **Literacy** (1997): 100%.

Major International Organizations: UN and all of its specialized agencies, OECD, EU, NATO.

Embassy: 3200 Whitehaven St. NW 20008; 234-4300.

The origin of Copenhagen dates back to ancient times, when the fishing and trading place named Havn (port) grew up on a cluster of islets, but Bishop Absalon (1128-1201) is regarded as the actual founder of the city.

Danes formed a large component of the Viking raiders in the early Middle Ages. The Danish kingdom was a major north European power until the 17th century, when it lost its land in southern Sweden. Norway was separated in 1815, and Schleswig-Holstein in 1864. Northern Schleswig was returned in 1920.

Voters ratified the Maastricht Treaty, the basic document of the European Union, in May 1993, after rejecting it in 1992.

The **Faroe Islands** in the North Atlantic, about 300 mi. NW of the Shetlands, and 850 mi. from Denmark proper, 18 inhabited, have an area of 540 sq. mi. and pop. (1997 est.) of 43,057. They are an administrative division of Denmark, self-governing in most matters. Torshavn is the capital.

Greenland (Kalaallit Nunaat)

Greenland, a huge island between the North Atlantic and the Polar Sea, is separated from the North American continent by Davis Strait and Baffin Bay. Its total area is 840,000 sq. mi., 84% of which is ice-capped. Most of the island is a lofty plateau 9,000 to 10,000 ft. in altitude. The average thickness of the cap is 1,000 ft. The population (1997 est.) is 58,768. Under the 1953 Danish constitution the colony became an integral part of the realm with representatives in the Folketing (Danish legislature). The Danish parliament, 1978, approved home rule for Greenland, effective May 1, 1979. With home rule, Greenlandic place names came into official use. The technically correct name for Greenland is now Kalaallit Nunaat; its capital is Nuuk, rather than Gothab. Fish is the principal export.

Djibouti
Republic of Djibouti
Jumhuriyah Djibouti

People: Population: 434,116. **Age distrib.** (%): <15: 43; 65+: 3. **Pop. density:** 49 per sq. mi. **Urban:** 82%. **Ethnic groups:** Somali 60%, Afar 35%. **Principal languages:** French, Arabic (both official); Afar, Somali. **Chief religions:** Muslim 94%, Christian 6%.

Geography: Area: 8,950 sq. mi. **Location:** On E coast of Africa, separated from Arabian Peninsula by the strategically vital strait of Bab el-Mandeb. **Neighbors:** Ethiopia on W and SW, Eritrea on NW, Somalia on SE. **Topography:** The territory, divided into a low coastal plain, mountains behind, and an interior plateau, is arid, sandy, and desolate. The climate is generally hot and dry. **Capital:** Djibouti (1995): 383,000.

Government: Type: Republic. **Head of state:** Pres. Hassan Gouled Aptidon; b 1916; in office: June 24, 1977. **Head of government:** Prem. Barkat Gourad Hamadou; in office: Sept. 30, 1978. **Local divisions:** 5 districts. **Defense: Active troop strength:** 9,600 est.

Economy: Based on service activities. **Arable land:** 0%. **Electricity prod.** (1995): 180 mil kWh.

Finance: Monetary unit: Franc (Aug. 1997: 176.95 = $1 US). **Gross domestic product** (1994 est.): $500 mil. **Per capita GDP:** $1,200. **Imports** (1994 est.): $384 mil; partners: France, UK. **Exports** (1994 est.): $184 mil; partners: Somalia 48%, Yemen 42%. **National budget** (1993 est.): $201 mil. **International reserves less gold** (Apr. 1997): $70.49 mil.

Transport: Railroad: Length: 60.2 mi. **Motor vehicles in use:** 13,500 passenger cars, 3,000 commercial vehicles. **Chief port:** Djibouti.

Communications: Television sets: 1 per 23 persons. **Radios:** 1 per 12 persons. **Telephones:** 1 per 77 persons.

Health: Life expectancy at birth (1997): 48.7 male; 52.6 female. **Births** (per 1,000 pop.): 42. **Deaths** (per 1,000 pop.): 15. **Natural increase:** 2.7%. **Infant mortality** (per 1,000 live births 1997): 105.

Education: Literacy (1995 est.): 46%.
Major International Organizations: UN, OAU, Arab League.
Embassy: Suite 515, 1156 15th St. NW 20005; 331-0270.

France gained control of the territory in stages between 1862 and 1900. As French Somaliland it became an overseas territory of France in 1945; in 1967 it was renamed the French Territory of the Afars and the Issas.

Ethiopia and Somalia have renounced their claims to the area, but each has accused the other of trying to gain control. There were clashes between Afars (ethnically related to Ethiopians) and Issas (related to Somalis) in 1976. Immigrants from both countries continued to enter the country up to independence, which came June 27, 1977.

French aid is the mainstay of the economy, as well as assistance from Arab countries. A peace accord Dec. 1994 ended a 3-year-long uprising by Afar rebels.

Dominica
Commonwealth of Dominica

People: Population: 83,226. **Age distrib.:** (%): <15: 28; 65+: 8. **Pop. density:** 287 per sq. mi. **Urban:** 70%. **Ethnic groups:** Nearly all African, some Carib. **Principal languages:** English (official), French patois. **Chief religions:** Roman Catholic 77%, Protestant 15%.

Geography: Area: 290 sq. mi. **Location:** In Eastern Caribbean, most northerly Windward Isl. **Neighbors:** Guadeloupe to N, Martinique to S. **Topography:** Mountainous, a central ridge running from N to S, terminating in cliffs; volcanic in origin, with numerous thermal springs; rich deep topsoil on leeward side, red tropical clay on windward coast. **Capital:** Roseau (1991 est.): 15,900.

Government: Type: Parliamentary democracy. **Head of state:** Pres. Crispin Anselm Sorhaindo; in office: Oct. 25, 1993. **Head of government:** Prime Min. Edison James; in office: June 14, 1995. **Local divisions:** 10 parishes.

Economy: Industries: Soap, tourism. **Chief crops:** Bananas, citrus fruits, mangoes, coconuts. **Minerals:** Pumice. **Other resources:** Forests. **Arable land:** 9%. **Electricity prod.** (1995): 37 mil kWh. **Labor force:** 40% agric.; 32% ind. & commerce; 28% services.

Finance: Monetary unit: East Caribbean Dollar (Aug. 1997: 2.70 = $1 US). **Gross domestic product** (1995 est.): $200 mil. **Per capita GDP:** $2,450. **Imports** (1993): $98.8 mil; partners: U.S. 25%, UK. **Exports** (1993): $48.3 mil; partners: UK 55%. **Tourism** (1994): $31 mil. **National budget** (FY 1995-96 est.): $95.8 mil. **International reserves less gold** (May 1997): $25.25 mil. **Consumer prices** (change in 1996): 1.7%.

Transport: Chief port: Roseau.
Communications: Television sets: 1 per 13 persons. **Telephones:** 1 per 4.0 persons.
Health: Life expectancy at birth (1997): 74.7 male; 80.6 female. **Births** (per 1,000 pop.): 18. **Deaths** (per 1,000 pop.): 5. **Natural increase:** 1.3%. **Hospital beds:** 1 per 298 persons. **Physicians:** 1 per 2,112 persons. **Infant mortality** (per 1,000 live births 1997): 9.
Education: Free compulsory: ages 5-15. **Literacy** (1993): 90%.
Major International Organizations: UN, OAS, the Commonwealth.

A British colony since 1805, Dominica was granted self-government in 1967. Independence was achieved Nov. 3, 1978.

Hurricane David struck, Aug. 30, 1979, devastating the island and destroying the banana plantations, Dominica's economic mainstay. Coups were attempted in 1980 and 1981.

Dominica participated in the 1983 U.S.-led invasion of Grenada.

Dominican Republic
República Dominicana

People: Population: 8,228,151. **Age distrib.** (%): <15: 34; 65+: 4. **Pop. density:** 438 per sq. mi. **Urban:** 63%. **Ethnic groups:** Mixed 73%, white 16%, black 11%. **Principal language:** Spanish (official). **Chief religions:** Roman Catholic 95%.

Geography: Area: 18,792 sq. mi. **Location:** In West Indies, sharing isl. of Hispaniola with Haiti. **Neighbors:** Haiti on W, Puerto Rico (U.S.) to E. **Topography:** The Cordillera Central range crosses the center of the country, rising to over 10,000 ft., highest in the Caribbean. The Cibao Valley to the N is major agricultural area. **Capital:** Santo Domingo. **Cities** (1993 est.): Santo Domingo 3,166,000; Santiago de los Caballeros 1,289,000*.

Government: Type: Republic. **Head of state:** Pres. Leonel Fernández; b Dec. 26, 1953; in office: Aug. 16, 1996. **Local**

divisions: 29 provinces and Santo Domingo. **Defense:** 1.4% of GDP (1994). **Active troop strength:** 24,500.

Economy: Industries: Sugar refining, cement, tourism. **Chief crops:** Sugar, cocoa, coffee, cotton, rice. **Minerals:** Nickel, bauxite, gold, silver. **Arable land:** 23%. **Livestock** (1996): cattle: 2.4 mil; pigs: 950,000. **Electricity prod.** (1995): 6.5 bil kWh. **Labor force:** 50% agric.; 32% serv. & govt.; 18% ind.

Finance: Monetary unit: Peso (Aug. 1997: 14.25 = $1 US). **Gross domestic product** (1995 est.): $26.8 bil. **Per capita GDP:** $3,400. **Imports** (1995): $2.9 bil; partners: U.S. 60%. **Exports** (1995): $837.7 mil; partners: U.S. 47.5%, EU 22%. **Tourism** (1994): $1.1 bil. **National budget** (1994 est.): $2.2 bil. **International reserves less gold** (June 1997): $364.4 mil. **Gold:** 18,000 oz t.

Transport: Railroad: Length: 470.1 mi. **Motor vehicles in use:** 120,000 passenger cars, 80,000 comm. vehicles. **Civil aviation:** 145.3 mil passenger-mi.; 4 airports. **Chief ports:** Santo Domingo, San Pedro de Macoris, Puerto Plata.

Communications: Television sets: 1 per 11 persons. **Radios:** 1 per 5.8 persons. **Telephones:** 1 per 14 persons. **Daily newspaper circ.:** 34 per 1,000 pop.

Health: Life expectancy at birth (1997): 67.2 male; 71.7 female. **Births** (per 1,000 pop.): 23. **Deaths** (per 1,000 pop.): 6. **Natural increase:** 1.7%. **Hospital beds:** 1 per 838 persons. **Physicians:** 1 per 1,052 persons. **Infant mortality** (per 1,000 live births 1997): 46.
Education: Compulsory: ages 7-14. **Literacy** (1995 est.): 82%.
Major International Organizations: UN (World Bank, IMF, FAO, WHO, WTO), OAS.
Embassy: 1715 22d St. NW 20008; 332-6280.

Carib and Arawak Indians inhabited the island of Hispaniola when Columbus landed in 1492. The city of Santo Domingo, founded 1496, is the oldest settlement by Europeans in the hemisphere and has the supposed ashes of Columbus in an elaborate tomb in its ancient cathedral.

The western third of the island was ceded to France in 1697. Santo Domingo itself was ceded to France in 1795. Haitian leader Toussaint L'Ouverture seized it, 1801. Spain returned intermittently 1803-21, as several native republics came and went. Haiti ruled again, 1822-44, and Spanish occupation occurred 1861-63.

The country was occupied by U.S. Marines from 1916 to 1924, when a constitutionally elected government was installed.

In 1930, Gen. Rafael Leonidas Trujillo Molina was elected president. Trujillo ruled brutally until his assassination in 1961. Pres. Joaquín Balaguer, appointed by Trujillo in 1960, resigned under pressure in 1962.

Juan Bosch, elected president in the first free elections in 38 years, was overthrown in 1963. On Apr. 24, 1965, a revolt was launched by followers of Bosch and others, including a few Communists. Four days later U.S. Marines intervened against pro-Bosch forces. Token units were later sent by 5 South American countries as a peacekeeping force. A provisional government supervised a June 1966 election, in which Balaguer defeated Bosch. Balaguer remained in office for most of the next 28 years, but his May 1994 reelection was widely denounced as fraudulent. He cut short his term and on June 30, 1996, Leonel Fernández was elected his successor.

Continued depressed world prices have affected the main export commodity, sugar.

Ecuador
Republic of Ecuador
República del Ecuador

People: Population: 11,690,535. **Age distrib.** (%): <15: 35; 65+: 5. **Pop. density:** 111 per sq. mi. **Urban:** 60%. **Ethnic groups:** Mestizo 55%, Indian 25%, Spanish 10%, African 10%. **Principal languages:** Spanish (official), Quechuan, other Amerindian. **Chief religions:** Roman Catholic 95%.

Geography: Area: 105,037 sq. mi. **Location:** In NW South America, on Pacific coast, astride the Equator. **Neighbors:** Colombia on N, Peru on E and S. **Topography:** Two ranges of Andes run N and S, splitting the country into 3 zones: hot, humid lowlands on the coast; temperate highlands between the ranges; and rainy, tropical lowlands to the E. **Capital:** Quito. **Cities:** Guayaquil 1,831,000; Quito 1,298,000*.

Government: Type: Republic. **Head of state:** Pres. Fabian Alarcón; b Apr. 14, 1947; in office: Feb. 11, 1997. **Local divisions:** 21 provinces. **Defense:** 2.1% of GDP (1995). **Active troop strength:** 57,100.

Economy: Industries: Oil, food processing, metalwork, textiles. **Chief crops:** Bananas (leading producer), coffee, rice, sugar, potatoes. **Minerals:** Oil, gas, copper, zinc, silver, gold. **Crude oil reserves** (1996): 2.1 bil bbls. **Other resources:**

Forests (a leading producer of balsawood), seafood. **Arable land:** 6%. **Livestock** (1996): cattle: 5.1 mil; pigs: 2.7 mil; sheep: 1.7 mil. **Fish catch** (1995): 581,860 metric tons. **Electricity prod.** (1995): 8.6 bil kWh. **Labor force:** 35% agric.; 28% services; 21% manuf.; 16% commerce.

Finance: Monetary unit: Sucre (Aug. 1997: 4,110 = $1 US). **Gross domestic product** (1995 est.): $44.6 bil. **Per capita GDP:** $4,100. **Imports** (1994): $3.7 bil; partners: U.S. 28%. **Exports** (1994): $4 bil; partners: U.S. 42%. **Tourism** (1994): $252 mil. **National budget** (1996 est.) $3.3 bil. **International reserves less gold** (June 1997): $2.29 bil. **Gold:** 414,000 oz t. **Consumer prices** (change in 1996): 24.4%.

Transport: Railroad: Length: 599.3 mi. **Motor vehicles in use:** 200,000 passenger cars, 280,000 comm. vehicles. **Civil aviation:** 875.6 mil passenger-mi.; 14 airports. **Chief ports:** Guayaquil, Manta, Esmeraldas, Puerto Bolivar.

Communications: Television sets: 1 per 11 persons. **Radios:** 1 per 3.1 persons. **Telephones:** 1 per 15 persons. **Daily newspaper circ.:** 72 per 1,000 pop.

Health: Life expectancy at birth (1997): 68.8 male; 74.2 female. **Births** (per 1,000 pop.): 25. **Deaths** (per 1,000 pop.): 5. **Natural increase:** 1.9%. **Hospital beds:** 1 per 623 persons. **Physicians:** 1 per 904 persons. **Infant mortality** (per 1,000 live births 1997): 33.

Education: Free and compulsory for 6 years between ages 6-14. **Literacy** (1995 est.): 90%.

Major International Organizations: UN (IMF, FAO, World Bank, WHO), OAS.

Embassy: 2535 15th St. NW 20009; 234-7200.

The region, which was the northern Inca empire, was conquered by Spain in 1533. Liberation forces defeated the Spanish May 24, 1822, near Quito. Ecuador became part of the Great Colombia Republic but seceded, May 13, 1830.

A peaceful transfer of power from military rule to democratic civilian government took place in 1979.

Since 1972, the economy has revolved around petroleum exports; oil revenues have declined since 1982, causing severe economic problems. Ecuador suspended interest payments for 1987 on its estimated $8.2 billion foreign debt following a Mar. 5-6 earthquake that left 20,000 homeless and destroyed a stretch of the country's main oil pipeline.

Ecuadoran Indians staged protests in the 1990s to demand greater rights. A border war with Peru flared from Jan. 26, 1995, until a truce took effect Mar. 1. Vice-Pres. Alberto Dahik resigned and fled Ecuador, Oct. 11, 1995, to avoid arrest on corruption charges. Elected president in a runoff, July 7, 1996, Abdalá Bucaram—a populist known as El Loco, or "The Crazy One"—imposed stiff price increases and other austerity measures. His rising unpopularity and erratic behavior led the National Congress, Feb. 6, 1997, to dismiss him for "mental incapacity." Bucaram went into exile, and Congress, on Feb. 11, confirmed its leader, Fabián Alarcón, as president for 18 months. Voters endorsed the actions in a referendum May 25.

The **Galapagos Islands,** pop. (1996 est.) 14,000, about 600 mi. to the W, are the home of huge tortoises and other unusual animals.

Egypt

Arab Republic of Egypt

Jumhuriyat Misr al-Arabiyah

People: Population: 64,791,891. **Age distrib** (%) <15: 36; 65+: 4. **Pop. density:** 168 per sq. mi. **Urban:** 45%. **Ethnic groups:** Eastern Hamitic stock (Egyptian, Bedouin, Berber) 99%, Greek, Nubian, Armenian. **Principal languages:** Arabic (official), English, French. **Chief religions:** Muslim (mostly Sunni) 94%, Coptic Christian and other 6%.

Geography: Area: 385,229 sq. mi. **Location:** Northeast corner of Africa. **Neighbors:** Libya on W, Sudan on S, Israel on E. **Topography:** Almost entirely desolate and barren, with hills and mountains in E and along Nile. The Nile Valley, where most of the people live, stretches 550 miles. **Capital:** Cairo. **Cities:** Cairo 9,690,000; Alexandria 3,584,000; Shubra El-Khemia 1,204,000*.

Government: Type: Republic. **Head of state:** Pres. Hosni Mubarak; b May 4, 1928; in office: Oct. 14, 1981. **Head of government:** Prime Min. Kamal al-Ganzouri; b 1933; in office: Jan. 4, 1996. **Local divisions:** 26 governorates. **Defense:** 8.2% of GDP (FY 1994-95 est.). **Active troop strength:** 440,000.

Economy: Industries: Textiles, tourism, chemicals, oil, food processing, cement. **Chief crops:** Cotton, rice, beans, fruits, grains, vegetables, corn. **Minerals:** Oil, gas, phosphates, gypsum, iron, manganese, limestone. **Crude oil reserves** (1996): 3.7 bil bbls. **Arable land:** 3%. **Livestock** (1996): sheep: 3.5 mil; goats: 3.25 mil; buffalo: 2.8 mil; cattle 2.7 mil. **Fish catch** (1995): 309,578 metric tons. **Electricity prod.** (1995): 48.5 bil kWh. **Labor force:** 34% agric.; 35% serv.

Finance: Monetary unit: Pound (Aug. 1997: 3.39 = $1 US). **Gross domestic product** (1994): $171 bil. **Per capita GDP:** $2,760. **Imports** (FY 1994-95): $15.2 bil; partners: U.S. 17%, Germany 10%. **Exports** (FY 1994-95): $5.4 bil; partners: Italy 12%, U.S. 11%. **Tourism** (1994): $1.4 bil. **National budget** (FY 1994-95 est.): $19.4 bil. **International reserves less gold** (Apr. 1997): $17.99 bil. **Gold:** 2.43 mil oz t. **Consumer prices** (change in 1996): 7.2%.

Transport: Railroads: Length: 2,950.4 mi. **Motor vehicles in use:** 1.2 mil passenger cars, 446,000 comm. vehicles. **Civil aviation:** 3.9 bil passenger-mi.; 14 airports. **Chief ports:** Alexandria, Port Said, Suez.

Communications: Television sets: 1 per 9.2 persons. **Radios:** 1 per 3.3 persons. **Telephones:** 1 per 22 persons. **Daily newspaper circ.:** 64 per 1,000 pop. (partial circ.).

Health: Life expectancy at birth (1997): 59.8 male; 63.8 female. **Births** (per 1,000 pop.): 28. **Deaths** (per 1,000 pop.): 9. **Natural increase:** 1.9%. **Hospital beds:** 1 per 515 persons. **Physicians:** 1 per 1,472 persons. **Infant mortality** (per 1,000 live births 1997): 71.

Education: Compulsory: ages 6-11. **Literacy** (1995 est.): 51%.

Major International Organizations: UN (IMF, FAO, WHO, World Bank, WTO), OAU, Arab League.

Embassy: 3521 International Ct. NW 20008; 895-5400.

Archaeological records of ancient Egyptian civilization date back to 4000 BC. A unified kingdom arose around 3200 BC, and extended its way south into Nubia and as far north as Syria. A high culture of rulers and priests was built on an economic base of serfdom, fertile soil, and annual flooding of the Nile banks.

Imperial decline facilitated conquest by Asian invaders (Hyksos, Assyrians). The last native dynasty fell in 341 BC to the Persians, who were in turn replaced by Greeks (Alexander and the Ptolemies), Romans, Byzantines, and Arabs, who introduced Islam and the Arabic language. The ancient Egyptian language is preserved only in the liturgy of the Coptic Christians.

Egypt was ruled as part of larger Islamic empires for several centuries. The Mamluks, a military caste of Caucasian origin, ruled Egypt from 1250 until defeat by the Ottoman Turks in 1517. Under Turkish sultans the khedive was hereditary viceroy had wide authority. Britain intervened in 1882 and took control of administration, though nominal allegiance to the Ottoman Empire continued until 1914.

The country was a British protectorate from 1914 to 1922. A 1936 treaty strengthened Egyptian autonomy, but Britain retained bases in Egypt and a condominium over the Sudan. Britain fought German and Italian armies from Egypt, 1940-42. In 1951 Egypt abrogated the 1936 treaty; the Sudan became independent in 1956.

The uprising of July 23, 1952, was led by the Society of Free Officers, who named Maj. Gen. Mohammed Naguib commander in chief and forced King Farouk to abdicate. When the republic was proclaimed June 18, 1953, Naguib became its first president and premier. Lt. Col. Gamal Abdel Nasser removed Naguib and became premier in 1954. In 1956, he was voted president. Nasser died in 1970 and was replaced by Vice Pres. Anwar Sadat.

The Aswan High Dam, completed 1971, provides irrigation for more than a million acres of land. Artesian wells, drilled in the Western Desert, reclaimed 43,000 acres, 1960-66.

When the state of Israel was proclaimed in 1948, Egypt joined other Arab nations invading Israel and was defeated.

After terrorist raids across its border, Israel invaded Egypt's Sinai Peninsula, Oct. 29, 1956. Egypt rejected a cease-fire demand by Britain and France; on Oct. 31 the 2 nations dropped bombs and on Nov. 5-6 landed forces. Egypt and Israel accepted a UN cease-fire; fighting ended Nov. 7.

A UN Emergency Force guarded the 117-mile-long border between Egypt and Israel until May 19, 1967, when it was withdrawn at Nasser's demand. Egyptian troops entered the Gaza Strip and the heights of Sharm el Sheikh and 3 days later closed the Strait of Tiran to all Israeli shipping. Full-scale war broke out June 5; before it ended under a UN cease-fire June 10, Israel had captured Gaza and the Sinai Peninsula, controlled the east bank of the Suez Canal, and reopened the gulf. After sporadic fighting, Israel and Egypt agreed, Aug. 7, 1970, to a new cease-fire.

In a surprise attack Oct. 6, 1973, Egyptian forces crossed the Suez Canal into the Sinai. (At the same time, Syrian forces attacked Israelis on the Golan Heights.) Egypt was supplied by a USSR military airlift; the U.S. responded with an airlift to Israel. Israel counterattacked, crossed the canal, surrounded Suez City. A UN cease-fire took effect Oct. 24.

A disengagement agreement was signed Jan. 18, 1974. Under it, Israeli forces withdrew from the canal's W bank; limited numbers of Egyptian forces occupied a strip along the E bank. A second accord was signed in 1975, with Israel yielding Sinai oil fields. Pres. Sadat's surprise visit to Jerusalem, Nov. 1977, opened the prospect of peace with Israel. On Mar. 26, 1979, Egypt and Israel signed a formal peace treaty, ending 30 years of war, and establishing diplomatic relations. Israel returned control of the Sinai to Egypt in Apr. 1982.

Tension between Muslim fundamentalists and Christians in 1981 caused street riots and culminated in a nationwide security crackdown in Sept. Pres Sadat was assassinated on Oct. 6; he was succeeded by Hosni Mubarak.

Egypt was a political and military supporter of the Allied forces in their defeat of Iraq in the Persian Gulf War, 1991.

Egypt saw a rising tide of Islamic fundamentalist violence in the 1990s. Egyptian security forces conducted raids against Islamic militants, some of whom were executed for terrorism. Naguib Mahfouz, winner of the 1988 Nobel Prize for Literature, was stabbed by Islamic militants Oct. 14, 1994. Pres. Mubarak escaped assassination in Ethiopia, June 26, 1995; Egypt blamed Sudan for the attack.

The **Suez Canal,** 103 mi. long, links the Mediterranean and Red seas. It was built by a French corporation 1859-69, but Britain obtained controlling interest in 1875. The last British troops were removed June 13, 1956. On July 26, Egypt nationalized the canal.

El Salvador
Republic of El Salvador
República de El Salvador

People: Population: 5,661,827. **Age distrib.** (%): <15: 37; 65+: 5. **Pop. density:** 697 per sq. mi. **Urban:** 45%. **Ethnic groups:** Mestizo 94%, Indian 5%. **Principal language:** Spanish (official). **Chief religions:** Roman Catholic 75%, many Protestant groups.

Geography: Area: 8,124 sq. mi. **Location:** In Central America. **Neighbors:** Guatemala on W, Honduras on N. **Topography:** A hot Pacific coastal plain in the south rises to a cooler plateau and valley region, densely populated. The N is mountainous, including many volcanoes. **Capital:** San Salvador: 1,214,000*.

Government: Type: Republic. **Head of state:** Pres. Armando Calderón Sol; b June 24, 1948; in office: June 1, 1994. **Local divisions:** 14 departments. **Defense:** 1% of GDP (1995). **Active troop strength:** 28,380.

Economy: Industries: Food and beverages, oil products, tobacco. **Chief crops:** Coffee, corn, sugar, rice. **Other resources:** Hydropower. **Arable land:** 27%. **Livestock** (1996): cattle: 1.3 mil; pigs: 400,000. **Electricity prod.** (1995): 3.6 bil kWh. **Labor force:** 34% agric.; 15% commerce; 14% manuf.; 13% govt.

Finance: Monetary unit: Colon (Aug. 1997: 8.76 = $1 US). **Gross domestic product** (1995 est.): $11.4 bil. **Per capita GDP:** $1,950. **Imports** (1995 est.): $3.3 bil; partners: U.S. 42%, Guatemala 11%. **Exports** (1995 est.): $1.6 bil; partners: U.S. 23%, Guatemala 22%. **Tourism** (1994): $86 mil. **National budget** (1992 est.): $890 mil. **International reserves less gold** (Apr. 1997): $993 mil. **Gold:** 469,000 oz t. **Consumer prices** (change in 1996): 9.8%.

Transport: Railroad: Length: 373.8 mi. **Motor vehicles in use:** 25,000 passenger cars, 37,000 comm. vehicles. **Civil aviation:** 976.8 mil passenger-mi. **Chief ports:** La Union, Acajutla.

Communications: Television sets: 1 per 12 persons. **Radios:** 1 per 2.3 persons. **Telephones:** 1 per 19 persons. **Daily newspaper circ.:** 50 per 1,000 pop.

Health: Life expectancy at birth (1997): 65.9 male; 72.8 female. **Births** (per 1,000 pop.): 27. **Deaths** (per 1,000 pop.): 6. **Natural increase:** 2.1%. **Hospital beds:** 1 per 588 persons. **Physicians:** 1 per 1,219 persons. **Infant mortality** (per 1,000 live births 1997): 30.

Education: Compulsory: ages 7-16. **Literacy** (1995 est.): 71.5%.

Major International Organizations: UN (IMF, WTO, WHO, FAO, World Bank, ILO), OAS.

Embassy: 2308 California St. NW 20008; 265-9671.

El Salvador became independent of Spain in 1821, and of the Central American Federation in 1839.

A fight with Honduras in 1969 over the presence of 300,000 Salvadoran workers left 2,000 dead.

A military coup overthrew the government of Pres. Carlos Humberto Romero in 1979, but the ruling military-civilian junta failed to quell a rebellion by leftist insurgents, armed by Cuba and Nicaragua. Extreme right-wing death squads organized to eliminate suspected leftists were blamed for thousands of deaths in the 1980s. The Reagan administration staunchly supported the government with military aid.

Voters turned out in large numbers in the May 1984 presidential election. Christian Democrat José Napoleon Duarte, a moderate, was victorious, with 54% of the vote.

The 12-year civil war ended Jan. 16, 1992, as the government and leftist rebels signed a formal peace treaty. The civil war had taken the lives of some 75,000 people. The treaty provided for military and political reforms.

Nine soldiers, including 3 officers, were indicted Jan. 1990 in the Nov. 1989 slaying of 6 Jesuit priests in San Salvador. Two of the officers received maximum 30-year jail sentences. They were released Mar. 20, 1993, when the National Assembly passed a sweeping amnesty.

Equatorial Guinea
Republic of Equatorial Guinea
República de Guinea Ecuatorial

People: Population: 442,516. **Age distrib.** (%): <15: 43; 65+: 4. **Pop. density:** 41 per sq. mi. **Urban:** 43%. **Ethnic groups:** Fang 83%, Bubi 10%. **Principal languages:** Spanish (official), Fang, Bubi. **Religion:** Predominantly Roman Catholic.

Geography: Area: 10,831 sq. mi. **Location:** Bioko Isl. off W Africa coast in Gulf of Guinea, and Rio Muni, mainland enclave. **Neighbors:** Gabon on S, Cameroon on E and N. **Topography:** Bioko Isl. consists of 2 volcanic mountains and a connecting valley. Rio Muni, with over 90% of the area, has a coastal plain and low hills beyond. **Capital:** Malabo (1991 est.): 58,000.

Government: Type: Republic. **Head of state:** Pres. Teodoro Obiang Nguema Mbasogo; b June 5, 1942; in office: Oct. 10, 1979. **Head of government:** Prime Min. Angel Serafin Seriche Dougan; in office: Mar. 29, 1996. **Local divisions:** 7 provinces. **Defense:** 2.2% of GNP (1994). **Active troop strength:** 1,320.

Economy: Industries: Fishing, sawmilling. **Chief crops:** Cocoa, coffee, rice, bananas, yams. **Minerals:** Oil. **Other resources:** Timber. **Arable land:** 8%. **Electricity prod.** (1995): 20 mil kWh. **Labor force:** 66% agric.; 23% serv.; 11% ind.

Finance: Monetary unit: CFA Franc (Aug. 1997: 610 = $1 US). **Gross domestic product** (1995 est.): $325 mil. **Per capita GDP:** $800. **Imports** (1993): $60 mil; partners: Cameroon 37%, Italy 17%. **Exports** (1993): $62 mil; partners: Japan 15%, Spain 12%. **National budget** (1992 est.): $36 mil.

Transport: Civil aviation: 4.3 mil passenger-mi. **Chief ports:** Malabo, Bata.

Communications: Television sets: 1 per 104 persons. **Radios:** 1 per 2.4 persons. **Telephones:** 1 per 159 persons.

Health: Life expectancy at birth (1997): 51.2 male; 55.8 female. **Births** (per 1,000 pop.): 39. **Deaths** (per 1,000 pop.): 14. **Natural increase:** 2.6%. **Hospital beds:** 1 per 350 persons. **Physicians:** 1 per 3,532 persons. **Infant mortality** (per 1,000 live births 1997): 96.

Education: Free and compulsory: ages 6-14. **Literacy** (1995 est.): 78.5%.

Major International Organizations: UN (IMF, FAO, WHO, World Bank), OAU.

Embassy: Suite 405, 1511 K St. NW 20005; 393-0525.

Fernando Po (now Bioko) Island was reached by Portugal in the late 15th century and ceded to Spain in 1778. Independence came Oct. 12, 1968. Riots occurred in 1969 over disputes between the island and the more backward Rio Muni province on the mainland. Masie Nguema Biyogo, a mainlander, became president for life in 1972.

Masie's reign was one of the most brutal in Africa, resulting in a bankrupted nation. Most of the nation's 7,000 Europeans emigrated. He was ousted in a military coup, Aug. 1979, and Teodoro Mbasogo, leader of the coup, became president. His regime eventually agreed to elections, held Nov. 21, 1993. These were nominally won by the ruling party, but boycotted by opposition parties that maintained the rules were rigged. A presidential election Feb. 25, 1996, was similarly flawed.

Eritrea
State of Eritrea

People: Population: 3,589,687. **Age distrib.** (%): <15: 43; 65+: 3. **Pop. density:** 79 per sq. mi. **Urban:** 17%. **Ethnic groups:** Tigrinya 50%, Tigre and Kunama 40%, Afar 4%. **Principal languages:** Tigrinya, Tigre. **Chief religions:** About evenly split between Muslim and Christian.

Geography: Area: 45,300 sq. mi. **Location:** In E Africa, on SW coast of Red Sea. **Neighbors:** Ethiopia on S, Djibouti on SE, Sudan on W. **Topography:** Includes many islands of the Dahlak Archipelago, low coastal plains in S, mountain range with peaks to 9,000 ft. in N. **Capital:** Asmara (1992): 400,000.

Government: Type: In transition. **Head of state:** Isaias Afwerki; b Feb. 2, 1946; in office: May 24, 1993. **Local divisions:** 8 provinces. **Defense: Active troop strength:** 48,000-55,000 est.

Economy: Industries: Food processing, textiles, fishing. **Chief crops:** Cotton, coffee, tobacco, lentils, sorghum. **Minerals:** Gold, potash, zinc, copper. **Livestock** (1996): sheep: 1.5 mil; goats: 1.4 mil; cattle: 1.3 mil. **Arable land:** 3%.

Transport: Railroad: Length: 190.6 mi.

Finance: Monetary unit: Birr (Aug. 1997: 7.20 = $1 US). **Gross domestic product** (1995 est.): $2 bil. **Per capita GDP:** $570. **Imports** (1995 est.): $420 mil. **Exports** (1995 est.): $33 mil.

Chief ports: Mitsiwa, Aseb.

Communications: Radios: 1 per 11 persons. **Telephones:** 1 per 208 persons.

Health (1997): **Life expectancy at birth:** 48.9 male; 52.4 female. **Births** (per 1,000 pop.): 44. **Deaths** (per 1,000 pop.): 15. **Natural increase:** 2.9%. **Physicians:** 1 per 36,000 persons.

Education: Compulsory: ages 7-13. **Literacy** (1994): 20%.

Major International Organizations: UN, OAU.

Embassy: Suite 400, 910 17th St. NW 20006; 429-1991.

Eritrea was part of the Ethiopian kingdom of Aksum. It was an Italian colony from 1890 to 1941, when it was captured by the British. Following a period of British and UN supervision, Eritrea was awarded to Ethiopia as part of a federation in 1952. Ethiopia annexed Eritrea as a province in 1962. This led to a 31-year struggle for independence, which ended when Eritrea formally declared itself an independent nation May 24, 1993. Legislative elections are scheduled for 1997.

Estonia
Republic of Estonia
Eesti Vabariik

People: Population: 1,444,721. **Age distrib.** (%): <15: 20; 65+: 14. **Pop. density:** 83 per sq. mi. **Urban:** 73%. **Ethnic groups:** Estonian 61.5%, Russian 30%. **Principal languages:** Estonian (official), Latvian, Lithuanian, Russian. **Chief religions:** Lutheran, Orthodox.

Geography: Area: 17,462 sq. mi. **Location:** E Europe, bordering the Baltic Sea and Gulf of Finland. **Neighbors:** Russia on E, Latvia on S. **Capital:** Tallinn (1995 est.): 434,763.

Government: Type: Republic. **Head of state:** Pres. Lennart Meri; b Mar. 29, 1929; in office: Oct. 5, 1992. **Head of government:** Prime Min. Mart Siimann; b 1946; in office: Feb. 27, 1997. **Local divisions:** 15 counties. **Defense:** 1.5% of GDP (1995). **Active troop strength:** 3,450.

Economy: Industries: Shipbuilding, electric motors, cement. **Chief crops:** Potatoes, fruits, vegetables. **Minerals:** Oil shale, phosphorites. **Other resources:** Dairy prods., peat. **Arable land:** 22%. **Livestock** (1996): pigs: 480,000; cattle: 415,000. **Electricity prod.** (1995): 8.1 bil kWh. **Labor force:** 42% ind. & constr., 20% agric. & forestry.

Finance: Monetary unit: Kroon (Aug. 1997: 14.58 = $1 US). **Gross domestic product** (1995 est.): $12.3 bil. **Per capita GDP:** $7,600. **Imports** (1995): $2.5 bil; partners: Finland 38%, Russia 15%. **Exports** (1995): $1.8 bil; partners: Finland 21%, Russia 18%. **National budget** (Jan.-Oct. 1995): $582 mil. **International reserves less gold** (June 1997): $620 mil. **Gold:** 8,000 oz. t. **Consumer prices** (change in 1996): 23.1%.

Transport: Railroads: Length: 632.2 mi. **Motor vehicles in use:** 338,000 passenger cars, 60,000 comm. vehicles. **Civil aviation:** 57.1 mil passenger-mi. **Chief port:** Tallinn.

Communications: Television sets: 1 per 2.7 persons. **Radios:** 1 per 2.1 persons. **Telephones:** 1 per 3.6 persons. **Daily newspaper circ.:** 242 per 1,000 pop.

Health: Life expectancy at birth (1997): 62.8 male; 74.1 female. **Births** (per 1,000 pop.): 12. **Deaths** (per 1,000 pop.): 14. **Natural increase:** −0.3%. **Hospital beds:** 1 per 119 persons. **Physicians:** 1 per 319 persons. **Infant mortality** (per 1,000 live births 1997): 17.

Education: Compulsory: ages 7-16. **Literacy** (1994): 100%.

Major International Organizations: UN (IMF, FAO, World Bank, WHO).

Embassy: 2131 Massachusetts Ave. NW 20008; 588-0101.

Estonia was a province of imperial Russia before World War I, was independent between World Wars I and II. It was conquered by the USSR in 1940 and was incorporated as the Estonian SSR. Estonia declared itself an "occupied territory," and proclaimed itself a free nation Mar. 1990. During an abortive Soviet coup, Estonia declared immediate full independence, Aug. 20, 1991; the Soviet Union recognized its independence in Sept. 1991. The first free elections in over 50 years were held Sept. 20, 1992. The last occupying Russian troops were withdrawn by Aug. 31, 1994.

Ethiopia
Federal Democratic Republic of Ethiopia
(Figures prior to 1993 include Eritrea)

People: Population: 58,732,577. **Age distrib.** (%): <15: 46; 65+: 3. **Pop. density:** 134 per sq. mi. **Urban:** 16%. **Ethnic groups:** Oromo 40%, Amhara and Tigre 32%, Sidamo 9%. **Principal languages:** Amharic (official), Tigrinya, Orominga. **Chief religions:** Muslim 45-50%, Ethiopian Orthodox 35-40%, animist 12%.

Geography: Area: 437,794 sq. mi. **Location:** In East Africa. **Neighbors:** Sudan on W, Kenya on S, Somalia and Djibouti on E, Eritrea on N. **Topography:** A high central plateau, between 6,000 and 10,000 ft. high, rises to higher mountains near the Great Rift Valley, cutting in from the SW. The Blue Nile and other rivers cross the plateau, which descends to plains on both W and SE. **Capital:** Addis Ababa: 2,431,000*.

Government: Type: Federal republic. **Head of state:** Pres. Negasso Gidada; in office: Aug. 22, 1995. **Head of government:** Prime Min. Meles Zenawi; b 1955; in office: Aug. 23, 1995. **Local divisions:** 9 administrative regions, 1 federal capital. **Defense:** 4.1% of GDP (FY 1994-95). **Active troop strength:** 120,000 est.

Economy: Industries: Food processing, chemicals, textiles. **Chief crops:** Coffee (60% of export earnings), oilseeds, grains. **Minerals:** Platinum, gold, copper. **Arable land:** 12%. **Livestock** (1996): cattle: 29.9 mil; sheep: 21.7 mil; goats: 16.7 mil. **Electricity prod.** (1995): 1.1 bil kWh. **Labor force:** 80% agric.

Finance: Monetary unit: Birr (Aug. 1997: 6.81 = $1 US). **Gross domestic product** (1995 est.): $24.2 bil. **Per capita GDP:** $400. **Imports** (1994 est.): $972 mil; partners: Saudi Arabia 19%. **Exports** (1994 est.): $296 mil; partners: Germany 20%, Japan 19%. **National budget** (FY 1993-94): $1.7 bil. **International reserves less gold** (June 1997): $583.3 mil. **Gold:** 24,000 oz t. **Consumer prices** (change in 1996): −5.1%.

Transport: Railroads: Length: 422.9 mi. **Motor vehicles in use:** 42,000 passenger cars, 30,000 comm. vehicles. **Civil aviation:** 997.9 mil passenger-mi.; 31 airports.

Communications: Television sets: 1 per 233 persons. **Radios:** 1 per 5.1 persons. **Telephones:** 1 per 401 persons.

Health: Life expectancy at birth (1997): 45.5 male; 47.8 female. **Births** (per 1,000 pop.): 46. **Deaths** (per 1,000 pop.): 18. **Natural increase:** 2.8%. **Infant mortality** (per 1,000 live births 1997): 122.

Education: Free and compulsory: ages 7-13. **Literacy** (1995 est.2): 35.5%.

Major International Organizations: UN (IMF, FAO, World Bank, WHO), OAU.

Embassy: 2134 Kalorama Rd. NW 20008; 234-2281.

Ethiopian culture was influenced by Egypt and Greece. The ancient monarchy was invaded by Italy in 1880 but maintained its independence until another Italian invasion in 1936. British forces freed the country in 1941.

The last emperor, Haile Selassie I, established a parliament and judiciary system in 1931 but barred all political parties.

A series of droughts in the 1970s killed hundreds of thousands. An army mutiny, strikes, and student demonstrations led to the dethronement of Selassie in 1974; he died Aug. 1975, while being held by the ruling junta. The junta pledged to form a one-party socialist state and instituted a successful land reform; opposition was violently suppressed. The influence of the Coptic Church, embraced in AD 330, was curbed, and the monarchy was abolished in 1975.

The regime, torn by bloody coups, faced uprisings by tribal and political groups in part aided by Sudan and Somalia. Ties with the U.S., once a major ally, deteriorated, while cooperation accords were signed with the USSR in 1977. In 1978, Soviet advisers and Cuban troops helped defeat Somalian forces. Ethiopia and Somalia signed a peace agreement in 1988.

A worldwide relief effort began in 1984, as an extended drought threatened the country with famine; up to a million people may have died as a result of starvation and disease. In 1988, victories by Eritrean guerrillas led the government to curtail the efforts of foreign aid workers in drought-stricken regions.

The Ethiopian People's Revolutionary Democractic Front (EPRDF), an umbrella group of 6 rebel armies, launched a major push against government forces, Feb. 1, 1991. In May, Pres. Mengistu Haile Mariam resigned and left the country. The EPRDF took over and set up a transitional government. Under a new constitution ratified Dec. 8, 1994, Ethiopia's first multi-party general elections were held in 1995.

Eritrea, a province on the Red Sea, declared its independence May 24, 1993.

Fiji
Republic of Fiji

People: Population: 792,441. **Age distrib.** (%): <15: 35; 65+: 3. **Pop. density:** 112 per sq. mi. **Urban:** 41%. **Ethnic**

groups: Fijian (Melanesian-Polynesian) 49%, Indian 46%, European. **Principal languages:** English (official), Fijian, Hindustani. **Chief religions:** Christian 52%, Hindu 38%, Muslim 8%.

Geography: Area: 7,055 sq. mi. **Location:** In western South Pacific O. **Neighbors:** Nearest are Vanuatu to W, Tonga to E. **Topography:** 322 islands (106 inhabited), many mountainous, with tropical forests and large fertile areas. Viti Levu, the largest island, has over half the total land area. **Capital:** Suva (1990 met.): 200,000.

Government: Type: Republic. **Head of state:** Pres. Ratu Sir Kamisese Mara; b May 13, 1920; in office: Jan. 18, 1994. **Head of government:** Prime Min. Sitiveni Rabuka; b Sept. 13, 1948; in office: June 2, 1992. **Local divisions:** 4 divisions, 1 dependency. **Defense:** 2.5% of GDP (1995). **Active troop strength:** 3,600 est.

Economy: Industries: Sugar refining, light industry, tourism. **Chief crops:** Sugar, bananas, coconuts. **Minerals:** Gold, copper. **Other resources:** Timber, fish. **Arable land:** 8%. **Electricity prod.** (1995): 545 mil kWh. **Labor force:** 67% subsistence agric.

Finance: Monetary unit: Dollar (Aug. 1997: 1.45 = $1.00 US). **Gross domestic product** (1995 est.): $4.7 bil. **Per capita GDP:** $6,100. **Imports** (1995): $864 mil; partners: Australia 30%, N.Z. 17%, Japan 13%. **Exports** (1995): $572 mil; partners: EU 26%, Australia 15%. **Tourism** (1994): $298 mil. **National budget** (1995 est.): $591 mil. **International reserves less gold** (Apr. 1997): $351.52 mil. **Gold:** 1,000 oz t. **Consumer prices** (change in 1996): 3.1%.

Transport: Railroads: Length: 370.7 mi. **Motor vehicles in use:** 30,000 passenger cars, 29,000 comm. vehicles. **Civil aviation:** 683.7 mil passenger-mi.; 13 airports with scheduled flights. **Chief ports:** Suva, Lautoka.

Communications: Television sets: 1 per 59 persons. **Radios:** 1 per 1.6 persons. **Telephones:** 1 per 12 persons. **Daily newspaper circ.:** 45 per 1,000 pop.

Health: Life expectancy at birth (1997): 63.7 male; 68.5 female. **Births** (per 1,000 pop.): 23. **Deaths** (per 1,000 pop.): 6. **Natural increase:** 1.7%. **Hospital beds:** 1 per 438 persons. **Physicians:** 1 per 2,161 persons. **Infant mortality** (per 1,000 live births 1997): 17.

Education: Literacy (1995 est.): 92%.

Major International Organizations: UN (IMF, FAO, WTO, World Bank, WHO).

Embassy: 2233 Wisconsin Ave. NW 20007; 337-8320.

A British colony since 1874, Fiji became an independent parliamentary democracy Oct. 10, 1970.

Cultural differences between the majority Indian community, descendants of contract laborers brought to the islands in the 19th century, and the less modernized native Fijians, who by law own 83% of the land in communal villages, have led to political polarization.

In 1987, a military coup ousted the government; order was restored May 21 under a compromise granting Lt. Col. Sitiveni Rabuka, the coup's leader, increased power. Rabuka staged a second coup Sept. 25 and declared Fiji a republic. Civilian government was restored in Dec. A new constitution favoring indigenous Fijians was issued July 25, 1990; amendments enacted in July 1997 made the constitution more equitable.

Finland
Republic of Finland
Suomen Tasavalta

People: Population: 5,109,148. **Age distrib.** (%): <15: 19; 65+: 14. **Pop. density:** 39 per sq. mi. **Urban:** 64%. **Ethnic groups:** Finn 94%, Swede, Lapp. **Principal languages:** Finnish, Swedish (both official). **Religion:** Evangelical Lutheran 89%.

Geography: Area: 130,559 sq. mi. **Location:** In northern Europe. **Neighbors:** Norway on N, Sweden on W, Russia on E. **Topography:** South and central Finland are mostly flat areas with low hills and many lakes. The N has mountainous areas, 3,000-4,000 ft. **Capital:** Helsinki. **Cities** (1996 est.): Helsinki 525,031; Espoo 191,247; Tampere 182,742.

Government: Type: Constitutional republic. **Head of state:** Pres. Martti Ahtisaari; b June 23, 1937; in office: Mar. 1, 1994. **Head of government:** Prime Min. Paavo Lipponen; b Apr. 23, 1941; in office: Apr. 13, 1995. **Local divisions:** 12 laanit (provinces). **Defense:** 1.6% of GDP (1995). **Active troop strength:** 32,500.

Economy: Industries: Metal prods., shipbuilding, wood processing, chemicals, textiles. **Chief crops:** Grains, sugar beets, potatoes. **Minerals:** Copper, iron, zinc. **Other resources:** Timber, dairy prods. **Arable land:** 8%. **Livestock** (1996): pigs: 1.4 mil; cattle: 1.2 mil. **Fish catch** (1993): 152,491 metric tons. **Electricity prod.** (1995): 58.6 bil kWh. **Labor force:** 46% ind., commerce & finance; 30% public serv.; 9% agric.

Finance: Monetary unit: Markka (Aug. 1997: 5.43 = $1 US). **Gross domestic product** (1995 est.): $92.4 bil. **Per capita GDP:** $18,200. **Imports** (1994): $23.2 bil; partners: Germany 15%. **Exports** (1994): $29.7 bil; partners: Germany 13%. **Tourism** (1994): $1.4 bil. **National budget** (1993 est.): $31.7 bil. **International reserves less gold** (June 1997): $10.29 bil. **Gold:** 1.6 mil oz t. **Consumer prices** (change in 1996): 0.6%.

Transport: Railroad: Length: 3,660.8 mi. **Motor vehicles in use:** 1.9 mil passenger cars, 280,000 comm. vehicles. **Civil aviation:** 4.2 bil passenger-mi.; 24 airports. **Chief ports:** Helsinki, Turku.

Communications: Television sets: 1 per 2.0 persons. **Radios:** 1 per 1.0 person. **Telephones:** 1 per 1.8 persons. **Daily newspaper circ.:** 473 per 1,000 pop.

Health: Life expectancy at birth (1997): 74.0 male; 77.3 female. **Births** (per 1,000 pop.): 11. **Deaths** (per 1,000 pop.): 11. **Natural increase:** –0.0. **Hospital beds:** 1 per 102 persons. **Physicians:** 1 per 371 persons. **Infant mortality** (per 1,000 live births 1997): 5.

Education: Free and compulsory: ages 7-16. **Literacy** (1997): 100%.

Major International Organizations: UN (IMF, FAO, World Bank, WHO, WTO), EU, OECD.

Embassy: 3301 Massachusetts Ave. NW 20008; 298-5800.

The early Finns probably migrated from the Ural area at about the beginning of the Christian era. Swedish settlers brought the country into Sweden, 1154 to 1809, when Finland became an autonomous grand duchy of the Russian Empire. Russian exactions created a strong national spirit; on Dec. 6, 1917, Finland declared its independence and in 1919 became a republic.

On Nov. 30, 1939, the Soviet Union invaded, and the Finns were forced to cede 16,173 sq. mi. of territory. After World War II, further cessions were exacted. In 1948, Finland signed a treaty of mutual assistance with the USSR; Finland and Russia nullified this treaty with a new pact in Jan. 1992.

Following approval by Finnish voters in an advisory referendum Oct. 16, 1994, Finland joined the European Union effective Jan. 1, 1995.

Aland, constituting an autonomous department, is a group of small islands, 590 sq. mi., in the Gulf of Bothnia, 25 mi. from Sweden, 15 mi. from Finland. Mariehamn is the principal port.

France
French Republic
République Française

People: Population: 58,040,230. **Age distrib.** (%): <15: 19; 65+: 16. **Pop. density:** 276 per sq. mi. **Urban:** 74%. **Ethnic groups:** Celtic and Latin; Teutonic, Slavic, North African, Indochinese, Basque minorities. **Principal languages:** French (official); minorities speak Breton, Alsatian German, Flemish, Italian, Basque, Catalan. **Religion:** Roman Catholic 90%.

Geography: Area: 210,026 sq. mi. **Location:** In western Europe, between Atlantic O. and Mediterranean Sea. **Neighbors:** Spain on S; Italy, Switzerland, Germany on E; Luxembourg, Belgium on N. **Topography:** A wide plain covers more than half of the country, in N and W, drained to W by Seine, Loire, Garonne rivers. The Massif Central is a mountainous plateau in center. In E are Alps (Mt. Blanc is tallest in W Europe, 15,771 ft.), the lower Jura range, and the forested Vosges. The Rhone flows from Lake Geneva to Mediterranean. Pyrenees are in SW, on border with Spain. **Capital:** Paris. **Cities:** Paris 9,523,000; Lyon 1,319,000; Marseilles 1,234,000; Lille 976,000*.

Government: Type: Republic. **Head of state:** Pres. Jacques Chirac; b Nov. 29, 1932; in office: May 17, 1995. **Head of government:** Prime Min. Lionel Jospin; b July 12, 1937; in office: June 3, 1997. **Local divisions:** 22 administrative regions containing 96 departments. **Defense:** 3.1% of GDP (1995). **Active troop strength:** 409,000.

Economy: Industries: Steel, chemicals, textiles, tourism, wine, perfume, aircraft, machinery, electronic equipment. **Chief crops:** Grains, corn, soybeans, fruits, vegetables. France is largest food producer, exporter, in W Europe. **Minerals:** Bauxite, iron, coal. **Crude oil reserves** (1995): 152 mil bbls. **Other resources:** Forests, dairy. **Arable land:** 32%. **Livestock** (1994): cattle: 20.1 mil; pigs: 13.4 mil; sheep: 10.5 mil. **Fish catch** (1995): 793,413 metric tons. **Electricity prod.** (1995): 467.5 bil kWh. **Labor force:** 62% services; 31% ind.; 7% agric.

Finance: Monetary unit: Franc (Aug. 1997: 6.10 = $1 US). **Gross domestic product** (1994): $1.08 tril. **Per capita GDP:** $18,670. **Imports** (1994): $238 bil; partners: Germany 18%, Italy 11%, U.S. 10%. **Exports** (1994): $249 bil; partners: Germany 19%, Italy 11%, Spain 11%. **Tourism** (1993): $23.4 bil. **National budget** (1993): $249.1 bil. **International reserves less gold** (June 1997): $28.97 bil. **Gold:** 81.85 mil oz t. **Consumer prices** (change in 1996): 2.0%.

Transport: Railroad: Length: 21,046.3 mi. **Motor vehicles:** in use: 24.4 mil passenger cars, 4.9 mil comm. vehicles. **Civil aviation:** 42.2 bil passenger-mi.; 61 airports with scheduled flights. **Chief ports:** Marseille, Le Havre, Bordeaux, Rouen.

Communications: Television sets: 1 per 1.7 persons. **Radios:** 1 per 1.1 persons. **Telephones:** 1 per 1.8 persons. **Daily newspaper circ.:** 237 per 1,000 pop.

Health: Life expectancy at birth (1996): 75 male; 83 female. **Births** (per 1,000 pop.): 11. **Deaths** (per 1,000 pop.): 9. **Natural increase:** 0.2%. **Hospital beds:** 1 per 86 persons. **Physicians:** 1 per 361 persons. **Infant mortality** (per 1,000 live births 1996): 6.

Education: Free and compulsory: ages 6-16. **Literacy** (1994): 99%.

Major International Organizations: UN and most of its specialized agencies, WTO, OECD, EU, NATO.

Embassy: 4101 Reservoir Rd. NW 20007; 944-6000.

Celtic Gaul was conquered by Julius Caesar 58-51 BC; Romans ruled for 500 years. Under Charlemagne, Frankish rule extended over much of Europe. After his death France emerged as one of the successor kingdoms.

The monarchy was overthrown by the French Revolution (1789-93) and succeeded by the First Republic; followed by the First Empire under Napoleon (1804-15), a monarchy (1814-48), the Second Republic (1848-52), the Second Empire (1852-70), the Third Republic (1871-1946), the Fourth Republic (1946-58), and the Fifth Republic (1958 to present).

France suffered severe losses in manpower and wealth in the first World War, 1914-18, when it was invaded by Germany. By the Treaty of Versailles, France exacted return of Alsace and Lorraine, French provinces seized by Germany in 1871. Germany invaded France again in May 1940, and signed an armistice with a government based in Vichy. After France was liberated by the Allies Sept. 1944, Gen. Charles de Gaulle became head of the provisional government, serving until 1946.

De Gaulle again became premier in 1958, during a crisis over Algeria, and obtained voter approval for a new constitution, ushering in the Fifth Republic. He became president Jan. 1959. Using strong executive powers, he promoted French economic and technological advances in the context of the European Economic Community and guarded French foreign policy independence.

France had withdrawn from Indochina in 1954, and from Morocco and Tunisia in 1956. Most of its remaining African territories were freed 1958-62. In 1966, France withdrew all its troops from the integrated military command of NATO, though 60,000 remained stationed in Germany.

In May 1968 rebellious students in Paris and other centers rioted, battled police, and were joined by workers who launched nationwide strikes. The government awarded pay increases to the strikers May 26. De Gaulle resigned from office in Apr. 1969, after losing a nationwide referendum on constitutional reform. Georges Pompidou, who was elected to succeed him, continued De Gaulle's emphasis on French independence from the two superpowers. After Pompidou's death, in 1974, Valery Giscard d'Estaing was elected president; he continued the basically conservative policies of his predecessors.

On May 10, 1981, France elected François Mitterrand, a Socialist, president. Under Mitterrand the government nationalized 5 major industries and most private banks. After 1986, however, when rightists won a narrow victory in the National Assembly, Mitterrand chose conservative Jacques Chirac as premier. A 2-year period of "cohabitation" ensued, and France began to pursue a privatization program in which many state-owned companies were sold. After Mitterrand was elected to a 2d 7-year term in 1988, he appointed a Socialist as premier. The center-right won a large majority in 1993 legislative elections, ushering in another period of "cohabitation" with a conservative premier.

In 1993, France set tighter rules for entry into the country and made it easier for the government to expel foreigners. In 1994, France sent troops to Rwanda in an effort to help protect civilians there from ongoing massacres. The international terrorist known as Carlos the Jackal (Ilich Ramirez Sánchez) was arrested in Sudan in Aug. 1994 and extradited to France, where he had been sentenced in absentia to life imprisonment.

Former conservative Prime Min. Jacques Chirac won the presidency in a runoff May 7, 1995. A series of terrorist bombings and bombing attempts began in summer 1995; Islamic extremists, opposed to France's support of the Algerian government and its struggle with Islamic fundamentalists, were believed responsible. In Sept. 1995, France stirred widespread protests by resuming nuclear tests in the South Pacific, after a 3-year moratorium; the tests ended Jan. 1996. In May Chirac promised to phase out military conscription, as part of a plan to restructure the armed forces.

Chirac cut government spending to help the French economy meet the budgetary goals set for the introduction of a common European currency. With unemployment at nearly 13%, legislative elections completed June 1, 1997, produced a decisive victory for the leftist parties. The result was a new period of "cohabitation," this time between a conservative president and a Socialist prime minister, Lionel Jospin.

The island of **Corsica**, in the Mediterranean W of Italy and N of Sardinia, is a territorial collectivity and region of France comprising 2 departments. It elects a total of 2 senators and 3 deputies to the French Parliament. Area: 3,369 sq. mi.; pop. (1996 est.): 258,000. The capital is Ajaccio, birthplace of Napoleon. Violence by Corsican separatist groups has hurt tourism, a leading industry on the island.

Overseas Departments

French Guiana is on the NE coast of South America with Suriname on the W and Brazil on the E and S. Its area is 33,399 sq. mi.; pop. (1997 est.): 156,946. Guiana sends one senator and 2 deputies to the French Parliament. Guiana is administered by a prefect and has a Council General of 16 elected members; capital is Cayenne.

The famous penal colony, Devil's Island, was phased out between 1938 and 1951. The European Space Agency maintains a satellite-launching center (established by France in 1964) in the city of Kourou.

Immense forests of rich timber cover 88% of the land. Fishing (especially shrimp), forestry, and gold mining are the most important industries.

Guadeloupe, in the West Indies' Leeward Islands, consists of 2 large islands, Basse-Terre and Grande-Terre, separated by the Salt River, plus Marie Galante and the Saintes group to the S and, to the N, Desirade, St. Barthelemy, and over half of St. Martin (the Netherlands' portion is called St. Maarten). A French possession since 1635, the department is represented in the French Parliament by 2 senators and 4 deputies; administration consists of a prefect (governor) and an elected general and regional councils.

Area of the islands is 687 sq. mi.; pop. (1997 est.) 412,614, mainly descendants of slaves; capital is Basse-Terre on Basse-Terre Island. The land is fertile; sugar, rum, and bananas are exported. Tourism is an important industry.

Martinique, the northernmost of the Windward Islands, in the West Indies, has been a possession since 1635, and a department since Mar. 1946. It is represented in the French Parliament by 2 senators and 4 deputies. The island was the birthplace of Napoleon's Empress Josephine.

It has an area of 436 sq. mi.; pop. (1997 est.) 403,531, mostly descendants of slaves. The capital is Fort-de-France (pop. 1991: 101,000). It is a popular tourist stop. The chief exports are rum, bananas, and petroleum products.

Réunion is a volcanic island in the Indian O. about 420 mi. E of Madagascar, and has belonged to France since 1665. Area, 970 sq. mi.; pop. (1997 est.) 692,204, 30% of French extraction. Capital: Saint-Denis. The chief export is sugar. It elects 5 deputies, 3 senators to the French Parliament.

Overseas Territorial Collectivities

Mayotte, claimed by Comoros and administered by France, voted in 1976 to become a territorial collectivity of France. An island NW of Madagascar, area is 144 sq. mi., pop. (1997 est.) 104,715. The capital is Mamoutzou.

St. Pierre and Miquelon, formerly an overseas territory (1816-1976) and department (1976-85), made the transition to territorial collectivity in 1985. It consists of 2 groups of rocky islands near the SW coast of Newfoundland, inhabited by fishermen. The exports are chiefly fish products. The St. Pierre group has an area of 10 sq. mi.; Miquelon, 83 sq. mi. Total pop. (1997 est.), 6,862. The capital is St. Pierre.

Both Mayotte and St. Pierre and Miquelon elect a deputy and a senator to the French Parliament.

Overseas Territories

Territory of **French Polynesia** comprises 130 islands widely scattered among 5 archipelagos in the South Pacific; administered by a Council of Ministers (headed by a president). Territorial Assembly and the Council have headquarters at Papeete, on Tahiti, one of the **Society Islands** (which include the **Windward** and **Leeward** islands). Two deputies and a senator are elected to the French Parliament.

Other groups are the **Marquesas Islands,** the **Tuamotu Archipelago,** including the **Gambier Islands,** and the **Austral Islands.**

Total area of the islands administered from Tahiti is 1,544 sq. mi.; pop. (1997 est.), 233,488, more than half on Tahiti. Tahiti is picturesque and mountainous with a productive coastline bearing coconuts, citrus fruits, pineapples, and vanilla. Cultured pearls are also produced.

Tahiti was visited by Capt. James Cook in 1769 and by Capt. Bligh in the *Bounty*, 1788-89. Its beauty impressed Herman Melville, Paul Gauguin, and Charles Darwin. Tahitians angered by French nuclear testing rioted Sept. 1995.

Territory of the **French Southern and Antarctic Lands** comprises **Adelie Land,** on Antarctica, and 4 island groups in the Indian O. Adelie, reached 1840, has a research station, a coastline of 185 mi., and tapers 1,240 mi. inland to the South Pole. The U.S. does not recognize national claims in Antarctica. There are 2 huge glaciers, Ninnis, 22 mi. wide, 99 mi. long, and Mentz, 11 mi. wide, 140 mi. long. The Indian O. groups are:

Kerguelen Archipelago, visited 1772, consists of one large and 300 small islands. The chief is 87 mi. long, 74 mi. wide, and has Mt. Ross, 6,429 ft. tall. Principal research station is Port-aux-Français. Seals often weigh 2 tons; there are blue whales, coal, peat, semiprecious stones. **Crozet Archipelago,** reached 1772, covers 195 sq. mi. Eastern Island rises to 6,560 ft. **Saint Paul,** in southern Indian O., has warm springs with earth at places heating to 120° to 390° F. **Amsterdam** is nearby; both produce cod and rock lobster.

Territory of **New Caledonia** and Dependencies is a group of islands in the Pacific O. about 1,115 mi. E of Australia and approx. the same distance NW of New Zealand. Dependencies are the **Loyalty Islands, Isle of Pines, Belep Archipelago,** and **Huon Islands.**

The largest island, New Caledonia, is 6,530 sq. mi. Total area of the territory is 8,548 sq. mi.; population (1997 est.) 191,003. The group was acquired by France in 1853.

The territory is administered by a High Commissioner. There is a popularly elected Territorial Congress. Two deputies and a senator are elected to the French Parliament. Capital: Noumea.

Mining is the chief industry. New Caledonia is one of the world's largest nickel producers. Other minerals found are chrome, iron, cobalt, manganese, silver, gold, lead, and copper. Agricultural products include yams, sweet potatoes, potatoes, manioc (cassava), corn, and coconuts.

In 1987, New Caledonia voters chose by referendum to remain within the French Republic. There were clashes between French and Melanesians (Kanaks) in 1988. Another referendum is scheduled for 1998.

Territory of the **Wallis and Futuna Islands** comprises 2 island groups in the SW Pacific S of Tuvalu, N of Fiji, and W of Western Samoa; became an overseas territory July 29, 1961. The islands have a total area of 106 sq. mi. and population (1997 est.) of 14,817. **Alofi,** attached to Futuna, is uninhabited. Capital: Mata-Utu. Chief products are copra, yams, taro roots, bananas, and coconuts. A senator and a deputy are elected to the French Parliament.

Gabon
Gabonese Republic
République Gabonaise

People: Population: 1,190,159. **Age distrib.** (%): <15: 34; 65+: 5. **Pop. density:** 12 per sq. mi. **Urban:** 51%. **Ethnic groups:** Fang, Eshira, Bapounou, Bateke, other Bantu, other Africans, Europeans. **Principal languages:** French (official), Bantu dialects. **Chief religions:** Mostly Christian, some Muslim and animist.

Geography: Area: 103,347 sq. mi. **Location:** On Atlantic coast of W central Africa. **Neighbors:** Equatorial Guinea and Cameroon on N, Congo on E and S. **Topography:** Heavily forested, the country consists of coastal lowlands; plateaus in N, E, and S; mountains in N, SE, and center. The Ogooue R. system covers most of Gabon. **Capital:** Libreville (1993 met.): 462,086.

Government: Type: Republic. **Head of state:** Pres. Omar Bongo; b Dec. 30, 1935; in office: Dec. 2, 1967. **Head of government:** Prime Min. Paulin Obame-Nguema; in office: Nov. 2, 1994. **Local divisions:** 9 provinces. **Defense:** 2.4% of GDP (1993). **Active troop strength:** 4,700 est.

Economy: Industries: Oil products, textiles, food and beverages. **Chief crops:** Cocoa, coffee, palm products. **Minerals:** Oil, manganese, uranium, iron, gold. **Crude oil reserves** (1996): 1.3 bil bbls. **Other resources:** Timber. **Arable land:** 1%. **Electricity prod.** (1995): 925 mil kWh. **Labor force:** 65% agric.; 30% ind. & commerce.

Finance: Monetary unit: CFA Franc (Aug. 1997: 610 = $1 US). **Gross domestic product** (1995 est.): $6 bil. **Per capita income:** $5,200. **Imports** (1994 est.): $800 mil; partners: France 35%. **Exports** (1994 est.): $2.1 bil; partners: U.S. 50%, France 16%. **National budget** (1993 est.): $1.6 bil. **Consumer prices** (change in 1996): 4.2%.

Transport: Railroads: Length: 403 mi. **Motor vehicles in use:** 23,000 passenger cars, 10,000 comm. vehicles. **Civil aviation:** 446.5 mil passenger-mi.; 23 airports with scheduled flights. **Chief ports:** Port-Gentil, Owendo, Libreville.

Communications: Television sets: 1 per 26 persons. **Radios:** 1 per 6.8 persons. **Telephones:** 1 per 41 persons.

Health: Life expectancy at birth (1997): 53.1 male; 59.1 female. **Births** (per 1,000 pop.): 28. **Deaths** (per 1,000 pop.):

13. **Natural increase:** 1.5%. **Infant mortality** (per 1,000 live births 1997): 88.

Education: Compulsory: ages 6-16. **Literacy** (1995 est.): 63%.

Major International Organizations: UN (WTO, FAO, WHO, IMF, World Bank), OAU, OPEC.

Embassy: Suite 200, 2034 20th St. NW 20009; 797-1000.

France established control over the region in the second half of the 19th century. Gabon became independent Aug. 17, 1960. A multiparty political system was introduced in 1990, and a new constitution was enacted Mar. 14, 1991. However, the reelection of longtime Pres. Omar Bongo, on Dec. 5, 1993, prompted rioting and charges of vote fraud. Under a revised constitution approved by referendum July 23, 1995, parliamentary elections were held in Dec. 1996.

Gabon is one of the most prosperous black African countries, thanks to abundant natural resources, foreign private investment, and government development programs.

The Gambia
Republic of The Gambia

People: Population: 1,248,085. **Age distrib.** (%): <15: 46; 65+: 3. **Pop. density:** 302 per sq. mi. **Urban:** 30%. **Ethnic groups:** Mandinka 42%, Fula 18%, Wolof 16%, other African. **Principal languages:** English (official), Mandinka, Wolof. **Chief religions:** Muslim 90%, Christian 9%.

Geography: Area: 4,127 sq. mi. **Location:** On Atlantic coast near W tip of Africa. **Neighbors:** Surrounded on 3 sides by Senegal. **Topography:** A narrow strip of land on each side of the lower Gambia R. **Capital:** Banjul (1993): 42,407.

Government: Type: Republic. **Head of state and government:** Yahya Jammeh; b May 25, 1965; in office: July 23, 1994. **Local divisions:** 5 divisions and Banjul. **Defense:** 3.8% of GDP (FY 1993-94). **Active troop strength:** 800.

Economy: Industries: Tourism, peanut processing. **Chief crops:** Peanuts (main export), rice. **Arable land:** 16%. **Fish catch** (1993): 20,000 metric tons. **Electricity prod.** (1995): 73 mil kWh. **Labor force:** 75% agric.; 19% ind., comm., serv.

Finance: Monetary unit: Dalasi (Aug. 1997: 10.46 = $1.00 US). **Gross domestic product** (1995 est.): $1.1 bil. **Per capita GDP:** $1,100. **Imports** (1994 est.): $209 mil; partners: Europe 57%. **Exports** (1994 est.): $35 mil; partners: Japan 60%. **Tourism** (1994): $27 mil. **National budget** (FY 1995-96 est.): $90 mil. **International reserves less gold** (Feb. 1997): $101.93 mil. **Consumer prices** (change in 1996): 1.1%.

Transport: Motor vehicles in use: 7,600 passenger cars, 3,100 comm. vehicles. **Civil aviation:** 31.1 mil passenger-mi. **Chief port:** Banjul.

Communications: Radios: 1 per 6.1 persons. **Telephones:** 1 per 58 persons.

Health: Life expectancy at birth (1997): 51.2 male; 55.8 female. **Births** (per 1,000 pop.): 44. **Deaths** (per 1,000 pop.): 13. **Natural increase:** 2.4%. **Hospital beds:** 1 per 1,475 persons. **Physicians:** 1 per 14,536 persons. **Infant mortality** (per 1,000 live births 1997): 79.

Education: Literacy (1995 est.): 39%.

Major International Organizations: UN (IMF, FAO, WTO, World Bank, WHO), OAU, the Commonwealth.

Embassy: Suite 1000, 1155 15th St. NW 20005; 785-1399.

The tribes of Gambia were at one time associated with the West African empires of Ghana, Mali, and Songhay. The area became Britain's first African possession in 1588.

Independence came Feb. 18, 1965; republic status within the Commonwealth was achieved in 1970. The country suffered from severe famine in the 1970s. After a coup attempt in 1981, The Gambia formed the confederation of Senegambia with Senegal that lasted until 1989.

On July 23, 1994, after 24 years in power, Pres. Dawda K. Jawara was deposed in a bloodless coup by a military officer, Yahya Jammeh. Jammeh barred political activity, detained potential opponents, and governed by decree. A new constitution was approved by referendum, Aug. 8, 1996. On Sept. 27 Jammeh won the presidential election. Parliamentary balloting on Jan. 2, 1997, completed the nominal return to civilian rule, but Jammeh retained a firm grip on power.

Georgia
Republic of Georgia
Sakartvelos Respublika

People: Population: 5,174,642. **Age distrib.** ($): <15: 22; 65+: 12. **Pop. density:** 193 per sq. mi. **Urban:** 59%. **Ethnic groups:** Georgian 70%, Armenian 8%, Russian 6%. **Principal languages:** Georgian (official), Russian. **Chief religions:** Georgian Orthodox 65%, Muslim 11%, Russian Orthodox 10%.

Geography: Area: 26,831 sq. mi. **Location:** In SW Asia, on E coast of Black Sea. **Neighbors:** Russia on N and NE, Turkey and Armenia on S, Azerbaijan on SE. **Topography:** Separated from Russia on NE by main range of the Caucasus Mts. **Capital:** Tbilisi (1994 est.): 1,342,000*.

Government: Type: Republic. **Head of state:** Pres. Eduard A. Shevardnadze; b Jan. 25, 1928; in office: Nov. 6, 1992. **Defense:** 3.1% of GNP (1993). **Active troop strength:** NA.

Economy: Industries: Manganese mining, steel, machinery. **Chief crops:** Citrus and other fruits, potatoes, corn, grapes, tea. **Minerals:** Manganese, coal. **Arable land:** 11%. **Livestock** (1996): cattle: 950,000; sheep: 760,000. **Electricity prod.** (1995): 6.6 bil kWh. **Labor force:** 31% ind., constr.; 25% agric.

Finance: Monetary unit: Lari (Aug. 1997: 1.20 = $1 U.S.). **Gross domestic product** (1995 est.): $6.2 bil. **Per capita GDP:** $1,080. **Imports** (1995): $250 mil. **Exports** (1995): $140 mil.

Transport: Railroads: Length: 975 mi. **Motor vehicles in use:** 442,000 passenger cars, 50,000 comm. vehicles. **Civil aviation:** 175.7 mil passenger-mi. **Chief ports:** Batumi, Sukhumi, Poti.

Communications: Radios: 1 per 1.8 persons. **Telephones:** 1 per 9.7 persons.

Health: Life expectancy at birth (1997): 63.6 male; 73.1 female. **Births** (per 1,000 pop.): 14. **Deaths** (per 1,000 pop.): 12. **Natural increase:** 0.2%. **Hospital beds:** 1 per 95 persons. **Physicians:** 1 per 182 persons. **Infant mortality** (per 1,000 live births 1997): 22.

Education: Literacy (1994): 99%.

Major International Organizations: UN, CIS, World Bank. **Embassy:** Suite 424, 1511 K St. NW 20005; 393-5959.

The region contained the ancient kingdoms of Colchis and Iberia. It was Christianized in the 4th century and conquered by Arabs in the 8th century. The region expanded to include area from the Black Sea to Caspian and parts of Armenia and Persia before its disintegration under the impact of Mongol and Turkish invasions. Its annexation by Russia in 1801 caused the Russian war with Persia, 1804-1813. Georgia entered the USSR in 1922 and became a constituent republic in 1936.

In 1989, strong nationalist feelings led the USSR to attempts at repression; Soviet troops attacked nationalist demonstrators in April, killing some 20 persons. Georgia declared independence Apr. 9, 1991. It became an independent state when the Soviet Union disbanded Dec. 26, 1991.

There was fighting during 1991 between rebel forces and loyalists of Pres. Zviad Gamsakhurdia, who fled the capital Jan. 6, 1992. The ruling Military Council picked former Soviet Foreign Minister Eduard A. Shevardnadze to chair a newly created State Council. An attempted coup by forces loyal to Gamsakhurdia was crushed June 24, 1992. Shevardnadze was later elected president. Gamsakhurdia died Jan. 1994, reportedly by suicide.

In Abkhazia, an autonomous region within Georgia, ethnic Abkhazis, reportedly aided by Russia, launched a bloody military campaign and, by late 1993, had gained control of much of the region. A cease-fire providing for Russian peacekeepers was signed in Moscow May 14, 1994.

On Feb. 3, 1994, Georgia signed agreements with Russia for economic and military cooperation. On Mar. 1, Georgia's Supreme Council ratified membership by Georgia in the Commonwealth of Independent States.

Shevardnadze was wounded by a car bomb Aug. 29, 1995, while on his way to Parliament to sign a new constitution. He was reelected president Nov. 5.

Germany
Federal Republic of Germany
Bundesrepublik Deutschland

People: Population: 84,068,216. **Age distrib.** (%): <15: 16; 65+: 15. **Pop. density:** 610 per sq. mi. **Urban:** 87%. **Ethnic groups:** German 95%, Turkish 2%. **Principal language:** German (official). **Chief religions:** Protestant 45%, Roman Catholic 37%.

Geography: Area: 137,830 sq. mi. **Location:** In central Europe. **Neighbors:** Denmark on N; Netherlands, Belgium, Luxembourg, France on W; Switzerland, Austria on S; Czech Rep., Poland on E. **Topography:** Germany is flat in N, hilly in contor and W, and mountainous in Bavaria in the S. Chief rivers are Elbe, Weser, Ems, Rhine, and Main, all flowing toward North Sea, and Danube, flowing toward Black Sea. **Capital:** Berlin. **Cities:** Essen 6,482,000; Frankfurt 3,605,000; Berlin 3,317,000; Düsseldorf 3,030,000; Cologne 2,984,000*.

Government: Type: Federal republic. **Head of state:** Pres. Roman Herzog; b Apr. 5, 1934; in office: July 1, 1994. **Head of government:** Chan. Helmut Kohl; b Apr. 3, 1930; in office: Oct.

1, 1982. **Local divisions:** 16 laender (states) with substantial powers. **Defense:** 1.5% of GDP (1995). **Active troop strength:** 358,400.

Economy: Industries: Steel, ships, vehicles, machinery, electronics, coal, chemicals, food and beverages. **Chief crops:** Grains, potatoes, sugar beets. **Minerals:** Coal, potash, lignite, iron, uranium. **Crude oil reserves** (1996): 385 mil bbls. **Arable land:** 34%. **Livestock** (1996): pigs: 23.7 mil; cattle: 15.9 mil; sheep: 2.4 mil. **Fish catch** (1995): 288,017 metric tons. **Electricity prod.** (1995): 495.875 bil kWh. **Labor force:** 41% ind.; 6% agric.

Finance: Monetary unit: Mark (Aug. 1997: 1.81 = $1 US). **Gross domestic product** (1995 est.): $1.45 tril. **Per capita GDP:** $17,900. **Imports** (1994): $362 bil; partners: EU 46%, U.S. 7%. **Exports** (1994): $437 bil; partners: EU 48%, U.S. 8%. **Tourism** (1994): $10.6 bil. **National budget** (1994): $780 bil. **International reserves less gold** (June 1997): $80.77 bil. **Gold:** 95.18 mil oz t. **Consumer prices** (change in 1996): 1.5%.

Transport: Railroads: Length: 27,302.9 mi. **Motor vehicles in use:** 40.5 mil passenger cars, 3.1 mil comm. vehicles. **Civil aviation:** 35.3 bil passenger-mi.; 28 airports with scheduled flights. **Chief ports:** Hamburg, Bremen, Bremerhaven, Lubeck, Rostock.

Communications: Television sets: 1 per 1.8 persons. **Radios:** 1 per 1.1 persons. **Telephones:** 1 per 2.0 persons. **Daily newspaper circ.:** 317 per 1,000 pop.

Health: Life expectancy at birth (1997): 73.0 male; 79.4 female. **Births** (per 1,000 pop.): 9. **Deaths** (per 1,000 pop.): 11. **Natural increase:** –0.2%. **Hospital beds:** 1 per 130 persons. **Physicians:** 1 per 298 persons. **Infant mortality** (per 1,000 live births 1997): 6.

Education: Compulsory: ages 6-15. **Literacy** (1993): 100%.

Major International Organizations: UN and all of its specialized agencies, EU, OECD, NATO.

Embassy: 4645 Reservoir Rd. NW 20007; 298-4000.

Germany is a central European nation originally composed of numerous states, with a common language and traditions, that were united in one country in 1871; Germany was split into 2 countries from the end of World War II until 1990, when it was reunified.

History and government. Germanic tribes were defeated by Julius Caesar, 55 and 53 BC, but Roman expansion N of the Rhine was stopped in AD 9. Charlemagne, ruler of the Franks, consolidated Saxon, Bavarian, Rhenish, Frankish, and other lands; after him the eastern part became the German Empire. The Thirty Years' War, 1618-1648, split Germany into small principalities and kingdoms. After Napoleon, Austria contended with Prussia for dominance, but lost the Seven Weeks' War to Prussia, 1866. Otto von Bismarck, Prussian chancellor, formed the North German Confederation, 1867.

In 1870 Bismarck maneuvered Napoleon III into declaring war. After the quick defeat of France, Bismarck formed the **German Empire** and on Jan. 18, 1871, in Versailles, proclaimed King Wilhelm I of Prussia German emperor (Deutscher kaiser).

The German Empire reached its peak before World War I in 1914, with 208,780 sq. mi., plus a colonial empire. After that war Germany ceded Alsace-Lorraine to France; West Prussia and Posen (Poznan) province to Poland; part of Schleswig to Denmark; lost all of its colonies and the ports of Memel and Danzig.

Republic of Germany, 1919-1933, adopted the Weimar constitution; met reparation payments and elected Friedrich Ebert and Gen. Paul von Hindenburg presidents.

Third Reich, 1933-1945, Adolf Hitler led the National Socialist German Workers' (Nazi) party after World War I. In 1923 he attempted to unseat the Bavarian government and was imprisoned. Pres. von Hindenburg named Hitler chancellor Jan. 30, 1933; on Aug. 3, 1934, the day after Hindenburg's death, the cabinet joined the offices of president and chancellor and made Hitler fuehrer (leader). Hitler abolished freedom of speech and assembly, and began a long series of persecutions climaxed by the murder of millions of Jews and others.

Hitler repudiated the Versailles treaty and reparations agreements. He remilitarized the Rhineland (1936) and annexed Austria (Anschluss, 1938). At Munich he made an agreement with Neville Chamberlain, British prime minister, which permitted Germany to annex part of Czechoslovakia. He signed a nonaggression treaty with the USSR, 1939. He declared war on Poland Sept. 1, 1939, precipitating World War II.

With total defeat near, Hitler committed suicide in Berlin Apr. 1945. The victorious Allies voided all acts and annexations of Hitler's Reich.

Division of Germany. Germany was sectioned into 4 zones of occupation, administered by the Allied Powers (U.S., USSR,

U.K., and France). The USSR took control of many E German states. The territory E of the so-called Oder-Neisse line was assigned to, and later annexed by, Poland. Northern East Prussia (now Kaliningrad) was annexed by the USSR. Administration of the remaining regions, in the W and S (which make up about two-thirds of present-day Germany), was split among the Western Allies.

There was also created the area of Greater Berlin, within but not part of the Soviet zone, administered by the 4 occupying powers under the Allied Command. In 1948 the USSR withdrew, established its single command in East Berlin, and cut off supplies. The Western Allies utilized a gigantic airlift to bring food to West Berlin, 1948-49.

In 1949, 2 separate German states were established; in May the zones administered by the Western Allies became West Germany, capital: Bonn; in Oct. the Soviet sector became East Germany, capital: East Berlin. West Berlin was considered an enclave of West Germany, although its status was disputed by the Soviet bloc.

East Germany. The German Democratic Republic (East Germany) was proclaimed in the Soviet sector of Berlin Oct. 7, 1949. It was proclaimed fully sovereign in 1954, but Soviet troops remained on grounds of security and the 4-power Potsdam agreement.

Coincident with the entrance of West Germany into the European defense community in 1952, the East German government decreed a prohibited zone 3 miles deep along its 600-mile border with West Germany and cut Berlin's telephone system in two. Berlin was further divided by erection of a fortified wall in 1961, after over 3 million East Germans had emigrated West; an exodus of refugees to the West continued, though on a smaller scale.

East Germany suffered severe economic problems at least until the mid-1960s. Then a "new economic system" was introduced, easing central planning controls and allowing factories to make profits provided they were reinvested in operations or redistributed to workers as bonuses. By the early 1970s, the economy was highly industrialized, and the nation was credited with the highest standard of living among Warsaw Pact countries. But growth slowed in the late 1970s, because of shortages of natural resources and labor, and a huge debt to lenders in the West. Comparison with the lifestyle in the West caused many of the young to leave the country.

The government firmly resisted following the USSR's policy of *glasnost,* but by Oct. 1989, was faced with nationwide demonstrations demanding reform. Pres. Erich Honecker, in office since 1976, was forced to resign, Oct. 18. On Nov. 4, the border with Czechoslovakia was opened and permission granted for refugees to travel to the West. On Nov. 9, the East German government announced its decision to open the border with the West, signaling the end of the "Berlin Wall," which was the supreme emblem of the cold war. On Aug. 23, 1990, the East German parliament agreed to formal unification with West Germany; this occurred Oct. 3.

West Germany. The Federal Republic of Germany (West Germany) was proclaimed May 23, 1949, in Bonn, after a constitution had been drawn up by a consultative assembly formed by representatives of the 11 laender (states) in the French, British, and American zones. Later reorganized into 9 units, the laender numbered 10 with the addition of the Saar, 1957. Berlin also was granted land (state) status, but the 1945 occupation agreements placed restrictions on it.

The occupying powers, the U.S., Britain, and France, restored civil status, Sept. 21, 1949. The Western Allies ended the state of war with Germany in 1951 (the U.S. resumed diplomatic relations July 2), while the USSR did so in 1955. The powers lifted controls and the republic became fully independent May 5, 1955.

Dr. Konrad Adenauer, Christian Democrat, was made chancellor Sept. 15, 1949, reelected 1953, 1957, 1961. Willy Brandt, heading a coalition of Social Democrats and Free Democrats, became chancellor Oct. 21, 1969. (He resigned May 1974 because of a spy scandal.)

In 1970 Brandt signed friendship treaties with the USSR and Poland. In 1971, the U.S., Britain, France, and the USSR signed an agreement on Western access to West Berlin. In 1972 East and West Germany signed their first formal treaty, implementing the agreement easing access to West Berlin. In 1973 a West Germany-Czechoslovakia pact normalized relations and nullified the 1938 "Munich Agreement."

West Germany experienced strong economic growth starting in the 1950s. The country led Europe in provisions for worker participation in the management of industry.

A NATO decision to deploy medium-range nuclear missiles in Western Europe sparked a demonstration by some 400,000 protesters in 1983. In 1989, Chancellor Helmut Kohl's call for early negotiations with the Soviets on reducing short-range missiles caused a rift with NATO allies.

In 1989, the changes in the East German government and opening of the Berlin Wall sparked talk of reunification of the 2 Germanys. In 1990, under Chancellor Kohl's leadership, West Germany moved rapidly to reunite with East Germany.

A New Era. As Communism was being rejected in East Germany, talks began concerning German reunification. At a meeting in Ottawa, Feb. 1990, the foreign ministers of the World War II "Big Four" Allied nations and of East Germany and West Germany reached agreement on a format for high-level talks on German reunification.

In May, NATO ministers adopted a package of proposals on reunification, including the inclusion of the united Germany as a full member of NATO and the barring of the new Germany from having its own nuclear, chemical, or biological weapons. In July, the USSR agreed to conditions that would allow Germany to become a member of NATO.

The 2 nations agreed to monetary unification under the West German mark beginning in July. The merger of the 2 Germanys took place Oct. 3, and the first all-German elections since 1932 were held Dec. 2.

In 1991, Berlin again became the capital of Germany; the seat of government was scheduled to shift from Bonn to Berlin over the course of about 10 years.

In 1992, neo-Nazi groups intensified their campaign against refugees. Parliament approved constitutional changes to restrict foreigners' rights to seek asylum in Germany, May 1993.

Germany's highest court ruled, July 12, 1994, that German troops could participate in international military missions abroad, when approved by Parliament. Ceremonies were held marking the final withdrawal of Russian troops from Germany, Aug. 31, 1994. Ceremonies were held the following week marking the final withdrawal of American, British, and French troops from Berlin. General elections Oct. 16, 1994, left Chancellor Helmut Kohl's governing coalition with a slim parliamentary majority. Eastern Germany received more than $1 trillion in public and private funds from western Germany between 1990 and 1995. On Oct. 31, 1996, after more than 14 years in office, Kohl surpassed Adenauer as Germany's longest-serving chancellor in the 20th century.

Helgoland, an island of 130 acres in the North Sea, was taken from Denmark by a British Naval Force in 1807 and later ceded to Germany to become part of Schleswig-Holstein province in return for rights in East Africa. The heavily fortified island was surrendered to UK, May 23, 1945, demilitarized in 1947, and returned to West Germany, Mar. 1, 1952. It is a free port.

Ghana
Republic of Ghana

People: Population: 18,100,703. **Age distrib.** (%): <15: 43; 65+: 3. **Pop. density:** 197 per sq. mi. **Urban:** 36%. **Ethnic groups:** Akan 44%, Moshi-Dagomba 16%, Ewe 13%, Ga 8%. **Principal languages:** English (official), Akan, Moshi-Dagomba, Ewe, Ga. **Chief religions:** Indigenous beliefs 38%, Muslim 30%, Christian 24%.

Geography: Area: 92,098 sq. mi. **Location:** On southern coast of W Africa. **Neighbors:** Côte d'Ivoire on W, Burkina Faso on N, Togo on E. **Topography:** Most of Ghana consists of low fertile plains and scrubland, cut by rivers and by the artificial Lake Volta. **Capital:** Accra: 1,673,000*.

Government: Type: Republic. **Head of state and government:** Pres. Jerry Rawlings; b 1947; in office: Dec. 31, 1981. **Local divisions:** 10 regions. **Defense:** 0.8% of GDP (1994). **Active troop strength:** 7,000.

Economy: Industries: Aluminum, light manufacturing. **Chief crops:** Cocoa, coffee, rice, cassava, peanuts, corn. **Minerals:** Gold, manganese, industrial diamonds, bauxite. **Other resources:** Timber, rubber. **Arable land:** 5%. **Livestock** (1996): goats: 3.3 mil; sheep: 3.3 mil; cattle: 1.7 mil. **Fish catch** (1995): 344,450 metric tons. **Electricity prod.** (1995): 6.1 bil kWh. **Labor force:** 55% agric.; 19% ind.; 15% sales, clerical.

Finance: Monetary unit: Cedi (Aug. 1997: 2,190 = $1 US). **Gross domestic product** (1995 est.): $25.1 bil. **Per capita GDP:** $1,400. **Imports** (1993 est.): $1.7 bil; partners: Germany 14%, UK 12%, U.S. 12%. **Exports** (1993 est.): $1 bil; partners: U.K. 16%, Italy 8%. **Tourism** (1994): $228 mil. **National budget** (1993): $1.2 bil. **International reserves less gold** (Feb. 1997): $873.3 mil. **Gold:** 275,000 oz t. **Consumer prices** (change in 1996): 34.0%.

Transport: Railroad: Length: 591.8 mi. **Motor vehicles in use:** 90,000 passenger cars, 45,000 comm. vehicles. **Civil aviation:** 296.8 mil passenger-mi.; 1 airport with scheduled flights. **Chief ports:** Tema, Takoradi.

Communications: Television sets: 1 per 11 persons. **Radios:** 1 per 4.4 persons. **Telephones:** 1 per 285 persons. **Daily newspaper circ.:** 18 per 1,000 pop.

Health: Life expectancy at birth (1997): 54.5 male; 58.6 female. **Births** (per 1,000 pop.): 34. **Deaths** (per 1,000 pop.):

11. **Natural increase:** 2.3%. **Hospital beds:** 1 per 791 persons. **Infant mortality** (per 1,000 live births 1997): 79.
Education: Compulsory: ages 6-16. **Literacy** (1995 est.): 64%.
Major International Organizations: UN and all of its specialized agencies, OAU, the Commonwealth.
Embassy: 3512 International Dr. NW 20008; 686-4520.

Named for an African empire along the Niger River, AD 400-1240, Ghana was ruled by Britain for 113 years as the Gold Coast. The UN in 1956 approved merger with the British Togoland trust territory. Independence came March 6, 1957. Republic status within the Commonwealth was attained in 1960.

Pres. Kwame Nkrumah built hospitals and schools, promoted development projects like the Volta R. hydroelectric and aluminum plants but ran the country into debt, jailed opponents, and was accused of corruption. A 1964 referendum gave Nkrumah dictatorial powers and set up a one-party socialist state.

Nkrumah was overthrown in 1966 by a police-army coup, which expelled Chinese and East German teachers and technicians. Elections were held in 1969, but 4 further coups occurred in 1972, 1978, 1979, and 1981. The 1979 and 1981 coups, led by Flight Lieut. Jerry Rawlings, were followed by suspension of the constitution and banning of political parties. A new constitution, which allowed for multiparty politics, was approved in April 1992.

In Feb. 1993 more than 1,000 people were killed in ethnic clashes in northern Ghana. Rawlings won the presidential election of Dec. 7, 1996. Kofi Annan, a career UN diplomat from Ghana, became UN secretary general on Jan. 1, 1997.

Greece
Hellenic Republic
Elliniki Dhimokratia

People: Population: 10,583,126. **Age distrib.** (%): <15: 16; 65+: 16. **Pop. density:** 208 per sq. mi. **Urban:** 59%. **Ethnic groups:** Greek 98%. (**Note:** Greek govt. states there are no ethnic divisions in Greece.) **Principal languages:** Greek (official), English, French. **Religion:** Greek Orthodox 98% (official).

Geography: Area: 50,949 sq. mi. **Location:** Occupies southern end of Balkan Peninsula in SE Europe. **Neighbors:** Albania, Macedonia, Bulgaria on N; Turkey on E. **Topography:** About 3/4 of Greece is nonarable, with mountains in all areas. Pindus Mts. run through the country N to S. The heavily indented coastline is 9,385 mi. long. Of over 2,000 islands, only 169 are inhabited, among them Crete, Rhodes, Milos, Kerkira (Corfu), Chios, Lesbos, Samos, Euboea, Delos, Mykonos. **Capital:** Athens. **Cities:** Athens 3,093,000; Thessaloníki 987,000*.

Government: Type: Parliamentary republic. **Head of state:** Pres. Costis Stefanopoulos; b 1926; in office: Mar. 8, 1995. **Head of government:** Prime Min. Costas Simitis; b June 23, 1936; in office: Jan. 18, 1996. **Local divisions:** 51 prefectures, 1 autonomous region. **Defense:** 4.6% of GDP (1995). **Active troop strength:** 168,300.

Economy: Industries: Tourism, textiles, chemicals, metals, wine, food processing. **Chief crops:** Grains, corn, sugar beets, cotton, tobacco, olives, grapes, citrus and other fruits, tomatoes. **Minerals:** Bauxite, lignite, magnesite, oil. **Arable land:** 23%. **Livestock** (1996): sheep: 9.6 mil; goats: 6.2 mil; pigs: 1.1 mil. **Fish catch** (1993): 199,607 metric tons. **Electricity prod.** (1995): 38.8 bil kWh. **Labor force:** 52% services; 25% ind.; 23% agric.

Finance: Monetary unit: Drachma (Aug. 1997: 285.08 = $1 US). **Gross domestic product** (1995 est.): $101.7 bil. **Per capita GDP:** $9,500. **Imports** (1994): $21.9 bil; partners: Germany 17%, Italy 17%, France 8%. **Exports** (1994): $8.8 bil; partners: Germany 21%, Italy 14%, UK 6%. **Tourism** (1994): $3.9 bil. **National budget** (1995 est.): $47 bil. **International reserves less gold** (June 1997): $15.39 bil. **Gold:** 3.47 mil oz t. **Consumer prices** (change in 1996): 8.2%.

Transport: Railroad: Length: 1,536.4 mi. **Motor vehicles in use:** 2.2 mil passenger cars, 901,000 comm. vehicles. **Civil aviation:** 5.2 bil passenger-mi.; 36 airports with scheduled flights. **Chief ports:** Piraeus, Thessaloníki, Patras.

Communications: Television sets: 1 per 4.9 persons. **Radios:** 1 per 2.4 persons. **Telephones:** 1 per 2.0 persons. **Daily newspaper circ.:** 156 per 1,000 pop.

Health: Life expectancy at birth (1997): 75.8 male; 81.0 female. **Births** (per 1,000 pop.): 10. **Deaths** (per 1,000 pop.). 10. **Natural increase:** 0.0. **Hospital beds:** 1 per 201 persons. **Physicians:** 1 per 259 persons. **Infant mortality** (per 1,000 live births 1997): 7.

Education: Free and compulsory: ages 6-15. **Literacy** (1993): 95%.

Major International Organizations: UN (WTO, FAO, World Bank, IMF, WHO, ILO), EU, NATO, OECD.
Embassy: 2221 Massachusetts Ave. NW 20008; 939-5800.

The achievements of ancient Greece in art, architecture, science, mathematics, philosophy, drama, literature, and democracy became legacies for succeeding ages. Greece reached the height of its glory and power, particularly in the Athenian city-state, in the 5th century BC.

Greece fell under Roman rule in the 2d and 1st centuries BC. In the 4th century AD it became part of the Byzantine Empire and, after the fall of Constantinople to the Turks in 1453, part of the Ottoman Empire.

Greece won its war of independence from Turkey 1821-1829, and became a kingdom. A republic was established 1924; the monarchy was restored, 1935, and George II, King of the Hellenes, resumed the throne. In Oct. 1940, Greece rejected an ultimatum from Italy. Nazi support resulted in its defeat and occupation by Germans, Italians, and Bulgarians. By the end of 1944 the invaders withdrew. Communist resistance forces were defeated by Royalist and British troops. A plebiscite again restored the monarchy.

Communists waged guerrilla war 1947-49 against the government but were defeated with the aid of the U.S. A period of reconstruction and rapid development followed, mainly with conservative governments under Premier Constantine Karamanlis. The Center Union, led by George Papandreou, won elections in 1963 and 1964, but King Constantine, who acceded in 1964, forced Papandreou to resign. A period of political maneuvers ended in the military takeover of April 21, 1967, by Col. George Papadopoulos. King Constantine tried to reverse the consolidation of the harsh dictatorship Dec. 13, 1967, but failed and fled to Italy. Papadopoulos was ousted Nov. 25, 1973.

Greek army officers serving in the National Guard of Cyprus staged a coup on the island July 15, 1974. Turkey invaded Cyprus a week later, precipitating the collapse of the Greek junta, which was implicated in the Cyprus coup. Democratic government returned (and in 1975 the monarchy was abolished).

The 1981 electoral victory of the Panhellenic Socialist Movement (Pasok) of Andreas Papandreou brought about substantial changes in Greece's internal and external policies. A scandal centered on George Kostokas, a banker and publisher, led to the arrest or investigation of leading Socialists, implicated Papandreou, and contributed to the defeat of the Socialists at the polls in 1989. However, Papandreou, who was narrowly acquitted Jan. 1992 of corruption charges, led the Socialists to a comeback victory in general elections Oct. 10, 1993.

Tensions between Greece and the Former Yugoslav Republic of Macedonia eased when the 2 countries agreed to normalize relations Sept. 13, 1995. The ailing Papandreou was replaced as prime minister by Costas Simitis, Jan. 18, 1996. Simitis led the Socialists to victory in the election of Sept. 22. The International Olympic Committee, Sept. 5, 1997, chose Athens to host the Summer Games in 2004.

Grenada

People: Population: 95,537. **Age distrib.** (%): <15: 45; 65+: 5. **Pop. density:** 718 per sq. mi. **Urban:** 36%. **Ethnic groups:** Mostly black African. **Principal languages:** English (official), French patois. **Chief religions:** Roman Catholic 53%, Protestant 38%.

Geography: Area: 133 sq. mi. **Location:** In Caribbean, 90 mi. N of Venezuela. **Neighbors:** Venezuela, Trinidid & Tobago to S; St. Vincent & the Grenadines to N. **Topography:** Main island is mountainous; country includes Carriacou and Petit Martinique islands. **Capital:** Saint George's (1991): 4,439.

Government: Type: Parliamentary democracy. **Head of state:** Queen Elizabeth II, represented by Gov.-Gen. Daniel Williams; b Nov. 4, 1935; in office: Aug. 8, 1996. **Head of government:** Prime Min.: Keith Mitchell; b Nov. 12, 1946; in office: June 22, 1995. **Local divisions:** 6 parishes and 1 dependency.

Economy: Industries: Tourism, textiles, spices. **Chief crops:** Nutmeg, bananas, cocoa, mace. **Arable land:** 15%. **Electricity prod.** (1995): 70 mil kWh. **Labor force:** 31% services; 24% agric.

Finance: Monetary unit: East Caribbean dollar (Aug. 1997: 2.70 = $1 US). **Gross domestic product** (1995 est.): $284 mil. **Per capita GDP:** $3,000. **Imports** (1995 est.): $162.2 mil; partners: Caricom 24%; U.S. 31%, UK 14%. **Exports** (1995 est.): $24.2 mil; partners: Caricom 32%; UK 20%. **Tourism** (1994): $60 mil. **National budget** (1996 est.): $126.7 mil. **International reserves less gold** (May 1997): $39.1 mil. **Consumer prices** (change in 1996): 1.9%.

Chief ports: Saint George's, Grenville.

Communications: Television sets: 1 per 3.0 persons. **Radios:** 1 per 1.7 persons. **Telephones:** 1 per 3.9 persons.

Health: Life expectancy at birth (1997): 68.6 male; 73.7 female. **Births** (per 1,000 pop.): 29. **Deaths** (per 1,000 pop.): 6. **Natural increase:** 2.3%. **Hospital beds:** 1 per 240 persons.

Physicians: 1 per 1,517 persons. **Infant mortality** (per 1,000 live births 1997): 12.
　　Education: Free and compulsory: ages 6-14. **Literacy** (1994): 85%.
　　Major International Organizations: UN (IMF, FAO, WTO, World Bank, WHO), OAS, the Commonwealth.
　　Embassy: 1701 New Hampshire Ave. NW 20009; 265-2561.

Columbus sighted the island 1498. First European settlers were French, 1650. The island was held alternately by France and England until final British occupation, 1784. Grenada became fully independent Feb. 7, 1974, during a general strike. It is the smallest independent nation in the western hemisphere.
　　On Oct. 14, 1983, a military coup ousted Prime Minister Maurice Bishop, who was put under house arrest, later freed by supporters, rearrested, and, finally, on Oct. 19, executed. U.S. forces, with a token force from 6 area nations, invaded Grenada, Oct. 25. Resistance from the Grenadian army and Cuban advisors was quickly overcome as most of the population welcomed the invading forces. U.S. troops left Grenada in June 1985.

Guatemala
Republic of Guatemala
República de Guatemala

People: Population: 11,558,407. **Age distrib.** (%): <15: 42; 65+: 4. **Pop. density:** 275 per sq. mi. **Urban:** 39%. **Ethnic groups:** Mestizo 56%, Amerindian 44%. **Principal languages:** Spanish (official), Mayan languages. **Religion:** Mostly Roman Catholic, some Protestant, traditional Mayan.
　　Geography: Area: 42,042 sq. mi. **Location:** In Central America. **Neighbors:** Mexico on N and W, El Salvador on S, Honduras and Belize on E. **Topography:** The central highland and mountain areas are bordered by the narrow Pacific coast and the lowlands and fertile river valleys on the Caribbean. There are numerous volcanoes in S, more than half a dozen over 11,000 ft. **Capital:** Guatemala City: 2,205,000*.
　　Government: Type: Republic. **Head of state and government:** Pres. Alvaro Arzú Irigoyen; b 1946; in office: Jan. 14, 1996. **Local divisions:** 22 departments. **Defense:** 1% of GDP (1994). **Active troop strength:** 44,200.
　　Economy: Industries: Furniture, rubber, textiles. **Chief crops:** Coffee, sugar, bananas, corn, cardamom. **Minerals:** Oil, nickel. **Crude oil reserves** (1996): 200 mil bbls. **Other resources:** Rare woods, fish, chicle. **Arable land:** 12%. **Livestock** (1996): cattle: 2.3 mil; pigs: 950,000. **Electricity prod.** (1995): 3.1 bil kWh. **Labor force:** 60% agric.; 13% serv.; 12% manuf.
　　Finance: Monetary unit: Quetzal (Aug. 1997: 6.08 = $1 US). **Gross domestic product** (1995 est.): $36.7 bil. **Per capita GDP:** $3,300. **Imports** (1995 est.): $2.85 bil; partners: U.S. 44%. **Exports** (1995 est.): $2.3 bil; partners: U.S. 30%. **Tourism** (1994): $258 mil. **National budget** (1996 est.): $1.88 bil. **International reserves less gold** (June 1997): $1.06 bil. **Gold:** 213,000 oz t. **Consumer prices** (change in 1996): 11.1%.
　　Transport: Railroads: Length: 549 mi. **Motor vehicles in use:** 102,000 passenger cars, 97,000 comm. vehicles. **Civil aviation:** 255.2 mil passenger-mi; 2 airports with scheduled flights. **Chief ports:** Puerto Barrios, San Jose.
　　Communications: Television sets: 1 per 19 persons. **Radios:** 1 per 15 persons. **Telephones:** 1 per 37 persons. **Daily newspaper circ.:** 23 per 1,000 pop.
　　Health: Life expectancy at birth (1997): 63.0 male; 68.4 female. **Births** (per 1,000 pop.): 33. **Deaths** (per 1,000 pop.): 7. **Natural increase:** 2.6%. **Infant mortality** (per 1,000 live births 1997): 49.
　　Education: Free and compulsory: ages 7-14. **Literacy** (1995 est.): 56%.
　　Major International Organizations: UN (IMF, FAO, WTO, WHO, World Bank), OAS.
　　Embassy: 2220 R St. NW 20008; 745-4952.

The old Mayan Indian empire flourished in what is today Guatemala for over 1,000 years before the Spanish.
　　Guatemala was a Spanish colony 1524-1821; briefly a part of Mexico and then of the U.S. of Central America, the republic was established in 1839.
　　Since 1945 when a liberal government was elected to replace the long-term dictatorship of Jorge Ubico, the country has seen a variety of military and civilian governments and periods of civil war. Dissident army officers seized power Mar. 23, 1982, denouncing a presidential election as fraudulent and pledging to restore "authentic democracy" to the nation. Political violence caused large numbers of Guatemalans to seek refuge in Mexico. Another military coup occurred Oct. 8, 1983. The nation returned to civilian rule in 1986.

The crisis-ridden government of Pres. Jorge Serrano Elías was ousted by the military June 1, 1993. Ramiro de León Carpio was elected president by Congress June 6. A UN report in March 1995 blamed state authorities for a majority of human rights violations in Guatemala.
　　A conservative businessman, Alvaro Arzú Irigoyen, won the presidency, Jan. 7, 1996. On Sept. 19 the Guatemalan government and leftist rebels approved a peace accord; the final agreement was signed Dec. 29. During more than 35 years of armed conflict, over 100,000 people were killed, another 40,000 "disappeared" and are presumed dead, and a million more became refugees.

Guinea
Republic of Guinea
République de Guinée

People: Population: 7,405,375. **Age distrib.** (%): <15: 44; 65+: 3. **Pop. density:** 78 per sq. mi. **Urban:** 30%. **Ethnic groups:** Peuhl 40%, Malinke 30%, Soussou 20%, smaller tribes 10%. **Principal languages:** French (official), Peuhl, Malinke, Soussou. **Chief religions:** Muslim 85%, Christian 8%.
　　Geography: Area: 94,926 sq. mi. **Location:** On Atlantic coast of W Africa. **Neighbors:** Guinea-Bissau, Senegal, Mali on N; Côte d'Ivoire on E; Liberia on S. **Topography:** A narrow coastal belt leads to the mountainous middle region, the source of the Gambia, Senegal, and Niger rivers. Upper Guinea, farther inland, is a cooler upland. The SE is forested. **Capital:** Conakry: 1.,558,000*.
　　Government: Type: Republic. **Head of state and government:** Pres. Gen. Lansana Conté; b 1934; in office: Apr. 5, 1984. **Local divisions:** 33 administrative regions. **Defense:** 1.6% of GDP (1994). **Active troop strength:** 9,700.
　　Economy: Industries: Mining, light manufacturing, agricultural processing. **Chief crops:** Bananas, pineapples, rice, palm kernels, coffee, cassava. **Minerals:** Bauxite, iron, diamonds, gold. **Arable land:** 6%. **Electricity prod.** (1995) 500 mil kWh. **Labor force:** 80% agric.; 11% ind. & commerce.
　　Finance: Monetary unit: Franc (Aug. 1997: 1,119 = $1 US). **Gross domestic product** (1995 est.): $6.5 bil. **Per capita GDP:** $1,020. **Imports** (1994 est.): $688 mil; partners: France 26%. **Exports** (1994 est.): $562 mil; partners: U.S. 23%. **National budget** (1990 est.): $708 mil. **International reserves less gold** (May 1997): $80.34 mil.
　　Transport: Railroads: Length: 674.4 mi. **Motor vehicles in use:** 23,000 passenger cars, 13,000 comm. vehicles. **Civil aviation:** 20.5 mil passenger-mi. **Chief port:** Conakry.
　　Communications: Television sets: 1 per 130 persons. **Radios:** 1 per 23 persons. **Telephones:** 1 per 607 persons.
　　Health: Life expectancy at birth (1997): 43.2 male; 48.0 female. **Births** (per 1,000 pop.): 42. **Deaths** (per 1,000 pop.): 18. **Natural increase:** 2.4%. **Physicians:** 1 per 7,445 persons. **Infant mortality** (per 1,000 live births 1997): 132.
　　Education: Free and compulsory: ages 7-13. **Literacy** (1995 est.): 36%.
　　Major International Organizations: UN and most of its specialized agencies, OAU, World Bank.
　　Embassy: 2112 Leroy Pl. NW 20008; 483-9420.

Part of the ancient West African empires, Guinea fell under French control 1849-98. Under Sékou Touré, it opted for full independence in 1958, and France withdrew all aid.
　　Touré turned to Communist nations for support and set up a militant one-party state. Thousands of opponents were jailed in the 1970s, in the aftermath of an unsuccessful Portuguese invasion. Many were tortured and killed.
　　The military took control in a bloodless coup after the March 1984 death of Touré. A new constitution was approved in 1991, but movement toward democracy was slow. When presidential elections were finally held, in Dec. 1993, the incumbent, Gen. Lansana Conté, was the official winner; outside monitors called the elections flawed. Parliamentary elections June 11, 1995, raised similar complaints. Conté suppressed an army mutiny in Conakry, Feb. 2-3, 1996.

Guinea-Bissau
Republic of Guinea-Bissau
Republica da Guiné-Bissau

People: Population: 1,178,584. **Age distrib.** (%): <15: 43; 65+: 3. **Pop. density:** 84 per sq. mi. **Urban:** 22%. **Ethnic groups:** Balanta 30%, Fula 20%, Manjaca 14%, Mandinga 13%. **Principal languages:** Portuguese (official), Criolo, tribal languages. **Chief religions:** Indigenous beliefs 65%, Muslim 30%, Christian 5%.
　　Geography: Area: 13,948 sq. mi. **Location:** On Atlantic coast of W Africa. **Neighbors:** Senegal on N, Guinea on E and

S. **Topography:** A swampy coastal plain covers most of the country; to the east is a low savanna region. **Capital:** Bissau (1991): 197,610.

Government: Type: Republic. **Head of state:** Pres. Joao Bernardo Vieira; b 1939; in office: Nov. 14, 1980. **Head of government:** Prime Min. Carlos Correia; in office: June 6, 1997. **Local divisions:** 9 regions. **Defense:** 4.5% of GDP (1994). **Active troop strength:** 9,250 est.

Economy: Chief crops: Peanuts, cashews, palm kernels, cotton, rice. **Minerals:** Bauxite, phosphates. **Arable land:** 11%. **Electricity prod.** (1995): 45 mil kWh. **Labor force:** 90% agric.

Finance: Monetary unit: CFA Franc (Aug. 1997: 610 = $1 US). **Gross domestic product** (1994 est.): $1 bil. **Per capita GDP:** $900. **Imports** (1994): $63 mil; partners: Thailand 30%, Portugal 22%. **Exports** (1994): $32 mil; partners: India 40%, Spain 38%. **National budget** (1991 est.): $44.8 mil. **International reserves less gold** (Mar. 1997): $16.41 mil. **Consumer prices** (change in 1996): 50.7%.

Transport: Motor vehicles in use: 4,000 passenger cars, 2,800 comm. vehicles. **Civil aviation:** 6.2 mil passenger-mi.; 2 airports with scheduled flights. **Chief port:** Bissau.

Communications: Radios: 1 per 25 persons. **Telephones:** 1 per 114 persons.

Health: Life expectancy at birth (1997): 47.1 male; 50.4 female. **Births** (per 1,000 pop.): 39. **Deaths** (per 1,000 pop.): 16. **Natural increase:** 2.3%. **Hospital beds:** 1 per 797 persons. **Infant mortality** (per 1,000 live births 1997): 114.

Education: Compulsory: ages 7-13. **Literacy** (1995 est.): 55%.

Major International Organizations: UN (World Bank), OAU.

Embassy: 918 16th St. NW 20006; 872-4222.

Portuguese mariners explored the area in the mid-15th century; the slave trade flourished in the 17th and 18th centuries, and colonization began in the 19th.

Beginning in the 1960s, an independence movement waged a guerrilla war and formed a government in the interior that achieved international support. Full independence came Sept. 10, 1974, after the Portuguese regime was overthrown.

The November 1980 coup gave Vieira absolute power. Vieira eventually initiated political liberalization; multiparty elections were held July 3, 1994.

Guyana
Co-operative Republic of Guyana

People: Population: 706,116. **Age distrib.** (%): <15: 32; 65+: 5. **Pop. density:** 9 per sq. mi. **Urban:** 36%. **Ethnic groups:** East Indian 51%, black and mixed 43%, Amerindian 4%. **Principal languages:** English (official), Amerindian dialects. **Chief religions:** Christian 57%, Hindu 33%, Muslim 9%.

Geography: Area: 83,044 sq. mi. **Location:** On N coast of South America. **Neighbors:** Venezuela on W, Brazil on S, Suriname on E. **Topography:** Dense tropical forests cover much of the land, although a flat coastal area up to 40 mi. wide, where 90% of the population lives, provides rich alluvial soil for agriculture. A grassy savanna divides the 2 zones. **Capital:** Georgetown (1992 est.): 248,500.

Government: Type: Republic. **Head of state:** Pres. Samuel Hinds; b Dec. 27, 1943; in office: Mar. 6, 1997. **Head of government:** Prime Min. Janet Jagan; b Oct. 20, 1920; in office: Mar. 17, 1997. **Local divisions:** 10 regions. **Defense:** 1.7% of GDP (1994). **Active troop strength:** 1,600 est.

Economy: Industries: Mining, textiles. **Chief crops:** Sugar, rice, citrus and other fruits. **Minerals:** Bauxite, gold, diamonds. **Other resources:** Timber, shrimp, dairy prods. **Arable land:** 3%. **Electricity prod.** (1995): 230 mil kWh. **Labor force:** 44.5% ind. & commerce; 34% agric.; 22% services.

Finance: Monetary unit: Dollar (Aug. 1997: 141 = $1 US). **Gross domestic product** (1995 est.): $1.6 bil. **Per capita GDP:** $2,200. **Imports** (1994): $456 mil; partners: U.S. 37%, Trin. & Tob. 13%. **Exports** (1994): $453 mil; partners: UK 33%, U.S. 31%. **National budget** (1995 est): $303 mil. **International reserves less gold** (May 1997): $323.5 mil.

Transport: Railroads: Length: 54.6 mi. **Motor vehicles in use:** 24,000 passenger cars, 9,000 comm. vehicles. **Civil aviation:** 139.1 mil passenger-mi. **Chief port:** Georgetown.

Communications: Television sets: 1 per 26 persons. **Radios:** 1 per 2.0 persons. **Telephones:** 1 per 19 persons. **Daily newspaper circ.:** 97 per 1,000 pop.

Health: Life expectancy at birth (1997): 56.9 male; 61.7 female. **Births** (per 1,000 pop.): 19. **Deaths** (per 1,000 pop.): 10. **Natural increase:** 0.9%. **Physicians:** 1 per 3,000 persons. **Infant mortality** (per 1,000 live births 1997): 51.

Education: Free and compulsory: ages 6-14. **Literacy** (1995 est.): 99%.

Major International Organizations: UN (WTO, ILO, FAO, WHO, IMF, World Bank), the Commonwealth, OAS.

Embassy: 2490 Tracy Pl. NW 20008; 265-6900.

Guyana became a Dutch possession in the 17th century, but sovereignty passed to Britain in 1815. Indentured servants from India soon outnumbered African slaves. Ethnic tension has affected political life.

Guyana became independent May 26, 1966. A Venezuelan claim to the western half of Guyana was suspended in 1970 but renewed in 1982; an agreement was reached in 1989. The Suriname border is disputed. The government has nationalized most of the economy, which has remained severely depressed.

The Port Kaituma ambush of U.S. Rep. Leo J. Ryan and others investigating mistreatment of American followers of the Rev. Jim Jones's People's Temple cult triggered a mass suicide-execution of 911 cultists at Jonestown in the Guyana jungle, Nov. 18, 1978.

The People's National Congress, the party in power since Guyana became independent, was voted out of office with the election of Cheddi Jagan in Oct. 1992. When Pres. Jagan died Mar. 6, 1997, Prime Min. Samuel Hinds succeeded him; his widow, Janet Jagan, became prime min. Mar. 17.

Haiti
Republic of Haiti
République d'Haïti

People: Population: 6,611,407. **Age distrib.** (%): <15: 43; 65+: 4. **Pop. density:** 618 per sq. mi. **Urban:** 32%. **Ethnic groups:** Black 95%. **Principal languages:** Haitian Creole, French (both official). **Chief religions:** Roman Catholic 80%, Protestant 16%; Voodoo widely practiced.

Geography: Area: 10,695 sq. mi. **Location:** In Caribbean, occupies western third of Isl. of Hispaniola. **Neighbors:** Dominican Republic on E, Cuba to W. **Topography:** About two-thirds of Haiti is mountainous. Much of the rest is semiarid. Coastal areas are warm and moist. **Capital:** Port-au-Prince 1,461,000*.

Government: Type: Republic. **Head of state:** Pres. René Préval; b Jan. 17, 1943; in office Feb. 7, 1996. **Head of government:** Prime Min. Rosny Smarth; b Oct. 19, 1940; in office: Mar. 6, 1996. **Local divisions:** 9 departments. **Defense:** 2.2% of GDP (1994). **Active security forces:** 3,000-4,000.

Economy: Industries: Sugar refining, textiles. **Chief crops:** Coffee, sugar, bananas, corn, rice. **Minerals:** Bauxite. **Arable land:** 20%. **Livestock** (1996): goats: 1.7 mil; cattle: 1.2 mil. **Fish catch** (1993): 5,600 metric tons. **Electricity prod.** (1995): 315 mil kWh. **Labor force:** 66% agric.; 25% services; 9% ind.

Finance: Monetary unit: Gourde (Aug. 1997: 16.81 = $1 US). **Gross domestic product** (1995 est.): $6.5 bil. **Per capita GDP:** $1,000. **Imports** (1995 est.): $537 mil; partners: U.S. 51%. **Exports** (1995 est.): $161 mil; partners: U.S. 81%. **National budget** (FY 1994-95): $299 mil. **International reserves less gold** (Apr. 1997): $121.4 mil. **Gold:** 19,000 oz t. **Consumer prices** (change in 1996): 17.1%.

Transport: Railroads: Length: 24.8 mi. **Motor vehicles in use:** 32,000 passenger cars, 21,000 comm. vehicles. **Chief ports:** Port-au-Prince, Les Cayes, Cap-Haitien.

Communications: Television sets: 1 per 208 persons. **Radios:** 1 per 20 persons. **Telephones:** 1 per 119 persons. **Daily newspaper circ.:** 6 per 1,000 pop.

Health: Life expectancy at birth (1997): 47.5 male; 51.6 female. **Births** (per 1,000 pop.): 33. **Deaths** (per 1,000 pop.): 15. **Natural increase:** 1.8%. **Hospital beds:** 1 per 994 persons. **Physicians:** 1 per 10,041 persons. **Infant mortality rate** (per 1,000 live births 1997): 102.

Education: Compulsory: ages 6-12. **Literacy** (1995 est.): 45%.

Major International Organizations: UN and most of its specialized agencies, OAS.

Embassy: 2311 Massachusetts Ave. NW 20008; 332-4090.

Haiti, visited by Columbus, 1492, and a French colony from 1697, attained its independence, 1804, following the rebellion led by former slave Toussaint L'Ouverture. Following a period of political violence, the U.S. occupied the country 1915-34.

Francois Duvalier was elected president in Sept. 1957; in 1964 he was named president for life. Upon his death in 1971, he was succeeded by his son, Jean Claude. Drought in 1975-77 brought famine, and Hurricane Allen in 1980 destroyed most of the rice, bean, and coffee crops. Following several weeks of unrest, President Jean Claude Duvalier fled Haiti aboard a U.S. Air Force jet Feb. 7, 1986, ending the 28-year dictatorship by the Duvalier family.

A military-civilian council headed by Gen. Henri Namphy assumed control. In 1987, voters approved a new constitution, but the Jan. 1988 elections were marred by violence and boycotted by the opposition. Gen. Namphy seized control, June 20, but was ousted by a military coup in Sept.

Father Jean-Bertrand Aristide was elected president Dec. 1990. In Sept. 1991, Aristide was arrested by the military and expelled from the country. Some 35,000 Haitian refugees were intercepted by the U.S. Coast Guard as they tried to enter the U.S., 1991-92. Most were returned to Haiti. There was a new upsurge of refugees starting in late 1993.

The UN imposed a worldwide oil, arms, and financial embargo on Haiti June 23, 1993. The embargo was suspended when the military agreed to Aristide's return to power on Oct. 30, but the military effectively blocked his return. After renewed sanctions, the UN Security Council authorized, July 31, 1994, an invasion of Haiti by a multinational force. With U.S. troops already en route, an invasion was averted, Sept. 18, by a new agreement for military leaders to step down and Aristide to resume office. As part of the agreement, thousands of U.S. troops began arriving in Haiti, Sept. 19. Aristide returned to Haiti and was restored in office Oct. 15. A UN peacekeeping force took over responsibility for Haiti as of Mar. 31, 1995.

Aristide transferred power to his elected successor, René Préval, on Feb. 7, 1996. The last U.S. combat troops left Haiti Apr. 17, but a small UN peacekeeping force remained. Prime Min. Rosny Smarth announced his resignation June 9, but Préval and parliament were unable to agree on a successor.

Honduras
Republic of Honduras
República de Honduras

People: Population: 5,751,384. **Age distrib.** (%): <15: 42; 65+: 3. **Pop. density:** 132 per sq. mi. **Urban:** 44%. **Ethnic groups:** Mestizo 90%, Indian 7%. **Principal language:** Spanish (official). **Chief religions:** Roman Catholic 97%.

Geography: Area: 43,433 sq. mi. **Location:** In Central America. **Neighbors:** Guatemala on W, El Salvador and Nicaragua on S. **Topography:** The Caribbean coast is 500 mi. long. Pacific coast, on Gulf of Fonseca, is 40 mi. long. Honduras is mountainous, with wide fertile valleys and rich forests. **Capital:** Tegucigalpa: 995,000*.

Government: Type: Republic. **Head of State:** Pres. Carlos Roberta Reina Idiaquez; b Mar. 13, 1926; in office: Jan. 27, 1994. **Local divisions:** 18 departments. **Defense:** 0.4% of GDP (1994). **Active troop strength:** 18,800.

Economy: Industries: Textiles, wood prods. **Chief crops:** Bananas, sugar, corn, citrus fruit. **Minerals:** Gold, silver, copper, lead, zinc, iron, antimony, coal. **Other resources:** Timber, fish. **Arable land:** 14%. **Livestock** (1996): cattle: 2.2 mil; pigs: 600,000. **Electricity prod.** (1995): 2.8 bil kWh. **Labor force:** 62% agric.; 20% services; 9% manuf.

Finance: Monetary unit: Lempira (Aug. 1997: 13.18 = $1 US). **Gross domestic product** (1995 est.): $10.8 bil. **Per capita GDP:** $1,980. **Imports** (1994): $1.1 bil; partners: U.S. 50%, Mexico 8%. **Exports** (1994): $843 mil; partners: U.S. 53%, Germany 11%. **Tourism** (1994): $33 mil. **National budget** (1993 est.): $668 mil. **International reserves less gold** (June 1997): $506.56 mil. **Gold:** 21,000 oz t. **Consumer prices** (change in 1996): 23.8%.

Transport: Railroads: Length: 369.5 mi. **Motor vehicles in use:** 41,000 passenger cars, 74,000 comm. vehicles. **Civil aviation:** 200.6 mil passenger-mi.; 8 airports with scheduled flights. **Chief ports:** Puerto Cortes, La Ceiba.

Communications: Television sets: 1 per 13 persons. **Radios:** 1 per 2.5 persons. **Telephones:** 1 per 35 persons. **Daily newspaper circ.:** 44 per 1,000 pop.

Health: Life expectancy at birth (1997): 66.4 male; 71.4 female. **Births** (per 1,000 pop.): 33. **Deaths** (per 1,000 pop.): 6. **Natural increase:** 2.7%. **Hospital beds:** 1 per 1,126 persons. **Physicians:** 1 per 1,586 persons. **Infant mortality** (per 1,000 live births 1997): 40.

Education: Free and compulsory: ages 7-13. **Literacy** (1995 est.): 73%.

Major International Organizations: UN, (IMF, FAO, WTO, World Bank, WHO, ILO), OAS.

Embassy: 3007 Tilden St. NW 20008; 966-7702.

Mayan civilization flourished in Honduras in the 1st millennium AD. Columbus arrived in 1502. Honduras became independent after freeing itself from Spain, 1821, and from the Fed. of Central America, 1838.

Gen. Oswaldo Lopez Arellano, president for most of the period 1963-75 by virtue of one election and 2 coups, was ousted by the army in 1975 over charges of pervasive bribery by United Brands Co. of the U.S. An elected civilian government took power in 1982. Some 3,200 U.S. troops were sent to Honduras after the Honduran border was violated by Nicaraguan forces, Mar. 1988.

Honduras is one of the poorest countries in the western hemisphere.

Hungary
Republic of Hungary
Magyar Köztársaság

People: Population: 9,935,774. **Age distrib.** (%): <15: 18; 65+: 14. **Pop. density:** 277 per sq. mi. **Urban:** 65%. **Ethnic groups:** Hungarian 89.9%, Gypsy 4%, German 2.6%. **Principal language:** Hungarian (Magyar; official). **Chief religions:** Roman Catholic 67.5%, Calvinist 20%, Lutheran 5%.

Geography: Area: 35,919 sq. mi. **Location:** In E central Europe. **Neighbors:** Slovakia, Ukraine on N; Austria on W; Slovenia, Yugoslavia, Croatia on S; Romania on E. **Topography:** The Danube R. forms the Slovak border in the NW, then swings S to bisect the country. The eastern half of Hungary is mainly a great fertile plain, the Alfold; the W and N are hilly. **Capital:** Budapest. **Cities** (1996 est.): Budapest 1,909,000; Debrecen 211,000; Miskolc 180,000.

Government: Type: Parliamentary democracy. **Head of state:** Pres. Arpad Goncz; b Feb. 10, 1922; in office: May 2, 1990. **Head of government:** Prime Min. Gyula Horn; b July 5, 1932; in office: July 15, 1994. **Local divisions:** 38 counties, 1 capital. **Defense:** 1.7% of GDP (1995). **Active troop strength:** 64,300.

Economy: Industries: Iron and steel, construction materials, processed foods, pharmaceuticals, vehicles. **Chief crops:** Wheat, corn, sunflowers, potatoes, sugar beets. **Minerals:** Bauxite, coal, gas. **Crude oil reserves** (1996): 120 mil bbls. **Arable land:** 51%. **Livestock** (1996): pigs: 5.0 mil; sheep: 977,000; cattle: 928,000. **Electricity prod.** (1995): 32.9 bil kWh. **Labor force:** 30% ind.; 16% agric.

Finance: Monetary unit: Forint (Aug. 1997: 194.53 = $1 US). **Gross domestic product** (1995 est.): $72.5 bil. **Per capita GDP:** $7,000. **Imports** (1995 est.): $15 bil; partners: Germany 23%, Austria 12%, Russia 12%. **Exports** (1995 est.): $13 bil; partners: Germany 28%, Austria 11%. **National budget** (1995): $13.8 bil. **Tourism** (1994): $1.4 bil. **International reserves less gold** (Mar. 1997): $8.56 bil. **Gold:** 101,000 oz t. **Consumer prices** (change in 1996): 23.5%.

Transport: Railroads: Length: 4,772.4 mi. **Motor vehicles in use:** 2.2 mil passenger cars, 310,000 comm. vehicles. **Civil aviation:** 1.0 bil. passenger-mi.; 1 airport with scheduled flights.

Communications: Television sets: 1 per 2.3 persons. **Radios:** 1 per 1.6 persons. **Telephones:** 1 per 5.4 persons. **Daily newspaper circ.:** 228 per 1,000 pop.

Health: Life expectancy at birth (1997): 64.4 male; 74.2 female. **Births** (per 1,000 pop.): 11. **Deaths** (per 1,000 pop.): 15. **Natural increase:** −0.4%. **Hospital beds:** 1 per 104 persons. **Physicians:** 1 per 280 persons. **Infant mortality** (per 1,000 live births 1997): 12.

Education: Compulsory: ages 6-16. **Literacy:** (1993): 99%.

Major International Organizations: UN (IMF, FAO, WHO, World Bank, WTO), OECD.

Embassy: 3910 Shoemaker St. NW 20008; 362-6730.

Earliest settlers, chiefly Slav and Germanic, were overrun by Magyars from the E. Stephen I (997-1038) was made king by Pope Sylvester II in AD 1000. The country suffered repeated Turkish invasions in the 15th-17th centuries. After the defeats of the Turks, 1686-1697, Austria dominated, but Hungary obtained concessions until it regained internal independence in 1867, with the emperor of Austria as king of Hungary in a dual monarchy with a single diplomatic service. Defeated with the Central Powers in 1918, Hungary lost Transylvania to Romania, Croatia and Bacska to Yugoslavia, Slovakia and Carpatho-Ruthenia to Czechoslovakia, all of which had large Hungarian minorities. A republic under Michael Karolyi and a bolshevist revolt under Bela Kun were followed by a vote for a monarchy in 1920 with Admiral Nicholas Horthy as regent.

Hungary joined Germany in World War II, and was allowed to annex most of its lost territories. Russian troops captured the country, 1944-1945. By terms of an armistice with the Allied powers Hungary agreed to give up territory acquired by the 1938 dismemberment of Czechoslovakia and to return to its borders of 1937.

A republic was declared Feb. 1, 1946; Zoltan Tildy was elected president. In 1947 the communists forced Tildy out.Premier Imre Nagy, who had been in office since mid-1953, was ousted for his moderate policy of favoring agriculture and consumer production, April 18, 1955.

In 1956, popular demands to oust Erno Gero, Communist Party secretary, and for formation of a government by Nagy, resulted in the latter's appointment Oct. 23; demonstrations against communist rule developed into open revolt. On Nov. 4 Soviet forces launched a massive attack against Budapest with 200,000 troops, 2,500 tanks and armored cars.

About 200,000 persons fled the country. Thousands were arrested and executed, including Nagy in June 1958. In the spring of 1963 the regime freed many captives from the 1956 revolt.

Hungarian troops participated in the 1968 Warsaw Pact invasion of Czechoslovakia. Major economic reforms were launched early in 1968, switching from a central planning system to one in which market forces and profit controlled much of production.

In 1989 Parliament passed legislation legalizing freedom of assembly and association as Hungary shifted away from communism. In Oct. the Communist Party was formally dissolved. The last Soviet troops left Hungary June 19, 1991. On July 8, 1997, NATO invited Hungary to become a full member of the alliance within 2 years.

Iceland
Republic of Iceland
Lýoveldio Ísland

People: Population: 272,550. **Age distrib.** (%): <15: 24; 65+: 12. **Pop. density:** 7 per sq. mi. **Urban:** 92%. **Ethnic groups:** Homogeneous, descendants of Norwegians, Celts. **Principal language:** Icelandic (Islenska; official). **Chief religions:** Evangelical Lutheran 96%.

Geography: Area: 39,699 sq. mi. **Location:** Isl. at N end of Atlantic O. **Neighbors:** Nearest is Greenland (Den.), to W. **Topography:** Recent volcanic origin. Three-quarters of the surface is wasteland: glaciers, lakes, a lava desert. There are geysers and hot springs, and the climate is moderated by the Gulf Stream. **Capital:** Reykjavík (1995 est.): 104,276.

Government: Type: Constitutional republic. **Head of state:** Pres. Olafur Ragnar Grímsson; b May 14, 1943; in office: Aug. 1, 1996. **Head of government:** Prime Min. David Oddsson; Jan. 17, 1948; in office: Apr. 30, 1991. **Local divisions:** 23 counties, 14 independent towns. **Defense:** Provided by U.S.-manned Icelandic Defense Force.

Economy: Industries: Fish products (some 75% of exports), aluminum. **Chief crops:** Potatoes, turnips. **Arable land:** 1%. **Livestock** (1996): sheep: 451,000. **Fish catch** (1995): 1.62 mil metric tons. **Electricity prod.** (1995): 4.9 bil kWh. **Labor force:** 60% commerce & services; 12.5% manuf.; 12% fish.

Finance: Monetary unit: Krona (Aug. 1997: 72.67 = $1 US). **Gross domestic product** (1995 est.): $5 bil. **Per capita GDP:** $18,800. **Imports** (1994): $1.5 bil; partners: EU 53%. **Exports** (1994): $1.6 bil; partners: EU 68%. **Tourism** (1994): $137 mil. **National budget** (1994 est.): $2.1 bil. **International reserves less gold** (June 1997): $480.2 mil. **Gold:** 49,000 oz t. **Consumer prices** (change in 1996): 2.3%.

Transport: Motor vehicles in use: 119,000 passenger cars, 16,000 comm. vehicles. **Civil aviation:** 1.4 bil passenger-mi.; 24 airports with scheduled flights. **Chief port:** Reykjavík.

Communications: Television sets: 1 per 2.9 persons. **Radios:** 1 per 1.3 persons. **Telephones:** 1 per 1.8 persons. **Daily newspaper circ.:** 515 per 1,000 pop.

Health: Life expectancy at birth (1997): 78.0 male; 83.0 female. **Births** (per 1,000 pop.): 17. **Deaths** (per 1,000 pop.): 6. **Natural increase:** 1.1%. **Hospital beds:** 1 per 95 persons. **Physicians:** 1 per 357 persons. **Infant mortality** (per 1,000 live births 1997): 4.

Education: Free and compulsory: ages 6-16. **Literacy** (1997): 100%.

Major International Organizations: UN (WTO, FAO, World Bank, IMF, WHO), NATO, EFTA, OECD.

Embassy: Suite, 1200, 1156 15th St. NW 20005; 265-6653.

Iceland was an independent republic from 930 to 1262, when it joined with Norway. Its language has maintained its purity for 1,000 years. Danish rule lasted from 1380-1918; the last ties with the Danish crown were severed in 1941. The Althing, or assembly, is the world's oldest surviving parliament.

India
Republic of India
Bharat

People: Population: 967,612,804. **Age distrib.** (%): <15: 34; 65+: 4. **Pop. density:** 792 per sq. mi. **Urban:** 27%. **Ethnic groups:** Indo Aryan 72%, Dravidian 25%, Mongoloid and other 3%. **Principal languages:** Hindi (official), English (associate official), 17 regional languages. **Chief religions:** Hindu 80%, Muslim 14%, Christian 2%, Sikh 2%.

Geography: Area: 1,222,243 sq. mi. **Location:** Occupies most of the Indian subcontinent in S Asia. **Neighbors:** Pakistan on W; China, Nepal, Bhutan on N; Myanmar, Bangladesh on E. **Topography:** The Himalaya Mts., highest in

world, stretch across India's northern borders. Below, the Ganges Plain is wide, fertile, and among the most densely populated regions of the world. The area below includes the Deccan Peninsula. Close to one quarter of the area is forested. The climate varies from tropical heat in S to near-Arctic cold in N. Rajasthan Desert is in NW; NE Assam Hills get 400 in. of rain a year. **Capital:** New Delhi. **Cities:** Bombay (Mumbai) 15,138,000; Calcutta 11,923,000; Delhi 9,948,000; Madras (Chennai) 6,002,000; Hyderabad 5,477,000; Bangalore 4,799,000*.

Government: Type: Federal republic. **Head of state:** Pres. Kocheril Raman Narayanan; b Oct. 17, 1920; in office: July 25, 1997. **Head of government:** Prime Min. Inder Kumar Gujral; b Dec. 4, 1919; in office: Apr. 21, 1997. **Local divisions:** 25 states, 7 union territories. **Defense:** 2.7% of GDP (FY 1995-96). **Active troop strength:** 1.145 mil.

Economy: Industries: Textiles, steel, processed foods, cement, machinery, chemicals, mining, autos. **Chief crops:** Rice, grains, sugar, spices, tea, cashews, cotton, potatoes, jute, linseed. **Minerals:** Coal, iron, manganese, mica, bauxite, titanium, chromite, diamonds, gas, oil. **Crude oil reserves** (1996): 4.3 bil bbls. **Other resources:** Rubber, timber. **Arable land:** 55%. **Livestock** (1996): cattle: 196 mil; goats: 120 mil; buffalo: 80.1 mil; sheep: 45.4 mil; pigs: 11.9 mil. **Fish catch** (1995): 4.9 mil metric tons. **Electricity prod.** (1995): 398.3 bil kWh. **Labor force:** 65% agric.

Finance: Monetary unit: Rupee (Aug. 1997: 36.12 = $1 US). **Gross domestic product** (1995 est.): $1.41 tril. **Per capita GDP:** $1,500. **Imports** (1995): $33.5 bil; partners: U.S. 10%, Germany 8%, Japan 7%. **Exports** (1995): $30.0 bil; partners: U.S. 19%, Japan 8%, Germany 7%. **Tourism** (1994): $2.3 bil. **National budget** (FY 1994-95): $54.9 bil. **International reserves less gold** (June 1997): $25.70 bil. **Gold:** 12.78 mil oz t. **Consumer prices** (change in 1996): 9.0%.

Transport: Railroad: Length: 38,788.9 mi. **Motor vehicles in use:** 3.5 mil passenger cars, 3.05 mil comm. vehicles. **Civil aviation:** 10.9 bil passenger-mi.; 66 airports with scheduled flights. **Chief ports:** Calcutta, Bombay (Mumbai), Kochi, Madras (Chennai), Vishakhapatnam.

Communications: Television sets: 1 per 25 persons. **Radios:** 1 per 12 persons. **Telephones:** 1 per 78 persons. **Daily newspaper circ.:** 21 per 1,000 pop.

Health: Life expectancy at birth (1997): 59.5 male; 60.8 female. **Births** (per 1,000 pop.): 25. **Deaths** (per 1,000 pop.): 9. **Natural increase:** 1.6%. **Hospital beds:** 1 per 1,357 persons. **Physicians:** 1 per 2,173 persons. **Infant mortality** (per 1,000 live births 1997): 69.

Education: Theoretically compulsory in 23 states to age 14. **Literacy** (1995 est.): 52%.

Major International Organizations: UN (IMF, FAO, WHO, WTO, World Bank), the Commonwealth.

Embassy: 2107 Massachusetts Ave. NW 20008; 939-7000.

India has one of the oldest civilizations in the world. Excavations trace the Indus Valley civilization back for at least 5,000 years. Paintings in the mountain caves of Ajanta, richly carved temples, the Taj Mahal in Agra, and the Kutab Minar in Delhi are among relics of the past.

Aryan tribes, speaking Sanskrit, invaded from the NW around 1500 BC, and merged with the earlier inhabitants to create classical Indian civilization.

Asoka ruled most of the Indian subcontinent in the 3d century BC, and established Buddhism. But Hinduism revived and eventually predominated. During the Gupta kingdom, 4th-6th century AD, science, literature, and the arts enjoyed a "golden age."

Arab invaders established a Muslim foothold in the W in the 8th century, and Turkish Muslims gained control of North India by 1200. The Mogul emperors ruled 1526-1857.

Vasco da Gama established Portuguese trading posts 1498-1503. The Dutch followed. The British East India Co. sent Capt. William Hawkins, 1609, to get concessions from the Mogul emperor for spices and textiles. Operating as the East India Co. the British gained control of most of India. The British parliament assumed political direction; under Lord Bentinck, 1828-35, rule by rajahs was curbed. After the Sepoy troops mutinied, 1857-58, the British supported the native rulers.

Nationalism grew rapidly after World War I. The Indian National Congress and the Muslim League demanded constitutional reform. A leader emerged in Mohandas K. Gandhi (called Mahatma, or Great Soul), born Oct. 2, 1869, assassinated Jan. 30, 1948. He advocated self-rule, nonviolence, and removal of the caste system of untouchability. In 1930 he launched "civil disobedience," including boycott of British goods and rejection of taxes without representation.

In 1935 Britain gave India a constitution providing a bicameral federal congress. Muhammad Ali Jinnah, head of the Muslim League, sought creation of a Muslim nation, Pakistan.

The British government partitioned British India into the dominions of India and Pakistan. India became a member of the

UN in 1945, a self-governing member of the Commonwealth in 1947, and a democratic republic, Jan. 26, 1950.

More than 12 million Hindu and Muslim refugees crossed the India-Pakistan borders in a mass transferral of some of the 2 peoples during 1947; about 200,000 were killed in communal fighting.

After Pakistan troops began attacks on Bengali separatists in East Pakistan, Mar. 25, 1971, some 10 million refugees fled into India. India and Pakistan went to war Dec. 3, 1971, on both the East and West fronts. Pakistan troops in the east surrendered Dec. 16; Pakistan agreed to a cease-fire in the west Dec. 17. In Aug. 1973 India released 93,000 Pakistanis held prisoner since 1971. The 2 countries resumed full relations in 1976.

Indira Gandhi, was named prime minister Jan. 19, 1966. Threatened with adverse court rulings and an opposition protest campaign, Gandhi invoked emergency provisions of the constitution June 1975. Thousands of opponents were arrested and press censorship imposed. These and other actions, including the enforcement of coercive birth control measures in some areas, were widely resented. Opposition parties, united in the Janata coalition, turned Gandhi's New Congress Party from power in federal and state parliamentary elections in 1977.

Gandhi became prime minister for the second time, Jan. 14, 1980. She was assassinated by 2 of her Sikh bodyguards Oct. 31, 1984, in response to the government suppression of a Sikh uprising in Punjab in June 1984, which included an assault on the Golden Temple at Amritsar, the holiest Sikh shrine. Widespread rioting followed the assassination. Thousands of Sikhs were killed and some 50,000 left homeless.

Rajiv, Indira Gandhi's son, replaced her as prime minister. He was swept from office in 1989 amid charges of incompetence and corruption. He was assassinated May 21, 1991, during an election campaign to regain the prime ministership.

Sikhs ignited several violent clashes during the 1980s. The government's May 1987 decision to bring the state of Punjab under the rule of the central government led to violence. Many died during a government siege of the Golden Temple, May 1988. Another trouble spot was Assam in NW India, where thousands were killed in ethnic violence in Feb. 1993; a renewed outburst in July 1994 led to more than 60 deaths there.

Nationwide riots followed the destruction of a 16th-century mosque by Hindu militants in Dec. 1992. In the biggest wave of criminal violence in Indian history, a series of bombings jolted Bombay and Calcutta, Mar. 12-19, 1993, killing more than 300.

Corruption scandals dominated Indian politics in the mid-1990s. After an inconclusive election, a Hindu nationalist party was unable to form a government, and a center-left coalition took office June 1, 1996. A Saudi jetliner and a Kazakh cargo plane collided in midair near New Delhi on Nov. 12, killing 349 passengers and crew.

Inder Kumar Gujral was sworn in Apr. 21, 1997, as India's 4th prime min. in less than a year. India's 1st lowest-caste pres., K. R. Narayanan, took office July 25. Mother Teresa of Calcutta, renowned for her work among the poor, died Sept. 5.

Sikkim, bordered by Tibet, Bhutan, and Nepal, formerly British protected, became a protectorate of India in 1950. Area, 2,740 sq. mi.; pop., 1994 est., 444,000; capital: Gangtok. In Sept. 1974, India's parliament voted to make Sikkim an associate Indian state, absorbing it into India.

Kashmir, a predominantly Muslim region in the NW, has been in dispute between India and Pakistan since 1947. A cease-fire was negotiated by the UN Jan. 1, 1949; it gave Pakistan control of one-third of the area, in the west and northwest, and India the remaining two-thirds, the Indian state of **Jammu and Kashmir,** which enjoys internal autonomy.

In the 1990s there were repeated clashes between Indian army troops and pro-independence demonstrators triggered by India's decision to impose central government rule; by 1996 the conflict had claimed at least 30,000 lives. The clashes strained relations between India and Pakistan, which India charged was aiding the Muslim separatists. In Sept. 1996, a pro-Indian-government party won a majority in assembly elections, the first held since separatist fighting began.

France, 1952-54, peacefully yielded to India its 5 colonies, former French India, comprising Pondicherry, Karikal, Mahe, Yanaon (which became **Pondicherry Union Territory,** area 190 sq. mi.; pop., 1994 est., 894,000) and Chandernagor (which was incorporated into the state of **West Bengal**).

Indonesia
Republic of Indonesia
Republik Indonesia

People: Population: 209,774,138. **Age distrib.** (%): <15: 31; 65+: 4. **Pop. density:** 283 per sq. mi. **Urban:** 36%. **Ethnic groups:** Javanese 45%, Sundanese 14%, Madurese 7.5%, Malay 7.5%. **Principal languages:** Bahasa Indonesian (Malay) (official), English, Dutch, Javanese. **Chief religions:** Muslim 87%, Protestant 6%.

Geography: Area: 741,052 sq. mi. **Location:** Archipelago SE of Asian mainland along the Equator. **Neighbors:** Malaysia on N, Papua New Guinea on E. **Topography:** Indonesia comprises over 13,500 islands (6,000 inhabited), including Java (one of the most densely populated areas in the world with over 2,000 persons per sq. mi.), Sumatra, Kalimantan (most of Borneo), Sulawesi (Celebes), and West Irian (Irian Jaya, the W half of New Guinea). Also: Bangka, Billiton, Madura, Bali, Timor. The mountains and plateaus on the major islands have a cooler climate than the tropical lowlands. **Capital:** Jakarta. **Cities:** Jakarta 8,621,000; Bandung 2,896,000; Surabaja 2,253,000*.

Government: Type: Republic. **Head of state:** Pres. Suharto; b June 8, 1921; in office: Mar. 6, 1967. **Local divisions:** 24 provinces, 2 special regions, 1 capital district. **Defense:** 1.4% of GNP (FY 1995-96). **Active troop strength:** 299,200.

Economy: Industries: Oil, gas, food processing, textiles, cement, light industry. **Chief crops:** Rice, cocoa, peanuts. **Minerals:** Nickel, tin, oil, bauxite, copper, gas. **Crude oil reserves** (1996): 5.0 bil bbls. **Other resources:** Rubber, timber. **Arable land:** 8%. **Livestock** (1996): goats: 14.3 mil; cattle: 11.9 mil; pigs: 7.8 mil; sheep: 7.7 mil. **Fish catch** (1995): 4.12 mil metric tons. **Electricity prod.** (1995): 60.4 bil kWh. **Labor force:** 55% agric.; 10% manuf.

Finance: Monetary unit: Rupiah (Aug. 1997: 2,824 = $1 US). **Gross domestic product** (1995 est.): $711 bil. **Per capita GDP:** $3,500. **Imports** (1994): $32 bil; partners: Japan 24%, U.S. 11%, Germany 8%. **Exports** (1994): $39.9 bil; partners: Japan 27%, U.S. 15%, Singapore 10%. **Tourism** (1994): $4.8 bil. **National budget** (FY 1996-97 est.): $38.1 bil. **International reserves less gold** (June 1997): $20.34 bil. **Gold:** 3.10 mil oz t. **Consumer prices** (change in 1996): 8.0%.

Transport: Railroads: Length: 4,010.4 mi. **Motor vehicles in use:** 1.9 mil passenger cars, 1.85 mil comm. vehicles. **Civil aviation:** 13.1 bil passenger-mi.; 81 airports. **Chief ports:** Jakarta, Surabaya, Palembang, Semarang, Ujungpandang.

Communications: Television sets: 1 per 16 persons. **Radios:** 1 per 6.8 persons. **Telephones:** 1 per 59 persons. **Daily newspaper circ.:** 20 per 1,000 pop.

Health: Life expectancy at birth (1997): 59.9 male; 64.3 female. **Births** (per 1,000 pop.): 23. **Deaths** (per 1,000 pop.): 8. **Natural increase:** 1.5%. **Hospital beds:** 1 per 1,650 persons. **Physicians:** 1 per 7,402 persons. **Infant mortality** (per 1,000 live births 1997): 61.

Education: Compulsory: ages 7-16. **Literacy** (1995 est.): 84%.

Major International Organizations: UN and all of its specialized agencies, ASEAN, OPEC, APEC.

Embassy: 2020 Massachusetts Ave. NW 20036; 775-5200.

Hindu and Buddhist civilization from India reached Indonesia nearly 2,000 years ago, taking root especially in Java. Islam spread along the maritime trade routes in the 15th century, and became predominant by the 16th century. The Dutch replaced the Portuguese as the area's most important European trade power in the 17th century, securing territorial control over Java by 1750. The outer islands were not finally subdued until the early 20th century, when the full area of present-day Indonesia was united under one rule for the first time.

Following Japanese occupation, 1942-45, nationalists led by Sukarno and Hatta declared independence. The Netherlands ceded sovereignty Dec. 27, 1949, after 4 years of fighting. A republic was declared, Aug. 17, 1950, with Sukarno as president. West Irian, on New Guinea, remained under Dutch control.

After the Dutch in 1957 rejected proposals for new negotiations over West Irian, Indonesia stepped up the seizure of Dutch property. A U.S. mediator's plan was adopted in 1962. In 1963 the UN turned the area over to Indonesia, which promised a plebiscite. In 1969, voting by tribal chiefs favored staying with Indonesia, despite an uprising and widespread opposition.

Sukarno suspended Parliament in 1960, and was named president for life in 1963. He made close alliances with Communist governments. Russian-armed Indonesian troops staged raids in 1964 and 1965 into Malaysia, whose formation Sukarno had opposed. (In 1966 Indonesia and Malaysia signed an agreement ending hostility.)

In 1965 an attempted coup in which several military officers were murdered was successfully put down. The regime blamed the coup on the Communist Party, some of whose members were known to have been involved. In its wake more than 300,000 alleged Communists were killed in army-initiated massacres.

Gen. Suharto, head of the army, was named president in 1968. With military backing he developed a strong government party, restricted the opposition, and allied the country with the West; meanwhile, oil exports spurred economic growth. Suharto was reelected for a 6th consecutive term in 1993. A riot in Jakarta, July 27, 1996, signaled rising popular discontent. The collapse of a fraudulent gold-mining venture at Busang, E Kalimantan, in Mar. 1997 cost investors more than $3 bil. In Sept. 1997 smoke from widespread forest fires in Indonesia created a major environmental hazard. A major plane crash near Medan airport, Sept. 26, 1997, killed 234 persons.

In Dec. 1975, Indonesia invaded **East Timor** as Portuguese rule collapsed there. Indonesia annexed it in 1976, despite international condemnation. Timorese opposition to continued Indonesian rule has been ruthlessly suppressed.

In 1997 smoke from forest fires in Indonesia and Malaysia blanketed large areas of SE Asia.

Iran
Islamic Republic of Iran
Jomhuri-ye Eslami-ye Iran

People: Population: 67,540,002. **Age distrib.** (%): <15: 44; 65+: 4. **Pop. density:** 107 per sq. mi. **Urban:** 60%. **Ethnic groups:** Persian 51%, Azerbaijani 24%, Kurd 7%. **Principal languages:** Persian (Farsi; official), Turkic, Kurdish, Luri. **Religion:** Shi'a Muslim 89%, Sunni Muslim 10%.

Geography: Area: 632,457 sq. mi. **Location:** Between the Middle East and S Asia. **Neighbors:** Turkey, Iraq on W; Armenia, Azerbaijan, Turkmenistan on N; Afghanistan, Pakistan on E. **Topography:** Interior highlands and plains surrounded by high mountains, up to 18,000 ft. Large salt deserts cover much of area, but there are many oases and forest areas. Most of the population inhabits the N and NW. **Capital:** Tehran. **Cities:** Tehran 6,836,000; Mashhad 2,016,000; Esfahan 1,924,000*.

Government: Type: Islamic republic. **Religious head:** Ayatollah Sayyed Ali Khamenei; b 1940; in office: June 4, 1989. **Head of state:** Pres. Mohammad Khatami; b 1943; in office: Aug. 3, 1997. **Local divisions:** 25 provinces. **Defense:** 2.4% of GNP (1994). **Active troop strength:** 513,000.

Economy: Industries: Oil, petrochemicals, cement, sugar refining, carpets. **Chief crops:** Grains, rice, fruits, nuts, sugar beets, cotton. **Minerals:** Chromium, coal, oil, gas. **Crude oil reserves** (1996): 93 bil bbls. **Other resources:** Gums, wool, silk, caviar. **Arable land:** 8%. **Livestock** (1996): sheep: 51.5 mil; goats: 25.8 mil; cattle: 8.5 mil. **Fish catch** (1995): 388,300 metric tons. **Electricity prod.** (1995): 79 bil kWh. **Labor force:** 33% agric.; 21% manuf.

Finance: Monetary unit: Rial (Aug. 1997: 3,000 = $1 US). **Gross domestic product** (1995 est.): $323.5 bil. **Per capita GDP:** $4,700. **Imports** (1994 est.): $13 bil; partners: Germany 14%, UAE 9%, Japan 8%. **Exports** (1994 est.): $16 bil; partners: Japan 13%, South Korea 6%. **National budget** (1990): $80 bil. **Consumer prices** (change in 1996): 28.9%.

Transport: Railroads: Length: 3,162.8 mi. **Motor vehicles in use:** 1.6 mil passenger cars, 589,000 comm. vehicles. **Civil aviation:** 3.3 bil passenger-mi.; 19 airports with scheduled flights. **Chief port:** Bandar-e Abbas.

Communications: Television sets: 1 per 16 persons. **Radios:** 1 per 4.2 persons. **Telephones:** 1 per 13 persons. **Daily newspaper circ.:** 18 per 1,000 pop.

Health: Life expectancy at birth (1997): 66.5 male; 69.2 female. **Births** (per 1,000 pop.): 33. **Deaths** (per 1,000 pop.): 6. **Natural increase:** 2.6%. **Hospital beds:** 1 per 650 persons. **Physicians:** 1 per 1,600 persons. **Infant mortality** (per 1,000 live births 1997): 51.

Education: Compulsory: ages 6-10. **Literacy** (1994 est.): 72%.

Major International Organizations: UN (IMF, FAO, World Bank, WHO), OPEC.

Iran was once called Persia. The Iranians, who supplanted an earlier agricultural civilization, came from the E during the 2d millennium BC; they were an Indo-European group related to the Aryans of India.

In 549 BC Cyrus the Great united the Medes and Persians in the Persian Empire, conquered Babylonia in 538 BC, restored Jerusalem to the Jews. Alexander the Great conquered Persia in 333 BC, but Persians regained their independence in the next century under the Parthians, themselves succeeded by Sassanian Persians in AD 226. Arabs brought Islam to Persia in the 7th century, replacing the indigenous Zoroastrian faith. After Persian political and cultural autonomy was reasserted in the 9th century, the arts and sciences flourished for several centuries.

Turks and Mongols ruled Persia in turn from the 11th century to 1502, when a native dynasty reasserted full independence. The British and Russian empires vied for influence in

the 19th century; Afghanistan was severed from Iran by Britain in 1857.

Reza Khan abdicated as shah, 1941, and was succeeded by his son, Mohammad Reza Pahlavi. Under his rule, Iran underwent economic and social change but political opposition was not tolerated.

Conservative Muslim protests led to 1978 violence. Martial law was declared in 12 cities Sept. 8. A military government was appointed Nov. 6 to deal with striking oil workers. The shah appointed Prime Min. Shahpur Bakhtiar to head a regency council in his absence. The shah left Iran Jan. 16, 1979.

Exiled religious leader Ayatollah Ruhollah Khomeini named a provisional government council in preparation for his return to Iran, Jan. 31. Clashes between Khomeini's supporters and government troops culminated in a rout of Iran's elite Imperial Guard Feb. 11, leading to the fall of Bakhtiar's government.

The Iranian revolution was marked by revolts among the ethnic minorities and by a continuing struggle between the clerical forces and westernized intellectuals and liberals. The Islamic Constitution established final authority to be vested in a Faghi, the Ayatollah Khomeini.

Iranian militants seized the U.S. embassy, Nov. 4, 1979, and took hostages including 62 Americans. Despite international condemnations and U.S. efforts, including an abortive Apr. 1980 rescue attempt, the crisis continued. The U.S. broke diplomatic relations with Iran, Apr. 7. The shah died in Egypt, July 27. The hostage drama finally ended Jan. 21, 1981, when an accord, involving the release of frozen Iranian assets, was reached.

A dispute over the Shatt al-Arab waterway that divides the two countries brought Iran and Iraq, Sept. 22, 1980, into open warfare. Iraqi planes attacked Iranian airfields including Tehran airport. Iranian planes bombed Iraqi bases. Iraqi troops occupied Iranian territory, including the port city of Khorramshahr in October. Iranian troops recaptured the city and drove Iraqi troops back across the border, May 1982. Iraq, and later Iran, attacked several oil tankers in the Persian Gulf during 1984.

In Nov. 1986 it became known that senior U.S. officials had secretly visited Iran and that the U.S. had provided arms in exchange for Iran's help in obtaining the release of U.S. hostages held by terrorists in Lebanon. The revelation sparked a major scandal in the Reagan administration.

A U.S. Navy warship shot down an Iranian commercial airliner, July 3, 1988, after mistaking it for an F-14 fighter jet; all 290 aboard the plane died. In Aug. 1988, Iran agreed to accept a UN resolution calling for a cease-fire with Iraq.

A major earthquake struck northern Iran June 21, 1990, killing more than 45,000, injuring 100,000, and leaving 400,000 homeless. Some one million Kurdish refugees fled from Iraq to Iran following the Persian Gulf War. To curb Iran's alleged support for international terrorism, the U.S. in 1996 authorized sanctions on foreign companies that invest there. Mohammad Khatami, a moderate Shiite Muslim cleric, was elected president on May 23, 1997, winning nearly 70% of the vote.

Iraq
Republic of Iraq
Al Jumhuriyah al Iraqiyah

People: Population: 22,219,289. **Age distrib.** (%): <15: 47; 65+: 3. **Pop. density:** 132 per sq. mi. **Urban:** 75%. **Ethnic groups:** Arab 75-80%, Kurd 15-20%, Turkoman. **Principal languages:** Arabic (official), Kurdish. **Chief religions:** Muslim 97% (Shi'a 60-65%, Sunni 32-37%).

Geography: Area: 167,975 sq. mi. **Location:** In the Middle East, occupying most of historic Mesopotamia. **Neighbors:** Jordan and Syria on W, Turkey on N, Iran on E, Kuwait and Saudi Arabia on S. **Topography:** Mostly an alluvial plain, including the Tigris and Euphrates rivers, descending from mountains in N to desert in SW. Persian Gulf region is marshland. **Capital:** Baghdad. **Cities:** Baghdad 4,336,000; Arbil 1,743,000; Mosul 879,000*.

Government: Type: Republic. **Head of state:** Pres. Saddam Hussein, b. Apr. 29, 1937; in office: July 16, 1979; also assumed post of prime minister, May 29, 1994. **Local divisions:** 18 provinces. **Defense:** 18% of GDP (1994 est.). **Active troop strength:** 382,500.

Economy: Industries: Textiles, petrochemicals, oil refining, cement. **Chief crops:** Grains, rice, dates, cotton. **Minerals:** Oil, gas. **Crude oil reserves** (1996): 112 bil bbls. **Other resources:** Wool, hides. **Arable land:** 12%. **Livestock** (1996): sheep: 5.0 mil; cattle: 1.0 mil. **Fish catch** (1993): 23,500 metric tons. **Electricity prod.** (1995): 26 bil kWh. **Labor force:** 48% services; 30% agric.; 22% ind.

Finance: Monetary unit: Dinar (Aug. 1997: 1,200 = $1 US). **Gross domestic product** (1995 est.): $41.1 bil. **Per capita**

GDP: $2,000. **Imports** (1994 est.): $1.9 bil; partners: U.S., Germany. **Exports** (1994 est.): $450 mil; partners: U.S., Brazil. **National budget** (1990): $35 bil.

Transport: Railroad: Length: 1,261.9 mi. **Motor vehicles in use:** 672,000 passenger cars, 368,000 comm. vehicles. **Civil aviation:** 12.4 mil passenger-mi. **Chief port:** Basra. **Communications: Television sets:** 1 per 13 persons. **Radios:** 1 per 4.6 persons. **Telephones:** 1 per 30 persons. **Daily newspaper circ.:** 27 per 1,000 pop.

Health: Life expectancy at birth (1997): 66.3 male; 68.5 female. **Births** (per 1,000 pop.): 43. **Deaths** (per 1,000 pop.): 6. **Natural increase:** 3.6%. **Hospital beds:** 1 per 704 persons. **Physicians:** 1 per 2,181 persons. **Infant mortality** (per 1,000 live births 1997): 58.

Education: Free and compulsory: ages 6-12. **Literacy** (1995 est.): 58%.

Major International Organizations: UN (IMF, ILO), Arab League, OPEC.

The Tigris-Euphrates valley, formerly called Mesopotamia, was the site of one of the earliest civilizations in the world. The Sumerian city-states of 3,000 BC originated the culture later developed by the Semitic Akkadians, Babylonians, and Assyrians.

Mesopotamia ceased to be a separate entity after the Persian, Greek, and Arab conquests. The latter founded Baghdad, from where the caliph ruled a vast empire in the 8th and 9th centuries. Mongol and Turkish conquests led to a decline in population, economy, cultural life, and the irrigation system.

Britain secured a League of Nations mandate over Iraq after World War I. Independence under a king came in 1932. A leftist, pan-Arab revolution established a republic in 1958, which oriented foreign policy toward the USSR. Most industry has been nationalized, and large land holdings broken up.

A local faction of the international Baath Arab Socialist party has ruled by decree since 1968. The USSR and Iraq signed an aid pact in 1972, and arms were sent along with several thousand advisers. The 1978 execution of 21 communists and a shift of trade to the West signalled a more neutral policy, straining relations with the USSR. In the 1973 Arab-Israeli war Iraq sent forces to aid Syria. Within a month of assuming power, Saddam Hussein instituted a bloody purge in the wake of a reported coup attempt against the new regime.

Years of battling with the Kurdish minority resulted in total defeat for the Kurds in 1975, when Iran withdrew support. The fighting led to Iraqi bombing of Kurdish villages in Iran, causing relations with Iran to deteriorate.

After skirmishing intermittently for 10 months over the sovereignty of the disputed Shatt al-Arab waterway that divides the two countries, Iraq and Iran entered into open warfare on Sept. 22, 1980. In the following days, there was heavy ground fighting around Abadan and the port of Khorramshahr, as Iraq launched an attack on Iran's oil-rich province of Khuzistan.

Israeli airplanes destroyed a nuclear reactor near Baghdad on June 7, 1981, claiming it could be used to produce nuclear weapons.

Iraq and Iran expanded their war to the Persian Gulf in Apr. 1984. There were several attacks on oil tankers. An Iraqi warplane launched a missile attack on the USS *Stark*, a U.S. Navy frigate on patrol in the Persian Gulf, May 17, 1987; 37 U.S. sailors died. Iraq apologized for the attack, claiming it was inadvertent. The fierce war ended Aug. 1988, when Iraq accepted a UN resolution for a cease-fire.

Iraq attacked and overran Kuwait Aug. 2, 1990, sparking an international crisis. The UN, Aug. 6, imposed a ban on all trade with Iraq and called on member countries to protect the assets of the legitimate government of Kuwait. Iraq declared Kuwait its 19th province, Aug. 28.

A U.S.-led coalition launched air and missile attacks on Iraq, Jan. 16, 1991, after the expiration of a UN Security Council deadline for Iraq to withdraw from Kuwait. Iraq retaliated by firing scud missiles at Saudi Arabia and Israel. The coalition began a ground attack to retake Kuwait Feb. 23. Iraqi forces showed little resistance and were soundly defeated in 4 days. Some 175,000 Iraqis were taken prisoner, and casualties were estimated at over 85,000. As part of the cease-fire agreement, Iraq agreed to scrap all poison gas and germ weapons and allow UN observers to inspect the sites. UN trade sanctions would remain in effect until Iraq complied with all terms.

In the aftermath of the war, there were revolts against Pres. Saddam Hussein throughout Iraq. In Feb., Iraqi troops drove Kurdish insurgents and civilians to the Iran and Turkey borders, causing a refugee crisis. The U.S. and allies established havens inside Iraq for the Kurds. Iraqi cooperation with UN weapons inspection teams was intermittent.

The U.S. launched a missile attack aimed at Iraq's intelligence headquarters in Baghdad June 26, 1993. The U.S. justified the attack by citing evidence that Iraq had sponsored a plot to kill former Pres. George Bush during his visit to Kuwait in Apr. 1993. In Aug. 1995, two of Saddam Hussein's sons-in-law, who held high positions in the Iraqi military, defected to Jordan; both were killed after returning to Iraq in Feb. 1996. After fighting between two Kurdish factions (one allied with Iraq, the other with Iran) erupted in the protected zone of northern Iraq, the Baghdad government intervened in the conflict by sending troops into Arbil, Aug. 31, 1996. The U.S. retaliated with missile strikes against air defense sites in the south. On Dec. 9 the UN allowed Baghdad to begin selling limited amounts of oil for food and medicine. Saddam Hussein's son Odai was seriously wounded in an assassination attempt in Baghdad Dec. 12.

Ireland

Éire

People: Population: 3,555,500. **Age distrib.** (%): <15: 23; 65+: 11. **Pop. density:** 131 per sq. mi. **Urban:** 58%. **Ethnic groups:** Celtic, English minority. **Principal languages:** English predominates, Irish (Gaelic) spoken by minority (both official). **Chief religions:** Roman Catholic 93%, Anglican 3%.

Geography: Area: 27,137 sq. mi. **Location:** In the Atlantic O. just W of Great Britain. **Neighbors:** United Kingdom (Northern Ireland) on E. **Topography:** Ireland consists of a central plateau surrounded by isolated groups of hills and mountains. The coastline is heavily indented by the Atlantic O. **Capital:** Dublin. **Cities** (1991 met.): Dublin 478,389; Cork 127,253.

Government: Type: Parliamentary republic. **Head of state:** Pres. Mary Robinson; b May 21, 1944; in office: Dec. 3, 1990 (resigned: Sept. 12, 1997). **Head of government:** Prime Min. Bertie Ahern; b Sept. 12, 1951; in office: June 26, 1997. **Local divisions:** 26 counties. **Defense:** 1.3% of GDP (1994). **Active troop strength:** 12,700.

Economy: Industries: Food processing, textiles, chemicals, brewing, machinery, tourism. **Chief crops:** Potatoes, grains, sugar beets, turnips. **Minerals:** Zinc, lead, gas, oil. **Arable land:** 14%. **Livestock** (1996): cattle: 6.4 mil; sheep: 5.8 mil; pigs: 1.5 mil. **Fish catch** (1995): 412,722 metric tons. **Electricity prod.** (1995): 16.6 bil kWh. **Labor force:** 57% services; 28% manuf. & constr.; 13.5% agric. & fish.

Finance: Monetary unit: Pound (Aug. 1997: 0.6775 = $1.59 US). **Gross domestic product** (1995 est.): $54.6 bil. **Per capita GDP:** $15,400. **Imports** (1994): $25.3 bil; partners: UK 36%, U.S. 18%, Germany 7%. **Exports** (1994): $29.9 bil; partners: UK 27%, Germany 14%, U.S. 9%. **Tourism** (1994): $1.8 bil. **National budget** (1994): $20.3 bil. **International reserves less gold** (June 1997): $7.58 bil. **Gold:** 360,000 oz t. **Consumer prices** (change in 1996): 1.7%.

Transport: Railroads: Length: 1,207.2 mi. **Motor vehicles in use:** 990,000 passenger cars, 240,000 comm. vehicles. **Civil aviation:** 3.1 bil passenger-mi.; 9 airports. **Chief ports:** Dublin, Cork.

Communications: Television sets: 1 per 3.3 persons. **Radios:** 1 per 1.6 persons. **Telephones:** 1 per 2.7 persons. **Daily newspaper circ.:** 170 per 1,000 pop.

Health: Life expectancy at birth (1997): 73.1 male; 78.6 female. **Births** (per 1,000 pop.): 13. **Deaths** (per 1,000 pop.): 9. **Natural increase:** 0.4%. **Hospital beds:** 1 per 255 persons. **Infant mortality** (per 1,000 live births 1997): 6.

Education: Compulsory: ages 6-15. **Literacy** (1993): 100%.

Major International Organizations: UN (WHO, FAO, WTO, IMF, World Bank), EU, OECD.

Embassy: 2234 Massachusetts Ave. NW 20008; 462-3939.

Celtic tribes invaded the islands about the 4th century BC; their Gaelic culture and literature flourished and spread to Scotland and elsewhere in the 5th century AD, the same century in which St. Patrick converted the Irish to Christianity. Invasions by Norsemen began in the 8th century, ended with defeat of the Danes by the Irish King Brian Boru in 1014. English invasions started in the 12th century; for over 700 years the Anglo-Irish struggle continued with bitter rebellions and savage repressions.

The Easter Monday Rebellion (1916) failed but was followed by guerrilla warfare and harsh reprisals by British troops, the "Black and Tans." The Dail Eireann, (Irish parliament), reaffirmed independence in Jan. 1919. The British offered dominion status to Ulster (6 counties) and southern Ireland (26 counties) Dec. 1921. The constitution of the Irish Free State, a British dominion, was adopted Dec. 11, 1922. Northern Ireland remained part of the United Kingdom.

A new constitution adopted by plebiscite came into operation Dec. 29, 1937. It declared the name of the state Eire in the Irish language (Ireland in the English) and declared it a sovereign democratic state.

(continued on page 785)

TRANSITION IN CHINA

Paramount leader Deng Xiaoping (left), the driving force behind China's economic modernization, died Feb. 19 at 92. Below, a procession carrying Deng's remains files out of a Beijing hospital, prior to the state funeral.

XINHUA/CHINE NOUVELLE/GAMMA LIAISON; (INSET) FORREST ANDERSON/GAMMA LIAISON

IVO LORENC/SYGMA

AP/WIDE WORLD PHOTOS

In another dramatic transition, China regained control of prosperous Hong Kong after 156 years of British rule. At left, the last colonial governor, Chris Patten, receives the British flag; at right, China's flag is raised, in handover ceremonies July 1.

WORLD EVENTS

A 7-month civil war in the former Zaire ended in May when rebel troops, shown above, took over the capital city after strongman Mobutu Sese Seko fled. Rebel leader Laurent Kabila (inset) was sworn in May 29 as president of the renamed Democratic Republic of the Congo. Mobutu himself died Sept. 7 in Morocco.

On Apr. 22, government troops stormed the Japanese ambassador's residence (left) in Lima, Peru, to rescue 72 hostages held by guerrillas for 126 days. All 14 guerrillas, 1 hostage, and 2 soldiers were killed. Above, troops help hostages escape.

In a tragedy mourned by literally billions of people, Diana, Princess of Wales, 36, was fatally injured Aug. 31 in a car crash (inset, right) in a Paris tunnel; also killed were her companion, Dodi Fayed, and the driver. Above, in ceremonies televised around the world, Diana's casket is carried into London's Westminster Abbey; standing by, left to right, are her former husband, Prince Charles; her son Prince Harry; her brother, Earl Spencer; her son Prince William; and the queen's husband, Prince Philip. Below, the "people's princess" meets Bosnian children during a visit to focus attention on land mines.

Tony Blair, with his family, waves to onlookers outside 10 Downing Street, after a landslide Labor Party election victory May 1 made him Britain's new prime minister.

Arts and Entertainment

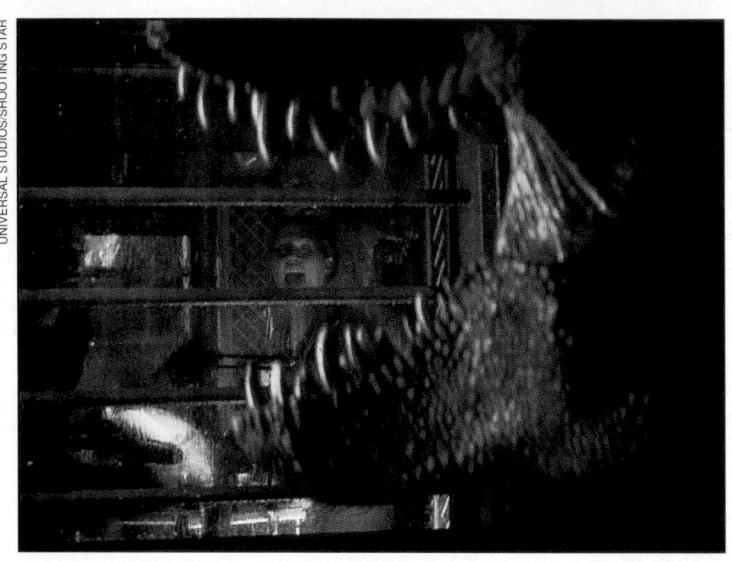

Dinosaurs were on the attack again in the summer of 1997, as *The Lost World,* a sequel to *Jurassic Park,* took in more than $225 million at the box office by September.

In 1997, *The English Patient,* starring Ralph Fiennes and Kristin Scott Thomas (above), won 9 Oscars, including best picture and best director. Only 2 films (*West Side Story* and *Ben Hur*) ever won more.

In an episode of the ABC sitcom *Ellen,* aired on Apr. 30, the title character, played by Ellen DeGeneres (left, in a scene with guest star Laura Dern), announced she was a lesbian. DeGeneres herself made a similar announcement earlier the same month.

At the age of only 14, LeAnn Rimes won two Grammy awards, including one for Best New Artist. She was the first country singer to win a Grammy in that category.

AP/WIDE WORLD PHOTOS

AP/WIDE WORLD PHOTOS

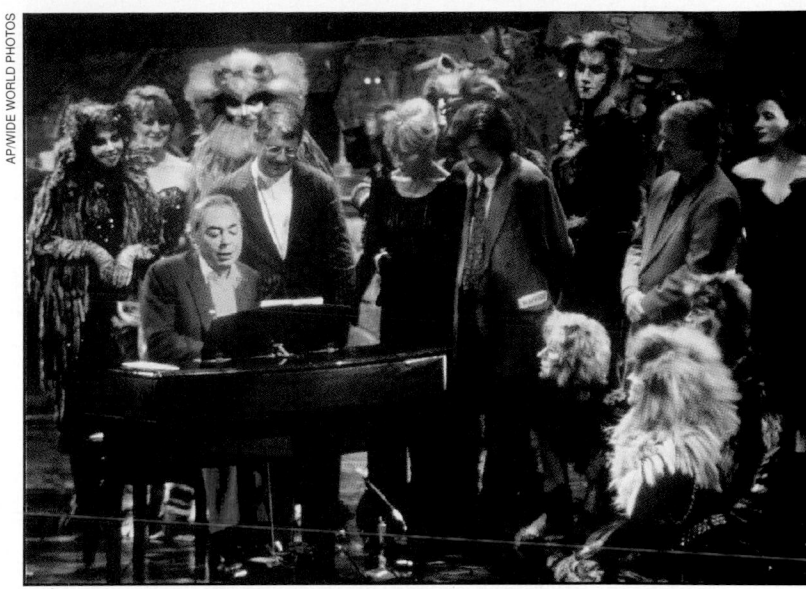

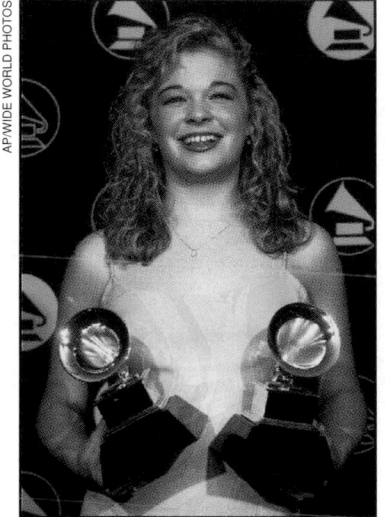

On June 19, the musical *Cats* became the longest-running Broadway show in history. Above, composer Andrew Lloyd Webber, at the piano, surrounded by the cast and others responsible for the show, plays a *Cats* song on stage following the record-breaking 6,138th performance.

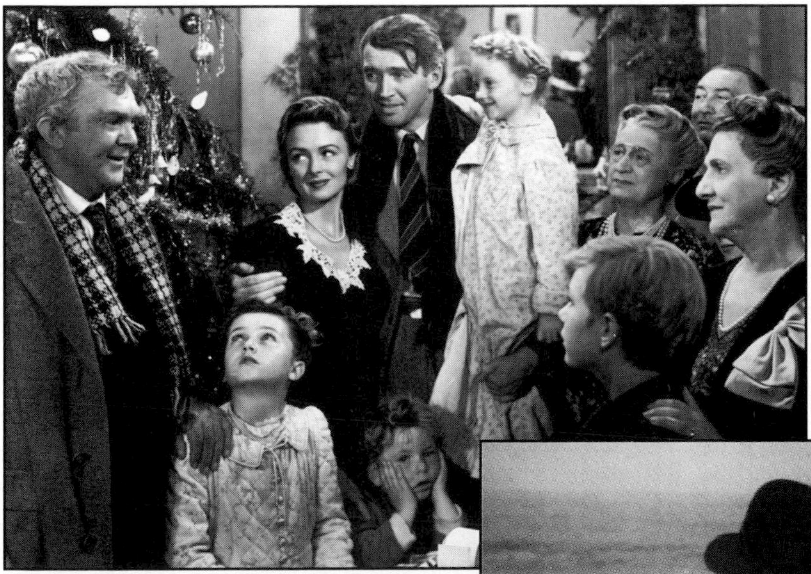

THE KOBAL COLLECTION

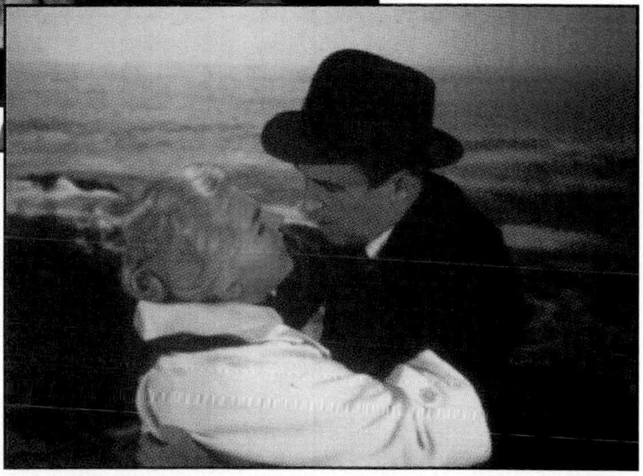

© 1996 UNIVERSAL CITY STUDIOS/THE KOBAL COLLECTION

An American legend passed into history with the death July 2 of actor Jimmy Stewart. Perhaps most beloved as the small-town banker (above, center) in *It's a Wonderful Life* (1946), he also appeared in a wide variety of other roles—as in Alfred Hitchcock's *Vertigo* (1958), at right.

SPORTS HIGHLIGHTS

Quarterback Brett Favre led the Green Bay Packers to victory in Super Bowl XXXI, Jan. 26, 1997, at the Louisiana Superdome in New Orleans. The Packers beat the New England Patriots, 35-21, to win their first NFL title in 29 years.

Chicago Bulls guard Michael Jordan, named MVP in the NBA Finals for the 5th time, goes up for a shot in Game 5. The Bulls defeated the Utah Jazz, 4 games to 2, to take their 5th NBA championship in 7 years.

On Apr. 13, 21-year-old Tiger Woods won the Masters with the lowest score in the tournament's history–270, or 18 under par. He was the youngest golfer to win it, and his margin of victory over his nearest opponent (12 strokes) was the biggest ever.

The sport of boxing was said to have sunk to a new low when Mike Tyson twice bit heavyweight champ Evander Holyfield's ears during Round 3 of their June 28 bout in Las Vegas. Besides being disqualified, Tyson was fined and barred from boxing in the state for a year.

The 1997 baseball season was dedicated to Jackie Robinson, who 50 years earlier broke the "color barrier" to become the first black player in the major leagues. Below, Robinson steals home for the Brooklyn Dodgers in the 1955 World Series against the New York Yankees.

On June 12, baseball teams from the two leagues faced each other for the first time in regular-season play. In the first interleague game to get under way, the San Francisco Giants edged out the Texas Rangers, 4-3, in Arlington, TX. Above, Giants shortstop Jose Vizcaino chases a grounder during the first inning.

SPORTS HIGHLIGHTS

Fourteen-year-old Tara Lipinski became the youngest world figure skating champion ever when she took the title on Mar. 22 in Lausanne, Switzerland. The previous month, she had become the youngest-ever U.S. figure skating champ.

Sixteen-year-old tennis sensation Martina Hingis became the youngest Wimbledon champion since 1887, and took 2 of the other 3 Grand Slam events–the Australian and U.S. opens.

The Detroit Red Wings swept the Philadelphia Flyers in 4 games to win their first Stanley Cup since 1955. Red Wings goalie Mike Vernon, in action at left, won the Conn Smythe Trophy as playoffs MVP.

On Dec. 21, 1948, an Irish law declared the country a republic rather than a dominion and withdrew it from the Commonwealth. The British Parliament recognized both actions, 1949, but reasserted its claim to incorporate the 6 northeastern counties in the United Kingdom. This claim has not been recognized by Ireland (see United Kingdom — Northern Ireland).

Irish governments have favored peaceful unification of all Ireland and have cooperated with Britain against terrorist groups. On Dec. 15, 1993, the Irish and British governments agreed on outlines of a peace plan to resolve the Northern Ireland issue. On Aug. 31, 1994, the Irish Republican Army announced a cease-fire; when peace talks lagged, however, the IRA returned to its terror campaign on Feb. 9, 1996. The IRA proclaimed a new cease-fire as of July 20, 1997, and peace talks resumed Sept. 15.

Ireland's first woman president, Mary Robinson, resigned Sept. 12 to become UN high commissioner for human rights.

Israel
State of Israel
Medinat Yisra'el

People: Population: 5,534,672. **Age distrib.** (%): <15: 28; 65+: 10. **Pop. density:** 702 per sq. mi. **Urban:** 91%. **Ethnic groups:** Jewish 82%, non-Jewish (mostly Arab) 18%. **Principal languages:** Hebrew (official), Arabic (used officially for Arab minority), English. **Chief religions:** Jewish 82%, Muslim (mostly Sunni) 14%.

Geography: Area: 7,876 sq. mi. **Location:** Middle East, on E end of Mediterranean Sea. **Neighbors:** Lebanon on N, Syria and Jordan on E, Egypt on W. **Topography:** The Mediterranean coastal plain is fertile and well-watered. In the center is the Judean Plateau. A triangular-shaped semi-desert region, the Negev, extends from south of Beersheba to an apex at the head of the Gulf of Aqaba. The E border drops sharply into the Jordan Rift Valley, including Lake Tiberias (Sea of Galilee) and the Dead Sea, which is 1,312 ft. below sea level, lowest point on the earth's surface. **Capital:** Jerusalem (most countries maintain their embassy in Tel Aviv). **Cities** (1996 est.): Jerusalem 591,400; Tel Aviv-Yafo 355,900; Haifa 252,300.

Government: Type: Republic. **Head of state:** Pres. Ezer Weizman; b June 15, 1924; in office: May 13, 1993. **Head of government:** Prime Min. Benjamin Netanyahu; b Oct. 21, 1949; in office: June 18, 1996. **Local divisions:** 6 districts. **Defense:** 9.8% of GDP (1996). **Active troop strength:** 175,000 est.

Economy: Industries: Diamond cutting, textiles, electronics, machinery, food processing. **Chief crops:** Citrus fruit, vegetables, cotton. **Minerals:** Copper, phosphates, bromide, potash, clay. **Arable land:** 17%. **Livestock** (1996): cattle: 379,000; sheep: 352,000. **Fish catch** (1993): 18,661 metric tons. **Electricity prod.** (1995): 28 bil kWh. **Labor force:** 29% public services; 22% ind.; 14% commerce.

Finance: Monetary unit: New Shekel (Aug. 1997: 3.52 = $1 US). **Gross domestic prod.** (1995 est.): $80.1 bil. **Per capita GDP:** $15,500. **Imports** (1995 est.): $40.1 bil; partners: U.S. 18.6%, Belgium 12.2%. **Exports** (1995 est.): $28.4 bil; partners: U.S. 30.1%. **Tourism** (1994): $2.3 bil. **National budget** (1996): $53 bil. **International reserves less gold** (June 1997): $17.86 bil. **Gold:** 9,000 oz t. **Consumer prices** (change in 1996): 11.3%.

Transport: Railroads: Length: 326.6 mi. **Motor vehicles in use:** 1.1 mil passenger cars, 273,000 comm. vehicles. **Civil aviation:** 6.0 bil passenger-mi.; 7 airports with scheduled flights. **Chief ports:** Haifa, Ashdod, Elat.

Communications: Television sets: 1 per 3.6 persons. **Radios:** 1 per 2.1 persons. **Telephones:** 1 per 2.4 persons. **Daily newspaper circ.:** 281 per 1,000 pop.

Health: Life expectancy at birth (1997): 76.3 male; 80.2 female. **Births** (per 1,000 pop.): 20. **Deaths** (per 1,000 pop.): 6. **Natural increase:** 1.4%. **Hospital beds:** 1 per 165 persons. **Physicians:** 1 per 212 persons. **Infant mortality** (per 1,000 live births 1997): 8.

Education: Free and compulsory: ages 5-16. **Literacy** (1994): 95%.

Major International Organizations: UN (WTO, IMF).

Embassy: 3514 International Dr. NW 20008; 364-5500.

Occupying the SW corner of the ancient Fertile Crescent, Israel contains some of the oldest known evidence of agriculture and of primitive town life. A more advanced civilization emerged in the 3d millennium BC. The Hebrews probably arrived early in the 2d millennium BC. Under King David and his successors (c.1000 BC-597 BC), Judaism was developed and secured. After conquest by Babylonians, Persians, and Greeks, an independent Jewish kingdom was revived, 168 BC, but Rome took effective control in the next century, suppressed Jewish revolts in AD 70 and AD 135, and renamed Judea Palestine, after the earlier coastal inhabitants, the Philistines.

Arab invaders conquered Palestine in 636. The Arabic language and Islam prevailed within a few centuries, but a Jewish minority remained. The land was ruled from the 11th century as a part of non-Arab empires by Seljuks, Mamluks, and Ottomans (with a crusader interval, 1098-1291).

After 4 centuries of Ottoman rule, during which the population declined to a low of 350,000 (1785), the land was taken in 1917 by Britain, which in the Balfour Declaration that year pledged to support a Jewish national homeland there, as foreseen by the Zionists. In 1920 a British Palestine Mandate was recognized; in 1922 the land east of the Jordan was detached.

Jewish immigration, begun in the late 19th century, swelled in the 1930s with refugees from the Nazis; heavy Arab immigration from Syria and Lebanon also occurred. Arab opposition to Jewish immigration turned violent in 1920, 1921, 1929, and 1936. The UN General Assembly voted in 1947 to partition Palestine into an Arab and a Jewish state. Britain withdrew in May 1948.

Israel was declared an independent state May 14, 1948; the Arabs rejected partition. Egypt, Jordan, Syria, Lebanon, Iraq, and Saudi Arabia invaded, but failed to destroy the Jewish state, which gained territory. Separate armistices with the Arab nations were signed in 1949; Jordan occupied the West Bank, Egypt occupied Gaza; neither granted Palestinian autonomy.

After persistent terrorist raids, Israel invaded Egypt's Sinai, Oct. 29, 1956, aided briefly by British and French forces. A UN cease-fire was arranged Nov. 6.

An uneasy truce between Israel and the Arab countries, supervised by a UN Emergency Force, prevailed until May 19, 1967, when the UN force withdrew at Egypt's demand. Egyptian forces reoccupied the Gaza Strip and closed the Gulf of Aqaba to Israeli shipping. In a 6-day war that started June 5, the Israelis took the Gaza Strip, occupied the Sinai Peninsula to the Suez Canal, and captured East Jerusalem, Syria's Golan Heights, and Jordan's West Bank. The fighting was halted June 10 by UN-arranged cease-fire agreements.

Egypt and Syria attacked Israel, Oct. 6, 1973 (Yom Kippur, most solemn day on the Jewish calendar). Israel counterattacked, driving the Syrians back, and crossed the Suez Canal.

A cease-fire took effect Oct. 24; a UN peacekeeping force went to the area. A disengagement agreement was signed Jan. 18, 1974. Israel withdrew from the canal's west bank. A second withdrawal was completed in 1976; Israel returned the Sinai to Egypt in 1982.

Israeli forces raided Entebbe, Uganda, July 3, 1976, and rescued 103 hostages seized by Arab and German terrorists.

In 1977, the conservative opposition, led by Menachem Begin, was voted into office for the first time. Egypt's Pres. Anwar al-Sadat visited Jerusalem Nov. 1977, and on Mar. 26, 1979, Egypt and Israel signed a formal peace treaty, ending 30 years of war and establishing diplomatic relations.

Israel invaded S Lebanon, Mar. 1978, following a Lebanon-based terrorist attack in Israel. Israel withdrew in favor of a 6,000-man UN force, but continued to aid Lebanese Christian militiamen. Violence on the Israeli-occupied West Bank rose in 1982 when Israel announced plans to build new Jewish settlements. Israel affirmed the entire city of Jerusalem as its capital, July 1980, encompassing the annexed East Jerusalem.

On June 7, 1981, Israeli jets destroyed an Iraqi atomic reactor near Baghdad that, Israel claimed, would have enabled Iraq to manufacture nuclear weapons.

Israeli jets bombed Palestine Liberation Organization (PLO) strongholds in Lebanon Apr.-May 1982. In reaction to the wounding of the Israeli ambassador to Great Britain, Israeli forces in a coordinated land, sea, and air attack invaded Lebanon, June 6, to destroy PLO strongholds in that country. Israeli forces encircled Beirut June 14. Following massive Israeli bombing of West Beirut, the PLO agreed to evacuate the city.

Israeli troops entered West Beirut after newly elected Lebanese Pres. Bashir Gemayel was assassinated on Sept. 14. Israel received widespread condemnation when Lebanese Christian forces, Sept. 16, entered two West Beirut refugee camps and slaughtered hundreds of Palestinian refugees.

In 1988, violence escalated over the Israeli military occupation of the West Bank and Gaza Strip, in a series of uprisings known as the intifada, Palestinian protesters defied Israeli troops, who forcibly retaliated. Israeli police and stone-throwing Palestinians clashed, Oct. 8, 1990, around the al-Aqsa mosque on the Temple Mount in Jerusalem; some 20 Palestinians died.

During the Persian Gulf War in early 1991, Iraq fired a series of scud missiles at Israel. The Labor Party of Yitzhak Rabin won a clear victory in elections held June 23, 1992.

Ongoing peace talks produced historic agreements between Israel and the Palestine Liberation Organization in Sept. 1993. The latter recognized Israel's right to exist, and Israel recognized the PLO as the representative of the Palestinians; the two sides then signed, Sept. 13, an agreement for limited Palestinian self-rule in Gaza and in the West Bank, beginning with the city of Jericho. An accord formally initiating self-rule was signed in Cairo, May 4, 1994. Israel and Jordan signed, July 25, 1994, in Washington, DC, a declaration ending their 46-year state of war; a formal peace treaty was signed Oct. 26. An accord between Israel and the PLO expanding Palestinian self-rule in the West Bank was signed Sept. 28, 1995.

Arab and Jewish extremists repeatedly challenged the peace process. A Jewish gunman opened fire on Arab worshippers at a mosque in Hebron, Feb. 25, 1994, killing at least 29 before he himself was killed. On Nov. 4, 1995, an Orthodox Jewish Israeli assassinated Rabin as he left a peace rally in Tel Aviv.

Support for Rabin's successor, Shimon Peres, was shaken by a series of suicide bombings and rocket attacks against Israel by Islamic militants. In Apr. 1996, Israel attacked suspected guerrilla bases in southern Lebanon. Emphasizing security issues, the candidate of the conservative Likud bloc, Benjamin Netanyahu, was elected prime minister on May 29.

On Sept. 24, Israel opened a tunnel entrance near a sacred Muslim site in Jerusalem, setting off several days of violence between Israeli soldiers and Palestinian demonstrators and police. Pres. Clinton hosted a summit meeting between Netanyahu and PLO leader Yasir Arafat Oct. 1-2, and peace talks were resumed. Israel and the PLO agreed Jan. 15, 1997, on a partial Israeli pullout from the West Bank city of Hebron. Two suicide bombings in a Jerusalem market July 30 left 15 people dead and more than 170 wounded.

Gaza: Population (1997 est.): **987,869. Area:** 140 sq. mi.
West Bank: Population (1997 est.): 1,495,683. **Area:** 2,270 sq. mi.

Italy
Italian Republic
Repubblica Italiana

People: Population: 57,534,088. **Age distrib.** (%): <15: 15; 65+: 17. **Pop. density:** 494 per sq. mi. **Urban:** 67%. **Ethnic groups:** Italian, small minorities of German, French, Slovene, Albanian, Greek. **Principal languages:** Italian (official), German, French, Slovene. **Chief religions:** Roman Catholic 98%.

Geography: Area: 116,341 sq. mi. **Location:** In S Europe, jutting into Mediterranean Sea. **Neighbors:** France on W, Switzerland and Austria on N, Slovenia on E. **Topography:** Occupies a long boot-shaped peninsula, extending SE from the Alps into the Mediterranean, with the islands of Sicily and Sardinia offshore. The alluvial Po Valley drains most of N. The rest of the country is rugged and mountainous, except for intermittent coastal plains, like the Campania, S of Rome. Apennine Mts. run down through center of peninsula. **Capital:** Rome. **Cities:** Milan 4,251,000; Naples 3,012,000; Rome 2,688,000.; Turin 1,294,000*.

Government: Type: Republic. **Head of state:** Pres. Oscar Luigi Scalfaro; b Sept. 9, 1918; in office: May 28, 1992. **Head of government:** Prime Min. Romano Prodi; b Aug. 9, 1939; in office: May 18, 1996. **Local divisions:** 20 regions with some autonomy, divided into 95 provinces. **Defense:** 1.9% of GDP (1995). **Active troop strength:** 325,150.

Economy: Industries: Tourism, steel, machinery, autos, textiles, shoes, clothing, chemicals. **Chief crops:** Grapes, olives, citrus fruits, vegetables, wheat. **Minerals:** Mercury, potash, sulphur. **Crude oil reserves** (1996): 685 mil bbls. **Arable land:** 32%. **Livestock** (1996): sheep: 10.5 mil; pigs: 8.0 mil; cattle: 7.0 mil; goats: 1.5 mil. **Fish catch** (1995): 609,768 metric tons. **Electricity prod.** (1995): 225.2 bil kWh. **Labor force:** 58% services; 32% ind.; 10% agric.

Finance: Monetary unit: Lira (Aug. 1997: 1,767.40 = $1 US). **Gross domestic product** (1994): $1.09 tril. **Per capita GDP:** $18,700. **Imports** (1994): $168.7 bil; partners: EU 56%, U.S. 5%. **Exports** (1994): $190.8 bil; partners: EU 53%, U.S. 8%. **Tourism** (1994): $23.9 bil. **National budget** (1994 est.): $431 bil. **International reserves less gold** (June 1997): $42.23 bil. **Gold:** 66.67 mil oz t. **Consumer prices** (change in 1996): 4.0%.

Transport: Railroads: Length: 11,774.8 mi. **Motor vehicles:** in use: 30.0 mil passenger cars, 2.8 mil comm. vehicles.

Civil aviation: 19.7 bil passenger-mi.; 31 airports. **Chief ports:** Genoa, Venice, Trieste, Palermo, Naples, La Spezia.

Communications: Television sets: 1 per 2.3 persons. **Radios:** 1 per 1.2 persons. **Telephones:** 1 per 2.3 persons. **Daily newspaper circ.:** 105 per 1,000 pop.

Health: Life expectancy at birth (1997): 75.0 male; 81.6 female. **Births** (per 1,000 pop.): 10. **Deaths** (per 1,000 pop.): 10. **Natural increase:** -0.0. **Hospital beds:** 1 per 147 persons. **Physicians:** 1 per 193 persons. **Infant mortality** (per 1,000 live births 1997): 7.

Education: Free and compulsory: ages 6-13. **Literacy** (1994): 97%.

Major International Organizations: UN and all of its specialized agencies, NATO, OECD, EU.

Embassy: 1601 Fuller St. NW 20009; 328-5500.

Rome emerged as the major power in Italy after 500 BC, dominating the Etruscans to the N and Greeks to the S. Under the Empire, which lasted until the 5th century AD, Rome ruled most of Western Europe, the Balkans, the Middle East, and N Africa. In 1988, archaeologists unearthed evidence showing Rome as a dynamic society in the 6th and 7th centuries BC.

After the Germanic invasions, lasting several centuries, a high civilization arose in the city-states of the N, culminating in the Renaissance. But German, French, Spanish, and Austrian intervention prevented the unification of the country. In 1859 Lombardy came under the crown of King Victor Emmanuel II of Sardinia. By plebiscite in 1860, Parma, Modena, Romagna, and Tuscany joined, followed by Sicily and Naples, and by the Marches and Umbria. The first Italian Parliament declared Victor Emmanuel king of Italy Mar. 17, 1861. Mantua and Venetia were added in 1866 as an outcome of the Austro-Prussian war. The Papal States were taken by Italian troops Sept. 20, 1870, on the withdrawal of the French garrison. The states were annexed to the kingdom by plebiscite. Italy recognized Vatican City as independent Feb. 11, 1929.

Fascism appeared in Italy Mar. 23, 1919, led by Benito Mussolini, who took over the government at the invitation of the king Oct. 28, 1922. Mussolini acquired dictatorial powers. He made war on Ethiopia and proclaimed Victor Emmanuel III emperor, defied the sanctions of the League of Nations, sent troops to fight for Franco against the Republic of Spain, and joined Germany in World War II.

After Fascism was overthrown in 1943, Italy declared war on Germany and Japan and contributed to the Allied victory. It surrendered conquered lands and lost its colonies. Mussolini was killed by partisans Apr. 28, 1945. Victor Emmanuel III abdicated May 9, 1946; his son Humbert II was king until June 10, when Italy became a republic after a referendum, June 2-3.

Since World War II, Italy has enjoyed growth in industrial output and living standards, in part a result of membership in the European Community (now European Union). Political stability has not kept pace with economic prosperity, and organized crime and corruption have been persistent problems.

Christian Democratic leader and former Prime Min. Aldo Moro was abducted and murdered in 1978 by Red Brigade terrorists. The wave of left-wing political violence, including other kidnappings and assassinations, continued into the 1980s.

In the early 1990s, scandals implicated some of Italy's most prominent politicians. In Mar. 1994 voting, under reformed election rules, right-wing parties won a majority, dislodging Italy's long-powerful Christian Democratic Party. After a series of short-lived governments, a coalition of center-left parties won the election of Apr. 21, 1996. Italy led a 7,000-member international peacekeeping force in Albania, Apr.-Aug. 1997. Two earthquakes in central Italy Sept. 26 killed 11 people, left about 12,000 homeless, and damaged priceless frescoes in Assisi.

Sicily, 9,926 sq. mi., pop. (1994 est.) 5,025,000, is an island 180 by 120 mi., seat of a region that embraces the island of **Pantelleria,** 32 sq. mi., and the **Lipari** group, 44 sq. mi., including 2 active volcanoes: **Vulcano,** 1,637 ft., and **Stromboli,** 3,038 ft. From prehistoric times Sicily has been settled by various peoples; a Greek state had its capital at Syracuse. Rome took Sicily from Carthage 215 BC. **Mt. Etna,** an 11,053-ft. active volcano, is its tallest peak.

Sardinia, 9,301 sq. mi., pop. (1994 est.) 1,657,000, lies in the Mediterranean, 115 mi. W of Italy and 7½ mi. S of Corsica. It is 160 mi. long, 68 mi. wide, and mountainous, with mining of coal, zinc, lead, copper. In 1720 Sardinia was added to the possessions of the Dukes of Savoy in Piedmont and Savoy to form the Kingdom of Sardinia. Giuseppe Garibaldi is buried on the nearby isle of Caprera. **Elba,** 86 sq. mi., lies 6 mi. W of Tuscany. Napoleon I lived in exile on Elba 1814-1815.

Jamaica

People: Population: 2,615,582. **Age distrib.** (%): <15: 32; 65+: 7. **Pop. density:** 616 per sq. mi. **Urban:** 54%. **Ethnic groups:** African 76%, Afro-European 15%, white, Chinese, East Indian. **Principal languages:** English (official), Jamaican Creole. **Chief religions:** Protestant 56%, Roman Catholic 5%, spiritual cults and other 39%.

Geography: Area: 4,244 sq. mi. **Location:** In West Indies. **Neighbors:** Nearest are Cuba to N, Haiti to E. **Topography:** The country is four-fifths covered by mountains. **Capital:** Kingston (1991 met.): 103,771.

Government: Type: Parliamentary democracy. **Head of state:** Queen Elizabeth II, represented by Gov.-Gen. Sir Howard Cooke; b Nov. 13, 1915; in office: Aug. 1, 1991. **Head of government:** Prime Min. Percival J. Patterson; b Apr. 10, 1935; in office: Mar. 30, 1992. **Local divisions:** 14 parishes. **Defense:** 0.7% of GNP (1994). **Active troop strength:** 3,320 est.

Economy: Industries: Sugar, bauxite mining, tourism. **Chief crops:** Sugar, coffee, bananas, potatoes, citrus fruits. **Minerals:** Bauxite, limestone, gypsum. **Arable land:** 19%. **Livestock** (1996): cattle: 450,000; goats: 440,000. **Fish catch** (1993): 10,764 metric tons. **Electricity prod.** (1995): 3.9 bil kWh. **Labor force:** 41% services; 22.5% agric.; 19% ind.

Finance: Monetary unit: Dollar (Aug. 1997: 35.75 = $1 US). **Gross domestic product** (1995 est.): $8.2 bil. **Per capita GDP:** $3,200. **Imports** (1995 est.): $2.7 bil; partners: U.S. 54%. **Exports** (1995 est.): $2 bil; partners: U.S. 47%. **Tourism** (1994): $919 mil. **National budget** (FY 1995-96 est.): $2 bil. **International reserves less gold** (Apr. 1997): $805.7 mil. **Consumer prices** (change in 1996): 26.4%.

Transport: Railroads: Length: 168.9 mi. **Motor vehicles in use:** 104,000 passenger cars, 22,000 comm. vehicles. **Civil aviation:** 880.0 mil passenger-mi.; 5 airports with scheduled flights. **Chief ports:** Kingston, Montego Bay.

Communications: Television sets: 1 per 7.0 persons. **Radios:** 1 per 2.3 persons. **Telephones:** 1 per 8.7 persons.

Health: Life expectancy at birth (1997): 72.8 male; 77.6 female. **Births** (per 1,000 pop.): 22. **Deaths:** (per 1,000 pop.): 6. **Natural increase:** 1.6%. **Hospital beds:** 1 per 492 persons. **Physicians:** 1 per 6,043 persons. **Infant mortality** (per 1,000 live births 1997): 15.

Education: Free and compulsory: ages 6-12. **Literacy** (1995 est.): 85%.

Major International Organizations: UN (World Bank, WTO), OAS, the Commonwealth.

Embassy: 1520 New Hampshire Ave. NW 20036; 452-0660.

Jamaica was visited by Columbus, 1494, and ruled by Spain (under whom Arawak Indians died out) until seized by Britain, 1655. Jamaica won independence Aug. 6, 1962.

In 1974 Jamaica sought an increase in taxes paid by U.S. and Canadian bauxite mines. The socialist government acquired 50% ownership of the companies' Jamaican interests in 1976, and was reelected that year. Rudimentary welfare state measures were passed. Relations with the U.S. improved greatly in the 1980s following the election of Edward Seaga, which marked the beginning of a more conservative era.

Japan

Nippon

People: Population: 125,716,637. **Age distrib.** (%): <15: 16; 65+: 15. **Pop. density:** 861 per sq. mi. **Urban:** 78%. **Ethnic groups:** Japanese 99.4%, other (mostly Korean) 0.6%. **Principal language:** Japanese. **Chief religions:** Buddhism, Shintoism shared by large majority.

Geography: Area: 145,850 sq. mi. **Location:** Archipelago off E coast of Asia. **Neighbors:** Russia to N, South Korea to W. **Topography:** Japan consists of 4 main islands: Honshu ("mainland"), 87,805 sq. mi.; Hokkaido, 30,144 sq. mi.; Kyushu, 14,114 sq. mi.; and Shikoku, 7,049 sq. mi. The coast, deeply indented, measures 16,654 mi. The northern islands are a continuation of the Sakhalin Mts. The Kunlun range of China continues into southern islands, the ranges meeting in the Japanese Alps. In a vast transverse fissure crossing Honshu E-W rises a group of volcanoes, mostly extinct or inactive, including 12,388 ft Mt. Fuji (Fujiyama) near Tokyo. **Capital:** Tokyo. **Cities** (1994): Tokyo 26,959,000, Osaka 10,609,000; Nagoya 3,213,000; Sapporo 1,710,000; Kyoto 1,703,000*.

Government: Type: Parliamentary democracy. **Head of state:** Emp. Akihito; b Dec. 23, 1933; in office: Jan. 7, 1989. **Head of government:** Prime Min. Ryutaro Hashimoto; b July 29, 1937; in office: Jan. 11, 1996. **Local divisions:** 47 prefectures. **Defense:** 1% of GDP (FY 1995-96). **Active troop strength:** 235,500.

Economy: Industries: Electrical & electronic equip., vehicles, machinery, metallurgy, chemicals, fishing. **Chief crops:** Rice, potatoes, sugar, sugar beets, cabbages, fruits. **Arable land:** 13%. **Livestock** (1996): pigs: 10.1 mil.; cattle: 4.9 mil. **Fish catch** (1995): 8,767,570 mil metric tons. **Electricity prod.** (1995): 930.6 bil kWh. **Labor force:** 54% services & trade; 33% manuf., mining, & constr.; 7% agric. & fish.

Finance: Monetary unit: Yen (Aug. 1997: 118.59 = $1 US). **Gross domestic product** (1995 est.): $2.68 tril. **Per capita GDP:** $21,300. **Imports** (1995): $336.1 bil; partners: SE Asia 25%, U.S. 22%, China 11%. **Exports** (1995): $442.8 bil; partners: SE Asia 38%, U.S. 27%. **Tourism** (1994): $3.5 bil. **National budget** (1995 est.): $829 bil. **International reserves less gold** (June 1997): $221.13 bil. **Gold:** 24.23 mil oz t. **Consumer prices** (change in 1996): 0.1%.

Transport: Railroads: Length: 16,460.2 mi. **Motor vehicles in use:** 44.7 mil passenger cars, 22.2 mil comm. vehicles. **Civil aviation:** 73.3 bil passenger-mi.; 73 airports with scheduled flights. **Chief ports:** Yokohama, Tokyo, Kobe, Osaka, Nagoya, Chiba, Kawasaki, Hakodate.

Communications: Television sets: 1 per 1.5 persons. **Radios:** 1 per 1.1 persons. **Telephones:** 1 per 2.0 persons. **Daily newspaper circ.:** 576 per 1,000 pop.

Health: Life expectancy at birth (1997): 76.7 male; 82.8 female. **Births** (per 1,000 pop.): 10. **Deaths** (per 1,000 pop.): 8. **Natural increase:** 0.2%. **Hospital beds:** 1 per 74 persons. **Physicians:** 1 per 546 persons. **Infant mortality** (per 1,000 live births 1997): 4.

Education: Free and compulsory: ages 6-15. **Literacy** (1997): 100%.

Major International Organizations: UN and all its specialized agencies, OECD.

Embassy: 2520 Massachusetts Ave. NW 20008; 939-6700.

According to Japanese legend, the empire was founded by Emperor Jimmu, 660 BC, but earliest records of a unified Japan date from 1,000 years later. Chinese influence was strong in the formation of Japanese civilization. Buddhism was introduced before the 6th century AD.

A feudal system, with locally powerful noble families and their samurai warrior retainers, dominated from 1192. Central power was held by successive families of shoguns (military dictators), 1192-1867, until recovered by Emperor Meiji, 1868. The Portuguese and Dutch had minor trade with Japan in the 16th and 17th centuries; U.S. Commodore Matthew C. Perry opened it to U.S. trade in a treaty ratified 1854. Japan fought China, 1894-95, gaining Taiwan. After war with Russia, 1904-5, Russia ceded S half of Sakhalin and gave concessions in China. Japan annexed Korea 1910. In World War I Japan ousted Germany from Shandong in China, took over German Pacific islands. Japan took Manchuria 1931, started war with China 1932. Japan launched war against the U.S. by attack on Pearl Harbor Dec. 7, 1941. The U.S. dropped atomic bombs on Hiroshima, Aug. 6, and Nagasaki, Aug. 9, 1945. Japan surrendered Aug. 14, 1945. Japan apologized Aug. 15, 1995, for its acts of "colonial rule and aggression" during World War II.

In a new constitution adopted May 3, 1947, Japan renounced the right to wage war; the emperor gave up claims to divinity; the Diet became the sole law-making authority.

The U.S. and 48 other non-communist nations signed a peace treaty and the U.S. a bilateral defense agreement with Japan, in San Francisco Sept. 8, 1951, restoring Japan's sovereignty as of April 28, 1952.

On June 26, 1968, the U.S. returned to Japanese control the Bonin Isls., Volcano Isls. (including Iwo Jima), and Marcus Isls. On May 15, 1972, Okinawa, the other Ryukyu Isls., and the Daito Isls. were returned by the U.S.; it was agreed the U.S. would continue to maintain military bases on Okinawa.

Industrialization was begun in the late 19th century. After World War II, Japan emerged as one of the most powerful economies in the world, and as a leader in technology.

The U.S. and EU member nations have criticized Japan for its restrictive policy on imports, which has given Japan a substantial trade surplus.

The Recruit scandal, the nation's worst political scandal since World War II, which involved illegal political donations and stock trading, led to the resignation of Premier Noboru Takeshita in May 1989. A series of scandals rocked Japan's financial sector in 1991.

Following new political scandals, the Liberal Democratic Party (LDP) was denied a majority in general elections July

18, 1993. The LDP had held power since it was founded in 1955. Morihiro Hosokawa, a reformer, was chosen prime minister Aug. 6; he initiated reforms but resigned Apr. 8, 1994, because of controversy over his financial connections. His replacement, Tsutomu Hata, resigned June 25, to be replaced by Japan's first Socialist premier since 1947-48, Tomiichi Murayama.

An earthquake in the Kobe area, Jan. 17, 1995, claimed more than 6,300 lives, injured nearly 35,000, and caused over $90 billion in property damage. On Mar. 20, a nerve gas attack in the Tokyo subway (blamed on a religious cult) killed 12 and injured thousands. Public anger at the rape of a 12-year-old Okinawa schoolgirl by 3 U.S. servicemen, Sept. 4, led the U.S. to begin reducing its military presence there.

Murayama resigned as prime minister, Jan. 5, 1996, and was replaced by Ryutaro Hashimoto of the LDP. He signed a joint security declaration with U.S. Pres. Bill Clinton in Tokyo, Apr. 17. The LDP increased its plurality in parliamentary elections Oct. 20.

Nagano is scheduled to host the Winter Olympics, Feb. 7-22, 1998.

Jordan
Hashemite Kingdom of Jordan
Al Mamlakah al Urduniyah al Hashimiyah

People: Population: 4,324,638. **Age distrib.** (%): <15: 44; 65+: 3. **Pop. density:** 125 per sq. mi. **Urban:** 72%. **Ethnic groups:** Arab 98%. **Principal language:** Arabic (official). **Chief religions:** Sunni Muslim 92%, Christian 8%.

Geography: Area: 34,342 sq. mi. **Location:** In Middle East. **Neighbors:** Israel on W, Saudi Arabia on S, Iraq on E, Syria on N. **Topography:** About 88% of Jordan is arid. Fertile areas are in W. Only port is on short Aqaba Gulf coast. Country shares Dead Sea (1,312 ft. below sea level) with Israel. **Capital:** Amman. **Cities:** Amman 483,000*.

Government: Type: Constitutional monarchy. **Head of state:** King Hussein I; b Nov. 14, 1935; in office: Aug. 11, 1952. **Head of government:** Prime Min. Abdul Salam Majali; b 1925; in office: Mar. 19, 1997. **Local divisions:** 8 governorates. **Defense:** 8.2% of GDP (1996). **Active troop strength:** 98,600 est.

Economy: Industries: Oil refining, cement, light manufacturing. **Chief crops:** Grains, olives, vegetables, fruits. **Minerals:** Phosphates, potash. **Arable land:** 4%. **Livestock** (1996): sheep: 2.1 mil. **Electricity prod.** (1995): 5 bil kWh. **Labor force:** 11% ind.; 10.5% commerce; 10% constr.; 9% transport, communications; 7% agric.; 52% other services.

Finance: Monetary unit: Dinar (Aug. 1997: 0.71 = $1 US). **Gross domestic product** (1995 est.): $19.3 bil. **Per capita GDP:** $4,700. **Imports** (1994): $3.8 bil; partners: Iraq 12%, U.S. 9%. **Exports** (1994): $1.4 bil; partners: Iraq 19%, India 11%. **Tourism** (1994): $582 mil. **National budget** (1996 est.): $2.5 bil. **International reserves less gold** (June 1997): $1.62 bil. **Gold:** 807,000 oz t. **Consumer prices** (change in 1996): 6.5%.

Transport: Railroads: Length: 419.8 mi. **Motor vehicles in use:** 168,000 passenger cars, 83,000 comm. vehicles. **Civil aviation:** 2.6 bil passenger-mi.; 2 airports with scheduled flights. **Chief port:** Aqaba.

Communications: Television sets: 1 per 13 persons. **Radios:** 1 per 4.1 persons. **Telephones:** 1 per 14 persons. **Daily newspaper circ.:** 48 per 1,000 pop.

Health: Life expectancy at birth (1997): 70.8 male; 74.7 female. **Births** (per 1,000 pop.): 36. **Deaths** (per 1,000 pop.): 4. **Natural increase:** 3.2%. **Hospital beds:** 1 per 651 persons. **Physicians:** 1 per 893 persons. **Infant mortality** (per 1,000 live births 1997): 31.

Education: Free and compulsory: ages 6-16. **Literacy** (1995 est.): 87%.

Major International Organizations: UN (WHO, IMF), Arab League.

Embassy: 3504 International Dr. NW 20008; 966-2664.

From ancient times to 1922 the lands to the E of the Jordan River were culturally and politically united with the lands to the W. Arabs conquered the area in the 7th century; the Ottomans took control in the 16th. Britain's 1920 Palestine Mandate covered both sides of the Jordan. In 1921, Abdullah, son of the ruler of Hejaz in Arabia, was installed by Britain as emir of an autonomous Transjordan, covering two-thirds of Palestine. An independent kingdom was proclaimed, 1946.

During the 1948 Arab-Israeli war the West Bank and East Jerusalem were added to the kingdom, which changed its name to Jordan. All these territories were lost to Israel in the 1967 war, which swelled the number of Arab refugees on the East Bank. A 1974 Arab summit conference designated the Palestine Liberation Organization as the sole representative of Arabs on the West Bank. In 1988 Jordan cut legal and administrative ties with the Israeli-occupied West Bank.

Some 700,000 refugees entered Jordan following Iraq's invasion of Kuwait, Aug. 1990. Jordan was viewed as supporting Iraq during the 1990-1991 Persian Gulf crisis.

Jordan and Israel officially agreed, July 25, 1994, to end their state of war; a formal peace treaty was signed Oct. 26.

Kazakhstan
Republic of Kazakhstan
Qazaqstan Respublikasy

People: Population: 16,898,572. **Age distrib.** (%): <15: 30; 65+: 7. **Pop. density:** 16 per sq. mi. **Urban:** 60%. **Ethnic groups:** Kazakh 42%, Russian 37%, Ukrainian 5%, German 5%. **Principal languages:** Kazakh (official), Russian. **Chief religions:** Muslim 47%, Russian Orthodox 44%.

Geography: Area: 1,052,100 sq. mi. **Location:** In Central Asia. **Neighbors:** Russia on N; China on E; Kyrgyzstan, Uzbekistan, Turkmenistan on S; Caspian Sea on W. **Topography:** Extends from the lower reaches of Volga in Europe to the Altay Mts. on the Chinese border. **Capital:** Almaty (Alma-Ata): 1,245,000*.

Government: Type: Republic. **Head of state:** Pres. Nursultan A. Nazarbayev; b July 6, 1940; in office: Apr. 1990. **Head of government:** Prime Min. Arkezhan Kazhgeldin; b Mar. 27, 1952; in office, Oct. 12, 1994. **Local divisions:** 19 oblystar, 1 city. **Defense:** 2.1% of GNP (1994). **Active troop strength:** 40,000 est.

Economy: Industries: Oil, steel, mining, agricultural machinery. **Chief crops:** Grain, cotton. **Minerals:** Oil, coal, iron, manganese, chrome ore, copper. **Arable land:** 15%. **Livestock** (1996): sheep: 19.2 mil; cattle: 6.9 mil; pigs: 1.6 mil. **Electricity prod.** (1995): 61.7 bil kWh. **Labor force:** 31% ind., constr.; 26% agric., for.

Finance: Monetary unit: Tenge (Aug. 1997: 75.80 = $1 US). **Gross domestic product** (1995 est.): $46.9 bil. **Per capita GDP:** $2,700. **Imports** (1995): $3.9 bil. **Exports** (1995): $5.1 bil. **International reserves less gold** (June 1997): $1.46 bil. **Gold:** 1.8 mil oz t. **Consumer prices** (change in 1996): 39.2%.

Transport: Railroads: Length: 8,595.3 mi. **Motor vehicles:** 1.0 mil passenger cars, 515,000 comm. vehicles. **Civil aviation:** 1.1 bil passenger-mi.; 12 airports with scheduled flights. **Chief ports:** Aqtau, Atyrau.

Communications: Radios: 1 per 2.7 persons. **Telephones:** 1 per 8.5 persons.

Health: Life expectancy at birth (1997): 58.7 male; 70.1 female. **Birth rate** (per 1,000 pop.): 19. **Death rate** (per 1,000 pop.): 10. **Natural increase:** 0.9%. **Hospital beds:** 1 per 81 persons. **Physicians:** 1 per 276 persons. **Infant mortality** (per 1,000 live births 1997): 62.

Education: Free and compulsory: ages 7-18. **Literacy** (1992): 98%.

Major International Organizations: UN (WHO, IMF), CIS. **Embassy:** 3421 Massachusetts Ave. NW 20008; 333-4504.

The region came under the Mongols in the 13th century and gradually came under Russian rule, 1730-1853. It was admitted to the USSR as a constituent republic 1936. Kazakhstan declared independence Dec. 16, 1991. It became an independent state when the Soviet Union dissolved Dec. 26, 1991. The party chief, Nursultan Nazarbayev, was elected president unopposed. In legislative elections Mar. 7, 1994, criticized by international monitors, his party won a sweeping victory. Kazakhstan agreed, Feb. 14, to dismantle nuclear missiles and adhere to the 1968 Nuclear Nonproliferation Treaty; the U.S. pledged increased aid. A referendum Apr. 29, 1995, extended Nazarbayev's term to Dec. 2000; a new draft constitution was approved in a referendum Aug. 30. Private land ownership was legalized Dec. 26. Plans were made to relocate government ministries, parliament, and the president from Almaty to Aqmola, which was to become the nation's new capital.

Kenya
Republic of Kenya
Jamhuri ya Kenya

People: Population: 28,803,085. **Age distrib.** (%): <15: 44; 65+: 3. **Pop. density:** 128 per sq. mi. **Urban:** 30%. **Ethnic groups:** Kikuyu 22%, Luhya 14%, Luo 13%, Kalenjin 12%, Kamba 11%, others including Asian, Arab, European. **Principal languages:** Swahili, English (both official), numerous indigenous languages. **Chief religions:** Protestant 38%, Roman Catholic 28%, indigenous beliefs 26%.

Geography: Area: 224,961 sq. mi. **Location:** E Africa, on coast of Indian O. **Neighbors:** Uganda on W, Tanzania on S, Somalia on E, Ethopia on N, Sudan on NW. **Topography:** The northern three-fifths of Kenya is arid. To the S, a low coastal area and a plateau varying from 3,000 to 10,000 ft. The Great Rift Valley enters the country N-S, flanked by high mountains. **Capital:** Nairobi. **Cities** (1991 est.): Nairobi 2,000,000; Mombasa 600,000.

Government: Type: Republic. **Head of state:** Pres. Daniel arap Moi, b. Sept. 2, 1924; in office: Aug. 22, 1978. **Local divisions:** Nairobi and 7 provinces. **Defense:** 1.9% of GDP (FY 1993-94). **Active troop strength:** 24,200.

Economy: Industries: Tourism, light industry, agricultural processing, oil refining. **Chief crops:** Coffee, corn, tea. **Minerals:** Gold, limestone, salt, rubies, fluorspar, garnets. **Other resources:** Timber, hides, dairy products. **Arable land:** 3%. **Livestock** (1996): cattle: 13.0 mil; goats: 7.4 mil; sheep: 5.6 mil. **Fish catch** (1995): 241,064 metric tons. **Electricity prod.** (1995): 3.6 bil kWh. **Labor force:** 75-80% agric.

Finance: Monetary unit: Shilling (Aug. 1997: 69.88 = $1 US). **Gross domestic product** (1995 est.): $36.8 bil. **Per capita GDP:** $1,300. **Imports** (1994): $2.2 bil; partners: EU 46%. **Exports** (1994): $1.6 bil; partners: EU 47%. **Tourism** (1994): $421 mil. **National budget** (1990 est.): $2.8 bil. **International reserves less gold** (June 1997): $923.6 mil. **Gold:** 80,000 oz t. **Consumer prices** (change in 1996): 8.8%.

Transport: Railroads: Length: 1,646.9 mi. **Motor vehicles in use:** 258,000 passenger cars, 66,000 comm. vehicles. **Civil aviation:** 1.1 bil passenger-mi.; 13 airports with scheduled flights. **Chief port:** Mombasa.

Communications: Television sets: 1 per 91 persons. **Radios:** 1 per 11 persons. **Telephones:** 1 per 111 persons.

Health: Life expectancy at birth (1997): 54.2 male; 54.6 female. **Births** (per 1,000 pop.): 32. **Deaths** (per 1,000 pop.): 11. **Natural increase:** 2.2%. **Hospital beds:** 1 per 734 persons. **Physicians:** 1 per 5,999 persons. **Infant mortality** (per 1,000 live births 1997): 55.

Education: Free and compulsory: ages 6-14. **Literacy** (1995 est.): 78%.

Major International Organizations: UN and all of its specialized agencies, OAU, the Commonwealth.

Embassy: 2249 R St. NW 20008; 387-6101.

Arab colonies exported spices and slaves from the Kenya coast as early as the 8th century. Britain obtained control in the 19th century. Kenya won independence Dec. 12, 1963, 4 years after the end of the violent Mau Mau uprising.

Kenya had steady growth in industry and agriculture under a modified private enterprise system, and enjoyed a relatively free political life. But stability was shaken in 1974-75, with opposition charges of corruption and oppression. Jomo Kenyatta, the country's leader since independence, died Aug. 22, 1978. He was succeeded by his vice president, Daniel arap Moi.

During the first half of the 1990s, Kenya suffered from widespread unemployment and high inflation. Tribal clashes in the western provinces claimed thousands of lives and left tens of thousands homeless. Pres. Moi won a third term in Dec. 1992 elections, which were marred by violence and fraud. Clashes in the Mombasa region, Aug. 1997, left more than 40 people dead.

Kiribati
Republic of Kiribati

People: Population: 82,449. **Pop. density:** 263 per sq. mi. **Urban:** 36%. **Ethnic groups:** Nearly all Micronesian, some Polynesian. **Principal languages:** English (official), Gilbertese. **Chief religions:** Roman Catholic 53%, Protestant 41%.

Geography: Area: 313 sq. mi. **Location:** 33 Micronesian islands (the Gilbert, Line, and Phoenix groups) in the mid-Pacific scattered in a 2-mil sq. mi. chain around the point where the International Date Line formerly cut the Equator. In 1997 the Date Line was moved to follow Kiribati's E border. **Neighbors:** Nearest are Nauru to SW, Tuvalu and Tokelau Isls. to S. **Topography:** Except Banaba (Ocean) Isl., all are low-lying, with soil of coral sand and rock fragments, subject to erratic rainfall. **Capital:** Tarawa (1990): 25,000.

Government: Type: Republic. **Head of state and government:** Pres. Teburoro Tito; in office: Oct. 1, 1994.

Economy: Industries: Fishing, handicrafts. **Chief crops:** Copra, taro, breadfruit, sweet potatoes, vegetables. **Electricity prod.** (1995): 7 mil kWh.

Finance: Monetary unit: Australian Dollar. **Gross domestic product** (1995 est.): $63 mil. **Per capita GDP:** $860. **National budget** (1995 est.): $54.3 mil.

Transport: Chief port: Tarawa. **Civil aviation:** 6.2 mil passenger-mi.

Communications: Radios: 1 per 4.8 persons. **Telephones:** 1 per 39 persons.

Health: Life expectancy at birth (1997): 60.6 male; 64.4 female. **Births** (per 1,000 pop.): 27. **Deaths** (per 1,000 pop.): 8. **Natural increase:** 1.9%. **Hospital beds:** 1 per 253 persons. **Physicians:** 1 per 7,687 persons.

Education: Free and compulsory: ages 6-14. **Literacy** (1993): 90%.

Major International Organizations: The Commonwealth.

A British protectorate since 1892, the Gilbert and Ellice Islands colony was completed with the inclusion of the Phoenix Islands, 1937. Self-rule was granted 1971; the Ellice Islands separated from the colony 1975 and became independent Tuvalu, 1978. Kiribati (pronounced *Kiribass*) independence was attained July 12, 1979. Under a treaty of friendship the U.S. relinquished its claims to several Line and Phoenix islands, including Christmas (Kiritimati), Canton, and Enderbury.

Tarawa Atoll was the scene of some of the bloodiest fighting in the Pacific during World War II.

Korea, North
Democratic People's Republic of Korea
Choson Minjujuui Inmin Konghwaguk

People: Population: 24,317,004. **Age distrib.** (%): <15: 30; 65+: 4. **Pop. density:** 513 per sq. mi. **Urban:** 62%. **Ethnic group:** Korean. **Principal language:** Korean (official). **Chief religions:** Activities almost nonexistent; traditionally Buddhism, Confucianism, Chondogyo.

Geography: Area: 47,399 sq. mi. **Location:** In northern E Asia. **Neighbors:** China and Russia on N, South Korea on S. **Topography:** Mountains and hills cover nearly all the country, with narrow valleys and small plains in between. The N and the E coasts are the most rugged areas. **Capital:** Pyongyang (1987 est.): 2.4 mil.

Government: Type: Communist state. **Leader:** Kim Jong Il; b Feb. 16, 1948; officially assumed post Oct. 8, 1997. **Local divisions:** 9 provinces, 3 special cities. **Defense** (1995 est.): 25-33% of GDP (1994). **Active troop strength:** 1.054 mil est.

Economy: Industries: Textiles, chemicals, machinery, food processing. **Chief crops:** Corn, potatoes, soybeans, rice. **Minerals:** Coal, lead, tungsten, zinc, graphite, magnesite, iron, copper, gold, salt, fluorspar. **Arable land:** 18%. **Livestock** (1996): pigs: 3.35 mil; cattle: 1.35 mil. **Fish catch** (1995): 1,850,000 metric tons. **Electricity prod.** (1995): 35.2 bil kWh. **Labor force:** 36% agric.

Finance: Monetary unit: Won (June 1996: 2.15 = $1 US). **Gross domestic product** (1995 est.): $21.5 bil. **Per capita GDP:** $920. **Imports** (1995): $1.5 bil; partners: China 34%, Japan 14%, Italy 8%. **Exports** (1995): $590 mil; partners: Japan 38%, China 24%, Germany 7%. **National budget** (1992 est.): $19.3 bil.

Transport: Railroads: Length: 3,052.2 mi. **Civil aviation:** 122.3 mil passenger-mi.; 1 airport with scheduled flights. **Chief ports:** Chongjin, Hamhung, Nampo.

Communications: Television sets: 1 per 23 persons. **Radios:** 1 per 7.9 persons. **Telephones:** 1 per 22 persons. **Daily newspaper circ.:** 213 per 1,000 pop.

Health: Life expectancy at birth (1997): 67.5 male; 73.9 female. **Births** (per 1,000 pop.): 22. **Deaths** (per 1,000 pop.): 5. **Natural increase:** 1.7%. **Hospital beds:** 1 per 74 persons. **Physicians:** 1 per 370 persons. **Infant mortality** (per 1,000 live births 1997): 25.

Education: Free and compulsory: ages 6-17. **Literacy** (1992): 95%.

Major International Organizations: UN (WHO).

The Democratic People's Republic of Korea was founded May 1, 1948, in the zone occupied by Russian troops after World War II. Its armies tried to conquer the south, 1950. After 3 years of fighting, with Chinese and U.S. intervention, a cease-fire was proclaimed.

Industry, begun by the Japanese during their 1910-45 occupation, and nationalized in the 1940s, had grown substantially, using North Korea's abundant mineral and hydroelectric resources.

In Mar. 1993, North Korea became the first nation to formally withdraw from the Nuclear Nonproliferation Treaty, the international pact designed to limit the spread of nuclear weapons. The nation suspended its withdrawal in June in reaction to threats of UN economic sanctions, but was widely believed to be developing nuclear weapons. The U.S. and North Korea reached an interim agreement, Aug. 13, 1994, intended to resolve the nuclear issue, and further negotiations followed.

Kim Il Sung, who in 1948 had been one of the founders of the state of North Korea and who had ruled over it for more than 40 years, died July 8, 1994. He was succeeded by his son, Kim Jong Il. North Korea suffered from defections by high officials, a deteriorating economy, and severe food shortages in the late 1990s.

Korea, South
Republic of Korea
Taehan Min'guk

People: Population: 45,948,811. **Age distrib.** (%): <15: 23; 65+: 6. **Pop. density:** 1,197 per sq. mi. **Urban:** 83%. **Ethnic group:** Korean. **Principal language:** Korean (official). **Chief religions:** Christianity 49%, Buddhism 47%.

Geography: Area: 38,375 sq. mi. **Location:** In northern E Asia. **Neighbors:** North Korea on N. **Topography:** The country is mountainous, with a rugged east coast. The western and southern coasts are deeply indented, with many islands and harbors. **Capital:** Seoul. **Cities:** Seoul 11,609,000; Pusan 4,038,000; Taegu 2,432,000*.

Government: Type: Republic, with power centralized in a strong executive. **Head of state:** Pres. Kim Young Sam; b Dec. 20, 1927; in office: Feb. 25, 1993. **Head of government:** Prime Min. Koh Kun; b Jan. 2, 1938; in office: Mar. 4, 1997. **Local divisions:** 9 provinces and 6 special cities. **Defense:** 3.3% of GNP (1996). **Active troop strength:** 660,000.

Economy: Industries: Electronics, autos, chemicals, ships, textiles, clothing. **Chief crops:** Rice, barley, vegetables. **Minerals:** Tungsten, coal, graphite. **Arable land:** 21%. **Livestock** (1996): pigs: 6.95 mil; cattle: 3.5 mil. **Fish catch:** (1995): 2,698,024 metric tons. **Electricity prod.** (1995): 174.5 bil kWh. **Labor force:** 52% services & other; 27% manuf. & mining; 21% agric.

Finance: Monetary unit: Won (Aug. 1997: 904 = $1 US). **Gross domestic product** (1995 est.): $591 bil. **Per capita GDP:** $13,000. **Imports** (1995): $135 bil; partners: Japan 24%, U.S. 23%. **Exports** (1995): $125 bil; partners: U.S. 19%, Japan 14%. **Tourism** (1994): $3.8 bil. **National budget** (1995 est.): $67 bil. **International reserves less gold** (June 1997): $34.07 bil. **Gold:** 327,000 oz t. **Consumer prices** (change in 1996): 5.0%.

Transport: Railroads: Length: 1,925.7 mi. **Motor vehicles in use:** 6.0 mil passenger cars, 2.5 mil comm. vehicles. **Civil aviation:** 24.6 bil passenger-mi.; 14 airports with scheduled flights. **Chief ports:** Pusan, Inchon.

Communications: Television sets: 1 per 3.1 persons. **Radios:** 1 per 1.0 person. **Telephones:** 1 per 2.4 persons. **Daily newspaper circ.:** 404 per 1,000 pop.

Health: Life expectancy at birth (1997): 70.0 male; 77.7 female. **Births** (per 1,000 pop.): 16. **Deaths** (per 1,000 pop.): 6. **Natural increase:** 1.1%. **Hospital beds:** 1 per 244 persons. **Physicians:** 1 per 817 persons. **Infant mortality** (per 1,000 live births 1997): 8.

Education: Free and compulsory: ages 6-12. **Literacy** (1995): 98%.

Major International Organizations: UN (WTO, IMF, WHO), APEC.

Embassy: 2450 Massachusetts Ave. NW 20008; 939-5600.

Korea, once called the Hermit Kingdom, has a recorded history since the 1st century BC. It was united in a kingdom under the Silla Dynasty, AD 668. It was at times associated with the Chinese empire; the treaty that concluded the Sino-Japanese war of 1894-95 recognized Korea's complete independence. In 1910 Japan forcibly annexed Korea as Chosun.

At the Potsdam conference, July 1945, the 38th parallel was designated as the line dividing the Soviet and the American occupation. Russian troops entered Korea Aug. 10, 1945, U.S. troops entered Sept. 8, 1945. The Soviet military organized socialists and Communists and blocked efforts to let the Koreans unite their country. *(See Index for Korean War.)*

The South Koreans formed the Republic of Korea in May 1948 with Seoul as the capital. Dr. Syngman Rhee was chosen president, but a movement spearheaded by college students forced his resignation Apr. 26, 1960.

In an army coup May 16, 1961, Gen. Park Chung Hee became chairman of the ruling junta. He was elected president, 1963; a 1972 referendum allowed him to be reelected for an unlimited series of 6-year terms. Park was assassinated by the chief of the Korean CIA, Oct. 26, 1979. In May 1980, Gen. Chun Doo Hwan, head of military intelligence, reinstated full martial law and ordered the brutal suppression of prodemocracy demonstrations in Kwangju.

In July 1972 South and North Korea agreed on a common goal of reunifying the 2 nations by peaceful means. But there was no sign of a thaw in relations between the two regimes until 1985, when they agreed to discuss economic issues.

On June 10, 1987, middle-class office workers, shopkeepers, and business executives joined students in antigovernment protests in Seoul calling for democratic reforms. Following weeks of rioting and violence, Chun, July 1, agreed to permit election of the next president by direct popular vote and other reforms. In Dec., Roh Tae Woo was elected president. In 1990, the nation's 3 largest political parties merged; some 100,000 students protested the merger as undemocratic.

Kim Young Sam took office in 1993 as the first civilian president since 1961. Convicted of mutiny, treason, and corruption, Chun was sentenced to death by a Seoul court, Aug. 26, 1996, for his role in the 1979 coup and 1980 Kwangju massacre; Roh received a 22-1/2 year prison sentence. On Dec. 16 an appeals court reduced Chun's sentence to life in prison, and Roh's to 17 years. The collapse in Jan. 1997 of the huge Hanbo steel firm triggered another round of corruption scandals.

Kuwait
State of Kuwait
Dawlat al Kuwayt

People: Population: 2,076,805. **Age distrib.** (%): <15: 33; 65+: 2. **Pop. density:** 301 per sq. mi. **Urban:** 97%. **Ethnic groups:** Kuwaiti 45%, other Arab 35%, Iranian. **Principal language:** Arabic (official). **Chief religions:** Muslim 85%.

Geography: Area: 6,880 sq. mi. **Location:** In Middle East, at N end of Persian Gulf. **Neighbors:** Iraq on N, Saudi Arabia on S. **Topography:** The country is flat, very dry, and extremely hot. **Capital:** Kuwait City. **Cities** (1995 est.): Kuwait City 276,915; al-Jahra 228,457.

Government: Type: Constitutional monarchy. **Head of state:** Emir Sheikh Jabir al-Ahmad al-Jabir as-Sabah; b 1928; in office: Jan. 1, 1978. **Head of government:** Prime Min. Sheikh Saad Abdulla as-Salim as-Sabah; b 1930; in office: Feb. 8, 1978. **Local divisions:** 5 governorates. **Defense:** 12.8% of GDP (FFY 1995-96). **Active troop strength:** 15,300.

Economy: Industries: Oil products. **Minerals:** Oil, gas. **Crude oil reserves** (1996): 96.5 bil bbls. **Arable land:** 0%. **Electricity prod.** (1995): 25 bil kWh. **Labor force:** 50% gov't. and social services; 25% industry and agric.

Finance: Monetary unit: Dinar (Aug. 1997: 0.30 = $1 US). **Gross domestic product** (1995 est.): $30.8 bil. **Per capita GDP:** $17,000. **Imports** (1995): $6.6 bil; partners: U.S. 16%, France 11%. **Exports** (1995): $10.5 bil; partners: India 16%, Saudi Arabia 16%. **Tourism** (1994): $101 mil. **National budget** (FY 1995-96 est.): $14.2 bil. **International reserves less gold** (June 1997): $3.29 bil. **Gold:** 2.54 mil oz t. **Consumer prices** (change in 1996): 3.2%.

Transport: Motor vehicles in use: 545,000 passenger cars, 155,000 comm. vehicles. **Civil aviation:** 2.8 bil passenger-mi.; 1 airport with scheduled flights. **Chief port:** Mina al-Ahmadi.

Communications: Television sets: 1 per 2.6 persons. **Radios:** 1 per 2.2 persons. **Telephones:** 1 per 4.4 persons. **Daily newspaper circ.:** 401 per 1,000 pop.

Health: Life expectancy at birth (1997): 73.9 male; 78.7 female. **Births** (per 1,000 pop.): 20. **Deaths** (per 1,000 pop.): 2. **Natural increase:** 1.7%. **Hospital beds:** 1 per 357 persons. **Physicians:** 1 per 533 persons. **Infant mortality** (per 1,000 live births 1997): 11.

Education: Free and compulsory: ages 6-14. **Literacy** (1995): 79%.

Major International Organizations: UN (World Bank, IMF, WTO), Arab League, OPEC.

Embassy: 2940 Tilden St. NW 20008; 966-0702.

Kuwait is ruled by the Al-Sabah dynasty, founded 1759. Britain ran foreign relations and defense from 1899 until independence in 1961. The majority of the population is non-Kuwaiti, with many Palestinians, and cannot vote.

Oil is the fiscal mainstay, providing most of Kuwait's income. Oil pays for free medical care, education, and social security. There are no taxes, except customs duties.

Kuwaiti oil tankers came under frequent attack by Iran because of Kuwait's support of Iraq in the Iran-Iraq War. In July 1987, U.S. Navy warships began escorting Kuwaiti tankers in the Persian Gulf.

Kuwait was attacked and overrun by Iraqi forces Aug. 2, 1990. The emir and senior members of the ruling family fled to Saudi Arabia to establish a government in exile. On Aug. 28, Iraq announced that Kuwait was its 19th province. Following several weeks of aerial attacks on Iraq and Iraqi forces in Kuwait, a U.S.-led coalition began a ground attack Feb. 23, 1991. By Feb. 27, Iraqi forces were routed and Kuwait liberated. Following liberation, there were reports of abuse of Palestinians and others suspected of collaborating with Iraqi occupiers. Kuwait spent more than $5 billion to repair oil installations damaged during 1990-91.

Former U.S. Pres. George Bush visited Kuwait, Apr. 14-16, 1993, and was honored as the leader of the Persian Gulf War alliance that expelled Iraqi troops. Kuwaiti authorities arrested 14 Iraqis and Kuwaitis for allegedly plotting to assassinate Bush during his visit. Thirteen were convicted and sentenced to prison or death, June 4, 1994.

Kyrgyzstan
Republic of Kyrgyzstan
Kyrgyz Respublikasy

People: Population: 4,540,185. **Age distrib. (%):** <15: 37; 65+: 6. **Pop density:** 59 per sq. mi. **Urban:** 39%. **Ethnic groups:** Kyrgyz 52%, Russian 22%, Uzbek 13%. **Principal languages:** Kyrgyz, Russian (both official). **Religion:** Predominantly Sunni Muslim.

Geography: Area: 76,600 sq. mi. **Location:** In Central Asia. **Neighbors:** Kazakhstan on N, China on E, Uzbekistan on W, Tajikistan on S. **Capital:** Bishkek (1994 est.) 597,000.

Government: Type: Republic. **Head of state:** Pres. Askar Akayev; b Nov. 10, 1944; in office: Oct. 28, 1990. **Head of government:** Prime Min. Apas Jumagulov; b 1934; in office: Dec. 14, 1993. **Local divisions:** 6 oblasts, 1 city. **Defense:** 4.9% of GNP (1995). **Active troop strength:** 7,000 est.

Economy: Industries: Textiles, mining, small machinery. **Chief crops:** Tobacco, cotton, fruits. **Minerals:** Gold, coal, oil. **Arable land:** 7%. **Livestock** (1996): sheep: 4.1 mil; cattle: 869,000. **Electricity prod.** (1995): 12.1 bil kWh. **Labor force:** 38% agric.; 21% ind.

Finance: Monetary unit: Som (Aug. 1997: 17.15 = $1 US). **Gross domestic prod.** (1995 est.): $5.4 bil. **Per capita GDP:** $1,140.

Transport: Railroads: Length: 229.8 mi. **Motor vehicles in use:** 164,000 passenger cars. **Civil aviation:** 352.7 mil passenger-mi.; 2 airports with scheduled flights. **Chief port:** Ysyk-Kol.

Communications: Telephones: 1 per 13 persons. **Daily newspaper circ.:** 11 per 1,000 pop.

Health: Life expectancy at birth (1997): 59.3 male; 68.9 female. **Birth rate** (per 1,000 pop.): 26. **Death rate** (per 1,000 pop.): 9. **Natural increase:** 1.7%. **Hospital beds:** 1 per 95 persons. **Physicians:** 1 per 319 persons. **Infant mortality** (per 1,000 live births 1997): 77.

Education: Compulsory: ages 6-15. **Literacy** (1993): 97%.

Major International Organizations: UN (IMF), CIS.

Embassy: 1511 K St. NW, Suite 706, 20005; 347-3732.

The region was inhabited around the 13th century by the K(yrgyz. It was annexed to Russia 1864. After 1917 it was nominally a Kara-Kyrgyz autonomous area, which was reorganized 1926, and made a constituent republic of the USSR in 1936. Kyrgyzstan declared independence Aug. 31, 1991. It became an independent state when the USSR disbanded Dec. 26, 1991. A constitution was adopted May 5, 1993. Reelected

Dec. 24, 1995, Pres. Askar Akayev gained approval by referendum of a constitutional amendment expanding his presidential powers, Feb. 10, 1996.

Laos
Lao People's Democratic Republic
Sathalanalat Paxathipatai Paxaxon Lao

People: Population: 5,116,959. **Age distrib. (%):** <15: 45; 65+: 3. **Pop. density:** 55 per sq. mi. **Urban:** 21%. **Ethnic groups:** Lao Loum 68%, Lao Theung 22%, Lao Soung (includes Hmong and Yao) 9%. **Principal languages:** Lao (official), French, English. **Chief religions:** Buddhism 60%, animist and other 40%.

Geography: Area: 91,429 sq. mi. **Location:** In Indochina Peninsula in SE Asia. **Neighbors:** Myanmar and China on N, Vietnam on E, Cambodia on S, Thailand on W. **Topography:** Landlocked, dominated by jungle. High mountains along the eastern border are the source of the E-W rivers slicing across the country to the Mekong R., which defines most of the western border. **Capital:** Vientiane (1990 met. est.): 442,000.

Government: Type: Communist. **Head of state:** Pres. Nouhak Phoumsavan; b Apr. 9, 1914; in office: Nov. 25, 1992. **Head of government:** Prime Min. Khamtai Siphandon; b Feb. 8, 1924; in office: Aug. 15, 1991. **Local divisions:** 16 provinces, 1 municipality. **Defense:** 8.1% of GDP (FY 1992-93). **Active troop strength:** 37,000.

Economy: Industries: Wood products, mining. **Chief crops:** Sweet potatoes, corn, cotton, opium, vegetables, coffee. **Minerals:** Gypsum, tin, gold. **Arable land:** 4%. **Livestock** (1996): pigs: 1.7 mil; buffalo: 1.2 mil; cattle: 1.1 mil. **Fish catch** (1993): 30,500 metric tons. **Electricity prod.** (1995): 900 mil kWh. **Labor force:** 80% agric.

Finance: Monetary unit: Kip (Aug. 1997: 1,300 = $1 US). **Gross domestic product** (1995 est.): $5.2 bil. **Per capita GDP:** $1,100. **Imports** (1995): $628 mil; partners: Thailand 45%, Japan 11%. **Exports** (1995): $348 mil; partners: Thailand 41%, Vietnam 25%. **International reserves less gold** (June 1997): $179.51 mil. **Gold:** 17,000 oz t.

Transport: Motor vehicles in use: 10,000 passenger cars, 10,000 comm. vehicles. **Civil aviation:** 28.6 mil passenger-mi.

Communications: Television sets: 1 per 119 persons. **Radios:** 1 per 7.9 persons. **Telephones:** 1 per 239 persons.

Health: Life expectancy at birth (1997): 51.6 male; 54.8 female. **Births** (per 1,000 pop.): 41. **Deaths** (per 1,000 pop.): 13. **Natural increase:** 2.8%. **Hospital beds:** 1 per 402 persons. **Physicians:** 1 per 3,555 persons. **Infant mortality** (per 1,000 live births 1997): 94.

Education: Compulsory for 5 years between ages 6-15. **Literacy** (1995): 57%.

Major International Organizations: UN (ASEAN, FAO, IMF, WHO).

Embassy: 2222 S St. NW 20008; 332-6416.

Laos became a French protectorate in 1893, but regained independence as a constitutional monarchy July 19, 1949.

Conflicts among neutralist, communist, and conservative factions created a chaotic political situation. Armed conflict increased after 1960.

The 3 factions formed a coalition government in June 1962, with neutralist Prince Souvanna Phouma as premier. A 14-nation conference in Geneva signed agreements, 1962, guaranteeing neutrality and independence. By 1964 the Pathet Lao had withdrawn from the coalition, and, with aid from North Vietnamese troops, renewed sporadic attacks. U.S. planes bombed the Ho Chi Minh trail, supply line from North Vietnam to Communist forces in Laos and South Vietnam.

In 1970 the U.S. stepped up air support and military aid. After Pathet Lao military gains, Souvanna Phouma in May 1975 ordered government troops to cease fighting; the Pathet Lao took control. The Lao People's Democratic Republic was proclaimed Dec. 3, 1975.

From the mid-1970s through the 1980s, the Laotian government relied on Vietnam for military and financial aid. Since easing its foreign investment laws in 1988, Laos has attracted more than $5 billion from Thailand, the U.S., and other nations. Laos was admitted to ASEAN on July 23, 1997.

Latvia
Republic of Latvia
Latvijas Republika

People: Population: 2,437,649. **Age distrib.** (%): <15: 20. 65+: 14. **Pop density:** 97 per sq. mi. **Urban:** 73%. **Ethnic groups:** Latvian 52%, Russian 34%. **Principal languages:** Latvian (official), Lithuanian, Russian. **Chief religions:** Lutheran, Roman Catholic, Russian Orthodox.

Geography: Area: 24,946 sq. mi. **Location:** E Europe, on the Baltic Sea. **Neighbors:** Estonia on N, Lithuania and Belarus on S, Russia on E. **Capital:** Riga: 921,000.*

Government: Type: Republic. **Head of state:** Pres. Guntis Ulmanis; b Sept 13, 1939; in office: July 7, 1993. **Head of government:** Prime Min. Guntars Krasts; b Oct. 16, 1957; in office: July 28, 1997. **Local divisions:** 26 counties, 7 municipalities. **Defense:** 3-5% of GDP (1994). **Active troop strength:** 8,000.

Economy: Industries: Machinery, vehicles, electric railway passenger cars. **Chief crops:** Grains, sugar beets, potatoes. **Arable land:** 27%. **Fish catch** (1994): 142,000 metric tons. **Electricity prod.** (1995): 4.1 bil kWh. **Labor force:** 41% ind. & constr.; 16% agric. & forestry.

Finance: Monetary unit: Lats (Aug. 1997: 0.58 = $1 US). **Gross domestic product** (1995 est.): $14.7 bil. **Per capita GDP:** $5,300. **Imports** (1994): $1.3 bil. **Exports** (1994): $1 bil. **International reserves less gold** (June 1997): $668.52 mil. **Gold:** 249,000 oz t. **Consumer prices** (change in 1996): 17.6%.

Transport: Railroads: Length: 1,497.9 mi. **Motor vehicles in use:** 252,000 passenger cars, 74,000 comm. vehicles. **Civil aviation:** 90.0 mil passenger-mi.; 1 airport with scheduled flights. **Chief port:** Riga.

Communications: Television sets: 1 per 2.2 persons. **Radios:** 1 per 1.5 persons. **Telephones:** 1 per 3.6 persons. **Daily newspaper circ.:** 228 per 1,000 pop.

Health: Life expectancy at birth (1997): 61.3 male, 73.4 female. **Births** (per 1,000 pop.): 12. **Deaths** (per 1,000 pop.): 15. **Natural increase:** −0.4%. **Hospital beds:** 1 per 83 persons. **Physicians:** 1 per 291 persons. **Infant mortality rates** (per 1,000 live births 1997): 21.

Education: Compulsory: ages 7-16. **Literacy** (1989): 100%. **Major International Organizations:** UN (IMF, WHO). **Embassy:** 4325 17th St. NW 20011; 726-8213.

Prior to 1918, Latvia was occupied by the Russians and Germans. It was an independent republic, 1918-39. The Aug. 1939 Soviet-German agreement assigned Latvia to the Soviet sphere of influence. It was officially accepted as part of the USSR on Aug. 5, 1940. It was overrun by the German army in 1941, but retaken in 1945.

During an abortive Soviet coup, Latvia declared independence, Aug. 21, 1991. The Soviet Union recognized Latvia's independence in Sept. 1991. The last Russian troops in Latvia withdrew by Aug. 31, 1994.

Lebanon
Republic of Lebanon
Al Jumhuriyah al Lubnaniyah

People: Population: 3,858,736. **Age distrib.** (%): <15: 35; 65+: 6. **Pop. density:** 976 per sq. mi. **Urban:** 88%. **Ethnic groups:** Arab 95%, Armenian 4%. **Principal languages:** Arabic, French (both official). **Chief religions:** Muslim 70%, Christian 30%.

Geography: Area: 3,950 sq. mi. **Location:** In Middle East, on E end of Mediterranean Sea. **Neighbors:** Syria on E, Israel on S. **Topography:** There is a narrow coastal strip, and 2 mountain ranges running N-S enclosing the fertile Beqaa Valley. The Litani R. runs S through the valley, turning W to empty into the Mediterranean. **Capital:** Beirut: 1,826,000*.

Government: Type: Republic. **Head of state:** Pres. Elias Hrawi; b 1926; in office: Nov. 24, 1989. **Head of government:** Prime Min. Rafiq al-Hariri; b 1944; in office: Oct. 31, 1992. **Local divisions:** 5 governorates. **Defense:** 5.5% of GDP (1994). **Active troop strength:** 48,900.

Economy: Industries: Banking, food products, textiles, cement, oil refining. **Chief crops:** Citrus fruits, olives, tobacco, grapes, vegetables. **Minerals:** Limestone, iron. **Arable land:** 21%. **Electricity prod.** (1995): 5 bil kWh. **Labor force:** 60% services, 28% industry; 12% agric.

Finance: Monetary unit: Pound (Aug. 1997: 1,540 = $1 US). **Gross domestic product** (1995 est.): $18.3 bil. **Per cap-**

ita **GDP:** $4,900. **Imports** (1995): $8.2 bil; partners: Italy 12%, France 8%, U.S. 8%. **Exports** (1995): $1.1 bil; partners: Saudi Arabia 8%, Switzerland 7%, U.A.E. 6%. **National budget** (1994): $3.2 bil. **International reserves less gold** (June 1997): $7.39 bil. **Gold:** 9.22 mil oz t.

Transport: Railroads: Length: 137.9 mi. **Motor vehicles in use:** 1.2 mil passenger cars, 85,000 comm. vehicles. **Civil aviation:** 986.1 mil passenger-mi.; 1 airport with scheduled flights. **Chief ports:** Beirut, Tripoli, Sidon.

Communications: Television sets: 1 per 2.8 persons. **Radios:** 1 per 1.1 persons. **Telephones:** 1 per 12 persons. **Newspaper circ.:** 172 per 1,000 pop.

Health: Life expectancy at birth (1997): 67.8 male; 73.0 female. **Births** (per 1,000 pop.): 28. **Deaths** (per 1,000 pop.): 6. **Natural increase:** 2.2%. **Hospital beds:** 1 per 83 persons. **Physicians:** 1 per 291 persons. **Infant mortality** (per 1,000 live births 1997): 35.

Education: Literacy (1995): 92%. **Major International Organizations:** UN, Arab League. **Embassy:** 2560 28th St. NW 20008; 939-6300.

Formed from 5 former Turkish Empire districts, Lebanon became an independent state Sept. 1, 1920, administered under French mandate 1920-41. French troops withdrew in 1946.

Under the 1943 National Covenant, all public positions were divided among the various religious communities, with Christians in the majority. By the 1970s, Muslims became the majority and demanded a larger political and economic role.

U.S. Marines intervened, May-Oct. 1958, during a Syrian-aided revolt. Continued raids against Israeli civilians, 1970-75, brought Israeli attacks against guerrilla camps and villages. Israeli troops occupied S Lebanon, Mar. 1978, and again in Apr. 1980.

An estimated 60,000 were killed and billions of dollars in damage inflicted in a 1975-76 civil war. Palestinian units and leftist Muslims fought against the Maronite militia, the Phalange, and other Christians. Several Arab countries provided political and arms support to the various factions, while Israel aided Christian forces. Up to 15,000 Syrian troops intervened in 1976, and fought Palestinian groups. Arab League troops from several nations tried to impose a cease-fire.

Clashes between Syrian troops and Christian forces erupted, Apr. 1, 1981, bringing to an end the cease-fire. By Apr. 22, fighting had also broken out between two Muslim factions. In July, Israeli air raids on Beirut killed or wounded some 800 persons.

Israeli forces invaded Lebanon June 6, 1982, in a coordinated land, sea, and air attack aimed at crushing strongholds of the Palestine Liberation Organization (PLO). Israeli and Syrian forces engaged in the Bekaa Valley. By June 14, Israeli troops had encircled Beirut. On Aug. 21, the PLO evacuated west Beirut following massive Israeli bombings of the city. Israeli troops entered west Beirut following the Sept. 14 assassination of newly elected Lebanese Pres. Bashir Gemayel. On Sept. 16, Lebanese Christian troops entered 2 refugee camps and massacred hundreds of Palestinian refugees. An agreement May 17, 1983, between Lebanon, Israel, and the U.S. (but not Syria) provided for the withdrawal of Israeli troops; at least 30,000 Syrian troops remained in Lebanon, and Israeli forces continued to occupy a "security zone" in the south.

In 1983, terrorist bombings became a way of life in Beirut as some 50 people were killed in an explosion at the U.S. Embassy, Apr. 18; 241 U.S. servicemen and 58 French soldiers died in separate Muslim suicide attacks, Oct. 23.

Kidnapping of foreign nationals by Islamic militants became common in the 1980s. U.S., British, French, and Soviet citizens were victims. All were released by 1992.

A treaty signed May 22, 1991, between Lebanon and Syria recognized Lebanon as a separate state for the first time since the 2 countries gained independence in 1943.

Israeli forces conducted air raids and artillery strikes against guerrilla bases and villages in S Lebanon, causing over 200,000 to flee their homes July 25-29, 1993. Some 500,000 civilians fled their homes in Apr. 1996 when Israel again struck suspected guerrilla bases in the south. Pope John Paul II visited Lebanon May 10-11, 1997.

Lesotho
Kingdom of Lesotho

People: Population: 2,007,814. **Age distrib.** (%): <15: 41; 65+: 5. **Pop. density:** 171 per sq. mi. **Urban:** 25%. **Ethnic groups:** Sotho 99.7%. **Principal languages:** English, Sesotho (both official). **Religion:** Christian 80%, indigenous beliefs 20%.

Geography: Area: 11,720 sq. mi. **Location:** In southern Africa. **Neighbors:** Completely surrounded by Republic of South Africa. **Topography:** Landlocked and mountainous, with altitudes ranging from 5,000 to 11,000 ft. **Capital:** Maseru (1995 est.): 400,200.

Government: Type: Modified constitutional monarchy. **Head of state:** King Letsie III; b July 17, 1963; in office: Feb. 7, 1996. **Head of government:** Ntsu Mokhehle; b Dec. 26, 1918; in office: Sept. 14, 1994. **Local divisions:** 10 districts. **Defense:** 1.9% of GNP (1994). **Active troop strength:** 2,000.

Economy: Industries: Food processing, textiles. **Chief crops:** Corn, grains, peas, beans. **Other resources:** Diamonds. **Arable land:** 10%. **Labor force:** 86% subsistence agric.

Finance: Monetary unit: Loti (June 1996: 4.34 = $1 US). **Gross domestic product** (1995 est.): $18.3 bil. **Per capita GDP:** $4,900. **Imports** (1995): $1 bil; partners: South Africa 83%; Asia 12%. **Exports** (1995): $142 mil; partners: South Africa 39%, EC 22%. **National budget** (FY 1994-95): $400 mil. **International reserves less gold** (Apr. 1997): $573.76 mil. **Consumer prices** (change in 1996): 9.3%.

Transport: Railroads: Length: 1.6 mi. **Motor vehicles in use:** 5,900 passenger cars, 18,000 comm. vehicles. **Civil aviation:** 5.6 mil passenger-mi.

Communications: Television sets: 1 per 100 persons. **Radios:** 1 per 30 persons. **Telephones:** 1 per 111 persons. **Daily newspaper circ.:** 17 per 1,000 pop.

Health: Life expectancy at birth (1997): 49.5 male; 53.9 female. **Births** (per 1,000 pop.): 32. **Deaths** (per 1,000 pop.): 14. **Natural increase:** 1.8%. **Hospital beds:** 1 per 765 persons. **Physicians:** 1 per 14,306 persons. **Infant mortality** (per 1,000 live births 1997): 80.

Education: Free and compulsory: ages 6-13. **Literacy** (1995): 71%.

Major International Organizations: UN (IMF, WTO, WHO), OAU, the Commonwealth.

Embassy: 2511 Massachusetts Ave. NW 20008; 797-5533.

Lesotho (once called Basutoland) became a British protectorate in 1868 when Chief Moshesh sought protection against the Boers. Independence came Oct. 4, 1966. Elections were suspended in 1970. Most of Lesotho's GNP is provided by citizens working in South Africa. Livestock raising is the chief industry; diamonds are the chief export.

South Africa imposed a blockade, Jan. 1, 1986, because of Lesotho's giving sanctuary to rebel groups fighting to overthrow the South African government. The blockade sparked a Jan 20 military coup, and was lifted, Jan. 25, when the new leaders agreed to expel the rebels.

In Mar. 1990, King Moshoeshoe was exiled by the military government. Letsie III became king Nov. 12. In Mar. 1993, Ntsu Mokhehle, a civilian, was elected prime minister, ending 23 years of military rule. After a series of violent disturbances, the king dismissed the Mokhele government Aug. 17, 1994; constitutional rule was restored Sept. 14. Letsie abdicated and Moshoeshoe was reinstated Jan. 25, 1995.

Moshoeshoe died in an automobile accident, Jan. 15, 1996, and was succeeded by Letsie Feb. 7.

Liberia
Republic of Liberia

People: Population: 2,602,068. **Age distrib.** (%): <15: 45; 65+: 4. **Pop. density:** 68 per sq. mi. **Urban:** 46%. **Ethnic groups:** Indigenous tribes 95%, Americo-Liberians 5%. **Principal languages:** English (official), tribal languages. **Chief religions:** Traditional beliefs 70%, Muslim 20%, Christian 10%.

Geography: Area: 38,250 sq. mi. **Location:** On SW coast of W Africa. **Neighbors:** Sierra Leone on W, Guinea on N, Côte d'Ivoire on E. **Topography:** Marshy Atlantic coastline rises to low mountains and plateaus in the forested interior; 6 major rivers flow in parallel courses to the ocean. **Capital:** Monrovia: 962,000*.

Government: Type: Republic. **Head of state:** Pres. Charles Taylor; b Jan. 29, 1948; in office: Aug. 2, 1997. **Local divisions:** 13 counties. **Defense:** 2.9% of GNP (1993).

Economy: Industries: Food processing, mining. **Chief crops:** Rice, cassava, coffee, cocoa, sugar. **Minerals:** Iron, diamonds, gold. **Other resources:** Rubber, timber. **Arable land:** 1%. **Fish catch** (1993): 7,782 metric tons. **Electricity prod.** (1995): 472 mil kWh. **Labor force:** 71% agric.; 11% serv.

Finance: Monetary unit: Dollar (Aug. 1997: 1.00 = $1 US). **Gross domestic product** (1994 est.): $2.3 bil. **Per capita GDP:** $770. **Imports** (1995): $5.9 bil; partners: Japan 33%; S. Korea 20%; Italy 9%. **Exports** (1995): $667 mil; partners: Belg.-Lux. 57%; Ukraine 12%; Greece 6%. **National budget** (1994 est.): $285 mil.

Transport: Railroads: Length: 304.3 mi. **Motor vehicles in use:** 17,000 passenger cars, 11,000 comm. vehicles. **Civil aviation:** 4.3 mil passenger-mi. **Chief ports:** Monrovia, Buchanan, Greenville.

Communications: Television sets: 1 per 53 persons. **Radios:** 1 per 4.4 persons. **Telephones:** 1 per 625 persons. **Daily newspaper circ.:** 14 per 1,000 pop.

Health: Life expectancy at birth (1997): 56.4 male; 61.7 female. **Births** (per 1,000 pop.): 42. **Deaths** (per 1,000 pop.): 12. **Natural increase:** 3.1%. **Infant mortality** (per 1,000 live births 1997): 106.

Education: Free and compulsory: ages 7-16. **Literacy** (1995): 38%.

Major International Organizations: UN and most of its specialized agencies, OAU.

Embassy: 5201 16th St. NW 20011; 723-0437.

Liberia was founded in 1822 by U.S. black freedmen who settled at Monrovia with the aid of colonization societies. It became a republic July 26, 1847, with a constitution modeled on that of the U.S. Descendants of freedmen dominated politics.

Charging rampant corruption, an Army Redemption Council of enlisted men staged a bloody predawn coup, April 12, 1980, in which Pres. Tolbert was killed and replaced as head of state by Sgt. Samuel Doe. Doe was chosen president in a disputed election, and survived a subsequent coup, in 1985.

A civil war began Dec. 1989. Rebel forces seeking to depose Pres. Doe made major territorial gains and advanced on the capital, June 1990. In Sept., Doe was captured and put to death. Despite the introduction of peacekeeping forces from several countries, factional fighting intensified, and a series of cease-fires failed. A transitional Council of State was instituted Sept. 1, 1995. Factional fighting flared up again in Apr. 1996, devastating Monrovia. On Sept. 3, 1996, Ruth Perry became modern Africa's first female head of state, leading another transitional government. By then, the civil war had claimed more than 150,000 lives and uprooted over half the population.

Former rebel leader Charles Taylor was elected president July 19, 1997, in Liberia's 1st national election in 12 years.

Libya
Socialist People's Libyan Arab Jamahiriya
Al Jamahiriyah al Arabiyah al Libiyah ash Shabiyah al Ishirakiyah

People: Population: 5,648,359. **Age distrib.** (%): <15: 48; 65+: 3. **Pop. density:** 8 per sq. mi. **Urban:** 86%. **Ethnic groups:** Arab-Berber 97%. **Principal language:** Arabic (official), Italian, English. **Religion:** Sunni Muslim 97%.

Geography: Area: 678,400 sq. mi. **Location:** On Mediterranean coast of N Africa. **Neighbors:** Tunisia, Algeria on W; Niger, Chad on S; Sudan, Egypt on E. **Topography:** Desert and semidesert regions cover 92% of the land, with low mountains in N, higher mountains in S, and a narrow coastal zone. **Capital:** Tripoli: 1,681,000*.

Government: Type: Islamic Arabic Socialist "Mass-State." **Leader:** Col. Muammar al-Qaddafi; b Sept. 1942; in power: Sept. 1969. **Local divisions:** 25 municipalities. **Defense:** 6.1% of GDP (1994 est.). **Active troop strength:** 65,000 est.

Economy: Industries: Oil, food processing, textiles. **Chief crops:** Dates, olives, citrus fruits, grapes, wheat. **Minerals:** Gypsum, oil, gas. **Crude oil reserves** (1996): 29.5 bil bbls. **Arable land:** 2%. **Livestock** (1996): sheep: 4.4 mil; goats: 800,000. **Electricity prod.** (1995): 17 bil kWh. **Labor force:** 31% ind.; 27% services; 24% govt.; 18% agric.

Finance: Monetary unit: Dinar (Aug. 1997: 0.38 = $1 US). **Gross domestic product** (1994 est.): $32.9 bil. **Per capita GDP:** $6,510. **Imports** (1995): $4.9 bil; partners: Italy 22%, Germany 14%. **Exports** (1995): $8.7 bil; partners: Italy 39%, Germany 16%, Spain 12%. **National budget** (1989): $9.8 bil. **International reserves less gold** (Jun. 1993): $5.9 bil. **Gold:** 3.6 mil oz t.

Transport: Motor vehicles in use: 448,000 passenger cars, 322,000 comm. vehicles. **Civil aviation:** 263.9 mil passenger-mi. **Chief ports:** Tripoli, Banghazi.

Communications: Television sets: 1 per 10 persons. **Radios:** 1 per 4.4 persons. **Telephones:** 1 per 17 persons. **Daily newspaper circ.:** 13 per 1,000 pop.

Health: Life expectancy at birth (1997): 62.8 male; 67.4 female. **Births** (per 1,000 pop.): 44. **Deaths** (per 1,000 pop.): 7. **Natural increase:** 3.6%. **Hospital beds:** 1 per 246 persons. **Physicians:** 1 per 948 persons. **Infant mortality** (per 1,000 live births 1997): 58.

Education: Compulsory: ages 6-15. **Literacy** (1995): 76%.

Major International Organizations: UN, Arab League, OAU, OPEC.

First settled by Berbers, Libya was ruled in succession by Carthage, Rome, the Vandals, and the Ottomans. Italy ruled from 1912, and Britain and France after WW II. Libya became an independent constitutional monarchy Jan. 2, 1952. In 1969 a junta led by Col. Muammar al-Qaddafi seized power.

Libya and Egypt fought several air and land battles along their border in July 1977. Chad charged Libya with military occupation of its uranium-rich northern region in 1977. Libyan troops were driven from their last major stronghold by Chad forces in 1987, leaving over $1 billion in military equipment behind.

Libya reportedly helped arm violent revolutionary groups in Egypt and Sudan and aided terrorists of various nationalities.

On Jan. 7, 1986, the U.S. imposed economic sanctions against Libya, ordered all Americans to leave that country, and froze all Libyan assets in the U.S. The U.S. commenced flight operations over the Gulf of Sidra, Jan. 27, and a U.S. Navy task force began conducting exercises in the Gulf, Mar. 23. When Libya fired antiaircraft missiles at American warplanes, the U.S. responded by sinking 2 Libyan ships and bombing a missile site in Libya. The U.S. withdrew from the Gulf, Mar. 27.

The U.S. accused Qaddafi of having ordered the Apr. 5, 1986, bombing of a West Berlin discotheque, which killed 3, including a U.S. serviceman. In response, the U.S. sent warplanes to attack terrorist-related targets in Tripoli and Banghazi, Libya, Apr. 14.

The UN imposed limited sanctions, Apr. 15, 1992, for Libya's failure to extradite 2 agents linked to the 1988 bombing of Pan American World Airways Flight 103 over Lockerbie, Scotland, and 4 others linked to an airplane bombing over Niger. Sanctions were tightened as of Dec. 1, 1993. In 1996 the U.S. authorized sanctions on foreign companies that invest in Libya.

Liechtenstein
Principality of Liechtenstein
Fürstentum Liechtenstein

People: Population: 31,461. **Age distrib.** (%): <15: 19; 65+: 11. **Pop. density:** 507 per sq. mi. **Urban:** 21%. **Ethnic groups:** Alemannic 95%. **Principal languages:** German (official), Alemannic dialect. **Chief religions:** Roman Catholic 87%, Protestant 8%.

Geography: Area: 62 sq. mi. **Location:** Central Europe, in the Alps. **Neighbors:** Switzerland on W, Austria on E. **Topography:** The Rhine Valley occupies one-third of the country, the Alps cover the rest. **Capital:** Vaduz (1995 est.): 5,067.

Government: Type: Hereditary constitutional monarchy. **Head of state:** Prince Hans-Adam II; b Feb 14, 1945; in office: Nov. 13, 1989. **Head of government:** Mario Frick; b May 8, 1965; in office: Dec. 15, 1993. **Local divisions:** 11 communes. **Defense:** Responsibility of Switzerland.

Economy: Industries: Precision instruments, electronics, textiles, ceramics. **Chief crops:** Vegetables, corn, wheat. **Arable land:** 25%. **Labor force:** 50% services; 48% industry, trade, constr.

Finance: Monetary unit: Swiss Franc. **Gross domestic product** (1990): $630 mil. **Per capita GDP:** $22,300. **National budget** (1995 est.): $442 mil.

Transport: Railroads: Length: 11.5 mi.

Communications: Television sets: 1 per 3.0 persons. **Radios:** 1 per 1.5 persons. **Telephones:** 1 per 1.6 persons. **Daily newspaper circ.:** 581 per 1,000 pop.

Health (1997): **Life expectancy at birth:** 76.1 male; 82.3 female. **Births** (per 1,000 pop.): 11. **Deaths** (per 1,000 pop.): 7. **Natural increase:** 0.5%. **Physicians:** 1 per 957 persons. **Infant mortality** (per 1,000 live births): 5.

Education: Compulsory: ages 7-16. **Literacy** (1997): 100%.

Major International Organizations: UN (WTO), EFTA.

Liechtenstein became sovereign in 1866. Austria administered Liechtenstein's ports up to 1920; Switzerland has admin-istered its postal services since 1921. Liechtenstein is united with Switzerland by a customs and monetary union. Taxes are low; many international corporations have headquarters there. Foreign workers comprise a third of the population.

Lithuania
Republic of Lithuania
Lietuvos Respublika

People: Population: 3,635,932. **Age distrib.** (%): <15: 21; 65+: 13. **Pop. density:** 144 per sq. mi. **Urban:** 73%. **Ethnic groups:** Lithuanian 80%, Russian 9%, Polish 8%. **Principal languages:** Lithuanian (official), Polish, Russian. **Chief religions:** Mostly Roman Catholic.

Geography: Area: 25,213 sq. mi. **Location:** In E Europe, on SE coast of Baltic. **Neighbors:** Latvia on N, Belarus on E, S, Poland and Russia on W. **Capital:** Vilnius. **Cities** (1994): Vilnius 578,700; Kaunas 419,000.

Government: Type: Republic. **Head of state:** Pres. Algirdas Brazauskas; b Sept. 22, 1932; in office: Feb. 25, 1993. **Head of government:** Prime Min. Gediminas Vagnorius; b June 10, 1957; in office: Nov. 28, 1996. **Local divisions:** 44 regions, 11 municipalities. **Defense:** 1% of GDP (1995). **Active troop strength:** 5,100 est.

Economy: Industries: Machinery, shipbuilding. **Chief crops:** Sugar beets, grain, potatoes, vegetables. **Arable land:** 49%. **Livestock** (1996): pigs: 1.15 mil, cattle: 1.1 mil. **Electricity prod.** (1995): 13.7 bil kWh. **Labor force:** 42% ind. & constr.; 18% agric.

Finance: Monetary unit: Litas (Aug. 1997: 3.99 = $1 US). **Gross domestic product** (1995 est.): $13.3 bil. **Per capita GDP:** $3,400. **Imports** (1995): $2.5 bil; partners: Russia 31%. **Exports** (1995): $2.2 bil; partners: Russia 20%; Belarus 11%. **National budget** (1995 est.): $206.2 mil. **International reserves less gold** (June 1997): $870.45 mil. **Gold:** 186,000 oz t. **Consumer prices** (change in 1996): 24.6%.

Transport: Railroads: Length: 1,243.2 mi. **Motor vehicles in use:** 653,000 passenger cars, 111,000 comm. vehicles. **Civil aviation:** 149.7 mil passenger-mi.; 3 airports with scheduled flights. **Chief port:** Klaipeda.

Communications: Television sets: 1 per 2.6 persons. **Radios:** 1 per 2.6 persons. **Telephones:** 1 per 3.9 persons. **Daily newspaper circ.:** 136 per 1,000 pop.

Health: Life expectancy at birth (1997): 62.6 male; 74.4 female. **Births** (per 1,000 pop.): 14. **Deaths** (per 1,000 pop.): 13. **Natural increase:** 0.1%. **Hospital beds:** 1 per 86 persons. **Physicians:** 1 per 225 persons. **Infant mortality** (per 1,000 live births 1997): 16.

Education: Free and compulsory: ages 6-12. **Literacy** (1989): 98%.

Major International Organizations: UN, EU.

Embassy: 2622 16th St. NW 20009; 234-5860.

Lithuania was occupied by the German army, 1914-18. It was annexed by the Soviet Russian army, but the Soviets were overthrown, 1919. Lithuania was a democratic republic until 1926 when the regime was ousted by a coup. In 1939, the Soviet-German treaty assigned most of Lithuania to the Soviet sphere of influence. It was annexed by the USSR Aug. 3, 1940. Lithuania formally declared its independence from the Soviet Union Mar. 11, 1990. During an abortive Soviet coup in Aug., the Western nations recognized Lithuania's independence, which was recognized by the Soviet Union in Sept. 1991.

The last Russian troops withdrew on Aug. 31, 1993. Lithuania applied to join the European Union, Dec. 8, 1995. The conservative Homeland Union defeated the former Communists in parliamentary elections Oct. 20 and Nov. 10, 1996.

Luxembourg
Grand Duchy of Luxembourg
Grand-Duché de Luxembourg

People: Population: 422,474. **Age distrib.** (%): <15: 18; 65+: 14. **Pop. density:** 422 per sq. mi. **Urban:** 90%. **Ethnic groups:** Mixture of French and Germans predominates. **Principal languages:** French, German, Luxembourgisch. **Chief religions:** Roman Catholic 97%.

Geography: Area: 999 sq. mi. **Location:** In W Europe. **Neighbors:** Belgium on W, France on S, Germany on E. **Topography:**

Heavy forests (Ardennes) cover N, S is a low, open plateau. **Capital:** Luxembourg (1995): 76,400.

Government: Type: Constitutional monarchy. **Head of state:** Grand Duke Jean; b Jan. 5, 1921; in office: Nov. 12, 1964. **Head of government:** Prime Min. Jean-Claude Juncker; b Dec. 9, 1954; in office: Jan. 19, 1995. **Local divisions:** 3 districts. **Defense:** 1% of GDP (1995). **Active troop strength:** 800.

Economy: Industries: Steel, chemicals, food processing, tires, banking, engineering, metal products. **Chief crops:** Grains, potatoes, wine grapes. **Arable land:** 24%. **Electricity prod.** (1995): 470 mil kWh. **Labor force:** 60% services; 37% ind.; 3% agric.

Finance: Monetary unit: Franc (Aug. 1997: 37.37 = $1 US). **Gross domestic product** (1995 est.): $10 bil. **Per capita GDP:** $24,800. **Tourism** (1994): $291 mil. **National budget** (1994): $4.1 bil. **International reserves less gold** (June 1997): $67.54 mil. **Gold:** 305,000 oz t. **Consumer prices** (change in 1996): 1.4%.

Transport: Railroads: Length: 170.8 mi. **Motor vehicles in use:** 232,000 passenger cars, 17,000 comm. vehicles. **Civil aviation:** 224.2 mil passenger-mi. **Chief port:** Mertert.

Communications: Television sets: 1 per 2.7 persons. **Radios:** 1 per 1.6 persons. **Telephones:** 1 per 1.8 persons. **Daily newspaper circ.:** 384 per 1,000 pop.

Health: Life expectancy at birth (1997): 75.8 male; 82.1 female. **Births** (per 1,000 pop.): 13. **Deaths** (per 1,000 pop.): 8. **Natural increase:** 0.5%. **Hospital beds:** 1 per 87 persons. **Physicians:** 1 per 469 persons. **Infant mortality** (per 1,000 live births 1997): 5.

Education: Compulsory: ages 6-15. **Literacy** (1995): 100%.

Major International Organizations: UN (WTO), OECD, EU, NATO.

Embassy: 2200 Massachusetts Ave. NW 20008; 265-4171.

Luxembourg, founded about 963, was ruled by Burgundy, Spain, Austria, and France from 1448 to 1815. It left the Germanic Confederation in 1866. Overrun by Germany in 2 world wars, Luxembourg ended its neutrality in 1948, when a customs union with Belgium and Netherlands was adopted.

Macedonia
Former Yugoslav Republic of Macedonia
Republika Makedonija

People: Population: 2,113,866. **Age distrib.** (%): <15: 22; 65+: 10. **Pop. density:** 216 per sq. mi. **Urban:** 60%. **Ethnic groups:** Macedonian 65%, Albanian 22%. **Principal languages:** Macedonian (official), Albanian, Turkish, Serbo-Croatian. **Chief religions:** Eastern Orthodox 67%, Muslim 30%.

Geography: Area: 9,781 sq. mi. **Location:** In SE Europe. **Neighbors:** Bulgaria on E, Greece on S, Albania on W, Serbia on N. **Capital:** Skopje (1994 cen.): 541,280.

Government: Type: Republic. **Head of state:** Pres. Kiro Gligorov; b May 3, 1917; in office: Jan. 27, 1991. **Head of government:** Prime Min. Branko Crvenkovski; b 1962; in office: Sept. 4, 1992. **Local divisions:** 34 counties. **Defense: Active troop strength:** 10,400.

Economy: Industries: Mining, textiles. **Chief crops:** Wheat, rice, cotton, tobacco. **Minerals:** Chromium, lead, zinc. **Arable land:** 5%. **Livestock** (1996): sheep: 2.0 mil. **Electricity prod.** (1995): 5.4 bil kWh. **Labor force:** 40% manuf. & mining.

Finance: Monetary unit: Dinar (Aug. 1997: 5.70 = $1 US). **Gross domestic product** (1995 est.): $1.9 bil. **Per capita GDP:** $880. **Imports** (1994): $1.5 bil. **Exports** (1994): $1.1 bil.

Transport: Railroads: Length: 434.1 mi. **Motor vehicles in use:** 263,000 passenger cars, 23,000 comm. vehicles. **Civil aviation:** 198.1 mil passenger-mi.; 1 airport with scheduled flights.

Communications: Television sets: 1 per 6.0 persons. **Radios:** 1 per 5.5 persons. **Telephones:** 1 per 6.1 persons. **Daily newspaper circ.:** 21 per 1,000 pop.

Health: Life expectancy at birth (1997): 70.0 male; 74.4 female. **Births** (per 1,000 pop.): 13. **Deaths** (per 1,000 pop.): 9. **Natural increase:** 0.5%. **Hospital beds:** 1 per 195 persons. **Physicians:** 1 per 437 persons. **Infant mortality** (per 1,000 live births 1997): 29.

Education: Literacy (1993): 89%. Free and compulsory: ages 7-15.

Major International Organizations: UN (IMF, WHO). **Embassy:** 3050 K St. NW 20007; 337-3063.

Macedonia, as part of a larger region also called Macedonia, was ruled by Muslim Turks from 1389 to 1912, when native Greeks, Bulgarians, and Slavs won independence. Serbia received the largest part of the territory, with the rest going to Greece and Bulgaria. In 1913, the area was incorporated into Serbia, which in 1918 became part of the Kingdom of Serbs, Croats, and Slovenes (later Yugoslavia). In 1946, Macedonia became a constituent republic of Yugoslavia.

Macedonia declared its independence Sept. 8, 1991, and was admitted to the UN under a provisional name in 1993. A UN force, which included several hundred U.S. troops, was deployed there to deter the warring factions in Bosnia from carrying their dispute into other areas of the Balkans.

In Feb. 1994 both Russia and the U.S. recognized Macedonia. Greece, which objected to Macedonia's use of what it considered a Hellenic name and symbols, imposed a trade blockade on the landlocked nation; the 2 countries agreed to normalize relations Sept. 13, 1995. A car bombing, Oct. 3, seriously injured Pres. Kiro Gligorov. Macedonia and Yugoslavia signed a treaty normalizing relations Apr. 8, 1996.

Madagascar
Republic of Madagascar
Repoblikan'i Madagasikara

People: Population: 14,061,627. **Age distrib.** (%): <15: 45; 65+: 3. **Pop. density:** 62 per sq. mi. **Urban:** 27%. **Ethnic groups:** 18 Malayo-Indonesian tribes (Merina 26%), with Arab and African presence. **Principal languages:** Malagasy, French (both official). **Chief religions:** Indigenous beliefs 52%, Christian 41%, Muslim 7%.

Geography: Area: 226,658 sq. mi. **Location:** In the Indian O., off the SE coast of Africa. **Neighbors:** Comoro Isls. to NW, Mozambique to W. **Topography:** Humid coastal strip in the E, fertile valleys in the mountainous center plateau region, and a wider coastal strip on the W. **Capital:** Antananarivo: **876,000*.**

Government: Type: Republic. **Head of state:** Pres. Didier Ratsiraka; b Nov. 4, 1936; in office: Jan. 31, 1997. **Head of government:** Pascal Rakotomavo; in office: Feb. 21, 1997. **Local divisions:** 6 provinces. **Defense:** 1% of GDP (1994). **Active troop strength:** 21,000 est.

Economy: Industries: Meat processing, textiles. **Chief crops:** Coffee, cloves, vanilla beans, rice, sugar, cassava, peanuts. **Minerals:** Chromite, graphite, coal, bauxite. **Arable land:** 4%. **Livestock** (1996): cattle: 10.3 mil; pigs: 1.6 mil; sheep: 1.3 mil. **Fish catch** (1993): 115,029 metric tons. **Electricity prod.** (1995): 595 mil kWh. **Labor force:** 86% agric.

Finance: Monetary unit: Franc (Aug. 1997: 5426.92 = $1 US). **Gross domestic product** (1995 est.): $11.4 bil. **Per capita GDP:** $820. **Imports** (1994): $510 mil; partners: France 30%, U.S. 6%, Germany 6%. **Exports** (1994): $240 mil; partners: France 27%, U.S. 16%. **Tourism** (1994): $54 mil. **National budget** (1991): $265 mil. **International reserves less gold** (June 1997): $253.1 mil. **Consumer prices** (change in 1996): 19.8%.

Transport: Railroads: Length: 548.3 mi. **Motor vehicles in use:** 48,000 passenger cars, 34,000 comm. vehicles. **Civil aviation:** 352.1 mil passenger-mi.; 19 airports with scheduled flights. **Chief ports:** Toamasina, Antsiranana, Mahajanga, Toliara.

Communications: Television sets: 1 per 50 persons. **Radios:** 1 per 5.2 persons. **Telephones:** 1 per 413 persons.

Health: Life expectancy at birth (1997): 51.4 male; 53.7 female. **Births** (per 1,000 pop.): 42. **Deaths** (per 1,000 pop.): 14. **Natural increase:** 2.8%. **Physicians:** 1 per 8,628 persons. **Infant mortality** (per 1,000 live births 1997): 92.

Education: Compulsory for 5 years between ages 6 and 13. **Literacy** (1995): 46%.

Major International Organizations: UN (WHO, IMF, WTO), OAU.

Embassy: 2374 Massachusetts Ave. NW 20008; 265-5525.

Madagascar was settled 2,000 years ago by Malayan-Indonesian people, whose descendants still predominate. A unified kingdom ruled the 18th and 19th centuries. The island became a French protectorate, 1885, and a colony 1896. Independence came June 26, 1960.

Discontent with inflation and French domination led to a coup in 1972. The new regime nationalized French-owned financial interests, closed French bases and a U.S. space-tracking station, and obtained Chinese aid. The government conducted a program of arrests, expulsion of foreigners, and repression of strikes, 1979.

In 1990, Madagascar ended a ban on multiparty politics that had been in place since 1975. Albert Zafy was elected president in 1993, ending the 17-year rule of Adm. Didier Ratsiraka. After Zafy was impeached by the legislature, Madagascar's constitutional court removed him from office, Sept. 5, 1996. Prime Min. Norbert Ratsirahonana then became interim president pending national elections, Nov. 3 and Dec. 29, in which Ratsiraka edged Zafy.

Malawi
Republic of Malawi

People: Population: 9,609,081. **Age distrib.** (%): <15: 46; 65+: 3. **Pop. density:** 210 per sq. mi. **Urban:** 14%. **Ethnic groups:** Chewa, Nyanja, Lomwe, other Bantu tribes. **Principal languages:** English, Chichewa (both official). **Chief religions:** Protestant 55%, Muslim 20%, Roman Catholic 20%.

Geography: Area: 45,747 sq. mi. **Location:** In SE Africa. **Neighbors:** Zambia on W, Mozambique on S and E, Tanzania on N. **Topography:** Malawi stretches 560 mi. N-S along Lake Malawi (Lake Nyasa), most of which belongs to Malawi. High plateaus and mountains line the Rift Valley the length of the nation. **Capital:** Lilongwe. **Cities** (1993 est.): Blantyre 446,800; Lilongwe 395,500.

Government: Type: Multiparty democracy. **Head of state and government:** Pres. Bakili Muluzi; b Mar. 17, 1943; in office: May 21, 1994. **Local divisions:** 24 districts. **Defense:** 1.1% of GNP (FY 1993-94). **Active troop strength:** 9,800.

Economy: Industries: Agricultural processing, cement. **Chief crops:** Tea, tobacco, sugar, cotton, corn, potatoes. **Arable land:** 25%. **Fish catch** (1993): 65,000 metric tons. **Electricity prod.** (1995): 800 mil kWh. **Labor force:** 43% agric.; 25% manuf. & commerce; 15% personal services.

Finance: Monetary unit: Kwacha (Aug. 1997: 17.36 = $1 US). **Gross domestic product** (1995 est.): $6.9 bil. **Per capita GDP:** $700. **Imports** (1994): $240 mil; partners: South Africa 31%, UK 23%, Japan 8%. **Exports** (1994): $365 mil; partners: Germany 16%, UK 16%, Japan 14%. **National budget** (1993): $674 mil. **International reserves less gold** (Apr. 1997): $146.17 mil. **Gold:** 13,000 oz t.

Transport: Railroads: Length: 490 mi. **Motor vehicles in use:** 15,000 passenger cars, 19,000 comm. vehicles. **Civil aviation:** 179.5 mil passenger-mi.

Communications: Radios: 1 per 4.4 persons. **Telephones:** 1 per 283 persons.

Health: Life expectancy at birth (1997): 34.9 male; 35.7 female. **Births** (per 1,000 pop.): 41. **Deaths** (per 1,000 pop.): 25. **Natural increase:** 1.6%. **Physicians:** 1 per 47,634 persons. **Infant mortality** (per 1,000 live births 1997): 139.

Education: Compulsory: ages 6-14. **Literacy** (1995): 56%.

Major International Organizations: UN (World Bank, WTO, IMF), OAU, the Commonwealth.

Embassy: 2408 Massachusetts Ave. NW 20008; 797-1007.

Bantus came in the 16th century, Arab slavers in the 19th. The area became the British protectorate Nyasaland in 1891. It became independent July 6, 1964, and a republic in 1966. After 3 decades as a one-party state under Pres. Hastings Kamuzu Banda, Malawi adopted a new constitution and, in multiparty elections held May 17, 1994, chose a new leader, Bakili Muluzi. Banda was acquitted, Dec. 23, 1995, of complicity in the deaths of 4 political opponents in 1983.

Malaysia

People: Population: 20,376,235. **Age distrib.** (%): <15: 36; 65+: 4. **Pop. density:** 159 per sq. mi. **Urban:** 54%. **Ethnic groups:** Malay and other indigenous 59%, Chinese 32%, Indian 9%. **Principal languages:** Malay (official), English, Chinese, Indian languages. **Chief religions:** Muslim, Hindu, Buddhist, Christian, local religions.

Geography: Area: 127,584 sq. mi. **Location:** On the SE tip of Asia, plus the N coast of the island of Borneo. **Neighbors:** Thailand on N, Indonesia on S. **Topography:** Most of W Malaysia is covered by tropical jungle, including the central mountain range that runs N-S through the peninsula. The western coast is marshy, the eastern, sandy. E Malaysia has a wide, swampy coastal plain, with interior jungles and mountains. **Capital:** Kuala Lumpur: 1,236,000*.

Government: Type: Federal parliamentary democracy with a constitutional monarch. **Head of state:** Paramount Ruler Tuanku Ja'afar ibni Al-Marhum Tuanku Abdul Rahman; b Jul. 19, 1922; in office: Apr. 26, 1994. **Head of government:** Prime Min. Datuk Seri Mahathir bin Mohamad; b Dec. 20, 1925; in office: July 16, 1981. **Local divisions:** 13 states and 2 federal terr. **Defense:** 2.9% of GDP (1995). **Active troop strength:** 114,500.

Economy: Industries: Rubber goods, logging, electronics. **Chief crops:** Palm oil (world's leading producer), rice, pepper. **Minerals:** Tin (a leading producer), oil, bauxite, iron. **Crude oil reserves** (1996): 4.0 bil bbls. **Other resources:** Rubber, timber. **Arable land:** 3%. **Livestock** (1996): pigs: 3.3 mil. **Fish catch** (1995): 1,238,795 metric tons. **Electricity prod.** (1995): 42 bil kWh. **Labor force:** 25% services & trade; 23% manuf.; 21% agric.

Finance: Monetary unit: Ringgit (Aug, 1997: 2.77 = $1 US). **Gross domestic product** (1995 est.): $193.6 bil. **Per capita GDP:** $9,800. **Imports** (1995): $72.2 bil; partners: Japan 27%, U.S. 17%, Singapore 14%. **Exports** (1995): $72 bil; partners: Singapore 21%, U.S. 21%, Japan 12%. **Tourism** (1994): $3.2 bil. **National budget** (1995 est.): $19.9 bil. **International reserves less gold** (Feb. 1997): $26.13 bil. **Gold:** 2.28 mil oz t. **Consumer prices** (change in 1996): 3.5%.

Transport: Railroads: Length: 1,121.5 mi. **Motor vehicles in use:** 2.6 mil passenger cars, 35,000 comm. vehicles. **Civil aviation:** 12.6 bil passenger-mi.; 36 airports. **Chief ports:** Kuantan, Kelang, Kota Kinabalu, Kuching.

Communications: Television sets: 1 per 6.4 persons. **Radios:** 1 per 2.3 persons. **Telephones:** 1 per 6.0 persons. **Daily newspaper circ.:** 142 per 1,000 pop.

Health: Life expectancy at birth (1997): 67.1 male; 73.2 female. **Births** (per 1,000 pop.): 26. **Deaths** (per 1,000 pop.): 5. **Natural increase:** 2.0%. **Hospital beds:** 1 per 586 persons. **Physicians:** 1 per 2,301 persons. **Infant mortality** (per 1,000 live births 1997): 23.

Education: Free and compulsory: ages 6-16. **Attendance:** 93% primary. **Literacy** (1995): 84%.

Major International Organizations: UN (World Bank, IMF, WTO), ASEAN, the Commonwealth.

Embassy: 2401 Massachusetts Ave. NW 20008; 328-2700.

European traders appeared in the 16th century; Britain established control in 1867. Malaysia was created Sept. 16, 1963. It included Malaya (which had become independent in 1957 after the suppression of Communist rebels), plus the formerly British Singapore, Sabah (N Borneo), and Sarawak (NW Borneo). Singapore was separated in 1965, in order to end tensions between Chinese, the majority in Singapore, and Malays in control of the Malaysian government.

A monarch is elected by a council of hereditary rulers of the Malayan states every 5 years.

Abundant natural resources have assured prosperity, and foreign investment has aided industrialization. Work on a new federal capital at Putrajaya, south of Kuala Lumpur, began in 1995. Sagging stock and currency prices forced the postponement of major development projects in Sept. 1997.

Maldives
Republic of Maldives
Divehi Jumhuriyya

People: Population: 280,391. **Age distrib.** (%): <15: 47; 65+: 3. **Pop. density:** 2,438 per sq. mi. **Urban:** 27%. **Ethnic groups:** Sinhalese, Dravidian, Arab, African. **Principal language:** Divehi (Sinhalese dialect; official). **Religion:** Sunni Muslim.

Geography: Area: 115 sq. mi. **Location:** In the Indian O., SW of India. **Neighbors:** Nearest is India on N. **Topography:** 19 atolls with 1,190 islands, 198 inhabited. None of the islands are over 5 sq. mi. in area, and all are nearly flat. **Capital:** Male (1995 est.): 62,973.

Government: Type: Republic. **Head of state:** Pres. Maumoon Abdul Gayoom; b Dec. 29, 1937; in office: Nov. 11, 1978. **Local divisions:** 19 districts.

Economy: Industries: Fish processing, tourism. **Chief crops:** Coconuts, corn, sweet potatoes. **Arable land:** 10%. **Fish catch** (1993): 89,938 metric tons. **Electricity prod.** (1995): 50 mil kWh. **Labor force:** 25% fishing & agric.; 16% trade; 15% manuf.

Finance: Monetary unit: Rufiyaa (Aug. 1997: 11.77 = $1 US). **Gross domestic product** (1994 est.): $390 mil. **Per capita GDP:** $1,560. **Imports** (1994 est.): $195 min.; partners: Singapore 52%, India 9%. **Exports** (1994 est.): $75 mil; partners: Sri Lanka 30%, UK 25%. **Tourism** (1994): $181 mil. **National budget** (1995 est.): $141 mil. **International reserves less gold** (June 1997): $95.25 mil. **Consumer prices** (change in 1996): 6.3%.

Transport: Civil aviation: 4.3 mil passenger-mi. **Chief port:** Male.

Communications: Television sets: 1 per 40 persons. **Radios:** 1 per 8.5 persons. **Telephones:** 1 per 18 persons.

Health: Life expectancy at birth (1997): 65.2 male; 68.6 female. **Births** (per 1,000 pop.): 41. **Deaths** (per 1,000 pop.): 6. **Natural increase:** 3.5%. **Hospital beds:** 1 per 1,192 persons. **Physicians:** 1 per 5,297 persons. **Infant mortality** (per 1,000 live births 1997): 44.

Education: Literacy (1995): 93%.

Major International Organizations: UN (WTO, WHO, IMF), the Commonwealth.

The islands had been a British protectorate since 1887. The country became independent July 26, 1965. Long a sultanate, the Maldives became a republic in 1968. Natural resources and tourism are being developed; however, the Maldives remains one of the world's poorest countries.

Mali
Republic of Mali
République du Mali

People: Population: 9,945,383. **Age distrib.** (%): <15: 48; 65+: 3. **Pop. density:** 20 per sq. mi. **Urban:** 28%. **Ethnic groups:** Mande (Bambara, Malinke, Sarakole) 50%, Peul 17%, Voltaic 12%, Songhai 6%, Tuareg and Moor 10%. **Principal languages:** French (official), Bambara, many other African languages. **Religion:** Muslim 90%, indigenous beliefs 9%.

Geography: Area: 482,077 sq. mi. **Location:** In the interior of W Africa. **Neighbors:** Mauritania, Senegal on W; Guinea, Côte d'Ivoire, Burkina Faso on S; Niger on E; Algeria on N. **Topography:** A landlocked grassy plain in the upper basins of the Senegal and Niger rivers, extending N into the Sahara. **Capital:** Bamako: 919,000*.

Government: Type: Republic. **Head of state:** Pres. Alpha Oumar Konare; b Feb. 2, 1946; in office: June 8, 1992. **Head of government:** Prime Min. Ibrahim Boubakar Keita; b Jan. 29, 1945; in office: Feb. 4, 1994. **Local divisions:** 8 regions. **Defense:** 2.2% of GDP (1994). **Active troop strength:** 7,350 est.

Economy: Chief crops: Millet, rice, peanuts, cotton. **Minerals:** Gold, phosphates, kaolin. **Arable land:** 2%. **Livestock** (1996): goats: 7.7 mil; cattle: 5.7 mil; sheep: 5.4 mil. **Fish catch** (1993): 64,354 metric tons. **Electricity prod.** (1995): 290 mil kWh. **Labor force:** 80% agric.; 19% services.

Finance: Monetary unit: CFA Franc (Aug. 1997: 610 = $1 US). **Gross domestic product** (1994): $5.4 bil. **Per capita GDP:** $600. **Imports** (1993): $842 mil; partners: Norway 28%, Côte d'Ivoire 18%. **Exports** (1993): $415 mil; partners: Norway 29%, Thailand 18%. **Tourism** (1994): $18 mil. **National budget** (1992): $697 mil. **International reserves less gold** (Mar. 1997): $411.2 mil. **Gold:** 19,000 oz t. **Consumer prices** (change in 1996): 6.8%.

Transport: Railroads: Length: 398.1 mi. **Motor vehicles in use:** 21,000 passenger cars, 8,600 comm. vehicles. **Civil aviation:** 133.5 mil passenger-mi. **Chief port:** Koulikoro.

Communications: Television sets: 1 per 769 persons. **Radios:** 1 per 23 persons. **Telephones:** 1 per 573 persons.

Health: Life expectancy at birth (1997): 45.5 male; 49.1 female. **Births** (per 1,000 pop.): 51. **Deaths** (per 1,000 pop.): 19. **Natural increase:** 3.2%. **Infant mortality** (per 1,000 live births 1997): 101.

Education: Free and compulsory: ages 7-16. **Literacy** (1995): 31%.

Major International Organizations: UN and most of its specialized agencies, OAU.

Embassy: 2130 R St. NW 20008; 332-2249.

Until the 15th century the area was part of the great Mali Empire. Timbuktu (Tombouctou) was a center of Islamic study. French rule was secured, 1898. The Sudanese Rep. and Senegal became independent as the Mali Federation June 20, 1960, but Senegal withdrew, and the Sudanese Rep. was renamed Mali.

Mali signed economic agreements with France and, in 1963, with Senegal. In 1968, a coup ended the socialist regime. Famine struck in 1973-74, killing as many as 100,000 people. Drought conditions returned in the 1980s.

The military, Mar. 26, 1991, overthrew the government of Pres. Amadou Toumani Traoré, who had been in power since 1968. Oumar Konare, a leader in the coup, was elected president, Apr. 26, 1992. A peace accord between the government and a Tuareg rebel group was signed in June 1994. Konare and his party won a series of flawed elections, Apr.-Aug. 1997.

Malta
Republic of Malta
Repubblika ta' Malta

People: Population: 379,365. **Age distrib.** (%): <15: 22; 65+: 11. **Pop. density:** 3,109 per sq. mi. **Urban:** 90%. **Ethnic groups:** Italian, Arab, Spanish, English. **Principal languages:** Maltese, English (both official). **Religion:** Roman Catholic 98%.

Geography: Area: 122 sq. mi. **Location:** In center of Mediterranean Sea. **Neighbors:** Nearest is Italy on N. **Topography:** Island of Malta is 95 sq. mi.; other islands in the group: Gozo, 26 sq. mi.; Comino, 1 sq. mi. The coastline is heavily indented. Low hills cover the interior. **Capital:** Valletta (1995 est.): 9,129.

Government: Type: Parliamentary democracy. **Head of state:** Pres. Ugo Mifsud Bonnici; b Nov. 8, 1932; in office: Apr. 4, 1994. **Head of government:** Prime Min. Alfred Sant; b Feb. 28, 1948; in office: Oct. 28, 1996. **Defense:** 1% of GDP (FY 1992-93). **Active troop strength:** 1,950.

Economy: Industries: Tourism, electronics, construction, textiles, food & beverages. **Chief crops:** Potatoes, tomatoes. **Arable land:** 38%. **Electricity prod.** (1995): $1.5 bil kWh. **Labor force:** 37% govt.; 26% services; 22% manuf.; 2% agric.

Finance: Monetary unit: Lira (Aug. 1997: .3950 = $2.75 US). **Gross domestic product** (1995 est.): $4.4 bil. **Per capita GDP:** $12,000. **Imports** (1994): $2.5 bil; partners: Italy 27%, Germany 18%, UK 15%. **Exports** (1994): $1.5 bil; partners: Italy 38%, Germany 14%, France 10%. **Tourism** (1994): $639 mil. **National budget** (FY 1994-95): $1.4 bil. **International reserves less gold** (Mar. 1997): 1.49 bil. **Gold:** 53,000 oz t. **Consumer prices** (change in 1996): 2.5%.

Transport: Motor vehicles in use: 117,000 passenger cars, 15,000 comm. vehicles. **Civil aviation:** 1.1 bil passenger-mi.; 1 airport with scheduled flights. **Chief port:** Valletta.

Communications: Television sets: 1 per 1.3 persons. **Radios:** 1 per 1.9 persons. **Telephones:** 1 per 2.2 persons.

Health: Life expectancy at birth (1997): 76.3 male; 81.2 female. **Births** (per 1,000 pop.): 15. **Deaths** (per 1,000 pop.): 7. **Natural increase:** 0.8%. **Hospital beds:** 1 per 172 persons. **Physicians:** 1 per 407 persons. **Infant mortality** (per 1,000 live births 1997): 6.

Education: Free and compulsory: ages 5-16. **Literacy** (1995): 91%.

Major International Organizations: UN (WTO, WHO, IMF), the Commonwealth.

Embassy: 2017 Connecticut Ave. NW 20008; 462-3611.

Malta was ruled by Phoenicians, Romans, Arabs, Normans, the Knights of Malta, France, and Britain (since 1814). It became independent Sept. 21, 1964. Malta became a republic in 1974. The withdrawal of the last British sailors, Apr. 1, 1979, ended 179 years of British military presence on the island. From 1971 to 1987, Malta was governed by the socialist Labor Party; it returned to office in 1996 after an interlude of Nationalist Party government.

Marshall Islands
Republic of the Marshall Islands

People: Population: 60,652. **Age. distrib.** (%): <15: 50; 65+: 2. **Pop. density:** 866 per sq. mi. **Urban:** 70%. **Ethnic groups:** Micronesian. **Principal languages:** English (official), Marshallese, Japanese. **Chief religions:** Protestant 90%.

Geography: Area: 70 sq. mi. **Location:** In N Pacific Ocean; composed of two 800-mi-long parallel chains of coral atolls. **Neighbors:** Nearest are Micronesia to W, Nauru and Kiribati to S. **Capital:** Majuro (1990 est.) 20,000.

Government: Type: Republic. **Head of state:** Pres. Imata Kabua; b May 20, 1943; in office: Jan. 22, 1997.

Economy: Agriculture and tourism are mainstays. **Electricity prod.** (1990): 80 mil kWh.

Finance: Monetary unit: U.S. Dollar. **Gross domestic product** (1995 est.): $94 mil. **Per capita GDP:** $1,680. **Imports** (1995): $70 mil. **Exports** (1995): $21 mil.

Transport: 23 airports with scheduled flights. **Civil aviation:** 25.5 mil passenger-mi. **Chief port:** Majuro.

Communications: Telephones: 1 per 18 persons.

Health: Life expectancy at birth (1997): 62.0 male; 65.0 female. **Births** (per 1,000 pop.): 46. **Deaths** (per 1,000 pop.): 7. **Natural increase:** 3.8%. **Physicians:** 1 per 2,309 persons. **Infant mortality** (per 1,000 live births 1997): 46.

Education: Compulsory: ages 6-14. **Literacy** (1994): 91%.

Major International Organizations: UN.
Embassy: 2433 Massachusetts Ave. NW 20008; 234-5414.

The Marshall Islands were a German possession until World War I and were administered by Japan between the World Wars. After WW II, they were administered as part of the UN Trust Territory of the Pacific Islands by the U.S.

The Marshall Islands secured international recognition as an independent nation on Sept. 17, 1991. Amata Kabua, the islands' first and only president since 1979, died Dec. 19, 1996. His cousin Imata Kabua was elected Jan. 13, 1997.

Mauritania
Islamic Republic of Mauritania
Al Jumhuriyah al Islamiyah al Muritaniyah

People: Population: 2,411,317. **Age distrib.** (%): <15: 48; 65+: 2. **Pop. density:** 6 per sq. mi. **Urban:** 53%. **Ethnic groups:** Mixed Maur/black 40%, Maur 30%, black 30%. **Principal languages:** Hasaniya Arabic, Wolof (both official), Pular, Soninke. **Chief religions:** Muslim.
Geography: Area: 398,000 sq. mi. **Location:** In NW Africa. **Neighbors:** Morocco on N, Algeria and Mali on E, Senegal on S. **Topography:** The fertile Senegal R. valley in the S gives way to a wide central region of sandy plains and scrub trees. The N is arid and extends into the Sahara. **Capital:** Nouakchott (1995 est.): 735,000.
Government: Type: Islamic republic. **Head of state:** Pres. Maaouya Ould Sidi Ahmed Taya; b 1943; in office: Apr. 18, 1992. **Head of government:** Prime Min. Cheikh El Afia Ould Mohamed Khouna; in office: Jan. 2, 1996. **Local divisions:** 12 regions, 1 capital district. **Defense:** 2.5% of GDP (1995). **Active troop strength:** 15,650 est.
Economy: Industries: Fish processing, iron mining. **Chief crops:** Dates, grain. **Minerals:** Iron ore, gypsum. **Livestock** (1996): sheep: 6.1 mil; goats: 4.1 mil; cattle: 1.1 mil; camels: 1.1 mil. **Fish catch** (1994): 296,627 metric tons. **Electricity prod.** (1995): 143 mil kWh. **Labor force:** 47% agric.; 29% services; 14% ind. & commerce.
Finance: Monetary unit: Ouguiya (Aug. 1997: 155 = $1 US). **Gross domestic product** (1995 est.): $2.8 bil. **Per capita GDP:** $1,200. **Imports** (1994): $352 mil; partners: France 23%. **Exports** (1994): $394 mil; partners: Japan 28%, Italy 15%. **International reserves less gold** (June 1997): $162.6 mil. **Gold:** 12,000 oz t. **Consumer prices** (change in 1996): 4.7%.
Transport: Railroads: Length: 437.2 mi. **Motor vehicles in use:** 8,000 passenger cars, 5,700 comm. vehicles. **Civil aviation:** 179.5 mil passenger-mi. **Chief ports:** Nouakchott, Nouad-hibou.
Communications: Television sets: 1 per 40 persons. **Radios:** 1 per 6.8 persons. **Telephones:** 1 per 246 persons.
Health: Life expectancy at birth (1997): 46.5 male; 52.6 female. **Births** (per 1,000 pop.): 47. **Deaths** (per 1,000 pop.): 15. **Natural increase:** 3.2%. **Physicians:** 1 per 11,085 persons. **Infant mortality** (per 1,000 live births 1997): 80.
Education: Literacy (1995): 38%.
Major International Organizations: UN (WTO, IMF, WHO), OAU, Arab League.
Embassy: 2129 Leroy Pl. NW 20008; 232-5700.

Mauritania was a French protectorate from 1903. It became independent Nov. 28, 1960 and annexed the south of former Spanish Sahara (now Western Sahara) in 1976. Saharan guerrillas of the Polisario Front stepped up attacks in 1977; 8,000 Moroccan troops and French bomber raids aided the government. Mauritania signed a peace treaty with the Polisario Front, 1980, resumed diplomatic relations with Algeria while breaking a defense treaty with Morocco, and renounced sovereignty over its share of Western Sahara. Opposition parties were legalized and a new constitution approved in 1991.

Mauritius
Republic of Mauritius

People: Population: 1,154,272. **Age distrib.** (%): <15: 27; 65+: 6. **Pop. density:** 1,464 per sq. mi. **Urban:** 41%. **Ethnic groups:** Indo-Mauritian 68%, Creole 27%. **Principal languages:** English (official), French, Creole, Hindi, Bhojpoori. **Chief religions:** Hindu 52%, Christian 28%, Muslim 17%.
Geography: Area: 788 sq. mi. **Location:** In the Indian O., 500 mi. E of Madagascar. **Neighbors:** Nearest is Madagascar to W. **Topography:** A volcanic island nearly surrounded by

coral reefs. A central plateau is encircled by mountain peaks. **Capital:** Port Louis (1994 est.): 144,776.
Government: Type: Republic. **Head of state:** Pres. Cassam Uteem; b Mar. 22, 1941; in office: June 30, 1992. **Head of government:** Prime Min. Navin Ramgoolam; b July 14, 1947; in office: Dec. 22, 1995. **Local divisions:** 9 districts, 3 dependencies. **Defense:** 0.4% of GDP (FY 1992-93). **Active troop strength:** 1,300 (paramilitary).
Economy: Industries: Tourism, textiles, food processing. **Chief crops:** Sugarcane, tea. **Arable land:** 54%. **Electricity prod.** (1995): 960 mil kWh. **Labor force:** 29% govt. services; 27% agric. & fishing; 22% manuf.
Finance: Monetary unit: Rupee (Aug. 1997: 21.65 = $1 US). **Gross domestic product** (1995 est.): $10.9 bil. **Per capita GDP:** $9,600. **Imports** (1994): $1.9 bil; partners: France 19%, South Africa 12%. **Exports** (1994): $1.3 bil; partners: UK 32%, France 20%, U.S. 18%. **Tourism** (1994): $356 mil. **National budget** (FY 1992-93): $567 mil. **International reserves less gold** (June 1997): $838.1 mil. **Gold:** 62,000 oz t. **Consumer prices** (change in 1996): 6.6%.
Transport: Motor vehicles in use: 54,000 passenger cars, 14,000 comm. vehicles. **Civil aviation:** 1.8 bil passenger-mi. **Chief port:** Port Louis.
Communications: Television sets: 1 per 4.5 persons. **Radios:** 1 per 2.7 persons. **Telephones:** 1 per 7.6 persons. **Daily newspaper circ.:** 68 per 1,000 pop.
Health: Life expectancy at birth (1997): 66.9 male; 74.5 female. **Births** (per 1,000 pop.): 19. **Deaths** (per 1,000 pop.): 7. **Natural increase:** 1.2%. **Hospital beds:** 1 per 351 persons. **Physicians:** 1 per 1,182 persons. **Infant mortality** (per 1,000 live births 1997): 17.
Education: Compulsory: ages 5-12. **Literacy** (1995): 83%.
Major International Organizations: UN and all of its specialized agencies, OAU, the Commonwealth.
Embassy: 4301 Connecticut Ave. NW, Suite 441, 20008; 244-1491.

Mauritius was uninhabited when settled in 1638 by the Dutch, who introduced sugarcane. France took over in 1721, bringing African slaves. Britain ruled from 1810 to Mar. 12, 1968, bringing Indian workers for the sugar plantations.

Mauritius formally severed its association with the British crown Mar. 12, 1992.

Mexico
United Mexican States
Estados Unidos Mexicanos

People: Population: 97,563,374. **Age distrib.** (%): <15: 36; 65+: 4. **Pop. density:** 129 per sq. mi. **Urban:** 74%. **Ethnic groups:** Mestizo 60%, Amerindian 30%, Caucasian 9%. **Principal languages:** Spanish (official), Amerindian languages. **Chief religions:** Roman Catholic 89%, Protestant 6%.
Geography: Area: 756,066 sq. mi. **Location:** In southern North America. **Neighbors:** U.S. on N, Guatemala and Belize on S. **Topography:** The Sierra Madre Occidental Mts. run NW-SE near the west coast; the Sierra Madre Oriental Mts. run near the Gulf of Mexico. They join S of Mexico City. Between the 2 ranges lies the dry central plateau, 5,000 to 8,000 ft. alt., rising toward the S, with temperate vegetation. Coastal lowlands are tropical. About 45% of land is arid. **Capital:** Mexico City. **Cities:** Mexico City 16,562,000; Guadalajara 3,430,000*.
Government: Type: Federal republic. **Head of state:** Pres. Ernesto Zedillo Ponce de León; b Dec. 27, 1951; in office: Dec. 1, 1994. **Local divisions:** 31 states, 1 federal district. **Defense:** 1% of GDP (1996). **Active troop strength:** 175,000.
Economy: Industries: Steel, chemicals, consumer durables, textiles, rubber, oil, tourism. **Chief crops:** Cotton, coffee, wheat, rice, beans, vegetables, corn. **Minerals:** Silver, lead, zinc, gold, oil, gas. **Crude oil reserves** (1996): 48.8 bil barrels. **Arable land:** 12%. **Livestock** (1996): cattle: 28.1 mil; pigs: 18.0 mil; goats: 10.5 mil; sheep: 6.0 mil. **Fish catch** (1995): 1,358,358 metric tons. **Electricity prod.** (1995): 145.2 bil kWh. **Labor force:** 32% services; 28% agric.; 15% commerce; 11% manuf.
Finance: Monetary unit: New Peso (Aug. 1997: 7.80 = $1 US). **Gross domestic product** (1995 est.): $721 bil. **Per capita GDP:** $7,700. **Imports** (1995): $72.5 bil; partners: U.S. 75%, Japan 5%. **Exports** (1994): $79.8 bil; partners: U.S. 84%, Canada 3%. **Tourism** (1994): $6.3 bil. **National budget** (1995 est.): $54 bil. **International reserves less gold** (June 1997): $23.78 bil. **Gold:** 231,000 oz t. **Consumer prices** (change in 1996): 34.4%.

Transport: Railroads: Length: 12,772.1 mi. Motor vehicles in use: 14.6 bil passenger cars, 3.75 mil comm. vehicles. Civil aviation: 11.9 bil passenger-mi.; 83 airports. Chief ports: Coatzacoalcos, Mazatlan, Tampico, Veracruz.

Communications: Television sets: 1 per 6.1 persons. Radios: 1 per 3.9 persons. Telephones: 1 per 10 persons. Daily newspaper circ.: 113 per 1,000 pop.

Health: Life expectancy at birth (1997): 70.4 male; 77.8 female. Births (per 1,000 pop.): 26. Deaths (per 1,000 pop.): 5. Natural increase: 2.1%. Hospital beds: 1 per 1,196 persons. Physicians: 1 per 613 persons. Infant mortality (per 1,000 live births 1997): 24.

Education: Free and compulsory: ages 6-12. Literacy (19954): 90%.

Major International Organizations: UN (IMF, WTO), OAS, OECD.

Embassy: 1911 Pennsylvania Ave. NW 20006; 728-1600.

Mexico was the site of advanced Indian civilizations. The Mayas, an agricultural people, moved up from Yucatan, built immense stone pyramids, invented a calendar. The Toltecs were overcome by the Aztecs, who founded Tenochtitlan AD 1325, now Mexico City. Hernando Cortes, Spanish conquistador, destroyed the Aztec empire, 1519-21.

After 3 centuries of Spanish rule the people rose, under Fr. Miguel Hidalgo y Costilla, 1810, Fr. Morelos y Payon, 1812, and Gen. Agustin Iturbide, who made himself emperor as Agustin I, 1821. A republic was declared in 1823.

Mexican territory extended into the present American Southwest and California until Texas revolted and established a republic in 1836; the Mexican legislature refused recognition but was unable to enforce its authority there. After numerous clashes, the U.S.-Mexican War, 1846-48, resulted in the loss by Mexico of the lands north of the Rio Grande.

French arms supported an Austrian archduke on the throne of Mexico as Maximilian I, 1864-67, but pressure from the U.S. forced France to withdraw. A dictatorial rule by Porfirio Diaz, president 1877-80, 1884-1911, led to fighting by rival forces until a new constitution, Feb. 5, 1917, provided social reform.

The Institutional Revolutionary Party (PRI) dominated politics from 1929 until the late 1990s. Radical opposition, including some guerrilla activity, was contained by strong measures.

Some gains in agriculture, industry, and social services have been achieved, but much of the work force is jobless or underemployed. The land is rich, but the rugged topography and lack of sufficient rainfall are major obstacles. Although economic prospects brightened with the discovery of vast oil reserves, inflation and a drop in world oil prices aggravated Mexico's economic problems in the 1980s.

Mexico reached agreement with the U.S. and Canada on the North American Free Trade Agreement (NAFTA) Aug. 12, 1992; it took effect Jan. 1, 1994.

Guerrillas of the Zapatista National Liberation Army (EZLN) launched an uprising, Jan. 1, 1994, in southern Mexico. A tentative peace accord was reached Mar. 2. The presidential candidate of the governing PRI, Luis Donaldo Colosio Murrieta, was assassinated at a political rally in Tijuana, Mar. 23. The new PRI candidate, Ernesto Zedillo Ponce de León, won election Aug. 21 and was inaugurated Dec. 1.

An austerity plan and pledges of U.S. aid saved Mexico's currency from collapse in early 1995. Popular Revolutionary Army guerrillas launched coordinated attacks on government targets in Aug. 1996. In elections July 6, 1997, the PRI failed to win a congressional majority for the first time since 1929.

Micronesia
Federated States of Micronesia

People: Population: 127,616. Pop. density: 470 per sq. mi. Urban: 28%. Ethnic groups: 9 ethnic Micronesian and Polynesian groups. Principal languages: English (official), Trukese, Pohnpeian. Chief religions: Roman Catholic 50%, Protestant 47%.

Geography: Area: 271 sq. mi. Location: Consists of 607 islands in the W Pacific Ocean. Capital: Palikir, on Pohnpei (1994 island pop.) 33,372.

Government: Type: Republic. Head of state: Jacob Nena; in office: May 8, 1997. Local divisions: 4 states.

Economy: Industries: Tourism, fish processing. Chief crops: Tropical fruits, vegetables, black, pepper.

Finance: Monetary unit: U.S. Dollar. Gross domestic product (1994 est.): $205 mil. Per capita GDP: $1,700. Imports (1994): $129 mil; partners: U.S. 56%, Japan 32%. Exports (1994): $79 mil; partners: Japan 80%, U.S. 9%.

Transport: 6 airports with scheduled flights.

Communications: Television sets: 1 per 15 persons. Radios: 1 per 1.5 persons. Telephones: 1 per 14 persons.

Health: Life expectancy at birth (1997): 66.2 male; 70.2 female. Births (per 1,000 pop.): 28. Deaths (per 1,000 pop.): 6. Natural increase: 2.2%. Hospital beds: 1 per 318 persons. Physicians: 1 per 2,069 persons. Infant mortality (per 1,000 live births 1997): 35.

Education: Compulsory: ages 6-14. Literacy (1991): 90%.

Major International Organizations: UN.

Embassy: 1725 N St. NW 20036; 223-4383.

The Federated States of Micronesia, formerly known as the Caroline Islands, was ruled successively by Spain, Germany, Japan, and the U.S. It was internationally recognized as an independent nation Sept. 17, 1991.

Moldova
Republic of Moldova
Republica Moldova

People: Population: 4,475,232. Age distrib. (%): <15: 26; 65+: 10. Pop. density: 343 per sq. mi. Urban: 52%. Ethnic groups: Moldovan/Romanian 65%, Ukrainian 14%, Russian 13%. Principal languages: Moldovan (official), Russian. Chief religions: Eastern Orthodox 99%.

Geography: Area: 13,012 sq. mi. Location: In E Europe. Neighbors: Romania on W; Ukraine on N, E, and S. Capital: Chisinau 765,000*.

Government: Type: Republic. Head of state: Pres. Petru Lucinschi; b Jan. 27, 1940; in office: Jan. 15, 1997. Head of government: Prime Min. Ion Clubuc; b 1943; in office: Jan. 24, 1997. Defense: 3% of GDP (1995). Active troop strength: 11,900.

Economy: Industries: Canning, wine making, tobacco. Chief crops: Grain, wine grapes. Minerals: Lignite, gypsum. Arable land: 50%. Livestock (1996): sheep: 1.3 mil; pigs: 1.0 mil. Electricity prod. (1995): 7.2 bil kWh.

Finance: Monetary unit: Leu (Aug. 1997: 4.52 = $1 US). Gross domestic product (1995 est.): $10.4 bil. Per capita GDP: $2,310. Imports (1995): $822 mil. Exports (1995): $720 mil. International reserves less gold (June 1997): $335.42 mil.

Transport: Railroads: Length: 824.7 mi. Motor vehicles in use: 169,000 passenger cars, 71,000 comm. vehicles. Civil aviation: 669.4 mil passenger-mi.; 1 airport with scheduled flights.

Communications: Television sets: 1 per 3.7 persons. Telephones: 1 per 7.7 persons. Daily newspaper circ.: 24 per 1,000 pop.

Health: Life expectancy at birth (1997): 61.0 male; 69.9 female. Births (per 1,000 pop.): 17. Deaths (per 1,000 pop.): 12. Natural increase: 0.5%. Hospital beds: 1 per 82 persons. Physicians: 1 per 250 persons. Infant mortality (per 1,000 live births 1997): 46.

Education: Compulsory: ages 7-16. Literacy (1995): 96%.

Major International Organizations: UN, CIS.

Embassy: 1511 K St. NW 20005; 783-3012.

In 1918, Romania annexed all of Bessarabia that Russia had acquired from Turkey in 1812 by the Treaty of Bucharest. In 1924, the Soviet Union established the Moldavian Autonomous Soviet Socialist Republic on the eastern bank of the Dniester. It was merged with the Romanian-speaking districts of Bessarabia in 1940 to form the Moldavian SSR.

During World War II, Romania, allied with Germany, occupied the area. It was recaptured by the USSR in 1944. Moldova declared independence Aug. 27, 1991. It became an independent state when the USSR disbanded Dec. 26, 1991.

Fighting erupted Mar. 1992 in the Dnestr (Dniester) region between Moldovan security forces and Slavic separatists—ethnic Russians and ethnic Ukrainians—who feared Moldova would merge with neighboring Romania. In a plebiscite on Mar. 6, 1994, voters in Moldova supported independence, without unification with Romania. Defying the Moldovan government, voters in the breakaway Dnestr region held legislative elections and approved a separatist constitution Dec. 24, 1995. Petru Lucinschi, a former Communist, won a presidential runoff election Dec. 1, 1996. A peace accord with Dnestr separatists was signed in Moscow May 8, 1997.

Monaco
Principality of Monaco
Principanté de Monaco

People: Population: 31,892. **Age distrib.** (%): <15: 17; 65+: 20. **Pop. density:** 42,522 per sq. mi. **Urban:** 100%. **Ethnic groups:** French 47%, Italian 16%, Monegasque 16%. **Principal languages:** French (official), English, Italian, Monegasque. **Chief religions:** Roman Catholic 95%.

Geography: Area: 1.95 sq. mi. **Location:** On the NW Mediterranean coast. **Neighbors:** France to W, N, E. **Topography:** Monaco-Ville sits atop a high promontory, the rest of the principality rises from the port up the hillside. **Capital:** Monaco.

Government: Type: Constitutional monarchy. **Head of state:** Prince Rainier III; b May 31, 1923; in office: May 9, 1949. **Head of government:** Min. of State Michel Lévêque; in office: Feb. 3, 1997. **Local divisions:** 4 quarters.

Economy: Industries: Tourism, gambling, chemicals, precision instruments, plastics.

Finance: Monetary unit: French Franc or Monégasque Franc. **Gross domestic product** (1994 est.): $788 mil. **Per capita GDP:** $25,000. **National budget** (1993 est.): $586 mil.

Transport: Railroads: Length: 1.1 mi. **Civil aviation:** 0.6 mil passenger-mi. **Chief port:** Monaco.

Communications: Television sets: 1 per 1.3 persons. **Radios:** 1 per 1.0 person. **Telephones:** 1 per 2.1 persons.

Health (1997): **Births** (per 1,000 pop.): 11. **Deaths** (per 1,000 pop.): 12. **Natural increase:** –0.1%. **Infant mortality** (per 1,000 live births): 7.

Major International Organizations: UN.

An independent principality for over 300 years, Monaco has belonged to the House of Grimaldi since 1297, except during the French Revolution. It was placed under the protectorate of Sardinia in 1815, and under that of France, 1861. The Prince of Monaco was an absolute ruler until a 1911 constitution.

Monaco's fame as a tourist resort is widespread. It is noted for its mild climate and magnificent scenery.

Mongolia
Mongol Uls

People: Population: 2,538,211. **Age distrib.** (%): <15: 38; 65+: 4. **Pop. density:** 4 per sq. mi. **Urban:** 61%. **Ethnic groups:** Mongol 90%. **Principal languages:** Khalka Mongolian (official). **Chief religions:** Traditionally Tibetan Buddhist.

Geography: Area: 604,800 sq. mi. **Location:** In E Central Asia. **Neighbors:** Russia on N, China on E, W, and S. **Topography:** Mostly a high plateau with mountains, salt lakes, and vast grasslands. Arid lands in the S are part of the Gobi Desert. **Capital:** Ulaanbaatar. **Cities** (1994): Ulaanbaatar 680,000; Darhan 85,800.

Government: Type: Republic. **Head of state:** Pres. Natsagiyn Bagabandi; in office: June 20, 1997. **Head of government:** Pres. Natsagiyn Bagatandi; b Apr. 22, 1950; in office: June 20, 1997. **Local divisions:** 18 provinces, 3 municipalities. **Defense:** 2.4% of GNP (1994). **Active troop strength:** 21,000.

Economy: Industries: Food processing, mining, construction materials. **Chief crops:** Grain, potatoes. **Minerals:** Coal, oil, tungsten, copper, molybdenum, gold, tin. **Arable land:** 1%. **Livestock** (1996): sheep: 13.7 mil; goats: 8.5 mil; cattle: 3.3 mil. **Electricity prod.** (1995): 3.2 bil kWh. **Labor force:** 40% agric.; 13% services; 12% manuf. & mining.

Finance: Monetary unit: Tugrik (Aug. 1997: 804.46 = $1 US). **Gross domestic product** (1995 est.): $4.9 bil. **Per capita GDP:** $1,970. **Imports** (1995): $473 mil; partners: Russia 52%, Japan 11%, China 10%. **Exports** (1995): $451 mil; partners: Japan 19%, Kazakhstan 15%. **International reserves less gold** (May 1997): $94.67 mil. **Gold:** 14,000 oz t. **Consumer prices** (change in 1996): 45.8%.

Transport: Railroads: Length: 1,197.3 mi. **Motor vehicles in use:** 28,000 passenger cars, 28,000 comm. vehicles. **Civil aviation:** 304.9 mil passenger-mi.

Communications: Television sets: 1 per 24 persons. **Radios:** 1 per 7.4 persons. **Telephones:** 1 per 31 persons. **Daily newspaper circ.:** 88 per 1,000 pop.

Health: Life expectancy at birth (1997): 59.1 male; 63.2 female. **Births** (per 1,000 pop.): 25. **Deaths** (per 1,000 pop.): 8. **Natural increase:** 1.6%. **Hospital beds:** 1 per 101 persons. **Physicians:** 1 per 401 persons. **Infant mortality** (per 1,000 live births 1997): 68.

Education: Compulsory: ages 6-16. **Literacy** (1991): 83%. **Major International Organizations:** UN (ILO, WHO, IMF). **Embassy:** 2833 M St. NW 20007; 333-7117.

One of the world's oldest countries, Mongolia reached the zenith of its power in the 13th century when Genghis Khan and his successors conquered all of China and extended their influence as far west as Hungary and Poland. In later centuries, the empire dissolved and Mongolia became a province of China.

With the advent of the 1911 Chinese revolution, Mongolia, with Russian backing, declared its independence. A Communist regime was established July 11, 1921.

In 1990, the Mongolian Communist Party yielded its monopoly on power. Free elections in July 1990 were won by the Communists. A new constitution took effect Feb. 12, 1992. A democratic alliance won legislative elections, June 30, 1996. A former Communist, Natsagiyn Bagabandi, won the presidential election May 18, 1997.

Morocco
Kingdom of Morocco
Al Mamlakah al Maghribiyah

People: Population: 30,391,423. **Age distrib.** (%): <15: 37; 65+: 4. **Pop. density:** 171 per sq. mi. **Urban:** 53%. **Ethnic groups:** Arab-Berber 99%. **Principal languages:** Arabic (official), Berber. **Chief religions:** Sunni Muslim 99%.

Geography: Area: 177,117 sq. mi. **Location:** On NW coast of Africa. **Neighbors:** Western Sahara on S, Algeria on E. **Topography:** Consists of 5 natural regions: mountain ranges (Riff in the N, Middle Atlas, Upper Atlas, and Anti-Atlas); rich plains in the W; alluvial plains in SW; well-cultivated plateaus in the center; a pre-Sahara arid zone extending from SE. **Capital:** Rabat. **Cities:** Casablanca 3,101,000; Rabat 1,293,000*.

Government: Type: Constitutional monarchy. **Head of state:** King Hassan II; b July 9, 1929; in office: Mar. 3, 1961. **Head of government:** Prime Min. Abdellatif Filali; b Jan. 26, 1928; in office: May 25, 1994. **Local divisions:** 36 provinces, 5 municipalities. **Defense:** 4.1% of GDP (1995). **Active troop strength:** 194,000.

Economy: Industries: Carpets, clothing, leather goods, mining, tourism. **Chief crops:** Grain, citrus fruits, grapes, olives. **Minerals:** Phosphates, iron ore, manganese, lead, zinc. **Arable land:** 18%. **Livestock** (1996): sheep: 16.0 mil; goats: 4.7 mil; cattle: 2.4 mil. **Fish catch** (1995): 845,201 metric tons. **Electricity prod.** (1995): 10.8 bil kWh. **Labor force:** 50% agric.; 26% services; 15% ind.

Finance: Monetary unit: Dirham (Aug. 1997: 9.77 = $1 US). **Gross domestic product** (1995 est.): $87.4 bil. **Per capita GDP:** $3,000. **Imports** (1994): $7.2 bil; partners: France 23%, Spain 9%, U.S. 9%. **Exports** (1994): $4 bil; partners: France 32%, Spain 9%, Japan 7%. **Tourism** (1994): $1.3 bil. **National budget** (1994): $8.9 bil. **International reserves less gold** (June 1997): $4.12 bil. **Gold:** 704,000 oz t. **Consumer prices** (change in 1996): 3.0%.

Transport: Railroads: Length: 1,184.2 mi. **Motor vehicles in use:** 957,000 passenger cars, 321,000 comm. vehicles. **Civil aviation:** 2.8 bil passenger-mi.; 12 airports. **Chief ports:** Tangier, Casablanca, Kenitra.

Communications: Television sets: 1 per 13 persons. **Radios:** 1 per 4.6 persons. **Telephones:** 1 per 23 persons. **Daily newspaper circ.:** 13 per 1,000 pop.

Health: Life expectancy at birth (1997): 68.0 male; 72.2 female. **Births** (per 1,000 pop.): 27. **Deaths** (per 1,000 pop.): 6. **Natural increase:** 2.1%. **Hospital beds:** 1 per 978 persons. **Physicians:** 1 per 2,923 persons. **Infant mortality** (per 1,000 live births 1997): 41.

Education: Compulsory: ages 7-13. **Literacy** (1995): 44%. **Major International Organizations:** UN (ILO, WTO, IMF, WHO), Arab League. **Embassy:** 1601 21st St. NW 20009; 462-7979.

Berbers were the original inhabitants, followed by Carthaginians and Romans. Arabs conquered in 683. In the 11th and 12th centuries, a Berber empire ruled all NW Africa and most of Spain from Morocco.

Part of Morocco came under Spanish rule in the 19th century; France controlled the rest in the early 20th. Tribal uprisings lasted from 1911 to 1933. The country became independent Mar. 2, 1956. Tangier, an internationalized seaport, was turned over to Morocco, 1956. Ifni, a Spanish enclave, was ceded in 1969.

Morocco annexed over 70,000 sq. mi. of phosphate-rich land Apr. 14, 1976, two-thirds of former Spanish Sahara (now Western Sahara), with the remainder annexed by Mauritania. Spain had withdrawn in February. Polisario, a guerrilla movement, proclaimed the region independent Feb. 27, and launched attacks with Algerian support. When Mauritania signed a treaty with the Polisario Front and gave up its portion of Western Sahara, Morocco occupied the area, 1980.

After years of bitter fighting, Morocco controlled the main urban areas, but the Polisario Front's guerrillas moved freely in the vast, sparsely populated deserts. The 2 sides signed a cease-fire in 1990. A UN-sponsored referendum on self-determination for Western Sahara has been repeatedly postponed. Pop. of **Western Sahara** (1997 est.) is 228,138; capital: Laayoune (El Aaiun).

Mozambique
Republic of Mozambique
República Popular de Moçambique

People: Population: 18,165,476. **Age distrib.** (%): <15: 45; 65+: 2. **Pop. density:** 57 per sq. mi. **Urban:** 35%. **Ethnic groups:** indigenous tribal groups. **Principal languages:** Portuguese (official), Makua, Malawi, Shona, Tsonga. **Chief religions:** Indigenous beliefs 50%, Christian 30%, Muslim 20%.

Geography: Area: 313,661 sq. mi. **Location:** On SE coast of Africa. **Neighbors:** Tanzania on N; Malawi, Zambia, Zimbabwe on W; South Africa, Swaziland on S. **Topography:** Coastal lowlands comprise nearly half the country with plateaus rising in steps to the mountains along the western border. **Capital:** Maputo: 2,212,000*.

Government: Type: Republic. **Head of state:** Pres. Joaquim Chissano; b Oct. 22, 1939; in office: Oct. 19, 1986. **Head of government:** Prime Min. Pascoal Mocumbi; b Apr. 10, 1941; in office: Dec. 21, 1994. **Local divisions:** 10 provinces. **Defense:** 7.3% of GDP (1993). **Active troop strength:** 11,000-30,000 est.

Economy: Industries: Chemicals, petroleum products, textiles. **Chief crops:** Cashews, cotton, sugar, corn, tea. **Minerals:** Coal, titanium. **Arable land:** 4%. **Livestock** (1996): cattle: 1.3 mil. **Fish catch** (1994): 24,170 metric tons. **Electricity prod.** (1995): 465 mil kWh. **Labor force:** 90% agric.

Finance: Monetary unit: Metical (Aug. 1997: 11,300 = $1 US). **Gross domestic product** (1995 est.): $12.2 bil. **Per capita GDP:** $700. **Imports** (1994): $1 bil; partners: South Africa 35%, UK 8%. **Exports** (1994): $150 mil; partners: Spain 22%, South Africa 15%. **National budget** (1992 est.): $607 mil. **Consumer prices** (change in 1996): 45.0%.

Transport: Railroads: Length: 1,944.4 mi. **Motor vehicles in use:** 84,000 passenger cars, 27,000 comm. vehicles. **Civil aviation:** 275.1 mil passenger-mi. **Chief ports:** Maputo, Beira, Nacala, Inhambane.

Communications: Television sets: 1 per 286 persons. **Radios:** 1 per 27 persons. **Telephones:** 1 per 291 persons.

Health: Life expectancy at birth (1997): 43.7 male; 46.0 female. **Births** (per 1,000 pop.): 44. **Deaths** (per 1,000 pop.): 18. **Natural increase:** 2.6%. **Hospital beds:** 1 per 1,231 persons. **Physicians:** 1 per 143,351 persons. **Infant mortality** (per 1,000 live births 1997): 123.

Education: Compulsory: ages 7-14. **Literacy** (1995): 40%.

Major International Organizations: UN (IMF, World Bank, WTO), OAU, the Commonwealth.

Embassy: 1990 M St. NW, Suite 570 20036; 293-7146.

The first Portuguese post on the Mozambique coast was established in 1505, on the trade route to the East. Mozambique became independent June 25, 1975, after a ten-year war against Portuguese colonial domination. The 1974 revolution in Portugal had paved the way for the orderly transfer of power to Frelimo (Front for the Liberation of Mozambique). Frelimo took over local administration Sept. 20, 1974, although opposed, in part violently, by some blacks and whites.

The new government, led by Maoist Pres. Samora Machel, provided for a gradual transition to a communist system. Economic problems included the emigration of most of the country's whites, a politically untenable economic dependence on white-ruled South Africa, and a large external debt.

In the 1980s, severe drought and civil war caused famine and heavy loss of life.

The ruling party formally abandoned Marxist-Leninism in 1989, and a new constitution, effective Nov. 30, 1990, provided for multiparty elections and a free-market economy.

On Oct. 4, 1992, a peace agreement was signed aimed at ending hostilities between the government and the rebel Mozambique National Resistance (MNR). Elections took place Oct. 27-28, 1994. Repatriation of 1.7 million Mozambican refugees officially ended June 1995.

Myanmar (*formerly* Burma)
Union of Myanmar
Pyidaungzu Myanma Naingngandaw

People: Population: 46,821,943. **Age distrib.** (%): <15: 37; 65+: 4. **Pop. density:** 179 per sq. mi. **Urban:** 26%. **Ethnic groups:** Burman (related to Tibetan) 68%, Shan 9%, Karen 7%, Rakhine 4%. **Principal languages:** Burmese (official). **Chief religions:** Buddhist 89%, Christian 4%, Muslim 4%.

Geography: Area: 261,228 sq. mi. **Location:** Between S and SE Asia, on Bay of Bengal. **Neighbors:** Bangladesh, India on W; China, Laos, Thailand on E. **Topography:** Mountains surround Myanmar on W, N, and E, and dense forests cover much of the nation. N-S rivers provide habitable valleys and communications, especially the Irrawaddy, navigable for 900 miles. The country has a tropical monsoon climate. **Capital:** Yangôn (Rangoon) 3,873,000*.

Government: Type: Military. **Head of state and government:** Gen. Than Shwe; b 1933; in office: Apr. 24, 1992. **Local divisions:** 7 states and 7 divisions. **Defense:** 3.1% of GDP (1992). **Active troop strength:** 321,000 est.

Economy: Industries: Mining, textiles, footwear, wood products, petroleum refining. **Chief crops:** Rice, sugarcane, corn, pulses. **Minerals:** Oil, lead, copper, tin, tungsten, precious stones. **Other resources:** Rubber, teakwood. **Arable land:** 15%. **Livestock** (1996): cattle: 9.9 mil; pigs: 2.9 mil; buffalo: 2.2 mil; goats: 1.2 mil. **Fish catch** (1995): 832,469 metric tons. **Electricity prod.** (1993): 3.6 bil kWh. **Labor force:** 65% agric.; 14% ind.; 10% trade.

Finance: Monetary unit: Kyat (Aug. 1997: 197 = $1 US). **Gross domestic product** (1995 est.): $47 bil. **Per capita GDP:** $1,000. **Imports** (FY 1994-95): $1.5 bil; partners: Japan 26%, China 16%. **Exports** (FY 1994-95): $879 mil; partners: Thailand 17%, Singapore 14%. **Tourism** (1994): $24 mil. **National budget** (1995 est.): $10 bil. **International reserves less gold** (May 1997): $177.3 mil. **Gold:** 231,000 oz t. **Consumer prices** (change in 1996): 16.3%.

Transport: Railroads: Length: 2,216.3 mi. **Motor vehicles in use:** 44,000 passenger cars, 42,000 comm. vehicles. **Civil aviation:** 86.9 mil passenger-mi.; 19 airports with scheduled flights. **Chief ports:** Yangôn, Bassein, Moulmein.

Communications: Television sets: 1 per 200 persons. **Radios:** 1 per 12 persons. **Telephones:** 1 per 317 persons. **Daily newspaper circ.:** 23 per 1,000 pop.

Health: Life expectancy at birth (1997): 54.9 male; 58.5 female. **Births** (per 1,000 pop.): 30. **Deaths** (per 1,000 pop.): 11. **Natural increase:** 1.8%. **Hospital beds:** 1 per 1,586 persons. **Physicians:** 1 per 3,554 persons. **Infant mortality** (per 1,000 live births 1997): 79.

Education: Free and compulsory: ages 5-10. **Literacy** (1995): 83%.

Major International Organizations: UN (World Bank, IMF, WTO), ASEAN.

Embassy: 2300 S St. NW 20008; 332-9044.

The Burmese arrived from Tibet before the 9th century, displacing earlier cultures, and a Buddhist monarchy was established by the 11th. Burma was conquered by the Mongol dynasty of China in 1272, then ruled by Shans as a Chinese tributary, until the 16th century.

Britain subjugated Burma in 3 wars, 1824-84, and ruled the country as part of India until 1937, when it became self-governing. Independence outside the Commonwealth was achieved Jan. 4, 1948.

Gen. Ne Win dominated politics from 1962 to 1988, first as military ruler then as constitutional president. His regime drove Indians from the civil service and Chinese from commerce. Socialization of the economy was advanced, isolation from foreign countries enforced. In 1987 Burma, once the richest nation in SE Asia, was granted less-developed status by the UN.

Ne Win resigned July 1988, following waves of antigovernment riots. Rioting and street violence continued, and in Sept. the military seized power, under Gen. Saw Maung. In 1989 the country's name was changed to Myanmar.

The first free multiparty elections in 30 years took place May 27, 1990, with the main opposition party winning a decisive victory, but the military refused to hand over power. A key opposition leader, Aung San Suu Kyi, awarded the Nobel Peace Prize in 1991, was held under house arrest from July 20, 1989, to July 10, 1995; after her release, the military government continued to harass and imprison her supporters. New U.S. economic sanctions took effect on May 21, 1997. Myanmar was admitted to ASEAN on July 23.

Namibia
Republic of Namibia

People: Population: 1,727,183. **Age distrib.** (%): <15: 43; 65+: 4. **Pop density:** 5 per sq. mi. **Urban:** 37%. **Ethnic groups:** Ovambo 50%, Kavangos 9%, Herero 7%, Damara 7%, Caucasian 7%. **Principal languages:** Afrikaans, English (official), German, indigenous languages. **Chief religions:** Lutheran 50%, other Christian 30%.

Geography: Area: 318,580 sq. mi. **Location:** In S Africa on the coast of the Atlantic Ocean. **Neighbors:** Angola on N, Botswana on E, South Africa on S. **Capital:** Windhoek (1992 est.): 161,000.

Government: Type: Republic. **Head of state:** Pres. Sam Nujoma; b May 12, 1929; in office: Mar. 21, 1990. **Head of government:** Prime Min. Hage Geingob; b Aug. 3, 1941; in office: Mar. 21, 1990. **Local divisions:** 13 regions. **Defense:** 2% of GDP (FY 1995-96). **Active troop strength:** 8,100 est.

Economy: Economy: Mining accounts for almost 25% of GDP. **Minerals:** Diamonds, copper, gold, tin, lead, uranium. **Livestock** (1996): sheep: 2.1 mil; cattle: 2.1 mil; goats: 1.7 mil. **Fish catch** (1995): 289,980 metric tons. **Electricity prod.** (1991): 1.3 bil kWh. **Labor Force:** 60% agric., 19% ind. & commerce.

Finance: Monetary unit: Dollar (Aug. 1997: 4.69 = $1 US). **Gross domestic product** (1994): $5.8 bil. **Per capital GDP:** $3,600. **Imports** (1993): $1.2 bil. **Exports** (1993): $1.3 bil. **Tourism** (1994): $184 mil. **National budget** (FY 1993-94): $1.05 bil. **International reserves less gold** (Apr. 1997): $161.71 mil. **Consumer prices** (change in 1996): 8.0%.

Transport: Railroads: Length: 1,479.2 mi. **Motor vehicles in use:** 61,000 passenger cars, 65,000 comm. vehicles. **Civil aviation:** 466.4 mil passenger-mi. **Chief ports:** Luderitz, Walvis Bay.

Communications: Television sets: 1 per 43 persons. **Radios:** 1 per 7.2 persons. **Telephones:** 1 per 20 persons.

Health: Life expectancy at birth (1997): 63.2 male; 66.6 female. **Births** (per 1,000 pop.): 37. **Deaths** (per 1,000 pop.): 8. **Natural increase:** 2.9%. **Hospital beds:** 1 per 216 persons. **Physicians:** 1 per 4,594 persons. **Infant mortality** (per 1,000 live births 1997): 46.

Education: Compulsory: ages 6-16. **Literacy** (1993): 76%.

Major International Organizations: UN (WTO, WHO, IMF), OAU, the Commonwealth.

Embassy: 1605 New Hampshire Ave. NW 20009; 986-0540.

Namibia was declared a protectorate by Germany in 1890 and officially called South-West Africa. South Africa seized the territory from Germany in 1915 during World War I; the League of Nations gave South Africa a mandate over the territory in 1920. In 1966, the Marxist South-West Africa People's Organization (SWAPO) launched a guerrilla war for independence.

In 1968 the UN General Assembly gave the area the name Namibia.

After many years of guerrilla warfare and failed diplomatic efforts, South Africa, Angola, and Cuba signed a U.S.-mediated agreement Dec. 22, 1988, to end South African administration of Namibia and provide for a cease-fire and transition to independence, in accordance with a 1978 UN plan. A separate accord between Cuba and Angola provided for a phased withdrawal of Cuban troops from Namibia. SWAPO later endorsed the plan. Elections were held for a constituent assembly, and a constitution providing for multiparty government was adopted Feb. 9, 1990. Namibia became an independent nation Mar. 21, 1990.

Walvis Bay, the principal deepwater port, had been turned over to South African administration in 1922. It remained in South African hands after independence, but South Africa turned control of the port back to Namibia, as of Mar. 1, 1994.

Nauru
Republic of Nauru

People: Population: 10,390. **Pop. density:** 1,267 per sq. mi. **Urban:** 100%. **Ethnic groups:** Nauruan 58%, other Pacific Islander 26%, Chinese 8%, European 8%. **Principal languages:** Nauruan (official), English. **Chief religions:** Predominantly Christian.

Geography: Area: 21 sq. mi. **Location:** In W Pacific O. just S of the Equator. **Neighbors:** Nearest is Kiribati to E. **Topography:** Mostly a plateau bearing high-grade phosphate deposits, surrounded by a sandy shore and coral reef in concentric rings. **Capital:** Govt. offices in district of Yaren.

Government: Type: Republic. **Head of state:** Pres. Kinza Clodumar; In office: Feb. 12, 1997. **Local divisions:** 14 districts.

Economy: Economy: Phosphate mining. **Electricity prod.** (1995): 30 mil kWh.

Finance: Monetary unit: Australian Dollar. **Gross domestic product** (1993): $100 mil. **GDP per capita:** $10,000.

Transport: Railroads: Length: 2.4 mi. **Civil aviation:** 127.9 mil passenger-mi.

Communications: Radios: 1 per 1.7 persons.

Health (1997): **Births** (per 1,000 pop.): 18. **Deaths** (per 1,000 pop.): 5. **Natural increase:** 1.3%. **Infant mortality** (per 1,000 live births): 41.

Education: Free and compulsory: ages 6-16. **Literacy** (1989): 99%.

The island was discovered in 1798 by the British but was formally annexed to the German Empire in 1886. After World War I, Nauru became a League of Nations mandate administered by Australia. During World War II the Japanese occupied the island and shipped 1,200 Nauruans to the fortress island of Truk as slave laborers.

In 1947 Nauru was made a UN trust territory, administered by Australia. It became an independent republic Jan. 31, 1968.

Phosphate exports have provided Nauru with per capita revenues that are among the highest in the Third World. Phosphate reserves, however, are expected to be depleted by 2000, and environmental damage from strip-mining has been severe.

Nepal
Kingdom of Nepal
Nepal Adhirajya

People: Population: 22,641,061. **Age distrib.** (%): <15: 42; 65+: 3. **Pop. density:** 398 per sq. mi. **Urban:** 11%. **Ethnic groups:** The many tribes are descendants of Indian, Tibetan, and Central Asian migrants. **Principal languages:** Nepali (official), numerous dialects. **Chief religions:** Hindu (official) 90%, Buddhist 5%, Muslim 3%.

Geography: Area: 56,827 sq. mi. **Location:** Astride the Himalaya Mts. **Neighbors:** China on N, India on S. **Topography:** The Himalayas stretch across the N, the hill country with its fertile valleys extends across the center, while the S border region is part of the flat, subtropical Ganges Plain. **Capital:** Kathmandu. **Cities** (1993 met. est.): Kathmandu 535,000; Lalitpur 190,000; Biratnagar 132,000.

Government: Type: Constitutional monarchy. **Head of state:** King Birendra Bir Bikram Shah Dev; b Dec. 28, 1945; in office: Jan. 31, 1972. **Head of government:** Prime Min. Surya Bahadur Thapa; in office: Oct. 6, 1997. **Local divisions:** 14 zones. **Defense:** 1.2% of GDP (FY 1992-93). **Active troop strength:** 43,000-50,000.

Economy: Industries: Sugar and jute mills, tourism. **Chief crops:** Jute, rice, grain. **Minerals:** Quartz. **Other resources:** Forests, hydroelectric power. **Arable land:** 17%. **Livestock** (1996): cattle: 6.8 mil; goats: 5.6 mil; buffalo: 3.3 mil. **Electricity prod.** (1995): 920 mil kWh. **Labor force:** 93% agric.

Finance: Monetary unit: Rupee (Aug. 1997: 57.25 = $1 US). **Gross domestic product** (1995 est.): $25.2 bil. **Per capita GDP:** $1,200. **Imports** (1995 est.): $1.4 bil; partners: India 41%, Singapore 32%, Japan 16%. **Exports** (1995 est.): $430 mil; partners: Germany 49%, U.S. 26%. **Tourism** (1994): $172 mil. **National budget** (FY 1994-95): $1.05 bil. **International reserves less gold** (Mar. 1997): $614.6 mil. **Gold:** 153,000 oz t. **Consumer prices** (change in 1996): 9.2%.

Transport: Railroads: Length: 62.7 mi. **Civil aviation:** 504.3 mil passenger-mi.; 24 airports with scheduled flights.

Communications: Television sets: 1 per 213 persons. **Radios:** 1 per 29 persons. **Telephones:** 1 per 276 persons.

Health: Life expectancy at birth (1997): 53.8 male; 54.5 female. **Births** (per 1,000 pop.): 37. **Deaths** (per 1,000 pop.): 12. **Natural increase:** 2.4%. **Hospital beds:** 1 per 3,898 persons. **Physicians:** 1 per 12,623 persons. **Infant mortality** (per 1,000 live births 1997): 77.

Education: Free and compulsory: ages 6-11. **Literacy** (1995): 28%.

Major International Organizations: UN (IMF).
Embassy: 2131 Leroy Pl. NW 20008; 667-4550.

Nepal was originally a group of petty principalities, the inhabitants of one of which, the Gurkhas, became dominant about 1769. In 1951 King Tribhubana Bir Bikram, member of the Shah family, ended the system of rule by hereditary premiers of the Ranas family, who had kept the kings virtual prisoners, and established a cabinet system of government.

Virtually closed to the outside world for centuries, Nepal is now linked to India and Pakistan by roads and air service and to Tibet by road. Polygamy, child marriage, and the caste system were officially abolished in 1963.

The government announced the legalization of political parties in 1990. Elections on Nov. 15, 1994, led to the installation of Nepal's first Communist government, which held power until a no-confidence vote Sept. 10, 1995.

Netherlands
Kingdom of the Netherlands
Koninkrijk der Nederlanden

People: Population: 15,653,091. **Age distrib.** (%): <15: 18; 65+: 13. **Pop. density:** 976 per sq. mi. **Urban:** 89%. **Ethnic groups:** Dutch 96%. **Principal language:** Dutch (official). **Chief religions:** Roman Catholic 34%, Protestant 25%.

Geography: Area: 16,033 sq. mi. **Location:** In NW Europe on North Sea. **Neighbors:** Germany on E, Belgium on S. **Topography:** The land is flat, an average alt. of 37 ft. above sea level, with much land below sea level reclaimed and protected by some 1,500 miles of dikes. Since 1920 the government has been draining the IJsselmeer, formerly the Zuider Zee. **Capital:** Amsterdam. **Cities** (1995 est.): Amsterdam 722,245; Rotterdam 599,414; The Hague 442,105.

Government: Type: Parliamentary democracy under a constitutional monarch. **Head of state:** Queen Beatrix; b Jan. 31, 1938; in office: Apr. 30, 1980. **Head of government:** Prime Min. Wim Kok; b Sept. 29, 1938; in office: Aug. 22, 1994. **Seat of govt.:** The Hague. **Local divisions:** 12 provinces. **Defense:** 2.1% of GDP (1995). **Active troop strength:** 63,100.

Economy: Industries: Metals, machinery, chemicals, oil refinery, diamond cutting, microelectronics, tourism. **Chief crops:** Grains, potatoes, sugar beets, vegetables, fruits, flowers. **Minerals:** Natural gas, oil. **Crude oil reserves** (1996): 88 mil bbls. **Arable land:** 26%. **Livestock** (1996): pigs: 14.0 mil; cattle: 4.6 mil; sheep: 2.0 mil. **Fish catch** (1995): 521,377 metric tons. **Electricity prod.** (1995): 76.2 bil kWh. **Labor force:** 73% services; 23% manuf. & constr.; 4% agric.

Finance: Monetary unit: Guilder (Aug. 1997: 2.04 = $1 US). **Gross domestic product** (1995 est.): $301.9 bil. **Per capita GDP:** $19,500. **Imports** (1995): $133 bil; partners: Germany 21%, Belgium-Lux. 11%, UK 9%, U.S. 9%. **Exports** (1995): $146 bil; partners: Germany 28%, Belgium-Lux. 13%, UK 9%. **Tourism** (1994): $5.6 bil. **National budget** (1992): $122.1 bil. **International reserves less gold** (June 1997): $27.09 bil. **Gold:** 27.07 mil oz t. **Consumer prices** (change in 1996): 2.1%.

Transport: Railroads: Length: 1,795.3 mi. **Motor vehicles in use:** 5.6 mil passenger cars, 657,000 comm. vehicles. **Civil aviation:** 26.4 bil passenger-mi.; 6 airports. **Chief ports:** Rotterdam, Amsterdam, IJmuiden.

Communications: Television sets: 1 per 2.0 persons. **Radios:** 1 per 1.1 persons. **Telephones:** 1 per 1.9 persons. **Daily newspaper circ.:** 334 per 1,000 pop.

Health: Life expectancy at birth (1997): 75.1 male; 80.8 female. **Births** (per 1,000 pop.): 12. **Deaths** (per 1,000 pop.): 9. **Natural increase:** 0.3%. **Hospital beds:** 1 per 178 persons. **Physicians:** 1 per 391 persons. **Infant mortality** (per 1,000 live births 1997): 5.

Education: Compulsory: ages 5-18. **Literacy** (1993): 100%.
Major International Organizations: UN and all of its specialized agencies, NATO, EU, OECD.
Embassy: 4200 Wisconsin Ave. NW 20016; 244-5300.

Julius Caesar conquered the region in 55 BC, when it was inhabited by Celtic and Germanic tribes.

After the empire of Charlemagne fell apart, the Netherlands (Holland, Belgium, Flanders) split among counts, dukes, and bishops, passed to Burgundy and thence to Charles V of Spain. His son, Philip II, tried to check the Dutch drive toward political freedom and Protestantism (1568-1573). William the Silent, prince of Orange, led a confederation of the northern provinces, called Estates, in the Union of Utrecht, 1579. The Estates retained individual sovereignty, but were represented jointly in the States-General, a body that had control of foreign affairs and defense. In 1581 they repudiated allegiance to Spain. The rise of the Dutch republic to naval, economic, and artistic eminence came in the 17th century.

The United Dutch Republic ended 1795 when the French formed the Batavian Republic. Napoleon made his brother Louis king of Holland, 1806; Louis abdicated 1810 when Napoleon annexed Holland. In 1813 the French were expelled. In 1815 the Congress of Vienna formed a kingdom of the Netherlands, including Belgium, under William I. In 1830, the Belgians seceded and formed a separate kingdom.

The constitution, promulgated 1814, and subsequently revised, provides for a hereditary constitutional monarchy.

The Netherlands maintained its neutrality in World War I, but was invaded and brutally occupied by Germany, 1940-45.

In 1949, after several years of fighting, the Netherlands granted independence to Indonesia. In 1963, West New Guinea (now Irian Jaya) was turned over to Indonesia. Immigration from former Dutch colonies has been substantial.

Although the Netherlands is heavily industrialized, its small farms export large quantities of pork and dairy foods. Rotterdam, located along the principal mouth of the Rhine, is one of the world's leading cargo ports. Canals, extendng over 3,400 miles, are important in transportation.

Netherlands Dependencies

The **Netherlands Antilles,** constitutionally on a level of equality with the Netherlands homeland within the kingdom, consist of 2 groups of islands in the West Indies. **Curaçao** and **Bonaire** are near the coast of Venezuela; **St. Eustatius, Saba,** and the southern part of **St. Maarten** are SE of Puerto Rico. The northern two-thirds of St. Maarten belongs to French Guadeloupe; the French call the island St. Martin. Total area of the 2 groups is 309 sq. mi., including Bonaire 111, Curaçao 171, St. Eustatius 8, Saba 5, St. Maarten (Dutch part) 13. St. Maarten suffered extensive damage from Hurricane Luis, Sept. 1995. Total pop. of the Netherlands Antilles (1997 est.) was 211,093. Willemstad, on Curaçao, is the capital. The principal industry is the refining of crude oil from Venezuela. Tourism is also an important industry, as is shipbuilding.

Aruba, about 26 mi. W of Curaçao, was separated from the Netherlands Antilles on Jan. 1, 1986; it is an autonomous member of the Netherlands, the same status as the Netherland Antilles. Area 75 sq. mi.; pop. (1997 est.) 68,031; capital Oranjestad. Chief industries are oil refining and tourism.

New Zealand

People: Population: 3,587,275. **Age distrib.** (%): <15: 23; 65+: 12. **Pop. density:** 34 per sq. mi. **Urban:** 86%. **Ethnic groups:** European (mostly British) 88%, Maori 9%. **Principal languages:** English (official), Maori. **Chief religions:** Anglican 24%, Presbyterian 18%, Roman Catholic 15%.

Geography: Area: 104,454 sq. mi. **Location:** In SW Pacific O. **Neighbors:** Nearest are Australia on W, Fiji and Tonga on N. **Topography:** Each of the 2 main islands (North and South Isls.) is mainly hilly and mountainous. The east coasts consist of fertile plains, especially the broad Canterbury Plains on South Isl. A volcanic plateau is in center of North Isl. South Isl. has glaciers and 15 peaks over 10,000 ft. **Capital:** Wellington. **Cities** (1996): Auckland 353,670; Christchurch 313,969; Wellington 158,275.

Government: Type: Parliamentary democracy. **Head of state:** Queen Elizabeth II, represented by Gov.-Gen. Dame Catherine Tizard; b Apr. 4, 1931; in office: Nov. 20, 1990. **Head of government:** Prime Min. Jim Bolger; b May 31, 1935; in office: Oct. 27, 1990. **Local divisions:** 93 counties, 12 towns and districts. **Defense:** 1% of GNP (FY 1993-94). **Active troop strength:** 9,870.

Economy: Industries: Food processing, textiles, machinery, fish, forest prods. **Chief crops:** Grains, potatoes, fruits. **Minerals:** Gold, gas, iron, coal. **Crude oil reserves** (1996): 135 mil bbls. **Other resources:** Wool, timber. **Arable land:** 2%. **Livestock** (1996): sheep: 48.8 mil; cattle: 8.8 mil. **Fish catch** (1995): 612,243 metric tons. **Electricity prod.** (1995): 30.7 bil kWh. **Labor force:** 65% services, 25% ind.; 10% agric.

Finance: Monetary unit: Dollar (Aug. 1997: 1.54 = $1 UO). **Gross domestic product** (1995 est.): $60.8 bil. **Per capita GDP:** $18,300. **Imports** (1995): $13.6 bil; partners: Australia 21%, U.S. 18%, Japan 16%. **Exports** (1995): $13.4 bil; partners: Australia 20%, Japan 15%; U.S. 12%. **Tourism** (1994): $1.4 bil. **National budget** (FY 1995-96): $20.3 bil. **Interna-**

tional reserves less gold (May 1997): $4.60 bil. Consumer prices (change in 1996): 2.3%.

Transport: Railroads: Length: 2,467.2 mi. Motor vehicles in use: 1.7 mil passenger cars; 353,000 comm. vehicles. Civil aviation: 10.5 bil passenger-mi.; 36 airports. Chief ports: Auckland, Christchurch, Wellington, Dunedin, Tauranga.

Communications: Television sets: 1 per 2.0 persons. Radios: 1 per 1.0 person. Telephones: 1 per 2.1 persons. Daily newspaper circ.: 297 per 1,000 pop.

Health: Life expectancy at birth (1997): 74.2 male; 80.6 female. Births (per 1,000 pop.): 15. Deaths (per 1,000 pop.): 8. Natural increase: 0.8%. Hospital beds: 1 per 146 persons. Physicians: 1 per 301 persons. Infant mortality (per 1,000 live births 1997): 7.

Education: Free and compulsory: ages 6-16. Literacy (1997): 100%.

Major International Organizations: UN (WTO, World Bank, IMF), the Commonwealth, OECD.

Embassy: 37 Observatory Cir. NW 20008; 328-4800.

The Maoris, a Polynesian group from the eastern Pacific, reached New Zealand before and during the 14th century. The first European to sight New Zealand was Dutch navigator Abel Janszoon Tasman, but Maoris refused to allow him to land. British Capt. James Cook explored the coasts, 1769-1770.

British sovereignty was proclaimed in 1840, with organized settlement beginning in the same year. Representative institutions were granted in 1853. Maori Wars ended in 1870 with British victory. The colony became a dominion in 1907, and is an independent member of the Commonwealth.

A progressive tradition in politics dates back to the 19th century, when New Zealand was internationally known for social experimentation. Private ownership is basic to the economy, but state ownership or regulation affects many industries. In recent years, the Labor and National parties have had alternating periods in power. The National Party, led by Jim Bolger, won general elections in 1990 and 1993. After inconclusive elections, Oct. 12, 1996, Bolger remained as prime minister, heading a National/New Zealand First party coalition.

The native Maoris number about 340,000. Six of 120 members of the House of Representatives are elected directly by the Maori people.

New Zealand comprises North Island, 44,702 sq. mi.; South Island, 58,384 sq. mi.; Stewart Island, 674 sq. mi.; Chatham Islands, 372 sq. mi.; and several groups of smaller islands.

In 1965, the Cook Islands (pop., 1997 est., 19,776; area 93 sq. mi.), located halfway between New Zealand and Hawaii, became self-governing although New Zealand retains responsibility for defense and foreign affairs. Niue attained the same status in 1974; it lies 400 mi. to W (pop., 1995 est., 1,800; area 100 sq. mi.). Tokelau (pop., 1995 est., 1,500; area 4 sq. mi.) comprises 3 atolls 300 mi. N of Samoa.

Ross Dependency, administered by New Zealand since 1923, comprises 160,000 sq. mi. of Antarctic territory.

Nicaragua

Republic of Nicaragua

República de Nicaragua

People: Population: 4,386,399. Age distrib. (%): <15: 44; 65+: 3. Pop. density: 86 per sq. mi. Urban: 63%. Ethnic groups: Mestizo 69%, white 17%, black 9%, Indian 5%. Principal languages: Spanish (official). Chief religions: Roman Catholic 95%.

Geography: Area: 50,893 sq. mi. Location: In Central America. Neighbors: Honduras on N, Costa Rica on S. Topography: Both Caribbean and Pacific coasts are over 200 mi. long. The Cordillera Mts., with many volcanic peaks, run NW-SE through the middle of the country. Between this and a volcanic range to the E lie Lakes Managua and Nicaragua. Capital: Managua (1995 est.) 1,124,000*.

Government: Type: Republic. Head of state and government: Pres. Arnoldo Alemán Lacayo; b Jan. 23, 1946; in office Jan. 10, 1997. Local divisions: 15 departments, 2 autonomous regions. Defense: 1.7% of GDP (1994). Active troop strength: 17,000 est.

Economy: Industries: Oil refining, food processing, chemicals, textiles. Chief crops: Bananas, cotton, fruit, coffee, sugar, corn, rice. Minerals: Gold, silver, copper, tungsten. Other resources: Forests, seafood. Arable land: 9%. Livestock (1996): cattle: 1.65 mil; pigs: 400,000.

Electricity prod. (1995): 1.8 bil kWh. Labor force: 44% agric.; 43% services; 13% ind.

Finance: Monetary unit: Gold Cordoba (Aug. 1997: 9.71 = $1 US). Gross domestic product (1995 est.): $7.1 bil. Per capita GDP: $1,700. Imports (1995 est.): $870 mil; partners: U.S. 25%, Venezuela 12%. Exports (1995 est.): $526 mil; partners: U.S. 43%, Germany 13%. National budget (1996 est.): $551 mil. International reserves less gold (May 1997): $336.63 mil. Consumer prices (change in 1996): 11.6%.

Transport: Motor vehicles in use: 72,000 passenger cars, 76,000 comm. vehicles. Civil aviation: 44.7 mil passenger-mi.; 10 airports with scheduled flights. Chief ports: Corinto, Puerto Sandino, San Juan del Sur.

Communications: Television sets: 1 per 15 persons. Radios: 1 per 3.8 persons. Telephones: 1 per 43 persons. Daily newspaper circ.: 30 per 1,000 pop.

Health: Life expectancy at birth (1997): 63.8 male; 68.6 female. Births (per 1,000 pop.): 33. Deaths (per 1,000 pop.): 6. Natural increase: 2.7%. Hospital beds: 1 per 914 persons. Physicians: 1 per 1,566 persons. Infant mortality (per 1,000 live births 1997): 44.

Education: Free and compulsory: ages 7-13. Literacy (1995): 66%.

Major International Organizations: UN and most of its specialized agencies, OAS.

Embassy: 1627 New Hampshire Ave. NW 20009; 939-6570.

Nicaragua, inhabited by various Indian tribes, was conquered by Spain in 1552. After gaining independence from Spain, 1821, Nicaragua was united for a short period with Mexico, then with the United Provinces of Central America, finally becoming an independent republic, 1838.

U.S. Marines occupied the country at times in the early 20th century, the last time from 1926 to 1933.

Gen. Anastasio Somoza Debayle was elected president 1967. He resigned 1972, but was elected president again in 1974. Martial law was imposed in Dec. 1974, after officials were kidnapped by the Marxist Sandinista guerrillas. Violent opposition spread to nearly all classes in 1978; nationwide strikes called against the government touched off a state of civil war. Months of simmering civil war ended when Somoza fled, July 19, 1979; he was assassinated in Paraguay in 1980.

Relations with the U.S. were strained as a result of Nicaragua's aid to leftist guerrillas in El Salvador and U.S. backing of anti-Sandinista contra guerrilla groups.

In 1983 the contras launched a major offensive; the Sandinistas imposed rule by decree. In 1985 the U.S. House rejected Pres. Reagan's request for military aid to the contras. The subsequent diversion of funds to the contras from the proceeds of a secret arms sale to Iran caused a major scandal in the U.S.

In a stunning upset, Violeta Barrios de Chamorro defeated Sandinista leader Daniel Ortega Saavedra in national elections, Feb. 25, 1990. Arnoldo Alemán Lacayo, a conservative former mayor of Managua, defeated Ortega in the presidential election of Oct. 20, 1996.

Niger

Republic of Niger

République du Niger

People: Population: 9,388,859. Age distrib. (%): <15: 48; 65+: 2. Pop. density: 18 per sq. mi. Urban: 19%. Ethnic groups: Hausa 56%, Djerma 22%, Fula 9%, Tuareg 8%. Principal languages: French (official), Hausa, Djerma. Religion: Sunni Muslim 80%.

Geography: Area: 496,900 sq. mi. Location: In the interior of N Africa. Neighbors: Libya, Algeria on N; Mali, Burkina Faso on W; Benin, Nigeria on S; Chad on E. Topography: Mostly arid desert and mountains. A narrow savanna in the S and the Niger R. basin in the SW contain most of the population. Capital: Niamey (1988): 391,876.

Government: Type: Republic. Head of state: Pres. Ibrahim Bare Mainassara; b 1949; in office: Jan. 27, 1996. Head of government: Prime Min. Ahmadou Boubacar Cissé; in office: Dec. 21, 1996. Local divisions: 7 departments, 1 capital district. Defense: 1.3% of GDP (FY 1992-93). Active troop strength: 5,300.

Economy: Chief crops: Peanuts, cowpeas, cotton. Minerals: Uranium, coal, iron. Arable land: 3%. Livestock (1996): goats: 5.9 mil; sheep: 3.8 mil; cattle: 2.0 mil. Electricity prod. (1995): 170 mil kWh. Labor force: 90% agric.

Finance: Monetary unit: CFA Franc (Aug. 1997: 610 = $1 US). **Gross domestic product** (1995 est.): $5.5 bil. **Per capita GDP:** $600. **Imports** (1994 est.): $234 mil; partners: France 23%. **Exports** (1994 est.): $232 mil; partners: France 77%, Nigeria 8%. **National budget** (1993): $400 mil. **International reserves less gold** (Mar. 1997): $91.1 mil. **Gold:** 11,000 oz t. **Consumer prices** (change in 1996): 5.3%.

Transport: Motor vehicles in use: 16,000 passenger cars, 18,000 comm. vehicles. **Civil aviation:** 133.5 mil passenger-mi.; 6 airports with scheduled flights.

Communications: Television sets: 1 per 204 persons. **Radios:** 1 per 16 persons. **Telephones:** 1 per 677 persons.

Health: Life expectancy at birth (1997): 41.4 male; 40.7 female. **Births** (per 1,000 pop.): 54. **Deaths** (per 1,000 pop.): 24. **Natural increase:** 3.0%. **Physicians:** 1 per 54,444 persons. **Infant mortality** (per 1,000 live births 1997): 116.

Education: Free and compulsory: ages 7-15. **Literacy** (1995): 14%.

Major International Organizations: UN (IMF, WHO, FAO), OAU.

Embassy: 2204 R St. NW 20008; 483-4224.

Niger was part of ancient and medieval African empires. European explorers reached the area in the late 18th century. The French colony of Niger was established 1900-22, after the defeat of Tuareg fighters, who had invaded the area from the N a century before. The country became independent Aug. 3, 1960. The next year it signed a bilateral agreement with France.

In 1993, Niger held its first free and open elections since independence; an opposition leader, Mahamane Ousmane, won the presidency. A peace accord Apr. 24, 1995, ended a Tuareg rebellion that began in 1990. A coup, Jan. 27, 1996, followed by a disputed presidential election in July, left the military in control of Niger.

Nigeria
Federal Republic of Nigeria

People: Population: 107,129,469. **Age distrib.** (%): <15: 45; 65+: 3. **Pop. density:** 300 per sq. mi. **Urban:** 40%. **Ethnic groups:** Hausa 21%, Yoruba 21%, Ibo 18%, Fulani 11%. **Principal languages:** English (official), Hausa, Yoruba, Ibo. **Chief religions:** Muslim (in N) 50%, Christian (in S) 40%.

Geography: Area: 356,669 sq. mi. **Location:** On the S coast of W Africa. **Neighbors:** Benin on W, Niger on N, Chad and Cameroon on E. **Topography:** 4 E-W regions divide Nigeria: a coastal mangrove swamp 10-60 mi. wide, a tropical rain forest 50-100 mi. wide, a plateau of savanna and open woodland, and semidesert in the N. **Capital:** Abuja. **Cities:** Lagos 10,287,000; Ibadan 1,484,000*.

Government: Type: In transition. **Head of state and government:** Pres. Gen. Sani Abacha; b 1943; in office: Nov. 17, 1993. **Local divisions:** 30 states, 1 federal capital territory. **Defense:** 1% of GDP (1992). **Active troop strength:** 77,100.

Economy: Industries: Crude oil (98% of exports), mining, food processing, textiles. **Chief crops:** Cocoa (main export crop), palm products, corn, rice, yams, cassava. **Minerals:** Oil, gas, coal, iron, limestone, columbite, tin. **Crude oil reserves** (1996): 15.5 bil bbls. **Other resources:** Timber, rubber, hides. **Arable land:** 31%. **Livestock** (1996): goats: 24.5 mil; cattle: 17.8 mil; sheep: 14.0 mil. **Fish catch** (1995): 388,101 metric tons. **Electricity prod.** (1995): 15.5 bil kWh. **Labor force:** 54% agric.; 19% ind., commerce, serv.; 15% govt.

Finance: Monetary unit: Naira (Aug. 1997: 85.20 = $1 US). **Gross domestic product** (1995 est.): $136 bil. **Per capita GDP:** $1,300. **Imports** (1993): $7.5 bil; partners: EU 50%, U.S. 13%. **Exports** (1993): $9.9 bil; partners: U.S. 52%, EU 34%. **Tourism** (1994): $34 mil. **National budget** (1994 est.): $6.4 bil. **International reserves less gold** (Dec. 1996): $7.97 bil. **Gold:** 687,000 oz t. **Consumer prices** (change in 1996): 29.3%.

Transport: Railroads: Length: 2,208.9 mi. **Motor vehicles in use:** 590,000 passenger cars, 364,000 comm. vehicles. **Civil aviation:** 611.7 mil passenger-mi.; 12 airports. **Chief ports:** Port Harcourt, Lagos, Warri, Calabar.

Communications: Television sets: 1 per 26 persons. **Radios:** 1 per 5.1 persons. **Telephones:** 1 per 275 persons. **Daily newspaper circ.:** 18 per 1,000 pop.

Health: Life expectancy at birth (1997): 53.3 male; 56.0 female. **Births** (per 1,000 pop.): 42. **Deaths** (per 1,000 pop.): 12. **Natural increase:** 3.0%. **Hospital beds:** 1 per 1,070 persons. **Physicians:** 1 per 4,496 persons. **Infant mortality** (per 1,000 live births 1997): 70.

Education: Free and compulsory: ages 6-15. **Literacy** (1995): 57%.

Major International Organizations: UN (WTO, IMO, WHO), OPEC, OAU, the Commonwealth (suspended Nov. 1995).

Embassy: 1333 16th St. NW 20036; 986-8400.

Early cultures in Nigeria date back to at least 700 BC. From the 12th to the 14th centuries, more advanced cultures developed in the Yoruba area, at Ife, and in the north, where Muslim influence prevailed.

Portuguese and British slavers appeared from the 15th-16th centuries. Britain seized Lagos, 1861, and gradually extended control inland until 1900. Nigeria became independent Oct. 1, 1960, and a republic Oct. 1, 1963.

On May 30, 1967, the Eastern Region seceded, proclaiming itself the Republic of Biafra, plunging the country into civil war. Casualties in the war were estimated at over 1 million, including many "Biafrans" (mostly Ibos) who died of starvation despite international efforts to provide relief. The secessionists, after steadily losing ground, capitulated Jan. 12, 1970.

Oil revenues have made possible a massive economic development program, largely using private enterprise, but agriculture has lagged.

After 13 years of military rule, the nation made a peaceful return to civilian government, Oct. 1979. However, military rule resumed, Dec. 31, 1983, as a coup ousted the democratically elected government. A second coup came in 1985. The new regime, headed by Gen. Ibrahim Babangida, promised elections but voided the result of a presidential election on June 23, 1993; riots followed and many were killed.

Babangida resigned and appointed a civilian to head an interim government, Aug. 26, 1993, but that government was ousted in a military coup, Nov. 17. On June 11, 1994, the presumed winner of the 1993 presidential election, Moshood Abiola, declared himself president; he was jailed June 23.

The execution, Nov. 10, 1995, of Ogoni playwright and environmentalist Ken Saro-Wiwa and 8 associates, accused in connection with the deaths of 4 political opponents, led to international sanctions against Nigeria, including suspension of its Commonwealth membership.

Norway
Kingdom of Norway
Kongeriket Norge

People: Population: 4,404,456. **Age distrib.** (%): <15: 19; 65+: 16. **Pop. density:** 35 per sq. mi. **Urban:** 73%. **Ethnic groups:** Germanic (Nordic, Alpine, Baltic), Lapps (minority). **Principal languages:** Norwegian (official). **Chief religions:** Evangelical Lutheran 88%.

Geography: Area: 125,050 sq. mi. **Location:** W part of Scandinavian peninsula in NW Europe (extends farther north than any European land). **Neighbors:** Sweden, Finland, Russia on E. **Topography:** A highly indented coast is lined with tens of thousands of islands. Mountains and plateaus cover most of the country, which is only 25% forested. **Capital:** Oslo. **Cities** (1996 met. est.): Oslo 487,908; Bergen 223,100.

Government: Type: Hereditary constitutional monarchy. **Head of state:** King Harald V; b Feb. 21, 1937; in office: Jan. 17, 1991. **Head of government:** Prime Min. Thorbjørn Jagland; b Nov. 5, 1950; in office: Oct. 25, 1996. **Local divisions:** 19 provinces. **Defense:** 2.9% of GDP (1995). **Active troop strength:** 30,000.

Economy: Industries: Wood & paper prods., shipbuilding, metals, chemicals, food processing, fish, oil, gas. **Chief crops:** Grains, potatoes. **Minerals:** Oil, gas, copper, pyrites, nickel, iron, zinc, lead. **Crude oil reserves** (1996): 11.2 bil bbls. **Arable land:** 3%. **Livestock** (1996): sheep: 2.4 mil; cattle: 1.0 mil; pigs: 725,000. **Fish catch** (1995): 2,807,540 metric tons. **Electricity prod.** (1995): 121.4 bil kWh. **Labor force:** 71% services; 23% industry.

Finance: Monetary unit: Krone (Aug. 1997: 7.49 = $1 US). **Gross domestic product** (1995 est.): $106.2 bil. **Per capita GDP:** $24,500. **Imports** (1994): $27.3 bil; partners: EU 69%. **Exports** (1994): $34.7 bil; partners: EU 78%. **Tourism** (1994): $2.2 bil. **National budget** (1994 est.): $53 bil. **International reserves less gold** (June 1997): $28.45 bil. **Gold:** 1.18 mil oz t. **Consumer prices** (change in 1996): 1.3%.

Transport: Railroads: Length: 2,500.8 mi. **Motor vehicles in use:** 1.7 mil passenger cars, 382,000 comm. vehicles. **Civil aviation:** 4.8 bil passenger-mi.; 48 airports. **Chief ports:** Bergen, Stavanger, Oslo, Kristiansand.

Communications: Television sets: 1 per 2.3 persons. **Radios:** 1 per 1.3 persons. **Telephones:** 1 per 1.8 persons. **Daily newspaper circ.:** 607 per 1,000 pop.

Health: Life expectancy at birth (1997): 74.8 male; 80.7 female. **Births** (per 1,000 pop.): 11. **Deaths** (per 1,000 pop.): 11. **Natural increase:** 0.1%. **Hospital beds:** 1 per 183 persons. **Physicians:** 1 per 299 persons. **Infant mortality** (per 1,000 live births 1997): 5.

Education: Compulsory: ages 6-16. **Literacy** (1994): 100%.

Major International Organizations: UN and all of its specialized agencies, NATO, OECD, EFTA.

Embassy: 2720 34th St. NW 20008; 333-6000.

The first ruler of Norway was Harald the Fairhaired, who came to power in AD 872. Between 800 and 1000, Norway's Vikings raided and occupied widely dispersed parts of Europe.

The country was united with Denmark 1381-1814, and with Sweden, 1814-1905. In 1905, the country became independent with Prince Charles of Denmark as king.

Norway remained neutral during World War I. Germany attacked Norway Apr. 9, 1940, and held it until liberation May 8, 1945. The country abandoned its neutrality after the war, and joined NATO. In a referendum Nov. 28, 1994, Norwegian voters rejected European Union membership.

Abundant hydroelectric resources provided the base for industrialization, giving Norway one of the highest living standards in the world. The country is a leading producer and exporter of crude oil, with extensive reserves in the North Sea. Norway's merchant marine is one of the world's largest.

Svalbard is a group of mountainous islands in the Arctic O., area 23,957 sq. mi., pop. (1995 est.) 2,900. The largest, Spitsbergen (formerly called West Spitsbergen), 15,060 sq. mi., seat of the governor, is about 370 mi. N of Norway. By a treaty signed in Paris, 1920, major European powers recognized the sovereignty of Norway, which incorporated it in 1925.

Jan Mayen, area 144 sq. mi., is a volcanic island located about 565 mi. WNW of Norway; it was annexed in 1929.

Oman
Sultanate of Oman
Saltanat 'Uman

People: Population: 2,264,590. **Age distrib.** (%): <15: 46; 65+: 3. **Pop. density:** 19 per sq. mi. **Urban:** 78%. **Ethnic groups:** Omani Arab 74%, Pakistani 19%. **Principal languages:** Arabic (official). **Chief religions:** Ibadhi Muslim 75%, other Muslim, Hindu.

Geography: Area: 118,150 sq. mi. **Location:** On SE coast of Arabian peninsula. **Neighbors:** United Arab Emirates, Saudi Arabia, Yemen on W. **Topography:** Oman has a narrow coastal plain up to 10 mi. wide, a range of barren mountains reaching 9,900 ft., and a wide, stony, mostly waterless plateau, avg. alt. 1,000 ft. Also, an exclave at the tip of the Musandam peninsula controls access to the Persian Gulf. **Capital:** Muscat (1993): 51,969.

Government: Type: Absolute monarchy. **Head of state and government:** Sultan Qabus bin Said; b Nov. 18, 1942; in office: July 23, 1970. **Local divisions:** 6 regions, 2 governorates. **Defense:** 13.7% of GDP (1996). **Active troop strength:** 43,500.

Economy: Industries: Oil, gas, construction. **Chief crops:** Dates, limes, vegetables, alfalfa, bananas. **Minerals:** Oil (87% of exports). **Arable land:** 2%. **Crude oil reserves** (1996): 5.1 bil bbls. **Fish catch** (1994): 118,571 metric tons. **Electricity prod.** (1995): 7.8 bil kWh. **Labor force:** 37% agric.

Finance: Monetary unit: Rial Omani (Aug. 1997: 0.39 = $1 US). **Gross domestic product** (1995 est.): $19.1 bil. **Per capita GDP:** $10,800. **Imports** (1994): $4.1 bil; partners: UAE 27%, Japan 20%, UK 15%. **Exports** (1994): $4.8 bil; partners: Japan 35%, South Korea 16%. **Tourism** (1994): $88 mil. **National budget** (1995 est.): $5.6 bil. **International reserves less gold** (Mar. 1997): $1.67 bil. **Gold:** 291,000 oz t.

Transport: Motor vehicles in use: 166,000 passenger cars, 84,000 comm. vehicles. **Civil aviation:** 1.7 bil passenger-mi.; 6 airports with scheduled flights. **Chief ports:** Matrah, Mina' al Fahl.

Communications: Television sets: 1 per 1.5 persons. **Radios:** 1 per 1.7 persons. **Telephones:** 1 per 13 persons.

Health: Life expectancy at birth (1997): 68.8 male; 72.9 female. **Births** (per 1,000 pop.): 38. **Deaths** (per 1,000 pop.): 4. **Natural increase:** 3.3%. **Hospital beds:** 1 per 550 persons. **Physicians:** 1 per 837 persons. **Infant mortality** (per 1,000 live births 1997): 26.

Education: Literacy (1993): 59%.

Major International Organizations: UN (World Bank, IMF), Arab League.

Embassy: 2535 Belmont Rd. NW 20008; 387-1980.

Oman was originally called Muscat and Oman. A long history of rule by other lands, including Portugal in the 16th century, ended with the ouster of the Persians in 1744. By the early 19th century, Muscat and Oman was one of the most important countries in the region, controlling much of the Persian and Pakistan coasts, and ruling far-away Zanzibar, which was separated in 1861 under British mediation.

British influence was confirmed in a 1951 treaty, and Britain helped suppress an uprising by traditionally rebellious interior tribes against control by Muscat in the 1950s.

On July 23, 1970, Sultan Said bin Taimur was overthrown by his son, who changed the nation's name to Sultanate of Oman.

Oil is the major source of income.

Oman opened its air bases to Western forces following the Iraqi invasion of Kuwait on Aug. 2, 1990.

Pakistan
Islamic Republic of Pakistan
Islami Jamhuriyah e Pakistan

People: Population: 132,185,299. **Age distrib.** (%): <15: 42; 65+: 4. **Pop. density:** 389 per sq. mi. **Urban:** 35%. **Ethnic groups:** Punjabi, Sindhi, Pashtun (Pathan), Balochi. **Principal languages:** Urdu, English (both official), Punjabi, Sindhi, Pashtu, Balochi. **Chief religions:** Sunni Muslim 77%, Shi'a Muslim 20%.

Geography: Area: 307,374 sq. mi. **Location:** In W part of South Asia. **Neighbors:** Iran on W, Afghanistan and China on N, India on E. **Topography:** The Indus R. rises in the Hindu Kush and Himalaya Mts. in the N (highest is K2, or Godwin Austen, 28,250 ft., 2d highest in world), then flows over 1,000 mi. through fertile valley and empties into Arabian Sea. Thar Desert, Eastern Plains flank Indus Valley. **Capital:** Islamabad. **Cities:** Karachi 9,733,000; Lahore 5,012,000; Faisalabad 1,845,000*.

Government: Type: Republic. **Head of state:** Pres. Sardar Farooq Ahmad Khan Leghari; b May 2, 1940; in office: Nov. 14, 1993. **Head of government:** Prime Min. Nawaz Sharif; b Dec. 25, 1949; in office: Feb. 17, 1997. **Local divisions:** 4 provinces, 1 capital territory, 1 territory. **Defense:** 5.3% of GDP (FY 1995-96). **Active troop strength:** 587,000.

Economy: Industries: Textiles, food processing, beverages. **Chief crops:** Rice, wheat, cotton. **Minerals:** Natural gas, iron. **Crude oil reserves** (1996): 208 mil bbls. **Arable land:** 23%. **Livestock** (1996): goats: 43.8 mil; sheep: 29.1 mil; buffalo: 20 mil; cattle: 19.0 mil. **Fish catch** (1995): 540,560 metric tons. **Electricity prod.** (1995): 57 bil kWh. **Labor force:** 46% agric.; 18% mining & manuf.; 17% services.

Finance: Monetary unit: Rupee (Aug. 1997: 40.48 = $1 US). **Gross domestic product** (1995 est.): $274 bil. **Per capita GDP:** $2,100. **Imports** (1995 est.): $10.7 bil; partners: Japan 12%, U.S. 11%, Malaysia 6%. **Exports** (1995 est.): $8.7 bil; partners: U.S. 14%, Japan 8%, Germany 8%. **Tourism** (1994): $117 mil. **National budget** (FY 1994-95): $12.4 bil. **International reserves less gold** (June 1997): $1.17 bil. **Gold:** 2.06 mil oz t. **Consumer prices** (change in 1996): 10.4%.

Transport: Railroads: Length: 5,069.2 mi. **Motor vehicles in use:** 770,000 passenger cars, 275,000 comm. vehicles. **Civil aviation:** 6.5 bil passenger-mi.; 34 airports with scheduled flights. **Chief port:** Karachi.

Communications: Television sets: 1 per 53 persons. **Radios:** 1 per 11 persons. **Telephones:** 1 per 61 persons. **Daily newspaper circ.:** 21 per 1,000 pop.

Health: Life expectancy at birth (1997): 58.0 male; 59.6 female. **Births** (per 1,000 pop.): 35. **Deaths** (per 1,000 pop.): 11. **Natural increase:** 2.4%. **Hospital beds:** 1 per 1,689 persons. **Physicians:** 1 per 2,064 persons. **Infant mortality** (per 1,000 live births 1997): 95.

Education: Literacy (1995): 38%.

Major International Organizations: UN (WTO, ILO, IMF, WHO), the Commonwealth.

Embassy: 2315 Massachusetts Ave. NW 20008; 939-6200.

Present-day Pakistan shares the 5,000-year history of the India-Pakistan subcontinent. At present-day Harappa and Mohenjo Daro, the Indus Valley Civilization, with large cities and elaborate irrigation systems, flourished c. 4,000-2,500 BC.

Aryan invaders from the NW conquered the region around 1,500 BC, forging a Hindu civilization that dominated Pakistan as well as India for 2,000 years.

Beginning with the Persians in the 6th century BC, and continuing with Alexander the Great and with the Sassanians, successive nations to the west ruled or influenced Pakistan, eventually separating the area from the Indian cultural sphere.

The first Arab invasion, AD 712, introduced Islam. Under the Mogul empire (1526-1857), Muslims ruled most of India, yielding to British encroachment and resurgent Hindus.

After World War I the Muslims of British India began agitation for minority rights in elections. Muhammad Ali Jinnah (1876-1948) was the principal architect of Pakistan. A leader of the Muslim League from 1916, he worked for dominion status for India; from 1940 he advocated a separate Muslim state.

When the British withdrew Aug. 14, 1947, the Islamic majority areas of India acquired self-government as Pakistan, with dominion status in the Commonwealth. Pakistan was divided into 2 sections, West Pakistan and East Pakistan. The 2 areas were nearly 1,000 mi. apart on opposite sides of India. Pakistan became a republic in 1956.

In Oct. 1958, Gen. Mohammad Ayub Khan took power in a coup. He was elected president in 1960, reelected in 1965. He resigned Mar. 25, 1969, after several months of violent rioting and unrest, most of it in East Pakistan, which demanded autonomy. The government was turned over to Gen. Agha Mohammad Yahya Khan and martial law was declared.

The Awami League, which sought regional autonomy for East Pakistan, won a majority in Dec. 1970 elections to a constituent assembly. In March 1971 Yahya postponed the assembly. Rioting and strikes broke out in the East.

On Mar. 25, 1971, government troops launched attacks in the East. The Easterners, aided by India, proclaimed the independent nation of Bangladesh. In months of widespread fighting, countless thousands were killed. Some 10 million Easterners fled into India.

Full-scale war between India and Pakistan had spread to both the East and West fronts by Dec. 3. Pakistan troops in the East surrendered Dec. 16; Pakistan agreed to a cease-fire in the West Dec. 17. On July 3, 1972, Pakistan and India signed a pact agreeing to withdraw troops from their borders and seek peaceful solutions to all problems.

Zulfikar Ali Bhutto, leader of the Pakistan People's Party, which had won the most West Pakistan votes in the Dec. 1970 elections, became president Dec. 20.

Bhutto was overthrown in a military coup July 1977. Convicted of complicity in a 1974 political murder, he was executed Apr. 4, 1979. More than 3 million Afghan refugees flooded into Pakistan after the USSR invaded Afghanistan Dec. 1979; more than 1.4 million remained in the mid-1990s.

Pres. Mohammad Zia ul-Haq was killed when his plane exploded in Aug. 1988. Following Nov. elections, Benazir Bhutto, the daughter of Zulfikar Ali Bhutto, was named prime minister, becoming the first woman leader of a Muslim nation. She was accused of corruption and dismissed by the president, Aug. 1990; her party was soundly defeated in Oct. 1990 elections, and Nawaz Sharif became prime minister. She regained power after elections in Oct. 1993. Opposition to Bhutto centered around Karachi, which was crippled by violent strikes and ethnic clashes during 1995 and 1996.

Bhutto's brother, Murtaza Bhutto, a leader in the opposition to Benazir, was killed by police on Sept. 20, 1996, when they tried to arrest him. Accusing the Bhutto government of corruption and mismanagement, Pres. Farooq Leghari appointed a caretaker prime minister Nov. 5. Bhutto's husband, Asif Ali Zardari, was charged Dec. 18 with complicity in Murtaza's death. Elections on Feb. 3, 1997, gave Sharif a parliamentary majority.

Palau
Republic of Palau
Belu'u era Belau

People: Population: 17,240. **Pop. density:** 91 per sq. mi. **Urban:** 72%. **Ethnic groups:** Polynesian, Malayan, Melanesian. **Principal languages:** English, Palauan (both official); Sonsorolese, Angaur, Japanese, Tobi (all official within certain Palauan states). **Chief religions:** Roman Catholic, Protestant, Modekngei.

Geography: Area: 188 sq. mi. **Location:** Archipelago (26 islands, more than 300 islets) in the W Pacific Ocean, about 530 mi SE of the Philippines. **Neighbors:** Micronesia to E, Indonesia to S. **Capital:** Koror (1992) 10,500. (Note: a new capital is being built on the island of Babelthuap.)

Government: Type. Republic. **Head of state:** Pres. Kuniwo Nakamura; in office: Nov. 4, 1992.

Economy: Industries: Tourism, fish. **Chief crops:** Coconuts, copra, cassava, sweet potatoes.

Finance: Monetary unit: U.S. Dollar. **Gross domestic product** (1994): $81.8 mil. **Per capita GDP:** $5,000.

Communications: Radios: 1 per 1.8 persons.

Health: Life expectancy at birth (1997): 69.1 male; 73.0 female. **Births** (per 1,000 pop.): 21. **Deaths** (per 1,000 pop.): 7. **Natural increase:** 1.4%. **Hospital beds:** 1 per 200 persons. **Physicians:** 1 per 1,518 persons. **Infant mortality** (per 1,000 live births 1997): 25.

Education: Compulsory: ages 6-14. **Literacy** (1990): 98%.

Major International Organizations: UN.

Embassy: 2000 L St. NW, Suite 407, 20036; 452-6814.

Spain acquired the Palau Islands in 1886 and sold them to Germany in 1899. Japan seized them in 1914. American forces occupied the islands in 1944; in 1947, they became part of the U.S.-administered UN Trust Territory of the Pacific Islands. In 1981 Palau became an autonomous republic; in 1993 the republic ratified a compact of free association with the U.S., which provides financial aid in return for U.S. use of Palauan military facilities over 15 years. Palau became an independent nation on Oct. 1, 1994.

Panama
Republic of Panama
República de Panamá

People: Population: 2,693,417. **Age distrib.** (%): <15: 32; 65+: 6. **Pop. density:** 92 per sq. mi. **Urban:** 56%. **Ethnic groups:** Mestizo 70%, West Indian 14%, white 10%, Indian 6%. **Principal languages:** Spanish (official), English. **Chief religions:** Roman Catholic 85%, Protestant 15%.

Geography: Area: 29,157 sq. mi. **Location:** In Central America. **Neighbors:** Costa Rica on W, Colombia on E. **Topography:** 2 mountain ranges run the length of the isthmus. Tropical rain forests cover the Caribbean coast and eastern Panama. **Capital:** Panama (est.): 967,000*.

Government: Type: Constitutional republic. **Head of state and government:** Pres. Ernesto Pérez Balladares; b June 29, 1946; in office: Sept. 1, 1994. **Local divisions:** 9 provinces, 1 territory. **Defense:** 1.0% of GDP (1993 est.). **Active troop strength:** 11,800 est.

Economy: Industries: Oil refining, international banking, construction. **Chief crops:** Bananas, rice, corn, sugar. **Minerals:** Copper. **Other resources:** Forests (mahogany), shrimp. **Arable land:** 6%. **Livestock** (1996): cattle: 1.5 mil; pigs: 261,000. **Electricity prod.** (1995): 3.6 bil kWh. **Labor force:** 32% govt. & community services; 27% agric. & fishing.

Finance: Monetary unit: Balboa (Aug. 1997: 1.00 = $1 US). **Gross domestic product** (1995 est.): $13.6 bil. **Per capita GDP:** $5,100. **Imports** (1995): $2.45 bil; partners: U.S. 40%. **Exports** (1995): $548 mil; partners: U.S. 39%. **Tourism** (1994): $244 mil. **National budget** (1995): $1.9 bil. **International reserves less gold** (May 1997): $1.86 bil. **Consumer prices** (change in 1996): 1.3%.

Transport: Railroads: Length: 220.5 mi. **Motor vehicles in use:** 111,000 passenger cars, 79,000 comm. vehicles. **Civil aviation:** 251.5 mil passenger-mi.; 10 airports with scheduled flights. **Chief ports:** Balboa, Cristobal.

Communications: Television sets: 1 per 5.9 persons. **Radios:** 1 per 4.4 persons. **Telephones:** 1 per 8.8 persons. **Daily newspaper circ.:** 62 per 1,000 pop.

Health: Life expectancy at birth (1997): 71.6 male; 77.1 female. **Births** (per 1,000 pop.): 22. **Deaths** (per 1,000 pop.): 5. **Natural increase:** 1.7%. **Hospital beds:** 1 per 363 persons. **Physicians:** 1 per 808 persons. **Infant mortality** (per 1,000 live births 1997): 25.

Education: Free and compulsory for 6 years between ages 6-15. **Literacy** (1995): 91%.

Major International Organizations: UN (IMF, IMO, World Bank), OAS.

Embassy: 2862 McGill Terrace NW 20008; 483-1407.

The coast of Panama was sighted by Rodrigo de Bastidas, sailing with Columbus for Spain in 1501, and was visited by Columbus in 1502. Vasco Nunez de Balboa crossed the isthmus and "discovered" the Pacific O. Sept. 13, 1513. Spanish colonies were ravaged by Francis Drake, 1572-95, and Henry Morgan, 1668-71. Morgan destroyed the old city of Panama which had been founded in 1519. Freed from Spain, Panama joined Colombia in 1821.

Panama declared its independence from Colombia Nov. 3, 1903, with U.S. recognition. U.S. naval forces deterred action by Colombia. Panama granted use, occupation, and control of the Canal Zone to the U.S. by treaty, ratified Feb. 26, 1904. In 1978, a new treaty provided for a gradual takeover by Panama of the canal, and withdrawal of U.S. troops, to be completed by 1999. U.S. payments were substantially increased in the interim.

President Delvalle was ousted by the National Assembly, Feb. 26, 1988, after he tried to fire the head of the Panama Defense Forces, Gen. Manuel Antonio Noriega. Noriega had been indicted by 2 U.S. federal grand juries on drug charges. A general strike followed. Despite U.S.-imposed economic sanctions Noriega remained in power. Voters went to the polls to elect a new president May 7, 1989. Norlega claimed victory, but foreign observers said that the opposition had won overwhelmingly. The government voided the election May 10, charging foreign interference. There was an attempted coup against Noriega Oct. 3.

U.S. troops invaded Panama Dec. 20, 1989, following a series of incidents, including the killing of a U.S. Marine by Panamanian soldiers. The operation had as its chief objective the capture of Noriega. He took refuge in the Vatican diplomatic mission, but surrendered to U.S. officials Jan. 3, 1990. He was convicted on 8 counts of racketeering and drug trafficking in a U.S. District Court in Miami, Florida, Apr. 9, 1992.

Papua New Guinea
Independent State of Papua New Guinea

People: Population: 4,496,221. **Age distrib.** (%): <15: 40; 65+: 3. **Pop. density:** 25 per sq. mi. **Urban:** 16%. **Ethnic groups:** Papuan (in S and interior), Melanesian (N, E). **Principal languages:** English (official), Tok Pisin, Motu. **Chief religions:** Protestant 44%, Roman Catholic 22%, indigenous beliefs 34%.

Geography: Area: 178,704 sq. mi. **Location:** SE Asia, occupying E half of island of New Guinea and about 600 nearby islands. **Neighbors:** Indonesia (West Irian) on W, Australia on S. **Topography:** Thickly forested mts. cover much of the center of the country, with lowlands along the coasts. Included are some islands of Bismarck and Solomon groups, such as the Admiralty Isls., New Ireland, New Britain, and Bougainville. **Capital:** Port Moresby. **Cities** (1991): Port Moresby 192,000; Lae 80,700.

Government: Type: Parliamentary democracy. **Head of state:** Queen Elizabeth II, represented by Gov. Gen. Wiwa Korowi; b July 7, 1948; in office: Oct. 4, 1991. **Head of government:** Prime Min. Bill Skate; b 1953; in office: July 22, 1997. **Local divisions:** 20 provinces. **Defense:** 0.9% of GDP (1995). **Active troop strength:** 3,700.

Economy: Chief crops: Coffee, coconuts, cocoa. **Minerals:** Gold, copper, silver. **Crude oil reserves** (1996): 275 mil bbls. **Arable land:** 0%. **Livestock** (1996): pigs: 1.0 mil. **Electricity prod.** (1995): 1.8 bil kWh. **Labor force:** 64% agric.

Finance: Monetary unit: Kina (Aug. 1997: 1.42 = $1 US). **Gross domestic product** (1995 est.): $10.2 bil. **Per capita GDP:** $2,400. **Imports** (1995 est.): $1.4 bil; partners: Australia 37%, Japan 15%; Singapore 14%. **Exports** (1995 est.): $2.4 bil; partners: Australia 36%; Japan 21%. **Tourism** (1994): $55 mil. **National budget** (1995 est.): $1.9 bil. **International reserves less gold** (Apr. 1997): $552.58 mil. **Gold:** 63,000 oz t. **Consumer prices** (change in 1996): 11.6%.

Transport: Motor vehicles in use: 20,000 passenger cars, 35,000 comm. vehicles. **Civil aviation:** 519.8 mil passenger-mi. **Chief ports:** Port Moresby, Lae.

Communications: Television sets: 1 per 345 persons. **Radios:** 1 per 13 persons. **Telephones:** 1 per 99 persons. **Daily newspaper circ.:** 15 per 1,000 pop.

Health: Life expectancy at birth (1997): 56.8 male; 58.6 female. **Births** (per 1,000 pop.): 33. **Deaths** (per 1,000 pop.): 10. **Natural increase:** 2.3%. **Hospital beds:** 1 per 234 persons. **Physicians:** 1 per 5,584 persons. **Infant mortality** (per 1,000 live births 1997): 59.

Education: Literacy (1995): 72%.

Major International Organizations: UN, the Commonwealth, APEC.

Embassy: 1615 New Hampshire Ave. NW 20009; 745-3680.

Human remains have been found in the interior of New Guinea dating back at least 10,000 years and possibly much earlier. Successive waves of peoples probably entered the country from Asia through Indonesia. Europeans visited in the 15th century, but land claims did not begin until the 19th century, when the Dutch took control of the island's western half.

The southern half of eastern New Guinea was first claimed by Britain in 1884, and transferred to Australia in 1905. The northern half was claimed by Germany in 1884, but captured in World War I by Australia, which was granted a League of Nations mandate and then a UN trusteeship over the area. The 2 territories were

administered jointly after 1949, were given self-government Dec. 1, 1973, and became independent Sept. 16, 1975.

The indigenous population consists of a huge number of tribes, many living in almost complete isolation with mutually unintelligible languages. Secessionist rebels have clashed with government forces on Bougainville since 1988. The country suffered from a severe drought in 1997.

Paraguay
Republic of Paraguay
República del Paraguay

People: Population: 5,651,634. **Age distrib.** (%): <15: 40; 65+: 4. **Pop. density:** 35 per sq. mi. **Urban:** 53%. **Ethnic groups:** Mestizo 95%, white & Amerindian 5%. **Principal languages:** Spanish (official), Guarani. **Chief religions:** Roman Catholic 90%.

Geography: Area: 157,048 sq. mi. **Location:** Landlocked country in central South America. **Neighbors:** Bolivia on N, Argentina on S, Brazil on E. **Topography:** Paraguay R. bisects the country. To E are fertile plains, wooded slopes, grasslands. To W is the Gran Chaco plain, with marshes and scrub trees. Extreme W is arid. **Capital:** Asunción 1,081,000*.

Government: Type: Republic. **Head of state:** Pres. Juan Carlos Wasmosy; b Dec. 15, 1938; in office: Aug. 15, 1993. **Local divisions:** 17 departments. **Defense:** 0.6% of GDP (1994). **Active troop strength:** 20,200.

Economy: Industries: Food processing, textiles, cement. **Chief crops:** Corn, cotton, soybeans, sugarcane. **Minerals:** Iron, manganese, limestone. **Other resources:** Forests. **Arable land:** 20%. **Livestock** (1996): cattle: 8.1 mil; pigs: 2.7 mil. **Electricity prod.** (1995): 40.1 bil kWh. **Labor force:** 45% agriculture.

Finance: Monetary unit: Guarani (Aug. 1997: 2,182 = $1 US). **Gross domestic product** (1995 est.): $17 bil. **Per capita GDP:** $3,200. **Imports** (1994): $2.1 bil; partners: Brazil 29%, US 22%. **Exports** (1995): $819 mil; partners: Brazil 46%, Germany 8%. **Tourism** (1994): $197 mil. **National budget** (1995 est.): $1.7 bil. **International reserves less gold** (June 1997): $824.68 mil. **Gold:** 35,000 oz t. **Consumer prices** (change in 1996): 9.8%.

Transport: Railroads: Length: 603.0 mi. **Motor vehicles in use:** 75,000 passenger cars, 50,000 comm. vehicles. **Civil aviation:** 766.9 mil passenger-mi; 5 airports with scheduled flights. **Chief port:** Asunción.

Communications: Television sets: 1 per 12 persons. **Radios:** 1 per 5.8 persons. **Telephones:** 1 per 30 persons. **Daily newspaper circ.:** 42 per 1,000 pop.

Health: Life expectancy at birth (1997): 72.6 male; 75.7 female. **Births** (per 1,000 pop.): 30. **Deaths** (per 1,000 pop.): 4. **Natural increase:** 2.6%. **Hospital beds:** 1 per 864 persons. **Physicians:** 1 per 1,406 persons. **Infant mortality** (per 1,000 live births 1997): 22.

Education: Compulsory: ages 7-20. **Literacy** (1995): 92%.

Major International Organizations: UN (IMF, WHO, WTO), OAS.

Embassy: 2400 Massachusetts Ave. NW 20008; 483-6960.

The Guarani Indians were settled farmers speaking a common language before the arrival of Europeans.

Visited by Sebastian Cabot in 1527 and settled as a Spanish possession in 1535, Paraguay gained its independence from Spain in 1811. It lost much of its territory to Brazil, Uruguay, and Argentina in the War of the Triple Alliance, 1865-1870. Large areas were won from Bolivia in the Chaco War, 1932-35.

Gen. Alfredo Stroessner, who had ruled since 1954, was ousted in a military coup led by Gen. Andrés Rodríguez on Feb. 3, 1989. Rodríguez was elected president May 1. Juan Carlos Wasmosy was elected president May 9, 1993, becoming the nation's first civilian head of state in many years. An army rebellion was averted in Apr. 1996.

Peru
Republic of Peru
República del Perú

People: Population: 24,949,512. **Age distrib.** (%): <15: 34; 65+: 5. **Pop. density:** 50 per sq. mi. **Urban:** 71%. **Ethnic groups:** Indian 45%, mestizo 37%, white 15%. **Principal languages:** Spanish, Quechua (both official), Aymara. **Chief religions:** Predominantly Roman Catholic.

Geography

Geography: Area: 496,225 sq. mi. **Location:** On the Pacific coast of South America. **Neighbors:** Ecuador, Colombia on N; Brazil, Bolivia on E; Chile on S. **Topography:** An arid coastal strip, 10 to 100 mi. wide, supports much of the population thanks to widespread irrigation. The Andes cover 27% of land area. The uplands are well-watered, as are the eastern slopes reaching the Amazon basin, which covers half the country with its forests and jungles. **Capital:** Lima. **Cities** (1993 met. est.): Lima 6,742,576; Arequipa 981,272; Callao 684,135.

Government: Type: Republic. **Head of state:** Pres. Alberto Fujimori; b July 28, 1938; in office: July 28, 1990. **Head of government:** Prime Min. Alberto Pandolfi Arbulu; b Aug. 20, 1940; in office: Apr. 3, 1996. **Local divisions:** 24 departments, 1 constitutional province. **Defense:** 1.6% of GDP (1996). **Active troop strength:** 125,000.

Economy: Industries: Fishing, mining, food processing, textiles. **Chief crops:** Cotton, sugar, coffee, rice. **Minerals:** Copper, silver, gold, iron, oil. **Crude oil reserves** (1996): 808 mil bbls. **Other resources:** Wool, sardines. **Arable land:** 3%. **Livestock** (1996): sheep: 12.6 mil; cattle: 4.55 mil; pigs: 2.45 mil; goats: 2.1 mil. **Fish catch** (1995): 8,943,208 metric tons. **Electricity prod.** (1995): 15.6 bil kWh. **Labor force:** 44% govt. and other services; 33% agric.; 19% ind.

Finance: Monetary unit: New Sol (Aug. 1997: 2.66 = $1 US). **Gross domestic product** (1995 est.): $87 bil. **Per capita GDP:** $3,600. **Imports** (1994): $5.6 bil; partners: U.S. 28%. **Exports** (1994): $4.1 bil; partners: U.S. 18%, Japan 10%. **Tourism** (1994): $402 mil. **National budget** (1996 est.): $9.3 bil. **International reserves less gold** (May 1997): $10.49 bil. **Gold:** 1.12 mil oz t. **Consumer prices** (change in 1996): 11.5%.

Transport: Railroads: Length: 1,267.5 mi. **Motor vehicles in use:** 472,000 passenger cars, 264,000 comm. vehicles. **Civil aviation:** 1.6 bil passenger-mi; 27 airports. **Chief ports:** Callao, Chimbote, Salaverry.

Communications: Television sets: 1 per 10 persons. **Radios:** 1 per 3.9 persons. **Telephones:** 1 per 21 persons. **Daily newspaper circ.:** 86 per 1,000 pop.

Health: Life expectancy at birth (1997): 67.4 male; 71.8 female. **Births** (per 1,000 pop.): 24. **Deaths** (per 1,000 pop.): 6. **Natural increase:** 1.8%. **Hospital beds:** 1 per 509 persons. **Physicians:** 1 per 1,116 persons. **Infant mortality** (per 1,000 live births 1997): 50.

Education: Free and compulsory: ages 6-16. **Literacy** (1995): 89%.

Major International Organizations: UN and all of its specialized agencies, OAS.

Embassy: 1700 Massachusetts Ave. NW 20036; 833-9860.

The powerful Inca empire had its seat at Cuzco in the Andes and covered most of Peru, Bolivia, and Ecuador, as well as parts of Colombia, Chile, and Argentina. Building on the achievements of 800 years of Andean civilization, the Incas had a high level of skill in architecture, engineering, textiles, and social organization.

A civil war had weakened the empire when Francisco Pizarro, Spanish conquistador, began raiding Peru for its wealth, 1532. In 1533 he seized the ruling Inca, Atahualpa, filled a room with gold as a ransom, then executed him and enslaved the natives.

Lima was the seat of Spanish viceroys until the Argentine liberator, José de San Martin, captured it in 1821; Spanish forces were ultimately routed by Simón Bolívar, 1824.

On Oct. 3, 1968, a military coup ousted Pres. Fernando Belaunde Terry. In 1968-74, the military government started socialist programs. Food shortages, escalating foreign debt, and strikes led to another coup, Aug. 29, 1976.

After 12 years of military rule, Peru returned to democratic leadership in 1980 but was plagued by economic problems and terrorism by leftist Shining Path (Sendero Luminoso) guerrillas.

Pres. Alberto Fujimori, elected in June 1990, dissolved the National Congress, suspended parts of the constitution, and initiated press censorship, Apr. 5, 1992. The leader of Shining Path was captured Sept. 12.

With the economy booming and signs of significant progress in curtailing guerrilla activity, Fujimori won reelection Apr. 9, 1995. Peru's repressive antiterrorism tactics, however, drew international criticism. On Dec. 17, 1996, leftist Tupac Amaru guerrillas infiltrated a reception at the Japanese ambassador's residence in Lima and took hundreds of hostages, most of whom were later released. Peruvian soldiers stormed the embassy Apr. 22, 1997, rescuing 71 of the remaining hostages; 1 hostage, 2 soldiers, and all 14 guerrillas were killed.

Philippines
Republic of the Philippines
Republika ng Pilipinas

People: Population: 76,103,564. **Age distrib.** (%): <15: 38; 65+: 4. **Pop. density:** 656 per sq. mi. **Urban:** 55%. **Ethnic groups:** Christian 92%, Muslim Malay 4%. **Principal languages:** Pilipino (based on Tagalog), English (both official). **Chief religions:** Roman Catholic 83%, Protestant 9%, Muslim 5%.

Geography: Area: 115,860 sq. mi. **Location:** An archipelago off the SE coast of Asia. **Neighbors:** Nearest are Malaysia and Indonesia on S, Taiwan on N. **Topography:** The country consists of some 7,100 islands stretching 1,100 mi. N-S. About 95% of area and population are on 11 largest islands, which are mountainous, except for the heavily indented coastlines and for the central plain on Luzon. **Capital:** Manila. **Cities** (1994): Manila 8,594,150; Quezon City 1,676,644.

Government: Type: Republic. **Head of state:** Pres. Fidel V. Ramos; b Mar. 18, 1928; in office: June 30, 1992. **Local divisions:** 15 regions, divided into 72 provinces. **Defense:** 1.4% of GNP (1995). **Active troop strength:** 107,500 est.

Economy: Industries: Food processing, textiles, chemicals, pharmaceuticals, wood prods. **Chief crops:** Sugar, rice, corn, pineapples, coconuts. **Minerals:** Cobalt, copper, gold, nickel, silver, oil. **Other resources:** Forests (40% of area). **Crude oil reserves** (1996): 213 mil bbls. **Arable land:** 26%. **Livestock** (1996): buffalo: 2.5 mil; pigs: 8.9 mil; goats: 2.8 mil; cattle: 2.1 mil. **Fish catch** (1995): 2,289,234 metric tons. **Electricity prod.** (1995): 25.7 bil kWh. **Labor force:** 46% agric.; 19% services; 16% ind. and comm.

Finance: Monetary unit: Peso (Aug. 1997: 30.23 = $1 US). **Gross domestic product** (1995 est.): $180 bil. **Per capita GDP:** $2,530. **Imports** (1995): $26.5 bil; partners: Japan 22%, U.S. 19%. **Exports** (1995): $17.4 bil; partners: U.S. 35%, Japan 16%. **Tourism** (1994): $2.3 bil. **National budget** (1995): $13.6 bil. **International reserves less gold** (Apr. 1997): $10.17 bil. **Gold:** 4.46 mil oz t. **Consumer prices** (change in 1996): 8.4%.

Transport: Railroads: Length: 309.9 mi. **Motor vehicles in use:** 573,000 passenger cars, 207,000 comm. vehicles. **Civil aviation:** 8.7 bil passenger-mi.; 21 airports with scheduled flights. **Chief ports:** Cebu, Manila, Iloilo, Davao.

Communications: Television sets: 1 per 2.1 persons. **Radios:** 1 per 6.9 persons. **Telephones:** 1 per 48 persons. **Daily newspaper circ.:** 65 per 1,000 pop.

Health: Life expectancy at birth (1997): 63.4 male; 69.1 female. **Births** (per 1,000 pop.): 29. **Deaths** (per 1,000 pop.): 7. **Natural increase:** 2.2%. **Hospital beds:** 1 per 780 persons. **Physicians:** 1 per 849 persons. **Infant mortality** (per 1,000 live births 1997): 35.

Education: Free and compulsory: ages 7-12. **Literacy** (1995): 95%.

Major International Organizations: UN (World Bank, IMF, WTO), ASEAN.

Embassy: 1600 Massachusetts Ave. NW 20036; 467-9300.

The Malay peoples of the Philippine Islands, whose ancestors probably migrated from Southeast Asia, were mostly hunters, fishers, and unsettled cultivators when first visited by Europeans.

The archipelago was visited by Magellan, 1521. The Spanish founded Manila, 1571. The islands, named for King Philip II of Spain, were ceded by Spain to the U.S. for $20 million, 1898, following the Spanish-American War. U.S. troops suppressed a guerrilla uprising in a brutal 6-year war, 1899-1905.

Japan attacked the Philippines Dec. 8, 1941, and occupied the islands during WW II. On July 4, 1946, independence was proclaimed in accordance with an act passed by the U.S. Congress in 1934. A republic was established.

On Sept. 21, 1972, Pres. Ferdinand Marcos declared martial law. Marcos proclaimed a new constitution, Jan. 17, 1973, with himself as president. His wife, Imelda, received wide powers in 1978 to supervise planning and development. Political corruption was widespread.

Martial law was lifted Jan. 17, 1981, but Marcos retained broad emergency powers. He was reelected in June to a new 6-year term as president.

The assassination of prominent opposition leader Benigno S. Aquino Jr., Aug. 21, 1983, sparked demonstrations calling for the resignation of Marcos. A bitter presidential election campaign ended Feb. 7, 1986, as elections were held amid allegations of widespread fraud. On Feb. 16, Marcos was declared the victor over Corazon Aquino, widow of the slain opposition leader. On

Feb. 24, Marcos declared a state of emergency as his military and religious support eroded. He ended his 20-year tenure as president Feb. 26 and fled the country. Aquino was recognized as president by the U.S. and other nations.

Aquino's government was plagued by a weak economy, widespread poverty, Communist and Muslim insurgencies, and lukewarm military support. Rebel troops seized military bases and TV stations and bombed the presidential palace, Dec. 1, 1989. Government forces defeated the attempted coup aided by air cover provided by U.S. F-4s. Aquino endorsed Fidel Ramos in the May 1992 presidential election, which he won.

The U.S. vacated the Subic Bay Naval Station at the end of 1992, ending its long military presence in the Philippines.

The government signed a cease-fire agreement, Jan. 30, 1994, with Muslim separatist guerrillas, but some rebels refused to abide by the accord. A new treaty providing for expansion and development of the autonomous Muslim region of southern Mindanao was signed Sept. 2, 1996, formally ending a rebellion that had claimed more than 120,000 lives since 1972.

Poland
Republic of Poland
Rzeczpospolita Polska

People: Population: 38,700,291. **Age distrib.** (%): <15: 22; 65+: 12. **Pop. density:** 320 per sq. mi. **Urban:** 64%. **Ethnic groups:** Polish 98%, German, Ukrainian, Byelorussian. **Principal language:** Polish (official). **Religion:** Roman Catholic 95%.

Geography: Area: 120,728 sq. mi. **Location:** On the Baltic Sea in E central Europe. **Neighbors:** Germany on W; Czech Rep., Slovakia on S; Lithuania, Belarus, Ukraine on E; Russia on N. **Topography:** Mostly lowlands forming part of the Northern European Plain. The Carpathian Mts. along the southern border rise to 8,200 ft. **Capital:** Warsaw. **Cities:** (1993): Katowice 3,425,000; Warsaw 2,219,000; Lodz 1,041,000*.

Government: Type: Republic. **Head of state:** Pres. Aleksander Kwasniewski; b Nov. 15, 1954; in office: Dec. 23, 1995. **Head of government:** Prime Min. Wlodzimierz Cimoszewicz; b Sept. 13, 1950; in office: Feb. 1, 1996. **Local divisions:** 49 provinces. **Defense:** 2.4% of GNP (1995). **Active troop strength:** 248,500.

Economy: Industries: Shipbuilding, chemicals, metals, machinery, food processing. **Chief crops:** Grains, potatoes, sugar beets. **Minerals:** Coal, copper, silver, lead, sulfur, natural gas. **Arable land:** 48%. **Livestock** (1996): pigs: 18.8 mil; cattle: 7.4 mil. **Fish catch** (1995): 451,346 metric tons. **Electricity prod.** (1995): 130.9 bil kWh. **Labor force:** 32% ind. & constr.; 28% agric.

Finance: Monetary unit: Zloty (Aug. 1997: 3.4 = $1 US). **Gross domestic product** (1995 est.): $226.7 bil. **Per capita GDP:** $5,800. **Imports** (1995 est.): $23.4 bil; partners: Germany 28%, Italy 8%. **Exports** (1995 est.): $22.2 bil; partners: Germany 36%, Netherlands 6%. **Tourism** (1994): $6.2 bil. **National budget** (1995 est.): $37.8 bil. **International reserves less gold** (June 1997): $19.38 bil. **Gold:** 904,000 oz t. **Consumer prices** (change in 1996): 20.2%.

Transport: Railroads: Length: 15,628.1 mi. **Motor vehicles in use:** 3.5 mil passenger cars, 430,000 comm. vehicles. **Civil aviation:** 2.3 bil passenger-mi.; 12 airports. **Chief ports:** Gdansk, Gdynia, Szczecin.

Communications: Television sets: 1 per 3.2 persons. **Radios:** 1 per 2.3 persons. **Telephones:** 1 per 6.7 persons. **Daily newspaper circ.:** 141 per 1,000 pop.

Health: Life expectancy at birth (1997): 68.1 male; 76.6 female. **Births** (per 1,000 pop.): 12. **Deaths** (per 1,000 pop.): 10. **Natural increase:** 0.2%. **Hospital beds:** 1 per 180 persons. **Physicians:** 1 per 436 persons. **Infant mortality** (per 1,000 live births 1997): 12.

Education: Free and compulsory: ages 7-14. **Literacy** (1994): 99%.

Major International Organizations: UN (WTO, WHO), OECD.

Embassy: 2640 16th St. NW 20009; 234-3800.

Slavic tribes in the area were converted to Latin Christianity in the 10th century. Poland was a great power from the 14th to the 17th centuries. In 3 partitions (1772, 1793, 1795) it was apportioned among Prussia, Russia, and Austria. Overrun by the Austro-German armies in World War I, it declared its independence on Nov. 11, 1918, and was recognized as independent by the Treaty of Versailles, June 28, 1919. Large territories to the east were taken in a war with Russia, 1921.

Germany and the USSR invaded Poland Sept. 1-27, 1939, and divided the country. During the war, some 6 million Polish citizens, half of them Jews, were killed by the Nazis. With Germany's defeat, a Polish government-in-exile in London was recognized by the U.S., but the USSR pressed the claims of a rival group. The election of 1947 was completely dominated by the Communists.

In compensation for 69,860 sq. mi. ceded to the USSR, 1945, Poland received approx. 40,000 sq. mi. of German territory E of the Oder-Neisse line comprising Silesia, Pomerania, West Prussia, and part of East Prussia.

In 12 years of rule by Stalinists, large estates were abolished, industries nationalized, schools secularized, and Roman Catholic prelates jailed. Farm production fell off. Harsh working conditions caused a riot in Poznan, June 28-29, 1956. A new Politburo, committed to a more independent Polish Communism, was named Oct. 1956, with Wladyslaw Gomulka as first secretary of the party. Collectivization of farms was ended. Gomulka agreed to permit religious liberty and religious publications, provided the church kept out of politics.

In Dec. 1970 workers in port cities rioted because of price rises and new incentive wage rules. On Dec. 20 Gomulka resigned as party leader; he was succeeded by Edward Gierek. The incentive rules were dropped; price rises were revoked.

After 2 months of labor turmoil had crippled the country, the Polish government, Aug. 30, 1980, met the demands of striking workers at the Lenin Shipyard, Gdansk. Among the 21 concessions granted were the right to form independent trade unions and the right to strike. By 1981, 9.5 mil workers had joined the independent trade union (Solidarity). Solidarity leaders proposed, Dec. 12, a nationwide referendum on establishing a non-Communist government if the government failed to agree to a series of demands.

Spurred by the fear of Soviet intervention, the government, Dec. 13, imposed martial law. Lech Walesa and other Solidarity leaders were arrested. The U.S. imposed economic sanctions, which were lifted when martial law was suspended Dec. 1982. On Apr. 5, 1989, an accord was reached between the government and opposition factions on a broad range of political and economic reforms including free elections. Candidates endorsed by Solidarity swept the parliamentary elections, June 4. Lech Walesa became president Dec. 22, 1990.

A radical economic program designed to transform the economy into a free-market system led to inflation and unemployment. In Sept. 1993 elections, former Communists and other leftists won a majority of seats in the lower house of Parliament. Walesa lost to a former Communist, Aleksander Kwasniewski, in a presidential runoff election, Nov. 19, 1995.

A new constitution was approved by referendum May 25, 1997. On July 8, Poland was invited to become a full member of NATO within 2 years. Flooding in July caused more than $1 billion in property damage. Solidarity won parliamentary elections held Sept. 21.

Portugal
Portuguese Republic
República Portuguesa

People: Population: 9,867,654. **Age distrib.** (%): <15: 17; 65+: 15. **Pop. density:** 277 per sq. mi. **Urban:** 36%. **Ethnic groups:** Homogeneous Mediterranean stock, small African minority. **Principal languages:** Portuguese (official). **Chief religions:** Roman Catholic 97%.

Geography: Area: 35,456 sq. mi., incl. the Azores and Madeira Islands. **Location:** At SW extreme of Europe. **Neighbors:** Spain on N, E. **Topography:** Portugal N of Tajus R., which bisects the country NE-SW, is mountainous, cool and rainy. To the S there are drier, rolling plains, and a warm climate. **Capital:** Lisbon. **Cities** (1993 met. est.): Lisbon 2,048,000; Porto 1,652,000.

Government: Type: Republic. **Head of state:** Pres. Jorge Sampaio; b Sept. 18, 1939; in office: Mar. 9, 1996. **Head of government:** Prime Min. Antonio Guterres; b Apr. 30, 1949; in office: Oct. 30, 1995. **Local divisions:** 18 districts, 2 autonomous regions, one dependency. **Defense:** 2.4% of GDP (1995). **Active troop strength:** 54,200.

Economy: Industries: Textiles, footwear, cork, chemicals, fish canning, wine, paper. **Chief crops:** Grains, potatoes, grapes, olives, fruits. **Minerals:** Tungsten, uranium, iron. **Other resources:** Forests (world leader in cork production). **Arable land:** 32%. **Livestock** (1996): sheep: 6.2 mil; pigs: 2.4 mil; cattle: 1.3 mil. **Fish catch** (1995): 265,508 metric tons. **Electricity prod.** (1995): 31.4 bil kWh. **Labor force:** 55% services; 24% manuf.; 11% agric., fish.

Finance: Monetary unit: Escudo (Aug. 1997: 183.75 = $1 US). **Gross domestic product** (1995 est.): $116.2 bil. **Per capita GDP:** $11,000. **Imports** (1995): $24.1 bil; partners: EU 71%. **Exports** (1995): $18.9 bil; partners: EU 75%. **Tourism** (1994): $3.8 bil. **National budget** (1994): $41 bil. **International reserves less gold** (Feb. 1997): $15.51 bil. **Gold:** 16.07 mil oz t. **Consumer prices** (change in 1996): 3.1%.

Transport: Railroads: Length: 1,905.2 mi. **Motor vehicles in use:** 2.6 mil passenger cars, 879,000 comm. vehicles. **Civil aviation:** 4.9 bil passenger-mi.; 14 airports. **Chief ports:** Lisbon, Setubal, Leixoes.

Communications: Television sets: 1 per 3.1 persons. **Radios:** 1 per 4.3 persons. **Telephones:** 1 per 2.8 persons. **Daily newspaper circ.:** 41 per 1,000 pop.

Health: Life expectancy at birth (1997): 71.8 male; 79.5 female. **Births** (per 1,000 pop.): 11. **Deaths** (per 1,000 pop.): 10. **Natural increase:** 0.0%. **Hospital beds:** 1 per 241 persons. **Physicians:** 1 per 343 persons. **Infant mortality** (per 1,000 live births 1997): 8.

Education: Free and compulsory: ages 6-15. **Literacy** (1995): 90%.

Major International Organizations: UN (WTO, IMF, WHO), NATO, EU, OECD.

Embassy: 2125 Kalorama Rd. NW 20008; 328-8610.

Portugal, an independent state since the 12th century, was a kingdom until a revolution in 1910 drove out King Manoel II and a republic was proclaimed.

From 1932 a strong, repressive government was headed by Premier Antonio de Oliveira Salazar. Illness forced his retirement in Sept. 1968.

On Apr. 25, 1974, the government was seized by a military junta led by Gen. Antonio de Spinola, who became president.

The new government reached agreements providing independence for Guinea-Bissau, Mozambique, Cape Verde Islands, Angola, and São Tomé and Príncipe. Banks, insurance companies, and other industries were nationalized.

Parliament approved, June 1, 1989, a package of reforms that did away with the socialist economy and created a "democratic" economy, denationalizing industries.

Azores Islands, in the Atlantic, 740 mi. W of Portugal, have an area of 868 sq. mi. and a pop. (1993 est.) of 238,000. A 1951 agreement gave the U.S. rights to use defense facilities in the Azores. The **Madeira Islands,** 350 mi. off the NW coast of Africa, have an area of 306 sq. mi. and a pop. (1993 est.) of 254,000. Both groups were offered partial autonomy in 1976.

Macau, area of 6 sq. mi., is an enclave, a peninsula and 2 small islands, at the mouth of the Xi (Pearl) R. in China. Portugal granted broad autonomy in 1976. In 1987, Portugal and China agreed Macau would revert to China in 1999. Macau, like Hong Kong, was guaranteed 50 years of noninterference in its way of life and capitalist system. Pop. (1997 est.): 502,325.

Qatar
State of Qatar
Dawlat Qatar

People: Population: 665,485. **Age distrib.** (%): <15: 29; 65+: 2. **Pop. density:** 150 per sq. mi. **Urban:** 92%. **Ethnic groups:** Arab 40%, Pakistani 18%, Indian 18%, Iranian 10%. **Principal languages:** Arabic (official), English. **Chief religions:** Muslim 95%.

Geography: Area: 4,416 sq. mi. **Location:** Middle East, occupying peninsula on W coast of Persian Gulf. **Neighbors:** Saudi Arabia on S. **Topography:** Mostly a flat desert, with some limestone ridges; vegetation of any kind is scarce. **Capital:** Doha (1992 est.): 313,639.

Government: Type: Traditional monarchy. **Head of state:** Emir Hamad bin Khalifa ath-Thani; b 1950; in office:, June 27, 1995. **Head of government:** Prime Min. Abdullah bin Khalifa ath-Thani; in office: Oct. 29, 1996. **Local divisions:** 9 municipalities. **Defense:** 3.9% of GNP (1993). **Active troop strength:** 11,800 est.

Economy: Industries: Oil production and refining, natural gas. **Crude oil reserves** (1996): 3.7 bil bbls. **Electricity prod.**

(1995): 5.8 bil kWh. **Labor force:** 51% serv.; 25% manuf. & constr.

Finance: Monetary unit: Riyal (Aug. 1997: 3.64 = $1 US). **Gross domestic product** (1994): $10.7 bil. **Per capita GDP:** $20,820. **Imports** (1994 est.): $2 bil; partners: Germany 14%, Japan 12%. **Exports** (1994 est.): $2.9 bil; partners: Japan 61%. **National budget** (FY 1995-96): $3.5 bil. **Gold** (May 1997): 204,000 oz t.

Transport: Civil aviation: 1.5 bil passenger-mi. **Chief ports:** Doha, Umm Said.

Communications: Television sets: 1 per 2.5 persons. **Radios:** 1 per 2.3 persons. **Telephones:** 1 per 4.5 persons.

Health: Life expectancy at birth (1997): 71.1 male; 76.2 female. **Births** (per 1,000 pop.): 20. **Deaths** (per 1,000 pop.): 4. **Natural increase:** 1.7%. **Hospital beds:** 1 per 509 persons. **Physicians:** 1 per 793 persons. **Infant mortality** (per 1,000 live births 1997): 19.

Education: Literacy (1995): 79%.

Major International Organizations: UN (FAO, IMF, World Bank, WTO), Arab League, OPEC.

Embassy: 600 New Hampshire Ave. NW 20037; 338-0111.

Qatar was under Bahrain's control until the Ottoman Turks took power, 1872 to 1915. In a treaty signed 1916, Qatar gave Great Britain responsibility for its defense and foreign relations. After Britain announced it would remove its military forces from the Persian Gulf area by the end of 1971, Qatar sought a federation with other British-protected states in the area; this failed and Qatar declared itself independent, Sept. 1, 1971. Crown Prince Hamad bin Khalifa ath-Thani ousted his father, Emir Khalifa bin Hamad ath-Thani, June 27, 1995.

Oil and natural gas revenues give Qatar a per capita income among the world's highest.

Romania

People: Population: 21,399,114. **Age distrib.** (%): <15: 19; 65+: 13. **Pop. density:** 233 per sq. mi. **Urban:** 56%. **Ethnic groups:** Romanian 89%, Hungarian 9%. **Principal languages:** Romanian (official), Hungarian, German. **Chief religions:** Romanian Orthodox 70%, Roman Catholic 6%, Protestant 6%.

Geography: Area: 92,043 sq. mi. **Location:** SE Europe, on the Black Sea. **Neighbors:** Moldova on E, Ukraine on N, Hungary and Yugoslavia on W, Bulgaria on S. **Topography:** The Carpathian Mts. encase the north-central Transylvanian plateau. There are wide plains S and E of the mountains, through which flow the lower reaches of the rivers of the Danube system. **Capital:** Bucharest. **Cities** (1994 met. est.): Bucharest 2,339,156; Iasi 815,368; Constanta 747,441.

Government: Type: Republic. **Head of state:** Pres. Emil Constantinescu; b Nov. 19, 1939; in office: Nov. 29, 1996. **Head of government:** Prime Min. Victor Ciorbea; in office: Dec. 12, 1996. **Local divisions:** 40 counties and 1 municipality. **Defense:** 3% of GDP (1995). **Active troop strength:** 228,400.

Economy: Industries: Mining, construction materials, metals, machinery, oil products, chemicals, food processing. **Chief crops:** Grains, grapes, sugar beets, potatoes. **Minerals:** Oil, gas, coal. **Crude oil reserves** (1996): 1.6 bil bbls. **Other resources:** Timber. **Arable land:** 43%. **Livestock** (1996): sheep: 10.4 mil; pigs: 8.0 mil; cattle: 3.5 mil. **Fish catch** (1993): 34,919 metric tons. **Electricity prod.** (1995): 55.2 bil kWh. **Labor force:** 33% agric.; 26% mining & manuf.

Finance: Monetary unit: Leu (Aug. 1997: 7,420 = $1 US). **Gross domestic product** (1995 est.): $105.7 bil. **Per capita GDP:** $4,600. **Imports** (1994): $7.1 bil; partners: EU 45%, Russia 14%. **Exports** (1994): $6.2 bil; partners: EU 50%, Russia 3%. **Tourism** (1994): $414 mil. **National budget** (1995 est.): $6.6 bil. **International reserves less gold** (Apr. 1997): $2.25 bil. **Gold:** $2.86 mil oz t. **Consumer prices** (change in 1996): 38.8%.

Transport: Railroads: Length: 7,063.3 mi. **Motor vehicles in use:** 2.0 mil passenger cars; 370,000 comm. vehicles. **Civil aviation:** 1.6 bil passenger-mi; 12 airports. **Chief ports:** Constanta, Braila.

Communications: Television sets: 1 per 5.0 persons. **Radios:** 1 per 4.9 persons. **Telephones:** 1 per 7.6 persons. **Daily newspaper circ.:** 297 per 1,000 pop.

Health: Life expectancy at birth (1997): 65.6 male; 73.8 female. **Births** (per 1,000 pop.): 10. **Deaths** (per 1,000 pop.): 12. **Natural increase:** –0.3%. **Hospital beds:** 1 per 105 persons. **Physicians:** 1 per 565 persons. **Infant mortality** (per 1,000 live births 1997): 23.

Education: Compulsory: ages 6-16. **Literacy** (1992): 97%.

Major International Organizations: UN (World Bank, IMF, WTO).

Embassy: 1607 23d St. NW 20008; 332-4846.

Romania's earliest known people merged with invading Proto-Thracians, preceding by centuries the Dacians. The Dacian kingdom was occupied by Rome, AD 106-271; people and language were Romanized. The principalities of Wallachia and Moldavia, dominated by Turkey, were united in 1859, became Romania in 1861. In 1877 Romania proclaimed independence from Turkey, and became an independent state by the Treaty of Berlin, 1878; a kingdom under Carol I, 1881; and a constitutional monarchy with a bicameral legislature, 1886.

Romania helped Russia in its war with Turkey, 1877-78. After World War I it acquired Bessarabia, Bukovina, Transylvania, and Banat. In 1940 it ceded Bessarabia and Northern Bukovina to the USSR, part of southern Dobrudja to Bulgaria, and northern Transylvania to Hungary.

In 1941, Prem. Marshal Ion Antonescu led Romania in support of Germany against the USSR. In 1944 he was overthrown by King Michael and Romania joined the Allies.

After occupation by Soviet troops a People's Republic was proclaimed, Dec. 30, 1947; Michael was forced to abdicate.

On Aug. 22, 1965, a new constitution proclaimed Romania a Socialist Republic. President Nicolae Ceausescu maintained an independent course in foreign affairs, but his domestic policies were repressive. All industry was state-owned, and state farms and cooperatives owned almost all the arable land.

On Dec. 16, 1989, security forces opened fire on antigovernment demonstrators in Timisoara; hundreds were buried in mass graves. Ceausescu declared a state of emergency as protests spread to other cities. On Dec. 21, in Bucharest, security forces fired on protesters. Army units joined the rebellion, Dec. 22, and a group known as the Council of National Salvation announced that it had overthrown the government. Fierce fighting took place between the army, which backed the new government, and forces loyal to Ceausescu.

Ceausescu and his wife were captured and, following a trial in which they were found guilty of genocide, were executed Dec. 25, 1989. Former Communists dominated the government in succeeding years. A new constitution providing for a multiparty system took effect Dec. 8, 1991. Many of Romania's state-owned companies were privatized in 1996. The former Communists were swept from power in elections Nov. 3 and 17.

Russia
Russian Federation
Rossiyskaya Federatsiya

People: Population: 147,987,101. **Age distrib.** (%): <15: 21; 65+: 12. **Pop. density:** 22 per sq. mi. **Urban:** 76%. **Ethnic groups:** Russians 82%, Tatar 4%. **Principal languages:** Russian (official), many others. **Chief religions:** Russian Orthodox, Muslim, others.

Geography: Area: 6,592,800 sq. mi., more than 76% of the total area of the former USSR and the largest country in the world. **Location:** Stretches from E Europe across N Asia to the Pacific O. **Neighbors:** Finland, Norway, Estonia, Latvia, Belarus, Ukraine on W; Georgia, Azerbaijan, Kazakhstan, China, Mongolia, North Korea on S; Kaliningrad exclave bordered by Poland on the S, Lithuania on the N and E. **Topography:** Russia contains every type of climate except the distinctly tropical, and has a varied topography. The European portion is a low plain, grassy in S, wooded in N, with Ural Mts. on the E, and Caucasus Mts. on the S. Urals stretch N-S for 2,500 mi. The Asiatic portion is also a vast plain, with mountains on the S and in the E; tundra covers extreme N, with forest belt below; plains, marshes are in W, desert in SW. **Capital:** Moscow. **Cities:** Moscow 9,269,000; St. Petersburg 5,132,000; Novosibirsk 1,476,000*.

Government: Type: Federation. **Head of state:** Pres. Boris Yeltsin; b Feb. 1, 1931; in office: July 10, 1991. **Head of government:** Prime Min. Viktor Chernomyrdin; b Apr. 9, 1938; in office: Dec. 14, 1992. **Local divisions:** 21 autonomous republics, 49 oblasts, 6 krays, 10 autonomous okrugs, 1 autonomous oblast. **Defense:** 12.4% of GNP (1994). **Active troop strength:** 1.27 mil est.

Economy: Industries: Steel, machinery, machine tools, vehicles, chemicals, mining, footwear, textiles, appliances, paper. **Chief crops:** Grains, sugar beets, potatoes, vegetables, sunflowers. **Minerals:** Manganese, mercury, potash, bauxite, cobalt, chromium, copper, coal, gold, lead, molybdenum, nickel, phosphates, silver, tin, tungsten, zinc, oil, gas, iron, potassium. **Crude oil reserves** (1996): 57 bil bbls. (all former USSR). **Other resources:** Forests. **Arable land:** 8%. **Live-**

stock (1996): cattle: 39.7 mil; sheep: 25.8 mil; pigs: 22.6 mil; goats: 2.2 mil. **Fish catch** (1995): 4,373,827 metric tons. **Electricity prod.** (1995): 843.6 bil kWh. **Labor force:** 84% production & serv.; 16% govt.

Finance: Monetary unit: Ruble (Aug. 1997: 5,815 = $1 US). **Gross domestic product** (1995 est.): $796 bil. **Per capita GDP:** $5,300. **Imports** (1995): $33 bil; partners: Germany 20%, U.S. 8%. **Exports** (1995): $66 bil; partners: Germany 9%, U.S. 7%. **Tourism** (1994): $1.2 bil. **National budget** (1996): $56.6 bil. **International reserves less gold** (May 1997): $15.88 bil. **Gold:** 13.77 mil oz t. **Consumer prices** (change in 1996): 47.6%.

Transport: Railroads: Length: 95,634.0 mi. **Motor vehicles in use:** 10.5 mil passenger cars, 407,000 comm. vehicles. **Civil aviation:** 40.5 bil passenger-mi.; 75 airports. **Chief ports:** St. Petersburg, Murmansk, Arkhangelsk.

Communications: Television sets: 1 per 2.7 persons. **Radios:** 1 per 2.9 persons. **Telephones:** 1 per 5.9 persons. **Daily newspaper circ.:** 267 per 1,000 pop.

Health: Life expectancy at birth (1997): 57.2 male; 70.7 female. **Births** (per 1,000 pop.): 11. **Deaths** (per 1,000 pop.): 16. **Natural increase:** –0.5%. **Hospital beds:** 1 per 80 persons. **Physicians:** 1 per 235 persons. **Infant mortality** (per 1,000 live births 1997): 24.

Education: Free and compulsory: ages 7-17. **Literacy** (1995): 99%.

Major International Organizations: UN (ILO, IMF, WHO), CIS. **Embassy:** 2650 Wisconsin Ave. NW 20007; 298-5700.

History. Slavic tribes began migrating into Russia from the W in the 5th century AD. The first Russian state, founded by Scandinavian chieftains, was established in the 9th century, centering in Novgorod and Kiev. In the 13th century the Mongols overran the country. It recovered under the grand dukes and princes of Muscovy, or Moscow, and by 1480 freed itself from the Mongols. Ivan the Terrible was the first to be formally proclaimed Tsar (1547). Peter the Great (1682-1725) extended the domain and, in 1721, founded the Russian Empire.

Western ideas and the beginnings of modernization spread through the huge Russian empire in the 19th and early 20th centuries. But political evolution failed to keep pace.

Military reverses in the 1905 war with Japan and in World War I led to the breakdown of the Tsarist regime. The 1917 Revolution began in March with a series of sporadic strikes for higher wages by factory workers. A provisional democratic government under Prince Georgi Lvov was established but was quickly followed in May by the second provisional government, led by Alexander Kerensky. The Kerensky government and the freely-elected Constituent Assembly were overthrown in a Communist coup led by Vladimir Ilyich Lenin Nov. 7.

Soviet Union

Lenin's death Jan. 21, 1924, resulted in an internal power struggle from which Joseph Stalin eventually emerged on top. Stalin secured his position at first by exiling opponents, but from the 1930s to 1953, he resorted to a series of "purge" trials, mass executions, and mass exiles to work camps. These measures resulted in millions of deaths, according to most estimates.

Germany and the Soviet Union signed a non-aggression pact Aug. 1939; Germany launched a massive invasion of the Soviet Union, June 1941. Notable heroic episode was the "900 days" siege of Leningrad (now St. Petersburg), lasting to Jan. 1944, and causing a million deaths; the city was never taken. Russian winter counterthrusts, 1941-42 and 1942-43, stopped the German advance. Turning point was the failure of German troops to take and hold Stalingrad (now Volgograd), Sept. 1942 to Feb. 1943. With British and U.S. Lend-Lease aid and sustaining great casualties, the Russians drove the German forces from eastern Europe and the Balkans in the next 2 years.

After Stalin died, Mar. 5, 1953, Nikita Khrushchev was elected first secretary of the Central Committee. In 1956 he condemned Stalin. "De-Stalinization" of the country was begun.

Under Khrushchev the open antagonism of Poles and Hungarians toward domination by Moscow was brutally suppressed in 1956. He advocated peaceful co-existence with the capitalist countries, but continued arming the Soviet Union with nuclear weapons. He aided the Cuban revolution under Fidel Castro but withdrew Soviet missiles from Cuba during confrontation by U.S. Pres. Kennedy, Sept.-Oct. 1962. Khrushchev was suddenly deposed, Oct. 1964, and replaced by Leonid I. Brezhnev.

In Aug. 1968 Russian, Polish, East German, Hungarian, and Bulgarian military forces invaded Czechoslovakia to put a curb on liberalization policies of the Czech government.

Massive Soviet military aid to North Vietnam in the late 1960s and early 1970s helped assure Communist victories throughout Indo-China. Soviet arms aid and advisers were sent to several African countries in the 1970s.

In Dec. 1979, Soviet forces entered Afghanistan to support that government against rebels. In Apr. 1988, the Soviets agreed to withdraw their troops, ending a futile 8-year war.

Mikhail Gorbachev was chosen gen. secy. of the Communist Party, Mar. 1985. He held 4 summit meetings with U.S. Pres. Ronald Reagan. In 1987, in Washington, a treaty was signed eliminating intermediate-range nuclear missiles from Europe.

In 1987, Gorbachev initiated a program of reforms, including expanded freedoms and the democratization of the political process, through openness (*glasnost*) and restructuring (*perestroika*). The reforms were opposed by some Eastern bloc countries and many old-line Communists in the USSR. Gorbachev faced economic problems as well as ethnic and nationalist unrest in the republics.

When an apparent coup against Gorbachev became known on Aug. 19, 1991, the pres. of the Russian Republic, Boris Yeltsin, denounced it and called for a general strike. Some 50,000 demonstrated at the Russian Parliament in support of Yeltsin. By Aug. 21, the coup had failed and Gorbachev was restored as president. On Aug. 24, Gorbachev resigned as leader of the Communist Party. Several republics declared their independence, including Russia, Ukraine, and Kazakhstan. On Aug. 29, the Soviet Parliament voted to suspend all activities of the Communist Party.

The Soviet Union officially broke up Dec. 26, 1991, one day after Gorbachev resigned. The Soviet hammer and sickle flying over the Kremlin was lowered and replaced by the flag of Russia, ending the domination of the Communist Party over all areas of national life since 1917.

Russian Federation

In a first major step in radical economic reform, Russia eliminated state subsidies of most goods and services, Jan. 1992. The effect was to allow prices to soar far beyond the means of ordinary workers. In June, Pres. Yeltsin and U.S. Pres. George Bush agreed to massive arms reductions.

Russia launched a drive to privatize thousands of large and medium-sized state-owned enterprises in 1993. Yeltsin narrowly survived an impeachment vote by the Congress of People's Deputies, Mar. 28. He received strong support from voters in a referendum Apr. 25, but he continued to face a legislature dominated by conservatives and former Communists.

On Sept. 21, 1993, Yeltsin called early elections and dissolved Parliament, which in turn declared him deposed. Anti-Yeltsin legislators then barricaded themselves in the Parliament building. On Oct. 3, anti-Yeltsin forces attacked some facilities in Moscow and broke into the Parliament building. Yeltsin ordered the army to attack and seize the building. About 140 people were killed in the fighting, according to medical authorities. More than 150 were arrested.

In elections Dec. 12, 1993, a Yeltsin-supported constitution was approved, but ultranationalists and Communist hard-liners made strong showings in legislative contests. In Dec. 1994 the Russian government sent troops into the breakaway republic of Chechnya. Grozny, the Chechen capital, fell in Feb. 1995 after heavy fighting, but Chechen rebels continued to resist.

Communists made further gains in parliamentary elections Dec. 17, 1995. Despite poor health, Yeltsin won a presidential runoff election over a Communist opponent, July 3, 1996. On Aug. 14, after rebels embarrassed the Russian military by retaking Grozny, Yeltsin gave his security chief, Alexander Lebed, broad powers to negotiate an end to the Chechnya war. Lebed and Chechen leaders signed a peace accord Aug. 31. On Oct. 17, Yeltsin dismissed Lebed for insubordination. Yeltsin survived quintuple-bypass heart surgery Nov. 5.

The last Russian troops remaining in Chechnya were pulled out in Jan. 1997. A revitalized Yeltsin revamped his cabinet in Mar. to strengthen the hand of reformers. On May 27, 1997, he signed a "founding act" increasing cooperation with NATO and paving the way for NATO to admit Eastern European countries.

Rwanda
Republic of Rwanda
Republika y'u Rwanda

People: Population: 7,737,537. **Age distrib.** (%): <15: 46; 65+: 3. **Pop. density:** 760 per sq. mi. **Urban:** 6%. **Ethnic groups:** Hutu 90%, Tutsi 19%, Twa (Pygmy) 1%. **Principal**

languages: French, Kinyarwanda (both official). **Chief religions:** Christian 74%, indigenous beliefs 25%, Muslim 1%.

Geography: Area: 10,169 sq. mi. **Location:** In E central Africa. **Neighbors:** Uganda on N, Congo-(formerly Zaire) on W, Burundi on S, Tanzania on E. **Topography:** Grassy uplands and hills cover most of the country, with a chain of volcanoes in the NW. The source of the Nile R. has been located in the headwaters of the Kagera (Akagera) R., SW of Kigali. **Capital:** Kigali (1993): 234,500.

Government: Type: Republic. **Head of state:** Pres. Pasteur Bizimungu; in office: July 19, 1994. **Head of government:** Prime Min. Pierre Claver Rwigema; in office: Aug. 31, 1995. **Local divisions:** 10 prefectures. **Defense:** 7% of GDP (1992). **Active troop strength:** 33,000+.

Economy: Industries: Mining, cement. **Chief crops:** Coffee, tea, bananas. **Minerals:** Tin, gold, wolframite. **Arable land:** 29%. **Electricity prod.** (1995): 169 mil kWh. **Labor force:** 93% agric.

Finance: Monetary unit: Franc (Aug. 1997: 295.50 = $1 US). **Gross domestic product** (1995 est.): $3.8 bil. **Per capita GDP:** $400. **Imports** (1994): $459 mil; partners: Belg.-Lux. 17%, Kenya 13%, France 7%. **Exports** (1994): $32 mil; partners: Germany 21%, Netherlands 19%. **National budget** (1992 est.): $453.7 mil. **International reserves less gold** (June 1997): $198.38 mil. **Consumer prices** (change in 1996): 7.4%.

Transport: Motor vehicles in use: 7,900 passenger cars, 2,000 comm. vehicles. **Civil aviation:** 1.2 mil passenger-mi. **Chief ports:** Gisenyi, Cyangugu.

Communications: Radios: 1 per 15 persons. **Telephones:** 1 per 530 persons.

Health: Life expectancy at birth (1997): 38.6 male; 39.6 female. **Births** (per 1,000 pop.): 39. **Deaths** (per 1,000 pop.): 21. **Natural increase:** 1.8%. **Infant mortality** (per 1,000 live births 1997): 119.

Education: Compulsory: ages 7-14. **Literacy** (1995): 61%.

Major International Organizations: UN (IMF, WHO, WTO), OAU.

Embassy: 1714 New Hampshire Ave. NW 20009; 232-2882.

For centuries, the Tutsi (an extremely tall people) dominated the Hutu (90% of the population). A civil war broke out in 1959 and Tutsi power was ended. Many Tutsi went into exile. A referendum in 1961 abolished the monarchic system. Rwanda, which had been part of the Belgian UN trusteeship of Rwanda-Urundi, became independent July 1, 1962.

In 1963 Tutsi exiles invaded in an unsuccessful coup; a large-scale massacre of Tutsi followed. Rivalries among Hutu led to a bloodless coup July 1973 in which Juvénal Habyarimana took power. After an invasion and coup attempt by Tutsi exiles in 1990, a multiparty democracy was established.

Renewed ethnic strife led to an Aug. 1993 peace accord between the government and rebels of the Tutsi-led Rwandan Patriotic Front (RPF). But after Habyarimana and the president of Burundi were killed Apr. 6, 1994, in a suspicious plane crash, massive violence broke out. At least 500,000 died in massacres, mainly of Tutsi by Hutu militias, and in civil warfare as the RPF sought power. An estimated 2 million Tutsi and Hutu fled to camps in Zaire (now Congo) and other countries, where many died of cholera and other natural causes. French troops under a UN mandate moved into SW Rwanda June 23 to establish a so-called safe zone. The RPF claimed victory, installing a government in July led by a moderate Hutu president. French troops pulled out Aug. 22. A UN peacekeeping mission ended Mar. 8, 1996, but a UN-sponsored tribunal and the Rwandan government continued to gather evidence against those responsible for genocide. More than 1 million refugees (mostly Hutu) flooded back to Rwanda from Tanzania and Zaire in Nov. and Dec. 1996.

Saint Kitts and Nevis
Federation of Saint Kitts and Nevis

People: Population: 41,803. **Age distrib.** (%): <15: 34; 65+: 6. **Pop. density:** 401 per sq. mi. **Urban:** 34%. **Ethnic groups:** Black African 95%. **Principal language:** English (official). **Chief religions:** Protestant 76%, Roman Catholic 11%.

Geography: Area: 104 sq. mi. **Location:** In the N part of the Leeward group of the Lesser Antilles in the E Caribbean Sea. **Neighbors:** Antigua and Barbuda to E. **Capital:** Basseterre (1994 est.): 12,600.

Government: Type: Constitutional monarchy. **Head of state:** Queen Elizabeth II, represented by Gov. Gen. Sir Cuthbert M. Sebastian; b Oct. 22, 1921; in office: Jan. 1, 1996. **Head of government:** Prime Min. Denzil Llewellyn Douglas; b Jan. 14, 1953; in office: July 3, 1995. **Local divisions:** 14 parishes.

Economy: Industries: Sugar (main industry), tourism. **Arable land:** 22%. **Electricity prod.** (1995): 81 mil kWh. **Labor force:** 69% services; 31% manuf.

Finance: Monetary unit: East Caribbean Dollar (Sept. 1997: 2.70 = $1 US). **Gross domestic product** (1995 est.): $220 mil. **Per capita GDP:** $5,380. **Tourism** (1994): $75 mil. **National budget** (1996 est.) $100 mil. **International reserves less gold** (May 1997): $38.37 mil. **Consumer prices** (change in 1996): 2.5%.

Chief ports: Basseterre, Charlestown.

Transport: Railroads: Length: 36.0 mi.

Communications: Television sets: 1 per 4.7 persons. **Telephones:** 1 per 2.8 persons.

Health (1997): **Life expectancy at birth:** 64.2 male; 70.4 female. **Births** (per 1,000 pop.): 23. **Deaths** (per 1,000 pop.): 9. **Natural increase:** 1.4%. **Hospital beds:** 1 per 142 persons. **Physicians:** 1 per 1,057 persons. **Infant mortality** (per 1,000 live births): 18.

Education: Compulsory for 12-13 years between ages 5-18. **Literacy** (1992): 90%.

Major International Organizations: UN (WTO), the Commonwealth, OAS.

Embassy: 3216 New Mexico Ave., NW 20016; 686-2636.

St. Kitts (formerly St. Christopher; known by the natives as Liamuiga) and Nevis were reached (and named) by Columbus in 1493. They were settled by Britain in 1623, but ownership was disputed with France until 1713. They were part of the Leeward Islands Federation, 1871-1956, and the Federation of the West Indies, 1958-62. The colony achieved self-government as an Associated State of the UK in 1967, and became fully independent Sept. 19, 1983.

Saint Lucia

People: Population: 159,639. **Age distrib.** (%): <15: 33; 65+: 5. **Urban:** 37%. **Pop. density:** 670 per sq. mi. **Ethnic groups:** African descent 90%. **Principal languages:** English (official), French patois. **Chief religions:** Roman Catholic 90%, Protestant 7%.

Geography: Area: 238 sq. mi. **Location:** In E Caribbean, 2d largest of the Windward Isls. **Neighbors:** Martinique to N, St. Vincent to S. **Topography:** Mountainous, volcanic in origin; Soufriere, a volcanic crater, in the S. Wooded mountains run N-S to Mt. Gimie, 3,145 ft., with streams through fertile valleys. **Capital:** Castries (1992 met. est.): 13,615.

Government: Type: Parliamentary democracy. **Head of state:** Queen Elizabeth II, represented by Gov.-Gen. Stanislaus Anthony James; b Nov. 13, 1919; in office: Oct. 10, 1988. **Head of government:** Prime Min. Kenny Anthony; b Jan. 8, 1951; in office: May 24, 1997. **Local divisions:** 11 quarters.

Economy: Industries: Clothing, beverages, tourism, manufacturing. **Chief crops:** Bananas, coconuts, cocoa, citrus fruits. **Other resources:** Forests. **Arable land:** 8%. **Electricity prod.** (1995): 110 mil kWh. **Labor force:** 43% agric.; 39% services; 18% ind. & commerce.

Finance: Monetary unit: East Caribbean Dollar (Sept. 1997: 2.70 = $1 US). **Gross domestic product** (1995 est.): $640 mil. **Per capita GDP:** $4,080. **Imports** (1993): $300 mil; partners: U.S. 37%, UK 13%. **Exports** (1993): $120 mil; partners: UK 50%, U.S. 27%. **Tourism** (1994): $224 mil. **International reserves less gold** (May 1997): $60.30 mil.

Transport: Motor vehicles in use: 11,000 passenger cars, 800 comm. vehicles. **Chief ports:** Castries, Vieux Fort.

Communications: Television sets: 1 per 5.3 persons. **Radios:** 1 per 1.3 persons. **Telephones:** 1 per 5.4 persons.

Health: Life expectancy at birth (1997): 66.7 male; 74.2 female. **Births** (per 1,000 pop.): 22. **Deaths** (per 1,000 pop.): 6. **Natural increase:** 1.6%. **Hospital beds:** 1 per 318 persons. **Physicians:** 1 per 2,235 persons. **Infant mortality** (per 1,000 live births 1997): 20.

Education: Compulsory: ages 5-15.**Literacy** (1993): 80%.

Major International Organizations: UN (IMF, WTO, ILO), the Commonwealth, OAS.

Embassy: 3216 New Mexico Ave. NW 20016; 364-6792.

St. Lucia was ceded to Britain by France at the Treaty of Paris, 1814. Self-government was granted with the West Indies Act, 1967. Independence was attained Feb. 22, 1979.

Saint Vincent and the Grenadines

People: Population: 119,092. **Pop. density:** 793 per sq. mi. **Urban:** 50%. **Ethnic groups:** Mainly African descent.

Principal languages: English (official), French patois. **Chief religions:** Anglican, Methodist, Roman Catholic.

Geography: Area: 150 sq. mi. **Location:** In the E Caribbean, St. Vincent (133 sq. mi.) and the northern islets of the Grenadines form a part of the Windward chain. **Neighbors:** St. Lucia to N, Barbados to E, Grenada to S. **Topography:** St. Vincent is volcanic, with a ridge of thickly wooded mountains running its length. **Capital:** Kingstown (1994): 15,924.

Government: Type: Constitutional monarchy. **Head of state:** Queen Elizabeth II, represented by Gov.-Gen. Sir David Jack; b July 16, 1918; in office: Sept. 20, 1989. **Head of government:** Prime Min. James Fitz-Allen Mitchell; b May 15, 1931; in office: July 30, 1984. **Local divisions:** 6 parishes.

Economy: Industries: Agriculture, tourism. **Chief crops:** Bananas, coconuts. **Arable land:** 38%. **Electricity prod.** (1995): 64 mil kWh. **Labor force:** 20% agric; 19% services.

Finance: Monetary unit: East Caribbean Dollar (Sept. 1997: 2.70 = $1 US). **Gross domestic product** (1995 est.): $240 mil. **Per capita GDP:** $2,060. **Tourism** (1994): $51 mil. **National budget** (1996 est.): $118 mil. **International reserves less gold** (May 1997): $26.13 mil. **Consumer prices** (change in 1996): 4.4%.

Transport: Motor vehicles in use: 4,900 passenger cars, 3,200 comm. vehicles. **Chief port:** Kingstown.

Communications: Television sets: 1 per 6.8 persons. **Radios:** 1 per 1.5 persons. **Telephones:** 1 per 6.1 persons.

Health (1997): **Life expectancy at birth:** 71.7 male; 74.8 female. **Births** (per 1,000 pop.): 19. **Deaths** (per 1,000 pop.): 5. **Natural increase:** 1.4%. **Physicians:** 1 per 2,708 persons. **Infant mortality** (per 1,000 live births): 16.

Education: Literacy (1992): 96%.

Major International Organizations: UN (WTO), OAS, the Commonwealth.

Embassy: 1717 Massachusetts Ave. NW 20036; 462-7806.

Columbus landed on St. Vincent on Jan. 22, 1498 (St. Vincent's Day). Britain and France both laid claim to the island in the 17th and 18th centuries; the Treaty of Versailles, 1783, finally ceded it to Britain. Associated State status was granted 1969; independence was attained Oct. 27, 1979.

Samoa *(formerly* Western Samoa)
Independent State of Samoa

People: Population: 219,509. **Age distrib.** (%): <15: 40; 65+: 4. **Pop. density:** 200 per sq. mi. **Urban:** 21%. **Ethnic groups:** Samoan (Polynesian) 93%, Euronesian (mixed) 7%. **Principal languages:** Samoan, English (both official). **Chief religions:** Christian 99.7%.

Geography: Area: 1,093 sq. mi. **Location:** In the S Pacific O. **Neighbors:** Nearest are Fiji to SW, Tonga to S. **Topography:** Main islands, Savaii (659 sq. mi.) and Upolu (432 sq. mi.), both ruggedly mountainous, and small islands Manono and Apolima. **Capital:** Apia (1991): 32,859.

Government: Type: Constitutional monarchy. **Head of state:** Malietoa Tanumafili II; b Jan. 4, 1913; in office: Jan. 1, 1962. **Head of government:** Prime Min. Tofilau Eti Alesana; in office: Apr. 11, 1988. **Local divisions:** 11 districts.

Economy: Industries: Timber, tourism. **Chief crops:** Coconuts, yams, bananas. **Other resources:** Hardwoods, fish. **Arable land:** 19%. **Electricity prod.** (1995): 65 mil kWh. **Labor force:** 65% agric.; 30% services; 5% industry.

Finance: Monetary unit: Tala (Aug. 1997: 2.49 = $1 US). **Gross domestic product** (1995 est.): $415 mil. **Per capita GDP:** $1,900. **Imports** (1992): $11.5 mil; partners: NZ 37%. **Exports** (1993): $6.4 mil; partners: NZ 34%; Australia 25%. **Tourism** (1994): $23 mil. **International reserves less gold** (May 1997): $62.47 mil. **Consumer prices** (change in 1996): 7.6%.

Transport: Motor vehicles in use: 1,100 passenger cars, 1,200 comm. vehicles. **Chief ports:** Apia, Asau.

Communications: Television sets: 1 per 26 persons. **Radios:** 1 per 2.2 persons. **Telephones:** 1 per 22 persons.

Health: Life expectancy at birth (1997): 66.7 male; 71.6 female. **Births** (per 1,000 pop.): 30. **Deaths** (per 1,000 pop.): 6. **Natural increase:** 2.5%. **Hospital beds:** 1 per 255 persons. **Physicians:** 1 per 2,682 persons. **Infant mortality** (per 1,000 live births 1997): 33.

Education: Free and compulsory: ages 6-16. **Literacy** (1989): 100%.

Major International Organizations: UN (IMF, World Bank), the Commonwealth.

Embassy: 820 2d Ave., Suite 800, New York, NY 10017; (212) 599-6196.

Samoa (formerly known as Western Samoa to distinguish it from American Samoa, a small U.S. territory) was a German colony, 1899 to 1914, when New Zealand landed troops and took over. It became a New Zealand mandate under the League of Nations and, in 1945, a New Zealand UN Trusteeship.

An elected local government took office in Oct. 1959 and the country became fully independent Jan. 1, 1962.

San Marino

Most Serene Republic of San Marino

Serenissima Repubblica di San Marino

People: Population: 24,714. **Age distrib.** (%): <15: 16; 65+: 16. **Pop. density:** 1,029 per sq. mi. **Urban:** 95%. **Ethnic groups:** Sammarinese 75%, Italian 23%. **Principal languages:** Italian. **Chief religions:** Predominantly Roman Catholic.

Geography: Area: 24 sq. mi. **Location:** In N central Italy near Adriatic coast. **Neighbors:** Completely surrounded by Italy. **Topography:** The country lies on the slopes of Mt. Titano. **Capital:** San Marino. **Cities** (1996 est.): Serravalle/Dogano 7,904; San Marino 4,357.

Government: Type: Republic. **Head of state:** Two co-regents appt. every 6 months. **Local divisions:** 9 municipalities. **Defense:** 1% of GDP (1992 est.).

Economy: Industries: Tourism, woolen goods, wine, cement, ceramics. **Chief crops:** Wheat, grapes, corn. **Arable land:** 17%.

Finance: Monetary unit: Italian Lira. **Gross domestic product** (1993): $380 mil. **Per capita GDP:** $15,800. **National budget** (1995 est.): $320 mil.

Communications: Radios: 1 per 1.7 persons. **Telephones:** 1 per 1.6 persons.

Health (1997): **Life expectancy at birth:** 77.4 male; 85.3 female. **Births** (per 1,000 pop.): 11. **Deaths** (per 1,000 pop.): 8. **Natural increase:** 0.3%. **Infant mortality** (per 1,000 live births): 6.

Education: Compulsory: ages 6-14. **Literacy** (1995): 98%.

Major International Organizations: UN.

San Marino claims to be the oldest state in Europe and to have been founded in the 4th century. A Communist-led coalition ruled 1947-57; a similar coalition ruled 1978-86. It has had a treaty of friendship with Italy since 1862.

São Tomé and Príncipe

Democratic Republic of São Tomé and Príncipe

República Democrática de São Tomé e Príncipe

People: Population: 147,865. **Age distrib.** (%): <15: 40; 65+: 5. **Pop. density:** 383 per sq. mi. **Urban:** 44%. **Ethnic groups:** Mesticos (Portuguese-African mixture), African minority (Angola, Mozambique immigrants). **Principal languages:** Portuguese (official). **Chief religions:** Roman Catholic, Protestant.

Geography: Area: 386 sq. mi. **Location:** In the Gulf of Guinea about 125 miles off W central Africa. **Neighbors:** Gabon, Equatorial Guinea to E. **Topography:** São Tomé and Príncipe islands, part of an extinct volcano chain, are both covered by lush forests and croplands. **Capital:** São Tomé (1993 est.): 43,000.

Government: Type: Republic. **Head of state:** Pres. Miguel Trovoada; b Dec. 27, 1936; in office: Apr. 3, 1991. **Head of government:** Prime Min. Raul Bragança Neto; in office: Nov. 19, 1996. **Local divisions:** 2 districts.

Economy: Chief crops: Cocoa, coconut products. **Arable land:** 1%. **Electricity prod.** (1995): 16 mil kWh.

Finance: Monetary unit: Dobra (Dec. 1996: 2,833 = $1 US). **Gross domestic product** (1994 est.): $138 mil. **Per capita GDP:** $1,000.

Transport: Civil aviation: 5 mil passenger-mi. **Chief ports:** São Tomé, Santo Antonio.

Communications: Television sets: 1 per 6.2 persons. **Radios:** 1 per 3.7 persons. **Telephone:** 1 per 52 persons.

Health: Life expectancy at birth (1997): 62.2 male; 66.1 female. **Births** (per 1,000 pop.): 34. **Deaths** (per 1,000 pop.): 8. **Natural increase:** 2.5%. **Physicians:** 1 per 1,881 persons. **Infant mortality** (per 1,000 live births 1997): 60.

Education: Compulsory for 4 years between ages 7-14. **Literacy** (1991): 73%.

Major International Organizations: UN, OAU.

The islands were discovered in 1471 by the Portuguese, who brought the first settlers—convicts and exiled Jews. Sugar planting was replaced by the slave trade as the chief economic activity until coffee and cocoa were introduced in the 19th century.

Portugal agreed, 1974, to turn the colony over to the Gabon-based Movement for the Liberation of São Tomé and Príncipe, which proclaimed as first president its East German-trained leader, Manuel Pinto da Costa. Independence came July 12, 1975. Democratic reforms were instituted in 1987. In 1991 Miguel Trovoada won the first free presidential election following da Costa's withdrawal. A military coup that ousted Trovoada Aug. 15, 1995, was reversed a week later after Angolan mediation. Trovoada defeated da Costa in a presidential runoff election, July 21, 1996.

Saudi Arabia

Kingdom of Saudi Arabia

Al Mamlakah al Arabiyah as Saudiyah

People: Population: 20,087,965. **Age distrib.** (%): <15: 43; 65+: 2. **Pop. density:** 23 per sq. mi. **Urban:** 84%. **Ethnic groups:** Arab 90%, Afro-Asian 10%. **Principal languages:** Arabic (official). **Chief religions:** Muslim 100%.

Geography: Area: 864,000 sq. mi. **Location:** Occupies most of Arabian Peninsula in Middle East. **Neighbors:** Kuwait, Iraq, Jordan on N; Yemen, Oman on S; United Arab Emirates, Qatar on E. **Topography:** Bordered by Red Sea on the W. The highlands on W, up to 9,000 ft., slope as an arid, barren desert to the Persian Gulf on the E. **Capital:** Riyadh. **Cities:** Riyadh 2,619,000; Jeddah 1,492,000; Mecca 777,000*.

Government: Type: Monarchy with council of ministers. **Head of state and government:** King Fahd ibn Abdul Aziz; b 1923; in office: June 13, 1982 (prime min. since 1982). **Local divisions:** 13 provinces. **Defense:** 8.5% of GDP (1996). **Active troop strength:** 105,500.

Economy: Industries: Oil, oil products. **Chief crops:** Dates, wheat, barley, citrus. **Minerals:** Oil, gas, gold, copper, iron. **Crude oil reserves** (1996): 261.5 bil barrels. **Arable land:** 1%. **Livestock** (1996): sheep: 7.8 mil; goats: 4.4 mil. **Electricity prod.** (1995): 65 bil kWh. **Labor force:** 40% govt.; 25% industry & oil; 30% services; 5% agric.

Finance: Monetary unit: Riyal (Aug. 1997: 3.75 = $1 US). **Gross domestic product** (1995 est.): $189 bil. **Per capita GDP:** $10,100. **Imports** (1994 est.): $21.3 bil; partners: US 21%, Japan 12%, UK 8%. **Exports** (1994 est.): $41.7 bil; partners: U.S. 17%, Japan 17%. **Tourism** (1994): $1.1 bil. **National budget** (1993 est.): $50 bil. **International reserves less gold** (May 1997): $9.28 bil. **Gold:** 4.60 mil oz t. **Consumer prices** (change in 1996): 1.2%.

Transport: Railroads: Length: 863.2 mi. **Motor vehicles in use:** 1.7 mil passenger cars, 1.1 mil comm. vehicles. **Civil aviation:** 11.3 bil passenger-mi.; 25 airports with scheduled flights. **Chief ports:** Jeddah, Ad Dammam, Ras Tanurah.

Communications: Television sets: 1 per 3.9 persons. **Radios:** 1 per 3.4 persons. **Telephones:** 1 per 10 persons. **Daily newspaper circ.:** 54 per 1,000 pop.

Health: Life expectancy at birth (1997): 67.7 male; 71.4 female. **Births** (per 1,000 pop.): 38. **Deaths** (per 1,000 pop.): 5. **Natural increase:** 3.3%. **Hospital beds:** 1 per 433 persons. **Physicians:** 1 per 612 persons. **Infant mortality** (per 1,000 live births 1997): 44.

Education: Literacy (1995): 63%.

Major International Organizations: UN (IMF, WHO, FAO), Arab League, OPEC.

Embassy: 601 New Hampshire Ave. NW 20037; 342-3800.

Before Muhammad, Arabia was divided among numerous warring tribes and small kingdoms and was at times dominated by larger Arabian and non-Arabian kingdoms. It was united for the first time by Muhammad, in the early 7th century AD. His successors conquered the entire Near East and North Africa, bringing Islam and the Arabic language. But Arabia itself soon returned to its former status.

Nejd, in central Arabia, long an independent state and center of the Wahhabi sect, fell under Turkish rule in the 18th century. In 1913 Ibn Saud, founder of the Saudi dynasty, overthrew the Turks and captured the Turkish province of Hasa in E Arabia; he took the Hejaz region in W Arabia in 1925 and most of Asir, in SW Arabia, by 1926. The discovery of oil in the 1930s transformed the new country.

Ibn Saud reigned until his death, Nov. 1953. Subsequent kings have been sons of Ibn Saud. The king exercises authority together with a Council of Ministers. The Islamic religious code is the law of the land. Alcohol and public entertainments are restricted, and women have an inferior legal status. There is no constitution and no parliament, although a Consultative Council was established by the king in 1993.

Saudi Arabia has often allied itself with the U.S. and other Western nations, and billions of dollars of advanced arms have been purchased from Britain, France, and the U.S.; however, Western support for Israel has often strained relations. Saudi units fought against Israel in the 1948 and 1973 Arab-Israeli wars. Beginning with the 1967 Arab-Israeli war, Saudi Arabia provided large annual financial gifts to Egypt; aid was later extended to Syria, Jordan, and Palestinian groups, as well as to other Islamic countries.

King Faisal played a leading role in the 1973-74 Arab oil embargo against the U.S. and other nations. Crown Prince Khalid was proclaimed king on Mar. 25, 1975, after the assassination of Faisal. Fahd became king on June 13, 1982, following Khalid's death.

The Hejaz contains the holy cities of Islam—Medina, where the Mosque of the Prophet enshrines the tomb of Muhammad, and Mecca, his birthplace. More than 2 million Muslims make pilgrimage to Mecca annually. In 1987, Iranians making a pilgrimage to Mecca clashed with anti-Iranian pilgrims and Saudi police; more than 400 were killed. Some 1,426 Muslim pilgrims died July 2, 1990, in a stampede in a pedestrian tunnel leading to Mecca. Nearly 300 pilgrims were killed in a stampede in Mecca, May 26, 1994. More than 340 pilgrims died in a tent fire near Mecca, Apr. 15, 1997.

Following Iraq's attack on Kuwait, Aug. 2, 1990, Saudi Arabia accepted the Kuwait royal family and more than 400,000 Kuwaiti refugees. King Fahd invited Western and Arab troops to deploy on its soil in support of Saudi defense forces. During the Persian Gulf War, 28 U.S. soldiers were killed when an Iraqi missile hit their barracks in Dhahran, Feb. 25, 1991. The nation's northern Gulf coastline suffered severe pollution as a result of Iraqi sabotage of the Kuwaiti oil fields. Islamic extremists were blamed for truck bombs that killed 7 (5 from the U.S.) at a military training center in Riyadh, Nov. 13, 1995, and 19 Americans at a base in Dhahran, June 25, 1996. U.S. officials repeatedly chided the Saudi government for failing to cooperate fully in the investigation.

Senegal
Republic of Senegal
République du Sénégal

People: Population: 9,403,546. **Age distrib.** (%): <15: 48; 65+: 3. **Pop. density:** 123 per sq. mi. **Urban:** 44%. **Ethnic groups:** Wolof 36%, Fulani 17%, Serer 17%, Diola 9%, Toucouleur 9%, Mandingo 9%. **Principal languages:** French (official), Wolof, Pulaar, Diola, Mandingo, others. **Chief religions:** Muslim 92%, indigenous beliefs 6%, Christian 2%.

Geography: Area: 75,951 sq. mi. **Location:** At W extreme of Africa. **Neighbors:** Mauritania on N, Mali on E, Guinea and Guinea-Bissau on S; surrounds Gambia on three sides. **Topography:** Low rolling plains cover most of Senegal, rising somewhat in the SE. Swamp and jungles are in SW. **Capital:** Dakar: 768,000*.

Government: Type: Republic. **Head of state:** Pres. Abdou Diouf; b Sept. 7, 1935; in office: Jan. 1, 1981. **Head of government:** Prime Min. Habib Thiam; b Jan 21, 1933; in office: Apr. 8, 1991. **Local divisions:** 10 regions. **Defense:** 2.1% of GDP (1996 est.). **Active troop strength:** 13,400 est.

Economy: Industries: Food processing, fishing. **Chief crops:** Peanuts, millet, rice. **Minerals:** Phosphates, iron. **Arable land:** 27%. **Livestock** (1996): sheep: 4.8 mil; goats: 3.25 mil; cattle: 2.9 mil. **Fish catch** (1995): 348,288 metric tons. **Electricity prod.** (1995): 730 mil kWh. **Labor force:** 77% subsistence agric.

Finance: Monetary unit: CFA Franc (Aug. 1997: 610 = $1 US). **Gross domestic product** (1995 est.): $14.5 bil. **Per capita GDP:** $1,600. **Imports** (1994 est.): $1.1 bil; partners: France 31%, Cote d'Ivoire 7%. **Exports** (1994 est.): $940 mil;

partners: France 28%, India 14%. **Tourism** (1994): $115 mil. **National budget** (1992): $1.2 bil. **International reserves less gold** (Mar. 1997): $353.6 mil. **Gold:** 29,000 oz t. **Consumer prices** (change in 1996): 2.8%.

Transport: Railroads: Length: 561.4 mi. **Motor vehicles in use:** 106,000 passenger cars, 48,000 comm. vehicles. **Civil aviation:** 139.1 mil passenger-mi. **Chief ports:** Dakar, Saint-Louis.

Communications: Television sets: 1 per 27 persons. **Radios:** 1 per 8.5 persons. **Telephones:** 1 per 102 persons.

Health: Life expectancy at birth (1997): 54.2 male; 59.8 female. **Births** (per 1,000 pop.): 45. **Deaths** (per 1,000 pop.): 11. **Natural increase:** 3.4%. **Hospital beds:** 1 per 1,041 persons. **Physicians:** 1 per 14,825 persons. **Infant mortality** (per 1,000 live births 1997): 63.

Education: Compulsory: ages 7-13. **Literacy** (1995): 33%.

Major International Organizations: UN and all of its specialized agencies, OAU.

Embassy: 2112 Wyoming Ave. NW 20008; 234-0540.

Portuguese settlers arrived in the 15th century, but French control grew from the 17th century. The last independent Muslim state was subdued in 1893. Dakar became the capital of French West Africa.

Independence as part, along with the Sudanese Rep., of the Mali Federation, came June 20, 1960. Senegal withdrew Aug. 20. French political and economic influence remained strong.

Senegal, Dec. 17, 1981, signed an agreement with The Gambia for confederation of the 2 countries, without loss of individual sovereignty, under the name of Senegambia. The confederation collapsed in 1989, although in 1991 the 2 nations signed a friendship and cooperation treaty.

Separatists in Casamance Province of S Senegal have clashed with government forces since 1982.

Seychelles
Republic of Seychelles

People: Population: 78,142. **Age distrib.** (%): <15: 30; 65+: 6. **Pop. density:** 443 per sq. mi. **Urban:** 55%. **Ethnic groups:** Seychellois (mixture of Asians, Africans, and French). **Principal languages:** English, French (both official), Creole. **Chief religions:** Roman Catholic 90%, Anglican 8%.

Geography: Area: 176 sq. mi. **Location:** In the Indian O. 700 miles NE of Madagascar. **Neighbors:** Nearest are Madagascar on SW, Somalia on NW. **Topography:** A group of 86 islands, about half of them composed of coral, the other half granite, the latter predominantly mountainous. **Capital:** Victoria (1993 est.): 25,000.

Government: Type: Republic. **Head of state:** Pres. France-Albert René, b. Nov. 16, 1935; in office: June 5, 1977. **Local divisions:** 23 districts. **Defense:** 4% of GDP (1990 est.). **Active troop strength:** 300.

Economy: Industries: Tourism, food processing, fishing. **Chief crops:** Coconuts, cinnamon, vanilla. **Arable land:** 4%. **Electricity prod.** (1995): 125 mil kWh. **Labor force:** 31% industry & comm.; 21% services; 20% govt.; 12% agric.

Finance: Monetary unit: Rupee (Aug. 1997: 5.10 = $1 US). **Gross domestic product** (1993 est.): $430 mil. **Per capita GDP:** $6,000. **Imports** (1993 est.): $261 mil; partners: Bahran 16%; Singapore 16%. **Exports** (1993 est.): $50 mil; partners: France 43%; UK 22%. **National budget** (1993): $263 mil. **Tourism** (1994): $103 mil. **International reserves less gold** (Feb.. 1997): $26.79 mil. **Consumer prices** (change in 1996): −1.2%.

Transport: Motor vehicles in use: 5,100 passenger cars, 2,000 comm. vehicles. **Civil aviation:** 425.4 mil passenger-mi. **Chief port:** Victoria.

Communications: Television sets: 1 per 11 persons. **Radios:** 1 per 2.0 persons. **Telephones:** 1 per 5.6 persons. **Daily newspaper circ.:** 44 per 1,000 pop.

Health: Life expectancy at birth (1997): 64.8 male; 74.5 female. **Births** (per 1,000 pop.): 21. **Deaths** (per 1,000 pop.): 7. **Natural increase:** 1.3%. **Hospital beds:** 1 per 180 persons. **Physicians:** 1 per 974 persons. **Infant mortality** (per 1,000 live births 1997): 12.

Education: Free and compulsory: ages 6-15. **Literacy** (1995): 84%.

Major International Organizations: UN, OAU, the Commonwealth.

Embassy: 820 2d Ave., New York, NY 10017; 212-687-9766.

The islands were occupied by France in 1768, and seized by Britain in 1794. Ruled as part of Mauritius from 1814, the

Seychelles became a separate colony in 1903. The ruling party had opposed independence as impractical, but pressure from the OAU and the UN became irresistible, and independence was declared June 29, 1976. The first president was ousted in a coup a year later by a socialist leader. A new constitution, approved June 1993, provided for a multiparty state.

Sierra Leone
Republic of Sierra Leone

People: Population: 4,891,546. **Age distrib.** (%): <15: 45; 65+: 3. **Pop. density:** 176 per sq. mi. **Urban:** 34%. **Ethnic groups:** Temne 30%, Mende 30%, other tribes 39%. **Principal languages:** English (official), tribal languages, Krio. **Chief religions:** Muslim 60%, indigenous beliefs 30%, Christian 10%.
Geography: Area: 27,699 sq. mi. **Location:** On W coast of W Africa. **Neighbors:** Guinea on N and E, Liberia on S. **Topography:** The heavily-indented, 210-mi. coastline has mangrove swamps. Behind are wooded hills, rising to a plateau and mountains in the E. **Capital:** Freetown. (1990 est.) 669,000.
Government: Type: In transition. **Head of state:** Maj. Johnny Paul Koromah; in office: May 25, 1997. **Local divisions:** 3 provinces, 1 area. **Defense:** 2.6% of GDP (FY 1992-93). **Active troop strength:** 14,200 est.
Economy: Industries: Mining, light manufacturing. **Chief crops:** Cocoa, coffee, palm kernels, rice. **Minerals:** Diamonds, titanium, bauxite. **Arable land:** 25%. **Fish catch** (1994): 62,568 metric tons. **Electricity prod.** (1995): 230 mil kWh. **Labor force:** 65% agric.; 35% ind. & serv.
Finance: Monetary unit: Leone (Aug 1997: 863 = $1 US). **Gross domestic product** (1994 est.): $4.4 bil. **Per capita GDP:** $960. **Imports** (1994): $150 mil; partners: U.S. 43%. **Exports** (1994): $115 mil; partners: U.S. 45%, UK 17%. **National budget** (1992 est.): $118 mil. **International reserves less gold** (Apr. 1997): $32.9 mil. **Consumer prices** (change in 1996): 23.2%.
Transport: Railroads: Length: 52.2 mi. **Motor vehicles in use:** 32,000 passenger cars, 12,000 comm. vehicles. **Civil aviation:** 41 mil passenger-mi. **Chief ports:** Freetown, Bonthe.
Communications: Television sets: 1 per 91 persons. **Radios:** 1 per 4.3 persons. **Telephones:** 1 per 271 persons.
Health: Life expectancy at birth (1997): 45.1 male; 51.1 female. **Births** (per 1,000 pop.): 47. **Deaths** (per 1,000 pop.): 18. **Natural increase:** 2.9 **Physicians:** 1 per 10,832 persons. **Infant mortality** (per 1,000 live births 1997): 133.
Education: Literacy (1995): 31%.
Major International Organizations: UN (IMF, WHO, WTO), the Commonwealth, OAU.
Embassy: 1701 19th St. NW 20009; 939-9261.

Freetown was founded in 1787 by the British government as a haven for freed slaves. Their descendants, known as Creoles, number more than 60,000.

Successive steps toward independence followed the 1951 constitution. Full independence arrived Apr. 27, 1961. Sierra Leone became a republic Apr. 19, 1971. A one-party state approved by referendum in 1978 brought political stability, but mismanagement and corruption plagued the economy.

Mutinous soldiers ousted Pres. Joseph Momoh Apr. 30, 1992. Another coup, Jan. 16, 1996, paved the way for multiparty elections and a return to civilian rule. A peace accord signed Nov. 30 with the Revolutionary United Front ended a civil war that had taken more than 10,000 lives in 5 years. A coup on May 25, 1997, met with widespread international opposition.

Singapore
Republic of Singapore

People: Population: 3,461,929. **Age distrib.** (%): <15: 22; 65+: 7. **Pop. density:** 13,847 per sq. mi. **Urban:** 100%. **Ethnic groups:** Chinese 76%, Malay 15%, Indian 6%. **Principal languages:** Chinese, Malay, Tamil, English (all official). **Chief religions:** Buddhist, Taoist, Muslim, Christian, Hindu.
Geography: Area: 250 sq. mi. **Location:** Off tip of Malayan Peninsula in SE Asia. **Neighbors:** Nearest are Malaysia on N, Indonesia on S. **Topography:** Singapore is a flat, formerly swampy island. The nation includes 40 nearby islets. **Capital:** Singapore 3,327,000*.
Government: Type: Republic. **Head of state:** Pres. Ong Teng Cheong; b Jan 22, 1936; in office: Sept. 2, 1993. **Head of**

government: Prime Min. Goh Chok Tong; b May 20, 1941; in office: Nov. 28, 1990. **Defense:** 4.3% of GDP (1995 est.). **Active troop strength:** 53,900 est.
Economy: Industries: Oil refining, electronics, banking, food and rubber processing, biotechnology. **Arable land:** 4%. **Fish catch** (1995): 9,941 metric tons. **Electricity prod.** (1995): 21 bil kWh. **Labor force:** 34% finance, business, other serv.; 26% manuf.; 23% commerce.
Finance: Monetary unit: Dollar (Aug. 1997: 1.50 = $1 US). **Gross domestic product** (1995 est.): $66.1 bil. **Per capita GDP:** $22,900. **Imports** (1995): $125.9 bil; partners: Japan 22%, Malaysia 16%, U.S. 15%. **Exports** (1995): $119.6 bil; partners: Malaysia 20%, U.S. 19%, Hong Kong 9%. **Tourism** (1994): $7.1 bil. **National budget** (FY 1995-96 est.): $12.9 bil. **International reserves** (May 1997): $80.43 bil. **Consumer prices** (change in 1996): 1.4%.
Transport: Railroads: Length: 24.0 mi. **Motor vehicles in use:** 324,000 passenger cars, 137,000 comm. vehicles. **Civil aviation:** 27.9 bil passenger-mi.; 1 airport. **Chief port:** Singapore.
Communications: Television sets: 1 per 2.6 persons. **Radios:** 1 per 1.6 persons. **Telephones:** 1 per 2.1 persons. **Daily newspaper circ.:** 364 per 1,000 pop.
Health: Life expectancy at birth (1997): 75.3 male; 81.7 female. **Births** (per 1,000 pop.): 16. **Deaths** (per 1,000 pop.): 5. **Natural increase:** 1.2%. **Hospital beds:** 1 per 281 persons. **Physicians:** 1 per 681 persons. **Infant mortality** (per 1,000 live births 1997): 5.
Education: Literacy (1995): 91%.
Major International Organizations: UN (WTO, IMF, WHO), the Commonwealth, ASEAN.
Embassy: 3501 International Pl. NW 20008; 537-3100.

Founded in 1819 by Sir Thomas Stamford Raffles, Singapore was a British colony until 1959, when it became autonomous within the Commonwealth. On Sept. 16, 1963, it joined with Malaya, Sarawak, and Sabah to form the Federation of Malaysia. Tensions between Malayans, dominant in the federation, and ethnic Chinese, dominant in Singapore, led to an accord under which Singapore became a separate nation, Aug. 9, 1965.

Singapore is one of the world's largest ports. Standards in health, education, and housing are high. International banking has grown. The government, dominated by a single party, has taken strong actions to suppress dissent.

Slovakia
Slovak Republic
Slovenská Republika

People: Population: 5,393,016. **Age distrib.** (%): <15: 22; +65: 11. **Pop. density:** 284 per sq. mi. **Urban:** 59%. **Ethnic groups:** Slovak 86%, Hungarian 11%. **Principal languages:** Slovak (official), Hungarian. **Chief religions:** Roman Catholic 60%, Protestant 8%.
Geography: Area: 18,933 sq. mi. **Location:** In E central Europe. **Neighbors:** Poland on N, Hungary on S, Austria and Czech Rep. on W, Ukraine on E. **Topography:** Mountains (Carpathians) in N, fertile Danube plane in S. **Capital:** Bratislava. **Cities** (1995 est.): Bratislava 450,776; Kosice 239,927.
Government: Type: Republic. **Head of state:** Pres. Michal Kovac; b Aug. 5, 1930; in office: Mar. 1993. **Head of government:** Prime Min. Vladimir Meciar; b July 26, 1942; in office: Dec. 13, 1994. **Local divisions:** 4 departments. **Defense:** 3% of GDP (1995). **Active troop strength:** 42,600 est.
Economy: Industries: Metal products, food and beverages, oil, chemicals. **Chief crops:** Grains, potatoes, sugar beets, hops, fruit. **Minerals:** Coal, iron, copper. **Livestock** (1996): pigs: 2.1 mil; cattle: 929,000. **Electricity prod.** (1995): 23.2 bil kWh. **Labor force:** 33% ind.; 12% agric.; 10% constr.
Finance: Monetary unit: Koruna (Aug. 1997: 34.70 = $1 US). **Gross domestic product** (1995 est.): $39 bil. **Per capita GDP:** $7,200. **Imports** (1995): $8.7 bil; partners: Czech Rep. 28%, Russia 17%. **Exports** (1995): $8.8 bil; parnters: Czech Rep. 35%, Germany 19%. **Tourism** (1994): $568 mil. **International reserves less gold** (June 1997): 2.96 bil. **Gold:** 1.29 mil oz t. **Consumer prices** (change in 1996): 5.8%.
Transport: Railroads: Length: 2,272.9 mi. **Motor vehicles in use:** 994,000 passenger cars, 94,000 comm. vehicles. **Civil aviation:** 7.5 mil passenger-mi.; 2 airports with scheduled flights. **Chief ports:** Bratislava, Komarno.
Communications: Television sets: 1 per 2.1 persons. **Radios:** 1 per 1.8 persons. **Telephones:** 1 per 4.8 persons. **Daily newspaper circ.:** 256 per 1,000 pop.

Health (1997): **Life expectancy at birth:** 69.1 male; 77.3 female. **Births** (per 1,000 pop.): 13. **Deaths** (per 1,000 pop.): 9. **Natural increase:** 0.3%. **Hospital beds:** 1 per 85 persons. **Physicians:** 1 per 290 persons. **Infant mortality** (per 1,000 live births): 11.
Education: Compulsory: ages 6-14. **Literacy** (1994): 100%.
Major International Organizations: UN (WTO, WHO, IMF).
Embassy: 2201 Wisconsin Ave. NW 20007; 965-5161.

Slovakia was originally settled by Illyrian, Celtic, and Germanic tribes and was incorporated into Great Moravia in the 9th century. It became part of Hungary in the 11th century. Overrun by Czech Hussites in the 15th century, it was restored to Hungarian rule in 1526. The Slovaks disassociated themselves from Hungary following World War I and joined the Czechs of Bohemia to form the Republic of Czechoslovakia, Oct. 28, 1918.
Germany invaded Czechoslovakia, 1939, and declared Slovakia independent. Slovakia rejoined Czechoslovakia in 1945.
Czechoslovakia split into 2 separate states—the Czech Republic and Slovakia—on Jan. 1, 1993. Slovakia, with its less developed economy, applied to join the European Union in 1995.

Slovenia
Republic of Slovenia
Republika Slovenija

People: Population: 1,945,998. **Age distrib.** (%): <15: 17; 65+: 13. **Pop. density:** 248 per sq. mi. **Urban:** 52%. **Ethnic groups:** Slovene 91%, Croat 3%. **Principal languages:** Slovenian (official), Serbo-Croatian. **Chief religions:** Roman Catholic 96%.
Geography: Area: 7,821 sq. mi. **Location:** In SE Europe. **Neighbors:** Italy on W, Austria on N, Hungary on NE, Croatia on SE, S. **Topography:** Mostly hilly; 42% of the land is forested. **Capital:** Ljubljana (1995 est.): 276,119.
Government: Type: Republic. **Head of state:** Pres. Milan Kucan; b Jan. 14, 1941; in office: Apr. 1990. **Head of government:** Prime Min. Janez Drnovsek; b May 1950; in office: May 14, 1992. **Local divisions:** 60 provinces. **Defense:** 3.6% of GDP (1995 est.). **Active troop strength:** 9,550.
Economy: Industries: Metallurgy, electronics, vehicles. **Minerals:** Coal, lead, zinc, mercury. **Chief crops:** Potatoes, hops, wheat. **Arable land:** 10%. **Livestock** (1996): pigs: 592,000; cattle: 496,000. **Electricity prod.** (1995): 11.6 bil kWh.
Finance: Monetary unit: Tolar (Aug. 1997: 166.19= $1 US). **Gross domestic product** (1995 est.): $22.6 bil. **Per capita GDP:** $11,000. **Imports** (1995 est.): $9.1 bil; partners: Germany 24%, Italy 17%. **Exports** (1995 est.): $8.3 bil; partners: Germany 31%, former Yugoslavia 14%. **Tourism** (1994): $932 mil. **International reserves less gold** (May 1997): $2.70 bil. **Gold:** 3,000 oz t. **Consumer prices** (change in 1996): 9.7%.
Transport: Railroads: Length: 745.8 mi. **Motor vehicles in use:** 657,000 passenger cars, 37,000 comm. vehicles. **Civil aviation:** 204.3 mil passenger-mi; 1 airport. **Chief ports:** Izola, Koper.
Communications: Television sets: 1 per 3.1 persons. **Radios:** 1 per 2.6 persons. **Telephones:** 1 per 3.2 persons. **Daily newspaper circ.:** 185 per 1,000 pop.
Health: Life expectancy at birth (1997): 71.5 male; 79.1 female. **Births** (per 1,000 pop.): 8. **Deaths** (per 1,000 pop.): 10. **Natural increase:** –0.1%. **Hospital beds:** 1 per 173 persons. **Physicians:** 1 per 943 persons. **Infant mortality** (per 1,000 live births 1997): 7.
Education: Free and compulsory: ages 5-15. **Literacy** (1993): 99%.
Major International Organizations: UN (WTO, WHO, IMF).
Embassy: 1525 New Hampshire Ave. NW 20036; 667-5363.

The Slovenes settled in their current territory during the period from the 6th to the 8th century. They fell under German domination as early as the 9th century. Modern Slovenian political history began after 1848 when the Slovenes, who were divided among several Austrian provinces, began their struggle for political and national unification. With the establishment of the Kingdom of Serbs, Croats, and Slovenes in 1918, this unification was largely achieved when the majority of the Slovenes entered the new state, which later became Yugoslavia.
Slovenia declared independence June 25, 1991, and joined the UN May 22, 1992. Linked by trade with the European Union, Slovenia applied for full membership June 10, 1996.

Solomon Islands

People: Population: 426,855. **Age distrib.** (%): <15: 45; 65+: 3.**Pop. density:** 38 per sq. mi. **Urban:** 18%. **Ethnic groups:** Melanesian 93%, Polynesian 4%. **Principal languages:** English (official); Melanesian, Papuan, Polynesian languages. **Chief religions:** Anglican 34%, Roman Catholic 19%, Baptist 17%, other Christian 26%.
Geography: Area: 10,954 sq. mi. **Location:** Melanesian Archipelago in the W Pacific O. **Neighbors:** Nearest is Papua New Guinea to W. **Topography:** 10 large volcanic and rugged islands and 4 groups of smaller ones. **Capital:** Honiara (1996 est.): 43,643.
Government: Type: Parliamentary democracy within the Commonwealth of Nations. **Head of state:** Queen Elizabeth II, represented by Gov.-Gen. Moses Pitakaka; in office: June 1994. **Head of government:** Prime Min. Bartholomew Ulufa'alu; in office: Aug. 27, 1997. **Local divisions:** 7 provinces and Honiara.
Economy: Industries: Copra, fishing. **Chief crops:** Coconuts, rice, cocoa, beans. **Minerals:** Gold, bauxite. **Other resources:** Forests. **Arable land:** 1%. **Fish catch** (1994): 39,000 metric tons. **Electricity prod.** (1995): 30 mil kWh. **Labor force:** 42% services 24% agric., forestry, fish.
Finance: Monetary unit: Dollar (Aug. 1997: 3.69 = $1 US). **Gross domestic product** (1992): $1 bil. **Per capita GDP:** $2,590. **Imports** (1993): $101 mil; partners: Australia 34%, Japan 16%. **Exports** (1993): $94 mil; partners: Japan 39%, UK 23%. **International reserves less gold** (Mar. 1997): $29.34 mil. **Consumer prices:** (change in 1996): 11.8%.
Transport: Civil aviation: 40.4 mil passenger-mi. 30 airports with scheduled flights.
Communications: Radios: 1 per 8.2 persons. **Telephones:** 1 per 58 persons.
Health: Life expectancy at birth (1997): 69.0 male; 74.1 female. **Births** (per 1,000 pop.): 37. **Deaths** (per 1,000 pop.): 4. **Natural increase:** 3.3%. **Hospital beds:** 1 per 1,208 persons. **Physicians:** 1 per 6,154 persons. **Infant mortality** (per 1,000 live births 1997): 25.
Education: Literacy (1994): 54%.
Major International Organizations: UN (WHO, IMF), the Commonwealth.

The Solomon Islands were sighted in 1568 by an expedition from Peru. Britain established a protectorate in the 1890s over most of the group, inhabited by Melanesians. The islands saw major World War II battles. Self-government came Jan. 2, 1976, and independence was formally attained July 7, 1978.

Somalia
Soomaaliya

People: Population: 9,940,232. **Age distrib.** (%): <15: 44; +65: 4. **Pop. density:** 40 per sq. mi. **Urban:** 26%. **Ethnic groups:** Mainly Somali. **Principal languages:** Somali (official), Arabic, Italian, English. **Chief religions:** Mainly Sunni Muslim.
Geography: Area: 246,000 sq. mi. **Location:** Occupies the eastern horn of Africa. **Neighbors:** Djibouti, Ethiopia, Kenya on W. **Topography:** The coastline extends for 1,700 mi. Hills cover the N; the center and S are flat. **Capital:** Mogadishu 997,000*.
Government: Type: In transition. **Local divisions:** 18 regions.
Economy: Chief crops: Sugar, bananas, sorghum, corn, mangoes. **Minerals:** Iron, tin, gypsum, bauxite, uranium. **Arable land:** 2%. **Livestock** (1996): sheep: 13.5 mil; goats: 12.5 mil; camels: 6.2 mil; cattle: 5.2 mil. **Fish catch** (1993): 14,850 metric tons. **Electricity prod.** (1995): 245 mil kWh. **Labor force:** 71% nomadic agric; 29% industry & services.
Finance: Monetary unit: Shilling (Aug. 1997: 4,000 = $1 US). **Gross domestic product** (1995 est.): $3.6 bil. **Per capita GDP:** $500. **Imports** (1991): $360 mil; partners: Italy 31%. **Exports** (1991): $86 mil; partners: Italy 29%, Suadi Arabia 23%.
Transport: Motor vehicles in use: 12,000 passenger cars, 12,000 comm. vehicles. **Civil aviation:** 86.9 mil passenger-mi. **Chief ports:** Mogadishu, Berbera.
Communications: Radios: 1 per 24 persons. **Telephones:** 1 per 605 persons.
Health (1997): **Life expectancy at birth:** 55.5 male; 56.2 female. **Births** (per 1,000 pop.): 44. **Deaths** (per 1,000 pop.): 13. **Natural increase:** 3.1%. **Infant mortality** (per 1,000 live births): 119.
Education: Free and compulsory: ages 6-14. **Literacy** (1990): 24%.
Major International Organizations: UN, OAU, Arab League.

British Somaliland (present-day N Somalia) was formed in the 19th century, as was Italian Somaliland (now central and S Somalia). Italy lost its African colonies in World War II. In 1949, the UN approved eventual independence for the former Italian colony (designated the UN Trust Territory of Somalia) after a 10-year period under Italian administration.

British Somaliland gained independence, June 26, 1960, and by prearrangement, merged July 1 with the trust territory of Somalia to create the independent Somali Republic (Somalia).

On Oct. 16, 1969, Pres. Abdi Rashid Ali Shirmarke was assassinated. On Oct. 21, a military group led by Maj. Gen. Muhammad Siad Barre seized power in a bloodless coup. In 1970, Barre declared the country a socialist state—the Somali Democratic Republic. In the following years most of the economy was nationalized.

Somalia has laid claim to Ogaden, the huge eastern region of Ethiopia, peopled mostly by Somalis. Ethiopia battled Somali rebels in 1977. Some 11,000 Cuban troops with Soviet arms defeated Somali army troops and ethnic Somali rebels in Ethiopia, 1978. As many as 1.5 mil refugees entered Somalia. Guerrilla fighting in Ogaden continued until 1988, when a peace agreement was reached with Ethiopia.

The civil war intensified again and Barre was forced to flee the capital, Jan. 1991. Fighting between rival factions caused 40,000 casualties in 1991 and 1992, and by mid-1992 the civil war, drought, and banditry combined to produce a famine that threatened some 1.5 million people with starvation. In July 1992 the UN secretary general declared Somalia to be a country without a government.

In Dec. 1992 the UN accepted a U.S. offer of troops to safeguard food delivery to the starving. The UN took control of the multinational relief effort from the U.S. May 4, 1993. While the operation helped alleviate the famine, efforts to reestablish order foundered, and there were significant U.S. and other casualties. The U.S. withdrew its peacekeeping forces Mar. 25, 1994. When the last UN troops pulled out Mar. 3, 1995, Mogadishu still had no functioning government, and armed factions controlled different parts of the country.

South Africa
Republic of South Africa

People: Population: 42,327,458. **Age distrib.** (%): <15: 40; 65+: 4. **Pop. density:** 89 per sq. mi. **Urban:** 50%. **Ethnic groups:** Black 75%, White 14%, Coloured 9%. **Principal languages:** 11 official languages incl. Afrikaans, English, Ndebele, Sotho. **Chief religions:** Mainly Christian; Hindu, Muslim minorities.

Geography: Area: 470,693 sq. mi. **Location:** At the southern extreme of Africa. **Neighbors:** Namibia, Botswana, Zimbabwe on N; Mozambique, Swaziland on E; surrounds Lesotho. **Topography:** The large interior plateau reaches close to the country's 2,700-mi. coastline. There are few major rivers or lakes; rainfall is sparse in W, more plentiful in E. **Capitals:** Cape Town (legislative), Pretoria (executive), and Bloemfontein (judicial). **Cities** Cape Town 2,727,000; Johannesburg 2,172,000; Pretoria 1,314,000*.

Government: Type: Federal republic with bicameral Parliament and universal suffrage. **Head of state:** Pres. Nelson Mandela; b July 18, 1918; in office: May 10, 1994. **Local divisions:** 9 provinces. **Defense:** 2.2% of GDP (FY 1995-96). **Active troop strength:** 137,900 est.

Economy: Industries: Mining, steel, chemicals, vehicles, machinery, textiles. **Chief crops:** Corn, grains, potatoes, sugar, fruit, tomatoes, grapes. **Minerals** Platinum, chromium; antimony, coal, iron, manganese, nickel, phosphates, tin, uranium, gem diamonds, copper, vanadium; world's largest producer of gold. **Other resources:** Wool, dairy products. **Arable land:** 10%. **Livestock** (1996): sheep: 29.0 mil; cattle: 13.0 mil; goats: 6.5 mil; pigs: 1.6 mil. **Fish catch** (1995): 575,177 metric tons. **Electricity prod.** (1995): 163.6 bil kWh. **Labor force:** 35% services; 30% agric.; 20% ind.

Finance: Monetary unit: Rand (Aug. 1997: 4.69 = $1 US). **Gross domestic product** (1995 est.): $215 bil. **Per capita GDP** $4,800. **Imports** (1995): $27 bil; partners: Germany 16%, U.S. 16%, UK 11%. **Exports** (1995): $27.9 bil; partners: Switz. 7%, UK 7%, U.S. 5%. **Tourism** (1994): $1.4 bil. **National budget** (FY 1994-95 est.): $38 bil. **International reserves less gold** (June 1997): $3.74 bil. **Gold:** 3.77 mil oz t. **Consumer prices** (change in 1996): 7.4%.

Transport: Railroads: Length: 13,308.7 mi. **Motor vehicles in use:** 3.95 mil passenger cars, 2.0 mil comm. vehicles. **Civil aviation:** 7.7 bil passenger-mi.; 27 airports. **Chief ports:** Durban, Cape Town, East London, Port Elizabeth.

Communications: Television sets: 1 per 9.9 persons. **Radios:** 1 per 3.2 persons. **Telephones:** 1 per 11 persons. **Daily newspaper circ.:** 33 per 1,000 pop.

Health: Life expectancy at birth (1997): 54.4 male; 58.2 female. **Births** (per 1,000 pop.): 27. **Deaths** (per 1,000 pop.): 12. **Natural increase:** 1.5%. **Hospital beds:** 1 per 260 persons. **Physicians:** 1 per 1,523 persons. **Infant mortality** (per 1,000 live births 1997): 53.

Education: Compulsory: ages 7-16. **Literacy** (1995): 82%.

Major International Organizations: UN (WTO), OAU, the Commonwealth.

Embassy: 3051 Massachusetts Ave. NW 20008; 232-4400.

Bushmen and Hottentots were the original inhabitants. Bantus, including Zulu, Xhosa, Swazi, and Sotho, had occupied the area from NE to S South Africa before the 17th century.

The Cape of Good Hope area was settled by Dutch, beginning in the 17th century. Britain seized the Cape in 1806. Many Dutch trekked north and founded 2 republics, the Transvaal and the Orange Free State. Diamonds were discovered, 1867, and gold, 1886. The Dutch (Boers) resented encroachments by the British and others; the Anglo-Boer War followed, 1899-1902. Britain won and, effective May 31, 1910, created the Union of South Africa, incorporating the British colonies of the Cape and Natal, the Transvaal and the Orange Free State. After a referendum, the Union became the Republic of South Africa, May 31, 1961, and withdrew from the Commonwealth.

With the election victory of Daniel Malan's National Party in 1948, the policy of separate development of the races, or apartheid, already existing unofficially, became official. Under apartheid, blacks were severely restricted to certain occupations, and paid far lower wages than whites for similar work. Only whites could vote or run for public office. Persons of Asian Indian ancestry and those of mixed race (Coloureds) had limited political rights. In 1959 the government passed acts providing the eventual creation of several Bantu nations or Bantustans on 13% of the country's land area, though most black leaders opposed the plan.

Protests against the apartheid system were brutally suppressed. At Sharpeville on Mar. 21, 1960, 69 black protesters were killed by government troops. At least 600 persons, mostly Bantus, were killed in 1976 riots protesting apartheid. In 1981, South Africa launched military operations in Angola and Mozambique to combat guerrilla groups. South African troops attacked the South West African People's Organization (SWAPO) guerrillas in Angola, Mar. 1982. South Africa and Mozambique signed a nonaggression pact in 1984.

A new constitution was approved by referendum, Nov. 1983, extending the parliamentary franchise to the Coloured and Asian minorities. Laws banning interracial sex and marriage were repealed in 1985.

In 1986, Nobel Peace Prize winner Bishop Desmond Tutu called for Western nations to apply sanctions against South Africa to force an end to apartheid. President P. W. Botha announced in Apr. the end to the nation's system of racial pass laws and offered blacks an advisory role in government. On May 19, South Africa attacked 3 neighboring countries—Zimbabwe, Botswana, Zambia—to strike at guerrilla strongholds of the black nationalist African National Congress (ANC). A nationwide state of emergency was declared June 12, giving almost unlimited power to the security forces. As confrontation between blacks and government increased, there was widespread support in Western nations for a complete trade embargo on South Africa.

Some 2 million South African black workers staged a massive strike, June 6-8, 1988. Pres. Botha, head of the government since 1978, resigned Aug. 14, 1989, and was replaced by F. W. de Klerk.

In 1990, the government lifted its ban on the ANC. On Feb. 11, black nationalist leader Nelson Mandela was freed after more than 27 years in prison. In Feb. 1991, Pres. de Klerk announced plans to end all apartheid laws.

In 1993 the nation's negotiating parties, led by the ANC and the National Party, agreed on basic principles for a new constitution, with elections in which all races could vote. Under the new system, South Africa's partially self-governing black territories, or "homelands," were dissolved and incorporated into a national system of 9 provinces.

In elections Apr. 26-29, 1994, the ANC won 62.7% of the vote, making Mandela president. The National Party won 20.4%. The Inkatha Freedom Party won 10.5% and control of the legislature in a mainly Zulu province. Fighting between the ANC and Inkatha (aided, during the apartheid era, by South

African defense forces) has killed more than 10,000 people in the Zulu region since the mid-1980s.

In 1995, Mandela appointed a truth commission, led by Desmond Tutu, to document human rights abuses under apartheid. A post-apartheid constitution, modified to meet the objections of the Constitutional Court, became law Dec. 10, 1996, with provisions to take effect over a 3-year period.

Spain
Kingdom of Spain
Reino de España

People: Population: 39,244,195. **Age distrib.** (%): <15: 16; 65+: 16. **Pop. density:** 200 per sq. mi. **Urban:** 77%. **Ethnic groups:** Mix of Mediterranean and Nordic types. **Principal languages:** Castilian Spanish (official), Catalan, Galician, Basque. **Chief religions:** Roman Catholic 99%.

Geography: Area: 195,364 sq. mi. **Location:** In SW Europe. **Neighbors:** Portugal on W, France on N. **Topography:** The interior is a high, arid plateau broken by mountain ranges and river valleys. The NW is heavily watered, the S has lowlands and a Mediterranean climate. **Capital:** Madrid. **Cities:** Madrid 4,072,000; Barcelona 2,819,000; Valencia 751,000*.

Government: Type: Constitutional monarchy. **Head of state:** King Juan Carlos I de Borbon y Borbon, b. Jan. 5, 1938; in office: Nov. 22, 1975. **Head of government:** Prime Min. José María Aznar; b Feb. 25, 1953; in office: May 5, 1996. **Local divisions:** 17 automonous communities. **Defense:** 1.4% of GDP (1995). **Active troop strength:** 206,800.

Economy: Industries: Machinery, metals, textiles, shoes, vehicles, processed foods, tourism. **Chief crops:** Grains, olives, grapes, citrus fruits, vegetables. **Minerals:** Lignite, uranium, lead, iron, copper, zinc, coal. **Other resources:** Forests. **Arable land:** 31%. **Livestock** (1996): sheep: 21.3 mil; pigs: 18.0 mil; cattle: 5.7 mil; goats: 2.5 mil. **Fish catch** (1995): 1,320,000 metric tons. **Electricity prod.** (1995): 154.1 bil kWh. **Labor force:** 53% serv.; 24% ind.; 14% agric.

Finance: Monetary unit: Peseta (Aug. 1997: 153.15 = $1 US). **Gross domestic product** (1995 est.): $565 bil. **Per capita GDP:** $14,300. **Imports** (1995): $110.0 bil; partners: EU 61%, U.S. 7%. **Exports** (1995): $85.0 bil; partners: EU 69%, U.S. 5%. **Tourism** (1994): $21.9 bil. **National budget** (1994 est.): $122.5 bil. **International reserves less gold** (June 1997): $63.42 bil. **Gold:** 15.63 mil oz t. **Consumer prices** (change in 1996): 3.6%.

Transport: Railroads: Length: 8,907.0 mi. **Motor vehicles in use:** 14.2 mil passenger cars, 3.1 mil comm. vehicles. **Civil aviation:** 16.6 bil passenger-mi.; 25 airports with scheduled flights. **Chief ports:** Barcelona, Bilbao, Valencia, Cartagena.

Communications: Television sets: 1 per 2.5 persons. **Radios:** 1 per 3.2 persons. **Telephones:** 1 per 2.6 persons. **Daily newspaper circ.:** 104 per 1,000 pop.

Health: Life expectancy at birth (1997): 75.2 male; 82.0 female. **Births** (per 1,000 pop.): 10. **Deaths** (per 1,000 pop.): 9. **Natural increase:** 0.1%. **Hospital beds:** 1 per 234 persons. **Physicians:** 1 per 246 persons. **Infant mortality** (per 1,000 live births 1997): 6.

Education: Free and compulsory: ages 6-16. **Literacy** (1995): 97%.

Major International Organizations: UN and all of its specialized agencies, NATO, OECD, EU.

Embassy: 2375 Pennsylvania Ave. NW 20037; 452-0100.

Spain was settled by Iberians, Basques, and Celts, partly overrun by Carthaginians, conquered by Rome c. 200 BC. The Visigoths, in power by the 5th century AD, adopted Christianity but by 711 lost to the Islamic invasion from Africa. Christian reconquest from the N led to a Spanish nationalism. In 1469 the kingdoms of Aragon and Castile were united by the marriage of Ferdinand II and Isabella I, and the last Moorish power was broken by the fall of the kingdom of Granada, 1492.

Spain obtained a colonial empire with the "discovery" of America by Columbus, 1492, the conquest of Mexico by Cortes, and Peru by Pizarro. It also controlled the Netherlands and parts of Italy and Germany. Spain lost its American colonies in the early 19th century. It lost Cuba, the Philippines, and Puerto Rico during the Spanish-American War, 1898.

Primo de Rivera became dictator in 1923. King Alfonso XIII revoked the dictatorship, 1930, but was forced to leave the country 1931. A republic was proclaimed, which disestablished the church, curtailed its privileges, and secularized education. A conservative reaction occurred 1933 but was followed by a

Popular Front (1936-1939) composed of socialists, Communists, republicans, and anarchists.

Army officers under Francisco Franco revolted against the government, 1936. In a destructive 3-year war, in which some one million died, Franco received massive help and troops from Italy and Germany, while the USSR, France, and Mexico supported the republic. War ended Mar. 28, 1939. Franco was named caudillo, leader of the nation. Spain was neutral in World War II, but its relations with fascist countries caused its exclusion from the UN until 1955.

In July 1969, Franco and the Cortes (Parliament) designated Prince Juan Carlos as the future king and chief of state. After Franco's death, Nov. 20, 1975, Juan Carlos was sworn in as king. He presided over the formal dissolution of the institutions of the Franco regime. In free elections June 1977, moderates and democratic socialists emerged as the largest parties.

In 1981 a coup attempt by right-wing military officers was thwarted by the king. The Socialist Workers' Party, under Felipe González Márquez, won 4 consecutive general elections, from 1982 to 1993, but yielded power to a coalition of conservative and regional parties after the election of Mar. 3, 1996.

Catalonia and the Basque country were granted autonomy, Jan. 1980, following overwhelming approval in home-rule referendums. Basque extremists, however, have continued their campaign for independence.

The **Balearic Islands** in the W Mediterranean, 1,927 sq. mi., are a province of Spain; they include **Majorca** (Mallorca; capital Palma de Mallorca), **Minorca, Cabrera, Ibiza,** and **Formentera.** The **Canary Islands,** 2,807 sq. mi., in the Atlantic W of Morocco, form 2 provinces, and include the islands of **Tenerife, Palma, Gomera, Hierro, Grand Canary, Fuerteventura,** and **Lanzarote;** Las Palmas and Santa Cruz are thriving ports. **Ceuta** and **Melilla,** small Spanish enclaves on Morocco's Mediterranean coast, gained limited autonomy in Sept. 1994.

Spain has sought the return of Gibraltar, in British hands since 1704.

Sri Lanka
Democratic Socialist Republic of Sri Lanka
Sri Lanka Prajathanthrika Samajavadi Janarajaya

People: Population: 18,762,075. **Age distrib.** (%): <15: 28; 65+: 6. **Pop. density:** 740 per sq. mi. **Urban:** 22%. **Ethnic groups:** Sinhalese 74%, Tamil 18%, Moor 7%. **Principal languages:** Sinhala, Tamil (both official), English. **Chief religions:** Buddhist 69%, Hindu 15%, Christian 8%, Muslim 8%.

Geography: Area: 25,332 sq. mi. **Location:** In Indian O. off SE coast of India. **Neighbors:** India on NW. **Topography:** The coastal area and the northern half are flat; the S-central area is hilly and mountainous. **Capital:** Colombo (1993 est.): 2,026,000.

Government: Type: Republic. **Head of state:** Pres. Chandrika Bandaranaike Kumaratunga; b June 29, 1945; in office: Nov. 12, 1994. **Head of government:** Prime Min. Sirimavo Bandaranaike; b Apr. 17, 1916; in office: Nov. 14, 1994. **Local divisions:** 8 provinces. **Defense:** 4.4% of GDP (1996). **Active troop strength:** 110,000-115,000 est.

Economy: Industries: Clothing, agric. processing, oil refining, textiles. **Chief crops:** Tea, coconuts, rice, sugar. **Minerals:** Graphite, limestone, gems, phosphates. **Other resources:** Forests, rubber. **Arable land:** 16%. **Livestock** (1996): cattle: 1.7 mil. **Fish catch** (1995): 235,929 metric tons. **Electricity prod.** (1995): 4.7 bil kWh. **Labor force:** 46% agric.; 13% mining & manuf.

Finance: Monetary unit: Rupee (Aug. 1997: 58.94 = $1 US). **Gross domestic product** (1995 est.): $65.6 bil. **Per capita GDP:** $3,600. **Imports** (1994): $4.8 bil; partners: Japan 12%, India 9%. **Exports** (1994): $3.2 bil; partners: U.S. 35%, UK 9%. **Tourism** (1994): $230 mil. **National budget** (1993): $3.6 bil. **International reserves less gold** (June 1997): $1.77 bil. **Gold:** 63,000 oz t. **Consumer prices** (change in 1996): 15.9%.

Transport: Railroads: Length: 921.6 mi. **Motor vehicles in use:** 210,000 passenger cars, 232,000 comm. vehicles. **Civil aviation:** 2.3 bil passenger-mi.; 1 airport. **Chief ports:** Colombo, Trincomalee, Galle.

Communications: Television sets: 1 per 20 persons. **Radios:** 1 per 5.0 persons. **Telephones:** 1 per 90 persons.

Health: Life expectancy at birth (1997): 70.0 male; 75.3 female. **Births** (per 1,000 pop.): 18. **Deaths** (per 1,000 pop.): 6. **Natural increase:** 1.2%. **Hospital beds:** 1 per 362 persons. **Physicians:** 1 per 5,203 persons. **Infant mortality** (per 1,000 live births 1997): 20.

Education: Free and compulsory: ages 5-15. **Literacy** (1995): 90%.

Major International Organizations: UN (World Bank, WTO, IMF), the Commonwealth.

Embassy: 2148 Wyoming Ave. NW 20008; 483-4025.

The island was known to the ancient world as Taprobane (Greek for copper-colored) and later as Serendip (from Arabic). Colonists from northern India subdued the indigenous Veddahs about 543 BC; their descendants, the Buddhist Sinhalese, still form most of the population. Hindu descendants of Tamil immigrants from southern India account for about one-fifth of the population. Parts were occupied by the Portuguese in 1505 and by the Dutch in 1658. The British seized the island in 1796. As Ceylon it became an independent member of the Commonwealth in 1948. On May 22, 1972, Ceylon became the Republic of Sri Lanka.

Prime Min. W. R. D. Bandaranaike was assassinated Sept. 25, 1959. In new elections, the Freedom Party was victorious under Mrs. Sirimavo Bandaranaike, widow of the former prime minister.

After May 1970 elections, Mrs. Bandaranaike became prime minister again. In 1971 the nation suffered economic problems and terrorist activities by ultra-leftists, thousands of whom were executed. Massive land reform and nationalization of foreign-owned plantations were undertaken in the mid-1970s. Mrs. Bandaranaike was ousted in 1977 elections. Presidential powers were increased in 1978 in an effort to restore stability.

Tensions between the Sinhalese and Tamil separatists erupted into violence in the early 1980s. Nearly 50,000 have died in the civil war, which continued in the late 1990s.

Pres. Ranasinghe Premadasa was assassinated May 1, 1993, by a Tamil rebel. Mrs. Bandaranaike's daughter, Chandrika Bandaranaike Kumaratunga, became prime minister after the Aug. 16, 1994, general elections. Elected president Nov. 9, Kumaratunga appointed her mother prime minister.

Sudan
Republic of the Sudan
Jumhuriyat as-Sudan

People: Population: 32,594,128. **Age distrib.** (%): <15: 46; 65+: 2. **Pop. density:** 33 per sq. mi. **Urban:** 32%. **Ethnic groups:** Black 52%, Arab 39%, Beja 6%. **Principal languages:** Arabic (official), Nubian, Ta Bedawie. **Chief religions:** Sunni Muslim 70%, indigenous beliefs 25%, Christians 5%.

Geography: Area: 966,499 sq. mi., the largest country in Africa. **Location:** At the E end of Sahara desert zone. **Neighbors:** Egypt on N; Libya, Chad, Central African Republic on W; Congo (formerly Zaire), Uganda, Kenya on S; Ethiopia, Eritrea on E. **Topography:** The N consists of the Libyan Desert in the W, and the mountainous Nubia Desert in E, with narrow Nile valley between. The center contains large, fertile, rainy areas with fields, pasture, and forest. The S has rich soil, heavy rain. **Capital:** Khartoum 2,249,000*.

Government: Type: Military. **Head of state and government:** Pres. Gen. Omar Hassan Ahmad Al-Bashir; b Jan. 1, 1944; in office: June 30, 1989. **Local divisions:** 9 states. **Defense:** 7.3% of GDP (FY 1993-94). **Active troop strength:** 89,000.

Economy: Industries: Cotton ginning, textiles, cement. **Chief crops:** Gum arabic, sorghum, cotton (main export), wheat. **Minerals:** Chromium, copper. **Crude oil reserves** (1996): 300 mil bbls. **Arable land:** 5%. **Livestock** (1996): sheep: 23.0 mil; cattle: 22.0 mil; goats: 16.5 mil; camels: 2.9 mil. **Electricity prod.** (1995): 1.3 bil kWh. **Labor force:** 80% agric.; 10% ind. & comm.; 6% govt.

Finance: Monetary unit: Pound (Aug. 1997: 1,615 = $1 US), Dinar (June 1996: 98 = $1 US). **Gross domestic product** (1995 est.): $25.0 bil. **Per capita GDP:** $800. **Imports** 1994-95: $1.1 bil; partners: Saudi Arabia 14%. **Exports** (1994-95): $444 mil; partners: Saudi Arabia 20%, UK 10%. **National budget** (1994): $1.1 bil. **International reserves less gold** (Nov. 1996): $102.8 mil.

Transport: Railroads: Length: 3,425.4 mi. **Motor vehicles in use:** 31,000 passenger cars, 36,000 comm. vehicles. **Civil aviation:** 381.9 mil passenger-mi.; 10 airports with scheduled flights. **Chief port:** Port Sudan.

Communications: Television sets: 1 per 13 persons. **Radios:** 1 per 3.9 persons. **Telephones:** 1 per 376 persons. **Daily newspaper circ.:** 23 per 1,000 pop.

Health: Life expectancy at birth (1997): 54.6 male; 56.5 female. **Births** (per 1,000 pop.): 41. **Deaths** (per 1,000 pop.): 11. **Natural increase:** 2.9%. **Physicians:** 1 per 10,000 persons. **Infant mortality** (per 1,000 live births 1997): 74.

Education: Literacy (1995): 46%.

Major International Organizations: UN (IMF, WHO, FAO), Arab League, OAU.

Embassy: 2210 Massachusetts Ave. NW 20008; 338-8565.

Northern Sudan, ancient Nubia, was settled by Egyptians in antiquity, and was converted to Coptic Christianity in the 6th century. Arab conquests brought Islam in the 15th century.

In the 1820s Egypt took over Sudan, defeating the last of earlier empires, including the Fung. In the 1880s a revolution was led by Muhammad Ahmad, who called himself the Mahdi (leader of the faithful), and his followers, the dervishes.

In 1898 an Anglo-Egyptian force crushed the Mahdi's successors. In 1951 the Egyptian Parliament abrogated its 1899 and 1936 treaties with Great Britain and amended its constitution to provide for a separate Sudanese constitution. Sudan voted for complete independence as a parliamentary government effective Jan. 1, 1956.

In 1969, a Revolutionary Council took power, but a civilian premier and cabinet were appointed; the government announced it would create a socialist state.

Economic problems plagued the nation in the 1980s and 1990s, aggravated by civil war and influxes of refugees from neighboring countries. After 16 years in power, Pres. Jaafar al-Nimeiry was overthrown in a bloodless military coup, Apr. 6, 1985. Sudan held its first democratic parliamentary elections in 18 years in 1986, but the elected government was overthrown in a bloodless coup June 30, 1989.

In the mid-1980s, rebels in the south (populated largely by black Christians and followers of tribal religions) took up arms against government domination by northern Sudan, predominantly Arab-Muslim. War and related famine cost an estimated 1.3 mil lives and displaced nearly 3 mil southerners by the mid-1990s.

In 1993, Amnesty International accused Sudan of practicing "ethnic cleansing" against the Nuba people in the South, and Sudan was among several countries cited for human rights violations by the UN Human Rights Commission Mar. 9, 1994. Egypt publicly blamed Sudan for an attempted assassination of Egyptian Pres. Hosni Mubarak in Ethiopia, June 26, 1995. Elections in Mar. 1996 were boycotted by opposition groups.

Suriname
Republic of Suriname
Republiek Suriname

People: Population: 443,446. **Age distrib.** (%): <15: 33; 65+: 5. **Pop. density:** 7 per sq. mi. **Urban:** 50%. **Ethnic groups:** Hindustani 37%, Creole 31%, Javanese 15%. **Principal languages:** Dutch (official), Sranang Tongo, English, Hindustani. **Chief religions:** Christian 48%, Hindu 27%, Muslim 20%.

Geography: Area: 63,251 sq. mi. **Location:** On N shore of South America. **Neighbors:** Guyana on W, Brazil on S, French Guiana on E. **Topography:** A flat Atlantic coast, where dikes permit agriculture. Inland is a forest belt; to the S, largely unexplored hills cover 75% of the country. **Capital:** Paramaribo (1993 est.): 200,970.

Government: Type: Republic. **Head of state:** Pres. Jules Wijdenbosch; b May 2, 1941; in office: Sept. 14, 1996. **Local divisions:** 10 districts. **Defense:** 1.1% of GNP (1993). **Active troop strength:** 1,800 est.

Economy: Industries: Aluminum, food processing. **Chief crops:** Rice, bananas, palm kernels. **Minerals:** Bauxite, iron. **Other resources:** Forests, fish, shrimp. **Arable land:** 0%. **Electricity prod.** (1995): 1.6 bil kWh.

Finance: Monetary unit: Guilder (Aug. 1997: 396 = $1 US). **Gross domestic product** (1995 est.): $1.3 bil. **Per capita GDP:** $2,950. **Imports** (1994): $350.2 mil; partners: U.S. 40%, Netherlands 24%. **Exports** (1994): $339.8 mil. partners: Norway 33%, Netherlands 27%, U.S. 13%. **Tourism** (1994): $11 mil. **National budget** (1994): $700 mil. **International reserves less gold** (June 1997): $88.72 mil. **Gold:** 134,000 oz t. **Consumer prices** (change in 1996): –0.7%.

Transport: Railroads: Length: 103.1 mi. **Motor vehicles in use:** 49,000 passenger cars, 17,000 comm. vehicles. **Civil aviation:** 336.0 mil passenger-mi. **Chief ports:** Paramaribo, Nieuw Nickerie.
Communications: Television sets: 1 per 7.1 persons. **Radios:** 1 per 1.5 persons. **Telephones:** 1 per 7.7 persons. **Daily newspaper circ.:** 103 per 1,000 pop.
Health (1997): **Life expectancy at birth:** 67.8 male; 73.0 female. **Births** (per 1,000 pop.): 24. **Deaths** (per 1,000 pop.): 6. **Natural increase:** 1.8%. **Physicians:** 1 per 1,348 persons. **Infant mortality** (per 1,000 live births): 28.
Education: Compulsory: ages 6-16. **Literacy** (1995): 93%.
Major International Organizations: UN (WHO, WTO, ILO, FAO, World Bank, IMF), OAS.
Embassy: 4301 Connecticut Ave. NW 20008; 244-7488.

The Netherlands acquired Suriname in 1667 from Britain, in exchange for New Netherlands (New York). The 1954 Dutch constitution raised the colony to a level of equality with the Netherlands and the Netherlands Antilles. Independence was granted Nov. 25, 1975, despite objections from East Indians. Some 40% of the population (mostly East Indians) immigrated to the Netherlands in the months before independence.

The National Military Council took control of the government, Feb. 1982. Civilian rule was restored in 1987, but political turmoil continued until 1992 disrupting the nation's economy.

Swaziland
Kingdom of Swaziland
Umbuso weSwatini

People: Population: 1,031,600. **Age distrib.** (%): <15: 46; 65+: 2. **Pop. density:** 153 per sq. mi. **Urban:** 32%. **Ethnic groups:** African 97%, European 3%. **Principal languages:** siSwati, English (both official). **Chief religions:** Christians 60%, indigenous beliefs 40%.
Geography: Area: 6,704 sq. mi. **Location:** In southern Africa, near Indian O. coast. **Neighbors:** South Africa on N, W, S; Mozambique on E. **Topography:** The country descends from W-E in broad belts, becoming more arid in the low veld region, then rising to a plateau in the E. **Capital:** Mbabane (1990 est.) 47,000.
Government: Type: Constitutional monarchy. **Head of state:** King Mswati 3d; b 1968; in office: Apr. 25, 1986. **Head of government:** Prime Min. Barnabas Sibusiso Dlamini; in office: July 26, 1996. **Local divisions:** 4 districts.
Economy: Industries: Wood pulp, mining. **Chief crops:** Sugar, corn, cotton, rice, pineapples, sugar, citrus fruits. **Minerals:** Asbestos, clay, coal. **Other resources:** Forests. **Arable land:** 11%. **Electricity prod.** (1995): 407 mil kWh. **Labor force:** More than 60% agric.
Finance: Monetary unit: Lilangeni (Aug. 1997: 4.69 = $1 US). **Gross domestic product** (1995 est.): $3.6 bil. **Per capita GDP:** $3,700. **Imports** (1994 est.): $827 mil; partners: South Africa 90%. **Exports** (1994 est.): $798 mil; partners: South Africa 50%. **Tourism** (1994): $29 mil. **National budget** (1994 est.): $410 mil. **International reserves less gold** (June 1997): $289.73 mil. **Consumer prices** (change in 1996): 12.5%.
Transport: Railroads: Length: 184.4 mi. **Motor vehicles in use:** 30,000 passenger cars, 9,000 comm. vehicles. **Civil aviation:** 29.8 mil passenger-mi.
Communications: Television sets: 1 per 50 persons. **Radios:** 1 per 6.1 persons. **Telephones:** 1 per 48 persons.
Health (1997): **Life expectancy at birth:** 53.7 male; 61.8 female. **Births** (per 1,000 pop.): 43. **Deaths** (per 1,000 pop.): 10. **Natural increase:** 3.2%. **Physicians:** 1 per 9,265 persons. **Infant mortality rate** (per 1,000 live births): 86.
Education: Literacy (1995): 77%.
Major International Organizations: UN (IMF, WTO, WHO, FAO), OAU, the Commonwealth.
Embassy: 3400 International Dr. NW 20008; 362-6683.

The royal house of Swaziland traces back 400 years, and is one of Africa's last ruling dynasties. The Swazis, a Bantu people, were driven to Swaziland from lands to the N by the Zulus in 1820. Their autonomy was later guaranteed by Britain and Transvaal (later part of South Africa), with Britain assuming control after 1903. Independence came Sept. 6, 1968. In 1973 the king repealed the constitution and assumed full powers.

A new constitution banning political parties took effect Oct. 13, 1978. As Swaziland slowly moved toward political reform, student and labor unrest grew in the mid-1990s.

Sweden
Kingdom of Sweden
Konungariket Sverige

People: Population: 8,946,193. **Age distrib.** (%): <15: 19; 65+: 17. **Pop. density:** 51 per sq. mi. **Urban:** 83%. **Ethnic groups:** Swedish 90%, Finnish 2%, Lappish, European immigrant. **Principal languages:** Swedish. **Chief religions:** Evangelical Lutheran (official) 94%.
Geography: Area: 173,732 sq. mi. **Location:** On Scandinavian Peninsula in N Europe. **Neighbors:** Norway on W, Denmark on S (across Kattegat), Finland on E. **Topography:** Mountains along NW border cover 25% of Sweden, flat or rolling terrain covers the central and southern areas, which include several large lakes. **Capital:** Stockholm. **Cities:** Stockholm 1,545,000; Göteborg 751,000*.
Government: Type: Constitutional monarchy. **Head of state:** King Carl XVI Gustaf; b Apr. 30, 1946; in office: Sept. 19, 1973. **Head of government:** Prime Min. Goran Persson; b June 20, 1949; in office: Mar. 22, 1996. **Local divisions:** 24 provinces. **Defense:** 2.5% of GDP (FY 1994-95). **Active troop strength:** 62,600.
Economy: Industries: Steel, machinery, precision instruments, vehicles, shipbuilding, paper. **Chief crops:** Grains, potatoes, sugar beets. **Minerals:** Zinc, iron, lead, copper, silver. **Other resources:** Forests (half the country); yield about 16% of exports. **Arable land:** 7%. **Livestock** (1996): cattle: 1.8 mil; pigs: 2.3 mil. **Fish catch** (1995): 412,153 metric tons. **Electricity prod.** (1995): 142.9 bil kWh. **Labor force:** 38% social & personal services; 21% manuf. & mining.
Finance: Monetary unit: Krona (Aug. 1997: 7.87 = $1 US). **Gross domestic product** (1995 est.): $177.3 bil. **Per capita GDP:** $20,100. **Imports** (1994): $51.8 bil; partners: EU 63%; U.S. 9%. **Exports** (1994): $61.2 bil; partners: EU 59%, U.S. 8%. **Tourism** (1994): $2.8 bil. **National budget** (FY 1995-96): $146.1 bil. **International reserves less gold** (June 1997): $14.25 bil. **Gold:** 4.8 mil oz t. **Consumer prices** (change in 1996): 0.5%.
Transport: Railroads: Length: 7,839.5 mi. **Motor vehicles in use:** 3.6 mil passenger cars, 322,000 comm. vehicles. **Civil aviation:** 5.8 bil passenger-mi.; 48 airports. **Chief ports:** Göteborg, Stockholm, Malmö.
Communications: Television sets: 1 per 2.1 persons. **Radios:** 1 per 1.1 persons. **Telephones:** 1 per 1.5 persons. **Daily newspaper circ.:** 483 per 1,000 pop.
Health: Life expectancy at birth (1997): 75.7 male; 80.7 female. **Births** (per 1,000 pop.): 11. **Deaths** (per 1,000 pop.): 11. **Natural increase:** –0.1. **Hospital beds:** 1 per 166 persons. **Physicians:** 1 per 394 persons. **Infant mortality** (per 1,000 live births 1997): 5.
Education: Compulsory: ages 6-15. **Literacy** (1995): 100%.
Major International Organizations: UN and all of its specialized agencies, EU, OECD.
Embassy: 1501 M St. NW 20005; 467-2600.

The Swedes have lived in present-day Sweden for at least 5,000 years, longer than nearly any other European people. Gothic tribes from Sweden played a major role in the disintegration of the Roman Empire. Other Swedes helped create the first Russian state in the 9th century.

The Swedes were Christianized from the 11th century, and a strong centralized monarchy developed. A parliament, the Riksdag, was first called in 1435, the earliest parliament on the European continent, with all classes of society represented.

Swedish independence from rule by Danish kings (dating from 1397) was secured by Gustavus I in a revolt, 1521-23; he built up the government and established the Lutheran Church. In the 17th century Sweden was a major European power, gaining most of the Baltic seacoast, but its international position subsequently declined.

The Napoleonic wars, 1799-1815, in which Sweden acquired Norway (it became independent 1905), were the last in which Sweden participated. Armed neutrality was maintained in both world wars.

More than 4 decades of Social Democratic rule ended in the 1976 parliamentary elections; the party returned to power in the 1982 elections. After Prime Min. Olof Palme was shot to death in Stockholm, Feb. 28, 1986, Ingvar Carlsson took office. Carl Bildt, a non-Socialist, became prime minister Oct. 1991, with a mandate to restore Sweden's economic competitiveness. The Social Democrats returned to power following 1994 elections.

Swedish voters approved membership in the European Union Nov. 13, 1994, and Sweden entered the EU as of Jan. 1, 1995. Carlsson retired and was succeeded by Goran Persson in Mar. 1996.

Switzerland
Swiss Confederation

People: Population: 7,248,984. **Age distrib.** (%): <15: 17; 65+: 15. **Pop. density:** 454 per sq. mi. **Urban:** 61%. **Ethnic groups:** German, French, Italian, Romansch. **Principal languages:** German, French, Italian (all official). **Chief religions:** Roman Catholic 48%, Protestant 44%.

Geography: Area: 15,940 sq. mi. **Location:** In the Alps Mts. in central Europe. **Neighbors:** France on W, Italy on S, Austria on E, Germany on N. **Topography:** The Alps cover 60% of the land area; the Jura, near France, 10%. Running between, from NE to SW, are midlands, 30%. **Capitals:** Bern (administrative), Lausanne (judicial). **Cities** (1995 est.): Zurich 342,872; Basel 175,561; Geneva 172,737; Bern 128,422.

Government: Type: Federal republic. **Head of government:** The president is elected by the Federal Assembly to a nonrenewable 1-year term. **Local divisions:** 20 full cantons, 6 half cantons. **Defense:** 1.4% of GDP (1995). **Active troop strength:** 3,300.

Economy: Industries: Machinery, chemicals, precision instruments, watches, textiles, foodstuffs (cheese, chocolate), banking, tourism. **Minerals:** Salt. **Other resources:** Hydropower potential, dairy products. **Arable land:** 10%. **Livestock** (1996): cattle: 1.8 mil; pigs: 1.6 mil. **Electricity prod.** (1995): 59.7 bil kWh. **Labor force:** 50% serv.; 33% ind. and crafts; 10% govt.

Finance: Monetary unit: Franc (Aug. 1997: 1.50 = $1 US). **Gross domestic product** (1995 est.): $158.5 bil. **Per capita GDP:** $22,400. **Imports** (1994): $68.2 bil; partners: EU 72%. **Exports** (1994): $69.6 bil; partners: EU 56%; U.S. 9%. **Tourism** (1994): $7.6 bil. **National budget** (1995): $36.9 bil. **International reserves less gold** (June 1997): $35.0 bil. **Gold:** 83.28 mil oz t. **Consumer prices** (change in 1996): 0.8%.

Transport: Railroads: Length: 3,551.5 mi. **Motor vehicles in use:** 3.2 mil passenger cars, 299,000 comm. vehicles. **Civil aviation:** 11.7 bil passenger-mi.; 5 airports with scheduled flights. **Chief port:** Basel.

Communications: Television sets: 1 per 2.4 persons. **Radios:** 1 per 1.2 persons. **Telephones:** 1 per 1.6 persons. **Daily newspaper circ.:** 409 per 1,000 pop.

Health: Life expectancy at birth (1997): 74.7 male; 80.7 female. **Births** (per 1,000 pop.): 11. **Deaths** (per 1,000 pop.): 10. **Natural increase:** 0.2%. **Hospital beds:** 1 per 134 persons. **Physicians:** 1 per 299 persons. **Infant mortality** (per 1,000 live births 1997): 5.

Education: Compulsory: ages 7-16. **Literacy** (1994): 100%. **Major International Organizations:** Many UN specialized agencies (though not a member), EFTA, OECD. **Embassy:** 2900 Cathedral Ave. NW 20008; 745-7900.

Switzerland, the Roman province of Helvetia, is a federation of 23 cantons (20 full cantons and 6 half cantons), 3 of which in 1291 created a defensive league and later were joined by other districts. Voters in the French-speaking part of Canton Bern voted for self-government, 1978; Canton Jura was created Jan. 1, 1979.

In 1648 the Swiss Confederation obtained its independence from the Holy Roman Empire. The cantons were joined under a federal constitution in 1848, with large powers of local control retained by each canton.

Switzerland has maintained an armed neutrality since 1815, and has not been involved in a foreign war since 1515. It is the seat of many UN and other international agencies.

Switzerland is a leading world banking center. In an effort to crack down on criminal transactions, the nation's strict bank-secrecy rules have been eased since 1990. Stung by accusations that assets seized by the Nazis and deposited in Swiss banks during World War II had not been properly returned, the government announced, March 5, 1997, a $4.7-billion fund to compensate victims of the Holocaust and other catastrophes.

Syria
Syrian Arab Republic
Al Jumhuriyah al Arabiyah as Suriyah

People: Population: 16,137,899. **Age distrib.** (%): <15: 46; 65+: 3. **Pop. density:** 225 per sq. mi. **Urban:** 53%. **Ethnic groups:** Arab 90%. **Principal languages:** Arabic (official), Kurdish, Armenian. **Chief religions:** Sunni Muslim 74%, other Muslims 16%, Christian 10%.

Geography: Area: 71,498 sq. mi. **Location:** Middle East, at E end of Mediterranean Sea. **Neighbors:** Lebanon and Israel on W, Jordan on S, Iraq on E, Turkey on N. **Topography:** Syria has a short Mediterranean coastline, then stretches E and S with fertile lowlands and plains, alternating with mountains and large desert areas. **Capital:** Damascus. **Cities:** Damascus 2,036,000; Aleppo 1,840,000*.

Government: Type: Republic (under military regime). **Head of state:** Pres. Hafez al-Assad; b Mar. 1930; in office: Feb. 22, 1971. **Head of government:** Prime Min. Mahmoud Zuabi; in office: Nov. 1, 1987. **Local divisions:** Damascus and 13 provinces. **Defense:** 8% of GDP (1994 est.). **Active troop strength:** 421,000 est.

Economy: Industries: Oil prods., textiles, food processing, tobacco, phosphate mining. **Chief crops:** Cotton, grains, olives, lentils, chickpeas. **Minerals:** Oil, phosphates, iron, gypsum. **Crude oil reserves** (1996): 2.5 bil bbls. **Other resources:** Wool, dairy prods. **Arable land:** 28%. **Livestock** (1996): sheep: 11.8 mil, goats: 1.2 mil. **Electricity prod.** (1995): 14.9 bil kWh. **Labor force:** 42% services; 36% ind. & constr.; 22% agric.

Finance: Monetary unit: Pound (Aug. 1997: 45 = $1 US). **Gross domestic product** (1995 est.): $91.2 bil. **Per capita GDP:** $5,900. **Imports** (1994): $5.4 bil; partners: EU 37%. **Exports** (1994): $3.5 bil; partners: EU 61%. **Tourism** (1994): $800 mil. **National budget** (1994 est.): $3.4 bil. **Gold:** 833,000 oz t. **Consumer prices** (change in 1996): 8.2%.

Transport: Railroads: Length: 1,240.8 mi. **Motor vehicles in use:** 120,000 passenger cars, 160,000 comm. vehicles. **Civil aviation:** 509.2 mil passenger-mi.; 5 airports with scheduled flights. **Chief ports:** Latakia, Tartus.

Communications: Television sets: 1 per 16 persons. **Radios:** 1 per 3.9 persons. **Telephones:** 1 per 16 persons. **Daily newspaper circ.:** 18 per 1,000 pop.

Health: Life expectancy at birth (1997): 66.2 male; 68.7 female. **Births** (per 1,000 pop.): 39. **Deaths** (per 1,000 pop.): 6. **Natural increase:** 3.3%. **Hospital beds:** 1 per 911 persons. **Physicians:** 1 per 966 persons. **Infant mortality** (per 1,000 live births 1997): 39.

Education: Compulsory: ages 6-12. **Literacy** (1995): 71%. **Major International Organizations:** UN (IMF, WHO, FAO), Arab League.

Embassy: 2215 Wyoming Ave. NW 20008; 232-6313.

Syria contains some of the most ancient remains of civilization. It was the center of the Seleucid empire, but later became absorbed in the Roman and Arab empires. Ottoman rule prevailed for 4 centuries, until the end of World War I.

The state of Syria was formed from former Turkish districts, separated by the Treaty of Sevres, 1920, and divided into the states of Syria and Greater Lebanon. Both were administered under a French League of Nations mandate 1920-1941.

Syria was proclaimed a republic by the occupying French Sept. 16, 1941, and exercised full independence effective Apr. 17, 1946. Syria joined in the Arab invasion of Israel in 1948.

Syria joined Egypt Feb. 1958 in the United Arab Republic but seceded Sept. 1961. The Socialist Baath party and military leaders seized power Mar. 1963. The Baath, a pan-Arab organization, became the only legal party. The government has been dominated by members of the minority Alawite sect.

In the Arab-Israeli war of June 1967, Israel seized and occupied the Golan Heights area inside Syria, from which Israeli settlements had for years been shelled by Syria. On Oct. 6, 1973, Syria joined Egypt in an attack on Israel. Arab oil states agreed in 1974 to give Syria $1 billion a year to aid anti-Israel moves. Some 30,000 Syrian troops entered Lebanon in 1976 to mediate in a civil war. They fought Palestinian guerrillas and, later, Christian militiamen. Syrian troops again battled Christian forces in Lebanon, Apr. 1981.

Following the June 6, 1982, Israeli invasion of Lebanon, Israeli planes destroyed 17 Syrian antiaircraft missile batteries in the Bekaa Valley, June 9. Some 25 Syrian planes were downed during the engagement. Israel and Syria agreed to a cease-fire June 11. In 1983, Syria backed the PLO rebels who ousted Yasir Arafat's forces from Tripoli.

Syria's role in promoting international terrorism led to the breaking of diplomatic relations with Great Britain and to limited sanctions by the European Community in 1986.

Syria condemned the Aug. 1990 Iraqi invasion of Kuwait and sent troops to help Allied forces in the Gulf War. In 1991, Syria accepted U.S. proposals for the terms of an Arab-Israeli peace conference. Syria subsequently participated in negotiations with Israel, but progress toward peace was slow.

Taiwan
Republic of China
Chung-hua Min-kuo

People: Population: 21,655,515. **Age distrib.** (%): <15: 23; 65+: 8. **Pop. density:** 1,550 per sq. mi. **Urban:** 75%. **Ethnic groups:** Taiwanese 84%, mainland Chinese 14%. **Principal languages:** Mandarin Chinese (official), Taiwanese. **Chief religions:** Buddhist, Taoist, Confucian 93%; Christian 4.5%.

Geography: Area: 13,969 sq. mi. **Location:** Off SE coast of China, between East and South China seas. **Neighbors:** Nearest is China. **Topography:** A mountain range forms the backbone of the island; the eastern half is very steep and craggy, the western slope is flat, fertile, and well cultivated. **Capital:** Taipei. **Cities** (1996 est.): Taipei 2,626,138; Kaohsiung 1.426,518 mil; Taichung 857,590.

Government: Type: Democracy. **Head of state and Nationalist Party chmn.:** Pres. Lee Teng-hui; b Jan. 15, 1923; in office: Jan. 13, 1988. **Head of government:** Prime Min. Vincent Siew; b Jan. 3, 1939, in office: Aug. 28, 1997. **Local divisions:** 16 counties, 5 municipalities, Taipei and Kaohsiung. **Defense:** 3.6% of GDP (FY 1996-97). **Active troop strength:** 376,000 est.

Economy: Industries: Textiles, clothing, electronics, processed foods, chemicals. **Chief crops:** Vegetables, rice, fruit, tea. **Minerals:** Coal, limestone, marble. **Arable land:** 24%. **Livestock** (1995): pigs: 10.5 mil. **Fish catch** (1995): 1,288,406 metric tons. **Electricity prod.** (1995): 121.8 bil kWh. **Labor force:** 49% services; 39% ind. & comm.; 11% agric.

Finance: Monetary unit: New Taiwan Dollar (Aug. 1997: 28.68 = $1 US). **Gross domestic product** (1995 est.): $290.5 bil. **Per capita GDP:** $13,510. **Imports** (1994): $85.1 bil; partners: Japan 30%, U.S. 22%. **Exports** (1994): $93 bil; partners: U.S. 28%, Hong Kong 22%, EU 15%. **Tourism** (1994): $3.2 bil. **National budget** (1991): $30.1 bil.

Transport: Railroads: Length: 2,856.6 mi. **Motor vehicles in use:** 4.1 mil passenger cars, 850,000 commercial vehicles. **Civil aviation:** 22.8 bil passenger-mi.; 13 airports. **Chief ports:** Kaohsiung, Chilung (Keelung), Hualien, Taichung.

Communications: Television sets: 1 per 3.0 persons. **Radios:** 1 per 2.5 persons. **Telephones:** 1 per 2.3 persons.

Health: Life expectancy at birth (1997): 73.7 male; 79.1 female. **Births** (per 1,000 pop.): 15. **Deaths** (per 1,000 pop.): 6. **Natural increase:** 0.9%. **Hospital beds:** 1 per 204 persons. **Physicians:** 1 per 864 persons. **Infant mortality** (per 1,000 live births 1997): 7.

Education: Free and compulsory: ages 6-15. **Literacy** (1994): 94%.

Major International Organizations: APEC

Large-scale Chinese immigration began in the 17th century. The island came under mainland control after an interval of Dutch rule, 1620-62. Taiwan (also called Formosa) was ruled by Japan 1895-1945. Two million Kuomintang supporters fled to Taiwan in 1949. Both the Taipei and Beijing governments consider Taiwan an integral part of China. Taiwan has resisted Beijing's efforts at reunification, including military pressure, but economic ties with the mainland expanded in the 1990s.

The U.S., upon its recognition of the People's Republic of China, Dec. 15, 1978, severed diplomatic ties with Taiwan. The U.S. maintains the unofficial American Institute in Taiwan, while Taiwan has an agency, the Taipei Economic and Cultural Representative Office, with field offices in Washington, DC, and other U.S. cities.

Land reform, government planning, U.S. aid and investment, and free universal education have brought huge advances in industry, agriculture, and living standards. In 1987 martial law was lifted after 38 years, and in 1991 the 43-year period of emergency rule ended. Taiwan held its first direct presidential election Mar. 23, 1996. The ruling Nationalist Party has faced increasing challenge from opposition parties.

Taiwan has one of the world's strongest economies and is among the 10 leading capital exporters.

The **Penghu Isls.** (Pescadores), 49 sq. mi., pop. (1995 est.) 92,000, lie between Taiwan and the mainland. **Quemoy** and **Matsu,** pop. (1995 est.) 52,000, lie just off the mainland.

Tajikistan
Republic of Tajikistan
Jumhurii Tojikiston

People: Population: 6,013,855. **Age distrib.** (%): <15: 43; 65+: 4. **Pop. density:** 108 per sq. mi. **Urban:** 32%. **Ethnic**

groups: Tajik 65%, Uzbek 25%. **Principal languages:** Tajik (official), Russian. **Chief religions:** Sunni Muslim 80%.

Geography: Area: 55,300 sq. mi. **Location:** Central Asia. **Neighbors:** Uzbekistan on N and W, Kyrgyzstan on N, China on E, Afghanistan on S. **Topography:** Mountainous region that contains the Pamirs, Trans-Alai mountain system. **Capital:** Dushanbe (1994 est.): 524,000.

Government: Type: Republic. **Head of state:** Pres. Imomali Rakhmonov; b Oct. 5, 1952; in office: Nov. 16, 1994. **Head of Government:** Yakhyo Azimov; b Dec. 4, 1947; in office: Feb. 8, 1996. **Local divisions:** 2 oblasts, 1 autonomous oblast. **Defense:** 3.4% of GDP (1994). **Active troop strength:** 5,000-7,000 est.

Economy: Industries: Aluminum, cement, mining. **Chief crops:** Cotton, barley, wheat, melons, vegetables. **Minerals:** Coal, lead, zinc. **Arable land:** 6%. **Livestock** (1996): sheep: 1.8 mil; cattle: 1.1 mil. **Electricity prod.** (1995): 14.7 bil kWh. **Labor force:** 51% agric. 17% serv.

Finance: Monetary unit: Ruble (Aug. 1997: 840 = $1 US). **Gross domestic product** (1995 est.): $6.4 bil. **Per capita GDP:** $1,040. **Imports** (1995): $690 mil; partners: Uzbekistan 34%, Russia 24%. **Exports** (1995): $707 mil; partners: Russia 42%, Uzbekistan 21%.

Transportation: Railroads: Length: 298.1 mi. **Motor vehicles in use:** 185,000 passenger cars, 3,600 comm. vehicles. **Civil aviation:** 1.4 bil passenger-mi.; 1 airport with scheduled flights.

Communications: Radios: 1 per 6.7 persons. **Telephones:** 1 per 22 persons. **Daily newspaper circ.:** 13 per 1,000 pop.

Health: Life expectancy at birth (1997): 61.0 male; 68.4 female. **Births** (per 1,000 pop.): 34. **Deaths** (per 1,000 pop.): 8. **Natural increase:** 2.6%. **Hospital beds:** 1 per 70 persons. **Physicians:** 1 per 265 persons. **Infant mortality** (per 1,000 live births 1997): 111.

Education: Compulsory for 9 years between ages 7-17. **Literacy** (1995): 100%.

Major International Organizations: UN, CIS.

There were settled societies in the region from about 3000 BC. Throughout history, it has undergone invasions by Iranians (Arabs who converted the population to Islam), Mongols, Uzbeks, Afghans, and Russians. The USSR gained control of the region 1918-25. In 1924, the Tajik ASSR was created within the Uzbek SSR. The Tajik SSR was proclaimed in 1929.

Tajikistan declared independence Sept. 9, 1991. It became an independent state when the Soviet Union disbanded Dec. 26, 1991. Conservative Communist Pres. Rakhmon Nabiyev was forced to resign, Sept. 1992, by a coalition of Islamic, nationalist, and Western-oriented parties.

Factional fighting led to the installation of a pro-Communist regime, Jan. 1993. A new constitution establishing a presidential system was approved by referendum Nov. 6, 1994. Clashes between Muslim rebels, reportedly armed by Afghanistan, and troops loyal to the government and supported by Russia, claimed at least 30,000 lives by mid-1997, despite a series of peace accords.

Tanzania
United Republic of Tanzania
Jamhuri ya Muungano wa Tanzania

People: Population: 29,460,753. **Age distrib.** (%): <15: 45; 65+: 3. **Pop. density:** 80 per sq. mi. **Urban:** 25%. **Ethnic groups:** African 99%. **Principal languages:** Swahili, English (both official), many others. **Chief religions:** Christians 45%, Muslims 35%, indigenous beliefs 20%.

Geography: Area: 364,017 sq. mi. **Location:** On coast of E Africa. **Neighbors:** Kenya, Uganda on N; Rwanda, Burundi, Congo (formerly Zaire) on W; Zambia, Malawi, Mozambique on S. **Topography:** Hot, arid central plateau, surrounded by the lake region in the W, temperate highlands in N and S, the coastal plains. Mt. Kilimanjaro, 19,340 ft., is highest in Africa. **Capital:** Dar-es-Salaam (capital is being moved to Dodoma). **Cities:** Dar-es-Salaam 1,747,000*.

Government: Type: Republic. **Head of state:** Pres. Benjamin William Mkapa; b Nov. 12, 1938; in office: Nov. 23, 1995. **Head of government:** Prime Min. Frederick Sumaye; in office: Nov. 28, 1995. **Local divisions:** 25 regions. **Defense:** 3.3% of GNP (1994). **Active troop strength:** 34,600 est.

Economy: Industries: Agricultural processing, mining, textiles. **Chief crops:** Sisal, cotton, coffee, tea, tobacco, corn, spices. **Minerals:** Tin, phospates, diamonds, gold. **Other resources:** Pyrethrum (insecticide made from chrysanthemums). **Arable land:** 5%. **Livestock** (1996): cattle: 13.4 mil; goats: 9.7

mil; **sheep:** 4.0 mil. **Fish catch** (1995): 360,000 metric tons. **Electricity prod.** (1995): 895 mil kWh. **Labor force:** 90% agric.; 10% ind. & comm.

Finance: Monetary unit: Shilling (Aug. 1997: 629.50 = $1 US). **Gross domestic product** (1995 est.): $23.1 bil. **Per capita GDP:** $800. **Imports** (1994): $1.4 bil; partners: UK 13%, Japan 10%, Italy 8%. **Exports** (1994): $462 mil; partners: Ger. 16%, UK 9%. **Tourism** (1994): $192 mil. **National budget** (1990): $631 mil. **International reserves less gold** (June 1997): $460.1 mil. **Consumer prices** (change in 1996): 19.7%.

Transport: Railroads: Length: 2,216.3 mi. **Motor vehicles in use:** 50,000 passenger cars; 78,000 comm. vehicles. **Civil aviation:** 102.5 mil passenger-mi.; 11 airports with scheduled flights. **Chief ports:** Dar-es-Salaam, Mtwara, Tanga.

Communications: Television sets: 1 per 476 persons. **Radios:** 1 per 38 persons. **Telephones:** 1 per 328 persons.

Health: Life expectancy at birth (1997): 40.3 male; 43.1 female. **Births** (per 1,000 pop.): 41. **Deaths** (per 1,000 pop.): 20. **Natural increase:** 2.1%. **Hospital beds:** 1 per 2,000 persons. **Physicians:** 1 per 22,900 persons. **Infant mortality** (per 1,000 live births 1997): 105.

Education: Free and compulsory: ages 7-14. **Literacy** (1995): 68%.

Major International Organizations: UN and all of its specialized agencies, OAU, the Commonwealth.

Embassy: 2139 R St. NW 20008; 939-6125.

The Republic of Tanganyika in E Africa and the island Republic of Zanzibar, off the coast of Tanganyika, both of which had recently gained independence, joined into a single nation, the United Republic of Tanzania, Apr. 26, 1964. Zanzibar retains internal self-government.

Until resigning as president in 1985, Julius K. Nyerere, a former Tanganyikan independence leader, dominated Tanzania's politics, which emphasized government planning and control of the economy, with single-party rule. In 1992 the constitution was amended to establish a multiparty system. Privatization of the economy was undertaken in the 1990s.

At least 500 people died when an overcrowded Tanzanian ferry sank in Lake Victoria, May 21, 1996. About 460,000 Rwandan refugees, mostly Hutu, returned from Tanzania to Rwanda in Dec. 1996.

Tanganyika. Arab colonization and slaving began in the 8th century AD; Portuguese sailors explored the coast by about 1500. Other Europeans followed.

In 1885 Germany established German East Africa of which Tanganyika formed the bulk. It became a League of Nations mandate and, after 1946, a UN trust territory, both under Britain. It became independent Dec. 9, 1961, and a republic within the Commonwealth a year later.

Zanzibar, the Isle of Cloves, lies 23 mi. off mainland Tanzania; area 640 sq. mi. and pop. (1990 est.) 375,000. The island of **Pemba,** 25 mi. to the NE, area 380 sq. mi. and pop. (1988 cen.) 265,000, is included in the administration.

Chief industry is cloves and clove oil production, of which Zanzibar and Pemba produce most of the world's supply.

Zanzibar was for centuries the center for Arab slave traders. Portugal ruled for 2 centuries until ousted by Arabs around 1700. Zanzibar became a British Protectorate in 1890; independence came Dec. 10, 1963. Revolutionary forces overthrew the Sultan Jan. 12, 1964. The new government ousted Western diplomats and newsmen, slaughtered thousands of Arabs, and nationalized farms. Union with Tanganyika followed.

Thailand

Kingdom of Thailand

Muang Thai *or* Prathet Thai

People: Population: 59,450,818. **Age distrib.** (%): <15: 25; 65+: 6. **Pop. density:** 300 per sq. mi. **Urban:** 20%. **Ethnic groups:** Thai 75%, Chinese 14%. **Principal languages:** Thai (official), English, Lao, Chinese, Malay. **Chief religions:** Buddhist 95%, Muslim 4%.

Geography: Area: 198,115 sq. mi. **Location:** On Indochinese and Malayan peninsulas in SE Asia. **Neighbors:** Myanmar on W and N, Laos on N, Cambodia on E, Malaysia on S. **Topography:** A plateau dominates the NE third of Thailand, dropping to the fertile alluvial valley of the Chao Phraya R. in the center. Forested mountains are in the N, with narrow fertile valleys. The S peninsula region is covered by rain forests. **Capital:** Bangkok 6,547,000*.

Government: Type: Constitutional monarchy. **Head of state:** King Bhumibol Adulyadej; b Dec. 5, 1927; in office: June 9, 1946. **Head of government:** Prime Min. Chavalit Yongchaiyudh; b May 15, 1932; in office: Nov. 25, 1996. **Local divisions:** 76 provinces. **Defense:** 2.5% of GNP (FY 1994-95). **Active troop strength:** 254,000.

Economy: Industries: Textiles, agric. processing, tourism. **Chief crops:** Rice (major export), corn, tapioca, sugarcane. **Minerals:** Among world's largest producers of tin and tungsten; gas. **Crude oil reserves** (1996): 295 mil bbls. **Other resources:** Forests (teak is exported), rubber, seafood. **Arable land:** 34%. **Livestock** (1996): cattle: 8.0 mil; buffalo: 4.8 mil; pigs: 4.0 mil. **Fish catch** (1995): 3,501,772 metric tons. **Electricity prod.** (1995): 77.5 bil kWh. **Labor force:** 57% agric.; 28% ind. & comm.; 15% serv. & govt.

Finance: Monetary unit: Baht (Aug. 1997: 34.17 = $1 US). **Gross domestic product** (1995 est.): $416.7 bil. **Per capita GDP:** $6,900. **Imports** (1994): $53.9 bil; partners: Japan 30%, U.S. 12%. **Exports** (1994): $45.1 bil; partners: U.S. 21%, Japan 17%. **Tourism** (1994): $5.8 bil. **National budget** (FY 1994-95): $28.4 bil. **International reserves less gold** (June 1997): $31.36 bil. **Gold:** 2.47 mil oz t. **Consumer prices** (change in 1996): 5.8%.

Transport: Railroads: Length: 2,870.9 mi. **Motor vehicles in use:** 1.35 mil passenger cars, 3.65 mil comm. vehicles. **Civil aviation:** 15.7 bil passenger-mi.; 25 airports with scheduled flights. **Chief ports:** Bangkok, Sattahip.

Communication: Television sets: 1 per 8.5 persons. **Radios:** 1 per 5.3 persons. **Telephones:** 1 per 17 persons. **Daily newspaper circ.:** 48 per 1,000 pop.

Health: Life expectancy at birth (1997): 65.1 male; 72.7 female. **Births** (per 1,000 pop.): 17. **Deaths** (per 1,000 pop.): 7. **Natural increase:** 1.0%. **Hospital beds:** 1 per 599 persons. **Physicians:** 1 per 4,245 persons. **Infant mortality** (per 1,000 live births 1997): 32.

Education: Compulsory: ages 6-15. **Literacy** (1995): 94%.

Major International Organizations: UN (WTO, World Bank), ASEAN, APEC.

Embassy: 1024 Wisconsin Ave. NW 20007; 944-3600.

Thais began migrating from southern China during the 11th century.

Thailand, known as Siam until 1939, is the only country in SE Asia never taken over by a European power, thanks to King Mongkut and his son King Chulalongkorn—who ruled from 1851 to 1910, modernized the country, and signed trade treaties with Britain and France. A bloodless revolution in 1932 limited the monarchy. Japan occupied the country in 1941.

The military took over the government in a bloody 1976 coup. Kriangsak Chomanan, prime minister, resigned Feb. 1980 because of soaring inflation, oil price increases, labor unrest, and growing crime. Vietnamese troops crossed the border but were repulsed by Thai forces in the 1980s.

Chatichai Choonhavan was chosen prime minister in a democratic election, Aug. 1988. In Feb. 1991, the military ousted Choonhavan in a bloodless coup. A violent crackdown on street demonstrations in May 1992 led to more than 50 deaths. After general elections July 2, 1995, Banharn Silpa-archa succeeded Chuan Leekpai as prime minister. AIDS reached epidemic proportions in Thailand in the mid-1990s.

General elections were held Nov. 17, 1996. Prime Min. Chavalit Yongchaiyudh formed a 6-party coalition and was appointed Nov. 25, just before Bill Clinton became the first U.S. president in 27 years to pay a state visit to Thailand. A steep downturn in the economy forced Thailand to seek more than $15 billion in emergency international loans in Aug. 1997. A reform constitution won legislative approval Sept. 27.

Togo

Republic of Togo

République Togolaise

People: Population: 4,735,610. **Age distrib.** (%): <15: 48; 65+: 2. **Pop. density:** 215 per sq. mi. **Urban:** 31%. **Ethnic groups:** Ewe, Mina, Kabye, 34 other tribes. **Principal languages:** French (official), Ewe, Mina, Dagomba, Kabye. **Chief religions:** Indigenous beliefs 70%, Christian 20%, Muslim 10%.

Geography: Area: 21,925 sq. mi. **Location:** On S coast of W Africa. **Neighbors:** Ghana on W, Burkina Faso on N, Benin on E. **Topography:** A range of hills running SW-NE splits Togo into 2 savanna plains regions. **Capital:** Lomé (1990 met. est.): 513,000.

Government: Type: Republic. **Head of state:** Pres. Gnassingbé Eyadéma; b Dec. 26, 1937; in office: Apr. 14, 1967. **Head of government:** Prime Min. Kwassi Klutsé; b July 29, 1945; in office: Aug. 20, 1996. **Local divisions:** 23 circumscriptions. **Defense:** 2.9% of GDP (1993). **Active troop strength:** 6,950 est.

Economy: Industries: Textiles, handicrafts, agric. processing. **Chief crops:** Coffee, cocoa, yams, cotton, millet, rice. **Minerals:** Phosphates, limestone. **Arable land:** 25%. **Livestock** (1996): goats: 1.9 mil; sheep: 1.2 mil. **Electricity prod.** (1995): 90 mil kWh. **Labor force:** 64% agric., 21% services.

Finance: Monetary unit: CFA Franc (Aug. 1997: 610 = $1 US). **Gross domestic product** (1995 est.): $4.1 bil. **Per capita GDP:** $900. **Imports** (1994): $212 mil; partners: EU 57%. **Exports** (1994): $162.2 mil; partners: EU 40%. **Tourism** (1994): $7 mil. **National budget** (1995 est.): $274 mil. **International reserves less gold** (Mar. 1997): $110.9 mil. **Gold:** 13,000 oz t. **Consumer prices** (change in 1995): 15.7%.

Transport: Railroads: Length: 326.0 mi. **Motor vehicles in use:** 18,000 passenger cars, 12,000 comm. vehicles. **Civil aviation:** 133.5 mil passenger-mi. **Chief port:** Lomé.

Communications: Television sets: 1 per 133 persons. **Radios:** 1 per 4.7 persons. **Telephones:** 1 per 191 persons.

Health: Life expectancy at birth (1997): 56.1 male; 60.6 female. **Births** (per 1,000 pop.): 46. **Deaths** (per 1,000 pop.): 10. **Natural increase:** 3.5%. **Hospital beds:** 1 per 640 persons. **Infant mortality** (per 1,000 live births 1997): 82.

Education: Compulsory: ages 6-12. **Literacy** (1995): 52%.

Major International Organizations: UN (WTO, IMF), OAU.

Embassy: 2208 Massachusetts Ave. NW 20008; 234-4212.

The Ewe arrived in southern Togo several centuries ago. The country later became a major source of slaves. Germany took control in 1884. France and Britain administered Togoland as UN trusteeships. The French sector became the republic of Togo Apr. 27, 1960.

The population is divided between Bantus in the S and Hamitic tribes in the N. Togo has actively promoted regional integration, as a means of stimulating the economy.

In Jan. 1993 police fired on antigovernment demonstrators, killing at least 22. Some 25,000 people fled to Ghana and Benin as a result of civil unrest. In Jan. 1994 at least 40 people were killed when gunmen reportedly attacked an army base. Further violence marred Togo's first multiparty legislative elections, held Feb. 1994.

Tonga
Kingdom of Tonga
Pule'anga Fakatu'i 'o Tonga

People: Population: 107,335. **Pop. density:** 370 per sq. mi. **Urban:** 42%. **Ethnic groups:** Polynesian, European. **Principal languages:** Tongan, English (both official). **Chief religions:** Mostly Christian (Free Wesleyan 43%, Roman Catholic 16%, Mormon 12%, Free Church of Tonga 11%, Church of Tonga 7%).

Geography: Area: 290 sq. mi. **Location:** In western South Pacific O. **Neighbors:** Nearest are Fiji to W, Samoa to NE. **Topography:** Tonga comprises 170 volcanic and coral islands, 36 inhabited. **Capital:** Nuku'alofa (1990 est.): 34,000.

Government: Type: Constitutional monarchy. **Head of state:** King Taufa'ahau Tupou IV; b July 4, 1918; in office: Dec. 16, 1965. **Head of Government:** Prime Min. Baron Vaea; in office: Aug. 22, 1991. **Local divisions:** 3 main island groups.

Economy: Industries: Tourism, fishing. **Chief crops:** Coconuts, copra, bananas, vanilla beans. **Arable land:** 25%. **Electricity prod.** (1995): 30 mil kWh. **Labor force:** 70% agric.

Finance: Monetary unit: Pa'anga (Aug. 1997: 1.24 = $1 US). **Gross domestic product** (1995 est.): $228 mil. **Per capita GDP:** $2,160. **Imports** (FY 1993-94): $57.8 mil; partners: N.Z. 44%, Australia 22%. **Exports** (FY 1993-94): $20.3 mil; partners: Japan 59%, U.S. 14%. **Tourism** (1994): $9 mil. **International reserves less gold** (Apr. 1997): $29.57 mil. **Consumer prices** (change in 1996): 3.0%.

Transport: Motor vehicles in use: 3,400 passenger cars, 3,900 comm. vehicles. **Civil aviation:** 6.8 mil passenger-mi.; 6 airports with scheduled flights. **Chief port:** Nuku'alofa.

Communications: Television sets: 1 per 63 persons. **Radios:** 1 per 1.8 persons. **Telephones:** 1 per 15 persons.

Health (1997): **Life expectancy at birth:** 67.3 male; 71.7 female. **Births** (per 1,000 pop.): 27. **Deaths** (per 1,000 pop.): 6. **Natural increase:** 2.1%. **Hospital beds:** 1 per 320 persons.

Physicians: 1 per 2,201 persons. **Infant mortality** (per 1,000 live births): 39.

Education: Free and compulsory: ages 5-14. **Literacy** (1992): 93%.

Major International Organizations: The Commonwealth.

The islands were first visited by the Dutch in the early 17th century. A series of civil wars ended in 1845 with establishment of the Tupou dynasty. In 1900 Tonga became a British protectorate. On June 4, 1970, Tonga became independent and a member of the Commonwealth.

Trinidad and Tobago
Republic of Trinidad and Tobago

People: Population: 1,273,141. **Age distrib.** (%): <15: 29; 65+: 6. **Pop. density:** 643 per sq. mi. **Urban:** 72%. **Ethnic groups:** Black 43%, East Indian 40%, mixed 14%. **Principal languages:** English (official), Hindi, French, Spanish. **Chief religions:** Roman Catholic 32%, Protestant 28%, Hindu 24%.

Geography: Area: 1,980 sq. mi. **Location:** In Caribbean, off E coast of Venezuela. **Neighbors:** Nearest is Venezuela to SW. **Topography:** Three low mountain ranges cross Trinidad E-W, with a well-watered plain between N and central ranges. Parts of E and W coasts are swamps. Tobago, 116 sq. mi., lies 20 mi. NE. **Capital:** Port-of-Spain (1992 est.): 52,451.

Government: Type: Parliamentary democracy. **Head of state:** Pres. Arthur N. R. Robinson; b Dec. 16, 1926; in office: Mar. 19, 1997. **Head of government:** Prime Min. Basdeo Panday; b May 25, 1933; in office: Nov. 9, 1995. **Local divisions:** 8 counties, 3 municipalities, 1 ward. **Defense:** 1.7% of GNP (1994). **Active troop strength:** 2,100.

Economy: Industries: Oil products, chemicals, tourism. **Chief crops:** Sugar, cocoa, coffee, citrus fruits, rice. **Minerals:** Asphalt, oil, gas. **Crude oil reserves** (1996): 551 mil bbls. **Arable land:** 14%. **Electricity prod.** (1995): 3.9 bil kWh. **Labor force:** 62% services; 11% agric.

Finance: Monetary unit: Dollar (Aug. 1997: 6.19 = $1 US). **Gross domestic product** (1995 est.): $16.2 bil. **Per capita GDP:** $12,100. **Imports** (1994): $996 mil; partners: U.S. 48%, Venezuela 10%. **Exports** (1995): $2.2 bil; partners: U.S. 48%. **Tourism** (1994): $80 mil. **National budget** (1996 est.): $1.63 bil. **International reserves less gold** (Feb. 1997): $531.3 mil. **Gold:** 54,000 oz t. **Consumer prices** (change in 1996): 3.4%.

Transport: Motor vehicles in use: 127,000 passenger cars, 26,000 comm. vehicles. **Civil aviation:** 2.6 bil passenger-mi.; 2 airports with scheduled flights. **Chief ports:** Port-of-Spain, Scarborough.

Communications: Television sets: 1 per 3.2 persons. **Radios:** 1 per 2.0 persons. **Telephones:** 1 per 6.2 persons. **Daily newspaper circ.:** 135 per 1,000 pop.

Health: Life expectancy at birth (1997): 68.1 male; 72.9 female. **Births** (per 1,000 pop.): 16. **Deaths** (per 1,000 pop.): 7. **Natural increase:** 0.9%. **Hospital beds:** 1 per 340 persons. **Physicians:** 1 per 1,191 persons. **Infant mortality** (per 1,000 live births 1997): 18.

Education: Free and compulsory: ages 6-12. **Literacy** (1995): 98%.

Major International Organizations: UN (WTO, IMF, WHO), the Commonwealth, OAS.

Embassy: 1708 Massachusetts Ave. NW 20036; 467-6490.

Columbus sighted Trinidad in 1498. A British possession since 1802, Trinidad and Tobago won independence Aug. 31, 1962. It became a republic in 1976.

The nation is one of the most prosperous in the Caribbean. Oil production has increased with offshore finds. Middle Eastern oil is refined and exported, mostly to the U.S.

In July 1990, some 120 Muslim extremists captured the Parliament building and TV station and took about 50 hostages, including Prime Min. Arthur N. R. Robinson, who was beaten, shot in the legs, and tied to explosives. After a 6-day siege, the rebels surrendered.

Basdeo Panday, the country's first prime minister of East Indian ancestry, took office Nov. 9, 1995. Robinson became president on Mar. 19, 1997.

Tunisia
Republic of Tunisia
Al Jumhuriyah at Tunisiyah

People: Population: 9,183,097. **Age distrib.** (%) <15: 33; 65+: 6. **Pop. density:** 144 per sq. mi. **Urban:** 63%. **Ethnic**

groups: Arab-Berber 98%. **Principal languages:** Arabic (official), French. **Chief religions:** Muslim 98%.

Geography: Area: 63,378 sq. mi. **Location:** On N coast of Africa. **Neighbors:** Algeria on W, Libya on E. **Topography:** The N is wooded and fertile. The central coastal plains are given to grazing and orchards. The S is arid, approaching Sahara Desert. **Capital:** Tunis: 1,722,000*.

Government: Type: Republic. **Head of state:** Pres. Gen. Zine al-Abidine Ben Ali; b Sept 3, 1936; in office: Nov. 7, 1987. **Head of government:** Prime Min. Hamed Karoui; b Dec. 30, 1927; in office: Sept. 27, 1989. **Local divisions:** 23 governorates. **Defense:** 2.8% of GDP (1995). **Active troop strength:** 35,000 est.

Economy: Industries: Food processing, textiles, oil products, mining, tourism. **Chief crops:** Grains, dates, olives, sugar beets, grapes. **Minerals:** Phosphates, iron, oil, lead, zinc. **Crude oil reserves** (1996): 308 mil bbls. **Arable land:** 20%. **Livestock** (1996): sheep: 6.4 mil; goats: 1.25 mil. **Fish catch** (1994): 87,000 metric tons. **Electricity prod.** (1995): 6.2 bil kWh. **Labor force:** 55% services; 23% industry; 22% agric.

Finance: Monetary unit: Dinar (Aug. 1997: 1.21 = $1 US). **Gross domestic product** (1994): $37.1 bil. **Per capita GDP:** $4,250. **Imports** (1994): $6.6 bil; partners: EU 70%. **Exports** (1994): $4.7 bil; partners: EU 75%. **Tourism** (1994): $1.3 bil. **National budget** (1993 est.): $5.5 bil. **International reserves less gold** (Apr. 1997): $1.52 bil. **Gold:** 217,000 oz t. **Consumer prices** (change in 1996): 3.7%.

Transport: Railroads: Length: 1,403.5 mi. **Motor vehicles in use:** 320,000 passenger cars, 184,000 comm. vehicles. **Civil aviation:** 1.2 bil passenger-mi.; 5 airports. **Chief ports:** Tunis, Sfax, Bizerte.

Communications: Television sets: 1 per 12 persons. **Radios:** 1 per 5.0 persons. **Telephones:** 1 per 17 persons. **Daily newspaper circ:** 46 per 1,000 pop.

Health: Life expectancy at birth (1997): 71.5 male; 74.3 female. **Births** (per 1,000 pop.): 24. **Deaths** (per 1,000 pop.): 5. **Natural increase:** 1.9%. **Hospital beds:** 1 per 556 persons. **Physicians:** 1 per 1,640 persons. **Infant mortality** (per 1,000 live births 1997): 34.

Education: Compulsory: ages 6-16. **Literacy** (1995): 67%.

Major International Organizations: UN (WTO), Arab League, OAU.

Embassy: 1515 Massachusetts Ave. NW 20005; 862-1850.

Site of ancient Carthage and a former Barbary state under the suzerainty of Turkey, Tunisia became a protectorate of France under a treaty signed May 12, 1881. The nation became independent Mar. 20, 1956, and ended the monarchy the following year. Habib Bourguiba, an independence leader, served as president until 1987, when he was deposed by his prime minister, Zine al-Abidine Ben Ali.

Tunisia has actively repressed Islamic fundamentalism.

Turkey
Republic of Turkey
Turkiye Cumhuriyeti

People: Population: 63,528,225. **Age distrib.** (%): <15: 31; 65+: 6. **Pop. density:** 211 per sq. mi. **Urban:** 71%. **Ethnic groups:** Turk 80%, Kurd 20%. **Principal languages:** Turkish (official), Kurdish, Arabic. **Chief religions:** Muslim 99.8%.

Geography: Area: 300,948 sq. mi. **Location:** Occupies Asia Minor, stretches into continental Europe; borders on Mediterranean and Black seas. **Neighbors:** Bulgaria, Greece on W; Georgia, Armenia on N; Iran on E; Iraq, Syria on S. **Topography:** Central Turkey has wide plateaus, with hot, dry summers and cold winters. High mountains ring the interior on all but W, with more than 20 peaks over 10,000 ft. Rolling plains are in W; mild, fertile coastal plains are in S, W. **Capital:** Ankara. **Cities:** Istanbul 7,911,000; Ankara 2,846,000; Izmir 2,052,000*.

Government: Type: Republic. **Head of state:** Pres. Suleyman Demirel; b 1924; in office: May 16, 1993. **Head of government:** Prime Min. Mesut Yilmaz; b 1947; in office: July 12, 1997. **Local divisions:** 79 provinces. **Defense:** 4% of GDP (1995). **Active troop strength:** 639,000.

Economy: Industries: Textiles, steel, mining, processed foods. **Chief crops:** Tobacco, grains, cotton, pulses, citrus, olives, sugar beets. **Minerals:** Antimony, chromium, mercury, copper, coal. **Crude oil reserves** (1996): 260 mil bbls. **Other resources:** Wool, silk, forests. **Arable land:** 30%. **Livestock** (1996): sheep: 35.6 mil; cattle: 11.9 mil; goats: 9.55 mil. **Fish catch** (1995): 652,183 metric tons. **Electricity prod.** (1995): 82.9 bil kWh. **Labor force:** 44% agric.; 41% serv.; 15% ind.

Finance: Monetary unit: Lira (Aug. 1997: 165,200 = $1 US). **Gross domestic product** (1995 est.): $345.7 bil. **Per capita GDP:** $5,500. **Imports** (1995): $35.7 bil; partners: Germany 16%, U.S. 10%. **Exports** (1995): $21.6 bil; partners: Germany 23%. **Tourism** (1994): $4.3 bil. **National budget** (1995): $35 bil. **International reserves less gold** (June 1997): $16.06 bil. **Gold:** 3.75 mil oz t. **Consumer prices** (change in 1996): 80.3%.

Transport: Railroads: Length: 6,449.7 mi. **Motor vehicles in use:** 3.1 mil passenger cars, 982,000 comm. vehicles. **Civil aviation:** 5.3 bil passenger-mi.; 26 airports with scheduled flights. **Chief ports:** Istanbul, Izmir, Mersin.

Communications: Television sets: 1 per 5.5 persons. **Radios:** 1 per 6.2 persons. **Telephones:** 1 per 4.7 persons. **Daily newspaper circ:** 44 per 1,000 pop.

Health: Life expectancy at birth (1997): 70.0 male; 74.9 female. **Births** (per 1,000 pop.): 22. **Deaths** (per 1,000 pop.): 5. **Natural increase:** 1.6%. **Hospital beds:** 1 per 450 persons. **Physicians:** 1 per 970 persons. **Infant mortality** (per 1,000 live births 1997): 41.

Education: Free and compulsory: ages 6-14. **Literacy** (1995): 82%.

Major International Organizations: UN (WTO, WHO, IMF), NATO, OECD.

Embassy: 1714 Massachusetts Ave. NW 20036; 659-8200.

Ancient inhabitants of Turkey were among the world's first agriculturalists. Such civilizations as the Hittite, Phrygian, and Lydian flourished in Asiatic Turkey (Asia Minor), as did much of Greek civilization. After the fall of Rome in the 5th century, Constantinople (now Istanbul) was the capital of the Byzantine Empire for 1,000 years. It fell in 1453 to Ottoman Turks, who ruled a vast empire for over 400 years.

Just before World War I, Turkey, or the Ottoman Empire, ruled what is now Syria, Lebanon, Iraq, Jordan, Israel, Saudi Arabia, Yemen, and islands in the Aegean Sea.

Turkey joined Germany and Austria in World War I and its defeat resulted in loss of much territory and fall of the sultanate. A republic was declared Oct. 29, 1923, with Mustafa Kemal (later Kemal Ataturk) as its first president. Ataturk led Turkey until his death in 1938. The Caliphate (spiritual leadership of Islam) was renounced in 1924.

Long embroiled with Greece over Cyprus, off Turkey's south coast, Turkey invaded the island July 20, 1974, after Greek officers seized the Cypriot government as a step toward unification with Greece. Turkey sought a new government for Cyprus, with Greek Cypriot and Turkish Cypriot zones. In reaction to Turkey's moves, the U.S. cut off military aid in 1975. Turkey, in turn, suspended the use of most U.S. bases. Aid was restored in 1978. There was a military takeover, Sept. 12, 1980.

Religious and ethnic tensions and active left and right extremists have caused endemic violence. Martial law, imposed in 1978, was lifted in 1984. The military formally transferred power to an elected Parliament in 1983.

Turkey was a member of the Allied forces that ousted Iraq from Kuwait, 1991. In the aftermath of the war, millions of Kurdish refugees fled to Turkey's border to escape Iraqi forces. The Turkish government mounted sporadic offensives against separatist Kurds in this border area and in N Iraq, causing heavy casualties among guerrillas and civilians.

Kurdish militants, demanding an independent state for the Kurds, raided Turkish diplomatic missions in some 25 Western European cities June 24, 1993. Tansu Ciller officially became Turkey's first woman prime minister July 5, 1993. The Welfare Party, an Islamic group, gained strength in the 1990s but was unable to form a government until June 1996, when it came to power in coalition with Ciller's True Path Party. The pro-Islamic government resigned June 18, 1997, under pressure from the military.

Turkmenistan
Republic of Turkmenistan
Turkmenistan Jumhuriyati

People: Population: 4,225,351. **Age distrib.** *%): <15: 39; 65+: 4. **Pop. density:** 22 per sq. mi. **Urban:** 45%. **Ethnic groups:** Turkmen 73%, Russian 10%, Uzbek 9%. **Principal languages:** Turkmen (official), Russian, Uzbek. **Chief religions:** Muslim 87%, Eastern Orthodox 11%.

Geography: Area: 188,500 sq. mi. **Neighbors:** Kazakhstan on N, Uzbekistan on N and E, Afghanistan and Iran on S. **Topography:** The Kara Kum Desert occupies 80% of the area. Bordered on W by Caspian Sea. **Capital:** Ashgabat (1994 est.): 518,000.

Government: Type: Republic. **Head of state:** Pres. Saparmurad Niyazov; b Feb. 18, 1940; in office: Oct. 27, 1990. **Local divisions:** 5 regions. **Defense:** 3% of GDP (1995). **Active troop strength:** 16,000-18,000.

Economy: Industries: Oil, natural gas, food processing, textiles. **Chief crops:** Grain, cotton, grapes. **Minerals:** Coal, sulfur, salt. **Arable land:** 2%. **Livestock** (1996): sheep: 6.15 mil; cattle: 1.2 mil. **Electricity prod.** (1995): 9.2 bil kWh. **Labor force:** 44% agric. & forestry; 20% ind. & constr.

Finance: Monetary unit: Manat (Aug. 1997: 5,200 = $1 US). **Gross domestic product** (1995 est.): $11.5 bil. **Per capita GDP:** $2,820. **Imports** (1994): $304 mil, excl. CIS. **Exports** (1994): $382 mil, excl. CIS.

Transport: Railroads: Length: 1,316.5 mi. **Civil aviation:** 970 mil passenger-mi. **Chief port:** Turkmenbashi.

Communications: Television sets: 1 per 5.6 persons. **Telephones:** 1 per 14 persons.

Health: Life expectancy at birth (1997): 56.9 male; 66.7 female. **Births** (per 1,000 pop.): 29. **Deaths** (per 1,000 pop.): 9. **Natural increase:** 2.0%. **Hospital beds:** 1 per 94 persons. **Physicians:** 1 per 315 persons. **Infant mortality** (per 1,000 live births 1997): 81.

Education: Literacy (1995): 100%.

Major International Organizations: UN (WHO, WTO), CIS.

Embassy: 1511 K St. NW, Suite 412 20005; 737-4800.

The region has been inhabited by Turkic tribes since the 10th century. It became part of Russian Turkestan in 1881, and a constituent republic of the USSR in 1925. Turkmenistan declared independence Oct. 27, 1991, and became an independent state when the USSR disbanded Dec. 26, 1991.

Extensive oil and gas reserves place Turkmenistan in a more favorable economic position than other former Soviet republics. A new rail line linking Iran and Turkmenistan was inaugurated May 13, 1996. Political power centered around the former Communist Party apparatus, and Pres. Saparmurad Niyazov became the object of a personality cult.

Tuvalu

People: Population: 10,297. **Age distrib.** (%): <15: 36; 65+: 5. **Pop. density:** 1,095 per sq. mi. **Urban:** 48%. **Ethnic groups:** Polynesian 96%. **Principal languages:** Tuvaluan, English. **Chief religions:** Church of Tuvalu (Congregationalist) 97%.

Geography: Area: 9.4 sq. mi. **Location:** 9 islands forming a NW-SE chain 360 mi. long in the SW Pacific O. **Neighbors:** Nearest are Kiribati to N, Fiji to S. **Topography:** The islands are all low-lying atolls, nowhere rising more than 15 ft. above sea level, composed of coral reefs. **Capital:** Funafuti Atoll (1991): 3,839.

Government: Head of state: Queen Elizabeth II, represented by Gov.-Gen. Tulaga Manuella; in office: June 1994. **Head of government:** Prime Min. Bikenibeu Paeniu; in office: Dec. 23, 1996.

Economy: Industries: Copra. **Chief crops:** Coconuts. **Other resources:** fish.

Finance: Monetary unit: Tuvalu Dollar, Australian Dollar. **Gross domestic product** (1995 est.): $7.8 mil. **Per capita GDP:** $800.

Transport: Chief port: Funafuti.

Health (1997): **Life expectancy at birth:** 62.4 male; 64.8 female. **Births** (per 1,000 pop.): 23. **Deaths** (per 1,000 pop.): 9. **Natural increase:** 1.4%. **Physicians:** 1 per 1,152 persons. **Infant mortality** (per 1,000 live births): 27.

Education: Compulsory: ages 7-17. **Literacy** (1990): 95%.

Major International Organizations: the Commonwealth.

The Ellice Islands separated from the British Gilbert and Ellice Islands Colony in 1975 and became Tuvalu; independence came Oct. 1, 1978.

Uganda
Republic of Uganda

People: Population: 20,604,874. **Age distrib.** (%): <15: 50; 65+: 2. **Pop. density:** 221 per sq. mi. **Urban:** 13%. **Ethnic groups:** Bantu, Nilotic, Nilo-Hamitic, Sudanic tribes. **Principal languages:** English (official), Luganda, Swahili. **Chief religions:** Christian 66%, indigenous beliefs 18%, Muslim 16%.

Geography: Area: 93,070 sq. mi. **Location:** In E Central Africa. **Neighbors:** Sudan on N, Congo (formerly Zaire) on

W, Rwanda and Tanzania on S, Kenya on E. **Topography:** Most of Uganda is a high plateau 3,000-6,000 ft. high, with high Ruwenzori range in W (Mt. Margherita 16,750 ft.), volcanoes in SW; NE is arid, W and SW rainy. Lakes Victoria, Edward, Albert form much of borders. **Capital:** Kampala: 954,000*.

Government: Type: Republic. **Head of state:** Pres. Yoweri Kaguta Museveni; b Mar. 1944; in office: Jan. 29, 1986. **Head of government:** Prime Min. Kintu Mosoke; in office: Nov. 18, 1994. **Local divisions:** 39 districts. **Defense:** 1.7% of budget (FY 1993-94). **Active troop strength:** 50,000 est.

Economy: Industries: Brewing, textiles, cement. **Chief crops:** Coffee, cotton, tea, corn, tobacco. **Minerals:** Copper, cobalt. **Arable land:** 23%. **Livestock** (1996): cattle: 5.2 mil; goats: 3.5 mil; sheep: 1.9 mil; pigs: 920,000. **Fish catch** (1995): 208,807 metric tons. **Electricity prod.** (1995): 807 mil kWh. **Labor force:** 80% agric.

Finance: Monetary unit: Shilling (Aug. 1997: 1,110 = $1 US). **Gross domestic product** (1995 est.): $16.8 bil. **Per capita GDP:** $900. **Imports** (1994-95): $1 bil.; partners: Kenya 23%, UK 10%. **Exports** (1994): $537 mil; partners: UK 21%, Belg.-Lux. 12%. **Tourism** (1994): $61 mil. **National budget** (1994-95 est.): $1.07 bil. **International reserves less gold** (Apr. 1997): $565.4 mil. **Consumer prices** (change in 1996): 7.2%.

Transport: Railroads: Length: 770.7 mi. **Motor vehicles in use:** 18,000 passenger cars, 25,000 comm. vehicles. **Civil aviation:** 32.3 mil passenger-mi. **Chief ports:** Entebbe, Jinja.

Communications: Television sets: 1 per 91 persons. **Radios:** 1 per 9.3 persons. **Telephones:** 1 per 440 persons.

Health: Life expectancy at birth (1997): 39.3 male; 40.1 female. **Births** (per 1,000 pop.): 45. **Deaths** (per 1,000 pop.): 21. **Natural increase:** 2.4%. **Infant mortality** (per 1,000 live births 1997): 98.

Education: Literacy (1995): 62%.

Major International Organizations: UN (WTO, WHO, IMF), OAU, the Commonwealth.

Embassy: 5911 16th St. NW 20011; 726-7100.

Britain obtained a protectorate over Uganda in 1894. The country became independent Oct. 9, 1962, and a republic within the Commonwealth a year later. In 1967, the traditional kingdoms, including the powerful Buganda state, were abolished and the central government strengthened. (In 1993 the government authorized restoration of the Buganda and other monarchies, but as ceremonial only.)

Gen. Idi Amin seized power from Prime Min. Milton Obote in 1971. As many as 300,000 of his opponents were reported killed in subsequent years. Amin was named president for life in 1976.

In 1972 Amin expelled nearly all of Uganda's 45,000 Asians. In 1973 the U.S. withdrew all diplomatic personnel. Amid worsening economic and domestic crises, Uganda's troops exchanged invasion attacks with long-standing foe Tanzania, 1978 to 1979. Tanzanian forces, coupled with Ugandan exiles and rebels, ended the dictatorial rule of Amin, Apr. 11, 1979.

Under a new constitution ratified Oct. 1995, nonparty presidential and legislative elections were held in 1996.

Ukraine
Ukrayina

People: Population: 50,684,635. **Age distrib.** (%): <15: 20; 65+: 14. **Pop. density:** 217 per sq. mi. **Urban:** 71%. **Ethnic groups:** Ukrainian 73%, Russian 22%. **Principal languages:** Ukrainian (official), Russian. **Chief religions:** Mostly Ukrainian Orthodox, some Ukrainian Catholic.

Geography: Area: 233,100 sq. mi. **Location:** In E Europe. **Neighbors:** Belarus on N; Russia on NE and E; Moldova and Romania on SW; Hungary, Slovakia, and Poland on W. **Topography:** Part of the E European plain. Mountainous areas include the Carpathians in the SW and Crimean chain in the S. Arable black soil constitutes a large part of the country. **Capital:** Kiev. **Cities:** Kiev (Kyiv) 2,812,000; Kharkov 1,681,000; mil; Dnipropetrovsk 1,231,000.

Government: Type: Constitutional republic. **Head of state:** Pres. Leonid Danylovich Kuchma; b Aug. 9, 1938; in office: July 19, 1994. **Head of government:** Prime Min. Valery Pustovoitenko; in office: July 16, 1997. **Local divisions:** 24 oblasts, 2 municipalities, 1 autonomous republic. **Defense:** Less than 2% of GDP (1996 est.). **Active troop strength:** 400,800 est.

Economy: Industries: Chemicals, machinery, food processing. **Chief crops:** Grains, sugar beets, vegetables. **Minerals:** Iron, manganese, coal, gas, oil, sulfur, nickel, salt. **Other resources:** Forests. **Arable land:** 56%. **Livestock** (1996): cattle: 15.6 mil; pigs: 12.3 mil; sheep: 2.1 mil. **Fish catch** (1995): 424,812 metric tons. **Electricity prod.** (1995): 180.1 bil kWh. **Labor force:** 33% ind. & constr.; 21% agric. & forestry.

Finance: Monetary unit: Hryvna (Aug. 1997: 1.83 = $1 US). **Gross domestic product** (1995 est.): $174.6 bil. **Per capita GDP:** $3,370. **Imports** (1995): $11.4 bil; partners: Russia 51%. **Exports** (1995): $11.6 bil; partners: Russia 44%. **Tourism** (1994): $230 mil. **National budget** (1990): $8 bil. **International reserves less gold** (Mar. 1997): $1.89 bil. **Gold:** 80,900 oz t. **Consumer prices** (change in 1996): 80.3%.

Transport: Railroads: Length: 14,500.4 mi. **Motor vehicles in use:** 4.5 mil passenger cars. **Civil aviation:** 803.6 mil passenger-mi.; 11 airports with scheduled flights. **Chief ports:** Odesa, Kiev, Berdiansk.

Communications: Television sets: 1 per 2.9 persons. **Radios:** 1 per 1.2 persons. **Telephones:** 1 per 6.2 persons. **Daily newspaper circ.:** 118 per 1,000 pop.

Health: Life expectancy at birth (1997): 61.9 male; 72.5 female. **Births** (per 1,000 pop.): 12. **Deaths** (per 1,000 pop.): 15. **Natural increase:** –0.3. **Hospital beds:** 1 per 81 persons. **Physicians:** 1 per 224 persons. **Infant mortality** (per 1,000 live births 1997): 22.

Education: Compulsory: ages 7-15. **Literacy** (1994): 98%.

Major International Organizations: UN, CIS.

Embassy: 3350 M St. NW 20007; 333-0606.

The ancient ancestors of Ukrainians, the Trypilians, flourished along the Dnieper River, Ukraine's main artery, from 6000-1000 BC. The Slavic ancestors of the Ukrainians inhabited modern Ukrainian territory well before the first century AD.

In the 9th century, the princes of Kiev established a strong state called Kievan Rus, which included much of present-day Ukraine. A strong dynasty was established, with ties to virtually all major European royal families. St. Vladimir the Great, ruler of Kievan Rus, accepted Christianity as the national faith in 988. At the crossroads of European trade routes, Kievan Rus reached its zenith under Yaroslav the Wise (1019-1054). Internal conflicts led to the disintegration of the Ukrainian state into principalities by the time of the Asian invasion of Europe in the 13th century. Mongol rule was supplanted by Poland and Lithuania in the 14th and 15th centuries. The N Black Sea coast and Crimea came under the control of the Turks in 1478.

Ukrainian Cossacks, starting in the late 16th century, waged numerous wars of liberation against the occupiers of Ukraine: Russia, Poland, and Turkey. By the late 18th century, Ukrainian independence was lost. Ukraine's neighbors once again divided its territory. At the turn of the 19th century, Ukraine was occupied by Russia and Austria-Hungary.

An independent Ukrainian National Republic was proclaimed on January 22, 1918. In 1921, Ukraine's neighbors occupied and divided Ukrainian territory. In 1922, Ukraine became a constituent republic of the USSR as the Ukrainian SSR. In 1932-33, the Soviet government engineered a man-made famine in eastern Ukraine, resulting in the deaths of 7-10 million Ukrainians.

In March 1939, independent Carpatho-Ukraine was the first European state to wage war against Nazi-led aggression in the region. During WW2 the Ukrainian nationalist underground and its Ukrainian Insurgent Army (UPA) fought both Nazi German and Soviet forces. The restoration of Ukrainian independence was declared on June 30, 1941. Over 5 million Ukrainians lost their lives during the war. With the reoccupation of Ukraine by Soviet troops in 1944 came a renewed wave of mass arrests, executions, and deportations of Ukrainians.

The world's worst nuclear power plant disaster occurred in Chernobyl, Ukraine, in April 1986.

Ukrainian independence was restored in Dec. 1991 with the dissolution of the Soviet Union. In the post-Soviet period Ukraine was burdened with a deteriorating economy.

Following a 1994 accord with Russia and the U.S., Ukraine's large nuclear arsenal was transferred to Russia for destruction. A new constitution legalizing private property and establishing Ukrainian as the sole official language was approved by parliament June 29, 1996. In May 1997, Russia and Ukraine resolved disputes over the Black Sea fleet and the future of Sevastopol and signed a long-delayed treaty of friendship and cooperation.

United Arab Emirates
Al Imarata al Arabiyah al Muttahidah

People: Population: 2,262,309. **Age distrib.** (%): <15: 33; 65+: 2. **Pop. density:** 70 per sq. mi. **Urban:** 84%. **Ethnic groups:** Arab, Iranian, Pakistani, Indian. **Principal languages:** Arabic (official), Persian, English, Hindi. **Chief religions:** Muslim 96%, Christian, Hindu.

Geography: Area: 32,280 sq. mi. **Location:** Middle East, on the S shore of the Persian Gulf. **Neighbors:** Saudi Arabia on W and S, Oman on E. **Topography:** A barren, flat coastal plain gives way to uninhabited sand dunes on the S. Hajar Mts. are on E. **Capital:** 799,000*.

Government: Type: Federation of emirates. **Head of state:** Pres. Zaid ibn Sultan an-Nahayan b. 1923; in office: Dec. 2, 1971. **Head of government:** Prime Min. Sheikh Maktum ibn Rashid al-Maktum; in office: Nov. 20, 1990. **Local divisions:** 7 autonomous emirates: Abu Dhabi, Ajman, Dubai, Fujaira, Ras al-Khaimah, Sharjah, Umm al-Qaiwain. **Defense:** 4.3% of GDP (1994). **Active troop strength:** 64,500 est.

Economy: Chief crops: Vegetables, dates. **Minerals:** Oil, natural gas. **Crude oil reserves** (1996): 98 bil bbls. **Arable land:** 0%. **Electricity prod.** (1995): 18 bil kWh. **Labor force:** 56% ind. and commerce; 6% agric.; 38% serv.

Finance: Monetary unit: Dirham (Aug. 1997: 3.67 = $1 US). **Gross domestic product** (1995 est.): $70.1 bil. **Per capita GDP:** $24,000. **Imports** (1994): $20 bil; partners: Japan 10%, UK 8%, **Exports** (1994): $21 bil; partners: Japan 40%. **National budget** (1995 est.): $4.9 bil. **International reserves less gold** (May 1997): $8.94 bil. **Gold:** 795,000 oz t.

Transport: Motor vehicles in use: 313,000 passenger cars, 73,000 comm. vehicles. **Civil aviation:** 5.13 bil passenger-mi.; 6 airports with scheduled flights. **Chief ports:** Dubai, Abu Dhabi.

Communications: Television sets: 1 per 9.3 persons. **Radios:** 1 per 3.2 persons. **Telephones:** 1 per 3.5 persons.

Health: Life expectancy at birth (1997): 73.2 male; 76.2 female. **Births** (per 1,000 pop.): 18. **Deaths** (per 1,000 pop.): 3. **Natural increase:** 1.5%. **Hospital beds:** 1 per 297 persons. **Physicians:** 1 per 720 persons. **Infant mortality** (per 1,000 live births 1997): 16.

Education: Compulsory: ages 6-12. **Literacy** (1995): 79%.

Major International Organizations: UN (World Bank, IMF, ILO, WTO), Arab League, OPEC.

Embassy: 3000 K St. NW, Suite 600 20007; 338-6500.

The 7 "Trucial Sheikdoms" gave Britain control of defense and foreign relations in the 19th century. They merged to become an independent state Dec. 2, 1971.

The Abu Dhabi Petroleum Co. was fully nationalized in 1975. Oil revenues have given the UAE one of the highest per capita GDPs in the world. International banking has grown in recent years.

United Kingdom
United Kingdom of Great Britain and Northern Ireland

People: Population: 58,610,182. **Age distrib.** (%): <15: 20; 65+: 16. **Pop. density:** 621 per sq. mi. **Urban:** 89%. **Ethnic groups:** English 81.5%, Scottish 9.6%, Irish 2.4%, Welsh 1.9%, Ulster 1.8%; West Indian, Indian, Pakistani, others 2.8%. **Principal languages:** English, Welsh, Scottish, Gaelic. **Chief religions:** Anglican, Roman Catholic, other Christian, Muslim.

Geography: Area: 94,251 sq. mi. **Location:** Off the NW coast of Europe, across English Channel, Strait of Dover, and North Sea. **Neighbors:** Ireland to W, France to SE. **Topography:** England is mostly rolling land, rising to Uplands of southern Scotland; Lowlands are in center of Scotland, granite Highlands are in N. Coast is heavily indented, especially on W. British Isles have milder climate than N Europe due to the Gulf Stream and ample rainfall. Severn, 220 mi., and Thames, 215 mi., are longest rivers. **Capital:** London. **Cities:** London 7,640,000; Birmingham 2,271,000; Manchester 2,252,000; Leeds 1,433,000; Liverpool 877,000*.

Government: Type: Constitutional monarchy. **Head of state:** Queen Elizabeth II; b Apr. 21, 1926, in office: Feb. 0, 1952. **Head of government:** Prime Min. Tony Blair; b May 6, 1953; in office: May 2, 1997. **Local divisions:** England and Wales: 47 counties, 7 metropolitan counties; Scotland: 9 regions, 3 island areas; Northern Ireland: 26 districts.

Defense: 3.1% of GDP (FY 1995-96). **Active troop strength:** 226,000.

Economy: Industries: Steel, metals, vehicles, shipbuilding, banking, textiles, chemicals, electronics, aircraft, machinery, distilling. **Chief crops:** Grains, sugar beets, potatoes, vegetables. **Minerals:** Coal, tin, oil, gas, limestone, iron, salt, clay. **Crude oil reserves** (1996): 4.5 bil bbls. **Arable land:** 29%. **Livestock** (1996): sheep: 28.8 mil; cattle: 11.6 mil; pigs: 7.4 mil. **Fish catch** (1995): 1,003,740 metric tons. **Electricity prod.** (1995): 306.6 bil kWh. **Labor force:** 63% services; 25% manuf. & constr.; 9% govt.

Finance: Monetary unit: Pound (Aug. 1997: 0.62 = $1 US). **Gross domestic product** (1993): $1.14 tril. **Per capita GDP:** $19,500. **Imports** (1994): $221.9 bil; partners: EU 55%, U.S. 12%. **Exports** (1994): $200.4 bil; partners: EU 56%, U.S. 13%. **Tourism** (1994): $15.2 bil. **National budget** (FY 1994-95 est.): $447.6 bil. **International reserves less gold** (Apr. 1997): $35.13 bil. **Gold:** 18.43 mil oz t. **Consumer prices** (change in 1996): 2.4%.

Transport: Railroads: Length: 10,905.4 mi. **Motor vehicles in use:** 24.3 mil passenger cars, 3.6 mil comm. vehicles. **Civil aviation:** 86.4 bil passenger-mi.; 50 airports with scheduled flights. **Chief ports:** London, Liverpool, Glasgow, Southampton, Cardiff, Belfast.

Communications: Television sets: 1 per 2.3 persons. **Radios:** 1 per 0.7 person. **Telephones:** 1 per 2.0 persons. **Daily newspaper circ.:** 351 per 1,000 pop.

Health: Life expectancy at birth (1997): 74.0 male; 79.3 female. **Births:** (per 1,000 pop.): 13. **Deaths:** (per 1,000 pop.): 11. **Natural increase:** 0.2%. **Hospital beds:** 1 per 205 persons. **Physicians:** 1 per 629 persons. **Infant mortality** (per 1,000 live births 1997): 6.

Education: Compulsory: ages 6-12. **Literacy** (1993): 100%. Compulsory: ages 5-16.

Major International Organizations: UN and all of its specialized agencies, NATO, EU, OECD, the Commonwealth.

Embassy: 3100 Massachusetts Ave. NW 20008; 462-1340.

The United Kingdom of Great Britain and Northern Ireland comprises England, Wales, Scotland, and Northern Ireland.

Queen and Royal Family. The ruling sovereign is Elizabeth II of the House of Windsor, born Apr. 21, 1926, elder daughter of King George VI. She succeeded to the throne Feb. 6, 1952, and was crowned June 2, 1953. She was married Nov. 20, 1947, to Lt. Philip Mountbatten, born June 10, 1921, former Prince of Greece. He was created Duke of Edinburgh, Earl of Merioneth, and Baron Greenwich, and given the title H.R.H., Nov. 19, 1947; he was given the title Prince of the United Kingdom and Northern Ireland Feb. 22, 1957. Prince Charles Philip Arthur George, born Nov. 14, 1948, is the Prince of Wales and heir apparent. His son, William Philip Arthur Louis, born June 21, 1982, is second in line to the throne.

Parliament is the legislative governing body for the United Kingdom, with certain powers over dependent units. It consists of 2 houses: The **House of Lords** includes 772 hereditary and 380 life peers and peeresses, 22 Lords of Appeal, 2 archbishops and 24 bishops of the Church of England. Total membership is 1,200. The **House of Commons** has 659 members, who are elected by direct ballot and divided as follows: England 529; Wales 40; Scotland 72; Northern Ireland 18.

Resources and Industries. Great Britain's major occupations are manufacturing and trade. Metals and metal-using industries contribute more than 50% of the exports. Of about 60 million acres of land in England, Wales, and Scotland, 46 million are farmed, of which 17 million are arable, the rest pastures.

Large oil and gas fields have been found in the North Sea. Commercial oil production began in 1975. There are large deposits of coal.

Britain imports all of its cotton, rubber, sulphur, about 80% of its wool, half of its food and iron ore, also certain amounts of paper, tobacco, chemicals. Manufactured goods made from these basic materials have been exported since the industrial age began. Main exports are machinery, chemicals, woolen and synthetic textiles, clothing, autos and trucks, iron and steel, locomotives, ships, jet aircraft, farm machinery, drugs, radio, TV, radar and navigation equipment, scientific instruments, arms, whisky.

Religion and Education. The Church of England is Protestant Episcopal. The queen is its temporal head, with rights of appointments to archbishoprics, bishoprics, and other offices. There are 2 provinces, Canterbury and York, each headed by an archbishop. The most famous church is Westminster Abbey (1050-1760), site of coronations, tombs of Elizabeth I, Mary, Queen of Scots, kings, poets, and of the Unknown Warrior.

The most celebrated British universities are Oxford and Cambridge, each dating to the 13th century. There are about 70 other universities.

History. Britain was part of the continent of Europe until about 6,000 BC, but migration of peoples across the English Channel continued long afterward. Celts arrived 2,500 to 3,000 years ago. Their language survives in Welsh, and Gaelic enclaves.

England was added to the Roman Empire in AD 43. After the withdrawal of Roman legions in 410, waves of Jutes, Angles, and Saxons arrived from German lands. They contended with Danish raiders for control from the 8th through 11th centuries. The last successful invasion was by French speaking Normans in 1066, who united the country with their dominions in France.

Opposition by nobles to royal authority forced King John to sign the Magna Carta in 1215, a guarantee of rights and the rule of law. In the ensuing decades, the foundations of the parliamentary system were laid.

English dynastic claims to large parts of France led to the Hundred Years War, 1338-1453, and the defeat of England. A long civil war, the War of the Roses, lasted 1455-85, and ended with the establishment of the powerful Tudor monarchy. A distinct English civilization flourished. The economy prospered over long periods of domestic peace unmatched in continental Europe. Religious independence was secured when the Church of England was separated from the authority of the pope in 1534.

Under Queen Elizabeth I, England became a major naval power, leading to the founding of colonies in the new world and the expansion of trade with Europe and the Orient. Scotland was united with England when James VI of Scotland was crowned James I of England in 1603.

A struggle between Parliament and the Stuart kings led to a bloody civil war, 1642-49, and the establishment of a republic under the Puritan Oliver Cromwell. The monarchy was restored in 1660, but the "Glorious Revolution" of 1688 confirmed the sovereignty of Parliament: a Bill of Rights was granted 1689.

In the 18th century, parliamentary rule was strengthened. Technological and entrepreneurial innovations led to the Industrial Revolution. The 13 North American colonies were lost, but replaced by growing empires in Canada and India. Britain's role in the defeat of Napoleon, 1815, strengthened its position as the leading world power.

The extension of the franchise in 1832 and 1867, the formation of trade unions, and the development of universal public education were among the drastic social changes that accompanied the spread of industrialization and urbanization in the 19th century. Large parts of Africa and Asia were added to the empire during the reign of Queen Victoria, 1837-1901.

Though victorious in World War I, Britain suffered huge casualties and economic dislocation. Ireland became independent in 1921, and independence movements became active in India and other colonies. The country suffered major bombing damage in World War II, but held out against Germany singlehandedly for a year after the fall of France in 1940.

Industrial growth continued in the postwar period, but Britain lost its leadership position to other powers. Labor governments passed socialist programs nationalizing some basic industries and expanding social security. The Conservative government of Prime Min. Margaret Thatcher, however, tried to increase the role of private enterprise. In 1987, Thatcher became the first British leader in 160 years to be elected to a 3d consecutive term as prime minister. Falling on unpopular times, she resigned as prime minister in Nov. 1990. Her successor, John Major, led Conservatives to an upset victory at the polls, Apr. 9, 1992.

The UK supported the UN resolutions against Iraq and sent military forces to the Persian Gulf War.

The Channel Tunnel linking Britain to the Continent was officially inaugurated May 6, 1994. Britain's relations with the European Union were frayed in 1996 when the EU banned British beef because of the threat of "mad cow" disease.

On May 1, 1997, the Labour Party swept into power in a landslide victory, the largest of any party since 1935. Labour Party leader Tony Blair, 43, became Britain's youngest prime minister since 1812. Diana, Princess of Wales, the divorced wife of Prince Charles and the mother of Prince William, died in a car crash in Paris, Aug. 31, and received an elaborate funeral in London, Sept. 6.

Wales

The Principality of Wales in western Britain has an area of 8,019 sq. mi. and a population (1992 est.) of 2,899,000. Cardiff is the capital, pop. (1994 est.) 299,000.

England and Wales are administered as a unit. Less than 20% of the population of Wales speak both English and Welsh; about 32,000 speak Welsh solely. A 1979 referendum rejected, 4-1, the creation of an elected Welsh assembly; a similar proposal passed by a razor-thin margin on Sept. 18, 1997.

Early Anglo-Saxon invaders drove Celtic peoples into the mountains of Wales, terming them Waelise (Welsh, or foreign). There they developed a distinct nationality. Members of the ruling house of Gwynedd in the 13th century fought England but were crushed, 1283. Edward of Caernarvon, son of Edward I of England, was created Prince of Wales, 1301.

Scotland

Scotland, a kingdom now united with England and Wales in Great Britain, occupies the northern 37% of the main British island, and the Hebrides, Orkney, Shetland, and smaller islands. Length 275 mi., breadth approx. 150 mi., area 30,418 sq. mi., population (1992 est.) 5,111,000.

The Lowlands, a belt of land approximately 60 mi. wide from the Firth of Clyde to the Firth of Forth, divide the farming region of the Southern Uplands from the granite Highlands of the North, contain 75% of the population and most of the industry. The Highlands, famous for hunting and fishing, have been opened to industry by many hydroelectric power stations.

Edinburgh, pop. (1994 est.) 442,000, is the capital. Glasgow, pop. (1994 est.) 681,000, is Britain's greatest industrial center. It is a shipbuilding complex on the Clyde and an ocean port. Aberdeen, pop. (1994 est.) 218,000, NE of Edinburgh, is a major port, center of granite industry, fish-processing, and North Sea oil exploration. Dundee, pop. (1993 est.) 170,000, NE of Edinburgh, is an industrial and fish-processing center. About 90,000 persons speak Gaelic as well as English.

History. Scotland was called Caledonia by the Romans who battled early Celtic tribes and occupied southern areas from the 1st to the 4th centuries. Missionaries from Britain introduced Christianity in the 4th century; St. Columba, an Irish monk, converted most of Scotland in the 6th century.

The Kingdom of Scotland was founded in 1018. William Wallace and Robert Bruce both defeated English armies 1297 and 1314, respectively.

In 1603 James VI of Scotland, son of Mary, Queen of Scots, succeeded to the throne of England as James I, and effected the Union of the Crowns. In 1707 Scotland received representation in the British Parliament, resulting from the union of former separate Parliaments. Its executive in the British cabinet is the Secretary of State for Scotland. The growing Scottish National Party urges independence. A 1979 referendum on the creation of an elected Scottish assembly was defeated, but a proposal to create a regional legislature with limited taxing authority passed by an overwhelming margin, Sept. 11, 1997.

Memorials of Robert Burns, Sir Walter Scott, John Knox, Mary, Queen of Scots draw many tourists, as do the beauties of the Trossachs, Loch Katrine, Loch Lomond, and abbey ruins.

Industries. Engineering products are the most important industry, with growing emphasis on office machinery, autos, electronics, and other consumer goods. Oil has been discovered offshore in the North Sea, stimulating on-shore support industries.

Scotland produces fine woolens, worsteds, tweeds, silks, fine linens, and jute. It is known for its special breeds of cattle and sheep. Fisheries have large hauls of herring, cod, whiting. Whisky is the biggest export.

The Hebrides are a group of c. 500 islands, 100 inhabited, off the W coast. The Inner Hebrides include **Skye, Mull,** and **Iona,** the last famous for the arrival of St. Columba, AD 563. The Outer Hebrides include **Lewis** and **Harris.** Industries include sheep raising and weaving. The **Orkney Islands,** c. 90, are to the NE. The capital is Kirkwall, on Pomona Isl. Fish curling, sheep raising, and weaving are occupations. NE of the Orkneys are the 200 **Shetland Islands,** 24 inhabited, home of Shetland pony. The Orkneys and Shetlands have become centers for the North Sea oil industry.

Northern Ireland

Six of the 9 counties of Ulster, the NE corner of Ireland, constitute Northern Ireland, with the parliamentary boroughs of Belfast and Londonderry. Area 5,452 sq. mi., pop. (1992 est.) 1,610,000, capital and chief industrial center, Belfast, pop. (1994 est.) 281,000.

Industries. Shipbuilding, including large tankers, has long been an important industry, centered in Belfast, the largest port. Linen manufacture is also important, along with apparel, rope, and twine. Growing diversification has added engineering products, synthetic fibers, and electronics. There are large numbers of cattle, hogs, and sheep. Potatoes, poultry, and dairy foods are also produced.

Government. An act of the British Parliament, 1920, divided Northern from Southern Ireland, each with a parliament and government. When Ireland became a dominion, 1921, and later a republic, Northern Ireland chose to remain a part of the United Kingdom. It elects 18 members to the British House of Commons.

During 1968-69, large demonstrations were conducted by Roman Catholics who charged they were discriminated against in voting rights, housing, and employment. The Catholics, a minority comprising about a third of the population, demanded abolition of property qualifications for voting in local elections. Violence and terrorism intensified, involving branches of the Irish Republican Army (outlawed in the Irish Republic), Protestant groups, police, and British troops.

A succession of Northern Ireland prime ministers pressed reform programs but failed to satisfy extremists on both sides. Between 1969 and 1994 more than 3,000 were killed in sectarian violence, many in England itself. Britain suspended the Northern Ireland parliament Mar. 30, 1972, and imposed direct British rule. A coalition government was formed in 1973 when moderates won election to a new one-house Assembly. But a Protestant general strike overthrew the government in 1974 and direct rule was resumed.

The turmoil and agony of Northern Ireland was dramatized in 1981 by the deaths of 10 imprisoned Irish nationalist hunger strikers in Maze Prison near Belfast. The inmates had starved themselves to death in an attempt to achieve status as political prisoners, but the British government refused to yield to their demands. In 1985, the Hillsborough agreement gave the Rep. of Ireland a voice in the governing of Northern Ireland; the accord was strongly opposed by Ulster loyalists. On Dec. 12, 1993, Britain and Ireland announced a declaration of principles aimed at leading to a political settlement in Northern Ireland.

On Aug. 31, 1994, the IRA announced a cease-fire, saying it would rely on political means to achieve its objectives; the IRA resumed its terrorist tactics on Feb. 9, 1996. Reinstatement of the IRA cease-fire as of July 20, 1997, led to the resumption of peace talks Sept. 15.

Education and Religion. Northern Ireland is about 58% Protestant, 42% Roman Catholic. Education is compulsory through age 15.

Channel Islands

The Channel Islands, area 75 sq. mi., pop. (1997 est.) 152,241, off the NW coast of France, the only parts of the one-time Dukedom of Normandy belonging to England, are Jersey, Guernsey and the dependencies of Guernsey — Alderney, Brechou, Great Sark, Little Sark, Herm, Jethou and Lihou. Jersey and Guernsey have separate legal existences and lieutenant governors named by the Crown. The islands were the only British soil occupied by German troops in World War II.

Isle of Man

The Isle of Man, area 227 sq. mi., pop. (1997 est.) 74,504, is in the Irish Sea, 20 mi. from Scotland, 30 mi. from Cumberland. It is rich in lead and iron. The island has its own laws and a lieutenant governor appointed by the Crown. The Tynwald (legislature) consists of the Legislative Council, partly elected, and House of Keys, elected. Capital: Douglas. Farming, tourism, and fishing (kippers, scallops) are chief occupations. Man is famous for the Manx tailless cat.

Gibraltar

Gibraltar, a dependency on the southern coast of Spain, guards the entrance to the Mediterranean. The Rock has been in British possession since 1704. The Rock is 2.75 mi. long, 3/4 of a mi. wide and 1,396 ft. in height; a narrow isthmus connects it with the mainland. Pop. (1997 est.) 28,913.

Gibraltar has historically been an object of contention between Britain and Spain. Residents voted with near unanimity to remain under British rule, in a 1967 referendum held in pursuance of a UN resolution on decolonization. A new constitution, May 30, 1969, increased Gibraltarian control of domestic affairs (the UK continues to handle defense and internal security matters). Following a 1984 agreement between Britain and Spain, the border, closed by Spain in 1969, was fully reopened in Feb. 1985. A UN General Assembly resolution requested Britain to end Gibraltar's colonial status by Oct. 1, 1996. No settlement has been reached.

British West Indies

Swinging in a vast arc from the coast of Venezuela NE, then N and NW toward Puerto Rico are the Leeward Islands, forming a coral and volcanic barrier sheltering the Caribbean from the open Atlantic. Many of the islands are self-governing British possessions. Universal suffrage was instituted 1951-54; ministerial systems were set up 1956-1960.

The **Leeward Islands** still associated with the UK are **Montserrat**, area 32 sq. mi., pop. (Sept. 1997 est.) 4,200, capital Plymouth; the **British Virgin Islands**, 59 sq. mi., pop. (1997 est.) 13,368, capital Road Town; and **Anguilla**, the most northerly of the Leeward Islands, 60 sq. mi., pop. (1997 est.) 10,785, capital The Valley. Montserrat has been devastated by the Soufrière Hills volcano, which began erupting July 18, 1995.

The three **Cayman Islands**, a dependency, lie S of Cuba, NW of Jamaica. Pop. (1997 est.) 36,153, most of it on Grand Cayman. It is a free port; in the 1970s Grand Cayman became a tax-free refuge for foreign funds and branches of many Western banks were opened there. Total area 102 sq. mi., capital Georgetown.

The **Turks and Caicos Islands** are a dependency at the SE end of the Bahama Islands. Of about 30 islands, only 6 are inhabited; area 193 sq. mi., pop. (1997 est.) 14,631; capital Grand Turk. Salt, shellfish, and conch shells are the main exports.

Bermuda

Bermuda is a British dependency governed by a royal governor and an assembly, dating from 1620, the oldest legislative body among British dependencies. Capital is Hamilton.

It is a group of about 150 small islands of coral formation, 20 inhabited, comprising 20.6 sq. mi. in the western Atlantic, 580 mi. E of North Carolina. Pop. (1997 est.) 62,569 (about 61% of African descent). Pop. density is high.

The U.S. maintains a NASA tracking facility; a U.S. naval air base was closed in 1995.

Tourism is the major industry; Bermuda boasts many resort hotels. The government raises most revenue from import duties. Exports: petroleum products, medicine. In a referendum Aug. 15, 1995, voters rejected independence by nearly a 3-to-1 majority.

South Atlantic

The **Falkland Islands**, a dependency, lie 300 mi. E of the Strait of Magellan at the southern end of South America.

The Falklands or Islas Malvinas include 2 large islands and about 200 smaller ones, area 4,700 sq. mi., pop. (1995 est.) 2,317, capital Stanley. The licensing of foreign fishing vessels has become the major source of revenue. Sheep-grazing is a main industry; wool is the principal export. There are indications of large oil and gas deposits. The islands are also claimed by Argentina, though 97% of inhabitants are of British origin. Argentina invaded the islands Apr. 2, 1982. The British responded by sending a task force to the area, landing their main force on the Falklands, May 21, and forcing an Argentine surrender at Port Stanley, June 14.

British Antarctic Territory, south of 60° S lat., formerly a dependency of the Falkland Isls., was made a separate colony in 1962 and includes the **South Shetland Islands**, the **South Orkneys**, and the Antarctic Peninsula. A chain of meteorological stations is maintained.

South Georgia and the South Sandwich Islands, formerly administered by the Falklands Isls., became a separate dependency in 1985. South Georgia, 1,450 sq. mi., with no permanent population, is about 800 mi. SE of the Falklands; the South Sandwich Isls., 130 sq. mi., are uninhabited, about 470 mi. SE of South Georgia.

St. Helena, an island 1,200 mi. off the W coast of Africa and 1,800 mi. E of South America, 47 sq. mi. and pop. (1997 est.) 6,803. Flax, lace, and rope-making are the chief industries. After Napoleon Bonaparte was defeated at Waterloo the Allies exiled him to St. Helena, where he lived from Oct. 16, 1815, to his death, May 5, 1821. Capital is Jamestown.

Tristan da Cunha is the principal of a group of islands of volcanic origin, total area 40 sq. mi., halfway between the Cape of Good Hope and South America. A volcanic peak 6,760 ft. high erupted in 1961. The 262 inhabitants were removed to England, but most returned in 1963. The islands are dependencies of St. Helena. Pop. (1993) 300.

Ascension is an island of volcanic origin, 34 sq. mi. in area, 700 mi. NW of St. Helena, through which it is administered. It is a communications relay center for Britain, and has a U.S. satellite tracking center. Pop. (1993) was 1,117, half of them communications workers. The island is noted for sea turtles.

Hong Kong (*See* China)

British Indian Ocean Territory

Formed Nov. 1965, embracing islands formerly dependencies of Mauritius or Seychelles: the Chagos Archipelago (including Diego Garcia), Aldabra, Farquhar, and Des Roches. The latter 3 were transferred to Seychelles, which became independent in 1976. Area 23 sq. mi. No permanent civilian population remains; the U.K. and the U.S. maintain a military presence.

Pacific Ocean

Pitcairn Island is in the Pacific, halfway between South America and Australia. The island was discovered in 1767 by Philip Carteret but was not inhabited until 23 years later when the mutineers of the *Bounty* landed there. The area is 1.7 sq. mi. and 1995 pop. was 54. It is a British dependency and is administered by a British High Commissioner in New Zealand and a local Council. The uninhabited islands of **Henderson, Ducie,** and **Oeno** are in the Pitcairn group.

United States

United States of America

People: Population: 267,954,767 (incl. 50 states & Dist. of Columbia). (**Note:** U.S. pop. figures may differ elsewhere in *The World Almanac*.) **Age distrib.** (%): <15: 22; 65+: 13. **Pop. density:** 72 per sq. mi. **Urban:** 76%.

Geography: Land area: 3,675,031 sq. mi. (incl. 50 states and DC). **Topography:** Vast central plain, mountains in west, hills and low mountains in east. **Capital:** Washington, D.C.

Government: Federal republic, strong democratic tradition. **Head of state:** Pres. Bill Clinton; b Aug. 19, 1946; in office: Jan. 20, 1993. **Administrative divisions:** 50 states and Dist. of Columbia. **Defense:** 3.8% of GDP (1995 est.). **Active troop strength:** 1.484 mil.

Economy: Minerals: Coal, copper, lead, molybdenum, phosphates, uranium, bauxite, gold, iron, mercury, nickel, potash, silver, tungsten, zinc. **Crude oil reserves** (1996): 22.4 bil bbls. **Arable land:** 20%. **Livestock** (1996): cattle: 103.8 mil; pigs: 58.2 mil; sheep: 8.5 mil; goats: 1.9 mil. **Fish catch** (1995): 6,834,419 metric tons. **Electricity prod.** (1995): 3.6 trl kWh.

Finance: Gross domestic product (1997): 7.17 tril. **Per capita GDP:** $27,607. **Imports** (1995): $749 bil; partners: Canada 19%, Japan 16%. **Exports** (1995): $685 bil; partners: Canada 19%, Japan 9%. **Tourism** (1994): $60.4 bil. **International reserves less gold** (May 1997): $57.0 bil. **Gold:** 261.72 mil oz t. **Consumer prices** (change in 1996): 2.9%.

Transport: Railroads: Length: 149,040.0 mi. **Motor vehicles in use:** 135.0 mil passenger cars, 65.5 mil comm. vehicles. **Civil aviation:** 510.6 bil passenger-mi.; 834 airports with scheduled flights.

Communications: Television sets: 1 per 1.2 persons. **Radios:** 1 per 0.5 person. **Telephones:** 1 per 1.6 persons. **Daily newspaper circ.:** 228 per 1,000 pop.

Health: Life expectancy at birth (1997): 72.8 male; 79.5 female. **Births** (per 1,000 pop.): 15. **Deaths** (per 1,000 pop.): 9. **Natural increase:** 0.6%. **Hospital beds:** 1 per 232 persons. **Physicians:** 1 per 381 persons. **Infant mortality** (per 1,000 live births 1997): 7.

Education: Free and compulsory: ages 7-16. **Literacy** (1994): 96%.

Major International Organizations: UN (WTO, ILO, IMF, WHO, FAO), OAS, NATO, OECD, APEC.

Uruguay
Oriental Republic of Uruguay
República Oriental del Uruguay

People: Population: 3,261,707. **Age distrib.** (%): <15: 24; 65+: 13. **Pop. density:** 47 per sq. mi. **Urban:** 91%. **Ethnic groups:** White (Iberians, Italians) 88%, mestizo 8%, black 4%. **Principal languages:** Spanish (official). **Chief religions:** Roman Catholic 66%.

Geography: Area: 68,037 sq. mi. **Location:** In southern South America, on the Atlantic O. **Neighbors:** Argentina on W, Brazil on N. **Topography:** Uruguay is composed of rolling, grassy plains and hills, well watered by rivers flowing W to Uruguay R. **Capital:** Montevideo: 1,325,000*.

Government: Type: Republic. **Head of state:** Pres. Julio María Sanguinetti Cairolo; Jan. 6, 1936; in office: Mar. 1, 1995. **Local divisions:** 19 departments. **Defense:** 1.5% of GDP (1994). **Active troop strength:** 25,600.

Economy: Industries: Meat packing, wool and hides, textiles, wine, oil refining. **Chief crops:** Corn, wheat, sugar, rice. **Arable land:** 8%. **Livestock** (1996): sheep: 19.3 mil; cattle: 11.4 mil. **Fish catch** (1994): 126,120 metric tons. **Electricity prod.** (1995): 7.6 bil kWh. **Labor force** 33% serv.; 25% govt.; 19% manuf.; 12% comm.; 11% agric.

Finance: Monetary unit: Peso (Aug. 1997: 9.67 = $1 US). **Gross domestic product** (1995 est.): $24.4 bil. **Per capita GDP:** $7,600. **Imports** (1995): $2.9 bil; partners: Brazil 26%, Argentina 24%. **Exports** (1995): $2.1 bil; partners: Brazil 26%, Argentina 20%. **Tourism** (1994): $632 mil. **National budget** (1994 est.): $3.37 bil. **International reserves less gold** (Apr. 1997): $1.17 bil. **Gold:** 1.75 mil oz t. **Consumer prices** (change in 1996): 28.3%

Transport: Railroads: Length: 1,285.5 mi. **Motor vehicles in use:** 445,000 passenger cars, 46,000 comm. vehicles. **Civil aviation:** 400.5 mil passenger-mi.; 1 airport. **Chief port:** Montevideo.

Communications: Television sets: 1 per 4.3 persons. **Radios:** 1 per 1.7 persons. **Telephones:** 1 per 5.1 persons. **Daily newspaper circ.:** 237 per 1,000 pop.

Health: Life expectancy at birth (1997): 72.1 male; 78.6 female. **Births** (per 1,000 pop.): 17. **Deaths** (per 1,000 pop.): 9. **Natural increase:** 0.8%. **Physicians:** 1 per 282 persons. **Infant mortality** (per 1,000 live births 1997): 15.

Education: Free and compulsory for 6 years between ages 6-14. **Literacy** (1995): 97%.

Major International Organizations: UN (WTO, IMF, WHO), OAS.

Embassy: 1918 F St. NW 20006; 331-1313.

Spanish settlers did not begin replacing the indigenous Charrua Indians until 1624. Portuguese from Brazil arrived later, but Uruguay was attached to the Spanish Viceroyalty of Rio de la Plata in the 18th century. Rebels fought against Spain beginning in 1810. An independent republic was declared Aug. 25, 1825.

Socialist measures were adopted as far back as 1911. The state owns the power, telephone, railroad, cement, oil-refining, and other industries.

Uruguay's standard of living was one of the highest in South America, and political and labor conditions among the freest. Economic stagnation, inflation, floods and drought, and a general strike in the late 1960s brought government attempts to strengthen the economy through devaluation of the peso and wage and price controls.

Terrorist activities led Pres. Juan María Bordaberry to agree to military control of his administration Feb. 1973. In June he abolished Congress and set up a Council of State in its place. Bordaberry was removed by the military in a 1976 coup. Civilian government was restored in 1985.

Uzbekistan
Republic of Uzbekistan
Uzbekiston Respublikasi

People: Population: 23,860,452. **Age distrib.** (%): <15: 40; 65+: 5. **Pop. density:** 138 per sq. mi. **Urban:** 41%. **Ethnic groups:** Uzbek 71%, Russian 8%. **Principal languages:** Uzbek (official), Russian. **Chief religions:** Mostly Sunni Muslim, some Eastern Orthodox.

Geography: Area: 172,700 sq. mi. **Location:** Central Asia. **Neighbors:** Kazakhstan on N and W, Kyrgyzstan and Tajikistan on E, Afghanistan and Turkmenistan on S. **Topography:** Mostly plains and desert. **Capital:** Tashkent 2,282,000*.

Government: Type: Republic. **Head of state:** Pres. Islam A. Karimov; b Jan. 30, 1938; in office: March 24, 1990. **Head of government:** Prime Min. Utkur Sultanov; in office: Dec. 1995. **Local divisions:** 12 regions, 1 autonomous republic, and Tashkent. **Defense: Active troop strength:** 29,000-30,000 est.

Economy: Industries: Machinery, food processing, natural gas, textiles. **Chief crops:** Vegetables, cotton, wheat. **Minerals:** Gas, oil, coal, gold, copper. **Arable land:** 10%. **Livestock** (1996): sheep: 8.7 mil; cattle: 5.2 mil. **Electricity prod.** (1995): 44.7 bil kWh. **Labor force:** 43% agric. & forestry; 22% ind. & constr.

Finance: Monetary unit: Som (Aug. 1997: 72.45 = $1 US). **Gross domestic product** (1995 est.): $54.7 bil. **Per capita GDP:** $2,370. **Imports** (1995): $2.9 bil; partners: Russia 59%, Kazakhstan 17%. **Exports** (1995): $3.1 bil; partners: Russia 53%, Kazakhstan 16%.

Transport: Railroads: Length: 2,148.7 mi. **Motor vehicles in use:** 865,000 passenger cars, 14,500 commercial vehicles. **Civil aviation:** 3.0 bil passenger-mi.; 9 airports with scheduled flights. **Chief port:** Termiz.

Communications: Television sets: 1 per 5.3 persons. **Radios:** 1 per 12 persons. **Telephones:** 1 per 13 persons.

Health: Life expectancy at birth (1997): 60.6 male; 69.1 female. **Births** (per 1,000 pop.): 29. **Deaths** (per 1,000 pop.): 8. **Natural increase:** 2.2%. **Hospital beds:** 1 per 118 persons. **Physicians:** 1 per 284 persons. **Infant mortality** (per 1,000 live births 1997): 79.

Education: Compulsory: ages 6-14. **Literacy** (1993): 97%.

Major International Organizations: UN, CIS.

Embassy: 1511 K St. NW 20005; 638-4266.

The region was overrun by the Mongols under Genghis Khan in 1220. In the 14th century, Uzbekistan became the center of a native empire—that of the Timurids. In later centuries Muslim feudal states emerged. Russian military conquest began in the 19th century.

The Uzbek SSR became a Soviet Union republic in 1925. Uzbekistan declared independence Aug. 29, 1991. It became an independent republic when the Soviet Union disbanded Dec. 26, 1991. Subsequently, the government of Uzbekistan was dominated by former Communists.

Vanuatu
Republic of Vanuatu
Ripablik blong Vanuatu

People: Population: 181,358. **Age distrib.** (%): <15: 40; 65+: 3. **Pop. density:** 38 per sq. mi. **Urban:** 19%. **Ethnic groups:** Melanesian 94%, some European, Asian, Pacific Islander. **Principal languages:** French, English, Bislama (all official). **Chief religions:** Presbyterian 37%, Anglican 15%, Roman Catholic 15%, other Christian 10%, indigenous beliefs 8%.

Geography: Area: 4,707 sq. mi. **Location:** SW Pacific, 1,200 mi. NE of Brisbane, Australia. **Neighbors:** Fiji to E, Solomon Isls. to NW. **Topography:** Dense forest with narrow coastal strips of cultivated land. **Capital:** Port-Vila (1993 est.): 26,100.

Government: Type: Republic. **Head of state:** Pres. Jean-Marie Leye; b 1932; in office: Mar. 2, 1994. **Head of government:** Prime Min. Serge Vohor; in office: Sept. 30, 1996. **Local divisions:** 6 provinces.

Economy: Industries: Fish-freezing, meat canneries, tourism. **Chief crops:** Copra, coconuts, cocoa, coffee. **Minerals:** Manganese. **Other resources:** Forests, cattle. **Fish catch** (1993): 2,925 metric tons. **Electricity prod.** (1995): 30 mil kWh.

Finance: Monetary unit: Vatu (Aug. 1997): 114.75 = $1 US). **Gross domestic product** (1994 est.): $210 mil. **Per capita GDP:** $1,220. **Imports** (1994 est.): $78.6 mil.; partners: Australia 41%, France 15%. **Exports** (1994 est.): $24.6 mil.; partners: EU 32%, Japan 29%. **Tourism** (1994): $55 mil. **International reserves less gold** (June 1997): $38.01 mil. **Consumer prices** (change in 1996): 0.9%.

Transport: Civil aviation: 88.8 mil passenger-mi.

Communications: Radios: 1 per 3.4 persons. **Telephones:** 1 per 40 persons.

Health (1997): **Life expectancy at birth:** 58.7 male; 62.6 female. **Births** (per 1,000 pop.): 30. **Deaths** (per 1,000 pop.): 9. **Natural increase:** 2.1%. **Hospital beds:** 1 per 450 persons. **Physicians:** 1 per 14,025 persons. **Infant mortality** (per 1,000 live births): 63.

Education: Literacy (1992): 53%.

Major International Organizations: UN, the Commonwealth.

The Anglo-French condominium of the New Hebrides, administered jointly by France and Great Britain since 1906, became the independent Republic of Vanuatu on July 30, 1980.

Vatican City (The Holy See)
Città del Vaticano (Santa Sede)

People: Population: 840. **Urban:** 100%. **Ethnic groups:** Italian, Swiss. **Principal languages:** Italian, Latin. **Chief religions:** Roman Catholic.

Geography: Area: 108.7 acres. **Location:** In Rome, Italy. **Neighbors:** Completely surrounded by Italy.

Monetary unit: Vatican Lira, Italian Lira (equal value).

Apostolic Nunciature in U.S.: 3339 Massachusetts Ave. NW 20008; 333-7121.

The popes for many centuries, with brief interruptions, held temporal sovereignty over mid-Italy (the so-called Papal States), comprising an area of some 16,000 sq. mi., with a population in the 19th century of more than 3 million. This territory was incorporated in the new Kingdom of Italy, the sovereignty of the pope being confined to the palaces of the Vatican and the Lateran in Rome and the villa of Castel Gandolfo, by an Italian law, May 13, 1871. This law also guaranteed to the pope and his successors a yearly indemnity of over $620,000. The allowance, however, remained unclaimed.

A Treaty of Conciliation, a concordat, and a financial convention were signed Feb. 11, 1929, by Cardinal Gasparri and Premier Mussolini. The documents established the independent state of Vatican City and gave the Catholic religion special status in Italy. The treaty (Lateran Agreement) was made part of the Constitution of Italy (Article 7) in 1947. Italy and the Vatican signed an agreement in 1984 on revisions of the concordat; the accord eliminated Roman Catholicism as the state religion and ended required religious education in Italian schools.

Vatican City includes St. Peter's, the Vatican Palace and Museum covering over 13 acres, the Vatican gardens, and neighboring buildings between Viale Vaticano and the Church. Thirteen buildings in Rome, outside the boundaries, enjoy extraterritorial rights; these buildings house congregations or officers necessary for the administration of the Holy See.

The legal system is based on the code of canon law, the apostolic constitutions, and laws especially promulgated for the Vatican City by the pope. The Secretariat of State represents the Holy See in its diplomatic relations. By the Treaty of Conciliation the pope is pledged to a perpetual neutrality unless his mediation is specifically requested. This, however, does not prevent the defense of the Church whenever it is persecuted.

The present sovereign of the State of Vatican City is the Supreme Pontiff John Paul II, Karol Wojtyla, born in Wadowice, Poland, May 18, 1920, elected Oct. 16, 1978 (the first non-Italian to be elected Pope in 456 years).

The U.S. restored formal relations in 1984 after the U.S. Congress repealed an 1867 ban on diplomatic relations with the Vatican. The Vatican and Israel agreed to establish formal relations Dec. 30, 1993.

Venezuela
Republic of Venezuela
República de Venezuela

People: Population: 22,396,407. **Age distrib.** (%): <15: 34; 65+: 4. **Pop. density:** 63 per sq. mi. **Urban:** 86%. **Ethnic groups:** Mestizo 67%, white (Spanish, Portuguese, Italian) 21%, black 10%, Indian 2%. **Principal languages:** Spanish (official). **Chief religions:** Roman Catholic 96%.

Geography: Area: 352,144 sq. mi. **Location:** On the Caribbean coast of South America. **Neighbors:** Colombia on W, Brazil on S, Guyana on E. **Topography:** Flat coastal plain and

Orinoco Delta are bordered by Andes Mts. and hills. Plains, called llanos, extend between mountains and Orinoco. Guyana Highlands and plains are S of Orinoco, which stretches 1,600 mi. and drains 80% of Venezuela. **Capital:** Caracas. **Cities:** Caracas 3,007,000; Maracaibo 1,603,000; Valencia 1,462,000*.

Government: Type: Federal republic. **Head of state:** Pres. Rafael Caldera; b Jan. 24, 1916; in office: Feb. 2, 1994. **Local divisions:** 21 states, 1 territory, 1 federal district, 1 federal dependency. **Defense:** 1.4% of GDP (1996). **Active troop strength:** 79,000.

Economy: Industries: Steel, oil products, textiles. **Chief crops:** Rice, corn, fruits, sugar. **Minerals:** Oil, gas, iron (extensive reserves and production); gold. **Crude oil reserves** (1996): 64.9 bil barrels. **Arable land:** 3%. **Livestock** (1996): cattle: 14.6 mil; goats: 3.2 mil; pigs: 2.85 mil; sheep: 1.2 mil. **Fish catch** (1995): 504,791 metric tons. **Electricity prod.** (1995): 74.0 bil kWh. **Labor force:** 63% services; 25% ind.; 12% agric.

Finance: Monetary unit: Bolivar (Aug. 1997: 496 = $1 US). **Gross domestic product** (1995 est.): $195.5 bil. **Per capita GDP:** $9,300. **Imports** (1995): $11.6 bil; partners: U.S. 40%. **Exports** (1995): $18.3 bil; partners: U.S. & P.R. 55%. **Tourism** (1994): $486 mil. **National budget** (1995 est.): $9.8 bil. **International reserves less gold** (May 1996): $13.22 bil. **Gold:** 11.46 mil oz t. **Consumer prices** (change in 1996): 99.9%.

Transport: Railroads: Length: 362.7 mi. **Motor vehicles in use:** 1.5 mil passenger cars, 512,000 comm. vehicles. **Civil aviation:** 4.0 bil passenger-mi.; 24 airports with scheduled flights. **Chief ports:** Maracaibo, La Guaira, Puerto Cabello.

Communications: Television sets: 1 per 6.1 persons. **Radios:** 1 per 2.3 persons. **Telephones:** 1 per 9.0 persons. **Daily newspaper circ.:** 215 per 1,000 pop.

Health: Life expectancy at birth (1997): 69.4 male; 75.6 female. **Births** (per 1,000 pop.): 24. **Deaths** (per 1,000 pop.): 5. **Natural increase:** 1.9%. **Hospital beds:** 1 per 382 persons. **Physicians:** 1 per 576 persons. **Infant mortality** (per 1,000 live births 1997): 29.

Education: Free and compulsory: ages 5-15. **Literacy** (1995): 91%.

Major International Organizations: UN (IMF, WTO, WHO, FAO), OAS, OPEC.

Embassy: 1099 30th St. NW 20007; 342-2214.

Columbus first set foot on the South American continent on the peninsula of Paria, Aug. 1498. Alonso de Ojeda, 1499, found Lake Maracaibo, and called the land Venezuela, or Little Venice, because natives had houses on stilts. Venezuela was under Spanish domination until 1821. The republic was formed after secession from the Colombian Federation in 1830.

Military strongmen ruled Venezuela for most of the 20th century. They promoted the oil industry; some social reforms were implemented. Since 1959, the country has had democratically elected governments.

Venezuela helped found the Organization of Petroleum Exporting Countries (OPEC). The government, Jan. 1, 1976, nationalized the oil industry with compensation. Oil accounts for much of total export earnings and the economy suffered a severe cash crisis in the 1980s and 1990s as a result of falling oil revenues. The government has attempted to reduce dependence on oil.

A coup attempt, led by midlevel military officers, was thwarted by loyalist troops Feb. 4, 1992. A second coup attempt was thwarted in Nov. Pres. Carlos Andrés Pérez was removed from office on corruption charges, May 1993; he was convicted, May 1996, of mismanaging a $17-million secret government security fund. Citing an economic crisis, Pres. Rafael Caldera, a populist elected Dec. 5, 1993, suspended many civil liberties June 27, 1994; constitutional rights were restored in most regions July 6, 1995.

Vietnam
Socialist Republic of Vietnam
Cong Hoa Xa Hoi Chu Nghia Viet Nam

People: Population: 75,123,880. **Age distrib.** (%): <15: 35; 65+: 5. **Pop. density:** 587 per sq. mi. **Urban:** 19%. **Ethnic groups:** Vietnamese 85-90%, Chinese 3%, Muong, Thai, Meo, Khmer, Man, Cham. **Principal languages:** Vietnamese (official), French, Chinese. **Chief religions:** Mainly Buddhist and Taoist; also Roman Catholic, indigenous beliefs.

Geography: Area: 127,816 sq. mi. **Location:** SE Asia, on the E coast of the Indochinese Peninsula. **Neighbors:** China on N, Laos and Cambodia on W. **Topography:** Vietnam is long and narrow, with a 1,400-mi. coast. About 22% of country is readily arable, including the densely settled Red R. valley in the N, narrow coastal plains in center, and the wide, often marshy Mekong R. Delta in the S. The rest consists of semi-arid plateaus and barren mountains, with some stretches of tropical rain forest. **Capital:** Hanoi. **Cities:** Ho Chi Minh City 3,521,000; Hanoi 1,236,000*.

Government: Type: Communist. **Head of state:** Pres. Tran Duc Luong; b May 1937; in office: Sept. 24, 1997. **Head of government:** Prime Min. Phan Van Khai; b Dec. 1933; in office: Sept. 25, 1997. **Local divisions:** 50 provinces, 3 municipalities. **Defense:** 2.7% of GDP (1995). **Active troop strength:** 572,000 est.

Economy: Industries: Food processing, textiles, chemical fertilizer. **Chief crops:** Rice, sugar, fruits, vegetables, cassava, corn. **Minerals:** Phosphates, coal, manganese, bauxite, chromate, oil. **Crude oil reserves** (1996): 600 mil bbls. **Other resources:** Forests. **Arable land:** 22%. **Livestock** (1996): pigs: 17.2 mil; cattle: 3.6 mil; buffalo: 3.0 mil. **Fish catch** (1995): 1,200,000 mil metric tons. **Electricity prod.** (1995): 12.3 bil kWh. **Labor force:** 65% agric.; 35% ind. and services.

Finance: Monetary unit: Dong (Aug. 1997: 11,669 = $1 US). **Gross domestic product** (1995 est.): $97 bil. **Per capita GDP:** $1,300. **Imports** (1995): $11.6 bil; partners: Singapore 17%, N.&S. Korea 13%. **Exports** (1995): $5.5 bil. partners: Japan 29%, Germany 9%. **Tourism** (1994): $85 mil. **National budget** (1995 est.): $5 bil.

Transport: Railroads: Length: 1,760.5 mi. **Motor vehicles in use:** 200,000. **Civil aviation:** 129.8 mil passenger-mi.; 12 airports with scheduled flights. **Chief ports:** Ho Chi Minh City, Haiphong, Da Nang.

Communications: Television sets: 1 per 23 persons. **Radios:** 1 per 9.6 persons. **Telephones:** 1 per 95 persons. **Daily newspaper circ.:** 8 per 1,000 pop.

Health: Life expectancy at birth (1997): 65.0 male; 69.9 female. **Births** (per 1,000 pop.): 22. **Deaths** (per 1,000 pop.): 7. **Natural increase:** 1.6%. **Hospital beds:** 1 per 366 persons. **Physicians:** 1 per 2,502 persons. **Infant mortality** (per 1,000 live births 1997): 37.

Education: Compulsory: ages 6-11. **Literacy** (1995): 94%.

Major International Organizations: UN (IMF, WHO, ASEAN). **Embassy:** 1233 20th St. NW 20036; 861-0737.

Vietnam's recorded history began in Tonkin before the Christian era. Settled by Viets from central China, Vietnam was held by China, 111 BC-AD 939, and was a vassal state during subsequent periods. Vietnam defeated the armies of Kublai Khan, 1288. Conquest by France began in 1858 and ended in 1884 with the protectorates of Tonkin and Annam in the N and the colony of Cochin-China in the S.

In 1940 Vietnam was occupied by Japan; nationalist aims gathered force. A number of groups formed the Vietminh (Independence) League, headed by Ho Chi Minh, Communist guerrilla leader. In Aug. 1945 the Vietminh forced out Bao Dai, former emperor of Annam, head of a Japan-sponsored regime. France, seeking to reestablish colonial control, battled Communist and nationalist forces, 1946-1954, and was defeated at Dienbienphu, May 8, 1954. Meanwhile, on July 1, 1949, Bao Dai had formed a State of Vietnam, with himself as chief of state, with French approval. China backed Ho Chi Minh.

A cease-fire signed in Geneva July 21, 1954, provided for a buffer zone, withdrawal of French troops from the North, and elections to determine the country's future. Under the agreement the Communists gained control of territory north of the 17th parallel, with its capital at Hanoi and Ho Chi Minh as president. South Vietnam came to comprise the 39 southern provinces. Some 900,000 North Vietnamese fled to South Vietnam.

On Oct. 26, 1955, Ngo Dinh Diem, premier of the interim government of South Vietnam, proclaimed the Republic of Vietnam and became its first president.

The North adopted a constitution Dec. 31, 1959, based on Communist principles and calling for reunification of all Vietnam. North Vietnam sought to take over South Vietnam beginning in 1954. Fighting persisted from 1956, with the Communist Vietcong, aided by North Vietnam, pressing war in the South. Northern aid to Vietcong guerrillas was intensified in 1959, and large-scale troop infiltration began in 1964, with Soviet and

Chinese arms assistance. Large Northern forces were stationed in border areas of Laos and Cambodia.

A serious political conflict arose in the South in 1963 when Buddhists denounced authoritarianism and brutality. This paved the way for a military coup Nov. 1-2, 1963, which overthrew Diem. Several other military coups followed.

In 1964, the U.S. began air strikes against North Vietnam. Beginning in 1965, the raids were stepped up and U.S. troops became combatants. U.S. troop strength in Vietnam, which reached a high of 543,400 in Apr. 1969, was ordered reduced by President Nixon in a series of withdrawals, beginning in June 1969. U.S. bombings were resumed in 1972-73.

A cease-fire agreement was signed in Paris Jan. 27, 1973 by the U.S., North and South Vietnam, and the Vietcong. It was never implemented.

North Vietnamese forces launched attacks against remaining government outposts in the Central Highlands in the first months of 1975. Government retreats turned into a rout, and the Saigon regime surrendered April 30. North Vietnam assumed control, and began transforming society along Communist lines.

The war's toll included—Combat deaths: U.S. 47,369; South Vietnam more than 200,000; other allied forces 5,225. Total U.S. fatalities numbered more than 58,000. Vietnamese civilian casualties were more than a million. Displaced war refugees in South Vietnam totaled more than 6.5 million.

The country was officially reunited July 2, 1976. The Northern capital, flag, anthem, emblem, and currency were applied to the new state. Nearly all major government posts went to officials of the former Northern government.

Heavy fighting with Cambodia took place, 1977-80, amid mutual charges of aggression and atrocities against civilians. Increasing numbers of Vietnamese civilians, ethnic Chinese, escaped the country, via the sea or the overland route across Cambodia. Vietnam launched an offensive against Cambodian refugee strongholds along the Thai-Cambodian border in 1985; they also engaged Thai troops.

Relations with China soured as 140,000 ethnic Chinese left Vietnam charging discrimination; China cut off economic aid. Reacting to Vietnam's invasion of Cambodia, China attacked 4 Vietnamese border provinces, Feb. 1979.

Vietnam announced reforms aimed at reducing central control of the economy in 1987, as many of the old revolutionary followers of Ho Chi Minh were removed from office.

Citing Vietnamese cooperation in returning remains of U.S. soldiers killed in the Vietnam War, the U.S. announced an end, Feb. 3, 1994, to a 19-year-old U.S. embargo on trade with Vietnam. The U.S. extended full diplomatic recognition to Vietnam July 11, 1995. The Communist Party replaced the country's ill and aging leadership in Sept. 1997.

Western Samoa

(See Samoa)

Yemen

Republic of Yemen

Al Jumhuriyah al Yamaniyah

People: Population: 13,972,477. **Age distrib.** (%): <15: 48; +65: 3. **Pop. density:** 67 per sq. mi. **Urban:** 34%. **Ethnic groups:** Arab, some Afro-Arab, South Asian. **Principal language:** Arabic (official). **Chief religions:** Mostly Muslim (Sha'fi-Sunni, Zaydi-Shi'a).

Geography: Area: 207,286 sq. mi. **Location:** Middle East, on the S coast of the Arabian Peninsula. **Neighbors:** Saudi Arabia on N, Oman on the E. **Topography:** A sandy coastal strip leads to well-watered fertile mountains in interior. **Capital:** Sanaa. **Cities:** (1995 est.) Sanaa 972,000; Aden 562,000.

Government: Type: Republic. **Head of state:** Pres. Ali Abdullah Saleh, b. 1942; in office: July 17, 1978. **Head of government:** Prime Min. Faraj Said bin Ghanem; in office: May 14, 1997. **Local divisions:** 17 governorates, Sanaa. **Defense:** 7.1% of GDP (1993). **Active troop strength:** 42,000.

Economy: Industries: Oil, food processing. **Chief crops:** Grains, fruits, qat, coffee, cotton. **Minerals:** Oil, salt. **Crude oil reserves** (1996): 4 bil bbls. **Arable land:** 6%. **Livestock** (1996): sheep: 3.7 mil; goats: 3.2 mil; cattle: 1.1 mil. **Fish catch** (1995): 86,811 metric tons. **Electricity prod.** (1995): 1.0 bil kWh.

Finance: Monetary unit: Rial (Aug. 1997: 134 = $1 US). **Gross domestic product** (1995 est.): $37.1 bil. **Per capita GDP:** $2,520. **Imports** (1994 est.): $1.8 bil; partners: U.S.

11%, UK 7%. **Exports** (1994 est.): $1.1 bil; partners: U.S. 17%, Japan 16%. **National budget** (1996 est.): $1.2 bil. **International reserves less gold** (Feb. 1997): $1.09 bil. **Gold:** 50,000 oz t.

Transport: Motor vehicles in use: 228,000 passenger cars, 282,000 commercial vehicles. **Civil aviation:** 734.6 mil passenger-mi.; 11 airports with scheduled flights. **Chief ports:** Al Hudaydah, Al Mukalla, Aden.

Communications: Television sets: 1 per 36 persons. **Radios:** 1 per 31 persons. **Telephones:** 1 per 81 persons.

Health: Life expectancy at birth (1997): 58.9 male; 61.8 female. **Births** (per 1,000 pop.): 45. **Deaths** (per 1,000 pop.): 9. **Natural increase:** 3.6%. **Hospital beds:** 1 per 1,591 persons. **Physicians:** 1 per 4,549 persons. **Infant mortality** (per 1,000 live births 1997): 68.

Education: Compulsory: ages 6-15. **Literacy** (1994): 43%.

Major International Organizations: UN (IMF, WHO), Arab League.

Embassy: 2600 Virginia Ave. NW 20037; 965-4760.

Yemen's territory once was part of the ancient Kindgom of Sheba, or Saba, a prosperous link in trade between Africa and India. A Biblical reference speaks of its gold, spices, and precious stones as gifts borne by the Queen of Sheba to King Solomon.

Yemen became independent in 1918, after years of Ottoman Turkish rule, but remained politically and economically backward. Imam Ahmed ruled 1948-1962. Army officers headed by Brig. Gen. Abdullah al-Salal declared the country to be the Yemen Arab Republic.

The Imam Ahmed's heir, the Imam Mohamad al-Badr, fled to the mountains where tribesmen joined royalist forces; internal warfare between them and the republican forces continued. About 150,000 people died in the fighting.

There was a bloodless coup Nov. 5, 1967. In April 1970 hostilities ended with an agreement between Yemen and Saudi Arabia. On June 13, 1974, an army group, led by Col. Ibrahim al-Hamidi, seized the government. He was assassinated in 1977.

Meanwhile, South Yemen won independence from Britain in 1967, formed out of the British colony of Aden and the British protectorate of South Arabia. It became the Arab world's only Marxist state, taking the name People's Democratic Republic of Yemen in 1970 and signing a friendship treaty with the USSR in 1979 that allowed for the stationing of Soviet troops.

More than 300,000 Yemenis fled from the south to the north after independence, contributing to 2 decades of hostility between the 2 states that flared into warfare twice in the 1970s.

An Arab League-sponsored agreement between North and South Yemen on unification of the 2 countries was signed Mar. 29, 1979. An agreement providing for widespread political and economic cooperation was signed in 1988.

The 2 countries were formally united on May 21, 1990, but regional clan-based rivalries led to full-scale civil war in 1994. Secessionists declared a breakaway state in S Yemen, May 21, 1994. However, northern troops captured the former southern capital of Aden in July. A new constitution was approved Sept. 28. Parliamentary elections were held Apr. 27, 1997.

Yugoslavia
Federal Republic of Yugoslavia
Savezna Republika Jugoslavija

(Data prior to 1992 include former republics Croatia, Slovenia, Bosnia and Herzegovina, and Macedonia.)

People: Population: 10,655,317. **Pop. density:** 269 per sq. mi. **Urban:** 57%. **Ethnic groups:** Serbian 63%, Albanian 14%, Montenegrin 6%. **Principal languages:** Serbo-Croatian (official) 95%, Albanian 5%. **Chief religions:** Orthodox 65%, Muslim 19%, Roman Catholic 4%.

Geography: Area: 39,449 sq. mi. **Location:** On the Balkan Peninsula in SE Europe. Present-day Yugoslavia consists of the former republics of Serbia and Montenegro. **Neighbors:** Croatia, Bosnia and Herzegovina on W; Hungary on N; Romania, Bulgaria on E; Albania, Macedonia on S. **Capital:** Belgrade 1,204,000*.

Government: Type: Republic. **Head of state:** Pres. Slobodan Milosevic; b Aug. 29, 1941; in office: July 23, 1997. **Head of government:** Prime Min. Radoje Kontic; b May 31, 1937; in

office: Dec. 29, 1992. **Local divisions:** 2 republics, 2 autonomous provinces. **Defense:** 4%-6% of GDP (1992 est.). **Active troop strength:** 113,900.

Economy: Industries: Steel, machinery, consumer goods, mining, electronics. **Chief crops:** Corn, grains, sugar beets, potatoes. **Minerals:** Oil, gas, coal, antimony, lead, nickel, gold, copper, chrome. **Arable land:** 30%. **Livestock** (1996): pigs: 4.4 mil; sheep: 2.7 mil; cattle: 1.9 mil. **Fish catch:** (1994): 6,465 metric tons. **Electricity prod.** (1994): 34 bil kWh. **Labor force:** 28% agric. & mining; 11% services.

Finance: Monetary unit: New Dinar (Aug. 1997: 6.15 = $1 US). **Gross domestic product** (1995 est.): $20.6 bil. **Per capita GDP:** $2,000. **Imports** (1992): $3.9 bil; partners: Germany 13%, Italy 7%. **Exports** (1992): $2.5 bil; partners: Germany 27%, former USSR 13%. **Tourism** (1994): $31 mil.

Transport: Motor vehicles in use: 2,459.2 mil passenger cars, 132,000 comm. vehicles. **Civil aviation:** 93 mil passenger-mi.; 5 airports. **Chief ports:** Bar, Novi Sad.

Communications: Television sets: 1 per 5.6 persons. **Radios:** 1 per 4.9 persons. **Telephones:** 1 per 5.2 persons. **Daily newspaper circ.:** 90 per 1,000 pop.

Health: Life expectancy at birth (1997): 69.2 male; 75.6 female. **Births** (per 1,000 pop.): 14. **Deaths** (per 1,000 pop.): 10. **Natural increase:** 0.4%. **Hospital beds:** 1 per 184 persons. **Physicians:** 1 per 502 persons. **Infant mortality** (per 1,000 live births 1997): 22.8.

Education: Free and compulsory: ages 7-15. **Literacy** (1995): 98%.

Major International Organizations: Some UN agencies (though not a member).

Embassy: 2410 California St. NW 20008; 462-6566.

Serbia, which had since 1389 been a vassal principality of Turkey, was established as an independent kingdom by the Treaty of Berlin, 1878. Montenegro, independent since 1389, also obtained international recognition in 1878. After the Balkan wars Serbia's boundaries were enlarged by the annexation of Old Serbia and Macedonia, 1913.

When the Austro-Hungarian empire collapsed after World War I, the Kingdom of the Serbs, Croats, and Slovenes was formed from the former provinces of Croatia, Dalmatia, Bosnia, Herzegovina, Slovenia, Vojvodina, and the independent state of Montenegro. The name was later changed to Yugoslavia.

Nazi Germany invaded in 1941. Many Yugoslav partisan troops continued to operate. Among these were the Chetniks led by Draja Mikhailovich, who fought other partisans led by Josip Broz, known as Marshal Tito. Tito, backed by the USSR and Britain from 1943, was in control by the time the Germans had been driven from Yugoslavia in 1945. Mikhailovich was executed July 17, 1946, by Tito regime.

A constituent assembly proclaimed Yugoslavia a republic Nov. 29, 1945. It became a federated republic Jan. 31, 1946, and Marshal Tito, a Communist, became head of the government. The Stalin policy of dictating to all Communist nations was rejected by Tito. He accepted economic aid and military equipment from the U.S. and received aid in foreign trade also from France and Britain. Tito supported the liberal government of Czechoslovakia in 1968 before the Soviet invasion.

Pres. Tito died May 4, 1980. After his death, Yugoslavia was governed by a collective presidency, with a rotating succession. On Jan. 22, 1990, the Communist Party renounced its leading role in society.

Croatia and Slovenia formally declared independence June 25, 1991. In Croatia, fighting began between Croats and ethnic Serbs. Serbia sent arms and medical supplies to the Serb rebels in Croatia. Croatian forces clashed with Yugoslavian army units and their Serb supporters.

The republics of Serbia and Montenegro proclaimed a new "Federal Republic of Yugoslavia" Apr. 17, 1992. Serbia, under Pres. Slobodan Milosevic, was the main supplier of arms to the ethnic Serb fighters in Bosnia and Herzegovina. The UN imposed sweeping international sanctions on the new Yugoslavia (Serbia and Montenegro) as a means of ending the bloodshed in Bosnia, May 30, 1992. On Aug. 4, 1994, Yugoslavia said it was cutting off support for Bosnian Serbs because they rejected an international partition plan for Bosnia. This prompted the UN to vote for a conditional easing of sanctions, Sept. 23, 1994.

A peace agreement initialed in Dayton, Ohio, Nov. 21, 1995, was signed in Paris, Dec. 14, by Milosevic and leaders of Bosnia and Croatia. In May 1996, a UN tribunal in the Netherlands began trying suspected war criminals from the former Yugoslavia. The UN lifted sanctions against Yugoslavia Oct. 1, 1996, after electons were held in Bosnia. Mass protests erupted when Milosevic refused to accept opposition victories in local elections Nov. 17; non-Communist governments took office in Belgrade and other cities in Feb. 1997. Barred from running for a 3d term as Serbian president, Milosevic had himself inaugurated as president of Yugoslavia on July 23.

Kosovo: An area in southern Serbia (4,203 sq. mi.), with a population of about 2,000,000, mostly Albanians. The capital is Pristina. The Albanian majority has declared its independence, which Serbia has not recognized.

Vojvodina: An area in northern Serbia (8,304 sq. mi.), with a population of about 2,000,000, mostly Serbian. The capital is Novi Sad.

Zaire
(See Congo)

Zambia
Republic of Zambia

People: Population: 9,349,975. **Age distrib.** (%): <15: 49; 65+: 3. **Pop. density:** 32 per sq. mi. **Urban:** 43%. **Ethnic groups:** African 99%, European 1%. **Principal languages:** English (official), Bantu dialects. **Chief religions:** Christian 50-75%, Hindu and Muslim 24-49%.

Geography: Area: 290,586 sq. mi. **Location:** In S central Africa. **Neighbors:** Congo (formerly Zaire) on N; Tanzania, Malawi, Mozambique on E; Zimbabwe, Namibia on S; Angola on W. **Topography:** Zambia is mostly high plateau country covered with thick forests, and drained by several important rivers, including the Zambezi. **Capital:** Lusaka 1,317,000*.

Government: Type: Republic. **Head of state:** Pres. Frederick Chiluba; b Apr. 30, 1943; in office: Nov. 2, 1991. **Local divisions:** 9 provinces. **Defense:** 2.7% of GDP (1995). **Active troop strength:** 21,600.

Economy: Chief crops: Corn, cassava, sugar. **Minerals:** Cobalt, copper, zinc, emeralds, gold, lead, silver, uranium, coal. **Arable land:** 7%. **Livestock** (1996): cattle: 2.6 mil. **Fish catch** (1993): 65,307 metric tons. **Electricity prod.** (1995): 7.8 bil kWh. **Labor force:** 85% agric.; 15% ind. and commerce.

Finance: Monetary unit: Kwacha (Aug. 1997: 1,323 = $1 US). **Gross domestic product** (1995 est.): $8.9 bil. **Per capita GDP:** $900. **Imports** (1995): $1.3 bil; South Africa 28%, UK 11%. **Exports** (1995): $1.2 bil; partners: Japan 18%, Saudi Arabia 13%. **Tourism** (1994): $43 mil. **National budget** (1991 est.): $767 mil. **International reserves less gold** (Mar. 1994): $207 mil. **Consumer prices** (change in 1996): 43.9%.

Transport: Railroads: Length: 1,343.8 mi. **Motor vehicles in use:** 96,000 passenger cars, 68,000 comm. vehicles. **Civil aviation:** 265.8 mil passenger-mi.; 8 airports with scheduled flights. **Chief port:** Mpulungu.

Communications: Television sets: 1 per 37 persons. **Radios:** 1 per 12 persons. **Telephones:** 1 per 123 persons. **Daily newspaper circ.:** 8 per 1,000 pop.

Health: Life expectancy at birth (1997): 35.6 male; 35.6 female. **Births** (per 1,000 pop.): 44. **Deaths** (per 1,000 pop.): 24. **Natural increase:** 2.0%. **Infant mortality** (per 1,000 live births 1997): 97.

Education: Compulsory: ages 7-14. **Literacy** (1995): 78%.

Major International Organizations: UN (WTO, IMF, WHO), OAU, the Commonwealth.

Embassy: 2419 Massachusetts Ave. NW 20008; 265-9717.

As Northern Rhodesia, the country was under the administration of the South Africa Company, 1889 until 1924, when the office of governor was established, and, subsequently, a legislature. The country became an independent republic within the Commonwealth Oct. 24, 1964.

After the white government of Rhodesia (now Zimbabwe) declared its independence from Britain Nov. 11, 1965, relations between Zambia and Rhodesia became strained.

As part of a program of government participation in major industries, a government corporation in 1970 took over 51% of the ownership of 2 foreign-owned copper-mining companies. Privately-held land and other enterprises were nationalized in 1975. In the 1980s and 1990s lowered copper prices hurt the economy and severe drought caused famine.

Food riots erupted in June 1990, as the nation suffered its worst violence since independence. Elections held Oct. 1991 brought an end to one-party rule. The new government made efforts to sell state enterprises, including the copper industry. Pres. Frederick Chiluba won reelection Nov. 18, 1996, but international observers cited harassment of opposition parties.

Zimbabwe
Republic of Zimbabwe

People: Population: 11,423,175. **Age distrib.** (%): <15: 44; 65+: 3. **Pop. density:** 75 per sq. mi. **Urban:** 33%. **Ethnic groups:** Shona 71%, Ndebele 16%. **Principal languages:** English (official), Shona, Sindebele. **Chief religions:** Syncretic (Christian-indigenous mix) 50%, Christian 25%, indigenous beliefs 24%.

Geography: Area: 150,872 sq. mi. **Location:** In southern Africa. **Neighbors:** Zambia on N, Botswana on W, South Africa on S, Mozambique on E. **Topography:** Zimbabwe is high plateau country, rising to mountains on eastern border, sloping down on the other borders. **Capital:** Harare 1,410,000*.

Government: Type: Republic. **Head of state:** Pres. Robert Mugabe; b Feb. 21, 1924; in office: Jan. 1, 1988. **Local divisions:** 8 provinces, 2 cities. **Defense:** 3.4% of GDP (FY 1995-96). **Active troop strength:** 43,000.

Economy: Industries: Clothing, mining, steel, chemicals. **Chief crops:** Tobacco, sugar, vegetables, corn. **Minerals:** Chromium, gold, nickel, asbestos, copper, iron, coal. **Arable land:** 7%. **Livestock** (1996): cattle: 4.65 mil; goats: 2.9 mil. **Electricity prod.** (1995): 7.1 bil kWh. **Labor force:** 70% agric.; 22% serv. & transport; 8% ind.

Finance: Monetary unit: Dollar (Aug. 1997: 11.60 = $1 US). **Gross domestic product** (1995 est.): $18.1 bil. **Per capita GDP:** $1,620. **Imports** (1995 est.): $1.8 bil; partners: South Africa 25%, UK 15%. **Exports** (1995 est.): $2.2 bil; partners: UK 14%, Germany 11%, South Africa 10%. **Tourism** (1994): $153 mil. **National budget** (FY 1992-93): $2.2 bil. **International reserves less gold** (June 1997): $447.0 mil. **Gold:** 600,000 oz t. **Consumer prices** (change in 1996): 21.4%.

Transport: Railroads: Length: 1,713.3 mi. **Motor vehicles in use:** 180,000 passenger cars, 90,000 comm. vehicles. **Civil aviation:** 413.6 mil passenger-mi.; 7 airports with scheduled flights. **Chief ports:** Binga, Kariba.

Communications: Television sets: 1 per 37 persons. **Radios:** 1 per 12 persons. **Telephones:** 1 per 71 persons. **Daily newspaper circ.:** 18 per 1,000 pop.

Health: Life expectancy at birth (1997): 40.9 male; 40.8 female. **Births** (per 1,000 pop.): 32. **Deaths** (per 1,000 pop.): 19. **Natural increase:** 1.3%. **Hospital beds:** 1 per 514 persons. **Physicians:** 1 per 6,909 persons. **Infant mortality** (per 1,000 live births 1997): 73.

Education: Compulsory: ages 7-13. **Literacy** (1995): 85%.

Major International Organizations: UN (IMF, WTO, World Bank), OAU, the Commonwealth.

Embassy: 1608 New Hampshire Ave. NW 20009; 332-7100.

Britain took over the area as Southern Rhodesia in 1923 from the British South Africa Co. (which, under Cecil Rhodes, had conquered it by 1897) and granted internal self-government. Under a 1961 constitution, voting was restricted to keep whites in power. On Nov. 11, 1965, Prime Min. Ian D. Smith announced his country's unilateral declaration of independence. Britain termed the act illegal and demanded that Zimbabwe (known as Rhodesia until 1980) broaden voting rights to provide for eventual rule by the black African majority.

Urged by Britain, the UN imposed sanctions, including embargoes on oil shipments to Zimbabwe. In May 1968, the UN Security Council ordered a trade embargo.

Intermittent negotiations between the government and various black nationalist groups failed to prevent increasing guerrilla warfare. An "internal settlement" signed Mar. 1978 in which Smith and 3 popular black leaders would share control of the government until a transfer of power to the black majority was rejected by guerrilla leaders.

In the country's first universal-franchise election, Apr. 21, 1979, Bishop Abel Muzorewa's United African National Council gained a bare majority control of the black-dominated Parliament. Britain, 1979, began efforts to normalize its relationship with Zimbabwe. A British cease-fire was accepted by all parties, Dec. 5. Independence was finally achieved Apr. 18, 1980.

Pres. Robert Mugabe declared Zimbabwe's drought a national disaster and appealed to foreign donors for food, money, and medicine, Mar. 6, 1992. An economic adjustment program caused widespread hardship. Mugabe was reelected Mar. 1996 after opposition candidates withdrew. An estimated 1 mil Zimbabweans have HIV, the virus that causes AIDS.

Area and Population of the World

Source: Bureau of the Census, U.S. Dept. of Commerce; prior to 1950, Rand McNally & Co.

Continent or Region	Area (1,000 sq. mi.)	% of Earth	Population (est., in thousands)							% World Total, 1997
			1650	1750	1850	1900	1950	1980	1997	
North America*	9,400	16.2	5,000	5,000	39,000	106,000	221,000	372,000	464,000	7.9
South America	6,900	11.9	8,000	7,000	20,000	38,000	111,000	242,000	329,000	5.6
Europe	3,800	6.6	100,000	140,000	265,000	400,000	392,000	484,000	508,000	8.7
Asia	17,400	30.1	335,000	476,000	754,000	932,000	1,411,000	2,601,000	3,477,000	59.4
Africa	11,700	20.2	100,000	95,000	95,000	118,000	229,000	470,000	750,000	12.8
Former USSR	—	—	—	—	—	—	180,000	266,000	293,000	5.0
Oceania, incl. Australia	3,300	5.7	2,000	2,000	2,000	6,000	12,000	23,000	29,000	0.5
Antarctica	5,400	9.3	Uninhabited							...
World	57,900	—	550,000	725,000	1,175,000	1,600,000	2,556,000	4,458,000	5,852,000	—

*Includes Mexico and the Caribbean. **Note:** Figures may not add to total because of independent rounding.

Leading Countries in Population and Area, 1997

China had the highest population in the world, with an estimated 1.2 billion inhabitants in mid-1997, more than one-fifth of the world's total population. India had some 968 million people and was expected to reach 1 billion by the end of the decade. The United States had the world's third-largest population, with about 268 million, followed by Indonesia, Brazil, and Russia. Russia is the largest country in land area, with over 6.5 million square miles, followed by Canada, China, the United States, and Brazil.

Population of the World's Largest Cities

Source: United Nations, Dept. for Economic and Social Information and Policy Analysis

The figures given here are United Nations estimates and projections, as revised in 1996, for "urban agglomerations"— that is, contiguous densely populated urban areas, not demarcated by administrative boundaries. These figures may not correspond to figures for cities in other parts of *The World Almanac*.

Rank	City, Country	Pop. (thousands) 1995	Pop. (thousands, projected) 2015	Annual growth rate (percent) 1990-1995	Percentage increase for: 1975-1995	Percentage increase for: 1995-2015	Pop. of city as percentage of: Total pop.[1]	Pop. of city as percentage of: Urban pop.[2]
1.	Tokyo, Japan	26,959	28,887	1.45	36.36	7.15	21.56	27.62
2.	Mexico City, Mexico	16,562	19,180	1.81	47.40	15.81	18.17	24.75
3.	Sao Paulo, Brazil	16,533	20,320	1.84	64.56	22.91	10.40	13.27
4.	New York City, U.S.	16,332	17,602	0.34	2.85	7.78	6.11	8.03
5.	Bombay (Mumbai), India	15,138	26,218	4.24	120.79	73.19	1.63	6.08
6.	Shanghai, China	13,584	17,969	0.36	18.71	32.28	1.11	3.68
7.	Los Angeles, U.S.	12,410	14,217	1.60	39.03	14.56	4.65	6.10
8.	Calcutta, India	11,923	17,305	1.81	51.15	45.14	1.28	4.79
9.	Buenos Aires, Argentina	11,802	13,856	1.15	29.07	17.40	33.95	38.54
10.	Seoul, South Korea	11,609	12,980	1.92	70.52	11.81	25.85	31.81
11.	Beijing, China	11,299	15,572	0.87	32.23	37.82	0.93	3.06
12.	Osaka, Japan	10,609	10,609	0.23	7.77	0.00	8.48	10.87
13.	Lagos, Nigeria	10,287	24,640	5.68	211.73	139.53	9.21	23.28
14.	Rio de Janeiro, Brazil	10,181	11,860	1.00	29.63	16.49	6.40	8.17
15.	Delhi, India	9,948	16,860	3.85	124.76	69.48	1.07	4.0

(1) Denotes percentage of the total population of the country in which the corresponding city is located. (2) Denotes the percentage of the total urban population of the country in which the corresponding city is located.

Current Population and Projections for All Countries: 1997, 2020, and 2050

Source: Bureau of the Census, U.S. Dept. of Commerce

(midyear figures, in thousands)

Country	1997	2020	2050	Country	1997	2020	2050
Afghanistan	23,738	43,050	76,231	Belgium	10,204	10,271	8,976
Albania	3,293	4,257	4,881	Belize	225	356	489
Algeria	29,830	44,783	58,880	Benin	5,902	11,920	22,171
Andorra	75	97	80	Bhutan	1,865	3,035	4,935
Angola	10,624	19,272	34,579	Bolivia	7,670	11,245	15,240
Antigua and Barbuda	66	80	79	Bosnia and Herzegovina	2,608	2,966	2,616
Argentina	35,798	46,393	56,357	Botswana	1,501	1,553	2,051
Armenia	3,466	3,665	3,956	Brazil	164,511	194,246	212,045
Australia	18,439	21,696	22,847	Brunei	308	490	705
Austria	8,054	8,262	7,070	Bulgaria	8,653	8,777	7,554
Azerbaijan	7,736	9,007	10,340	Burkina Faso	10,891	16,569	29,515
Bahamas	262	314	327	Burundi	6,053	10,197	18,555
Bahrain	603	870	1,098	Cambodia	11,164	20,208	37,301
Bangladesh	125,340	172,041	210,624	Cameroon	14,678	25,896	48,083
Barbados	258	284	276	Canada	29,123	34,753	37,086
Belarus	10,440	11,059	10,711	Cape Verde	394	512	545

Country	1997	2020	2050
Central African Republic	3,342	4,780	7,865
Chad	7,166	12,831	22,504
Chile	14,508	17,535	18,333
China	1,221,592	1,413,251	1,397,559
Colombia	37,418	49,266	55,798
Comoros	590	1,249	2,383
Congo (formerly Zaire)	47,440	91,548	182,567
Congo Republic	2,583	3,817	5,856
Costa Rica	3,534	5,044	6,321
Côte d'Ivoire	14,986	24,155	42,347
Croatia	5,027	4,821	4,063
Cuba	10,999	11,699	10,565
Cyprus	753	936	1,058
Czech Republic	10,319	10,271	8,994
Denmark	5,269	5,458	4,831
Djibouti	434	751	1,329
Dominica	83	96	103
Dominican Republic	8,228	11,152	13,459
Ecuador	11,691	16,546	20,815
Egypt	64,792	92,350	117,736
El Salvador	5,662	7,852	10,814
Equatorial Guinea	443	783	1,394
Eritrea	3,590	7,596	13,102
Estonia	1,445	1,370	1,300
Ethiopia	58,733	100,813	180,949
Fiji	792	1,037	1,285
Finland	5,109	5,075	4,388
France	58,470	61,375	54,798
Gabon	1,190	1,675	2,518
Gambia, The	1,248	2,399	4,038
Georgia	5,175	5,205	5,346
Germany	84,068	88,870	74,680
Ghana	18,101	26,516	34,324
Greece	10,583	11,076	9,335
Grenada	96	141	210
Guatemala	11,558	18,131	25,147
Guinea	7,405	11,836	20,034
Guinea-Bissau	1,179	1,925	2,970
Guyana	706	685	702
Haiti	6,611	9,328	12,345
Honduras	5,751	9,042	12,528
Hungary	9,936	9,103	8,140
Iceland	273	325	354
India	967,613	1,289,473	1,564,237
Indonesia	209,774	276,017	330,566
Iran	67,540	104,282	142,336
Iraq	22,219	46,260	85,537
Ireland	3,556	3,570	3,458
Israel	5,535	7,439	8,961
Italy	57,534	55,665	45,544
Jamaica	2,616	3,213	3,712
Japan	125,717	123,620	102,010
Jordan	4,325	7,529	11,362
Kazakhstan	16,899	18,408	20,823
Kenya	28,803	35,236	45,061
Kiribati	82	98	100
Korea, North	24,317	30,969	33,711
Korea, South	45,949	53,451	52,625
Kuwait	2,077	3,560	4,124
Kyrgyzstan	4,540	6,257	8,840
Laos	5,117	8,923	13,844
Latvia	2,438	2,212	2,066
Lebanon	3,859	5,748	7,713
Lesotho	2,008	2,693	3,692
Liberia	2,602	5,737	10,992
Libya	5,648	12,391	27,036
Liechtenstein	31	36	31
Lithuania	3,636	3,646	3,524
Luxembourg	422	523	466
Macedonia	2,114	2,296	2,153
Madagascar	14,062	25,988	48,327
Malawi	9,609	10,719	14,788
Malaysia	20,376	29,830	39,743
Maldives	280	554	949
Mali	9,945	20,427	43,296
Malta	379	450	460
Marshall Islands	61	144	348
Mauritania	2,411	4,859	9,301
Mauritius	1,154	1,440	1,614
Mexico	97,563	136,096	170,280
Micronesia	128	143	143
Moldova	4,475	5,000	5,025
Monaco	33	34	34
Mongolia	2,538	3,393	4,057
Morocco	30,391	44,519	58,375
Mozambique	18,165	30,392	47,805
Myanmar	46,822	67,501	92,952
Namibia	1,727	3,267	6,004
Nauru	10	12	12
Nepal	22,641	37,767	58,971
Netherlands	15,653	16,490	14,283
New Zealand	3,587	4,326	4,561
Nicaragua	4,386	6,973	9,714
Niger	9,389	17,983	33,896
Nigeria	107,129	205,160	386,339
Norway	4,404	4,632	4,131
Oman	2,265	4,731	8,644
Pakistan	132,185	198,722	260,245
Palau	17	21	24
Panama	2,693	3,619	4,418
Papua New Guinea	4,496	7,044	10,049
Paraguay	5,652	9,474	14,186
Peru	24,950	33,226	38,014
Philippines	76,104	112,963	150,272
Poland	38,700	40,833	38,705
Portugal	9,868	10,005	8,755
Qatar	665	1,121	1,882
Romania	21,399	20,135	18,104
Russia	147,987	149,632	142,887
Rwanda	7,738	11,040	18,928
Saint Kitts and Nevis	42	57	69
Saint Lucia	160	202	227
Saint Vincent and the Grenadines	119	146	163
Samoa (formerly Western Samoa)	220	341	471
San Marino	25	27	27
São Tomé and Príncipe	148	232	318
Saudi Arabia	20,088	43,255	97,120
Senegal	9,404	19,497	39,690
Seychelles	78	89	96
Sierra Leone	4,892	9,690	18,369
Singapore	3,462	4,330	4,589
Slovakia	5,393	5,837	5,591
Slovenia	1,946	1,856	1,513
Solomon Islands	427	767	1,158
Somalia	9,940	18,955	32,546
South Africa	42,327	45,023	53,442
Spain	39,244	39,758	33,833
Sri Lanka	18,762	22,877	24,154
Sudan	32,594	58,621	93,625
Suriname	443	598	710
Swaziland	1,032	2,128	4,754
Sweden	8,946	9,515	8,523
Switzerland	7,249	7,802	6,734
Syria	16,138	28,926	43,463
Taiwan	21,656	25,155	24,817
Tajikistan	6,014	10,019	16,958
Tanzania	29,461	40,102	64,556
Thailand	59,451	69,298	69,741
Togo	4,736	10,146	20,725
Tonga	107	128	156
Trinidad and Tobago	1,273	1,409	1,447
Tunisia	9,183	12,751	15,723
Turkey	63,528	85,643	103,649
Turkmenistan	4,225	6,380	9,321
Tuvalu	10	15	20
Uganda	20,605	30,872	53,886
Ukraine	50,685	49,038	45,833
United Arab Emirates	2,262	3,286	4,057
United Kingdom	58,610	59,289	54,313
United States	267,955	323,052	394,241
Uruguay	3,262	3,811	4,256
Uzbekistan	23,860	36,628	55,250
Vanuatu	181	266	347
Venezuela	22,396	30,876	37,773
Vietnam	75,124	99,153	119,464
Yemen	13,972	29,469	55,179
Yugoslavia	10,655	11,067	10,308
Zambia	9,350	13,022	23,564
Zimbabwe	11,423	11,344	14,657
Regions			
Asia	3,477,122	4,492,834	5,267,544
Africa	750,081	1,221,607	2,049,953
Europe	508,401	521,138	458,012
South America	329,162	414,151	474,568
North America	464,490	589,065	720,371
Former Soviet Union	293,052	317,621	342,400
Oceania, incl. Australia	29,294	37,057	42,773
World[1]	**5,851,569**	**7,593,379**	**9,355,701**

(1) Figures may not add to total because of rounding and exclusion of certain pseudo-national entities.

Estimated HIV Infection and Reported AIDS Cases

Source: UNAIDS Program, United Nations

Studies, primarily in industrialized nations, have indicated that about 60% of adults infected by the human immunodeficiency virus (HIV) will develop acquired immune deficiency syndrome (AIDS) within 12-13 years of becoming infected; progression of the disease might be more rapid in developing countries. It is expected that the vast majority of HIV-infected persons will eventually develop AIDS. Survival after the onset of AIDS is estimated by UNAIDS to be about 3 years, on the average, in industrialized countries and less than 1 year in developing countries. About 75-85% of adult HIV infections worldwide have been transmitted through unprotected sexual intercourse. As of June 30, 1996, a total of 1,393,649 AIDS cases had been officially reported, a 19% increase from the 1,169,811 reported on June 30, 1995. The actual number of AIDS cases worldwide is estimated to be more than 7.7 million—5½ times the number of reported cases—because of underdiagnosis, underreporting, and reporting delays in different countries. UNAIDS estimates more than 3.1 million new HIV infections occurred in 1996. Since the start of the global epidemic in the late 1970s, about 27.9 million people have been infected by HIV and about 5.8 million have died, including 1.3 million children.

Estimated Current and Cumulative HIV/AIDS Cases by Region, Mid-1996

Region	Current cases[1]	Cumulative cases[2]	Pct. of adults[3]	Region	Current cases[1]	Cumulative cases[2]	Pct. of adults[3]
North America.......	780,000	1,200,000	3.7	Sub-Saharan Africa ..	14,000,000	19,000,000	63.0
Caribbean	270,000	330,000	1.3	E. Europe/Central Asia	30,000	31,000	0.1
Latin America	1,300,000	1,600,000	6.0	South/Southeast Asia	4,800,000	5,000,000	23.0
Western Europe	470,000	640,000	2.2	East Asia/Pacific	35,000	36,000	0.2
North Africa/Middle				Australasia	13,000	23,000	0.1
East	200,000	220,000	0.9	World	21,800,000	27,900,000	100[4]

(1) Adults and children living with HIV/AIDS. (2) Since the late 1970s. (3) Percentage of total number of adults living with HIV. (4) Details do not add to total because of rounding.

The World's Refugees

Source: *World Refugee Survey 1997*, U.S. Committee for Refugees, a nonprofit corp. The refugees in this table include only those who are in need of protection and/or assistance and generally do not include refugees who have permanently settled in other countries.

(as of Dec. 31, 1996; only countries hosting 50,000 or more refugees are listed)

Place of asylum	Mostly from	Number	Place of asylum	Mostly from	Number
Total Africa		**3,684,000**	Azerbaijan	Armenia, Uzbekistan	249,150[1]
Algeria	Western Sahara, Mali, Niger...	114,000[1]	Croatia.......	Bosnia and Herzegovina, Yugo-	
Congo[2].......	Rwanda, Angola, Sudan, Bu-			slavia[3]..........	167,000
	rundi, Uganda	455,000[1]	Germany	Bosnia and Herzegovina ...	436,400[1]
Côte d'Ivoire ...	Liberia	320,000	Russia	Former USSR	484,000[1]
Ethiopia	Somalia, Sudan, Djibouti, Kenya	328,000[1]	Sweden	Bosnia and Herzegovina ...	60,500[1]
Guinea	Liberia, Sierra Leone	650,000[1]	Yugoslavia[3] ...	Croatia, Bosnia and Herzegovina	450,000[1]
Kenya........	Somalia, Sudan, Ethiopia.....	186,000[1]			
Liberia	Sierra Leone	100,000[1]	**Total Middle East.**		**5,841,000**
Senegal	Mauritania	51,000	Gaza Strip	Palestinians	716,900
Sudan	Eritrea, Ethiopia, Chad	395,000[1]	Iran	Afghanistan, Iraq..........	2,020,000[1]
Tanzania	Rwanda, Burundi, Congo[2]	335,000[1]	Iraq	Palestinians, Iran, Turkey.....	114,400
Uganda	Sudan, Congo[2], Rwanda	225,000	Jordan	Palestinians	1,362,500
Zambia	Angola, Congo[2]	126,000	Lebanon......	Palestinians	355,100
			Saudi Arabia...	Palestinians, Iraq	257,850
Total Americas and the Caribbean.		**233,000**	Syria	Palestinians	384,400
United States ..	Cuba, various other	129,600	West Bank	Palestinians	532,400
			Yemen.......	Somalia, Palestinians	54,600
Total East Asia and the Pacific		**450,000**			
China	Vietnam, Myanmar	294,100[1]	**Total South and Central Asia.**		**1,795,000**
Thailand.....	Myanmar, Laos	95,850	India........	Tibet, Sri Lanka, Bangladesh,	
				Bhutan, Afghanistan, Myanmar	352,200[1]
Total Europe and Former Soviet Republics		**2,479,000**	Nepal........	Bhutan, Tibet	109,800
Armenia	Azerbaijan................	150,000[1]	Pakistan......	Afghanistan, India, Iraq, Somalia	1,215,700[1]
Austria	Bosnia and Herzegovina	80,000[1]	**Total Refugees**		**14,482,000**

(1) Significant variance among sources in number reported. (2) Formerly Zaire. (3) Serbia/Montenegro.

Principal Sources of Refugees

Palestinians............	3,718,500[1]	Sierra Leone	350,000[1]	Angola	220,000[1]
Afghanistan............	2,628,550[1]	Eritrea...............	343,100[1]	Tajikistan	215,600[1]
Bosnia and Herzegovina ..	1,006,450[1]	Croatia...............	300,000[1]	Armenia	197,000[1]
Liberia	755,000[1]	Vietnam..............	288,000	Myanmar	184,300[1]
Iraq..................	608,500[1]	Burundi	285,000[1]	Tibet.................	128,000
Somalia	467,100[1]	Rwanda	257,000[1]	Bhutan	121,800[1]
Sudan................	433,700	Azerbaijan	238,000[1]	Congo (formerly Zaire)....	116,800

(1) Significant variance among sources in number reported.

U.S. Immigration Law

Source: Immigration and Naturalization Service, U.S. Dept. of Justice

Most U.S. regulations affecting immigration were modified in the Immigration and Nationality Act of 1952, which has been amended several times since then. The most recent major amendments were made through the Immigration Act of 1990, signed by Pres. George Bush on Nov. 29, 1990. New provisions, enacted as part of an omnibus spending bill signed by Pres. Bill Clinton on Sept. 30, 1996, focused mainly on illegal immigration. However, rules for sponsorship of legal immigrants were changed under the 1996 legislation.

The Immigration Act of 1990 raised the total number of numerically limited immigrants entering the U.S. annually in fiscal year 1992-94 to 700,000 (excluding refugees whose admission numbers are announced annually and some others not subject to limitation). Beginning in fiscal year 1995, the number dropped from 700,000 to 675,000, subject to adjustment based largely on the number of visas issued in the previous year. In fiscal year 1997, allowable visas were to be distributed as follows:

- 226,000 for family immigrants;
- 140,000 for employment-based immigrants;
- 55,000 for "diversity immigrants."

Immediate Relatives (Family Immigrants)

Fiscal year 1992-94: 465,000 minus the number of "immediate relatives" admitted the previous fiscal year, plus any numbers unused by the employment-based preference system. During this period, the number of family-sponsored visas could not fall below 226,000 (10,000 visas higher than the previous allocation). If visa availability dipped below this new floor, the shortfall was made up from the category below.

During this period, 55,000 additional visas were made available to the spouses and children of aliens legalized under the Immigration Reform and Control Act (IRCA) of 1986.

Fiscal year 1995 and beyond: 480,000 minus the number of "immediate relatives" admitted during the previous fiscal year, plus any unused numbers under the employment-based preference system. The number of family-sponsored visas cannot drop below a floor of 226,000.

Family Preference System

First preference—unmarried sons and daughters of U.S. citizens: 23,400 visas in FY 1997 plus unused visas from the 4th preference.

Second preference—spouses and unmarried children of Lawful Permanent Residents (LPRs): 114,200 visas, plus any visas available above the floor of 226,000 family preference visas, plus any unused visas from the previous preference.

The category is subdivided as follows: A minimum of 77% of the visas allocated to the category goes to the spouses and minor children of LPRs; 75% of the visas are issued without regard to per country ceilings; these visas are distributed in the order in which the petitions were filed. A maximum of 23% of the category visa allocation goes to the unmarried sons and daughters of LPRs. This group of visas continues to be subject to per country ceilings.

Third preference—married sons and daughters of U.S. citizens; 23,400 visas plus unused visas from all earlier preferences.

Fourth preference—brothers and sisters of U.S. citizens: 65,000 plus unused visas from all earlier preferences.

Employment-Based Immigrants

The law allows a total of 140,000 plus, beginning in fiscal year 1994, any unused numbers under the family-sponsored system. These visas are distributed as follows:

First preference—Priority Workers—28.6% of the employment-based limit plus visas unused by the fourth and fifth employment-based preferences—"investors" and "special immigrants." The category is subdivided as follows: (1) extraordinary ability, demonstrated by sustained national or international acclaim, in the sciences, arts, education, business, and athletics; no U.S. employer required; (2) professors and researchers, seeking to enter in senior positions; U.S. employer required; (3) executives and managers of multinationals—requires one year of prior service with the firm during the preceding 3 years; the terms are extensively defined; U.S. employer required.

Second preference—Professionals with advanced degrees and aliens of exceptional ability—28.6% of the employment-based limit plus any unused "priority worker" visas. A U.S. employer and labor certification are required—although the Attorney General can waive both requirements. Members of the professions with advanced degrees or exceptional ability in the sciences, arts, or business. The possession of a degree, certificate, or license is not by itself considered sufficient evidence of exceptional ability.

Third preference—Skilled workers, professionals, and "other workers"—40,000 visas plus any visas unused by the 2 previous categories. Requires a U.S. employer and labor certification. Skilled work-ers must be in an occupation that requires at least 2 years training or experience. Professionals need a bachelor's degree. "Other workers" refers to unskilled workers. Their numbers are limited to no more than 10,000 visas per year.

Fourth preference—Special immigrants—7.1% of the employment-based limit. This category includes ministers of religion and persons working for religious organizations for at least 2 years*, foreign medical graduates, employees of the U.S. government abroad including certain employees of the U.S. mission in Hong Kong who file for admission as special immigrants before Jan. 1, 2002, retired employees of international organizations, etc.

*As of Oct., Congress was debating if non-ministerial religious workers should be eliminated from this category.

Fifth preference—7.1% of the employment-based limit—7,000 for investors of $1 million in urban areas and 3,000 for investors of no less than $500,000 in rural or high-unemployment areas. The Attorney General may increase the required investment amount up to $3 million for high employment areas. Investment must create employment for at least 10 U.S. workers.

Diversity Immigrant (DV) Category

Since FY 1995, the Immigration and Nationality Act has allowed 55,000 immigrant visas each fiscal year, distributed by lottery, to provide immigration opportunities for persons from countries other than the principal sources of current immigration to the U.S. DV visas are divided among six geographic regions. Not more than 3,850 visas (7% of the 55,000 visa limit) may be provided to immigrants from any one country.

The allotment of FY 1999 visa numbers for each region was as follows: Africa, 21,409; Asia, 7,254; Europe, 23,024; North America (Bahamas), 8; South America, Central America, and the Caribbean, 2,468; and Oceania, 837.

The FY 1999 DV registration mail-in was to be held Oct. 24-Nov. 24, 1997. During this one-month period, the National Visa Center in Portsmouth, NH, expected to receive between 6 to 7 million qualified entries. An additional 1.5 million entries received during those dates are expected to be disqualified for not providing the requested information or following published guidelines. Winners of visas will be notified between Apr. and July 1998.

In order to issue all 55,000 visas in FY 1999, the National Visa Center plans to register about 100,000 persons, both principal applicants and their spouses and children. Those selected will be sent instructions on how to apply for an immigrant visa. During the visa interview, applicants must provide proof of a high school education or its equivalent, or must show two years of work experience within the past five years in an occupation which requires at least two years of training or experience. Those selected need to act on their immigrant visa applications quickly. As soon as the 55,000 visas are issued, the program for FY 1999 ends.

Sponsorship of Immigrants

Under the 1996 immigration law, sponsors of an immigrant entering the country as an immediate relative or as an employment-based immigrant who will be employed by either a relative or a relative's company must earn at least 125% of the poverty level. If the sponsor does not earn enough, a cosponsor may be found who will accept joint responsibility for the immigrant. Persons who are active members of the U.S. armed forces need earn only 100% of the poverty level to be accepted as sponsors.

The sponsor must sign a legally binding affidavit of support for an immigrant, which would be enforceable until the immigrant either became a citizen or worked and paid taxes for 40 quarters as determined by the Social Security Administration.

Naturalization: How to Become an American Citizen

Source: Federal Statutes

A person who desires to be naturalized as a citizen of the United States may obtain the necessary application form as well as detailed information from the nearest office of the Immigration and Naturalization Service or from the clerk of a court handling naturalization cases.

An applicant must be at least 18 years old and must have been a lawful resident of the United States continuously for 5 years. For husbands and wives of U.S. citizens the period is 3 years in most instances. Special provisions apply to certain veterans of the armed forces.

An applicant must have been physically present in the country for at least half of the required 5 years' residence.

Every applicant for naturalization must:

(1) demonstrate an understanding of the English language, including an ability to read, write, and speak words in ordinary usage in English (persons physically unable to do so and persons who, on the examination date, are over 55 years of age and have been lawful permanent residents of the United States for 15 years or more, or who are over 50 and have been residents 20 or more years, are exempt);

(2) have been a person of good moral character, attached to the principles of the Constitution, and well disposed to the good order and happiness of the United States for 5 years just before filing the petition or for whatever other period of residence is required in the par-ticular case and continue to be such a person until admitted to citizenship; and

(3) demonstrate a knowledge and understanding of the fundamentals of the history, and the principles and form of government, of the United States. This can be done at private, designated testing entities or at the interview before an immigration examiner.

At the interview the applicant may be represented by a lawyer or social service agency. If action is favorable, there is a swearing in ceremony conducted administratively or judicially. At that ceremony the following oath of allegiance is administered:

I hereby declare, on oath, that I absolutely and entirely renounce and abjure all allegiance and fidelity to any foreign prince, potentate, state or sovereignty, to whom or which I have heretofore been a subject or citizen; that I will support and defend the Constitution and laws of the United States of America against all enemies, foreign and domestic; that I will bear true faith and allegiance to the same; that I will bear arms on behalf of the United States when required by the law; that I will perform noncombatant service in the armed forces of the United States when required by the law; that I will perform work of national importance under civilian direction when required by the law; and that I take this obligation freely without any mental reservation or purpose of evasion; so help me God.

Major International Organizations

(as of Sept. 1997)

Asia-Pacific Economic Cooperation Group (APEC), founded Nov. 1989 as a forum to further cooperation on trade and investment between nations of the region and the rest of the world. Members in 1997 were Australia, Brunei, Canada, Chile, China, Indonesia, Japan, Malaysia, Mexico, New Zealand, Papua New Guinea, Philippines, Singapore, South Korea, Taiwan, Thailand, and the United States. Headquarters: Singapore.

Association of Southeast Asian Nations (ASEAN), formed in 1967 to promote economic, social, and cultural cooperation and development among states of the Southeast Asian region. Members in 1997 were Brunei, Indonesia, Laos, Malaysia, Myanmar, Philippines, Singapore, Thailand, and Vietnam. Annual ministerial meetings set policy; a central Secretariat in Jakarta and specialized intergovernmental committees work in trade, transportation, communications, agriculture, science, finance, and culture. Headquarters: Jakarta.

Caribbean Community and Common Market (CARICOM), established July 4, 1973. Its function is to further cooperation in economics, health, education, culture, science and technology, and tax administration, as well as the coordination of foreign policy. Member nations in 1997 were Antigua and Barbuda, Bahamas (Community only), Barbados, Belize, Dominica, Grenada, Guyana, Jamaica, Montserrat, Saint Kitts and Nevis, Saint Lucia, Saint Vincent and the Grenadines, Suriname, and Trinidad and Tobago. Headquarters: Georgetown, Guyana.

Commonwealth of Independent States (CIS), created Dec. 1991 upon the disbanding of the Soviet Union. It is made up of 12 of the 15 former Soviet constituent republics. Members in 1997 were Armenia, Azerbaijan, Belarus, Georgia, Kazakhstan, Kyrgyzstan, Moldova, Russia, Tajikistan, Turkmenistan, Ukraine, and Uzbekistan. The commonwealth is not in itself a state but an alliance of fully independent states. Commonwealth policy is set through coordinating bodies such as a Council of Heads of State and Council of Heads of Government. The capital of the commonwealth is Minsk, Belarus.

The Commonwealth, originally called the British Commonwealth of Nations, and then the Commonwealth of Nations, an association of nations and dependencies loosely joined by a common interest based on having been parts of the old British Empire. The British monarch is the symbolic head of the Commonwealth.

There are 53 self-governing independent nations in the Commonwealth, plus various colonies and protectorates. As of 1997, members were the United Kingdom of Great Britain and Northern Ireland and 15 other nations recognizing the British monarch, represented by a governor-general, as their head of state: Antigua and Barbuda, Australia, The Bahamas, Barbados, Belize, Canada, Grenada, Jamaica, New Zealand, Papua New Guinea, Saint Kitts and Nevis, Saint Lucia, Saint Vincent and the Grenadines, Solomon Islands, and Tuvalu (special member); and 38 countries with their own heads of state: Bangladesh, Botswana, Brunei, Cameroon, Cyprus, Dominica, The Gambia, Ghana, Guyana, India, Kenya, Kiribati, Lesotho, Malawi, Malaysia, The Maldives, Malta, Mauritius, Mozambique, Namibia, Nauru (special member), Nigeria (suspended Nov. 1995), Pakistan, Samoa, Seychelles, Sierra Leone, Singapore, South Africa, Sri Lanka, Swaziland, Tanzania, Tonga, Trinidad and Tobago, Tuvalu (special member), Uganda, Vanuatu, Zambia, and Zimbabwe.

The Commonwealth facilitates consultation among member states through meetings of prime ministers and finance ministers, and through a permanent Secretariat. Members consult on economic, scientific, educational, financial, legal, and military matters, and try to coordinate policies. Headquarters: London.

European Union (EU)—known as the European Community (EC) until 1994—the collective designation of three organizations with common membership: the European Economic Community (Common Market), the European Coal and Steel Community, and the European Atomic Energy Community (Euratom). The 15 full members in 1997 were Austria, Belgium, Denmark, Finland, France, Germany, Greece, Ireland, Italy, Luxembourg, Netherlands, Portugal, Spain, Sweden, and United Kingdom. Austria, Finland, and Sweden entered the EU on Jan. 1, 1995; Norway was scheduled to join at the same time, but Norwegian citizens in a Nov. 1994 referendum voted against membership. Some 70 nations in Africa, the Caribbean, and the Pacific are affiliated under the Lomé Convention.

A merger of the 3 communities' executives went into effect July 1, 1967, though the component organizations date back to 1951 and 1958. The Council of Ministers, European Commission, European Parliament, and European Court of Justice comprise the permanent structure. The EU aims to integrate the economies, coordinate social developments, and bring about political union of the democratic states of Europe. Effective Dec. 31, 1992, there are no restrictions on the movement of goods, services, capital, workers, and tourists within the EU. There are also common agricultural, fisheries, and nuclear research policies.

Leaders of the member nations (12 at the time) met Dec. 9-11, 1991, in Maastricht, the Netherlands. Treaties on monetary union and political union and accompanying protocols agreed upon by the leaders:

- Committed the organization to launching a common currency for at least some nations by 1999. Britain and, later, Denmark were allowed to "opt out" of joining.
- Sought to establish common foreign policies for the members.
- Laid the groundwork for a common defense policy.
- Expanded the policy issues in which the organization would have a voice.
- Gave the organization a leading role in social policy. Britain was not included in this plan.
- Pledged increased aid for the 4 poorest member nations—Ireland, Greece, Spain, and Portugal.
- Slightly increased the powers of the 567-member European Parliament.

The treaties went into effect Nov. 1, 1993, following ratification by all 12 members.

European Free Trade Association (EFTA), created May 3, 1960, to promote expansion of free trade. By Dec. 31, 1966, tariffs and quotas between member nations had been eliminated. Members of the EFTA entered into free trade agreements with the EU in 1972 and 1973. In 1992 the EFTA and EU concluded an agreement to create a single market—with free flow of goods, services, capital, and labor—encompassing nations of the two organizations. Members in 1997 were Iceland, Liechtenstein, Norway, and Switzerland. Many former EFTA members are now EU members. Headquarters: Geneva.

Group of Seven (G-7), organization of seven major industrial democracies who meet periodically to discuss world economic and other issues. Established Sept. 22, 1985. Members are Canada, France, Germany, Italy, Japan, United Kingdom, and the United States. At its annual economic summit in June 1997 Russia participated in discussions; the entire group was informally referred to as "The Eight."

International Criminal Police Organization (Interpol), created June 13, 1956, to ensure and promote the widest possible mutual assistance between all police authorities within the limits of the law existing in the different countries and in the spirit of the Universal Declaration of Human Rights. There were 177 members (independent nations), plus 14 subbureaus (dependencies), in 1997.

League of Arab States (Arab League), created Mar. 22, 1945. The League promotes economic, social, political, and military cooperation and mediates disputes among the Arab states; it represents Arab states in certain international negotiations. Members in 1997 were Algeria, Bahrain, Comoros, Djibouti, Egypt, Iraq, Jordan, Kuwait, Lebanon, Libya, Mauritania, Morocco, Oman, Palestine (considered an independent state by the League), Qatar, Saudi Arabia, Somalia, Sudan, Syria, Tunisia, United Arab Emirates, and Yemen. Headquarters: Cairo.

North Atlantic Treaty Organization (NATO), created by treaty (signed Apr. 4, 1949; in effect Aug. 24, 1949). Members in 1997 were Belgium, Canada, Denmark, France, Germany, Greece, Iceland, Italy, Luxembourg, Netherlands, Norway, Portugal, Spain, Turkey, United Kingdom, and United States. The members agreed to settle disputes by peaceful means; to develop their individual and collective capacity to resist armed attack; to regard an attack on one as an attack on all; and to take necessary action to repel an attack under Article 51 of the United Nations Charter.

The NATO structure consists of a Council, the Defense Planning Committee, the Military Committee (consisting of 2 commands: Allied Command Europe, Allied Command Atlantic), the Nuclear Planning Group, and the Canada-U.S. Regional Planning Group. France detached itself from the military command structure in 1966.

With the dissolution of the Soviet Union and the end of the cold war in the early 1990s, NATO members sought to modify the organization's mission, putting greater stress on political action and creating a rapid deployment force to react to local crises. NATO has proceeded cautiously toward extending membership to former Eastern bloc nations, because of Russia's sensitivity to the issue. By the end of 1995, 27 nations, including Russia and other former Soviet republics, had joined with NATO in the so-called Partnership for Peace (PfP; drafted Dec. 1993), which provided for limited joint military exercises, peace-keeping missions, and information exchange. On July 8, 1997, 3 former Warsaw Pact members, Hungary, Poland, and the Czech Republic, were invited to join NATO, with formal accession taking place in 1999 after ratification of the accession protocols by the 16 NATO member states.

In Dec. 1995, a NATO-led multinational force was deployed to help keep the peace during the political reconstruction of Bosnia and Herzegovina. Headquarters: Brussels.

Organization of African Unity (OAU), formed May 25, 1963, by 32 African countries (53 members in 1997) to promote peace and security as well as economic and social development. It holds annual conferences of heads of state. Headquarters: Addis Ababa, Ethiopia.

Organization of American States (OAS), formed in Bogotá, Colombia, Apr. 30, 1948. It has a Permanent Council, Inter-American Council for Integral Development, Juridical Committee, and Commission on Human Rights. The Permanent Council can call meetings of foreign ministers to deal with urgent security matters. A General Assembly meets annually. A secretary general and assistant are elected for 5-year terms. There are 35 members, each with one vote in the various organizations: Antigua and Barbuda, Argentina, The Bahamas, Barbados, Belize, Bolivia, Brazil, Canada, Chile, Colombia,

Costa Rica, Cuba, Dominica, Dominican Republic, Ecuador, El Salvador, Grenada, Guatemala, Guyana, Haiti, Honduras, Jamaica, Mexico, Nicaragua, Panama, Paraguay, Peru, Saint Kitts and Nevis, Saint Lucia, Saint Vincent and the Grenadines, Suriname, Trinidad and Tobago, United States, Uruguay, and Venezuela. In 1962, the OAS suspended Cuba from OAS activities but not from membership. Headquarters: Washington, DC.

Organization for Economic Cooperation and Development (OECD), established Sept. 30, 1961, to promote the economic and social welfare in its member countries, and to stimulate and harmonize efforts on behalf of developing nations. The OECD also collects and disseminates relevant economic and environmental information. Members in 1997 were Australia, Austria, Belgium, Canada, Czech Republic, Denmark, Finland, France, Germany, Greece, Hungary, Iceland, Ireland, Italy, Japan, Luxembourg, Mexico, Netherlands, New Zealand, Norway, Poland, Portugal, South Korea, Spain, Sweden, Switzerland, Turkey, United Kingdom, and the United States. Headquarters: Paris.

Organization of Petroleum Exporting Countries (OPEC), created Sept. 14, 1960. The group attempts to set world oil prices by controlling oil production. It is also involved in advancing members' interests in trade and development dealings with industrialized oil-consuming nations. Members in 1997 were Algeria, Indonesia, Iran, Iraq, Kuwait, Libya, Nigeria, Qatar, Saudi Arabia, United Arab Emirates, and Venezuela. Headquarters: Vienna.

Organization for Security and Cooperation in Europe (OSCE), established in 1972 as the Conference on Security and Cooperation in Europe; current name adopted Jan. 1, 1995. The group, formed by NATO and Warsaw Pact members, is interested in furthering East-West relations through a commitment to nonaggression and human rights as well as cooperation in economics, science and technology, cultural exchange, and environmental protection. There were 54 member states in 1997. Headquarters: Vienna.

United Nations

The 52d regular session of United Nations General Assembly opened in Sept. 1997.

UN headquarters is in New York, NY, between First Ave. and Roosevelt Drive and E. 42d St. and E. 48th St. The General Assembly Bldg., Secretariat, Conference and Library bldgs. are interconnected.

Some 53,300 people work in the UN system, which includes the Secretariat and 28 other organizations.

The UN has a post office originating its own stamps.

Proposals to establish an organization of nations for maintenance of world peace led to the United Nations Conference on International Organization at San Francisco, Apr. 25-June 26, 1945, where the charter of the United Nations was drawn up. It was signed June 26 by 50 nations, and by Poland, one of the original 51 UN members, on Oct. 15, 1945. The charter came into effect Oct. 24, 1945, upon ratification by the perma-

nent members of the Security Council and a majority of other signatories.

Purposes: To maintain international peace and security; to develop friendly relations among nations; to achieve international cooperation in solving economic, social, cultural, and humanitarian problems and in promoting respect for human rights and fundamental freedoms; to be a center for harmonizing the actions of nations in attaining these common ends.

Visitors to the UN: Headquarters is open to the public every day of the year except Christmas and New Year's Day. Guided tours are given approximately every half hour from 9:15 AM to 4:45 PM daily, except on weekends during January and February. Groups of 12 or more persons should write to the Group Program Unit, Visitors' Service, Room GA-56, United Nations, New York, NY 10017, or telephone (212) 963-4440. Children under 5 are not permitted on tours.

Roster of the United Nations

The 185 members of the United Nations, with the years in which they became members; as of Sept. 1997

Member	Year	Member	Year	Member	Year	Member	Year
Afghanistan	1946	Brunei	1984	Djibouti	1977	Haiti	1945
Albania	1955	Bulgaria	1955	Dominica	1978	Honduras	1945
Algeria	1962	Burkina Faso	1960	Dominican Republic	1945	Hungary	1955
Andorra	1993	Burundi	1962	Ecuador	1945	Iceland	1946
Angola	1976	Cambodia[1]	1955	Egypt[4]	1945	India	1945
Antigua and Barbuda	1981	Cameroon	1960	El Salvador	1945	Indonesia[5]	1950
Argentina	1945	Canada	1945	Equatorial Guinea	1968	Iran	1945
Armenia	1992	Cape Verde	1975	Eritrea	1993	Iraq	1945
Australia	1945	Central African Republic	1960	Estonia	1991	Ireland	1955
Austria	1955	Chad	1960	Ethiopia	1945	Israel	1949
Azerbaijan	1992	Chile	1945	Fiji	1970	Italy	1955
Bahamas	1973	China[2]	1945	Finland	1955	Jamaica	1962
Bahrain	1971	Colombia	1945	France	1945	Japan	1956
Bangladesh	1974	Comoros	1975	Gabon	1960	Jordan	1955
Barbados	1966	Congo, Democratic Republic of the (Zaire)	1960	Gambia, The	1965	Kazakhstan	1992
Belarus	1945	Congo, Republic of the	1960	Georgia	1992	Kenya	1963
Belgium	1945	Germany	1973	Korea, North	1991
Belize	1981	Costa Rica	1945	Ghana	1957	Korea, South	1991
Benin	1960	Côte d'Ivoire	1960	Greece	1945	Kuwait	1963
Bhutan	1971	Croatia	1992	Grenada	1974	Kyrgyzstan	1992
Bolivia	1945	Cuba	1945	Guatemala	1945	Laos	1955
Bosnia and Herzegovina	1992	Cyprus	1960	Guinea	1958	Latvia	1991
Botswana	1966	Czech Republic[3]	1993	Guinea-Bissau	1974	Lebanon	1945
Brazil	1945	Denmark	1945	Guyana	1966	Lesotho	1966

Member	Year	Member	Year	Member	Year	Member	Year
Liberia	1945	Namibia	1990	Saint Lucia	1979	Syria[4]	1945
Libya	1955	Nepal	1955	Saint Vincent and		Tajikistan	1992
Liechtenstein	1990	Netherlands	1945	the Grenadines	1980	Tanzania[10]	1961
Lithuania	1991	New Zealand	1945	Samoa (formerly West-		Thailand	1946
Luxembourg	1945	Nicaragua	1945	ern Samoa)	1976	Togo	1960
Macedonia[6]	1993	Niger	1960	San Marino	1992	Trinidad and Tobago	1962
Madagascar	1960	Nigeria	1960	São Tomé and Príncipe	1975	Tunisia	1956
Malawi	1964	Norway	1945	Saudi Arabia	1945	Turkey	1945
Malaysia[7]	1957	Oman	1971	Senegal	1960	Turkmenistan	1992
Maldives	1965	Pakistan	1947	Seychelles	1976	Uganda	1962
Mali	1960	Palau	1994	Sierra Leone	1961	Ukraine	1945
Malta	1964	Panama	1945	Singapore[7]	1965	United Arab Emirates	1971
Marshall Islands	1991	Papua New Guinea	1975	Slovakia[3]	1993	United Kingdom	1945
Mauritania	1961	Paraguay	1945	Slovenia	1992	United States	1945
Mauritius	1968	Peru	1945	Solomon Islands	1978	Uruguay	1945
Mexico	1945	Philippines	1945	Somalia	1960	Uzbekistan	1992
Micronesia	1991	Poland	1945	South Africa[9]	1945	Vanuatu	1981
Moldova	1992	Portugal	1955	Spain	1955	Venezuela	1945
Monaco	1993	Qatar	1971	Sri Lanka	1955	Vietnam	1977
Mongolia	1961	Romania	1955	Sudan	1956	Yemen[11]	1947
Morocco	1956	Russia[8]	1945	Suriname	1975	Yugoslavia[12]	1945
Mozambique	1975	Rwanda	1962	Swaziland	1968	Zambia	1964
Myanmar (Burma)	1948	Saint Kitts and Nevis	1983	Sweden	1946	Zimbabwe	1980

(1) Cambodia's seat in the General Assembly was declared vacant in Sept. 1997, after a dispute over which faction should be seated, following a July 1997 coup. (2) The General Assembly voted in 1971 to expel the Chinese government on Taiwan and admit the Beijing government in its place. (3) Czechoslovakia, which split into the separate nations of the Czech Republic and Slovakia on Jan. 1, 1993, was a UN member from 1945 to 1992. (4) Egypt and Syria were original members of the UN. In 1958, the United Arab Republic was established by a union of Egypt and Syria and continued as a single member of the UN. In 1961, Syria resumed its separate membership. (5) Indonesia withdrew from the UN in 1965 and rejoined in 1966. (6) Admitted under the provisional name of The Former Yugoslav Republic of Macedonia. (7) Malaya joined the UN in 1957. In 1963, its name was changed to Malaysia following the accession of Singapore, Sabah, and Sarawak. Singapore became an independent UN member in 1965. (8) The Union of Soviet Socialist Republics was an original member of the UN from 1945. After the USSR's dissolution in 1991, Russia informed the UN it would be continuing the USSR's membership in the Security Council and all other UN organs with the support of the Commonwealth of Independent States (comprised of most of the former Soviet republics). (9) In 1994, the General Assembly accepted the credentials of the South African delegation, which had been rejected for 24 years because of the country's former apartheid policies. (10) Tanganyika was a member of the UN from 1961 and Zanzibar was a member from 1963. Following the ratification in 1964 of Articles of Union between Tanganyika and Zanzibar, the United Republic of Tanganyika and Zanzibar continued as a single member of the UN, later changing its name to United Republic of Tanzania. (11) The Yemen Arab Republic was admitted in 1947; the People's Republic of Yemen, in 1967. The two nations merged in 1990. (12) The Socialist Federal Republic of Yugoslavia became a member in 1945. After four of its six republics (Bosnia and Herzegovina, Croatia, Macedonia, and Slovenia) declared independence in 1991-92, the two remaining republics, Montenegro and Serbia, reconstituted themselves as the Federal Republic of Yugoslavia, which assumed Yugoslavia's UN seat Apr. 8, 1992. In Sept. 1992, the General Assembly decided the Federal Republic of Yugoslavia should apply for membership as it could not automatically take the seat of the former Yugoslavia.

United Nations Secretaries General

Year	Secretary, Nation	Year	Secretary, Nation	Year	Secretary, Nation
1946	Trygve Lie, Norway	1972	Kurt Waldheim, Austria	1992	Boutros Boutros-Ghali, Egypt
1953	Dag Hammarskjold, Sweden				
1961	U Thant, Burma	1982	Javier Perez de Cuellar, Peru	1997	Kofi Annan, Ghana

U.S. Representatives to the United Nations

The U.S. Representative to the United Nations is the Chief of the U.S. Mission to the United Nations in New York and holds the rank and status of Ambassador Extraordinary and Plenipotentiary (A.E.P.).

Year	Representative	Year	Representative	Year	Representative
1946	Edward R. Stettinius, Jr.	1968	James Russell Wiggins	1979	Donald McHenry
1946	Herschel V. Johnson (act.)	1969	Charles W. Yost	1981	Jeane J. Kirkpatrick
1947	Warren R. Austin	1971	George Bush	1985	Vernon A. Walters
1953	Henry Cabot Lodge, Jr.	1973	John A. Scali	1989	Thomas R. Pickering
1960	James J. Wadsworth	1975	Daniel P. Moynihan	1992	Edward J. Perkins
1961	Adlai E. Stevenson	1976	William W. Scranton	1993	Madeleine K. Albright
1965	Arthur J. Goldberg	1977	Andrew Young	1997	Bill Richardson
1968	George W. Ball				

Organization of the United Nations

The text of the UN Charter may be obtained from the Public Inquiries Unit, Department of Public Information, United Nations, New York, NY 10017. (212) 963-4475.

General Assembly. The General Assembly is composed of representatives of all the member nations. Each nation is entitled to one vote.

The General Assembly meets in regular annual sessions and in special session when necessary. Special sessions are convoked by the secretary general at the request of the Security Council or of a majority of the members of the UN.

On important questions a two-thirds majority of members present and voting is required; on other questions a simple majority is sufficient.

The General Assembly must approve the budget and apportion expenses among members. A member in arrears can lose its vote if the amount of arrears equals or exceeds the amount of the contributions due for the preceding 2 full years.

Security Council. The Security Council consists of 15 members, 5 with permanent seats. The remaining 10 are elected for 2-year terms by the General Assembly; they are not eligible for immediate reelection.

Permanent members of the Council are: China, France, Russia, United Kingdom, and the United States.

Nonpermanent members are: (with terms expiring Dec. 31, 1997) Chile, Egypt, Guinea-Bissau, Poland, Republic of Korea; and (with terms expiring Dec. 31, 1998) Costa Rica, Japan, Kenya, Portugal, and Sweden.

The Security Council has the primary responsibility within the UN for maintaining international peace and security. The Council may investigate any dispute that threatens international peace and security.

Any member of the UN at UN headquarters may, if invited by the Council, participate in its discussions and a nation not a member of the UN may appear if it is a party to a dispute.

Decisions on procedural questions are made by an affirmative vote of 9 members. On all other matters the affirmative vote of 9 members must include the concurring votes of all permanent members; it is this clause which gives rise to the so-called veto power of permanent members. A party to a dispute must refrain from voting.

The Security Council directs the various peacekeeping forces deployed throughout the world.

Economic and Social Council. The Economic and Social Council consists of 54 members elected by the General Assembly for 3-year terms of office. The council is responsible under the General Assembly for carrying out the functions of the United Nations with regard to international economic, social, cultural, educational, health, and related matters. The council meets once a year.

Trusteeship Council. The administration of trust territories was under UN supervision; however, all 11 Trust Territories have attained their right to self-determination. The work of the Council has, therefore, been suspended.

Secretariat. The Secretary General is the chief administrative officer of the UN. He may bring to the attention of the Security Council any matter that threatens international peace. He reports to the General Assembly.

Budget: The General Assembly approved a total budget for 1997-98 of $2.61 billion.

International Court of Justice (World Court). The International Court of Justice is the principal judicial organ of the United Nations. All members are *ipso facto* parties to the statute of the Court. Other states may become parties to the Court's statute.

The jurisdiction of the Court comprises cases which the parties submit to it and matters especially provided for in the charter or in treaties. The Court gives advisory opinions and renders judgments. Its decisions are binding only between the parties concerned and in respect to a particular dispute. If any party to a case fails to heed a judgment, the other party may have recourse to the Security Council.

The 15 judges are elected for 9-year terms by the General Assembly and the Security Council. Retiring judges are eligible for reelection. The Court remains permanently in session, except during vacations. All questions are decided by majority. The Court sits in The Hague, Netherlands.

Selected Specialized and Related Agencies

These agencies are autonomous, with their own memberships and organs, and have a functional relationship or working agreement with the UN (headquarters), except for UNICEF and UNHCR, which report directly to the Economic and Social Council and to the General Assembly.

Food and Agriculture Organization (FAO), aims to increase production from farms, forests, and fisheries; improve food distribution and marketing, nutrition, and the living conditions of rural people. (Viale delle Terme di Caracalla, 00100 Rome, Italy.)

International Atomic Energy Agency (IAEA), aims to promote the safe, peaceful uses of atomic energy. (Vienna International Centre, PO Box 100, A-1400, Vienna, Austria.)

International Bank for Reconstruction and Development (IBRD) (World Bank), provides loans and technical assistance for economic development projects in developing member countries; encourages cofinancing for projects from other public and private sources. The IBRD has 3 affiliates: (1) The **International Development Association (IDA)** provides funds for development projects on concessionary terms to poorer developing member countries. (2) The **International Finance Corporation (IFC)** promotes the growth of the private sector in developing member countries; encourages the development of local capital markets; stimulates the international flow of private capital. (3) The **Multilateral Investment Guarantee Agency (MIGA)** promotes private investment in developing countries; guarantees investments to protect investors from noncommercial risks, such as war or nationalization; advises governments on attracting private investment. (1818 H St., NW, Washington, DC 20433.)

International Civil Aviation Org. (ICAO), promotes international civil aviation standards and regulations. (1000 Sherbrooke St. W., Montreal, Quebec, Canada H3A 2R2.)

International Fund for Agricultural Development (IFAD), aims to mobilize funds for agricultural and rural projects in developing countries. (107 Via del Seratico, 00142 Rome, Italy.)

International Labor Org. (ILO), aims to promote employment; improve labor conditions and living standards. (4 route de Morillons, CH-1211 Geneva 22, Switzerland.)

International Maritime Org. (IMO), aims to promote cooperation on technical matters affecting international shipping. (4 Albert Embankment, London SE1 7SR, England.)

International Monetary Fund (IMF), aims to promote international monetary cooperation and currency stabilization and expansion of international trade. (700 19th St., NW, Washington, DC 20431.)

International Telecommunication Union (ITU), establishes international regulations for radio, telegraph, telephone, and space radio-communications, allocates radio frequencies. (Place des Nations, 1211 Geneva 20, Switzerland.)

United Nations Children's Fund (UNICEF), provides aid and development assistance to programs for children and mothers in developing countries. (3 UN Plaza, New York, NY 10017.)

United Nations Educational, Scientific, and Cultural Org. (UNESCO), aims to promote collaboration among nations through education, science, and culture. (7 Place de Fontenoy, 75352 Paris 07SP, France.)

United Nations High Commissioner for Refugees (UNHCR), provides essential assistance for refugees. (Place des Nations, 1211 Geneva 10, Switzerland.)

Universal Postal Union (UPU), aims to perfect postal services and promote international collaboration. (Weltpoststrasse 4, 3000 Berne, 15 Switzerland.)

World Health Org. (WHO), aims to aid the attainment of the highest possible level of health. (1211 Geneva 27, Switzerland.)

World Intellectual Property Org. (WIPO), seeks to protect, through international cooperation, literary, industrial, scientific, and artistic works. (34, Chemin des Colom Bettes, 1211 Geneva, Switzerland.)

World Meteorological Org. (WMO), aims to coordinate and improve world meteorological work. (41, Avenue Giuseppe-Motta, Case Postale 2300, 1211 Geneva 2, Switzerland.)

World Trade Org. (WTO), replacing the General Agreement on Tariffs and Trade (GATT), is the major body overseeing international trade. The WTO administers trade agreements and treaties, examines the trade regimes of members, keeps track of various trade measures and statistics, and attempts to settle trade disputes. (Centre William Rappard, 154 rue de Lausanne, 1211 Geneva 21, Switzerland.)

Geneva Conventions

The Geneva Conventions are 4 international treaties governing the protection of civilians in time of war, the treatment of prisoners of war, and the care of the wounded and sick in the armed forces. The first convention, covering the sick and wounded, was concluded in Geneva, Switzerland, in 1864; it was amended and expanded in 1906. A third convention, in 1929, covered prisoners of war. Outrage at the treatment of prisoners and civilians during World War II by some belligerents, notably Germany and Japan, prompted the conclusion, in Aug. 1949, of 4 new conventions. Three of these restated and strengthened the previous conventions, and the fourth codified general principles of international law governing the treatment of civilians in wartime.

The 1949 convention for civilians provided for special safeguards for the following: wounded persons, children under 15, pregnant women, and the elderly. Discrimination was forbidden on racial, religious, national, or political grounds. Torture, collective punishment, reprisals, the unwarranted destruction of property, and the forced use of civilians for an occupier's armed forces were also prohibited.

Also included in the new 1949 treaties was a pledge to treat prisoners humanely, feed them adequately, and deliver relief supplies to them. They were not to be forced to disclose more than minimal information.

Most countries have formally accepted all or most of the humanitarian conventions as binding. A nation is not free to withdraw its ratification of the conventions during wartime. However, there is no permanent machinery in place to apprehend, try, or punish violators.

Ambassadors and Envoys

"Envoys from the United States" as of Aug. 1997. "Envoys to the United States" as of Sept. 1997. The address of U.S. embassies abroad is the appropriate foreign capital. The U.S. does not have diplomatic relations with the following countries: Cuba[1], Iran[2], Iraq[3], Libya[4], Liechtenstein, North Korea, and Taiwan[5]. There are informal relations with Bhutan.

Countries	Envoys from United States	Envoys to United States
Afghanistan	None	Yar Mohammad Mohabbat, Chargé
Albania	Marisa R. Lino, Amb.	Lublin Dilja, Amb.
Algeria	Ronald E. Neumann, Amb.	Ramtane Lamamra, Amb.
Andorra	None	Juli Minoves Triquell, Amb.
Angola	Donald K. Steinberg, Amb.	Antonio dos Santos Franca, Amb.
Antigua & Barbuda	Jeanette W. Hyde, Amb.	Lionel A. Hurst, Amb.
Argentina	Vacancy	Diego Ramiro Guelar, Amb.
Armenia	Peter Tomsen, Amb.	Rouben Robert Shugarian, Amb.
Australia	Genta Hawkins Holmes, Amb.	Andrew S. Peacock, Amb.
Austria	Swanee G. Hunt, Amb.	Helmut Tuerk, Amb.
Azerbaijan	Stan Escudero, Amb.	Hafiz Mir Jalal Oglu Pashayev, Amb.
Bahamas	Sidney Williams, Amb.	Arlington Griffith Butler, Amb.
Bahrain	David M. Ransom, Amb.	Muhammad Abdul Ghaffar, Amb.
Bangladesh	John Holzman, Amb.	K.M. Shehabuddin, Amb.
Barbados	Jeanette W. Hyde, Amb.	Courtney N. M. Blackman, Amb.
Belarus	Daniel Speckhard, Amb.	Valery V. Tsepkalo, Amb.
Belgium	Alan J. Blinken, Amb.	Andre Adam, Amb.
Belize	George C. Bruno, Amb.	James S. Murphy, Amb.
Benin	John M. Yates, Amb.	Lucien Tonoukouin, Amb.
Bolivia	Curt W. Kamman, Amb.	Fernando Cossio, Amb.
Bosnia and Herzegovina	Richard D. Kauzlarich, Amb.	Sven Alkalaj, Amb.
Botswana	Robert Krueger, Amb.	Archibald Mooketsa Mogwe, Amb.
Brazil	Melvyn Levitsky, Amb.	Paulo Tarso Flecha de Lima, Amb.
Brunei	Glen R. Rase, Amb.	Pengiran Anak Dato Puteh, Amb.
Bulgaria	Avis T. Bohlen, Amb.	Snejana Damianova Botoucharova, Amb.
Burkina Faso	Sharon P. Wilkinson, Amb.	Gaetan R. Ouedraogo, Amb.
Burundi	Morris N. Hughes Jr., Amb.	Henri Simbakwira, Chargé
Cambodia	Kenneth M. Quinn, Amb.	Huoth Var, Amb.
Cameroon	Charles H. Twining, Amb.	Jerome Mendouga, Amb.
Canada	Gordon Giffin, Amb.	Raymond A. J. Chretien, Amb.
Cape Verde	Lawrence N. Benedict, Amb.	Corentino Virgillio Santos, Amb.
Central African Republic	Mosina H. Jordan, Amb.	Henry Koba, Amb.
Chad	David C. Halsted, Amb.	Ahmat Mahamat-Saleh, Amb.
Chile	Gabriel Guerra-Mondragon, Amb.	John Biehl, Amb.
China	Jim Sasser, Amb.	Li Daoyu, Amb.
Colombia	Myles R. Rene Frechette, Amb.	Juan Carlos Esguerra, Amb.
Comoros	Harold W. Geisel, Amb.	Vacancy
Congo, Dem. Rep. of the (formerly Zaire)	Daniel H. Simpson, Amb.	Mukendi Tambo a Kabila, Chargé
Congo Republic	Aubrey Hooks, Amb.	Dieudonne Antoine Ganga, Amb.
Costa Rica	Peter Jon de Vos, Amb.	Sonia Picado, Amb.
Côte d'Ivoire	Lannon Walker, Amb.	Koffi Moise Koumoue, Amb.
Croatia	Peter W. Galbraith, Amb.	Miomir Zuzul, Amb.
Cyprus	Kenneth C. Brill, Amb.	Andros A. Nicolaides, Amb.
Czech Republic	Jenonne R. Walker, Amb.	Alexandr Vondra, Amb.
Denmark	Edward E. Elson, Amb.*	K. Erik Tygesen, Amb.
Djibouti	Lange Schermerhorn*	Roble Olhaye, Amb.
Dominica	Jeanette W. Hyde, Amb.	None
Dominican Republic	Donna J. Hrinak, Amb.	Bernardo Vega, Amb.
Ecuador	Leslie M. Alexander, Amb.	Alberto F. Maspons, Amb.
Egypt	Edward S. Walker, Amb.	Ahmed Maher El Sayed, Amb.
El Salvador	Anne W. Patterson, Amb.	Rene A. Leon, Amb.
Equatorial Guinea	Charles H. Twining, Amb.	Pastor Micha Ondo Bile, Amb.
Eritrea	John F. Hicks Sr., Amb.	Semere Russon, Amb.
Estonia	Lawrence P. Taylor, Amb.	Grigore-Kalev Stoicescu, Amb.
Ethiopia	David H. Shinn, Amb.	Berhane Gebre-Christos, Amb.
Fiji	Don Lee Gevirtz, Amb.	Napolioni Masirewa, Amb.
Finland	Derek Shearer, Amb.	Jaakko Laajava, Amb.
France	Felix Rohatyn, Amb.	Francois V. Bujon, Amb.
Gabon	Elizabeth Raspolic, Amb.	Paul Boundoukou-Latha, Amb.
Gambia, The	Gerald W. Scott, Amb.	Crispin Grey Johnson, Amb.
Georgia	William H. Courtney, Amb.	Tedo Japaridze, Amb.
Germany	John Kornblum, Amb.	Juergen Chrobog, Amb.
Ghana	Edward Brynn, Amb.	Nana Effah-Apenteng, Chargé
Greece	Thomas M. Tolliver Niles, Amb.	Loucas Tsilas, Amb.
Grenada	Jeanette W. Hyde, Amb.	Denis G. Antoine, Amb.
Guatemala	Donald J. Planty, Amb.	Pedro Miguel Lamport, Amb.
Guinea	Tibor P. Nagy Jr., Amb.	Mohamed Aly Thiam, Amb.
Guinea-Bissau	Peggy Blackford, Amb.	Rufino Jose Mendes, Amb.
Guyana	James Mack, Amb.	Mohammed Ali Odeen Ishmael, Amb.
Haiti	William L. Swing, Amb.	Jean Casimir, Amb.
Honduras	James F. Creagan, Amb.	Roberto Flores Bermudez, Amb.
Hungary	Donald M. Blinken, Amb.	Gyorgy Banlaki, Amb.
Iceland	Day Olin Mount, Amb.	Einar Benediktsson, Amb.
India	Frank G. Wisner, Amb.	Naresh Chandra, Amb.
Indonesia	J. Stapleton Roy, Amb.	Arifin Mohamad Siregar, Amb.
Ireland	Jean Kennedy Smith, Amb.	Sean O'Huiginn, Amb.
Israel	Martin S. Indyk, Amb.	Eliahu Ben-Elissar, Amb.
Italy	Reginald Bartholomew, Amb.	Ferdinando Salleo, Amb.
Jamaica	Jerome G. Cooper, Amb.	Richard Leighton Bernal, Amb.
Japan	Tom Foley*	Kunihiko Saito, Amb.
Jordan	Wesley W. Egan, Amb.	Marwan Jamil Muasher, Amb.
Kazakhstan	A. Elizabeth Jones, Amb.	Bolat K. Nurgaliyev, Amb.
Kenya	Prudence Bushnell, Amb.	Benjamin Edgar Kipkorir, Amb.

Countries	Envoys from United States	Envoys to United States
Kiribati	Joan M. Plaisted, Amb.	None
Korea, South	Steven Bosworth*	Kun Woo Park, Amb.
Kuwait	Ryan C. Crocker, Amb.	Mohammed Sabah Al-Salim Al-Sabah, Amb.
Kyrgyzstan	Anne Sigmund, Amb.	Almas Chukin, Chargé
Laos	Wendy Jean Chamberlin, Amb.	Hiem Phommachanh, Amb.
Latvia	Larry C. Napper, Amb.	Ojars Eriks Kalnins, Amb.
Lebanon	Richard H. Jones, Amb.	Mohamad Baha Chatah, Amb.
Lesotho	Bismarck Myrick, Amb.	Eunice M. Bulane, Amb.
Liberia	William B. Milam, Chargé	Konah Blackett, Chargé
Lithuania	Keith Smith, Amb.	Alfonsas Eidintas, Amb.
Luxembourg	Clay Constantinou, Amb.	Alphonse Berns, Amb.
Macedonia	Christopher R. Hill, Amb.	Lubica Z. Acevska, Amb.
Madagascar	Vicki J. Huddleston, Amb.	Pierrot J. Rajaonarivelo, Amb.
Malawi	Peter R. Chaveas, Amb.	Willie Chokani, Amb.
Malaysia	John R. Malott, Amb.	Dato Dali Mahmud Hashim, Amb.
Maldives	A. Peter Burleigh, Amb.	None
Mali	David P. Rawson, Amb.	Cheick Oumar Diarrah, Amb.
Malta	Vacancy.	Mark Anthony Micallef, Amb.
Marshall Islands	Joan M. Plaisted, Amb.	Banny de Brum, Amb.
Mauritania	Dorothy Myers Sampas, Amb.	Ahmed Ould Sid Ahmed, Amb.
Mauritius	Harold W. Geisel, Amb.	Chitmansing Jesseramsing, Amb.
Mexico	Vacancy.	Jesus Silva Herzog, Amb.
Micronesia	Vacancy.	Jesse B. Marehalau, Amb.
Moldova	John T. Stewart, Amb.	Nicolae Tau, Amb.
Mongolia	Al LaPorta*	Jalbuu Choinhor, Chargé
Morocco	Marc C. Ginsberg, Amb.	Mohamed Benaissa, Amb.
Mozambique	Dean Curran*	Marcos G. Namashulua, Amb.
Myanmar	Kent M.Wiedemann, Chargé.	Tin Winn, Amb.
Namibia	George F. Ward Jr., Amb.	Veiccoh K. Nghiwete, Amb.
Nauru	Don Lee Gevirtz, Amb.	None
Nepal	Ralph Frank, Amb.	Bhekh Bahadur Thapa, Amb.
Netherlands	K. Terry Dornbush, Amb.	Adriaan P. Jacobovits de Szeged, Amb.
New Zealand	Josiah Horton Beeman, Amb.	L. John Wood, Amb.
Nicaragua	Lino Gutierrez, Amb.	Francisco Aguirre Sacasa, Amb.
Niger	Charles O. Cecil, Amb.	Joseph Diatta, Amb.
Nigeria	Walter C. Carrington, Amb.	Wakili Hassan Adamu, Amb.
Norway	Thomas A. Loftus, Amb.	Tom Eric Vraalsen, Amb.
Oman	Frances D. Cook, Amb.	Abdulla Moh'd. Aqeel Al-Dhahab, Amb.
Pakistan	Thomas W. Simons Jr., Amb.	Riaz H. Khokhar, Amb.
Palau	Thomas C. Hubbard, Amb.	David Orrukem, Chargé
Panama	William J. Hughes, Amb.	Eduardo Morgan Gonzalez, Amb.
Papua New Guinea	Arma Jane Karaer, Amb.	Nagora Bogan, Amb.
Paraguay	Maura Harty, Amb.	Jorge G. Prieto, Amb.
Peru	Dennis C. Jett, Amb.	Ricardo V. Luna, Amb.
Philippines	Thomas C. Hubbard, Amb.	Raul Chaves Rabe, Amb.
Poland	Nicholas Andrew Rey, Amb.	Jerzy Kozminski, Amb.
Portugal	Elizabeth Frawley Bagley, Amb.	Fernando Andresen Guimaraes, Amb.
Qatar	Patrick N. Theros, Amb.	Saad Mohamed Al Kobaisi, Amb.
Romania	Alfred H. Moses, Amb.	Mircea Dan Geoana, Amb.
Russia	James Collins, Amb.	Yuli M. Vorontsov, Amb.
Rwanda	Robert E. Gribbin III, Amb.	Theogene N. Rudasingwa, Amb.
St. Kitts & Nevis	Jeanette W. Hyde, Amb.	Osbert W. Liburd, Amb.
St. Lucia	Jeanette W. Hyde, Amb.	Dr. Joseph Edsel Edmunds, Amb.
St. Vincent and the Grenadines	Jeanette W. Hyde, Amb.	Kingsley C.A. Layne, Amb.
Samoa (formerly Western Samoa)	Josiah Horton Beeman, Amb.	Tuiloma Neroni Slade, Amb.
São Tomé and Príncipe	Elizabeth Raspolic, Amb.	Vacancy
Saudi Arabia	Wyche Fowler Jr., Amb.	Prince Bandar Bin Sultan, Amb.
Senegal	Dane Farnsworth Smith Jr., Amb.	Mamadou Mansour Seck, Amb.
Seychelles	Harold W. Geisel, Amb.	Claude S. Morel, Chargé
Sierra Leone	John L. Hirsch, Amb.	John Ernest Leigh, Amb.
Singapore	Timothy A. Chorba, Amb.	Heng-Chee Chan, Amb.
Slovakia	Ralph R. Johnson, Amb.	Branislav Lichardus, Amb.
Slovenia	Victor Jackovich, Amb.	Ernest Petric, Amb.
Solomon Islands	Arma Jane Karaer, Amb.	Rex Stephen Horoi, Amb.
South Africa	James A. Joseph, Amb.	Franklin Sonn, Amb.
Spain	Richard N. Gardner, Amb.	Antonio Oyarzabal, Amb.
Sri Lanka	A. Peter Burleigh, Amb.	M. Neetha Geethangani de Silva, Chargé
Sudan	Timothy M. Carney, Amb.	Mahdi Ibrahim Mohamed, Amb.
Suriname	Dennis K. Hays, Amb.	Arnold T. Halfhide, Amb.
Swaziland	Alan R. McKee, Amb.	Mary M. Kanya, Amb.
Sweden	Thomas L. Siebert, Amb.	Rolf Ekeus, Amb.
Switzerland	Madeleine May Kunin, Amb.	Alfred Defago, Amb.
Syria	Christopher W. S. Ross, Amb.	Walid Al-Moualem, Amb.
Tajikistan	R. Grant Smith, Amb.	None
Tanzania	Brady Anderson, Amb.	Mustafa Salim Nyang'anyi, Amb.
Thailand	William H. Itoh, Amb.	Nitya Pibulsonggram, Amb.
Togo	Johnny Young, Amb.	Kossivi Osseyi, Amb.
Tonga	Don Lee Gevirtz, Amb.	Akosita Fineanganofo, Amb.
Trinidad and Tobago	Brian J. Donnelly, Amb.	Corinne Averille McKnight, Amb.
Tunisia	Mary Ann Casey, Amb.	Azouz Ennifar, Amb.
Turkey	Mark Parris*	Nuzhet Kandemir, Amb.
Turkmenistan	Michael W. Cotter, Amb.	Halil Ugur, Amb.
Tuvalu	Don Lee Gevirtz, Amb.	None
Uganda	E. Michael Southwick, Amb.	Edith Grace Ssempala, Amb.
Ukraine	William Green Miller, Amb.	Yuri M. Shcherbak, Amb.
United Arab Emirates	David C. Litt, Amb.	Mohammad bin Hussain Al-Shaali, Amb.
United Kingdom	Philip Lader, Amb.	Sir John Olav Kerr, Amb.
Uruguay	Thomas J. Dodd, Amb.	Alvaro Mario Diez de Medina, Amb.

Countries	Envoys from United States	Envoys to United States
Uzbekistan	Stanley Tuemler Escudero, Amb.	Sodiq Safaev, Amb.
Vanuatu	Arma Jane Karaer, Amb.	None
Vatican City (The Holy See)	Raymond Leo Flynn, Amb.	Most Rev. Agostino Cacciavillan, Pro-Nuncio
Venezuela	John F. Maisto, Amb.	Pedro Luis Echeverria, Amb.
Vietnam	Pete Peterson, Amb.	Bang Le, Amb.
Yemen	David G. Newton, Amb.	Abdulwahab A. Al-Hajjri, Amb.
Yugoslavia	Richard M. Miles, Chargé	Nebojsa Vujovic, Chargé
Zambia	Arlene Render, Amb.	Dunstan Weston Kamana, Amb.
Zimbabwe	Johnnie Carson, Amb.	Amos Bernard Muvengwa Midzi, Amb.

Special Missions: U.S. Mission to NATO, Brussels—Robert E. Hunter, A.E.P.; U.S. Mission to the European Union, Brussels—A. Vernon Weaver, A.E.P.; U.S. Mission to the UN, New York—Bill Richardson, A.E.P.; U.S. Mission to the European Office of the UN, Geneva—Vacant; U.S. Mission to the OECD, Paris—David L. Aaron, Amb.; U.S. Mission to the Organization of American States, Washington—Harriet C. Babbitt, Amb.; U.S. Mission to the Vienna Office of the UN—John B. Ritch III, Amb.

(1) Relations severed in 1961; limited ties restored in 1977. (2) U.S. severed relations in Apr. 1980. (3) Operations temporarily suspended. (4) Embassy closed in May 1980. U.S. closed the Libyan mission in May 1981. (5) Relations severed in 1978; unofficial relations are maintained. *Ambassador designate.

Codes for International Direct Dial Calling From the U.S.

Station-to-station: 011 + country code (below) + city code (if required) + local number.
Person-to-person (operator-assisted, collect calls, credit card calls, and calls billed to another number): 01 + country code (below) + city code (if required) + local number.
For countries or territories not listed, contact your long distance company.

Country/Territory	Code	Country/Territory	Code	Country/Territory	Code	Country/Territory	Code
Afghanistan	93	Cape Verde	238	Israel	972	Poland	48
Albania	355	Cayman Islands	345*	Italy	39	Portugal	351
Algeria	213	Central African Rep.	236	Jamaica[2]	809*	Puerto Rico	787*
American Samoa	684	Chad	235	Japan	81	Qatar	974
Andorra	376	Chile	56	Jordan	962	Romania	40
Angola	244	China	86	Kazakhstan	7	Russia	7
Anguilla	264*	Colombia	57	Kenya	254	Rwanda	250
Antarctica (Scott		Comoros	269	Kiribati	686	St. Kitts & Nevis	869*
Base)	64240	Congo (formerly		Korea, North	850	St. Lucia	758*
Antigua & Barbuda	268*	Zaire)	243	Korea, South	82	St. Vincent & the	
Argentina	54	Congo Republic	242	Kuwait	965	Grenadines[3]	809*
Armenia	374	Costa Rica	506	Kyrgyzstan	7	Samoa (formerly	
Aruba	297	Côte d'Ivoire	225	Laos	856	Western Samoa)	685
Ascension Island	247	Croatia	385	Latvia	371	San Marino	378
Australia	61	Cuba	53	Lebanon	961	São Tomé & Príncipe	239
Austria	43	Cyprus	357	Lesotho	266	Saudi Arabia	966
Azerbaijan	994	Czech Republic	42	Liberia	231	Senegal	221
Bahamas	242*	Denmark	45	Libya	218	Seychelles	248
Bahrain	973	Djibouti	253	Liechtenstein	4175	Sierra Leone	232
Bangladesh	880	Dominica	767*	Lithuania	370	Singapore	65
Barbados	246*	Dominican Republic	809*	Luxembourg	352	Slovakia	42
Belarus	375	Ecuador	593	Macau	853	Slovenia	386
Belgium	32	Egypt	20	Macedonia	389	Solomon Islands	677
Belize	501	El Salvador	503	Madagascar	261	Somalia	252
Benin	229	Equatorial Guinea	240	Malawi	265	South Africa	27
Bermuda	441*	Eritrea	291	Malaysia	60	Spain	34
Bhutan	975	Estonia	372	Maldives	960	Sri Lanka	94
Bolivia	591	Ethiopia	251	Mali	223	Sudan	249
Bosnia & Herze-		Falkland Islands	500	Malta	356	Suriname	597
govina	387	Fiji	679	Marshall Islands	692	Swaziland	268
Botswana	267	Finland	358	Martinique	596	Sweden	46
Brazil	55	France	33	Mauritania	222	Switzerland	41
Brunei	673	French Antilles	596	Mauritius	230	Syria	963
Bulgaria	359	French Guiana	594	Mexico	52	Taiwan	886
Burkina Faso	226	French Polynesia	689	Micronesia	691	Tajikistan	7
Burundi	257	Gabon	241	Moldova	373	Tanzania	255
Cambodia	855	Gambia, The	220	Monaco	377	Thailand	66
Cameroon	237	Georgia	995	Mongolia	976	Togo	228
Canada		Germany	49	Montserrat	664*	Tonga	676
Alberta	403*	Ghana	233	Morocco	21	Trinidad & Tobago	868*
British Columbia	250*	Gibraltar	350	Mozambique	258	Tunisia	216
Vancouver	604*	Greece	30	Myanmar	95	Turkey	90
Manitoba	204*	Greenland	299	Namibia	264	Turkmenistan	7
New Brunswick	506*	Grenada	473*	Nauru	674	Turks & Caicos Isls.	649*
Newfoundland	709*	Guadeloupe	590	Nepal	977	Tuvalu	688
NW Territories	867*	Guam	671*	Netherlands	31	Uganda	256
Nova Scotia	902*	Guantanamo Bay	5399	New Caledonia	687	Ukraine	380
Ontario		Guatemala	502	New Zealand	64	United Arab Emirates	971
London	519*	Guinea	224	Nicaragua	505	United Kingdom	44
North Bay	705*	Guinea-Bissau	245	Niger	227	Uruguay	598
Ottawa	613*	Guyana	592	Nigeria	234	Uzbekistan	7
Thunder Bay	807*	Haiti	509	N. Mariana Isls.	670*	Vanuatu	678
Toronto Metro	416*	Honduras	504	Norway	47	Vatican City	379
Toronto Vicinity	905*	Hong Kong	852	Oman	968	Venezuela	58
Prince Edward Isl.	902*	Hungary	36	Pakistan	92	Vietnam	84
Quebec		Iceland	354	Palau	680	Virgin Islands, British	284*
Montreal[1]	514*	India	91	Panama	507	Virgin Islands, U.S.	340*
Quebec City	418*	Indonesia	62	Papua New Guinea	675	Yemen	967
Sherbrooke	819*	Iran	98	Paraguay	595	Yugoslavia	381
Saskatchewan	306*	Iraq	964	Peru	51	Zambia	260
Yukon Territory	867*	Ireland	353	Philippines	63	Zimbabwe	263

* These numbers are area codes. Follow Domestic Dialing instructions: dial "1" + area code + number you are calling. (1) In June 1998, area code for a portion of Montreal will change to 450. (2) Area code will change to 876 on a date not determined as of Sept. 1997. (3) Area code will change to 784 on a date not determined as of Sept. 1997.

SPORTS
Ten Most Dramatic Sports Events of 1997

Tiger Woods continued to astonish the golf world, scoring a record 12-stroke victory in the Masters tournament at Augusta, GA, Apr. 13. Woods, who won the event in his first year as a professional, set several other tournament records. Besides winning by the largest margin ever, Woods, at age 21, was the youngest golfer ever to win the Masters and shot the lowest score (270) in the history of the event. He was the first African-American and first Asian-American to win any of the four major tournaments in men's professional golf.

With a come-from-behind 11-inning victory in game 7, the Florida Marlins, who had finished second in the National League's Eastern Division, defeated the Cleveland Indians, 4 games to 3, to become the first wild card team to win the World Series. The Series featured high-scoring games, fielding lapses, and a game (Oct. 22 in Cleveland) played in snow showers and the coldest temperatures in Series history.

The Green Bay Packers won Super Bowl XXXI, their first Super Bowl in 29 years, handily defeating the New England Patriots, 35-21, Jan. 26, 1997, in New Orleans, LA. It was the 13th Super Bowl in a row won by an NFC team. Kickoff/punt returner Desmond Howard became the first special teams player chosen as Super Bowl MVP.

The Chicago Bulls again showed championship poise, as they defeated the Utah Jazz in 6 games in the NBA Finals in June and gained their 5th title in 7 years. Michael Jordan picked up his second straight and record 5th Finals MVP award.

On June 7 the Detroit Red Wings ended a 42-year drought by finishing off a four-game sweep of the Philadelphia Flyers to win the NHL's Stanley Cup Finals. Detroit goaltender Mike Vernon won the Conn Smythe Trophy as playoff MVP. The victory was soured, however, when a limousine carrying some members of the team crashed, June 13, seriously injuring Vladimir Kostantinov, one of the Red Wings' star players.

Boxing received a severe black eye, June 28, in Las Vegas, NV, when Mike Tyson twice bit the ears of defending WBA heavyweight champion Evander Holyfield in the third round of their title bout. Tyson (who felt he had been head-butted earlier in the fight) was disqualified. Holyfield retained his title, and Tyson, on July 9, was banned from boxing in Nevada for one year by the Nevada State Athletic Commission. The commission also fined Tyson $3,000,000; both penalties were the maximum allowed under Nevada boxing rules.

Two professional women's basketball leagues closed out their inaugural seasons in 1997. The American Basketball League (ABL), which began play in Oct. 1996, wrapped up its season Mar. 11, with the Columbus Quest winning the championship. The Women's National Basketball Association (WNBA), backed by the NBA, played a summer schedule beginning June 21, drawing enthusiastic crowds and much media attention. On Aug. 30 the Houston Comets beat the New York Liberty to gain the WNBA championship.

Martina Hingis of Switzerland captured three of tennis's Grand Slam events in 1997 and in March became the youngest women's tennis player to be ranked number one in the world. Hingis won the women's singles title at the Australian Open in January, Wimbledon in July, and the U.S. Open in September.

The University of Florida Gators, Jan. 2, beat the Florida State Seminoles in the Sugar Bowl, 52-20, to gain the number one ranking in the final polls of top NCAA Division I football teams. Gators quarterback Danny Wuerffel, the Heisman Trophy winner, was named the game's outstanding player.

Royal Air Force pilot Andy Green broke the sound barrier on land for the first time and achieved a record land speed of 763.035 mph in Black Rock Desert, NV, Oct. 15. Green's Thrust SSC car was powered by two Rolls-Royce engines.

OLYMPICS
Summary Olympic Games in 1996

Atlanta, GA, U.S., July 19-Aug. 4, 1996

On July 19, former boxing great Muhammad Ali lit the flame inaugurating the Centennial Olympic Games, the 26th Olympiad. About 10,750 athletes gathered for 17 days to compete for medals in a record 271 events; athletes from 197 nations and territories participated (25 more than in any previous Olympics). A bomb attack, July 27, at Centennial Olympic Park led to 2 deaths and injured more than 100, casting a somber mood on the 2d week of the games—still, the spirit of competition prevailed.

Outstanding athletes and teams of the 1996 games included: Kerri Strug, who ignored an ankle injury to lead the U.S. women's gymnastics team to a gold medal; the U.S. women's basketball, softball, and soccer teams; the U.S. men's basketball team (Dream Team), who again breezed to a gold; U.S. runner Michael Johnson, who won the 200 and 400 meters; France's Marie-Jose Perec, winner of the women's 200 and 400 meters; Canada's Donovan Bailey, who set a world record in the 100-meter run; Dan O'Brien of the U.S., who won the decathlon, after not even qualifying for the 1992 Olympics; U.S. swimmer Amy Van Dyken, who won 4 gold medals; Ireland's Michelle Smith, winner of 3 gold medals in swimming; China's Fu Mingxia, who swept both women's diving events; marathon runner Josia Thugwane, who became South Africa's first black gold medalist; Russian Aleksandr Karelin, who won his 3d consecutive gold in Greco-Roman wrestling's super-heavyweight class; and Carl Lewis, who won his 4th consecutive gold medal in the long jump.

The U.S. won the most medals, 101, and the most gold medals, 44. Germany finished 2d in the medal count with 65, while Russia was 3d in total medals with 63, and 2d in gold medals with 26.

Final Medal Standings

Country	G	S	B	T	Country	G	S	B	T	Country	G	S	B	T
United States	44	32	25	101	Norway	2	2	3	7	Uzbekistan	0	1	1	2
Germany	20	18	27	65	Denmark	4	1	1	6	Georgia	0	0	2	2
Russia	26	21	16	63	Turkey	4	1	1	6	Morocco	0	0	2	2
China	16	22	12	50	New Zealand	3	2	1	6	Trinidad				
Australia	9	9	23	41	Belgium	2	2	2	6	& Tobago	0	0	2	2
France	15	7	15	37	Nigeria	2	1	3	6	Burundi	1	0	0	1
Italy	13	10	12	35	Jamaica	1	3	2	6	Costa Rica	1	0	0	1
South Korea	7	15	5	27	South Africa	3	1	1	5	Ecuador	1	0	0	1
Cuba	9	8	8	25	North Korea	2	1	2	5	Hong Kong	1	0	0	1
Ukraine	9	2	12	23	Ireland	3	0	1	4	Syria	1	0	0	1
Canada	3	11	8	22	Finland	1	2	1	4	Azerbaijan	0	1	0	1
Hungary	7	4	10	21	Indonesia	1	1	2	4	Bahamas	0	1	0	1
Romania	4	7	9	20	Yugoslavia	1	1	2	4	Latvia	0	1	0	1
Netherlands	4	5	10	19	Algeria	2	0	1	3	Philippines	0	1	0	1
Poland	7	5	5	17	Ethiopia	2	0	1	3	Taiwan	0	1	0	1
Spain	5	6	6	17	Iran	1	1	1	3	Tonga	0	1	0	1
Bulgaria	3	7	5	15	Slovakia	1	1	1	3	Zambia	0	1	0	1
Brazil	3	3	9	15	Argentina	0	2	1	3	India	0	0	1	1
Great Britain	1	8	6	15	Austria	0	1	2	3	Israel	0	0	1	1
Belarus	1	6	8	15	Armenia	1	1	0	2	Lithuania	0	0	1	1
Japan	3	6	5	14	Croatia	1	1	0	2	Mexico	0	0	1	1
Czech Rep.	4	3	4	11	Portugal	1	0	1	2	Moldova	0	1	1	2
Kazakhstan	3	4	4	11	Thailand	1	0	1	2	Mongolia	0	0	1	1
Greece	4	4	0	8	Namibia	0	2	0	2	Mozambique	0	0	1	1
Sweden	2	4	2	8	Slovenia	0	2	0	2	Puerto Rico	0	0	1	1
Kenya	1	4	3	8	Malaysia	0	1	1	2	Tunisia	0	0	1	1
Switzerland	4	3	0	7	Moldova	0	1	1	2	Uganda	0	0	1	1

Sites of Summer Olympic Games

1896	Athens, Greece	1924	Paris, France	1960	Rome, Italy	1984	Los Angeles, U.S.
1900	Paris, France	1928	Amsterdam, Netherlands	1964	Tokyo, Japan	1988	Seoul, South Korea
1904	St. Louis, U.S.	1932	Los Angeles, U.S.	1968	Mexico City, Mexico	1992	Barcelona, Spain
1906*	Athens, Greece	1936	Berlin, Germany	1972	Munich, W. Germany	1996	Atlanta, U.S.
1908	London, England	1948	London, England	1976	Montreal, Canada	2000	Sydney, Australia
1912	Stockholm, Sweden	1952	Helsinki, Finland	1980	Moscow, USSR	2004	Athens, Greece
1920	Antwerp, Belgium	1956	Melbourne, Australia				

*Games not recognized by International Olympic Committee. Games 6 (1916), 12 (1940), and 13 (1944) were not celebrated.

Summer Olympic Games Champions, 1896-1996

(*Indicates Olympic record)

The 1980 games were boycotted by 62 nations, including the U.S. The 1984 games were boycotted by the USSR and by most Eastern bloc nations. East and West Germany competed separately 1968-88. The 1992 Unified Team consisted of 12 former Soviet republics. The 1992 Independent Olympic Participants (I.O.P.) were athletes from Serbia, Montenegro, and Macedonia.

Track and Field — Men

100-Meter Run

1896	Thomas Burke, United States	12s
1900	Francis W. Jarvis, United States	11.0s
1904	Archie Hahn, United States	11.0s
1908	Reginald Walker, South Africa	10.8s
1912	Ralph Craig, United States	10.8s
1920	Charles Paddock, United States	10.8s
1924	Harold Abrahams, Great Britain	10.6s
1928	Percy Williams, Canada	10.8s
1932	Eddie Tolan, United States	10.3s
1936	Jesse Owens, United States	10.3s
1948	Harrison Dillard, United States	10.3s
1952	Lindy Remigino, United States	10.4s
1956	Bobby Morrow, United States	10.5s
1960	Armin Hary, Germany	10.2s
1964	Bob Hayes, United States	10.0s
1968	Jim Hines, United States	9.95s
1972	Valery Borzov, USSR	10.14s
1976	Hasely Crawford, Trinidad	10.06s
1980	Allan Wells, Great Britain	10.25s
1984	Carl Lewis, United States	9.99s
1988	Carl Lewis, United States	9.92s
1992	Linford Christie, Great Britain	9.96s
1996	Donovan Bailey, Canada	9.84s*

200-Meter Run

1900	Walter Tewksbury, United States	22.2s
1904	Archie Hahn, United States	21.6s
1908	Robert Kerr, Canada	22.6s
1912	Ralph Craig, United States	21.7s
1920	Allan Woodring, United States	22s
1924	Jackson Scholz, United States	21.6s
1928	Percy Williams, Canada	21.8s
1932	Eddie Tolan, United States	21.2s
1936	Jesse Owens, United States	20.7s
1948	Mel Patton, United States	21.1s
1952	Andrew Stanfield, United States	20.7s
1956	Bobby Morrow, United States	20.6s
1960	Livio Berruti, Italy	20.5s
1964	Henry Carr, United States	20.3s
1968	Tommie Smith, United States	19.83s
1972	Valeri Borzov, USSR	20.00s
1976	Donald Quarrie, Jamaica	20.23s
1980	Pietro Mennea, Italy	20.19s
1984	Carl Lewis, United States	19.80s
1988	Joe DeLoach, United States	19.75s
1992	Mike Marsh, United States	20.01s
1996	Michael Johnson, United States	19.32s*

400-Meter Run

1896	Thomas Burke, United States	54.2s
1900	Maxey Long, United States	49.4s
1904	Harry Hillman, United States	49.2s
1908	Wyndham Halswelle, Great Britain, walkover	50s
1912	Charles Reidpath, United States	48.2s
1920	Bevil Rudd, South Africa	49.6s
1924	Eric Liddell, Great Britain	47.6s
1928	Ray Barbuti, United States	47.8s
1932	William Carr, United States	46.2s
1936	Archie Williams, United States	46.5s
1948	Arthur Wint, Jamaica	46.2s

1952	George Rhoden, Jamaica	45.9s
1956	Charles Jenkins, United States	46.7s
1960	Otis Davis, United States	44.9s
1964	Michael Larrabee, United States	45.1s
1968	Lee Evans, United States	43.8s
1972	Vincent Matthews, United States	44.66s
1976	Alberto Juantorena, Cuba	44.26s
1980	Viktor Markin, USSR	44.60s
1984	Alonzo Babers, United States	44.27s
1988	Steven Lewis, United States	43.87s
1992	Quincy Watts, United States	43.50s
1996	Michael Johnson, United States	43.49s*

800-Meter Run

1896	Edwin Flack, Australia	2m. 11s
1900	Alfred Tysoe, Great Britain	2m. 1.2s
1904	James Lightbody, United States	1m. 56s
1908	Mel Sheppard, United States	1m. 52.8s
1912	James Meredith, United States	1m. 51.9s
1920	Albert Hill, Great Britain	1m. 53.4s
1924	Douglas Lowe, Great Britain	1m. 52.4s
1928	Douglas Lowe, Great Britain	1m. 51.8s
1932	Thomas Hampson, Great Britain	1m. 49.8s
1936	John Woodruff, United States	1m. 52.9s
1948	Mal Whitfield, United States	1m. 49.2s
1952	Mal Whitfield, United States	1m. 49.2s
1956	Thomas Courtney, United States	1m. 47.7s
1960	Peter Snell, New Zealand	1m. 46.3s
1964	Peter Snell, New Zealand	1m. 45.1s
1968	Ralph Doubell, Australia	1m. 44.3s
1972	Dave Wottle, United States	1m. 45.9s
1976	Alberto Juantorena, Cuba	1m. 43.50s
1980	Steve Ovett, Great Britain	1m. 45.40s
1984	Joaquim Cruz, Brazil	1m. 43.00s
1988	Paul Ereng, Kenya	1m. 43.45s
1992	William Tanui, Kenya	1m. 43.66s
1996	Vebjoern Rodal, Norway	1m. 42.58s*

1,500-Meter Run

1896	Edwin Flack, Australia	4m. 33.2s
1900	Charles Bennett, Great Britain	4m. 6.2s
1904	James Lightbody, United States	4m. 5.4s
1908	Mel Sheppard, United States	4m. 3.4s
1912	Arnold Jackson, Great Britain	3m. 56.8s
1920	Albert Hill, Great Britain	4m. 1.8s
1924	Paavo Nurmi, Finland	3m. 53.6s
1928	Harry Larva, Finland	3m. 53.2s
1932	Luigi Beccali, Italy	3m. 51.2s
1936	Jack Lovelock, New Zealand	3m. 47.8s
1948	Henri Eriksson, Sweden	3m. 49.8s
1952	Joseph Barthel, Luxembourg	3m. 45.2s
1956	Ron Delany, Ireland	3m. 41.2s
1960	Herb Elliott, Australia	3m. 35.6s
1964	Peter Snell, New Zealand	3m. 38.1s
1968	Kipchoge Keino, Kenya	3m. 34.9s
1972	Pekka Vasala, Finland	3m. 36.3s
1976	John Walker, New Zealand	3m. 39.17s
1980	Sebastian Coe, Great Britain	3m. 38.4s
1984	Sebastian Coe, Great Britain	3m. 32.53s*
1988	Peter Rono, Kenya	3m. 35.96s
1992	Fermin Cacho Ruiz, Spain	3m. 40.12s
1996	Noureddine Morceli, Algeria	3m. 35.78s

5,000-Meter Run

1912	Hannes Kolehmainen, Finland	14m. 36.6s
1920	Joseph Guillemot, France	14m. 55.6s
1924	Paavo Nurmi, Finland	14m. 31.2s
1928	Willie Ritola, Finland	14m. 38s
1932	Lauri Lehtinen, Finland	14m. 30s
1936	Gunnar Hockert, Finland	14m. 22.2s
1948	Gaston Reiff, Belgium	14m. 17.6s
1952	Emil Zatopek, Czechoslovakia	14m. 6.6s
1956	Vladimir Kuts, USSR	13m. 39.6s
1960	Murray Halberg, New Zealand	13m. 43.4s
1964	Bob Schul, United States	13m. 48.8s
1968	Mohamed Gammoudi, Tunisia	14m. 05.0s
1972	Lasse Viren, Finland	13m. 26.4s
1976	Lasse Viren, Finland	13m. 24.76s
1980	Miruts Yifter, Ethiopia	13m. 21.0s
1984	Said Aouita, Morocco	13m. 05.59s*
1988	John Ngugi, Kenya	13m. 11.70s
1992	Dieter Baumann, Germany	13m. 12.52s
1996	Venuste Niyongabo, Burundi	13m. 07.96s

10,000-Meter Run

1912	Hannes Kolehmainen, Finland	31m. 20.8s
1920	Paavo Nurmi, Finland	31m. 45.8s
1924	Willie Ritola, Finland	30m. 23.2s
1928	Paavo Nurmi, Finland	30m. 18.8s
1932	Janusz Kusocinski, Poland	30m. 11.4s
1936	Ilmari Salminen, Finland	30m. 15.4s
1948	Emil Zatopek, Czechoslovakia	29m. 59.6s
1952	Emil Zatopek, Czechoslovakia	29m. 17.0s
1956	Vladimir Kuts, USSR	28m. 45.6s
1960	Pyotr Bolotnikov, USSR	28m. 32.2s
1964	Billy Mills, United States	28m. 24.4s
1968	Naftali Temu, Kenya	29m. 27.4s
1972	Lasse Viren, Finland	27m. 38.4s
1976	Lasse Viren, Finland	27m. 40.38s
1980	Miruts Yifter, Ethiopia	27m. 42.7s
1984	Alberto Cova, Italy	27m. 47.54s
1988	Brahim Boutaib, Morocco	27m. 21.46s
1992	Khalid Skah, Morocco	27m. 46.70s
1996	Haile Gebrselassie, Ethiopia	27m. 07.34s*

110-Meter Hurdles

1896	Thomas Curtis, United States	17.6s
1900	Alvin Kraenzlein, United States	15.4s
1904	Frederick Schule, United States	16s
1908	Forrest Smithson, United States	15s
1912	Frederick Kelly, United States	15.1s
1920	Earl Thomson, Canada	14.8s
1924	Daniel Kinsey, United States	15s
1928	Sydney Atkinson, South Africa	14.8s
1932	George Saling, United States	14.6s
1936	Forrest Towns, United States	14.2s
1948	William Porter, United States	13.9s
1952	Harrison Dillard, United States	13.7s
1956	Lee Calhoun, United States	13.5s
1960	Lee Calhoun, United States	13.8s
1964	Hayes Jones, United States	13.6s
1968	Willie Davenport, United States	13.3s
1972	Rod Milburn, United States	13.24s
1976	Guy Drut, France	13.30s
1980	Thomas Munkelt, E. Germany	13. 39s
1984	Roger Kingdom, United States	13.20s
1988	Roger Kingdom, United States	12.98s
1992	Mark McCoy, Canada	13.12s
1996	Allen Johnson, United States	12.95s*

400-Meter Hurdles

1900	J.W.B. Tewksbury, United States	57.6s
1904	Harry Hillman, United States	53s
1908	Charles Bacon, United States	55s
1920	Frank Loomis, United States	54s
1924	F. Morgan Taylor, United States	52.6s
1928	Lord Burghley, Great Britain	53.4s
1932	Robert Tisdall, Ireland	51.7s
1936	Glenn Hardin, United States	52.4s
1948	Roy Cochran, United States	51.1s
1952	Charles Moore, United States	50.8s
1956	Glenn Davis, United States	50.1s
1960	Glenn Davis, United States	49.3s
1964	Rex Cawley, United States	49.6s
1968	Dave Hemery, Great Britain	48.12s

1972	John Akii-Bua, Uganda	47.82s
1976	Edwin Moses, United States	47.64s
1980	Volker Beck, E. Germany	48.70s
1984	Edwin Moses, United States	47.75s
1988	Andre Phillips, United States	47.19s
1992	Kevin Young, United States	46.78s*
1996	Derrick Adkins, United States	47.54s

400-Meter Relay

1912	Great Britain	42.4s
1920	United States	42.2s
1924	United States	41s
1928	United States	41s
1932	United States	40s
1936	United States	39.8s
1948	United States	40.6s
1952	United States	40.1s
1956	United States	39.5s
1960	Germany (U.S. disqualified)	39.5s
1964	United States	39.0s
1968	United States	38.2s
1972	United States	38.19s
1976	United States	38.33s
1980	USSR	38.26s
1984	United States	37.83s
1988	USSR (U.S. disqualified)	38.19s
1992	United States	37.40s*
1996	Canada	37.69s

1,600-Meter Relay

1908	United States	3m. 29.4s
1912	United States	3m. 16.6s
1920	Great Britain	3m. 22.2s
1924	United States	3m. 16s
1928	United States	3m. 14.2s
1932	United States	3m. 8.2s
1936	Great Britain	3m. 9s
1948	United States	3m. 10.4s
1952	Jamaica	3m. 03.9s
1956	United States	3m. 04.8s
1960	United States	3m. 02.2s
1964	United States	3m. 00.7s
1968	United States	2m. 56.16s
1972	Kenya	2m. 59.8s
1976	United States	2m. 58.65s
1980	USSR	3m. 01.1s
1984	United States	2m. 57.91s
1988	United States	2m. 56.16s
1992	United States	2m. 55.74s*
1996	United States	2m. 55.99s

3,000-Meter Steeplechase

1920	Percy Hodge, Great Britain	10m. 0.4s
1924	Willie Ritola, Finland	9m. 33.6s
1928	Toivo Loukola, Finland	9m. 21.8s
1932	Volmari Iso-Hollo, Finland	10m. 33.4s
	(About 3,450 m; extra lap by error.)	
1936	Volmari Iso-Hollo, Finland	9m. 3.8s
1948	Thore Sjoestrand, Sweden	9m. 4.6s
1952	Horace Ashenfelter, United States	8m. 45.4s
1956	Chris Brasher, Great Britain	8m. 41.2s
1960	Zdzislaw Krzyszkowiak, Poland	8m. 34.2s
1964	Gaston Roelants, Belgium	8m. 30.8s
1968	Amos Biwott, Kenya	8m. 51s
1972	Kipchoge Keino, Kenya	8m. 23.6s
1976	Anders Garderud, Sweden	8m. 08.2s
1980	Bronislaw Malinowski, Poland	8m. 09.7s
1984	Julius Korir, Kenya	8m. 11.8s
1988	Julius Kariuki, Kenya	8m. 05.51s*
1992	Matthew Birir, Kenya	8m. 08.84s
1996	Joseph Keter, Kenya	8m. 07.12s

20-Kilometer Walk

1956	Leonid Spirin, USSR	1h. 31m. 27.4s
1960	Vladimir Golubnichy, USSR	1h. 33m. 7.2s
1964	Kenneth Mathews, Great Britain	1h. 29m. 34.0s
1968	Vladimir Golubnichy, USSR	1h. 33m. 58.4s
1972	Peter Frenkel, E. Germany	1h. 26m. 42.4s
1976	Daniel Bautista, Mexico	1h. 24m. 40.6s
1980	Maurizio Damilano, Italy	1h. 23m. 35.5s
1984	Ernesto Canto, Mexico	1h. 23m. 13.0s
1988	Josef Pribilinec, Czechoslovakia	1h. 19m. 57.0s*
1992	Daniel Plaza Montero, Spain	1h. 21m. 45.0s
1996	Jefferson Perez, Ecuador	1h. 20m. 7s

50-Kilometer Walk

1932	Thomas W. Green, Great Britain	4h. 50m. 10s
1936	Harold Whitlock, Great Britain	4h. 30m. 41.4s
1948	John Ljunggren, Sweden	4h. 41m. 52s
1952	Giuseppe Dordoni, Italy	4h. 28m. 07.8s
1956	Norman Read, New Zealand	4h. 30m. 42.8s
1960	Donald Thompson, Great Britain	4h. 25m. 30s
1964	Abdon Pamich, Italy	4h. 11m. 12.4s
1968	Christoph Hohne, E. Germany	4h. 20m. 13.6s
1972	Bern Kannenberg, W. Germany	3h. 56m. 11.6s
1980	Hartwig Gauter, E. Germany	3h. 49m. 24.0s
1984	Raul Gonzalez, Mexico	3h. 47m. 26.0s
1988	Vayachslav Ivanenko, USSR	3h. 38m. 29.0s*
1992	Andrei Perlov, Unified Team	3h. 50m. 13.0s
1996	Robert Korzeniowski, Poland	3h. 43m. 30s

Marathon

1896	Spiridon Loues, Greece	2h. 58m. 50s
1900	Michel Theato, France	2h. 59m. 45s
1904	Thomas Hicks, United States	3h. 28m. 63s
1908	John J. Hayes, United States	2h. 55m. 18.4s
1912	Kenneth McArthur, South Africa	2h. 36m. 54.8s
1920	Hannes Kolehmainen, Finland	2h. 32m. 35.8s
1924	Albin Stenroos, Finland	2h. 41m. 22.6s
1928	A.B. El Ouafi, France	2h. 32m. 57s
1932	Juan Zabala, Argentina	2h. 31m. 36s
1936	Kijung Son, Japan (Korean)	2h. 29m. 19.2s
1948	Delfo Cabrera, Argentina	2h. 34m. 51.6s
1952	Emil Zatopek, Czechoslovakia	2h. 23m. 03.2s
1956	Alain Mimoun, France	2h. 25m.
1960	Abebe Bikila, Ethiopia	2h. 15m. 16.2s
1964	Abebe Bikila, Ethiopia	2h. 12m. 11.2s
1968	Mamo Wolde, Ethiopia	2h. 20m. 26.4s
1972	Frank Shorter, United States	2h. 12m. 19.8s
1976	Waldemar Cierpinski, E. Germany	2h. 09m. 55s
1980	Waldemar Cierpinski, E. Germany	2h. 11m. 03s
1984	Carlos Lopes, Portugal	2h. 09m. 21s*
1988	Gelindo Bordin, Italy	2h. 10m. 32s
1992	Hwang Young-Cho, S. Korea	2h. 13m. 23s
1996	Josia Thugwane, South Africa	2h. 12m. 36s

High Jump

1896	Ellery Clark, United States	5ft. 11 1-4 in.
1900	Irving Baxter, United States	6ft. 2 4-5 in.
1904	Samuel Jones, United States	5ft. 11 in.
1908	Harry Porter, United States	6ft. 3 in.
1912	Alma Richards, United States	6ft. 4 in.
1920	Richmond Landon, United States	6ft. 4 in.
1924	Harold Osborn, United States	6ft. 6 in.
1928	Robert W. King, United States	6ft. 4 1-2 in.
1932	Duncan McNaughton, Canada	6ft. 5 5-8 in.
1936	Cornelius Johnson, United States	6ft. 8 in.
1948	John L. Winter, Australia	6ft. 6 in.
1952	Walter Davis, United States	6ft. 8.32 in.
1956	Charles Dumas, United States	6ft. 11 1-2 in.
1960	Robert Shavlakadze, USSR	7ft. 1 in.
1964	Valery Brumel, USSR	7ft. 1 3-4 in.
1968	Dick Fosbury, United States	7ft. 4 1-4 in.
1972	Yuri Tarmak, USSR	7ft. 3 3-4 in.
1976	Jacek Wszola, Poland	7ft. 4 1-2 in.
1980	Gerd Wessig, E. Germany	7ft. 8 3-4 in.
1984	Dietmar Mogenburg, W. Germany	7ft. 8 1-2 in.
1988	Guennadi Avdeenko, USSR	7ft. 9 1-2 in.
1992	Javier Sotomayor, Cuba	7ft. 8 in.
1996	Charles Austin, United States	7ft. 10 in.*

Long Jump

1896	Ellery Clark, United States	20ft. 10 in.
1900	Alvin Kraenzlein, United States	23ft. 6 3-4 in.
1904	Myer Prinstein, United States	24ft. 1 in.
1908	Frank Irons, United States	24ft. 6 1-2 in.
1912	Albert Gutterson, United States	24ft. 11 1-4 in.
1920	William Petterssen, Sweden	23ft. 5 1-2 in.
1924	DeHart Hubbard, United States	24ft. 5 in.
1928	Edward B. Hamm, United States	25ft. 4 1-2 in.
1932	Edward Gordon, United States	25ft. 3-4 in.
1936	Jesse Owens, United States	26ft. 5 1-2 in.
1948	William Steele, United States	25ft. 8 in.
1952	Jerome Biffle, United States	24ft. 10 in.
1956	Gregory Bell, United States	25ft. 8 1-4 in.
1960	Ralph Boston, United States	26ft. 7 3-4 in.
1964	Lynn Davies, Great Britain	26ft. 5 3-4 in.
1968	Bob Beamon, United States	29ft. 2 1-2 in.*
1972	Randy Williams, United States	27ft. 1-2 in.
1976	Arnie Robinson, United States	27ft. 4 1-2 in.

1980	Lutz Dombrowski, E. Germany	28ft. 1-4 in.
1984	Carl Lewis, United States	28ft. 1-4 in.
1988	Carl Lewis, United States	28ft. 7 1-4 in.
1992	Carl Lewis, United States	28ft. 5 1-2 in.
1996	Carl Lewis, United States	27ft. 10 3-4 in.

Triple Jump

1896	James Connolly, United States	44ft. 11 3-4 in.
1900	Myer Prinstein, United States	47ft. 5 3-4 in.
1904	Myer Prinstein, United States	47 ft.
1908	Timothy Ahearne, Great Britain, Ireland	48ft. 11 1-4 in.
1912	Gustaf Lindblom, Sweden	48ft. 5 1-4 in.
1920	Vilho Tuulos, Finland	47ft. 7 in.
1924	Anthony Winter, Australia	50ft. 11 1-4 in.
1928	Mikio Oda, Japan	49ft. 11 in.
1932	Chuhei Nambu, Japan	51ft. 7 in.
1936	Naoto Tajima, Japan	52ft. 6 in.
1948	Arne Ahman, Sweden	50ft. 6 1-4 in.
1952	Adhemar da Silva, Brazil	53ft. 2 3-4 in.
1956	Adhemar da Silva, Brazil	53ft. 7 3-4 in.
1960	Jozef Schmidt, Poland	55ft. 2 in.
1964	Jozef Schmidt, Poland	55ft. 3 1-2 in.
1968	Viktor Saneev, USSR	57ft. 3-4 in.
1972	Viktor Saneev, USSR	56ft. 11 in.
1976	Viktor Saneev, USSR	56ft. 8 3-4 in.
1980	Jaak Uudmae, USSR	56ft. 11 1-4 in.
1984	Al Joyner, United States	56ft. 7 1-2 in.
1988	Hristo Markov, Bulgaria	57ft. 9 1-4 in.
1992	Mike Conley, United States	57ft. 10 1-4 in.
1996	Kenny Harrison, United States	59ft. 4 1-4 in.*

Discus Throw

1896	Robert Garrett, United States	95ft. 7 1-2 in.
1900	Rudolf Bauer, Hungary	118ft. 3 in.
1904	Martin Sheridan, United States	128ft. 10 1-2 in.
1908	Martin Sheridan, United States	134ft. 2 in.
1912	Armas Taipale, Finland	148ft. 3 in.
	Both hands—Armas Taipale, Finland	271ft. 10 1-4 in.
1920	Elmer Niklander, Finland	146ft. 7 in.
1924	Clarence Houser, United States	151ft. 4 in.
1928	Clarence Houser, United States	155ft. 3 in.
1932	John Anderson, United States	162ft. 4 in.
1936	Ken Carpenter, United States	165ft. 7 in.
1948	Adolfo Consolini, Italy	173ft. 2 in.
1952	Sim Iness, United States	180ft. 6.85 in.
1956	Al Oerter, United States	184ft. 10 1-2 in.
1960	Al Oerter, United States	194ft. 2 in.
1964	Al Oerter, United States	200ft. 1 1-2 in.
1968	Al Oerter, United States	212ft. 6 1-2 in.
1972	Ludvik Danek, Czechoslovakia	211ft. 3 in.
1976	Mac Wilkins, United States	221ft. 5.4 in.
1980	Viktor Rashchupkin, USSR	218ft. 8 in.
1984	Rolf Dannenberg, W. Germany	218ft. 6 in.
1988	Jurgen Schult, E. Germany	225ft. 9 1-4 in.
1992	Romas Ubartas, Lithuania	213ft. 7 3-4 in.
1996	Lars Riedel, Germany	227ft. 8 in.*

Hammer Throw

1900	John Flanagan, United States	163ft. 1 in.
1904	John Flanagan, United States	168ft. 1 in.
1908	John Flanagan, United States	170ft. 4 1-4 in.
1912	Matt McGrath, United States	179ft. 7 1-8 in.
1920	Pat Ryan, United States	173ft. 5 5-8 in.
1924	Fred Tootell, United States	174ft. 10 1-8 in.
1928	Patrick O'Callaghan, Ireland	168ft. 7 1-2 in.
1932	Patrick O'Callaghan, Ireland	176ft. 11 1-8 in.
1936	Karl Hein, Germany	185ft. 4 in.
1948	Imre Nemeth, Hungary	183ft. 11 1-2 in.
1952	Jozsef Csermak, Hungary	197ft. 11 9-16 in.
1956	Harold Connolly, United States	207ft. 3 1-2 in.
1960	Vasily Rudenkov, USSR	220ft. 1 5-8 in.
1964	Romuald Klim, USSR	228ft. 9 1-2 in.
1968	Gyula Zsivotsky, USSR	240ft. 8 in.
1972	Anatoli Bondarchuk, USSR	247ft. 8 in.
1976	Yuri Syedykh, USSR	254ft. 4 in.
1980	Yuri Syedykh, USSR	268ft. 4 1-2 in.
1984	Juha Tiainen, Finland	256ft. 2 in.
1988	Sergei Litinov, USSR	278ft. 2 1-2 in.*
1992	Andrey Abduvaliyev, Unified Team	270ft. 9 1-2 in.
1996	Balazs Kiss, Hungary	266ft. 6 in.

Javelin Throw

1908	Erik Lemming, Sweden	178ft. 7 1-2 in.
	Held in middle—Erik Lemming, Sweden	179ft. 10 1-2 in.

1912	Erik Lemming, Sweden	198ft. 11 1-4 in.
	Both hands, Julius Saaristo, Finland	358ft. 11 7-8 in.
1920	Jonni Myyra, Finland	215ft. 9 3-4 in.
1924	Jonni Myyra, Finland	206ft. 6 3-4 in.
1928	Eric Lundkvist, Sweden	218ft. 6 1-8 in.
1932	Matti Jarvinen, Finland	238ft. 6 in.
1936	Gerhard Stoeck, Germany	235ft. 8 5-16 in.
1948	Tapio Rautavaara, Finland	228ft. 10 1-2 in.
1952	Cy Young, United States	242ft. 0.79 in.
1956	Egil Danielson, Norway	281ft. 2 1-4 in.
1960	Viktor Tsibulenko, USSR	277ft. 8 3-8 in.
1964	Pauli Nevala, Finland	271ft. 2 1-2 in.
1968	Janis Lusis, USSR	295ft. 7 1-4 in.
1972	Klaus Wolfermann, W. Germany	296ft. 10 in.
1976	Miklos Nemeth, Hungary	310ft. 4 in.
1980	Dainis Kula, USSR	299ft. 2 3-8 in.
1984	Arto Haerkoenen, Finland	284ft. 8 in.
1988	Tapio Korjus, Finland	276ft. 6 in.
1992	Jan Zelezny, Czechoslovakia	294ft. 2 in.*(a)
1996	Jan Zelezny, Czech Republic	289ft. 3 in.

(a) New records were kept after javelin was modified in 1986.

Pole Vault

1896	William Hoyt, United States	10ft. 10 in.
1900	Irving Baxter, United States	10ft. 10 in.
1904	Charles Dvorak, United States	11ft. 5 3-4 in.
1908	A. C. Gilbert, United States	
	Edward Cook Jr., United States	12ft. 2 in.
1912	Harry Babcock, United States	12ft. 11 1-2 in.
1920	Frank Foss, United States	13ft. 5 in.
1924	Lee Barnes, United States	12ft. 11 1-2 in.
1928	Sabin W. Carr, United States	13ft. 9 1-4 in.
1932	William Miller, United States	14ft. 1 3-4 in.
1936	Earle Meadows, United States	14ft. 3 1-4 in.
1948	Guinn Smith, United States	14ft. 1 1-4 in.
1952	Robert Richards, United States	14ft. 11 in.
1956	Robert Richards, United States	14ft. 11 1-2 in.
1960	Don Bragg, United States	15ft. 5 in.
1964	Fred Hansen, United States	16ft. 8 3-4 in.
1968	Bob Seagren, United States	17ft. 8 1-2 in.
1972	Wolfgang Nordwig, E. Germany	18ft. 1-2 in.
1976	Tadeusz Slusarski, Poland	18ft. 1-2 in.
1980	Wladyslaw Kozakiewicz, Poland	18ft. 11 1-2 in.
1984	Pierre Quinon, France	18ft. 10 1-4 in.
1988	Sergei Bubka, USSR	19ft. 4 1-4 in.
1992	Maksim Tarassov, Unified Team	19ft. 1-4 in.
1996	Jean Galfione, France	19ft. 5 in.*

16-lb. Shot Put

1896	Robert Garrett, United States	36ft. 9 3-4 in.
1900	Richard Sheldon, United States	46ft. 3 1-4 in.

1904	Ralph Rose, United States	48ft. 7 in.
1908	Ralph Rose, United States	46ft. 7 1-2 in.
1912	Pat McDonald, United States	50ft. 4 in.
	Both hands—Ralph Rose, United States	90ft. 5 1-2 in.
1920	Ville Porhola, Finland	48ft. 7 1-4 in.
1924	Clarence Houser, United States	49ft. 2 1-4 in.
1928	John Kuck, United States	52ft. 3-4 in.
1932	Leo Sexton, United States	52ft. 6 in.
1936	Hans Woellke, Germany	53ft. 1 3-4 in.
1948	Wilbur Thompson, United States	56ft. 2 in.
1952	Parry O'Brien, United States	57ft. 1-2 in.
1956	Parry O'Brien, United States	60ft. 11 1-4 in.
1960	William Nieder, United States	64ft. 6 3-4 in.
1964	Dallas Long, United States	66ft. 8 1-2 in.
1968	Randy Matson, United States	67ft. 4 3-4 in.
1972	Wladyslaw Komar, Poland	69ft. 6 in.
1976	Udo Beyer, E. Germany	69ft. 3-4 in.
1980	Vladimir Kiselyov, USSR	70ft. 1-2 in.
1984	Alessandro Andrei, Italy	69ft. 9 in.
1988	Ulf Timmermann, E. Germany	73ft. 8 3-4 in.*
1992	Michael Stulce, United States	71ft. 2 1-4 in.
1996	Randy Barnes, United States	70ft. 11 1-4 in.

Decathlon

1912	Hugo Wieslander, Sweden	7,724.49 pts.(a)
1920	Helge Lovland, Norway	6,804.35 pts.
1924	Harold Osborn, United States	7,710.77 pts.
1928	Paavo Yrjola, Finland	8,053.29 pts.
1932	James Bausch, United States	8,462.23 pts.
1936	Glenn Morris, United States	7,900 pts.
1948	Robert Mathias, United States	7,139 pts.
1952	Robert Mathias, United States	7,887 pts.
1956	Milton Campbell, United States	7,937 pts.
1960	Rafer Johnson, United States	8,392 pts.
1964	Willi Holdorf, Germany	7,887 pts.(b)
1968	Bill Toomey, United States	8,193 pts.
1972	Nikolai Avilov, USSR	8,454 pts.
1976	Bruce Jenner, United States	8,617 pts.
1980	Daley Thompson, Great Britain	8,495 pts.
1984	Daley Thompson, Great Britain	8,798 pts.*(c)
1988	Christian Schenk, E. Germany	8,488 pts.
1992	Robert Zmelik, Czechoslovakia	8,611 pts.
1996	Dan O'Brien, United States	8,824 pts.

(a) Jim Thorpe of the U.S. won the 1912 Decathlon with 8,413 pts. but was disqualified and had to return his medals because he had played professional baseball prior to the Olympic games. The medals were restored posthumously in 1982. (b) Former point systems used prior to 1964. (c) Scoring change effective Apr. 1985; Thompson's readjusted score is 8,847 pts.

Track and Field—Women

100-Meter Run

1928	Elizabeth Robinson, United States	12.2s
1932	Stella Walsh, Poland (a)	11.9s
1936	Helen Stephens, United States	11.5s
1948	Francina Blankers-Koen, Netherlands	11.9s
1952	Marjorie Jackson, Australia	11.5s
1956	Betty Cuthbert, Australia	11.5s
1960	Wilma Rudolph, United States	11.0s
1964	Wyomia Tyus, United States	11.4s
1968	Wyomia Tyus, United States	11.0s
1972	Renate Stecher, E. Germany	11.07s
1976	Annegret Richter, W. Germany	11.08s
1980	Lyudmila Kondratyeva, USSR	11.6s
1984	Evelyn Ashford, United States	10.97s
1988	Florence Griffith-Joyner, United States	10.54s*
1992	Gail Devers, United States	10.82s
1996	Gail Devers, United States	10.94s

(a) A 1980 autopsy determined that Walsh was a man.

200-Meter Run

1948	Francina Blankers-Koen, Netherlands	24.4s
1952	Marjorie Jackson, Australia	23.7s
1956	Betty Cuthbert, Australia	23.4s
1960	Wilma Rudolph, United States	24.0s
1964	Edith McGuire, United States	23.0s
1968	Irena Szewinska, Poland	22.5s
1972	Renate Stecher, E. Germany	22.40s
1976	Barbel Eckert, E. Germany	22.37s

1980	Barbel Wockel, E. Germany	22.03s
1984	Valerie Brisco-Hooks, United States	21.81s
1988	Florence Griffith-Joyner, United States	21.34s*
1992	Gwen Torrence, United States	21.81s
1996	Marie-Jose Perec, France	22.12s

400-Meter Run

1964	Betty Cuthbert, Australia	52s
1968	Colette Besson, France	52s
1972	Monika Zehrt, E. Germany	51.08s
1976	Irena Szewinska, Poland	49.29s
1980	Marita Koch, E. Germany	48.88s
1984	Valerie Brisco-Hooks, United States	48.83s
1988	Olga Bryzgina, USSR	48.65s
1992	Marie-Jose Perec, France	48.83s
1996	Marie-Jose Perec, France	48.25s*

800-Meter Run

1928	Lina Radke, Germany	2m. 16.8s
1960	Ludmila Shevtsova, USSR	2m. 4.3s
1964	Ann Packer, Great Britain	2m. 1.1s
1968	Madeline Manning, United States	2m. 0.9s
1972	Hildegard Falck, W. Germany	1m. 58.6s
1976	Tatyana Kazankina, USSR	1m. 54.94s
1980	Nadezhda Olizarenko, USSR	1m. 53.5s*
1984	Doina Melinte, Romania	1m. 57.6s
1988	Sigrun Wodars, E. Germany	1m. 56.10s
1992	Ellen Van Langen, Netherlands	1m. 55.54s
1996	Svetlana Masterkova, Russia	1m. 57.73s

1,500-Meter Run

1972	Lyudmila Bragina, USSR	4m. 01.4s
1976	Tatyana Kazankina, USSR	4m. 05.48s
1980	Tatyana Kazankina, USSR	3m. 56.6s
1984	Gabriella Dorio, Italy	4m. 03.25s
1988	Paula Ivan, Romania	3m. 53.96s*
1992	Hassiba Boulmerka, Algeria	3m. 55.30s
1996	Svetlana Masterkova, Russia	4m. 00.83s

3,000-Meter Run

1984	Maricica Puica, Romania	8m. 35.96s
1988	Tatyana Samolenko, USSR	8m. 26.53s*
1992	Elena Romanova, Unified Team	8m. 46.04s

5,000-Meter Run

1996	Wang Junxia, China	14m. 59.88s*

10,000-Meter Run

1988	Olga Boldarenko, USSR	31m. 44.69s
1992	Derartu Tulu, Ethiopia	31m. 06.02s
1996	Fernanda Ribeiro, Portugal	31m. 01.63s*

100-Meter Hurdles

1972	Annelie Ehrhardt, E. Germany	12.59s
1976	Johanna Schaller, E. Germany	12.77s
1980	Vera Komisova, USSR	12.56s
1984	Benita Brown-Fitzgerald, United States	12.84s
1988	Jordanka Donkova, Bulgaria	12.38s*
1992	Paraskevi Patoulidou, Greece	12.64s
1996	Ludmila Enquist, Sweden	12.58s

400-Meter Hurdles

1984	Nawal el Moutawakil, Morocco	54.61s
1988	Debra Flintoff-King, Australia	53.17s
1992	Sally Gunnell, Great Britain	53.23s
1996	Deon Hemmings, Jamaica	52.82s*

400-Meter Relay

1928	Canada	48.4s
1932	United States	46.9s
1936	United States	46.9s
1948	Netherlands	47.5s
1952	United States	45.9s
1956	Australia	44.5s
1960	United States	44.5s
1964	Poland	43.6s
1968	United States	42.8s
1972	West Germany	42.81s
1976	East Germany	42.55s
1980	East Germany	41.60s*
1984	United States	41.65s
1988	United States	41.98s
1992	United States	42.11s
1996	United States	41.95s

1,600-Meter Relay

1972	East Germany	3m. 23s
1976	East Germany	3m. 19.23s
1980	USSR	3m. 20.02s
1984	United States	3m. 18.29s
1988	USSR	3 m. 15.18s*
1992	Unified Team	3m. 20.20s
1996	United States	3m. 20.91s

10 Kilometer Walk

1992	Chen Yueling, China	44m. 32s
1996	Elena Nikolayeva, Russia	41m. 49s*

Marathon

1984	Joan Benoit, United States	2h. 24m. 52s*
1988	Rosa Mota, Portugal	2h. 25m. 40s
1992	Valentina Yegorova, Unified Team	2h. 32m. 41s
1996	Fatuma Roba, Ethiopia	2h. 26m. 05s

High Jump

1928	Ethel Catherwood, Canada	5ft. 2 1-2 in.
1932	Jean Shiley, United States	5ft. 5 1-4 in.
1936	Ibolya Csak, Hungary	5ft. 3 in.
1948	Alice Coachman, United States	5ft. 6 1-8 in.
1952	Esther Brand, South Africa	5ft. 5 3-4 in.
1956	Mildred L. McDaniel, United States	5ft. 9 1-4 in.
1960	Iolanda Balas, Romania	6ft. 3-4 in.
1964	Iolanda Balas, Romania	6ft. 2 3-4 in.
1968	Miloslava Reskova, Czechoslovakia	5ft. 11 1-2 in.
1972	Ulrike Meyfarth, W. Germany	6ft. 4 in.
1976	Rosemarie Ackermann, E. Germany	6ft. 3 3-4 in.
1980	Sara Simeoni, Italy	6ft. 5 1-2 in.
1984	Ulrike Meyfarth, W. Germany	6ft. 7 1-2 in.
1988	Louise Ritter, United States	6ft. 8 in.
1992	Heike Henkel, Germany	6ft. 7 1-2 in.
1996	Stefka Kostadinova, Bulgaria	6ft. 8 3-4 in.*

Long Jump

1948	Olga Gyarmati, Hungary	18ft. 8 1-4 in.
1952	Yvette Williams, New Zealand	20ft. 5 3-4 in.
1956	Elzbieta Krzeskinska, Poland	20ft. 9 3-4 in.
1960	Vyera Krepkina, USSR	20ft. 10 3-4 in.
1964	Mary Rand, Great Britain	22ft. 2 1-4 in.
1968	Viorica Viscopoleanu, Romania	22ft. 4 1-2 in.
1972	Heidemarie Rosendahl, W. Germany	22ft. 3 in.
1976	Angela Voigt, E. Germany	22ft. 3-4 in.
1980	Tatyana Kolpakova, USSR	23ft. 2 in.
1984	Anisoara Stanciu, Romania	22ft. 10 in.
1988	Jackie Joyner-Kersee, United States	24ft. 3 1-2 in.*
1992	Heike Drechsler, Germany	23ft. 5 1-4 in.
1996	Chioma Ajunwa, Nigeria	23ft. 4 1-2 in.

Triple Jump

1996	Inessa Kravets, Ukraine	50ft. 3 1-2 in. *

Discus Throw

1928	Helena Konopacka, Poland	129ft. 11 3-4 in.
1932	Lillian Copeland, United States	133ft. 2 in.
1936	Gisela Mauermayer, Germany	156ft. 3 in.
1948	Micheline Ostermeyer, France	137ft. 6 1-2 in.
1952	Nina Romaschkova, USSR	168ft. 8 in.
1956	Olga Fikotova, Czechoslovakia	176ft. 1 in.
1960	Nina Ponomareva, USSR	180ft. 8 1-4 in.
1964	Tamara Press, USSR	187ft. 10 in.
1968	Lia Manoliu, Romania	191ft. 2 in.
1972	Faina Melnik, USSR	218ft. 7 in.
1976	Evelin Schlaak, E. Germany	226ft. 4 in.
1980	Evelin Jahl, E. Germany	229ft. 6 in.
1984	Ria Stalman, Netherlands	214ft. 5 in.
1988	Martina Hellmann, E. Germany	237ft. 2 1-4 in.*
1992	Maritza Marten Garcia, Cuba	222ft. 10 in.
1996	Ilke Wyludda, Germany	228ft. 6 in.

Javelin Throw

1932	"Babe" Didrikson, United States	143ft. 4 in.
1936	Tilly Fleischer, Germany	148ft. 2 3-4 in.
1948	Herma Bauma, Austria	149ft. 6 in.
1952	Dana Zatopkova, Czechoslovakia	165ft. 7 in.
1956	Inese Jaunzeme, USSR	176ft. 8 in.
1960	Elvira Ozolina, USSR	183ft. 8 in.
1964	Mihaela Penes, Romania	198ft. 7 1-2 in.
1968	Angela Nemeth, Hungary	198ft. 1-2 in.
1972	Ruth Fuchs, E. Germany	209ft. 7 in.
1976	Ruth Fuchs, E. Germany	216ft. 4 in.
1980	Maria Colon, Cuba	224ft. 5 in.
1984	Tessa Sanderson, Great Britain	228ft. 2 in.
1988	Petra Felke, E. Germany	245 ft.*
1992	Silke Renke, Germany	224ft. 2 1-2 in.
1996	Heli Rantanen, Finland	222ft. 11 in.

Shot Put (8 lb., 13 oz.)

1948	Micheline Ostermeyer, France	45ft. 1 1-2 in.
1952	Galina Zybina, USSR	50ft. 1 3-4 in.
1956	Tamara Tishkyevich, USSR	54ft. 5 in.
1960	Tamara Press, USSR	56ft. 10 in.
1964	Tamara Press, USSR	59ft. 6 1-4 in.
1968	Margitta Gummel, E. Germany	64ft. 4 in.
1972	Nadezhda Chizova, USSR	69ft.
1976	Ivanka Hristova, Bulgaria	69ft. 5 1-4 in.
1980	Ilona Slupianek, E. Germany	73ft. 6 1-4 in.*
1984	Claudia Losch, W. Germany	67ft. 2 1-4 in.
1988	Natalya Lisovskaya, USSR	72ft. 11 1-2 in.
1992	Svetlana Kriveleva, Unified Team	69ft. 1 1-2in.
1996	Astrid Kumbernuss, Germany	67ft. 5 1-2in.

Heptathlon

1984	Glynis Nunn, Australia	6,390 pts.	1992	Jackie Joyner-Kersee, United States	7,044 pts.
1988	Jackie Joyner-Kersee, United States	7,215 pts.*	1996	Ghada Shouaa, Syria	6,780 pts.

Swimming and Diving—Men

50-Meter Freestyle

1988	Matt Biondi, U.S.	22.14
1992	Aleksandr Popov, Unified Team	21.91*
1996	Aleksandr Popov, Russia	22.13

100-Meter Freestyle

1896	Alfred Hajos, Hungary	1:22.2
1904	Zoltan de Halmay, Hungary (100 yards)	1:02.8
1908	Charles Daniels, U.S.	1:05.6
1912	Duke P. Kahanamoku, U.S.	1:03.4
1920	Duke P. Kahanamoku, U.S.	1:01.4
1924	John Weissmuller, U.S.	59.0
1928	John Weissmuller, U.S.	58.6
1932	Yasuji Miyazaki, Japan	58.2
1936	Ferenc Csik, Hungary	57.6
1948	Wally Ris, U.S.	57.3
1952	Clark Scholes, U.S.	57.4
1956	Jon Henricks, Australia	55.4
1960	John Devitt, Australia	55.2
1964	Don Schollander, U.S.	53.4
1968	Mike Wenden, Australia	52.2
1972	Mark Spitz, U.S.	51.22
1976	Jim Montgomery, U.S.	49.99
1980	Jorg Woithe, E. Germany	50.40
1984	Rowdy Gaines, U.S.	49.80
1988	Matt Biondi, U.S.	48.63*
1992	Aleksandr Popov, Unified Team	49.02
1996	Aleksandr Popov, Russia	48.74

200-Meter Freestyle

1968	Mike Wenden, Australia	1:55.2
1972	Mark Spitz, U.S.	1:52.78
1976	Bruce Furniss, U.S.	1:50.29
1980	Sergei Kopliakov, USSR	1:49.81
1984	Michael Gross, W. Germany	1:47.44
1988	Duncan Armstrong, Australia	1:47.25
1992	Yevgeny Sadovyi, Unified Team	1:46.70*
1996	Danyon Loader, New Zealand	1:47.63

400-Meter Freestyle

1904	C. M. Daniels, U.S. (440 yards)	6:16.2
1908	Henry Taylor, Great Britain	5:36.8
1912	George Hodgson, Canada	5:24.4
1920	Norman Ross, U.S.	5:26.8
1924	John Weissmuller, U.S.	5:04.2
1928	Albert Zorilla, Argentina	5:01.6
1932	Clarence Crabbe, U.S.	4:48.4
1936	Jack Medica, U.S.	4:44.5
1948	William Smith, U.S.	4:41.0
1952	Jean Boiteux, France	4:30.7
1956	Murray Rose, Australia	4:27.3
1960	Murray Rose, Australia	4:18.3
1964	Don Schollander, U.S.	4:12.2
1968	Mike Burton, U.S.	4:09.0
1972	Brad Cooper, Australia	4:00.27
1976	Brian Goodell, U.S.	3:51.93
1980	Vladimir Salnikov, USSR	3:51.31
1984	George DiCarlo, U.S.	3:51.23
1988	Ewe Dassler, E. Germany	3:46.95
1992	Yevgeny Sadovyi, Unified Team	3:45.00*
1996	Danyon Loader, New Zealand	3:47.97

1,500-Meter Freestyle

1908	Henry Taylor, Great Britain	22:48.4
1912	George Hodgson, Canada	22:00.0
1920	Norman Ross, U.S.	22:23.2
1924	Andrew Charlton, Australia	20:06.6
1928	Arne Borg, Sweden	19:51.8
1932	Kusuo Kitamura, Japan	19:12.4
1936	Noboru Terada, Japan	19:13.7
1948	James McLane, U.S.	19:18.5
1952	Ford Konno, U.S.	18:30.3
1956	Murray Rose, Australia	17:58.9

1960	Jon Konrads, Australia	17:19.6
1964	Robert Windle, Australia	17:01.7
1968	Mike Burton, U.S.	16:38.9
1972	Mike Burton, U.S.	15:52.58
1976	Brian Goodell, U.S.	15:02.40
1980	Vladimir Salnikov, USSR	14:58.27
1984	Michael O'Brien, U.S.	15:05.20
1988	Vladimir Salnikov, USSR	15:00.40
1992	Kieren Perkins, Australia	14:43.48*
1996	Kieren Perkins, Australia	14:56.40

100-Meter Backstroke

1904	Walter Brack, Germany (100 yds.)	1:16.8
1908	Arno Bieberstein, Germany	1:24.6
1912	Harry Hebner, U.S.	1:21.2
1920	Warren Kealoha, U.S.	1:15.2
1924	Warren Kealoha, U.S.	1:13.2
1928	George Kojac, U.S.	1:08.2
1932	Masaji Kiyokawa, Japan	1:08.6
1936	Adolph Kiefer, U.S.	1:05.9
1948	Allen Stack, U.S.	1:06.4
1952	Yoshi Oyakawa, U.S.	1:05.4
1956	David Thiele, Australia	1:02.2
1960	David Thiele, Australia	1:01.9
1968	Roland Matthes, E. Germany	58.7
1972	Roland Matthes, E. Germany	56.58
1976	John Naber, U.S.	55.49
1980	Bengt Baron, Sweden	56.33
1984	Rick Carey, U.S.	55.79
1988	Daichi Suzuki, Japan	55.05
1992	Mark Tewksbury, Canada	53.98*
1996	Jeff Rouse, U.S.	54.10

200-Meter Backstroke

1964	Jed Graef, U.S.	2:10.3
1968	Roland Matthes, E. Germany	2:09.6
1972	Roland Matthes, E. Germany	2:02.82
1976	John Naber, U.S.	1:59.19
1980	Sandor Wladar, Hungary	2:01.93
1984	Rick Carey, U.S.	2:00.23
1988	Igor Polianski, USSR	1:59.37
1992	Martin Lopez-Zubero, Spain	1:58.47*
1996	Brad Bridgewater, U.S.	1:58.54

100-Meter Breaststroke

1968	Don McKenzie, U.S.	1:07.7
1972	Nobutaka Taguchi, Japan	1:04.94
1976	John Hencken, U.S.	1:03.11
1980	Duncan Goodhew, Great Britain	1:03.44
1984	Steve Lundquist, U.S.	1:01.65
1988	Adrian Moorhouse, Great Britain	1:02.04
1992	Nelson Diebel, U.S.	1:01.50
1996	Fred Deburghgraeve, Belgium	1:00.60*

200-Meter Breaststroke

1908	Frederick Holman, Great Britain	3:09.2
1912	Walter Bathe, Germany	3:01.8
1920	Haken Malmroth, Sweden	3:04.4
1924	Robert Skelton, U.S.	2:56.6
1928	Yoshiyuki Tsuruta, Japan	2:48.8
1932	Yoshiyuki Tsuruta, Japan	2:45.4
1936	Tetsuo Hamuro, Japan	2:41.5
1948	Joseph Verdeur, U.S.	2:39.3
1952	John Davies, Australia	2:34.4
1956	Masura Furukawa, Japan	2:34.7
1960	William Mulliken, U.S.	2:37.4
1964	Ian O'Brien, Australia	2:27.8
1968	Felipe Munoz, Mexico	2:28.7
1972	John Hencken, U.S.	2:21.55
1976	David Wilkie, Great Britain	2:15.11
1980	Robertas Zhulpa, USSR	2:15.85
1984	Victor Davis, Canada	2:13.34
1988	Jozsef Szabo, Hungary	2:13.52
1992	Mike Barrowman, U.S.	2:10.16*
1996	Norbert Rozsa, Hungary	2:12.57

100-Meter Butterfly

1968	Doug Russell, U.S.	55.9
1972	Mark Spitz, U.S.	54.27
1976	Matt Vogel, U.S.	54.35
1980	Par Arvidsson, Sweden	54.92
1984	Michael Gross, W. Germany	53.08
1988	Anthony Nesty, Suriname	53.00
1992	Pablo Morales, U.S.	53.32
1996	Denis Pankratov, Russia	52.27*

200-Meter Butterfly

1956	William Yorzyk, U.S.	2:19.3
1960	Michael Troy, U.S.	2:12.8
1964	Kevin J. Berry, Australia	2:06.6
1968	Carl Robie, U.S.	2:08.7
1972	Mark Spitz, U.S.	2:00.70
1976	Mike Bruner, U.S.	1:59.23
1980	Sergei Fesenko, USSR.	1:59.76
1984	Jon Sieben, Australia	1:57.04
1988	Michael Gross, W. Germany	1:56.94
1992	Mel Stewart, U.S.	1:56.26*
1996	Denis Pankratov, Russia	1:56.51

200-Meter Individual Medley

1968	Charles Hickcox, U.S.	2:12.0
1972	Gunnar Larsson, Sweden	2:07.17
1984	Alex Baumann, Canada	2:01.42
1988	Tamas Darnyi, Hungary	2:00.17
1992	Tamas Darnyi, Hungary	2:00.76
1996	Attila Czene, Hungary	1:59.91*

400-Meter Individual Medley

1964	Dick Roth, U.S.	4:45.4
1968	Charles Hickcox, U.S.	4:48.4
1972	Gunnar Larsson, Sweden	4:31.98
1976	Rod Strachan, U.S.	4:23.68
1980	Aleksandr Sidorenko, USSR	4:22.89
1984	Alex Baumann, Canada	4:17.41
1988	Tamas Darnyi, Hungary	4:14.75
1992	Tamas Darnyi, Hungary	4:14.23*
1996	Tom Dolan, U.S.	4:14.90

400-Meter Freestyle Relay

1964	United States	3:31.2
1968	United States	3:31.7
1972	United States	3:26.42
1984	United States	3:19.03
1988	United States	3:16.53
1992	United States	3:16.74
1996	United States	3:15.41*

800-Meter Freestyle Relay

1908	Great Britain	10:55.6
1912	Australia	10:11.6
1920	United States	10:04.4
1924	United States	9:53.4
1928	United States	9:36.2
1932	Japan	8:58.4
1936	Japan	8:51.5
1948	United States	8:46.0
1952	United States	8:31.1
1956	Australia	8:23.6
1960	United States	8:10.2
1964	United States	7:52.1
1968	United States	7:52.33

1972	United States	7:35.78
1976	United States	7:23.22
1980	USSR	7:23.50
1984	United States	7:15.69
1988	United States	7:12.51
1992	Unified Team	7:11.95*
1996	United States	7:14.84

400-Meter Medley Relay

1960	United States	4:05.4
1964	United States	3:58.4
1968	United States	3:54.9
1972	United States	3:48.16
1976	United States	3:42.22
1980	Australia	3:45.70
1984	United States	3:39.30
1988	United States	3:36.93
1992	United States	3:36.93
1996	United States	3:34.84*

Springboard Diving

		Points
1908	Albert Zurner, Germany	85.5
1912	Paul Guenther, Germany	79.23
1920	Louis Kuehn, U.S	675.40
1924	Albert White, U.S.	97.46
1928	Pete Desjardins, U.S.	185.04
1932	Michael Galitzen, U.S.	161.38
1936	Richard Degener, U.S.	163.57
1948	Bruce Harlan, U.S.	163.64
1952	David Browning, U.S.	205.29
1956	Robert Clotworthy, U.S.	159.56
1960	Gary Tobian, U.S.	170.00
1964	Kenneth Sitzberger, U.S.	159.90
1968	Bernie Wrightson, U.S.	170.15
1972	Vladimir Vasin, USSR	594.09
1976	Phil Boggs, U.S.	619.52
1980	Aleksandr Portnov, USSR	905.02
1984	Greg Louganis, U.S.	754.41
1988	Greg Louganis, U.S.	730.80
1992	Mark Lenzi, U.S.	676.53
1996	Xiong Ni, China	701.46

Platform Diving

		Points
1904	Dr. G.E. Sheldon, U.S.	12.75
1908	Hjalmar Johansson, Sweden	83.75
1912	Erik Adlerz, Sweden	73.94
1920	Clarence Pinkston, U.S.	100.67
1924	Albert White, U.S.	97.46
1928	Pete Desjardins, U.S.	98.74
1932	Harold Smith, U.S.	124.80
1936	Marshall Wayne, U.S.	113.58
1948	Sammy Lee, U.S.	130.05
1952	Sammy Lee, U.S.	156.28
1956	Joaquin Capilla, Mexico	152.44
1960	Robert Webster, U.S.	165.56
1964	Robert Webster, U.S.	148.58
1968	Klaus Dibiasi, Italy	164.18
1972	Klaus Dibiasi, Italy	504.12
1976	Klaus Dibiasi, Italy	600.51
1980	Falk Hoffmann, E. Germany	835.65
1984	Greg Louganis, U.S.	710.91
1988	Greg Louganis, U.S.	638.61
1992	Sun Shuwei, China	677.31
1996	Dmitri Sautin, Russia	692.34

Swimming and Diving—Women

50-Meter Freestyle

1988	Kristin Otto, E. Germany	25.49
1992	Yang Wenyi, China	24.76*
1996	Amy Van Dyken, U.S.	24.87

100-Meter Freestyle

1912	Fanny Durack, Australia	1:22.2
1920	Ethelda Bleibtrey, U.S.	1:13.6
1924	Ethel Lackie, U.S.	1:12.4
1928	Albina Osipowich, U.S.	1:11.0
1932	Helene Madison, U.S.	1:06.8
1936	Hendrika Mastenbroek, Holland	1:05.9

1948	Greta Andersen, Denmark	1:06.3
1952	Katalin Szoke, Hungary	1:06.8
1956	Dawn Fraser, Australia	1:02.0
1960	Dawn Fraser, Australia	1:01.2
1964	Dawn Fraser, Australia	59.5
1968	Jan Henne, U.S.	1:00.0
1972	Sandra Neilson, U.S.	58.59
1976	Kornelia Ender, E. Germany	55.65
1980	Barbara Krause, E. Germany	54.79
1984	(tie) Carrie Steinseifer, U.S.	55.92
	Nancy Hogshead, U.S.	55.92
1988	Kristin Otto, E. Germany	54.93
1992	Zhuang Yong, China	54.64
1996	Li Jingyi, China	54.50*

200-Meter Freestyle

1968	Debbie Meyer, U.S.	2:10.5
1972	Shane Gould, Australia.	2:03.56
1976	Kornelia Ender, E. Germany	1:59.26
1980	Barbara Krause, E. Germany	1:58.33
1984	Mary Wayte, U.S.	1:59.23
1988	Heike Friedrich, E. Germany	1:57.65*
1992	Nicole Haislett, U.S.	1:57.90
1996	Claudia Poll, Costa Rica	1:58.16

400-Meter Freestyle

1924	Martha Norelius, U.S.	6:02.2
1928	Martha Norelius, U.S.	5:42.8
1932	Helene Madison, U.S.	5:28.5
1936	Hendrika Mastenbroek, Netherlands	5:26.4
1948	Ann Curtis, U.S.	5:17.8
1952	Valerie Gyenge, Hungary	5:12.1
1956	Lorraine Crapp, Australia	4:54.6
1960	Susan Chris von Saltza, U.S.	4:50.6
1964	Virginia Duenkel, U.S.	4:43.3
1968	Debbie Meyer, U.S.	4:31.8
1972	Shane Gould, Australia.	4:19.44
1976	Petra Thuemer, E. Germany	4:09.89
1980	Ines Diers, E. Germany	4:08.76
1984	Tiffany Cohen, U.S.	4:07.10
1988	Janet Evans, U.S.	4:03.85*
1992	Dagmar Hase, Germany.	4:07.18
1996	Michelle Smith, Ireland	4:07.25

800-Meter Freestyle

1968	Debbie Meyer, U.S.	9:24.0
1972	Keena Rothhammer, U.S.	8:53.68
1976	Petra Thuemer, E. Germany	8:37.14
1980	Michelle Ford, Australia	8:28.90
1984	Tiffany Cohen, U.S.	8:24.95
1988	Janet Evans, U.S.	8:20.20*
1992	Janet Evans, U.S.	8:25.52
1996	Brooke Bennett, U.S.	8:27.89

100-Meter Backstroke

1924	Sybil Bauer, U.S.	1:23.2
1928	Marie Braun, Netherlands	1:22.0
1932	Eleanor Holm, U.S.	1:19.4
1936	Dina Senff, Netherlands	1:18.9
1948	Karen Harup, Denmark.	1:14.4
1952	Joan Harrison, South Africa.	1:14.3
1956	Judy Grinham, Great Britain	1:12.9
1960	Lynn Burke, U.S.	1:09.3
1964	Cathy Ferguson, U.S.	1:07.7
1968	Kaye Hall, U.S.	1:06.2
1972	Melissa Belote, U.S.	1:05.78
1976	Ulrike Richter, E. Germany	1:01.83
1980	Rica Reinisch, E. Germany	1:00.86
1984	Theresa Andrews, U.S.	1:02.55
1988	Kristin Otto, E. Germany	1:00.89
1992	Krisztina Egerszegi, Hungary	1:00.68*
1996	Beth Botsford, U.S.	1:01.19

200-Meter Backstroke

1968	Pokey Watson, U.S.	2:24.8
1972	Melissa Belote, U.S.	2:19.19
1976	Ulrike Richter, E. Germany	2:13.43
1980	Rica Reinisch, E. Germany	2:11.77
1984	Jolanda De Rover, Netherlands	2:12.38
1988	Krisztina Egerszegi, Hungary	2:09.29
1992	Krisztina Egerszegi, Hungary	2:07.06*
1996	Krisztina Egerszegi, Hungary	2:07.83

100-Meter Breaststroke

1968	Djurdjica Bjedov, Yugoslavia	1:15.8
1972	Cathy Carr, U.S.	1:13.58
1976	Hannelore Anke, E. Germany	1:11.16
1980	Ute Geweniger, E. Germany	1:10.22
1984	Petra Van Staveren, Netherlands	1:09.88
1988	Tania Dangalakova, Bulgaria	1:07.95
1992	Elena Roudkovskaia, Unified Team	1:08.00
1996	Penny Heyns, South Africa	1:07.70*

200-Meter Breaststroke

1924	Lucy Morton, Great Britain.	3:33.2
1928	Hilde Schrader, Germany.	3:12.6
1932	Clare Dennis, Australia	3:06.3
1936	Hideko Maehata, Japan.	3:03.6
1948	Nelly Van Vliet, Netherlands	2:57.2
1952	Eva Szekely, Hungary	2:51.7
1956	Ursula Happe, Germany	2:53.1
1960	Anita Lonsbrough, Great Britain.	2:49.5
1964	Galina Prozumenschikova, USSR	2:46.4
1968	Sharon Wichman, U.S.	2:44.4
1972	Beverly Whitfield, Australia	2:41.71
1976	Marina Koshevaia, USSR	2:33.35
1980	Lina Kachushite, USSR	2:29.54
1984	Anne Ottenbrite, Canada.	2:30.38
1988	Silke Hoerner, E. Germany	2:26.71
1992	Kyoko Iwasaki, Japan	2:26.65
1996	Penny Heyns, South Africa	2:25.41*

100-Meter Butterfly

1956	Shelley Mann, U.S.	1:11.0
1960	Carolyn Schuler, U.S.	1:09.5
1964	Sharon Stouder, U.S.	1:04.7
1968	Lynn McClements, Australia	1:05.5
1972	Mayumi Aoki, Japan	1:03.34
1976	Kornelia Ender, E. Germany	1:00.13
1980	Caren Metschuck, E. Germany	1:00.42
1984	Mary T. Meagher, U.S.	59.26
1988	Kristin Otto, E. Germany	59.00
1992	Qian Hong, China.	58.62*
1996	Amy Van Dyken, U.S.	59.13

200-Meter Butterfly

1968	Ada Kok, Netherlands	2:24.7
1972	Karen Moe, U.S.	2:15.57
1976	Andrea Pollack, E. Germany.	2:11.41
1980	Ines Geissler, E. Germany	2:10.44
1984	Mary T. Meagher, U.S.	2:06.90*
1988	Kathleen Nord, E. Germany	2:09.51
1992	Summer Sanders, U.S.	2:08.67
1996	Susan O'Neill, Australia	2:07.76

200-Meter Individual Medley

1968	Claudia Kolb, U.S.	2:24.7
1972	Shane Gould, Australia	2:23.07
1984	Tracy Caulkins, U.S.	2:12.64
1988	Daniela Hunger, E. Germany	2:12.59
1992	Lin Li, China.	2:11.65*
1996	Michelle Smith, Ireland	2:13.93

400-Meter Individual Medley

1964	Donna de Varona, U.S.	5:18.7
1968	Claudia Kolb, U.S.	5:08.5
1972	Gail Neall, Australia	5:02.97
1976	Ulrike Tauber, E. Germany	4:42.77
1980	Petra Schneider, E. Germany.	4:36.29*
1984	Tracy Caulkins, U.S.	4:39.24
1988	Janet Evans, U.S.	4:37.76
1992	Krisztina Egerszegi, Hungary	4:36.54
1996	Michelle Smith, Ireland	4:39.18

400-Meter Freestyle Relay

1912	Great Britain.	5:52.8
1920	United States	5:11.6
1924	United States	4:58.8
1928	United States	4:47.6
1932	United States	4:38.0
1936	Netherlands	4:36.0
1948	United States	4:29.2
1952	Hungary	4:24.4
1956	Australia	4:17.1
1960	United States	4:08.9
1964	United States	4:03.8
1968	United States	4:02.5
1972	United States	3:55.19
1976	United States	3:44.82
1980	East Germany	3:42.71
1984	United States	3:43.43
1988	East Germany	3:40.63
1992	United States	3:39.46
1996	United States	3:39.29*

800-Meter Freestyle Relay

1996	United States	7:59.87*

400-Meter Medley Relay

1960	United States	4:41.1
1964	United States	4:33.9
1968	United States	4:28.3
1972	United States	4:20.75
1976	East Germany	4:07.95
1980	East Germany	4:06.67
1984	United States	4:08.34
1988	East Germany	4:03.74
1992	United States	4:02.54*
1996	United States	4:02.88

Springboard Diving

		Points
1920	Aileen Riggin, U.S.	539.90
1924	Elizabeth Becker, U.S.	474.50
1928	Helen Meany, U.S.	78.62
1932	Georgia Coleman U.S.	87.52
1936	Marjorie Gestring, U.S.	89.27
1948	Victoria M. Draves, U.S.	108.74
1952	Patricia McCormick, U.S.	147.30
1956	Patricia McCormick, U.S.	142.36
1960	Ingrid Kramer, Germany	155.81
1964	Ingrid Engel-Kramer, Germany	145.00
1968	Sue Gossick, U.S.	150.77

1972	Micki King, U.S.	450.03
1976	Jenni Chandler, U.S.	506.19
1980	Irina Kalinina, USSR	725.91
1984	Sylvie Bernier, Canada	530.70
1988	Gao Min, China	580.23
1992	Gao Min, China	572.40
1996	Fu Mingxia, China	547.68

Platform Diving

		Points
1912	Greta Johansson, Sweden	39.90
1920	Stefani Fryland-Clausen, Denmark	34.60
1924	Caroline Smith, U.S.	33.20
1928	Elizabeth B. Pinkston, U.S.	31.60
1932	Dorothy Poynton, U.S.	40.26
1936	Dorothy Poynton Hill, U.S.	33.93
1948	Victoria M. Draves, U.S.	68.87
1952	Patricia McCormick, U.S.	79.37
1956	Patricia McCormick, U.S.	84.85
1960	Ingrid Kramer, Germany	91.28
1964	Lesley Bush, U.S.	99.80
1968	Milena Duchkova, Czech.	109.59
1972	Ulrika Knape, Sweden	390.00
1976	Elena Vaytsekhouskaya, USSR	406.59
1980	Martina Jaschke, E. Germany	596.25
1984	Zhou Jihong, China.	435.51
1988	Xu Yanmei, China	445.20
1992	Fu Mingxia, China	461.43
1996	Fu Mingxia, China	521.58

Boxing

Light Flyweight (106 lbs)

1968	Francisco Rodriguez, Venezuela
1972	Gyorgy Gedo, Hungary
1976	Jorge Hernandez, Cuba
1980	Shamil Sabyrov, USSR
1984	Paul Gonzalez, U.S.
1988	Ivailo Hristov, Bulgaria
1992	Rogelio Marcelo, Cuba
1996	Daniel Petrov, Bulgaria

Flyweight (112 lbs)

1904	George Finnegan, U.S.
1920	William Di Gennara, U.S.
1924	Fidel LaBarba, U.S.
1928	Antal Kocsis, Hungary
1932	Istvan Enekes, Hungary
1936	Willi Kaiser, Germany
1948	Pascual Perez, Argentina
1952	Nathan Brooks, U.S.
1956	Terence Spinks, Great Britain
1960	GyulaTorok, Hungary
1964	Fernando Atzori, Italy
1968	Ricardo Delgado, Mexico
1972	Georgi Kostadinov, Bulgaria
1976	Leo Randolph, U.S.
1980	Peter Lessov, Bulgaria
1984	Steve McCrory, U.S.
1988	Kim Kwang Sun, S. Korea
1992	Su Choi Choi, N. Korea
1996	Maikro Romero, Cuba

Bantamweight (119 lbs)

1904	Oliver Kirk, U.S.
1908	A. Henry Thomas, Great Britain
1920	Clarence Walker, South Africa
1924	William Smith, South Africa
1928	Vittorio Tamagnini, Italy
1932	Horace Gwynne, Canada
1936	Ulderico Sergo, Italy
1948	Tibor Csik, Hungary
1952	Pentti Hamalainen, Finland
1956	Wolfgang Behrendt, E. Germany
1960	Oleg Grigoryev, USSR
1964	Takao Sakurai, Japan
1968	Valery Sokolov, USSR
1972	Orlando Martinez, Cuba
1976	Yong-Jo Gu, N. Korea
1980	Juan Hernandez, Cuba

1984	Maurizio Stecca, Italy
1988	Kennedy McKinney, U.S.
1992	Joel Casamayor, Cuba
1996	Istvan Kovacs, Hungary

Featherweight (126 lbs)

1904	Oliver Kirk, U.S.
1908	Richard Gunn, Great Britain
1920	Paul Fritsch, France
1924	John Fields, U.S.
1928	Lambertus van Klaveren, Netherlands
1932	Carmelo Robledo, Argentina
1936	Oscar Casanovas, Argentina
1948	Ernesto Formenti, Italy
1952	Jan Zachara, Czechoslavakia
1956	Vladimir Safronov, USSR
1960	Francesco Musso, Italy
1964	Stanislav Stephashkin, USSR
1968	Antonin Roldan, Mexico
1972	Boris Kousnetsov, USSR
1976	Angel Herrera, Cuba
1980	Rudi Fink, E. Germany
1984	Meldrick Taylor, U.S.
1988	Giovanni Parisi, Italy
1992	Andreas Tews, Germany
1996	Somluck Kamsing, Thailand

Lightweight (132 lbs)

1904	Harry Spanger, U.S.
1908	Frederick Grace, Great Britain
1920	Samuel Mosberg, U.S.
1924	Hans Nielsen, Denmark
1928	Carlo Orlandi, Italy
1932	Lawrence Stevens, South Africa
1936	Imre Harangi, Hungary
1948	Gerald Dreyer, South Africa
1952	Aureliano Bolognesi, Italy
1956	Richard McTaggart, Great Britain
1960	Kazimierz Pazdzior, Poland
1964	Jozef Grudzien, Poland
1968	Ronald Harris, U.S.
1972	Jan Szczepanski, Poland
1976	Howard Davis, U.S.
1980	Angel Herrera, Cuba
1984	Pernell Whitaker, U.S.
1988	Andreas Zuelow, E. Germany
1992	Oscar De La Hoya, U.S.
1996	Hocine Soltani, Algeria

Light Welterweight (140 lbs)

1952	Charles Adkins, U.S.
1956	Vladimir Yengibaryan, USSR
1960	Bohumil Nemecek, Czechoslavakia
1964	Jerzy Kulej, Poland
1968	Jerzy Kulej, Poland
1972	Ray Seales, U.S.
1976	Ray Leonard, U.S.
1980	Patrizio Oliva, Italy
1984	Jerry Page, U.S.
1988	Viatcheslav Janovski, USSR
1992	Hector Vinent, Cuba
1996	Hector Vinent, Cuba

Welterweight (147 lbs)

1904	Albert Young, U.S.
1920	Albert Schneider, Canada
1924	Jean Delarge, Belgium
1928	Edward Morgan, New Zealand
1932	Edward Flynn, U.S.
1936	Sten Suvio, Finland
1948	Julius Torma, Czechoslavakia
1952	Zygmunt Chychla, Poland
1956	Nicolae Linca, Romania
1960	Giovanni Benvenuti, Italy
1964	Marian Kasprzyk, Poland
1968	Manfred Wolke, E. Germany
1972	Emilio Correa, Cuba
1976	Jochen Bachfeld, E. Germany
1980	Andres Aldama, Cuba
1984	Mark Breland, U.S.
1988	Robert Wangila, Kenya
1992	Michael Carruth, Ireland
1996	Oleg Saitov, Russia

Light Middleweight (157 lbs)

1952	Laszlo Papp, Hungary
1956	Laszlo Papp, Hungary
1960	Wilbert McClure, U.S.
1964	Boris Lagutin, USSR
1968	Boris Lagutin, USSR
1972	Dieter Kottysch, W. Germany
1976	Jerzy Rybicki, Poland
1980	Armando Martinez, Cuba
1984	Frank Tate, U.S.
1988	Park Si Hun, S. Korea
1992	Juan Lemus, Cuba
1996	David Reid, U.S.

Middleweight (165 lbs)

1904	Charles Mayer, U.S.
1908	John Douglas, Great Britain
1920	Harry Mallin, Great Britain
1924	Harry Mallin, Great Britain
1928	Piero Toscani, Italy
1932	Carmen Barth, U.S.
1936	Jean Despeaux, France
1948	Laszlo Papp, Hungary
1952	Floyd Patterson, U.S.
1956	Gennady Schatkov, USSR
1960	Edward Crook, U.S.
1964	Valery Popenchenko, USSR
1968	Christopher Finnegan, Great Britain
1972	Vyacheslav Lemechev, USSR
1976	Michael Spinks, U.S.
1980	Jose Gomez, Cuba
1984	Joon-Sup Shin, S. Korea
1988	Henry Maske, E. Germany
1992	Ariel Hernandez, Cuba
1996	Ariel Hernandez, Cuba

Light Heavyweight (179 lbs)

1920	Edward Eagan, U.S.
1924	Harry Mitchell, Great Britain

1928	Victor Avendano, Argentina
1932	David Carstens, South Africa
1936	Roger Michelot, France
1948	George Hunter, South Africa
1952	Norvel Lee, U.S.
1956	James Boyd, U.S.
1960	Cassius Clay, U.S.
1964	Cosimo Pinto, Italy
1968	Dan Poznyak, USSR
1972	Mate Parlov, Yugoslavia
1976	Leon Spinks, U.S.
1980	Slobodan Kacar, Yugoslavia
1984	Anton Josipovic, Yugoslavia
1988	Andrew Maynard, U.S.
1992	Torsten May, Germany
1996	Vassili Jirov, Kazakhstan

Heavyweight (201 lbs)

1984	Henry Tillman, U.S.
1988	Ray Mercer, U.S.
1992	Felix Savon, Cuba
1996	Felix Savon, Cuba

Super Heavyweight (Unlimited)
(known as heavyweight, 1904-80)

1904	Samuel Berger, U.S.
1908	Albert Oldham, Great Britain
1920	Ronald Rawson, Great Britain
1924	Otto von Porat, Norway
1928	Arturo Rodriguez Jurado, Argentina
1932	Santiago Lovell, Argentina
1936	Herbert Runge, Germany
1948	Rafael Inglesias, Argentina
1952	H. Edward Sanders, U.S.
1956	T. Peter Rademacher, U.S.
1960	Franco De Piccoli, Italy
1964	Joe Frazier, U.S.
1968	George Foreman, U.S.
1972	Teofilo Stevenson, Cuba
1976	Teofilo Stevenson, Cuba
1980	Teofilo Stevenson, Cuba
1984	Tyrell Biggs, U.S.
1988	Lennox Lewis, Canada
1992	Roberto Balado, Cuba
1996	Vladimir Klitchko, Ukraine

Other Summer Olympics Gold Medal Winners in 1996

Archery
Men's 70-Meter Individual—Justin Huish, U.S.
Men's Team—U.S.
Women's 70-Meter Individual—Kim Kyung Wook, S. Korea
Women's Team—S. Korea

Badminton
Men's Singles—Poul-Erik Hoyer-Larsen, Denmark
Men's Doubles—Rexy Mainaky & Ricky Subagja, Indonesia
Women's Singles—Bang Soo Hyun, S. Korea
Women's Doubles—Ge Fei & Gu Jun, China
Mixed Doubles—Gil Young Ah & Kim Dong Moon, S. Korea

Baseball
G-Cuba; S-Japan; B-U.S.

Basketball
Men—G-U.S.; S-Yugoslavia; B-Lithuania.
Women—G-U.S.; S-Brazil; B-Australia.

Beach Volleyball
Men—Karch Kiraly & Kent Steffes, U.S.
Women—Jackie Silva & Sandra Pires, Brazil

Canoe/Kayak
Men
Kayak Slalom—Oliver Fix, Germany
Kayak 500M Singles—Antonio Rossi, Italy
Kayak 500M Doubles—Kay Bluhm & Torsten Gutsche, Germany
Kayak 1,000M Singles—Knut Holmann, Norway
Kayak 1,000M Doubles—Antonio Rossi & Daniele Scarpa, Italy
Kayak 1,000M Fours—G-Germany; S-Hungary; B-Russia
Canoe Slalom Singles—Michal Martikan, Slovakia
Canoe Slalom Doubles—France
Canoe 500M Singles—Martin Doktor, Czech Rep.
Canoe 500M Doubles—Csaba Horvath & Gyorgy Kolonics, Hungary
Canoe 1,000M Singles—Martin Doktor, Czech Rep.
Canoe 1,000M Doubles—Andreas Dittmer & Gunar Kirchbach, Germany

Women
Kayak Slalom—Stepnka Hilgertova, Czech Rep.
Kayak 500M Singles—Rita Koban, Hungary
Kayak 500M Doubles—Agneta Andersson & Susanne Gunnarsson, Sweden
Kayak 500M Fours—G-Germany; S-Switzerland; B-Sweden

Cycling
Men
Individual Road Race—Pascal Richard, Switzerland
Sprint—Jens Fiedler, Germany
Individual Points Race—Silvio Martinello, Italy
4KM Team Pursuit—G-France; S-Russia; B-Australia
4KM Individual Pursuit—Andrea Collinelli, Italy
1KM Time Trial—Florian Rousseau, France

Individual Time Trial—Miguel Indurain, Spain
Cross-Country—Bart Jan Brentjens, Netherlands
Women
Individual Road Race—Jeannie Longo-Ciprelli, France
Sprint—Felicia Ballanger, France
Individual Points Race—Nathalie Lancien, France
Individual Pursuit—Antonella Bellutti, Italy
Individual Time Trial—Zulfiya Zabirova, Russia
Cross-Country—Paola Pezzo, Italy

Equestrian
Individual Three-Day Event—Blyth Tait, New Zealand
Team Three-Day Event—Australia
Individual Dressage—Isabell Werth, Germany
Team Dressage—Germany
Individual Jumping—Ulrich Kirchoff, Germany
Team Jumping—Germany

Fencing
Men
Individual Foil—Alessandro Puccini, Italy
Team Foil—Russia
Individual Saber—Stanislas Pozdnyakov, Russia
Team Saber—Russia
Individual Épée—Aleksandr Beketov, Russia
Team Épée—Italy

Women
Individual Foil—Laura Badea, Romania
Team Foil—Italy
Individual Épée—Laura Flessel, France
Team Épée—France

Field Hockey
Men—G-Netherlands; S-Spain; B-Australia
Women—G-Australia; S-S. Korea; B-Netherlands

Gymnastics
Men
Floor Exercise—Ioannis Melissanidis, Greece
Horizontal Bar—Andreas Wecker, Germany
Parallel Bars—Rustam Sharipov, Ukraine
Pommel Horse—Li Donghua, Switzerland
Rings—Yuri Chechi, Italy
Vault—Aleksei Nemov, Russia
Individual All-Around—Li Xiaoshuang, China
Team—G-Russia; S-China; B-Ukraine.

Women
Balance Beam—Shannon Miller, U.S.
Floor Exercise—Lilia Podkopayeva, Ukraine
Uneven Bars—Svetlana Chorkina, Russia
Vault—Simona Amanar, Romania
Individual All-Around—Lilia Podkopayeva, Ukraine
Team—G-U.S.; S-Russia; B-Romania.

Rhythmic Gymnastics
Individual All-Around—Yekaterina Serebryanskaya, Ukraine
Team—G-Spain; S-Bulgaria; B-Russia

Judo
Men
132 Pounds—Tadahiro Nomura, Japan
143 Pounds—Udo Quellmalz, Germany
157 Pounds—Kenzo Nakamura, Japan
172 Pounds—Djamel Bouras, France
190 Pounds—Jeon Ki Young, S. Korea
209 Pounds—Pawel Nastula, Poland
Heavyweight—David Douillet, France

Women
106 Pounds—Kye Sun Hi, N. Korea
115 Pounds—Marie-Claire Restoux, France
123 Pounds—Driulis Gonzalez, Cuba
134 Pounds—Yuko Emoto, Japan
146 Pounds—Cho Min Sun, S. Korea
159 Pounds—Ulla Werbrouck, Belgium
Over 159 Pounds—Sun Fuming, China

Modern Pentathlon
Aleksandr Parygin, Kazakhstan

Rowing
Men
Single Sculls—Xeno Müller, Switzerland
Double Sculls—Italy
Lightweight Double Sculls—Switzerland
Quadruple Sculls—Germany
Coxless Pairs—Great Britain
Coxless Fours—Australia
Lightweight Coxless Fours—Denmark
Coxed Eights—Netherlands

Women
Single Sculls—Yekaterina Khodotovich, Belarus
Double Sculls—Canada
Lightweight Double Sculls—Romania
Quadruple Sculls—Germany
Coxless Pairs—Australia
Coxed Eights—Romania

Shooting
Men
Air Pistol—Roberto Di Donna, Italy
Trap—Michael Diamond, Australia
Air Rifle—Artem Khadzhibekov, Russia
Free Pistol—Boris Kokorev, Russia
Double Trap—Russell Mark, Australia
Rapid Fire Pistol—Ralf Schumann, Germany
Rifle Prone—Christian Klees, Germany
Running Game Target—Yang Ling, China
Three-Position Rifle—Jean-Pierre Amat, France
Skeet—Ennio Falco, Italy

Women
Air Pistol—Olga Klochneva, Russia
Three-Position Rifle—Aleksandra Ivosev, Yugoslavia
Double Trap—Kim Rhode, U.S.
Sport Pistol—Li Duihong, China
Air Rifle—Renata Mauer, Poland

Soccer
Men—G-Nigeria; S-Argentina; B-Brazil
Women—G-U.S.; S-China; B-Norway

Softball
G-U.S.; S-China; B-Australia

Synchronized Swimming
G-U.S.; S-Canada; B-Japan

Table Tennis
Men's Singles—Liu Guoliang, China
Men's Doubles—Kong Linghui & Liu Guoliang, China

Women's Singles—Deng Yaping, China
Women's Doubles—Deng Yaping & Qiao Hong, China

Team Handball
Men—G-Croatia; S-Sweden; B-Spain
Women—G-Denmark; S- S. Korea; B-Hungary

Tennis
Men's Singles—Andre Agassi, U.S.
Men's Doubles—Todd Woodbridge & Mark Woodforde, Australia
Women's Singles—Lindsey Davenport, U.S.
Women's Doubles—Gigi Fernandez & Mary Joe Fernandez, U.S.

Volleyball
Men—G-Netherlands; S-Italy; B-Yugoslavia
Women—G-Cuba; S-China; B- Brazil

Water Polo
G-Spain; S-Croatia; B- Italy

Weight Lifting
119 Pounds—Halil Mutlu, Turkey
130 Pounds—Tang Ningsheng, China
141 Pounds—Naim Suleymanoglu, Turkey
154 Pounds—Zhan Xugang, China
161½ Pounds—Pablo Lara, Cuba
183 Pounds—Pyrros Dimas, Greece
200½ Pounds—Aleksei Petrov, Russia
218 Pounds— Akakide Kakhiashvilis, Greece
238 Pounds—Timur Taimazov, Ukraine
Over 238 Pounds—Andrei Chemerkin, Russia

Wrestling
Freestyle
105½ Pounds—Kim Il, N. Korea
114½ Pounds—Valentin Jordanov, Bulgaria
125½ Pounds—Kendall Cross, U.S.
136½ Pounds—Tom Brands, U.S.
149½ Pounds—Vadim Bogiev, Russia
163 Pounds—Bouvaisa Satiev, Russia
180½ Pounds—Khadzhimurad Magomedov, Russia
198 Pounds—Rasul Khadem, Iran
220 Pounds—Kurt Angle, U.S.
286 Pounds—Mahmut Demir, Turkey

Greco-Roman
105½ Pounds—Sim Kwan Ho, S. Korea
114½ Pounds—Armen Nazaryan, Armenia
125½ Pounds—Yuri Melnichenko, Kazakhstan
136½ Pounds—Wlodzimierz Zwadzki, Poland
149½ Pounds—Ryszard Wolny, Poland
163 Pounds—Feliberto Ascuy Aguilera, Cuba
180½ Pounds—Hamza Yerlikiya, Turkey
198 Pounds—Vyacheslav Oleynyk, Ukraine
220 Pounds—Andrzej Wronski, Poland
286 Pounds—Aleksandr Karelin, Russia

Yachting
Open
Laser—Robert Scheidt, Brazil
Soling—G-Germany; S-Russia; B-U.S.
Star—G-Brazil; S-Sweden; B-Australia
Tornado—G-Spain; S-Australia; B-Brazil

Men
Finn—Mateusz Kusznierewicz, Poland
Mistral—Nikolaos Kaklamanakis, Greece
470—G-Ukraine; S-Great Britain; B-Portugal

Women
Europe—Kristine Rough, Denmark
Mistral—Lee Lai-Shan, Hong Kong
470—G-Spain; S-Japan; B-Ukraine.

History of the Olympic Games

The modern Olympic Games, first held in Athens, Greece, in 1896, were the result of efforts by Baron Pierre de Coubertin, a French educator, to promote interest in education and culture and to foster better international understanding through love of athletics. His source of inspiration was the ancient Greek Olympic Games, most notable of the 4 Panhellenic celebrations. The games were combined patriotic, religious, and athletic festivals held every 4 years. The first such recorded festival was held in 776 BC, the date from which the Greeks began to keep their calendar by "Olympiads," or 4-year spans between the games. The first Olympiad is said to have consisted merely of a 200-yd foot race near the small city of Olympia, but the games gained in scope and became demonstrations of national pride. Only Greek citizens—amateurs—could participate. Winners received laurel, wild olive, and palm wreaths and were accorded special privileges. Under the Roman emperors, the games deteriorated into professional carnivals and circuses. Emperor Theodosius banned them in AD 394.

Baron de Coubertin enlisted 13 nations to send athletes to the first modern Olympics in 1896; now athletes from nearly 200 nations and territories compete. Winter Olympic Games were started in 1924.

Winter Olympic Games
Sites of Winter Olympic Games

1924 Chamonix, France	**1948** St. Moritz, Switzerland	**1988** Calgary, Alberta
1928 St. Moritz, Switzerland	**1952** Oslo, Norway	**1992** Albertville, France
1932 Lake Placid, New York	**1956** Cortina d'Ampezzo, Italy	**1994** Lillehammer, Norway
1936 Garmisch-Partenkirchen, Germany	**1960** Squaw Valley, California	**1998** Nagano, Japan
	1964 Innsbruck, Austria	**1968** Grenoble, France	**2002** Salt Lake City, Utah
	1972 Sapporo, Japan	
	1976 Innsbruck, Austria	
	1980 Lake Placid, New York	
	1984 Sarajevo, Yugoslavia	

Winter Olympic Games in 1994
Lillehammer, Norway, Feb. 12-27, 1994

The 17th Olympic Winter Games were held in 1994 only 2 years after the previous games, because of an International Olympic Committee decision to switch to a 2-year cycle between Summer and Winter Olympics. The 18th Winter Games will be held in 1998 (in Nagano, Japan). The 1994 Winter Games, held in Lillehammer, Norway, featured 1,884 athletes from 67 countries, including 11 former Soviet republics competing as independent countries. Athletes from host-country Norway, whose speed skater Johann Olav Koss broke 3 Olympic records, won a games-high 26 medals. Germany placed 2d, with 24; Russia had the most golds (11). U.S. speed skater Bonnie Blair took home 2 gold medals, for a career total of 5 gold medals, the most of any female American Olympian. Team USA captured 13 medals, more than in any previous Olympic Winter Games.

For the first time, the U.S. Olympic Committee rewarded athletes' superior performances by handing out prizes— $15,000 for a gold medal, $10,000 for a silver, $7,500 for a bronze, and $5,000 for a fourth-place finish.

Final Medal Standings

	Gold	Silver	Bronze	Total		Gold	Silver	Bronze	Total
Norway	10	11	5	**26**	France	0	1	4	**5**
Germany	9	7	8	**24**	Netherlands	0	1	3	**4**
Russia	11	8	4	**23**	Sweden	2	1	0	**3**
Italy	7	5	8	**20**	Kazakhstan	1	2	0	**3**
U.S.	6	5	2	**13**	China	0	1	2	**3**
Canada	3	6	4	**13**	Slovenia	0	0	3	**3**
Switzerland	3	4	2	**9**	Ukraine	1	0	1	**2**
Austria	2	3	4	**9**	Belarus	0	2	0	**2**
S. Korea	4	1	1	**6**	Great Britain	0	0	2	**2**
Finland	0	1	5	**6**	Uzbekistan	1	0	0	**1**
Japan	1	2	2	**5**	Australia	0	0	1	**1**

Winter Olympic Games Champions, 1924-1994

In 1992, the Unified Team represented the former Soviet republics of Russia, Ukraine, Belarus, Kazakhstan, and Uzbekistan.

Bobsledding
(Driver in parentheses)

	4-Man Bob	**Time**
1924	Switzerland (Eduard Scherrer)	5:45.54
1928	United States (William Fiske) (5-man)	3:20.50
1932	United States (William Fiske)	7:53.68
1936	Switzerland (Pierre Musy)	5:19.85
1948	United States (Francis Tyler)	5:20.10
1952	Germany (Andreas Ostler)	5:07.84
1956	Switzerland (Franz Kapus)	5:10.44
1964	Canada (Victor Emery)	4:14.46
1968	Italy (Eugenio Monti) (2 races)	2:17.39
1972	Switzerland (Jean Wicki)	4:43.07
1976	E. Germany (Meinhard Nehmer)	3:40.43
1980	E. Germany (Meinhard Nehmer)	3:59.92
1984	E. Germany (Wolfgang Hoppe)	3:20.22
1988	Switzerland (Ekkehard Fasser)	3:47.51
1992	Austria (Ingo Appelt)	3:53.90
1994	Germany (Wolfgang Hoppe)	3:27.28

	2-Man Bob	**Time**
1932	United States (Hubert Stevens)	8:14.74
1936	United States (Ivan Brown)	5:29.29
1948	Switzerland (F. Endrich)	5:29.20
1952	Germany (Andreas Ostler)	5:24.54
1956	Italy (Dalla Costa)	5:30.14
1964	Great Britain (Anthony Nash)	4:21.90
1968	Italy (Eugenio Monti)	4:41.54
1972	W. Germany (Wolfgang Zimmerer)	4:57.07
1976	E. Germany (Meinhard Nehmer)	3:44.42
1980	Switzerland (Erich Schaerer)	4:09.36
1984	E. Germany (Wolfgang Hoppe)	3:25.56
1988	USSR (Janis Kipours)	3:54.19
1992	Switzerland (Gustav Weber)	4:03.26
1994	Switzerland (Gustav Weber)	3:30.81

Luge

	Men's Singles	**Time**
1964	Thomas Keohler, Germany	3:26.77
1968	Manfred Schmid, Austria	2:52.48
1972	Wolfgang Scheidel, E. Germany	3:27.50
1976	Detlef Guenther, E. Germany	3:27.688
1980	Bernhard Glass, E. Germany	2:54.796
1984	Paul Hildgartner, Italy	3:04.258
1988	Jens Mueller, E. Germany	3:05.548
1992	Georg Hackl, Germany	3:02.363
1994	Georg Hackl, Germany	3:21.571

	Men's Pairs	**Time**
1964	Austria	1:41.62
1968	E. Germany	1:35.85
1972	Italy, E. Germany (tie)	1:28.35
1976	E. Germany	1:25.604
1980	E. Germany	1:19.331
1984	W. Germany	1:23.620
1988	E. Germany	1:31.940
1992	Germany	1:32.053
1994	Italy	1:36.720

	Women's Singles	**Time**
1964	Ortun Enderlein, Germany	3:24.67
1968	Erica Lechner, Italy	2:28.66
1972	Anna M. Muller, E. Germany	2:59.18
1976	Margit Schumann, E. Germany	2:50.621
1980	Vera Zozulya, USSR	2:36.537
1984	Steffi Martin, E. Germany	2:46.570
1988	Steffi Walter, E. Germany	3:03.973
1992	Doris Neuner, Austria	3:06.696
1994	Gerda Weissensteiner, Italy	3:15.517

Biathlon

	Men's 10 Kilometers	**Time**
1980	Frank Ullrich, E. Germany	32:10.69
1984	Eirik Kvalfoss, Norway	30:53.80
1988	Frank-Peter Roetsch, E. Germany	25:08.10
1992	Mark Kirchner, Germany	26:02.30
1994	Serguei Tchepikov, Russia	28:07.00

	Men's 20 Kilometers	**Time**
1960	Klas Lestander, Sweden	1:33:21.6
1964	Vladimir Melanin, USSR	1:20:26.8
1968	Magnar Solberg, Norway	1:13:45.9
1972	Magnar Solberg, Norway	1:15:55.50
1976	Nikolai Kruglov, USSR	1:14:12.26
1980	Anatoly Aljabiev, USSR	1:08:16.31
1984	Peter Angerer, W. Germany	1:11:52.7
1988	Frank-Peter Roetsch, E. Germany	0:56:33.33
1992	Yevgeny Redkine, Unified Team	0:57:34.4
1994	Serguei Tarasov, Russia	0:57:25.3

	Men's 30-Kilometer Relay	**Time**
1968	USSR, Norway, Sweden (40 km)	2:13:02.4
1972	USSR, Finland, E. Germany (40 km)	1:51:44.92
1976	USSR, Finland, E. Germany (40 km)	1:57:55.64
1980	USSR, E. Germany, W. Germany	1:34:03.27
1984	USSR, Norway, W. Germany	1:38:51.70
1988	USSR, W. Germany, Italy	1:22:30.00

Men's 30-Kilometer Relay (continued)	**Time**
1992 Germany, Unified Team, Sweden....	1:24:43.50
1994 Germany, Russia, France	1:30:22.1

Women's 7.5 Kilometers	**Time**
1992 Anfissa Restsova, Unified Team	24:29.20
1994 Myriam Bedard, Canada	26:08.8

Women's 15 Kilometers	**Time**
1992 Antje Misersky, Germany........	51:47.2
1994 Myriam Bedard, Canada	52:06.6

Women's 22.5-Kilometer Relay	**Time**
1992 France, Germany, Unified Team....	1:15:55.6

Women's 30-Kilometer Relay	**Time**
1994 Russia, Germany, France	1:47:19.5

Figure Skating
Men's Singles

1908†	Ulrich Salchow, Sweden
1920†	Gillis Grafstrom, Sweden
1924	Gillis Grafstrom, Sweden
1928	Gillis Grafstrom, Sweden
1932	Karl Schaefer, Austria
1936	Karl Schaefer, Austria
1948	Richard Button, U.S.
1952	Richard Button, U.S.
1956	Hayes Alan Jenkins, U.S.
1960	David W. Jenkins, U.S.
1964	Manfred Schnelldorfer, Germany
1968	Wolfgang Schwartz, Austria
1972	Ondrej Nepela, Czechoslovakia
1976	John Curry, Great Britain
1980	Robin Cousins, Great Britain
1984	Scott Hamilton, U.S.
1988	Brian Boitano, U.S.
1992	Viktor Petrenko, Unified Team
1994	Aleksei Urmanov, Russia

Women's Singles

1908†	Madge Syers, Great Britain
1920†	Magda Julin-Mauroy, Sweden
1924	Herma von Szabo-Planck, Austria
1928	Sonja Henie, Norway
1932	Sonja Henie, Norway
1936	Sonja Henie, Norway
1948	Barbara Ann Scott, Canada
1952	Jeanette Altwegg, Great Britain
1956	Tenley Albright, U.S.
1960	Carol Heiss, U.S.
1964	Sjoukje Dijkstra, Netherlands
1968	Peggy Fleming, U.S.
1972	Beatrix Schuba, Austria
1976	Dorothy Hamill, U.S.
1980	Anett Poetzsch, E. Germany
1984	Katarina Witt, E. Germany
1988	Katarina Witt, E. Germany
1992	Kristi Yamaguchi, U.S.
1994	Oksana Baiul, Ukraine

Pairs

1908†	Anna Hubler & Heinrich Burger, Germany
1920†	Ludovika & Walter Jakobsson, Finland
1924	Helene Engelman & Alfred Berger, Austria
1928	Andree Joly & Pierre Brunet, France
1932	Andree Joly & Pierre Brunet, France
1936	Maxi Herber & Ernst Baier, Germany
1948	Micheline Lannoy & Pierre Baugniet, Belgium
1952	Ria and Paul Falk, Germany
1956	Elisabeth Schwartz & Kurt Oppelt, Austria
1960	Barbara Wagner & Robert Paul, Canada
1964	Ludmila Beloussova & Oleg Protopopov, USSR
1968	Ludmila Beloussova & Oleg Protopopov, USSR
1972	Irina Rodnina & Alexei Ulanov, USSR
1976	Irina Rodnina & Aleksandr Zaitzev, USSR
1980	Irina Rodnina & Aleksandr Zaitzev, USSR
1984	Elena Valova & Oleg Vassiliev, USSR
1988	Ekaterina Gordeeva & Sergei Grinkov, USSR
1992	Natalia Mishkutienok & Artur Dimitriev, Unified Team
1994	Ekaterina Gordeeva & Sergei Grinkov, Russia

Ice Dancing

1976	Ludmila Pakhomova & Aleksandr Gorschkov, USSR
1980	Natalya Linichuk & Gennadi Karponosov, USSR
1984	Jayne Torvill & Christopher Dean, Great Britain
1988	Natalia Bestemianova & Andrei Bukin, USSR
1992	Marina Klimova & Sergei Ponomarenko, Unified Team
1994	Oksana Grichtchuk & Yevgeny Platov, Russia

(†) Event was held at Summer Olympics.

Ice Hockey

1920†	Canada, U.S., Czechoslovakia
1924	Canada, U.S., Great Britain
1928	Canada, Sweden, Switzerland
1932	Canada, U.S., Germany
1936	Great Britain, Canada, U.S.
1948	Canada, Czechoslovakia, Switzerland
1952	Canada, U.S., Sweden
1956	USSR, U.S., Canada
1960	U.S., Canada, USSR
1964	USSR, Sweden, Czechoslovakia
1968	USSR, Czechoslovakia, Canada
1972	USSR, U.S., Czechoslovakia
1976	USSR, Czechoslovakia, W. Germany
1980	U.S., USSR, Sweden
1984	USSR, Czechoslovakia, Sweden
1988	USSR, Finland, Sweden
1992	Unified Team, Canada, Czechoslovakia
1994	Sweden, Canada, Finland

(†) Event was held at Summer Olympics.

Alpine Skiing
Men's Downhill

		Time
1948	Henri Oreiller, France	2:55.0
1952	Zeno Colo, Italy	2:30.8
1956	Anton Sailer, Austria.	2:52.2
1960	Jean Vuarnet, France............	2:06.0
1964	Egon Zimmermann, Austria.......	2:18.16
1968	Jean-Claude Killy, France	1:59.85
1972	Bernhard Russi, Switzerland	1:51.43
1976	Franz Klammer, Austria	1:45.73
1980	Leonhard Stock, Austria	1:45.50
1984	Bill Johnson, U.S..	1:45:59
1988	Pirmin Zurbriggen, Switzerland	1:59.63
1992	Patrick Ortlieb, Austria	1:50.37
1994	Tommy Moe, U.S.	1:45.75

Men's Super Giant Slalom

		Time
1988	Franck Piccard, France.	1:39.66
1992	Kjetil-Andre Aamodt, Norway.....	1:13.04
1994	Markus Wasmeier, Germany.....	1:32.53

Men's Giant Slalom

		Time
1952	Stein Eriksen, Norway	2:25.0
1956	Anton Sailer, Austria.	3:00.1
1960	Roger Staub, Switzerland	1:48.3
1964	Francois Bonlieu, France	1:46.71
1968	Jean-Claude Killy, France........	3:29.28
1972	Gustavo Thoeni, Italy	3:09.62
1976	Heini Hemmi, Switzerland	3:26.97
1980	Ingemar Stenmark, Sweden	2:40.74
1984	Max Julen, Switzerland	2:41.18
1988	Alberto Tomba, Italy	2:06:37
1992	Alberto Tomba, Italy	2:06.98
1994	Markus Wasmeier, Germany.......	2:52.46

Men's Slalom

		Time
1948	Edi Reinalter, Switzerland	2:10.3
1952	Othmar Schneider, Austria	2:00.0
1956	Anton Sailer, Austria.	3:14.7
1960	Ernst Hinterseer, Austria.	2:08.9
1964	Josef Stiegler, Austria.	2:11.13
1968	Jean-Claude Killy, France	1:39.73
1972	Francisco Fernandez Ochoa, Spain..	1:49.27
1976	Piero Gros, Italy	2:03.29
1980	Ingemar Stenmark, Sweden	1:44.26
1984	Phil Mahre, U.S..	1:39.41
1988	Alberto Tomba, Italy	1:39.47
1992	Finn Christian Jagge, Norway	1:44.39
1994	Thomas Stangassinger, Austria.....	2:02.02

Men's Combined

		Time
1988	Hubert Strolz, Austria	36.55 (pts.)
1992	Josef Polig, Italy................	14.58 (pts.)
1994	Lasse Kjus, Norway	3:17.53

Women's Downhill

		Time
1948	Hedi Schlunegger, Switzerland	2:28.3
1952	Trude Jochum-Beiser, Austria	1:47.1
1956	Madeleine Berthod, Switzerland ...	1:40.7
1960	Heidi Biebl, Germany	1:37.6
1964	Christl Haas, Austria.	1:55.39
1968	Olga Pall, Austria.	1:40.87
1972	Marie Therese Nadig, Switzerland ...	1:36.68
1976	Rosi Mittermaier, W. Germany.....	1:46.16
1980	Annemarie Proell Moser, Austria ...	1:37.52
1984	Michela Figini, Switzerland	1:13.36
1988	Marina Kiehl, W. Germany	1:25.86
1992	Kerrin Lee-Gartner, Canada	1:52.55
1994	Katja Seizinger, Germany	1:35.93

Women's Super Giant Slalom

		Time
1988	Sigrid Wolf, Austria.	1:19.03
1992	Deborah Compagnoni, Italy.	1:21.22
1994	Diann Roffe-Steinrotter, U.S.	1:22.15

Women's Giant Slalom

		Time
1952	Andrea Mead Lawrence, U.S.	2:06.8
1956	Ossi Reichert, Germany	1:56.5

1960	Yvonne Ruegg, Switzerland	1:39.9
1964	Marielle Goitschel, France	1:52.24
1968	Nancy Greene, Canada	1:51.97
1972	Marie Therese Nadig, Switzerland	1:29.90
1976	Kathy Kreiner, Canada	1:29.13
1980	Hanni Wenzel, Liechtenstein (2 runs)	2:41.66
1984	Debbie Armstrong, U.S.	2:20.98
1988	Vreni Schneider, Switzerland	2:06.49
1992	Pernilla Wiberg, Sweden	2:12.74
1994	Deborah Compagnoni, Italy	2:30.97

Women's Slalom — Time

1948	Gretchen Fraser, U.S.	1:57.2
1952	Andrea Mead Lawrence, U.S.	2:10.6
1956	Renee Colliard, Switzerland	1:52.3
1960	Anne Heggtveigt, Canada	1:49.6
1964	Christine Goitschel, France	1:29.86
1968	Marielle Goitschel, France	1:25.86
1972	Barbara Cochran, U.S.	1:31.24
1976	Rosi Mittermaier, W. Germany	1:30.54
1980	Hanni Wenzel, Liechtenstein	1:25.09
1984	Paoletta Magoni, Italy	1:36.47
1988	Vreni Schneider, Switzerland	1:36.69
1992	Petra Kronberger, Austria	1:32.68
1994	Vreni Schneider, Switzerland	1:56.01

Women's Combined — Time

1988	Anita Wachter, Austria	29.25 (pts.)
1992	Petra Kronberger, Austria	2.55 (pts.)
1994	Pernilla Wiberg, Sweden	3:05.16

Freestyle Skiing

Men's Moguls — Points

1992	Edgar Grospiron, France	25.81
1994	Jean-Luc Brassard, Canada	27.24

Men's Aerials — Points

1994	Andreas Schoenbaechler, Switzerland	234.67

Women's Moguls — Points

1992	Donna Weinbrecht, U.S.	23.69
1994	Stine Lise Hattestad, Norway	25.97

Women's Aerials — Points

1994	Lina Tcherjazova, Uzbekistan	166.84

Nordic Skiing

Cross-Country Events

Men's 10 Kilometers (6.2 miles) — Time

1992	Vegard Ulvang, Norway	27:36.0
1994	Bjorn Daehlie, Norway	24:20.1

Men's 15 Kilometers (9.3 miles) — Time

1924	Thorleif Haug, Norway	1:14:31
1928	Johan Grottumsbraaten, Norway	1:37:01
1932	Sven Utterstrom, Sweden	1:23:07
1936	Erik-August Larsson, Sweden	1:14:38
1948	Martin Lundstrom, Sweden	1:13:50
1952	Hallgeir Brenden, Norway	1:01:34
1956	Hallgeir Brenden, Norway	49:39.0
1960	Haakon Brusveen, Norway	51:55.5
1964	Eero Maentyranta, Finland	50:54.1
1968	Harald Groenningen, Norway	47:54.2
1972	Sven-Ake Lundback, Sweden	45:28.24
1976	Nikolai Balukov, USSR	43:58.47
1980	Thomas Wassberg, Sweden	41:57.63
1984	Gunde Svan, Sweden	41:25.6
1988	Mikhail Deviatiarov, USSR	41:18.9
1992	Bjorn Daehlie, Norway	38:01.9
1994	Bjorn Daehlie, Norway	35:48.8

(Note: approx. 18-km course 1924-1952)

Men's 30 Kilometers (18.6 miles) — Time

1956	Veikko Hakulinen, Finland	1:44:06.0
1960	Sixten Jernberg, Sweden	1:51:03.9
1964	Eero Maentyranta, Finland	1:30:50.7
1968	Franco Nones, Italy	1:35:39.2
1972	Vyacheslav Vedenine, USSR	1:36:31.15
1976	Sergei Saveliev, USSR	1:30:29.38
1980	Nikolai Zimyatov, USSR	1:27:02.80
1984	Nikolai Zimyatov, USSR	1:28:56.3
1988	Aleksei Prokourorov, USSR	1:24:26.3
1992	Vegard Ulvang, Norway	1:22:27.8
1994	Thomas Alsgaard, Norway	1:12:26.4

Men's 50 kilometers (31.2 miles) — Time

1924	Thorleif Haug, Norway	3:44:32.0
1928	Per Erik Hedlund, Sweden	4:52:03.0
1932	Veli Saarinen, Finland	4:28:00.0
1936	Elis Wiklund, Sweden	3:30:11.0
1948	Nils Karlsson, Sweden	3:47:48.0
1952	Veikko Hakulinen, Finland	3:33:33.0
1956	Sixten Jernberg, Sweden	2:50:27.0
1960	Kalevi Hamalainen, Finland	2:59:06.3
1964	Sixten Jernberg, Sweden	2:43:52.6
1968	Ole Ellefsaeter, Norway	2:28:45.8

1972	Paal Tyldum, Norway	2:43:14.75
1976	Ivar Formo, Norway	2:37:30.05
1980	Nikolai Zimyatov, USSR	2:27:24.60
1984	Thomas Wassberg, Sweden	2:15:55.8
1988	Gunde Svan, Sweden	2:04:30.9
1992	Bjorn Daehlie, Norway	2:03:41.5
1994	Vladimir Smirnov, Kazakhstan	2:07:20.3

Men's 40-Kilometer Relay — Time

1936	Finland, Norway, Sweden	2:41:33.0
1948	Sweden, Finland, Norway	2:32:08.0
1952	Finland, Norway, Sweden	2:20:16.0
1956	USSR, Finland, Sweden	2:15:30.0
1960	Finland, Norway, USSR	2:18:45.6
1964	Sweden, Finland, USSR	2:18:34.6
1968	Norway, Sweden, Finland	2:08:33.5
1972	USSR, Norway, Switzerland	2:04:47.94
1976	Finland, Norway, USSR	2:07:59.72
1980	USSR, Norway, Finland	1:57:03.46
1984	Sweden, USSR, Finland	1:55:06.30
1988	Sweden, USSR, Czechoslovakia	1:43:58.60
1992	Norway, Italy, Finland	1:39:26.00
1994	Italy, Norway, Finland	1:41:15.00

Women's 5 Kilometers (approx. 3.1 miles)

1964	Claudia Boyarskikh, USSR	17:50.5
1968	Toini Gustafsson, Sweden	16:45.2
1972	Galina Koulacova, USSR	17:00.50
1976	Helena Takalo, Finland	15:48.69
1980	Raisa Smetanina, USSR	15:06.92
1984	Marja-Liisa Haemaelainen, Finland	17:04.0
1988	Marjo Matikainen, Finland	15:04.0
1992	Marjut Lukkarinen, Finland	14:13.8
1994	Ljubov Egorova, Russia	14:08.8

Women's 10 Kilometers (6.2 miles) — Time

1952	Lydia Wideman, Finland	41:40.0
1956	Lyubov Kosyreva, USSR	38:11.0
1960	Maria Gusakova, USSR	39:46.6
1964	Claudia Boyarskikh, USSR	40:24.3
1968	Toini Gustafsson, Sweden	36:46.5
1972	Galina Koulacova, USSR	34:17.82
1976	Raisa Smetanina, USSR	30:13.41
1980	Barbara Petzold, E. Germany	30:31.54
1984	Marja-Liisa Haemaelainen, Finland	31:44.2
1988	Vida Ventsene, USSR	30:08.3
1992	Lyubov Egorova, Unified Team	25:53.7
1994	Lyubov Egorova, Russia	27:30.1

Women's 15 Kilometers (9.3 miles) — Time

1992	Lyubov Egorova, Unified Team	42:20.8
1994	Manuela Di Centa, Italy	39:44.5

Women's 30 Kilometers (18.6 miles) — Time

1992	Stefania Belmondo, Italy	1:22:30.1
1994	Manuela Di Centa, Italy	1:25:41.6

Women's 20-Kilometer Relay — Time

1956	Finland, USSR, Sweden (15 km)	1:09:01.0
1960	Sweden, USSR, Finland (15 km)	1:04:21.4
1964	USSR, Sweden, Finland (15 km)	59:20.2
1968	Norway, Sweden, USSR (15 km)	57:30.0
1972	USSR, Finland, Norway (15 km)	48:46.15
1976	USSR, Finland, E. Germany	1:07:49.75
1980	E. Germany, USSR, Norway	1:02:11.1
1984	Norway, Czechoslovakia, Finland	1:06:49.7
1988	USSR, Norway, Finland	59:51.1
1992	United Team, Norway, Italy	59:34.8
1994	Russia, Norway, Italy	57:12.5

Combined Cross-Country & Jumping (Men)

Nordic Combined — Points

1924	Thorleif Haug, Norway	453.800
1928	Johan Grottumsbraaten, Norway	427.800
1932	Johan Grottumsbraaten, Norway	446.000
1936	Oddbjorn Hagen, Norway	430.300
1948	Heikki Hasu, Finland	448.800
1952	Simon Slattvik, Norway	451.621
1956	Sverre Stenersen, Norway	455.000
1960	Georg Thoma, Germany	457.952
1964	Tormod Knutsen, Norway	469.280
1968	Franz Keller, W. Germany	449.040
1972	Ulrich Wehling, E. Germany	413.340
1976	Ulrich Wehling, E. Germany	423.390
1980	Ulrich Wehling, E. Germany	432.200
1984	Tom Sandberg, Norway	422.595
1988	Hippolyt Kempf, Switzerland	235.8
1992	Fabrice Guy, France	426.470
1994	Fred Barre Lundberg, Norway	457.970

Team Nordic Combined — Time

1988	W. Germany, Switzerland, Austria	1:20:46.0
1992	Japan, Norway, Austria	1:23:36.5
1994	Japan, Norway, Switzerland	1,368.860 (pts.)

Ski Jumping (Men)

Normal Hill

Year	Champion	Points
1964	Veikko Kankkonen, Finland	229.9
1968	Jiri Raska, Czechoslovakia	216.5
1972	Yukio Kasaya, Japan	244.2
1976	Hans-Georg Aschenbach, E. Germany	252.0
1980	Toni Innauer, Austria	266.3
1984	Jens Weissflog, E. Germany	215.2
1988	Matti Nykaenen, Finland	230.5
1992	Ernst Vettori, Austria	222.8
1994	Espen Bredesen, Norway	282.0

Large Hill

Year	Champion	Points
1924	Jacob Tullin Thams, Norway	18.960
1928	Alfred Andersen, Norway	19.208
1932	Birger Ruud, Norway	228.1
1936	Birger Ruud, Norway	232.0
1948	Petter Hugsted, Norway	228.1
1952	Arnfinn Bergmann, Norway	226.0
1956	Antti Hyvarinen, Finland	227.0
1960	Helmut Recknagel, Germany	227.2
1964	Toralf Engan, Norway	230.7
1968	Vladimir Beloussov, USSR	231.3
1972	Wojciech Fortuna, Poland	219.9
1976	Karl Schnabl, Austria	234.8
1980	Jouko Tormanen, Finland	271.0
1984	Matti Nykaenen, Finland	231.2
1988	Matti Nykaenen, Finland	224.0
1992	Toni Nieminen, Finland	239.5
1994	Jens Weissflog, Germany	274.5

Team Large Hill

Year	Champion	Points
1988	Finland, Yugoslavia, Norway	634.4
1992	Finland, Austria, Czechoslovakia	644.4
1994	Germany, Japan, Austria	970.1

Speed Skating

Men's 500 Meters

Year	Champion	Time
1924	Charles Jewtraw, U.S.	0:44.0
1928	Thunberg, Finland & Evensen, Norway (tie)	0:43.4
1932	John A. Shea, U.S.	0:43.4
1936	Ivar Ballangrud, Norway	0:43.4
1948	Finn Helgesen, Norway	0:43.1
1952	Kenneth Henry, U.S.	0:43.2
1956	Evgeniy Grishin, USSR	0:40.2
1960	Evgeniy Grishin, USSR	0:40.2
1964	Terry McDermott, U.S.	0:40.1
1968	Erhard Keller, W. Germany	0:40.3
1972	Erhard Keller, W. Germany	0:39.44
1976	Evgeny Kulikov, USSR	0:39.17
1980	Eric Heiden, U.S.	0:38.03
1984	Sergei Fokichev, USSR	0:38.19
1988	Uwe-Jens Mey, E. Germany	0:36.45
1992	Uwe-Jens Mey, Germany	0:37.14
1994	Aleksandr Golubev, Russia	0:36.33

Men's 1,000 Meters

Year	Champion	Time
1976	Peter Mueller, U.S.	1:19.32
1980	Eric Heiden, U.S.	1:15.18
1984	Gaetan Boucher, Canada	1:15.80
1988	Nikolai Guiliaev, USSR	1:13.03
1992	Olaf Zinke, Germany	1:14.85
1994	Dan Jansen, U.S.	1:12.43

Men's 1,500 Meters

Year	Champion	Time
1924	Clas Thunberg, Finland	2:20.8
1928	Clas Thunberg, Finland	2:21.1
1932	John A. Shea, U.S.	2:57.5
1936	Charles Mathiesen, Norway	2:19.2
1948	Sverre Farstad, Norway	2:17.6
1952	Hjalmar Andersen, Norway	2:20.4
1956	Grishin, & Mikhailov, both USSR (tie)	2:08.6
1960	Aas, Norway & Grishin, USSR (tie)	2:10.4
1964	Ants Anston, USSR	2:10.3
1968	Cornelis Verkerk, Netherlands	2:03.4
1972	Ard Schenk, Netherlands	2:02.96
1976	Jan Egil Storholt, Norway	1:59.38
1980	Eric Heiden, U.S.	1:55.44
1984	Gaetan Boucher, Canada	1:58.36
1988	Andre Hoffmann, E. Germany	1:52.06
1992	Johann Koss, Norway	1:54.81
1994	Johann Koss, Norway	1:51.29

Men's 5,000 Meters

Year	Champion	Time
1924	Clas Thunberg, Finland	8:39.0
1928	Ivar Ballangrud, Norway	8:50.5
1932	Irving Jaffee, U.S.	9:40.8
1936	Ivar Ballangrud, Norway	8:19.6
1948	Reidar Liaklev, Norway	8:29.4
1952	Hjalmar Andersen, Norway	8:10.6
1956	Boris Shilkov, USSR	7:48.7
1960	Viktor Kosichkin, USSR	7:51.3

Year	Champion	Time
1964	Knut Johannesen, Norway	7:38.4
1968	F. Anton Maier, Norway	7:22.4
1972	Ard Schenk, Netherlands	7:23.61
1976	Sten Stensen, Norway	7:24.48
1980	Eric Heiden, U.S.	7:02.29
1984	Sven Tomas Gustafson, Sweden	7:12.28
1988	Tomas Gustafson, Sweden	6:44.63
1992	Geir Karlstad, Norway	6:59.97
1994	Johann Koss, Norway	6:34.96

Men's 10,000 Meters

Year	Champion	Time
1924	Julius Skutnabb, Finland	18:04.8
1928	Event not held, thawing of ice	
1932	Irving Jaffee, U.S.	19:13.6
1936	Ivar Ballangrud, Norway	17:24.3
1948	Ake Seyffarth, Sweden	17:26.3
1952	Hjalmar Andersen, Norway	16:45.8
1956	Sigvard Ericsson, Sweden	16:35.9
1960	Knut Johannesen, Norway	15:46.6
1964	Jonny Nilsson, Sweden	15:50.1
1968	Jonny Hoeglin, Sweden	15:23.6
1972	Ard Schenk, Netherlands	15:01.35
1976	Piet Kleine, Netherlands	14:50.59
1980	Eric Heiden, U.S.	14:28.13
1984	Igor Malkov, USSR	14:39.90
1988	Tomas Gustafson, Sweden	13:48.20
1992	Bart Veldkamp, Netherlands	14:12.12
1994	Johann Koss, Norway	13:30.55

Women's 500 Meters

Year	Champion	Time
1960	Helga Haase, Germany	0:45.9
1964	Lydia Skoblikova, USSR	0:45.0
1968	Ludmila Titova, USSR	0:46.1
1972	Anne Henning, U.S.	0:43.33
1976	Sheila Young, U.S.	0:42.76
1980	Karin Enke, E. Germany	0:41.78
1984	Christa Rothenburger, E. Germany	0:41.02
1988	Bonnie Blair, U.S.	0:39.10
1992	Bonnie Blair, U.S.	0:40.33
1994	Bonnie Blair, U.S.	0:39.25

Women's 1,000 Meters

Year	Champion	Time
1960	Klara Guseva, USSR	1:34.1
1964	Lydia Skoblikova, USSR	1:33.2
1968	Carolina Geijssen, Netherlands	1:32.6
1972	Monika Pflug, W. Germany	1:31.40
1976	Tatiana Averina, USSR	1:28.43
1980	Natalya Petruseva, USSR	1:24.10
1984	Karin Enke, E. Germany	1:21.61
1988	Christa Rothenburger, E. Germany	1:17.65
1992	Bonnie Blair, U.S.	1:21.90
1994	Bonnie Blair, U.S.	1:18.74

Women's 1,500 Meters

Year	Champion	Time
1960	Lydia Skoblikova, USSR	2:52.2
1964	Lydia Skoblikova, USSR	2:22.6
1968	Kaija Mustonen, Finland	2:22.4
1972	Dianne Holum, U.S.	2:20.85
1976	Galina Stepanskaya, USSR	2:16.58
1980	Anne Borckink, Netherlands	2:10.95
1984	Karin Enke, E. Germany	2:03.42
1988	Yvonne van Gennip, Netherlands	2:00.68
1992	Jacqueline Boerner, Germany	2:05.87
1994	Emese Hunyady, Austria	2:02.19

Women's 3,000 Meters

Year	Champion	Time
1960	Lydia Skoblikova, USSR	5:14.3
1964	Lydia Skoblikova, USSR	5:14.9
1968	Johanna Schut, Netherlands	4:56.2
1972	Christina Baas-Kaiser, Netherlands	4:52.14
1976	Tatiana Averina, USSR	4:45.19
1980	Bjoerg Eva Jensen, Norway	4:32.13
1984	Andrea Schoene, E. Germany	4:24.79
1988	Yvonne van Gennip, Netherlands	4:11.94
1992	Gunda Niemann, Germany	4:19.90
1994	Svetlana Bazhanova, Russia	4:17.43

Women's 5,000 Meters

Year	Champion	Time
1988	Yvonne van Gennip, Netherlands	7:14.13
1992	Gunda Niemann, Germany	7:31.57
1994	Claudia Pechstein, Germany	7:14.37

Short-Track Speed Skating

Men's 1,000 Meters

Year	Champion	Time
1992	Kim Ki-Hoon, S. Korea	1:30.76
1994	Kim Ki-Hoon, S. Korea	1:34.57

Men's 5,000-Meter Relay

Year	Champion	Time
1992	S. Korea, Canada, Japan	7:14.02
1994	Italy, U.S., Australia	7:11.74

Women's 500 Meters

Year	Champion	Time
1992	Cathy Turner, U.S.	47:04
1994	Cathy Turner, U.S.	45.98

Women's 3,000-Meter Relay

Year	Champion	Time
1992	Canada, U.S., Unified Team	4:36.62
1994	S. Korea, Canada, U.S.	4:26.64

Olympic Information

Symbol: Five rings or circles, linked together to represent the sporting friendship of all peoples. The rings also symbolize 5 geographic areas—Europe, Asia, Africa, Australia, and America. Each ring is a different color—blue, yellow, black, green, and red.

Flag: The symbol of the 5 rings on a plain white background.

Motto: "Citius, Altius, Fortius." Latin meaning "faster, higher, braver," or in a more modern rendering, "swifter, higher, stronger." The motto was coined by Father Didon, a French educator, in 1895.

Creed: "The most important thing in the Olympic Games is not to win but to take part, just as the most important thing in life is not the triumph but the struggle. The essential thing is not to have conquered but to have fought well."

Oath: An athlete of the host country recites the following at the opening ceremony. "In the name of all competitors I promise that we will take part in these Olympic Games, respecting and abiding by the rules which govern them, in the true spirit of sportsmanship for the glory of sport and the honor of our teams." Both the oath and the creed were composed by Baron Pierre de Coubertin, the founder of the modern Games.

Flame: Symbolizes the continuity between the ancient and modern Games. The modern version of the flame was adopted in 1936. The torch used to kindle the flame is first lit by the sun's rays at Olympia, Greece, and then carried to the site of the Games by relays of runners. Ships and planes are used when necessary.

TRACK AND FIELD
World Track and Field Records
As of Oct. 1997

The International Amateur Athletic Federation, the world body of track and field, recognizes only records in metric distances, except for the mile. *Record pending.

Men's Records
Running

Event	Record	Holder	Country	Date	Where made
100 meters	9.84 s.	Donovan Bailey	Canada	July 27, 1996	Atlanta, GA
200 meters	19.32 s.	Michael Johnson	U.S.	Aug. 1, 1996	Atlanta, GA
400 meters	43.29 s.	Harry "Butch" Reynolds	U.S.	Aug. 17, 1988	Zurich
800 meters	*1 m., 41.11 s.	Wilson Kipketer	Denmark	Aug. 24, 1997	Cologne, Germany
1,000 meters	2 m., 12.18 s.	Sebastian Coe	Gr. Britain	July 11, 1981	Oslo
1,500 meters	3 m., 27.37 s.	Noureddine Morceli	Algeria	July 12, 1995	Nice, France
1 mile	3 m., 44.39 s.	Noureddine Morceli	Algeria	Sept. 5, 1993	Rieti, Italy
2,000 meters	4 m., 47.88 s.	Noureddine Morceli	Algeria	July 3, 1995	Paris
3,000 meters	7 m., 20.67 s.	Daniel Komen	Kenya	Sept. 1, 1996	Rieti, Italy
5,000 meters	*12 m., 39.74 s.	Daniel Komen	Kenya	Aug. 22, 1997	Brussels
10,000 meters	*26 m., 27.85 s.	Paul Tergat	Kenya	Aug. 22,1997	Brussels
20,000 meters	56 m., 55.6 s.	Arturo Barrios	Mexico	Mar. 30, 1991	La Fleche, France
25,000 meters	1 hr., 13 m., 55.8 s.	Toshihiko Seko	Japan	Mar. 22, 1981	Christchurch, New Zealand
3,000 meter stpl.	*7 m., 55.72 s.	Bernard Barmasai	Kenya	Aug. 24, 1997	Cologne, Germany
Marathon	2 hr., 6 m., 50 s.	Belayneh Dinsamo	Ethiopia	Apr. 17, 1988	Rotterdam

Hurdles

Event	Record	Holder	Country	Date	Where made
110 meters	12.91 s.	Colin Jackson	Gr. Britain	Aug. 20, 1993	Stuttgart, Germany
400 meters	46.78 s.	Kevin Young	U.S.	Aug. 6, 1992	Barcelona

Relay Races

Event	Record	Holder	Country	Date	Where made
400 mtrs. (4x100)	37.40 s.	(Marsh, Burrell, Mitchell, Lewis)	U.S.	Aug. 8, 1992	Barcelona
		(Drummond, Cason, Mitchell, Burrell)	U.S.	Aug. 21, 1993	Stuttgart, Germany
800 mtrs. (4×200)	1 m., 18.68 s.	(Marsh, Burrell, Heard, Lewis)	U.S.	Apr. 17, 1994	Walnut, CA
1,600 mtrs. (4×400)	2 m., 54.29 s.	(Valmon, Watts, Reynolds, Johnson)	U.S.	Aug. 22, 1993	Stuttgart, Germany
3,200 mtrs. (4×800)	7 m., 03.89 s.	(Elliott, Cook, Cram, Coe)	Gr. Britain	Aug. 30, 1982	London

Field Events

Event	Record	Holder	Country	Date	Where made
High jump	8 ft., ½ in.	Javier Sotomayor	Cuba	July 27, 1993	Salamanca, Spain
Long jump	29 ft., 4½ in.	Mike Powell	U.S.	Aug. 30, 1991	Tokyo
Triple jump	60 ft., ¼ in.	Jonathan Edwards	Gr. Britain	Aug. 7, 1995	Göteborg, Sweden
Pole vault	20 ft., 1¾ in.	Sergei Bubka	Ukraine	July 31, 1994	Sestriere, Italy
16-lb. shot put	75 ft., 10¼ in.	Randy Barnes	U.S.	May 20, 1990	Los Angeles, CA
Discus	243 ft.	Juergen Schult	E. Germany	June 6, 1986	E. Germany
Javelin	323 ft., 1 in.	Jan Zelezny	Czech Rep.	May 25, 1996	Jena, Germany
16-lb. hammer	284 ft., 7 in.	Yuri Sedykh	USSR	Aug. 30, 1986	Stuttgart, W. Germany
Decathlon	8,891 pts.	Dan O'Brien	U.S.	Sept. 4-5, 1992	Talence, France

Women's Records
Running

Event	Record	Holder	Country	Date	Where made
100 meters	10.49 s.	Florence Griffith Joyner	U.S.	July 16, 1988	Indianapolis, IN
200 meters	21.34 s.	Florence Griffith Joyner	U.S.	Sept. 29, 1988	Seoul
400 meters	47.60 s.	Marita Koch	E. Germany	Oct. 6, 1985	Canberra, Australia
800 meters	1 m., 53.28 s.	Jarmila Kratochvilova	Czechoslovakia	July 26, 1983	Munich
1,000 meters	2 m., 28.98 s.	Svetlana Masterkova	Russia	Aug. 23, 1996	Brussels

(continued)

Event	Record	Holder	Country	Date	Where made
1,500 meters.....	3 m., 50.46 s.	Qu Yunxia............	China	Sept. 11, 1993	Beijing
1 mile	4 m., 12.56 s.	Svetlana Masterkova	Russia........	Aug. 14, 1996	Zurich
2,000 meters.....	5 m., 25.36 s.	Sonia O'Sullivan	Ireland........	July 8, 1994	Edinburgh
3,000 meters.....	8 m., 06.11 s.	Wang Junxia..........	China	Sept. 13, 1993	Beijing
5,000 meters.....	14 m., 36.45 s.	Fernanda Ribeiro......	Portugal.......	July 22, 1995	Hechtel, Belgium
10,000 meters....	29 m., 31.78 s.	Wang Junxia..........	China	Sept. 8, 1993	Beijing
Marathon	2 h., 21 m., 06 s. ...	Ingrid Kristiansen.....	Norway	Apr. 21, 1985	London

Hurdles

Event	Record	Holder	Country	Date	Where made
100 meters	12.21 s.	Yordanka Donkova	Bulgaria........	Aug. 20, 1988	Bulgaria
400 meters	52.61 s.	Kim Batten	U.S.	Aug. 11, 1995	Göteborg, Sweden

Field Events

Event	Record	Holder	Country	Date	Where made
High jump	6 ft., 10¼ in.	Stefka Kostadinova	Bulgaria.....	Aug. 30, 1987	Rome
Long jump......	24 ft., 8¼ in.	Galina Chistyakova	USSR	June 11, 1988	Leningrad
Triple jump	50 ft., 10¼ in.	Inessa Kravets	Ukraine	Aug. 10, 1995	Göteborg, Sweden
Pole vault	14 ft., 11 in.	Emma George.........	Australia	Feb. 20, 1997	Melbourne
Shot put	74 ft., 3 in.	Natalya Lisovskaya	USSR	June 7, 1987	Moscow
Discus	252 ft........	Gabriele Reinsch......	E. Germany	July 9, 1988	E. Germany
Hammer	239 ft., 8 in.	Olga Kuzenkova	Russia.....	June 22, 1997	Munich
Javelin	262 ft., 5 in.	Petra Felke	E. Germany	Sept. 9, 1988	E. Germany
Heptathlon	7,291 pts........	Jackie Joyner-Kersee....	U.S.	Sept. 23-24, 1988	Seoul

Relay Races

Event	Record	Holder	Country	Date	Where made
400 mtrs. (4×100) .	41.37 s.	(Gladisch, Rieger, Auerswald, Goehr)	E. Germany	Oct. 6, 1985	Canberra, Australia
800 mtrs. (4×200) .	1 m., 28.15 s.	(Goehr, Mueller, Woeckel, Koch)	E. Germany	Aug. 9, 1980	Jena, E. Germany
1,600 mtrs. (4×400) .	3 m., 15.17 s.	(Ledovskaya, Nazarova, Pinigina, Bryzgina)	USSR	Oct. 1, 1988	Seoul
3,200 mtrs. (4×800) .	7 m., 50.17 s.	(Olizarenko, Gurina, Borisova, Podyalovskaya)	USSR	Aug. 5, 1984	Moscow

World Track and Field Indoor Records

As of Oct. 1997

The International Amateur Athletic Federation began recognizing world indoor track and field records as official on Jan. 1, 1987. Prior to that, there were only unofficial world indoor bests. World indoor bests set prior to Jan. 1, 1987, are subject to approval as world records providing they meet the prescribed IAAF world records criteria, including drug testing. To be accepted as a world indoor record, a performance must meet the same criteria as a world record outdoors except that a track performance cannot be set on an indoor track larger than 200 meters.

Men

Event	Record	Holder	Country	Date	Where made
50 meters	5.56	Donovan Bailey	Canada.........	Feb. 9, 1996	Reno, NV
60 meters	6.41	Andre Cason......	U.S.	Feb. 14, 1992	Madrid
200 meters	19.92	Frankie Fredericks ..	Namibia	Feb. 18, 1996	Lievin, France
400 meters	44.63	Michael Johnson ...	U.S.	Mar. 4, 1995	Atlanta, GA
800 meters	1:42.67	Wilson Kipketer	Denmark.....	Mar. 9, 1997	Paris
1,000 meters....	2:15.26......	Noureddine Morceli .	Algeria	Feb. 22, 1992	Birmingham, England
1,500 meters....	3:31.18......	Hicham el-Guerrouj .	Morocco	Feb. 2, 1997	Stuttgart, Germany
1 mile	3:48.45......	Hicham el-Guerrouj .	Morocco	Feb. 12, 1997	Ghent, Belgium
3,000 meters....	7:30.72......	Haile Gebrselassie.	Ethiopia	Feb. 4, 1996	Stuttgart, Germany
5,000 meters....	12:59.04.....	Haile Gebrselassie..	Ethiopia	Feb. 20, 1997	Stockholm
50-meter hurdles .	6.25	Mark McKoy	Canada.....	Mar. 5, 1986	Kobe, Japan
60-meter hurdles .	7.30	Colin Jackson	Gr. Britain	Mar. 6, 1994	Sindelfingen, Germany
High jump	7 ft., 11¼ in. .	Javier Sotomayor ..	Cuba	Mar. 4, 1989	Budapest
Pole vault	20 ft., 2 in. .	Sergei Bubka	Ukraine	Feb. 21, 1993	Donyetsk, Ukraine
Long jump......	28 ft., 10¼ in. .	Carl Lewis	U.S.	Jan. 27, 1984	New York, NY
Triple jump	58 ft., 6 in. .	Eliecer Urrutia	Cuba	Mar. 1, 1997	Sindelfingen, Germany
Shot put	74 ft., 4¼ in. .	Randy Barnes	U.S.	Jan. 20, 1989	Los Angeles, CA

Women

Event	Record	Holder	Country	Date	Where made
50 meters	5.96	Irina Privalova	Russia........	Feb. 9, 1995	Madrid
60 meters	6.92	Irina Privalova	Russia........	Feb. 9, 1995	Madrid
		Irina Privalova	Russia........	Feb. 11, 1993	Madrid
200 meters	21.87	Merlene Ottey	Jamaica	Feb. 13, 1993	Lievin, France
400 meters	49.59	Jarmila Kratochvilova .	Czechoslovakia...	Mar. 7, 1982	Milan, Italy
800 meters	1:56.40......	Christine Wachtel ..	E. Germany.	Feb. 13, 1988	Vienna
1,000 meters....	2:31.23......	Maria Mutola	Mozambique ...	Feb. 25, 1996	Stockholm
1,500 meters....	4:00.27......	Doina Melinte	Romania	Feb. 9, 1990	E. Rutherford, NJ
1 mile	4:17.14......	Doina Melinte	Romania	Feb. 9, 1990	E. Rutherford, NJ
3,000 meters....	8:33.82......	Elly van Hulst	Netherlands ...	Mar. 4, 1989	Budapest
5,000 meters....	15:03.17.....	Liz McColgan	Gr. Britain	Feb. 22, 1992	Birmingham, England
50-meter hurdles .	6.58	Cornelia Oschkenat ..	E. Germany.....	Feb. 20, 1988	Berlin
60-meter hurdles .	7.69	Lyudmila Narozhilenko	USSR...........	Feb 4, 1990	Chelyabinsk, USSR
High jump	6 ft., 9½ in. .	Heike Henkel	Germany.....	Feb. 8, 1992	Karlsruhe, Germany
Pole vault	14 ft., 5¼ in. .	Emma George.....	Australia	Dec. 10, 1996	Melbourne
Long jump......	24 ft., 2¼ in. .	Heike Drechsler.....	E. Germany.....	Feb. 13, 1988	Vienna
Triple jump	49 ft., 3¾ in. .	Yolanda Chen	Russia	Mar. 11, 1995	Barcelona
Shot put	73 ft., 10 in. .	Helena Fibingerova ..	Czechoslovakia...	Feb. 19, 1977	Czechoslovakia

NATIONAL FOOTBALL LEAGUE

NFL 1996-97: Records in Rushing, Receiving, and Kicking; Oilers to Tennessee

Marcus Allen of Kansas City set the record for most rushing touchdowns in a career, with 112, eclipsing Walter Payton's 110. Detroit's Barry Sanders, enroute to his 3d NFL rushing title, became the first player to rush for over 1,500 yards in 3 consecutive seasons. San Francisco's Jerry Rice became the first to haul in 1,000 career receptions. New York Jets kicker Nick Lowery became the career leader in field goals with 383, while Carolina kicker John Kasay set a single-season mark with 37. The Houston Oilers became the Tennessee Oilers before the 1997 season and will play home games at the Liberty Bowl in Memphis until 1999, when a new stadium in Nashville is to be completed.

Final 1996 Standings

American Football Conference

Eastern Division

	W	L	T	Pct.	Pts.	Opp.
New England	11	5	0	.689	418	313
Buffalo*	10	6	0	.625	319	266
Indianapolis*	9	7	0	.563	317	334
Miami	8	8	0	.500	339	325
N.Y. Jets	1	15	0	.063	279	454

Central Division

	W	L	T	Pct.	Pts.	Opp.
Pittsburgh	10	6	0	.625	344	257
Jacksonville*	9	7	0	.563	325	335
Cincinnati	8	8	0	.500	372	369
Houston	8	8	0	.500	345	319
Baltimore	4	12	0	.250	371	441

Western Division

	W	L	T	Pct.	Pts.	Opp.
Denver	13	3	0	.813	391	275
Kansas City	9	7	0	.563	297	300
San Diego	8	8	0	.500	310	376
Oakland	7	9	0	.438	340	293
Seattle	7	9	0	.438	317	376

National Football Conference

Eastern Division

	W	L	T	Pct.	Pts.	Opp.
Dallas	10	6	0	.625	286	250
Philadelphia*	10	6	0	.625	363	341
Washington	9	7	0	.563	364	312
Arizona	7	9	0	.438	300	397
N.Y. Giants	6	10	0	.375	242	297

Central Division

	W	L	T	Pct.	Pts.	Opp.
Green Bay	13	3	0	.813	456	210
Minnesota*	9	7	0	.563	298	315
Chicago	7	9	0	.438	283	305
Tampa Bay	6	10	0	.375	221	293
Detroit	5	11	0	.313	302	368

Western Division

	W	L	T	Pct.	Pts.	Opp.
Carolina	12	4	0	.750	367	218
San Francisco*	12	4	0	.750	398	257
St. Louis	6	10	0	.375	303	409
Atlanta	3	13	0	.188	309	461
New Orleans	3	13	0	.188	229	339

* Wild card team.

AFC Playoffs—Pittsburgh 42, Indianapolis 14; Jacksonville 30, Buffalo 27; New England 28, Pittsburgh 3; Jacksonville 30, Denver 27; New England 20, Jacksonville 6.

NFC Playoffs—Dallas 40, Minnesota 15; San Francisco 14, Philadelphia 0; Green Bay 35, San Francisco 14; Carolina 26, Dallas 17; Green Bay 30, Carolina 13.

Super Bowl—Green Bay 35, New England 21.

National Football League Champions

Year	East Winner (W-L-T)	West Winner (W-L-T)	Playoff
1933	New York Giants (11-3-0)	Chicago Bears (10-2-1)	Chicago Bears 23, New York 21
1934	New York Giants (8-5-0)	Chicago Bears (13-0-0)	New York 30, Chicago Bears 13
1935	New York Giants (9-3-0)	Detroit Lions (7-3-2)	Detroit 26, New York 7
1936	Boston Redskins (7-5-0)	Green Bay Packers (10-1-1)	Green Bay 21, Boston 6
1937	Washington Redskins (8-3-0)	Chicago Bears (9-1-1)	Washington 28, Chicago Bears 21
1938	New York Giants (8-2-1)	Green Bay Packers (8-3-0)	New York 23, Green Bay 17
1939	New York Giants (9-1-1)	Green Bay Packers (9-2-0)	Green Bay 27, New York 0
1940	Washington Redskins (9-2-0)	Chicago Bears (8-3-0)	Chicago Bears 73, Washington 0
1941	New York Giants (8-3-0)	Chicago Bears (10-1-1)(a)	Chicago Bears 37, New York 9
1942	Washington Redskins (10-1-1)	Chicago Bears (11-0-0)	Washington 14, Chicago Bears 6
1943	Washington Redskins (6-3-1)(a)	Chicago Bears (8-1-1)	Chicago Bears, 41, Washington 21
1944	New York Giants (8-1-1)	Green Bay Packers (8-2-0)	Green Bay 14, New York 7
1945	Washington Redskins (8-2-0)	Cleveland Rams (9-1-0)	Cleveland 15, Washington 14
1946	New York Giants (7-3-1)	Chicago Bears (8-2-1)	Chicago Bears 24, New York 14
1947	Philadelphia Eagles (8-4-0)(a)	Chicago Cardinals (9-3-0)	Chicago Cardinals 28, Philadelphia 21
1948	Philadelphia Eagles (9-2-1)	Chicago Cardinals (11-1-0)	Philadelphia 7, Chicago Cardinals 0
1949	Philadelphia Eagles (11-1-0)	Los Angeles Rams (8-2-2)	Philadelphia 14, Los Angeles 0
1950	Cleveland Browns (10-2-0)(a)	Los Angeles Rams (9-3-0)(a)	Cleveland 30, Los Angeles 28
1951	Cleveland Browns (11-1-0)	Los Angeles Rams (8-4-0)	Los Angeles 24, Cleveland 17
1952	Cleveland Browns (8-4-0)	Detroit Lions (9-3-0)(a)	Detroit 17, Cleveland 7
1953	Cleveland Browns (11-1-0)	Detroit Lions (10-2-0)	Detroit 17, Cleveland 16
1954	Cleveland Browns (9-3-0)	Detroit Lions (9-2-1)	Cleveland 56, Detroit 10
1955	Cleveland Browns (9-2-1)	Los Angeles Rams (8-3-1)	Cleveland 38, Los Angeles 14
1956	New York Giants (8-3-1)	Chicago Bears (9-2-1)	New York 47, Chicago Bears 7
1957	Cleveland Browns (9-2-1)	Detroit Lions (8-4-0)(a)	Detroit 59, Cleveland 14
1958	New York Giants (9-3-0)(a)	Baltimore Colts (9-3-0)	Baltimore 23, New York 17(b)
1959	New York Giants (10-2-0)	Baltimore Colts (9-3-0)	Baltimore 31, New York 16
1960	Philadelphia Eagles (10-2-0)	Green Bay Packers (8-4-0)	Philadelphia 17, Green Bay 13
1961	New York Giants (10-3-1)	Green Bay Packers (11-3-0)	Green Bay 37, New York 0
1962	New York Giants (12-2-0)	Green Bay Packers (13-1-0)	Green Bay 16, New York 7
1963	New York Giants (11-3-0)	Chicago Bears (11-1-2)	Chicago 14, New York 10
1964	Cleveland Browns (10-3-1)	Baltimore Colts (12-2-0)	Cleveland 27, Baltimore 0
1965	Cleveland Browns (11-3-0)	Green Bay Packers (10-3-1)(a)	Green Bay 23, Cleveland 12
1966	Dallas Cowboys (10-3-1)	Green Bay Packers (12-2-0)	Green Bay 34, Dallas 27

(a) Won divisional playoff. (b) Won at 8:15 of sudden death overtime period.

Year	Conference	Division	Winner (W-L-T)	Playoffs(c)
1967	East	Century	Cleveland Browns (9-5-0)	Dallas 52, Cleveland 14
		Capitol	Dallas Cowboys (9-5-0)	
	West	Central	Green Bay Packers (9-4-1)	Green Bay 28, Los Angeles 7
		Coastal	Los Angeles Rams (11-1-2)(a)	Green Bay 21, Dallas 17

(continued)

Year	Conference	Division	Winner (W-L-T)	Playoffs(c)
1968	East	Century	Cleveland Browns (10-4-0)	Cleveland 31, Dallas 20
		Capitol	Dallas Cowboys (12-2-0)	
	West	Central	Minnesota Vikings (8-6-0)	Baltimore 24, Minnesota 14
		Coastal	Baltimore Colts (13-1-0)	Baltimore 34, Cleveland 0
1969	East	Century	Cleveland Browns (10-3-1)	Cleveland 38, Dallas 14
		Capitol	Dallas Cowboys (11-2-1)	
	West	Central	Minnesota Vikings (12-2-0)	Minnesota 23, Los Angeles 20
		Coastal	Los Angeles Rams (11-3-0)	Minnesota 27, Cleveland 7
1970	American	Eastern	Baltimore Colts (11-2-1)	Baltimore 17, Cincinnati 0
		Central	Cincinnati Bengals (8-6-0)	Oakland 21, Miami* 14
		Western	Oakland Raiders (8-4-2)	Baltimore 27, Oakland 17
	National	Eastern	Dallas Cowboys (10-4-0)	Dallas 5, Detroit* 0
		Central	Minnesota Vikings (12-2-0)	San Francisco 17, Minnesota 14
		Western	San Francisco 49ers (10-3-1)	Dallas 17, San Francisco 10
1971	American	Eastern	Miami Dolphins (10-3-1)	Miami 27, Kansas City* 24
		Central	Cleveland Browns (9-5-0)	Baltimore 20, Cleveland 3
		Western	Kansas City Chiefs (10-3-1)	Miami 21, Baltimore 0
	National	Eastern	Dallas Cowboys (11-3-0)	Dallas 20, Minnesota 12
		Central	Minnesota Vikings (11-3-0)	San Francisco 24, Washington* 20
		Western	San Francisco 49ers (9-5-0)	Dallas 14, San Francisco 3
1972	American	Eastern	Miami Dolphins (14-0-0)	Miami 20, Cleveland* 14
		Central	Pittsburgh Steelers (11-3-0)	Pittsburgh 13, Oakland 7
		Western	Oakland Raiders (10-3-1)	Miami 21, Pittsburgh 17
	National	Eastern	Washington Redskins (11-3-0)	Washington 16, Green Bay 3
		Central	Green Bay Packers (10-4-0)	Dallas* 30, San Francisco 28
		Western	San Francisco 49ers (8-5-1)	Washington 26, Dallas* 3
1973	American	Eastern	Miami Dolphins (12-2-0)	Miami 34, Cincinnati 16
		Central	Cincinnati Bengals (10-4-0)	Oakland 33, Pittsburgh* 14
		Western	Oakland Raiders (9-4-1)	Miami 27, Oakland 10
	National	Eastern	Dallas Cowboys (10-4-0)	Dallas 27, Los Angeles 16
		Central	Minnesota Vikings (12-2-0)	Minnesota 27, Washington* 20
		Western	Los Angeles Rams (12-2-0)	Minnesota 27, Dallas 10
1974	American	Eastern	Miami Dolphins (11-3-0)	Oakland 28, Miami 26
		Central	Pittsburgh Steelers (10-3-1)	Pittsburgh 32, Buffalo* 14
		Western	Oakland Raiders (12-2-0)	Pittsburgh 24, Oakland 13
	National	Eastern	St. Louis Cardinals (10-4-0)	Minnesota 30, St. Louis 14
		Central	Minnesota Vikings (10-4-0)	Los Angeles 19, Washington* 10
		Western	Los Angeles Rams (10-4-0)	Minnesota 14, Los Angeles 10
1975	American	Eastern	Baltimore Colts (10-4-0)	Pittsburgh 28, Baltimore 10
		Central	Pittsburgh Steelers (12-2-0)	Oakland 31, Cincinnati* 28
		Western	Oakland Raiders (11-3-0)	Pittsburgh 16, Oakland 10
	National	Eastern	St. Louis Cardinals (11-3-0)	Dallas* 17, Minnesota 14
		Central	Minnesota Vikings (12-2-0)	Los Angeles 35, St. Louis 23
		Western	Los Angeles Rams (12-2-0)	Dallas* 37, Los Angeles 7
1976	American	Eastern	Baltimore Colts (11-3-0)	Pittsburgh 40, Baltimore 14
		Central	Pittsburgh Steelers (10-4-0)	Oakland 24, New England* 21
		Western	Oakland Raiders (13-1-0)	Oakland 24, Pittsburgh 7
	National	Eastern	Dallas Cowboys (11-3-0)	Minnesota 35, Washington* 20
		Central	Minnesota Vikings (11-2-1)	Los Angeles 14, Dallas 12
		Western	Los Angeles Rams (10-3-1)	Minnesota 24, Los Angeles 13
1977	American	Eastern	Baltimore Colts (10-4-0)	Oakland* 37, Baltimore 31
		Central	Pittsburgh Steelers (9-5-0)	Denver 34, Pittsburgh 21
		Western	Denver Broncos (12-2-0)	Denver 20, Oakland* 17
	National	Eastern	Dallas Cowboys (12-2-0)	Dallas 37, Chicago* 7
		Central	Minnesota Vikings (9-5-0)	Minnesota 14, Los Angeles 7
		Western	Los Angeles Rams (10-4-0)	Dallas 23, Minnesota 6
1978	American	Eastern	New England Patriots (11-5-0)	Pittsburgh 33, Denver 10
		Central	Pittsburgh Steelers (14-2-0)	Houston* 31, New England 14
		Western	Denver Broncos (10-6-0)	Pittsburgh 34, Houston* 5
	National	Eastern	Dallas Cowboys (12-4-0)	Dallas 27, Atlanta* 20
		Central	Minnesota Vikings (8-7-1)	Los Angeles 34, Minnesota 10
		Western	Los Angeles Rams (12-4-0)	Dallas 28, Los Angeles 0
1979	American	Eastern	Miami Dolphins (10-6-0)	Houston* 17, San Diego 14
		Central	Pittsburgh Steelers (12-4-0)	Pittsburgh 34, Miami 14
		Western	San Diego Chargers (12-4-0)	Pittsburgh 27, Houston* 13
	National	Eastern	Dallas Cowboys (11-5-0)	Tampa Bay 24, Philadelphia* 17
		Central	Tampa Bay Buccaneers (10-6-0)	Los Angeles 21, Dallas 19
		Western	Los Angeles Rams (9-7-0)	Los Angeles 9, Tampa Bay 0
1980	American	Eastern	Buffalo Bills (11-5-0)	San Diego 20, Buffalo 14
		Central	Cleveland Browns (11-5-0)	Oakland* 14, Cleveland 12
		Western	San Diego Chargers (11-5-0)	Oakland* 34, San Diego 27
	National	Eastern	Philadelphia Eagles (12-4-0)	Philadelphia 31, Minnesota 16
		Central	Minnesota Vikings (9-7-0)	Dallas* 30, Atlanta 27
		Western	Atlanta Falcons (12-4-0)	Philadelphia 20, Dallas* 7
1981	American	Eastern	Miami Dolphins (11-4-1)	San Diego 41, Miami 38
		Central	Cincinnati Bengals (12-4-0)	Cincinnati 28, Buffalo* 21
		Western	San Diego Chargers (10-6-0)	Cincinnati 27, San Diego 7
	National	Eastern	Dallas Cowboys (12-4-0)	Dallas 38, Tampa Bay 0
		Central	Tampa Bay Buccaneers (9-7-0)	San Francisco 38, N.Y. Giants* 24
		Western	San Francisco 49ers (13-3-0)	San Francisco 28, Dallas 27
1982(d)	American		Los Angeles Raiders (8-1-0)	Strike-shortened season (see
	National		Washington Redskins (8-1-0)	playoff results below)

AFC playoffs—Miami 28, New England 13; L.A. Raiders 27, Cleveland 10; N.Y. Jets 44, Cincinnati 17; San Diego 31, Pittsburgh 28; N.Y. Jets 17, L.A. Raiders 14; Miami 34, San Diego 13; Miami 14, N.Y. Jets 0. **NFC playoffs**—Washington 31, Detroit 7; Green Bay 41, St. Louis 16; Dallas 30, Tampa Bay 17; Minnesota 30, Atlanta 24; Washington 21, Minnesota 7; Dallas 37, Green Bay 26; Washington 31, Dallas 17. **AFC Champion**—Miami Dolphins. **NFC Champion**—Washington Redskins.

Year	Conference	Division	Winner (W-L-T)	Playoffs(c)
1983.........	American ...	Eastern	Miami Dolphins (12-4-0)	Seattle* 27, Miami 20
		Central	Pittsburgh Steelers (10-6-0)	L.A. Raiders 38, Pittsburgh 10
		Western.....	Los Angeles Raiders (12-4-0)	L.A. Raiders 30, Seattle* 14
	National....	Eastern	Washington Redskins (14-2-0)	Washington 51, L.A. Rams* 7
		Central	Detroit Lions (9-7-0)	San Francisco 24, Detroit 23
		Western.....	San Francisico 49ers (10-6-0)....	Washington 24, San Francisco 21
1984.......	American ...	Eastern	Miami Dolphins (14-2-0)	Miami 31, Seattle* 10
		Central	Pittsburgh Steelers (9-7-0)	Pittsburgh 24, Denver 17
		Western.....	Denver Broncos (13-3-0)	Miami 45, Pittsburgh 28
	National....	Eastern	Washington Redskins (11-5-0)	Chicago 23, Washington 19
		Central	Chicago Bears (10-6-0)	San Francisco 21, N.Y. Giants* 10
		Western.....	San Francisco 49ers (15-1-0)	San Francisco 23, Chicago 0
1985.......	American ...	Eastern	Miami Dolphins (12-4-0)	New England* 27, L.A. Raiders 20
		Central	Cleveland Browns (8-8-0)	Miami 24, Cleveland 21
		Western.....	Los Angeles Raiders (12-4-0)	New England* 31, Miami 14
	National....	Eastern	Dallas Cowboys (10-6-0)	Chicago 21, N.Y. Giants* 0
		Central	Chicago Bears (15-1-0)	L.A. Rams 20, Dallas 0
		Western.....	Los Angeles Rams (11-5-0)	Chicago 24, L.A. Rams 0
1986.......	American ...	Eastern	New England Patriots (11-5-0)	Denver 22, New England 17
		Central	Cleveland Browns (12-4-0)	Cleveland 23, N.Y. Jets* 20
		Western.....	Denver Broncos (11-5-0)	Denver 23, Cleveland 20
	National....	Eastern	New York Giants (14-2-0)	N.Y. Giants 49, San Francisco 3
		Central	Chicago Bears (14-2-0)	Washington* 27, Chicago 13
		Western.....	San Francisco 49ers (10-5-1)	N.Y. Giants 17, Washington* 0
1987.......	American ...	Eastern	Indianapolis Colts (9-6-0)	Cleveland 38, Indianapolis 21
		Central	Cleveland Browns (10-5-0)	Denver 34, Houston* 10
		Western.....	Denver Broncos (10-4-1)	Denver 38, Cleveland 33
	National....	Eastern	Washington Redskins (11-4-0)	Washington 21, Chicago 17
		Central	Chicago Bears (11-4-0)	Minnesota* 36, San Francisco 24
		Western.....	San Francisco 49ers (13-2-0)	Washington 17, Minnesota* 10
1988.......	American ...	Eastern	Buffalo Bills (12-4-0).........	Buffalo 17, Houston* 10
		Central	Cincinnati Bengals (12-4-0)	Cincinnati 21, Seattle 13
		Western.....	Seattle Seahawks (9-7-0)........	Cincinnati 21, Buffalo 10
	National....	Eastern	Philadelphia Eagles (10-6-0)	Chicago 20, Philadelphia 12
		Central	Chicago Bears (12-4-0)	San Francisco 34, Minnesota* 9
		Western.....	San Francisco 49ers (10-6-0)	San Francisco 28, Chicago 3
1989.......	American ...	Eastern	Buffalo Bills (9-7-0)	Cleveland 34, Buffalo 30
		Central	Cleveland Browns (9-6-1)	Denver 24, Pittsburgh* 23
		Western.....	Denver Broncos (11-5-0)	Denver 37, Cleveland 21
	National....	Eastern	New York Giants (12-4-0)	San Francisco 41, Minnesota 13
		Central	Minnesota Vikings (10-6-0)	L.A. Rams* 19, N.Y. Giants 13
		Western.....	San Francisco 49ers (14-2-0)	San Francisco 30, L.A. Rams* 3
1990.......	American ...	Eastern	Buffalo Bills (13-3-0).........	L.A. Raiders 20, Cincinnati 10
		Central	Cincinnati Bengals (9-7-0)	Buffalo 44, Miami* 34
		Western.....	Los Angeles Raiders (12-4-0)	Buffalo 51, L.A. Raiders 3
	National....	Eastern	New York Giants (13-3-0)	San Francisco 28, Washington* 10
		Central	Chicago Bears (11-5-0)	N.Y. Giants 31, Chicago 3
		Western.....	San Francisco 49ers (14-2-0)	N.Y. Giants 15, San Francisco 13
1991.......	American ...	Eastern	Buffalo Bills (13-3-0).........	Denver 26, Houston 24
		Central	Houston Oilers (11-5-0)	Buffalo 37, Kansas City* 14
		Western.....	Denver Broncos (12-4-0)	Buffalo 10, Denver 7
	National....	Eastern	Washington Redskins (14-2-0)	Washington 24, Atlanta* 7
		Central	Detroit Lions (12-4-0)	Detroit 38, Dallas* 6
		Western.....	New Orleans Saints (11-5-0).....	Washington 41, Detroit 10
1992.......	American ...	Eastern	Miami Dolphins (11-5-0)	Miami 31, San Diego 0
		Central	Pittsburgh Steelers (11-5-0)	Buffalo* 24, Pittsburgh 3
		Western.....	San Diego Chargers (11-5-0)	Buffalo* 29, Miami 10
	National....	Eastern	Dallas Cowboys (13-3-0)	Dallas 34, Philadelphia* 10
		Central	Minnesota Vikings (11-5-0)	San Francisco 20, Washington* 13
		Western.....	San Francisco 49ers (14-2-0)	Dallas 30, San Francisco 20
1993.......	American ...	Eastern	Buffalo Bills (12-4-0)...........	Buffalo 29, L.A. Raiders* 23
		Central	Houston Oilers (12-4-0)	Kansas City 28, Houston 20
		Western.....	Kansas City Chiefs (11-5-0)	Buffalo 30, Kansas City 13
	National....	Eastern	Dallas Cowboys (12-4-0)	Dallas 27, Green Bay* 17
		Central	Detroit Lions (10-6-0)	San Francisco 44, N.Y. Giants* 3
		Western.....	San Francisco 49ers (10-6-0)	Dallas 38, San Francisco 21
1994.......	American ...	Eastern	Miami Dolphins (10-6-0).........	Pittsburgh 29, Cleveland* 9
		Central	Pittsburgh Steelers (12-4-0)	San Diego 22, Miami 21
		Western.....	San Diego Chargers (11-5-0)	San Diego 17, Pittsburgh 13
	National....	Eastern	Dallas Cowboys (12-4-0)	San Francisco 44, Chicago* 15
		Central	Minnesota Vikings (10-6-0).......	Dallas 35, Green Bay* 9
		Western.....	San Francisco 49ers (13-3-0)	San Francisco 38, Dallas 28
1995.......	American ...	Eastern	Buffalo Bills (10-6-0)...........	Indianapolis* 10, Kansas City 7
		Central	Pittsburgh Steelers (11-5-0)	Pittsburgh 40, Buffalo 21
		Western.....	Kansas City Chiefs (13-3-0)	Pittsburgh 20, Indianapolis* 16
	National....	Eastern	Dallas Cowboys (12-4-0)	Dallas 30, Philadelphia* 11
		Central	Green Bay Packers (11-5-0)	Green Bay 27, San Francisco 17
		Western.....	San Francisco 49ers (11-5-0)	Dallas 38, Green Bay 27
1996.......	American ...	Eastern	New England Patriots (11-5-0)	Jacksonville* 30, Denver 27
		Central	Pittsburgh Steelers (10-6-0)	New England 28, Pittsburgh 3
		Western.....	Denver Broncos (13-3-0)	New England 20, Jacksonville* 6
	National....	Eastern	Dallas Cowboys (10-6-0)	Green Bay 35, San Francisco* 14
		Central	Green Bay Packers (13-3-0)	Carolina 26, Dallas 17
		Western.....	Carolina Panthers (12-4-0)	Green Bay 30, Carolina 13

*Wild card team. (c) From 1978 on, only the final 2 conference playoff rounds are shown. (d) A strike shortened the 1982 season from 16 to 9 games. The top 8 teams in each conference played in a tournament to determine the conference champion.

Green Bay Packers Defeat New England Patriots in Super Bowl XXXI

The Green Bay Packers, appearing in their first Super Bowl since 1968, defeated the New England Patriots, 35-21, Jan. 26, 1997, in New Orleans, LA. The Packers played an all-around solid game, but the star of the game, no doubt, was kick-off/punt returner Desmond Howard, who had a record-setting 99-yard kickoff return for a touchdown. Howard set several other Super Bowl records, including most total return yards (244), and became the first special teams player to be selected Super Bowl MVP. The Packer victory was the 13th consecutive Super Bowl win for an NFC team.

Score by Quarters

New England.......	14	0	7	0—21	
Green Bay.........	10	17	8	0—35	

Scoring

Green Bay—Rison 54 yd. pass from Favre (Jacke kick)
Green Bay—Jacke 37 yd. field goal
New England—Byars 1 yd. pass from Bledsoe (Vinatieri kick)
New England—Coates 4 yd. pass from Bledsoe (Vinatieri kick)
Green Bay—Freeman 81 yd. pass from Favre (Jacke kick)
Green Bay—Jacke 31 yd. field goal
Green Bay—Favre 2 yd. run (Jacke kick)
New England—Martin 18 yd. run (Vinatieri kick)
Green Bay—Howard 99 yd. kickoff return (Chmura pass from Favre)

Individual Statistics

Rushing — New England, Martin 11-42, Bledsoe 1-1, Meggett 1-0. Green Bay, Levens 14-61, Bennett 17-40, Favre 4-12, Henderson 1-2.
Passing — New England, Bledsoe 25-48-4-253. Green Bay, Favre 14-27-0-246.
Receiving — New England, Coates 6-67, Glenn 4-62, Byars 4-42, Jefferson 3-34, Martin 3-28, Meggett 3-8, Brisby

2-12. Green Bay, Freeman 3-105, Levens 3-23, Rison 2-77, Henderson 2-14, Chmura 2-13, Jackson 1-10, Bennett 1-4.

Team Statistics

	New England	Green Bay
First downs................	16	16
Total yards................	257	323
Rushes-yards..............	13-43	36-115
Passing yards, net.........	214	208
Punt returns-yards...........	4-30	6-90
Kickoff returns-yards.......	6-135	4-154
Interception returns-yards......	0-0	4-24
Comp.-att.-int..............	25-48-4	14-27-0
Field goals made-attempts.....	0-0	2-3
Sacked-yards lost...........	5-39	5-38
Punts-average..............	8-45.1	7-42.7
Fumbles-lost..............	0-0	0-0
Penalties-yards............	2-22	3-41
Time of possession.........	25:45	34:15

Attendance—72,301. Time—3:21.

Super Bowls

	Year	Winner	Loser	Winning coach	Site
I	1967	Green Bay Packers, 35	Kansas City Chiefs, 10	Vince Lombardi	Los Angeles Coliseum, CA
II	1968	Green Bay Packers, 33	Oakland Raiders, 14	Vince Lombardi	Orange Bowl, Miami, FL
III	1969	New York Jets, 16	Baltimore Colts, 7	Weeb Ewbank	Orange Bowl, Miami, FL
IV	1970	Kansas City Chiefs, 23	Minnesota Vikings, 7	Hank Stram	Tulane Stadium, New Orleans, LA
V	1971	Baltimore Colts, 16	Dallas Cowboys, 13	Don McCafferty	Orange Bowl, Miami, FL
VI	1972	Dallas Cowboys, 24	Miami Dolphins, 3	Tom Landry	Tulane Stadium, New Orleans, LA
VII	1973	Miami Dolphins, 14	Washington Redskins, 7	Don Shula	Los Angeles Coliseum, CA
VIII	1974	Miami Dolphins, 24	Minnesota Vikings, 7	Don Shula	Rice Stadium, Houston, TX
IX	1975	Pittsburgh Steelers, 16	Minnesota Vikings, 6	Chuck Noll	Tulane Stadium, New Orleans, LA
X	1976	Pittsburgh Steelers, 21	Dallas Cowboys, 17	Chuck Noll	Orange Bowl, Miami, FL
XI	1977	Oakland Raiders, 32	Minnesota Vikings, 14	John Madden	Rose Bowl, Pasadena, CA
XII	1978	Dallas Cowboys, 27	Denver Broncos, 10	Tom Landry	Superdome, New Orleans, LA
XIII	1979	Pittsburgh Steelers, 35	Dallas Cowboys, 31	Chuck Noll	Orange Bowl, Miami, FL
XIV	1980	Pittsburgh Steelers, 31	Los Angeles Rams, 19	Chuck Noll	Rose Bowl, Pasadena, CA
XV	1981	Oakland Raiders, 27	Philadelphia Eagles, 10	Tom Flores	Superdome, New Orleans, LA
XVI	1982	San Francisco 49ers, 26	Cincinnati Bengals, 21	Bill Walsh	Silverdome, Pontiac, MI
XVII	1983	Washington Redskins, 27	Miami Dolphins, 17	Joe Gibbs	Rose Bowl, Pasadena, CA
XVIII	1984	Los Angeles Raiders, 38	Washington Redskins, 9	Tom Flores	Tampa Stadium, FL
XIX	1985	San Francisco 49ers, 38	Miami Dolphins, 16	Bill Walsh	Stanford Stadium, Palo Alto, CA
XX	1986	Chicago Bears, 46	New England Patriots, 10	Mike Ditka	Superdome, New Orleans, LA
XXI	1987	New York Giants, 39	Denver Broncos, 20	Bill Parcells	Rose Bowl, Pasadena, CA
XXII	1988	Washington Redskins, 42	Denver Broncos, 10	Joe Gibbs	San Diego Stadium, CA
XXIII	1989	San Francisco 49ers, 20	Cincinnati Bengals, 16	Bill Walsh	Joe Robbie Stadium, Miami, FL
XXIV	1990	San Francisco 49ers, 55	Denver Broncos, 10	George Seifert	Superdome, New Orleans, LA
XXV	1991	New York Giants, 20	Buffalo Bills, 19	Bill Parcells	Tampa Stadium, FL
XXVI	1992	Washington Redskins, 37	Buffalo Bills, 24	Joe Gibbs	Metrodome, Minneapolis, MN
XXVII	1993	Dallas Cowboys, 52	Buffalo Bills, 17	Jimmy Johnson	Rose Bowl, Pasadena, CA
XXVIII	1994	Dallas Cowboys, 30	Buffalo Bills, 13	Jimmy Johnson	Georgia Dome, Atlanta, GA
XXIX	1995	San Francisco 49ers, 49	San Diego Chargers, 26	George Seifert	Joe Robbie Stadium, Miami, FL
XXX	1996	Dallas Cowboys, 27	Pittsburgh Steelers, 17	Barry Switzer	Sun Devil Stadium, Tempe, AZ
XXXI	1997	Green Bay Packers, 35	New England Patriots, 21	Mike Holmgren	Superdome, New Orleans, LA

Super Bowl MVPs

1967	Bart Starr, Green Bay	1978	Randy White, Harvey Martin, Dallas	1988	Doug Williams, Washington
1968	Bart Starr, Green Bay	1979	Terry Bradshaw, Pittsburgh	1989	Jerry Rice, San Francisco
1969	Joe Namath, N.Y. Jets	1980	Terry Bradshaw, Pittsburgh	1990	Joe Montana, San Francisco
1970	Len Dawson, Kansas City	1981	Jim Plunkett, Oakland	1991	Ottis Anderson, N.Y. Giants
1971	Chuck Howley, Dallas	1982	Joe Montana, San Francisco	1992	Mark Rypien, Washington
1972	Roger Staubach, Dallas	1983	John Riggins, Washington	1993	Troy Aikman, Dallas
1973	Jake Scott, Miami	1984	Marcus Allen, L.A. Raiders	1994	Emmitt Smith, Dallas
1974	Larry Csonka, Miami	1985	Joe Montana, San Francisco	1995	Steve Young, San Francisco
1975	Franco Harris, Pittsburgh	1986	Richard Dent, Chicago	1996	Larry Brown, Dallas
1976	Lynn Swann, Pittsburgh	1987	Phil Simms, N.Y. Giants	1997	Desmond Howard, Green Bay
1977	Fred Biletnikoff, Oakland				

American Football League Champions

Year	Eastern Division	Western Division	Playoff
1960	Houston Oilers (10-4-0)............	Los Angeles Chargers (10-4-0)....	Houston 24, Los Angeles 16
1961	Houston Oilers (10-3-1)............	San Diego Chargers (12-2-0)......	Houston 10, San Diego 3
1962	Houston Oilers (11-3-0)............	Dallas Texans (11-3-0)...........	Dallas 20, Houston 17 (2 overtimes)
1963	Boston Patriots (7-6-1)(a)...........	San Diego Chargers (11-3-0)......	San Diego 51, Boston 10
1964	Buffalo Bills (12-2-0).............	San Diego Chargers (8-5-1)......	Buffalo 20, San Diego 7
1965	Buffalo Bills (10-3-1).............	San Diego Chargers (9-2-3)......	Buffalo 23, San Diego 0
1966	Buffalo Bills (9-4-1).............	Kansas City Chiefs (11-2-1)......	Kansas City 31, Buffalo 7
1967	Houston Oilers (9-4-1).............	Oakland Raiders (13-1-0).......	Oakland 40, Houston 7
1968	New York Jets (11-3-0).............	Oakland Raiders (12-2-0)(b)......	New York 27, Oakland 23
1969	New York Jets (10-4-0)............	Oakland Raiders (12-1-1)........	Kansas City 17, Oakland 7(c)

(a) Defeated Buffalo Bills in divisional playoff. (b) Defeated Kansas City Chiefs in divisional playoff. (c) Kansas City Chiefs defeated New York Jets and Oakland Raiders defeated Houston Oilers in divisional playoffs.

American Football Conference Leaders

(American Football League, 1960-69)

Passing / Pass-Receiving

Player, team	Atts	Com	YG	TD	Year	Player, team	Ct	YG	TD
Jack Kemp, L.A. Chargers	406	211	3,018	20	1960	Lionel Taylor, Denver	92	1,235	12
George Blanda, Houston	362	187	3,330	36	1961	Lionel Taylor, Denver	100	1,176	4
Len Dawson, Dallas Texans	310	189	2,759	29	1962	Lionel Taylor, Denver	77	908	4
Tobin Rote, San Diego	286	170	2,510	20	1963	Lionel Taylor, Denver	78	1,101	10
Len Dawson, Kansas City	354	199	2,879	30	1964	Charley Hennigan, Houston	101	1,546	8
John Hadl, San Diego	348	174	2,798	20	1965	Lionel Taylor, Denver	85	1,131	6
Len Dawson, Kansas City	284	159	2,527	26	1966	Lance Alworth, San Diego	73	1,383	13
Daryle Lamonica, Oakland	425	220	3,228	30	1967	George Sauer, N.Y. Jets	75	1,189	6
Len Dawson, Kansas City	224	131	2,109	17	1968	Lance Alworth, San Diego	68	1,312	10
Greg Cook, Cincinnati	197	106	1,854	15	1969	Lance Alworth, San Diego	64	1,003	4
Daryle Lamonica, Oakland	356	179	2,516	22	1970	Marlin Briscoe, Buffalo	57	1,036	8
Bob Griese, Miami	263	145	2,089	19	1971	Fred Biletnikoff, Oakland	61	929	9
Earl Morrall, Miami	150	83	1,360	11	1972	Fred Biletnikoff, Oakland	58	802	7
Ken Stabler, Oakland	260	163	1,997	14	1973	Fred Willis, Houston	57	371	1
Ken Anderson, Cincinnati	328	213	2,667	18	1974	Lydell Mitchell, Baltimore Colts	72	544	2
Ken Anderson, Cincinnati	377	228	3,169	21	1975	Reggie Rucker, Cleveland	60	770	3
						Lydell Mitchell, Baltimore Colts	60	554	4
Ken Stabler, Oakland	291	194	2,737	27	1976	MacArthur Lane, Kansas City	66	686	1
Bob Griese, Miami	307	180	2,252	22	1977	Lydell Mitchell, Baltimore Colts	71	620	4
Terry Bradshaw, Pittsburgh	368	207	2,915	28	1978	Steve Largent, Seattle	71	1,168	8
Dan Fouts, San Diego	530	332	4,082	24	1979	Joe Washington, Baltimore Colts	82	750	3
Brian Sipe, Cleveland	554	337	4,132	30	1980	Kellen Winslow, San Diego	89	1,290	9
Ken Anderson, Cincinnati	479	300	3,754	29	1981	Kellen Winslow, San Diego	88	1,075	10
Ken Anderson, Cincinnati	309	218	2,495	12	1982	Kellen Winslow, San Diego	54	721	6
Dan Marino, Miami	296	173	2,210	20	1983	Todd Christensen, L.A. Raiders	92	1,247	12
Dan Marino, Miami	564	362	5,084	48	1984	Ozzie Newsome, Cleveland	89	1,001	5
Ken O'Brien, N.Y. Jets	488	297	3,888	25	1985	Lionel James, San Diego	86	1,027	6
Dan Marino, Miami	623	378	4,746	44	1986	Todd Christensen, L.A. Raiders	95	1,153	8
Bernie Kosar, Cleveland	389	241	3,033	22	1987	Al Toon, N.Y. Jets	68	976	5
Boomer Esiason, Cincinnati	388	223	3,572	28	1988	Al Toon, N.Y. Jets	93	1,067	5
Boomer Esiason, Cincinnati	455	258	3,525	28	1989	Andre Reed, Buffalo	88	1,312	9
Jim Kelly, Buffalo	346	219	2,829	24	1990	Haywood Jeffires, Houston	74	1,048	8
						Drew Hill, Houston	74	1,019	5
Jim Kelly, Buffalo	474	304	3,844	33	1991	Haywood Jeffires, Houston	100	1,181	7
Warren Moon, Houston	346	224	2,521	18	1992	Haywood Jeffires, Houston	90	913	9
John Elway, Denver	551	348	4,030	25	1993	Reggie Langhorne, Indianapolis	85	1,038	3
Dan Marino, Miami	615	385	4,453	30	1994	Ben Coates, New England	96	1,174	7
Jim Harbaugh, Indianapolis	314	200	2,575	17	1995	Carl Pickens, Cincinnati	99	1,234	17
John Elway, Denver	466	287	3,328	26	1996	Carl Pickens, Cincinnati	100	1,180	12

Scoring / Rushing

Player, team	TD	PAT	FG	Pts	Year	Player, team	Yds	Atts	TD
Gene Mingo, Denver	6	33	18	123	1960	Abner Haynes, Dallas Texans	875	156	9
Gino Cappelletti, Boston	8	48	17	147	1961	Billy Cannon, Houston	948	200	6
Gene Mingo, Denver	4	32	27	137	1962	Cookie Gilchrest, Buffalo	1,096	214	13
Gino Cappelletti, Boston	2	35	22	113	1963	Clem Daniels, Oakland	1,099	215	3
Gino Cappelletti, Boston	7	36	25	155	1964	Cookie Gilchrest, Buffalo	981	230	6
Gino Cappelletti, Boston	9	27	17	132	1965	Paul Lowe, San Diego	1,121	222	7
Gino Cappelletti, Boston	6	35	16	119	1966	Jim Nance, Boston	1,458	299	11
George Blanda, Oakland	0	56	20	116	1967	Jim Nance, Boston	1,216	269	7
Jim Turner, N.Y. Jets	0	43	34	145	1968	Paul Robinson, Cincinnati	1,023	238	8
Jim Turner, N.Y. Jets	0	33	32	129	1969	Dick Post, San Diego	873	182	6
Jan Stenerud, Kansas City	0	26	30	116	1970	Floyd Little, Denver	901	209	3
Garo Yepremian, Miami	0	33	28	117	1971	Floyd Little, Denver	1,133	284	6
Bobby Howfield, N.Y. Jets	0	40	27	121	1972	O.J. Simpson, Buffalo	1,251	292	6
Roy Gerela, Pittsburgh	0	36	29	123	1973	O.J. Simpson, Buffalo	2,003	332	12
Roy Gerela, Pittsburgh	0	33	20	93	1974	Otis Armstrong, Denver	1,407	263	9
O.J. Simpson, Buffalo	23	0	0	138	1975	O.J. Simpson, Buffalo	1,817	329	16
Toni Linhart, Baltimore Colts	0	49	20	109	1976	O.J. Simpson, Buffalo	1,503	290	8
Errol Mann, Oakland	0	39	20	99	1977	Mark van Eeghen, Oakland	1,273	324	7
Pat Leahy, N.Y. Jets	0	41	22	107	1978	Earl Campbell, Houston	1,450	302	13
John Smith, New England	0	46	23	115	1979	Earl Campbell, Houston	1,697	368	19
John Smith, New England	0	51	26	129	1980	Earl Campbell, Houston	1,934	373	13
Jim Breech, Cincinnati	0	49	22	115	1981	Earl Campbell, Houston	1,376	361	10
Nick Lowery, Kansas City	0	37	26	115					
Marcus Allen, L.A. Raiders	14	0	0	84	1982	Freeman McNeil, N.Y. Jets	786	151	6
Gary Anderson, Pittsburgh	0	38	27	119	1983	Curt Warner, Seattle	1,446	335	13
Gary Anderson, Pittsburgh	0	45	24	117	1984	Earnest Jackson, San Diego	1,179	296	8
Gary Anderson, Pittsburgh	0	40	33	139	1985	Marcus Allen, L.A. Raiders	1,759	380	11
Tony Franklin, New England	0	44	32	140	1986	Curt Warner, Seattle	1,481	319	13
Jim Breech, Cincinnati	0	25	24	97	1987	Eric Dickerson, L.A. Rams-Ind.	1,288*	283	6
Scott Norwood, Buffalo	0	33	32	129	1988	Eric Dickerson, Indianapolis	1,659	388	14
David Treadwell, Denver	0	39	27	120	1989	Christian Okoye, Kansas City	1,480	370	12
Nick Lowery, Kansas City	0	37	34	139	1990	Thurman Thomas, Buffalo	1,297	271	11
Pete Stoyanovich, Miami	0	28	31	121	1991	Thurman Thomas, Buffalo	1,407	288	7
Pete Stoyanovich, Miami	0	34	30	124	1992	Barry Foster, Pittsburgh	1,690	390	11
Jeff Jaeger, L.A. Raiders	0	27	35	132	1993	Thurman Thomas, Buffalo	1,315	355	6
John Carney, San Diego	0	33	34	135	1994	Chris Warren, Seattle	1,545	333	9
Norm Johnson, Pittsburgh	0	39	34	141	1995	Curtis Martin, New England	1,487	368	14
Cary Blanchard, Indianapolis	0	27	36	135	1996	Terrell Davis, Denver	1,538	345	13

*1,011 AFC yards led conference.

National Football Conference Leaders
(National Football League, 1960-69)

Passing

Player, team	Atts	Com	YG	TD	Year
Milt Plum, Cleveland	250	151	2,297	21	1960
Milt Plum, Cleveland	302	177	2,416	18	1961
Bart Starr, Green Bay	285	178	2,438	12	1962
Y.A. Tittle, N.Y. Giants	367	221	3,145	36	1963
Bart Starr, Green Bay	272	163	2,144	15	1964
Rudy Bukich, Chicago	312	176	2,641	20	1965
Bart Starr, Green Bay	251	156	2,257	14	1966
Sonny Jurgensen, Washington	508	288	3,747	31	1967
Earl Morrall, Baltimore Colts	317	182	2,909	26	1968
Sonny Jurgensen, Washington	442	274	3,102	22	1969
John Brodie, San Francisco	378	223	2,941	24	1970
Roger Staubach, Dallas	211	126	1,882	15	1971
Norm Snead, N.Y. Giants	325	196	2,307	17	1972
Roger Staubach, Dallas	286	179	2,428	23	1973
Sonny Jurgensen, Washington	167	107	1,185	11	1974
Fran Tarkenton, Minnesota	425	273	2,994	25	1975
James Harris, L.A. Rams	158	91	1,460	8	1976
Roger Staubach, Dallas	361	210	2,620	18	1977
Roger Staubach, Dallas	413	231	3,190	25	1978
Roger Staubach, Dallas	461	267	3,586	27	1979
Ron Jaworski, Philadelphia	451	257	3,529	27	1980
Joe Montana, San Francisco	488	311	3,565	19	1981
Joe Thiesmann, Washington	252	161	2,033	13	1982
Steve Bartkowski, Atlanta	432	274	3,167	22	1983
Joe Montana, San Francisco	432	279	3,630	28	1984
Joe Montana, San Francisco	494	303	3,653	27	1985
Tommy Kramer, Minnesota	372	208	3,000	24	1986
Joe Montana, San Francisco	398	266	3,054	31	1987
Wade Wilson, Minnesota	332	204	2,746	15	1988
Joe Montana, San Francisco	386	271	3,521	26	1989
Phil Simms, N.Y. Giants	311	184	2,284	15	1990
Steve Young, San Francisco	279	180	2,517	17	1991
Steve Young, San Francisco	402	268	3,465	25	1992
Steve Young, San Francisco	462	314	4,023	29	1993
Steve Young, San Francisco	461	324	3,969	35	1994
Brett Favre, Green Bay	570	359	4,413	38	1995
Steve Young, San Francisco	316	214	2,410	14	1996

Pass-Receiving

Player, team	Ct	YG	TD	Year
Raymond Berry, Baltimore Colts	74	1,298	10	1960
Jim Phillips, L.A. Rams	78	1,092	5	1961
Bobby Mitchell, Washington	72	1,384	11	1962
Bobby Joe Conrad, St.L. Cardinals	73	967	10	1963
Johnny Morris, Chicago	93	1,200	10	1964
Dave Parks, San Francisco	80	1,344	12	1965
Charley Taylor, Washington	72	1,119	12	1966
Charley Taylor, Washington	70	990	9	1967
Clifton McNeil, San Francisco	71	994	7	1968
Dan Abramowicz, New Orleans	73	1,015	7	1969
Dick Gordon, Chicago	71	1,026	13	1970
Bob Tucker, N.Y. Giants	59	791	4	1971
Harold Jackson, Philadelphia	62	1,048	4	1972
Harold Carmichael, Philadelphia	67	1,116	9	1973
Charles Young, Philadelphia	63	696	3	1974
Chuck Foreman, Minnesota	73	691	9	1975
Drew Pearson, Dallas	58	806	6	1976
Ahmad Rashad, Minnesota	51	681	2	1977
Rickey Young, San Francisco	88	704	5	1978
Ahmad Rashad, Minnesota	80	1,156	9	1979
Earl Cooper, San Francisco	83	567	4	1980
Dwight Clark, San Francisco	85	1,105	4	1981
Dwight Clark, San Francisco	60	913	5	1982
Roy Green, St. Louis Cardinals	78	1,227	14	1983
Charlie Brown, Washington	78	1,225	8	
Earnest Gray, N.Y. Giants	78	1,139	5	
Art Monk, Washington	106	1,372	7	1984
Roger Craig, San Francisco	92	1,016	6	1985
Jerry Rice, San Francisco	86	1,570	15	1986
J.T. Smith, St. Louis Cardinals	91	1,117	8	1987
Henry Ellard, L.A. Rams	86	1,414	10	1988
Sterling Sharpe, Green Bay	90	1,423	12	1989
Jerry Rice, San Francisco	100	1,502	13	1990
Michael Irvin, Dallas	93	1,523	8	1991
Sterling Sharpe, Green Bay	108	1,461	13	1992
Sterling Sharpe, Green Bay	112	1,274	11	1993
Cris Carter, Minnesota	122	1,256	7	1994
Herman Moore, Detroit	123	1,686	14	1995
Jerry Rice, San Francisco	108	1,254	8	1996

Scoring

Player, team	TD	PAT	FG	Pts	Year
Paul Hornung, Green Bay	15	41	15	176	1960
Paul Hornung, Green Bay	10	41	15	146	1961
Jim Taylor, Green Bay	19	0	0	114	1962
Don Chandler, N.Y. Giants	0	52	18	106	1963
Lenny Moore, Baltimore Colts	20	0	0	120	1964
Gale Sayers, Chicago	22	0	0	132	1965
Bruce Gossett, L.A. Rams	0	29	28	113	1966
Jim Bakken, St. Louis Cardinals	0	36	27	117	1967
Leroy Kelly, Cleveland	20	0	0	120	1968
Fred Cox, Minnesota	0	43	26	121	1969
Fred Cox, Minnesota	0	35	30	125	1970
Curt Knight, Washington	0	27	29	114	1971
Chester Marcol, Green Bay	0	29	33	128	1972
David Ray, L.A. Rams	0	40	30	130	1973
Chester Marcol, Green Bay	0	19	25	94	1974
Chuck Foreman, Minnesota	22	0	0	132	1975
Mark Moseley, Washington	0	31	22	97	1976
Walter Payton, Chicago	16	0	0	96	1977
Frank Corral, L.A. Rams	0	31	29	118	1978
Mark Moseley, Washington	0	39	25	114	1979
Ed Murray, Detroit	0	35	27	116	1980
Ed Murray, Detroit	0	46	25	121	1981
Rafael Septien, Dallas	0	40	27	121	
Wendell Tyler, L.A. Rams	13	0	0	78	1982
Mark Moseley, Washington	0	62	33	161	1983
Ray Wersching, San Francisco	0	56	25	131	1984
Kevin Butler, Chicago	0	51	31	144	1985
Kevin Butler, Chicago	0	36	28	120	1986
Jerry Rice, San Francisco	23	0	0	138	1987
Mike Cofer, San Francisco	0	40	27	121	1988
Mike Cofer, San Francisco	0	49	29	136	1989
Chip Lohmiller, Washington	0	41	30	131	1990
Chip Lohmiller, Washington	0	56	31	149	1991
Morten Andersen, New Orleans	0	33	29	120	1992
Chip Lohmiller, Washington	0	30	30	120	
Jason Hanson, Detroit	0	28	34	130	1993
Fuad Reveiz, Minnesota	0	30	34	132	1994
Emmitt Smith, Dallas	22	0	0	132	
Emmitt Smith, Dallas	25	0	0	150	1995
John Kasay, Carolina	0	34	37	145	1996

Rushing

Player, team	Yds	Atts	TD	Year
Jim Brown, Cleveland	1,257	215	9	1960
Jim Brown, Cleveland	1,408	305	8	1961
Jim Taylor, Green Bay	1,474	272	19	1962
Jim Brown, Cleveland	1,863	291	12	1963
Jim Brown, Cleveland	1,446	280	7	1964
Jim Brown, Cleveland	1,544	289	17	1965
Gale Sayers, Chicago	1,231	229	8	1966
Leroy Kelly, Cleveland	1,205	235	11	1967
Leroy Kelly, Cleveland	1,239	248	16	1968
Gale Sayers, Chicago	1,032	236	8	1969
Larry Brown, Washington	1,125	237	5	1970
John Brockington, Green Bay	1,105	216	4	1971
Larry Brown, Washington	1,216	285	8	1972
John Brockington, Green Bay	1,144	265	3	1973
Lawrence McCutcheon, L.A. Rams	1,109	236	3	1974
Jim Otis, St. Louis Cardinals	1,076	269	5	1975
Walter Payton, Chicago	1,390	311	13	1976
Walter Payton, Chicago	1,852	339	14	1977
Walter Payton, Chicago	1,395	333	11	1978
Walter Payton, Chicago	1,610	369	14	1979
Walter Payton, Chicago	1,460	317	6	1980
George Rogers, New Orleans	1,674	378	13	1981
Tony Dorsett, Dallas	745	177	5	1982
Eric Dickerson, L.A. Rams	1,808	390	18	1983
Eric Dickerson, L.A. Rams	2,105	379	14	1984
Gerald Riggs, Atlanta	1,719	397	10	1985
Eric Dickerson, L.A. Rams	1,821	404	11	1986
Charles White, L.A. Rams	1,374	324	11	1987
Herschel Walker, Dallas	1,514	361	5	1988
Barry Sanders, Detroit	1,470	280	14	1989
Barry Sanders, Detroit	1,304	255	13	1990
Emmitt Smith, Dallas	1,563	365	12	1991
Emmitt Smith, Dallas	1,713	373	18	1992
Emmitt Smith, Dallas	1,486	283	9	1993
Barry Sanders, Detroit	1,883	331	7	1994
Emmitt Smith, Dallas	1,773	377	25	1995
Barry Sanders, Detroit	1,553	307	11	1996

1996 NFL Individual Leaders
American Football Conference
Passing

	Att	Comp	Pct comp	Yds	Avg gain	Long	TD	Pct TD	Int	Rating points
John Elway, Denver	466	287	61.6	3,328	7.14	51	26	5.6	14	89.2
Vinny Testaverde, Baltimore	549	325	59.2	4,177	7.61	86td	33	6.0	19	88.7
Dan Marino, Miami	373	221	59.2	2,795	7.49	74td	17	4.6	9	87.8
Mark Brunell, Jacksonville	557	353	63.4	4,367	7.84	62	19	3.4	20	84.0
Drew Bledsoe, New England	623	373	59.9	4,086	6.56	84td	27	4.3	15	83.7
Jeff Hostetler, Oakland	402	242	60.2	2,548	6.34	62td	23	5.7	14	83.2
Jeff Blake, Cincinnati	549	308	56.1	3,624	6.60	61td	24	4.4	14	80.3
Chris Chandler, Houston	320	184	57.5	2,099	6.56	63td	16	5.0	11	79.7
Stan Humphries, San Diego	416	232	55.8	2,670	6.42	63td	18	4.3	13	76.7
Jim Harbaugh, Indianapolis	405	232	57.3	2,630	6.49	51	13	3.2	11	76.3
Jim Kelly, Buffalo	379	222	58.6	2,810	7.41	67td	14	3.7	19	73.2
Mike Tomczak, Pittsburgh	401	222	55.4	2,767	6.90	70td	15	3.7	17	71.8

Rushing

	Att	Yds	Avg	Long	TD
Terrell Davis, Denver	345	1,538	4.5	71td	13
Jerome Bettis, Pittsburgh	320	1,431	4.5	50td	11
Eddie George, Houston	335	1,368	4.1	76	8
Adrian Murrell, N.Y. Jets	301	1,249	4.1	78	6
Curtis Martin, New England	316	1,152	3.6	57	14
Karim Abdul-Jabbar, Miami	307	1,116	3.6	29	11
Thurman Thomas, Buffalo	281	1,033	3.7	36	8
Napoleon Kaufman, Oakland	150	874	5.8	77	1
Chris Warren, Seattle	203	855	4.2	51	5
Garrison Hearst, Cincinnati	225	847	3.8	24	0

Pass Receiving

	No	Yds	Avg	Long	TD
Carl Pickens, Cincinnati	100	1,180	11.8	61td	12
Terry Glenn, New England	90	1,132	12.6	37td	6
Tim Brown, Oakland	90	1,104	12.3	42td	9
Tony Martin, San Diego	85	1,171	13.8	55	14
Keenan McCardell, Jacksonville	85	1,129	13.3	52	3
Wayne Chrebet, N.Y. Jets	84	909	10.8	44	3
Jimmy Smith, Jacksonville	83	1,244	15.0	62	7
Shannon Sharpe, Denver	80	1,062	13.3	51	10
Michael Jackson, Baltimore	76	1,201	15.8	86td	14
O. J. McDuffie, Miami	74	918	12.4	36	8

Scoring—Non-Kickers

	TD	Rush	Pass	2 Pt	Pts
Curtis Martin, New England	17	14	3	1	104
Terrell Davis, Denver	15	13	2	0	90
Michael Jackson, Baltimore	14	0	14	2	88
Tony Martin, San Diego	14	0	14	0	84
Carl Pickens, Cincinnati	12	0	12	1	74

Scoring—Kickers

	PAT	FG	Long	Pts
Cary Blanchard, Indianapolis	27/27	36/40	52	135
Al Del Greco, Houston	35/35	32/38	56	131
Adam Vinatieri, New England	39/42	27/35	50	120
John Carney, San Diego	31/31	29/36	53	118
Mike Hollis, Jacksonville	27/27	30/36	53	117
Todd Peterson, Seattle	27/27	28/34	54	111
Doug Pelfrey, Cincinnati	41/41	23/28	49	110

	PAT	FG	Long	Pts
Jason Elam, Denver	46/46	21/28	51	109
Cole Ford, Oakland	36/36	24/31	47	108
Norm Johnson, Pittsburgh	37/37	23/30	49	106

Interceptions

	No	Yds	Avg	Long	TD
Tyrone Braxton, Denver	9	128	14.2	69td	1
Ashley Ambrose, Cincinnati	8	63	7.9	31td	1
Terrell Buckley, Miami	6	164	27.3	91td	1
Rod Woodson, Pittsburgh	6	121	20.2	43td	1
Mark Collins, Kansas City	6	45	7.5	23	0

Kickoff Returns

	No	Yds	Avg	Long	TD
Tamarick Vanover, Kansas City	33	854	25.9	97td	1
Mel Gray, Houston	50	1,224	24.5	88	0
Vaughn Hebron, Denver	45	1,099	24.4	59	0
Irving Spikes, Miami	28	681	24.3	59	0
Aaron Bailey, Indianapolis	43	1,041	24.2	95td	1

Punt Returns

	No	Yds	Avg	Long	TD
Darrien Gordon, San Diego	36	537	14.9	81td	1
Rod Smith, Denver	23	283	12.3	36	0
Todd Kinchen, Denver	26	300	11.5	40	0
Dave Meggett, New England	52	588	11.3	60td	1
Chris Hudson, Jacksonville	32	348	10.9	60	0

Punting

	No	Yds	Long	Avg
John Kidd, Miami	78	3,611	63	46.3
Chris Gardocki, Indianapolis	68	3,105	61	45.7
Darren Bennett, San Diego	87	3,967	66	45.6
Lee Johnson, Cincinnati	80	3,630	67	45.4
Brian Hansen, N.Y. Jets	74	3,293	69	44.5

Sacks

	No
Bruce Smith, Buffalo	13.5
Michael McCrary, Seattle	13.5
Chad Brown, Pittsburgh	13.0
Mike Sinclair, Seattle	13.0
Derrick Thomas, Kansas City	13.0
Alfred Williams, Denver	13.0

National Football Conference
Passing

	Att	Comp	Pct comp	Yds	Avg gain	Long	TD	Pct TD	Int	Rating points
Steve Young, San Francisco	316	214	67.7	2,410	7.63	52	14	4.4	6	97.2
Brett Favre, Green Bay	543	325	59.9	3,899	7.18	80td	39	7.2	13	95.8
Brad Johnson, Minnesota	311	195	62.7	2,258	7.26	82td	17	5.5	10	89.4
Ty Detmer, Philadelphia	401	238	59.4	2,911	7.26	42	15	3.7	13	80.8
Troy Aikman, Dallas	465	296	63.7	3,126	6.72	61	12	2.6	13	80.1
Kerry Collins, Carolina	364	204	56.0	2,454	6.74	55	14	3.8	9	79.4
Gus Frerotte, Washington	470	270	57.4	3,453	7.35	52td	12	2.6	11	79.3
Dave Krieg, Chicago	377	226	59.9	2,278	6.04	53td	14	3.7	12	76.3
Kent Graham, Arizona	274	146	53.3	1,624	5.93	69	12	4.4	7	75.1
Scott Mitchell, Detroit	437	253	57.9	2,917	6.68	62td	17	3.9	17	74.9
Bobby Hebert, Atlanta	489	294	60.2	3,152	6.46	57	22	4.5	25	72.9
Tony Banks, St. Louis	368	192	52.2	2,544	6.91	77td	15	4.1	15	71.0

Rushing

	Att	Yds	Avg	Long	TD
Barry Sanders, Detroit	307	1,553	5.1	54td	11
Ricky Watters, Philadelphia	353	1,411	4.0	56td	13
Terry Allen, Washington	347	1,353	0.0	10td	21
Emmitt Smith, Dallas	327	1,204	3.7	42	12
Anthony Johnson, Carolina	300	1,120	3.7	29	6
Jamal Anderson, Atlanta	232	1,055	4.5	32td	5
Edgar Bennett, Green Bay	222	899	4.0	23	2
Rodney Hampton, N.Y. Giants	254	827	3.3	25	1
Raymont Harris, Chicago	194	748	3.9	23	4
Robert Smith, Minnesota	162	692	4.3	57	3

Receiving

	No	Yds	Avg	Long	TD
Jerry Rice, San Francisco	108	1,254	11.6	39	8
Herman Moore, Detroit	106	1,296	12.2	50td	9
Larry Centers, Arizona	99	766	7.7	39	7
Cris Carter, Minnesota	96	1,163	12.1	43td	10
Brett Perriman, Detroit	94	1,021	10.9	44	5

(continued)

	No	Yds	Avg	Long	TD
Irving Fryar, Philadelphia	88	1,195	13.6	42	11
Isaac Bruce, St. Louis	84	1,338	15.9	70	7
Curtis Conway, Chicago	81	1,049	13.0	58td	7
Bert Emanuel, Atlanta	75	921	12.3	53	6
Jake Reed, Minnesota	72	1,320	18.3	82td	7

Scoring—Non-Kickers

	TD	Rush	Pass	2 Pt	Pts
Terry Allen, Washington......	21	21	0	0	126
Emmitt Smith, Dallas........	15	12	3	0	90
Ricky Watters, Philadelphia ...	13	13	0	0	78
Irving Fryar, Philadelphia ...	11	0	11	0	66
Eddie Kennison, St. Louis	11	0	9	0	66[1]
Barry Sanders, Detroit	11	11	0	0	66

(1) Includes 2 returns for touchdowns.

Scoring—Kickers

	PAT	FG	Long	Pts
John Kasay, Carolina.........	34/35	37/45	53	145
Jeff Wilkins, San Francisco....	40/40	30/34	49	130
Chris Boniol, Dallas.........	24/25	32/36	52	120
Scott Blanton, Washington ...	40/40	26/32	53	118
Gary Anderson, Philadelphia ..	40/40	25/29	46	115
Chris Jacke, Green Bay	51/53	21/27	53	114
Morten Andersen, Atlanta ...	31/31	22/29	54	97
Scott Sisson, Minnesota.....	30/30	22/29	44	96
Brad Daluiso, N.Y. Giants	22/22	24/27	46	94
Michael Husted, Tampa Bay...	18/19	25/32	50	93

Interceptions

	No	Yds	Avg	Long	TD
Keith Lyle, St. Louis.........	9	152	16.9	68	0
Eugene Robinson, Green Bay..	6	107	17.8	39	0
Marquez Pope, San Francisco .	6	98	16.3	55td	1

	No	Yds	Avg	Long	TD
Aeneas Williams, Arizona.....	6	89	14.8	65td	1
Donnell Woolford, Chicago ...	6	37	6.2	28td	1

Kickoff Returns

	No	Yds	Avg	Long	TD
Michael Bates, Carolina	33	998	30.2	93td	1
Herschel Walker, Dallas	27	779	28.9	89	0
Tyrone Hughes, New Orleans .	70	1,791	25.6	58	0
Glyn Milburn, Detroit	64	1,627	25.4	65	0
Derrick Witherspoon, Phila. ..	53	1,271	24.0	97td	2

Punt Returns

	No	Yds	Avg	Long	TD
Desmond Howard, Green Bay .	58	875	15.1	92td	3
Eddie Kennison, St. Louis ...	29	423	14.6	78td	2
Winslow Oliver, Carolina	52	598	11.5	84td	1
Brian Mitchell, Washington...	23	258	11.2	71	0
Eric Metcalf, Atlanta	27	296	11.0	39	0

Punting

	No	Yds	Long	Avg
Matt Turk, Washington.......	75	3,386	63	45.1
Sean Landeta, St. Louis......	78	3,491	70	44.8
Todd Sauerbrun, Chicago.....	78	3,491	72	44.8
Tommy Thompson, San Francisco	73	3,217	65	44.1
Jeff Feagles, Arizona.........	76	3,328	68	43.8

Sacks

	No
Kevin Greene, Carolina.......	14.5
Lamar Lathon, Carolina.......	13.5
William Fuller, Philadelphia ...	13.0
Roy Barker, San Francisco	12.5
Simeon Rice, Arizona........	12.5

NFL MVP, Defensive Player of the Year, and Rookie of the Year

The Most Valuable Player is one of many awards given out annually by the Associated Press. The George Halas Trophy is awarded to the outstanding defensive player as chosen by a panel of sports experts. Rookie of the Year is one of many awards given out annually by *The Sporting News*. Many other organizations give out annual awards honoring the NFL's finest players.

Most Valuable Player

1957	Jim Brown, Cleveland
1958	Gino Marchetti, Baltimore Colts
1959	Charley Conerly, N.Y. Giants
1960	Norm Van Brocklin, Philadelphia; Joe Schmidt, Detroit
1961	Paul Hornung, Green Bay
1962	Jim Taylor, Green Bay
1963	Y.A. Tittle, N.Y. Giants
1964	John Unitas, Baltimore Colts
1965	Jim Brown, Cleveland
1966	Bart Starr, Green Bay
1967	John Unitas, Baltimore Colts
1968	Earl Morrall, Baltimore Colts
1969	Roman Gabriel, L.A. Rams
1970	John Brodie, San Francisco
1971	Alan Page, Minnesota
1972	Larry Brown, Washington
1973	O.J. Simpson, Buffalo
1974	Ken Stabler, Oakland
1975	Fran Tarkenton, Minnesota
1976	Bert Jones, Baltimore
1977	Walter Payton, Chicago
1978	Terry Bradshaw, Pittsburgh
1979	Earl Campbell, Houston
1980	Brian Sipe, Cleveland
1981	Ken Anderson, Cincinnati
1982	Mark Moseley, Washington
1983	Joe Theismann, Washington
1984	Dan Marino, Miami
1985	Marcus Allen, L.A. Raiders
1986	Lawrence Taylor, N.Y. Giants
1987	John Elway, Denver
1988	Boomer Esiason, Cincinnati
1989	Joe Montana, San Francisco
1990	Joe Montana, San Francisco
1991	Thurman Thomas, Buffalo
1992	Steve Young, San Francisco
1993	Emmitt Smith, Dallas
1994	Steve Young, San Francisco
1995	Brett Favre, Green Bay
1996	Brett Favre, Green Bay

Defensive Player of the Year

1966	Larry Wilson, St. Louis
1967	Deacon Jones, Los Angeles
1968	Deacon Jones, Los Angeles
1969	Dick Butkus, Chicago
1970	Dick Butkus, Chicago
1971	Carl Eller, Minnesota
1972	Joe Greene, Pittsburgh
1973	Alan Page, Minnesota
1974	Joe Greene, Pittsburgh
1975	Curley Culp, Houston
1976	Jerry Sherk, Cleveland
1977	Harvey Martin, Dallas
1978	Randy Gradishar, Denver
1979	Lee Roy Selmon, Tampa Bay
1980	Lester Hayes, Oakland
1981	Joe Klecko, N.Y. Jets
1982	Mark Gastineau, N.Y. Jets
1983	Jack Lambert, Pittsburgh
1984	Mike Haynes, L.A. Raiders
1985	Howie Long, L.A. Raiders; Andre Tippett, New England
1986	Lawrence Taylor, N.Y. Giants
1987	Reggie White, Philadelphia
1988	Mike Singletary, Chicago
1989	Tim Harris, Green Bay
1990	Bruce Smith, Buffalo
1991	Pat Swilling, New Orleans
1992	Junior Seau, San Diego
1993	Bruce Smith, Buffalo
1994	Deion Sanders, San Francisco
1995	Bryce Paup, Buffalo
1996	Bruce Smith, Buffalo

Rookie of the Year

1964	Charley Taylor, Washington
1965	Gale Sayers, Chicago
1966	Tommy Nobis, Atlanta
1967	Mel Farr, Detroit
1968	Earl McCullouch, Detroit
1969	Calvin Hill, Dallas
1970	NFC: Bruce Taylor, San Francsico
	AFC: Dennis Shaw, Buffalo
1971	NFC: John Brockington, Green Bay
	AFC: Jim Plunkett, New England
1972	NFC: Chester Marcol, Green Bay
	AFC: Franco Harris, Pittsburgh
1973	NFC: Chuck Foreman, Minnesota
	AFC: Boobie Clark, Cincinnati
1974	NFC: Wilbur Jackson, San Francisco
	AFC: Don Woods, San Diego
1975	NFC: Steve Bartkowski, Atlanta
	AFC: Robert Brazile, Houston
1976	NFC: Sammy White, Minnesota
	AFC: Mike Haynes, New England
1977	NFC: Tony Dorsett, Dallas
	AFC: A. J. Duhe, Miami
1978	NFC: Al Baker, Detroit
	AFC: Earl Campbell, Houston
1979	NFC: Ottis Anderson, St. Louis
	AFC: Jerry Butler, Buffalo
1980	Billy Sims, Detroit
1981	George Rogers, New Orleans
1982	Marcus Allen, L.A. Raiders
1983	Dan Marino, Miami
1984	Louis Lipps, Pittsburgh
1985	Eddie Brown, Cincinnati
1986	Rueben Mayes, New Orleans
1987	Robert Awalt, St. Louis
1988	Keith Jackson, Philadelphia
1989	Barry Sanders, Detroit
1990	Richmond Webb, Miami
1991	Mike Croel, Denver
1992	Santana Dotson, Tampa Bay
1993	Jerome Bettis, L.A. Rams
1994	Marshall Faulk, Indianapolis
1995	Curtis Martin, New England
1996	Eddie George, Houston

NFL Head Coaches at the Start of the 1997 Season

AFC

Baltimore—Ted Marchibroda
Buffalo—Marv Levy
Cincinnati—Bruce Coslet
Denver—Mike Shanahan
Indianapolis—Lindy Infante
Jacksonville—Tom Coughlin
Kansas City—Marty Schottenheimer
Miami—Jimmy Johnson
New England—Pete Carroll
N.Y. Jets—Bill Parcells
Oakland—Joe Bugel
Pittsburgh—Bill Cowher
San Diego—Kevin Gilbride
Seattle—Dennis Erickson
Tennessee—Jeff Fisher

NFC

Arizona—Vince Tobin
Atlanta—Dan Reeves
Carolina—Dom Capers
Chicago—Dave Wannstedt
Dallas—Barry Switzer
Detroit—Bobby Ross
Green Bay—Mike Holmgren
Minnesota—Dennis Green
New Orleans—Mike Ditka
N.Y. Giants—Jim Fassel
Philadelphia—Ray Rhodes
St. Louis—Dick Vermeil
San Francisco—Steve Mariucci
Tampa Bay—Tony Dungy
Washington—Norv Turner

Number One NFL Draft Choices, 1936-97

Year	Team	Player, Pos., College	Year	Team	Player, Pos., College
1936	Philadelphia	Jay Berwanger, HB, Chicago	1967	Baltimore Colts	Bubba Smith, DT, Michigan St.
1937	Philadelphia	Sam Francis, FB, Nebraska	1968	Minnesota	Ron Yary, T, USC
1938	Cleveland Rams	Corbett Davis, FB, Indiana	1969	Buffalo	O.J. Simpson, RB, USC
1939	Chicago Cards	Ki Aldrich, C, TCU	1970	Pittsburgh	Terry Bradshaw, QB, La.Tech
1940	Chicago Cards	George Cafego, HB, Tennessee	1971	New England	Jim Plunkett, QB, Stanford
1941	Chicago Bears	Tom Harmon, HB, Michigan	1972	Buffalo	Walt Patulski, DE, Notre Dame
1942	Pittsburgh	Bill Dudley, HB, Virginia	1973	Houston	John Matuszak, DE, Tampa
1943	Detroit	Frank Sinkwich, HB, Georgia	1974	Dallas	Ed "Too Tall" Jones, DE, Tenn. St.
1944	Boston Yanks	Angelo Bertelli, QB, Notre Dame	1975	Atlanta	Steve Bartkowski, QB, Cal.
1945	Chicago Cards	Charley Trippi, HB, Georgia	1976	Tampa Bay	Lee Roy Selmon, DE, Oklahoma
1946	Boston Yanks	Frank Dancewicz, QB, Notre Dame	1977	Tampa Bay	Ricky Bell, RB, USC
1947	Chicago Bears	Bob Fenimore, HB, Okla. A&M	1978	Houston	Earl Campbell, RB, Texas
1948	Washington	Harry Gilmer, QB, Alabama	1979	Buffalo	Tom Cousineau, LB, Ohio St.
1949	Philadelphia	Chuck Bednarik, C, Penn	1980	Detroit	Billy Sims, RB, Oklahoma
1950	Detroit	Leon Hart, E, Notre Dame	1981	New Orleans	George Rogers, RB, S.Carolina
1951	N.Y. Giants	Kyle Rote, HB, SMU	1982	New England	Kenneth Sims, DT, Texas
1952	L.A. Rams	Bill Wade, QB, Vanderbilt	1983	Baltimore Colts	John Elway, QB, Stanford
1953	San Francisco	Harry Babcock, E, Georgia	1984	New England	Irving Fryar, WR, Nebraska
1954	Cleveland	Bobby Garrett, QB, Stanford	1985	Buffalo	Bruce Smith, DE, Va.Tech
1955	Baltimore Colts	George Shaw, QB, Oregon	1986	Tampa Bay	Bo Jackson, RB, Auburn
1956	Pittsburgh	Gary Glick, DB, Col. A&M	1987	Tampa Bay	Vinny Testaverde, QB, Miami (FL)
1957	Green Bay	Paul Hornung, QB, Notre Dame	1988	Atlanta	Aundray Bruce, LB, Auburn
1958	Chicago Cards	King Hill, QB, Rice	1989	Dallas	Troy Aikman, QB, UCLA
1959	Green Bay	Randy Duncan, QB, Iowa	1990	Indianapolis	Jeff George, QB, Illinois
1960	L.A. Rams	Billy Cannon, HB, LSU	1991	Dallas	Russell Maryland, DL, Miami (FL)
1961	Minnesota	Tommy Mason, HB, Tulane	1992	Indianapolis	Steve Emtman, DL, Washington
1962	Washington	Ernie Davis, HB, Syracuse	1993	New England	Drew Bledsoe, QB, Washington St.
1963	L.A. Rams	Terry Baker, QB, Oregon St.	1994	Cincinnati	Dan Wilkinson, DT, Ohio St.
1964	San Francisco	Dave Parks, E, Texas Tech	1995	Cincinnati	Ki-Jana Carter, RB, Penn State
1965	N.Y. Giants	Tucker Frederickson, HB, Auburn	1996	N.Y. Jets	Keyshawn Johnson, WR, USC
1966	Atlanta	Tommy Nobis, LB, Texas	1997	St. Louis	Orlando Pace, T, Ohio St.

First-Round Selections in the 1997 NFL Draft

	Team	Player	Pos	College		Team	Player	Pos	College
1.	St. Louis	Orlando Pace	T	Ohio St.	16.	Tampa Bay	Reidel Anthony	WR	Florida
2.	Oakland	Darrell Russell	DT	USC	17.	Washington	Kenard Lang	DE	Miami (FL)
3.	Seattle	Shawn Springs	CB	Ohio St.	18.	Tennessee	Kenny Holmes	DE	Miami (FL)
4.	Baltimore	Peter Boulware	DE	Florida St.	19.	Indianapolis	Tarik Glenn	T	California
5.	Detroit	Bryant Westbrook	DB	Texas	20.	Minnesota	Dwayne Rudd	LB	Alabama
6.	Seattle	Walter Jones	T	Florida St.	21.	Jacksonville	Renaldo Wynn	DT	Notre Dame
7.	N.Y. Giants	Ike Hilliard	WR	Florida	22.	Dallas	David LaFleur	TE	Louisiana St.
8.	N.Y. Jets	James Farrior	LB	Virginia	23.	Buffalo	Antowain Smith	RB	Houston
9.	Arizona	Tom Knight	CB	Iowa	24.	Pittsburgh	Chad Scott	DB	Maryland
10.	New Orleans	Chris Naeole	G	Colorado	25.	Philadelphia	Jon Harris	DE	Virginia
11.	Atlanta	Michael Booker	DB	Nebraska	26.	San Francisco	Jim Druckenmiller	QB	Virginia Tech
12.	Tampa Bay	Warrick Dunn	RB	Florida St.	27.	Carolina	Rae Carruth	WR	Colorado
13.	Kansas City	Tony Gonzalez	TE	California	28.	Denver	Trevor Pryce	DT	Clemson
14.	Cincinnati	Reinard Wilson	LB	Florida St.	29.	New England	Chris Canty	DB	Kansas St.
15.	Miami	Yatil Green	WR	Miami (FL)	30.	Green Bay	Ross Verba	T	Iowa

Pro Football Hall of Fame, Canton, Ohio

(1997 inductees are in **bold**)

Herb Adderley	Willie Davis	**Mike Haynes**	Dante Lavelli	Merlin Olsen
Lance Alworth	Len Dawson	Ed Healey	Bobby Layne	Jim Otto
Doug Atkins	Dan Dierdorf	Mel Hein	Alphonse "Tuffy" Leemans	Steve Owen
Morris "Red" Badgro	Mike Ditka	Ted Hendricks	Bob Lilly	Alan Page
Lem Barney	Art Donovan	Wilbur "Pete" Henry	Larry Little	Clarence "Ace" Parker
Cliff Battles	Tony Dorsett	Arnold Herber	Vince Lombardi	Jim Parker
Sammy Baugh	John "Paddy" Driscoll	Bill Hewitt	Sid Luckman	Walter Payton
Chuck Bednarik	Bill Dudley	Clarke Hinkle	Roy "Link" Lyman	Joe Perry
Bert Bell	Glen "Turk" Edwards	Elroy "Crazylegs" Hirsch	John Mackey	Pete Pihos
Bobby Bell	Weeb Ewbank	Paul Hornung	Tim Mara	Hugh "Shorty" Ray
Raymond Berry	Tom Fears	Ken Houston	**Wellington Mara**	Dan Reeves
Charles Bidwell	Jim Finks	Cal Hubbard	Gino Marchetti	Mel Renfro
Fred Biletnikoff	Ray Flaherty	Sam Huff	George Preston Marshall	John Riggins
George Blanda	Len Ford	Lamar Hunt	Ollie Matson	Jim Ringo
Mel Blount	Dr. Daniel Fortmann	Don Hutson	Don Maynard	Andy Robustelli
Terry Bradshaw	Dan Fouts	Jimmy Johnson	George McAfee	Art Rooney
Jim Brown	Frank Gatski	John Henry Johnson	Mike McCormack	Pete Rozelle
Paul Brown	Bill George	Charlie Joiner	Hugh McElhenny	Bob St. Clair
Roosevelt Brown	Joe Gibbs	David "Deacon" Jones	Johnny "Blood" McNally	Gale Sayers
Willie Brown	Frank Gifford	Stan Jones	Mike Michalske	Joe Schmidt
Buck Buchanan	Sid Gillman	Henry Jordan	Wayne Millner	Tex Schramm
Dick Butkus	Otto Graham	Sonny Jurgensen	Bobby Mitchell	Lee Roy Selmon
Earl Campbell	Red Grange	Leroy Kelly	Ron Mix	Art Shell
Tony Canadeo	Bud Grant	Walt Kiesling	Lenny Moore	Don Shula
Joe Carr	Joe Greene	Frank "Bruiser" Kinard	Marion Motley	O.J. Simpson
Guy Chamberlin	Forrest Gregg	Earl "Curly" Lambeau	George Musso	Jackie Smith
Jack Christiansen	Bob Griese	Jack Lambert	Bronko Nagurski	Bart Starr
Earl "Dutch" Clark	Lou Groza	Tom Landry	Joe Namath	Roger Staubach
George Connor	Joe Guyon	Dick "Night Train" Lane	Earle "Greasy" Neale	Ernie Stautner
Jim Conzelman	George Halas	Jim Langer	Ernie Nevers	Jan Stenerud
Lou Creekmur	Jack Ham	Willie Lanier	Ray Nitschke	Ken Strong
Larry Csonka	John Hannah	Steve Largent	Chuck Noll	Joe Stydahar
Al Davis	Franco Harris	Yale Lary	Leo Nomellini	Fran Tarkenton

(continued)

Charley Taylor	Charley Trippi	Norm Van Brocklin	Bob Waterfield	Larry Wilson
Jim Taylor	Emlen Tunnell	Steve Van Buren	**Mike Webster**	Kellen Winslow
Jim Thorpe	Clyde "Bulldog" Turner	Doak Walker	Arnie Weinmeister	Alex Wojciechowicz
Y.A. Tittle	Johnny Unitas	Bill Walsh	Randy White	Willie Wood
George Trafton	Gene Upshaw	Paul Warfield	Bill Willis	

Future Sites of the Super Bowl

No.	Site	Date	No.	Site	Date
XXXII	Qualcomm Stadium, San Diego, CA	Jan. 25, 1998	XXXIV	Georgia Dome, Atlanta, GA	Jan. 30, 2000
XXXIII	Pro Player Stadium, Miami, FL	Jan. 31, 1999	XXXV	Houlihan's Stadium, Tampa, FL	Jan. 28, 2001

All-Time NFL Coaching Victories
(at end of 1996 season; *active through 1996)

			Regular Season				Career			
Coach	Years	Teams	W	L	T	Pct	W	L	T	Pct
Don Shula	33	Colts, Dolphins	328	156	6	.676	347	173	6	.665
George Halas	40	Bears	318	148	31	.671	324	151	31	.671
Tom Landry	29	Cowboys	250	162	6	.605	270	178	6	.601
Curly Lambeau	33	Packers, Cardinals, Redskins	226	132	22	.624	229	134	22	.623
Chuck Noll	23	Steelers	193	148	1	.566	209	156	1	.572
Chuck Knox	22	Rams, Bills, Seahawks	186	147	1	.558	193	158	1	.550
Paul Brown	21	Browns, Bengals	166	100	6	.621	170	108	6	.609
Bud Grant	18	Vikings	158	96	5	.620	168	108	5	.607
Steve Owen	23	Giants	151	100	17	.595	153	108	17	.581
Dan Reeves*	16	Broncos, Giants	141	106	1	.571	149	113	1	.568
Marv Levy*	16	Chiefs, Bills	137	102	0	.573	148	110	0	.574
Joe Gibbs	12	Redskins	124	60	0	.674	140	65	0	.683
Hank Stram	17	Chiefs, Saints	131	97	10	.571	136	100	10	.573
Weeb Ewbank	20	Colts, Jets	130	129	7	.502	134	130	7	.507
M. Schottenheimer*	13	Browns, Chiefs	125	73	1	.631	130	83	1	.610
Sid Gillman	18	Rams, Chargers, Oilers	122	99	7	.550	123	104	7	.541
Bill Parcells*	12	Giants, Patriots	109	81	1	.573	119	86	1	.580
George Allen	12	Rams, Redskins	116	47	5	.705	118	54	5	.681
Don Coryell	14	Cardinals, Chargers	111	83	1	.572	114	89	1	.561
John Madden	10	Raiders	103	32	7	.750	112	39	7	.731
Mike Ditka	11	Bears	106	62	0	.631	112	68	0	.622

All-Time Professional (NFL and AFL) Football Records
(at end of 1996 season; *active through 1996)
Leading Lifetime Rushers

Player	League	Yrs	Att	Yards	Avg	Player	League	Yrs	Att	Yards	Avg
Walter Payton	NFL	13	3,838	16,726	4.4	Ottis Anderson	NFL	14	2,562	10,273	4.0
Eric Dickerson	NFL	11	2,996	13,259	4.4	Emmitt Smith*	NFL	7	2,334	10,160	4.4
Tony Dorsett	NFL	12	2,936	12,739	4.3	Earl Campbell	NFL	8	2,187	9,407	4.3
Jim Brown	NFL	9	2,359	12,312	5.2	Jim Taylor	NFL	10	1,941	8,597	4.4
Franco Harris	NFL	13	2,949	12,120	4.1	Joe Perry	NFL	14	1,737	8,378	4.8
Marcus Allen*	NFL	15	2,898	11,738	4.1	Herschel Walker*	NFL	11	1,948	8,205	4.2
Barry Sanders*	NFL	8	2,384	11,725	4.9	Roger Craig	NFL	11	1,991	8,189	4.1
John Riggins	NFL	14	2,916	11,352	3.9	Gerald Riggs	NFL	10	1,989	8,188	4.1
O.J. Simpson	AFL-NFL	11	2,404	11,236	4.7	Larry Csonka	AFL-NFL	11	1,891	8,081	4.3
Thurman Thomas*	NFL	9	2,566	10,762	4.2	Freeman McNeil	NFL	12	1,798	8,074	4.5

Most Yards Gained, Season — 2,105, Eric Dickerson, Los Angeles Rams, 1984.
Most Yards Gained, Game — 275, Walter Payton, Chicago Bears vs. Minnesota Vikings, Nov. 20, 1977.
Most Touchdowns Rushing, Career — 112, Marcus Allen, Los Angeles Raiders-Kansas City Chiefs, 1982-1996.
Most Touchdowns Rushing, Season — 25, Emmitt Smith, Dallas Cowboys, 1995.
Most Touchdowns Rushing, Game — 6, Ernie Nevers, Chicago Cardinals vs. Chicago Bears, Nov. 28, 1929.
Most Rushing Attempts, Game — 45, Jamie Morris, Washington Redskins vs. Cincinnati Bengals, Dec. 17, 1988 (overtime).
Longest Run From Scrimmage — 99 yds., Tony Dorsett, Dallas Cowboys vs. Minnesota Vikings, Jan. 3, 1983 (touchdown).

Leading Lifetime Passers
(minimum 1,500 attempts)

Player	League	Yrs	Att	Comp	Yds	Pts†	Player	League	Yrs	Att	Comp	Yds	Pts†
Steve Young*	NFL	12	3,192	2,059	25,479	96.2	Jeff Hostetler*	NFL	11	2,194	1,278	15,531	82.1
Joe Montana	NFL	15	5,391	3,409	40,551	92.3	Ken Anderson	NFL	16	4,475	2,654	32,838	81.9
Brett Favre*	NFL	6	2,693	1,667	18,724	88.6	Bernie Kosar*	NFL	12	3,365	1,994	23,301	81.8
Dan Marino*	NFL	14	6,904	4,134	51,636	88.3	Danny White	NFL	13	2,950	1,761	21,959	81.7
Jim Kelly*	NFL	11	4,779	2,874	35,467	84.4	Dave Krieg*	NFL	17	5,288	3,092	37,946	81.5
Roger Staubach	NFL	11	2,958	1,685	22,700	83.4	Warren Moon*	NFL	13	6,000	3,514	43,787	81.0
Troy Aikman*	NFL	8	3,178	2,000	22,733	83.0	Neil O'Donnell*	NFL	7	2,059	1,179	14,014	80.5
Neil Lomax	NFL	8	3,153	1,817	22,771	82.7	Scott Mitchell*	NFL	6	1,507	853	10,516	80.5
Sonny Jurgensen	NFL	18	4,262	2,433	32,224	82.6	Bart Starr	NFL	16	3,149	1,808	24,718	80.5
Len Dawson	NFL-AFL	19	3,741	2,136	28,711	82.6	Ken O'Brien	NFL	11	3,602	2,110	25,094	80.4

†Rating points based on performances in the following categories: Percentage of completions, percentage of touchdown passes, percentage of interceptions, and average gain per pass attempt.

Most Yards Gained, Career — 51,636, Dan Marino, Miami Dolphins, 1983-1996.
Most Yards Gained, Season — 5,084, Dan Marino, Miami Dolphins, 1984.
Most Yards Gained, Game — 554, Norm Van Brocklin, Los Angeles Rams vs. New York Yankees, Sept. 18, 1951 (27 completions in 41 attempts).
Most Touchdowns Passing, Career — 369, Dan Marino, Miami Dolphins, 1983-1996.
Most Touchdowns Passing, Season — 48, Dan Marino, Miami Dolphins, 1984.
Most Touchdowns Passing, Game — 7, Sid Luckman, Chicago Bears vs. New York Giants, Nov. 14, 1943; Adrian Burk, Philadelphia Eagles vs. Washington Redskins, Oct. 17, 1954; George Blanda, Houston Oilers vs. New York Titans, Nov. 19, 1961; Y.A. Tittle, New York Giants vs. Washington Redskins, Oct. 28, 1962; Joe Kapp, Minnesota Vikings vs. Baltimore Colts, Sept. 28, 1969.
Most Passes Completed, Career — 4,134, Dan Marino, Miami Dolphins, 1983-1996.
Most Passes Completed, Season — 404, Warren Moon, Houston Oilers, 1991.
Most Passes Completed, Game — 45, Drew Bledsoe, New England Patriots vs. Minnesota Vikings, Nov. 13, 1994 (overtime).

Leading Lifetime Receivers

Player	League	Yrs	No	Yds	Avg	Player	League	Yrs	No	Yds	Avg
Jerry Rice*	NFL	12	1,050	16,377	15.6	Irving Fryar*	NFL	13	650	10,111	15.6
Art Monk	NFL	16	940	12,721	13.5	Charley Taylor	NFL	13	649	9,110	14.0
Steve Largent	NFL	14	819	13,089	16.0	Drew Hill	NFL	14	634	9,831	15.5
Henry Ellard*	NFL	14	775	13,177	17.0	Don Maynard	AFL-NFL	15	633	11,834	18.7
Andre Reed*	NFL	12	766	10,884	14.2	Raymond Berry	NFL	13	631	9,275	14.7
James Lofton	NFL	16	764	14,004	18.3	Sterling Sharpe	NFL	7	595	8,134	13.7
Charlie Joiner	AFL-NFL	18	750	12,146	16.2	Michael Irvin*	NFL	9	591	9,500	16.1
Gary Clark	NFL	11	699	10,856	15.5	Harold Carmichael	NFL	14	590	8,985	15.2
Cris Carter*	NFL	10	667	8,367	12.5	Fred Biletnikoff	AFL-NFL	14	589	8,974	15.2
Ozzie Newsome	NFL	13	662	7,980	12.1	Bill Brooks*	NFL	11	583	8,001	13.7

Most Yards Gained, Career — 16,377, Jerry Rice, San Francisco 49ers, 1985-1996.
Most Yards Gained, Season — 1,848, Jerry Rice, San Francisco 49ers, 1995.
Most Yards Gained, Game — 336, Willie "Flipper" Anderson, Los Angeles Rams vs. New Orleans, Nov. 26, 1989 (overtime).
Most Pass Receptions, Season — 123, Herman Moore, Detroit Lions, 1995.
Most Pass Receptions, Game — 18, Tom Fears, Los Angeles Rams vs. Green Bay Packers, Dec. 3, 1950 (189 yards).
Most Touchdown Passes, Career — 154, Jerry Rice, San Francisco 49ers, 1985-1996.
Most Touchdown Passes, Season — 22, Jerry Rice, San Francisco 49ers, 1987.
Most Touchdown Passes, Game — 5, Bob Shaw, Chicago Cardinals vs. Baltimore Colts, Oct. 2, 1950; Kellen Winslow, San Diego Chargers vs. Oakland Raiders, Nov. 22, 1981; Jerry Rice, San Francisco 49ers vs. Atlanta Falcons, Oct. 14, 1990.

Leading Lifetime Scorers

Player	League	Yrs	TD	PAT	FG	Total	Player	League	Yrs	TD	PAT	FG	Total
George Blanda	AFL-NFL	26	9	943	335	2,002	Mark Moseley	NFL	16	0	482	300	1,382
Nick Lowery*	NFL	18	0	562	383	1,711	Jim Bakken	NFL	17	0	534	282	1,380
Jan Stenerud	AFL-NFL	19	0	580	373	1,699	Fred Cox	NFL	15	0	519	282	1,365
Gary Anderson*	NFL	15	0	488	356	1,556	Lou Groza	NFL	17	1	641	234	1,349
Morten Andersen*	NFL	15	0	472	355	1,537	Jim Breech	NFL	14	0	517	243	1,246
Eddie Murray	NFL	16	0	498	325	1,473	Chris Bahr	NFL	14	0	490	241	1,213
Pat Leahy	NFL	18	0	558	304	1,470	Kevin Butler*	NFL	12	0	404	257	1,175
Norm Johnson*	NFL	15	0	552	300	1,452	Gino Cappelletti	AFL-NFL	11	42	350	176	1,130
Jim Turner	AFL-NFL	16	1	521	304	1,439	Ray Wersching	NFL	15	0	456	222	1,122
Matt Bahr	NFL	17	0	522	300	1,422	Al Del Greco*	NFL	13	0	403	236	1,111

Most Points, Season — 176, Paul Hornung, Green Bay Packers, 1960 (15 TDs, 41 PATs, 15 FGs).
Most Points, Game — 40, Ernie Nevers, Chicago Cardinals vs. Chicago Bears, Nov. 28, 1929 (6 TDs, 4 PATs).
Most Touchdowns, Career — 165, Jerry Rice, San Francisco 49ers, 1985-1996 (10 rushing, 154 pass receptions, 1 fumble recovery).
Most Touchdowns, Season — 25, Emmitt Smith, Dallas Cowboys, 1995 (25 rushing).
Most Touchdowns, Game — 6, Ernie Nevers, Chicago Cardinals vs. Chicago Bears, Nov. 28, 1929 (6 rushing); Dub Jones, Cleveland Browns vs. Chicago Bears, Nov. 25, 1951 (4 rushing, 2 pass receptions); Gale Sayers, Chicago Bears vs. San Francisco 49ers, Dec. 12, 1965 (4 rushing, 1 pass reception, 1 punt return).
Most Points After Touchdown, Season — 66, Uwe von Schamann, Miami Dolphins, 1984.
Most Consecutive Points After Touchdown — 234, Tommy Davis, San Francisco 49ers, 1959-1969.
Most Field Goals, Career — 383, Nick Lowery, New England Patriots-Kansas City Chiefs-New York Jets, 1978, 1980-1996.
Most Field Goals, Season — 37, John Kasay, Carolina Panthers, 1996.
Most Field Goals, Game — 7, Jim Bakken, St. Louis Cardinals vs. Pittsburgh Steelers, Sept. 24, 1967; Rich Karlis, Minnesota Vikings vs. Los Angeles Rams, Nov. 5, 1989 (overtime); Chris Boniol, Dallas Cowboys vs. Green Bay Packers, Nov. 18, 1996.
Longest Field Goal — 63 yds., Tom Dempsey, New Orleans Saints vs. Detroit Lions, Nov. 8, 1970.

Defensive Records

Most Interceptions, Career — 81, Paul Krause, Washington Redskins-Minnesota Vikings, 1964-1979.
Most Interceptions, Season — 14, Dick "Night Train" Lane, Los Angeles Rams, 1952.
Most Touchdowns, Career — 9, Ken Houston, Houston Oilers-Washington Redskins, 1967-1980.
Most Touchdowns, Season — 4, Ken Houston, Houston Oilers, 1971; Jim Kearney, Kansas City Chiefs, 1972; Eric Allen, Philadelphia Eagles, 1993.
Most Sacks, Career (Since 1982) — 165.5, Reggie White, Philadelphia Eagles-Green Bay Packers, 1985-1996.
Most Sacks, Season (Since 1982) — 22, Mark Gastineau, New York Jets, 1984.
Most Sacks, Game (Since 1982) — 7, Derrick Thomas, Kansas City Chiefs vs. Seattle Seahawks, Nov. 11, 1990.

NFL Stadiums

Team—Stadium, Location, Turf (Year Built)	Capacity	Team—Stadium, Location, Turf (Year Built)	Capacity
Bears—Soldier Field, Chicago, IL, G (1924)	66,944	Jets—Giants Stad.[6], E. Rutherford, NJ, A (1976)	77,716
Bengals—Cinergy Field[1], Cincinnati, OH, A (1970)	60,389	Lions—Pontiac Silverdome, MI, A (1975)	80,368
Bills—Rich Stad., Buffalo, NY, A (1973)	80,091	Oilers—Liberty Bowl Mem. Stad., Memphis, TN, G (1964)	62,380
Broncos—Denver Mile High Stad., CO, G (1948)	76,078	Packers—Lambeau Field, Green Bay, WI, G (1957)	60,790
Buccaneers—Houlihan's Stad.[2], Tampa, FL, G (1967)	74,301	Panthers—Ericsson Stad.[8], Charlotte, NC, G (1996)	72,520
Cardinals—Sun Devil Stad., Tempe, AZ, G (1958)	73,243	Patriots—Foxboro Stad., MA, G (1971)	60,292
Chargers—Qualcomm Stad.[3], San Diego, CA, G (1967)	71,000	Raiders—Oakland-Alameda Cty. Coliseum, CA, G (1966)	62,500
Chiefs—Arrowhead Stad., Kansas City, MO, G (1972)	79,101	Rams—Trans World Dome, St. Louis, MO, A (1995)	66,000
Colts—RCA Dome, Indianapolis, IN, A (1983)	60,599	Ravens—Memorial Stad., Baltimore, MD, G (1924)	65,000
Cowboys—Texas Stad., Irving, TX, A (1971)	65,812	Redskins—Jack Kent Cooke Stad., Raljon, MD, G (1997)	78,600
Dolphins—Pro Player Stad.[4], Miami, FL, G (1987)	74,916	Saints—Louisiana Superdome, New Orleans, A (1975)	69,729
Eagles—Veterans Stad., Philadelphia, PA, A (1971)	65,352	Seahawks—Kingdome, Seattle, WA, A (1976)	66,400
Falcons—Georgia Dome, Atlanta, GA, A (1992)	71,280	Steelers—Three Rivers Stad., Pittsburgh, PA, A (1970)	59,600
49ers—3Com Park[5], San Francisco, CA, G (1960)	70,270	Vikings—Metrodome, Minneapolis, MN, A (1982)	64,035
Giants—Giants Stad.[6], E. Rutherford, NJ, A (1976)	78,148		
Jaguars—ALLTEL Stad.[7], Jacksonville, FL, G (1995)	73,000		

G=Grass. A=Artificial turf. Stad.=Stadium. (1) Formerly Riverfront Stadium. (2) Formerly Tampa Stadium. (3) Formerly San Diego Jack Murphy Stadium. (4) Formerly Joe Robbie Stadium. (5) Formerly Candlestick Park; full name: 3Com Park at Candlestick Point. (6) Although Giants and Jets both play at Giants Stadium, capacities differ because extra seating is made available for Giants games. (7) Formerly Jacksonville Municipal Stadium. (8) Formerly Carolinas Stadium.

The Sporting News 1996 NFL All-Pro Team

Offense—QB: Brett Favre, Green Bay. RB: Barry Sanders, Detroit; Terrell Davis, Denver. WR: Jerry Rice, San Francisco; Herman Moore, Detroit. TE: Shannon Sharpe, Denver. T: William Roaf, New Orleans; Gary Zimmerman, Denver. G: Larry Allen, Dallas; Randall McDaniel, Minnesota. C: Dermontti Dawson, Pittsburgh. **Defense**—LB: Chad Brown, Pittsburgh; Junior Seau, San Diego; Lamar Lathon, Carolina. DE: Bruce Smith, Buffalo; Alfred Williams, Denver. DT: Bryant Young, San Francisco; John Randle, Minnesota. CB: Deion Sanders, Dallas; Dale Carter, Kansas City. S: LeRoy Butler, Green Bay; Darren Woodson, Dallas. **Special Teams**—K: Cary Blanchard, Indianapolis. P: Chris Gardocki, Indianapolis. PR: Desmond Howard, Green Bay. KR: Michael Bates, Carolina.

CANADIAN FOOTBALL LEAGUE
Grey Cup Championship Game

1954 Edmonton Eskimos 26, Montreal Alouettes 25	1976 Ottawa Rough Riders 23, Saskatchewan Roughriders 20
1955 Edmonton Eskimos 34, Montreal Alouettes 19	1977 Montreal Alouettes 41, Edmonton Eskimos 6
1956 Edmonton Eskimos 50, Montreal Alouettes 27	1978 Edmonton Eskimos 20, Montreal Alouettes 13
1957 Hamilton Tiger-Cats 32, Winnipeg Blue Bombers 7	1979 Edmonton Eskimos 17, Montreal Alouettes 9
1958 Winnipeg Blue Bombers 35, Hamilton Tiger-Cats 28	1980 Edmonton Eskimos 48, Hamilton Tiger-Cats 10
1959 WInnipeg Blue Bombers 21, Hamilton Tiger-Cats 7	1981 Edmonton Eskimos 26, Ottawa Rough Riders 23
1960 Ottawa Rough Riders 16, Edmonton Eskimos 6	1982 Edmonton Eskimos 32, Toronto Argonauts 16
1961 Winnipeg Blue Bombers 21, Hamilton Tiger-Cats 14	1983 Toronto Argonauts 18, British Columbia Lions 17
1962 Winnipeg Blue Bombers 28, Hamilton Tiger-Cats 27	1984 Winnipeg Blue Bombers 47, Hamilton Tiger-Cats 17
1963 Hamilton Tiger-Cats 21, British Columbia Lions 10	1985 British Columbia Lions 37, Hamilton Tiger-Cats 24
1964 British Columbia Lions 34, Hamilton Tiger-Cats 24	1986 Hamilton Tiger-Cats 39, Edmonton Eskimos 15
1965 Hamilton Tiger-Cats 22, Winnipeg Blue Bombers 16	1987 Edmonton Eskimos 38, Toronto Argonauts 36
1966 Saskatchewan Roughriders 29, Ottawa Rough Riders 14	1988 Winnipeg Blue Bombers 22, British Columbia Lions 21
1967 Hamilton Tiger-Cats 24, Saskatchewan Roughriders 1	1989 Saskatchewan Roughriders 43, Hamilton Tiger-Cats 40
1968 Ottawa Rough Riders 24, Calgary Stampeders 21	1990 Winnipeg Blue Bombers 50, Edmonton Eskimos 11
1969 Ottawa Rough Riders 29, Saskatchewan Roughriders 11	1991 Toronto Argonauts 36, Calgary Stampeders 21
1970 Montreal Alouettes 23, Calgary Stampeders 10	1992 Calgary Stampeders 24, Winnipeg Blue Bombers 10
1971 Calgary Stampeders 14, Toronto Argonauts 11	1993 Edmonton Eskimos 33, Winnipeg Blue Bombers 23
1972 Hamilton Tiger-Cats 13, Saskatchewan Roughriders 10	1994 British Columbia Lions 26, Baltimore Football Club* 23
1973 Ottawa Rough Riders 22, Edmonton Eskimos 18	1995 Baltimore Stallions 37, Calgary Stampeders 20
1974 Montreal Alouettes 20, Edmonton Eskimos 7	1996 Toronto Argonauts 43, Edmonton Eskimos 37
1975 Edmonton Eskimos 9, Montreal Alouettes 8	

*Baltimore's team nickname had not been determined at this time.

1996 CFL Review: Ottawa Disbands, Divisional Alignment Changes

The 120-year old Ottawa Rough Riders suspended operations following the 1996 season. The CFL continued in 1997 with 8 teams with the Winnipeg Blue Bombers playing in the Eastern Division. For the 1996 season the CFL returned to its traditional format, featuring an East-West divisional alignment. In 1995, the league had adopted a different alignment, featuring a Northern Division with 9 Canadian-based teams and a Southern Division with 5 U.S.-based expansion teams. But after that season the 1995 CFL-champion Baltimore Stallions moved to Montreal—and reintroduced the name Alouettes—while the other U.S.-based teams suspended operations.

1996 Final Standings

Western Division	W	L	T	Pct	PF	PA	Eastern Division	W	L	T	Pct	PF	PA
Calgary Stampeders	13	5	0	.722	608	375	Toronto Argonauts	15	3	0	.833	556	359
Edmonton Eskimos	11	7	0	.611	459	354	Montreal Alouettes	12	6	0	.667	536	467
Winnipeg Blue Bombers	9	9	0	.500	421	495	Hamilton Tiger-Cats	8	10	0	.444	426	576
Saskatchewan Roughriders	5	13	0	.278	360	498	Ottawa Rough Riders	3	15	0	.167	352	524
British Columbia Lions	5	13	0	.278	410	483							

1996 Playoff Results

Western Division—Edmonton 68, Winnipeg 7; Edmonton 15, Calgary 12
Eastern Division—Montreal 22, Hamilton 11; Toronto 43, Montreal 7
Grey Cup—Toronto 43, Edmonton 37

All-Time CFL Records
(through 1996 season; *active during 1996)

Longest Run—The Canadian Football League features 3 downs, 12 players on a side, and a field that is 110 yards long. George Dixon of the Montreal Alouettes made full use of the field with a 109-yard run against Ottawa on Sept. 2, 1963. Willie Fleming of the British Columbia Lions did the same against Edmonton on Oct. 17, 1964.

Leading Lifetime Rushers

	Yrs	No	Yds	Avg	Long	TDs		Yrs	No	Yds	Avg	Long	TDs
George Reed, Sask.	13	3,243	16,116	5.0	71	134	Earl Lunsford, Calg.	6	1,199	6,994	5.8	85	55
Johnny Bright, Calg.-Edm.	13	1,969	10,909	5.5	90	69	Dick Shatto, Tor.	12	1,322	6,958	5.3	67	39
Normie Kwong, Calg.-Edm.	13	1,745	9,022	5.2	60	78	*Tracy Ham, Edm.-Tor.-Balt./Mtl.	10	878	6,870	7.8	80	52
Leo Lewis, Wpg.	11	1,351	8,861	6.5	92	48	*Damon Allen, Edm.-Ott.-Ham.-Mps.-B.C.	12	960	6,775	7.1	51	56
Dave Thelen, Ott.-Tor.	9	1,530	8,463	5.5	77	47							
Jim Everson, B.C.-Ott.	7	1,460	7,060	4.8	68	37							

Leading Lifetime Passers

	Yrs	Att	Comp	Yds	Pct	Avg	Long	TDs
Ron Lancaster, Ott.-Sask.	19	6,233	3,384	50,535	54.3	14.9	102	333
Matt Dunigan, Edm.-B.C.-Tor.-Wpg.-Bhm.-Ham.	14	5,476	3,057	43,857	55.8	14.3	89	306
Tom Clements, Ott.-Sask.-Ham.-Wpg.	12	4,657	2,807	39,041	60.3	13.9	105	252
Kent Austin, Sask.-B.C.-Tor.-Wpg.	10	4,700	2,709	36,030	57.6	13.3	107	198
*Doug Flutie, B.C.-Calg.-Tor.	7	4,181	2,545	35,850	60.9	14.1	106	223
Dieter Brock, Wpg.-Ham.	11	4,535	2,602	34,830	57.4	13.4	98	210
*Damon Allen, Edm.-Ott.-Ham.-Mps.-B.C.	12	4,372	2,289	33,558	52.4	14.7	102	194
*Tracy Ham, Edm.-Tor-Balt./Mtl.	10	3,945	2,103	32,405	53.3	15.4	85	229
Tom Burgess, Ott.-Sask.-Wpg.	10	4,034	2,118	30,308	52.5	14.3	104	190
Sam Etcheverry, Mtl.	7	2,829	1,630	25,582	57.6	15.7	109	183

Leading Lifetime Receivers

	Yrs	No	Yds		Yrs	No	Yds
Ray Elgaard, Sask.	14	830	13,198	Tony Gabriel, Ham.-Ont.	11	614	9,832
Brian Kelly, Edm.	9	575	11,169	Rocky DiPietro, Ham.	14	706	9,762
Tom Scott, Wpg.-Edm.-Calg.	11	649	10,837	Terry Evanshen, Mtl.-Calg.-Ham.-Tor.	14	600	9,697
Tommy Joe Coffey, Edm.-Ham.-Tor.	14	650	10,320	*Earl Winfield, Ham.	10	544	9,657
*Allen Pitts, Calg.	8	643	10,140	*Don Narcisse, Sask.	10	713	9,601

COLLEGE FOOTBALL

Florida Defeats Florida State in the Sugar Bowl, Chosen 1996 National Champions

The University of Florida Gators chomped on the Florida State Seminoles, 52-20, in the Sugar Bowl in New Orleans, LA, Jan. 2, 1997. They were subsequently chosen as the top college football team in the country by both the Associated Press and the USA Today/CNN college football polls, thereby clinching the NCAA Division I football title—a first for the Gators. The victory avenged Florida's only loss of the 1996 season; the Seminoles beat Florida, 24-21, on Nov. 30, in Tallahassee. Gator quarterback Danny Wuerffel, the 1996 Heisman Trophy winner, passed for 306 yards and 3 touchdowns in the Sugar Bowl and was selected the game's Most Valuable Player.

National College Football Champions, 1936-96

The unofficial national champion as selected each year by the AP poll of writers and the USA Today/CNN (until 1991 the UPI) poll of coaches. When the polls disagree, both teams are listed. The AP poll originated in 1936, and the UPI poll in 1950.

1936 Minnesota	1951 Tennessee	1966 Notre Dame	1982 Penn St.
1937 Pittsburgh	1952 Michigan St.	1967 Southern Cal	1983 Miami (FL)
1938 Texas Christian	1953 Maryland	1968 Ohio St.	1984 Brigham Young
1939 Texas A&M	1954 Ohio St., UCLA	1969 Texas	1985 Oklahoma
1940 Minnesota	1955 Oklahoma	1970 Nebraska, Texas	1986 Penn St.
1941 Minnesota	1956 Oklahoma	1971 Nebraska	1987 Miami (FL)
1942 Ohio St.	1957 Auburn, Ohio St.	1972 Southern Cal	1988 Notre Dame
1943 Notre Dame	1958 Louisiana St.	1973 Notre Dame, Alabama	1989 Miami (FL)
1944 Army	1959 Syracuse	1974 Oklahoma, Southern Cal	1990 Colorado, Georgia Tech
1945 Army	1960 Minnesota	1975 Oklahoma	1991 Miami (FL), Washington
1946 Notre Dame	1961 Alabama	1976 Pittsburgh	1992 Alabama
1947 Notre Dame	1962 Southern Cal	1977 Notre Dame	1993 Florida St.
1948 Michigan	1963 Texas	1978 Alabama, Southern Cal	1994 Nebraska
1949 Notre Dame	1964 Alabama	1979 Alabama	1995 Nebraska
1950 Oklahoma	1965 Alabama, Mich. St.	1980 Georgia	1996 Florida
		1981 Clemson	

1996 Final Associated Press and USA Today/CNN NCAA Football Polls

	Associated Press				USA Today/CNN		
Rank	Team[1]	Rank	Team[1]	Rank	Team[1]	Rank	Team[1]
1.	Florida (12-1)	14.	Miami (FL) (9-3)	1.	Florida	14.	Miami (FL)
2.	Ohio St. (11-1)	15.	Northwestern (9-3)	2.	Ohio St.	15.	Washington
3.	Florida St. (11-1)	16.	Washington (9-3)	3.	Florida St.	16.	Northwestern
4.	Arizona St. (11-1)	17.	Kansas St. (9-3)	4.	Arizona St.	17.	Kansas St.
5.	Brigham Young (14-1)	18.	Iowa (9-3)	5.	Brigham Young	18.	Iowa
6.	Nebraska (11-2)	19.	Notre Dame (8-3)	6.	Nebraska	19.	Syracuse
7.	Penn St. (11-2)	20.	Michigan (8-4)	7.	Penn St.	20.	Michigan
8.	Colorado (10-2)	21.	Syracuse (9-3)	8.	Colorado	21.	Notre Dame
9.	Tennessee (10-2)	22.	Wyoming (10-2)	9.	Tennessee	22.	Wyoming
10.	North Carolina (10-2)	23.	Texas (8-5)	10.	North Carolina	23.	Texas
11.	Alabama (10-3)	24.	Auburn (8-4)	11.	Alabama	24.	Army
12.	LSU (10-2)	25.	Army (10-2)	12.	Virginia Tech	25.	Auburn
13.	Virginia Tech (10-2)			13.	LSU		

(1) Team records include bowl games. Won-loss records for teams in USA Today/CNN poll can be found in AP poll.

Annual Results of Major Bowl Games

(Dates indicate the year that the game was played; bowl games are generally played in late December or early January.)

Rose Bowl, Pasadena, CA

1902	(Jan.) Michigan 49, Stanford 0	1943	Georgia 9, UCLA 0	1971	Stanford 27, Ohio St. 17
1916	Washington St. 14, Brown 0	1944	Southern Cal 29, Washington 0	1972	Stanford 13, Michigan 12
1917	Oregon 14, Pennsylvania 0	1945	Southern Cal 25, Tennessee 0	1973	Southern Cal 42, Ohio St. 17
1918	Service teams	1946	Alabama 34, Southern Cal 14	1974	Ohio St. 42, Southern Cal 21
1919	Service teams	1947	Illinois 45, UCLA 14	1975	Southern Cal 18, Ohio St. 17
1920	Harvard 7, Oregon 6	1948	Michigan 49, Southern Cal 0	1976	UCLA 23, Ohio St. 10
1921	California 28, Ohio St. 0	1949	Northwestern 20, California 14	1977	Southern Cal 14, Michigan 6
1922	Wash. & Jeff. 0, California 0	1950	Ohio St. 17, California 14	1978	Washington 27, Michigan 20
1923	Southern Cal 14, Penn St. 3	1951	Michigan 14, California 6	1979	Southern Cal 17, Michigan 10
1924	Navy 14, Washington 14	1952	Illinois 40, Stanford 7	1980	Southern Cal 17, Ohio St. 16
1925	Notre Dame 27, Stanford 10	1953	Southern Cal 7, Wisconsin 0	1981	Michigan 23, Washington 6
1926	Alabama 20, Washington 19	1954	Mich. St. 28, UCLA 20	1982	Washington 28, Iowa 0
1927	Alabama 7, Stanford 7	1955	Ohio St. 20, Southern Cal 7	1983	UCLA 24, Michigan 14
1928	Stanford 7, Pittsburgh 6	1956	Mich. St. 17, UCLA 14	1984	UCLA 45, Illinois 9
1929	Georgia Tech 8, California 7	1957	Iowa 35, Oregon St. 19	1985	Southern Cal 20, Ohio St. 17
1930	Southern Cal 47, Pittsburgh 14	1958	Ohio St. 10, Oregon 7	1986	UCLA 45, Iowa 28
1931	Alabama 24, Wash. St. 0	1959	Iowa 38, California 12	1987	Arizona St. 22, Michigan 15
1932	Southern Cal 21, Tulane 12	1960	Washington 44, Wisconsin 8	1988	Mich. St. 20, Southern Cal 17
1933	Southern Cal 35, Pittsburgh 0	1961	Washington 17, Minnesota 7	1989	Michigan 22, Southern Cal 14
1934	Columbia 7, Stanford 0	1962	Minnesota 21, UCLA 3	1990	Southern Cal 17, Michigan 10
1935	Alabama 29, Stanford 13	1963	Southern Cal 42, Wisconsin 37	1991	Washington 46, Iowa 34
1936	Stanford 7, SMU 0	1964	Illinois 17, Washington 7	1992	Washington 34, Michigan 14
1937	Pittsburgh 21, Washington 0	1965	Michigan 34, Oregon St. 7	1993	Michigan 38, Washington 31
1938	California 13, Alabama 0	1966	UCLA 14, Mich. St. 12	1994	Wisconsin 21, UCLA 16
1939	Southern Cal 7, Duke 3	1967	Purdue 14, Southern Cal 10	1995	Penn St. 38, Oregon 20
1940	Southern Cal 14, Tennessee 0	1968	Southern Cal 14, Indiana 3	1996	Southern Cal 41, Northwestern 32
1941	Stanford 21, Nebraska 13	1969	Ohio St. 27, Southern Cal 16	1997	Ohio St. 20, Arizona St. 17
1942*	Oregon St. 20, Duke 16	1970	Southern Cal 10, Michigan 3		

*Played at Durham, NC.

Orange Bowl, Miami, FL

1935	(Jan.) Bucknell 26, Miami (FL) 0	1956	Oklahoma 20, Maryland 6	1978	Arkansas 31, Oklahoma 6
1936	Catholic U. 20, Mississippi 19	1957	Colorado 27, Clemson 21	1979	Oklahoma 31, Nebraska 24
1937	Duquesne 13, Mississippi St. 12	1958	Oklahoma 48, Duke 21	1980	Oklahoma 24, Florida St. 7
1938	Auburn 6, Michigan St. 0	1959	Oklahoma 21, Syracuse 6	1981	Oklahoma 18, Florida St. 17
1939	Tennessee 17, Oklahoma 0	1960	Georgia 14, Missouri 0	1982	Clemson 22, Nebraska 15
1940	Georgia Tech 21, Missouri 7	1961	Missouri 21, Navy 14	1983	Nebraska 21, LSU 20
1941	Mississippi St. 14, Georgetown 7	1962	LSU 25, Colorado 7	1984	Miami (FL) 31, Nebraska 30
1942	Georgia 40, TCU 26	1963	Alabama 17, Oklahoma 0	1985	Washington 28, Oklahoma 17
1943	Alabama 37, Boston Coll. 21	1964	Nebraska 13, Auburn 7	1986	Oklahoma 25, Penn St. 10
1944	LSU 19, Texas A&M 14	1965	Texas 21, Alabama 17	1987	Oklahoma 42, Arkansas 8
1945	Tulsa 26, Georgia Tech 12	1966	Alabama 39, Nebraska 28	1988	Miami (FL) 20, Oklahoma 14
1946	Miami (FL) 13, Holy Cross 6	1967	Florida 27, Georgia Tech 12	1989	Miami (FL) 23, Nebraska 3
1947	Rice 8, Tennessee 0	1968	Oklahoma 26, Tennessee 24	1990	Notre Dame 21, Colorado 6
1948	Georgia Tech 20, Kansas 14	1969	Penn St. 15, Kansas 14	1991	Colorado 10, Notre Dame 9
1949	Texas 41, Georgia 28	1970	Penn St. 10, Missouri 3	1992	Miami (FL) 22, Nebraska 0
1950	Santa Clara 21, Kentucky 13	1971	Nebraska 17, LSU 12	1993	Florida St. 27, Nebraska 14
1951	Clemson 15, Miami (FL) 14	1972	Nebraska 38, Alabama 6	1994	Florida St. 18, Nebraska 16
1952	Georgia Tech 17, Baylor 14	1973	Nebraska 40, Notre Dame 6	1995	Nebraska 24, Miami (FL) 17
1953	Alabama 61, Syracuse 6	1974	Penn St. 16, LSU 9	1996	Florida St. 31, Notre Dame 26
1954	Oklahoma 7, Maryland 0	1975	Notre Dame 13, Alabama 11	1996	(Dec.) Nebraska 41, Virginia
1955	Duke 34, Nebraska 7	1976	Oklahoma 14, Michigan 6		Tech 21
		1977	Ohio St. 27, Colorado 10		

Sugar Bowl, New Orleans, LA

1935	(Jan.) Tulane 20, Temple 14	1956	Georgia Tech 7, Pittsburgh 0	1977	(Jan.) Pittsburgh 27, Georgia 3
1936	TCU 3, LSU 2	1957	Baylor 13, Tennessee 7	1978	Alabama 35, Ohio St. 6
1937	Santa Clara 21, LSU 14	1958	Mississippi 39, Texas 7	1979	Alabama 14, Penn St. 7
1938	Santa Clara 6, LSU 0	1959	LSU 7, Clemson 0	1980	Alabama 24, Arkansas 9
1939	TCU 15, Carnegie Tech 7	1960	Mississippi 21, LSU 0	1981	Georgia 17, Notre Dame 10
1940	Texas A&M 14, Tulane 13	1961	Mississippi 14, Rice 6	1982	Pittsburgh 24, Georgia 20
1941	Boston Col. 19, Tennessee 13	1962	Alabama 10, Arkansas 3	1983	Penn St. 27, Georgia 23
1942	Fordham 2, Missouri 0	1963	Mississippi 17, Arkansas 13	1984	Auburn 9, Michigan 7
1943	Tennessee 14, Tulsa 7	1964	Alabama 12, Mississippi 7	1985	Nebraska 28, LSU 10
1944	Georgia Tech 20, Tulsa 18	1965	LSU 13, Syracuse 10	1986	Tennessee 35, Miami (FL) 7
1945	Duke 29, Alabama 26	1966	Missouri 20, Florida 18	1987	Nebraska 30, LSU 15
1946	Oklahoma A&M 33, St. Mary's 13	1967	Alabama 34, Nebraska 7	1988	Syracuse 16, Auburn 16
1947	Georgia 20, N. Carolina 10	1968	LSU 20, Wyoming 13	1989	Florida St. 13, Auburn 7
1948	Texas 27, Alabama 7	1969	Arkansas 16, Georgia 2	1990	Miami (FL) 33, Alabama 25
1949	Oklahoma 14, N. Carolina 6	1970	Mississippi 27, Arkansas 22	1991	Tennessee 23, Virginia 22
1950	Oklahoma 35, LSU 0	1971	Tennessee 34, Air Force 13	1992	Notre Dame 39, Florida 28
1951	Kentucky 13, Oklahoma 7	1972	Oklahoma 40, Auburn 22	1993	Alabama 34, Miami (FL) 13
1952	Maryland 28, Tennessee 13	1972*	(Dec.) Oklahoma 14, Penn St. 0	1994	Florida 41, West Virginia 7
1953	Georgia Tech 24, Mississippi 7	1973	Notre Dame 24, Alabama 23	1995	Florida St. 23, Florida 17
1954	Georgia Tech 42, West Virginia 19	1974	Nebraska 13, Florida 10	1995	(Dec.) Virginia Tech 28, Texas 10
1955	Navy 21, Mississippi 0	1975	Alabama 13, Penn St. 6	1997	(Jan.) Florida 52, Florida St. 20

* Penn St. awarded game by forfeit.

Fiesta Bowl, Tempe, AZ

1971	(Dec.) Arizona St. 45, Florida St. 38	1979	Pittsburgh 16, Arizona 10	1989	Notre Dame 34, W. Virginia 21
1972	Arizona St. 49, Missouri 35	1980	Penn St. 31, Ohio St. 19	1990	Florida St. 41, Nebraska 17
1973	Arizona St. 28, Pittsburgh 7	1982	(Jan.) Penn St. 26, USC 10	1991	Louisville 34, Alabama 7
1974	Okla. St. 16, Brigham Young 6	1983	Arizona St. 32, Oklahoma 21	1992	Penn St. 42, Tennessee 17
1975	Arizona St. 17, Nebraska 14	1984	Ohio St. 28, Pittsburgh 23	1993	Syracuse 26, Colorado 22
1976	Oklahoma 41, Wyoming 7	1985	UCLA 39, Miami (FL) 37	1994	Arizona 29, Miami (FL) 0
1977	Penn St. 42, Arizona St. 30	1986	Michigan 27, Nebraska 23	1995	Colorado 41, Notre Dame 24
1978	UCLA 10, Arkansas 10	1987	Penn St. 14, Miami (FL) 10	1996	Nebraska 62, Florida 24
		1988	Florida St. 31, Nebraska 28	1997	Penn St. 38, Texas 15

Cotton Bowl, Dallas, TX

1937	(Jan.) TCU 16, Marquette 6	1958	Navy 20, Rice 7	1978	Notre Dame 38, Texas 10
1938	Rice 28, Colorado 14	1959	TCU 0, Air Force 0	1979	Notre Dame 35, Houston 34
1939	St. Mary's 20, Texas Tech 13	1960	Syracuse 23, Texas 14	1980	Houston 17, Nebraska 14
1940	Clemson 6, Boston Coll. 3	1961	Duke 7, Arkansas 6	1981	Alabama 30, Baylor 2
1941	Texas A&M 13, Fordham 12	1962	Texas 12, Mississippi 7	1982	Texas 14, Alabama 12
1942	Alabama 29, Texas A&M 21	1963	LSU 13, Texas 0	1983	SMU 7, Pittsburgh 3
1943	Texas 14, Georgia Tech 7	1964	Texas 28, Navy 6	1984	Georgia 10, Texas 9
1944	Randolph Field 7, Texas 7	1965	Arkansas 10, Nebraska 7	1985	Boston Coll. 45, Houston 28
1945	Oklahoma A&M 34, TCU 0	1966	LSU 14, Arkansas 7	1986	Texas A&M 36, Auburn 16
1946	Texas 40, Missouri 27	1966	(Dec.) Georgia 24, SMU 9	1987	Ohio St. 28, Texas A&M 12
1947	Arkansas 0, LSU 0	1968	(Jan.) Texas A&M 20, Alabama 16	1988	Texas A&M 35, Notre Dame 10
1948	SMU 13, Penn St. 13			1989	UCLA 17, Arkansas 3
1949	SMU 21, Oregon 13	1969	Texas 36, Tennessee 13	1990	Tennessee 31, Arkansas 27
1950	Rice 27, North Carolina 13	1970	Texas 21, Notre Dame 17	1991	Miami (FL) 46, Texas 3
1951	Tennessee 20, Texas 14	1971	Notre Dame 24, Texas 11	1992	Florida St. 10, Texas A&M 2
1952	Kentucky 20, TCU 7	1972	Penn St. 30, Texas 6	1993	Notre Dame 28, Texas A&M 3
1953	Texas 16, Tennessee 0	1973	Texas 17, Alabama 13	1994	Notre Dame 24, Texas A&M 21
1954	Rice 28, Alabama 6	1974	Nebraska 19, Texas 3	1995	Southern Cal. 55, Tex. Tech 14
1955	Georgia Tech 14, Arkansas 6	1975	Penn St. 41, Baylor 20	1996	Colorado 38, Oregon 6
1956	Mississippi 14, TCU 13	1976	Arkansas 31, Georgia 10	1997	Brigham Young 19, Kansas St. 15
1957	TCU 28, Syracuse 27	1977	Houston 30, Maryland 21		

Sun Bowl, El Paso, TX (John Hancock Bowl, 1989-93)

1936	(Jan.) Hardin-Simmons 14, New Mexico St. 14	1938	West Virginia 7, Texas Tech 6	1942	Tulsa 6, Texas Tech 0
1937	Hardin-Simmons 34, Texas Mines 6	1939	Utah 26, New Mexico 0	1943	2d Air Force 13, Hardin-Simmons 7
		1940	Catholic U. 0, Arizona St. 0	1944	Southwestern (TX) 7, New Mexico 0
		1941	Western Reserve 26, Arizona St. 13		

1945	Southwestern (TX) 35, U. of Mexico 0	1960	New Mexico St. 20, Utah St. 13	1978	Texas 42, Maryland 0
1946	New Mexico 34, Denver 24	1961	Villanova 17, Wichita 9	1979	Washington 14, Texas 7
1947	Cincinnati 18, Virginia Tech 6	1962	West Texas St. 15, Ohio U. 14	1980	Nebraska 31, Mississippi St. 17
1948	Miami (OH) 13, Texas Tech 12	1963	Oregon 21, SMU 14	1981	Oklahoma 40, Houston 14
1949	West Virginia 21, Texas Mines 12	1964	Georgia 7, Texas Tech 0	1982	North Carolina 26, Texas 10
1950	Texas Western 33, Georgetown 20	1965	Texas Western 13, TCU 12	1983	Alabama 28, SMU 7
1951	West Texas St. 14, Cincinnati 13	1966	Wyoming 28, Florida St. 20	1984	Maryland 28, Tennessee 27
1952	Texas Tech 25, Pacific (CA) 14	1967	UTEP 14, Mississippi 7	1985	Georgia 13, Arizona 13
1953	Pacific (CA) 26, S. Mississippi 7	1968	Auburn 34, Arizona 10	1986	Alabama 28, Washington 6
1954	Texas Western 37, S. Miss. 14	1969	Nebraska 45, Georgia 6	1987	Oklahoma St. 35, West Virginia 33
1955	Texas Western 47, Florida St. 20	1970	Georgia Tech. 17, Texas Tech 9	1988	Alabama 29, Army 28
1956	Wyoming 21, Texas Tech 14	1971	LSU 33, Iowa St. 15	1989	Pittsburgh 31, Texas A&M 28
1957	Geo. Washington 13, Texas Western 0	1972	North Carolina 32, Texas Tech 28	1990	Michigan St. 17, USC 16
		1973	Missouri 34, Auburn 17	1991	UCLA 6, Illinois 3
1958	Louisville 34, Drake 20	1974	Mississippi St. 26, North Carolina 24	1992	Baylor 20, Arizona 15
1958	(Dec.) Wyoming 14, Hardin-Simmons 6	1975	Pittsburgh 33, Kansas 19	1993	Oklahoma 41, Texas Tech 10
		1977	(Jan.) Texas A&M 37, Florida 14	1994	Texas 35, North Carolina 31
1959	New Mexico St. 28, N. Texas St. 8	1977	(Dec.) Stanford 24, LSU 14	1995	Iowa 38, Washington 18
				1996	Stanford 38, Michigan St. 0

Gator Bowl, Jacksonville, FL

1946	(Jan.) Wake Forest 26, S. Carolina 14	1961	Penn St. 30, Georgia Tech 15	1979	N. Carolina 17, Michigan 15
1947	Oklahoma 34, N. Carolina St. 13	1962	Florida 17, Penn St. 7	1980	Pittsburgh 37, S. Carolina 9
1948	Maryland 20, Georgia 20	1963	N. Carolina 35, Air Force 0	1981	N. Carolina 31, Arkansas 27
1949	Clemson 24, Missouri 23	1965	(Jan.) Florida St. 36, Okla.19	1982	Florida St. 31, West Virginia 12
1950	Maryland 20, Missouri 7	1965	(Dec.) Georgia Tech 31, Texas Tech 21	1983	Florida 14, Iowa 6
1951	Wyoming 20, Washington & Lee 7			1984	Oklahoma St. 21, S. Carolina 14
		1966	Tennessee 18, Syracuse 12	1985	Florida St. 34, Oklahoma St. 23
1952	Miami (FL) 14, Clemson 0	1967	Penn St. 17, Florida St. 17	1986	Clemson 27, Stanford 21
1953	Florida 14, Tulsa 13	1968	Missouri 35, Alabama 10	1987	LSU 30, S. Carolina 13
1954	Texas Tech 35, Auburn 13	1969	Florida 14, Tennessee 13	1989	(Jan.) Georgia 34, Michigan St. 27
1954	(Dec.) Auburn 33, Baylor 13	1971	(Jan.) Auburn 35, Mississippi 28		
1955	Vanderbilt 25, Auburn 13	1971	(Dec.) Georgia 7, N. Carolina 3	1989	(Dec.) Clemson 27, W. Virginia 7
1956	Georgia Tech 21, Pittsburgh 14	1972	Auburn 24, Colorado 3	1991	(Jan.) Michigan 35, Mississippi 3
1957	Tennessee 3, Texas A&M 0	1973	Texas Tech 28, Tenn. 19	1991	(Dec.) Oklahoma 48, Virginia 14
1958	Mississippi 7, Florida 3	1974	Auburn 27, Texas 3	1992	Florida 27, N. Carolina St. 10
1960	(Jan.) Arkansas 14, Georgia Tech 7	1975	Maryland 13, Florida 0	1993	Alabama 24, N. Carolina 10
		1976	Notre Dame 20, Penn St. 9	1994	Tennessee 45, Virginia Tech 23
		1977	Pittsburgh 34, Clemson 3	1996	(Jan.) Syracuse 41, Clemson 0
1960	(Dec.) Florida 13, Baylor 12	1978	Clemson 17, Ohio St. 15	1997	N. Carolina 20, W. Virginia 13

Outback Bowl, Tampa, FL (Hall of Fame Bowl Until 1996)

1986	(Dec.) Boston Coll. 27, Georgia 24	1990	Auburn 31, Ohio St. 14	1994	Michigan 42, N. Carolina St. 7
		1991	Clemson 30, Illinois 0	1995	Wisconsin 34, Duke 20
1988	(Jan.) Michigan 28, Alabama 24	1992	Syracuse 24, Ohio St. 17	1996	Penn St. 43, Auburn 14
1989	Syracuse 23, LSU 10	1993	Tennessee 38, Boston Coll. 23	1997	Alabama 17, Michigan 14

Liberty Bowl, Memphis, TN

1959	(Dec.) Penn St. 7, Alabama 0	1971	Tennessee 14, Arkansas 13	1984	Auburn 21, Arkansas 15
1960	Penn St. 41, Oregon 12	1972	Georgia Tech 31, Iowa St. 30	1985	Baylor 21, LSU 7
1961	Syracuse 15, Miami (FL) 14	1973	N. Carolina St. 31, Kansas 18	1986	Tennessee 21, Minnesota 14
1962	Oregon St. 6, Villanova 0	1974	Tennessee 7, Maryland 3	1987	Georgia 20, Arkansas 17
1963	Mississippi St. 16, N. Carolina St. 12	1975	USC 20, Texas A&M 0	1988	Indiana 34, S. Carolina 10
		1976	Alabama 36, UCLA 6	1989	Mississippi 42, Air Force 29
1964	Utah 32, West Virginia 6	1977	Nebraska 21, N. Carolina 17	1990	Air Force 23, Ohio St. 11
1965	Mississippi 13, Auburn 7	1978	Missouri 20, LSU 15	1991	Air Force 38, Mississippi St. 15
1966	Miami (FL) 14, Virginia Tech 7	1979	Penn St. 9, Tulane 6	1992	Mississippi 13, Air Force 0
1967	N. Carolina St. 14, Georgia 7	1980	Purdue 28, Missouri 25	1993	Louisville 18, Michigan St. 7
1968	Mississippi 34, Virginia Tech 17	1981	Ohio St. 31, Navy 28	1994	Illinois 30, East Carolina 0
1969	Colorado 47, Alabama 33	1982	Alabama 21, Illinois 15	1995	East Carolina 19, Stanford 13
1970	Tulane 17, Colorado 3	1983	Notre Dame 19, Boston Coll. 18	1996	Syracuse 30, Houston 17

Copper Bowl, Tucson, AZ

1989	(Dec.) Arizona 17, N. Carolina St. 10	1991	Indiana 24, Baylor 0	1994	Brigham Young 31, Oklahoma 6
		1992	Washington St. 31, Utah 28	1995	Texas Tech 55, Air Force 41
1990	California 17, Wyoming 15	1993	Kansas St. 52, Wyoming 17	1996	Wisconsin 38, Utah 10

Independence Bowl, Shreveport, LA

1976	(Dec.)McNeese St. 20, Tulsa 16	1983	Air Force 9, Mississippi 3	1990	Louisiana Tech 34, Maryland 34
1977	Louisiana Tech 24, Louisville 14	1984	Air Force 23, Virginia Tech 7	1991	Georgia 24, Arkansas 15
1978	E. Carolina 35, Louisiana Tech 13	1985	Minnesota 20, Clemson 13	1992	Wake Forest 39, Oregon 35
1979	Syracuse 31, McNeese St. 7	1986	Mississippi 20, Texas Tech 17	1993	Virginia Tech 45, Indiana 20
1980	So. Mississippi 16, McNeese St. 14	1987	Washington 24, Tulane 12	1994	Virginia 20, Texas Christian 10
1981	Texas A&M 33, Oklahoma St. 16	1988	So. Mississippi 38, UTEP 18	1995	LSU 45, Michigan St. 26
1982	Wisconsin 14, Kansas St. 3	1989	Oregon 27, Tulsa 24	1996	Auburn 32, Army 29

Florida Citrus Bowl, Orlando, FL (Tangerine Bowl Until 1983)

1947	(Jan.) Catawba 31, Maryville 6	1957	West Texas St. 20, So. Miss. 13	1964	E. Carolina 14, Massachusetts 13
1948	Catawba 7, Marshall 0	1958	East Texas St. 10, So. Miss. 9	1965	E. Carolina 31, Maine 0
1949	Murray St. 21, Sul Ross St. 21	1958	(Dec.) East Texas St. 26, Missouri Valley 7	1966	Morgan St. 14, West Chester 6
1950	St. Vincent 7, Emory & Henry 6			1967	Tenn.-Martin 25, West Chester 8
1951	Morris Harvey 35, Emory & Henry 14	1960	(Jan.) Middle Tennessee 21, Presbyterian 12	1968	Richmond 49, Ohio U. 42
1952	Stetson 35, Arkansas St. 20			1969	Toledo 56, Davidson 33
1953	East Texas St. 33, Tenn. Tech 0	1960	(Dec.) Citadel 27, Tenn. Tech 0	1970	Toledo 40, William & Mary 12
1954	East Texas St. 7, Arkansas St. 7	1961	Lamar 21, Middle Tennessee 14	1971	Toledo 28, Richmond 3
1955	Neb.-Omaha 7, E. Kentucky 6	1962	Houston 49, Miami (OH) 21	1972	Tampa 21, Kent St. 18
1956	Juniata 6, Missouri Valley 6	1963	Western Ky. 27, Coast Guard 0	1973	Miami (OH) 16, Florida 7

(continued)

1974	Miami (OH) 21, Georgia 10
1975	Miami (OH) 20, S. Carolina 7
1976	Okla. St. 49, Brigham Young 21
1977	Florida St. 40, Texas Tech 17
1978	N. Carolina St. 30, Pittsburgh 17
1979	LSU 34, Wake Forest 10
1980	Florida 35, Maryland 20
1981	Missouri 19, So. Mississippi 17

1982	Auburn 33, Boston College 26
1983	Tennessee 30, Maryland 23
1984	Georgia 17, Florida St. 17
1985	Ohio St. 10, Brigham Young 7
1987	(Jan.) Auburn 16, USC 7
1988	Clemson 35, Penn St. 10
1989	Clemson 13, Oklahoma 6
1990	Illinois 31, Virginia 21

1991	Georgia Tech 45, Nebraska 21
1992	California 37, Clemson 13
1993	Georgia 21, Ohio St. 14
1994	Penn St. 31, Tennessee 13
1995	Alabama 24, Ohio St. 17
1996	Tennessee 20, Ohio St. 14
1997	Tennessee 48, Northwestern 28

Peach Bowl, Atlanta, GA

1968	(Dec.) LSU 31, Florida St. 27
1969	W. Virginia 14, S. Carolina 3
1970	Arizona St. 48, N. Carolina 26
1971	Mississippi 41, Georgia Tech 18
1972	N. Carolina St. 49, W. Virginia 13
1973	Georgia 17, Maryland 16
1974	Vanderbilt 6, Texas Tech 6
1975	W. Virginia 13, N. Carolina St. 10
1976	Kentucky 21, N. Carolina 0
1977	N. Carolina St. 24, Iowa St. 14
1978	Purdue 41, Georgia Tech. 21

1979	Baylor 24, Clemson 18
1981	(Jan.) Miami (FL) 20, Virginia Tech 10
1981	(Dec.) W. Virginia 26, Florida 6
1982	Iowa 28, Tennessee 22
1983	Florida St. 28, N. Carolina 3
1984	Virginia 27, Purdue 22
1985	Army 31, Illinois 29
1986	Va. Tech 25, N. Carolina St. 24
1988	(Jan.) Tennessee 28, Indiana 22
1988	(Dec.) N. Carolina St. 28, Iowa 23

1989	Syracuse 19, Georgia 18
1990	Auburn 27, Indiana 23
1992	(Jan.) E. Carolina 37, N. Carolina St. 34
1993	N. Carolina 21, Mississippi St. 17
1993	(Dec.) Clemson 14, Kentucky 13
1995	(Jan.) N. Carolina St. 28, Mississippi St. 24
1995	(Dec.) Virginia 34, Georgia 27
1996	LSU 10, Clemson 7

Holiday Bowl, San Diego, CA

1978	(Dec.) Navy 23, Brigham Young 16
1979	Indiana 38, Brigham Young 37
1980	Brigham Young 46, SMU 45
1981	Brigham Young 38, Washington St. 36
1982	Ohio St. 47, Brigham Young 17

1983	Brigham Young 21, Missouri 17
1984	Brigham Young 24, Michigan 17
1985	Arkansas 18, Arizona St. 17
1986	Iowa 39, San Diego St. 38
1987	Iowa 20, Wyoming 19
1988	Oklahoma St. 62, Wyoming 14
1989	Penn St. 50, Brigham Young 39

1990	Texas A&M 65, Brigham Young 14
1991	Iowa 13, Brigham Young 13
1992	Hawaii 27, Illinois 17
1993	Ohio St. 28, Brigham Young 21
1994	Michigan 24, Colorado St. 14
1995	Kansas St. 54, Colorado St. 21
1996	Colorado 33, Washington 21

Aloha Bowl, Honolulu, HI

1982	(Dec.) Washington 21, Md. 20
1983	Penn St. 13, Washington 10
1984	SMU 27, Notre Dame 20
1985	Alabama 24, USC 3
1986	Arizona 30, North Carolina 21

1987	UCLA 20, Florida 16
1988	Washington St. 24, Houston 22
1989	Michigan St. 33, Hawaii 13
1990	Syracuse 28, Arizona 0
1991	Georgia Tech 18, Stanford 17

1992	Kansas 23, Brigham Young 20
1993	Colorado 41, Fresno St. 30
1994	Boston Coll. 12, Kansas St. 7
1995	Kansas 51, UCLA 30
1996	Navy 42, California 38

Carquest Bowl, Miami, FL (Blockbuster Bowl Until 1993)

1990	(Dec.) Florida St. 24, Penn St. 17
1991	Alabama 30, Colorado 25

1993	(Jan.) Stanford 24, Penn St. 3
1994	Boston Coll. 31, Virginia 13
1995	S. Carolina 24, W. Virginia 21

1995	(Dec.) N. Carolina 20, Arkansas 10
1996	Miami (FL) 31, Virginia 21

Las Vegas Bowl, Las Vegas, NV

1992	(Dec.) Bowling Green 35, Nevada 34

1993	Utah St. 42, Ball St. 33
1994	UNLV 52, Central Michigan 24

1995	Toledo 40, Nevada 37 (OT)
1996	Nevada 18, Ball St. 15

Alamo Bowl, San Antonio, TX

1993	(Dec.) California 37, Iowa 3
1994	Washington St. 10, Baylor 3

1995	Texas A&M 22, Michigan 20
1996	Iowa 27, Texas Tech 0

Selected College Division I Football Teams

(1996 record does not include bowl games or Division I-AA playoff games; coaches at the start of 1997 season)

Team	Nickname	Team colors	Conference	Coach	1996 record (W-L)
Air Force	Falcons	Blue & silver	Western Athletic	Fisher DeBerry	6-5
Akron	Zips	Blue & gold	Mid-American	Lee Owens	4-7
Alabama	Crimson Tide	Crimson & white	Southeastern	Mike DuBose	9-3
Arizona	Wildcats	Cardinal & navy	Pacific Ten	Dick Tomey	5-6
Arizona State	Sun Devils	Maroon & gold	Pacific Ten	Bruce Snyder	11-0
Arkansas	Razorbacks	Cardinal & white	Southeastern	Danny Ford	4-7
Arkansas State	Indians	Scarlet & black	Independent	Joe Hollis	4-7
Army	Cadets, Black Knights	Black, gold, gray	Independent	Bob Sutton	10-1
Auburn	Tigers	Burnt orange & navy	Southeastern	Terry Bowden	7-4
Ball State	Cardinals	Cardinal & white	Mid-American	Bill Lynch	8-3
Baylor	Bears	Green & gold	Big Twelve	Dave Roberts	4-7
Boston College	Eagles	Maroon & gold	Big East	Tom O'Brien	5-7
Boston University	Terriers	Scarlet & white	Atlantic Ten	Tom Masella	1-10
Bowling Green	Falcons	Orange & brown	Mid-American	Gary Blackney	4-7
Brigham Young (BYU)	Cougars	Royal blue & white	Western Athletic	LaVell Edwards	13-1
Brown	Bears	Brown, cardinal, white	Ivy League	Mark Whipple	5-5
California	Golden Bears	Blue & gold	Pacific Ten	Tom Holmoe	6-5
Central Michigan	Chippewas	Maroon & gold	Mid-American	Dick Flynn	5-6
Cincinnati	Bearcats	Red & black	Conference USA	Rick Minter	6-5
Citadel	Bulldogs	Blue & white	Southern	Don Powers	4-7
Clemson	Tigers	Purple & orange	Atlantic Coast	Tommy West	7-4
Colgate	Red Raiders	Maroon	Patriot League	Dick Biddle	6-5
Colorado	Buffaloes	Silver, gold & black	Big Twelve	Rick Neuheisel	9-2
Colorado State	Rams	Green & gold	Western Athletic	Sonny Lubick	7-5
Columbia	Lions	Columbia blue & white	Ivy League	Ray Tellier	8-2
Cornell	Big Red	Carnelian & white	Ivy League	Jim Hofher	4-6
Dartmouth	Big Green	Dartmouth green & white	Ivy League	John Lyons	10-0
Delaware	Fightin' Blue Hens	Blue & gold	Atlantic Ten	Tubby Raymond	8-3
Delaware State	Hornets	Red & blue	Mid-Eastern Athletic	John McKenzie	3-8
Duke	Blue Devils	Royal blue & white	Atlantic Coast	Fred Goldsmith	0-11
East Carolina	Pirates	Purple & gold	Conference USA	Steve Logan	8-3
East Tennessee State	Buccaneers	Blue & gold	Southern	Paul Hamilton	9-2

Team	Nickname	Team colors	Conference	Coach	1996 record (W-L)
Eastern Illinois	Panthers	Blue & gray	Ohio Valley	Bob Spoo	8-3
Eastern Kentucky	Colonels	Maroon & white	Ohio Valley	Roy Kidd	6-5
Eastern Michigan	Eagles	Dark green & white	Mid-American	Rick Rasnick	3-8
Eastern Washington	Eagles	Red & white	Big Sky	Mike Kramer	6-5
Florida	Gators	Orange & blue	Southeastern	Steve Spurrier	11-1
Florida A&M	Rattlers	Orange & green	Mid-Eastern Athletic	Billy Joe	9-2
Florida State	Seminoles	Garnet & gold	Atlantic Coast	Bobby Bowden	11-0
Fresno State	Bulldogs	Cardinal & blue	Western Athletic	Pat Hill	4-7
Furman	Paladins	Purple & white	Southern	Bobby Johnson	8-3
Georgia	Bulldogs	Red & black	Southeastern	Jim Donnan	5-6
Georgia Southern	Eagles	Blue & white	Southern	Paul Johnson	4-7
Georgia Tech	Yellow Jackets	Old gold & white	Atlantic Coast	George O'Leary	5-6
Grambling	Tigers	Black & gold	Southwestern	Eddie Robinson	3-8
Harvard	Crimson	Crimson, black, white	Ivy League	Tim Murphy	4-6
Hawaii	Rainbow Warriors	Green & white	Western Athletic	Fred vonAppen	2-10
Holy Cross	Crusaders	Royal purple	Patriot League	Dan Allen	2-9
Houston	Cougars	Scarlet & white	Conference USA	Kim Helton	7-4
Howard	Bison	Blue, white & red	Mid-Eastern Athletic	Steve Wilson	9-2
Idaho	Vandals	Silver & gold	Big West	Chris Tormey	6-5
Idaho State	Bengals	Orange & black	Big Sky	Tom Walsh	4-7
Illinois	Fighting Illini	Orange & blue	Big Ten	Ron Turner	2-9
Illinois State	Redbirds	Red & white	Gateway	Todd Berry	3-8
Indiana	Fightin' Hoosiers	Cream & crimson	Big Ten	Cam Cameron	3-8
Indiana State	Sycamores	Blue & white	Gateway	Dennis Raetz	6-5
Iowa	Hawkeyes	Old gold & black	Big Ten	Hayden Fry	8-3
Iowa State	Cyclones	Cardinal & gold	Big Twelve	Dan McCarney	2-9
Jackson State	Tigers	Blue & white	Southwestern	James Carson	10-1
James Madison	Dukes	Purple & gold	Atlantic Ten	Alex Wood	7-4
Kansas	Jayhawks	Crimson & blue	Big Twelve	Terry Allen	4-7
Kansas State	Wildcats	Purple & white	Big Twelve	Bill Snyder	9-2
Kent	Golden Flashes	Navy blue & gold	Mid-American	Jim Corrigall	2-9
Kentucky	Wildcats	Blue & white	Southeastern	Hal Mumme	4-7
Lafayette	Leopards	Maroon & white	Patriot League	Bill Russo	5-5
Lehigh	Engineers, Mountain Hawks	Brown & white	Patriot League	Kevin Higgins	5-6
Liberty	Flames	Red, white, blue	Independent	Sam Rutigliano	5-6
Louisiana State (LSU)	Fighting Tigers	Purple & gold	Southeastern	Gerry DiNardo	9-2
Louisiana Tech	Bulldogs	Red & blue	Independent	Gary Crowton	6-5
Louisville	Cardinals	Red, black, white	Conference USA	Ron Cooper	5-6
Maine	Black Bears	Blue & white	Atlantic Ten	Jack Cosgrove	7-4
Marshall	Thundering Herd	Green & white	Mid-American	Bob Pruett	11-0
Maryland	Terrapins	Red, white, black, gold	Atlantic Coast	Ron Vanderlinden	5-6
Massachusetts	Minutemen	Maroon & white	Atlantic Ten	Mike Hodges	6-5
McNeese State	Cowboys	Blue & gold	Southland	Bobby Keasler	3-8
Memphis	Tigers	Blue & gray	Conference USA	Rip Scherer	4-7
Miami (Florida)	Hurricanes	Orange, green, white	Big East	Butch Davis	8-3
Miami (Ohio)	RedHawks	Red & white	Mid-American	Randy Walker	6-5
Michigan	Wolverines	Maize & blue	Big Ten	Lloyd Carr	8-3
Michigan State	Spartans	Green & white	Big Ten	Nick Saban	6-5
Middle Tennessee St.	Blue Raiders	Blue & white	Ohio Valley	Boots Donnelly	6-5
Minnesota	Golden Gophers	Maroon & gold	Big Ten	Glen Mason	4-7
Mississippi	Rebels	Cardinal red & navy	Southeastern	Tommy Tuberville	5-6
Mississippi State	Bulldogs	Maroon & white	Southeastern	Jackie Sherrill	5-6
Mississippi Valley State	Delta Devils	Green & white	Southwestern	Larry Dorsey	7-4
Missouri	Tigers	Old gold & black	Big Twelve	Larry Smith	5-6
Montana	Grizzlies	Copper, silver, gold	Big Sky	Mick Dennehy	11-0
Montana State	Bobcats	Blue & gold	Big Sky	Cliff Hysell	6-5
Morehead State	Eagles	Blue & gold	Independent	Matt Ballard	6-4
Morgan State	Bears	Blue & orange	Mid-Eastern Athletic	Stump Mitchell	4-7
Murray State	Racers	Blue & gold	Ohio Valley	Denver Johnson	10-1
Navy	Midshipmen	Navy blue & gold	Independent	Charlie Weatherbie	8-3
Nebraska	Cornhuskers	Scarlet & cream	Big Twelve	Tom Osborne	10-2
Nevada	Wolf Pack	Silver & blue	Big West	Jeff Tisdel	8-3
Nev.-Las Vegas (UNLV)	Rebels	Scarlet & gray	Western Athletic	Jeff Horton	1-11
New Hampshire	Wildcats	Blue & white	Atlantic Ten	Bill Bowes	8-3
New Mexico	Lobos	Cherry & silver	Western Athletic	Dennis Franchione	6-5
New Mexico State	Aggies	Crimson & white	Big West	Tony Samuel	1-10
Nicholls St.	Colonels	Red & gray	Southland	Darren Barbier	8-3
North Carolina	Tar Heels	Carolina blue & white	Atlantic Coast	Mack Brown	9-2
North Carolina A & T	Aggies	Blue & gold	Mid-Eastern Athletic	Bill Hayes	8-3
North Carolina State	Wolfpack	Red & white	Atlantic Coast	Mike O'Cain	3-8
North Texas	Eagles	Green & white	Big West	Matt Simon	5-6
Northeast Louisiana	Indians	Maroon & gold	Independent	Ed Zaunbrecher	5-6
Northeastern	Huskies	Red & black	Atlantic Ten	Barry Gallup	6-5
Northern Arizona	Lumberjacks	Blue & gold	Big Sky	Steve Axman	9-2
Northern Illinois	Huskies	Cardinal & black	Mid-American	Joe Novak	1-10
Northern Iowa	Panthers	Purple & old gold	Gateway	Mike Dunbar	10-1
Northwestern	Wildcats	Purple & white	Big Ten	Gary Barnett	9-2
Northwestern State	Demons	Purple & white	Southland	Sam Goodwin	6-5
Notre Dame	Fighting Irish	Gold & blue	Independent	Bob Davie	8-3
Ohio	Bobcats	Ohio green & white	Mid-American	Jim Grobe	6-6
Ohio State	Buckeyes	Scarlet & gray	Big Ten	John Cooper	10-1
Oklahoma	Sooners	Crimson & cream	Big Twelve	John Blake	3-8
Oklahoma State	Cowboys	Orange & black	Big Twelve	Bob Simmons	5-6
Oregon	Ducks	Green & yellow	Pacific Ten	Mike Bellotti	6-5
Oregon State	Beavers	Orange & black	Pacific Ten	Mike Riley	2-9

(continued)

Team	Nickname	Team colors	Conference	Coach	1996 record (W-L)
Penn State	Nittany Lions	Blue & white	Big Ten	Joe Paterno	10-2
Pennsylvania	Red & Blue, Quakers	Red & blue	Ivy League	Al Bagnoli	5-5
Pittsburgh	Panthers	Blue & gold	Big East	Walt Harris	4-7
Princeton	Tigers	Orange & black	Ivy League	Steve Tosches	3-7
Purdue	Boilermakers	Old gold & black	Big Ten	Joe Tiller	3-8
Rhode Island	Rams	Light & dark blue, white	Atlantic Ten	Floyd Keith	4-6
Rice	Owls	Blue & gray	Western Athletic	Ken Hatfield	7-4
Richmond	Spiders	Red & blue	Atlantic Ten	Jim Reid	2-9
Rutgers	Scarlet Knights	Scarlet	Big East	Terry Shea	2-9
Sam Houston State	Bearkats	Orange & white	Southland	Ron Randleman	4-7
Samford	Bulldogs	Crimson & blue	Independent	Pete Hurt	6-5
San Diego State	Aztecs	Scarlet & black	Western Athletic	Ted Tollner	8-3
San Jose State	Spartans	Gold, white, blue	Western Athletic	Dave Baldwin	3-9
South Carolina	Fighting Gamecocks	Garnet & black	Southeastern	Brad Scott	6-5
South Carolina State	Bulldogs	Garnet & blue	Mid-Eastern Athletic	Willie E. Jeffries	4-6
SE Missouri State	Indians	Red & black	Ohio Valley	John Mumford	3-8
Southern-Baton Rouge	Jaguars	Blue & gold	Southwestern	Pete Richardson	7-4
Southern California (USC)	Trojans	Cardinal & gold	Pacific Ten	John Robinson	6-6
Southern Illinois	Salukis	Maroon & white	Gateway	Jan Quarless	5-6
Southern Methodist (SMU)	Mustangs	Red & blue	Western Athletic	Mike Cavan	5-6
Southern Mississippi	Golden Eagles	Black & gold	Conference USA	Jeff Bower	8-3
SW Missouri State	Bears	Maroon & white	Gateway	Del Miller	7-4
SW Texas State	Bobcats	Maroon & gold	Southland	Bob DeBesse	5-6
SW Louisiana	Ragin' Cajuns	Vermilion & white	Independent	Nelson Stokley	5-6
Stanford	Cardinal	Cardinal & white	Pacific Ten	Tyrone Willingham	6-5
Stephen F. Austin State	Lumberjacks	Purple & white	Southland	John Pearce	7-4
Syracuse	Orangemen	Orange	Big East	Paul Pasqualoni	8-3
Temple	Owls	Cherry & white	Big East	Ron Dickerson	1-10
Tennessee	Volunteers	Orange & white	Southeastern	Phillip Fulmer	9-2
Tennessee-Chattanooga	Mocs	Navy blue & gold	Southern	Buddy Green	3-8
Tennessee-Martin	Skyhawks	Orange, white, blue	Ohio Valley	Jim Marshall	1-10
Tennessee State	Tigers	Royal blue & white	Ohio Valley	L. C. Cole	4-7
Tennessee Tech	Golden Eagles	Purple & gold	Ohio Valley	Mike Hennigan	5-6
Texas	Longhorns	Burnt orange & white	Big Twelve	John Mackovic	8-4
Texas A & M	Aggies	Maroon & white	Big Twelve	R. C. Slocum	6-6
Texas Christian (TCU)	Horned Frogs	Purple & white	Western Athletic	Pat Sullivan	4-7
Texas Southern	Tigers	Maroon & gray	Southwestern	Bill Thomas	7-4
Texas Tech	Red Raiders	Scarlet & black	Big Twelve	Spike Dykes	7-4
Toledo	Rockets	Blue & gold	Mid-American	Gary Pinkel	7-4
Towson State	Tigers	Gold & white	Patriot League	Gordy Combs	6-4
Troy State	Trojans	Cardinal, gray, black	Southland	Larry Blakeney	10-1
Tulane	Green Wave	Olive green & sky blue	Conference USA	Tommy Bowden	2-9
Tulsa	Golden Hurricane	Blue & gold	Western Athletic	David Rader	4-7
UCLA	Bruins	Blue & gold	Pacific Ten	Bob Toledo	5-6
Utah	Utes	Crimson & white	Western Athletic	Ron McBride	8-3
Utah State	Aggies	Navy blue & white	Big West	John L. Smith	6-5
UTEP (Texas-El Paso)	Miners	Orange, blue, white	Western Athletic	Charlie Bailey	2-9
Vanderbilt	Commodores	Black & gold	Southeastern	Woody Widenhofer	2-9
Villanova	Wildcats	Blue & white	Atlantic Ten	Andy Talley	8-3
Virginia	Cavaliers	Orange & blue	Atlantic Coast	George Welsh	7-4
Virginia Military Inst. (VMI)	Keydets	Red, white & yellow	Southern	Ted Cain	3-8
Virginia Tech	Gobblers, Hokies	Orange & maroon	Big East	Frank Beamer	10-1
Wake Forest	Demon Deacons	Old gold & black	Atlantic Coast	Jim Caldwell	3-8
Washington	Huskies	Purple & gold	Pacific Ten	Jim Lambright	9-2
Washington State	Cougars	Crimson & gray	Pacific Ten	Mike Price	5-6
Weber State	Wildcats	Royal purple & white	Big Sky	Dave Arslanian	7-4
West Virginia	Mountaineers	Old gold & blue	Big East	Don Nehlen	8-3
Western Carolina	Catamounts	Purple & gold	Southern	Bill Bleil	4-7
Western Illinois	Leathernecks	Purple & gold	Gateway	Randy Ball	9-2
Western Kentucky	Hilltoppers	Red & white	Independent	Jack Harbaugh	7-4
Western Michigan	Broncos	Brown & gold	Mid-American	Gary Darnell	2-9
William & Mary	Tribe	Green, gold, silver	Atlantic Ten	Jimmye Laycock	9-2
Wisconsin	Badgers	Cardinal & white	Big Ten	Barry Alvarez	7-5
Wyoming	Cowboys	Brown & yellow	Western Athletic	Dana Dimel	10-2
Yale	Bulldogs, Elis	Yale blue & white	Ivy League	Jack Siedlecki	2-8
Youngstown State	Penguins	Red & white	Gateway	Jim Tressel	8-3

Heisman Trophy Winners

Awarded annually to the nation's outstanding college football player by the Downtown Athletic Club.

1935 Jay Berwanger, Chicago, HB	1952 Billy Vessels, Oklahoma, HB	1969 Steve Owens, Oklahoma, RB
1936 Larry Kelley, Yale, E	1953 John Lattner, Notre Dame, HB	1970 Jim Plunkett, Stanford, QB
1937 Clinton Frank, Yale, HB	1954 Alan Ameche, Wisconsin, FB	1971 Pat Sullivan, Auburn, QB
1938 David O'Brien, Texas Christian, QB	1955 Howard Cassady, Ohio St., HB	1972 Johnny Rodgers, Nebraska, RB-WR
1939 Nile Kinnick, Iowa, HB	1956 Paul Hornung, Notre Dame, QB	1973 John Cappelletti, Penn St., RB
1940 Tom Harmon, Michigan, HB	1957 John Crow, Texas A & M, HB	1974 Archie Griffin, Ohio St., RB
1941 Bruce Smith, Minnesota, HB	1958 Pete Dawkins, Army, HB	1975 Archie Griffin, Ohio St., RB
1942 Frank Sinkwich, Georgia, HB	1959 Billy Cannon, LSU, HB	1976 Tony Dorsett, Pittsburgh, RB
1943 Angelo Bertelli, Notre Dame, QB	1960 Joe Bellino, Navy, HB	1977 Earl Campbell, Texas, RB
1944 Leslie Horvath, Ohio St., QB	1961 Ernest Davis, Syracuse, HB	1978 Billy Sims, Oklahoma, RB
1945 Felix Blanchard, Army, FB	1962 Terry Baker, Oregon St., QB	1979 Charles White, USC, RB
1946 Glenn Davis, Army, HB	1963 Roger Staubach, Navy, QB	1980 George Rogers, S. Carolina, RB
1947 John Lujack, Notre Dame, QB	1964 John Huarte, Notre Dame, QB	1981 Marcus Allen, USC, RB
1948 Doak Walker, SMU, HB	1965 Mike Garrett, USC, HB	1982 Herschel Walker, Georgia, RB
1949 Leon Hart, Notre Dame, E	1966 Steve Spurrier, Florida, QB	1983 Mike Rozier, Nebraska, RB
1950 Vic Janowicz, Ohio St., HB	1967 Gary Beban, UCLA, QB	1984 Doug Flutie, Boston College, QB
1951 Richard Kazmaier, Princeton, HB	1968 O. J. Simpson, USC, RB	1985 Bo Jackson, Auburn, RB

1986	Vinny Testaverde, Miami, QB	1990	Ty Detmer, BYU, QB	1994	Rashaan Salaam, Colorado, RB
1987	Tim Brown, Notre Dame, WR	1991	Desmond Howard, Michigan, WR	1995	Eddie George, Ohio St., RB
1988	Barry Sanders, Oklahoma St., RB	1992	Gino Torretta, Miami, QB	1996	Danny Wuerffel, Florida, QB
1989	Andre Ware, Houston, QB	1993	Charlie Ward, Florida St., QB		

Outland Award Winners

Honoring the outstanding interior lineman selected by the Football Writers Association of America.

1946	George Connor, Notre Dame, T	1963	Scott Appleton, Texas, T	1980	Mark May, Pittsburgh, OT
1947	Joe Steffy, Army, G	1964	Steve Delong, Tennessee, T	1981	Dave Rimington, Nebraska, C
1948	Bill Fischer, Notre Dame, G	1965	Tommy Nobis, Texas, G	1982	Dave Rimington, Nebraska, C
1949	Ed Bagdon, Michigan St., G	1966	Loyd Phillips, Arkansas, T	1983	Dean Steinkuhler, Nebraska, G
1950	Bob Gain, Kentucky, T	1967	Ron Yary, Southern Cal, T	1984	Bruce Smith, Virginia Tech, DT
1951	Jim Weatherall, Oklahoma, T	1968	Bill Stanfill, Georgia, T	1985	Mike Ruth, Boston College, NG
1952	Dick Modzelewski, Maryland, T	1969	Mike Reid, Penn St., DT	1986	Jason Buck, BYU, DT
1953	J. D. Roberts, Oklahoma, G	1970	Jim Stillwagon, Ohio St., MG	1987	Chad Hennings, Air Force, DT
1954	Bill Brooks, Arkansas, G	1971	Larry Jacobson, Nebraska, DT	1988	Tracy Rocker, Auburn, DT
1955	Calvin Jones, Iowa, G	1972	Rich Glover, Nebraska, MG	1989	Mohammed Elewonibi, BYU, G
1956	Jim Parker, Ohio St., G	1973	John Hicks, Ohio St., OT	1990	Russell Maryland, Miami (FL), DT
1957	Alex Karras, Iowa, T	1974	Randy White, Maryland, DE	1991	Steve Emtman, Washington, DT
1958	Zeke Smith, Auburn, G	1975	Lee Roy Selmon, Oklahoma, DT	1992	Will Shields, Nebraska, G
1959	Mike McGee, Duke, T	1976	Ross Browner, Notre Dame, DE	1993	Rob Waldrop, Arizona, NG
1960	Tom Brown, Minnesota, G	1977	Brad Shearer, Texas, DT	1994	Zach Wiegert, Nebraska, OT
1961	Merlin Olsen, Utah St., T	1978	Greg Roberts, Oklahoma, G	1995	Jonathan Ogden, UCLA, OT
1962	Bobby Bell, Minnesota, T	1979	Jim Ritcher, N. Carolina St., C	1996	Orlando Pace, Ohio St., OT

All-Time Division I-A Percentage Leaders

(Classified as Division I-A for the last 10 years; record includes bowl games; ties computed as half won and half lost)

	Years	Won	Lost	Tied	Pct.	Bowl Games† W	L	T
Notre Dame	108	746	222	42	.759	13	8	0
Michigan	117	764	254	36	.737	13	15	0
Alabama*	102	713	253	43	.728	28	17	3
Oklahoma	102	673	259	53	.710	20	11	1
Texas	104	713	284	33	.708	17	18	2
Ohio St.	107	690	272	53	.706	13	16	0
Nebraska.	107	709	292	40	.700	17	18	0
USC.	104	653	265	54	.700	25	13	0
Penn St.	110	706	296	41	.697	21	10	2
Tennessee*	100	666	283	52	.691	21	16	0
Florida St. *	50	347	180	17	.653	16	8	2
Central Michigan . . .	96	498	271	36	.641	0	2	0
Washington*	107	585	321	50	.638	12	10	1
Army	107	607	341	51	.633	2	2	0
Miami (OH)	108	566	319	44	.633	5	2	0
LSU*	103	594	338	47	.631	13	16	1
Arizona St	84	464	269	24	.629	9	6	1
Georgia	103	606	349	54	.627	15	14	3
Auburn*	104	583	344	47	.623	13	10	2
Colorado	107	588	353	36	.620	9	12	0
Miami (FL)	70	438	268	19	.617	11	11	0
Bowling Green	78	407	257	52	.605	2	3	0
Texas A&M	102	574	370	48	.603	11	10	0
Syracuse.	107	608	393	49	.602	10	6	1
UCLA.	78	454	297	37	.600	10	9	1

*Includes games forfeited or changed by action of NCAA Council and/or Committee on Infractions. †Major bowl games only; that is, team's opponent was classified as a major college team that season or at the time of the bowl game.

College Football Coach of the Year

The Division I-A Coach of the Year has been selected by the American Football Coaches Assn. since 1935 and selected by the Football Writers Assn. of America since 1957. When polls disagree, both winners are indicated.

1935	Lynn Waldorf, Northwestern	1961	Paul "Bear" Bryant, Ala. (AFCA);	1977	Don James, Washington (AFCA);
1936	Dick Harlow, Harvard		Darrell Royal, Texas (FWAA)		Lou Holtz, Arkansas (FWAA)
1937	Edward Mylin, Lafayette	1962	John McKay, USC	1978	Joe Paterno, Penn St.
1938	Bill Kern, Carnegie Tech	1963	Darrell Royal, Texas	1979	Earle Bruce, Ohio St.
1939	Eddie Anderson, Iowa	1964	Ara Parseghian, Notre Dame, &	1980	Vince Dooley, Georgia
1940	Clark Shaughnessy, Stanford		Frank Broyles, Arkansas(AFCA);	1981	Danny Ford, Clemson
1941	Frank Leahy, Notre Dame		Ara Parseghian (FWAA)	1982	Joe Paterno, Penn St.
1942	Bill Alexander, Georgia Tech	1965	Tommy Prothro, UCLA (AFCA);	1983	Ken Hatfield, Air Force (AFCA);
1943	Amos Alonzo Stagg, Pacific		Duffy Daugherty, Mich. St. (FWAA)		Howard Schnellenberger, Miami
1944	Carroll Widdoes, Ohio St.	1966	Tom Cahill, Army		(FL) (FWAA)
1945	Bo McMillin, Indiana	1967	John Pont, Indiana	1984	LaVell Edwards, Brigham Young
1946	Earl "Red" Blaik, Army	1968	Joe Paterno, Penn St. (AFCA);	1985	Fisher De Berry, Air Force
1947	Fritz Crisler, Michigan		Woody Hayes, Ohio St. (FWAA)	1986	Joe Paterno, Penn St.
1948	Bennie Oosterbaan, Michigan	1969	Bo Schembechler, Michigan	1987	Dick MacPherson, Syracuse
1949	Bud Wilkinson, Oklahoma	1970	Charles McClendon, LSU, &	1988	Don Nehlen, W. Virginia (AFCA);
1950	Charlie Caldwell, Princeton		Darrell Royal, Texas (AFCA);		Lou Holtz, Notre Dame (FWAA)
1951	Chuck Taylor, Stanford		Alex Agase, Northwestern (FWAA)	1989	Bill McCartney, Colorado
1952	Biggie Munn, Michigan St.	1971	Paul "Bear" Bryant, Alabama (AFCA);	1990	Bobby Ross, Georgia Tech
1953	Jim Tatum, Maryland		Bob Devaney, Nebraska (FWAA)	1991	Don James, Washington
1954	Henry "Red" Sanders, UCLA	1972	John McKay, USC	1992	Gene Stallings, Alabama
1955	Duffy Daugherty, Michigan St	1973	Paul "Bear" Bryant, Alabama (AFCA);	1993	Barry Alvarez, Wisconsin (AFCA);
1956	Bowden Wyatt, Tennessee		Johnny Majors, Pittsburgh (FWAA)		Terry Bowden, Auburn (FWAA)
1957	Woody Hayes, Ohio St.	1974	Grant Teaff, Baylor	1994	Tom Osborne, Nebraska (AFCA);
1958	Paul Dietzel, LSU	1975	Frank Kush, Arizona St. (AFCA);		Rich Brooks, Oregon (FWAA)
1959	Ben Schwartzwalder, Syracuse		Woody Hayes, Ohio St. (FWAA)	1995	Gary Barnett, Northwestern
1960	Murray Warmath, Minnesota	1976	Johnny Majors, Pittsburgh	1996	Bruce Snyder, Arizona St.

All-Time Division I-A Coaching Victories (Including Bowl Games)

Paul "Bear" Bryant	323	*Hayden Fry	222	Fielding Yost	196
Glenn "Pop" Warner	319	*Lou Holtz	216	Howard Jones	194
Amos Alonzo Stagg	314	Jess Neely	207	John Vaught	190
*Joe Paterno	289	Warren Woodson	203	John Heisman	185
*Bobby Bowden	270	Eddie Anderson	201	Johnny Majors	185
*Tom Osborne	242	Vince Dooley	201	Darrell Royal	184
Woody Hayes	238	Jim Sweeney	200	Gil Dobie	180
Bo Schembechler	234	Dana Bible	198	Carl Snavely	180
*LaVell Edwards	228	Dan McGugin	197	Jerry Claiborne	179

Coaches active in 1997 are denoted by an asterisk (*). Eddie Robinson of Grambling State Univ. holds the record for most college football victories, with 405 at the end of the 1996 season.

College Football Conference Champions

Atlantic Coast

1980	North Carolina
1981	Clemson
1982	Clemson
1983	Maryland
1984	Maryland
1985	Maryland
1986	Clemson
1987	Clemson
1988	Clemson
1989	Virginia, Duke
1990	Georgia Tech
1991	Clemson
1992	Florida St.
1993	Florida St.
1994	Florida St.
1995	Virginia, Florida St.
1996	Florida St.

Ivy

1980	Yale
1981	Yale, Dartmouth
1982	Harvard, Dartmouth, Penn
1983	Harvard, Penn
1984	Penn
1985	Penn
1986	Penn
1987	Harvard
1988	Penn, Cornell
1989	Yale, Princeton
1990	Cornell, Dartmouth
1991	Dartmouth
1992	Dartmouth, Princeton
1993	Penn
1994	Penn
1995	Princeton
1996	Dartmouth

Big Eight*

1980	Oklahoma
1981	Nebraska
1982	Nebraska
1983	Nebraska
1984	Nebraska, Oklahoma
1985	Oklahoma
1986	Oklahoma
1987	Oklahoma
1988	Nebraska
1989	Colorado
1990	Colorado
1991	Nebraska, Colorado
1992	Nebraska
1993	Nebraska
1994	Nebraska
1995	Nebraska

Big Ten

1980	Michigan
1981	Iowa, Ohio St.
1982	Michigan
1983	Illinois
1984	Ohio St.
1985	Iowa
1986	Michigan, Ohio St.
1987	Michigan St.
1988	Michigan
1989	Michigan
1990	Iowa, Illinois, Michigan, Michigan St.
1991	Michigan
1992	Michigan
1993	Ohio St., Wisconsin
1994	Penn St.
1995	Northwestern
1996	Ohio St., Northwestern

Mid-American Athletic

1980	Central Michigan
1981	Toledo
1982	Bowling Green
1983	Northern Illinois
1984	Toledo
1985	Bowling Green
1986	Miami (OH)
1987	E. Michigan
1988	W. Michigan
1989	Ball St.
1990	Central Michigan
1991	Bowling Green
1992	Bowling Green
1993	Ball St.
1994	Central Michigan
1995	Toledo
1996	Ball St.

Southern

1980	Furman
1981	Furman
1982	Furman
1983	Furman
1984	Tenn.-Chattanooga
1985	Furman
1986	Appalachian St.
1987	Appalachian St.
1988	Marshall, Furman
1989	Furman
1990	Furman
1991	Appalachian St.
1992	Citadel
1993	Georgia Southern
1994	Marshall
1995	Appalachian St.
1996	Marshall

Southeastern

1980	Georgia
1981	Georgia, Alabama
1982	Georgia
1983	Auburn
1984	Florida (title vacated)
1985	Tennessee
1986	LSU
1987	Auburn
1988	Auburn, LSU
1989	Ala., Tenn., Auburn
1990	Tennessee
1991	Florida
1992	Alabama
1993	Florida
1994	Florida
1995	Florida
1996	Florida

Southwest*

1980	Baylor
1981	Texas
1982	SMU
1983	Texas
1984	SMU, Houston
1985	Texas A&M
1986	Texas A&M
1987	Texas A&M
1988	Arkansas
1989	Arkansas
1990	Texas
1991	Texas A&M
1992	Texas A&M
1993	Texas A&M
1994	Baylor, Rice, Texas, Texas Christian, Texas Tech
1995	Texas

Pacific Ten

1980	Washington
1981	Washington
1982	UCLA
1983	UCLA
1984	USC
1985	UCLA
1986	Arizona St.
1987	UCLA, USC
1988	USC
1989	USC
1990	Washington
1991	Washington
1992	Washington, Stanford
1993	UCLA, Arizona, USC
1994	Oregon
1995	USC, Washington
1996	Arizona St.

Western Athletic

1980	Brigham Young (BYU)
1981	Brigham Young
1982	Brigham Young
1983	Brigham Young
1984	Brigham Young
1985	Brigham Young, Air Force
1986	San Diego St.
1987	Wyoming
1988	Wyoming
1989	Brigham Young
1990	Brigham Young
1991	Brigham Young
1992	Hawaii, Brigham Young, Fresno St.
1993	Wyoming, Fresno St., BYU
1994	Colorado St.
1995	Colorado St., Air Force, Utah, BYU
1996	Brigham Young

Big West

1980	Long Beach St.
1981	San Jose St.
1982	Fresno St.
1983	Cal St.-Fullerton
1984	Cal St.-Fullerton
1985	Fresno St.
1986	San Jose St.
1987	San Jose St.
1988	Fresno St.
1989	Fresno St.
1990	San Jose St.
1991	San Jose St., Fresno St.
1992	Nevada
1993	SW Louisiana, Utah St.
1994	Nevada, SW Louisiana, Nevada-Las Vegas
1995	Nevada
1996	Nevada, Utah St.

Big East

1991	Miami (FL), Syracuse
1992	Miami (FL)
1993	West Virginia
1994	Miami (FL)
1995	Virginia Tech, Miami (FL)
1996	Virginia Tech, Miami (FL), Syracuse

Big 12*

1996	Texas

Conference USA

1996	Southern Mississippi, Houston

(*) After the 1995 season, the Big Eight and Southwest conferences disbanded. In 1996 all former Big Eight Conference teams joined with 4 of the 8 Southwest Conference teams to form the Big 12 Conference.

NATIONAL HOCKEY LEAGUE

1996-97 NHL Review: Mario Lemieux Retires, Whalers Move, League to Expand

Mario Lemieux, the 6th-leading scorer in NHL history, played in his last game on Apr. 26, 1997. Lemieux, 31, played 12 years in the league; his retirement was widely attributed to health problems, including two back surgeries and Hodgkin's disease (diagnosed in 1993). In Sept., less than 6 months after his retirement, Lemieux was elected to the Hockey Hall of Fame after the Hall waived the usual 3-year wait. The Hartford Whalers moved to Raleigh, NC, and became the Carolina Hurricanes; they will play in Greensboro, NC, for 2 years before moving to a new arena in Raleigh. On June 25, the NHL Board of Governors approved a plan to add 4 new franchises to the 26-team league by the year 2001; the cities selected were: Nashville, TN; Atlanta, GA; Columbus, OH; St. Paul, MN.

Final Standings 1996-97

Eastern Conference

Northeast Division

	W	L	T	GF	GA	PTS
Buffalo	40	30	12	237	208	92
Pittsburgh	38	36	8	285	280	84
Ottawa	31	36	15	226	234	77
Montreal	31	36	15	249	276	77
Hartford	32	39	11	226	256	75
Boston	26	47	9	234	300	61

Atlantic Division

	W	L	T	GF	GA	PTS
New Jersey	45	23	14	231	182	104
Philadelphia	45	24	13	274	217	103
Florida	35	28	19	221	201	89
N.Y. Rangers	38	34	10	258	231	86
Washington	33	40	9	214	231	75
Tampa Bay	32	40	10	217	247	74
N.Y. Islanders	29	41	12	240	250	70

Western Conference

Central Division

	W	L	T	GF	GA	PTS
Dallas	48	26	8	252	198	104
Detroit	38	26	18	253	197	94
Phoenix	38	37	7	240	243	83
St. Louis	36	35	11	236	239	83
Chicago	34	35	13	223	210	81
Toronto	30	44	8	230	273	68

Pacific Division

	W	L	T	GF	GA	PTS
Colorado	49	24	9	277	205	107
Anaheim	36	33	13	245	233	85
Edmonton	36	37	9	252	247	81
Vancouver	35	40	7	257	273	77
Calgary	32	41	9	214	239	73
Los Angeles	28	43	11	214	268	67
San Jose	27	47	8	211	278	62

Detroit Red Wings Win Stanley Cup Championship

The Detroit Red Wings won the 1997 Stanley Cup as they swept the Philadelphia Flyers in the final round of the playoffs, ending a 42-year drought. Detroit goaltender Mike Vernon won the Conn Smythe Trophy as most valuable player in the playoffs.

Stanley Cup Playoff Results

Eastern Conference

New Jersey defeated Montreal 4 games to 1
Buffalo defeated Ottawa 4 games to 3
Philadelphia defeated Pittsburgh 4 games to 1
N.Y. Rangers defeated Florida 4 games to 1
N.Y. Rangers defeated New Jersey 4 games to 1
Philadelphia defeated Buffalo 4 games to 1
Philadelphia defeated N.Y. Rangers 4 games to 1

Western Conference

Colorado defeated Chicago 4 games to 2
Edmonton defeated Dallas 4 games to 3
Detroit defeated St. Louis 4 games to 2
Anaheim defeated Phoenix 4 games to 3
Colorado defeated Edmonton 4 games to 1
Detroit defeated Anaheim 4 games to 0
Detroit defeated Colorado 4 games to 2

Finals

Detroit defeated Philadelphia 4 games to 0 (4-2, 4-2, 6-1, 2-1)

Stanley Cup Champions Since 1927

Year	Champion	Coach	Final opponent	Year	Champion	Coach	Final opponent
1927	Ottawa	Dave Gill	Boston	1962	Toronto	Punch Imlach	Chicago
1928	N.Y. Rangers	Lester Patrick	Montreal	1963	Toronto	Punch Imlach	Detroit
1929	Boston	Cy Denneny	N.Y. Rangers	1964	Toronto	Punch Imlach	Detroit
1930	Montreal	Cecil Hart	Boston	1965	Montreal	Toe Blake	Chicago
1931	Montreal	Cecil Hart	Chicago	1966	Montreal	Toe Blake	Detroit
1932	Toronto	Dick Irvin	N.Y. Rangers	1967	Toronto	Punch Imlach	Montreal
1933	N.Y. Rangers	Lester Patrick	Toronto	1968	Montreal	Toe Blake	St. Louis
1934	Chicago	Tommy Gorman	Detroit	1969	Montreal	Claude Ruel	St. Louis
1935	Montreal Maroons	Tommy Gorman	Toronto	1970	Boston	Harry Sinden	St. Louis
1936	Detroit	Jack Adams	Toronto	1971	Montreal	Al MacNeil	Chicago
1937	Detroit	Jack Adams	N.Y. Rangers	1972	Boston	Tom Johnson	N.Y. Rangers
1938	Chicago	Bill Stewart	Toronto	1973	Montreal	Scotty Bowman	Chicago
1939	Boston	Art Ross	Toronto	1974	Philadelphia	Fred Shero	Boston
1940	N.Y. Rangers	Frank Boucher	Toronto	1975	Philadelphia	Fred Shero	Buffalo
1941	Boston	Cooney Weiland	Detroit	1976	Montreal	Scotty Bowman	Philadelphia
1942	Toronto	Hap Day	Detroit	1977	Montreal	Scotty Bowman	Boston
1943	Detroit	Jack Adams	Boston	1978	Montreal	Scotty Bowman	Boston
1944	Montreal	Dick Irvin	Chicago	1979	Montreal	Scotty Bowman	N.Y. Rangers
1945	Toronto	Hap Day	Detroit	1980	N.Y. Islanders	Al Arbour	Philadelphia
1946	Montreal	Dick Irvin	Boston	1981	N.Y. Islanders	Al Arbour	Minnesota
1947	Toronto	Hap Day	Montreal	1982	N.Y. Islanders	Al Arbour	Vancouver
1948	Toronto	Hap Day	Detroit	1983	N.Y. Islanders	Al Arbour	Edmonton
1949	Toronto	Hap Day	Detroit	1984	Edmonton	Glen Sather	N.Y. Islanders
1950	Detroit	Tommy Ivan	N.Y. Rangers	1985	Edmonton	Glen Sather	Philadelphia
1951	Toronto	Joe Primeau	Montreal	1986	Montreal	Jean Perron	Calgary
1952	Detroit	Tommy Ivan	Montreal	1987	Edmonton	Glen Sather	Philadelphia
1953	Detroit	Dick Irvin	Boston	1988	Edmonton	Glen Sather	Boston
1954	Detroit	Tommy Ivan	Montreal	1989	Calgary	Terry Crisp	Montreal
1955	Detroit	Jimmy Skinner	Montreal	1990	Edmonton	John Muckler	Boston
1956	Montreal	Toe Blake	Detroit	1991	Pittsburgh	Bob Johnson	Minnesota
1957	Montreal	Toe Blake	Boston	1992	Pittsburgh	Scotty Bowman	Chicago
1958	Montreal	Toe Blake	Boston	1993	Montreal	Jacques Demers	Los Angeles
1959	Montreal	Toe Blake	Toronto	1994	N.Y. Rangers	Mike Keenan	Vancouver
1960	Montreal	Toe Blake	Toronto	1995	New Jersey	Jacques Lemaire	Detroit
1961	Chicago	Rudy Pilous	Detroit	1996	Colorado	Marc Crawford	Florida
				1997	Detroit	Scotty Bowman	Philadelphia

Individual Leaders, 1996-97

Points

Mario Lemieux, Pittsburgh, 122; Teemu Selanne, Anaheim, 109; Paul Kariya, Anaheim, 99; Wayne Gretzky, N.Y. Rangers, 97; John LeClair, Philadelphia, 97.

Goals

Keith Tkachuk, Phoenix, 52; Teemu Selanne, Anaheim, 51; John LeClair, Philadelphia, 50; Mario Lemieux, Pittsburgh, 50; Zigmund Palffy, N.Y. Islanders, 48.

Assists

Wayne Gretzky, N.Y. Rangers, 72; Mario Lemieux, Pittsburgh, 72; Ron Francis, Pittsburgh, 63; Steve Yzerman, Detroit, 63; Doug Weight, Edmonton, 61.

Power-play goals

Brendan Shanahan, Har.-Det., 20; Ryan Smith, Edmonton, 20; Paul Kariya, Anaheim, 15; Mario Lemieux, Pittsburgh, 15; Keith Jones, Was.-Col., 14; Andrei Kovalenko, Edmonton, 14.

Shorthanded goals

Michael Peca, Buffalo, 6; Trent Klatt, Philadelphia, 5; Mark Messier, N.Y. Rangers, 5; Mike Modano, Dallas, 5; many tied with 4.

Shooting percentage

(minimum 82 shots)

Miroslav Satan, Edm.-Buf., 21.0; Jaromir Jagr, Pittsburgh, 20.1; Martin Gelinas, Vancouver, 19.8; Andrei Kovalenko, Edmonton, 19.6; Teemu Selanne, Anaheim, 18.7.

Plus/Minus

John LeClair, Philadelphia, 44; Mike Modano, Dallas, 43; Dave Andreychuk, New Jersey, 38; Vladimir Konstantinov, Detroit, 38; Darryl Sydor, Dallas, 37.

Goaltending Leaders

(minimum 25 games)

Goals against average

Martin Brodeur, New Jersey, 1.88; Andy Moog, Dallas, 2.15; Jeff Hackett, Chicago, 2.16; Dominik Hasek, Buffalo, 2.27; John Vanbiesbrouck, Florida, 2.29.

Wins

Patrick Roy, Colorado 38; Martin Brodeur, New Jersey, 37; Dominik Hasek, Buffalo, 37; Grant Fuhr, St. Louis, 33; Mike Richter, N.Y. Rangers, 33.

Save percentage

Dominik Hasek, Buffalo, .930; Jeff Hackett, Chicago, .927; Martin Bordeur, New Jersey, .927; Patrick Roy, Colorado, .923; Guy Hebert, Anaheim, .919; John Vanbiesbrouck, Florida, .919.

Shutouts

Martin Brodeur, New Jersey, 10; Nikolai Khabibulin, Phoenix, 7; Patrick Roy, Colorado, 7; Curtis Joseph, Edmonton, 6; Chris Osgood, Detroit, 6.

Individual Scoring, 1996-97

(40 or more games played; *played for more than one team during 1996-97; g—denotes goalie; E= even)

Mighty Ducks of Anaheim

	GP	G	A	Pts	PIM-	+/-
Teemu Selanne	78	51	58	109	34	28
Paul Kariya	69	44	55	99	6	36
Steve Rucchin	79	19	48	67	24	26
Dmiitri Mironov*	77	13	39	52	101	16
Jari Kurri*	82	13	22	35	12	−13
Brian Bellows*	69	16	15	31	22	−15
Kevin Todd	65	9	21	30	44	−7
Joe Sacco	77	12	17	29	35	1
J.J. Daigneault*	66	5	23	28	58	E
Darren Van Impe	74	4	19	23	90	3
Jean-Francios Jomphe	64	7	14	21	53	−9
Ted Drury	73	9	9	18	54	−9
Bobby Dollas	79	4	14	18	55	17
Warren Rychel	70	10	7	17	218	6
Dave Karpa	69	2	11	13	210	11
Ken Baumgartner	67	0	11	11	182	E
Jason Marshall	73	1	9	10	140	6
Mark Janssens*	66	2	6	8	137	−13
Guy Hebert (g)	67	0	1	1	4	—

Coach—Ron Wilson

Boston Bruins

	GP	G	A	Pts	PIM-	+/-
Jozef Stumpel	78	21	55	76	14	−22
Ted Donato	67	25	26	51	37	−9
Ray Bourque	62	19	31	50	18	−11
Jason Allison*	72	8	26	34	34	−6
Rob DiMaio	72	13	15	28	82	−21
Don Sweeney	82	3	23	26	39	−5
Jean Yves Roy	52	10	15	25	22	−8
Landon Wison*	49	8	12	20	72	−5
Sheldon Kennedy	56	8	10	18	30	−17
Barry Richter	50	5	13	18	32	−7
Brett Harkins	44	4	14	18	8	−3
Jeff Odgers	80	7	8	15	197	−15
Troy Mallette	68	6	8	14	155	−8
Kyle McLaren	58	5	9	14	54	−9
Mattias Timander	41	1	8	9	14	−9
Trent McCleary	59	3	5	8	33	−16
Dean Chynoweth	57	0	3	3	171	−12
Jim Carey* (g)	59	0	0	0	2	—

Coach—Steve Kasper

Buffalo Sabres

	GP	G	A	Pts	PIM-	+/-
Derek Plante	82	27	26	53	24	14
Brian Holzinger	81	22	29	51	54	9
Donald Audette	73	28	22	50	48	−6
Michael Peca	79	20	29	49	80	26
Jason Dawe	81	22	26	48	32	14
Dixon Ward	79	13	32	45	36	17
Matthew Barnaby	68	19	24	43	249	16
Miroslav Satan*	76	25	13	38	26	−3
Garry Galley	71	4	34	38	102	10
Michal Grosek	82	15	21	36	71	25
Alexei Zhitnik	80	7	28	35	95	10
Randy Burridge	55	10	21	31	20	17
Richard Smehlik	62	11	19	30	43	19
Darryl Shannon	82	4	19	23	112	23
Mike Wilson	77	2	9	11	51	13
Rob Ray	82	7	3	10	286	3
Jay McKee	43	1	9	10	35	3
Bob Boughner	77	1	7	8	225	12
Brad May	42	3	4	7	106	−8
Wayne Primeau	45	2	4	6	64	−2
Dominik Hasek (g)	67	0	3	3	30	—

Coach—Ted Nolan

Calgary Flames

	GP	G	A	Pts	PIM-	+/-
Theoren Fleury	81	29	38	67	104	−12
Dave Gagner	82	27	33	60	48	2
German Titov	79	22	30	52	36	−12
Jarome Iginla	82	21	29	50	37	−4
Marty McInnis*	80	23	26	49	22	−8
Jonas Hoglund	68	19	16	35	12	−4
Corey Millen	61	11	15	26	32	−19
Cory Stillman	58	6	20	26	14	−6
Aaron Gavey*	57	8	11	19	46	−12
Todd Hlushko	58	7	11	18	49	−2
Ronnie Stern	79	7	10	17	157	−4
Yves Racine	46	1	15	16	24	4
Tommy Albelin	72	4	11	15	14	−8
Todd Simpson	82	1	13	14	208	−14
Ed Ward	40	5	8	13	49	−3
Mike Sullivan	67	5	6	11	10	−11
Glen Featherstone*	54	3	8	11	106	−1
Joel Bouchard	76	4	5	9	49	−23
Cal Hulse	63	1	6	7	91	−2
Trevor Kidd (g)	55	0	2	2	16	—

Coach—Pierre Page

Chicago Blackhawks

	GP	G	A	Pts	PIM-	+/-
Tony Amonte	81	41	36	77	64	35
Alexei Zhamnov	74	20	42	62	56	18
Chris Chelios	72	10	38	48	112	16
Eric Daze	71	22	19	41	16	−4
Murray Craven	75	8	27	35	12	E
Ulf Dahlen*	73	14	19	33	18	−2
Eric Weinrich	81	7	25	32	62	19
Kevin Miller	69	14	17	31	62	−10
Ethan Moreau	82	15	16	31	123	13
Jeff Shantz	69	9	21	30	28	11
Gary Suter	82	7	21	28	70	−4
Denis Savard	64	9	18	27	60	−10
Sergei Krivokrasov	67	13	11	24	42	−1
James Black	64	12	11	23	20	6
Bob Probert	82	9	14	23	326	−3
Keith Carney	81	3	15	18	62	26

	GP	G	A	Pts	PIM-	+/-
Michal Sykora*	63	3	14	17	69	4
Jim Cummins	65	6	6	12	199	4
Enrico Ciccone	67	2	2	4	233	−1
Cam Russell	44	1	1	2	65	−8
Jeff Hackett (g)	41	0	1	1	6	—

Coach—Craig Hartsburg

Colorado Avalanche

	GP	G	A	Pts	PIM-	+/-
Peter Forsberg	65	28	58	86	73	31
Joe Sakic	65	22	52	74	34	−10
Sandis Ozolinsh	80	23	45	68	88	4
Valeri Kamensky	68	28	38	66	38	5
Adam Deadmarsh	78	33	27	60	136	8
Keith Jones*	78	25	23	48	118	3
Scott Young	72	18	19	37	14	−5
Eric Lacroix	81	18	18	36	26	16
Mike Ricci	63	13	19	32	59	−3
Claude Lemieux	45	11	17	28	43	−4
Rene Corbet	76	12	15	27	67	14
Mike Keane	81	10	17	27	63	2
Stephane Yelle	79	9	17	26	38	1
Jon Klemm	80	9	15	24	37	12
Uwe Krupp	60	4	17	21	48	12
Adam Foote	78	2	19	21	135	16
Aaron Miller	56	5	12	17	15	15
Alexei Gusarov	58	2	12	14	28	4
Sylvain Lefebvre	71	2	11	13	30	12
Brent Severyn	66	1	4	5	193	−6
Patrick Roy (g)	62	0	1	1	15	—

Coach—Marc Crawford

Dallas Stars

	GP	G	A	Pts	PIM-	+/-
Mike Modano	80	35	48	83	42	43
Pat Verbeek	81	17	36	53	128	3
Joe Nieuwendyk	66	30	21	51	32	−5
Darryl Sydor	82	8	40	48	51	37
Benoit Hogue	73	19	24	43	54	8
Jere Lehtinen	63	16	27	43	2	26
Sergei Zubov	78	13	30	43	24	19
Dave Reid	82	19	20	39	10	12
Jamie Lagenbrunner	76	13	26	39	51	−2
Greg Adams	50	21	15	36	2	27
Todd Harvey	71	9	22	31	142	19
Brent Gilchrist	67	10	20	30	24	6
Derian Hatcher	63	3	19	22	97	8
Guy Carbonneau	73	5	16	21	36	9
Neil Broten*	42	8	12	20	12	−4
Grant Ledyard	67	1	15	16	61	31
Craig Ludwig	77	2	11	13	62	17
Bob Bassen	46	5	7	12	41	5
Richard Matvichuk	57	5	7	12	87	1
Bill Huard	40	5	6	11	105	5
Grant Marshall	56	6	4	10	98	5
Mike Lalor	55	1	1	2	42	3
Andy Moog (g)	48	0	1	1	12	—

Coach—Ken Hitchcock

Detroit Red Wings

	GP	G	A	Pts	PIM-	+/-
Brendan Shanahan*	81	47	41	88	131	32
Steve Yzerman	81	22	63	85	78	22
Sergei Fedorov	74	30	33	63	30	29
Nicklas Lidstrom	79	15	42	57	30	11
Igor Larionov	64	12	42	54	26	31
Darren McCarty	68	19	30	49	126	14
Vyacheslav Kozlov	75	23	22	45	46	21
Larry Murphy*	81	9	36	45	20	3
Tomas Sandstrom*	74	18	24	42	69	6
Vladimir Konstantinov	77	5	33	38	151	38
Martin Lapointe	78	16	17	33	167	−14
Viacheslav Fetisov	64	5	23	28	76	26
Kris Draper	76	8	5	13	73	−11
Doug Brown	49	6	7	13	8	−3
Bob Rouse	70	4	9	13	58	8
Mathieu Dadenault	65	3	9	12	28	−10
Jamie Pushor	75	4	7	11	129	1
Tomas Holmstrom	47	6	3	9	33	−10
Kirk Maltby	66	3	5	8	75	3
Tim Taylor	44	3	4	7	52	−6
Aaron Ward	49	2	5	7	52	−9
Chris Osgood (g)	47	0	2	2	6	—

Coach—Scotty Bowman

Edmonton Oilers

	GP	G	A	Pts	PIM-	+/-
Doug Weight	80	21	61	82	80	1
Ryan Smyth	82	39	22	61	76	−7
Andrei Kovalenko	74	32	27	59	81	−5
Jason Arnott	67	19	38	57	92	−21

	GP	G	A	Pts	PIM-	+/-
Mariusz Czerkawski	76	26	21	47	16	E
Kelly Buchberger	81	8	30	38	159	4
Todd Marchant	79	14	19	33	44	11
Mike Grier	79	15	17	32	45	7
Boris Mironov	55	6	26	32	85	2
Rem Murray	82	11	20	31	16	9
Dean McAmmond	57	12	17	29	28	−15
Mats Lingren	69	11	14	25	12	−7
Daniel McGillis	73	6	16	22	52	2
Drew Bannister*	65	4	14	18	44	−23
Bryan Marchment	71	3	13	16	132	13
Kevin Lowe	64	1	13	14	50	−1
Luke Richardson	82	1	11	12	91	9
Curtis Joseph (g)	72	0	2	2	20	—

Coach—Ron Low

Florida Panthers

	GP	G	A	Pts	PIM-	+/-
Ray Sheppard	68	29	31	60	4	4
Scott Mellanby	82	27	29	56	170	7
Robert Svehla	82	13	32	45	86	2
Kirk Muller*	76	21	19	40	89	−25
Radek Dvorak	78	18	21	39	30	−2
Rob Niedermayer	60	14	24	38	54	4
Johan Garpenlov	53	11	25	36	47	10
Bill Lindsay	81	11	23	34	120	1
Dave Lowry	77	15	14	29	51	2
Martin Straka	55	7	22	29	12	9
Per Gustafsson	58	7	22	29	22	11
Tom Fitzgerald	71	10	14	24	64	7
Gord Murphy	80	8	15	23	51	3
Ed Jovanovski	61	7	16	23	172	−1
Brian Skrudland	51	5	13	18	48	4
Jody Hull	67	10	6	16	4	1
Mike Hough	69	8	6	14	48	12
Terry Carkner	70	0	14	14	96	−4
Rhett Warrener	62	4	9	13	88	20
Paul Laus	77	0	12	12	313	13
Chris Wells	47	2	6	8	42	5
John Vanbiesbrouck (g)	57	0	2	2	8	—

Coach—Doug MacLean

Hartford Whalers

	GP	G	A	Pts	PIM-	+/-
Geoff Sanderson	82	36	31	67	29	−9
Andrew Cassels	81	22	24	66	46	−16
Derek King*	82	26	33	59	22	−6
Keith Primeau	75	26	26	51	151	−3
Kevin Dineen	78	19	29	48	141	−6
Nelson Emerson	66	9	29	38	34	−21
Steven Rice	78	21	14	35	59	−11
Glen Wesley	68	6	26	32	40	E
Steve Chiasson*	65	8	22	30	39	−21
Jeff O'Neill	72	14	16	30	40	−24
Sami Kapanen	45	13	12	25	2	6
Robert Kron	68	10	12	22	10	−18
Curtis Leschyshyn*	77	4	18	22	38	−18
Paul Ranheim	67	10	11	21	18	−18
Adam Burt	71	2	11	13	79	−13
Kevin Haller*	62	2	11	13	85	−12
Kent Manderville	44	6	5	11	18	3
Chris Murray*	64	5	3	8	124	−7
Alexander Godynyuk	55	1	6	7	41	−10
Marek Malik	47	1	5	6	50	5
Stu Grimson*	76	2	2	4	218	−8
Sean Burke (g)	66	0	6	6	16	—

Coach—Paul Maurice

Los Angeles Kings

	GP	G	A	Pts	PIM-	+/-
Dimitri Khristich	75	19	37	56	38	8
Ray Ferraro	81	25	21	46	112	−22
Vladimir Tsyplakov	67	16	23	39	12	8
Kevin Stevens	69	14	20	34	96	−27
Vitali Yachmenev	65	10	22	32	10	−9
Rob Blake	62	8	23	31	82	−28
Glen Murray*	77	16	14	30	32	−21
Kai Nurminen	67	16	11	27	22	−3
Yanic Perreault	41	11	14	25	20	E
Philippe Boucher	60	7	18	25	25	E
Ian Laperriere	62	8	15	23	102	−25
Mattias Norstrom	80	1	21	22	84	−4
Sean O'Donnell	55	5	12	17	144	−13
Brad Smyth*	52	9	8	17	76	−10
Dan Bylsma	79	3	6	9	32	−15
Aki Berg	41	2	6	8	24	−9
Steven Finn	54	2	3	5	84	−8
Matt Johnson	52	1	3	4	194	−4
Doug Zmolek	57	1	0	1	116	−22
Byron Dafoe (g)	40	0	0	0	0	—
Stephane Fiset (g)	44	0	2	2	2	—

Coach—Larry Robinson

Montreal Canadiens

	GP	G	A	Pts	PIM-	+/−
Vincent Damphousse....	82	27	54	81	82	−6
Mark Recchi...........	82	34	46	80	58	−1
Brian Savage..........	81	23	37	60	39	−14
Saku Koivu...........	50	17	39	56	38	7
Martin Rucinsky.......	70	28	27	55	62	1
Stephane Richer.......	63	22	24	46	32	E
Valeri Bure..........	64	14	21	35	6	4
Vladimir Malakhov.....	65	10	20	30	43	3
Shane Corson*........	58	8	16	24	104	−9
Stephane Quintal......	71	7	15	22	100	1
Dave Manson*........	75	4	18	22	187	−26
Turner Stevenson......	65	8	13	21	97	−14
Scott Thornton........	73	10	10	20	128	−19
Darcy Tucker.........	73	7	13	20	110	−5
Marc Bureau..........	43	6	9	15	16	4
David Wilkie.........	61	6	9	15	63	−9
Patrice Brisebois......	49	2	13	15	24	−7
Peter Popovic........	78	1	13	14	32	9
Jassen Cullimore*.....	52	2	6	8	44	2
Jocelyn Thibault (g)	61	0	0	0	0	—
Coach—Mario Tremblay						

New Jersey Devils

	GP	G	A	Pts	PIM-	+/−
Doug Gilmour*........	81	22	60	82	68	2
Bobby Holik..........	82	23	39	62	54	24
Dave Andreychuk......	82	27	34	61	48	38
John MacLean.........	80	29	25	54	49	11
Bill Guerin...........	82	29	25	54	95	−2
Brian Rolston........	81	18	27	45	20	6
Valeri Zelepukin......	71	14	24	38	36	−10
Scott Niedermayer.....	81	5	30	35	64	−4
Steve Thomas........	57	15	19	34	46	9
Denis Pederson.......	70	12	20	32	62	7
Randy McKay.........	77	9	18	27	109	15
Scott Stevens.........	79	5	19	24	70	26
Shawn Chambers......	73	4	17	21	19	17
Dave Ellett*..........	76	6	15	21	40	−6
Bob Carpenter.......	62	4	15	19	14	6
Lyle Odelein.........	79	3	13	16	110	16
Peter Zezel*.........	53	4	12	16	16	10
Jay Pandolfo.........	46	6	8	14	6	−1
Ken Daneyko.........	77	2	7	9	70	24
Kevin Dean..........	28	2	4	6	6	2
Martin Brodeur (g)	67	0	4	4	8	—
Coach—Jacques Lemaire						

New York Islanders

	GP	G	A	Pts	PIM-	+/−
Zigmund Palffy	80	48	42	90	43	21
Travis Green	79	23	41	64	38	−5
Robert Reichel*.......	82	21	41	62	26	5
Bryan Smolinski.......	64	28	28	56	25	9
Bryan Berard........	82	8	40	48	86	1
Niklas Andersson......	74	12	31	43	57	4
Bryan McCabe........	82	8	20	28	165	−2
Todd Bertuzzi........	64	10	13	23	68	−3
Kenny Jonsson........	81	3	18	21	24	10
Claude Lapointe	73	13	5	18	49	−12
Scott Lachance	81	3	11	14	47	−7
Derek Armstrong	50	6	7	13	33	−8
Dan Plante	67	4	9	13	75	−6
Randy Wood..........	65	6	5	11	61	−7
Brent Hughes	51	7	3	10	57	−4
Doug Houda	70	2	8	10	99	1
Paul Kruse*..........	62	6	2	8	141	−9
Steve Webb	41	1	4	5	144	−10
Richard Pilon	52	1	4	5	179	4
Tommy Salo (g)........	58	0	1	1	4	—
Coach—Mike Milbury, Rick Bowness						

New York Rangers

	GP	G	A	Pts	PIM-	+/−
Wayne Gretzky	82	25	72	97	28	12
Mark Messier.........	71	36	48	84	88	12
Brian Leetch	82	20	58	78	40	31
Adam Graves	82	33	28	61	66	10
Niklas Sundstrom......	82	24	28	52	20	23
Luc Robitaille........	69	24	24	48	48	16
Alexander Karpovtsev ...	77	9	29	38	59	1
Alexei Kovalev	45	13	22	35	42	11
Bruce Driver	79	5	25	30	48	8
Patrick Flatley	68	10	12	22	26	6
Ulf Samuelsson.......	73	6	11	17	138	3

	GP	G	A	Pts	PIM-	+/−
Bill Berg	67	8	6	14	37	2
Daniel Goneau	41	10	3	13	10	−5
Jeff Beukeboom	80	3	9	12	167	22
Darren Langdon	60	3	6	9	195	−1
Mike Eastwood*.......	60	2	10	12	14	−1
Doug Lidster.........	48	3	4	7	24	10
Russ Courtnall*.......	61	11	24	35	26	1
Esa Tikkanen*.......	76	13	17	30	72	−9
Eric Cairns..........	40	0	1	1	147	−7
Shane Churla.........	45	0	1	1	106	−10
Mike Richter (g)	61	0	0	0	4	—
Coach—Colin Campbell						

Ottawa Senators

	GP	G	A	Pts	PIM-	+/−
Alexei Yashin	82	35	40	75	44	−7
Daniel Alfredsson	76	24	47	71	30	5
Alexandre Daigle	82	26	25	51	33	−33
Steve Duchesne	78	19	28	47	38	−9
Randy Cunneyworth	76	12	24	36	99	−7
Andreas Dackell	79	12	19	31	8	−6
Shawn McEachern	65	11	20	31	18	−5
Wade Redden	82	6	24	30	41	1
Sergei Zholtok	57	12	16	28	19	−2
Tom Chorske	68	18	8	26	16	−1
Shaun Van Allen	80	11	14	25	35	−8
Bruce Gardiner	60	11	10	21	49	4
Jason York	75	4	17	21	67	−8
Janne Laukkanen	76	3	18	21	76	−14
Denny Lambert	80	4	16	20	217	−4
Radek Bonk	53	5	13	18	14	−4
Lance Pitlick........	66	5	5	10	91	2
Frank Musil	57	0	5	5	58	6
Damian Rhodes (g).....	50	0	2	2	2	—
Coach—Jacques Martin						

Philadelphia Flyers

	GP	G	A	Pts	PIM-	+/−
John LeClair..........	82	50	47	97	58	44
Eric Lindros	52	32	47	79	136	31
Rod Brind'Amour	82	27	32	59	41	2
Mikael Renberg	77	22	37	59	65	36
Eric Desjardins.......	82	12	34	46	50	25
Trent Klatt	76	24	21	45	20	9
Janne Niinimaa.......	77	4	40	44	58	12
Paul Coffey*.........	57	9	25	34	38	11
Dale Hawerchuk	51	12	22	34	32	9
Shjon Podein	82	14	18	32	41	7
Joel Otto	78	13	19	32	99	12
Chris Therien	71	2	22	24	64	27
Pat Falloon..........	52	11	12	23	10	−8
Danius Zubrus	68	8	13	21	22	3
Karl Dykhuis	62	4	15	19	35	6
John Druce	43	7	8	15	12	−5
Petr Svoboda	67	2	12	14	94	10
Daniel Lacroix	74	7	1	8	163	−1
Scott Daniels	56	5	3	8	237	2
Dan Kordic..........	75	1	4	5	210	−1
Ron Hextall (g)	55	0	0	0	43	—
Coach—Terry Murray						

Phoenix Coyotes

	GP	G	A	Pts	PIM-	+/−
Keith Tkachuk	81	52	34	86	228	−1
Jeremy Roenick	72	29	40	69	115	−7
Mike Gartner	82	32	31	63	38	−11
Oleg Tverdovsky	82	10	45	55	30	−5
Craig Janney	77	15	38	53	26	−1
Cliff Ronning	69	19	32	51	26	−9
Dallas Drake	63	17	19	36	52	−11
Teppo Numminen......	82	2	25	27	28	−3
Darrin Shannon	82	11	13	24	41	4
Bob Corkum	80	9	11	20	40	−7
Mike Stapleton	55	4	11	15	36	−4
Gerald Diduck*.......	67	2	12	14	63	−7
Kris King	81	3	11	14	185	−7
Shane Doan	63	4	8	12	49	−3
Jeff Finley	65	3	7	10	40	−8
Jim Johnson	55	3	7	10	74	5
Igor Korolev	41	3	7	10	28	−5
Murray Baron*.......	79	1	7	8	122	−20
Jim McKenzie........	65	5	3	8	200	−5
Nikolai Khabibulin (g) ...	72	0	3	3	16	—
Coach—Don Hay						

Pittsburgh Penguins

	GP	G	A	Pts	PIM-	+/-
Mario Lemieux.	76	50	72	122	65	27
Jaromir Jagr	63	47	48	95	40	22
Ron Francis	81	27	63	90	20	7
Petr Nedved	74	33	38	71	66	-2
Ed Olczyk*	79	25	30	55	51	-18
Kevin Hatcher	80	15	39	54	103	11
Stu Barnes*	81	19	30	49	26	-23
Fredrik Olausson*	71	9	29	38	32	16
Jason Woolley	60	6	30	36	30	4
Greg Johnson*	75	13	19	32	26	-18
Alex Hicks*	73	7	21	28	90	-5
Darius Kasparaitis*	75	2	21	23	100	17
Joe Mullen	54	7	15	22	4	E
Garry Valk*	70	10	11	21	78	-8
Joe Dziedzic	59	9	9	18	63	-4
Mike Stapleton.	55	4	11	15	36	-4
Andreas Johansson*	42	4	9	13	20	-12
Dave Roche	61	5	5	10	155	-13
Chris Tamer	45	2	4	6	131	-25
Craig Muni	64	0	4	4	36	6
Tyler Wright	45	2	2	4	70	-7
Francois Leroux.	59	0	3	3	81	3
Ken Wregget (g)	46	0	1	1	6	—

Coach—Eddie Johnston, Craig Patrick

St. Louis Blues

	GP	G	A	Pts	PIM-	+/-
Pierre Turgeon*	78	26	59	85	14	8
Brett Hull.	77	42	40	82	10	-9
Geoff Courtnall	82	17	40	57	86	3
Joe Murphy	75	20	25	45	69	-1
Jim Campbell	68	23	20	43	68	3
Al MacInnis	72	13	30	43	65	2
Stephane Matteau	74	16	20	36	50	11
Chris Pronger	79	11	24	35	143	15
Harry York.	74	14	18	32	24	1
Igor Kravchuk	82	4	24	28	35	7
Robert Petrovicky	44	7	12	19	10	2
Scott Pellerin	54	8	10	18	35	12
Craig Conroy	61	6	11	17	43	E
Ricard Persson*	54	4	8	12	45	-2
Craig MacTavish	50	2	5	7	33	-12
Mike Peluso*	64	2	5	7	226	E
Sergio Momesso*	40	1	3	4	48	-6
Marc Bergevin	82	0	4	4	53	-9
Tony Twist	64	1	2	3	121	-8
Grant Fuhr (g)	73	0	2	2	6	—

Coach—Mike Keenan, Jimmy Roberts, Joel Quenneville

San Jose Sharks

	GP	G	A	Pts	PIM-	+/-
Owen Nolan	72	31	32	63	155	-19
Jeff Friesen.	82	28	34	62	75	-8
Bernie Nicholls	65	12	33	45	63	-21
Viktor Kozlov	78	16	25	41	40	-16
Tony Granato	76	25	15	40	159	-7
Darren Turcotte	65	16	21	37	16	-8
Andrei Nazarov	60	12	15	27	222	-4
Stephen Guolla	43	13	8	21	14	-10
Todd Gill.	79	0	21	21	101	-20
Greg Hawgood	63	6	12	18	69	-22
Marcus Ragnarsson.	69	3	14	17	63	-18
Marty McSorley	57	4	12	16	186	-6
Doug Bodger	81	1	15	16	64	-14
Shean Donovan	73	9	6	15	42	-18
Al Iafrate.	38	6	9	15	91	-10
Bob Errey*	66	4	8	12	47	-5
Ron Sutter.	78	5	7	12	65	-8
Dody Wood.	44	3	2	5	193	-3
Tim Hunter	46	0	4	4	135	E
Todd Ewen	51	0	2	2	162	-5
Ed Belfour* (g)	46	0	0	0	34	—
Kelly Hrudey (g).	48	0	0	0	0	—

Coach—Al Sims

Tampa Bay Lightning

	GP	G	A	Pts	PIM-	+/-
Chris Gratton.	82	30	32	62	201	-28
Dino Ciccarelli.	77	35	25	60	116	11
John Cullen	70	18	37	55	95	-14
Rob Zamuner	82	17	33	50	56	3
Roman Hamrlik	79	12	28	40	57	-29
Shawn Burr	74	14	21	35	106	5
Alexander Selivanov	69	15	18	33	61	-3

	GP	G	A	Pts	PIM-	+/-
Daymond Langkow	79	15	13	28	35	1
Patrick Poulin	73	12	14	26	56	-16
Bill Houlder.	79	4	21	25	30	16
Brian Bradley	35	7	17	24	16	2
Mikael Andersson	70	5	14	19	8	1
Jeff Norton*	75	2	16	18	58	-7
Paul Ysebaert.	39	5	12	17	4	1
Jason Wiemer	63	9	5	14	134	-13
David Shaw	57	1	10	11	72	1
Jeff Toms	34	2	8	10	10	2
Cory Cross	72	4	5	9	95	6
Igor Ulanov	59	1	7	8	108	2
Rudy Poeschek	60	0	6	6	120	-3
Jamie Huscroft*	52	0	5	5	151	-2
Brantt Myhres.	47	3	1	4	136	1
Rick Tabaracci* (g)	62	0	1	1	12	—

Coach—Terry Crisp

Toronto Maple Leafs

	GP	G	A	Pts	PIM-	+/-
Mats Sundin.	82	41	53	94	59	6
Wendel Clark	65	30	19	49	75	-2
Sergei Berezin	73	25	16	41	2	-3
Steve Sullivan*	54	13	25	38	37	14
Todd Warriner	75	12	21	33	41	-3
Tie Domi	80	11	17	28	275	-17
Mike Craig	65	7	13	20	62	-20
Darby Hendrickson	64	11	6	17	47	-20
Jamie Baker	58	8	8	16	28	-2
Dimitri Yushkevich	74	4	10	14	56	-24
Rob Zetter	48	2	12	14	51	8
Fredrik Modin	76	6	7	13	24	-14
Jamie Macoun	73	1	10	11	93	-14
Jason Smith*	78	1	7	8	54	-12
Felix Potvin (g)	74	0	3	3	19	—

Coach—Mike Murphy

Vancouver Canucks

	GP	G	A	Pts	PIM-	+/-
Alexander Mogilny	76	31	42	73	18	9
Martin Gelinas	74	35	33	68	42	6
Pavel Bure	63	23	32	55	40	-14
Mike Ridley	75	20	32	52	42	E
Markus Naslund	78	21	20	41	30	-15
Trevor Linden.	49	9	31	40	27	5
Mike Sillinger	78	17	20	37	25	-3
Jyrki Lumme.	66	11	24	35	32	8
Brian Noonan*	73	12	22	34	34	-3
David Roberts	58	10	17	27	51	11
Dave Babych	78	5	22	27	38	-2
Sergei Nemchinov*	69	8	16	24	16	9
Adrian Aucoin	70	5	16	21	63	E
Bret Hedican	67	4	15	19	51	-3
Scott Walker.	64	3	15	18	132	2
Steve Staios*	63	3	14	17	91	-24
Chris Joseph	63	3	13	16	62	-21
Donald Brashear*	69	8	5	13	245	-8
Gino Odjick	70	5	8	13	371	-5
Leif Rohlon	40	2	8	10	8	4
Dana Murzyn	61	1	7	8	118	7
Kirk McLean (g)	44	0	2	2	2	—

Coach—Tom Renney

Washington Capitals

	GP	G	A	Pts	PIM-	+/-
Adam Oates*	80	22	60	82	14	-5
Peter Bondra	77	46	31	77	72	7
Dale Hunter	82	14	32	46	125	-2
Joe Juneau	58	15	27	42	8	-11
Steve Konowalchuk	78	17	25	42	67	-3
Phil Housley	77	11	29	40	24	-10
Rick Tocchet*	53	21	19	40	98	-3
Sergei Gonchar	57	13	17	30	36	-11
Andrei Nikolishin*	71	9	19	28	32	3
Sylvain Cote	57	6	18	24	28	11
Kelly Miller	77	10	14	24	33	4
Michal Pivonka	54	7	16	23	22	-15
Chris Simon	42	9	13	22	165	-1
Calle Johansson	65	6	11	17	16	-2
Todd Krygier	47	5	11	16	37	-10
Ken Klee	80	3	8	11	115	-5
Joe Reekie	65	1	8	9	107	8
Mike Eagles	70	1	7	8	42	-4
Mark Tinordi	56	2	6	8	118	3
Craig Berube	80	4	3	7	218	-11
Bill Ranford* (g)	55	0	1	1	7	—

Coach—Jim Schoenfeld

Individual Goaltending, 1996-97

(25 or more games played; ranked by goals against average)

Player	GP	GAA	W	L	T	SO	SV%	Player	GP	GAA	W	L	T	SO	SV%
Brodeur, N.J.	67	1.88	37	14	13	10	.927	Salo, N.Y.I.	58	2.82	20	27	8	5	.904
Moog, Dal.	48	2.15	28	13	5	3	.913	Khabibulin, Pho.	72	2.83	30	33	6	7	.908
Hackett, Chi.	41	2.16	19	18	4	2	.927	Kidd, Cgy.	55	2.84	21	23	6	4	.900
Hasek, Buf.	67	2.27	37	20	10	5	.930	Belfour, Chi.-S.J.	46	2.89	14	24	6	2	.901
Vanbiesbrouck, Fla.	57	2.29	27	19	10	2	.919	Roloson, Cgy.	31	2.89	9	14	3	1	.897
Osgood, Det.	47	2.30	23	13	9	6	.910	Thibault, Mon.	61	2.90	22	24	11	1	.910
Roy, Col.	62	2.32	38	15	7	7	.923	Joseph, Edm.	72	2.93	32	29	9	6	.907
Fitzpatrick, Fla	30	2.36	8	9	9	0	.914	Lalime, Pit.	39	2.94	21	12	2	3	.913
Vernon, Det.	33	2.43	13	11	8	0	.899	Schwab, T.B.	31	3.04	11	12	1	2	.897
Snow, Phi.	35	2.52	14	8	8	2	.903	Carey, Was.-Bos.	59	3.08	22	31	3	1	.886
Dunham, N.J.	26	2.55	8	7	1	2	.906	Fichaud, N.Y.I.	34	3.10	9	14	4	0	.899
Hextall, Phi.	55	2.56	31	16	5	5	.897	Dafoe, L.A.	40	3.11	13	17	5	0	.905
Kolzig, Was.	29	2.59	8	15	4	2	.906	Potvin, Tor.	74	3.15	27	36	7	0	.908
Hebert, Ana.	67	2.67	29	25	12	4	.919	Hrudey, S.J.	48	3.19	16	24	5	0	.889
Richter, N.Y.R.	61	2.68	33	22	6	4	.917	Fiset, L.A.	44	3.19	13	24	5	4	.906
Irbe, S.J.	35	2.69	17	12	3	3	.893	McLean, Van.	44	3.21	21	18	3	0	.889
Burke, Hfd.	51	2.69	22	22	6	4	.914	Wregget, Pit.	46	3.25	17	17	6	2	.902
Tabaracci, Cgy.-T.B	62	2.70	22	29	6	5	.903	Ranford, Was.	55	3.25	20	23	10	2	.887
Rhodes, Ott.	50	2.72	14	20	14	1	.890	Hirsch, Van.	39	3.27	12	20	4	2	.894
Fuhr, St.L.	73	2.72	33	27	11	3	.901	Tallas, Bos.	28	3.33	8	12	1	1	.882
Terreri, S.J.-Chi.	29	2.73	10	11	5	0	.901	Muzzatti, Hfd.	31	3.43	9	13	5	0	.888
Tugnutt, Ott.	37	2.80	17	15	1	3	.895								

All-Time Leading Scorers

Player	Goals	Assists	Points	Player	Goals	Assists	Points
Wayne Gretzky*	862	1,843	2,705	Jari Kurri*	596	780	1,376
Gordie Howe	801	1,049	1,850	John Bucyk	556	813	1,369
Marcel Dionne	731	1,040	1,771	Ray Bourque*	362	1,001	1,363
Phil Esposito	717	873	1,590	Guy Lafleur	560	793	1,353
Mark Messier*	575	977	1,552	Ron Francis*	403	944	1,347
Mario Lemieux*	613	881	1,494	Steve Yzerman*	539	801	1,340
Stan Mikita	541	926	1,467	Denis Savard*	473	865	1,338
Paul Coffey*	381	1,063	1,444	Gilbert Perreault	512	814	1,326
Bryan Trottier	524	901	1,425	Mike Gartner*	696	612	1,308
Dale Hawerchuk*	518	891	1,409	Alex Delvecchio	456	825	1,281

Note: Through end of 1996-97 season.* Active at end of 1996-97 season.

Most NHL Goals in a Season

Player	Team	Season	Goals	Player	Team	Season	Goals
Wayne Gretzky	Edmonton	1981-82	92	Jari Kurri	Edmonton	1984-85	71
Wayne Gretzky	Edmonton	1983-84	87	Bret Hull	St. Louis	1991-92	70
Brett Hull	St. Louis	1990-91	86	Mario Lemieux	Pittsburgh	1987-88	70
Mario Lemieux	Pittsburgh	1988-89	85	Bernie Nicholls	Los Angeles	1988-89	70
Phil Esposito	Boston	1970-71	76	Mike Bossy	N.Y. Islanders	1978-79	69
Alexander Mogilny	Buffalo	1992-93	76	Mario Lemieux	Pittsburgh	1992-93	69
Teemu Selanne	Winnipeg	1992-93	76	Mario Lemieux	Pittsburgh	1995-96	69
Wayne Gretzky	Edmonton	1984-85	73	Mike Bossy	N.Y. Islanders	1980-81	68
Brett Hull	St. Louis	1989-90	72	Phil Esposito	Boston	1973-74	68
Wayne Gretzky	Edmonton	1982-83	71	Jari Kurri	Edmonton	1985-86	68

Art Ross Trophy (Leading Scorer)

1927	Bill Cook, N.Y. Rangers	1951	Gordie Howe, Detroit	1975	Bobby Orr, Boston
1928	Howie Morenz, Montreal	1952	Gordie Howe, Detroit	1976	Guy Lafleur, Montreal
1929	Ace Bailey, Toronto	1953	Gordie Howe, Detroit	1977	Guy Lafleur, Montreal
1930	Cooney Weiland, Boston	1954	Gordie Howe, Detroit	1978	Guy Lafleur, Montreal
1931	Howie Morenz, Montreal	1955	Bernie Geoffrion, Montreal	1979	Bryan Trottier, N.Y. Islanders
1932	Harvey Jackson, Toronto	1956	Jean Beliveau, Montreal	1980	Marcel Dionne, Los Angeles
1933	Bill Cook, N.Y. Rangers	1957	Gordie Howe, Detroit	1981	Wayne Gretzky, Edmonton
1934	Charlie Conacher, Toronto	1958	Dickie Moore, Montreal	1982	Wayne Gretzky, Edmonton
1935	Charlie Conacher, Toronto	1959	Dickie Moore, Montreal	1983	Wayne Gretzky, Edmonton
1936	Dave Schriner, N.Y. Americans	1960	Bobby Hull, Chicago	1984	Wayne Gretzky, Edmonton
1937	Dave Schriner, N.Y. Americans	1961	Bernie Geoffrion, Montreal	1985	Wayne Gretzky, Edmonton
1938	Gordie Drillon, Toronto	1962	Bobby Hull, Chicago	1986	Wayne Gretzky, Edmonton
1939	Toe Blake, Montreal	1963	Gordie Howe, Detroit	1987	Wayne Gretzky, Edmonton
1940	Milt Schmidt, Boston	1964	Stan Mikita, Chicago	1988	Mario Lemieux, Pittsburgh
1941	Bill Cowley, Boston	1965	Stan Mikita, Chicago	1989	Mario Lemieux, Pittsburgh
1942	Bryan Hextall, N.Y. Rangers	1966	Bobby Hull, Chicago	1990	Wayne Gretzky, Los Angeles
1943	Doug Bentley, Chicago	1967	Stan Mikita, Chicago	1991	Wayne Gretzky, Los Angeles
1944	Herbie Cain, Boston	1968	Stan Mikita, Chicago	1992	Mario Lemieux, Pittsburgh
1945	Elmer Lach, Montreal	1969	Phil Esposito, Boston	1993	Mario Lemieux, Pittsburgh
1946	Max Bentley, Chicago	1970	Bobby Orr, Boston	1994	Wayne Gretzky, Los Angeles
1947	Max Bentley, Chicago	1971	Phil Esposito, Boston	1995	Jaromir Jagr, Pittsburgh
1948	Elmer Lach, Montreal	1972	Phil Esposito, Boston	1996	Mario Lemieux, Pittsburgh
1949	Roy Conacher, Chicago	1973	Phil Esposito, Boston	1997	Mario Lemieux, Pittsburgh
1950	Ted Lindsay, Detroit	1974	Phil Esposito, Boston		

James Norris Memorial Trophy (Outstanding Defenseman)

1954	Red Kelly, Detroit	1965	Pierre Pilote, Chicago	1976	Denis Potvin, N.Y. Islanders
1955	Doug Harvey, Montreal	1966	Jacques Laperriere, Montreal	1977	Larry Robinson, Montreal
1956	Doug Harvey, Montreal	1967	Harry Howell, N.Y. Rangers	1978	Denis Potvin, N.Y. Islanders
1957	Doug Harvey, Montreal	1968	Bobby Orr, Boston	1979	Denis Potvin, N.Y. Islanders
1958	Doug Harvey, Montreal	1969	Bobby Orr, Boston	1980	Larry Robinson, Montreal
1959	Tom Johnson, Montreal	1970	Bobby Orr, Boston	1981	Randy Carlyle, Pittsburgh
1960	Doug Harvey, Montreal	1971	Bobby Orr, Boston	1982	Doug Wilson, Chicago
1961	Doug Harvey, Montreal	1972	Bobby Orr, Boston	1983	Rod Langway, Washington
1962	Doug Harvey, N.Y. Rangers	1973	Bobby Orr, Boston	1984	Rod Langway, Washington
1963	Pierre Pilote, Chicago	1974	Bobby Orr, Boston	1985	Paul Coffey, Edmonton
1964	Pierre Pilote, Chicago	1975	Bobby Orr, Boston	1986	Paul Coffey, Edmonton

1987	Ray Bourque, Boston	1991	Ray Bourque, Boston	1995	Paul Coffey, Detroit
1988	Ray Bourque, Boston	1992	Brian Leetch, N.Y. Rangers	1996	Chris Chelios, Chicago
1989	Chris Chelios, Montreal	1993	Chris Chelios, Chicago		
1990	Ray Bourque, Boston	1994	Ray Bourque, Boston	1997	Brian Leetch, N.Y. Rangers

Vezina Trophy (Outstanding Goalie)*

1927	George Hainsworth, Montreal	1952	Terry Sawchuk, Detroit	1975	Bernie Parent, Philadelphia
1928	George Hainsworth, Montreal	1953	Terry Sawchuk, Detroit	1976	Ken Dryden, Montreal
1929	George Hainsworth, Montreal	1954	Harry Lumley, Toronto	1977	Dryden, Larocque, Montreal
1930	Tiny Thompson, Boston	1955	Terry Sawchuk, Detroit	1978	Dryden, Larocque, Montreal
1931	Roy Worters, N.Y. Americans	1956	Jacques Plante, Montreal	1979	Dryden, Larocque, Montreal
1932	Charlie Gardiner, Chicago	1957	Jacques Plante, Montreal	1980	Sauve, Edwards, Buffalo
1933	Tiny Thompson, Boston	1958	Jacques Plante, Montreal	1981	Sevigny, Larocque, Herron,
1934	Charlie Gardiner, Chicago	1959	Jacques Plante, Montreal		Montreal
1935	Lorne Chabot, Chicago	1960	Jacques Plante, Montreal	1982	Bill Smith, N.Y. Islanders
1936	Tiny Thompson, Boston	1961	John Bower, Toronto	1983	Pete Peeters, Boston
1937	Normie Smith, Detroit	1962	Jacques Plante, Montreal	1984	Tom Barrasso, Buffalo
1938	Tiny Thompson, Boston	1963	Glenn Hall, Chicago	1985	Pelle Lindbergh, Philadelphia
1939	Frank Brimsek, Boston	1964	Charlie Hodge, Montreal	1986	John Vanbiesbrouck, N.Y.
1940	Dave Kerr, N.Y. Rangers	1965	Sawchuk, Bower, Toronto		Rangers
1941	Turk Broda, Toronto	1966	Worsley, Hodge, Montreal	1987	Ron Hextall, Philadelphia
1942	Frank Brimsek, Boston	1967	Hall, DeJordy, Chicago	1988	Grant Fuhr, Edmonton
1943	Johnny Mowers, Detroit	1968	Worsley, Vachon, Montreal	1989	Patrick Roy, Montreal
1944	Bill Durnan, Montreal	1969	Hall, Plante, St. Louis	1990	Patrick Roy, Montreal
1945	Bill Durnan, Montreal	1970	Tony Esposito, Chicago	1991	Ed Belfour, Chicago
1946	Bill Durnan, Montreal	1971	Giacomin, Villemure, N.Y.	1992	Patrick Roy, Montreal
1947	Bill Durnan, Montreal		Rangers	1993	Ed Belfour, Chicago
1948	Turk Broda, Toronto	1972	Esposito, Smith, Chicago	1994	Dominik Hasek, Buffalo
1949	Bill Durnan, Montreal	1973	Ken Dryden, Montreal	1995	Dominik Hasek, Buffalo
1950	Bill Durnan, Montreal	1974	Bernie Parent, Philadelphia;	1996	Jim Carey, Washington
1951	Al Rollins, Toronto		Tony Esposito, Chicago	1997	Dominik Hasek, Buffalo

*Before 1982, awarded to the goalie or goalies who played a minimum of 25 games for the team that allowed the fewest goals; since 1982, awarded to the outstanding goalie.

Calder Memorial Trophy (Rookie of the Year)

1933	Carl Voss, Detroit	1954	Camille Henry, N.Y. Rangers	1976	Bryan Trottier, N.Y. Islanders
1934	Russ Blinco, Montreal	1955	Ed Litzenberger, Chicago	1977	Willi Plett, Atlanta
	Maroons	1956	Glenn Hall, Detroit	1978	Mike Bossy, N.Y. Islanders
1935	Dave Schriner, N.Y. Americans	1957	Larry Regan, Boston	1979	Bobby Smith, Minnesota
1936	Mike Karakas, Chicago	1958	Frank Mahovlich, Toronto	1980	Ray Bourque, Boston
1937	Syl Apps, Toronto	1959	Ralph Backstrom, Montreal	1981	Peter Stastny, Quebec
1938	Cully Dahlstrom, Chicago	1960	Bill Hay, Chicago	1982	Dale Hawerchuk, Winnipeg
1939	Frank Brimsek, Boston	1961	Dave Keon, Toronto	1983	Steve Larmer, Chicago
1940	Kilby Macdonald, N.Y. Rangers	1962	Bobby Rousseau, Montreal	1984	Tom Barrasso, Buffalo
1941	John Quilty, Montreal	1963	Kent Douglas, Toronto	1985	Mario Lemieux, Pittsburgh
1942	Grant Warwick, N.Y. Rangers	1964	Jacques Laperriere, Montreal	1986	Gary Suter, Calgary
1943	Gaye Stewart, Toronto	1965	Roger Crozier, Detroit	1987	Luc Robitaille, Los Angeles
1944	Gus Bodnar, Toronto	1966	Brit Selby, Toronto	1988	Joe Nieuwendyk, Calgary
1945	Frank McCool, Toronto	1967	Bobby Orr, Boston	1989	Brian Leetch, N.Y. Rangers
1946	Edgar Laprade, N.Y. Rangers	1968	Derek Sanderson, Boston	1990	Sergei Makarov, Calgary
1947	Howie Meeker, Toronto	1969	Danny Grant, Minnesota	1991	Ed Belfour, Chicago
1948	Jim McFadden, Detroit	1970	Tony Esposito, Chicago	1992	Pavel Bure, Vancouver
1949	Pentti Lund, N.Y. Rangers	1971	Gilbert Perreault, Buffalo	1993	Teemu Selanne, Winnipeg
1950	Jack Gelineau, Boston	1972	Ken Dryden, Montreal	1994	Martin Brodeur, New Jersey
1951	Terry Sawchuk, Detroit	1973	Steve Vickers, N.Y. Rangers	1995	Peter Forsberg, Quebec
1952	Bernie Geoffrion, Montreal	1974	Denis Potvin, N.Y. Islanders	1996	Daniel Alfredsson, Ottawa
1953	Gump Worsley, N.Y. Rangers	1975	Eric Vail, Atlanta	1997	Bryan Berard, N.Y. Islanders

Lady Byng Memorial Trophy (Most Gentlemanly Player)

1925	Frank Nighbor, Ottawa	1950	Edgar Laprade, N.Y. Rangers	1974	John Bucyk, Boston
1926	Frank Nighbor, Ottawa	1951	Red Kelly, Detroit	1975	Marcel Dionne, Detroit
1927	Billy Burch, N.Y. Americans	1952	Sid Smith, Toronto	1976	Jean Ratelle, N.Y.R.-Boston
1928	Frank Boucher, N.Y. Rangers	1953	Red Kelly, Detroit	1977	Marcel Dionne, Los Angeles
1929	Frank Boucher, N.Y. Rangers	1954	Red Kelly, Detroit	1978	Butch Goring, Los Angeles
1930	Frank Boucher, N.Y. Rangers	1955	Sid Smith, Toronto	1979	Bob MacMillan, Atlanta
1931	Frank Boucher, N.Y. Rangers	1956	Earl Reibel, Detroit	1980	Wayne Gretzky, Edmonton
1932	Joe Primeau, Toronto	1957	Andy Hebenton, N.Y. Rangers	1981	Rick Kehoe, Pittsburgh
1933	Frank Boucher, N.Y. Rangers	1958	Camille Henry, N.Y. Rangers	1982	Rick Middleton, Boston
1934	Frank Boucher, N.Y. Rangers	1959	Alex Delvecchio, Detroit	1983	Mike Bossy, N.Y. Islanders
1935	Frank Boucher, N.Y. Rangers	1960	Don McKenney, Boston	1984	Mike Bossy, N.Y. Islanders
1936	Doc Romnes, Chicago	1961	Red Kelly, Toronto	1985	Jari Kurri, Edmonton
1937	Marty Barry, Detroit	1962	Dave Keon, Toronto	1986	Mike Bossy, N.Y. Islanders
1938	Gordie Drillon, Toronto	1963	Dave Keon, Toronto	1987	Joe Mullen, Calgary
1939	Clint Smith, N.Y. Rangers	1964	Ken Wharram, Chicago	1988	Mats Naslund, Montreal
1940	Bobby Bauer, Boston	1965	Bobby Hull, Chicago	1989	Joe Mullen, Calgary
1941	Bobby Bauer, Boston	1966	Alex Delvecchio, Detroit	1990	Brett Hull, St. Louis
1942	Syl Apps, Toronto	1967	Stan Mikita, Chicago	1991	Wayne Gretzky, Los Angeles
1943	Max Bentley, Chicago	1968	Stan Mikita, Chicago	1992	Wayne Gretzky, Los Angeles
1944	Clint Smith, Chicago	1969	Alex Delvecchio, Detroit	1993	Pierre Turgeon, N.Y. Islanders
1945	Bill Mosienko, Chicago	1970	Phil Goyette, St. Louis	1994	Wayne Gretzky, Los Angeles
1946	Toe Blake, Montreal	1971	John Bucyk, Boston	1995	Ron Francis, Pittsburgh
1947	Bobby Bauer, Boston	1972	Jean Ratelle, N.Y. Rangers	1996	Paul Kariya, Anaheim
1948	Buddy O'Connor, N.Y. Rangers	1973	Gil Perreault, Buffalo	1997	Paul Kariya, Anaheim
1949	Bill Quackenbush, Detroit				

Frank J. Selke Trophy (Best Defensive Forward)

1978	Bob Gainey, Montreal	1985	Craig Ramsay, Buffalo	1991	Dirk Graham, Chicago
1979	Bob Gainey, Montreal	1986	Troy Murray, Chicago	1992	Guy Carbonneau, Montreal
1980	Bob Gainey, Montreal	1987	Dave Poulin, Philadelphia	1993	Doug Gilmour, Toronto
1981	Bob Gainey, Montreal	1988	Guy Carbonneau, Montreal	1994	Sergei Fedorov, Detroit
1982	Steve Kasper, Boston	1989	Guy Carbonneau, Montreal	1995	Ron Francis, Pittsburgh
1983	Bobby Clarke, Philadelphia	1990	Rick Meagher, St. Louis	1996	Sergei Federov, Detroit
1984	Doug Jarvis, Washington			1997	Michael Peca, Buffalo

Hart Memorial Trophy (MVP)

1927	Herb Gardiner, Montreal	1950	Chuck Rayner, N.Y. Rangers	1974	Phil Esposito, Boston
1928	Howie Morenz, Montreal	1951	Milt Schmidt, Boston	1975	Bobby Clarke, Philadelphia
1929	Roy Worters, N.Y. Americans	1952	Gordie Howe, Detroit	1976	Bobby Clarke, Philadelphia
1930	Nels Stewart, Montreal Maroons	1953	Gordie Howe, Detroit	1977	Guy Lafleur, Montreal
		1954	Al Rollins, Chicago	1978	Guy Lafleur, Montreal
1931	Howie Morenz, Montreal	1955	Ted Kennedy, Toronto	1979	Bryan Trottier, N.Y. Islanders
1932	Howie Morenz, Montreal	1956	Jean Beliveau, Montreal	1980	Wayne Gretzky, Edmonton
1933	Eddie Shore, Boston	1957	Gordie Howe, Detroit	1981	Wayne Gretzky, Edmonton
1934	Aurel Joliat, Montreal	1958	Gordie Howe, Detroit	1982	Wayne Gretzky, Edmonton
1935	Eddie Shore, Boston	1959	Andy Bathgate, N.Y. Rangers	1983	Wayne Gretzky, Edmonton
1936	Eddie Shore, Boston	1960	Gordie Howe, Detroit	1984	Wayne Gretzky, Edmonton
1937	Babe Siebert, Montreal	1961	Bernie Geoffrion, Montreal	1985	Wayne Gretzky, Edmonton
1938	Eddie Shore, Boston	1962	Jacques Plante, Montreal	1986	Wayne Gretzky, Edmonton
1939	Toe Blake, Montreal	1963	Gordie Howe, Detroit	1987	Wayne Gretzky, Edmonton
1940	Ebbie Goodfellow, Detroit	1964	Jean Beliveau, Montreal	1988	Mario Lemieux, Pittsburgh
1941	Bill Cowley, Boston	1965	Bobby Hull, Chicago	1989	Wayne Gretzky, Los Angeles
1942	Tom Anderson, N.Y. Americans	1966	Bobby Hull, Chicago	1990	Mark Messier, Edmonton
1943	Bill Cowley, Boston	1967	Stan Mikita, Chicago	1991	Brett Hull, St. Louis
1944	Babe Pratt, Toronto	1968	Stan Mikita, Chicago	1992	Mark Messier, N.Y. Rangers
1945	Elmer Lach, Montreal	1969	Phil Esposito, Boston	1993	Mario Lemieux, Pittsburgh
1946	Max Bentley, Chicago	1970	Bobby Orr, Boston	1994	Sergei Fedorov, Detroit
1947	Maurice Richard, Montreal	1971	Bobby Orr, Boston	1995	Eric Lindros, Philadelphia
1948	Buddy O'Connor, N.Y. Rangers	1972	Bobby Orr, Boston	1996	Mario Lemieux, Pittsburgh
1949	Sid Abel, Detroit	1973	Bobby Clarke, Philadelphia	1997	Dominik Hasek, Buffalo

Conn Smythe Trophy (MVP in Playoffs)

1965	Jean Beliveau, Montreal	1976	Reg Leach, Philadelphia	1987	Ron Hextall, Philadelphia
1966	Roger Crozier, Detroit	1977	Guy Lafleur, Montreal	1988	Wayne Gretzky, Edmonton
1967	Dave Keon, Toronto	1978	Larry Robinson, Montreal	1989	Al MacInnis, Calgary
1968	Glenn Hall, St. Louis	1979	Bob Gainey, Montreal	1990	Bill Ranford, Edmonton
1969	Serge Savard, Montreal	1980	Bryan Trottier, N.Y. Islanders	1991	Mario Lemieux, Pittsburgh
1970	Bobby Orr, Boston	1981	Butch Goring, N.Y. Islanders	1992	Mario Lemieux, Pittsburgh
1971	Ken Dryden, Montreal	1982	Mike Bossy, N.Y. Islanders	1993	Patrick Roy, Montreal
1972	Bobby Orr, Boston	1983	Billy Smith, N.Y. Islanders	1994	Brian Leetch, N.Y. Rangers
1973	Yvan Cournoyer, Montreal	1984	Mark Messier, Edmonton	1995	Claude Lemieux, New Jersey
1974	Bernie Parent, Philadelphia	1985	Wayne Gretzky, Edmonton	1996	Joe Sakic, Colorado
1975	Bernie Parent, Philadelphia	1986	Patrick Roy, Montreal	1997	Mike Vernon, Detroit

NCAA HOCKEY CHAMPIONS

1948	Michigan	1961	Denver	1973	Wisconsin	1985	RPI
1949	Boston College	1962	Michigan Tech	1974	Minnesota	1986	Michigan State
1950	Colorado College	1963	North Dakota	1975	Michigan Tech	1987	North Dakota
1951	Michigan	1964	Michigan	1976	Minnesota	1988	Lake Superior St.
1952	Michigan	1965	Michigan Tech	1977	Wisconsin	1989	Harvard
1953	Michigan	1966	Michigan State	1978	Boston Univ.	1990	Wisconsin
1954	RPI	1967	Cornell	1979	Minnesota	1991	N. Michigan
1955	Michigan	1968	Denver	1980	North Dakota	1992	Lake Superior St.
1956	Michigan	1969	Denver	1981	Wisconsin	1993	Maine
1957	Colorado College	1970	Cornell	1982	North Dakota	1994	Lake Superior St.
1958	Denver	1971	Boston Univ.	1983	Wisconsin	1995	Boston Univ.
1959	North Dakota	1972	Boston Univ.	1984	Bowling Green	1996	Michigan
1960	Denver					1997	North Dakota

LACROSSE

Lacrosse Champions in 1997

World Lacrosse Championship (1994; held every 4 years)— Manchester, England, July 30: U.S. 21, Australia 7.

U.S. Club Lacrosse Association Championship—Syracuse, NY, June 15: Long Island-Hofstra 16, Chesapeake Toyota 15.

Mill Pro Indoor Lacrosse Championship—Buffalo, NY, April 12: Rochester 15, Buffalo 12.

NCAA Division I Championship—College Park, MD, May 26: Princeton 19, Maryland 7.

NCAA Division II Championship—Garden City, NY, May 10: New York Tech 18, Adelphi 11.

NCAA Division III Championship—College Park, MD, May 25: Nazareth 15, Washington College 14 (OT).

NCAA Division I All-Star Game—Hempstead, NY, June 8: South 18, North 16.

National Junior College Championship—Essex, MD, May 11: Nassau (NY) C.C. 22, Herkimer (NY) C.C. 11.

Women's World Cup—Edogaua, Japan, May 4: USA 3, Australia 2 (OT).

NCAA Women's Division I Championship—Bethlehem, PA, May 18: Maryland 8, Loyola 7.

NCAA Women's Division III Championship—Bethlehem, PA, May 18: Middlebury 14, College of New Jersey 8.

NCAA Division I All America Team

Attack: Jon Hess, Princeton; Doug Knight, Virginia; Casey Powell, Syracuse; Michael Watson, Virginia. (4 men selected for the 3 attack positions.)

Midfield: David Curry, Virginia; Jim Gonnella, Duke; Lorne Smith, Princeton.

Defense: John Gagliardi, Johns Hopkins; Brian Kuczma, Johns Hopkins; David Stilley, Duke.

Goal: Greg Cattrano, Brown.

Coach of the Year: Jack McGetrick, Hartford.

NCAA Division I Lacrosse Champions

Year	Champion	Year	Champion	Year	Champion	Year	Champion
1971	Cornell	1978	Johns Hopkins	1985	Johns Hopkins	1992	Princeton
1972	Virginia	1979	Johns Hopkins	1986	North Carolina	1993	Syracuse
1973	Maryland	1980	Johns Hopkins	1987	Johns Hopkins	1994	Princeton
1974	Johns Hopkins	1981	North Carolina	1988	Syracuse	1995	Syracuse
1975	Maryland	1982	North Carolina	1989	Syracuse	1996	Princeton
1976	Cornell	1983	Syracuse	1990	vacated	1997	Princeton
1977	Cornell	1984	Johns Hopkins	1991	North Carolina		

THOROUGHBRED RACING
Triple Crown Winners

Since 1920, colts have carried 126 lb in triple crown events; fillies, 121 lb.

(Kentucky Derby, Preakness, and Belmont Stakes)

Year	Horse	Jockey	Trainer	Year	Horse	Jockey	Trainer
1919	Sir Barton	J. Loftus	H. G. Bedwell	1946	Assault	W. Mehrtens	M. Hirsch
1930	Gallant Fox	E. Sande	J. Fitzsimmons	1948	Citation	E. Arcaro	H. A. Jones
1935	Omaha	W. Sanders	J. Fitzsimmons	1973	Secretariat	R. Turcotte	L. Laurin
1937	War Admiral	C. Kurtsinger	G. Conway	1977	Seattle Slew	J. Cruguet	W. H. Turner, Jr.
1941	Whirlaway	E. Arcaro	B. A. Jones	1978	Affirmed	S. Cauthen	L. S. Barrera
1943	Count Fleet	J. Longden	G. D. Cameron				

Kentucky Derby

Churchill Downs, Louisville, KY; inaugurated 1875; distance 1-1/4 mi; 1-1/2 mi until 1896. 3-year-olds.
Best time: 1:59.2, by Secretariat, 1973.

Year	Winner	Jockey	Year	Winner	Jockey	Year	Winner	Jockey
1875	Aristides	O. Lewis	1916	George Smith	J. Loftus	1957	Iron Liege	W. Hartack
1876	Vagrant	R. Swim	1917	Omar Khayyam	C. Borel	1958	Tim Tam	I. Valenzuela
1877	Baden Baden	W. Walker	1918	Exterminator	W. Knapp	1959	Tomy Lee	W. Shoemaker
1878	Day Star	J. Carter	1919	Sir Barton	J. Loftus	1960	Venetian Way	W. Hartack
1879	Lord Murphy	C. Schauer	1920	Paul Jones	T. Rice	1961	Carry Back	J. Sellers
1880	Fonso	G. Lewis	1921	Behave Yourself	C. Thompson	1962	Decidedly	W. Hartack
1881	Hindoo	J. McLaughlin	1922	Morvich	A. Johnson	1963	Chateaugay	B. Baeza
1882	Apollo	B. Hurd	1923	Zev	E. Sande	1964	Northern Dancer	W. Hartack
1883	Leonatus	W. Donohue	1924	Black Gold	J. D. Mooney	1965	Lucky Debonair	W. Shoemaker
1884	Buchanan	I. Murphy	1925	Flying Ebony	E. Sande	1966	Kauai King	D. Brumfield
1885	Joe Cotton	E. Henderson	1926	Bubbling Over	A. Johnson	1967	Proud Clarion	R. Ussery
1886	Ben Ali	P. Duffy	1927	Whiskery	L. McAtee	1968	Dancer's Image (a)	R. Ussery
1887	Montrose	I. Lewis	1928	Reigh Count	C. Lang	1969	Majestic Prince	W. Hartack
1888	Macbeth II	G. Covington	1929	Clyde Van Dusen	L. McAtee	1970	Dust Commander	M. Manganello
1889	Spokane	T. Kiley	1930	Gallant Fox	E. Sande	1971	Canonero II	G. Avila
1890	Riley	I. Murphy	1931	Twenty Grand	C. Kurtsinger	1972	Riva Ridge	R. Turcotte
1891	Kingman	I. Murphy	1932	Burgoo King	E. James	1973	Secretariat	R. Turcotte
1892	Azra	A. Clayton	1933	Brokers Tip	D. Meade	1974	Cannonade	A. Cordero
1893	Lookout	E. Kunze	1934	Cavalcade	M. Garner	1975	Foolish Pleasure	J. Vasquez
1894	Chant	F. Goodale	1935	Omaha	W. Saunders	1976	Bold Forbes	A. Cordero
1895	Halma	J. Perkins	1936	Bold Venture	I. Hanford	1977	Seattle Slew	J. Cruguet
1896	Ben Brush	W. Simms	1937	War Admiral	C. Kurtsinger	1978	Affirmed	S. Cauthen
1897	Typhoon II	F. Garner	1938	Lawrin	E. Arcaro	1979	Spectacular Bid	R. Franklin
1898	Plaudit	W. Simms	1939	Johnstown	J. Stout	1980	Genuine Risk*	J. Vasquez
1899	Manuel	F. Taral	1940	Gallahadion	C. Bierman	1981	Pleasant Colony	J. Velasquez
1900	Lieut. Gibson	J. Boland	1941	Whirlaway	E. Arcaro	1982	Gato del Sol	E. Delahoussaye
1901	His Eminence	J. Winkfield	1942	Shut Out	W. D. Wright	1983	Sunny's Halo	E. Delahoussaye
1902	Alan-a-Dale	J. Winkfield	1943	Count Fleet	J. Longden	1984	Swale	L. Pincay
1903	Judge Himes	H. Booker	1944	Pensive	C. McCreary	1985	Spend a Buck	A. Cordero
1904	Elwood	F. Prior	1945	Hoop, Jr.	E. Arcaro	1986	Ferdinand	W. Shoemaker
1905	Agile	J. Martin	1946	Assault	W. Mehrtens	1987	Alysheba	C. McCarron
1906	Sir Huon	R. Troxler	1947	Jet Pilot	E. Guerin	1988	Winning Colors*	G. Stevens
1907	Pink Star	A. Minder	1948	Citation	E. Arcaro	1989	Sunday Silence	P. Valenzuela
1908	Stone Street	A. Pickens	1949	Ponder	S. Brooks	1990	Unbridled	C. Perret
1909	Wintergreen	V. Powers	1950	Middleground	W. Boland	1991	Strike the Gold	C. Antley
1910	Donau	F. Herbert	1951	Count Turf	C. McCreary	1992	Lil E. Tee	P. Day
1911	Meridian	G. Archibald	1952	Hill Gail	E. Arcaro	1993	Sea Hero	J. Bailey
1912	Worth	C.H. Shilling	1953	Dark Star	H. Moreno	1994	Go for Gin	C. McCarron
1913	Donerail	R. Goose	1954	Determine	R. York	1995	Thunder Gulch	G. Stevens
1914	Old Rosebud	J. McCabe	1955	Swaps	W. Shoemaker	1996	Grindstone	J. Bailey
1915	Regret*	J. Notter	1956	Needles	D. Erb	1997	Silver Charm	G. Stevens

(a) Dancer's Image was disqualified from purse money after tests disclosed that he had run with a pain-killing drug, phenylbutazone, in his system. All wagers were paid on Dancer's Image. Forward Pass was awarded first place money.
The Kentucky Derby has been won 5 times by 2 jockeys: Eddie Arcaro, 1938, 1941, 1945, 1948, and 1952; and Bill Hartack, 1957, 1960, 1962, 1964, and 1969. It was won 4 times by Willie Shoemaker, 1955, 1959, 1965, and 1986; and 3 times by each of 4 jockeys: Isaac Murphy, 1884, 1890, and 1891; Earle Sande, 1923, 1925, and 1930; Angel Cordero, 1974, 1976, and 1985; and Gary Stevens, 1988, 1995, and 1997. *Regret, Genuine Risk, and Winning Colors are the only fillies to have won the Derby.

Preakness

Pimlico, Baltimore, MD; inaugurated 1873; distance 1-3/16 mi. 3-year-olds. Best time: 1:53.2, by Tank's Prospect (1985) and Louis Quatorze (1996).

Year	Winner	Jockey	Year	Winner	Jockey	Year	Winner	Jockey
1873	Survivor	G. Barbee	1889	Buddhist	G. Anderson	1908	Royal Tourist	E. Dugan
1874	Culpepper	M. Donohue	1890	Montague	W. Martin	1909	Effendi	W. Doyle
1875	Tom Ochiltree	L. Hughes	1894	Assignee	F. Taral	1910	Layminster	R. Estep
1876	Shirley	G. Barbee	1895	Belmar	F. Taral	1911	Watervale	E. Dugan
1877	Cloverbrook	C. Holloway	1896	Margrave	H. Griffin	1912	Colonel Holloway	C. Turner
1878	Duke of Magenta	C. Holloway	1897	Paul Kauvar	C. Thorpe	1913	Buskin	J. Butwell
1879	Harold	L. Hughes	1898	Sly Fox	W. Simms	1914	Holiday	A. Schuttinger
1880	Grenada	L. Hughes	1899	Half Time	R. Clawson	1915	Rhine Maiden	D. Hoffman
1881	Saunterer	W. Costello	1900	Hindus	H. Spencer	1916	Damrosch	L. McAtee
1882	Vanguard	W. Costello	1901	The Parader	F. Landry	1917	Kalitan	E. Haynes
1883	Jacobus	G. Barbee	1902	Old England	L. Jackson	1918	War Cloud	J. Loftus
1884	Knight of Ellersle	S. H. Fisher	1900	Flocarline	W. Gannon		Jack Hare, Jr.	C. Peak
1885	Tecumseh	J. McLaughlin	1903	Bryn Mawr	E. Hildebrand	1919	Sir Barton	J. Loftus
1886	The Bard	S. H. Fisher	1905	Cairngorm	W. Davis	1920	Man o' War	C. Kummer
1887	Dunboyne	W. Donohue	1906	Whimsical	W. Miller	1921	Broomspun	F. Coltiletti
1888	Refund	F. Littlefield	1907	Don Enrique	G. Mountain			*(continued)*

Year	Winner	Jockey	Year	Winner	Jockey	Year	Winner	Jockey
1922	Pillory	L. Morris	1948	Citation	E. Arcaro	1973	Secretariat	R. Turcotte
1923	Vigil	B. Marinelli	1949	Capot	T. Atkinson	1974	Little Current	M. Rivera
1924	Nellie Morse	J. Merimee	1950	Hill Prince	E. Arcaro	1975	Master Derby	D. McHargue
1925	Coventry	C. Kummer	1951	Bold	E. Arcaro	1976	Elocutionist	J. Lively
1926	Display	J. Malben	1952	Blue Man	C. McCreary	1977	Seattle Slew	J. Cruguet
1927	Bostonian	A. Abel	1953	Native Dancer	E. Guerin	1978	Affirmed	S. Cauthen
1928	Victorian	R. Workman	1954	Hasty Road	J. Adams	1979	Spectacular Bid	R. Franklin
1929	Dr. Freeland	L. Schaefer	1955	Nashua	E. Arcaro	1980	Codex	A. Cordero
1930	Gallant Fox	E. Sande	1956	Fabius	W. Hartack	1981	Pleasant Colony	J. Velasquez
1931	Mate	G. Ellis	1957	Bold Ruler	E. Arcaro	1982	Aloma's Ruler	J. Kaenel
1932	Burgoo King	E. James	1958	Tim Tam	I. Valenzuela	1983	Deputed Testamony	D. Miller
1933	Head Play	C. Kurtsinger	1959	Royal Orbit	W. Harmatz	1984	Gate Dancer	A. Cordero
1934	High Quest	R. Jones	1960	Bally Ache	R. Ussery	1985	Tank's Prospect	P. Day
1935	Omaha	W. Saunders	1961	Carry Back	J. Sellers	1986	Snow Chief	A. Solis
1936	Bold Venture	G. Woolf	1962	Greek Money	J.L. Rotz	1987	Alysheba	C. McCarron
1937	War Admiral	C. Kurtsinger	1963	Candy Spots	W. Shoemaker	1988	Risen Star	E. Delahoussaye
1938	Dauber	M. Peters	1964	Northern Dancer	W. Hartack	1989	Sunday Silence	P. Valenzuela
1939	Challedon	G. Seabo	1965	Tom Rolfe	R. Turcotte	1990	Summer Squall	P. Day
1940	Bimelech	F.A. Smith	1966	Kauai King	D. Brumfield	1991	Hansel	J. Bailey
1941	Whirlaway	E. Arcaro	1967	Damascus	W. Shoemaker	1992	Pine Bluff	C. McCarron
1942	Alsab	B. James	1968	Forward Pass	I. Valenzuela	1993	Prairie Bayou	M. Smith
1943	Count Fleet	J. Longden	1969	Majestic Prince	W. Hartack	1994	Tabasco Cat	P. Day
1944	Pensive	C. McCreary	1970	Personality	E. Belmonte	1995	Timber Country	P. Day
1945	Polynesian	W.D. Wright	1971	Canonero II	G. Avila	1996	Louis Quatorze	P. Day
1946	Assault	W. Mehrtens	1972	Bee Bee Bee	E. Nelson	1997	Silver Charm	G. Stevens
1947	Faultless	D. Dodson						

Belmont Stakes

Belmont Park, Elmont, NY; inaugurated 1867; distance 1-1/2 mi. 3-year-olds. Best time: 2:24, Secretariat, 1973.

Year	Winner	Jockey	Year	Winner	Jockey	Year	Winner	Jockey
1867	Ruthless	J. Gilpatrick	1910	Sweep	J. Butwell	1955	Nashua	E. Arcaro
1868	General Duke	R. Swim	1913	Prince Eugene	R. Troxler	1956	Needles	D. Erb
1869	Fenian	C. Miller	1914	Luke McLuke	M. Buxton	1957	Gallant Man	W. Shoemaker
1870	Kingfisher	W. Dick	1915	The Finn	G. Byrne	1958	Cavan	P. Anderson
1871	Harry Bassett	W. Miller	1916	Friar Rock	E. Haynes	1959	Sword Dancer	W. Shoemaker
1872	Joe Daniels	J. Rowe	1917	Hourless	J. Butwell	1960	Celtic Ash	W. Hartack
1873	Springbok	J. Rowe	1918	Johren	F. Robinson	1961	Sherluck	B. Baeza
1874	Saxon	G. Barbee	1919	Sir Barton	J. Loftus	1962	Jaipur	W. Shoemaker
1875	Calvin	R. Swim	1920	Man o' War	C. Kummer	1963	Chateaugay	B. Baeza
1876	Algerine	W. Donohue	1921	Grey Lag	E. Sande	1964	Quadrangle	M. Ycaza
1877	Cloverbrook	C. Holloway	1922	Pillory	C. H. Miller	1965	Hail to All	J. Sellers
1878	Duke of Magenta	L. Hughes	1923	Zev	E. Sande	1966	Amberoid	W. Boland
1879	Spendthrift	S. Evans	1924	Mad Play	E. Sande	1967	Damascus	W. Shoemaker
1880	Grenada	L. Hughes	1925	American Flag	A. Johnson	1968	Stage Door Johnny	H. Gustines
1881	Saunterer	T. Costello	1926	Crusader	A. Johnson	1969	Arts and Letters	B. Baeza
1882	Forester	J. McLaughlin	1927	Chance Shot	E. Sande	1970	High Echelon	J. L. Rotz
1883	George Kinney	J. McLaughlin	1928	Vito	C. Kummer	1971	Pass Catcher	W. Blum
1884	Panique	J. McLaughlin	1929	Blue Larkspur	M. Garner	1972	Riva Ridge	R. Turcotte
1885	Tyrant	P. Duffy	1930	Gallant Fox	E. Sande	1973	Secretariat	R. Turcotte
1886	Inspector B.	J. McLaughlin	1931	Twenty Grand	C. Kurtsinger	1974	Little Current	M. Rivera
1887	Hanover	J. McLaughlin	1932	Faireno	T. Malley	1975	Avatar	W. Shoemaker
1888	Sir Dixon	J. McLaughlin	1933	Hurryoff	M. Garner	1976	Bold Forbes	A. Cordero
1889	Eric	W. Hayward	1934	Peace Chance	W. D. Wright	1977	Seattle Slew	J. Cruguet
1890	Burlington	S. Barnes	1935	Omaha	W. Saunders	1978	Affirmed	S. Cauthen
1891	Foxford	E. Garrison	1936	Granville	J. Stout	1979	Coastal	R. Hernandez
1892	Patron	W. Hayward	1937	War Admiral	C. Kurtsinger	1980	Temperence Hill	E. Maple
1893	Comanche	W. Simms	1938	Pasteurized	J. Stout	1981	Summing	G. Martens
1894	Henry of Navarre	W. Simms	1939	Johnstown	J. Stout	1982	Conquistador Cielo	L. Pincay
1895	Belmar	F. Taral	1940	Bimelech	F. A. Smith	1983	Caveat	L. Pincay
1896	Hastings	H. Griffin	1941	Whirlaway	E. Arcaro	1984	Swale	L. Pincay
1897	Scottish Chieftain	J. Scherrer	1942	Shut Out	E. Arcaro	1985	Creme Fraiche	E. Maple
1898	Bowling Brook	F. Littlefield	1943	Count Fleet	J. Longden	1986	Danzig Connection	C. McCarron
1899	Jean Bereaud	R. R. Clawson	1944	Bounding Home	G. L. Smith	1987	Bet Twice	C. Perret
1900	Ildrim	N. Turner	1945	Pavot	E. Arcaro	1988	Risen Star	E. Delahoussaye
1901	Commando	H. Spencer	1946	Assault	W. Mehrtens	1989	Easy Goer	P. Day
1902	Masterman	J. Bullman	1947	Phalanx	R. Donoso	1990	Go and Go	M. Kinane
1903	Africander	J. Bullman	1948	Citation	E. Arcaro	1991	Hansel	J. Bailey
1904	Delhi	G. Odom	1949	Capot	T. Atkinson	1992	A.P. Indy	E. Delahoussaye
1905	Tanya	E. Hildebrand	1950	Middleground	W. Boland	1993	Colonial Affair	J. Krone
1906	Burgomaster	L. Lyne	1951	Counterpoint	D. Gorman	1994	Tabasco Cat	P. Day
1907	Peter Pan	G. Mountain	1952	One Count	E. Arcaro	1995	Thunder Gulch	G. Stevens
1908	Colin	J. Notter	1953	Native Dancer	E. Guerin	1996	Editor's Note	R. Douglas
1909	Joe Madden	E. Dugan	1954	High Gun	E. Arcaro	1997	Touch Gold	C. McCarron

Annual Leading Jockey—Money Won

Year	Jockey	Dollars	Year	Jockey	Dollars	Year	Jockey	Dollars
1957	Bill Hartack	$3,060,501	1971	Laffit Pincay, Jr.	$3,784,377	1984	Chris McCarron	$12,045,813
1958	Willie Shoemaker	2,961,693	1972	Laffit Pincay, Jr.	3,225,827	1985	Laffit Pincay, Jr.	13,353,299
1959	Willie Shoemaker	2,843,133	1973	Laffit Pincay, Jr.	4,093,492	1986	Jose Santos	11,329,297
1960	Willie Shoemaker	2,123,961	1974	Laffit Pincay, Jr.	4,251,060	1987	Jose Santos	12,375,433
1961	Willie Shoemaker	2,690,819	1975	Braulio Baeza	3,695,198	1988	Jose Santos	14,877,298
1962	Willie Shoemaker	2,916,844	1976	Angel Cordero, Jr.	4,709,500	1989	Jose Santos	13,838,389
1963	Willie Shoemaker	2,526,925	1977	Steve Cauthen	6,151,750	1990	Gary Stevens	13,881,198
1964	Willie Shoemaker	2,649,553	1978	Darrel McHargue	6,029,885	1991	Chris McCarron	14,441,083
1965	Braulio Baeza	2,582,702	1979	Laffit Pincay, Jr.	8,193,535	1992	Kent Desormeaux	14,193,006
1966	Braulio Baeza	2,951,022	1980	Chris McCarron	7,663,300	1993	Mike Smith	14,024,815
1967	Braulio Baeza	3,088,888	1981	Chris McCarron	8,397,604	1994	Mike Smith	15,979,820
1968	Braulio Baeza	2,835,108	1982	Angel Cordero, Jr.	9,483,590	1995	Jerry Bailey	16,311,876
1969	Jorge Velasquez	2,542,315	1983	Angel Cordero, Jr.	10,116,697	1996	Jerry Bailey	19,465,376
1970	Laffit Pincay, Jr.	2,626,526						

Breeders' Cup

The Breeders' Cup was inaugurated in 1984 and consists of 7 races at one track on one day late in the year to determine Thoroughbred racing's champion contenders. It has been held at the following locations:

1984	Hollywood Park, CA	1989	Gulfstream Park, FL	1993	Santa Anita Park, CA
1985	Aqueduct Racetrack, NY	1990	Belmont Park, NY	1994	Churchill Downs, KY
1986	Santa Anita Park, CA	1991	Churchill Downs, KY	1995	Belmont Park, NY
1987	Hollywood Park, CA	1992	Gulfstream Park, FL	1996	Woodbine Racetrack, Ontario
1988	Churchill Downs, KY				

Juvenile
Distances: 1 mi 1984-85, 1987; 1-1/16 mi 1986 and since 1988

Year		Jockey	Year		Jockey	Year		Jockey
1984	Chief's Crown	D. MacBeth	1989	Rhythm	C. Perret	1993	Brocco	G. Stevens
1985	Tasso	L. Pincay, Jr.	1990	Fly So Free	J. Santos	1994	Timber Country	P. Day
1986	Capote	L. Pincay, Jr.	1991	Arazi	P. Valenzuela	1995	Unbridled's Song	M. Smith
1987	Success Express	J. Santos	1992	Gilded Time	C. McCarron	1996	Boston Harbor	J. Bailey
1988	Is It True	L. Pincay, Jr.						

Juvenile Fillies
Distances: 1 mi 1984-85, 1987; 1-1/16 mi 1986 and since 1988

Year		Jockey	Year		Jockey	Year		Jockey
1984	*Outstandingly	W. Guerra	1989	Go for Wand	R. Romero	1993	Phone Chatter	L. Pincay, Jr.
1985	Twilight Ridge	J. Velasquez	1990	Meadow Star	J. Santos	1994	Flanders	P. Day
1986	Brave Raj	P. Valenzuela	1991	Pleasant Stage	E. Delahoussaye	1995	My Flag	J. Bailey
1987	Epitome	P. Day	1992	Eliza	P. Valenzuela	1996	Storm Song	C. Perret
1988	Open Mind	A. Cordero, Jr.						

*By disqualification.

Sprint
Distance: 6 furlongs

Year		Jockey	Year		Jockey	Year		Jockey
1984	Eillo	C. Perret	1989	Dancing Spree	A. Cordero, Jr.	1993	Cardmania	E. Delahoussaye
1985	Precisionist	C. McCarron	1990	Safely Kept	C. Perret	1994	Cherokee Run	M. Smith
1986	Smile	J. Vasquez	1991	Sheikh Albadou	P. Eddery	1995	Desert Stormer	K. Desormeaux
1987	Very Subtle	P. Valenzuela	1992	Thirty Slews	E. Delahoussaye	1996	Lit De Justice	C. Nakatani
1988	Gulch	A. Cordero, Jr.						

Mile

Year		Jockey	Year		Jockey	Year		Jockey
1984	Royal Heroine	F. Toro	1989	Steinlen	J. Santos	1993	Lure	M. Smith
1985	Cozzene	W. Guerra	1990	Royal Academy	L. Piggott	1994	Barathea	L. Dettori
1986	Last Tycoon	Y. St.-Martin	1991	Opening Verse	P. Valenzuela	1995	Ridgewood Pearl	J. Murtagh
1987	Miesque	F. Head	1992	Lure	M. Smith	1996	Da Hoss	G. Stevens
1988	Miesque	F. Head						

Distaff
Distances: 1-1/4 mi 1984-87; 1-1/8 mi since 1988

Year		Jockey	Year		Jockey	Year		Jockey
1984	Princess Rooney	E. Delahoussaye	1988	Personal Ensign	R. Romero	1993	Hollywood Wildcat	E. Delahoussaye
1985	Life's Magic	A. Cordero, Jr.	1989	Bayakoa	L. Pincay, Jr.	1994	One Dreamer	G. Stevens
1986	Lady's Secret	P. Day	1990	Bayakoa	L. Pincay, Jr.	1995	Inside Information	M. Smith
1987	Sacahuista	R. Romero	1991	Dance Smartly	P. Day			
			1992	Paseana	C. McCarron	1996	Jewel Princess	C. Nakatani

Turf
Distance: 1-1/2 mi

Year		Jockey	Year		Jockey	Year		Jockey
1984	Lashkari	Y. St.-Martin	1988	Great Communicator	R. Sibille	1992	Fraise	P. Valenzuela
1985	Pebbles	P. Eddery	1989	Prized	E. Delahoussaye	1993	Kotashaan	K. Desormeaux
1986	Manila	J. Santos	1990	In The Wings	G. Stevens	1994	Tikkanen	M. Smith
1987	Theatrical	P. Day	1991	Miss Alleged	E. Legrix	1995	Northern Spur	C. McCarron
						1996	Pilsudski	W. Swinburn

Classic
Distance: 1-1/4 mi

Year		Jockey	Year		Jockey	Year		Jockey
1984	Wild Again	P. Day	1989	Sunday Silence	C. McCarron	1992	A.P. Indy	E. Delahoussaye
1985	Proud Truth	J. Velasquez	1990	Unbridled	P. Day	1993	Arcangues	J. Bailey
1986	Skywalker	L. Pincay, Jr.	1991	Black Tie Affair	J. Bailey	1994	Concern	J. Bailey
1987	Ferdinand	W. Shoemaker				1995	Cigar	J. Bailey
1988	Alysheba	C. McCarron				1996	Alphabet Soup	C. McCarron

Eclipse Awards

The Eclipse Awards, honoring the Horse of the Year and other champions of the sport, began in 1971 and are sponsored by the *Daily Racing Form*, the Thoroughbred Racing Associations, and the National Turf Writers Assn. Prior to 1971, the DRF (1936-70) and the TRA (1950-70) issued separate selections for horse of the year.

Eclipse Awards for 1996

Horse of the Year—Cigar
2-year-old colt or gelding—Boston Harbor
2-year-old filly—Storm Song
3-year-old colt or gelding—Skip Away
3-year-old filly—Yanks Music
Older male (4-year-olds & up)—Cigar
Older female (4-year-olds & up)—Jewel Princess
Male turf horse—Singspiel

Turf filly or mare—Wandesta
Sprinter—Lit De Justice
Steeplechase horse—Correggio
Trainer—William I. Mott
Jockey—Jerry Bailey
Apprentice jockey—Neil Poznansky
Breeder—Farnsworth Farms
Owner—Allen Paulson

Horse of the Year

Year	Horse	Year	Horse	Year	Horse	Year	Horse
1936	Granville	1952	One Count (DRF)	1966	Buckpasser	1981	John Henry
1937	War Admiral		Native Dancer (TRA)	1967	Damascus	1982	Conquistador Cielo
1938	Seabiscuit	1953	Tom Fool	1968	Dr. Fager	1983	All Along
1939	Challedon	1954	Native Dancer	1969	Arts and Letters	1984	John Henry
1940	Challedon	1955	Nashua	1970	Fort Marcy (DRF)	1985	Spend A Buck
1941	Whirlaway	1956	Swaps		Personality (TRA)	1986	Lady's Secret
1942	Whirlaway	1957	Bold Ruler (DRF)	1971	Ack Ack	1987	Ferdinand
1943	Count Fleet		Dedicate (TRA)	1972	Secretariat	1988	Alysheba
1944	Twilight Tear	1958	Round Table	1973	Secretariat	1989	Sunday Silence
1945	Busher	1959	Sword Dancer	1974	Forego	1990	Criminal Type
1946	Assault	1960	Kelso	1975	Forego	1991	Black Tie Affair
1947	Armed	1961	Kelso	1976	Forego	1992	A.P. Indy
1948	Citation	1962	Kelso	1977	Seattle Slew	1993	Kotashaan
1949	Capot	1963	Kelso	1978	Affirmed	1994	Holy Bull
1950	Hill Prince	1964	Kelso	1979	Affirmed	1995	Cigar
1951	Counterpoint	1965	Roman Brother (DRF)	1980	Spectacular Bid	1996	Cigar
			Moccasin (TRA)				

HARNESS RACING
Harness Horse of the Year
(Chosen by the U.S. Trotting Assn. and the U.S. Harness Writers Assn.)

Year	Horse	Year	Horse	Year	Horse	Year	Horse
1947	Victory Song	1960	Adios Butler	1973	Sir Dalrae	1985	Nihilator
1948	Rodney	1961	Adios Butler	1974	Delmonica Hanover	1986	Forrest Skipper
1949	Good Time	1962	Su Mac Lad	1975	Savoir	1987	Mack Lobell
1950	Proximity	1963	Speedy Scot	1976	Keystone Ore	1988	Mack Lobell
1951	Pronto Don	1964	Bret Hanover	1977	Green Speed	1989	Matt's Scooter
1952	Good Time	1965	Bret Hanover	1978	Abercrombie	1990	Beach Towel
1953	Hi Lo's Forbes	1966	Bret Hanover	1979	Niatross	1991	Precious Bunny
1954	Stenographer	1967	Nevele Pride	1980	Niatross	1992	Artsplace
1955	Scott Frost	1968	Nevele Pride	1981	Fan Hanover	1993	Staying Together
1956	Scott Frost	1969	Nevele Pride	1982	Cam Fella	1994	Cam's Card Shark
1957	Torpid	1970	Fresh Yankee	1983	Cam Fella	1995	CR Kay Suzie
1958	Emily's Pride	1971	Albatross	1984	Fancy Crown	1996	Continentalvictory
1959	Bye Bye Byrd	1972	Albatross				

The Hambletonian (3-year-old trotters)

Year	Winner	Driver	Year	Winner	Driver
1965	Egyptian Candor	Del Cameron	1982	Speed Bowl	Tommy Haughton
1966	Kerry Way	Frank Ervin	1983	Duenna	Stanley Dancer
1967	Speedy Streak	Del Cameron	1984	Historic Freight	Ben Webster
1968	Nevele Pride	Stanley Dancer	1985	Prakas	Bill O'Donnell
1969	Lindy's Pride	Howard Beissinger	1986	Nuclear Kosmos	Ulf Thoresen
1970	Timothy T	John Simpson, Sr.	1987	Mack Lobell	John Campbell
1971	Speedy Crown	Howard Beissinger	1988	Armbro Goal	John Campbell
1972	Super Bowl	Stanley Dancer	1989	Park Avenue Joe	Ron Waples
1973	Flirth	Ralph Baldwin	1990	Harmonious	John Campbell
1974	Christopher T	Bill Haughton	1991	Giant Victory	Jack Moiseyev
1975	Bonefish	Stanley Dancer	1992	Alf Palema	Mickey McNicholl
1976	Steve Lobell	Bill Haughton	1993	American Winner	Ron Pierce
1977	Green Speed	Bill Haughton	1994	Victory Dream	Michel Lachance
1978	Speedy Somolli	Howard Beissinger	1995	Tagliabue	John Campbell
1979	Legend Hanover	George Sholty	1996	Continentalvictory	Michel Lachance
1980	Burgomeister	Bill Haughton	1997	Malabar Man	Malvern Burroughs
1981	Shiaway St. Pat	Ray Remmen			

BOWLING
Professional Bowlers Association
Hall of Fame

Performance				
Bill Allen	Mike Durbin	Mike McGrath	Brian Voss	E. A. "Bud" Fisher
Glenn Allison	Buzz Fazio	Amleto Monacelli	Wayne Webb	Lou Frantz
Earl Anthony	Dave Ferraro	David Ozio	Dick Weber	Harry Golden
Barry Asher	Skee Foremsky	George Pappas	Billy Welu	Ted Hoffman, Jr.
Mike Aulby	Jim Godman	Johnny Petraglia	Walter Ray Williams, Jr.	John Jowdy
Ray Bluth	Johnny Guenther	Dick Ritger	Wayne Zahn	Joe Kelley
Roy Buckley	Billy Hardwick	Mark Roth	**Meritorious service**	Larry Lichstein
Nelson Burton, Jr.	Tommy Hudson	Jim St. John	Joe Antenora	Steve Nagy
Don Carter	Dave Husted	Carmen Salvino	John Archibald	Chuck Pezzano
Pat Colwell	Don Johnson	Ernie Schlegel	Chuck Clemens	Jack Reichert
Steve Cook	Joe Joseph	Bob Strampe	Eddie Elias	Joe Richards
Dave Davis	Larry Laub	Harry Smith	Frank Esposito	Chris Schenkel
Gary Dickinson	Mike Limongello	Dave Soutar	Dick Evans	Lorraine Stilzlein
	Don McCune	Jim Stefanich	Raymond Firestone	Al Thompson
				Roger Zeller

Tournament of Champions

Year	Winner	Year	Winner	Year	Winner	Year	Winner
1965	Billy Hardwick	1974	Earl Anthony	1982	Mike Durbin	1990	Dave Ferraro
1966	Wayne Zahn	1975	Dave Davis	1983	Joe Berardi	1991	David Ozio
1967	Jim Stefanich	1976	Marshall Holman	1984	Mike Durbin	1992	Marc McDowell
1968	Dave Davis	1977	Mike Berlin	1985	Mark Williams	1993	George Branham, 3d
1969	Jim Godman	1978	Earl Anthony	1986	Marshall Holman	1994	Norm Duke
1970	Don Johnson	1979	George Pappas	1987	Pete Weber	1995	Mike Aulby
1971	Johnny Petraglia	1980	Wayne Webb	1988	Mark Williams	1996	Dave D'Entremont
1972	Mike Durbin	1981	Steve Cook	1989	Del Ballard, Jr.	1997	John Gant
1973	Jim Godman						

PBA Leading Money Winners

Total winnings are from PBA, ABC Masters, and BPAA All-Star tournaments only and do not include numerous other tournaments or earnings from special television shows and matches.

Year	Bowler	Amount	Year	Bowler	Amount	Year	Bowler	Amount
1962	Don Carter	$49,972	1975	Earl Anthony	$107,585	1987	Pete Weber	$175,491
1963	Dick Weber	46,333	1976	Earl Anthony	110,833	1988	Brian Voss	225,485
1964	Bob Strampe	33,592	1977	Mark Roth	105,583	1989	Mike Aulby	298,237
1965	Dick Weber	47,674	1978	Mark Roth	134,500	1990	Amleto Monacelli	204,775
1966	Wayne Zahn	54,720	1979	Mark Roth	124,517	1991	David Ozio	225,585
1967	Dave Davis	54,165	1980	Wayne Webb	116,700	1992	Marc McDowell	174,215
1968	Jim Stefanich	67,377	1981	Earl Anthony	164,735	1993	Walter Ray Williams, Jr.	296,370
1969	Billy Hardwick	64,160	1982	Earl Anthony	134,760			
1970	Mike McGrath	52,049	1983	Earl Anthony	135,605	1994	Norm Duke	273,753
1971	Johnny Petraglia	85,065	1984	Mark Roth	158,712	1995	Mike Aulby	219,792
1972	Don Johnson	56,648	1985	Mike Aulby	201,200	1996	Walter Ray Williams, Jr.	241,330
1973	Don McCune	69,000	1986	Walter Ray Williams, Jr.	145,550			
1974	Earl Anthony	99,585						

Leading PBA Averages by Year

Year	Bowler	Average	Year	Bowler	Average	Year	Bowler	Average
1962	Don Carter	212.844	1975	Earl Anthony	219.060	1987	Marshall Holman	216.801
1963	Billy Hardwick	210.346	1976	Mark Roth	215.970	1988	Mark Roth	218.036
1964	Ray Bluth	210.512	1977	Mark Roth	218.174	1989	Pete Weber	215.432
1965	Dick Weber	211.895	1978	Mark Roth	219.834	1990	Amleto Monacelli	218.158
1966	Wayne Zahn	208.663	1979	Mark Roth	221.662	1991	Norm Duke	218.208
1967	Wayne Zahn	212.342	1980	Earl Anthony	218.535	1992	Dave Ferraro	219.702
1968	Jim Stefanich	211.895	1981	Mark Roth	216.699	1993	Walter Ray Williams, Jr.	222.980
1969	Bill Hardwick	212.957	1982	Marshall Holman	212.844			
1970	Nelson Burton, Jr.	214.908	1983	Earl Anthony	216.645	1994	Norm Duke	222.830
1971	Don Johnson	213.977	1984	Marshall Holman	213.911	1995	Mike Aulby	225.490
1972	Don Johnson	215.290	1985	Mark Baker	213.718	1996	Walter Ray Williams, Jr.	225.370
1973	Earl Anthony	215.799	1986	John Gant	214.378			
1974	Earl Anthony	219.394						

American Bowling Congress

ABC Masters Tournament Champions

Year	Winner	Year	Winner	Year	Winner
1980	Neil Burton, St. Louis, MO	1986	Mark Fahy, Chicago, IL	1992	Ken Johnson, N. Richmond Hills, TX
1981	Randy Lightfoot, St. Charles, MO	1987	Rick Steelsmith, Wichita, KS		
1982	Joe Berardi, Brooklyn, NY	1988	Del Ballard, Jr., Richardson, TX	1993	Norm Duke, Oklahoma City, OK
1983	Mike Lastowski, Havre de Grace, MD	1989	Mike Aulby, Indianapolis, IN	1994	Steve Fehr, Cincinnati, OH
		1990	Chris Warren, Dallas, TX	1995	Mike Aulby, Indianapolis, IN
1984	Earl Anthony, Dublin, CA	1991	Doug Kent, Canandaigua, NY	1996	Ernie Schlegel, Vancouver, WA
1985	Steve Wunderlich, St. Louis, MO			1997	Jason Queen, Decatur, IL

Champions in 1997

Singles Event—John Socha, New Berlin, WI
Doubles Event—Rob Stueber and Paul Zuehkle, Oshkosh, WI
All Events—Jeff Richgels, Oregon, WI

Regular Team—Dan Ottman Enterprises, Troy, MI
Booster Team—Pinsetter Lanes No. 1., West Point, MS

Most Sanctioned 300 Games

Bob Learn, Jr., Erie, PA 54	Jason Hurd, Tulare, CA 34	Mitch Jabczenski, Detroit, MI 27
Mike Whalin, Cincinnati, OH 52	Keith Bruening, St. Charles, MO. . . 33	Steve Levering, Landisville, PA . . . 27
Jim Johnson, Jr., Wilmington, DE. . 52	Ron Woolet, Louisville, KY 33	Elvin Mesger, Sullivan, MO 27
Joe Jimenez, Saginaw, MI 48	John Chako, Jr., Larksville, PA. . . . 32	Mark Stibora, Cleveland, OH 27
Robert Faragon, Albany, NY 43	John Delp III, West Lawn, PA. 32	Anthony Juliano, Margate, FL. 26
Jerry Kessler, Dayton, OH 41	Steve Gehringer, Reading, PA 32	Jerome Penxa, Detroit, MI 26
Ralph Burley, Jr., Dayton, OH 41	Doug Spicer, W. Bloomfield, MI . . . 32	Dave Soutar, Kansas City, MO. . . . 25
Bob Buckery, McAdoo, PA. 41	Woody Crist, Williamsport, PA 31	Gary Barney, St. Louis, MO 25
Jeff Jensen, Wichita, KS 40	Alan Hulsizer, Reading, PA 31	Kevin Lickers, Wilkes-Barre, PA . . . 25
Ken Hall, Schenectady, NY 37	Randy Choat, Granite City, IL. 30	Brian Burgess, Fond du Lac, WI. . . 24
Bob Johnson, Dayton, OH 36	Richard (Skip) Vigars. 30	Paul Cannon, Binghamton, NY. . . . 24
John Wilcox, Jr., Shavertown, PA. . 36	Ron Bohnert, Cincinnati, OH 28	Paul Masminster, Cincinnati, OH . . 24
Eric Roddy, New Orleans, LA. 35	Tim Zelger, Red Lion, PA. 28	Tony Torrice, Wolcott, CT 24
Jim Ewald, Jr., Louisville, KY 34		

Women's International Bowling Congress

Champions in 1997

Queens Tournament—Sandra Jo Odom, Coldwater, MI
Singles Event—Jan Schmidt, Rochelle, IL
All Events—Kendra Cameron, Gambrills, MD

Doubles Event—Jennifer Klekamp, Cleves, OH, and Regina Snodgrass, Versailles, IN
Team—(tie) Here 4 Beer II, Glendale, AZ, and Contour Power Grips, Vallejo, CA

Most Sanctioned 300 Games

Tish Johnson, Panorama City, CA	27	Leanne Barrette, Youkon, OK . . . 19	Betty Morris, Stockton, CA 12
Vicki Fischel, Wheat Ridge, CO . .	21	Aleta Sill, Dearborn, MI 18	Donna Adamek, Apple Valley, CA	11
Jeanne Maiden-Naccarato, Tacoma, WA.	21	Cheryl Daniels, Detroit, MI 15	Robin Romeo, Van Nuys, CA. . . .	9
		Cindy Coburn-Carroll, Tonawanda, NY 14	

FIGURE SKATING

U.S. Champions | World Champions

Men	Women	Year	Men	Women
Dick Button	Tenley Albright	1952	Dick Button, U.S.	Jacqueline du Bief, France
Hayes Jenkins	Tenley Albright	1953	Hayes Jenkins, U.S.	Tenley Albright, U.S.
Hayes Jenkins	Tenley Albright	1954	Hayes Jenkins, U.S.	Gundi Busch, W. Germany
Hayes Jenkins	Tenley Albright	1955	Hayes Jenkins, U.S.	Tenley Albright, U.S.
Hayes Jenkins	Tenley Albright	1956	Hayes Jenkins, U.S.	Carol Heiss, U.S.
Dave Jenkins	Carol Heiss	1957	Dave Jenkins, U.S.	Carol Heiss, U.S.
Dave Jenkins	Carol Heiss	1958	Dave Jenkins, U.S.	Carol Heiss, U.S.
Dave Jenkins	Carol Heiss	1959	Dave Jenkins, U.S.	Carol Heiss, U.S.
Dave Jenkins	Carol Heiss	1960	Alain Giletti, France	Carol Heiss, U.S.
Bradley Lord	Laurence Owen	1961	none	none
Monty Hoyt	Barbara Roles Pursley	1962	Don Jackson, Canada	Sjoukje Dijkstra, Netherlands
Tommy Litz	Lorraine Hanlon	1963	Don McPherson, Canada	Sjoukje Dijkstra, Netherlands
Scott Allen	Peggy Fleming	1964	Manfred Schnelldorfer, W. Germany	Sjoukje Dijkstra, Netherlands
Gary Visconti	Peggy Fleming	1965	Alain Calmat, France	Petra Burka, Canada
Scott Allen	Peggy Fleming	1966	Emmerich Danzer, Austria	Peggy Fleming, U.S.
Gary Visconti	Peggy Fleming	1967	Emmerich Danzer, Austria	Peggy Fleming, U.S.
Tim Wood	Peggy Fleming	1968	Emmerich Danzer, Austria	Peggy Fleming, U.S.
Tim Wood	Janet Lynn	1969	Tim Wood, U.S.	Gabriele Seyfert, E. Germany
Tim Wood	Janet Lynn	1970	Tim Wood, U.S.	Gabriele Seyfert, E. Germany
John Misha Petkevich	Janet Lynn	1971	Ondrej Nepela, Czechoslovakia	Beatrix Schuba, Austria
Ken Shelley	Janet Lynn	1972	Ondrej Nepela, Czechoslovakia	Beatrix Schuba, Austria
Gordon McKellen, Jr.	Janet Lynn	1973	Ondrej Nepela, Czechoslovakia	Karen Magnussen, Canada
Gordon McKellen, Jr.	Dorothy Hamill	1974	Jan Hoffmann, E. Germany	Christine Errath, E. Germany
Gordon McKellen, Jr.	Dorothy Hamill	1975	Sergei Volkov, USSR	Dianne de Leeuw, Neth.-U.S.
Terry Kubicka	Dorothy Hamill	1976	John Curry, Gr. Britain	Dorothy Hamill, U.S.
Charles Tickner	Linda Fratianne	1977	Vladimir Kovalev, USSR	Linda Fratianne, U.S.
Charles Tickner	Linda Fratianne	1978	Charles Tickner, U.S.	Anett Poetzsch, E. Germany
Charles Tickner	Linda Fratianne	1979	Vladimir Kovalev, USSR	Linda Fratianne, U.S.
Charles Tickner	Linda Fratianne	1980	Jan Hoffmann, E. Germany	Anett Poetzsch, E. Germany
Scott Hamilton	Elaine Zayak	1981	Scott Hamilton, U.S.	Denise Biellmann, Switzerland
Scott Hamilton	Rosalynn Sumners	1982	Scott Hamilton, U.S.	Elaine Zayak, U.S.
Scott Hamilton	Rosalynn Sumners	1983	Scott Hamilton, U.S.	Rosalynn Sumners, U.S.
Scott Hamilton	Rosalynn Sumners	1984	Scott Hamilton, U.S.	Katarina Witt, E. Germany
Brian Boitano	Tiffany Chin	1985	Aleksandr Fadeev, USSR	Katarina Witt, E. Germany
Brian Boitano	Debi Thomas	1986	Brian Boitano, U.S.	Debi Thomas, U.S.
Brian Boitano	Jill Trenary	1987	Brian Orser, Canada	Katarina Witt, E. Germany
Brian Boitano	Debi Thomas	1988	Brian Boitano, U.S.	Katarina Witt, E. Germany
Christopher Bowman	Jill Trenary	1989	Kurt Browning, Canada	Midori Ito, Japan
Todd Eldredge	Jill Trenary	1990	Kurt Browning, Canada	Jill Trenary, U.S.
Todd Eldredge	Tonya Harding	1991	Kurt Browning, Canada	Kristi Yamaguchi, U.S.
Christopher Bowman	Kristi Yamaguchi	1992	Viktor Petrenko, Ukraine	Kristi Yamaguchi, U.S.
Scott Davis	Nancy Kerrigan	1993	Kurt Browning, Canada	Oksana Baiul, Ukraine
Scott Davis	vacant[1]	1994	Elvis Stojko, Canada	Yuka Sato, Japan
Todd Eldredge	Nicole Bobek	1995	Elvis Stojko, Canada	Chen Lu, China
Rudy Galindo	Michelle Kwan	1996	Todd Eldredge, U.S.	Michelle Kwan, U.S.
Todd Eldredge	Tara Lipinski	1997	Elvis Stojko, Canada	Tara Lipinski, U.S.

(1) Tonya Harding was stripped of title.

JAMES E. SULLIVAN MEMORIAL TROPHY WINNERS

The James E. Sullivan Memorial Trophy, named after the former president of the AAU and inaugurated in 1930, is awarded annually by the AAU to the athlete who "by his or her performance, example and influence as an amateur, has done the most during the year to advance the cause of sportsmanship."

Year	Winner	Sport	Year	Winner	Sport	Year	Winner	Sport
1930	Bobby Jones	Golf	1954	Mal Whitfield	Track	1978	Tracy Caulkins	Swimming
1931	Barney Berlinger	Track	1955	Harrison Dillard	Track	1979	Kurt Thomas	Gymnastics
1932	Jim Bausch	Track	1956	Patricia McCormick	Diving	1980	Eric Heiden	Speed Skating
1933	Glenn Cunningham	Track	1957	Bobby Joe Morrow	Track			
1934	Bill Bonthron	Track	1958	Glenn Davis	Track	1981	Carl Lewis	Track
1935	Lawson Little	Golf	1959	Parry O'Brien	Track	1982	Mary Decker	Track
1936	Glenn Morris	Track	1960	Rafer Johnson	Track	1983	Edwin Moses	Track
1937	Don Budge	Tennis	1961	Wilma Rudolph Ward	Track	1984	Greg Louganis	Diving
1938	Don Lash	Track				1985	Joan Benoit Samuelson	Marathon
1939	Joe Burk	Rowing	1962	James Beatty	Track	1986	Jackie Joyner-Kersee	Track
1940	Greg Rice	Track	1963	John Pennel	Track			
1941	Leslie MacMitchell	Track	1964	Don Schollander	Swimming	1987	Jim Abbott	Baseball
1942	Cornelius Warmerdam	Track	1965	Bill Bradley	Basketball	1988	Florence Griffith Joyner	Track
1943	Gilbert Dodds	Track	1966	Jim Ryun	Track			
1944	Ann Curtis	Swimming	1967	Randy Matson	Track	1989	Janet Evans	Swimming
1945	Doc Blanchard	Football	1968	Debbie Meyer	Swimming	1990	John Smith	Wrestling
1946	Arnold Tucker	Football	1969	Bill Toomey	Track	1991	Mike Powell	Track
1947	John Kelly, Jr.	Rowing	1970	John Kinsella	Swimming	1992	Bonnie Blair	Speed Skating
1948	Robert Mathias	Track	1971	Mark Spitz	Swimming			
1949	Dick Button	Skating	1972	Frank Shorter	Track	1993	Charlie Ward	Football, Basketball
1950	Fred Wilt	Track	1973	Bill Walton	Basketball			
1951	Rev. Robert Richards	Track	1974	Rick Wohlhutter	Track	1994	Dan Jansen	Speed Skating
			1975	Tim Shaw	Swimming			
1952	Horace Ashenfelter	Track	1976	Bruce Jenner	Track	1995	Bruce Baumgartner	Wrestling
1953	Dr. Sammy Lee	Diving	1977	John Naber	Swimming	1996	Michael Johnson	Track

DIRECTORY OF SPORTS ORGANIZATIONS
Major League Baseball
Internet Site: http://www.majorleaguebaseball.com
Note: Teams and leagues as of 1997 season. *Expansion team; begins play in 1998 season.

Commissioner's Office
350 Park Ave.
New York, NY 10022

National League
National League Office
350 Park Ave.
New York, NY 10022

Arizona Diamondbacks*
PO Box 2095
Phoenix, AZ 85001

Atlanta Braves
PO Box 4064
Atlanta, GA 30302

Chicago Cubs
1060 W. Addison St.
Chicago, IL 60613

Cincinnati Reds
100 Cinergy Ave.
Cincinnati, OH 45202

Colorado Rockies
2001 Blake St.
Denver, CO 80205

Florida Marlins
2267 NW 199th St.
Miami, FL 33056

Houston Astros
PO Box 288
Houston, TX 77001

Los Angeles Dodgers
1000 Elysian Park Ave.
Los Angeles, CA 90012

Montreal Expos
PO Box 500, Station M
Montreal, Que. H1V 3P2

New York Mets
123-01 Roosevelt Ave.
Flushing, NY 11368

Philadelphia Phillies
PO Box 7575
Philadelphia, PA 19101

Pittsburgh Pirates
PO Box 7000
Pittsburgh, PA 15212

St. Louis Cardinals
250 Stadium Plaza
St. Louis, MO 63102

San Diego Padres
PO Box 2000
San Diego, CA 92112

San Francisco Giants
3Com Park
San Francisco, CA 94124

American League
American League Office
350 Park Ave.
New York, NY 10022

Anaheim Angels
PO Box 2000
Anaheim, CA 92803

Baltimore Orioles
333 W. Camden St.
Baltimore, MD 21201

Boston Red Sox
4 Yawkey Way
Boston, MA 02215

Chicago White Sox
333 W. 35th St.
Chicago, IL 60616

Cleveland Indians
2401 Ontario St.
Cleveland, OH 44115

Detroit Tigers
Tiger Stadium
Detroit, MI 48216

Kansas City Royals
P.O. Box 419969
Kansas City, MO 64141

Milwaukee Brewers
P.O. Box 3099
Milwaukee, WI 53201

Minnesota Twins
501 Chicago Ave. South
Minneapolis, MN 55415

New York Yankees
Yankee Stadium
Bronx, NY 10451

Oakland Athletics
7677 Oakport, Ste. 200
Oakland, CA 94621

Seattle Mariners
PO Box 4100
Seattle, WA 98104

Tampa Bay Devil Rays*
One Stadium Dr.
St. Petersburg, FL 33705

Texas Rangers
PO Box 90111
Arlington, TX 76011

Toronto Blue Jays
1 Blue Jays Way, Ste. 3200
Toronto, Ont. M5V 1J1

National Basketball Association
Internet Site: http://www.nba.com

League Office
645 5th Ave.
New York, NY 10022

Atlanta Hawks
One CNN Center, Ste. 405
Atlanta, GA 30303

Boston Celtics
151 Merrimac St.
Boston, MA 02114

Charlotte Hornets
100 Hive Dr.
Charlotte, NC 28217

Chicago Bulls
1901 W. Madison St.
Chicago, IL 60612

Cleveland Cavaliers
1 Center Court
Cleveland, OH 44115

Dallas Mavericks
777 Sports St.
Dallas, TX 75207

Denver Nuggets
1635 Clay St.
Denver, CO 80204

Detroit Pistons
Two Championship Dr.
Auburn Hills, MI 48326

Golden State Warriors
1011 Broadway
Oakland, CA 94607

Houston Rockets
Two Greenway Plaza, Ste. 400
Houston, TX 77046

Indiana Pacers
300 E. Market St.
Indianapolis, IN 46204

Los Angeles Clippers
3939 S. Figueroa St.
Los Angeles, CA 90037

Los Angeles Lakers
3900 W. Manchester Blvd.
Inglewood, CA 90306

Miami Heat
One SE 3d Ave., Ste. 2300
Miami, FL 33131

Milwaukee Bucks
1001 N. 4th St.
Milwaukee, WI 53203

Minnesota Timberwolves
600 1st Ave. North
Minneapolis, MN 55403

New Jersey Nets
405 Murray Hill Parkway
E. Rutherford, NJ 07073

New York Knickerbockers
Two Pennsylvania Plaza
New York, NY 10121

Orlando Magic
One Magic Place
Orlando, FL 32801

Philadelphia 76ers
1 CoreStates Complex
Philadelphia, PA 19148

Phoenix Suns
201 E. Jefferson
Phoenix, AZ 85004

Portland Trail Blazers
One Center Ct., Ste. 200
Portland, OR 97227

Sacramento Kings
One Sports Parkway
Sacramento, CA 95834

San Antonio Spurs
100 Montana St.
San Antonio, TX 78203

Seattle SuperSonics
190 Queen Anne Ave. N
Seattle, WA 98109

Toronto Raptors
20 Bay St., Ste. 1702
Toronto, Ont. M5J 2N8

Utah Jazz
301 W. South Temple
Salt Lake City, UT 84101

Vancouver Grizzlies
800 Griffiths Way
Vancouver, B.C. V6B 6G1

Washington Wizards
US Airways Arena
Landover, MD 20785

National Hockey League
Internet Site: http://www.nhl.com

League Headquarters
1251 Ave. of the Americas
New York, NY 10020-1198

Mighty Ducks of Anaheim
2695 E. Katella Ave.
Anaheim, CA 92803

Boston Bruins
One FleetCenter, Ste. 250
Boston, MA 02114

Buffalo Sabres
One Seymour H. Knox III Plaza
Buffalo, NY 14203

Calgary Flames
PO Box 1540, Station M
Calgary, Alta. T2P 3B9

Carolina Hurricanes
5000 Aerial Ctr., Ste. 100
Morrisville, NC 27560

Chicago Blackhawks
1901 W. Madison St.
Chicago, IL 60612

Colorado Avalanche
1635 Clay St.
Denver, CO 80204

Dallas Stars
211 Cowboys Parkway
Irving, TX 75063

Detroit Red Wings
600 Civic Center Dr.
Detroit, MI 48226

Edmonton Oilers
Edmonton Coliseum
Edmonton, Alta. T5B 4M9

Florida Panthers
100 NE Third Ave.
Fort Lauderdale, FL 33301

Los Angeles Kings
3900 W. Manchester Blvd.
Inglewood, CA 90305

Montreal Canadiens
1260 rue de La Gauchetiere, Ouest
Montreal, Que. H3B 5E8

New Jersey Devils
PO Box 504
E. Rutherford, NJ 07073

(continued)

National Hockey League (*continued*)

New York Islanders
Nassau Veterans Memorial
  Coliseum
Uniondale, NY 11553

New York Rangers
2 Pennsylvania Plaza
New York, NY 10121

Ottawa Senators
1000 Palladium Dr.
Kanata, Ont. K2V 1A5

Philadelphia Flyers
CoreStates Center
Philadelphia, PA 19148

Phoenix Coyotes
2 N. Central, Ste. 1930
Phoenix, AZ 85004

Pittsburgh Penguins
66 Mario Lemieux Place
Pittsburgh, PA 15219

St. Louis Blues
1401 Clark Ave.
St. Louis, MO 63103

San Jose Sharks
525 W. Santa Clara St.
San Jose, CA 95113

Tampa Bay Lightning
401 Channels Dr.
Tampa, FL 33602

Toronto Maple Leafs
60 Carlton St.
Toronto, Ont. M5B 1L1

Vancouver Canucks
800 Griffiths Way
Vancouver, B.C. V6B 6G1

Washington Capitals
1 Harry S Truman Dr.
Landover, MD 20785

National Football League

Internet Site: http://www.nfl.com

League Office
280 Park Avenue
New York, NY 10017

Arizona Cardinals
PO Box 888
Phoenix, AZ 85001

Atlanta Falcons
One Falcon Place
Suwanee, GA 30174

Baltimore Ravens
11001 Owings Mills Blvd.
Owings Mills, MD 21117

Buffalo Bills
One Bills Drive
Orchard Park, NY 14127

Carolina Panthers
800 S. Mint St.
Charlotte, NC 28202

Chicago Bears
1000 Football Dr.
Lake Forest, IL 60045

Cincinnati Bengals
One Bengals Dr.
Cincinnati, OH 45204

Dallas Cowboys
One Cowboys Parkway
Irving, TX 75063

Denver Broncos
13655 Broncos Parkway
Englewood, CO 80112

Detroit Lions
1200 Featherstone Rd.
Pontiac, MI 48342

Green Bay Packers
1265 Lombardi Ave.
Green Bay, WI 54304

Indianapolis Colts
PO Box 535000
Indianapolis, IN 46253

Jacksonville Jaguars
One ALLTELL Stadium Place
Jacksonville, FL 32202

Kansas City Chiefs
One Arrowhead Drive
Kansas City, MO 64129

Miami Dolphins
7500 SW 30th St.
Davie, FL 33314

Minnesota Vikings
9520 Viking Dr.
Eden Prairie, MN 55344

New England Patriots
60 Washington St.
Foxboro, MA 02035

New Orleans Saints
5800 Airline Highway
Metairie, LA 70003

New York Giants
Giants Stadium
E. Rutherford, NJ 07073

New York Jets
1000 Fulton Ave.
Hempstead, NY 11550

Oakland Raiders
1220 Harbor Bay Parkway
Alameda, CA 94502

Philadelphia Eagles
3501 S. Broad St.
Philadelphia, PA 19148

Pittsburgh Steelers
300 Stadium Circle
Pittsburgh, PA 15212

St. Louis Rams
One Rams Way
St. Louis County, MO 63045

San Diego Chargers
PO Box 609609
San Diego, CA 92160

San Francisco 49ers
4949 Centennial Blvd.
Santa Clara, CA 95054

Seattle Seahawks
11220 NE 53d St.
Kirkland, WA 98033

Tampa Bay Buccaneers
One Buccaneer Place
Tampa, FL 33607

Tennessee Oilers
7640 Hwy 70 South
Nashville, TN 37221

Washington Redskins
PO Box 17247
Washington, DC 20041

Other Sports Organizations

Amateur Athletic Union
PO Box 10000
Lake Buena Vista, FL 32830

Amateur Softball Assn.
2801 NE 50th St.
Oklahoma City, OK 73111

American Basketball League
1900 Embarcadero Rd., Ste. 110
Palo Alto, CA 94303

American Horse Shows Assn.
220 E. 42d St.
New York, NY 10017

American Kennel Club
51 Madison Ave.
New York, NY 10010

Canadian Football League
110 Eglinton Ave. W
Toronto, Ont. M4R 1A3

CART
755 W. Big Beaver Rd.
Troy, MI 48084

Intl. Game Fish Assn.
1301 E. Atlantic Blvd.
Pompano Beach, FL 33060

LPGA
100 International Golf Dr.
Daytona Beach, FL 32124

Little League Baseball
PO Box 3485
Williamsport, PA 17701

Major League Soccer
110 E. 42d St., Ste. 1000
New York, NY 10017

NASCAR
PO Box 2875
Daytona Beach, FL 32120

NCAA
6201 College Blvd.
Overland Park, KS 66211 ·

National Rifle Assn.
11250 Waples Mill Rd.
Fairfax, VA 22030

Pro Bowlers Assn.
PO Box 5118
Akron, OH 44334

PGA
100 Ave. of the Champions
Palm Beach Gardens, FL 33410

Pro Rodeo Cowboys Assn.
101 Pro Rodeo Dr.
Colorado Springs, CO 80919

Special Olympics
1325 G St., NW
Washington, DC 20005

Thoroughbred Racing Assns.
420 Fair Hill Dr.
Elkton, MD 21921

USA Track & Field
PO Box 120
Indianapolis, IN 46206

U.S. Auto Club
4910 W. 16th St.
Speedway, IN 46224

U.S. Figure Skating Assn.
20 First St.
Colorado Springs, CO 80906

U.S. Olympic Committee
One Olympic Plaza
Colorado Springs, CO 80909

U.S. Skiing Assn.
PO Box 100
Park City, UT 84060

U.S. Soccer Federation
1801 S. Prairie Ave.
Chicago, IL 60616

U.S. Swimming
One Olympic Plaza
Colorado Springs, CO 80909

U.S. Tennis Assn.
70 W. Red Oak Lane
White Plains, NY 10604

U.S. Trotting Assn.
750 Michigan Ave.
Columbus, OH 43215

WNBA
645 5th Ave.
New York, NY 10022

NCAA WRESTLING CHAMPIONS

Year	Champion	Year	Champion	Year	Champion	Year	Champion	Year	Champion
1964	Oklahoma State	1971	Oklahoma State	1978	Iowa	1985	Iowa	1991	Iowa
1965	Iowa State	1972	Iowa State	1979	Iowa	1986	Iowa	1992	Iowa
1966	Oklahoma State	1973	Iowa State	1980	Iowa	1987	Iowa State	1993	Iowa
1967	Michigan State	1974	Oklahoma	1981	Iowa	1988	Arizona State	1994	Oklahoma State
1968	Oklahoma State	1975	Iowa	1982	Iowa	1989	Oklahoma State	1995	Iowa
1969	Iowa State	1976	Iowa	1983	Iowa	1990	Oklahoma State	1996	Iowa
1970	Iowa State	1977	Iowa State	1984	Iowa			1997	Iowa

SWIMMING
World Swimming Records
As of Oct. 1997

Men's Records

Distance	Time	Holder	Country	Where made	Date
Freestyle					
50 meters	0:21.81	Tom Jager	U.S.	Nashville, TN	Mar. 24, 1990
100 meters	0:48.21	Alexander Popov	Russia	Monte Carlo	June 18, 1994
200 meters	1:46.69	Giorgio Lamberti	Italy	Bonn	Aug. 15, 1989
400 meters	3:43.80	Kieren Perkins	Australia	Rome	Sept. 9, 1994
800 meters	7:46.00	Kieren Perkins	Australia	Victoria, Canada	Aug. 24, 1994
1,500 meters	14:41.66	Kieren Perkins	Australia	Victoria, Canada	Aug. 24, 1994
Breaststroke					
100 meters	1:00.60	Fred DeBurghgraeve	Belguim	Atlanta, GA	July 20, 1996
200 meters	2:10.16	Mike Barrowman	U.S.	Barcelona	July 29, 1992
Butterfly					
100 meters	0:52.27	Denis Pankratov	Russia	Atlanta, GA	July 24, 1996
200 meters	1:55.22	Denis Pankratov	Russia	Canet, France	June 14, 1995
Backstroke					
100 meters	0:53.86	Jeff Rouse	U.S.	Barcelona	July 29, 1992
200 meters	1:56.57	Martin Lopez-Zubero	Spain	Tuscaloosa, AL	Nov. 23, 1991
Individual Medley					
200 meters	1:58.16	Jani Sievinen	Finland	Rome	Sept. 11, 1994
400 meters	4:12.30	Tom Dolan	U.S.	Rome	Sept. 6, 1994
Freestyle Relays					
400 m. (4×100)	3:15.11	(Fox, Hudepohl, Olsen, Hall)	U.S.	Atlanta, GA	Aug. 12, 1995
800 m. (4×200)	7:11.95	(Lepikov, Pychenko, Taianovitch, Sadovyi)	Unified Team	Barcelona	July 27, 1992
Medley Relay					
400 m. (4×100)	3:34.84	(Rouse, Linn, Henderson, Hall, Jr.)	U.S.	Atlanta, GA	July 26, 1996

Women's Records

Distance	Time	Holder	Country	Where made	Date
Freestyle					
50 meters	0:24.51	Jingyi Le	China	Rome	Sept. 11, 1994
100 meters	0:54.01	Jingyi Le	China	Rome	Sept. 5, 1994
200 meters	1:56.78	Franziska Van Almsick	Germany	Rome	Sept. 6, 1994
400 meters	4:03.85	Janet Evans	U.S.	Seoul	Sept. 22, 1988
800 meters	8:16.22	Janet Evans	U.S.	Tokyo	Aug. 20, 1989
1,500 meters	15:52.10	Janet Evans	U.S.	Orlando, FL	Mar. 26, 1988
Breaststroke					
100 meters	1:07.02	Penny Heyns	South Africa	Atlanta, GA	July 21, 1996
200 meters	2:24.76	Rebecca Brown	Australia	Queensland, Australia	Mar. 16, 1994
Butterfly					
100 meters	0:57.93	Mary T. Meagher	U.S.	Brown Deer, WI	Aug. 16, 1981
200 meters	2:05.96	Mary T. Meagher	U.S.	Brown Deer, WI	Aug. 13, 1981
Backstroke					
100 meters	1:00.16	Cihong He	China	Rome	Sept. 10, 1994
200 meters	2:06.62	Krisztina Egerszegi	Hungary	Athens	Aug. 25, 1991
Individual Medley					
200 meters	2:11.65	Li Lin	China	Barcelona	July 30, 1992
400 meters	4:36.10	Petra Schneider	E. Germany	Guayaquil, Ecuador	Aug. 1, 1982
Freestyle Relays					
400 m. (4×100)	3:37.91	(Jingyi Le, Shan Ying, Ying Le, Lu Bin)	China	Rome	Sept. 7, 1994
800 m. (4×200)	7:55.47	(Stellmach, Strauss, Mohring, Friedrich)	E. Germany	Strasbourg, France	Aug. 18, 1987
Medley Relay					
400 m. (4×100)	4:01.67	(Cihong He, Guohong Dai, Limin Liu, Jingyi Le)	China	Rome	Sept. 10, 1994

NATIONAL BASKETBALL ASSOCIATION

1996-97 NBA Review: Bulls Still on Top, Malone wins MVP, Washington Wizardry

The Chicago Bulls won their 5th NBA Championship in 7 years, a feat accomplished by only 2 other teams (the Boston Celtics and Minneapolis Lakers). Michael Jordan gained another scoring title in the regular season and won the MVP award in the Finals. This year's runner up, the Utah Jazz, showed much improvement, led by Karl Malone, the regular season MVP. The Washington Bullets in an effort to improve their image changed the team moniker to the Wizards.

Final Standings, 1996-97 Season

Eastern Conference

Atlantic Division

	W	L	Pct	GB
Miami	61	21	.744	—
New York	57	25	.695	4
Orlando	45	37	.549	16
Washington	44	38	.537	17
New Jersey	26	56	.317	35
Philadelphia	22	60	.268	39
Boston	15	67	.183	46

Central Division

	W	L	Pct	GB
Chicago	69	13	.841	—
Atlanta	56	26	.683	13
Charlotte	54	28	.659	15
Detroit	54	28	.659	15
Cleveland	42	40	.512	27
Indiana	39	43	.476	30
Milwaukee	33	49	.402	36
Toronto	30	52	.366	39

Western Conference

Midwest Division

	W	L	Pct	GB
Utah	64	18	.780	—
Houston	57	25	.695	7
Minnesota	40	42	.488	24
Dallas	24	58	.293	40
Denver	21	61	.256	43
San Antonio	20	62	.244	44
Vancouver	14	68	.171	50

Pacific Division

	W	L	Pct	GB
Seattle	57	25	.695	—
L.A. Lakers	56	26	.683	1
Portland	49	33	.598	8
Phoenix	40	42	.488	17
L.A. Clippers	36	46	.439	21
Sacramento	34	48	.415	23
Golden State	30	52	.366	27

NBA Regular Season Individual Highs in 1996-97

Most minutes played, season — 3,362: Glen Rice, Charlotte.

Most points, game — 51: Michael Jordan, Chicago v. New York, Jan. 21.

Most field goals made, game — 24: Hakeem Olajuwon, Houston v. Denver, Jan. 30.

Most field goal attempts, game — 40: Hakeem Olajuwon, Houston v. Denver, Jan. 30.

Most 3-point field goals made, game — 9: Steve Smith, Atlanta v. Seattle, Mar. 14.

Most 3-point field goal attempts, game — 15: 3 times, most recently by Steve Smith, Atlanta v. Seattle, Mar. 14.

Most free throws made, game — 22: Latrell Sprewell, Golden State at L.A. Clippers, Mar. 10.

Most rebounds, game — 33: Charles Barkley, Houston at Phoenix, Nov. 2.

Most offensive rebounds, season — 320: Dennis Rodman, Chicago.

Most defensive rebounds, season — 682: Ervin Johnson, Denver.

Most assists, game — 23: Nick Van Exel, L.A. Lakers at Vancouver, Jan. 5.

Most steals, game — 10: Clyde Drexler, Houston v. Sacramento, Nov. 1.

Most blocked shots, game — 12: Vlade Divac, Charlotte v. New Jersey, Feb. 12.

Most personal fouls, season — 320: Shawn Kemp, Seattle.

Most games disqualified, season — 11: Walt Williams, Toronto; Shawn Kemp, Seattle.

Bulls Win 5th Championship in 7 Years, Defeating Utah in 6 Games

In June 1997, the Chicago Bulls won their 5th NBA championship in 7 years and 2d in a row, defeating the Utah Jazz, 4 games to 2. The victory capped a year in which the Bulls won 69 regular-season games. Chicago lost a total of only 4 games in its playoff run. Utah made the series interesting, winning 2 games in a row after dropping the first 2 in Chicago. Michael Jordan, who averaged 32.3 points per game, was named NBA Finals MVP for a record 5th time.

Chicago Bulls

	FG A-M	FT A-M	Reb O-T	Ast	Avg
Jordan	158-72	55-42	9-42	36	32.3
Pippen	95-40	36-28	12-50	21	20.0
Kukoc	37-15	10-8	2-19	16	8.0
Longley	33-20	5-1	11-23	7	6.8
Williams	36-17	13-7	6-20	5	6.8
Harper	32-11	6-4	8-27	14	4.8
Kerr	25-9	4-4	1-5	7	4.3
Rodman	20-5	8-3	10-46	9	2.3
Buechler	8-4	2-1	3-7	2	1.7
Brown	5-1	2-2	0-1	1	0.8
Caffey	0-0	0-0	2-2	1	0.0

Utah Jazz

	FG A-M	FT A-M	Reb O-T	Ast	Avg
Malone	122-54	58-35	19-62	21	23.8
Stockton	62-31	26-22	3-24	53	15.0
Hornacek	58-22	26-22	4-21	13	12.0
Russell	59-23	8-7	6-35	4	11.3
Foster	21-10	13-12	4-21	4	5.5
Eisley	22-11	10-9	0-4	15	5.3
Ostertag	25-10	12-6	18-44	2	4.3
Anderson	19-6	6-4	2-7	2	4.3
Morris	17-8	0-0	1-10	1	3.5
Carr	22-9	0-0	2-10	5	3.0
Keefe	3-1	2-1	1-7	1	0.8

1997 NBA Playoff Results

Eastern Conference

Chicago defeated Washington 3 games to 0
Miami defeated Orlando 3 games to 2
New York defeated Charlotte 3 games to 0
Atlanta defeated Detroit 3 games to 2
Chicago defeated Atlanta 4 games to 1
Miami defeated New York 4 games to 3
Chicago defeated Miami 4 games to 1

Western Conference

Utah defeated L.A. Clippers 3 games to 0
Seattle defeated Phoenix 3 games to 2
Houston defeated Minnesota 3 games to 0
L.A. Lakers defeated Portland 3 games to 1
Utah defeated L.A. Lakers 4 games to 1
Houston defeated Seattle 4 games to 3
Utah defeated Houston 4 games to 2

Championship

Chicago defeated Utah 4 games to 2 (84-82, 97-85, 93-104, 73-78, 90-88, 90-86)

NBA Finals MVP

1969	Jerry West, Los Angeles	1979	Dennis Johnson, Seattle	1988	James Worthy, L.A. Lakers
1970	Willis Reed, New York	1980	Magic Johnson, Los Angeles	1989	Joe Dumars, Detroit
1971	Lew Alcindor (Kareem Abdul-Jabbar), Milwaukee	1981	Cedric Maxwell, Boston	1990	Isiah Thomas, Detroit
		1982	Magic Johnson, Los Angeles	1991	Michael Jordan, Chicago
1972	Wilt Chamberlain, Los Angeles	1983	Moses Malone, Philadelphia	1992	Michael Jordan, Chicago
1973	Willis Reed, New York	1984	Larry Bird, Boston	1993	Michael Jordan, Chicago
1974	John Havlicek, Boston	1985	Kareem Abdul-Jabbar, L.A. Lakers	1994	Hakeem Olajuwon, Houston
1975	Rick Barry, Golden State			1995	Hakeem Olajuwon, Houston
1976	Jo Jo White, Boston	1986	Larry Bird, Boston	1996	Michael Jordan, Chicago
1977	Bill Walton, Portland	1987	Magic Johnson, L.A. Lakers	1997	Michael Jordan, Chicago
1978	Wes Unseld, Washington				

NBA Scoring Leaders

Year	Scoring champion	Pts	Avg	Year	Scoring champion	Pts	Avg
1947	Joe Fulks, Philadelphia	1,389	23.2	1972	Kareem Abdul-Jabbar, Milwaukee	2,822	34.8
1948	Max Zaslofsky, Chicago	1,007	21.0	1973	Nate Archibald, Kans. City-Omaha	2,719	34.0
1949	George Mikan, Minneapolis	1,698	28.3	1974	Bob McAdoo, Buffalo	2,261	30.6
1950	George Mikan, Minneapolis	1,865	27.4	1975	Bob McAdoo, Buffalo	2,831	34.5
1951	George Mikan, Minneapolis	1,932	28.4	1976	Bob McAdoo, Buffalo	2,427	31.1
1952	Paul Arizin, Philadelphia	1,674	25.4	1977	Pete Maravich, New Orleans	2,273	31.1
1953	Neil Johnston, Philadelphia	1,564	22.3	1978	George Gervin, San Antonio	2,232	27.2
1954	Neil Johnston, Philadelphia	1,759	24.4	1979	George Gervin, San Antonio	2,365	29.6
1955	Neil Johnston, Philadelphia	1,631	22.7	1980	George Gervin, San Antonio	2,585	33.1
1956	Bob Pettit, St. Louis	1,849	25.7	1981	Adrian Dantley, Utah	2,452	30.7
1957	Paul Arizin, Philadelphia	1,817	25.6	1982	George Gervin, San Antonio	2,551	32.3
1958	George Yardley, Detroit	2,001	27.8	1983	Alex English, Denver	2,326	28.4
1959	Bob Pettit, St. Louis	2,105	29.2	1984	Adrian Dantley, Utah	2,418	30.6
1960	Wilt Chamberlain, Philadelphia	2,707	37.9	1985	Bernard King, New York	1,809	32.9
1961	Wilt Chamberlain, Philadelphia	3,033	38.4	1986	Dominique Wilkins, Atlanta	2,366	30.3
1962	Wilt Chamberlain, Philadelphia	4,029	50.4	1987	Michael Jordan, Chicago	3,041	37.1
1963	Wilt Chamberlain, San Francisco	3,586	44.8	1988	Michael Jordan, Chicago	2,868	35.0
1964	Wilt Chamberlain, San Francisco	2,948	36.5	1989	Michael Jordan, Chicago	2,633	32.5
1965	Wilt Chamberlain, San Fran., Phi.	2,534	34.7	1990	Michael Jordan, Chicago	2,753	33.6
1966	Wilt Chamberlain, Philadelphia	2,649	33.5	1991	Michael Jordan, Chicago	2,580	31.5
1967	Rick Barry, San Francisco	2,775	35.6	1992	Michael Jordan, Chicago	2,404	30.1
1968	Dave Bing, Detroit	2,142	27.1	1993	Michael Jordan, Chicago	2,541	32.6
1969	Elvin Hayes, San Diego	2,327	28.4	1994	David Robinson, San Antonio	2,383	29.8
1970	Jerry West, Los Angeles	2,309	31.2	1995	Shaquille O'Neal, Orlando	2,315	29.3
1971	Lew Alcindor (Kareem Abdul-Jabbar), Milwaukee	2,596	31.7	1996	Michael Jordan, Chicago	2,465	30.4
				1997	Michael Jordan, Chicago	2,431	29.6

NBA Most Valuable Player

1956	Bob Pettit, St. Louis	1977	Kareem Abdul-Jabbar, Los Angeles
1957	Bob Cousy, Boston	1978	Bill Walton, Portland
1958	Bill Russell, Boston	1979	Moses Malone, Houston
1959	Bob Pettit, St. Louis	1980	Kareem Abdul-Jabbar, Los Angeles
1960	Wilt Chamberlain, Philadelphia	1981	Julius Erving, Philadelphia
1961	Bill Russell, Boston	1982	Moses Malone, Houston
1962	Bill Russell, Boston	1983	Moses Malone, Philadelphia
1963	Bill Russell, Boston	1984	Larry Bird, Boston
1964	Oscar Robertson, Cincinnati	1985	Larry Bird, Boston
1965	Bill Russell, Boston	1986	Larry Bird, Boston
1966	Wilt Chamberlain, Philadelphia	1987	Magic Johnson, L.A. Lakers
1967	Wilt Chamberlain, Philadelphia	1988	Michael Jordan, Chicago
1968	Wilt Chamberlain, Philadelphia	1989	Magic Johnson, L.A. Lakers
1969	Wes Unseld, Baltimore	1990	Magic Johnson, L.A. Lakers
1970	Willis Reed, New York	1991	Michael Jordan, Chicago
1971	Lew Alcindor (Kareem Abdul-Jabbar), Milwaukee	1992	Michael Jordan, Chicago
1972	Kareem Abdul-Jabbar, Milwaukee	1993	Charles Barkley, Phoenix
1973	Dave Cowens, Boston	1994	Hakeem Olajuwon, Houston
1974	Kareem Abdul-Jabbar, Milwaukee	1995	David Robinson, San Antonio
1975	Bob McAdoo, Buffalo	1996	Michael Jordan, Chicago
1976	Kareem Abdul-Jabbar, Los Angeles	1997	Karl Malone, Utah

NBA Champions 1947-97

	Regular season		Playoffs		
Year	Eastern Conference	Western Conference	Winner	Coach	Runner-up
1947	Washington Capitols	Chicago Stags	Philadelphia	Ed Gottlieb	Chicago
1948	Philadelphia Warriors	St. Louis Bombers	Baltimore	Buddy Jeannette	Philadelphia
1949	Washington Capitols	Rochester	Minneapolis	John Kundla	Washington
1950	Syracuse	Minneapolis	Minneapolis	John Kundla	Syracuse
1951	Philadelphia Warriors	Minneapolis	Rochester	Lester Harrison	New York
1952	Syracuse	Rochester	Minneapolis	John Kundla	New York
1953	New York	Minneapolis	Minneapolis	John Kundla	New York
1954	New York	Minneapolis	Minneapolis	John Kundla	Syracuse
1955	Syracuse	Ft. Wayne	Syracuse	Al Cervi	Ft. Wayne
1956	Philadelphia Warriors	Ft. Wayne	Philadelphia	George Senesky	Ft. Wayne
1957	Boston	St. Louis	Boston	Red Auerbach	St. Louis
1958	Boston	St. Louis	St. Louis	Alex Hannum	Boston
1959	Boston	St. Louis	Boston	Red Auerbach	Minneapolis
1960	Boston	St. Louis	Boston	Red Auerbach	St. Louis
1961	Boston	St. Louis	Boston	Red Auerbach	St. Louis
1962	Boston	Los Angeles	Boston	Red Auerbach	Los Angeles
1963	Boston	Los Angeles	Boston	Red Auerbach	Los Angeles
1964	Boston	San Francisco	Boston	Red Auerbach	San Francisco
1965	Boston	Los Angeles	Boston	Red Auerbach	Los Angeles
1966	Philadelphia	Los Angeles	Boston	Red Auerbach	Los Angeles
1967	Philadelphia	San Francisco	Philadelphia	Alex Hannum	San Francisco

(continued)

	Regular season			Playoffs		
Year	Eastern Conference	Western Conference	Winner	Coach		Runner-up
1968	Philadelphia	St. Louis	Boston	Bill Russell		Los Angeles
1969	Baltimore	Los Angeles	Boston	Bill Russell		Los Angeles
1970	New York	Atlanta	New York	Red Holzman		Los Angeles

Year	Atlantic	Central	Midwest	Pacific	Winner	Coach	Runner-up
1971	New York	Baltimore	Milwaukee	Los Angeles	Milwaukee	Larry Costello	Baltimore
1972	Boston	Baltimore	Milwaukee	Los Angeles	Los Angeles	Bill Sharman	New York
1973	Boston	Baltimore	Milwaukee	Los Angeles	New York	Red Holzman	Los Angeles
1974	Boston	Capital	Milwaukee	Los Angeles	Boston	Tom Heinsohn	Milwaukee
1975	Boston	Washington	Chicago	Golden State	Golden State	Al Attles	Washington
1976	Boston	Cleveland	Milwaukee	Golden State	Boston	Tom Heinsohn	Phoenix
1977	Philadelphia	Houston	Denver	Los Angeles	Portland	Jack Ramsay	Philadelphia
1978	Philadelphia	San Antonio	Denver	Portland	Washington	Dick Motta	Seattle
1979	Washington	San Antonio	Kansas City	Seattle	Seattle	Len Wilkens	Washington
1980	Boston	Atlanta	Milwaukee	Los Angeles	Los Angeles	Paul Westhead	Philadelphia
1981	Boston	Milwaukee	San Antonio	Phoenix	Boston	Bill Fitch	Houston
1982	Boston	Milwaukee	San Antonio	Los Angeles	Los Angeles	Pat Riley	Philadelphia
1983	Philadelphia	Milwaukee	San Antonio	Los Angeles	Philadelphia	Billy Cunningham	Los Angeles
1984	Boston	Milwaukee	Utah	Los Angeles	Boston	K.C. Jones	Los Angeles
1985	Boston	Milwaukee	Denver	L.A. Lakers	L.A. Lakers	Pat Riley	Boston
1986	Boston	Milwaukee	Houston	L.A. Lakers	Boston	K.C. Jones	Houston
1987	Boston	Atlanta	Dallas	L.A. Lakers	L.A. Lakers	Pat Riley	Boston
1988	Boston	Detroit	Denver	L.A. Lakers	L.A. Lakers	Pat Riley	Detroit
1989	New York	Detroit	Utah	L.A. Lakers	Detroit	Chuck Daly	L.A. Lakers
1990	Philadelphia	Detroit	San Antonio	L.A. Lakers	Detroit	Chuck Daly	Portland
1991	Boston	Chicago	San Antonio	Portland	Chicago	Phil Jackson	L.A. Lakers
1992	Boston	Chicago	Utah	Portland	Chicago	Phil Jackson	Portland
1993	New York	Chicago	Houston	Phoenix	Chicago	Phil Jackson	Phoenix
1994	New York	Atlanta	Houston	Seattle	Houston	Rudy Tomjanovich	New York
1995	Orlando	Indiana	San Antonio	Phoenix	Houston	Rudy Tomjanovich	Orlando
1996	Orlando	Chicago	San Antonio	Seattle	Chicago	Phil Jackson	Seattle
1997	Miami	Chicago	Utah	Seattle	Chicago	Phil Jackson	Utah

NBA Coach of the Year, 1963-97

1963	Harry Gallatin, St. Louis Hawks	1975	Phil Johnson, Kansas City-Omaha Kings	1987	Mike Schuler, Portland Trail Blazers
1964	Alex Hannum, San Francisco Warriors	1976	Bill Fitch, Cleveland Cavaliers	1988	Doug Moe, Denver Nuggets
1965	Red Auerbach, Boston Celtics	1977	Tom Nissalke, Houston Rockets	1989	Cotton Fitzsimmons, Phoenix Suns
1966	Dolph Schayes, Philadelphia 76ers	1978	Hubie Brown, Atlanta Hawks	1990	Pat Riley, Los Angeles Lakers
1967	Johnny Kerr, Chicago Bulls	1979	Cotton Fitzsimmons, Kansas City Kings	1991	Don Chaney, Houston Rockets
1968	Richie Guerin, St. Louis Hawks	1980	Bill Fitch, Boston Celtics	1992	Don Nelson, Golden State Warriors
1969	Gene Shue, Baltimore Bullets	1981	Jack McKinney, Indiana Pacers	1993	Pat Riley, New York Knicks
1970	Red Holzman, New York Knicks	1982	Gene Shue, Washington Bullets	1994	Lenny Wilkens, Atlanta Hawks
1971	Dick Motta, Chicago Bulls	1983	Don Nelson, Milwaukee Bucks	1995	Del Harris, Los Angeles Lakers
1972	Bill Sharman, Los Angeles Lakers	1984	Frank Layden, Utah Jazz	1996	Phil Jackson, Chicago Bulls
1973	Tom Heinsohn, Boston Celtics	1985	Don Nelson, Milwaukee Bucks	1997	Pat Riley, Miami Heat
1974	Ray Scott, Detroit Pistons	1986	Mike Fratello, Atlanta Hawks		

NBA All-League and All-Defensive Teams, 1996-97

All-League Team		Position	All-Defensive Team	
First team	Second team		First team	Second team
Karl Malone, Utah	Scottie Pippen, Chicago	Forward	Scottie Pippen, Chicago	Anthony Mason, Charlotte
Grant Hill, Detroit	Glen Rice, Charlotte	Forward	Karl Malone, Utah	P. J. Brown, Miami
Hakeem Olajuwon, Houston	Patrick Ewing, New York	Center	Dikembe Mutombo, Atlanta	Hakeem Olajuwon, Houston
Michael Jordan, Chicago	Gary Payton, Seattle	Guard	Michael Jordan, Chicago	Mookie Blaylock, Atlanta
Tim Hardaway, Miami	Mitch Richmond, Sacramento	Guard	Gary Payton, Seattle	John Stockton, Utah

NBA Statistical Leaders, 1996-97

Scoring

(Minimum 70 games or 1,400 pts)

	G	FG	FT	Pts	Avg
Jordan, Chicago	82	920	480	2,431	29.6
Malone, Utah	82	864	521	2,249	27.4
Rice, Charlotte	79	722	464	2,115	26.8
Richmond, Sacramento	81	717	457	2,095	25.9
Sprewell, Golden State	80	649	493	1,938	24.2
Iverson, Philadelphia	76	625	382	1,787	23.5
Olajuwon, Houston	78	727	351	1,810	23.2
Ewing, New York	78	655	439	1,751	22.4
Gill, New Jersey	82	644	427	1,789	21.8
Payton, Seattle	82	706	254	1,785	21.8

Rebounds per Game

(Minimum 70 games or 800 rebounds)

	G	Off	Def	Tot	Avg
Rodman, Chicago	55	320	563	883	16.1
Mutombo, Atlanta	80	268	661	929	11.6
Mason, Charlotte	73	186	643	829	11.4
Er. Johnson, Denver	82	231	682	913	11.1
Ewing, New York	78	175	659	834	10.7
Webber, Washington	72	238	505	743	10.3
Baker, Milwaukee	78	267	537	804	10.3
Vaught, L.A. Clippers	82	222	595	817	10.0
Kemp, Seattle	81	275	532	807	10.0
T. Hill, Cleveland	74	259	477	736	9.9
Malone, Utah	82	193	616	809	9.9

Field Goal Percentage

(Minimum 300 field goals made)

	FGM	FGA	Pct
Muresan, Washington	327	541	.604
T. Hill, Cleveland	357	595	.600
Wallace, Portland	380	681	.558
O'Neal, L.A. Lakers	552	991	.557
Mullin, Golden State	438	792	.553
Malone, Utah	864	1,571	.550
Stockton, Utah	416	759	.548
D. Davis, Indiana	370	688	.538
Manning, Phoenix	426	795	.536
Trent, Portland	361	674	.536

Free Throw Percentage
(Minimum 125 free throws made)

	FTM	FTA	Pct
Price, Golden State	155	171	.906
Brandon, Cleveland	268	297	.902
Hornacek, Utah	293	326	.899
Pierce, Denver-Charlotte	139	155	.897
Elie, Houston	207	231	.896
Miller, Indiana	418	475	.880
Sealy, L.A. Clippers	254	290	.876
Hawkins, Seattle	258	295	.875
Martin, L.A. Clippers	218	250	.872
Rice, Charlotte	464	535	.867
Dumas, Detroit	222	256	.867

3-Point Field Goal Percentage
(Minimum 50 goals made)

	FG	FGA	Pct
Rice, Charlotte	207	440	.470
Kerr, Chicago	110	237	.464
K. Johnson, Phoenix	89	202	.441
Dumars, Detroit	166	384	.432
Richmond, Sacramento	204	477	.428
Miller, Indiana	229	536	.427
Curry, Charlotte	126	296	.426
Mills, Detroit	175	415	.422
Elie, Houston	120	286	.420
Lenard, Miami	183	442	.414

Assists
(Minimum 70 games or 400 assists)

	G	No	Avg
M. Jackson, Denver-Indiana	82	935	11.4
Stockton, Utah	82	860	10.5
K. Johnson, Phoenix	70	653	9.3
Kidd, Dallas-Phoenix	55	496	9.0
Strickland, Washington	82	727	8.9
Stoudamire, Toronto	81	709	8.8
T. Hardaway, Miami	81	695	8.6
Van Exel, L.A. Lakers	79	672	8.5
Pack, New Jersey-Dallas	54	452	8.4
Marbury, Minnesota	67	522	7.8

Steals
(Minimum 70 games or 125 steals)

	G	No	Avg
Blaylock, Atlanta	78	212	2.72
Christie, Toronto	81	201	2.48
Payton, Seattle	82	197	2.40
Jones, L.A. Lakers	80	189	2.36
Fox, Boston	76	167	2.20
Wesley, Boston	74	162	2.19
Iverson, Philadelphia	76	157	2.07
Stockton, Utah	82	166	2.02
Anthony, Vancouver	65	129	1.98
Anderson, Portland	82	162	1.98

Blocked Shots
(Minimum 70 games or 100 blocked shots)

	G	Blk	Avg
Bradley, New Jersey-Dallas	73	248	3.40
Mutombo, Atlanta	80	264	3.30
O'Neal, L.A. Lakers	51	147	2.88
Mourning, Miami	66	189	2.86
Er. Johnson, Denver	82	227	2.77
Ewing, New York	78	189	2.42
Divac, Charlotte	81	180	2.22
Olajuwon, Houston	78	173	2.22
Garnett, Minnesota	77	163	2.12
Camby, Toronto	63	130	2.06

NBA Rookie of the Year

Year	Player
1953	Don Meineke, Ft. Wayne
1954	Ray Felix, Baltimore
1955	Bob Pettit, Milwaukee
1956	Maurice Stokes, Rochester
1957	Tom Heinsohn, Boston
1958	Woody Sauldsberry, Philadelphia
1959	Elgin Baylor, Minneapolis
1960	Wilt Chamberlain, Philadelphia
1961	Oscar Robertson, Cincinnati
1962	Walt Bellamy, Chicago
1963	Terry Dischinger, Chicago
1964	Jerry Lucas, Cincinnati
1965	Willis Reed, New York
1966	Rick Barry, San Francisco
1967	Dave Bing, Detroit
1968	Earl Monroe, Baltimore
1969	Wes Unseld, Baltimore
1970	Lew Alcindor, Milwaukee
1971	Dave Cowens, Boston; Geoff Petrie, Portland (tie)
1972	Sidney Wicks, Portland
1973	Bob McAdoo, Buffalo
1974	Ernie DiGregorio, Buffalo
1975	Keith Wilkes, Golden State
1976	Alvan Adams, Phoenix
1977	Adrian Dantley, Buffalo
1978	Walter Davis, Phoenix
1979	Phil Ford, Kansas City
1980	Larry Bird, Boston
1981	Darrell Griffith, Utah
1982	Buck Williams, New Jersey
1983	Terry Cummings, San Diego
1984	Ralph Sampson, Houston
1985	Michael Jordan, Chicago
1986	Patrick Ewing, New York
1987	Chuck Person, Indiana
1988	Mark Jackson, New York
1989	Mitch Richmond, Golden State
1990	David Robinson, San Antonio
1991	Derrick Coleman, New Jersey
1992	Larry Johnson, Charlotte
1993	Shaquille O'Neal, Orlando
1994	Chris Webber, Golden State
1995	Grant Hill, Detroit; Jason Kidd, Dallas (tie)
1996	Damon Stoudamire, Toronto
1997	Allen Iverson, Philadelphia

NBA Individual Statistics, 1996-97
(more than 600 minutes played; *played for more than one team during 1996-97)

Atlanta Hawks

	Min	FG%	FT%	Reb	Ast	Pts	Avg
Smith	2818	.429	.847	238	305	1445	20.1
Laettner	3140	.486	.816	720	223	1486	18.1
Blaylock	3056	.432	.753	413	463	1354	17.4
Mutombo	2973	.527	.705	929	110	1066	13.3
Corbin	2305	.422	.796	294	124	666	9.5
James	945	.408	.833	81	21	356	6.7
Recasner	1207	.423	.879	115	94	405	5.7
Barry	965	.407	.804	99	115	285	4.9
Newbill	850	.440	.385	204	24	100	1.4
Coach—Lenny Wilkens							

Boston Celtics

	Min	FG%	FT%	Reb	Ast	Pts	Avg
Walker	2970	.425	.631	741	262	1435	17.5
Wesley	2991	.468	.781	264	537	1240	16.8
Fox	2650	.456	.787	394	286	1174	15.4
Williams	2435	.456	.752	329	129	1078	15.0
Day	2277	.398	.773	330	117	1178	14.5
Radja	874	.440	.718	211	48	349	14.0
Barros	708	.435	.860	48	81	300	12.5
Conlon	1614	.471	.842	323	104	574	7.8
Szabo	662	.446	.738	165	17	153	2.2
Coach—M.L. Carr							

Charlotte Hornets

	Min	FG%	FT%	Reb	Ast	Pts	Avg
Rice	3362	.477	.867	318	160	2115	26.8
Mason	3143	.525	.745	829	414	1186	16.2
Curry	2078	.459	.803	211	118	1008	14.8
Divac	2840	.494	.683	725	301	1024	12.6
Pierce*	1250	.481	.897	121	80	659	11.0
Geiger	1044	.489	.701	258	58	437	8.9
Bogues	1880	.460	.844	141	469	522	8.0
Delk	867	.465	.824	99	99	332	5.4
Smith	1291	.409	.644	94	150	346	5.0
Royal*	858	.425	.803	154	25	218	3.5
Coach—Dave Cowens							

Chicago Bulls

	Min	FG%	FT%	Reb	Ast	Pts	Avg
Jordan	3106	.486	.833	482	352	2431	29.6
Pippen	3095	.474	.701	531	467	1656	20.2
Kukoc	1610	.471	.770	261	256	754	13.2
Longley	1472	.456	.792	332	141	537	9.1
Kerr	1861	.533	.806	130	175	662	8.1
Caffey	1405	.532	.659	301	89	549	7.3
Harper	1740	.456	.707	193	191	480	6.3
Rodman	1947	.449	.569	883	170	311	5.7
Brown	1057	.420	.679	111	133	341	4.7
Wennington	783	.498	.830	129	41	280	4.6
Buechler	703	.367	.357	126	60	139	1.8
Coach—Phil Jackson							

Cleveland Cavaliers

	Min	FG%	FT%	Reb	Ast	Pts	Avg
Brandon ..	2868	.438	.902	301	490	1519	19.5
Mills	3167	.453	.842	497	198	1072	13.4
Hill	2582	.600	.633	736	92	955	12.9
Phills	2375	.428	.718	245	233	866	12.6
Ferry.....	2633	.429	.851	337	151	870	10.6
Sura.....	2269	.431	.614	308	390	755	9.2
Potapenko.	1238	.440	.736	217	40	465	5.8
West.....	959	.556	.482	186	19	227	3.2
Lang.....	843	.420	.729	127	33	171	2.7

Coach—Mike Fratello

Dallas Mavericks

	Min	FG%	FT%	Reb	Ast	Pts	Avg
Finley* ...	2790	.444	.808	372	224	1249	15.0
Pack*....	1782	.392	.807	146	452	771	14.3
Bradley*..	2288	.449	.654	611	52	961	13.2
Danilovic*.	1789	.435	.801	136	102	702	12.5
Strickland .	759	.398	.813	90	68	297	10.6
Harper ...	2210	.444	.742	137	321	753	10.0
Reeves*...	1432	.391	.747	119	226	516	8.2
Green* ...	2492	.483	.650	656	69	597	7.2
Walker ...	602	.444	.649	147	17	214	5.0
O'Bannon*	809	.333	.886	148	39	235	3.7

Coach—Jim Cleamons

Denver Nuggets

	Min	FG%	FT%	Reb	Ast	Pts	Avg
L. Ellis....	2002	.439	.773	386	131	1203	21.9
McDyess..	2565	.463	.708	537	106	1352	18.3
D. Ellis...	2940	.414	.817	293	165	1361	16.6
Stith	1788	.416	.863	217	133	774	14.9
Er. Johnson	2599	.520	.615	913	71	582	7.1
B. Thompson*	1055	.399	.632	96	180	445	6.6
Goldwire* .	1188	.397	.782	84	219	387	6.5
Smith* ...	765	.423	.867	44	116	300	6.3
Hammonds	1758	.480	.721	401	64	506	6.2
Askew*...	838	.435	.795	98	90	239	5.6
Allen*....	943	.353	.583	98	152	228	3.0

Coach—Bernie Bickerstaff; Dick Motta

Detroit Pistons

	Min	FG%	FT%	Reb	Ast	Pts	Avg
Hill	3147	.496	.711	721	583	1710	21.4
Dumars...	2923	.440	.867	191	318	1158	14.7
Hunter ...	3023	.404	.778	233	154	1166	14.2
Thorpe ...	2661	.532	.653	622	133	1036	13.1
Mills	1997	.444	.829	377	99	857	10.8
Ratliff	1292	.531	.698	256	13	439	5.8
McKie*...	1625	.411	.836	221	161	433	5.2
Long.....	1166	.447	.750	222	39	326	5.0
Curry	1217	.448	.898	119	43	318	3.9

Coach—Doug Collins

Golden State Warriors

	Min	FG%	FT%	Reb	Ast	Pts	Avg
Sprewell ..	3353	.449	.843	366	507	1938	24.2
Smith	3086	.454	.814	679	125	1493	18.7
Mullin	2733	.553	.864	317	322	1143	14.5
Price.....	1876	.447	.906	179	342	793	11.3
Armstrong.	1020	.453	.861	74	126	389	7.9
Marshall...	1022	.413	.622	276	54	444	7.3
Coles	1183	.389	.755	118	149	311	6.1
DeClercq..	1065	.520	.603	298	32	375	5.3
Burrell*...	939	.362	.750	158	74	294	5.2
Spencer* .	1558	.489	.584	416	22	372	5.1
Fuller	949	.429	.691	249	24	304	4.1

Coach—Rick Adelman

Houston Rockets

	Min	FG%	FT%	Reb	Ast	Pts	Avg
Olajuwon..	2852	.510	.787	716	236	1810	23.2
Barkley ...	2009	.484	.694	716	248	1016	19.2
Drexler ...	2271	.442	.750	373	354	1114	18.0
Elie......	2687	.497	.896	235	310	909	11.7
Willis.....	1964	.481	.693	561	71	842	11.2
Maloney ..	2386	.441	.763	160	303	767	9.4
E. Johnson*	913	.442	.809	138	52	424	8.2
Mack	904	.401	.833	106	58	292	5.6
Harrington.	860	.549	.605	198	18	273	4.8
Bullard...	1025	.401	.735	117	67	320	4.5
Livingston .	981	.437	.646	94	155	251	3.9

Coach—Rudy Tomjanovich

Indiana Pacers

	Min	FG%	FT%	Reb	Ast	Pts	Avg
Miller	2966	.444	.880	286	273	1751	21.6
Smits.....	1518	.486	.797	361	67	887	17.1
A. Davis..	2335	.481	.666	598	65	858	10.5
D. Davis..	2589	.538	.428	772	59	832	10.4
Best.....	2064	.442	.756	166	318	754	9.9
Jackson*..	3054	.426	.789	395	935	812	9.9
McKey ...	1449	.391	.724	241	135	400	8.0
Rose.....	1188	.456	.750	121	155	482	7.3
Ferrell	1115	.472	.617	141	66	394	6.4
Dampier..	1052	.390	.637	294	43	370	5.1

Coach—Larry Brown

Los Angeles Clippers

	Min	FG%	FT%	Reb	Ast	Pts	Avg
Vaught...	2838	.500	.702	817	110	1220	14.9
Sealy....	2456	.396	.876	238	165	1079	13.5
Rogers...	2480	.462	.663	411	222	1072	13.2
Martin ...	1820	.407	.872	113	339	893	10.9
Outlaw...	2195	.609	.504	454	157	625	7.6
Barry	1094	.409	.817	110	154	442	7.5
Murray...	1295	.416	.739	233	57	549	7.4
Wright ...	1936	.481	.587	471	49	561	7.3
Dehere...	1053	.386	.824	95	158	470	6.4
Piatkowski	747	.450	.821	105	52	388	6.0
Richardson	1065	.381	.605	98	169	330	5.6

Coach—Bill Fitch

Los Angeles Lakers

	Min	FG%	FT%	Reb	Ast	Pts	Avg
O'Neal ...	1941	.557	.484	640	159	1336	26.2
Jones....	2998	.438	.819	326	270	1374	17.2
Van Exel.	2937	.402	.825	226	672	1206	15.3
Campbell .	2516	.469	.711	615	126	1148	14.9
McCloud*.	1493	.412	.822	179	109	658	10.3
Horry	1395	.436	.667	237	110	423	7.8
Bryant ...	1103	.417	.819	132	91	539	7.6
Kersey ...	1766	.432	.602	363	89	476	6.8
Scott	1440	.430	.841	118	99	526	6.7
Knight ...	1156	.509	.620	319	39	342	4.8
Blount ...	1009	.514	.675	276	35	241	4.2
Fisher ...	921	.397	.658	97	119	309	3.9
Rooks ...	735	.470	.700	163	42	265	3.8

Coach—Del Harris

Miami Heat

	Min	FG%	FT%	Reb	Ast	Pts	Avg
T. Hardaway	3136	.415	.799	277	695	1644	20.3
Mourning .	2320	.534	.642	656	104	1310	19.8
Lenard ...	2111	.459	.819	217	161	897	12.3
Mashburn*	2164	.385	.702	294	204	822	11.9
Majerle ...	1264	.406	.678	162	116	390	10.8
Austin....	1881	.502	.664	478	101	792	9.7
Brown.....	2592	.457	.732	670	92	761	9.5
Askins ...	1773	.433	.672	271	75	384	4.9
Crotty....	659	.513	.844	47	102	232	4.8

Coach—Pat Riley

Milwaukee Bucks

	Min	FG%	FT%	Reb	Ast	Pts	Avg
G. Robinson	3114	.465	.791	502	248	1689	21.1
Baker....	3159	.505	.687	804	211	1637	21.0
Allen	2532	.430	.823	326	210	1102	13.4
Douglas ..	2316	.502	.667	193	427	764	9.7
Newman .	2060	.450	.765	186	116	715	8.7
Gilliam ...	2050	.471	.768	497	53	691	8.6
Perry	1595	.474	.745	124	247	562	6.9
Lang	1194	.464	.721	278	25	274	5.3
Brown* ...	757	.506	.671	148	28	204	2.9

Coach—Chris Ford

Minnesota Timberwolves

	Min	FG%	FT%	Reb	Ast	Pts	Avg
Gugliotta...	3131	.442	.820	702	335	1672	20.6
Garnett ...	2995	.499	.754	618	236	1309	17.0
Marbury ...	2324	.408	.727	184	522	1057	15.8
Mitchell ...	2044	.446	.759	326	79	766	9.3
Robinson ..	1309	.407	.684	112	126	572	8.3
Garrett....	1665	.573	.696	495	38	542	8.0
West	1920	.467	.681	148	113	531	7.8
Porter	1568	.416	.765	176	295	568	6.9
Carr......	830	.461	.767	113	48	337	6.1
Vrankovic..	766	.561	.676	168	14	181	3.4
Parks.....	961	.510	.605	195	34	252	3.3

Coach—Flip Saunders

New Jersey Nets

	Min	FG%	FT%	Reb	Ast	Pts	Avg
Gill	3199	.443	.797	499	326	1789	21.8
Gatling* . .	1283	.525	.717	370	28	891	19.0
Kittles	3012	.426	.771	319	249	1347	16.4
Jackson* . .	2831	.431	.813	411	316	1226	15.9
Cassell* . .	1714	.430	.845	182	305	967	15.9
J. Williams . .	1432	.409	.590	553	51	550	13.4
Massenburg	1954	.485	.631	517	23	568	7.2
McDaniel . .	1170	.389	.730	318	65	346	5.6
Montross* . .	1828	.456	.339	518	61	339	4.3
Kleine*	848	.406	.737	203	35	168	2.8

Coach—John Calipari

New York Knickerbockers

	Min	FG%	FT%	Reb	Ast	Pts	Avg
Ewing	2887	.488	.754	834	156	1751	22.4
Houston . .	2681	.423	.803	240	179	1197	14.8
Starks	2042	.431	.769	205	217	1061	13.8
L. Johnson	2613	.512	.693	393	174	976	12.8
Oakley	2873	.488	.808	781	221	864	10.8
Childs	2076	.414	.758	191	398	605	9.3
B. Williams	1496	.537	.642	397	53	465	6.3
Ward	1763	.395	.760	220	326	409	5.2
Wallace . . .	787	.517	.718	155	37	325	4.8

Coach—Jeff Van Gundy

Orlando Magic

	Min	FG%	FT%	Reb	Ast	Pts	Avg
A. Hardaway	2221	.447	.820	263	332	1210	20.5
Seikaly . . .	2615	.507	.714	701	92	1277	17.3
Grant	2496	.515	.715	600	163	845	12.6
Scott	2166	.398	.792	203	139	823	12.5
Anderson .	2163	.397	.404	304	182	757	12.0
G. Wilkins .	2202	.426	.716	173	173	848	10.6
Strong . . .	2004	.447	.803	519	73	699	8.5
Shaw	1867	.366	.793	194	319	552	7.2
Armstrong .	1010	.383	.868	76	175	411	6.1

Coach—Brian Hill; Richie Adubato

Philadelphia 76ers

	Min	FG%	FT%	Reb	Ast	Pts	Avg
Iverson	3045	.416	.702	312	567	1787	23.5
Stackhouse . .	3166	.407	.766	338	253	1679	20.7
Coleman . . .	2102	.435	.745	593	193	1032	18.1
Weatherspoon	2949	.491	.738	679	140	1003	12.2
MacLean	733	.447	.660	140	37	402	10.9
Davis	1705	.469	.673	323	135	639	8.5
Walters	1041	.455	.790	107	113	402	6.8
Williams	1317	.509	.691	397	41	362	5.8
Harris	813	.381	.702	71	50	293	5.4
Overton	634	.426	.938	68	101	217	3.6
Cage	1247	.468	.463	320	43	151	1.8

Coach—Johnny Davis

Phoenix Suns

	Min	FG%	FT%	Reb	Ast	Pts	Avg
K. Johnson	2658	.496	.852	253	653	1410	20.1
Ceballos* .	1426	.457	.747	330	64	729	14.6
Chapman .	1833	.443	.832	181	182	898	13.8
Manning . .	2134	.536	.721	469	173	1040	13.5
Person . . .	2326	.453	.798	292	123	1080	13.5
Kidd*	1964	.403	.679	249	496	599	10.9
Bryant	1018	.553	.704	212	47	380	9.3
Williams . .	2137	.490	.672	562	100	541	8.0
Tisdale . . .	778	.426	.625	120	20	346	6.5
Meyer* . . .	708	.443	.719	145	19	266	4.9
Nash	684	.423	.824	63	138	213	3.3

Coach—Cotton Fitzsimmons; Danny Ainge

Portland Trail Blazers

	Min	FG%	FT%	Reb	Ast	Pts	Avg
Anderson .	3081	.427	.768	363	584	1436	17.5
Rider	2563	.464	.812	304	198	1223	16.1
Wallace . . .	1892	.558	.638	419	74	938	15.1
C. Robinson	3077	.426	.696	321	261	1224	15.1
Sabonis . .	1762	.498	.777	547	146	928	13.4
Trent	1918	.536	.699	428	87	882	10.8
Augmon* .	942	.477	.711	138	56	279	4.7
Dudley . . .	1840	.430	.474	593	41	317	3.9

Coach—P.J. Carlesimo

Sacramento Kings

	Min	FG%	FT%	Reb	Ast	Pts	Avg
Richmond .	3125	.454	.861	319	338	2095	25.9
Abdul-Rauf	2131	.445	.846	122	189	1031	13.7
Polynice . .	2893	.457	.562	772	178	1025	12.5
Williamson	1992	.498	.689	326	124	915	11.6
Owens . . .	1995	.467	.697	392	187	724	11.0
Grant	607	.440	.778	142	28	252	10.5
Edney	1376	.384	.823	113	226	485	6.9

	Min	FG%	FT%	Reb	Ast	Pts	Avg
Smith	2526	.539	.496	769	191	532	6.6
Gamble . .	953	.430	.700	107	77	307	5.0
Hurley . . .	632	.368	.698	38	146	143	2.9

Coach—Garry St. Jean; Eddie Jordan

San Antonio Spurs

	Min	FG%	FT%	Reb	Ast	Pts	Avg
D. Wilkins . .	1945	.417	.803	402	119	1145	18.2
Elliott	1393	.422	.755	190	124	582	14.9
Maxwell . . .	2068	.375	.744	159	153	929	12.9
Del Negro . .	2243	.467	.868	210	231	886	12.3
Johnson . . .	2472	.477	.690	147	513	800	10.5
Williams . . .	1345	.509	.645	206	91	588	9.0
Perdue	1918	.568	.579	638	38	565	8.7
Herrera	1837	.433	.686	340	50	597	8.0
Alexander . .	1454	.396	.736	123	254	577	7.2
Anderson . .	1659	.496	.667	448	34	322	3.9
Feick*	624	.357	.507	214	26	151	3.7

Coach—Bob Hill; Gregg Popovich

Seattle SuperSonics

	Min	FG%	FT%	Reb	Ast	Pts	Avg
Payton . . .	3213	.476	.715	378	583	1785	21.8
Kemp	2750	.510	.742	807	156	1516	18.7
Schrempf .	2192	.492	.801	394	266	1022	16.8
Hawkins . .	2755	.464	.875	320	250	1139	13.9
Perkins . .	1976	.439	.817	300	103	889	11.0
Cummings	828	.486	.695	183	39	370	8.2
McMillan .	798	.409	.655	118	140	169	4.6
Stewart . .	982	.444	.720	171	52	300	4.3
McIlvaine .	1477	.471	.495	330	23	314	3.8
Wingate . .	929	.416	.825	74	80	236	3.6
Ehlo	848	.351	.500	110	68	214	3.5
Snow	775	.451	.712	70	159	199	3.0

Coach—George Karl

Toronto Raptors

	Min	FG%	FT%	Reb	Ast	Pts	Avg
Stoudamire	3311	.401	.823	330	709	1634	20.2
Williams . .	2647	.427	.765	367	197	1199	16.4
Camby . . .	1897	.482	.693	394	97	935	14.8
Christie . . .	3127	.417	.775	432	315	1176	14.5
Rogers . . .	1397	.525	.600	304	37	551	9.8
Jones	2421	.480	.818	680	84	616	7.8
Wright	1009	.400	.511	186	28	390	6.5
Davis	623	.402	.739	40	34	181	5.0
Miller* . . .	1152	.517	.608	306	87	294	4.8
Rozier* . . .	737	.454	.508	234	31	189	4.5

Coach—Darrell Walker

Utah Jazz

	Min	FG%	FT%	Reb	Ast	Pts	Avg
Malone . . .	2998	.550	.755	809	368	2249	27.4
Hornacek .	2592	.482	.899	241	361	1191	14.5
Stockton . .	2896	.548	.846	228	860	1183	14.4
Russell . . .	2525	.479	.701	331	123	873	10.8
Carr	1460	.483	.780	195	74	603	7.4
Ostertag . .	1818	.515	.678	565	27	559	7.3
Anderson . .	1066	.462	.687	179	49	386	5.9
Eisley	1083	.451	.787	84	198	368	4.5
Morris	977	.408	.722	162	43	314	4.3
Keefe	915	.513	.689	216	32	235	3.8
Foster . . .	920	.453	.831	187	31	278	3.5

Coach—Jerry Sloan

Vancouver Grizzlies

	Min	FG%	FT%	Reb	Ast	Pts	Avg
Abdur-Rahim	2802	.453	.746	555	175	1494	18.7
Reeves . .	2777	.486	.704	610	160	1213	16.2
Peeler . . .	2291	.398	.820	247	256	1041	14.5
Anthony . .	1863	.393	.730	184	407	616	9.5
Lynch	1059	.471	.619	261	76	342	8.3
B. Edwards	1439	.397	.817	189	114	478	7.8
Moten . . .	1214	.388	.646	119	129	447	6.7
Rogers . . .	1848	.505	.574	386	46	543	6.6
Mayberry .	1952	.403	.630	134	329	410	5.1
Robinson .	681	.379	.615	71	65	188	4.6
Chilcutt . .	662	.436	.591	156	47	182	3.4

Coach—Brian Winters; Stu Jackson

Washington Bullets

	Min	FG%	FT%	Reb	Ast	Pts	Avg
Webber . .	2806	.518	.565	743	331	1445	20.1
Howard . . .	3324	.486	.756	652	311	1570	19.1
Strickland .	2997	.466	.738	335	727	1410	17.2
Muresan . .	1849	.604	.618	481	29	777	10.6
Cheaney .	2411	.505	.693	268	114	837	10.6
Murray . . .	1814	.425	.990	950	70	817	10.8
Whitney . .	1117	.421	.832	104	182	430	5.2
Jackson . .	1133	.407	.768	132	65	374	5.0
Grant	1604	.411	.769	256	68	316	4.1

Coach—Jim Lynam; Bernie Bickerstaff

1997 NBA Player Draft, First-Round Picks

	Team	Player, College
1.	San Antonio	Tim Duncan, Wake Forest
2.	Philadelphia	Keith Van Horn[1], Utah
3.	Boston	Chauncey Billups, Colorado
4.	Vancouver	Antonio Daniels, Bowling Green
5.	Denver	Tony Battie, Texas Tech
6.	Boston	Ron Mercer, Kentucky
7.	New Jersey	Tim Thomas, Villanova
8.	Golden State	Adonal Foyle, Colgate
9.	Toronto	Tracy McGrady, Mt. Zion Christian Academy
10.	Milwaukee	Danny Fortson[2], Cincinnati
11.	Sacramento	Olivier Saint-Jean, San Jose State
12.	Indiana	Austin Croshere, Providence
13.	Cleveland	Derek Anderson, Kentucky
14.	L.A. Clippers	Maurice Taylor, Michigan
15.	Dallas	Kelvin Cato[3], Iowa State
16.	Cleveland	Brevin Knight, Stanford
17.	Orlando	Johnny Taylor, Tenn.-Chattanooga
18.	Portland	Chris Anstey, SE Melbourne Magic (NBL)
19.	Detroit	Scot Pollard, Kansas
20.	Minnesota	Paul Grant, Wisconsin
21.	New Jersey	Anthony Parker, Bradley
22.	Atlanta	Ed Gray, California
23.	Seattle	Bobby Jackson[4], Minnesota
24.	Houston	Rodrick Rhodes, USC
25.	New York	John Thomas, Minnesota
26.	Miami	Charles Smith, New Mexico
27.	Utah	Jacque Vaughn, Kansas
28.	Chicago	Keith Booth, Maryland

Note: Washington gave up its 1997 first-round draft pick (17th overall) as compensation for re-signing free agent Juwan Howard in 1996. (1) Traded with Don MacLean, Michael Cage, Lucious Harris to New Jersey for Jim Jackson, Eric Montross, Tim Thomas, and Anthony Parker. (2) Traded with Johnny Newman and Joe Wolf to Denver for Ervin Johnson. (3) Traded to Portland for Chris Antsey. (4) Traded to Denver for James Cotton and 1998 second-round draft pick.

Number-One First-Round NBA Draft Picks, 1966-97

Year	Team	Player, college
1966	New York	Cazzie Russell, Michigan
1967	Detroit	Jimmy Walker, Providence
1968	Houston	Elvin Hayes, Houston
1969	Milwaukee	Lew Alcindor[1], UCLA
1970	Detroit	Bob Lanier, St. Bonaventure
1971	Cleveland	Austin Carr, Notre Dame
1972	Portland	LaRue Martin, Loyola-Chicago
1973	Philadelphia	Doug Collins, Illinois St.
1974	Portland	Bill Walton, UCLA
1975	Atlanta	David Thompson[2], N.C. State
1976	Houston	John Lucas, Maryland
1977	Milwaukee	Kent Benson, Indiana
1978	Portland	Mychal Thompson, Minnesota
1979	L.A. Lakers	Magic Johnson, Michigan St.
1980	Golden State	Joe Barry Carroll, Purdue
1981	Dallas	Mark Aguirre, DePaul
1982	L.A. Lakers	James Worthy, North Carolina
1983	Houston	Ralph Sampson, Virginia
1984	Houston	Akeem Olajuwon, Houston
1985	New York	Patrick Ewing, Georgetown
1986	Cleveland	Brad Daugherty, North Carolina
1987	San Antonio	David Robinson, Navy
1988	L.A. Clippers	Danny Manning, Kansas
1989	Sacramento	Pervis Ellison, Louisville
1990	New Jersey	Derrick Coleman, Syracuse
1991	Charlotte	Larry Johnson, UNLV
1992	Orlando	Shaquille O'Neal, LSU
1993	Orlando	Chris Webber[3], Michigan
1994	Milwaukee	Glenn Robinson, Purdue
1995	Golden State	Joe Smith, Maryland
1996	Philadelphia	Allen Iverson, Georgetown
1997	San Antonio	Tim Duncan, Wake Forest

(1) Later Kareem Abdul-Jabbar. (2) Signed with Denver of the ABA. (3) Traded to Golden State.

All-Time NBA Statistical Leaders

(At the start of the 1997-98 season. *Player active in 1996-97 season.)

Scoring Average
(Minimum 400 games or 10,000 pts)

	G	Pts.	Avg
*Michael Jordan	848	26,920	31.7
Wilt Chamberlain	1,045	31,419	30.1
Elgin Baylor	846	23,149	27.4
Jerry West	932	25,192	27.0
Bob Pettit	792	20,880	26.4
George Gervin	791	20,708	26.2
*Karl Malone	980	25,592	26.1
Oscar Robinson	1,040	26,710	25.7
*David Robinson	563	14,366	25.5
*Dominique Wilkins	1,047	26,534	25.3

Field Goal Percentage
(Minimum 2,000 field goals made)

	FGA	FGM	Pct.
Artis Gilmore	9,570	5,732	.599
*Mark West	4,264	2,491	.584
*Shaquille O'Neal	6,513	3,760	.577
Steve Johnson	4,965	2,841	.572
Darryl Dawkins	6,079	3,477	.572
James Donaldson	5,442	3,105	.571
Jeff Ruland	3,734	2,105	.564
Kareem Abdul-Jabbar	28,307	15,837	.559
Kevin McHale	12,334	6,830	.554
*Otis Thorpe	11,155	6,154	.552

Free Throw Percentage
(Minimum 1,200 free throws made)

	FTA	FTM	Pct.
*Mark Price	2,259	2,048	.907
Rick Barry	4,243	3,818	.900
Calvin Murphy	3,864	3,445	.892
Scott Skiles	1,741	1,548	.889
Larry Bird	4,471	3,960	.886
Bill Sharman	3,559	3,143	.883
*Reggie Miller	4,597	4,034	.877
*Ricky Pierce	3,819	3,346	.876
Kiki Vandeweghe	3,997	3,484	.872
Jeff Malone	3,383	2,947	.871

Points

Kareem Abdul-Jabbar	38,387
Wilt Chamberlain	31,419
Moses Malone	27,409
Elvin Hayes	27,313
*Michael Jordan	26,920
Oscar Robertson	26,710
*Dominique Wilkins	26,534
John Havlicek	26,395
Alex English	25,613
*Karl Malone	25,592

Games Played

*Robert Parish	1,611
Kareem Abdul-Jabbar	1,560
Moses Malone	1,329
Elvin Hayes	1,303
John Havlicek	1,270
*Buck Williams	1,266
Paul Silas	1,254
Alex English	1,193
James Edwards	1,168
Tree Rollins	1,156

Assists

*John Stockton	12,170
Magic Johnson	10,141
Oscar Robertson	9,887
Isiah Thomas	9,061
Maurice Cheeks	7,392
Lenny Wilkens	7,211
Bob Cousy	6,955
Guy Rodgers	6,917
*Mark Jackson	6,825
Nate Archibald	6,476

Field Goals Made

Kareem Abdul-Jabbar	15,837
Wilt Chamberlain	12,681
Elvin Hayes	10,976
Alex English	10,659
John Havlicek	10,513
*Michael Jordan	10,081
*Dominique Wilkins	9,913
*Robert Parish	9,614
*Karl Malone	9,510
Oscar Robertson	9,508

Rebounds

Wilt Chamberlain	23,924
Bill Russell	21,620
Kareem Addul-Jabbar	17,440
Elvin Hayes	16,279
Moses Malone	16,212
*Robert Parish	14,715
Nate Thurmond	14,464
Walt Bellamy	14,241
Wes Unseld	13,769
Jerry Lucas	12,942

Basketball Hall of Fame, Springfield, MA
(1997 inductees are in **bold**)

PLAYERS
Abdul-Jabbar, Kareem
Archibald, Nate
Arizin, Paul
Barlow, Thomas
Barry, Rick
Baylor, Elgin
Beckman, John
Bellamy, Walt
Belov, Sergei
Bing, Dave
Blazejowski, Carol
Borgmann, Bennie
Bradley, Bill
Brennan, Joseph
Cervi, Al
Chamberlain, Wilt
Cooper, Charles
Cosic, Kresimir
Cousy, Bob
Cowens, Dave
Crawford, Joan
Cunningham, Billy
Curry, Denise
Davies, Bob
DeBernardi, Forrest
DeBusschere, Dave
Dehnert, Dutch
Donovan, Anne
Endacott, Paul
English, Alex
Erving, Julius
Foster, Bud
Frazier, Walt
Friedman, Max
Fulks, Joe
Gale, Lauren
Gallatin, Harry
Gates, Pop
Gervin, George
Gola, Tom
Goodrich, Gail
Greer, Hal
Gruenig, Ace
Hagan, Cliff
Hanson, Victor
Harris, Luisa

Havlicek, John
Hawkins, Connie
Hayes, Elvin
Heinsohn, Tom
Holman, Nat
Howell, Bailey
Hyatt, Chuck
Issel, Dan
Jeannette, Buddy
Johnson, William
Johnston, Neil
Jones, K.C.
Jones, Sam
Krause, Moose
Kurland, Bob
Lanier, Bob
Lapchick, Joe
Lieberman-Cline,
  Nancy
Lovellette, Clyde
Lucas, Jerry
Luisetti, Hank
Macauley, Ed
Maravich, Pete
Martin, Slater
McCracken, Branch
McCracken, Jack
McDermott, Bobby
McGuire, Dick
Meyers, Ann
Mikan, George
Mikkelsen, Vern
Miller, Cheryl
Monroe, Earl
Murphy, Calvin
Murphy, Stretch
Page, Pat
Pettit, Bob
Phillip, Andy
Pollard, Jim
Ramsey, Frank
Reed, Willis
Robertson, Oscar
Roosma, John S.
Russell, Bill
Russell, Honey

Schayes, Adolph
Schmidt, Ernest
Schommer, John
Sedran, Barney
Semjonova, Uljana
Sharman, Bill
Steinmetz, Christian
Thompson, Cat
Thompson, David
Thurmond, Nate
Twyman, Jack
Unseld, Wes
Vandivier, Fuzzy
Wachter, Edward
Walton, Bill
Wanzer, Bobby
West, Jerry
White, Nera
Wilkens, Lenny
Wooden, John
Yardley, George

COACHES
Allen, Phog
Anderson, Harold
Auerbach, Red
Barry, Sam
Blood, Ernest
Cann, Howard
Carlson, Dr. H. C.
Carnesecca, Lou
Carnevale, Ben
Carril, Pete
Case, Everett
Crum, Denny
Daly, Chuck
Dean, Everett
Diaz-Miguel, Antonio
Diddle, Edgar
Drake, Bruce
Gaines, Clarence
Gardner, Jack
Gill, Slats
Gomelsky, Aleksandr
Harshman, Marv
Haskins, Don
Hickey, Edgar
Hobson, Howard

Holzman, Red
Iba, Hank
Julian, Alvin
Keaney, Frank
Keogan, George
Knight, Bob
Kundla, John
Lambert, Ward
Litwack, Harry
Loeffler, Kenneth
Lonborg, Dutch
McCutchan, Arad
McGuire, Al
McGuire, Frank
McLendon, John
Meanwell, Dr. W. E.
Meyer, Ray
Miller, Ralph
Newell, Pete
Ramsay, Jack
Rubini, Cesare
Rupp, Adolph
Sachs, Leonard
Shelton, Everett
Smith, Dean
Taylor, Fred
Wade, Margaret
Watts, Stan
Wooden, John
Woolpert, Phil

REFEREES
Enright, James
Hepbron, George
Hoyt, George
Kennedy, Matthew
Leith, Lloyd
Mihalik, Red
Nucatola, John
Quigley, Ernest
Shirley, J. Dallas
Strom, Earl
Tobey, David
Walsh, David

CONTRIBUTORS
Abbott, Senda B.
Bee, Clair

Brown, Walter
Bunn, John
Douglas, Bob
Duer, Al O.
Fagan, Cliff
Fisher, Harry
Fleisher, Larry
Gottlieb, Edward
Gulick, Dr. L. H.
Harrison, Lester
Hepp, Dr. Ferenc
Hickox, Edward
Hinkle, Tony
Irish, Ned
Jones, R. W.
Kennedy, Walter
Liston, Emil
Mokray, Bill
Morgan, Ralph
Morgenweck, Frank
Naismith, Dr. James
O'Brien, John
O'Brien, Larry
Olsen, Harold
Podoloff, Maurice
Porter, H. V.
Reid, William
Ripley, Elmer
St. John, Lynn
Saperstein, Abe
Schabinger, Arthur
Stagg, Amos Alonzo
Stankovic, Boris
Steitz, Edward
Taylor, Chuck
Teague, Bertha
Tower, Oswald
Trester, Arthur
Wells, Clifford
Wilke, Lou

TEAMS
First Team
Original Celtics
Buffalo Germans
Renaissance

All-Time NBA Coaching Victories
(At the start of the 1997-98 season. *Active through 1996-97 season.)

Coach	W-L	Pct.	Coach	W-L	Pct.
Lenny Wilkens*	1,070-876	.550	Mike Fratello*	503-402	.556
Red Auerbach	938-479	.662	Del Harris*	489-430	.532
Dick Motta*	935-1,017	.479	Phil Jackson*	483-173	.736
Bill Fitch*	927-1,041	.471	Kevin Loughery	474-662	.417
Jack Ramsay	864-783	.525	Alex Hannum	471-412	.533
Pat Riley*	859-360	.705	Billy Cunningham	454-196	.698
Don Nelson	851-629	.575	George Karl*	442-305	.592
Cotton Fitzsimmons*	832-775	.518	Larry Costello	430-300	.589
Gene Shue	784-861	.477	Tom Heinsohn	427-263	.619
John MacLeod	707-657	.518	John Kundla	423-302	.583
Red Holzman	696-604	.535	Rick Adelman*	357-252	.586
Doug Moe	628-529	.543	Hubie Brown	341-410	.454
Larry Brown*	624-480	.565	Bill Russell	341-290	.540
Jerry Sloan*	577-359	.616	Bill Sharman	333-240	.581
Chuck Daly	564-379	.598	Jim Lynam*	328-392	.456
Alvin Attles	557-518	.518	Richie Guerin	327-291	.529
K.C. Jones	522-252	.674	Al Cervi	326-241	.575

NBA Home Courts

Team	Name (built)	Capacity	Team	Name (built)	Capacity
Atlanta	Georgia Dome (1997);	21,570/34,821	Milwaukee	Bradley Center (1988)	18,717
	Georgia Tech (1956)	9,300	Minnesota	Target Center (1990)	19,006
Boston	FleetCenter (1995)	18,624	New Jersey	Continental Airlines Arena (1981)	20,049
Charlotte	Charlotte Coliseum (1988)	24,042	New York	Madison Square Garden (1968)	19,763
Chicago	United Center (1994)	21,711	Orlando	Orlando Arena (1989)	17,248
Cleveland	Gund Arena (1994)	20,562	Philadelphia	CoreStates Center (1996)	20,444
Dallas	Reunion Arena (1980)	18,042	Phoenix	America West Arena (1992)	19,023
Denver	McNichols Sports Arena (1975)	17,171	Portland	The Rose Garden (1995)	21,538
Detroit	Palace of Auburn Hills (1988)	21,454	Sacramento	ARCO Arena (1988)	17,317
Golden State	Oakland Arena (1997)	19,200	San Antonio	Alamodome (1993)	20,662/34,215
Houston	The Summit (1975)	16,285	Seattle	KeyArena (1995)	17,072
Indiana	Market Square Arena (1974)	16,530	Toronto	SkyDome (1989)	20,125/35,000
L.A. Clippers	L.A. Memorial Sports Arena (1959);	16,021	Utah	Delta Center (1991)	19,911
	Arrowhead Pond of Anaheim (1992)	18,211	Vancouver	Bear Country at GM Place (1995)	19,193
L.A. Lakers	The Great Western Forum (1967)	17,505	Washington	US Airways Arena (1973)	18,756
Miami	Miami Arena (1988)	15,200			

WOMEN'S PROFESSIONAL BASKETBALL

Women's National Basketball Association

The Women's National Basketball Association (WNBA), which is backed by the National Basketball Association, tipped off its inaugural season on June 21, 1997. The initial eight teams, located in cities that already have NBA franchises, feature former women's Olympic and college stars. To avoid direct competition with the NBA season, the WNBA had a summer schedule, beginning after the NBA playoffs. The teams played a 28-game regular season schedule that lasted 10 weeks, and on Aug. 30, 1997, the Houston Comets became the first championship team of the new league.

Because of its success in its first year, the WNBA already has plans for expansion. The league's Operating Committee announced a plan to add two expansion teams for the 1998 season. The teams were to be operated by the Detroit Pistons and the Washington Wizards, and were to be granted franchises on the condition that they secured pledges for at least 3,000 season tickets before Nov. 10, 1997. On Nov. 11, the committee was to vote on this recommendation as well as a proposal for two additional franchises in 1999. The league also announced that it will add two games to the regular season and change the format of the playoffs beginning in the 1997-98 season. The first WNBA All-Star Game was scheduled to take place during the 1999 season.

WNBA Final Standings, 1997 Season

Eastern Conference	W	L	Pct	GB	Western Conference	W	L	Pct	GB
Houston Comets	18	10	.643	—	Phoenix Mercury	16	12	.571	—
New York Liberty	17	11	.607	1	Los Angeles Sparks	14	14	.500	2
Cleveland Rockers	15	13	.536	3	Sacramento Monarchs	10	18	.357	6
Charlotte Sting	15	13	.536	3	Utah Starzz	7	21	.250	9

WNBA Playoff Semifinals

Houston 70, Charlotte 54
New York 59, Phoenix 41

WNBA Championship

Houston 65, New York 51
MVP, championship series — Cynthia Cooper, Houston

WNBA Regular Season Individual Highs in 1997

Most minutes played — 1,051: Chantel Tremitiere, Sacramento.
Most points — 621: Cynthia Cooper, Houston.
Highest field goal percentage — .618: Zheng Haixia, Los Angeles.
Highest 3-point field goal percentage — .435: Eva Nemcova, Cleveland.
Highest free throw percentage — .898: Bridget Pettis, Phoenix.
Most rebounds — 266: Lisa Leslie, Los Angeles.
Most assists — 172: Teresa Weatherspoon, New York.
Most steals — 85: Teresa Weatherspoon, New York.
Most blocked shots — 63: Elena Baranova, Utah.
MVP — Cynthia Cooper, Houston.
Coach of the year — Van Chancellor, Houston.

American Basketball League

The American Basketball League (ABL) began its first season of play on Oct. 18, 1996, with eight teams playing a 40-game schedule. The season ended on Feb. 20, 1997, and the Columbus Quest captured the first ever ABL championship, Mar. 11, after a grueling five-game series against the Richmond Rage.

The ABL's 1997-98 season opened on Oct. 12, with nine teams including the expansion Long Beach StingRays. The Richmond Rage moved to Philadelphia before the start of the 1997-98 season.

ABL Final Standings, 1996-97 Season

East	W	L	Pct	GB	West	W	L	Pct	GB
Columbus Quest	31	9	.775	—	Colorado Xplosion	25	15	.625	—
Richmond Rage	21	19	.525	10	San Jose Lasers	18	22	.450	7
Atlanta Glory	18	22	.450	13	Seattle Reign	17	23	.425	8
New England Blizzard	16	24	.350	15	Portland Power	14	26	.350	11

ABL Playoff Semifinals

Richmond defeated Colorado 2 games to 0
Columbus defeated San Jose 2 games to 0

ABL Championship Series

Columbus defeated Richmond 3 games to 2

ABL Regular Season Individual Highs in 1996-97

Most points — 847: Carolyn Jones, New England.
Highest field goal percentage — .587: Missy Masley, Atlanta.
Highest 3-point field goal percentage — .479: Shannon Johnson, Columbus.
Highest free throw percentage — .872: Niesa Johnson, Atlanta.
Most rebounds — 400: Natalie Williams, Portland.
Most assists — 320: Dawn Staley, Richmond.
Most steals — 177: Debbie Black, Colorado.
Most blocked shots — 58: Taj McWilliams, Richmond.
MVP — Nikki McCray, Columbus.
Coach of the year — Brian Agler, Columbus.
Defensive player of the year — Debbie Black, Colorado.

COLLEGE BASKETBALL
Final NCAA Division I Conference Standing, 1996-97
(*conference tournament champion; †conference does not hold a tournament)

America East
	Conference W	L	Overall W	L
Boston U.*	17	1	25	5
Drexel	16	2	22	9
Hartford	11	7	17	11
Hofstra	9	9	12	15
Delaware	8	10	15	16
Vermont	7	11	14	13
Northeastern	6	12	7	20
Maine	6	12	11	20
New Hampshire	5	13	7	20
Towson St.	5	13	9	19

Atlantic Coast
	Conf. W	L	Overall W	L
Duke	12	4	24	9
Wake Forest	11	5	24	7
North Carolina*	11	5	28	7
Clemson	9	7	23	10
Maryland	9	7	21	11
Virginia	7	9	18	13
Florida St.	6	10	20	12
North Carolina St.	4	12	17	15
Georgia Tech	3	13	9	18

Atlantic 10
Eastern Division
	Conf. W	L	Overall W	L
St. Joseph's (PA)*	13	3	26	7
Rhode Island	12	4	20	10
Massachusetts	11	5	19	14
Temple	10	6	20	11
St. Bonaventure	5	11	14	14
Fordham	1	15	6	21

Western Division
	Conf. W	L	Overall W	L
Xavier (OH)	13	3	23	6
George Washington	8	8	15	14
Virginia Tech	7	9	15	16
Dayton	6	10	13	14
Duquesne	5	11	9	18
La Salle	5	11	10	17

Big East
Big East 7
	Conf. W	L	Overall W	L
Georgetown	11	7	20	10
Providence	10	8	24	12
Pittsburgh	10	8	18	15
Syracuse	9	9	19	13
Miami (FL)	9	9	16	13
Rutgers	5	13	11	16
Seton Hall	5	13	10	18

Big East 6
	Conf. W	L	Overall W	L
Villanova	12	6	24	10
Boston College*	12	6	22	9
West Virginia	11	7	21	10
Notre Dame	8	10	16	14
St. John's (NY)	8	10	13	14
Connecticut	7	11	18	15

Big Sky
	Conf. W	L	Overall W	L
Northern Arizona	14	2	21	7
Montana*	11	5	21	11
Montana St.	10	6	16	14
Weber St.	9	7	15	13
Idaho St.	8	6	14	13
Cal. St. Northridge	8	8	14	15
Portland St.	6	10	9	17
E. Washington	3	13	7	19
Cal. St. Sacramento	2	14	3	23

Big South
	Conf. W	L	Overall W	L
Liberty	11	3	23	9
N.C.-Asheville	11	3	18	10
Radford	8	6	15	13
Charleston So.*	7	7	17	13
Coastal Carolina	6	8	11	16
N.C.-Greensboro	6	8	10	20
Winthrop	5	9	12	15
Md.-Balt. County	2	12	5	22

Big Ten†
	Conf. W	L	Overall W	L
Minnesota	16	2	31	4
Iowa	12	6	22	10
Purdue	12	6	18	12
Illinois	11	7	22	10
Wisconsin	11	7	18	10
Indiana	9	9	22	11
Michigan	9	9	24	11
Michigan St.	9	9	17	12
Ohio St.	5	13	10	17
Penn St.	3	15	10	17
Northwestern	2	16	7	22

Big 12
	Conf. W	L	Overall W	L
Kansas*	15	1	34	2
Colorado	11	5	22	10
Iowa St.	10	6	22	9
Texas Tech	10	6	19	9
Texas	10	6	18	12
Oklahoma	9	7	19	11
Oklahoma St.	7	9	17	15
Nebraska	7	9	18	15
Baylor	6	10	18	12
Missouri	5	11	16	17
Kansas St.	3	13	10	17
Texas A&M	3	13	9	18

Big West
Eastern Division
	Conf. W	L	Overall W	L
Utah St.	12	4	20	9
Nevada	12	4	21	10
New Mexico St.	12	4	19	9
Boise St.	9	7	14	13
Idaho	5	11	13	17
North Texas	5	11	10	16

Western Division
	Conf. W	L	Overall W	L
Pacific (CA)*	12	4	24	6
Long Beach St.	9	7	13	14
UC Santa Barbara	7	9	12	15
Cal. St. Fullerton	6	10	13	14
Cal. Poly SLO	6	10	14	16
UC Irvine	1	15	1	25

Colonial Athletic
	Conf. W	L	Overall W	L
Old Dominion*	10	6	22	11
N.C.-Wilmington	10	6	16	14
East Carolina	9	7	17	10
Va. Commonwealth	9	7	14	13
William & Mary	8	8	12	16
James Madison	8	8	16	13
American	7	9	11	16
Richmond	7	9	13	15
George Mason	4	12	10	17

Conference USA
Red Division
	Conf. W	L	Overall W	L
Tulane	11	3	20	11
Ala.-Birmingham	7	7	18	14
Southern Mississippi	6	8	12	15
South Florida	2	12	8	19

White Division
	Conf. W	L	Overall W	L
N.C.-Charlotte	10	4	22	9
Memphis	10	4	16	15
Louisville	9	5	26	9
Houston	3	11	11	16

Blue Division
	Conf. W	L	Overall W	L
Cincinnati	12	2	26	8
Marquette*	9	5	22	9
St. Louis	4	10	11	18
DePaul	1	13	3	23

Ivy Group†
	Conf. W	L	Overall W	L
Princeton	14	0	24	4
Dartmouth	10	4	18	9
Harvard	10	4	17	9
Pennsylvania	8	6	12	14
Cornell	7	7	15	11
Yale	3	11	10	16
Brown	3	11	4	22
Columbia	1	13	0	20

Metro Atlantic Athletic
	Conf. W	L	Overall W	L
Iona	11	3	22	8
Canisius	10	4	17	12
Loyola (MD)	10	4	13	14
St. Peter's	9	5	13	15
Niagara	5	9	11	17
Manhattan	5	9	9	18
Siena	4	10	9	18
Fairfield*	2	12	11	19

Mid-American
	Conf. W	L	Overall W	L
Bowling Green	13	5	22	10
Miami (OH)*	13	5	21	9
Ohio	12	6	17	10
Eastern Michigan	11	7	22	10
Ball St.	9	9	16	13
Western Michigan	9	9	14	14
Kent	7	11	9	18
Toledo	6	12	13	14
Akron	6	12	8	18
Central Michigan	4	14	7	19

Mid-Continent
	Conf. W	L	Overall W	L
Valparaiso*	13	3	24	7
Western Illinois	11	5	19	10
Buffalo	11	5	17	11
Troy St.	10	6	16	11
Northeastern Illinois	8	8	16	12
Mo.-Kansas City	7	9	10	17
Youngstown St.	4	12	9	18
Central Conn. St.	4	12	8	19
Chicago St.	4	12	4	23

Mid-Eastern Athletic
	Conf. W	L	Overall W	L
Coppin St.*	15	3	22	9
South Carolina St.	12	6	14	14
North Carolina A&T	11	7	15	13
Bethune-Cookman	9	9	12	16
Morgan St.	8	10	9	18
Florida A&M	8	10	8	19
Hampton	7	11	8	19
Delaware St.	7	11	7	20
Howard	7	11	7	20
Md.-East. Shore	6	12	11	17

Midwestern Collegiate
	Conf. W	L	Overall W	L
Butler*	12	4	23	10
Detroit	11	5	16	13
Ill.-Chicago	11	5	15	14
Wis.-Green Bay	10	6	14	14
Loyola (IL)	7	9	12	15
Northern Illinois	6	10	12	15
Cleveland St.	6	10	9	19
Wright St.	5	11	7	20
Wis.-Milwaukee	4	12	8	20

Missouri Valley
	Conf. W	L	Overall W	L
Illinois St.*	14	4	24	6
Bradley	12	6	17	13
Southwest Mo. St.	12	6	24	9
Northern Iowa	11	7	16	12
Evansville	11	7	17	14
Creighton	10	8	15	15
Wichita St.	8	10	14	13
Indiana St.	6	12	12	16
Southern Illinois	6	12	13	17
Drake	0	18	2	26

Northeast
	Conf. W	L	Overall W	L
LIU-Brooklyn*	15	3	21	9
Fairleigh Dickinson	13	5	18	10
Monmouth (NJ)	12	6	18	11
Rider	10	8	14	14
Mt. St. Mary's (MD)	10	8	14	13
St. Francis (PA)	9	9	12	15
St. Francis (NY)	7	11	13	15
Wagner	7	11	10	17
Marist	4	14	6	22
Robert Morris	3	15	4	23

Ohio Valley

	Conference W	Conference L	Overall W	Overall L
Murray St.*	12	6	20	10
Austin Peay	12	6	17	14
Middle Tenn. St.	11	7	19	12
Tennessee Tech.	10	8	15	13
Eastern Illinois	9	9	12	18
Southeast Mo. St.	9	9	12	18
Tennessee-Martin	8	10	11	16
Tennessee St.	7	11	9	18
Eastern Kentucky	6	12	8	18
Morehead St.	6	12	8	19

Pacific-10†

	Conference W	Conference L	Overall W	Overall L
UCLA	15	3	24	8
California	12	6	23	9
Stanford	12	6	22	8
Southern Cal.	12	6	17	11
Arizona	11	7	25	9
Washington	10	8	17	11
Oregon	8	10	17	11
Washington St.	5	13	13	17
Oregon St.	3	15	7	20
Arizona St.	2	16	10	20

Patriot League

	Conference W	Conference L	Overall W	Overall L
Navy*	10	2	20	9
Bucknell	9	3	18	11
Colgate	8	4	12	16
Holy Cross	5	7	8	19
Lafayette	5	7	11	17
Army	4	8	10	16
Lehigh	1	11	1	26

Southeastern

Eastern Division

	Conference W	Conference L	Overall W	Overall L
South Carolina	15	1	24	8
Kentucky*	13	3	35	5
Georgia	10	6	24	9
Vanderbilt	9	7	19	12
Florida	5	11	13	17
Tennessee	4	12	11	16

Western Division

	Conference W	Conference L	Overall W	Overall L
Mississippi	11	5	20	9
Arkansas	8	8	18	14
Auburn	6	10	16	15
Alabama	6	10	17	14
Mississippi St.	6	10	12	18
LSU	3	13	10	20

Southern

Northern Division

	Conference W	Conference L	Overall W	Overall L
Marshall	10	4	20	9
Davidson	10	4	18	10
Appalachian St.	8	6	14	14
VMI	7	7	12	16
East Tennessee St.	2	12	7	20

Southern Division

	Conference W	Conference L	Overall W	Overall L
Tenn.-Chattanooga*	11	3	24	11
Western Carolina	7	7	14	13
Citadel	6	8	13	14
Georgia Southern	5	9	10	18
Furman	4	10	10	17

Southland

	Conference W	Conference L	Overall W	Overall L
Northeast Lousiana	10	6	14	14
Southwest Tex. St.*	10	6	16	13
McNeese St.	10	6	18	12
Northwestern St.	8	8	13	15
Stephen F. Austin	8	8	12	15
Texas-Arlington	8	8	12	15
Nicholls St.	7	9	10	16
Sam Houston St.	7	9	8	18
Texas-San Antonio	4	12	9	17

Southwestern Athletic

	Conference W	Conference L	Overall W	Overall L
Mississippi Val.	11	3	19	10
Jackson St.*	9	5	14	16
Alcorn St.	8	6	11	17
Prairie View	7	7	10	17
Texas Southern	6	8	12	16
Grambling	5	9	10	17
Southern University	5	9	10	17
Alabama St.	5	9	8	21

Sun Belt

	Conference W	Conference L	Overall W	Overall L
New Orleans	14	4	22	7
South Alabama*	14	4	23	7
Ark.-Little Rock	11	7	18	11
Lamar	10	8	15	12
Louisiana Tech.	10	8	15	14
Western Kentucky	9	9	12	15
Southwestern La.	9	9	12	16
Arkansas St.	8	10	15	12
Jacksonville	4	14	5	23
Tex.-Pan American	1	17	3	25

Trans America Athletic

East Division

	Conference W	Conference L	Overall W	Overall L
Charleston (SC)*	16	0	29	3
Florida International	12	4	16	13
Florida Atlantic	11	5	16	11
Campbell	8	8	11	16
Stetson	5	11	9	18
Central Florida	4	12	7	19

West Division

	Conference W	Conference L	Overall W	Overall L
Samford	11	5	19	9
Jacksonville St.	9	7	10	17
Southeastern La.	7	9	10	18
Georgia St.	6	10	10	17
Centenary (LA)	6	10	9	18
Mercer	1	15	3	23

West Coast

	Conference W	Conference L	Overall W	Overall L
Santa Clara	10	4	16	11
St. Mary's (CA)*	10	4	23	8
San Francisco	9	5	16	13
San Diego	8	6	17	11
Gonzaga	8	6	15	12
Portland	4	10	9	18
Pepperdine	4	10	6	21
Loyola Marymount	3	11	7	21

Western Athletic

Pacific Division

	Conference W	Conference L	Overall W	Overall L
Hawaii	12	4	21	8
Fresno St.	12	4	20	12
UNLV	11	5	22	10
Colorado St.	10	6	20	9
Wyoming	8	8	12	16
San Jose St.	5	11	13	14
San Diego St.	4	12	12	15
Air Force	2	14	7	19

Mountain Division

	Conference W	Conference L	Overall W	Overall L
Utah*	15	1	29	4
Tulsa	12	4	24	10
New Mexico	11	5	25	8
Texas Christian	7	9	22	13
Southern Methodist	7	9	16	12
UTEP	6	10	13	13
Rice	6	10	12	15
Brigham Young	0	16	1	25

Independents

	W	L
Oral Roberts	21	7
Southern Utah	9	17
Wofford	7	20

All-Time Winningest College Teams by Percentage

School	Years	Won	Lost	Pct.	School	Years	Won	Lost	Pct.
Kentucky	94	1,685	525	.762	Louisville	83	1,325	696	.656
North Carolina	87	1,675	595	.738	DePaul	74	1,175	618	.655
UNLV	39	811	294	.734	Indiana	97	1,410	755	.651
UCLA	78	1,399	603	.699	Notre Dame	92	1,414	762	.650
Kansas	99	1,630	710	.697	Utah	89	1,346	728	.649
St. John's (NY)	90	1,532	696	.688	Temple	101	1,475	804	.647
Syracuse	96	1,451	683	.680	Weber State	35	640	351	.646
Western Kentucky	78	1,356	650	.676	Purdue	99	1,355	750	.644
Duke	92	1,516	749	.669	Illinois	92	1,321	736	.642
Arkansas	74	1,268	662	.657	Villanova	77	1,256	705	.640

Major College Basketball Tournaments

The National Invitation Tournament (NIT), first played in 1938, is the nation's oldest basketball tournament. The first National Collegiate Athletic Association (NCAA) national championship tournament was played a year later. Selections for both tournaments are made in Mar., with the NCAA selecting first from among the top Division I teams.

National Invitation Tournament Champions

Year	Champion	Year	Champion	Year	Champion	Year	Champion
1938	Temple	1953	Seton Hall	1968	Dayton	1983	Fresno State
1939	Long Island Univ.	1954	Holy Cross	1969	Temple	1984	Michigan
1940	Colorado	1955	Duquesne	1970	Marquette	1985	UCLA
1941	Long Island Univ.	1956	Louisville	1971	North Carolina	1986	Ohio State
1942	West Virginia	1957	Bradley	1972	Maryland	1987	Southern Mississippi
1943	St. John's	1958	Xavier (Ohio)	1973	Virginia Tech	1988	Connecticut
1944	St. John's	1959	St. John's	1974	Purdue	1989	St. John's
1945	De Paul	1960	Bradley	1975	Princeton	1990	Vanderbilt
1946	Kentucky	1961	Providence	1976	Kentucky	1991	Stanford
1947	Utah	1962	Dayton	1977	St. Bonaventure	1992	Virginia
1948	St. Louis	1963	Providence	1978	Texas	1993	Minnesota
1949	San Francisco	1964	Bradley	1979	Indiana	1994	Villanova
1950	CCNY	1965	St. John's	1980	Virginia	1995	Virginia Tech
1951	Brigham Young	1966	Brigham Young	1981	Tulsa	1996	Nebraska
1952	LaSalle	1967	Southern Illinois	1982	Bradley	1997	Michigan

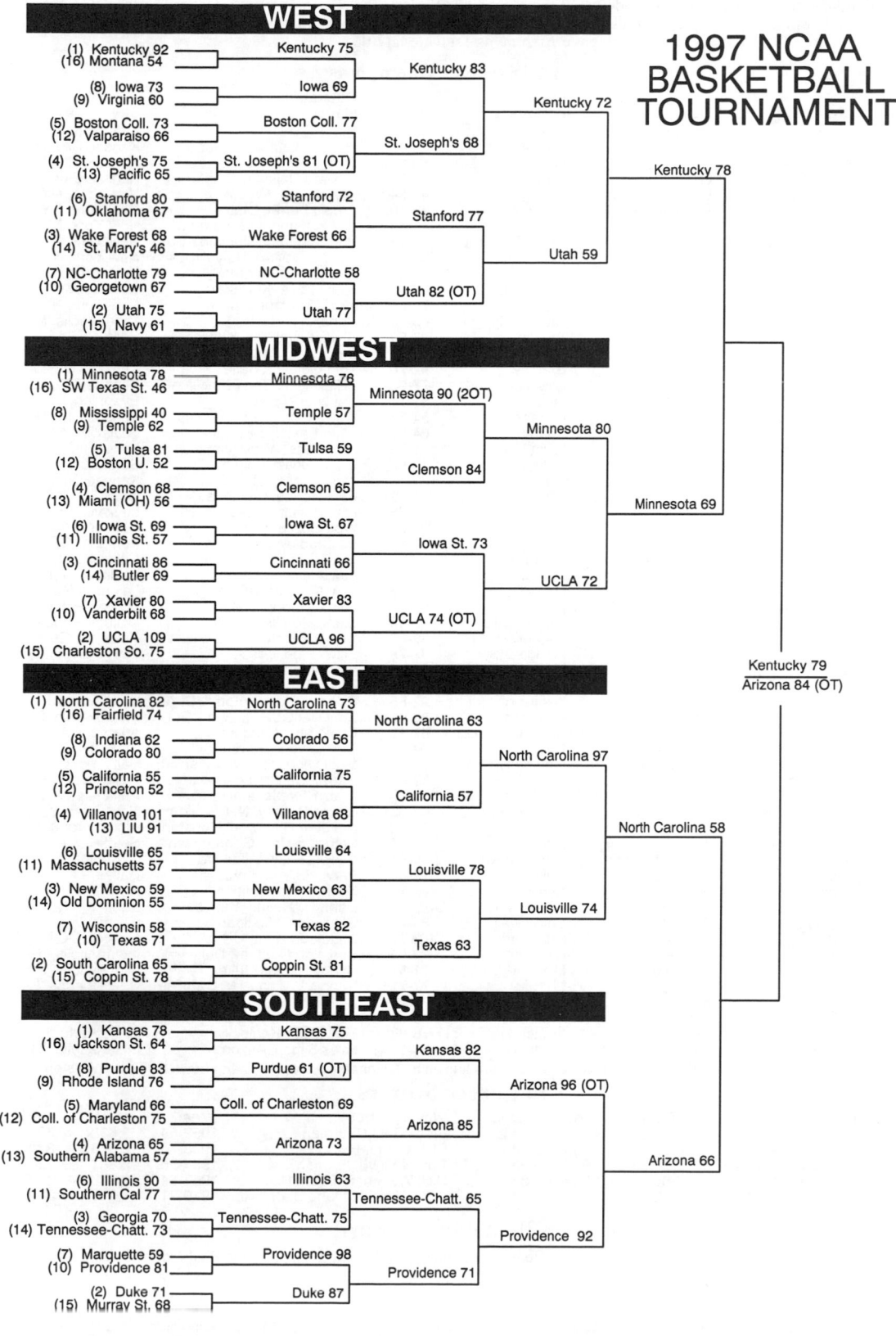

1997 NCAA BASKETBALL TOURNAMENT

WEST

(1) Kentucky 92 / (16) Montana 54 — Kentucky 75
(8) Iowa 73 / (9) Virginia 60 — Iowa 69
Kentucky 83

(5) Boston Coll. 73 / (12) Valparaiso 66 — Boston Coll. 77
(4) St. Joseph's 75 / (13) Pacific 65 — St. Joseph's 81 (OT)
St. Joseph's 68

Kentucky 72

(6) Stanford 80 / (11) Oklahoma 67 — Stanford 72
(3) Wake Forest 68 / (14) St. Mary's 46 — Wake Forest 66
Stanford 77

(7) NC-Charlotte 79 / (10) Georgetown 67 — NC-Charlotte 58
(2) Utah 75 / (15) Navy 61 — Utah 77
Utah 82 (OT)

Utah 59

Kentucky 78

MIDWEST

(1) Minnesota 78 / (16) SW Texas St. 46 — Minnesota 76
(8) Mississippi 40 / (9) Temple 62 — Temple 57
Minnesota 90 (2OT)

(5) Tulsa 81 / (12) Boston U. 52 — Tulsa 59
(4) Clemson 68 / (13) Miami (OH) 56 — Clemson 65
Clemson 84

Minnesota 80

(6) Iowa St. 69 / (11) Illinois St. 57 — Iowa St. 67
(3) Cincinnati 86 / (14) Butler 69 — Cincinnati 66
Iowa St. 73

(7) Xavier 80 / (10) Vanderbilt 68 — Xavier 83
(2) UCLA 109 / (15) Charleston So. 75 — UCLA 96
UCLA 74 (OT)

UCLA 72

Minnesota 69

Kentucky 79
Arizona 84 (OT)

EAST

(1) North Carolina 82 / (16) Fairfield 74 — North Carolina 73
(8) Indiana 62 / (9) Colorado 80 — Colorado 56
North Carolina 63

(5) California 55 / (12) Princeton 52 — California 75
(4) Villanova 101 / (13) LIU 91 — Villanova 68
California 57

North Carolina 97

(6) Louisville 65 / (11) Massachusetts 57 — Louisville 64
(3) New Mexico 59 / (14) Old Dominion 55 — New Mexico 63
Louisville 78

(7) Wisconsin 58 / (10) Texas 71 — Texas 82
(2) South Carolina 65 / (15) Coppin St. 78 — Coppin St. 81
Texas 63

Louisville 74

North Carolina 58

SOUTHEAST

(1) Kansas 78 / (16) Jackson St. 64 — Kansas 75
(8) Purdue 83 / (9) Rhode Island 76 — Purdue 61 (OT)
Kansas 82

(5) Maryland 66 / (12) Coll. of Charleston 75 — Coll. of Charleston 69
(4) Arizona 65 / (13) Southern Alabama 57 — Arizona 73
Arizona 85

Arizona 96 (OT)

(6) Illinois 90 / (11) Southern Cal 77 — Illinois 63
(3) Georgia 70 / (14) Tennessee-Chatt. 73 — Tennessee-Chatt. 75
Tennessee-Chatt. 65

(7) Marquette 59 / (10) Providence 81 — Providence 98
(2) Duke 71 / (15) Murray St. 68 — Duke 87
Providence 71

Providence 92

Arizona 66

Arizona Defeats Kentucky in Overtime to Win the 1997 NCAA Men's Basketball Championship

The University of Arizona Wildcats defeated the Kentucky Wildcats, 84-79, in overtime, to capture the NCAA men's basketball championship, Mar. 31, at Indianapolis, IN. Arizona was led by junior guard Miles Simon, who scored 30 points and made 14 of 17 free throws. The victory gave Arizona its 1st national title.

NCAA Division I Champions

Year	Champion	Coach	Final opponent	Score	Outstanding player	Site
1939	Oregon	Howard Hobson	Ohio St.	46-33	None	Evanston, IL
1940	Indiana	Branch McCracken	Kansas	60-42	Marvin Huffman, Indiana	Kansas City, MO
1941	Wisconsin	Harold Foster	Washington St.	39-34	John Kotz, Wisconsin	Kansas City, MO
1942	Stanford	Everett Dean	Dartmouth	53-38	Howard Dallmar, Stanford	Kansas City, MO
1943	Wyoming	Everett Shelton	Georgetown	46-34	Ken Sailors, Wyoming	New York, NY
1944	Utah	Vadal Peterson	Dartmouth	42-40[1]	Arnold Ferrin, Utah	New York, NY
1945	Oklahoma St.[2]	Henry Iba	NYU	49-45	Bob Kurland, Oklahoma St.	New York, NY
1946	Oklahoma St.[2]	Henry Iba	North Carolina	43-40	Bob Kurland, Oklahoma St.	New York, NY
1947	Holy Cross	Alvin Julian	Oklahoma	58-47	George Kaftan, Holy Cross	New York, NY
1948	Kentucky	Adolph Rupp	Baylor	58-42	Alex Groza, Kentucky	New York, NY
1949	Kentucky	Adolph Rupp	Oklahoma St.	46-36	Alex Groza, Kentucky	Seattle, WA
1950	CCNY	Nat Holman	Bradley	71-68	Irwin Dambrot, CCNY	New York, NY
1951	Kentucky	Adolph Rupp	Kansas St.	68-58	None	Minneapolis, MN
1952	Kansas	Forrest Allen	St. John's	80-63	Clyde Lovellette, Kansas	Seattle, WA
1953	Indiana	Branch McCracken	Kansas	69-68	B.H. Born, Kansas	Kansas City, MO
1954	La Salle	Kenneth Loeffler	Bradley	92-76	Tom Gola, La Salle	Kansas City, MO
1955	San Francisco	Phil Woolpert	LaSalle	77-63	Bill Russell, San Francisco	Kansas City, MO
1956	San Francisco	Phil Woolpert	Iowa	83-71	Hal Lear, Temple	Evanston, IL
1957	North Carolina	Frank McGuire	Kansas	54-53[1]	Wilt Chamberlain, Kansas	Kansas City, MO
1958	Kentucky	Adolph Rupp	Seattle	84-72	Elgin Baylor, Seattle	Louisville, KY
1959	California	Pete Newell	West Virginia	71-70	Jerry West, West Virginia	Louisville, KY
1960	Ohio St.	Fred Taylor	California	75-55	Jerry Lucas, Ohio St.	San Francisco, CA
1961	Cincinnati	Edwin Jucker	Ohio St.	70-65[1]	Jerry Lucas, Ohio St.	Kansas City, MO
1962	Cincinnati	Edwin Jucker	Ohio St.	71-59	Paul Hogue, Cincinnati	Louisville, KY
1963	Loyola (IL)	George Ireland	Cincinnati	60-58[1]	Art Heyman, Duke	Louisville, KY
1964	UCLA	John Wooden	Duke	98-83	Walt Hazzard, UCLA	Kansas City, MO
1965	UCLA	John Wooden	Michigan	91-80	Bill Bradley, Princeton	Portland, OR
1966	Texas-El Paso[3]	Don Haskins	Kentucky	72-65	Jerry Chambers, Utah	College Park, MD
1967	UCLA	John Wooden	Dayton	79-64	Lew Alcindor, UCLA	Louisville, KY
1968	UCLA	John Wooden	North Carolina	78-55	Lew Alcindor, UCLA	Los Angeles, CA
1969	UCLA	John Wooden	Purdue	92-72	Lew Alcindor, UCLA	Louisville, KY
1970	UCLA	John Wooden	Jacksonville	80-69	Sidney Wicks, UCLA	College Park, MD
1971	UCLA	John Wooden	Villanova*	68-62	Howard Porter, Villanova*	Houston, TX
1972	UCLA	John Wooden	Florida St.	81-76	Bill Walton, UCLA	Los Angeles, CA
1973	UCLA	John Wooden	Memphis St.	87-66	Bill Walton, UCLA	St. Louis, MO
1974	North Carolina St.	Norm Sloan	Marquette	76-64	David Thompson, N.C. St.	Greensboro, NC
1975	UCLA	John Wooden	Kentucky	92-85	Richard Washington, UCLA	San Diego, CA
1976	Indiana	Bob Knight	Michigan	86-68	Kent Benson, Indiana	Philadelphia, PA
1977	Marquette	Al McGuire	North Carolina	67-59	Butch Lee, Marquette	Atlanta, GA
1978	Kentucky	Joe Hall	Duke	94-88	Jack Givens, Kentucky	St. Louis, MO
1979	Michigan St.	Jud Heathcote	Indiana St.	75-64	Magic Johnson, Michigan St.	Salt Lake City, UT
1980	Louisville	Denny Crum	UCLA*	59-54	Darrell Griffith, Louisville	Indianapolis, IN
1981	Indiana	Bob Knight	North Carolina	63-50	Isiah Thomas, Indiana	Philadelphia, PA
1982	North Carolina	Dean Smith	Georgetown	63-62	James Worthy, N. Carolina	New Orleans, LA
1983	North Carolina St.	Jim Valvano	Houston	54-52	Hakeem Olajuwon, Houston	Albuquerque, NM
1984	Georgetown	John Thompson	Houston	84-75	Patrick Ewing, Georgetown	Seattle, WA
1985	Villanova	Rollie Massimino	Georgetown	66-64	Ed Pinckney, Villanova	Lexington, KY
1986	Louisville	Denny Crum	Duke	72-69	Pervis Ellison, Louisville	Dallas, TX
1987	Indiana	Bob Knight	Syracuse	74-73	Keith Smart, Indiana	New Orleans, LA
1988	Kansas	Larry Brown	Oklahoma	83-79	Danny Manning, Kansas	Kansas City, MO
1989	Michigan	Steve Fisher	Seton Hall	80-79[1]	Glen Rice, Michigan	Seattle, WA
1990	UNLV	Jerry Tarkanian	Duke	103-73	Anderson Hunt, UNLV	Denver, CO
1991	Duke	Mike Krzyzewski	Kansas	72-65	Christian Laettner, Duke	Indianapolis, IN
1992	Duke	Mike Krzyzewski	Michigan	71-51	Bobby Hurley, Duke	Minneapolis, MN
1993	North Carolina	Dean Smith	Michigan	77-71	Donald Williams, N. Carolina	New Orleans, LA
1994	Arkansas	Nolan Richardson	Duke	76-72	Corliss Williamson, Arkansas	Charlotte, NC
1995	UCLA	Jim Harrick	Arkansas	89-78	Ed O'Bannon, UCLA	Seattle, WA
1996	Kentucky	Rick Pitino	Syracuse	76-67	Tony Delk, Kentucky	E. Rutherford, NJ
1997	Arizona	Lute Olson	Kentucky	84-79[1]	Miles Simon, Arizona	Indianapolis, IN

*Declared ineligible after the tournament. (1) Overtime. (2) Then known as Oklahoma A&M. (3) Then known as Texas Western.

Top Career Scorers

Player, school	Years	Points	Avg.	Player, school	Years	Points	Avg.
Pete Maravich, LSU	1968-70	3,667	44.2	Frank Selvy, Furman	1952-54	2,538	32.5
Austin Carr, Notre Dame	1969-71	2,560	34.6	Rick Mount, Purdue	1968-70	2,323	32.3
Oscar Robertson, Cincinnati	1958-60	2,973	33.8	Darrell Floyd, Furman	1954-56	2,281	32.1
Calvin Murphy, Niagara	1968-70	2,548	33.1	Nick Werkman, Seton Hall	1962-64	2,273	32.0
Dwight Lamar, SW Louisiana	1972-73	1,862	32.7	Willie Humes, Idaho State	1970-71	1,510	31.5

John R. Wooden Award

Awarded annually to the nation's outstanding college basketball player by the United States Basketball Writers Assn.

1977	Marques Johnson, UCLA	1984	Michael Jordan, North Carolina	1991	Larry Johnson, UNLV
1978	Phil Ford, North Carolina	1985	Chris Mullin, St. John's	1992	Christian Laettner, Duke
1979	Larry Bird, Indiana State	1986	Walter Berry, St. John's	1993	Calbert Cheaney, Indiana
1980	Darrell Griffith, Louisville	1987	David Robinson, Navy	1994	Glenn Robinson, Purdue
1981	Danny Ainge, Brigham Young	1988	Danny Manning, Kansas	1995	Ed O'Bannon, UCLA
1982	Ralph Sampson, Virginia	1989	Sean Elliott, Arizona	1996	Marcus Camby, Massachusetts
1983	Ralph Sampson, Virginia	1990	Lionel Simmons, La Salle	1997	Tim Duncan, Wake Forest

Selected Division I Basketball Coaches in 1997[1]

College	Coach	College	Coach	College	Coach
Akron	Dan Hipsher	Indiana St.	Royce Waltman	Rice	Willis Wilson
Alabama	David Hobbs	Iowa	Tom Davis	Richmond	John Beilein
Alabama-Birmingham	Murry Bartow	Iowa St.	Tim Floyd	Rutgers	Kevin Bannon
American	Art Perry	James Madison	Sherman Dillard	St. Bonaventure	Jim Baron
Arizona	Lute Olson	Kansas	Roy Williams	St. John's (NY)	Fran Fraschilla
Arizona St.	Don Newman	Kansas St.	Tom Asbury	St. Joseph's (PA)	Phil Martelli
Arkansas	Nolan Richardson	Kent	Gary Waters	St. Louis	Charlie Spoonhour
Army	Pat Harris	Kentucky	Tubby Smith	St. Mary's (CA)	Dave Bollwinkei
Auburn	Cliff Ellis	Long Beach St.	Wayne Morgan	St. Peter's	Rodger Blind
Austin Peay	Dave Loos	LSU	John Brady	San Diego	Brad Holland
Ball St.	Ray McCallum	Louisville	Denny Crum	San Diego St.	Fred Trenkle
Baylor	Harry Miller	Loyola (IL)	Ken Burmeister	San Francisco	Phil Mathews
Boise St.	Rod Jensen	Loyola Marymount	Charles Bradley	San Jose St.	Stan Morrison
Boston College	Jim O'Brien	Manhattan	John Leonard	Santa Clara	Dick Davey
Bowling Green	Dan Dakich	Marquette	Mike Deane	Seton Hall	Tommy Amaker
Bradley	Jim Molinari	Maryland	Gary Williams	South Carolina	Eddie Fogler
Brigham Young	Steve Cleveland	Massachusetts	James "Bruiser" Flint	South Florida	Seth Greenberg
Brown	Frank Dobbs	Memphis	Tic Price	SE Missouri St.	Gary Garner
Butler	Barry Collier	Miami (FL)	Leonard Hamilton	USC	Henry Bibby
California	Ben Braun	Miami (OH)	Charlie Coles	Southern Illinois	Rich Herrin
Cal. St. Fullerton	Bob Hawking	Michigan	To be announced	SMU	Mike Dement
UC Irvine	Pat Douglas	Michigan St.	Tom Izzo	Southern Mississippi	James Green
UC Santa Barbara	Jerry Pimm	Middle Tenn. St.	Randy Wiel	SW Missouri St.	Steve Alford
Central Michigan	Jay Smith	Minnesota	Clem Haskins	Stanford	Mike Montgomery
Cincinnati	Bob Huggins	Mississippi	Rob Evans	Syracuse	Jim Boeheim
Clemson	Rick Barnes	Mississippi St.	Richard Williams	Temple	John Chaney
Cleveland St.	Rollie Massimino	Missouri	Norm Stewart	Tennessee	Jerry Green
Colgate	Jack Bruen	Montana	Blaine Taylor	Tennessee St.	Frankie Allen
Colorado	Ricardo Patton	Montana St.	Mick Durham	Tennessee Tech	Frank Harrell
Colorado St.	Stew Morrill	Morehead St.	Kyle Macy	Tenn.-Chattanooga	Henry Dickerson
Columbia	Armond Hill	Mt. St. Mary's (MD)	Jim Phelan	Tennessee-Martin	Calvin C. Luther
Connecticut	Jim Calhoun	Murray St.	Mark Gottfried	Texas	Tom Penders
Cornell	Scott Thompson	Nebraska	Danny Nee	Texas A&M	Tony Barone
Creighton	Dana Altman	Nevada	Pat Foster	Texas Christian	Billy Tubbs
Dartmouth	Dave Faucher	UNLV	Bill Bayno	Texas-Arlington	Eddie McCarter
Dayton	Oliver Purnell	New Mexico	Dave Bliss	UTEP	Don Haskins
DePaul	Pat Kennedy	New Mexico St.	Lou Henson	Texas Southern	Robert Moreland
Detroit	Perry Watson	Nicholls St.	Rickey Broussard	Toledo	Stan Joplin
Drake	Kurt Kanaskie	North Carolina	Bill Guthridge	Tulane	Perry Clark
Drexel	Bill Herrion	North Carolina A&T	Roy Thomas	Tulsa	Bill Self
Duke	Mike Krzyzewski	North Carolina St.	Herb Sendek	UCLA	Steve Lavin
E. Carolina	Joe Dooley	N.C.-Charlotte	Melvin Watkins	Utah	Rick Majerus
E. Illinois	Rick Samuels	N.C.-Greensboro	Randy Peele	Utah St.	Larry Eustachy
E. Kentucky	Scott Perry	N.C.-Wilmington	Jerry Wainwright	Valparaiso	Homer Drew
E. Michigan	Milton Barnes	N. Arizona	Ben Howland	Vanderbilt	Jan van Breda Kolff
E. Washington	Steve Aggers	N. Illinois	Brian Hammel	Villanova	Steve Lappas
Evansville	Jim Crews	N. Iowa	Eldon Miller	Virginia	Jeff Jones
Florida	Billy Donovan	Northwestern	Kevin O'Neill	Va. Commonwealth	Sonny Smith
Florida International	Shakey Rodriquez	Notre Dame	John MacLeod	Virginia Tech	Bobby Hussey
Florida St.	Steve Robinson	Ohio	Larry Hunter	Wake Forest	Dave Odom
Fresno St.	Jerry Tarkanian	Ohio St.	Jim O'Brien	Washington	Bob Bender
George Mason	Jim Larranaga	Oklahoma	Kelvin Sampson	Washington St.	Kevin Eastman
Geo. Washington	Mike Jarvis	Oklahoma St.	Eddie Sutton	Weber St.	Ron Abegglen
Georgetown	John Thompson	Old Dominion	Jeff Capel	West Virginia	Gale Catlett
Georgia	Ron Jirsa	Oregon	Ernie Kent	W. Illinois	Jim Kerwin
Georgia Tech	Bobby Cremins	Oregon St.	Eddie Payne	W. Kentucky	Matt Kilcullen
Gonzaga	Dan Monson	Pacific (CA)	Bob Thomason	W. Michigan	Bob Donewald
Harvard	Frank Sullivan	Pennsylvania	Fran Dunphy	Wichita St.	Randy Smithson
Hawaii	Riley Wallace	Penn St.	Jerry Dunn	William & Mary	Charlie Woollum
Houston	Alvin Brooks	Pepperdine	Lorenzo Romar	Wisconsin	Dick Bennett
Idaho	David Farrar	Pittsburgh	Ralph Willard	Wis.-Green Bay	Mike Heideman
Idaho St.	Herb Williams	Portland	Rob Chavez	Wright St.	Ed Schilling
Illinois	Lon Kruger	Princeton	Bill Carmody	Wyoming	Larry Shyatt
Illinois-Chicago	Jimmy Collins	Providence	Pete Gillen	Xavier (OH)	Skip Prosser
Illinois St.	Kevin Stallings	Purdue	Gene Keady	Yale	Dick Kuchen
Indiana	Bob Knight	Rhode Island	Jim Harrick		

(1) As of mid-Oct.

Most Coaching Victories in the NCAA Tournament Through 1997

Coach, school(s), years	Wins	Tournaments	Coach, school(s), years	Wins	Tournaments
Dean Smith, North Carolina, 1967-97 ...	65	27	Jerry Tarkanian, Long Beach State and UNLV, 1970-91	31	13
John Wooden, UCLA, 1950-75	47	16			
Denny Crum, Louisville, 1972-97	42	21	Adolph Rupp, Kentucky, 1942-72	30	20
Bob Knight, Indiana, 1973-97	40	21	Lute Olson, Iowa and Arizona, 1979-97 ..	28	18
Mike Krzyzewski, Duke, 1984-97	40	13	Jim Boeheim, Syracuse, 1977-97	27	17
John Thompson, Georgetown, 1975-97 ..	34	20			

Women's College Basketball

Tennessee Defeats Old Dominion, Takes Its Fifth NCAA Women's Championship

The University of Tennessee Lady Volunteers beat the Old Dominion Lady Monarchs, 68-59, to win their 2d consecutive NCAA Division I Women's Basketball Championship, Mar. 30, 1997, in Cincinnati, OH. The victory gave Tennessee a record 5 national championships in the last 11 years. In the quarterfinals, the Lady Vols, who had lost 10 games during the season, upset previously undefeated Connecticut, who were ranked number one. Tennessee sophomore forward Chamique Holdsclaw, who scored 24 points in the title game, was named the tournament's most outstanding player.

NCAA Division I Women's Champions

Year	Champion	Coach	Final opponent	Score	Outstanding player	Site
1982	Louisiana Tech	Sonja Hogg	Cheyney	76-62	Janice Lawrence, La. Tech	Norfolk, VA
1983	USC	Linda Sharp	Louisiana Tech	69-67	Cheryl Miller, USC	Norfolk, VA
1984	USC	Linda Sharp	Tennessee	72-61	Cheryl Miller, USC	Los Angeles, CA
1985	Old Dominion	Marianne Stanley	Georgia	70-65	Tracy Claxton, Old Dominion	Austin, TX
1986	Texas	Jody Conradt	USC	97-81	Clarissa Davis, Texas	Lexington, KY
1987	Tennessee	Pat Summitt	Louisiana Tech	67-44	Tonya Edwards, Tennessee	Austin, TX
1988	Louisiana Tech	Leon Barmore	Auburn	56-54	Erica Westbrooks, La. Tech	Tacoma, WA
1989	Tennessee	Pat Summitt	Auburn	76-60	Bridgette Gordon, Tennessee	Tacoma, WA
1990	Stanford	Tara VanDerveer	Auburn	88-81	Jennifer Azzi, Stanford	Knoxville, TN
1991	Tennessee	Pat Summitt	Virginia	70-67*	Dawn Staley, Virginia	New Orleans, LA
1992	Stanford	Tara VanDerveer	W. Kentucky	78-62	Molly Goodenbour, Stanford	Los Angeles, CA
1993	Texas Tech	Marsha Sharp	Ohio St.	84-82	Sheryl Swoopes, Texas Tech	Atlanta, GA
1994	North Carolina	Sylvia Hatchell	Louisiana Tech	60-59	Charlotte Smith, North Carolina	Richmond, VA
1995	Connecticut	Geno Auriemma	Tennessee	70-64	Rebecca Lobo, Connecticut	Minneapolis, MN
1996	Tennessee	Pat Summitt	Georgia	83-65	Michelle Marciniak, Tennessee	Charlotte, NC
1997	Tennessee	Pat Summitt	Old Dominion	68-59	Chamique Holdsclaw, Tennessee	Cincinnati, OH

* Overtime.

Wade Trophy

Awarded by the National Assn. for Girls and Women in Sport for academics, community service, and player performance in basketball.

Year	Player, school	Year	Player, school	Year	Player, school
1978	Carol Blazejowski, Montclair St.	1985	Cheryl Miller, USC	1991	Daedra Charles, Tennessee
1979	Nancy Lieberman, Old Dominion	1986	Kamie Ethridge, Texas	1992	Susan Robinson, Penn St.
1980	Nancy Lieberman, Old Dominion	1987	Shelly Pennefeather, Villanova	1993	Karen Jennings, Nebraska
1981	Lynette Woodard, Kansas	1988	Teresa Weatherspoon, Louisiana Tech	1994	Carol Ann Shudlick, Minnesota
1982	Pam Kelly, Louisiana Tech			1995	Rebecca Lobo, Connecticut
1983	LaTaunya Pollard, Long Beach St.	1989	Clarissa Davis, Texas	1996	Jennifer Rizzotti, Connecticut
1984	Janice Lawrence, Louisiana Tech	1990	Jennifer Azzi, Stanford	1997	DeLisha Milton, Florida

Top Women's Career Scorers

(Minimum 1,500 points; ranked by average)

Player, school	Years	Points	Avg.	Player, school	Years	Points	Avg.
Patricia Hoskins, Mississippi Valley State	1985-89	3,122	28.4	Joyce Walker, LSU	1981-84	2,906	24.8
Sandra Hodge, New Orleans	1981-84	2,860	26.7	Tarcha Hollis, Grambling	1988-91	2,058	24.2
Lorri Bauman, Drake	1981-84	3,115	26.0	Karen Pelphrey, Marshall	1983-86	2,746	24.1
Andrea Congreaves, Mercer	1989-93	2,796	25.9	Erma Jones, Bethune-Cookman	1982-84	2,095	24.1
Valorie Whiteside, Appalachian State	1984-88	2,944	25.4	Cheryl Miller, USC	1983-86	3,018	23.6

SKIING

World Cup Alpine Champions

Men

Year		Year		Year	
1967	Jean Claude Killy, France	1977	Ingemar Stenmark, Sweden	1987	Pirmin Zurbriggen, Switzerland
1968	Jean Claude Killy, France	1978	Ingemar Stenmark, Sweden	1988	Pirmin Zurbriggen, Switzerland
1969	Karl Schranz, Austria	1979	Peter Luescher, Switzerland	1989	Marc Girardelli, Luxembourg
1970	Karl Schranz, Austria	1980	Andreas Wenzel, Liechtenstein	1990	Pirmin Zurbriggen, Switzerland
1971	Gustavo Thoeni, Italy	1981	Phil Mahre, U.S.	1991	Marc Girardelli, Luxembourg
1972	Gustavo Thoeni, Italy	1982	Phil Mahre, U.S.	1992	Paul Accola, Switzerland
1973	Gustavo Thoeni, Italy	1983	Phil Mahre, U.S.	1993	Marc Girardelli, Luxembourg
1974	Piero Gros, Italy	1984	Pirmin Zurbriggen, Switzerland	1994	Kjetil Andre Aamodt, Norway
1975	Gustavo Thoeni, Italy	1985	Marc Girardelli, Luxembourg	1995	Alberto Tomba, Italy
1976	Ingemar Stenmark, Sweden	1986	Marc Girardelli, Luxembourg	1996	Lasse Kjus, Norway
				1997	Luc Alphand, France

Women

Year		Year		Year	
1967	Nancy Greene, Canada	1977	Lise-Marie Morerod, Switzerland	1987	Maria Walliser, Switzerland
1968	Nancy Greene, Canada	1978	Hanni Wenzel, Liechtenstein	1988	Michela Figini, Switzerland
1969	Gertrud Gabl, Austria	1979	Annemarie Proell Moser, Austria	1989	Vreni Schneider, Switzerland
1970	Michele Jacot, France	1980	Hanni Wenzel, Liechtenstein	1990	Petra Kronberger, Austria
1971	Annemarie Proell, Austria	1981	Marie-Theres Nadig, Switzerland	1991	Petra Kronberger, Austria
1972	Annemarie Proell, Austria	1982	Erika Hess, Switzerland	1992	Petra Kronberger, Austria
1973	Annemarie Proell, Austria	1983	Tamara McKinney, U.S.	1993	Anita Wachter, Austria
1974	Annemarie Proell, Austria	1984	Erika Hess, Switzerland	1994	Vreni Schneider, Switzerland
1975	Annemarie Proell, Austria	1985	Michela Figini, Switzerland	1995	Vreni Schneider, Switzerland
1976	Rose Mittermaier, W. Germany	1986	Maria Walliser, Switzerland	1996	Katja Seizinger, Germany
				1997	Pernilla Wiberg, Sweden

FISHING
Selected IGFA Saltwater & Freshwater All-Tackle World Records
Source: International Game Fish Association; records confirmed to Oct. 15, 1997

Saltwater Fish Records

Species	Weight	Where caught	Date	Angler
Albacore	88 lbs. 2 oz.	Gran Canaria, Canary Islands	Nov. 19, 1977	Siegfried Dickemann
Amberjack, greater.	155 lbs. 10 oz.	Challenger Bank, Bermuda	June 24, 1981	Joseph Dawson
Barracuda, great	85 lbs.	Christmas Island, Kiribati	Apr. 11, 1992	John Helfrich
Barracuda, Mexican. . . .	21 lbs.	Phantom Isle, Costa Rica	Mar. 27, 1987	E. Greg Kent
Barracuda, Pacific	7 lbs. 11 oz.	Catalina Island, CA	May 22, 1994	Jim Kingsmill
Bass, barred sand	13 lbs. 3 oz.	Huntington Beach, CA	Aug. 29, 1988	Robert Halal
Bass, black sea	9 lbs. 8 oz.	Virginia Beach, VA	Jan. 9, 1987	Joe Mizelle Jr.
		Virginia Beach, VA	Dec. 2, 1990	Jack G. Stallings
Bass, giant sea	563 lbs. 8 oz.	Anacaba Island, CA	Aug. 20, 1968	James D. McAdam Jr.
Bass, redeye	8 lbs. 12 oz.	Apalachicola River, FL	Jan. 28, 1995	Carl W. Davis
Bass, striped	78 lbs. 8 oz.	Atlantic City, NJ	Sept. 21, 1982	Albert McReynolds
Bluefish.	31 lbs. 12 oz.	Hatteras Inlet, NC	Jan. 30, 1972	James M. Hussey
Bonefish	19 lbs.	Zululand, South Africa	May 26, 1962	Brian W. Batchelor
Bonito, Atlantic	18 lbs. 4 oz.	Faial Island, Azores	July 8, 1953	D. Gama Higgs
Bonito, Pacific	14 lbs. 12 oz.	San Benitos Island, Mexico	Oct. 12, 1980	Jerome Rilling
Cabezon.	23 lbs.	Juan De Fuca Strait, WA	Aug. 4, 1990	Wesley Hunter
Cobia	135 lbs. 9 oz.	Shark Bay, Australia	July 9, 1985	Peter W. Goulding
Cod, Atlantic	98 lbs. 12 oz.	Isle of Shoals, NH	June 8, 1969	Alphonse Bielevich
Cod, Pacific.	30 lbs.	Andrew Bay, AK	June 7, 1984	Donald Vaughn
Conger	133 lbs. 4 oz.	Berry Head, S. Devon, England	June 5, 1995	Vic Evans
Dolphin	87 lbs.	Papagallo Gulf, Costa Rica	Sept. 25, 1976	Manuel Salazar
Drum, black.	113 lbs. 1 oz.	Lewes, DE	Sept. 15, 1975	Gerald Townsend
Drum, red	94 lbs. 2 oz.	Avon, NC	Nov. 7, 1984	David Deuel
Eel, American	9 lbs. 4 oz.	Cape May, NJ	Nov. 9, 1995	Jeff Pennick
Eel, marbled	36 lbs. 1 oz.	Hazelmere Dam, South Africa	June 10, 1984	Ferdie van Nooten
Flounder, southern.	20 lbs. 9 oz.	Nassau Sound, FL	Dec. 23, 1983	Larenza Mungin
Flounder, summer	22 lbs. 7 oz.	Montauk, NY	Sept. 15, 1975	Charles Nappi
Grouper, Warsaw.	436 lbs. 12 oz.	Gulf of Mexico, Destin, FL	Dec. 22, 1985	Steve Haeusler
Halibut, Atlantic	255 lbs. 4 oz.	Gloucester, MA	July 28, 1989	Sonny Manley
Halibut, California	53 lbs. 4 oz.	Santa Rosa Island, CA	July 7, 1988	Russell Harmon
Halibut, Pacific.	395 lbs.	Unalaska Bay, Bering Sea	June 21, 1995	Michael James Golat
Jack, crevalle	57 lbs. 5 oz.	Barra do Kwanza, Angola	Oct. 10, 1992	Cam Nicolson`
Jack, horse-eye	24 lbs. 8 oz.	Miami, FL	Dec. 20, 1982	Tito Schnau
Jack, Pacific crevalle . . .	29 lbs. 8 oz.	Playa Zancudo, Costa Rica	Jan. 1, 1994	Ronald C. Snody
Jewfish	680 lbs.	Fernandina Beach, FL	May 20, 1961	Lynn Joyner
Kawakawa	29 lbs.	Clarion Island, Mexico	Dec. 17, 1986	Ronald Nakamura
Lingcod.	69 lbs.	Langara Island, British Columbia	June 16, 1992	Murray Romer
Mackerel, cero.	17 lbs. 2 oz.	Islamorada, FL	Apr. 5, 1986	G. Michael Mills
Mackerel, king	90 lbs.	Key West, FL	Feb. 16, 1976	Norton Thomton
Mackerel, Spanish	13 lbs.	Ocracoke Inlet, NC	Nov. 4, 1987	Robert Cranton
Marlin, Atlantic blue	1,402 lbs. 2 oz.	Vitoria, Brazil	Feb. 29, 1992	Paulo Amorim
Marlin, black	1,560 lbs.	Cabo Blanco, Peru	Aug. 4, 1953	Alfred C. Glassell Jr.
Marlin, Pacific blue	1,376 lbs.	Kaaiwi Pt., Kona, HI	May 31, 1982	Jay W. deBeaubien
Marlin, striped	494 lbs.	Tutukaka, New Zealand	Jan. 16, 1986	Bill Boniface
Marlin, white	181 lbs. 14 oz.	Vitoria, Brazil	Dec. 8, 1979	Evandro Luiz Coser
Permit	53 lbs. 4 oz.	Lake Worth Inlet, FL	Mar. 25, 1994	Roy Brooker
Pollack, European	27 lbs. 6 oz.	Salcombe, Devon, England	Jan. 16, 1986	Robert Milkins
Pollock	50 lbs.	Saltraumen, Norway	Nov. 30, 1995	Thor-Magnus Lekang
Pompano, African	50 lbs. 8 oz.	Daytona Beach, FL	Apr. 21, 1990	Tom Sargent
Roosterfish	114 lbs.	La Paz, Baja Cal., Mexico	June 1, 1960	Abe Sackheim
Runner, blue	8 lbs. 7 oz.	Port Aransas, TX	Feb. 13, 1995	Allen E. Windecker
Runner, rainbow	37 lbs. 9 oz.	Clarion Island, Mexico	Nov. 21, 1991	Tom Pfleger
Sailfish, Atlantic	141 lbs. 1 oz.	Luanda, Angola	Feb. 19, 1994	Alfredo de Sousa Neves
Sailfish, Pacific	221 lbs.	Santa Cruz Island, Ecuador	Feb. 12, 1947	C. W. Stewart
Seabass, white	83 lbs. 12 oz.	San Felipe, Mexico	Mar. 31, 1953	L. C. Baumgardner
Seatrout, spotted	17 lbs. 7 oz.	Ft. Pierce, FL	May 11, 1995	Graig F. Carson
Shark, bigeye thresher . .	802 lbs.	Tutukaka, New Zealand	Feb. 8, 1981	Dianne North
Shark, bignose	369 lbs. 14 oz.	Markham R., Papua New Guinea	Oct. 23, 1993	Lester Rohrlach
Shark, blue	437 lbs.	Catherine Bay, N.S.W., Australia	Oct. 2, 1976	Peter Hyde
Shark, great hammerhead	991 lbs.	Sarasota, FL	May 30, 1982	Allen Ogle
Shark, Greenland	1,708 lbs. 9 oz.	Trondheimsfjord, Norway	Oct. 18, 1987	Terje Nordtvedt
Shark, man-eater or white	2,664 lbs.	Ceduna, S.A., Australia	Apr. 21, 1959	Alfred Dean
Shark, porbeagle	507 lbs.	Caithness, Scotland	Mar. 9, 1993	Christopher Bennet
Shark, shortfin mako . . .	1,115 lbs.	Black River, Mauritius	Nov. 16, 1988	Patrick Guillanton
Shark, tiger	1,780 lbs.	Cherry Grove, SC	June 14, 1964	Walter Maxwell
Shark, tope	98 lbs. 8 oz.	Santa Monica, CA	Oct. 20, 1994	Fred Oakley
Sheepshead	21 lbs. 4 oz.	New Orleans, LA	Apr. 16, 1982	Wayne Deselle
Skipjack, black.	26 lbs.	Thetis Bank, Baja Cal., Mexico	Oct. 23, 1991	Clifford Hamaishi
Snapper, cubera	121 lbs. 8 oz.	Cameron, LA	July 5, 1982	Mike Hebert
Snapper, red	46 lbs. 8 oz.	Destin, FL	Oct. 1, 1985	E. Lane Nichols 3d
Snook, common.	53 lbs. 10 oz.	Parismina Ranch, Costa Rica	Oct. 18, 1978	Gilbert Ponzi
Spearfish, Mediterranean	90 lbs. 13 oz.	Madeira Island, Portugal	June 2, 1980	Joseph Larkin
Swordfish	1,182 lbs.	Iquique, Chile	May 7, 1953	L. Marron
Tarpon	283 lbs. 4 oz.	Sherbro Island, Sierra Leone	Apr. 16, 1991	Yvon Sebag
Tautog	24 lbs.	Wachapreague, VA	Aug. 25, 1987	Gregory Bell
Trevally, bigeye	18 lbs. 1 oz.	Clipperton Island, France	May 12, 1990	Robonon Mille
Trevally, giant	145 lbs. 8 oz.	Makona, Maui, HI	Mar. 28, 1991	Russell Mori
Tuna, Atlantic bigeye . . .	375 lbs. 8 oz.	Ocean City, MD	Aug. 26, 1977	Cecil Browne
Tuna, blackfin	42 lbs. 8 oz.	Marathon Humps, Duck Key, FL	May 21, 1995	Shawn Snyder

(continued)

Species	Weight	Where caught	Date	Angler
Tuna, bluefin	1,496 lbs.	Aulds Cove, Nova Scotia	Oct. 26, 1979	Ken Fraser
Tuna, longtail	79 lbs. 2 oz.	Montague Isl., N.S.W., Australia	Apr. 12, 1982	Tim Simpson
Tuna, Pacific bigeye	435 lbs.	Cabo Blanco, Peru	Apr. 17, 1957	Dr. Russel Lee
Tuna, skipjack	45 lbs. 4 oz.	Flathead Bank, Baja Cal., Mexico	Nov. 16, 1996	Brian Evans
Tuna, southern bluefin	348 lbs. 5 oz.	Whakatane, New Zealand	Jan. 16, 1981	Rex Wood
Tuna, yellowfin	388 lbs. 12 oz.	San Benedicto Island, Mexico	Apr. 1, 1977	Curt Wiesenhutter
Tunny, little	35 lbs. 2 oz.	Cap de Garde, Algeria	Dec. 14, 1988	Jean Yves Chatard
Wahoo	155 lbs. 8 oz.	San Salvador, Bahamas	Apr. 3, 1990	William Bourne
Weakfish	19 lbs. 2 oz.	Jones Beach Inlet, NY	Oct. 11, 1984	Dennis Rooney
		Delaware Bay, DE	May 20, 1989	William Thomas
Yellowtail, California	79 lbs. 4 oz.	Alijos Rocks, Baja Cal., Mexico	July 2, 1991	Robert Walker
Yellowtail, southern	114 lbs. 10 oz.	Tauranga, New Zealand	Feb. 5, 1984	Mike Godfrey

Freshwater Fish Records

Species	Weight	Where caught	Date	Angler
Barramundi	63 lbs. 2 oz.	Normah River, Australia	Apr. 28, 1991	Scott Barnsley
Bass, largemouth	22 lbs. 4 oz.	Montgomery Lake, GA	June 2, 1932	George W. Perry
Bass, peacock	27 lbs.	Rio Negro, Brazil	Dec. 4, 1994	Gerald "Doc" Lawson
Bass, rock	3 lbs.	York River, Ontario	Aug. 1, 1974	Peter Gulgin
Bass, smallmouth	10 lbs. 14 oz.	Dale Hollow Lake, KY	Apr. 24, 1969	John T. Gorman
Bass, Suwannee	3 lbs. 14 oz.	Suwannee River, FL	Mar. 2, 1985	Ronnie Everett
Bass, white	6 lbs. 13 oz.	Lake Orange, VA	July 31, 1989	Ronald Sprouse
Bass, whiterock	25 lbs. 8 oz.	Lake Chatuge, GA	May 1, 1995	David C. Hobby
Bass, yellow	2 lbs. 4 oz.	Lake Monroe, IN	Mar. 27, 1977	Donald L. Stalker
Bluegill	4 lbs. 12 oz.	Ketona Lake, AL	Apr. 9, 1950	T. S. Hudson
Bowfin	21 lbs. 8 oz.	Florence, SC	Jan. 29, 1980	Robert Harmon
Buffalo, bigmouth	70 lbs. 5 oz.	Bussey Brake, Bastrop, LA	Apr. 21, 1980	Delbert Sisk
Buffalo, black	55 lbs. 8 oz.	Cherokee Lake, TN	May 3, 1984	Edward McLain
Buffalo, smallmouth	68 lbs. 8 oz.	Lake Hamilton, AR	May 16, 1984	Jerry Dolezal
Bullhead, brown	5 lbs. 11 oz.	Cedar Creek, FL	Mar. 28, 1995	Robert Bengis
Bullhead, yellow	4 lbs. 4 oz.	Mormon Lake, AZ	May 11, 1984	Emily Williams
Burbot	18 lbs. 11 oz.	Angenmanalren, Sweden	Oct. 22, 1996	Margit Agren
Carp, common	75 lbs. 11 oz.	Lac de St. Cassien, France	May 21, 1987	Leo van der Gugten
Catfish, blue	109 lbs. 4 oz.	Cooper River, SC	Mar. 14, 1991	George Lijewski
Catfish, channel	58 lbs.	Santee-Cooper Res., SC	July 7, 1964	W. B. Whaley
Catfish, flathead	91 lbs. 4 oz.	Lake Lewisville, TX	Mar. 28, 1982	Mike Rogers
Catfish, white	18 lbs. 14 oz.	Withlacoochee River, FL	Sept. 21, 1991	Jim Miller
Char, Arctic	32 lbs. 9 oz.	Tree River, Canada	July 30, 1981	Jeffrey Ward
Crappie, white	5 lbs. 3 oz.	Enid Dam, MS	July 31, 1957	Fred L. Bright
Dolly Varden	18 lbs. 9 oz.	Mashutuk River, AK	July 13, 1993	Richard B. Evans
Dorado	51 lbs. 5 oz.	Toledo (Corrientes), Argentina	Sept. 27, 1984	Armando Giudice
Drum, freshwater	54 lbs. 8 oz.	Nickajack Lake, TN	Apr. 20, 1972	Benny E. Hull
Gar, alligator	279 lbs.	Rio Grande, TX	Dec. 2, 1951	Bill Valverde
Gar, Florida	21 lbs. 3 oz.	Boca Raton, FL	June 3, 1981	Jeff Sabol
Gar, longnose	50 lbs. 5 oz.	Trinity River, TX	July 30, 1954	Townsend Miller
Gar, shortnose	5 lbs. 12 oz.	Rend Lake, IL	July 6, 1995	Donna K. Willmert
Gar, spotted	9 lbs. 12 oz.	Lake Mexia, TX	Apr. 7, 1994	Rick Rivard
Grayling, Arctic	5 lbs. 15 oz.	Katseyedie River, N.W.T.	Aug. 16, 1967	Jeanne P. Branson
Inconnu	53 lbs.	Pah River, AK	Aug. 20, 1986	Lawrence Hudnall
Kokanee	9 lbs. 6 oz.	Okanagan Lake, Vernon, B.C.	June 18, 1988	Norm Kuhn
Muskellunge	67 lbs. 8 oz.	Lake Court Oreilles, WI	July 24, 1949	Cal Johnson
Muskellunge, tiger	51 lbs. 3 oz.	Lac Vieux-Desert, WI-MI	July 16, 1919	John Knobla
Perch, Nile	191 lbs. 8 oz.	Lake Victoria, Kenya	Sept. 5, 1991	Andy Davison
Perch, white	4 lbs. 12 oz.	Messalonskee Lake, ME	June 4, 1949	Mrs. Earl Small
Perch, yellow	4 lbs. 3 oz.	Bordentown, NJ	May, 1865	Dr. C. C. Abbot
Pickerel, chain	9 lbs. 6 oz.	Homerville, GA	Feb. 17, 1961	Baxley McQuaig Jr.
Pike, northern	55 lbs. 1 oz.	Lake of Grefeern, W. Germany	Oct. 16, 1986	Lothar Louis
Redhorse, greater	9 lbs. 3 oz.	Salmon River, Pulaski, NY	May 11, 1985	Jason Wilson
Redhorse, silver	11 lbs. 7 oz.	Plum Creek, WI	May 29, 1985	Neal Long
Salmon, Atlantic	79 lbs. 2 oz.	Tana River, Norway	1928	Henrik Henriksen
Salmon, chinook	97 lbs. 4 oz.	Kenai River, AK	May 17, 1985	Les Anderson
Salmon, chum	32 lbs.	Behm Canal, AK	June 7, 1985	Fredrick Thynes
Salmon, coho	33 lbs. 4 oz.	Salmon River, Pulaski, NY	Sept. 27, 1989	Jerry Lifton
Salmon, pink	13 lbs. 1 oz.	St. Mary's River, Ontario	Sept. 23, 1992	Ray Higaki
Salmon, sockeye	15 lbs. 3 oz.	Kenai River, AK	Aug. 9, 1987	Stan Roach
Sauger	8 lbs. 12 oz.	Lake Sakakawea, ND	Oct. 6, 1971	Mike Fischer
Shad, American	11 lbs. 4 oz.	Connecticut River, MA	May 19, 1986	Bob Thibodo
Sturgeon, beluga	224 lbs. 13 oz.	Guryev, Kazakhstan	May 3, 1993	Merete Lehne
Sturgeon, white	468 lbs.	Benicia, CA	July 9, 1983	Joey Pallotta 3d
Sunfish, green	2 lbs. 2 oz.	Stockton Lake, MO	June 18, 1971	Paul M. Dilley
Sunfish, redbreast	1 lb. 12 oz.	Suwannee River, FL	May 29, 1984	Alvin Buchanan
Sunfish, redear	5 lbs. 3 oz.	Sacramento, CA	June 27, 1994	Anthony H. White
Tigerfish, giant	97 lbs.	Zaire River, Kinshasa, Zaire	July 9, 1988	Raymond Houtmans
Tilapia	6 lbs. 5 oz.	Lake Aranal, Costa Rica	Feb. 10, 1995	Marvin C. Smith
Trout, Apache	5 lbs. 3 oz.	Apache Res., AZ	May 29, 1991	John Baldwin
Trout, brook	14 lbs. 8 oz.	Nipigon River, Ontario	July 1916	Dr. W. J. Cook
Trout, brown	40 lbs. 4 oz.	Little Red River, AR	May 9, 1992	Howard "Rip" Collins
Trout, bull	32 lbs.	Lake Pend Oreille, ID	Oct. 27, 1949	N. L. Higgins
Trout, cutthroat	41 lbs.	Pyramid Lake, NV	Dec. 1925	John Skimmerhorn
Trout, golden	11 lbs.	Cooks Lake, WY	Aug. 5, 1948	Charles S. Reed
Trout, lake	66 lbs. 8 oz.	Great Bear Lake, N.W.T.	July 19, 1991	Rodney Harback
Trout, rainbow	42 lbs. 2 oz.	Bell Island, AK	June 22, 1970	David Robert White
Trout, tiger	20 lbs. 13 oz.	Lake Michigan, WI	Aug. 12, 1978	Pete Friedland
Walleye	25 lbs.	Old Hickory Lake, TN	Aug. 2, 1960	Mabry Harper
Warmouth	2 lbs. 7 oz.	Yellow River, Holt, FL	Oct. 19, 1985	Tony D. Dempsey
Whitefish, lake	14 lbs. 6 oz.	Meaford, Ontario	May 21, 1984	Dennis Laycock
Whitefish, mountain	5 lbs. 6 oz.	Rioh River, Saskatchewan	June 15, 1988	John Bell
Whitefish, round	6 lbs.	Putahow River, Manitoba	June 14, 1984	Allen Ristori
Zander	25 lbs. 2 oz.	Trosa, Sweden	June 12, 1986	Harry Lee Tennison

GOLF
United States Open Winners

Year[1]	Winner	Year[1]	Winner	Year[1]	Winner	Year[1]	Winner
1903	Willie Anderson	1927	Tommy Armour	1953	Ben Hogan	1975	Lou Graham
1904	Willie Anderson	1928	John Farrell	1954	Ed Furgol	1976	Jerry Pate
1905	Willie Anderson	1929	Bobby Jones*	1955	Jack Fleck	1977	Hubert Green
1906	Alex Smith	1930	Bobby Jones*	1956	Cary Middlecoff	1978	Andy North
1907	Alex Ross	1931	Wm. Burke	1957	Dick Mayer	1979	Hale Irwin
1908	Fred McLeod	1932	Gene Sarazen	1958	Tommy Bolt	1980	Jack Nicklaus
1909	George Sargent	1933	John Goodman*	1959	Billy Casper	1981	David Graham
1910	Alex Smith	1934	Olin Dutra	1960	Arnold Palmer	1982	Tom Watson
1911	John McDermott	1935	Sam Parks, Jr.	1961	Gene Littler	1983	Larry Nelson
1912	John McDermott	1936	Tony Manero	1962	Jack Nicklaus	1984	Fuzzy Zoeller
1913	Francis Ouimet*	1937	Ralph Guldahl	1963	Julius Boros	1985	Andy North
1914	Walter Hagen	1938	Ralph Guldahl	1964	Ken Venturi	1986	Ray Floyd
1915	Jerome Travers*	1939	Byron Nelson	1965	Gary Player	1987	Scott Simpson
1916	Chick Evans*	1940	Lawson Little	1966	Billy Casper	1988	Curtis Strange
1919	Walter Hagen	1941	Craig Wood	1967	Jack Nicklaus	1989	Curtis Strange
1920	Edward Ray	1946	Lloyd Mangrum	1968	Lee Trevino	1990	Hale Irwin
1921	Jim Barnes	1947	L. Worsham	1969	Orville Moody	1991	Payne Stewart
1922	Gene Sarazen	1948	Ben Hogan	1970	Tony Jacklin	1992	Tom Kite
1923	Bobby Jones*	1949	Cary Middlecoff	1971	Lee Trevino	1993	Lee Janzen
1924	Cyril Walker	1950	Ben Hogan	1972	Jack Nicklaus	1994	Ernie Els
1925	Willie MacFarlane	1951	Ben Hogan	1973	Johnny Miller	1995	Corey Pavin
1926	Bobby Jones*	1952	Julius Boros	1974	Hale Irwin	1996	Steve Jones
						1997	Ernie Els

* Amateur. (1) 1917-18 and 1942-45 not played.

Professional Golfer's Association Championship Winners

Year[1]	Winner	Year[1]	Winner	Year[1]	Winner	Year[1]	Winner
1922	Gene Sarazen	1941	Victor Ghezzi	1961	Jerry Barber	1979	David Graham
1923	Gene Sarazen	1942	Sam Snead	1962	Gary Player	1980	Jack Nicklaus
1924	Walter Hagen	1944	Bob Hamilton	1963	Jack Nicklaus	1981	Larry Nelson
1925	Walter Hagen	1945	Byron Nelson	1964	Bob Nichols	1982	Ray Floyd
1926	Walter Hagen	1946	Ben Hogan	1965	Dave Marr	1983	Hal Sutton
1927	Walter Hagen	1947	Jim Ferrier	1966	Al Geiberger	1984	Lee Trevino
1928	Leo Diegel	1948	Ben Hogan	1967	Don January	1985	Hubert Green
1929	Leo Diegel	1949	Sam Snead	1968	Julius Boros	1986	Bob Tway
1930	Tommy Armour	1950	Chandler Harper	1969	Ray Floyd	1987	Larry Nelson
1931	Tom Creavy	1951	Sam Snead	1970	Dave Stockton	1988	Jeff Sluman
1932	Olin Dutra	1952	James Turnesa	1971	Jack Nicklaus	1989	Payne Stewart
1933	Gene Sarazen	1953	Walter Burkemo	1972	Gary Player	1990	Wayne Grady
1934	Paul Runyan	1954	Melvin Harbert	1973	Jack Nicklaus	1991	John Daly
1935	Johnny Revolta	1955	Doug Ford	1974	Lee Trevino	1992	Nick Price
1936	Denny Shute	1956	Jack Burke	1975	Jack Nicklaus	1993	Paul Azinger
1937	Denny Shute	1957	Lionel Hebert	1976	Dave Stockton	1994	Nick Price
1938	Paul Runyan	1958	Dow Finsterwald	1977	Lanny Wadkins	1995	Steve Elkington
1939	Henry Picard	1959	Bob Rosburg	1978	John Mahaffey	1996	Mark Brooks
1940	Byron Nelson	1960	Jay Hebert			1997	Davis Love III

(1) 1943 not played.

Masters Golf Tournament Winners

Year[1]	Winner	Year[1]	Winner	Year[1]	Winner	Year[1]	Winner
1934	Horton Smith	1952	Sam Snead	1967	Gay Brewer, Jr.	1982	Craig Stadler
1935	Gene Sarazen	1953	Ben Hogan	1968	Bob Goalby	1983	Seve Ballesteros
1936	Horton Smith	1954	Sam Snead	1969	George Archer	1984	Ben Crenshaw
1937	Byron Nelson	1955	Cary Middlecoff	1970	Billy Casper	1985	Bernhard Langer
1938	Henry Picard	1956	Jack Burke	1971	Charles Coody	1986	Jack Nicklaus
1939	Ralph Guldahl	1957	Doug Ford	1972	Jack Nicklaus	1987	Larry Mize
1940	Jimmy Demaret	1958	Arnold Palmer	1973	Tommy Aaron	1988	Sandy Lyle
1941	Craig Wood	1959	Art Wall Jr.	1974	Gary Player	1989	Nick Faldo
1942	Byron Nelson	1960	Arnold Palmer	1975	Jack Nicklaus	1990	Nick Faldo
1946	Herman Keiser	1961	Gary Player	1976	Ray Floyd	1991	Ian Woosnam
1947	Jimmy Demaret	1962	Arnold Palmer	1977	Tom Watson	1992	Fred Couples
1948	Claude Harmon	1963	Jack Nicklaus	1978	Gary Player	1993	Bernhard Langer
1949	Sam Snead	1964	Arnold Palmer	1979	Fuzzy Zoeller	1994	Jose Maria Olazabal
1950	Jimmy Demaret	1965	Jack Nicklaus	1980	Seve Ballesteros	1995	Ben Crenshaw
1951	Ben Hogan	1966	Jack Nicklaus	1981	Tom Watson	1996	Nick Faldo
						1997	Tiger Woods

(1) 1943-45 not played.

British Open Winners

Year[1]	Winner	Year[1]	Winner	Year[1]	Winner	Year[1]	Winner
1931	Tommy Armour	1953	Ben Hogan	1968	Gary Player	1983	Tom Watson
1932	Gene Sarazen	1954	Peter Thomson	1969	Tony Jacklin	1984	Seve Ballesteros
1933	Denny Shute	1955	Peter Thomson	1970	Jack Nicklaus	1985	Sandy Lyle
1934	Henry Cotton	1956	Peter Thomson	1971	Lee Trevino	1986	Greg Norman
1935	Alf Perry	1957	Bobby Locke	1972	Lee Trevino	1987	Nick Faldo
1936	Alf Padgham	1958	Peter Thomson	1973	Tom Weiskopf	1988	Seve Ballesteros
1937	T.H. Cotton	1959	Gary Player	1974	Gary Player	1989	Mark Calcavecchia
1938	R.A. Whitcombe	1960	Kel Nagle	1975	Tom Watson	1990	Nick Faldo
1939	Richard Burton	1961	Arnold Palmer	1976	Johnny Miller	1991	Ian Baker-Finch
1946	Sam Snead	1962	Arnold Palmer	1977	Tom Watson	1992	Nick Faldo
1947	Fred Daly	1963	Bob Charles	1978	Jack Nicklaus	1993	Greg Norman
1948	Henry Cotton	1964	Tony Lema	1979	Seve Ballesteros	1994	Nick Price
1949	Bobby Locke	1965	Peter Thomson	1980	Tom Watson	1995	John Daly
1950	Bobby Locke	1966	Jack Nicklaus	1981	Bill Rogers	1996	Tom Lehman
1951	Max Faulkner	1967	Roberto de Vicenzo	1982	Tom Watson	1997	Justin Leonard
1952	Bobby Locke						

(1) 1940-45 not played.

Professional Golf Tournaments in 1997
(through mid-Oct.)
Men

Date	Event	Winner	Score	Prize
Jan. 12	Mercedes Championships, Carlsbad, CA.	Tiger Woods	*†202	$216,000
Jan. 19	Bob Hope Chrysler Classic, Indian Wells, CA.	John Cook	327	270,000
Jan. 25	Phoenix Open, Scottsdale, AZ	Steve Jones	258	270,000
Feb. 2	AT&T Pebble Beach National Pro Am, Pebble Beach, CA	Mark O'Meara	268	342,000
Feb. 9	Buick Invitational of CA, La Jolla, CA	Mark O'Meara	275	270,000
Feb. 16	United Airlines Hawaiian Open, Honolulu, HI	Paul Stankowski	*271	216,000
Feb. 23	Tucson Chrysler Classic, Tucson, AZ	Jeff Sluman	275	234,000
Mar. 2	Nissan Open, Pacific Palisades, CA	Nick Faldo	272	252,000
Mar. 9	Doral-Ryder Open, Miami, FL.	Steve Elkington	275	324,000
Mar. 16	Honda Classic, Coral Springs, FL	Stuart Appleby	274	270,000
Mar. 23	Bay Hill Invitational, Orlando, FL.	Phil Mickelson	272	270,000
Mar. 30	The Players Championship, Ponte Vedra Beach, FL	Steve Elkington	272	630,000
Apr. 6	Freeport-McDermott Classic, New Orleans, LA	Brad Faxon	272	270,000
Apr. 13	Masters Tournament, Augusta, GA.	Tiger Woods	T270	486,000
Apr. 20	MCI Classic, Hilton Head Island, SC	Nick Price	269	270,000
Apr. 27	Greater Greensboro Chrysler Classic, Greensboro, NC	Frank Nobilo	*274	342,000
May 4	Shell Houston Open, The Woodlands, TX	Phil Blackmar	*276	288,000
May 11	BellSouth Classic, Duluth, GA	Scott McCarron	274	270,000
May 18	GTE Byron Nelson Classic, Irving, TX	Tiger Woods	263	324,000
May 23	MasterCard Colonial, Fort Worth, TX.	David Frost	265	288,000
June 2	Memorial Tournament, Dublin, OH	Vijay Singh	†202	342,000
June 8	Kemper Open, Potomac, MD	Justin Leonard	274	270,000
June 15	U.S. Open, Bethesda, MD	Ernie Els	276	465,000
June 22	Buick Classic, Rye, NY	Ernie Els	268	270,000
June 29	FedEx St. Jude Classic, Memphis, TN.	Greg Norman	268	270,000
July 6	Motorola Western Open, Lemont, IL	Tiger Woods	275	360,000
July 13	Quad City Classic, Coal Valley, IL.	David Toms	265	243,000
July 20	British Open, Troon, Scotland, United Kingdom	Justin Leonard	272	418,875
July 20	Deposit Guaranty Golf Classic, Madison, MS.	Billy Ray Brown	271	180,000
July 27	Canon Greater Hartford Open, Cromwell, CT.	Stewart Cink	267	270,000
Aug. 3	Sprint International, Castle Rock, CO	Phil Mickelson	T48 pts.	306,000
Aug. 10	Buick Open, Grand Blanc, MI	Vijay Singh	273	270,000
Aug. 17	PGA Championship, Mamaroneck, NY	Davis Love III	269	470,000
Aug. 24	NEC World Series of Golf, Akron, OH	Greg Norman	273	396,000
Aug. 24	Greater Vancouver Open, Surrey, British Columbia	Mark Calcavecchia	265	270,000
Aug. 31	Greater Milwaukee Open, Milwaukee, WI	Scott Hoch	268	234,000
Sept. 7	Bell Canadian Open, Montreal, Quebec	Steve Jones	275	270,000
Sept. 14	CVS-Charity Classic, Sutton, MA	Loren Roberts	266	216,000
Sept. 21	LaCantera Texas Open, San Antonio, TX	Tim Herron	271	252,000
Sept. 28	B.C. Open, Endicott, NY	Gabriel Hjertstedt	275	234,000
Oct. 5	Buick Challenge, Pine Mountain, GA.	Davis Love III	267	216,000
Oct. 12	Michelob Championship at Kingsmill, Williamsburg, VA	David Duval	273	74,400
Oct. 19	Walt Disney World/Oldsmobile Classic, Lake Buena Vista, FL	David Duval	*270	270,000

Women

Date	Event	Winner	Score	Prize
Jan. 12	Chrysler-Plymouth Tournament of Champions, Ft. Lauderdale, FL	Annika Sorenstam	272	$115,000
Jan. 19	HealthSouth Inaugural, Orlando, FL	Michelle McGann	*207	90,000
Feb. 9	Diet Dr. Pepper National Pro-Am, W. Palm Beach, FL	Kelly Robbins	*271	75,000
Feb. 16	Los Angeles Women's Championship, Glendale, CA	Terry-Jo Myers	206	97,500
Feb. 22	Cup Noodles Hawaiian Ladies Open, Kapolei, Oahu, HI	Annika Sorenstam	206	97,500
Mar. 2	Alpine Australian Ladies Masters, Queensland, Australia	Gail Graham	273	97,500
Mar. 16	Welch's/Circle K Championship, Tucson, AZ	Donna Andrews	273	75,000
Mar. 23	Standard Register PING, Phoenix, AZ.	Laura Davies	*277	127,500
Mar. 30	Nabisco Dinah Shore Classic, Rancho Mirage, CA.	Betsy King	276	135,000
Apr. 6	Longs Drugs Challenge, Lincoln, CA.	Annika Sorenstam	*285	75,000
Apr. 20	Susan G. Komen International, Murrells Inlet, SC.	Karrie Webb	276	75,000
Apr. 27	Chick-Fil-A Charity Championship, Stockbridge, GA.	Nancy Lopez	†137	82,500
May 4	Sprint Titleholders Championship, Daytona Beach, FL	Tammie Green	274	180,000
May 11	Sara Lee Classic, Old Hickory, TN	Terry-Jo Myers	*207	101,250
May 18	McDonald's LPGA Championship, Wilmington, DE	Chris Johnson	*281	180,000
May 25	LPGA Corning Classic, Corning, NY	Rosie Jones	*277	97,500
May 25	JCPenney/LPGA Skins Game, Frisco, TX	Annika Sorenstam	8 skins	220,000
June 1	Michelob Light Classic, St. Louis, MO	Annika Sorenstam	277	90,000
June 8	Oldsmobile Classic, East Lansing, MI	Pat Hurst	279	90,000
June 15	First Bank-Edina Realty LPGA Classic, Maple Grove, MN.	Danielle Ammaccapane	208	90,000
June 22	Rochester International, Pittsford, NY	Penny Hammel	279	90,000
June 29	ShopRite LPGA Classic, Somers Point, NJ	Michelle McGann	201	135,000
July 6	Jamie Farr Kroger Classic, Sylvania, OH	Kelly Robbins	265	105,000
July 13	U.S. Women's Open, Cornelius, OR	Alison Nicholas	274	232,500
July 20	JAL Big Apple Classic, New Rochelle, NY	Michele Redman	272	112,500
July 27	Giant Eagle LPGA Classic, Warren, OH	Tammie Green	*203	90,000
Aug. 3	du Maurier Classic, Oakville, Ontario.	Colleen Walker	278	180,000
Aug. 10	Friendly's Classic, Agawam, MA.	Deb Richard	277	82,500
Aug. 17	Weetabix Women's British Open, Sunningdale, England.	Karrie Webb	269	129,938
Aug. 24	Star Bank LPGA Classic, Beavercreek, OH	Colleen Walker	203	82,500
Sept. 1	State Farm Rail Classic, Springfield, IL	Cindy Figg-Currier	*200	90,000
Sept. 7	The Safeway LPGA Golf Championship, Portland, OR	Chris Johnson	206	82,500
Sept. 14	SAFECO Classic, Kent, WA	Karrie Webb	272	82,500
Sept. 21	PING Welch's Championship, Canton, MA	Liselotte Neumann	276	82,500
Sept. 28	Fieldcrest Cannon Classic, Charlotte, NC	Wendy Ward	265	82,500
Oct. 5	CoreStates Betsy King Classic, Kutztown, PA	Annika Sorenstam	274	90,000
Oct. 19	World Championship of Women's Golf, Seoul, S. Korea	Juli Inkster	*280	131,000

* Won playoff. (†) Shortened because of weather. (T) Tournament record.

Ryder Cup in 1997

A team of professional golfers from Europe defeated the U.S. team, 14½-13½, Sept. 26-28 at Valderrama Golf Club in Sotogrande, Spain, to retain the Ryder Cup.

U.S. Women's Open Golf Champions

Year	Winner	Year	Winner	Year	Winner	Year	Winner
1948	"Babe" Zaharias	1961	Mickey Wright	1973	Susie Maxwell Berning	1985	Kathy Baker
1949	Louise Suggs	1962	Murle Lindstrom	1974	Sandra Haynie	1986	Jane Geddes
1950	"Babe" Zaharias	1963	Mary Mills	1975	Sandra Palmer	1987	Laura Davies
1951	Betsy Rawls	1964	Mickey Wright	1976	JoAnne Carner	1988	Liselotte Neumann
1952	Louise Suggs	1965	Carol Mann	1977	Hollis Stacy	1989	Betsy King
1953	Betsy Rawls	1966	Sandra Spuzich	1978	Hollis Stacy	1990	Betsy King
1954	"Babe" Zaharias	1967	Catherine Lacoste*	1979	Jerilyn Britz	1991	Meg Mallon
1955	Fay Crocker	1968	Susie Maxwell Berning	1980	Amy Alcott	1992	Patty Sheehan
1956	Mrs. K. Cornelius	1969	Donna Caponi	1981	Pat Bradley	1993	Lauri Merten
1957	Betsy Rawls	1970	Donna Caponi	1982	Janet Alex	1994	Patty Sheehan
1958	Mickey Wright	1971	JoAnne Carner	1983	Jan Stephenson	1995	Annika Sorenstam
1959	Mickey Wright	1972	Susie Maxwell Berning	1984	Hollis Stacy	1996	Annika Sorenstam
1960	Betsy Rawls					1997	Alison Nicholas

*Amateur

PGA Leading Money Winners

Year	Player	Dollars	Year	Player	Dollars	Year	Player	Dollars
1946	Ben Hogan	$42,556	1963	Arnold Palmer	$128,230	1980	Tom Watson	$530,808
1947	Jimmy Demaret	27,936	1964	Jack Nicklaus	113,284	1981	Tom Kite	375,699
1948	Ben Hogan	36,812	1965	Jack Nicklaus	140,752	1982	Craig Stadler	446,462
1949	Sam Snead	31,593	1966	Billy Casper	121,944	1983	Hal Sutton	426,668
1950	Sam Snead	35,758	1967	Jack Nicklaus	188,988	1984	Tom Watson	476,260
1951	Lloyd Mangrum	26,088	1968	Billy Casper	205,168	1985	Curtis Strange	542,321
1952	Julius Boros	37,032	1969	Frank Beard	175,223	1986	Greg Norman	653,296
1953	Lew Worsham	34,002	1970	Lee Trevino	157,037	1987	Curtis Strange	925,941
1954	Bob Toski	65,819	1971	Jack Nicklaus	244,490	1988	Curtis Strange	1,147,644
1955	Julius Boros	65,121	1972	Jack Nicklaus	320,542	1989	Tom Kite	1,395,278
1956	Ted Kroll	72,835	1973	Jack Nicklaus	308,362	1990	Greg Norman	1,165,477
1957	Dick Mayer	65,835	1974	Johnny Miller	353,201	1991	Corey Pavin	979,430
1958	Arnold Palmer	42,407	1975	Jack Nicklaus	323,149	1992	Fred Couples	1,344,188
1959	Art Wall, Jr.	53,167	1976	Jack Nicklaus	266,438	1993	Nick Price	1,478,557
1960	Arnold Palmer	75,262	1977	Tom Watson	310,653	1994	Nick Price	1,499,927
1961	Gary Player	64,540	1978	Tom Watson	362,429	1995	Greg Norman	1,654,959
1962	Arnold Palmer	81,448	1979	Tom Watson	462,636	1996	Tom Lehman	1,780,159

LPGA Leading Money Winners

Year	Player	Dollars	Year	Player	Dollars	Year	Player	Dollars
1954	Patty Berg	$16,011	1969	Carol Mann	$49,152	1983	JoAnne Carner	$291,404
1955	Patty Berg	16,492	1970	Kathy Whitworth	30,235	1984	Betsy King	266,771
1956	Marlene Hagge	20,235	1971	Kathy Whitworth	41,181	1985	Nancy Lopez	416,472
1957	Patty Berg	16,272	1972	Kathy Whitworth	65,063	1986	Pat Bradley	492,021
1958	Beverly Hanson	12,629	1973	Kathy Whitworth	82,854	1987	Ayako Okamoto	466,034
1959	Betsy Rawls	26,774	1974	JoAnne Carner	87,094	1988	Sherri Turner	347,255
1960	Louise Suggs	16,892	1975	Sandra Palmer	94,805	1989	Betsy King	654,132
1961	Mickey Wright	22,236	1976	Judy Rankin	150,734	1990	Beth Daniel	863,578
1962	Mickey Wright	21,641	1977	Judy Rankin	122,890	1991	Pat Bradley	763,118
1963	Mickey Wright	31,269	1978	Nancy Lopez	189,813	1992	Dottie Mochrie	693,335
1964	Mickey Wright	29,800	1979	Nancy Lopez	215,987	1993	Betsy King	595,992
1965	Kathy Whitworth	28,658	1980	Beth Daniel	231,000	1994	Laura Davies	687,201
1966	Kathy Whitworth	33,517	1981	Beth Daniel	206,977	1995	Annika Sorenstam	666,533
1967	Kathy Whitworth	32,937	1982	JoAnne Carner	310,399	1996	Karrie Webb	1,002,000
1968	Kathy Whitworth	48,379						

RIFLE AND PISTOL INDIVIDUAL CHAMPIONSHIPS

Source: National Rifle Association

National Outdoor Rifle and Pistol Championships in 1997

Smallbore Rifle Prone—Lones W. Wigger, USA, Colorado Springs, CO, 6399-527X

Civilian Smallbore Rifle Prone—Lones W. Wigger, Colorado Springs, CO, 6399-527X

Woman Smallbore Rifle Prone—Carolyn D. Millard-Sparks, Dunwoody, GA, 6392-526X

Smallbore Rifle NRA 3-Position—MAJ Steve C. Goff, USA, Columbus, GA, 2295-82X

Civilian Smallbore Rifle NRA 3-Position—Kenneth M. Benyo, Allentown, PA, 2277-108X

Woman Smallbore Rifle NRA 3-Position—2LT Kimberly N. Howe, USAR, Alexandria, PA, 2213-73X

High Power Rifle—G. D. Tubb, Canadian, TX, 2378-99X

Civilian High Power Rifle—G. D. Tubb, Canadian, TX, 2378-99X

Woman High Power Rifle—Nancy H. Tompkins-Gallagher, Prescott, AZ, 2361-101X

Pistol—SGT Jason E. Meidinger, USMC, Montecello, NY, 2654-140X

Civilian Pistol—Jerry Chaney, Lily, KY, 2639-122X

Woman Pistol—SFC Ruby Fox, USAR, Parker, AZ, 2570-106X

National Indoor Rifle and Pistol Championships in 1997

Smallbore Rifle 4-Position—Lance S. Hopper, Phenix City, AL, 800

Woman Smallbore Rifle 4-Position—Suzanne M. Mitchell, Englewood, CO, 796

Smallbore Rifle NRA 3-Position—Stephen Goff, Columbus, GA, 1196

Woman Smallbore Rifle NRA 3-Position—Sara R. Haas-Parra, Springfield, OR, 1164

International Smallbore Rifle—Glen A. Dubis, Columbus, GA, 1186

Woman International Smallbore Rifle—Wanda R. Jewell, Columbus, GA, 1178

Air Rifle—Kenneth A. Johnson, Marshfield, MA, 591

Woman Air Rifle—Tammie L. Forester, North Haven, CT, 587

Conventional Pistol—Allen E. Putzer, Spencer, WI, 897

Woman Conventional Pistol—Barbara J. Scotto, Malverne, NY, 856

International Free Pistol—Gary F. Spear, Harpursville, NY, 553

Woman International Free Pistol—Sandra Utasy, Columbus, GA, 534

International Standard Pistol—Scott S. Lorenz, Lynnwood, WA, 571

Woman International Standard Pistol—C. Carthew, Niagara Falls, NY, 530

Air Pistol—Neal Caloia, Cottage Grove, OR, 578

Woman Air Pistol—Sandra Utasy, Columbus, GA, 552

NRA Bianchi Cup National Action Pistol Championships in 1997

Action Pistol—Bruce Piatt, Montvale, NJ, 1920-181X

Woman Action Pistol—Sharon Edington, Columbus, GA, 1906-142X

Junior Action Pistol—Jason Scallen, Gillette, NY, 1910-162X

NOTABLE SPORTS PERSONALITIES

Henry (Hank) Aaron, b. 1934: Milwaukee-Atlanta outfielder hit record 755 home runs, led NL 4 times; record 2,297 RBIs.

Kareem Abdul-Jabbar, b. 1947: Milwaukee, L.A. Lakers center; MVP 6 times; leading scorer twice; playoff MVP, 1971, 1985; all-time leading NBA scorer.

Troy Aikman, b. 1966: quarterback led Dallas Cowboys to Super Bowl wins in 1993-94, 1996; Super Bowl MVP, 1993.

Grover Cleveland Alexander (1887-1950): pitcher won 374 NL games; pitched 16 shutouts, 1916.

Muhammad Ali, b. 1942: 3-time heavyweight champion.

Mario Andretti, b. 1940: won Indy 500, 1969; Grand Prix champ, 1978.

Eddie Arcaro, b. 1916: jockey rode 4,779 winners including the Kentucky Derby 5 times; the Preakness and Belmont Stakes 6 times each.

Henry Armstrong (1912-1988): boxer held feather-, welter-, lightweight titles simultaneously, 1937-38.

Arthur Ashe (1943-1993): U.S. singles champ, 1968; Wimbledon champ, 1975.

Red Auerbach, b. 1917: coached Boston Celtics to 9 NBA championships.

Donovan Bailey, b. 1967: Canadian Olympic gold medalist in 100 meters (set world record), 1996.

Ernie Banks, b. 1931: Chicago Cubs slugger hit 512 NL homers; twice MVP.

Roger Bannister, b. 1929: Briton ran first sub 4-minute mile, May 6, 1954.

Rick Barry, b. 1944: NBA scoring leader, 1967; ABA, 1969.

Sammy Baugh, b. 1914: Washington Redskins quarterback held numerous records upon retirement after 16 pro seasons.

Elgin Baylor, b. 1934: L.A. Lakers forward; 1st team all-star 10 times.

Boris Becker, b. 1967: German tennis star; won U.S. Open 1989; Wimbledon champ 3 times.

Jean Beliveau, b. 1931: Montreal Canadiens center scored 507 goals; twice MVP.

Johnny Bench, b. 1947: Cincinnati Reds catcher; MVP twice; led league in home runs twice, RBIs 3 times.

Patty Berg, b. 1918: won more than 80 golf tournaments; AP Woman Athlete-of-the-Year 3 times.

Yogi Berra, b. 1925: N.Y. Yankees catcher; MVP 3 times; played in 14 World Series.

Matt Biondi, b. 1965: swimmer won 5 gold medals at 1988 Olympics.

Larry Bird, b. 1956: Boston Celtics forward; chosen MVP 1984-86; Playoff MVP, 1984, 1986.

George Blanda, b. 1927: quarterback, kicker; 26 years as active player, scoring record 2,002 points.

Wade Boggs, b. 1958: AL batting champ, 1983, 1985-88.

Barry Bonds, b. 1964: outfielder was NL MVP 1990, 1992-93; 2d player in 40 home runs/40 stolen bases club, 1996.

Bjorn Borg, b. 1956: led Sweden to first Davis Cup, 1975; Wimbledon champion 5 times.

Mike Bossy, b. 1957: N.Y. Islanders right wing scored more than 50 goals 8 times.

Ray Bourque, b. 1960: Boston Bruins defenseman won Norris Trophy 5 times.

Terry Bradshaw, b. 1948; Pittsburgh Steelers quarterback led team to 4 Super Bowl titles.

George Brett, b. 1953: Kansas City Royals infielder led AL in batting, 1976, 1980, 1990; MVP, 1980.

Lou Brock, b. 1939: St. Louis Cardinals outfielder stole NL record 118 bases, 1974; led NL 8 times.

Jim Brown, b. 1936: Cleveland Browns fullback ran for 12,312 career yards; MVP 3 times.

Paul Brown (1908-1991), football owner, coach; led Cleveland Browns to 3 NFL championships.

Paul "Bear" Bryant (1913-1983), college football coach with 323 victories.

Sergei Bubka, b. 1963: Ukrainian pole vaulter; first to clear 20 feet both indoors and outdoors; gold medal, 1988 Olympics.

Maria Bueno, b. 1939: U.S. singles champ 4 times; Wimbledon champ 3 times.

Dick Butkus, b. 1942: Chicago Bears linebacker twice chosen best NFL defensive player.

Dick Button, b. 1929: figure skater won 1948, 1952 Olympic gold medals; world titlist, 1948-52.

Roy Campanella (1921-1993): Brooklyn Dodgers catcher; MVP 3 times.

Earl Campbell, b. 1955: NFL running back; MVP 1978-80.

Rod Carew, b. 1945: AL infielder won 7 batting titles; MVP, 1977.

Steve Carlton, b. 1944: NL pitcher won 20 games 5 times, Cy Young award 4 times.

Billy Casper, b. 1931: PGA Player-of-the-Year 3 times; U.S. Open champ twice.

Wilt Chamberlain, b. 1936: center was NBA leading scorer 7 times; MVP 4 times; scored 100 pts in a game, 1962.

Bobby Clarke, b. 1949: Philadelphia Flyers center led team to 2 Stanley Cup championships; MVP 3 times.

Roger Clemens, b. 1962: Boston Red Sox pitcher; AL MVP 1986; Cy Young award 1986, 1987, 1991; twice struck out record 20 batters in a game.

Roberto Clemente (1934-1972): Pittsburgh Pirates outfielder won 4 batting titles; MVP, 1966.

Ty Cobb (1886-1961): Detroit Tigers outfielder had record .367 lifetime batting average, 12 batting titles.

Sebastian Coe, b. 1956: Briton won Olympic 1,500-meter run, 1980, 1984.

Nadia Comaneci, b. 1961: Romanian gymnast won 3 gold medals, achieved 7 perfect scores, 1976 Olympics.

Maureen Connolly (1934-1969): won tennis "grand slam," 1953; AP Woman-Athlete-of-the-Year 3 times.

Jimmy Connors, b. 1952: U.S. singles champ 5 times; Wimbledon champ twice.

James J. Corbett (1866-1933): heavyweight champion, 1892-97; credited with being the first "scientific" boxer.

Angel Cordero, b. 1942: leading money winner, 1976, 1982-83; rode 3 Kentucky Derby winners.

Margaret Smith Court, b. 1942: Australian tennis great won U.S. Open 5 times, Wimbledon 3 times; 24 grand slam titles.

Bob Cousy, b. 1928: Boston Celtics guard led team to 6 NBA championships; MVP, 1957.

Dizzy Dean (1911-1974): colorful pitcher for St. Louis Cardinals "Gashouse Gang" in the '30s; MVP, 1934.

Oscar De La Hoya, b. 1972: boxer won lightweight title, 1995; super lightweight title, 1996; welterweight title, 1997.

Jack Dempsey (1895-1983): heavyweight champ, 1919-26.

Gail Devers, b. 1966: sprinter won Olympic gold medals in 100-meter run 1992, 1996.

Eric Dickerson, b. 1960: running back ran for NFL record 2,105 yds., 1984; led NFC 3 times, AFC twice.

Joe DiMaggio, b. 1914: N.Y. Yankees outfielder hit safely in record 56 consecutive games, 1941; AL MVP 3 times.

Dale Earnhardt, b. 1951: auto racer was NASCAR Winston Cup champion 7 times.

Stefan Edberg, b. 1966: U.S. singles champ 1991, 1992; Wimbledon champ 1988, 1990.

Gertrude Ederle, b. 1906: first woman to swim English Channel, broke existing men's record, 1926.

Julius Erving, b. 1950: MVP and leading scorer in ABA 3 times; NBA MVP, 1981.

Phil Esposito, b. 1942: NHL scoring leader 5 times.

Janet Evans, b. 1971: swimmer won 3 Olympic gold medals, 1988, 1 in 1992.

Chris Evert, b. 1954: U.S. Open tennis champ 6 times, Wimbledon champ 3 times.

Ray Ewry (1873-1937): track-and-field star won 8 gold medals, 1900, 1904, and 1908 Olympics.

Nick Faldo, 1957: British golfer won Masters, British Open 3 times each.

Juan Fangio (1911-1995): World Grand Prix champion 5 times.

Brett Favre, b. 1969: quarterback led Green Bay Packers to Super Bowl win, 1997; NFL regular-season MVP, 1995, 1996.

Bob Feller, b. 1918: Cleveland Indians pitcher won 266 games; pitched 3 no-hitters, 12 one-hitters.

Peggy Fleming, b. 1948: world figure skating champion, 1966-68; gold medalist 1968 Olympics.

Whitey Ford, b. 1928: N.Y. Yankees pitcher won record 10 World Series games.

George Foreman, b. 1949: heavyweight champion, 1973-74, 1994-95; at 45, the oldest to win a heavyweight title.

Dick Fosbury, b. 1947: high jumper won 1968 Olympic gold medal; developed the "Fosbury Flop."

Jimmie Foxx (1907-1967): Red Sox, Athletics slugger; MVP 3 times; triple crown, 1933.

A.J. Foyt, b. 1935: won Indy 500 4 times; U.S. Auto Club champ 7 times.

Joe Frazier, b. 1944: heavyweight champion, 1970-73.

Lou Gehrig (1903-1941): N.Y. Yankees 1st baseman played 2,130 consecutive games; MVP, 1927, 1936; triple crown, 1934; AL record 184 RBIs, 1931.

George Gervin, b. 1952: top NBA scorer, 1978-80, 1982.

Althea Gibson, b. 1927: twice U.S. and Wimbledon singles champ.

Bob Gibson, b. 1935: St. Louis Cardinals pitcher won Cy Young award twice; struck out 3,117 batters.

Marc Girardelli, b. 1963: Luxembourg skier won 5 World Cup titles.

Jeff Gordon, b. 1971: race car driver was youngest of the modern era to win the NASCAR Winston Cup, 1995.

Steffi Graf, b. 1969: German won tennis "grand slam," 1988; U.S. champ 5 times; Wimbledon champ 7 times.

Otto Graham, b. 1921: Cleveland Browns quarterback; all-pro 4 times.

Red Grange (1903-1991): All-America at Univ. of Illinois 1923-25; played for Chicago Bears, 1925-35.

Joe Greene, b. 1946: Pittsburgh Steelers lineman; twice NFL outstanding defensive player.

Wayne Gretzky, b. 1961: leading scorer in NHL history; MVP, 1980-87, 1989.

Ken Griffey Jr., b. 1969: Seattle Mariner outfielder led AL in home runs, 1994, 1997; 8 gold gloves.

Lefty Grove (1900-1975): pitcher won 300 AL games; 20-game winner 8 times.

Tony Gwynn, b. 1960: 8-time NL batting champ, 1984, 1987-89, 1994-97.

Walter Hagen (1892-1969): won PGA championship 5 times; British Open 4 times.

George Halas (1895-1983): founder-coach of Chicago Bears; won 5 NFL championships.

Scott Hamilton, b. 1958: U.S. and world figure skating champion, 1981-84; Olympic gold medalist, 1984.

Bill Hartack, b. 1932: jockey rode 5 Kentucky Derby winners.

John Havlicek, b. 1940: Boston Celtics forward scored more than 26,000 NBA points.

Dominik Hasek, b. 1965: Buffalo Sabres goalie won Vezina Trophy, 1994-95, 1997; NHL MVP, 1997.

Rickey Henderson, b. 1958: outfielder stole record 130 bases, 1982; record lifetime steals; AL MVP, 1990.

Sonja Henie (1912-1969): world champion figure skater, 1927-36; Olympic gold medalist, 1928, 1932, 1936.

Martina Hingis, b. 1980: youngest woman to hold No. 1 tennis ranking; won Australian Open, Wimbledon, U.S. Open, 1997.

Ben Hogan (1912-1997): won 4 U.S. Open championships, 2 PGA, 2 Masters.

Evander Holyfield, b. 1962: 3-time heavyweight champion.

Rogers Hornsby (1896-1963): NL 2d baseman batted record .424 in 1924; twice won triple crown; batting leader, 1920-25.

Paul Hornung, b. 1935: Green Bay Packers runner-placekicker scored record 176 points, 1960.

Gordie Howe, b. 1928: hockey forward; NHL MVP 6 times; scored 801 goals in 26 NHL seasons.

Carl Hubbell (1903-1988): N.Y. Giants pitcher; 20-game winner 5 consecutive years, 1933-37.

Bobby Hull, b. 1939: NHL all-star 10 times; MVP 1965-66.

Brett Hull, b. 1964: St. Louis Blues forward led NHL in goals, 1990-92; MVP 1991.

Catfish Hunter, b. 1946: pitched perfect game, 1968; 20-game winner 5 times.

Don Hutson (1913-1997): Green Bay Packers receiver caught 99 NFL touchdown passes.

Reggie Jackson, b. 1946: slugger led AL in home runs 4 times; MVP, 1973; hit 5 World Series home runs, 1977.

Earvin (Magic) Johnson, b. 1959: NBA MVP 1987, 1989, 1990; Playoff MVP 1980, 1982, 1987; 2d in career assists.

Jack Johnson (1878-1946): heavyweight champion, 1910-15.

Michael Johnson, b. 1967: won Olympic gold medals in 200-meter (shattered world record) and 400-meter run, 1996.

Walter Johnson (1887-1946): Washington Senators pitcher won 416 games; record 110 shutouts.

Bobby Jones (1902-1971): won "grand slam of golf" 1930; U.S. Amateur champ 5 times, U.S. Open champ 4 times.

Michael Jordan, b. 1963: NBA leading scorer, 1987-93, 1996-97; MVP, 1988, 1991-92, 1996; Playoff MVP, 1991-93, 1996-97.

Florence Griffith Joyner, b. 1959: sprinter won 3 gold medals at 1988 Olympics.

Jackie Joyner-Kersee, b. 1962; Olympic gold medalist in heptathlon, 1988, 1992.

Duke Kahanamoku (1890-1968): swimmer won 1912, 1920 Olympic gold medals in 100-meter freestyle; surfing pioneer.

Harmon Killebrew, b. 1936: Minnesota Twins slugger led AL in home runs 6 times; 573 lifetime.

Jean Claude Killy, b. 1943: French skier won 3 1968 Olympic gold medals.

Ralph Kiner, b. 1922: Pittsburgh Pirates slugger led NL in home runs 7 consecutive years, 1946-52.

Billie Jean King, b. 1943: U.S. singles champ 4 times; Wimbledon champ 6 times.

Bob Knight, b. 1940: Indiana U. basketball coach led team to NCAA championships, 1976, 1981, 1987.

Olga Korbut, b. 1955: Soviet gymnast won 3 1972 Olympic gold medals.

Sandy Koufax, b. 1935: Dodgers pitcher won Cy Young award 3 times; lowest ERA in NL, 1962-66; pitched 4 no-hitters, one a perfect game.

Guy Lafleur, b. 1951: forward led NHL in scoring 3 times; MVP, 1977, 1978.

Tom Landry, b. 1924: Dallas Cowboys head coach 1960-88.

Rod Laver, b. 1938: Australian won tennis "grand slam" twice, 1962, 1969; Wimbledon champ 4 times.

Mario Lemieux, b. 1965: 6-time NHL leading scorer; MVP, 1988, 1993, 1996; Playoff MVP, 1991-92.

Ivan Lendl, b. 1960: U.S. Open tennis champ, 1985-87.

Sugar Ray Leonard, b. 1956: boxer held titles in 5 different weight classes.

Carl Lewis, b. 1961: track-and-field star won 9 Olympic gold medals in sprinting and the long jump.

Tara Lipinski, b. 1982: youngest woman to win U.S. and world figure skating championships, 1997.

Vince Lombardi (1913-1970): Green Bay Packers coach led team to 5 NFL championships and 2 Super Bowl victories.

Greg Louganis, b. 1960: won Olympic gold medals in both springboard and platform diving, 1984, 1988.

Joe Louis (1914-1981): heavyweight champion, 1937-49.

Sid Luckman, b. 1916: Chicago Bears quarterback led team to 4 NFL championships; MVP, 1943.

Connie Mack (1862-1956): Philadelphia Athletics manager, 1901-50; won 9 pennants, 5 championships.

Greg Maddux, b. 1966: NL pitcher won 4 consecutive Cy Young awards, 1992-95.

Karl Malone, b. 1963: Utah Jazz forward was MVP, 1997; 10-time All-Star; 25,000+ career points.

Moses Malone, b. 1955: NBA center was MVP 1979, 1982-83.

Mickey Mantle (1931-1995): N.Y. Yankees outfielder; triple crown, 1956; 18 World Series home runs; MVP 3 times.

Pete Maravich (1948-1988): guard scored NCAA record 44.2 ppg during collegiate career; led NBA in scoring, 1977.

Rocky Marciano (1923-1969): heavyweight champion, 1952-56; retired undefeated.

Dan Marino, b. 1961: Miami Dolphins quarterback passed for NFL record 5,084 yds and 48 touchdowns, 1984; holds career NFL records for touchdowns, yds passing, completions.

Roger Maris (1934-1985): N.Y. Yankees outfielder hit record 61 home runs, 1961; MVP, 1960 and 1961.

Eddie Mathews, b. 1931: Milwaukee-Atlanta 3d baseman hit 512 career home runs.

Christy Mathewson (1880-1925): N.Y. Giants pitcher won 373 games.

Bob Mathias, b. 1930: decathlon gold medalist, 1948, 1952.

Willie Mays, b. 1931: N.Y.-S.F. Giants center fielder hit 660 home runs, led NL 4 times; had 3,283 hits; twice MVP.

Willie McCovey, b. 1938: S.F. Giants slugger hit 521 home runs; led NL 3 times; MVP, 1969.

John McEnroe, b. 1959: U.S. Open tennis champ, 1979-81, 1984; Wimbledon champ, 1981, 1983-84.

John McGraw (1873-1934): N.Y. Giants manager led team to 10 pennants, 3 championships.

Mark McGwire, b. 1963: 1st baseman led major leagues with 52 home runs in 1996, 58 (34 AL, 24 NL) in 1997.

Mark Messier, b. 1961: center chosen NHL MVP, 1990 and 1992; Conn Smythe Trophy, 1984.

George Mikan, b. 1924: Minn. Lakers center considered the best basketball player of the first half of the century.

Stan Mikita, b. 1940: Chicago Black Hawks center led NHL in scoring 4 times; MVP twice.

Joe Montana, b. 1956: S.F. 49ers quarterback was Super Bowl MVP, 1982, 1985, 1990.

Archie Moore, b. 1913: light-heavyweight champion, 1952-62.

Howie Morenz (1902-1937): Montreal Canadiens forward considered the best hockey player of first half of the century.

Eddie Murray, b. 1956: durable slugger was 3d player to combine 3,000+ hits with 500+ home runs.

Stan Musial, b. 1920: St. Louis Cardinals star won 7 NL batting titles; MVP 3 times.

Bronko Nagurski (1908-1990): Chicago Bears fullback and tackle; gained more than 4,000 yds. rushing.

Joe Namath, b. 1943: N.Y. Jets quarterback was Super Bowl MVP, 1969.

Martina Navratilova, b. 1956: Wimbledon champ 9 times, U.S. champ 1983-84, 1986-87.

Byron Nelson, b. 1912: won 11 consecutive golf tournaments in 1945; twice Masters and PGA titlist.

Ernie Nevers (1903-1976): Stanford star selected the best college fullback to play between 1919-69.

John Newcombe, b. 1943: Australian twice U.S. Open tennis champ; Wimbledon titlist 3 times.

Jack Nicklaus, b. 1940: PGA Player-of-the-Year, 1967, 1972; leading money winner 8 times; won Masters 6 times.

Chuck Noll, b. 1931: coach led Pittsburgh Steelers to 4 Super Bowl titles.

Paavo Nurmi (1897-1973): Finnish distance runner won 6 Olympic gold medals, 1920, 1924, 1928.

Al Oerter, b. 1936: discus thrower won gold medal at 4 consecutive Olympics, 1956-68.

Hakeem Olajuwon, b. 1963: Houston Rockets center was NBA MVP 1994, Playoffs MVP 1994-95; career leader in blocked shots.

Shaquille O'Neal, b. 1972: NBA center was rookie of the year, 1993; scoring leader, 1995.

Bobby Orr, b. 1948: Boston Bruins defenseman; Norris Trophy 8 times; led NHL in scoring twice, assists 5 times.

Mel Ott (1909-1958): N.Y. Giants outfielder hit 511 home runs; led NL 6 times.

Jesse Owens (1913-1980): track and field star won 4 1936 Olympic gold medals.

Satchel Paige (1906-1982): pitcher starred in Negro leagues, 1924-48; entered major leagues at age 42.

Arnold Palmer, b. 1929: golf's first $1 million winner; won 4 Masters, 2 British Opens.

Jim Palmer, b. 1945: Baltimore Orioles pitcher; Cy Young award 3 times; 20-game winner 8 times.

Joe Paterno, b. 1926: winningest active NCAA football coach; led Penn St. to 2 national titles, 1982, 1986.

Floyd Patterson, b. 1935: twice heavyweight champion.

Walter Payton, b. 1954: Chicago Bears running back has most rushing yards in NFL history; top NFC rusher, 1976-80.

Pele, b. 1940: Brazilian soccer star scored 1,281 goals during 22-year career.

Bob Pettit, b. 1932: first NBA player to score 20,000 points; twice NBA scoring leader.

Richard Petty, b. 1937: NASCAR national champ 7 times; 7-time Daytona 500 winner.

Laffit Pincay Jr., b. 1946: leading money-winning jockey, 1970-74, 1979, 1985.

Jacques Plante (1929-1986): goalie, 7 Vezina trophies; first goalie to wear a mask in a game.

Kirby Puckett, b. 1961: Minn. Twins outfielder won AL batting title, 1989; led AL in hits, 1987-89, 1992; RBIs, 1994.

Willis Reed, b. 1942: N.Y. Knicks center; MVP, 1970; Playoff MVP, 1970, 1973.

Jerry Rice, b. 1962: S.F. 49ers receiver; Super Bowl MVP, 1989; NFL record for career touchdowns, receptions.

Maurice Richard, b. 1921: Montreal Canadiens forward scored 544 regular season goals, 82 playoff goals.

Branch Rickey (1881-1965): executive helped break baseball's color barrier, 1947; initiated farm system, 1919.

Pat Riley, b. 1945: coached L.A. Lakers to 4 NBA titles.

Cal Ripken Jr., b. 1960: Baltimore Orioles shortstop; AL MVP 1983, 1991; broke Lou Gehrig's record for most consecutive games played, 1995.

Oscar Robertson, b. 1938: guard averaged career 25.7 points per game; 3d most career assists; MVP, 1964.

Brooks Robinson, b. 1937: Baltimore Orioles 3d baseman played in 4 World Series; MVP, 1964; 16 gold gloves.

Frank Robinson, b. 1935: slugger was MVP in both NL and AL; triple crown, 1966; 586 lifetime home runs; first black manager in majors.

Jackie Robinson (1919-1972): broke baseball's color barrier with Brooklyn Dodgers, 1947; MVP, 1949.

Sugar Ray Robinson (1920-1989): middleweight champion 5 times, welterweight champion.

Knute Rockne (1888-1931): Notre Dame football coach, 1918-31; revolutionized game by stressing forward pass.

Dennis Rodman, b. 1961: eccentric forward led NBA in rebounding 1991-97.

Pete Rose, b. 1941: won 3 NL batting titles; hit safely in 44 consecutive games, 1978; has most career hits, 4,256.

Patrick Roy, b. 1965: Montreal-Colorado goalie was 3-time Vezina Trophy winner, Playoffs MVP 1993.

Wilma Rudolph (1940-1994): sprinter won 3 1960 Olympic gold medals.

Adolph Rupp (1901-77): winningest NCAA basketball coach; led Kentucky to 4 national titles, 1948-49, 1951, 1958.

Bill Russell, b. 1934: Boston Celtics center led team to 11 NBA titles; MVP 5 times; first black coach of major pro sports team.

Babe Ruth (1895-1948): N.Y. Yankees outfielder hit 60 home runs, 1927; 714 lifetime; led AL 12 times.

Johnny Rutherford, b. 1938: auto racer won 3 Indy 500s.

Nolan Ryan, b. 1947: pitcher struck out record 383 batters, 1973; record 5,714 career; pitched record 7 no-hitters; won 324 major league games.

Pete Sampras, b. 1971: tennis star won U.S. Open, Wimbledon 4 times each.

Barry Sanders, b. 1968: running back was Heisman Trophy winner, 1988; NCAA single-season records for rushing yds, touchdowns; led NFL in rushing, 1990, 1994, 1996.

Gene Sarazen, b. 1902: won PGA championship 3 times, U.S. Open twice; developer of sand wedge.

Gale Sayers, b. 1943: Chicago Bears back twice led NFL in rushing.

Mike Schmidt, b. 1949: Phillies 3d baseman led NL in home runs 8 times; 548 lifetime; NL MVP, 1980, 1981, 1986.

Tom Seaver, b. 1944: pitcher won NL Cy Young award 3 times; won 311 major league games.

Monica Seles, b. 1973: U.S. Open tennis champ 1991, 1992.

Willie Shoemaker, b. 1931: jockey rode 4 Kentucky Derby and 5 Belmont Stakes winners; leading career money winner.

Eddie Shore (1902-1985): Boston Bruins defenseman; MVP 4 times, first-team all-star 7 times.

Don Shula, b. 1930: all-time winningest NFL coach.

Al Simmons (1902-1956): AL outfielder batted .334 lifetime.

O.J. Simpson, b. 1947: running back rushed for 2,003 yds., 1973; AFC leading rusher 4 times.

George Sisler (1893-1973): St. Louis Browns 1st baseman had record 257 hits, 1920; batted .340 lifetime.

Dean Smith, b. 1931: North Carolina basketball coach has most career NCAA Division I tournament victories.

Emmitt Smith, b. 1969: Dallas Cowboys running back led NFL in rushing, 1991-93, 1995; NFL and Super Bowl MVP, 1993; record 25 rushing touchdowns, 1995.

Lee Smith, b. 1957: relief pitcher, all-time saves leader, 478.

Sam Snead, b. 1912: PGA and Masters champ 3 times each.

Warren Spahn, b. 1921: pitcher won 363 NL games; 20-game winner 13 times; Cy Young award, 1957.

Tris Speaker (1885-1958): AL outfielder batted .344 over 22 seasons; hit record 793 career doubles.

Mark Spitz, b. 1950: swimmer won 7 1972 Olympic gold medals.

Amos Alonzo Stagg (1862-1965): coached Univ. of Chicago football team for 41 years, including 5 undefeated seasons; introduced huddle, man-in-motion, and end-around play.

Bart Starr, b. 1934: Green Bay Packers quarterback led team to 5 NFL titles and 2 Super Bowl victories.

Roger Staubach, b. 1942: Dallas Cowboys quarterback; leading NFC passer 5 times.

Casey Stengel (1890-1975): managed Yankees to 10 pennants, 7 championships, 1949-60.

Jackie Stewart, b. 1939: Scot auto racer retired with 27 Grand Prix victories.

John Stockton, b. 1962: Utah Jazz guard is NBA career leader in assists, steals; NBA assists leader, 1988-96.

John L. Sullivan (1858-1918): last bareknuckle heavyweight champion, 1882-1892.

Fran Tarkenton, b. 1940: quarterback is 2d in career touchdown passes, passing yds.

Lawrence Taylor, b. 1959: linebacker led N.Y. Giants to 2 Super Bowl titles; played in 10 Pro Bowls.

Frank Thomas, b. 1968: Chicago White Sox 1st baseman was AL MVP, 1993-94; won AL batting title, 1997.

Jim Thorpe (1888-1953): football All-America, 1911, 1912; won pentathlon and decathlon, 1912 Olympics.

Bill Tilden (1893-1953): U.S. singles champ 7 times; played on 11 Davis Cup teams.

Y.A. Tittle, b. 1926: N.Y. Giants quarterback; MVP, 1961, 1963.

Lee Trevino, b. 1939: golfer won U.S., British Open twice.

Bryan Trottier, b. 1956: center played on 6 Stanley Cup championship teams.

Wyomia Tyus, b. 1945: sprinter won 1964, 1968 Olympic 100-meter dash.

Johnny Unitas, b. 1933: Baltimore Colts quarterback passed for more than 40,000 yds; MVP, 1957, 1967.

Al Unser, b. 1939: Indy 500 winner 4 times.

Bobby Unser, b. 1934: Indy 500 winner 3 times.

Norm Van Brocklin (1926-1983): quarterback passed for game record 554 yds., 1951; MVP, 1960.

Honus Wagner (1874-1955): Pittsburgh Pirates shortstop won 8 NL batting titles.

Tom Watson, b. 1949: golfer won British Open 5 times.

Johnny Weissmuller (1903-1984): swimmer won 52 national championships, 5 Olympic gold medals; set 67 world records.

Jerry West, b. 1938: L.A. Lakers guard had career average 27 points per game; first team all-star 10 times.

Reggie White, b. 1961: defensive end is all-time NFL sack leader; Defensive Player of the Year, 1987.

Kathy Whitworth, b. 1939: women's golf leading money winner 8 times; first woman to earn more than $300,000.

Lenny Wilkens, b. 1937: winningest coach in NBA history.

Ted Williams, b. 1918: Boston Red Sox outfielder won 6 batting titles; last major leaguer to hit over .400: .406 in 1941; twice won triple crown; .344 lifetime batting average.

Katarina Witt, b. 1965: German figure skater; won Olympic gold medal, 1984, 1988.

John Wooden, b. 1910: coached UCLA basketball team to 10 national championships.

Tiger Woods, b. 1975: only golfer to win 3 consecutive U.S. Amateur titles, 1994-96; won Masters, 1997.

Mickey Wright, b. 1935: won LPGA championship 4 times, Vare Trophy 5 times; twice AP Woman-Athlete-of-the-Year.

Carl Yastrzemski, b. 1939: Boston Red Sox slugger won 3 batting titles; triple crown, 1967.

Cy Young (1867-1955): pitcher won record 511 games.

Steve Young, b. 1961: San Francisco 49ers quarterback led NFL in passing, 1991-94, 1996; Super Bowl MVP, 1995.

Babe Didrikson Zaharias (1914-1956): track star won 2 1932 Olympic gold medals; won numerous golf tournaments.

TENNIS
U.S. Open Champions
Men's Singles

Year	Champion	Final opponent	Year	Champion	Final opponent
1910	William Larned	T. C. Bundy	1954	E. Victor Seixas Jr.	Rex Hartwig
1911	William Larned	Maurice McLoughlin	1955	Tony Trabert	Ken Rosewall
1912	Maurice McLoughlin	Wallace Johnson	1956	Ken Rosewall	Lewis Hoad
1913	Maurice McLoughlin	Richard Williams	1957	Malcolm Anderson	Ashley Cooper
1914	Richard Williams	Maurice McLoughlin	1958	Ashley Cooper	Malcolm Anderson
1915	William Johnston	Maurice McLoughlin	1959	Neale A. Fraser	Alejandro Olmedo
1916	Richard Williams	William Johnston	1960	Neale A. Fraser	Rod Laver
1917	R. L. Murray	N. W. Niles	1961	Roy Emerson	Rod Laver
1918	R. L. Murray	Bill Tilden	1962	Rod Laver	Roy Emerson
1919	William Johnston	Bill Tilden	1963	Rafael Osuna	F. A. Froehling 3d
1920	Bill Tilden	William Johnston	1964	Roy Emerson	Fred Stolle
1921	Bill Tilden	Wallace Johnson	1965	Manuel Santana	Cliff Drysdale
1922	Bill Tilden	William Johnston	1966	Fred Stolle	John Newcombe
1923	Bill Tilden	William Johnston	1967	John Newcombe	Clark Graebner
1924	Bill Tilden	William Johnston	1968	Arthur Ashe	Tom Okker
1925	Bill Tilden	William Johnston	1969	Rod Laver	Tony Roche
1926	Rene Lacoste	Jean Borotra	1970	Ken Rosewall	Tony Roche
1927	Rene Lacoste	Bill Tilden	1971	Stan Smith	Jan Kodes
1928	Henri Cochet	Francis Hunter	1972	Ilie Nastase	Arthur Ashe
1929	Bill Tilden	Francis Hunter	1973	John Newcombe	Jan Kodes
1930	John Doeg	Francis Shields	1974	Jimmy Connors	Ken Rosewall
1931	H. Ellsworth Vines	George Lott	1975	Manuel Orantes	Jimmy Connors
1932	H. Ellsworth Vines	Henri Cochet	1976	Jimmy Connors	Bjorn Borg
1933	Fred Perry	John Crawford	1977	Guillermo Vilas	Jimmy Connors
1934	Fred Perry	Wilmer Allison	1978	Jimmy Connors	Bjorn Borg
1935	Wilmer Allison	Sidney Wood	1979	John McEnroe	Vitas Gerulaitis
1936	Fred Perry	Don Budge	1980	John McEnroe	Bjorn Borg
1937	Don Budge	Baron G. von Cramm	1981	John McEnroe	Bjorn Borg
1938	Don Budge	C. Gene Mako	1982	Jimmy Connors	Ivan Lendl
1939	Robert Riggs	S. Welby Van Horn	1983	Jimmy Connors	Ivan Lendl
1940	Don McNeill	Robert Riggs	1984	John McEnroe	Ivan Lendl
1941	Robert Riggs	F. L. Kovacs	1985	Ivan Lendl	John McEnroe
1942	F. R. Schroeder Jr.	Frank Parker	1986	Ivan Lendl	Miloslav Mecir
1943	Joseph Hunt	Jack Kramer	1987	Ivan Lendl	Mats Wilander
1944	Frank Parker	William Talbert	1988	Mats Wilander	Ivan Lendl
1945	Frank Parker	William Talbert	1989	Boris Becker	Ivan Lendl
1946	Jack Kramer	Thomas Brown Jr.	1990	Pete Sampras	Andre Agassi
1947	Jack Kramer	Frank Parker	1991	Stefan Edberg	Jim Courier
1948	Pancho Gonzales	Eric Sturgess	1992	Stefan Edberg	Pete Sampras
1949	Pancho Gonzales	F. R. Schroeder Jr.	1993	Pete Sampras	Cedric Pioline
1950	Arthur Larsen	Herbert Flam	1994	Andre Agassi	Michael Stich
1951	Frank Sedgman	E. Victor Seixas Jr.	1995	Pete Sampras	Andre Agassi
1952	Frank Sedgman	Gardnar Mulloy	1996	Pete Sampras	Michael Chang
1953	Tony Trabert	E. Victor Seixas Jr.	1997	Patrick Rafter	Greg Rusedski

Women's Singles

Year	Champion	Final opponent	Year	Champion	Final opponent
1926	Molla B. Mallory	Elizabeth Ryan	1962	Margaret Smith	Darlene Hard
1927	Helen Wills	Betty Nuthall	1963	Maria Bueno	Margaret Smith
1928	Helen Wills	Helen Jacobs	1964	Maria Bueno	Carole Graebner
1929	Helen Wills	M. Watson	1965	Margaret Smith	Billie Jean Moffitt
1930	Betty Nuthall	L. A. Harper	1966	Maria Bueno	Nancy Richey
1931	Helen Wills Moody	E. B. Whittingstall	1967	Billie Jean King	Ann Haydon Jones
1932	Helen Jacobs	Carolin A. Babcock	1968	Virginia Wade	Billie Jean King
1933	Helen Jacobs	Helen Wills Moody	1969	Margaret Smith Court	Nancy Richey
1934	Helen Jacobs	Sarah H. Palfrey	1970	Margaret Smith Court	Rosemary Casals
1935	Helen Jacobs	Sarah Palfrey Fabyan	1971	Billie Jean King	Rosemary Casals
1936	Alice Marble	Helen Jacobs	1972	Billie Jean King	Kerry Melville
1937	Anita Lizana	Jadwiga Jedrzejowska	1973	Margaret Smith Court	Evonne Goolagong
1938	Alice Marble	Nancye Wynne	1974	Billie Jean King	Evonne Goolagong
1939	Alice Marble	Helen Jacobs	1975	Chris Evert	Evonne Goolagong
1940	Alice Marble	Helen Jacobs	1976	Chris Evert	Evonne Goolagong
1941	Sarah Palfrey Cooke	Pauline Betz	1977	Chris Evert	Wendy Turnbull
1942	Pauline Betz	Louise Brough	1978	Chris Evert	Pam Shriver
1943	Pauline Betz	Louise Brough	1979	Tracy Austin	Chris Evert Lloyd
1944	Pauline Betz	Margaret Osborne	1980	Chris Evert Lloyd	Hana Mandlikova
1945	Sarah Palfrey Cooke	Pauline Betz	1981	Tracy Austin	Martina Navratilova
1946	Pauline Betz	Doris Hart	1982	Chris Evert Lloyd	Hana Mandlikova
1947	Louise Brough	Margaret Osborne	1983	Martina Navratilova	Chris Evert Lloyd
1948	Margaret Osborne duPont	Louise Brough	1984	Martina Navratilova	Chris Evert Lloyd
1949	Margaret Osborne duPont	Doris Hart	1985	Hana Mandlikova	Martina Navratilova
1950	Margaret Osborne duPont	Doris Hart	1986	Martina Navratilova	Helena Sukova
1951	Maureen Connolly	Shirley Fry	1987	Martina Navratilova	Steffi Graf
1952	Maureen Connolly	Doris Hart	1988	Steffi Graf	Gabriela Sabatini
1953	Maureen Connolly	Doris Hart	1989	Steffi Graf	Martina Navratilova
1954	Doris Hart	Louise Brough	1990	Gabriela Sabatini	Steffi Graf
1955	Doris Hart	Patricia Ward	1991	Monica Seles	Martina Navratilova
1956	Shirley Fry	Althea Gibson	1992	Monica Seles	Arantxa Sanchez Vicario
1957	Althea Gibson	Louise Brough	1000	Steffi Graf	Helena Sukova
1958	Althea Gibson	Darlene Hard	1994	Arantxa Sanchez Vicario	Steffi Graf
1959	Maria Bueno	Christine Truman	1995	Steffi Graf	Monica Seles
1000	Darlene Hard	Maria Bueno	1996	Steffi Graf	Monica Seles
1961	Darlene Hard	Ann Haydon	1997	Martina Hingis	Venus Williams

All-England Champions, Wimbledon

Men's Singles

Year	Champion	Final opponent	Year	Champion	Final opponent
1933	Jack Crawford	Ellsworth Vines	1968	Rod Laver	Tony Roche
1934	Fred Perry	Jack Crawford	1969	Rod Laver	John Newcombe
1935	Fred Perry	Gottfried von Cramm	1970	John Newcombe	Ken Rosewall
1936	Fred Perry	Gottfried von Cramm	1971	John Newcombe	Stan Smith
1937	Donald Budge	Gottfried von Cramm	1972	Stan Smith	Ilie Nastase
1938	Donald Budge	Wilfred Austin	1973	Jan Kodes	Alex Metreveli
1939	Bobby Riggs	Elwood Cooke	1974	Jimmy Connors	Ken Rosewall
1940-45	not held		1975	Arthur Ashe	Jimmy Connors
1946	Yvon Petra	Geoff E. Brown	1976	Bjorn Borg	Ilie Nastase
1947	Jack Kramer	Tom P. Brown	1977	Bjorn Borg	Jimmy Connors
1948	Bob Falkenburg	John Bromwich	1978	Bjorn Borg	Jimmy Connors
1949	Ted Schroeder	Jaroslav Drobny	1979	Bjorn Borg	Roscoe Tanner
1950	Budge Patty	Frank Sedgman	1980	Bjorn Borg	John McEnroe
1951	Dick Savitt	Ken McGregor	1981	John McEnroe	Bjorn Borg
1952	Frank Sedgman	Jaroslav Drobny	1982	Jimmy Connors	John McEnroe
1953	Vic Seixas	Kurt Nielsen	1983	John McEnroe	Chris Lewis
1954	Jaroslav Drobny	Ken Rosewall	1984	John McEnroe	Jimmy Connors
1955	Tony Trabert	Kurt Nielsen	1985	Boris Becker	Kevin Curren
1956	Lew Hoad	Ken Rosewall	1986	Boris Becker	Ivan Lendl
1957	Lew Hoad	Ashley Cooper	1987	Pat Cash	Ivan Lendl
1958	Ashley Cooper	Neale Fraser	1988	Stefan Edberg	Boris Becker
1959	Alex Olmedo	Rod Laver	1989	Boris Becker	Stefan Edberg
1960	Neale Fraser	Rod Laver	1990	Stefan Edberg	Boris Becker
1961	Rod Laver	Chuck McKinley	1991	Michael Stich	Boris Becker
1962	Rod Laver	Martin Mulligan	1992	Andre Agassi	Goran Ivanisevic
1963	Chuck McKinley	Fred Stolle	1993	Pete Sampras	Jim Courier
1964	Roy Emerson	Fred Stolle	1994	Pete Sampras	Goran Ivanisevic
1965	Roy Emerson	Fred Stolle	1995	Pete Sampras	Boris Becker
1966	Manuel Santana	Dennis Ralston	1996	Richard Krajicek	MaliVai Washington
1967	John Newcombe	Wilhelm Bungert	1997	Pete Sampras	Cedric Pioline

Women's Singles

Year	Champion	Year	Champion	Year	Champion	Year	Champion
1946	Pauline Betz	1959	Maria Bueno	1972	Billie Jean King	1985	Martina Navratilova
1947	Margaret Osborne	1960	Maria Bueno	1973	Billie Jean King	1986	Martina Navratilova
1948	Louise Brough	1961	Angela Mortimer	1974	Chris Evert	1987	Martina Navratilova
1949	Louise Brough	1962	Karen Hantze-Susman	1975	Billie Jean King	1988	Steffi Graf
1950	Louise Brough	1963	Margaret Smith	1976	Chris Evert	1989	Steffi Graf
1951	Doris Hart	1964	Maria Bueno	1977	Virginia Wade	1990	Martina Navratilova
1952	Maureen Connolly	1965	Margaret Smith	1978	Martina Navratilova	1991	Steffi Graf
1953	Maureen Connolly	1966	Billie Jean King	1979	Martina Navratilova	1992	Steffi Graf
1954	Maureen Connolly	1967	Billie Jean King	1980	Evonne Goolagong	1993	Steffi Graf
1955	Louise Brough	1968	Billie Jean King	1981	Chris Evert Lloyd	1994	Conchita Martinez
1956	Shirley Fry	1969	Ann Haydon-Jones	1982	Martina Navratilova	1995	Steffi Graf
1957	Althea Gibson	1970	Margaret Smith Court	1983	Martina Navratilova	1996	Steffi Graf
1958	Althea Gibson	1971	Evonne Goolagong	1984	Martina Navratilova	1997	Martina Hingis

Davis Cup Challenge Round

Year	Result	Year	Result	Year	Result
1900	United States 3, British Isles 0	1933	Great Britain 3, France 2	1968	United States 4, Australia
1901	(not played)	1934	Great Britain 4, United States 1	1969	United States 5, Romania 0
1902	United States 3, British Isles 2	1935	Great Britain 5, United States 0	1970	United States 5, W. Germany 0
1903	British Isles 4, United States 1	1936	Great Britain 3, Australia 2	1971	United States 3, Romania 2
1904	British Isles 5, Belgium 0	1937	United States 4, Great Britain 1	1972	United States 3, Romania 2
1905	British Isles 5, United States 0	1938	United States 3, Australia 2	1973	Australia 5, United States 0
1906	British Isles 5, United States 0	1939	Australia 3, United States 2	1974	South Africa (default by India)
1907	Australia 3, British Isles 2	1940-45	(not played)	1975	Sweden 3, Czechoslovakia 2
1908	Australasia 3, United States 2	1946	United States 5, Australia 0	1976	Italy 4, Chile 1
1909	Australasia 5, United States 0	1947	United States 4, Australia 1	1977	Australia 3, Italy 1
1910	(not played)	1948	United States 5, Australia 0	1978	United States 4, Great Britain 1
1911	Australasia 5, United States 0	1949	United States 4, Australia 1	1979	United States 5, Italy 0
1912	British Isles 3, Australasia 2	1950	Australia 4, United States 1	1980	Czechoslovakia 4, Italy 1
1913	United States 3, British Isles 2	1951	Australia 3, United States 2	1981	United States 3, Argentina 1
1914	Australasia 3, United States 2	1952	Australia 4, United States 1	1982	United States 4, France, 1
1915-18	(not played)	1953	Australia 3, United States 2	1983	Australia 3, Sweden 2
1919	Australasia 4, British Isles 1	1954	United States 3, Australia 2	1984	Sweden 4, United States 1
1920	United States 5, Australasia 0	1955	Australia 5, United States 0	1985	Sweden 3, W. Germany 2
1921	United States 5, Japan 0	1956	Australia 5, United States 0	1986	Australia 3, Sweden 2
1922	United States 4, Australasia 1	1957	Australia 3, United States 2	1987	Sweden 5, India 0
1923	United States 4, Australasia 1	1958	United States 3, Australia 2	1988	W. Germany 4, Sweden 1
1924	United States 5, Australasia 0	1959	Australia 3, United States 2	1989	W. Germany 3, Sweden 2
1925	United States 5, France 0	1960	Australia 4, Italy 1	1990	United States 3, Australia 2
1926	United States 4, France 1	1961	Australia 5, Italy 0	1991	France 3, United States 1
1927	France 3, United States 2	1962	Australia 5, Mexico 0	1992	United States 3, Switzerland 1
1928	France 4, United States 1	1963	United States 3, Australia 2	1993	Germany 4, Australia 1
1929	France 3, United States 2	1964	Australia 3, United States 2	1994	Sweden 4, Russia 1
1930	France 4, United States 1	1965	Australia 4, Spain 1	1995	United States 3, Russia 2
1931	France 3, Great Britain 2	1966	Australia 4, India 1	1996	France 3, Sweden 2
1932	France 3, United States 2	1967	Australia 4, Spain 1		

French Open Singles Champions

Year	Men	Women	Year	Men	Women
1969	Rod Laver	Margaret Smith Court	1984	Ivan Lendl	Martina Navratilova
1970	Jan Kodes	Margaret Smith Court	1985	Mats Wilander	Chris Evert Lloyd
1971	Jan Kodes	Evonne Goolagong	1986	Ivan Lendl	Chris Evert Lloyd
1972	Andres Gimeno	Billie Jean King	1987	Ivan Lendl	Steffi Graf
1973	Ilie Nastase	Margaret Smith Court	1988	Mats Wilander	Steffi Graf
1974	Bjorn Borg	Chris Evert	1989	Michael Chang	Arantxa Sanchez Vicario
1975	Bjorn Borg	Chris Evert	1990	Andres Gomez	Monica Seles
1976	Adriano Panatta	Sue Barker	1991	Jim Courier	Monica Seles
1977	Guillermo Vilas	Mima Jausovec	1992	Jim Courier	Monica Seles
1978	Bjorn Borg	Virginia Ruzici	1993	Sergi Bruguera	Steffi Graf
1979	Bjorn Borg	Chris Evert Lloyd	1994	Sergi Bruguera	Arantxa Sanchez Vicario
1980	Bjorn Borg	Chris Evert Lloyd	1995	Thomas Muster	Steffi Graf
1981	Bjorn Borg	Hana Mandlikova	1996	Yevgeny Kafelnikov	Steffi Graf
1982	Mats Wilander	Martina Navratilova	1997	Gustavo Kuerten	Iva Majoli
1983	Yannick Noah	Chris Evert Lloyd			

Australian Open Singles Champions

Year*	Men	Women	Year*	Men	Women
1969	Rod Laver	Margaret Smith Court	1983	Mats Wilander	Martina Navratilova
1970	Arthur Ashe	Margaret Smith Court	1984	Mats Wilander	Chris Evert Lloyd
1971	Ken Rosewall	Margaret Smith Court	1985	Stefan Edberg	Martina Navratilova
1972	Ken Rosewall	Virginia Wade	1986	Not held	Not held
1973	John Newcombe	Margaret Smith Court	1987	Stefan Edberg	Hana Mandlikova
1974	Jimmy Connors	Evonne Goolagong	1988	Mats Wilander	Steffi Graf
1975	John Newcombe	Evonne Goolagong	1989	Ivan Lendl	Steffi Graf
1976	Mark Edmondson	Evonne Goolagong	1990	Ivan Lendl	Steffi Graf
1977	Roscoe Tanner	Kerry Reid	1991	Boris Becker	Monica Seles
	Vitas Gerulaitis	Evonne Goolagong	1992	Jim Courier	Monica Seles
1978	Guillermo Vilas	Chris O'Neill	1993	Jim Courier	Monica Seles
1979	Guillermo Vilas	Barbara Jordan	1994	Pete Sampras	Steffi Graf
1980	Brian Teacher	Hana Mandlikova	1995	Andre Agassi	Mary Pierce
1981	Johan Kriek	Martina Navratilova	1996	Boris Becker	Monica Seles
1982	Johan Kriek	Chris Evert Lloyd	1997	Pete Sampras	Martina Hingis

* Two tournaments were held in 1977 (Jan. & Dec.). Tournament was moved back to Jan. in 1987, so no championship was decided in 1986.

AUTO RACING

Indianapolis 500 Winners

Year	Winner, Car (Chassis-Engine)	MPH	Year	Winner, Car (Chassis-Engine)	MPH
1911	Ray Harroun, Marmon	74.602	1958	Jimmy Bryan, Salih-Offy	133.791
1912	Joe Dawson, National	78.719	1959	Rodger Ward, Watson-Offy	135.857
1913	Jules Goux, Peugeot	75.933	1960	Jim Rathmann, Watson-Offy	138.767
1914	Rene Thomas, Delage	82.474	1961	A.J. Foyt Jr., Trevis-Offy	139.130
1915	Ralph DePalma, Mercedes	89.840	1962	Rodger Ward, Watson-Offy	140.293
1916	Dario Resta, Peugeot	84.001	1963	Parnelli Jones, Watson-Offy	143.137
1917-18	race not held		1964	A.J. Foyt Jr., Watson-Offy	147.350
1919	Howdy Wilcox, Peugeot	88.050	1965	Jim Clark, Lotus-Ford	150.686
1920	Gaston Chevrolet, Frontenac	88.618	1966	Graham Hill, Lola-Ford	144.317
1921	Tommy Milton, Frontenac	89.621	1967	A.J. Foyt Jr., Coyote-Ford	151.207
1922	Jimmy Murphy, Duesenberg-Miller	94.484	1968	Bobby Unser, Eagle-Offy	152.882
1923	Tommy Milton, Miller	90.954	1969	Mario Andretti, Hawk-Ford	156.867
1924	L.L. Corum-Joe Boyer, Duesenberg	98.234	1970	Al Unser, P.J. Colt-Ford	155.749
1925	Peter DePaolo, Duesenberg	101.127	1971	Al Unser, P.J. Colt-Ford	157.735
1926	Frank Lockhart, Miller	95.904	1972	Mark Donohue, McLaren-Offy	162.962
1927	George Souders, Duesenberg	97.545	1973	Gordon Johncock, Eagle-Offy	159.036
1928	Louie Meyer, Miller	99.482	1974	Johnny Rutherford, McLaren-Offy	158.589
1929	Ray Keech, Miller	97.585	1975	Bobby Unser, Eagle-Offy	149.213
1930	Billy Arnold, Summers-Miller	100.448	1976	Johnny Rutherford, McLaren-Offy	148.725
1931	Louis Schneider, Stevens-Miller	96.629	1977	A.J. Foyt Jr., Coyote-Foyt	161.331
1932	Fred Frame, Wetteroth-Miller	104.144	1978	Al Unser, Lola-Cosworth	161.363
1933	Louie Meyer, Miller	104.162	1979	Rick Mears, Penske-Cosworth	158.899
1934	Bill Cummings, Miller	104.863	1980	Johnny Rutherford, Chaparral-Cosworth	142.862
1935	Kelly Petillo, Wetteroth-Offy	106.240	1981	Bobby Unser, Penske-Cosworth	139.084
1936	Louie Meyer, Stevens-Miller	109.069	1982	Gordon Johncock, Wildcat-Cosworth	162.029
1937	Wilbur Shaw, Shaw-Offy	113.580	1983	Tom Sneva, March-Cosworth	162.117
1938	Floyd Roberts, Wetteroth-Miller	117.200	1984	Rick Mears, March-Cosworth	163.612
1939	Wilbur Shaw, Maserati	115.035	1985	Danny Sullivan, March-Cosworth	152.982
1940	Wilbur Shaw, Maserati	114.277	1986	Bobby Rahal, March-Cosworth	170.722
1941	Floyd Davis-Mauri Rose, Wetteroth-Offy	115.117	1987	Al Unser, March-Cosworth	162.175
1942-45	race not held		1988	Rick Mears, Penske-Chevy Indy V8	144.809
1946	George Robson, Adams-Sparks	114.820	1989	Emerson Fittipaldi, Penske-Chevy Indy V8	167.581
1947	Mauri Rose, Deidt-Offy	116.338	1990	Arie Luyendyk, Lola-Chevy Indy V8	185.981*
1948	Mauri Rose, Deidt-Offy	119.814	1991	Rick Mears, Penske-Chevy Indy V8	176.457
1949	Bill Holland, Deidt-Offy	121.327	1992	Al Unser Jr., Galmer-Chevy Indy V8A	134.477
1950	Johnnie Parsons, Kurtis-Offy	124.002	1993	Emerson Fittipaldi, Penske-Chevy Indy V8C	157.207
1951	Lee Wallard, Kurtis-Offy	126.244			
1952	Troy Ruttman, Kuzma-Offy	128.922	1994	Al Unser Jr., Penske-Mercedes Benz	160.872
1953	Bill Vukovich, KK500A-Offy	128.740	1995	Jacques Villeneuve, Reynard-Ford Cosworth XB	153.616
1954	Bill Vukovich, KK500A-Offy	130.840			
1955	Bob Sweikert, KK500C-Offy	128.213			
1956	Pat Flaherty, Watson-Offy	128.490	1996	Buddy Lazier, Reynard-Ford Cosworth	147.956
1957	Sam Hanks, Salih-Offy	135.601	1997	Arie Luyendyk, G Force-Aurora	145.827

*Race record. **Note:** The race was less than 500 mi in the following years: 1916 (300 mi), 1926 (400 mi), 1950 (345 mi), 1973 (332.5 mi), 1975 (435 mi), 1976 (255 mi).

IndyCar Champions

(U.S. Auto Club Champions prior to 1979; Championship Auto Racing Teams [CART] Champions, 1979-96)

Year	Driver	Year	Driver	Year	Driver	Year	Driver
1960	A. J. Foyt	1970	Al Unser	1980	Johnny Rutherford	1989	Emerson Fittipaldi
1961	A. J. Foyt	1971	Joe Leonard	1981	Rick Mears	1990	Al Unser Jr.
1962	Rodger Ward	1972	Joe Leonard	1982	Rick Mears	1991	Michael Andretti
1963	A. J. Foyt	1973	Roger McCluskey	1983	Al Unser	1992	Bobby Rahal
1964	A. J. Foyt	1974	Bobby Unser	1984	Mario Andretti	1993	Nigel Mansell
1965	Mario Andretti	1975	A. J. Foyt	1985	Al Unser	1994	Al Unser Jr.
1966	Mario Andretti	1976	Gordon Johncock	1986	Bobby Rahal	1995	Jacques Villeneuve
1967	A. J. Foyt	1977	Tom Sneva	1987	Bobby Rahal	1996	Jimmy Vasser
1968	Bobby Unser	1978	Tom Sneva	1988	Danny Sullivan	1997	Alex Zanardi
1969	Mario Andretti	1979	Rick Mears				

Notable One-Mile Land Speed Records

Andy Green, a Royal Air Force pilot, broke the sound barrier and set the first supersonic world speed record on land, Oct. 15, 1997, in Black Rock Desert, NV. Green, driving a car built by Richard Noble, had 2 runs at an average speed of 763.035 mph, as calculated according to the rules of the Federation Internationale Automobiliste (FIA). This record and speed exceeded the speed of sound, calculated at 751.251 mph for this time. On Sept. 25, Green had set a new world mark at 714.144 mph, which eclipsed the old record of 633.468. Both 1997 records were recorded by the United States Auto Club, with official world recognition by the FIA pending.

Date	Driver	Car	MPH	Date	Driver	Car	MPH
1/26/06	Marriott	Stanley (Steam)	127.659	11/19/37	Eyston	Thunderbolt 1	311.42
3/16/10	Oldfield	Benz	131.724	9/16/38	Eyston	Thunderbolt 1	357.5
4/23/11	Burman	Benz	141.732	8/23/39	Cobb	Railton	368.9
2/12/19	DePalma	Packard	149.875	9/16/47	Cobb	Railton-Mobil	394.2
4/27/20	Milton	Dusenberg	155.046	8/5/63	Breedlove	Spirit of America	407.45
4/28/26	Parry-Thomas	Thomas Spl.	170.624	10/27/64	Arfons	Green Monster	536.71
3/29/27	Seagrave	Sunbeam	203.790	11/15/65	Breedlove	Spirit of America	600.601
4/22/28	Keech	White Triplex	207.552	10/23/70	Gabelich	Blue Flame	622.407
3/11/29	Seagrave	Irving-Napier	231.446	10/9/79	Barrett	Budweiser Rocket	638.637*
2/5/31	Campbell	Napier-Campbell	246.086	10/4/83	Noble	Thrust 2	633.468
2/24/32	Campbell	Napier-Campbell	253.96	9/25/97	Green	Thrust SSC	714.144
2/22/33	Campbell	Napier-Campbell	272.109	10/15/97	Green	Thrust SSC	763.035
9/3/35	Campbell	Bluebird Special	301.13				

*Not recognized as official by sanctioning bodies.

24 Hours of Le Mans Race in 1997

Michele Alboreto (Italy), Stefan Johansson (Sweden), and Tom Kristensen (Denmark) drove their Joest TWR-Porsche to victory in the 1997 "24 Hours of Le Mans" race, June 15. They traveled 3,052.45 miles at an average of 126.9 mph.

World Grand Prix Champions

Year	Driver	Year	Driver	Year	Driver
1951	Juan Fangio, Argentina	1967	Denis Hulme, New Zealand	1983	Nelson Piquet, Brazil
1952	Alberto Ascari, Italy	1968	Graham Hill, England	1984	Niki Lauda, Austria
1953	Alberto Ascari, Italy	1969	Jackie Stewart, Scotland	1985	Alain Prost, France
1954	Juan Fangio, Argentina	1970	Jochen Rindt, Austria	1986	Alain Prost, France
1955	Juan Fangio, Argentina	1971	Jackie Stewart, Scotland	1987	Nelson Piquet, Brazil
1956	Juan Fangio, Argentina	1972	Emerson Fittipaldi, Brazil	1988	Ayrton Senna, Brazil
1957	Juan Fangio, Argentina	1973	Jackie Stewart, Scotland	1989	Alain Prost, France
1958	Mike Hawthorne, England	1974	Emerson Fittipaldi, Brazil	1990	Ayrton Senna, Brazil
1959	Jack Brabham, Australia	1975	Niki Lauda, Austria	1991	Ayrton Senna, Brazil
1960	Jack Brabham, Australia	1976	James Hunt, England	1992	Nigel Mansell, Britain
1961	Phil Hill, United States	1977	Niki Lauda, Austria	1993	Alain Prost, France
1962	Graham Hill, England	1978	Mario Andretti, United States	1994	Michael Schumacher, Germany
1963	Jim Clark, Scotland	1979	Jody Scheckter, South Africa	1995	Michael Schumacher, Germany
1964	John Surtees, England	1980	Alan Jones, Australia	1996	Damon Hill, England
1965	Jim Clark, Scotland	1981	Nelson Piquet, Brazil	1997	Jacques Villeneuve, Canada
1966	Jack Brabham, Australia	1982	Keke Rosberg, Finland		

Grand Prix Races for Formula 1 Cars in 1997

Date	Grand Prix	Winner, car	Date	Grand Prix	Winner, car
3/9	Australian	David Coulthard, McLaren-Mercedes	7/27	German	Gerhard Berger, Benetton-Renault
3/30	Brazilian	Jacques Villeneuve, Williams-Renault	8/10	Hungarian	Jacques Villeneuve, Williams-Renault
4/13	Argentinian	Jacques Villeneuve, Williams-Renault	8/24	Belgian	Michael Schumacher, Ferrari
4/27	San Marino	Heinz-Harald Frentzen, Williams-Renault	9/7	Italian	David Coulthard, McLaren-Mercedes
5/11	Monaco	Michael Schumacher, Ferrari	9/21	Austrian	Jacques Villeneuve, Williams-Renault
5/25	Spanish	Jacques Villeneuve, Williams-Renault	9/28	Luxembourg	Jacques Villeneuve, Williams-Renault
6/15	Canadian	Michael Schumacher, Ferrari	10/12	Japanese	Michael Schumacher, Ferrari
6/29	French	Michael Schumacher, Ferrari	10/26	European	Mika Hakkinen, McLaren-Mercedes
7/13	British	Jacques Villeneuve, Williams-Renault			

NASCAR Racing
Winston Cup Champions

Year	Driver	Year	Driver	Year	Driver	Year	Driver
1949	Red Byron	1959	Lee Petty	1969	David Pearson	1979	Richard Petty
1950	Bill Rexford	1960	Rex White	1970	Bobby Isaac	1980	Dale Earnhardt
1951	Herb Thomas	1961	Ned Jarrett	1971	Richard Petty	1981	Darrell Waltrip
1952	Tim Flock	1962	Joe Weatherly	1972	Richard Petty	1982	Darrell Waltrip
1953	Herb Thomas	1963	Joe Weatherly	1973	Benny Parsons	1983	Bobby Allison
1954	Lee Petty	1964	Richard Petty	1974	Richard Petty	1984	Terry Labonte
1955	Tim Flock	1965	Ned Jarrett	1975	Richard Petty	1985	Darrell Waltrip
1956	Buck Baker	1966	David Pearson	1976	Cale Yarborough	1986	Dale Earnhardt
1957	Buck Baker	1967	Richard Petty	1977	Cale Yarborough	1987	Dale Earnhardt
1958	Lee Petty	1968	David Pearson	1978	Cale Yarborough	1988	Bill Elliott

Daytona 500 Winners

Year	Driver, car	Avg. MPH	Year	Driver, car	Avg. MPH
1959	Lee Petty, Oldsmobile	135.521	1979	Richard Petty, Oldsmobile	143.977
1960	Junior Johnson, Chevrolet	124.740	1980	Buddy Baker, Oldsmobile	177.602
1961	Marvin Panch, Pontiac	149.601	1981	Richard Petty, Buick	169.651
1962	Fireball Roberts, Pontiac	152.529	1982	Bobby Allison, Buick	153.991
1963	Tiny Lund, Ford	151.566	1983	Cale Yarborough, Pontiac	155.979
1964	Richard Petty, Plymouth	154.334	1984	Cale Yarborough, Chevrolet	150.994
1965	Fred Lorenzen, Ford (a)	141.539	1985	Bill Elliott, Ford	172.265
1966	Richard Petty, Plymouth (b)	160.627	1986	Geoff Bodine, Chevrolet	148.124
1967	Mario Andretti, Ford	146.926	1987	Bill Elliott, Ford	176.263
1968	Cale Yarborough, Mercury	143.251	1988	Bobby Allison, Buick	137.531
1969	Lee Roy Yarborough, Ford	160.875	1989	Darrell Waltrip, Chevrolet	148.466
1970	Pete Hamilton, Plymouth	149.601	1990	Derrike Cope, Chevrolet	165.761
1971	Richard Petty, Plymouth	144.456	1991	Ernie Irvan, Chevrolet	148.148
1972	A. J. Foyt, Mercury	161.550	1992	Davey Allison, Ford	160.256
1973	Richard Petty, Dodge	157.205	1993	Dale Jarrett, Chevrolet	154.972
1974	Richard Petty, Dodge (c)	140.894	1994	Sterling Marlin, Chevrolet	156.931
1975	Benny Parsons, Chevrolet	153.649	1995	Sterling Marlin, Chevrolet	141.710
1976	David Pearson, Mercury	152.181	1996	Dale Jarrett, Ford	154.308
1977	Cale Yarborough, Chevrolet	153.218	1997	Jeff Gordon, Chevrolet	148.295
1978	Bobby Allison, Ford	159.730			

(a) 322.5 mi. (b) 495 mi. (c) 450 mi.

Winston Cup Series Races in 1997

Date	Race, site	Winner	Car	Prize
Feb. 9	*Busch Clash of '97, Daytona Beach, FL	Jeff Gordon	Chevrolet	$54,000
Feb. 13	*Gatorade Twin 125s, Daytona Beach, FL	Dale Jarrett/	Ford/	50,589/
		Dale Earnhardt	Chevrolet	40,589
Feb. 16	Daytona 500, Daytona Beach, FL	Jeff Gordon	Chevrolet	456,999
Feb. 23	Goodwrench Service 400, Rockingham, NC	Jeff Gordon	Chevrolet	93,115
Mar. 2	Pontiac Excitement 400, Richmond, VA	Rusty Wallace	Ford	86,775
Mar. 9	PRIMESTAR 500, Atlanta, GA	Dale Jarrett	Ford	137,650
Mar. 23	TranSouth Financial 400, Darlington, SC	Dale Jarrett	Ford	142,860
Apr. 6	Interstate Batteries 500, Fort Worth, TX	Jeff Burton	Ford	354,350
Apr. 13	Food City 500, Bristol, TN	Jeff Gordon	Chevrolet	83,640
Apr. 20	Goody's Headache Powder 500, Martinsville, VA	Jeff Gordon	Chevrolet	99,225
May 4	Save Mart Supermarkets 300, Sonoma, CA	Mark Martin	Ford	113,995
May 10	Winston 500, Talladega, AL	Mark Martin	Ford	92,220
May 17	*Winston Open, Charlotte, NC	Ricky Craven	Chevrolet	28,000
May 17	*The Winston, Charlotte, NC	Jeff Gordon	Chevrolet	207,500
May 25	Coca-Cola 600, Charlotte, NC	Jeff Gordon	Chevrolet	432,400
June 1	Miller 500, Dover, DE	Rickey Rudd	Ford	95,255
June 8	Pocono 500, Pocono, PA	Jeff Gordon	Chevrolet	166,080
June 15	Miller 400, Brooklyn, MI	Ernie Irvan	Ford	93,830
June 22	NAPA's California 500, Fontana, CA	Jeff Gordon	Chevrolet	144,600
July 5	Pepsi 400, Daytona Beach, FL	John Andretti	Ford	109,525
July 13	Jiffy Lube 300, Loudon, NH	Jeff Burton	Ford	117,875
July 20	Pennsylvania 500, Long Pond, PA	Dale Jarrett	Ford	104,570
Aug. 2	Brickyard 400, Indianapolis, IN	Rickey Rudd	Ford	571,000
Aug. 10	The Bud at The Glen, Watkins Glen, NY	Jeff Gordon	Chevrolet	139,120
Aug. 17	ITW DeVilbiss 400, Brooklyn, MI	Mark Martin	Ford	93,045
Aug. 23	Goody's Headache Powder 500, Bristol, TN	Dale Jarrett	Ford	101,500
Aug. 31	Mountain Dew Southern 500, Darlington, SC	Jeff Gordon	Chevrolet	131,330
Sept. 6	Exide Select Batteries 400, Richmond, VA	Dale Jarrett	Ford	91,490
Sept. 14	CMT 300, Louden, NH	Jeff Gordon	Chevrolet	188,625
Sept. 21	MBNA 400, Dover, DE	Mark Martin	Ford	195,305
Sept. 28	Hanes 500, Martinsville, VA	Jeff Burton	Ford	78,675
Oct. 5	UAW-GM Quality 500, Charlotte, NC	Dale Jarrett	Ford	130,000
Oct. 12	Sears DieHard 500, Talladega, AL	Terry Labonte	Chevrolet	116,725

*Denotes nonpoint event.

RODEO

Pro Rodeo Championship Standings in 1996

Event	Winner	Money won	Event	Winner	Money won
All Around	Joe Beaver, Huntsville, TX	$166,103	Steer Roping	Guy Allen, Lovington, NM	$66,739
Saddle Bronc	Billy Etbauer, Ree Heights, SD	190,257	Team Roping	Steve Purcella, Hereford, TX (head) &	
Bareback	Mark Garrett, Spearfish, SD	139,868		Steve Northcott, Odessa, TX (heel)	91,069
Bull Riding	Terry West, Henryetta, OK	125,425	Barrel Racing	Kristie Peterson, Elbert, CO	170,083
Calf Roping	Fred Whitfield, Hockley, TX	155,336	Wrangler		
Steer Wrestling	Chad Bedell, Jensen, UT	120,784	Bullfighting	Mike Matt, Billings, MT	46,018

Pro Rodeo Cowboy All-Around Champions

Year	Winner	Money won	Year	Winner	Money won
1972	Phil Lyne, George West, TX	$60,852	1984	Dee Pickett, Caldwell, ID	$122,618
1973	Larry Mahan, Dallas, TX	64,447	1985	Lewis Feild, Elk Ridge, UT	130,347
1974	Tom Ferguson, Miami, OK	66,929	1986	Lewis Feild, Elk Ridge, UT	166,042
1975	Leo Camarillo, Oakdale, CA	50,300	1987	Lewis Feild, Elk Ridge, UT	144,335
	Tom Ferguson, Miami, OK	50,300	1988	Dave Appleton, Arlington, TX	121,546
1976	Tom Ferguson, Miami, OK	87,908	1989	Ty Murray, Odessa, TX	134,806
1977	Tom Ferguson, Miami, OK	76,730	1990	Ty Murray, Stephenville, TX	213,772
1978	Tom Ferguson, Miami, OK	103,734	1991	Ty Murray, Stephenville, TX	244,230
1979	Tom Ferguson, Miami, OK	96,272	1992	Ty Murray, Stephenville, TX	225,992
1980	Paul Tierney, Rapid City, SD	105,568	1993	Ty Murray, Stephenville, TX	297,896
1981	Jimmie Cooper, Monument, NM	105,862	1994	Ty Murray, Stephenville, TX	246,170
1982	Chris Lybbert, Coyote, CA	123,709	1995	Joe Beaver, Huntsville, TX	141,753
1983	Roy Cooper, Durant, OK	153,391	1996	Joe Beaver, Huntsville, TX	166,103

BOXING
Champions by Classes

There are many governing bodies in boxing, including the World Boxing Council, World Boxing Assn., International Boxing Federation, World Boxing Org., U.S. Boxing Assn., North American Boxing Federation, and European Boxing Union. Others are recognized by TV networks and the print media. All the governing bodies have their own champions and assorted boxing divisions. The following are the recognized champions— as of Oct. 15, 1997—in the principal divisions of the WBC, WBA, and IBF.

Class, Weight limit	WBC	WBA	IBF
Heavyweight	Lennox Lewis, U.K.	Evander Holyfield, U.S.	Michael Moorer, U.S.
Cruiserweight (190 lb)	Marcelo Dominguez, Argentina	Nate Miller, U.S.	Uriah Grant, Jamaica
Light Heavyweight (175 lb)	Roy Jones Jr., U.S.	Louis Del Valle, U.S.	William Guthrie, U.S.
Super Middleweight (168 lb)	Robin Reid, U.K.	Frank Liles, U.S.	Charles Brewer, U.S.
Middleweight (160 lb)	Keith Holmes, U.S.	Julio Cesar Green, U.S.	Bernard Hopkins, U.S.
Jr. Middleweight (154 lb)	Terry Norris, U.S.	Laurent Boudouani, France	Raul Marquez, U.S.
Welterweight (147 lb)	Oscar De La Hoya, U.S.	Ike Quartey, Ghana	Felix Trinidad, Puerto Rico
Jr. Welterweight (140 lb)	Vacant	Khalid Rahilou, France	Vince Phillips, U.S.
Lightweight (135 lb)	Steve Johnston, U.S.	Orzubek Nazarov, Russia	Shane Mosely, U.S.
Jr. Lightweight (130 lb)	Genaro Hernandez, U.S.	Choi Yong Soo, South Korea	Arturo Gatti, U.S.
Featherweight (126 lb)	Luisito Espinoza, Philippines	Wilfredo Vasquez, Puerto Rico	Vacant
Jr. Featherweight (122 lb)	Erik Morales, Mexico	Vacant	Vuyani Bungu, South Africa
Bantamweight (118 lb)	S. Singmanassuk, Thailand	Nana Yw Konadu, Ghana	Tim Austin, U.S.
Jr. Bantamweight (115 lb)	Gerry Penalosa, Philippines	Yokthai Sithoar, Thailand	Johnny Tapia, U.S.
Flyweight (112 lb)	Chatchai Sasakul, Thailand	Jose Bonilla, Venezuela	Mark Johnson, U.S.
Jr. Flyweight (108 lb)	Saman Sorjaturong, Thailand	Pichitnoi C. Siriwat, Thailand	Vacant
Strawweight (105 lb)	Ricardo Lopez, Mexico	Rosendo Alvarez, Nicaragua	Ratanapol S. Vorapin, Thailand

Ring Champions by Years

(*abandoned the title or was stripped of it; IBF champions listed only for heavyweight division)

Heavyweights

1882-1892	John L. Sullivan (a)
1892-1897	James J. Corbett (b)
1897-1899	Robert Fitzsimmons
1899-1905	James J. Jeffries* (c)
1905-1906	Marvin Hart
1906-1908	Tommy Burns
1908-1915	Jack Johnson
1915-1919	Jess Willard
1919-1926	Jack Dempsey
1926-1928	Gene Tunney*
1928-1930	Vacant
1930-1932	Max Schmeling
1932-1933	Jack Sharkey
1933-1934	Primo Carnera
1934-1935	Max Baer
1935-1937	James J. Braddock
1937-1949	Joe Louis*
1949-1951	Ezzard Charles
1951-1952	Joe Walcott
1952-1956	Rocky Marciano*
1956-1959	Floyd Patterson
1959-1960	Ingemar Johansson
1960-1962	Floyd Patterson
1962-1964	Sonny Liston
1964-1967	Cassius Clay* (Muhammad Ali) (d)
1970-1973	Joe Frazier
1973-1974	George Foreman
1974-1978	Muhammad Ali
1978	Leon Spinks (WBC*, WBA) (e); Ken Norton (WBC); Larry Holmes (WBC); Muhammad Ali* (WBA)
1978-1983	Larry Holmes* (WBC) (f)
1979-1980	John Tate (WBA)
1980-1982	Mike Weaver (WBA)
1982-1983	Michael Dokes (WBA)
1983	Gerrie Coetzee (WBA); Larry Holmes (IBF) (f)
1984	Tim Witherspoon (WBC); Pinklon Thomas (WBC); Greg Page (WBA)
1985-1986	Tony Tubbs (WBA)
1985-1987	Michael Spinks* (IBF)
1986	Tim Witherspoon (WBA); Trevor Berbick (WBC); Mike Tyson (WBC); James "Bone-crusher" Smith (WBA)
1986-1987	James "Bonecrusher" Smith (WBA)
1987	Mike Tyson (WBC, WBA); Tony Tucker (IBF)
1987-1990	Mike Tyson (WBC, WBA, IBF)
1990	James "Buster" Douglas (WBA, WBC, IBF)
1990-1992	Evander Holyfield (WBA, WBC, IBF)
1992-1993	Riddick Bowe (WBA, IBF, WBC*)
1992-1994	Lennox Lewis (WBC)
1993-1994	Evander Holyfield (WBA, IBF)
1994	Michael Moorer (WBA, IBF); Oliver McCall (WBC); George Foreman (WBA*, IBF*)
1995	Bruce Seldon (WBA); Frank Bruno (WBC); Frans Botha* (IBF)
1996	Mike Tyson (WBC*, WBA); Michael Moorer (IBF); Evander Holyfield (WBA)
1997	Lennox Lewis (WBC)

(a) London Prize Ring (bare knuckle champion). (b) First Marquis of Queensberry champion. (c) Jeffries abandoned the title (1905) and designated Marvin Hart and Jack Root as logical contenders. Hart defeated Root in 12 rounds (1905) and in turn was defeated by Tommy Burns (1906), who laid claim to the title. Jack Johnson defeated Burns (1908) and was recognized as champion. He clinched the title by defeating Jeffries in an attempted comeback (1910). (d) Title declared vacant by the WBA and other groups in 1967 after Ali's refusal to fulfill his military obligation. Joe Frazier was recognized as champion by 6 states, Mexico, and South America. Jimmy Ellis was declared champion by the WBA. Frazier KOd Ellis, Feb. 16, 1970. (e) After Spinks defeated Ali, the WBC recognized Ken Norton as champion. Ali defeated Spinks in a rematch to win the WBA title and subsequently retired in 1979. (f) Holmes relinquished the WBC title in Dec. 1983 and immediately began fighting as champion of the newly formed IBF.

Light Heavyweights

1903	Jack Root, George Gardner
1903-1905	Bob Fitzsimmons
1905-1912	Philadelphia Jack O'Brien*
1912-1916	Jack Dillon
1916-1920	Battling Levinsky
1920-1922	George Carpentier
1922-1923	Battling Siki
1923-1925	Mike McTigue
1925-1926	Paul Berlenbach
1926-1927	Jack Delaney*
1927-1929	Tommy Loughran*
1930-1934	Maxey Rosenbloom
1934-1935	Bob Olin
1935-1939	John Henry Lewis*
1939	Melio Bettina
1939-1941	Billy Conn*
1941	Anton Christoforidis (won NBA title)
1941-1948	Gus Lesnevich, Freddie Mills
1948-1950	Freddie Mills
1950-1952	Joey Maxim
1952-1960	Archie Moore
1961-1962	Vacant
1962-1963	Harold Johnson
1963-1965	Willie Pastrano
1965-1966	Jose Torres
1966-1968	Dick Tiger
1968-1974	Bob Foster*
1974-1977	John Conteh (WBC); Victor Galindez (WBA)
1977-1978	Miguel Cuello (WBC)
1978	Mike Rossman (WBA); Mate Parlov (WBC); Marvin Johnson (WBC)
1979	Matthew Saad Muhammad (WBC); Victor Galindez (WBA); Marvin Johnson (WBA)
1980	Eddie Mustafa Muhammad (WBA)
1981	Michael Spinks (WBA); Dwight Braxton (WBC)
1983-1985	Michael Spinks*
1985	J. B. Williamson (WBC)
1986	Marvin Johnson (WBA); Dennis Andries (WBC)
1987	Thomas Hearns* (WBC); Leslie Stewart (WBA); Virgil Hill (WBA); Don Lalonde (WBC)
1988	Ray Leonard* (WBC)
1989	Dennis Andries (WBC); Jeff Harding (WBC)

1990	Dennis Andries (WBC)
1991	Thomas Hearns (WBA); Jeff Harding (WBC)
1992	Iran Barkley* (WBA); Virgil Hill (WBA)
1994-1995	Mike McCallum (WBC)
1995-1996	Fabrice Tiozzo* (WBC)
1996-1997	Roy Jones Jr. (WBC)
1997	Montell Griffin (WBC); Darius Michalczewski* (WBA); Roy Jones Jr. (WBC); Lou Del Valle (WBA)

Middleweights

1884-1891	Jack "Nonpareil" Dempsey
1891-1897	Bob Fitzsimmons*
1897-1907	Tommy Ryan*
1907-1908	Stanley Ketchel, Billy Papke
1908-1910	Stanley Ketchel
1911-1913	vacant
1913	Frank Klaus; George Chip
1914-1917	Al McCoy
1917-1920	Mike O'Dowd
1920-1923	Johnny Wilson
1923-1926	Harry Greb
1926-1931	Tiger Flowers; Mickey Walker
1931-1932	Gorilla Jones (NBA)
1932-1937	Marcel Thil
1938	Al Hostak (NBA); Solly Krieger (NBA)
1939-1940	Al Hostak (NBA)
1941-1947	Tony Zale
1947-1948	Rocky Graziano
1948	Tony Zale; Marcel Cerdan
1949-1951	Jake LaMotta
1951	Ray Robinson; Randy Turpin; Ray Robinson*
1953-1955	Carl (Bobo) Olson
1955-1957	Ray Robinson
1957	Gene Fullmer; Ray Robinson; Carmen Basilio
1958	Ray Robinson
1959	Gene Fullmer (NBA); Ray Robinson (NY)
1960	Gene Fullmer (NBA); Paul Pender (NY and MA)
1961	Gene Fullmer (NBA); Terry Downes (NY, MA, Europe)
1962	Gene Fullmer; Dick Tiger (NBA); Paul Pender (NY and MA)*
1963	Dick Tiger (universal)
1963-1965	Joey Giardello
1965-1966	Dick Tiger
1966-1967	Emile Griffith
1967	Nino Benvenuti
1967-1968	Emile Griffith
1968-1970	Nino Benvenuti
1970-1977	Carlos Monzon*
1977-1978	Rodrigo Valdez
1978-1979	Hugo Corro
1979-1980	Vito Antuofermo
1980	Alan Minter; Marvin Hagler
1987	Ray Leonard* (WBC); Thomas Hearns (WBC); Sumbu Kalambay (WBA)
1988-1989	Iran Barkley (WBC)
1989	Mike McCallum* (WBA); Roberto Duran (WBC)
1991-1993	Julian Jackson (WBC)
1992-1993	Reggie Johnson (WBA)
1993	Gerald McClellan (WBC); John David Jackson* (WBA)
1994-1995	Jorge Castro (WBA)
1995	Julian Jackson (WBC); Quincy Taylor (WBC); Shinji Takehara (WBA)
1996	Keith Holmes (WBC); William Joppy (WBA)
1997	Julio Cesar Green (WBA)

Welterweights

1892-1894	Mysterious Billy Smith
1894-1896	Tommy Ryan
1896	Kid McCoy*
1900	Rube Ferns; Matty Matthews
1901	Rube Ferns
1901-1904	Joe Walcott
1904-1906	Dixie Kid; Joe Walcott; Honey Mellody
1907-1911	Mike Sullivan
1911-1915	Vacant
1915-1919	Ted Lewis
1919-1922	Jack Britton
1922-1926	Mickey Walker
1926	Pete Latzo
1927-1929	Joe Dundee
1929	Jackie Fields
1930	Jack Thompson; Tommy Freeman
1931	Tommy Freeman; Jack Thompson; Lou Brouillard
1932	Jackie Fields
1933	Young Corbett; Jimmy McLarnin
1934	Barney Ross; Jimmy McLarnin
1935-1938	Barney Ross
1938-1940	Henry Armstrong
1940-1941	Fritzie Zivic
1941-1946	Fred Cochrane
1946	Marty Servo*; Ray Robinson (a)
1946-1950	Ray Robinson*

1951	Johnny Bratton (NBA)
1951-1954	Kid Gavilan
1954-1955	Johnny Saxton
1955	Tony De Marco; Carmen Basilio
1956	Carmen Basilio; Johnny Saxton; Carmen Basilio
1957	Carmen Basilio*
1958-1960	Virgil Akins, Don Jordan
1960	Benny Paret
1961	Emile Griffith; Benny Paret
1962	Emile Griffith
1963	Luis Rodriguez; Emile Griffith
1964-1966	Emile Griffith*
1966-1969	Curtis Cokes
1969-1970	Jose Napoles; Billy Backus
1971-1975	Jose Napoles
1975-1976	John Stracey (WBC); Angel Espada (WBA)
1976-1979	Carlos Palomino (WBC); Jose Cuevas (WBA)
1979	Wilfredo Benitez (WBC); Sugar Ray Leonard (WBC)
1980	Roberto Duran (WBC); Thomas Hearns (WBA); Sugar Ray Leonard (WBC)
1981-1982	Sugar Ray Leonard*
1983-1985	Donald Curry (WBA); Milton McCrory (WBC)
1985-1986	Donald Curry
1986-1987	Lloyd Honeyghan (WBC)
1987	Mark Breland (WBA); Marlon Starling (WBA); Jorge Vaca (WBC).
1988-1989	Tomas Molinares (WBA); Lloyd Honeyghan (WBC)
1989-1990	Marlon Starling (WBC); Mark Breland (WBA)
1990-1991	Maurice Blocker (WBC); Aaron Davis (WBA)
1991	Meldrick Taylor (WBA); Simon Brown (WBC); Buddy McGirt (WBC)
1992-1994	Crisanto Espana (WBA)
1993-1997	Pernell Whitaker (WBC)
1994-	Ike Quartey (WBA)
1997-	Oscar De La Hoya (WBC)

(a) Robinson gained the title by defeating Tommy Bell in an elimination agreed to by the New York Commission and the NBA. Both claimed Robinson waived his title when he won the middleweight crown from LaMotta in 1951.

Lightweights

1896-1899	Kid Lavigne
1899-1902	Frank Erne
1902-1908	Joe Gans
1908-1910	Battling Nelson
1910-1912	Ad Wolgast
1912-1914	Willie Ritchie
1914-1917	Freddie Welsh
1917-1925	Benny Leonard*
1925	Jimmy Goodrich; Rocky Kansas
1926-1930	Sammy Mandell
1930	Al Singer; Tony Canzoneri
1930-1933	Tony Canzoneri
1933-1935	Barney Ross*
1935-1936	Tony Canzoneri
1936-1938	Lou Ambers
1938	Henry Armstrong
1939	Lou Ambers
1940	Lew Jenkins
1941-1943	Sammy Angott
1944	S. Angott (NBA); J. Zurita (NBA)
1945-1951	Ike Williams (NBA: later universal)
1951-1952	James Carter
1952	Lauro Salas; James Carter
1953-1954	James Carter
1954	Paddy De Marco; James Carter
1955	James Carter; Bud Smith
1956	Bud Smith; Joe Brown
1956-1962	Joe Brown
1962-1965	Carlos Ortiz
1965	Ismael Laguna
1965-1968	Carlos Ortiz
1968-1969	Teo Cruz
1969-1970	Mando Ramos
1970	Ismael Laguna; Ken Buchanan (WBA)
1971	Mando Ramos (WBC); Pedro Carrasco (WBC)
1972-1979	Roberto Duran* (WBA)
1972	Pedro Carrasco; Mando Ramos; Chango Carmona; Rodolfo Gonzalez (all WBC)
1974-1976	Guts Ishimatsu (WBC)
1976-1977	Esteban De Jesus (WBC)
1979	Jim Watt (WBC); Ernesto Espana (WBA)
1980	Hilmer Kenty (WBA)
1981	Alexis Arguello (WBC); Sean O'Grady (WBA); Arturo Frias (WBA)
1982-1984	Ray Mancini (WBA)
1983-1984	Edwin Rosario (WBC)
1984	Livingstone Bramble (WBA); Jose Luis Ramirez (WBC)
1985-1986	Hector (Macho) Camacho (WBC)
1986	Edwin Rosario (WBA); Jose Luis Ramirez (WBC)
1987-1989	Julio Cesar Chavez (WBA)

1989-1990	Edwin Rosario (WBA); Pernell Whitaker (WBC)
1990	Juan Nazario (WBA)
1990-1992	Pernell Whitaker*
1992	Joey Gamache (WBA); Tony Lopez (WBA)
1992-1996	Miguel Angel Gonzalez* (WBC)
1993	Dingaan Thobela (WBA); Orzubek Nazarov (WBA)
1996-1997	Jean-Baptiste Mendy (WBC)
1997	Steve Johnston (WBC)

Featherweights

1892-1900	George Dixon (disputed)
1900-1901	Terry McGovern; Young Corbett*
1901-1912	Abe Attell
1912-1923	Johnny Kilbane
1923	Eugene Criqui; Johnny Dundee
1923-1925	Johnny Dundee*
1925-1927	Kid Kaplan*
1927-1928	Benny Bass; Tony Canzoneri
1928-1929	Andre Routis
1929-1932	Battling Battalino*
1932-1934	Tommy Paul (NBA)
1933-1936	Freddie Miller
1936-1937	Petey Sarron
1937-1938	Henry Armstrong*
1938-1940	Joey Archibald (a)
1940-1941	Harry Jeffra
1942-1948	Willie Pep
1948-1949	Sandy Saddler
1949-1950	Willie Pep
1950-1957	Sandy Saddler*
1957-1959	Hogan (Kid) Bassey
1959-1963	Davey Moore

1963-1964	Sugar Ramos
1964-1967	Vicente Saldivar*
1968-1971	Paul Rojas (WBA); Sho Saijo (WBA)
1971-1972	Antonio Gomez (WBA); Kuniaki Shibada (WBC)
1972	Ernesto Marcel* (WBA); Clemente Sanchez* (WBC); Jose Legra (WBC)
1973-1974	Eder Jofre (WBC)
1974	Ruben Olivares (WBA); Alexis Arguello (WBA); Bobby Chacon (WBC)
1975	Ruben Olivares (WBC); David Kotey (WBC)
1976-1980	Danny Lopez (WBC)
1977-1978	Rafael Ortega (WBA)
1978	Cecilio Lastra (WBA); Eusebio Pedrosa (WBA)
1980-1982	Salvador Sanchez (WBC)
1982-1984	Juan LaPorte (WBC)
1984	Wilfredo Gomez (WBC); Azumah Nelson (WBC)
1985-1986	Barry McGuigan (WBA)
1986-1987	Steve Cruz (WBA)
1987-1991	Antonio Esparragoza (WBA)
1988-1990	Jeff Fenech (WBC)
1990-1991	Marcos Villasana (WBC)
1991-1993	Park Yung Kyun (WBA); Paul Hodkinson (WBC)
1993	Goyo Vargas (WBC); Kevin Kelley (WBC); Eloy Rojas (WBA)
1995	Alejandro Gonzalez (WBC); Manuel Medina (WBC); Luisito Espinosa (WBC)
1996-1997	Wilfredo Vasquez (WBA)

(a) After Petey Scalzo knocked out Archibald in an overweight match and was refused a title bout, the NBA named Scalzo champion. NBA title succession: Scalzo, 1938-1941; Richard Lemos, 1941; Jackie Wilson, 1941-1943; Jackie Callura, 1943; Phil Terranova, 1943-1944; Sal Bartolo, 1944-1946.

History of Heavyweight Championship Bouts

(bouts in which title changed hands)

1889—July 8—John L. Sullivan def. Jake Kilrain, 75, Richburg, MS. (Last championship bare knuckles bout.)

1892—Sept. 7—James J. Corbett def. John L. Sullivan, 21, New Orleans. (Big gloves used for first time.)

1897—Bob Fitzsimmons def. James J. Corbett, 14, Carson City, NV.

1899—June 9—James J. Jeffries def. Bob Fitzsimmons, 11, Coney Island, NY. (Jeffries retired as champion in 1905.)

1905—July 3—Marvin Hart KOd Jack Root, 12, Reno, NV. (Jeffries refereed and presented the title to the victor. Jack O'Brien also claimed the title.)

1906—Feb. 23—Tommy Burns def. Marvin Hart, 20, Los Angeles.

1908—Dec. 26—Jack Johnson KOd Tommy Burns, 14, Sydney, Australia. (Police halted contest.)

1915—April 5—Jess Willard KOd Jack Johnson, 26, Havana, Cuba.

1919—July 4—Jack Dempsey KOd Jess Willard, Toledo, OH. (Willard failed to answer bell for 4th round.)

1926—Sept. 23—Gene Tunney def. Jack Dempsey, 10, Philadelphia. (Tunney retired as champion in 1928.)

1930—June 12—Max Schmeling def. Jack Sharkey, 4, New York. (Sharkey fouled Schmeling in a bout generally considered to have resulted in the election of a successor to Tunney.)

1932—June 21—Jack Sharkey def. Max Schmeling, 15, New York.

1933—June 29—Primo Carnera KOd Jack Sharkey, 6, New York.

1934—June 14—Max Baer KOd Primo Carnera, 11, New York.

1935—June 13—James J. Braddock def. Max Baer, 15, New York.

1937—June 22—Joe Louis KOd James J. Braddock, 8, Chicago. (Louis retired as champion in 1949.)

1949—June 22—Ezzard Charles def. Joe Walcott, 15, Chicago; NBA recognition only.

1951—July 18—Joe Walcott KOd Ezzard Charles, 7, Pittsburgh.

1952—Sept. 23—Rocky Marciano KOd Joe Walcott, 13, Philadelphia. (Marciano retired as champion in 1956.)

1956—Nov. 30—Floyd Patterson KOd Archie Moore, 5, Chicago.

1959—June 26—Ingemar Johansson KOd Floyd Patterson, 3, New York.

1960—June 20—Floyd Patterson KOd Ingemar Johansson, 5, New York. (Patterson was 1st heavyweight to regain title.)

1962—Sept. 25—Sonny Liston KOd Floyd Patterson, 1, Chicago.

1964—Feb. 25—Cassius Clay (Muhammad Ali) KOd Sonny Liston, 7, Miami Beach, FL. (In 1967, Ali was stripped of his title by the WBA and others for refusing military service.)

1970—Feb. 16—Joe Frazier KOd Jimmy Ellis, 5, New York. (Frazier def. Ali in 15 rounds, Mar. 8, 1971, in New York.)

1973—Jan. 22—George Foreman KOd Joe Frazier, 2, Kingston, Jamaica.

1974—Oct. 30—Muhammad Ali KOd George Foreman, 8, Zaire.

1978—Feb. 15—Leon Spinks def. Muhammad Ali, 15, Las Vegas. (WBC recognized Ken Norton as champion after Spinks refused to fight him before his rematch with Ali.)

1978—June 9—(WBC) Larry Holmes def. Ken Norton, 15, Las Vegas. (Holmes gave up title in Dec. 1983.)

1978—Sept. 15—(WBA) Muhammad Ali def. Leon Spinks, 15, New Orleans. (Ali retired as champion in 1979.)

1979—Oct. 20—(WBA) John Tate def. Gerrie Coetzee, 15, Pretoria, South Africa.

1980—Mar. 31—(WBA) Mike Weaver KOd John Tate, 15, Knoxville, TN.

1982—Dec. 10—(WBA) Michael Dokes KOd Mike Weaver, 1, Las Vegas.

1983—Sept. 23—(WBA) Gerrie Coetzee KOd Michael Dokes, 10, Richfield, OH.

1983—In Dec., Larry Holmes relinquished the WBC title and was named champion of the newly formed IBF.

1984—Mar. 9—(WBC) Tim Witherspoon def. Greg Page, 12, Las Vegas.

1984—Aug. 31—(WBC) Pinklon Thomas def. Tim Witherspoon, 12, Las Vegas.

1984—Dec. 2—(WBA) Greg Page KOd Gerrie Coetzee, 8, Sun City, Bophuthatswana.

1985—Apr. 29—(WBA) Tony Tubbs def. Greg Page, 15, Buffalo, NY.

1985—Sept. 21—(IBF) Michael Spinks def. Larry Holmes, 15, Las Vegas. (Spinks relinquished title in Feb. 1987.)

1986—Jan. 17—(WBA) Tim Witherspoon def. Tony Tubbs, 15, Atlanta, GA.

1986—Mar. 23—(WBC) Trevor Berbick def. Pinklon Thomas, 12, Miami.

1986—Nov. 22—(WBC) Mike Tyson KOd Trevor Berbick, 2, Las Vegas.

1986—Dec. 12—(WBA) James "Bonecrusher" Smith KOd Tim Witherspoon, 1, New York.

1987—Mar. 7—(WBA, WBC) Mike Tyson def. James "Bonecrusher" Smith, 12, Las Vegas.

1987—May 30—(IBF) Tony Tucker KO'd James "Buster" Douglas, 10, Las Vegas.

1987—Aug. 1—(WBA, WBC, IBF) Mike Tyson def. Tony Tucker, 12, Las Vegas. (Tyson became undisputed champion.)

1990—Feb. 11—(WBA, WBC, IBF) James "Buster" Douglas KOd Mike Tyson, 10, Tokyo.

1990—Oct. 25—(WBA, WBC, IBF) Evander Holyfield KOd James "Buster" Douglas, 3, Las Vegas.

1992—Nov. 13—(WBA, WBC, IBF) Riddick Bowe def. Evander Holyfield, 12, Las Vegas. (Lennox Lewis was later named WBC champion when Bowe refused to fight him.)

1993—Nov. 6—(WBA, IBF) Evander Holyfield def. Riddick Bowe, 12, Las Vegas.
1994—Apr. 22—(WBA, IBF) Michael Moorer def. Evander Holyfield, 12, Las Vegas.
1994—Sept. 24—(WBC) Oliver McCall KOd Lennox Lewis, 2, London.
1994—Nov. 5—(WBA, IBF) George Foreman KOd Michael Moorer, 10, Las Vegas. (In Mar. 1995, Foreman was stripped of the WBA title. In June, Foreman relinquished the IBF title.)
1995—Sept. 2—(WBC) Frank Bruno def. Oliver McCall, 12, London.

1995—Dec. 9—(IBF) Frans Botha def. Axel Schulz, 12, Las Vegas. (Botha was subsequently stripped of title.)
1996—Mar. 16—(WBC) Mike Tyson KOd Frank Bruno, 3, Las Vegas.
1996—June 22—(IBF) Michael Moorer def. Axel Schulz, 12, Dortmund, Germany.
1996—Sept. 7—(WBA, WBC) Mike Tyson KOd Bruce Seldon, 1, Las Vegas. (Tyson was subsequently stripped of the WBC title.)
1996—Nov. 9—(WBA) Evander Holyfield KOd Mike Tyson, 11, Las Vegas.
1997—Feb. 7—(WBC) Lennox Lewis KOd Oliver McCall, 5, Las Vegas.

YACHTING
The America's Cup

In the 1995 America's Cup match, the New Zealand yacht *Black Magic 1* defeated the U.S. yacht *Young America* 5-0 in the waters off San Diego, CA. It was only the 2d time since 1851 (the 1st since 1983) that the U.S. lost the Cup. *Black Magic 1* was skippered by Russell Coutts. The next competition was scheduled for 1999-2000 in New Zealand.

Competition for the America's Cup grew out of the first contest to establish a world yachting championship, one of the carnival features of the London Exposition of 1851. The race, open to all classes of yachts from all over the world, covered a 60-mile course around the Isle of Wight; the prize was a cup worth about $500, donated by the Royal Yacht Squadron of England, known as the "America's Cup" because it was first won by the U.S. yacht *America*.

Winners of the America's Cup

1851	America
1870	Magic defeated Cambria, England, (1-0)
1871	Columbia (first three races) and Sappho (last two races) defeated Livonia, England, (4-1)
1876	Madeline defeated Countess of Dufferin, Canada, (2-0)
1881	Mischief defeated Atalanta, Canada, (2-0)
1885	Puritan defeated Genesta, England, (2-0)
1886	Mayflower defeated Galatea, England, (2-0)
1887	Volunteer defeated Thistle, Scotland, (2-0)
1893	Vigilant defeated Valkyrie II, England, (3-0)
1895	Defender defeated Valkyrie III, England, (3-0)
1899	Columbia defeated Shamrock, England, (3-0)
1901	Columbia defeated Shamrock II, England, (3-0)
1903	Reliance defeated Shamrock III, England, (3-0)
1920	Resolute defeated Shamrock IV, England, (3-2)
1930	Enterprise defeated Shamrock V, England, (4-0)
1934	Rainbow defeated Endeavour, England, (4-2)
1937	Ranger defeated Endeavour II, England, (4-0)
1958	Columbia defeated Sceptre, England, (4-0)
1962	Weatherly defeated Gretel, Australia, (4-1)
1964	Constellation defeated Sovereign, England, (4-0)
1967	Intrepid defeated Dame Pattie, Australia, (4-0)
1970	Intrepid defeated Gretel II, Australia, (4-1)
1974	Courageous defeated Southern Cross, Australia, (4-0)
1977	Courageous defeated Australia, Australia, (4-0)
1980	Freedom defeated Australia, Australia, (4-1)
1983	Australia II, Australia, defeated Liberty, (4-3)
1987	Stars & Stripes defeated Kookaburra III, Australia, (4-0)
1988	Stars & Stripes defeated New Zealand, New Zealand, (2-0)
1992	America[3] defeated Il Moro di Venezia, Italy, (4-1)
1995	Black Magic 1, New Zealand, defeated Young America, (5-0)

POWER BOATING
American Power Boat Assn. Gold Cup Champions

Year	Boat	Driver	Year	Boat	Driver
1975	Pay 'N Pak	George Henley	1987	Miller American	Chip Hanauer
1976	Miss U.S.	Tom D'Eath	1988	Circus Circus	Chip Hanauer
1977	Atlas Van Lines	Bill Muncey	1989	Miss Budweiser	Tom D'Eath
1978	Atlas Van Lines	Bill Muncey	1990	Miss Budweiser	Tom D'Eath
1979	Atlas Van Lines	Bill Muncey	1991	Winston Eagle	Mark Tate
1980	Miss Budweiser	Dean Chenoweth	1992	Miss Budweiser	Chip Hanauer
1981	Miss Budweiser	Dean Chenoweth	1993	Miss Budweiser	Chip Hanauer
1982	Atlas Van Lines	Chip Hanauer	1994	Smokin' Joe's	Mark Tate
1983	Atlas Van Lines	Chip Hanauer	1995	Miss Budweiser	Chip Hanauer
1984	Atlas Van Lines	Chip Hanauer	1996	Pico American Dream	Dave Villwock
1985	Miller American	Chip Hanauer	1997	Miss Budweiser	Dave Villwock
1986	Miller American	Chip Hanauer			

DOGS
Westminster Kennel Club

Year	Best-in-show	Breed	Owner(s)
1987	Ch. Covy Tucker Hill's Manhattan	German Shepherd	Shirley Braunstein & Jane Firestone
1988	Ch. Great Elms Prince Charming II	Pomeranian	Skip Piazza & Olga Baker
1989	Ch. Royal Tudor's Wild As The Wind	Doberman	Sue & Art Kemp, Richard & Carolyn Vida, Beth Wilhite
1990	Ch. Wendessa Crown Prince	Pekingese	Ed Jenner
1991	Ch. Whisperwind on a Carousel	Poodle	Joan & Frederick Hartsock
1992	Ch. Registry's Lonesome Dove	Fox Terrier	Marion & Sam Lawrence
1993	Ch. Salilyn's Condor	English Springer Spaniel	Donna & Roger Herzig
1994	Ch. Chidley Willum	Norwich Terrier	Ruth Cooper & Patricia Lussier
1995	Ch. Gaelforce Post Script	Scottish Terrier	Dr. Vandra Huber & Dr. Joe Kinnarney
1996	Ch. Clussexx Country Sunrise	Clumber Spaniel	Judith & Richard Zaleski
1997	Ch. Parsifal Di Casa Netzer	Standard Schnauzer	Rita Holloway & Gabrio Del Torre

Iditarod Trail Sled Dog Race in 1997

Martin Buser won the 1997 Iditarod Trail Sled Dog Race, Mar. 11, with a time of 9 days, 8 hours, 31 minutes. For winning the 1,100-mile race from Anchorage to Nome, AK, Buser received $50,000 in prize money, as well as a $38,000 truck. Buser also won the race in 1992 and 1994. Doug Swingley, winner of the 1995 Iditarod, finished second.

CYCLING
Tour de France in 1997

On July 27, Jan Ullrich became the first German cyclist to win the Tour de France, the world's most prestigious bicycle race. His margin of victory in the 84th Tour de France was 9 minutes, 9 seconds, and he completed the 21-stage, 2,455-mile (3,950-km) race in a total time of 100 hours, 30 minutes, 35 seconds. Richard Virenque of France finished second. The 23-year-old Ullrich, who finished second in the 1996 Tour, was the eighth-oldest ever to win the race.

BASEBALL

1997: Interleague Play Introduced, Marlins Win Series, McGwire's 20/20 Club

The 1997 Major League Baseball season featured interleague games for the first time, with teams playing 15 or 16 games against opponents outside their league. The Florida Marlins and Montreal Expos benefited the most from the interleague schedule, both posting 12-3 marks against the American League. Florida also made it to the playoffs in only its fifth year of existence, qualifying for the wild card spot in the National League. With a dramatic 11th-inning victory over Cleveland in game 7 of the World Series, Florida became the first wild card team to win the Series and the expansion team that took the fewest years to become world champions. The Baltimore Orioles became the third American League team to lead their division or league from opening day until season's end, matching the 1927 New York Yankees and the 1984 Detroit Tigers. Last year's new team record for home runs in a season was broken by the Milwaukee Brewers, who hit 264 in 1997, and the Colorado Rockies set a new National League high with 242. Mark McGwire became the first player since Babe Ruth to hit 50 or more home runs in back-to-back seasons; McGwire also became the first player to hit 20 home runs in both leagues in one season. Roger Clemens, who signed with the Toronto Blue Jays in the off-season, was the first American League pitcher since Hal Newhouser in 1945 to lead the league in victories (21), earned run average (2.05), and strikeouts (292, a career high). Tony Gwynn of the San Diego Padres won his eighth National League batting title, matching Honus Wagner's NL record.

Major League Pennant Winners, 1901–1968

	National League						American League				
Year	Winner	Won	Lost	Pct	Manager	Year	Winner	Won	Lost	Pct	Manager
1901	Pittsburgh	90	49	.647	Clarke	1901	Chicago	83	53	.610	Griffith
1902	Pittsburgh	103	36	.741	Clarke	1902	Philadelphia	83	53	.610	Mack
1903	Pittsburgh	91	49	.650	Clarke	1903	Boston	91	47	.659	Collins
1904	New York	106	47	.693	McGraw	1904	Boston	95	59	.617	Collins
1905	New York	105	48	.686	McGraw	1905	Philadelphia	92	56	.622	Mack
1906	Chicago	116	36	.763	Chance	1906	Chicago	93	58	.616	Jones
1907	Chicago	107	45	.704	Chance	1907	Detroit	92	58	.613	Jennings
1908	Chicago	99	55	.643	Chance	1908	Detroit	90	63	.588	Jennings
1909	Pittsburgh	110	42	.724	Clarke	1909	Detroit	98	54	.645	Jennings
1910	Chicago	104	50	.675	Chance	1910	Philadelphia	102	48	.680	Mack
1911	New York	99	54	.647	McGraw	1911	Philadelphia	101	50	.669	Mack
1912	New York	103	48	.682	McGraw	1912	Boston	105	47	.691	Stahl
1913	New York	101	51	.664	McGraw	1913	Philadelphia	96	57	.627	Mack
1914	Boston	94	59	.614	Stallings	1914	Philadelphia	99	53	.651	Mack
1915	Philadelphia	90	62	.592	Moran	1915	Boston	101	50	.669	Carrigan
1916	Brooklyn	94	60	.610	Robinson	1916	Boston	91	63	.591	Carrigan
1917	New York	98	56	.636	McGraw	1917	Chicago	100	54	.649	Rowland
1918	Chicago	84	45	.651	Mitchell	1918	Boston	75	51	.595	Barrow
1919	Cincinnati	96	44	.686	Moran	1919	Chicago	88	52	.629	Gleason
1920	Brooklyn	93	60	.604	Robinson	1920	Cleveland	98	56	.636	Speaker
1921	New York	94	56	.614	McGraw	1921	New York	98	55	.641	Huggins
1922	New York	93	61	.604	McGraw	1922	New York	94	60	.610	Huggins
1923	New York	95	58	.621	McGraw	1923	New York	98	54	.645	Huggins
1924	New York	93	60	.608	McGraw	1924	Washington	92	62	.597	Harris
1925	Pittsburgh	95	58	.621	McKechnie	1925	Washington	96	55	.636	Harris
1926	St. Louis	89	65	.578	Hornsby	1926	New York	91	63	.591	Huggins
1927	Pittsburgh	94	60	.610	Bush	1927	New York	110	44	.714	Huggins
1928	St. Louis	95	59	.617	McKechnie	1928	New York	101	53	.656	Huggins
1929	Chicago	98	54	.645	McCarthy	1929	Philadelphia	104	46	.693	Mack
1930	St. Louis	92	62	.597	Street	1930	Philadelphia	102	52	.662	Mack
1931	St. Louis	101	53	.656	Street	1931	Philadelphia	107	45	.704	Mack
1932	Chicago	90	64	.584	Grimm	1932	New York	107	47	.695	McCarthy
1933	New York	91	61	.599	Terry	1933	Washington	99	53	.651	Cronin
1934	St. Louis	95	58	.621	Frisch	1934	Detroit	101	53	.656	Cochrane
1935	Chicago	100	54	.649	Grimm	1935	Detroit	93	58	.616	Cochrane
1936	New York	91	62	.597	Terry	1936	New York	102	51	.667	McCarthy
1937	New York	95	57	.625	Terry	1937	New York	102	52	.662	McCarthy
1938	Chicago	89	63	.586	Hartnett	1938	New York	99	53	.651	McCarthy
1939	Cincinnati	97	57	.630	McKechnie	1939	New York	106	45	.702	McCarthy
1940	Cincinnati	100	53	.654	McKechnie	1940	Detroit	90	64	.584	Baker
1941	Brooklyn	100	54	.649	Durocher	1941	New York	101	53	.656	McCarthy
1942	St. Louis	106	48	.688	Southworth	1942	New York	103	51	.669	McCarthy
1943	St. Louis	105	49	.682	Southworth	1943	New York	98	56	.636	McCarthy
1944	St. Louis	105	49	.682	Southworth	1944	St. Louis	89	65	.578	Sewell
1945	Chicago	98	56	.636	Grimm	1945	Detroit	88	65	.575	O'Neill
1946	St. Louis	98	58	.628	Dyer	1946	Boston	104	50	.675	Cronin
1947	Brooklyn	94	60	.610	Shotton	1947	New York	97	57	.630	Harris
1948	Boston	91	62	.595	Southworth	1948	Cleveland	97	58	.626	Boudreau
1949	Brooklyn	97	57	.630	Shotton	1949	New York	97	57	.630	Stengel
1950	Philadelphia	91	63	.591	Sawyer	1950	New York	98	56	.636	Stengel
1951	New York	98	59	.624	Durocher	1951	New York	98	56	.636	Stengel
1952	Brooklyn	96	57	.627	Dressen	1952	New York	95	59	.617	Stengel
1953	Brooklyn	105	49	.682	Dressen	1953	New York	99	52	.656	Stengel
1954	New York	97	57	.630	Durocher	1954	Cleveland	111	43	.721	Lopez
1955	Brooklyn	98	55	.641	Alston	1955	New York	96	58	.623	Stengel
1956	Brooklyn	93	61	.604	Alston	1956	New York	97	57	.630	Stengel
1957	Milwaukee	95	59	.617	Haney	1957	New York	98	56	.636	Stengel
1958	Milwaukee	92	62	.597	Haney	1958	New York	92	62	.597	Stengel
1959	Los Angeles	88	68	.564	Alston	1959	Chicago	94	60	.610	Lopez
1960	Pittsburgh	95	59	.617	Murtaugh	1960	New York	97	57	.630	Stengel
1961	Cincinnati	93	61	.604	Hutchinson	1961	New York	109	53	.673	Houk
1962	San Francisco	103	62	.624	Dark	1962	New York	96	66	.593	Houk
1963	Los Angeles	99	63	.611	Alston	1963	New York	104	57	.646	Houk
1964	St. Louis	93	69	.574	Keane	1964	New York	99	63	.611	Berra
1965	Los Angeles	97	65	.599	Alston	1965	Minnesota	102	60	.630	Mele
1966	Los Angeles	95	67	.586	Alston	1966	Baltimore	97	63	.606	Bauer
1967	St. Louis	101	60	.627	Schoendienst	1967	Boston	92	70	.568	Williams
1968	St. Louis	97	65	.599	Schoendienst	1968	Detroit	103	59	.636	Smith

Major League Pennant Winners, 1969-1997
National League

Year	Winner					East					West			Pennant winner

Year	Winner (East)	W	L	Pct	Manager	Winner (West)	W	L	Pct	Manager	Pennant winner
1969	N.Y. Mets	100	62	.617	Hodges	Atlanta	93	69	.574	Harris	New York
1970	Pittsburgh	89	73	.549	Murtaugh	Cincinnati	102	60	.630	Anderson	Cincinnati
1971	Pittsburgh	97	65	.599	Murtaugh	San Francisco ..	90	72	.556	Fox	Pittsburgh
1972	Pittsburgh	96	59	.619	Virdon	Cincinnati	95	59	.617	Anderson	Cincinnati
1973	N.Y. Mets	82	79	.509	Berra	Cincinnati	99	63	.611	Anderson	New York
1974	Pittsburgh	88	74	.543	Murtaugh	Los Angeles ...	102	60	.630	Alston	Los Angeles
1975	Pittsburgh	92	69	.571	Murtaugh	Cincinnati	108	54	.667	Anderson	Cincinnati
1976	Philadelphia ..	101	61	.623	Ozark	Cincinnati	102	60	.630	Anderson	Cincinnati
1977	Philadelphia ..	101	61	.623	Ozark	Los Angeles ...	98	64	.605	Lasorda	Los Angeles
1978	Philadelphia ..	90	72	.556	Ozark	Los Angeles ...	95	67	.586	Lasorda	Los Angeles
1979	Pittsburgh	98	64	.605	Tanner	Cincinnati	90	71	.559	McNamara	Pittsburgh
1980	Philadelphia ..	91	71	.562	Green	Houston	93	70	.571	Virdon	Philadelphia
1981(a)	Philadelphia ..	34	21	.618	Green	Los Angeles ...	36	21	.632	Lasorda	(c)
1981(b)	Montreal	30	23	.566	Williams, Fanning	Houston	33	20	.623	Virdon	Los Angeles
1982	St. Louis	92	70	.568	Herzog	Atlanta	89	73	.549	Torre	St. Louis
1983	Philadelphia ..	90	72	.556	Corrales, Owens	Los Angeles ...	91	71	.562	Lasorda	Philadelphia
1984	Chicago	96	65	.596	Frey	San Diego.....	92	70	.568	Williams	San Diego
1985	St. Louis	101	61	.623	Herzog	Los Angeles ...	95	67	.586	Lasorda	St. Louis
1986	N.Y. Mets	108	54	.667	Johnson	Houston	96	66	.593	Lanier	New York
1987	St. Louis	95	67	.586	Herzog	San Francisco ..	90	72	.556	Craig	St. Louis
1988	N.Y. Mets	100	60	.625	Johnson	Los Angeles ...	94	67	.584	Lasorda	Los Angeles
1989	Chicago	93	69	.571	Zimmer	San Francisco ..	92	70	.568	Craig	San Francisco
1990	Plttsburgh	95	67	.586	Leyland	Cincinnati	91	71	.562	Piniella	Cincinnati
1991	Pittsburgh	98	64	.605	Leyland	Atlanta	94	68	.580	Cox	Atlanta
1992	Pittsburgh	96	66	.593	Leyland	Atlanta	98	64	.605	Cox	Atlanta
1993	Philadelphia ..	97	65	.599	Fregosi	Atlanta	104	58	.642	Cox	Philadelphia

Year	Division	Winner	W	L	Pct.	Manager	Playoffs	Pennant Winner
1994(d)	East	Montreal	74	40	.649	Alou	—	—
	Central	Cincinnati	66	48	.579	Johnson		
	West	Los Angeles	58	56	.509	Lasorda		
1995	East	Atlanta	90	54	.625	Cox	Atlanta 3, Colorado* 1	Atlanta
	Central	Cincinnati	85	59	.590	Johnson	Cincinnati 3, Los Angeles 0	
	West	Los Angeles	78	66	.542	Lasorda	Atlanta 4, Cincinnati 0	
1996	East	Atlanta	96	66	.593	Cox	Atlanta 3, Los Angeles* 0	Atlanta
	Central	St. Louis	88	74	.543	La Russa	St. Louis 3, San Diego 0	
	West	San Diego	91	71	.562	Bochy	Atlanta 4, St. Louis 3	
1997	East	Atlanta	101	61	.623	Cox	Atlanta 3, Houston 0	Florida (e)
	Central	Houston	84	78	.519	Dierker	Florida 3, San Francisco 0	
	West	San Francisco	90	72	.556	Baker	Florida* 4, Atlanta 2	

American League

Year	Winner (East)	W	L	Pct	Manager	Winner (West)	W	L	Pct	Manager	Pennant winner
1969	Baltimore	109	53	.673	Weaver	Minnesota....	97	65	.599	Martin	Baltimore
1970	Baltimore	108	54	.667	Weaver	Minnesota....	98	64	.605	Rigney	Baltimore
1971	Baltimore	101	57	.639	Weaver	Oakland	101	60	.627	Williams	Baltimore
1972	Detroit	86	70	.551	Martin	Oakland	93	62	.600	Williams	Oakland
1973	Baltimore	97	65	.599	Weaver	Oakland	94	68	.580	Williams	Oakland
1974	Baltimore	91	71	.562	Weaver	Oakland	90	72	.556	Dark	Oakland
1975	Boston	95	65	.594	Johnson	Oakland	98	64	.605	Dark	Boston
1976	New York	97	62	.610	Martin	Kansas City ..	90	72	.556	Herzog	New York
1977	New York	100	62	.617	Martin	Kansas City ..	102	60	.630	Herzog	New York
1978	New York	100	63	.613	Martin, Lemon	Kansas City ..	92	70	.568	Herzog	New York
1979	Baltimore	102	57	.642	Weaver	California	88	74	.543	Fregosi	Baltimore
1980	New York	103	59	.636	Howser	Kansas City ..	97	65	.599	Frey	Kansas City
1981(a)	New York	34	22	.607	Michael	Oakland	37	23	.617	Martin	(c)
1981(b)	Milwaukee	31	22	.585	Rodgers	Kansas City ..	30	23	.566	Frey, Howser	New York
1982	Milwaukee	95	67	.586	Rodgers, Kuenn	California	93	69	.574	Mauch	Milwaukee
1983	Baltimore	98	64	.605	Altobelli	Chicago	99	63	.611	La Russa	Baltimore
1984	Detroit	104	58	.642	Anderson	Kansas City ..	84	78	.519	Howser	Detroit
1985	Toronto	99	62	.615	Cox	Kansas City ..	91	71	.562	Howser	Kansas City
1986	Boston	95	66	.590	McNamara	California	92	70	.568	Mauch	Boston
1987	Detroit	98	64	.605	Anderson	Minnesota....	85	77	.525	Kelly	Minnesota
1988	Boston	89	73	.549	McNamara, Morgan	Oakland	104	58	.642	La Russa	Oakland
1989	Toronto	89	73	.549	Williams, Gaston	Oakland	99	63	.611	La Russa	Oakland
1990	Boston	88	74	.543	Morgan	Oakland	103	59	.636	La Russa	Oakland
1991	Toronto	91	71	.562	Gaston	Minnesota....	95	67	.586	Kelly	Minnesota
1992	Toronto	96	66	.593	Gaston	Oakland	96	66	.593	La Russa	Toronto
1993	Toronto	95	67	.586	Gaston	Chicago	94	68	.580	Lamont	Toronto

Year	Division	Winner	W	L	Pct.	Manager	Playoffs	Pennant Winner
1994(d)	East	New York	70	43	.619	Showalter	—	—
	Central	Chicago	67	46	.593	Lamont		
	West	Texas	52	62	.456	Kennedy		
1995	East	Boston	86	58	.597	Kennedy	Cleveland 3, Boston 0	Cleveland
	Central	Cleveland	100	44	.694	Hargrove	Seattle 3, New York* 2	
	West	Seattle	79	66	.545	Piniella	Cleveland 4, Seattle 2	
1996	East	New York	92	70	.568	Torre	Baltimore* 3, Cleveland 1	New York
	Central	Cleveland	99	62	.615	Hargrove	New York 3, Texas 1	
	West	Texas	90	72	.556	Oates	New York 4, Baltimore* 1	
1997	East	Baltimore	98	64	.605	Johnson	Baltimore 3, Seattle 1	Cleveland
	Central	Cleveland	86	75	.534	Hargrove	Cleveland 0, New York* 2	
	West	Seattle	90	72	.556	Piniella	Cleveland 4, Baltimore 2	

*Wild card team. (a) First half. (b) Second half. (c) Montreal, L.A., N.Y. Yankees, and Oakland won the divisional playoffs. (d) In Aug. 1994, a players' strike began that caused the cancellation of the remainder of the season, the playoffs, and the World Series. Teams listed as division "winners" for 1994 were leading their divisions at the time of the strike. (e) Florida manager: Jim Leyland.

The Sporting News Gold Glove Awards in 1997

National League
Greg Maddux, Atlanta, pitcher
Charles Johnson, Florida, catcher
J. T. Snow, San Francisco, first base
Craig Biggio, Houston, second base
Ken Caminiti, San Diego, third base
Rey Ordonez, New York, shortstop
Barry Bonds, San Francisco, outfield
Raul Mondesi, Los Angeles, outfield
Larry Walker, Colorado, outfield

American League
Mike Mussina, Baltimore, pitcher
Ivan Rodriguez, Texas, catcher
Rafael Palmeiro, Baltimore, first base
Chuck Knoblauch, Minnesota, second base
Matt Williams, Cleveland, third base
Omar Vizquel, Cleveland, shortstop
Jim Edmonds, Anaheim, outfield
Ken Griffey Jr., Seattle, outfield
Bernie Williams, New York, outfield

The following are the players at each position who have won the most Gold Gloves since the award was instituted in 1957.

Pitcher:	Jim Kaat	16	Second base:	Ryne Sandberg	9	Outfield:	Roberto Clemente	12
	Bob Gibson	9		Bill Mazeroski	8		Willie Mays	12
Catcher:	Johnny Bench	10		Frank White	8		Al Kaline	10
	Bob Boone	7	Third base:	Brooks Robinson	16		Paul Blair	8
				Mike Schmidt	10		Dwight Evans	8
First base:	Keith Hernandez	11	Shortstop:	Ozzie Smith	13		Garry Maddox	8
	Don Mattingly	9		Luis Aparicio	9		Ken Griffey Jr.	8

Home Run Leaders

Note: **Boldface** indicates the all-time, single-season record for each league.

National League

Year	Player, Team	HR
1901	Sam Crawford, Cincinnati	16
1902	Thomas Leach, Pittsburgh	6
1903	James Sheckard, Brooklyn	9
1904	Harry Lumley, Brooklyn	9
1905	Fred Odwell, Cincinnati	9
1906	Timothy Jordan, Brooklyn	12
1907	David Brain, Boston	10
1908	Timothy Jordan, Brooklyn	12
1909	Red Murray, New York	7
1910	Fred Beck, Boston; Frank Schulte, Chicago	10
1911	Frank Schulte, Chicago	21
1912	Henry Zimmerman, Chicago	14
1913	Gavvy Cravath, Philadelphia	19
1914	Gavvy Cravath, Philadelphia	19
1915	Gavvy Cravath, Philadelphia	24
1916	Dave Robertson, N.Y.; Fred (Cy) Williams, Chi.	12
1917	Dave Robertson, N.Y.; Gavvy Cravath, Phi.	12
1918	Gavvy Cravath, Philadelphia	8
1919	Gavvy Cravath, Philadelphia	12
1920	Cy Williams, Philadelphia	15
1921	George Kelly, New York	23
1922	Rogers Hornsby, St. Louis	42
1923	Cy Williams, Philadelphia	41
1924	Jacques Fournier, Brooklyn	27
1925	Rogers Hornsby, St. Louis	39
1926	Hack Wilson, Chicago	21
1927	Hack Wilson, Chicago; Cy Williams, Philadelphia	30
1928	Hack Wilson, Chicago; Jim Bottomley, St. Louis	31
1929	Chuck Klein, Philadelphia	43
1930	**Hack Wilson, Chicago**	**56**
1931	Chuck Klein, Philadelphia	31
1932	Chuck Klein, Philadelphia; Mel Ott, New York	38
1933	Chuck Klein, Philadelphia	28
1934	Rip Collins, St. Louis; Mel Ott, New York	35
1935	Walter Berger, Boston	34
1936	Mel Ott, New York	33
1937	Mel Ott, New York; Joe Medwick, St. Louis	31
1938	Mel Ott, New York	36
1939	John Mize, St. Louis	28
1940	John Mize, St. Louis	43
1941	Dolph Camilli, Brooklyn	34
1942	Mel Ott, New York	30
1943	Bill Nicholson, Chicago	29
1944	Bill Nicholson, Chicago	33
1945	Tommy Holmes, Boston	28
1946	Ralph Kiner, Pittsburgh	23
1947	Ralph Kiner, Pittsburgh; John Mize, New York	51
1948	Ralph Kiner, Pittsburgh; John Mize, New York	40
1949	Ralph Kiner, Pittsburgh	54
1950	Ralph Kiner, Pittsburgh	47
1951	Ralph Kiner, Pittsburgh	42
1952	Ralph Kiner, Pittsburgh; Hank Sauer, Chicago	37
1953	Ed Mathews, Milwaukee	47
1954	Ted Kluszewski, Cincinnati	49
1955	Willie Mays, New York	51
1956	Duke Snider, Brooklyn	43
1957	Hank Aaron, Milwaukee	44
1958	Ernie Banks, Chicago	47
1959	Ed Mathews, Milwaukee	46
1960	Ernie Banks, Chicago	41
1961	Orlando Cepeda, San Francisco	46
1962	Willie Mays, San Francisco	49
1963	Hank Aaron, Milwaukee; Willie McCovey, S.F.	44

American League

Year	Player, Team	HR
1901	Napoleon Lajoie, Philadelphia	13
1902	Socks Seybold, Philadelphia	16
1903	Buck Freeman, Boston	13
1904	Harry Davis, Philadelphia	10
1905	Harry Davis, Philadelphia	8
1906	Harry Davis, Philadelphia	12
1907	Harry Davis, Philadelphia	8
1908	Sam Crawford, Detroit	7
1909	Ty Cobb, Detroit	9
1910	Jake Stahl, Boston	10
1911	J. Franklin Baker, Philadelphia	9
1912	J. Franklin Baker, Philadelphia; Tris Speaker, Boston	10
1913	J. Franklin Baker, Philadelphia	13
1914	J. Franklin, Baker, Philadelphia	9
1915	Robert Roth, Chicago-Cleveland	7
1916	Wally Pipp, New York	12
1917	Wally Pipp, New York	9
1918	Babe Ruth, Boston; Tilly Walker, Philadelphia	11
1919	Babe Ruth, Boston	29
1920	Babe Ruth, New York	54
1921	Babe Ruth, New York	59
1922	Ken Williams, St. Louis	39
1923	Babe Ruth, New York	41
1924	Babe Ruth, New York	46
1925	Bob Meusel, New York	33
1926	Babe Ruth, New York	47
1927	Babe Ruth, New York	60
1928	Babe Ruth, New York	54
1929	Babe Ruth, New York	46
1930	Babe Ruth, New York	49
1931	Babe Ruth, Lou Gehrig, New York	46
1932	Jimmie Foxx, Philadelphia	58
1933	Jimmie Foxx, Philadelphia	48
1934	Lou Gehrig, New York	49
1935	Jimmie Foxx, Philadelphia; Hank Greenberg, Detroit	36
1936	Lou Gehrig, New York	49
1937	Joe DiMaggio, New York	46
1938	Hank Greenberg, Detroit	58
1939	Jimmie Foxx, Boston	35
1940	Hank Greenberg, Detroit	41
1941	Ted Williams, Boston	37
1942	Ted Williams, Boston	36
1943	Rudy York, Detroit	34
1944	Nick Etten, New York	22
1945	Vern Stephens, St. Louis	24
1946	Hank Greenberg, Detroit	44
1947	Ted Williams, Boston	32
1948	Joe DiMaggio, New York	39
1949	Ted Williams, Boston	43
1950	Al Rosen, Cleveland	37
1951	Gus Zernial, Chicago-Philadelphia	33
1952	Larry Doby, Cleveland	32
1953	Al Rosen, Cleveland	43
1954	Larry Doby, Cleveland	32
1955	Mickey Mantle, New York	37
1956	Mickey Mantle, New York	52
1957	Roy Sievers, Washington	42
1958	Mickey Mantle, New York	42
1959	Rocky Colavito, Cleve.; Harmon Killebrew, Wash.	42
1960	Mickey Mantle, New York	40
1961	**Roger Maris, New York**	**61**
1962	Harmon Killebrew, Minnesota	48
1963	Harmon Killebrew, Minnesota	45

Year	National League — Player, Team	HR	Year	American League — Player, Team	HR
1964	Willie Mays, San Francisco	47	1964	Harmon Killebrew, Minnesota	49
1965	Willie Mays, San Francisco	52	1965	Tony Conigliaro, Boston	32
1966	Hank Aaron, Atlanta	44	1966	Frank Robinson, Baltimore	49
1967	Hank Aaron, Atlanta	39	1967	Carl Yastrzemski, Boston; Harmon Killebrew, Minn.	44
1968	Willie McCovey, San Francisco	36	1968	Frank Howard, Washington	44
1969	Willie McCovey, San Francisco	45	1969	Harmon Killebrew, Minnesota	49
1970	Johnny Bench, Cincinnati	45	1970	Frank Howard, Washington	44
1971	Willie Stargell, Pittsburgh	48	1971	Bill Melton, Chicago	33
1972	Johnny Bench, Cincinnati	40	1972	Dick Allen, Chicago	37
1973	Willie Stargell, Pittsburgh	44	1973	Reggie Jackson, Oakland	32
1974	Mike Schmidt, Philadelphia	36	1974	Dick Allen, Chicago	32
1975	Mike Schmidt, Philadelphia	38	1975	George Scott, Milwaukee; Reggie Jackson, Oakland	36
1976	Mike Schmidt, Philadelphia	38	1976	Graig Nettles, New York	32
1977	George Foster, Cincinnati	52	1977	Jim Rice, Boston	39
1978	George Foster, Cincinnati	40	1978	Jim Rice, Boston	46
1979	Dave Kingman, Chicago	48	1979	Gorman Thomas, Milwaukee	45
1980	Mike Schmidt, Philadelphia	48	1980	Reggie Jackson, New York; Ben Oglivie, Milwaukee	41
1981	Mike Schmidt, Philadelphia	31	1981	Bobby Grich, California; Tony Armas, Oakland; Dwight Evans, Boston; Eddie Murray, Baltimore	22
1982	Dave Kingman, New York	37	1982	Gorman Thomas, Milwaukee; Reggie Jackson, Cal.	39
1983	Mike Schmidt, Philadelphia	40	1983	Jim Rice, Boston	39
1984	Mike Schmidt, Phi.; Dale Murphy, Atlanta	36	1984	Tony Armas, Boston	43
1985	Dale Murphy, Atlanta	37	1985	Darrell Evans, Detroit	40
1986	Mike Schmidt, Philadelphia	37	1986	Jesse Barfield, Toronto	40
1987	Andre Dawson, Chicago	49	1987	Mark McGwire, Oakland	49
1988	Darryl Strawberry, New York	39	1988	Jose Canseco, Oakland	42
1989	Kevin Mitchell, San Francisco	47	1989	Fred McGriff, Toronto	36
1990	Ryne Sandberg, Chicago	40	1990	Cecil Fielder, Detroit	51
1991	Howard Johnson, New York	38	1991	Cecil Fielder, Detroit; Jose Canseco, Oakland	44
1992	Fred McGriff, San Diego	35	1992	Juan Gonzalez, Texas	43
1993	Barry Bonds, San Francisco	46	1993	Juan Gonzalez, Texas	46
1994	Matt Williams, San Francisco	43	1994	Ken Griffey Jr., Seattle	40
1995	Dante Bichette, Colorado	40	1995	Albert Belle, Cleveland	50
1996	Andres Galarraga, Colorado	47	1996	Mark McGwire, Oakland	52
1997[1]	Larry Walker, Colorado	49	1997[1]	Ken Griffey Jr., Seattle	56

(1) In 1997, Mark McGwire lead the Major Leagues with 58 home runs, splitting time between the Oakland Athletics (AL), 34, and the St. Louis Cardinals (NL), 24.

Runs Batted In Leaders

Note: **Boldface** indicates the all-time, single-season record for each league.

Year	National League — Player, Team	RBI	Year	American League — Player, Team	RBI
1907	Sherwood Magee, Philadelphia	85	1907	Ty Cobb, Detroit	116
1908	Honus Wager, Pittsburgh	109	1908	Ty Cobb, Detroit	108
1909	Honus Wager, Pittsburgh	100	1909	Ty Cobb, Detroit	107
1910	Sherwood Magee, Philadelphia	123	1910	Sam Crawford, Detroit	120
1911	Frank Schulte, Chicago	121	1911	Ty Cobb, Detroit	144
1912	Henry Zimmerman, Chicago	103	1912	J. Franklin Baker, Philadelphia	133
1913	Gavvy Cravath, Philadelphia	128	1913	J. Franklin Baker, Philadelphia	126
1914	Sherwood Magee, Philadelphia	103	1914	Sam Crawford, Detroit	104
1915	Gavvy Cravath, Philadelphia	115	1915	Sam Crawford, Detroit; Robert Veach, Detroit	112
1916	Henry Zimmerman, Chicago-NewYork	83	1916	Del Pratt, St. Louis	103
1917	Henry Zimmerman, New York	102	1917	Robert Veach, Detroit	103
1918	Sherwood Magee, Philadelphia	76	1918	Robert Veach, Detroit	78
1919	Hi Myers, Boston	73	1919	Babe Ruth, Boston	114
1920	George Kelly, N.Y.; Rogers Hornsby, St. Louis	94	1920	Babe Ruth, New York	137
1921	Rogers Hornsby, St. Louis	126	1921	Babe Ruth, New York	171
1922	Rogers Hornsby, St. Louis	152	1922	Ken Williams, St. Louis	155
1923	Emil Meusel, New York	125	1923	Babe Ruth, New York	131
1924	George Kelly, New York	136	1924	Goose Goslin, Washington	129
1925	Rogers Hornsby, St. Louis	143	1925	Bob Meusel, New York	138
1926	Jim Bottomley, St. Louis	120	1926	Babe Ruth, New York	145
1927	Paul Waner, Pittsburgh	131	1927	Lou Gehrig, New York	175
1928	Jim Bottomley, St. Louis	136	1928	Babe Ruth, New York; Lou Gehrig, New York	142
1929	Hack Wilson, Chicago	159	1929	Al Simmons, Philadelphia	157
1930	**Hack Wilson, Chicago**	**190**	1930	Lou Gehrig, New York	174
1931	Chuck Klein, Philadelphia	121	**1931**	**Lou Gehrig, New York**	**184**
1932	Don Hurst, Philadelphia	143	1932	Jimmie Foxx, Philadelphia	169
1933	Chuck Klein, Philadelphia	120	1933	Jimmie Foxx, Philadelphia	163
1934	Mel Ott, New York	135	1934	Lou Gehrig, New York	165
1935	Walter Berger, Boston	130	1935	Hank Greenberg, Detroit	170
1936	Joe Medwick, St. Louis	138	1936	Hal Trosky, Cleveland	162
1937	Joe Medwick, St. Louis	154	1937	Hank Greenberg, Detroit	183
1938	Joe Medwick, St. Louis	122	1938	Jimmie Foxx, Boston	175
1939	Frank McCormick, Cincinnati	128	1939	Ted Williams, Boston	145
1940	John Mize, St. Louis	137	1940	Hank Greenberg, Detroit	150
1941	Adolph Camilli, Brooklyn	120	1941	Joe DiMaggio, New York	125
1942	John Mize, New York	110	1942	Ted Williams, Boston	137
1943	Bill Nicholson, Chicago	128	1943	Rudy York, Detroit	118
1944	Bill Nicholson, Chicago	122	1944	Vern Stephens, St. Louis	109
1945	Dixie Walker, Brooklyn	124	1945	Nick Etten, New York	111
1946	Enos Slaughter, St. Louis	130	1946	Hank Greenberg, Detroit	127
1947	John Mize, New York	138	1947	Ted Williams, Boston	114
1948	Stan Musial, St. Louis	131	1948	Joe DiMaggio, New York	155
1949	Ralph Kiner, Pittsburgh	127	1949	Ted Williams, Bos., Vern Stephens, Bos.	159
1950	Del Ennis, Philadelphia	126	1950	Walt Dropo, Bos.; Vern Stephens, Bos.	144
1951	Monte Irvin, New York	121	1951	Gus Zernial, Chicago-Philadelphia	129
1952	Hank Sauer, Chicago	121	1952	Al Rosen, Cleveland	105

(continued)

National League

Year	Player, Team	RBI
1953	Roy Campanella, Brooklyn	142
1954	Ted Kluszewski, Cincinnati	141
1955	Duke Snider, Brooklyn	136
1956	Stan Musial, St. Louis	109
1957	Hank Aaron, Milwaukee	132
1958	Ernie Banks, Chicago	129
1959	Ernie Banks, Chicago	143
1960	Hank Aaron, Milwaukee	126
1961	Orlando Cepeda, San Francisco	142
1962	Tommy Davis, Los Angeles	153
1963	Hank Aaron, Milwaukee	130
1964	Ken Boyer, St. Louis	119
1965	Deron Johnson, Cincinnati	130
1966	Hank Aaron, Atlanta	127
1967	Orlando Cepeda, St. Louis	111
1968	Willie McCovey, San Francisco	105
1969	Willie McCovey, San Francisco	126
1970	Johnny Bench, Cincinnati	148
1971	Joe Torre, St. Louis	137
1972	Johnny Bench, Cincinnati	125
1973	Willie Stargell, Pittsburgh	119
1974	Johnny Bench, Cincinnati	129
1975	Greg Luzinski, Philadelphia	120
1976	George Foster, Cincinnati	121
1977	George Foster, Cincinnati	149
1978	George Foster, Cincinnati	120
1979	Dave Winfield, San Diego	118
1980	Mike Schmidt, Philadelphia	121
1981	Mike Schmidt, Philadelphia	91
1982	Dale Murphy, Atlanta; Al Oliver, Montreal	109
1983	Dale Murphy, Atlanta	121
1984	Gary Carter, Montreal; Mike Schmidt, Phi.	106
1985	Dave Parker, Cincinnati	125
1986	Mike Schmidt, Philadelphia	119
1987	Andre Dawson, Chicago	137
1988	Will Clark, San Francisco	109
1989	Kevin Mitchell, San Francisco	125
1990	Matt Williams, San Francisco	122
1991	Howard Johnson, New York	117
1992	Darren Daulton, Philadelphia	109
1993	Barry Bonds, San Francisco	123
1994	Jeff Bagwell, Houston	116
1995	Dante Bichette, Colorado	128
1996	Andres Galarraga, Colorado	150
1997	Andres Galarraga, Colorado	140

American League

Year	Player, Team	RBI
1953	Al Rosen, Cleveland	145
1954	Larry Doby, Cleveland	126
1955	Ray Boone, Detroit; Jackie Jensen, Boston	116
1956	Mickey Mantle, New York	130
1957	Roy Sievers, Washington	114
1958	Jackie Jensen, Boston	122
1959	Jackie Jensen, Boston	112
1960	Roger Maris, New York	112
1961	Roger Maris, New York	142
1962	Harmon Killebrew, Minnesota	126
1963	Dick Stuart, Boston	118
1964	Brooks Robinson, Baltimore	118
1965	Rocky Colavito, Cleveland	108
1966	Frank Robinson, Baltimore	122
1967	Carl Yastrzemski, Boston	121
1968	Ken Harrelson, Boston	109
1969	Harmon Killebrew, Minnesota	140
1970	Frank Howard, Washington	126
1971	Harmon Killebrew, Minnesota	119
1972	Dick Allen, Chicago	113
1973	Reggie Jackson, Oakland	117
1974	Jeff Burroughs, Texas	118
1975	George Scott, Milwaukee	109
1976	Lee May, Baltimore	109
1977	Larry Hisle, Minnesota	119
1978	Jim Rice, Boston	139
1979	Don Baylor, California	139
1980	Cecil Cooper, Milwaukee	122
1981	Eddie Murray, Baltimore	78
1982	Hal McRae, Kansas City	133
1983	Cecil Cooper, Milwaukee; Jim Rice, Boston	126
1984	Tony Armas, Boston	123
1985	Don Mattingly, New York	145
1986	Joe Carter, Cleveland	121
1987	George Bell, Toronto	134
1988	Jose Canseco, Oakland	124
1989	Ruben Sierra, Texas	119
1990	Cecil Fielder, Detroit	132
1991	Cecil Fielder, Detroit	133
1992	Cecil Fielder, Detroit	124
1993	Albert Belle, Cleveland	129
1994	Kirby Puckett, Minnesota	112
1995	Albert Belle, Cleveland; Mo Vaughn, Boston	126
1996	Albert Belle, Cleveland	148
1997	Ken Griffey Jr., Seattle	147

Batting Champions

Note: **Boldface** name and team indicates the all-time, single-season record for each league.

National League

Year	Player	Club	Avg.
1901	Jesse C. Burkett	St. Louis	.382
1902	Clarence Beaumont	Pittsburgh	.357
1903	Honus Wagner	Pittsburgh	.355
1904	Honus Wagner	Pittsburgh	.349
1905	James Seymour	Cincinnati	.377
1906	Honus Wagner	Pittsburgh	.339
1907	Honus Wagner	Pittsburgh	.350
1908	Honus Wagner	Pittsburgh	.354
1909	Honus Wagner	Pittsburgh	.339
1910	Sherwood Magee	Philadelphia	.331
1911	Honus Wagner	Pittsburgh	.334
1912	Henry Zimmerman	Chicago	.372
1913	Jacob Daubert	Brooklyn	.350
1914	Jacob Daubert	Brooklyn	.329
1915	Larry Doyle	New York	.320
1916	Hal Chase	Cincinnati	.339
1917	Edd Roush	Cincinnati	.341
1918	Zach Wheat	Brooklyn	.335
1919	Edd Roush	Cincinnati	.321
1920	Rogers Hornsby	St. Louis	.370
1921	Rogers Hornsby	St. Louis	.397
1922	Rogers Hornsby	St. Louis	.401
1923	Rogers Hornsby	St. Louis	.384
1924	**Rogers Hornsby**	**St. Louis**	**.424**
1925	Rogers Hornsby	St. Louis	.403
1926	Eugene Hargrave	Cincinnati	.353
1927	Paul Waner	Pittsburgh	.380
1928	Rogers Hornsby	Boston	.387
1929	Lefty O'Doul	Philadelphia	.398
1930	Bill Terry	New York	.401
1931	Chick Hafey	St. Louis	.349
1932	Lefty O'Doul	Brooklyn	.368
1933	Chuck Klein	Philadelphia	.368
1934	Paul Waner	Pittsburgh	.362
1935	Arky Vaughan	Pittsburgh	.385
1936	Paul Waner	Pittsburgh	.373
1937	Joe Medwick	St. Louis	.374
1938	Ernie Lombardi	Cincinnati	.342
1939	John Mize	St. Louis	.349

American League

Year	Player	Club	Avg.
1901	**Napoleon Lajoie**	**Philadelphia**	**.422**
1902	Ed Delahanty	Washington	.376
1903	Napoleon Lajoie	Cleveland	.355
1904	Napoleon Lajoie	Cleveland	.381
1905	Elmer Flick	Cleveland	.306
1906	George Stone	St. Louis	.358
1907	Ty Cobb	Detroit	.350
1908	Ty Cobb	Detroit	.324
1909	Ty Cobb	Detroit	.377
1910	Ty Cobb*	Detroit	.385
1911	Ty Cobb	Detroit	.420
1912	Ty Cobb	Detroit	.410
1913	Ty Cobb	Detroit	.390
1914	Ty Cobb	Detroit	.368
1915	Ty Cobb	Detroit	.369
1916	Tris Speaker	Cleveland	.386
1917	Ty Cobb	Detroit	.383
1918	Ty Cobb	Detroit	.382
1919	Ty Cobb	Detroit	.384
1920	George Sisler	St. Louis	.407
1921	Harry Heilmann	Detroit	.394
1922	George Sisler	St. Louis	.420
1923	Harry Heilmann	Detroit	.403
1924	Babe Ruth	New York	.378
1925	Harry Heilmann	Detroit	.393
1926	Henry Manush	Detroit	.378
1927	Harry Heilmann	Detroit	.398
1928	Goose Goslin	Washington	.379
1929	Lew Fonseca	Cleveland	.369
1930	Al Simmons	Philadelphia	.381
1931	Al Simmons	Philadelphia	.390
1932	Dale Alexander	Detroit-Boston	.367
1933	Jimmie Foxx	Philadelphia	.356
1934	Lou Gehrig	New York	.363
1935	Buddy Myer	Washington	.349
1936	Luke Appling	Chicago	.388
1937	Charlie Gehringer	Detroit	.371
1938	Jimmie Foxx	Boston	.349
1939	Joe DiMaggio	New York	.381

National League				American League		
Year	Player	Club	Avg.	Year	Player	Club	Avg.
1940	Debs Garms	Pittsburgh	.355	1940	Joe DiMaggio	New York	.352
1941	Pete Reiser	Brooklyn	.343	1941	Ted Williams	Boston	.406
1942	Ernie Lombardi	Boston	.330	1942	Ted Williams	Boston	.356
1943	Stan Musial	St. Louis	.357	1943	Luke Appling	Chicago	.328
1944	Dixie Walker	Brooklyn	.357	1944	Lou Boudreau	Cleveland	.327
1945	Phil Cavarretta	Chicago	.355	1945	George Stirnweiss	New York	.309
1946	Stan Musial	St. Louis	.365	1946	Mickey Vernon	Washington	.353
1947	Harry Walker	St.L.-Phi.	.363	1947	Ted Williams	Boston	.343
1948	Stan Musial	St. Louis	.376	1948	Ted Williams	Boston	.369
1949	Jackie Robinson	Brooklyn	.342	1949	George Kell	Detroit	.343
1950	Stan Musial	St. Louis	.346	1950	Billy Goodman	Boston	.354
1951	Stan Musial	St. Louis	.355	1951	Ferris Fain	Philadelphia	.344
1952	Stan Musial	St. Louis	.336	1952	Ferris Fain	Philadelphia	.327
1953	Carl Furillo	Brooklyn	.344	1953	Mickey Vernon	Washington	.337
1954	Willie Mays	New York	.345	1954	Roberto Avila	Cleveland	.341
1955	Richie Ashburn	Philadelphia	.338	1955	Al Kaline	Detroit	.340
1956	Hank Aaron	Milwaukee	.328	1956	Mickey Mantle	New York	.353
1957	Stan Musial	St. Louis	.351	1957	Ted Williams	Boston	.388
1958	Richie Ashburn	Philadelphia	.350	1958	Ted Williams	Boston	.328
1959	Hank Aaron	Milwaukee	.355	1959	Harvey Kuenn	Detroit	.353
1960	Dick Groat	Pittsburgh	.325	1960	Pete Runnels	Boston	.320
1961	Roberto Clemente	Pittsburgh	.351	1961	Norm Cash	Detroit	.361
1962	Tommy Davis	Los Angeles	.346	1962	Pete Runnels	Boston	.326
1963	Tommy Davis	Los Angeles	.326	1963	Carl Yastrzemski	Boston	.321
1964	Roberto Clemente	Pittsburgh	.339	1964	Tony Oliva	Minnesota	.323
1965	Roberto Clemente	Pittsburgh	.329	1965	Tony Oliva	Minnesota	.321
1966	Matty Alou	Pittsburgh	.342	1966	Frank Robinson	Baltimore	.316
1967	Roberto Clemente	Pittsburgh	.357	1967	Carl Yastrzemski	Boston	.326
1968	Pete Rose	Cincinnati	.335	1968	Carl Yastrzemski	Boston	.301
1969	Pete Rose	Cincinnati	.348	1969	Rod Carew	Minnesota	.332
1970	Rico Carty	Atlanta	.366	1970	Alex Johnson	California	.329
1971	Joe Torre	St. Louis	.363	1971	Tony Oliva	Minnesota	.337
1972	Billy Williams	Chicago	.333	1972	Rod Carew	Minnesota	.318
1973	Pete Rose	Cincinnati	.338	1973	Rod Carew	Minnesota	.350
1974	Ralph Garr	Atlanta	.353	1974	Rod Carew	Minnesota	.364
1975	Bill Madlock	Chicago	.354	1975	Rod Carew	Minnesota	.359
1976	Bill Madlock	Chicago	.339	1976	George Brett	Kansas City	.333
1977	Dave Parker	Pittsburgh	.338	1977	Rod Carew	Minnesota	.388
1978	Dave Parker	Pittsburgh	.334	1978	Rod Carew	Minnesota	.333
1979	Keith Hernandez	St. Louis	.344	1979	Fred Lynn	Boston	.333
1980	Bill Buckner	Chicago	.324	1980	George Brett	Kansas City	.390
1981	Bill Madlock	Pittsburgh	.341	1981	Carney Lansford	Boston	.336
1982	Al Oliver	Montreal	.331	1982	Willie Wilson	Kansas City	.332
1983	Bill Madlock	Pittsburgh	.323	1983	Wade Boggs	Boston	.361
1984	Tony Gwynn	San Diego	.351	1984	Don Mattingly	New York	.343
1985	Willie McGee	St. Louis	.353	1985	Wade Boggs	Boston	.368
1986	Tim Raines	Montreal	.334	1986	Wade Boggs	Boston	.357
1987	Tony Gwynn	San Diego	.370	1987	Wade Boggs	Boston	.363
1988	Tony Gwynn	San Diego	.313	1988	Wade Boggs	Boston	.366
1989	Tony Gwynn	San Diego	.336	1989	Kirby Puckett	Minnesota	.339
1990	Willie McGee	St. Louis	.335	1990	George Brett	Kansas City	.329
1991	Terry Pendleton	Atlanta	.319	1991	Julio Franco	Texas	.341
1992	Gary Sheffield	San Diego	.330	1992	Edgar Martinez	Seattle	.343
1993	Andres Galarraga	Colorado	.370	1993	John Olerud	Toronto	.363
1994	Tony Gwynn	San Diego	.394	1994	Paul O'Neill	New York	.359
1995	Tony Gwynn	San Diego	.368	1995	Edgar Martinez	Seattle	.356
1996	Tony Gwynn	San Diego	.353	1996	Alex Rodriguez	Seattle	.358
1997	Tony Gwynn	San Diego	.372	1997	Frank Thomas	Chicago	.347

*Some baseball researchers have determined that Ty Cobb actually hit .382 in 1910, while Napoleon Lajoie, Cleveland, hit .383.

Cy Young Award Winners

Year	Player, Team	Year	Player, Team	Year	Player, Team
1956	Don Newcombe, Dodgers	1973	(NL) Tom Seaver, Mets	1985	(NL) Dwight Gooden, Mets
1957	Warren Spahn, Braves		(AL) Jim Palmer, Orioles		(AL) Bret Saberhagen, Royals
1958	Bob Turley, Yankees	1974	(NL) Mike Marshall, Dodgers	1986	(NL) Mike Scott, Astros
1959	Early Wynn, White Sox		(AL) Jim (Catfish) Hunter, A's		(AL) Roger Clemens, Red Sox
1960	Vernon Law, Pirates	1975	(NL) Tom Seaver, Mets	1987	(NL) Steve Bedrosian, Phillies
1961	Whitey Ford, Yankees		(AL) Jim Palmer, Orioles		(AL) Roger Clemens, Red Sox
1962	Don Drysdale, Dodgers	1976	(NL) Randy Jones, Padres	1988	(NL) Orel Hershiser, Dodgers
1963	Sandy Koufax, Dodgers		(AL) Jim Palmer, Orioles		(AL) Frank Viola, Twins
1964	Dean Chance, Angels	1977	(NL) Steve Carlton, Phillies	1989	(NL) Mark Davis, Padres
1965	Sandy Koufax, Dodgers		(AL) Sparky Lyle, Yankees		(AL) Bret Saberhagen, Royals
1966	Sandy Koufax, Dodgers	1978	(NL) Gaylord Perry, Padres	1990	(NL) Doug Drabek, Pirates
1967	(NL) Mike McCormick, Giants		(AL) Ron Guidry, Yankees		(AL) Bob Welch, A's
	(AL) Jim Lonborg, Red Sox	1979	(NL) Bruce Sutter, Cubs	1991	(NL) Tom Glavine, Braves
1968	(NL) Bob Gibson, Cardinals		(AL) Mike Flanagan, Orioles		(AL) Roger Clemens, Red Sox
	(AL) Dennis McLain, Tigers	1980	(NL) Steve Carlton, Phillies	1992	(NL) Greg Maddux, Cubs
1969	(NL) Tom Seaver, Mets		(AL) Steve Stone, Orioles		(AL) Dennis Eckersley, A's
	(AL) (tie) Dennis McLain, Tigers	1981	(NL) Fernando Valenzuela, Dodgers	1993	(NL) Greg Maddux, Braves
	Mike Cuellar, Orioles		(AL) Rollie Fingers, Brewers		(AL) Jack McDowell, White Sox
1970	(NL) Bob Gibson, Cardinals	1982	(NL) Steve Carlton, Phillies	1994	(NL) Greg Maddux, Braves
	(AL) Jim Perry, Twins		(AL) Pete Vuckovich, Brewers		(AL) David Cone, Royals
1971	(NL) Ferguson Jenkins, Cubs	1983	(NL) John Denny, Phillies	1995	(NL) Greg Maddux, Braves
	(AL) Vida Blue, A's		(AL) LaMarr Hoyt, White Sox		(AL) Randy Johnson, Mariners
1972	(NL) Steve Carlton, Phillies	1984	(NL) Rick Sutcliffe, Cubs	1996	(NL) John Smoltz, Braves
	(AL) Gaylord Perry, Indians		(AL) Willie Hernandez, Tigers		(AL) Pat Hentgen, Blue Jays

Most Valuable Player
National League

Year	Player, team	Year	Player, team	Year	Player, team
1931	Frank Frisch, St. Louis	1953	Roy Campanella, Brooklyn	1975	Joe Morgan, Cincinnati
1932	Charles Klein, Philadelphia	1954	Willie Mays, New York	1976	Joe Morgan, Cincinnati
1933	Carl Hubbell, New York	1955	Roy Campanella, Brooklyn	1977	George Foster, Cincinnati
1934	Dizzy Dean, St. Louis	1956	Don Newcombe, Brooklyn	1978	Dave Parker, Pittsburgh
1935	Gabby Hartnett, Chicago	1957	Hank Aaron, Milwaukee	1979	Willie Stargell, Pittsburgh
1936	Carl Hubbell, New York	1958	Ernie Banks, Chicago	(tie)	Keith Hernandez, St. Louis
1937	Joe Medwick, St. Louis	1959	Ernie Banks, Chicago	1980	Mike Schmidt, Philadelphia
1938	Ernie Lombardi, Cincinnati	1960	Dick Groat, Pittsburgh	1981	Mike Schmidt, Philadelphia
1939	Bucky Walters, Cincinnati	1961	Frank Robinson, Cincinnati	1982	Dale Murphy, Atlanta
1940	Frank McCormick, Cincinnati	1962	Maury Wills, Los Angeles	1983	Dale Murphy, Atlanta
1941	Dolph Camilli, Brooklyn	1963	Sandy Koufax, Los Angeles	1984	Ryne Sandberg, Chicago
1942	Mort Cooper, St. Louis	1964	Ken Boyer, St. Louis	1985	Willie McGee, St. Louis
1943	Stan Musial, St. Louis	1965	Willie Mays, San Francisco	1986	Mike Schmidt, Philadelphia
1944	Martin Marion, St. Louis	1966	Roberto Clemente, Pittsburgh	1987	Andre Dawson, Chicago
1945	Phil Cavarretta, Chicago	1967	Orlando Cepeda, St. Louis	1988	Kirk Gibson, Los Angeles
1946	Stan Musial, St. Louis	1968	Bob Gibson, St. Louis	1989	Kevin Mitchell, San Francisco
1947	Bob Elliott, Boston	1969	Willie McCovey, San Francisco	1990	Barry Bonds, Pittsburgh
1948	Stan Musial, St. Louis	1970	Johnny Bench, Cincinnati	1991	Terry Pendleton, Atlanta
1949	Jackie Robinson, Brooklyn	1971	Joe Torre, St. Louis	1992	Barry Bonds, Pittsburgh
1950	Jim Konstanty, Philadelphia	1972	Johnny Bench, Cincinnati	1993	Barry Bonds, San Francisco
1951	Roy Campanella, Brooklyn	1973	Pete Rose, Cincinnati	1994	Jeff Bagwell, Houston
1952	Hank Sauer, Chicago	1974	Steve Garvey, Los Angeles	1995	Barry Larkin, Cincinnati
				1996	Ken Caminiti, San Diego

American League

Year	Player, team	Year	Player, team	Year	Player, team
1931	Lefty Grove, Philadelphia	1953	Al Rosen, Cleveland	1975	Fred Lynn, Boston
1932	Jimmie Foxx, Philadelphia	1954	Yogi Berra, New York	1976	Thurman Munson, New York
1933	Jimmie Foxx, Philadelphia	1955	Yogi Berra, New York	1977	Rod Carew, Minnesota
1934	Mickey Cochrane, Detroit	1956	Mickey Mantle, New York	1978	Jim Rice, Boston
1935	Hank Greenberg, Detroit	1957	Mickey Mantle, New York	1979	Don Baylor, California
1936	Lou Gehrig, New York	1958	Jackie Jensen, Boston	1980	George Brett, Kansas City
1937	Charley Gehringer, Detroit	1959	Nellie Fox, Chicago	1981	Rollie Fingers, Milwaukee
1938	Jimmie Foxx, Boston	1960	Roger Maris, New York	1982	Robin Yount, Milwaukee
1939	Joe DiMaggio, New York	1961	Roger Maris, New York	1983	Cal Ripken, Jr., Baltimore
1940	Hank Greenberg, Detroit	1962	Mickey Mantle, New York	1984	Willie Hernandez, Detroit
1941	Joe DiMaggio, New York	1963	Elston Howard, New York	1985	Don Mattingly, New York
1942	Joe Gordon, New York	1964	Brooks Robinson, Baltimore	1986	Roger Clemens, Boston
1943	Spurgeon Chandler, New York	1965	Zoilo Versalles, Minnesota	1987	George Bell, Toronto
1944	Hal Newhouser, Detroit	1966	Frank Robinson, Baltimore	1988	Jose Canseco, Oakland
1945	Hal Newhouser, Detroit	1967	Carl Yastrzemski, Boston	1989	Robin Yount, Milwaukee
1946	Ted Williams, Boston	1968	Denny McLain, Detroit	1990	Rickey Henderson, Oakland
1947	Joe DiMaggio, New York	1969	Harmon Killebrew, Minnesota	1991	Cal Ripken, Jr., Baltimore
1948	Lou Boudreau, Cleveland	1970	John (Boog) Powell, Baltimore	1992	Dennis Eckersley, Oakland
1949	Ted Williams, Boston	1971	Vida Blue, Oakland	1993	Frank Thomas, Chicago
1950	Phil Rizzuto, New York	1972	Dick Allen, Chicago	1994	Frank Thomas, Chicago
1951	Yogi Berra, New York	1973	Reggie Jackson, Oakland	1995	Mo Vaughn, Boston
1952	Bobby Shantz, Philadelphia	1974	Jeff Burroughs, Texas	1996	Juan Gonzalez, Texas

Rookie of the Year

1947—Combined selection—Jackie Robinson, Brooklyn, 1b; 1948—Combined selection—Alvin Dark, Boston, N.L., ss

National League

Year	Player, team	Year	Player, team	Year	Player, team
1949	Don Newcombe, Brooklyn, p	1966	Tommy Helms, Cincinnati, 2b	1981	Fernando Valenzuela, Los Angeles, p
1950	Sam Jethroe, Boston, of	1967	Tom Seaver, New York, p	1982	Steve Sax, Los Angeles, 2b
1951	Willie Mays, New York, of	1968	Johnny Bench, Cincinnati, c	1983	Darryl Strawberry, New York, of
1952	Joe Black, Brooklyn, p	1969	Ted Sizemore, Los Angeles, 2b	1984	Dwight Gooden, New York, p
1953	Jim Gilliam, Brooklyn, 2b	1970	Carl Morton, Montreal, p	1985	Vince Coleman, St. Louis, of
1954	Wally Moon, St. Louis, of	1971	Earl Williams, Atlanta, c	1986	Todd Worrell, St. Louis, p
1955	Bill Virdon, St. Louis, of	1972	Jon Matlack, New York, p	1987	Benito Santiago, San Diego, c
1956	Frank Robinson, Cincinnati, of	1973	Gary Matthews, S.F., of	1988	Chris Sabo, Cincinnati, 3b
1957	Jack Sanford, Philadelphia, p	1974	Bake McBride, St. Louis, of	1989	Jerome Walton, Chicago, of
1958	Orlando Cepeda, S.F., 1b	1975	John Montefusco, S.F., p	1990	Dave Justice, Atlanta, 1b
1959	Willie McCovey, S.F., 1b	1976	Butch Metzger, San Diego, p	1991	Jeff Bagwell, Houston, 1b
1960	Frank Howard, Los Angeles, of	(tie)	Pat Zachry, Cincinnati, p	1992	Eric Karros, Los Angeles, 1b
1961	Billy Williams, Chicago, of	1977	Andre Dawson, Montreal, of	1993	Mike Piazza, Los Angeles, c
1962	Ken Hubbs, Chicago, 2b	1978	Bob Horner, Atlanta, 3b	1994	Raul Mondesi, Los Angeles, of
1963	Pete Rose, Cincinnati, 2b	1979	Rick Sutcliffe, Los Angeles, p	1995	Hideo Nomo, Los Angeles, p
1964	Richie Allen, Philadelphia, 3b	1980	Steve Howe, Los Angeles, p	1996	Todd Hollandsworth, Los Angeles, of
1965	Jim Lefebvre, Los Angeles, 2b				

American League

Year	Player, team	Year	Player, team	Year	Player, team
1949	Roy Sievers, St. Louis, of	1965	Curt Blefary, Baltimore, of	1980	Joe Charboneau, Cleveland, of
1950	Walt Dropo, Boston, 1b	1966	Tommie Agee, Chicago, of	1981	Dave Righetti, New York, p
1951	Gil McDougald, New York, 3b	1967	Rod Carew, Minnesota, 2b	1982	Cal Ripken, Jr., Baltimore, ss
1952	Harry Byrd, Philadelphia, p	1968	Stan Bahnsen, New York, p	1983	Ron Kittle, Chicago, of
1953	Harvey Kuenn, Detroit, ss	1969	Lou Piniella, Kansas City, of	1984	Alvin Davis, Seattle, 1b
1954	Bob Grim, New York, p	1970	Thurman Munson, New York, c	1985	Ozzie Guillen, Chicago, ss
1955	Herb Score, Cleveland, p	1971	Chris Chambliss, Cleveland, 1b	1986	Jose Canseco, Oakland, of
1956	Luis Aparicio, Chicago, ss	1972	Carlton Fisk, Boston, c	1987	Mark McGwire, Oakland, 1b
1957	Tony Kubek, New York, if-of	1973	Al Bumbry, Baltimore, of	1988	Walt Weiss, Oakland, ss
1958	Albie Pearson, Washington, of	1974	Mike Hargrove, Texas, 1b	1989	Gregg Olson, Baltimore, p
1959	Bob Allison, Washington, of	1975	Fred Lynn, Boston, of	1990	Sandy Alomar, Jr., Cleveland, c
1960	Ron Hansen, Baltimore, ss	1976	Mark Fidrych, Detroit, p	1991	Chuck Knoblauch, Minnesota, 2b
1961	Don Schwall, Boston, p	1977	Eddie Murray, Baltimore, dh	1992	Pat Listach, Milwaukee, ss
1962	Tom Tresh, New York, if-of	1978	Lou Whitaker, Detroit, 2b	1993	Tim Salmon, California, of
1963	Gary Peters, Chicago, p	1979	John Castino, Minnesota, 3b	1994	Bob Hamelin, Kansas City, dh
1964	Tony Oliva, Minnesota, of	(tie)	Alfredo Griffin, Toronto, ss	1995	Marty Cordova, Minnesota, of
				1996	Derek Jeter, New York, ss

National League Final Standings, 1997

Eastern Division

	W	L	Pct.	GB	Home	vs. East	vs. Central	vs. West	vs. AL
Atlanta	101	61	.623	—	50-31	29-19	38-17	26-18	8-7
Florida*	92	70	.568	9	52-29	25-23	34-21	21-23	12-3
New York	88	74	.543	13	50-31	29-19	34-21	18-26	7-8
Montreal	78	84	.481	23	45-36	18-30	26-29	22-22	12-3
Philadelphia	68	94	.420	33	38-43	19-29	26-29	18-26	5-10

Central Division

	W	L	Pct.	GB	Home	vs. East	vs. Central	vs. West	vs. AL
Houston.	84	78	.519	—	46-35	27-28	31-17	22-22	4-11
Pittsburgh	79	83	.488	5	43-38	26-29	24-24	22-22	7-8
Cincinnati.	76	86	.469	8	40-41	23-32	24-24	20-24	9-6
St. Louis	73	89	.451	11	41-40	21-34	20-28	24-20	8-7
Chicago.	68	94	.420	16	42-39	20-35	21-27	18-26	9-6

Western Division

	W	L	Pct.	GB	Home	vs. East	vs. Central	vs. West	vs. AL
San Francisco . . .	90	72	.556	—	48-33	31-24	27-28	22-14	10-6
Los Angeles	88	74	.543	2	47-34	32-23	29-26	18-18	9-7
Colorado	83	79	.512	7	47-34	30-25	31-24	13-23	9-7
San Diego	76	86	.469	14	39-42	22-33	27-28	19-17	8-8

*Wild card team.

National League Playoff Results, 1997

Division Series
Atlanta defeated Houston 3 games to 0 (2-1,13-3, 4-1)
Florida defeated San Francisco 3 games to 0 (2-1, 7-6, 6-2)

Championship Series
Florida defeated Atlanta 4 games to 2 (5-3, 1-7, 5-2, 0-4, 2-1, 7-4)

National League Statistics, 1997
(Individual Statistics: Batting—at least 150 at-bats; Pitching—at least 70 innings or 10 saves)

Team Batting

	Avg	AB	R	H	HR	RBI
Colorado	.288	5,603	923	1,611	239	869
San Diego . . .	.271	5,609	795	1,519	152	761
Atlanta	.270	5,528	791	1,490	174	755
Los Angeles . .	.268	5,544	742	1,488	174	706
Chicago.	.263	5,489	687	1,444	127	642
New York	.262	5,524	777	1,448	153	741
Pittsburgh. . . .	.262	5,507	724	1,441	129	686
Florida.	.259	5,439	740	1,410	136	703
Houston.	.259	5,502	777	1,427	133	720
Montreal	.258	5,526	691	1,423	172	659
San Francisco .	.258	5,480	784	1,414	172	746
Philadelphia . .	.255	5,443	668	1,390	116	622
St. Louis	.255	5,524	689	1,409	144	653
Cincinnati	.253	5,484	651	1,386	142	612

Team Pitching

	ERA	IP	H	BB	SO	Sv
Atlanta.	3.18	1,465.2	1,319	450	1,196	37
Los Angeles. . . .	3.63	1,459.1	1,325	546	1,232	45
Houston	3.67	1,459.0	1,379	511	1,138	37
Florida	3.83	1,446.2	1,353	639	1,188	39
St. Louis	3.90	1,457.1	1,425	535	1,133	39
New York	3.95	1,459.1	1,452	504	982	49
Montreal	4.14	1,447.0	1,365	557	1,138	37
Pittsburgh	4.28	1,436.0	1,503	560	1,080	41
Cincinnati	4.42	1,449.0	1,408	558	1,159	49
San Francisco. . .	4.42	1,444.0	1,490	579	1,041	45
Chicago	4.44	1,429.0	1,451	590	1,072	37
Philadelphia. . . .	4.87	1,420.1	1,441	616	1,209	35
San Diego	4.99	1,450.0	1,581	596	1,059	43
Colorado.	5.25	1,432.2	1,698	566	870	38

Atlanta Braves

Batting	AB	R	H	HR	RBI	SB	AVG
Lofton	493	90	164	5	48	27	.333
Blauser	519	90	160	17	70	5	.308
C. Jones	597	100	176	21	111	20	.295
Lopez	414	52	122	23	68	1	.295
Tucker	499	80	141	14	56	12	.283
Colbrunn	54	3	15	2	9	0	.278
McGriff	564	77	156	22	97	5	.277
Klesko	467	67	122	24	84	4	.261
Graffanino	186	33	48	8	20	6	.258
Lemke	351	33	86	2	26	2	.245
A. Jones	399	60	92	18	70	20	.231
Perez	191	20	41	6	18	0	.215

Pitching	W	L	ERA	IP	H	BB	SO	Sv
Maddux	19	4	2.20	232.2	200	20	177	0
Glavine	14	7	2.90	240.0	197	79	152	0
Neagle	20	5	2.97	233.1	204	49	172	0
Smoltz	15	12	3.02	256.0	234	63	241	0
Wohlers	5	7	3.50	69.1	57	38	92	33

Manager—Bobby Cox

Chicago Cubs

Batting	AB	R	H	HR	RBI	SB	AVG
Grace	555	87	177	13	78	2	.319
Hansen	151	19	47	3	21	1	.311
Johnson.	410	60	126	5	39	20	.307
Glanville	474	79	142	4	35	19	.300
Orie	364	40	100	8	44	2	.275
Hernandez	183	33	50	7	26	2	.273
Alexander	248	37	66	3	22	13	.266
Sandberg	447	54	118	12	64	7	.264
Houston	196	15	51	2	28	1	.260
Servais	385	36	100	6	45	0	.260
Sosa	642	90	161	36	119	22	.251
Sanchez	205	14	51	1	12	4	.249

Pitching	W	L	ERA	IP	H	BB	SO	Sv
Tapani	9	3	3.39	85.0	77	23	55	0
M. Clark	14	8	3.82	205.0	213	59	123	0
Bottenfield	2	3	3.86	84.0	83	26	71	0
Gonzalez	11	9	4.25	144.0	126	69	93	0
Trachsel	8	12	4.51	201.1	225	69	160	0
Foster	10	7	4.61	146.1	141	66	118	0
Adams	2	9	4.62	74.0	91	40	64	18

Manager—Jim Riggleman

Cincinnati Reds

Batting	AB	R	H	HR	RBI	SB	AVG
Stynes	198	31	69	6	28	11	.348
Nunnally	201	38	64	13	35	7	.318
Larkin	224	34	71	4	20	14	.317
Morris	333	42	92	1	33	3	.276
D. Sanders	465	53	127	5	23	56	.273
Harris	238	32	65	3	28	4	.273
Taubensee	254	26	68	10	34	0	.268
Oliver	349	28	90	14	43	1	.258
R. Sanders	312	52	79	19	56	13	.253
Goodwin	265	27	67	1	12	22	.253
Greene	495	62	125	26	91	6	.253
Perez	297	44	75	16	52	5	.253
B. Boone.......	443	40	99	7	46	5	.223
Reese..........	397	48	87	4	26	25	.219

Pitching	W	L	ERA	IP	H	BB	SO	Sv
Shaw	4	2	2.38	94.2	79	12	74	42
Sullivan......	5	3	3.24	97.1	79	30	96	1
Tomko	11	7	3.43	126.0	106	47	95	0
Belinda......	1	5	3.71	99.1	84	33	114	1
Mercker	8	11	3.92	144.2	135	62	75	0
Remlinger....	8	8	4.14	124.0	100	60	145	2
Burba	11	10	4.73	160.0	157	73	131	0
Morgan......	9	12	4.78	162.0	165	49	103	0
Smiley	9	10	5.23	117.0	139	31	94	0
Schourek	5	8	5.42	84.2	78	38	59	0

Manager—Ray Knight; Jack McKeon

Colorado Rockies

Batting	AB	R	H	HR	RBI	SB	AVG
Walker	568	143	208	49	130	33	.366
Galarraga	600	120	191	41	140	15	.318
Bichette	561	81	173	26	118	6	.308
Castilla	612	94	186	40	113	2	.304
J. Reed.........	256	43	76	17	47	2	.297
McCracken	325	69	95	3	36	28	.292
Perez	313	46	91	5	31	4	.291
Burks	424	91	123	32	82	7	.290
Weiss	393	52	106	4	38	5	.270
Manwaring	337	22	76	1	27	1	.226
Vander Wal.....	92	7	16	1	11	1	.174

Pitching	W	L	ERA	IP	H	BB	SO	Sv
Astacio	12	10	4.14	202.1	200	61	166	0
Bailey	9	10	4.29	191.0	210	70	84	0
DiPoto	5	3	4.70	95.2	108	33	74	16
Thomson.....	7	9	4.71	166.1	193	51	106	0
Holmes......	9	2	5.34	89.1	113	36	70	3
Castillo	12	12	5.42	184.1	220	69	126	0
Ritz..........	6	8	5.87	107.1	142	46	56	0
Wright.......	8	12	6.25	149.2	198	71	59	0

Manager—Don Baylor

Florida Marlins

Batting	AB	R	H	HR	RBI	SB	AVG
Counsell	164	20	49	1	16	1	.299
Bonilla	562	77	167	17	96	6	.297
Alou	538	88	157	23	115	9	.292
Eisenreich.......	293	36	82	2	34	0	.280
Renteria	617	90	171	4	52	32	.277
Abbott..........	252	35	69	6	30	3	.274
Daulton	395	68	104	14	63	6	.263
Johnson	416	43	104	19	63	0	.250
Sheffield	444	86	111	21	71	11	.250
White	265	37	65	6	34	13	.245
Cangelosi	192	28	47	1	12	5	.245
Conine	405	46	98	17	61	2	.242
Castillo	263	27	63	0	8	16	.240

Pitching	W	L	ERA	IP	H	BB	SO	Sv
Brown.......	16	8	2.69	237.1	214	66	205	0
Jernandez....	9	3	3.18	96.1	81	38	72	0
Fernandez....	17	12	3.59	220.2	193	69	183	0
Pall..........	0	0	3.86	2.1	3	1	0	0
Nen	9	3	3.89	74.0	72	40	81	35
Leiter	11	9	4.34	151.1	133	91	132	0
Helling	2	6	4.38	76.0	61	48	53	0
Saunders	4	6	4.61	111.1	99	64	102	0

Manager—Jim Leyland

Houston Astros

Batting	AB	R	H	HR	RBI	SB	AVG
Spiers	291	51	93	4	48	10	.320
Biggio	619	146	191	22	81	47	.309
Bagwell	566	109	162	43	135	31	.286
Carr.	192	34	53	4	17	11	.276
Bell	493	67	136	15	71	15	.276
Eusebio........	164	12	45	1	18	0	.274
Ausmus	425	45	113	4	44	14	.266
Gutierrez	303	33	79	3	34	5	.261
Gonzalez.......	550	78	142	10	68	10	.258
Berry	301	37	77	8	43	1	.256
Abreau.........	188	22	47	3	26	7	.250
Bogar.	241	30	60	4	30	4	.249
Howard	255	24	63	3	22	1	.247
Mouton	180	24	38	3	23	9	.211

Pitching	W	L	ERA	IP	H	BB	SO	Sv
Kile	19	7	2.57	255.2	208	94	205	0
Wagner	7	8	2.85	66.1	49	30	106	23
Holt	8	12	3.52	209.2	211	61	95	0
Garcia	9	8	3.69	158.2	155	52	120	1
Hampton	15	10	3.83	223.0	217	77	139	0
Reynolds	9	10	4.23	181.0	189	47	152	0
Lima	1	6	5.28	75.0	79	16	63	2

Manager—Larry Dierker

Los Angeles Dodgers

Batting	AB	R	H	HR	RBI	SB	AVG
Piazza	556	104	201	40	124	5	.362
Mondesi........	616	95	191	30	87	32	.310
Guerro.........	357	39	104	4	32	6	.291
Butler..........	343	52	97	0	18	15	.283
Young	622	106	174	8	61	45	.280
Nixon	175	30	48	1	18	12	.274
Cedeno	194	31	53	3	17	9	.273
Zeile	575	89	154	31	90	8	.268
Karros	628	86	167	31	104	15	.266
Gange	514	49	129	9	57	2	.251
Hollandsworth ...	296	39	73	4	31	5	.247

Pitching	W	L	ERA	IP	H	BB	SO	Sv
Valdes	10	11	2.65	196.2	171	47	140	0
Park..........	14	8	3.38	192.0	149	70	166	0
Candiotti	10	7	3.60	135.0	128	40	89	0
Martinez......	10	5	3.64	133.2	123	68	120	0
Nomo........	14	12	4.25	207.1	193	92	233	0
Worrell.......	2	6	5.28	59.2	60	23	61	35

Manager—Bill Russell

Montreal Expos

Batting	AB	R	H	HR	RBI	SB	AVG
Segui..........	459	75	141	21	68	1	.307
Guerrero	325	44	98	11	40	3	.302
Lansing	572	86	161	20	70	11	.281
Fletcher	310	39	86	17	55	1	.277
Grudzielanek	649	76	177	4	51	25	.273
White..........	592	84	160	28	82	16	.270
Strange	327	40	84	12	47	0	.257
McGuire........	199	22	51	3	17	1	.256
Santangelo.	350	56	87	5	31	8	.249
Vidro	169	19	42	2	17	1	.249
Rodriguez	476	55	116	26	83	3	.244
Widger.........	278	30	65	7	37	2	.234
Orsulak	150	13	34	1	7	0	.227

Pitching	W	L	ERA	IP	H	BB	SO	Sv
Martinez......	17	8	1.90	241.1	158	67	305	0
Valdes	4	4	3.13	95.0	84	39	54	2
Telford	4	6	3.24	89.0	77	33	61	1
Hermanson ...	8	8	3.69	158.1	134	66	136	0
Urbina	5	8	3.78	64.1	52	29	84	27
Perez.........	12	13	3.88	206.2	206	48	110	0
Juden	11	5	4.22	130.0	125	57	107	0
Bullinger......	7	12	5.56	155.1	165	74	87	0

Manager—Felipe Alou

New York Mets

Batting	AB	R	H	HR	RBI	SB	AVG
Alfonzo	518	84	163	10	72	11	.315
Olerud	524	90	154	22	102	0	.294
Huskey	471	61	135	24	81	8	.287
Baerga	467	53	131	9	52	2	.281
M. Franco	163	21	45	5	21	1	.276
Hundley	417	78	114	30	86	2	.273
Lopez	178	19	48	1	19	2	.270
Gilkey	518	85	129	18	78	7	.249
Everett	443	58	110	14	57	17	.248
Ochoa	238	31	58	3	22	3	.244
McRae	562	86	136	11	43	17	.242
Ordonez	356	35	77	1	33	11	.216

Pitching	W	L	ERA	IP	H	BB	SO	Sv
J. Franco	5	3	2.55	60.0	49	20	53	36
Reed	13	9	2.89	208.1	186	31	113	0
McMichael	7	10	2.98	87.2	73	27	81	7
Lidle	7	2	3.53	81.2	86	20	54	2
Jones	15	9	3.63	193.1	177	63	125	0
Bohanon	6	4	3.82	94.1	95	34	66	0
Mlicki	8	12	4.00	193.2	194	76	157	0
Wendell	3	5	4.36	76.1	68	53	64	5
Renoso	6	3	4.53	91.1	95	29	47	0
Rojas	0	6	4.64	85.1	78	36	93	15

Manager—Bobby Valentine

St. Louis Cardinals

Batting	AB	R	H	HR	RBI	SB	AVG
McGee	300	29	90	3	38	8	.300
DeShields	572	92	169	11	58	55	.295
Lankford	465	94	137	31	98	21	.295
Mabry	388	40	110	5	36	0	.284
Clayton	576	75	153	9	61	30	.266
Young	333	38	86	5	34	6	.258
McGwire	174	38	44	24	42	2	.253
Gaetti	502	63	126	17	69	7	.251
Lampkin	229	28	56	7	22	2	.245
Difelice	260	16	62	4	30	1	.238
Gant	502	68	115	17	62	14	.229

Pitching	W	L	ERA	IP	H	BB	SO	Sv
Frascatore	5	2	2.48	80.0	74	33	58	0
Al. Benes	9	9	2.89	161.2	128	68	160	0
An. Benes	10	7	3.10	177.0	149	61	175	0
Morris	12	9	3.19	217.0	208	69	149	0
Stottlemyre	12	9	3.88	181.0	155	65	160	0
Eckersley	1	5	3.91	53.0	49	8	45	36
Osborne	3	7	4.93	80.1	84	23	51	0
Valenzuela	2	12	4.96	89.0	106	46	61	0
Petkovsek	4	7	5.06	96.0	109	31	51	2

Manager—Tony La Russa

Philadelphia Phillies

Batting	AB	R	H	HR	RBI	SB	AVG
Morandini	553	83	163	1	39	16	.295
Barron	189	22	54	4	24	0	.286
Rolen	561	93	159	21	92	16	.283
Stocker	504	51	134	4	40	11	.266
Jordan	177	19	47	6	30	0	.266
Cummings	314	35	83	4	31	2	.264
Jefferies	476	68	122	11	48	12	.256
Brogna	543	68	137	20	81	12	.252
Otero	151	20	38	0	3	0	.252
Lieberthal	455	59	112	20	77	3	.246
Amaro	175	18	41	2	21	1	.234

Pitching	W	L	ERA	IP	H	BB	SO	Sv
Schilling	17	11	2.97	254.1	208	58	319	0
Stephenson	8	6	3.15	117.0	104	38	81	0
Bottalico	2	5	3.65	74.0	68	42	89	34
Spradin	4	8	4.74	81.2	86	27	67	1
Green	4	4	4.93	76.2	72	45	58	0
Beech	4	9	5.07	136.2	147	57	120	0
Leiter	10	17	5.67	182.2	216	64	148	0
Maduro	3	7	7.23	71.0	83	41	31	0

Manager—Terry Francona

San Diego Padres

Batting	AB	R	H	HR	RBI	SB	AVG
Gwynn	592	97	220	17	119	12	.372
Joyner	455	59	149	13	83	3	.327
Caminiti	486	92	141	26	90	11	.290
Sweeney	164	16	46	2	23	2	.280
Henderson	288	63	79	6	27	29	.274
Flaherty	439	38	120	9	46	4	.273
Q. Veras	539	74	143	3	45	33	.265
Finley	560	101	146	28	92	15	.261
Gomez	522	62	132	5	54	5	.253
Cianfrocco	220	25	54	4	26	7	.245
Jones	152	24	37	7	25	7	.243
Vaughn	361	60	78	18	57	7	.216

Pitching	W	L	ERA	IP	H	BB	SO	Sv
Hoffman	6	4	2.66	81.1	59	24	111	37
Ashby	9	11	4.13	200.2	207	49	144	0
Hamilton	12	7	4.25	192.2	199	69	124	0
Smith	7	6	4.81	118.0	120	52	68	1
Worrell	4	8	5.16	106.1	116	50	81	3
Hitchcock	10	11	5.20	161.0	172	55	106	0
Cunnane	6	3	5.81	91.1	114	49	79	0
Bergman	2	4	6.09	99.0	126	38	74	0

Manager—Bruce Bochy

Pittsburgh Pirates

Batting	AB	R	H	HR	RBI	SB	AVG
Ward	167	33	59	7	33	4	.353
Randa	443	58	134	7	60	4	.302
Young	333	59	100	18	74	11	.300
Dunston	490	71	147	14	57	32	.300
Kendall	486	71	143	8	49	18	.294
Martin	423	64	123	13	59	23	.291
Smith	193	29	55	9	35	3	.285
Womack	641	85	178	6	50	60	.278
Polcovich	245	37	67	4	21	2	.273
Guillen	498	58	133	14	70	1	.267
Sveum	306	30	80	12	47	0	.261
Allensworth	369	55	94	3	43	14	.255
M. Johnson	219	30	47	4	29	1	.215

Pitching	W	L	ERA	IP	H	BB	SO	Sv
Loiselle	1	5	3.10	72.2	76	24	66	29
Cordova	11	8	3.63	178.2	75	49	121	0
Wilkins	9	5	3.69	75.2	65	33	47	2
Loaiza	11	11	4.13	196.1	214	56	122	0
Cooke	9	15	4.30	167.1	184	77	109	0
Lieber	11	14	4.49	188.1	193	51	160	0
Schmidt	10	9	4.60	187.2	193	76	136	0

Manager—Gene Lamont

San Francisco Giants

Batting	AB	R	H	HR	RBI	SB	AVG
Mueller	390	51	114	7	44	4	.292
Bonds	532	123	155	40	101	37	.291
Javier	440	69	126	8	50	25	.286
Snow	531	81	149	28	104	6	.281
Johnson	179	19	50	11	27	0	.279
Hamilton	460	78	124	5	43	15	.270
Lewis	341	50	91	10	42	3	.267
Vizcaino	568	77	151	5	50	8	.266
Hill	398	47	104	11	64	7	.261
Berryhill	167	17	43	3	23	0	.257
Kent	580	90	145	29	121	11	.250
Wilkins	190	18	37	6	23	0	.195

Pitching	W	L	ERA	IP	H	BB	SO	Sv
Estes	19	5	3.18	201.0	162	100	181	0
Rueter	13	6	3.45	190.2	194	51	115	0
Beck	7	4	3.47	70.0	67	8	53	37
Tavarez	6	4	3.87	88.1	91	34	38	0
Mulholland	6	13	4.24	186.2	190	51	99	0
Gardner	12	9	4.29	180.1	188	57	136	0
Henry	4	5	4.71	70.2	70	41	69	3
Rapp	5	8	4.83	141.2	158	72	92	0
VanLandingham	4	7	4.96	89.0	80	59	52	0

Manager—Dusty Baker

American League Final Standings, 1997

Eastern Division

	W	L	Pct.	GB	Home	vs. East	vs. Central	vs. West	vs. NL
Baltimore	98	64	.605	—	46-35	25-23	33-22	32-12	8-7
New York*	96	66	.593	2	47-33	29-19	38-17	24-20	5-10
Detroit	79	83	.488	19	42-39	21-27	26-29	24-20	8-7
Boston	78	84	.481	20	39-42	22-26	28-27	22-22	6-9
Toronto	76	86	.469	22	42-39	23-25	29-26	20-24	4-11

Central Division

	W	L	Pct.	GB	Home	vs. East	vs. Central	vs. West	vs. NL
Cleveland.	86	75	.534	—	44-37	27-28	31-16	19-25	9-6
Chicago	80	81	.497	6	45-36	25-30	26-21	21-23	8-7
Milwaukee	78	83	.484	8	47-33	27-28	22-25	21-23	8-7
Minnesota	68	94	.420	18½	35-46	17-38	22-26	22-22	7-8
Kansas City	67	94	.416	19	33-47	25-30	17-30	19-25	6-9

Western Division

	W	L	Pct.	GB	Home	vs. East	vs. Central	vs. West	vs. NL
Seattle	90	72	.556	—	45-36	30-25	32-23	21-15	7-9
Anaheim	84	78	.519	6	46-36	25-30	30-25	25-11	4-12
Texas	77	85	.475	13	39-42	21-34	31-24	15-21	10-6
Oakland	65	97	.401	25	35-46	22-33	25-30	11-25	7-9

*Wild card team.

American League Playoff Results, 1997

Division Series

Baltimore defeated Seatlle 3 games to 1 (9-3, 9-3, 2-4, 3-1)
Cleveland defeated New York 3 games to 2 (6-8, 7-5, 1-6, 3-2, 4-3)

Championship Series

Cleveland defeated Baltimore 4 games to 2 (0-3, 5-4, 2-1 [12], 8-7, 2-4, 1-0 [11])

American League Statistics, 1997

(Individual Statistics: Batting—at least 150 at-bats; Pitching—at least 70 innings or 10 saves)

Team Batting

	Avg	AB	R	H	HR	RBI
Boston . . .	.291	5,779	850	1,683	185	810
New York . .	.287	5,710	891	1,636	161	846
Cleveland . .	.286	5,556	868	1,589	220	810
Seattle . . .	.280	5,614	925	1,574	264	890
Texas	.274	5,653	807	1,548	187	773
Chicago . . .	.273	5,491	779	1,498	158	740
Anaheim . .	.272	5,628	829	1,531	161	775
Minnesota . .	.270	5,634	772	1,522	132	730
Baltimore . .	.268	5,584	812	1,498	196	780
Kansas City .	.264	5,599	747	1,478	158	711
Milwaukee . .	.260	5,444	681	1,415	135	643
Oakland . . .	.260	5,589	763	1,451	197	714
Detroit . . .	.258	5,481	784	1,415	176	743
Toronto . . .	.244	5,473	655	1,333	147	627

Team Pitching

	ERA	IP	H	BB	SO	Sv
New York . .	3.84	1,467.2	1,463	532	1,165	51
Baltimore . .	3.91	1,461.0	1,404	563	1,139	59
Toronto . . .	3.92	1,442.2	1,452	497	1,150	35
Milwaukee .	4.24	1,423.2	1,419	541	1,012	44
Anaheim . .	4.52	1,454.2	1,506	605	1,050	39
Detroit . . .	4.56	1,445.2	1,476	552	982	42
Texas	4.69	1,428.2	1,593	541	925	33
Kansas City	4.71	1,443.0	1,530	531	961	29
Cleveland .	4.73	1,425.2	1,528	575	1,036	39
Chicago . .	4.74	1,422.1	1,505	575	961	52
Seattle . . .	4.79	1,447.2	1,500	598	1,207	38
Boston . . .	4.88	1,448.2	1,567	610	987	40
Minnesota .	5.02	1,434.0	1,596	495	908	30
Oakland . .	5.49	1,445.1	1,734	642	953	38

Anaheim Angels

Batting	AB	R	H	HR	RBI	SB	AVG
Anderson . . .	624	76	189	8	92	10	.303
Erstad.	539	99	161	16	77	23	.299
Salmon.	582	95	172	33	129	9	.296
Edmonds . . .	502	82	146	26	80	5	.291
Hollins	572	101	165	16	85	16	.288
Phillips	534	96	147	8	57	13	.275
Howell	174	25	45	14	34	1	.259
Alicea.	388	59	98	5	37	22	.253
DiSarcina . . .	549	52	135	4	47	7	.246
Kreuter	255	25	59	5	21	0	.231
Murray	160	13	35	3	15	1	.219

Pitching	W	L	ERA	IP	H	BB	SO	Sv
Percival.	5	5	3.46	52.0	40	22	72	27
Harris	5	4	3.62	79.2	82	38	56	0
Hasegawa. . .	3	7	3.93	116.2	118	46	83	0
Finley	13	6	4.23	164.0	152	65	155	0
Dickson.	13	9	4.29	203.2	236	56	115	0
Hill	9	12	4.55	190.0	194	95	106	0
Watson	12	12	4.93	199.0	220	73	141	0
Springer	9	9	5.18	194.2	199	73	75	0

Manager—Terry Collins

Baltimore Orioles

Batting	AB	R	H	HR	RBI	SB	AVG
Alomar.	412	64	137	14	60	9	.333
Davis.	158	29	48	8	25	6	.304
Baines.	452	55	136	16	67	0	.301
Anderson.	590	97	170	18	73	18	.288
Surhoff.	528	80	150	18	88	1	.284
Berroa.	561	88	159	26	90	4	.283
Ripken.	615	79	166	17	84	1	.270
Hammonds	397	71	105	21	55	15	.264
Hoiles	320	45	83	12	49	1	.259
Webster.	259	29	66	7	37	0	.255
Palmeiro	614	95	156	38	110	5	.254
Reboulet	228	26	54	4	27	3	.237
Bordick	509	55	120	7	46	0	.236
Tarasco.	166	26	34	7	26	2	.205

Pitching	W	L	ERA	IP	H	BB	SO	Sv
Myers	2	3	1.51	59.2	47	22	56	45
Benitez	4	5	2.45	73.1	49	43	106	9
Rhodes	10	3	3.02	95.1	75	26	102	1

Pitching	W	L	ERA	IP	H	BB	SO	Sv
Mussina	15	8	3.20	224.2	197	54	218	0
Key	16	10	3.43	212.1	210	82	141	0
Erickson	16	7	3.69	221.2	218	61	131	0
Kamieniecki	10	6	4.01	179.1	179	67	109	0
Boskie	6	6	6.43	77.0	95	26	50	1

Manager—Davey Johnson

Boston Red Sox

Batting	AB	R	H	HR	RBI	SB	AVG
Jefferson	489	74	156	13	67	1	.319
Vaughn	527	91	166	35	96	2	.315
Frye	404	56	126	3	51	19	.312
O'Leary	499	65	154	15	80	0	.309
Valentin	575	95	176	18	77	7	.306
Garciaparra	684	122	209	30	98	22	.306
Naehring	259	38	74	9	40	1	.286
Cordero	570	82	160	18	72	1	.281
Hatteberg	350	46	97	10	44	0	.277
Bragg	513	65	132	9	57	10	.257
Haselman	212	22	50	6	26	0	.236
Pride	164	22	35	3	20	6	.213

Pitching	W	L	ERA	IP	H	BB	SO	Sv
Henry	7	3	3.52	84.1	89	19	51	6
Gordon	6	10	3.74	182.2	155	78	159	11
Wakefield	12	15	4.25	201.1	193	87	151	0
Wasdin	4	6	4.40	124.2	121	38	84	0
Sele	13	12	5.38	177.1	196	80	122	0
Suppan	7	3	5.69	112.1	140	36	67	0
Avery	6	7	6.42	96.2	127	49	51	0

Manager—Jimy Williams

Chicago White Sox

Batting	AB	R	H	HR	RBI	SB	AVG
F. Thomas	530	110	184	35	125	1	.347
Martin	213	24	64	2	27	1	.300
Martinez	504	78	144	12	55	12	.286
Belle	634	90	174	30	116	4	.274
Durham	634	106	172	11	53	33	.271
Mouton	242	26	65	5	23	4	.269
Ventura	183	27	48	6	26	0	.262
Cameron	379	63	98	14	55	23	.259
Fabregas	360	33	93	7	51	1	.258
Guillen	490	59	120	4	52	5	.245
Snopek	298	27	65	5	35	3	.218

Pitching	W	L	ERA	IP	H	BB	SO	Sv
Hernandez	5	1	2.44	48.0	38	24	47	27
Karchner	3	1	2.91	52.2	50	26	30	15
Alvarez	9	8	3.03	145.2	126	55	110	0
McElroy	1	3	3.84	75.0	73	22	62	1
D. Darwin	4	8	4.13	113.1	130	31	62	0
Baldwin	12	15	5.27	200.0	205	83	140	0
Drabek	12	11	5.74	169.1	170	69	85	0
Navarro	9	14	5.79	209.2	267	73	142	0

Manager—Terry Bevington

Cleveland Indians

Batting	AB	R	H	HR	RBI	SB	AVG
Justice	495	84	163	33	101	3	.329
Ramirez	561	99	184	26	88	2	.328
Alomar	451	63	146	21	83	0	.324
Roberts	431	63	130	4	44	18	.302
Borders	159	17	47	4	15	0	.296
Thome	496	104	142	40	102	1	.286
Fernandez	409	55	117	11	44	6	.286
Vizquel	565	89	158	5	49	43	.280
Giles	377	62	101	17	61	13	.268
Seitzer	198	27	53	2	24	0	.268
Williams	596	86	157	32	105	12	.263
Grissom	558	74	146	12	66	22	.262

Pitching	W	L	ERA	IP	H	BB	SO	Sv
Mesa	4	4	2.40	82.1	83	28	69	16
M. Jackson	2	5	3.24	75.0	59	29	74	15
Nagy	15	11	4.28	227.0	253	77	149	0
Wright	8	3	4.38	90.1	81	35	63	0
Hershiser	14	6	4.47	195.1	199	69	107	0
Ogea	8	9	4.99	126.1	139	47	80	0
Colon	4	7	5.65	94.0	107	45	66	0

Pitching	W	L	ERA	IP	H	BB	SO	Sv
Lopez	3	7	6.93	76.2	101	40	63	0

Manager—Mike Hargrove

Detroit Tigers

Batting	AB	R	H	HR	RBI	SB	AVG
Higginson	546	94	163	27	101	12	.299
Clark	580	105	160	32	117	1	.276
Fryman	595	90	163	22	102	16	.274
Hamelin	318	47	86	18	52	2	.270
Hunter	658	112	177	4	45	74	.269
Easley	527	97	139	22	72	28	.264
Casanova	304	27	74	5	24	1	.243
Cruz	436	35	105	2	40	3	.241
Nevin	251	32	59	9	35	0	.235
Nieves	359	46	82	20	64	1	.228

Pitching	W	L	ERA	IP	H	BB	SO	Sv
Thompson	15	11	3.02	223.1	188	66	151	0
Jones	5	4	3.09	70.0	60	35	70	31
Brocail	3	4	3.23	78.0	74	36	60	2
Blair	16	8	4.17	175.0	186	46	90	0
Sager	3	4	4.18	84.0	81	24	53	3
Moehler	11	12	4.67	175.1	198	61	97	0
Miceli	3	2	5.01	82.2	77	38	79	3
Sanders	6	14	5.86	139.2	152	62	120	2

Manager—Buddy Bell

Kansas City Royals

Batting	AB	R	H	HR	RBI	SB	AVG
Offerman	424	59	126	2	39	9	.297
Bell	573	89	167	21	92	10	.291
Davis	477	71	133	30	90	6	.279
Damon	472	70	130	8	48	16	.275
Benitez	191	22	51	8	21	2	.267
Palmer	542	70	139	23	86	2	.256
Sweeney	240	30	58	7	31	3	.242
Howard	162	24	39	1	13	2	.241
King	543	84	129	28	112	16	.238
Macfarlane	257	34	61	8	35	0	.237
Dye	263	26	62	7	22	2	.236
Paquette	252	26	58	8	33	2	.230
Cooper	159	12	32	3	15	1	.201

Pitching	W	L	ERA	IP	H	BB	SO	Sv
Appier	9	13	3.40	235.2	215	74	196	0
Montgomery	1	4	3.49	59.1	53	18	48	14
Pichardo	3	5	4.22	49.0	51	24	34	11
Rosado	9	12	4.69	203.1	208	73	129	0
Belcher	13	12	5.02	213.1	242	70	113	0
Pittsley	5	8	5.46	112.0	120	54	52	0
Rusch	6	9	5.50	170.1	206	52	116	0
Bones	4	7	5.97	78.1	102	25	36	0

Manager—Bob Boone; Tony Muser

Milwaukee Brewers

Batting	AB	R	H	HR	RBI	SB	AVG
Cirillo	580	74	167	10	82	4	.288
Loretta	418	56	120	5	47	5	.287
Levis	200	19	57	1	19	1	.285
Burnitz	494	85	139	27	85	20	.281
Nilsson	554	71	154	20	81	2	.278
Vina	324	37	89	4	28	8	.275
Franco	430	68	116	7	44	15	.270
Jackson	211	26	55	5	36	4	.261
Valentin	494	58	125	17	58	19	.253
Williams	566	73	143	10	41	23	.253
Mieske	253	39	63	5	21	1	.249
Jaha	162	25	40	11	26	1	.247
Voigt	151	20	37	8	22	1	.245
Matheny	320	29	78	4	32	0	.244
Newfield	157	14	36	1	18	0	.229

Pitching	W	L	ERA	IP	H	BB	SO	SV
Jones	6	6	2.02	80.1	62	9	82	36
Wickman	7	6	2.73	95.2	89	41	78	1
Fetters	1	5	3.45	70.1	62	33	62	6
Adamson	5	3	3.54	76.1	78	19	56	0
Mercedes	7	10	3.79	159.0	146	53	80	0
McDonald	8	7	4.06	133.0	120	36	110	0
Florie	4	4	4.33	75.0	71	12	60	0
Karl	10	13	4.47	193.1	212	67	119	0
D'Amico	9	7	4.71	135.2	139	43	94	0
Eldred	13	15	4.99	202.0	207	89	122	0

Manager—Phil Garner

Minnesota Twins

Batting	AB	R	H	HR	RBI	SB	AVG
Molitor	538	63	164	10	89	11	.305
Coomer	523	63	156	13	85	4	.298
Knoblauch	611	117	178	9	58	62	.291
Colbrunn	217	24	61	5	26	1	.281
Meares	439	63	121	10	60	7	.276
Brede	190	25	52	3	21	7	.274
Myers	165	24	44	5	28	0	.267
Becker	443	61	117	10	45	17	.264
Hocking	253	28	65	2	25	3	.257
Steinbach	447	60	111	12	54	6	.248
Lawton	460	74	114	14	60	7	.248
Cordova	378	44	93	15	51	5	.246
Walker	156	15	37	3	16	7	.237
Stahoviak	275	33	63	10	33	5	.229

Pitching	W	L	ERA	IP	H	BB	SO	Sv
Swindell	7	4	3.58	115.2	102	25	75	1
Aguilera	5	4	3.82	68.1	65	22	68	26
Radke	20	10	3.87	239.2	238	48	174	0
Tewksbury	8	13	4.22	168.2	200	31	92	0
Trombley	2	3	4.37	82.1	77	31	74	1
Ritchie	2	3	4.58	74.2	87	28	44	0
Rodriguez	3	6	4.62	142.1	147	60	65	0
Robertson	8	12	5.69	147.0	169	70	69	0
Hawkins	6	12	5.84	103.1	134	47	58	0
Aldred	2	10	7.68	77.1	102	28	33	0

Manager—Tom Kelly

New York Yankees

Batting	AB	R	H	HR	RBI	SB	AVG
Williams	509	107	167	21	100	15	.328
O'Neill	553	89	179	21	117	10	.324
Raines	271	56	87	4	38	8	.321
Sojo	215	27	66	2	25	3	.307
Stanley	347	61	103	16	65	0	.297
Martinez	594	96	176	44	141	3	.296
Boggs	353	55	103	4	28	0	.292
Jeter	654	116	190	10	70	23	.291
Curtis	349	59	99	15	55	12	.284
Whiten	215	34	57	5	24	4	.265
Girardi	398	38	105	1	50	2	.264
Fielder	361	40	94	13	61	0	.260
Hayes	353	39	91	11	53	3	.258
Posada	188	29	47	6	25	1	.250
Incaviglia	154	19	38	5	12	0	.247

Pitching	W	L	ERA	IP	H	BB	SO	Sv
Rivera	6	4	1.88	71.2	65	20	68	43
Cone	12	6	2.82	195.0	155	86	222	0
Nelson	3	7	2.86	78.2	53	37	81	2
Pettitte	18	7	2.88	240.1	233	65	166	0
Wells	16	10	4.21	218.0	239	45	156	0
Mendoza	8	6	4.24	133.2	157	28	82	2
Gooden	9	5	4.91	106.1	116	53	66	0
Rogers	6	7	5.65	145.0	161	62	78	0

Manager—Joe Torre

Oakland Athletics

Batting	AB	R	H	HR	RBI	SB	AVG
Magadan	271	38	82	4	30	1	.303
Stairs	352	62	105	27	73	3	.298
Giambi	519	66	152	20	81	0	.293
Mayne	256	29	74	6	22	1	.289
Williams	201	30	58	3	22	0	.289
McGwire	366	48	104	34	81	1	.284
Bournigal	222	29	62	1	20	2	.279
McDonald	236	47	62	4	14	13	.263
Mashore	279	55	69	3	18	5	.247
Spiezio	538	58	131	14	65	9	.243
Brito	172	17	41	2	14	1	.238
Canseco	388	56	91	23	74	8	.235
Bellhorn	224	33	51	6	19	7	.228
Young	175	22	39	5	15	1	.223
Brosius	479	59	97	11	41	9	.203
Batista	188	22	38	4	18	2	.202

Pitching	W	L	ERA	IP	H	BB	SO	Sv
Taylor	3	4	3.82	73.0	70	36	66	23
Small	9	5	4.28	96.2	109	40	57	4
Haynes	3	6	4.42	73.1	74	40	65	0
Rigby	1	7	4.87	77.2	92	22	34	0
Oquist	4	6	5.02	107.2	111	43	72	0
Prieto	6	8	5.04	125.0	155	70	90	0
Mohler	1	10	5.13	101.2	116	54	66	1
Karsay	3	12	5.77	132.2	166	47	92	0

Pitching	W	L	ERA	IP	H	BB	SO	Sv
Reyes	3	4	5.82	77.1	101	25	43	0
Wengert	5	11	6.04	134.0	177	41	68	2
Telgheder	4	6	6.06	101.0	134	35	55	0

Manager—Art Howe

Seattle Mariners

Batting	AB	R	H	HR	RBI	SB	AVG
E. Martinez	542	104	179	28	108	2	.330
Griffey	608	125	185	56	147	15	.304
Rodriguez	587	100	176	23	84	29	.300
Cora	574	105	172	11	54	6	.300
Blowers	150	22	44	5	20	0	.293
Kelly	368	58	107	12	59	9	.291
Ducey	143	25	41	5	10	3	.287
Amaral	190	34	54	1	21	12	.284
R. Davis	420	57	114	20	63	6	.271
Wilson	508	66	137	15	74	7	.270
Sorrento	457	68	123	31	80	0	.269
Buhner	540	104	131	40	109	0	.243
Gates	151	18	36	3	20	0	.238
Tinsley	122	12	24	0	6	2	.197

Pitching	W	L	ERA	IP	H	BB	SO	Sv
Johnson	20	4	2.28	213.0	147	77	291	0
Timlin	6	4	3.22	72.2	69	20	45	10
Fassero	16	9	3.61	234.1	226	84	189	0
Spoljaric	0	3	3.69	70.2	61	36	70	3
Ayala	10	5	3.82	96.2	91	41	92	8
Moyer	17	5	3.86	188.2	187	43	113	0
Olivares	6	10	4.97	177.1	191	81	103	0
Slocumb	0	9	5.16	75.0	84	49	64	27
Wolcott	5	6	6.03	100.0	129	29	58	0
Lira	5	11	6.34	110.2	132	55	73	0
Charlton	3	8	7.27	69.1	89	47	55	14

Manager—Lou Piniella

Texas Rangers

Batting	AB	R	H	HR	RBI	SB	AVG
W. Clark	393	56	128	12	51	0	.326
Greer	601	112	193	26	87	9	.321
Rodriguez	597	98	187	20	77	7	.313
Stevens	426	58	128	21	74	1	.300
Gonzalez	533	87	158	42	131	0	.296
Cedeno	365	49	103	4	36	3	.282
Leyritz	379	58	105	11	64	2	.277
Ripken	203	18	56	3	24	0	.276
McLemore	349	47	91	1	25	7	.261
Goodwin	574	90	149	2	39	50	.260
Tatis	223	29	57	8	29	3	.256
Buford	366	49	82	8	39	18	.224
Gil	317	35	71	5	31	1	.224
Newson	169	23	36	10	23	3	.213

Pitching	W	L	ERA	IP	H	BB	SO	Sv
Wetteland	7	2	1.94	65.0	43	21	63	31
Patterson	10	6	3.42	71.0	70	23	69	1
Oliver	13	12	4.20	201.1	213	82	104	0
Burkett	9	12	4.56	189.1	240	30	139	0
Witt	12	12	4.82	209.0	245	74	121	0
Whiteside	4	1	5.08	72.2	85	26	44	0
Santana	4	6	6.75	104.0	141	49	64	0

Manager—Johnny Oates

Toronto Blue Jays

Batting	AB	R	H	HR	RBI	SB	AVG
Green	429	57	123	16	53	14	.287
Stewart	168	25	48	0	22	10	.286
Merced	368	45	98	9	40	7	.266
Delgado	519	79	136	30	91	0	.262
Nixon	401	54	105	1	26	47	.262
Cruz	395	59	98	26	68	7	.248
Santiago	341	31	83	13	42	1	.243
Gonzalez	426	46	102	12	35	15	.239
Duncan	339	36	80	1	25	6	.236
Carter	612	76	143	21	102	8	.234
Sprague	504	63	115	14	48	0	.228
Garcia	350	29	77	3	23	11	.220
O'Brien	225	22	49	4	27	0	.218
Brumfield	174	22	36	2	20	4	.207

Pitching	W	L	ERA	IP	H	BB	SO	Sv
Quantrill	6	7	1.94	88.0	103	17	56	5
Clemens	21	7	2.05	264.0	204	68	292	0
Escobar	3	2	2.90	31.0	28	19	36	14
Hentgen	15	10	3.68	264.0	253	71	160	0
Williams	9	14	4.35	194.2	201	66	124	0
Carpenter	3	7	5.09	81.1	108	37	55	0
Person	5	10	5.61	128.1	125	60	99	0

Manager—Cito Gaston, Mel Queen

National Baseball Hall of Fame and Museum, Cooperstown, NY

Aaron, Hank	Conlan, Jocko	Hafey, Chick	Lombardi, Ernie	Rusie, Amos
Alexander, Grover Cleveland	Connolly, Thomas H.	Haines, Jesee	Lopez, Al	Ruth, Babe
Alston, Walt	Connor, Roger	Hamilton, Bill	Lyons, Ted	Schalk, Ray
Anson, Cap	Coveleski, Stan	Hanlon, Ned	Mack, Connie	Schmidt, Mike
Aparicio, Luis	Crawford, Sam	Harridge, Will	MacPhail, Larry	Schoendienst, Red
Appling, Luke	Cronin, Joe	Harris, Bucky	Mantle, Mickey	Seaver, Tom
Ashburn, Richie	Cummings, Candy	Hartnett, Gabby	Manush, Henry	Sewell, Joe
Averill, Earl	Cuyler, Kiki	Heilmann, Harry	Maranville, Rabbit	Simmons, Al
Baker, Home Run	Dandridge, Ray	Herman, Billy	Marichal, Juan	Sisler, George
Bancroft, Dave	Day, Leon	Hooper, Harry	Marquard, Rube	Slaughter, Enos
Banks, Ernie	Dean, Dizzy	Hornsby, Rogers	Mathews, Eddie	Snider, Duke
Barlick, Al	Delahanty, Ed	Hoyt, Waite	Mathewson, Christy	Spahn, Warren
Barrow, Edward G.	Dickey, Bill	Hubbard, Cal	Mays, Willie	Spalding, Albert
Beckley, Jake	DiHigo, Martin	Hubbell, Carl	McCarthy, Joe	Speaker, Tris
Bell, Cool Papa	DiMaggio, Joe	Huggins, Miller	McCarthy, Thomas	Stargell, Willie
Bench, Johnny	Doerr, Bobby	Hulbert, William	McCovey, Willie	Stengel, Casey
Bender, Chief	Drysdale, Don	Hunter, Catfish	McGinnity, Joe	Terry, Bill
Berra, Yogi	Duffy, Hugh	Irvin, Monte	McGowan, Bill	Thompson, Sam
Bottomley, Jim	Durocher, Leo	Jackson, Reggie	McGraw, John	Tinker, Joe
Boudreau, Lou	Evans, Billy	Jackson, Travis	McKechnie, Bill	Traynor, Pie
Bresnahan, Roger	Evers, John	Jenkins, Ferguson	Medwick, Joe	Vance, Dazzy
Brock, Lou	Ewing, Buck	Jennings, Hugh	Mize, Johnny	Vaughan, Arky
Brouthers, Dan	Faber, Urban	Johnson, Byron	Morgan, Joe	Veeck, Bill
Brown, Mordecai (Three Finger)	Feller, Bob	Johnson, William (Judy)	Musial, Stan	Waddell, Rube
Bulkeley, Morgan C.	Ferrell, Rick	Johnson, Walter	Newhouser, Hal	Wagner, Honus
Bunning, Jim	Fingers, Rollie	Joss, Addie	Nichols, Kid	Wallace, Roderick
Burkett, Jesse C.	Flick, Elmer H.	Kaline, Al	**Niekro, Phil**	Walsh, Ed
Campanella, Roy	Ford, Whitey	Keefe, Timothy	O'Rourke, James	Waner, Lloyd
Carew, Rod	Foster, Andrew (Rube)	Keeler, William	Ott, Mel	Waner, Paul
Carey, Max	Foster, Bill	Kell, George	Paige, Satchel	Ward, John
Carlton, Steve	**Fox, Nellie**	Kelley, Joe	Palmer, Jim	Weaver, Earl
Cartwright, Alexander	Foxx, Jimmie	Kelly, George	Pennock, Herb	Weiss, George
Chadwick, Henry	Frick, Ford	Kelly, King	Perry, Gaylord	Welch, Mickey
Chance, Frank	Frisch, Frank	Killebrew, Harmon	Plank, Ed	**Wells, Willie**
Chandler, Happy	Galvin, Pud	Kiner, Ralph	Radbourn, Charlie	Wheat, Zach
Charleston, Oscar	Gehrig, Lou	Klein, Chuck	Reese, Pee Wee	Wilhelm, Hoyt
Chesbro, John	Gehringer, Charles	Klem, Bill	Rice, Sam	Williams, Billy
Clarke, Fred	Gibson, Bob	Koufax, Sandy	Rickey, Branch	Williams, Ted
Clarkson, John	Gibson, Josh	Lajoie, Napoleon	Rixey, Eppa	Williams, Vic
Clemente, Roberto	Giles, Warren	Landis, Kenesaw M.	Rizzuto, Phil (Scooter)	Wilson, Hack
Cobb, Ty	Gomez, Lefty	**Lasorda, Tom**	Roberts, Robin	Wright, George
Cochrane, Mickey	Goslin, Goose	Lazzeri, Tony	Robinson, Brooks	Wright, Harry
Collins, Eddie	Greenberg, Hank	Lemon, Bob	Robinson, Frank	Wynn, Early
Collins, James	Griffith, Clark	Leonard, Buck	Robinson, Jackie	Yastrzemski, Carl
Combs, Earle	Grimes, Burleigh	Lindstrom, Fred	Robinson, Wilbert	Yawkey, Tom
Comiskey, Charles A.	Grove, Lefty	Lloyd, Pop	Roush, Edd	Young, Cy
			Ruffing, Red	Youngs, Ross

Note: 1997 inductees are in **bold**.

Hall of Famers Chosen in First Year of Eligibility[1]

1962	Jackie Robinson, Bob Feller	**1977**	Ernie Banks	**1983**	Brooks Robinson	**1990**	Jim Palmer, Joe Morgan
1966	Ted Williams	**1979**	Willie Mays	**1985**	Lou Brock	**1991**	Rod Carew
1969	Stan Musial	**1980**	Al Kaline	**1986**	Willie McCovey	**1992**	Tom Seaver
1972	Sandy Koufax	**1981**	Bob Gibson	**1988**	Willie Stargell	**1993**	Reggie Jackson
1973	Warren Spahn	**1982**	Hank Aaron,	**1989**	Johnny Bench,	**1994**	Steve Carlton
1974	Mickey Mantle		Frank Robinson		Carl Yastrzemski	**1995**	Mike Schmidt

(1) Player must generally be retired for five complete seasons before being eligible for induction. List does not include players inducted in 1936 (the first year the Hall of Fame began): Ty Cobb, Walter Johnson, Christy Mathewson, Babe Ruth, and Honus Wagner. Four players, Babe Ruth (1936), Lou Gehrig (1939), Joe DiMaggio (1955), and Roberto Clemente (1973), were inducted less than five years after retirement or, in Clemente's case, death.

All-Star Baseball Games, 1933-1997

Year	Winner, Score	Host team	Year	Winner, Score	Host team	Year	Winner, Score	Host team
1933*	American, 4-2	Chicago (AL)	1956*	National, 7-3	Washington	1975	National, 6-3	Milwaukee
1934*	American, 9-7	New York (NL)	1957*	American, 6-5	St. Louis	1976	National, 7-1	Philadelphia
1935*	American, 4-1	Cleveland	1958*	American, 4-3	Baltimore	1977	National, 7-5	New York (AL)
1936*	National, 4-3	Boston (NL)	1959*	National, 5-4	Pittsburgh	1978	National, 7-3	San Diego
1937*	American, 8-3	Washington	1959*	American, 5-3	Los Angeles	1979	National, 7-6	Seattle
1938*	National, 4-1	Cincinnati	1960*	National, 5-3	Kansas City	1980	National, 4-2	Los Angeles
1939*	American, 3-1	New York (AL)	1960*	National, 6-0	New York (AL)	1981	National, 5-4	Cleveland
1940*	National, 4-0	St. Louis (NL)	1961*	National, 5-4 [1]	San Francisco	1982	National, 4-1	Montreal
1941*	American, 7-5	Detroit	1961*	Called–rain, 1-1	Boston	1983	American, 13-3	Chicago (AL)
1942*	American, 3-1	New York (NL)	1962*	National, 3-1 [1]	Washington	1984	National, 3-1	San Francisco
1943	American, 5-3	Philadelphia (AL)	1962*	American, 9-4	Chicago (NL)	1985	National, 6-1	Minnesota
1944	National, 7-1	Pittsburgh	1963*	National, 5-3	Cleveland	1986	American, 3-2	Houston
1945	(Not played)		1964*	National, 7-4	New York (NL)	1987	National, 2-0 [3]	Oakland
1946*	American, 12-0	Boston (AL)	1965*	National, 6-5	Minnesota	1988	American, 2-1	Cincinnati
1947*	American, 2-1	Chicago (NL)	1966*	National, 2-1 [1]	St. Louis	1989	American, 5-3	California
1948*	American, 5-2	St. Louis (AL)	1967*	National, 2-1 [5]	California	1990	American, 2-0	Chicago (NL)
1949*	American, 11-7	Brooklyn	1968	National, 1-0	Houston	1991	American, 4-2	Toronto
1950*	National, 4-3 [4]	Chicago (AL)	1969*	National, 9-3	Washington	1992	American, 13-6	San Diego
1951*	National, 8-3	Detroit	1970	National, 5-4 [2]	Cincinnati	1993	American, 9-3	Baltimore
1952*	National, 3-2	Philadelphia (NL)	1971	American, 6-4	Detroit	1994	National, 8-7 [1]	Pittsburgh
1953*	National, 5-1	Cincinnati	1972	National, 4-3	Atlanta	1995	National, 3-2	Texas
1954*	American, 11-9	Cleveland	1973	National, 7-1	Kansas City	1996	National, 6-0	Philadelphia
1955*	National, 6-5 [2]	Milwaukee	1974	National, 7-2	Pittsburgh	1997	American, 3-1	Cleveland

*Denotes day game. (1) 10 innings. (2) 12 innings. (3) 13 innings. (4) 14 innings. (5) 15 innings.

Major League Leaders in 1997

American League

Batting
F. Thomas, Chicago, .347; E. Martinez, Seattle, .330; Justice, Cleveland, .329; Ramirez, Cleveland, .328; B. Williams, New York, .328.

Runs
Griffey, Seattle, 125; Garciaparra, Boston, 122; Knoblauch, Minnesota, 117; Jeter, New York, 116; B. Hunter, Detroit, 112; Greer, Texas, 112.

Runs Batted In
Griffey, Seattle, 147; Martinez, New York, 141; J. Gonzalez, Texas, 131; Salmon, Anaheim, 129; F. Thomas, Chicago, 125.

Hits
Garciaparra, Boston, 209; Greer, Texas, 193; Jeter, New York, 190; Anderson, Anaheim, 189; Rodriguez, Texas, 187.

Doubles
Valetin, Boston, 47; Cirillo, Milwaukee, 46; Belle, Chicago, 45; Garciaparra, Boston, 44; Delgado, Toronto, 42; Greer, Texas, 42; O'Neill, New York, 42.

Triples
Garciaparra, Boston, 11; Knoblauch, Minnesota, 10; Burnitz, Milwaukee, 8; Damon, Kansas City, 8; Alicea, Anaheim, 7; Anderson, Baltimore, 7; Hunter, Detroit, 7; Jeter, New York, 7; Stewart, Toronto, 7.

Home Runs[1]
Griffey, Seattle, 56; Martinez, New York, 44; J. Gonzalez, Texas, 42; Buhner, Seattle, 40; Thome, Cleveland, 40.

Stolen Bases
Hunter, Detroit, 74; Knoblauch, Minnesota, 62; Goodwin, K.C.-Tex., 50; Nixon, Toronto, 47; Vizquel, Cleveland, 43.

Pitching (Most wins: W-L, ERA, Pct.)
Clemens, Toronto, 21-7, 2.05, .750; Johnson, Seattle, 20-4, 2.28, .833; Radke, Minnesota, 20-10, 3.87, .666; Pettitte, New York, 18-7, 2.88, .720; Moyer, Seattle, 17-5, 3.86, .773.

Strikeouts
Clemens, Toronto, 292; Johnson, Seattle, 291; Cone, New York, 222; Mussina, Baltimore, 218; Appier, Kansas City, 196.

Saves
Myers, Baltimore, 45; Rivera, New York, 43; Jones, Milwaukee, 36; Jones, Detroit, 31; Wetteland, Texas, 31.

National League

Batting
Gwynn, San Diego, .372; Walker, Colorado, .366; Piazza, Los Angeles, .362; Lofton, Atlanta, .333; Joyner, San Diego, .327.

Runs
Biggio, Houston, 146; Walker, Colorado, 143; Bonds, San Francisco, 123; Galarraga, Colorado, 120; Bagwell, Houston, 109.

Runs Batted In
Galarraga, Colorado, 140; Bagwell, Houston, 135; Walker, Colorado, 130; Piazza, Los Angeles, 124; Kent, San Francisco, 121.

Hits
Gwynn, San Diego, 220; Walker, Colorado, 208; Piazza, Los Angeles, 201; Biggio, Houston, 191; Galarraga, Colorado, 191.

Doubles
Grudzielanek, Montreal, 54; Gwynn, San Diego, 49; Walker, Colorado, 46; Lansing, Montreal, 45; Mondesi, Los Angeles, 42.

Triples
DeShields, St. Louis, 14; Perez, Colorado, 10; Guerrero, Los Angeles, 9; Randa, Pittsburgh, 9; Womack, Pittsburgh, 9.

Home Runs[1]
Walker, Colorado, 49; Bagwell, Houston, 43; Galarraga, Colorado, 41; Bonds, San Francisco, 40; Castilla, Colorado, 40; Piazza, Los Angeles, 40.

Stolen Bases
Womack, Pittsburgh, 60; D. Sanders, Cincinnati, 56; DeShields, St. Louis, 55; Biggio, Houston, 47; Young, Col.-L.A., 45.

Pitching (Most wins: W-L, ERA, Pct.)
Neagle, Atlanta, 20-5, 2.97, .800; Maddux, Atlanta, 19-4, 2.20, .826; Estes, San Francisco, 19-5, 3.18, .792; Kile, Houston, 19-7, 2.57, .731; Martinez, Montreal, 17-8, 1.90, .680.

Strikeouts
Schilling, Philadelphia, 319; Martinez, Montreal, 305; Smoltz, Atlanta, 241; Nomo, Los Angeles, 233; Brown, Florida, 205; Kile, Houston, 205.

Saves
Shaw, Cincinnati, 42; Beck, San Francisco, 37; Hoffman, San Diego, 37; Eckersley, St. Louis, 36; J. Franco, New York, 36.

(1) Mark McGwire lead the Major Leagues with 58 home runs, splitting them between the Oakland Athletics (AL), 34, and the St. Louis Cardinals (NL), 24.

McGwire Sets Home Run Pace

Mark McGwire became only the second player in Major League Baseball history to hit 50 or more home runs in two consecutive seasons. McGwire hit 52 in 1996 playing for the Oakland Athletics, and in 1997 he hit a combined total of 58 with Oakland and the St. Louis Cardinals. Playing for the New York Yankees, Babe Ruth achieved this feat twice in his illustrious career. In 1920, Ruth hit 54 home runs, and he hit 59 in 1921. After Ruth set the record for most home runs in a season in 1927 (60), a record that would not be broken until Roger Maris hit 61 in 1961, he followed with 54 home runs in 1928.

McGwire also had the distinction of becoming the only player to hit 20 or more home runs in both leagues in one year, 34 with the Oakland Athletics and 24 with the St. Louis Cardinals. McGwire finished in the top ten home run leaders (ninth overall) in the American League, although he was traded to St. Louis on July 31.

Earned Run Average Leaders

	National League					American League			
Year	Player, club	G	IP	ERA	Year	Player, club	G	IP	ERA
1977	John Candelaria, Pittsburgh	33	231	2.34	1977	Frank Tanana, California	31	241	2.54
1978	Craig Swan, New York	29	207	2.43	1978	Ron Guidry, New York	35	274	1.74
1979	J. R. Richard, Houston	38	292	2.71	1979	Ron Guidry, New York	33	236	2.78
1980	Don Sutton, Los Angeles	32	212	2.21	1980	Rudy May, New York	41	175	2.47
1981	Nolan Ryan, Houston	21	149	1.69	1981	Steve McCatty, Oakland	22	186	2.32
1982	Steve Rogers, Montreal	35	277	2.40	1982	Rick Sutcliffe, Cleveland	34	216	2.96
1983	Atlee Hammaker, San Francisco	23	172	2.25	1983	Rick Honeycutt, Texas	25	174	2.42
1984	Alejandro Pena, Los Angeles	28	199	2.48	1984	Mike Boddicker, Baltimore	34	261	2.79
1985	Dwight Gooden, New York	35	276	1.53	1985	Dave Stieb, Toronto	36	265	2.48
1986	Mike Scott, Houston	37	275	2.22	1986	Roger Clemens, Boston	33	254	2.48
1987	Nolan Ryan, Houston	34	211	2.76	1987	Jimmy Key, Toronto	36	261	2.76
1988	Joe Magrane, St. Louis	24	165	2.18	1988	Allan Anderson, Minnesota	30	202	2.45
1989	Scott Garrelts, San Francisco	30	193	2.28	1989	Bret Saberhagen, Kansas City	36	262	2.16
1990	Danny Darwin, Houston	48	162	2.21	1990	Roger Clemens, Boston	31	228	1.93
1991	Dennis Martinez, Montreal	31	222	2.39	1991	Roger Clemens, Boston	35	271	2.62
1992	Bill Swift, San Francisco	30	164	2.08	1992	Roger Clemens, Boston	32	246	2.41
1993	Greg Maddux, Atlanta	36	267	2.36	1993	Kevin Appier, Kansas City	34	238	2.56
1994	Greg Maddux, Atlanta	25	202	1.56	1994	Steve Ontiveros, Oakland	27	115	2.65
1995	Greg Maddux, Atlanta	28	209	1.63	1995	Randy Johnson, Seattle	30	214	2.48
1996	Kevin Brown, Florida	32	233	1.89	1996	Juan Guzman, Toronto	27	187	2.93
1997	Pedro Martinez, Montreal	31	241	1.90	1997	Roger Clemens, Toronto	34	264	2.05

ERA is computed by multiplying earned runs allowed by 9, then dividing by innings pitched.

Marlins Defeat Indians 4 Games to 3 in the 1997 World Series

In Oct. 1997 the Florida Marlins became the first wild card team to win the World Series, defeating the Cleveland Indians 4 games to 3. The Marlins, who entered the National League in 1993, also became the youngest new franchise in baseball history to win the title, by taking the seventh game of a see-saw series in the 11th inning. The teams split the first two games in Florida, then traveled north for three frigid games in Cleveland. Florida took the third and fifth games, sandwiching a Cleveland victory in game 4. After the Indians forced a deciding game 7 with a win in game 6 back in Florida, the Marlins, two outs from defeat, tied game 7 in the bottom of the ninth and went on to win two innings later to take the Series. Rookie pitcher Livan Hernandez, who picked up two of the Marlins' four victories, was named the series MVP.

Game One: Marlins 7, Indians 4

Cleveland	ab	r	h	bi	Florida	ab	r	h	bi
Roberts 2b	4	1	2	0	White cf	4	0	0	0
Vizquel ss	4	0	0	0	Renteria ss	4	0	0	1
Ramirez rf	3	1	1	1	Sheffield rf	2	1	0	0
Justice lf	4	0	2	1	Bonilla 3b	3	2	2	0
Williams 3b	5	0	1	0	Daulton 1b	2	1	1	0
Thome 1b	5	1	1	1	Conine 1b	2	0	1	1
Alomar c	5	0	1	0	Alou lf	3	1	1	3
Grissom cf	3	1	2	0	Johnson c	3	1	1	1
Hershiser p	2	0	0	0	Counsell 2b	3	1	1	0
Juden p	0	0	0	0	Hernandez p	2	0	0	0
Branson ph	1	0	0	0	Cook p	0	0	0	0
Plunk p	0	0	0	0	Powell p	0	0	0	0
Giles p	1	0	1	1	Cangelosi ph	1	0	0	0
Assenmacher p	0	0	0	0	Nen p	0	0	0	0
Totals	37	4	11	4	Totals	29	7	7	6

Cleveland	1	0	0	0	1	1	0	1	0—4
Florida	0	0	1	4	2	0	0	0	x—7

Cleveland	ip	h	r	er	bb	so
Hershiser L, 0-1	4.1	6	7	7	4	2
Juden	0.2	0	0	0	2	0
Plunk	2.0	1	0	0	1	1
Assenmacher	1.0	0	0	0	0	2
Florida						
Hernandez W, 1-0	5.2	8	3	3	2	5
Cook	1.2	0	0	0	1	2
Powell	0.2	1	1	1	2	1
Nen S, 1	1	2	0	0	0	2

E - Sheffield (1). LOB - Cleveland 12, Florida 6. 2B - Roberts 2 (2), Grissom (1), Giles (1), Counsell (1). HR - Ramirez (1), Thome (1), Alou (1), Johnson (1). RBI - Justice (1), Ramirez (1), Thome (1), Giles (1), Renteria (1), Alou 3 (3), Johnson (1), Conine (1). S - Vizquel, Hernandez.

How runs were scored—One in Cleveland first: Roberts doubled. Justice singled scoring Roberts.

One in Florida third: Counsell doubled. Hernandez sacrificed Counsell to third. Renteria grounded out scoring Counsell.

Four in Florida fourth: Bonilla walked. Daulton hit an infield single sending Bonilla to second. Alou homered scoring Bonilla and Daulton. Johnson homered.

One in Cleveland fifth: Ramirez homered

Two in Florida fifth: Sheffield walked. Bonilla singled sending Sheffield to third. Conine singled scoring Sheffield and sending Bonilla to second. Alou grounded into a fielder's choice moving, Bonilla to third. Juden threw a wild pitch allowing Bonilla to score.

One in Cleveland sixth: Thome homered.

One in Cleveland eighth: Grissom walked. Giles tripled scoring Grissom.

Game Two: Indians 6, Marlins 1

Cleveland	ab	r	h	bi	Florida	ab	r	h	bi
Roberts 2b	3	0	1	2	White cf	5	0	2	0
Fernandez ph-2b	2	0	2	0	Renteria ss	4	1	2	0
Vizquel ss	4	1	2	0	Sheffield rf	2	0	1	0
Ramirez rf	5	0	0	0	Bonilla 3b	4	0	0	0
Justice lf	3	0	1	1	Conine 1b	3	0	1	1
Williams 3b	4	2	2	0	Daulton ph-1b	1	0	0	0
Thome 1b	4	0	1	0	Alou lf	4	0	2	0
Alomar c	4	2	2	2	Johnson c	3	0	0	0
Grissom cf	4	1	3	1	Zaun ph	1	0	0	0
Ogea p	2	0	0	0	Counsell 2b	3	0	0	0
Jackson p	1	0	0	0	Brown p	2	0	0	0
Mesa p	0	0	0	0	Heredia p	0	0	0	0
Totals	36	6	14	6	Eisenreich ph	1	0	0	0
					Alfonseca p	0	0	0	0
					Floyd ph	1	0	0	0
					Totals	34	1	8	1

Cleveland	1	0	0	0	3	2	0	0	0—6
Florida	1	0	0	0	0	0	0	0	0—1

Cleveland	ip	h	r	er	bb	so
Ogea W, 1-0	6.2	7	1	1	1	4
Jackson	1.1	1	0	0	0	1
Mesa	1	0	0	0	1	1
Florida						
Brown L, 0-1	6	10	6	6	2	4
Heredia	1	1	0	0	0	1
Alfonseca	2	3	0	0	0	0

E - None. LOB - Cleveland 6, Florida 9. 2B - Vizquel (1), Fernandez (1), Renteria (1), Alou 2 (2), White (1). HR - Alomar (1). RBI - Justice 1 (2), Grissom (1), Roberts 2 (2), Alomar 2 (2), Conine 1 (2). CS - Justice (1). S - Ogea.

How runs were scored—One in Cleveland first: Vizquel doubled. Justice singled scoring Vizquel.

One in Florida first: Renteria singled. Sheffield was hit by a pitch moving Renteria to second. Conine singled scoring Renteria.

Three in Cleveland fifth: Williams singled. Alomar singled sending Williams to second. Grissom singled scoring Williams and sending Alomar to second. Ogea sacrificed Alomar to third and Grissom to second. Roberts singled scoring Alomar and Grissom.

Two in Cleveland sixth: Williams reached on a fielder's choice. Alomar homered scoring Williams.

Game Three: Marlins 14, Indians 11

Florida	ab	r	h	bi	Cleveland	ab	r	h	bi
White cf	5	0	1	0	Roberts lf	5	1	1	2
Renteria ss	4	2	2	1	Vizquel ss	4	0	0	1
Sheffield rf	5	2	3	5	Ramirez rf	5	0	1	1
Bonilla 3b	5	1	1	2	Justice dh	3	2	0	0
Daulton 1b	4	3	2	1	Williams 3b	5	0	1	1
Conine 1b	0	0	0	0	Alomar c	3	2	2	1
Alou lf	5	0	0	0	Giles ph	0	1	0	0
Eisenreich dh	3	1	2	2	Thome 1b	4	3	2	2
Abbott ph-dh	1	0	0	0	Fernandez 2b	4	0	1	1
Floyd ph-dh	0	1	0	0	Grissom cf	3	2	2	1
Johnson c	5	2	3	0	Totals	36	11	10	10
Counsell 2b	5	2	2	1					
Totals	42	14	16	12					

Florida	1	0	1	1	0	2	2	0	7—14
Cleveland	2	0	0	3	2	0	0	0	4—11

Florida	ip	h	r	er	bb	so
Leiter	4.2	6	7	4	6	3
Heredia	2.1	0	0	0	1	0
Cook W, 1-0	1	1	0	0	0	1
Nen	1	3	4	4	2	1
Cleveland						
Nagy	6	6	5	5	4	5
Anderson	0.1	1	1	1	0	0
Jackson	0.2	2	1	1	1	0
Assenmacher	0.2	3	0	0	0	1
Plunk L, 0-1	0.2	2	4	3	2	1
Morman	0.1	0	2	0	1	1
Mesa	0.1	2	1	1	0	0

E - Leiter (1), Bonilla 2 (2), Grissom (1), Thome (1), Fernandez (1). LOB - Florida 9, Cleveland 9. 2B - Sheffield (1), Roberts 1 (3). HR - Sheffield (1), Daulton (1), Eisenreich (1), Thome 1 (2). RBI - Sheffield 5 (5), Daulton (1), Eisenreich 2 (2), Renteria 1 (2), Counsell (1), Bonilla 2 (2), Williams (1), Alomar 1 (3), Vizquel (1), Ramirez 1 (2), Thome 2 (3), Fernandez (1), Grissom 1 (2), Roberts 2 (4). S - Roberts. SF - Fernandez.

How runs were scored—One in Florida first: Sheffield homered.

Two in Cleveland first: Roberts reached on error. Vizquel grounded out moving Roberts to second. Justice walked. Williams singled scoring Roberts and sending Justice to third. Alomar singled scoring Justice.

One in Florida third: Johnson singled. White walked moving Johnson to second. Renteria walked loading the bases. Sheffield walked scoring Johnson.

One in Florida fourth: Daulton homered.

Three in Cleveland fourth: Alomar walked. Thome walked moving Alomar to second. Fernandez flied out advancing both Alomar and Thome. Grissom walked loading the bases. Vizquel walked scoring Alomar and advancing Thome and Grissom. Ramirez hit an infield single scoring Thome and sending Grissom to third and Vizquel to second. Grissom scored on a throwing error.

Two in Cleveland fifth: Alomar hit an infield single. Thome homered scoring Alomar.

Two in Florida sixth: Daulton walked. Eisenreich homered scoring Daulton.

Two in Florida seventh: Counsell singled. White grounded out moving Counsell to second. Renteria singled scoring Counsell. Sheffield doubled scoring Renteria.

Seven in Florida ninth: Bonilla walked. Daulton singled sending Bonilla to third. Daulton advanced to second on throw to third. Throw to third hits Bonilla for an error and Bonilla scores, Daulton goes to third. Floyd was intentionally walked. Daulton scores on a fielding error. Johnson singled sending Floyd to third. Counsell reaches on an error scoring Floyd and moving Johnson to second. Renteria walked sending Johnson to third and Counsell to second. Sheffield singled scoring Johnson and Counsell and sending Renteria to second. Sheffield and Renteria advance on a wild pitch. Bonilla singled scoring Renteria and Sheffield.

Four in Cleveland ninth: Justice walked. Giles walked sending Justice to second. Thome singled loading the bases. Fernandez hit a sacrifice fly scoring Justice. Grissom singled scoring Giles and sending Thome to second. Roberts doubled scoring Thome and Grissom.

Game Four: Indians 10, Marlins 3

Florida	ab	r	h	bi	Cleveland	ab	r	h	bi
White cf	4	0	0	0	Roberts lf	4	0	1	0
Renteria ss	4	0	1	0	Giles lf	1	0	1	1
Sheffield rf	3	0	0	0	Vizquel ss	5	2	2	0
Bonilla 3b	4	0	0	0	Ramirez rf	4	2	1	2
Daulton 1b	3	2	2	0	Justice dh	3	2	1	0
Alou lf	3	1	1	2	Williams 3b	3	3	3	2
Eisenreich dh	2	0	2	1	Alomar c	5	0	3	3
Arias ph-dh	1	0	0	0	Thome 1b	4	0	1	0
Johnson c	4	0	0	0	Fernandez 2b	5	1	2	1
Counsell 2b	2	0	0	0	Grissom cf	4	0	0	0
Abbott ph	1	0	0	0	**Totals**	**38**	**10**	**15**	**9**
Totals	**31**	**3**	**6**	**3**					

Florida	0	0	0	1	0	2	0	0	0—3
Cleveland	3	0	3	0	0	1	1	2	x—10

	ip	h	r	er	bb	so
Florida						
Saunders L, 0-1	2	7	6	6	3	2
Alfonseca	3	3	0	0	0	4
Vosberg	2	3	2	2	2	1
Powell	1	2	2	2	1	0
Cleveland						
Wright W, 1-0	6	5	3	3	5	5
Anderson S, 1	3	1	0	0	0	2

E - Saunders (1), Renteria (1). LOB - Florida 6, Cleveland 10. 2B - Daulton (1), Alomar (1), Roberts 1 (4). HR - Alou 1 (2), Ramirez 1 (2), Williams (1). RBI - Eisenreich 1 (3), Alou 2 (5), Ramirez 2 (4), Alomar 3 (6), Giles 1 (2), Williams 2 (3). SB - Counsell (1), Vizquel (1). CS - Giles (1).

How runs were scored—Three in Cleveland first: Vizquel singled. Ramirez homered scoring Vizquel. Williams singled. Alomar doubled scoring Williams.

Three in Cleveland third: Ramirez walked. Ramirez advanced to second on an error. Justice hit an infield single sending Ramirez to third. Ramirez scored and Justice moved to second on an error. Williams walked. Alomar singled scoring Justice and sending Williams to second. Fernandez singled scoring Williams.

One in Florida fourth: Daulton doubled. Alou walked. Eisenreich singled scoring Daulton.

Two in Florida sixth: Daulton walked. Alou homered scoring Daulton.

One in Cleveland sixth: Vizquel singled and stole second. Justice walked. Williams walked moving Vizquel to third and Justice to second. Alomar hit into a fielder's choice scoring Vizquel.

One in Cleveland seventh: Fernandez singled. Grissom grounded out moving Fernandez to second. Giles singled scoring Fernandez.

Two in Cleveland eighth: Justice walked. Williams homered scoring Justice.

Game Five: Marlins 8, Indians 7

Florida	ab	r	h	bi	Cleveland	ab	r	h	bi
White cf	4	0	2	2	Roberts 2b	3	1	0	0
Renteria ss	5	0	1	0	Vizquel ss	4	1	1	0
Sheffield rf	5	1	2	0	Ramirez rf	5	0	1	0
Bonilla 3b	4	1	1	0	Justice dh	5	0	1	2
Arias pr-3b	0	1	0	0	Williams 3b	3	2	1	0
Daulton dh	5	1	2	0	Thome 1b	4	2	2	1
Alou lf	5	2	3	4	Alomar c	5	1	2	4
Conine 1b	5	1	1	0	Giles lf	1	0	0	0
Johnson c	5	1	3	2	Grissom cf	4	0	1	0
Counsell 2b	2	0	0	0	**Totals**	**34**	**7**	**9**	**7**
Totals	**40**	**8**	**15**	**8**					

Florida	0	2	0	0	0	4	0	1	1—8
Cleveland	0	1	3	0	0	0	0	0	3—7

	ip	h	r	er	bb	so
Florida						
Hernandez W, 2-0	8	7	6	5	8	2
Nen S, 2	1	2	1	0	0	1
Cleveland						
Hershiser L, 0-2	5.2	9	6	6	2	3
Morman	0	0	0	0	1	0
Plunk	0.1	0	0	0	1	1
Juden	1.1	2	1	1	0	0
Assenmacher	0.2	1	0	0	0	1
Mesa	1	3	1	1	0	1

E - Hernandez (1), Counsell (1). LOB - Florida 9, Cleveland 9. 2B - Daulton 1 (2), White 2 (3), Bonilla (1). 3B - Thome (1). HR - Alou 1 (3), Alomar 1 (2). RBI - Johnson 2 (3), White 2 (3), Alou 4 (9), Alomar 4 (10), Justice 2 (4), Thome 1 (4). SB - Alou (1), Daulton (1). S - Vizquel.

How runs were scored—Two in Florida second: Daulton doubled. Conine grounded out sending Daulton to third. Johnson singled scoring Daulton. Counsell walked sending Johnson to second. White doubled scoring Johnson.

One in Cleveland second: Thome tripled. Alomar singled scoring Thome.

Three in Cleveland third: Williams walked. Thome walked. Alomar homered scoring Williams and Thome.

Four in Florida sixth: Sheffield singled. Bonilla walked. Alou homered scoring Sheffield and Bonilla. Conine singled. Johnson singled. Counsell walked loading the bases. White walked scoring Conine.

One in Florida eighth: Alou hit an infield single. Alou stole second. Conine grounded out sending Alou to third. Johnson singled scoring Alou.

One in Florida ninth: Bonilla doubled to right. Arias ran for Bonilla. Daulton singled sending Arias to third. Alou singled scoring Arias.

Three in Cleveland ninth: Roberts reached on an error. Vizquel singled sending Roberts to third. Vizquel moved to second without a throw from catcher. Justice singled scoring Roberts and Vizquel. Williams reached on a fielder's choice. Williams moved to second on a throwing error. Thome singled scoring Williams.

Game Six: Indians 4, Marlins 1

Cleveland	ab	r	h	bi	Florida	ab	r	h	bi
Roberts 2b	3	0	1	0	White cf	5	0	3	0
Fernandez 2b	1	0	1	0	Renteria ss	5	0	0	0
Vizquel ss	4	1	1	0	Sheffield rf	3	0	0	0
Ramirez rf	1	0	0	2	Bonilla 3b	4	0	0	0
Justice lf	4	0	0	0	Conine lf	2	0	0	0
Williams 3b	4	1	1	0	Eisenreich ph-1b	1	0	0	0
Thome 1b	3	1	0	0	Alou lf	3	1	1	0
Alomar c	3	0	0	0	Johnson c	4	0	2	0
Grissom cf	3	0	0	0	Counsell 2b	4	0	1	0
Ogea p	2	1	2	2	Brown p	1	0	0	0
Jackson p	0	0	0	0	Daulton ph	1	0	0	1
Assenmacher p	0	0	0	0	Heredia p	0	0	0	0
Seitzer ph	1	0	0	0	Cangelosi ph	1	0	1	0
Mesa p	0	0	0	0	Powell p	0	0	0	0
Totals	**30**	**4**	**7**	**4**	Vosberg p	0	0	0	0
					Floyd ph	1	0	0	0
					Totals	**34**	**1**	**8**	**1**

Cleveland	0	2	1	0	1	0	0	0	0—4
Florida	0	0	0	0	1	0	0	0	0—1

	ip	h	r	er	bb	so
Cleveland						
Ogea W, 2-0	5	4	1	1	2	1
Jackson	2	2	0	0	2	2
Assenmacher	1	1	0	0	0	1
Mesa S, 1	1	1	0	0	0	1
Florida						
Brown L, 0-2	5	5	4	4	3	2
Heredia	2	0	0	0	0	4
Powell	1	2	0	0	1	0
Vosberg	1	0	0	0	1	1

E - None. LOB - Cleveland 5, Florida 11. 2B - Vizquel 1 (2), Ogea (1), Williams (1). 3B - White (1). RBI - Ogea 2 (2), Ramirez 2 (6), Daulton 1 (2). SB - Vizquel 2 (3), White (1). CS - Roberts (1). SF - Ramirez 2, Daulton 1.

How runs were scored—Two in Cleveland second: Williams hit an infield single. Thome walked sending Williams to second. Grissom walked loading the bases. Ogea singled scoring Williams and Thome.

One in Cleveland third: Vizquel doubled. Vizquel stole third. Ramirez hit a sacrifice fly scoring Vizquel.

One in Cleveland fifth: Ogea doubled. Roberts singled sending Ogea to third. Ramirez hit a sacrifice fly scoring Ogea.

One in Florida fifth: Alou singled. Johnson singled sending Alou to second. Counsell grounded into a fielder's choice moving Alou to third. Daulton hit a sacrifice fly scoring Alou.

Game Seven: Marlins 3, Indians 2 (11 innings)

Cleveland	ab	r	h	bi	Florida	ab	r	h	bi
Vizquel ss	5	0	1	0	White cf	6	0	0	0
Fernandez 2b	5	0	2	2	Renteria ss	5	0	3	1
Ramirez rf	3	0	0	0	Sheffield rf	4	0	1	0
Justice lf	5	0	0	0	Daulton 1b	3	0	0	0
Williams 3b	2	0	0	0	Conine ph-1b	1	0	0	0
Alomar c	5	0	1	0	Nen p	0	0	0	0
Thome 1b	4	1	1	0	Cangelosi ph	1	0	0	0
Grissom cf	4	1	1	0	Powell p	0	0	0	0
Wright p	2	0	0	0	Alou rf	5	1	1	0
Assenmacher p	0	0	0	0	Bonilla 3b	5	1	2	1
Jackson p	0	0	0	0	Johnson c	4	0	1	0
Anderson p	0	0	0	0	Zaun pr-c	1	0	0	0
Giles ph	1	0	0	0	Counsell 2b	3	1	0	1
Mesa p	0	0	0	0	Leiter p	0	0	0	0
Nagy p	0	0	0	0	Cook p	0	0	0	0
Totals	**36**	**2**	**6**	**2**	Floyd p	0	0	0	0
					Abbott ph	1	0	0	0
					Alfonseca p	0	0	0	0
					Heredia p	0	0	0	0
					Eisenreich 1b	1	0	0	0
					Totals	**40**	**3**	**8**	**3**

Cleveland	0	0	2	0	0	0	0	0	0	0	0—2
Florida	0	0	0	0	0	1	0	1	0	1	1—3

	ip	h	r	er	bb	so
Cleveland						
Wright	6.1	2	1	1	5	7
Assenmacher	0.2	0	0	0	0	1
Jackson	0.2	0	0	0	0	1
Anderson	0.1	0	0	0	0	0
Mesa	1.2	4	1	1	0	2
Nagy L, 0-1	1	2	1	0	1	0
Florida						
Leiter	6	4	2	2	4	7
Cook	1	0	0	0	0	2
Alfonseca	1.1	0	0	0	1	1
Heredia	0	1	0	0	0	0
Nen	1.2	0	0	0	0	3
Powell W, 1-0	1	1	0	0	1	0

E - Ramirez (1), Fernandez 1 (2). LOB - Cleveland 8, Florida 12. 2B - Renteria 1 (2). HR - Bonilla (1). RBI - Fernandez 2 (4), Bonilla 1 (3), Counsell 1 (2), Renteria 1 (3). SB - Vizquel 2 (5). S - Wright 1. SF - Counsell 1.

How runs were scored—Two in Cleveland third: Thome walked. Grissom singled sending Thome to second. Wright sacrificed advancing both runners. Fernandez singled scoring Thome and Grissom.

One in Florida seventh: Bonilla homered.

One in Florida ninth: Alou singled. Johnson singled sending Alou to third. Counsell hit a sacrifice fly scoring Alou.

One in Florida eleventh: Bonilla singled. Counsell reached on an error, and Bonilla moved to third. Eisenreich was intentionally walked moving Counsell to second. White grounded into a fielder's choice moving Counsell to third, Bonilla forced out at home. Renteria singled scoring Counsell.

World Series Results, 1903-1997

1903	Boston AL 5, Pittsburgh NL 3	1935	Detroit AL 4, Chicago NL 2	1966	Baltimore AL 4, Los Angeles NL 0
1904	No series	1936	New York AL 4, New York NL 2	1967	St. Louis NL 4, Boston AL 3
1905	New York NL 4, Philadelphia AL 1	1937	New York AL 4, New York NL 1	1968	Detroit AL 4, St. Louis NL 3
1906	Chicago AL 4, Chicago NL 2	1938	New York AL 4, Chicago NL 0	1969	New York NL 4, Baltimore AL 1
1907	Chicago NL 4, Detroit AL 0, 1 tie	1939	New York AL 4, Cincinnati NL 0	1970	Baltimore AL 4, Cincinnati NL 1
1908	Chicago NL 4, Detroit AL 1	1940	Cincinnati NL 4, Detroit AL 3	1971	Pittsburgh NL 4, Baltimore AL 3
1909	Pittsburgh NL 4, Detroit AL 3	1941	New York AL 4, Brooklyn NL 1	1972	Oakland AL 4, Cincinnati NL 3
1910	Philadelphia AL 4, Chicago NL 1	1942	St. Louis NL 4, New York AL 1	1973	Oakland AL 4, New York NL 3
1911	Philadelphia AL 4, New York NL 2	1943	New York AL 4, St. Louis NL 1	1974	Oakland AL 4, Los Angeles NL 1
1912	Boston AL 4, New York NL 3, 1 tie	1944	St. Louis NL 4, St. Louis AL 2	1975	Cincinnati NL 4, Boston AL 3
1913	Philadelphia AL 4, New York NL 1	1945	Detroit AL 4, Chicago NL 3	1976	Cincinnati NL 4, New York AL 0
1914	Boston NL 4, Philadelphia AL 0	1946	St. Louis NL 4, Boston AL 3	1977	New York AL 4, Los Angeles NL 2
1915	Boston AL 4, Philadelphia NL 1	1947	New York AL 4, Brooklyn NL 3	1978	New York AL 4, Los Angeles NL 2
1916	Boston AL 4, Brooklyn NL 1	1948	Cleveland AL 4, Boston NL 2	1979	Pittsburgh NL 4, Baltimore AL 3
1917	Chicago AL 4, New York NL 2	1949	New York AL 4, Brooklyn NL 1	1980	Philadelphia NL 4, Kansas City AL 2
1918	Boston AL 4, Chicago NL 2	1950	New York AL 4, Philadelphia NL 0	1981	Los Angeles NL 4, New York AL 2
1919	Cincinnati NL 5, Chicago AL 3	1951	New York AL 4, New York NL 2	1982	St. Louis NL 4, Milwaukee AL 3
1920	Cleveland AL 5, Brooklyn NL 2	1952	New York AL 4, Brooklyn NL 3	1983	Baltimore AL 4, Philadelphia NL 1
1921	New York NL 5, New York AL 3	1953	New York AL 4, Brooklyn NL 2	1984	Detroit AL 4, San Diego NL 1
1922	New York NL 4, New York AL 0, 1 tie	1954	New York NL 4, Cleveland AL 0	1985	Kansas City AL 4, St. Louis NL 3
1923	New York AL 4, New York NL 2	1955	Brooklyn NL 4, New York AL 3	1986	New York NL 4, Boston AL 3
1924	Washington AL 4, New York NL 3	1956	New York AL 4, Brooklyn NL 3	1987	Minnesota AL 4, St. Louis NL 3
1925	Pittsburgh NL 4, Washington AL 3	1957	Milwaukee NL 4, New York AL 3	1988	Los Angeles NL 4, Oakland AL 1
1926	St. Louis NL 4, New York AL 3	1958	New York AL 4, Milwaukee NL 3	1989	Oakland AL 4, San Francisco NL 0
1927	New York AL 4, Pittsburgh NL 0	1959	Los Angeles NL 4, Chicago AL 2	1990	Cincinnati NL 4, Oakland AL 0
1928	New York AL 4, St. Louis NL 0	1960	Pittsburgh NL 4, New York AL 3	1991	Minnesota AL 4, Atlanta NL 3
1929	Philadelphia AL 4, Chicago NL 1	1961	New York AL 4, Cincinnati NL 1	1992	Toronto AL 4, Atlanta NL 2
1930	Philadelphia AL 4, St. Louis NL 2	1962	New York AL 4, San Francisco NL 3	1993	Toronto AL 4, Philadelphia NL 2
1931	St. Louis NL 4, Philadelphia AL 3	1963	Los Angeles NL 4, New York AL 0	1994	No series
1932	New York AL 4, Chicago NL 0	1964	St. Louis NL 4, New York AL 3	1995	Atlanta NL 4, Cleveland AL 2
1933	New York NL 4, Washington AL 1	1965	Los Angeles NL 4, Minnesota AL 3	1996	New York AL 4, Atlanta NL 2
1934	St. Louis NL 4, Detroit AL 3			1997	Florida NL 4, Cleveland AL 3

All-Time Major League Leaders
(*player active at end of 1997 season)

Games		At Bats		Runs Batted In		Stolen Bases	
Pete Rose	3,562	Pete Rose	14,053	Hank Aaron	2,297	Rickey Henderson*	1,231
Carl Yastrzemski	3,308	Hank Aaron	12,364	Babe Ruth	2,213	Lou Brock	938
Hank Aaron	3,298	Carl Yastrzemski	11,988	Cap Anson	2,076	Billy Hamilton	912
Ty Cobb	3,035	Ty Cobb	11,434	Lou Gehrig	1,995	Ty Cobb	892
Eddie Murray*	3,026	Eddie Murray*	11,336	Stan Musial	1,951	Tim Raines*	795
Stan Musial	3,026	Robin Yount	11,008	Ty Cobb	1,937	Vince Coleman*	752
Willie Mays	2,992	Dave Winfield	11,003	Jimmie Foxx	1,922	Eddie Collins	744
Dave Winfield	2,973	Stan Musial	10,972	Eddie Murray*	1,915	Arlie Latham	739
Rusty Staub	2,951	Willie Mays	10,881	Willie Mays	1,903	Max Carey	738
Brooks Robinson	2,896	Brooks Robinson	10,654	Mel Ott	1,860	Honus Wagner	722
Runs		**Strikeouts**		**Shutouts**		**Saves**	
Ty Cobb	2,246	Nolan Ryan	5,714	Walter Johnson	110	Lee Smith	478
Hank Aaron	2,174	Steve Carlton	4,136	Grover C. Alexander	90	Dennis Eckersley*	389
Babe Ruth	2,174	Bert Blyleven	3,701	Christy Mathewson	79	Jeff Reardon	367
Pete Rose	2,165	Tom Seaver	3,640	Cy Young	76	John Franco*	359
Willie Mays	2,062	Don Sutton	3,574	Eddie Plank	69	Rollie Fingers	341
Cap Anson	1,996	Gaylord Perry	3,534	Warren Spahn	63	Randy Myers*	319
Stan Musial	1,949	Walter Johnson	3,509	Nolan Ryan	61	Tom Henke	311
Rickey Henderson*	1,913	Phil Niekro	3,342	Tom Seaver	61	Rich Gossage	310
Lou Gehrig	1,888	Ferguson Jenkins	3,192	Bert Blyleven	60	Bruce Sutter	300
Tris Speaker	1,882	Bob Gibson	3,117	Don Sutton	58	Doug Jones*	278

All-Time Home Run Leaders

Player	HR	Player	HR	Player	HR	Player	HR
Hank Aaron	755	Ted Williams	521	Dave Kingman	442	Dwight Evans	385
Babe Ruth	714	Ernie Banks	512	Andre Dawson	438	Frank Howard	382
Willie Mays	660	Ed Mathews	512	Billy Williams	426	Jim Rice	382
Frank Robinson	586	Mel Ott	511	Darrell Evans	414	Orlando Cepeda	379
Harmon Killebrew	573	Eddie Murray*	504	Duke Snider	407	Tony Perez	379
Reggie Jackson	563	Lou Gehrig	493	Al Kaline	399	Joe Carter*	378
Mike Schmidt	548	Stan Musial	475	Dale Murphy	398	Norm Cash	377
Mickey Mantle	536	Willie Stargell	475	Graig Nettles	390	Carlton Fisk	376
Jimmy Foxx	534	Dave Winfield	465	Johnny Bench	389	Barry Bonds*	374
Willie McCovey	521	Carl Yastrzemski	452	Mark McGwire*	387	Rocky Colavito	374

Players With 3,000 Major League Hits

Player	Hits	Player	Hits	Player	Hits
Pete Rose	4,256	Honus Wagner	3,415	Paul Waner	3,152
Ty Cobb	4,189	Eddie Collins	3,315	Robin Yount	3,142
Hank Aaron	3,771	Willie Mays	3,283	Dave Winfield	3,110
Stan Musial	3,630	Eddie Murray*	3,255	Rod Carew	3,053
Tris Speaker	3,514	Nap Lajoie	3,242	Lou Brock	3,023
Carl Yastrzemski	3,419	Paul Molitor*	3,178	Al Kaline	3,007
Cap Anson	3,418	George Brett	3,154	Roberto Clemente	3,000

Pitchers With 300 Major League Wins

Cy Young	511	Warren Spahn	363	Steve Carlton	329	Don Sutton	324	Old Hoss Radbourn	309
Walter Johnson	417	Kid Nichols	361	John Clarkson	328	Phil Niekro	318	Mickey Welch	307
Grover Alexander	373	Pud Galvin	360	Eddie Plank	326	Gaylord Perry	314	Lefty Grove	300
Christy Mathewson	373	Tim Keefe	342	Nolan Ryan	324	Tom Seaver	311	Early Wynn	300

Baseball Stadiums[1]

National League

Team	Stadium (year opened)	Surface	Home run distances (ft.)			Seating capacity
			LF	Center	RF	
Arizona Diamondbacks ..	Bank One Ballpark (1998)[2]	Grass	328	402	335	48,569
Atlanta Braves.........	Turner Field (1997)	Grass	335	401	330	50,528
Chicago Cubs.........	Wrigley Field (1914)	Grass	355	400	353	38,765
Cincinnati Reds.......	Cinergy Field (1970)..............	Artificial	330	404	330	52,952
Colorado Rockies	Coors Field (1995)	Grass	347	415	350	50,000
Florida Marlins	Pro Player Stadium (1987)	Grass	335	410	345	48,000
Houston Astros	The Astrodome (1965)	Artificial	325	400	325	54,370
Los Angeles Dodgers....	Dodger Stadium (1962)	Grass	330	395	330	56,000
Montreal Expos	Olympic Stadium (1976)	Artificial	325	404	325	46,500
New York Mets	Shea Stadium (1964)	Grass	338	410	338	55,601
Philadelphia Phillies.....	Veterans Stadium (1971)	Artificial	330	408	330	62,530
Pittsburgh Pirates	Three Rivers Stadium (1970)	Artificial	335	400	335	47,972
St. Louis Cardinals......	Busch Stadium (1966)	Grass	330	402	330	57,000
San Diego Padres	Qualcomm Stadium (1967)	Grass	327	405	327	46,510
San Francisco Giants....	3Com Park at Candlestick Point (1960) .	Grass	335	400	328	63,000

American League

Team	Stadium (year opened)	Surface	LF	Center	RF	Seating capacity
Anaheim Angels	Anaheim Stadium (1966)	Grass	333	404	333	64,593
Baltimore Orioles........	Oriole Park at Camden Yards (1992)...	Grass	333	400	318	48,188
Boston Red Sox	Fenway Park (1912)...............	Grass	315	420	302	33,871
Chicago White Sox	Comiskey Park (1991)	Grass	347	400	347	44,321
Cleveland Indians	Jacobs Field (1994)	Grass	325	405	325	42,400
Detroit Tigers...........	Tiger Stadium (1912)	Grass	340	440	325	52,416
Kansas City Royals	Kauffman Stadium (1973)...........	Grass	330	400	330	40,625
Milwaukee Brewers	County Stadium (1953).............	Grass	315	402	315	53,192
Minnesota Twins	Hubert H. Humphrey Metrodome (1982)	Artificial	343	408	327	56,783
New York Yankees	Yankee Stadium (1923)	Grass	312	410	310	57,545
Oakland A's...........	Oakland Coliseum (1968)	Grass	330	400	330	43,012
Seattle Mariners	The Kingdome (1976).	Artificial	331	405	312	59,856
Tampa Bay Devil Rays ...	Tropicana Field (1990)[3]	Artificial	315	410	322	45,200
Texas Rangers	The Ballpark in Arlington (1994)	Grass	332	400	325	49,178
Toronto Blue Jays	SkyDome (1989)	Artificial	328	400	328	50,516

(1) As of 1997 season, except for expansion teams Arizona and Tampa Bay, beginning play in 1998. (2) To be completed Apr. 1, 1998. (2) Renovations (to meet Major League Baseball regulations) to be completed Apr. 1, 1998.

Cal Ripken, Jr., Extends His Consecutive Games Record

On Sept. 6, 1995, Baltimore Orioles shortstop Cal Ripken, Jr., played in his 2,131st consecutive game to break Lou Gehrig's record, which had stood for over 56 years and was thought by many to be unbreakable. At the end of the 1997 season Ripken's streak was still alive. Here is a comparison of some of their statistics during their respective streaks:

Lou Gehrig		Cal Ripken, Jr.
June 1, 1925	Streak began	May 30, 1982
April 30, 1939	Streak ended	—
2,130	Consecutive games played	2,477
7,938	At bats	9,642
2,700	Hits	2,674
492	Home Runs	370
1,984	Runs Batted In	1,433
.340	Batting Average	.277

Major League Franchise Shifts and Additions

1953—Boston Braves (NL) became Milwaukee Braves.
1954—St. Louis Browns (AL) became Baltimore Orioles.
1955—Philadelphia Athletics (AL) became Kansas City Athletics.
1958—New York Giants (NL) became San Francisco Giants.
1958—Brooklyn Dodgers (NL) became Los Angeles Dodgers.
1961—Washington Senators (AL) became Minnesota Twins.
1961—Los Angeles Angels (renamed California Angels in 1965 and Anaheim Angels in 1997) enfranchised by the American League.
1961—Washington Senators enfranchised by the American League (a new team, replacing the former Washington club, whose franchise was moved to Minneapolis-St. Paul).
1962—Houston Colt .45's (renamed the Houston Astros in 1965) enfranchised by the National League.
1962—New York Mets enfranchised by the National League.

1966—Milwaukee Braves (NL) became Atlanta Braves.
1968—Kansas City Athletics (AL) became Oakland Athletics.
1969—Kansas City Royals and Seattle Pilots enfranchised by the American League; Montreal Expos and San Diego Padres enfranchised by the National League.
1970—Seattle Pilots became Milwaukee Brewers.
1971—Washington Senators became Texas Rangers (Dallas-Fort Worth area).
1977—Toronto Blue Jays and Seattle Mariners enfranchised by the American League.
1993—Colorado Rockies (Denver) and Florida Marlins (Miami) enfranchised by the National League.
1998—Tampa Bay Devil Rays to begin play in the American League; Arizona Diamondbacks (Phoenix) to begin play in the National League (both teams enfranchised in 1995).

NCAA Baseball Champions

1960	Minnesota	1970	USC	1980	Arizona	1989	Wichita St.
1961	USC	1971	USC	1981	Arizona St.	1990	Georgia
1962	Michigan	1972	USC	1982	Miami (FL)	1991	LSU
1963	USC	1973	USC	1983	Texas	1992	Pepperdine
1964	Minnesota	1974	USC	1984	Cal. St.-Fullerton	1993	LSU
1965	Arizona St.	1975	Texas	1985	Miami (FL)	1994	Oklahoma
1966	Ohio St.	1976	Arizona	1986	Arizona	1995	Cal. St.-Fullerton
1967	Arizona St.	1977	Arizona St.	1987	Stanford	1996	LSU
1968	USC	1978	USC	1988	Stanford	1997	LSU
1969	Arizona St.	1979	Cal. St.-Fullerton				

Little League World Series

The Little League World Series is played annually in Williamsport, PA. The team from Guadalupe, Mexico, won the 1997 Little League World Series by defeating the team from Mission Viejo, CA, 5-4, on Aug. 22. Guadalupe, the first Mexican team to win the Series since 1958, scored 4 runs in the 6th inning to cap a come-from-behind victory.

Year	Winning / Losing Team	Score	Year	Winning / Losing Team	Score	Year	Winning / Losing Team	Score
1947	Williamsport, PA; Lock Haven, PA	16-7	1963	Granada Hills, CA; Stratford, CT	2-1	1981	Taiwan; Tampa, FL	4-2
1948	Lock Haven, PA; St. Petersburg, FL	6-5	1964	Staten Island, NY; Mexico	4-0	1982	Kirkland, WA; Taiwan	6-0
1949	Hammonton, NJ; Pensacola, FL	5-0	1965	Windsor Locks, CT; Ontario, Canada	3-1	1983	Marietta, GA; Dominican Rep.	3-1
1950	Houston, TX; Bridgeport, CT	2-1	1966	Houston, TX; W. New York, NJ	8-2	1984	South Korea; Altamonte Springs, FL	6-2
1951	Stamford, CT; Austin, TX	3-0	1967	Tokyo, Japan; Chicago, IL	4-1	1985	South Korea; Mexico	7-1
1952	Norwalk, CT; Monongahela, PA	4-3	1968	Osaka, Japan; Richmond, VA	1-0	1986	Taiwan; Tucson, AZ	12-0
1953	Birmingham, AL; Schenectady, NY	1-0	1969	Taiwan; Santa Clara, CA	5-0	1987	Chinese Taipei; Irvine, CA	21-1
1954	Schenectady, NY; Colton, CA	7-5	1970	Wayne, NJ; Campbell, CA	2-0	1988	Chinese Taipei; Pearl City, HI	10-0
1955	Morrisville, PA; Merchantville, NJ	4-3	1971	Taiwan; Gary, IN	12-3	1989	Trumbull, CT; Chinese Taipei	5-2
1956	Roswell, NM; Delaware, NJ	3-1	1972	Taiwan; Hammond, IN	6-0	1990	Chinese Taipei; Shippensburg, PA	9-0
1957	Mexico; La Mesa, CA	4-0	1973	Taiwan; Tucson, AZ	12-0	1991	Chinese Taipei; Danville, CA	11-0
1958	Mexico; Kankakee, IL	10-1	1974	Taiwan; Red Bluff, CA	12-1	1992	Long Beach, CA; Philippines	6-0
1959	Hamtramck, MI; Auburn, CA	12-0	1975	Lakewood, NJ; Tampa, FL	4-3	1993	Long Beach, CA; Panama	3-2
1960	Levittown, PA; Ft. Worth, TX	5-0	1976	Tokyo, Japan; Campbell, CA	10-3	1994	Venezuela; Northridge, CA	4-3
1961	El Cajon, CA; El Campo, TX	4-2	1977	Taiwan; El Cajon, CA	7-2	1995	Taiwan; Spring, TX	17-3
1962	San Jose, CA; Kankakee, IL	3-0	1978	Taiwan; Danville, CA	11-1	1996	Taiwan; Cranston, RI	13-3
			1979	Taiwan; Campbell, CA	2-1	1997	Mexico; Mission Viejo, CA	5-4
			1980	Taiwan; Tampa, FL	4-3			

SPECIAL OLYMPICS

Special Olympics is an international program of year-round sports training and athletic competition for children and adults with mental retardation. All 50 U.S. states, Washington, DC, and Guam have chapter offices. In addition, there are accredited Special Olympics programs in nearly 150 countries. Persons wishing to volunteer or find out more about Special Olympics can contact Special Olympics International Headquarters, 1325 G St. NW, Suite 500, Washington, DC 20005, or access the Special Olympics web site at http://www.specialolympics.org

1997 Special Olympic World Winter Games/1999 Special Olympic World Summer Games

The 6th Special Olympic World Winter Games were held Feb. 2-8, 1997, in Toronto and Collingwood, Ont., Canada. Nearly 2,000 athletes from 75 countries participated, along with approx. 500 coaches, 1,500 volunteers, and 2,000 family and friends. Athletes competed in Alpine Skiing, Cross-Country Skiing, Floor Hockey, Figure Skating, Speed Skating, and Snow-Shoeing (the last not official).

The 10th Special Olympic World Summer Games were scheduled to be held June 26-July 4, 1999, in Raleigh-Durham/Chapel Hill, NC. Over 7,000 athletes and coaches from 150 countries were expected to participate, competing in 19 sports.

CHESS

World Chess Champions

Source: U.S. Chess Federation

Chess dates back to antiquity, its exact origin unknown. The best players of their time, regarded by later generations as world champions, were François Philidor, Alexandre Deschappelles, Louis de la Bourdonnais, all France; Howard Staunton, England; Adolph Anderssen, Germany; and Paul Morphy, U.S. In 1866 Wilhelm Steinitz defeated Adolph Anderssen and claimed the world champion title. Official world champions since the title was first used follow:

1866-1894	Wilhelm Steinitz, Austria	**1948-1957**	Mikhail Botvinnik, USSR	**1972-1975**	Bobby Fischer, U.S. (b)
1894-1921	Emanuel Lasker, Germany	**1957-1958**	Vassily Smyslov, USSR	**1975-1985**	Anatoly Karpov, USSR
1921-1927	Jose R. Capablanca, Cuba	**1958-1959**	Mikhail Botvinnik, USSR	**1985-1993**	Garry Kasparov, USSR/Russia (c)
1927-1935	Alexander A. Alekhine, France	**1960-1961**	Mikhail Tal, USSR	**1993-**	Garry Kasparov, Russia (PCA)
1935-1937	Max Euwe, Netherlands	**1961-1963**	Mikhail Botvinnik, USSR		
1937-1946	Alexander A. Alekhine, France (a)	**1963-1969**	Tigran Petrosian, USSR	**1993-**	Anatoly Karpov, Russia (FIDE)
		1969-1972	Boris Spassky, USSR		

(a) After Alekhine died in 1946, the title was vacant until 1948, when Botvinnik won the 1st championship match sanctioned by the International Chess Federation (FIDE). (b) Defaulted championship after refusal to accept FIDE rules for a championship match, Apr. 1975. (c) Kasparov broke with FIDE, Feb. 26, 1993. FIDE stripped Kasparov of his title Mar. 23. Kasparov defeated Nigel Short of Great Britain in a world championship match played Sept.-Oct. 1993 under the auspices of a new organization the two had founded, the Professional Chess Association (PCA). FIDE held a championship match between Anatoly Karpov (Russia) and Jan Timman (the Netherlands), which Karpov won in Nov. 1993. **Recent matches:** In Feb. 1996, Kasparov defeated Deep Blue (3 wins, 1 loss, 2 draws), a computer designed by IBM, in the 1st multigame regulation match between a world chess champion and a computer. In a May 1997 rematch, however, Kasparov was soundly defeated by the computer; he scored 1 win, 2 losses, 3 draws. Karpov successfully defended the FIDE title in June-July 1996 against 1991 U.S. chess champion Gata Kamsky of New York City, 10½ to 7½. **Further information:** More information on chess and chess champions may be accessed on the U.S. Chess Federation's Internet site: http://www.uschess.org

BOSTON MARATHON

Lameck Aguta of Kenya won the 1997 Boston Marathon, Apr. 21, with a time of 2 hours, 10 minutes, 34 seconds. Among the women, Fatuma Roba of Ethiopia became the first African woman to finish first in the event, with a time of 2 hours, 26 minutes, 23 seconds.

GYMNASTICS

World Gymnastics Championships in 1997

On Sept. 5, Svetlana Khorkina of Russia won the women's all-around title at the World Gymnastics Championship, held in Lausanne, Switzerland, with a score of 38.636. Ivan Ivankov of Belarus won the men's all-around title with a score of 56.887.

SOCCER
Major League Soccer

Major League Soccer (MLS), a U.S. league that began play in 1996, ended its second season in Oct. 1997. The league planned to expand from ten to twelve teams for the 1998 season. The new teams, the Fusion and the Fire, will be located in Miami and Chicago, respectively. The league also announced that it had concluded a television package providing for broadcasts of MLS games on ESPN and ABC beginning in 1998.

1997 Final Standings

Eastern Conference	W	So	L	GF	GA	Pts	Western Conference	W	So	L	GF	GA	Pts
Washington D.C. United	21	4	11	70	53	55	Kansas City Wizards	21	7	11	57	51	49
Tampa Bay Mutiny	17	3	15	55	60	45	Los Angeles Galaxy	16	2	16	55	44	44
Columbus Crew	15	3	17	42	41	39	Dallas Burn	16	3	16	55	49	42
New England Revolution	15	4	17	40	53	37	Colorado Rapids	14	2	18	50	59	38
NY/NJ MetroStars	13	2	19	43	53	35	San Jose Clash	12	3	20	55	59	30

Note: 3 points for a regulation-time win, 1 point for a shootout win. So= shootout win.

1997 MLS Individual Statistical Leaders

Leading Scorers (2 points for a goal, 1 point for an assist)

	Name	Team	Games	Goals	Assists	Points
1.	Preki	Kansas City	27	12	17	41
2.	Jaime Moreno	Washington D.C.	20	16	8	40
3.	Raul Diaz Arce	Washington D.C.	22	15	6	36
4.	Ronald Cerritos	San Jose	22	12	10	34
5.	Giovanni Savarese	New York/New Jersey	29	14	4	32
6.	Dante Washington	Dallas	30	12	6	30
7.	Lawrence Lozzano	San Jose	29	10	10	30
8.	Damian	Dallas	19	11	7	29
9.	Mark Chung	Kansas City	32	10	8	28
10.	Chris Henderson	Colorado	30	7	14	28

Goalkeeping Leaders (minimum 1,395 minutes)

	Name	Team	Games	Minutes	Shots	Saves	GA	GAA	Wins	Loses
1.	Brad Friedel	Columbus	29	2,609	168	131	35	1.21	14	15
2.	Walter Zenga	New England	22	1,980	110	79	28	1.27	15	7
3.	Jorge Campos	Los Angeles	19	1,584	85	60	23	1.31	12	5
4.	Marcus Hahnemann	Colorado	25	2,157	144	111	37	1.54	13	11
5.	Mike Ammann	Kansas City	29	2,597	157	110	45	1.56	21	8
6.	Mark Dodd	Dallas	30	2,700	240	183	48	1.60	14	16
7.	Tony Meola	New York/New Jersey	30	2,683	207	147	48	1.61	12	18
8.	David Kramer	San Jose	21	1,832	115	84	33	1.62	7	14
9.	Dave Salzwedel	San Jose	20	1,678	115	71	35	1.88	7	11
10.	Mark Dougherty	Tampa Bay	25	2,143	150	108	45	1.89	15	8

Note: GA = goals against; GAA = goals against average.

1997 MLS Awards

MVP: Preki, Kansas City Wizards
Defender of the year: Eddie Pope, Washington D.C. United
Coach of the year: Bruce Arena, Washington D.C. United
Goalkeeper of the year: Brad Friedel, Columbus Crew
Rookie of the year: Mike Duhaney, Tampa Bay Mutiny
Goal of the year: Marco Etcheverry, Washington D.C. United

1997 MLS Playoff Results

Eastern Conference
Washington D.C. defeated New England 2 games to 0
Columbus defeated Tampa Bay 2 games to 0
Washington D.C. defeated Columbus 2 games to 0

Western Conference
Dallas defeated Los Angeles 2 games to 0
Colorado defeated Kansas City 2 games to 0
Colorado defeated Dallas 2 games to 0

1997 MLS Cup
Washington D.C. United 2, Colorado Rapids 1

The World Cup

In 1994 the World Cup, emblematic of international soccer supremacy, was held in the U.S. for the first time. Brazil captured an unprecedented 4th World Cup by defeating Italy on July 17, 1994, at the Rose Bowl stadium in Pasadena, CA. For the first time ever, the final was decided in the tie-breaking, penalty-kick round, in which Brazil outscored Italy 3-2, after neither team had been able to score in 90 minutes of regulation time and an additional 30 minutes of extra time. The 1998 World Cup was scheduled to be held in France, and the 2002 World Cup is scheduled to be held jointly in Japan and South Korea. Winners and sites for previous World Cup tournaments follow:

Year	Winner	Final opponent	Site	Year	Winner	Final opponent	Site
1930	Uruguay	Argentina	Uruguay	1970	Brazil	Italy	Mexico
1934	Italy	Czechoslovakia	Italy	1974	W. Germany	Netherlands	W. Germany
1938	Italy	Hungary	France	1978	Argentina	Netherlands	Argentina
1950	Uruguay	Brazil	Brazil	1982	Italy	W. Germany	Spain
1954	W. Germany	Hungary	Switzerland	1986	Argentina	W. Germany	Mexico
1958	Brazil	Sweden	Sweden	1990	W. Germany	Argentina	Italy
1962	Brazil	Czechoslovakia	Chile	1994	Brazil	Italy	U.S.
1966	England	W. Germany	England				

CRIME

Crime in U.S. Down Overall in 1996

Serious crimes reported to law enforcement agencies in the U.S. decreased 3% in 1996 compared with 1995, according to *Uniform Crime Reports* figures released by the Federal Bureau of Investigation. The decrease continued the trend of recent years; overall crime was down 1% in 1995, 1% in 1994, 2% in 1993, and 3% in 1992.

Serious crime is measured by the Crime Index, which is composed of 4 violent and 4 property crimes. Violent crime dropped 7% in 1996, and property crime, 2%.

All 4 violent crimes in the Crime Index decreased. Murder fell 9%, robbery decreased by 8%, aggravated assault declined 6%, and forcible rape dropped by 2%.

In the property-crime category, motor vehicle theft was down 5%, burglary fell 4%, and larceny-theft decreased by 1%. Sufficient data are not available to estimate totals for arson.

Declines in overall Crime Index totals occurred in 3 regions (8% in the West, 7% in the Northeast, and 1% in the Midwest); crime in the South increased by 1%.

Cities with more than 1 million inhabitants showed the largest decline, 6%. Cities with populations from 250,000 to 499,999, those with 100,000 to 249,999, and those with 50,000 to 99,999 inhabitants experienced a 4% decrease. The crime data for the 2-year period of 1995 and 1996 show that suburban counties experienced a 4% decrease in their crime level, while rural counties reported a 2% decline.

U.S. Crime Index Trends

Source: FBI, *Uniform Crime Reports*, 1996

(percentage change 1996 over 1995, offenses known to the police)

Population group and area	No. of agen-cies[1]	Population (thou-sands)	Crime Index (total)	Vio-lent crime[3]	Prop-erty crime[4]	Mur-der	Forc-ible rape	Rob-bery	Aggra-vated assault	Bur-glary	Lar-ceny/ theft	Motor ve-hicle theft
Total U.S.			−3	−7	−2	−9	−2	−8	−6	−4	−1	−5
Cities[2]:												
Over 1,000,000	10	22,285	−6	−8	−5	−13	−1	−10	−7	−7	−4	−7
500,000 to 999,999	17	10,967	−3	−5	−2	−3	−5	−5	−4	−3	−2	−2
250,000 to 499,999	37	13,423	−4	−7	−3	−13	−2	−8	−7	−4	−2	−7
100,000 to 249,999	147	21,674	−4	−7	−4	−12	−4	−8	−7	−5	−2	−7
50,000 to 99,999	320	21,769	−4	−8	−4	−8	+1	−8	−9	−5	−3	−4
25,000 to 49,999	590	20,446	−2	−6	−2	−6	−1	−6	−6	−4	−1	−4
10,000 to 24,999	1,436	22,582	−1	−5	0	−10	+1	−1	−7	−2	0	0
Under 10,000	5,228	18,434	−1	−6	−1	−1	−2	−3	−8	−1	0	0
Counties[2]:												
Suburban	1,108	46,151	−4	−8	−3	−9	−6	−6	−9	−6	−2	−6
Rural[5]	2,127	23,155	−2	−5	−2	−6	−6	−2	−5	−3	−1	0
Areas[2]:												
Suburban area[6]	5,452	87,516	−3	−7	−3	−8	−4	−5	−8	−5	−1	−5

(1) Law-enforcement agencies. (2) For these categories, index trend figures are based on data from approximately 83% of agencies that reported for both 1995 and 1996. (3) Violent crimes are murder, forcible rape, robbery, and aggravated assault. (4) Property crimes are burglary, larceny-theft, and motor vehicle theft. Data for property crime of arson are not included. (5) Includes state police agencies with no county breakdowns. (6) Includes suburban city and county law enforcement agencies within metropolitan areas but not central cities. Suburban cities and counties are also included in other groups.

Crime Index Trends by Geographic Region

Source: FBI, *Uniform Crime Reports*, 1996

(percentage change 1996 over 1995, offenses known to the police)

Region	Crime Index (total)	Violent crime	Property crime[1]	Mur-der	Forcible rape	Rob-bery	Aggra-vated assault	Burglary	Larceny-theft	Motor vehicle theft
Total U.S.	−3	−7	−2	−9	−2	−8	−6	−4	−1	−5
Northeast	−7	−9	−6	−13	0	−11	−8	−9	−5	−8
Midwest	−1	−8	0	−7	−5	−9	−7	−2	0	−1
South	+1	−3	+2	−7	0	−3	−3	+1	+2	0
West	−8	−9	−7	−13	−3	−8	−10	−8	−6	12

NA=Not available. (1) Data for arson not included.

Crime Index Trends, 1992-96

Source: FBI, *Uniform Crime Reports*, 1996

(percentage change over previous year)

Year	Crime Index (total)	Violent crime	Property crime[1]	Mur-der	Forcible rape	Rob-bery	Aggra-vated assault	Burglary	Larceny-theft	Motor vehicle theft
1992	−3	+1	−4	−4	+2	−2	+3	−6	−3	−3
1993	−2	0	−2	+3	−4	−2	+1	−5	−1	−3
1994	−1	−3	−1	−5	−4	−6	1	1	−1	−2
1995	−1	−1	−1	−7	−6	−7	−3	−5	+1	−5
1996	−3	−7	−2	−9	−2	−8	−6	−4	−1	−5

NA=Not available. (1) Data for arson not included.

Crime in the U.S., 1977-96

Source: FBI, *Uniform Crime Reports*, 1996

Population[1]	Crime Index (total)[2]	Violent crime	Property crime[3]	Murder and non-negligent man-slaughter	Forcible rape	Robbery	Burglary	Larceny-theft
Population by year				Number of reported offenses				
1977–216,332,000	10,984,500	1,029,580	9,955,000	19,120	63,500	412,610	3,071,500	5,905,700
1978–218,059,000	11,209,000	1,085,550	10,123,400	19,560	67,610	426,930	3,128,300	5,991,000
1979–220,099,000	12,249,500	1,208,030	11,041,500	21,460	76,390	480,700	3,327,700	6,601,000
1980–225,349,264	13,408,300	1,344,520	12,063,700	23,040	82,990	565,840	3,795,200	7,136,900
1981–229,146,000	13,423,800	1,361,820	12,061,900	22,520	82,500	592,910	3,779,700	7,194,400
1982–231,534,000	12,974,400	1,322,390	11,652,000	21,010	78,770	553,130	3,447,100	7,142,500
1983–233,981,000	12,108,600	1,258,090	10,850,500	19,310	78,920	506,570	3,129,900	6,712,800
1984–236,158,000	11,881,800	1,273,280	10,608,500	18,690	84,230	485,010	2,984,400	6,591,900
1985–238,740,000	12,431,400	1,328,800	11,102,600	18,980	88,670	497,870	3,073,300	6,926,400
1986–241,077,000	13,211,900	1,489,170	11,722,700	20,610	91,460	542,780	3,241,400	7,257,200
1987–243,400,000	13,508,700	1,484,000	12,024,700	20,100	91,110	517,700	3,236,200	7,499,900
1988–245,807,000	13,923,100	1,566,220	12,356,900	20,680	92,490	542,970	3,218,100	7,705,900
1989–248,239,000	14,251,400	1,646,040	12,605,400	21,500	94,500	578,330	3,168,200	7,872,400
1990–248,709,873	14,475,600	1,820,130	12,655,500	23,440	102,560	639,270	3,073,900	7,945,700
1991–252,177,000	14,872,900	1,911,770	12,961,100	24,700	106,590	687,730	3,157,200	8,142,200
1992–255,082,000	14,438,200	1,932,270	12,505,900	23,760	109,060	672,480	2,979,900	7,915,200
1993–257,908,000	14,144,800	1,926,020	12,218,800	24,530	106,010	659,870	2,834,800	7,820,900
1994–260,341,000	13,989,500	1,857,670	12,131,900	23,330	102,220	618,950	2,712,800	7,879,800
1995–262,755,000[4]	13,862,700	1,798,790	12,063,900	21,610	97,470	580,510	2,593,800	7,997,700
1996–265,284,000	13,473,600	1,682,280	11,791,300	19,650	95,770	537,050	2,501,500	7,894,600
Percent change: number of offenses								
1996/1995	–2.8	–6.5	–2.3	–9.1	–1.7	–7.5	–3.6	–1.3
1996/1992	–6.7	–12.9	–5.7	–17.3	–12.2	–20.1	–16.1	–0.3
1996/1987	–0.3	+13.4	–1.9	–2.2	+5.1	+3.7	–22.7	+5.3
Year				Rate per 100,000 inhabitants				
1977	5,077.6	475.9	4,601.7	8.8	29.4	190.7	1,419.8	2,729.9
1978	5,140.3	497.8	4,642.5	9.0	31.0	195.8	1,434.6	2,747.4
1979	5,565.5	548.9	5,016.6	9.7	34.7	218.4	1,511.9	2,999.1
1980	5,950.0	596.6	5,353.3	10.2	36.8	251.1	1,684.1	3,167.0
1981	5,858.2	594.3	5,263.9	9.8	36.0	258.7	1,649.5	3,139.7
1982	5,603.6	571.1	5,032.5	9.1	34.0	238.9	1,488.8	3,084.8
1983	5,175.0	537.7	4,637.4	8.3	33.7	216.5	1,337.7	2,868.9
1984	5,031.3	539.2	4,492.1	7.9	35.7	205.4	1,263.7	2,791.3
1985	5,207.1	556.6	4,650.5	7.9	37.1	208.5	1,287.3	2,901.2
1986	5,480.4	617.7	4,862.6	8.6	37.9	225.1	1,344.6	3,010.3
1987	5,550.0	609.7	4,940.3	8.3	37.4	212.7	1,329.6	3,081.3
1988	5,664.2	637.2	5,027.1	8.4	37.6	220.9	1,309.2	3,134.9
1989	5,741.0	663.1	5,077.9	8.7	38.1	233.0	1,276.3	3,171.3
1990	5,820.3	731.8	5,088.5	9.4	41.2	257.0	1,235.9	3,194.8
1991	5,897.8	758.1	5,139.7	9.8	42.3	272.7	1,252.0	3,228.8
1992	5,660.2	757.5	4,902.7	9.3	42.8	263.6	1,168.2	3,103.0
1993	5,484.4	746.8	4,737.6	9.5	41.1	255.9	1,099.2	3,032.4
1994	5,373.5	713.6	4,660.0	9.0	39.3	237.7	1,042.0	3,026.7
1995[4]	5,275.9	684.6	4,591.3	8.2	37.1	220.9	987.1	3,043.8
1996	5,078.9	634.1	4,444.8	7.4	36.1	202.4	943.0	2,975.9
Percent change: rate per 100,000 inhabitants								
1996/1995	–3.7	–7.4	–3.2	–9.8	–2.7	–8.4	–4.5	–2.2
1996/1992	–10.3	–16.3	–9.3	–20.4	–15.7	–23.2	–19.3	–4.1
1996/1987	–8.5	+4.0	–10.0	–10.8	–3.5	–4.8	–29.1	–3.4

Note: All rates were calculated on the offenses before rounding. (1) Populations are Bureau of the Census provisional estimates as of July 1, except 1980 and 1990, which are the decennial census counts. (2) Because of rounding, violent and property crime may not add to total. Not all categories of violent and property crime appear separately. (3) Data for arson not included. (4) The 1995 figures have been adjusted.

Law Enforcement Officers

Source: FBI, *Uniform Crime Reports*, 1996

The U.S. law enforcement community employed an average of 2.4 full-time officers for every 1,000 inhabitants as of Oct. 31, 1996. Including full-time civilians, the overall law enforcement employee rate was 3.3 per 1,000 inhabitants, according to 13,025 city, county, and state police agencies. These agencies collectively offered law enforcement service covering a population of about 265 million, employing 595,170 officers and 234,668 civilians.

The law enforcement employee average for all cities nationwide was 3.0 per 1,000 inhabitants. The highest city law enforcement employee average was 4.0 per 1,000 inhabitants, in cities with populations of 250,000 or more. Rural and suburban counties averaged full-time law enforcement employee rates of 4.3 and 3.8 per 1,000 population, respectively.

Regionally, the law enforcement employee rate was 3.4 in the Northeast and the South, 2.7 in the Midwest, and 2.5 in the West.

Nationally, males constituted 90 percent of all sworn employees. Ninety-three percent of the officers in rural counties were males, and in suburban counties males accounted for 88 percent.

Civilians made up 28 percent of the total U.S. law enforcement employee force. They represented 22 percent of the police employees in cities, 37 percent of those in rural counties, and 38 percent in suburban counties.

Fifty-five law enforcement officers were feloniously slain in the line of duty in 1996, 19 fewer than in 1995. Another 45 officers were killed as a result of accidents occurring while performing official duties.

Crime Rates by Region, Geographic Division, and State, 1996

Source: FBI, *Uniform Crime Reports*, 1996

(rate per 100,000)

Area	Total	Violent crime[1]	Property crime[2]	Murder	Rape	Robbery	Aggra-vated assault	Burglary	Larceny-theft	Motor vehicle theft
United States total	5,078.9	634.1	4,444.8	7.4	36.1	202.4	388.2	943.0	2,975.9	525.9
Northeast	3,898.7	555.4	3,343.3	5.4	24.9	232.2	293.0	691.2	2,180.5	471.6
New England	3,777.9	447.1	3,330.9	3.0	27.2	111.3	305.6	726.1	2,176.2	428.6
Connecticut	4,227.7	412.0	3,815.6	4.8	23.1	169.6	214.6	842.2	2,484.1	489.4
Maine	3,394.1	124.9	3,269.2	2.0	20.9	23.5	78.5	748.4	2,377.9	142.9
Massachusetts	3,837.1	642.2	3,194.9	2.6	29.0	127.7	482.9	704.1	1,962.6	528.2
New Hampshire	2,823.5	118.2	2,705.3	1.7	34.8	27.3	54.4	435.7	2,118.0	151.6
Rhode Island	3,993.5	347.2	3,646.4	2.5	29.0	83.2	232.4	821.7	2,360.3	464.3
Vermont	3,002.9	121.2	2,881.7	1.9	27.0	15.4	76.9	673.0	2,058.4	150.3
Middle Atlantic	3,940.9	593.3	3,347.6	6.2	24.1	274.4	288.6	679.0	2,182.1	486.6
New Jersey	4,332.9	531.5	3,801.4	4.2	24.7	235.8	266.7	791.9	2,428.2	581.3
New York	4,132.3	727.0	3,405.3	7.4	23.0	340.0	356.7	713.9	2,197.0	494.4
Pennsylvania	3,392.5	432.5	2,960.1	5.7	25.3	201.1	200.4	551.4	1,996.5	412.2
Midwest	4,664.0	536.6	4,127.5	6.4	38.1	161.3	330.8	817.3	2,867.3	442.8
East North Central	4,765.6	592.1	4,173.5	7.0	39.5	184.8	360.9	833.6	2,850.5	489.5
Illinois	5,315.8	886.2	4,429.6	10.0	34.2	279.4	562.6	913.2	3,026.2	490.2
Indiana	4,498.2	537.0	3,961.2	7.2	34.1	124.1	371.6	783.8	2,752.6	424.9
Michigan	5,117.5	635.3	4,482.2	7.5	57.0	176.2	394.6	895.4	2,886.3	700.5
Ohio	4,455.7	428.7	4,027.0	4.8	41.3	164.1	218.4	835.4	2,784.1	407.5
Wisconsin	3,821.4	252.7	3,568.7	4.0	21.0	96.6	131.1	588.3	2,634.5	345.9
West North Central	4,424.1	405.5	4,018.6	4.8	34.9	105.9	259.8	778.9	2,907.0	332.8
Iowa	3,648.9	272.5	3,376.4	1.9	19.7	45.1	205.9	664.6	2,520.8	191.1
Kansas	4,681.7	413.8	4,268.0	6.6	42.6	96.3	268.3	981.3	3,038.3	248.4
Minnesota	4,463.1	338.8	4,124.3	3.6	50.0	115.6	169.7	762.5	2,977.1	384.8
Missouri	5,084.0	590.9	4,493.0	8.1	29.2	170.6	383.1	894.2	3,151.1	447.7
Nebraska	4,436.6	434.7	4,001.8	2.9	27.1	63.7	341.1	614.5	3,045.7	341.6
North Dakota	2,669.1	84.0	2,585.1	2.2	24.1	11.0	46.7	309.2	2,085.9	190.1
South Dakota	2,969.9	177.2	2,792.8	1.2	41.0	18.9	116.1	557.0	2,121.9	113.9
South	5,727.0	706.8	5,020.2	9.0	40.4	203.3	454.1	1,128.5	3,368.2	523.5
South Atlantic	6,081.8	777.8	5,304.0	8.9	39.3	234.6	494.9	1,180.8	3,574.0	549.1
Delaware	4,894.9	668.3	4,226.6	4.3	62.6	179.9	421.5	804.1	2,988.3	434.2
District of Columbia	11,896.7	2,469.8	9,426.9	73.1	47.9	1,186.7	1,162.1	1,809.9	5,779.9	1,837.0
Florida	7,497.4	1,051.0	6,446.3	7.5	52.1	289.2	702.2	1,521.2	4,204.5	720.6
Georgia	6,309.7	638.7	5,671.0	8.6	32.1	205.4	392.8	1,114.8	3,927.7	628.5
Maryland	6,061.9	931.2	5,130.7	11.6	37.6	393.2	488.8	992.3	3,427.0	711.4
North Carolina	5,526.2	588.1	4,938.1	8.5	31.3	163.9	384.5	1,345.6	3,257.0	335.5
South Carolina	6,214.1	996.9	5,217.2	9.0	49.2	172.0	766.7	1,283.8	3,505.0	428.5
Virginia	3,968.3	341.3	3,627.0	7.5	26.7	122.6	184.5	588.1	2,760.1	278.8
West Virginia	2,483.4	210.1	2,273.3	3.8	19.6	40.4	146.3	546.5	1,549.8	176.9
East South Central	4,580.3	562.2	4,018.1	9.1	37.6	162.5	353.0	1,001.7	2,585.7	430.6
Alabama	4,820.1	565.4	4,254.7	10.4	32.7	166.7	355.6	1,002.1	2,886.7	365.8
Kentucky	3,166.3	320.5	2,845.8	5.9	31.7	93.8	189.2	688.4	1,896.3	261.1
Mississippi	4,522.9	488.3	4,034.6	11.1	36.1	134.2	306.8	1,132.4	2,551.5	350.8
Tennessee	5,449.3	774.0	4,675.4	9.5	46.5	223.7	494.3	1,163.5	2,864.8	647.1
West South Central	5,783.9	671.1	5,112.8	9.2	43.6	174.9	443.5	1,113.5	3,466.0	533.3
Arkansas	4,699.2	524.3	4,174.9	8.7	41.7	114.1	359.8	953.2	2,908.8	312.9
Louisiana	6,838.8	929.1	5,909.7	17.5	41.5	276.6	593.5	1,295.8	3,982.3	631.6
Oklahoma	5,652.9	597.1	5,055.8	6.8	46.8	106.6	436.9	1,255.6	3,317.4	482.9
Texas	5,708.9	644.4	5,064.5	7.7	43.8	171.5	421.4	1,068.5	3,447.4	548.6
West	5,528.5	691.5	4,837.0	7.7	37.1	218.6	428.2	1,003.0	3,168.2	665.8
Mountain	5,863.9	516.6	5,347.3	7.0	41.1	129.5	339.0	1,034.2	3,747.7	565.4
Arizona	7,067.0	631.5	6,435.5	8.5	31.2	167.8	424.0	1,256.3	4,252.5	926.7
Colorado	5,118.5	404.5	4,714.0	4.7	46.2	98.2	255.4	900.8	3,415.5	397.8
Idaho	4,012.5	267.2	3,745.3	3.6	26.3	20.3	217.0	709.1	2,848.8	187.5
Montana	4,493.6	161.0	4,332.7	3.9	27.1	29.7	100.3	558.4	3,518.5	255.7
Nevada	5,992.0	811.3	5,180.7	13.7	53.4	307.6	436.6	1,220.1	3,262.3	698.3
New Mexico	6,602.3	840.6	5,761.7	11.5	63.5	162.4	603.2	1,376.9	3,802.6	582.2
Utah	5,985.9	331.9	5,654.0	3.2	41.8	68.9	218.1	848.3	4,377.1	428.6
Wyoming	4,254.1	249.7	4,004.4	3.3	29.1	20.4	196.9	662.0	3,203.3	139.1
Pacific	5,400.8	758.0	4,642.9	8.0	35.5	252.4	462.1	991.1	2,947.8	704.0
Alaska	5,450.4	727.7	4,722.7	7.4	65.6	117.0	537.7	843.2	3,386.7	492.9
California	5,207.8	862.7	4,345.1	9.1	32.1	295.6	525.8	979.4	2,605.1	760.6
Hawaii	6,584.5	280.6	6,304.0	3.4	27.5	135.6	114.0	1,079.5	4,620.0	604.5
Oregon	5,996.6	463.1	5,533.6	4.0	39.7	133.3	207.0	900.0	4,014.3	531.0
Washington	5,909.4	431.2	5,478.2	4.6	51.1	119.0	256.4	1,057.6	9,090.5	322.2

Note: Offense totals are based on all reporting agencies and estimates for unreported areas. Totals may not add because of rounding. (1) Violent crimes are murder, forcible rape, robbery, and aggravated assault. (2) Property crimes are burglary, larceny-theft, and motor vehicle theft. Data are not included for the property crime of arson.

State and Federal Prison Population; Death Penalty

Source: Prison population: Bureau of Justice Statistics, U.S. Dept. of Justice, Dec. 31, 1996;
Death penalty: Bureau of Justice Statistics, as of Dec. 31, 1995

The total number of prisoners under the jurisdiction of federal or state correctional authorities at year-end 1996 was estimated at a record high of 1,182,169. According to Bureau of Justice Statistics estimates, the states and the District of Columbia added 50,582 prisoners in 1996; the federal system, 5,294. The 1996 growth rate of 5.0% was below the average annual growth rate since 1985 (8.1%), and below the percentage increase recorded in 1995 (6.8%). The total increase (55,876) was the 2d lowest of the 1990s, after the 1991 increase of 51,640. The 1996 increase translated into a nationwide need to confine an additional 1,075 inmates per week, compared with 1,386 per week in 1995. Prisoners with a sentence of more than 1 year accounted for 96% of the total prison population at the end of 1996.

	Sentenced to more than 1 yr		% change 1995–96	Under sentence of death	Death penalty, 1995	
	Advance 1996	Final 1995			Executions	Death penalty
U.S. total	1,138,187	1,085,369	4.9%	3,054	56	—
Federal institutions	88,815	83,663	6.2	8	0	Yes
State institutions	1,049,372	1,001,706	4.8	3,046	56	38
Northeast	159,243	154,959	2.8	211	2	—
Connecticut	10,301	10,418	−1.1	5	0	Yes
Maine	1,401	1,326	5.7			No
Massachusetts	10,903	10,355	5.3			No
New Hampshire	2,071	2,014	2.8	0	0	Yes
New Jersey	27,490	27,066	1.6	10	0	Yes
New York	69,709	68,489	1.8	0	0	Yes
Pennsylvania	34,531	32,410	6.5	196	2	Yes
Rhode Island	2,030	1,833	10.7			No
Vermont	807	1,048	−23.0			No
Midwest	203,285	192,147	5.8	459	11	—
Illinois	38,852	37,658	3.2	154	5	Yes
Indiana	16,801	16,046	4.7	46	0	Yes
Iowa	6,342	5,906	7.4			No
Kansas	7,756	7,054	10.0	0	0	Yes
Michigan	42,349	41,112	3.0			No
Minnesota	5,158	4,846	6.4			No
Missouri	21,999	19,134	15.0	92	6	Yes
Nebraska	3,212	3,006	6.9	10	0	Yes
North Dakota	650	544	19.5			No
Ohio	46,174	44,663	3.4	155	0	Yes
South Dakota	2,064	1,841	12.1	2	0	Yes
Wisconsin	11,928	10,337	15.4			No
South	459,294	446,958	2.8	1,693	41	—
Alabama	21,107	20,130	4.9	143	2	Yes
Arkansas	8,992	9,021	−0.3	38	2	Yes
Delaware	3,119	2,980	4.7	14	1	Yes
District of Columbia	8,659	9,042	−4.2			No
Florida	63,746	63,866	−0.2	362	2	Yes
Georgia	34,328	34,168	0.5	98	2	Yes
Kentucky	12,910	12,060	7.0	28	0	Yes
Louisiana	26,779	25,195	6.3	57	1	Yes
Maryland	20,980	20,450	2.6	13	0	Yes
Mississippi	13,576	12,251	10.8	49	0	Yes
North Carolina	27,945	27,914	0.1	139	2	Yes
Oklahoma	19,593	18,151	7.9	129	3	Yes
South Carolina	19,758	19,015	3.9	67	1	Yes
Tennessee	15,626	15,206	2.8	96	0	Yes
Texas	132,383	127,766	3.6	404	19	Yes
Virginia	27,062	27,260	−0.7	56	5	Yes
West Virginia	2,730	2,483	9.9			No
West	27,550	207,642	9.6	683	2	—
Alaska	2,311	2,042	13.2			No
Arizona	21,603	20,291	6.5	117	1	Yes
California	144,386	131,745	9.6	420	0	Yes
Colorado	12,438	11,063	12.4	4	0	Yes
Hawaii	2,954	2,590	14.1			No
Idaho	3,834	3,328	15.2	19	0	Yes
Montana	2,073	1,999	3.7	6	1	Yes
Nevada	8,215	7,713	6.5	75	0	Yes
New Mexico	4,506	3,925	14.8	3	0	Yes
Oregon	7,316	6,515	12.3	20	0	Yes
Utah	3,913	3,428	14.1	10	0	Yes
Washington	12,518	11,608	7.8	9	0	Yes
Wyoming	1,483	1,395	6.3	0	0	Yes

Note: The advance count of prisoners is conducted in Jan. and may be revised. Prisoner counts for 1995 may differ from those reported in previous publications.

Sentences vs. Time Served for Selected Crimes

Source: Bureau of Justice Statistics, *Prison Sentences and Time Served for Violence,* Apr. 1995

The following is a comparison of the average maximum sentence lengths (excluding both life and death sentences) and the actual time served for selected state-court convictions.

Type of offense	Average sentence	Avg. time served[1]	Type of offense	Average sentence	Avg. time served[1]
All violent	7 years, 5 months	3 years, 7 months	Robbery	7 years, 11 months	3 years, 8 months
Homicide	12 years, 5 months	5 years, 11 months	Sexual assault	6 years	2 years, 11 months
Rape	9 years, 9 months	5 years, 5 months	Assault	5 years, 1 month	2 years, 5 months
Kidnapping	8 years, 8 months	4 years, 4 months	Other	5 years	2 years, 4 months

(1) Includes jail credit and prison time.

Prison Situation Among the States and in the Federal System, 1996

Source: *Prisoners in 1996,* Bureau of Justice Statistics, U.S. Dept. of Justice; year-end 1996.

The 10 largest total prison populations, 1996	Number of inmates	The 10 highest incarceration rates, 1996	Prisoners per 100,000 residents[1]	The 10 largest % increases in prison population			
				1995–96	% increase	1991–96	% increase
California	147,712	Texas	686	North Dakota	18.8	Texas	156.2
Texas	132,383	Louisiana	615	New Mexico	15.8	Wisconsin	63.7
Federal system	105,544	Oklahoma	591	Idaho	15.2	North Carolina	62.4
New York	69,709	South Carolina	532	Missouri	15.0	Mississippi	60.5
Florida	63,763	Nevada	502	Wisconsin	14.8	Iowa	53.0
Ohio	46,174	Mississippi	498	Utah	14.1	New Mexico	51.5
Michigan	42,349	Alabama	492	Rhode Island	12.7	South Dakota	50.2
Illinois	38,852	Arizona	481	Mississippi	12.7	Utah	50.1
Georgia	35,139	Georgia	462	Hawaii	12.7	Hawaii	48.6
Pennsylvania	34,537	California	451	Colorado	12.4	Minnesota	48.6

(1) Prisoners with sentences of more than 1 year. The Federal Bureau of Prisons and the District of Columbia are excluded.

Executions, by State and Method, 1977-95

Source: Bureau of Justice Statistics, *Capital Punishment 1995,* Dec. 1995

State	No.	Method of Execution					State	No.	Method of Execution				
		Lethal injection	Electrocution	Lethal gas	Firing squad	Hanging			Lethal injection	Electrocution	Lethal gas	Firing squad	Hanging
Total U.S.	313	180	121	9	1	2	South Carolina	5	1	4			
Texas	104	104					Arizona	4	3		1		
Florida	36		36				Mississippi	4			4		
Virginia	29	5	24				Utah	4	3			1	
Louisiana	22	2	20				Indiana	3		3			
Georgia	20		20				California	2			2		
Missouri	17	17					Pennsylvania	2	2				
Alabama	12		12				Washington	2					2
Arkansas	11	10	1				Idaho	1	1				
North Carolina	8	7		1			Maryland	1	1				
Illinois	7	7					Montana	1	1				
Oklahoma	6	6					Nebraska	1		1			
Delaware	5	5					Wyoming	1	1				
Nevada	5	4		1									

Note: This table shows execution methods used since 1977. Lethal injection was used in 58% of the executions carried out. Eight states—Arizona, Arkansas, Louisiana, Nevada, North Carolina, South Carolina, Utah, and Virginia—have employed 2 methods.

Total Estimated Arrests,[1] 1996

Source: FBI, *Uniform Crime Reports,* 1996

Total[2]	15,168,100	Weapons: carrying, possessing, etc.	216,200
Murder and nonnegligent manslaughter	19,020	Prostitution and commercialized vice	99,000
Forcible rape	33,050	Sex offenses (except forcible rape	
Robbery	156,270	and prostitution)	95,800
Aggravated assault	521,570	Drug abuse violations	1,506,200
Burglary	364,800	Gambling	21,000
Larceny–theft	1,486,300	Offenses against family and children	149,800
Motor vehicle theft	175,400	Driving under the influence	1,467,300
Arson	19,000	Liquor laws	677,400
Violent crimes[3]	**729,900**	Drunkenness	718,700
Property crime[4]	**2,045,600**	Disorderly conduct	842,600
Crime Index total[2, 5]	**2,775,500**	Vagrancy	27,800
Other assaults	1,329,000	All other offenses	3,786,700
Forgery and counterfeiting	121,600	Suspicion (not included in totals)	4,900
Fraud	465,000	Curfew and loitering law violations	185,100
Embezzlement	15,700	Runaways	195,900
Stolen property: buying, receiving, possessing	151,100		
Vandalism	320,900		

(1) Arrest totals are based on all reporting agencies and estimates for unreported areas. (2) Because of rounding, figures may not add to totals. (3) Violent crimes are murder, forcible rape, robbery, and aggravated assault. (4) Property crimes are burglary, larceny-theft, motor vehicle theft, and arson. (5) Includes arson.

Federal Bureau of Investigation

The Federal Bureau of Investigation was created July 26, 1908, and was referred to as Office of Chief Examiner. It became the Bureau of Investigation (Mar. 16, 1909), United States Bureau of Investigation (July 1, 1932), Division of Investigation (Aug. 10, 1933), and Federal Bureau of Investigation (July 1, 1935).

Director	Assumed office	Director	Assumed office
Stanley W. Finch	July 26, 1908	William D. Ruckelshaus, act.	Apr. 27, 1973
A(lexander) Bruce Bielaski	Apr. 30, 1912	Clarence M. Kelley	July 9, 1973
William E. Allen, act.	Feb. 10, 1919	William H. Webster	Feb. 23, 1978
William J. Flynn	July 1, 1919	John E. Otto, act.	May 26, 1987
William J. Burns	Aug. 22, 1921	William S. Sessions	Nov. 2, 1987
J. Edgar Hoover, act.	May 10, 1924	Floyd I. Clarke, act.	July 19, 1993
J. Edgar Hoover	Dec. 10, 1924	Louis J. Freeh	Sept. 1, 1993
L. Patrick Gray, act.	May 3, 1972		

VITAL STATISTICS
Annual Report for the Year 1996
Source: National Center for Health Statistics, U.S. Dept. of Health and Human Services

Highlights
Provisional data for 1996 reported by the National Center for Health Statistics show that the U.S. infant mortality rate reached a record low (7.2 infant deaths per 1,000 live births). Life expectancy reached an all-time high of 76.1 years. Marriage and divorce rates both continued to decline, and the rate of natural increase declined slightly.

Births
An estimated 3,914,953 babies were born in the U.S. in 1996, an increase of less than 1% from the 3,899,589 births in 1995. The birthrate was slightly lower than the rate for the preceding year (14.76 per 1,000 population as compared to 14.83). The fertility rate (the number of live births per 1,000 women aged 15-44 years) for 1996 was 65.7, slightly higher than the rate for 1995 (65.6).

Deaths
The provisional count of deaths during 1996 was 2,322,265, less than 1% more than in the previous year (2,312,132). The death rate of 875.4 deaths per 100,000 population was slightly lower than the 1995 death rate of 880.0. The infant mortality rate of 7.2 infant deaths per 1,000 live births was 5% lower than the rate of 7.6 for 1995.

Natural Increase
As a result of natural increase, the excess of births over deaths, an estimated 1,592,688 persons were added to the population in 1996. The rate was 6.0 per 1,000 population, slightly lower than for 1995, and the lowest since 1976 (5.9). The steady rate of natural increase was due to similar slight declines in the birth and death rates.

Marriages
An estimated 2,344,000 marriages were performed in 1996, less than 1% higher than in 1995 (2,336,000). The marriage rate for 1996 (8.8 per 1,000 population) was 1% lower than in 1995 (8.9). This rate has generally declined since the early 1980s and is currently the lowest rate since 1963 (8.8).

Divorces
About 1,150,000 divorces were granted in the U.S. in 1996, 2% fewer than the number for 1995 (1,169,000), and 5% fewer than the all-time high of 1,215,000 in 1992. The divorce rate per 1,000 population in 1996 (4.3) was 2% lower than the rate for 1995 (4.4) and was the lowest divorce rate in over 2 decades.

Births and Deaths in the U.S.
Source: National Center for Health Statistics, U.S. Dept. of Health and Human Services

Year	Births Total number	Births Rate	Deaths Total number	Deaths Rate
1960	4,257,850	23.7	1,711,982	9.5
1970	3,731,386	18.4	1,921,031	9.5
1980	3,612,258	15.9	1,989,841	8.7
1990	4,158,212	16.7	2,148,463	8.6
1991	4,110,907	16.3	2,169,518	8.6
1992	4,065,014	15.9	2,175,613	8.5
1993	4,000,240	15.5	2,268,000	8.8
1994	3,952,767	15.2	2,278,994	8.8
1995	3,899,589	14.8	2,312,132	8.8
1996 (P)	3,914,953	14.8	2,322,265	8.8

(P) = provisional data. **Note:** Refers only to events occurring within the U.S. Excludes fetal deaths. Rates per 1,000 population enumerated as of Apr. 1 for 1960 and 1970; estimated as of July 1 for all other years. Beginning 1970 excludes births and deaths occurring to nonresidents of the U.S. Data include revisions.

MILLENNIUM FACT BOX

Facts About Americans—Historical Comparisons

Life in the U.S. has changed considerably since 1900. The population has increased by nearly 250%, birth and death rates have both plummeted, and life expectancy has risen sharply. Fewer people are getting married, more are getting divorced (although the divorce rate has recently been declining), and families are smaller. The numbers of physicians and dentists have risen more than sixfold.

	1900	1996[1]
Population	76,212,168	265,283,783
Births	2,461,653	3,914,953
Birth rate (per 1,000 population)	32.3	14.8
Death rate (per 1,000 population)	17.2[2]	8.8
Marriages	685,101	2,344,000
Marriage rate (per 1,000 population)	9.3	8.8
Divorces	55,751	1,150,000
Divorce rate (per 1,000 population)	0.7	4.3
Years of life expected at birth	47.3	76.1
Male	46.3	73.0
Female	48.3	79.0
Number of households	15,964,000	98,990,000[3]
Persons per household	4.77	2.65[3]
Number of physicians	119,749	737,764
Physicians per 100,000 population	157	278
Number of dentists	25,189	156,800[4]
Dentists per 100,000 population	33	61[4]

(1) Some statistics are estimated or provisional. (2) For 1900, the death rate is based on incomplete totals, from states and localities reporting to the National Office of Vital Statistics; a total U.S. death figure is not available. (3) 1995 figure. (4) 1994 figure.

Births and Deaths, by States and Regions, 1995-96

Source: National Center for Health Statistics, U.S. Dept. of Health and Human Services

Area	Live births 1995 Number	Rate	1996 Number	Rate	Deaths 1995 Number	Rate	1996 Number	Rate
New England	178,775	13.4	171,393	12.8	120,461	9.1	119,119	8.9
Maine	14,006	11.3	13,718	11.0	11,625	9.4	11,035	8.9
New Hampshire	15,069	13.1	14,125	12.2	9,244	8.1	9,114	7.8
Vermont	6,780	11.6	6,773	11.5	5,031	8.6	4,885	8.3
Massachusetts	85,045	14.0	80,165	13.2	55,965	9.2	55,328	9.1
Rhode Island	12,695	12.8	12,601	12.7	9,640	9.7	9,574	9.7
Connecticut	45,180	13.8	44,011	13.4	28,956	8.9	29,183	8.9
Middle Atlantic	531,123	13.9	535,193	14.0	371,192	9.7	364,233	9.5
New York	264,253	14.5	271,569	14.9	168,140	9.2	162,875	9.0
New Jersey	115,116	14.5	113,713	14.2	74,974	9.4	71,895	9.0
Pennsylvania	151,754	12.6	149,911	12.4	128,078	10.6	129,463	10.7
East North Central ...	625,045	14.4	624,455	14.3	395,210	9.1	394,908	9.1
Ohio	155,568	14.0	152,233	13.6	105,799	9.5	105,213	9.4
Indiana	84,188	14.5	83,417	14.3	52,514	9.1	54,321	9.3
Illinois	185,442	15.7	184,526	15.6	108,735	9.2	106,355	9.0
Michigan	132,783	13.9	137,518	14.3	83,394	8.7	83,972	8.8
Wisconsin	67,064	13.1	66,761	12.9	44,768	8.7	45,047	8.7
West North Central ..	253,754	13.8	253,702	13.7	170,443	9.3	168,223	9.1
Minnesota	62,752	13.6	63,657	13.7	37,028	8.0	36,804	7.9
Iowa	36,399	12.8	34,838	12.2	25,897	9.1	26,315	9.2
Missouri	74,946	14.1	73,132	13.6	55,599	10.5	53,697	10.0
North Dakota	8,719	13.6	8,396	13.0	6,099	9.5	5,753	8.9
South Dakota	10,574	14.5	10,081	13.8	6,901	9.5	6,314	8.6
Nebraska	23,159	14.1	23,355	14.1	15,284	9.3	15,472	9.4
Kansas	37,205	14.5	40,243	15.6	23,655	9.2	23,868	9.3
South Atlantic	655,356	13.9	658,995	13.8	436,204	9.3	440,186	9.2
Delaware	10,013	14.0	10,142	14.0	6,151	8.6	6,443	8.9
Maryland	72,198	14.3	71,042	14.0	41,004	8.1	41,965	8.3
District of Columbia .	8,943	16.1	8,240	15.2	6,653	12.0	6,317	11.6
Virginia	89,948	13.6	89,149	13.4	52,989	8.0	52,847	7.9
West Virginia	20,954	11.5	19,621	10.7	19,887	10.9	19,106	10.5
North Carolina	102,165	14.2	106,261	14.5	65,132	9.0	66,357	9.1
South Carolina	49,841	13.6	50,568	13.7	32,570	8.9	34,603	9.4
Georgia	113,196	15.7	114,603	15.6	58,230	8.1	58,802	8.0
Florida	188,098	13.3	189,369	13.2	153,588	10.8	153,746	10.7
East South Central ...	223,287	13.9	229,159	14.2	158,420	9.9	156,908	9.7
Kentucky	51,015	13.2	52,545	13.5	38,319	9.9	37,550	9.7
Tennessee	73,892	14.1	73,658	13.8	50,658	9.7	49,934	9.4
Alabama	61,182	14.4	61,514	14.4	42,254	10.0	42,668	10.0
Mississippi	37,198	13.8	41,442	15.3	27,189	10.1	26,756	9.9
West South Central ..	480,765	16.6	463,073	15.8	239,795	8.3	235,943	8.1
Arkansas	34,340	13.8	35,876	14.3	25,960	10.4	25,666	10.2
Louisiana	67,376	15.5	66,291	15.2	39,348	9.1	40,460	9.3
Oklahoma	45,894	14.0	45,151	13.7	32,852	10.0	33,224	10.1
Texas	333,155	17.7	315,755	16.5	141,635	7.5	136,593	7.1
Mountain	240,966	15.3	254,829	15.8	113,880	7.2	121,162	7.5
Montana	11,230	12.9	10,797	12.3	7,646	8.8	7,710	8.8
Idaho	17,735	15.2	18,868	15.9	8,488	7.3	8,685	7.3
Wyoming	6,293	13.1	6,198	12.9	3,781	7.9	3,610	7.5
Colorado........	49,938	13.3	47,610	12.5	24,852	6.6	25,853	6.8
New Mexico	27,142	16.1	27,173	15.9	12,475	7.4	12,325	7.2
Arizona	68,434	15.9	79,530	18.0	33,633	7.8	39,005	8.8
Utah...........	38,870	19.8	41,214	20.6	10,814	5.5	11,077	5.5
Nevada	21,324	13.9	23,439	14.6	12,191	7.9	12,897	8.0
Pacific	713,738	17.0	695,959	16.4	302,091	7.2	310,475	7.3
Washington	78,160	14.3	79,808	14.4	40,582	7.4	39,493	7.1
Oregon	42,953	13.6	43,798	13.7	28,011	8.9	28,293	8.8
California	564,156	17.9	543,832	17.1	223,521	7.1	232,266	7.3
Alaska	10,081	16.7	10,176	16.8	2,450	4.1	2,562	4.2
Hawaii	18,388	15.6	18,345	15.5	7,527	6.4	7,861	6.6

Note: Data are provisional estimates, reported by state of residence. Figures include revisions, and so may differ from those previously published. Rates for births and deaths are per 1,000 population.

Infant Deaths and Infant Mortality Rates, for Selected Causes, 1996-97

Source: National Center for Health Statistics, U.S. Dept. of Health and Human Services

Age and cause of death	1997 Number	Rate	1996 Number	Rate	Age and cause of death	1997 Number	Rate	1996 Number	Rate
Total, under 1 year	27,800	718.0	29,000	752.5	Birth trauma	150	3.9	200	5.2
Under 28 days	18,330	473.6	18,340	476.9	Intrauterine hypoxia and				
28 days to 11 months ...	9,450	244.2	10,560	274.6	birth asphyxia	520	13.4	460	12.0
Certain gastrointestinal					Respiratory distress				
diseases	250	6.5	170	4.4	syndrome	1,380	35.7	1,220	31.7
Pneumonia and					Other conditions				
influenza	310	8.0	340	8.8	originating around				
Congenital anomalies	6,620	171.1	5,990	155.8	the time of birth	6,890	178.0	7,850	204.1
Disorders relating to short					Sudden infant death				
gestation and unspecified					syndrome	2,500	64.6	2,910	75.7
low birthweight	3,610	93.3	3,370	87.6	All other causes	5,560	143.7	6,400	166.4

Note: Data are provisional, estimated from a 10% sample of deaths for a 12-month period ending in Jan. of the year cited. Rates are on an annual basis per 100,000 live births. Because of rounding of estimates, figures may not add to totals.

Infant Mortality Rates, by Race and Sex, 1960-95[1]

Source: National Center for Health Statistics, U.S. Dept. of Health and Human Services

	All races			White			Black		
Year	Both sexes	Male	Female	Both sexes	Male	Female	Both sexes	Male	Female
1960	26.0	29.3	22.6	22.9	26.0	19.6	44.3	49.1	39.4
1970	20.0	22.4	17.5	17.8	20.0	15.4	32.6	36.2	29.0
1980	12.6	13.9	11.2	11.0	12.3	9.6	21.4	23.3	19.4
1981	11.9	13.1	10.7	10.5	11.7	9.2	20.0	21.7	18.3
1982	11.5	12.8	10.2	10.1	11.2	8.9	19.6	21.5	17.7
1983	11.2	12.3	10.0	9.7	10.8	8.6	19.2	21.1	17.2
1984	10.8	11.9	9.6	9.4	10.5	8.3	18.4	19.8	16.9
1985	10.6	11.9	9.3	9.3	10.6	8.0	18.2	19.9	16.5
1986	10.4	11.5	9.1	8.9	10.0	7.8	18.0	20.0	16.0
1987	10.1	11.2	8.9	8.6	9.6	7.6	17.9	19.6	16.0
1988	10.0	11.0	8.9	8.5	9.5	7.4	17.6	19.0	16.1
1989	9.8	10.8	8.8	8.1	9.0	7.1	18.6	20.0	17.2
1990	9.2	10.3	8.1	7.6	8.5	6.6	18.0	19.6	16.2
1991	8.9	10.0	7.8	7.3	8.3	6.3	17.6	19.4	15.7
1992	8.5	9.4	7.6	6.9	7.7	6.1	16.8	18.4	15.3
1993	8.4	9.3	7.4	6.8	7.6	6.0	16.5	18.3	14.7
1994	8.0	8.8	7.2	6.6	7.2	5.9	15.8	17.5	14.1
1995	7.6	8.3	6.8	6.3	7.0	5.6	15.1	16.3	13.9

(1) Final data. Rates per 1,000 live births.

The 10 Leading Causes of Death, 1996[1]

Source: National Center for Health Statistics, U.S. Dept. of Health and Human Services

Rank	Cause of death	Number	Death rate[2]	Percentage of total deaths
	All causes	2,322,421	875.4	100.0
1.	Heart disease	733,834	276.6	31.6
2.	Cancer	544,278	205.2	23.4
3.	Stroke	160,431	60.5	6.9
4.	Chronic obstructive lung diseases and allied conditions	106,146	40.0	4.6
5.	Accidents and adverse effects	93,874	35.4	4.0
	Motor vehicle accidents	43,449	16.4	1.9
	All other accidents and adverse effects	50,425	19.0	2.2
6.	Pneumonia and influenza	82,579	31.1	3.6
7.	Diabetes mellitus	61,559	23.2	2.7
8.	Human immunodeficiency virus (HIV) infection[3]	32,655	12.3	1.4
9.	Suicide	30,862	11.6	1.3
10.	Chronic liver disease and cirrhosis	25,135	9.5	1.1

(1) Data are preliminary and may vary somewhat from other sources. (2) Per 100,000 population. (3) HIV is the virus that causes AIDS.

U.S. Abortion Patients, by Selected Characteristics, 1994-95

Source: Alan Guttmacher Institute, New York, NY

Characteristic	% distribution		Characteristic	% distribution	
	Abortion patients	All women 15-44[1]		Abortion patients	All women 15-44[1]
Age group[2]			**Religion[3]**		
15-17	8.8	8.8	Protestant	37.4	53.9
18-19	11.5	5.7	Catholic	31.3	30.9
20-24	32.8	15.2	Jewish	1.3	1.2
25-29	21.4	16.1	Other	6.3	8.1
30-34	14.4	18.8	None	23.7	5.0
35-39	7.5	18.6	**Born again/Evangelical**		
40 years and older..	2.3	16.8	Yes	18.0	46.0
Race			No	82.0	54.0
White	61.3	81.2	**Education**		
Black	31.1	14.0	8th grade or less ...	4.2	4.7
Other	7.6	4.9	9th-11th grade ...	16.9	16.4
Ethnicity			H.S. graduate or GED.	30.4	30.1
Hispanic	20.2	10.6	Some college or		
Non-Hispanic	79.8	89.4	associate's degree.	34.9	30.0
Marital status			College graduate ...	13.7	16.8
Married	18.4	49.9	**Enrolled in school**		
Separated	7.2	3.3	Yes	30.3	24.6
Divorced	9.4	8.6	No	69.7	75.4
Widowed	0.5	0.7	**Currently employed**		
Never married	64.4	37.5	Yes	66.2	65.6
Cohabiting			No	33.8	34.4
Yes	20.2	5.8	**Family income**		
No/married	79.8	94.2	Less than $15,000 ..	28.7	15.4
Number of live births			$15,000-$29,999 ...	19.5	20.6
0	45.4	41.2	$30,000-$59,999 ...	38.0	35.9
1	24.7	18.2	$60,000 or greater ..	13.8	23.1
2	17.8	23.8	**Medicaid coverage**		
3	7.7	11.1	Yes	26.5	12.9
4 or more	4.4	5.8	No	73.5	87.1
Region of residence			**Intend more children**		
Metropolitan	88.5	79.6	Yes	66.0	47.8
Nonmetropolitan ...	11.5	20.4	No	34.0	52.2

(1) Data for 1994 except Medicaid status (1993), religion (1993-95), and childbearing intention (1990 intention by age, applied to 1994 population). (2) Not included are patients under the age of 15, who make up 1.2%. (3) Based on women 18-44 years of age. **Note:** Percents may not add to 100 because of rounding.

Suicides by Age, Race, and Sex, 1995

Source: National Center for Health Statistics, U.S. Dept. of Health and Human Services

	All ages	1-14 yrs.	15-24 yrs.	25-34 yrs.	35-44 yrs.	45-54 yrs.	55-64 yrs.	65-74 yrs.	75-84 yrs.	85 yrs. & over	Age not stated
All races, both sexes[1] .	31,284	337	4,784	6,292	6,467	4,532	2,804	2,960	2,311	785	12
Male	25,369	260	4,132	5,234	5,080	3,465	2,214	2,393	1,938	642	11
Female	5,915	77	652	1,058	1,387	1,067	590	567	373	143	1
White, both sexes	28,187	289	4,003	5,420	5,842	4,225	2,622	2,784	2,230	761	11
Male	22,853	223	3,459	4,514	4,584	3,228	2,073	2,262	1,873	627	10
Female	5,334	66	544	906	1,258	997	549	522	357	134	1
Black, both sexes	2,231	31	552	633	484	222	121	118	56	13	1
Male	1,878	25	492	535	391	184	99	91	50	10	1
Female	353	6	60	98	93	38	22	27	6	3	(—)

(—) = Data represent zero. **Note:** Data are provisional, estimated from a 10% sample of deaths. Because of rounding of estimates, figures may not add to totals. (1) "All races" includes races other than white and black.

Living Arrangements of Children, 1970-95

Source: Bureau of the Census, U.S. Dept. of Commerce

(as of Mar.; excludes persons under 18 years of age who maintained households or resided in group quarters)

Race, Hispanic origin, and year	Number (1,000)	Both parents	Mother only Total	Divorced	Married spouse absent	Single[1]	Widowed	Father only	Neither parent
White									
1970	58,790	90	8	3	3	Z	2	1	2
1980	52,242	83	14	7	4	1	2	2	2
1990	51,390	79	16	8	4	3	1	3	2
1991	51,918	79	17	8	5	3	1	3	2
1993	53,042	77	17	8	4	4	1	4	2
1994	54,775	76	18	8	4	4	1	3	3
1995	55,315	76	18	8	5	4	1	3	3
Black									
1970	9,422	59	30	5	16	4	4	2	10
1980	9,375	42	44	11	16	13	4	2	12
1990	10,018	38	51	10	12	27	2	4	8
1991	10,209	36	54	10	11	31	2	4	7
1993	10,649	36	54	10	12	31	1	3	7
1994	11,169	33	53	10	12	30	1	4	10
1995	11,301	33	52	11	11	29	2	4	11
Hispanic[2]									
1970	4,006[3]	78	NA	NA	NA	NA	NA	NA	NA
1980	5,459	75	20	6	8	4	2	2	4
1990	7,174	67	27	7	10	8	2	3	3
1991	7,462	66	27	7	10	9	2	3	4
1993	7,773	64	28	7	9	11	1	4	4
1994	9,483	64	28	6	9	11	2	4	5
1995	9,842	63	28	8	9	10	1	4	4

NA=Not available. Z = Less than 0.5%. (1) Never married. (2) Hispanic persons may be of any race. (3) All persons under 18 years old.

Cigarette Use[1] by Adults 18 and Older

Source: National Health Interview Survey, 1994, American Cancer Society

Category	% Men	% Women	% Total	Category	% Men	% Women	% Total
Age				American Indian/			
18-24	29.8	25.2	27.5	Alaskan Native[2] ..	53.7	33.1	42.2
25-44	32.3	27.8	30.0	Asian/Pacific Islander .	20.4	7.5	13.9
45-64	28.3	22.8	25.5	**Years of education[3]**			
65 or older	13.2	11.1	12.0	8 or less	30.4	17.8	23.7
Race/Ethnicity				9-11	45.8	32.1	38.2
White	28.0	24.7	26.3	12	33.2	27.3	29.8
Black	33.9	21.8	27.2	13-15	28.4	23.3	25.7
Hispanic	24.3	15.2	19.5	16 or more.........	13.8	10.4	12.3
				Total...............	**28.2**	**23.1**	**25.5**

(1) Percent of persons in each category who reported having smoked more than 100 cigarettes in 1994. (2) Estimates should be interpreted with caution because of the small sample sizes. (3) Persons aged 25 and older.

Drug Use in the General U.S. Population

Source: Substance Abuse and Mental Health Services Administration (SAMHSA), U.S. Dept. of Health and Human Services

According to the Substance Abuse and Mental Health Services Administration's 1996 National Household Survey on Drug Abuse, an estimated 74 mil Americans 12 years of age and older (35%) had used an illicit drug at least once during their lifetimes, 11% used one during the previous year, and 6% used one in the month before the survey was conducted. Among those 25 years of age and under, an estimated 1.6 mil used cocaine (including crack) and 9.5 mil used marijuana at least once within the previ-

ous year. Among those 26 years of age and over, 2.4 mil used cocaine (including crack) and 8.9 mil used marijuana at least once within the previous year.

The Substance Abuse and Mental Health Services Administration's Drug Abuse Warning Network reported an estimated 531,800 drug-related episodes in hospital emergency departments nationwide in 1995. The rate of these episodes per 100,000 population increased 37% from 167 in 1990 to 229 in 1995.

Drug Use: America's Middle and High School Students

Source: *Monitoring the Future,* Univ. of Michigan Inst. for Social Research and National Inst. on Drug Abuse

Drug use among American young people continued to rise in 1996, according to the results of the University of Michigan's 22d annual survey of American high school seniors and 6th annual survey of 8th and 10th graders. Since the increase in illicit drug use among 8th graders began in 1991, the proportion of 8th graders taking illicit drugs in the 12 months prior to the survey has more than doubled (from 11% to 24%). Since 1992, when the rise began for 10th and 12th graders, the proportion of 10th graders using illicit drugs in the prior 12 months has nearly doubled (from 20% to 38%), and among 12th graders, the proportion has increased by about half (from 27% to 40%).

Marijuana remained the most commonly used illegal drug among the 3 grade levels. In 1996, the proportion of students that reported using marijuana in the past year rose to 18% of 8th graders, 34% of 10th graders, and 36% of 12th graders. Use of marijuana on a daily basis also increased. Nearly 1 in 20 high school seniors (4.9%) and roughly 1 in every 30 10th graders (3.5%) was a daily user.

Use of LSD and other hallucinogens, tranquilizers, and stimulants also continued to drift upward. After a steady increase in the use of inhalants since 1992, their use decreased in 1996 among the 3 grade levels. Although heroin use remained rather low, levels of use in 1996 were 2 to 2½ times higher than they had been a few years earlier. The use of alcohol remained high but stable for all grade levels in 1996. Prevalence of cigarette smoking rose again in 1996. About 21% of 8th graders, 30% of 10th graders, and 34% of 12th graders reported having smoked during the 30 days before they responded to the survey.

In 1996, about 15,000 seniors in 139 public and private high schools participated in the survey, along with 16,000 10th graders in 133 schools and 18,000 8th graders in 152 schools. It should be noted that the surveys missed the 15% of a class group that drops out of school early and the 16-19% who are absentees. These populations have higher rates of drug use overall.

Drug Use: America's High School Seniors, 1975-96

Source: *Monitoring the Future,* Univ. of Michigan Inst. for Social Research and National Inst. on Drug Abuse

Percentage ever used

	Class of 1975	Class of 1980	Class of 1985	Class of 1990	Class of 1991	Class of 1992	Class of 1993	Class of 1994	Class of 1995	Class of 1996	'95-'96 change
Marijuana/hashish	47.3	60.3	54.2	40.7	36.7	32.6	35.3	38.2	41.7	44.9	+3.2
Inhalants	NA	11.9	15.4	18.0	17.6	16.6	17.4	17.7	17.4	16.6	−0.8
Inhalants adjusted[1] . . .	NA	17.3	18.1	18.5	18.0	17.0	17.7	18.3	17.8	NA	NA
Amyl & butyl nitrites .	NA	11.1	7.9	2.1	1.6	1.5	1.4	1.7	1.5	1.8	+0.3
Hallucinogens	16.3	13.3	10.3	9.4	9.6	9.2	10.9	11.4	12.7	14.0	+1.3
Hallucinogens adjusted[2]	NA	15.6	12.1	9.7	10.0	9.4	11.3	11.7	13.1	NA	NA
LSD	11.3	9.3	7.5	8.7	8.8	8.6	10.3	10.5	11.7	12.6	+0.9
PCP	NA	9.6	4.9	2.8	2.9	2.4	2.9	2.8	2.7	4.0	+1.3
Cocaine	9.0	15.7	17.3	9.4	7.8	6.1	6.1	5.9	6.0	7.1	+1.1
Crack	NA	NA	NA	3.5	3.1	2.6	2.6	3.0	3.0	3.3	+0.3
Heroin[3]	2.2	1.1	1.2	1.3	0.9	1.2	1.1	1.2	1.6	1.8	+0.2
Other opiates[4]	9.0	9.8	10.2	8.3	6.6	6.1	6.4	6.6	7.2	8.2	+1.0
Stimulants[4,5]	22.3	26.4	26.2	17.5	15.4	13.9	15.1	15.7	15.3	15.3	0
Sedatives[4]	18.2	14.9	11.8	7.5	6.7	6.1	6.4	7.3	7.6	NA	NA
Barbiturates[4]	16.9	11.0	9.2	6.8	6.2	5.5	6.3	7.0	7.4	7.6	+0.2
Methaqualone[4].	8.1	9.5	6.7	2.3	1.3	1.6	0.8	1.4	1.2	2.0	+0.8
Tranquilizers[4]	17.0	15.2	11.9	7.2	7.2	6.0	6.4	6.6	7.1	7.2	+0.1
Alcohol	90.4	93.2	92.2	89.5	88.0	87.5	87.0	80.4[6]	80.7[6]	79.2[6]	−1.5
Cigarettes	73.6	71.0	68.8	64.4	63.1	61.8	61.9	62.0	64.2	63.5	−0.7

NA=Not available. (1) Adjusted for underreporting of amyl and butyl nitrites. (2) Adjusted for underreporting of PCP. (3) Reflects use with or without injection. (4) Includes only drug use that was not under a doctor's orders. (5) Adjusted for overreporting of the nonprescription stimulants. (6) Data for 1994, 1995, and 1996 are not directly comparable to prior years.

Alcohol Use by 8th and 12th Graders, 1980-96

Source: *Monitoring the Future,* Univ. of Michigan Inst. for Social Research and National Inst. on Drug Abuse

	1980	1985	1986	1987	1988	1989	1990	1991	1992	1993	1994	1995	1996
Alcohol[1]					Percent using in the month before the survey								
All 12th graders.	72.0	65.9	65.3	66.4	63.9	60.0	57.1	54.0	51.3	48.6	50.1	51.3	50.8
Male.	77.4	69.8	69.0	69.9	68.0	65.1	61.3	58.4	55.8	54.2	55.5	55.7	54.8
Female.	66.8	62.1	61.9	63.1	59.9	54.9	52.3	49.0	46.8	43.4	45.2	47.0	46.9
White	75.8	70.2	70.2	71.8	69.5	65.3	62.2	57.7	56.0	53.4	54.8	54.8	54.7
Black	47.7	43.6	40.4	38.5	40.9	38.1	32.9	34.4	29.5	35.1	33.1	37.4	35.7
All 8th graders	—	—	—	—	—	—	—	25.1	26.1	24.3	25.5	24.6	26.2
Male.	—	—	—	—	—	—	—	26.3	26.3	25.3	26.5	25.0	26.6
Female.	—	—	—	—	—	—	—	23.8	25.9	28.7	24.7	24.0	25.8
White	—	—	—	—	—	—	—	26.0	27.3	25.1	25.4	25.4	27.7
Black	—	—	—	—	—	—	—	17.8	19.2	17.7	20.2	17.3	19.0
Binge drinking[2]					Percent in the 2 weeks before the survey								
All 12th graders.	41.2	36.7	36.8	37.5	34.7	33.0	32.2	29.8	27.9	27.5	28.2	29.8	30.2
Male.	52.1	45.3	46.1	46.1	43.0	41.2	39.1	37.8	35.6	34.6	37.0	36.9	37.0
Female.	30.5	28.2	28.1	29.2	26.5	24.9	24.4	21.2	20.3	20.7	20.2	23.0	23.5
White	44.6	40.1	40.5	41.2	38.8	36.9	36.2	32.9	31.3	31.3	31.7	32.9	34.0
Black	17.0	16.7	16.1	15.5	14.9	16.6	11.6	11.8	10.8	14.6	14.2	15.5	15.1
All 8th graders	—	—	—	—	—	—	—	12.9	13.4	13.5	14.5	14.5	15.6
Male.	—	—	—	—	—	—	—	14.3	13.9	14.8	16.0	15.1	16.5
Female.	—	—	—	—	—	—	—	11.4	12.8	12.3	13.0	13.9	14.5
White	—	—	—	—	—	—	—	12.6	12.9	12.4	13.4	14.5	15.7
Black	—	—	—	—	—	—	—	9.9	9.3	11.9	11.8	10.0	10.9

(—) = Data not available. **Note**: *Monitoring the Future* study excludes high school dropouts (about 15% of the age group during the 1980s) and absentees (about 16-19% of high school students). High school dropouts and absentees have higher alcohol usage than those included in the survey. (1) In 1993 the alcohol question was changed to indicate that a "drink" meant "more than a few sips." (2) Five or more drinks in a row at least once in the prior 2-week period.

Principal Types of Accidental Deaths, 1970-96

Source: National Safety Council

Year	Motor vehicle	Falls	Poison (solid, liquid)	Drowning	Fires, burns	Ingestion of food, object	Firearms	Poison (gases)
1970......	54,633	16,926	3,679	7,860	6,718	2,753	2,406	1,620
1975......	45,853	14,896	4,694	8,000	6,071	3,106	2,380	1,577
1980......	53,172	13,294	3,089	7,257	5,822	3,249	1,955	1,242
1985......	45,901	12,001	4,091	5,316	4,938	3,551	1,649	1,079
1990......	46,814	12,313	5,055	4,685	4,175	3,303	1,416	748
1991......	43,536	12,662	5,698	4,818	4,120	3,240	1,441	736
1992......	40,982	12,646	6,449	3,542	3,958	3,182	1,409	633
1993......	41,893	13,141	7,877	3,807	3,900	3,160	1,521	660
1994......	42,524	13,450	8,309	3,942	3,986	3,065	1,356	685
1995......	43,363	13,600	9,400	4,300	3,800	2,900	1,200	600
1996......	43,300	14,100	9,800	3,900	3,200	3,000	1,400	600

Death rates per 100,000 population

Year	Motor vehicle	Falls	Poison (solid, liquid)	Drowning	Fires, burns	Ingestion of food, object	Firearms	Poison (gases)
1970......	26.8	8.3	1.8	3.9	3.3	1.4	1.2	0.8
1975......	21.3	6.9	2.2	3.7	2.8	1.4	1.1	0.7
1980......	23.4	5.9	1.4	3.2	2.6	1.4	0.9	0.5
1985......	19.3	5.0	1.7	2.2	2.1	1.5	0.7	0.5
1990......	18.8	4.9	2.0	1.9	1.7	1.3	0.6	0.3
1991......	17.3	5.0	2.3	1.8	1.6	1.3	0.6	0.3
1992......	16.1	5.0	2.5	1.4	1.6	1.2	0.6	0.2
1993......	16.3	5.1	3.1	1.5	1.5	1.2	0.6	0.3
1994......	16.3	5.2	3.2	1.5	1.5	1.2	0.5	0.3
1995......	16.5	5.2	3.6	1.6	1.4	1.1	0.5	0.2
1996......	16.3	5.3	3.7	1.5	1.7	1.1	0.5	0.2

Note: There were 14,100 other accidental deaths in 1996; the most frequently occurring types were medical and surgical complications, machinery, air transport, water transport (except drownings), mechanical suffocation, and excessive cold.

Motor Vehicle Accidents

Source: National Safety Council

Motor vehicle deaths in 1996 were virtually unchanged from levels in 1995. Of the 177,800,000 licensed drivers in 1996, about 89.5 mil (50.3%) were men and 88.3 mil (49.7%) were women.

Male drivers were involved in more fatal accidents than female drivers in 1996. About 42,300 men and 15,100 women drivers were involved in fatal accidents.

About 11.4 mil male drivers and 7.5 mil female drivers were involved in all types of accidents in 1996. However, since males account for about 64% of the miles driven each year, according to the latest estimates, and females for 36%, women have higher accident involvement rates. At least part of the difference in accident involvement rates between men and women may be due to differences

in the time, place, and circumstance of driving experienced by both groups of drivers. Accident rates were 75 per 10 million miles driven for men and 84 per 10 million miles driven for women.

About 40% of all traffic fatalities in 1995 involved an intoxicated or alcohol-impaired driver or nonoccupant. Of these 17,274 alcohol-related traffic fatalities, an estimated 13,564 occurred in accidents in which a driver or nonoccupant was intoxicated, and the remainder involved a driver or nonoccupant who had been drinking but was not legally intoxicated. Alcohol was also a factor in about 7% of all traffic accidents, both fatal and nonfatal, in 1995. In 1985 alcohol-related fatalities accounted for 52% of all traffic deaths.

	Death total 1996	Percentage change from 1995	Death rate 1996[1]
All motor vehicle accidents	43,300	(2)	16.3
Collision between motor vehicles	19,300	+3	7.3
Collision with fixed object	12,000	+1	4.5
Pedestrian accidents	6,100	−9	2.3
Noncollision accidents	4,600	+2	1.7
Collision with pedalcycle	800	−11	0.3
Collision with railroad train	400	−20	0.2
Other collision (animal, animal-drawn vehicles)	100	0	(3)

(1) Deaths per 100,000 population. (2) Change was less than 0.5%. (3) Death rate was less than 0.05.

Improper Driving Reported in Accidents, 1995-96

Source: National Safety Council

Type	Percentage of fatal accidents 1995	1996	Percentage of injury accidents 1995	1996	Percentage of all accidents 1995	1996
Improper driving	**68.1**	**69.1**	**73.5**	**87.1**	**75.5**	**87.4**
Speed too fast or unsafe	19.8	17.6	13.9	13.5	14.0	14.3
Right of way	15.2	15.7	25.5	29.1	22.9	23.6
Failed to yield	10.2	10.1	18.1	20.2	17.0	17.2
Passed stop sign	3.0	2.1	5.0	1.3	4.0	1.2
Disregarded signal	2.2	3.5	2.4	7.6	1.9	5.2
Drove left of center	9.1	8.1	2.4	2.3	2.2	2.1
Improper overtaking	1.5	1.2	1.3	1.1	1.5	1.2
Made improper turn	2.3	4.1	2.8	4.1	4.2	5.7
Followed too closely	0.5	0.9	7.0	9.9	7.2	9.6
Other improper driving	19.7	21.5	20.7	27.1	20.0	30.9
No improper driving stated . . .	**31.9**	**30.9**	**26.5**	**12.9**	**24.5**	**12.6**

Note: Based on reports from 11 state traffic authorities. When a driver was under the influence of alcohol or drugs, the accident was considered a result of the driver's physical condition—not a driving error. For this reason, accidents in which the driver was reported to be under the influence are classified under "no improper driving."

Deaths Involving Firearms, by Age, 1994[1]

Source: National Safety Council

	All ages	Under 5	5-14	15-24	25-44	45-64	65-74	75 & over
Total firearms deaths	**38,166**	**107**	**762**	**10,954**	**15,402**	**6,184**	**2,349**	**2,408**
Male	32,694	62	571	9,809	12,905	5,119	2,039	2,189
Female	5,472	45	191	1,145	2,497	1,065	310	219
Accidents	**1,356**	**34**	**151**	**540**	**398**	**141**	**46**	**46**
Male	1,192	23	131	504	333	121	40	40
Female	164	11	20	36	65	20	6	6
Suicides	**18,765**	**0**	**188**	**3,344**	**6,796**	**4,240**	**2,010**	**2,187**
Male	16,287	0	140	2,988	5,736	3,588	1,791	2,044
Female	2,478	0	48	356	1,060	652	219	143
Homicides	**17,527**	**71**	**395**	**6,881**	**8,017**	**1,728**	**278**	**157**
Male	14,766	38	274	6,141	6,672	1,357	195	89
Female	2,761	33	121	740	1,345	371	83	68
Undetermined[2]	**518**	**2**	**28**	**189**	**191**	**75**	**15**	**18**
Male	449	1	26	176	164	53	3	16
Female	69	1	2	13	27	22	2	2

(1) Figures exclude firearms deaths by legal intervention. These deaths totaled 339 in 1994. (2) "Undetermined" means that the intention involved (whether accident, suicide, or homicide) could not be determined.

Home Accident Deaths, 1950-96

Source: National Safety Council

Year	Total	Falls	Poison (solid, liquid)	Fires, burns[1]	Suffoc., Ingesting object	Firearms	Suffoc., mechanical	Poison (gases)	All other
1950	29,000	14,800	1,300	5,000	([2])	950	1,600	1,250	4,100
1960	28,000	12,300	1,350	6,350	1,850	1,200	1,500	900	2,550
1970	27,000	9,700	3,000	5,600	1,800[3]	1,400[3]	1,100[3]	1,100	3,300[3]
1980	22,800	7,100	2,500	4,800	2,000	1,100	500	700	4,100[4]
1990	21,500	6,700	4,000	3,400	2,300	800	600	500	3,200
1991	22,100	6,900	4,500	3,400	2,200	800	700	500	3,100
1992	24,000	7,700	4,800	3,700	1,500	1,000	700	400	4,200
1993	26,100	7,900	6,000	3,700	1,700	1,100	700	500	4,500
1994[5]	26,300	8,100	6,300	3,700	1,600	900	800	500	4,400
1995[5]	26,300	7,900	7,400	3,500	1,400	700	700	400	4,300
1996[6]	26,500	8.200	7,800	2,900	1,500	800	600	400	4,300

(1) Includes deaths resulting from conflagration, regardless of nature of injury. (2) Included under "All other" category. (3) Data for this year and subsequent years not comparable with data from previous years because of classification changes. (4) Includes about 1,000 deaths attributed to summer heat wave. (5) Revised figures. The National Safety Council adopted the count from the Bureau of Labor Statistics Census of Fatal Occupational Injuries for all work-related unintentional injuries, retroactive to 1992 data. (6) Data for 1996 are preliminary.

Worldwide Airline Fatalities, 1980-96

Source: National Safety Council

Year	Aircraft accidents[1]	Passenger deaths	Death rate[2]	Year	Aircraft accidents[1]	Passenger deaths	Death rate[2]
1980	22	814	0.14	1989	27	817	0.08
1981	21	362	0.06	1990	22	440	0.04
1982	26	764	0.13	1991	25	510	0.05
1983	20	809	0.13	1992	25	990	0.09
1984	16	223	0.03	1993	31	801	0.07
1985	22	1,066	0.15	1994	24	732	0.06
1986	17	331	0.04	1995	22	557	0.04
1987	24	890	0.10	1996[3]	22	1,132	0.08
1988	25	699	0.08				

(1) Those involving one or more passenger fatalities only. (2) Passenger deaths per 100 mil passenger mi. (3) Preliminary figures.

Cost of Unintentional Injuries, 1996

Source: National Safety Council, estimates

The cost of. . .	is equivalent to. . .
. . .all injuries ($444.1 bil)	68 cents of every dollar paid in 1996 federal personal income taxes,
or	58 cents of every dollar spent on food in the U.S. in 1996.
. . .motor vehicle accidents ($176.1 bil)	purchasing 680 gallons of gasoline per registered vehicle in the U.S.,
or	a $20,700 rebate on each new car sold in 1996.
. . .work injuries ($121.0 bil)	50 cents of every dollar of 1996 corporate dividends to stockholders,
or	19 cents of every dollar of 1996 pre-tax corporate profits.
. . .home injuries ($95.7 bil)	an $82,400 rebate on each new single-family home built in 1996,
or	42 cents of every dollar of property taxes paid in 1996.
. . .public injuries[1] ($65.3 bil)	a $7.2 million grant to each public library in the U.S.,
or	an $83,400 bonus for each police officer and firefighter.

(1) Any injuries that occur in public places or places used in a public way and not involving motor vehicles.

U.S. Fires, 1996

Source: National Fire Protection Assn.

Fires
- Public fire departments responded to 1,975,000 fires in 1996, an increase of 0.5% from 1995.
- There were 578,500 structure fires in 1996, an increase of 0.9% from the 1995 figure.
- 74% of all structure fires, or 428,000 fires, occurred in residential properties.
- There were 413,500 vehicle fires in 1996, an increase of 1.7% from the previous year.
- There were 983,000 fires in outside properties, a decrease of 0.3% from 1995.
- The South had the highest fire incident rate in the country, with 9.0 fires per 1,000 population.

Civilian deaths
- There were 4,990 civilian fire deaths in 1996, an increase of 8.8% from 1995.
- The number of deaths from fire in the home increased by 10.9% to 4,035.
- About 81% of all fire deaths occurred in the home.
- The South had the highest fire death rate, with 26.1 civilian deaths per million population, followed by the North Central region, with 18.7 deaths per million.
- Nationwide, someone died in a fire every 105 minutes.

Civilian injuries
- There were an estimated 25,550 civilian fire injuries in 1996, virtually no change from 1995. This estimate is low because of underreporting of civilian fire injuries to the fire service.
- Residential properties were the site of 19,300 civilian fire injuries, or 75.5% of injuries overall; 2,575 injuries, or 10.1%, occurred in nonresidential structure fires.

- The Northeast had the highest regional injury rate in the U.S., with 121.5 civilian injuries per million population. The next highest rate was in the North Central region, with 103.7 injuries per million.
- Nationwide, a civilian was injured in a fire every 21 minutes.

Property damage
- Property damage resulting from fires increased in 1996 by 5.5%, to an estimated $9.406 billion.
- Structure fires resulted in 84% of all property damage, or $7.933 billion.
- 63% of all structure property loss occurred in residential properties, accounting for $4.962 billion.
- The Northeast had the highest property loss rate in the U.S.—$42.1 per person—followed by the North Central region, with $38.6 per person.

Incendiary and suspicious fires
- 14.8% of all structure fires, or an estimated 85,500 fires, were deliberately set or are suspected of having been deliberately set. This represents an increase of 5.5% from 1995.
- Incendiary or suspicious structure fires resulted in 520 civilian deaths. The unusually large decrease of 29.7% from the previous year reflects the 168 civilians killed in the explosion and fire at the Alfred P. Murrah Federal Office Building in Oklahoma City on Apr. 19, 1995. Incendiary or suspicious fires caused $1.405 billion in property damage, or 17.7% of all property loss from structure fires.
- The number of vehicle fires of incendiary or suspicious origin in 1996 was 47,000, no change from 1995. They caused an estimated $202 million in property damage, which is a 15.4% increase from the year before.

Physicians by Age, Sex, and Specialty, 1996

Source: American Medical Assn., as of Dec. 31, 1996

	Total Physicians[1]		Under 35 yrs		35-44 yrs		45-54 yrs		55-64 yrs	
	Male	Female	Male	Female	Male	Female	Male	Female	Male	Female
All Specialties	580,377	157,387	85,657	47,348	153,865	58,888	137,398	29,948	88,665	10,833
Aerospace Medicine	550	38	67	8	164	17	134	10	104	2
Allergy & Immunology	3,048	745	190	112	785	308	969	222	641	57
Anesthesiology	26,750	6,568	4,688	1,473	10,721	2,660	6,131	1,497	3,369	696
Cardiovascular Disease	17,895	1,342	1,943	291	6,349	651	5,346	283	2,834	81
Child Psychiatry	3,448	2,167	306	332	1,006	858	1,083	600	658	252
Colon/Rectal Surgery	962	56	65	12	325	35	317	7	149	2
Dermatology	6,248	2,606	682	767	1,509	1,153	2,055	498	1,278	136
Diagnostic Radiology	16,223	3,820	3,445	1,274	5,553	1,632	4,624	736	1,992	142
Emergency Medicine	16,492	3,538	3,256	1,160	6,044	1,503	5,285	693	1,277	137
Family Practice	46,964	15,337	7,693	5,610	16,675	6,508	12,535	2,388	5,138	582
Forensic Pathology	373	133	17	7	111	62	99	39	87	17
Gastroenterology	8,960	758	1,104	189	3,340	390	2,885	150	1,197	25
General Practice	14,441	2,454	220	82	1,238	548	2,723	827	3,638	545
General Preventive Med.	1,010	497	95	82	301	234	277	109	178	42
General Surgery	34,490	3,453	7,728	1,713	8,080	1,184	7,828	439	6,399	81
Internal Medicine	92,038	30,087	20,293	10,973	29,321	12,214	23,237	5,097	11,321	1,276
Medical Genetics	130	88	10	6	36	40	48	28	26	12
Neurological Surgery	4,708	216	802	71	1,284	101	1,114	38	1,011	4
Neurology	9,362	2,233	1,173	535	3,184	998	2,900	513	1,475	152
Nuclear Medicine	1,170	256	90	36	280	99	366	69	294	39
Obstetrics/Gynecology	26,559	11,865	3,207	4,346	6,552	4,689	7,689	1,954	5,693	646
Occupational Medicine	2,575	487	55	33	585	221	696	144	507	59
Ophthalmology	15,423	2,354	2,108	729	4,288	1,033	4,182	415	3,255	128
Orthopedic Surgery	21,803	718	3,835	252	6,436	328	5,658	103	4,110	21
Otolaryngology	8,296	732	1,441	300	2,213	303	2,077	103	1,845	18
Pathology-Anat./Clin.	12,974	4,977	1,480	1,034	3,386	1,920	3,385	1,212	2,908	570
Pediatric Cardiology	1,029	328	143	92	365	126	259	58	169	32
Pediatrics	29,098	24,271	5,190	8,275	8,606	8,931	7,934	4,800	4,438	1,636
Physical Med./Rehab.	3,934	1,829	867	502	1,524	652	815	423	404	170
Plastic Surgery	5,395	503	437	85	1,762	256	1,712	118	1,097	29
Psychiatry	27,831	10,586	2,395	1,821	6,273	3,834	7,643	2,774	6,173	1,301
Public Health	1,249	440	14	14	197	119	336	107	289	84
Pulmonary Diseases	6,141	683	365	128	2,340	349	2,342	141	783	38
Radiation Oncology	2,881	803	451	205	1,008	305	741	205	466	67
Radiology	7,181	1,000	477	125	1,224	367	1,592	295	2,493	146
Thoracic Surgery	2,249	54	200	7	776	32	439	13	500	2
Urological Surgery	9,763	238	1,333	102	2,403	110	2,709	27	2,272	0
Other	5,075	888	49	14	844	264	1,273	264	1,348	177
Unspecified	6,774	3,285	4,225	2,289	1,521	709	540	190	235	61

(1) Includes physicians 65 and older, those living in U.S. possessions, those "Inactive," "Not Classified," and "Address Unknown."

U.S. Health Expenditures, 1965-95

Source: *Health, United States, 1996-97,* National Center for Health Statistics, U.S. Dept. of Health and Human Services

Type of expenditure	1965	1970	1975	1980	1985	1990	1992	1993	1994	1995
				Amount in billions						
Total	$41.1	$73.2	$130.7	$247.2	$428.2	$697.5	$834.2	$892.1	$937.1	$988.5
				Percent distribution						
Health services & supplies	91.6	92.7	93.6	95.3	96.2	96.5	96.7	96.7	96.8	96.9
Personal health care	85.5	87.1	87.6	87.8	87.9	88.1	88.8	88.2	88.3	88.9
Hospital care	34.1	38.2	40.2	41.5	39.3	36.8	36.6	36.2	35.7	35.4
Physician services	19.9	18.5	18.3	18.3	19.5	21.0	21.1	20.5	20.3	20.4
Dentist services	6.8	6.4	6.1	5.4	5.1	4.5	4.4	4.4	4.5	4.6
Nursing home care	3.6	5.8	6.6	7.1	7.2	7.3	7.5	7.5	7.7	7.9
Other professional services	2.1	1.9	2.1	2.6	3.9	5.0	5.0	5.2	5.2	5.3
Home health care	0.2	0.3	0.5	1.0	1.3	1.9	2.4	2.6	2.8	2.9
Drugs & other medical nondurables	14.3	12.0	10.0	8.7	8.7	8.6	8.5	8.4	8.3	8.4
Vision products & other medical durables	2.4	2.2	2.0	1.5	1.6	1.5	1.4	1.4	1.4	1.4
Other personal health care	2.0	1.8	1.9	1.6	1.4	1.6	1.8	2.0	2.3	2.5
Program administration & net cost of health insurance	4.7	3.7	3.8	4.8	5.6	5.5	5.1	5.7	5.4	4.8
Government public health activities[1]	1.5	1.8	2.2	2.7	2.7	2.8	2.8	2.8	3.0	3.2
Research & construction	8.4	7.3	6.4	4.7	3.8	3.5	3.3	3.3	3.2	3.1
Noncommercial research	3.7	2.7	2.5	2.2	1.8	1.8	1.7	1.6	1.7	1.7
Construction	4.7	4.6	3.9	2.5	2.0	1.8	1.6	1.6	1.6	1.4
			Average annual % change from previous year shown							
All expenditures	—	12.2	12.3	13.6	11.6	10.2	9.4	6.9	5.1	5.5
Health services & supplies	—	12.5	12.5	14.0	11.8	10.3	9.5	7.0	5.1	5.6
Personal health care	—	12.7	12.4	13.6	11.6	10.3	9.8	6.3	5.2	6.1
Hospital care	—	14.8	13.4	14.3	10.4	8.8	9.1	5.9	3.6	4.5
Physician services	—	10.6	12.0	13.6	13.1	11.8	9.6	4.0	4.4	5.8
Dentist services	—	10.8	11.2	10.9	10.2	7.8	8.3	6.0	7.3	8.9
Nursing home care	—	23.4	15.5	15.3	11.7	10.7	10.6	7.6	8.1	7.5
Other professional services	—	10.2	14.2	18.4	21.2	15.8	10.2	10.0	6.1	7.0
Home health care	—	19.7	23.2	30.7	18.9	18.4	22.3	17.1	14.4	8.6
Drugs & other medical nondurables	8.4		8.1	10.7	11.4	10.1	9.0	5.4	3.6	7.3
Vision products & other medical durables	10.2		9.5	8.1	12.4	9.2	6.7	5.1	2.8	7.2
Other personal health care	—	9.5	13.8	10.2	8.8	12.9	17.0	16.4	21.6	14.9
Program administration & net cost of health insurance	—	7.1	12.5	19.2	15.0	10.2	5.2	19.1	-0.5	-5.8
Government public health activities[1]	—	17.0	16.8	18.1	11.5	11.0	9.3	7.9	11.6	11.3
Research & construction	—	9.2	9.4	6.8	7.1	8.4	6.0	5.3	4.9	0.8
Noncommercial research	—	5.1	11.2	10.4	7.5	9.3	7.7	2.2	9.3	5.0
Construction	—	12.1	8.3	4.1	6.7	7.6	4.2	8.7	0.5	-3.8

Note: Numbers may not add to totals because of rounding. (1) Includes personal care services delivered by government public health agencies.

Ownership of Life Insurance in the U.S. and Assets of U.S. Life Insurance Companies, 1940-96

Source: American Council of Life Insurance

(millions of dollars)

Year	Purchases of life insurance Ordinary	Group	Industrial	Total	Insurance in force Ordinary	Group	Industrial	Credit	Total	Assets
1940	6,689	691	3,350	10,730	79,346	14,938	20,866	380	115,530	30,802
1950	17,326	6,068	5,402	28,796	149,116	47,793	33,415	3,844	234,168	64,020
1960	52,883	14,645	6,880	74,408	341,881	175,903	39,563	29,101	586,448	119,576
1970	122,820	63,690[1]	6,612	193,122[1]	734,730	551,357	38,644	77,392	1,402,123	207,254
1975	188,003	95,190[1]	6,729	289,922[1]	1,083,421	904,695	39,423	112,032	2,139,571	289,304
1980	385,575	183,418	3,609	572,602	1,760,474	1,579,355	35,994	165,215	3,541,038	479,210
1985	910,944	319,503	722	1,231,169	3,247,289	2,561,595	28,250	215,973	6,053,107	825,901
1987	986,660	365,529	324	1,352,513	4,139,071	3,043,782	26,668	242,977	7,452,498	1,044,459
1989	1,020,719	420,707	252	1,441,678	4,939,964	3,469,498	24,446	260,107	8,694,015	1,299,756
1990	1,069,660	459,271	220	1,529,151	5,366,982	3,753,506	24,071	248,038	9,392,597	1,408,208
1991	1,041,508	573,953[1]	198	1,615,659[1]	5,677,777	4,057,606	22,475	228,478	9,986,336	1,551,201
1992	1,048,135	440,143	222	1,488,500	5,941,810	4,240,919	20,973	202,090	10,405,792	1,664,531
1993	1,101,327	576,823	149	1,678,299	6,428,434	4,456,338	20,451	199,518	11,104,741	1,839,127
1994	1,107,216	549,984	232	1,657,432	6,835,239	4,608,746	20,145	209,491	11,673,621	1,942,273
1995	1,101,032	499,024	317	1,600,373	7,547,537	4,777,912	19,971	231,251	12,576,677	2,143,544
1996[2]	1,118,335	581,366	—	1,699,701	8,337,188	5,158,538	18,899	245,679	13,760,304	2,323,546

(1) Includes Servicemen's Group Life Insurance, which amounted to $17.1 billion in 1970, $1.7 billion in 1975, and $166.7 billion in 1991. (2) Beginning with 1996 figures, the 2 categories "Ordinary" and "Industrial" purchases were combined into 1 category called "Individual," which is the sum of the 2 former categories (given here under "Ordinary").

Health Insurance Coverage,[1] by State, 1996

Source: Bureau of the Census, U.S. Dept. of Commerce, Mar. 1997 Current Population Survey; in thousands

State	Total population	Covered by insurance	Not covered	% not covered	State	Total population	Covered by insurance	Not covered	% not covered
AL....	4,276	3,726	550	12.9	MT....	912	788	124	13.6
AK....	658	569	89	13.5	NE....	1,673	1,483	190	11.4
AZ....	4,801	3,642	1,159	24.1	NV....	1,636	1,381	255	15.6
AR....	2,607	2,041	566	21.7	NH....	1,142	1,033	109	9.5
CA....	32,367	25,853	6,514	20.1	NJ....	7,863	6,546	1,317	16.7
CO....	3,884	3,240	644	16.6	NM....	1,847	1,435	412	22.3
CT....	3,353	2,985	368	11.0	NY....	18,397	15,265	3,132	17.0
DE....	734	636	98	13.4	NC....	7,263	6,103	1,160	16.0
DC....	539	459	80	14.8	ND....	630	568	62	9.8
FL....	14,376	11,654	2,722	18.9	OH....	11,266	9,974	1,292	11.5
GA....	7,399	6,080	1,319	17.8	OK....	3,354	2,784	570	17.0
HI	1,174	1,073	101	8.6	OR....	3,239	2,743	496	15.3
ID	1,186	990	196	16.5	PA....	11,896	10,763	1,133	9.5
IL	11,848	10,511	1,337	11.3	RI	940	847	93	9.9
IN	5,681	5,081	600	10.6	SC....	3,711	3,077	634	17.1
IA	2,900	2,565	335	11.6	SD....	706	639	67	9.5
KS....	2,572	2,280	292	11.4	TN....	5,543	4,702	841	15.2
KY....	3,896	3,295	601	15.4	TX....	19,237	14,557	4,680	24.3
LA....	4,268	3,378	890	20.9	UT....	1,998	1,758	240	12.0
ME....	1,204	1,058	146	12.1	VT....	587	522	65	11.1
MD....	5,088	4,507	581	11.4	VA....	6,491	5,680	811	12.5
MA....	6,158	5,392	766	12.4	WA....	5,642	4,881	761	13.5
MI	9,596	8,739	857	8.9	WV....	1,748	1,487	261	14.9
MN....	4,709	4,229	480	10.2	WI	5,219	4,781	438	8.4
MS....	2,797	2,279	518	18.5	WY ...	488	422	66	13.5
MO ...	5,291	4,591	700	13.2	**U.S....**	**266,793**	**225,077**	**41,716**	**15.6**

(1) For all ages, including those 65 or over, an age group largely covered by Medicare.

Persons Not Covered by Health Insurance, by Selected Characteristics, 1996

Source: Bureau of the Census, U.S. Dept. of Commerce, Mar. 1997 Current Population Survey; in thousands

Characteristic	Number	Percent	Characteristic	Number	Percent
Total not covered	41,716	15.6	Black.........................	7,419	21.7
Sex			Asian or Pacific Islander	2,124	21.1
Male	22,328	17.1	Hispanic origin[1]	9,974	33.6
Female....................	19,388	14.2	**Education[2]**		
Age			No high school diploma	9,118	25.1
Under 18 years..............	10,555	14.8	High school graduate, no college...	11,344	17.4
18 to 24 years..............	7,217	28.9	Some college, no degree	5,964	15.7
25 to 34 years..............	8,973	22.3	Associate degree..............	1,486	11.1
35 to 44 years..............	7,151	16.3	Bachelor's degree or higher	3,250	7.6
45 to 64 years..............	7,483	13.7	**Work experience[3]**		
65 years and over............	336	1.1	Worked during year	23,279	17.4
Nativity			Worked full-time...............	17,867	16.3
Native	33,066	13.7	Worked part-time..............	5,411	22.4
Foreign-born.................	8,650	33.6	Did not work	7,547	25.3
Naturalized citizen............	1,556	17.2	**Household income**		
Not a citizen	7,094	42.4	Less than $25,000	18,470	24.3
Race and Hispanic origin			$25,000-$49,000	13,585	16.6
White........................	31,728	14.4	$50,000-$74,999	5,630	10.0
White, not of Hispanic origin....	22,093	11.5	$75,000 or more	4,030	7.6

(1) Persons of Hispanic origin may be of any race. (2) Persons aged 18 years and over. (3) Persons aged 18-64.

Health Coverage for Persons Under 65, by Characteristics, 1989-95

Source: *Health, United States, 1996-97,* National Center for Health Statistics, U.S. Dept. of Health and Human Services

	Private insurance				Medicaid				Not covered[1]			
	1989	1993[2]	1994	1995[3]	1989	1993[2]	1994	1995[3]	1989	1993[2]	1994	1995[3]
					Percent of population							
Age												
Under 15 years	71.7	65.6	63.0	64.7	11.4	18.9	19.8	20.7	15.9	14.8	16.1	14.2
15-44 years	76.6	70.6	69.9	70.8	4.4	6.4	6.7	7.2	18.1	21.6	22.0	20.7
45-64 years	83.3	80.7	80.5	80.1	3.4	3.4	3.6	4.6	10.6	12.3	12.2	11.5
Race and Hispanic origin[4]												
White, non-Hispanic	83.0	78.6	77.4	78.2	3.6	5.8	6.2	6.9	12.1	13.9	14.6	13.4
Black, non-Hispanic........	59.3	51.5	52.4	53.5	17.1	23.2	23.8	24.9	21.8	23.0	21.1	19.9
All Hispanic	50.6	48.6	48.7	47.2	10.5	16.2	17.4	20.0	31.3	34.2	32.9	31.5
Family income[4]												
Less than $14,000	34.6	26.0	24.7	24.3	26.6	37.2	38.0	40.8	37.3	35.3	35.0	33.5
$14,000-$24,999..........	71.4	60.1	54.0	55.7	4.8	10.5	12.3	13.6	21.4	27.5	30.4	28.0
$25,000-$34,999..........	87.9	80.9	78.4	75.4	1.2	2.4	3.5	4.8	9.3	13.8	15.6	17.2
$35,000-$49,999..........	92.4	89.4	88.5	87.7	0.8	1.3	1.3	2.4	5.6	7.8	8.7	8.3
$50,000 or more	95.7	93.9	92.7	93.6	0.4	0.4	0.7	0.7	3.2	4.6	5.6	4.6
Geographic region[4]												
Northeast.................	83.4	76.2	74.8	75.1	5.8	9.3	10.2	11.1	10.3	14.3	14.7	13.8
Midwest.................	81.9	77.7	77.3	77.4	7.1	9.9	9.4	9.8	10.7	11.7	12.3	12.0
South...................	71.8	66.1	65.3	65.9	5.7	9.3	10.2	11.2	20.0	21.9	21.4	20.1
West...................	72.1	68.1	65.4	68.9	7.2	10.4	11.0	11.6	19.1	19.9	21.0	19.4

Note: Data based on household interviews of a sample of the civilian noninstitutionalized population. Percents do not add to 100 because other types of health insurance (e.g., Medicare, military) are not shown, and persons with both private insurance and Medicaid appear in both columns. (1) Includes persons not covered by private insurance, Medicaid, Medicare, or military plans. (2) July 1 to Dec. 31, 1993. The questionnaire changed in 1993. (3) Jan. 1-June 30, 1995; preliminary data. (4) Age adjusted.

Physician Contacts Per Person, by Selected Characteristics, 1987-94

Source: *Health United States 1995*, National Center for Health Statistics, U.S. Dept. of Health and Human Services

	1987	1988	1989	1990	1991	1992	1993	1994
Total[1,2]	5.4	5.3	5.3	5.5	5.6	5.9	6.0	6.0
Age								
Under 15 years	4.5	4.6	4.6	4.5	4.7	4.6	4.9	4.6
Under 5 years	6.7	7.0	6.7	6.9	7.1	6.9	7.2	6.8
5-14 years	3.3	3.3	3.5	3.2	3.4	3.4	3.6	3.4
15-44 years	4.6	4.7	4.6	4.8	4.7	5.0	5.0	5.0
45-64 years	6.4	6.1	6.1	6.4	6.6	7.2	7.1	7.3
65 years and over	8.9	8.7	8.9	9.2	10.4	10.6	10.9	11.3
65-74 years	8.4	8.4	8.2	8.5	9.2	9.7	9.9	10.3
75 years and over	9.7	9.2	9.9	10.1	12.3	12.1	12.3	12.7
Sex								
Male[1]	4.6	4.6	4.8	4.7	4.9	5.1	5.2	5.2
Female[1]	6.0	6.0	5.9	6.1	6.3	6.6	6.7	6.7
Race								
White[1]	5.5	5.5	5.5	5.6	5.8	6.0	6.0	6.1
Black[1]	5.1	4.8	4.9	5.1	5.2	5.9	6.0	5.7
Family income[1,3]								
Less than $14,000	6.8	6.2	6.3	6.3	6.8	7.3	7.3	7.6
$14,000-$24,999	5.6	5.3	5.2	5.6	5.6	6.0	5.7	5.9
$25,000-$34,999	5.2	5.0	5.5	5.2	5.5	5.7	6.0	5.8
$35,000-$49,999	5.2	5.5	5.2	5.7	5.8	5.9	6.0	6.2
$50,000 or more	5.4	5.5	6.0	5.6	5.8	5.8	5.8	6.0
Geographic region[1]								
Northeast	5.2	5.0	5.3	5.2	5.4	5.9	5.9	5.9
Midwest	5.6	5.4	5.4	5.3	5.8	5.9	6.2	6.0
South	5.1	5.2	5.3	5.6	5.5	5.8	5.7	5.6
West	5.5	5.9	5.5	5.6	5.9	6.1	6.0	6.4
Location of residence[1]								
Within MSA	5.5	5.5	5.4	5.6	5.8	6.0	6.1	6.0
Outside MSA	4.8	4.9	5.2	4.9	5.1	5.6	5.6	5.7

MSA = metropolitan statistical area. **Note:** Data based on household interviews of a sample of the civilian noninstitutionalized population. (1) Age adjusted. (2) Includes all other races not shown separately and unknown family income. (3) Family income categories for 1989-94. Income categories for 1987 are the following: less than $10,000; $10,000-$14,999; $15,000-$19,999; $20,000-$34,999; and $35,000 or more. Income categroies for 1988 are less than $13,000; $13,000-$18,999; $19,000-$24,999; $25,000-$44,999; and $45,000 or more.

Top 20 Reasons Given by Patients for Emergency Room Visits, 1995

Source: National Center for Health Statistics, U.S. Dept. of Health and Human Services

Principal reason for visit	No. of visits (1,000)	Percent of total	Principal reason for visit	No. of visits (1,000)	Percent of total
All visits	96,545	100.0	Pain, site not referable to a specific body system	1,789	1.9
Stomach and abdominal pain, cramps, and spasms	5,940	6.2	Vomiting	1,781	1.8
Chest pain and related symptoms	4,892	5.1	Labored or difficult breathing (dyspnea)	1,729	1.8
Fever	4,609	4.8	Injury, other and unspecified type—head, neck and face	1,640	1.7
Injury—upper extremity	2,679	2.6	Laceration and cuts—facial area	1,614	1.7
Cough	2,422	2.5	Accident, not otherwise specified	1,527	1.6
Symptoms referable to throat	2,210	2.3	Hand and finger(s) injury	1,381	1.4
Shortness of breath	2,179	2.3	Skin rash	1,321	1.4
Headache, pain in head	2,161	2.2	Motor vehicle accident, type of injury unspecified	1,303	1.3
Earache or ear infection	1,905	2.0	Neck symptoms	1,193	1.2
Back symptoms	1,889	2.0	All other reasons	50,381	52.2

Top 20 Reasons Given by Patients for Physicians' Office Visits, 1995

Source: National Center for Health Statistics, U.S. Dept. of Health and Human Services

Principal reason for visit	Number of visits (1,000)	Percentage distribution Total	Female	Male
All visits	697,082	100.0	100.0	100.0
General medical examination	47,315	6.8	7.0	6.4
Cough	25,630	3.7	3.4	4.1
Progress visit, not otherwise specified	21,235	3.0	2.8	3.4
Postoperative visit	20,449	2.9	2.9	2.9
Routine prenatal examination	17,729	2.5	4.3	NA
Symptoms referable to throat	16,502	2.4	2.5	2.1
Earache or ear infection	13,030	1.9	1.7	2.1
Back symptoms	12,975	1.9	1.7	2.1
Fever	12,661	1.8	1.6	2.2
Stomach pain, cramps, and spasms	12,341	1.8	2.0	1.4
Well-baby examination	12,193	1.7	1.6	2.0
Vision dysfunctions	10,544	1.5	1.5	1.6
Head cold, upper respiratory infection (coryza)	10,272	1.5	1.5	1.4
Skin rash	10,240	1.5	1.3	1.7
Headache, pain in head	9,626	1.4	1.6	1.0
Knee symptoms	9,455	1.4	1.3	1.4
Nasal congestion	9,319	1.3	1.2	1.5
Hypertension	9,269	1.3	1.4	1.3
Depression	9,011	1.3	1.5	1.0
Chest pain and related symptoms	8,235	1.2	1.2	1.2
All other reasons	399,051	57.2	56.0	59.2

NA = not applicable.

Drugs Most Frequently Prescribed in Physicians' Offices, 1995

Source: National Center for Health Statistics, U.S. Dept. of Health and Human Services; Physicians' Desk Reference; in thousands

Rank	Name of drug and principal generic substance[1]	Number of times prescribed	Therapeutic use
1.	Amoxicillin	19,676	Antibiotic
2.	Lasix (furosemide)	12,712	Diuretic, antihypertensive
3.	Premarin (estrogens)	12,352	Estrogen replacement therapy
4.	Amoxil (amoxicillin)	11,662	Antibiotic
5.	Tylenol (acetaminophen)	11,604	Analgesic
6.	Synthroid (levothyroxine)	10,303	Thyroid hormone therapy
7.	Prednisone	9,950	Steroid replacement therapy, anti-inflammatory agent
8.	Zantac (ranitidine)	9,060	Duodenal or gastric ulcer
9.	Proventil (albuterol)	7,702	Bronchodilator
10.	Lanoxin (digoxin)	7,108	Congestive heart failure, irregular heartbeat
11.	Motrin (ibuprofin)	7,055	Anti-inflammatory agent
12.	Keflex (cephalexin)	6,953	Antibiotic
13.	Vasotec (enalapril)	6,738	Antihypertensive
14.	Coumadin (crystalline warfarin sodium)	6,466	Anticoagulant
15.	Allergy relief or shots	6,327	Diagnostics
16.	Cardizem (ditiazem)	6,319	Angina/calcium channel blocking agent
17.	Xanax (alprazolam)	6,314	Anxiety disorders
18.	Biaxin (clarithromycin)	6,204	Antibiotic
19.	Provera (medroxyprogesterone acetate)	6,170	Progestin replacement therapy
20.	Prozac (fluoxetine hydrochloride)	5,995	Antidepressant
	All other	749,462	

(1) The trade or generic name used by the physician on the prescription or other medical records. The use of trade names is for identification only and does not imply endorsement by the Public Health Service or the U.S. Dept. of Health and Human Services.

Enrollment in Health Maintenance Organizations (HMOs), 1976-96

Source: *Health, United States, 1996-97*, National Center for Health Statistics, U.S. Dept. of Health and Human Services

	1976	1980	1985[1]	1989	1990	1991	1992	1993	1994	1995	1996
	Number of enrolled in millions										
Total	6.0	9.1	21.0	31.9	33.0	34.0	36.1	38.4	42.2	46.2	52.5
Model type[2]											
Individual practice association[3]	0.4	1.7	6.4	13.5	13.7	13.6	14.7	15.3	16.1	17.4	21.7
Group[4]	5.6	7.4	14.6	18.3	19.3	17.1	16.5	15.4	13.6	12.9	13.5
Mixed	—	—	—	—	—	3.3	4.9	7.7	12.5	15.9	17.2
Federal program[5]											
Medicaid[6]	—	0.3	0.6	1.0	1.2	1.4	1.7	1.7	2.6	3.5	8.5
Medicare	—	0.4	1.1	1.8	1.8	2.0	2.2	2.2	2.5	2.9	3.7
	Percent of population enrolled in HMOs										
Total	2.8	4.0	8.9	13.0	13.4	13.6	14.3	15.1	16.1	17.7	19.9
Geographic region											
Northeast	2.0	3.1	7.9	13.8	14.6	15.4	16.1	18.0	19.5	20.9	23.8
Midwest	1.5	2.8	9.7	12.9	12.6	12.7	12.8	13.2	13.7	14.4	16.2
South	0.4	0.8	3.8	7.1	7.1	7.1	7.8	8.4	9.4	11.2	13.2
West	9.7	12.2	17.3	22.6	23.2	23.8	24.7	25.1	26.4	29.0	30.7

Note: Data are as of June 30 in 1976-80, Dec. 31 in 1985, Jan. 1 in 1989-96. Medicaid enrollment in 1989-90 as of June 30. HMOs in Guam not included prior to 1995. Open-ended enrollment in HMO plans, amounting to 6 million on Jan. 1, 1996, not included in this table. (1) Increases partly due to changes in reporting methods. (2) Eleven HMOs with 35,000 enrollment did not report model type in 1976. (3) This type of HMO contracts with an association of physicians from various settings (a mixture of solo and group practices) to provide health services. (4) Group includes staff, group, and network model types. (5) Enrollment by Medicaid or Medicare beneficiaries, where the Medicaid or Medicare program contracts directly with the HMO to pay the premium. (6) Data for 1989 and later include enrollment in managed-care health insuring organizations.

Years of Life Expected at Birth

Source: National Center for Health Statistics

Year[1]	All Races Total	All Races Male	All Races Female	White Total	White Male	White Female	Black and Other Total	Black and Other Male	Black and Other Female
1920	54.1	53.6	54.6	54.9	54.4	55.6	45.3	45.5	45.2
1930	59.7	58.1	61.6	61.4	59.7	63.5	48.1	47.3	49.2
1940	62.9	60.8	65.2	64.2	62.1	66.6	53.1	51.5	54.9
1950	68.2	65.6	71.1	69.1	66.5	72.2	60.8	59.1	62.9
1960	69.7	66.6	73.1	70.6	67.4	74.1	63.6	61.1	66.3
1965	70.2	66.8	73.7	71.0	67.6	74.7	64.1	61.1	67.4
1970	70.8	67.1	74.7	71.7	68.0	75.6	65.3	61.3	69.4
1975	72.6	68.8	76.6	73.4	69.5	77.3	68.0	63.7	72.4
1976	72.9	69.1	76.8	73.6	69.9	77.5	68.4	64.2	72.7
1977	73.3	69.5	77.2	74.0	70.2	77.9	68.9	64.7	73.2
1978	73.5	69.6	77.3	74.1	70.4	78.0	68.1	63.7	72.4
1979	73.9	70.0	77.8	74.6	70.8	78.4	69.8	65.4	74.1
1980	73.7	70.0	77.5	74.4	70.7	78.1	69.5	65.3	73.6
1981	74.2	70.4	77.8	74.8	71.1	78.4	70.3	66.2	74.4
1982	74.5	70.9	78.1	75.1	71.5	78.7	70.9	66.8	74.9
1983	74.6	71.0	78.1	75.2	71.7	78.7	70.9	67.0	74.7
1984	74.7	71.2	78.2	75.3	71.8	78.7	71.1	67.2	74.9
1985	74.7	71.2	78.2	75.3	71.9	78.7	67.0	64.8	69.3
1986	74.8	71.3	78.3	75.4	72.0	78.8	70.9	66.8	74.9
1987	75.0	71.5	78.4	75.6	72.2	78.9	66.9	65.0	69.1
1988	74.9	71.5	78.3	75.6	72.3	78.9	70.8	66.7	74.8
1989	75.1	71.7	78.5	75.9	72.5	79.2	70.9	66.7	74.9
1990	75.4	71.8	78.8	76.1	72.9	79.4	71.2	67.0	75.2
1991	75.5	72.0	78.9	76.3	72.9	79.2	71.5	67.4	75.5
1992	75.5	72.1	78.9	76.4	73.0	79.5	71.7	67.5	75.8
1993	75.5	72.1	78.9	76.3	73.0	79.5	71.5	67.4	75.5
1994	75.7	72.4	79.0	76.5	73.3	79.6	71.7	67.5	75.8
1995	75.8	72.5	78.9	76.5	73.4	79.6	71.9	67.9	75.7
1996[p]	76.1	73.0	79.0	76.8	73.8	79.6	72.6	68.8	76.2

p = preliminary. (1) Data prior to 1940 for death-registration states only.

Estimated New Cancer Cases and Deaths, by Sex, for Leading Sites, 1997

Source: American Cancer Society

The estimates of expected new cancer cases are offered as a rough guide and should not be regarded as definitive. They exclude basal and squamous cell skin cancers and in situ carcinomas except in bladder. Carcinoma in situ of the breast accounts for about 30,000 new cases annually, and melanoma carcinoma in situ accounts for about 17,300 new cases annually. More than 900,000 basal and squamous cell skin cancers occur annually. About 2,100 nonmelanoma skin cancer deaths are included among the deaths in all sites expected in 1997.

Estimated New Cases

Both sexes		Women		Men	
All Sites	1,257,800	All Sites	596,600	All Sites	661,200
Prostate	209,900	Breast	180,200	Prostate	209,900
Breast	181,600	Lung	79,800	Lung	98,300
Lung	178,100	Colorectal	64,800	Colorectal	66,400
Colorectal	131,200	Uterus	34,900	Bladder	39,500
Non-Hodgkin's lymphoma	53,600	Ovary	26,800	Non-Hodgkin's lymphoma	30,300

Estimated Deaths

Both sexes		Women		Men	
All Sites	560,000	All Sites	265,900	All Sites	294,100
Lung	160,400	Lung	66,000	Lung	94,400
Colorectal	54,900	Breast	43,900	Prostate	41,800
Breast	44,190	Colorectal	27,900	Colorectal	27,000
Prostate	41,800	Pancreas	14,600	Pancreas	13,500
Pancreas	28,100	Ovary	14,200	Non-Hodgkin's lymphoma	12,400

Trends in Cancer Death Rates, 1971-73 and 1991-93

Source: American Cancer Society

Sites	Sex	Death rate[1] 1971-73	1991-93	Percentage change	Number of deaths 1973	Number of deaths 1993
All Sites	Male	204.5	219.0	7	190,487	279,375
	Female	132.0	142.0	8	159,110	250,529
Brain	Male	4.7	5.1	9	4,650	6,551
	Female	3.2	3.5	9	3,661	5,442
Breast	Male	0.3	0.2	−33	293	355
	Female	26.8	26.4	−1	31,850	43,555
Cervix	Female	5.6	2.9	−48	6,041	4,583
Colon and rectum	Male	25.3	22.3	−12	22,680	28,199
	Female	20.0	15.1	−25	24,823	29,206
Esophagus	Male	5.0	6.2	24	4,768	7,813
	Female	1.4	1.5	7	1,723	2,637
Hodgkin's disease	Male	1.9	0.7	−63	1,732	900
	Female	1.1	0.4	−64	1,188	674
Leukemia	Male	8.9	8.4	−6	8,262	10,873
	Female	5.3	4.9	−8	6,216	8,834
Lung	Male	61.3	73.5	20	59,082	92,493
	Female	12.7	32.9	159	15,706	56,234
Melanoma	Male	2.0	3.2	60	1,964	4,128
	Female	1.3	1.5	15	1,465	2,584
Non-Hodgkin's lymphoma	Male	5.8	8.1	40	5,473	10,458
	Female	3.9	5.3	36	4,747	10,028
Ovary	Female	8.6	7.8	−9	9,885	12,870
Pancreas	Male	11.1	10.0	−10	10,380	12,669
	Female	6.7	7.3	9	8,273	13,776
Prostate	Male	21.4	26.8	25	18,830	34,865
Stomach	Male	10.4	6.6	−37	9,178	8,229
	Female	5.0	3.0	−40	6,020	5,621
Urinary bladder	Male	7.2	5.7	−21	6,481	7,474
	Female	2.2	1.7	−23	2,855	3,488
Uterus	Female	4.7	3.4	−28	5,686	6,098

Note: Even though some death rates declined or remained stable, the number of deaths increased because the population has become larger and older. The U.S. population increased 22% from 1973 to 1993. (1) Death rates are per 100,000 persons and were adjusted to the age distribution of the 1970 U.S. census population.

Cardiovascular Diseases Statistical Summary, 1995

Source: American Heart Association, Dallas, TX

Prevalence[1] — 57,900,000 Americans had one or more forms of heart and blood vessel disease.

- high blood pressure — 50,000,000
- coronary heart disease — 13,900,000
- stroke — 4,000,000
- rheumatic heart disease — 1,400,000

Hypertension (high blood pressure) — afflicts 50,000,000 Americans age 6 and above, including about 1 in 4 adults.

Mortality — 960,592 in 1995 (41.5% of all deaths).

- Someone died from cardiovascular disease every 33 seconds in the U.S. in 1995.

Congenital or inborn heart defects —

- Mortality from such heart defects was 5,001 in 1995.

Coronary heart disease (heart attack) — caused 481,287 deaths in 1995.

- 13,900,000 people alive today have a history of heart attack and/or angina pectoris.
- As many as 1,500,000 Americans had heart attacks in 1995, about one-third of them fatal.

Stroke — killed about 157,991 Americans in 1995; afflicted 4,000,000.

Rheumatic heart disease — killed 5,147 in 1995; afflicted 1,400,000.

(1) Estimate based on new methodology and does not indicate a lowering of the estimate from past years.

AIDS Deaths and New AIDS Cases in the U.S., 1985-96

Source: *Health, United States, 1996-97; HIV/AIDS Surveillance Report,* Vol. 8, No. 2, covering through 1996; National Center for Health Statistics, U.S. Dept. of Health and Human Services

	All years[1]	1985	1990	1991	1992	1993	1994	1995	1996
Total Deaths	362,004	6,971	31,466	36,458	40,807	43,889	47,636	45,765	25,695
			New AIDS Cases						
All races	581,429	8,167	41,612	43,601	45,806	102,412	77,388	71,293	69,151
Male									
All males, 13 years and older[2]	488,300	7,517	36,350	37,589	39,097	85,575	63,069	57,439	54,653
White, not Hispanic	247,461	4,763	20,925	20,840	20,840	43,479	29,630	26,377	23,341
Black, not Hispanic	151,413	1,707	10,267	11,121	12,150	28,376	22,515	21,093	20,199
Hispanic	83,923	988	4,760	5,446	5,626	12,655	10,129	9,203	10,337
American Indian[3]	1,300	7	80	86	104	306	200	198	166
Asian or Pacific Islander[4]	3,643	49	263	258	294	657	522	483	480
13-19 years	1,744	28	108	103	91	365	230	234	217
20-29 years	83,255	1,507	6,962	6,564	6,492	14,677	9,703	8,445	NA
30-39 years	224,412	3,589	16,739	17,356	17,900	39,036	29,045	25,987	NA
40-49 years	127,195	1,636	8,878	9,559	10,307	22,942	17,294	16,417	NA
50-59 years	38,059	597	2,653	2,899	3,072	6,451	5,089	4,770	NA
60 years and over	13,635	160	1,010	1,108	1,235	2,104	1,708	1,586	NA
Female									
All females, 13 years and over[2]	85,500	522	4,537	5,345	5,961	15,969	13,344	13,109	13,820
White, not Hispanic	20,026	141	1,223	1,340	1,478	4,058	3,105	3,075	2,888
Black, not Hispanic	47,367	280	2,543	3,105	3,402	9,109	7,865	7,671	8,147
Hispanic	17,330	98	733	854	1,010	2,627	2,279	2,236	2,629
American Indian[3]	244	2	9	11	18	58	40	39	41
Asian or Pacific Islander[4]	447	1	19	24	40	99	49	74	81
13-19 years	1,010	4	65	54	56	198	176	154	186
20-29 years	19,649	176	1,120	1,228	1,388	3,728	2,948	2,681	NA
30-39 years	39,314	233	2,077	2,521	2,732	7,539	6,010	6,013	NA
40-49 years	17,797	45	783	986	1,235	3,218	3,090	3,107	NA
50-59 years	4,967	26	273	338	340	854	775	815	NA
60 years and over	2,763	38	219	218	210	432	345	339	NA
Children									
All children, under 13 years[2] .	7,629	128	725	667	748	868	975	745	678
White, not Hispanic	1,369	26	160	143	129	150	142	118	98
Black, not Hispanic	4,409	84	387	406	483	533	636	482	429
Hispanic	1,770	18	169	112	129	175	182	134	145
American Indian[3]	25	–	5	2	3	3	2	2	3
Asian or Pacific Islander[4]	41	–	4	4	1	4	11	5	1
Under 1 year	NA	63	316	267	328	348	352	269	NA
1-12 years	NA	65	409	400	420	520	623	476	NA

NA=Not available. **Note:** The definition of AIDS cases for reporting purposes was expanded in 1985, 1987, and 1993, as more was learned about the spectrum of human immunodeficiency virus-associated diseases. Data exclude residents of U.S. territories. Figures are updated periodically because of reporting delays. (1) Revised figures; includes cases and deaths prior to 1985 and for years not shown. (2) Total includes persons whose ethnicity was not known. (3) Includes Aleut and Eskimo. (4) Includes Chinese, Japanese, Filipino, Hawaiian and part-Hawaiian, and other Asian or Pacific Islander.

New AIDS Cases in the U.S., 1985-96, by Transmission Category

Source: *HIV/AIDS Surveillance Report,* Vol. 8, No. 2, covering through 1996; National Center for Health Statistics, U.S. Dept. of Health and Human Services

Transmission category	All years[1]	1985	1990	1991	1992	1993	1994	1995	1996
All males, 13 years and older	488,300	7,517	36,350	37,589	39,097	85,575	63,069	57,439	54,653
Men who have sex with men	287,576	5,370	23,860	23,936	24,482	49,716	35,283	30,721	27,316
Injecting drug use	107,784	1,101	6,958	7,628	8,045	20,113	15,127	13,203	12,333
Men who have sex with men and injecting drug use	37,152	650	2,781	3,029	3,125	7,001	4,242	3,503	2,967
Hemophilia/coagulation disorder	4,269	68	331	305	325	1,050	478	420	301
Heterosexual contact[2]	17,040	31	717	880	1,239	3,016	2,767	2,710	3,299
Sex with injecting drug user	6,561	25	458	489	628	1,188	915	888	879
Transfusion[3]	4,534	104	453	389	349	613	385	354	281
Undetermined[4]	29,945	193	1,250	1,422	1,532	4,066	4,787	6,528	8,156
All females, 13 years and older	85,500	522	4,537	5,345	5,961	15,969	13,344	13,109	13,820
Injecting drug use	38,575	285	2,323	2,780	2,960	7,974	5,813	5,157	4,694
Hemophilia/coagulation disorder	174	3	13	14	10	30	27	24	17
Heterosexual contact[2].	32,724	119	1,538	1,883	2,282	6,048	5,347	5,210	5,522
Sex with injecting drug user	15,182	82	1,035	1,176	1,320	2,770	1,997	1,843	1,911
Transfusion[3]	3,354	63	336	239	262	499	323	282	270
Undetermined[4]	10,673	52	327	429	447	1,418	1,834	2,436	3,317

Note: The definition of AIDS cases for reporting purposes was expanded in 1985, 1987, and 1993, as more was learned about the spectrum of human immunodeficiency virus-associated diseases. Data exclude residents of U.S. territories. Figures are updated periodically because of reporting delays. (1) Includes cases prior to 1985 and for years not shown. (2) Includes persons who have had heterosexual contact with a person with human immunodeficiency virus (HIV) infection or at risk of HIV infection. (3) Receipt of blood transfusion, blood components, or tissue. (4) Includes persons for whom risk information is incomplete, persons still under investigation, men reported only to have had heterosexual contact with prostitutes, and interviewed persons for whom no specific risk is identified.

QUICK REFERENCE INDEX

QUICK REFERENCE SPORTS INDEX

For complete Index, see pp. 4-32.